CANADIAN ALMANAC & DIRECTORY 1997

Also Published by ...
Copp Clark Professional

ASSOCIATIONS CANADA 1996/97: An Encyclopedic Directory/ Un Répertoire encyclopédique
1500 pages, 8 1/2 x 11, Paperback
6th edition, April, 1996

ISBN 1 895021 21 9

Over 20,000 entries profile Canadian and international organizations active in Canada. Over 3,000 subject classifications index activities, professions and interests served by associations. Includes listings of NGO's, institutes, coalitions, social agencies, federations, foundations, trade unions, fraternal orders, political parties. Organizational profiles are included for major organizations. Entries typically include professional staff, elected officials, membership profiles, services provided, resource centres, publications and convention details. Subject, geographic, alphabetic, executive name, acronym, mailing list indexes are included for easy reference.

CANADIAN ENVIRONMENTAL DIRECTORY 1996/97
1400 Pages, 8 1/2 X 11, Paperback
6th edition, June, 1996

ISBN 1 895021 23 5

The complete network of government agencies, associations, law firms, consulting firms, research and educational establishments involved in environment-related activities. A variety of indexes assist in locating specific subjects and issues with links to government and association contacts at all levels. Information Services provide a select bibliography, journalists, conferences, trade shows, awards, funding programs. A Directory of Products & Services categorizes the country's major suppliers of products and services.

THE REGISTER OF CANADIAN HONOURS/ Registre des distinctions honorifiques canadiennes
448 pages, 8 1/2 x 11, illustrated, hardcover.
1991

ISBN 1 895021 01 4 - regular edition.
ISBN 1 895021 06 5 - deluxe leatherbound edition.

This authorized directory of Canada's honours system includes listings of all members of The Order of Canada with their citations; The Order of Military Merit; Decorations for Bravery with the record of deeds; Exemplary Service and all other medals. Colour inserts depict all medals and their order of precedence. All armorial bearings created by the Canadian Heraldic Authority are included.

CANADIAN ALMANAC & DIRECTORY 1997

COPP CLARK PROFESSIONAL

Toronto

Distribution

U.S.A. and its possessions: Gale Research Company, Book Tower, Detroit, Michigan 48226
U.K. and Europe: William Snyder Publishing Associates, 5, Five Mile Dr., Oxford OX2 8HT, England
Australia and New Zealand: D.W. Thorpe, 271-273 Lane Cove Road, North Ryde, 2113, Australia

© Copp Clark Professional 1996

All rights reserved. No part of the material covered by this copyright may be reproduced in any form or by any means (whether electronic, mechanical or photographic) for storage in retrieval systems, tapes, discs, or for making multiple copies without the written permission of the publisher.

EDITORIAL DIRECTOR:	Ann Marie Aldighieri
EDITORS:	Peter Asselstine
	Beata Kulesza
	Ward McBurney
	Anthony Sraka
	Susan Traer
FACT CHECKER:	John Whiteman
SYSTEMS MANAGER:	Ruth Watkins
PRODUCTION CO-ORDINATOR:	Dana Bailey
MARKETING MANAGER:	Ian MacRae
MARKETING ASSOC.:	Sarah Gencey

Astronomical Calculations: John R. Percy, Ph.D.
British & Commonwealth Honours: Maj. (Ret.) Richard K. Malott, C.D., M.Sc., B.A., F.R.P.S.C.
Forms of Address: Michael Measures

Design by *Artplus*
Colour Section Layout, Brenda Barratt, The Brenwill Workshop
Translations by *In Other Words...*

Every effort has been made to ensure that the information contained in this book is accurate and complete on publication date. The publisher cannot be held liable for errors or omissions.

Users of the *Almanac* are invited to make suggestions concerning information that might be added to future editions or changes to the presentation of listings and information that might make the book more useful. Please contact the Editor.

ISBN 1-895021-26-X

Copp Clark Professional
200 Adelaide St. West, 3rd Fl., Toronto, ON M5H 1W7
(416) 597-1616; Fax (416) 597-1617; Email: info@mail.CanadaInfo.com;
URL: http://www.canadainfo.com

Printed and bound in Canada by Tri-Graphic Printing (Ottawa) Ltd.

Canadian Cataloguing in Publication Data
The National Library of Canada has catalogued this publication as follows:

Main entry under title:

Canadian almanac & directory

Annual.
101st- year; 1948-
Also available on microfiche from: Toronto: Micromedia.
1SSN 0068-8193
ISBN 1-895021-26-X

1. Almanacs, Canadian. 2. Canada - Directories.
AY414.C2   971'.0025   C75-032392-2

Dedicated to all Editors and contributors
19th century editors not identified
Pre-1924 Arnold W. Thomas
1924-34 Arnold W. Thomas & Horace C. Corner
1935-47 Horace C. Corner
1948-49 Horace C. Corner & Marsh Jeanneret
1950-53 Marsh Jeanneret & Beatrice Logan
1954-58 Beatrice Logan
1959-61 Copp Clark Editorial Staff
1962-66 Ann Gardner
1967-90 Susan (Walters) Bracken
1991-93 Liba Berry
1994- Ann Marie Aldighieri

PRIME MINISTER · PREMIER MINISTRE

It is a pleasure to take this opportunity to extend greetings to the *Canadian Almanac & Directory* on the occasion of its 150th anniversary celebration.

This sesqui-centennial gives you cause to reflect upon the valuable service that you have provided for a century-and-a-half. Your commitment and dedication to compiling and circulating the most up-to-date information about Canadian institutions, organizations, and prominent citizens has proven to be a fine research tool for generations of students, a valuable source of general reference information, and a window on Canada for an international audience.

As Canada's social and political institutions evolve, the *Canadian Almanac & Directory* remains an effective sourcebook that reflects our dynamic heritage.

I commend the publishers and staff - past and present - for maintaining a tradition of excellence. And extend my very best wishes for continued success in the years to come.

C'est un réel plaisir pour moi de féliciter le *Canadian Almanac & Directory* à l'occasion de son 150e anniversaire.

Après un siècle et demi de fonctionnement, il y a tout lieu de réfléchir sur le précieux service que vous rendez. Grâce à votre engagement et votre dévouement dans la compilation et la distribution des informations les plus récentes sur les institutions, les organisations et les personnalités canadiennes, vous avez créé un excellent outil de recherche pour des générations d'étudiants, une source précieuse d'informations générales et une fenêtre sur le Canada pour un auditoire international.

À mesure que les institutions sociales et politiques du Canada évoluent, le *Canadian Almanac & Directory* demeure un guide de référence efficace qui témoigne du dynamisme de notre patrimoine.

Je tiens à féliciter les éditeurs et les employés d'hier et d'aujourd'hui d'avoir conservé une tradition d'excellence. Recevez mes meilleurs vœux de succès dans les années à venir.

OTTAWA
1996

OTTAWA
1996

PREFACE

It is a pleasure to have been invited to write the preface for this very special anniversary edition of the *Canadian Almanac & Directory*.

The fact of 150 years of publishing without interruption is a noteworthy achievement in itself. But the *Almanac & Directory* is recognized for much more than its longevity. This is the work that is generally acknowledged as our country's most valuable source of basic reference information, a source that librarians across the country regard as a veritable bible of quick information.

In my early days as a librarian, I turned to this "bible" almost daily. I knew that this was the place to find accurate answers to factual questions swiftly. There was, and is, nowhere better in drawing a fast picture and in placing it in its historical perspective. The *Almanac* never disappointed me. The information I needed was always there, succinct, current and easy to find.

My reference staff at the National Library today are just as appreciative of the *Canadian Almanac & Directory*'s timeliness and reliability and regard it as the first, sometimes the only, stop required in a quest for information on such topics as the nature of government bodies, cultural institutions, Canadians symbols and customs regulations or a variety of statistics, such as election results, marriage and death rates or the number of Canadians who own personal computers.

I wonder whether Scobie and Balfour realized, when they began publishing the *Almanac & Directory* in Toronto in 1847, that it would become the reference source of first resort for so many or for so long. I think they would have been gratified to see their commitment to ensuring the availability of fundamental facts upheld & presented so effectively.

Through its 150 years, the *Canadian Almanac & Directory* has remained true to its original objective of being an immediate source of current factual information. It reflects the past by providing historical context. It keeps abreast of the times and changes content, style and format as necessary. For example, a CD-ROM version of the *Almanac* is now available, and last year's edition included a website directory and "Who's Who" of key officials and organizations on the Canadian information highway. You will see further changes in this year's edition, but that is no more than all who use it regularly and rely on it heavily have come to expect from Canada's premier reference source.

My sincere congratulations to all involved with publishing the *Canadian Almanac & Directory*, past and present. Long may it continue to serve the many information seekers who rely on it!

Marianne Scott
National Librarian

INTRODUCTION

In 1838, when Hugh Scobie started the *British Colonist* newspaper, his chief concern was to keep the Tory government of the day off-guard. His liberal-conservative views often in support of Presbyterian causes provided for a lively news sheet. The newspaper presses also allowed for commercial printing and publishing which he combined with bookselling to create a viable business in early Toronto. As an extension of both his journalistic and publishing interests, Scobie and partner Balfour, together with John Simpson, published the first Canadian "Almanack" in 1847. This volume is the 150th annual edition of Scobie's work.

When Scobie died in 1853 his business was eventually purchased by employees Walter Copp & Henry Clark who began trading under their own names in 1873. The *Canadian Almanac & Directory* continues under the copyright of Copp Clark Professional, in every respect the firm that Scobie started in early Toronto.

To celebrate this sesquicentennial, we have published a facsimile of the first edition under the original title, *The Canadian Mercantile Almanack for 1847* etc. In that first slim volume, the editors set out the information of the day to provide citizens with lists of officials, post offices, churches, associations and other general items much in the manner of today. Editorial comments were often added, as in describing the Judge Advocate-General of Great Britain, Charles Buller, Esq., "who, it is understood, also performs the duties of an Under-Secretary of the Colonies." Interestingly, the entire British government and the Government of Canada were both presented in 5 pages of well-spaced type.

When Scobie, Balfour and Simpson began the *Almanac,* type was still assembled by hand. It wasn't until 1886 that a point system for measuring type was established in North America. Advances that led to hot-metal typesetters and motorized printing presses in the early twentieth century would no doubt have improved the methods used by Almanac editors to maintain current, accurate data. However, the electronic information age exploding at the end of the 20th century has changed forever every facet of information provision.

In 1989, we began the electronic databasing of the many card-indexes and notebooks so lovingly coddled by generations of editors. Susan Bracken, editor for 23 years, 1967-90, surpassed in service only by the 25+ years editorship of Horace C. Corner, devised an ingenious system of files, notebooks, folders and ledgers that worked as well as any early IBM mainframe. But by the late 80's the sheer volume of changes overwhelmed that ingenuity. Consider that you could reach anyone in the 1940's by sending a letter to a simple street address or by phoning a four or five digit number. That person is much more accessible today but one needs suite, street address, postal code, phone, phone extension, fax, email and website numbers ... the ideal information block for the electronic relational database. Storing, sorting and checking made easier.

The unending demand for currency of information spurred by the World Wide Web is a close concern of all *Canadian Almanac* staff. Our website, CanadaInfo.com, receives thousands of visits every month. All staff contribute to updating and monitoring the site. Our CD-ROM version, now in its third edition, is perhaps a precursor to instant access: a time when the electronic *Almanac* will give you daily changes! This *Almanac* and every subsequent edition will reflect the changing nature of information processing and our continued commitment to the high editorial standards of Hugh Scobie and the generations who followed his lead.

Throughout our stewardship of this work we have consulted with users to determine new needs and we have been eager to correct reported errors or omissions. Since 1989, the amount of information in this volume has expanded by more than 50%. Indeed, in 1996 we reached the limit of a binder's ability to guarantee a strong case for the more than 1,500 pages. This 150th edition marks a departure in format that allows us to increase type-size and better display the ever-growing information. We enter into this change with a great deal of fore-thought and sincerely hope that you will find the new size agreeable. We apologize in advance if it necessitates a library shelf adjustment.

Frederick David Wardle
Publisher

Ann Marie Aldighieri
Editor

ACKNOWLEDGEMENTS

I would like to take the opportunity of the 150th edition of the Almanac to express the editorial staff's thanks to several contributors whose expertise is sought yearly:

Dr. John Percy, Ph.D., University of Toronto (Astronomical Information, Calendars)

Major (Retd.) Richard K. Malott, C.D., M.Sc., B.A., F.R.P.S.C. (British & Commonwealth Honours, Canadian Honours)

Michael Measures (Forms of Address)

Mary de Bellefeuille-Percy and Juliane Martin, Government House (Canadian Honours System, Flags, Coats of Arms, Emblems, Governors General)

Joann Morton and Barbara King, Statistics Canada (Statistics)

Linda Crawley, Linda Crawley Designs

Joan Saint-Pierre, In Other Words (French translation)

In addition, I would like to acknowledge Stephen Delroy, Curator of the House of Commons, for permission to reproduce the official portraits of the Prime Ministers, the National Archives for photographs of the Prime Ministers, Canadian Heritage for permission to reproduce flags, coats of arms and emblems from their publication *Symbols of Nationhood*, the Liberal Party of Canada, Joe Clark & Associates, the National Speakers Bureau; Brenda Barratt; and Artplus, for the *Almanac*'s new look.

As always, we thank the thousands who respond to our annual requests for information; your comments, suggestions and corrections are welcome at any time. Finally, personal thanks to the in-house editorial, systems and production team--you've done it again.

AMA

INTRODUCTION

En 1838, lorsque Hugh Scobie lança le *British Colonist*, son but principal était de garder le gouvernement conservateur de l'époque sur le qui-vive. Ses vues libérales-conservatrices, souvent appuyant les causes presbytériennes, étaient la source d'un journal vivant et stimulant. Les presses du journal permettaient aussi l'impression commerciale et l'impression de livres; combinant ces activités avec la vente de livres, M. Scobie créa un commerce viable dans la ville de Toronto. Comme extension à ses intérêts de journaliste et d'éditeur, Hugh Scobie, avec John Simpson, publia le premier *Canadian Almanack* en 1847. Ce volume-ci est la 150eme édition annuelle de l'ouvrage de M. Scobie.

Lorsque M. Scobie mourut en 1853, son commerce fut éventuellement acheté par ses employés Walter Copp & Henry Clark qui, en 1873, ont commencé à faire affaire sous leurs propres noms. Le *Canadian Almanac & Directory* continu d'être publié sous les droits d'auteur de Copp Clark Professional, l'entreprise qui, à tous les égards, est celle fondée par M. Scobie dans la ville de Toronto de l'époque.

Pour célébrer ce 150eme anniversaire, nous avons publié un fac-similé de la première édition sous son titre original, *The Canadian Mercantile Almanack for 1847*. Dans ce premier volume très mince, les éditeurs publient les renseignements du jour et donnent aux citoyens une liste des officiels, des bureaux de poste, des églises, des associations et autres renseignements généraux, assez près de ce qui se fait aujourd'hui. Des commentaires étaient souvent ajoutés, comme cette description d'un juge de Grande-Bretagne, Charles Buller, Esq., "qui, selon ce que nous comprenons, rempli aussi les fonctions de sous-secrétaire aux Colonies". Il est intéressant de noter que tout le gouvernement britannique ainsi que le gouvernement du Canada étaient tous deux présentés sur cinq pages où le caractère d'imprimerie était bien aéré.

Lorsque MM. Scobie et Simpson ont commencé l'*Almanac*, les caractères d'imprimerie étaient encore assemblés à la main. Ce ne fut qu'en 1886 qu'un système de points devint la mesure des caractères d'imprimerie en Amérique du Nord. Les progrès qui ont amené les procédés plus évolués de Linotype et de presses motorisées du début du vingtième siècle ont sans doute aidé les éditeurs de l'*Almanac* à améliorer les moyens utilisés pour maintenir la pertinence et la précision de leurs données. Cependant, l'explosion de l'ère de l'information électronique de la fin du 20eme siècle a changé à tout jamais les multiples facettes de la gestion de l'information.

En 1989, nous avons commencé la collecte sur informatique des données amassées sur fiches et carnets de note et protégées avec amour par des générations de rédacteurs et rédactrices en chef. Susan Bracken, rédactrice en chef durant 23 ans, de 1967 à 1990, n'est dépassée en années de service que par les 35 années comme rédacteur d'Horace C. Corner, durant la première moitié de ce siècle. Elle mit sur pieds un ingénieux système de fiches, carnets de notes, chemises et grand livre qui fonctionnait aussi bien que n'importe quel ordinateur IBM de l'époque. Mais, vers la fin des années `80, le volume stupéfiant des changements vint à bout de cette ingéniosité. Pensez que, vers 1940, on pouvait rejoindre à peu près n'importe qui en postant une lettre à une simple adresse de rue ou en composant un numéro de téléphone à quatre ou cinq chiffres. Cette personne est beaucoup plus facile à rejoindre aujourd'hui mais il nous faut une adresse de rue, une suite, un code postal, un numéro de téléphone, un numéro de poste, de télécopieur, une adresse électronique et une adresse web... tous des renseignements sur mesure pour une banque de donnée électronique. L'entreposage, le triage et la vérification à son meilleur.

La demande sans cesse croissante pour des renseignements courants, poussée par l'avènement du World Wide Web, est un aspect dont tous les employés du *Canadian Almanac* sont conscients. Notre site Web, CanadaInfo.com, reçoit chaque mois plusieurs milliers de visites. Tous les employés voient à la mise à jour et à la surveillance du site. Notre version sur CD-ROM, qui en est maintenant à sa troisième édition, est peut-être un précurseur de l'accès instantané: une époque où l'*Almanac* vous donnera les changements sur une base quotidienne! Cette édition et les éditions subséquentes refléteront cette nature changeante du processus de gestion de l'information et notre implication continue à rencontrer les hauts standards établis par Hugh Scobie et les générations qui ont suivi son exemple.

Tout au long de notre implication dans ce travail, nous avons consulté les utilisateurs afin de déterminer leurs besoins et nous avons corrigé avec diligence les erreurs et les omissions. Depuis 1989, le nombre de renseignements contenus dans ce volume s'est accru de plus de 50%. De fait, en 1996, nous avons atteint la limite où on pouvait nous garantir une reliure solide pour nos plus de 1 500 pages. Cette 150eme édition marque une modification au format, ce qui nous permet de grossir le caractère employé et de mieux présenter l'information toujours croissante. Ce changement est le résultat d'une réflexion antérieure intense et nous espérons sincèrement que ce nouveau format vous plaira. Nous nous excusons à l'avance si ce changement exige que vous rajustiez une tablette de votre bibliothèque.

Frederick David Wardle
Éditeur

Ann Marie Aldighieri
Rédactrice en chef

RECONNAISSANCES

Je voudrais profiter de cette occasion que me donne cette 150eme publication pour exprimer les remerciements de l'équipe de rédaction aux nombreux collaborateurs dont nous sollicitons l'expertise à chaque année:

Dr. John Percy, Ph.D., Université de Toronto (Renseignements astronomiques, calendriers)

Major (Retd.) K. Malott, C.D., M.Sc., B.A., F.R.P.S.C. (titres honorifiques britanniques et du Commonwealth, titres honorifiques canadiens)

Michael Measures (Formules d'appel)

Mary de Bellefeuille-Percy et Juliane Martin de la Chancellerie (Système honorifique canadien, drapeaux, armoiries, emblèmes, gouverneurs général)

Joann Morton et Barbara King, Statistiques Canada (Statistiques)

Linda Crawley, Linda Crawley Designs

Joan Saint-Pierre, In Other Words (Traduction française)

De plus, j'aimerais mentionner Stephen Delroy, curateur de la Chambre des communes, pour la permission de reproduire les portraits officiels du Premier ministre; les Archives nationales pour les photographies des Premiers ministres; le Patrimoine canadien pour la permission de reproduire les drapeaux, les armoiries et les emblèmes de leur publication *Symbols of Nationhood*; le parti Libéral du Canada; Joe Clark & Associates; le National Speakers Bureau; Brenda Barratt; et Art Plus pour la nouvelle présentation de l'*Almanac*.

Comme toujours, nous remercions les milliers de personnes qui répondent à nos requêtes annuelles de renseignements; vos commentaires, vos suggestions et vos corrections sont les bienvenus en tout temps. Pour terminer, mes remerciements personnels à l'équipe de rédaction et de production interne - - vous avez réussi encore une fois!

AMA

CONTENTS

See ADDENDA at the back of this book for late changes & additional information.

SECTION 1: Almanac & Miscellany
Astronomical Calculations & Almanac • Canadian Precedence and Titles • Canadian Honours List • British & Commonwealth Honours • Forms of Address • Abbreviations • Customs, Election, Liquor and Marriage Regulations • Postal Information • Canadian Flags, Coats of Arms & Emblems • Governors General • Prime Ministers • Provincial Emblems and Birds • Canadian Honours • Canadian Statistics • Weights and Measures • Distances • Air Line Companies and Railroad Companies • Exhibition and Show Planners • Exhibitions, Shows and Events • Major Canadian Awards

SECTION 2: Organizations
Religious Denominations & Organizations • Associations • Trade Unions and Associations of Workers • Foundations

SECTION 3: Government Directory
Quick Reference • Government of Canada • Provincial Governments • Territorial Governments • Foreign Governments Compared • The Queen & Royal Family • The Commonwealth • The Francophonie • International Organizations • Foreign Diplomats In Canada • Canadian Diplomats Abroad

SECTION 4: Municipal Directory
Municipalities in Canada • Major Cities in detail • Major Regional Governments

SECTION 5: Communications & Information Management
Libraries • Archives • Book Publishers • Newspapers • Magazines • AM and FM Radio Stations, TV Stations and Cable Companies • Freenets • Online Service Providers • Website Directory

SECTION 6: Arts & Culture
Museums • Art Galleries • Performing Arts • Botanical Gardens • Aquaria • Zoos

SECTION 7: Business & Finance
Banks, Trust Companies, Mortgage & Loan Companies • Investment Fund Managers • Stock Exchanges • Insurance Companies • Boards of Trade/Chambers of Commerce • Consultant Lobbyists • Major Canadian Companies

SECTION 8: Health Directory
Hospitals & Health Care Facilities

SECTION 9: Education Directory
School Boards • Universities & Colleges • Private & Specialized Schools

SECTION 10: Legal Directory
Courts and Judges • Registrars in Bankruptcy • Law Firms in Canada

---

SECTION 1: Almanach et Miscellanées
Almanach et calculs d'astronomie • Drapeaux et insignes du Canada • Oiseaux et fleurs, emblèmes provinciaux • Protocole de préséance et appels utilisés • Décorations et titres honorifiques canadiens • Règlements douaniers • Réglementation concernant les électeurs, le mariage et l'alcool • Formules d'appel • Abréviations • Renseignements postaux • Premiers Ministres • Gouverneurs-Général • Statistiques canadiennes • Poids et mesures • Distances • Compagnies de transport aérien et ferroviaire • Planificateurs de foires commerciales • Foires agricoles, commerciales et événements spéciaux • Prix et citations

SECTION 2: Organisations
Dénominations et organisations religieuses • Associations • Associations et syndicats ouvriers • Fondations

SECTION 3: Répertoire des Gouvernements
Index de référence des services gouvernementaux • Gouvernement du Canada • Gouvernements des provinces • Gouvernements des territoires • La Reine et la Famille royale • Nations du Commonwealth • La Francophonie • Comparaison du Gouvernement du Canada et Gouvernements étrangers • Corps diplomatiques et consulaires: ambassadeurs/ambassades et hauts commissaires au Canada • Diplomates canadiens à l'étranger • Bureaux des organismes internationaux

SECTION 4: Répertoire des Municipalités
Municipalités du Canada • Principales villes en détail • Communautés urbaines principales

SECTION 5: Communications et Gestion de l'Information
Bibliothèques • Archives • Éditeurs de livres • Journaux • Périodiques • Stations de radio AM et FM, stations de télévision et câblodistributeurs • Fournisseurs de services Internet • Répertoire Internet

SECTION 6: Art et Culture
Musées • Galeries d'art • Art de Réprésentation • Jardins zoologiques et botaniques, aquariums

SECTION 7: Commerce et Finance
Banques, Sociétés de fiducie • Investissements des fonds mutuels • Bourses • Compagnies d'Assurances • Chambres de commerce et d'industrie • Lobbyistes • Sociétés canadiennes principales

SECTION 8: Répertoire des Hôpitaux et Soins de Santé
Hôpitaux et services de santé

SECTION 9: Répertoire de l'Éducation
Répertoire des services et institutions d'enseignement

SECTION 10: Répertoire Juridique
Cours et juges • Bureaux d'avocats du Canada • Registraires en Faillite

TOPICAL TABLE OF CONTENTS

For detailed references, *see* Index.

For late changes, *see* Addenda.

Abbreviations, Honours & Titles
Academic & Professional 1-35
Astronomical 1-1
Business 1-39
Forms of Address 1-33
Honours & Decorations 1-26
Order of Canada **15**, 1-26
Table of Precedence 1-25
Table to Titles 1-26

Associations & Societies 2-8

Broadcasting & Communication
AM Radio Stations 5-199
Associations 2-28
Awards 1-93
Book Publishers 5-115
Cable TV Companies 5-223
Cdn. Radio-Television & Telecommunications
 Commission 3-61
FM Radio Stations 5-206
Forms of Address 1-33
Magazines 5-159
Newspapers 5-130
Online Service Providers 5-230
Postal Information 1-43
Radio Stations 5-198
TV Stations 5-213
Websites 5-233, 5-239

Churches & Religious Organizations 2-2
Websites 5-258

Citizenship & Bravery Awards 1-28, 1-95, **16**

Commerce & Finance
Advertising Organizations 2-10
Accountants' Associations 2-8
Associations 2-33, 2-69
Awards 1-94
Bank of Canada 3-55
Banking Institutions 7-1
Better Business Bureaus 2-33
Boards of Trade 7-23
Business Development Bank of Canada 3-55
Business Information (Government) 3-6
Business Publications 5-159, 5-162
Canadian Commercial Corporation 3-57
Chambers of Commerce 7-23
Consumer Price Index 1-54
Convention Planners 1-68
Custom Brokers Society 2-34

Economic Associations 2-44
Financial Analyst's Council 2-69
Financial Corporations Association 2-69
Financial Executives' Institute 2-70
Government Finance Departments 3-16
Insurance Companies 7-13
Investment Fund Managers 7-4
Major Canadian Companies 7-40
Marketing Organizations 2-10
Meeting Organizers 1-68
Mortgage & Loan Companies 7-4
Stock Exchanges 7-9
Tax Court of Canada 10-2
Trade Unions 2-195
Trust Companies 7-3
Websites 5-236

Cultural Directory
Archives 5-111
Art Galleries 6-29
Arts Associations 2-24
Awards 1-96
Book Publishers 5-115
Botanical Gardens 6-45
Dance Associations 6-41
Government Cultural Departments 3-3
Journalism Awards 1-102
Language, Linguistics, Literature Assns 2-111
Libraries 5-1
Literary Awards 1-104
Museums 6-1
Music Associations 6-37
Native Peoples' Associations 2-132
Performing Arts Awards 1-108
Theatre Organizations 6-35
Visual Arts Associations 2-190
Visual Arts Awards 1-96
Websites 5-233
Writers Organizations 2-193
Zoological Gardens 6-44

Education Directory
Directory by province, including Boards of Education, Post Secondary Institutions, Technical & Vocational Colleges, & Private Schools.

 Alberta 9-1
 British Columbia 9-6
 Manitoba 9-13
 New Brunswick 9-17
 Newfoundland & Labrador 9-19
 Northwest Territories 9-21
 Nova Scotia 9-21
 Ontario 9-23
 Prince Edward Island 9-41
 Québec 9-41
 Saskatchewan 9-51

 Yukon 9-55
Associations 2-45
Awards 1-97
Government Education Departments 3-13
Journals 5-195
Websites 5-242

Electoral Districts
Places in 4-1
List of (with Eligible Voters, & Elected Members):
 Alberta 3-93
 British Columbia 3-106
 Federal 3-47
 Manitoba 3-121
 New Brunswick 3-132
 Newfoundland & Labrador 3-141
 Northwest Territories 3-150
 Nova Scotia 3-155
 Ontario 3-166
 Prince Edward Island 3-187
 Québec 3-194
 Saskatchewan 3-211
 Yukon 3-221

Engineering
Awards 1-111
Organizations 2-57

Environmental
Awards 1-99
Government Environment Departments 3-15
Organizations 2-59
Websites 5-258

Foreign & International
Ambassadors & Embassies in Canada 3-248
Canadian Consulates 3-259
Canadian Embassies 3-259
Canadian/Foreign Government
 Equivalency Table 3-226
Foreign Government Departments
 & Agencies 3-230
Commonwealth Nations 3-247
Consular Agents in Canada 3-248
International Agencies 3-247
Royal Family 3-246

Geographic Information
Area of Canada 1-63
Area of Cities (*see* Government, Municipal-Large Cities
 Directory - below)
Area of Provinces (*see* Government, Provincial - below)
Canals & Locks 1-64
Climatic Data 1-65

Distances in Canada. 1-66
Population of Cities, Towns & Villages 4-1
Population of Provinces 1-47
Time Zones 1-3

Government Directory
Awards 1-103
Canadian Diplomats 3-248
Canadian/Foreign Government
    Equivalency Table. 3-226
Foreign Government Departments
    & Agencies 3-230
Foreign Government Diplomats 3-248
Lobbyists, Consultant 7-35
Quick Reference. 3-1
Websites 5-244

Federal
Information Services 3-18
Governor General 3-43
Privy Council 3-43
Senate. 3-44
House of Commons 3-45

Agriculture & Agri-food 3-52
Archives 3-78
Auditor General 3-54
Bank of Canada 3-55
Business Development Bank of Canada 3-55
Canada Mortgage & Housing
    Corporation 3-55
Canada Post Corporation 3-56
Canadian Broadcasting Corporation 3-56
Canadian Heritage 3-58
Citizenship & Immigration 3-62
Correctional Service 3-63
Defence. 3-79
Elections 3-64
Environment. 3-64
Finance 3-66
Fisheries & Oceans. 3-67
Foreign Affairs & International Trade 3-68
Health 3-71
Human Resources Development 3-72
Indian & Northern Affairs. 3-73
Industry 3-74
Justice. 3-77
NAFTA Secretariat 3-84
Natural Resources 3-81
Parks. 3-58
Passport Information. 3-70
Ports 3-56
Public Service Commission 3-84
Public Works & Government Services 3-85
Radio-Television & Communication 3-61
RCMP 3-88
Research Council 3-80
Revenue 3-86
Solicitor General. 3-88
Statistics Canada 3-89
Status of Women 3-90
Transport. 3-90
Treasury Board. 3-91
Veterans Affairs 3-92

Provincial/Territorial
Information Services. 3-18

Directory by province, including Cabinet, Members of Legislature, Government Departments with addresses, phone & Fax numbers, & chief personnel, Crown Corporations & Agencies
    Alberta 3-92
    British Columbia 3-105
    Manitoba 3-120
    New Brunswick. 3-131
    Newfoundland & Labrador 3-140
    Northwest Territories. 3-150
    Nova Scotia 3-154
    Ontario 3-164
    Prince Edward Island 3-187
    Québec. 3-193
    Saskatchewan. 3-210
    Yukon. 3-221

Municipal
Directory by province, including Cities, Towns and other Municipalities, with population, electoral districts, addresses & names of Clerks, & showing counties where applicable
    Alberta 4-1
    British Columbia 4-12
    Manitoba 4-18
    New Brunswick 4-24
    Newfoundland & Labrador 4-29
    Northwest Territories 4-37
    Nova Scotia 4-39
    Ontario 4-42
    Prince Edward Island 4-74
    Québec. 4-77
    Saskatchewan. 4-134
    Yukon. 4-152
Large Cities Directory 4-153
Regional Governments Directory 4-171

Historical & General Information
Archives (Government). 3-20
Associations & Societies 2-95
Astronomical Calculations 1-1
Birds, Official Provincial. 9
Birth & Death Rates. 1-48, 1-59
Canadian Awards 1-92
Coats of Arms. **1**, **9**
Constitutional Repatriation (Participants). 1-25
Customs Regulations. 1-39
Election Regulations 1-41
Fathers of Confederation 1-25
Flags **8**
Floral Emblems. **9**
Governors General since 1867. . . . . **2**
Liquor Regulations 1-41
Marriage Regulations 1-42
National Anthem 1-25
Order of Canada 15, 1-26
Political Organizations 2-141
Population 1-47, 1-58
Prime Ministers since 1867 . . . . **4**
Queen & Royal Family 3-245
Standard Holidays 1-24
Statistics 1-47
Weights & Measures 1-60

Hospitals & Health Care Facilities
Awards 1-101

Dental Organizations 2-39
Federal Government Hospitals 3-71
Government Health Departments 3-19
Hospital Associations 2-99
Hospitals 8-1
Magazines 5-168, 5-183
Medical Associations 2-80
Nurses' Associations 2-135
Websites 5-250

Legal
Attorneys General (Justice Departments) 3-23
Awards 1-103
Canadian Judicial Council. 3-61
Courts & Judges, Sheriffs etc.
    Alberta 10-2
    British Columbia. 10-4
    Federal Court of Canada 10-1
    Manitoba. 10-6
    New Brunswick 10-7
    Newfoundland & Labrador 10-8
    Northwest Territories 10-8
    Nova Scotia 10-9
    Ontario 10-10
    Prince Edward Island 10-14
    Québec 10-15
    Saskatchewan 10-20
    Yukon 10-21
Supreme Court of Canada 10-1
Tax Court of Canada 10-2
Law Societies 2-113
Law Firms 10-22
Magazines. 5-170
Official Receivers 10-21
Solicitors General (Departments) 3-36
Websites 5-255

Postal Information 1-43

Religious Organizations &
Denominations 2-2
Websites 5-258

Sports
Awards 1-112
Organizations 2-172
Websites 5-256

Tourism
Associations 2-183
Chambers of Commerce 7-23
Government Tourism Departments 3-37
Magazines 5-176, 5-190
Parks 3-29

Transportation
Associations 2-188
Air Line Companies 1-67
Canals & Locks 1-64
Government Transportation Departments . . . 3-38
Magazines 5-176
Railway Companies 1-67
Websites 5-261

ALPHABETICAL FASTFINDER

Abbreviations 1-35	Federal Government 3-43	O Canada 1-25
Air Line Companies 1-67	Flags **1, 8**	Official Receivers 10-21
Alberta Government 3-92	Floral Emblems **9**	Online Service Providers 5-230
Archives 5-111	Foreign Government Departments	Ontario Government 3-164
Area of Canada 1-63	& Agencies 3-230	Order of Canada **15**, 1-26
Armorial Bearings **1, 9**	Foreign Government Equivalency Table 3-226	
Art Galleries 6-29	Forms of Address 1-33	Population 1-47, 5-1
Associations 2-8	Foundations 2-208	Postal Information 1-43
Astronomy 1-1	Freenets 5-232	Precedence 1-25
Awards 1-92		Prime Ministers 3-43, **4**
	Government 3-43	Prince Edward Island Government 3-187
Banks 7-1	Government Equivalency	Privy Council 3-43
Birds, Official Provincial **9**	Table (Cdn./Foreign) 3-226	Publishers 5-115
Boards of Trade 7-23	Government Quick Reference Table 3-1	
Book Publishers 5-115	Government Lobbyists (Consultant) 7-35	Québec Government 3-193
Botanical Gardens 6-45	Governors General **2**, 3-43	Queen & Royal Family 3-245
British Columbia Government 3-105		
Broadcasting Networks 5-198	High Commissions in Canada 3-248	Radio Stations 5-198
	Holidays 1-24	Railway Companies .1-67
Cable TV Companies 5-223	Honours & Decorations **15**, 1-26	Religious Organizations & Denominations 2-2
Canadian Consuls & Embassies 3-259	Hospitals 8-1	
Canadian Government 3-43	House of Commons 3-45	Saskatchewan Government 3-210
Canadian High Commissions 3-259		School Boards & Schools 9-1
Canals and Locks 1-64	Imports & Exports 1-55	Senate 3-44
Chambers of Commerce 7-23	Insurance Companies 7-13	Statistics 1-47
Churches 2-2		Stock Exchanges 7-9
Cities and Towns 4-1	Judges 10-1	Supreme Court of Canada 10-1
City Government 4-153		
Consuls in Canada 3-248	Lawyers 10-22	Tax Court of Canada 10-2
Consultant Lobbyists 7-35	Libraries 5-1	Television Stations .5-213
Consumer Price Index 1-54	Lobbyists, Consultant 7-35	Time Zones 1-3
Convention Planners 1-68		Trade Unions 2-195
Courts and Judges 10-1	Magazines 5-159	Trust Companies 7-3
Crown Corporations (Federal) 3-52	Major Canadian Companies 7-40	
Customs Regulations 1-39	Manitoba Government 3-120	Universities 9-1
	Meeting Organizers 1-68	
Diplomats 3-248	Municipalities 4-1	Websites 5-233
Distances in Canada 1-66	Museums 6-1	Weights & Measures 1-60
Educational Institutions 9-1	New Brunswick Government 3-131	Yukon Government .3-221
Electoral Districts 4-1	Newfoundland & Labrador Government 3-140	
Embassies in Canada 3-248	Newspapers 5-130	Zoological Gardens .6-44
	Northwest Territories Government 3-150	
Federal Court of Canada 10-1	Nova Scotia Government 3-154	

Page numbers in boldface refer to the illustrated section following page 1-46.

TABLE DES MATIÈRES PAR SUJETS

Pour référence detailée *voir* l'Index.

Pour modifications de dernière heure *voir* l'Addenda.

Abréviations, titres honorifiques et autres
Astronomie 1-1
Commerce. 1-39
Diplômes et professions 1-35
Formules d'appel 1-33
Ordre du Canada **15**, 1-26
Protocole de préséance 1-25
Table de titres 1-26
Titre honorifiques et décorations 1-26

Agences internationales
Bureaux au Canada 3-248
Famille royale. 3-246
Missions canadiennes à/au. 3-259

Art et culture
Associations autochtones 2-132
Associations de langues, linguistiques
  et littéraires 2-111
Associations musicales. 6-37
Archives 5-111
Associations artistiques 2-24
Associations de Danse 6-41
Bibliothèques. 5-1
Départements des affaires culturelles 3-3
Éditeurs de livres 5-115
Galeries d'art. 6-29
Jardins botaniques. 6-45
Jardins zoologiques 6-44
Musées 6-1
Organisations d'écrivains 2-193
Organisations théâtrales 6-35
Prix aux arts d'interprétation 1-108
Prix aux arts visuels 1-96
Prix et citations 1-96
Prix au journalisme. 1-102
Prix littéraires 1-104
Sites web. 5-233

Associations et sociétés 2-8

Circonscriptions électorales
Par endroits. 4-1
Liste des membres élus (et le nombre d'électeurs):
  Alberta. 3-92
  Colombie-Britannique. 3-105
  Fédéral 3-43
  Île-du-Prince-Édouard 3-187
  Manitoba. 3-120
  Nouveau-Brunswick. 3-131
  Nouvelle-Écosse. 3-154
  Ontario 3-164
  Québec 3-193
  Terre-Neuve. 3-140
  Territoires du Nord-Ouest 3-150

  Saskatchewan 3-210
  Yukon. 3-221

Commerce et finance
Associations 2-33, 2-69
Association des compagnies financières
  canadiennes 2-69
Associations de comptables. 2-8
Association de courtiers en douane 2-34
Associations d'économique 2-44
Banque du Canada 3-55
Banque de développement du Canada 3-55
Bourses 7-9
Bureaux d'éthique commerciale 2-33
Chambres de commerce 7-23
Compagnies d'assurances. 7-13
Conseil canadien des analystes financiers . . . 2-69
Corporation commerciale canadienne. 3-57
Cour canadienne de l'impôt 10-2
Indice des prix à la consommation 1-54
Institut des dirigeants financiers du Canada . . 2-70
Institutions bancaires 7-1
Investissement des fonds mutuels 7-4
Ministères des finances. 3-16
Organisations de marketing/publicité 2-10
Planification de congrès 1-68
Prix et citations 1-94
Publications commerciales 5-159, 5-162
Planification de réunions 1-68
Sites web. 5-236
Sociétés canadiennes principales. 7-40
Sociétés de fiducie 7-3
Sources d'informations pour commerce
  (Gouvernement) 3-6
Syndicats ouvriers. 2-195

Décorations civiles, citations pour
bravoure 1-28, 1-95, **16**

Diffusion et communication
Associations. 2-28
Câblodistributeurs. 5-223
Éditeurs de livres 5-115
Formules d'appel 1-33
Journaux. 5-159
Prix et citations 1-93
Publications 5-130
Renseignements postaux. 1-43
Sites web. 5-233, 5-239
Stations de radio. 5-198
Stations radio AM 5-199
Stations radio FM 5-206
Stations de télévision. 5-213

Enseignement
Répertoire par provinces, comprenant les conseils scolaires, les institutions d'enseignement secondaire, les collèges d'enseignement technique et d'enseignement professionnel, les écoles privées.
  Alberta 9-1
  Colombie-Britannique. 9-6
  Île-du-Prince-Édouard 9-41
  Manitoba 9-13
  Nouveau-Brunswick. 9-17
  Nouvelle-Écosse 9-21
  Ontario 9-23
  Québec 9-41
  Terre-Neuve 9-21
  Territoires du Nord-Ouest 9-21
  Saskatchewan. 9-51
  Yukon 9-55
Associations 2-45
Départements d'éducation 3-13
Prix et citations 1-97
Publications. 5-195
Sites web 5-242

Environnement
Départements gouvernementaux 3-15
Organisations 2-59
Prix et citations 1-99
Sites web 5-258

Géographie
Étendue du Canada 1-63
Étendue des provinces (voir Gouvernements
  provinciaux, plus bas)
Étendue des villes (voir Gouvernements municipaux,
  grandes villes, plus bas)
Canaux et écluses 1-64
Climat et températures. 1-65
Fuseaux horaires 1-3
Populations des provinces 1-47
Populations des villes et villages 4-1
Tableau de distances canadiennes 1-66

Hôpitaux et soins de santé
Associations médicales 2-80
Associations d'infirmier(ière)s 2-135
Associations de services hospitaliers. 2-99
Départements gouvernementaux de santé . . 3-19
Hôpitaux. 8-1
Hôpitaux sous juridiction fédérale 3-71
Organisations de soins dentaires 2-39
Prix et citations 1-101
Publications. 5-168, 5-183
Sites web 5-250

Ingénierie
Organisations......................... 2-57
Prix et citations 1-111

International et étranger
Ambassadeurs et ambassades au Canada.. 3-248
Ambassades canadiennes à l'étranger..... 3-259
Consulats canadiens.................. 3-259
Consulats au Canada 3-248
Gouvernements canadien et étrangers:
  Table de comparaison.............. 3-226
Gouvernements étrangers............. 3-230
Nations du Commonwealth 3-247

Juridique
Barreaux et sociétés juridiques 2-113
Bureaux d'avocats 10-22
Conseil canadien de la Magistrature 3-61
Cour canadienne de l'impôt 10-2
Cour fédérale du Canada 10-1
Cour suprême du Canada 10-1
Cours et juges, shérif, etc.
  Alberta............................ 10-2
  Colombie-Britannique............... 10-4
  Île-du-Prince-Édouard.............. 10-14
  Manitoba.......................... 10-6
  Nouveau-Brunswick................ 10-7
  Nouvelle-Écosse................... 10-9
  Ontario........................... 10-10
  Québec........................... 10-15
  Terre-Neuve....................... 10-8
  Territoires du Nord-Ouest 10-8
  Saskatchewan 10-20
  Yukon 10-21
Prix 1-103
Publications 5-170
Séquestres officiels 10-21
Solliciteurs général (bureaux) 3-36
Sites web 5-255

Religions et organisations religieuses 2-2
Sites web 5-258

Renseignements historiques et généraux
Archives gouvernementales 3-20
Armoiries............................. **1**
Associations et sociétés 2-95
Calculs d'astronomie 1-1
Drapeaux............................. **8**
Fêtes et congés 1-24
Fleurs, emblèmes..................... **9**
Gouverneurs généraux depuis 1867 ..... **2**
Hymne national 1-25
Oiseaux, emblèmes des provinces......... **9**
Ordre du Canada **15**, 1-26
Organisations politiques 2-141
Pères de la Confédération 1-25
Poids et mesures 1-60
Population 1-47, 1-58
Premiers ministres depuis 1867 .... **4**

Prix et citations du Canada 1-92
Qualifications d'un électeur 1-41
Rapatriement de la Constitution (participants) . 1-25
Réglementation de l'alcool............. 1-41
Réglementation du mariage 1-42
Règlements douaniers................. 1-39
Reine et Famille royale 3-245
Statistiques.......................... 1-47
Taux de naissances et de décès...... 1-48, 1-59

Renseignements postaux 1-43

Répertoire des gouvernements
Gouvernements canadien et étrangers: Table de
  comparaison..................... 3-226
Lobbyistes 7-35
Prix et citations 1-103
Référence rapide...................... 3-1
Sites web 5-244

Fédéral
Services de renseignements 3-18
Conseil privé......................... 3-43
Sénat 3-44
Chambre des communes................ 3-45
Affaires étrangères et commerce international 3-68
Affaires indiennes et du Nord Canada..... 3-73
Agriculture et Agro-alimentaire 3-52
Anciens combattants.................. 3-92
Archives 3-78
Banque du Canada 3-55
Banque de développement du Canada ... 3-55
Citoyenneté et Immigration 3-62
Commission de la Fonction publique 3-84
Conseil de la recherche................ 3-80
Conseil du Trésor 3-91
Défense 3-79
Développement des ressources humaines ... 3-72
Élections............................ 3-64
Environnement 3-64
Finance 3-66
Gendarmerie Royale 3-88
Gouverneur général................... 3-43
Industrie............................ 3-74
Justice 3-77
Parcs 3-58
Passeports, renseignements 3-70
Patrimoine (canadien) 3-58
Pêches et Océans 3-67
Ports 3-56
Radiodiffusion et télécommunications...... 3-61
Ressources naturelles 3-81
Revenu 3-86
Santé 3-71
Service correctionnels 3-63
Société canadienne d'hypothèques
  et de logement 3-55
Société canadienne des postes 3-56
Société Radio Canada 3-56
Solliciteur général 3-88
Statistique Canada 3-89
Transport 3-90

Travaux Publics et services gouvernementaux .3-85
Vérificateur général 3-54

Provinciaux
Services de renseignements 3-18
Répertoire par province comprenant les membres du cabinet et de la législature; les divers ministères, services, sociétés de la Couronne et agences, avec noms du personnel cadre, adresse, numéros de téléphone et de télécopieur
  Alberta 3-92
  Colombie-Britannique............... 3-105
  Île-du-Prince-Édouard.............. 3-187
  Manitoba.......................... 3-120
  Nouveau-Brunswick................ 3-131
  Nouvelle-Écosse................... 3-154
  Ontario........................... 3-164
  Québec........................... 3-193
  Terre-Neuve....................... 3-140
  Territoires du Nord-Ouest 3-150
  Saskatchewan 3-210
  Yukon 3-221

Municipaux
Répertoire par provinces comprenant les villes, villages et autre municipalités avec population, circonscriptions électorales, le nom du secrétaire, l'adresse et le comté
  Alberta 4-1
  Colombie-Britannique............... 4-12
  Île-du-Prince-Édouard.............. 4-74
  Manitoba.......................... 4-18
  Nouveau-Brunswick................ 4-24
  Nouvelle-Écosse................... 4-39
  Ontario........................... 4-42
  Québec........................... 4-77
  Saskatchewan 4-134
  Terre-Neuve....................... 4-29
  Territoires du Nord-Ouest 4-37
  Yukon 4-152
Répertoire des grandes villes 4-153
Répertoires des Communautés urbaines 4-171

Sports
Organisations 2-172
Prix et citations 1-112
Sites web 5-256

Tourisme
Associations 2-183
Chambres de commerce 7-23
Départements gouvernementaux de tourisme .3-37
Publications.................... 5-176, 5-190

Transport
Associations 2-188
Canaux et écluses 1-64
Compagnies ferroviaires 1-67
Compagnies de transport aérien 1-67
Ministères des transports 3-38
Publications 5-176
Sites web 5-261

RAPIDINDEX ALPHABÉTIQUE

Abréviations 1-35	Églises 2-2	Oiseaux, emblèmes des provinces **9**
Alberta, gouvernement 3-92	Enseignement, institutions d'. 9-1	Ontario, gouvernement. 3-164
Ambassades au Canada. 3-248	Étendue du Canada. 1-63	Ordre du Canada 15, 1-26
Ambassades canadiennes 3-259		
Appel, formules d' 1-33	Fédéral, gouvernement 3-43	Poids et mesures 1-60
Archives 5-111	Ferroviaires, compagnies. 1-67	Population 5-1, 1-47
Armoiries. **1, 9**	Fêtes 6-24	Postes, renseignements 1-43
Associations 2-8	Fiducie, sociétés de 7-3	Préséance, protocole de 1-25
Assurances, compagnies d' 7-13	Fleurs, emblèmes **9**	Premiers ministres 3-43, **4**
Astronomie 1-1	Fondations 2-208	Prix et citations 1-92
Avocats 10-22	Fournisseurs de services internet 5-230	Publications 5-159
	Fuseaux horaires 1-3	
Banques 7-1		Québec, gouvernement 3-193
Bibliothèques 5-1	Galeries d'art 6-29	Quotidiens 5-130
Botaniques, jardins 6-45	Gouvernement 3-43	
Bourses 7-9	Gouvernements canadien et étrangers: Table de	Radiodiffusion, réseaux et stations 5-198
	comparaison 3-226	Reine et Famille royale 3-245
Câblodistributeurs 5-223	Gouvernement, table de référence rapide 3-1	Religions, organisations et dénominations 2-2
Canada, gouvernement du 3-43	Gouverneurs général **2**	Réunions, planificateurs de 1-68
Canaux et écluses 1-64	Hauts-commissaires au Canada 3-248	
Circonscriptions électorales 4-1	Hauts-commissaires canadiens 3-259	Saskatchewan, gouvernement 3-210
Chambre des communes 3-45	Hôpitaux 8-1	Sénat 3-44
Chambres de commerce 7-23		Sociétés canadiennes principales 7-40
Colombie-Britannique, gouvernement 3-105	Île-du-Prince-Édouard, gouvernement 3-187	Sociétés de la Couronne (fédéral) 3-52
Congés 1-24	Importations et exportations 1-55	Statistiques 1-47
Congrès, planification de 1-68	Indice des prix à la consommation 1-54	Syndicats ouvriers 2-195
Conseil privé 3-43		Syndics officiels 10-21
Conseils scolaires et écoles 9-1	Journaux 5-130, 5-159	
Consuls canadiens 3-259	Juges 10-1	Télévision, stations de 5-213
Consuls au Canada 3-248		Terre-Neuve, gouvernement 3-140
Cour canadienne de l'impôt 10-2	Livres, éditeurs 5-115	Territoires du Nord-Ouest, gouvernement . . .3-150
Cour fédérale du Canada 10-1	Lobbyistes 7-35	Titres honorifiques 1-26
Cour suprême du Canada 10-1		Transport aérien 1-67
Cours et juges 10-1	Manitoba, gouvernement 3-120	
	Municipalités 4-1	Universités 9-1
Diplomates 3-248	Musées 6-1	
Distances routières 1-66		Villes et villages 4-1
Drapeaux **1, 8**	Nouveau-Brunswick, gouvernement 3-131	Villes, gouvernement 4-153
	Nouvelle-Écosse, gouvernement 3-154	Yukon, gouvernement 3-221
Écoles 9-1		
Éditeurs 5-115	O Canada 1-25	Zoologiques, jardins 6-44

Les numéros de page en caractères gros font référence à la section illustrée qui suit la page 1-46.

GUIDE TO THE ALMANAC'S REORGANIZATION

Information in this year's edition has been organized into ten new sections: Almanac & Miscellany; Organizations Directory; Government Directory; Municipalities Directory; Communications & Information Management Directory; Arts & Culture Directory; Business & Finance Directory; Health Directory; Education Directory; Legal Directory.

The following lists changes and relocation of major sections of the Almanac, where they differ from the 1996 edition.

1996 Edition	Current Edition
Section 1:	
Financial Institutions	Section 7
Libraries	Section 5
Art Galleries	Section 6
Archives	Section 5
Museums	Section 6
Zoos, Botanical Gardens, Aquaria	Section 6
Book Publishers	Section 5
Newspapers	Section 5
Magazines	Section 5
Radio, TV & Cable stations	Section 5
Boards of Trade/Chambers of Commerce	Section 7
Exhibition Planners	Section 1 (unchanged)
Exhibitions, Shows & Events	Section 1 (unchanged)
Airline & Railway Companies	Section 1 (unchanged)
Hospitals & Health Care Facilities	Section 8
Online Directory (Freenets, Websites etc.)	Section 5
Section 2:	
Organizations (unchanged)	
Section 3:	
Education	Section 9
Section 4:	
Government	Section 3
except for Lobbyists	Section 7
Section 5:	
Municipal Government	Section 4
Section 6:	
(Governors General, Prime Ministers, Flags, Coats of Arms, Emblems, selected Orders & Decorations are found in a special colour section, following page 1-46)	Section 1
Section 7:	
Legal	Section 10

NEW IN THIS EDITION

Historical Statistics, selected from previous editions of the Almanac	Section 1
Canadian/Foreign Government Equivalency Table: Major Trading Partners, their Departments, Agencies compared with Canadian counterparts. Complete listings for each of the fifteen foreign governments.	Section 3
Maps of major regional centres: Greater Vancouver, Ottawa-Hull, Metropolitan Montréal & Toronto	Section 4
Online Service Providers	Section 5
Performing Arts Companies	Section 6
Major Canadian Companies	Section 7
Index to selected University Faculties & Schools	Section 9
Map of 1848 Upper Canada; reproduced from the 1848 edition of the Almanac	Inside Back Cover

For specific pages, refer to the General Index at the back of the book.

SECTION 1

ALMANAC & MISCELLANY

ASTRONOMY IN CANADA	1	FORMS OF ADDRESS	33	WEIGHTS & MEASURES	60
THE CALENDAR	2	ABBREVIATIONS	35	LAND & FRESHWATER AREAS OF	
STANDARD TIME	3	CUSTOMS REGULATIONS FOR CANADIANS		CANADA	63
ASTRONOMICAL TABLES	6	RETURNING FROM ABROAD	39	CLIMATE	65
FIXED AND MOVABLE FESTIVALS AND		ELECTION REGULATIONS	41	DISTANCES BETWEEN MAJOR POINTS IN	
ANNIVERSARIES	24	LIQUOR REGULATIONS	41	CANADA	66
FATHERS OF CONFEDERATION	25	MARRIAGE REGULATIONS	42	AIRLINE AND RAILWAY COMPANIES	67
CANADIAN HONOURS SYSTEM	26	POSTAL INFORMATION	43	EXHIBITIONS, SHOWS & EVENTS	72
BRITISH AND COMMONWEALTH HONOURS	29	STATISTICAL INFORMATION	47	CANADIAN AWARDS	92

See ADDENDA at the back of this book for late changes & additional information.

ASTRONOMICAL CALCULATIONS

Prepared for this publication by John R. Percy, Ph.D., of the David Dunlap Observatory and Erindale College, University of Toronto.

ASTRONOMY IN CANADA

Canada possesses a number of major observatories and research institutes devoted to one phase or other of astronomical research. Some of these are operated by the National Research Council of Canada, others by Canadian universities.

Astronomical research in the National Research Council is carried out by the Herzberg Institute of Astrophysics, which operates the following observatories: the Dominion Astrophysical Observatory at Victoria, with telescopes of 1.8 m (72") and 1.2 m (48") apertures; the Dominion Radio Astrophysical Observatory near Penticton which has, among others, a 26 m (85') paraboloid; and the Ottawa River Solar Observatory. The National Research Council also maintains Canada's Time Service in its Division of Physics.

A number of Canadian universities offer graduate training in astronomy: Victoria, British Columbia (Vancouver); Alberta (Edmonton); Calgary; Western Ontario (London); Waterloo; McMaster (Hamilton); York (Toronto); Toronto; Queen's (Kingston); Montréal; Laval (Québec); and St. Mary's (Halifax). Most of these have some local facilities for observational and theoretical studies, and all of them have access to national facilities in Canada and elsewhere. Among the major observatories operated by Canadian universities are: an infrared telescope opened in 1987 by the University of Calgary; a 1.2 m (48") telescope at the University of Western Ontario; a 1.9 m (74") telescope at the University of Toronto's David Dunlap Observatory in Richmond Hill and a 0.6 m (24") telescope at its Las Campanas Observatory in the Chilean Andes; and a 1.5 m (60") telescope at the Mont Megantic Observatory operated by the University of Montréal and Laval University. There is also a Canadian Institute of Theoretical Astrophysics located at the University of Toronto.

Canadian astronomers also have access to a 3.6 m optical telescope atop Mauna Kea on the island of Hawaii at an elevation of nearly 4200 m. This telescope is shared both as to cost and operation by Canada, France and the state of Hawaii. Canadian astronomers also share (with the Netherlands and the UK) in the operation of the James Clerk Maxwell telescope, a sophisticated millimetre-wave radio telescope at the same site. Canada is a partner, along with several other countries, in Project Gemini, a project to build two 8-m telescopes, one in Hawaii and one in Chile.

Observatories

Observatories are open to the public as follows:

BURKE-GAFFNEY OBSERVATORY, St. Mary's University, Halifax NS B3H 3C3. Public tours are held on the 1st & 3rd Sat. of each month at 7:00 p.m. (Nov. - Mar.) or 9:00 p.m. (Apr. - Oct.), weather permitting. Tours are held every Saturday evening from June through September. Mon. evenings or daytime groups by arrangement. 902/420-5633, 5896.

CANADA-FRANCE-HAWAII TELESCOPE, Mauna Kea, Hawaii, USA: 808/885-7944. By appointment only.

CLIMENHAGA OBSERVATORY, Dept. of Physics & Astronomy, University of Victoria, PO Box 3055, Victoria BC V8W 3P6. 604/721-7747.

DAVID DUNLAP OBSERVATORY, Richmond Hill ON L4C 4Y6. Wed. mornings: 10:00 a.m.; Sat. evenings Apr. - Oct., by reservation. 905/884-2112.

DOMINION ASTROPHYSICAL OBSERVATORY, 5071 West Saanich Road, Victoria BC V8X 3X3. May - Aug.: daily 9:15 a.m.-4:30 p.m.; Sept. -Apr.: Mon. - Fri., 9:15 a.m. - 4:30 p.m.; public observing, Sat. evenings, Apr. - Oct. inclusive. 604/363-0001.

DOMINION RADIO ASTROPHYSICAL OBSERVATORY, Penticton BC V2A 6K3. Conducted Tours: Sun., July - Aug.: 2:00 - 5:00 p.m. Visitors' Centre open year round during daylight hours. 604/490-4355.

HUME CRONYN OBSERVATORY, Department of Astronomy, University of Western Ontario, London ON N6A 3K7. Summer open houses (slide show, followed by viewing of the sky through the 25 cm refractor when the weather is suitable) are held each Saturday night from mid-May until the end of August, 8:30 - 11:00 p.m. A winter public night program is available to groups and individuals by appointment. 519/661-3183.

NATIONAL MUSEUM OF SCIENCE AND TECHNOLOGY, 1867 St. Laurent Blvd., Ottawa ON K1G 5A3. 38 cm refractor (from the former Dominion Observatory), Starlab planetarium. "Discover the Universe" by appointment only, rain or shine. Oct. - May: Group tours, Mon., Tues., Wed., Thurs.; phone for dates and times of public visits throughout the year. 613/991-9219.

OBSERVATOIRE ASTRONOMIQUE DU MONT MEGANTIC, Notre-Dame-des-Bois PQ J0B 2E0. Summer programs. 514/343-6718.

SCIENCE NORTH SOLAR OBSERVATORY, 100 Ramsey Lake Rd., Sudbury ON P3E 5S9. Open every day except Christmas Day, Boxing Day & New Year's Day. 705/522-3701.

GORDON MACMILLAN SOUTHAM OBSERVATORY, 1100 Chestnut St., Vancouver BC V6J 3J9. Open Fri., Sat., Sun. and statutory holidays: 12:00 - 5:00 p.m., 7:00 - 11:00 p.m., weather and volunteer staff permitting. Extended hours during school holidays. 604/738-STAR.

UNIVERSITY OF BRITISH COLUMBIA OBSERVATORY, 2219 Main Mall, Vancouver BC V6T 1Z4. Clear Saturday evenings, year round. 604/822-6186. Tours by appointment: 604/822-2217; Fax: 604/822-6047.

UNIVERSITY OF SASKATCHEWAN OBSERVATORY, Dept. of Physics, Saskatoon SK S7N 5E2. Saturday evening programs year round, if clear; times vary. School groups by appointment. 306/966-6429.

YORK UNIVERSITY OBSERVATORY, 4700 Keele St., North York ON M3J 1P3. Public viewing most Wednesday evenings. 416/736-2100, ext.77773 (recorded message).

Canadian Almanac & Directory 1997

There are the following planetariums, mostly with daily shows:

ALBERTA SCIENCE CENTRE/CALGARY CENTENNIAL PLANETARIUM, Calgary AB. 403/237-STAR (program information).

DORAN PLANETARIUM, Laurentian University, Sudbury ON. 705/675-1151, ext.2227 (reservations).

PLANETARIUM DE MONTRÉAL, Montréal PQ. 514/872-4530.

EDMONTON SPACE AND SCIENCE CENTRE, Edmonton AB. Recorded astronomy information: 403/493-9000/4254.

THE HALIFAX PLANETARIUM, Halifax NS. 902/424-7353.

THE LOCKHART PLANETARIUM, University of Manitoba, Winnipeg MB. 204/474-9785.

H.R. MACMILLAN PLANETARIUM, Vancouver BC. 604/738-STAR.

MANITOBA PLANETARIUM, Winnipeg MB. 204/956-2830.

W.J. MCCALLION PLANETARIUM, Dept. of Physics and Astronomy, McMaster University, 1280 Main Street West, Hamilton ON L8S 4M1. 905/525-9140, ext.27777; Fax: 905/546-1252.

ONTARIO SCIENCE CENTRE, Toronto ON. 416/696-3127.

Many of Canada's professional astronomers and most of Canada's enthusiastic amateur astronomers and telescope makers are members of the Royal Astronomical Society of Canada (see index) which has 22 Centres across Canada, and which celebrated its centenary in 1990.

Most of Canada's professional astronomers belong to the Canadian Astronomical Society (see index).

THE CALENDAR

The calendar is a method of identifying the passage of time and thereby regulating our civil life and religious observances.

Days, months, and years are based on astronomical periods. The day is the time it takes the earth to make one revolution on its axis, the month is associated with the period of orbiting of the moon around the earth, while the year has to do with the orbiting of the earth around the sun.

Many religious ideas and observances have been connected with the changes of the moon, and in ancient times the calendar took account of the moon rather than the seasons. From new moon to new moon is 29.530 days, and from one spring equinox to the next is 365.24219 days. Since the two are incommensurable, the modern calendar disregards the moon, except insofar as our months are roughly equal to a lunation.

The Week

The division of the week is found only among Aryan nations and in nations and in regions into which they have penetrated. The day is, for convenience, divided into 24 equal parts and is the period of a single rotation of the earth upon its own axis.

A solar or astronomical day commences at midnight, and is divided into two equal portions of 12 hours each — those before noon being termed (A.M.) those after noon (P.M.).

The Chinese week consists of 5 days, which are named after iron, wood, water, feathers and earth; they divide the day into 12 parts of 2 hours each.

The Anglo-Saxons named the days of the week after the following deities: Sunday, the Sun; Monday, the Moon; Tuesday, Tuesco (God of War); Wednesday, Woden (God of Storms); Thursday, Thor (God of Thunder); Friday, Freya (Goddess of Love); Saturday, Saturn (God of Time).

The word week is from Wikon (German); = change, succession.

The Julian Calendar

When Julius Caesar came to power, the Roman Calendar was hopelessly confused. With the advice of the Alexandrian astronomer Sosigenes, Julius Caesar established the Julian Calendar. The length of the year was taken as 365 1/4 days, and in order to account for the 1/4 day, an extra day was added every fourth year. From 45 B.C. each month has had its present number of days. In the old Roman Calendar which was based on the moon an extra month was inserted to straighten out the difference between twelve lunations 354.37 days, and 355 days, which they called a year. This was inserted when necessary after February 23rd. In the Julian Calendar the extra day was added by repeating the sixth day before the Kalends (1st) of March, whence comes our word bissextile for leap year.

No very significant change was made till the reform by Pope Gregory XIII in A.D. 1582.

The Julian Calendar is known as the "Old Style" whereas the calendar as improved by Pope Gregory is known as the "New Style". The difference between the two is now 13 days.

The Gregorian Calendar

In that the Solar Year is 11 minutes, 12 seconds less than the Julian Year of 365 1/4 days, it followed in course of years that the Julian Calendar became inaccurate by several days, and in 1582 this difference amounted to 10 days. Pope Gregory XIII, at the suggestion of Aloysius Lilus, an astronomer of Naples, determined to rectify this, and devised the Calendar now known as the Gregorian Calendar. He dropped or cancelled these 10 days — October 5th being called October 15th — and made centurial years leap years only once in 4 centuries; so that whilst 1700, 1800 and 1900 were to be ordinary years 2000, would be leap year. This modification brought the Gregorian year into such close exactitude with the solar year that there is only a difference of 26 seconds, which amounts to a day in 3,323 years. This is the "New Style". The Gregorian Calendar was adopted in Italy, France, Spain, Portugal and Poland in 1582, by most of the German Roman Catholic states, Holland and Flanders in 1583, Hungary in 1587. The adoption in Switzerland began in 1584 and was not completed till 1812. The German and Dutch Protestant states generally, along with Denmark adopted it in 1700, British dominions in 1752, Sweden in 1753, Japan in 1873, China in 1912, Bulgaria in 1915, Soviet Russia in 1918, Yugoslavia in 1919, Romania and Greece in 1924, Turkey in 1927. The rules for Easter have not, however, been adopted by those oriental churches that are not subject to the Papacy.

The difference between the two "Styles" will remain 13 days until A.D. 2100.

The Jewish Calendar

The Jewish Calendar from the institution of the Mosaic Law downward was a lunar one, consisting of twelve months. The cycles of religious feasts commencing with the Passover depended not only on the month but on the moon; the 14th of the month of Abid or Nisan was coincident with the full moon; and the new moons themselves were the occasions of regular festivals; the commencement of the month was generally determined by observations of the new moon, but twelve lunar months would make but 354 1/2 days, the years would be short twelve days of the true year and it was necessary that an additional month, Veader, be inserted about every third year.

The modern Jewish Calendar is based on fixed rules and not on observation. A common year may contain 353, 354 or 355 days and the leap year 383, 384 or 385 days. The intercalary month always contains 30 days and is inserted next before the month Adar which name and place it takes, Adar itself called second Adar or Veadar. Tishri 1 is the Jewish New Year and it cannot be a Sunday, Wednesday or Friday. Tishri 1 is not necessarily the day of new moon but is governed by a mean new moon which is calculated from the value of a mean lunation. It is complicated as compared with the Gregorian Calendar. The intercalary month is introduced seven times in every nineteen years.

The identification of the Jewish months with our own cannot be effected with precision on account of the variations existing between the lunar and solar month.

The Muslim Calendar

The Muslim Calendar is called also the calendar of Hegira (i.e. Migration) and is attributed to the primary migration of Mohammed, the Prophet of Islam, on July 16th, 622 A.D. from Mecca, his native city in the land of Hejaz, Arabia, to the city of Medina in the north of the same land. In Medina the Prophet and Founder of the Islamic Faith died and was buried.

Each year consists of 12 lunar months and, since no intercalation is made, the months go round the seasons in between 32 and 33 years.

Far Eastern Calendars

The ancient Chinese calendar is a lunar calendar, divided into 12 months of either 29 or 30 days. It is synchronized with the solar calendar by the addition of extra months as required. The four-day Chinese New Year (Hsin Nien) begins at the first new moon over China after the sun enters Aquarius, and may fall between January 21 and February 19. The calendar runs on a 60-year cycle, and each year has both a number and a name: 1997 (Ox), 1998 (Tiger), 1999 (Hare/Rabbit), 2000 (Dragon), 2001 (Snake). The three-day Vietnamese New Year (Tet) and the three-to-four-day Korean festival Suhl are set by the same new moon. The Japanese calendar uses the Gregorian date of new year, but with a different epoch.

The Hindu Calendar

The Hindu calendar contains both lunar and solar elements, and is therefore complex. Furthermore, each lunar month is divided into two halves: the dark half (full moon to new moon) and the bright half (new moon to full moon). For some Hindus (primarily South Indian), the lunar month begins on the day following the new moon; for others (primarily North Indian), it begins on the day following the full moon. Likewise, the calculation of the date of the New Year varies. There are some holidays which are set by the solar calendar, as well as several which are set by the lunar calendar.

The Indian Calendar

Various religious groups in India have their own calendars (see The Muslim Calendar, and The Hindu Calendar, above). The Indian civil calendar sets the New Year on March 22 in a common year, and on March 21 in a leap year. The years are reckoned according to the native Saka historical era.

The Zoroastrian Calendar

The Zoroastrian calendar is solar, and consists of 12 months of 30 days; five additional days called "gatha" bring the total days in a year to 365. The calculation of the date of the New Year varies among the various Zoroastrian groups.

The Baha'i Calendar

The Baha'i calendar is astronomically fixed, commencing at the vernal equinox. The calendar is solar, and consists of 19 months of 19 days, with the addition of four or five days to bring the total to 365 or 366.

US Civil Calendar 1997

New Year's Day	Wed. Jan. 1
Martin Luther King's Birthday	Mon. Jan. 20
Lincoln's Birthday	Wed. Feb. 12
Washington's Birthday	Mon. Feb. 17
Memorial Day	Mon. May 26
Independence Day	Fri. July 4
Labor Day	Mon. Sept. 1

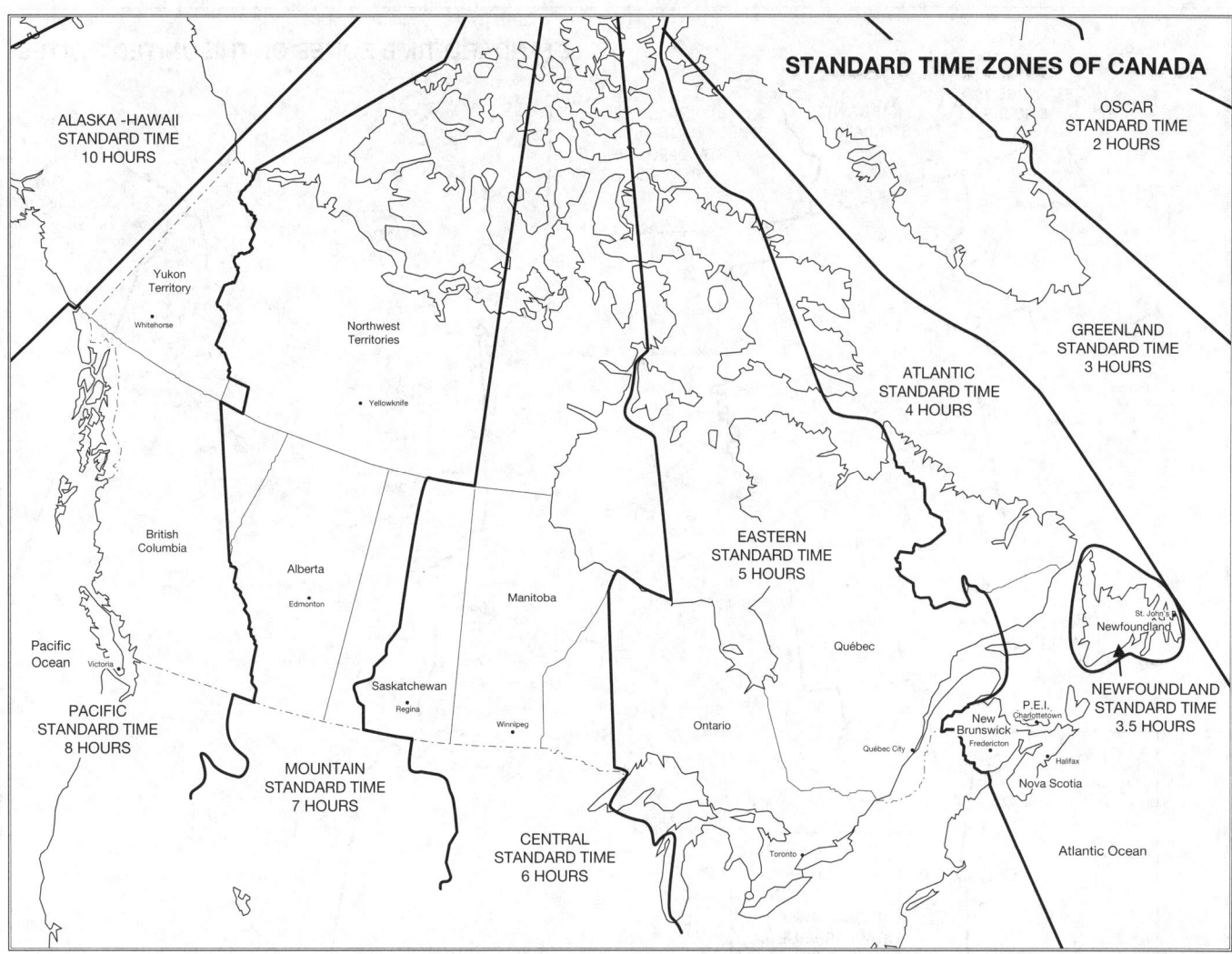

Columbus Day ....Mon. Oct. 13
Election Day ....Tue. Nov. 4
Veterans Day ....Tue. Nov. 11
Thanksgiving Day ....Thu. Nov. 27

United Kingdom Civil Calendar 1997
Accession of Queen Elizabeth II ..Thu. Feb. 6
St. David (Wales) ....Sat. Mar. 1
Commonwealth Day ....Mon. Mar. 10
St. Patrick (Ireland) ....Mon. Mar. 17
Birthday of Queen Elizabeth II ...Mon. Apr. 21
St. George (England) ....Wed. Apr. 23
Coronation Day ....Mon. June 2
Birthday of Prince Philip,
  Duke of Edinburgh ....Tue. June 10
The Queen's Official Birthday ....Sat. June 14
Remembrance Sunday ....Sun. Nov. 9
Birthday of the Prince of Wales ...Fri. Nov. 14
St. Andrew (Scotland) ....Sun. Nov. 30

EPOCHS

The year 5758 of the Jewish era begins at sunset on Oct. 1, 1997, Gregorian Calendar.

The year 1418 of the Mohammedan era, or the era of the Hegira, begins at sunset on May 8, 1997, Gregorian Calendar.

The year 4634 of the Chinese era begins on Feb. 7, 1997.

The year 2657 of the Japanese era begins on Jan. 1, 1997.

The year 1919 of the Indian (Saka) era begins on Mar. 22, 1997.

January 1, 1997, Julian Calendar, corresponds to January 14, 1997, Gregorian Calendar.

The 46th year of the reign of Queen Elizabeth II begins on February 6, 1997.

The 131st year of the Dominion of Canada begins July 1, 1997.

The 222nd year of the Independence of the United States of America begins July 4, 1997.

The Julian Day 2,450,450 begins at Greenwich mean noon January 1, 1997, Gregorian Calendar.

THE SEASONS 1997
Eastern Standard Time
Spring begins .... March 20th .....08 h 55 m
Summer begins ...... June 21st ....03 h 20 m
Autumn begins ...... Sept. 22nd ......18 h 56 m
Winter begins........ Dec. 21st ....15 h 07 m

Eastern Standard time applies in Ontario and Québec. Newfoundland time is 1 1/2 hours later than Eastern Standard time; in the Maritime Provinces, on Atlantic time, time is 1 hour later; in Manitoba and the eastern half of Saskatchewan, on Central time, time is 1 hour earlier; in Alberta and the western half of Saskatchewan, on Mountain time, time is 2 hours earlier; in British Columbia, on Pacific time, time is 3 hours earlier.

STANDARD TIME

Owing to the great breadth of Canada the difference in solar time in various parts of the country is adjusted by the creation of Standard Time Zones, one hour in width, fixed between arbitrary lines running approximately north and south, 15° of longitude apart, the time observed in each zone being an exact, except for Newfoundland, number of hours slow from Greenwich.

Example: When it is 8 a.m. by Pacific Time it is 12 noon by Atlantic Time and 4 p.m. at Greenwich.

There are six zones divided as follows, reckoning from Greenwich:

Newfoundland Standard Time: Newfoundland, excluding Labrador, 3 1/2 hours slow.

Atlantic Standard Time/60th Meridian Time: Labrador, New Brunswick, Nova Scotia, Prince Edward Island, and those parts of Québec and Northwest Territories east of the 63rd Meridian, 4 hours slow.

Eastern Standard Time/75th Meridian Time: Québec west of the 63rd Meridian and Ontario as far west as the 90th Meridian; Northwest Territories between the 68th and 85th Meridian, 5 hours slow.

Central Standard Time/90th Meridian Time: Ontario west of the 90th Meridian, Manitoba, easterly part of Saskatchewan and Northwest Territories between the 85th and 102nd Meridian, 6 hours slow.

Mountain Standard Time/105th Meridian Time: Eastern Saskatchewan (in winter); throughout Alberta and in Northwest Territories west of the 102nd Meridian, 7 hours slow.

Pacific Standard Time/120th Meridian Time: Throughout most of British Columbia and in the Yukon, 8 hours slow.

Railways and airways make up their schedules according to Standard Time in winter and Daylight Saving Time in summer. Solar time around the globe varies four minutes with each degree of longitude.

Canadian Almanac & Directory 1997

1-4 TIME ZONES

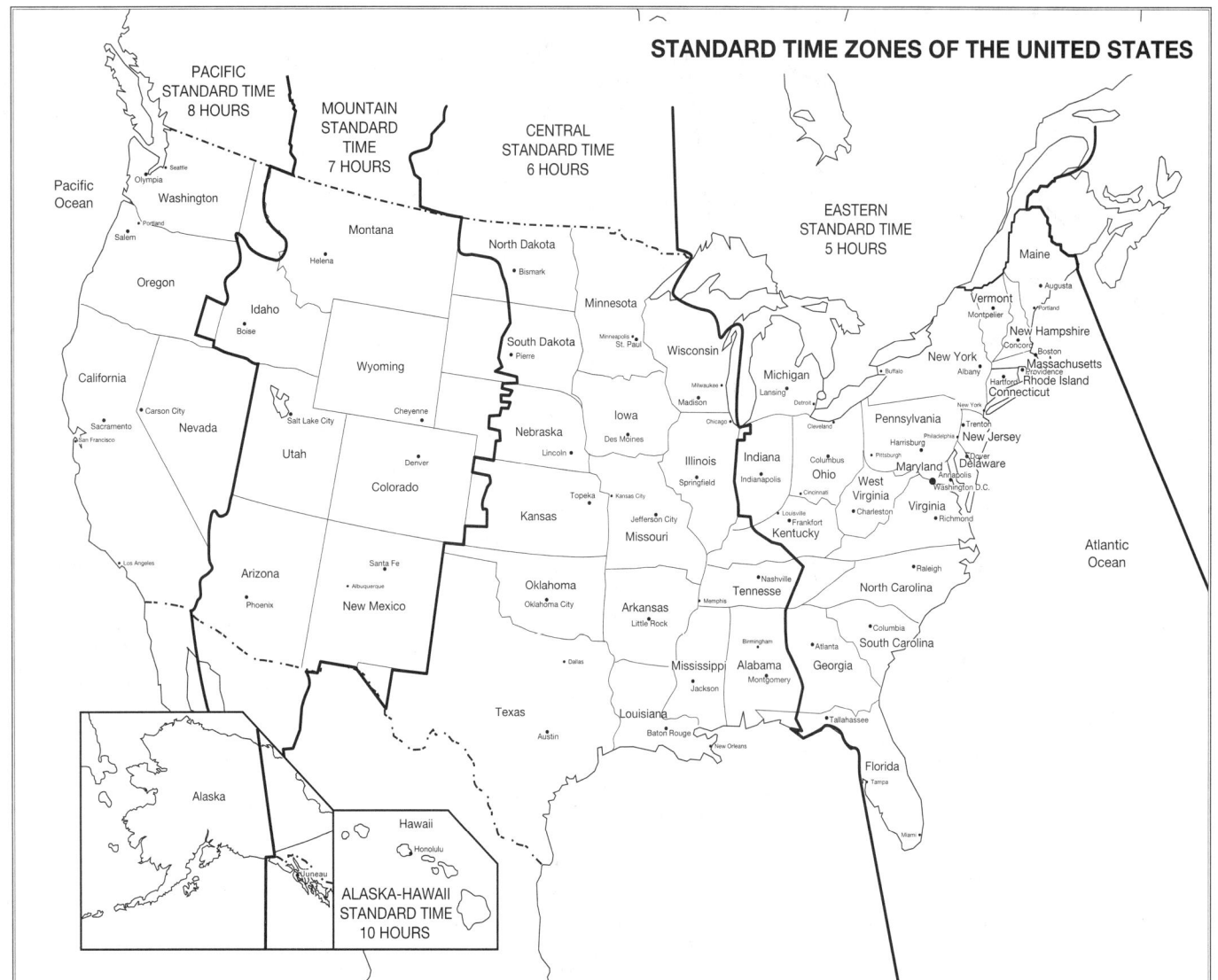

Canadian Almanac & Directory 1997

TIME ZONES 1-5

INTERNATIONAL TIME ZONES

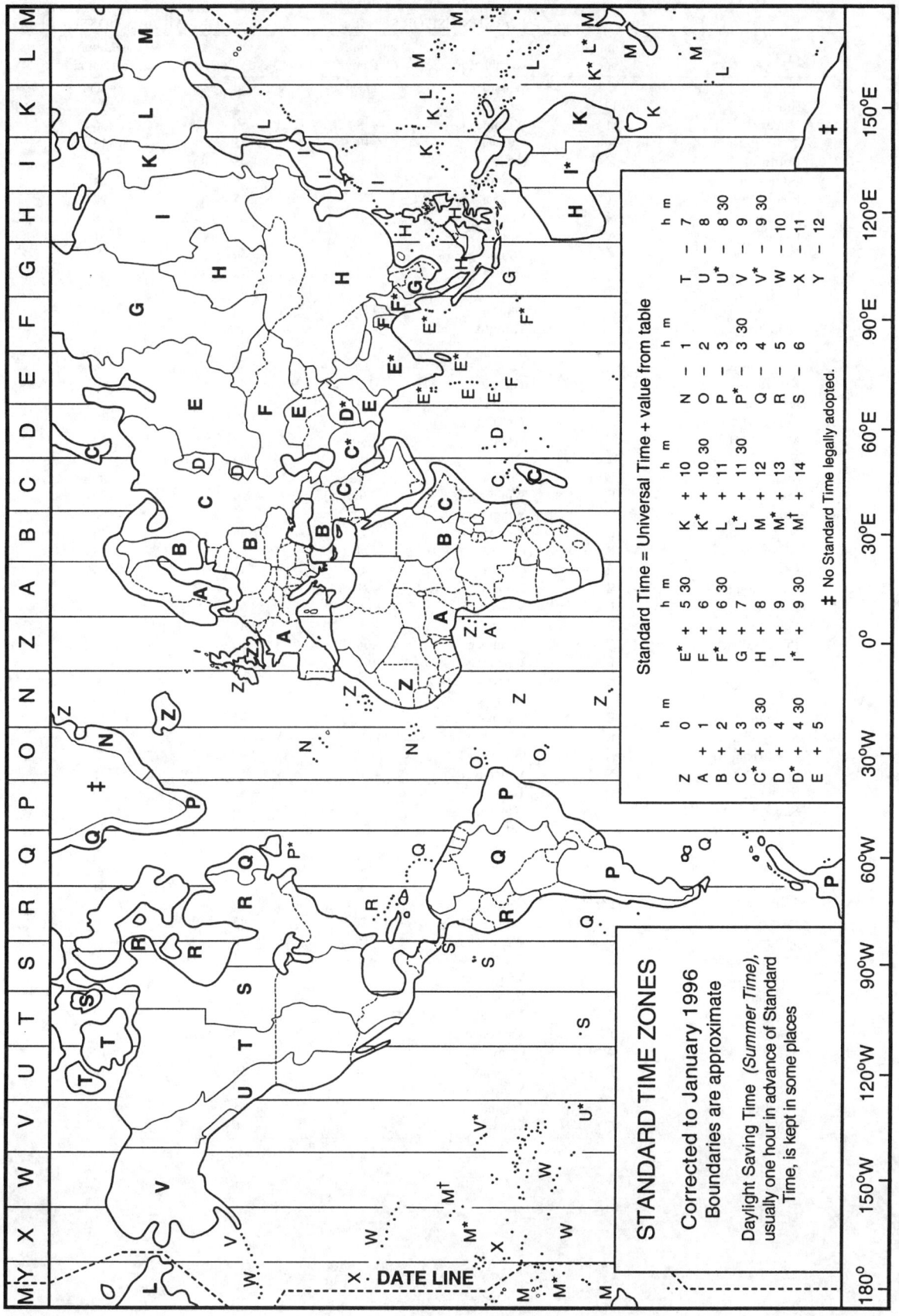

TABLE FOR FINDING APPROXIMATE STANDARD TIME OF SUNRISE, SUNSET, MOONRISE, MOONSET, FOR CANADIAN CITIES AND TOWNS

PLACE	Time Zone	FOR SUNRISE OR SUNSET Take value for	and apply correction	FOR MOONRISE OR MOONSET Take value for	and apply correction
Brandon	C	Winnipeg	+11m	50°	+40m
Brantford	E	Toronto	+ 4	45	+21
Calgary	M	Winnipeg	+ 8	50	+36
Charlottetown	A	Ottawa	+10	45	+13
Cornwall	E	Ottawa	- 4	45	- 1
Edmonton	M	Winnipeg	+ 6	50	+34
Fredericton	A	Ottawa	+24	45	+27
Gander	N	Vancouver	- 4	50	+ 8
Glace Bay	A	Ottawa	- 3	45	0
Goose Bay	A	Winnipeg	-26	50	- 2
Granby	E	Ottawa	-12	45	- 9
Guelph	E	Toronto	+ 3	45	+21
Halifax	A	Ottawa	+11	45	+14
Hamilton	E	Toronto	+ 2	45	+21
Hull	E	Ottawa	0	45	+ 3
Kapuskasing	E	Vancouver	+17	50	+30
Kingston	E	Toronto	-12	45	+ 6
Kitchener	E	Toronto	+ 4	45	+22
London	E	Toronto	+ 8	45	+25
Medicine Hat	M	Winnipeg	- 4	50	+22
Moncton	A	Ottawa	+16	45	+19
Montréal	E	Ottawa	- 9	45	- 6
Moosonee	E	Winnipeg	- 6	50	+23
Moose Jaw	C	Winnipeg	+34	50	+62
Niagara Falls	E	Toronto	- 1	45	+16
North Bay	E	Ottawa	+14	45	+18
Ottawa	E	Ottawa	0	45	+ 3
Owen Sound	E	Ottawa	+21	45	+24
Penticton	P	Vancouver	-14	50	- 2
Peterborough	E	Toronto	- 4	45	+13
Prince Albert	C	Winnipeg	+36	50	+64
Prince Rupert	P	Winnipeg	+12	50	+40
Québec	E	Ottawa	-18	45	-15
Regina	C	Winnipeg	+30	50	+58
St. Catharines	E	Toronto	0	45	+17
St. Hyacinthe	E	Ottawa	-11	45	- 8
Saint John, NB	A	Ottawa	+22	45	+24
St. John's NF	N	Vancouver	-11	50	+ 1
Sarnia	E	Toronto	+12	45	+30
Saskatoon	C	Winnipeg	+38	50	+66
Sault Ste. Marie	E	Ottawa	+34	45	+37
Shawinigan	E	Ottawa	-12	45	- 9
Sherbrooke	E	Ottawa	-14	45	-12
Stratford	E	Toronto	+ 6	45	+24
Sudbury	E	Ottawa	+21	45	+24
Sydney	A	Ottawa	- 2	45	+ 1
The Pas	C	Winnipeg	+16	50	+44
Trois-Rivières	E	Ottawa	-12	45	- 9
Thunder Bay	E	Vancouver	+44	50	+57
Timmins	E	Vancouver	+13	50	+25
Toronto	E	Toronto	0	45	+18
Trail	P	Vancouver	-22	50	-10
Truro	A	Ottawa	+10	45	+13
Vancouver	P	Vancouver	0	50	+12
Victoria	P	Vancouver	+ 2	50	+14
Windsor	E	Toronto	+14	45	+32
Winnipeg	C	Winnipeg	0	50	+28

AZIMUTHS OF THE POINTS OF RISING AND SETTING OF THE SUN FOR LATITUDES 43°N TO 52°N

In Degrees East of North for Rising and West of North for Setting

			43°N	44°N	45°N	46°N	47°N	48°N	49°N	50°N	51°N	52°N
Jan. 2	and	Dec. 11	122	123	124	124	125	126	127	127	128	129
Jan. 10	and	Dec. 3	121	121	122	123	123	124	125	126	127	127
Jan. 16	and	Nov. 27	119	120	120	121	122	122	123	124	125	126
Jan. 21	and	Nov. 22	118	118	119	120	120	121	121	122	123	124
Jan. 25	and	Nov. 17	116	117	117	118	119	119	120	120	121	122
Jan. 29	and	Nov. 14	115	115	116	116	117	118	118	119	119	120
Feb. 2	and	Nov. 10	114	114	114	115	115	116	116	117	118	118
Feb. 5	and	Nov. 6	112	113	113	113	114	114	115	115	116	116
Feb. 9	and	Nov. 3	111	111	111	112	112	113	113	114	114	115
Feb. 12	and	Oct. 31	109	110	110	110	111	111	112	112	113	113
Feb. 15	and	Oct. 28	108	108	109	109	109	110	110	110	111	111
Feb. 18	and	Oct. 25	107	107	107	107	108	108	108	109	109	110
Feb. 20	and	Oct. 22	105	105	106	106	106	106	107	107	108	108
Feb. 23	and	Oct. 19	104	104	104	104	105	105	105	106	106	106
Feb. 26	and	Oct. 17	102	103	103	103	103	104	104	104	104	105
Mar. 1	and	Oct. 14	101	101	101	102	102	102	102	102	103	103
Mar. 3	and	Oct. 11	100	100	100	100	100	100	101	101	101	101
Mar. 6	and	Oct. 9	98	98	98	99	99	99	99	99	100	100
Mar. 8	and	Oct. 6	97	97	97	97	97	97	98	98	98	98
Mar. 11	and	Oct. 4	95	96	96	96	96	96	96	96	96	96
Mar. 13	and	Oct. 1	94	94	94	94	94	94	95	95	95	95
Mar. 16	and	Sept. 28	93	93	93	93	93	93	93	93	93	93
Mar. 18	and	Sept. 26	91	91	91	91	91	92	92	92	92	92
Mar. 21	and	Sept. 23	90	90	90	90	90	90	90	90	90	90
Mar. 23	and	Sept. 21	89	89	89	89	89	88	88	88	88	88
Mar. 26	and	Sept. 18	87	87	87	87	87	87	87	87	87	87
Mar. 28	and	Sept. 16	86	86	86	86	86	86	85	85	85	85
Mar. 31	and	Sept. 13	85	84	84	84	84	84	84	84	84	84
Apr. 3	and	Sept. 10	83	83	83	83	83	83	82	82	82	82
Apr. 5	and	Sept. 8	82	82	82	81	81	81	81	81	80	80
Apr. 8	and	Sept. 5	80	80	80	80	80	80	79	79	79	79
Apr. 11	and	Sept. 2	79	79	79	78	78	78	78	78	77	77
Apr. 13	and	Aug. 30	78	77	77	77	77	76	76	76	76	75
Apr. 16	and	Aug. 28	76	76	76	76	75	75	75	74	74	74
Apr. 19	and	Aug. 25	75	75	74	74	74	73	73	73	72	72
Apr. 22	and	Aug. 22	73	73	73	73	72	72	72	71	71	70
Apr. 25	and	Aug. 19	72	72	71	71	71	70	70	70	69	69
Apr. 28	and	Aug. 16	71	70	70	70	69	69	68	68	67	67
May 1	and	Aug. 12	69	69	69	68	68	67	67	66	66	65
May 5	and	Aug. 9	68	67	67	67	66	66	65	65	64	63
May 8	and	Aug. 5	66	66	66	65	65	64	64	63	62	62
May 12	and	Aug. 2	65	65	64	64	63	62	62	61	61	60
May 16	and	July 28	64	63	63	62	61	61	60	60	59	58
May 21	and	June 24	62	62	61	60	60	59	59	58	57	56
May 26	and	June 19	61	60	60	59	58	58	57	56	55	54
June 1	and	July 12	59	59	58	57	57	56	55	54	53	53
June 10	and	July 3	58	57	56	56	55	54	53	53	52	51

AZIMUTH OF THE SUN AT RISING AND SETTING

Only twice a year, namely about March 21 and September 23, does the sun rise and set more or less exactly in the east and west respectively. It is of interest and sometimes of value to know the position of Sunrise and Sunset at other times. The table above tabulates these in degrees east of north and west of north for Sunrise and Sunset respectively for a selection of latitudes and dates. For latitudes and dates other than those tabulated take simple proportions.

REFERENCES

The tables and charts in the *Canadian Almanac* are intended for simple astronomical observations. To make more extensive observations the following are recommended: *The Observer's Handbook* (obtainable from the Royal Astronomical Society of Canada, 136 Dupont St., Toronto, ON M5R 1V2); *Astronomical Phenomena* (obtainable from The Superintendent of Documents, U.S. Government Printing Office, Washington, D.C.). See also "Suggestions for Further Reading".

NOTES ON THE ASTRONOMICAL TABLES

The purpose of the following notes is to explain those tables which are not self-explanatory and to illustrate how they may be used for places other than those specified.

These tables give Standard Times of Sunrise and Sunset for the four Canadian cities listed. When Daylight Saving Time is in effect, of course, one hour must be added to the listed times. The calculations are for the upper limb (edge) of the sun and for the astronomical (sea) horizon. Accordingly the actual observation of Sunrise or Sunset will differ from the tabulated value if the observer is below or above the level of his visible horizon at the point of Sunrise or Sunset.

The listed times of Moonrise and Moonset have been calculated for places at the stated latitudes and for longitude 5 hours west.

To obtain the approximate times of Sunrise, Sunset, Moonrise and Moonset for other Canadian cities and towns proceed as indicated in the table on page 1-6. The errors for Sunrise and Sunset by this approximate method will seldom exceed 10 minutes in winter and summer or 4 minutes in spring and fall, and for Moonrise and Moonset they will seldom exceed 15 minutes.

The tables have been calculated using a computer program written by Li Sen, using algorithms given in *Astronomy with your Personal Computer* (second edition), by Peter Duffett-Smith (Cambridge University Press, 1990).

1-8 SOLAR AND LUNAR TABLES

JANUARY 1997

Last Quarter	1 d	20 h	45 m
New Moon	8 d	23 h	26 m
First Quarter	15 d	15 h	02 m
Full Moon	23 d	10 h	11 m
Last Quarter	31 d	14 h	40 m

Moon's Phases E.S.T.

SUNRISE AND SUNSET / MOONRISE AND MOONSET (Local Mean Time)

Day of Yr.	Day of Mo.	Day of Wk.	Ottawa E.S.T. Rises	Sets	Toronto E.S.T. Rises	Sets	Winnipeg C.S.T. Rises	Sets	Vancouver P.S.T. Rises	Sets	Lat. 45° Rises	Sets	Lat. 50° Rises	Sets	Day of Wk.	Day of Mo.
			h m	h m	h m	h m	h m	h m	h m	h m	h m	h m	h m	h m		
1	1	Wed	7 42	16 30	7 51	16 51	8 26	16 38	8 07	16 25	-- --	11 30	-- --	11 28	Wed	1
2	2	Thu	7 42	16 30	7 51	16 52	8 26	16 39	8 07	16 26	0 22	11 59	0 25	11 54	Thu	2
3	3	Fri	7 42	16 31	7 51	16 53	8 26	16 40	8 07	16 27	1 23	12 29	1 30	12 21	Fri	3
4	4	Sat	7 42	16 32	7 51	16 54	8 26	16 41	8 07	16 28	2 27	13 04	2 37	12 53	Sat	4
5	5	Sun	7 42	16 33	7 51	16 55	8 25	16 42	8 06	16 29	3 32	13 44	3 45	13 30	Sun	5
6	6	Mon	7 42	16 34	7 51	16 56	8 25	16 44	8 06	16 30	4 37	14 31	4 52	14 16	Mon	6
7	7	Tue	7 42	16 35	7 51	16 57	8 25	16 45	8 06	16 31	5 41	15 27	5 57	15 11	Tue	7
8	8	Wed	7 42	16 36	7 50	16 58	8 24	16 46	8 05	16 33	6 41	16 31	6 57	16 15	Wed	8
9	9	Thu	7 41	16 37	7 50	16 59	8 24	16 47	8 05	16 34	7 35	17 42	7 49	17 28	Thu	9
10	10	Fri	7 41	16 39	7 50	17 00	8 23	16 49	8 04	16 35	8 22	18 56	8 34	18 45	Fri	10
11	11	Sat	7 41	16 40	7 49	17 01	8 23	16 50	8 04	16 37	9 04	20 11	9 12	20 04	Sat	11
12	12	Sun	7 40	16 41	7 49	17 02	8 22	16 51	8 03	16 38	9 41	21 25	9 46	21 22	Sun	12
13	13	Mon	7 40	16 42	7 49	17 04	8 22	16 53	8 03	16 39	10 15	22 37	10 16	22 38	Mon	13
14	14	Tue	7 39	16 43	7 48	17 05	8 21	16 54	8 02	16 41	10 48	23 47	10 45	23 51	Tue	14
15	15	Wed	7 39	16 45	7 48	17 06	8 20	16 56	8 01	16 42	11 20	-- --	11 15	-- --	Wed	15
16	16	Thu	7 38	16 46	7 47	17 07	8 19	16 57	8 00	16 44	11 54	0 54	11 45	1 02	Thu	16
17	17	Fri	7 38	16 47	7 47	17 09	8 19	16 59	8 00	16 45	12 30	2 00	12 18	2 10	Fri	17
18	18	Sat	7 37	16 48	7 46	17 10	8 18	17 00	7 59	16 47	13 10	3 02	12 55	3 15	Sat	18
19	19	Sun	7 36	16 50	7 45	17 11	8 17	17 02	7 58	16 48	13 53	4 00	13 37	4 15	Sun	19
20	20	Mon	7 36	16 51	7 45	17 12	8 16	17 03	7 57	16 50	14 40	4 54	14 24	5 10	Mon	20
21	21	Tue	7 35	16 53	7 44	17 14	8 15	17 05	7 56	16 51	15 31	5 43	15 15	5 59	Tue	21
22	22	Wed	7 34	16 54	7 43	17 15	8 14	17 07	7 55	16 53	16 25	6 27	16 11	6 41	Wed	22
23	23	Thu	7 33	16 55	7 42	17 16	8 13	17 08	7 54	16 54	17 21	7 05	17 09	7 18	Thu	23
24	24	Fri	7 32	16 57	7 42	17 18	8 11	17 10	7 53	16 56	18 18	7 40	18 09	7 51	Fri	24
25	25	Sat	7 32	16 58	7 41	17 19	8 10	17 11	7 52	16 58	19 16	8 11	19 09	8 19	Sat	25
26	26	Sun	7 31	16 59	7 40	17 20	8 09	17 13	7 50	16 59	20 14	8 40	20 10	8 45	Sun	26
27	27	Mon	7 30	17 01	7 39	17 22	8 08	17 15	7 49	17 01	21 12	9 07	21 12	9 09	Mon	27
28	28	Tue	7 29	17 02	7 38	17 23	8 07	17 16	7 48	17 02	22 11	9 34	22 14	9 33	Tue	28
29	29	Wed	7 28	17 04	7 37	17 24	8 05	17 18	7 47	17 04	23 11	10 01	23 17	9 58	Wed	29
30	30	Thu	7 26	17 05	7 36	17 26	8 04	17 20	7 45	17 06	-- --	10 31	-- --	10 24	Thu	30
31	31	Fri	7 25	17 07	7 35	17 27	8 02	17 22	7 44	17 07	0 12	11 02	0 21	10 53	Fri	31

FEBRUARY 1997

New Moon	7 d	10 h	06 m
First Quarter	14 d	03 h	58 m
Full Moon	22 d	05 h	27 m

Moon's Phases E.S.T.

SUNRISE AND SUNSET / MOONRISE AND MOONSET (Local Mean Time)

Day of Yr.	Day of Mo.	Day of Wk.	Ottawa E.S.T. Rises	Sets	Toronto E.S.T. Rises	Sets	Winnipeg C.S.T. Rises	Sets	Vancouver P.S.T. Rises	Sets	Lat. 45° Rises	Sets	Lat. 50° Rises	Sets	Day of Wk.	Day of Mo.
			h m	h m	h m	h m	h m	h m	h m	h m	h m	h m	h m	h m		
32	1	Sat	7 24	17 08	7 34	17 28	8 01	17 23	7 43	17 09	1 14	11 39	1 26	11 26	Sat	1
33	2	Sun	7 23	17 09	7 33	17 30	8 00	17 25	7 41	17 11	2 18	12 21	2 32	12 06	Sun	2
34	3	Mon	7 22	17 11	7 31	17 31	7 58	17 27	7 40	17 12	3 20	13 10	3 36	12 54	Mon	3
35	4	Tue	7 21	17 12	7 30	17 33	7 57	17 28	7 38	17 14	4 21	14 08	4 37	13 52	Tue	4
36	5	Wed	7 19	17 14	7 29	17 34	7 55	17 30	7 37	17 16	5 17	15 14	5 33	14 59	Wed	5
37	6	Thu	7 18	17 15	7 28	17 35	7 53	17 32	7 35	17 17	6 08	16 27	6 22	16 14	Thu	6
38	7	Fri	7 17	17 17	7 27	17 37	7 52	17 34	7 34	17 19	6 54	17 42	7 04	17 33	Fri	7
39	8	Sat	7 15	17 18	7 25	17 38	7 50	17 35	7 32	17 21	7 34	18 59	7 41	18 54	Sat	8
40	9	Sun	7 14	17 20	7 24	17 39	7 49	17 37	7 31	17 22	8 12	20 15	8 15	20 14	Sun	9
41	10	Mon	7 13	17 21	7 23	17 41	7 47	17 39	7 29	17 24	8 46	21 29	8 46	21 32	Mon	10
42	11	Tue	7 11	17 23	7 21	17 42	7 45	17 40	7 27	17 26	9 20	22 40	9 16	22 47	Tue	11
43	12	Wed	7 10	17 24	7 20	17 43	7 43	17 42	7 25	17 27	9 55	23 48	9 47	24 00	Wed	12
44	13	Thu	7 08	17 26	7 19	17 45	7 42	17 44	7 24	17 29	10 31	-- --	10 21	24 00	Thu	13
45	14	Fri	7 07	17 27	7 17	17 46	7 40	17 46	7 22	17 31	11 10	0 53	10 57	1 06	Fri	14
46	15	Sat	7 05	17 28	7 16	17 48	7 38	17 47	7 20	17 32	11 52	1 54	11 37	2 08	Sat	15
47	16	Sun	7 04	17 30	7 14	17 49	7 36	17 49	7 19	17 34	12 38	2 49	12 22	3 05	Sun	16
48	17	Mon	7 02	17 31	7 13	17 50	7 34	17 51	7 17	17 36	13 28	3 40	13 12	3 56	Mon	17
49	18	Tue	7 01	17 33	7 11	17 52	7 33	17 52	7 15	17 37	14 20	4 25	14 05	4 40	Tue	18
50	19	Wed	6 59	17 34	7 10	17 53	7 31	17 54	7 13	17 39	15 15	5 05	15 02	5 19	Wed	19
51	20	Thu	6 57	17 36	7 08	17 54	7 29	17 56	7 11	17 41	16 12	5 41	16 01	5 53	Thu	20
52	21	Fri	6 56	17 37	7 07	17 56	7 27	17 57	7 09	17 42	17 09	6 14	17 01	6 22	Fri	21
53	22	Sat	6 54	17 38	7 05	17 57	7 25	17 59	7 07	17 44	18 07	6 43	18 02	6 49	Sat	22
54	23	Sun	6 53	17 40	7 03	17 58	7 23	18 01	7 05	17 46	19 06	7 11	19 04	7 15	Sun	23
55	24	Mon	6 51	17 41	7 02	18 00	7 21	18 03	7 04	17 47	20 04	7 38	20 06	7 39	Mon	24
56	25	Tue	6 49	17 43	7 00	18 01	7 19	18 04	7 02	17 49	21 04	8 06	21 08	8 03	Tue	25
57	26	Wed	6 47	17 44	6 59	18 02	7 17	18 06	7 00	17 51	22 04	8 34	22 11	8 28	Wed	26
58	27	Thu	6 46	17 45	6 57	18 03	7 15	18 08	6 58	17 52	23 05	9 05	23 15	8 56	Thu	27
59	28	Fri	6 44	17 47	6 55	18 05	7 13	18 09	6 56	17 54	-- --	9 39	-- --	9 27	Fri	28

Canadian Almanac & Directory 1997

SOLAR AND LUNAR TABLES 1-9

MARCH 1997

Last Quarter	2 d	04 h	38 m
New Moon	8 d	20 h	15 m
First Quarter	15 d	19 h	06 m
Full Moon	23 d	23 h	45 m
Last Quarter	31 d	14 h	38 m

Moon's Phases E.S.T.

SUNRISE AND SUNSET / MOONRISE AND MOONSET (Local Mean Time)

Day of Yr.	Day of Mo.	Day of Wk.	Ottawa E.S.T. Rises	Sets	Toronto E.S.T. Rises	Sets	Winnipeg C.S.T. Rises	Sets	Vancouver P.S.T. Rises	Sets	Lat. 45° Rises	Sets	Lat. 50° Rises	Sets	Day of Wk.	Day of Mo.
			h m	h m	h m	h m	h m	h m	h m	h m	h m	h m	h m	h m		
60	1	Sat	6 42	17 48	6 54	18 06	7 11	18 11	6 54	17 55	0 06	10 17	0 19	10 04	Sat	1
61	2	Sun	6 40	17 50	6 52	18 07	7 09	18 12	6 52	17 57	1 07	11 02	1 22	10 47	Sun	2
62	3	Mon	6 39	17 51	6 50	18 09	7 07	18 14	6 50	17 59	2 07	11 54	2 23	11 38	Mon	3
63	4	Tue	6 37	17 52	6 49	18 10	7 05	18 16	6 48	18 00	3 03	12 54	3 19	12 38	Tue	4
64	5	Wed	6 35	17 54	6 47	18 11	7 03	18 17	6 46	18 02	3 55	14 01	4 09	13 47	Wed	5
65	6	Thu	6 33	17 55	6 45	18 12	7 01	18 19	6 44	18 03	4 42	15 13	4 54	15 02	Thu	6
66	7	Fri	6 31	17 56	6 43	18 14	6 58	18 21	6 42	18 05	5 24	16 29	5 33	16 21	Fri	7
67	8	Sat	6 30	17 58	6 42	18 15	6 56	18 22	6 39	18 07	6 03	17 45	6 08	17 42	Sat	8
68	9	Sun	6 28	17 59	6 40	18 16	6 54	18 24	6 37	18 08	6 40	19 00	6 41	19 00	Sun	9
69	10	Mon	6 26	18 00	6 38	18 17	6 52	18 26	6 35	18 10	7 15	20 16	7 13	20 21	Mon	10
70	11	Tue	6 24	18 02	6 36	18 19	6 50	18 27	6 33	18 11	7 50	21 28	7 44	21 37	Tue	11
71	12	Wed	6 22	18 03	6 35	18 20	6 48	18 29	6 31	18 13	8 27	22 37	8 18	22 49	Wed	12
72	13	Thu	6 20	18 05	6 33	18 21	6 46	18 30	6 29	18 14	9 06	23 42	8 54	24 00	Thu	13
73	14	Fri	6 19	18 06	6 31	18 22	6 44	18 32	6 27	18 16	9 48	-- --	9 34	24 00	Fri	14
74	15	Sat	6 17	18 07	6 29	18 24	6 41	18 34	6 25	18 18	10 34	0 41	10 18	1 00	Sat	15
75	16	Sun	6 15	18 08	6 27	18 25	6 39	18 35	6 23	18 19	11 23	1 35	11 07	1 51	Sun	16
76	17	Mon	6 13	18 10	6 26	18 26	6 37	18 37	6 21	18 21	12 15	2 22	12 00	2 38	Mon	17
77	18	Tue	6 11	18 11	6 24	18 27	6 35	18 38	6 18	18 22	13 09	3 05	12 56	3 19	Tue	18
78	19	Wed	6 09	18 12	6 22	18 28	6 33	18 40	6 16	18 24	14 05	3 42	13 54	3 54	Wed	19
79	20	Thu	6 07	18 14	6 20	18 30	6 31	18 41	6 14	18 25	15 02	4 15	14 54	4 25	Thu	20
80	21	Fri	6 05	18 15	6 18	18 31	6 28	18 43	6 12	18 27	16 00	4 46	15 54	4 53	Fri	21
81	22	Sat	6 03	18 16	6 17	18 32	6 26	18 45	6 10	18 28	16 58	5 14	16 55	5 19	Sat	22
82	23	Sun	6 01	18 18	6 15	18 33	6 24	18 46	6 08	18 30	17 57	5 42	17 58	5 43	Sun	23
83	24	Mon	6 00	18 19	6 13	18 35	6 22	18 48	6 06	18 31	18 57	6 09	19 01	6 08	Mon	24
84	25	Tue	5 58	18 20	6 11	18 36	6 20	18 49	6 04	18 33	19 58	6 37	20 04	6 33	Tue	25
85	26	Wed	5 56	18 22	6 09	18 37	6 18	18 51	6 01	18 34	20 59	7 07	21 08	7 00	Wed	26
86	27	Thu	5 54	18 23	6 08	18 38	6 15	18 52	5 59	18 36	22 01	7 40	22 12	7 30	Thu	27
87	28	Fri	5 52	18 24	6 06	18 39	6 13	18 54	5 57	18 37	23 01	8 17	23 16	8 04	Fri	28
88	29	Sat	5 50	18 25	6 04	18 41	6 11	18 56	5 55	18 39	23 59	9 00	-- --	8 45	Sat	29
89	30	Sun	5 48	18 27	6 02	18 42	6 09	18 57	5 53	18 40	-- --	9 48	0 16	9 32	Sun	30
90	31	Mon	5 46	18 28	6 00	18 43	6 07	18 59	5 51	18 42	0 56	10 44	1 13	10 28	Mon	31

APRIL 1997

New Moon	7 d	06 h	02 m
First Quarter	14 d	12 h	00 m
Full Moon	22 d	15 h	33 m
Last Quarter	29 d	21 h	37 m

Moon's Phases E.S.T.

SUNRISE AND SUNSET / MOONRISE AND MOONSET (Local Mean Time)

Day of Yr.	Day of Mo.	Day of Wk.	Ottawa E.S.T. Rises	Sets	Toronto E.S.T. Rises	Sets	Winnipeg C.S.T. Rises	Sets	Vancouver P.S.T. Rises	Sets	Lat. 45° Rises	Sets	Lat. 50° Rises	Sets	Day of Wk.	Day of Mo.
			h m	h m	h m	h m	h m	h m	h m	h m	h m	h m	h m	h m		
91	1	Tue	5 44	18 29	5 59	18 44	6 05	19 00	5 49	18 44	1 48	11 46	2 03	11 31	Tue	1
92	2	Wed	5 43	18 31	5 57	18 45	6 02	19 02	5 47	18 45	2 35	12 54	2 48	12 41	Wed	2
93	3	Thu	5 41	18 32	5 55	18 46	6 00	19 03	5 45	18 47	3 18	14 05	3 28	13 56	Thu	3
94	4	Fri	5 39	18 33	5 53	18 48	5 58	19 05	5 42	18 48	3 57	15 19	4 04	15 14	Fri	4
95	5	Sat	5 37	18 34	5 51	18 49	5 56	19 07	5 40	18 50	4 33	16 34	4 36	16 32	Sat	5
96	6	Sun	5 35	18 36	5 50	18 50	5 54	19 08	5 38	18 51	5 08	17 49	5 08	17 51	Sun	6
97	7	Mon	5 33	18 37	5 48	18 51	5 52	19 10	5 36	18 53	5 43	19 03	5 39	19 09	Mon	7
98	8	Tue	5 31	18 38	5 46	18 52	5 50	19 11	5 34	18 54	6 20	20 15	6 12	20 24	Tue	8
99	9	Wed	5 30	18 40	5 44	18 54	5 48	19 13	5 32	18 56	6 58	21 23	6 47	21 36	Wed	9
100	10	Thu	5 28	18 41	5 43	18 55	5 45	19 14	5 30	18 57	7 40	22 27	7 26	22 42	Thu	10
101	11	Fri	5 26	18 42	5 41	18 56	5 43	19 16	5 28	18 59	8 25	23 25	8 10	23 41	Fri	11
102	12	Sat	5 24	18 43	5 39	18 57	5 41	19 17	5 26	19 00	9 14	-- --	8 58	-- --	Sat	12
103	13	Sun	5 22	18 45	5 38	18 58	5 39	19 19	5 24	19 02	10 06	0 16	9 50	0 32	Sun	13
104	14	Mon	5 20	18 46	5 36	19 00	5 37	19 21	5 22	19 03	11 01	1 01	10 46	1 16	Mon	14
105	15	Tue	5 19	18 47	5 34	19 01	5 35	19 22	5 20	19 05	11 57	1 41	11 44	1 54	Tue	15
106	16	Wed	5 17	18 49	5 33	19 02	5 33	19 24	5 18	19 06	12 54	2 16	12 44	2 27	Wed	16
107	17	Thu	5 15	18 50	5 31	19 03	5 31	19 25	5 16	19 08	13 51	2 47	13 44	2 56	Thu	17
108	18	Fri	5 13	18 51	5 29	19 04	5 29	19 27	5 14	19 09	14 49	3 17	14 45	3 22	Fri	18
109	19	Sat	5 12	18 52	5 28	19 06	5 27	19 28	5 12	19 11	15 48	3 44	15 47	3 47	Sat	19
110	20	Sun	5 10	18 54	5 26	19 07	5 25	19 30	5 10	19 12	16 48	4 12	16 50	4 11	Sun	20
111	21	Mon	5 08	18 55	5 24	19 08	5 23	19 31	5 08	19 14	17 48	4 39	17 54	4 36	Mon	21
112	22	Tue	5 07	18 56	5 23	19 09	5 21	19 33	5 06	19 15	18 50	5 09	18 58	5 02	Tue	22
113	23	Wed	5 05	18 58	5 21	19 10	5 19	19 35	5 04	19 17	19 52	5 41	20 04	5 32	Wed	23
114	24	Thu	5 03	18 59	5 20	19 12	5 17	19 36	5 03	19 18	20 54	6 17	21 08	6 05	Thu	24
115	25	Fri	5 02	19 00	5 18	19 13	5 15	19 38	5 01	19 20	21 55	6 58	22 11	6 44	Fri	25
116	26	Sat	5 00	19 01	5 17	19 14	5 14	19 39	4 59	19 21	22 53	7 45	23 09	7 29	Sat	26
117	27	Sun	4 58	19 03	5 15	19 15	5 12	19 41	4 57	19 23	23 46	8 39	-- --	8 22	Sun	27
118	28	Mon	4 57	19 04	5 14	19 16	5 10	19 42	4 55	19 24	-- --	9 39	0 00	9 23	Mon	28
119	29	Tue	4 55	19 05	5 12	19 17	5 08	19 44	4 54	19 26	0 34	10 43	0 48	10 30	Tue	29
120	30	Wed	4 54	19 07	5 11	19 19	5 06	19 45	4 52	19 27	1 17	11 52	1 28	11 42	Wed	30

Canadian Almanac & Directory 1997

1-10 SOLAR AND LUNAR TABLES

MAY 1997	New Moon .... 6 d 15 h 47 m First Quarter .... 14 d 05 h 55 m Full Moon .... 22 d 04 h 13 m Last Quarter .... 29 d 02 h 51 m	Moon's Phases E.S.T.

SUNRISE AND SUNSET / MOONRISE AND MOONSET (Local Mean Time)

Day of Yr.	Day of Mo.	Day of Wk.	Ottawa E.S.T. Rises	Sets	Toronto E.S.T. Rises	Sets	Winnipeg C.S.T. Rises	Sets	Vancouver P.S.T. Rises	Sets	Lat. 45° Rises	Sets	Lat. 50° Rises	Sets	Day of Wk.	Day of Mo.
			h m	h m	h m	h m	h m	h m	h m	h m	h m	h m	h m	h m		
121	1	Thu	4 52	19 08	5 09	19 20	5 05	19 47	4 50	19 29	1 56	13 03	2 04	12 56	Thu	1
122	2	Fri	4 51	19 09	5 08	19 21	5 03	19 48	4 48	19 30	2 32	14 15	2 36	14 12	Fri	2
123	3	Sat	4 49	19 10	5 07	19 22	5 01	19 50	4 47	19 32	3 06	15 28	3 07	15 28	Sat	3
124	4	Sun	4 48	19 12	5 05	19 23	4 59	19 51	4 45	19 33	3 39	16 40	3 37	16 45	Sun	4
125	5	Mon	4 46	19 13	5 04	19 25	4 58	19 53	4 43	19 35	4 14	17 52	4 08	18 00	Mon	5
126	6	Tue	4 45	19 14	5 03	19 26	4 56	19 54	4 42	19 36	4 51	19 02	4 41	19 13	Tue	6
127	7	Wed	4 43	19 15	5 01	19 27	4 54	19 56	4 40	19 38	5 31	20 09	5 18	20 23	Wed	7
128	8	Thu	4 42	19 17	5 00	19 28	4 53	19 57	4 39	19 39	6 14	21 11	6 00	21 26	Thu	8
129	9	Fri	4 41	19 18	4 59	19 29	4 51	19 59	4 37	19 40	7 02	22 06	6 46	22 22	Fri	9
130	10	Sat	4 39	19 19	4 57	19 30	4 50	20 00	4 36	19 42	7 54	22 55	7 38	23 11	Sat	10
131	11	Sun	4 38	19 20	4 56	19 31	4 48	20 02	4 34	19 43	8 48	23 38	8 33	23 52	Sun	11
132	12	Mon	4 37	19 21	4 55	19 32	4 47	20 03	4 33	19 45	9 45	-- --	9 31	-- --	Mon	12
133	13	Tue	4 35	19 23	4 54	19 34	4 45	20 05	4 31	19 46	10 42	0 15	10 31	0 27	Tue	13
134	14	Wed	4 34	19 24	4 53	19 35	4 44	20 06	4 30	19 47	11 40	0 48	11 32	0 58	Wed	14
135	15	Thu	4 33	19 25	4 52	19 36	4 42	20 07	4 29	19 49	12 38	1 18	12 33	1 25	Thu	15
136	16	Fri	4 32	19 26	4 51	19 37	4 41	20 09	4 27	19 50	13 36	1 46	13 34	1 50	Fri	16
137	17	Sat	4 31	19 27	4 50	19 38	4 40	20 10	4 26	19 51	14 35	2 14	14 36	2 14	Sat	17
138	18	Sun	4 30	19 28	4 49	19 39	4 38	20 12	4 25	19 53	15 36	2 41	15 40	2 39	Sun	18
139	19	Mon	4 29	19 30	4 48	19 40	4 37	20 13	4 23	19 54	16 37	3 09	16 44	3 04	Mon	19
140	20	Tue	4 28	19 31	4 47	19 41	4 36	20 14	4 22	19 55	17 40	3 40	17 50	3 32	Tue	20
141	21	Wed	4 27	19 32	4 46	19 42	4 35	20 16	4 21	19 57	18 43	4 15	18 56	4 03	Wed	21
142	22	Thu	4 26	19 33	4 45	19 43	4 34	20 17	4 20	19 58	19 46	4 54	20 01	4 40	Thu	22
143	23	Fri	4 25	19 34	4 44	19 44	4 33	20 18	4 15	19 59	20 46	5 39	21 03	5 24	Fri	23
144	24	Sat	4 24	19 35	4 43	19 45	4 31	20 19	4 14	20 00	21 42	6 32	21 59	6 15	Sat	24
145	25	Sun	4 23	19 36	4 43	19 46	4 30	20 20	4 13	20 01	22 33	7 31	22 48	7 15	Sun	25
146	26	Mon	4 22	19 37	4 42	19 47	4 29	20 22	4 12	20 03	23 18	8 35	23 31	8 21	Mon	26
147	27	Tue	4 21	19 38	4 41	19 48	4 28	20 23	4 11	20 04	24 00	9 43	-- --	9 32	Tue	27
148	28	Wed	4 21	19 39	4 41	19 49	4 28	20 24	4 10	20 05	-- --	10 54	0 08	10 45	Wed	28
149	29	Thu	4 20	19 40	4 40	19 50	4 27	20 25	4 09	20 06	0 35	12 05	0 41	12 00	Thu	29
150	30	Fri	4 19	19 41	4 39	19 50	4 26	20 26	4 09	20 07	1 08	13 16	1 11	13 15	Fri	30
151	31	Sat	4 18	19 42	4 39	19 51	4 25	20 27	4 08	20 08	1 41	14 26	1 40	14 29	Sat	31

JUNE 1997	New Moon .... 5 d 02 h 04 m First Quarter .... 12 d 23 h 51 m Full Moon .... 20 d 14 h 09 m Last Quarter .... 27 d 07 h 42 m	Moon's Phases E.S.T.

SUNRISE AND SUNSET / MOONRISE AND MOONSET (Local Mean Time)

Day of Yr.	Day of Mo.	Day of Wk.	Ottawa E.S.T. Rises	Sets	Toronto E.S.T. Rises	Sets	Winnipeg C.S.T. Rises	Sets	Vancouver P.S.T. Rises	Sets	Lat. 45° Rises	Sets	Lat. 50° Rises	Sets	Day of Wk.	Day of Mo.
			h m	h m	h m	h m	h m	h m	h m	h m	h m	h m	h m	h m		
152	1	Sun	4 18	19 43	4 38	19 52	4 24	20 28	4 07	20 09	2 14	15 37	2 09	15 43	Sun	1
153	2	Mon	4 17	19 44	4 38	19 53	4 24	20 29	4 07	20 10	2 49	16 46	2 41	16 56	Mon	2
154	3	Tue	4 17	19 44	4 37	19 54	4 23	20 30	4 06	20 11	3 26	17 53	3 15	18 06	Tue	3
155	4	Wed	4 16	19 45	4 37	19 54	4 22	20 31	4 05	20 12	4 07	18 56	3 53	19 12	Wed	4
156	5	Thu	4 16	19 46	4 37	19 55	4 22	20 32	4 05	20 13	4 52	19 55	4 37	20 11	Thu	5
157	6	Fri	4 15	19 47	4 36	19 56	4 21	20 33	4 04	20 13	5 42	20 47	5 26	21 03	Fri	6
158	7	Sat	4 15	19 47	4 36	19 56	4 21	20 34	4 04	20 14	6 36	21 33	6 20	21 48	Sat	7
159	8	Sun	4 15	19 48	4 36	19 57	4 21	20 34	4 03	20 15	7 32	22 14	7 17	22 27	Sun	8
160	9	Mon	4 14	19 49	4 35	19 58	4 20	20 35	4 03	20 16	8 30	22 49	8 17	22 59	Mon	9
161	10	Tue	4 14	19 49	4 35	19 58	4 20	20 36	4 03	20 16	9 28	23 20	9 18	23 28	Tue	10
162	11	Wed	4 14	19 50	4 35	19 59	4 20	20 36	4 03	20 17	10 26	23 49	10 19	23 54	Wed	11
163	12	Thu	4 14	19 51	4 35	19 59	4 19	20 37	4 02	20 18	11 24	-- --	11 20	-- --	Thu	12
164	13	Fri	4 13	19 51	4 35	20 00	4 19	20 38	4 02	20 18	12 23	0 16	12 22	0 18	Fri	13
165	14	Sat	4 13	19 52	4 35	20 00	4 19	20 38	4 02	20 19	13 22	0 43	13 24	0 42	Sat	14
166	15	Sun	4 13	19 52	4 35	20 01	4 19	20 39	4 02	20 19	14 22	1 10	14 28	1 06	Sun	15
167	16	Mon	4 13	19 53	4 35	20 01	4 19	20 39	4 02	20 19	15 24	1 39	15 33	1 33	Mon	16
168	17	Tue	4 13	19 53	4 35	20 01	4 19	20 39	4 02	20 20	16 27	2 12	16 39	2 02	Tue	17
169	18	Wed	4 13	19 53	4 35	20 02	4 19	20 40	4 02	20 20	17 30	2 48	17 45	2 36	Wed	18
170	19	Thu	4 13	19 54	4 35	20 02	4 19	20 40	4 02	20 20	18 33	3 31	18 49	3 16	Thu	19
171	20	Fri	4 14	19 54	4 35	20 02	4 19	20 40	4 02	20 21	19 33	4 21	19 49	4 04	Fri	20
172	21	Sat	4 14	19 54	4 35	20 02	4 19	20 41	4 03	20 21	20 27	5 18	20 43	5 01	Sat	21
173	22	Sun	4 14	19 54	4 36	20 03	4 16	20 41	4 03	20 21	21 16	6 22	21 30	6 07	Sun	22
174	23	Mon	4 14	19 55	4 36	20 03	4 16	20 41	4 03	20 21	21 59	7 31	22 10	7 18	Mon	23
175	24	Tue	4 14	19 55	4 36	20 03	4 16	20 41	4 03	20 21	22 37	8 42	22 45	8 33	Tue	24
176	25	Wed	4 15	19 55	4 37	20 03	4 17	20 41	4 04	20 21	23 20	9 55	23 16	9 49	Wed	25
177	26	Thu	4 15	19 55	4 37	20 03	4 17	20 41	4 04	20 21	23 45	11 07	23 46	11 04	Thu	26
178	27	Fri	4 15	19 55	4 37	20 03	4 18	20 41	4 05	20 21	-- --	12 17	-- --	12 19	Fri	27
179	28	Sat	4 16	19 55	4 38	20 03	4 18	20 41	4 05	20 21	0 18	13 27	0 15	13 33	Sat	28
180	29	Sun	4 16	19 55	4 38	20 03	4 19	20 40	4 06	20 21	0 51	14 36	0 44	14 45	Sun	29
181	30	Mon	4 17	19 55	4 39	20 03	4 19	20 40	4 06	20 21	1 26	15 42	1 17	15 54	Mon	30

Canadian Almanac & Directory 1997

SOLAR AND LUNAR TABLES 1-11

	JULY 1997	New Moon .... First Quarter .... Full Moon .... Last Quarter............	4 d 12 d 19 d 26 d	13 h 16 h 22 h 13 h	40 m 44 m 20 m 28 m	Moon's Phases E.S.T.

Day of Yr.	Day of Mo.	Day of Wk.	Ottawa E.S.T. Rises	Sets	Toronto E.S.T. Rises	Sets	Winnipeg C.S.T. Rises	Sets	Vancouver P.S.T. Rises	Sets	Lat. 45° Rises	Sets	Lat. 50° Rises	Sets	Day of Wk.	Day of Mo.
			h m	h m	h m	h m	h m	h m	h m	h m	h m	h m	h m	h m		
182	1	Tue	4 17	19 55	4 39	20 03	4 20	20 40	4 07	20 20	2 05	16 46	1 52	17 00	Tue	1
183	2	Wed	4 18	19 54	4 40	20 02	4 21	20 40	4 08	20 20	2 48	17 46	2 33	18 02	Wed	2
184	3	Thu	4 18	19 54	4 40	20 02	4 21	20 39	4 08	20 20	3 35	18 40	3 19	18 56	Thu	3
185	4	Fri	4 19	19 54	4 41	20 02	4 22	20 39	4 09	20 19	4 26	19 29	4 10	19 44	Fri	4
186	5	Sat	4 20	19 54	4 42	20 02	4 23	20 38	4 10	20 19	5 21	20 11	5 06	20 25	Sat	5
187	6	Sun	4 20	19 53	4 42	20 01	4 24	20 38	4 11	20 18	6 18	20 48	6 05	21 00	Sun	6
188	7	Mon	4 21	19 53	4 39	20 01	4 24	20 37	4 11	20 18	7 16	21 21	7 06	21 31	Mon	7
189	8	Tue	4 18	19 52	4 40	20 00	4 25	20 37	4 12	20 17	8 15	21 51	8 07	21 58	Tue	8
190	9	Wed	4 19	19 52	4 41	20 00	4 26	20 36	4 13	20 17	9 13	22 19	9 08	22 23	Wed	9
191	10	Thu	4 19	19 51	4 41	19 59	4 27	20 35	4 14	20 16	10 11	22 46	10 09	22 46	Thu	10
192	11	Fri	4 20	19 51	4 42	19 59	4 28	20 35	4 15	20 15	11 10	23 13	11 11	23 10	Fri	11
193	12	Sat	4 21	19 50	4 43	19 58	4 29	20 34	4 16	20 14	12 09	23 40	12 13	23 35	Sat	12
194	13	Sun	4 22	19 50	4 44	19 58	4 30	20 33	4 17	20 14	13 09	-- --	13 16	24 00	Sun	13
195	14	Mon	4 23	19 49	4 48	19 57	4 31	20 32	4 18	20 13	14 10	0 06	14 20	-- --	Mon	14
196	15	Tue	4 24	19 48	4 49	19 56	4 32	20 31	4 19	20 12	15 12	0 40	15 25	0 34	Tue	15
197	16	Wed	4 25	19 48	4 50	19 56	4 34	20 30	4 20	20 11	16 15	1 19	16 30	1 05	Wed	16
198	17	Thu	4 29	19 47	4 51	19 55	4 35	20 29	4 21	20 10	17 16	2 04	17 32	1 49	Thu	17
199	18	Fri	4 30	19 46	4 52	19 54	4 36	20 28	4 23	20 09	18 14	2 58	18 30	2 41	Fri	18
200	19	Sat	4 31	19 45	4 53	19 53	4 41	20 27	4 28	20 08	19 06	3 59	19 21	3 43	Sat	19
201	20	Sun	4 32	19 44	4 54	19 53	4 42	20 26	4 29	20 07	19 54	5 11	20 06	4 57	Sun	20
202	21	Mon	4 33	19 43	4 55	19 52	4 43	20 25	4 30	20 06	20 35	6 23	20 44	6 12	Mon	21
203	22	Tue	4 34	19 42	4 56	19 51	4 45	20 24	4 31	20 05	21 13	7 38	21 18	7 30	Tue	22
204	23	Wed	4 35	19 41	4 57	19 50	4 46	20 22	4 32	20 03	21 48	8 52	21 49	8 49	Wed	23
205	24	Thu	4 37	19 40	4 58	19 49	4 47	20 21	4 34	20 02	22 21	10 06	22 19	10 06	Thu	24
206	25	Fri	4 38	19 39	4 59	19 48	4 49	20 20	4 35	20 01	22 55	11 18	22 49	11 22	Fri	25
207	26	Sat	4 39	19 38	5 00	19 47	4 50	20 19	4 36	20 00	23 29	12 27	23 21	12 35	Sat	26
208	27	Sun	4 40	19 37	5 01	19 46	4 51	20 17	4 38	19 58	-- --	13 35	23 55	13 46	Sun	27
209	28	Mon	4 41	19 36	5 02	19 45	4 53	20 16	4 39	19 57	0 00	14 39	-- --	14 53	Mon	28
210	29	Tue	4 42	19 35	5 03	19 44	4 54	20 14	4 40	19 56	0 44	15 40	0 29	15 55	Tue	29
211	30	Wed	4 43	19 34	5 04	19 42	4 55	20 13	4 42	19 54	1 28	16 35	1 13	16 51	Wed	30
212	31	Thu	4 44	19 32	5 05	19 41	4 57	20 11	4 43	19 53	2 18	17 25	2 01	17 41	Thu	31

	AUGUST 1997	New Moon .... First Quarter .... Full Moon .... Last Quarter................	3 d 11 d 18 d 24 d	05 h 07 h 05 h 21 h	14 m 42 m 55 m 24 m	Moon's Phases E.S.T.

Day of Yr.	Day of Mo.	Day of Wk.	Ottawa E.S.T. Rises	Sets	Toronto E.S.T. Rises	Sets	Winnipeg C.S.T. Rises	Sets	Vancouver P.S.T. Rises	Sets	Lat. 45° Rises	Sets	Lat. 50° Rises	Sets	Day of Wk.	Day of Mo.
			h m	h m	h m	h m	h m	h m	h m	h m	h m	h m	h m	h m		
213	1	Fri	4 45	19 31	5 06	19 40	4 58	20 10	4 44	19 51	3 11	18 09	2 55	18 24	Fri	1
214	2	Sat	4 47	19 30	5 07	19 39	5 00	20 08	4 46	19 50	4 10	18 48	3 56	19 01	Sat	2
215	3	Sun	4 48	19 29	5 08	19 37	5 01	20 07	4 47	19 48	5 08	19 23	4 56	19 33	Sun	3
216	4	Mon	4 49	19 27	5 09	19 36	5 02	20 05	4 48	19 47	6 06	19 54	5 57	20 01	Mon	4
217	5	Tue	4 50	19 26	5 11	19 35	5 04	20 03	4 50	19 45	7 04	20 22	6 58	20 27	Tue	5
218	6	Wed	4 51	19 25	5 12	19 34	5 05	20 02	4 51	19 43	8 02	20 49	7 59	20 51	Wed	6
219	7	Thu	4 52	19 23	5 13	19 32	5 07	20 00	4 53	19 42	9 00	21 16	9 00	21 15	Thu	7
220	8	Fri	4 54	19 22	5 14	19 31	5 08	19 58	4 54	19 40	9 59	21 43	10 01	21 39	Fri	8
221	9	Sat	4 55	19 20	5 15	19 29	5 10	19 57	4 55	19 38	10 57	22 12	11 03	22 05	Sat	9
222	10	Sun	4 56	19 19	5 16	19 28	5 11	19 55	4 57	19 37	11 57	22 43	12 06	22 33	Sun	10
223	11	Mon	4 57	19 17	5 17	19 27	5 12	19 53	4 58	19 35	12 57	23 19	13 09	23 06	Mon	11
224	12	Tue	4 58	19 16	5 18	19 25	5 14	19 51	5 00	19 33	13 58	24 00	14 12	23 45	Tue	12
225	13	Wed	5 00	19 14	5 19	19 24	5 15	19 49	5 01	19 31	14 59	-- --	15 15	-- --	Wed	13
226	14	Thu	5 01	19 13	5 21	19 22	5 17	19 48	5 03	19 29	15 57	0 40	16 14	0 28	Thu	14
227	15	Fri	5 02	19 11	5 22	19 21	5 18	19 46	5 04	19 28	16 52	1 40	17 07	1 23	Fri	15
228	16	Sat	5 03	19 09	5 23	19 19	5 20	19 44	5 05	19 26	17 42	2 48	17 55	2 32	Sat	16
229	17	Sun	5 04	19 08	5 24	19 18	5 21	19 42	5 07	19 24	18 27	3 58	18 37	3 45	Sun	17
230	18	Mon	5 06	19 06	5 25	19 16	5 23	19 40	5 08	19 22	19 07	5 12	19 14	5 03	Mon	18
231	19	Tue	5 07	19 05	5 26	19 14	5 24	19 38	5 10	19 20	19 44	6 29	19 48	6 23	Tue	19
232	20	Wed	5 08	19 03	5 27	19 13	5 26	19 36	5 11	19 18	20 20	7 45	20 19	7 44	Wed	20
233	21	Thu	5 09	19 01	5 28	19 11	5 27	19 34	5 13	19 16	20 54	9 00	20 50	9 03	Thu	21
234	22	Fri	5 11	18 59	5 30	19 10	5 29	19 32	5 14	19 14	21 30	10 13	21 22	10 20	Fri	22
235	23	Sat	5 12	18 58	5 31	19 08	5 30	19 30	5 15	19 12	22 07	11 24	21 57	11 33	Sat	23
236	24	Sun	5 13	18 56	5 32	19 06	5 32	19 28	5 17	19 10	22 48	12 31	22 34	12 43	Sun	24
237	25	Mon	5 14	18 54	5 33	19 05	5 33	19 26	5 18	19 08	23 32	13 33	23 16	13 48	Mon	25
238	26	Tue	5 15	18 52	5 34	19 03	5 35	19 24	5 20	19 06	-- --	14 31	24 00	14 47	Tue	26
239	27	Wed	5 17	18 51	5 35	19 01	5 36	19 22	5 21	19 04	0 15	15 22	-- --	15 38	Wed	27
240	28	Thu	5 18	18 49	5 36	18 59	5 38	19 20	5 23	19 02	1 07	16 08	0 51	16 23	Thu	28
241	29	Fri	5 19	18 47	5 37	18 58	5 39	19 18	5 24	19 00	2 05	16 49	1 51	17 02	Fri	29
242	30	Sat	5 20	18 45	5 39	18 56	5 41	19 16	5 26	18 58	3 02	17 24	2 49	17 35	Sat	30
243	31	Sun	5 21	18 43	5 40	18 54	5 42	19 14	5 27	18 56	3 59	17 56	3 49	18 05	Sun	31

Canadian Almanac & Directory 1997

1-12 SOLAR AND LUNAR TABLES

SEPTEMBER 1997

Moon Phase	Day	Hour	Minute
New Moon	1 d	18 h	52 m
First Quarter	9 d	20 h	31 m
Full Moon	16 d	13 h	50 m
Last Quarter	23 d	08 h	35 m

Moon's Phases E.S.T.

SUNRISE AND SUNSET / MOONRISE AND MOONSET (Local Mean Time)

Day of Yr.	Day of Mo.	Day of Wk.	Ottawa E.S.T. Rises	Sets	Toronto E.S.T. Rises	Sets	Winnipeg C.S.T. Rises	Sets	Vancouver P.S.T. Rises	Sets	Lat. 45° Rises	Sets	Lat. 50° Rises	Sets	Day of Wk.	Day of Mo.
			h m	h m	h m	h m	h m	h m	h m	h m	h m	h m	h m	h m		
244	1	Mon	5 23	18 42	5 41	18 52	5 44	19 11	5 28	18 54	4 57	18 26	4 50	18 31	Mon	1
245	2	Tue	5 24	18 40	5 42	18 51	5 45	19 09	5 30	18 52	5 55	18 53	5 51	18 56	Tue	2
246	3	Wed	5 25	18 38	5 43	18 49	5 47	19 07	5 31	18 50	6 53	19 20	6 52	19 20	Wed	3
247	4	Thu	5 26	18 36	5 44	18 47	5 48	19 05	5 33	18 48	7 52	19 47	7 53	19 44	Thu	4
248	5	Fri	5 28	18 34	5 45	18 45	5 49	19 03	5 34	18 46	8 50	20 15	8 55	20 09	Fri	5
249	6	Sat	5 29	18 32	5 46	18 44	5 51	19 01	5 36	18 44	9 49	20 45	9 57	20 36	Sat	6
250	7	Sun	5 30	18 30	5 48	18 42	5 52	18 59	5 37	18 41	10 48	21 18	10 59	21 07	Sun	7
251	8	Mon	5 31	18 29	5 49	18 40	5 54	18 56	5 38	18 39	11 48	21 56	12 01	21 42	Mon	8
252	9	Tue	5 32	18 27	5 50	18 38	5 55	18 54	5 40	18 37	12 47	22 40	13 02	22 24	Tue	9
253	10	Wed	5 34	18 25	5 51	18 36	5 57	18 52	5 41	18 35	13 44	23 30	14 00	23 14	Wed	10
254	11	Thu	5 35	18 23	5 52	18 35	5 58	18 50	5 43	18 33	14 39	-- --	14 55	-- --	Thu	11
255	12	Fri	5 36	18 21	5 53	18 33	6 00	18 48	5 44	18 31	15 30	0 24	15 44	0 09	Fri	12
256	13	Sat	5 37	18 19	5 54	18 31	6 01	18 46	5 46	18 29	16 16	1 34	16 28	1 20	Sat	13
257	14	Sun	5 38	18 17	5 55	18 29	6 03	18 43	5 47	18 27	16 58	2 45	17 07	2 34	Sun	14
258	15	Mon	5 40	18 15	5 57	18 27	6 04	18 41	5 49	18 24	17 37	4 00	17 42	3 52	Mon	15
259	16	Tue	5 41	18 13	5 58	18 25	6 06	18 39	5 50	18 22	18 13	5 17	18 15	5 13	Tue	16
260	17	Wed	5 42	18 11	5 59	18 24	6 07	18 37	5 51	18 20	18 49	6 34	18 47	6 34	Wed	17
261	18	Thu	5 43	18 09	6 00	18 22	6 09	18 35	5 53	18 18	19 25	7 50	19 19	7 54	Thu	18
262	19	Fri	5 45	18 07	6 01	18 20	6 10	18 32	5 54	18 16	20 03	9 04	19 54	9 12	Fri	19
263	20	Sat	5 46	18 05	6 02	18 18	6 12	18 30	5 56	18 14	20 43	10 15	20 31	10 27	Sat	20
264	21	Sun	5 47	18 04	6 03	18 16	6 13	18 28	5 57	18 11	21 27	11 22	21 13	11 36	Sun	21
265	22	Mon	5 48	18 02	6 04	18 14	6 15	18 26	5 59	18 09	22 15	12 23	21 59	12 39	Mon	22
266	23	Tue	5 49	18 00	6 06	18 12	6 16	18 24	6 00	18 07	23 06	13 18	22 50	13 34	Tue	23
267	24	Wed	5 51	17 58	6 07	18 11	6 18	18 21	6 02	18 05	24 00	14 06	23 45	14 22	Wed	24
268	25	Thu	5 52	17 56	6 08	18 09	6 19	18 19	6 03	18 03	-- --	14 49	-- --	15 03	Thu	25
269	26	Fri	5 53	17 54	6 09	18 07	6 21	18 17	6 05	18 01	0 56	15 26	0 43	15 38	Fri	26
270	27	Sat	5 54	17 52	6 10	18 05	6 22	18 15	6 06	17 59	1 53	15 59	1 42	16 08	Sat	27
271	28	Sun	5 56	17 50	6 11	18 03	6 24	18 13	6 07	17 56	2 51	16 29	2 43	16 35	Sun	28
272	29	Mon	5 57	17 48	6 12	18 02	6 25	18 10	6 09	17 54	3 49	16 57	3 44	17 00	Mon	29
273	30	Tue	5 58	17 46	6 14	18 00	6 27	18 08	6 10	17 52	4 47	17 24	4 45	17 24	Tue	30

OCTOBER 1997

Moon Phase	Day	Hour	Minute
New Moon	1 d	11 h	52 m
First Quarter	9 d	07 h	22 m
Full Moon	15 d	22 h	46 m
Last Quarter	22 d	23 h	48 m
New Moon	31 d	05 h	01 m

Moon's Phases E.S.T.

SUNRISE AND SUNSET / MOONRISE AND MOONSET (Local Mean Time)

Day of Yr.	Day of Mo.	Day of Wk.	Ottawa E.S.T. Rises	Sets	Toronto E.S.T. Rises	Sets	Winnipeg C.S.T. Rises	Sets	Vancouver P.S.T. Rises	Sets	Lat. 45° Rises	Sets	Lat. 50° Rises	Sets	Day of Wk.	Day of Mo.
			h m	h m	h m	h m	h m	h m	h m	h m	h m	h m	h m	h m		
274	1	Wed	5 59	17 44	6 15	17 58	6 28	18 06	6 12	17 50	5 45	17 51	5 46	17 48	Wed	1
275	2	Thu	6 01	17 42	6 16	17 56	6 30	18 04	6 13	17 48	6 44	18 18	6 48	18 13	Thu	2
276	3	Fri	6 02	17 41	6 17	17 54	6 31	18 02	6 15	17 46	7 43	18 48	7 50	18 39	Fri	3
277	4	Sat	6 03	17 39	6 18	17 53	6 33	18 00	6 16	17 44	8 42	19 20	8 52	19 09	Sat	4
278	5	Sun	6 04	17 37	6 19	17 51	6 35	17 58	6 18	17 42	9 42	19 56	9 54	19 43	Sun	5
279	6	Mon	6 06	17 35	6 21	17 49	6 36	17 55	6 19	17 40	10 41	20 37	10 55	20 22	Mon	6
280	7	Tue	6 07	17 33	6 22	17 47	6 38	17 53	6 21	17 37	11 38	21 24	11 54	21 08	Tue	7
281	8	Wed	6 08	17 31	6 23	17 45	6 39	17 51	6 22	17 35	12 32	22 18	12 48	22 02	Wed	8
282	9	Thu	6 10	17 29	6 24	17 44	6 41	17 49	6 24	17 33	13 23	23 18	13 38	23 04	Thu	9
283	10	Fri	6 11	17 28	6 25	17 42	6 42	17 47	6 25	17 31	14 09	-- --	14 22	-- --	Fri	10
284	11	Sat	6 12	17 26	6 27	17 40	6 44	17 45	6 27	17 29	14 51	0 25	15 02	0 12	Sat	11
285	12	Sun	6 13	17 24	6 28	17 39	6 45	17 43	6 28	17 27	15 30	1 35	15 37	1 26	Sun	12
286	13	Mon	6 15	17 22	6 29	17 37	6 47	17 41	6 30	17 25	16 06	2 49	16 10	2 43	Mon	13
287	14	Tue	6 16	17 20	6 30	17 35	6 49	17 39	6 32	17 23	16 42	4 05	16 41	4 03	Tue	14
288	15	Wed	6 17	17 19	6 32	17 34	6 50	17 37	6 33	17 21	17 17	5 21	17 13	5 23	Wed	15
289	16	Thu	6 19	17 17	6 33	17 32	6 52	17 35	6 35	17 19	17 54	6 37	17 47	6 43	Thu	16
290	17	Fri	6 20	17 15	6 34	17 30	6 53	17 33	6 36	17 17	18 34	7 51	18 23	8 01	Fri	17
291	18	Sat	6 21	17 13	6 35	17 29	6 55	17 31	6 38	17 15	19 18	9 03	19 04	9 15	Sat	18
292	19	Sun	6 23	17 12	6 36	17 27	6 57	17 29	6 39	17 13	20 05	10 09	19 50	10 24	Sun	19
293	20	Mon	6 24	17 10	6 38	17 25	6 58	17 27	6 41	17 12	20 56	11 08	20 40	11 25	Mon	20
294	21	Tue	6 25	17 08	6 39	17 24	7 00	17 25	6 42	17 10	21 51	12 01	21 35	12 17	Tue	21
295	22	Wed	6 27	17 07	6 40	17 22	7 01	17 23	6 44	17 08	22 48	12 47	22 33	13 01	Wed	22
296	23	Thu	6 28	17 05	6 42	17 21	7 03	17 21	6 46	17 06	23 45	13 26	23 33	13 39	Thu	23
297	24	Fri	6 29	17 03	6 43	17 19	7 05	17 19	6 47	17 04	-- --	14 01	-- --	14 11	Fri	24
298	25	Sat	6 31	17 02	6 44	17 18	7 06	17 17	6 49	17 02	0 43	14 32	0 34	14 39	Sat	25
299	26	Sun	6 32	17 00	6 45	17 16	7 08	17 15	6 50	17 00	1 41	15 00	1 35	15 05	Sun	26
300	27	Mon	6 34	16 58	6 47	17 15	7 10	17 14	6 52	16 59	2 39	15 27	2 36	15 29	Mon	27
301	28	Tue	6 35	16 57	6 48	17 13	7 11	17 12	6 54	16 57	3 37	15 54	3 37	15 53	Tue	28
302	29	Wed	6 36	16 55	6 49	17 12	7 13	17 10	6 55	16 55	4 36	16 21	4 39	16 17	Wed	29
303	30	Thu	6 38	16 54	6 51	17 10	7 15	17 08	6 57	16 54	5 35	16 50	5 41	16 43	Thu	30
304	31	Fri	6 39	16 52	6 52	17 09	7 16	17 07	6 58	16 52	6 35	17 21	6 44	17 11	Fri	31

Canadian Almanac & Directory 1997

SOLAR AND LUNAR TABLES 1-13

	NOVEMBER 1997		First Quarter	7 d	16 h	43 m		Moon's Phases E.S.T.
			Full Moon	14 d	09 h	12 m		
			Last Quarter	21 d	18 h	58 m		
			New Moon	29 d	21 h	14 m		

SUNRISE AND SUNSET / MOONRISE AND MOONSET (Local Mean Time)

Day of Yr.	Day of Mo.	Day of Wk.	Ottawa E.S.T. Rises	Sets	Toronto E.S.T. Rises	Sets	Winnipeg C.S.T. Rises	Sets	Vancouver P.S.T. Rises	Sets	Lat. 45° Rises	Sets	Lat. 50° Rises	Sets	Day of Wk.	Day of Mo.
			h m	h m	h m	h m	h m	h m	h m	h m	h m	h m	h m	h m		
305	1	Sat	6 40	16 51	6 53	17 08	7 18	17 05	7 00	16 50	7 36	17 56	7 47	17 43	Sat	1
306	2	Sun	6 42	16 49	6 54	17 06	7 20	17 03	7 02	16 49	8 36	18 36	8 50	18 21	Sun	2
307	3	Mon	6 43	16 48	6 56	17 05	7 21	17 02	7 03	16 47	9 34	19 21	9 50	19 05	Mon	3
308	4	Tue	6 45	16 47	6 57	17 04	7 23	17 00	7 05	16 45	10 29	20 13	10 46	19 56	Tue	4
309	5	Wed	6 46	16 45	6 58	17 03	7 25	16 58	7 07	16 44	11 21	21 11	11 37	20 55	Wed	5
310	6	Thu	6 47	16 44	7 00	17 01	7 26	16 57	7 08	16 42	12 08	22 14	12 22	22 00	Thu	6
311	7	Fri	6 49	16 43	7 01	17 00	7 28	16 55	7 10	16 41	12 50	23 21	13 02	23 10	Fri	7
312	8	Sat	6 50	16 41	7 02	16 59	7 29	16 54	7 11	16 39	13 28	-- --	13 37	-- --	Sat	8
313	9	Sun	6 52	16 40	7 04	16 58	7 31	16 52	7 13	16 38	14 04	0 31	14 09	0 24	Sun	9
314	10	Mon	6 53	16 39	7 05	16 57	7 33	16 51	7 15	16 37	14 38	1 43	14 40	1 40	Mon	10
315	11	Tue	6 54	16 38	7 06	16 56	7 34	16 49	7 16	16 35	15 12	2 57	15 10	2 57	Tue	11
316	12	Wed	6 56	16 37	7 08	16 55	7 36	16 48	7 18	16 34	15 47	4 11	15 41	4 15	Wed	12
317	13	Thu	6 57	16 35	7 09	16 54	7 38	16 47	7 19	16 33	16 25	5 25	16 16	5 33	Thu	13
318	14	Fri	6 59	16 34	7 10	16 53	7 39	16 45	7 21	16 31	17 06	6 38	16 54	6 49	Fri	14
319	15	Sat	7 00	16 33	7 12	16 52	7 41	16 44	7 23	16 30	17 52	7 48	17 37	8 02	Sat	15
320	16	Sun	7 01	16 32	7 13	16 51	7 43	16 43	7 24	16 29	18 42	8 52	18 26	9 08	Sun	16
321	17	Mon	7 03	16 31	7 14	16 50	7 44	16 42	7 26	16 28	19 37	9 50	19 20	10 06	Mon	17
322	18	Tue	7 04	16 30	7 15	16 49	7 46	16 41	7 27	16 27	20 34	10 40	20 19	10 56	Tue	18
323	19	Wed	7 05	16 29	7 17	16 48	7 47	16 40	7 29	16 26	21 33	11 23	21 19	11 37	Wed	19
324	20	Thu	7 07	16 28	7 18	16 47	7 49	16 38	7 30	16 25	22 32	12 01	22 21	12 12	Thu	20
325	21	Fri	7 08	16 28	7 19	16 47	7 50	16 37	7 32	16 24	23 30	12 33	23 23	12 42	Fri	21
326	22	Sat	7 09	16 27	7 20	16 46	7 52	16 36	7 33	16 23	-- --	13 03	-- --	13 09	Sat	22
327	23	Sun	7 11	16 26	7 22	16 45	7 53	16 35	7 35	16 22	0 29	13 30	0 24	13 33	Sun	23
328	24	Mon	7 12	16 25	7 23	16 45	7 55	16 35	7 36	16 21	1 27	13 57	1 25	13 57	Mon	24
329	25	Tue	7 13	16 25	7 24	16 44	7 56	16 34	7 38	16 20	2 25	14 23	2 27	14 21	Tue	25
330	26	Wed	7 15	16 24	7 25	16 43	7 58	16 33	7 39	16 19	3 24	14 51	3 29	14 45	Wed	26
331	27	Thu	7 16	16 23	7 26	16 43	7 59	16 32	7 40	16 19	4 24	15 21	4 32	15 12	Thu	27
332	28	Fri	7 17	16 23	7 28	16 42	8 01	16 31	7 42	16 18	5 25	15 55	5 36	15 43	Fri	28
333	29	Sat	7 18	16 22	7 29	16 42	8 02	16 31	7 43	16 17	6 26	16 33	6 40	16 19	Sat	29
334	30	Sun	7 20	16 22	7 30	16 42	8 03	16 30	7 44	16 17	7 26	17 17	7 42	17 01	Sun	30

	DECEMBER 1997		First Quarter	7 d	01 h	09 m		Moon's Phases E.S.T.
			Full Moon	13 d	21 h	37 m		
			Last Quarter	21 d	16 h	43 m		
			New Moon	29 d	11 h	57 m		

SUNRISE AND SUNSET / MOONRISE AND MOONSET (Local Mean Time)

Day of Yr.	Day of Mo.	Day of Wk.	Ottawa E.S.T. Rises	Sets	Toronto E.S.T. Rises	Sets	Winnipeg C.S.T. Rises	Sets	Vancouver P.S.T. Rises	Sets	Lat. 45° Rises	Sets	Lat. 50° Rises	Sets	Day of Wk.	Day of Mo.
			h m	h m	h m	h m	h m	h m	h m	h m	h m	h m	h m	h m		
335	1	Mon	7 21	16 21	7 31	16 41	8 05	16 30	7 46	16 16	8 25	18 07	8 41	17 50	Mon	1
336	2	Tue	7 22	16 21	7 32	16 41	8 06	16 29	7 47	16 16	9 19	19 04	9 35	18 48	Tue	2
337	3	Wed	7 23	16 20	7 33	16 41	8 07	16 29	7 48	16 15	10 08	20 06	10 23	19 52	Wed	3
338	4	Thu	7 24	16 20	7 34	16 41	8 09	16 28	7 50	16 15	10 52	21 12	11 05	21 01	Thu	4
339	5	Fri	7 25	16 20	7 35	16 40	8 10	16 28	7 51	16 14	11 31	22 21	11 41	22 13	Fri	5
340	6	Sat	7 26	16 20	7 36	16 40	8 11	16 28	7 52	16 14	12 07	23 32	12 14	23 27	Sat	6
341	7	Sun	7 27	16 19	7 37	16 40	8 12	16 27	7 53	16 14	12 41	-- --	12 44	-- --	Sun	7
342	8	Mon	7 28	16 19	7 38	16 40	8 13	16 27	7 54	16 14	13 13	0 43	13 13	0 41	Mon	8
343	9	Tue	7 29	16 19	7 39	16 40	8 14	16 27	7 55	16 14	13 46	1 54	13 42	1 57	Tue	9
344	10	Wed	7 30	16 19	7 40	16 40	8 15	16 27	7 56	16 13	14 21	3 06	14 13	3 12	Wed	10
345	11	Thu	7 31	16 19	7 41	16 40	8 16	16 27	7 57	16 13	14 59	4 17	14 48	4 27	Thu	11
346	12	Fri	7 32	16 19	7 42	16 40	8 17	16 27	7 58	16 13	15 41	5 27	15 28	5 40	Fri	12
347	13	Sat	7 33	16 19	7 42	16 40	8 18	16 27	7 59	16 14	16 29	6 34	16 13	6 49	Sat	13
348	14	Sun	7 34	16 19	7 43	16 41	8 19	16 27	8 00	16 14	17 21	7 35	17 04	7 51	Sun	14
349	15	Mon	7 35	16 20	7 44	16 41	8 20	16 27	8 01	16 14	18 17	8 30	18 01	8 46	Mon	15
350	16	Tue	7 35	16 20	7 45	16 41	8 21	16 27	8 01	16 14	19 16	9 17	19 02	9 32	Tue	16
351	17	Wed	7 36	16 20	7 45	16 41	8 21	16 28	8 02	16 14	20 17	9 58	20 05	10 11	Wed	17
352	18	Thu	7 37	16 20	7 46	16 42	8 22	16 28	8 03	16 15	21 17	10 33	21 07	10 43	Thu	18
353	19	Fri	7 37	16 21	7 47	16 42	8 23	16 28	8 03	16 15	22 16	11 04	22 10	11 12	Fri	19
354	20	Sat	7 38	16 21	7 47	16 43	8 23	16 29	8 04	16 15	23 15	11 33	23 11	11 37	Sat	20
355	21	Sun	7 39	16 22	7 48	16 43	8 24	16 29	8 04	16 16	-- --	12 00	-- --	12 01	Sun	21
356	22	Mon	7 39	16 22	7 48	16 44	8 24	16 30	8 05	16 17	0 13	12 26	0 13	12 24	Mon	22
357	23	Tue	7 40	16 23	7 49	16 44	8 25	16 30	8 05	16 17	1 11	12 53	1 14	12 48	Tue	23
358	24	Wed	7 40	16 23	7 49	16 45	8 25	16 31	8 06	16 18	2 10	13 21	2 17	13 14	Wed	24
359	25	Thu	7 40	16 24	7 49	16 45	8 25	16 32	8 06	16 18	3 10	13 53	3 20	13 42	Thu	25
360	26	Fri	7 41	16 24	7 50	16 46	8 26	16 32	8 06	16 19	4 11	14 28	4 23	14 15	Fri	26
361	27	Sat	7 41	16 25	7 50	16 47	8 26	16 33	8 07	16 20	5 12	15 09	5 27	14 54	Sat	27
362	28	Sun	7 41	16 26	7 50	16 47	8 26	16 34	8 07	16 21	6 12	15 57	6 29	15 41	Sun	28
363	29	Mon	7 42	16 27	7 51	16 48	8 26	16 35	8 07	16 22	7 10	16 52	7 26	16 36	Mon	29
364	30	Tue	7 42	16 27	7 51	16 49	8 26	16 36	8 07	16 22	8 02	17 54	8 18	17 38	Tue	30
365	31	Wed	7 42	16 28	7 51	16 50	8 26	16 37	8 07	16 23	8 50	19 01	9 04	18 48	Wed	31

Canadian Almanac & Directory 1997

PRINCIPAL (MEAN) ELEMENTS OF THE SOLAR SYSTEM

Object	Equatorial Diameter (miles)	Equatorial Diameter (km)	Mass (earth=1)	Axial Rotation (days)	Magnitude at brightest	Mean Dist. from Sun (mill. miles)	Mean Dist. from Sun (mill. km)	Per. of Revol.	Eccentricity	Inclination (deg.)
Sun	865,000	1,392,000	332,946	24.7**	-26.8					
Moon	2,159	3,475	0.0123	27.3217	-12.6					
Mercury	3,032	4,879	0.0553	58.646	-1.9	36.0	57.9	88.0d	.206	7.0
Venus	7,521	12,104	0.8150	243.019***	-4.7	67.2	108.2	224.7	.007	3.4
Earth	7,926	12,756	1.0000	0.9973		93.0	149.6	365.3	.017	
Mars	4,222	6,794	0.1074	1.0260	-2.8	141.6	227.9	687.0	.093	1.9
Jupiter	88,846*	142,984*	317.833	0.410**	-2.5	483.7	778	11.86y	.048	1.3
Saturn	74,898*	120,536*	95.159	0.44401	-0.4	888	1,429	29.42	.056	2.5
Uranus	31,763*	51,118*	14.500	0.71833***	+5.7	1,786	2,875	83.75	.046	0.8
Neptune	30,775*	49,528*	17.204	0.67125	+7.6	2,799	4,504	163.7	.009	1.8
Pluto	1,430	2,302	0.0025	6.3872***	+14.0	3,676	5,916	248.0	.249	17.1

*at pressure 1 bar (101.325 kPa)   ** at equator   *** retrograde

PLANETARY CONFIGURATIONS, 1997
UNIVERSAL (GREENWICH) TIME

	d	h			d	h	
January	2	00	Earth at Perihelion (distance 147,095,000 km)	July	5	04	Mercury 5° S. of Pollux
	2	01	Mercury in inferior conjunction		21	07	Neptune at opposition (distance 4,358,000,000 km)
	12	14	Mercury 3° N. of Venus		23	01	Venus 1.2° N. of Regulus
	12	21	Mercury stationary		27	00	Mercury 0.5° S. of Regulus
	17	13	Neptune in conjunction with Sun		29	19	Uranus at opposition (distance 2,814,000,000 km)
	19	13	Jupiter in conjunction with Sun	August	2	19	Saturn stationary
	24	05	Mercury at greatest elongation W. (25°)		2	23	Mars 1.7° N. of Spica
	24	14	Uranus in conjunction with Sun		4	00	Mercury at greatest elongation E. (27°)
February	1	11	Venus 1.0° S. of Neptune		9	14	Jupiter at opposition (distance 605,7000,000 km)
	6	00	Venus 0.3° S. of Jupiter		16	05	Pluto stationary
	6	18	Mars stationary		17	03	Mercury stationary
	7	12	Venus 0.2° S. of Uranus		31	14	Mercury in inferior conjunction
	7	20	Mercury 1.4° S. of Neptune	September	2	00	Eclipse of Sun (page 1-22)
	12	14	Mercury 1.0° S. of Jupiter		6	05	Venus 1.9° N. of Spica
	13	00	Mercury 0.9° S. of Uranus		9	06	Mercury stationary
	16	08	Jupiter 0.2° N. of Uranus		16	19	Eclipse of Moon (page 1-22)
March	9	01	Eclipse of Sun (page 1-22)		16	22	Mercury at greatest elongation W. (18°)
	10	06	Pluto stationary		23	00	Equinox. Northern autumn begins
	11	16	Mercury in superior conjunction	October	8	07	Jupiter stationary
	17	08	Mars in opposition		8	22	Neptune stationary
	20	14	Equinox. Northern spring begins		10	04	Saturn at opposition (distance 1,255,000,000 km)
	20	17	Mars closest approach (distance 98,642,000 km)		13	21	Mercury in superior conjunction
	24	05	Eclipse of Moon (page 1-22)		14	14	Uranus stationary
	30	22	Saturn in conjunction with Sun		16	22	Venus 1.7° N. of Antares
April	2	14	Venus in superior conjunction		26	23	Venus 2° S. of Mars
	6	01	Mercury at greatest elongation E. (19°)	November	6	07	Venus at greatest elongation E. (47°)
	15	05	Mercury stationary		14	04	Mercury 2° N. of Antares
	25	11	Mercury in inferior conjunction		27	17	Pluto in conjunction with Sun
	29	06	Mars stationary		28	16	Mercury at greatest elongation E. (22°)
May	1	23	Neptune stationary	December	7	16	Mercury stationary
	7	18	Mercury stationary		7	20	Venus 3° S. of Neptune
	13	09	Uranus stationary		11	23	Venus at greatest brilliancy (-4.7)
	19	08	Venus 6° N. of Aldebaran		15	19	Mars 1.6° S. of Neptune
	22	23	Mercury at greatest elongation W. (25°)		17	08	Mercury in inferior conjunction
	25	10	Pluto at opposition (distance 4,336,000,000 km)		17	11	Saturn stationary
June	10	11	Jupiter stationary		21	20	Solstice. Northern winter begins
	14	14	Mercury 5° N. of Aldebaran		22	11	Venus 1.1° N. of Mars
	21	08	Solstice. Northern summer begins		25	14	Venus stationary
	23	23	Venus 5° S. of Pollux		26	20	Mars 0.6° S. of Uranus
	25	19	Mercury in superior conjunction		27	13	Mercury stationary
July	4	19	Earth at aphelion (distance 152,104,000 km)				

This table includes configurations involving the sun, planets, and bright zodiacal stars. The meaning of the terms is as follows:

Aphelion: the point at which a planet is furthest from the sun.

Conjunction: in the same direction as another object--the sun, unless otherwise stated. Mercury and Venus can be at inferior conjunction (closer than the sun) or superior conjunction (beyond the sun).

Elongation: the angle between the planet and the sun.

Opposition: opposite another object (the sun, unless otherwise stated).

Perihelion: the point at which a planet is closest to the sun.

Stationary: motionless relative to the background stars. Because of the orbital motions of the planet and the earth, the planet normally moves eastward or westward relative to the background stars. At the moment when its motion changes from eastward to westward, or vice versa, the planet is said to be stationary.

SYMBOLS AND ABBREVIATIONS

SUN, MOON AND PLANETS

☉	The Sun	♃	Jupiter
☾	The Moon	♄	Saturn
☿	Mercury	♅	Uranus
♀	Venus	♆	Neptune
⊕	The Earth	♇	Pluto
♂	Mars		

SIGNS OF THE ZODIAC

1.	♈	Aries	7.	♎	Libra	N.	North	′	Minutes of Arc
2.	♉	Taurus	8.	♏	Scorpius	S.	South	″	Seconds of Arc
3.	♊	Gemini	9.	♐	Sagittarius	E.	East	h	Hours
4.	♋	Cancer	10.	♑	Capricornus	W.	West	m	Minutes of Time
5.	♌	Leo	11.	♒	Aquarius	°	Degrees	s	Seconds of Time
6.	♍	Virgo	12.	♓	Pisces				

METEORS, METEORITES, AND METEOR SHOWERS

A *meteor* or "shooting star" appears momentarily in the sky when a particle from beyond the earth enters the earth's atmosphere at a high velocity. Most visible meteors are caused by particles smaller than a grape or marble, and these small particles are completely vaporized in the atmosphere at a height of about 80 km. A spectacular meteor, known as a *fire-ball*, is caused by a larger body which may fall to the earth's surface in one or more pieces. Particles seen thus to fall, or subsequently found by analysis to be of this nature, are called *meteorites*.

Meteorites may be divided into two main classes-- the irons, which are almost pure nickel-iron, and the stones. Any freshly-fallen meteorite is characterized by a dark, smooth crust caused by the fusion of the outer part.

Meteors may be observed on any clear, moonless night at an average rate of about five an hour. At times *meteor showers* occur, when meteors are seen with much greater frequency and appear to radiate from a particular part of the sky which is called the *radiant*. This is an effect of perspective, the radiant being the vanishing point of the parallel tracks of the meteors. Meteor showers usually repeat themselves annually, and in some cases have been associated with the orbits of comets. When the earth passes through or near the orbit of a comet it can intercept the small particles (meteoroids) which cause meteors. The principal meteor showers for the northern hemisphere are listed below.

The study of meteors and meteorites adds to our knowledge of the nature and origin of the solar system and also to our knowledge of the earth's outer atmosphere.

Comet Hale-Bopp

Comet Hale-Bopp was discovered independently on July 23, 1996, by two US amateur astronomers, Alan Hale and Thomas Bopp. From measurements of the position of the comet over the next few weeks, astronomers were able to determine its orbit, and predict its position and brightness into the future. These predictions suggest that Comet Hale-Bopp will reach maximum brightness around April 1, 1997, when it will be one of the brightest comets of the century. It will be even brighter than Comet Hyakutake, which was discovered by Yuji Hyakutake on January 30, 1996, and which passed only a few million kilometres from Earth on March 25, 1996. That comet was easily visible, even from urban locations, as it drifted through the northern sky in late March. Comet Hale-Bopp was visible with binoculars in early 1996 and, as it moves past the glare of the sun in January 1997, it should be easily visible to the unaided eye. In February and March, it moves from Aquila through Cygnus to Andromeda, reaching the brightness of Jupiter by the end of March (though the comet will be a fuzzy patch, rather than a point of light like a planet or star). In the first two weeks of April, it moves from Andromeda to Perseus, remaining easily visible until the Moon becomes a problem around the middle of the month. Look low in the north-west, in the early evening sky. Binoculars are helpful, even when the comet can be seen without them. Predictions of comet brightnesses are notoriously unreliable but, so far, Comet Hale-Bopp is "on track" to becoming the astronomical event of 1997.

MAPS OF THE NIGHT SKY

The maps on the next six pages cover the northern sky. Stars are shown down to a magnitude of 4.5 or 5, i.e. those which are readily apparent to the unaided eye on a reasonably dark night.

The maps are drawn for 45°N latitude, but are useful for latitudes several degrees north or south of this. They show the hemisphere of sky visible to an observer at various times of the year. Because the aspect of the night sky changes continuously with both longitude and time, while time zones change discontinuously with both longitude and time of year, it is not possible to state simply when, in general, a particular observer will find that his or her sky fits exactly one of the six maps. The month indicated below each map is the time of year when the map will match the "late evening" sky. On any particular night, successive maps will represent the sky as it appears every four hours later. For example, at 2 or 3 am on a March night, the May map should be used. Just after dinner on a January night, the November map will be appropriate. The centre of each map is the zenith, the point directly overhead; the circumference is the horizon. To identify the stars, hold the map in front of you so that the part of the horizon which you are facing (west, for instance) is downward. (The four letters around the periphery of each map indicate compass directions.)

On the maps, stars forming the usual constellation patterns are linked by straight lines, constellation names being given in upper case letters. The names in lower case are those of first magnitude stars, except Algol and Mira which are famous variable stars, and Polaris which is near the north celestial pole. Small clusters of dots indicate the positions of bright star clusters, nebulae, or galaxies. Although a few of these are just visible to the naked eye, and most can be located in binoculars, a telescope is needed for good views of these objects. The pair of wavy, dotted lines indicates roughly the borders of the Milky Way. Small asterisks locate the directions of the galactic centre (GC), the north galactic pole (NGP), and the south galactic pole (SGP). Two dashed lines appear on each of the six maps. The one with the more dashes is the celestial equator. Tick marks along this indicate hours of right ascension, the odd hours being labelled. The line with fewer dashes is the ecliptic, the apparent annual path of the Sun across the heavens. Letters along this line indicate the approximate position of the Sun at the beginning of each month. Also located along the ecliptic are the vernal equinox (VE), summer solstice (SS), autumnal equinox (AE), and winter solstice (WS). Moon and the other eight planets are found near the ecliptic, but since their motions are not related in a simple way to our year, it is not feasible to show them on a general set of maps.

The text above, and the six star charts on the following pages, were prepared by Professor Roy L. Bishop, Editor of the annual *Observer's Handbook of the Royal Astronomical Society of Canada* (RASC). They are copyright RASC 1996. They are used here with the kind permission of Professor Bishop and the RASC.

PRINCIPAL ANNUAL METEOR SHOWERS FOR THE NORTHERN HEMISPHERE (UNIVERSAL TIME)

Shower	Location of Radiant	Date of Maximum Frequency	Hourly Number	Duration (in days)
Quadrantids	Bootes	Jan. 4	40	1
Lyrids	Lyra	Apr. 22	15	2
Eta Aquarids	Aquarius	May 4	20	3
Delta Aquarids	Aquarius	July 28	20	--
Perseids	Perseus	Aug. 12	50	5
Orionids	Orion	Oct. 22	25	2
Taurids	Taurus	Nov. 3	15	--
Leonids	Leo	Nov. 17	15	--
Geminids	Gemini	Dec. 14	50	3
Ursids	Ursa Minor	Dec. 23	15	2
Quadranids	Bootes	Jan. 3/98	40	1

1-16 THE NAKED-EYE PLANETS FOR 1997

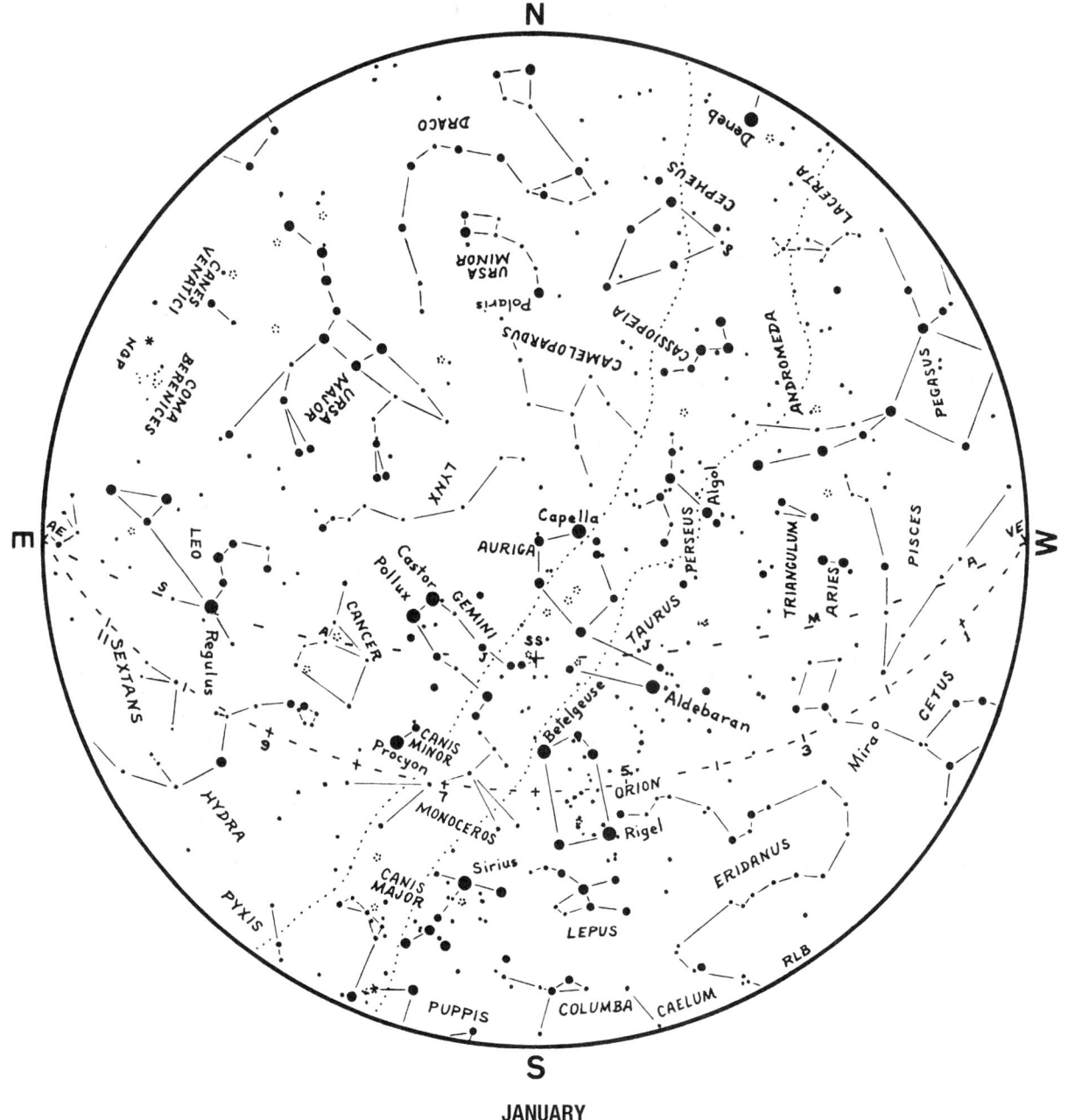

JANUARY

THE NAKED-EYE PLANETS FOR 1997

The planets do *not* appear on the bimonthly star maps. They move slowly, relative to the background stars, near the *ecliptic*, which *is* shown on the maps. Mercury is never more than about 25° from the sun. Venus is very bright and is never more than about 45° from the sun. Mars is reddish. Jupiter is bright. Mercury, Mars and Saturn are comparable in brightness with the brightest stars.

January

MERCURY may be visible, late in the month, low in the southeast, just before sunrise. It is close to Venus on the 12th.

VENUS may be visible, early in the month, low in the southeast, just before sunrise. It is close to Mercury on the 12th.

MARS, moving through Virgo, rises in the southeast before midnight, and is west of south by sunrise.

JUPITER is not visible this month.

SATURN, in Pisces, is visible in the southwest at sunset, and sets a few hours later.

February

MERCURY may be visible, early in the month, very low in the southeast, just before sunrise. It is close to Jupiter on the 12th.

VENUS may be visible, at the beginning of the month, very low in the southeast, just before sunrise. It is close to Jupiter on the 6th.

MARS, in Virgo, rises in mid-evening, and is visible for the rest of the night. It is brightening rapidly as it approaches opposition to the sun.

JUPITER, in Capricorn, is visible, late in the month, low in the southeast, just before sunrise. It is very close to Venus on the 6th, but will be difficult to see at that time.

SATURN, in Pisces, is visible low in the southwest at sunset, and sets a few hours later.

Canadian Almanac & Directory 1997

THE NAKED-EYE PLANETS FOR 1997

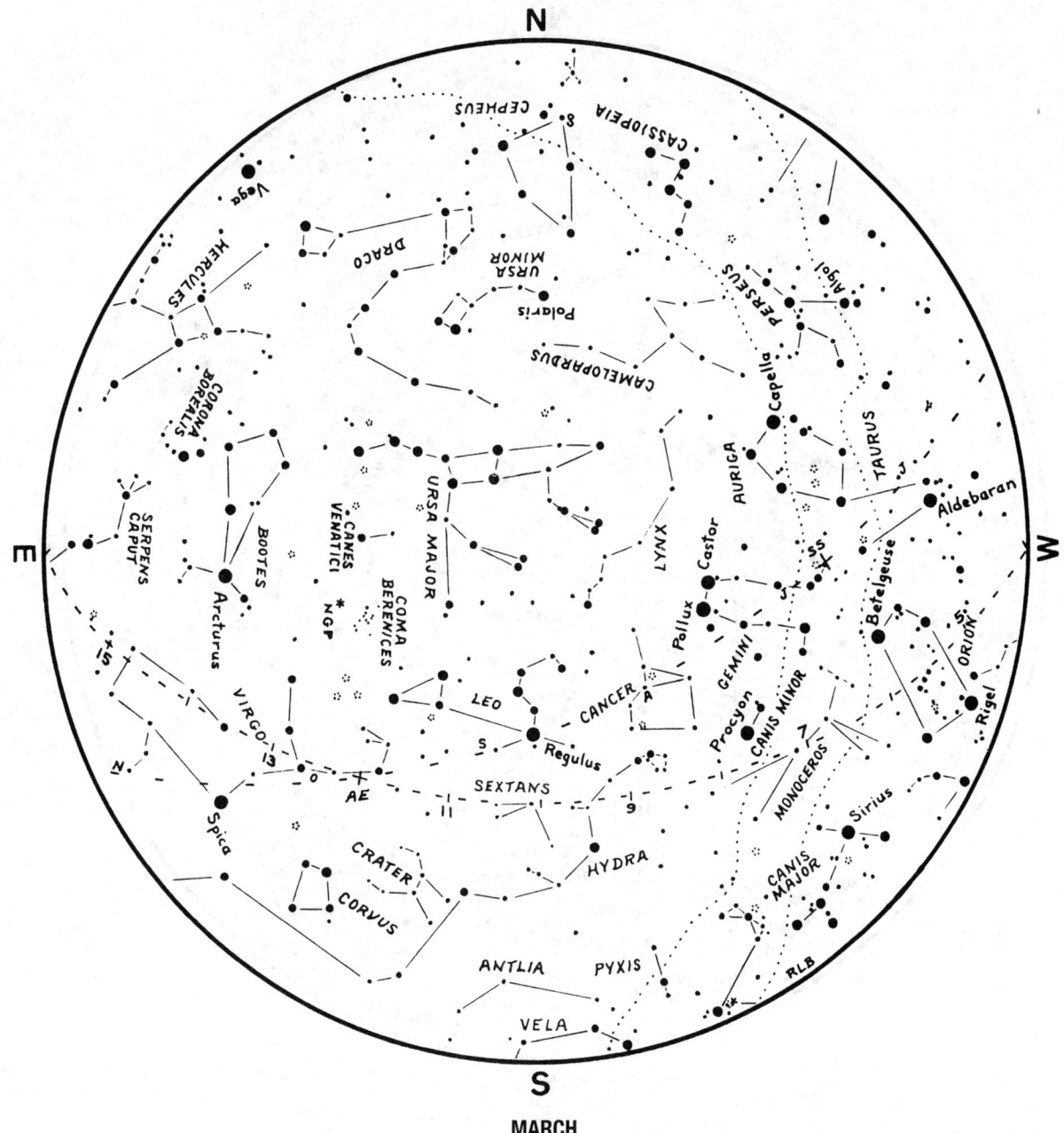

MARCH

THE NAKED-EYE PLANETS FOR 1997

The planets do *not* appear on the bimonthly star maps. They move slowly, relative to the background stars, near the *ecliptic*, which *is* shown on the maps. Mercury is never more than about 25° from the sun. Venus is very bright and is never more than about 45° from the sun. Mars is reddish. Jupiter is bright. Mercury, Mars and Saturn are comparable in brightness with the brightest stars.

March

MERCURY may be visible, at the end of the month, very low in the southwest, just after sunset.

VENUS is not visible this month.

MARS moves into Leo late in the month. It is at opposition to the sun on the 17th. It rises at about sunset, and is visible all night.

JUPITER, in Capricorn, is visible, very low in the southeast, just before sunrise.

SATURN may be visible at the beginning of the month, very low in the southwest, just after sunset.

April

MERCURY is visible during the first half of the month, very low in the west, just after sunset.

VENUS is not visible this month.

MARS, in Leo, rises before sunset, and is visible most of the night.

JUPITER, in Capricorn, is visible, low in the southeast, just before sunrise.

SATURN, in Cetus, may be visible at the end of the month (but with great difficulty), very low in the southeast, just before sunrise.

Canadian Almanac & Directory 1997

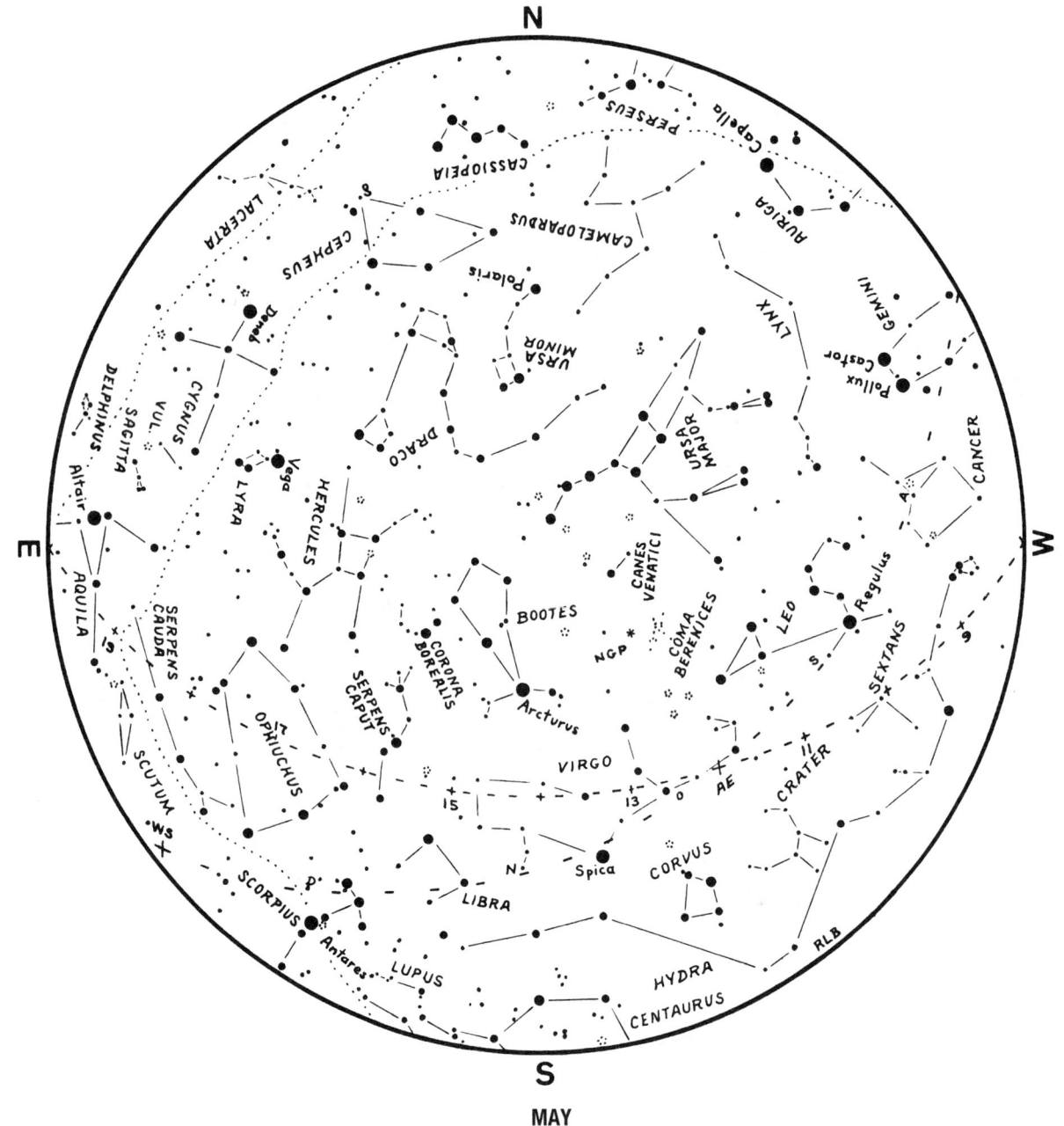

MAY

THE NAKED-EYE PLANETS FOR 1997

The planets do *not* appear on the bimonthly star maps. They move slowly, relative to the background stars, near the *ecliptic*, which *is* shown on the maps. Mercury is never more than about 25° from the sun. Venus is very bright and is never more than about 45° from the sun. Mars is reddish. Jupiter is bright. Mercury, Mars and Saturn are comparable in brightness with the brightest stars.

May

MERCURY may be visible late in the month, with great difficulty, very low in the southeast, just before sunrise.

VENUS may be visible at the end of the month, with difficulty, very low in the west, just after sunset.

MARS, in Leo, is high in the south at sunset, and sets after midnight.

JUPITER, in Capricorn, rises around midnight, and is low in the south by sunrise.

SATURN, in Pisces, may be visible with difficulty, very low in the east, just before sunrise.

June

MERCURY may be visible at the beginning of the month, with great difficulty, very low in the southeast, just before sunrise.

VENUS may be visible (especially later in the month), very low in the west, just after sunset.

MARS moves from Leo into Virgo early in the month. It is in the south at sunset, and sets about midnight.

JUPITER, in Capricorn, rises about midnight, and is visible for the rest of the night.

SATURN, in Pisces, rises after midnight, and is approaching south by sunrise.

Canadian Almanac & Directory 1997

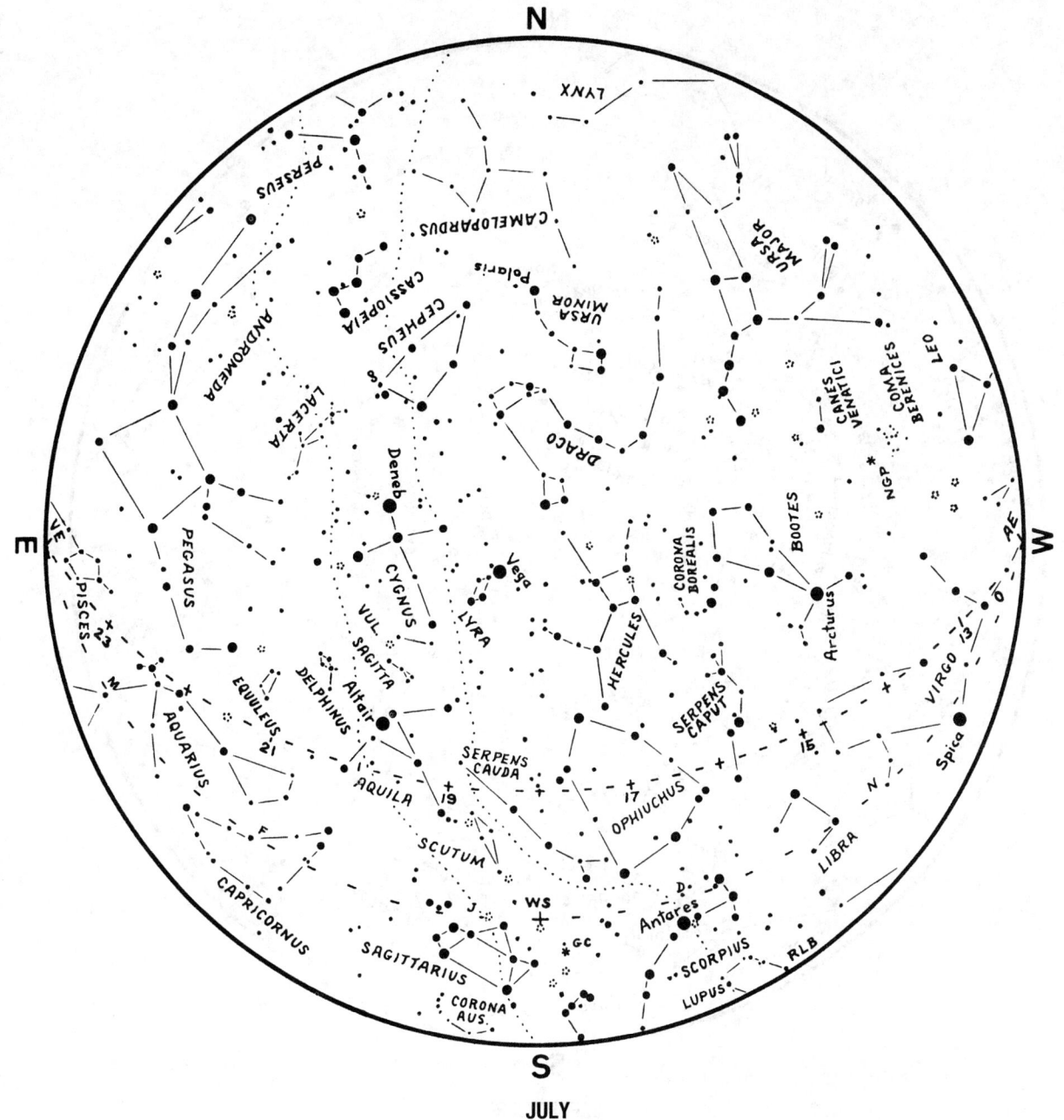

JULY

THE NAKED-EYE PLANETS FOR 1997

The planets do *not* appear on the bimonthly star maps. They move slowly, relative to the background stars, near the *ecliptic*, which *is* shown on the maps. Mercury is never more than about 25° from the sun. Venus is very bright and is never more than about 45° from the sun. Mars is reddish. Jupiter is bright. Mercury, Mars and Saturn are comparable in brightness with the brightest stars.

July

MERCURY may be visible in the last half of the month, very low in the west, just after sunset. It is close to Regulus on the 27th.

VENUS is bright, and becoming more visible, but it is still very low in the west at sunset. It is close to Regulus on the 23rd.

MARS, in Virgo, is west of south at sunset, and sets a few hours later.

JUPITER, in Capricorn, rises after sunset, and is visible for the rest of the night.

SATURN, in Pisces, rises after midnight, and is in the southeast at sunrise.

August

MERCURY may be visible early in the month, with great difficulty, very low in the west, just after sunset.

VENUS is visible, very low in the west, just after sunset.

MARS moves from Virgo into Libra late in the month, passing close to Spica on the 2nd. It is visible, low in the west at sunset, and sets a few hours later.

JUPITER, in Capricorn, rises about sunset, and is visible all night. It is opposite the sun on the 9th.

SATURN, in Pisces, rises before midnight, and is visible for the rest of the night.

1-20 THE NAKED-EYE PLANETS FOR 1997

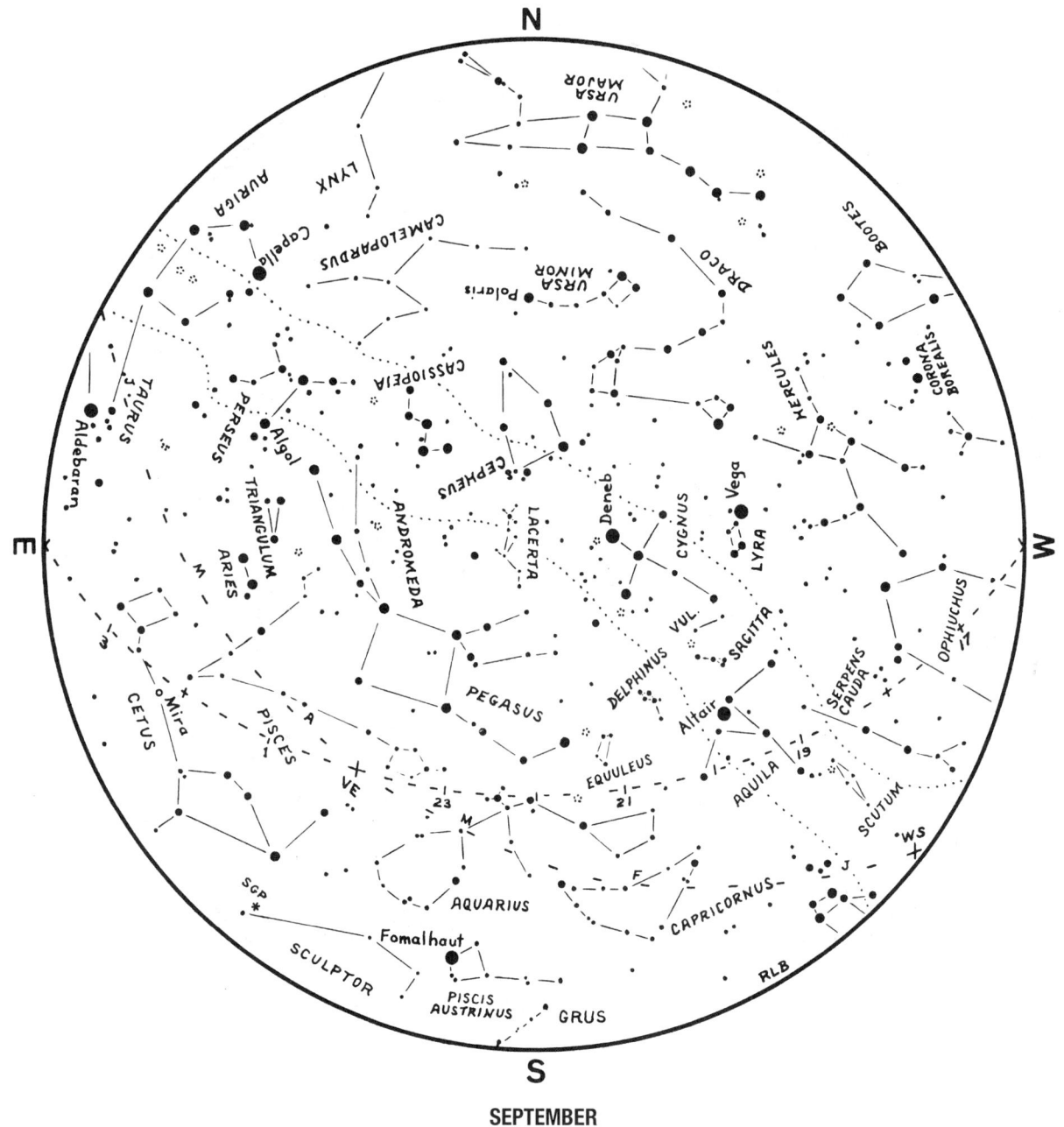

SEPTEMBER

THE NAKED-EYE PLANETS FOR 1997

The planets do *not* appear on the bimonthly star maps. They move slowly, relative to the background stars, near the *ecliptic*, which *is* shown on the maps. Mercury is never more than about 25° from the sun. Venus is very bright and is never more than about 45° from the sun. Mars is reddish. Jupiter is bright. Mercury, Mars and Saturn are comparable in brightness with the brightest stars.

September

MERCURY is visible in the middle of the month, very low in the east, just before sunrise.

VENUS is a brilliant object, low in the west, just after sunset.

MARS moves from Libra into Scorpius late in the month. It is visible, low in the southwest at sunset, and it sets a few hours later.

JUPITER, in Capricorn, is low in the southeast at sunset, and is visible most of the night.

SATURN, in Pisces, rises shortly after sunset, and is visible for the rest of the night.

October

MERCURY is not visible this month.

VENUS is a brilliant object, low in the southwest, just after sunset. It is close to Antares on the 16th, and to Mars on the 26th.

MARS moves from Scorpius into Ophiuchus in mid-month, passing near Antares on the 11th. It is low in the southwest, just after sunset, and sets a few hours later. On the 26th, it is near Venus.

JUPITER, in Capricorn, is low in the south at sunset, and sets about midnight.

SATURN, in Pisces, is opposite the sun on the 10th. It rises about sunset, and is visible all night.

Canadian Almanac & Directory 1997

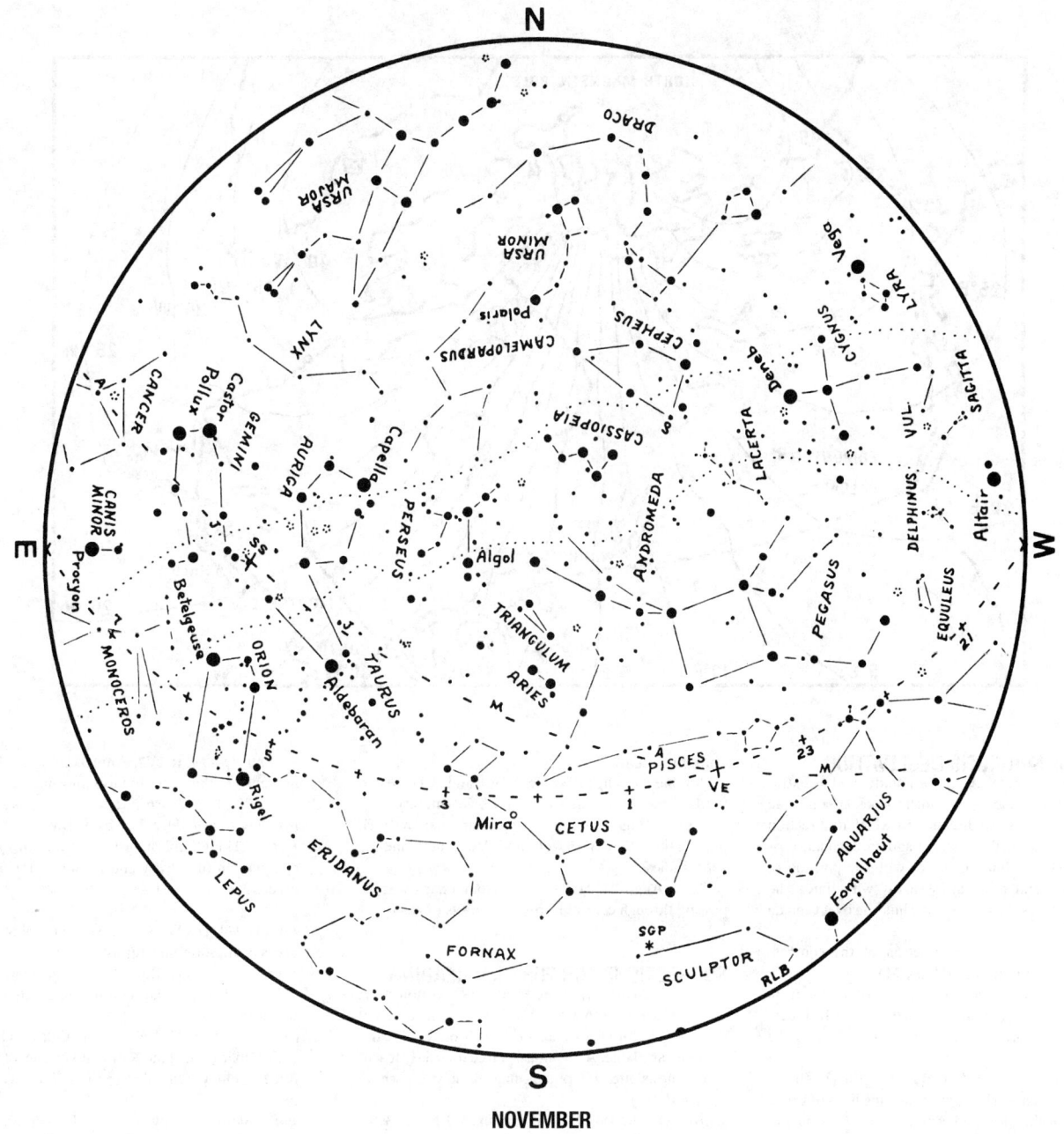

NOVEMBER

THE NAKED-EYE PLANETS FOR 1997

The planets do *not* appear on the bimonthly star maps. They move slowly, relative to the background stars, near the *ecliptic*, which *is* shown on the maps. Mercury is never more than about 25° from the sun. Venus is very bright and is never more than about 45° from the sun. Mars is reddish. Jupiter is bright. Mercury, Mars and Saturn are comparable in brightness with the brightest stars.

November

MERCURY may be visible at the end of the month, with great difficulty, very low in the southwest, just after sunset.

VENUS is a brilliant object, low in the southwest, just after sunset; it sets a few hours later.

MARS moves from Ophiuchus into Sagittarius early in the month, and is close to Venus. It is visible, low in the southwest, after sunset, and sets a few hours later.

JUPITER, in Capricorn, is a bright object in the southwestern sky at sunset; it sets a few hours later.

SATURN, in Pisces, is approaching south at sunset, and sets after midnight.

December

MERCURY may be visible at the beginning of the month, with great difficulty, very low in the southwest, just after sunset.

VENUS is a brilliant object, low in the southwest, after sunset; it sets a few hours later. It is close to Mars on the 22nd.

MARS moves from Sagittarius into Capricorn late in the month. It is visible low in the southwest, after sunset, and sets a few hours later. It is close to Venus on the 22nd.

JUPITER, in Capricorn, is visible low in the southwest, after sunset, and sets a few hours later.

SATURN, in Pisces, is high in the south at sunset, and sets about midnight.

1-22 CHART OF MAGNETIC DECLINATION

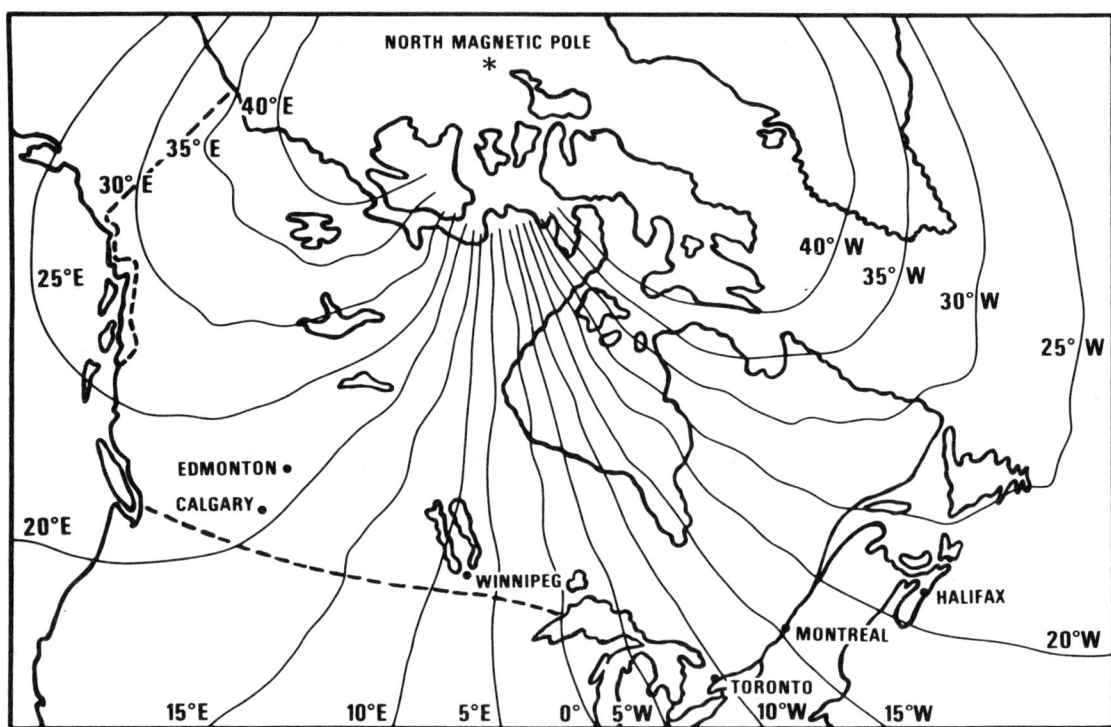

CHART OF MAGNETIC DECLINATION

A compass needle, even when unaffected by extraneous magnetic fields, does not in general point due north. The amount and direction by which its direction differs from true north is called magnetic declination or variation. The declination varies with the position of the observer and also varies slowly with time. The above chart gives the values of declination over Canada as of 1980.

Example: What is the direction of the compass needle at the southern tip of Lake Manitoba?

From the chart this point is about 3/4 of the way from the line of 5°E declination towards the line of 10°E declination. Therefore the declination is 9°E, i.e., the needle points 9° east of true north.

The Isogonic Map of Canada MCR 701 (1980), revised every 5 years, a large map showing lines of Equal Magnetic Declination and Annual Change is obtainable from the Canada Map Office, 615 Booth St., Ottawa ON K1A 0E9.

ECLIPSES DURING 1997

In 1997, there will be four eclipses, two of the Sun, and two of the Moon.

1. **A total eclipse of the Sun** on March 8-9, visible from northeast Asia. Although the total phases are not visible from North America, some of the partial phases are visible from parts of BC, the Yukon, and the NWT.

2. **A partial eclipse of the Moon** on March 24. The beginning of the umbral phase is visible from North America except Alaska and Northwest Canada and the end is visible from North America except the Aleutian Islands. The magnitude of the eclipse (the fraction of the moon's diameter in the earth's shadow) is 0.924.

3. **A partial eclipse of the Sun** on September 1-2, visible from Australia, New Zealand, and parts of Antarctica, but not from North America.

4. **A total eclipse of the Moon** on September 16, not visible in North America.

Looking Ahead:

Among the eclipses visible in 1998 and 1999 are two total eclipses of the sun which may be of interest:

1. On February 26, 1998, visible from a narrow track passing through parts of Colombia, Venezuela, and the West Indies.

2. On August 11, 1999, visible from a narrow track passing through central Europe and parts of Asia.

SUGGESTIONS FOR FURTHER READING

Astronomical Society of the Pacific, 390 Ashton Ave., San Francisco CA USA 94112. Excellent source of astronomical slides and other such material; catalogue available. Also publish a free quarterly teachers' newsletter (to obtain, mail request on school letterhead).

Astronomy, PO Box 1612, Waukesha WI USA 53187. Popular non-technical monthly magazine for general astronomy readers.

The Backyard Astronomer's Guide, by Terence Dickinson & Alan Dyer. Camden House Publishing, 1991. The best guide to equipment & techniques.

The Beginner's Observing Guide, by Leo Enright. Royal Astronomical Society of Canada, 136 Dupont St., Toronto ON M5R 1V2. A simple but serious introduction to the night sky. (3rd edition: 1996-2000)

The Cold Light of Dawn, by Richard Jarrell. University of Toronto Press, 1988. An authoritative and comprehensive history of Canadian astronomy.

Exploring the Night Sky, by Terence Dickinson. Camden House Publishing, 1987. An award-winning guide, especially for young people.

Looking Up, by Peter Broughton. Dundurn Press, 1993. A history of the Royal Astronomical Society of Canada, illustrated.

Nightwatch, by Terence Dickinson. Camden House Publishing, 1989. Excellent introduction to the night sky.

Observer's Handbook, edited by Roy L. Bishop. Royal Astronomical Society of Canada, 136 Dupont St., Toronto ON M5R 1V2. Annual guide to sky phenomena & other astronomical information.

Project SPICA: A Teacher Resource to Enhance Astronomy Education, edited by N. Butcher Ball et al. Kendall/Hunt Publishing Co., 1994. An excellent compilation of activity and resources for teaching grades 3 to 12.

Sky Atlas 2000.0, by Wil Tirion. Sky Publishing. A popular sky atlas for amateur astronomers.

Sky & Telescope, PO Box 9111, Belmont MA USA 02178-9111. A popular monthly magazine for amateur astronomers.

SkyNews. PO Box 9724, Station T, Ottawa ON K1G 5A3. Publication of the National Museum of Science & Technology; general astronomy from a Canadian perspective.

Summer Stargazing, by Terence Dickinson. Firefly Books, 1996. A practical, user-friendly guide.

The Universe at your Fingertips, edited by Andrew Fraknoi et al. Astronomical Society of the Pacific, 390 Ashton Avenue, San Francisco CA USA 94112. Another excellent collection of teaching activities & resources.

CANADIAN ASTRONOMY WEB SITES

Almost all of the astronomical institutions mentioned on page 1-1, and many of the branches of the Royal Astronomical Society of Canada, have sites on the World Wide Web. They can be accessed from the following key sites:

Canadian Astronomical Society: http://www.astro.umontreal.ca/~casca

Department of Astronomy, University of Toronto: http://www.astro.utoronto.ca/home.html

Royal Astronomical Society of Canada: http://www.stmarys.ca/rasc/nat

Canadian Almanac & Directory 1997

PERPETUAL CALENDAR
(Table for Determining the Weekday of a Given Date)

In the YEAR table, locate the first two figures of the given year (lower left) and the last two figures (upper right) and take the number at the intersection.

With that number, enter the MONTH table, and take the number at the intersection with the given month. Note the special columns for January and February in the case of a bissextile (leap) year.

With that number, enter the DAY OF THE MONTH table. The weekday is found at the intersection with the given day of the month.

Example: 1970 March 7

	00	01	02	03	—	04	05
	06	07	—	08	09	10	11
	—	12	13	14	15	—	16
	17	18	19	—	20	21	22
	23	—	24	25	26	27	—
	28	29	30	31	—	32	33
	34	35	—	36	37	38	39
	—	40	41	42	43	—	44
	45	46	47	—	48	49	50
	51	—	52	53	54	55	—
	56	57	58	59	—	60	61
	62	63	—	64	65	66	67
	—	68	69	70	71	—	72
	73	74	75	—	76	77	78
	79	—	80	81	82	83	—
	84	85	86	87	—	88	89
	90	91	—	92	93	94	95
YEAR	—	96	97	98	99		

0	7	14	17	21	6	0	1	2	3	4	5
1	8	15 *J*			5	6	0	1	2	3	4
2	9		18	22	4	5	6	0	1	2	3
3	10				3	4	5	6	0	1	2
4	11	15 *G*	19	23	2	3	4	5	6	0	1
5	12	16	20	24	1	2	3	4	5	6	0
6	13				0	1	2	3	4	5	6

J: until 1582 October 4 inclusively (Julian Calendar)
G: from 1582 October 15 onwards (Gregorian Calendar)
Example: In the first table, we find 5 at the intersection of 19 and 70.

MONTH	May	Feb. (B) Aug.	Feb. March Nov.	June	Sept. Dec.	Jan. (B) April July	Jan. Oct.
1	2	3	4	5	6	0	1
2	3	4	5	6	0	1	2
3	4	5	6	0	1	2	3
4	5	6	0	1	2	3	4
5	6	0	1	2	3	4	5
6	0	1	2	3	4	5	6
0	1	2	3	4	5	6	0

(B) = Bissextile (leap) year
Example: In the second table, we find 1 at the intersection of 5 and March.

DAY OF MONTH	1 8 15 22 29	2 9 16 23 30	3 10 17 24 31	4 11 18 25	5 12 19 26	6 13 20 27	7 14 21 28
1	Sun.	Mon.	Tue.	Wed.	Thur.	Fri.	Sat.
2	Mon.	Tue.	Wed.	Thur.	Fri.	Sat.	Sun.
3	Tue.	Wed.	Thur.	Fri.	Sat.	Sun.	Mon.
4	Wed.	Thur.	Fri.	Sat.	Sun.	Mon.	Tue.
5	Thur.	Fri.	Sat.	Sun.	Mon.	Tue.	Wed.
6	Fri.	Sat.	Sun.	Mon.	Tue.	Wed.	Thu.
0	Sat.	Sun.	Mon.	Tue.	Wed.	Thu.	Fri.

Example: In the third table, we find *Saturday* at the intersection of 1 and 7.

Reprinted from *Astronomical Tables of the Sun, Moon and Planets*, by Jean Meeus (Willmann-Bell Inc., 1983), with the permission of the publisher.

Canadian Almanac & Directory 1997

FIXED AND MOVABLE FESTIVALS AND ANNIVERSARIES
(Gregorian Calendar)

	1997			1998			1999			2000			2001		
JANUARY begins on	Wed.			Thu.			Fri.			Sat.			Mon.		
New Year's Day	We	Jan.	1	Th	Jan.	1	Fr	Jan.	1	Sa	Jan.	1	Mo	Jan.	1
Circumcision	We	Jan.	1	Th	Jan.	1	Fr	Jan.	1	Sa	Jan.	1	Mo	Jan.	1
Mary Mother of God	We	Jan.	1	Th	Jan.	1	Fr	Jan.	1	Sa	Jan.	1	Mo	Jan.	1
Epiphany	Mo	Jan.	6	Tu	Jan.	6	We	Jan.	6	Th	Jan.	6	Sa	Jan.	6
Church Unity Week begins on	Su	Jan.	19	Su	Jan.	18	Su	Jan.	24	Su	Jan.	23	Su	Jan.	21
FEBRUARY begins on	Sat.			Sun.			Mon.			Tue.			Thu.		
Lunar New Year (Chinese, etc.)	Fr	Feb.	7	We	Jan.	28	Mo	Feb.	15	Fr	Feb.	4	Sa	Feb.	24
Ash Wednesday	We	Feb.	12	We	Feb.	25	We	Feb.	17	We	Mar.	8	We	Feb.	28
St. Valentine's Day	Fr	Feb.	14	Sa	Feb.	14	Su	Feb.	14	Mo	Feb.	14	We	Feb.	14
First Sunday of Lent	Su	Feb.	16	Su	Mar.	1	Su	Feb.	28	Su	Mar.	12	Su	Mar.	4
MARCH begins on	Sat.			Sun.			Mon.			Wed.			Thu.		
St. David	Sa	Mar.	1	Su	Mar.	1	Mo	Mar.	1	We	Mar.	1	Th	Mar.	1
World Day of Prayer	Fr	Mar.	7	Fr	Mar.	6	Fr	Mar.	5	Fr	Mar.	3	Fr	Mar.	2
Passion Sunday	Su	Mar.	16	Su	Mar.	29	Su	Mar.	21	Su	Apr.	9	Su	Apr.	1
St. Patrick	Mo	Mar.	17	Tu	Mar.	17	We	Mar.	17	Fr	Mar.	17	Sa	Mar.	17
St. Joseph (Patron Saint of Canada)	We	Mar.	19	Th	Mar.	19	Fr	Mar.	19	Su	Mar.	19	Mo	Mar.	19
Palm Sunday	Su	Mar.	23	Su	Apr.	5	Su	Mar.	28	Su	Apr.	16	Su	Apr.	8
Annunciation	Tu	Mar.	25	We	Mar.	25	Th	Mar.	25	Sa	Mar.	25	Su	Mar.	25
Good Friday	Fr	Mar.	28	Fr	Apr.	10	Fr	Apr.	2	Fr	Apr.	21	Fr	Apr.	13
Easter Sunday	Su	Mar.	30	Su	Apr.	12	Su	Apr.	4	Su	Apr.	23	Su	Apr.	15
APRIL begins on	Tue.			Wed.			Thu.			Sat.			Sun.		
Daylight Savings Time begins	Su	Apr.	6	Su	Apr.	5	Su	Apr.	4	Su	Apr.	2	Su	Apr.	1
First Day of Passover (Pesach)	Tu	Apr.	22	Sa	Apr.	11	Th	Apr.	1	Th	Apr.	20	Su	Apr.	8
St. George	We	Apr.	23	Th	Apr.	23	Fr	Apr.	23	Su	Apr.	23	Mo	Apr.	23
MAY begins on	Thu.			Fri.			Sat.			Mon.			Tue.		
Rogation Sunday	Su	May	4	Su	May	17	Su	May	9	Su	May	28	Su	May	20
Ascension	Th	May	8	Th	May	21	Th	May	13	Th	June	1	Th	May	24
Islamic New Year*	Fr	May	9	Tu	Apr.	28	Sa	Apr.	17	Th	Apr.	6	Mo	Mar.	26
Mother's Day	Su	May	11	Su	May	10	Su	May	9	Su	May	14	Su	May	13
Ascension Sunday	Su	May	11	Su	May	24	Su	May	16	Su	June	4	Su	May	27
Pentecost (Whit Sunday)	Su	May	18	Su	May	31	Su	May	23	Su	June	11	Su	June	3
Victoria Day	Mo	May	19	Mo	May	18	Mo	May	24	Mo	May	22	Mo	May	21
Trinity Sunday	Su	May	25	Su	June	7	Su	May	30	Su	June	18	Su	June	10
Corpus Christi (Thursday)	Th	May	29	Th	June	11	Th	June	3	Th	June	22	Th	June	14
JUNE begins on	Sun.			Mon.			Tue.			Thu.			Fri.		
Corpus Christi (Sunday)	Su	June	1	Su	June	14	Su	June	6	Su	June	25	Su	June	17
Sacred Heart of Jesus	Fr	June	6	Fr	June	19	Fr	June	11	Fr	June	30	Fr	June	22
Pentecost (Shavuoth)	We	June	11	Su	May	31	Fr	May	21	Fr	June	9	Mo	May	28
Father's Day	Su	June	15	Su	June	21	Su	June	20	Su	June	18	Su	June	17
St. John Baptist	Tu	June	24	We	June	24	Th	June	24	Sa	June	24	Su	June	24
St. Peter and St. Paul	Su	June	29	Mo	June	29	Tu	June	29	Th	June	29	Fr	June	29
JULY begins on	Tue.			Wed.			Thu.			Sat.			Sun.		
Canada Day	Tu	July	1	We	July	1	Th	July	1	Sa	July	1	Su	July	1
AUGUST begins on	Fri.			Sat.			Sun.			Tue.			Wed.		
Transfiguration	We	Aug.	6	Th	Aug.	6	Fr	Aug.	6	Su	Aug.	6	Mo	Aug.	6
Assumption	Fr	Aug.	15	Sa	Aug.	15	Su	Aug.	15	Tu	Aug.	15	We	Aug.	15
SEPTEMBER begins on	Mon.			Tue.			Wed.			Fri.			Sat.		
Labour Day	Mo	Sept.	1	Mo	Sep.	7	Mo	Sept.	6	Mo	Sept.	4	Mo	Sept.	3
St. Michael	Mo	Sept.	29	Tu	Sep.	29	We	Sept.	29	Fr	Sept.	29	Sa	Sept.	29
OCTOBER begins on	Wed.			Thu.			Fri.			Sun.			Mon.		
Hebrew New Year	Th	Oct.	2	Mo	Sep.	21	Sa	Sept.	11	Sa	Sept.	30	Th	Sept.	18
Day of Atonement (Yom Kippur)	Sa	Oct.	11	We	Sep.	30	Mo	Sept.	20	Mo	Oct.	9	Th	Sept.	27
Thanksgiving	Mo	Oct.	13	Mo	Oct.	12	Mo	Oct.	11	Mo	Oct.	9	Mo	Oct.	8
First Day of Feast of Tabernacles (Sukkoth)	Th	Oct.	16	Mo	Oct.	5	Sa	Sept.	25	Sa	Oct.	14	Tu	Oct.	2
Daylight Savings Time ends	Su	Oct.	26	Su	Oct.	25	Su	Oct.	31	Su	Oct.	29	Su	Oct.	28
NOVEMBER begins on	Sat.			Sun.			Mon.			Wed.			Thu.		
All Saints Day	Sa	Nov.	1	Su	Nov.	1	Mo	Nov.	1	We	Nov.	1	Th	Nov.	1
Remembrance Day	Tu	Nov.	11	We	Nov.	11	Th	Nov.	11	Sa	Nov.	11	Su	Nov.	11
St. Andrew	Su	Nov.	30	Mo	Nov.	30	Tu	Nov.	30	Th	Nov.	30	Fr	Nov.	30
First Sunday in Advent	Su	Nov.	30	Su	Nov.	29	Su	Nov.	28	Su	Dec.	3	Su	Dec.	2
DECEMBER begins on	Mon.			Tue.			Wed.			Fri.			Sat.		
First Day in Hanukah	We	Dec.	24	Mo	Dec.	14	Sa	Dec.	4	Fr	Dec.	22	Mo	Dec.	10
Christmas Day	Th	Dec.	25	Fr	Dec.	25	Sa	Dec.	25	Mo	Dec.	25	Tu	Dec.	25
Last Day of Year	Wed.			Thu.			Fri.			Sun.			Mon.		

*These are tabular dates of the Islamic New Year; the new year begins at sunset on the day before. According to Islamic custom, the date of the new year is actually set by the direct observation of the new crescent moon.

STANDARD HOLIDAYS in Canada include the following: New Year's Day, Good Friday, Canada Day, Labour Day, Christmas Day, and any other day so proclaimed by the Governor General of Canada, or the Lieutenants Governor of the Provinces. Additionally, Provincial Holidays include:

ALBERTA: Victoria Day, Thanksgiving Day, Remembrance Day, Alberta Family Day (third Monday in February)
BRITISH COLUMBIA: Victoria Day, Thanksgiving Day, Remembrance Day, British Columbia Day (usually the first Monday in August)
MANITOBA: Victoria Day, Thanksgiving Day, Remembrance Day
NEW BRUNSWICK: New Brunswick Day
NORTHWEST TERRITORIES: Victoria Day, Thanksgiving Day, Remembrance Day, Civic Holiday (usually first Monday in August)
NOVA SCOTIA: Remembrance Day
ONTARIO: Victoria Day, Thanksgiving Day, Boxing Day
QUÉBEC: Victoria Day, Thanksgiving Day, St-Jean-Baptiste Day (June 24)
SASKATCHEWAN: Victoria Day, Thanksgiving Day, Remembrance Day, Saskatchewan Day
YUKON: Victoria Day, Thanksgiving Day, Remembrance Day, Discovery Day (being the third Monday in August)

Canadian Almanac & Directory 1997

NATIONAL ANTHEM: O CANADA

From "Chapter 5, Statues of Canada 1980; proclaimed July 1, 1980." Composed by Calixa Lavallée; French lyrics written by Judge Adolphe-Basile Routhier; English lyrics written by Robert Stanley Weir (with some changes incorporated in 1967).

O Canada! Our home and native land!
True patriot love in all thy sons command.
With glowing hearts we see thee rise, The True North strong and free!
From far and wide, O Canada, We stand on guard for thee.
God keep our land glorious and free!
O Canada, we stand on guard for thee.
O Canada, we stand on guard for thee.

O Canada! Terre de nos aïeux!
Ton front est ceint de fleurons glorieux!
Car ton bras sait porter l'épée, Il sait porter la croix!
Ton histoire est une épopée Des plus brillants exploits.
Et ta valeur, de foi trempée,
Protégera nos foyers et nos droits,
Protégera nos foyers et nos droits.

FATHERS OF CONFEDERATION

Three conferences helped to pave the way for Confederation — those held at Charlottetown (September, 1864), Québec City (October, 1864) and London (December, 1866). As all the delegates who were at the Charlottetown conferences were also in attendance at Québec, the following list includes the names of all those who attended one or more of the three conferences.

*Hewitt Bernard was John A. Macdonald's private secretary. He served as secretary of both the Québec and London conferences.

DELEGATES TO THE CONFEDERATION CONFERENCES, 1864-1866

LEGEND: Charlottetown, 1 September, 1864   C
Québec, 10 October, 1864   Q
London, 4 December, 1866   L

CANADA
John A. Macdonald	C Q L
George E. Cartier	C Q L
Alexander T. Galt	C Q L
William McDougall	C Q L
Hector L. Langevin	C Q L
George Brown	C Q
Thomas D'Arcy McGee	C Q
Alexander Campbell	C Q
Sir Etienne P. Taché	Q
Oliver Mowat	Q
J.C. Chapais	Q
James Cockburn	Q
W.P. Howland	L
*Hewitt Bernard	

NOVA SCOTIA
Charles Tupper	C Q L
William A. Henry	C Q L
Jonathan McCully	C Q L
Adams G. Archibald	C Q L
Robert B. Dickey	Q
J.W. Ritchie	L

NEW BRUNSWICK
Samuel L. Tilley	C Q L
J.M. Johnson	C Q L
William H. Steeves	C Q
E.B. Chandler	C Q
John Hamilton Gray	C Q
Peter Mitchell	Q L
Charles Fisher	Q L
R.D. Wilmot	L

PRINCE EDWARD ISLAND
John Hamilton Gray	C Q
Edward Palmer	C Q
William H. Pope	C Q
A.A. Macdonald	C Q
George Coles	C Q
T.H. Haviland	Q
Edward Whelan	Q

NEWFOUNDLAND
F.B.T. Carter	Q
Ambrose Shea	Q

PARTICIPANTS TO THE FIRST MINISTERS' CONSTITUTIONAL CONFERENCE ON PATRIATION OF THE CONSTITUTION

(held in Ottawa from September 2 to 5, 1981)

The Right Honourable Pierre Elliott Trudeau, P.C., Q.C., M.P., Prime Minister of Canada;
The Honourable William G. Davis, Q.C., Premier of Ontario;
The Honourable René Lévesque, Premier of Québec;
The Honourable John M. Buchanan, Q.C., Premier of Nova Scotia;
The Honourable Richard B. Hatfield, Premier of New Brunswick;
The Honourable Sterling R. Lyon, Q.C., Premier of Manitoba;
The Honourable W.R. Bennett, Premier of British Columbia;
The Honourable J. Angus MacLean, P.C., D.F.C., C.D., Premier of Prince Edward Island;
The Honourable Allan Blakeney, Q.C., Premier of Saskatchewan;
The Honourable Peter Lougheed, Q.C., Premier of Alberta;
The Honourable Brian Peckford, Premier of Newfoundland.

TABLE OF PRECEDENCE FOR CANADA

(As revised on June 8, 1993)

1. The Governor General of Canada or the Administrator of the Government of Canada. (Notes 1, 2 and 2.1).
2. The Prime Minister of Canada. (Note 3).
3. The Chief Justice of Canada. (Note 4).
4. The Speaker of the Senate.
5. The Speaker of the House of Commons.
6. Ambassadors, High Commissioners, Ministers Plenipotentiary. (Note 5).
7. Members of the Cabinet with relative precedence governed by the date of their appointment to the Queen's Privy Council for Canada.
8. The Leader of the Opposition. (Subject to Note 3).
9. The Lieutenant Governor of Ontario;
   The Lieutenant Governor of Québec;
   The Lieutenant Governor of Nova Scotia;
   The Lieutenant Governor of New Brunswick;
   The Lieutenant Governor of Manitoba;
   The Lieutenant Governor of British Columbia;
   The Lieutenant Governor of Prince Edward Island;
   The Lieutenant Governor of Saskatchewan;
   The Lieutenant Governor of Alberta;
   The Lieutenant Governor of Newfoundland (Note 6).
10. Members of the Queen's Privy Council for Canada, not of the Cabinet, in accordance with the date of their appointment to the Privy Council.
11. Premiers of the Provinces of Canada in the same order as Lieutenant Governors. (Note 6).
12. The Commissioner of the Northwest Territories;
    The Commissioner of the Yukon Territory
13. Government Leader of the Northwest Territories;
    The Government Leader of the Yukon Territory
14. Representatives of Faith Communities. (Note 7).
15. Puisne Judges of the Supreme Court of Canada.
16. The Chief Justice and the Associate Chief Justices of the Federal Court of Canada.
17. (a) Chief Justices of the highest court of each province and territory;
    (b) Chief Justices and Associate Chief Justices of the other superior courts of the provinces and territories; with precedence within sub-categories (a) and (b) governed by the date of appointment as chief justice.
18. (a) Judges of the Federal Court of Canada.
    (b) Puisne Judges of the superior courts of the provinces and territories.
    (c) The Chief Judge of the Tax Court of Canada;
    (d) The Associate Chief Judge of the Tax Court of Canada;
    (e) Judges of the Tax Court of Canada; with precedence within each sub-category governed by date of appointment.
19. Senators of Canada.
20. Members of the House of Commons.
21. Consuls General of countries without diplomatic representation.
22. The Chief of the Defence Staff and the Commissioner of the Royal Canadian Mounted Police. (Note 8).
23. Speakers of Legislative Assemblies, within their Provinces and Territory.
24. Members of the Executive Councils, within their Provinces and Territory.
25. Judges of Provincial and Territorial Courts, within their Province and Territory.
26. Members of Legislative Assemblies, within their Provinces and Territory.

NOTES

1. The presence of The Sovereign in Canada does not impair or supersede the authority of the Governor General to perform the functions delegated to him under the Letters Patent. The Governor General, under all circumstances, should be accorded precedence immediately after The Sovereign.
2. Precedence to be given immediately after the Chief Justice of Canada to former Governors General, with relative precedence among them governed by the date of their leaving office.
2.1 Precedence to be given immediately after the former Governors General to surviving spouses of deceased former Governors General (applicable only where the spouse was married to the Governor General during the latter's term of office), with relative precedence among them governed by the dates on which the deceased former Governor General left office.
3. Precedence to be given immediately after the surviving spouses of deceased former Governors General referred to in Note 2.1 to former Prime Ministers, with relative precedence governed by the date of their first assumption of office.
4. Precedence to be given immediately after former Prime Ministers to former Chief Justices of Canada, with relative precedence among them governed by the dates of their appointment as Chief Justice of Canada.

Canadian Almanac & Directory 1997

5. Precedence among Ambassadors and High Commissioners, who rank equally, to be determined by the date of the presentation of their credentials. Precedence to be given to Chargés d'Affaires immediately after Ministers Plenipotentiary.
6. This provision does not apply to such ceremonies and occasions as are of a provincial nature.
7. The religious dignitaries will be senior Canadian representatives of faith communities having a significant presence in a relevant jurisdiction. The relevant precedence of the representatives of faith communities is to be governed by the date of their assumption in their present office, their representatives being given the same relative precedence.
8. This precedence to be given to the Chief of the Defence Staff and the Commissioner of the R.C.M.P. on occasions when he has official functions to perform, otherwise the Chief of the Defence Staff and the Commissioner of the R.C.M.P. to have equal precedence with Deputy Ministers with their relative position to be determined according to the respective dates of their appointments to office. The relative precedence of the Chief of the Defence Staff and R.C.M.P. Commissioner, Deputy Ministers and other high officials of the public service to be determined from time to time by the Secretary of State of Canada in consultation with the Prime Minister.

TABLE OF TITLES TO BE USED IN CANADA

(As revised June 18, 1993)

1. The Governor General of Canada to be styled "Right Honourable" for life and to be styled "His Excellency" and his wife "Her Excellency", or "Her Excellency" and her husband "His Excellency", as the case may be, while in office.
2. The Lieutenant Governor of a Province to be styled "Honourable" for life and to be styled "His Honour" and his wife "Her Honour", or "Her Honour" and her husband "His Honour", as the case may be, while in office.
3. The Prime Minister of Canada to be styled "Right Honourable" for life.
4. The Chief Justice of Canada to be styled "Right Honourable" for life.
5. Privy Councillors of Canada to be styled "Honourable" for life.
6. Senators of Canada to be styled "Honourable" for life.
7. The Speaker of the House of Commons to be styled "Honourable" while in office.
8. The Commissioner of a Territory to be styled "Honourable" while in office.
9. Puisne Judges of the Supreme Court of Canada and Judges of the Federal Courts and the Tax Court of Canada as well as the Judges of the undermentioned Courts in the Provinces and Territories:
    Ontario — Court of Appeal and the Ontario Court of Justice (General Division)
    Québec — The Court of Appeal and the Superior Court of Québec
    Nova Scotia — The Court of Appeal and the Supreme Court of Nova Scotia
    New Brunswick — The Court of Appeal and the Court of Queen's Bench of New Brunswick
    Manitoba — The Court of Appeal and the Court of Queen's Bench for Manitoba
    British Columbia — The Court of Appeal and the Supreme Court of British Columbia
    Prince Edward Island — The Supreme Court of Prince Edward Island
    Saskatchewan — The Court of Appeal and the Court of Queen's Bench for Saskatchewan
    Alberta — The Court of Appeal and the Court of Queen's Bench of Alberta
    Newfoundland — The Supreme Court of Newfoundland
    Northwest Territories — The Supreme Court of Northwest Territories
    Yukon Territory — The Supreme Court of Yukon to be styled "Honourable" while in office.
    (b) The Judges of the County and District Courts to be styled "Honourable" while in office.
10. Presidents and Speakers of the Legislative Assemblies of the Provinces and Territories to be styled "Honourable" while in office.
11. Members of the Executive Councils of the Provinces and Territories to be styled "Honourable" while in office.
12. Judges of Provincial and Territorial Courts (appointed by the Provincial and Territorial Governments) to be styled "Honourable" while in office.
13. The following are eligible to be granted permission by the Governor General, in the name of Her Majesty The Queen, to retain the title of "Honourable" after they have ceased to hold office:
    (a) Speakers of the House of Commons;
    (b) Commissioners of Territories;
    (c) Judges designated in item 9.
14. The title "Right Honourable" is granted for life to the following eminent Canadians:
    The Right Honourable Martial Asselin
    The Right Honourable Ellen L. Fairclough
    The Right Honourable Francis Alvin George Hamilton
    The Right Honourable Donald F. Mazankowski, P.C., M.P.
    The Right Honourable Jean-Luc Pepin
    The Right Honourable John Whitney Pickersgill

The Right Honourable Robert Lorne Stanfield

CANADIAN HONOURS SYSTEM

For some years after Confederation, awards were made of a few hereditary honours and some knighthoods and companionships in orders of chivalry, and this policy continued until the end of the first World War.

From 1919 until 1933 no titular honours were granted. There was a brief revival of the defunct honours policy during the Conservative administration of R.B. Bennett, and several distinctions were awarded 1934-35, but the prohibition was reinstated with the return of the Liberals to office in 1935. Consequently, at the outset of WWII Canadians in the armed services were not entitled to receive awards in the order of chivalry for which other Commonwealth personnel were eligible. A parliamentary committee appointed in 1943 recommended that the ban on nontitular honours be lifted, clearing the way for members of the military and civilians to receive recognition for wartime services.

The hundredth anniversary of Confederation, July 1st, 1967, was the occasion on which the Order of Canada was created as the first component of a distinctly Canadian honours system. More information concerning Order, Decorations and Medals (as well as various Governor General's awards) may be obtained by writing to: Public Information Directorate, Government House, 1 Sussex Dr., Ottawa ON K1A 0A1.

HERALDRY

Coats-of-arms, flags, badges and other heraldic devices are marks of honour and symbols of identity, authority and, in some cases, sovereignty. Each is granted by the Crown under an exercise of the Sovereign's prerogative to create heraldic honours.

Until June 4, 1988, Canadian corporations and individuals wishing to bear lawful arms petitioned the Sovereign's traditional heraldic officers in London and Edinburgh. On that date, by Royal Letters Patent, the Queen transferred the exercise of her heraldic prerogative, as Queen of Canada, to the Governor General who now heads a new office, the Canadian Heraldic Authority. With the act, heraldry, which has a long history in Canada, has been fully patriated.

These vice-regal responsibilities are administered by Canadian officers of arms appointed by commission under the Governor General's privy seal: the Herald Chancellor (the Secretary to the Governor General), the Deputy Herald Chancellor (the Deputy Secretary, Chancellery) and the Chief Herald of Canada (Director, Heraldry). He is assisted by three officers of arms: Saint-Laurent, Athabaska and Fraser heralds, and one officer of arms extraordinary, Dauphin Herald.

New heraldic emblems are granted, and existing ones registered, by the Chief Herald upon receipt of an enabling Warrant from the Herald Chancellor or the Deputy Herald Chancellor acting on behalf of the Governor General. Grants and registrations are made by Letters Patent, documents that set out the Governor General's heraldic responsibilities, describe the emblem granted, and feature a representation of the Governor General's personal arms. To ensure a lasting record, the newly granted and registered emblems are entered in Canada's national armorial, the Public Register of Arms, Flags and Badges of Canada. Since the Authority was created, hundreds of petitions have been received from every part of the country, most for new grants of arms.

CANADIAN HONOURS LIST

ORDER OF CANADA

As mentioned above, the Order of Canada was created July 1, 1967, and celebrates its thirtieth anniversary on July 1, 1997. Her Majesty The Queen is Sovereign of the Order of Canada and the Governor General is, by virtue of that office, Chancellor and Principal Companion. She is assisted in the administration of the Order by an Advisory Council which comprises:
a) the Chief Justice of Canada (Chairman)
b) the Clerk of the Privy Council
c) Deputy Minister, Canadian Heritage
d) the Chair of the Canada Council
e) the President of the Royal Society of Canada
f) the Chair of the Board of the Association of Universities and Colleges of Canada
g) where considered appropriate by the Governor General, not more than two other members can be appointed for three-year terms.

The Secretary to the Governor General is, by his/her office, Secretary General of the Order.

The Order of Canada is designed to honour Canadian citizens for outstanding achievement and service to the country or to humanity at large and also for distinguished service in particular localities and fields of activity. The Order comprises three levels of membership: Companion, Officer, Member. Up to 15 Companions may be appointed annually, but the total number of living Companions may not exceed 165. Up to 50 Officers and 100 Members may be appointed annually with no over-all limit.

The Order includes no titles of honour and confers no special privileges, hereditary or otherwise. Awards are made solely on the basis of merit. Members of the Order are entitled to place after their names the letters "C.C." for Companions, "O.C." for Officers, and "C.M." for Members.

Any person or organization may make nominations for appointment to the Order by writing to the Chancellery, Rideau Hall, Ottawa. The Advisory Council submits to the Governor General lists of those nominees who, in the opinion of the Council, are of greatest merit. Appointments to the Order are made by the Sovereign of the Order on the recommendation of the Governor General as Chancellor of the Order, under an instrument sealed with the Seal of the Order.

Non-Canadians whom the Government desires to honour may be accorded honourary membership in the Order. **See page 15 for colour reproductions of the Order of Canada.**

Companions of the Order of Canada/Compagnons de l'Ordre du Canada (C.C.)
14* indicates a promotion within the Order
(Appointed November 15, 1995)
Pierrette Alarie, C.C., Victoria, BC*
Louis Applebaum, C.C., Don Mills, ON*
Léopold Simoneau, C.C., Victoria, BC*
(Appointed May 9, 1996)
The Hon. John Lang Nichol, C.C., Vancouver, BC*
Huguette Oligny, C.C., Montréal, PQ*
Charles Robert Scriver, C.C., Montréal, PQ*

Officers of the Order of Canada/Officiers de l'Ordre du Canada (O.C.)
(Appointed November 15, 1995)
Harvey Barkun, O.C., Rockcliffe, ON
Donald W. Baxter, O.C., Montréal, PQ
André Bérard, O.C., Montréal, PQ
The Hon. Sidney L. Buckwold, O.C., Saskatoon, SK
Jean Davignon, O.C., Montréal, PQ
Abel Joseph Diamond, O.C., Toronto, AB
John Douglas Morecroft Griffin, O.C., Toronto, ON
Thomas Ranald Ide, O.C., Scarborough, ON
Norman David Inkster, O.C., Toronto, ON
The Hon. David C. (See-Chai) Lam, C.V.O., O.C., Vancouver, BC*
Carroll A. Laurin, O.C., Montréal, PQ
Arthur A. May, O.C., St. John's, NF
G. Wallace F. McCain, O.C., Fredericton, NB
Jean E. Pigott, O.C., Ottawa, ON
John Peter Lee Roberts, O.C., Calgary, AB*
Verna Huffman Splane, O.C., Vancouver, BC
Denis A. St-Onge, O.C., Ottawa, ON
Michel Vennat, O.C., Montréal, PQ
Bryce Weir, O.C., Chicago, IL & Edmonton, AB
(Appointed May 9, 1996)
Charles E. Beaulieu, O.C., Ste-Foy, PQ
André Bisson, O.C., Baie d'Urfé, PQ*
The Hon. Rosemary Brown, P.C., O.C., O.B.C., Vancouver, BC
Mona L. Campbell, O.C., Toronto, ON
"Stompin' Tom" Connors, O.C., Ballinafad, ON
Purdy Crawford, O.C., Toronto, ON
The Hon. Barnett J. Danson, P.C., O.C., Toronto, ON
Léon Dion, O.C., O.Q., Sillery, PQ
The Hon. André Dubé, O.C., Québec, PQ
Jean-Pierre Ferland, O.C., Montréal, PQ
Kenneth W. Harrigan, O.C., Oakville, ON
Jane Jacobs, O.C., Toronto, ON
Arthur Sackville Labatt, O.C., Toronto, ON
Geddy Lee, O.C., Toronto, ON
Alex Lifeson, O.C., Richmond Hill, ON
W. Thomas Molloy, O.C., Saskatoon, SK
Desmond Morton, O.C., Montréal, PQ
Neil E. Peart, O.C., Toronto, ON
Lloyd Montgomery Pidgeon, O.C., M.B.E., Kingston, ON
John Edward Poole, O.C., Edmonton, AB
David W. Strangway, O.C., Vancouver, BC
Robert Henry Thorlarkson, O.C., Headingley, MB
Cardinal Jean-Claude Turcotte, O.C., St. John's, NF
Victor L. Young, O.C., St. John's, NF

Members of the Order of Canada/Membres de l'Ordre du Canada (C.M.)
(Appointed November 15, 1995)
Nabil N. Antaki, C.M., Québec, PQ
Barbara Bettine Barrett, C.M., St. John's NF
Eric A. Barton, C.M., Toronto, ON
Luc Beauregard, C.M., Montréal, PQ
Jack Bell, C.M., O.B.C., Vancouver, BC
Frances Belzberg, C.M., Vancouver, BC
Gordon Brown, C.M., Westmount, PQ
Bonnie Laura McClung Cappucino, C.M., Maxville, ON
Fred Cappucino, C.M., Maxville, ON
Walter Curlook, C.M., Noumea, New Caledonia & Toronto, ON
Omer Deslauriers, C.M., Toronto, ON
Olive Patricia Dickason, C.M., Edmonton, AB
Ronald Dunkley, C.M., Waterloo, ON
Gordon Charles Emberley, C.M., Lac Du Bonnet, MB
Lorette Gallant, C.M., Moncton, NB
Yhetta Miriam Gold, C.M., Winnipeg, MB
Calvin Carl Gotlieb, C.M., Toronto, ON
Cora deYong Greenaway, C.M., Dartmouth, NS
Margaret Pictou LaBillois, C.M., Restigouche County, NB
Arthur Lamothe, C.M., Montréal, PQ
Roy Oliver Lindseth, C.M., Calgary, AB
Bob Lowery, C.M., Thompson, MB
Col. The Hon. Jack Marchall, C.M., C.D., Ottawa, ON
Judith Maxwell, C.M., Ottawa, ON
John Duncan McKellar, C.M., Toronto, ON
L. Jacques Ménard, C.M., Outremont, PQ
Kamal Midha, C.M., Saskatoon, SK
Donald Oliver Mills, C.M., Dartmouth, NS
Christopher Newton, C.M., Niagara-on-the-Lake, ON
Lena Kokom Nottaway, C.M., Rapid Lake, PQ
William Andrew O'Neil, C.M., London, England & Nepean, ON
Margaret Anchoretta Ormsby, C.M., O.B.C., Vernon, BC
Charles Thomas Peacocke, C.M., Edmonton, AB
Walter Podiluk, C.M., Saskatoon, SK
Jan Rubes, C.M., Toronto, ON
David Smith, C.M., Ottawa, ON
Donald James Smith, C.M., London, ON
Ernest Alvia (Smokey) Smith, V.C., C.M., C.D., Vancouver, BC
David F. Sobey, C.M., Stellarton, NS
Richard Beverly Splane, C.M., Vancouver, BC
Edna Staebler, C.M., Waterloo, ON
Joseph Manuel Tanenbaum, C.M., Toronto, ON
William Aubrey Tetley, C.M., Montréal, PQ
Walter B. Tilden, C.M., Toronto, ON
Armand Viau, C.M., Aylmer, PQ
Norman E. Webster, C.M., Montréal, PQ
(Appointed May 9, 1996)
Charles Anderson, C.M., Edmonton, AB
Margaret Weir Andrekson, C.M., Edmonton, AB
Evelyn Mary Atkinson, C.M., Vancouver, BC
George Balcan, C.M., Hampstead, PQ
Gerald Bales, C.M., London, ON
Christopher Richard Barnes, C.M., Victoria, BC
Jacques Beaudoin, C.M., Verchères, PQ
Jocelyn Beaudoin, C.M., Montréal PQ
Claude R. Brochu, C.M., Montréal, PQ
John F. Bulloch, C.M., North York, ON
William Collins, C.M., Calgary, AB
Ernest Coombs, C.M., Pickering, ON
Leslie L. Dan, C.M., North York, ON
Robert Davidson, C.M., O.B.C., Richmond, BC
William Andrew Dimma, C.M. Toronto, ON
Angèle Dubeau, C.M., Westmount, PQ
David Charles Earle, C.M., Toronto, ON
Paul Gauthier, C.M., Québec, PQ
James Gillies, C.M., North York, ON
Daniel Alexander Gillis, C.M., Riyadh, Arabia
John G.H. Halstead, C.M., Ottawa, ON
Charles Harold Hantho, C.M., Islington, ON
Jean McEachran Jones, C.M., Dundas, ON
Walter H. Kaasa, C.M., Edmonton, AB
Doris Knight, C.M., Regina, SK
Robinson Koilpillai, C.M., Edmonton, AB
Walter Oscar Kupsch, C.M., Saskatoon, SK
Mary Jo Leddy, C.M., Toronto, ON
Gilles Marcotte, C.M., Montréal, PQ
Frederic Shaw Martin, C.M., Aylmer, PQ
Col. The Hon. William John McKeag, C.M., C.D., Winnipeg, MB
Robert Patrick Barten Paine, C.M., Navan, ON
Winston Trevor Payne, C.M., Beaconsfield, PQ
William Burton Pearson, C.M., D.F.C., Ariss, ON
Gordon William Gavin Penrose, C.M., Scarborough, ON
Evelyn Agnes Pepper, C.M., Ottawa, ON
Michel Perron, C.M., Montréal, PQ
George S. Petty, C.M., Montréal, PQ
Beryl Potter, C.M., O.Ont., Scarborough, ON
The Hon. Marion Loretta Reid, C.M., Breadalbane, PE
Gordon Smith, C.M., West Vancouver, BC
Percy Starr, C.M., Klemtu, BC
Peter Stursberg, C.M., West Vancouver, BC
Antonio Tascona, C.M., Winnipeg, MB
Donald Garth Woodside, C.M., North York, ON

ORDER OF MILITARY MERIT
July 1, 1997 marks the twenty-fifth anniversary of the Order of Military Merit. The Order was created on July 1, 1972 to recognize meritorious service and devotion to duty by members of the Canadian Forces. The Order has three grades of membership: Commander (C.M.M.), Officer (O.M.M.) and Member (M.M.M.). The annual number of appointments is limited to one-tenth of one percent of the number of persons in the Canadian Forces in the preceding year. **See page 15 for colour reproductions of the Order of Military Merit.**

Commanders of the Order of Military Merit/ Commandeurs de l'Ordre du mérite militaire (C.M.M.)
(Appointed September 6, 1995)
L.Gen. J.M. Baril, C.M.M., M.S.M., C.D., St-Hubert, PQ*
L.Gen. J.E. Boyle, C.M.M., C.D., Ottawa, ON*
M.Gen. W.A. Clay, C.M.M., C.D., Ottawa, ON
M.Gen. E.W. Linden, C.M.M., C.D., Ottawa, ON
B.Gen. A.R. Macdonald, C.M.M., C.D., St-Hubert, PQ
Rear-Adm. R.D. Moore, C.M.M., C.D., Norfolk, VA, USA

Officers of the the Order of Military Merit/Officiers de l'Ordre du mérite militaire (O.M.M.)
(Appointed September 6, 1995)
Capt.(N) R.W. Allen, O.M.M., M.S.C., C.D., Halifax & Dartmouth, NS
L.Cdr. D.W. Bancroft, O.M.M., C.D., Victoria, BC
Col. J.S.R. Bastien, O.M.M., C.D., Bagotville & St-Louis-de-Terrebonne, PQ
Col. W.J.Brewer, O.M.M., C.D., Ottawa, ON & St-Bruno, PQ
Capt.(N) B.R. Brown, O.M.M., C.D., Ottawa & Watford, ON
L.Col. R.C. Coleman, O.M.M., C.D., St-Hubert, PQ & Toronto, Ottawa, ON
L.Col. J.D.M.G. Couture, O.M.M., C.D., Montréal & St-Bruno, PQ
L.Col. J.W. Craig, O.M.M., C.D., Ottawa, ON & New Westminster, BC
Col. C.K. Ford, O.M.M., C.D., Ottawa, ON & Winnipeg, MB
Cdr. D.J. Gallina, O.M.M., C.D., Halifax, NS & Niagara Falls, ON
L.Col. J.-R.R. Guilbault, O.M.M., C.D., Ottawa, ON
Cdr. R.P. Harrison, O.M.M., C.D., Toronto, ON & Victoria, BC
Col. T.M. Hearn, O.M.M., C.D., Ottawa, ON & Harbour Grace, NF
Col. A.W. Kalbfleisch, O.M.M., C.D., Ottawa, ON & Moose Jaw, SK
Maj. H.A. Kochaanski, O.M.M., C.D., Zagreb, Croatia & Regina, SK
Maj. J.J.-M.G. Larose, O.M.M., C.D., Ottawa, ON & Montréal, PQ
L.Col. J.G. Lindsay, O.M.M., C.D., Ottawa, ON
L.Col. D.J. MacLean, O.M.M., C.D., Wainwright, AB & Brockville, ON

Canadian Almanac & Directory 1997

Maj. W.D. Mahoney, O.M.M., C.D., Greenwood, NS & St. John's NF
K.A. McCrimmon, O.M.M., C.D., Westwin, MB & Windsor, ON
Col. J.C. Muise, O.M.M., C.D., Ottawa, ON & Cheticamp, NB
L.Col. M.B. Murphy, O.M.M., C.D., Shearwater & Wolfville, NS
Maj. N.D. Nolan, O.M.M., C.D., Kingston & Toronto, ON
Maj. V.R. Paddon, O.M.M., C.D., Hamilton & Brantford, ON
L.Col. R.J. Palmer, O.M.M., C.D., Ottawa, ON & Dartmouth, NS
Cdr. E.R. Paquette, O.M.M., C.D., Esquimalt, BC & Québec, PQ
L.Col. D.D. Peart, O.M.M., C.D., Tyndall, FL, USA & Brantford, ON
Col. A.M. Pellerin, O.M.M., C.D., Rome, Italy & Verdun, PQ
Col. J. Stewart, O.M.M., C.D., Ottawa, ON & Vancouver, BC
Col. R.B. Ward, O.M.M., C.D., Halifax & New Glasgow, NS
L.Col. R.A.E. Williams, O.M.M., C.D., Calgary, AB

Members of the Order of Military Merit/Membres de l'Ordre du mérite militaire (M.M.M.)
(Appointed September 6, 1995)

Petty Officer 1st Class P. Agostini, M.M.M., C.D., Victoria, BC & Hamilton, ON
Chief Petty Officer 2nd Class S. Ambrose, M.M.M., C.D., Halifax, NS & Montréal, PQ
Chief Warrant Officer J.G.G.J.-P. Archambault, M.M.M., C.D., Bagotville & Montréal, PQ
Master Warrant Officer D.W. Armstrong, M.M.M., C.D., Cold Lake, AB & Hedley, BC
Master Warrant Officer C.E. Asher, M.M.M., C.D., Halifax NS & Winnipeg, MB
Master Warrant Officer H.P.E. Aucoin, M.M.M., C.D., Belgium & Cheticamp, NS
Warrant Officer R.J. Baker, M.M.M., C.D., Tyndall, FL, USA & Ottawa, ON
Capt. R.M. Barry, M.M.M., C.D., Goose Bay & St. John's, NF
Master Warrant Officer D.P. Batchelor, M.M.M., C.D., Westwin & Gretna, MB
Chief Warrant Officer J.H. Bentley, M.M.M., C.D., Petawawa, ON & Glace Bay, NS
Chief Warrant Officer J.-M. Bernatchez, M.M.M., C.D., Borden, ON & Rivière-au-Renard, PQ
Chief Warrant Officer J.S. Boutet, M.M.M., C.D., St-Hubert & Île-Maligne, Lac-St-Jean, PQ
Chief Warrant Officer E.G. Brown, M.M.M., C.D., Toronto, ON
Master Warrant Officer J.M. Caron, M.M.M., C.D., Halifax, NS & Grimsby, PQ
Chief Warrant Officer R.M. Charest, M.M.M., C.D., St-Hubert & St-Raphael-d'Albertville, PQ
Chief Warrant Officer J.Y.R. Chartrand, M.M.M., C.D., Chilliwack, BC & St-Hubert, PQ
Chief Warrant Officer R.W. Cook, M.M.M., C.D., Cold Lake, AB & Spryfield, NS
Chief Warrant Officer J.F.D. Couture, M.M.M., C.D., Ottawa, ON & Montréal, PQ
Chief Petty Officer 1st Class L.A. Crepin, M.M.M., C.D., Ottawa, ON & Dartmouth, NS
Capt. D.W. Cull, M.M.M., C.D., Gagetown, NB & Cobalt, ON
Warrant Officer J.-É. Deslauriers, M.M.M., C.D., Valcartier & Buckingham, PQ
Chief Warrant Officer G. Dorfschmidt, M.M.M., C.D., Ottawa, ON & Bourlamaque, PQ
Warrant Officer R.R.J. Dumas, M.M.M., C.D., North Bay & Hanmer, ON
Master Warrant Officer G.A. Evans, M.M.M., C.D., Suffield & Medicine Hat, AB

Petty Officer 1st Class W.M. Flanagan, M.M.M., C.D., Westwin, MB & Angus, ON
Capt. L.B. Gebhart, M.M.M., C.D., Chilliwack & Esquimalt, BC
Sgt. J.H.C. Guérin, M.M.M., C.D., Courcelette & LaPrairie, PQ
Chief Petty Officer 2nd Class J.A. Hall, M.M.M., C.D., Saint John, NB & Wheatley, ON
Chief Petty Officer 2nd Class R.A. Hardy, M.M.M., C.D., Halifax, NS & New Richmond, PQ
Chief Warrant Officer J.L. Hessian, M.M.M., C.D., Ottawa, ON & New Glasgow, NS
Master Warrant Officer R.W.J. Hollingworth, M.M.M., C.D., Bagotville & Hull, PQ
Capt. J.D.G. Labrecque, M.M.M., C.D., Québec, PQ
Master Warrant Officer J.M. Laviolette, M.M.M., C.D., Winnipeg, MB
Chief Petty Officer 2nd Class S.J. Lawrence, M.M.M., C.D., Victoria, BC & St. John's, NF
Master Warrant Officer J.R.R. Leblanc, M.M.M., C.D., Gagetown, NB & MacKayville, PQ
Chief Warrant Officer J.S.D. Lebrun, Kingston, ON & Québec, PQ
Chief Petty Officer 1st Class E.W. MacBean, M.M.M., C.D., Victoria, BC & MOntréal, PQ
Petty Officer 1st Class D.S. MacCormac, M.M.M., C.D., Halifax, NS & Victoria, BC
Chief Warrant Officer J.A.A. Maillet, M.M.M., C.D., St-Hubert & St-Norbert, PQ
Master Warrant Officer D.J. Maltais, M.M.M., C.D., Moose Jaw, SK & Dalhousie, NB
Master Warrant Officer J.F.C. Martin, M.M.M., C.D., Cold Lake, AB & Québec, PQ
Capt. J.G.L. Massé, M.M.M., C.D., Québec & Amqui, PQ
Chief Warrant Officer B.J. Moss, M.M.M., C.D., Oetawawa, ON & Gambo, NF
Chief Warrant Officer J.S. Mossop, M.M.M., C.D., Gagetown & Burton, NB
Capt. A.J. O'Keefe, M.M.M., C.D., Kingston, ON & Montréal, PQ
Chief Warrant Officer D.D. Paul, M.M.M., C.D., Petawawa, ON & Halifax, NS
Chief Petty Officer 2nd Class G.E. Peaker, M.M.M., C.D., Victoria, BC
Chief Warrant Officer G.A. Plant, M.M.M., C.D., Esquimalt, BC & Lethbridge, AB
Master Warrant Officer T.M.R. Raymond, M.M.M., C.D., Borden, ON & Luseland, SK
Capt. C.K.H.S. Romain, M.M.M., C.D., Jerusalem, Israel & Vinton, PQ
Master Warrant Officer R.W. Ryan, M.M.M., C.D., Sydney, NS
Chief Warrant Officer J.R. Savoie, M.M.M., C.D., Ottawa, ON & Rogersville, NB
Chief Warrant Officer O.P. Shapka, M.M.M., C.D., Shearwater, NS & Vegreville, AB
Chief Petty Officer 2nd Class G.L. Shute, M.M.M., C.D., Halifax & Musquodoboit Harbour, NS
Chief Petty Officer 1st Class A.D. Skaalrud, M.M.M., C.D., Esquimalt, BC & Carseland, AB
Chief Warrant Officer D.W. Smith, M.M.M., C.D., Greenwood, NS & Hamilton, ON
Warrant Officer C. Thériault, M.M.M., C.D., St-Hubert & Rimouski, PQ
Warrant Officer G.W. Thoms, M.M.M., C.D., North Bay, ON & Boyd's Cove, NF
Chief Warrant Officer J.C.R. Trépanier, M.M.M., C.D., Ottawa, ON & Shawinigan, PQ
Chief Warrant Officer G.J. Vader, M.M.M., C.D., Cold Lake, AB & Penticton, BC
Chief Warrant Officer R.P. Van Iderstine, M.M.M., C.D., Moncton & Port Elgin, NB
Capt. J.E. Vaughan, M.M.M., C.D., Goose Bay, NF & Saint John, NB
Chief Warrant Officer N.D. Walker, M.M.M., C.D., Shilo, MB & Alder Point, NS

Chief Petty Officer 1st Class G.J. Westlake, M.M.M., C.D., Esquimalt, BC & Halifax, NS
Chief Petty Officer 1st Class M.D.K. Whalen, M.M.M., C.D., Victoria, BC & Newcastle, NB
Chief Warrant Officer P.J. Wonderham, M.M.M., C.D., Washington, DC, USA & Calgary, AB
Master Warrant Officer W. Yates, M.M.M., C.D., Ottawa & Stoney Creek, ON

CANADIAN BRAVERY DECORATIONS/ DÉCORATIONS CANADIENNES POUR ACTES DE BRAVOURE

In 1997, the Decorations for Bravery celebrate their twenty-fifth year of honouring those who have risked their lives to save or protect others. The Decorations for Bravery, consisting of the Cross of Valour, the Star of Courage and the Medal of Bravery were instituted and created on May 10, 1972. They may be awarded to Canadian citizens or to non-Canadians who have performed an act of bravery in Canada, or outside Canada if the act was in Canada's interest. The Decorations for Bravery may be awarded posthumously.

The Cross of Valour is awarded for acts of the most conspicuous courage in circumstances of extreme peril. The Star of Courage is awarded for acts of conspicuous courage in circumstances of great peril. The Medal of Bravery is awarded for acts of bravery in hazardous circumstances. **See page 16 for colour reproductions of the Canadian Bravery Decorations.**

Star of Courage/Étoile du courage (S.C.)
(Date of Announcement, August 10, 1995)
Corp. James Patrick Dickson, Port Coquitlam, BC
(Date of Announcement, January 10, 1996)
Alexander Leslie Lee, Ancaster, ON
Thaddeus Moonias, Thunder Bay, ON
(Date of Announcement, June 24, 1996)
Master Corp. Robert Clarence Andrew Fisher, Victoria, BC
(Date of Announcement, July 31, 1996)
Mary Ona Bjornson, Antigonish, NS

Medal of Bravery/Médaille de la bravoure (M.B.)
(Date of Announcement, August 10, 1995)
Constable Yvan Béliveau, Duvernay, Laval, PQ
Constable Gilles Bouchard, Montréal, PQ
Constable Sylvain Charbonneau, Montréal, PQ
Staff Sargeant Paul J. Giffin, Port Coquitlam, BC
Robert Giguère, St-Georges-de-Beauce, PQ
(Date of Announcement, November 8, 1995)
Alexander Dunbar, Bowmanville, ON
Constable Lynn Duncan, Verdun, PQ
Paul R. Fazekas, Red Lake, ON
Craig R. Garner, Niagara Falls, ON
Raymond Gionet, Niagara Falls, ON
Ronald Gould, Jr., Scoudouc, NB
Joseph Noel Richard Groulx, Plantagenet, ON
Sgt. Robert S. Guthrie, Leduc, AB
Jean-Claude Landry, Rimouski, PQ
Marc-André Ouellet, Montréal-Nord, PQ
Denis Rhéal Robert, Orleans, ON
Darrell Paul Robertson, Lashburn, SK
Paul Michael Semple, Toronto, ON (Posthumous)
William Van Dongen, Niagara Falls, ON
(Date of Announcement, January 10, 1996)
Constable Kimberly Anne Ashford, Langley, BC
Constable Thaddeus Atlookan, Thunder Bay, ON
Paul Anthony Bassi, Mount Hope, ON
Jean-François Beaulieu, Foster, PQ
Sgt. Marc Bédard, Carleton Place, ON
Gary J. Bolton, Peterborough, ON
Mikel Brennan, Wendover, ON (Posthumous)
Sgt. Marc Brunelle, Kanata, ON
Jacques Carrière, L'Ange Gardien, PQ
Kenneth Grant Chesebrough, Gananoque, ON
Benoît Desroches, Laval, PQ
Constable Luc Fleurant, Val David, PQ
Carl Gilbert, St-Liboire, PQ

Jean-Phillipe Gilbert, St-Liboire, PQ
William Hudon, Ville LaSalle, PQ
Dave Lucas, Belleville, ON
Constable George Makowski, M.B., Vancouver, BC
Constable Serge Rioux, St-Hippolyte, PQ
Glenn Romain, Fort-Coulonge, PQ
Mario Thibeault, Buckingham, PQ
Constable Terrance Trytten, North Vancouver, BC
Michael Vardon, Ville LaSalle, PQ
Constable Richard Peter Walton, North Vancouver, BC

(Date of Announcement, March 13, 1996)
Major Simon Toby Wass Bridge, London, UK

(Date of Announcement, March 21, 1996)
Tammy Benn, Woodville, ON
Tara Benn, Woodville, ON
Annell Bings, Aachen, Germany
Scott Joseph Patrick Brown, Arnprior, ON
Warrant Officer Darryl Hunter Crowell, Denwood AB
Capt. Wayne Desjardins, Timmins, ON
Stanley Houle, Peerless, AB
Sgt. Gregory William Janes, Petawawa, ON
Peter Karo, Nanaimo, BC
Earl Okemow, Peerless Lake, AB

(Date of Announcement, June 24, 1996)
Charles Cliffort Abray, Edmonton, AB
Anne Berberi, Laval, PQ
Yvon Blain, Kuujjuaq, PQ
Robert Charles Fitzgerald, Guelph, ON
Adam George Forrest, Acton, ON
David Forrest, Kuujjuaq, PQ
Constable Philip Gavin Francis, Cambridge, ON
Lawrence Henry Hansen, Prince Rupert, BC
Brian Douglas Jeffrey, White Rock, BC
Michel Lemire, Kuujjuaq, PQ
James Allan (Kim) Martin, Pickering, ON
Amy Jeannine Matthews, Lepreau, NB
Robert M. Pedersen, Calgary, AB
Maj. Keith David Sawatzky, North York, ON
Brian Schmelzer, Medicine Hat, AB
Donald Norman Schofield, Edmonton, AB
Denis Tessier, St-Rédempteur, PQ
Jennifer Anne Wilked, Lepreau, NB

(Date of Announcement, July 31, 1996)
Stanley Hutchings, Prince Rupert, BC
Kelly Kramil, Bolton, ON
Gregory David McKay, North Vancouver, BC
John Charles Parkin, Courtenay, BC
Ronda Sparkes, Scarborough, ON
Robert Michael Sheridan, Lillooet, BC
Christopher Brian Speed, Toronto, ON

MERITORIOUS SERVICE DECORATIONS/ DÉCORATIONS POUR SERVICE MÉRITOIRE

Approved by Her Majesty the Queen on July 10, 1991, the Meritorious Service Decorations were created to honour Canadians & foreigners (military & civil) for commendable actions performed on or after June 11, 1984.

The Meritorious Service Cross (Military Division) is awarded for the performance of a military deed or a military activity in an outstandingly professional manner or of a rare high standard that brings considerable benefit or great honour to the Canadian Forces.

The Meritorious Service Cross (Civil Division) is awarded for the performance of a deed or activity in an outstandingly professional manner or of an uncommonly high standard that brings considerable benefit or great honour to Canada.

The Meritorious Service Medal (Military Division) is awarded for the performance of a military deed or a military activity in a highly professional manner or of a very high standard that brings benefit or honour to the Canadian Forces.

The Meritorious Service Medal (Civil Division) is awarded for the performance of a deed or activity in a highly professional manner or of a very high standard that brings benefit or honour to Canada. **See page 16 for colour reproductions of the Meritorius Service Decorations.**

Meritorious Service Cross/M.S.C. (Civil)/La Croix du service méritoire (civile)
(Date of Announcement, May 2, 1995)
Sheila Wilson, Paisley, Scotland

Meritorious Service Cross/M.S.C. (Military)/La Croix du service méritoire (militaire)
(Date of Announcement, April 24, 1995)
Sgt. Thomas Joachim Hoppe, Calgary, AB
(Date of Announcement, April 18, 1995)
Maj. André Rioux, C.D., Beloeil, PQ
(Date of Announcement, April 19, 1995)
Sgt. Gary Paul Stevenson, C.D., St. John's, NF & Courcelette, PQ
(Date of Announcement, April 25, 1995)
L.Col. James Thomas Calvin, C.D., Oshawa & Ottawa, ON
(Date of Announcement, May 2, 1995)
Col. John Albin Almstrom, C.D., Zagreb, Yugoslavia
M.Gen. John Archie MacInnis, C.D., Halifax & Inverness, NS
Col. George Joseph Oehring, C.D., St-Hubert, PQ
Maj. Francis Roy Thomas, C.D., Nepean & Ottawa, ON
(Date of Announcement, May 5, 1995)
Gen. Gordon R. Sullivan, USA

Meritorious Service Medal/M.S.M. (Civil)/La Médaille du service méritoire (civile)
(Date of Announcement, April 19, 1995)
Bernard Nourry, Caen, France
(Date of Announcement, April 20, 1995)
Blake Desjardins, Sudbury, ON
Donald McNeil Donaldson, Lively ON
Terrance Larocque, Garson, ON
Michael Ouellette, Sudbury, ON
(Date of Announcement, April 21, 1995)
Isabelle Brasseur, Brossard, PQ
Lloyd Edgar Eisler, Jr., Boucherville, PQ
Marnie McBean, Toronto, ON
Alan Morrow, London, ON
Elvis Stojko, Richmond Hill, ON
(Date of Announcement, May 2, 1995)
George Frederick Anderson, Stroud, ON
Virginie Larivière, St-Polycarpe, PQ
Denis Ouellet, Dolbeau, PQ (Posthumous)
Edmund Carroll Whiteside, Kraainem, Belgium

Meritorious Service Medal M.S.M. (Military)/La Médaille du service méritoire (militaire)
(Date of Announcement, April 19, 1995)
Cpl. Michel Gonin, Sherbrooke, PQ
(Date of Announcement, May 2, 1995)
Maj. Joseph Jocelyn Yvan Bouchard, C.D., Anse St-Jean & St-Hubert, PQ
Maj. Joseph Roland Maurice Gaetan Royer, C.D., Chilliwack, BC & Zagreb, Yugoslavia
(Date of Announcement, May 4, 1995)
Sgt. John Joseph Raymond Butler, Petawawa, ON
(Date of Announcement, May 9,1995)
Capt. Owen L. Hanam, C.D., Cape Breton, NS
Maj. Robert Raymond Henderson, C.D., Halifax, NS (Posthumous)
Maj. Walter Charles Sweetman, C.D., Peterborough, ON (Posthumous)
(Date of Announcement, May 11, 1995)
Pte. Phillip Badanai, Thunder Bay & Petawawa, ON

BRITISH AND COMMONWEALTH HONOURS

In earlier times Canadians could receive hereditary titles, knighthoods and other such honours under the British system of honours, and this is still the case with Canadians who pursue careers in Britain. Furthermore, the Canadian military system of decorations was based on the British system and many Canadians hold such honours as a result of service in Canadian, British or other Commonwealth forces. While Canada has developed its own honours system, honours are still from time to time granted by the Sovereign to Canadians for, among other things, service to the Commonwealth.

VICTORIA CROSS (V.C.)
L.Col. C.C.I. Merritt, V.C.
Sgt. E. A. Smith, V.C.

The Victoria Cross was founded by Queen Victoria at the close of the Crimean campaign, 1856, but made retroactive to 1854. It is described as a Maltese cross, made of gun metal, with a Royal Crest in the centre and underneath it an escroll bearing the inscription "For Valour". It is awarded, irrespective of rank, to members of any branch of Her Majesty's services, either in the British Forces or those of any Commonwealth realm, dominion, colony or dependency, the Mercantile Marine, nurses or staffs of hospitals, or to civilians of either sex while serving in either regular or temporary capacity during naval, military, or air force operations. It is awarded only "for most conspicuous bravery or some daring or pre-eminent act of valour or self-sacrifice or extreme devotion to duty in the presence of the enemy." For additional conduct of similar bravery, a Bar is added. The ribbon was formerly red for the Army and blue for the Navy, but it is now red (a dull crimson) for all services. Since June 17th, 1943, the financial responsibility for a stipend to Canadian recipients has been assumed by the Canadian Government. Ninety-six V.C.s have been awarded to Canadians or to foreigners serving in Canadian or Commonwealth forces.

GEORGE CROSS (G.C.)
Gordon Love Bastion, G.C., M.B.E.
A.R.C. Butson, G.C., O.M.M., O.St.J., C.D., M.A., M.D., F.R.C.S. (Eng.), F.R.C.S.C.C.
John McClymont, G.C.

In 1940, King George VI instituted the George Cross for civilians and members of the services alike, male or female, who performed "acts of the greatest heroism or of the most conspicuous courage in circumstances of extreme danger." This decoration — the second highest Commonwealth award for bravery — is a plain silver cross bearing in the centre a representation of Saint George slaying the dragon and the words: "For Gallantry". The ribbon is garter blue. Eleven Canadians, and a Bermudian serving in a Canadian unit, have won the G.C. Not all were members of the armed forces.

ROYAL HONOURS (COMMONWEALTH)
The Order of Baronets, the lowest Hereditary rank, was instituted in 1611; a Baronet is designated "Sir John Smith, Baronet" — the abbreviation Bt. is used in Court Circulars and has been generally adopted in lieu of "Bart." Taking precedence of Baronets are members of The Most Honourable Privy Council, who are addressed "Right Honourable."
The Most Noble Order of the Garter, instituted 1349. — K.G.
The Most Ancient and Most Noble Order of the Thistle, instituted 1687. — K.T.
The Most Honourable Order of the Bath, instituted in 1399, and revived in 1725, is divided into three classes — Knights Grand Cross, G.C.B.; Knights Commanders, K.C.B.; and Companions, C.B.

Canadian Almanac & Directory 1997

The Order of Merit, O.M., carries no title.

The Most Distinguished Order of St. Michael and St. George, instituted in 1818, has three classes — Knights Grand Cross, G.C.M.G.; Knights Commanders, K.C.M.G.; Companions, C.M.G.

The Most Eminent Order of the Indian Empire instituted 1877, has three classes, — Knights Grand Commanders, G.C.I.E.; Knights Commanders, K.C.I.E.;Companions, C.I.E. (This Order has not been conferred since 1947.)

The Royal Victorian Order, instituted in 1896, has five classes — Knights Grand Cross, G.C.V.O.; Knights Commanders, K.C.V.O.; Commanders, C.V.O.; Members 4th and 5th classes — M.V.O. Ribbon; blue with red and white edges.

The Most Excellent Order of the British Empire, instituted in 1917, has five classes — Knights (or Dames) Grand Cross, G.B.E.; Knights Commanders, K.B.E.; Dames Commanders, D.B.E.; Commanders, C.B.E.; Officers, O.B.E.; and Members, M.B.E. Ribbon (Military) Rose pink, pearl grey edging, vertical pearl stripe in centre; (Civil) Rose pink, pearl grey edging and no central vertical stripe.

Knights Bachelors are gentlemen unconnected with any order who have received the honour of Knighthood, and are entitled to the prefix "Sir". They rank immediately after Knights Commanders of the British Empire.

The Companions of Honour, C.H., instituted in 1917 rank immediately after Knights (Dames) Grand Cross of the Order of the British Empire. Membership is limited and carries no title.

In all Orders of Knighthood the Knights Grand Cross and the Knights Commanders have the prefix "Sir" with the initials of their class following the name. Companions and Members bear no title, but have the letters C.B., C.M.G., L.V.O., M.V.O., as the case may be, attached to their names.

The Garter, the Thistle, The Order of Merit and the Royal Victorian Order are all in the personal bestowal of the Sovereign. Appointments to the other Orders are made by Her Majesty on recommendation of the Prime Ministers of Commonwealth countries who wish to secure such appointments. Premiers of individual Australian states may also make recommendations.

MARQUESS

The Most Hon. the Marquess of Exeter, Michael Anthony Cecil, 8th Marquess

The Most Hon. the Marquess of Ely, Charles John Tottenham, 8th Marquess

EARLS

The Right Hon. the Earl of Egmont, Frederick George Moore Perceval, 11th Earl and 15th Baronet

The Right Hon. the Earl Grey, Richard Fleming George Charles Grey, 6th Earl

The Right Hon. the Earl Winterton, Donald David Turnour, 8th Earl

VISCOUNTS

The Right Hon. the Viscount Charlemont, John Day Caulfeild, 14th Viscount

The Right Hon. the Viscount Galway, L.Cdr. George Rupert Monckton, R.C.N. (Retd.), 12th Viscount

The Right Hon. the Viscount Greenwood, Sir David Henry Hamar Greenwood, Bt., F.R.G.S., 2nd Viscount

The Right Hon. the Viscount Hardinge, Charles Henry Nicholas Hardinge, 6th Viscount

OLD CANADIAN TITLE

The title of Baron de Longueuil existed prior to the Treaty of Paris (1763), and was duly recognized by Queen Victoria pursuant to that treaty.

Baron de Longueuil, Raymond Grant de Longueuil, 11th Baron

BARONS

The Right Hon. the Lord Aylmer, Michael Anthony Aylmer, 13th Baron

The Right Hon. the Lord Beaverbrook, Maxwell William Henry Aitken, 3rd Baron and 3rd Baronet

The Right Hon. the Lord Chatfield, Ernle David Lewis Chatfield, 2nd Baron

The Right Hon. the Lord Martonmere, John Stephen Robinson, 2nd Baron

The Right Hon. the Lord Morris, Michael David Morris, 3rd Baron

The Right Hon. the Lord Rodney, George Brydges, 10th Baron and 10th Baronet

The Right Hon. the Lord Shaughnessy, William Graham Shaughnessy, 3rd Baron

The Right Hon. the Lord Strathcona and Mount Royal, Hon. Col. Donald Euan Palmer Howard, 4th Baron

The Right Hon. the Lord Thomson of Fleet, Kenneth Roy Thomson, 2nd Baron

BARONETS

Sir Richard Aylmer (16th Bt.)
Sir Christopher Hilaro Barlow (7th Bt.)
Sir Harold Boulton (4th Bt.)
Sir Alexander Boyd (3rd Bt.)
Sir Theodore Brinckman (6th Bt.)
Maj. Sir Hervey Bruce (7th Bt.)
Sir Lauder Brunton (3rd Bt.)
Sir Herbert Burbidge (5th Bt.)
Sir Michael Butler (3rd Bt.)
Sir Robert Cave-Brown-Cave (16th Bt.)
Sir George Reginald Chaytor (8th Bt.)
Sir Arthur Chetwynd (8th Bt.)
Sir John Davis (3rd Bt.)
Sir David Dyke (10th Bt.)
Sir David Flavelle (3rd Bt.)
The Revd. Sir Christopher Gibson, Bt., C.P. (4th Bt.)
Sir George Philip Grant-Suttie (8th Bt.)
Sir Philip Grotrian (3rd Bt.)
Sir Charles Gunning C.D., (8th Bt.)
Sir Charles Knowles (7th Bt.)
Sir Peter Johnson (7th Bt.)
Sir Peter Lambert (10th Bt.)
Sir Richard Latham (3rd Bt.)
Sir Edwin MacGregor (7th Bt.)
Sir Roderick McQuhae MacKenzie (12th Bt.)
Sir Robert Morris (10th Bt.)
Sir Richard Musgrave (7th Bt.)
Sir Christopher Oakes (3rd Bt.)
Sir Christopher Philipson-Stow, D.F.C. (5th Bt.)
Sir James Piers (11 Bt.)
Sir Francis Price, Bt. (7th Bt.)
Sir Christopher Robinson (8th Bt.)
Sir John James Michael Laud Robinson (11th Bt.)
Sir Julian Rose (5th Bt.)
Sir Charles Rugge-Price (9th Bt.)
Sir John Samuel (5th Bt.)
Sir Robert Shaw (7th Bt.)
Sir John Simeon (7th Bt.)
Sir Thomas Staples (15th Bt.)
The Rev. Sir Michael Stonhouse (19th Bt.)
Sir Adrian Stott (4th Bt.)
Sir John Stracey (9th Bt.)
Sir Philip Stuart (9th Bt.)
Sir Richard Sullivan (9th Bt.)
Sir Robert Synge (8th Bt.)
Sir Rodney Touche (2nd Bt.)
Sir Charles Hibbert Tupper (5th Bt.)
Sir Christopher Wells, M.D. (3rd Bt.)
Sir Donald Williams (10th Bt.)

Knight Grand Cross of the Most Honourable Order of the Bath (G.C.B.)

Air Chief Marshal Sir David Evans, G.C.B., C.B.E.

Knight Grand Cross of the Most Distinguished Order of St. Michael and St. George (G.C.M.G.)

Sir John Shaw Rennie, G.C.M.G., O.B.E.

Knight Grand Cross or Dame Grand Cross of the Most Excellent Order of the British Empire (G.B.E.)

Sir Peter Gadsden, G.B.E.
Sir Francis Aimé Vallat, G.B.E., K.C.M.G., Q.C.

Member of the Order of the Companions of Honour (C.H.)

Pierre Elliott Trudeau, C.C., C.H., P.C.

Knight Commander of the Most Honourable Order of the Bath (K.C.B.)

Air Marshal Sir Richard Nelson, K.C.B., O.B.E., M.D.

Knight Commander of the Most Distinguished Order of St. Michael and St. George (K.C.M.G.)

Sir Edwin Leather, K.C.M.G, K.C.V.O.

Knight Commander of the Royal Victorian Order (K.C.V.O.)

Sir Conrad Swan, K.C.V.O.

Knight Commander of the Most Excellent Order of the British Empire (K.B.E.)

Sir David Bate, K.B.E.
Hon. Sir Nigel Bowen, K.B.E.

KNIGHTS BACHELOR

Sir Graham Day
Sir Stanley Matthews, C.B.E.
Sir Neil Shaw

Companion of the Most Honourable Order of the Bath (C.B.)

Air Vice-Marshal George Brookes, C.B., O.B.E.
M.Gen. Bertram Meryl Hoffmeister, C.B., C.B.E., D.S.O.

Companion of the Most Distinguished Order of St. Michael and St. George (C.M.G.)

H.J. Carmichael, C.M.G.
Edmond Cloutier, C.M.G., B.A., L.Ph.
Eleanor Emery, C.M.G.
Donovan Bartley Finn, C.M.G., M.Sc., Ph.D., F.R.S.C., F.C.I.C.
George H. McIvor, C.M.G.
Hector Brown McKinnon, C.C., C.M.G.
Alexander Ross, C.M.G.
Reginald McCartney Samples, C.M.G., D.S.O., O.B.E.
Joseph Emile St. Laurent, C.M.G.
Ivor Otterbein Smith, C.M.G., O.B.E.

Companion of the Most Eminent Order of the Indian Empire (C.I.E.)

Maj. Frederick Wernham Gerrard, C.I.E.
Capt. John Ryland, C.I.E., R.C.N.
Maj. Frederick Augustus Berrill Sheppard, C.I.E., O.B.E.

Commander of the Royal Victorian Order (C.V.O.)

Leopold Henry Amyot, C.V.O.
Col. John Gilbert Bourne, C.V.O., C.D.
Henry E. Davis, C.V.O., C.M.
Michel Gauvin, C.V.O., D.S.O.
John Reginald Gorman, C.V.O., C.B.E., M.C.
The Hon. David C. Lam, C.V.O., C.M., K.St.J., O.B.C., B.A.(Econ.), M.B.A., L.L.D., D.Mil.Sc., D.H.L., D.H.
Veronica Jane Langton, C.V.O.
Hartland Molson MacDougall, C.V.O.
Capt. Donald Curtis McKinnon, C.V.O., C.D., R.C.N.
Cdr. G.J. Manson, C.V.O., C.D., R.C.N.
John Crosbie Perlin, C.V.O.
Peter Michael Pitfield, C.V.O., P.C., Q.C.
M.Gen. Roy A. Reid, C.V.O., C.M., M.C., C.D.
L.Cdr. Lawrence James Wallace, C.V.O., O.C., O.B.C., R.C.N.V.R.

Commander of the Order of the British Empire (C.B.E.)

William Eric Adams, C.B.E.

James Pomeroy Anderson, C.B.E.
Brig. Gerald Gardiner Anglin, C.B.E., M.C., E.D.
Brig. Walter A. Bean, C.B.E., E.D., C.D.
Brig. John Arthur Watson Bennett, C.B.E., C.D.
Brig. John Francis Bingham, C.B.E.
Brig. Dudley Kingdon Black, C.B.E., D.S.O.
M.Gen. Mortimer Patrick Bogert, C.B.E., D.S.O.
George Herbert Bowler, C.B.E.
Garrett Brownrigg, C.B.E.
John Burke, C.B.E.
Alfred Charpentier, C.B.E.
Howard Brown Chase, C.B.E.
John Horrell Collier-Wright, C.B.E.
L.Gen. Samuel Findlay Clark, C.B.E., C.D.
Brig. Frederick Graham Coleman, C.B.E.
Air Cdre. Martin Costello, C.B.E., R.C.A.F.
Brig. J. A. de Lalanne, C.B.E., M.C., E.D.
V.Adm. Harry George De Wolf, C.B.E., D.S.O., D.S.C., R.C.N.
Air Marshal Clarence Rupert Dunlap, C.B.E., C.D., R.C.A.F.
Philip Sydney Fisher, O.C., C.B.E., D.S.O., D.S.C., D.C.L., LL.D.
Conrad Trelawny Fitz-Gerald, C.B.E., M.D.
Brig. Frank James Fleury, C.B.E.
Charles Gavsie, C.B.E., Q.C.
Gerald Godsoe, C.B.E., Q.C.
Alexander Grant, C.B.E.
Joseph Ernest Gregoire, C.B.E.
Frank Sydney Grisdale, C.B.E.
Raymond Gushue, O.C., C.B.E., Q.C.
M.Gen. Lewis John Harris, C.B.E.
Wallace Bruce Haughan, C.B.E.
Brig. Robert James Henderson, C.B.E.
Harold Ferguson Hodgson, C.B.E.
Capt. Francis Deschamps Howie, C.B.E., D.S.O., R.N.
Alexander George Irvine, C.B.E.
Eric Campbell Judd, C.B.E., M.V.O.
Lester Millman Keachie, C.B.E., Q.C.
Capt. Thomas Douglas Kelly, C.B.E., R.C.N.R.
M.Gen. George Kitching, C.B.E., D.S.O., M.C.
Allan Collingwood Travers Lewis, C.B.E., Q.C.
Col. Edward Raymond Lewis, C.B.E.
Wilfrid Bennett Lewis, C.B.E.
Gordon Clapp Lindsay, C.B.E.
Air Vice-Marshal Ralph Edward McBurney, C.B.E., C.D., R.C.A.F.
John Struthers McNeil, C.B.E.
E.J. Mackie, C.B.E.
Raymond Charles Manning, C.B.E.
John Emile Marks, C.B.E.
Walter Melvill Marshall, C.B.E.
James Matson, C.B.E.
Ronald Henry Moray Mavor, C.B.E.
Air Chief Marshal Frank Robert Miller, C.B.E., C.D., R.C.A.F.
Edwin Mirvish, O.C., C.B.E.
E.C. O'Brien, C.B.E.
Air Vice-Marshal Walter Alyn Orr, C.B.E., C.D., R.C.A.F.
Luke William Pearsall, C.B.E.
M.Gen. Matthew Howard Somers Penhale, C.B.E., C.D.
Cyril Horace Frederick Pierrepont, C.B.E., E.D.
Air Vice-Marshal John Lawrence Plant, C.B.E., A.F.C., R.C.A.F.
Louis Rasminsky, C.C., C.B.E.
M.Gen. Norman Elliott Rodger, C.B.E.
James Joseph Alexander Ross, C.B.E., C.D.
T.H. Savage, C.B.E.
Lynn Seymour, C.B.E.
Air Vice-Marshal Douglas McCully Smith, C.B.E., C.D.
Brig. Gerald Lucian Morgan Smith, C.B.E., C.D.
George Spence, C.B.E., LL.D.
William Leonard O'Brien Stallard, C.B.E.
Basil Otto Stevenson, C.B.E.
Air Cdre. Stanley Gibson Tackaberry, C.B.E.

Kenneth Wiffin Taylor, O.C., C.B.E.
George Gamlin Thomas, C.B.E.
Lyman Trumbull, C.B.E.
L.Gen. Geoffrey Walsh, C.B.E., D.S.O., C.D.
M.Gen. Arthur Egbert Wrinch, C.B.E., C.D.
Henry Wrong, C.B.E.

IMPERIAL SERVICE ORDER (I.S.O.)
George Clayton Anderson
Robert Albert Andison
Arthur Barnstead
Avila Bedard
Peter Cooligan
Henri Fortier
Frank Henry French
Arthur Leigh Jolliffe
Edward Jost
Louis MacMillan
Walter Clifton Ronson
David John Scott
Ivan Vallee

ROYAL VICTORIAN CHAIN
Bestows no precedence; currently not held by anyone.

ORDER OF PRECEDENCE OF ORDERS, DECORATIONS AND MEDALS

(as revised November, 1994)

SEQUENCE 1
1. The sequence for wearing the insignia of Canadian orders, decorations and medals is, and the post-nominal letters associated with such orders, decorations and medals as approved by Orders in Council are:

Victoria Cross (V.C.)
Cross of Valour (C.V.)

NATIONAL ORDERS
Companion of the Order of Canada (C.C.)
Commander of the Order of Military Merit (C.M.M.)
Commander of the Royal Victorian Order (C.V.O.)
Officer of the Order of Canada (O.C.)
Officer of the Order of Military Merit (O.M.M.)
Lieutenant of the Royal Victorian Order (L.V.O.)
Member of the Order of Canada (C.M.)
Member of the Order of Military Merit (M.M.M.)
Member of the Royal Victorian Order (M.V.O.)
The Most Venerable Order of the Hospital of St. John of Jerusalem (All Grades) (no post-nominal letters)

PROVINCIAL ORDERS
Ordre national du Québec (G.O.Q., O.Q., C.Q.)
The Saskatchewan Order of Merit (S.O.M.)
The Order of Ontario (O.Ont.)
The Order of British Columbia (O.B.C.)
Alberta Order of Excellence (A.O.E.)

DECORATIONS
Star of Military Valour (S.M.V.)
Star of Courage (S.C)
Meritorious Service Cross (M.S.C.)
Medal of Military Valour (M.M.V.)
Medal of Bravery (M.B.)
Meritorious Service Medal (M.S.M.)
Royal Victorian Medal (R.V.M.)

WAR MEDALS
1939-1945 Star
Atlantic Star
Air Crew Europe Star
Africa Star
Pacific Star
Burma Star
Italy Star
France and Germany Star
Defence Medal
Canadian Volunteer Service Medal (C.V.S.M.)/Newfoundland Volunteers War Service Medal (N.V.W.S.M.)
War Medal (1939-1945)
Korea Medal
Canadian Volunteer Service Medal for Korea (C.V.S.M.K.)
Gulf and Kuwait Medal

SPECIAL SERVICE MEDAL (S.S.M.) WITH BARS FOR:
Pakistan (1989-1990)
Alert
Humanitas
NATO/ORAN
Peace/Paix

UNITED NATIONS MEDALS
UN Service (Korea) (1950-1954)
UN Emergency Force (1956-1967)
UN Truce Supervision Organization in Palestine (1948-) (U.N.T.S.O.) and Observer Group in Lebanon (1958)
UN Military Observation Group in India and Pakistan (1949-1979) (U.N.M.O.G.I.P.)
UN Organization in Congo (1960-1964)
UN Temporary Executive Authority in West New Guinea (1962-1963) (U.N.T.E.A.)
UN Yemen Observation Mission (1963-1964) (U.N.Y.O.M.)
UN Force in Cyprus (1965-1993) (U.N.F.C.Y.P.)
UN India Pakistan Observation Mission (1965-1966) (U.N.M.O.G.I.P.)
UN Emergency Force Middle East (1973-1979)
UN Disengagement Observation Force Golan Heights (1974-) (U.N.D.O.F.)
UN Interim Force in Lebanon (1978) (U.N.F.I.L.)
UN Iran/Iraq Military Observation Group (1989) (U.N.I.M.O.G.)
UN Transition Assistance Group (Namibia) (1989-1990) (U.N.T.A.G.)
UN Observer Group in Central America (1989-1992) (U.N.U.C.A.)
UN Iraq/Kuwait Observer Mission (1991) (U.N.I.K.O.M.)
UN Angola Verification Mission II (1991-1993) (U.N.A.V.E.M.)
UN Mission for the Referendum in Western Sahara (1991) (M.I.N.U.R.S.O.)
UN Observer Mission in El Salvador (1991) (O.N.U.S.A.L.)
UN Protection Force (Yugoslavia) (1992-) (U.N.P.R.O.F.O.R.)
UN Advance Mission in Cambodia (1992) (U.N.A.M.I.C.)
UN Transitional Authority in Cambodia (1992-1993) (U.N.T.A.C.)
UN Operation in Somalia (1992-1994) (O.N.U.S.O.M.)
UN Operation in Mozambique (1992-) (U.N.U.M.O.Z.)
UN Assistance Mission in Rwanda (1993-) (U.N.I.M.I.R.)

INTERNATIONAL COMMISSION MEDALS
International Commission for Supervision and Control (Indo-China) (1954-73)
International Commission for Control and Supervision (Vietnam) (1973)
Multinational Force and Observers (Sinai 1987-)
European Community Monitor Mission (Yugoslavia) (1991-)

COMMEMORATIVE MEDALS
Canadian Centennial Medal (1967)

Queen Elizabeth II's Silver Jubilee Medal (1977)
125th Anniversary of the Confederation of Canada Medal (1992)

LONG SERVICE AND GOOD CONDUCT MEDALS
RCMP Long Service Medal
Canadian Forces Decoration (C.D.)

EXEMPLARY SERVICE MEDALS
Police Exemplary Service Medal
Corrections Exemplary Service Medal
Fire Services Exemplary Service Medal
Canadian Coast Guard Exemplary Service Medal
Emergency Medical Services Exemplary Service Medal (created August 3, 1994)

OTHER MEDALS
Queen's Medal for Champion Shot
Service Medal of the Most Venerable Order of the Hospital of St. John of Jerusalem
2. The Bar to the Special Service Medal is worn centred on the ribbon. If there is more than one Bar, they are spaced evenly on the ribbon with the most recent uppermost.
3. Commonwealth orders, decorations and medals, the award of which is approved by the Government of Canada, are worn after Canadian orders, decorations and medlas listed in Section 1, the precedence in each category being set by the date of appointment or award.
4. Foreign orders, decorations and medals, the award of which is approved by the Government of Canada, are worn after those referred to in Sections 1 and 3, the precedence in each category being set by date of appointment or award.
5. The Newfoundland Volunteer War Service Medal has the same precedence as the Canadian Volunteer Service Medal.
6. The insignia of orders, decorations and medals not listed in this directive, as well as foreign awards, the award of which has not been approved by the Government of Canada, will not be mounted or worn in conjunction with orders, decorations and medals listed in this directive.
The insignia of orders, decorations and medals shall not be worn by anyone other than the recipient of such order, decoration or medal.

SEQUENCE 2
NOTWITHSTANDING THE ABOVE, a person who, **prior to 1 June, 1972** was a member of a British Order or the recipient of a British decoration or medal referred to in this section should wear the insignia, decoration or medal, together with the insignia of any Canadian Order or any Canadian decoration or medal that the recipient is entitled to wear, in the following sequence:
Victoria Cross (V.C.)
George Cross (G.C.)
Cross of Valour (C.V.)
Order of Merit (O.M.)
Order of the Companions of Honour (C.H.)
Companion of the Order of Canada (C.C.)
Commander of the Order of Military Merit (C.M.M.)
Officer of the Order of Canada (O.C.)
Companion of the Order of the Bath (C.B.)
Companion of the Order of St. Michael and St. George (C.M.G.)
Commander of the Royal Victorian Order (C.V.O.)
The Most Venerable Order of the Hospital of St. John of Jerusalem (All Grades) (No post-nominals)
Commander of the Order of the British Empire (C.B.E.)
Distinguished Service Order (D.S.O.)
Officer of the Order of Military Merit (O.M.M.)
Lieutenant of the Royal Victorian Order (L.V.O.)
Officer of the Order of the British Empire (O.B.E.)
Imperial Service Order (I.S.O.)
Member of the Order of Canada (C.M.)

Member of the Order of Military Merit (M.M.M.)
Member of the Royal Victorian Order (M.V.O.)
Member of the Order of the British Empire (M.B.E.)
Member of the Royal Red Cross (R.R.C.)
Distinguished Service Cross (D.S.C.)
Military Cross (M.C.)
Distinguished Flying Cross (D.F.C.)
Air Force Cross (A.F.C.)
Star of Courage (S.C.)
Meritorious Service Cross (M.S.C.)
Medal of Bravery (M.B.)
Meritorious Service Medal (M.S.M.)
Associate of the Royal Red Cross (A.R.R.C.)
Distinguished Conduct Medal (D.C.M.)
Conspicuous Gallantry Medal (C.G.M.)
George Medal (G.M.)
Distinguished Service Medal (D.S.M.)
Military Medal (M.M.)
Distinguished Flying Medal (D.F.M.)
Air Force Medal (A.F.M.)
Queen's Gallantry Medal (Q.G.M.)
Royal Victorian Medal (R.V.M.)
British Empire Medal (B.E.M.)

WAR MEDALS
Africa General Service Medal (1902-1956)
India General Service Medal (1908-1935)
Naval General Service Medal (1915-1962)
India General Service Medal (1936-39)
General Service Medal - Army and Air Force (1918-1962)
1914 Star
1914-15 Star
British War Medal (1914-18)
Mercantile Marine War Medal (1914-18)
Victory Medal (1914-18)
Territorial Force War Medal (1914-19)
1939-45 Star
Atlantic Star
Air Crew Europe Star
Africa Star
Pacific Star
Burma Star
Italy Star
France and Germany Star
Defence Medal
Canadian Volunteer Service Medal
War Medal (1939-45)
Korea Medal
Canadian Volunteer Service Medal for Korea
Gulf and Kuwait Medal
NOTE: Newfoundland Volunteer War Service Medal has the same precedence as the Canadian Volunteer Service Medal.

UNITED NATIONS MEDALS
As in Sequence 1.

INTERNATIONAL COMMISSION MEDALS
As in Sequence 1.

POLAR MEDALS
In order of date awarded.

COMMEMORATIVE MEDALS
King George V's Silver Jubilee Medal (1935)
King George VI's Coronation Medal (1937)
Queen Elizabeth II's Coronation Medal (1953)
Canadian Centennial Medal (1967)
Queen Elizabeth II's Silver Jubilee Medal (1977)
125th Anniversary of the Confederation of Canada Medal (1992)

LONG SERVICE AND GOOD CONDUCT MEDALS
Army Long Service and Good Conduct Medal
Naval Long Service and Good Conduct Medal
Air Force Long Service and Good Conduct Medal
RCMP Long Service Medal

Volunteer Officer's Decoration (V.D.)
Volunteer Long Service Medal
Colonial Auxiliary Forces Officer's Decoration (V.D.)
Colonial Auxiliary Forces Long Service Medal
Efficiency Decoration (E.D.)
Efficiency Medal
Naval Volunteer Reserve Decoration (V.R.D.)
Naval Volunteer Reserve Long Service and Good Conduct Medal
Air Efficiency Award
The Queen's Medal for Champion Shot
Canadian Forces Decoration (C.D.)
Exemplary Service Medals as in Sequence 1.
Other Medals as in Sequence 1.

COMMONWEALTH (less U.K.) ORDERS, DECORATIONS AND MEDALS,
the award of which must be approved by the Government of Canada, are worn after those listed above in the sequence of Orders, Decorations and Medals, the precedence in each category by date of appointment or award.

ALL OTHER FOREIGN AWARDS APPROVED BY THE GOVERNMENT OF CANADA,
the award of which is approved by the Government of Canada, are worn after those listed above in the sequence of Orders, Decorations and Medals, the precedence in each category by date of appointment or award.
The numerous Orders, Decorations and Medals not listed above and those Foreign Awards for which official approval has not be granted will not be mounted or worn in conjunction with the official awards.
The insignia of Orders, Decorations and Medals may not been worn by anyone other than the recipient.

ABBREVIATIONS INDICATING HONOURS AND DECORATIONS
A.F.C. – Air Force Cross. Ribbon, wide diagonal stripes of white and red.
A.F.M. – Air Force Medal. Ribbon, narrow diagonal stripes of white and red.
A.M. – Albert Medal, gold (Sea). Ribbon, nine alternate narrow stripes of blue and white.
Albert Medal, gold (Land). Ribbon, nine alternate narrow stripes of red and white.
Albert Medal, bronze (Sea). Ribbon, blue ground with two wide stripes of white.
Albert Medal, bronze (Land). Ribbon, red ground with two wide stripes of white.
B.E.M. – British Empire Medal.
Bt. – Baronet
C.B. – Companion of the Most Honourable Order of the Bath.
C.B.E. – Commander of the Order of the British Empire.
C.C. – Companion of the Order of Canada.
C.D. – Canadian Forces Decoration.
C.G.M. – Conspicuous Gallantry Medal; Navy and Air Force. It carries a cash grant. The Navy Medal ribbon is white with dark blue edges; the Air Force ribbon is light blue with dark blue edges.
C.H. – Member of the Order of the Companions of Honour.
C.I.E. – Companion of the Most Eminent Order of the Indian Empire.
C.M. – Member of the Order of Canada.
C.M.G. – Companion of the Most Distinguished Order of St. Michael and St. George.
C.M.M. – Commander of the Order of Military Merit.
C.S.I. – Companion of the Most Exalted Order of the Star of India.
C.V. – Cross of Valour.
C.V.O. – Commander of the Royal Victorian Order.
D.C.M. – Distinguished Conduct Medal. Ribbon, red ground, dark blue stripe in centre.

D.F.C. – Distinguished Flying Cross. Ribbon, wide diagonal stripes of violet and white.
D.F.M. – Distinguished Flying Medal. Ribbon, narrow diagonal stripes of white and violet.
D.S.C. – Distinguished Service Cross. Ribbon, three broad bands, dark blue, white, dark blue.
D.S.M. – Distinguished Service Medal.
D.S.O. – Companion of the Distinguished Service Order. Instituted 1886. Ribbon, dark red with dark blue stripe at each end.
E.D. – Canadian Efficiency Decoration for Officers of Military Auxiliary Forces.
E.M. – Edward Medal. Posthumous award.
E.M. – Efficiency Medal.
G.B.E. – Knight Grand Cross or Dame Grand Cross of the Most Excellent Order of the British Empire.
G.C. – George Cross.
G.C.B. – Knight Grand Cross of the Most Honourable Order of the Bath.
G.C.I.E. – Knight Grand Commander of the Most Eminent Order of the Indian Empire.
G.C.M.G. – Knight Grand Cross of the Most Distinguished Order of St. Michael and St. George.
G.C.S.I. – Knight Grand Commander of the Most Exalted Order of the Star of India.
G.C.V.O. – Knight Grand Cross of the Royal Victorian Order.
G.M. – George Medal.
I.S.M. – Imperial Service Medal.
I.S.O. – Companion of the Imperial Service Order. Instituted 1902.
K.B.E. – Knight Commander of the Most Excellent Order of the British Empire.
K.C.B. – Knight Commander of the Most Honourable Order of the Bath.
K.C.I.E. – Knight Commander of the Most Eminent Order of the Indian Empire.
K.C.M.G. – Knight Commander of the Most Distinguished Order of St. Michael and St. George.
K.C.S.I. – Knight Commander of the Most Exalted Order of the Star of India.
K.C.V.O. – Knight Commander of the Royal Victorian Order.
K.G. – Knight of the Most Noble Order of the Garter.
K.P. – Knight of the Most Illustrious Order of St. Patrick.
Kt. – Knight Bachelor.
K.T. – Knight of the Most Ancient and Most Noble Order of the Thistle.
L.V.O. – Lieutenant of the Royal Victorian Order
M.B. – Medal of Bravery.
M.B.E. – Member of the Order of the British Empire.
M.C. – Military Cross. Instituted 1915. Ribbon, white with broad band of blue in centre.
M. du C. – Canada Medal.
M.M. – Military Medal.
M.M.M. – Member of the Order of Military Merit.
M.V.O. – Member of the Royal Victorian Order.
M.S.C. – Meritorious Service Cross
M.S.M. – Meritorious Service Medal
O.B.E. – Officer of the Order of the British Empire.
O.C. – Officer of the Order of Canada.
O.M. – Member of the Order of Merit.
O.M.M. – Officer of the Order of Military Merit.
P.C. – Privy Counsellor.
R.R.C. – Royal Red Cross. Instituted 1883. Ribbon, dark blue with narrow band of dark red at each end.
R.V.M. – Royal Victorian Medal
S.C. – Star of Courage.
U.E. – Unity of Empire. Descendants of United Empire Loyalists.
V.C. – Victoria Cross.
V.D. – Auxiliary Forces (Volunteer) Officers' Decoration.
V.R.D. – Naval Volunteer Reserve Decoration

FORMS OF ADDRESS

The "Salutation and Closing" portions below have been used with the permission of the copyright holder, Michael Measures, from the book "Styles of Address" by Howard Measures. The content of each such portion is listed in order of diminishing formality.

GOVERNMENT

THE GOVERNOR GENERAL OF CANADA:

Address — His/Her Excellency The Governor General, Government House, Ottawa.
Address — His/Her Excellency the Rt. Hon. (name), P.C., C.C., Governor General of Canada, Government House, Ottawa
  Salutation and Closing —
    (Sir/Madam)
    I have the honour to be, Sir/Madam,
  Your Excellency's obedient servant,
  or, (Dear Governor General)
    Believe me, Your Excellency,
  Yours sincerely,
  or, (My dear Governor General)
    With kind regards,
  Yours very sincerely,
  Note: If the Governor General has military and other titles, the title His/Her Excellency precedes the others. If the Governor General is a Prince or a Royal Duke, the title His Royal Highness and the salutation Your Royal Highness are used instead of His Excellency and Your Excellency. The wife/husband of the Governor General is accorded the title Her/His Excellency. The Governor General and spouse together — Their Excellencies.

LIEUTENANT GOVERNOR OF A PROVINCE:

Address — His/Her Honour, The Lieutenant Governor of (the Province of) _____ , Government House, _____ . or,
Address — His/Her Honour the Hon. (name), Lieutenant Governor of (the Province of) _____ , Government House, _____ .
  Salutation and Closing —
    (Sir)
    I am, Your Honour,
  Yours very truly,
  or, (Dear Sir/Madam),
    Yours sincerely,
  or, (My dear Lieutenant Governor)
    I am, my dear Lieutenant Governor
  Yours sincerely,
  or, (Dear Mr., Mrs., Miss, ...)
    With kind regards,
  Yours sincerely,
  Note: A lieutenant governor of a province of Canada retains the title Honourable for life.

THE PRIME MINISTER OF CANADA:

Address — The Right Honourable John/Jean M. Blank, P.C., M.P., Prime Minister of Canada, Ottawa.
  Salutation and Closing —
    (Dear Sir/Madam)
    Yours very truly,
  or, (Dear Mr./Madam Prime Minister)
    Yours sincerely,
  or, (Dear Prime Minister)
    With kind regards,
  Yours sincerely,
  Note: The Prime Minister of Canada is a member of the Queen's Privy Council for Canada and has the title "The Right Honourable" for life.

THE PREMIER OF A PROVINCE OF CANADA:

Address — The Honourable John/Jean M. Blank, M.L.A., Premier of (the Province of) _____ ,
  Salutation and Closing —
    (Dear Sir/Madam)
    Yours very truly,
  or, (My dear Premier)
    Believe me, my dear Premier, Yours sincerely,
  or, (Dear Mr., Mrs., Miss, ...)
    With kindest regards,
  Yours sincerely,
  Note: The Premier of a Province of Canada has the title "The Honourable" during his or her term of office. The Premier is head of the government of the Province, i.e., the First Minister; he or she is generally the President of the Executive Council of the Province. In Québec the Premier is styled "Prime Minister" instead of "Premier."

MEMBER OF THE FEDERAL CABINET, MEMBER OF THE PRIVY COUNCIL NOT OF THE CABINET, AND MEMBER OF THE EXECUTIVE COUNCIL OF A PROVINCE:

Address — The Honourable John/Jean M. Blank, Minister of,.
  Salutation and Closing —
    (Dear Sir) (Dear Madam)
    Yours very truly,
  or, (Dear Mr. ...) (Dear Mrs., Miss, ...)
    With kind regards,
  Yours sincerely,
  Note: If also a member of the United Kingdom Privy Council, he or she is addressed "The Right Honourable" for life. The letters P.C. are placed after the names of members of the Privy Council of Canada but not of the United Kingdom unless he/she is a peer. One member of the Cabinet addressing another uses the salutation "My dear Colleague". Members of the Privy Council of Canada are appointed, and have the title "The Honourable", for life. Members of Executive Councils of the Provinces have the title of Honourable only during their terms of office.

MEMBER OF THE SENATE:

Address — The Honourable John M. Blank, or The Honourable Jean M. Blank, The Senate, Ottawa.
  Salutation and Closing —
    (Dear Sir/Madam)
    Yours very truly,
  or, (Dear Senator ...)
    I am, dear Senator ...
  Yours sincerely,
  or, (My dear Senator)
    Believe me,
  Yours sincerely,
  Note: A senator who is a member of the Canadian Privy Council is addressed "Senator the Honourable John/Jean M. Blank". A Senator who is a member of the United Kingdom Privy Council is addressed "Senator the Right Honourable John/Jean M. Blank".

MEMBER OF THE HOUSE OF COMMONS:

Address — Mr./Mrs. or Miss John/Jean M. Blank, M.P., House of Commons, Ottawa.
  Salutation and Closing —
    (Dear Sir) (Dear Madam)
    Yours very truly,
  or, (Dear Mr. ...) (Dear Mrs., Miss, ...)
    Yours sincerely,

DEPUTY MINISTER OF A DEPARTMENT:

Address — Mr./Mrs. or Miss John/Jean M. Blank, Deputy Minister of _____ .
  Salutation and Closing —
    (Sir/Madam)
    Yours truly,
  or, (Dear Sir/Madam)
    Yours sincerely,
  or, (Dear Mr., Mrs., Miss, ...)
    With kind regards,
  Yours sincerely,

MEMBER OF A PROVINCIAL LEGISLATURE:

Address — Mr./Mrs. or Miss John/Jean M. Blank, M.L.A., Member of the Legislative Assembly, (Legislative Bldgs., Edmonton; Parliament Bldgs., Victoria; Legislative Bldg., Winnipeg; Legislative Bldg., Fredericton;Confederation Bldg., St. John's; Province House, Halifax; Parliament Bldgs.,Toronto; Province Bldg., Charlottetown; Hotel du gouvernement, Québec; Legislative Bldgs., Regina).

Salutation and Closing —
    (Dear Sir/Madam)
    Yours very truly,
or, (Dear Mr., Mrs., Miss, ...)
    Believe me,
    Yours sincerely,
Note: In the case of the Province of Québec use M.N.A.; Ontario use M.P.P.; Newfoundland and Nova Scotia use M.H.A. instead of M.L.A.

MAYOR OF A CITY OR TOWN:

If the name is used:
    Address — His Worship Mayor John M. Blank, *or* Her Worship Mayor Joan M. Blank, City Hall.
If the name is not used:
    His Worship the Mayor of. Her Worship the Mayor of.
Salutation and Closing —
    (Dear Sir) (Dear Madam)
    Yours very truly,
or, (Dear Mr. Mayor) (Dear Madam Mayor)
    Believe me, dear Mr./Madam Mayor,
    Yours sincerely, JUDGES

CANADA:

In Canada there are two broad classes of courts — superior courts and county (or district) courts. Judges of the superior courts are addressed "The Honourable Mr./Madam Justice _____ " and judges of the county or district courts are addressed "The Honourable _____ , Judge." The Supreme Court of Canada and the Federal Court of Canada are also superior courts. The Supreme Courts of the Yukon and the Northwest Territories are superior courts.

There are two classes of Chief Justices — The Chief Justice of Canada or of a province on the one hand, and the Chief Justice of a court on the other. The Chief Justice of the Supreme Court of Canada is styled the Chief Justice of Canada; similarly, there is a Chief Justice for each of the provinces. Other courts in the provinces, namely, the trial courts, usually have a Chief Justice also and he or she is known as the Chief Justice of that court.

CHIEF JUSTICE:

The Chief Justice of Canada:
    Address — The Right Honourable The Chief Justice of Canada, Supreme Court of Canada, Ottawa.
    Or — The Right Honourable _____ , P.C., Chief Justice of Canada, Ottawa.
Salutation and Closing —
    (Sir/Madam)
    I am, Sir/Madam,
    Yours very truly,
or, (Dear Sir/Madam)
    Yours faithfully,
or, (Dear Mr./Madam Chief Justice)
    Yours sincerely,
Chief Justice of a Province or Territory:
    Address — The Honourable _____ , Chief Justice of _____ ,
Salutation and Closing —
    (Sir/Madam)
    I am, Sir/Madam,
    Yours very truly,
or, (Dear Sir/Madam)
    I am, Sir/Madam,
    Yours sincerely,
or, (Dear Mr./Madam Chief Justice)

    Believe me, dear Mr./Madam Chief Justice,
    Yours sincerely,

JUDGES:

Supreme Court of Canada, Federal Court of Canada, Courts of Appeal, Courts of the Queen's Bench, Superior Court of the Province of Québec, Supreme Courts of the Provinces and Territories:
    Address — The Honourable Mr. Justice John M. Blank, *or* The Honourable Madam Justice Jean M. Blank.
Salutation and Closing —
    (Sir) (Madam)
    I am, Sir/Madam,
    Yours very truly,
or, (Dear Mr./Madam Justice ...)
    Believe me,
    Dear Mr./Madam Justice ...
    Yours sincerely,

JUDGES:

County and District Courts:
    Address — The Honourable John/Jean M. Blank, Judge,
Salutation and Closing —
    (Sir/Madam)
    I am, Sir/Madam,
    Yours very truly,
or, (Dear Judge Smith)
    Believe me, dear Judge Smith,
    Yours sincerely,

RELIGION

Anglican Church of Canada

ARCHBISHOP:

Address — The Most Reverend _____ , D.D., Archbishop of _____ .
Salutation and Closing —
    (Most Reverend Sir)
    I have the honour to be,
    Most Reverend Sir,
    Your obedient servant,
or, (Dear Archbishop)
    Yours sincerely,

BISHOP:

Address — The Right Reverend _____ , D.D., Bishop of _____ .
Salutation and Closing —
    (Right Reverend Sir)
    I am, Right Reverend Sir,
    Respectfully yours,
or, (Dear Bishop ...)
    Believe me, dear Bishop ...
    Yours sincerely,
or, (My dear Bishop)
    Believe me, my dear Bishop,
    Yours sincerely,

ARCHDEACON:

Address — The Venerable The Archdeacon of _____ , *or*, The Venerable Archdeacon _____ .
Salutation and Closing —
    (Venerable Sir)
    I am, Venerable Sir,
    Yours sincerely,
or, (Dear Mr. Archdeacon)
    I am, dear Mr. Archdeacon,
    Yours sincerely,

DEAN:

Address — The Very Reverend John M. Blank, Dean of _____ .
Salutation and Closing —
    (Very Reverend Sir)

    I am, Very Reverend Sir,
    Yours very truly,
or, (Dear Mr. Dean)
    Believe me, dear Mr. Dean,
    Yours sincerely,

CANON:

Address — The Reverend Canon John M. Blank,
Salutation and Closing —
    (Reverend Sir)
    Yours very truly,
or, (Dear Canon ...)
    Believe me, dear Canon ...
    Yours faithfully,

Minister of Religion

Address — The Reverend John M. Blank,
Salutation and Closing —
    (Sir)
    I am, Reverend Sir, (or, Sir),
    Yours very truly,
or, (Reverend Sir)
    Yours sincerely,
or, (Dear Mr. ...)
    Believe me, dear Mr. ...
    Yours sincerely,

Moderator (Canada)

Address — The Right Reverend _____ , D.D., Moderator of the _____ Church,
Salutation and Closing —
    (Right Reverend Sir)
    I am, Right Reverend Sir,
    Yours sincerely,
or, (Dear Dr. ...)
    Believe me, dear Dr. ...
    Yours sincerely,

Roman Catholic

CARDINAL:

Address — His Eminence John Cardinal Blank, Archbishop of _____ .
Salutation and Closing —
    (Your Eminence)
    I have the honour to be, Your Eminence,
    Your obedient servant,
or, (Your Eminence)
    I am, Your Eminence,
    Yours sincerely,
or, (Dear Cardinal ...)
    Believe me, dear Cardinal ...
    Yours sincerely,

ARCHBISHOP:

Address — The Most Reverend John M. Blank, Archbishop of _____ .
Salutation and Closing —
    (Your Excellency)
    I have the honour to be,
    Your Excellency,
    Respectfully yours,
    (ecclesiastical use).
or, (Most Reverend Sir)
    I am, Most Reverend Sir,
    Yours very truly,
or, (Dear Archbishop)
    Yours sincerely,

BISHOP:

Address — The Most Reverend John M. Blank, Bishop of _____ *(ecclesiastical use).*
or, The Right Reverend John M. Blank, Bishop of _____ .
Salutation and Closing —
    (Your Excellency)
    I am, Your Excellency,
    Respectfully yours,

(ecclesiastical use).
or, (Right Reverend Sir)
  I am, Right Reverend Sir,
Yours sincerely,
or, (Dear Bishop ...)
  Believe me, dear Bishop ...
Yours sincerely,
or, (Dear Bishop)
  With kind regards, dear Bishop,
Sincerely yours,

MONSIGNOR:
Address — The Right Reverend John M. Blank.
Salutation and Closing —
  (Right Reverend Monsignor)
  I am, Right Reverend Monsignor,
Yours sincerely,
or, (My dear Monsignor ...)
  Believe me, my dear Monsignor ...
Yours sincerely,

CANON:
Address — The Very Reverend John M. Blank.
Salutation and Closing —
  (Very Reverend Canon)
  Very truly yours,
or, (My dear Canon ...)
  Sincerely yours,

MOTHER SUPERIOR:
Address — The Reverend Mother Superior, The Congregation of _____.
Salutation and Closing —
  (Dear Madam)
  I am, dear Madam,
Yours respectfully,
or, (Reverend Mother Superior)
  I remain,
Reverend Mother Superior,
Yours sincerely,
or, (Dear Mother Superior)
  Believe me, dear Mother Superior,
Yours sincerely,

Priest
Address — The Reverend John M. Blank.
Salutation and Closing —
  (Reverend Sir)
  Yours sincerely,
or, (Dear Father ...)
  Believe me, dear Father ...
Yours sincerely,

Jewish

CHIEF RABBI:
Address — The Very Reverend John M. Blank, Chief Rabbi.
Salutation and Closing —
  (Dear Sir)
  I remain, Sir,
Yours very truly,
or, (Dear Chief Rabbi)
  I am, dear Chief Rabbi,
Sincerely yours,

RABBI:
Address — The Reverend Rabbi John M. Blank.
Salutation and Closing —
  (Dear Sir)
  I am, Sir,
Yours very truly,
or, (Dear Rabbi ...)
  I am, my dear Rabbi ...
Yours sincerely,

PROFESSIONAL

ADVOCATE, NOTARY, PHYSICIAN, DENTIST, CHARTERED ACCOUNTANT, OPTOMETRIST, ETC.:
Address — John/Jean M. Blank, Esq., Q.C., John/Jean M. Blank, Esq., Advocate; Dr. John/Jean M. Blank, or J.M. Blank, Esq., M.D. (*Never* use both Dr. and M.D.); Dr. John/Jean M. Blank, or J.M. Blank, Esq., D.D.S. (*Never* use both Dr. and D.D.S.); J.M. Blank, Esq., C.A.; Optometrist John/Jean M. Blank, or J.M. Blank, O.D., or Dr. John/Jean M. Blank.
Salutation and Closing —
  (Dear Sir/Madam)
  Yours very truly,

DIPLOMATIC

AMBASSADORS of foreign countries in Canada:
Address — His/Her Excellency John/Jean M. Blank, Ambassador of _____, Ottawa.
Salutation and Closing —
  (Excellency)
  Accept, Excellency, the assurances of my highest consideration (*formal diplomatic usage*).
or, (Excellency)
  Yours very truly,
or, (Dear Mr./Madam Ambassador)
  I am, dear Mr./Madam Ambassador,
Yours sincerely,
or, (Dear Mr., Mrs., Miss, ...)
  I am, dear Mr., Mrs., Miss, ...
Yours sincerely,

HIGH COMMISSIONERS of British Commonwealth countries in Canada:
Address — His/Her Excellency John/Jean M. Blank, High Commissioner for _____, Ottawa.
Salutation and Closing —
  (Your Excellency)
  Accept, Your Excellency, the assurances of my highest consideration (*formal diplomatic usage*).
or, (Dear Sir/Madam)
  Yours sincerely,
or, (Dear High Commissioner)
  Believe me, dear High Commissioner,
Yours sincerely,
or, (Dear Mr., Mrs., Miss, ...)
  With kind regards,
Yours very sincerely,

MINISTERS PLENIPOTENTIARY of foreign countries in Canada:
Address — His/Her Excellency John/Jean M. Blank, Minister of _____, Ottawa.
Salutation and Closing —
  (Excellency)
  Accept, Excellency, the assurances of my highest consideration (*formal diplomatic usage*).
or, (Dear Mr./Madam Minister)
  I remain, dear Mr./Madam Minister,
Yours sincerely,
or, (Dear Mr., Mrs., Miss, ...)
  Believe me, dear Mr., Mrs., Miss, ...
Yours sincerely,

CANADIAN AMBASSADORS abroad from a Canadian citizen:
Address — Mr./Mrs. or Miss John/Jean M. Blank, Canadian Ambassador to _____, _____.
Salutation and Closing —
  (Dear Sir/Madam)
  Yours very truly,
or, (Dear Ambassador)
  I am, dear Ambassador,
Yours sincerely,
or, (Dear Mr., Mrs., Miss, ...)
  With kind regards,
Yours sincerely,

CANADIAN AMBASSADORS abroad from a foreign citizen:
Address — His/Her Excellency John/Jean M. Blank, Canadian Ambassador to _____, _____.
Salutation and Closing —
  (Your Excellency)
  Accept, Your Excellency, the (renewed) assurances of my highest consideration (*formal diplomatic usage*).
or, (Dear Mr./Madam Ambassador)
  I am, dear Mr./Madam Ambassador,
Yours sincerely,
or, (Dear Mr., Mrs., Miss, ...)
  I am, dear Mr., Mrs., Miss, ...
Yours sincerely,

CANADIAN HIGH COMMISSIONERS abroad:
Address — Mr./Mrs. or Miss John/Jean M. Blank, High Commissioner for Canada.
Salutation and Closing —
  (Dear Sir/Madam)
  Yours very truly,
or, (Dear High Commissioner)
  Believe me, dear High Commissioner,
Yours sincerely,
or, (Dear Mr., Mrs., Miss, ...)
  With kind regards,
Yours sincerely,

CANADIAN MINISTERS PLENIPOTENTIARY abroad from a Canadian citizen:
Address — Mr./Mrs. or Miss John/Jean M. Blank, Canadian Minister to _____, _____.
Salutation and Closing —
  (Sir/Madam)
  I am, Sir/Madam,
Yours very truly,
or, (Dear Sir/Madam)
  Yours very truly,
or, (Dear Mr., Mrs., Miss, ...)
  With kind regards,
Yours sincerely,

CANADIAN MINISTERS PLENIPOTENTIARY abroad from a foreign citizen:
Address — His/Her Excellency John/Jean M. Blank, Canadian Minister to _____, _____.
Salutation and Closing —
  (Your Excellency)
  Accept, Your Excellency, the (renewed) assurances of my highest consideration (*formal diplomatic usage*).
or, (Dear Mr./Madam Minister)
  I remain, dear Mr./Madam Minister,
Yours sincerely,
or, (Dear Mr., Mrs., Miss, ...)
  Believe me, dear Mr., Mrs., Miss, ...
Yours sincerely,

ABBREVIATIONS

Indicating Academic, Ecclesiastical and other Degrees, membership in Societies and Institutions, military ranks, etc., appearing in the Canadian Almanac and Directory. For other lists of abbreviations, see Index.

A.A.C.C.A.	Associate of Association of Certified Accountants & Corporate Accountants (British)
A.A.C.I.	Accredited Appraiser Canadian Institute
A.A.E.	Associate of Accountants' & Executives' Corp. of Canada
A.A.G.O.	-- of the American Guild of Organists
A.A.S.A.	-- of the Alberta Society of Artists
A.B.	Bachelor of Arts, American (Artium Baccalaureus)

Canadian Almanac & Directory 1997

A.C.	"Advanced Certification" Canadian Association of Medical Radiation Technologists	B.A.A.	-- of Applied Arts	B.Sc.Dom.	Baccalauréat en Sciences Domestiques
		B.Acc.	-- of Accountancy	B.Sc.F. (B.S.F.)	Bachelor of Science in Forestry
		B.Adm. (B.Admin.)	-- of Administration	B.Sc.F.E.	-- of Science in Forestry Engineering
A.C.A.	Associate of Institute of Chartered Accountants (Eng.)			B.Sc.H.	Bachelier en Sciences Hospitalières
		B.Adm.Pub.	-- Baccalauréat spécialisé en administration publique	B.Sc.N. (or B.S.N. or B.Sc. (Nurs.))	Bachelor of Science in Nursing
A.C.C.O.	-- of Canadian College of Organists				
AccS.C.R.P.	-- of Canadian Public Relations Society Inc.	B.Ae.E. (B.Aero.E.)	Bachelor of Aeronautical Engineering	B.Sc.(OT) (or B.Sc.(Occ.Ther.))	-- of Science in Occupational Therapy
A.C.D.	Archaeologiae Christianae Doctor	B.A.I.	-- of Engineering (U. of Dublin)	B.Sc.Phm. (B.S.P.)	-- of Science in Pharmacy
A.C.G.I.	Associate of the City & Guilds of London Institute	B.A.L.S.	-- of Arts in Library Science		
		B.A.O.	-- of Obstetrics	B.Sc.Soc.	-- of Social Science
A.C.I.C.	-- of Canadian Institute of Chemistry	B.Arch.	-- in Architecture	B.S.C.E.	-- of Science in Civil Engineering
A.C.Inst.M.	-- of the Institute of Marketing	B.A.S. (B.A.Sc.)	-- of Applied Science	B.S.Ed.	-- of Science in Education
A.C.I.S.	-- of Chartered Institute of Secretaries (British)			B.S.E.E.	-- of Science in Electrical Engineering
		B.A.S.M.	-- of Arts, Master of Science	B.S.S.	-- of Social Sciences
A.C.S.M.	-- of Cambourne School of Mines	B.A.Theo.	-- of Arts in Theology	B.S.W.	-- of Social Work (or Welfare)
Adm.	Admiral	B.B.A.	-- of Business Administration	B.Tech.	-- of Technology
A.F.R.A.S. (A.F.R.Ae.S.)	Fellow of the Royal Aeronautical Society	B.C.D.	Bachelier en Chirurgie Dentale	B.Th.	-- of Theology
		B.C.E.	Bachelor of Civil Engineering	B.T.S.	-- of Technological Science (Edinburgh)
Ag. de l'U (Paris)	Honorary Professor of University of Paris (Agrégé de l'Université Paris)	B.Ch. (Ch.B.)	-- in Surgery (British)		
		B.Ch.E.	-- in Chemical Engineering (American)	B.V.Sc.	-- of Veterinary Science
Ag. de Phil.	Professor of Philosophy (Agrégé en Philosophie Louvain)			C.A.	Chartered Accountant
		B.C.L.	-- of Civil Law (or Canon Law)	C.A.A.P.	Certified Advertising Agency Practitioner
A.G.S.M.	Associate of the Guildhall School of Music (British)	B.Com. (B. Comm.)	-- of Commerce		
				C.A.E.	-- Association Executive
A.I.C.	-- of the Institute of Chemistry (British)	B.Comp.Sc.	-- of Computer Science	C.A.E./c.a.é.	Chartered Account Executive
		B.D.	-- of Divinity	C.A.P.	Certificat d'Aptitude Pedagogique
A.I.I.C.	-- of the Insurance Institute of Canada	B.D.C.	Bachelier en droit canonique	Capt. (or Capt.(N))	Captain (or Captain (Naval))
A.K.C.	-- of King's College (London)	B.Des.	Bachelor of Design		
A.L.C.M.	-- of London (Canada) Conservatory of Music	B.D.S.	-- of Dental Surgery (British)	C.B.E.	Commander, Order of the British Empire
		B.E. (B.Eng.)	-- of Engineering		
A.L.S.	Commissioned Alberta Land Surveyor	B.Ed. (B.E.A.D.)	-- of Education	C.B.V.	Chartered Business Valuator
A.M.	Master of Arts (Artium Magister)			C.C.	Chartered Cartographer
A.M.E.I.C.	Associate Member of the Engineering Institute of Canada	B.E.D.S.	-- of Environmental Design Studies	C.C.	Companion, Order of Canada
		B.E.E.	-- of Electrical Engineering (American)	C.D.	Canadian Forces Decoration
A.M.I.C.E.	-- Member of the Institution of Civil Engineers (British)			Cdr.	Commander
		B. en Ph.	Bachelier en Philosophie	C.E.	Civil Engineer
A.M.I.E.E.	-- Member of the Institute of Electrical Engineers	B. en Sc. Com.	-- en Science Commerciale	Cer.E.	Ceramic Engineer
		B.E.S.	Bachelor of Environmental Sciences (or Studies)	C.E.S.	Certificat d'Études Secondaires (La Sorbonne)
A.M.I.Mech.E.	-- Member of the Institution of Mechanical Engineers (British)				
		B. ès A.	Bachelier ès Arts	C.F.A.	Chartered Financial Analyst
A.Mus.	-- of Music	B. ès L.	-- ès Lettres	C.F.P.	Chartered Financial Planner
A.P.A.	-- Member of the Institute of Accredited Public Accountants (British)	B. ès Sc.	-- ès Science	C.G.A.	Certified General Accountant
		B. ès Sc. App.	-- ès Science Appliquée	Chan.	Chanoine (Canon)
A.P.H.A.	-- Member of the Public Health Association (British)	B.F.	Bachelor of Forestry (American)	C.H.E.	Certified Health Executive
		B.F.A.	-- of Fine Arts	Chem. Ing.	Ingénieur Chimiste Diplomé (Swiss Fed. Inst. Technology)
A.P.R.	Accredited Member of the Canadian Public Relations Society	B.Gen.	Brigadier-General		
		B.H.E. (B.H.Ec.)	Bachelor of Home Economics	C.I.F.	Canadian Institute of Forestry
A.R.A.	Associate of the Royal Academy (honorary)			C.I.M.	Certificate in Management
		B.H.Sc.	-- of Household Science	C.I.M.	Certified Industrial Manager
A.R.C.D.	-- of the Royal College of Dancing	B.J.	-- of Journalism	C.I.S.&P.	Canadian Inst. of Surveying & Photogrammetry
A.R.C.M.	-- of the Royal College of Music	B.J.C.	-- in Canon Law		
A.R.C.O.	-- of the Royal College of Organists (Canadian)	B.L.	-- in Literature (or of Laws)	C.L.A.	Canadian Library Association
		B.L.A.	-- of Landscape Architecture	C.L.S.	Canada Land Surveyor
A.R.C.S. (A.R.C.Sc.)	-- of the Royal College of Science	B.Litt.	-- of Literature (American & British)	C.L.U.	Chartered Life Underwriter
		B.L.S.	-- of Library Science	C.M.	Master in Medicine (British)
A.R.C.T.	-- of the Royal Conservatory of Music of Toronto	B.M.	-- of Medicine	C.M.	Member, Order of Canada
		B.Mus.	-- of Music	C.M.A.	Certified Management Accountant (or Canadian Medical Association or Canadian Management Association)
A.R.C.V.S.	-- of the Royal College of Veterinary Surgeons	B.M.V.	Bachelier en Médecine Vétérinaire		
		B.N.	Bachelor of Nursing		
A.R.D.I.O.	-- of Registered Interior Designers of Ontario	B.N.Sc.	-- of Nursing Science		
		B. Paed. (Péd.)	-- of Pedagogy	C.M.C.	Certified Management Consultant
A.R.D.S.	-- of the Royal Drawing Society (London, Eng.)	B.P.A.	-- of Public Administration	Cmd.O.	Commissioned Officer
		B.P.E.	-- of Physical Education	Cmdre.	Commodore
A.R.I.B.A.	-- of the Royal Institute of British Architects	B.Ph. (B.Phil.)	-- of Philosophy	C.M.M.	Certified Municipal Manager (Ontario)
		B.P.H.E.	-- of Physical & Health Education		
A.R.I.C.	-- of the Royal Institute of Chemistry	B.Ps.	Baccalauréat en Psychologie	C.M.M.	Commander, Order of Military Merit
A.R.S.H.	-- of the Royal Society of Health	Br.	Brother	C.O.A.	Certified Office Administrator
A.R.S.M.	-- of the Royal School of Mines	B.S.	Bachelor of Science (or of Surgery) (American)	Col.	Colonel
A.R.S.M.	-- of the Royal School of Music			C.P.A.	Certified Public Accountant
A.Sc.T.	Applied Science Technologist	B.S.A.	-- of Science in Agriculture (or in Accounting, or in Administration)	C.P.C.	-- Personnel Consultant
Assoc. Inst. M.M.	Associate of the Institute of Mining and Metallurgy (British)			C.P.M.	Certificate in Personnel Management
		B.Sc.	-- of Science	C.P.P.M.A.	-- in Public Personnel Management Association
A.T.C.L.	-- of Trinity College, London (Eng.)	B.Sc.A.	Bachelier ès science appliquées		
A.T.C.M.	-- of the Toronto Conservatory of Music	B.Sc.B.	-- en Bibliothéconomie	C.P.P.O.	Certified Public Purchasing Officer
		B.Sc.(CE)	Bachelor of Science in Civil Engineering	C.P.P.	-- Professional Purchaser
A.Th.	-- in Theology			C.R. (c.r.)	Conseiller de la Reine (Queen's Counsel)
B.A.	Bachelor of Arts	B.Sc.Com.	-- of Commercial Science		

Canadian Almanac & Directory 1997

C.R.A.	Canadian Residential Appraiser
C.S.R.	Chartered Stenographic Reporter
C.T.C.	Certified Travel Counsellor
C.Tech.	-- Technician
C.W.O.	Chief Warrant Officer
D.A.	Doctor of Arts (honorary)
D.A.	-- of Archaeology (Laval)
D.Arch.	-- of Architecture
D.A.Sc.	-- in Applied Sciences
D.C.	-- of Chiropractic
D.C.D.	Docteur en Chirurgie Dentale
D.Ch.	Doctor of Surgery (British)
D.Ch.E.	-- of Chemical Engineering (American)
D.C.L.	-- of Civil Law (or Canon Law)
D.D.	-- of Divinity
D.D.C.	Doctorat Droit Canonique
D. de l'Un.	-- de l'Université
D.D.S.	Doctor of Dental Surgery (British)
D.D.T.	-- of Drugless Therapy
D.Ed.	-- of Education
D.Eng.	-- of Engineering
D. en Méd. Vet.	Docteur en Médecine Vetérinaire
D. en Ph.	-- en Philosophie
D. ès L.	-- ès Lettres (Doctor of Letters)
D. ès Sc. App.	Doctor of Applied Science
D.F.	-- of Forestry (American)
D.F.A.	-- of Fine Arts (often honorary)
D.F.Sc.	-- of Financial Science (Laval)
D.I.C.	Diploma of Membership of Imperial College of Science & Technology (British)
Dip. Bact.	-- in Bacteriology
Dip. d'É.	Diplome d'Études
Dip. de l'U. (P)	Diploma of the U. of Paris
Dip. d'É. Sup. or Dip.E.S.	Diplome d'Études Supérieures, Paris
Dip. Ing.	Diploma in Engineering
D.Jour	Doctor of Journalism
D. Lit. (D. Litt.)	-- of Letters (or Literature)
D.L.O.	Diploma in Laryngology & Otology
D.L.S.	Dominion Land Surveyor (or Doctor of Library Science)
D.M.	Doctorat Médecine
D.M.D.	Doctor of Dental Medicine
D. Ms.	-- in Missionology
D. Mus.	Doctorat en Musique
D.M.R. (D. or T.)	Diploma in Medical Radiology (Royal Coll. of Surgeons, London)
D.M.T.	-- in Tropical Medicine
D.M.T. & H. (Eng.)	-- in Tropical Medicine & Hygiene
D.N.S. D.N.Sc.	Doctor of Nursing Science
D.O.	-- of Osteopathy
Doct. Arch.	-- of Christian Archaeology (Pontifical Institute, Rome)
D. Paed. (Péd.)	-- of Paedagogy
D.P.E.	Diploma in Physical Education
D.Ph. (D.Phil. or Ph.D.)	Doctor of Philosophy
D.P.Ec.	-- of Political Economy
D.P.H.	-- (or Diploma) in Public Health
D.Ps. (D.Psy.)	-- of Psychologie
D.P.Sc.	-- of Political Science
D. Psych.	-- (or Diploma) in Psychiatry
D.P.T.	-- of Physio-Therapy
Dr.	Doctor
D.R.	Doctor of Radiology
Dr.Com.Sc.	-- of Commercial Science
Dr. de l'U. (P)	-- of the U. of Paris
Dr. ès Lettres	-- of Letters (History of Literature)
Dr. jur.	-- of Law (Dr. Juris)
Dr. rer. pol.	-- of Political Economy (Dr. Rerum Politicarum) (Docteur des Sciences Politiques)
D.S.A. (D.Sc.A.)	Docteur ès science appliqués
D.Sc.	Doctor of Science
D.Sc.Mil.	-- of Military Science
D.S.L.	-- of Sacred Letters
D.Sc.Com.	-- of Commercial Science
D.Sc.Fin.	-- of Financial Science
D.Sc.Nat.	-- in Natural Science
D.Sc.Soc.	-- of Social Science
D.Th.	-- of Theology
D.V.M. (D.M.V.)	-- of Veterinary Medicine
D.V.Sc.	-- of Veterinary Science
Ed.D.	-- of Education
Ed.M.	Master of Education (Harvard)
E.E.	Electrical Engineer
E.M.	Mining Engineer
E.T.C.M.	Graduate of Eastern Townships Conservatory of Music
F.A.A.O.	Fellow of the American Academy of Optometry
F.A.A.O.Dip.	Diplomatic Fellow of the American Academy of Optometry
F.A.C.D.	Fellow of the American College of Dentists
F.A.C.O.	-- of the American College of Organists
F.A.C.P.	-- of the American College of Physicians
F.A.C.R.	-- of the American College of Radiology
F.A.C.S.	-- of the American College of Surgeons
F.A.E.	-- of the Accountants' & Executives' Corp. of Canada
F.A.G.S.	-- of the American Geographical Society
F.A.I.A.	-- of the American Institute of Actuaries
	-- of the American Institute of Architects
F.A.I.A.	Association of International Accountants
F.A.O.U.	Fellow of the American Ornithologists Union
F.A.P.H.A.	-- of the American Public Health Association
F.A.P.S.	-- of the American Physical Society
F.A.S.	-- of the Actuarial Society
F.B.A.	-- of the British Academy (honorary)
F.B.O.A.	-- of British Association of Optometrists
F.C.A.	-- of the Institute of Chartered Accountants (British)
F.C.B.A.	-- of Canadian Bankers' Association
F.C.C.A.	-- of the Association of Certified Accountants
F.C.C.O.	-- of the Canadian College of Organists
F.C.C.T.	-- of the Canadian College of Teachers
F.C.C.U.I.	-- of the Canadian Credit Union Institute
F.C.G.I.	-- of the City & Guilds of London Institute
F.C.I.	-- of the Canadian Credit Institute
F.C.I.C.	-- of the Chemical Institute of Canada
F.C.I.I.	-- of the Chartered Insurance Institute (British)
F.C.I.S.	-- of the Chartered Institute of Secretaries (British)
F.C.O.G.	-- of the College of Obstetricians & Gynaecologists (British)
F.C.A.M.R.T.	-- of Canadian Association of Medical Radiation Technologists
F.C.S.I.	-- of the Canadian Securities Institute
F.C.T.C.	-- of the Canadian Institute of Travel Counsellors
F.E.	Forest Engineer
F.E.I.C.	Fellow of the Engineering Institute of Canada
F.F.A.	-- of the Faculty of Actuaries (Scotland)
F.F.R.	-- of the Faculty of Radiologists (British)
F.G.S.	-- of the Geological Society (British)
F.G.S.A.	-- of the Geological Society of America
F.I.A.	-- of the Institute of Actuaries (British)
F.I.C.	-- of the Institute of Chemistry
F.I.C.B.	-- of the Institute of Canadian Bankers
F.I.C.E.	-- of the Institution of Civil Engineers
F.I.E.E.	-- of the Institution of Electrical Engineers
F.I.I.C.	-- of the Insurance Institute of Canada
F.I.L.	-- of the Institute of Linguists (British)
F.L.A.	-- of the Library Association (England)
F.M.S.A.	-- of the Mineralogical Society of America
Fr.	Father
F.R.A.I.	Fellow of the Royal Anthropological Institute
F.R.A.I.C.	-- of the Royal Architectural Institute of Canada
F.R.A.M.	-- of the Royal Academy of Music
F.R.A.S.	-- of the Royal Astronomical Society
F.R.C.C.O.	-- of the Royal Canadian College of Organists
F.R.C.M.	-- of the Royal College of Music
F.R.C.O.	-- of the Royal College of Organists
F.R.C.O.G.	-- of the Royal College of Obstetricians & Gynaecologists
F.R.C.P.	-- of the Royal College of Physicians of London
F.R.C.P.(C)	-- of the College of Physicians of Canada
or (E) or (I) or (Glas)	-- of the College of Physicians of Edinburgh or of Ireland or of Glasgow
F.R.C.S.	-- of the Royal College of Surgeons of England
F.R.C.S.(C)	-- of the Royal College of Surgeons of Canada
or (E) or (I) or (Glas)	-- of the Royal College of Surgeons of Edinburgh or of Ireland or of Glasgow
F.R.G.S.	-- of the Royal Geographical Society
F.R.Hist.S.	-- of the Royal Historical Society
F.R.Hort.S.	-- of the Royal Horticultural Society
F.R.I.B.A.	-- of the Royal Institute of British Architects
F.R.I.C.	-- of the Royal Institute of Chemistry
F.R.I.C.S.	-- of the Royal Institution of Chartered Surveyors
F.R.M.C.M.	-- of Royal Manchester College of Music
F.R.M.S. (F.R.Met.S.)	-- of the Royal Meteorological Society
F.R.S.	-- of the Royal Society (honorary)
F.R.S.A.	-- of the Royal Society of Arts
F.R.S.C.	-- of the Royal Society of Canada
F.R.S.E.	-- of the Royal Society of Edinburgh
F.R.S.H.	-- of the Royal Society of Health
F.R.S.L.	-- of the Royal Society of Literature
F.S.A.	-- of the Society of Actuaries (or of Antiquaries) (honorary)
F.S.M.A.C.	-- of the Society of Management Accountants of Canada
F.S.S.	-- of the Royal Statistical Society
F.T.C.L.	-- of Trinity College of Music (London)
F.Z.S.	-- of the Zoological Society (British)
Gen.	General
G.J.	Graduate Jeweller
H.A.R.C.V.S.	Honorary Associate of Royal College of Veterinary Surgeons
Ing.E.T.P.	Diplome de l'École Spéciale des Travaux Publiques
J.C.B.	Bachelor of Canon Law
J.C.D.	Doctor of Canon Law (or of Civil Law)

Canadian Almanac & Directory 1997

J.C.L.	Licentiate in Canon Law (Juris Canonici Licentiatus)	M.A.Sc. (M.A.S.)	-- of Applied Science	M.R.A.I.C.	Member of the Royal Architectural Institute of Canada
J.D.	Doctor of Jurisprudence	M.A.S.C.E.	Member of the American Society of Civil Engineers	M.R.C.O.G.	-- of the Royal College of Obstetricians & Gynaecologists
J.D.S.	-- of Juridical Science	M.A.S.M.E.	-- of the American Society of Mechanical Engineers	M.R.C.P.	-- of the Royal College of Physicians
Jr.	Junior	M.Aust. I.M.	-- of the Australian Institute of Mining & Metallurgy	M.R.C.P.(E) or (I) or (Glas)	-- of the Royal College of Physicians of Edinburgh (or Ireland or Glasgow)
J.U.L.	Licentiate of Law in Utroque (both Civil & Canon Law)	M.B.	Bachelor of Medicine (British)	M.R.C.S.	-- of the Royal College of Surgeons
Jur.M.	Master of Jurisprudence	M.B.A.	Master in Business Administration	M.R.C.S.(E)	-- of the Royal College of Surgeons of Edinburgh
Jur. utr. Dr.	Juris utriusque doctor, Equiv. to LL.D.	M.C.E.	-- of Civil Engineering	M.R.C.V.S.	-- of the Royal College of Veterinary Surgeons
L.A.B.	Licentiate of the Assoc. Bd. of Royal Schools of Music (London, Eng.)	M.Ch. (Ch.M.)	-- of Surgery (British)	M.R.M.	Master of Resource Management
L.Cdr.	Lieutenant-Commander	M.Ch.E.	-- of Chemical Engineering (American)	M.R.S.C.	Member of the Royal Society of Canada
L.C.L.	Licentiate in Canon Law	M.C.I.	Member of the Credit Institute	M.R.S.H.	-- of the Royal Society of Health
L.C.M.I.	-- of the Cost & Management Institute	M.C.I.C.	-- of the Chemical Institute of Canada	M.R.S.T.	-- of the Royal Society of Teachers
L.Col.	Lieutenant-Colonel	M.C.I.F.	-- of the Canadian Institute of Forestry	M.S.	Master of Surgery (British)
L.D.C.	Licencié ès Droit Canonique	M.C.I.M.	-- of the Canadian Institute of Mining	M.S.A.	-- of Science in Agriculture
L.D.S.	Licentiate in Dental Surgery (British)	M.C.I.M.M.	-- of the Canadian Institute of Mining & Metallurgy	M.Sc.	-- of Science
L. ès L.	Licencié ès Lettres	M.C.Inst.M.	-- of the Canadian Institute of Marketing	M.Sc.A.	-- of Applied Science
L. ès Sc.	-- ès Sciences	M.C.L.	Master of Civil Law	M.Sc.C.E.	-- of Science in Civil Engineering
L.Gen.	Lieutenant-General	M.Com.	-- of Commerce	M.Sc.F.	-- of Science in Forestry
L.G.S.M.	Licentiate of the Guildhall School of Music & Drama (London, Eng.)	M.Comp.	-- of Canon Law	M.Sc.(Med.)	-- of Science in Medicine
Litt.D.	Doctor of Letters (or Literature)	M.Comp.Sc.	-- of Computer Science	M.Sc.N. (M.S.N.)	-- of Science in Nursing
Litt.L.	Licence ès Lettres	M.D.	Doctor of Medicine		
Litt.M.	Master of Letters (or Literature)	M.D.C.	Master of Canon Law	M.Sc.Phm.	-- of Science in Pharmacy
L.J.C.	Licentiatus Juris Canonici	M.D.C.M.	Doctor of Medicine & Master of Surgery	M.Sc.Soc.	-- in Social Sciences
L.L.	License in Civil Law			M.S.Ed.	-- of Science in Education
LL.B.	Bachelor of Laws (Legum Baccalaureus)	M.Des.	Master of Design	M.S.Litt.	-- of Sacred Letters
LL.D.	Doctor of Laws (usually honorary)	M.Div.	-- of Divinity	M.S.P.E.	McGill School of Physical Education
LL.L.	Licence en droit	M.D.S.	-- of Dental Surgery (British)	M.S.R.C.	Membre Société Royale du Canada
LL.M.	Master of Law	M.D.V.	Doctor of Veterinary Medicine	M.S.S.	Master of Social Science
L. Mus.	Licentiate in Music	Me	Maître	M.S.W.	-- of Social Work
L.M.U.S.	-- in Music of the Univ. of Saskatchewan	M.E.	Master of Mechanical Engineering	M.U.Dr.	Medecinae Universae Doctor (Prague) (Dentistry & Medicine)
		M.Ed. (M.A.Ed.)	-- of Education	M.U.P.	Master of Planning
L. Mus. T.C.L.	-- in General Musicianship of Trinity College, London			M.U.R.P.	-- of Urban & Rural Planning
L.Péd.	Licence en Pédagogie	M.E.D.S.	-- of Environmental Design Studies	Mus. Bac. (Mus.B.)	Bachelor of Music
L.Ph.	-- en Philosophie	M.E.E.	-- of Electrical Engineering (American)		
L.Psych.	Licencié en Psychologie			Mus. Doc. (Mus.D.)	Doctor of Music
L.R.A.M.	Licentiate of the Royal Academy of Music (London)	M.E.I.C.	Member of the Engineering Institute of Canada		
L.R.C.M.	-- of the Royal College of Music (London)	M.Eng.	Master of Engineering	Mus. G. Paed.	Musicae Graduatus Paedagogus (Graduate Teacher in Music)
L.R.C.P.	-- of the Royal College of Physicians	M.F.	-- of Forestry	Mus.M.	Master of Music
L.R.C.S.	-- of the Royal College of Surgeons	M.F.A.	-- of Fine Arts	M.V.	Médécin Vétérinaire
L.R.C.T.	-- of the Royal Conservatory of Toronto	M.Gen.	Major-General	M.V.Sc.	Master of Veterinary Science
		Mgr.	Monsignor (or Manager or Monseigneur)	N.D.A.	National Diploma in Agriculture (Royal Ag. Soc. of Engineering)
L.R.E.	-- in Religious Education				
L.R.S.M.	-- of the Royal Schools of Music (London)	M.H.A.	Master of Health (or Hospital) Administration	N.D.D.	National Diploma in Dairying (Scotland)
L.S.	Land Surveyor	M.H.E. (M.H.Ec.)	-- of Home Economics	N.P.	Notary Public
L.S.A.	Licentiate in Agricultural Science			O.A.	Officier d'Académie (France)
L.Sc.Com.	-- in Commercial Science	M.I.C.E.	Member of the Institution of Civil Engineers (British)	O.C.	Order of Canada
L.Sc.O.	Licence en optométrie			O.D.	Doctor of Optometry
L.S.Sc.	Licentiate in Sacred Scriptures	M.I.C.I.A.	-- of Industrial, Commercial & Institutional Accountants	O.I.P.	Officier de l'Instruction Publique
L.Sc.Soc.	Licence in Social Science			O.L.S.	Ontario Land Surveyor
L.S.T.	Licentiate in Sacred Theology	M.I.E.E.	-- of the Institution of Electrical Engineers (British)	O.M.M.	Officer, Order of Military Merit
Lt. (or Lt.(N)	Lieutenant (or Lieutenant (Naval))			O.S.A.	Ontario Society of Artists
L.T.C.L.	-- of Trinity College of Music (London)	M.I.M.M.	-- of the Institute of Mining & Metallurgy (British)	P.C.	Privy Councillor
L.T.C.M.	-- of the Toronto Conservatory of Music			P.D.	Doctor of Parapsychology
		M.I.N.A.	-- of the Institute of Naval Architects	P.E.	Professional Engineer
L.Th	Licentiate in Theology	M.I.R.E.	-- of the Institute of Radio Engineers	P.Eng.	Registered Professional Engineer
M.	Monsieur	M.J.	Master of Journalism	Ph.B.	Bachelor of Philosophy
M.A.	Master of Arts	M.Litt.	-- of Letters (or Literature)	Ph.C.	Philosopher of Chiropractic
M.Acc.	-- of Accountancy	M.L.I.S.	-- of Library & Information Science	Ph.D.	Doctor of Philosophy
M.A.C.F.	Membre de l'Académie canadienne-française	M.L.S.	-- of Library Science (or Licentiate in Medieval Studies)	Ph.T.D.	Physical Therapy Doctor
				Ph.L.	Licentiate in Philosophy
M.Ae.E.	Master of Aeronautical Engineering	M.M. (M.Mus.)	-- of Music	P.L.S.	Professional Legal Secretary
M.A.I.E.E.	Member of American Institute of Electrical Engineers	M.M.M.	Member, Order of Military Merit	P.Mgr.	-- Manager
		M.N. (M.Nurs.)	Master of Nursing	P.P.	-- Purchaser
M.A.I.M.E.	-- of American Institute of Mining Engineers	M.P.	-- of Planning	P.P.B.	-- Public Buyer
		M.P.	Member of Parliament	Prof.	Professor
Maj.	Major	M.P.E.	Master of Physical Education	P.T.I.C.	Patent & Trade Mark Institute of Canada
M.A.L.S.	Master of Arts in Library Science	M.Ph. (M.Phil.)	-- of Philosophy		
M.A.P.	Maîtrise en administration publique	M.P.M.	-- of Pest Management	Q.A.A.	Qualified Administrative Assistant
M.Arch.	Master of Architecture	M.P.P.	Member of Provincial Parliament	Q.C.	Queen's Counsel
M.A.S.	-- of Archival Studies	M.Ps. (M.Psy.)	Master of Psychology	Q.L.S.	Québec Land Surveyor

Canadian Almanac & Directory 1997

R.A.	Royal Academy (honorary)
R.Adm.	Rear-Admiral
R.A.M.	Royal Academy of Music (Budapest)
R.A.S.	Royal Aeronautical Society
R.B.A.	Royal Society of British Artists
R.C.A.	Royal Canadian Academy of Arts
R.C.A.M.	Royal College & Academy of Music (Budapest)
R.C.M.	Royal Conservatory of Music (Leipzig)
R.E.	Royal Engineers
Rev.	Reverend
R.F.P.	Registered Financial Planner
R.M.S.	Royal Society of Miniature Painters
R.M.T.	Registered Music Teacher
R.N.	-- Nurse
R.O.I.	Royal Institute of Oil Painters
R.P.	Member of the Royal Society of Portrait Painters
R.P.	Révérend Père (Reverend Father)
R.P.A.	Registered Public Accountant
R.P.Bio.	-- Professional Biologist
R.P.Dt.	-- Professional Dietitian
R.P.F.	-- Professional Forester
R.R.L.	-- Record Librarian
R.S.H.	Royal Society of Health
R.S.W.	Registered Specification Writer
R.T.	-- Technician of the Cdn. Association of Medical Radiation Technologists
S.C.	Senior Counsel (Eire) equivalent of Q.C.
Sc.D.	Doctorat ès Sciences
Sc.L.	Licence ès Sciences
Sc. Soc. B.	Bachelier Science Sociale
Sc. Soc. D.	Doctor of Social Science
Sc. Soc. L.	License in Social Science
S.J.	Society of Jesus
S.L.S.	Saskatchewan Land Surveyor
S.Lt.	Sub-Lieutenant
S.M.	Master of Science
Sr.	Senior
Sr.	Sister
S.S.B.	Bachelier en Science Sacrée
S.S.C.	Sculptors' Society of Canada
S.S.L.	Licentiate in Sacred Scripture
S.T.B. (S.Th.B.)	Bachelor of Sacred Theology
S.T.D. (S.Th.D.)	Doctor of Sacred Theology
S.T.L. (S.Th.L.)	Sacrae Theologiae Licentiatus (Licentiate in Sacred Theology)
S.T.M.	Master of Sacred Theology
T.C.L.	Trinity College, London
T.M.M.G.	Teacher, Massage & Medical Gymnastics
Th.D.	Doctor of Theology
V.Adm.	Vice-Admiral
V.G.	Vicar-General
V.S.	Veterinary Surgeon

BUSINESS AND SHIPPING ABBREVIATIONS

As shipping terms vary in different countries, insurance or shipping agents should be consulted.

For other lists of abbreviations, academic, etc., see Index.

a/c	Account
Ad val.	Ad valorem
avoir.	Avoirdupois
bbl.	Barrel
B/L.	Bill of Lading
b.m.	Board Measure
B.O.	Buyer's Option
B/P.	Bills Payable
B/R.	Bills Receivable
B/S.	Bill of Sale
c.	Hundred
C or Cent.	Centigrade
cf.	Compare
C. and F.	Cost & Freight
Cie	Compagnie
c.i.f.	Cost insurance & freight
C.L.	Car Load (of freight)
Co.	Company
C.O.D.	Cash on Delivery
C. of F.	Cost of Freight
Cr.	Credit
C.W.O.	Cash with Order
Cwt.	Hundredweight
D/A.	Documents Attached, also Deposit Account
Dis. (Disct.)	Discount
Dl. (or Tl.)	Double (or triple) first class
D.O.A.	Deliver Documents on Acceptance of Draft
D.O.P.	Deliver Documents on Payment of Draft
Dr.	Debit
D.V.	God willing (Deo volente)
e.g.	For example (exempli gratia)
E.&O.E.	Errors & omissions excepted
Est. Wt.	Estimated Weight
et seq.	And the following (et sequens)
Ex. Div.	Without Dividend
Ex-Warehouse	Purchaser pays carriage charges & assumes risks from seller's warehouse
F.	Fahrenheit
F.a.a.	Free of Average (marine insurance)
F.A.S.	Free Alongside (Seller assumes risks & delivers goods to alongside of steamer free of carriage charges)
F.O.B.	Free on Board (Purchaser pays carriage charges & assumes risks from point specified)
F.P.A.	Free of Particular Average (Insured can recover only for a total loss, subject to other conditions of the contract)
Franco.	Pre-paid free of expense to point specified
G.A.	General Average (All owners of cargo & vessel share in any loss arising from expense incurred to preserve ship & contents from greater loss)
gm.	Grammes
gr.	Grain; grains, or gross
ibid.	In the same place (ibidem)
i.e.	That is (id est)
Inc.	Incorporated
Int.	Interest
K.D.	Knocked down
lb. (libra)	Pound
L/C.	Letter of Credit
L.C.L.	Less than Car Load (of freight)
Limited; Ltd.	Limited Liability (Shareholders are "limited" in liability to the amount of their subscribed stock in certain companies)
L.P.	List Price
M.	Thousand (Mille)
MS., MSS.	Manuscript(s)
N.E.S. (N.O.P.)	Not Otherwise Provided For (Customs)
N.O.S.	Not Otherwise Specified
N.S.F.	Not Sufficient Funds (re cheques)
Nstd.	Nested
O.K.	Correct
op. cit.	In the work quoted (opere citato)
O.R.	At Owner's Risk
O.R.B.	At Owner's Risk of Breakage
oz.	Ounce
P.A.	Particular Average (As used in Marine Insurance, means damage to the goods caused by perils insured against & named in the contract. This form is often written with a Franchise Clause, & means there will be no claim unless the loss exceeds the percentage named)
P/A.	Power of Attorney
P & D.	Pick Up & Deliver
pp.	Pages
Pro forma	As a Matter of Form
P.S.	Postscript
q.v.	Which see (quod vide)
R.R.	Rural Route (Postal delivery)
S.B.	Shipping Bill
s.s.	Steamship
s/o	Ship's Option, weight or measurement
S.U.	Set Up (meaning article is complete)
T.B.L.	Through Bill of Lading
Tare	Weight of Container (Deducting tare from "gross weight" gives "net weight")
Ton	2,000 (short ton) or 2,240 (long ton) lbs. avoirdupois. A cubic ton in marine freight = 40 cubic feet
Ton wt/M.	Ton, weight or measurement (ship's option)
vide	See
viz	Namely; to wit (videlicet)

CUSTOMS REGULATIONS FOR CANADIANS RETURNING FROM ABROAD

Canadians returning to Canada may bring any amount of goods into the country subject to duties and any provincial or territorial assessments, with the exception of restricted items. Duties represent duty, excise taxes and the Goods & Services Tax (GST). Provincial and territorial taxes are not included in duties unless a relationship has been established between the federal government and a province or territory whereby the federal government collects the provincial or territorial taxes, levies and fees on their behalf.

Goods included in personal exemptions must be for personal or household use, souvenirs or gifts. Goods brought in for commercial use, or on behalf of another person do not qualify and are subject to full duties.

On your return to Canada, you must declare all goods acquired (purchases, gifts, awards, prizes, and purchases made at Canadian or foreign duty-free shops and still in your possession) and repairs or modifications you made to your vehicle, vessel or aircraft while outside Canada.

Personal Exemptions

To qualify for personal exemptions you must be:
- Canadian resident returning from a trip abroad;
- former resident of Canada returning to live in Canada; or
- temporary resident of Canada.

Children and infants qualify for personal exemptions as long as the goods are for the use of the child or infant. The parent or guardian makes the customs declaration for the child.

Personal exemptions are applicable after the following minimum absences:

1. After an absence of 24 hours or more: up to a value of $50 in total (with the exception of tobacco and alcoholic beverages) any number of times a year. If the value of the goods exceeds $50 you pay duty on the full value (exemption cannot be claimed). The goods must accompany you on your return to Canada. A written declaration may be necessary.

2. After an absence of 48 hours or more: up to $200 in total any number of times in a year. You may have

to make a written declaration. The goods must accompany you on your return to Canada.

3. After an absence of seven days or more: up to $500 any number of times in a year. You may have to make a written declaration. Goods you claim under this exemption may follow you by mail or other means, with the exception of alcoholic beverages or tobacco. You require a Form E24, "Returning Persons Declaration", obtainable from a customs officer, to claim your goods when they arrive. Goods must be claimed within 40 days of their arrival in Canada; duty is then payable, along with a processing fee. You may pay the duty and then apply to Revenue Canada for a refund (if the personal exemption applies) or refuse delivery; following a review that determines if the goods are eligible for free importation, the goods will be released to you without an assessment.

Persons residing outside Canada for part of the year are considered to be residents of Canada and are entitled to the above personal exemptions.

Exemptions cannot be transferred to another person or combined with another person's personal exemption. You cannot combine a 24-hour ($50) or 48-hour ($200) or the seven-day ($500) exemption when claiming an exemption. Nor can you carry over an unused portion of an exemption for another period of absence.

Tobacco & Alcohol

Tobacco & alcoholic beverages must accompany you in your hand or checked luggage and may be included in the 48-hour ($200) or the seven-day ($500) exemptions, but not in the 24-hour ($50) exemption. You must meet the age requirements set by the province or territory where you enter Canada. In addition the following conditions apply:

1. You may bring in up to 200 cigarettes, 50 cigars or cigarillos, 400 tobacco sticks and 400 grams of manufactured tobacco. Duty must be paid on anything above this allowance, plus any applicable provincial or territorial limits or assessments.

2. You may include up to 1.14 litres (40 ounces) of wine or liquor, or 24 335 ml (12-ounce) cans or bottles (8.5 litres) of beer or ale. Wine coolers are classified as wine; beer coolers are classified as beer. Beer or wine that contains 0.5% alcohol by volume or less is not classifed as an alcoholic beverage, so no quantity limits apply. You may bring in more than this allowance of alcohol anywhere in Canada (with the exception of the Northwest Territories) as long as the quantities are within the limits set by the province. In most cases you must carry the allowance with you. If bringing in more than the free allowance, you must pay customs and provincial/territorial assessments; check with the appropriate provincial/territorial liquor control agency prior to leaving Canada for more information.

Gifts

While abroad, you may send gifts duty-free and tax-free to recipients in Canada. The gift must be valued at $60 or less and cannot be an alcoholic beverage, tobacco product or advertising material. Gifts in excess of $60 require duty payment by the recipient on the excess amount. Gifts that accompany you on your return to Canada must be included in your personal exemption, while gifts you send from abroad are not included. Some conditions apply; contact your nearest Revenue Canada customs office for details.

Prizes & Awards

In most cases, you pay regular duty on prizes or awards received outside Canada. Contact Revenue Canada customs offices for more information.

Paying Duties

Duties my be paid by cash or travellers' cheques. Personal cheques are also acceptable (for amounts of $2500 or less and with proper identification); VISA and MasterCard are accepted at most customs locations.

For information on duty rates for particular items, contact your nearest Revenue Canada customs office.

Special Duty Rate

After any trip abroad of 48 hours or longer you are entitled to a special duty rate on goods worth up to $300 more than your personal exemption. The goods must accompany you. The special duty rate does not apply to tobacco or alcoholic beverages. The special duty rate for goods not eligible under NAFTA, when combined with the GST, works out to about 15%.

NAFTA Special Duty Rate

Goods qualify for a lower duty rate under NAFTA if they are:
- for personal use; and
- marked as made in the U.S., Mexico or Canada; or
- not marked or labelled to indicate they were made anywhere other than in the U.S., Mexico or Canada.

If you do not qualify for a personal exemption or if you exceed your exemption limit, you will have to pay GST over and above applicable duty or taxes on the portion not eligible under your exemption.

United States: The special duty rate on eligible goods will be reduced annually until 1998, when only GST will apply. The special duty rates, when combined with the GST rounded to the nearest half percent are: 8.5% (1996), 8% (1997), 7% (1998).

Mexico: The special duty rate for eligible goods, when combined with the GST, is 8% (1995 rate). The combined rate will decrease each year until 2003, when only the GST will apply.

For information on goods eligible for the special duty rate under NAFTA, contact your nearest Revenue Canada customs office.

Regular Duty Rates

If you do not qualify for a personal exemption, or you exceed your exemption limit, you will pay GST over and above all duties, taxes and assessments that apply on the portion not eligible under your exemption. The rates vary according to the goods, their country of origin and the country from which you are importing them.

GATT (General Agreement on Tariffs & Trade)

Since January 1, 1995, duty on a wide range of products originating in non-NAFTA countries has been eliminated or will be reduced to zero within the next ten years. NAFTA goods also qualify for the GATT rate, so if the rate on the goods you are importing is lower under GATT than under NAFTA, the lower rate will automatically by applied.

Value for Duty/Foreign Sales Tax

Value for duty is the amount used to calculate duty and is generally the price you paid for the item. Foreign sales tax is included in the price and forms part of the value of the item. However, if the foreign sales tax is eligible for reimbursement, the tax does not have to be included in the price of the item you are importing.

Declaration

When returning to Canada by commercial aircraft, a traveller declaration card is distributed for completion before arrival. The cards are also used at some locations for people arriving by train, vessel or bus. If arriving by a private vehicle (eg., automobile), you must make an oral declaration unless you are claiming the $500 exemption.

Customs officials are legally entitled to examine luggage; you are responsible for opening, unpacking and repacking the luggage. Retain receipts of purchases and repairs made to verify length of stay and value of goods or repairs. Failure to declare or a false declaration may result in the seizure of goods. Penalties range from 25 to 80% of the value of the seized goods. Vehicles used to transport unlawfully imported goods may also be seized, with a penalty imposed before the vehicle can be returned. Commodities such as alcohol and tobacco are seized and not returned.

Restrictions

Firearms: Contact a Revenue Canada customs office.

Explosives, fireworks, ammunition: You require authorization and you may also need a permit. Contact Chief Inspector of Explosives Division, Natural Resources Canada, 580 Booth St., Ottawa ON K1A 0E4, 613/995-2388.

Motor Vehicles: Import restrictions apply to most used or second-hand cars, generally from countries other than the United States. Under NAFTA, restrictions do not apply to vehicles imported from the U.S.; special duty rates, as outlined above, apply. Duty rates on vehicles drop annually, until they become duty-free in 1998 (excise tax and GST continue to apply in the usual way). Under NAFTA, customs restrictions continue to apply to vehicles imported from Mexico until 2009, when you will be able to import vehicles ten years or older. The age restriction will drop every second year until the restriction is dropped altogether in 2019. Vehicles imported from Mexico become duty-free in 2003. Under Transport Canada restrictions, all imported vehicles less than fifteen years old must comply with Canadian federal safety and emission standards. The person importing the vehicle is responsible for ensuring it meets the standards. For information, contact: Road Safety & Motor Vehicle Regulation Directorate, Transport Canada, 344 Slater St., 13th Fl., Ottawa ON K1A 0N5, 613/998-2174, 1-800-333-0558 (outside Ottawa area). Your vehicle may be subject to provincial or territorial sales tax; contact your provincial or territorial department of motor vehicles for information. In addition, you may need to meet some requirements in the country from which the vehicle is being exported.

Import Controls: Certain goods are monitored for their effect on Canadian manufacturers. You may need a permit to import, even if you qualify for a personal exemption. For information, contact Export & Import Permits Bureau, Dept. of Foreign Affairs & International Trade, Ottawa ON K1A 0G2, 613/952-1362.

Meat, dairy products, fresh fruit & vegetables: Complex requirements & restrictions exist; some importation of meat & dairy products from the U.S. is allowed. Limits exist for small amounts or for foodstuffs you can import under your personal exemption; if above those limits, duty ranges from 150 to 350% and you may require an agricultural inspection certificate. Contact regional Revenue Canada customs offices.

Cultural property: Antiquities or cultural objects of significance in the country of origin cannot be imported into Canada. For information, contact Movable Cultural Property, Cultural Development & Heritage, Dept. of Canadian Heritage, #500, 300 Slater St., Ottawa, ON K1A 0C8, 613/990-4161, Fax: 613/954-8826.

Agricultural products: Restrictions exist on live animals & animal products, meat & poultry products, dairy products, egg & egg products, fresh fruit & vegetables, seeds & grains, animal feeds, plant & plant products, forestry products, soil & fertilizers, pest control products, biological products. Contact a district office of the Food Production & Inspection Branch, Agriculture & Agri-Food Canada.

Endangered species: Canada is a signatory to an international agreement restricting the sale, trade or movement of a large number of endangered animals, birds, reptiles, fish, insects and certain forms of plant life; the restrictions also apply to their parts or products made from their parts. For information, contact Convention Administrator, Canadian Wildlife Service, Environment Canada, Ottawa ON K1A 0H3, 819/997-1840.

Canadian Almanac & Directory 1997

Appeals

Disagreements about the amount of duty paid should be directed to your nearest Revenue Canada customs office; if not satisfactorily resolved, a formal appeal may be undertaken. If goods have been seized and you disagree with the action taken, you must notify Revenue Canada in writing within 30 days of the seizure date of your intention to appeal.

Precautions

Carry proper identification and identification for children travelling with you; customs officials look for missing children and may ask questions about the children travelling with you.

"Identification of Articles for Temporary Exportation": Revenue Canada customs offices offer a free identification program for valuables; a list of your valuables (excluding jewellery) and their serial numbers on a wallet-sized form will show customs officials that the items were previously purchased in Canada or that you lawfully imported them prior to your current time abroad. In the case of jewellery, carry an appraisal of the item(s) from a gemologist, jeweller or insurance agent, together with a signed and dated photograph and a written declaration that the items in the photograph are those described in the appraisal report. If previously imported, carry a copy of the customs receipt.

If you take any item outside Canada and modify it, it is considered to be a new item and its full value will need to be declared. Similarly, under Canadian law, any repairs or modifications to a vehicle that increase its value, improve its condition or modify it while abroad may require that you pay duty on its full value on your return to Canada. This does not apply to incidental repairs to keep the car in operational condition while abroad, although you may be required to pay duty on the repairs and parts. A special provision is available that waives duties payable in such cases. Contact Revenue Canada for information.

Regional Customs Offices

Atlantic	902/426-2911
Québec	418/648-4445
Montréal Region	514/283-9900
Northern Ontario	613/993-0534
(after 4:30 pm & weekends)	613/998-3326
Southern Ontario	416/973-8022
(weekends & holidays)	416/676-3643
Hamilton Region	905/308-8715, 1-800-361-5603
Windsor Region	519/257-6400
Prairies	204/983-6004
Calgary Region	403/292-8750, 4660
Pacific	604/666-0545
Website	http://www.revcan.ca

ELECTION REGULATIONS

According to the Canada Elections Act, and subject to certain exceptions, the general rule as to the franchise of electors at a federal election is that every person in Canada is qualified as an elector if such person

(a) is of the full age of 18 years;
(b) is a Canadian citizen; and
(c) is ordinarily resident in Canada on the enumeration date.

Among persons disqualified are certain officials charged with administering the elections, individuals who have lost their right to vote for a specified period for the commission of an election-related offence, and persons imprisoned in a correctional institute serving a sentence of two years or more.

Writs for an election (general or by-election) are issued at least 47 days before the date fixed for polling day.

Similar qualifications apply in the Provinces and Territories, although for provincial and territorial elections there is usually a residence requirement of either six or twelve months before the date of the issue of the writ of election. The age requirement is 18 years.

To contact election officers see Index, "Elections, Govt. Info. Sources".

LIQUOR REGULATIONS

For names of personnel of the various Liquor Control Boards see index "Liquor Board, Commission, or Control."

Alberta

Spirits, wines & beers (liquors) are sold in private retail liquor stores.

Liquor in unopened bottles may be sold by licensed hotels to persons who are not disqualified under the Act, for consumption off the premises (off-sales). Some restrictions may apply.

Legal drinking age is 18 years.

Liquor may be sold in licensed premises whose primary source of business is the sale of food or liquor. Liquor may also be sold in a licensed canteen, club, racetrack stadium (except where prohibited by local by-law), at professional sports or entertainment events, recreational facility, theatre, post-secondary institution, senior citizens' institution, traveller's lounge, aircraft, bus, train or water excursion craft for consumption on the premises.

Licensees may purchase liquor from private retail liquor stores & warehouse under certain conditions. Licenses are normally issued for a maximum two-year period. Fees vary with the type of license.

Alberta Gaming & Liquor Commission, 50 Corriveau Ave., St. Albert AB T8N 3T5 – 403/447-8737; Fax: 403/447-8908.

British Columbia

The Liquor Control & Licensing Branch administers the Liquor Control & Licensing Act & Regulations & is responsible for:
- Issuing, renewing & transferring licenses for the sale of liquor;
- Licensing breweries, distilleries, wineries & their agents;
- Inspecting licensed premises;
- Approving & monitoring advertising of beer, wine & liquor;
- Enforcing the Liquor Control & Licensing Act & Regulations.

The Branch issues 10 types of liquor licenses for the sale of liquor. Each type of license has different licensing requirements.

"A" licenses, mainly hotels, resorts & clubs;
"B" restaurants;
"C" cabarets;
"D" neighbourhood public houses;
"E" stadium & concert hall;
"F" marine public house;
"G" & "H" licensee retail stores or cold beer & wine stores;
"I" restoration public house;
"J" winery lounge license.

British Columbia Liquor Control & Licensing Branch, 1019 Wharf St., Victoria BC V8W 2Y9

The Liquor Distribution Branch is solely responsible for the selection, purchasing, pricing & distribution of all alcoholic beverages (wines, spirits & beer) throughout British Columbia, in a retail store system & to license holders. A portfolio of approximately 1,900 products is offered for sale to persons 19 years & older in more than 200 government liquor stores & over 70 agency stores in the province.

British Columbia Liquor Distribution Branch, 3200 E. Broadway, Vancouver, BC V5M 1Z6 – 604/254-5711; TLX 04-53470

Manitoba

Persons over the age of 18 years & who are not otherwise prohibited may purchase & consume spirits, wine & beer in premises licensed by the Liquor Control Commission. Further, those persons may purchase from a Liquor Control Commission store, liquor vendor or specialty wine store for consumption in a residence.

Beer may also be purchased from beer vendor depots located in most hotels throughout the province.

Parents dining with their children may purchase alcoholic beverages for the latter, for consumption with meals, only in licensed restaurants, dining rooms, cocktail lounges or cabarets.

Beverage rooms & cocktail rooms must be vacated within 30 minutes after the hour at which sale of liquor must cease.

Manitoba Liquor Control Commission, 1555 Buffalo Place, PO Box 1023, Winnipeg MB R3C 2X1 – 204/284-2501; Fax: 204/475-7666

New Brunswick

Intoxicating liquor is sold in sealed packages at Liquor Stores. Where a permit &/or a license has been obtained, liquor may be sold by the glass in dining rooms, restaurants, taverns, cabarets, lounges, beverage rooms, & clubs. Age of majority is 19.

New Brunswick Liquor Corp., PO Box 20787, Fredericton NB E3B 5B8 – 506/452-6826; Fax: 506/452-9890

Newfoundland

The importation, manufacture, & sale of Alcoholic Beverages through Retail Liquor outlets is the responsibility of the Newfoundland Liquor Corp.

The Newfoundland Liquor Corporation is also responsible for the issuing of all licenses, including those to manufacture & to sell packaged beer, & enforcement of regulations including, but not limited, to the following:

All liquor sold upon licensed premises shall be consumed thereon.

All liquor served in licensed premises shall be dispensed from the original container in which the liquor is purchased from or under the authority of the Liquor Corp.

The drinking age in Newfoundland is 19 years.

Nfld. Liquor Corp., PO Box 8750, Stn A, St. John's NF A1B 3V1 – 709/724-1100; Fax: 709/754-0321; TLX: 016-4923.

Northwest Territories

The Northwest Territories Act, Chapter 331 of the Revised Statutes of Canada, 1952, authorizes the Commissioner in Council of the Northwest Territories to make acts respecting intoxicants.

The Liquor Licensing Board, established under Part I of the Liquor Act, controls the conduct of licensees & operation of licensed premises; grants, renews & transfers licenses &, after a hearing, may cancel or suspend licenses. There are presently twelve types of licenses issued by the Board. Part I also provides for plebiscites to be held concerning new liquor license applications & also concerning restriction or prohibition in a community.

Part II of the Liquor Act establishes a Liquor Commission. The Minister responsible for this Part may designate his powers to the Liquor Commission to operate liquor stores & to purchase, sell & distribute liquor in the Northwest Territories. The Liquor Commission operates liquor warehouses in Iqaluit & Yellowknife. Through agency agreements, private contractors operate retail liquor stores on behalf of the Liquor Commission in Fort Simpson, Fort Smith, Hay River, Inuvik,

Canadian Almanac & Directory 1997

Yellowknife, Norman Wells & liquor warehouses in Hay River & Inuvik.

Northwest Territories Liquor Commission, PO Box 1130, Hay River NT X0E 0R0

Nova Scotia

All liquor is sold through Government Stores. Generally local option vote applies.

Eating establishment liquor licenses, lounges, clubs & cabarets serve spirits, draught beer, bottled beer & wine.

Beverage Rooms in "wet" areas may serve draught beer, bottled beer & wine.

The legal minimum drinking age is 19 years.

Nova Scotia Liquor License Bd., #401, 277 Pleasant St., Dartmouth NS B2Y 4B7 – 902/469-6160; Fax: 902/465-6557

Nova Scotia Liquor Commission, PO Box 8720, Stn A, Halifax NS B3K 5M4 – 902/454-5841; Fax: 902/453-1153

Ontario

In accordance with the provisions of the Liquor Control Act of Ontario, the Liquor Control Board buys wine, spirits & beer from all over the world for distribution & sale to Ontario consumers & licensed establishments.

To provide this service, the LCBO operates five major regional storage & distribution centres which supply more than 600 retail liquor stores. Through this vast network, over 3,000 products are available to consumers either by direct purchase or special order. As an additional service, customers can obtain products from around the world, that are not available in Ontario, through an LCBO private stock order.

The LCBO also operates a number of special outlets, known as Vintages stores, which offer consumers a wide variety of premium wines, spirits & special releases. Vintages products are also available in special sections of many regular LCBO stores. In addition, consumers can order from the full list of Vintages items at any LCBO outlet.

In the interests of consumer protection, the LCBO also regularly tests all alcoholic beverages sold in Ontario. This "quality control" testing ensures that all products carried by LCBO stores, Ontario winery stores & Brewers Retail outlets comply with the standards required under the Federal Food & Drug Act & Regulations.

Pursuant to the Liquor License Act of Ontario, the Liquor License Board of Ontario is responsible for the licensing & inspecting of approved premises which sell liquor (spirits, wine or beer) to the general public for on-premises consumption. Liquor may be sold in licensed premises in municipalities where the municipal electors have decided in favour of such sale. In addition, Special Occasion Permits are issued for occasional use only & not for private profit. Special events include weddings, receptions, banquets, charitable fundraisers, & community festivals. The LLBO also licenses manufacturers to sell to the LCBO & approves all liquor advertising pursuant to the Advertising Guidelines.

The drinking age in Ontario is 19.

The Liquor License Bd. of Ont., 55 Lake Shore Blvd. East, Toronto ON M5E 1A4 – 416/326-0308

Liquor Control Bd. of Ont., 55 Lake Shore Blvd. East, Toronto ON M5E 1A4 – 416/864-2400; Fax: 416/864-2476; URL: http//www.lcbo.com

Prince Edward Island

Spirits, wines & beer in sealed packages may be purchased at Commission Stores throughout the Province by any person over the age of 19 who is not otherwise disqualified.

Spirits by the glass, & beer & wine by the open bottle or glass, may be purchased in dining rooms, cocktail lounges, clubs & military canteens licensed by the Commission.

Prince Edward Island Liquor Control Commission, 3 Garfield St., PO Box 967, Charlottetown PE C1A 7M4 – 902/368-5710; Fax: 902/368-5735

Québec

Spirits & wines are sold by Québec Liquor Corporation stores only.

Spirits, beer & wine may be sold to the public by restaurants, bars & clubs under permit for consumption on the premises. Taverns may sell beer & cider. Pubs may sell beer, draught wine & cider.

A licensed grocery store may sell beer & certain designated wines & the product must not be consumed on the premises.

Persons under the age of 18 years old cannot be admitted into bars, pubs & taverns & at no time may alcoholic beverages be sold to them in other establishments.

Régie des Alcools, des courses et des jeux, 1, rue Notre-Dame est, Montréal PQ H2Y 1B6 – 514/873-3577; 1281, boul Charest ouest, Québec PQ G1N 2C9 – 418/643-7667

Saskatchewan

The Saskatchewan Liquor & Gaming Authority, a Treasury Board Crown corporation, regulates liquor & gaming activities in the province. It is responsible for the control, sale & distribution of liquor in the province, & also licenses & regulates bingos, raffles, casinos, & breakopen tickets. The Liquor & Gaming Authority also controls the Video Lottery Terminal network through the province.

The minimum drinking age is 19.

Saskatchewan Liquor & Gaming Authority, PO Box 5054, Regina SK S4P 3M3 – 306/787-4213; Fax: 306/787-8468

Yukon Territory

The Yukon Act, Chapter Y-2 of the Revised Statutes of Canada, 1970, authorizes the Commissioner in Executive Council, Yukon Territory, to make acts respecting intoxicants.

By virtue of Chapter 105 cited as the Liquor Act, established the laws governing the importation, distributing, licensing & retailing of alcoholic beverages in Yukon.

The formation of the Yukon Liquor Corporation by means of amendments to the Liquor Act came into force on April 1st, 1977. The separation as a Corporate entity resulted in increased responsibility & full accountability in all areas except major government policy.

The five members of the Board of Directors are appointed by the Commissioner in executive council to hold office at pleasure.

The President & Chief Executive Officer of the Corporation, is charged with the general direction, supervision & control of the Corporation & the administration of the Act.

Yukon Liquor Corp., 9031 Quartz Road, Whitehorse YT Y1A 4P9 – 403/667-5245; Fax: 403/668-7806

MARRIAGE REGULATIONS

Divorce Act in Canada

Divorce grounds in Canada, under the Divorce Act, 1985:

Breakdown of marriage, established by:
  Spouses intentionally living separate and apart at least one year with the idea that the marriage is over,
  or
  Since the marriage, either spouse has:
  Committed adultery, or
  Treated the other spouse with physical or mental cruelty rendering continued cohabitation intolerable.

Alberta

Marriageable age:
  --Without parental consent: 18 years
  --With parental consent: 16 years
  --A female, under the age of 16, may be married without parental consent & proof that she is the mother of a living child or proof that she is expecting a child.

Blood Test: not required

Waiting Period: None. Marriage Licence is valid immediately & is valid for 3 months (from date of issuance).

Licence fee: $40.00

Civic Marriage ceremony fee: $50.00

British Columbia

Marriageable age:
  --Without parental consent: 19 years
  With parental consent: 16 to 18 years
  --A court order of consent: under 16 years

Blood test: not required

Waiting period for licence: none

Marriage Licence: $75.00

Civil Marriage Ceremony: $80.25

Manitoba

Marriageable age:
  --Without parental consent: 18 years
  --With parental consent: 16 years (Persons under 16 years of age can be married only with the consent of a judge of the Family Court.)

Blood test: not required

Waiting period for licence: none

Waiting period after issuance of licence: 24 hours (This may be waived by person performing ceremony.)

Licence fee: $50.00. Licence valid for 3 months.

New Brunswick

Marriageable age:
  --Without parental consent: 18 years
  --With parental consent: under 18 years
  --Under 16 years: a declaration of a Judge of the Court of Queen's Bench that the proposed marriage may take place is necessary.

Blood test: not required

Waiting period for licence: none

Licence fee: $100.00

Newfoundland

Marriageable age:
  --Greater than or equal to 19 years: without parental consent
  --Greater than or equal to 18 years: without parental consent in certain circumstances
  --Greater than or equal to 16 years and less than 19 years: with the applicable parental, guardian or Director of Child Welfare consent (Consent may be dispensed within exceptional cases.)
  --Less than 16 years: where by reason of pregnancy a judge issues a licence

Blood test: not required

Licence fee: $20.00

Northwest Territories

Marriageable age:
  --Without parental consent: 19 years
  --At least 18 years of age if
  (a) parent whose consent is required is not a resident of the NWT & minor has been a resident of the NWT for 12 months
  (b) minor has been living apart from his or her parents (or guardian) and has not received financial aid from the parents (or guardian) for not less than 6 months preceding the date of delivery of a

prescribed statutory declaration to the member of the clergy who is to proclaim the banns or to the issuer of marriage licences;
(c) father & mother of minor are dead & minor has no guardian;
(d) parents (surviving parent) of minor are (is) patients (patient) in a mental institution & minor has no guardian.
--With parental consent: 15 years
Blood test: not required
Waiting period for licence: none
Licence fee: $25.00

Nova Scotia
Marriageable age:
--Without parental consent: 19 years or over
--With parental consent, or if a widow, widower, or divorcee: 16 years
--With court order: under 16 years
Blood test: not required
Waiting period for licence: 5 days
Licence fee: $100.00

Ontario
Marriageable age:
--Without parental consent: 18 years
--With parental consent: 16 years
Blood test: not required
Waiting period after issuance of licence: none
Licence fee: $53.00
Fee for solemnization of marriage by judge or justice of the peace: $53.00

Prince Edward Island
Marriageable age:
--Without parental consent: 18 years
--With parental consent: under 18 years
Other requirements: birth certificates and Social Insurance Numbers; in the case of a widow or widower, death certificate; in the case of a divorced person, certified copy of the Decree Absolute or Certificate of Divorce
Waiting period for licence: none
Licence fee: $100.00

Québec
Marriageable age:
--Minimum age: 16 years
(ref.: art. 373, Code Civil du Québec)
--Moreover, a minor (under 18 years of age) must have the authorization of his or her parent(s) or tutor to get married.
Blood test: not required
Waiting period for licence: none
Fee for civil marriage: $183.47 (taxes included)

Saskatchewan
Marriageable age:
--Without parental consent: 18 years
--With parental consent: 16 to 18 years
--With parental and court consent: under 16 years
Blood test: not required
Licence fee: $50.00

Yukon Territory
Marriageable age:
--Without parental consent: 19 years (In the case of an 18 year old person who has lived apart from his parents/guardians for at least 6 months and received no financial aid from them during that time, no consent is needed.)
Blood test: not required
Waiting period for licence: none
Waiting period after issuance of licence: 24 hours
Licence fee: $20.00

POSTAL INFORMATION

Services & rates quoted are as of September 1, 1996. Check with a local Canada Post postal outlet for more details.

COMMUNICATIONS SERVICES

LETTERMAIL RATES FOR DELIVERY IN CANADA

Includes letters, postcards, greeting cards and business correspondence.

Up to 30 g $0.45
(standard lettermail)
Over 30 g to 50 g 0.71
Up to 30 g 0.58
(non-coded lettermail; business mail only)
Over 30 g to 50 g 0.82
Up to 100 g 0.90
(other lettermail incl. non-standard & oversize)
Over 100 g to 200 g 1.45
Over 200 g to 500 g 2.05

Oversize Letter Rates apply to all letters with any dimension greater than 24.5 cm (length) x 15 cm (width) x .5 mm (thickness), but not greater than 38 cm (length) x 27 cm (width) x 2 cm (thickness). Maximum weight for Lettermail is 500g. Items with any dimension exceeding the maximum dimension for Oversize Lettermail or exceeding 500g must be paid at parcel rates.

Incentive Rates are available under sales agreements for customers whose mailing meets standard volume, frequency & preparation conditions. For details, please contact a Canada Post Corp. representative.

BUSINESS REPLY MAIL (CANADA)

This service allows the mailer's current & potential clients to correspond with them by mail at no charge. The user of the service must enter into an Agreement with Canada Post & abide by standards outlined for this product. Business Reply Mail pieces consist of cards or envelopes on which a Business Reply indicia is printed as well as the name & address of the mailer. All Business Reply Mail applications are subject to an annual administrative fee.

CONTRACT CERTIFIED MAIL (CANADA)

Contract Certified is an optional service for domestic Lettermail products available by Sales Agreements only. The recipient's signature is automatically returned to the sender as legal proof of delivery and a copy is retained at the office of delivery for 24 months. There is no computerized information retrieval for this option.

Contract Certified Mail consists of a prepaid envelope which has a computer track perforated edge for efficient bulk preparation by the mailer. An adhesive label is located in the upper left hand corner of the envelope which serves as the sender's return address label and is affixed to the Acknowledgement of Receipt (AR) card by the delivery employee.

Lettermail service standards (2 days local, 3 days regional & 4 days national) apply to Contract Certified items. Standards are measured from date of acceptance to the date of first delivery attempt. See Service Performance below for more details.

Contract Certified items can be deposited at any postal outlet or in street letter boxes. Contract Certified is available on an order basis at any retail outlet or through the National Philatelic Centre in Antigonish by calling 1-800-565-4362.

Contract Certified envelopes are sold in packs of 100 up to 10 packs (1,000). For purchases over 10 packs, there are volume discounts available.

The price for 1 to 5 packs is $396.00 per pack and $345.00 per pack for 6 to 10 packs.

SPECIAL SERVICES:

TRACE MAIL (CANADA)

Common to all of the Trace Mail options, is the ability of Canada Post to provide immediate response to customer inquiries for delivery status information on items to be delivered in Canada. Customers are able to obtain delivery status information through a 1-800 number.

REGISTERED MAIL (CANADA)

Add-on service to Lettermail items that do not require the extra security or indemnity of the Security Registered product. The mailer will be provided with a proof of mailing & a signature will be obtained from the addressee or his/her representative before the delivery is completed. The fee is $3.15 plus applicable Lettermail postage. Upon payment of the appropriate fee, the acknowledgement of receipt service is also available.

SECURITY REGISTERED MAIL

Security Registered involves a high security processing stream making the product ideal for mailing lettermail items or parcels with an insurable value. The product provides proof of mailing, signature upon delivery, & an option of having a copy of the recipient's signature returned to the mailer.

The fee for Security Registered within Canada is $5.60 plus the applicable lettermail rate. The Xpresspost rates plus the Security Registered service fee determine the rate for parcels.

Fees to the USA - $5.60 plus the applicable postage which includes a base indemnity of $100. Additional indemnity is available for $1.00 up to $1,000.

Fees for other international destinations - $5.60 plus the applicalbe postage which includes a maximum indemnity of $60.

PROOF OF DELIVERY (CANADA)

Add-on service to Regular Post Service that provides delivery confirmation via Canada Post's automated telephone inquiry system. The fee is $1.00 per item & includes $100 indemnity coverage. Additional coverage may be purchased for $0.45 for each additional $100 up to a maximum of $1,000.

ACKNOWLEDGEMENT OF RECEIPT CARDS (CANADA)

a) At time of mailing $0.90
b) Subsequent to the mailing (Canada only) . $1.60
Acknowledgement of Receipt (AR) Int'l & USA: at time of mailing only $0.90

SPECIAL DELIVERY

Special Delivery to the USA is $4.50 plus applicable postage & can be used for expedited delivery of letters, postcards, & small airmail packets.

Special Delivery to most international destinations is $4.50 plus applicable postage & can be used for expedited delivery of letters, postcards, small airmail packets, & airmail printed papers.

LITERATURE FOR THE BLIND (CANADA)

The following items can be mailed free of postage when bearing the label or words "Literature for the Blind" on the top right hand corner of the address: Items impressed in Braille or similar raised type; plates for printing literature for the blind; tapes & records posted by the blind in Canada for delivery in Canada; recording tapes, records, special writing paper intended solely for use of the blind when mailed by or addressed to a recognized institution for the blind.

OMNIPOST

OmniPost is a unique computer-based message delivery system that lets you send Lasermailr, Faxmail, and E-Mail from your personal computer. OmniPost assists small- and medium-sized businesses to send letters, sales reports, or invoices by hard copy, fax, or electronic mail. For details about the OmniPost service and rates, call our customer service representative 1 (800) 363-4763.

ELECTRONIC LETTERMAIL

Electronic Lettermail is a one-stop, computerized mail production and delivery service. Electronic Lettermail is used by businesses, financial institutions, and government organizations that require high volume, highly personalized mailings of invoices, statements and time-sensitive notices. Electronic Lettermail is a secure and confidential service. For details about Electronic Lettermail service and rates, call our customer service representative at 1 (800) 363-4763.

ELECTRONIC ADMAIL

Electronic Admail is a one-stop computerized mail production and delivery service for businesses who routinely mail large volumes of advertising material, solicitations, notices and bulletins. Mailings can be as personalized and customized as you like. The message and mailing list is transmitted to Canada Post by modem, diskette or magnetic tape. Once you approve the mailing, Canada Post transmits the data to regional production centres across Canada, where the mailing is laser printed, inserted, and delivered according to letter carrier routes. For details about Electronic Admail service and rates, call our customer service representative at 1 (800) 363-4763.

DOCUPOST

DocuPost is a business document storage, retrieval and distribution service, and is the ideal way to handle routine document requests. DocuPost combines the technologies of fax and electronic mail with Canada Post's existing delivery structure and extensive database capacity. Any information - text, graphic or audio - can be stored and distributed by DocuPost. Customers then have a one-stop service accessible by fax 24 hours a day 7 days a week, or by phone during business hours. DocuPost is ideal for frequent, routine requests such as catalogues, application forms, price lists or schedules For details about DocuPost service and rates, call our customer service representative at 1 (800) 363-4763.

HYBRID DATA INTERCHANGE

Canada Post's HDI Services offer electronic communication between organizations regardless of their electronic capabilities. HDI converts data from paper, fax or any electronic file format to EDI transactions or from EDI or almost any electronic file format to physical documents. Paper documents are scanned and converted to images. Those images, along with faxed documents then undergo data extraction, accuracy validation and conversion to appropriate formats based on Canada Post's directory of receiver preferences. HDI Services acts as a communication bridge between trading partners with different technological capabilities. For details about the HDI Service and rates, call our customer service representative at 1 (800) 363-4763.

VALUE-ADDED SERVICES:

ADDRESS ACCURACY - LIST VALIDATION AND CORRECTION

Canada Post can validate your mailing lists and correct addresses. Mailing lists and rented lists can also be purged to eliminate duplicates, or remove addresses of people who do not wish to receive advertising direct mail.

RETURNED MAIL MANAGEMENT

Returned Mail Management reduces the frustration and expense caused by undelivered mail. Canada Post creates your mail piece with a barcode, and as undeliverables are returned to a Canada Post centre, the barcode is scanned and generates an electronic report which, if you choose can include a "reason code".

Canadian Almanac & Directory 1997

HIGHLIGHT COLOUR:

Colour adds a simple, cost-effective attention-grabbing feature to direct mail and other materials. Colour choices include red, green, blue, magenta and cyan.

CERTIFIED PLUS

Certified Plus provides assurance that your mail was delivered. Receivers sign an Acknowledgement of Receipt card which can be returned to you, or Canada Post can notify you electronically that your mail has been delivered to the recipient or duly authorized representative.

REGISTERED PLUS

Registered Plus meets the demand of governments and businesses that need legally binding proof that their documents were delivered. Each mail piece is inserted into a barcoded registered envelope at the time of production. Canada Post issues a proof of mailing manifest in hard copy and electronic format. Items can be traced by calling the customer service 1-800 number up to two years after delivery.

REMITMAIL

Businesses provide Canada Post with tapes of their invoice files, and the invoices are sent to individuals via Electronic Lettermail. Payments are remitted to Canada Post's processing centre, and Canada Post deposits the payments into your company's bank account and provide status reports - all electronically. Remitmail can also process survey results, questionnaires, requests for information and other services.

More information on all these Value-Added services is available through our customer service centre at 1(800) 363-4763.

GOODS DISTRIBUTION SERVICES:

PRIORITY COURIER

Priority Courier is a fully featured, domestic courier service providing next business day delivery between most major centres and an on-time delivery guarantee. It also offers 10:00 a.m., Saturday & evening pickup & delivery options and a range of Advance Purchase Products. Information regarding delivery status & additional product information is available from local Priority Courier centres or by calling the 1-800 number listed below. International courier service is offered through the SkyPak product, with trace capabilities to more than 200 countries.

Priority Courier: 1-800-661-3434
Locally:
Edmonton: 403/944-3100
Halifax: 902/494-4848
Ottawa/Hull: 613/526-3278
London: 519/645-4355
Montréal: 514/633-8483
Québec City: 418/624-6521
Vancouver: 604/482-4000
Winnipeg: 204/987-5400
Toronto: 416/673-3278

XPRESSPOST

XPRESSPOST is an affordable, simple to use delivery service for packages and documents which provides an on-time delivery guarantee and confirmation of delivery. Positioned right in the middle between Priority Courier & Regular Post in terms of price, service & features, XPRESSPOST offers next business day local; two business day regional/national delivery between major Canadian centres and a full range of Advance Purchase Products. Customers can verify delivery of their items or obtain product information by calling 1-800-565-5880.

REGULAR POST

Regular Post is the most economical, domestic, ground parcel service. There are two delivery service levels available. Expedited service is the our fastest ground service providing an on-time delivery guarantee (next business day local, 2-5 business day regional and 5-7 business day national between major centres) and a full range of Advance Purchase Parcel Labels. Regular service is for non time-sensitive shipments (3-12 business days) and offers the most economical rates.

PHOTOMAIL (CANADA)

The photomail rate is limited to photographic discs, films, negatives, prints or slides mailed in Canada for delivery in Canada to or from a film processor.
a) When posted by any person to a film processor
 1) Items not exceeding 2 cm in thickness may be sent at lettermail rates.
 2) Per item up to 250 g $1.85
 3) be at least 130 mm long by 90 mm wide
 4) be no more than 380 mm long by 270 mm wide
 3) All other items exceeding 2 cm in thickness . . . . Parcel rates
 4) When posted by any person to a film processor as an item of business reply mail exceeding 2 cm in thickness or 250 g. . . . . available on contract
b) When posted by a film processor to any person
 1) Items not exceeding 2 cm in thickness may be sent at lettermail rates
 2) Per item up to 250 g $1.15
 3) All other items exceeding 2 cm in thickness or 250 g . . . . Parcel rates

ADMAIL (Advertising Mail)

Addressed Admail must bear the correct postal code & meet size & weight requirements. Rates are based on volume & level of mail preparation. Letter Carrier Presort requires an LCP Sales Agreement. Using the National distribution Guide requires the use of a Statement of Mailing. All mailings (LC, NDG) must be accompanied by a complete Statement of Mailing.

Unaddressed Admail offers delivery of advertising material & samples bearing no specific address other than but not required the word "Householder" or "Occupant". Discounted prices are available based on large volume single mailings or based on an annual volume commitment.

PUBLICATIONS MAIL

Publications mail includes newspapers & periodicals, posted in Canada for delivery in Canada and consisting of at least two (2) sheets published in a regular page format (not in the form of a circular letter). Publications must be registered with Canada Post. Direct bag (for international mailings only) rates available for large quantities mailed to the same addressee. Commercial options offer lower rates to customers who meet mail preparation & presortation requirements. For details, please inquire at a postal outlet.

OTHER SERVICES:

INSURANCE FEES

Insurance is a service where Canada Post provides compensation for the loss, rifling or damage of mailable items if the requirements of indemnity subjects are met.

Not available for parcels within Canada (use Proof of Delivery).
a) Within Canada (except parcels)
 Insurance up to $100 . . . . $0.45
 and $0.45 for each additional $100 coverage up to a maximum $1,000.
b) To the USA (parcels only)
 Insurance up to $100 . . . . $1.00
 and $1.00 for each additional $100 coverage up to a maximum of $1,000.
c) To international destinations (parcels only)
 Insurance up to $100 . . . . $1.00
 and $1.00 for each additional $100 coverage up to a maximum of $1,000.

POSTAL INFORMATION 1-45

C.O.D. FEE (CANADA)
C.O.D. is a service for Regular Post and Xpresspost only. An amount due to the sender, up to a maximum of $1,000, is collected from the addressee upon delivery of the item. Customers wishing to use C.O.D. on document size items must pay the appropriate Xpresspost rate plus the C.O.D. fee.

The fee is $3.50 (no basic indemnity) plus appropriate postage and indemnity can be purchased at $0.45 per $100 up to $1,000.

MONEY ORDER FEES
A Money Order is a funds transmission document which may be purchased for values not exceeding $999.99 in Cdn$ and U.S.$ and 100 sterling at postal outlets. Money orders are to be drawn in Canadian currency for payment in CANADA & the following countries:

Anguilla, Antigua & Barbuda, Bahamas, Barbados, Belize, Cayman Islands, Dominica, Fiji, Grenada, Haiti, Jamaica, Nevis, St. Kitts, St. Lucia, St. Vincent & Grenadines, Trinidad & Tobago. The fee is as follows:
Up to $999.99 maximum $2.00

Money orders are to be drawn in U.S. currency for payment in the UNITED STATES. The fee is as follows:
Up to $999.99 maximum $3.50

In the UNITED KINGDOM & GUYANA. The fee is as follows:
From 100 maximum $4.50

Money orders are to be drawn in Canadian currency for all other countries except Poland (U.S. currency) & requires the preparation of a Canadian Postal Money Order Advice form which must accompany the money to be sent to the Ottawa Money Order Exchange office using a pre-addressed envelope. The fee is as follows:
Up to $999.99 maximum $5.00

REDIRECTION SERVICE CHARGE
Redirected mail is mail that cannot be delivered as addressed because the addressee has moved. However, if a Change Of Address (COA) has been filed by the addressee the mail can be redirected to the new address. Customers who plan to move should complete a Change of Address Notification (COAN) form available at all postal outlets and the appropriate fee.

Canada
A - For Consumers
a) Where redirection is requested to an address in Canada for each six month period $30.00
The customer may purchase 1 additional service periods at the current rate.
B - For Businesses / Non-residential addresses
a) For first six-month period $130.00
b) For a six month renewal period prior to cancellation of the original request (maximum 1 additional service periods) $130.00

Change of Address Announcement Cards, used by the public to notify their correspondents, are available at postal outlets & require Lettermail postage.

There is no charge when filing a request for redirection of mail on behalf of a deceased person's estate.

Outside Canada
For Consumers: $60.00 for each six month period. A maximum of 1 additional service period may be purchased at the current rate.
For Businesses: $300.00 for each six month period.

TEMPORARY REDIRECTION
Customers must complete the Change of Address Notification Form. Within Canada the fee is $9.00 per month, minimum 3 months, and $18.00 per month outside Canada. For businesses, the Temporary Redirection service costs $65.00 per month, when redirection is requested to an address within Canada, and $150.00 per month for outside Canada.

Outside of Canada for Consumers:

Initial fee $27.00 & $9.00 for each additional month if requested prior to expiration of the original request (up to 3 month service).

HOLD MAIL SERVICE (CANADA)
Customers must complete "Request to Hold the Mail" & pay a fee of $3.00 a week or any part thereof (minimum 2 weeks) for consumers or $5.50 a day for businesses (minimum of 5 days).

MAIL MANAGEMENT SERVICES (MMS)
Mail Management Services are designed to assist business, government and institutions in areas which are not core competencies, yet have a significant impact on business activities, costs and service to customers. MMS will provide management services and advisory services, and provide customized solutions. MMS expertise is in mail generation, fulfillment, distribution, and other related business processes. For details about Mail Management Services, call our customer service representative at 1 (800) 363-4763.

RATES TO THE UNITED STATES (its Territories & Possessions):

LETTERMAIL
Weight Steps
Up to & including 30 g $0.52
Over 30 g to 50 g 0.77
Oversize letter rates (max. 500g)
Up to & including 100 g 1.17
100 g to 200 g 2.23
Over 200 g to 500 g 3.80
Lettermail more than 27 cm (width) x 38 cm (length) x 2 cm (thickness) up to 105 cm longest side x 200 cm (longest side plus girth)
Up to an including 250 g 3.60
Over 250 g to 500 kg 4.85

USA Incentive Lettermail offers Canadian mailers significant postage savings & improved service performance linked to volume, & quality of mail preparation. For various USA Incentive Lettermail rates, please inquire at a postal outlet.

PRINTED PAPERS (US)
Weight Steps . . . . Surface Mail
Up to & including 30 g 0.52
Over 30 g to 100 g 0.96
Over 100 g to 200 g 1.43
Over 200 g to 300 g 2.00
Over 300 g to 400 g 2.70
Over 400 g to 500 g 3.55
Over 500 g to 1 kg 6.20
"M" bags (direct bags) of printed papers - $6.20 for the first kilogram plus $2.50 for each additional kilogram or fraction up to 30 kg (surface only).

SMALL PACKETS (US)
Weight Steps . . . . Surface Mail . . . . . Air Mail
Up to & including 250 g . . . . $2.30 . . . . $3.60
Over 250 g to 500 g . . . . 3.55 . . . . 4.85
Over 500 g to 1 kg . . . . 6.20 . . . . 8.55

PARCEL SERVICE (US)
Parcel rate (surface) starts at $6.30 depending on destination for the first 1.5 kg. For details inquire at a postal outlets.

Parcel rate (air) starts $11.50 for the first half kilogram. For details inquire at a postal outlet.

Parcels are subject to customs inspection & must bear a properly completed customs document (43-074-013). Completion of the customs document in English is preferred.

INTERNATIONAL REPLY COUPONS
International Reply Coupons may be purchased in Canada for $3.50 each & are exchangeable in any countries of the Universal Postal Union for the minimum postage payable for an unregistered letter upon presentation of a sufficient number of reply coupons. An International Reply Coupon is exchangeable at any Canadian post outlet for $0.90 in Canadian postage stamps.

INTERNATIONAL RATES
All countries except the U.S.A., its Territories & Possessions, Canadian Forces post offices & Fleet Mail Offices.

LETTERMAIL
Weight Steps . . . . Air Mail
Up to & including 20 g $0.90
Over 20 g to 50 g 1.37
Over 50 g to 100g 2.25
Over 100 g to 250 g 5.05
Over 250 g to 500 g 9.90
Over 500 g to 1 kg 18.55
Over 1 kg to 2 kg 37.10

AEROGRAMMES & POSTCARDS
All countries . . . . $0.90 each

PRINTED PAPERS (INTERNATIONAL)
The Printed Papers service includes printed paper, "M" bags (directed bags) for printed paper & books. Fees are for "M" bags of printed papers - surface only: $7.20 for the first kilogram & $3.85 for each additional kilogram or fraction up to 30 kg maximum.

Weight Steps	Air Mail	Surface Mail
Up to & including 20 g	$0.73	$0.52
Over 20 g to 50 g	1.16	0.80
Over 50 g to 100 g	2.20	1.44
Over 100 g to 250 g	4.10	2.60
Over 250 g to 500 g	8.05	4.10
Over 500 g to 1 kg	16.10	7.20
Over 1 kg to 2 kg	26.80	10.20

SMALL PACKETS INTERNATIONAL
Weight Steps	Air Mail	Surface Mail
Up to & including 100 g	$2.20	$1.44
Over 100 g to 250 g	4.10	2.60
Over 250 g to 500 g	8.05	4.10
Over 500 g to 1 kg	16.10	7.20
Over 1 kg to 2 kg	26.80	10.20

PARCEL SERVICE (INTERNATIONAL)
International Air & Surface parcel rates depend on the weight & destination. For details, please inquire at a postal outlet.

The prohibitions, restrictions, conditions, requirements & rates vary from country to country. For details, please inquire at a postal outlet.

INTERNATIONAL REPLY COUPONS
See U.S.A. Rates

GENERAL INFORMATION:

SERVICE PERFORMANCE
Canada Post Corporation is committed to consistently delivery properly prepared lettermail as follows:
within two business days, for letters whose destination is within the same major urban centre;
within three business days for letters whose destination is in a major urban centre in the same province;
in no more than four business days, for letters whose destination is in another major urban centre in another province.

Service performance evaluation conducted by an outside party reveal that the Corporation is consistently meeting its targets 97% of the time.

POSTAGE NOT REQUIRED
No postage is required on mail addressed to the Governor General, or Secretary to the Governor Gen-

Canadian Almanac & Directory 1997

POSTAL INFORMATION

eral, the Speaker or the Clerk of the Senate or House of Commons, the parliamentary librarian or associate parliamentary librarian, members of the Senate & members of the House of Commons.

RETURN TO SENDER PROGRAM

Unpaid or shortpaid mail is mail for which the postage or fees have not been paid or fully paid. Lettermail & Parcels, with or without special services (such as Insurance, Security Registered, Registered, XPRESS-POST (domestic mail only), COD) are returned to sender for the collection of adequate postage, instead of penalizing the addressee.

PROHIBITED ARTICLES

It is forbidden to post for delivery or transmission by or through Canada Post any prohibited items. Prohibited items are defined as any item which is prohibited by law or which contains products or substances that could harm Canada Post employees, soil or damage equipment or other shipments. For a complete list of items please consult a Canada Post Customer Service representative or visit your local postal outlet.

POSTAL CODE DIRECTORY

Postal code directories are available for purchase by sending an $14.00 (plus applicable taxes) cheque or money order, payable to Canada Post Corporation to the National Philatelic Centre (address below) or by calling 1-800-565-4362. Postal code information is also available through the Corporation's web site on the Internet. Please see the electronic address below.

PROVINCIAL SYMBOLS

Standard two-letter postal abbreviations for the provinces & territories are as follows:

Alberta . . . . AB
British Columbia . . . . BC
Manitoba. . . . . MB
New Brunswick . . . . NB
Newfoundland & Labrador . . . . . . NF
Northwest Territories . . . . NT
Nova Scotia. . . . . NS
Ontario . . . . ON
Prince Edward Island . . . . PE
Québec . . . . QC
Saskatchewan . . . . SK
Yukon Territory. . . . . YT

PHILATELIC SERVICES

Philatelic products such as stamps, official first day covers, postal stationary of philatelic quality, Annual & Heritage Souvenir Collections & Commemorative Stamp Packs are available at most post offices, at special philatelic counters or by ordering through the Corporation's mail order service.

A quarterly booklet titled "Collections of Canada" provides descriptions & details of these products & may be requested from:

National Philatelic Centre, Canada Post Corporation, 75 St. Ninians St., Antigonish NS B2G 2R8; 1-800-565-4362.

CUSTOMER SERVICE

Further information on Canada Post's products & services can be obtained through your local postal outlets, postal directory, your local customer service representative, or by calling one of the following numbers:

Toll Free (English): 1-800-267-1177
Toll Free (French): 1-800-267-1155
Hearing Impaired with
    TTY-Teletyping: 1-800-267-2797
Montréal: 514/344-8822
Toronto: 416/979-8822

Customers may also contact Canada Post via the Internet : http://www.mailposte.ca

E-Mail: service@mailposte.ca

Canada Post Corporation, 2701 Riverside Dr/., Ottawa ON K1A 0B1

MAP OF CANADA

Legend
- Each letter represents the first character of the area postal code.
- Each number represents the telephone/fax area code

Canadian Almanac & Directory 1997

THE ROYAL ARMS OF CANADA BY PROCLAMATION OF KING GEORGE V IN 1921

The Royal Arms of Canada were established by proclamation of King George V on 21 November, 1921. On the advice of the Prime Minister of Canada, Her Majesty the Queen approved, on 12 July, 1994, that the arms be augmented with a ribbon bearing the motto of the Order of Canada, DESIDERANTES MELIOREM PATRIAM – "They desire a better country".

This coat of arms was developed by a special committee appointed by Order in Council and is substantially based on a version of the Royal Arms of the United Kingdom, featuring the historic arms of England and Scotland. To this were added the old arms of Royal France and the historic emblem of Ireland, the harp of Tara, thus honouring many of the founding European peoples of modern Canada. To mark these arms as Canadian, the three red maple leaves on a field of white were added.

The supporters, and the crest, above the helmet, are also versions of elements of the Royal Arms of the United Kingdom, including the lion of England and unicorn of Scotland. The lion holds the Union Jack and the unicorn, the banner of Royal France. The crowned lion holding the maple leaf, which is the Royal Crest of Canada, has, since 1981, also been the official symbol of the Governor General of Canada, the Sovereign's representative.

At the base of the Royal Arms are the floral emblems of the founding nations of Canada, the English Rose, the Scottish Thistle, the French Lily and the Irish Shamrock.

The motto — A MARI USQUE AD MARE — "From sea to sea" — is an extract from the Latin version of verse 8 of the 72nd Psalm — "He shall have dominion also from sea to sea, and from the river unto the ends of the earth."

THE NATIONAL FLAG

The National Flag of Canada, otherwise known as the Canadian Flag, was approved by Parliament and proclaimed by Her Majesty Queen Elizabeth II to be in force as of February 15, 1965. It is described as a red flag of the proportions two by length and one by width, containing in its centre a white square the width of the flag, bearing a single red maple leaf. Red and white are the official colours of Canada, as approved by the proclamation of King George V appointing Arms for Canada in 1921. The Flag is flown on land at all federal government buildings, airports, and military bases within and outside Canada, and may appropriately be flown or displayed by individuals and organizations. The Flag is the proper national colours for all Canadian ships and boats; and it is the flag flown on Canadian Naval vessels.

The Flag is flown daily from sunrise to sunset. However, it is not contrary to etiquette to have the Flag flying at night. No flag, banner or pennant should be flown or displayed above the Canadian Flag. Flags flown together should be approximately the same size and flown from separate staffs at the same height. When flown on a speaker's platform, it should be to the right of the speaker. When used in the body of an auditorium; it should be to the right of the audience. When two or more than three flags are flown together, the Flag should be on the left as seen by spectators in front of the flags. When three flags are flown together, the Canadian Flag should occupy the central position.

A complete set of rules for flying the Canadian Flag can be obtained from the Department of Canadian Heritage.

Canadian Almanac & Directory 1997

GOVERNORS GENERAL OF CANADA SINCE CONFEDERATION
(WITH DATE APPOINTED)

The Viscount Monck, G.C.M.G.
June 1, 1867

Lord Lisgar, G.C.M.G.
Dec. 29, 1868

**The Earl of Dufferin,
K.P., G.C.B., G.C.S.I., G.C.M.G.,
G.C.I.E.**
May 22, 1872

**The Marquess of Lorne,
K.T., G.C.M.G., G.C.V.O.**
Oct. 5, 1878

**The Marquess of Lansdowne,
K.G., G.C.S.I., G.C.M.G., G.C.I.E.**
Aug. 18, 1883

**Lord Stanley of Preston,
K.G., G.C.B., G.C.V.O.**
May 1, 1888

**The Earl of Aberdeen,
K.T., G.C.M.G., G.C.V.O.**
May 22, 1893

**The Earl of Minto,
K.G., G.C.S.I., G.C.M.G., G.C.I.E.**
July 30, 1898

**The Earl Grey,
G.C.B., G.C.M.G., G.C.V.O.**
Sept. 26, 1904

**H.R.H. The Duke of Connaught,
K.G., K.T., K.P., G.M.B., G.C.S.I.,
G.C.M.G., G.C.I.E., G.C.V.O.,
G.B.E., T.D.**
Mar. 21, 1911

**The Duke of Devonshire,
K.G., G.C.M.G., G.C.V.O., T.D.**
Aug. 19, 1916

**Lord Byng of Vimy,
G.C.B., G.C.M.G., M.V.O.**
Aug. 2, 1921

**The Viscount Willingdon of Ratton,
G.C.S.I., G.C.M.G., G.C.I.E., G.B.E.**
Aug. 5, 1926

**The Earl of Bessborough,
G.C.M.G.**
Feb. 9, 1931

Canadian Almanac & Directory 1997

Baron Tweedsmuir of Elsfield,
G.C.M.G., G.C.V.O., C.H.
Aug. 10, 1935

Major-General The Earl of Athlone,
K.G., G.C.B., G.C.M.G., G.C.V.O.,
D.S.O.
Apr. 3, 1940

Field Marshal The Viscount
Alexander of Tunis,
K.G., G.C.B., O.M., G.C.M.G., C.S.I.,
D.S.O., M.C., A.D.C.
Aug. 1, 1945

The Rt. Hon. Vincent Massey,
P.C., C.C., C.H.
Jan. 24, 1952

Major General
The Rt. Hon. Georges-P. Vanier,
D.S.O., M.C., C.D.
Aug. 1, 1959

The Rt. Hon. Roland Michener,
P.C., C.C., C.M.M., C.D., Q.C.
Mar. 25, 1967

The Rt. Hon. Jules Léger,
P.C., C.C., C.M.M., C.D.
Oct. 5, 1973

The Rt. Hon.
Edward Richard Schreyer,
P.C., C.C., C.M.M., C.D.
Dec. 7, 1978

The Rt. Hon. Jeanne Sauvé,
P.C., C.C., C.M.M., C.D.
Dec. 23, 1983

The Rt. Hon.
Ramon John Hnatyshyn,
P.C., C.C., C.M.M., C.D., Q.C.
Oct. 6, 1989

The Rt. Hon. Roméo LeBlanc,
P.C., C.C., C.M.M., C.D.
Nov. 22, 1994

Credit: Photos of Governors General reproduced with the permission of Government House.

CANADIAN PRIME MINISTERS
(WITH PARTY AFFILIATION AND TIME IN OFFICE)

**Rt. Hon. Sir John A. Macdonald
(Conservative)**
July 1, 1867 to Nov. 5, 1873
Oct. 17, 1878 to June 6, 1891

PHOTO CREDIT: William James Topley/National
Archives of Canada/PA-027013

**Hon. Alexander MacKenzie
(Liberal)**
Nov. 7, 1873 to Oct. 16, 1878

PHOTO CREDIT: William James Topley/National
Archives of Canada/PA-026308

**Hon. Sir John J. Abbott
(Conservative)**
June 16, 1891 to Nov. 24, 1892

PHOTO CREDIT: William James Topley/National
Archives of Canada/PA-033933

**Rt. Hon. Sir John S. D. Thompson
(Conservative)**
Dec. 5, 1892 to Dec. 12, 1894

PHOTO CREDIT: National Archives of Canada/
C-000698

**Hon. Sir Mackenzie Bowell
(Conservative)**
Dec. 21, 1894 to April 27, 1896

PHOTO CREDIT: William James Topley/National
Archives of Canada/PA-027159

**Rt. Hon. Sir Charles Tupper
(Conservative)**
May 1, 1896 to July 8, 1896

PHOTO CREDIT: National Archives of Canada
/PA-027743

**Rt. Hon. Sir Wilfrid Laurier
(Liberal)**
July 11, 1896 to Oct. 6, 1911

PHOTO CREDIT:William James Topley/National
Archives of Canada/C-001971

Rt. Hon. Sir Robert L. Borden
Oct. 10, 1911 to Oct. 12, 1917
(Conservative Administration)
Oct. 12, 1917 to July 10, 1920
(Unionist Administration)

PHOTO CREDIT: William James Topley/National
Archives of Canada/PA-028128

Rt. Hon. Arthur Meighen
July 10, 1920 to Dec. 29, 1921
(Unionist "National Liberal
and Conservative Party")
June 29, 1926 to Sept. 25, 1926
(Conservative)

PHOTO CREDIT: William James Topley/National
Archives of Canada/PA-026987

**Rt. Hon.
William Lyon Mackenzie King
(Liberal)**
Dec. 29, 1921 to June 28, 1926
Sept. 25, 1926 to Aug. 6, 1930
Oct. 23, 1935 to Nov. 15, 1948

PHOTO CREDIT: National Archives of
Canada/C-027645

**Rt. Hon. Richard Bedford Bennett
(Conservative)
(Became Viscount Bennett, 1941)**
Aug. 7, 1930 to Oct. 23, 1935

PHOTO CREDIT: National Archives of
Canada/C-000687

Canadian Almanac & Directory 1997

PRIME MINISTERS 5

**Rt. Hon. Louis Stephen St. Laurent
(Liberal)**
Nov. 15, 1948 to June 21, 1957

PHOTO CREDIT: National Archives of Canada
/C-010461

**Rt. Hon. John G. Diefenbaker
(Progressive Conservative)**
June 21, 1957 to April 22, 1963

PHOTO CREDIT: Paul Horsdal/National Archives of
Canada/PA-130070

**Rt. Hon. Lester Bowles Pearson
(Liberal)**
April 22, 1963 toApril 20, 1968

PHOTO CREDIT: Ashley-Crippen Studio/National
Archives of Canada/PA-126393

**Rt. Hon. Pierre Elliott Trudeau
(Liberal)**
April 20, 1968 to June 4, 1979
Mar. 3, 1980 to June 30, 1984

PHOTO CREDIT: National Archives of Canada
/C-046600

**Rt. Hon. Charles Joseph Clark
(Progressive Conservative)**
June 4, 1979 to Mar. 3, 1980

PHOTO CREDIT: Mia & Klaus

**Rt. Hon. John Napier Turner
(Liberal)**
June 30, 1984 to Sept. 17, 1984

PHOTO CREDIT: Courtesy of the Liberal Party
of Canada

**Rt. Hon. Martin Brian Mulroney
(Progressive Conservative)**
Sept. 17, 1984 to June 25, 1993

PHOTO CREDIT: Robert Cooper/National Archives of
Canada/PA-152416

**Rt. Hon. Kim Campbell
(Progressive Conservative)**
June 25, 1993 to Nov. 4, 1993

PHOTO CREDIT: Courtesy of the National
Speakers Bureau

**Rt. Hon. Jean Chrétien
(Liberal)**
Nov. 4, 1993 to —

PHOTO CREDIT: Courtesy of the
Prime Minister's Office

Canadian Almanac & Directory 1997

6 PRIME MINISTERS

PORTRAITS OF PRIME MINISTERS IN THE HOUSE OF COMMONS

Reproduced with the permission of the Curator, House of Commons

Hon. Alexander Mackenzie
Credit: John Wycliffe Lowes Forster/National Archives of Canada/C-116811

Sir Charles Tupper
Credit: Victor A. Long/National Archives of Canada/C-116813

Sir John Alexander Macdonald
Credit: Henry Sandham/National Archives of Canada/C-025743

Sir Wilfrid Laurier
Credit: John Wentworth Russell/National Archives of Canada/C-116814

Sir John Thompson
Credit: John Wycliffe Lowes Forster/National Archives of Canada/C-116812

Sir Robert Borden
Credit: Kenneth Keith Forbes/National Archives of Canada/C-116815

Canadian Almanac & Directory 1997

PRIME MINISTERS 7

Rt. Hon. John G. Diefenbaker
Credit: Arthur Edward Cleeve Horne/National Archives of Canada/C-116820

Rt. Hon. William Lyon Mackenzie King
Credit: Frank O. Salisbury/National Archives of Canada/C-116818

Rt. Hon. Lester Bowles Pearson
Credit: Hugh Seaforth MacKenzie /National Archives of Canada /C-116821

Rt. Hon. Louis St. Laurent
Credit: Audrey Watts McNaughton/National Archives of Canada/C-116819

Rt. Hon. Richard Bedford Bennett
Credit: Kenneth Keith Forbes/National Archives of Canada/C-116817

Rt. Hon. Arthur Meighen
Credit: George Ernest Fosbery/National Archives of Canada/C-116816

Canadian Almanac & Directory 1997

THE ROYAL UNION FLAG
The Royal Union Flag, generally known as the Union Jack, was approved by Parliament on December 18, 1964 for continued use in Canada as a symbol of Canada's membership in the Commonwealth of Nations and of her allegiance to the Crown. It will, where physical arrangements make it possible, be flown along with the National Flag at federal buildings, airports, and military bases and establishments within Canada on the date of the official observance of the Queen's birthday, the Anniversary of the Statute of Westminster (December 11th), Commonwealth Day (second Monday in March), and on the occasions of Royal Visits and certain Commonwealth gatherings in Canada.

QUEEN'S PERSONAL CANADIAN FLAG
In 1962, Her Majesty The Queen adopted a personal flag specifically for use in Canada. The design comprises the Arms of Canada with The Queen's own device in the centre. The device – the initial "E" surmounted by the St. Edward's Crown within a chaplet of roses – is gold on a blue background.

When the Queen is in Canada, this flag is flown, day and night, at any building in which She is in residence. Generally, the flag is also flown behind the saluting base when She conducts troop inspections, on all vehicles in which She travels, and on Her Majesty's Canadian ships (HMCS) when the Queen is aboard.

FLAG OF THE GOVERNOR GENERAL
The Governor General's standard is a blue flag with the crest of the Arms of Canada in its centre. A symbol of the Sovereignty of Canada, the crest is made of a gold lion passant imperially crowned, on a wreath of the official colours of Canada, holding in its right paw a red maple leaf. The standard was approved by Her Majesty The Queen on February 23, 1981. The Governor General's personal standard flies whenever the incumbent is in residence, and takes precedence over all other flags in Canada, except The Queen's.

CANADIAN ARMED FORCES BADGE
The Canadian Armed Forces Badge was sanctioned by Her Majesty Queen Elizabeth II in May 1967. The description is as follows:

Within a wreath of ten stylized maple leaves Red, a cartouche medium Blue edge Gold, charged with a foul anchor Gold, surmounted by Crusader's Swords in Saltire Silver and blue, pommelled and hilted Gold; and in front an eagle volant affront head to the sinister Gold, the whole ensigned with a Royal Crown proper.

The Canadian Forces Badge replaces the badges of the Royal Canadian Navy, the Canadian Army, and the Royal Canadian Air Force.

Canadian Almanac & Directory 1997

ALBERTA

The Arms of the Province of Alberta were granted by Royal Warrant on May 30, 1907. On July 30th, 1980, the Arms were augmented as follows: Crest: Upon a Helm with a Wreath Argent and Gules a Beaver couchant upholding on its back the Royal Crown both proper; Supporters: On the dexter side a Lion Or armed and langued Gules and on the sinister side a Pronghorn Antelope (Antilocapra americana) proper; the Compartment comprising a grassy mount with the Floral Emblem of the said Province of Alberta the Wild Rose (Rosa acicularis) growing therefrom proper; Motto: FORTIS ET LIBER (Strong and Free) to be borne and used together with the Arms upon Seals, Shields, Banners, Flags or otherwise according to the Laws of Arms.

In 1958 the Government of Alberta authorized the design and use of an offical flag. A flag bearing the Armorial Ensign on a royal ultramarine blue background was adopted and the Flag Act proclaimed June 1st, 1968. Proportions of the flag are two by length and one by width with the Armorial Ensign seven-elevenths of the width of the flag carried in the centre. The flag may be used by citizens of the Province and others in a manner befitting its dignity and importance but no other banner or flag that includes the Armorial Ensign may be assumed or used.

Floral Emblem: Wild Rose (Rosa Acicularis). Chosen in the Floral Emblem Act of 1930.

Provincial Bird: Great horned owl (budo virginianus). Adopted May 3, 1977.

BRITISH COLUMBIA

The shield of British Columbia was granted by Royal Warrant on March 31, 1906. On October 15th, 1987, the shield was augmented by Her Majesty Queen Elizabeth II. The crest and supporters have become part of the provincial Arms through usage. The heraldic description is as follows: Crest: Upon a Helm with a Wreath Argent and Gules the Royal Crest of general purpose of Our Royal Predecessor Queen Victoria differenced for Us and Our Successors in right of British Columbia with the Lion thereof garlanded about the neck with the Provincial Flower that is to say the Pacific Dogwood (Cornus nuttallii) with leaves all proper Mantled Gules doubled Argent; Supporters: On the dexter side a Wapiti Stag (Cervus canadensis) proper and on the sinister side a Bighorn Sheep Ram (Oviscanadensis) Argent armed and unguled Or; Compartment: Beneath the Shield a Scroll entwined with Pacific Dogwood flowers slipped and leaved proper inscribed with the Motto assigned by the said Warrant of Our Royal Predecessor King Edward VII that is to say SPLENDOR SINE OCCASU, (splendour without diminishment).

The flag of British Columbia was authorized by an Order-in-Council of June 27, 1960. The Union Jack symbolizes the province's origins as a British colony, and the crown at its centre represents the sovereign power linking the nations of the Commonwealth. The sun sets over the Pacific Ocean. The original design of the flag was located in 1960 by Hon. W. A. C. Bennett at the College of Arms in London.

Floral Emblem: Pacific Dogwood (Cornus Nuttallii, Audubon). Adopted under the Floral Emblem Act, 1956.

Provincial Bird: Steller's jay. Adopted November 19, 1987.

Canadian Almanac & Directory 1997

MANITOBA

The Arms of the Province of Manitoba were granted by Royal Warrant on May 10, 1905, augmented by warrant of the Governor General on October 23, 1992. The description is as follows: above the familiar shield of 1905 is a helmet and mantling; above the helmet is the Crest, including the beaver holding a prairie crocus, the province's floral emblem. On the beaver's back is the royal crown. The left supporter is a unicorn wearing a collar bearing a decorative frieze of maple leaves, the collar representing Manitoba's position as Canada's "keystone" province. Hanging from the collar is a wheel of a Red River cart. The right supporter is a white horse, and its collar of bead and bone honours First Peoples. The supporters and the shield rest on a compartment representing the province's rivers and lakes, grain fields and forests, composed of the provincial tree, the white spruce, and seven prairie crocuses. At the base is a Latin translation of the phrase "Glorious and Free."

The flag of the Province of Manitoba was adopted under The Provincial Flag Act, assented to May 11, 1965, and proclaimed into force on May 12, 1966. It incorporates parts of the Royal Armorial Ensigns, namely the Union and Red Ensign; the badge in the fly of the flag is the shield of the arms of the province.

Description: A flag of the proportions two by length and one by width with the Union Jack occupying the upper quarter next the staff and with the shield of the armorial bearings of the province centred in the half farthest from the staff.

Floral Emblem: Pasque Flower, known locally as Prairie Crocus (Anemone Patens). Adopted 1906.

Provincial Bird: Great gray owl. Adopted July 16, 1987.

NEW BRUNSWICK

The Arms of New Brunswick were granted by Royal Warrant on May 26, 1868. The motto SPEM REDUXIT (hope restored) was added by Order-in-Council in 1966. The description is as follows: The upper third of the shield is red and features a gold lion, symbolizing New Brunswicks' ties to Britain. The lion is also found in the arms of the Duchy of Brunswick in Germany, the ancestral home of King George III. The lower part of the shield displays an ancient galley with oars in action. It could be interpreted as a reference to the importance of both shipbuilding and seafaring to New Brunswick in those days. It is also based on the design of the province's original great seal which featured a sailing ship on water. The shield is supported by two white-tailed deer wearing collars of Indian wampum. From one is suspended the Royal Union Flag (the Union Jack), from the other the fleur-de-lis to indicate the province's British and French background. The crest consists of an Atlantic Salmon leaping from a coronet of gold maple leaves and bearing St. Edward's Crown on its back. The base, or compartment, is a grassy mound with fiddleheads as well as purple violets, the provincial floral emblem. The motto: "Spem Reduxit" is taken from the first great seal of the province.

The flag of New Brunswick, adopted by Proclamation on February 24, 1965, is based on the Arms of the province. The chief and charge occupy the upper one-third of the flag, and the remainder of the armorial bearings occupy the lower two-thirds. The proportion is four by length and two and one half by width.

Floral Emblem: Purple Violet (Viola Cuculata). Adopted by Order-in-Council, December 1, 1936, at the request of the New Brunswick Women's Institute.

Provincial Bird: Black-capped chickadee. Adopted August 1983.

Canadian Almanac & Directory 1997

NEWFOUNDLAND

The Arms of Newfoundland were granted by Royal Letters Patent dated January 1, 1637 by King Charles I. The heraldic description is as follows: Gules, a Cross Argent, in the first and fourth quarters a Lion passant guardant crowned Or, in the second and third quarters an Unicorn passant Argent armed and crined Or, gorged with a Coronet and a Chain affixed thereto reflexed of the last. Crest: on a wreath Or and Gules a Moose passant proper. Supporters: two Savages of the clime armed and apparelled according to their guise when they go to war. The motto reads QUAERITE PRIMEREGNUM DEI (seek ye first the kingdom of God).

The official flag of Newfoundland, adopted in 1980, has primary colours of Red, Gold and Blue, against a White background. The Blue section on the left represents Newfoundland's Commonwealth heritage and the Red and Gold section on the right represents the hopes for the future with the arrow pointing the way. The two triangles represent the mainland and island parts of the province.

Floral Emblem: Pitcher Plant (Sarracenia Purpurea). Adopted June 1954.

Provincial Bird: Atlantic puffin. Proposed, but not officially adopted.

NOVA SCOTIA

The Arms of the Province of Nova Scotia were granted to the Royal Province in 1625 by King Charles I. The complete Armorial Achievement includes the Arms, surmounted by a royal helm with a blue and silver scroll or mantling representing the Royal cloak. Above is the crest of heraldic symbols: two joined hands, one armoured and the other bare, supporting a spray of laurel for peace and thistle for Scotland. On the left is the mythical royal unicorn and on the right a 17th century representation of the North American Indian. The motto reads MUNIT HAEC ET ALTERA VINCIT (one defends and the other conquers). Entwined with the thistle of Scotland at the base is the mayflower, added in 1929, as the floral emblem of Nova Scotia.

The flag of the Province of Nova Scotia is a blue St. Andrew's Cross on a white field, with the Royal Arms of Scotland mounted thereon. The width of the flag is three-quarters of the length.

The flag was originally authorized by Charles I in 1625. In 1929, on petition of Nova Scotia, a Royal Warrant of King George V was issued, revoking the modern Arms and ordering that the original Arms granted by Charles I be borne upon (seals) shields, banners, and otherwise according to the laws of Arms.

Floral Emblem: Trailing Arbutus, also known as Mayflower (Epigaea Repens). Adopted April 1901.

Provincial Bird: Osprey. Adopted Spring, 1994.

Canadian Almanac & Directory 1997

ONTARIO

The Arms of the Province of Ontario were granted by Royal Warrants on May 26, 1868 (shield), and February 27, 1909 (crest and supporters). The heraldic description is as follows: Vert, a Sprig of three leaves of Maple slipped Or on a Chief Argent the Cross of St. George. Crest: upon a wreath Vert and Or a Bear passant Sable. The supporters are on the dexter side, a Moose, and on the sinister side a Canadian Deer, both proper. The motto reads: UT INCEPIT FIDELIS SIC PERMANET (loyal in the beginning, so it remained).

The flag of the Province of Ontario was adopted under the Flag Act of May 21, 1965. It incorporates parts of the Royal Armorial Ensigns, namely the Union and Red Ensign; the badge in the fly of the flag is the shield of the Arms of the province. The flag is of the proportions two by length and one by width, with the Union Jack occupying the upper quarter next the staff and the shield of the armorial bearings of the province centred in the half farthest from the staff.

Floral Emblem: White Trillium (Trillium Grandiflorum). Adopted March 25, 1937.

Provincial Bird: Common loon. Proposed, but not officially adopted.

PRINCE EDWARD ISLAND

The Arms of the Province of Prince Edward Island were granted by Royal Warrant, May 30, 1905. The heraldic description is as follows: Argent on an Island Vert, to the sinister an Oak Tree fructed, to the dexter thereof three Oak saplings sprouting all proper, on a Chief Gules a Lion passant guardant Or. The motto reads: PARVA SUB INGENTI (the small under the protection of the great).

The flag of the Province of Prince Edward Island was authorized by an Act of the Legislative Assembly, March 24, 1964. The design of the flag is that part of the Arms contained within the shield, but is of rectangular shape, with a fringe of alternating red and white. The chief and charge of the Arms occupies the upper one-third of the flag, and the remainder of the Arms occupies the lower two-thirds. The proportions of the flag are six, four, and one-quarter in relation to the fly, the hoist, and the depth of the fringe.

Floral Emblem: Lady's Slipper (Cypripedium Acaule). Designated as the province's floral emblem by the Legislative Assembly in 1947. A more precise botanical name was included in an amendment to the Floral Emblem Act in 1965.

Provincial Bird: Blue Jay (cyanocitta cristata) was designated as avian emblem by the Provincial Emblems Acts, May 13, 1977.

Canadian Almanac & Directory 1997

PROVINCIAL FLAGS, ARMS & EMBLEMS **13**

QUÉBEC

The Arms of the Province of Québec were granted by Queen Victoria, May 26, 1868, and revised by a Provincial Order-in-Council on December 9, 1939. The heraldic description is as follows: Tierced in fess: Azure, three Fleurs-de-lis Or; Gules, a Lion passant guardant Or armed and langued Azure; Or, a Sugar Maple sprig with three leaves Vert veined Or. Surmounted with the Royal Crown. Below the shield a scroll argent, surrounded by a bordure Azure, inscribed with the motto JE ME SOUVIENS Azure.

The official flag of the Province of Québec was adopted by a Provincial Order-in-Council of January 21, 1948. It is a white cross on a sky blue ground, with the fleur-de-lis in an upright position on the blue ground in each of the four quarters. The proportion is six units wide by four units deep.

Floral Emblem: White Garden (Madonna) Lily (Lilium Candidum). Adopted under the Floral Emblem Act, 1963.

Provincial Bird: Snowy owl. Adopted December 17, 1987.

SASKATCHEWAN

The complete armorial bearings of the Province of Saskatchewan were granted by Royal Warrant on September 16, 1986, through augmentation of the original shield of arms granted by King Edward VII on August 25, 1906. The heraldic description is as follows: Shield: Vert three Garbs in fesse Or, on a Chief of the last a Lion passant guardant Gules. Crest: Upon a Helm with a Wreath Argent and Gules a Beaver upholding with its back Our Royal Crown and holding in the dexter fore-claws a Western Red Lily (Lilium philadelphicumandinum) slipped all proper Mantled Gules doubled Argent. Supporters: On the dexter side a Lion Or gorged with a Collar of Prairie Indian beadwork proper and dependent therefrom a six-pointed Mullet faceted Argent fimbriated and garnished Or charged with a Maple Leaf Gules and on the sinister side a White tailed deer (Odocoileus virginianus) proper gorged with a like Collar and dependent therefrom a like Mullet charged with a Western Red Lily slipped and leaved proper. Motto: Beneath the Shield a Scroll entwined with Western Red Lilies slipped and leaved proper inscribed with the Motto MULTIS E GENTIBUS VIRES.

The official flag was dedicated on September 22, 1969, and features the Arms of the province in the upper quarter nearest the staff, with the Western Red Lily, in the half farthest from the staff. The upper green portion represents forests, while the gold symbolizes prairie wheat fields. The basic design was adopted from the prize-winning entry of Anthony Drake of Hodgeville from a province-wide flag design competition.

Floral Emblem: Western Red Lily (Lilium philadelphicum var. andinum). Adopted April 8, 1941.

Provincial Bird: Prairie sharp-tailed grouse. Adopted March 30, 1945.

Canadian Almanac & Directory 1997

NORTHWEST TERRITORIES

The Arms of the Northwest Territories were approved by Her Majesty Queen Elizabeth II on February 24, 1956. The crest consists of two gold narwhals guarding a compass rose, symbolic of the magnetic north pole. The white upper third of the shield represents the polar ice pack and is crossed by a wavy blue line portraying the Northwest Passage. The tree line is reflected by the diagonal line separating the red and green segments of the lower portion of the shield: the green symbolizing the forested areas south of the tree line, and the red standing for the barren lands north of it. The important bases of northern wealth, minerals and fur, are represented by gold billets in the green portion and the mask of a white fox in the red.

The official flag of the Northwest Territories was adopted by the Territorial Council on January 1, 1969. Blue panels at either side of the flag represent the lakes and waters of the Territories. The white centre panel, equal in width to the two blue panels combined, symbolizes the ice and snow of the North. In the centre of the white portion is the shield from the Arms of the Territories.

Floral Emblem: Mountain Avens (Dryas Integrifolia). Adopted by the Council on June 7, 1957.

Provincial Bird: Gyrfalcon. Adopted June 1990.

YUKON

The Arms of the Yukon, granted by Queen Elizabeth II on February 24, 1956, have the following explanation: The wavy white and blue vertical stripe represents the Yukon River and refers also to the rivers and creeks where gold was discovered. The red spire-like forms represent the mountainous country, and the gold discs the mineral resources. The St. George's Cross is in reference to the early explorers and fur traders from Great Britain, and the roundel in vair in the centre of the cross is a symbol for the fur trade. The crest displays a Malamute dog, an animal which has played an important part in the early history of the Yukon.

The Yukon flag, designed by Lynn Lambert, a Haines Junction student, was adopted by Council in 1967. It is divided into thirds: green for forests, white for snow, and blue for water.

The flag consists of three vertical panels, the centre panel being one and one-half times the width of each of the other two panels. The panel adjacent to the mast is coloured green, the centre panel is coloured white and has the Yukon Crest disposed above a symbolic representation of the floral emblem of the territory, epilobium augustifolium, (fireweed), and the panel on the fly is coloured blue. The stem and leaves of the floral emblem are coloured green, and the flowers thereof are coloured red. The Yukon Crest is coloured red and blue, with the Malamute dog coloured black.

Floral Emblem: Fireweed (Epilobium Angustifolium). Adopted November 16, 1957.

Provincial Bird: Common raven. Adopted October 28, 1985.

Canadian Almanac & Directory 1997

CANADIAN HONOURS 15

ORDER OF CANADA

Companions of the Order of Canada   Members of the Order of Canada   Officers of the Order of Canada

ORDER OF MILITARY MERIT

Officers of the the Order of Military Merit   Commanders of the Order of Military Merit   Members of the Order of Military Merit

Canadian Almanac & Directory 1997

CANADIAN BRAVERY DECORATIONS

Star of Courage   Cross of Valour   Medal of Bravery

MERITORIOUS SERVICE DECORATIONS

**Meritorious Service Cross
Obverse (Military Version)**

**Meritorious Service Medal
Reverse (Civil Version)**

Canadian Almanac & Directory 1997

STATISTICAL INFORMATION

See page 1-58 for a selection of statistics taken from past editions of the *Canadian Almanac*.

CANADIAN POPULATION AND PERCENTAGE DISTRIBUTION BY PROVINCES AND TERRITORIES, 1961 TO 1991 (CENSUS)

PROVINCE AND TERRITORY	1961 / %	1971 / %	1981 / %	1991[1] / %
Newfoundland	457,853	522,104	567,681	568,474
	2.51	2.42	2.33	2.08
Prince Edward Island	104,629	111,641	122,506	129,765
	0.58	0.52	0.50	0.46
Nova Scotia	737,007	788,960	847,442	899,942
	4.04	3.66	3.48	3.30
New Brunswick	597,936	634,557	696,403	723,900
	3.28	2.94	2.86	2.65
Québec	5,259,211	6,027,764	6,438,403	6,895,963
	28.84	27.95	26.44	25.26
Ontario	6,236,092	7,703,106	8,625,107	10,084,885
	34.19	35.71	35.43	36.9
Manitoba	921,686	988,247	1,026,241	1,091,942
	5.05	4.58	4.21	4.00
Saskatchewan	925,181	926,242	968,313	988,928
	5.07	4.29	3.97	3.62
Alberta	1,331,944	1,627,874	2,237,724	2,545,553
	7.30	7.55	9.19	9.33
British Columbia	1,629,082	2,184,621	2,744,467	3,282,061
	8.93	10.13	11.27	12.02
Yukon	14,628	18,388	23,153	27,797
	0.08	0.09	0.09	0.10
Northwest Territories	22,998	34,807	45,741	57,649
	0.13	0.16	0.18	0.21
TOTALS	18,238,247	21,568,311	24,343,181	27,296,859
100	100	100	100	100
Rural	5,537,857	5,157,525	5,907,254	6,389,724
Urban	12,700,390	16,410,785	18,435,927	20,907,135

1. Excluding incompletely enumerated Indian reserves and Indian settlements.

Comparison of the 1991 Census data with data from earlier censuses is affected by a change in the definition of the 1991 Census population. Persons in Canada, on student authorizations, employment authorizations, minister's permits, and as refugee claimants were enumerated in the 1991 Census but not in previous censuses. These persons are referred to as non-permanent residents. Source: Census of Canada

POPULATION OF METROPOLITAN AREAS AS OF JUNE 4, 1991 CENSUS WITH THOSE OF THE 1986 CENSUS

	1991	1986[1]
Calgary, AB	754,033	671,453[2]
Chicoutimi-Jonquière, PQ	160,928	158,468[2]
Edmonton, AB	839,924	774,026
Halifax, NS	320,521	295,922
Hamilton, ON	599,760	557,029
Kitchener, ON	356,421	311,195
London, ON	381,522	342,302
Montréal, PQ	3,127,242	2,921,357
Oshawa, ON	240,104	203,543
Ottawa-Hull, ON, PQ	920,857	819,263
Ontario (part)	693,900	619,049
Québec (part)	226,957	200,214
Québec, PQ	645,550	603,267
Regina, SK	191,692	186,521
St. John, NB	124,981	121,265
Saskatoon, SK	210,023	200,665
Sherbrooke, PQ	139,194	129,960
St. Catharines-Niagara, ON	364,552	343,258
St. John's, NF	171,859	161,901
Sudbury, ON	157,613	148,877
Thunder Bay, ON	124,427	122,217
Toronto, ON	3,893,046	3,431,981[2]
Trois-Rivières, PQ	136,303	128,888
Vancouver, BC	1,602,502	1,380,729
Victoria, BC	287,897	255,225[2]
Windsor, ON	262,075	253,988
Winnipeg, MB	652,354	625,304

1. Based on 1991 limits.
2. Adjusted Figure due to boundary change.

Source: Census of Canada

VITAL STATISTICS COMPARED WITH MACROREGIONS AND REGIONS 1990-95

MACRO REGIONS AND REGIONS	BIRTH RATE 0/000	DEATH RATE 0/000
World	25	9
Africa	42	14
Eastern Africa	46	16
Middle Africa	46	15
Northern Africa	31	9
Southern Africa	32	9
Western Africa	46	16
Northern America	16	9
Latin America	26	7
Caribbean	24	8
Central America	30	6
South America	25	7
Asia	25	8
Eastern Asia	18	7
South Central Asia	31	10
South Eastern Asia	27	8
Western Asia	32	7
Europe	12	11
Eastern Europe	12	12
Northern Europe	14	11
Southern Europe	11	10
Western Europe	12	11
Oceania	19	8
Australia and New Zealand	15	8
Melanesia	32	9
Micronesia	33	6
Polynesia	31	6

Source: Statistical Yearbook (Fortieth issue) - United Nations

BIRTH AND DEATH RATES, CANADA 1994

PROVINCE	LIVE BIRTHS Number	Rate[2]	DEATHS Number	Rate[2]	INFANT DEATHS[1] Number	Rate[3]
Newfoundland	6,339	10.9	4,050	7.0	52	8.2
Prince Edward Island	1,716	12.8	1,114	8.3	11	6.4
Nova Scotia	11,099	11.9	7,770	8.3	67	6.0
New Brunswick	8,978	11.8	5,917	7.8	48	5.3
Québec	90,578	12.4	51,366	7.0	506	5.6
Ontario	147,068	13.4	77,487	7.1	879	6.0
Manitoba	16,480	14.6	9,148	8.1	115	7.0
Saskatchewan	14,038	13.9	8,308	8.2	125	8.9
Alberta	39,796	14.7	15,613	5.8	294	7.4
British Columbia	46,998	12.8	25,939	7.1	297	6.3
Yukon	442	14.9	124	4.2	1	2.3
Northwest Territories	1,580	24.4	241	3.7	23	15.6
TOTALS	385,112	13.2	207,077	7.1	2,418	6.3

1. Children under one year of age.
2. Rate per 1,000 population.
3. Rate per 1,000 live births.

Source: Statistics Canada, Catalogue 84-210, Births and Deaths

DEATHS, CANADA, 1994

	DEATHS BOTH SEXES	FEMALES	MALES	RATE[1] BOTH SEXES	FEMALES	MALES
Canada	207,077	97,335	109,742	6.8	5.3	8.7
Newfoundland	4,050	1,781	2,269	7.8	6.0	9.9
Prince Edward Island	1,114	508	606	6.9	5.2	9.2
Nova Scotia	7,770	3,637	4,133	7.3	5.7	9.6
New Brunswick	5,917	2,767	3,150	7.1	5.5	9.2
Québec	51,366	23,947	27,419	6.9	5.3	9.2
Ontario	77,487	37,271	40,216	6.7	5.4	8.6
Manitoba	9,148	4,390	4,758	6.7	5.3	8.6
Saskatchewan	8,308	3,795	4,513	6.4	4.9	8.2
Alberta	15,613	7,026	8,587	6.5	5.1	8.4
British Columbia	25,939	12,093	13,846	6.4	5.1	8.0
Yukon	124	39	85	9.5	6.8	12.2
Northwest Territories	241	81	160	8.9	6.9	11.5

1. Per 1,000 population

Source: Statistics Canada, Catalogue 84-210, Births and Deaths

LEADING CAUSES OF DEATH, 1993

FEMALE CAUSE	RANK	NUMBER	PERCENT	RATE[1]
Diseases of the circulatory system	1	38,381	40.2	262.9
Ischaemic heart disease		19,667	20.6	134.7
Stroke		8,951	9.4	61.3
Cancer	2	25,709	26.9	176.1
Lung		5,130	5.4	35.1
Breast		4,779	5.0	32.7
Respiratory diseases	3	8,082	8.5	55.4
Pneumonia and influenza		3,759	3.9	25.8
Other chronic airways obstruction		2,374	2.5	16.3
Accidents and adverse effects	4	4,277	4.5	29.3
Accidents falls		1,215	1.3	8.3
Motor vehicle accidents		1,128	1.2	7.7
Diseases of the digestive system	5	3,624	3.8	24.8
Chronic liver disease and cirrhosis		768	0.8	5.3
Noninfective enteritis and colitis		565	0.6	3.9
Endocrine diseases, etc.	6	3,425	3.6	23.5
Diabetes mellitus		2,682	2.8	18.4
Fluid, electrolyte and acid-base balance		249	0.3	1.7
Diseases of the nervous system	7	3,153	3.3	21.6
Alzheimer's disease		1,563	1.6	10.7
Parkinson's disease		470	0.5	3.2
Mental disorders	8	2,234	2.3	15.3
Senile and presenile dementia		1,031	1.1	7.1
Alcoholic psychoses, etc.		154	0.2	1.1
All other causes		6,620	6.9	45.4
ALL CAUSES		95,505	100.0	654.3

MALE CAUSE	RANK	NUMBER	PERCENT	RATE[1]
Diseases of the circulatory system	1	40,512	37.0	282.4
Ischaemic heart disease		25,100	22.9	175.0
Stroke		6,478	5.9	45.2
Cancer	2	30,483	27.9	212.5
Lung		9,983	9.1	69.6
Prostate		3,582	3.3	25.0
Respiratory diseases	3	9,971	9.1	69.5
Other chronic airways obstruction		4,257	3.9	29.7
Pneumonia and influenza		3,288	3.0	22.9
Accidents and adverse effects	4	9,292	8.5	64.8
Suicide		3,014	2.8	21.0
Motor vehicle accidents		2,445	2.2	17.0
Diseases of the digestive system	5	3,931	3.6	27.4
Chronic liver disease and cirrhosis		1,469	1.3	10.2
Gastrointestinal haemorrhage		388	0.4	2.6
Endocrine diseases, etc.	6	2,955	2.7	20.6
Diabetes mellitus		2,339	2.1	16.3
Fluid, electrolyte and acid-base balance		194	0.2	1.4
Diseases of the nervous system	7	2,586	2.4	18.0
Alzheimer's disease		849	0.8	5.9
Parkinson's disease		540	0.5	3.8
Infectious and parasitic diseases	8	2,266	2.1	15.8
HIV infection		1,474	1.3	10.3
Septicaemia		385	0.4	2.7
All other causes		7,408	6.7	51.8
ALL CAUSES		109,404	100.0	762.8

1. Per 100,000 population

Source: Statistics Canada, Centre for Health Statistics.

MARRIAGES, 1994

	CANADA	NFLD.	P.E.I.	N.S.	N.B.	QUÉ	ONT.	MAN.	SASK.	ALTA.	B.C.	YUKON	N.W.T.
Marriages	159,959	3,318	850	5,374	4,219	24,985	66,694	6,585	5,689	18,096	23,739	169	241
Marriage Rate [1]	5.5	5.7	6.3	5.8	5.6	3.4	6.1	5.8	5.6	6.7	6.5	5.7	3.7
Mean age at marriage:													
Grooms	32.6	30.4	31.9	32.5	31.9	32.9	32.6	31.7	31.3	32.0	33.7	35.6	32.5
Brides	30.1	28.1	29.7	30.1	29.5	30.4	30.2	29.1	28.7	29.5	30.8	31.6	29.7
Mean age at marriage of single persons:													
Grooms	28.8	27.9	28.3	28.6	28.0	29.3	28.9	28.3	27.9	28.4	29.2	31.0	29.9
Brides	26.9	26.1	31.3	26.6	26.0	27.4	27.1	26.1	25.6	26.1	27.1	27.9	27.6
Mean age at marriage of divorced persons:													
Grooms	42.1	41.0	41.5	41.9	42.8	43.8	41.7	41.1	40.7	41.3	42.9	45.5	43.1
Brides	38.6	37.2	40.0	38.8	38.4	40.1	38.4	37.6	37.4	37.7	38.9	38.5	39.0

1. Per 1,000 population

Source: Statistics Canada Catalogue 84-212, Marriages

MOTHER TONGUE, 1991

LANGUAGE	MOTHER TONGUE
English	16,454,515
French	6,623,235
Italian	538,690
German	490,650
Chinese	516,875
Spanish	187,615
Portuguese	220,630
Ukrainian	201,315
Polish	200,395
Dutch	146,420
Punjabi	147,265
Arabic	119,255
Greek	132,980
Tagalog	115,980
Vietnamese	83,630
Hindi	40,575
Hungarian	83,915
Cree	82,070
Russian	38,030
Gujari	42,175

Source: Statistics Canada, Catalogue 96-304, 1991 Census Highlights

RELIGION, 1991

	TOTAL POPULATION
All religions	26,994,040
Catholic	12,335,255
Protestant	9,780,715
United Church	3,093,120
Anglican	2,188,110
Presbyterian	636,295
Lutheran	636,205
Baptist	663,360
Pentecostal	436,435
Eastern Orthodox	387,390
Jewish	318,070
Eastern non-Christian	747,455
Islam	253,260
Buddist	163,415
Hindu	157,010
Sikh	147,440
Para-religious	28,160
No religious affiliation	3,386,365

Source: Statistics Canada, Catalogue 96-304, 1991 Census Highlights

LABOUR FORCE ESTIMATES, ANNUAL AVERAGES

	POPULATION AGED 15 AND OVER	LABOUR FORCE TOTAL	EMPLOYMENT	UNEMPLOYMENT	PARTICIPATION RATE	UNEMPLOYMENT RATE	EMPLOYMENT/ POPULATION RATIO
	(000's)		(000'S)		(%)	(%)	(%)
1949	9,268	5,055	4,913	141	54.5	2.8	53.0
1959	11,605	6,242	5,870	372	53.8	6.0	50.6
1969	14,162	8,194	7,832	362	57.9	4.4	55.3
1970	14,528	8,395	7,919	476	57.8	5.7	54.5
1971	14,872	8,639	8,104	535	58.1	6.2	54.5
1972	15,186	8,897	8,344	553	58.6	6.2	54.9
1973	15,526	9,276	8,761	515	59.7	5.5	56.4
1974	15,924	9,639	9,125	514	60.5	5.3	57.3
1975	16,323	9,974	9,284	690	61.1	6.9	56.9
1976	16,701	10,203	9,477	726	61.1	7.1	56.7
1977	17,051	10,500	9,651	849	61.6	8.1	56.6
1978	17,377	10,895	9,987	908	62.7	8.3	57.5
1979	17,702	11,231	10,395	836	63.4	7.4	58.7
1980	18,053	11,573	10,708	865	64.1	7.5	59.3
1981	18,368	11,899	11,001	898	64.8	7.5	59.9
1982	18,608	11,926	10,618	1,308	64.1	11.0	57.1
1983	18,805	12,109	10,675	1,434	64.4	11.8	56.8
1984	18,996	12,316	10,932	1,384	64.8	11.2	57.5
1985	19,190	12,532	11,221	1,311	65.3	10.5	58.5
1986	19,397	12,746	11,531	1,215	65.7	9.5	59.4
1987	19,642	13,011	11,861	1,150	66.2	8.8	60.4
1988	19,890	13,275	12,245	1,031	66.7	7.8	61.6
1989	20,968	14,151	12,086	1,065	67.5	7.5	62.4
1990	21,227	14,329	13,165	1,164	67.3	8.1	61.9
1991	21,613	14,408	12,916	1,492	66.7	10.4	59.8
1992	21,986	14,482	12,842	1,640	65.9	11.3	58.4
1993	22,315	14,663	13,015	1,649	65.5	11.2	58.2
1994	22,717	14,832	13,292	1,541	65.3	10.4	58.5
1995	23,027	14,928	13,506	1,422	64.8	9.5	58.6

Source: Statistics Canada, Catalogue 71-220, Labour Force Annual Averages

EMPLOYMENT BY DETAILED OCCUPATION, CANADA, ANNUAL AVERAGES, 1991 TO 1995

	1990	1991	1992	1993	1994	1995
			THOUSANDS			
All Occupation	13,165	12,916	12,842	13,015	13,292	13,506
Managerial and other professional	3,961	4,081	4,095	4,238	4,331	4,449
Managerial and administrative	1,697	1,735	1,735	1,769	1,773	1,901
Other professional	2,264	2,347	2,359	2,469	2,558	2,548
Natural sciences, engineering and mathematics	487	517	483	514	532	547
Social sciences	258	275	288	293	316	297
Religion	35	30	29	34	36	33
Teaching	568	582	629	627	652	647
Medicine and health	664	699	692	730	732	730
Artistic, literary and recreational	251	243	239	272	290	294
Clerical	2,192	2,122	2,083	2,043	2,004	1,969
Sales	1,271	1,247	1,274	1,275	1,326	1,339
Service	1,735	1,721	1,749	1,801	1,826	1,846
Primary occupations	619	621	595	613	597	606
Farming, horticulture & animal husbandry	464	470	455	474	448	452
Fishing and trapping	39	44	37	39	38	30
Forestry and logging	52	50	52	51	58	65
Mining and quarrying	64	58	51	50	53	59
Processing machining and fabricating etc.	1,677	1,528	1,487	1,486	1,548	1,618
Processing	388	359	340	341	337	356
Machining	229	192	194	187	209	219
Fabricating, assembling and repairing	1,060	977	953	958	1,002	1,043
Construction	783	697	670	669	698	689
Transport equipment operating	493	474	466	461	498	519
Material handling and other crafts	434	425	423	427	465	470
Material handling	276	266	264	273	305	308
Other crafts	158	159	160	154	160	162

Source: Statistics Canada, Catalogue 71-220, Labour Force Annual Averages

Canadian Almanac & Directory 1997

LABOUR FORCE PARTICIPATION RATES OF WOMEN BY AGE AND EDUCATION, CANADA, 1991

EDUCATION	TOTAL	15-19	20-24	25-34	35-44	45-54	55-64	65 & OVER
Total	59.9	47.5	81.1	78.5	79.6	71.9	39.2	5.7
Less than Grade 9	24.3	24.5	44.6	48.5	56.0	49.5	25.2	3.5
Grade 9-13 without certificate or diploma	46.9	37.6	64.1	65.5	71.3	65.8	37.4	5.1
Grade 9-13 with certificate or diploma	64.3	57.1	80.5	75.9	79.1	73.6	42.0	6.7
Trades certificate or diploma[1]	72.0	71.8	86.7	81.1	82.8	79.4	50.9	8.2
Some university or other non-university without certificate or diploma[2]	71.5	78.0	83.3	78.9	80.6	76.9	47.2	7.9
University or other non-university with Certificate or diploma[3]	77.9	81.0	90.2	87.2	87.2	83.5	54.4	9.7
University degree	83.3	72.7	88.4	88.9	88.0	88.3	59.9	14.2

1. Includes persons with a trades certificate or diploma only and persons with other non-university education and a trades certificate or diploma.
2. Includes persons with some university education (with or without other non-university education) with a trades certificate or diploma.
3. Does not include persons with other non-university education and a trades certificate or diploma, or persons with some university education (with or without other non-university education) with a trades certificate or diploma.

Source: 1991 Census of Canada, unpublished data, Labour Household Survey Analysis Division

EMPLOYED PERSONS WITH DISABILITIES, AGED 15 TO 64, BY SEX, BY OCCUPATION, CANADA (1986/1991)

OCCUPATION	FEMALES 1986	FEMALES 1991	MALES 1986	MALES 1991
Total-all occupations	269,530	472,640	442,030	633,565
Upper level managers	605	2,155	8,130	9,375
Middle and other managers	9,995	30,915	31,240	42,720
Professionals	34,605	61,015	37,595	42,195
Semi-professionals and technicians	17,710	18,875	14,305	27,715
Supervisors	6,450	10,815	11,270	8,890
Foremen/women	1,500	2,415	15,130	21,725
Clerical workers	79,325	121,345	26,130	41,145
Sale workers	23,650	32,850	33,685	36,320
Service workers	31,950	65,285	24,365	33,990
Skilled crafts and trades	2,940	7,180	66,715	73,120
Semi-skilled manual workers	15,375	13,665	66,835	99,690
Other manual workers	30,025	36,605	86,180	116,405
Not stated	15,395	69,520	20,460	80,270

Figures suppressed. The coefficient of variation of the estimate is higher than 33.3%. Sampling error is between 16.5% & 33.3%; use with caution.

Source: Statistics Canada, Post-Censal Surveys Progam

MINIMUM HOURLY WAGE RATES FOR EXPERIENCED ADULT WORKERS, YOUNG WORKERS & STUDENTS

JURISDICTION	EXPERIENCED ADULT WORKERS (INCLUDING DOMESTICS)	EFFECTIVE DATE	YOUNG WORKERS & STUDENTS [1]	EFFECTIVE DATE
Federal	Same as adult minimum wage rate in each provincial & territorial jurisdiction on July 17, 1996	17/07/96	Employees under 17; same as the adult minimum wage rate in each provincial and territorial jurisdiction on July 1, 1996	01/07/96
Alberta	$5.00	01/04/92	Employees under 18 attending school: $4.50	01/04/92
British Columbia	$7.00	01/10/95	Abolished	01/03/95
Manitoba	$5.40	01/01/96	Abolished	01/03/91
New Brunswick	$5.50	01/07/96		
Newfoundland [2]	$5.00	01/09/96		
	$5.25	01/04/97		
Nova Scotia	$5.15	01/01/93	Abolished	01/01/93
	$5.35	01/10/96		
	$5.50	01/02/97		
Ontario	$6.85	01/01/95	Students under 18 emplyed for not more than 28 hours in a week or during a school holiday: $6.40	01/01/95
Prince Edward Island	$5.15	01/09/95	Abolished	01/01/93
	$5.40	01/10/96		
Québec	$6.45	01/10/95		
	$6.70	01/10/96		
Saskatchewan	$5.35	01/12/92		
Northwest Territories [2]	$6.50	01/04/91	Employees under 16: $6.00	01/04/91
	$7.00 [3]	01/04/91	$6.50 [3]	01/04/91
Yukon Territory	$6.86	01/10/95		

1. Alberta, Ontario & the Northwest Territories have special rates for young workers or students.
2. Sixteen years of age & over.
3. For areas distant from the NWT highway system.

Source: Human Resources Development Canada, External Cooperation Division, September 1996

Canadian Almanac & Directory 1997

AVERAGE EARNINGS OF MEN & WOMEN IN CANADA[1]

	1983	1984	1985	1986	1987	1988	1989	1990	1991	1992	1993	1994
Males[2] $	30,100	29,453	30,152	30,609	30,832	31,509	31,598	31,231	30,311	30,194	29,599	31,087
Females[2] $	16,532	16,889	16,940	17,569	17,772	18,080	18,634	18,712	18,655	19,269	18,936	19.359
Males[3] $	40,051	38,954	39,115	39,361	39,820	40,302	40,113	40,242	39,859	40,189	39,433	40,717
Females[3]$	25,868	25,541	25,403	25,905	26,257	26,323	26,409	27,207	27,742	28,868	28,392	28,423

1. Constant (1994) dollars.
2. All earners.
3. Full year full time workers.

Source: Statistics Canada, Catalogue 13-217, Earnings of Men & Women

AVERAGE FAMILY INCOME, 1991/1992/1994

	1991 $	1992 $	1994$
Canada	51,856	52,504	52,858
Newfoundland	40,250	40,933	41,474
Prince Edward Island	43,171	44,519	45,369
Nova Scotia	44,113	45,541	45,436
New Brunswick	42,914	45,049	44,530
Québec	47,960	48,060	48,488
Ontario	56,727	57,071	57,482
Manitoba	46,214	49,545	48,809
Saskatchewan	45,685	47,720	46,507
Alberta	53,999	53,538	54,344
British Columbia	53,602	55,089	55,358

Source: Statistics Canada, Catalogue 13-208, Family Income

AVERAGE HOUSEHOLD EXPENDITURE 1990/1992

	1990 $	1992 $
Food	5,977	5,686
Shelter	8,229	8,102
Household operation	1,907	1,974
Household furnishings and equipment	1,425	1,372
Clothing	2,596	2,222
Transportation	5,603	5,640
Health Care	848	867
Personal Care	887	844
Recreation	2,358	2,300
Reading materials & other printed matter	272	248
Education	424	430
Tobacco products & alcoholic beverages	1,276	1,410
Gifts & contributions	1,734	1,464
Miscellaneous	1,294	1,322

Source: Statistics Canada, Catalogue 62-555, Family Expenditure in Canada, Household Surveys Division

NEW HOUSING PRICE INDEXES ANNUAL AVERAGES[1]
1986 = 100

	CANADA	ATLANTIC PROVINCES	QUÉBEC	ONTARIO	PRAIRIE PROVINCES	BRITISH COLUMBIA
1986	97.2	99.5	97.7	95.3	99.3	99.9
1987	113.6	102.8	110.9	121.5	103.1	103.0
1988	123.0	106.1	121.6	133.2	106.8	108.8
1989	134.7	109.8	126.7	150.1	108.7	121.3
1990	138.7	110.8	130.3	151.4	119.1	131.2
1991	125.1	113.1	131.1	128.5	117.9	117.5
1992	124.6	114.2	130.3	125.9	117.3	123.0
1993	125.2	115.6	130.5	123.5	122.9	127.9
1994	125.5	117.2	131.0	122.8	125.9	127.8
1995	124.8	119.8	133.0	123.8	126.4	119.5
1996	121.6	119.8	132.4	121.7	126.8	109.1

1. Twenty cities, house only.

Source: Statistics Canada, Prices, CANSIM- Time Series D698201, D698798, D6988803, D698804, D698805, D698809

HOME COMPUTERS & COMPUTER MODEMS

	1994					1995				
ESTIMATES IN THOUSANDS	TOTAL HOUSEHOLDS	HOME COMPUTERS[1] WITH	WITHOUT	COMPUTER MODEMS[2] WITH	WITHOUT	TOTAL HOUSEHOLDS	HOME COMPUTERS[1] WITH	WITHOUT	COMPUTER MODEMS[2] WITH	WITHOUT
Canada	10,387	2,594	7,792	872	9,514	11,243	3,238	8,006	1,355	1,883
Newfoundland	183	28	154	7	175	194	38	156	14	24
Prince Edward Island	48	6	42	--	46	50	8	42	4	4
Nova Scotia	332	60	272	23	309	357	80	277	33	47
New Brunswick	255	41	215	13	243	286	57	229	25	32
Québec	2,720	530	2,189	146	2,574	2,937	691	2,245	246	445
Ontario	3,820	1,078	2,742	378	3,442	4,143	1,346	2,797	602	743
Manitoba	397	74	323	23	374	419	104	315	37	66
Saskatchewan	361	76	285	22	339	385	90	295	30	61
Alberta	928	270	658	97	831	1,009	345	665	158	187
British Columbia	1,344	430	913	162	1,182	1,463	479	984	205	274

1. Excludes systems which can only be used to play games or are used exclusively for business purposes.
2. Includes internal & external units.
-- Amount too small to be expressed.

Source: Statistics Canada, Catalogue 64-202, Household Facilities and Equipment

CONSUMER PRICE INDEX
1973 - 1995; January 1995- August 1996
(1986 = 100)

	Food	Shelter	Household Operations & Furnishings	Clothing & Footwear	Transportation	Health & Personal Care	Recreation, Reading & Education	Alcohol Beverages & Tobacco Products	All-items Index
1973	33.5	37.0	--	47.4	32.8	37.5	43.0	29.4	36.0
1974	39.0	40.3	--	51.9	36.1	40.7	46.8	31.0	39.9
1975	44.0	44.3	--	55.0	40.3	45.4	51.7	34.8	44.2
1976	45.2	49.2	--	58.1	44.7	49.3	54.8	37.2	47.5
1977	48.9	53.8	--	62.0	47.8	52.9	57.3	39.9	51.3
1978	56.5	57.9	--	64.4	50.6	56.7	59.6	43.1	55.9
1979	63.9	61.9	65.2	70.3	55.5	61.9	63.7	46.2	61.0
1980	70.8	66.9	71.1	78.6	62.6	68.0	69.7	51.4	67.2
1981	78.9	75.3	78.6	84.2	74.1	75.4	76.8	58.0	75.5
1982	84.6	84.7	86.9	88.9	84.5	83.4	83.4	67.0	83.7
1983	87.7	90.2	91.6	92.5	88.7	89.2	88.8	75.5	88.5
1984	92.6	93.8	94.6	94.7	92.5	92.7	91.8	81.6	92.4
1985	95.2	97.1	97.1	97.3	96.9	95.9	95.6	89.4	96.0
1986	100.0	100.0	100.0	100.0	100.0	100.0	100.0	100.0	100.0
1987	104.4	104.0	102.9	104.2	103.6	105.0	105.4	106.7	104.4
1988	107.2	108.6	106.8	109.6	105.6	109.6	111.3	114.6	108.6
1989	111.1	114.3	110.7	114.1	111.1	114.4	116.2	125.2	114.0
1990	115.7	119.5	112.9	117.3	117.3	120.0	121.3	136.1	119.5
1991	121.2	124.7	117.3	128.4	119.4	128.4	130.2	159.5	126.2
1992	120.8	126.4	117.9	129.5	121.8	131.3	131.9	169.0	128.1
1993	122.8	128.0	119.0	130.8	125.7	134.8	135.3	171.7	130.4
1994	123.3	128.5	119.3	131.8	131.3	136.1	139.3	143.6	130.7
1995	126.3	134.0	121.6	131.8	138.1	135.9	142.9	143.5	133.5
1995									
Jan.	125.6	133.7	120.3	131.5	135.5	136.1	138.3	141.0	132.1
Feb.	126.4	133.7	120.7	133.3	136.1	136.1	139.6	141.2	132.7
Mar.	126.2	133.9	121.2	132.6	136.6	135.8	141.0	142.4	133.0
Apr.	127.6	133.4	121.4	133.4	137.3	135.9	141.1	142.7	133.4
May	126.8	133.9	121.6	131.7	138.8	135.9	142.5	143.6	133.7
June	127.1	134.1	121.3	130.8	138.8	135.8	142.6	143.9	133.7
July	127.1	134.1	121.5	130.2	138.9	136.1	145.4	144.0	134.0
Aug.	125.9	134.1	121.7	131.5	138.2	135.9	145.3	144.1	133.8
Sept	125.5	134.1	122.2	132.7	138.7	135.4	146.2	144.2	133.9
Oct	125.6	134.0	122.4	132.3	138.2	135.8	145.0	144.7	133.8
Nov	125.5	134.2	122.2	132.2	139.7	135.7	145.2	144.9	134.1
Dec.	126.1	134.3	122.2	129.0	140.4	135.8	142.5	144.7	133.9
1996									
Jan.	127.6	134.3	123.2	130.1	140.5	135.9	142.0	144.9	134.2
Feb.	126.8	134.3	123.5	132.0	140.4	136.0	142.9	145.3	134.4
Mar.	127.1	134.2	124.0	132.7	141.7	136.0	143.6	145.4	134.9
Apr.	128.3	134.1	123.9	132.0	143.1	136.7	144.0	145.5	135.3
May	127.8	134.2	124.0	131.5	144.9	136.7	145.7	146.3	135.7
June	128.6	134.0	124.5	129.4	143.8	136.5	145.8	146.5	135.6
July	128.3	134.1	124.5	129.5	142.4	136.6	149.2	146.3	135.6
Aug.	127.9	133.9	124.7	131.0	142.7	136.8	149.1	146.3	135.7

Source: Statistics Canada, Catalogue 62-001 The Consumer Price Index

PRINCIPAL TRADING PARTNERS IN 1995

COUNTRIES	IMPORTS	EXPORTS
	Millions of Dollars	
United States	150,873	196,486
Japan	12,095	11,899
United Kingdom	5,476	3,757
Germany	4,800	3,165
Korea South	3,204	2,697
France	3,122	1,889
Italy	3,271	1,776
China, People's Republic of	4,638	3,292
Taiwan	2,791	1,686
Mexico	5,350	1,110
Netherlands	948	1,590
Norway	2,314	762
Belgium	728	1,842
Hong Kong	1,304	1,380
Switzerland	902	533

Source: Statistics Canada, International Trade Division

The export figures in the Imports and Exports table are total exports (see following page), the Principal Trading Partners table features domestic export figures.

IMPORTS AND EXPORTS - CANADA

Value of merchandise imported and exported during the twelve months ended December 31st, 1995.

COMMONWEALTH AND PREFERENTIAL COUNTRIES	IMPORTS (millions of dollars)	EXPORTS (millions of dollars)
Australia	1,282	1,221
Bahamas	16	21
Bahrain	1	17
Bangladesh	100	90
Barbados	17	34
Belize	11	4
Bermuda	4	38
Cyprus	1	20
Fiji	29	1
Gibraltar	-	-
Ghana	12	18
Guyana	171	8
Hong Kong	1,304	1,760
India	541	439
Ireland	565	199
Jamaica	200	103
Kenya	19	18
Malawi	2	6
Malaysia	1,548	571
Malta	47	4
Mauritius	22	3
New Zealand	298	185
Nigeria	584	26
Pakistan	204	125
Papua, N.G.	1	4
Qatar	-	11
Sierra Leone	5	-
Singapore	1,309	499
South Africa	417	333
Sri Lanka	76	21
Tanzania, United Republic of	3	13
Trinidad and Tobago	18	102
Uganda	8	11
United Kingdom	5,476	3,878
Zambia	4	10
Zimbabwe	10	17

FOREIGN COUNTRIES	IMPORTS	EXPORTS
Albania Republic	1	2
Algeria	347	530
Angola	12	4
Argentina	169	237
Austria	536	296
Azerbaijin Republic	-	-
Belarus Republic	8	1
Belgium	728	1,863
Benin	-	6
Bolivia	22	11
Brazil	1,038	1,301
Bulgaria	51	7
Burkino Faso	-	2
Cameroon	10	17
Chile	278	387
China, People's Republic of	4,638	3,463
Colombia	372	392
Costa Rica	163	46
Côte d'Ivoire	28	13
Cuba	320	277
Czech Republic	75	66
Denmark	334	143
Dominican Republic	71	78
Ecuador	137	78
Egypt	43	153
El Salvador	18	22
Estonia Republic	12	6
Ethiopia	7	10
Finland	455	221
France	3,122	1,952
Gabon	-	1
Germany	4,800	3,309
Greece	66	122
Greenland	2	6
Guatemala	93	41

FOREIGN COUNTRIES (continued)	IMPORTS (millions of dollars)	EXPORTS (millions of dollars)
Guinea	13	4
Haiti	2	29
Honduras	49	20
Hungary	45	42
Iceland	59	17
Indonesia	597	662
Iran, Islamic Republic of	121	430
Iraq	-	-
Israel	240	236
Italy	3,271	1,838
Japan	12,095	12,053
Kazakhstan, Republic of	11	2
Korea, North	-	1
Korea, South	3,204	2,730
Kuwait	-	64
Kyrgyzstan, Republic of	1	8
Laos Peoples Democratic Republic	2	-
Latvia, Republic of	6	7
Lebanon	4	57
Liberia	-	-
Libyan Arab Jamahiriya	-	70
Lithuania, Republic of	24	3
Luxembourg	37	10
Madagascar	14	1
Mali	8	9
Mexico	5,350	1,141
Morocco	70	189
Mozambique	-	17
Myanmar	14	1
Nepal	4	4
Netherlands	948	1,663
Netherlands Antilles	65	37
Nicaragua	10	9
Niger	8	1
Norway	2,314	773
Oman (Muscat)	-	24
Panama	22	51
Paraguay	3	14
Peru	96	144
Philippines	497	328
Poland	120	179
Portugal	215	94
Romania	59	21
Russia Federation	498	208
Saudi Arabia	501	521
Senegal	1	10
Slovakia	29	14
Somalia	-	1
Spain	706	628
St. Pierre and Miquelon	-	32
Sudan	-	2
Surinam	-	4
Sweden	1,305	343
Switzerland	902	550
Syrian Arab Republic	27	21
Taiwan	2,791	1,721
Thailand	1,013	578
Togo	45	1
Tunisia	4	106
Turkey	150	288
Ukraine	17	46
United Arab Emirates	5	199
United States	150,873	209,888
Uruguay	24	25
Uzbekistan, Republic	6	1
Venezuela	670	800
Viet Nam	76	34
Yemen	-	18
Yugoslavia (Former)	-	1
Zaire	44	37
Total (all countries)	225,695	264,207

Source: Statistics Canada, Catalogue 65-202, Imports, Merchandise Trade; Statistics Canada, Catalogue 65-203, Exports, Merchandise Trade

Note: Dash (-) in the above table indicates imports/exports less than $1 million.

STATISTICS OF GROWTH AND PROGRESS IN CANADA

GROWTH STATISTICS: AGRICULTURE/FISHERIES

	POPULATION [1]	WHEAT PRODUCTION [2]	TOTAL CANADIAN CROPS [2,3]	FARM CASH RECEIPTS FOR TOTAL PRODUCTS [2]	FARM CASH RECEIPTS FOR LIVESTOCK & LIVESTOCK PRODUCTS [2,4]	DAIRY PRODUCTS INDUSTRY [5] VALUE OF SHIPMENTS	FISHERIES PRODUCTION [5,6]
		'000 BUSHELS	'000 ACRES	$000,000	$000,000		
1985	25,165 (ID)	891,076	111,863	8,100	9,803	6,410,570	2,337,990
1986	25,309 (C)	1,152,260	110,420	7,875	10,248	6,667,646	2,928,808
1987	25,617 (PD)	953,340	110,484	7,342	10,619	6,883,944	3,164,390
1988	25,909 (PD)	584,691	111,492	8,291	10,698	7,195,000	3,204,826
1989	26,240 (PD)	911,071	112,063	8,764	10,843	7,349,000	2,857,530
1990	26,610 (PD)	1,179,373	111,486	8,873	11,210	7,530,676	2,967,120
1991	27,296 (C)	1,173,802	110,702	8,726	10,854	7,576,415	2,935,130
1992	28,120 (PD)	1,097,853	111,601	8,541	11,330	7,461,886	2,877,970
1993	28,946 (PR)	1,000,594	112,715	8,997	12,276	7,318,954	3,017,850
1994	29,251 (PR)	858,100	113,531	11,482 (R)	12,493 (R)	7,412,945 (R)	-- -- --
1995	29,606 (PR)	934,465	---	12,826	12,670	7,824,250 (P)	-- -- --

1. Statistics Canada, Catalogue 91-213 Annual Demographic Statistics
2. Statistics Canada, Agriculture Division
3. Includes grains, specialty crops, summerfallow, hay and improved pasture area.
4. Total livestock and livestock products (including poultry and animals on fur farms).
5. Statistics Canada, Industry Division
6. New series beginning in 1977 includes marketed values for sea fisheries only.

-- Not available

(ID) Final intercensal estimates (PD) Final Postcensal estimates (PP) Preliminary Postcensal estimates

(C) Census Population (PR) Updated Postcensal estimates (R) Revised (P) Preliminary

GROWTH STATISTICS: PRODUCTION OF SELECTED MINERALS/METALS

	PIG IRON PRODUCTION	CRUDE PETROLEUM	COPPER TONS	NICKEL TONS)	NATURAL GAS MILLION CU. FT.	IRON ORE	ZINC TONS	ASBESTOS TONS	CEMENT	VALUE OF TOTAL MINERAL PRODUCTION
	'000 metric tonnes	'000 BBL cubic metres	'000 kgs)	'000 kgs	'000 cubic metres)	'000 tons metric tonnes	'000 kgs	metric tonnes	'000 tons metric tonnes	$000,000
1985	9,665	85,564	738,637	169,971	84,344	39,502	1,049,275	750	10,192	44,734
1986	9,249	85,468	698,527	163,639	71,896	36,167	988,173	662	10,611	32,447
1987	9,719	89,149	794,149	189,086	78,267	37,702	1,157,936	665	12,603	36,342
1988	9,498	93,806	758,478	198,744	90,911	39,934	1,370,000	710	12,350	36,955
1989	10,138	90,641	704,432	95,554	96,117	39,445	1,272,854	701	12,591	39,259
1990	7,346	90,279	771,443	195,004	98,771	35,670	1,179,300	686	11,745	40,778
1991	8,268	89,788	780,362	188,098	105,244	35,421	1,083,008	686	9,372	35,190
1992	8,621	93,256	761,694	177,555	116,664	31,582	1,195,736	587	8,598	35,404
1993	8,633	97,342	709,650	178,529	128,817	33,228	990,727	523	9,394	36,564
1994(R)	8,106	110,452	590,784	141,974	138,856	36,416	976,309	531	10,584	41,150
1995(P)	8,464	114,802	704,863	166,842	148,481	37,130	1,093,541	511	10,722	43,367

Sources: Statistics Canada, Catalogue 41-001 Primary Iron and Steel; Statistics Canada, 26-202 Canada's Mineral Production

(P) Preliminary Estimates (R) Revised

GROWTH STATISTICS: IMPORTS & EXPORTS

	EXPORTS (INCLUDING RE-EXPORTS)	IMPORTS	IMPORTS OF RAW SUGAR, CANE [1]	IMPORTS OF CRUDE NATURAL RUBBER (EXCLUDING LATEX) [1]	IMPORTS OF RAW COTTON [1]	IMPORTS OF CRUDE PETROLEUM
	$000,000	$000,000	'000 kg	'000 kg	'000kg	'000 cubic metres
1985	119,475	104,355	982	101,657	50,144	15,862,657
1986	120,669	112,511	1,090	91,302	58,332	20,166,763
1987	125,087	116,238	740	96,563	48,538	21,767,007
1988	138,498	131,171	732	81,206	40,666	23,475,727
1989	138,701	135,191	611	82,870	47,277	28,300,175
1990	148,979	136,245	911	75,116	39,197	31,846,753
1991	146,006	135,461	823	68,388	43,306	30,822,958
1992	162,823	148,017	891	81,500	44,876	29,383,477
1993	187,515	170,121	997	61,418	46,063	32,957,060
1994	226,475 (R)	202,737 (R)	995	101,814	44,961	36,237,601
1995	264,207	225,695	919	115,606	50,347	39,866,227

1. From 1988, based on Harmonized System

Sources: Statistics Canada, Catalogue 65-202 Exports Merchandise Trade; Statistics Canada, Catalogue 65-203 Imports Merchandise Trade; Statistics Canada, Catalogue 65-007 Imports By Commodity

Canadian Almanac & Directory 1997

GROWTH STATISTICS: TRANSPORT/TRANSPORTATION

	RAILWAY GROSS REVENUE [1]	RAILWAY OPERATING EXPENSES [1]	TONNE KILOMETRES REVENUE FREIGHT [1]	MOTOR VEHICLE REGISTRATION
	$000,000	$000,000	'000,000	'000
1985	7,452	7,179	231,977	14,819
1986	7,377	7,243	236,331	15,336
1987	7,717	7,325	261,704	15,794
1988	7,778	7,291	263,635	16,336
1989	7,234	7,176	240,519	16,720
1990	6,875	6,737	239,807	16,981
1991	7,015	7,013	252,939	17,223
1992	6,748	7,013	243,662	17,412
1993	6,859	6,904	249,854	17,586
1994	7,370 (R)	7,021(R)	280,481(R)	17,794
1995	7,062	7,415	271,032	--

1. 7 major railways representing about 95% of the industry in terms of operating revenues and other performance indicators.

Sources: Statistics Canada, Catalogue 52-003 Railway Operating Statistics; Statistics Canada, Catalogue 53-219, Road Motor Vehicles

(R) Revised

GROWTH STATISTICS: FINANCIAL

	BANK OF CANADA NOTES IN CIRCULATION	CHARTERED BANKS [1] ASSETS	LIABILITIES EXCLUDING CAPITAL RESERVES	DEMAND DEPOSITS	NOTICE DEPOSITS	TOTAL LOANS	LIFE INSURANCE [2] NET AMOUNT LIFE INSURANCE IN FORCE DEC.31 [2]	FEDERAL FINANCE TOTAL GROSS REVENUE [3]	TOTAL GROSS EXPENDITURE [3]	NET DEBT [4]
	$000,000	$000,000	$000,000	$000,000	$000,000	$000,000	$000,000	$000,000	$000,000	$000,000
1985	16,672	443,761	423,555	19,267	164,149	308,767	693,310	78,055(R)	115,039	202,104(R)
1986	17,911	467,972	444,495	20,123	177,464	315,891	776,718	83,060	116,911	239,888
1987	19,447	486,384	463,038	22,532	192,910	332,846	833,013	90,145	120,826	270,873
1988	21,032	508,652	475,792	24,424	215,281	344,748	843,142	103,089	130,720	298,103
1989	22,093	550,939	522,339	24,526	248,031	382,785	923,359	109,506	136,334	326,484
1990	22,970	609,867	577,807	24,015	270,944	420,830	1,008,526	120,748	148,748	354,848
1991	24,481	635,912	599,518	35,082	146,211	437,916	1,078,607	127,112	158,971	386,785
1992	25,609	677,650	642,126	41,332	141,420	470,464	1,123,191	129,170	167,141	421,316
1993	27,237	753,992	716,795	46,016	142,085	507,394	1,123,619	132,210	171,405	461,685
1994	28,329	841,037(R)	799,284	51,370	140,282	550,444	1,234,746	129,365	171,039	503,766
1995	28,778	912,069	869,187	57,533	135,563	586,711	-- -- --	136,982(R)	174,216(R)	541,128(R)
1996								145,453(E)	177,703(E)	573,378(E)

1. As of December of each year
2. Compiled by the Office of the Superientendent of Financial Institutions Canada. Includes federally registered companies and societies. Does not include provincial companies and excludes annuities.
3. Fiscal Year ended March 31.
4. As at March 31.

Source: Bank of Canada

(R) Revised   (E) Estimate

GROWTH STATISTICS: INDUSTRIAL/TELEPHONE/POSTAL

	INDUSTRY PRODUCT PRICE INDEX FOR MANUFACTURING	INDUSTRIAL [R] AGGREGATE [1]	STRIKES AND LOCKOUTS EMPLOYEES AFFECTED	DAYS NOT WORKED	TOTAL TELEPHONE ACCESS LINES	REVENUE FROM POSTAL OPERATIONS [2]
	1986=100	$	'000	'000	'000	$000
1985	99.2				15,974	2,500,248
1986	100.0	425.16	484	7,152	12,948	2,757,674
1987	102.8	441.23	582	3,812	13,444	2,970,056
1988	107.2	460.67	207	4,899	13,976	3,138,552
1989	109.4	484.23	444	3,701	14,648	3,411,216
1990	109.7	506.24	271	5,079	15,296	3,579,843
1991	108.6	529.48	253	2,516	15,815	3,739,000
1992	109.1	547.98	149	2,109	16,247	3,921,000
1993	112.7	557.94	101	1,519	16,716	4,118,000
1994	119.2 (R)	568.27	81	1,606 (R)	17,250	4,748,000
1995	128.8	573.75	163	1,607	--	--

1. Average weekly Earnings (including overtime) for all employees (Canada)
2. Fiscal year ended March 31.

Sources: Statistics Canada, Catalogue 62-011 Industry Price Indexes; Annual Estimates of Employment, Earnings and Hours, Statistics Canada, Labour Division.; Human Resources Development Canada; Catalogue 56-203 Telephone Statistics; Statistics Canada, Public Institutions Division

(R) Revised

Canadian Almanac & Directory 1997

HISTORICAL STATISTICS

The following statistics are drawn from Canadian Almanacs from the year 1852 onward. Detailed statistics did not appear in the Almanac until the 1860s. The sampling below is meant to illustrate the basic topics of birth, death, marriage and faith, from just after Confederation to the period following the Second World War.

POPULATION FIGURES FROM THE 19TH CENTURY
From *Scobie's Canadian Almanac and Repository of Useful Knowledge for the Year 1852*

PROVINCE	1848	1850
Lower Canada	770,000	791,000
Upper Canada	725,000	791,000
TOTALS	1,495,000	1,582,000

THE RELATION BETWEEN POPULATION AND ACREAGE
From *The Canadian Almanac and Repository of Useful Knowledge for the Year 1868*

PROVINCE	Area in square miles (approx.)	Acres surveyed to Dec. 31, 1866	Acres disposed of by sale & free grants to Dec. 31, 1866	Population in Jan. 1861	Annual rate of increase between census of Jan. 1852 & Jan. 1861	Population in Jan. 1867 assuming the same rate of increase
Upper Canada	121,260	25,031,838	21,746,655	1,396,091	4.34%	1,802,037
Lower Canada	210,020	25,871,502	19,284,734	1,111,566	2.5%	1,288,884
TOTALS	331,280	50,903,340	41,031389	2,507,657	----	3,090,921

IMMIGRATION AT CONFEDERATION
From *The Canadian Almanac and Repository of Useful Knowledge for the Year 1868*

Whence	No. of Vessels	Cabin Passengers	Steerage Passengers	Births on Passage	Deaths on passage	Deaths in quarantine
England	58	1,247	5,994	1	7	----
Ireland	6	153	2,077	----	----	----
Scotland	14	164	2,059	----	1	----
Germany	11	----	3,408	15	83	10
Norway & Sweden	57	----	13,550	38	73	9
Other Countries	7	----	125	1	1	----

CANADIAN POPULATION & PERCENTAGE DISTRIBUTION BY PROVINCES & TERRITORIES, 1871 TO 1951 (CENSUS)

PROVINCE OR TERRITORY	1871	1881	1891	1901	1911	1921	1931	1941	1951
Newfoundland	----	----	----	----	----	----	----	----	361,416
%	----	----	----	----	----	----	----	----	2.58
Prince Edward Island	94,021	108,891	109,078	103,259	93,728	88,615	88,038	95,047	98,429
%	2.55	----	2.25	1.92	1.30	1.01	0.85	0.83	0.70
Nova Scotia	387,800	440,572	450,396	459,574	492,338	523,837	512,846	577,962	642,584
%	10.51	----	9.32	8.56	6.83	5.96	4.94	5.02	4.59
New Brunswick	285,594	321,233	321,263	331,120	351,889	387,876	408,219	457,401	515,697
%	7.74	----	6.65	6.16	4.88	4.41	3.94	3.97	3.68
Québec	1,191,516	1,359,027	1,488,535	1,648,898	2,003,232	2,360,665	2,874,255	3,331,882	4,055,681
%	32.30	----	30.80	30.70	27.83	26.86	27.70	28.96	28.95
Ontario	1,620,851	1,926,922	2,114,321	2,182,947	2,523,274	2,933,662	3,431,683	3,787,655	4,597,542
%	43.94	----	43.74	40.64	35.07	33.39	33.07	32.92	32.82
Manitoba	25,228	62,260	152,506	255,211	455,614	610,118	700,139	729,744	776,541
%	0.68	----	3.16	4.75	6.40	6.94	6.75	6.34	5.54
Saskatchewan	----	----	----	91,279	492,432	757,510	921,785	895,992	831,728
%	----	----	----	1.70	6.84	8.62	8.88	7.79	5.94
Alberta	----	----	----	73,022	374,663	588,454	731,605	796,169	939,501
%	----	----	----	1.36	5.19	6.70	7.05	6.92	6.71
British Columbia	36,247	49,459	98,173	178,657	392,480	524,582	694,263	817,861	1,165,210
%	0.98	----	2.03	3.33	5.45	5.97	6.69	7.11	8.32
Yukon	----	----	----	27,219	8,512	4,157	4,230	4,914	9,096
%	----	----	----	0.51	0.12	0.05	0.04	0.04	0.06
Northwest Territories	48,000	56,446	98,967	20,129	18,481	7,988	9,723	12,028	16,004
%	1.30	----	2.05	0.37	0.09	0.09	0.09	0.10	0.11
TOTALS	3,689,257	4,324,810	4,833,239	5,371,315	7,206,643	8,787,949	10,376,786	11,506,655	14,009,429

Canadian Almanac & Directory 1997

BIRTH & DEATH RATES, CANADA, 1933

PROVINCE	LIVE BIRTHS Number	LIVE BIRTHS Rate	DEATHS Number	DEATHS Rate	INFANT DEATHS Rate
Alberta	16,009	21.1	5,328	7.0	60.3
British Columbia	9,552	13.4	6,210	8.7	45.9
Manitoba	13,304	18.4	5,455	7.6	63.4
New Brunswick	10,037	23.9	4,908	11.7	81.8
Nova Scotia	11,120	21.3	6,022	11.5	71.1
Ontario	63,597	18.0	35,293	10.0	59.8
Prince Edward Island	1,946	21.9	1,032	11.6	60.6
Québec	76,920	25.9	31,636	10.7	94.5
Saskatchewan	20,119	21.2	6,017	6.3	61.1
TOTALS	222,604	20.9	101,901	9.6	73.1

All Rates are per 1,000 (live births, population).

BIRTH & DEATH RATES, CANADA, 1963

PROVINCE	LIVE BIRTHS Number	LIVE BIRTHS Rate	DEATHS Number	DEATHS Rate	INFANT DEATHS Rate
Alberta	38,467	27.4	9,444	6.7	24
British Columbia	37,478	22.1	15,029	8.9	23
Manitoba	22,751	23.9	7,928	8.3	25
New Brunswick	15,771	25.7	4,815	7.8	28
Newfoundland	15,443	32.1	3,183	6.6	38
Northwest Territories	1,161	48.4	266	11.1	104
Nova Scotia	18,976	25.1	6,367	8.4	27
Ontario	155,089	24.1	53,617	8.3	23
Prince Edward Island	2,949	27.6	979	9.1	21
Québec	133,640	24.4	38,217	7.0	30
Saskatchewan	23,543	25.2	7,441	8.0	27
Yukon	499	33.3	81	5.4	32

All Rates are per 1,000 (live births, population).

CANADA'S "CONJUGAL CONDITION" Or, the Birth of Divorce, 1871-1911

CLASSES	SEX	1871	1881	1891	1901	1911
Sex	Male	1,764,311	2,188,854	2,460,471	2,751,708	3,821,995
	Female	1,721,450	2,135,956	2,372,768	2,619,607	3,384,648
	Total	3,485,761	4,324,810	4,833,239	5,371,315	7,206,643
Single	Male	1,183,787	1,447,414	1,601,541	1,748,582	2,369,766
	Female	1,099,216	1,336,982	1,451,851	1,564,011	1,941,886
	Total	2,283,003	2,784,396	3,053,392	3,312,593	4,311,652
Married	Male	543,037	690,544	796,153	928,952	1,331,853
	Female	542,339	689,540	791,902	904,091	1,251,468
	Total	1,085,376	1,380,084	1,588,055	1,833,043	2,583,321
Widowed	Male	37,487	50,895	62,777	73,837	89,154
	Female	79,895	109,435	129,015	151,181	179,656
	Total	117,382	160,330	191,792	225,018	268,810
Divorced	Male	----	----	----	337	839
	Female	----	----	----	324	691
	Total	----	----	----	661	1,530

COMMERCIAL FAILURES, BEFORE, DURING AND AFTER THE GREAT DEPRESSION

PROVINCES	1927	1929	1932	1936	1938	1941	1943
Alberta	62	68	89	53	24	24	1
British Columbia	112	40	193	40	7	18	8
Manitoba	201	124	170	90	56	43	8
New Brunswick	42	37	72	16	26	18	3
Nova Scotia	65	45	76	36	27	21	4
Ontario	648	437	879	432	245	200	42
P.E.I.	4	0	5	8	2	6	0
Québec	729	636	1,352	526	337	449	100
Saskatchewan	130	74	132	37	35	103	20

POPULATION OF CANADA BY RELIGIONS [1]			
Religions	Census 1931	Census 1921	Census 1911
Adventists	16,026	14,179	10,406
Anglicans	1,635,615	1,407,780	1,043,017
Baptists	443,341	421,730	382,720
Brethren	13,472	11,580	9,278
Buddhists	15,784	11,281	10,012
Christians	11,527	17,142	17,421
Christian Science	18,436	13,826	5,073
Church of Christ Disciples	15,811	13,107	14,554
Confucians	24,087	27,114	14,562
Congregationalists	694	30,730	34,054
Doukhobors	14,913	12,648	10,493
Evangelical Association	22,213	13,905	10,595
Greek Orthodox[2]	102,389	169,832	88,507
Intl. Bible Students Assn.	13,552	6,678	925
Jews	155,614	125,197	74,564
Lutherans	394,194	286,458	229,864
Mennonites & Hutterites	88,736	58,797	44,625
Methodists	[3]	1,159,246	1,079,993
Mormons	22,005	19,622	15,971
No Religion	21,071	21,739	26,027
Pentecostal	26,301	7,003	513
Presbyterians	870,728	1,409,406	1,116,071
Protestants	23,296	30,753	30,265
Roman Catholic[4]	4,285,388	3,389,626	2,833,041
Salvation Army	30,716	24,733	18,834
United Church	2,017,375	8,728	
Not stated	16,042	19,259	32,490
Pagans	5,008	6,778	11,840
All other sects	72,452	49,072	40,928
TOTAL POPULATION	10,376,786	8,787,949	7,206,643

1. This table lists denominations with over 10,000 adherents.
2. Greek Orthodox and Greek Catholic combined under the term "Greek Church" in 1921. In the 1931 Census, Greek Catholics are included with Roman Catholics.
3. Included in "United Church of Canada."
4. Includes 186,654 Greek Catholics.

WEIGHTS & MEASURES

THE INTERNATIONAL SYSTEM OF UNITS (SI) (BASE & SUPPLEMENTARY UNITS)

With the permission of the Canadian Standards Association, material is reproduced from CSA Standard CAN/CSA-Z234.1-89 (Canadian Metric Prqactice Guide), which is copyrighted by CSA, 178 Rexdale Blvd., Etobicoke, ON M9W 1R3. While use of this material has been authorized, CSA shall not be responsible for the manner in which the information is presented, nor for any interpretations thereof.

BASE UNITS

The International System of Units includes two classes of units: seven base units, and derived units. The base units are seven precisely defined units used internationally for teaching and scientific research.

SI BASE UNITS		
Quantity	Name	Symbol
length	metre	m
mass	kilogram	kg
time	second	s
electric current	ampere	A
thermodynamic temperature	kelvin	K
amount of substance	mole	mol
luminous intensity	candela	cd

SI PREFIXES		
Multiplying Factor	Prefix	Symbol
$1\ 000\ 000\ 000\ 000\ 000\ 000 = 10^{18}$	exa	E
$1\ 000\ 000\ 000\ 000\ 000 = 10^{15}$	peta	P
$1\ 000\ 000\ 000\ 000 = 10^{12}$	tera	T
$1\ 000\ 000\ 000 = 10^{9}$	giga	G
$1\ 000\ 000 = 10^{6}$	mega	M
$1\ 000 = 10^{3}$	kilo	k
$100 = 10^{2}$	hecto	h
$10 = 10^{1}$	deca	da
$0.1 = 10^{-1}$	deci	d
$0.01 = 10^{-2}$	centi	c
$0.001 = 10^{-3}$	milli	m
$0.000\ 001 = 10^{-6}$	micro	μ
$0.000\ 000\ 001 = 10^{-9}$	nano	n
$0.000\ 000\ 000\ 001 = 10^{-12}$	pico	p
$0.000\ 000\ 000\ 000\ 001 = 10^{-15}$	femto	f
$0.000\ 000\ 000\ 000\ 000\ 001 = 10^{-18}$	atto	a

SI Prefixes and their symbols given in the above table are used to form names and symbols of decimal multiples or sub-multiples of SI units.

SI DERIVED UNITS WITH SPECIAL NAMES

Name	Symbol	Typical Form[1]	In Base Units	Quantity
becquerel	Bq	s^{-1}	s^{-1}	activity of radionuclides
coulomb	C	s•A	s•A	quantity of electricity, electric charge
degree Celsius	°C	K	K	Celsius Temperature [2]
farad	F	C/V	$m^{-2}•kg^{-1}•s^4•A^2$	electric capacitance
gray	Gy	J/kg	$m^2•s^{-2}$	absorbed dose of ionizing radiation
henry	H	Wb/A	$m^2•kg•s^{-2}•A^{-2}$	inductance
hertz	Hz	s^{-1}	s^{-1}	frequency [3]
joule	J	N•m	$m^2•kg•s^{-2}$	energy, work, quantity of heat
lumen	lm	cd•sr	cd	luminous flux
lux	lx	lm/m^2	$m^{-2}•cd$	illuminance
newton	N	$m•kg/s^2$	$m•kg•s^{-2}$	force
ohm	Ω	V/A	$m^2•kg•s^{-3}•A^{-2}$	electric resistance
pascal	Pa	N/m^2	$m^{-1}•kg•s^{-2}$	pressure, stress
radian	rad	m/m	$m•m^{-1} = 1$	plane angle
siemens	S	A/V	$m^{-2}•kg^{-1}•s^3•A^2$	electric conductance
sievert	Sv	J/kg	$m^2•s^{-2}$	dose equivalent of ionizing radiation
steradian	sr	m^2/m^2	$m^2•m^{-2} = 1$	solid angle
tesla	T	Wb/m^2	$kg•s^{-2}•A^{-1}$	magnetic flux density
volt	V	W/A	$m^2•kg•s^{-3}•A^{-1}$	electric potential, potential difference, electromotive force
watt	W	J/s	$m^2•kg•s^{-3}$	power, radiant flux
weber	Wb	V•s	$m^2•kg•s^{-2}•A^{-1}$	magnetic flux

1. The formulae for derived units are not necessarily unique. For example, the volt may be defined as one joule per coulomb.
2. The Celsius temperature scale (previously called Centigrade, but renamed to avoid confusion with "centigrade", associated with the centesimal system of angular measurement) is the commonly used scale, except for certain scientific and technological purposes where the thermodynamic temperature scale is preferred. Note the use of uppercase C for Celsius.
3. The SI unit of frequency, the hertz, is one cycle per second. The reciprocal of the frequency is the period. The hertz should not be used as a measure of discrete items per unit of time, e.g. 5 boxes per second on an assembly line would not be referred to as 5 hertz, but may be referred to in terms of the reciprocal second i.e. $5s^{-1}$.

EXAMPLE OF SI DERIVED UNITS WITHOUT SPECIAL NAMES

Name	Typical Form	In Base Units	Quantity
ampere per metre	A/m	$A•m^{-1}$	magnetic field strength
ampere per square metre	A/m^2	$A•m^{-2}$	current density
candela per square metre	cd/m^2	$cd•m^{-2}$	luminance
coulomb per cubic metre	C/m^3	$m^{-3}•s•A$	electric charge density
coulomb per kilogram	C/kg	$A•s•kg^{-1}$	exposure
coulomb per square metre	C/m^2	$m^{-2}•s•A$	surface density of charge, flux density
cubic metre	m^3	m^3	volume
cubic metre per kilogram	m^3/kg	$m^3•kg^{-1}$	specific volume
farad per metre	F/m	$m^{-3}•kg^{-1}•s^4•A^2$	permittivity
gray per second	Gy/s	$m^2•s^{-3}$	absorbed dose rate
henry per metre	H/m	$m•kg•s^{-2}•A^{-2}$	permeability
joule per cubic metre	J/m^3	$m^{-1}•kg•s^{-2}$	energy density
joule per kelvin	J/K	$m^2•kg•s^{-2}•K^{-1}$	heat capacity, entropy
joule per kilogram kelvin	J/(kg•K)	$m^2•s^{-2}•K^{-1}$	specific heat capacity, specific entropy
joule per kilogram	J/kg	$m^2•s^{-2}$	specific energy
joule per mole	J/mol	$m^2•kg•s^{-2}•mol^{-1}$	molar energy
joule per mole kelvin	J/(mol•K)	$m^2•kg•s^{-2}•K^{-1}•mol^{-1}$	molar entropy, molar heat capacity
kilogram per cubic metre	kg/m^3	$kg•m^{-3}$	density, mass density
metre per second	m/s	$m•s^{-1}$	speed - linear
metre per second squared	m/s^2	$m•s^{-2}$	acceleration - linear
mole per cubic metre	mol/m^3	$mol•m^{-3}$	concentration (of amount of substance)
newton metre	N•m	$m^2•kg•s^{-2}$	moment of force
newton per metre	N/m	$kg•s^{-2}$	surface tension
pascal second	Pa•s	$m^{-1}•kg•s^{-1}$	dynamic viscosity
radian per second	rad/s	s^{-1}	- angular
radian per second squared	rad/s^2	s^{-2}	- angular
reciprocal metre	m^{-1}	m^{-1}	wave number*
square metre	m^2	m^2	area
square metre per second	m^2/s	$m^2•s^{-1}$	kinematic viscosity
volt per metre	V/m	$m•kg•s^{-3}•A^{-1}$	electric field strength
watt per metre kelvin	W/(m•K)	$m•kg•s^{-3}•K^{-1}$	thermal conductivity
watt per square metre	W/m^2	$kg•s^{-3}$	heat flux density, irradiance
watt per square metre steradian	$W/(m^2•sr)$	$kg•s^{-3}$	radiance
watt per steradian	W/sr	$m^2•kg•s^{-3}$	radiant intensity

Canadian Almanac & Directory 1997

WEIGHTS & MEASURES

UNITS PERMITTED FOR USE WITH THE SI

Quantity	Name	Symbol	Definition [1]
time	minute	min	1 min = **60** s [2]
	hour	h	1 h = **3600** s [2]
	day	d	1 d = **86 400** s [2]
	year	a	
plane angle	degree	°	1° = (π/**180**) rad [3]
	minute	'	1' = (π/**10 800**) rad [3]
	second	"	1" = (π/**648 000**) rad [3]
	revolution	r	1 r = **2π** rad [4]
area	hectare	ha	1 ha = **1** hm² = **10 000** m² [5]
volume	litre	L	1 L = **1** dm³ [6]
mass	metric ton or tonne	t	1 t = **1000** kg [7] = **1** Mg
linear density	tex	tex	1 tex = **1 x 10⁻⁶** kg/m [8]
energy	electronovolt	eV	* [9]
mass of atom	unified atomic mass unit	u	* [10]
length	astronomical unit parsec	pc	* [11, 12]

1. Conversion factors that are exact are shown in boldface.
2. These sysmbols are used only in the sense of duration of time & not for expressing the time of day.
3. No space is left between these symbols & the last digit of a number. The unit "degree", with its decimal subdivisions, is used when the unit "radian" is not suitable.
4. The designations revolution per minute (r/min) and revolution per second (r/s) are widely used in connection with rotating machinery.
5. Because of the need for a unit similar to the acre, the hectare will continue to be recognized as a unit for use in surveying & agriculture.
6. The international symbol for litre is L or l. In order to avoid possible confusion with the number one, the "L" is preferred in Canada.
7. Care must be taken in the interpretation of the word "tonne" when it occurs in French text of Canadian origin, where the meaning may be a "ton of 2000 pounds".
8. The tex is used only in the textile industry.
9. One electronvolt is the kinetic energy acquired by an electron in passing through a potential difference of 1V in vacuum.
10. The unified atomic mass unit is equal to the fraction 1/12 of the mass of an atom of the nuclide ^{12}C.
11. The astronomical symbol does not have an international symbol; abbreviations are used (e.g. AU in English, UA in French). The astronomical unit of distance is the length of the radius of the unperturbed circular orbit of a body of negligible mass moving around the sun with a sidereal angular velocity of 0.017 202 098 950 radian per day of 86 400 ephemeris seconds.
12. 1 parsec (pc) is the distance at which 1 astronomical unit subtends an angle of 1 second of arc.

CONVERSION OF UNITS TO THE INTERNATIONAL SYSTEM OF UNITS (SI)

Area
1 acre	=0.404 685 6 ha
1 arpent (French measure)*	=0.341 889 4 ha
1 circular mil	=506.7 x 10-6 m²
1 legal subdivision (40 acres)	=0.161 874 2 km²
1 perch (French measure)*	=34.188 94 m²
1 rood (1210 square yards)	=0.101 171 4 ha
1 section (1 mile square, 640 acres)	=2.589 988 km²
1 square foot	=929.030 4 cm²
1 square foot (French measure)*	=1 055.214 cm²
1 square inch	=645.16 mm²
1 square mile	=2.589 988 km²
1 square yard	=0.836 127 4 m²
1 township (36 sections)	=93.239 57 km²

* Measures formerly used to describe certain land in the Province of Québec

Energy
1 British thermal unit (Btu) (International Table)	= 1.055 056 kJ
1 British thermal unit (Btu) (mean)	= 1.055 87 kJ
1 British thermal unit (Btu) (thermochemical)	= 1.054 35 kJ
1 British thermal unit (Btu) (39° F)	= 1.059 67 kJ
1 British thermal unit (Btu) (59° F, 15° C)	= 1.054 80 kJ
1 British thermal unit (Btu) (60.5° F)	= 1.054 615 kJ
1 Calorie (dietetic)	= 4.185 5 kJ
1 calorie (International Table)	= 4.186 8 J
1 calorie (thermochemical)	= 4.184 J
1 calorie (15° C)	= 4.185 5 J
1 calorie (15° C)	= 4.185 8 J
1 electronovolt	= 0.160 217 7 aJ
1 erg	= 0.1 μJ
1 foot poundal	= 42.140 11 mJ
1 foot pound-force	= 1.355 818 J
1 horsepower hour	= 2.684 520 MJ
1 kilowatt hour	= 3.6 MJ
1 therm	= 105.506 MJ
1 ton (nuclear equivalent of TNT)	= 4.2 GJ
1 watt hour	= 3.6 kJ
1 watt second	= 1 J

Force
1 dyne	=10 μN
1 kilogram-force	= 9.806 65 N
1 kilopond	= 9.806 65 N
1 kip (thousand pounds force)	= 4.448 222 kN
1 ounce-force	= 0.278 013 9 N
1 poundal	= 0.138 255 0 N
1 pound-force	= 4.448 222 N

Length
1 angstrom	=0.1 nm
1 arpent (French measure)*	=58.471 31 m
1 astronomical unit	=149.597 870 Gm
1 chain (66 feet)	=20.116 8 m
1 ell (45 inches)	=1.143 m
1 fathom	=1.828 8 m
1 fermi	=1 fm
1 foot	=0.304 8 m
1 foot (French measure)*	=0.324 840 6 m
1 foot (US survey, limited usage)	=0.304 800 6 m
1 furlong	=0.201 168 km
1 inch	=25.4 mm
1 league (Intl. nautical)	=5.556 km
1 league (UK nautical)	=5.559 552 km
1 league (US)	=4.828 032 km
1 light year	=9.460 528 Pm
1 link (1/100 chain)	=0.201 168 m
1 microinch	=25.4 nm
1 micron	=1 μm
1 mil (0.001 inch)	=25.4 μm
1 mile	=1.609 344 km
1 mile (Intl. nautical)	=1.852 km
1 mile (UK nautical)	=1.853 184 km
1 mile (US nautical)	=1.852 km
1 parsec	=30.856 78 Pm
1 perch	=5.029 2 m
1 perch (French measure)*	=5.847 130 8 m
1 pica (printers)	=4.217 518 mm
1 point (printers)	=0.351 459 8 mm
1 pole	=5.029 2 m
1 rod	=5.029 2 m
1 yard	=0.914 4 m

Mass
1 carat	=200 mg
1 cental (100 lb)	=45.359 237 kg
1 coal tub (100 lb, Newfoundland)	=45.359 237 kg
1 drachm (apothecary)	=3.887 935 g
1 dram (apothecary, US)	=3.887 935 g
1 dram (avoirdupois)	=1.771 845 g
1 gamma	=1 μg
1 grain	=64.798 91 mg
1 hundredweight (100 lb)	=45.359 237 kg
1 hundredweight (long 112 lb, UK)	=50.802 35 kg
1 ounce (avoirdupois)	=28.349 523 g
1 ounce (troy or apothecary)	=31.103 476 8 g
1 metric carat	=200 mg
1 pennyweight	=1.555 174 g
1 pound (avoirdupois)	=0.453 592 37 kg
1 pound (troy or apothecary)	=373.241 721 6 g
1 quarter (28 lb, UK)	=12.700 58 kg
1 scruple (apothecary, 20 grains)	=1.295 978 g
1 slug	=14.593 90 kg
1 stone (14 lb, UK)	=6.350 293 kg
1 ton (2240 lb, UK)	=1.016 046 908 8 Mg
1 ton (short, 2000 lb)	=0.907 184 74 Mg
1 unified atomic mass	=1.660 540 x 10-27 kg

Power
1 Btu (IT) per hour	=0.293 071 1 W
1 Btu (thermochemical) per hour	=0.292 875 1 W
1 Btu (thermochemical) per minute	=17.572 50 W
1 Btu (thermochemical) per second	=1.054 350 kW
1 foot pound-force per hour	=0.376 616 1 mW
1 foot pound-force per minute	=22.596 97 mW
1 foot pound-force per second	=1.355 818 W

1 horsepower (boiler)	=9.809 50 kW
1 horsepower (electric)	=746 W
1 horsepower (metric, cheval vapeur)	=735.498 75 W
1 horsepower (water)	=746.043 W
1 horsepower (550 ft•lbf/s)	=745.699 9 W

Pressure or Stress (Force per Area)

1 atmosphere, standard	=101.325 kPa (=760 torr)
1 atmosphere, technical	=98.066 5 kPa (=1 kgf/cm^2)
1 bar	=100 kPa
1 foot of water (39.2° F, 4° C)	=2.988 98 kPa
1 inch of mercury (conventional 32° F)	=3.386 39 kPa
1 inch of mercury (60° F)	=3.376 85 kPa
1 inch of mercury (68° F, 20° C)	=3.374 11 kPa
1 inch of water (conventional)	=249.088 9 Pa
1 inch of water (39.2° F, 4° C)	=249.082 Pa
1 inch of water (60° F)	=248.843 Pa
1 inch of water (68° F, 20° C)	=248.641 Pa
1 ksi (1000 lbf/in2)	=6.894 757 MPa
1 poundal /square foot	=1.488 164 Pa
1 pound-force/square foot	=47.880 26 Pa
1 pound-force/square inch (psi)	=6.894 757 kPa
1 ton-force/square inch	=13.789 514 MPa
1 ton-force (UK)/square inch	=15.444 3 MPa
1 torr	=133.322 4 Pa

Temperature

Celsius temperature	= temperature in kelvins − 273.15
Fahrenheit temperature	= 1.8 (Celsius temperature) + 32
Fahrenheit temperature	= 1.8 (temperature in kelvins) − 459.67
Rankine temperature	= 1.8 (temperature in kelvins)

Velocity (Speed)

1 foot per hour	=84.666 67 µm/s =304.8 mm/h
1 foot per minute	=5.08 mm/s =304.8 mm/min
1 foot per second	=304.8 mm/s
1 inch per minute	=25.4 mm/min
1 inch per second	=25.4 mm/s
1 knot (International)	=1.852 km/h =0.514 444 4 m/s
1 knot (UK)	=1.853 184 km/h
1 mile per hour	=0.447 04 m/s =1.609 344 km/h
1 mile per minute	=26.822 4 m/s

Volume

1 acre foot	=1233.482 m^3
1 barrel (oil, 42 US gallons)	=0.158 987 3 m^3
1 barrel (US dry, 7056 in^3	=0.115 627 1 m^3
1 barrel	=95.471 03 dm^3
(US dry, cranberries, 5826 in^3	
1 barrel (36 UK gallons)	=0.163 659 2 m^3
1 board foot [a]	=2.359 737 dm^3
1 bushel	=36.368 72 dm^3
1 bushel (US dry, 2150.42 in^3	=35.239 07 dm^3
1 cord	=3.624 556 m^3
(128 ft^3, 4 ft x 4 ft x 8 ft, stacked wood)	
1 cubic foot	=28.316 85 dm^3
1 cubic inch	=16.387 064 cm^3
1 cubic yard	=0.764 554 9 m^3
1 cunit (100 ft^3, solid wood)	=2.831 685 m^3
1 cup	=250 cm^3
1 demiard	=0.284 130 6 dm^3
1 drop (1/100 teaspoon)	=0.05 cm^3
1 fluid dram	=3.551 633 cm^3
1 fluid dram (US measure)	=3.696 691 cm^3
1 fluid ounce	=28.413 062 cm^3
1 fluid ounce (US)	=29.573 53 cm^3
1 gallon	=4.546 09 dm^3
1 gallon (US)	=3.785 412 dm^3
1 gill	=0.142 065 dm^3
1 gill (US)	=0.118 294 dm^3
1 herring barrel	=145.474 9 dm^3
1 herring tub	=72.737 44 dm^3
1 hogshead	=245.488 9 dm^3
a lambda	=1 mm^3
1 minim	=59.193 9 mm^3
1 minim (US)	=61.611 52 mm^3
1 peck	=9.092 180 dm^3
1 peck (US dry)	=8.809 768 dm^3
1 Petrograd standard (165 ft^3, sawn timber)	=4.672 280 m^3
1 pint	=0.568 261 2 dm^3
1 pint (US dry)	=0.550 610 5 dm^3
1 pint (US liquid)	=0.473 176 5 dm^3
1 quart	=1.136 522 dm^3
1 quart (US dry)	=1.101 221 dm^3
1 quart (US liquid)	=0.946 352 9 dm^3
1 salt cart	=490.977 7 dm^3
1 salt tub	=81.829 62 dm^3
1 sand barrel	=81.829 62 dm^3
1 tablespoon	=15 cm^3
1 teaspoon	=5 cm^3
1 ton (register)	=2.831 685 m^3

a. The board foot is nominally 1x12x12 = 144 in^3. However, the actual volume of wood is about 2/3 of the nominal quality.
b. This applies to stacked wood, comprising wood, bark, & airspace, to a total volume of 128 ft^3.
c. Also referred to as the "imperial gallon".

MEASURES HAVING FORMER HOUSEHOLD USAGE

1 cup (Canadian, 8 fluid ounces)	=227 cm^3
1 cup (US, 8 fluid ounces)	=236 cm^3
1 cup (UK, 10 fluid ounces)	=284 cm^3
1 tablespoon =14.21 cm^3 (Canadian, 1/2 fluid ounce)	
1 tablespoon (UK, 5/8 fluid ounce)	=17.8 cm^3
1 tablespoon (US, 1/2 fluid ounce)	=14.8 cm^3
1 teaspoon (1/6 fluid ounce)	=4.74 cm^3
1 teaspoon (UK, 5/24 fluid ounce)	=5.92 cm^3
1 teaspoon (US, 1/6 fluid ounce)	=4.93 cm^3
*1 cm^3	=1 ml

LAND & FRESHWATER AREAS OF CANADA

Province or Territory	Land (km^2)	Freshwater (km^2)	Total Area (km^2)	Percentage of Total Area
Newfoundland	371,690	34,030	405,720	4.1
Island of Newfoundland*	105,700	5,690	111,390	1.1
Prince Edward Island	5,660	—	5,660	0.1
Nova Scotia	52,840	2,650	55,490	0.6
New Brunswick	72,090	1,350	73,440	0.7
Québec	1,356,790	183,890	1,540,680	15.5
Ontario	891,190	177,390	1,068,580	10.7
Manitoba	548,360	101,590	649,950	6.5
Saskatchewan	570,700	81,630	652,330	6.5
Alberta	644,390	16,800	661,190	6.6
British Columbia	929,730	18,070	947,800	9.5
Yukon Territory	478,970	4,480	483,450	4.8
Northwest Territories	3,293,020	133,300	3,426,320	34.4
Districts of Franklin *	1,423,560	19,430	1,442,990	14.5
Keewatin *	575,470	25,120	600,590	6.0
Mackenzie *	1,293,990	88,750	1,382,740	13.9
Canada	9,215,430	755,180	9,970,610	100.0

*Indicates portion of total.

Canadian Almanac & Directory 1997

CANADIAN HERITAGE — NAVIGATION CANALS

Name	Location	Length of Channel (km)	Locks No.	Minimum Dimensions Length (m)	Width (m)	Depth (m)
Atlantic Area						
St. Peters	St. Peter's Bay to Bras d'Or Lakes, Cape Breton, NS	0.80	1	91.44	14.45	4.88
Richelieu River						
St-Ours	St. Ours, PQ	0.10	1	99.6	13.41	3.66
Chambly	Chambly to St-Jean, PQ	18.96	9	33.52	6.70	1.98
Ottawa & Rideau/Cataraqui Rivers						
Ste-Anne-de-Bellevue	Junction of St. Lawrence & Ottawa River	0.19	1	54.86	12.9	2.74
Carillon	Carillon Rapids, Ottawa River	0.8	1	54.86	12.9	2.7**
Rideau	Ottawa to Kingston	202.0	45	27.4	8.5	1.22**
	Lower Rideau Lake to Perth (Tay Br.)	10.0	2	27.4	8.5	1.22**
Lake Ontario to Georgian Bay						
Trent-Severn Waterway	Trenton to Rice Lake	91.7	18	46.9	9.75	2.4
	Rice Lake to Kirkfield	180.8	15	31.4	9.75	1.8
	Kirkfield to Gamebridge	18.31	5	36.5	9.75	1.8
	Gamebridge to Port Severn	96.3	5	25.6	7.0	1.8
	Sturgeon Lake to Lindsay (Scugog Br.)	29.19	1	36.5	9.75	1.2
	Lindsay to Port Perry (Scugog Br.)	42.9	—	—	—	1.2
Murray	Lake Ontario to Bay of Quinte	12.1	—	—	—	2.9

Vessels drawing > 1.5 m must contact the TSW Peterborough (705/742-9267)
Overhead clearance 6.7 m
* Marine railway lift 17.3 m
** Vessels drawing > 1.22 m or with larger dimensions than above, are advised to contact the Rideau Canal (Superintendent, 613/283-5170)

FACTORS GOVERNING THE TRANSIT OF VESSELS THROUGH THE ST. LAWRENCE SEAWAY LOCKS, CANALS & CHANNELS BETWEEN MONTRÉAL & LAKE ERIE

Channel widths vary from a minimum of 61 m between bridge abutments & canals flanked by two embankments, to at least 137 m in open reaches.
Minimum vertical overhead clearance of structures & cables crossing the Seaway is 36 m above high water.

MAXIMUM VESSEL DIMENSIONS

Length   222.50 m overall
Beam   23.15 m extreme breadth excluding permanent fenders

The channels & canals in the deep waterway between Port of Montréal & Lake Erie are designed to a minimum controlling depth of 8.23 m.
In the Seaway canals the maximum permitted draught will be currently prescribed by the St. Lawrence Seaway Authority & the St. Lawrence Seaway Development Corporation.
The present maximum permissible draught is 79.5 dm.

Lock	Normal Lift in Metres	Useable Length in Metres	Width in Metres	Useable Length Lower Ent. in Metres	Useable Length Upper Ent. in Metres
St-Lambert (Montréal Harbour)	4.5	222.5	24.38	653	458
Côte Ste-Catherine	10.0	222.5	24.38	319	318
Lower Beauharnois	12.2	222.5	24.38	379	503
Upper Beauharnois	11.3	222.5	24.38	503	575
Snell	14.0	222.5	24.38	449	212
Eisenhower	11.8	222.5	24.38	210	330
Iroquois	0.2	222.5	24.38	236	671

Minimum depth on Lock Gate Sills is 9.14 m.

WELLAND CANAL LOCKS

Lock No.	Type	Useable Length in Metres	Width in Metres	Normal Lift in Metres	Mileage From Port Weller (Nautical Miles)*	Useable Length Lower Ent. in Metres	Useable Length Upper Ent. in Metres
1	Single	222.5	24.38	14	1.7	840	448
2	Single	222.5	24.38	14	3.2	458	507
3	Single	222.5	24.38	14	5.5	445	459
4	Double	222.5	24.38	15	6.8	223	—
5	Double	222.5	24.38	15	6.8	—	—
6	Double	222.5	24.38	13	6.8	—	—
7	Single	222.5	24.38	14	7.5	306	601
8	Single	350.0	24.38	2	21.3	342	382.5

*Distances are shown in nautical miles in keeping with an international maritime agreement. One nautical mile equals 1.852 km.

CLIMATE

Temperature Data for Representative Stations in Canada
Temperature in Degrees Celsius

Station (Airport)	Elevation (metres)	Annual	Jan.	Apr.	July	Oct.	Extreme Max.*	Extreme Min.* (m)	Last in Spring	First in Fall
Newfoundland:										
St. John's	140	4.8	-3.9	1.2	15.5	6.9	30.6	-23.3	June 1	Oct. 11
Prince Edward Island:										
Charlottetown Int.	55	5.4	-7.1	2.3	18.3	8.1	34.4	-28.1	May 16	Oct. 15
Nova Scotia:										
Halifax Int.	145	6.1	-6.0	3.3	18.2	8.6	34.5	-26.1	May 12	Oct. 15
Sydney	62	5.7	-4.7	2.0	17.7	8.4	35.0	-25.6	May 23	Oct. 14
Yarmouth	43	6.9	-2.7	4.7	16.3	9.5	30.0	-21.1	May 2	Oct. 21
New Brunswick:										
Chatham	34	4.8	-9.7	3.0	19.2	7.1	37.8	-35.0	May 19	Sept. 23
Fredericton	20	5.4	-9.2	4.1	19.3	7.5	37.2	-37.2	May 19	Sept. 23
St. John	109	5.0	-7.8	3.2	16.9	7.6	34.5	-36.7	May 16	Oct. 3
Quebec:										
Arvida	102	3.0	-15.0	2.9	18.4	6.1	35.6	-41.7	May 21	Sept. 20
Montréal Int. (Dorval)	36	6.2	-10.2	5.7	20.9	8.7	37.8	-37.8	May 3	Oct. 8
Point au Pere	8	3.1	-11.1	1.7	16.1	5.6	32.2	-36.1	May 22	Sept. 26
Québec	73	4.1	-12.1	3.3	19.1	6.6	32.0	-36.1	May 13	Sept. 28
Schefferville	522	-4.8	-22.8	-7.2	12.6	-1.4	31.7	-50.6	June 17	Sept. 3
Sherbrooke	241	4.0	-11.7	3.6	17.8	6.6	33.3	-40.0	June 2	Sept. 10
Ontario:										
Kapuskasing	226	0.5	-18.6	0.5	16.8	4.4	36.7	-44.4	May 10	Sept. 2
London	278	7.3	-6.6	6.4	20.3	9.4	36.7	-31.7	May 10	Oct. 5
Ottawa Int.	114	5.7	-10.9	5.6	20.6	8.1	37.8	-36.1	May 7	Oct. 2
Thunder Bay	199	2.3	-15.4	2.5	17.6	5.7	37.2	-41.1	May 30	Sept. 12
Toronto Int.	173	7.3	-6.7	6.2	20.6	9.3	38.3	-31.1	May 8	Oct. 5
Manitoba:										
Churchill	29	-7.2	-27.5	-10.1	11.8	-1.5	33.9	-45.4	June 24	Sept. 9
The Pas	271	-0.6	-22.7	0.0	17.7	3.6	36.7	-49.4	May 24	Sept. 17
Winnipeg Int.	239	2.2	-19.3	3.4	19.6	6.1	40.6	-45.0	May 23	Sept. 22
Saskatchewan:										
Prince Albert	428	0.1	-21.5	1.9	17.4	3.7	37.8	-50.0	June 1	Sept. 5
Regina	577	2.2	-17.9	3.3	18.9	5.2	43.3	-50.0	May 24	Sept. 11
Alberta:										
Beaverlodge CDA	732	1.6	-15.9	2.6	15.2	4.4	36.7	-47.8	May 24	Sept. 7
Calgary Int.	1,084	3.4	-11.8	3.3	16.4	5.5	36.1	-45.0	May 25	Sept. 15
Edmonton Int.	707	1.6	-16.5	3.2	15.8	4.7	35.0	-48.3	May 25	Sept. 8
British Columbia:										
Kamloops	346	8.3	-6.1	9.1	20.8	8.4	41.7	-37.2	May 4	Oct. 1
Prince George	676	3.3	-12.1	4.3	15.1	4.8	34.3	-50.0	June 6	Aug. 31
Prince Rupert	34	6.7	-0.2	5.4	12.8	7.9	32.2	-21.1	May 11	Oct. 15
Vancouver Int.	3	9.8	2.5	8.8	17.3	10.0	33.3	-17.8	Mar. 31	Nov. 3
Victoria Gonzales HTS	69	10.0	4.1	9.1	15.4	10.8	35.0	-15.6	Apr. 8	Oct. 29
Yukon Territory:										
Dawson	324	-5.1	-30.7	-1.6	15.6	-4.0	35.0	-58.3	May 28	Aug. 28
Whitehorse	703	-1.2	-20.7	0.3	14.1	0.6	34.4	-52.2	June 8	Aug. 30
Northwest Territories:										
Frobisher Bay	34	-9.3	-25.6	-14.3	7.6	-5.0	24.4	-45.6	June 28	Aug. 27
Inuvik	68	-9.8	-29.6	-14.3	13.6	-8.1	31.7	-56.7	June 23	Aug. 14
Resolute	67	-16.6	-32.1	-23.1	4.1	-15.1	18.3	-52.2	July 10	July 20
Yellowknife	205	-5.4	-28.8	-6.9	16.3	-1.6	32.2	-51.1	May 27	Sept. 16

* Temperature extremes are for the total period of record to 1980

Precipitation Data for Representative Stations in Canada
Temperature in Degrees Celsius

Average Total Precipitation (mm.)

Station	Jan.	Feb.	Mar.	Apr.	May	June	July	Aug.	Sept.	Oct.	Nov.	Dec.	Ann.	Aver. Ann. Snowfall (cm)
St. John's	155.8	140.1	131.9	115.6	101.8	85.6	75.3	121.6	116.7	145.5	162.5	161.2	1513.6	359.4
Charlottetown Int.	116.8	97.4	95.3	81.8	83.6	79.9	84.3	88.1	86.3	106.4	120.5	129.0	1169.4	330.6
Halifax Int.	152.8	135.5	128.4	114.8	106.4	89.4	94.2	111.3	93.7	133.5	152.5	180.1	1490.6	271.0
Sydney	149.0	123.6	131.4	102.0	95.2	82.1	81.4	101.3	87.2	122.7	160.4	163.6	1399.9	317.9
Yarmouth	141.0	114.2	98.5	96.3	92.4	81.3	77.8	97.3	89.4	116.5	134.7	142.2	1281.6	208.3
Chatham	98.8	86.8	97.1	84.5	81.9	82.0	91.0	83.5	85.2	95.6	102.4	107.9	1096.7	333.1
Fredericton	103.3	89.7	84.7	79.9	83.1	85.0	88.8	87.0	86.8	97.1	106.1	117.8	1109.3	290.4
St. John	148.8	115.7	114.1	107.7	107.7	94.2	103.4	102.0	111.8	127.7	145.7	166.0	144.4	292.7
Arvida	62.6	57.2	48.9	45.6	66.8	89.7	120.7	96.2	102.1	69.3	68.5	80.7	908.3	271.2
Montréal Int. (Dorval)	72.0	65.2	73.6	74.1	65.6	82.2	90.0	91.9	88.4	75.5	81.0	86.7	946.2	235.1
Point au Pere	75.6	62.7	66.3	52.4	71.4	60.5	78.7	78.4	81.5	75.9	67.9	79.3	850.6	292.9
Québec	89.8	78.1	82.0	72.8	86.9	109.9	116.6	117.1	119.4	90.7	97.1	113.6	1174.0	343.4
Schefferville	46.9	43.0	41.6	45.4	49.4	73.7	96.8	98.2	75.6	49.0	65.7	49.0	768.7	386.5
Sherbrooke	71.1	61.7	73.2	74.3	86.8	98.7	117.4	121.1	101.8	87.1	90.2	91.7	1075.1	322.6
Kapuskasing	53.6	43.0	55.4	53.2	74.3	84.7	96.3	92.5	94.4	77.4	80.1	53.3	858.2	319.9
London	75.2	60.5	75.1	81.2	66.9	73.6	72.4	80.3	78.6	73.4	84.7	87.5	909.4	208.8
Ottawa Int.	1.0	60.3	67.5	69.1	67.9	73.4	85.9	88.4	79.3	68.1	77.7	80.7	879.3	227.3
Thunder Bay	40.9	28.3	45.0	50.7	73.3	76.6	75.4	83.1	89.1	54.8	52.9	41.7	711.8	213.0
Toronto Int.	50.4	46.0	61.1	70.0	66.0	67.1	71.4	76.8	63.5	61.8	62.7	64.7	761.5	131.2
Churchill	15.3	13.1	18.1	22.9	31.9	43.5	45.6	58.3	50.9	43.0	38.8	20.9	402.3	195.5
The Pas	18.0	15.4	23.6	27.4	37.3	63.0	70.2	57.5	57.3	33.2	28.8	22.0	453.7	170.0
Winnipeg Int.	21.3	17.5	22.7	38.5	65.7	80.1	75.9	75.2	53.3	30.9	25.2	19.2	525.5	125.5
Prince Albert	16.6	14.9	19.2	22.0	39.4	69.1	65.3	52.1	39.4	21.6	17.0	21.8	398.4	121.7
Regina	16.6	16.1	17.8	23.7	46.4	79.6	53.3	44.8	36.7	18.8	13.5	16.7	384.0	115.7
Beaverlodge CDA	33.0	25.4	24.6	19.3	39.0	68.4	64.0	63.8	42.0	28.6	26.8	32.1	467.0	195.2
Calgary Int.	16.2	15.5	16.1	32.6	48.7	89.4	65.4	55.4	38.2	17.6	12.7	16.0	423.8	152.5
Edmonton Int.	24.4	17.6	16.0	20.2	42.2	76.7	91.6	78.2	45.7	15.4	16.7	21.9	466.6	137.9
Kamloops	31.6	16.0	9.7	10.4	18.4	29.9	22.5	27.5	21.4	15.2	22.0	32.2	265.5	91.5
Prince George	57.4	39.2	36.8	27.4	47.3	66.9	59.7	68.2	58.7	59.2	50.5	57.0	628.3	241.7
Prince Rupert	27.5	222.1	200.8	190.0	139.5	129.5	103.0	158.4	233.4	366.5	268.4	284.1	2523.2	151.7
Vancouver Int.	153.8	123.2	101.0	59.6	51.6	45.2	32.0	41.1	67.1	114.0	150.1	182.4	1112.6	60.4
Victoria Gonzales HTS	110.7	73.6	46.9	30.4	19.3	20.1	13.4	21.0	33.5	63.4	95.7	119.2	647.2	32.0
Dawson	16.5	15.7	10.1	9.7	21.1	38.8	47.2	44.0	28.2	28.7	21.5	24.6	306.1	137.1
Whitehorse	17.7	13.3	13.5	9.5	12.9	30.7	33.9	37.9	30.3	21.5	19.8	20.2	261.2	136.6
Frobisher Bay	26.1	23.3	23.3	26.4	25.3	39.4	63.3	58.9	46.0	44.1	34.4	22.1	432.6	255.5
Inuvik	17.9	10.5	12.0	14.8	17.6	23.5	33.6	43.6	23.9	33.4	17.9	17.4	266.1	176.6
Resolute	3.3	3.0	3.0	5.9	8.1	12.1	22.5	31.1	18.0	13.8	5.7	4.9	131.4	83.8
Yellowknife	13.3	11.2	12.4	10.3	17.2	16.8	33.8	44.0	30.5	34.5	24.5	18.2	266.7	135.4

*1 in. = 25.4 mm.; 2.54 cm.

Canadian Almanac & Directory 1997

1-66 DISTANCES BETWEEN MAJOR POINTS IN CANADA

AIRLINE COMPANIES

Advance Air Charters
35 McTavish Place NE, Calgary AB T2E 7J7
403/291-3462; Fax: 403/291-4208
Vice-President, Operations, Capt. J.A. Hucal

Aer Lingus
122 East 42nd St., New York NY USA 10168
Toll Free: 1-800-223-6537

Aeroflot, Russian International Airlines
615, boul de Maisonneuve ouest, Montréal PQ H3A 1L8
514/288-2125; Fax: 514/288-5973; Telex: 05-25821
General Manager, G. Matveyev

Aerolineas Argentinas
#802, 1235 Bay St., Toronto ON M5R 3K4
Toll Free: 1-800-688-0008

Air Canada
Air Canada Centre, PO Box 14000, Stn St-Laurent, Montréal PQ H4Y 1H4
514/422-5772; Fax: 514/422-5798; URL: http://www.aircanada.ca
President/CEO, Lamar Durrett

Air Charter Systems
780, boul Magenta, Farnham PQ J2N 1B8
514/293-3656; Fax: 514/293-5169; Toll Free: 1-800-363-9270
President, Edward C.C. Peagram

Air Club International
#205, 11905, route Cargo A-3, Mirabel PQ J7N 1H1
514/476-3555; Fax: 514/476-9818
Vice-President, Flight Operations, Jean Côté

Air France
#1510, 2000, rue Mansfield, Montréal PQ H3A 3A3
514/847-1106; Fax: 514/285-8994; Telex: 05-25304
General Manager for Canada, Michel J. Guiral, 514/285-5010

Air India
#908, 390 Bay St., Toronto ON M5H 2Y2
416/865-1030; Fax: 416/865-0716

Air Jamaica Ltd.
55 St. Clair Ave West, Toronto ON M4V 1K6
416/927-0081; Fax: 416/927-1524
Regional Manager, George de Mercado

Air Liberté
1125, boul de Maisonneuve ouest, Montréal PQ H3A 3B6
514/985-2586; Fax: 514/985-2588

Air Transat
11600, rue Cargo A-1, Mirabel PQ J7N 1G9
514/476-1011; Fax: 514/476-0338
Vice-President, Operations, Capt. Pierre Ménard

Alitalia
2055, rue Peel, Montréal PQ H3A 1V8
514/842-8241; Fax: 514/842-5651
General Manager for Canada, Vincenzo Ursino

American Airlines Inc.
Lester B. Pearson Airport, PO Box 6005, Stn Toronto AMF, Mississauga ON L5P 1B6
905/612-7266; Fax: 905/612-0144; URL: http://www.amrcorp.com
General Manager, Toronto, A.W. Pliszka

Austrian Airlines
17-20, White Stone Expressway, White Stone NY USA 11357
Toll Free: 1-800-843-0002

Avianca
(Aerovias Nacionales de Colombia)
#1102, 1 St. Clair Ave. West, Toronto ON M4V 1K6
416/969-8817; Fax: 416/969-9926

British Airways
#100, 4120 Yonge St., North York ON M2P 2B8
416/250-0250; Fax: 416/250-1921
Vice-President/General Manager, John Wood

BWIA International Airways
#401, 40 Holly St., Toronto ON M4S 3C3
416/440-0112; Fax: 416/440-1899
Regional Manager, Sales & Service (Canada), Carletta Davis

Canada 3000 Airlines Limited
27 Fasken Dr., Toronto ON M9W 1K6
416/674-0257; Fax: 416/674-0256
Vice-President, Operations, Capt. D.V. Thompson

Canadian Airlines International Ltd./Lignes Aériennes Canadien International ltée
#2800, 700 - 2 St. SW, Calgary AB T2P 2W2
403/294-2000; Fax: 403/294-2066; URL: http://www.cdnair.ca
Chairman, Rhys T. Eyton

Condor Flugdienst
PO Box 66178, Chicago IL USA 60666
312/686-8440

Continental Airlines
#500, 3663 Houston Pkwy., Houston TX USA 77032
Toll Free: 1-800-231-0856

Cubana
#405, 4, Place Ville-Marie, Montréal PQ H3B 2E7
514/871-1222; Fax: 514/871-1227

Czech Airlines
#1510, 401 Bay St., Toronto ON M5H 2Y4
416/363-3174; Fax: 416/363-0239; Email: csa@baxter.net; URL: http://www.baxter.net/csa
Regional Director, Antonin Jakubse

Delta Air Lines Inc.
#110, 3300, Place Côte Vertu ouest, Montréal PQ H4P 2B7
514/856-7600; Fax: 514/337-8976

El Al Israel Airlines
555, boul René-Lévesque ouest, Montréal PQ H2Z 1B1
514/875-8910; Fax: 514/393-9170

Finnair
#402, 20 York Mills Rd., North York ON M2P 2C2
416/222-0740; Fax: 416/222-5004; Telex: 065-23360
Manager, Canadian Division, Christina Massé

Iberia
1235 Bay St., 8th Fl., Toronto ON M5R 3K4
416/964-6645; Fax: 416/964-7684

Icelandair
#410, 5950 Symphony Woods Rd., Columbia MD USA 21044
Toll Free: 1-800-223-5500

Japan Airlines
#2110, 130 Adelaide St. West, Toronto ON M5H 3P5
416/364-7229; Fax: 416/364-6107; Toll Free: 1-800-525-3663
District Passenger Sales Manager, Tatsuo Kameda

KLM Royal Dutch Airlines
#2501, 777 Bay St., Toronto ON M5G 2C8
416/204-5137; Fax: 416/204-5180
General Manager, Canada, Nico Wiering

Korean Air
55 University Ave., Toronto ON M5J 2H7
416/862-8250; Fax: 416/862-2105

LOT - Polish Airlines
#680, 2000, rue Peel, Montréal PQ H3A 2W5
514/844-2674; Fax: 514/844-7339
General Manager, Henryk Rosinski

Lufthansa German Airlines
55 Yonge St., 10th Fl., Toronto ON M5E 1J4
416/360-3615; Fax: 416/360-3605
Canadian Vice-President, Rolf Kaptur

Northern Thunderbird Air Inc.
(NT Air)
4245 Hangar Rd., Prince George BC V1N 4M6
250/963-9611; Fax: 250/963-8422; Toll Free: 1-800-963-9611
President/Manager, Vernon Martin

Northwest Airlines
5101 Northwest Dr., St. Paul MN USA 55111-3034
612/726-2111; Toll Free: 1-800-225-2525; URL: http://www.nwa.com

Olympic Airways
#503, 80 Bloor St. West, Toronto ON M5S 2V1
416/964-7137; Fax: 416/920-3686

PIA Pakistan International Airlines
#437, 131 Bloor St. West, Toronto ON M5S 1R1
416/926-8747; Fax: 416/926-0507

Qantas Airways
#1705, 1111 West Georgia St., Vancouver BC V6E 4M3
604/684-1055; Fax: 604/684-8617; Toll Free: 1-800-227-4500
Manager, Canada, William Duplak

Royal Aviation Inc.
#503, 6700, Côte de Liesse, Montréal PQ H4T 1E3
514/739-7000; Fax: 514/739-7993
Vice-President, Operations & Maintenance, Maurice Dahan

Royal Jordanian
45 St. Clair Ave. West, Toronto ON M4V 1K9
416/962-3955; Fax: 416/960-9162

SABENA Belgian World Airlines
#730, 1001, boul de Maisonneuve ouest, Montréal PQ H3A 3C9
514/845-2165; Fax: 514/845-1978
Canadian General Manager, Willy Charniaux

Skyservice
5501 Electra Rd., PO Box 160, Toronto AMF ON L5P 1B1
905/677-3300; Fax: 905/678-5654; Email: keith_levia@skysrvs.com
Director, Flight Operations, Capt. Arnie MacLeish

Swissair
#502, 2 Bloor St. West, Toronto ON M4W 3E2
416/960-4290; Fax: 416/960-4295

TAP - Air Portugal
#1410, 1801, av McGill College, Montréal PQ H3A 2N4
514/849-6163; Fax: 514/844-1322; Toll Free: 1-800-361-0699
General Manager, Canada, Lidia Marques

TimeAir
PO Box 423, Lethbridge AB T1J 3Z1
403/329-0355; Fax: 403/327-1229
General Manager, T.A. Kapty

Trans North Air
Airport Hangar C, Whitehorse Airport, 917 Alaska Hwy., Whitehorse YT Y1A 3E4
403/668-2177; Fax: 403/668-3420
President, R.F. Connelly

Trans Provincial Airlines
PO Box 280, Prince Rupert BC V8J 3P6
250/627-1341; Fax: 250/627-8307
General Manager, Gene Storey

United Airlines
#310, 180 Bloor St. West, Toronto ON M5S 2V6
416/923-2740; Fax: 416/923-4853
District Sales Manager, Patrick K. Dunne

US Air
#100, 4120 Yonge St., Toronto ON M2P 2B8
Toll Free: 1-800-428-4322
Canadian Sales Manager, Carle Chadillon

Varig
(Viacao Aerea Rio-Grandense)
#1108, 77 Bloor St. West, Toronto ON M5S 1M2
416/926-9511; Toll Free: 1-800-468-2744

Viasa
(Venezolana Int'l de Aviacion)
#802, 1235 Bay St., Toronto ON M5R 3K2
Toll Free: 1-800-468-4272

RAILWAY COMPANIES

Algoma Central Railway Inc.
PO Box 9500, Sault Ste Marie ON P6A 6Y1
705/541-2905; Fax: 705/541-2909; URL: http://www.mcs.net/~dsdawdy/Canpass/acr/soo_her.html
Executive Representative, W.J. McComb

Canadian Almanac & Directory 1997

Rail service, Sault Ste. Marie to Hearst, Ont.
Amtrak (National Railroad Passenger Corporation)
  4 South Tower, 30th & Market Streets, Philadelphia PA USA 19104
  215/349-1699; Fax: 215/349-4565
  Senior Director, System Operating Rules, C.W. Autro
BC Rail Ltd.
  PO Box 8770, Vancouver BC V6B 4X6
  604/986-2012; Fax: 604/984-5265; URL: http://www.mcs.net/~dsdawdy/Canpass/bcr/bcr.html
  President/CEO, Paul J. McElligott
  Full & intermodal service with CP & CN connections
  1,388 miles of track operated; 107 locomotives; 10,361 freight cars
Burlington Northern (Manitoba) Ltd.
  963 Lindsay St., Winnipeg MB R3N 1X6
  204/453-4415; Fax: 204/477-0046
  President, J.R. Galassi
Burlington Northern Railroad
  400 Brunette Ave., New Westminster BC V3L 3E8
  604/520-5200; Fax: 604/520-5206
  Chair/CEO, Gerald Grinstein
  25,000 miles (181 miles in Canada); 58,343 railcars; 2,505 power
Canada & Gulf Terminal Railway Company/Le Chemin de fer de Matane et du Golfe
  206, rue Hébert, CP 578, Mont-Joli PQ G5H 3L3
  418/775-4373; Fax: 418/775-8661
  General Director, Pierre Chalifour
  30 miles; 1 locomotive
Cape Breton & Central Nova Scotia Railway
  PO Box 4444, Port Hawkesbury NS B0E 2V0
  902/625-5715; Fax: 902/625-5722
  General Manager, M.H. Westerfield
Cartier Railway Company/Chemin de Fer Cartier (QCM Railway)
  Rte. 138, Port Cartier PQ G5B 2H3
  514/285-2064; Fax: 514/285-1978
  President/CEO, Guy Dufresne
  416 km; 32 locomotives; 1,365 cars
Central Western Railway
  Webber Centre, #1420, 5555 Calgary Trail South, Edmonton AB T6H 5P9
  403/448-5855; Fax: 403/439-5658
  President/COO, T. Payne
CN North America - Division of Canadian National Railway Company/CN Amérique du Nord
  PO Box 8100, Stn A, Montréal PQ H3C 3N4
  514/399-4937; Fax: 514/399-6910
  Chair, David G.A. McLean
  22,471 km of main line track (includes Grand Trunk Corp., CN's rail network in US); 1,672 diesel locomotives; 62,230 freight cars
Consolidated Rail Corporation (ConRail)
  #14A, 2001 Market St., PO Box 41414, Philadelphia PA USA 19101-1414
  215/209-5583; Fax: 215/209-5582
  Chairman/President/CEO, James A. Hagen
  66 route miles in Québec, from New York-Québec border to Montréal. Includes owned lines, leased lines & trackage rights. Total route miles US & Canada, 13,068
CP Rail System
  (Canadian Pacific Railway)
  CP 6042, Succ A, Montréal PQ H3C 3E4
  514/395-6850; Fax: 514/395-7165
  Senior Vice-President, J.A. Linn
CSX Transportation Inc.
  12780 Levan Rd., Livonia MI USA 48150
  313/464-4948; Fax: 313/464-4893
  Chairman, R.J. Kirk
  166 miles in Canada
Devco Railway
  (Cape Breton Development Corporation)
  PO Box 2500, Sydney NS B1P 6K9
  902/564-7613; Fax: 902/564-7608
  General Manager, Transportation & Processing, Al McNeil
  88 miles; 10 locomotives; 550 cars
Esquimalt & Nanaimo Railway
  #800, 200 Granville St., Vancouver BC V6C 2R3
  604/643-3250; Fax: 604/643-3274
  Express Co.-Canadian Pacific
  195 miles (equipment included with CP Rail)
Essex Terminal Railwy Co.
  1601 Lincoln Rd., PO Box 24025, Windsor ON N8Y 4Y9
  519/973-8222; Fax: 519/973-7234
  President, B.G. McKeown
  Freight only; 24 miles of main track (CN CP CSX NS connect); 5 locomotives; 5 cars
GO Transit
  #600, 20 Bay St., Toronto ON M5J 2W3
  416/869-3600, ext.504; Fax: 416/869-3525; URL: http://www.mcs.net/~dsdawdy/Canpass/go/go_top.html
  Executive Director, Operations, J.A. Brown
Goderich-Exeter Railway Company Ltd.
  1 Maitland Rd., Goderich ON N7A 2W9
  519/524-4024; Fax: 519/524-4026
  General Manager, A.E. Parker
Greater Winnipeg Water District Railway
  598 Plinguet St., Winnipeg MB R2J 2W7
  204/986-4118; Fax: 204/237-6207
  Railway Supervisor, D.E. Carr
  Express Co.-None
  92 miles; 3 locomotives; 150 cars
New Brunswick Southern Railway Company Limited
  11 Gifford Rd., PO Box 5666, Saint John NB E2L 5B6
  506/635-2200; Fax: 506/635-2239
  Manager, S. Smith
Norfolk Southern Corporation
  185 Spring St. SW, Atlanta GA USA 30303
  404/529-1824; Fax: 404/529-1948
  General Manager, L.D. Hale Jr.
  Operating Subsidiaries: Norfolk Southern Railway Co., North American Van Lines
  Track miles 14,842 (245 miles in Canada); 2, 140 locomotives; 12,051 road haul equipment
Ontario Northland Transportation Commission
  555 Oak St. East, North Bay ON P1B 8L3
  705/472-4500; Fax: 705/476-5598; URL: http://www.mcs.net/~dsdawdy/Canpass/onr/onr.html
  Chairman, M. Rukavina
  (Owned by Province of Ontario)
  700 miles; 26 locomotives; 700 cars
Québec North Shore & Labrador Railway Company/Chemin de fer QNS&L
  CP 1000, Sept-Îles PQ G4R 4L5
  418/968-7495; Fax: 418/968-7498; URL: http://www.mcs.net/~dsdawdy/Canpass/qnsl/qnsl.html
  General Manager, M. Duclos
Roberval & Saguenay Railway Company/Compagnie du Chemin de Fer Roberbal Saguenay
  CP 1277, Arvida PQ G7S 4K8
  418/699-2433; Fax: 418/699-3300
  Superintendent, Railway Services, G. Grenon
  Express Co.-None (Canadian National Railway connects)
  54 miles; 14 locomotives; 193 cars
Southern Railway of British Columbia Limited
  2102 River Dr., New Westminster BC V3M 6S3
  604/521-1966; Fax: 604/526-0914
  President, R. Stoeckly
  (freight only)
  75 miles; 19 locomotives; 475 cars
Via Rail Canada Inc.
  CP 8116, Succ A, Montréal PQ H3C 3N3
  514/871-6190; Fax: 514/871-6641; URL: http://www.mcs.net/~dsdawdy/Canpass/via/via.html
  Chair, Marc Lefrançois
  (passenger services only)
Wabush Mines
  CP 878, Sept-Îles PQ G4R 4L4
  418/964-3000; Fax: 418/962-9876
  General Manager, D.K. Honsberger
  Wabush Mines represents both the Arnaud Railway Company & the Wabush Lake Railway
White Pass & Yukon Route
  PO Box 435, Skagway AK USA 98840
  907/983-2214; Fax: 907/983-2658
  Vice-President, Alaska Operations, Marvin P. Taylor
  Express Co.-None
  110 miles; 23 locomotives; 450 cars
Wisconsin Central Ltd.
  One O'Hare Center, 6250 North River Rd., Rosemont IL USA 60018
  708/318-4601; Fax: 708/318-4628
  President, E.A. Burkhardt

MEETING, CONFERENCE, EXHIBIT & EVENT PLANNERS

ALBERTA

CALGARY

Avatar Productions (1989) Ltd., #222, 8 Parkdale Cres. NW, Calgary AB T2N 3T8 – 403/270-7274; Fax: 403/270-8739 – President, Judy Markle

Canadian National Sportsmen's Shows, #340, 1032 - 17 Ave. SW, Calgary AB T2T 0A5 – 403/245-9008; Fax: 403/245-5100 – Wolfgang Ortner

Creative Outlet Ltd., #202, 222 - 58 Ave. SW, Calgary AB T2H 2S3 – 403/255-5511; Fax: 403/255-5512 – President, Jeff Eichler

Details - Convention & Event Management Inc., #320, 1000 Centre St. North, Calgary AB T2E 7W6 – 403/277-7377; Fax: 403/277-1399 – Contact, Jean Silzer, C.M.P.

First Nations Conferences Inc., PO Box 1240, Stn M, Calgary AB T2P 2L2 – 403/261-3022; Fax: 403/261-5676; Email: aboriginalcongress@discoveryweb.com; URL: http://www.aboriginalnet.com/congress – President, Edmund A. Oliverio

Industrial Trade & Consumer Shows Inc., #2450, 101 - 6th Ave SW, Calgary AB T2P 3P4 – 403/266-8700; Fax: 403/266-6814 – Contact, Steve Henrich

Johnson & Bell Association Management Services Inc., #204, 8 Parkdale Cres. NW, Calgary AB T2N 3T8 – 403/270-7868; Fax: 403/270-2981 – President, Bill Johnson

Maureen Payne & Associates, #225, 602 - 11 Ave. SW, Calgary AB T2R 1J8 – 403/266-5880; Fax: 403/262-4997 – President, Maureen Payne

Panex Show Services, 120 - 9 Ave. SE, Calgary AB T2G 0P3 – 403/261-8551, 8552; Fax: 403/261-8554 – Western Canada Manager, Terry Symington

Southex Exhibitions, #300, 999 - 8 St. SW, Calgary AB T2R 1N7 – 403/244-6111; Fax: 403/245-8649; URL: http://www.southex.com – Pat Atkinson

Trade Show Managers Inc., 5512, 4 St. NW, PO Box 64024, Calgary AB T2K 6J0 – 403/274-8858; Fax: 403/274-9388; Email: slmorrow@aca.ucalgary.ca – Contact, Sandra Morrow

EDMONTON

Cameo Convention Consultants Ltd., 7418 - 182 St., Edmonton AB T5T 2G7 – 403/481-6268; Fax: 403/243-0666 – President, Mamie Bercov

Conference Services, Dept. of Housing & Food Services, #44, Lister Hall, Edmonton AB T6G 2H6 – 403/492-4281; Fax: 403/492-7032; Email: conference.services@ualberta.ca; URL: http://www.nfs.ualberta.ca – Conference Services Coordinator, Michelle Hoyle

Dominion Trade Show Management Inc., 4614 - 97 St., Edmonton AB T6E 4M7 – 403/436-8000; Fax: 403/436-8009 – Marketing Representative, Cathy Chaney

Edmonton Convention Planners, 18828 - 80 Ave., Edmonton AB T5T 5B4 – 403/486-4589; Fax: 403/486-4589 – Principal & General Manager, Lois Zapf

Eu-Anna Hospitality, #302, 17304 - 105 Ave., Edmonton AB T5S 1G4 – 403/481-8819; Fax: 403/489-0939 – President, Brian Calnan

The Event Coordinators, 10977 - 141 St., Edmonton AB T5M 1T5 – 403/453-6962; Fax: 403/455-9029 – President, John Hohol

Harold Smith Travel, 10104 - 103 Ave., Edmonton AB T5J 0H8 – 403/429-3420; Fax: 403/424-7144 – Contact, Floyd Morphy

Maureen Payne & Associates, #610, 9925 - 109 St., Edmonton AB T5K 2J8 – 403/429-2511; Fax: 403/429-6172 – Senior Communications Consultant, David L. Young

Meetings Alberta Canada, Canada City Centre, 10155 - 102 St., 4th Fl., Edmonton AB T5J 4L6 – 905/427-1905; Fax: 905/422-5123; Toll Free: 1-800-661-8888 – Director, D. Lane

Western Convention Consulting Services Ltd., 15016 - 77 Ave., Edmonton AB T5R 3B3 – 403/487-8102; Fax: 403/487-2417 – President, Christine McLaren

LETHBRIDGE

University of Lethbridge, Conference Services, 4401 University Dr., Lethbridge AB T1K 3M4 – 403/329-2244; Fax: 403/329-5166; Email: confserv@chess.ancil.uleth.ca – Conference Associate, Robin Gardner

SAINT ALBERT

The Great Alberta Hospitality Company Ltd., 22 Estate Cr., St. Albert AB T8N 5X2 – 403/460-7207; Fax: 403/460-4699 – General Manager, Jill Douglas

BRITISH COLUMBIA

BURNABY

Canadian National Sportsmen's Shows (1989) Ltd., #501, 4190 Lougheed Hwy., Burnaby BC V5C 6A8 – 604/294-1313; Fax: 604/294-4740 – Show Manager, Jim Carslake

Southex Exhibitions, 4285 Canada Way, Burnaby BC V5G 1H2 – 604/433-5121; Fax: 604/433-9549; Toll Free: 1-800-633-8332 – Vice-President, Western Region, Fred Barnes

COQUITLAM

Classic Consulting International Inc., #201, 931 Brunette Ave., Coquitlam BC V3K 6T5 – 604/527-1045; Fax: 604/527-1046 – Managing Director, Dawn Williams

KAMLOOPS

Classic Moment Creative Events, 1255 Delta Ave., Kamloops BC V2B 3Y4 – 250/376-7934; Fax: 250/376-7927 – Event Producer/Owner, Judy Basso

Showest Management Inc., PO Box 300, Kamloops BC V2C 5K6 – 250/851-2145; Fax: 250/851-0551 – President, Gerry K. Hartley

RICHMOND

Creative Conventions Inc., 6191 Madrona Cres., Richmond BC V7C 2T3 – 604/277-1512 – Contact, Tim Enno

Levy Show Service Ltd., #3A, 11180 River Rd., Richmond BC V6X 1Z5 – 604/273-6332; Fax: 604/273-6374 – General Manager, Henry Levy

VANCOUVER

Cantrav West Services Ltd., #300, 238 - 2nd Ave. East, Vancouver BC V5T 1B7 – 604/879-0950; Fax: 604/879-0949; Email: cantrav@cantrav.com; URL: http://www.cantrav.com – Contact, Janice Cann

Congress Canada, 827 West Pender St., Vancouver BC V6C 3G8 – 604/682-2199; Fax: 604/689-5284 – President, Pam Graham

Contacts Pacific Services Inc., #280, 1090 West Georgia St., Vancouver BC V6E 3V7 – 604/683-2174; Fax: 604/688-6972; Toll Free: 1-800-661-4646 – Contact, George Bartel

Events by Design Inc., #601, 325 Howe St., Vancouver BC V6C 1Z7 – 604/669-7175; Fax: 604/669-7083 – Director/Partner, Janna Shillington

The Famous Events Group, #504, 68 Water St., Vancouver BC V6B 1A4 – 604/689-3448, 649-6944; Fax: 604/689-5245 – President, Richard Lowy

International Conference Services, #604, 850 West Hastings St., Vancouver BC V6C 1E1 – 604/681-2153; Fax: 604/681-1049 – President, Franziska Kaltenegger

MMG Meeting Management Group Ltd., #502, 1155 West Georgia St., Vancouver BC V6E 4E6 – 604/681-5701; Fax: 604/681-8601 – Director, Gail Edwards

Passport Planners, #308, 1345 Comox St., Vancouver BC V6E 4E4 – 604/687-3277; Fax: 604/687-2123 – President, George Brakey

Square Feet Northwest Event Management Inc., 1030 Mainland St., Vancouver BC V6B 2T4 – 604/683-4393; Fax: 604/688-0270; Email: mgmt@sqftevent.com – Blaine Woit

Taylordel Production Line Ltd., #200, 1865 Marine Dr. West, Vancouver BC V7V 1J7 – 604/922-3371; Fax: 604/922-3371 – Show Coordinator, Nicole Copley

Venue West Ltd., #645, 375 Water St., Vancouver BC V6B 5C6 – 604/681-5226; Fax: 604/681-2503 – B. Lou Cox

West Coast Music Conference, #203, 1104 Hornby St., Vancouver BC V6Z 1V8 – 604/684-9338; Fax: 604/684-9337 – Contact, Woody Turnquist

Westcoast Agenda, #708, 1755 Robson St., Vancouver BC V6G 3B7 – 604/688-8584; Fax: 604/669-9611 – Meeting Planner, Donna Reid

VICTORIA

Conference Management, Division of Continuing Studies, University of Victoria, PO Box 3030, Victoria BC V8W 3N6 – 250/721-8465; Fax: 250/721-8774; Email: morourke@castle.uvic.ca; URL: http://www.uvcs.uvic.ca/confman.htm – Contact, Mary O'Rourke

Connections Victoria Ltd., PO Box 40046, Victoria BC V8W 3N3 – 250/382-0332; Fax: 250/382-2076; Email: connvic@octonet.com; URL: http://www.octonet.com/connvic/ – Managing Director, Ann Moxley

Evergreen Exhibitions Ltd., 830D Pembrooke St., Victoria BC V8T 1H9 – 250/386-7469; Fax: 250/386-1431 – President, A.J. Chartrand

WEST VANCOUVER

Pacific Promotions Ltd., 138 Stevens Dr., West Vancouver BC V7S 1C4 – 604/925-3333, 2222; Fax: 604/925-4454 – President, David M. Frinton

WESTBANK

Home Business Exhibitions, 2956 Shannon Lake Rd., Westbank BC V4T 1T6 – 250/768-9561

WHISTLER

Destination Leisure Productions Ltd., PO Box 720, Whistler BC V0N 1B0 – 604/938-3350; Fax: 604/938-3485 – Managing Director, Laurin Kyle Boyle

WHITE ROCK

M. Van Keken & Associates Ltd., #303, 15047 Marine Dr., White Rock BC V4B 1C5 – 604/535-0944; Fax: 604/535-2744 – President/Executive Producer, Martin Van Keken

MANITOBA

BRANDON

Brandon Economic Development Board, 1043 Rosser Ave., Brandon MB R7A 0L5 – 204/728-3287; Fax: 204/727-2040; Email: bedb@docker.com; URL: http://www.docker.com/brandon.html – General Manager, Don Allan

WINNIPEG

Berkowitz Ltd., #242, 375 York Ave., Winnipeg MB R3C 3J3 – 204/957-7312; Fax: 204/943-0397 – Contact, Ivan Berkowitz

Frontline Associates, 676 Borebank St., Winnipeg MB R3N 1G2 – 204/254-2293; Fax: 204/489-2739

Hank Hartloper Agency, #2, 1575 Seel Ave., Winnipeg MB R3T 1C8 – 204/925-5711; Fax: 204/925-6643 – Owner, Hank Hartloper

IN-KA Meeting Planners, #202, 16 Albert St., Winnipeg MB R3B 1G4 – 204/949-1653; Fax: 204/956-1700 – Contact, Gail Hall

NEW BRUNSWICK

SAINT JOHN

Global Convention Services, PO Box 2329, Saint John NB E2L 3V6 – 506/658-0506; Fax: 506/658-0750 – General Manager, Ian Galbraith

Master Promotions Ltd., PO Box 565, Saint John NB E2L 3Z8 – 506/658-0018; Fax: 506/658-0750 – Show Manager, Sydney Jane Brittain

NEWFOUNDLAND

CONCEPTION BAY

McCarthy's Party, Tour & Convention Services Topsail, General Delivery, Topsail, Conception Bay NF A0A 3Y0 – 709/781-2244; Fax: 709/781-2233 – President, Regina McCarthy

GANDER

Atlantic Expositions Ltd, PO Box 402, Gander NF A1V 1W8 – 709/651-3315; Fax: 709/256-4051 – Manager, Keith Brown

ST. JOHN'S

The Fulcrum Group, #301, 140 Water St., St. John's NF A1C 6H6 – 709/753-1015; Fax: 709/753-1016

NOVA SCOTIA

DARTMOUTH

Creative Convention Consultants, 11 Pettipas Dr., Unit M, Dartmouth NS B3B 4K1 – 902/468-9101; Fax: 902/468-8938 – President, David M. Alexander

Denex Group Inc., Burnside Industrial Park, 192 Joseph Zatzman Dr., Dartmouth NS B3B 1N4 – 902/468-4999; Fax: 902/468-2795; Email: denman@new-edge.ca – President, Jon Denman

Meetings Plus Ltd., 4 Applewood Lane, Dartmouth NS B2X 2Z6 – 902/462-1929; Fax: 902/462-4275; Email: amirault@netcom.ca – President, Leslie Amirault

HALIFAX

A.B. Thompson Associates Ltd., PO Box 9410, Stn A, Halifax NS B3K 5S3 – 902/425-2445; Fax: 902/425-2441; Toll Free: 1-800-200-PATH; Email: pathfndr@fox.nstn.ca – Contact, John Sutherland

Brooks Diamond Productions, World Trade & Convention Centre, #507, 1800 Argyle St., Halifax NS B3J 3N8 – 902/422-7000; Fax: 902/422-2929 – Vice-President, Sheri Jones

MEETING, CONFERENCE, EXHIBIT & EVENT PLANNERS

DMS Enterprises Ltd., 5647 Morris St., Halifax NS B3J 1C4 – 902/425-5656 – Coordinator, Donna Susnick

Downeast Entertainment & Meeting Specialists, #116, 1585 Barrington St., Halifax NS B3J 1Z8 – 902/423-1974; Fax: 902/429-8002; Email: dwneast@fox.nstn.ca – Contact, Bill Norton

Lewis Conference Services International, Richmond Terminal, Pier 9, 3295 Barrington St., Halifax NS B3K 5X8 – 902/492-4988; Fax: 902/492-4781 – Contact, Trudy Lewis

M & J Tour Guide & Receptive Services, #102, 6960 Mumford Rd., Halifax NS B3L 4P1 – 902/455-9001; Fax: 902/455-7838 – Contact, Ian Brown

On Site Meeting Planners Ltd., PO Box 2627, Stn M, Halifax NS B3J 3P7 – 902/461-0230; Fax: 902/465-2233 – President, Lynn Buckley

ONTARIO

AJAX
Metropolitan Promotions, PO Box 193, Ajax ON L1S 3C3 – 905/428-7610; Fax: 905/428-7046 – Show Manager, Tom Glaesser

ASHBURN
Bar Hodgson Productions Inc., 8780 Baldwin St., RR#1, Ashburn ON L0B 1A0 – 905/427-4201; Fax: 905/655-3812 – President, Bar Hodgson

BRAMPTON
Creative Meeting & Marketing Services, 74 Mara Cres., Brampton ON L6V 4B7 – 905/456-0438; Fax: 905/456-9429 – Ingrid Norrish

BURLINGTON
Meeting Management Services Inc., 2267 Abbotsbury St., Burlington ON L7P 4H7 – 905/335-7993; Fax: 905/332-1587; Email: rdewar@ibm.net – Ronald F. Dewar

CARP
Beverley Anderson & Associates Ltd., 978 Spruce Ridge Rd., Carp ON K0A 1L0 – 613/831-7151; Fax: 613/831-7151 – President, Beverley Anderson

CONCORD
Multimedia Trade Shows Inc., #7, 70 Villarboit Cres., Concord ON L4K 4C7 – 905/660-2491; Fax: 905/660-2492 – President, Bruce Cole

CUMBERLAND
Larabie Entertainment Productions, 2491 Ferry Rd., Cumberland ON K4C 1C6 – 613/833-3256; Fax: 613/834-7073 – Contact, Ted Larabie

EXETER
AIS Communications Ltd., 145 Thames Rd. West, Exeter ON N0M 1S3 – 519/235-2400; Fax: 519/235-0798 – Contact, Peter Phillips

GRIMSBY
Toronto Show Promotions, PO Box 217, Grimsby ON L3M 4G3 – 905/945-2775; Fax: 905/945-3199 – Doug Jarvis

HAMILTON
About Town - Event & Meeting Planners, 494 Mary St., Hamilton ON L8L 4X4 – 905/529-6956; Fax: 905/529-1108 – Owner, Joan Balinson

Kelly-Alexander Inc., 875 Main St. West, Hamilton ON L8S 4R1 – 905/522-9422; Fax: 905/529-2242 – Show Manager, Paul McNair

Lakeshore Productions Inc., 875 Main St. West, Hamilton ON L8S 4R1 – 905/522-6117; Fax: 905/529-2242 – Show Manager, Karen McHarb

HAVELOCK
Neveu Productions Inc., PO Box 659, Havelock ON K0L 1Z0 – 705/778-2275; Fax: 705/778-2275; Toll Free: 1-800-461-6568 – Carolyn Neveu

KINGSTON
Events & Management Plus Inc., 190 Railway St., PO Box 1570, Kingston ON K7L 5C8 – 613/531-9210; Fax: 613/531-0626; Email: events@adan.kingston.net – Owner, E. Hooper

LONDON
London Show Productions, RR#5, London ON N6A 4B9 – 519/455-5888; Fax: 519/455-7780 – President, Arthur Bacon

Martha E. Murray Event Coordination, 274 Grosvenor St., London ON N6A 1Y8 – 519/675-0301; Fax. 519/675-0350

MARKHAM
Canadian Tel-A-Views Ltd., #12, 115 Apple Creek Blvd., Markham ON L3R 6C9 – 905/477-2677; Fax: 905/477-7872; Toll Free: 1-800-891-4859 – President, Fred Cox

Hugh Wilson & Associate Consultants Ltd., #204, 500 Alden Rd., Markham ON L3R 5H5 – 905/475-7531; Fax: 905/475-1916 – Contact, Emoke Nadai

Marketer Shows Inc., #635, 7305 Woodbine Ave., Markham ON L3R 3V7 – 905/473-7009; Fax: 905/473-5217 – Terrence Kehoe

Meridican Travel Inc., #1, 7225 Woodbine Ave., Markham ON L3R 1A3 – 905/477-7700; Fax: 905/477-7580 – President, Anthony Byron

MISSISSAUGA
Automotive Video Productions, #17, 5004 Timberlea Blvd., Mississauga ON L4W 5C5 – 416/206-1304; Fax: 416/206-1170; Toll Free: 1-800-275-4287 – President, Ron Baker

Custom Show Management Inc., #300, 2085 Hurontario St., Mississauga ON L5A 4G1 – 905/949-5550; Fax: 905/949-6903 – Show Manager, Brian McLean

Frank Teepell & Associates Meeting Consultants, International Inc., #26, 1724 The Chase, Mississauga ON L5M 4P2 – 905/828-0930 – President, Frank Teepell

Kerrwil Show & Conference Group, 395 Matheson Blvd. East, Mississauga ON L4Z 2H2 – 905/890-1846; Fax: 905/890-5769 – Manager, Anita Schachter

Lakeview Publications, #27, 1200 Aerowood Dr., Mississauga ON L4W 2S7 – 905/624-8100; Fax: 905/624-1760 – President, Robert C. Luton

Meetings Professional International - Toronto, 6519B Mississauga Rd., Mississauga ON L5N 1A6 – 905/567-9591; Fax: 905/567-9961 – Executive Director, Leslie Wright

Ontario Trade Shows Ltd., #8, 1606 Sedlescomb Dr., Mississauga ON L4X 1M6 – 905/625-7070; Fax: 905/625-4856 – Alexander Donald

Opportunities Canada, #42, 2550 Goldenridge Rd., Mississauga ON L4X 2S3 – 905/277-5600; Fax: 905/277-3397 – Sales Manager, Cheryl Higgins

Travel Trust International Canada, #300, 2810 Matheson Blvd. East, Mississauga ON L4W 4X7 – 905/629-9975; Fax: 905/629-0361 – Manager, Corporate Planning Group, Doreen Ostrowski

Winexpo Productions Inc., #11, 5080 Timberlea Blvd., Mississauga ON L4W 4M2 – 905/629-7469; Fax: 905/629-3823; URL: http://www.toronto.com/winexpo – General Manager, Megan Parry

NEPEAN
Intertrade Associates Inc., #250, 1511 Merivale Rd., Nepean ON K2G 3J3 – 613/224-3013; Fax: 613/224-4533; Toll Free: 1-888-662-6660 – Show Manager, Kevin McWhinnie

OAKVILLE
Jenkins Show Productions, 1076 Skyvalley Cr., Oakville ON L6M 3L2 – 905/827-4632; Fax: 905/827-8139; Toll Free: 1-800-465-1073 – President, Dave Jenkins

Premier Consumer Shows, City Parent Newsmagazine, 467 Speers Rd., Oakville ON L6K 3S4 – 905/815-0017; Fax: 905/815-0511 – Show Coordinator, Brenda Harris

Protocol International, 377 Yale Cres., Oakville ON L6L 3L6 – 905/825-8061; Fax: 905/825-4149; Email: 74117.733@compuserve.com – Director, Joy Fox

Ten Star Productions Inc., 155 Castle Cr., Oakville ON L6J 5H4 – 905/845-2644; Fax: 905/333-1097 – Show Manager, Roberta Said

OTTAWA
Conference Coll Inc., 1138 Sherman Dr., Ottawa ON K2C 2M4 – 613/224-1741(bus.); 225-4229(res.); Fax: 613/224-9685; Email: cci@sce.carleton.ca – President, Marg Coll

Connelly Business Exhibitions Inc., #214, 2487 Kaladar Ave., Ottawa ON K1V 8B9 – 613/731-9850; Fax: 613/731-2407 – Vice-President, Marketing, Dan Hamilton

DeLaurier Brown Associates, #20, 99 - 5th Ave., Ottawa ON K1S 5P5 – 613/823-6986; Fax: 613/823-6992 – President, Jean Brown

Golden Planners Inc., #404, 126 York St., Ottawa ON K1N 5T5 – 613/594-8226; Fax: 613/565-2173 – Contact, Hélène Lamadeleine

Impact Management International, #250, 2415 Holly Lane, Ottawa ON K1V 7P2 – 613/523-0974 – Contact, Sheila McKirdy

Intertask Ltd., 275 Bay St., Ottawa ON K1R 5Z5 – 613/238-4075; Fax: 613/238-3805 – President, Paul Akehurst

The Organizing Solution Inc., 174 Hickory St., Ottawa ON K1Y 3T6 – 613/724-9900; Fax: 613/724-4851; Toll Free: 1-800-363-4988 – President, Patti Mordasewicz

Player Expositions International, 255 Clemow Ave., Ottawa ON K1S 2B5 – 613/567-6408; Fax: 613/567-2718 – Show Organizer, Halina Player

Richmor Enterprises, #201, 251 Laurier Ave. West, Ottawa ON K1P 5J6 – 613/563-0093; Fax: 613/236-4351 – Conference Manager, Marion G. Fuller

Rolly Hammond Productions (1985) Inc., #201, 135 York, Ottawa ON K1N 5T4 – 613/234-2886; Fax: 613/234-3377 – Contact, Nathaly Pinchuk

Southex Exhibitions Inc., #440, 47 Clarence St., Ottawa ON K1N 9K1 – 613/232-0766; Fax: 613/238-4827 – Group Show Manager, Ray Fahey

Taylor & Associates Convention Management, 676 Shefford Ct., Ottawa ON K1J 6X3 – 613/747-0262; Fax: 613/745-1846 – President, April Taylor

The Willow Group, 582 Somerset West, Ottawa ON K1R 5K2 – 613/237-2324; Fax: 613/237-9900; Email: moreinfo@thewillowgroup.com; URL: http://thewillowgroup.com/willow/ – Contact, Benoit Comeau

PETERBOROUGH
Dawn Morris Productions Inc., #3, 1434 Chemong Rd., RR#1, Peterborough ON K9J 6X2 – 705/741-2536; Fax: 705/741-2539; Email: cifes@dawnmorris.on.ca; URL: http://www.dawnmorris.on.ca – Show Manager, Lesley Nicholson

RICHMOND HILL
Eagle-Com. Inc., 22 Dunvegan Dr., Richmond Hill ON L4C 6K1 – 905/882-7571; Fax: 905/882-7579 – Meetings & Conference Consultant, Julie Nurse

STOUFFVILLE
The Profile Group, #301, 37 Sandiford Dr., Stouffville ON L4A 7X5 – 905/640-7700; Fax: 905/640-7714

MEETING, CONFERENCE, EXHIBIT & EVENT PLANNERS

SUDBURY
DAC Marketing Ltd., PO Box 2837, Stn A, Sudbury ON P3A 5J3 – 705/673-5588; Fax: 705/525-0626 – President, Darren A. Ceccarelli

THORNHILL
Sheldon Kagan Productions Ltd., #14, 7420 Bathurst St., Thornhill ON L4J 6X4 – 905/882-5888

TORONTO
1071269 Ontario Inc., PO Box 1500-1288, Etobicoke ON M9C 4V5 – 416/620-6620; Fax: 416/621-6688 – Monique Trotter

Accent Toronto Inc./Insight Planners, One Sultan St., Toronto ON M5S 1L6 – 416/944-3631

Aldel Ltd., 1126B The Queensway, Etobicoke ON M8Z 1P7 – 416/259-3713; Fax: 416/259-8566 – Contact, Jim Clare

Backyard Living Productions, PO Box 1500-1288, Etobicoke ON M9C 4V5 – 416/620-6620; Fax: 416/621-6688 – Shirley Trotter

Barslow Communications & Marketing, 65 Helena Ave., Toronto ON M6G 2H3 – 416/653-4986; Fax: 416/653-2291; Email: barslow@to.org – President/CEO, Joyce Barslow

Base Services Canada Inc., #301, 250 Consumers Rd., North York ON M2J 4V6 – 416/494-1440; Fax: 416/495-8723; Email: base@onramp.ca – President, Brian Lechem

Business & Industry Services, 205 Humber College Blvd., Toronto ON M9W 5L7 – 416/675-5020; Fax: 416/675-6681 – Director, Ingrid A. Norrish

The Canadian Institute, 1329 Bay St., 3rd Fl., Toronto ON M5R 2C4 – 416/927-0718; Fax: 416/927-1061, 966-0175 – Contact, Hayley Colt

Canadian National Sportsmen's Shows (1989) Ltd., #202, 703 Evans Ave., Toronto ON M5C 5E9 – 416/695-0311; Fax: 416/695-0381 – President, Walter Oster

Canadian Shows & Special Events Inc., #1801, One Yonge St., Toronto ON M5E 1W7 – 416/363-1292; Fax: 416/369-0515 – Show Director, Brian Miles

Communiqué Group Inc., 370 King St. West, Toronto ON M5V 2J9 – 416/593-1212; Fax: 416/593-7008 – President, Geoff Genovese

Congress Canada, #100, 49 Bathurst St., Toronto ON M5V 2P2 – 416/504-4500; Fax: 416/504-4505; Email: sales@congresscan.com – President, Pam Graham

Contemporary Craft Shows Ltd., 37 Langley Ave., Toronto ON M4K 3V9 – 416/465-2379; Fax: 416/465-2379 – Casey Sadaka

Convention Planners International Inc., #302, 234 Eglinton Ave. East, Toronto ON M4P 1K5 – 416/482-2992; Fax: 416/482-2714 – Aubrey Harmes

Corporate Events Management Inc., #803, 1 Toronto St., Toronto ON M5C 2V6 – 416/869-0141; Fax: 416/869-1660 – Principal, Jacqueline Peake

Creative Consulting, #2510, 44 St. Joseph St., Toronto ON M4Y 2W4 – 416/929-5135; Fax: 416/929-5135 – President, Christine Z. Adelhardt, C.M.P.

Creative Events Management, 55 Vansco Rd., Toronto ON M8Z 5Z8 – 416/259-1346; Fax: 416/259-2053 – President, Margi Taylor

Crossroads Entertainment & Event Corporation, #100, 1815 Yonge St., Toronto ON M4T 2A4 – 416/488-5000; Fax: 416/488-7511 – President, Suzanne Bristow

Distinctive Meetings & Occasions, #408, 4576 Yonge St., North York ON M2N 6N4 – 416/441-9238; Fax: 416/441-9278 – President, Angela Tomsic

Farewell Tours, #420, 48 Yonge St., Toronto ON M5E 1G6 – 416/366-3901; Fax: 416/363-5561 – Contact, Nagel Andrews

Genigraphics Canada Inc., #400, 49 Spadina Ave., Toronto ON M5V 2J1 – 416/595-1335 – Contact, Michael Turney

Glavin & Associates, #301, 40 Holly St., Toronto ON M4S 3C3 – 416/482-3030; Fax: 416/482-3051; Email: glavin@magic.ca – Contact, Ingrid Rubin

Harold Taylor Enterprises Ltd., #110, 2175 Sheppard Ave. East, North York ON M2J 1W8 – 416/491-2897; Fax: 416/491-1670

H.D. Shield & Associates Ltd., 25 Bradgate Rd., North York ON M3B 1J6 – 416/444-5225; Fax: 416/444-8268 – Show Coordinator, Patrick Shield

Hospitality Toronto, 468 Balliol St., 5th Fl., Toronto ON M4S 1E2 – 416/487-7789; Fax: 416/487-3857 – President, Maureen Lorimer

Hospitality Tours, 180 Bloor St. West, Main Concourse, Toronto ON M5S 2V6 – 416/968-3481; Fax: 416/968-9053

Impact Event Management, 358 Danforth Ave., PO Box 65060, Toronto ON M4K 3Z2 – 416/461-5306; Fax: 416/461-8460 – Donald Nausbaum

InAdvance, 59 Hogarth Ave., Toronto ON M4K 1K2 – 416/465-1430; Fax: 416/462-3750 –

Incentives International Inc., 160 Bloor St. East, Toronto ON M4W 1B9 – 416/928-5829; Fax: 416/928-7798 – President, J. Duff Shaw, C.M.P., C.I.T.E.

International Conferences & Expositions Inc., #285, 144 Front St. West, Toronto ON M5J 2L7 – 416/581-8797; Fax: 416/591-8539

International Show Productions Inc., 36 Fallingbrook Dr., Scarborough ON M1N 1B6 – 416/691-2852; Fax: 416/691-2891 – Steve Nichols

International Tradeshow Services Inc., 20 Butterick Rd., Toronto ON M8W 3Z8 – 416/252-7791; Fax: 416/252-9848; Email: jimm@intltradeshows.com; URL: http://www.intltradeshows.com – President, James K. Mahon

JPdL Multi Management Inc., #2550, 55 King St. West, PO Box 77, Toronto ON M5K 1E7 – 416/784-5735; Fax: 416/784-0808 – Regional Director, Rosemary Blackbyrne

Kerbel Communications Inc., 40 Holly St., 6th Fl., Toronto ON M4S 3C3 – 416/489-1414; Fax: 416/489-9940; Toll Free: 1-800-625-3625; Email: kerbel@inforamp.net – Event Manager, Shari Koladich

Klanside Inc., 401 Magnetic Dr., Unit 21, North York ON M3J 3H9 – 416/661-2056; Fax: 416/661-2904

The Mariposa Group Inc., 147 Liberty St., Toronto ON M6K 3G3 – 416/588-6699; Fax: 416/532-7736 – CEO, Greg Cochrane

MCC Planners Inc. (Meetings, Conventions, Conferences), #201N, 310 North Queen St., Toronto ON M9C 1K4 – 416/621-6622; Fax: 416/621-0363 – President, Marsha Jones

Meteor Show Productions Inc., 298 Sheppard Ave. East, North York ON M2N 3B1 – 416/229-2060; Fax: 416/223-2826; Email: weil@meteorshows.com; URL: http://www.meteorshows.com – President, Ralph Weil

Michael Caplan Entertainment Toronto Inc., 777 The Queensway, Unit E, Toronto ON M8Z 1N4 – 416/503-3000; Fax: 416/503-0002 – Contact, Ronnie Caplan

MW Productions, #4, 88 Courcelette Rd., Scarborough ON M1N 2T2 – 416/691-6526; Fax: 416/691-6928; Toll Free: 1-800-267-4529; Email: ron.mackenzie@mwprod.com; URL: http://www.mwprod.com – Ron MacKenzie

Ontario Marketing Productions, 109 Scollard St., Toronto ON M5R 1G4 – 416/961-2999; Fax: 416/961-1157 – Contact, Linda Watt

Ontario Out of Doors Magazine, 777 Bay St., 6th Fl., Toronto ON M5W 1A7 – 416/596-5908; Fax: 416/596-2517; Email: 102677.1125@compuserve.com; URL: http://www.cyberplex.com/fishontario – Show Manager, Lynda Watson

Ontario Tour & Travel Services Ltd., 134 Jarvis St., Toronto ON M5B 2B5 – 416/869-3759; Fax: 416/869-0284 – President/Owner, John Ryan

Perdue Show Management, 378 Evans Ave., Etobicoke ON M8Z 1K6 – 416/503-8240; Fax: 416/503-8130 – President, Elizabeth Fairley

Peter Milne Consulting, 88 Patterson Ave., Scarborough ON M1L 3Y4 – 416/694-6059; Fax: 416/694-6059 – President, Peter Milne

Plesman Expositions & Conferences Inc., 2005 Sheppard Ave. East, 4th Fl., North York ON M2J 5B1 – 416/497-9562; Fax: 416/497-9427; Toll Free: 1-800-387-5012; URL: http://www.netcon.plesman.com – Show Coordinator, Sean Wainwright

Pro-Show, Trade Show Management, #102, 33 Isabella St., Toronto ON M4Y 2P7 – 416/960-8739; Fax: 416/960-1854 – Show Manager, Dan Joyce

Promex Productions Inc., 118 Indian Rd., 2nd Fl., Toronto ON M6R 2V4 – 416/531-2121; Fax: 416/531-2194 – Show Manager, Angela Abromaitis

Reed Exhibition Companies Inc., 3761 Victoria Park Ave., Scarborough ON M1W 3S2 – 416/491-7565; Fax: 416/491-5088

Ryerson Polytechnic University, 350 Victoria St., Toronto ON M5B 2K3 – 416/979-5184; Fax: 416/979-5148 – Program Director, Continuing Education, Diana E. Hennessy

Show Fest Productions Inc., #5, 60 St. Clair Ave. West, Toronto ON M4V 1M7 – 416/925-4533; Fax: 416/925-7701 – David Carter

Showcase Marketing Ltd., #410, 1110 Sheppard Ave. East, North York ON M2K 2W2 – 416/512-1305; Fax: 416/512-9998 – Paul Newdick

Sierra Corporate Productions Inc., #302, 102 Atlantic Ave., Toronto ON M6K 1X9 – 416/531-8757; Fax: 416/531-2602 – President, Bill Greenbaum

Sightlines Productions Ltd., #129, 6 Lansing Sq., North York ON M2J 1T5 – 416/499-5068; Fax: 416/492-4108 – President, Frank Bayley

Southex Exhibitions, 1450 Don Mills Rd., North York ON M3B 2X7 – 416/445-6641; Fax: 416/442-2207 –

Sparkling Concepts - Brilliant Events Inc., #100, 2005 Sheppard Ave. East, Willowdale, North York ON M2J 2B4 – 416/502-9578; Fax: 416/490-0173 – President, D'Arcy G. Moran

Toronto International Bicycle Show, #1801, 1 Yonge St., Toronto ON M5E 1W7 – 416/363-1292; Fax: 416/369-0515 – Show Manager, Josie Graziosi

Two Plus One Group, #611, 220 Duncan Mill Rd., North York ON M3B 3J5 – 416/510-0114; Fax: 416/510-0165 – President, Alice Chee

York Expositions, #803, 1 Toronto St., Toronto ON M5C 2V6 – 416/869-1156; Fax: 416/869-1660 – George Przybylowski

UTOPIA
Marty Kay Productions Inc., RR#1, Utopia ON L0M 1T0 – 705/424-2668; Fax: 705/424-5202 – Contact, Marty Kay

QUÉBEC

BROSSARD
Yves Barré & Associés, 6940, rue Barry, Brossard PQ J4Z 1V1 – 514/443-3131; Fax: 514/443-8415 – Président, Yves Barré

HULL
Communications Show, CP 1241, Succ B, Hull PQ J8X 3X7 – 418/877-8898; Fax: 418/877-9711 – Président, Roch Gamache

LONGUEUIL
Marcel Gaudreault, Consultant, 1431, Bourgeoys, Longueuil PQ J4M 1Z5 – 514/647-5530; Fax: 514/647-1031 – Président, Marcel Gaudreault

MONTREAL
AFLD Consultants Inc., 3565, rue Edgar Leduc, Lachine PQ H8T 3L5 – 514/639-6806; Fax: 514/639-6629 – Show Manager, Lucie Desharnais

Canadian Almanac & Directory 1997

Canadian National Sportsmen's Shows (1989) Ltd., #1630, 1155, rue Metcalfe, Montréal PQ H3B 2V6 – 514/866-5409; Fax: 514/866-4092 – Show Manager, Diane Laporte

Clarkson-Conway Inc., CP 216, Succ Place Bonaventure, Montréal PQ H5A 1A9 – 514/861-9694; Fax: 514/392-1577 – General Manager, Marilyn Meikle

Communications Savoir Faire, 4119, rue Sherbrooke ouest, Montréal PQ H3Z 1B6 – 514/935-7776; Fax: 514/935-3825 – Président, Gina Roitman

Coplanor Congrès inc., #600, 511, Place d'Armes, Montréal PQ H2Y 2W7 – 514/848-1133; Fax: 514/288-6469; Email: conf@coplanor.qc.ca – Executive Director, Carol Langevin

Expour Inc., 9200, boul Henri-Bourassa ouest, Montréal PQ H4S 1L5 – 514/334-3976; Fax: 514/334-1180; Toll Free: 1-800-668-3976 – Président, C. Guevremont

Gerry Lou & Associates, #211, 1224, rue Stanley, Montréal PQ H3B 2S7 – 514/878-2530; Fax: 514/878-2532 – Director, Client Services, Guylaine Pauld

GroupExpo, 101, rue Laurier ouest, Montréal PQ H2T 2N6 – 514/272-0606; Fax: 514/272-6699

International Motivation & Incentive Consultants, 5427 Robert Burns St., Montréal PQ H4W 2B5 – 514/482-3553; Fax: 514/482-9785; Telex: ITT 4951939 – President, Stephen P. Libman

JPdL Multi Management Inc., #609, 1410, rue Stanley, Montréal PQ H3A 1P8 – 514/287-1070; Fax: 514/287-1248; Toll Free: 1-800-361-1070 – Président, Jean-Paul de Lavison

Kenness Canada Inc., 1210, rue Sherbrooke ouest, Montréal PQ H3A 1H6 – 514/284-0864; Fax: 514/284-2968 – President, Danielle Pollack

Maestro Innovations, #500, 1410, rue Stanley, Montréal PQ H3A 1P8 – 514/287-1465; Fax: 514/843-5680 – Vice-President, Joan Macklin

Martin International, #2910, 500, Place des Armes, Montréal PQ H2Y 2W2 – 514/288-3931; Fax: 514/288-0641 – General Manager, Lorraine Boisvenue

McGill University Conference Office, #490, Tour Ouest, 550, rue Sherbrooke ouest, Montréal PQ H3A 1B9 – 514/398-3770; Fax: 514/398-4854; Email: MCO@ums1.ian.mcgill.ca; URL: http://www.mcgill.ca/mco – Contact, Joan Gross

Multicom International Montréal, Place Bonaventure, Door 4, PO Box 523, Montréal PQ H5A 1C3 – 514/875-2789; Fax: 514/272-8879; Telex: 05-268769 – President, Sigrid Chatel

P.R. Charette Inc., 35, Promenade Westland, Montréal-Ouest PQ H4X 1M3 – 514/489-8671; Fax: 514/487-3230 – Contact, Bob Charette

Promexpo Inc., 801, rue Sherbrooke est, 10e étage, Montréal PQ H2L 1K7 – 514/527-9221; Fax: 514/527-8449 – General Manager, Vic Côté

Sensix Communications & Events Inc., #201, 8225 Mayrand Ave., Montréal PQ H4P 2C7 – 514/739-2309; Fax: 514/342-1682 – Sales Director, Hélène Gibbens

Sheldon Kagan International Ltd., 95, McConnell, Dorval PQ H9S 5L9 – 514/631-2160; Fax: 514/631-4430 – President, Sheldon Kagan

Sorelcomm (1985) Inc., #704, 4446 St. Lawrence Blvd., Montréal PQ H2W 1Z5 – 514/499-8920; Fax: 514/499-8921 – President, Denise L. Duhaime

QUEBEC

Forum Québec, 30, rue Grande Allée ouest, Québec PQ G1R 2G6 – 418/524-8093; Fax: 418/529-1172

Omnitour, 105, Côte de la Montagne, Québec PQ G1R 4P3 – 418/692-1223; Fax: 418/692-4537 – Président, Jacques Morissette

Pro-Expo Inc., #115, 200, rue St-Jean-Baptiste, Québec PQ G2E 5E8 – 418/871-6130; Fax: 418/871-3831 – President, Gaétan Marcoux

Les Promotions André Pageau Inc., 1627, boul St-Joseph, Québec PQ G2K 1H1 – 418/623-3383; Fax: 418/623-5033 – Président, André Pageau

SAINT LAMBERT

Destination à la Carte inc., #24, 680, av Victoria, Mezzanine, Saint-Lambert PQ J4P 3S1 – 514/466-9342; Fax: 418/465-9949 – Président, Ken Ondrick

SASKATCHEWAN

REGINA

Dawn Redmond & Associates Ltd., 2352 Smith St., Regina SK S4P 2P6 – 306/781-7300; Fax: 306/565-0881 – President, Dawn Redmond-Bradley

Dimension 11 Consulting Ltd., 2301 - 15th Ave., Regina SK S4P 1A3 – 306/586-2315; Fax: 306/721-6602; Toll Free: 1-800-303-2315; Email: dim11@unibase.com – Contact, Sherry Knight

Merle Kennedy Consulting Inc., 3623 McCallum Ave., Regina SK S4S 0S6 – 306/586-0081 – Contact, Merle Kennedy

SASKATOON

Saskatoon Prairieland Exhibition Corporation, PO Box 6010, Saskatoon SK S7K 4E4 – 306/931-7149; Fax: 306/931-7886 – General Manager, Ed Sikorski

EXHIBITIONS, SHOWS & EVENTS

The following list includes Consumer & Trade shows, Public Events, Conferences, Festivals arranged by category of interest. The addresses given are the office addresses of associations/sponsors. Focus is on events of an ongoing annual or biennial nature. The lists are not complete, but are fairly representative of shows held throughout Canada. Users are cautioned that dates or venues may alter.

ACCOUNTING

The Bottom Line, Reed Exhibition Companies Inc., 3761 Victoria Park Ave., Scarborough ON M1W 3S2 – 416/491-7565; Fax: 416/491-5088 – September

National Conference, Society of Management Accountants of Canada, #850, 120 King St. West, PO Box 176, Hamilton ON L8N 3C3 – 905/525-4100; 416/847-0373 (Toronto line); Fax: 905/525-4533; Email: http://www.cma-canada.org – President, Stan E. Whiteley, CMA, FCMA – July 15-18 1997 – St. John's NF

ADVERTISING

Great Ideas, Festival Trade Shows, PO Box 1985, Kitchener ON N2G 4R9 – 519/571-8881; Fax: 519/571-8883 – Annual trade show, summer

The Motivational Marketing Expo, Southex Exhibitions, 1450 Don Mills Rd., North York ON M3B 2X7 – 416/445-6641; Fax: 416/442-2207 – Show Manager, Ross Horton – Annual trade show, September – Metro Toronto Convention Centre

National Convention & Trade Show, Canadian Direct Marketing Association, #607, One Concorde Gate, North York ON M3C 3N6 – 416/391-2362; Fax: 416/441-4062; Email: kbrasch@cdma.org; URL: http://www.cdma.org – Show Manager, Linda Kuschnir – Annual. Direct marketing & tele-marketing, May 13-16 1997 – World Trade & Convention Centre, Halifax NS

AGRICULTURE see FARM BUSINESS/AGRICULTURE

AIR SHOWS/AVIATION

Abbotsford International Airshow, PO Box 361, Abbotsford BC V2S 4N9 – 604/859-9211; Fax: 604/852-6093 – Contact, Leanne Martel – Large static display. Four/five hour flying show, August

Aeroheritage Hamilton International Airshow, #866, 150 King St. East, Hamilton ON L8N 1B2 – 905/528-4425; Fax: 905/528-8499 – General Manager, Al Lutchin – June

Airshow, International Air Show Society of Whitehorse, PO Box 5108, Whitehorse YT Y1A 4S3 – 403/667-2148 – May – Whitehorse YT

Airshow Canada, PO Box 6, Abbotsford BC V2S 4N9 – 604/852-4600; Fax: 604/852-3704 – Held in conjunction with the Canadian Business Aircraft Association Exhibition – Annual trade show & symposium, August

Armed Forces Day, Harman Field, Stephenville NF A2N 2Y7 – 709/643-9123 – July

Canadian International Airshow, Press Bldg., Exhibition Place, 2nd Fl., Toronto ON M6K 3C3 – 416/393-6061, 6062; Fax: 416/393-6259 – Coordinator, Deborah Day – Annually, three days of the Labour Day Weekend

CFB Comox Airshow, CFB Comox, Lazo BC V0R 2K0 – 250/339-8391 – Contact, Major Don Harrington – Biennial, even-numbered years, August 1998

Festival of Flight, c/o, PO Box 280, Gander NF A1V 1W6 – 709/651-2656 – A celebration of Gander's aviation history, July

Fredericton International Air Show, PO Box 130, Fredericton NB E3B 4Y7 – 506/452-9500; Fax: 506/452-9509 – Richard Bagley – May

Friendship Festival Air Show, 1133 Benner Rd., Fort Erie ON L2A 4N8 – 905/871-2529 – Annual, July

G.T. Rowan Anniversary Air Show, PO Box 779, La Ronge SK S0J 1L0 – 306/425-3497; Fax: 306/425-4328 – June

Kamloops Air Show, PO Box 866, Kamloops BC V2C 5M8 – 250/828-1404 – Chair, Holly Schwieger – August

Lethbridge International Airshow, 1610 - 15 Ave. South, Lethbridge AB T1K 0W7 – 403/328-7605 – Annual, August

London International Airshow, 26 Duncan Cres., London ON N5V 4E8 – 519/659-3298; URL: http://www.airshow.org/lias.html – June

National Capital Airshow, #250, 108 Airport Service Rd., Gloucester ON K1V 9B4 – 613/526-1030; Fax: 613/526-1035 – July

Saskatchewan Air Show, PO Box 5000, Moose Jaw SK S6H 7Z8 – 306/694-2600; Fax: 306/694-2602; Tollfree: 1-800-461-7469 – Capt. Andrew Mackenzie – July

Shearwater International Air Show, PO Box 218, Shearwater NS B0J 3A0 – 902/465-2725; Fax: 902/466-1796 – Canada's largest annual military air show. Industrial displays, static aircraft, flying display, marching bands, August

Vanderhoof International Airshow, PO Box 1248, Vanderhoof BC V0J 3A0 – 250/567-3144 – July

Victoria Airshow, #15, 9600 Canora Rd., Sidney BC V8L 4R1 – 250/656-3337; Fax: 250/655-3766 – August

Yarmouth International Air Show, PO Box 441, Yarmouth NS B5A 4B4 – 902/742-8134 – Biennial

ANTIQUES

Annual Consumer Show, Ontario Steam & Antique Preservers Association, 5511 3rd Line, RR#1, Milton ON L9T 2X5 – 905/878-3205 – Secretary, Gordon Rayner – Parades, races, competitions, toy shows, Aug. 29 – Sept. 1 1997 – Milton Fairgrounds, Milton ON

Blue Mountain's Antiques Show, Blue Mountain Promotions, #1323N, 6455 Macleod Trail, PO Box 30009, Calgary AB T2H 2V8 – 403/264-0792; Fax: 403/755-4081 – John Humphrey – Semi-annual (Spring & Fall) antiques & collectibles show – Calgary AB
Capital Antique Show, Antiquités Obsession Ltée, 1886, rue Notre-Dame ouest, Montréal PQ H3J 1M6 – 514/933-6375 – Robert Ness – Annual consumer show, March – Ottawa ON
Carswell Collectables Antiques Show & Sale, Carswell Collectables, PO Box 1036, Red Deer AB T4N 6S5 – 403/324-2943; Fax: 403/347-7633 – Rae Carswell – Consumer shows in Lacombe & Red Deer
Depression Glass Show & Sale, Hacking Antiques, 1026 Forestwood Dr., Mississauga ON L8H 7S7 – 905/277-1221 – Edith Hacking – Semi-annual consumer show – Toronto ON
Spring Sale of Antiques & Collectibles, PO Box 3691, Regina SK S4P 3N8 – 306/522-7580 – Sale Coordinator, Noreeta Finn – April
Toronto Antique Show, c/o Exhibition Place, Toronto ON M6K 3C3 – 416/939-8437
Toronto Collectibles Extravaganza, Toronto Show Promotions, PO Box 217, Grimsby ON L3M 4G3 – 905/945-2775; Fax: 905/945-3199 – Doug Jarvis – Annual; nostalgia & antique show, October – Toronto ON
Toronto International Toy Collectors Show, Toronto Show Promotions, PO Box 217, Grimsby ON L3M 4G3 – 905/945-2775; Fax: 905/945-3199 – Doug Jarvis – Annual; antique & collectible childhood memorabilia, November – Toronto ON
The Toronto Toy Show, Toronto Show Promotions, PO Box 217, Grimsby ON L3M 4G3 – 905/945-2775; Fax: 905/945-3199 – Doug Jarvis – Annual consumer show; antique & collectible childhood memorabilia, April – Toronto ON
Yesteryear Heritage Fair, Nepean Sportsplex, 101 Centrepointe Dr., Nepean ON K2G 5K7 – 613/727-6641; Fax: 613/727-6613 – Projects Co-ordinator, Billie Swartzack – February – Ottawa ON

APPAREL see FASHION

ARCHITECTURE see CONSTRUCTION & BUILDING PRODUCTS

ART/ARTS
see also First Night; Crafts; Music; Events
Arnold Mikelson Festival of Arts, 13743 - 16 Ave., White Rock BC V4A 1P7 – 604/536-6460
Banff Festival of the Arts, The Banff Centre, PO Box 1020, Banff AB T0L 0C0 – 403/762-6300 – Early June to late August
Fringe Theatre Event, 10330 - 84 Ave., Edmonton AB T6E 2G9 – 403/448-9000 – General Manager, Shannon Paddon – August
Manitoba Holiday Festival of the Arts, PO Box 147, Neepawa MB R0J 1H0 – 204/476-2927 – Doreen Sage – Classes, workshops for all ages. First two weeks of July
Nova Scotia Folk Art Festival, RR#3, East LaHave, Bridgewater NS B4V 2W2 – 902/766-4382 – Patricia Wyllie – August – Lunenburg NS
Shakespeare on the Saskatchewan Festival, PO Box 1646, Saskatoon SK S7K 3R8 – 306/653-2300; Fax: 306/653-2357 – General Manager, Dawn Martin – July/August
Teen Festival of the Arts, c/o Citadel Theatre, 9828 - 101A Ave., Edmonton AB T5J 3C6 – 403/426-4811 – July
Toronto Indoor Art Show, c/o Artfocus Magazine, PO Box 1063, Stn F, Toronto ON M4V 2T7 – 416/925-5564 – Annual consumer show, October (Displays of art, photos, sculpture, mixed media)

Winnipeg Fringe Festival, Manitoba Theatre Centre, 174 Market Ave., Winnipeg MB R3B 0P8 – 204/956-1340 – Craig Walls – July
Women in View, 314 Powell St., Vancouver BC V6A 1G4 – 604/685-6684; Fax: 604/685-6649; URL: http://www.ffa.ucalgary.ca/vca/wmnvie.htm – Executive Director, Dawn Brennan – Multi-disciplinary festival, January – Vancouver BC

AUTOMOTIVE
Auto Expo, DAC Marketing Ltd., PO Box 2837, Stn A, Sudbury ON P3A 5J3 – 705/673-5588; Fax: 705/525-0626 – President, Darren A. Ceccarelli
Autorama, 16 Wakefield Cres., London ON N5X 1Z7 – 519/451-5368 – Show Producer, Don Cook – Annual consumer show. Custom built autos, hot rods, race cars, antiques, classics, commercial exhibitors, February
Autorama, D&R Promotions, 2568 Carp Rd., Carp ON N6A 4G8 – 613/686-2200; Fax: 613/686-2202 – Doug McDougall – Annual consumer show, April – Ottawa ON
Big Rig National Truck Show, 490 Bethune St., Peterborough ON K92 3Z3 – 705/743-6671 – President, Kim Wallace – Annual consumer & trade show. Truck trailers, truck bodies, parts & accessories, engine power train components, service shop equipment, & supplies, truck & stock car race, June – Cayuga Speedway, Caledonia ON
Calgary International Auto & Truck Show, Calgary Motor Dealers Association, 3320 - 9 St. SE, Calgary AB T2G 3C3 – 403/287-3893; Fax: 403/243-0666 – Executive Manager, Jack Thompson – Annual consumer show: new vehicle displays, March – Calgary AB
Cam-Expo Québec, Pro-Expo Inc., #115, 200, rue St-Jean-Baptiste, Québec PQ G2E 5E8 – 418/871-6130; Fax: 418/871-3831 – President, Gaétan Marcoux – Biennial trade & consumer show, November
Canadian International Auto Show, Toronto Automobile Dealers Association, 85 Renfrew Dr., Markham ON L3R 0N9 – 905/940-2800; Fax: 905/940-2804 – Show Manager, Tom Tonks – Annual consumer show. New cars, classics, prototypes, motorsport & aftermarket products, Feb. 14-23 1997 – Metro Toronto Convention Centre & Skydome, Toronto ON
Canadian International Automotive Show, Automotive Industries Association of Canada, 1272 Wellington St., Ottawa ON K1Y 3A7 – 613/728-5821; Fax: 613/728-6021; Email: aia@aiacanada.com; URL: http://www.aftmkt.com – Vice-President, Yaroslav Zajac – Biennial trade show, April 25-27 1998 – International Centre, Toronto ON
Canadian International Motorcycle Super Show, Bar Hodgson Productions Inc., 8780 Baldwin St., RR#1, Ashburn ON L0B 1A0 – 905/427-4201; Fax: 905/655-3812 – President, Bar Hodgson – Annual consumer show, January – International Centre, Toronto ON
The Canadian Motorcycle Business Show, Bar Hodgson Productions Inc., 8780 Baldwin St., RR#1, Ashburn ON L0B 1A0 – 905/427-4201; Fax: 905/655-3812 – President, Bar Hodgson – Annual trade show, January – International Centre, Toronto ON
The Canadian Truck Show, AGM & Conference, Manitoba Trucking Association, 25 Bunting St., Winnipeg MB R2X 2P5 – 204/632-6600; Fax: 204/694-7134 – Show Contact, Bob Wilks – Biennial trade show. HD trucks, equipment, RMO supplies & related services, April 24-26 1997 – Winnipeg Convention Centre, Winnipeg MB
Car & Accessory Show, Greater Charlottetown Chamber of Commerce, 127 Kent St., PO Box 67, Charlottetown PE C1A 7K2 – 902/628-2000; Fax: 902/368-3570 – Ernest J. Dorion – Annual consumer show – Charlottetown PE

Chevy Weekend Challenge, Pro-Show, Trade Show Management, #102, 33 Isabella St., Toronto ON M4Y 2P7 – 416/960-8739; Fax: 416/960-1854 – Show Manager, Dan Joyce – Annual consumer show. Custom cars, hot rods, products & services, July – London ON
Classic Car Show, 2021 Wiggins Ave., Saskatoon SK S7J 1W2 – 306/343-0567 – Annie McDonald – 1955-1957 Chevrolets, Chev & GMC Trucks, Corvettes, Pontiacs, August
Cloverdale Fall RV Sale, Recreation Vehicle Dealers Association of British Columbia, #201, 19623 - 56 Ave., Langley BC V3A 3X7 – 604/533-4200; Fax: 604/533-0795 – Contact, Lynn Thompson – Annually, September
Collector's Car Club Annual Car Show, PO Box 3562, Regina SK S4P 3L7 – 306/525-5117 – David G. Bobinski – June
Edmonton International Auto & Truck Show, Edmonton Motor Dealers Association, 9249 - 48 St., Edmonton AB T6B 2R9 – 403/468-9552; Fax: 403/465-6201 – Show Manager, Elaine Babiy – Annual consumer show, March
Expo-Moto Montréal, Turbopress Inc., #600A, 5000, rue Buchan, Montréal PQ H4P 1T2 – 514/738-9439; Fax: 514/738-4929 – Contact, Roger Saint-Laurent – Montréal PQ
Expocam, Southex Exhibitions, 1450 Don Mills Rd., North York ON M3B 2X7 – 416/445-6641; Fax: 416/442-2207 – Show Manager, Margaret Johnston – Biennial trade show. Trucks, trailers, bodies, heavy duty parts & services & accessories, engine & power train components, service shop equipment, October 1997 – Montréal PQ
Hamilton International Auto Show, Kelly-Alexander Inc., 875 Main St. West, Hamilton ON L8S 4R1 – 905/522-9422; Fax: 905/529-2242 – Show Manager, Paul McNair – November – Copps Coliseum, Hamilton ON
Kelowna RV Show, Recreation Vehicle Dealers Association of British Columbia, #201, 19623 - 56 Ave., Langley BC V3A 3X7 – 604/533-4200; Fax: 604/533-0795 – Contact, Lynn Thompson – Annually, April – Kelowna BC
London International Auto Show, c/o The London Free Press, PO Box 2337, London ON N6A 4G3 – 519/667-4537; Fax: 519/667-4523 – Contact, Debra Mitchell – Annual consumer show, November
Molson Indy Vancouver at Pacific Place, 765 Pacific Blvd. South, Vancouver BC V6B 4Y9 – 604/684-4639; Fax: 604/684-1482 – Contact, Rena Shanaman – Annual Indy car race & show, August
Montréal International Auto Show, 2335, rue Guénette, St-Laurent PQ H4R 2E9 – 514/331-6571; Fax: 514/331-2045 – Directrice générale, Diane Bélair – Annual consumer show. New cars, light trucks, accessories, January – Olympic Stadium, Montréal PQ
The Motor Home & Trailer Show, Holger Enge Promotions, 204 Richmond St. West, Toronto ON M5H 2K1 – 416/777-1672; Fax: 416/777-1674 – Holger Enge – Annual consumer show; recreational vehicles, March – Mississauga ON
National Motorcycle Swap Meet & Bike Show, Neveu Productions Inc., PO Box 659, Havelock ON K0L 1Z0 – 705/778-2275; Fax: 705/778-2275; Tollfree: 1-800-461-6568 – President, Robert Neveu – Annual consumer show. Retail motorcycle show & sale, March – Queen Elizabeth Bldg., Exhibition Place, Toronto ON
Ottawa-Hull International Auto Show, Ottawa-Hull International Auto Show Inc., 234, boul Gingras, Fossambault-sur-le-Lac PQ G0A 3N0 – 418/875-1883; Fax: 418/875-1715 – Richard Cantin – Annual consumer show, January – Ottawa ON
Pacific International Auto & Light Truck Show, 882 Homer St., Vancouver BC V6B 2W5 – 604/669-3342; Fax: 604/669-3372 – Show Manager, Julia

Blockberger – Annual consumer show. New autos, related products & services, educational activities, aftermarket, January

Performance World Custom Car Show, Pro-Show, Trade Show Management, #102, 33 Isabella St., Toronto ON M4Y 2P7 – 416/960-8739; Fax: 416/960-1854 – Contact, Larry King – Annual consumer show, March

R.V. Exposition & Sale, Recreation Vehicle Dealers Association of Alberta, 11217 - 143 St., Edmonton AB T5M 3P8 – 403/455-8562; Fax: 403/453-3927 – Executive Vice-President, John Milligan – Annual consumer show held in Calgary & Edmonton

R.V. Super Sale, Recreation Vehicle Dealers Association of Manitoba, 58 Leger Cres., Winnipeg MB R3X 1J4 – 204/256-6119; Fax: 204/256-6119 – Manager, Susan Andree – Annual consumer show, March – Winnipwg MB

Salon Auto-Sport, Compagnie d'expositions d'automobiles du Québec, CP 53025, Québec PQ G1J 5K3 – 418/667-9009; Fax: 418/667-9009 – Jacques Picard – Annual sport car consumer show, April – Québec PQ

Salon de l'Auto de Québec/Québec City Auto Show, #325, 5600, boul des Galeries, Québec PQ G2K 2H6 – 418/624-2290; Fax: 418/624-4929 – General Manager, Jean-Guy Bégin – Consumer show, March – PEPS of Laval University, Québec PQ

Salon de la Moto de Montréal, Turbopress Inc., #600A, 5000, rue Buchan, Montréal PQ H4P 1T2 – 514/738-9439; Fax: 514/738-4929 – Contact, Roger Saint-Laurent – Annual consumer show, February – Montréal PQ

Salon de la Moto de Québec, Turbopress Inc., #600A, 5000, rue Buchan, Montréal PQ H4P 1T2 – 514/738-9439; Fax: 514/738-4929 – Contact, Roger Saint-Laurent – Annual consumer show, February – Québec PQ

Salon international des Véhicules récréatifs de Québec, Pro-Expo Inc., #115, 200, rue St-Jean-Baptiste, Québec PQ G2E 5E8 – 418/871-6130; Fax: 418/871-3831 – President, Gaétan Marcoux – Annual show, March

Snowbird RV Show & Sale, Recreation Vehicle Dealers Association of British Columbia, #201, 19623 - 56 Ave., Langley BC V3A 3X7 – 604/533-4200; Fax: 604/533-0795 – Contact, Lynn Thompson – Annually, October

Speedorama, Speedorama Shows Inc., PO Box 442, Ajax ON L1S 3C5 – 905/427-2100; Fax: 905/427-2158 – Show Manager, Mike Shane – Annual trade & consumer show. Customs, hot rods, motorcycles, commercial exhibitors, feature cars, racing personalities, February

Toronto Expo-Moto, Turbopress Inc., #600A, 5000, rue Buchan, Montréal PQ H4P 1T2 – 514/738-9439; Fax: 514/738-4929 – Contact, Roger Saint-Laurent

Toronto International Spring Bike Show, Bar Hodgson Productions Inc., 8780 Baldwin St., RR#1, Ashburn ON L0B 1A0 – 905/427-4201; Fax: 905/655-3812 – President, Bar Hodgson, April – International Centre, Toronto ON

Toronto RV Show, Ontario Recreation Vehicle Dealers Association, PO Box 270, Brechin ON L0K 1B0 – 705/484-0295; Fax: 705/484-5740 – Executive Director, William A. Mallatratt – Annual consumer show, January 1997 – Exhibition Place, Toronto ON

Trade Show, Canadian Automobile Dealers Association, 85 Renfrew Dr., Markham ON L3R 0N9 – 905/940-4959; Fax: 905/940-6870; Tollfree: 1-800-463-5289 – President, Kenneth R. Graydon – Feb. 1997 – Atlanta GA

Truckcan, Southex Exhibitions, 1450 Don Mills Rd., North York ON M3B 2X7 – 416/445-6641; Fax: 416/442-2207 – Show Manager, Chris Seeney – Biennial trade show. Trucks, trailers, bodies, heavy duty parts & accessories, engine & power train components, service shop equipment, signs & decals, October – International Centre, Mississauga ON

Truxpo '98, British Columbia Trucking Association, PO Box 381, Port Coquitlam BC V3C 4K6 – 604/942-3200; Fax: 604/942-3191; Tollfree: 1-800-565-2282 – Show Manager, Jerry Peters – Biennial trade show, Oct. 1-3 1998 – Abbotsford BC

Vancouver Island Bicycle & Motorcycle Show, VIEX Events Ltd., #2, 31 Bushby St., Victoria BC V8S 1B3 – 250/370-2983; Fax: 250/370-1733 – Sales & Marketing Director, Patrick Doyle – Annual consumer show, March – Victoria BC

Vancouver RV Show, Recreation Vehicle Dealers Association of British Columbia, #201, 19623 - 56 Ave., Langley BC V3A 3X7 – 604/533-4200; Fax: 604/533-0795 – Contact, Lynn Thompson – Annual consumer show, March – Vancouver BC

Vancouver Summer Motorcycle Show, Canadian National Sportsmen's Shows (1989) Ltd., #501, 4190 Lougheed Hwy., Burnaby BC V5C 6A8 – 604/294-1313; Fax: 604/294-4740 – Show Contact, Paul McGeachie – Annual consumer show, July – Vancouver BC

Wheels Auto Show & Sale, Thunder Bay Chamber of Commerce Trade Show, 857 North May St., Thunder Bay ON P7C 3S2 – 807/622-9882; Fax: 807/622-7752 – Show Manager, Arleene Mapledoram – Annual consumer show, February – Thunder Bay ON

World of Wheels, Master Promotions Ltd., PO Box 565, Saint John NB E2L 3Z8 – 506/658-0018; Fax: 506/658-0750 – Show Manager, Sydney Jane Brittain – Saint John NB

World of Wheels Show, Championship Auto Shows of Canada Inc., 6841 North Rochester Rd., Rochester NY 48306 – 810/650-5560; Fax: 810/650-5571 – Contact, Tom Williams – Annual consumer show. Sports & vintage cars. Held in Calgary, Edmonton, Winnipeg.

BOATING

Calgary Boat & Sportsmen's Show, Canadian National Sportsmen's Shows, #340, 1032 - 17 Ave. SW, Calgary AB T2T 0A5 – 403/245-9008; Fax: 403/245-5100 – Wolfgang Ortner – Annual consumer show, February – Roundup Centre, Stampede Park, Calgary AB

Classic Boat Festival, c/o Chamber of Commerce, 525 Fort St., Victoria BC V8W 1E8 – 250/385-7766 – Annually, September

Edmonton Boat & Sportsmen's Show, Canadian National Sportsmen's Shows, #340, 1032 - 17 Ave. SW, Calgary AB T2T 0A5 – 403/245-9008; Fax: 403/245-5100 – Wolfgang Ortner – Annual consumer show, March – Northlands Agricom, Edmonton AB

Fraser Valley Boat & Sportsmen's Show, Square Feet Northwest Event Management Inc,, 1030 Mainland St., Vancouver BC V6B 2T4 – 604/683-4393; Fax: 604/688-0270; Email: mgmt@sqftevent.com – Blaine Woit – Annual consumer show, March – Fraser Valley Trade & Exhibition Centre, Abbotsford BC

Halifax International Boat Show, Master Promotions Ltd., PO Box 565, Saint John NB E2L 3Z8 – 506/658-0018; Fax: 506/658-0750 – Show Manager, Sydney Jane Brittain – Annual consumer show, February – Halifax NS

London International Boat Show, 743 Wellington Rd. South, London ON N6A 4L5 – 519/686-3121; Fax: 519/686-3658 – General Manager, Jeff Guy – Consumer show, March – London ON

Muskoka Boat Show, 20 Edgevalley Dr., Etobicoke ON M9A 4N7 – Show Manager, Henry Timothy – Annual trade & consumer show, July – Barrie Arena Complex, Barrie ON

New Brunswick International Boat Show, Master Promotions Ltd., PO Box 565, Saint John NB E2L 3Z8 – 506/658-0018; Fax: 506/658-0750 – Show Manager, Sydney Jane Brittain – Annual consumer show, March – Exhibition Harbour Station, Saint John NB

Ottawa Boat & Sportsmen's Show/Ottawa Cottage Show, Canadian National Sportsmen's Shows (1989) Ltd., #202, 703 Evans Ave., Toronto ON M5C 5E9 – 416/695-0311; Fax: 416/695-0381 – Show Manager, Sherri Verdec – Annual consumer show. Boating, hunting, fishing, travel, February – Civic Centre, Lansdowne Park

Player's Ltd. Powerboat Championships, 375 York Ave., PO Box 229, Winnipeg MB R3C 3J3 – 204/982-6233 – Contact, Melanie Rennie

Sudbury Boat & Sportsmen's Show, DAC Marketing Ltd., PO Box 2837, Stn A, Sudbury ON P3A 5J3 – /05/673-5588, Fax: 705/525-0626 – President, Darren A. Ceccarelli – Annual consumer show, March

Toronto In-water Boat Show & Sale, #810, 310 Front St. East, Toronto ON M5V 3B5 – 416/591-6772; Fax: 416/591-3582 – September – Toronto ON

Toronto International Boat Show, #810, 310 Front St. West, Toronto ON M5V 3B5 – 416/591-6772; Fax: 416/591-3582 – Manager, Carol Bell – Annual consumer show: North America's largest boat show, January

Vancouver International Boat Show, Canadian National Sportsmen's Shows (1989) Ltd., #501, 4190 Lougheed Hwy., Burnaby BC V5C 6A8 – 604/294-1313; Fax: 604/294-4740 – Show Manager, Jim Carslake – Annual consumer show. Sail & powerboats, sailboards, inflatables, canoes, marine electronics, charters, sailing schools, travels, February – BC Place Stadium, Vancouver BC

BOOKS

Annual Conference & Trade Show, Ontario Library Association, #303, 100 Lombard St., Toronto ON M5C 1M3 – 416/363-3388; Fax: 416/941-9581; Email: jgilbert@interlog.com – Executive Director, Larry Moore – November

CLA Conference, Canadian Library Association, #602, 200 Elgin St., Ottawa ON K2P 1L5 – 613/232-9625; Fax: 613/563-9895; Email: ai077@freenet.carleton.ca – Events Coordinator, Susanne Fletcher – June 19-22 1997 – Ottawa ON

Convention & Trade Show, Canadian Booksellers Association, 301 Donlands Ave., Toronto ON M4J 3R8 – 416/467-7883; Fax: 416/467-7886; Email: enquiries@cbabook.org; URL: http://www.cbabook.org – Executive Director, John Finlay, CAE – Annual trade show, June 22-25 1997 – Metro Toronto Convention Centre, Toronto ON

Ideashop Conference & Exposition, Ontario School Library Association, #303, 100 Lombard St., Toronto ON M5C 1M3 – 416/363-3388; Fax: 416/941-9581; Email: jgilbert@interlog.com – President, Elizabeth Kerr – January 1997 – Toronto ON

Montréal Book Fair/Salon du livre de Montréal, Salon du livre de Montréal, #202, 480, boul St-Laurent, Montréal PQ H2Y 3Y7 – 514/845-2365; Fax: 514/845-7119 – Exhibits Manager, Noreen Bélanger – Annual consumer show, November – Montréal PQ

Salon du Livre de Québec, #203, 1026, rue St-Jean, Québec PQ G1R 1R7 – 418/692-5420; Fax: 418/692-0794 – General Manager, Denis Lebrun – Annual consumer show, October – Québec PQ

Vancouver International Writers Festival, 1243 Cartwright St., Vancouver BC V6H 4B7 – 604/681-6330; Fax: 604/681-8400; URL: http://www.ffa.ucalgary.ca/vca/vanwri.htm – General Manager, Hazel Currie – Five-day literary arts festival, October – Vancouver BC

The Word on the Street, 8680 Cambie St., Vancouver BC V6P 6M9 – 604/323-7148; Fax: 604/323-2600; URL: http://www.ffa.ucalgary.ca/vca/wordon.htm – Executive Director, Anne McWilliam – Annual book & magazine fair, September – Vancouver BC

BRIDAL

Canada's Bridal Show, Galaxy 2000, 30 Pemican Ct., 2nd Fl., Weston ON M9M 2Z3 – 905/264-7000; Fax: 905/264-7300 – Lorie Sansone – Annual consumer show. Bridal fashion shows, gifts, florists, photography, entertainment, travel, January – Toronto ON

National Bridal Show, Klanside Inc., 401 Magnetic Dr., Unit 21, North York ON M3J 3H9 – 416/661-2056; Fax: 416/661-2904 – Kathy O'Hara – Annual consumer show. Fashion shows, seminars & wedding-related exhibitors, February – Exhibition Place, Toronto ON

Le Salon de la Mariée, Sheldon Kagan International Ltd., 95, McConnell, Dorval PQ H9S 5L9 – 514/631-2160; Fax: 514/631-4430 – President, Sheldon Kagan – Annual consumer show, January – Palais des Congrès, Montréal PQ

Le Salon National des Futurs Mariés, Salon International des Futures Mariés Inc., #2, 1179, boul Décarie, St-Laurent PQ H4L 3M8 – 514/748-2015; Fax: 514/748-2427 – Mike S. Homsy – Annual consumer show, January – Montréal PQ

The Total Wedding Show, Ten Star Productions Inc., 155 Castle Cr., Oakville ON L6J 5H4 – 905/845-2644; Fax: 905/333-1097 – Show Manager, Roberta Said – Annual consumer show, January

Wedding Dreams, Bingemans Conference & Recreation Centre, 1380 Victoria St. North, Kitchener ON N2B 3E2 – 519/744-1555; Fax: 519/744-1985 – Contact, Doris Hauck – Annual consumer show. Fashion shows, wedding exhibits, January

Wedding Wishes, Thunder Bay Chamber of Commerce Trade Show, 857 North May St., Thunder Bay ON P7C 3S2 – 807/622-9882; Fax: 807/622-7752 – Show Manager, Arleene Mapledoram – Annual consumer show, November – Thunder Bay ON

BUSINESS

Annual Business Expo, DAC Marketing Ltd., PO Box 2837, Stn A, Sudbury ON P3A 5J3 – 705/673-5588; Fax: 705/525-0626 – President, Darren A. Ceccarelli

Annual Conference & Trade Show, Canadian Society of Association Executives, #1104, 40 University Ave., Toronto ON M5J 1T1 – 416/596-6433; Fax: 416/596-7994 – Executive Vice-President, Wayne Amundson, CAE – July 12-15 1997 – Hamilton ON

Business Expo, Saskatoon Chamber of Commerce, 345 - 3 Ave. South, Saskatoon SK S7K 1M6 – 306/244-2151; Fax: 306/244-8366 – President, Ken Ziegler – October

Business Start-up Exhibition, Martin International, #2910, 500, Place des Armes, Montréal PQ H2Y 2W2 – 514/288-3931; Fax: 514/288-0641 – General Manager, Lorraine Boisvenue – Consumer show, January

Business to Business Exposition, Corporate Events Management Inc., #803, 1 Toronto St., Toronto ON M5C 2V6 – 416/869-0141; Fax: 416/869-1660 – Principal, Jacqueline Peake – Trade show, March

Business World Exhibition, Martin International, #2910, 500, Place des Armes, Montréal PQ H2Y 2W2 – 514/288-3931; Fax: 514/288-0641 – General Manager, Lorraine Boisvenue – Trade show. International showcase, technology shows, finance, advertising, small business, home office, January

Canadian Business Hall of Fame, Junior Achievement of Canada, One Westside Dr., Toronto ON M9C 1B2 – 416/622-4602; Fax: 416/622-6861; Tollfree: 1-800-265-0699 – President/CEO, Colin P. Campbell – Consumer trade show. Showcase of student-manufactured products, April

Canadian National Franchising Exposition, Opportunities Canada, #42, 2550 Goldenridge Rd., Mississauga ON L4X 2S3 – 905/277-5600; Fax: 905/277-3397 – Sales Manager, Cheryl Higgins – Consumer show. Franchising opportunities, February

Careers Marketplace, Martin International, #2910, 500, Place des Armes, Montréal PQ H2Y 2W2 – 514/288-3931; Fax: 514/288-0641 – General Manager, Lorraine Boisvenue – Annual consumer show. Technological & scientific job market; franchising; office equipment, January

Cash & Treasury Management Conference, Treasury Management Association of Canada, #1010, 8 King St. East, Toronto ON M5C 1B5 – 416/367-8500; Fax: 416/367-3240; Email: tmac@inforamp.net; URL: http://www.tmac.ca./ – Manager of Administration, Patricia Wood – Annual trade show. Bank products, communication systems, financial software, pension management, brokers, dealers, stock exchanges, commercial paper & computers, Oct. 18-22 1997 – Palais des Congrès, Montréal PQ

Central Manitoba Trade Fair, c/o Chamber of Commerce, 160 Saskatchewan Ave. West, Portage la Prairie MB R1N 0M1 – 204/857-7778

Expo Emploi/Job Expo, Prométhée Communications, 3460, rue St-Hubert, Montréal PQ H2L 3Z7 – 514/843-9698; Fax: 514/843-9785 – Consumer show, March

Expo International, Blackpages Network Inc., #1201, 347 Bay St., Toronto ON M5H 2R7 – 416/364-1900; Fax: 416/366-5385 – Tony Ukonga – Annual trade & consumer show; business networking show for ethnic communities, October – Toronto ON

Financial Forum, #235, 180 Shirreff Ave., North Bay ON P1B 7K9 – 705/495-4215; Fax: 705/495-4414 – Contact, Steve Kizell – Annual consumer show, February

Financial Solutions, Canadian Tel-A-Views Ltd., #12, 115 Apple Creek Blvd., Markham ON L3R 6C9 – 905/477-2677; Fax: 905/477-7872; Tollfree: 1-800-891-4859 – President, Fred Cox – Held in Calgary & Ottawa, January/February

Franchise & Business Opportunities Expo, Prestige Promotions, PO Box 135, Etobicoke ON M9C 4V2 – 905/238-3320; Fax: 905/277-3397 – Bob Sinclair – Held in Kitchener, London, Ottawa, Toronto, Moncton, Halifax, Winnipeg, Vancouver, Victoria. Annual consumer shows

The Home Office Show & Telecommuting Show, Corporate Events Management Inc., #803, 1 Toronto St., Toronto ON M5C 2V6 – 416/869-0141; Fax: 416/869-1660 – Principal, Jacqueline Peake – Annual trade & consumer show, March/April

Home-Based Business & Opportunities Shows, Home Business Exhibitions, 2956 Shannon Lake Rd., Westbank BC V4T 1T6 – 250/768-9561 – Annually in Edmonton, Calgary, Vancouver & Abbotsford

The London Business-To-Business Show, Jenkins Show Productions, 1076 Skyvalley Cr., Oakville ON L6M 3L2 – 905/827-4632; Fax: 905/827-8139; Tollfree: 1-800-465-1073 – President, Dave Jenkins, February – London Convention Centre, London ON

The Metro Business Show, Corporate Events Management Inc., #803, 1 Toronto St., Toronto ON M5C 2V6 – 416/869-0141; Fax: 416/869-1660 – Principal, Jacqueline Peake – Annual trade show for business owners, managers, administrators, April – Metro Toronto Convention Centre, Toronto ON

Metro North Business Show & Conference, Canadian Tel-A-Views Ltd., #12, 115 Apple Creek Blvd., Markham ON L3R 6C9 – 905/477-2677; Fax: 905/477-7872; Tollfree: 1-800-891-4859 – President, Fred Cox – Annual consumer show. Products & services for business, plus franchising & dealership opportunities, September/October

Ottawa Business Show, Connelly Business Exhibitions Inc., #214, 2487 Kaladar Ave., Ottawa ON K1V 8B9 – 613/731-9850; Fax: 613/731-2407 – Vice-President, Marketing, Dan Hamilton – Annual trade show. Office equipment & systems, computers, communications, financial & investment services, advertising & marketing products; local, national & international, May – Ottawa ON

Salon international de la franchise et des réseaux d'affaires/International Franchising & Business Network Show, Promexpo Inc., 801, rue Sherbrooke est, 10e étage, Montréal PQ H2L 1K7 – 514/527-9221; Fax: 514/527-8449 – Jacques Lasnier – Annual consumer show, October

Saving & Investment Marketplace, Martin International, #2910, 500, Place des Armes, Montréal PQ H2Y 2W2 – 514/288-3931; Fax: 514/288-0641 – General Manager, Lorraine Boisvenue – Annual trade & consumer show. RRSPs, mutual funds, real estate tax shelters, January

Services & Suppliers Exposition, Human Resources Professionals Association of Ontario, #1902, 2 Bloor St. West, Toronto ON M4W 3E2 – 416/923-2324 (Office & Resource Line); Fax: 416/923-7264; Tollfree: 1-800-387-1311 – Trade Show Manager, Marta Pawych – Annual trade show, February

Thunder Bay Chamber of Commerce Trade Show, 857 North May St., Thunder Bay ON P7C 3S2 – 807/622-9882; Fax: 807/622-7752 – Show Manager, Arleene Mapledoram – Annual trade & consumer show, May

Vancouver Island Business Opportunity Show, Evergreen Exhibitions Ltd., 830D Pembrooke St., Victoria BC V8T 1H9 – 250/386-7469; Fax: 250/386-1431 – President, A.J. Chartrand, February

Vancouver Island Business Trade Show, Greater Nanaimo Chamber of Commerce, 777 Poplar St., Nanaimo BC V9S 2H7 – 250/753-1191; Fax: 250/754-5186 – Executive Director, Jane Hutchins – Annual trade show, March – Nanaimo BC

Yukon Trade Show, PO Box 4044, Whitehorse YT Y1A 3S9 – 403/668-7979 – Contact, Al Dibbs – Annually, April – Mount McIntyre Recreation Centre & Takhini Arena

CARS see AUTOMOTIVE

CHEMISTRY

Canadian Society of Clinical Chemists Annual Meeting, Events & Management Plus Inc., 190 Railway St., PO Box 1570, Kingston ON K7L 5C8 – 613/531-9210; Fax: 613/531-0626; Email: events@adan.kingston.net – Owner, E. Hooper – July – Halifax NS

CHILDREN

A Children's Festival, 5200 Robinson St., St. Catharines ON L2G 2A2 – 905/641-3012 – Annual three day festival. Over 60 educational & scientific exhibits, live entertainment & stage shows

Calgary International Children's Festival, Calgary Centre for Performing Arts, 205 - 8 Ave. SE, Calgary AB T2G 0K9 – 403/294-7414 – May

Canadian Juvenile Products Trade Show, Canadian Toy Association, PO Box 294, Kleinburg ON L0J 1C0 – 905/893-1689; Fax: 905/893-2392 – Executive Director, Sheila Edmondson – January

Children's Kaleidoscope, 2749 Kingsway Dr., Kitchener ON N2C 1A7 – 519/893-6200; Fax: 519/893-9034

City Parent Family Show, Premier Consumer Shows, City Parent Newsmagazine, 467 Speers Rd., Oakville ON L6K 3S4 – 905/815-0017; Fax: 905/815-0511 – Show Coordinator, Brenda Harris – Annual consumer show, June – Toronto ON

Edmonton International Children's Festival, c/o Citadel Theatre, 9828 - 101A Ave., Edmonton AB T5J 3C6 – 403/428-4811 – May

Northern Saskatchewan International Children's Festival, PO Box 1642, Saskatoon SK S7K 3R8 – 306/664-3378 – Artistic Co-Director, Cass Cozens – Annually, June. Four day international festival of the performing arts for children

The Parents & Kids Show, York Expositions, #803, 1 Toronto St., Toronto ON M5C 2V6 – 416/869-1156; Fax: 416/869-1660 – George Przybylowski – Annual consumer shows held in Toronto & Vancouver; products & services for children under 12 years of age, November

Regina International Children's Festival, 2201 Hamilton St., Regina SK S4P 2E7 – 306/352-7655; Fax: 306/525-6947 – Producer, Christa Donaldson – Annually, June. Four day festival & cultural activities for children

Vancouver Children's Festival, #302, 601 Cambie St., Vancouver BC V6B 2P1 – 604/687-7697; Fax: 604/669-3613 – President & Executive Producer, Ernie Fladell – Annually in May

Winnipeg International Children's Festival, #300, 112 Market Ave., Winnipeg MB R3B 0P4 – 204/958-4730 – Executive Director, James Turk – Annually, June. Six days of performances & hands-on activities

CHRISTMAS CRAFTS *see* **CRAFTS**

CLEANING

Can-Clean, Canadian Sanitation Supply Association, #G10, 300 Mill Rd., Etobicoke ON M9C 4W7 – 416/620-9320; Fax: 416/620-7199; Email: cssa@the_wire.com – Executive Director, Diane Gosling – April – Toronto ON

CLATA Update '98: Canadian Launderers & Dry Cleaners Exposition, International Tradeshow Services Inc., 20 Butterick Rd., Toronto ON M8W 3Z8 – 416/252-7791; Fax: 416/252-9848; Email: jimm@intltradeshows.com; URL: http://www.intltradeshows.com – Glenn Watermann – Quadrennial trade show, April 1998 – Exhibition Place, Toronto ON

COMMUNICATIONS

Annual Conference, Canadian Association of Broadcasters, #306, 350 Sparks St., PO Box 627, Stn B, Ottawa ON K1P 5S2 – 613/233-4035; Fax: 613/233-6961; URL: http://www.cab-acr.ca – President & CEO, Michael McCabe – Annual trade show

CCBE Broadcast Equipment Trade Show, c/o Secretariat, CCBE, 1466 Kalligan Court, Mississauga ON L4X 1A8 – 905/566-9654; Fax: 905/270-5521 – George Roach – Annual trade show

Inter Comm, CAPA Ventures International Ltd., #500, 1190 Melville St., Vancouver BC V6E 3W1 – 604/669-1090; Fax: 604/682-5703 – Project Director, Will Fong – Biennial trade show. Exhibition & congress on telecommunications, February 1997

MultiMedia, Multimedia Trade Shows Inc., #7, 70 Villarboit Cres., Concord ON L4K 4C7 – 905/660-2491; Fax: 905/660-2492 – President, Bruce Cole – Annual trade show featuring film & video production, electronic design & visual communications, June – Metro Toronto Convention Centre, Toronto ON

Production '97, c/o Production APIIS Inc., 1276, rue Amherst, Montréal PQ H2L 3K8 – 514/842-5333; Fax: 514/842-6717 – Contact, Claudine Letourneau – Annual trade show, May

Salon des communications canadien/Canadian Communications Show, Communications Show, CP 1241, Succ B, Hull PQ J8X 3X7 – 418/877-8898; Fax: 418/877-9711 – Président, Roch Gamache – November

Showcase on Production, Multimedia Trade Shows Inc., #7, 70 Villarboit Cres., Concord ON L4K 4C7 – 905/660-2491; Fax: 905/660-2492 – Jai Cole – Annual trade show. Film, video, television, broadcast, audio visual, sound & multimedia production

TeleCon - CBTA Exposition & Conference, International Tradeshow Services Inc., 20 Butterick Rd., Toronto ON M8W 3Z8 – 416/252-7791; Fax: 416/252-9848; Email: jimm@intltradeshows.com; URL: http://www.intltradeshows.com – Show Manager, Glen Waterman – Annual trade show, September

Televolution, MW Productions, #4, 88 Courcelette Rd., Scarborough ON M1N 2T2 – 416/691-6526; Fax: 416/691-6928; Tollfree: 1-800-267-4529; Email: ron.mackenzie@mwprod.com; URL: http://www.mwprod.com – Ron MacKenzie – Annual trade show, March – Metro Toronto Convention Centre, Toronto ON

Televolution East, MW Productions, #4, 88 Courcelette Rd., Scarborough ON M1N 2T2 – 416/691-6526; Fax: 416/691-6928; Tollfree: 1-800-267-4529; Email: ron.mackenzie@mwprod.com; URL: http://www.mwprod.com – Ron MacKenzie – Annual trade show. Telecommunications equipment, October – Saint John NB

VICOM, Multimedia Trade Shows Inc., #7, 70 Villarboit Cres., Concord ON L4K 4C7 – 905/660-2491; Fax: 905/660-2492 – President, Bruce Cole

VoicePower, #808, 15 Gervais Dr., North York ON M3C 1Y8 – 416/449-7229; Fax: 416/449-8944 – Contact, Jacob Gordon – Annual conference & trade show of the voice/fax processing industry

COMPUTERS

Atlantic Canada Business & Computer Show, Denex Group Inc., Burnside Industrial Park, 192 Joseph Zatzman Dr., Dartmouth NS B3B 1N4 – 902/468-4999; Fax: 902/468-2795; Email: denman@newedge.ca – President, Jon Denman – Annual, September – Halifax NS

Calgary Business Computer Show, Industrial Trade & Consumer Shows Inc., #2450, 101 - 6th Ave SW, Calgary AB T2P 3P4 – 403/266-8700; Fax: 403/266-6814 – Contact, Steve Henrich – Annual trade show & conference. Computer products & information, management technology, including hardware, software, open systems, multimedia, peripherals; home-based office & mobile office products, October – Stampede Park, Calgary AB

Canadian Conference & Showcase on Object Technology, Plesman Expositions & Conferences Inc., 2005 Sheppard Ave. East, 4th Fl., North York ON M2J 5B1 – 416/497-9562; Fax: 416/497-9427; Tollfree: 1-800-387-5012; URL: http://www.netcon.plesman.com – Show Coordinator, Sean Wainwright – Annual trade & consumer show, November – Toronto ON

Canadian Integrated Manufacturing & Design Show, Reed Exhibition Companies Inc., 3761 Victoria Park Ave., Scarborough ON M1W 3S2 – 416/491-7565; Fax: 416/491-5088

CIDC, York Expositions, #803, 1 Toronto St., Toronto ON M5C 2V6 – 416/869-1156; Fax: 416/869-1660 – George Przybylowski – Annual trade show, December – Toronto ON

COMDEX/Canada, The Interface Group, 300 First Ave., Needham MA 02194-2722 – 617/449-6600, 416/283-3334; Fax: 617/449-6617 – Richard Schwab – Annual trade show & conference (July) in up-scale information systems for volume buyers of computer & communications products; also COMDEX/Pacific Rim in Vancouver (January) & COMDEX/Québec in Montréal (October)

ComputerFest/NetFest, Show Fest Productions Inc., #5, 60 St. Clair Ave. West, Toronto ON M4V 1M7 – 416/925-4533; Fax: 416/925-7701 – David Carter – Consumer show (April, Sept., Nov.). Microcomputers, internet services, accessories & services, virtual reality – Toronto ON

Edmonton Computer & Business Show, Industrial Trade & Consumer Shows Inc., #2450, 101 - 6th Ave SW, Calgary AB T2P 3P4 – 403/266-8700; Fax: 403/266-6814 – Contact, Steve Henrich – Annual trade show: hardware, software, office equipment, networking, peripherals, integrated systems, October – Edmonton Convention Centre, Edmonton AB

Electronic Design Showcase, Multimedia Trade Shows Inc., #7, 70 Villarboit Cres., Concord ON L4K 4C7 – 905/660-2491; Fax: 905/660-2492 – Jai Cole – Annual trade show. Design communications, including graphic design, publication & art direction, electronic design, prepress, typography, illustration, printing & service bureau services, May

Executive Symposium & Showcase on Open Client/Server Computing, Plesman Expositions & Conferences Inc., 2005 Sheppard Ave. East, 4th Fl., North York ON M2J 5B1 – 416/497-9562; Fax: 416/497-9427; Tollfree: 1-800-387-5012; URL: http://www.netcon.plesman.com – Show Coordinator, Sean Wainwright – Annual trade & consumer show, May

Focus on Video, Promex Productions Inc., 118 Indian Rd., 2nd Fl., Toronto ON M6R 2V4 – 416/531-2121; Fax: 416/531-2194 – Show Manager, Angela Abromaitis – Annual trade show. Video hardware, software, accessories & systems, September

La Foire du Micro-Ordinateur, c/o Gestion Micro-Québec, 726, av Glazier, Vanier PQ G1M 2Z2 – 418/527-6648; Fax: 418/527-2067 – Annual consumer show, November

LAN Expo, The Interface Group, 300 First Ave., Needham MA 02194-2722 – 617/449-6600, 416/283-3334; Fax: 617/449-6617 – Richard Schwab – Annual trade show, July – Toronto ON

MacWorld Expo Canada, c/o Aedile Enterprises Inc., #212, 385 The West Mall, Etobicoke ON M9C 1E7 – 416/620-1078 – Contact, Tony Paul – Annual trade & consumer show, September

Micro Expo, ABBA Computer Corp., #G-06, 360, rue Notre-Dame ouest, Montréal PQ H2Y 1T9 – 514/844-0502; Fax: 514/849-9517 – Show Coordinator, Claude Thibault – Annual consumer show

National Factory Automation Show, Reed Exhibition Companies Inc., 3761 Victoria Park Ave., Scarborough ON M1W 3S2 – 416/491-7565; Fax: 416/491-5088 – Show Manager, Glen Chiasson – Annual trade show alternating between Toronto & Montréal, September

Netcon, Plesman Expositions & Conferences Inc., 2005 Sheppard Ave. East, 4th Fl., North York ON M2J 5B1 – 416/497-9562; Fax: 416/497-9427; Tollfree: 1-800-387-5012; URL: http://www.netcon.plesman.com – Show Coordinator, Sean Wainwright – Annual trade show for computer networking & connectivity; also Montréal, Ottawa, Calgary, Vancouver, September – Toronto ON

Ontario Computer Fairs, 185 Macdonell Ave., Toronto ON M6R 2A4 – 416/535-3761; Fax: 416/535-8091 – Annual consumer shows throughout the province

Vancouver Island Computer Show, VIEX Events Ltd., #2, 31 Bushby St., Victoria BC V8S 1B3 – 250/370-2983; Fax: 250/370-1733 – Sales & Marketing Director, Patrick Doyle – Annual consumer show, October – Victoria BC

VARDEX Exhibition & Conference, Reed Exhibition Companies Inc., 3761 Victoria Park Ave., Scarbor-

ough ON M1W 3S2 – 416/491-7565; Fax: 416/491-5088 – Show Manager, Janet Whidett – Annual trade show, May – Toronto ON
Virtual Reality World, Multimedia Trade Shows Inc., #7, 70 Villarboit Cres., Concord ON L4K 4C7 – 905/660-2491; Fax: 905/660-2492 – President, Bruce Cole
Windows World, The Interface Group, 300 First Ave., Needham MA 02194-2722 – 617/449-6600, 416/283-3334; Fax: 617/449-6617 – Richard Schwab – Annual trade show. Windows products, tools, platforms, July – Metro Toronto Convention Centre, Toronto ON

CONSTRUCTION & BUILDING PRODUCTS

Atlantic Building Materials Show, Atlantic Building Supply Dealers Association, #203, 95 Foundry St., Moncton NB E1C 5H7 – 506/858-0700; Fax: 506/859-0064; Tollfree: 1-800-561-7114 – Executive Director, John J. Ward – Annual trade show, March – Moncton Coliseum/Agrena Complex, Moncton NB
BOMEX, York Expositions, #803, 1 Toronto St., Toronto ON M5C 2V6 – 416/869-1156; Fax: 416/869-1660 – George Przybylowski – September – Ottawa Congress Centre, Ottawa ON
Buildex, RK Communications, #306, 1755 West Broadway, Vancouver BC V6J 4S5 – 604/739-2112; Fax: 604/739-2124 – Bruce Jones – Annual trade show, February
Buildtech Ottawa, Intertrade Associates Inc., #250, 1511 Merivale Rd., Nepean ON K2G 3J3 – 613/224-3013; Fax: 613/224-4533; Tollfree: 1-888-662-6660 – Show Manager, Kevin McWhinnie – January – Ottawa Civic Centre, Ottawa ON
Canadian Construction Show, Southex Exhibitions, 1450 Don Mills Rd., North York ON M3B 2X7 – 416/445-6641; Fax: 416/442-2207 – Beverley Morden – Annual trade show, February – International Centre, Toronto ON
Canadian Home Centre Show, Southex Exhibitions, 1450 Don Mills Rd., North York ON M3B 2X7 – 416/445-6641; Fax: 416/442-2207 – Show Manager, Geddis Ruttan – Annual trade show. Hardware, lumber & building materials, November/December
Canadian Rental Mart, AIS Communications Ltd., 145 Thames Rd. West, Exeter ON N0M 1S3 – 519/235-2400; Fax: 519/235-0798 – Contact, Peter Phillips – Annual trade show. Construction equipment, power tools & party goods, March – International Centre, Toronto ON
CanGlass, AIS Communications Ltd., 145 Thames Rd. West, Exeter ON N0M 1S3 – 519/235-2400; Fax: 519/235-0798 – Contact, Peter Phillips – Annual trade show. Architecture, auto glass, June – Royal Constellation Hotel, Toronto ON
Construct Canada, York Expositions, #803, 1 Toronto St., Toronto ON M5C 2V6 – 416/869-1156; Fax: 416/869-1660 – George Przybylowski – Annual trade show. Products, technologies, services for building design & construction, November/December – Metro Toronto Convention Centre, Toronto ON
Equipexpo, Communications Vero Inc., #404, 1600, boul Henri-Bourassa ouest, Montréal PQ H3M 3E2 – 514/332-8376; Toronto: 416/967-9291; Fax: 514/332-2666 – Pierre-Yves Verronneau – Biennial trade show, May
Expo-Rencontre Contech Inc., 257, rue Saint-Jean, Longueuil PQ J4H 2X4 – 514/646-1833; Fax: 514/646-3918 – Show Manager, Lise Monette – Annual trade show, October in Montréal, & November in Québec City
IDEAS - Industry Directed Educational Action Seminars & Shows, IDEAS, CP 400, Succ Victoria, Montréal PQ H3Z 2V8 – 514/489-4941; Fax: 514/489-5505 – Show Coordinator, Joyce Crandall – Annual trade show. Building product seminars; conferences & trade show; renovations, roofing, windows, doors, exterior & interior building products, February
Ottawa Buildings Show, York Expositions, #803, 1 Toronto St., Toronto ON M5C 2V6 – 416/869-1156; Fax: 416/869-1660 – George Przybylowski – Trade show, October – Ottawa Congress Centre, Ottawa ON
PM Expo, York Expositions, #803, 1 Toronto St., Toronto ON M5C 2V6 – 416/869-1156; Fax: 416/869-1660 – George Przybylowski – Trade show for property managers, November/December – Metro Toronto Convention Centre, Toronto ON
RoofTech, York Expositions, #803, 1 Toronto St., Toronto ON M5C 2V6 – 416/869-1156; Fax: 416/869-1660 – George Przybylowski – Biennial trade show, April 1997 – Metro Toronto Convention Centre, Toronto ON
Salon Constructo, 1500, boul Jules-Poitras, Saint-Laurent PQ H4N 1X7 – 514/745-5720; Fax: 514/339-2267 – Show Manager, Mark Perlstein – Annual trade show, November

COSMETICS

Beauty Convention, Allied Beauty Association, #1001, 2 Sheppard Ave. East, PO Box 42, North York ON M2N 5Y7 – 416/225-2359; Fax: 416/223-3610 – Marc Speir – Annual trade shows held in major cities across Canada; beauty & hair products
Esthetics 2000, #14, 1380 Matheson Blvd. East, Mississauga ON L4W 4P8 – 905/238-6875; Fax: 905/238-6876 – Annual trade show, May

CRAFTS

Annual Christmas Fair, Prince Edward Island Crafts Council, 156 Richmond St., Charlottetown PE C1A 1H9 – 902/892-5152; Fax: 902/628-8740; URL: http://www.crafts-council.pe.ca/index.html – November – Confederation Centre, Charlottetown PE
Art Market, Art Market Productions, PO Box 385, Banff AB T0L 0C0 – 403/762-2345 – Marlene Loney – Annual consumer show; art & craft sale, November – Calgary AB
Atlantic Craft Trade Show, Nova Scotia Economic Renewal Agency, PO Box 519, Halifax NS B3J 2R7 – 902/424-4212; Fax: 902/424-5739 – Trade Officer, Peter L. Giffin – Annual trade show. Juried craft & giftware products, February
Bazaart, MacKenzie Art Gallery, 3475 Albert St., Regina SK S4S 6X6 – 306/522-4242; Fax: 306/569-8191 – Bonnie Schaffer – Juried outdoor art show & sale; complete range of crafts
Cameo's Canadian Spring Craft Sale, Cameo Convention Consultants Ltd., 7418 - 182 St., Edmonton AB T5T 2G7 – 403/481-6268; Fax: 403/243-0666 – President, Mamie Bercov – Annual consumer show, April
Cameo's Christmas Craft Sale, Cameo Convention Consultants Ltd., 7418 - 182 St., Edmonton AB T5T 2G7 – 403/481-6268; Fax: 403/243-0666 – President, Mamie Bercov – Annual consumer show, November
Canada Day Craft Show, Festival Trade Shows, PO Box 1985, Kitchener ON N2G 4R9 – 519/571-8881; Fax: 519/571-8883 – Howard Gallup – Annual consumer show, July
Canadian Sewing & Needlecraft Annual Trade Show, Canadian Sewing & Needlecraft Association, #204, 224 Merton St., Toronto ON M4S 1A1 – 416/482-7724; Fax: 416/482-2862 – Contact, Eva Gramsch – April 26-28 1997 – Toronto International Centre, Mississauga ON
Christmas Arts & Craft Gift Sales, DAC Marketing Ltd., PO Box 2837, Stn A, Sudbury ON P3A 5J3 – 705/673-5588; Fax: 705/525-0626 – President, Darren A. Ceccarelli – Annual consumer shows. Various locations throughout Ontario
Christmas at the Forum - Festival of Crafts, Antiques, Art & Foods, DMS Enterprises Ltd., 5647 Morris St., Halifax NS B3J 1C4 – 902/425-5656 – Coordinator, Donna Susnick – Annual consumer show, November
Circle Craft Christmas Market, c/o Pacific Canadian Craft Shows Ltd., #101, 1765 - 8 Ave. West, Vancouver BC V6J 5C6 – 604/737-9050; Fax: 604/736-2186 – Producer, Paul Yard
Country Decorating & Collectibles Show & Sale, Synergic Media Ltd., RR#4, Uxbridge ON L9P 1R4 – 905/649-2480; Fax: 905/649-1022 – Show Producer, Ian Russell – Consumer show held in March, July & November – Markham Fairgrounds, Markham ON
Craft Christmas Gift Sale, Nepean Sportsplex, 101 Centrepointe Dr., Nepean ON K2G 5K7 – 613/727-6641; Fax: 613/727-6613 – Projects Co-ordinator, Billie Swartzack – Annual consumer show, November
Craft Fairs, Newfoundland & Labrador Crafts Development Association, Devon House, 59 Duckworth St., St. John's NF A1C 1E6 – 709/753-2749; Fax: 709/753-2766; Email: anne_manuel@port-hole.entnet.nf.ca – Executive Director, Anne Manuel – St. John's (July, October, November); Corner Brook (November)
The Craft Guild of Mississauga Annual Show & Sale, 1444 Dundas Cres., Mississauga ON L5C 1E9 – 905/890-0496 – November
Craft-Ex, DAC Marketing Ltd., PO Box 2837, Stn A, Sudbury ON P3A 5J3 – 705/673-5588; Fax: 705/525-0626 – President, Darren A. Ceccarelli – Annual consumer show, April – North Bay ON
Crafts & More, Canadian Craft & Hobby Association, 4404 - 12 St. NE, PO Box 44, Calgary AB T2E 6K9 – 403/291-0559; Fax: 403/291-0675; Email: parentp@cadvision.com – Executive Director, Patrice Baron-Parent – Annual consumer shows held in Toronto (March) & Calgary (May)
Craftworld, Cryderman Productions, 136 Thames St., Chatham ON N7L 2Y8 – 519/351-8344; Fax: 519/351-8345 – John Cryderman – Semi-annual shows in Chatham, Kitchener, London, Sarnia; annual shows in Stratford, Surrey
Creative Sewing & Needlework Festival, #200, 2900 John St., Markham ON L3R 5G3 – 905/470-7057; Fax: 905/470-0547 – President, Rita Gramsch – Semi-annual consumer shows, April & November. In association with the Canadian Sewing & Needlecraft Association. Other locations include Halifax, Winnipeg & Calgary – Toronto ON
Elegance Christmas Craft Show, Contemporary Craft Shows Ltd., 37 Langley Ave., Toronto ON M4K 3V9 – 416/465-2379; Fax: 416/465-2379 – Casey Sadaka – November
The Guild, Dante Club, 1330 London Rd., Sarnia ON N7S 1P7 – 519/542-5453 – November
Hill Potters Guild Sale, 530 Carrville Rd., Richmond Hill ON L4C 6E6 – 905/884-0327 – Sales twice a year, Spring & Fall
Holiday Show & Sale, 80 Woodlawn Ave. East, Toronto ON M4T 1C1 – 416/964-0758 – November
Mennonite Christmas Festival, York Quay Centre, 235 Queen's Quay West, Toronto ON M5J 2G8 – 416/973-3000 – December
Metro Toronto Christmas Gift Show & Sale, Metro Toronto Christmas Show, Lawrence Plaza, PO Box 54045, Toronto ON M6A 3B7 – 416/789-1925 – Annual consumer show, December – Skydome, Toronto ON
Na'Amat Pioneer Women Bazaar & Auction at Toronto International Centre, Mississauga, c/o 272 Codsell Ave., North York ON M3H 3X2 – 416/636-5425 – Annually, October/November
The National Hobby & Craft Show, Canadian Shows & Special Events Inc., #1801, One Yonge St., Toronto

ON M5E 1W7 – 416/363-1292; Fax: 416/369-0515 – Show Director, Brian Miles – Annual consumer show for all age groups, February – Automotive Building, Exhibition Place, Toronto ON

One of a Kind Christmas Canadian Craft Show & Sale, The Canadian Craft Show Ltd., 21 Grenville St., Toronto ON M4Y 1A1 – 416/960-3680; Fax: 416/923-5624 – Show Coordinator, Patti Stewart – Annual consumer show, November/December – Toronto ON

One of a Kind Springtime Canadian Craft Show & Sale, The Canadian Craft Show Ltd., 21 Grenville St., Toronto ON M4Y 1A1 – 416/960-3680; Fax: 416/923-5624 – Show Coordinator, Patti Stewart – Annual consumer show, March/April – Automotive Building, Exhibition Place, Toronto ON

ORIGINALS - The Spring Craft Sale, Southex Exhibitions Inc., #440, 47 Clarence St., Ottawa ON K1N 9K1 – 613/232-0766; Fax: 613/238-4827 – Show Manager, Tom Gamble – Consumer show, April – Civic Centre, Lansdowne Park, Ottawa ON

Ottawa Christmas Craft Sale, Southex Exhibitions Inc., #440, 47 Clarence St., Ottawa ON K1N 9K1 – 613/232-0766; Fax: 613/238-4827 – Show Manager, Tom Gamble – Consumer show, December – Civic Centre, Lansdowne Park, Ottawa ON

Pine Tree Potters Sale, 22 Church St., Aurora ON L4G 1G4 – 905/727-1278 – April & November

Plein Art Québec, Conseil des métiers d'art du Québec, 378, rue St-Paul ouest, Montréal PQ H2Y 2A6 – 514/287-7555; Fax: 514/287-9923 – Directeur général, Yvan Gauthier – Annual consumer show, August – Québec PQ

Quilt Canada 1998, Canadian Quilters Association, PO Box 22010, RPO Herongate, Ottawa ON K1V 0C2; URL: http://www.nt.net/~giselef/cqaacc1.htm – President, Virginia Newey, 705/969-8720, Email: newey@cyberbeach.net – Biennial conference

Salon des métiers d'arts, Conseil des métiers d'art du Québec, 378, rue St-Paul ouest, Montréal PQ H2Y 2A6 – 514/287-7555; Fax: 514/287-9923 – Directeur général, Yvan Gauthier – Annual consumer show, December – Montréal PQ

Saskatchewan Handcraft Festival, 813 Broadway Ave., Saskatoon SK S7N 1B5 – 306/653-3616 – Annual three-day festival, July – Battleford SK

Sew Creative! Craft & Quilting Show, Hank Hartloper Agency, #2, 1575 Seel Ave., Winnipeg MB R3T 1C8 – 204/925-5711; Fax: 204/925-6643 – Owner, Hank Hartloper – Shows in Edmonton, Winnipeg, Saskatoon, Vancouver

Signatures in Christmas Craft, Contemporary Craft Shows Ltd., 37 Langley Ave., Toronto ON M4K 3V9 – 416/465-2379; Fax: 416/465-2379 – Casey Sadaka – Annual consumer show, December

Signatures Québec, Contemporary Craft Shows Ltd., 37 Langley Ave., Toronto ON M4K 3V9 – 416/465-2379; Fax: 416/465-2379 – Casey Sadaka – Annual consumer show, November – Québec PQ

Springtime at the Forum - Festival of Crafts, Antiques, Art & Foods, DMS Enterprises Ltd., 5647 Morris St., Halifax NS B3J 1C4 – 902/425-5656 – Coordinator, Donna Susnick – Annual consumer show, May – Halifax NS

Sundog Handcraft Fair, PO Box 7183, Saskatoon SK S7K 4J1 – 306/374-1893 – Coordinator, Wendy Hayes – Juried two-day craft market plus continuous stage acts & gourmet food court. Annually, first weekend of December

Victoria Christmas Gift Show, Evergreen Exhibitions Ltd., 830D Pembrooke St., Victoria BC V8T 1H9 – 250/386-7469; Fax: 250/386-1431 – President, A.J. Chartrand – Annual consumer show, November – Victoria BC

Victoria County Craft Guild Annual County Creations, 159 Colborne St. West, Lindsay ON K9V 5Z8 – 705/324-7311 – November

Victoria Park Arts/Crafts Fair, 100 Westmorland St., Moncton NB E1C 5B2 – 506/853-3516 – Contact, Christine Connor – Annually, August

Wintergreen, 813 Broadway Ave., Saskatoon SK S7N 1B5 – 306/653-3616 – Annual. Three day Christmas craft market, November – Regina SK

YWCA Quilt Fair, 35 Highfield St., Moncton NB E1C 5N1 – 506/855-4349 – Contact, Barbara Brown – April

DANCE see MUSIC

DECORATING see HOME SHOWS

DENTAL

Annual Spring Meeting, Ontario Dental Association, 4 New St., Toronto ON M5R 1P6 – 416/922-3900; Fax: 416/922-9005 – Coordinator, Diana Thorneycroft – May 8-20 1997 – Metro Toronto Convention Centre, Toronto ON

Convention & Show, Canadian Association of Orthodontists, #310, 2175 Sheppard Ave. East, North York ON M2J 1W8 – 416/491-3186; Fax: 416/491-1670 – Administrator, Diane Gaunt – October 1996

Winter Clinic, Toronto Academy of Dentistry, #902, 170 Bloor St. West, Toronto ON M5S 1T9 – 416/967-5649; Fax: 416/967-5081 – Executive Administrator, Raisyl Wagman – Annual trade show, November – Metro Toronto Convention Centre, Toronto ON

ELECTRICAL/ELECTRONICS

Armed Forces Communications Electronics Association Show, Richmor Enterprises, #201, 251 Laurier Ave. West, Ottawa ON K1P 5J6 – 613/563-0093; Fax: 613/236-4351 – Conference Manager, Marion G. Fuller – April – Congress Centre, Ottawa ON

The Canadian Consumer Electronics Exposition, PO Box 1500-1288, Etobicoke ON M9C 4V5 – 416/620-6620; Fax: 416/621-6688 – Shirley Trotter – Annual trade & consumer show, September

Canadian High Technology Show, Reed Exhibition Companies Inc., 3761 Victoria Park Ave., Scarborough ON M1W 3S2 – 416/491-7565; Fax: 416/491-5088 – Group Show Manager, Mike Sweetman – Annual (Toronto) & biennial (Ottawa) trade show. Electronic components, robotics, communications systems

Electrical Showcase '97, Manitoba Electrical League, #14, 395 Berry St., Winnipeg MB R3J 1N6 – 204/885-3668; Fax: 204/885-3678 – Executive Director, Larry McLennan – Triennial trade show, April 15-16 1997 – Winnipeg Convention Centre, Winnipeg MB

ElectroTech West, Lakeview Publications, #27, 1200 Aerowood Dr., Mississauga ON L4W 2S7 – 905/624-8100; Fax: 905/624-1760 – President, Robert C. Luton – Biennial trade show. Electronic components, May

Eptech, Lakeview Publications, #27, 1200 Aerowood Dr., Mississauga ON L4W 2S7 – 905/624-8100; Fax: 905/624-1760 – President, Robert C. Luton – Trade show held in various locations. Electronic components, systems

ExpoLectria, Corporation des maîtres électriciens du Québec, #100, 5925, boul Décarie, Montréal PQ H3W 3C9 – 514/738-2184; Fax: 514/738-2192; Tollfree: 1-800-361-9061 – Directeur général et secrétaire executif, Yvon Guilbault – Annual trade show, mai 1997 – Montréal PQ

ENVIRONMENT

Calgary Environmental Tradeshow & Conference, Southex Exhibitions, #300, 999 - 8 St. SW, Calgary AB T2R 1N7 – 403/244-6111; Fax: 403/245-8649; URL: http://www.southex.com – Pat Atkinson – Annual international forum for environmental & pollution control industry, Oct. 21-22 1997 – Calgary AB

Canadian Environmental Technology Showcase, Reed Exhibition Companies Inc., 3761 Victoria Park Ave., Scarborough ON M1W 3S2 – 416/491-7565; Fax: 416/491-5088 – Annual trade show, May – Place Bonaventure, Montréal PQ

CETECH - Canadian Environmental Technology Pavilion, Reed Exhibition Companies Inc., 3761 Victoria Park Ave., Scarborough ON M1W 3S2 – 416/491-7565; Fax: 416/491-5088 – Environmental products, technology & services; part of Canadian Manufacturing Week, October – International Centre, Toronto ON

Globe '98 International Trade Fair & Conference on Business & the Environment, The Globe Foundation of Canada, #504, 999 Canada Place, Vancouver BC V6C 3E1 – 604/775-1994; Fax: 604/666-8123; Email: info@globe.apfnet.org; URL: http://www.globe.ca – President & CEO, John Wiebe – Sixth in a biennial series of trade fairs & conferences on developing the business of the environment; only major international event in North America for the environment industry, the corporate sector & the finance & investment community; offers exhibitors access to the Asia Pacific, North American & Latin American marketplaces., March 17-20 1998 – Vancouver Trade & Convention Centre, Vancouver BC

International Environment & Economy Crossroads, 1431, Bourgeoys, Longueuil PQ J4M 1Z4 – 514/647-5530; Fax: 514/647-1031 – Show Manager, Marcel Gaudreault – Annual trade & consumer show. Innovation showcase, four-day conference & gala, May

Toronto Environmental Tradeshow & Conference, Southex Exhibitions, #300, 999 - 8 St. SW, Calgary AB T2R 1N7 – 403/244-6111; Fax: 403/245-8649; URL: http://www.southex.com – Pat Atkinson – Annual trade show; environmental technology, products & services, May 6-7 1997 – International Centre, Toronto ON

ETHNIC see MULTICULTURAL

EVENTS

see also Specific categories for events such as winter carnivals, music festivals, rodeos, exhibitions, etc.

Altona Sunflower Festival, PO Box 1630, Altona MB R0G 0B0 – 204/324-6468 – Annual, July

Atlantic Canada Bicycle Rally, PO Box 1555, Stn M, Halifax NS B3J 2Y3 – 902/423-2453 – Fary Conrod – Largest bicycle event in Atlantic Canada, August – Tatamagouche NS

Benson & Hedges Inc. Symphony of Fire, c/o 1500 Don Mills Rd., North York ON M3B 3L1 – Annual fireworks competitions at Montreal, Toronto & Vancouver

Billy Barker Days, PO Box 4441, Quesnel BC V2J 3J4 – 250/992-1234

Blossom Festival, c/o, PO Box 268, Creston BC V0B 1G0 – 250/428-4342 – May

Brockville Riverfest, Waterfront, c/o, PO Box 1341, Brockville ON K6V 5Y6 – 613/342-8975 – June

Canadian National Strawberry Festival, c/o Chamber of Commerce, 160 Saskatchewan Ave. West, Portage La Prairie MB R1N 0M1 – 204/239-1113 – July

The Canadian Tulip Festival, PO Box 394, Stn A, Ottawa ON K1N 8V4 – 613/562-1480 – May

Canadian Turtle Derby, c/o Radio CJRB, PO Box 1220, Boissevain MB R0K 0E0 – 204/534-6000 – Contact, Ivan Strain – Annually, July

Charleswood In-Motion Days, 363 Laxdale Rd., Winnipeg MB R3R 0W5 – 204/837-7356 – Chairman, Ed

McTaggart – Annually, June. Business displays, stage performances, carnival, youth soccer tournament

Charlottetown Festival, 145 Richmond St., Charlottetown PE C1A 1J1 – 902/566-1267; Fax: 902/566-4648; Tollfree: 1-800-565-0278 – Annually, June - September. Musical & dramatic entertainment

CHIN International Picnic, Exhibition Place, Toronto ON M6K 3C3 – 416/531-9991 – June/July

Chocolate Fest, PO Box 5002, St. Stephen NB E3L 2X5 – 506/465-5616 – Annually, August

Colonial Harvest Week Festival, Craigflower Farmhouse, c/o Heritage Properties Branch, 800 Johnston St., 5th Fl., Victoria BC V8V 1X4 – 250/387-4697 – October

Discovery Days, PO Box 308, Dawson City YT Y0B 1G0 – 403/993-5434; Fax: 403/993-5237 – Contact, Peter G. Menzies – August

Exploit's Valley Salmon Festival, Grand-Falls-Windsor NF – 709/489-2728 – Music, horse show, dance, salmon dinner; largest festival in Newfoundland, July

Feast of St. Louis, PO Box 160, Louisbourg NS B0A 1M0 – 902/733-2280 – Asst. Chief, Visitor Services, Rose Anne Poirier – Eighteenth-century celebrations in honour of St. Louis, August – Louisbourg NS

Festival by the Sea, PO Box 6848, Stn A, Saint John NB E2L 4S3 – 506/632-0086; Fax: 506/632-0994 – General Manager, Gary D. Arthurs, C.A. – Annually, August. Performing arts. Ten days

Festival du Voyageur, 768, av Taché, Winnipeg MB R2H 2C4 – 204/237-7692; Fax: 204/233-7576 – Communications Officer, Debbie Guénette-Lavigne – Annually, February. Ten day winter festival celebrating the voyageur & fur trade era

Gold Fever Follies, c/o, PO Box 1725, Rossland BC V0G 1Y0 – 250/362-5666 – July

Gold Panning Championships, Taylor BC V0C 2K0 – 250/789-3392 – Annually, August long weekend

Halifax Highland Games, 7 Tay Ave., Dartmouth NS B2X 1K5 – Bob Findlay – July – Halifax NS

Harvestfest, 355 Main St., Yarmouth NS B5A 1E7 – 902/742-7885; Fax: 902/742-5215 – Contact, Narinder Singh – October. Feast, ox haul, farmers' market

Heritage Canoe Festival, (Lift Lock), c/o Friends of the Trent Severn, PO Box 572, Peterborough ON K9J 6Z6 – 705/742-2251 – Annually, February

Humber Valley Strawberry Festival, PO Box 989, Deer Lake NF A0K 2E0 – 709/635-3861; Fax: 709/635-5103 – Co-ordinator, Glenda Garnier – July

Icelandic Festival of Manitoba, 281 Wildwood Ave., Winnipeg MB R3T 0E5 – 204/284-2169

International Freedom Festival, Dieppe Park, c/o 500 Riverside Dr. West, Windsor ON N9A 5K6 – 519/252-7264 – June/July

Just for Laughs Festival, 51, rue Sherbrooke ouest, Montréal PQ H2X 1X2 – 514/845-3155; Fax: 514/845-4140; URL: http://www.hahaha.com – Contact, Robin Altman – July. 250 comics from 17 countries

Kitchener-Waterloo Oktoberfest, 17 Benton St., PO Box 1053, Kitchener ON N2G 4G1 – 519/576-0571; Fax: 519/742-3072; URL: http://www.sentex.net/oktoberfest – Annually, October. Bavarian festival: foods, entertainment, parades

Labrador Straits Bakeapple Folk Festival, PO Box 22, Forteau NF A0K 2P0 – 709/931-2908; Fax: 709/931-2306 – Annually, August

Leacock Heritage Festival, c/o 150 Front St. South, Orillia ON L3V 4S7 – 705/325-3261 – July/August

Louis Riel Day, 216 - 1st Ave. North, Saskatoon SK S7K 3W3 – 306/665-8600; Fax: 306/665-9210 – Promotion Manager, Bruce Acton – Annually, July

Manitoba Oktoberfest, 375 York Ave., 2nd Fl., Winnipeg MB R3C 3J3 – 204/956-1720 – Director of Sales & Marketing, Terry O'Reilly

Minto Coal Mining Festival, PO Box 7, Minto NB E0E 1J0 – 506/327-3383 – Contact, Rose Collette – June

Northern Manitoba Trappers' Festival, Inc., PO Box 475, The Pas MB R9A 1K6 – 204/623-2912 – Annually, February

Northwest Territorial Days, c/o, PO Box 668, North Battleford SK S9A 2Y9 – 306/445-2024 – July

Nova Scotia Gaelic Mod, PO Box 9, Baddeck NS B0E 1B0 – 902/295-3411 – Sam McPhee – Four-day festival, August – Gaelic College, St. Ann's NS

Nova Scotia International Tattoo, PO Box 3233 South, Halifax NS B3J 3H5 – 902/420-1114; Fax: 902/423-6621 – Assistant Producer, George Tibbetts – Annually, June/July

Okanagan Wine Festival, 185 Lakeshore Dr., Penticton BC V2A 1B7 – 250/493-4055 – Annually, end September or beginning October

Oktoberfest, 375 York Ave., Winnipeg MB R3C 3J3 – 204/956-1720; Fax: 204/943-0310 – Director of Sales & Marketing, Terry O'Reilly – September

Penticton Peach Festival, c/o 184 West Lakeshore Dr., Penticton BC V2A 1B7 – 250/493-4055 – August

Peterborough Summer Festival of Lights, c/o City Hall, 500 George St. North, Peterborough ON K9H 3R9 – 705/876-4611 – June to August every Wednesday & Saturday evenings at Crary Park

Pictou Lobster Carnival, PO Box 1480, Pictou NS B0K 1H0 – 902/485-5150 – Gerard McIsaac – Annual, July

Pile O Bones Sunday, c/o Regina Exhibition Association, PO Box 167, Regina SK S4P 2Z6 – 306/781-9200 – July

Québec International Summer Festival, 160, rue St-Paul, CP 25, Québec PQ G1K 7A1 – 418/692-4540 – Contact, Gilles Laforce – Entertainment in the streets & parks of Old Québec

Royal St. John's Regatta, St. John's NF – 709/576-8511 – North America's oldest continuing sporting event, August – St. John's NF

Sam Steele Days, c/o, PO Box 115, Cranbrook BC V1C 4H6 – 250/426-4161

Seafest, PO Box 577, Yarmouth NS B5A 4B4 – 902/742-7585; Fax: 902/742-5215 – Darlene Nickerson – Rum running, dory races, seafood, July – Yarmouth NS

Selkirk's Festival on the Red, PO Box 177, Selkirk MB R1A 2B2 – 204/482-3304

Shediac Lobster Festival, PO Box 1923, Shediac NB E0A 3G0 – 506/532-1122; Fax: 506/532-1122 – Annually, July

Shelburne County Lobster Festival, PO Box 280, Shelburne NS B0T 1W0 – 902/875-3544; Fax: 902/875-1278 – Annually, June

Shelburne Founder's Days, PO Box 699, Shelburne NS B0T 1W0 – 902/875-3873; Fax: 902/875-3932 – Annually, July

Shippagan Provincial Fisheries Festival, PO Box 1004, Shippagan NB E0B 2P0 – 506/336-8726 – Secretary, Claire Robichaud – Annually, July

Steinbach Pioneer Days, c/o Peter Goertzen, PO Box 1136, Steinbach MB R0A 2A0 – 204/326-9661

Storytelling Festival, c/o The Storytellers' School of Toronto, 412A College St., Toronto ON M5T 1T3 – Held annually at North York Library for two days, February

Summer Festival, c/o #1, 171 Main St. South, Newmarket ON L3Y 3Y9 – 905/895-5193 – June/July

Summerfest: Edmonton Street Performances Festival, #901, 10136 - 100 St., Edmonton AB T5J 0P1 – 403/425-5162 – July 4

Threshermen's Show & Seniors' Festival, PO Box 98, Yorkton SK S3N 2V6 – 306/783-8361 – Chairman, Susan Mandzluk – Annually, August

Trinity Conception Fair, c/o Harbour Grace Stadium, Harbour Grace NF A0A 2M0 – 709/945-5140 – Chairman, Gordon Pike – Annually, September

Welland Rose Festival, c/o Chamber of Commerce, 32 East Main St., Welland ON L3B 3W3 – 905/732-6603 – Annually, June. Rose show, lobsterfest, sporting events, moonlight canal cruises, juried art show, seniors' events, multi-cultural dancers, day-in-the-park, craft show, fishing derby, children's events, grand parade

Winnipeg Beach Boardwalk Summer Festival, Winnipeg Beach MB R0C 3G0 – 204/389-2698 – Norma Giller

World Gold-Panning Championships, Klondike Visitors Association, PO Box 389, Dawson City YT Y0B 1G0 – 403/993-5575 – July

Yukon Sourdough Rendezvous, PO Box 5108, Whitehorse YT Y1A 4S3 – 403/667-2148 – Annually. Dog sled races, mad trapper competitions, leg wrestling, flour packing, swede sawing, tug-of-war, fiddle show, February

EXHIBITIONS

see also **Farm Business/Agriculture, Rodeos**

Buffalo Days Exhibition, Regina Exhibition Park, PO Box 167, Regina SK S4P 2Z6 – 306/781-9200; Fax: 306/565-3443 – Tom Mullin – August

Calgary Exhibition & Stampede, PO Box 1060, Stn M, Calgary AB T2P 2K8 – 403/261-0101; Fax: 403/265-7197; Tollfree: 1-800-661-1260 – General Manager, Steve Edwards – Annual city-wide festival; agricultural exhibits, July – Stampede Fairgrounds, Calgary AB

Canadian Lakehead Exhibition, 425 Northern Ave., Thunder Bay ON P7C 2V7 – 807/622-6473; Fax: 807/623-5540 – Administrative Clerk, Dulcie Wavryk – Annually, June

Canadian National Exhibition, Canadian National Exhibition Association, Exhibition Place, Toronto ON M6K 3C3 – 416/393-6000; Fax: 416/393-6259 – General Manager, Peter Moore – Annual public show, Aug. - Sept. – Exhibition Place, Toronto ON

Edmonton's Klondike Days Exposition, PO Box 1480, Edmonton AB T5J 2N5 – 403/471-7210; Fax: 403/471-8176 – Contact, Bob Gray – Annual consumer show, July – Northlands Exposition Grounds

Expo Québec, La Commission de l'Exposition provinciale de Québec, 2205, av du Colisée, Québec PQ G1L 4W7 – 418/691-7110; Fax: 418/691-7249 – General Manager, André Savard – Annual exhibition. Industrial, agricultural, food, August – City Fairgrounds, Québec PQ

Fredericton Exhibition, PO Box 235, Stn A, Fredericton NB E3B 4Y9 – 506/458-8819 – Contact, Brian Embleton – Annual, September

Grand Ole Atlantic National Exhibition, PO Box 284, Saint John NB E2L 3Y2 – 506/633-2020; Fax: 506/633-0802 – Contact, Alma Walsh – Annual, August

Home Town Fair, c/o Moose Jaw Exhibition Co. Ltd., PO Box 1467, Moose Jaw SK S6H 4R3 – 306/692-2723 – Annually, June

Interior Provincial Exhibition, PO Box 490, Armstrong BC V0E 1B0 – 250/546-9406; Fax: 250/546-6181 – Manager, Mike McCarty – Annual consumer agricultural fair & show, September

Kamloops Exhibition, 479 Chilcotin St., Kamloops BC V2H 1G4 – 250/828-3590 – Annual agricultural fair & show, September

Lindsay Central Exhibition, 37 Adelaide St. North, Lindsay ON K9V 4K8 – 705/324-5551; Fax: 705/324-8111 – Secretary, John Lester – Annual consumer agricultural fair & show, September

Manitoba Stampede & Exhibition, PO Box 849, Morris MB R0G 1K0 – 204/746-2552; Fax: 204/746-2900 – Contact, Ron Janke – Annually, July. Five days

Markham Agricultural Fair, 10801 McCowan Rd., Markham ON L3P 3J3 – 905/642-3247 – Manager, David Morrison – Annual consumer show, September/October

Canadian Almanac & Directory 1997

Medicine Hat Exhibition & Stampede, PO Box 1298, Medicine Hat AB T1A 7N1 – 403/527-1234 – General Manager, Dann Sodero – Annual consumer show, August

Niagara Regional Exhibition, 1100 Niagara St. North, Welland ON L3C 1M6 – 905/735-6413 – Annual consumer agricultural fair & show, September

Northwest Roundup & Exhibition, PO Box 116, Swan River MB R0L 1Z0 – 204/734-3718

Nova Scotia Provincial Exhibition, PO Box 192, Truro NS B2N 5C5 – 902/893-9222 – Paul R. Roy – Agricultural exhibition, August – Bible Hill NS

Pacific National Exhibition, PO Box 69020, Vancouver BC V5K 4W3 – 604/253-2311; Fax: 604/251-7726 – Public Relations Manager, Roger Young – Annual event; agricultural competitions, parade, Aug. - Sept. – Exhibition Park, Vancouver BC

Prince Albert Exhibition, Prince Albert Exhibition Association, PO Box 1538, Prince Albert SK S6V 5T1 – 306/764-1711, 8265 – President, John Prins – Annual, August – Prince Albert SK

Provincial Exhibition of Manitoba, #3, 1175 - 18th St., Brandon MB R7A 7C5 – 204/726-3590; Fax: 204/725-0202 – General Manager, Dave Wowchuk – Annual summer fair & pro rodeo, June – Keystone Centre, Brandon MB

Red River Exhibition, Red River Exhibition Association, 876 St. James St., Winnipeg MB R3G 3J7 – 204/772-9464; Fax: 204/775-9695 – Manitoba's largest fair & single-site entertainment event. Annually, 10 days, last two weeks in June

Regina Buffalo Days Exhibition, Regina Exhibition Association Ltd., PO Box 167, Regina SK S4P 2Z6 – 306/781-9200; Fax: 306/565-3443 – Secretary, Isabel Sheltgen – Annual consumer show, July – Exhibition Grounds, Regina SK

Saskatoon Exhibition, Saskatoon Prairieland Exhibition Corporation, PO Box 6010, Saskatoon SK S7K 4E4 – 306/931-7149; Fax: 306/931-7886 – General Manager, Ed Sikorski – Commercial exhibits & agricultural shows, July – Prairieland Exhibition Centre, Saskatoon SK

FARM BUSINESS/AGRICULTURE
see also Exhibitions, Rodeos

Ag-Expo, Lethbridge & District Exhibition, 3401 Parkside Dr. South, Lethbridge AB T1J 4R3 – 403/328-4491; Fax: 403/320-8139 – Agricultural Coordinator, Twyla Gurr – Annual agricultural exhibition which includes the North American seed fair, March

Agritrade, Red Deer Chamber of Commerce, 3017 Gaetz Ave., Red Deer AB T4N 5Y6 – 403/347-4491; Fax: 403/343-6188 – Contact, Pat Kennedy – Annual, November

AgVenture, Medicine Hat & District Chamber of Commerce, 413 - 6th Ave. SE, Medicine Hat AB T1A 2S7 – 403/527-5214; Fax: 403/527-5182 – President, Barry Miskuski – March – Cypress Centre, Medicine Hat AB

Alberta Beef Congress, Red Deer Chamber of Commerce, 3017 Gaetz Ave., Red Deer AB T4N 5Y6 – 403/347-4491; Fax: 403/343-6188 – Contact, Pat Kennedy – Annual trade & consumer show, June – Red Deer AB

Alberta Pork Congress, Red Deer Chamber of Commerce, 3017 Gaetz Ave., Red Deer AB T4N 5Y6 – 403/347-4491; Fax: 403/343-6188 – Contact, Pat Kennedy – Annual trade & consumer show, June

Annual Convention & Trade Show, Canadian Association of Agri-Retailers, #107, 1090 Waverley St., Winnipeg MB R3T 0P4 – 204/989-9300; Fax: 204/989-9306 – Executive Director, Jacqueline Ryrie – February – Regina Exhibition Park, Regina SK

Atlantic Farm Mechanization Show, PO Box 686, Moncton NB E1C 8M7 – 506/856-9898; Fax: 506/532-9179 – Show Manager, Theresa McGuire – Biennial consumer show, March 1997 – Maritime Coliseum, Agrena Complex, Moncton NB

Atlantic Winter Fair, Prospect Court, RR#2, PO Box 3, Armdale NS B3L 4J2 – 902/876-8221; Fax: 902/876-8551 – Contact, David Coombes – Annual consumer exhibition, October

Canada Dairy Expo, Saskatoon Prairieland Exhibition Corporation, PO Box 6010, Saskatoon SK S7K 4E4 – 306/931-7149; Fax: 306/931-7886 – General Manager, Ed Sikorski – Largest national dairy cattle show & sale; comprehensive dairy industry exhibitions; trade show, April – Prairieland Exhibition Centre, Saskatoon SK

Canadian International Farm Equipment Show, Dawn Morris Productions Inc., #3, 1434 Chemong Rd., RR#1, Peterborough ON K9J 6X2 – 705/741-2536; Fax: 705/741-2539; Email: cifcs@dawnmorris.on.ca; URL: http://www.dawnmorris.on.ca – Show Manager, Lesley Nicholson – Annual trade show, February – Toronto ON

Canadian Western Agribition, Canadian Western Agribition Association, Regina Exhibition Park, Canada Centre Bldg., 2nd Fl., PO Box 3535, Regina SK S4P 3J8 – 306/565-0565; Fax: 306/757-9963; URL: http://www.sasknet.com/corporate/Agribition/ – Wayne Gamble – Annual trade & consumer show, November – Exhibition Park, Regina SK

Chinook Livestock Classic, Lethbridge & District Exhibition, 3401 Parkside Dr. South, Lethbridge AB T1J 4R3 – 403/328-4491; Fax: 403/320-8139 – Agricultural Coordinator, Twyla Gurr – Annual purebred beef cattle show, October – Exhibition Grounds, Lethbridge AB

Estevan Farmer's Day, c/o Estevan Chamber of Commerce, 1102 - 4th St., Estevan SK S4A 0W7 – 306/634-2828 – Manager, Linda Bouey – Annually, March

Fall Fair, Provincial Exhibition of Manitoba, #3, 1175 - 18th St., Brandon MB R7A 7C5 – 204/726-3590; Fax: 204/725-0202 – General Manager, Dave Wowchuk – Ag Ex, Winter Expressions, MRCA Rodeo finals, November – Keystone Centre, Brandon MB

Farmers' Field Day & Open House, c/o St. John's Research Station, Agriculture Canada, Brookfield Rd., St. John's NF A1E 3Y3 – 709/772-4619; Fax: 709/772-6064 – Coordinator, Frank Hender – Annually, late August

Food & Livestock Show, PO Box 8700, St. John's NF A1B 4J6 – 709/729-6716; Fax: 709/729-6046 – Coordinator, Denise Murphy – Annually, September/October

International Plowing Match & Farm Machinery Show, Ontario Plowmen's Association, 367 Woodlawn Rd. West, Guelph ON N1H 7K9 – 519/767-1967; Fax: 519/661-7569; Tollfree: 1-800-661-7569 – General Manager, John Fennell – Annual, Sept. 16-20 1997 – Barrie ON

International Potato Technology Exposition, Master Promotions Ltd., PO Box 565, Saint John NB E2L 3Z8 – 506/658-0018; Fax: 506/658-0750 – Show Manager, Mark Cusack – February – Civic Centre, Charlottetown PE

International Salon of Farm Machinery, Les Productions Jacqueline Vézina inc., #3000, 926, St-Maurice, Montréal PQ H3C 1L7 – 514/861-8241; Fax: 514/861-8246 – Présidente, Jacqueline Vézina

Manager & Crop Products Residues, Saskatchewan Soil Conservation Association Inc., PO Box 1360, Indian Head SK S0G 2K0 – 306/695-4235; Fax: 306/695-4236 – Blair McClinton – Annual trade show. Farm equipment, soil conservation, February – Regina SK

Norfolk County Fair & Horse Show, Norfolk County Agricultural Society, 172 South Dr., Simcoe ON N3Y 1G6 – 519/426-7280 – Secretary-Manager, S.J. Culver – Annual consumer show, October – Simcoe ON

Northlands Farmfair, c/o, PO Box 1480, Edmonton AB T5J 2N5 – 403/471-7210 – Annually, November

Nova Scotia 4-H Show, c/o NS Dept. of Agriculture & Marketing, PO Box 550, Truro NS B2N 5E3 – 902/893-6585, ext.310; Fax: 902/895-7693 – Supervisor, Elizabeth Crouse – Annual consumer show, September

Ontario Dairy Expo, Western Fair Association, PO Box 4550, Stn D, London ON N5W 5K3 – 519/438-7203; Fax: 519/679-3124 – Annual trade show, August – London ON

Ottawa Winter Fair, 466 Pleasant Park Rd., Ottawa ON K1H 5N1 – 613/733-6218 – Contact, Margaret Harrison – October

Paris Fall Fair, PO Box 124, Paris ON N3L 3E7 – 519/442-2823; Fax: 519/442-5121 – Secretary, Harold Edgar – Annual Labour Day weekend consumer show

Perth County Farm Progress Show, Perth County Agricultural Week, 20 Glastonbury Dr., PO Box 901, Stratford ON N5A 6W3 – 519/271-5130; Fax: 519/271-5832 – Manager, Brian Gropp – Annual consumer show, February

Potato Festival, PO Box 800, Grand Falls NB E0J 1M0 – 506/473-3080 – June

Poultry Industry Conference & Exhibition, Western Fair Association, PO Box 4550, Stn D, London ON N5W 5K3 – 519/438-7203; Fax: 519/679-3124 – Annual trade show, April – Western Fairgrounds, London ON

Prairie Ventures, Saskatoon Prairieland Exhibition Corporation, PO Box 6010, Saskatoon SK S7K 4E4 – 306/931-7149; Fax: 306/931-7886 – General Manager, Ed Sikorski – Annual consumer show. Livestock, February – Saskatoon SK

Provincial Livestock Show, c/o NB Dept. of Agriculture, PO Box 6000, Fredericton NB E3B 5H1 – 506/453-6610 – Contact, Deborah Graye – Annual, September

Royal Agricultural Winter Fair, Royal Agricultural Winter Fair Association, Coliseum, Exhibition Place, Toronto ON M6K 3C3 – 416/393-6400; Fax: 416/393-6488; Email: rwfair@io.org; URL: http://www.royalfair.org – CEO, David E. Garrick – Annual consumer show. World's largest indoor agricultural fair & equestrian event, November – Exhibition Place, Toronto ON

Royal Manitoba Winter Fair, Provincial Exhibition of Manitoba, #3, 1175 - 18th St., Brandon MB R7A 7C5 – 204/726-3590; Fax: 204/725-0202 – General Manager, Dave Wowchuk – Annual consumer show; agricultural machinery, products & services; horse shows, March – Keystone Centre, Brandon MB

Salon Agro-Alimentaire, Association des étudiants de l'Université Laval, #0110, Cité Universitaire, Pavillon Paul Comptoi, Ste-Foy PQ G1K 7P4 – 418/656-2131; Fax: 418/656-2610 – Yves Chagnon – Annual consumer show, February – Québec PQ

Salon de l'Agriculteur, CP 123, St-Hyacinthe PQ J2S 7B4 – 514/771-1226; Fax: 514/771-1226 – Florent Fortier – Annual trade show. Agricultural products, January – St-Hyacinthe PQ

Summerside Agricultural Exhibition, PO Box 1295, Summerside PE C1N 4K2 – 902/436-7139, 8324 – Colleen Marsh – September

Western Canada Farm Progress Show, PO Box 167, Regina SK S4P 2Z6 – 306/781-9200; Fax: 306/781-9396 – Show Administrator, David Fiddler – Annual consumer & trade show, June – Regina Exhibition Park, Regina SK

Western Canadian Crop Production Show, Saskatoon Prairieland Exhibition Corporation, PO Box 6010, Saskatoon SK S7K 4E4 – 306/931-7149; Fax: 306/931-7886 – General Manager, Ed Sikorski – Annual consumer show, January – Saskatoon SK

Western Fair, Western Fair Association, PO Box 4550, Stn D, London ON N5W 5K3 – 519/438-7203;

Fax: 519/679-3124 – Annual consumer show, September – Queen's Park, London ON

Western Farm Fair Show, Western Fair Association, PO Box 4550, Stn D, London ON N5W 5K3 – 519/438-7203; Fax: 519/679-3124 – Annual consumer show, March – Western Fairgrounds, London ON

Western Nova Scotia Exhibition, PO Box 425, Yarmouth NS B5A 4B3 – 902/742-8222; Fax: 902/742-0458 – Frank Anderson – Six-day agricultural fair & talent competition, July or Aug. – Yarmouth NS

Whoop Up Bull Show & Sale, Lethbridge & District Exhibition, 3401 Parkside Dr. South, Lethbridge AB T1J 4R3 – 403/328-4491; Fax: 403/320-8139 – Agricultural Coordinator, Twyla Gurr – Show & sale of purebred bulls, March

FASHION

Imprinted Sportswear Show, Miller Freeman Expositions, #500, 13760 Noel Rd., Dallas TX 75240 – 214/239-3060; Fax: 214/419-7855; Tollfree: 1-800-527-0207 – Annual trade show, April – Toronto ON

Luggage, Leathergoods, Handbags & Accessories, Pro-Show, Trade Show Management, #102, 33 Isabella St., Toronto ON M4Y 2P7 – 416/960-8739; Fax: 416/960-1854 – Show Manager, Dan Joyce – Annual trade show

Mode Accessories Show, Two Plus One Group, #611, 220 Duncan Mill Rd., North York ON M3B 3J5 – 416/510-0114; Fax: 416/510-0165 – President, Alice Chee – Semi-annual trade show (January & August) – Queen Elizabeth Building, Exhibition Place, Toronto ON

National Apparel Technology Show/Salon National de la Technologie du Vêtement, P.R. Charette Inc., 35, Promenade Westland, Montréal-Ouest PQ H4X 1M3 – 514/489-8671; Fax: 514/487-3230 – Contact, Bob Charette – May – Palais de Congrès de Montréal, Montréal PQ

Ontario Fashion Exhibitors Inc. Fashion Market, Ontario Fashion Exhibitors Inc., #219, 111 Peter St., Toronto ON M5V 2H1 – 416/596-2401; Fax: 416/596-1808 – Marketing Director, Lynn Radmore – Trade show held four times annually. Women's fashions & accessories; children's wear

FESTIVALS *see* **EVENTS**

FILM & VIDEO FESTIVALS/SPECIAL EVENTS

Alberta Film & Television Awards, Alberta Motion Picture Industries Association, 606 Midland Walwyn Tower, Edmonton Centre, Edmonton AB T5J 2Z2 – 403/944-0707; Fax: 403/426-3057 – President, Andy Thomson, 403/482-2022 – February

Annual Awards, Canadian Society of Cinematographers, #602, 235 Carlaw Ave., Toronto ON M4M 2S1 – 416/466-5013 – Contact, Jennifer Hietala

Atlantic Film & Video Producers Conference, PO Box 2726, Charlottetown PE C1A 8C3 – 902/892-3131; Fax: 902/566-1724 – June

Atlantic Film Festival/Festival du Film de l'Atlantique, Atlantic Film Festival, 2015 Gottingen St., Halifax NS B3K 3B1 – 902/422-3456; Fax: 902/422-4006; URL: http://www.ccn.cs.dal.ca/Culture/AFF/AFF-Home.html – Director, Constance Moffit – Films & videos. Competition, seminars & workshops, September – Halifax NS

The B Festival, #1111, 40 Alexander St., Toronto ON M4W 1B5 – 416/927-8651; Fax: 416/480-9528

Banff Festival of Mountain Films, 107 Tunnel Mountain Dr., PO Box 1020, Stn 38, Banff AB T0L 0C0 – 403/762-6125; Fax: 403/762-6277; Email: MFF@BanffCentre.ab.ca; URL: http://www.banffcentre.ab.ca/MFF/index.html – Annual festival, November – Banff Centre, Banff AB

Banff Television Festival, PO Box 1020, Banff AB T0L 0C0 – 403/762-3060; Fax: 403/762-5357 – President/Festival Director, Jerry Ezekiel – Television films & programs. Competition, seminars & workshops, June – Banff AB

Canadian International Annual Film Festival, 25 Eugenia St., Barrie ON L4M 1P6 – 705/737-2729; Fax: 705/726-4655 – Director, Ben Andrews – Judging takes place in June (categories: Independent Filmmakers, Film Students, Amateurs); Festival in the fall

Le Carrousel international du film de Rimouski, CP 1462, Rimouski PQ G5L 8M3 – 418/722-0103; Fax: 418/724-9504 – Directrice générale, Sylvie Blanchette – Films for children. Competition, workshops, September – Rimouski PQ

Cinémental - Le Festival de Films francophones au Manitoba, 245 Main St., PO Box 113, Winnipeg MB R2H 3B4 – 204/231-0907; Fax: 204/983-0742 – Coordinator, Martine Bordeleau – People's choice award – St-Boniface MB

Colloque de l'Association québécoise des études cinématographiques, 335, boul de Maisonneuve est, Montréal PQ H2X 1K1 – 514/842-9763; Fax: 514/842-1816 – November

Festival de l'audiovisuel, CP 68, Succ Ahuntsic, Montréal PQ H3L 3W5 – 514/334-4084 – May/June

Festival du cinéma francophone international en Acadie, #29, 140 Botsford St., Moncton NB E1C 4X4 – 506/855-6050; Fax: 506/857-3070 – Coordinator, Judith Hamel – Francophone feature films. People's choice awards, seminars, September – Moncton NB

Festival du cinéma international de Ste-Thérèse, 100, rue Duquet, Ste-Thérèse PQ J7E 3G6 – 514/434-0387, 430-3120; Fax: 514/434-7868 – Coordonnateur, Réjean St-Pierre – Last week in September

Festival du cinéma international en Abitibi-Témiscamingue, 215, av Mercier, Rouyn-Noranda PQ J9X 5W8 – 819/762-6212; Fax: 819/762-6762; URL: http://www.telebec.qc.ca/fciat/ – Executive Director, Jacques Matte – Features, medium-length & short films. Competition; regional jury award for short or medium-length film; people's choice award for feature & animation – Rouyn-Noranda PQ

Festival du film étudiant canadien/Canadian Student Film Festival, Festival du film étudiant canadien, #H-109, 1455, boul de Maisonneuve ouest, Montréal PQ H3G 1M8 – 514/848-3878; Fax: 514/848-3886 – Coordonnatrice, Danièle Cauchard – Films & videos by Canadian students. Film competition, August – Montréal PQ

Festival international du film de Baie-Comeau, 70, av Michel-Hémon, Baie-Comeau PQ G4Z 2A5 – 418/296-8379; Fax: 418/296-8399 – Coordinator, André Thalabot – Feature films, people's choice awards, January – Baie-Comeau PQ

Festival International du Film sur l'Art, #406, 640, rue Saint-Paul ouest, Montréal PQ H3C 1L9 – 514/874-1637; Fax: 514/874-9929 – Directeur général, René Rozon – Films & videos on visual & performing arts. Competition, March – Montréal PQ

Festival international du nouveau cinéma et de la vidéo/Montréal International Festival of New Cinema & Video, Festival international du nouveau cinéma et de la vidéo, 3726, boul St-Laurent, Montréal PQ H2X 2V8 – 514/843-4725, 4711; Fax: 514/843-4631 – Directeur, Claude Chamberlan – New trends in cinema & video. Competition, Québec Critics' awards for feature & short films. Jury award for video production, October – Montréal PQ

Festival of Festivals, 2 Carlton St., 16th Fl., Toronto ON M5B 1J3 – 416/967-7371; Fax: 416/967-9477; URL: http://www.bell.ca/toronto/filmfest – Managing Director, Suzanne Weiss – Features & theatrical shorts. Competition. Awards for excellence in Canadian production. People's choice & film critics awards. Symposium, workshops, sales office, September – Toronto ON

Film Studies Association of Canada Conference, Film Studies Association of Canada, Film Studies Program, Dept. of History in Art, Univ. of Victoria, PO Box 1700, Victoria BC V8W 2Y2; URL: http://www.film.queensu.ca/FSAC/Home.html – Sec.-Treas., Lianne McLarty – May/June annually, held at a different university each year

Filmex, 1204, rue Ste-Catherine est, Montréal PQ H2L 2G9 – 514/525-0057; Fax: 514/525-4616 – March/April

Five Days of Canadian Independent Cinema, #303, 4067, boul Saint-Laurent, Montréal PQ H2W 1Y7 – 514/845-7442; Fax: 514/849-1231 – Coordinator, Peter Sandmark – Biennial. Canadian independent films & videos. Forum, November 1998 – Montréal PQ

Genie, Gemini, Gémeaux Awards, Academy of Canadian Cinema & Television, 158 Pearl St., Toronto ON M5H 1L3 – 416/591-2040; Fax: 416/591-2157; Tollfree: 1-800-644-5194; URL: http://www.academy.ca – CEO, Maria Topalovich – Annual awards show

Guelph International Film Festival, 15 University Ave. East, Guelph ON N1G 2W5 – 519/824-4120, ext.6918; Fax: 519/767-0756 – Coordinator, L. Grubach – Annual event exploring the medium of "Third Cinema", held in September

Image & Nation gaie et lesbienne, festival international du cinéma et de vidéo de Montréal, CP 1595, Succ Place de P, Montréal PQ H2W 2R6 – 514/526-7221 – Autumn

Images du futur, Exposition internationale d'art, de Nouvelles Technologies et de Communication, #101, 15, rue de la Commune ouest, Montréal PQ H2Y 2C6 – 514/849-1612; Fax: 514/982-0064 – Président, Hervé Fischer – May to September, annually. The "International Computer Animation Competition" is part of Images du futur

Images Festival of Independent Film & Video, #448, 401 Richmond St. West, Toronto ON M5V 3A8 – 416/971-8405; Fax: 416/971-7412; Email: images@interlog; URL: http://www.interlog.com/~images/ – Executive Director, Dierdre Logue – Annual. Independent films & videos. Workshops, April – Toronto ON

In-Sight: Festival of Women's Films, 9722 - 102 St., 2nd Fl., Edmonton AB T5K 0X4 – 403/448-0703; Fax: 403/495-6412 – Coordinator, Nancy Poole – Biennial. Women's films & videos. Seminars, November 1998 – Edmonton AB

Indian Summer, World Festival of Aboriginal Motion Pictures, c/o, PO Box 1280, Pincher Creek AB T0K 1W0 – 403/627-4813; Fax: 403/627-4957 – September

International Film Festival of Québec City, #50, 35, rue Dalhousie, Québec PQ G1K 8W6 – 418/694-9920; Fax: 418/694-0632 – Coordinator, Marie Talbot – Feature films. Competition, people's choice awards, September – Québec PQ

International Images Film Festival, 106 Murray St., Peterborough ON K9H 2S5 – 705/745-1380; Fax: 705/745-8710 – Annual event held for two weeks, in October-November

International Short Film Festival of Montréal, #326, 4205, rue St-Denis, Montréal PQ H1V 3R2 – 514/285-4515; Fax: 514/285-2886 – Administrative Director, Paul-Jacques Hulot – Short films & videos by amatuer & non-professional filmmakers. Competition, seminars, January – Montréal PQ

L'Annuelle des Professionnels des Industries de L'Image et du Son/Image & Sound Industries Annual Conference & Forum, 1276, rue Amherst, Montréal PQ H2L 3K8 – 514/842-5333; Fax: 514/842-6717 – May

Les Journées du Cinéma Africain et Créole, 67, rue Ste-Catherine ouest, 5e étage, Montréal PQ H2X 1Z7 – 514/284-3322; Fax: 514/845-0631 – President, Gérard Le Chêne – Competition. Films by & about African & Creole peoples, April – Montréal PQ

Les Rendez-vous du cinéma québécois, 4545, av Pierre-De Coubertin, CP 1000, Succ M, Montréal PQ H1V 3R2 – 514/252-3021; Fax: 514/251-8038 – Directeur, Michel Coulombe – Restrospective of recent Québec productions. Competition, February – Montréal PQ

Local Heroes, 10022 - 103 St., 3rd Fl., Edmonton AB T5J 0X2 – 403/421-4084; Fax: 403/425-8098 – Executive Director, Jane Miller – Feature, medium-length & short films. Workshops, February – Edmonton AB

Making Scenes Film & Video Festival, National Gallery of Canada; URL: http://fox.nstn.ca/~scenes/ – Annual lesbian & gay film & video festival, May – National Gallery of Canada, Ottawa ON

La Mondiale de films et vidéos réalisé par des femmes, 709, rue du Roi, Québec PQ G1K 2V6 – 418/647-0147; Fax: 418/648-9201 – Coordinator, Hélène Roy – Biennial. Women's films & videos. Competition, seminars, March or April – Québec PQ

Montreal International Chinese Film Festival/Festival international du cinéma chinois de Montréal, #393, 1600, de Lorimier, Montréal PQ H2K 3W5 – 514/527-3981; Fax: 514/521-7081 – Coordinator, Suzanne Girard – Film screenings: Vancouver, mid-May, Montréal, end of May, Toronto, early June, Ottawa/Hull, early June. Exhibition: Montréal, mid-May to early June

Ottawa International Animation Festival, Canadian Film Institute, 2 Daly Ave., Ottawa ON K1N 6E2 – 613/232-6727; Fax: 613/232-6315 – Director, Tom Knott – Biennial. Animation films & videos. Workshops & panels, September – Ottawa ON

Saskatchewan Film & Video Showcase, 2431 - 8th Ave., Regina SK S4R 5J7 – 306/525-9899; Fax: 306/569-1818 – President, Jack Walton – Retrospective of recent Saskatchewan productions. Competition, forum & workshops, November – Regina SK

Silence Elles Tournent, Cinéma Femmes Montréal, #1414, 555, boul René-Lévesque, Montréal PQ H2Z 1B1 – 514/389-0010; Fax: 514/395-6012 – Director, Isabelle Jutras – Women's film & videos. Competition, workshops, April – Montréal PQ

St. John's Women's Film & Video Festival, PO Box 984, St. John's NF A1C 5C2 – 709/772-0359; Fax: 709/772-4808 – Festival Director, Alyson Dyer – Women's films & videos. Workshops & panels, October – St. John's NF

Sudbury Film Festival, #217, 40 Elm St., Sudbury ON P3C 1S8 – 705/688-1234; Fax: 705/688-1351 – Executive Director, Cam Haynes – Features, medium-length & short films. Competition, awards for best Canadian, international & Ontario films. Workshops, September – Sudbury ON

Summer Institute of Film & Television/Rencontre Estivale ciné-vidéo, Summer Institute of Film & Television, Algonquin College, 2 Daly Ave., 2nd Fl., Ottawa ON K1P 6E3 – 613/727-4723, ext.6150; Fax: 613/733-6170 – Coordinator, Lawry Trevor-Deutsch – Features, medium-length & short films. Workshops, June – Ottawa ON

Vancouver International Film Festival, #410, 1008 Homer St., Vancouver BC V6B 2X1 – 604/685-0260; Fax: 604/688-8221; Email: viff@viff.org; URL: http://www.viff.org/viff – Executive Director, Alan Franey – Features, medium-length & short films. Competition; jury award for best Canadian screenplay; people's choice award for most popular foreign film & for most popular Canadian film. Trade forum, October – Vancouver BC

World Film Festival, Montréal World Film Festival, #H-109, 1455, boul de Maisonneuve ouest, Montréal PQ H3G 1M8 – 514/848-3883; Fax: 514/848-3886;
Email: ffm@interlink.net; URL: http://www.ffm-montreal.org/ – President & Executive Director, Serge Losique – Features, medium-length & short films. Competition, symposium, markets, August – Montréal PQ

Yorkton Short Film & Video Festival, 49 Smith St. East, Yorkton SK S3N 0H4 – 306/782-7077; Fax: 306/782-1550 – Finance Director, Rob Dewhirst – Canadian short films & videos. Competition, seminars & workshops, May – Yorkton SK

FIRST NIGHT CELEBRATIONS

Calgary First Night Festival Society, 700 - 6 Ave. SW, Calgary AB T2P 0T8 – 403/269-6483; Fax: 403/265-5491 – Producer, Kathleen Specht

First Night Banff, c/o Banff Allied Arts Council, PO Box 1343, Banff AB T0L 0C0 – 403/762-8562; Fax: 403/762-4286 – General Manager, Special Events, Judy Anderson-Hansen

First Night Comox Valley, c/o Comox Valley Chamber of Commerce, 2040 Cliffe Ave., Courtenay BC V9N 2L3 – 250/338-1210; Fax: 250/334-1384 – Coordinator, Liz Wouters

First Night Edmonton Festival Society, #266, 9777 - 102 Ave., Edmonton AB T5J 4G9 – 403/448-9200; Fax: 403/426-7608 – Producer, Josh Keller

First Night Kamloops, PO Box 1166, Kamloops BC V2C 6H3 – 250/374-4634; Fax: 250/374-4621 – Executive Director, Marg Marshall

First Night Maple Ridge, 11925 Haney Pl., Maple Ridge BC V2X 6G2 – 604/463-5244; Fax: 604/463-8336 – Marilyn Jollymore

First Night Ottawa-Carleton, c/o Sparks Street Mall Management Board, 151 Sparks St., 2nd Fl., Ottawa ON K1P 5E3 – 613/230-0984; Fax: 613/230-7671 – Executive Director, Ken Dale

First Night Penticton, c/o City of Penticton, 325 Power St., Penticton BC V2A 5K9 – 250/490-2426; Fax: 250/490-2427 – Contact, Barry Reid

First Night Prince George, PO Box 386, Prince George BC V2L 4S2 – 250/562-2437; Fax: 250/562-1798 – Helen Leckie

First Night Qualicum Beach, PO Box 154, Qualicum Beach BC V9K 1S7 – 250/752-6841 – Margot Cyr

First Night Saint John, PO Box 6355, Stn A, Saint John NB E2L 4R8 – 506/658-2990; Fax: 506/632-6118 – Contact, Neil Jacobsen

First Night Toronto, #116-58, 65 Front St. West, Toronto ON M5J 1E6 – 416/362-3692; Fax: 416/362-4430 – Producer, Laurel Smith-Devlin

First Night Vancouver, c/o Pacific National Exhibition, PO Box 69020, Vancouver BC V5K 4W3 – 604/253-2311; Fax: 604/251-7726 – Division Manager, Hammy McClymont

First Night Victoria Celebration of the Arts Society, c/o #710, 1175 Douglas St., Victoria BC V8W 2E1 – 250/382-2160; Fax: 250/655-3655 – Producer, Debora Johns

First Night Whistler, 4010 Whistler Way, Whistler BC V0N 1B4 – 604/932-3928; Fax: 604/932-7231 – Contact, Maureen Douglas

Gabriola First Night Arts Society, PO Box 217, Gabriola BC V0R 1X0 – 250/247-9901; Fax: 250/247-9915 – President, Alan Howardson

FISHING/AQUACULTURE

Adams River Sockeye Salmon Run, PO Box 101, Celesta BC V0E 1L0 – 250/955-6279 – October

Atlantic Aquaculture Fair, Master Promotions Ltd., PO Box 565, Saint John NB E2L 3Z8 – 506/658-0018; Fax: 506/658-0750 – Show Manager, Sydney Jane Brittain – Canada's largest aquaculture event, June – St. Andrews NB

Eastern Canadian Fisheries Exposition, Master Promotions Ltd., PO Box 565, Saint John NB E2L 3Z8 – 506/658-0018; Fax: 506/658-0750 – General Manager, Keith Peacock – April – Yarmouth NS

Flin Flon Trout Festival, PO Box 751, Flin Flon MB R8A 1N6 – 204/687-5166, June – Flin Flon MB

Great Northern Pike Festival, PO Box 160, Nipawin SK S0E 1E0 – 306/356-8692 – June & mid-August – Lynn Lake MB

Nova Scotia Fisheries Exhibition & Fishermen's Reunion, PO Box 308, Lunenburg NS B0J 2C0 – 902/634-3025 – August

Salmon Festival, c/o, PO Box 234, Campbellton NB E3N 3G4 – 506/753-7767 – July

Seafood Festival, PO Box 1220, Shippagan NB E0B 2P0 – 506/336-4116 – June

South West Nova Fisheries Exposition, PO Box 425, Yarmouth NS B5A 4B3 – 902/742-8222; Fax: 902/742-0458 – Frank Anderson – Occupational & recreational technology & equipment, April – Yarmouth NS

FLOWERS/LANDSCAPING/GARDENING

CAN WEST Hortic. Show, British Columbia Nursery Trades Association, #101, 5830 - 176A St., Surrey BC V3S 4E3 – 604/574-7772; Fax: 604/574-7773 – Show Director, Jane Stock – September

Canadian Garden & Flower Show, Klanside Inc., 401 Magnetic Dr., Unit 21, North York ON M3J 3H9 – 416/661-2056; Fax: 416/661-2904 – Show Manager, Kathy O'Hara – Annual consumer show, March/April

Canadian Interior Landscape Conference, Royal Botanical Gardens, 680 Plains Rd. West, PO Box 399, Hamilton ON L8N 3H8 – 905/527-1158; Tollfree: 1-800-668-9449 – Annual trade show & conference

Flower & Vegetable Show, Newfoundland Horticultural Society, PO Box 84, Goulds NF A1S 1G3 – 709/737-8590; Fax: 709/772-6064 – President, Ron Taggart – August – St. John's NF

Garden & Flower Festival, 9 Woodbridge Rd., Hamilton ON L8K 3C6 – 905/547-7135; Fax: 905/547-7135 – Publicity Director, Christine Whitlock – Annual consumer show, February. Floral & landscaping exhibits, & conservation, ecology & the environment

Garden Club of Toronto Flower Show, Civic Garden Centre, 777 Lawrence Ave. East, North York ON M3C 1P2 – 416/447-5218 – President, Barbara Brown – Annually, March

Gardenscape, Saskatoon Prairieland Exhibition Corporation, PO Box 6010, Saskatoon SK S7K 4E4 – 306/931-7149; Fax: 306/931-7886 – Maurice Neault – Annual consumer show. Care & creation of yards & gardens; displays, exhibits, information & demonstrations, March – Jubilee Bldg., Prairieland Exhibition Centre, Saskatoon SK

Hamilton & Burlington Rose Society Show, Royal Botanical Gardens, 680 Plains Rd. West, PO Box 399, Hamilton ON L8N 3H8 – 905/527-1158; Tollfree: 1-800-668-9449 – June

Hamilton Orchid Show, Royal Botanical Gardens, 680 Plains Rd. West, PO Box 399, Hamilton ON L8N 3H8 – 905/527-1158; Tollfree: 1-800-668-9449 – March

Ikenobo Ikebana Japanese Flower Show, Royal Botanical Gardens, 680 Plains Rd. West, PO Box 399, Hamilton ON L8N 3H8 – 905/527-1158; Tollfree: 1-800-668-9449 – September

Landscape Ontario Annual Congress, Landscape Ontario Horticultural Trades Association, 7856 Fifth Line South, RR#4, Milton ON L9T 2X8 – 905/875-1805; Fax: 905/875-3942 – Executive Director, Tony DiGiovanni – Annual trade show, Jan. 14-16 1997 – Toronto ON

The Landscaping Show/Salon de l'aménagement extérieur, Promexpo Inc., 801, rue Sherbrooke est, 10e étage, Montréal PQ H2L 1K7 – 514/527-9221; Fax: 514/527-8449 – General Manager, Vic Côté – Annual consumer show

London Orchid Show, c/o Wonderland Gardens, 284 Wonderland Rd. South, London ON N6K 1L3 – 519/432-7759

Manitoba Horticulture Industry Days, 676 Borebank St., Winnipeg MB R3N 1G2 – 204/254-2293 – Coordinator, Carmen Neufeld – Annual trade show, November. Floral & nursery stock, computers, seed, chemicals, equipment

Milne House Garden Club Annual Flower Show, c/o Civic Garden Centre, 777 Lawrence Ave. East, North York ON M3C 1P2 – 416/449-3664 – June

Provincial Rose Show, 6955 Ward Ave., Halifax NS B3L 2K3 – 902/453-6801 – Marjorie Fowler – Competitive show for rose growers in Nova Scotia, July – Spring Garden Place, Halifax NS

Richmond Garden Club Horticultural Show, 8280 Colonial Dr., Richmond BC V7C 4T4 – 604/271-6487 – August

Saskatoon Horticultural Society Annual Show, 1420 Alexander Ave., Saskatoon SK S7K 3B9 – 306/652-8864 – Contact, Amanda Ryce – August

South Burnaby Garden Club, 15675 - 91 Ave., Surrey BC V4N 2X2 – 604/434-2100 – Secretary, D. Heys – September

Spring Flower Exhibition, Newfoundland Horticultural Society, PO Box 84, Goulds NF A1S 1G3 – 709/737-8590; Fax: 709/772-6064 – President, Ron Taggart, May – Oxen Pond, Memorial University, St. John's NF

Violets in New Scotland, c/o African Violet Society, 45 Shea St., Lower Sackville NS B4C 2B2 – 902/865-8612 – Lois Wiseman

Winnipeg Home, Garden, Pool & Patio Show, Hank Hartloper Agency, #2, 1575 Seel Ave., Winnipeg MB R3T 1C8 – 204/925-5711; Fax: 204/925-6643 – Owner, Hank Hartloper – Annual consumer show. Gardening & landscaping, power equipment, swimming pools & garden structures, March – Winnipeg MB

Winnipeg International Horticultural Show, c/o 54 Lochinvar Ave., Winnipeg MB R2J 1R4 – 204/253-4022 – B. Hildebrand – Mid August

FOOD & BEVERAGE
see also **Hospitality Industry**

AGM, Canadian Institute of Food Science & Technology, #1105, 191 The West Mall, Etobicoke ON M9C 5K8 – 416/626-3140; Fax: 416/620-5392 – Ingredients, lab services & other services for food manufacturers, August

AGM & Hostex Show, Ontario Restaurant Association, #1201, 121 Richmond St. West, Toronto ON M5H 2K1 – 416/359-0533; Fax: 416/359-0531; Tollfree: 1-800-668-8906 – Contact, Jane Anderson – October – International Centre, Mississauga ON

Annual Spring Show & National Conference, Canadian Health Food Association, 370 Steelcase Rd. East, Markham ON L3R 1G2 – 905/479-6939; Fax: 905/479-1516 – Executive Director, Bill Reynolds – Annual trade show, February

ARFEX – Alberta Restaurant & Foodservices Exposition, Alberta Restaurant & Foodservices Association, 10085 - 166 St., Edmonton AB T5P 4Y1 – 403/444-9494; Fax: 403/481-8727; Tollfree: 1-800-461-9762 – President, Elizabeth Kuhnel – Annual, April

Bakery & Pastry Exhibition, Communications Vero Inc., #404, 1600, boul Henri-Bourassa ouest, Montréal PQ H3M 3E2 – 514/332-8376; Toronto: 416/967-9291; Fax: 514/332-2666 – Pierre-Yves Verronneau – Biennial show, October 1997 – Palais des Congrès, Montréal PQ

Bakery Showcase, PH#3, 3300 Don Mills Rd., North York ON M2J 4X7 – 416/490-7910; Fax: 416/490-6931 – Sec.-Treas., Alex Telfer – Biennial trade show, October – Toronto ON

Brew & Wine Food Fest, Lakeshore Productions Inc., 875 Main St. West, Hamilton ON L8S 4R1 – 905/522-6117; Fax: 905/529-2242 – Show Manager, Karen McHarb – Annual consumer show, April – Convention Centre, Hamilton ON

Canadian Automatic Merchandising Show, Canadian Automatic Merchandising Association, PO Box 778, Stn Q, Toronto ON M4T 2N7 – 416/932-2262; Fax: 416/932-3732 – Executive Director, C. Davenport – May

Canadian Fine Food Show, Meteor Show Productions Inc., 298 Sheppard Ave. East, North York ON M2N 3B1 – 416/229-2060; Fax: 416/223-2826; Email: weil@meteorshows.com; URL: http://www.meteorshows.com – President, Ralph Weil – Annual trade show, May 25-27 1997

Canadian Food & Beverage Show, Canadian Restaurant & Foodservices Association, 316 Bloor St. West, Toronto ON M5S 1W5 – 416/923-8416; Fax: 416/923-1450; Tollfree: 1-800-387-5649; Email: 102447.3104@compuserve.com – Director of Expositions, Pawla Lunney – Annual trade show, Feb. 1997 – International Centre, Toronto ON

Canadian Food Technology Show, 850 Boundary Rd., Cornwall ON K6H 5R5 – 613/936-2698; Fax: 613/936-2716 – Annual trade show, June

FAB - Food & Beverage Shows, #105, 10544 - 114 St., Edmonton AB T5H 3J7 – 403/420-6336; Fax: 403/426-7862 – Contact, Rick Young – Annual consumer show. Food, wine & other spirits tasting, seminars, & entertainment, March

Flavour: Atlantic Canada's Food, Wine & Vacation Show, Denex Group Inc., Burnside Industrial Park, 192 Joseph Zatzman Dr., Dartmouth NS B3B 1N4 – 902/468-4999; Fax: 902/468-2795; Email: denman@newedge.ca – President, Jon Denman – Annual consumer show, April

Food & Hospitality Show, Restaurant & Foodservices Association of British Columbia & the Yukon, #140, 475 West Georgia St., Vancouver BC V6B 4H9 – 604/669-2239; Fax: 604/669-6175; Tollfree: 1-800-663-4482; URL: http://www.yes.net/RFABCY/ – Show Coordinator, George Acs – Annual trade show, Apr. 6-8 1997 – Vancouver BC

Food Pacific, c/o BC Pavilion Corporation, 777 Pacific Blvd. South, Vancouver BC V6B 4Y8 – 604/684-3663; Fax: 604/661-3412 – Biennial trade show. Seafood, specialty foods, produce & floriculture, beverages, August 1998

The Good Food Festival Market, 117 Evelyn Ave., Toronto ON M6J 4G7 – 416/766-2880; Fax: 416/762-9942 – Manager, Lynda Chubak – Annual consumer festival, May – Automotive Bldg., Exhibition Place

Gourmet Food & Wine Expo, Winexpo Productions Inc., #11, 5080 Timberlea Blvd., Mississauga ON L4W 4M2 – 905/629-7469; Fax: 905/629-3823; URL: http://www.toronto.com/winexpo – General Manager, Megan Parry – Consumer show, November – Metro Toronto Convention Centre, Toronto ON

Grocery Showcase Canada '97, Canadian Federation of Independent Grocers, #902, 2235 Sheppard Ave. East, North York ON M2J 5B5 – 416/492-2311; Fax: 416/492-2347; Tollfree: 1-800-661-2344 – President, John F.T. Scott – Annual trade show, Oct. 26-28 1997 – Metro Toronto Convention Centre, Toronto ON

Grocery Showcase West '97, Canadian Federation of Independent Grocers, #902, 2235 Sheppard Ave. East, North York ON M2J 5B5 – 416/492-2311; Fax: 416/492-2347; Tollfree: 1-800-661-2344 – President, John F.T. Scott – Annual trade show, Mar. 9-10 1997 – Vancouver Trade & Convention Centre, Vancouver BC

International Food Festival, Fort George Park, 1188 - 6th Ave., Prince George BC V2L 3M6 – 250/563-8525 – August

International Wine & Food Festival, 255 Clemow Ave., Ottawa ON K1S 2B5 – 613/236-9931 – Contact, Hubert de Gonneville – Annual consumer & trade show. New products, celebrity cooking demos, wine competitions, November

Okanagan Wine Festival, 185 Lakeshore Dr., Penticton BC V2A 1B7 – 250/490-8866; Fax: 250/492-6119 – Held annually at various Okanagan Valley locations

Ottawa Wine & Food Show, Player Expositions International, 255 Clemow Ave., Ottawa ON K1S 2B5 – 613/567-6408; Fax: 613/567-2718 – Show Organizer, Halina Player – Annual trade & consumer show, November

Rendez-vous Hôtel Restaurant 97, Association des fournisseurs d'hôtels et restaurants inc., 2435, rue Guénette, Saint Laurent PQ H4R 2E9 – 514/334-5161; Fax: 514/334-1279; Tollfree: 1-800-567-2347 – Trésorier, Raymond Mayrand – 9-11 fév. 1997 – Place Bonaventure, Montréal PQ

SIVS International Wine & Spirits Show / Salon International des Vins et Spiriteux, #1100, 300, Léo Pariseau, CP 159, Montréal PQ H2W 2N9 – 514/289-9669; Fax: 514/289-8711; Tollfree: 1-800363-2806 – General Manager, Alain Bellefeuille – Biennial consumer show. Sale by the bottle or case of alcoholic beverages & private stocks, March

SSA International - Super Salon de l'alimentation, #1100, 300, rue Léo Pariseau, CP 159, Montréal PQ H2W 2N9 – 514/289-9669; Fax: 514/289-8711; Tollfree: 1-800-363-2806 – Director, Sales & Operations, Bill Saad – Annual trade show for the food retail industry including food & beverage products & store equipment, April

Toronto Wine & Cheese Show, Meteor Show Productions Inc., 298 Sheppard Ave. East, North York ON M2N 3B1 – 416/229-2060; Fax: 416/223-2826; Email: weil@meteorshows.com; URL: http://www.meteorshows.com – President, Ralph Weil – Annual consumer show, March – Toronto ON

FOOTWEAR

Canadian International Footwear Exposition/Salon International Canadien de la Chaussure, 4101, rue Sherbrooke ouest, Montréal PQ H3Z 1A8 – 514/937-8118; Fax: 514/937-7066 – Exposition Coordinator, Lina Romano – Semi-annual trade show. Footwear, handbags, small leather goods, accessories, store fixtures, retail bags, trade publications

FOREST INDUSTRY

Canadian Forestry Exhibition, Denex Group Inc., Burnside Industrial Park, 192 Joseph Zatzman Dr., Dartmouth NS B3B 1N4 – 902/468-4999; Fax: 902/468-2795; Email: denman@newedge.ca – President, Jon Denman – Biennial trade show. Heavy equipment; transportations; logging equipment; mill equipment & supplies; occupational services & equipment; woodlots & tree growers; contractors; educational & government organizations; ancillary services, March 14-16 1997 – Fredericton NB

Demo '97, Canadian Pulp & Paper Association, Sun Life Building, 1155, rue Metcalfe, 19e étage, Montréal PQ H3B 4T6 – 514/866-6621; Fax: 514/866-3035 – Asst. Manager, Wayne Novak – Active demonstrations of all types of industrial woodlands equipment. Harvesting, silviculture, transportation & handling, September 1997

Exfor, Canadian Pulp & Paper Association, Sun Life Building, 1155, rue Metcalfe, 19e étage, Montréal PQ H3B 4T6 – 514/866-6621; Fax: 514/866-3035 – President, Forest Products Ltd., E.B. Eddy – Largest

Canadian Almanac & Directory 1997

annual exhibition & conference devoted to the manufacturing of pulp & paper products
Forest Expo, PO Box 2535, Prince George BC V2N 2S6 – 250/563-8833; Fax: 250/563-3697 – Show Manager, Trudy May – Annually, May
Nova Scotia Forestry Exhibition, PO Box 1149, Middleton NS B0S 1P0 – 902/825-4344; Fax: 902/825-4634 – Contact, Diane LeGard – Annually, June. "Great Canadian Lumberjack Show", "Nova Scotia Power Saw Championships", arm wrestling, horse & ox pulls
Truck Loggers Association Convention & Trade Show, The Truck Loggers Association, #725, 815 Hastings St. West, Vancouver BC V6C 1B4 – 604/684-4291; Fax: 604/684-7134 – Office Manager, Dave Webster – Annual trade & consumer show, January – Vancouver BC
Wood Tech '98, Southex Exhibitions, 4285 Canada Way, Burnaby BC V5G 1H2 – 604/433-5121; Fax: 604/433-9549; Tollfree: 1-800-633-8332 – Show Manager, Peter Henderson – Biennial logging trade show, September 1998

FUNERALS
Canadian Funeral Trade Show, PO Box 97507, Scarborough ON M1C 4Z1 – 416/281-5460; Fax: 416/282-9095 – Executive Director, Brenda Broughton – Annual trade show, May

FURNITURE *see* **HOME SHOWS**

GARDENING *see* **FLOWERS**

GIFTS & JEWELLERY
Alberta Fall Gift Show, Southex Exhibitions, 4285 Canada Way, Burnaby BC V5G 1H2 – 604/433-5121; Fax: 604/433-9549; Tollfree: 1-800-633-8332 – Show Manager, Peter Henderson – Annual trade show: giftware, stationery, kitchenware, luggage & leathergoods, pottery, china, glass & jewellery, August – Edmonton AB
Alberta Spring Gift Show, Southex Exhibitions, 4285 Canada Way, Burnaby BC V5G 1H2 – 604/433-5121; Fax: 604/433-9549; Tollfree: 1-800-633-8332 – Show Manager, Peter Henderson – Annual trade show: giftware, stationery, kitchenware, luggage & leathergoods, pottery, china, glass & jewellery, February – Edmonton AB
Expo-Achats Bijouterie/Jewellery Buy Mart, Corporation des bijoutiers du Québec, #0.1, 7585, rue Lacordaire, St-Léonard PQ H1S 2A6 – 514/251-2410; Fax: 514/251-1702 – Directrice générale, Lise Petitpas, August – Palais des Congrès, Montréal PQ
The Last Minute Christmas Show & Sale, PO Box 54045, Toronto ON M6A 3B7 – 416/789-1925 – December – International Centre, Mississauga ON
Montréal Fall Gift Show/Le Salon du Cadeau - Montréal - Automne, Southex Exhibitions, 1450 Don Mills Rd., North York ON M3B 2X7 – 416/445-6641; Fax: 416/442-2207 – Show Manager, Margaret Johnston – Annual trade show. Giftware, stationery, kitchenware, luggage & leathergoods, pottery, china, glass, jewellery, August – Montréal PQ
Montréal Spring Gift Show/Le Salon du Cadeau - Montréal - Printemps, Southex Exhibitions, 1450 Don Mills Rd., North York ON M3B 2X7 – 416/445-6641; Fax: 416/442-2207 – Show Manager, Margaret Johnston – Annual trade show. Giftware, stationery, kitchenware, luggage & leathergoods, pottery, china, glass, jewellery, March – Montréal PQ
Ontario North Gift Show, North Bay Chamber of Commerce, PO Box 747, North Bay ON P1A 8J8 – 705/472-8480; Fax: 705/472-8027 – Contact, Lisa Lassman – Annual trade show, April
Toronto Spring Gift Show, Southex Exhibitions, 1450 Don Mills Rd., North York ON M3B 2X7 – 416/445-6641; Fax: 416/442-2207 – Show Manager, Mary Carton – Annual trade show. Giftware, stationery, kitchenware, luggage & leathergoods, pottery, china, glass, jewellery, February – Toronto ON
Treasures, Heirloom Arts & Crafts Show, Synergic Media Ltd., RR#4, Uxbridge ON L9P 1R4 – 905/649-2480; Fax: 905/649-1022 – Show Producer, Ian Russell – Consumer show held in March & November – Markham Fairgrounds, Markham ON
Vancouver Fall Gift Show, Southex Exhibitions, 4285 Canada Way, Burnaby BC V5G 1H2 – 604/433-5121; Fax: 604/433-9549; Tollfree: 1-800-633-8332 – Show Manager, Peter Henderson – Annual trade show. Giftware, housewares, luggage & leathergoods, jewellery, September – Vancouver BC
Vancouver Island Gift Show, #2, 31 Bushby St., Victoria BC V8S 1B3 – 250/370-2983; Fax: 250/380-1733 – Annual trade show
Vancouver Spring Gift Show, Southex Exhibitions, 4285 Canada Way, Burnaby BC V5G 1H2 – 604/433-5121; Fax: 604/433-9549; Tollfree: 1-800-633-8332 – Show Manager, Peter Henderson – Annual trade show. Giftwares, housewares, luggage & leathergoods, jewellery, March – Vancouver BC
Victoriana - A Celebration of Elegance, Perdue Show Management, 378 Evans Ave., Etobicoke ON M8Z 1K6 – 416/503-8240; Fax: 416/503-8130 – Show Manager, Sandra Durbach – Spring & winter shows – King Edward Hotel, Toronto ON

GOVERNMENT
Government Technology Exhibition & Conference, Connelly Business Exhibitions Inc., #214, 2487 Kaladar Ave., Ottawa ON K1V 8B9 – 613/731-9850; Fax: 613/731-2407 – Vice-President, Marketing, Dan Hamilton – September
Québec Municipalities Show/Salon de la municipalité du Québec, Promexpo Inc., 801, rue Sherbrooke est, 10e étage, Montréal PQ H2L 1K7 – 514/527-9221; Fax: 514/527-8449 – General Manager, Ginette Gauthier – Annual trade show. Consultant services, environment, recreation, culture, GIS, April 1997
Saskatchewan Urban Municipalities Association Convention, Saskatchewan Urban Municipalities Association, #200, 1819 Cornwall St., Regina SK S4P 2K4 – 306/525-3727; Fax: 306/565-3552 – Convention Coordinator, Jennie Avram – Annual trade show. Sewer & water information, municipal educational displays, road signs, etc., January 1997

GRAPHIC ARTS
Canadian Community Newspapers Association Convention, Canadian Community Newspapers Association, #206, 90 Eglinton Ave. East, Toronto ON M4P 2Y3 – 416/482-1090; Fax: 416/482-1908; Email: ccna@sentex.net; URL: http://www.sentex.net/~ccna – Executive Director, Michael Anderson – Annual trade show, July 23-26 1997 – Whistler BC
Graphic Trade, Southex Exhibitions, 1450 Don Mills Rd., North York ON M3B 2X7 – 416/445-6641; Fax: 416/442-2207 – – Biennial trade show for graphic arts industry, November 1997 – Toronto ON
Ontario Community Newspapers Association Convention, Ontario Community Newspapers Association, 1184 Speers Rd., Oakville ON L6J 5A8 – 905/844-0184; Fax: 905/844-2769; Email: info@ocna.org; URL: http://www.ocna.org – Executive Director, Don Lamont – Annual trade show, March – Toronto ON
Print Ontario '98, Ontario Trade Shows Ltd., #8, 1606 Sedlescomb Dr., Mississauga ON L4X 1M6 – 905/625-7070; Fax: 905/625-4856 – Show Manager, Alexander Donald – Biennial trade show, November 1998 – Automotive Building, Exhibition Place, Toronto ON

HAIRDRESSING
Educational Hair Dressing Show, Allied Beauty Association, #1001, 2 Sheppard Ave. East, PO Box 42, North York ON M2N 5Y7 – 416/225-2359; Fax: 416/223-3610 – Executive Director, Marc Speir – Held in various locations, September/October

HARDWARE
Canadian Hardware/Housewares/Home Improvement Show, Canadian Retail Hardware Association, 6800 Campobello Rd., Mississauga ON L5N 2L8 – 905/821-3470; Fax: 905/821-8946; Tollfree: 1-800-268-3965; Email: crha@crha.com – Executive Director, Thomas M. Ross – Annual trade & consumer show, Feb. 2-4 1997 – Exhibition Place, Toronto ON
Montreal Hardware & Home Centre Show, #202, 814, boul Guimond, Longueuil PQ J4G 1T5 – 514/646-5799; Fax: 514/646-7099 – General Manager, Maurice Rheaume – Trade show
The Western Show, Canadian Hardware & Housewares Manufacturers' Association, #101, 1335 Morningside Ave., Scarborough ON M1B 5M4 – 416/282-0022; Fax: 416/282-0027 – Show Manager, Maureen Hizaka, October – BC Place Stadium, Vancouver BC

HEALTH
Annual Health Conference & Exhibition, Manitoba Health Organizations, #600, 360 Broadway, Winnipeg MB R3C 4G6 – 204/942-6591; Fax: 204/956-1373 – President, Ronald G. Birt – Nov. 5-7 1997 – Winnipeg Convention Centre, Winnipeg MB
Whole Life Expo, 356 Dupont Ave., Toronto ON M5R 1V9 – Julia Woodford – Annual consumer show. Herbal & natural products, November – Metro Toronto Convention Centre, Toronto ON

HEATING, PLUMBING & AIR CONDITIONING
see also Hardware
CEX '98, H.D. Shield & Associates Ltd., 25 Bradgate Rd., North York ON M3B 1J6 – 416/444-5225; Fax: 416/444-8268 – Show Coordinator, Patrick Shield – Biennial trade show. Heating, ventilation, plumbing, air conditioning & refrigeration, March 27-29 1998
CIPHEX '97 - West, Canadian Institute of Plumbing & Heating, #330, 295 The West Mall, Etobicoke ON M9C 4Z4 – 416/695-0447; Fax: 416/695-0450 – Elizabeth McCullough, Show Manager – Trade show; HVAC industries, Oct. 19-20 1997 – Northlands Park, Edmonton AB
Climatex, Corporation des maîtres entrepreneurs en réfrigération du Québec, #301, 6525, boul Décarie, Montréal PQ H3W 3E3 – 514/735-1131; Fax: 514/735-3509 – Sylvain Roy – Annual trade show, March – Montréal PQ
MécanExpo-Ciphex, Corporation des maîtres mécaniciens en tuyauterie du Québec, 8175, rue St-Laurent, Montréal PQ H2P 2M1 – 514/382-2668 – Agente de formation, Linda Campeau – Biennial trade show, Apr. 24-26 1997 – Place Bonaventure, Montréal PQ

HOBBIES
see also Crafts

Annual Maritime Arms Collectors Association Antique Arms Show, PO Box 3666, Halifax (South) NS B3J 3K6 – 902/422-5979 – September

Annual Stamp Exhibition & Sale of Stamps, Coins & Sports Cards, Regina Philatelic Club, 2601 Coronation St., PO Box 1891, Regina SK S4P 3E1 – 306/586-8152 – Feb. 25-26 – Regina SK

Montréal Hobby & Craft Show, CP 343, Succ Notre-Dame, Montréal PQ H4A 3P5 – 514/484-9414; Fax: 514/485-6579 – Annual consumer show, October

Montréal Show, Canadian Stamp Dealers' Association, PO Box 1123, Stn Adelaide, Toronto ON M5C 2K5 – 416/653-9885 – President, John Sheffield, 519/681-3420, Fax: 519/668-6872 – April & November 1997 – South Hall, Place Bonaventure, Montréal PQ

National Stamp Show, Canadian Stamp Dealers' Association, PO Box 1123, Stn Adelaide, Toronto ON M5C 2K5 – 416/653-9885 – President, John Sheffield, 519/681-3420, Fax: 519/668-6872 – April & November 1997 – Queen Elizabeth Bldg., Exhibition Place, Toronto ON

Saskatchewan Gun Collectors' Association Gun & Collectables Show, PO Box 1334, Regina SK S4P 3B8 – 306/545-2909 – Contact, Ted Cook – Twice a year (winter & summer)

Sport Card & Memorabilia Show, PO Box 79720, Stn A, Etobicoke ON M9N 3W9 – 416/244-5156; Fax: 416/244-4787 – Al Sinclair – Semi-annual show

Toronto Model Railway Show, 25 Lippincott St. West, Etobicoke ON M9N 1B3 – 416/249-4563 – Show Coordinator, Jack Bell – Annual consumer show, March

HOME SHOWS

Atlantic National Home Show, Master Promotions Ltd., PO Box 565, Saint John NB E2L 3Z8 – 506/658-0018; Fax: 506/658-0750 – Show Manager, Brian McKiel – Annual consumer show, March – Saint John NB

BC Fall Home Show, Southex Exhibitions, 4285 Canada Way, Burnaby BC V5G 1H2 – 604/433-5121; Fax: 604/433-9549; Tollfree: 1-800-633-8332 – Show Manager, Murat Olcay – Annual consumer show, October

BC Home & Garden Show, Southex Exhibitions, 4285 Canada Way, Burnaby BC V5G 1H2 – 604/433-5121; Fax: 604/433-9549; Tollfree: 1-800-633-8332 – Show Manager, Murat Olcay – Annual trade & consumer show, February

BC Interior Home & Garden Show, Showest Management Inc., PO Box 300, Kamloops BC V2C 5K6 – 250/851-2145; Fax: 250/851-0551 – Show Manager, Gerry Hartley – Annual consumer show, February/March

Better Living Home Show, Lakeshore Productions Inc., 875 Main St. West, Hamilton ON L8S 4R1 – 905/522-6117; Fax: 905/529-2242 – Show Manager, Karen McHarb – January – Convention Centre, Hamilton ON

Bridge City Cosmopolitan Home Show, Bridge City Cosmopolitan Club, PO Box 351, Saskatoon SK S7K 3L3 – 306/653-1888 – Terry Akister, February – Saskatchewan Place, Saskatoon SK

Burlington Lifestyle Home Show, Jenkins Show Productions, 1076 Skyvalley Cr., Oakville ON L6M 3L2 – 905/827-4632; Fax: 905/827-8139; Tollfree: 1-800-465-1073 – President, Dave Jenkins – Annual consumer show, April – Burlington ON

Calgary Renovation Show, Young Marketing Services Inc., #105, 10544 - 114 St., Edmonton AB T5H 3J7 – 403/423-4060; Fax: 403/426-7862 – Show Manager, Rick Young – Annual consumer show, January – Stampede Park, Calgary AB

Canadian Pool, Spa & Patio Show, "Splish Splash", c/o The Profile Group, #301, 37 Sandiford Dr., Stouffville ON L4A 7X5 – 905/640-7700; Fax: 905/640-7714 – Show Manager, George Zarras – Annual consumer show. Pools, spas, patios, decks, fencing & related leisure products, February

Central Pool & Spa Conference & Expo, National Spa & Pool Institute of Canada, #5, 7370 Bramalea Rd., Mississauga ON L5S 1N6 – 905/676-1591; Fax: 905/676-1598; Tollfree: 1-800-879-7066 – Show Manager, Nancy Lumb – Annual trade show, Dec. 3-4 1997 – Regal Constellation Hotel, Toronto ON

Colchester County Home Show, Master Promotions Ltd., PO Box 565, Saint John NB E2L 3Z8 – 506/658-0018; Fax: 506/658-0750 – Show Manager, Brian McKeil, April – Legion Stadium, Truro NS

The Cottage Show, 718 Wilson Ave., North York ON M3K 1E2 – 416/633-7872; Fax: 416/633-8223 – Risa Freeman – Annual consumer show. Building products & furnishings, February – Exhibition Place, Toronto ON

Cottagefest, Jenkins Show Productions, 1076 Skyvalley Cr., Oakville ON L6M 3L2 – 905/827-4632; Fax: 905/827-8139; Tollfree: 1-800-465-1073 – President, Dave Jenkins – Annual consumer show. Cottage country businesses; cottage-related products & services, June

Decor Showcase, c/o Canadian Decorating Products Association, #5, 7895 Tranmere Dr., Mississauga ON L5S 1V9 – 905/678-0331; Fax: 905/678-0335 – Contact, Dawn Lee – Annual trade show. Home decorating products, paint & coatings, sundries, wallcovering, window treatments, decorative fabrics & floor coverings, March

Design Forum, Perdue Show Management, 378 Evans Ave., Etobicoke ON M8Z 1K6 – 416/503-8240; Fax: 416/503-8130 – President, Elizabeth Fairley – Annual home furnishings trade show, August

Edmonton Home Show, Young Marketing Services Inc., #105, 10544 - 114 St., Edmonton AB T5H 3J7 – 403/423-4060; Fax: 403/426-7862 – Show Manager, Rick Young – Annual consumer show, September – Edmonton AB

Edmonton Renovation Show, Young Marketing Services Inc., #105, 10544 - 114 St., Edmonton AB T5H 3J7 – 403/423-4060; Fax: 403/426-7862 – Show Manager, Rick Young – Annual consumer show, January – Edmonton Northlands, Edmonton AB

Expo Habitat Québec, Association provinciale des constructeurs d'habitations Québec, 2825, boul Wilfrid-Hamel, Québec PQ G1P 2H9 – 418/682-3353; Fax: 418/682-3851 – Mildred Charlton – February – Patinodrome, Ste-Foy PQ

Fraser Valley Home & Garden Show, Southex Exhibitions, 4285 Canada Way, Burnaby BC V5G 1H2 – 604/433-5121; Fax: 604/433-9549; Tollfree: 1-800-633-8332 – Vice-President, Western Region, Fred Barnes – Annual consumer show, March – Abbotsford BC

Fredericton Spring Lifestyles, Master Promotions Ltd., PO Box 565, Saint John NB E2L 3Z8 – 506/658-0018; Fax: 506/658-0750 – Show Manager, Brian McKeil – March/April – Capital Exhibit Centre, Fredericton NB

Hamilton Home Show, Ontario Marketing Productions, 109 Scollard St., Toronto ON M5R 1G4 – 416/961-2999; Fax: 416/961-1157 – Contact, Linda Watt – Annual consumer show, March – Hamilton Convention Centre, Hamilton ON

Home Renovation Show, DAC Marketing Ltd., PO Box 2837, Stn A, Sudbury ON P3A 5J3 – 705/673-5588; Fax: 705/525-0626 – President, Darren A. Ceccarelli – Consumer show, April

Home, Garden & Leisure Show, Medicine Hat & District Chamber of Commerce, 413 - 6th Ave. SE, Medicine Hat AB T1A 2S7 – 403/527-5214; Fax: 403/527-5182 – Anna Steckle – Consumer show, March – Cypress Centre, Stampede Park, Medicine Hat AB

Indoor Living Show, Southex Exhibitions, 1450 Don Mills Rd., North York ON M3B 2X7 – 416/445-6641; Fax: 416/442-2207 – Show Manager, Arnie Hingston – Annual consumer show, October

International Home & Garden Show, Showcase Marketing Ltd., #410, 1110 Sheppard Ave. East, North York ON M2K 2W2 – 416/512-1305; Fax: 416/512-9998 – Paul Newdick – Annual consumer show, March

International Home Show, Showcase Marketing Ltd., #410, 1110 Sheppard Ave. East, North York ON M2K 2W2 – 416/512-1305; Fax: 416/512-9998 – Paul Newdick – Annual consumer show, November – International Centre, Toronto ON

Kitchener-Waterloo HomExpo, Ontario Marketing Productions, 109 Scollard St., Toronto ON M5R 1G4 – 416/961-2999; Fax: 416/961-1157 – Contact, Linda Watt – Consumer show, February – Kitchener Memorial Auditorium, Kitchener ON

The London Convention Centre Fall Home Show, Jenkins Show Productions, 1076 Skyvalley Cr., Oakville ON L6M 3L2 – 905/827-4632; Fax: 905/827-8139; Tollfree: 1-800-465-1073 – President, Dave Jenkins, October – London ON

London Home & Garden Show, London Show Productions, RR#5, London ON N6A 4B9 – 519/455-5888; Fax: 519/455-7780 – President, Arthur Bacon – Consumer show, April – London ON

The London Home Builders' Association Lifestyle Home Show, Jenkins Show Productions, 1076 Skyvalley Cr., Oakville ON L6M 3L2 – 905/827-4632; Fax: 905/827-8139; Tollfree: 1-800-465-1073 – President, Dave Jenkins – February – London ON

Mall Home Shows, Jenkins Show Productions, 1076 Skyvalley Cr., Oakville ON L6M 3L2 – 905/827-4632; Fax: 905/827-8139; Tollfree: 1-800-465-1073 – President, Dave Jenkins – Shows at shopping centres throughout Ontario in March, October, November

Markham Home Show, Canadian Tel-A-Views Ltd., #12, 115 Apple Creek Blvd., Markham ON L3R 6C9 – 905/477-2677; Fax: 905/477-7872; Tollfree: 1-800-891-4859 – Lynn McVey – October

Metro East Home Show, Metropolitan Promotions, PO Box 193, Ajax ON L1S 3C3 – 905/428-7610; Fax: 905/428-7046 – Show Manager, Tom Glaesser – February – Metro East Trade Centre, Pickering ON

Metro Home Show, Southex Exhibitions, 1450 Don Mills Rd., North York ON M3B 2X7 – 416/445-6641; Fax: 416/442-2207 – Show Manager, Norm Shulz – Annual consumer show, January – Metro Toronto Convention Centre, Toronto ON

The Metro West Fall Home Show, Jenkins Show Productions, 1076 Skyvalley Cr., Oakville ON L6M 3L2 – 905/827-4632; Fax: 905/827-8139; Tollfree: 1-800-465-1073 – President, Dave Jenkins – October – Oakville ON

Miramichi Lifestyle, Master Promotions Ltd., PO Box 565, Saint John NB E2L 3Z8 – 506/658-0018; Fax: 506/658-0750 – Brian McKeil – April – Miramichi Civic Centre, Miramichi NB

Montréal Kitchen & Bath Expo, Interface Design, 5318, boul St-Laurent, Montréal PQ H2T 1S1 – 514/273-4030; Fax: 514/273-3649 – Présidente, Ginette Gadoury – Montréal PQ

Montréal National Home Show/Salon National de l'habitation de Montréal, Promexpo Inc., 801, rue Sherbrooke est, 10e étage, Montréal PQ H2L 1K7 – 514/527-9221; Fax: 514/527-8449 – Michele Tessier – Annual consumer show, February/March – Montréal PQ

National Home Show, Southex Exhibitions, 1450 Don Mills Rd., North York ON M3B 2X7 – 416/445-6641; Fax: 416/442-2207 – Show Manager, Maureen Eck-

Canadian Almanac & Directory 1997

ford – Annual consumer show, April – Coliseum Bldg., Exhibition Place, Toronto ON
National Kitchen & Bath Showcase, Southex Exhibitions, 1450 Don Mills Rd., North York ON M3B 2X7 – 416/445-6641; Fax: 416/442-2207 – Show Manager, Maureen Eckford – April – Automotive Bldg., Exhibition Place, Toronto ON
Niagara Lifestyle Home Show, Jenkins Show Productions, 1076 Skyvalley Cr., Oakville ON L6M 3L2 – 905/827-4632; Fax: 905/827-8139; Tollfree: 1-800-465-1073 – President, Dave Jenkins – Annual consumer show, April – Garden City/Rex Stimers Arena, St Catharines ON
Nova Scotia Ideal Home Shows, Denex Group Inc., Burnside Industrial Park, 192 Joseph Zatzman Dr., Dartmouth NS B3B 1N4 – 902/468-4999; Fax: 902/468-2795; Email: denman@newedge.ca – Group Show Manager, Bev Campbell – Consumer shows held in April & September
Oakville Lifestyle Home Show, Jenkins Show Productions, 1076 Skyvalley Cr., Oakville ON L6M 3L2 – 905/827-4632; Fax: 905/827-8139; Tollfree: 1-800-465-1073 – President, Dave Jenkins – Annual consumer show, April – Glen Abbey Recreation Centre, Oakville ON
Ontario Home & Food Show, Intertrade Associates Inc., #250, 1511 Merivale Rd., Nepean ON K2G 3J3 – 613/224-3013; Fax: 613/224-4533; Tollfree: 1-888-662-6660 – Show Manager, Kevin McWhinnie – February – Toronto ON
Ottawa Fall Home Show, Southex Exhibitions Inc., #440, 47 Clarence St., Ottawa ON K1N 9K1 – 613/232-0766; Fax: 613/238-4827 – Show Manager, Paul Le Guerrier – Annual consumer show, September – Civic Centre, Lansdowne Park, Ottawa ON
Ottawa Spring Home Show, Southex Exhibitions Inc., #440, 47 Clarence St., Ottawa ON K1N 9K1 – 613/232-0766; Fax: 613/238-4827 – Show Manager, Paul Le Guerrier – Annual consumer show, April – Civic Centre, Lansdowne Park, Ottawa ON
PEI Provincial Home Show, Master Promotions Ltd., PO Box 565, Saint John NB E2L 3Z8 – 506/658-0018; Fax: 506/658-0750 – Show Manager, Mark Cusack – March – Charlottetown PE
Pool & Patio Show, c/o Bingemans Conference & Recreation Centre, 1380 Victoria St. North, Kitchener ON N2B 3E2 – 519/744-1555; Fax: 519/744-1985 – Marketing Manager, Brian Banks – Annual consumer show. Pools, spas, decks, landscaping, patio furniture. Manufacturers & services, March
Québec National Home Show/Salon National de l'habitation de Québec, Promexpo inc., 801, rue Sherbrooke est, 10e étage, Montréal PQ H2L 1K7 – 514/527-9221; Fax: 514/528-8449 – General Manager, Audrey Robitaille – Annual consumer show, March – Québec PQ
Red Deer Home Ideas, #201, 7819 - 50 Ave., Red Deer AB T4P 1M8 – 403/346-5321; Fax: 403/342-1301 – Contact, Marilyn Hummel – Annual, February
Renovations - The Kitchen, Bath & Window Show, Southex Exhibitions Inc., #440, 47 Clarence St., Ottawa ON K1N 9K1 – 613/232-0766; Fax: 613/238-4827 – Show Manager, Paul Le Guerrier – Annual trade & consumer show, January – Civic Centre, Lansdowne Park, Ottawa ON
Saint John Home & Garden Show, Master Promotions Ltd., PO Box 565, Saint John NB E2L 3Z8 – 506/658-0018; Fax: 506/658-0750 – Show Manager, Sydney Jane Brittain – Saint John NB
Salmon Arm Home & Recreation Show, Romana Frey & Associates, 2905 - 30 Ave., Vernon BC V1T 2B8 – 250/542-9957; Fax: 250/545-1011 – Show Manager, Gerry Hartley – Annual consumer show
Salon international du mueble de Toronto/Toronto International Home Furnishings Market, Association des fabricants de meubles du Québec inc., #101, 1111, rue St-Urbain, Montréal PQ H2Z 1Y6 – 514/866-3631; Fax: 514/871-9900 – Director of Exhibitions, Rita Hanson – Annual trade & consumer show, January – International Centre, Toronto ON
Sarnia CHOK Home & Recreation Show, Sarnia CHOK, 148 North Front St., Sarnia ON N7T 7K5 – 519/336-1070 – Show Manager, Penni Steele – Annual consumer show, May – Clearwater Arena, Sarnia ON
Selkirk Homelife Show, Home Life Exhibitions, 122 Fairlane Ave., Winnipeg MB R2Y 0B1 – 204/889-5777; Fax: 204/832-5666 – General Manager, A.W. Mann – Consumer show, February – Selkirk MB
Showcase, Medicine Hat & District Chamber of Commerce, 413 - 6th Ave. SE, Medicine Hat AB T1A 2S7 – 403/527-5214; Fax: 403/527-5182 – Jeanette Frost – Annual consumer show, October – Cypress Centre, Stampede Park, Medicine Hat AB
Showmart - Home & Leisure Show, c/o CHWK, PO Box 386, Chilliwack BC V2P 6J7 – 604/795-5711; Fax: 604/795-6643 – Sales, Steve Hemenway – Annual consumer show, February
Sudbury Spring Home Show, DAC Marketing Ltd., PO Box 2837, Stn A, Sudbury ON P3A 5J3 – 705/673-5588; Fax: 705/525-0626 – President, Darren A. Ceccarelli – Consumer show, March/April – Garson Arena, Sudbury ON
Victoria Home Expo, Evergreen Exhibitions Ltd., 830D Pembrooke St., Victoria BC V8T 1H9 – 250/386-7469; Fax: 250/386-1431 – President, A.J. Chartrand – Annual, February/March – Victoria BC
Western Canada Kitchen & Bath Expo, Hank Hartloper Agency, #2, 1575 Seel Ave., Winnipeg MB R3T 1C8 – 204/925-5711; Fax: 204/925-6643 – Owner, Hank Hartloper – Annual consumer show, January – Winnipeg Convention Centre, Winnipeg MB
Western Canadian Pool & Spa Conference & Expo, National Spa & Pool Institute of Canada, #5, 7370 Bramalea Rd., Mississauga ON L5S 1N6 – 905/676-1591; Fax: 905/676-1598; Tollfree: 1-800-879-7066 – Executive Director, Nancy Lumb – Annual trade & consumer show, February

HORSES
The Masters Show Jumping Show, Spruce Meadows, RR#9, Calgary AB T2J 5G5 – 403/974-4200 – Contact, Sharon McLennan – Annual consumer show. Includes Equi-Fair, Alberta Breeds for the World, Festival of Nations, September
Royal Red Arabian Horse Show, PO Box 167, Regina SK S4P 2Z6 – 306/781-9200; Fax: 306/565-3443 – Lee Kennedy – Annual, August
Thoroughbred & Quarter Horse Live Racing, Whoop-Up Park, 3401 - 6 Ave. South, Lethbridge AB T1J 1G6 – 403/328-4491; Fax: 403/320-8139 – Contact, Twyla Gurr – Annual fall event
Whoop Up Spring Quarter Horse Show, Lethbridge & District Exhibition, 3401 Parkside Dr. South, Lethbridge AB T1J 4R3 – 403/328-4491; Fax: 403/320-8139 – Agricultural Coordinator, Twyla Gurr – Annual trade & consumer show, April

HORTICULTURE see FLOWERS

HOSPITAL
Convention, Provincial Health Authorities of Alberta, 44 Capital Blvd., #200, 10044 - 108 St. NW, Edmonton AB T5J 3S7 – 403/426-8502; Fax: 403/424-4309 – Coordinator, Christine Y. Chepyha – Annual trade show, November
Convention & Exhibition, Ontario Hospital Association, #2800, 200 Front St. West, Toronto ON M5V 3L1 – 416/205-1300; Fax: 416/205-1301 – Maria Batt – Annual trade show, Nov. 3-5 1997 – Metro Toronto Convention Centre; Holiday Inn, Toronto ON
Hopitex - Health Care Show/Salon Santé, AFLD Consultants Inc., 3565, rue Edgar Leduc, Lachine PQ H8T 3L5 – 514/639-6806; Fax: 514/639-6629 – Show Manager, Lucie Desharnais – Annual trade show, May

HOSPITALITY INDUSTRY (HOTEL, MOTEL, RESTAURANT)
see also Food & Beverage
ACCEX Accommodation Exhibition, Motels Ontario, RR#6, 347 Pido Rd., Unit 2, Peterborough ON K9J 6X7 – 705/745-4982; Fax: 705/745-4983; Tollfree: 1-800-461-1972 – President, Bob Gravel – Annual trade show, November
Annual Convention & Exposition, British Columbia & Yukon Hotels Association, 948 Howe St., 2nd Fl., Vancouver BC V6Z 1N9 – 604/681-7164; Fax: 604/681-7649; Tollfree: 1-800-663-3153; URL: http://www.fleethouse.com/fhcanada/bc-acco.htm – Event Coordinator, Marilyn Pierlet – Annual trade show, November
ApEx '97, Atlantic Provinces Restaurant & Foodservices Association, PO Box 3118, Dartmouth NS B2W 4Y3 – 902/434-3767; Fax: 902/434-5224 – Show Manager, Ellen Scanlon – Annual trade show, Mar. 23-25 1997 – Exhibition Park, Halifax NS
HostEx, Canadian Restaurant & Foodservices Association, 316 Bloor St. West, Toronto ON M5S 1W5 – 416/923-8416; Fax: 416/923-1450; Tollfree: 1-800-387-5649; Email: 102447.3104@compuserve.com – Chairman, Paul Hollands – Annual trade show, October
Salon Rendez-vous, Association des fournisseurs d'hôtels et restaurants inc., 2435, rue Guénette, Saint Laurent PQ H4R 2E9 – 514/334-5161; Fax: 514/334-1279; Tollfree: 1-800-567-2347 – Trésorier, Raymond Mayrand – Annual trade show, February – Montréal PQ
Salon Reste-Hôte, Association des restaurateurs du Québec, 2485, rue Sherbrooke est, Montréal PQ H2K 1E8 – 514/527-9801; Fax: 514/527-3066; Tollfree: 1-800-463-9801 – Exhibits Manager, F. Gadbois – Annual trade show. Equipment, services & food products for restaurants, hotels & institutions, March – Québec PQ

IMPORT/EXPORT
The British Show, c/o Banner Promotions, PO Box 724, Niagara Falls ON L2E 6V5 – Annual consumer show – Exhibition Place, Toronto ON
World Trade '97, Canadian International Trade Association, #611, 2 Carlton St., Toronto ON M5B 1J3 – 416/351-9728; Fax: 416/351-9911 – President, Sydney King – Annual trade show. Agents & distributors locator & recruiter show, Oct. 23 1997 – Toronto ON

INDUSTRIAL
Atlantic Industrial Exhibition, Reed Exhibition Companies Inc., 3761 Victoria Park Ave., Scarborough ON M1W 3S2 – 416/491-7565; Fax: 416/491-5088 – Show Manager, Tracy McKnight – Biennial trade show; Moncton (1997) & Moncton (1998), September
Halifax Industrial Exhibition, Reed Exhibition Companies Inc., 3761 Victoria Park Ave., Scarborough ON M1W 3S2 – 416/491-7565; Fax: 416/491-5088 – Annual trade show; machine tools, September
IndEX, c/o Western Canadian Industry Exhibition Association Inc., 1939 Elph, Regina SK S4T 3N3 – 306/

757-6891; Fax: 306/347-8595 – Biennial industrial trade show, construction, manufacturing, advanced technology, transportation, mining

Industrial Expo New Brunswick, Master Promotions Ltd., PO Box 565, Saint John NB E2L 3Z8 – 506/658-0018; Fax: 506/658-0750 – Show Manager, Mark Cusack – May – Saint John NB

Industrial Expo Nova Scotia, Master Promotions Ltd., PO Box 565, Saint John NB E2L 3Z8 – 506/658-0018; Fax: 506/658-0750 – Mark Cusack – Biennial show, May 1997 – The Forum Complex, Halifax NS

Intermat '97, Intermat '95, c/o, CP 282, Laval-des-Rapides PQ H7N 4Z9 – 514/382-5280; Fax: 514/382-5280 – Contact, Stephanie Vonka – Biennial international material handling convention & educational forum (material handling, packaging, robotics, automation, warehousing, integrated material handling systems, services, consulting, education)

Montréal Fabricating & Machine Tool Show/Le Salon du Travail des Métaux et de la Machine Outil de Montréal, Reed Exhibition Companies Inc., 3761 Victoria Park Ave., Scarborough ON M1W 3S2 – 416/491-7565; Fax: 416/491-5088 – National Accounts Manager, Bob Mathieu – Biennial trade show, May 1998 – Montréal PQ

Plant Maintenance & Engineering Show/Le Salon Industriel de la Maintenance et de l'Ingenierie, Reed Exhibition Companies Inc., 3761 Victoria Park Ave., Scarborough ON M1W 3S2 – 416/491-7565; Fax: 416/491-5088 – Show Manager, Bob Mathieu – Annual trade show, May – Montréal PQ

Salon industriel de l'Estrie, Les Promotions André Pageau Inc., 1627, boul St-Joseph, Québec PQ G2K 1H1 – 418/623-3383; Fax: 418/623-5033 – Président, André Pageau – Biennial trade show, September 1997 – Sherbrooke PQ

Salon Industriel de la Mauricie Bois-Francs, Les Promotions André Pageau Inc., 1627, boul St-Joseph, Québec PQ G2K 1H1 – 418/623-3383; Fax: 418/623-5033 – Président, André Pageau – Biennial trade show, April 1998 – Trois-Rivières PQ

Salon Industriel de Québec, Les Promotions André Pageau Inc., 1627, boul St-Joseph, Québec PQ G2K 1H1 – 418/623-3383; Fax: 418/623-5033 – Président, André Pageau – Biennial trade show, October 1998 – Québec PQ

Salon Industriel du Saguenay/Lac-St-Jean, Les Promotions André Pageau Inc., 1627, boul St-Joseph, Québec PQ G2K 1H1 – 418/623-3383; Fax: 418/623-5033 – Président, André Pageau – Biennial, May 1997 – Chicoutimi PQ

Southwestern Ontario Industrial Show, Reed Exhibition Companies Inc., 3761 Victoria Park Ave., Scarborough ON M1W 3S2 – 416/491-7565; Fax: 416/491-5088 – Trade show, May

Vancouver Industrial Exhibition, Reed Exhibition Companies Inc., 3761 Victoria Park Ave., Scarborough ON M1W 3S2 – 416/491-7565; Fax: 416/491-5088 – Show Manager, Sharon Freedman – Biennial trade show, April 1998 – Vancouver BC

Weld Expo Canada, Reed Exhibition Companies Inc., 3761 Victoria Park Ave., Scarborough ON M1W 3S2 – 416/491-7565; Fax: 416/491-5088 – Show Manager, Terry Lynn Weiss – Trade show, October

Windsor Mold Show, Reed Exhibition Companies Inc., 3761 Victoria Park Ave., Scarborough ON M1W 3S2 – 416/491-7565; Fax: 416/491-5088 – Show Manager, Charlene Jennings – Biennial trade show, October 1998 – Cioccaro Club, Windsor ON

INSURANCE
Annual Convention, Insurance Brokers Association of Ontario, 90 Eglinton Ave. East, 2nd Fl., Toronto ON M4P 2Y3 – 416/488-7422; Fax: 416/488-7526 – Executive Director, Robert J. Carter – Annual trade show, Oct. 22-24 1997 – Sheraton Centre, Toronto ON

INTERIOR DESIGN/DECORATING
see also Home Shows

Designers' Weekend, Venue West Ltd., #645, 375 Water St., Vancouver BC V6B 5C6 – 604/681-5226; Fax: 604/681-2503 – President, Betty Fata – Annual trade show, February

IIDEX - International Interior Design Exposition, Association of Registered Interior Designers of Ontario, 717 Church St., Toronto ON M4W 2M5 – 416/921-2127; Fax: 416/921-3660; Tollfree: 1-800-334-1180 – Contact, Cathy Clark – November – Metro Toronto Convention Centre, Toronto ON

International Decor Showcase, Canadian Decorating Products Association, #5, 7895 Tranmere Dr., Mississauga ON L5S 1V9 – 905/678-0331; Fax: 905/678-0335 – Show Manager, Mary Schooley – February – Automotive Bldg., Exhibition Place, Toronto ON

SIDIM - Montréal International Interior Design Show, Interface Design, 5318, boul St-Laurent, Montréal PQ H2T 1S1 – 514/273-4030; Fax: 514/273-3649 – Présidente, Ginette Gadoury – Trade & consumer show, May – Montréal PQ

JEWELLERY see GIFTS

LANDSCAPING see FLOWERS

LEGAL
Technology for Lawyers/Technologie juridique, Canadian Society for the Advancement of Legal Technology, #200, 20 Toronto St., Toronto ON M5C 2B8 – 416/663-5290; Fax: 416/663-6502; URL: http://www.io.org/~csalt/csalt.htm – Conference Coordinator, Tricia W. Sands – Annual two-day event open to public. Application of technology to the practice of law, April

LEISURE see SPORTS & RECREATION

LIGHTING
International Lighting Exposition, Kerrwil Show & Conference Group, 395 Matheson Blvd. East, Mississauga ON L4Z 2H2 – 905/890-1846; Fax: 905/890-5769 – Manager, Anita Schachter – Biennial trade show. Residential, commercial, industrial, landscape, emergency lighting, September – Metro Toronto Convention Centre, Toronto ON

LOGISTICS
Logistech - The International Materials Handling & Distribution Show, Southex Exhibitions, 1450 Don Mills Rd., North York ON M3B 2X7 – 416/445-6641; Fax: 416/442-2207 – Show Manager, Glen Cooper – Biennial trade show, September 1998

MACHINERY & MANUFACTURING
see also Industrial

Canadian Machine Tool Show, Reed Exhibition Companies Inc., 3761 Victoria Park Ave., Scarborough ON M1W 3S2 – 416/491-7565; Fax: 416/491-5088 – Show Manager, Elaine Dale Harris – Biennial trade show, September 1997 – Toronto ON

MAGAZINES
Magazines, Ontario Trade Shows Ltd., #8, 1606 Sedlescomb Dr., Mississauga ON L4X 1M6 – 905/625-7070; Fax: 905/625-4856 – Doug Bennet – Annual conference & trade show for publishing professionals, May or June – Toronto ON

MARINE
see also Boating

Canadian Shipbuilding & Offshore Exhibition, Shipbuilding Association of Canada, #1502, 222 Queen St., Ottawa ON K1P 5V9 – 613/232-7127; Fax: 613/238-5519 – Director, Administration & Finance, Joy MacPherson – Annual trade show, February – Ottawa ON

Toronto International Boat Show, The National Marine Manufacturers Association, #810, 310 Front St. West, Toronto ON M5V 3B5 – 416/591-6772; Fax: 416/591-3582 – Manager, Carol Bell – Jan. 13-21 1997 – Exhibition Place, Toronto ON

Toronto International Marine Trade Show, The National Marine Manufacturers Association, #810, 310 Front St. West, Toronto ON M5V 3B5 – 416/591-6772; Fax: 416/591-3582 – Manager, Carol Bell, January – Toronto ON

MARKETING see ADVERTISING

MATERIALS HANDLING see LOGISTICS

MEDICAL
Annual Congress, Canadian Society of Laboratory Technologists, PO Box 2830, Stn A, Hamilton ON L8N 3N8 – 905/528-8642; Fax: 905/528-4968; URL: http://cslt.com/ – Executive Director, E. Valerie Booth – Annual trade show, June 15-20 1997 – Prince Edward Hotel, Charlottetown PE

Annual Meeting, Canadian Paediatric Society, Children's Hospital of Eastern Ontario, 401 Smyth Rd., Ottawa ON K1H 8L1 – 613/737-2728; Fax: 613/737-2794 – Executive Vice-President, Dr. Victor Marchessault – June 25-29 1997 – Halifax NS

Annual Scientific & Business Meeting, College of Family Physicians of Canada, 2630 Skylark Ave., Mississauga ON L4W 5A4 – 905/629-1600; Fax: 905/629-4810 – Meeting Planner, Beverly Davies – Nov. 14-16 1996 – Toronto Marriott Eaton Centre, Toronto ON

Canadian Cardiovascular Society Annual Scientific Meeting & Exhibition, Venue West Ltd., #645, 375 Water St., Vancouver BC V6B 5C6 – 604/681-5226; Fax: 604/681-2503 – President, Betty Fata – Trade show, October

COS Annual Meeting & Exhibition, Canadian Ophthalmological Society, #610, 1525 Carling Ave., Ottawa ON K1Z 8R9 – 613/729-6779; Fax: 613/729-7209; Tollfree: 1-800-267-5763 – Executive Director, Hubert Drouin – June 13-16 1997 – Québec Convention Centre, Québec PQ

Mayfest, Canadian Hearing Society, 271 Spadina Rd., Toronto ON M5R 2V3 – 416/964-9595; TTY: 416/964-0023; Fax: 416/928-2525; Tollfree: 1-800-465-4327; Email: info@chs.ca; URL: http://www.chs.ca – President, Keith Golem – Latest innovations & access for deaf, deafened & hard of hearing people, May – Toronto ON

Medical & Surgical Exposition, The Royal College of Physicians & Surgeons of Canada, 774 Echo Dr., Ottawa ON K1S 5N8 – 613/730-8177; Fax: 613/730-8833; Tollfree: 1-800-668-3740 – Executive Director, Gilles D. Hurteau – Annual trade show, Sept. 25-28 1997 – Vancouver Trade & Convention Centre, Vancouver BC

Canadian Almanac & Directory 1997

MILITARY

ARMX '97, 310 Dupont St., Toronto ON M5R 1V9 – 416/968-7252; Fax: 416/968-2377 – Contact, Wolfgang Schmidt – Biennial. Aerospace & defence equipment exhibition for the Canadian government. Seminars on training & simulation. International exhibitions, May

MINING & MINERALS

International Convention & Trade Show, Prospectors & Developers Association of Canada, 34 King St. East, 9th Fl., Toronto ON M5C 2X8 – 416/362-1969; Fax: 416/362-0101 – Technical & Convention Manager, Rita D Plaskett – Annual trade show: exploration & development industries, universities, governments, March 1997

MOTORCYCLES *see* **AUTOMOTIVE**

MULTICULTURAL

Acadian Festival, Caraquet NB E0B 1K0 – 506/727-6515 – August

Can-Irish Harmony: Canada's Irish Festival on the Miramichi, Irish Canadian Cultural Association of New Brunswick, 109 Roy Ave., Miramichi NB E1V 3N8 – 506/622-4007; Fax: 506/773-5997 – President, Farrell McCarthy – July – Miramichi NB

Canada's National Ukrainian Festival, 119 Main St. South, Dauphin MB R7N 1K4 – 204/638-5645; Fax: 204/638-5851 – Manager, Pat Maksymchuk – Annual. Three days of song, dance, music, costume, cuisine, culture, August

Caribana, 171 Carlton St., Toronto ON M5A 2K3 – 416/925-5435 – Annually, late July - Aug. Ten days. Caribbean music, entertainment, parades & culture

Carrousel of the Nations, c/o 370 Victoria Ave., Windsor ON N9A 4M6 – 519/255-1127 – Annually. Thirty ethnocultural villages, June

Celebration Multicultural Festival, Multicultural Association of Nova Scotia, #901, 1809 Barrington St., Halifax NS B3J 3K8 – 902/423-6534; Fax: 902/422-0881 – Executive Director, Barbara Campbell – Annual festival, June – Dartmouth NS

Edmonton Heritage Festival, #200, 9562 - 82 Ave., Edmonton AB T6C 2W5 – 403/433-3378; Fax: 403/433-9097 – Annually. Two days. Forty or more ethnic pavilions, August

Fall Festival, London Museum of Archaeology, 1600 Attawandaron Rd., London ON N6G 3M6 – 519/473-1360 – Annually. Food, arts & crafts, games, September

Festival Acadien de Clare, PO Box 282, Meteghan NS B0W 2J0 – 902/645-3168; Fax: 902/769-2408 – Annually. Five days. Musical, cultural, sports, July

Le Festival de l'Escaouette, a/s Les Trois Pignons, PO Box 430, Cheticamp NS B0E 1H0 – 902/224-2642 – Assistant Manager, Daniel Aucoin – Annually. Acadian folklore, traditions, culture, August

Festival de la Francophonie, PO Box 1498, Tracadie NB E0C 2B0 – 506/395-9746 – June 30 – July 4

Foire Brayonne, c/o Box 338, Edmundston NB E3V 3K9 – 506/739-6608 – July/August. Brayon heritage festival

Folkfest, 233 Ave. C South, Saskatoon SK S7M 1N3 – 306/931-0100; Fax: 306/665-3421 – Coordinator, Deneen Gudjonson – Annual. Three days. Twenty or more ethnic pavilions, August

Folklorama - Canada's Cultural Celebration, 375 York Ave., Winnipeg MB R3C 3J3 – 204/982-6221; Fax: 204/943-1956 – Director, Claudette Leclerc – Annual. Fourteen days. More than forty ethnic pavilions, August

Folklore Festival, Fort William Gardens, 901 East Miles St., Thunder Bay ON P7C 1J9 – 807/345-0551 – Annual. More than twenty ethnic pavilions, May

Franco-Ontarien Festival, Major's Hill Park, c/o PO Box 287, Stn A, Ottawa ON K1M 8V2 – 613/230-0056 – Annual. Outdoor concerts, entertainment, international foods, June

Loyalist Days, c/o Delta Hotel, #207, 39 King St., Saint John NB E2L 4W3 – 506/634-8123 – July

Manitoba Highland Gathering, PO Box 59, Selkirk MB R1A 2B1 – 204/757-2365 – Annual, July

Metro International Caravan, 253 Adelaide St. West, Toronto ON M5H 1Y2 – 416/977-0466 – Annual. Nine days. Ethnic pavilions, June

MOSAIC - Regina's Annual Festival of Cultures, Regina Multicultural Council, 2144 Cornwall St., Regina SK S4P 2K7 – 306/757-5990; Fax. 306/780-9407 – Executive Director, Sharon Amyotte – Annual. Three days. Twenty ethno-cultural pavilions, June

Opasquiak Indian Days, PO Box 297, The Pas MB R9A 1K8 – 204/623-5483 – Caroline Constant – Traditional native events, August

Red Deer Highland Games, 5205B - 54 Ave., Red Deer AB T4N 5E5 – 403/342-6203 – June

Ukrainian Pysanka Festival, c/o PO Box 877, Vegreville AB T9C 1R9 – 403/632-2771 – Music, folk art, Pysanka writing, Easter egg painting, July

Vesna Festival, 205 Sturgeon Pl., Saskatoon SK S7K 4C5 – 306/931-8659 – Don Gabruch – Annual Spring celebration. Two days of entertainment, dancing, cultural demonstrations & displays. "The World's Largest Ukrainian Cabaret", May

MUSIC

Aberfoyle Old Time Fiddler's Contest, c/o, PO Box 1268, Guelph ON N1H 6N6 – September

Annual Northeastern Fiddling & Step Dancing Championships, Community Centre, Mattawa ON P0H 1V0 – 705/744-2789

Annual Olde Tyme Fiddling Contest, Memorial Centre, Blind River ON P0R 1B0 – 705/356-2555 – July

Atlantic Jazz Festival, PO Box 33043, Halifax NS B3L 4T6 – 902/422-8221 – Contact, Susan Hunter – July

Big Valley Jamboree, 200 Lakeshore Dr., Regina SK S4P 3V7 – 306/565-4500; Fax: 306/565-3274 – Louise Yates – July. Country music

Brandon Folk Music & Arts Festival, PO Box 2047, Brandon MB R7A 6S8 – 204/727-3928 – Contact, Scott Stewart – Annually, August

Canadian Open Old Time Fiddler's Contest, Sports Complex, c/o, PO Box 27, Shelburne ON L0N 1S0 – 519/925-3013

Central Canada's Fiddlers' Festival, PO Box 10, Austin MB R0H 0C0 – 204/637-2354 – Contact, Terry Farley

Classical Music Festival, c/o, PO Box 181, Whistler BC V0N 1B0 – 604/932-3928 – August

CMX - The Canadian Music Exposition, #533, 67 Mowat Ave., Toronto ON M6K 3E3 – 416/533-9417; Fax: 416/533-0367 – Contact, Kathleen Miller – Annually, Spring

Dawson City Music Festival, PO Box 456, Dawson City YT Y0B 1G0 – 403/993-5584 – Annually, July

Dockside Ceilidh, c/o 89 King St., North Sydney NS B2A 2T3 – 902/794-3772 – President, Northside Highland Dancers' Association, Kay Batherson – Daily, summer. Cultural music & entertainment at Marine Atlantic Ferry Terminal

Downtowners Optimist Band Festival, 1544 Albert St., Regina SK S40 2S4 – 306/757-7172; Fax: 306/757-0577 – Co-Chairman, Greg Way – Annually, March. Band & vocal jazz festival

Edmonton Folk Music Festival, PO Box 4130, Edmonton AB T6E 4T2 – 403/429-1899 – August. Blues, jazz, country, Celtic, bluegrass. arts & crafts

Elora Festival, c/o, PO Box 990, Elora ON N0B 1S0 – 519/846-0331 – July - Aug. Choral & contemporary Canadian music

Festival International de Jazz de Montréal, 822, rue Sherbrooke est, Montréal PQ H2L 1K4 – 514/523-FEST; Fax: 514/525-5609; URL: http://www.montrealjazzfestival.worldlinx.com/ – Contact, Caroline Jamet – Annual. Over 1,500 musicians & 350 shows, July – Montréal PQ

Festival Mondial de Folklore de Drummondville, 405, rue Saint-Jean, Drummondville PQ J2B 5L7 – 819/472-1184; Fax: 819/474-6585 – Contact, Maurice Rhéaume – July. Ten days, over 20 countries, 300 shows

Folk on the Rocks, PO Box 326, Yellowknife NT X1A 2N3 – 403/920-7806 – Annual. Two days. Inuit, Dene, other northern & southern folk groups, July

Huronia Open Fiddle & Step Dance Contest, Centennial Arena, c/o 575 Dominion Ave., Midland ON L4R 1R2 – 705/526-4770 – July

International Festival of Baroque Music, PO Box 644, Lameque NB E0B 1V0 – 506/344-5846; Fax: 506/344-2296 – Early music festival with five productions in July (Northeastern New Brunswick, on Lameque Island)

International Jazz Festival, 435 West Hastings St., Vancouver BC V6B 1L4 – 604/682-0706 – June

Jazz City International Festival, 10516 - 77 Ave., Edmonton AB T6E 1N1 – 403/432-7166 – Annually June. Ten days

Kamloops Big Band Spectacular, c/o Kamloops Parks & Recreation Services, 7 Victoria St., Kamloops BC V2C 1A2 – 250/828-3552; Fax: 250/372-1573 – Contact, K. Sean-Smith – May

Kamloops Bluegrass Country Music Festival, Tyee Park, 694 Steinky Pl., Kamloops BC V2B 7L7 – 250/579-9162

Kinsmen International Band & Choral Festival, Moose Jaw Kinsmen Club, PO Box 883, Moose Jaw SK S6H 4P5 – 306/693-5933 – Russ McKnight – 3,000 musicians, evening concerts, parade. Annual, May – Moose Jaw SK

Kiwanis Music Festival of Greater Toronto, #501, 100 Adelaide St. West, Toronto ON M5H 1S3 – 416/363-3238

Maritime Old Time Fiddling Contest & Jamboree, PO Box 3037, Dartmouth East NS B2W 4Y3 – 902/434-5466 – James Delaney – July

Miramichi Folk Song Festival, PO Box 13, Miramichi NB E1V 3M2 – 506/773-4469 – August

Newfoundland & Labrador Folk Festival, c/o Tourism St. John's, PO Box 908, St. John's NF A1C 5P3 – 709/576-8508 – August. Traditional Newfoundland & Labrador music & dance

Northern Lights Festival, Bell Park Amphitheatre, c/o, PO Box 1236, Stn B, Sudbury ON P3E 4S7 – 705/674-5512 – July

Nova Scotia Bluegrass Oldtime Music Festival, 119 Victoria St. West, Amherst NS B4H 1C7 – 902/667-9629 – Wilson Moore – Annually, July. Three days

Nova Scotia Kiwanis Music Festival, PO Box 1623, Halifax NS B3J 2Z1 – 902/423-6147 – Sharon Holland – Adjudicated music festival & closing concert, February – Halifax NS

Old Time Fiddle & Step Dancing Championships, Memorial Centre, c/o, PO Box 365, Pembroke ON K8A 6X6 – 613/584-3377 – August

Ottawa International Jazz Festival, Confederation Park, c/o, PO Box 3104, Stn D, Ottawa ON K1P 6H7 – 613/594-3580 – July

Regina Folk Festival, PO Box 1203, Regina SK S4P 3B4 – 306/757-7684; Fax: 306/525-4009; URL: http://bfsmedia.com/RBCS/rff96/ – Contact, Karen Haggman – Annually, June. Three days

Canadian Almanac & Directory 1997

EXHIBITIONS, SHOWS & EVENTS — RODEOS 1-89

Royal Canadian Big Band Music Festival, c/o 201 King St., London ON N6A 1C9 – 519/663-9467 – Annually, Canada Day

Saskatchewan Jazz Festival, PO Box 1593, Saskatoon SK S7K 3R3 – 306/652-1421; Fax: 306/934-5014; URL: http://www.sasknet.com/jazz/ – Manager, Kristine Magnus – June - July – Saskatoon SK

Scotia Festival of Music, #317, 1541 Barrington St., Halifax NS B3J 1Z5 – 902/429-9467 – Contact, Christopher Wilcox – Annually, May. Chamber music

Sound of Music Festival, c/o Parks & Recreation Dept., City Hall, Burlington ON L7R 3Z6 – 905/335-7704 – June

Southwestern Ontario Fiddle & Step Dance Championships, Coliseum, c/o 88 Wellington St., Stratford ON N5A 2L2 – 519/271-6115 – June

TerrifVic Dixieland Jazz Party, #211, 633 Courtney St., Victoria BC V8W 1B9 – 250/381-5277 – Annually, April

Vancouver Folk Music Festival, 3271 Main St., Vancouver BC V5V 3M6 – 604/879-2931; Fax: 604/879-4315; URL: http://www.ffa.ucalgary.ca/vca/canfol.htm – Executive Director, Brent Gibson – Annual festival, July – Vancouver BC

Victoriaville International Festival of New Music, CP 460, Victoriaville PQ G6P 6T3 – 819/752-7912 – Contact, Michel Levasseur – May

Welcome to the Ceilidh, 2360 Armcrescent West, Halifax NS B3L 3E3 – 902/422-3143 – Contact, Anita MacDougall – Annually, June. Highland, national & choreographed Scottish dancers

Western Canada Olde Tyme Fiddling Championship, 841 - 8th Ave. NE, Swift Current SK S9H 2R6 – 306/773-8924 – Contact, Don MacRae – Annual, September

Winnipeg Folk Festival, 264 Taché Ave., Winnipeg MB R2H 1Z9 – 204/231-0096; URL: http://www.magic.mb.ca/~wff/ – Annually, July

Winnipeg Jazz Festival, #501, 100 Arthur St., Winnipeg MB R3B 1H3 – 204/942-1654; URL: http://www.xpressnet.com/~cohenm/jazzwpg/ – Neal Kimelman – June

OFFICE EQUIPMENT

COMDA Product Show, Canadian Office Machine Dealers Association, #204, 3464 Kingston Rd., Scarborough ON M1M 1R5 – 416/261-1607; Fax: 416/261-1679 – Executive Director, Don Vickery

The COPA Show, Canadian Office Products Association, #911, 1243 Islington Ave., Toronto ON M8X 1Y9 – 416/239-2737; Fax: 416/239-1553 – Manager, Conference services, Gerald Petkau – Annual trade show. Office products, furniture, equipment

OIL & GAS

Calgary Oil & Gas Show, Southex Exhibitions, #300, 999 - 8 St. SW, Calgary AB T2R 1N7 – 403/244-6111; Fax: 403/245-8649; URL: http://www.southex.com – Pat Atkinson – Biennial trade show. Petroleum & natural gas products, services & technology; exploration, production, transmission, processing, marketing, June 1997 – Roundup Centre, Stampede Park, Calgary AB

Fort McMurray Oil Sands Tradeshow, Southex Exhibitions, #300, 999 - 8 St. SW, Calgary AB T2R 1N7 – 403/244-6111; Fax: 403/245-8649; URL: http://www.southex.com – Pat Atkinson – Biennial trade show; products, services & technology for the mining & processing of oil sands, Sept. 1-2 1998 – MacDonald Island Centre, Fort McMurray AB

Offshore Newfoundland Oil & Gas Exhibition, Atlantic Expositions Ltd, PO Box 402, Gander NF A1V 1W8 – 709/651-3315; Fax: 709/256-4051 – Manager, Keith Brown – Annual trade show, June – St. John's NF

PACKAGING

Pac-Ex, Packaging Association of Canada, #330, 2255 Sheppard Ave. East, North York ON M2J 4Y1 – 905/490-7860; Fax: 905/490-7844 – Show Manager, Steve Utting – Biennial trade show, Sept. 9-11 1997 – International Centre, Toronto ON

Packaging Forum/Forum d'Emballage, Packaging Association of Canada, #330, 2255 Sheppard Ave. East, North York ON M2J 4Y1 – 905/490-7860; Fax: 905/490-7844 – Show Manager, Steve Utting – Biennial trade show, May 1997

PARENTS see CHILDREN

PETS

All About Pets, William Peddie Show Productions Inc., 21 Lorraine Gardens, Etobicoke ON M9B 4Z5 – 416/231-9992; Fax: 416/233-9725 – Show Manager, Gregory Williams – Annual consumer show, April – Toronto ON

PIJAC Canada National Pet & Trade Show, PIJAC Canada, #1001, 4 King St. West, Toronto ON M5H 1B6 – 416/364-9317; Fax: 416/364-9118; Tollfree: 1-800-667-7452 – Show Committee Chair, Bob Stevens – Annual trade show, September – Toronto ON

PHARMACEUTICALS

International Conference, Canadian Pharmaceutical Association, 1785 Alta Vista Dr., 2nd Fl., Ottawa ON K1G 3Y6 – 613/523-7877; Fax: 613/523-0445; Tollfree: 1-800-917-9489 – Executive Director, L.C. Fevang – Aug. 31 - Sept. 5 1997 – Vancouver Trade & Convention Centre, Vancouver BC

PLASTICS & RUBBER

Expoplast, Society of the Plastics Industry of Canada, #500, 5925 Airport Rd., Mississauga ON L4V 1W1 – 905/678-7748; Fax: 905/678-0774 – Show Manager, Jack McLean – Triennial trade show: plastics machinery, raw materials suppliers, mold makers, processors, fabricators, auxilliary equipment, October 1997

Plast-ex, Society of the Plastics Industry of Canada, #500, 5925 Airport Rd., Mississauga ON L4V 1W1 – 905/678-7748; Fax: 905/678-0774 – President, Pierre Dubois – Triennial trade show, May 1998

PSYCHIC PHENOMENA

ESP Psychic Expo, Impact Event Management, 358 Danforth Ave., PO Box 65060, Toronto ON M4K 3Z2 – 416/461-5306; Fax: 416/461-8460 – Donald Nausbaum – Annual consumer show. Psychics, astrologers, natural healing, crystals, books, tapes, computers, October

International Psychic & Astrology Expo, Impact Event Management, 358 Danforth Ave., PO Box 65060, Toronto ON M4K 3Z2 – 416/461-5306; Fax: 416/461-8460 – Donald Nausbaum – Consumer show. Astrologers, tarot card readers, holistic health, computers, April – Toronto ON

Psychic, Mystics & Seers Fair, Impact Event Management, 358 Danforth Ave., PO Box 65060, Toronto ON M4K 3Z2 – 416/461-5306; Fax: 416/461-8460 – Donald Nausbaum – Consumer show. Psychics, astrologers, tarot card readers, holistic health, computers, February – Queen Elizabeth Bldg., Exhibition Place, Toronto ON

PULP & PAPER PROCESSING

Exfor, Clarkson-Conway Inc., CP 216, Succ Place Bonaventure, Montréal PQ H5A 1A9 – 514/861-9694; Fax: 514/392-1577 – General Manager, Marilyn Meikle – Annual exhibition of the Technical Section, Canadian Pulp & Paper Association, January 1997 – Montréal PQ

Pacific Paper Expo, Papermaker Magazine, #900, 1130 West Pender St., Vancouver BC V6E 4A4 – 604/891-5615; Fax: 604/683-8202 – Laurie Grant – Biennial trade show, October 1997

REAL ESTATE

National Annual Conference, The Canadian Real Estate Association, Minto Place, The Canada Bldg., #1600, 344 Slater St., Ottawa ON K1R 7Y3 – 613/237-7111; Fax: 613/234-2567; Email: info@crea.ca; URL: http://www.mls.ca/crea.ca – Coordinator, Gail McHardy – Annual trade show, October

National Canadian Condominium Conference, #501, 366 Adelaide St. West, Toronto ON M5V 1R9 – 416/585-2552; Fax: 416/585-9741 – Conference Coordinator, Renée Ayache – Annual trade conference. Property management, legal issues, insurance, etc., October

Real Estate Show, Martin International, #2910, 500, Place des Armes, Montréal PQ H2Y 2W2 – 514/288-3931; Fax: 514/288-0641 – General Manager, Lorraine Boisvenu – Annual consumer show. Commercial real estate, professional services, financing & insuring, vacation homes, luxury homes, homes of the future. Québec City & Montréal, January

The Real Estate Show, York Expositions, #803, 1 Toronto St., Toronto ON M5C 2V6 – 416/869-1156; Fax: 416/869-1660 – George Przybylowski – Annual show, November/December – Metro Toronto Convention Centre, Toronto ON

RECREATIONAL VEHICLES see AUTOMOTIVE; SPORTS & RECREATION

RENTALS

Canadian Rental Mart, AIS Communications Ltd., 145 Thames Rd. West, Exeter ON N0M 1S3 – 519/235-2400; Fax: 519/235-0798 – Contact, Peter Phillips – January

RODEOS

see also Exhibitions, Farm Business/Agriculture

Agribition Rodeo, c/o Public Relations Office, Canadian Western Agribition, PO Box 353, Regina SK S4P 3J8 – 306/565-0565; Fax: 306/757-9963 – Annually, November

Budweiser Pro Tour Rodeo Finals, c/o, PO Box 6010, Saskatoon SK S7K 4E4 – 306/931-7149 – Annually, October. Three days

Canadian Firefighters Rodeo, PO Box 1886, Virden MB R0M 2C0 – 204/748-2587

CCA Finals Rodeo, c/o Canadian Cowboys Association, PO Box 1877, Lloydminster SK S9V 1N4 – 306/825-7116 – Annually, October. Four days

Hometown Rodeo, c/o Moose Jaw Exhibition Co. Ltd., PO Box 1467, Moose Jaw SK S6H 4R3 – 306/692-2723 – Annually, April & September

Manitoba Threshermen's Reunion & Stampede, PO Box 10, Austin MB R0H 0C0 – 204/637-2354

Canadian Almanac & Directory 1997

Maple Creek Cowtown Rodeo, PO Box 1091, Maple Creek SK S0N 1N0 – 306/662-3667 – Jim Montgomery – Annually, May

Ponoka Annual Stampede, Stampede Park, Ponoka AB T0C 2H0 – 403/783-0100 – June

Williams Lake Stampede, c/o 1148 South Broadway, Williams Lake BC V2G 1A2 – 250/392-5025

RVS see AUTOMOTIVE; SPORTS & RECREATION

SAFETY

Annual Conference, Canadian Association of Chiefs of Police, #1908, 112 Kent St., Ottawa ON K1P 5P2 – 613/233-1106; Fax: 613/233-6960 – Executive Director, Fred Schultz – August 1997 Fredericton NB

Conference, Canada Safety Council, 1020 Thomas Spratt Place, Ottawa ON K1G 5L5 – 613/739-1535; Fax: 613/739-1566 – President, Émile-J. Thérien – Annual trade show. Safety-related products & services for workplace, traffic, home & leisure, May

Health & Safety '97 Conference & Trade Show, Industrial Accident Prevention Association Ontario, Eaton Tower, 250 Yonge St., 28th Fl., Toronto ON M5B 2N4 – 416/506-8888; Fax: 416/506-8880; Tollfree: 1-800-669-4939 – Executive Vice-President & General Manager, Maureen C. Shaw – April 21-23 1997 – Regal Constellation Hotel, Toronto ON

SCIENCE

Annual Meeting, Canadian Federation of Biological Societies, #104, 1750 Courtwood Cres., Ottawa ON K2C 2B5 – 613/225-8889; Fax: 613/225-9621; Email: cfbs@hpb.hwc.ca – President, Dr. Judy Anderson – June 18-21 1997 – Québec PQ

Mines & Minerals Symposia, c/o Ministry of Northern Development & Mines, #A3, 933 Ramsey Lake R, Sudbury ON P3E 6B5 – 705/670-5627; Fax: 705/670-5622 – Annual trade show & seminar in April (Northern Ontario) & December (Toronto)

SENIOR CITIZENS

The GoodAge Show, Pro-Show, Trade Show Management, #102, 33 Isabella St., Toronto ON M4Y 2P7 – 416/960-8739; Fax: 416/960-1854 – Marketing Director, Larry Cohen – Annual consumer show, May – Toronto ON

Great Canadian Maturity Show & Travel Show, Premier Consumer Shows, City Parent Newsmagazine, 467 Speers Rd., Oakville ON L6K 3S4 – 905/815-0017; Fax: 905/815-0511 – Show Coordinator, Brenda Harris – Semi-annual consumer show in April & October (Toronto); various annual shows in Ontario centres

Salon des Aînés et Salon Vacances Loisirs, Expositions André Guillemette, #302, 2900, rue Quatre-Bourgeois, Ste-Foy PQ G1N 1Y4 – 418/657-7949; Fax: 418/650-6393 – André Guillemette – Annual consumer show; travel & other services for seniors, May

Salon International des Aînés, Salon international des Aînés, 4728C, de Mentana, Montréal PQ H2J 3B9 – 514/523-1873

The Time of Your Life Seniors Show, Taylordel Production Line Ltd., #200, 1865 Marine Dr. West, Vancouver BC V7V 1J7 – 604/922-3371; Fax: 604/922-3371 – Show Coordinator, Nicole Copley – Consumer show, May

Yorton Threshermen's Show & Seniors' Festival, Yorkton Threshermen's Show & Seniors' Festival, Western Development Museum, PO Box 98, Yorkton SK S3N 2V6 – 306/783-8361 – Event Chairman, Susan Mandziuk – Annual, July – Western Development Museum, Yorkton SK

SEWING see CRAFTS

SPORTS & RECREATION

see also Boating; Automotive, for combined auto/RV shows

Alberta Camping & Cottage Show, Uniglobe International Exhibitions Ltd., #240, 4936 - 87 St., Edmonton AB T6E 5W3 – 403/469-2400; Fax: 403/469-1398 – President, Tom McCaffrey – Annual consumer show; products & services related to camping, cottage & tourist industry; held in Edmonton (Feb.) & Calgary (Mar.)

All Canada Goose Shoot, PO Box 21, Lundar MB R0C 1Y0 – 204/762-5789 – Fred Burdett

Atlantic Canada Snowmobile Show, Snowtime, #131, 449 University Ave., Charlottetown PE C1A 8K3 – 902/892-0040; Fax: 902/892-9646 – Art Gennis – Annual trade & consumer show, October

Atlantic Outdoor Sports & RV Show, PO Box 2968, Dartmouth East NS B2W 4Y2 – 902/827-3572 – Manager, Darrelyn Sapp – Annual consumer show. Trailer & motor homes, 4x4s, tent trailers, boats, motors, hunting, fishing & camping, tourism & sporting goods, March

Calgary Ski & Snowboard Show, Canadian National Sportsmen's Shows, #340, 1032 - 17 Ave. SW, Calgary AB T2T 0A5 – 403/245-9008; Fax: 403/245-5100 – Wolfgang Ortner – Annual consumer show, November – Max Bell Centre, Calgary AB

Campex, Ontario Private Campground Association, RR#5, Owen Sound ON N4K 5N7 – 519/371-3393; Fax: 519/371-5315; Email: opca@bmts.com – Managing Director, Marcel Gobeil – Trade show, October – London ON

Canadian Bicycle Dealer Trade Show, Canadian Shows & Special Events Inc., #1801, One Yonge St., Toronto ON M5E 1W7 – 416/363-1292; Fax: 416/369-0515 – Show Manager, Carl Bastedo – Annual trade show; bicycles & bicycle accessories, September

Canadian Hunting & Shooting Sports Trade Show, Canadian Sporting Arms & Ammunition Association, PO Box 235, Cobourg ON K9A 4K5 – 905/373-1623; Fax: 905/373-1706; Email: showgun@eagle.ca; URL: http://www.eagle.ca/showgun – Executive Director, René J.J. Roberge – Annual trade show, Feb. 22-24 1997 – Hull Convention Centre, Hull PQ

Canadian Power Toboggan Championship, PO Box 22, Beausejour MB R0E 0C0 – 204/268-2049 – Annual, March

Canoe Expo, c/o The Profile Group, #301, 37 Sandiford Dr., Stouffville ON L4A 7X5 – 905/640-7700; Fax: 905/640-7714 – Show Producer, George Zarras – Annual consumer show. Canoes, kayaks, location camps & outfitters, April

CHALLENGE - Canada's Sports, Fitness & Music Show, 65 Helena Ave., Toronto ON M6G 2H3 – 416/652-1302; Fax: 416/653-2291 – Executive Producer, Joyce Barslow – Annual consumer show. Health & fitness, leisure, fashion, April

Cottage & Country Living Show, Square Feet Northwest Event Management Inc., 1030 Mainland St., Vancouver BC V6B 2T4 – 604/683-4393; Fax: 604/688-0270; Email: mgmt@sqftevent.com – Blaine Woit – Annual consumer show, January – Vancouver BC

Fall Hunting Show, Ontario Out of Doors Magazine, 777 Bay St., 6th Fl., Toronto ON M5W 1A7 – 416/596-5908; Fax: 416/596-2517; Email: 102677.1125@compuserve.com; URL: http://www.cyberplex.com/fishontario – Show Manager, Lynda Watson – Annual consumer show: hunting equipment, dog trials, "World Calling Contest"; shooting range; seminars, Sept. 5-7 1997

The Great Outdoors Show, c/o Bingemans Conference & Recreation Centre, 1380 Victoria St. North, Kitchener ON N2B 3E2 – 519/744-1555; Fax: 519/744-1985 – Contact, John Bingeman – Annual consumer show, Jan./Feb. Hunting & fishing equipment, charters, boats, campgrounds

Hamilton Travelcamping Show, Ontario Recreation Vehicle Dealers Association, PO Box 270, Brechin ON L0K 1B0 – 705/484-0295; Fax: 705/484-5740 – Executive Director, William A. Mallatratt – Annual consumer show. RVs, trailers, truck campers, campgrounds, etc., February

Ironman Canada Triathlon Championship, 522 Dawson Ave., Penticton BC V2A 3N8 – 250/490-8787; Fax: 250/490-8788 – Annual three-day trade expo staged as part of the events prior to the Ironman race

Kelowna RV Show, c/o Recreation Dealers Association of BC, #201, 19623 - 56 Ave., Langley BC V3A 3X7 – 604/533-4200; Fax: 604/533-0795 – Marketing Manager, Lynn Thompson – Annual consumer show. RV dealers, RV lifestyle, parks & destinations, April

London Sports Show, PO Box 4550, London ON N5W 5K3 – 519/438-7203; Fax: 519/679-3124 – Annual consumer show. Fishing, golf, hockey, baseball, February

London Sports Show, Western Fair Association, PO Box 4550, Stn D, London ON N5W 5K3 – 519/438-7203; Fax: 519/679-3124 – Annual consumer show, February – Western Fairgrounds, London ON

MISE - Montréal International Sports Exhibition, Canadian Sporting Goods Association, #510, 455, rue Saint-Antoine ouest, Montréal PQ H2Z 1J1 – 514/393-1132; Fax: 514/393-9513 – President & CEO, Yves Paquette – Annual trade show, February

The Montréal Golf & Travel Show, International Show Productions Inc., 36 Fallingbrook Dr., Scarborough ON M1N 1B6 – 416/691-2852; Fax: 416/691-2891 – Steve Nichols – Annual consumer show, March

NSIA Ski, Snowboard & Outdoor Trade Show, National Ski Industries Association, #340, 8250, boul Decarie, Montréal PQ H4P 2P5 – 514/737-1672; Fax: 514/737-0724 – Executive Director, Carol Hopper – Annual trade show, February

"One Big Canadian Show"; Fall Market & BTAC Outdoor Show, Canadian Sporting Goods Association, #510, 455, rue Saint-Antoine ouest, Montréal PQ H2Z 1J1 – 514/393-1132; Fax: 514/393-9513 – President & CEO, Yves Paquette – Annual trade show, September – Toronto Congress Centre, Toronto ON

Ottawa Ski & Travel Show, Intertrade Associates Inc., #250, 1511 Merivale Rd., Nepean ON K2G 3J3 – 613/224-3013; Fax: 613/224-4533; Tollfree: 1-888-662-6660 – Marketing Manager, Martin Charlton – Consumer show, November

Outdoor Sports & Leisure Show, DAC Marketing Ltd., PO Box 2837, Stn A, Sudbury ON P3A 5J3 – 705/673-5588; Fax: 705/525-0626 – President, Darren A. Ceccarelli – March – New Sudbury Centre, Sudbury ON

Outfitters Hunting & Fishing Show, Expour Inc., 9200, boul Henri-Bourassa ouest, Montréal PQ H4S 1L5 – 514/334-3976; Fax: 514/334-1180; Tollfree: 1-800-668-3976 – Président, C. Guevremont – Held in Montréal & Québec City, March

Pool, Spa & Patio Show, Backyard Living Productions, PO Box 1500-1288, Etobicoke ON M9C 4V5 – 416/620-6620; Fax: 416/621-6688 – Shirley Trotter – March – International Centre, Toronto ON

Red Deer Sportsman Show, Westerner Exposition Association, 4847A - 19 St., Red Deer AB T4R 2N7 – 403/343-7800; Fax: 403/341-4699 – General Manager, Larry Johnstone – Annual consumer show, March – Western Exposition Grounds, Red Deer AB

Salon Camping, Plein Air, Chasse et Pêche de Montréal/Montréal Sportsmen's Show, Canadian National Sportsmen's Shows (1989) Ltd., #1630, 1155, rue Metcalfe, Montréal PQ H3B 2V6 – 514/866-5409; Fax: 514/866-4092 – Show Manager, Diane Laporte – Annual consumer show: camping, fishing, hunting, RVs, tourism, April – Place Bonaventure, Montréal PQ

Salon Camping, Plein Air, Chasse et Pêche de Québec/Québec City Sportsmen's Show, Canadian National Sportsmen's Shows (1989) Ltd., #1630, 1155, rue Metcalfe, Montréal PQ H3B 2V6 – 514/866-5409; Fax: 514/866-4092 – Show Manager, Diane Laporte – Annual consumer show: camping, fishing, hunting, RVs, tourism, March – Parc de l'Exposition, Québec PQ

Salon Sports Plein Air Outaouais/The Outaouais Sports Outdoors Exhibition, Salon Sports Plein Air Outaouais/The Outaouais Sports Outdoor Exhibition, CP 1151, Succ B, Hull PQ J8X 3X7 – 819/457-2063; Fax: 819/457-1805 – Promoter, Gyslaine Sarrasin – Annual consumer show. Outfitters & nautical section, February – Robert Guertin Arena, Hull PQ

Ski Atlantic, Denex Group Inc., Burnside Industrial Park, 192 Joseph Zatzman Dr., Dartmouth NS B3B 1N4 – 902/468-4999; Fax: 902/468-2795; Email: denman@newedge.ca – Show Manager, Bob Dunnington – Consumer show, September

Sports, Recreation & Leisure Trade Show, c/o South East Alberta Travel & Convention Association, PO Box 605, Medicine Hat AB T1A 7G5 – 403/527-6422; Fax: 403/528-2683 – Annual consumer show, February

Sportsorama, Sports, Recreation, Travel & Leisure Show, PO Box 605, Medicine Hat AB T1A 7G5 – 403/527-6422; Fax: 403/528-2682 – Executive Director, Glenda Leitch – Annual consumer show. Fashion shows, sports & fishing demonstrations, February

The Spring Fishing Show, Ontario Out of Doors Magazine, 777 Bay St., 6th Fl., Toronto ON M5W 1A7 – 416/596-5908; Fax: 416/596-2517; Email: 102677.1125@compuserve.com; URL: http://www.cyberplex.com/fishontario – Show Manager, Lynda Watson – Annual consumer show, Feb. 14-16 1997 – International Centre, Toronto ON

Squamish Days (Loggers' Sports), Squamish BC V0N 3G0 – 604/892-9244

The Summer Holiday Show/Salon Vacances et Loisir d'été, Promexpo Inc., 801, rue Sherbrooke est, 10e étage, Montréal PQ H2L 1K7 – 514/527-9221; Fax: 514/527-8449 – General Manager, Maguy Rigaud – Annual consumer show held in Montréal & Québec, April

Supertrax International Snowmobilers Show, Marketer Shows Inc., #635, 7305 Woodbine Ave., Markham ON L3R 3V7 – 905/473-7009; Fax: 905/473-5217 – Terrence Kehoe – Annual consumer show, October – Markham ON

The Toronto Golf & Travel Show, International Show Productions Inc., 36 Fallingbrook Dr., Scarborough ON M1N 1B6 – 416/691-2852; Fax: 416/691-2891 – Steve Nichols – Annual consumer show, March

Toronto International Bicycle Show, #1801, 1 Yonge St., Toronto ON M5E 1W7 – 416/363-1292; Fax: 416/369-0515 – Show Manager, Josie Graziosi – March – Automotive Bldg., Exhibition Place, Toronto ON

Toronto Ski & Snowboard Show, Canadian National Sportsmen's Shows (1989) Ltd., #202, 703 Evans Ave., Toronto ON M5C 5E9 – 416/695-0311; Fax: 416/695-0381 – Show Manager, Tim Kennedy – Annual consumer show, October – Automotive Building, Exhibition Place, Toronto ON

Toronto Sportsmen's Show, Canadian National Sportsmen's Shows (1989) Ltd., #202, 703 Evans Ave., Toronto ON M5C 5E9 – 416/695-0311; Fax: 416/695-0381 – Show Manager, Robert Grainger – Annual consumer show, March – Coliseum Building, Exhibition Place, Toronto ON

Vancouver Fishing & Outdoor Show, Square Feet Northwest Event Management Inc., 1030 Mainland St., Vancouver BC V6B 2T4 – 604/683-4393; Fax: 604/688-0270; Email: mgmt@sqftevent.com – Bruce Guerin – Annual consumer show, January – Vancouver BC

Vancouver Island Sportsman Show, Evergreen Exhibitions Ltd., 830D Pembrooke St., Victoria BC V8T 1H9 – 250/386-7469; Fax: 250/386-1431 – President, A.J. Chartrand – Annual consumer show, February – Victoria BC

Vancouver Ski Show, Vancouver Ski Foundation, #306, 1367 West Broadway, Vancouver BC V6H 4A9 – 604/878-0754; Fax: 604/878-0754 – Producer, Valerie Lang – Annual consumer show, October – BC Place Stadium, Vancouver BC

Vancouver Sportsmen's Show, Canadian National Sportsmen's Shows (1989) Ltd., #501, 4190 Lougheed Hwy., Burnaby BC V5C 6A8 – 604/294-1313; Fax: 604/294-4740 – Show Manager, Jim Carslake – Annual consumer show, February/March – Pacific National Exhibition, Vancouver BC

STAMPEDES see RODEOS

THEATRE see ARTS

TOYS & GAMES

The Bear Fair, Trade Show Managers Inc., 5512, 4 St. NW, PO Box 64024, Calgary AB T2K 6J0 – 403/274-8858; Fax: 403/274-9388; Email: slmorrow@aca.ucalgary.ca – Contact, Sandra Morrow – October – Calgary AB

Canadian Toy & Decoration Fair, Canadian Toy Association, PO Box 294, Kleinburg ON L0J 1C0 – 905/893-1689; Fax: 905/893-2392 – Executive Director, Sheila Edmondson – Annual trade show, January

Salon international de la Video et di Divertissement familial, Yves Barré & Associés, 6940, rue Barry, Brossard PQ J4Z 1V1 – 514/443-3131; Fax: 514/443-8415 – Président, Yves Barré – November – Place Bonaventure, Montréal PQ

Teddy Collectors, Trade Show Managers Inc., 5512, 4 St. NW, PO Box 64024, Calgary AB T2K 6J0 – 403/274-8858; Fax: 403/274-9388; Email: slmorrow@aca.ucalgary.ca – Contact, Sandra Morrow – March – White Rock BC

TRANSPORTATION
see also **Automotive**

Annual Convention & Trade Show, Ontario School Bus Association, #100, 295 The West Mall, Etobicoke ON M9C 4Z4 – 416/695-9965; Fax: 416/695-9977 – Events Coordinator, Rebecca Jasas – Annual conference & trade show. Safety, fuel economy, buses & accessories, computers, July – Toronto ON

Transfreight, c/o Groupe Bomart, #103, 7493 Trans Canada Hwy., St-Laurent PQ H4T 1T3 – 514/337-9043; Fax: 514/337-1862 – Contact, Jean-Pierre Emmanuel – Annual multimodal transportation trade show & conference, September

TRAVEL & TOURISM

Canadian Meetings & Incentive Travel Symposium & Trade Show, 777 Bay St., 5th Fl., Toronto ON M5W 1A7 – 416/596-5165; Fax: 416/596-5810 – Richard Elliott – Annual trade show & conference, August

The London Travel Show, Motivations International Inc., 14 Rowan Ave., Toronto ON M4N 2X9 – 416/481-6384; Fax: 416/483-6791 – Coordinator, John Stephenson – Semi-annual consumer show (March & October) – London ON

Southwestern Ontario Golf & Vacation Show, Western Fair Association, PO Box 4550, Stn D, London ON N5W 5K3 – 519/438-7203; Fax: 519/679-3124 – Annual consumer show; equipment, destinations, demonstrations, February – London ON

The Travel & Leisure Show, Lindan M. Toole Consulting Ltd., #508, 174 Spadina Ave., Toronto ON M5T 2C2 – 416/360-5514; Fax: 416/360-4383 – Show Producer, Lindan M. Toole – Annual trade & consumer show, April

The Travel & Vacation Show, Player Expositions International, 255 Clemow Ave., Ottawa ON K1S 2B5 – 613/567-6408; Fax: 613/567-2718 – Show Organizer, Halina Player – Annual consumer show, April – Ottawa ON

Travel Technology Conference & Trade Show, Baxter Travel Group, 310 Dupont St., Toronto ON M5R 1V9 – 416/968-7252; Fax: 416/968-2377 – Special Projects Manager, Alan Crockford – Annual trade show, March

TRUCKS see AUTOMOTIVE

VIDEO see COMMUNICATIONS

WINTER CARNIVALS

Banff/Lake Louise Winter Festival, PO Box 1260, Banff AB T0L 0C0 – 403/762-1200 – February

Bon Soo Winter Carnival, PO Box 781, Sault Ste. Marie ON P6A 5N3 – 705/759-3000 – Late January/early February. Ten days

Bracebridge Winter Carnival, c/o, PO Box 578, Bracebridge ON P1L 1T8 – 705/645-8121 – February

Calgary Winter Festival, #710, 237 - 8 Ave. SE, Calgary AB T2G 5C3 – 403/268-2688 – February

Carnaval de Québec, 290, rue Joly, Quebec PQ G1L 1N8 – 418/626-3716 – Eleven days, major winter event, February

Carnaval-Souvenir de Chicoutimi, 67, Jacques-Cartier ouest, Chicoutimi PQ G7J 1E9 – 418/543-4438; Fax: 418/543-4884 – Ten days, major winter event, February

Charlottetown Winter Carnival, PO Box 3027, Charlottetown PE C1A 7N9 – 902/892-5708 – February

Conception Bay South Winterfest, Conception Bay South NF – 709/834-2093 – February

Corner Brook Winter Carnival, c/o, PO Box 886, Corner Brook NF A2H 6H6 – 709/634-4039 – Annually, 10 days, February

Elliot Lake Winterfest, c/o, PO Box 1, Elliot Lake ON P5A 1Z5 – 705/461-7233 – February

Fête des Neiges, Parc des Îles, Île Notre-Dame, CP 805, Succ C, Montréal PQ H2L 4L6 – 514/872-0210; Fax: 514/872-9315 – Ten day major winter event. Sports, cultural, ice sculptures, February

Hamilton Winterfest, c/o 555 Bay St. North, Hamilton ON L8L 1H1 – 905/546-4646 – February

Huntsville Winter Wonderfest, c/o, PO Box 1470, Huntsville ON P0A 1K0 – 705/789-8113 – February

Jasper in January, c/o, PO Box 98, Jasper AB T0E 1E0 – 403/852-3858; Fax: 403/852-4932 – January

Kapuskasing Winter Carnival, 88 Riverside Dr., Kapuskasing ON P5N 1B3 – 705/335-2341 – February & March

Kirkland Lake Winter Carnival, c/o PO Bag 1757, Kirkland Lake ON P2N 3P4 – 705/567-9361 – March

Labrador City Winter Carnival, PO Box 1237, Wabush NF A0R 1B0 – 709/944-3602; Fax: 709/282-5106

Mount Pearl Frosty Festival, Mount Pearl NF – 709/748-1008 – February

Canadian Almanac & Directory 1997

Nova Scotia Smelt Tournament, 2228 Conquerall Rd., Bridgewater NS B4V 2W3 – 902/543-7090; Fax: 902/543-7966 – Largest ice fishing tournament, Eastern Canada, February

Peterborough Snofest, c/o 135 George St. North, Peterborough ON K9J 3G6 – 705/748-8827 – January

Prince Albert Winter Festival, PO Box 1388, Prince Albert SK S6V 5S9 – 306/764-7595 – February

Red Deer Family Winter Fest, c/o Recreation & Culture Dept., PO Box 5008, Red Deer AB T4N 3T4 – 403/342-6100, 346-0180 – February

Regina Waskimo Winter Festival, PO Box 7111, Regina SK S4P 3S7 – 306/522-3661 – Annual – February

Richmond Hill Winter Carnival, c/o, PO Box 155, Richmond Hill ON L4C 4Y2 – 905/737-6101 – January

Riverview Winter Carnival, 30 Honour House Court, Riverview NB E1B 3Y9 – 506/387-2037; Fax: 506/387-7455 – February

Salmon Arm Winterfest, c/o, PO Box 669, Salmon Arm BC V1E 4N8 – 250/832-6247 – January

Saskatoon Winterfest, c/o Meewasin Valley Authority, 402 - 3rd Ave. South, Saskatoon SK S7K 3G5 – 306/665-6887

Sudbury Snowflake Festival, c/o 100 Elm St., Sudbury ON P3C 1T5 – 705/523-2006 – February

Vernon Winter Carnival, 3303 - 35th Ave., Vernon BC V1T 2T5 – 250/545-2236; Fax: 250/545-0006 – February

Winterfest, Gander NF – 709/651-2930 – February

Winterlude, 161 Laurier Ave. West, Ottawa ON K1P 6J6 – 613/239-5145; Fax: 613/239-5333 – Ten days. Major winter event. Rideau Canal skating, snow & ice sculptures, figure skating shows, North America's largest & unique winter playground for children "Sub Zero Connection", Triathlon, 10 km run, February

Winterlude, Grand Falls-Windsor NF – 709/489-2728 – February

WOMEN

Calgary Woman's Show, Avatar Productions (1989) Ltd., #222, 8 Parkdale Cres. NW, Calgary AB T2N 3T8 – 403/270-7274; Fax: 403/270-8739 – President, Judy Markle – Annual consumer show: products & services, October – Calgary AB

Toronto Women's Show, Toronto Women's Show Inc., PO Box 6465, Stn A, Toronto ON M5W 1X3 – 905/274-0888; Fax: 905/274-0434 – Show Manager, Brian MacLean – Annual consumer show, March – Queen Elizabeth Bldg., Exhibition Place, Toronto ON

Women in Focus, Classic Moment Creative Events, 1255 Delta Ave., Kamloops BC V2B 3Y4 – 250/376-7934; Fax: 250/376-7927 – Event Producer/Owner, Judy Basso – Annual spring trade show, work shops

Women on the Go, Custom Show Management Inc., #300, 2085 Hurontario St., Mississauga ON L5A 4G1 – 905/949-5550; Fax: 905/949-6903 – Show Manager, Brian McLean – Consumer show. Food, fashion, investments, health, March

Women's Showcase, PO Box 29217, London ON N6K 1M6 – 519/472-8565 – Contact, Diann Vail – Annual consumer show, winter. Fashion, health, business, home

World of Women, 3017 - 50 Ave., Red Deer AB T4N 5Y6 – 403/347-4491; Fax: 403/343-6188 – Contact, Tricia Kennedy – September

WOOD/WOODWORKING

The Brantford Woodshow, PO Box 852, Brantford ON N3T 5R7 – 519/449-2444; Fax: 519/449-2445 – Manager, Paul Fulcher – Annual consumer show, November

Calgary Woodworking Expo, DJC Enterprises, PO Box 49128, Calgary AB T2C 3W5 – 403/236-0192; Fax: 403/236-5834 – Donna Capiak – Annual trade & consumer show, January – Calgary AB

Salon Industriel du Bois Ouvre, Reed Exhibition Companies Inc., 3761 Victoria Park Ave., Scarborough ON M1W 3S2 – 416/491-7565; Fax: 416/491-5088 – Show Coordinator, Elaine Nichol – Biennial trade show, September 1998 – Montréal PQ

Salon Techni Bois, Les Promotions André Pageau Inc., 1627, boul St-Joseph, Québec PQ G2K 1H1 – 418/623-3383; Fax: 418/623-5033 – Président, André Pageau – Biennial trade show, May 1998 – Québec PQ

Wood Expo, Southex Exhibitions, 1450 Don Mills Rd., North York ON M3B 2X7 – 416/445-6641; Fax: 416/442-2207 – Annual trade show, September

Woodworking Machinery & Supply Expo, Reed Exhibition Companies Inc., 3761 Victoria Park Ave., Scarborough ON M1W 3S2 – 416/491-7565; Fax: 416/491-5088 – Show Coordinator, Elaine Nichol – Biennial trade show; industrial woodworking & furniture manufacturing equipment, systems, supplies & finishing machinery, October 1997

Woodworking Show, Cryderman Productions, 136 Thames St., Chatham ON N7L 2Y8 – 519/351-8344; Fax: 519/351-8345 – John Cryderman – Annual consumer show held in various locations (Edmonton, Ottawa, Surrey); woodworking products

CANADIAN AWARDS

(including Scholarships, Grants, Bursaries)

Awards are listed under the following categories:

Advertising & Public Relations	1-92
Agriculture & Farming	1-92
Broadcasting & Film	1-93
Business & Trade	1-94
Citizenship & Bravery	1-95
Culture, Visual Arts & Architecture	1-96
Educational	1-97
Environmental	1-99
Health & Medical	1-101
Journalism	1-102
Legal, Governmental, Public Administration	1-103
Literary Arts, Books & Libraries	1-104
Performing Arts	1-108
Public Affairs	1-110
Scientific, Engineering, Technical	1-111
Sports & Recreation	1-112

NOTE: Contact people for awards are listed at the end of the award description, where available.

ADVERTISING & PUBLIC RELATIONS

The Advertising & Design Club of Canada
#207, 109 Vanderhoof Ave., Toronto ON M4G 2H7
416/423-4113; Fax: 416/422-3762

The Advertising & Design Club of Canada Awards
Main categories of awards are: Advertising/Broadcast, Multimedia, Advertising/Print, Graphic Design & Editorial; winners receive gold awards, silver awards or merit awards

Association of Canadian Advertisers Inc. / Association canadienne des annonceurs
South Tower, #307, 175 Bloor St. East, Toronto ON M4W 3R8
416/964-3805; Fax: 416/964-0771; Toll Free: 1-800-565-0109; Email: aca@sympatico.ca

ACA Gold Medal
Established in 1941 to encourage high standards of personal achievement in advertising - for introducing new concepts or techniques, for significantly improving existing practices, or for enhancing the stature of advertising

Canadian Direct Marketing Association / Association canadienne du marketing direct
#607, One Concorde Gate, North York ON M3C 3N6
416/391-2362; Fax: 416/441-4062; Email: kbrasch@cdma.org; URL: http://www.cdma.org

RSVP Awards
21 categories of direct response awards, including Canada Post's Vic Perry Award for the best direct mail campaign of the year; Director's Choice Award for the company judged by the CDMA Board of Directors to have made the most outstanding contribution to direct marketing industry; Dream Team Award recognizes excellence among direct marketing suppliers; open to both CDMA members & non-members; direct response campaigns from all media are considered

Institute of Canadian Advertising
#500, 2300 Yonge St., PO Box 2350, Toronto ON M4P 1E4
416/482-1396; Fax: 416/481-1856; Toll Free: 1-800-567-7422; Email: ica@goodmedia.com; URL: http://www1.goodmedia.com/ica/

Cassie Awards
Established 1993; jointly administered with the Association of Canadian Advertisers; Cassies - an acronym for Canadian Advertising Success Stories - are judged on their effectiveness in attaining the advertiser's objectives; 10 gold awards presented bi-annually

Marketing Magazine
777 Bay St., 5th Fl., Toronto ON M5W 1A7
416/596-5858; Fax: 416/593-3170

The Marketing Awards
Annual advertising awards offering 20 Gold Awards in the following categories: television/cinema, radio, magazine, newspaper, transit, business press, direct mail, outdoor, point-of-purchase/interior store design, multimedia campaign, & public service. Silver Awards, Bronze Awards, & Certificates of Excellences are also awarded. Entries must have run in the previous year & must have been conceived & created by people working in English in the Canadian advertising business

Outdoor Advertising Association of Canada / L'Association canadienne de l'affichage extérieur
#100, 21 St. Clair Ave. East, Toronto ON M4T 1L9
416/968-3435; Fax: 416/968-0154

Billi Awards
Established in 1978, the awards recognize creative excellence in English outdoor ad design, primarily in billboard & transit-shelter formats

Le Publicité club de Montréal
4316, boul Saint-Laurent, 4e étage, Montréal PQ H2W 1Z3
514/842-5681; Email: pubclub@cam.org; URL: http://www.pcm.montreal.qc.ca/

Les Prix coq d'or
Definitive French language advertising awards

AGRICULTURE & FARMING

Canadian Society of Animal Science / Société canadienne de zootechnie
#907, 151 Slater St., Ottawa ON K1P 5H4
613/232-9459; Fax: 613/594-5190

Canadian Animal Industries Award in Extension & Public Service
Recognizes outstanding service to the animal industries of Canada in technology transfer, leadership & education in animal production

Canadian Association of Animal Breeder's Award for Excellence in Genetics & Physiology
Recognizes excellence in teaching, research, or extension in the area of animal breeding or physiology

Shurgain Award for Excellence in Nutrition & Meat Sciences
Awarded to recognize excellence in teaching, research, or extension in the area of animal nutrition or meat science

Provincial Exhibition of Manitoba
#3, 1175 - 18th St., Brandon MB R7A 7C5
204/726-3590; Fax: 204/725-0202

Royal Manitoba Winter Fair Awards
Prizes given in various categories for best of show for agricultural products, animals & crops; several equestrian events offer prizes for best in competition

Royal Agricultural Winter Fair Association / Foire agricole royale d'hiver
Coliseum, Exhibition Place, Toronto ON M6K 3C3
416/393-6400; Fax: 416/393-6488; Email: rwfair@io.org;
  URL: http://www.royalfair.org

Agricultural Awards
Grand Champion is the highest honour in the following categories: dairy, beef, sheep, goats, swine, market livestock, field crops, vegetables, honey & maple, poultry, jams/jellies/pickles, dairy products, square dancing, fiddling, fleece wool, rabbits, & eight youth activities

Breeding Horse Awards
17 sections award prizes in this category

Performance Horse Awards
35 divisions & classes offer prizes; Leading International Rider is the highest honour in the horse show

ARCHITECTURE see CULTURE, VISUAL ARTS & ARCHITECTURE

ART see CULTURE, VISUAL ARTS & ARCHITECTURE

BRAVERY see CITIZENSHIP & BRAVERY

BROADCASTING & FILM

Academy of Canadian Cinema & Television / Académie canadienne du cinéma et de la télévision
158 Pearl St., Toronto ON M5H 1L3
416/591-2040; Fax: 416/591-2157; Toll Free: 1-800-644-5194; URL: http://www.academy.ca

Prix Gémeaux
For excellence & achievement in French-language television production; held annually & presented in 50 categories covering Programs, Performance & Crafts; nominations & voting by peer groups composed of academy members

The Gemini Awards
The nationally telecast awards for excellence & achievement in Canadian television production are awarded annually & presented to winners in more than 50 categories covering Best Program, Best Performance & Best Craft, as well as three special awards following nomination & voting by a peer group

The Genie Awards
The nationally telecast Genie Awards celebrate excellence in Canadian cinema. The annual awards cover 21 categories from Best Picture to Best Sound, as well as the Air Canada Award for outstanding contribution to the business of filmmaking, the Golden Reel award for the top Canadian box office gross. Special achievement awards are voted by members of the academy. The Claude Jutra Award for Direction of a First Feature Film was added in 1993

Alberta Motion Picture Industries Association
606 Midland Walwyn Tower, Edmonton Centre, Edmonton AB T5J 2Z2
403/944-0707; Fax: 403/426-3057

Alberta Film & Television Awards
Annual awards established in 1973; "Rosies" presented to Albertans responsible for creating outstanding film & television works; presentation alternates between Calgary & Edmonton

Billington Awards
Lifetime achievement in the motion picture industry in Alberta

The Alliance for Children & Television / Alliance pour l'enfant et la télévision
#205, 344 Dupont St., Toronto ON M5R 1V9
416/515-0466; Fax: 416/515-0467; Email: acttv@interlog.com

Awards of Excellence
For children's TV programs produced in Canada

Banff Television Festival
PO Box 219, Banff AB T0L 0C0
403/678-9260; Fax: 403/678-9269; Email: banfftv@screen.com; URL: http://www.cochran.com/banfftv

Banff Rockie Awards
Annual televisions awards for: made-for-TV-movies; mini-series; continuing series; short dramas; comedies; social & political documentaries; popular science programs; arts documentaries; performance specials & children's programs. Also a grand prize winner & two special jury awards. All entries must be made for television & either in English or French

Canwest Global Outstanding Achievement Award
Given annually to an individual, organization or production unit for exceptional achievement

Canadian Association of Broadcasters / Association canadienne des radiodiffuseurs
#306, 350 Sparks St., PO Box 627, Stn B, Ottawa ON K1P 5S2
613/233-4035; Fax: 613/233-6961; URL: http://www.cab-acr.ca

BBM Scholarship
Established in 1986; $2,500 awarded annually to a student in a course of study at a Canadian university or post-secondary institution who has demonstrated achievement in & knowledge of statistical &/or quantitative research methodology

Gold Ribbon Awards
Awarded for: Broadcast Excellence, Canadian Radio Station Promotion, Canadian Talent Development, Canadian TV Program Promotion, Community Service, Engineering Achievement, News, News Series, & Public Affairs & Documentation; awarded to AM, FM &/or television stations or networks

Radio-mutuel Bursary
Established 1975; a $5,000 award offered by Radio-mutuel Network; open to any French-speaking Canadian citizen interested in improving radio &/or television skills through university training or the equivalent (on a full-time basis) in a Canadian institution

Ruth Hancock Memorial Scholarship
$1,500 award established jointly in 1975 by the Broadcast Executives Society & the CTV Television Network in cooperation with C.A.B; presented annually to three Canadian students enrolled in recognized communications courses

T.J.(Jim) Allard Broadcast Journalism Scholarship
Established 1983; $2,500 awarded annually to the student who best combines academic achievement with natural talent

Canadian Conference of the Arts / Conférence canadienne des arts
189 Laurier Ave. West, Ottawa ON K1N 6P1
613/238-3561; Fax: 613/238-4849; Toll Free: 1-800-463-3561; Email: ccarts@globalx.net

Rogers Communications Inc. Media Award for Coverage of the Arts
Established 1991; recognizes & appreciates the consistent &/or innovative creation & production of arts programming in the Canadian electronic media; nominations are made by CCA members & by media colleagues

Canadian Film & Television Production Association / Association canadienne de production de film et télévision
#806, 175 Bloor St. East, Toronto ON M4W 3R8
416/927-8942; Fax: 416/922-4038

Chetwynd Award for Entrepreneurial Excellence
Sponsored by Atlantis Films & presented to an individual or partnership that has demonstrated private sector entrepreneurial achievement in the motion picture &/or television industry

Jack Chisholm Award for Lifetime Contribution
Sponsored by Kodak Canada & presented to an individual who has demonstrated noteworthy contributions to the success & progress of the motion picture &/or television industry

Canadian Heritage
Jules Léger Bldg., 6th Fl., 25 Eddy St., Hull PQ K1A 0H3
819/997-76032

Jeanne Sauvé Award for Women in Communications
Established in 1994; jointly administered by the Department of Canadian Heritage & Canadian Women in Radio & Television; the award takes the form of three-month internships with Canadian Heritage enabling the winners to gain first-hand knowledge & insight into federal communications policy & legislation – Contact, Alison Taylor, 819/990-4152

Canadian International Annual Film/Video Festival
25 Eugenia St., Barrie ON L4M 1P6
705/737-2729

Canadian International Annual Film/Video Awards
Awards in three categories: amateur film/video maker; independent film/video maker, & pre-professional students of film/video

The Canadian Network for the Advancement of Research, Industry & Education
#470, 410 Laurier Ave. West, Ottawa ON K1P 6H5
613/660-3634; Fax: 613/660-3806; Email: info@canarie.ca; URL: http://www.canarie.ca

Canada's National Iway Award
Awards recognize accomplishments of individuals who have demonstrated leadership in the development of Canada's emerging information society in the following categories: Product Development for an individual who has demonstrated creativity & leadership in the design & implementation of a product which supports the development & application of the Information Highway in Canada; Education/Public Awareness for an individual who has initiated uses of Canada's Information Highway that improve the quality, effectiveness, access to &/or outcome of education & training programs in educational institutions; Government Services for an individual who has initiated uses of Canada's Information Highway that save time & taxpayer dollars in the conduct of government operations. Co-sponsored by the Canadian Advanced Technology Association

Canadian Scene News Services for the Ethnic Media
#301, 73 Simcoe St., Toronto ON M5J 1W9

Canadian Almanac & Directory 1997

416/593-0439; Fax: 416/593-0448
Canadian Scene Awards
Established 1991 to mark the 40th anniversary of the multilingual news service; one plaque is given to an individual for an article &/or a radio/television program best promoting intercultural understanding

Canadian Society of Cinematographers
#602, 235 Carlaw Ave., Toronto ON M4M 2S1
416/466-5013
Canadian Society of Cinematography Awards
Twelve awards given annually: Best Commercial Cinematography; Best Documentary Cinematography; Best Dramatic Short; Best Industrial Cinematography; Best TV Series Cinematography; Best Unique Cinematography; The Bill Hilson Award for Outstanding Achievement; The Fuji Award; The Kodak New Century Award; The Roy Tash Newsfilm Award; The Stan Clinton News Essay Award, & The Telefilm Canada Student Cinematography Award

Festival international du court métrage de Montréal / Montréal International Short Film Festival
#326, 4205, rue St-Denis, Montréal PQ H2J 2K9
514/285-4515; Fax: 514/285-2886
International Animation Competition
The following prizes are awarded for the best international animated short film (includes Canadian entries): Grand Prize of $1,000 to the director; TV 5 Kaleidoscope Prize, & Public Prize
International Competition
The following prizes are awarded for the best international short films (includes Canadian entries): Grand Prize, $2,000 for the director; Société Radio-Canada Prize; Best Screenplay; Youth Prize; Public Prize; C/FP Prize
Long Night of the Short
Prize given for the most bizarre film
Québec University Competition & Québec College Competition
Prizes given for the best short film produced by university students & the best produced by college students

ITVA CANADA
PO Box 1156, Stn Adelaide, Toronto ON M5C 2K5
416/733-3757; Fax: 416/733-1741; Email: itvacda@informap.net
ITVA Canada Awards
Variety of awards presented annually including: Best Script, Best Editing, Technical Imagery, Production Achievement, Student Achievement & Training Award

National Screen Institute - Canada / Institute national des arts de l'écran - Canada
10022 - 103 St., 3rd Fl., Edmonton AB T5J 0X2
403/421-4084; Fax: 403/425-8098; Toll Free: 1-800-480-4084; Email: filmhero@nsi-canada.ca; URL: http://www.nsi-canada.ca
Drama Prize
This national competition for emerging filmmakers has three components - competition, production/training, exhibition; the completed productions are premiered at the Local Heroes Film Festival
Six teams receive prizes of $6,000 each towards the production of a 10 minute dramatic film, augmented by up to $5,500 in equipment & services sponsorships; as well, an established filmmaker in their area acts as the production's mentor & assists in script development, fundraising & finding distribution opportunities

Société Radio-Canada
Service des émissions culturelles
1400, boul René-Lévesque est, 15e étage, Montréal PQ H2L 2M2
514/597-4510; Fax: 514/597-4807; URL: http://www.src-mtl.com/

Concours d'oeuvres dramatiques radiophoniques de Radio-Canada
Ce concours a été lancé en 1972 par Radio-Canada dans le but de susciter la création d'oeuvres dramatiques écrites spécialement pour la radio; les oeuvres doivent être conçues et rédigées en vue d'une création radiophonique de 30 minutes (1er prix 2 500 $, 2e prix 1 500 $) et de 15 minutes (1er prix 1 500 $, 2e prix 1 000 $)
Concours de nouvelles de Radio-Canada
Nature du prix: 1er prix 2 000 $, 2e prix 1 500 $, et 3e prix 1 000 $

Toronto International Film Festival / Festival international du film de Toronto
2 Carlton St., 16th Fl., Toronto ON M5B 1J3
416/967-7371; Fax: 416/967-9477; URL: http://www.bell.ca/toronto/filmfest
Air Canada People's Choice Award
Sponsored by Air Canada & voted best film of the festival by festival audiences
Metro Media Award & FIPRESCI Award
Metro Media Award is voted by the press corps at the festival, & the FIPRESCI Award is voted by the international film critics attending the festival
NFB - John Spotton Award for Best Canadian Short Film
Sponsored by the National Film Board, the award carries a prize of $2,500 towards the filmmaker's next film with an additional $2,500 in film processing from the NFB
Toronto-City Award for Best Canadian Feature Film
Jointly sponsored by the City of Toronto & Citytv; $25,000 awarded to the Best Canadian Feature Film

TVOntario
2180 Yonge St., PO Box 200, Stn Q, Toronto ON M4T 2T1
416/484-2600; Fax: 416/484-2725; URL: http://www.tvo.org/
Prix TVOntario Awards
Established 1991 to showcase the best educational broadcasters in Canada, the United States & abroad; awarded every two years

BUSINESS & TRADE

Alberta Economic Development & Tourism
Commerce Place, 4th Fl., 10155 - 102 St., Edmonton AB T5J 4L6
403/427-6291; Fax: 403/422-9127; Email: kellejer@censsw.gov.ab.ca
The Alberta Business Awards of Distinction
Seven annual awards in the following categories: Business Service Award of Distinction for achievement for a business providing services to businesses; Environment Business Award of Distinction for a business demonstrating outstanding achievement in developing &/or marketing products or services preventing environment degradation; Export Award of Distinction for a business which has demonstrated outstanding achievement in exporting outside Alberta; Manufacturers Award of Distinction; Marketing Award of Distinction; Small Business Award of Distinction, & Tourism Award of Distinction for outstanding achievement in promoting tourism in Alberta

Caldwell Partners
64 Prince Artnur Ave., Toronto ON M5R 1B4
416/920-7702; Fax: 416/922-8646
Outstanding CEO of the Year Award
The annual award takes into consideration the candidate's leadership, innovation, business achievements, corporate performance, social responsibility, sense of vision & global competitiveness
Top 40 Under 40
Established in 1996 & sponsored by CIBC, Canadian Airlines, CTV, the Financial Post & Caldwell Partners; recognizes 40 of Canada's new entrepreneurs, executives & professionals who have reached a level of success but haven't yet reached 40 years of age - Contact: 1-800-688-5540

Canadian Association of Family Enterprise / Association canadienne des enterprises familiales
CAFE - UC
1163 Sylvester St., PO Box 136, Lefroy ON L0L 1W0
800/760-8882; Fax: 800/760-8883; URL: http://www.cafe-uc.on.ca/
CAFE-Jaguar Award for Family Enterprise of the Year
Established to recognize the importance of family enterprise; looks at: job creation, technological advancement, environment, innovation & entrepeneurial success; open to any family enterprise, private or publicly owned

The Conference Board of Canada
255 Smyth Rd., Ottawa ON K1N 6C3
613/526-3280; Fax: 613/526-4857
National Awards for Excellence in Business-Education Partnership
Awarded to partnerships that have a demonstrated record of success in promoting the importance of science, technology &/or mathematics; linking education & the world of work, promoting teacher development, encouraging students to stay in school, expanding vocational &/or appreticeship training – Contact, Bonnie Coulombe

Entrepreneur of the Year Institute
Ernst & Young Tower, TD Centre, 222 Bay St., PO Box 251, Toronto ON M5K 1J7
416/943-3144; Fax: 416/943-3767; Toll Free: 1-800-268-3937
Entrepreneur of the Year
Founded in 1994 & co-sponsored by Ernest & Young, Canadian Business magazine, Bank of Montréal, Nesbitt Burns, McCarthy Tétrault, & Air Canada, the awards recognize successful business owners & also promote the beneficial impact the entrepreneurial spirit has on Canada's local & national economies; nominees must be owner-managers who are primarily responsible for the recent performance of their company; regional winners are honoured in fall banquets across the country & the national Entrepreneur of the Year award recipients are announced in October or November

The Financial Post
333 King St. East, Toronto ON M5A 4N2
416/350-6200; Fax: 416/350-6201
Financial Post Annual Reports Awards
Presented annually in 12 industry categories for excellence in communicating with shareholders & the public

Foreign Affairs & International Trade Canada
Canada Export Award Program, Intl. Trade Centres & Export Education, 125 Sussex Dr., Tower C, 5th Fl., Ottawa ON K1A 0G2
Fax: 613/996-8688; Toll Free: 1-800-267-8376
Canada Export Award
Honours those firms from across Canada who have demonstrated superior performance in the export arena
Open to all firms or divisions of firms resident in Canada, that have been exporting goods or services for three or more years; this includes trading houses & banks, as well as transport, market research, packaging & promotion firms; selection is based on but not limited to the extent to which the firm has shown significant increases in its export sales, success in breaking into new markets, success in introducing export products into world markets; other achievements by firms in export markets that contribute to Canada's economic

well-being or to the reputation of the organization as a world-class exporter will also be considered
Award is a plaque bearing the Canada Export Award logo & a brief citation of the firm's accomplishments; firms receiving an award are welcome to use the logo on their letterhead, advertisements & other promotional material for a period of up to three years after its presentation; national & local promotion will be given to firms receiving the award

The Group for Design in Business
c/o The Design Exchange, 234 Bay St., PO Box 18, Toronto ON M5K 1B2
416/368-3626; Fax: 416/367-9743
Financial Post Design Effectiveness Awards
Awards offered in the following categories: Design of Consumer Products, Design of Business & Industrial Products, Interactive Design, Package Design, Marketing Communications Design, Design of Corporate or Brand Identities, Architectural Design, Design of Public & Recreational Spaces, & Design of Retail & Entertainment Environments. Also Best of Show & Environmental Innovation awards

National Quality Institute / Institut national de la qualité
#1540, 360 Albert St., Ottawa ON K1R 7X7
613/237-4111; Fax: 613/237-7171; Toll Free: 1-800-263-9648; Email: info@nqionline.com; URL: http://www.nqi.com
Canada Awards for Excellence
Previously called the Canada Awards for Business Excellence & established by the Government of Canada in 1984, the awards have been expanded to recognize excellence in Education, Government & Health Care; those who apply for the Canada Awards for Excellence will receive a confidential assessment & written feedback report from the examiners on how far their organization has travelled on the road to excellence
Winners receive export assistance to help them access world markets, exposure through national advertising, & lifetime use of the Canada Awards for Excellence logo on corporate literature & products

National Transportation Week Inc.
2323 St. Laurent Blvd., Ottawa ON K1G 4K6
613/736-1350; Fax: 613/736-1395
Award of Achievement
Established 1987; awarded to those who have brought about positive & measurable developments of significant & lasting benefit to transportation in Canada
Award of Excellence
Established 1975; for an outstanding contribution to the betterment of the transportation industry

Ontario Fashion Exhibitors Inc.
#219, 111 Peter St., Toronto ON M5V 2H1
416/596-2401; Fax: 416/596-1808
The Judy Awards
Established 1958; presented every two years to honour retailers, the media, shopping centres, & manufacturers for their outstanding contribution to the Canadian fashion industry

University of Alberta
Faculty of Business, 25 University Campus NW, Calgary AB T6G 2E8
403/492-5693; Fax: 403/492-2997; URL: http://www.registrar.ualberta.ca/awards/awards.html
Canadian Business Leader Award
Annual award recognizes distinguished professional achievements & contributions to the community

The Women's Entrepreneurship Program
The Joseph L. Rotman Centre for Management, Univ. of Toronto, 105 George St., Toronto ON M5S 3E6
416/978-5703; Fax: 416/978-5433; Email: mbaprog@fmgmt.mgmt.utoronto.ca; URL: http://www.mgmt.utoronto.ca
Canadian Woman Entrepreneur of the Year Awards
Start-Up Award for a woman in business at least three years, but less than five, whose venture provides a product, service or marketing strategy that is innovative & supported by a solid plan for growth; Lifetime Achievement Award for a woman who has owned her business for at least 20 years; Quality Plus Award for demonstrated ability to develop & maintain excellence; Impact on Local Economy Award for a woman who has contributed significantly to the development of local economy through her business; International Competitiveness Award for a company that has increased sales by developing global markets, & Turnaround Award for a woman who has applied management skills to revitalize a declining or moribund business

CINEMA see BROADCASTING & FILM

CITIZENSHIP & BRAVERY

Bridgestone/Firestone Canada Inc.
#400, 5770 Hurontario St., Mississauga ON L5R 3G5
905/890-1990; Fax: 905/890-1991
National Truck Hero Award
Established 1956; endorsed by the Canada Safety Council, the Traffic Injury Research Foundation & the trucking industry; designed to promote highway safety by focusing public attention on acts of bravery performed by professional Canadian truck drivers in the course of their daily work

The Canadian Council of Christians & Jews / Conseil canadien des chrétiens et des juifs
#600, 44 Victoria St., Toronto ON M5C 1Y2
416/364-3101; Fax: 416/364-5705; Toll Free: 1-800-663-1848; Email: cccj@interlog.com; URL: http://www.interlog.com/~cccj/
Good Servant Medal
Created to commemorate the retirement of Richard D. Jones, O.C., LL.D., after 30 years of continuous service to CCCJ, as founder & principal officer, 1947-1977; recognizes individuals who have rendered extraordinary service to their community beyond the call of duty without seeking public recognition

The Canadian Council of the Blind / Le Conseil canadien des aveugles
#405, 396 Cooper St., Ottawa ON K2P 2H7
613/567-0311; Fax: 613/567-2728
Book of Fame Citation
The Book of Fame was donated to the Council in 1958 by the disbanded Comrades Club of Toronto; it contains the names & citations of outstanding blind Canadians selected yearly by the eight divisions & the National Board of Directors of the Council; each recipient of a citation is presented with a framed photograph of the appropriate page in the book

Canadian Decorations for Bravery
Canadian Decorations Advisory Committee, Rideau Hall, One Sussex Drive, Ottawa ON K1A 0A1
613/993-8200; Fax: 613/990-7636
Canadian Decorations for Bravery
The Canadian Honours System provides three decorations for Bravery to express the nation's gratitude to those people who risk their lives to save or protect others, defying in the process the instinct for self-preservation. See the Canadian Honours List in this section for a list of recent recipients

Canadian Native Arts Foundation / Fondation canadienne des arts autochtones
#508, 77 Mowat Ave., Toronto ON M6K 3E3
416/588-3328; Fax: 416/588-9198
National Aboriginal Achievement Awards
Established in 1993 & awarded to aboriginal achievers from the First Nations, Inuit & Metis communities; nominees are outstanding achievers working in any occupational area

The Duke of Edinburgh's Award
#406, 207 Queens Quay West, PO Box 124, Toronto ON M5J 1A7
416/203-0674; Fax: 416/203-0676
Young Canadians Challenge
Established in Canada in 1963 with His Royal Highness Prince Philip as Patron, the award recognizes personal achievement in a voluntary program of activities by young people in the age range of 14-25
Open to all Canadian youth; young people participate independently or through youth groups, clubs, schools, etc.; program is operated throughout Canada, with divisional offices located in each of the ten provinces
Award is in the form of a pin & an inscribed certificate representing Gold, Silver, & Bronze levels; Gold awards are presented by His Excellency The Governor General of Canada, or a member of the Royal Family, at national awards ceremonies

The National Citizens' Coalition
#907, 100 Adelaide St. West, Toronto ON M5H 1S3
416/869-3838; Fax: 416/869-1891
The Colin M. Brown Freedom Medal
Established 1987; a medal is awarded annually to an individual who best typified the principles of political & economic freedom which the Coalition espouses

National Transportation Week Inc.
2323 St. Laurent Blvd., Ottawa ON K1G 4K6
613/736-1350; Fax: 613/736-1395
Award of Valor
Established 1979; awarded for "an exemplary act of bravery in perilous circumstances"

Ontario Ministry of Citizenship, Culture & Recreation
Ontario Honours & Awards
77 Bloor St. West, 15th Fl., Toronto ON M7A 2R9
416/314-7526; Fax: 416/314-7743
The Ontario Medal for Firefighters Bravery
Established 1976 to recognize acts of superlative courage & bravery performed in the line of duty by members of Ontario's firefighting forces
The Ontario Medal for Good Citizenship
Established 1973 to recognize & pay tribute to citizens who, through their selflessness, humanity & kindness, make Ontario a better province in which to live
The Ontario Medal for Police Bravery
Established 1976 to recognize acts of superlative courage & bravery performed in the line of duty by members of Ontario's police forces
The Order of Ontario
Established 1986 to recognize those men & women who have rendered service of the greatest distinction & of singular excellence in all fields of endeavour benefiting society in Ontario & elsewhere

The Royal Bank of Canada
1, Place Ville-Marie, 4e étage sud, Montréal PQ H3C 3A9
514/874-8549; Fax: 514/874-3890
Royal Bank Award
Established 1967 to acknowledge the accomplishments of Canadian citizens, or persons living in Canada, whose unique work has benefited society at large
Candidate must be a Canadian citizen or a person domiciled in Canada; award may be shared & not necessarily conferred each year; institutions & corporations are not eligible; award consists of a gold medal & $125,000 to the winner & $125,000 to be donated to the winner's charity of choice

Canadian Almanac & Directory 1997

St. John Ambulance / Ambulance Saint-Jean
312 Laurier Ave. East, Ottawa ON K1N 6P6
613/236-7461; Fax: 613/236-2425
St. John Life Saving Medals
Awarded to individuals who, in a conspicuous act of gallantry, have endangered their lives to save a life

Toronto Life Fashion Magazine
59 Front St. East, 3rd Fl., Toronto ON M5E 1B3
416/364-3333; Fax: 416/861-1169
Women Who Make a Difference
Awarded annually to Toronto area women who have had noteworthy success in their field & who have made a vital contribution to life in the city; awards are given in the following categories: Business Professional, Community Affairs, Entrepreneur, Media, Performing Arts, Sports, & Visual Arts – Contact, Publicity & Promotion Director, Susan Elliot

United Nations Association in Canada / Association canadienne pour les Nations-Unies
#900, 130 Slater St., Ottawa ON K1P 6E2
613/232-5751; Fax: 613/563-2455; Email: unac@magi.com
Pearson Peace Medal
Awarded to a Canadian who has contibuted significantly to humanitarian causes

YTV Canada Inc.
64 Jefferson Ave., Unit 18, Toronto ON M6K 3H3
416/534-1191; Fax: 416/533-0346
YTV Achievement Awards
Recognize outstanding accomplishments & contributions made to society by young Canadians (19 years or younger) in: Acting, Band, Bravery, Dance, Entrepreneurship, Environmental, Innovation, Instrumental, Public Service, Specialty Performance, Sports, Terry Fox Award (for spirit & determination), Visual Arts, Vocal, & Writing
$3,000 & a statuette presented on the YTV awards show each spring

COMMUNICATIONS see JOURNALISM

CRAFTS see CULTURE, VISUAL ARTS & ARCHITECTURE

CULTURE, VISUAL ARTS & ARCHITECTURE

Arts Foundation of Greater Toronto
#402, 151 John St., Toronto ON M5V 2T2
416/597-8223; Fax: 416/597-6956
The Toronto Arts Awards
Awarded annually to encourage & promote the creative arts in Toronto; award recipients must be Canadian citizens, landed immigrants or long-term residents of Canada & must show that they have had an ongoing association with Toronto & have contributed significantly to the arts & culture of the city
Eight awards of $2,500 to purchase or commission an original work by a less-established Toronto artist are presented covering the following disciplines: media arts, writing & publishing, performing arts, music, visual arts, architecture & design, & two for lifetime achievement

The Canada Council / Conseil des Arts du Canada
350 Albert St., PO Box 1047, Ottawa ON K1P 5V8
613/566-4365; Fax: 613/566-4390; Toll Free: 1-800-263-5588
Note: At the time of going to press, the awards program at the Canada Council was being reviewed & changes may be made. Please contact the Council directly for more detailed information.

Bell Canada Award in Video Art
$10,000 awarded annually to a Canadian video artist who has made an exceptional contribution to the advancement of video art in Canada & to the development of video languages & practices in his/her videotapes or video installations
Candidates are nominated by three professional curators &/or critics who are specialists in Canadian video art, to be appointed annually by the Media Arts Section of the Canada Council; the winner is selected by the jury of professional video artists convened to assess the Arts Grant "A" applications in video art
Canada Council Molson Prizes
Two prizes of $50,000 each awarded annually to distinguished Canadians, one in the arts, one in social sciences & humanities; to acknowledge Canadian citizens whose contributions have enriched the cultural or intellectual heritage of Canada & to encourage Canadians honoured with this distinction to continue contributing to the cultural & intellectual heritage of Canada
Applications are not solicited or received; the laureates are simply invited to accept the honour
Duke & Duchess of York Prize in Photography
Endowed by the Government of Canada in 1986 on the occasion of Prince Andrew's marriage; awarded annually to a professional Canadian artist for personal creative work or advanced study in photography; winner is chosen from the recipients of the "B" Grants in photography
The prize covers living expenses, project costs, & travel expenses of up to $17,000
J.B.C. Watkins Award
A bequest from the estate of the late John B.C. Watkins, provides special grants, equivalent in value to an Arts Grant "B", to professional Canadian artists in any field who are graduates of a Canadian university or postsecondary art institution or training school; preference is given to those who wish to carry out their postgraduate studies in Denmark, Norway, Sweden or Iceland, but applications are accepted for studies in any country
Applications must be submitted to the Arts Awards Service of the Canada Council
Joseph S. Stauffer Prizes
Three Canadian artists are designated annually by the Canada Council, one in each of the fields of music, visual arts & literature; the prizes are made to honour the memory of the benefactor whose bequest to the Canada Council enables it to "encourage young Canadians of outstanding promise or potential"
Petro-Canada Award
Endowed by Petro-Canada in 1987 to celebrate the centenary of engineering in Canada; awarded biennially to a professional Canadian artist who has demonstrated outstanding & innovative use of new technology in the media arts; winner receives $10,000
Prix de Rome in Architecture
Established 1987; designed to recognize the work of a Canadian citizen actively engaged in the field of contemporary architecture whose career is well under way & whose personal work shows exceptional talent
In addition to a grant of $20,000 for living expenses & working costs, the winner has the use of a live-in studio on the Piazza Sant'Appolonia in the Trastevere quarter of Rome for one year
Ronald J. Thom Award for Early Design Achievement
$10,000 awarded biennially to a Canadian citizen in the early stages of his/her career who demonstrates both outstanding creative talent & exceptional potential in architectural design
Sensitivity to architecture's allied arts, crafts & professions in the context of the integrated building environment must be evident in all work; applications must be submitted to the Arts Awards Service of the Canada Council
Victor Martyn Lynch-Staunton Awards
Each year the Canada Council designates a few Canadian artists who have been awarded Arts Grants "A"

as holders of Victor Martyn Lynch-Staunton Awards; this designation is made to honour the memory of the benefactor whose bequest to the Council enables it to increase the number of grants in this category

Canadian Conference of the Arts / Conférence canadienne des arts
189 Laurier Ave. West, Ottawa ON K1N 6P1
613/238-3561; Fax: 613/238-4849; Toll Free: 1-800-463-3561; Email: ccarts@globalx.net
Diplôme d'Honneur
Established in 1954; presented annually to Canadians who have contributed outstanding service to the arts; recipients have included Vincent Massey, Wilfrid Pelletier, Maureen Forrester, Floyd Chalmers, Gabrielle Roy, Glenn Gould, Alfred Pellan, Bill Reid, Antonine Maillet

Canadian Crafts Council / Conseil canadien des métiers d'art
189 Laurier Ave. East, Ottawa ON K1N 6P1
613/235-8200; Fax: 613/235-7425
Prix Saidye Bronfman Award
$20,000 awarded annually to an outstanding crafts person in Canada, nominated by CCC members – Contact, Administrative Manager, Mireille Gratton

Canadian Historical Association / Société historique du Canada
395 Wellington St., Ottawa ON K1A 0N3
613/233-7885; Fax: 613/567-3110; Email: 74143.1061@compuserve.com
Albert B. Corey Prize
Established 1966 & jointly sponsored by the CHA & the American Historical Association; $1,000 awarded every two years to the best book dealing with the history of Canadian-American relations or the history of both countries
The Wallace K. Ferguson Prize
Established 1979; $1,000 awarded annually for a outstanding work in a field of history other than Canadian

The City of Toronto
Dept. of the City Clerk, City Hall, 100 Queen St. West, Toronto ON M5H 2N2
416/392-7494; Fax: 416/392-1446
City of Toronto Fashion Awards
A series of awards including: Designer of the Year, Industry Achievement, Couturier, Most Promising Fashion Graduate & Most Promising New Designer – Contact, Laurie Belzak, 416/392-7571
Urban Design Awards
Awarded every two years for urban development in Toronto – Contact, Planning & Development Dept., 416/392-1526

Conseil de la vie française en Amérique
56, rue Saint-Pierre, 1er étage, Québec PQ G1K 4A1
418/692-1150; Fax: 418/692-4578
L'Ordre de la fidélité française
Établi en 1947; destiné à reconnaître les mérites exceptionnels d'un francophone ayant apporté une contribution significative au progrès des francophones et à la promotion des facteurs de vie et de la culture française en Amérique du Nord
Prix littéraire Champlain
1 500 $; vise à encourager en Amérique du Nord la production littéraire chez les francophones qui vivent à l'extérieur du Québec, d'une part, et à susciter chez les Québécois un intérêt pour les francophones qui sont en situation de minorité hors du Québec en Amérique du Nord

Heritage Canada
412 MacLaren St., PO Box 1358, Stn B, Ottawa ON K1P 5R4
613/237-1066; Fax: 613/237-5987; Email: hercanot@interserv.com

Achievement Awards
Established 1989, these awards recognize individuals or groups for achievements in the conservation of heritage in the natural or cultural environments; designed to be presented jointly by Heritage Canada & established provincial or territorial umbrella groups or associations that are members of Heritage Canada & that have juried awards programs & awards ceremonies; each group or association, called a partner, will be fully responsible for choosing its candidate within prescribed criteria & eligibility rules; in this way, Heritage Canada also recognizes these partners for their dedication & commitment to excellence in heritage preservation

Gabrielle Léger Award
Recognizes outstanding work in architectural conservation in Canada; this is an annual national award to an individual who has contributed outstanding community service in the cause of heritage conservation

Lieutenant Governor's Award
Established 1979 to recognize outstanding work in architectural conservation on a provincial level by an individual or group

It must be demonstrated that the applicant's continuous efforts in the field of heritage conservation have benefited the province where the foundation's annual meeting is being held; applicants must be sponsored by an organized heritage group &/or elected officials at any level of government

Ontario Arts Council / Conseil des arts de l'Ontario
#600, 151 Bloor St. West, Toronto ON M5S 1T6
416/961-1660; Fax: 416/961-7796; Toll Free: 1-800-387-0058; Email: oac@gov.on.ca

Emerging Artists Award
$7,500 award established by the K.M. Hunter Charitable Foundation; the winners are selected from a batch of applicants recommended by Ontario Arts Council juries; awards rotate each year through film, photography, video, dance, literature, theatre, music & visual arts

Lieutenant-Governor's Awards
Approximately $75,000 to be awarded annually for the visual & performing arts that recognize institutional achievements rather than celebrating particular productions or artists; established in 1995

The Jean A. Chalmers Award for Crafts
Annual award of $20,000 honours individual Canadian craftspersons whose work continues to influence creativity & to set significant standards for innovation & excellence

The Jean A. Chalmers Award for Visual Arts
Annual award of $20,000 recognizes individual Canadian artists who have created a substantial body of work which influences creativity

The Venture Fund
Assists in artistic projects that embody a sense of challenge, experimentation or risk

PEI Council of the Arts
151 Richmond St., Charlottetown PE C1A 1H7
902/368-4410; Fax: 902/368-4418

Senior Arts Award
$5,000 awarded every two years to a PEI professional artist with an accumulated body of work who has contributed in general to art in PEI

Québec Ministère de la culture et des communications
225, Grande Allée est, Bloc V, 3e étage, Québec PQ G1R 5G5
418/643-2183; Fax: 418/643-3310

Les Prix du Québec:
Prix Albert-Tessier
$30,000, a silver medal & a scroll awarded for excellence in cinema

Prix Gérard-Morisset
$30,000, a silver medal & scroll awarded for excellence in heritage

Prix Paul-Émile-Borduas
$30,000, a silver medal & a scroll awarded for excellence in architecture, design, visual arts, & crafts

Royal Architectural Institute of Canada / Institut royal d'architecture du Canada
#330, 55 Murray St., Ottawa ON K1N 5M3
613/241-3600; Fax: 613/241-5750; URL: http://www.aecinfo.com/raic/index.html

Governor General's Medals for Architecture
Defined by the Governor General for recognition of outstanding achievement in the field of Canadian architecture

RAIC Allied Arts Medal
Established 1953; silver medals awarded at intervals of not less than one year & not more than three years for outstanding achievement in the arts which are allied to architecture, such as mural paintings, sculpture, decoration, stained glass, industrial design

RAIC Gold Medal
Established 1930; gold medals awarded annually in recognition of a person of science or letters related to architecture & the arts, in addition to an architect, for great achievement & contribution to the architectural profession

The Royal Society of Canada / La Société royale du Canada
#308, 225 Metcalfe St., Ottawa ON K2P 1P9
613/991-6990; Fax: 613/991-6996; Email: adminrsc@rsc.ca; URL: http://library.utoronto.ca/www/rsc/

Centenary Medal
Established 1982; awarded at irregular intervals in recognition of achievements in scholarship & research

Sir John William Dawson Medal
Established 1985; $2,000 & a silver medal awarded for important & sustained contributions by one individual in at least two different fields in the general areas of interest of the society or in a broad domain that transcends the usual disciplinary boundaries

The J.B. Tyrrell Historical Medal
Established 1927; awarded at least every two years for outstanding work in the history of Canada

Social Sciences & Humanities Research Council of Canada
350 Albert St., 10th Fl., PO Box 1610, Ottawa ON K1P 6G4
613/992-0530; Fax: 613/992-1787

The Jules & Gabrielle Léger Fellowship
To support experienced scholars, Canadian or resident in Canada, who wish to undertake research & writing on the historical contribution of the Crown & its representatives, federal & provincial, to the political, constitutional, cultural, intellectual & social life of the country, including comparisons between Canadian & Commonwealth systems

Award is for $50,000; a research & travel allowance of up to $10,000 is available

La Société Saint-Jean-Baptiste de Montréal
82, rue Sherbrooke ouest, Montréal PQ H2X 1X3
514/843-8851; Fax: 514/844-6369

Prix Esdras-Minville
Established 1978; $1,500 & a medal awarded annually to a French Canadian in recognition of outstanding achievement in Human Science (History, Sociology, Economics, Politics, etc.) in serving the higher interests of the French Canadian people

Prix Philippe-Hébert
Established 1971; $1,500 & a medal awarded annually to a French Canadian in recognition of outstanding achievement in the plastic arts in serving the higher interests of the French Canadian people

Prix Victor-Morin
Established 1962; $1,500 & a medal awarded annually to a French Canadian in recognition of outstanding achievement in theatre, television, or film, in serving the higher interests of the French Canadian people

Studio Magazine
124 Galaxy Blvd., Rexdale ON M9W 4Y6
416/675-1999; Fax: 416/675-6093

Studio Magazine Awards Program
Annual awards for: graphic design, art direction, illustration, photography, printing, TV commercials/video, & student work

Toronto Arts Council
141 Bathurst St., Toronto ON M5V 2R2
416/392-6800; Fax: 416/392-6920

Margo Bindhardt Award
The $5,000 annual award recognizes persons whose leadership & vision, through their creative work or activism, have had a significant impact on the arts & arts awareness in Toronto

Yorkdale Shopping Centre
#412, One Yorkdale Rd., Toronto ON M6A 3A1
416/789-3261

Yorkdale Designer of the Year Award
Annual award of $10,000; fashion designer must be Canadian & have presented at least six collections; second award of $2,500 for designing a special theme outfit for the annual fall show at Yorkdale – Contact, Fruitman Communications Group, 416/628-8366

Yorkdale New Designer Discovery Award
Annual award of $5,000 & use of a cart/kiosk in the mall for one month (value $2,500) for the best new fashion designer; must have a collection of at least 10 outfits & a minimum of three years experience in the fashion industry; second award of $2,500 for designing a special theme outfit for the annual spring fashion show at Yorkdale – Contact, Fruitman Communications Group, 416/638-8366

DANCE see PERFORMING ARTS

DRAMA see PERFORMING ARTS

EDUCATIONAL

Alberta Education
Devonian Building, West Tower, 11160 Jasper Ave., Edmonton AB T5K 0L2
403/422-9327; Fax: 403/422-4199

Excellence in Teaching Awards
Recognizes outstanding Alberta teachers; honours creative, innovative & effective teaching; focuses public attention on the teaching profession; involves Albertans in celebrating teaching excellence

Alberta Heritage Scholarship Fund
Students Finance Board, Baker Centre, 9th Fl., 10025 - 106 St., Edmonton AB T5J 4P9
403/427-8640
32 scholarships & awards are available in various fields of study

Association for Media & Technology in Education in Canada / Association des média et de la technologie en éducation au Canada
#1318, 3-1750 The Queensway, Etobicoke ON M9C 5H5
URL: http://www.camosun.bc.ca/~amtec/

AMTEC Leadership Award & the EMPDAC Achievement Award
Two awards recognize outstanding individual achievement & leadership in the field of educational media & technology

Canadian Almanac & Directory 1997

Association of Canadian Universities for Northern Studies / Association universitaire canadienne d'études nordiques
#405, 17 York St., Ottawa ON K1N 9J6
613/562-0515; Fax: 613/562-0533
Royal Canadian Geographical Society Studentship in Northern Geography
Based on academic excellence; $10,000 awarded to a graduate student engaged in northern geographical research
Studentships in Northern Studies
Research culminating in a thesis or similar document involving direct northern experience; $10,000 for students enrolled in graduate & undergraduate degree programs or other courses of study recognized at a Canadian university with special relevance to Canada's northern territories & adjacent regions

Association of Universities & Colleges of Canada / Association des universités et collèges du Canada
#600, 350 Albert St., Ottawa ON K1R 1B1
613/563-1236; Fax: 613/563-9745; URL: http://www.aucc.ca/
C.D. Howe Memorial Foundation Engineering Awards
Two $6,000 scholarships (one male, one female) for students who have completed the first year of an engineering program
C.D. Howe Scholarship Program
Two $5,000 scholarships open to all disciplines but for students from Thunder Bay or the following school boards: Lakehead, Lakehead District R.C., Lake Superior, North of Superior District R.C., Geraldton, Geraldton District R.C., Nipigon-Red Rock, & Hornepayne
Emergency Prepardness Canada Research Fellowship in Honour of Stuart Nesbitt White
Provides support of up to $10,000 per annum for research in the area of disaster/emergency research & planning; preference is given to applicants who hold a Master's degree & who are planning research in the following fields: Urban & Regional Planning, Economics, Earth Sciences, Risk Analysis & Management, Systems Science, Social Sciences, Business Administration & Health Administration – Contact, Micheline Léger, 613/563-1236, ext.266; fax: 613/563-9745; email: mleger@aucc.ca
Fessenden-Trott Awards
Four $9,000 scholarships open to all disciplines; restricted to Atlantic provinces universities in 1996, Ontario in 1997, & to Western in 1998
Frank Knox Memorial Fellowship Program
Up to two $13,000 US awards, plus tuition fees & health insurance for Canadian citizens who have graduated from a AUCC member institution & wish to study at Harvard in the following disciplines: arts & sciences (including engineering), business administration, design, divinity studies, education, law, public administration, medicine, dental medicine & public health
National Defence Scholarship Program in Military & Strategic Studies
Offers awards for studies relevant to current & future national security problems in all their dimensions & in a wide range of disciplines: Program for M.A. & Ph.D., $13,000 master's & $16,000 doctorate; Military & Strategic Studies Language Program, $16,000 plus tuition fees up to $8,000; R.B. Byers Post-Doctoral Fellowship Program, up to $25,000 for a Ph.D. or equivalent for further studies; Military & Strategic Studies Internship Program, up to $16,000 to help recent graduates obtain work experiences in strategic studies by working for a year in this field in the non-governmental or private sectors
Queen Elizabeth Silver Jubilee Endowment Fund for Study in a Second Official Language Award Program
Six $5,000 (plus travel costs) scholarships open to all disciplines, except translations, for students studying in their second language

Association des professionnels en ressources humaines du Québec / Association of Human Resources Professionals of the Province of Québec
#820, av 1253 McGill Collège, Montréal PQ H3B 2Y5
514/879-1636; Fax: 514/879-1722
Inter-University Excellence Contest
Established in 1987 to promote teaching of human resources management in Québec universities that prepared students for the job market; open to students at Québec universities
Annual prizes of $2,000, $1,500 & $1,000

BC Ministry of Education, Skills & Training
Parliament Bldgs., Victoria BC V8V 1X4
250/387-3165
Governor General's Academic Medal Award
Established to encourage academic students; awards medals to students achieving the highest academic standing in the graduating class
Lieutenant Governor's Silver Medal Award
Each college & institute in BC is eligible to present one medal each year to a student who has excelled academically, & has contributed to the life of their college, institute, or community
Premier's Excellence Award
Award provides a $5,000 bursary to the top all-around graduating Grade 12 student in each of the 15 college regions in BC who will attend one of the province's post-secondary institutions
United World College Scholarships
The Government of BC funds 14 World College Scholarships annually; each scholarship is valued at $16,500; each year seven new scholarships are funded in addition to seven scholarships to students returning for their second year of study; students attending United World Colleges follow a two-year program leading to the International Baccalaureate, accepted by major international universities as equivalent to the final year of senior secondary school & first year university

Black Business & Professional Association
#203, 675 King St. West, Toronto ON M5V 1M9
416/504-4097; Fax: 416/504-7343
Harry Jerome Scholarships
Five annual awards of $2,000 aimed at helping young people who may lack resources for further education

Boys & Girls Clubs of Canada
Boys & Girls Clubs of Ontario
346 Main St. East, Hamilton ON L8N 1J1
905/521-4441; Fax: 905/521-3062; Email: bgco@freenet.hamilton.on.ca
Scholarship Program
Founded in 1992 with a donation from the Roy C. Hill Foundation, the program has gradually grown & has received funding from the Trillium Non-Profit Ventures for Youth, Star Aerospace, Kellogg's, Campbells Soup Company Ltd., IBM Canada, Prudential Life Insurance of America (Canadian Operations), Hollinger & the Toronto Raptors Foundation. The program provides scholarships to youth members on the basis of financial need & entrance into post secondary educational institutions
$500 to $2,000 for a total of $40,000 in 1996

The Canada Council / Conseil des Arts du Canada
350 Albert St., PO Box 1047, Ottawa ON K1P 5V8
613/566-4365; Fax: 613/566-4390; Toll Free: 1-800-263-5588
John G. Diefenbaker Award
Funded by the Government of Canada, this annual award honours the memory of former Prime Minister John G. Diefenbaker; it enables a German scholar to spend up to 12 months in Canada to pursue research in any of the disciplines in the social sciences & humanities; candidates must be nominated by university departments or research institutes in Canada
Value of full award is $75,000; in addition, the Social Sciences & Humanities Research Council of Canada provides a travel allowance of up to $20,000

Canada Post Corporation
#N0610, 2701 Riverside Dr., Ottawa ON K1A 0B1
613/734-7610; Fax: 613/734-8814
Flight for Freedom Awards
Five annual award categories recognize the contributions of businesses, literacy organizations, educators, & individuals to the cause of literacy in Canada: the Governor General's Flight for Freedom Award to a literacy organization, the Government of Canada Literacy Innovation Award, Corporate Canada Literacy Award to a business/industry, Literacy Education Award (one English, one French) to an educator & Individual Achievement Award (one English, one French) for participation in a community literacy program

Canadian Sociology & Anthropology Association / Société canadienne de sociologie et d'anthropologie
1455, boul de Maisonneuve ouest, Montréal PQ H3G 1M8
514/848-8780; Fax: 514/848-4539; Email: csaa@vax2.concordia.ca
John Porter Award
Recognizes the best sociology book published in Canada in the past three years
Special Contribution Awards
Given to recognize the work of eminent sociologists

Canadian Teachers' Federation / Fédération canadienne des enseignantes et enseignants
110 Argyle Ave., Ottawa ON K2P 1B4
613/232-1505; Fax: 613/232-1886; Email: info@ctf-fce.ca; URL: http://www.ctf-fce.ca
Hilroy Fellowship Program
Twenty-eight awards given each year to encourage & reward active classroom teachers who have developed new ideas for the improvement of teaching practices; awarded through annual competition
Twenty provincial & one territorial award in the amount of $2,500 each; six national awards for Great Merit in the amount of $5,000 each & one national award for Outstanding Merit in the amount of $10,000

CIDA Awards Program
Canadian Bureau for International Education
#1100, 220 Laurier Ave. West, Ottawa ON K1P 5Z9
613/237-4820; Fax: 613/237-1073;
Email: HAlmednrades@CBIE.ca; LMcLachlan@CBIE.ca
Awards for Canadians
A program funded by CIDA & managed by the Canadian Bureau for International Education; CIDA wishes to increase the number of Canadian professionals capable of working in the international arena by providing funding up to $25,000 for short-term, overseas work experiences
Must possess a university degree, college diploma or professional designation, have a minimum of seven years work experience, two years of which have involved using specific skills necessary to undertake the proposed project. For information on fields of specialization & eligible countries, contact CIDA Communications Branch, 200 Promenade du Portage, Hull PQ K1A 0G4; 819/997-5006; Fax: 819/953-6088. Other information & applications should be sent to the BCIE at the above address

The City of Toronto
Dept. of the City Clerk, City Hall, 100 Queen St. West, Toronto ON M5H 2N2
416/392-7494; Fax: 416/392-1446

City of Toronto Scholarships
Awarded each year on Civic Honours Day (on the anniversary of the incorporation of Toronto in March)
Aboriginal Health Scholarship (University of Toronto)
Awarded to Aboriginal students for academic excellence in post-secondary health education
The George Brown College Scholarship
To commemorate the visit of Her Majesty Queen Elizabeth II in 1973; awarded to the most deserving student from a Toronto secondary school entering the business administration course at George Brown College, & who is qualifying himself/herself for employment relating to municipal government
The National Ballet School Scholarships
To commemorate the visit of Her Majesty Queen Elizabeth The Queen Mother in 1981; awarded to the most deserving student pursuing a career in ballet
Toronto Sesquicentennial Scholarship in Public Health Nursing (University of Toronto)
To commemorate the visit of Her Majesty Queen Elizabeth II in 1984; awarded to the most deserving baccalaureate student at the University of Toronto who is deemed most likely to contribute to public health nursing in Toronto
Women's Studies Scholarship (University of Toronto)
Established 1985; awarded annually to the undergraduate student deemed most likely to contribute to studies on the status of women, community studies & public policy, & who is most deserving of such assistance

The Commonwealth of Learning
Pacific Centre, Box 10428, #1700, 777 Dunsmuir St., PO Box 10428, Vancouver BC V7Y 1K4
604/775-8200; Telex: 04507508 COMLEARN; Fax: 604/775-8210; Email: info@col.org; URL: http://www.col.org
COL/ICDE Awards of Excellence
Recognizes individual & institutional achievement in distance education

Foundation for Educational Exchange Between Canada & the United States
#2015, 350 Albert St., Ottawa ON K1R 1A4
613/237-5366; Fax: 613/237-2029; Email: av551@freenet.carleton.ca; URL: http://www.usis.canada.usia.gov/fulbrigh.htm
Canada-US Fulbright Program
To expand research, teaching & study opportunities for Canadian & American faculty & students engaged in the study of Canada, the United States & the relationship between the two countries; based on academic excellence & the merit of the applicant's proposed project; awards given annually for study in a number of different fields including conservation, ecology, environmental management, resource analysis & environmental policy. Applicants must relocate from the U.S. to Canada, or Canada to the U.S.
$15,000 US for graduate students; $25,000 US for faculty

Insitute of Environmental Studies
#1016, 33 Wilcocks St., Toronto ON M5S 3E8
416/978-7077; Fax: 416/978-3884
Canadian Environmental Directory Publisher's Award
First awarded in 1996; annual award to a student in environmental studies

International Council for Canadian Studies / Conseil international d'études canadiennes
2 Daly Ave., Ottawa ON K1N 6E2
613/789-7834; Fax: 613/232-2495; Email: contact@iccs-ciec.ca; URL: http://www.iccs-ciec.ca/
Barton Awards
Maximum of $14,000 per year for M.A. or Ph.D. for study of international peace & security

The Japan Foundation, Toronto
#213, 131 Bloor St. West, Toronto ON M5S 1R1
416/966-1600; Fax: 416/966-9773; Email: jftor@interlog.com
Offers a broad range of programs designed to further cultural exchange with Japan, with an emphasis on Japanese studies at the post-secondary level & Japanese language study, including:
The Japan Foundation Fellowships
Scholars, researchers, artists & other professionals are provided an opportunity to conduct research or pursue projects in Japan. Term of award is from two to 14 months, depending on category; annual application deadline is Dec. 1 for funding year beginning the following April 1

Ontario Centre for Materials Research
PO Box 1146, Kingston ON K7L 4Y5
613/545-6519; Fax: 613/545-6510; Email: mcgeerj@post.queensu.ca; URL: http://www.queensu.ca/ocmr
Cooperative Research Awards
$17,000 for a Ph.D. student of materials science; needs industry sponsor; tenable only at Ottawa, McMaster, Queen's, Toronto, Waterloo or Western Ontario
Industrial Practice Scholarship Awards
$20,000 for a M.Sc. student for materials research; tenable only at Ottawa, McMaster, Queen's, Toronto, Waterloo or Western Ontario

Ontario Council on Graduate Studies
#203, 444 Yonge St., Toronto ON M5B 2H4
416/979-2165; Fax: 416/979-8635
John Charles Polanyi Prizes
In honour of the achievement of John Charles Polanyi, co-recipient of the 1986 Nobel Prize in Chemistry, the Government of Ontario has established a fund to provide annually up to five prizes to persons continuing to post-doctoral studies at an Ontario university

Ontario Ministry of Education & Training
Student Support Branch
189 Red River Rd., PO Box 4500, Stn P, Thunder Bay ON P7B 6G9
Queen Elizabeth II Ontario Scholarships
Provides funding of $15,000 for study in the area of planning, geography & environmental studies for those nearing the completion of a Ph.D., particularly in their final year of research & writing; a personal interview in required – Contact, Graduate Scholarship Officer, Gerry Vibert, 807/343-7257; Fax: 807/343-7278

The Royal Society of Canada / La Société royale du Canada
#308, 225 Metcalfe St., Ottawa ON K2P 1P9
613/991-6990; Fax: 613/991-6996; Email: adminrsc@rsc.ca; URL: http://library.utoronto.ca/www/rsc/
Innis-Gérin Medal
Established 1966; awarded every two years for a distinguished & sustained contribution to the literature of the social sciences including human geography & social psychology
NATO Fellowship Programme
To promote study & research leading to publication on the common interests, traditions & outlook of the countries of the North Atlantic Alliance; for social science researchers
Pierre Chauveau Medal
Established 1951; awarded every two years (since 1966) for a distinguished contribution to knowledge in the humanities other than Canadian literature & Canadian history
Sir Arthur Sims Scholarship
Established 1952; aims to encourage Canadian students to undertake postgraduate work in Great Britain; it may be awarded for outstanding merit & promise in any subject of the humanities, social sciences, or natural sciences

SaskPower
PO Box 220, Beauval SK S0M 0G0
306/288-2258; Fax: 306/288-4667
Northern Enterprise Fund Scholarship Program
To promote entrepreneurial spirit in Northern Saskatchewan by providing scholarships to students enrolled in courses related to business or based on occupational shortages in the north
Five $2,500 university scholarships & five $2,500 institute scholarships are awarded to full-time students who are permanent residents of the SaskPower Northern Enterprise Fund Administration District; priority will be given to applicants showing intention of returning to, or remaining in the north

Yukon Government
PO Box 2703, Whitehorse YT Y1A 2C6
403/667-5127; Fax: 403/667-6339
Innovations in Education Awards
Awarded to individuals or groups that have demonstrated innovation, superior dedication or outstanding service to education in the Yukon; winners may receive a $2,000 education bursary & a specially commissioned artwork

ENGINEERING see SCIENTIFIC, ENGINEERING, TECHNICAL

ENVIRONMENTAL

Alberta Emerald Foundation for Environmental Excellence
#600, 12220 Stony Plain Rd., Edmonton AB T5J 3L2
403/413-9629; Toll Free: 1-800-219-8329
Emerald Awards
Awarded to Albertans who have made a significant contribution to the protection or enhancement of the environment
Nominations are open to individual, not-for-profit organizations, business & industry, communities & government, educational institutions & volunteer organizations excelling in environmental achievements

Alberta Environmental Protection
Natural Resources Service
9915 - 108 St., 10th Fl., Edmonton AB T5K 2C9
403/427-6749; Fax: 403/422-6068
Order of the Big Horn
Fish & wildlife conservation awards presented to individuals, organizations & corporations for their outstanding contributions to fish & wildlife conservation in Alberta – Contact, Program Manager, Vonn Bricker

Atlantic Salmon Federation / Fédération du saumon atlantique
PO Box 429, St. Andrews NB E0G 2X0
506/529-4581; Fax: 506/529-4438; Email: atlsal@nbnet.nb.ca; URL: http://www.flyfishing.com/asf/
Olin Fellowship
$1,000-$3,000 fellowships offered annually to individuals seeking to improve their knowledge or skills in fields dealing with current problems in biology, management, or conservation of Atlantic salmon & its habitat; the fellowship may be applied toward a wide range of endeavours such as graduate work, sabbatical research, management experience, etc.; tenable at any accredited university or research laboratory, or in an active management program
Roll of Honour
Presented annually to individuals who exhibit outstanding commitment to salmon conservation at the grassroots level

BC Ministry of Environment, Lands & Parks
Public Affairs & Communications Branch
810 Blanshard St., 1st Fl., Victoria BC V8V 1X4

250/387-9422; Fax: 250/356-6464
Minister's Environmental Awards
Awarded for identifying, reducing, solving or avoiding an environmental problem; demonstrating consistently responsible environmental management practices; promoting active concern for the enhancement & protection of the environment; or improving public awareness & understanding of an environmental problem or solution
Categories include individual citizen, youth group, non-profit organization, community or municipality, business or industry, environmental education, communications or media; by nomination. Selection of award winners is made by the Minister

Canadian Heritage
Jules Léger Bldg., 6th Fl., 25 Eddy St., Hull PQ K1A 0H3
819/997-7603
Parks Canada Awards
Established in 1978, presented to individuals & groups in recognition of their exceptional or innovative achievement in the conservation of Canada's natural & cultural heritage in at least one of the following areas: policy development; research & education; resource management; public awareness, & responsible action & stewardship
Open to individuals, groups, corporations, other levels of government & educational institutions involved in the conservation of natural or cultural heritage

Canadian Industrial Innovation Centre
156 Columbia St. West, Waterloo ON N2L 3L3
519/885-5870; Fax: 519/885-5729; Toll Free: 1-800-265-4559; Email: info@innovationcentre.ca; URL: http://www.innovationcentre.ca
Green-vention Awards
The contest awards $1,000 each to the top two inventors whose innovations will improve or assist in environmentally friendly activities; its goal is to raise public awareness of the issues involved & the efforts Canadian innovators are making to provide global solutions
Inventions must be used in the clean-up/protection/conservation of the environment, decrease pollution levels or educate people on pro-environmental practices; each invention must be submitted to the Inventor's Assistance Program, Critical Factor Assessment Process & receive a positive rating; judging occurs in April

Canadian Land Reclamation Association / Association canadienne de réhabilitation des sites dégradés
PO Box 61047, RPO Kensington, Calgary AB T2N 4S6
403/289-9435; Fax: 403/289-9435
The Noranda Award
Presented annually by the association on behalf of Noranda Mines Inc. in recognition of superior research or field work in reclamation; not restricted to members

Canadian Nature Federation / Fédération canadienne de la nature
#520, One Nicholas St., Ottawa ON K1N 7B7
613/562-3447; Fax: 613/562-3371; Toll Free: 1-800-267-4088; Email: cnf@web.apc.org; URL: http://www.web.apc.org~cnf
Douglas H. Pimlott Award
Given in recognition of outstanding lifetime achievement in wildlife conservation

Canadian Wildlife Federation / Fédération canadienne de la faune
2740 Queensview Dr., Ottawa ON K2B 1A2
613/721-2286; Fax: 613/721-2902; Toll Free: 1-800-563-9453

Canadian Conservation Achievement Awards Program:
Canadian Outdoorsman of the Year Award
Presented annually to an outdoorsperson who has demonstrated an active commitment to conservation in Canada
Roderick Haig-Brown Memorial Award
Awarded annually to an individual who has made a significant contribution to furthering the sport of angling &/or conservation & wise use of Canada's recreational fisheries resources
Roland Michener Conservation Award
A trophy is given annually in recognition of an individual's outstanding achievement in the field of conservation in Canada

Conservation Council of Ontario / Le Conseil de conservation de l'Ontario
#506, 489 College St., Toronto ON M6G 1A5
416/969-9637; Fax: 416/960-8053; Email: cco@web.apc.org
The Lieutenant Governor's Conservation Award
Recognizes outstanding accomplishments in the conservation & protection of Ontario's natural environment; three categories of awards: individuals, non-profit/non-governmental organizations, & corporate/institutional or business associations

Energy Probe Research Foundation
225 Brunswick Ave., Toronto ON M5S 2M6
416/964-9223; Fax: 416/964-8239; Toll Free: 1-800-263-2784
The Margaret Laurence Fund
Grants & scholarships are made to foster an understanding of peace & the environment upon which the fate of the planet rests
Recipients of the grants & scholarships are limited to students, authors, researchers, & publishers, working with the foundation in collaborative projects approved by the directors

Environment Canada
Inquiry Centre
351 St. Joseph Blvd., Hull PQ K1A 0H3
819/997-2800; Fax: 819/953-2225; Toll Free: 1-800-668-6767; Email: enviroinfo@ec.gc.ca; URL: http://www.doe.ca
The Canadian Healthy Environment Awards:
Arts, Media & Communcations
Awarded to a Canadian author, journalist, broadcaster, filmmaker or performer whose work has significantly broadened Canadian's awareness of environmental issues
Corporate Environmental Leadership
Offered in recognition of innovative &/or exemplary environmental conduct by a Canadian corporation, institution or association (industrial or other); the winner of this award will have shown that ecological concerns can be reflected in economic decisions, & that profit-based operations can sustain themselves without contributing to environmental destruction
The nominee must be a corporate entity & must show how the company has protected the environment or conserved natural resources
Environmental Leadership by a Municipality
Award recognizes an innovative &/or exemplary environmental policy, project or activity of a municipality
Lifetime Achievement
Awarded to a Canadian citizen for a lifetime dedication to the environment
Non-Profit Organization
Awarded to a non-government, non-profit Canadian group, or Canadian branch of an international organization focusing on environmental issues or which has developed a program that deals with an environment-related topic & which has made an outstanding contribution to the protection of Canada's environment

Youth Leadership
Awarded to an outstanding young person who has demonstrated true leadership in an environmental activity & who is recognized as an inspiration amongst his/her peers
Any young Canadian between the ages of 13 to 20 years

The Financial Post
333 King St. East, Toronto ON M5A 4N2
416/350-6200; Fax: 416/350-6201
Environment Awards for Business:
Business Partnership Award
Awarded for environmental partnerships between business & community organizations that contribute to the reduction or elimination of pollution; sponsored by Syncrude Canada Ltd.
Document Management Award
Awarded for minimizing the environmental impact from office operations through the progressive use of technologies & processes that effectively manage documents to reduce or eliminate paper
Education Award
Awarded for an educational awareness program aimed at students or consumers to raise their awareness of the environment & environmental issues
Environmental Management Award
Awarded for the integration of ecological considerations into organizational decision-making
Environmental Technology Award
Awarded for the development of new Canadian technology either contributing to the reduction or elimination of pollution at its source or providing for cost effective remediation of environmental contamination
Product Stewartship Award
Awarded for organizations that have applied a product life cycle approach to the development of products or services in order to minimize the environmental impact resulting from the manufacture, use & disposal of products

George Cedric Metcalf Charitable Foundation
105 Pears Ave., Toronto ON M5R 1S9
416/926-0366
George Cedric Metcalf Charitable Foundation
Support for charitable organizations concerned with social services, arts/culture, education, environment, wildlife, & international development. Projects may be in Canada or in developing countries through Canadian-based organizations
Canadian registered charities only
Range: $500 to $45,000; median grant: $5,000 – Contact, Coordinator, Josie Romita

International Development Research Centre / Centre de recherches pour le développement international
250 Albert St., 10th Fl., PO Box 8500, Ottawa ON K1G 3H9
613/236-6163; Fax: 613/563-0815; Email: info@idrc.ca; URL: http://www.idrc.ca/index.html
John G. Bene Fellowship in Social Forestry
$7,000 awarded to M.Sc. or Ph.D. students interested in social sciences combined with forestry or agroforestry from an international development perspective; must spend at least part of thesis research overseas
Young Canadian Researchers Award
$20,000 per year provided for M.Sc. & Ph.D research in the areas of sustainable & equitable development in the following themes: intergrating environmental, social & economic policies; technology & the environment; food systems under stress; information & communication for environment & development; health & the environment; biodiversity

Manitoba Heritage Federation Inc.
21 - 2nd Ave. NW, 2nd Fl., Dauphin MB R7N 1H1
204/638-9154; Fax: 204/638-0683; Email: 76766.35@compuserve.com

D.L. Campbell Award
Recognizes outstanding achievement of an individual to support, enhance & promote heritage for all Manitobans
Heritage Preservation Award
Recognizes a project or work concerned with preserving Manitoba's heritage
Outstanding Contribution to Manitoba's Heritage
Awarded to one recipient from any of seven heritage disciplines who has made an outstanding contribution to Manitoba's heritage

Manitoba Sustainable Development Coordination Unit
#305, 155 Carlton St., Winnipeg MB R3C 3H8
204/945-1124; Fax: 204/945-0090
The Award of Excellence Program for Sustainable Development
Awarded to Manitobans (groups or individuals) for undertaking projects which exemplify the fundamental principles & guidelines of sustainable development

Newfoundland & Labrador Department of Environment & Labour
Public Relations Office
Confederation Bldg., PO Box 8700, St. John's NF A1B 4J6
709/729-3394; Email: TRYAN@env.gov.nf.ca; URL: http://www.gov.nf.ca
Environmental Awards Program
Sponsored & managed by the Department & administered by the Newfoundland & Labrador Women's Institutes, the awards, which began in 1990, recognize people from all walks of life who have contributed in a meaningful way to the preservation, protection, & restoration of the environment – Contact, Newfoundland & Labrador Women's Institutes, Executive Director, Sylvia Manning, 709/753-8780

OH & S Canada Magazine & Southam Information & Technology Group
c/o Occupational Health, Safety & Environment Group, 1450 Don Mills Rd., North York ON M3B 2X7
416/445-6641
Awards of Excellence
To recognize & honour outstanding contributions & innovations by Canadian occupational health & safety individuals or corporations; awards include: Lifetime Achievement Award, Professional of the Year Award, Most Promising Professional Award, Most Significant Individual Contribution Award, Training Award, Outstanding Contribution - Labour - Award, Best Occupational, Health & Safety Program - Company Award, Most Innovative Product or Service Award (Special Supplier Award)
Each winner receives $1,000 & an OSH trophy – Contact, Conference Coordinator, Sue Mogg

Recycling Council of Ontario / Conseil du recyclage de l'Ontario
#504, 489 College St., Toronto ON M6G 1A5
416/960-1025; Fax: 416/960-8053; Toll Free: 1-800-263-2849; Email: rco@web.apc.org; URL: http://www.web.apc.org/rco
Ontario Waste Minimization Awards
A series of awards for outstanding achievement in recycling: includes 3Rs initiatives in commercial, industrial & institutional settings; Outstanding Municipal, Non-profit Organization, Recycling Program Operator; Outstanding School Program & Outstanding Market Development

The Royal Society of Canada / La Société royale du Canada
#308, 225 Metcalfe St., Ottawa ON K2P 1P9
613/991-6990; Fax: 613/991-6996; Email: adminrsc@rsc.ca; URL: http://library.utoronto.ca/www/rsc/

Miroslaw Romanowski Medal
Established in 1993; $2,000 & a medal awarded every year in recognition of noteworthy contributions in the environmental sciences

Wildlife Habitat Canada / Habitat faunique Canada
#200, 7 Hinton Ave. North, Ottawa ON K1Y 4P1
613/722-2090; Fax: 613/722-3318; Email: jladd@whc.ca
Graduate Scholarship Program
$10,000 for two years for a Master's degree & $12,000 for three years for a Ph.D. for student research in the area of conservation of wildlife habitat

FILM see BROADCASTING & FILM

GOVERNMENTAL see LEGAL, GOVERNMENTAL, PUBLIC ADMINISTRATION

HEALTH & MEDICAL

Canada Safety Council / Conseil canadien de la sécurité
1020 Thomas Spratt Place, Ottawa ON K1G 5L5
613/739-1535; Fax: 613/739-1566
Dr. Stuart Wiberg Memorial Safety Award
Presented annually to an individual who has made an outstanding contribution to the field of public safety, primarily in a voluntary capacity
Gold/Silver Seal Certificates
Established by the Canadian Industrial Safety Association to stimulate interest in the prevention of occupational accidents & diseases & to recognize meritorious achievement in resolving safety issues; the award certificates are available on a non-competitive basis for in-plant recognition of a company's own injury-free record
Occupational Safety & Health Achievement Award
Provides visible recognition to individuals for outstanding contributions to the prevention of death, injury & disease in the Canadian workplace

Canadian Association of Medical Radiation Technologists / Association canadienne des technologues en radiation médicale
#601, 294 Albert St., Ottawa ON K1P 6E6
613/234-0012; Fax: 613/234-1097
CAMRT Awards
Administers awards for students & registered technologists including; Dr. M. Mallett Student Award, Dr. Petrie Memorial Award, George Reason Memorial Cup, The Hood Award, CAMRT Student Achievement Award & the Philips Rose Bowl

Canadian Centre on Substance Abuse / Centre canadien de lutte contre l'alcoolisme et les toxicomanies
#300, 75 Albert St., Ottawa ON K1P 5E7
613/235-4048; Fax: 613/235-8101; Email: ccsa@fox.nstn.ca; URL: http://www.ccsa.ca/default.htm
Award of Distinction
To recognize Canadian achievements in the substance abuse field; one award is given every year to an individual or organization that has had a clear imnpact on reducing harm associated with alcohol & other drugs on a national level
An original bronze sculpture & $1,000; in addition, the centre presents bronze medallions to all nominees not selected for the national award

Canadian Healthcare Association / Association canadienne des soins de santé
#100, 17 York St., Ottawa ON K1N 9J6
613/241-8005; Fax: 613/241-5055

Award of Excellence for Service & Leadership
Established 1949 as the "George Findlay Stephens Memorial Award" & renamed in 1991; awarded in recognition of noteworthy service in health care leadership at the national level in Canada

Canadian Nurses Association / Association des infirmières et infirmiers du Canada
50 Driveway, Ottawa ON K2P 1E2
613/237-2133; Fax: 613/237-3520
CNA Media Awards
Annual awards for media reports that foster public understanding of the values & objectives of the Canadian health system & the manner in which the various participants in the system perform their respective roles

Canadian Nurses Foundation / Fondation des infirmières et infirmiers du Canada
50 Driveway, Ottawa ON K2P 1E2
613/237-2133; Fax: 613/237-3520
Ross Award for Nursing Leadership
Recognizes an outstanding leader in the field of Canadian nursing, for a major contribution to nursing research or education in any of its aspects

Canadian Orthopaedic Association / Association canadienne d'orthopédie
#421, 1440, rue Sainte-Catherine ouest, Montréal PQ H3G 1R8
514/874-9003; Fax: 514/874-0464
J. Edouard Samson Award
Medal & $15,000 awarded for outstanding orthopaedic research by a young investigator; paper presented at the annual meeting of the Canadian Orthopaedic Research Society

Canadian Society of Hospital Pharmacists / Société canadienne des pharmaciens d'hôpitaux
#350, 1145 Hunt Club Rd., Ottawa ON K1V 0Y3
613/736-9733; Fax: 613/736-5660; Email: bleslie@worldlink.ca; URL: http://www.cshp.ca/~cshp
Horner Travel Award
$3,000 is awarded to two hospital pharmacists to travel outside Canada to study new techniques in research
Parke Davis Award
$2,000 is awarded for original scholarly papers, demonstrating significant innovations & developments in the pharmacist's contributions to the health care of geriatric patients &/or patients in rehabilitation programs or long-term health care facilities
Sandoz Award
$1,500 is awarded for original scholarly papers in pharmacoeconomic research

Canadian Society of Laboratory Technologists / Société canadienne des technologistes de laboratoire
PO Box 2830, Stn A, Hamilton ON L8N 3N8
905/528-8642; Fax: 905/528-4968; URL: http://cslt.com/
CSLT Awards
The association administers the following awards for students & graduate medical laboratory technologists: Award in Cytotechnology; Award of Merit; Clinical Microbiology Award; Cytology-Histology Award; Founders' Fund Award; Gold Medal Award; Graduate of the Year Award; Harold Amy Award; Hematology Award; Histotechnology Award; Immunohematology Award; Microbiology Award; Med-Chem Laboratories Clinical Chemistry Award, & Fisher Scientific Clinical Chemistry Award

Canadian Veterinary Medical Association / Association canadienne des vétérinaires
339 Booth St., Ottawa ON K1R 7K1
613/236-1162; Fax: 613/236-9681

The CVMA Humane Award
Established 1987 to encourage care & well-being of animals; awarded to an individual (veterinarian or non-veterinarian) whose work is judged to have contributed significantly to the welfare of animals; $1,000 & a plaque awarded

The Schering Veterinary Award
Established 1985 to enhance progress in large animal medicine & surgery; award made to a veterinarian whose work in large animal practice, clinical research or basic sciences is judged to have contributed significantly to the advancement of large animal medicine, surgery & theriogenology, including herd health management; $1,000 & a plaque awarded

The Small Animal Practitioner Award
Established 1987 to encourage progress in the field of small animal medicine & surgery; awarded to a veterinarian whose work in small animal practice, clinical research or basic sciences is judged to have contributed significantly to the advancement of small animal practice, including the advancement of the public's knowledge of the responsibilities of pet ownership; $1,000 & a plaque awarded

Catholic Health Association of Canada / Association catholique canadienne de la santé
1247 Kilborn Pl., Ottawa ON K1H 6K9
613/731-7148; Fax: 613/731-7797

Performance Citation Award
Established 1981; awarded annually to an individual who makes an outstanding contribution to health care in a Christian context, who exhibits exemplary leadership of a national effort at building the Christian community & unselfish dedication to others

College of Family Physicians of Canada / Collège des médecins de famille du Canada
2630 Skymark Ave., Mississauga ON L4W 5A4
905/629-0900; Fax: 905/629-0893

D.I. Rice Merit Award
$5,000, plus travel expenses awarded annually to a renowned leader in family medicine to allow travel for a period of approximately one month in order to engage in educational activities

D.M. Robb Research Award
$2,500 awarded annually to a community-based family physician to conduct research in family medicine

Family Physician of the Year Award
Sponsored by McNeil Pharmaceuticals (Canada) Ltd; awarded to physicians who have been in family practice for a minimum of 15 years & members of the college for at least 10 years, & who have made outstanding contributions to family medicine, to their communities & to the college
$1,000 plus travel costs & accommodation for the recipient & spouse to attend the assembly at which the award is presented

Easter Seals/March of Dimes National Council / Conseil National des Timbres de Pâques et de la Parade des dix sous
#511, 90 Eglinton Ave. East, Toronto ON M4P 2Y3
416/932-8382; Fax: 416/932-9844

The Easter Seals Canada Award

The Keith S. Armstrong Award
Established 1976; plaque awarded to recognize & pay tribute to an individual employed in a non-government rehabilitation organization who, over a period of years, has provided exceptional service in the interests of physically handicapped persons

The March of Dimes/Ability Fund Canada Award

The Sun Life Group Benefits Award

The Walter Dinsdale Award
Established 1982; plaque awarded to an individual or organization for outstanding achievement in the area of technical aids for the benefit of disabled persons

Canadian Almanac & Directory 1997

The Whipper Watson Award
Awarded to an individual or business that has made significant progress in integrating people with disabilities into the workplace

Epilepsy Canada / Epilepsie Canada
#745, 1470, rue Peel, Montréal PQ H3A 1T1
514/845-7855; Fax: 514/845-7866; Toll Free: 1-800-860-5499; Email: epilepsy@generation.net; URL: http://www.generation.net/~epilepsy/

Epilepsy Canada/Parke-Davis Canada Research Fellowship
To develop expertise in clinical or basic epilepsy research & to enhance the quality of care for epilepsy patients in Canada; $35,000 awarded annually to a Ph.D. or M.D. for clinical research at a Canadian institution; designed as a training program & not intended for those holding faculty appointments

Medical Research Council of Canada
Holland Cross, Tower B, 5th Fl., 1600 Holland St., Ottawa ON K1A 0W9
613/954-1812; Fax: 613/954-1800; Email: dsaintjean@hpb.hwx.xa; URL: http://www.hwc.ca:8100/

Michael Smith Award for Excellence
A medal plus $50,000 research grant awarded annually to an outstanding Canadian researcher who has demonstrated innovation, creativity & dedication to health research

Planned Parenthood Federation of Canada / Fédération pour le planning des naissances du Canada
#430, One Nicholas St., Ottawa ON K1N 7B7
613/241-4474; Fax: 613/241-7550; Email: ppfed@web.apc.org

Norman Barwin Scholarship
Established 1987; $2,500 awarded to a full-time graduate student in the field of reproductive health

The Royal College of Physicians & Surgeons of Canada / Le Collège royal des médecins et chirurgiens du Canada
774 Echo Dr., Ottawa ON K1S 5N8
613/730-8177; Fax: 613/730-8833; Toll Free: 1-800-668-3740

The Royal College of Physicians & Surgeons of Canada Medals
Established 1946; $5,000 & a bronze medal awarded annually for original scientific work judged best in the Division of Medicine, & the Division of Surgery; the purpose of the awards is to provide national recognition to original work by young clinicians & investigators

The Royal Society of Canada / La Société royale du Canada
#308, 225 Metcalfe St., Ottawa ON K2P 1P9
613/991-6990; Fax: 613/991-6996; Email: adminrsc@rsc.ca; URL: http://library.utoronto.ca/www/rsc/

Jason A. Hannah Medal
Established 1976; $1,500 & a bronze medal awarded annually for an important publication in the history of medicine

The McLaughlin Medal
$1,500 & a medal awarded annually for important research of sustained excellence in any branch of medical science

HERITAGE see CULTURE

HISTORY see CULTURE

HORTICULTURE see AGRICULTURE & FARMING

JOURNALISM

Alberta Weekly Newspapers Association
Terrace Plaza, #360, 4445 Calgary Trail South, Edmonton AB T6H 5R7
403/434-8746; Fax: 403/438-8356

Arts in Print Awards
Recognizes excellence in coverage of the arts by Alberta's weekly newspapers; awards totalling $3,000 are offered in partnership with the Alberta Foundation for the Arts

Association québécoise des éditeurs de magazines
4316, boul Saint-Laurent, Montréal PQ H2W 1Z3
514/499-9847; Fax: 514/842-2422

Grands Prix du Magazines du Québec
Des prix annuels sont remises dans les catégories suivantes: Articles; Arts visuels; Texte et images; Publicité, et Promotion

Atlantic Journalism Awards
PO Box 1010, Dartmouth NS B2Y 4R1
902/420-6934, 422-1271, ext.158

Journalism Awards
A program of the University of King's College School of Journalism established in 1981 to recognize excellence & achievement in work by Atlantic Canadian journalists; covers work in English or French; 8 award categories featuring work published or broadcast in the news media of Atlantic Canada
Winners in individual categories will receive an awards certificate & $300; Journalist of the Year will be selected from the winners of the individual categories & will receive a certificate & $500

Canadian Association of Journalists / L'Association canadienne des journalistes
St. Patrick's Building, Carleton University, 1125 Colonel By Dr., Ottawa ON K1S 5B6
613/526-8061; Fax: 613/521-3904; Email: cf408@freenet.carleton.ca; URL: http://freenet.carleton.ca/freeport/prof.assoc/caj/menu; http://www.ncf.carleton.ca/freeport/prof.assoc/caj/menu

The CAJ Awards
$1,000 awards presented for the top investigative report published or broadcast in the following media: Newspaper (open category), Newspaper (circulation under 25,000), Magazine, Network, Regional TV, Network Radio, Regional Radio

Canadian Business Press
40 Shields Crt., Unionville ON L3R 0M5
905/946-8889

Kenneth Wilson Awards
Recognize excellence in writing & graphic design in specialized business/professional publications; open to all business publications, regardless of CBP membership, that are published in English &/or French; all awards, except the Harvey Southam Editorial Career Award, require an entry fee

Canadian Community Newspapers Association
#206, 90 Eglinton Ave. East, Toronto ON M4P 2Y3
416/482-1090; Fax: 416/482-1908; Email: ccna@sentex.net; URL: http://www.sentex.net/~ccna

General Excellence Competitions Awards
Awards are presented to newspapers for general excellence by circulation category, & include presentations to the Best All-Round Newspaper, Best Front Page, & Best Editorial Page in both broadsheet & tabloid categories

Premier Awards
Awards are presented in the following categories: Outstanding Columnist, Local Cartoon, Editorial Writing,

Community Service, Agricultural Special Edition, House Ad, Reporter Initiative, News Story
Special Competitions Awards
Awards are given in following areas: Best Spot News Photo, Best Feature Photo, Best Sports Photo, Best Christmas Edition, Best Sports Page, Best Special Section, Best Historical Story, Best Newspaper Promotion, Best Feature Story, Best Photo Essay, Best Advertising Idea

Canadian Conference of the Arts / Conférence canadienne des arts
189 Laurier Ave. West, Ottawa ON K1N 6P1
613/238-3561; Fax: 613/238-4849; Toll Free: 1-800-463-3561; Email: ccarts@globalx.net
Imperial Oil Award for Excellence in Arts Journalism
Established in 1988; this $1,000 award is meant to encourage wider coverage of the arts & to recognize print & broadcast journalists who have consistently given the arts good & thoughtful coverage; nominations can be made by CAA members & by media colleagues

Canadian Daily Newspaper Association / Association canadienne des quotidiens
#1100, 890 Yonge St., Toronto ON M4W 3P4
416/923-3567; Fax: 416/923-7206; Email: bcantley@fox.nstn.ca; URL: http://fox.nstn.ca/~bcantley/cdna.html
National Newspaper Awards/Concours canadien de journalisme
Awards are presented annually in early spring in 15 categories: Spot News Reporting, Enterprise Reporting, Special Project, Layout & Design, Critical Writing, Sports Writing, Feature Writing, Cartooning, Columns, Business Reporting, International Reporting, Spot News Photography, Feature Photography, Sports Photography, Editorial Writing
Eligible are those employed by or freelance for daily newspapers or wire services in French or English; awards are governed by an independent board of governors consisting of newspaper & pubilc representatives
Winners receive $2,000 plus certificates; two runners-up in each category receive citations of merit

Canadian Science Writers' Association / Association canadienne des rédacteurs scientifiques
PO Box 75, Stn A, Toronto ON M5W 1A2
416/928-9624; Fax: 416/960-0528; Email: cswa@interlog.com; URL: http://www.interlog.com/~cswa
Canadian Forest Service-Ontario Journalism Award
Open to print journalists who have published an article concerning some aspect of forestry in Ontario during the previous calendar year
Greg Clark Outdoor Writing Award
Open to Canadian print entries for work appearing in an Ontario publication during the previous year & related to natural resources in Ontario

Canadian Society of Magazine Editors
c/o Canadian Living, #100, 25 Sheppard Ave. West, North York ON M2N 6S7
416/596-5177
The Editors Choice Awards
Awards are presented in three categories: fewer than 50,000 circulation; 50,000-250,000 circulation; more than 250,000 circulation

Electronic Link
#324, 885 Don Mills Rd., Don Mills ON M4C 1V9
416/510-0909; Fax: 416/510-0913; Email: elink@interlog.com
Digital Art & Design Awards
Established in 1995, awards are given in three categories: Static, images, products or packaging involving illustration, digital photo-manipulation, design, model-ing & rendering; Dynamic, anything involving motion, but not interactive (including animation, video & special effects); & Interactive, multimedia projects, including games, corporate presentations, promotions & on-line publishing

International Development Research Centre / Centre de recherches pour le développement international
250 Albert St., 10th Fl., PO Box 8500, Ottawa ON K1G 3H9
613/236-6163; Fax: 613/563-0815; Email: info@idrc.ca; URL: http://www.idrc.ca/index.html
Fellowship in Journalism with L'Agence Périscoop Multimédia
$30,000 fellowship awarded
Internship with Gemini News Service
$30,000 provided for an internship with Gemini News Service

The Martin Wise Goodman Trust
c/o Dian Kesler-Corneil, One Yonge St., Toronto ON M5E 1D9
416/869-4545; Fax: 416/869-4183
The Martin Wise Goodman Canadian Nieman Fellowship
Provides a mid-career opportunity for full-time news or editorial employees or photographers with newspapers, press services, radio, television or magazines to study & broaden their intellectual horizons; must have at least three years professional experience
A fellowship at Harvard University for the academic year worth approximately $40,000

National Magazine Awards Foundation / Fondation nationale des prix du magazine canadien
#207, 109 Vanderhoof Ave., Toronto ON M4G 2H7
416/422-1358; Fax: 416/422-3762
National Magazine Awards
Awards are presented annually in 26 categories including Personal Journalism, Arts & Entertainment, Humour, Business, Science, Health & Medicine, Sports & Recreation, Fiction, Poetry, Travel, Magazine Illustration, Photojournalism, Art Direction, Magazine Covers, & Photography; all above awards go to individual magazine writers, photographers, illustrators, or art directors; Magazine of the Year recognizes continual overall excellence, The President's Medal is awarded to an article from the text categories & offers a prize of $3,000; The Foundation Award for Outstanding Achievement was introduced in 1990 & recognizes an individual's innovation & creativity through career-long contributions to the magazine industry
Awards are gold or silver scrolls with $1,500 & $500 cash prizes respectively

La Société Saint-Jean-Baptiste de Montréal
82, rue Sherbrooke ouest, Montréal PQ H2X 1X3
514/843-8851; Fax: 514/844-6369
Prix Olivar-Asselin
Established 1955; $1,500 & a medal awarded annually to a French Canadian in recognition of outstanding achievement in journalism in serving the higher interests of the French Canadian people

Toronto Press Club
276 King St. West, Toronto ON M5V 1H9
416/408-3550
Canadian News Hall of Fame
Toronto Press Club is custodian of the Hall of Fame dedicated to those people who have contributed regularly to journalism as staffers
National Newspaper Awards
Established 1949; awarded annually to print men & women employed regularly on the staffs of Canadian daily newspapers
Norman DePoe Memorial Scholastic Fund
A bursary awards program to students in the media

Western Canadian Magazine Awards Foundation
3898 Hillcrest Ave., North Vancouver BC V7R 4B6
604/984-7525; Fax: 604/985-6262
The Western Magazine Awards
Twenty-six categories of awards for editorial excellence in Western Canadian magazine writing, photography, illustration & art direction

Western Ontario Newspaper Awards
225 Fairway Rd., PO Box R1200, Kitchener ON N2G 4E5
519/894-2231, ext.602
Ford Motor Company of Canada Limited Trophies
Family Section Feature Writing Trophy; Ford Spot News Photography Trophy; Ford Feature Photography Trophy; Ford Trophy for Writing Excellence
Southam Newspapers Trophies
Southam Business Writing Trophy; Southam Spot News Trophy; Sandy Baird Humourous Writing Trophy; K.J. Strachan Editorial Writing Trophy, & Southam Sports Photography Trophy
Special Awards & Trophies
C.B. Schmidt Award; John E. Motz Memorial Trophy; Joan May Memorial Trophy; Richard Sutton Memorial Trophy; Winnifred M. Stokes Hill Memorial Trophy; Gene Florcyk Memorial Award; Edward J. Hayes Award; Windsor Star Trophy; Walter J. Blackburn Award; Sault Star Award; Larry N. Smith Award; Norma R. Bidwell Award; Robert J. Hanley Award; Press Institute of Canada Award; Jack Bowman Memorial Award; The Del Bell Trophy; Carl Morgan Award, & the Martha G. Blackburn Award

LANGUAGES see CULTURE

LEGAL, GOVERNMENTAL, PUBLIC ADMINISTRATION

Alberta Human Rights & Citizenship Commission
Standard Life, #1600, 10405 Jasper Ave., Edmonton AB T5J 4R7
403/427-7661
Alberta Human Rights Award
A citation & a specially commissioned glass trophy awarded to the individual who made a significant contribution to the promotion of human rights in Alberta

Alberta Justice
Public Security Division
10365 - 97 St., 10th Fl., Edmonton AB T5J 3W7
403/427-3457; Fax: 403/422-0248
Crime Prevention Awards
Awards recognize the contributions of individuals, businesses, & special interest groups towards establishing & maintaining safer communities; awards are presented in three categories: individuals, businesses, & community programs/organizations; nominees must play a role in establishing, coordinating or maintaining a specific crime prevention practice in their community
– Contact, Gloria Ohrt, Manager, Family Violence & Crime Prevention

Crime Prevention Ontario
240 Leighland Ave., Oakville ON L6H 3H6
905/844-4594; Fax: 905/844-3608; Toll Free: 1-800-668-0261
Crime Prevention Ontario Community Awards
Established 1984; awards recognize outstanding contributions made by community organizations, volunteers, police services & individual police officers, in the prevention of crime in Ontario; participation is open to all residents of Ontario, to organizations operating in Ontario, & to Ontario police services

Certificates are presented at regional ceremonies held throughout the province from Ontario Crime Prevention Week in November to mid-March the following year – Contact, Marni Amodeo

Crime Prevention Ontario Provincial Awards

Awarded to the best of the Crime Prevention Ontario Community Award winners; plaques presented by the Solicitor General at the Annual Crime Prevention Ontario Symposium in April each year

Government Finance Officers Association of the US & Canada
#800, 180 North Michigan Ave., Chicago IL 60601
312/977-9700; Fax: 312/977-4806

The Canadian Award for Financial Reporting

Established in 1990; goal of the program is to encourage municipal governments throughout Canada to publish high-quality financial reports & to provide peer recognition & technical guidance for officials preparing these reports; awards are valid for one year & may be granted in successive years to qualified governments; submissions & judging are conducted in either English or French

The Distinguished Budget Presentation Award

Established 1984; recognizes excellence in governmental budgeting by state, provincial & local governments in the US & Canada; awards are valid for one year & may be granted successively to qualified organizations

Institute of Public Administration of Canada / Institut d'administration publique du Canada
#305, 150 Eglinton Ave. East, Toronto ON M4P 1E8
416/932-3666; Fax: 416/923-3667

IPAC/Coopers & Lybrand Award for Innovative Management

Awarded in recognition of outstanding organizational achievement in the public sector

Vanier Medal

A gold medal is awarded annually as a mark of distinction & exceptional achievement to a person who has shown outstanding leadership in public administration in Canada

Justice Canada
Programs Directorate, Justice Bldg., Ottawa ON K1A 0H8
613/957-4344

Civil Law/Common Law Exchange Program

To give civil & common law students from across Canada the opportunity to learn about & compare Canada's two legal systems; the program also promotes bilingualism within educational & cultural activities
Open to individuals enrolled in a three-year law program in a Canadian university; preference is given to students in their second & third year of law studies
A scholarship of $1,500 is awarded to participants who successfully complete both sessions of the program; all travel & living expenses associated with the program are paid & each student receives an incidental expense allowance

Legal Studies for Aboriginal People Program

A grants & scholarship program to encourage Metis & Non-Status Indians to enter the legal profession by providing financial assistance through a pre-law orientation course & a three-year scholarship program
Open to Aboriginal People (Metis & Non-Status Indians)

Professional Institute of The Public Service of Canada / Institut professionnel de la Fonction publique du Canada
53 Auriga Dr., Nepean ON K2E 8C3
613/228-6310; Fax: 613/228-9048; Toll Free: 1-800-267-0446

Professional Institute Gold Medals

Established 1937; two gold medals are presented biennially. Those eligible are scientific, professional, or technical workers or groups of workers employed by the federal, provincial or municipal government services of Canada who have made a contribution of outstanding importance to national or world well-being in either pure or applied science or in some field outside pure or applied science

Society of Composers, Authors & Music Publishers of Canada / Société canadienne des auteurs, compositeurs et éditeurs de musique
41 Valleybrook Dr., North York ON M3B 2S6
416/445-8700; Fax: 416/445-7108; Toll Free: 1-800-557-6226

Gordon F. Henderson/SOCAN Copyright Competition

$2,000 presented annually to a law student or articling lawyer for an essay on the subject of copyright & music

LITERARY ARTS, BOOKS & LIBRARIES

Alberta Foundation for the Arts
Beaver House, 10158 - 103 St., 5th Fl., Edmonton AB T5J 0X6
403/427-9968; Fax: 403/422-1162

Alberta New Fiction Competition

Established 1971 & awarded every two years; must be resident of Alberta; award winning book is purchased by the Foundation for the 307 libraries in Alberta

Alberta Playwriting Competition

Alberta Write for Radio Competition

Jon Whyte Memorial Essay Prize

The Alberta Writing for Youth Competition

Established 1980 & awarded every two years; first prize for best publishable manuscript is $4,500 for a resident of Alberta; the Foundation purchases 307 copies of the winning title for presentation to libraries in Alberta

Tommy Banks Award

Annual award recognizes achievements of high school band conductors; co-sponsored by the Alberta Stage & Concert Band Festival Association

Association des écrivains des langue français
14, rue Broussais, F75014 Paris
1/43-21-95-99

Prix France-Québec Jean-Hamelin

Fondé en 1965 par l'ADELF avec la collaboration de la Délégation générale du Québec à Paris; le prix est attribué à une écrivain québécois d'expression français, soit pour un ouvrage publié depuis janvier de l'année précédente
Le lauréat reçoit une bourse de 5 000 FF offerte par le gouvernement du Québec; les frais de voyage et de séjour du lauréat en France sont offerts par le gouvernement français

Association pour l'avancement des sciences et des techniques de la documentation
202, 3414, av du Parc, Montréal PQ H2X 2H5
514/281-5012; Fax: 514/281-8219; Email: info@asted.org; URL: http://www.asted.org

Prix Marie-Claire-Daveluy

Established 1970; awarded annually to encourage young authors to write for young people & to promote the production of Canadian writing for young people
Open to any French-speaking person between the ages of 15 & 20; must be a resident of Canada; prize of $500 for 15-17 year, & $500 for 18-20 years

Book Publishers Association of Alberta
#123, 10523 - 100 Ave., Edmonton AB T5J 0A8
403/424-5060; Fax: 403/424-7943; Email: bpaa@planet.eon.net

The Alberta Book Industry Awards

To recognize outstanding achievements in Alberta publishing; five awards are given - Alberta Publisher of the Year, Alberta Book of the Year, Alberta Book Design Award, Alberta Book Promotion Award, Alberta Educational Book of the Year
Stone carvings by Brian Clark are presented & kept by the winner in the award year & exchanged for plaques the following year

Books In Canada
427 Mount Pleasant Rd., Toronto ON M4S 2L8
416/489-4755; Fax: 416/489-6045; Email: binc@intacc.web.net

Smith Books/Books in Canada First Novel Award

Established 1976 by Books in Canada magazine; co-sponsored by Smith Books to promote & encourage Canadian writing
Winner receives $5,000 & his/her books are made available in Smith bookstores across Canada

British Columbia Historical Federation
PO Box 746, Grand Forks BC V0H 1H0
250/442-3865

Writing Awards

Established 1983; Lieutenant-Governor's Medal for Historical Writing, three Certificates of Merit, & cash awards given annually to authors of best books on any facet of BC history

The Canada Council / Conseil des Arts du Canada
350 Albert St., PO Box 1047, Ottawa ON K1P 5V8
613/566-4365; Fax: 613/566-4390; Toll Free: 1-800-263-5588

Canada-Japan Book Award

$10,000 awarded annually for a book in English or French about Japan by a Canadian author, or for a book by a Japanese author translated by a Canadian into English or French
The translated work or the work by the Canadian author must have been published during the year preceding the award; authors of eligible books may apply for this award to the Writing & Publishing Section of the Canada Council; winner is announced in the spring

The Governor General's Literary Awards

$10,000 each awarded annually to the best English-language & best French-language work in each of the following categories: children's literature (text & illustration), drama, fiction, poetry, non-fiction, & translation
Books must be by Canadian authors, illustrators & translators, published in Canada or abroad during the previous year; in the case of translation, the original work must also be a Canadian-authored title; juries select the winning titles from the books submitted by the publishers; a formal application from the publisher is required

Canadian Association of Children's Librarians
c/o Canadian Library Association, #602, 200 Elgin St., Ottawa ON K2P 1L5
613/232-9625; Fax: 613/563-9895; Email: ai077@freenet.carleton.ca

Amelia Frances Howard-Gibbon Illustrators Medal

Established 1971; a silver medal awarded annually for outstanding illustrations in a children's book published in Canada; the illustrator must be a Canadian or a Canadian resident

Book of the Year for Children Medal

A silver medal awarded annually for the outstanding children's book published during the calendar year; book must have been written by a Canadian or a resident of Canada

Canadian Association of College & University Libraries
c/o Canadian Library Association, #602, 200 Elgin St., Ottawa ON K2P 1L5
613/232-9625; Fax: 613/563-9895

Innovation Achievement Award

To recognize academic libraries which, through innovation in ongoing programs/services or in a special event/project, have contributed to academic librarian-

ship & library development; a framed acknowledgement & a $1,500 gift certificate is offered for the vendor of the institution's choice
Outstanding Academic Librarian Award
Awarded to a librarian who has made a notable contribution to the field of academic librarianship

Canadian Association of Public Libraries
c/o Brentwood Branch, Etobicoke Public Library, 36 Brentwood Rd. North, Etobicoke ON M8X 2B5
416/394-5245; Fax: 416/394-5257
Outstanding Public Library Service Award
Awarded annually for outstanding service in the field of public librarianship

Canadian Authors Association
27 Doxsee Ave. North, Campbellford ON K0L 1L0
705/653-0323; Fax: 705/653-0593
Canadian Authors Association/Air Canada Award
To encourage younger (30 years old or under) Canadian writers of promise; Air Canada offers the winner two return tickets anywhere within its system
Work may be published in any form; nominations are made by CAA branches & other writers organizations
The CAA Literary Awards
A program originally begun in 1937 as the Governor-General's medals for literature, these awards were reinstituted in 1975, & are funded by Harlequin Enterprises (Toronto); meant "to honour the writing that achieves literary excellence without sacrificing popular appeal" in prose fiction, prose nonfiction, poetry & drama; $5,000 & silver medal awarded
The Vicky Metcalfe Awards
Awarded annually for works of interest to Canadian youth; given to stimulate writing for children; presented annually at CAA conference
Cash prize of $10,000 (fiction, nonfiction, or picture book); $3,000 (short story for children published in magazine, periodical or anthology published in the calendar year); $1,000 (editor of a winning story if published in a Canadian book or periodical)

Canadian Booksellers Association
301 Donlands Ave., Toronto ON M4J 3R8
416/467-7883; Fax: 416/467-7886; Email: enquiries@cbabook.org; URL: http://www.cbabook.org
Barry Britnell Award
Presented annually to the bookseller of the year
Best Author of the Year
Presented annually to an author who has produced a substantial body of work & has made a significant contribution to the Canadian book industry
Publisher of the Year
Recognizes overall achievement with special reference to elements of particular concern to the bookselling community

The Canadian Children's Book Centre
35 Spadina Rd., Toronto ON M5R 2S9
416/975-0010; Fax: 416/975-1839; Email: ccbc@lglobal.com; URL: http://www.lglobal.com/~ccbc/
The Geoffrey Bilson Award for Historical Fiction
Rewards excellence in outstanding work of historical fiction for young people by a Canadian author, published in previous calendar year; categories are: writer, bookseller, children's books specialist, historian, librarian; award is in the amount of $1,000

Canadian Historical Association / Société historique du Canada
395 Wellington St., Ottawa ON K1A 0N3
613/233-7885; Fax: 613/567-3110; Email: 74143.1061@compuserve.com
François-Xavier Garneau Medal
The Senior CHA Prize; $2,500 & a life membership in CHA awarded every five years to a book which represents an outstanding Canadian contribution to history

Sir John A. Macdonald Prize
Established 1976; $1,000 awarded annually for the non-fiction work of Canadian history "judged to have made the most significant contribution to an understanding of the Canadian past"

Canadian Library Association
#602, 200 Elgin St., Ottawa ON K2P 1L5
613/232-9625; Fax: 613/563-9895; Email: ai077@freenet.carleton.ca
Dafoe Scholarship
$1,750 awarded annually to a student entering an accredited Canadian library school
H.W. Wilson Scholarship
$2,000 presented annually to a student entering an accredited Canadian library school
Howard V. Phalin - World Book Scholarship in Library Science
$2,500 scholarship given annually to be used for a program of study or series of courses either leading to a further library degree or related library work in which the candidate is currently engaged
Young Adult Canadian Book Award
Sponsored by Roots Canada; presented to recognize the best English-language fiction for young adults by a Canadian author

Canadian Library Trustees Association
c/o Canadian Library Association, #602, 200 Elgin St., Ottawa ON K2P 1L5
613/232-9625; Fax: 613/563-9895
Achievement in Literacy Award
Through this award, CLTA endorses the initiatives of the public library systems which have structured literacy programs as a component of library services to the community

Canadian School Library Association
c/o Canadian Library Association, #602, 200 Elgin St., Ottawa ON K2P 1L5
613/232-9625; Fax: 613/563-9895
Grolier Award for Research in School Librarianship in Canada
$1,000 awarded to support theoretical & applied research that advances the field of school librarianship
Margaret B. Scott Award of Merit
Awarded annually to recognize outstanding achievement in school librarianship in Canada
National Book Service Teacher-Librarian of the Year Award
To honour a school-based teacher-librarian who has made an outstanding contribution to school librarianship by planning & implementing an exemplary school library program based on a collaborative model; award is sponsored by Maclean Hunter Library Services

Canadian Science Writers' Association / Association canadienne des rédacteurs scientifiques
PO Box 75, Stn A, Toronto ON M5W 1A2
416/928-9624; Fax: 416/960-0528; Email: cswa@interlog.com; URL: http://www.interlog.com/~cswa
Science in Society Journalism Awards
Open to Canadian journalists in all media for work appearing in the previous calendar year; categories include newspapers, magazines, trade publications, radio, television, children's books & general books; awards total $12,000

Carousel Magazine
UC Room 274, University of Guelph, Guelph ON N1G 2W1
519/824-4120, ext.6748; Fax: 519/673-9603; Email: daniel@uoguelph.ca
Carousel Writing Contest
First awarded in 1996, $400 prize for fiction & $400 prize for poetry

CBC Radio / Saturday Night Literary Competition
PO Box 500, Stn A, Toronto ON M5W 1E6
416/205-3311
CBC Radio/Saturday Night Literary Awards
Established 1993; annual $10,000 awards for short story, personal essay & poetry; winning works are published in Saturday Night & broadcast on Between The Covers on CBC Radio

Christie Brown & Co.
2150 Lakeshore Blvd. West, Toronto ON M8V 1A3
416/503-6000; Fax: 416/503-6010
Mr. Christie's Book Award
Prizes total $45,000 & are awarded to the best children's book (one English & one French) in three age categories: ages four to eight; nine to 11, & 12 & over; the author &/or illustrator must be Canadian, & the books must be written/illustrated for children

The City of Toronto
Dept. of the City Clerk, City Hall, 100 Queen St. West, Toronto ON M5H 2N2
416/392-7494; Fax: 416/392-1446
Book Awards
In 1973, City Council established a Book Award Selection Committee to select an annual winner or winners of a literary prize; committee selects a short list of nominees whose books are about Toronto & published in the preceding year

Coopers & Lybrand
5160 Yonge S., North York ON M2N 6L3
416/224-2140; Fax: 416/229-3183
National Business Book Award
Established 1985; annual prize of $10,000 awarded to author of book containing key material on business in Canada

Corporation des bibliothécaires professionnels du Québec / Corporation of Professional Librarians of Québec
#320, 307, rue Ste-Catherine ouest, Montréal PQ H2X 2A3
514/845-3327; Fax: 514/845-1618; Email: cbpq@interlink.net
Merite annuel de la CBPQ - Bibliothécaire professionnel(le)
Stimuler et reconnaître l'excellence parmi les membres; attirer l'attention des médias sur les récipiendaires de cette distinction honorifique et sur la nature des réalisations primées; orienter des perceptions; le prix comporte les volets suivants: distinction honorifique, remise d'une épinglette en or, publicité entourant l'événement

Corporation du Grand Prix de la science-fiction et du fantastique québécois
3194, terrasse Sagard, Longueuil PQ J4L 3J9
514/674-0869
Grand Prix de la science-fiction et du fantastique québécois
Institué en 1984, une bourse de 2 500 $ finacée par la Société des arts et de la culture de Longueuil est remise au lauréat

The Crime Writers of Canada
3007 Kingston Rd., PO Box 113, Scarborough ON M1M 1P1
416/782-3116; Fax: 416/789-4680; Email: ap113@torfree.net; URL: http://www.swifty.com/cwc/cwchome.htm
The Arthur Ellis Awards
Established 1984; awarded annually in the following categories: the best Canadian crime novel, best non-fiction, best first novel, & best short story
The Derrick Murdoch Award
Established 1984; presented to an individual or organization which has made a significant & lasting contribution to the craft of crime writing in Canada

Le Fondation Émile-Nelligan
261, rue Bloomfiled, Outremont PQ H2V 3R6
514/522-0652
Prix Gilles-Corbeil
Ce prix (100 000 $) décerné pour la première fois en 1990, est triennal; le candidat doit être l'auteur d'une oeuvre écrite en français et citoyen du Canada ou des États-Unis

Fondation Les Forges
3231, rue Notre-Dame ouest, CP 232, Pointe-du-Lac PQ G0X 1Z0
819/379-9813; Fax: 819/376-0774
Grand Prix de poésie de la Fondation Les Forges
Le Fesitval international de la poésie remet une bourse de 5 000 $ au lauréat lors de l'ouverture officielle du festival; le candidat doit: être de citoyenneté canadienne et avoir déjà publié trois ouvrages de poésie chez un éditeur reconnu
Prix Piché de poésie - Le Sortilège
Les bourse sont offertes par la Société des alcools du Québec; 1er prix, 2 000 $, 2e prix, 500 $; le candidat doit être de citoyenneté canadienne et n'avoir jamais publié d'ouvrage de poésie chez un éditeur reconnu

The Giller Prize
c/o Kelly Duffin, 21 Steepleview Cres., Richmond Hill ON L4C 9R1
905/508-5146; Fax: 905/508-4469
The Giller Prize
$25,000 award to the author of the best Canadian novel or collection of short stories published in English

Harbourfront Reading Series
#100, 410 Queens Quay West, Toronto ON M5V 2Z3
416/973-4760; Fax: 416/954-4323
The Harbourfront Festival Prize
A cash award & a shopping allowance for purchase of office equipment totalling $11,000 for a Canadian writer who has made a significant contribution to the literary community; sponsored by OE a division of Canon Inc.

International Board on Books for Young People - Canadian Section / Union internationale pour les livres de jeunesse
c/o Canadian Children's Book Centre, 35 Spadina Rd., Toronto ON M5R 2S9
416/975-0010; Fax: 416/975-1839
Claude Aubry Award
$1,000 awarded biennially for distinguished contributions to Canadian children's literature by a librarian, teacher, author, illustrator, publisher, bookseller, or editor
Elizabeth Mrazik-Cleaver Picture Book Award
$1,000 awarded for distinguished Canadian picture book illustration; submissions to Children's Literature Service, National Library of Canada, 395 Wellington St., Ottawa, ON K1A 0N4
Frances E. Russell Award
Awarded to initiate & encourage research in children's literature in Canada; award is in the amount of $1,000

The League of Canadian Poets
The Writers' Centre, 54 Wolseley St., 3rd Fl., Toronto ON M5T 1A5
416/504-1657; Fax: 416/703-0059; Email: league@io.org
Gerald Lampert Award
Established 1979; $1,000 awarded annually for excellence in a first book of poetry, written by a Canadian citizen or landed immigrant, & published in the preceding year
National Poetry Contest Prizes
There is no limit on the number of poems a person may submit; poems should be previously unpublished & under 75 lines in length
First Prize: $1,000; Second: $750; Third: $500; the three winners, plus 47 finalists, are also published in the contest anthology
Pat Lowther Memorial Award
$1,000 awarded annually for excellence in a book of poetry, written by a Canadian female citizen or landed immigrant, & published in the preceding year

The Lionel Gelber Prize
c/o Manager, Lionel Gelber Prize, 410 Queen's Quay West, Toronto ON M5V 2Z3
416/973-4760
The Lionel Gelber Prize
This $50,000 prize is one of the largest of its kind in the world; a legacy of Lionel Gelber, internationalist writer who died in 1989 & who was much acclaimed for his service to Canada; the prize is "designed to stimulate authors of any nationality who write about international relations, & to encourage the audience for these books to grow"
For books published in English, must be copyrighted in the year in which the prize is awarded; books must be published or accessible in Canada; submissions by publishers only

Literary Translators' Association of Canada / Association des traducteurs et traductrices littéraires du Canada
3492, rue Laval, Montréal PQ H2X 3C8
514/849-8540
Glassco Translation Prize
$500 & one year's membership in the association awarded annually for a translator's first work in book-length literary translation into French or English, published in Canada during the previous calendar year

Manitoba Writers' Guild
#206, 100 Arthur St., Winnipeg MB R3B 1H3
204/942-6134; Fax: 204/942-5754
John Hirsch Award for Most Promising Manitoba Writer
$2,500 awarded annually to the most promising Manitoba writer working in poetry, fiction, creative non-fiction or drama
Manitoba Book Publishers' Award
For the best overall design in Manitoba book publishing
McNally Robinson Award for Manitoba Book of the Year
$2,500 to the Manitoba author judged to have written the best book in the calendar year

McClelland & Stewart
#900, 481 University Ave., Toronto ON M5G 2E9
416/598-1114; Fax: 416/598-7764
The Journey Prize
"The Journey Prize Anthology" presents accomplished selections from 13 outstanding new Canadian writers; one of these is chosen as winner
$10,000 cash prize donated by James Michener; the journal that submitted the winning piece will be awarded $2,000 by M&S

The Municipal Chapter of Toronto IODE
#205, 40 St. Clair Ave. East, Toronto ON M4T 1M9
416/925-5078; Fax: 416/925-5127
IODE Book Award
Established in 1975; an inscribed scroll & not less than $1,000 awarded annually to the author or illustrator of the best children's book written or illustrated by a Canadian resident in Toronto or surrounding area & published by a Canadian publisher within the preceding 12 months

The National Chapter of Canada IODE
#254, 40 Orchard View Blvd., Toronto ON M4R 1B9
416/487-4416; Fax: 416/487-4417
National Chapter of Canada IODE Violet Downey Book Award
$3,000 awarded annually for the best English-language book, containing at least 500 words of text in any category suitable for children aged 13 & under

Nova Scotia Library Association
c/o Nova Scotia Provincial Library, 3770 Kempt Rd., Halifax NS B3K 4X8
902/453-2810; Fax: 902/422-0633
Ann Connor Brimer Award
$500 awarded to the author of fiction or non-fiction books published in Canada currently in print & intended for children up the age of 15; writer must be residing in Atlantic Canada – Contact, Heather Mackenzie, Halifax City Regional Library, 5381 Spring Garden Rd., Halifax NS B3J 1E9

Ontario Arts Council / Conseil des arts de l'Ontario
#600, 151 Bloor St. West, Toronto ON M5S 1T6
416/961-1660; Fax: 416/961-7796; Toll Free: 1-800-387-0058; Email: oac@gov.on.ca
Floyd S. Chalmers Canadian Play Award
Four $10,000 awards may be given annually for outstanding plays performed in Metropolitan Toronto
Ruth Schwartz Children's Book Award
Two awards presented annually; $3,000 for best picture book & $2,000 for best young adult/middle reader book; in conjunction with the Canadian Booksellers Association
The Chalmers Canadian Children's Play Awards
Established 1973; awarded annually to recognize outstanding new Canadian plays for young audiences performed in the Metropolitan Toronto area; $10,000 for an outstanding play & $5,000 each for two runners-up

Ontario Library Association / Association des bibliothèques de l'Ontario
#303, 100 Lombard St., Toronto ON M5C 1M3
416/363-3388; Fax: 416/941-9581; Email: jgilbert@interlog.com
Silver Birch Awards
Reading program for children in Ontario in grades 4, 5 & 6, established in 1994 (approximately 12,000 children take part); children register through their school or public library to read 22 Canadian books, half fiction & half non-fiction; those who have read five of the books can then vote for their favourite; winners receive a tactile image of a silver birch tree

Ontario Ministry of Citizenship, Culture & Recreation
Ontario Publishing Centre, 77 Bloor St. West, 2nd Fl., Toronto ON M7A 2R9
416/314-7745
Trillium Book Award/Prix Trillium
Awarded annually to an Ontario author of a book of excellence; the winning book must have been published within the preceding 12 months; books in English or French in any genre are eligible; winner receives $12,000 & the publisher receives $2,500

PEI Council of the Arts
151 Richmond St., Charlottetown PE C1A 1H7
902/368-4410; Fax: 902/368-4418
Island Literary Awards
Established in 1987 in recognition of Island writers in six categories: Short Story, Poetry, Children's Literature, Novels or Historical Works, Creative Writing for Children, Playwriting; an additional award is made "for distinguished contribution to the literary arts"; awards of $500, $200 & $100

Periodical Marketers of Canada
South Tower, #1007, 175 Bloor St. East, Toronto ON M4W 3R8
416/968-7218; Fax: 416/968-6182

Canadian Letters Awards
Established 1977 in recognition of outstanding Canadian writing; a total of $5,000 in cash prizes is awarded annually in the following categories: Paperback Book Non-Fiction, Magazine, Public Affairs, Business & Finance, Science & Medicine, Fiction, Personality Feature, Humour, Arts & Entertainment, Cover Design, Magazine & Paperback Book, Special Recognition, Book of the Year, Author of the Year

Phoenix Community Works Foundation
316 Dupont St., Toronto ON M5R 1V9
416/964-7919; Fax: 416/964-6941
The bp nichol Chap-book Award
$1,000 awarded for the best poetry chap-book in English, published in Canada; entries must be from 10-48 pages in length

Prism International
#E462, Dept. of Creative Writing, UBC, 1866 Main Mall, Vancouver BC V6T 1Z1
604/822-2514; Email: prism@unixg.ubc.ca
Prism Short Fiction Contest
$3,000 in prizes for annual short fiction contest

Québec Ministère de la culture et des communications
225, Grande Allée est, Bloc V, 3e étage, Québec PQ G1R 5G5
418/643-2183; Fax: 418/643-3310
Les Prix du Québec:
Prix Athanase-David
La plus haute distinction du gouvernement du Québec en littérature; le lauréat reçoit 30 000 $ et une médaille en argent; attribué annuellement pour l'ensemble de l'oeuvre littéraire d'un créateur québécois

Québec Ministère des Relations internationales
Édifice Hector-Fabre, 525, boul René-Lévesque, Québec PQ G1R 5R2
Prix Québec-Paris
Originellement appelé Prix France-Canada, ce prix a été fondé en 1958 par la Commission culturelle de l'Association France-Canada, á laquelle s'est associée, dès a création en 1961, la Délégation générale du Québec; le prix est attribué à un écrivain d'expression français, québécois ou canadien français, dont l'ouvrage a été publié au Canada ou en France au cours de l'année pour laquelle le prix et attribué
Le lauréat reçoit une bourse de 2 000 $ offerts par le gouvernement du Québec, plus une contribution de 4 000 FF offerte par la Ville de Paris; de plus, le gouvernement français prend en charge les frais de voyage et de séjour en France du lauréat – Contact, Direction générale France, 418/649-2330
Prix Québec/Wallonie-Bruxelles du livre de la jeunesse
Le prix a été créé en 1978 dans le but d'encourager le developpement de la littérature de jeunesse at de faire connaître aux deux communautés, québécoise et français de Belgique, leur production respective; le prix est de 105 000 FB ou 3 500 $, auxquels s'ajoute une aide financière à l'éditeur de 180 000 FB ou 6 000 $ – Contact, Direction générale de l'Europe, 418/649-2308

Québec Society for the Promotion of English Language Literature / Société québecoise pour la promotion de la littérature de la langue anglaise
1200 Atwater Ave., Montréal PQ H3Z 1X6
514/933-0878; Fax: 514/933-0878
QSPELL Prizes
Established 1988; awards three annual prizes of $2,000 each to honour literary excellence: The A.M. Klein poetry prize, The Hugh MacLennan fiction prize & a non-fiction award
Books can be submitted by publishers or authors; three copies, accompanied by entry form & $10 registration fee per title; authors must have lived in Québec three of the past five years

Real Estate Institute of Canada / Institut canadien de l'immeuble
#208, 5407 Eglinton Ave. West, Toronto ON M9C 5K6
416/695-9000; Fax: 416/695-7230
Morguard Literary Awards
Co-sponsored by REIC & Morguard Investments Limited, this competition is open to any topic pertaining to the Canadian real estate industry; subject matter may include, but is not limited to, real estate law, architecture, legislation, property management, appraisal, & ethics; competition consists of two categories, including academic writers & practising industry lay writers
An award of $2,000 is presented to the winner in each category, & the winning submissions will be featured in a future edition of Contact

The Royal Society of Canada / La Société royale du Canada
#308, 225 Metcalfe St., Ottawa ON K2P 1P9
613/991-6990; Fax: 613/991-6996; Email: adminrsc@rsc.ca; URL: http://library.utoronto.ca/www/rsc/
Lorne Pierce Medal
Established 1926; awarded every two years for an achievement of special significance & conspicuous merit in imaginative or critical literature written in either English or French, & preferably dealing with a Canadian subject

Salon du livre de Québec
#203, 1026, rue Saint-Jean, Québec PQ G1R 1R7
418/692-5420; Fax: 418/692-0794
Les Prix littéraires Desjardins
Des prix de 2 000 $ sont offerts dans les catégories suivantes: roman, poésie, littérature pour la jeunesse, essai, et nouvelle, conte, récit pour les citoyens canadiens au Québec
Prix des libraires du Québec
Ce prix fut créé en 1993; il souligne l'excellence d'un roman québécois par sa qualité d'écriture et son originalité; une bourse de 2 000 $ est offerte au lauréat par Le Journal de Québec

Saskatchewan Book Awards
PO Box 1921, Regina SK S4P 3E1
306/569-1585; Fax: 306/569-4187
Brenda MacDonald Riches First Book Award
$1,000 to the author of the best first book by a Saskatchewan writer; sponsored by the Saskatchewan Writers Guild
Children's Literature Award
$1,000 awarded to the author of the best book of children's literature by a Saskatchewan author; sponsored by SaskTel
City of Regina Book Award
$1,000 to the author of the best book by a Regina writer
Fiction Award
$1,000 presented to the author of the best book of fiction (novel or short fiction) by a Saskatchewan author
Non-Fiction Award
$1,000 award sponsored by Wascana Energy for the best book of non-fiction by a Saskatchewan author
Poetry Award
$1,000 awarded to the best book of poetry by a Saskatchewan author
Saskatchewan Award for Publishing
A commemorative plaque for the publisher & a certificate for the author presented to the best book published in Saskatchewan; judged on overall quality of design, production, marketing, content & significance
Saskatchewan Book of the Year Award
Sponsored by Regina News-Midwest News; $1,000 awarded to the author of a book in one of the following categories: children's books, drama, fiction, non-fiction or poetry

Saskatchewan First Peoples Publishing Award
Commemorative certificates for the writer & publisher of the best book with First Nations, Metis, or non-status Indian content written, or in the case of an anthology, edited by a person of First Nations, Metis, or non-status Indian descent; based on the quality of publisher's craft, editing, & literary or artistic value
Saskatchewan Publishing in Education Award
Commemorative certificates for the writer or editor & publisher of the best books produced as an educational resource, judged on the quality of the publisher's craft, editing & its value to eduators at primary, secondary or post secondary levels

Saskatchewan Library Association
PO Box 3388, Regina SK S4P 3H1
306/780-9413; Fax: 306/780-9447; Email: sla@pleis.lib.sk.ca
The Frances Morrison Award
Awarded for outstanding service to libraries
The Mary Donaldson Award
Awarded for excellence to a student studying at a library education institution in Saskatchewan

Saskatchewan Writers Guild Inc.
PO Box 3986, Regina SK S4P 3R9
306/757-6310; Fax: 306/565-8554; URL: http://bailey2.unibase.com/~grain/SWG_Homepage.html
City of Regina Writing Award
$4,000 to a Regina writer to reward merit & enable a writer to work on a specific writing project; funded by the City of Regina Arts Commission & administered by the SWG
SWG Annual Literary Awards
Offers over $5,000 in prizes for original work in five categories; awards excellence in work by Saskatchewan writers of original, unpublished works; each year the contest features a manuscript competition offering three prizes of $1,000 each for book-length works, with the genre rotating through drama, fiction, non-fiction & poetry. Three prizes of $150 & honourable mentions of $75 are available in the short categories of poetry, short fiction, non-fiction & children's literature

La Société Saint-Jean-Baptiste de Montréal
82, rue Sherbrooke ouest, Montréal PQ H2X 1X3
514/843-8851; Fax: 514/844-6369
Prix Duvernay
Le prix a été crée en 1944 afin de signaler les mérites d'un compatriote dont la compétence et le rayonnement dans le domaine intellectuel et littéraire servent les intérêts supérieurs de la nation québécoise; le prix est de 3 000 $, accompagne une médaille, et est attribué à tous les trois ans

Stephen Leacock Associates
PO Box 854, Orillia ON L3V 6K8
705/325-6546
Stephen Leacock Memorial Medal
Established 1946 to encourage the writing & publishing of humorous works in Canada; given annually for the best Canadian book of humour published in the preceding year
Winner receives the medal & a cash award of $5,000 donated by Manulife Bank of Canada
The Order of Mariposa
Awarded occasionally to someone who has contributed significantly to humour in Canada

Stephen Leacock Heritage Festival
PO Box 2305, Orillia ON L3V 6S3
705/325-3261
Leacock Limerick Awards
Annual cash award of $1,000 for best limerick with 2nd & 3rd place prizes; entries must include $5 registration fee; winners announced Aug 1.

Union des écrivaines et écrivains québécois
La Maison des écrivains, 3492, av Laval, Montréal PQ H2X 3C8
514/849-8540; Fax: 514/849-6239; Email: UNEQ@login.net
Les Grands Prix du Journal de Montréal
Des prix annuels de 2 000 $ dans trois catégories (poésie, fiction et drame)
Prix Émile Nelligan
Le prix est accordé à un poète nord-américain de langue français de 35 ans ou moins
5 000 $ et une médaille à l'effigie du poète sont remises par la Fondation Émile-Nelligan
Prix Molson de l'Académie des lettres du Québec
Attribué à l'automne de chaque année à un roman paru dans les douze mois précédant le premier juin
Le Prix (5 000 $) couronne un roman de langue française, publié au Québec ou ailleurs, dont l'auteur est québécois ou canadien, membre ou non de l'Union des écrivaines et écrivains québécois

University of British Columbia
President's Office, 6328 Memorial Rd., Vancouver BC V6T 1Z2
604/822-8310; Fax: 604/822-3134
Medal for Canadian Biography
Established 1952; awarded annually for the best biography written either about or by a Canadian & published in the preceding year

Ville de Montréal
Service de la culture
5650, d'Iberville, 5e étage, Montréal PQ H2G 3E4
514/872-5579
Grand Prix du livre de Montréal
Le prix est offert par la Ville de Montréal à l'auteur ou aux co-auteurs d'un ouvrage de langue française ou anglaise, pour la facture exceptionnelle et l'apport original de cette publication; le prix consiste en une bourse de 10 000 $ pour un résident de la Communauté urbaine de Montréal

West Coast Book Prize Society
#700, 1033 Davie St., Vancouver BC V6E 1M7
604/687-2405; Fax: 604/687-2405
BC Book Prizes:
Established 1985; awards of $2,000 presented to winners in each of six categories; the the book may have been published anywhere in the world; $15 fee per entry:
Dorothy Livesay Poetry Prize
Awarded to the author of the best work of poetry; the writer must have lived in BC for three of the preceding five years
The Bill Duthie Booksellers' Choice Prize
Awarded for the best book in terms of public appeal, initiative, design, production & content; the book must have been published in BC
The Ethel Wilson Fiction Prize
Awarded to the author of the best work of fiction; the writer must have lived in BC for three of the preceding five years
The Hubert Evans Non-Fiction Prize
Awarded to the author of the best original non-fiction literary work (philosophy, belles lettres, biography, history, etc.); the writer must have lived in BC for three of the preceding five years
The Roderick Haig-Brown Regional Prize
Awarded to the author of the book that contributes most to the enjoyment & understanding of BC; the book may deal with any aspect of the province & should epitomize the BC experience
The Sheila A. Egoff Children's Prize
Awarded to the author of the best book for young people aged 16 & under; the author or illustrator must have lived in BC for three of the preceding five years

Writers Guild of Alberta
Percy Page Centre, 11759 Groat Rd., 3rd Fl., Edmonton AB T5M 3K6
403/422-8174; Fax: 403/422-2663; Toll Free: 1-800-665-5354
Annual Awards Program
Established 1982 to recognize excellence in writing by Alberta authors; published books may be entered in any of the following categories: Children's Literature (any genre), Drama, Novel, Non-Fiction, Poetry, Short Fiction; winners receive leather-bound copy of their book & $500 cash award

The Writers' Development Trust
The Writers' Centre, #201, 24 Ryerson Ave., Toronto ON M5T 2P3
416/504-8222; Fax: 416/504-9090
The Gordon Montador Award
Established 1993; $2,000 awarded annually for the year's best book on contemporary social issues
The Marian Engel Award
Established 1986; $10,000 awarded annually for outstanding prose writing by a Canadian woman

Writers' Federation of Nova Scotia
#901, 1809 Barrington St., Halifax NS B3J 3K8
902/423-8116; Fax: 902/422-0881
Evelyn Richardson Memorial Literary Trust Award
Established 1978 to recognize outstanding work in non-fiction by a Nova Scotian writer (native or resident); award consists of $800 & a trophy
Thomas H. Raddall Atlantic Fiction Prize

The Writers' Union of Canada
24 Ryerson Ave., Toronto ON M5T 2P3
416/703-8982; Fax: 416/703-0826; Email: twuc@the_wire.com; URL: http://www.swifty.com/twuc
Short Prose Competiton for Developing Writers

MEDICAL see HEALTH & MEDICAL

MULTICULTURAL see CITIZENSHIP & BRAVERY

MUSIC see PERFORMING ARTS

PERFORMING ARTS

Alberta Heritage Scholarship Fund
Students Finance Board, Baker Centre, 9th Fl., 10025 - 106 St., Edmonton AB T5J 4P9
403/427-8640
Alberta Foundation for the Arts Scholarships
Five awards of $10,000 at graduate level for study in music, drama, dance & the visual arts & up to $50,000 is available to assist Alberta artists to further their training through non-academic short-term courses & internship or apprenticeship programs

Alberta Recording Industries Association
#208, 10136 - 100 St., Edmonton AB T5J 0P1
403/428-3372; Fax: 403/426-0188; Toll Free: 1-800-465-3117
ARIA Craft Awards
Annual awards in the following categories: Recording Engineer of the Year, Record Producer of the Year, Recording Studio of the Year, Record Company of the Year, Publishing Company of the Year, Best Compilation Album of the Year, Best Album Design of the Year, Best Music Score of the Year, Best Music Video, Best Booking Agent, Manager of the Year, & Musician of the Year
ARIA Performance Awards
Annual awards for Alberta artists in the following categories: People's Choice Award, Female Recording Artist of the Year, Male Recording Artist of the Year, Group Recording of the Year, Most Promising Artist, Best Pop/Light Rock, Best Rock/Heavy Metal, Best Alternative, Best Country, Best Blues/R&B/Soul, Best Roots/Traditional/Ethnic, Best Rap/Dance/Rhythm, Best Jazz, Best Classical, Best Children's, Songwriter/Composer of the Year, Single of the Year, Album of the Year, Award of Distinction, & Award of Excellence

The Banff Centre
PO Box 1020, Banff AB T0M 0E0
403/762-6193; Fax: 403/762-6444
The Clifford E. Lee Choreography Award
Established 1978; awarded annually in recognition of outstanding Canadian choreography & jointly sponsored by the Banff Centre & the Edmonton-based Clifford E. Lee Foundation
Winner receives a $5,000 cash prize & a commission to mount a new work for premiere at the Banff Festival of the Arts – Contact, George Ross

The Canada Council / Conseil des Arts du Canada
350 Albert St., PO Box 1047, Ottawa ON K1P 5V8
613/566-4414, ext.5041; Fax: 613/566-4418; Toll Free: 1-800-263-5588
Glenn Gould Prize
The $50,000 international prize is awarded every three years to an individual who has earned international recognition as the result of a highly exceptional contribution to music & its communication, through any of the communications technologies
Individuals from a broad range of fields, including musical creation or performance, film, video, television, radio & recordings, musical theatre, & writing are eligible; candidates may not put forward their own nomination; they must be nominated by three specialists in the particular field or a related one
Healey Willan Prize
$5,000 awarded every two years to the Canadian amateur choir that gives the most convincing performance in terms of musicianship, technique & program in the CBC National Radio Competition for Amateur Choirs
Jacqueline Lemieux Prize
$3,000 awarded twice annually to the most talented Canadian candidate in each of the two Arts Grant "B" competitions in dance
Jean-Marie Beaudet Award
$1,000 awarded annually to a young Canadian orchestra conductor selected by the Music Advisory Committee of the Music Section of the Canada Council from among staff conductors with Canadian orchestras
Jules Léger Prize for New Chamber Music
Designed to encourage Canadian composers to write for chamber music groups & to foster the performance of Canadian chamber music by these groups; The Canada Council funds the award & selects the jury of musicians to study the submitted scores; the CBC broadcasts the winning work of its English- and French-language stereo networks; submissions to The Canadian Music Centre, 20 St. Joseph St., Toronto ON M4Y 1J9
Award consists of $7,500 & a trophy designed by the Québec sculptor Louis Archambault
Peter Dwyer Scholarships
Annual scholarships totalling $20,000 awarded to the most promising students at the National Ballet School & the National Theatre School
Robert Fleming Prizes
The annual $1,500 prize in memory of Robert Fleming is intended to encourage the careers of young creators of music; winners are selected from the competitors for the Arts Award "B" Grants in music composition
Sir Ernest MacMillan Memorial Prize in Choral Conducting
Provided by the Toronto Mendelssohn Choir Foundation & awarded annually to a Canadian candidate selected from among the competitors for Arts Awards grants in choral conducting; prize is valued at $1,000
Sylva Gelber Foundation Award
Established 1981; approximately $15,000 awarded annually to the most talented Canadian artist under the

age of 30 in the Arts Grants "B" competition for performers in classical music
Virginia P. Moore Award
Approximately $25,000 awarded annually to a young Canadian classical musician, instrumentalist, or conductor; the prize is intended to assist a young performer in furthering his/her career & is awarded on the recommendation of the Music Advisory Committee of the Music & Opera Section of the Canada Council
The winner must have received a Canada Council grant from a Council juried program to qualify for the award

Canadian Academy of Recording Arts & Sciences / Académie canadienne des arts et des sciences de l'enregistrement
124 Merton St., 3rd Fl., Toronto ON M4S 2Z2
416/485-3135; Fax: 416/485-4978
Juno Awards
Annual awards for: Album of the Year, Single of the Year, Bestselling Album (foreign/domestic), Bestselling Francophone Album, Female Vocalist of the Year, Male Vocalist of the Year, Group of the Year, Instrumental Artist(s) of the Year, Best New Solo Artist, Best New Group, Songwriter of the Year, Country Female Vocalist of the Year, Country Male Vocalist of the Year, Country Group or Duo of the Year, Best Children's Album, Best Roots & Traditional Album (one award Solo, one Group), Best Classical Album: Solo or Chamber Ensemble, Best Classical Album: Large Ensemble or Soloist(s) with Large Ensemble Accompaniment, Best Classical Album: Vocal or Choral Performance, Best Classical Composition, Best Contemporary Jazz Album, Best Mainstream Jazz Album, Best R&B/Soul Recording, Best Dance Recording, Best Rock Album, Best Rap Recording, Best Rap Recording, Best Reggae Recording, Best Blues/Gospel Album, Best Music of Aboriginal Canada Recording, Best Global Recording, Best Alternative Album
Also: Producer of the Year, Recording Engineer of the Year, Best Video, Best Album Design, Hall of Fame Award, Levi's Entertainer of the Year, Walt Grealis Special Achievement Award, & Global Achievement Award (not awarded every year)

Canadian Broadcasting Corporation
CBC Radio Music, PO Box 500, Stn A, Toronto ON M5W 1E6
416/205-7384
CBC Radio Competition for Young Performers
Held every two years as a competition for young Canadian singers & instrumentalists; there are five categories: voice, piano, strings, woodwinds & brass, & a special category from time to time; voice & piano categories, & woodwinds, bass & strings rotate biennially; open to Canadian citizens or landed immigrants between the ages of 15 & 30
First prize is $5,000; 2nd prize is $3,000; special prize of $2,000 (for the best performance of a Canadian work)
National Radio Competition for Amateur Choirs
Established 1975; awarded biennially; prizes offered in following categories: Children's, Youth, Large, Adult Mixed Chamber, Adult Equal Voice, Traditional & Ethno-Cultural, & Contemporary Choral Music
Nine first prizes of $1,500 each; nine 2nd prizes of $1,000 each; $500 for best performance of a Canadian work
National Radio Competition for Young Composers
Established 1973; competition sponsored every two years by CBC & the Canada Council; entrants must be Canadian citizens or landed immigrants, 30 years of age or under, & must not be employees of the CBC
Up to seven prizes are given: three 1st prizes of $5,000 each; three 2nd prizes of $4,000 each; a $5,000 Grand Prize; a performance of the winning works is given on CBC English & French radio networks

Canadian Country Music Association / Association de la musique country canadienne
#127, 3800 Steeles Ave. West, Woodbridge ON L4L 4G9
905/850-1144; Fax: 905/856-1633
Music Awards & Citations
Awards in 10 categories are presented annually to outstanding performers; 21 citations honour individuals & organizations that have made a significant contribution to country music

Canadian Theatre Critics Association / Association des critiques de théâtre du Canada
#2100, 181 University Ave., Toronto ON M5H 3M7
416/367-8896; Fax: 416/367-5992
The Nathan Cohen Award
Named in honour of the distinguished theatre critic of the Toronto Star; award is presented annually to help recognize high critical standards & to give encouragement to those working professionally in the field of theatre criticism
Entry categories in the English language division are: reviews of up to 750 words; reviews, profiles & other theatrical features of 750 words to a maximum of 3,000 words; up to three items may be submitted in either or both categories; one winner will be chosen from each category; each of the two winners receives a cheque for $500 & a framed certificate

Concours international de musique de Montréal / Montréal International Music Competition
Place des Arts, 1501, rue Jeanne-Mance, Montréal PQ H2X 1Z9
514/285-4380; Fax: 514/285-4266
Montreal International Music Competition
The competition rotates annually from piano to violin to voice; the prize is $15,000

Council for Business & the Arts in Canada / Conseil pour le monde des affaires et des arts du Canada
#1507, 401 Bay St., PO Box 7, Toronto ON M5H 2Y4
416/869-3016; Fax: 416/869-0435
Edmund C. Bovey Award
To recognize individual members of the business community who contribute leadership, time, money & expertise to the arts
A sculpture to the winner & $20,000 distributed to the arts in a way specified by the winner
Financial Post Awards for Business in the Arts
Established in 1979 to encourage the corporate sector's involvement with the visual & performing arts in Canada & to recognize this involvement

Dance Ontario Association
179 Richmond St. West, Toronto ON M5V 1V3
416/204-1083; Fax: 416/204-1085; Email: danceont@io.org
Dance Ontario Award
Recognizes a lifetime commitment to dance

Dreamspeakers Festival Society
9914 - 76 Ave., Edmonton AB T6E 1K7
403/439-3456; Fax: 403/439-2066
Aboriginal Film Awards
Established in 1996 to recognize outstanding achievement in the aboriginal filmmaking industry

Governor General's Performing Arts Foundation
PO Box 1534, Stn B, Ottawa ON K1P 5W1
613/947-0631; Fax: 613/996-2828
Governor General's Performing Arts Awards
Established in 1992; honours six performing artists for their lifetime achievement & contribution to the cultural enrichment of Canada; each recipient is awarded $10,000 & a commemorative medal
Ramon John Hnatyshyn Award for Voluntarism in the Performing Arts
Recognizes outstanding service to the performing arts; the recipient is presented with a specially commissioned artwork by Canadian glass artist Daniel Crichton
The National Arts Centre Award
Recognizes work of an extraordinary nature & significance in the performing arts by an individual artist &/or company in the past performance year; recipients receive a $10,000 cash award donated by the NAC Foundation & an original sculpture by Stephen Braithwaite

The Jazz Report
14 London St., Toronto ON M6G 1M5
416/533-2813
The Jazz Report Awards
Established 1993; annual awards in 36 categories determined by readers & contributors to the quarterly

The National Music Festival / Festival national de musique
1034 Chestnut Ave., Moose Jaw SK S6H 1A6
306/693-7087; Fax: 306/693-7087
Competition Awards
Ten separate provincial competitions are held throughout May & June & the winners of these compete for national honours each August in a different province each year; the Festival is underwritten as a public service by the Canadian Imperial Bank of Commerce, & organized by the Federation of Canadian Music Festivals, in cooperation with the hosting provincial association
Cash awards of $2,000, $1,000 & $500 are presented to first, second, & third place winners in each of six categories: Voice, Piano, Strings, Woodwinds, Brass, Chamber Groups; Grand Award of $7,500 is given to the best performer at the Grand Award Competition of the six winners

Ontario Arts Council / Conseil des arts de l'Ontario
#600, 151 Bloor St. West, Toronto ON M5S 1T6
416/961-1660; Fax: 416/961-7796; Toll Free: 1-800-387-0058; Email: oac@gov.on.ca
Heinz Unger Award for Conducting
Established 1968 & awarded biennially to honour the memory of the York Concert Society music director; administered by the Music Office of the Ontario Arts Council in cooperation with the Association of Canadian Orchestras
Jean A. Chalmers Award for Creativity in Dance
Biennial award of $20,000; honours an individual who has made an outstanding contribution to nuturing creativity in dance in Canada
Jean A. Chalmers Award for Distinction in Choreography
Established 1994; biennial $20,000 award honours prominent choreographers who have created a substantial body of work
Jean A. Chalmers Awards for Musical Composition
Established in 1993; two annual awards of $10,000 presented together; the Composers Award honours a Canadian composer of an outstanding work in a particular genre; the Presenters Award is given to an Ontario-based producer or commissioner of a new Canadian work in a particular genre
John Adaskin Memorial Fund
Established in memorial of the Canadian Music Centre's first executive secretary; supports a project that encourages the promotion & development of Canadian music in the school system
Leslie Bell Scholarship for Choral Conducting
Established 1973; up to $2,000 awarded biennially in competition; the purpose of the award is to help young emerging choral conductors in Ontario further their

studies in the choral music field either in Canada or abroad; competition organized by the Ontario Choral Federation

The Chalmers Performing Arts Training Grants
Assist qualified professional performing artists to undertake intensive study projects or professional upgrading with outstanding master teachers or at highly-regarded institutions

The Jean A. Chalmers Choreographic Award
$10,000 national award is presented every two years to honour choreographers of outstanding potential

The Jean A. Chalmers National Music Award
Annual $20,000 award recognizes individual performers or ensembles making an outstanding contribution to Canadian musical creativity

The John Hirsch Director's Award
Established in 1993; awarded every three years to promising theatre directors

The Pauline McGibbon Award
Annual award of $7,000; alternates between designers, directors & production craftspersons

The Vida Peene Fund
Provides assistance to projects which benefit the orchestra community as a whole

Tim Sims Encouragement Fund
Established in 1995; $1,000 to be awarded annually to a promising young comedic performer or troupe

Québec Ministère de la culture et des communications
225, Grande Allée est, Bloc V, 3e étage, Québec PQ G1R 5G5
418/643-2183; Fax: 418/643-3310

Les Prix du Québec:

Prix Denise-Pelletier
$30,000, a silver medal & scroll awarded for excellence in performing arts

RPM Weekly
6 Brentcliffe Rd., Toronto ON M4G 3Y2
416/425-0257; Fax: 416/425-8629

Big Country Awards
Annual awards to honour achievement by Canadian country music singers & composers; winners are selected by subscribers to the music trade magazine

La Société Saint-Jean-Baptiste de Montréal
82, rue Sherbrooke ouest, Montréal PQ H2X 1X3
514/843-8851; Fax: 514/844-6369

Prix Calixa-Lavallee
Established 1959; $1,500 & a medal awarded annually to a French Canadian in recognition of outstanding achievement in music in serving the higher interests of the French Canadian people

Society of Composers, Authors & Music Publishers of Canada / Société canadienne des auteurs, compositeurs & éditeurs de musique
41 Valleybrook Dr., North York ON M3B 2S6
416/445-8700; Fax: 416/445-7108; Toll Free: 1-800-557-6226

SOCAN Awards
Established 1990 for the purpose of recognizing SOCAN creators & their contribution to Canadian music; presented at the annual Awards Dinner; only SOCAN member writers, composers & music publishers are eligible

SOCAN Awards for Young Composers
Total of $16,500 awarded to encourage & recognize the creative talents of upcoming Canadian composers; The Sir Ernest MacMillan Awards for compositions for no fewer than 13 performers; The Serge Garant Awards for compositions for a minimum of three performers; The Pierre Mercure Awards for solo or duet compositions; The Hugh Le Caine Awards for compositions realized on tape with electronic means; The Godfrey Ridout Awards for choral compositions of any variety

Toronto Theatre Alliance
#403, 720 Bathurst St., Toronto ON M5S 2R4
416/536-6468; Fax: 416/536-3463; Email: tta@idirect.com

Dora Mavor Moore Awards
Established 1979; celebrating excellence in Toronto theatre, 35 awards in large, medium & small theatre divisions plus Theatre for Young Audiences & New Choreography

PUBLIC ADMINISTRATION see LEGAL, GOVERNMENTAL, PUBLIC ADMINISTRATION

PUBLIC AFFAIRS

B'nai Brith Canada
15 Hove St., North York ON M3H 4Y8
416/633-6224; Fax: 416/630-2159; Email: bnai_brith@uarr.org; URL: http://www.canada.ibm.net/bnaibrith

Award of Merit & Humanitarian Awards
Established 1981; presented annually at gala dinner dances in major communities across Canada
Selection of honourees based on outstanding achievement in their chosen fields as well as personal commitment over the years to the overall betterment of Canadian society with specific abiding concern for young people

The Canadian Council of Christians & Jews / Conseil canadien des chrétiens et des juifs
#600, 44 Victoria St., Toronto ON M5C 1Y2
416/364-3101; Fax: 416/364-5705; Toll Free: 1-800-663-1848; Email: cccj@interlog.com; URL: http://www.interlog.com/~cccj/

Human Relations Award
Made to outstanding Canadians who have made a significant contribution towards bringing people together regardless of race, religion, or social status, in an atmosphere of understanding & respect; the award is made annually & is approved by a National Nominating Committee from the Board of Directors of CCCJ

Canadian Council of Professional Engineers / Conseil canadien des ingénieurs professionnels
#401, 116 Albert St., Ottawa ON K1P 5G3
613/232-2474; Fax: 613/230-5759; Email: lmacdon@fox.nstn.ns.ca

The Meritorious Service Award for Community Service
Recognizes outstanding service & dedication to Canadian society through voluntary participation in community organizations, government-sponsored activities, or humanitarian work

The Canadian Council of the Blind / Le Conseil canadien des aveugles
#405, 396 Cooper St., Ottawa ON K2P 2H7
613/567-0311; Fax: 613/567-2728

Award of Merit
Established 1952; presented to a Canadian, blind or sighted, who has rendered outstanding work for the blind
A gold medal & clasp, a specially printed & bound citation & honorary life membership in the CCB

The City of Toronto
Dept. of the City Clerk, City Hall, 100 Queen St. West, Toronto ON M5H 2N2
416/392-7494; Fax: 416/392-1446

Access Award
Established 1982; presented to a group or organization which has made a significant contribution toward improving the quality of life for the city's disabled residents; the award honours those who are sensitive to the access needs of the disabled when planning structures or programs (this could include consideration of access requirements in the design of new or renovated buildings, a job creation campaign, a transportation system, recreational program, etc.)

Civic Award of Merit
Established 1956; awarded to individuals who have attained distinction & renown in various fields of endeavour; award is in the form of an acrylic obelisk with medallion

Constance E. Hamilton Award
This award commemorates the Privy Council of Great Britain granting women status as persons in 1929; award is named after the first woman member of City Council; recipients are persons who have made a significant contribution to securing equitable treatment for Toronto women

William P. Hubbard Race Relations Award
Named for Toronto's first visible minority Member of Council & Acting Mayor, this award honours persons who have made a voluntary contribution to racial harmony in Toronto; award was presented for the first time in 1990

Government of Newfoundland & Labrador
The Premier's Office, PO Box 8700, St. John's NF A1B 4J6
709/729-3570; Fax: 709/729-5875

The Premier's Award for Access & Awareness
Designed to reflect the aims & objectives of National Access Awareness Week; it is intended to recognize those exceptional individuals, organizations, & businesses that have made outstanding contributions to access & awareness for visible & nonvisible minorities

Ontario Ministry of Citizenship, Culture & Recreation - Seniors' Issues Group
76 College St., 6th Fl., Toronto ON M7A 1N3
416/327-2433; Fax: 416/327-2425; Toll Free: 1-800-267-7329

Ontario Senior Achievement Award
Presented annually to Ontario residents who have made a significant contribution to their communities after reaching 65 years of age; nominations may be made by any individual or organization – Contact, Kate Clark

Planned Parenthood Federation of Canada / Fédération pour le planning des naissances du Canada
#430, One Nicholas St., Ottawa ON K1N 7B7
613/241-4474; Fax: 613/241-7550; Email: ppfed@web.apc.org

Phyllis Harris Scholarship
$2,500 towards full-time study at a Canadian university for students who have worked or volunteered in the general field of human sexuality who intend to work for a degree in the field of family planning or population issues

Québec Ministère de l'industrie, du commerce, de la science et de la technologie
Direction de la diffusion de la science et de la technologie
710, place D'Youville, 3e étage, Québec PQ G1R 4Y4
418/691-8018

Prix Léon-Gérin
$30,000, a silver medal & a scroll awarded for excellence in human sciences – Contact, Secrétariat des Prix du Québec dans le domaine scientifique

Status of Women Canada
#700, 360 Albert St., Ottawa ON K1A 1C3
613/995-7835; Fax: 613/943-2386

Governor General's Award in Commemoration of Persons Case
Established 1979 to celebrate the 50th anniversary of the "Persons Case" which resulted in women being declared "persons" & thus eligible for appointment to

the Senate; annual awards recognize contributions by individuals toward promoting the equality of women in Canada

PUBLIC RELATIONS see ADVERTISING & PUBLIC RELATIONS

RADIO see BROADCASTING & FILM

RECREATION see SPORTS & RECREATION

SCIENTIFIC, ENGINEERING, TECHNICAL

Association of Universities & Colleges of Canada / Association des universités et collèges du Canada
#600, 350 Albert St., Ottawa ON K1R 1B1
613/563-1236; Fax: 613/563-9745; URL: http://www.aucc.ca/
Petro-Canada Graduate Research Award Program
Established by Petro-Canada to recognize academic excellence & to support & encourage graduate research in specialized fields of study relating to the petroleum industry; up to four awards of $10,000 for students working towards a Master's or Doctoral degree in sciences, engineering, social sciences & business administration who show the relevance of their plans to the oil & gas industry

The Canada Council / Conseil des Arts du Canada
350 Albert St., PO Box 1047, Ottawa ON K1P 5V8
613/566-4310; Fax: 613/566-4418; Toll Free: 1-800-263-5588
Isaak Walton Killam Memorial Prizes
Three prizes valued at $50,000 each are given annually to eminent Canadian scholars in recognition of a distinguished career in & contribution to the natural sciences, the health sciences, & engineering; candidates must be nominated by three experts in their particular field

Canadian Aeronautics & Space Institute / Institut aéronautique et spatial du Canada
#818, 130 Slater St., Ottawa ON K1P 6E2
613/234-0191; Fax: 613/234-9039; Email: ab144@freenet.carleton.ca; URL: http://www.ncf.carleton.ca/freeport/prof.assoc/casi/menu
C.D. Howe Award
Established 1966; a silver plaque presented annually for achievement in the fields of planning, policy making & overall leadership in Canadian aeronautics & space activities
McCurdy Award
Established 1954; a silver medal & trophy presented annually for outstanding achievement in art, science & engineering relating to aeronautics & space
Romeo Vachon Award
Established 1969; bronze plaque awarded annually for outstanding contribution of a practical nature to the art, science, & engineering of aeronautics & space in Canada
Trans-Canada (McKee) Trophy
Canada's oldest aviation award established 1927; presented annually except when no qualified recipient is nominated for outstanding achievement in the field of air operations

Canadian Council of Professional Engineers / Conseil canadien des ingénieurs professionnels
#401, 116 Albert St., Ottawa ON K1P 5G3
613/232-2474; Fax: 613/230-5759; Email: lmacdon@fox.nstn.ns.ca
Canadian Engineers' Gold Medal Award
Established 1972; a national award designed to bestow distinction on outstanding engineers in Canada & to recognize exceptional achievements in their chosen fields, irrespective of any affiliation with a given society, institute or association; the presentation of this award is also designed to assist in the furtherance of public understanding of the role of the engineer in Canadian society
ENCON Insurance Managers Inc.
$5,000 to a professional engineer wishing to pursue studies in the area of engineering failure investigation &/or materials testing
Manulife Financial Scholarship
Offers three scholarships of $10,000 each annually to provide financial assistance to engineers returning to university for further study or research in engineering-related courses
Meloche Monnex Scholarship
Two scholarships of $5,000 each to provide financial assistance to engineers returning to university to further study or research in a field other than engineering; field of study chosen should favour the acquisition of knowledge pertinent to enhancing the performance of the candidate in the engineering profession
The Young Engineer Achievement Award
Designed to bestow distinction on young outstanding engineers in Canada & to recognize exceptional achievements in their chosen fields, irrespective of any affiliation with a given society, institute or association; the presentation of this award is also designed to promote public understanding of the role of the professional engineer in Canadian society

Canadian Information Processing Society / Association Canadienne de L'Informatique
#106, 430 King St. West, Toronto ON M5V 1L5
416/593-4040; Fax: 416/593-5184; Email: info@cips.ca; URL: http://cips.ca
Canadian Information Technology Innovation
For organizations or individuals who have demonstrated innovation in information technology; both commercial & non-commercial innovations are eligible
Canadian Software Systems
For a software system, originating in Canada, that has had a significant effect, as evidenced by new concepts, market acceptance, increased competitiveness, or influence on later software developments; the award may be for a product or project, & given to an organization or group

Canadian Institute of Forestry / Institut forestier du Canada
#606, 151 Slater St., Ottawa ON K1P 5H3
613/234-2242; Fax: 613/234-6181; Email: 103741.553@compuserve.com; URL: http://www.episet/cif
Canadian Forestry Achievement Award
Established 1966 & presented annually in recognition of superior accomplishments in forestry research &/or in recognition of outstanding administrative leadership in management, education, research, & affairs of professional & scientific societies
Canadian Forestry Scientific Achievement Award
Established 1980; presented annually in recognition of superior accomplishments in scientific forestry
International Forestry Achievement Award
Established 1980; presented in recognition of outstanding achievement in international forestry

Canadian Institute of Mining, Metallurgy & Petroleum / Institut canadien des mines, de la métallurgie et du pétrole
#1210, 3400, boul de Maisonneuve ouest, Montréal PQ H3Z 3B8
514/939-2710; Fax: 514/939-2714
CIM Awards
The institute administers 26 awards recognizing achievement in mining, metallurgy & petroleum industries

Canadian Society for Chemical Engineering / Société canadienne du génié chimique
#550, 130 Slater St., Ottawa ON K1P 6E2
613/232-6252; Fax: 613/232-5862; Email: cscxt@acadvm1.uottawa.ca; URL: http://fox.nstn.ca/~cic_adm/csche.html
The Canadian Society for Chemical Engineering Awards
Offers several awards & scholarships in chemical engineering or industrial chemistry

Canadian Society for Chemistry / Société canadienne de chimie
#550, 130 Slater St., Ottawa ON K1P 6E2
613/232-6252; Fax: 613/232-5862; Email: cic.adm@fox.nstn.ca; URL: http://fox.nstn.ca/~cic_adm/csc.html
The Canadian Society for Chemistry Awards
Several awards & scholarships are offered in organic chemistry, inorganic, bio-organic, analytical, pure or applied, physical, medicinal, & electrochemistry

The Chemical Institute of Canada / Institut de chimie du Canada
#550, 130 Slater St., Ottawa ON K1P 6E2
613/232-6252; Fax: 613/232-5862; Email: cscxt@acadvm1.uottawa.ca; cic_adm@fox.nstn.ca; URL: http://fox.nstn.ca/~cic_adm/
Chemical Institute of Canada Awards
The institute administers several awards & scholarships in chemistry, chemical engineering, & macromolecular science or engineering, including the following:

E.W.R. Steacie Memorial Fund / Fondation E.W.R. Steacie
c/o Steacie Institute for Molecular Sciences, NRC Canada, 100 Sussex Dr., Ottawa ON K1A 0R6
613/990-0968, 993-1212; Fax: 613/954-5242; URL: http://www.sims.nrc.ca/sims/prize.htm
The Steacie Prize
Canada's most prestigious award for young scientists & engineers; named to honour the memory of Edgar William Richard Steacie, a physical chemist & former President of the National Research Council of Canada; established 1963; awarded annually to a person up to 40 years of age for outstanding scientific work in a Canadian context; winner receives a certificate & $8,000 – Contact, Dr. W. Siebrand

The Engineering Institute of Canada / Institut canadien des ingénieurs
1980 Ogilvie Rd., PO Box 27078, RPO Gloucester Ctr, Gloucester ON K1J 9L9
613/742-5185; Fax: 613/742-5189; Email: eic@nrc.ca
The Sir John Kennedy Medal
Established in 1927 in commemoration of the great services rendered in the field of engineering by Sir John Kennedy, a past president of the EIC; medal is awarded by the council in recognition of outstanding merit in the profession or of noteworthy contributions to the science of engineering or to the benefit of the institute

Ernest C. Manning Awards Foundation
#3900, 421 - 7th Ave. SW, Calgary AB T2P 4K9
403/266-7571; Fax: 403/266-8154
The Manning Awards
Given annually to Canadian innovators who have conceived & developed new concepts, procedures, processes or products of benefit to Canada; awards may be in any area of activity
One $100,000 Principal Award; one $25,000 Award of Distinction; two $5,000 Innovation prizes, & four $4,000 Young Canadian Innovation Awards

Natural Sciences & Engineering Research Council of Canada / Conseil de recherches en sciences naturelles et en génie
350 Albert St., Ottawa ON K1R 1A4
613/996-1898; Fax: 613/992-5337

Canadian Almanac & Directory 1997

Canada Gold Medal for Science & Engineering

Awarded to an individual in recognition of sustained & outstanding contributions to Canadian research in natural sciences & engineering; award will be made for any activity of exceptional importance that leads to the enhancement of the research enterprise in Canada - such activities may include contributions to knowledge, the application of existing knowledge, to the novel solution of practical problems, the promotion or management of research activity

The accomplishments for which the award is given must have been carried out in Canada & achieved over a substantial period of time; persons from any sector (academic, business & industry, or government) are eligible; current members of council are not eligible; awardee's performance in relation to the cited achievements must demonstrate an exceptional degree of ability & application of such qualities as expertise, creativity, imagination, leadership

The E.W.R. Steacie Memorial Fellowships

Awarded to enhance the career development of outstanding & promising scientists & engineers who are staff members of Canadian universities; successful fellows are relieved of any teaching & administrative duties, enabling them to devote themselves to research; up to four fellowships are awarded annually for a one or two-year period; fellowships are held at a Canadian university or affiliated research institution

Steacie fellows receive their normal university salary, which is paid by NSERC, & are eligible for NSERC grants

Québec Ministère de l'industrie, du commerce, de la science et de la technologie

Direction de la diffusion de la science et de la technologie
710, place D'Youville, 3e étage, Québec PQ G1R 4Y4
418/691-8018

Prix Armand-Frappier

$30,000, a silver medal & a scroll presented to recognize the career of a scientist who, in addition to having achieved excellence in his own research, has made exceptional contributions to the development of Québec's research institutions, & has promoted research or increased the Québec public's interest in science & technology – Contact, Secrétariat des Prix du Québec dans le domaine scientifique

Prix Marie-Victorin

$30,000, a silver medal & a scroll awarded for excellence in pure & applied science – Secrétariat des Prix du Québec dans le domaine scientifique

Prix Wilder-Penfield

$30,000, a silver medal & a scroll awarded for excellence in the biomedical domain; recognized disciplines include medical science, natural science, & engineering – Secrétariat des Prix du Québec dans le domaine scientifique

Royal Astronomical Society of Canada / Société royale d'astronomie du Canada

136 Dupont St., Toronto ON M5R 1V2
416/924-7973; Fax: 416/924-7973

Chant Medal

Established 1940 in appreciation of the great work of the late Prof. C.A. Chant in furthering the interests of astronomy in Canada; silver medal is awarded no more than once a year to an amateur astronomer resident in Canada on the basis of the value of the work which he/she has carried out in astronomy & closely allied fields of original investigation

Ken Chilton Prize

Established 1977; plaque awarded annually to an amateur astronomer resident in Canada, in recognition of a significant piece of work carried out or published during the year

The Royal Canadian Geographical Society / Société géographique royale du Canada

39 McArthur Ave., Vanier ON K1L 8L7
613/745-4629; Fax: 613/744-0947

The Gold Medal

Established 1972; to recognize a particular achievement of one or more individuals in the field of geography, or a significant national or international event – Coordinator, Society Programs, Karen Hallquist

The Massey Medal

Established 1959; awarded annually for outstanding personal achievement in the exploration, development, or description of the geography of Canada

The Royal Society of Canada / La Société royale du Canada

#308, 225 Metcalfe St., Ottawa ON K2P 1P9
613/991-6990; Fax: 613/991-6996; Email: adminrsc@rsc.ca; URL: http://library.utoronto.ca/www/rsc/

Bancroft Award

Established 1968; $1,500 & a presentation scroll awarded every two years for publication, instruction, & research in the earth sciences that have conspicuously contributed to public understanding & appreciation of the subject

Eadie Medal

Established 1975; $1,500 & a bronze medal awarded annually in recognition of major contributions to any field in engineering or applied science

John L. Synge Award

Established 1986; $1,500 & a diploma awarded at irregular intervals for outstanding research in any of the branches of mathematics

Rutherford Memorial Medals: Chemistry & Physics

Established 1980; two medals & $1,500 each awarded annually for outstanding research, one in chemistry, one in physics

The Flavelle Medal

Established 1924; awarded every two years (since 1966) for an outstanding contribution to biological science during the preceding 10 years or for significant additions to a previous outstanding contribution to biological science

The Henry Marshall Tory Medal

Established 1941; awarded every two years (since 1947) for outstanding research in a branch of astronomy, chemistry, mathematics, physics, or an allied science

The McNeil Medal

$1,500 bursary & a medal awarded to encourage communication of science to students & the public

Willet G. Miller Medal

Established 1943; awarded every two years for outstanding research in any branch of the earth sciences

Science Council of British Columbia

#800, 4710 Kingsway, Burnaby BC V5H 4M2
604/438-2752; Fax: 604/438-6564; Toll Free: 1-800-665-7222; Email: info@scbc.org; URL: http://www.scbc.org

BC Science & Technology Awards

Up to six gold medals awarded each year for outstanding achievements by BC scientists, engineers, industrial innovators & science communicators. The awards are: Industrial Innovation, Business/Education Partnership, Solutions Through Research, New Frontiers in Research, Cecil Green Award for Technology Entrepreneurship, Science Council Chairman's Award for Career Achievement, & Eve Savory Award for Science Communication

Society of the Chemical Industry - Canadian Section

c/o Praxair Canada Inc., One City Centre Dr., Mississauga ON L5B 1M2
905/803-1600; Fax: 905/803-1690

Canada Medal Award

Established 1939; awarded every two years for outstanding services in the Canadian chemical industry; recipient delivers an address at a meeting of the society

International Award

Established 1976; award is presented in recognition of outstanding service in the chemical industry in the international sphere, preferably to Canadians or persons who have contributed measurably to the Canadian chemical scene

SPORTS & RECREATION

Canadian Amateur Boxing Association / Association canadienne de boxe amateur

#711, 1600 James Naismith Dr., Gloucester ON K1B 5N4
613/748-5611; Fax: 613/748-5740

Canadian Amateur Boxing Association Awards

Best Amateur Boxer of the Year; Outstanding Canadian Boxer of the Year; Best International Boxer Canada Cup Award; Best Team Boxer Canada Cup Award

Canadian Association for Health, Physical Education, Recreation & Dance / Association canadienne pour la santé, l'éducation physique, le loisir et la danse

#809, 1600 James Naismith Dr., Gloucester ON K1B 5N4
613/748-5622; Fax: 613/748-5737; URL: http://www.cdnsport.ca/activeliving/cahperd/index.html

R. Tait McKenzie Awards of Honour

Instituted at the Montreal Convention in 1948, this is the most prestigious award presented by CAHPER; named after the distinguished Canadian physician, sculptor & physical educator, Dr. Robert Tait McKenzie; candidate shall have performed distinguished, meritorious service as a recognized leader regionally & nationally in his/her field

Canadian Association for the Advancement of Women & Sport & Physical Activity / Association canadienne pour l'avancement des femmes du sport et de l'activité physique

#308A, 1600 James Naismith Dr., Gloucester ON K1B 5N4
613/748-5793; Fax: 613/748-5775; URL: http://infoweb.magi.com/~wmnsport/index.html

Breakthrough Awards

Annual awards in recognition of women's achievements in sports

Canadian Curling Association / Association canadienne de curling

#803, 1600 James Naismith Dr., Gloucester ON K1B 5N4
613/748-5628; Fax: 613/748-5713; Email: cdn.curling@rtm.cdnsport.ca; URL: http://www.cdnsport.ca/curling

Award of Achievement

Commemorative plaque presented in recognition of individuals who have contributed significantly to any aspect of Canadian curling operations

Ray Kingsmith/Canadian Airlines International Executive of the Year

Two CAI international passes & an engraved plaque awarded to an individual who parallels the level of involvement & commitment exemplified by Ray Kingsmith

Canadian Sport Council / Conseil canadien du sport

#301A, 1600 James Naismith Dr., Gloucester ON K1B 5N4
613/748-5670; Fax: 613/748-5732; URL: http://cansport.magi.com/cansport

Allsport Insurance Marketing Ltd. Award
Awarded to Canada's most outstanding volunteer sport/recreation administrator in Canada with not less than 10 years service

Bruce Taylor Memorial Award
A trophy is awarded to an individual deemed to have made an outstanding lifetime contribution to amateur sport in a builder capacity, at the provincial, national, or international level, or a combination of all three

Canadian Airlines Athlete of the Month
Each month winners are chosen by a selection committee of the federation & receive a commemorative plaque & an airline pass to any Canadian Airlines destination in the world

Dick Ellis Trophy
Trophy is awarded to Canada's most outstanding national amateur team of the year

Elaine Tanner Trophy
Established 1972; trophy is awarded to Canada's most outstanding junior (under 20 years old) amateur female athlete of the year

Johnny F. Bassett Memorial Award
Presented by the Government of Canada through the Dept. of Canadian Heritage; presented to a citizen of the Canadian sport community who has displayed a combination of sporting excellence & community work

Norton H. Crowe Award
Established 1932; a medal is awarded to Canada's most outstanding amateur male athlete of the year selected from nominations from sport governing bodies; considerations are performance, sportsmanship & good character

Sylvie Fréchette Award
Honours an individual for the level of competitive achievement & for the ability to deal with exceptional circumstances with dignity & courage

The Corporate Award
Presented annually to the corporation deemed to have made the most significant contribution to the development of sport in Canada

The Doug Gilbert Award
Presented annually to a member of the written & electronic sports media who has given significant coverage & support to amateur sport

Tom Longboat Award
Awarded occasionally by National Indian Brotherhood to male/female athlete of the year

Velma Springstead Award
Established 1934; a silver bowl awarded to Canada's most outstanding amateur female athlete of the year; considerations are performance, sportsmanship & good character

Viscount Alexander Trophy
A trophy is awarded to Canada's most outstanding junior (under 20 years old) amateur male athlete of the year

Ontario Ministry of Citizenship, Culture & Recreation
Recreation Programs Branch, 77 Bloor St. West, 8th Fl., Toronto ON M7A 2R9
416/314-7696; Fax: 416/314-7458

Corps d'Elite Ontario Award
Established 1986; designed to acknowledge those residents of Ontario whose voluntary efforts have had a significant impact on the development of recreation in Ontario

La Société Saint-Jean-Baptiste de Montréal
82, rue Sherbrooke ouest, Montréal PQ H2X 1X3
514/843-8851; Fax: 514/844-6369

Prix Maurice-Richard
Established 1979; $1,500 & a medal awarded annually to a French Canadian in recognition of outstanding achievement in sports & athletics in serving the higher interests of the French Canadian people

Swimming/Natation Canada
#503, 1600 James Naismith Dr., Gloucester ON K1B 5N4
613/748-5673; Fax: 613/748-5715

Female/Male Athlete of the Year
Best international athlete of the year in terms of points; winner receives a plaque & gift

Recognition of Disabled Athletes
Awards made to disabled swimmers who win medals internationally for Canada; must be member of Swimming/Natation Canada

TECHNICAL see SCIENTIFIC, ENGINEERING, TECHNICAL

TELEVISION see BROADCASTING & FILM

THEATRE see PERFORMING ARTS

TRADE see BUSINESS & TRADE

VISUAL ARTS see CULTURE, VISUAL ARTS & ARCHITECTURE

VOLUNTEERISM see CITIZENSHIP & BRAVERY

WRITING see LITERARY ARTS, BOOKS & LIBRARIES

SECTION 2

ORGANIZATIONS DIRECTORY

RELIGIOUS DENOMINATIONS	**2**
RELIGIOUS ORGANIZATIONS	**6**
ORGANIZATIONS	**8**
TRADE UNIONS	**195**
CANADIAN FOUNDATIONS	**208**

See ADDENDA at the back of this book for late changes & additional information.

ACCOUNTING	2-8
ADDICTION	2-10
ADVERTISING & MARKETING	2-10
AGRICULTURE & FARMING	2-12
AIDS	2-16
ANIMAL BREEDING	2-19
ANIMALS & ANIMAL SCIENCE	2-21
ANTIQUES	2-23
ARCHAEOLOGY	2-23
ARCHITECTURE	2-24
ARTS	2-24
AUTOMOTIVE	2-25
AVIATION & AEROSPACE	2-27
BROADCASTING	2-28
BUILDING & CONSTRUCTION	2-30
BUSINESS	2-33
CHEMICAL INDUSTRY	2-35
CHILDBIRTH	2-36
CHILDREN & YOUTH	2-36
CITIZENSHIP & IMMIGRATION	2-37
CONSUMERS	2-38
CULTURE	2-38
DENTAL	2-39
DISABLED PERSONS	2-41
DRILLING	2-44
ECONOMICS	2-44
EDUCATION	2-45
ELECTRONICS & ELECTRICITY	2-54
EMERGENCY RESPONSE	2-55
EMPLOYMENT & HUMAN RESOURCES	2-55
ENERGY	2-56
ENGINEERING & TECHNOLOGY	2-57
ENVIRONMENTAL	2-59
EQUIPMENT & MACHINERY	2-65
EVENTS	2-66
FASHION & TEXTILES	2-67
FILM & VIDEO	2-68
FINANCE	2-69
FISHERIES & FISHING INDUSTRY	2-71
FOOD & BEVERAGE INDUSTRY	2-72
FORESTRY & FOREST PRODUCTS	2-74
FRATERNAL	2-75
FUNERAL SERVICES	2-76
FUR TRADE	2-77
GALLERIES & MUSEUMS	2-77
GAS & OIL	2-78
GEMS & JEWELLERY	2-78
GOVERNMENT & PUBLIC ADMINISTRATION	2-79
HEALTH & MEDICAL	2-80
HEATING, AIR CONDITIONING, PLUMBING	2-94
HISTORY, HERITAGE, GENEALOGY	2-95
HOMOSEXUALITY	2-98
HORTICULTURE, GARDENING, LANDSCAPE ARCHITECTURE	2-98
HOSPITALS	2-99
HOUSING	2-101
HUMAN RIGHTS & CIVIL LIBERTIES	2-102
INFORMATION TECHNOLOGY	2-103
INSURANCE INDUSTRY	2-104
INTERIOR DESIGN	2-106
INTERNATIONAL COOPERATION/ INTERNATIONAL RELATIONS	2-107
LABOUR RELATIONS	2-110
LANGUAGE, LINGUISTICS, LITERATURE	2-111
LAW	2-113
LIBRARIES & ARCHIVES	2-116
MANAGEMENT & ADMINISTRATION	2-120
MANUFACTURING & INDUSTRY	2-122
MARINE TRADES	2-124
MENTAL HEALTH	2-125
MILITARY & VETERANS	2-126
MINES & MINERAL RESOURCES	2-127
MULTICULTURALISM	2-128
NATIVE PEOPLES	2-132
NATURALISTS	2-134
NURSING	2-135
PACKAGING	2-138
PATENTS & COPYRIGHT	2-138
PHARMACEUTICAL	2-139
PHOTOGRAPHY	2-140
PLANNING & DEVELOPMENT	2-140
POLITICS	2-141
POULTRY & EGGS	2-142
PRINTING INDUSTRY & GRAPHIC ARTS	2-143
PRISONERS & EX-OFFENDERS	2-143
PUBLIC UTILITIES	2-143
PUBLISHING	2-143
REAL ESTATE	2-146
RECREATION, HOBBIES & GAMES	2-149
REPRODUCTIVE ISSUES	2-154
RESEARCH & SCHOLARSHIP	2-154
RESTAURANTS & FOOD SERVICES	2-157
RETAIL TRADE	2-158
SAFETY & ACCIDENT PREVENTION	2-158
SCIENTIFIC	2-161
SENIOR CITIZENS	2-163
SERVICE CLUBS	2-164
SOCIAL RESPONSE/SOCIAL SERVICES	2-165
SPORTS	2-172
STANDARDS & TESTING	2-181
STEEL & METAL INDUSTRIES	2-181
SURVEYING & MAPPING	2-182
TAXATION	2-183
TELECOMMUNICATIONS	2-183
TOURISM & TRAVEL	2-183
TRADE	2-187
TRANSPORTATION & SHIPPING	2-188
VISUAL ART, CRAFTS, FOLK ARTS	2-190
WOMEN	2-191
WRITERS & EDITORS	2-193

Canadian Almanac & Directory 1997

RELIGIOUS DENOMINATIONS

Ahmadiyya Movement in Islam (Canada)/ Mouvement Ahmadiyya en Islam (Canada) (1966)
10610 Jane St., Maple, ON L6A 1S1
905/832-2669, Fax: 905/832-3220, Email: info@islam.ahmadiyya.org
President & Missionary-in-Charge, Naseem Mahdi
General Secretary, Malik Lal Khan
Secretary External Affairs, Hasanat Ahmad Syed
Publications: Ahmadiyya Gazette

The Anglican Church of Canada/L'Église anglicane (ACC) (1893)
Anglican Church House, 600 Jarvis St., Toronto, ON M4Y 2J6
416/924-9192; Book Centre: 924-1332, Fax: 416/968-7983
Primate of the Anglican Church of Canada, The Most Rev. Michael Peers, B.A., L.Th., D.D.
Treasurer, Robert G. Armstrong, C.A.
Publications: Anglican Journal/Journal Anglican; Anglican Church Directory
Diocese of the Arctic: Bishop, The Rt. Rev. J. Christopher R. Williams, 1055 Avenue Rd., Toronto, ON M5N 2C8, 416/481-2263, Fax: 416/487-4948
Diocese of British Columbia: Bishop, The Rt. Rev. Barry Jenks; Bishop's Secretary, Jennifer M. Oliver, 912 Vancouver St., Victoria, BC V8V 3V7, 250/386-7781, Fax: 250/386-4013
Diocese of Calgary: Bishop, The Rt. Rev. Barry Curtis, 3015 Glencoe Rd. SW, Calgary, AB T2S 2L9, 403/243-3673, Fax: 403/243-2182
Diocese of Eastern Newfoundland & Labrador: Bishop, The Rt. Rev. Donald F. Harvey, 19 King's Bridge Rd., St. John's, NF A1C 3K4, 709/576-6697, Fax: 709/576-7122
Diocese of Fredericton: Bishop, The Rt. Rev. George C. Lemmon, 115 Church St., Fredericton, NB E3B 4C8, 506/459-1801, Fax: 506/459-8475
Diocese of Montréal: Bishop, The Rt. Rev. Andrew S. Hutchison; Bishop's Secretary, Marilyn Wiseman, 1444, av Union, Montréal, PQ H3A 2B8, 514/843-6577, Fax: 514/843-6344
Diocese of Nova Scotia: Bishop, The Rt. Rev. A.G. Peters; Bishop's Secretary, Margaret Hunter, 5732 College St., Halifax, NS B3H 1X3, 902/420-0717, Fax: 902/425-0717
Diocese of Ontario: Bishop, The Rt. Rev. Peter R. Mason; Office Manager, Twila Niemi, 90 Johnson St., Kingston, ON K7L 1X7, 613/544-4774, Fax: 613/547-3745
Diocese of Saskatchewan: Bishop, The Rt. Rev. Anthony Burton, PO Box 1088, Prince Albert, SK S6V 5S6, 306/763-2455, Fax: 306/764-5172
Diocese of Toronto: Bishop, The Rt. Rev. Terence E. Finlay; Bishop's Secretary, Margaret Banks, 135 Adelaide St. East, Toronto, ON M5C 1L8, 416/363-6021, Fax: 416/363-7678
Diocese of the Yukon: Bishop, The Rt. Rev. Ronald C. Ferris; Administrative Officer, Arlene Kubica, PO Box 4247, Whitehorse, YT Y1A 3T3, 403/667-7746, Fax: 403/667-6125

The Antiochan Orthodox Christian Archdiocese of North America (1905)
St. George's Orthodox Church, #555, 575, rue Jean Talon est, Montréal, PQ H2R 1T8
514/276-8533, Fax: 514/276-6740
His Eminence Metropolitan, Philip Saliba
Archpriest, Antony Gabriel

The Apostolic Church in Canada
27 Castlefield Ave., Toronto, ON M4R 1G3
416/489-0453

President, Rev. John Kristensen
National Secretary/Missionary Secretary, Rev. J. Karl Thomas

Apostolic Church of Pentecost of Canada Inc. (ACOP) (1921)
General Office, #200, 809 Manning Rd. NE, Calgary, AB T2E 7M9
306/273-5777, Fax: 306/273-8102
Moderator, Rev. Gil Killam
Clerk, Leonard K. Larsen
Missionary Chairman, Rev. Brian Cooper
Publications: Harvestime; Focus

Armenian Evangelical Church
c/o Armenian Evangelical Union of North America, 42 Glenforest Rd., Toronto, ON M4N 1Z8
Contact, Rev. Y. Sarmazian

Armenian Holy Apostolic Church - Canadian Diocese (AHAC) (1984)
615, av Stuart, Outremont, PQ H2V 3H2
514/276-9479, Fax: 514/276-9960
Archbishop, His Eminence Hovnan W. Derderian
Publications: Noragenounk
Affiliates: Canadian Council of Churches

Associated Gospel Churches of Canada/ Association des églises évangélique (AGC) (1925)
3430 South Service Rd., Burlington, ON L7N 3T9
905/634-8184, Fax: 905/634-6283
President, Dr. Donald Hamilton
Moderator, Rev. Stan R. Sadlier
Publications: Advance Magazine
Affiliates: World Relief; World Team; UFM International; Evangelical Fellowship of Canada
Eastern Office: 5500, rue Grenier, Saint-Hubert, PQ J3Y 1N7, 514/678-6345
Western Office: 1613 Early Dr., Saskatoon, SK S7H 3K1, 306/477-2321

Atlantic Canada Association of Free Will Baptists (1898)
RR#6, Woodstock, NB E0J 2B0
506/325-9381
Moderator, Licentiate Oral McAffee

The Baha'i Faith in Canada (1844)
Baha'i National Centre, 7200 Leslie St., Thornhill, ON L3T 6L8
905/889-8168, Fax: 905/889-8184, Telex: 06 96413, Email: nsacan@interlog.com
General Secretary, Reginald Newkirk
Public Affairs, Gerald Filson, Ph.D
Publications: Baha'i Canada
Affiliates: Baha'i International Community

Baptist General Conference of Canada (BGC) (1981)
4306 - 97 St., Edmonton, AB T6E 5R9
403/438-9127, Fax: 403/435-2478
Executive Director, Abe Funk
Office Administrator, Ruth Arnold
Publications: BGC Canada News
Baptist General Conference in Alberta: District Executive Minister, Dr. Cal Netterfield, 5011 - 122A St., Edmonton, AB T6H 3S8, 403/438-9126, Fax: 403/438-5258
British Columbia Baptist Conference: District Executive Minister, Rev. Walter W. Wieser, 7600 Glover Rd., Langley, BC V3A 6H4, 604/888-2246, Fax: 604/888-0046

Brethren in Christ (1788)
2619 Niagara Pkwy., Fort Erie, ON L2A 2Z4
905/871-9991, Fax: 905/871-6330
Bishop, Dale Shaw

Secretary, Betty Albraht
Treasurer, Doug Winger
Publications: Evangelical Visitor

British Methodist Episcopal Church Conference of Canada (1856)
460 Shaw St., Toronto, ON M6G 3L3
416/534-3831; Fax: 905/383-6856
General Superintendent, Rt. Rev. Dr. D.D. Rupwate
Clerk, M. Jones
Affiliates: Canadian Council of Churches

Buddhist Churches of Canada
4860 Garry St., Richmond, BC V7A 2B2
604/272-3330, Fax: 604/272-6865

Canadian Baptist Ministries/Ministères Baptist Canadiens (1912)
Canadian Baptist Place, 7185 Millcreek Dr., Mississauga, ON L5N 5R4
905/821-3533, Fax: 905/826-3441, Email: cbmadmin@inforamp.com
URL: http://www.inforamp.net/~cbmcomp
General Secretary, Rev. David K. Phillips
Communications, David Rogelstad
Publications: The Enterprise; Infomission, m.
Affiliates: Baptist World Alliance

BAPTIST CONVENTION OF ONTARIO & QUÉBEC (BCOQ) (1887)
#414, 195 The West Mall, Etobicoke, ON M9C 5K1
416/622-8600, Fax: 416/622-2308
Executive Minister, Rev. John Wilton
Publications: The Canadian Baptist; BCOQ Directory, a.

THE BAPTIST UNION OF WESTERN CANADA (BUWC) (1908)
#605, 999 - 8 St. SW, Calgary, AB T2R 1J5
403/228-9559, Fax: 403/228-9048
Executive Minister, Rev. G. Fisher
Publications: Share; Baptist Union Yearbook
Affiliates: Baptist World Alliance

UNION D'ÉGLISES BAPTISTES FRANÇAISES AU CANADA/UNION OF FRENCH BAPTIST CHURCHES IN CANADA (UEBF) (1969)
2285, av Papineau, Montréal, PQ H2K 4J5
514/526-6643, Téléc: 514/526-9269
Executive Officer, Dr. J. Boillat
Publications: Le Trait d'Union
Organisation(s) affiliée(s): Alliance Baptiste Mondiale

UNITED BAPTIST CONVENTION OF THE ATLANTIC PROVINCES/LA CONVENTION BAPTISTE DES PROVINCES DE L'ATLANTIQUE (UBCAP) (1906)
Atlantic United Baptist Convention
1655 Manawagonish Rd., Saint John, NB E2M 3Y2
506/635-1922, Fax: 506/635-0366
Executive Minister/Editor of the Year Book, Dr. E.M. Thompson
Director of Administration/Treasurer, Daryl W. Mackenzie
Publications: The Atlantic Baptist
Affiliates: Baptist World Alliance

Canadian Conference of Mennonite Brethren Churches
#3, 169 Riverton Ave., Winnipeg, MB R2L 2E5
204/669-6575, Fax: 204/654-1865
Executive Minister, Reuben Pauls

Canadian Convention of Southern Baptists (1987)
PO Box 300, Cochrane, AB T0L 0W0
403/932-5688, Fax: 403/932-4937, Email: 70420,2230@compuserve.com
Executive Director, Allen E. Schmidt
President, Rev. Ray Woodard
Publications: The Baptist Horizon
Affiliates: Southern Baptist Convention

Canadian Council for Conservative Judaism (CCCJ) (1982)
#112, 1520 Steeles Ave., Concord, ON L4K 3B9
905/738-1717, Fax: 905/738-1331, Email: 71263.302@compuserve.com
President, David Greenberg
Executive Secretary, Rhonda Schild
Publications: CCCJ/Mercaz/Masorti Update
Affiliates: United Synagogue of Conservative Judaism; World Council of Synagogues

Canadian Council for Reform Judaism
36 Atkinson Ave., Thornhill, ON L4J 8C9
905/709-2275, Fax: 905/709-1895
President, Charles Rothschild

Canadian Council of Reform Rabbis
c/o Temple Binai Tikvav, 1607 - 90 Ave. SW, Calgary, AB T2V 4V7
613/224-1802
Contact, Rabbi Jordan Goldsom

Canadian District of the Moravian Church in America, Northern Province
2304 - 38 St., Edmonton, AB T6L 4K9
403/467-6745, Fax: 403/467-0411
President, Ruth Humphreys

Canadian Friends Service Committee (CFSC) (1931)
Religious Society of Friends
60 Lowther Ave., Toronto, ON M5R 1C7
416/920-5213
Coordinator, Peter Chapman
Clerk, Mona Callin
Publications: Quaker Concern
Canadian Yearly Meeting: 91A Fourth Ave., Ottawa, ON K1S 2L1, 613/235-8553, Fax: 613/235-8553

Canadian Islamic Organization Inc. (1985)
2069 Kempton Park Dr., Mississauga, ON L5M 2Z4
905/820-4655, Fax: 905/820-0382
General Secretary, Fareed Ahmad Khan

The Canadian Orthodox Church/L'Église Orthodoxe canadienne (COC) (1970)
37323 Hawkins Pickle Rd., Dewdney, BC V0M 1H0
604/826-9336, Fax: 604/820-9758
Archbishop, Lazar Puhalo
Publications: Canadian Orthodox Missionary; Synakis: Canadian Orthodox Journal of Theology, q.
Affiliates: The Nemanjic Institute for Serbo-Byzantine Studies; Centre for Canadian Orthodox Studies

Canadian Unitarian Council/Conseil Unitarien du Canada (CUC) (1960)
Unitarian Church
#706, 188 Eglinton Ave. East, Toronto, ON M4P 2X7
416/489-4121, Fax: 416/489-9010, Email: cuc@web.apc.org
Executive Director, Ellen K. Campbell
Administrator, Carol Dahlquist
Publications: The Canadian Unitarian
Affiliates: Unitarian Universalist Association; International Association for Religious Freedom; International Council of Unitarians & Universities

Christian Brethren Church in the Province of Québec/l'Église des frères chrétiens dans la Province du Québec (CBCPQ) (1942)
Plymouth Brethren
358, rue Wellington sud, Sherbrooke, PQ J1H 5E4
819/820-1693, Fax: 819/821-9287
Secretary, Norman Buchanan

Christian Church (Disciples of Christ) in Canada/Église Chrétienne (Disciples du Christ) au Canada (DISCAN) (1922)
PO Box 64, Guelph, ON N1H 6J6
519/823-5190, Fax: 519/823-5766
Executive Regional Minister, Rev. Dr. Robert W. Steffer
Moderator, Rev. Mervin Bailey
Publications: The Canadian Disciple
Affiliates: The Christian Church (Disciples of Christ) in USA

The Christian & Missionary Alliance in Canada/Alliance chrétienne et missionaire au Canada (C&MA) (1972)
The Alliance Church
#510, 105 Gordon Baker Rd., PO Box 7900, Stn B, North York, ON M2K 2R6
416/492-8775, Fax: 416/492-7708, Email: cmacan@interlog.com
President, Dr. Arnold Cook
Vice-President, Canadian Ministries, Dr. C. Stuart Lightbody
Vice-President, Finance, M.H. Quigg
Vice-President, Personnel/Missions, Rev. Wally Albrecht
Vice-President, General Services, K.R. Paton
Publications: Briefing; Inside Story, s-a.; Alliance Life, bi-m.; Canadian Alliance News, 3 pa; Alliance Men in Action, s-a.; CMAC Official Directory, a.; Prayer Directory, a.; CMAC Yearbook; CMAC Statistical Report, a.; Prayer Line, m.; Praise & Prayer, m.
Affiliates: Alliance World Fellowship - International
Canadian Midwest District Office: District Superintendent, Rev. Bill Parsons, 2950 Arens Rd. East, Regina, SK S4V 1N8, 306/586-3549, Fax: 306/584-0399
Canadian Pacific District Office: District Superintendent, Rev. Brian Thom, #201, 11471 Blacksmith Pl., Richmond, BC V7A 4T7, 604/277-1983, Fax: 604/277-2003
Eastern & Central Canadian District Offices: Superintendent, Central Canadian District, Rev. David Lewis; Superintendent, Eastern Canadian District, Rev. Douglas Wiebe, 155 Panin Rd., Burlington, ON L7V 1A1, 905/639-9615, Fax: 905/634-7044
St. Lawrence District Office: District Superintendent, Rev. Yvan Fournier, #201, 964, rue Mainguy, Ste-Foy, PQ G1V 3S4, 418/659-3313, Fax: 418/659-4306
Western Canadian District Office: District Superintendent, Rev. Arnold Downey, 907A - 9 Ave. SW, Calgary, AB T2P 1L3, 403/265-7900, Fax: 403/265-4599

Christian Reformed Church in North America (CRCNA) (1857)
2850 Kalamazoo Ave. SE, Grand Rapids, MI 49560 USA
616/241-1691, Fax: 616/246-0834
General Secretary, Dr. David H. Engelhard
Executive Director of Ministries, Dr. Peter Borgdorff
Publications: The Banner
Affiliates: National Association of Evangelicals; North American Presbyterian & Reformed Council
Canada: Executive Secretary, Rev. Arie G. Van Eek; Canadian Director, Christian Reformed World Relief, Ray Elgersma; Christian Reformed World Missions, A.L. Karsten, 3475 Mainway, PO Box 5070, Burlington, ON L7R 3Y8, 905/336-2920, Fax: 905/336-8344

Christian Science (1879)
The First Church of Christ, Scientist, 175 Huntington Ave., Boston, MA 02115 USA
617/450-3301, Fax: 617/450-3325
Manager, Committee on Publication, Victor Westberg
Manager, Communications Division, Norm Bleichman, 617/450-3309
Publications: The Christian Science Journal; The Christian Science Monitor, daily; The Herald of Christian Science, m.; The Christian Science Sentinel, w.

The Church Army in Canada (1929)
Headquarters & College of Evangelism, 397 Brunswick Ave., Toronto, ON M5R 2Z2
416/924-9279, Fax: 416/924-2931
National Director, Bruce Smith
Warden, The Rev. Duke Vipperman
Publications: The Crusader
Affiliates: Anglican Church of Canada

Church of God, Anderson (1920)
Eastern Canada, 38 James St., Dundas, ON L9H 2J6
905/627-5236, Email: jr_wiebe@ecunet.org
Chairperson, Jim Wiebe
Publications: The Messenger
Affiliates: Church of God, Anderson, Indiana
Western Canada Assembly: Chairperson, Jack Wagner; Church Service/Mission Coordinator, John D. Campbell, 4717 - 56th St., Camrose, AB T4V 2C4, 403/672-0722, Fax: 403/672-6888

Church of God of Prophecy in Canada
RR#2, Brampton, ON L6V 1A1
905/843-2379
National Overseer, Canada East, Bishop Wade H. Phillips
National Overseer, Canada West, Bishop Vernon Van Deventer
Publications: Canadian Trumpeter (Canada West); Torch Light (Canada East)

Church of Jesus Christ of Latter-Day Saints (Mormons)
PO Box 641, North York, ON M3C 2T6
416/424-2485, Fax: 416/424-3326
Director, Jim Darden
Director, Elaine Darden

Church of The Nazarene Canada (1902)
#7, 3800 - 19 St. NE, Calgary, AB T2E 6V2
403/250-5166, Fax: 403/250-5183
Administrator, Dr. Neil E. Hightower
Chairman, Dr. William Stewart
Vice-Chairman, Dr. Charles Muxworthy
Secretary, Rev. Clair MacMillan
Publications: Spotlight

Conference of Mennonites in Canada (CMC) (1903)
600 Shaftesbury Blvd., Winnipeg, MB R3P 0M4
204/888-6781, Fax: 204/831-5675, Email: cmc@mbnet.mb.ca
General Secretary, Helmut Harder
Publications: Nexus

Congregational Christian Churches in Canada (CCCC) (1821)
#202, 222 Fairview Dr., Brantford, ON N3T 2W9
519/751-0606, Fax: 519/751-0852
Executive Director, Rev. W. Riegert
Publications: Communications

The Coptic Orthodox Church (Canada)
St. Mark's Coptic Orthodox Church, 41 Glendinning Ave., Scarborough, ON M1W 3E2
416/494-4449, Fax: 416/494-2631
Archpriest, Fr. M.A. Marcos
Publications: Coptologia

L'Église Réformée du Québec
5377, Maréchal-Joffre, Charny, PQ G6X 3C9
Courrier électronique: Farel@qbc.clic.net
Secrétaire, François Cordey
Publications: En Lui

Organisation(s) affiliée(s): Christian Reformed Church; Presbyterian Church of North America

Estonian Evangelical Lutheran Church (EELK) (1950)
383 Jarvis St., Toronto, ON M5B 2C7
416/923-5172, Fax: 416/923-5688
Archbishop, Rev. Udo Petersoo
Publications: Eesti Kirik
Affiliates: Lutheran World Federation; World Council of Churches

The Evangelical Alliance Mission of Canada Inc. (TEAM) (1969)
PO Box 56030, RPO Airways, Calgary, AB T2E 8K5
403/250-2140, Fax: 403/291-2857
Canadian Director, Rev. Norman Niemeyer
Publications: TEAM Horizons; Wherever, 3 pa; TEAM Prayer Directory, a.

Evangelical Covenant Church of Canada
245 - 21st St. East, Prince Albert, SK S6V 1L9
306/922-3449, Fax: 306/922-5414
Superintendent, Rev. Jerome Johnson
Publications: The Covenant Messenger

Evangelical Fellowship of Canada/Alliance évangélique du Canada (EFC) (1964)
PO Box 3745, Markham, ON L3S 0Y4
905/479-5885, Fax: 905/479-4742, Email: efc@efc-canada.com
URL: http://www.efc-canada.com
President, Brian C. Stiller
Corporate Affairs Director, Lorna A. Cheetham
Publications: Faith Today; Canada Watch, q.; Canada Watch Bulletin, q.

Evangelical Lutheran Church in Canada (ELCIC) (1986)
1512 St. James St., Winnipeg, MB R3H 0L2
204/786-6707, Fax: 204/783-7548
Secretary, Rev. Leon C. Gilbertson
Bishop, Rev. Telmor G. Sartison
Publications: Canada Lutheran
Affiliates: The Lutheran World Federation; World Council of Churches
The Lutheran Council in Canada: President, Rev. Dr. Edwin Lehman; Vice-President, Bishop Telmor Sartison, 1512 St. James St., Winnipeg, MB R3H 0L2, 204/783-7548
British Columbia Synod: Bishop, Marlin B. Aadland, Ph.D., 80 - 10 Ave. East, New Westminster, BC V3L 4R5, 604/524-1318, Fax: 604/524-9255
Eastern Synod: Bishop, Rev. William D. Huras, #340, 50 Queen St. North, Kitchener, ON N2H 6P4, 519/743-1461, Fax: 519/743-4291
Manitoba/Northwestern Ontario Synod: Rev. Richard M. Smith, #201, 3657 Roblin Blvd., Winnipeg, MB R3R 0E2, 204/889-3760, Fax: 204/896-0272
Saskatchewan Synod: Bishop, Rev. Allan A. Grundahl, Bessborough Towers, #707, 601 Spadina Cres. East, Saskatoon, SK S7K 3G8, 306/244-2474, Fax: 306/664-8677
Synod of Alberta & the Territories: Bishop, Rev. P. Kristenson, 10014 - 81 Ave., Edmonton, AB T6E 1W8, 403/439-2636, Fax: 403/433-6623

Evangelical Mennonite Conference (1812)
PO Box 1268, Steinbach, MB R0A 2A0
204/326-6401, Fax: 204/326-1613, Email: emconf@mts.net
Executive Secretary, Don Thiessen
Publications: Messenger
Affiliates: Mennonite Central Committee

Evangelical Mennonite Mission Conference (EMMC) (1959)
PO Box 52059, Stn Niakwa, Winnipeg, MB R2M 5P9

204/253-7929, Fax: 204/256-7384
Executive Secretary, Henry Dueck
Publications: The Recorder

Fellowship of Evangelical Baptist Churches in Canada
679 Southgate Dr., Guelph, ON N1G 4S2
519/821-4830, Fax: 519/821-9829, Email: 103227.1369@compuserve.com
President, Rev. Terry Cuthbert
Publications: Evangelical Baptist

Foursquare Gospel Church of Canada (1981)
#100, 8459 - 160th St., Surrey, BC V3S 3T9
604/543-8414, Fax: 604/543-8417, Email: fgcc@portal.ca
President/General Supervisor, Timothy J. Peterson
Publications: Foursquare World Advance

Free Methodist Church in Canada/Église méthodiste libre au Canada (1880)
4315 Village Centre Ct., Mississauga, ON L4Z 1S2
905/848-2600, Fax: 905/848-2603, Email: fmccan@inforamp.net
President, Bishop Gary R. Walsh
Secretary, David N. Ashton
Treasurer, Brian R. Cooke
Publications: The Free Methodist Herald
Affiliates: Evangelical Fellowship of Canada; Canadian Council of Christian Charities; World Methodist Council

Fung Loy Kok Institute of Taoism
1376 Bathurst St., 2nd Fl., Toronto, ON M5R 3J1
416/656-7479

General Church of the New Jerusalem in Canada
279 Burnhamthorpe Rd., Etobicoke, ON M9B 1Z6
519/748-5802, Fax: 519/748-6435
Rev. Michael D. Gladish

Greek Orthodox Church (Canada)
Greek Orthodox Diocese of Toronto, 27 Teddington Park Ave., Toronto, ON M4N 2C4
416/322-5055, Fax: 416/485-5929
Bishop of Toronto (Canada), The Rt. Rev. Sotirios Athanassoulas
Publications: The Orthodox Way

Independent Assemblies of God - Canada
1211 Lancaster St., London, ON N5V 2L4
519/451-1751
General Secretary, Rev. Harry O. Wuerch
Publications: The Canadian Mantle

Inter-Varsity Christian Fellowship of Canada (IVCF) (1929)
#17, 40 Vogell Rd., Richmond Hill, ON L4B 3N6
905/884-6880, Fax: 905/884-6550, Toll Free: 1-800-668-9766, Email: ivcfnat@hookup.net
General Director, James E. Berney
Chairperson, David Bogart
Publications: The Intercessor
Affiliates: International Fellowship of Evangelical Students; Evangelical Fellowship of Canada; Canadian Council of Christian Charities; Coalition for Religious Freedom in Education

ISKCON Toronto - Hare Krishna Movement (1966)
International Society for Krishna Consciousness
243 Avenue Rd., Toronto, ON M5R 2J6
416/922-5415, Fax: 416/964-9509
Director, Kala Das
Publications: Back to Godhead

Italian Pentecostal Church of Canada
6724 Fabre, Montréal, PQ H2G 2Z6
514/593-1944, Fax: 514/593-1835

General Superintendent, Rev. Daniel Ippolito
General Secretary, John Della Foresta
Publications: Voce Evangelica

Mennonite Central Committee Canada (MCCC) (1963)
134 Plaza Dr., Winnipeg, MB R3T 5K9
204/261-6381, Fax: 204/269-9875
URL: http://www.mennonitecc.ca/mcc
Executive Director, Marv Frey, Email: MF@mennonitecc.ca
Affiliates: Conference of Mennonites in Canada; Canadian Conference of Mennonite Brethren Churches; Canadian Conference of the Brethren in Christ Church; Evangelical Mennonite Brethren Conference; Evangelical Mennonite Mission Conference; Mennonite Conference of Eastern Canada; Northwest Mennonite Conference; Old Colony Mennonite Church; Sommerfelder Mennonite Church; Evangelical Mennonite Conference
MCC Alberta: Executive Director, Dick Neufeld, 76 Skyline Cres. NE, Calgary, AB T2K 5X7, 403/275-6935, Fax: 403/275-3711
MCC British Columbia: Executive Director, Ed Janzen, 31872 South Fraser Way, PO Box 2038, Clearbrook, BC V2T 3T8, 604/850-6639, Fax: 604/850-8734, Email: mccbc@web.apc.org
MCC Canada Ottawa Office: #803, 63 Sparks St., Ottawa, ON K1P 5A6, 613/238-7224, Fax: 613/238-7611, Email: mccott@web.apc.org
MCC Manitoba: Executive Director, Peter Peters, 134 Plaza Dr., Winnipeg, MB R3T 5K9, 204/261-6381, Fax: 204/269-9875
MCC Ontario: Executive Director, Dave Worth, 50 Kent Ave., Kitchener, ON N2G 3R1, 519/745-8458, Fax: 519/745-0064, Email: mccon@web.apc.org
MCC Saskatchewan: Executive Director, Werner Froese, 600 - 45 St. West, Saskatoon, SK S7L 5W9, 306/665-2555, Fax: 306/665-5564

Mennonite Conference of Eastern Canada (MCEC) (1988)
4489 King St. East, RR#3, Kitchener, ON N2G 3W6
Moderator, Ron Sawatsky

New Apostolic Church - Canada
65 Northfield Dr., PO Box 1615, Waterloo, ON N2J 4J2
519/884-2862, Fax: 519/884-3438, Telex: 06955333
President, M. Kraus
Treasurer, K.A. Storer

New Life League (1986)
PO Box 4083, Ponoka, AB T4J 1R5
403/783-6986, Fax: 403/783-6986
Director, Cliff Reimer
Treasurer, Don Hogman
Publications: Newsletter

North American Baptist Conference - Canadian Headquarters
11525 - 23 Ave., Edmonton, AB T6J 4T3
403/438-8852, Fax: 403/434-9170, Email: rberg@enabel.ccinet.ab.ca
Rev. Ron Berg
Publications: NAB Today
Affiliates: Edmonton Baptist Seminary; North American Baptist College

Northwest Mennonite Conference
9505 - 79 St., Edmonton, AB T6C 2S1
403/468-1003, Fax: 403/465-7313
Moderator, Jim Miller
Publications: Northwest Mennonite Conference Newsletter

The Old Holy Catholic Church in Canada (OHCC) (1939)
Sancta Vetus Catholica Ecclesia Canadiensis
PO Box 899, Hawkesbury, ON K6A 3E1
613/632-1210, Fax: 613/632-4812
Presiding Archbishop, Rainer Laufers
Chancellor, Rev. Fr. Ryan Perkins
Publications: OHCC Newsletter

Old Order Amish Church
c/o Heritage Historical Library, RR#4, Aylmer West, ON N5H 2R3
Contact, David Luthy

Orthodox Church in America - Archdiocese of Canada (OCA ADOC) (1902)
Office of the Bishop, PO Box 179, Spencerville, ON K0E 1X0
613/925-5226, Fax: 613/925-5221
HG Bishop Seraphim (Storheim)
Publications: Canadian Orthodox Messenger
Bishop's Office West: Dn. Andrew Piasta, Box 24, Site 5, RR#2, Winterburn, AB T0E 2N0, 403/987-4833, Fax: 403/987-4500
Chancery: Chancellor, Archpriest John Tkachuk, CP 1390, Succ Place Bonaventure, Montréal, PQ H5A 1H3, 514/481-5093, Fax: 514/481-2256

Orthodox Missionary Church of Canada (OMCC) (1968)
Sts. Cyril & Methodius Parish, #514, 186 King St., London, ON N6A 1C7
519/438-0734
URL: http://phobos.astro.uwo.ca/~arenburg/omcc.html
Missionary Vicar, The Very Rev. Andrei Bazilsky
Publications: Orthodoxy for Canada
Affiliates: Autocephalous Holy Orthodox Church of America

Patriarchal Parishes of the Russian Orthodox Church in Canada (1897)
St. Barbara's Russian Orthodox Cathedral, 10105 - 96th St., Edmonton, AB T5H 2G3
403/422-0277
Administrator, Rt. Rev. Bishop Mark

The Pentecostal Assemblies of Canada/Les Assemblées de la Pentecôte du Canada (PAoC) (1919)
6745 Century Ave., Mississauga, ON L5N 6P7
905/542-7400, Fax: 905/542-7313, Email: wmorrow@paoc.org
General Superintendent, Rev. William D. Morrow
Sec.-Treas., Rev. David Ball
Publications: The Pentecostal Testimony
Affiliates: World Pentecost; Pentecostal Fellowship of North America

Pentecostal Assemblies of Newfoundland (PAON) (1925)
PO Box 8248, St. John's, NF A1B 3N4
709/753-6314, Fax: 709/753-4945
General Superintendent, Roy D. King
Publications: Good Tidings
Affiliates: Pentecostal Fellowship of North America

Polish National Catholic Church of Canada
St. John's Cathedral, 186 Cowan Ave., Toronto, ON M6K 2N6
416/532-8249, Fax: 416/532-4653
Bishop Administrator, The Rt. Rev. Thaddeus Peplowski

Presbyterian Church in Canada/Église Presbytérienne au Canada (PCC) (1875)
50 Wynford Dr., North York, ON M3C 1J7
416/441-1111, Fax: 416/441-2825
Moderator, Tamiko Corbett, B.A.
Principal Clerk, The Rev. Dr. T. Gemmell, B.A., B.D., D.D.
Deputy Clerk, Barbara M. McLean
Deputy Clerk, The Rev. Dr. Tony Plomp, B.A., B.D., D.D.
General Secretary, Life & Mission Agency, The Rev. J.P. Morrison
General Secretary, Service Agency, Rev. K.A. Hincke
Chief Financial Officer, Donald A. Taylor
Principal, Knox College, Toronto, Dr. A. Van Seters
Principal, Presbyterian College, Montréal, Dr. W.J. Klempa
WMS President, The Rev. Rosemary Doran
AMS President, Marlene Sinnis
Executive Director, Women's Missionary Society, Charlotte Brown
Publications: The Presbyterian Record; Glad Tidings

The Reformed Episcopal Church of Canada - Diocese of Eastern Canada
58 Cedar Ave., PO Box 2532, New Liskeard, ON P0J 1P0
705/647-4565, Fax: 705/647-5429
President, Bishop Rt. Rev. Michael Fedechko

The Reformed Episcopal Church of Canada - Diocese of Western Canada (1874)
626 Blanshard St., Victoria, BC V8W 3G6
250/383-8915, Fax: 250/383-8916
Bishop, Rt. Rev. Charles W. Dorrington
Publications: The Grape Vine

Regional Synod of Canada Inc. - Reformed Church in America (RSC) (1993)
Reformed Church Centre, RR#4, Cambridge, ON N1R 5S5
519/622-1777, Fax: 519/622-1993, Email: RSCMoerman@aol.com
Executive Secretary, Rev. James Moerman
Publications: The Pioneer
Affiliates: The Reformed Church in America - HQ: New York, NY, USA

Reorganized Church of Jesus Christ of Latter Day Saints (Canada) (RLDS) (1830)
Saints' Church
390 Speedvale Ave. East, Guelph, ON N1E 1N5
519/822-4150, Fax: 519/822-4151
Bishop of Canada & Regional Bishop, Jim Poirier
Regional President, Larry Windland
Publications: Saint's Herald

Roman Catholic Church in Canada
Apostolic Nunciature, 724 Manor Ave., Ottawa, ON K1M 0E3
613/746-4914, Fax: 613/746-4786
Apostolic Pro-Nuncio to Canada, Most Reverend Carlo Curis
Counsellor, Msgr. Vito Rallo, P.H.
Secretary of the Apostolic Nunciature, Rev. Henri-Marie Guindon, S.M.M.
Assemblée des évêques du Québec: Secrétaire général, Clément Vigneault, 1225, boul St-Joseph est, Montréal, PQ H2J 1L7, 514/274-4323, Téléc: 514/274-4383
Atlantic Episcopal Assembly: Contact, Most Rev. J. Faber MacDonald, PO Box 771, Grand Falls-Windsor, NF A2A 2M4, 709/489-2778
Canadian Conference of Catholic Bishops: President, Rev. Jean-Guy Hamelin; General Secretary, Msgr. V. James Weisgerber; M. Éhilius Goulet, 90 Parent Ave., Ottawa, ON K1N 7B1, 613/241-9461, Fax: 613/241-8117; URL: http://www.cam.org/~cccb/
Ontario Conference of Catholic Bishops: General Secretary, Tom Reilly, #800, 10 St. Mary St., Toronto, ON M4V 1P9, 416/923-1423, Fax: 416/923-1509
Ordinariat militaire du Canada: Evêque, André Vallée, p.m.é; Aumônier général, B.Gen. Jean Pelletier, Ordinaire militaire, 1247, Place Kilborn, Ottawa, ON K1H 6K9, 613/990-7824, Téléc: 613/991-1056
The Western Catholic Conference: President, Most Rev. Paul O'Byrne, 1916 - 2 St. SW, Calgary, AB T2S 1S3, 403/228-4501, Fax: 403/228-7704

Romanian Orthodox Church in America (Canadian Parishes)
St. Demetrios Romanian Orthodox Church, 103 Furby St., Winnipeg, MB R3C 2A4
204/775-6472
Contact, Rev. Father Victor Malanca, Res: 284-0956
Treasurer, Terry Holunga, Res: 775-6973
Publications: Credinta - the Faith

The Salvation Army in Canada (1882)
Territorial Headquarters, Canada & Bermuda, 2 Overlea Blvd., Toronto, ON M4H 1P4
416/425-2111, Fax: 416/422-6157
Territorial Commander, Commissioner Donald Kerr
Chief Secretary, Colonel John Busby
Field Secretary, Personnel, Lt.Col. John Carew
Program Secretary, Lt.Col. Ralph Stanley
Secretary, Business Administration, Lt.Col. Clyde Moore
Assistant Chief Secretary, Lt.Col. William Wilson
Secretary, Social Services, Major Ray Moulton
Editor-in-Chief & Literary Secretary, Major Edward Forster
Education Secretary, Major Cecil Cooper
Financial Secretary, Major Glen Shepherd
Government Relations Officer & Director of Overseas Projects, Lt.Col. Elva Jolley
President, C.B.C.C., Winnipeg, Major Lloyd Hetherington
Principal, C.F.O.T., Toronto, Major Douglas Moore
Principal, C.F.O.T., St. John's, Major David Hiscock
Property Secretary, Major Donald Copple
Trade Secretary, Major Ronald Goodyear
Secretary, Ministry to Women, Major Mary Moore
Secretary, League of Mercy, Lt.Col. Verna Carew
Secretary, Music, Brian Burditt
Secretary, Public Relations, Lt.-Col. Melvin Bond
Secretary, Youth, Major Gregory Simmonds
Publications: The War Cry; En Avant, w.; The Young Soldier, w.; Sally Ann, m.; The Edge, m.; Horizons, bi-m.

Serbian Orthodox Church - Diocese of Canada (1983)
RR#3, Campbellville, ON L0P 1B0
905/878-0043, Fax: 905/878-1909
Serbian Orthodox Bishop of Canada, His Grace The Rt. Rev. Georgije Djokic
Publications: Istocnik

Seventh-Day Adventist Church in Canada
1148 King St. East, Oshawa, ON L1H 1H8
905/433-0011, Fax: 905/433-0982
President, Orville Parchment
Sec.-Treas., Robert Lemon
Director, Brian Ford
Director, C. Sabot
Director, K. Doukmetzian
Director, J. Saliba
Publications: Canadian Adventist Messenger

The Society of Saint Peter the Apostle (1889)
3329 Danforth Ave., Scarborough, ON M1L 4T3
416/699-7077, Fax: 416/699-9019, Email: missions@eda.net
URL: http://www.eda.net~mission
National Director, Sr. L. Spencer

The Spiritual Science Fellowship of Canada (1977)
Spiritualist Yoga Fellowship
PO Box 1387, Stn H, Montréal, PQ H3G 2N3
514/937-8539, Fax: 514/937-5380
President, Marilyn Zwaig Rossner, Ph.D.
Publications: SSF Events
Affiliates: International Council of Community Churches

Student Christian Movement of Canada/ Mouvement d'étudiant(e)s chrétien(ne)s (SCM) (1921)
#C3, 310 Danforth Ave., Toronto, ON M4K 1N6
416/463-4312
General Secretary, Jean Ann Ledwell
Publications: All Things New

Ukrainian Orthodox Church of Canada
9 St. John's Ave., Winnipeg, MB R2W 1G8
204/586-3093, Fax: 204/582-5241
Primate, The Most Rev. Metropolitan Fedak Wasyly
Auxillary Bishop, Rt. Rev. Yurij Kalistchuk
Archbishop, Rt. Rev. John Stinka
Chairman of the Presidium, Very Rev. Fr. William Makarenko
Publications: The Herald

Union of Spiritual Communities of Christ
Orthodox Doukhobors in Canada
PO Box 760, Grand Forks, BC V0H 1H0
250/442-8252, Fax: 250/442-3433
Chairperson, Andrew Evin
Administrator, S.W. Babakaiff
Publications: Iskra

Union of the Vietnamese Buddhist Churches in Canada (1983)
4450, av Van Horne, Montréal, PQ H3S 1S1
514/733-3841, Fax: 514/733-5860
Président, Ven Thich Thiên Nghi
Publications: Hoa Dao Magazine

The United Brethren Church in Canada (1856)
501 Whitelaw Rd., Guelph, ON N1K 1E7
519/836-0180, Fax: 519/837-2219
President, Rev. Brian K. Magnus
Treasurer, Bryan Winger
Secretary, Joan Sider
Publications: U.B.
Affiliates: Evangelical Fellowship of Canada

The United Church of Canada/Église Unie du Canada (UCC) (1925)
3250 Bloor St. West, Etobicoke, ON M8X 2Y4
416/231-5931, Fax: 416/231-3103, Info Line: 416/231-7680
Moderator/General Council, Marion Best
General Secretary, Virginia Coleman
Publications: The United Church Observer; Mandate, bi-m.; The United Church of Canada Yearbook & Directory, a.
Conferences
Alberta & Northwest Conference: Executive Secretary, Rev. Dr. George H. Rodgers, 9911 - 48 Ave., Edmonton, AB T6E 5V6, 403/435-3995, Fax: 403/438-3317
All Native Circle Conference: Speaker, Rev. Grafton Antone, #18, 399 Berry St., Winnipeg, MB R2W 4X3, 204/831-0740, Fax: 204/837-9703
Bay of Quinte Conference: Executive Secretary, Rev. David M. Iverson, 218 Barrie St., Kingston, ON K7L 3K3, 613/549-2503, Fax: 613/549-1050
British Columbia Conference: Executive Secretary, Rev. Brian D. Thorpe, #200, 1955 West 4 Ave., Vancouver, BC V6J 1M7, 604/734-0434, Fax: 604/734-7024

Hamilton Conference: PO Box 100, Carlisle, ON L0R 1H0, 905/659-3343, Fax: 905/659-7766
London Conference: Executive Secretary, Rev. W. Peter Scott, 359 Windermere Rd., London, ON N6G 2K3, 519/672-1930, Fax: 519/439-2800
Manitoba & Northwestern Ontario Conference: Executive Secretary, H. Dianne Cooper, 120 Maryland St., Winnipeg, MB R3G 1L1, 204/786-8911, Fax: 204/774-0159
Manitou Conference: Executive Secretary, Rev. J. Stewart Bell, 1402 Regina St., North Bay, ON P1B 2L5, 705/474-3350, Fax: 705/497-3597
Maritime Conference: Executive Secretary, Rev. Robert H. Mills, PO Box 1560, Sackville, NB E0A 3C0, 506/536-1334, Fax: 506/536-2900
Montréal & Ottawa Conference: Executive Secretary, Rev. Tad Mitsui, 225 - 50 Ave., Lachine, PQ H8T 2T7, 514/634-7015, Fax: 514/634-2489
Newfoundland & Labrador Conference: Executive Secretary, Rev. Boyd L. Hiscock, 320 Elizabeth Ave., St. John's, NF A1B 1T9, 709/754-0386, Fax: 709/754-8336
Saskatchewan Conference: Executive Secretary, Rev. Wilbert R. Wall, 418A McDonald St., Regina, SK S4N 6E1, 306/721-3311, Fax: 306/721-3171
Toronto Conference: Executive Secretary, Rev. Albion Wright, 65 Mayall Ave., North York, ON M3L 1E7, 416/241-2677, Fax: 416/241-2689

Watch Tower Bible & Tract Society of Canada
Jehovah's Witnesses
PO Box 4100, Georgetown, ON L7G 4Y4
905/873-4100, Fax: 905/873-4554
Executive Director, Kenneth A. Little
Information Officer, Warren Shewfelt
Publications: The Watchtower; Awake, s-m.

The Wesleyan Church of Canada (1897)
Central Canada District, #101, 3 Applewood Dr., Belleville, ON K8P 4E3
613/966-7527, Fax: 613/968-6190
District Superintendent, Rev. Donald E. Hodgins
Publications: Clarion
Atlantic District: District Superintendent, Ray Barnwell Sr., PO Box 20, Sussex, NB E0E 1P0, 506/433-1007, Fax: 506/432-6668

RELIGIOUS ORGANIZATIONS

Africa Inland Mission International (Canada)/ Mission à l'intérieur de l'Afrique (Canada) (AIM) (1895)
AIM Canada
1641 Victoria Park Ave., Scarborough, ON M1R 1P8
416/751-6077, Fax: 416/751-3467, Email: aim-can@ai-mint.org
Director, Dr. John Brown
Personnel Director, Robert Cousins
Publications: Africa Inland Mission International

Association of Christian Churches in Manitoba/ Association des les églises chrétiennes du Manitoba (ACCM) (1990)
484 Maryland St., Winnipeg, MB R3G 1M5
204/774-3143
Rev. Ted Chell

Association des parents catholiques du Québec (APCQ) (1966)
#406, 7400, boul Saint-Laurent, Montréal, PQ H2R 2Y1
514/276-8068; 8075, Téléc: 514/984-2595
Présidente, Jocelyene St.-Cyr
Publications: Famille - Québec
Organisation(s) affiliée(s): Organisation internationale de l'enseignement catholique (OIEO)

Association of Regular Baptist Churches (1957)
130 Gerrard St. East, Toronto, ON M5A 3T4
416/925-3261, Fax: 416/925-8305
President, Rev. Stephen Kring
Secretary, Rev. W.P. Bauman
Publications: The Gospel Witness

Atlantic Ecumenical Council of Churches (1951)
c/o Immaculate Conception Church, Saint-Louis, PQ C0B 1Z0
902/882-2622
President, David Luker
Secretary, Rev. Arthur Pendergast
Publications: Friends of AEC

The Bible Holiness Movement/Mouvement de sainteté biblique (1949)
PO Box 223, Stn A, Vancouver, BC V6C 2M3
250/498-3895
Bishop-General (International Leader), Evangelist Wesley H. Wakefield
Publications: Hallelujah
Affiliates: Religious Freedom of Council of Christian Minorities; Christians Concerned for Racial Equality

The Bible League of Canada/Société canadienne pour la distribution de la Bible (1949)
PO Box 5037, Burlington, ON L7R 3Y8
905/319-9500, Fax: 905/319-0484, Toll Free: 1-800-363-9673, Email: bibleag@worldchat.com
Executive Director, J.G. Klomps
President, J. Walhout
Publications: The Bible League Report
Affiliates: The Bible League

Buddhist Association of Canada
1330 Bloor St. West, Toronto, ON M6H 1P2
416/537-1342, Fax: 416/537-1342
Chairman, Dr. Clement Wong

Canada's National Bible Hour (1925)
PO Box 1210, St Catharines, ON L2R 7A7
905/684-1401
Founder, Ernest C. Manning
President, James O. Blackwood

Canadian African Missions Foundation
251 Head St. North, Simcoe, ON N3Y 3X8
519/426-0511, Fax: 519/426-1149
Vice-President, Jeff Campbell
Affiliates: Association of Faith Churches & Ministries (Canada)

Canadian Bible Society/Société biblique canadienne (1804)
10 Carnforth Rd., Toronto, ON M4A 2S4
416/757-4171, Fax: 416/757-3376, Toll Free: 1-800-465-2425
General Secretary, Dr. Rev. Floyd C. Babcock
Executive Director & Finance, Wallis Sherwin
Director, Ministry Funding, Barbara Walkden
Director, Secteur francophone, Serge Rhéaume, 514/524-7873
Director, Scripture Translations, Harold Fehderau, 519/741-8285, Fax: 519/741-8357
Publications: Canadian Bible Society Newsletter

Canadian Centre for Ecumenism/Centre canadien d'oecuménisme (1963)
2065, rue Sherbrooke ouest, Montréal, PQ H3H 1G6
514/937-9176, Fax: 514/937-2684
Director, Fr. Philippe Thibodeau
Chairman, Richard Bowie
Publications: Ecumenism/Oecumenisme
Affiliates: Canadian Conference of Catholic Bishops

Canadian Centre for Law & Justice (1993)
1318 Wellington St., PO Box 36038, Ottawa, ON K1Y 4V3
613/778-7718, Fax: 613/778-3443

Canadian Chapter of the International Council of Community Churches/Section canadienne du conseil international des églises communautaires (CCICCC) (1989)
30 Briermoor Cres., Ottawa, ON K1T 3G7
Fax: 613/738-7835
URL: http://www.geocities.com/Heartland/3285
General Superintendent for Canada, Bishop S.A. Thériault, Ph.D., Th.D.
Sec.-Treas., The Rev. J. Venne, L.Th.
Publications: CCICC Info SCCIEC
Affiliates: World Council of Churches; National Council of Churches
English-speaking Sector: Rev. Leona Hartman, O.Tr., PO Box 1387, Stn A, Montréal, PQ H3G 2N3, 514/937-8359
French-speaking Sector: Rev. Jacques Lefebvre, SPS, CP 403, Succ. A, Hull, PQ J8Y 6M9, 613/238-2213

The Canadian Churches' Forum for Global Ministries/Le forum des églises canadiennes pour les ministères globaux (1921)
11 Madison Ave., Toronto, ON M5R 2S2
416/924-9351, Fax: 416/924-5356, Email: ccforum@web.apc.org
Coordinator, Outreach & Communication, Robert Faris
Coordinator, Education & Training, Kevin Anderson
Coordinator, Finance & Administration, Mary Lou Smith
Publications: Focus
Affiliates: Canadian Council of Churches

The Canadian Council of Christians & Jews/Conseil canadien des chrétiens et des juifs (CCCJ) (1947)
#600, 44 Victoria St., Toronto, ON M5C 1Y2
416/364-3101, Fax: 416/364-5705, Toll Free: 1-800-663-1848, Email: cccj@interlog.com
URL: http://www.interlog.com/~cccj/
National Executive Director, Elyse Graff
Affiliates: International Council of Christians & Jews

The Canadian Council of Churches/Conseil canadien des églises (CCC) (1944)
#201, 40 St. Clair Ave. East, Toronto, ON M4T 1M9
416/921-4152, Fax: 416/921-7478
President, Dr. Alexandra Johnston
Interim General Secretary, Rev. Robert H. Mills
Publications: Entre nous
Affiliates: Members include Anglican Church of Canada, Armenian Orthodox Church, Baptist Convention of Ontario & Quebec, Canadian Conference of Catholic Bishops, Christian Church (Disciples of Christ), Coptic Orthodox Church, Ethiopian Orthodox Church, Greek Orthodox Church, Evangelical Lutheran Church in Canada, Orthodox Church in America, Polish National Catholic Church of Canada, Presbyterian Church in Canada, Reformed Church in America (Ont.), Religious Society of Friends, Salvation Army, United Church, Ukrainian Orthodox Church

Canadian Council of Muslim Women/Conseil canadien des femmes musulmanes (CCMW) (1982)
PO Box 128, Seba Beach, AB T0E 2B0
403/797-3855, Fax: 403/439-5088
Founding President, Dr. Lila Fahlman
Publications: The Muslim Woman
Affiliates: World Council of Muslim Women

Canadian Lutheran World Relief (CLWR) (1946)
1080 Kingsbury Ave., Winnipeg, MB R2P 1W5
204/694-5602, Fax: 204/694-5460, Toll Free: 1-800-661-2597, Email: clwr@mbnet.mb.ca
Executive Director, David E. Hardy

Canadian-Muslim Civil Liberties Association/Association canadienne-musulman des libertés civiles (CMCLA) (1995)
#200, 200 Consumers Rd., North York, ON M2J 4R4
416/496-9666, Fax: 416/496-9530
President, Faisal M. Kutty
Treasurer, Imran Yousuf
Vice-President, Fayaz Karin
Public Relations, Sajidah Kutty
Communications, Irfan Khan
Fundraising, Sagib Meer
Publications: CMCLA News; CMCLA Alert
Affiliates: Council on American Islamic Relations

Canadian Religious Conference/Conférence religieuse canadienne (CRC) (1954)
324 Laurier Ave. East, Ottawa, ON K1N 6P6
613/236-0824, Fax: 613/236-0825, Email: crch@web.apc.org
Publications: CRC Bulletin

Canadian Theological Society
Wycliffe College, 5 Hoskin Ave., Toronto, ON M5S 1H7
403/596-2439, Fax: 403/979-1471
Secretary, Prof. Brian Walsh

Canadian Tract Society (1970)
26 Hale St., PO Box 2156, Brampton, ON L6T 3S4
905/457-4559, Fax: 905/457-4559
Publications: Order Form

Catholic Biblical Association of Canada (CBAC) (1974)
3275 St. Clair Ave. East, Scarborough, ON M1L 1W2
416/285-9552, Fax: 416/285-9174
Executive Director, Jocelyn Monette
Publications: The Word Is Life
Affiliates: Catholic Biblical Federation

Child Evangelism Fellowship of Canada/Association de l'évangelisation des enfants (CEF) (1937)
PO Box 165, Winnipeg, MB R3C 2G9
204/943-2774, Email: 103442.1544@compuserve.com
National Director, Don Collins
Chairman, Jim Pride
Publications: Evangelizing Today's Child
Affiliates: Child Evangelism Fellowship Inc.; CEF of Nations

Christian Aid Mission (CAM) (1953)
201 Stanton St., Fort Erie, ON L2A 3N8
905/871-1773, Fax: 905/871-5165, Email: info@christianaid.ca
URL: http://www.christianaid.ca
President, James S. Eagles
Publications: Christian Mission; Prayerline

Christian Children's Fund of Canada
1027 McNicoll Ave., Scarborough, ON M1W 3X2
416/495-1174, Fax: 416/495-9395, Telex: 06-986703
National Director, Peter G. Harris

Christian Reformed World Relief Committee of Canada (CRWRC) (1962)
3475 Mainway, PO Box 5070, Burlington, ON L7R 3Y8
905/336-2920, Fax: 905/336-8344, Toll Free: 1-800-730-3490, Email: dejongw@crcnet.mhs.compuserve.com
Director, Wayne Dejong

Coordinator of Communications, Rachel Boehm Van Harmelen
Coordinator of Church Relations, Rick DeGraaf
Publications: In Touch
Affiliates: Christian Reformed World Relief Committee

Council of Muslim Communities of Canada
#1010, 4 Forest Lawn Way, North York, ON M2N 5X8
416/512-2106, Fax: 416/512-2106
President, Hanny Hassan
Coordinator, Muin Muinuddin
Publications: Islam Canada

Ecumenical Coalition for Economic Justice/Coalition oecuménique pour la justice économique (1973)
#402, 77 Charles St. West, Toronto, ON M5R 2S2
416/921-4615, Fax: 416/922-1419, Email: gattfly@web.apc.org
Publications: Economic Justice Report
Affiliates: Canadian Council of Churches

Federation of Islamic Associations
73 Patricia Ave., North York, ON M2M 1J1
416/222-2794, Fax: 416/674-8168
President, Ayube Ally

Focus on The Family (Canada) Association (1982)
PO Box 9800, Vancouver, BC V6B 4G3
604/684-8333, Fax: 604/684-8653
President, Geoffrey Still
Publications: Focus on the Family; Teachers in Focus

Gideons International in Canada (1911)
501 Imperial Rd. North, Guelph, ON N1H 6T9
519/823-1140, Fax: 519/767-1913
Executive Director, Graham Sawer
Publications: The Canadian Gideon

Global Outreach Mission Inc. (1943)
PO Box 1210, St Catharines, ON L2R 7A7
905/684-1401
President, James O. Blackwood
Sec.-Treas., Douglas Waters
Comptroller, Alvin Voth
Affiliates: Interdenominational Foreign Mission Association

Gospel Missionary Union of Canada (GMU) (1949)
2121 Henderson Hwy., Winnipeg, MB R2G 1P8
204/338-7831, Fax: 204/339-3321
Vice-President, Canadian Ministries, John Harder
Treasurer, Grant Morrison, CMA
Publications: The Gospel Message

Habitat for Humanity Canada (HFHC) (1985)
40 Albert St., Waterloo, ON N2L 3S2
519/885-4565, Fax: 519/885-5225, Toll Free: 1-800-667-5137, Email: hfhc@sentex.net
President & CEO, Wilmer Martin
Publications: Habitat Spirit

Holy Childhood Association (1843)
Children Helping Children
3329 Danforth Ave., Unit D, Scarborough, ON M1L 4T3
416/699-7077, Fax: 416/699-9019
Associate Director, Margaret T. Tipping

Jesuit Fathers & Brothers (1540)
Society of Jesus
69 Marmaduke St., Toronto, ON M6R 1T3
416/763-4664, Fax: 416/763-4666
National Superior, Rev. David E. Nazar, S.J.
Assistant to the National Superior, Rev. Geoffrey B. Williams, S.J.
Publications: Compass

2-8 ORGANIZATIONS—ACCOUNTING

CANADIAN JESUIT MISSIONS
1190 Danforth Ave., Toronto, ON M4J 1M6
416/465-1824, Fax: 416/465-1825
CEO, Michael Murray, S.J.
Director, Dr. Jim Thompson
International Executive Officer, J.P. Horigan

THE JESUIT CENTRE FOR SOCIAL FAITH & JUSTICE (1979)
947 Queen St. East, Toronto, ON M4M 1J9
416/469-1123, Fax: 416/469-3579
Director, Kevin Arsenault
Coordinator, Bob Jeffcott
Publications: The Moment Refugee Update; Central America Update, bi-m.

The Missionary Union of the Clergy & Religious (1916)
3329 Danforth Ave., Scarborough, ON M1L 4T3
416/699-7077, Fax: 416/699-9019, Email: missions@eda.net
URL: http://www.eda.net~missions
National Director, Sr. L. Spencer

Multifaith Action Society (1973)
385 Boundary Road, Vancouver, BC V5K 4S1
604/291-1865
Coordinator, Joan Craker
President, Rev. Dr. Phillip Hewett
Publications: Multifaith News; The Multifaith Calendar

OMF International - Canada (1865)
Overseas Missionary Fellowship
5759 Coopers Ave., Mississauga, ON L4Z 1R9
905/568-9971, Fax: 905/568-9974, Email: gdykema@cproject.com
National Director, Rev. William Fietje
Director, Administration & Finance, Ron Adams
Publications: East Asia Millions
Affiliates: Evangelical Fellowship of Canada

Operation Mobilization Canada (1966)
Send the Light
104 Culham St., Oakville, ON L6H 1G5
905/338-8106, Fax: 905/849-3501
Director, Steve Hawkins
Publications: Canadian Monthly

Organisation catholique canadienne pour le développement et la paix/Canadian Catholic Organization for Development & Peace (OCCDP) (1967)
Développement et Paix
5633, rue Sherbrooke est, Montréal, PQ H1N 1A3
514/257-8711, Téléc: 514/257-8497, Courrier électronique: devp@web.net
Directeur général, Fabien Leboeuf
Président, Raymond Boucher
Publications: Information; Solidarités, 5 fois par an; Global Village Voice, q.
Organisation(s) affiliée(s): Asia Partnership for Human Development; Coopération internationale pour le développement et la solidarité

Society for the Propagation of the Faith for Canada (1822)
English Sector, 3329 Danforth Ave., Unit D, Scarborough, ON M1L 4T3
416/699-7077, Fax: 416/699-9019, Email: missions@eda.net
URL: http://www.eda.net~missions
National Director, Sr. L. Spencer
Publications: Missions Today

OEUVRE PONTIFICALE DE LA PROPAGATION DE LA FOI - SECTEUR FRANÇAIS DU CANADA
2269, ch Saint-Louis, Sillery, PQ G1T 1R5
418/687-9531, Téléc: 418/687-9057

Directeur national, Jean-Marc Daoust
Publications: Univers

Taskforce on the Churches & Corporate Responsibility/Comité inter-Églises sur les responsabilités des corporations (TCCR) (1975)
129 St. Clair Ave. West, Toronto, ON M4V 1N5
416/923-1758, Fax: 416/927-7554, Email: tccr@web.apc.org
Coordinator, Daniel M. Gennarelli
Publications: TCCR Mailing
Affiliates: Anglican Church of Canada; Canadian Conference of Catholic Bishops; Evangelical Lutheran Church in Canada; Presbyterian Church in Canada; Religious Society of Friends (Quakers); United Church of Canada; CUSO; YWCA

Unitarian Service Committee of Canada/Comité du service unitaire du Canada (1945)
USC Canada
#705, 56 Sparks St., Ottawa, ON K1P 5B1
613/234-6827, Fax: 613/234-6842
CEO, John Martin
Director, Canadian Operations, Friederike Knabe
Director of Finance, Mary Forbes
Publications: 56 Sparks
BC Provincial Office: Provincial Coordinator, Shary Bartlett, #402, 207 West Hastings, Vancouver, BC V6H 1H7, 604/682-0486, Fax: 604/682-0486
Ontario Provincial Office: Provincial Coordinator, Jonquil Brunker, PO Box 2303, Stn B, Kitchener, ON N2H 6M2, 519/749-0411, Fax: 519/749-0411

VISION TV Canada's Faith Network (1988)
80 Bond St., Toronto, ON M5B 1X2
416/368-3194, Fax: 416/368-9774, Email: visiontv@web.apc.org
President & CEO, Fil Fraser
Vice-President, Programming & Development, Peter Flemington
Vice-President, Production & Presentation, Rita Deverell
Director, Finance & Administration, Susan Bower
Publications: Great Viewers' Guide; Social Justice Calendar, bi-m.; Faith Matters Calendar, bi-m.

World Congress of Faiths (1936)
2 Market St., Oxford OX1 3EF UK
086/520-2751, Fax: 086/520-2746
Chair, Rev. Marcus Braybrooke
Hon. Sec.-Treas., David Potter
Publications: World Faiths Encounter

ORGANIZATIONS

(Including Associations, Societies, Institutes, Research Organizations, Relief Agencies, Support Groups and Centres)

ABORIGINAL PEOPLES see **NATIVE PEOPLES**

ABORTION see **REPRODUCTIVE ISSUES**

ACCIDENT PREVENTION see **SAFETY & ACCIDENT PREVENTION**

ACCOUNTING

Canadian Academic Accounting Association/Association canadienne des professeurs de comptabilité (CAAA) (1976)
Faculty of Management, University of Toronto, #850, 120 King St. West, PO Box 176, Hamilton, ON L8N 3C3

905/525-1884, Fax: 905/525-3046
Administrative Officer, Vittoria Fortunato
President, Dan Thornton
Publications: Canadian Accounting Education & Research News; Contemporary Accounting Research, q.
Affiliates: American Accounting Association

Canadian Association of Certified Executive Accountants (CACEA) (1988)
#240, 2415 Holly Lane, Ottawa, ON K1V 7P2
613/521-0620, Fax: 613/521-1185
Administrator, Susan Singh
Publications: Official Newsletter
Affiliates: Canadian Society of Business Practitioners; Canadian Institute of Financial Accountants

Canadian Comprehensive Auditing Foundation/Fondation canadienne pour la vérification intégrée (CCAF) (1980)
#210, 55 Murray St., Ottawa, ON K1N 5M3
613/241-6900, Fax: 613/241-6900
Executive Director, J.P. Boisclair, FCA, CMC
Publications: CCAF Update

Canadian Institute of Chartered Accountants/Institut canadien des comptables agréés (CICA)
Chartered Accountants of Canada
277 Wellington St. West, Toronto, ON M5V 3H2
416/977-3222, Fax: 416/977-8585
URL: http://www.cica.ca/
President, Michael Rayner, FCA
Chair, Ron Gage
Executive Vice-President, E. Charlene Valiquette, CA
Vice-President, Communications, Randall Pearce
Publications: CA Magazine
Affiliates: International Accounting Standards Committee; International Federation of Accountants

ATLANTIC SCHOOL OF CHARTERED ACCOUNTANCY
PO Box 489, Halifax, NS B3J 2R7
902/425-7974, Fax: 902/423-9784
Executive Director, J.D. Trainor, C.A.

CHARTERED ACCOUNTANTS INSTITUTE OF BERMUDA (1973)
PO Box 1625, Hamilton HM GX Bermuda
809/292-7479, Fax: 809/295-3121
Executive Director, Sandra Mayor

INSTITUTE OF CHARTERED ACCOUNTANTS OF ALBERTA
Edmonton Centre, 901 Toronto Dominion Tower, Edmonton, AB T5J 2Z1
403/424-7391, Fax: 403/425-8766
Executive Director, S.J. Glover, FCA

INSTITUTE OF CHARTERED ACCOUNTANTS OF BRITISH COLUMBIA (ICABC) (1905)
1133 Melville St., Vancouver, BC V6E 4E5
604/681-3264, Fax: 604/681-1523, Toll Free: 1-800-663-2677, Email: exec.dir@sfu.ca
URL: http://www.ica.bc.ca
Executive Director/Executive Vice-President, R.W. McCloy, FCA
Publications: CommuniCAtion Magazine

INSTITUTE OF CHARTERED ACCOUNTANTS OF MANITOBA (1886)
#1200, 363 Broadway, Winnipeg, MB R3C 3N9
204/942-8248, Fax: 204/943-7119
Executive Vice-President, G.B. Hannaford
Publications: Folio

INSTITUTE OF CHARTERED ACCOUNTANTS OF NEWFOUNDLAND (1949)
CA Newfoundland
570 Newfoundland Dr., PO Box 103, St. John's, NF A1A 5B1
709/753-7566, Fax: 709/753-3609
Executive Director, Nina Adey

INSTITUTE OF CHARTERED ACCOUNTANTS OF THE NORTHWEST TERRITORIES
PO Box 2433, Yellowknife, NT X1A 2P8
403/873-3680, Fax: 403/920-4135
Administrative Assistant, Dorothy Davis

INSTITUTE OF CHARTERED ACCOUNTANTS OF NOVA SCOTIA
#1104, 1791 Barrington St., Halifax, NS B3J 3L1
902/425-3291, Fax: 902/423-4505
Executive Director, Ross Towler, FCA

INSTITUTE OF CHARTERED ACCOUNTANTS OF ONTARIO/INSTITUT DES COMPTABLES AGRÉÉS DE L'ONTARIO (ICAO) (1879)
69 Bloor St. East, Toronto, ON M4W 1B3
416/962-1841, Fax: 416/962-8900, Toll Free: 1-800-387-0735, Email: exof@icao.on.ca
URL: http://www.icao.on.ca
Chief Executive Officer, David A. Wilson, MBA, FCA
Director of the Executive Office, Brendan Wycks, MBA
Publications: CheckMark

INSTITUTE OF CHARTERED ACCOUNTANTS OF PRINCE EDWARD ISLAND (1921)
PO Box 301, Charlottetown, PE C1A 7K7
902/894-4290, Fax: 902/894-4791
Executive Director, Edison Shea, C.A.
Publications: Bottom Line

INSTITUTE OF CHARTERED ACCOUNTANTS OF SASKATCHEWAN
#900, 1867 Hamilton St., Regina, SK S4P 2C2
306/359-1010, Fax: 306/569-8288
Executive Director, Nola Dianne Jooristy
Publications: CHAFF

NEW BRUNSWICK INSTITUTE OF CHARTERED ACCOUNTANTS/ INSTITUT DES COMPTABLES AGRÉÉS DU NOUVEAU-BRUNSWICK (NBICA) (1916)
93 Prince William St., 4th Fl., Saint John, NB E2L 2B2
506/634-1588, Fax: 506/634-1015
Executive Director, J. Blackier, CA
Publications: Interim Report

ORDRE DES COMPTABLES AGRÉÉS DU QUÉBEC (OCAQ) (1880)
680, rue Sherbrooke ouest, 7e étage, Montréal, PQ H3A 2S3
514/288-3256, Téléc: 514/843-8375, Ligne sans frais: 1-800-363-4688
URL: http://www.uquebec.ca/comptables/agrees
Directeur général et secrétaire, Gérard Caron, FCA
Président, Jean-Pierre Dubeau
Directrice des communications, Francine Cléroux
Publications: Bilans; Répertoire de cours, semi-annuel

Canadian Institute of Financial Accountants (1988)
2380 Holly Lane, 2nd Fl., Ottawa, ON K1V 7P2
613/521-0620, Fax: 613/521-1185
President, Andrew Yeung
Publications: Newsletter
Affiliates: Canadian Association of Certified Executive Accountants

Canadian Insurance Accountants Association/ Association canadienne des comptables d'assurance
173 Durant Ave., Toronto, ON M4J 4W5
416/869-3670
Membership Coordinator, Linda Berkis

Certified General Accountants Association of Canada (1913)
CGA - Canada
#700, 1188 Georgia St. West, Vancouver, BC V6E 4A2
604/669-3555, Fax: 604/689-5845
URL: http://www.cga-canada.org
President & COO, Guy Legault, B.Sc., MBA, FCGA, CAE
Chairman & CEO, Ruby J. Howard, FCGA
Communications Manager, Edward Downing
Publications: CGA Magazine
Affiliates: International Federation of Accountants Council (IFAC); Confederation of Asian & Pacific Accountants (CAPA); International Accounting Standards Committee

CERTIFIED GENERAL ACCOUNTANTS ASSOCIATION OF ALBERTA
CGA - Alberta
#1410, 555 - 4 Ave. SW, Calgary, AB T2P 3E7
403/299-1300, Fax: 403/299-1339
Director, Communications, Corinne Wilkinson, 403/299-1326
Publications: Insight

CERTIFIED GENERAL ACCOUNTANTS ASSOCIATION OF ONTARIO
CGA - Ontario
240 Eglinton Ave. East, Toronto, ON M4P 1K8
416/322-6520, Fax: 416/322-6481, Toll Free: 1-800-668-1454
Executive Director, G.W. Fuller, FCGA
President & CEO, J. Brian Heaney, FCGA
Executive Vice-President, John C. Wright, FCGA
Manager, Public Relations, Roberta Greenberg

ATLANTIC REGION EDUCATION ASSOCIATION
236 St. George St., PO Box 5100, Moncton, NB E1C 8R2
506/857-2204

CERTIFIED GENERAL ACCOUNTANTS ASSOCIATION OF BRITISH COLUMBIA
CGA - British Columbia
1555 - 8th Ave. West, Vancouver, BC V6J 1T5
604/732-1211, Fax: 604/732-1252
Executive Director, R.W. Caulfield
Public Relations Coordinator, Maureen Sydor

CERTIFIED GENERAL ACCOUNTANTS ASSOCIATION OF MANITOBA (1973)
4 Donald St. South, Winnipeg, MB R3L 2T7
204/477-1256, Fax: 204/453-7176, Toll Free: 1-800-282-8001
Executive Director, L.W. Hampson, FCGA
Publications: Newsletter

CERTIFIED GENERAL ACCOUNTANTS ASSOCIATION OF NEW BRUNSWICK/ASSOCIATION DES COMPTABLES GÉNÉRAUX LICENCIÉS DU NOUVEAU-BRUNSWICK (1962)
CGA - New Brunswick
236 St. George St., PO Box 1395, Moncton, NB E1C 8T6
506/857-0939, Fax: 506/855-0887
President, Murray Lambert, BA, CGA
Administrative Assistant, Trudy Dryden
Publications: CGA-NB Newsletter

CERTIFIED GENERAL ACCOUNTANTS ASSOCIATION OF NEWFOUNDLAND
CGA - Newfoundland
685 Water St. West, PO Box 5010, St. John's, NF A1C 5V3
709/579-1863, Fax: 709/579-0838
President, Judy Summers, CGA

CERTIFIED GENERAL ACCOUNTANTS ASSOCIATION OF THE NORTHWEST TERRITORIES (1977)
CGA - Northwest Territories
PO Box 128, Yellowknife, NT X1A 2N1
403/873-5620, Fax: 403/873-4469
Executive Director, Angie Dumbrille, B.Sc.
Publications: Northern Accounts

CERTIFIED GENERAL ACCOUNTANTS ASSOCIATION OF NOVA SCOTIA
CGA - Nova Scotia
#416, 5251 Duke St., Halifax, NS B3J 1P3
902/425-4923, Fax: 902/425-4983
President, G. Angus MacGillivray, BBA, CGA

CERTIFIED GENERAL ACCOUNTANTS ASSOCIATION OF PRINCE EDWARD ISLAND
CGA - Prince Edward Island
178 Fitzroy St., 2nd Fl., PO Box 812, Charlottetown, PE C1A 7L9
902/892-3787, Fax: 902/368-3627
President, Mary McAskill, CGA

CERTIFIED GENERAL ACCOUNTANTS ASSOCIATION OF SASKATCHEWAN (1978)
CGA - Saskatchewan
4 - 2345 Ave. C North, Saskatoon, SK S7L 5Z5
306/955-4622, Fax: 306/373-9219, Toll Free: 1-800-667-5745
Executive Director, Howard L. Janzen, FCGA
Publications: CGA Saskatchewan Newsletter

CERTIFIED GENERAL ACCOUNTANTS ASSOCIATION OF YUKON
CGA - Yukon
PO Box 5358, Whitehorse, YT Y1A 4Z2
403/668-4461, Toll Free: 1-800-565-1211
President, Elaine Carlyle, CGA
Publications: Newsletter

CGA - CANADA RESEARCH FOUNDATION (CGARF) (1981)
#700, 1188 West Georgia St., Vancouver, BC V6E 4A2
604/669-3555, Fax: 604/689-5845
President, Jean Précourt
Manager of Research, Stephen Spector, CGA, MA
Publications: Research Review
Affiliates: American Accounting Association; Canadian Academic Accounting Association

ORDRE DES COMPTABLES GÉNÉRAUX LICENCIÉS DU QUÉBEC (1908)
CGA - Québec
#450, 445, boul St-Laurent, Montréal, PQ H2Y 2Y7
514/861-1823, Téléc: 514/861-7661, Ligne sans frais: 1-800-463-0163
Directeur général, Marcel Godbout Lavoie, CGA
Directrice des communications, France Goyette
Publications: Bulletin CGA

Guild of Industrial, Commercial & Institutional Accountants/Guilde des comptables industriels, commerciaux et institutionnels (1961)
Guild of ICIA
PO Box 7, Stn C, Toronto, ON M6J 3M7
905/278-7846, Fax: 905/795-0621
President, Norbert Bajcar, FICIA
Registrar, Garfield Brown, FICIA
Publications: Guild of ICIA Journal

Institute of Internal Auditors/Institut des vérificateurs internes (IIA) (1941)
249 Maitland Ave., Altamonte Springs, FL 32701-4201 USA
407/830-7600, Fax: 407/831-5171
International President, William G. Bishop III, CIA
Publications: Internal Auditor; IIA Today, bi-m.; Pistas de Auditoria; IIA Educator

Petroleum Accountants Society of Canada (1953)
#750, 700 - 4 Ave. SW, Calgary, AB T2P 3J4
403/262-4744, Fax: 403/266-1525, Email: petasocc@cadvision.com
URL: http://www.cadvision.com/pasc
President, Murray Montgomery
Secretary, Bill Bruggencate
Treasurer, John Topping
Publications: The Ledger

Society of Management Accountants of Canada/ Société des comptables en management du Canada (SMAC) (1920)
#850, 120 King St. West, PO Box 176, Hamilton, ON L8N 3C3
905/525-4100; 416/847-0373 (Toronto line), Fax: 905/525-4533, Email: http://www.cma-canada.org

President, Stan E. Whiteley, CMA, FCMA
Chairperson, Robert Stuart, CMA, FCMA
Publications: CMA, the Management Accounting Magazine
Affiliates: Confederation of Asian & Pacific Accountants; International Federation of Accountants

CERTIFIED MANAGEMENT ACCOUNTANTS SOCIETY OF BRITISH COLUMBIA (CMA) (1945)
#1575, 650 West Georgia St., PO Box 11548, Vancouver, BC V6B 4W7
250/687-5891, Fax: 250/687-6688, Toll Free: 1-800-663-9646
Executive Vice-President, W.C. Easton, BA, CAE, FCMA
Publications: CMA Update

ORDRE DES COMPTABLES EN MANAGEMENT ACCRÉDITÉS DU QUÉBEC (1941)
715, square Victoria, 3e étage, Montréal, PQ H2Y 2H7
514/849-1155, Téléc: 514/849-9674, Ligne sans frais: 1-800-263-5390
Président/Directeur général, François Renauld, CMA
Publications: Elite C.M.A.

SOCIETY OF MANAGEMENT ACCOUNTANTS OF ALBERTA (1944)
One Palliser Sq., #1800, 125 - 9 Ave. SE, Calgary, AB T2G 0P6
403/269-5341, Fax: 403/262-5477, Toll Free: 1-800-332-1106
Executive Director, Janice C. Kobelsky, CMA
Publications: Management Accounter

SOCIETY OF MANAGEMENT ACCOUNTANTS OF THE ATLANTIC PROVINCES
Purdy's Tower 2, Box 42, #1309, 1969 Upper Water St., Halifax, NS B3J 3R7
902/422-5836, Fax: 902/423-1605
Executive Director, G.D. Pollock, Ph.D.

SOCIETY OF MANAGEMENT ACCOUNTANTS OF MANITOBA (1947)
#808, 386 Broadway, Winnipeg, MB R3C 3R6
204/943-1538, 1539, Fax: 204/947-3308, Toll Free: 1-800-841-7148
Executive Director, Steve Vieweg

SOCIETY OF MANAGEMENT ACCOUNTANTS OF THE NORTHWEST TERRITORIES
PO Box 512, Yellowknife, NT X1A 2N4
403/873-2875, Fax: 403/920-2503
Executive Director, Nieta World
Publications: CMA News

SOCIETY OF MANAGEMENT ACCOUNTANTS OF ONTARIO (1941)
#300, 70 University Ave., Toronto, ON M5J 2M4
416/977-7741, Fax: 416/977-6079, Toll Free: 1-800-387-2991, Email: info@cma-ontario.org
URL: http://www.cma-ontario.org
Executive Director, R.W. Dye, FCMA
President, Teresa Fortney, CMA
Vice-President, Wm. Ballios, CMA
Treasurer, Terry Pringle, CMA
Secretary, Angela Holtham, CMA
Publications: The Management Accountants Handbook; Directions

SOCIETY OF MANAGEMENT ACCOUNTANTS OF SASKATCHEWAN (1929)
#111, 2001 Cornwall St., Regina, SK S4P 3X9
306/359-6461, Fax: 306/347-8580
Executive Director, John Hartney, B.A., B. Admin., CMA

SOCIETY OF MANAGEMENT ACCOUNTANTS OF THE YUKON (SMAY) (1975)
PO Box 4823, Whitehorse, YT Y1A 4N6
403/668-3388, Fax: 403/668-2402

ACTUARIES see INSURANCE INDUSTRY

ADDICTION

Addiction Research Foundation/Fondation de la recherche sur la toxicomanie (ARF) (1949)
33 Russell St., Toronto, ON M5S 2S1
416/595-6000, Fax: 416/595-5017, Info Line: 416/595-6111, Toll Free: 1-800-463-6273, Email: sanohelp@arf.org
URL: http://www.arf.org
President, Dr. Perry Kendall
Publications: The Journal
Affiliates: World Health Organization; United Nations; International Council of Alcohol & Addiction; International Labour Organization

Addictions Foundation of Manitoba
1031 Portage Ave., Winnipeg, MB R3G 0R8
204/944-6200, Fax: 204/786-7768
Executive Director, Herb Thompson

Adult Children of Alcoholics (ACA)
20 Bloor St. East, PO Box 75061, Toronto, ON M4W 3T3
416/593-5147
Contact, Dianne Dogherty
Publications: Serenity

Against Drunk Driving (ADD) (1983)
The Neil Gray Memorial Fund
PO Box 397, Stn A, Brampton, ON L6V 2L3
905/793-4233, Fax: 905/793-4233
Co-Chair, John Hymers
Co-Chair, Tom Tumilty
Office Manager, Kathleen Close
Publications: ADDvisor Newsletter; Grieving Process; Operation Lookout Network News
Affiliates: Ontario Community Council on Impaired Driving

Al-Anon Family Groups
National Public Information Canada/Information publique nationale du Canada
1712 Avenue Rd., PO Box 54533, North York, ON M5M 4N5
416/366-4072, Toll Free: 1-800-443-4525

Alcoholics Anonymous (AA)
#202, 234 Eglinton Ave. East, Toronto, ON M4P 1K5
416/487-5591, Fax: 416/487-5855
Office Manager, Carole Keenan

Canadian Association for Children of Alcoholics (CACOA) (1986)
c/o The Hospital for Sick Children, 555 University Ave., Toronto, ON M5G 1X8
416/813-5629, Fax: 416/813-5619
President, John Phin
Publications: CACOA Newsletter

Canadian Centre on Substance Abuse/Centre canadien de lutte contre l'alcoolisme et les toxicomanies (CCSA)
#300, 75 Albert St., Ottawa, ON K1P 5E7
613/235-4048, Fax: 613/235-8101, Email: ccsa@fox.nstn.ca
URL: http://www.ccsa.ca/default.htm
CEO, Jacques LeCavalier
Director, Policy & Research, Dr. Eric Single
Director, Communications, Richard Garlick
Publications: Action News
Policy & Research Unit: Banting Institute, #207, 100 College St., Toronto, ON M5G 1L5, 416/978-1772, Fax: 416/971-1365

Concerns, Canada (1934)
Alcohol & Drug Concerns, Inc.
#112H, 4500 Sheppard Ave. East, Scarborough, ON M1S 3R6
416/293-3400, Fax: 416/293-1142
CEO, Karl N. Burden
President, Keith Farraway
Publications: Concerns

Council on Drug Abuse (CODA)
#17, 698 Weston Rd., Toronto, ON M6N 3R3
416/763-1491, Fax: 416/767-6859
President, Frederick J. Burford
Secretary, Wendy Gidge
Treasurer, G. Ernest Jackson
Chairman, Frank C. Buckley
Publications: CODA

The Council for a Drug-Free Workplace/Le Conseil pour une entreprise sans drogues (1989)
44 King St. West, 12th Fl., Toronto, ON M5H 1H1
416/866-3699, Fax: 416/933-2388, Toll Free: 1-800-563-5000
Executive Director, Jacques Perras
Publications: Taking a Stand

MADD Canada (1982)
Mothers Against Drunk Driving
#36, 5160 Explorer Dr., Mississauga, ON L4W 4T7
905/624-5364, Fax: 905/624-8920
Chairman, Dave King
Administrator, L. Waywell
Publications: MADD Canada Report

Narcotics Anonymous (1953)
PO Box 5700, Toronto, ON M5W 1N8
416/691-9519
Chairperson, Public Information, Philip Horgan
Publications: Narcotics Anonymous

Parents Against Drugs (PAD) (1983)
7 Hawksdale Rd., North York, ON M3K 1W3
416/395-4970, Fax: 416/395-4972
Executive Director, Diane Buhler
Chairman, Michelle DiCarlo
Publications: PAD Parent Handbook
Affiliates: Council on Drug Abuse

Physicians for a Smoke-Free Canada/Médecins pour un Canada sans fumée (1985)
PO Box 4849, Stn E, Ottawa, ON K1S 5J1
613/233-4878, Fax: 613/748-0835
Executive Director, Catherine A. Rudick
Affiliates: International Organization of Consumers Unions

ADMINISTRATION see MANAGEMENT & ADMINISTRATION

ADVERTISING & MARKETING

Advertising Agency Association of Alberta
#2401, 10104 - 103 Ave., Edmonton, AB T5J OH8
403/424-5944, Fax: 403/428-0970
President, Russell B. Hakes

Advertising Agency Association of British Columbia (AAABC)
#1723, 595 Burrard St., PO Box 49122, Vancouver, BC V7X 1J1
604/682-1291, Fax: 604/682-1291
President, Steve Vrlak

Advertising Agency Print Production Association (AAPPA)
1881 Yonge St, PO Box 48027, Toronto, ON M4S 3C4

President, Jane Sallows, 416/480-6678
Publications: PPA Update

The Advertising & Design Club of Canada (1948)
#207, 109 Vanderhoof Ave., Toronto, ON M4G 2H7
416/423-4113, Fax: 416/422-3762
President, Doug Robinson
Publications: Directions

Agency Owners Roundtable (AOR) (1979)
RR#1, Brandy Crest Rd., Port Carling, ON P0B 1J0
705/764-8791, Fax: 705/764-8735
Executive Director/Sec.-Treas., R.A. McCall
Publications: AOR News Bulletin

American Marketing Association (AMA) (1937)
#200, 250 South Wacker Dr., Chicago, IL 60606-5819 USA
312/648-0536, Fax: 312/993-7542
Contact, Anne Carey
Publications: Marketing Management; Marketing Research, q.; Marketing News, bi-weekly; Journal of Marketing, q.; Journal of Marketing Research, q.; Journal of Health Care Marketing, q.; Journal of Public Policy and Marketing, biennial; Services Marketing Today, bi-m.
British Columbia Chapter: Member Recruitment, Celina Benndorf, #122, 980 West First St., North Vancouver, BC V7P 3N4, 604/986-5050, Fax: 604/988-5226
Calgary Chapter: Contact, Edith Wenzel, #1000, 734 - 7th Ave. SW, Calgary, AB T2P 3P8, 403/269-3734, Fax: 403/237-8186
Montréal Chapter: President, Pierre Trudel, 4316, boul St-Laurent, Montréal, PQ H2W 1Z3, 514/499-1391, Fax: 514/842-2422
Ottawa Chapter: President, Ken Lambert, PO Box 224, Stn B, Ottawa, ON K1P 1C4, 613/786-1166
Toronto Chapter: Association Manager, Renée Auer, 246 Sherbourne St., Toronto, ON M5A 2S1, 416/413-0170, Fax: 416/413-0485

Association of Canadian Advertisers Inc./ Association canadienne des annonceurs (ACA) (1914)
South Tower, #307, 175 Bloor St. East, Toronto, ON M4W 3R8
416/964-3805, Fax: 416/964-0771, Toll Free: 1-800-565-0109, Email: aca@sympatico.ca
President & CEO, Ronald S. Lund
Chair, Katherine Macmillan
Vice-President, Marketing, Joan Curran
Publications: ACA News

ASSOCIATION CANADIENNE DES ANNONCEURS INC.
1080, Côte du Beaver Hall, Montréal, PQ H2Z 1S8
514/861-0422, Téléc: 514/861-7740
Vice-président principal, Maurice Brisebois

Audit Bureau of Circulations (ABC) (1914)
Canadian Member Service Office, #850, 151 Bloor St. West, Toronto, ON M5S 1S4
416/962-5840, Fax: 416/962-5844
Senior Vice-President, Canada, Robert White
Supervisor, Canadian Member Services, Marian C. Robertson

Canadian Advertising Foundation/Fondation canadienne de la publicité (CAF) (1957)
#402, 350 Bloor St. East, Toronto, ON M4W 1H5
416/961-6311, Fax: 416/961-7904
CEO/President, Linda Nagel, CAE
Chairman, Peter Elwood
Publications: Pulse
Advertising Standards Council - Atlantic Region: PO Box 3112, Halifax, NS B3J 3G6
Advertising Standards Council - BC Region: PO Box 3005, Vancouver, BC V6B 3X5, 604/681-2674
Advertising Standards Council - Saskatchewan: Chairman, Gus Sanheim, PO Box 1322, Regina, SK S4P 3B8
Alberta Advertising Standards Council - Calgary: 215 - 16 St. SE, PO Box 2400, Stn M, Calgary, AB T2P 0W8
Le Conseil des normes de la publicité: Directeur général, Niquette Delage, #130, 4823 rue Sherbrooke ouest, Montréal, PQ H3Z 1G7, 514/931-8060, Téléc: 514/931-2797

Canadian Advertising Research Foundation/ Fondation canadienne de recherche en publicité (CARF) (1949)
South Tower, #307, 175 Bloor St. East, Toronto, ON M4W 3R8
416/964-3832, Fax: 416/964-0771
Administrative Board Assistant, Shirley Uyesugi
Chairman, John Chaplin

Canadian Association of Marketing Research Organizations/Association canadienne des organisations de recherche en marketing (CAMRO) (1975)
#1105, 191 The West Mall, Etobicoke, ON M9C 5K8
416/620-7420, Fax: 416/620-5392, Email: bbandc@enterprise.ca
Executive Director, Dave Stark
Association Coordinator, Laurie Watson
Publications: CAMRO News

Canadian Automatic Merchandising Association/ L'Association Canadienne d'Auto-Distribution (CAMA) (1953)
PO Box 778, Stn Q, Toronto, ON M4T 2N7
416/932-2262, Fax: 416/932-3732
Executive Director, C. Davenport
Publications: CAMA Update

Canadian Direct Marketing Association/ Association canadienne du marketing direct (CDMA) (1967)
#607, One Concorde Gate, North York, ON M3C 3N6
416/391-2362, Fax: 416/441-4062, Email: kbrasch@cdma.org
URL: http://www.cdma.org
President/CEO, John R. Gustavson
Director of Communications, Scott McClellan
Membership Sales & Marketing Manager, Gilles Latour
Publications: Communicator
Affiliates: European Direct Marketing Association; Direct Marketing Association - USA

Canadian Institute of Marketing/Institut canadien du marketing (CIM) (1982)
41 Capital Dr., Nepean, ON K2G 0E7
613/727-0954, Fax: 613/228-8398
National Chair, Roger Walsh
Director General, John Harte
National Vice-Chair, Jim Schauer
Publications: Communicate; CIM Information Letter
Affiliates: Affiliated with 13 other Institutes of Marketing around the world

Canadian Media Directors' Council
c/o SMW Advertising, 565 Bloor St. East, Toronto, ON M4V 1L5
416/925-7733
President, Sue Jaffe

Canadian Outdoor Measurement Bureau (COMB)
#302, 1300 Yonge St., Toronto, ON M4T 1X3
416/968-3823, Fax: 416/968-0154
Manager, Danielle Parent

Canadian Print Marketers Association/ Association canadienne des courtiers en imprimerie (CPMA) (1991)
#4, 110 West Beaver Creek Rd., Richmond Hill, ON L4B 1J9
905/764-6116, Fax: 905/764-6904
Director, David F. Fleiner
Publications: Newsline

Canadian Telemarketing Association
36 Adelaide St. East., PO Box 1113, Toronto, ON M5C 2K5
416/581-1236, ext.29, Fax: 416/599-5058, Toll Free: 1-800-363-4822
Executive Director, Don MacLeod

Chartered Institute of Marketing Management of Ontario (CIMMO) (1988)
19 Bartley Dr., RR#3, Caledon East, ON L0N 1E0
905/880-2964, Fax: 905/880-1970, Email: goodall@netcom.ca
Chairman, Nigel Goodall

Conseil des directeurs médias du Québec (CDMQ)
143, rue des Intendants, Varennes, PQ J3X 2C3
514/652-6834, Téléc: 514/652-6283
Secretaire, Michelle Valiquette

Industrial Marketing & Research Association of Canada/Association canadienne de recherche et marketing industriel (IMRAC)
Box 100-3, 2 Bloor St. West, Toronto, ON M4W 3E2
416/967-1537
President, Ross Vermilyea
Publications: IMRAC Newsletter

Institute of Canadian Advertising
#500, 2300 Yonge St., PO Box 2350, Toronto, ON M4P 1E4
416/482-1396, Fax: 416/481-1856, Toll Free: 1-800-567-7422; Email: ica@goodmedia.com
President, Rupert T.R. Brendon
Director, Education Services, Janice Schenk

Mediawatch/Evaluation-médias
#204, 517 Wellington St. West, Toronto, ON M5V 1G1
416/408-2065, Fax: 416/408-2069
Executive Director, Linda Hawke
Publications: The Bulletin

National Advertising Benevolent Society (NABS) (1983)
South Tower, #307, 175 Bloor St. East, Toronto, ON M4W 3R8
416/962-0446, Fax: 416/944-3797, Toll Free: 1-800-661-6227, Email: nabs@inforamp.net
URL: http://www.partnersweb.com/NABS
Executive Director, Patricia Crosbie
President, Sandy Muir
Publications: NABS News
NABS Atlantic: Contact, Jean Dixon, 2584 Agricola St., Halifax, NS B3K 4C4, 902/494-1084, Fax: 902/422-1199
NABS West: General Manager, Michael Godin, #401, 68 Water St., Vancouver, BC V6B 1A4, 604/688-3087, Fax: 604/689-7167

National Association of Major Mail Users, Inc./ Association nationale des grands usagers postaux inc. (NAMMU) (1983)
CP 481, Succ Desjardins, Montréal, PQ H5B 1B6
905/278-6737, Fax: 905/278-7357
President, Don McArthur
Publications: NAMMU Bulletin; ANGUP Bulletin

Newspaper Marketing Bureau Inc.
#201, 10 Bay St., Toronto, ON M5J 2R8

2-12 ORGANIZATIONS — AGRICULTURE & FARMING

416/364-3744, Fax: 416/363-2568
President, John Finneran
Montréal Office: #1328, 2020, rue University, Montréal, PQ H3A 2A5, 514/282-1542, Fax: 514/843-4354
Vancouver Office: Marketing Manager, Elena Dunn, #1005, 1166 Alberni St., Vancouver, BC V6E 3Z3, 604/669-8796, Fax: 604/683-1240

Outdoor Advertising Association of Canada/ L'Association canadienne de l'affichage extérieur (OAAC) (1903)
#100, 21 St. Clair Ave. East, Toronto, ON M4T 1L9
416/968-3435, Fax: 416/968-0154
Executive Assistant, Brenda Carroll
Publications: Outdoor Views

Print Measurement Bureau (PMB)
#1502, 77 Bloor St. West, Toronto, ON M5S 1M2
416/961-3205, Fax: 416/961-5052
President, John Chaplin
Director of Operations, Joanne Van der Burgt

Professional Marketing Research Society/ Association professionnelle de recherche en marketing (PMRS) (1960)
#110, 2175 Sheppard Ave. East, Toronto, ON M2J 1W8
416/493-4080, Fax: 416/491-1670
President, Mike Nestler
Adminstrator, Jennifer Rogers
Publications: Imprints; Canadian Journal of Marketing Research, a.

Promotional Products Association of Canada Inc./Association de la publicité par l'objet du Canada (PPAC) (1956)
#305, 4920, boul de Maisonneuve ouest, Montréal, PQ H3Z 1N1
514/489-5359, Fax: 514/489-7760, Toll Free: 1-800-489-8741
Executive Director, Kurt Reckziegel
Communications Coordinator, Carol Phillips
Publications: Image News/Nouvelles Image

Le publicité club de Montréal (PCM)
4316, boul Saint-Laurent, 4e étage, Montréal, PQ H2W 1Z3
514/842-5681, Courrier électronique: pubclub@cam.org
URL: http://www.pcm.montreal.qc.ca/
Président, Alain Richard
Secrétaire-trésorier, Georges E. Gaucher

Radio Marketing Bureau (RMB) (1961)
146 Yorkville Ave., Toronto, ON M5R 1C2
416/922-5757, Fax: 416/922-6542, Toll Free: 1-800-667-2346
President/CEO, Brian M. Jones
Affiliates: Radio Advisory Board of Canada
Ottawa Office: Senior Vice-President, T. Leadman, PO Box 3914, Stn C, Ottawa, ON K1Y 4M5, 613/729-7474, Fax: 613/725-2642

Sign Association of Canada
#500, 7030 Woodbine Ave., Markham, ON L3R 1A2
905/470-9787, Fax: 905/470-8993
General Manager, E.D. Gagnon

Society of Ontario Advertising Agencies (SOAA) (1970)
#205, 660 Eglinton Ave. West, Toronto, ON M5N 1C3
416/782-8908, Fax: 416/782-8908
Contact, Rita Otis
Publications: Meeting Notice

Telemarketing Industry Association (TIA) (1991)
PO Box 27018, Dieppe, NB E1A 4X0
Toll Free: 1-800-267-2822

Canadian Almanac & Directory 1997

Publications: Newsletter

Trans-Canada Advertising Agency Network (T-CAAN) (1963)
3390 Bayview Ave., North York, ON M2M 3S3
416/221-8883, Fax: 416/221-8260
President, Phil Chant
Managing Director, W.S. Whitehead
Publications: T-CAAN 'Tattler'
Affiliates: Inter-Market Association of Advertising Agencies - USA

AEROSPACE INDUSTRY see AVIATION & AEROSPACE

AGRICULTURE & FARMING
see also Animal Breeding; Poultry & Eggs

Agricultural Groups Concerned About Resources & the Environment
AGCare
491 Eglinton Ave. West, 5th Fl., Toronto, ON M5N 3A2
416/485-7330, Fax: 416/485-9528
Chairman, Jeff Wilson
Vice-Chairman, Bill Allison, Jr.
2nd Vice-Chairman, James Fischer
Technical Advisor, Michael Mazur
Communications Advisor, Terry Boland
Public Information Coordinator, Mary Wiley, Bus: 519/837-1326, Res: 519/837-1674
Secretary, Dave Armitage
Publications: AGCare Update
Affiliates: Ontario Soybean Growers' Marketing Board; Ontario Fruit & Vegetable Growers' Association; Ontario Corn Producers' Association; Ontario Wheat Producers' Marketing Board; Ontario Bean Producers' Marketing Board; Ontario Seed Growers' Association; Ontario Red Wheat Association; Ontario Soil & Crop Improvement Association; Ontario Federation of Agriculture; Flowers Canada (Ontario); Ontario Flue-Cured Tobacco Growers' Marketing Board

Agricultural Institute of Canada/Institut agricole du Canada (AIC) (1920)
141 Laurier Ave. West, 11th Fl., Ottawa, ON K1P 5J3
613/232-9459, Fax: 613/594-5190
Executive Director, Roy Carver
Publications: AgriScience
Affiliates: Canadian Economics & Farm Management Society; Canadian Consulting Agrologists' Association; Canadian Pest Management Society; Canadian Society of Agronomy; Canadian Society of Animal Science; Canadian Society of Extension; Canadian Society for Horticultural Science; Canadian Society of Soil Science; Canadian Society of Agrometeorology; British Columbia Institute of Agrologists; Alberta Institute of Agrologists; Saskatchewan Institute of Agrologists; Manitoba Institute of Agrologists; Ontario Institute of Agrologists; New Brunswick Institute of Agrologists; Nova Scotia Institute of Agrologists; PEI Institute of Agrologists; Newfoundland/Labrador Institute of Agrologists

ALBERTA INSTITUTE OF AGROLOGISTS
PO Box 5097, Airdrie, AB T4B 2B2
403/948-1231, Fax: 403/948-3141
President, Roger Lore
Publications: Calgary News Brief

BRITISH COLUMBIA INSTITUTE OF AGROLOGISTS
#302, 34252 Marshall Rd., Abbotsford, BC V2S 5E4
604/855-9291, Fax: 604/853-3556
Registrar, Garth Bean

MANITOBA INSTITUTE OF AGROLOGISTS (MIA) (1950)
16 Lowell Pl., Winnipeg, MB R3T 4H8
204/275-3721, Fax: 204/261-6565
Executive Director, Lee Anne Murphy, P.Ag.
Publications: The Manitoba Agrologist

NEW BRUNSWICK INSTITUTE OF AGROLOGISTS/L'INSTITUT DES AGRONOMES DU NOUVEAU-BRUNSWICK (NBIA)
PO Box 3479, Stn B, Fredericton, NB E3B 5H2
506/453-2717
Registrar, Evans N. Estabrooks
Publications: NBIA Newsletter

NEWFOUNDLAND & LABRADOR INSTITUTE OF AGROLOGISTS
PO Box 978, Mount Pearl, NF A1N 3C9
709/772-4170
President, Edward Woodrow
Sec. Treas., Gary Bishop

NOVA SCOTIA INSTITUTE OF AGROLOGISTS (NSIA) (1953)
Nova Scotia Agricultural College, PO Box 550, Truro, NS B2N 5E3
902/893-6520, Fax: 902/893-6393
Registrar, Dave Livingstone
Publications: NSIA Newsletter

ONTARIO INSTITUTE OF AGROLOGISTS (1960)
#203, 173 Woolwich St., Guelph, ON N1H 3V4
519/837-2820, Fax: 519/837-2820
Executive Director, Ruth Friendship-Keller
President, Jack Riddell
Publications: OIA Newsletter
Affiliates: Ontario Farm Animal Council; Conservation Council of Ontario

PRINCE EDWARD ISLAND INSTITUTE OF AGROLOGISTS (PEIIA)
PO Box 2712, Charlottetown, PE C1A 8C3
902/629-1229, Fax: 902/629-1229
President, Les Haliday
Sec.-Treas., Maria MacDonald
Publications: Newsletter

SASKATCHEWAN INSTITUTE OF AGROLOGISTS (SIA) (1946)
#100, 2103 Airport Dr., Saskatoon, SK S7L 6W2
306/242-2606, Fax: 306/244-4055
Executive Director, Glen Hass, P.Ag.
Publications: Agrologist

Alberta Association of Agricultural Societies (AAAS)
J.G. O'Donoghue Building, #201, 7000 - 113 St., Edmonton, AB T6H 5T6
403/427-2174, Fax: 403/438-3362
President, John Fraser
Administrator, Wendy Pruden
Publications: AG Society News

Alberta Canola Producers Commission (1989)
#170, 14315 - 118 Ave., Edmonton, AB T5L 4S6
403/452-6487, Fax: 403/451-6933
General Manager, H. Bruce Jeffery
Chairman, Reece Kindt
Publications: Alberta Canola Grower

Alberta Conservation Tillage Society (ACTS) (1978)
PO Box 326, Carbon, AB T0M 0L0
403/572-3600, Fax: 403/572-3605, Toll Free: 1-800-251-6846
President, Andy Wierenga
Vice-President, Spencer Hilton
Vice-President, Walter MacKoway
Treasurer, John Graham
Executive Manager, Russell Evans
Publications: The Conservation Tillage News
Affiliates: Alberta Wheat Pool

Alberta Milk Producers' Society (1989)
14904 - 121A Ave., Edmonton, AB T5V 1A3

403/453-5942, Fax: 403/455-2196
General Manager, Bob Tchir

Alberta Wheat Pool (AWP) (1923)
505 - 2 St. SW, PO Box 2700, Calgary, AB T2P 2P5
403/290-4910, Fax: 403/290-5550
URL: http://fis.awp.com
Director, Corporate Affairs, Dale Riddell
Affiliates: Prairie Pools Inc.; Prairie Sun Grains; Western Cooperative Fertilizers Ltd.; XCANGrain Pool Ltd.

Association of British Columbia Grape Growers (ABCGG) (1960)
#5, 1864 Spall Rd., Kelowna, BC V1Y 4R1
250/762-4652, Fax: 250/862-8870,
Email: bcgrapegrowers@awinc.com
Secretary, Connie Bielert

Association des jeunes ruraux du Québec (AJRQ) (1974)
#304, 1140, rue Taillon, Québec, PQ G1N 3T9
418/681-4847, Téléc: 418/654-0451, Courrier électronique: lynx@cmg.qc.ca
Directeur général, Maurice Le Pesant
Publications: Info-Rural
Organisation(s) affiliée(s): Conseil des 4-H du Canada

Association professionnelle des meuniers du Québec/Québec Feed Manufacturer's Association (APMQ) (1963)
#115, 2323, boul Versant nord, Ste-Foy, PQ G1N 4P4
418/688-9227, Téléc: 418/688-3575
Directeur général, André J. Pilon
Publications: Le Meunier

Association des technologistes agro-alimentaires inc./Agricultural Technologists Association Inc. (ATA) (1964)
3230, rue Sicotte, CP 308, Saint-Hyacinthe, PQ J2S 7B6
514/774-8969
Secrétaire exécutive, Marie Cloutier
Publications: Contact

Atlantic Dairy Council (ADC)
PO Box 9410, Stn A, Halifax, NS B3K 5S3
902/425-2445, Fax: 902/425-2441, Email: pathfndr@fox.nstn.ca
Executive Secretary, John K. Sutherland

Atlantic Farmers Council (1937)
PO Box 750, Moncton, NB E1C 8N5
506/858-6555, Fax: 506/858-6379
Executive Secretary, John Eaton
Contact, Liz Rattray

BC Milk Producers Association
846 Broughton St., Victoria, BC V8W 1E4
250/383-7171, Fax: 250/383-5031
Secretary, Andy Dolberg

Beef Information Centre
Head Office, #100, 2233 Argentia Rd., Toronto, ON L5N 2X7
905/821-4900, Fax: 905/821-4915
Executive Manager, Carolyn McDonell
National Public Relations Manager, Marg Thibeault

British Columbia Certified Seed Potato Growers' Association (1920)
4119 - 40 St., Ladner, BC V4K 3N2
604/946-8138
Secretary, Noel Roddick

British Columbia Fruit Growers' Association
1473 Water St., Kelowna, BC V1Y 1J6
250/762-5226, Fax: 250/861-9089
General Manager, Stephen Thomson

Canada Grains Council
#330, 360 Main St., Winnipeg, MB R3C 3Z3
204/942-2254
Chairman, Andrew Patterson

Canadian 4-H Council/Conseil des 4-H du Canada (1933)
#208, 1690 Woodward Dr., Ottawa, ON K2C 3R8
613/723-4444, Fax: 613/723-0745
Executive Director, Mike Nowosad
President, Keith Wilkinson
Publications: Forum; 4-H Council Directory, a.
Affiliates: Canadian 4-H Foundation; National 4-H Council (USA)
Member Councils
Alberta: Head, Home Economics & 4H Branch, R.T. (Ted) Youck, Alberta Agriculture, J.G. O'Donoghue Bldg., #200, 7000 - 113 St., Edmonton, AB T6H 5T6, 403/427-4462, Fax: 403/422-7755
British Columbia: Manager, Youth Development Farm, Gordon Bryant, P.Ag., #101, 3547 Skaha Lake Rd., Penticton, BC V2A 7K2, 250/492-1320, Fax: 250/492-1309, Email: gbryant@galaxy.gov.bc.ca
Manitoba: Chief, Youth Section/Marketing, Shaunda Rossington, Manitoba Agriculture, #916, 401 York Ave., Winnipeg, MB R3C 0P8, 204/945-4526, Fax: 204/945-6134
New Brunswick: Director, Communications & Education Branch, Serge Michaud, NB Department of Agriculture, PO Box 6000, Fredericton, NB E3B 5H1, 506/453-2666, Fax: 506/453-7978
Newfoundland: 4-H Youth Program Specialist, Robyn Moss, Dept. of Forest Resources & Agrifoods, Manitoba Dr., PO Box 569, Clarenville, NF A0E 1J0, 709/466-2558, Fax: 709/466-3644
Nova Scotia: 4-H & Rural Youth Supervisor, Elizabeth Crouse, P.Ag., Nova Scotia Dept. of Agriculture & Marketing, MacRae Library, 137 College Rd., Truro, NS B2N 5E3, 902/893-6587, Fax: 902/895-7693, Email: ecrouse@es.nsac.ns.ca
Ontario: 4-H Program Consultant, Cathy Wilson Pinkney, Ontario Ministry of Agriculture, Food & Rural Affairs, PO Box 1030, Guelph, ON N1H 6N1, 519/767-3150, Fax: 519/837-3049
PEI: 4-H Administrator, Heather Tweedy, PEI Dept. of Agriculture, Fisheries & Forestry, 420 University Ave., Charlottetown, PE C1A 7N8, 902/368-4833, Fax: 902/368-7204, Email: j.macquara@peinet.pe.ca
Saskatchewan: Executive Director, Janice Myers, Rural Service Centre, 3735 Thatcher Ave., Saskatoon, SK S7K 2H6, 306/933-7729, Fax: 306/933-7352

Canadian Agricultural Hall of Fame Association/Temple canadien de la renommée agricole (CAHFA) (1960)
c/o Ontario Institute of Agrologists, #203, 173 Woolwich St., Guelph, ON N1H 3V4
519/837-2820
Sec.-Treas., R. Friendship-Keller, P.Ag.

Canadian Co-operative Association (CCA) (1987)
#400, 275 Bank St., Ottawa, ON K2P 2L6
613/238-6711, Fax: 613/567-0658, Email: support@wopcca.com
Executive Director, Lynden Hillier
Executive Assistant, Cathi Wilkins

Canadian Consulting Agrologists Association/L'Association canadienne des agronomes-conseils (CCAA) (1973)
11 Lynnhaven Cres., Nepean, ON K2E 5K3
613/224-4471, Fax: 613/224-0785
Manager, Henry F. Heald, P.Ag.
President, Ralph Ashmead, P.Ag., CAC
Publications: CCAA Directory; CCAA News, q.

Canadian Federation of Agriculture/Fédération canadienne de l'agriculture (CFA) (1935)
#1101, 75 Albert St., Ottawa, ON K1P 5E7
613/236-3633, 9997, Fax: 613/236-5749
Executive Director/Treasurer, Sally Rutherford
President, Jack Wilkinson
Communications Coordinator, Joyce Henry
Publications: Update
Affiliates: BC Federation of Agriculture; Unifarm (Alberta); Keystone Agricultural Producers (Manitoba); Ontario Federation of Agriculture; L'Union des producteurs agricoles (Québec); Coopérative fédérée de Québec; NB Federation of Agriculture; NS Federation of Agriculture; PEI Federation of Agriculture; Canadian Chicken Marketing Agency; Canadian Egg Producers Council; Canadian Egg Marketing Agency; Canadian Turkey Marketing Agency; Dairy Farmers of Canada; Canadian Horticultural Council; Prairie Pools Inc.; Canadian Broiler Hatching Egg Marketing Agency; Canadian Sugar Beet Producers Association; Labrador & Nfld. Federation of Agriculture

BRITISH COLUMBIA FEDERATION OF AGRICULTURE (BCFA) (1935)
846 Broughton St., Victoria, BC V8W 1E4
250/383-7171, Fax: 250/383-5031
Jake Jansen
Publications: Country Life

CANADIAN SUGAR BEET PRODUCERS' ASSOCIATION (CSBPA) (1943)
PO Box 190, Taber, AB T0K 2G0
403/223-1110, Fax: 403/223-1022
Ron Hanzel
Affiliates: World Association of Beet & Cane Growers

COOPÉRATIVE FÉDÉRÉE DU QUÉBEC (CFQ)
#200, 9001, boul de l'Acadie, Montréal, PQ H4N 3H7
514/384-6450, Téléc: 514/384-8772
Directeur général, Mario Dumais

DAIRY FARMERS OF CANADA/LES PRODUCTEURS LAITIERS DU CANADA (1934)
#1101, 75 Albert St., Ottawa, ON K1P 5E7
613/236-9997, Fax: 613/236-5749
Executive Director, Richard Doyle
President, Peter Oosterhoff
Vice-President, John Core
Administrative Assistant, Elizabeth Medwenitsch
Publications: DFC Newsletter; Facts & Figures at a Glance, a.

GROUPE LACTEL, SOCIÉTÉ EN COMMANDITE (1990)
1205, rue Ampére, Boucherville, PQ J4B 7M6
514/449-6113, Téléc: 514/449-6297
Directeur général, Jean-François Robert
Directeur, Affaires institutionnelles, André Roy
Publications: LACTuel

KEYSTONE AGRICULTURAL PRODUCERS (KAP) (1985)
437 Assiniboine Ave., Winnipeg, MB R3C 0Y5
204/943-2509, Fax: 204/957-1742
General Manager, Craig Douglas
Publications: KAP News

NEW BRUNSWICK FEDERATION OF AGRICULTURE/FÉDÉRATION D'AGRICULTURE DU NOUVEAU-BRUNSWICK (NBFA) (1876)
#201, 1115 Regent St., Fredericton, NB E3B 3X2
506/452-8101, Fax: 506/452-1085
President, Maarten van Ord
Office Manager, Nicole Arseneau
Publications: NBFA Journal; Farm Talk

NOVA SCOTIA FEDERATION OF AGRICULTURE (NSFA)
PO Box 784, Truro, NS B2N 5E8
902/893-2293, Fax: 902/893-7063
Executive Director, Dermott English

2-14 ORGANIZATIONS — AGRICULTURE & FARMING

ONTARIO FEDERATION OF AGRICULTURE
#500, 491 Eglinton Ave. West, Toronto, ON M5N 3A2
416/485-3333, Fax: 416/485-9027
CEO, Carl H. Sulliman
President, Roger George
General Manager, Douglas J.R. Lisle
Publications: Farm & Country Journal
Affiliates: AG Care

PRAIRIE POOLS INC.
#724, 90 Sparks St., Ottawa, ON K1P 5B4
613/594-4976, Fax: 613/232-7043
Contact, Gordon Pugh

PRINCE EDWARD ISLAND FEDERATION OF AGRICULTURE
Farm Centre, 420 University Ave., Charlottetown, PE C1A 7Z5
902/892-6913, Fax: 902/368-7204
Contact, Anne Boswall

UNIFARM
14815 - 119 Ave., Edmonton, AB T5L 4W2
403/451-5912, Fax: 403/453-2669
Executive Director, W.J. Plosz

Canadian Feed Industry Association/Association canadienne des industries de l'alimentation animale (CFIA) (1929)
#625, 325 Dalhousie St., Ottawa, ON K1N 7G2
613/241-6421, Fax: 613/241-7970
General Manager, Christine Mercier
Chairman, Glenn Ravnsborg
Manager, Technical Services, Nancy Fischer
Publications: CFIA Newsletter
Affiliates: Canola Council of Canada; Canada Grains Council; Canadian Egg Marketing Agency; Canadian Chicken Marketing Agency; Canadian Turkey Marketing Agency

Canadian Feed Information Centre (CFIC) (1986)
PO Box 1251, Swift Current, SK S9H 3X4
306/773-5401, Fax: 306/773-3955
Contact, Dr. J.E. Knipfel

Canadian Honey Council/Conseil canadien du miel (1940)
PO Box 1566, Nipawin, SK S0E 1E0
306/862-3844, Fax: 306/862-5122, Toll Free: 1-800-663-2827
Sec.-Treas., Linda Gane
Publications: Hive Lights; Canadian Honey Council Information Letter; Canadian Honey Council Statistical Material
Affiliates: Apimondia

Canadian Honey Packers' Association
530, rang Nault, Victoriaville, PQ G6P 7R5
819/758-3877, Fax: 819/758-9386
President, Jean Marc Labonté
Affiliates: Canadian Honey Council

Canadian Mushroom Growers' Association/Association des champignonnistes du Canada (CMGA) (1955)
26 Alderbrook Dr., Nepean, ON K2H 5W5
613/820-6302, Fax: 613/820-6009
President, Lyle Whithan
Executive Vice-President, H.R. Taylor
Publications: Mushroom World; CMGA Roster, a.

Canadian Organic Growers Inc. (COG) (1975)
PO Box 6408, Stn J, Ottawa, ON K2A 3Y6
613/256-1848, Fax: 613/256-4453
President, Jeff Johnstone
Vice-President, Tomàs Nimmo, 705/444-0923
Membership Secretary, Kathy Lamarche

Canadian Almanac & Directory 1997

Publications: COGnition; Directory of Organic Agriculture; Organic Field Crop Handbook; Organic Field Crop
Affiliates: International Federation of Organic Agriculture Movements; Organic Trade Association

Canadian Pest Management Society/Société canadienne de lutte contre les organismes nuisibles (CPMS) (1954)
Agriculture Canada, PO Box 1000, Agassiz, BC V0M 1A0
604/796-2221, Fax: 604/796-0359, Email: brookes@bcrsag.agr.ca
Sec.-Treas., Victoria R. Brookes
Publications: Canadian Pest Management Society Newsletter
Affiliates: Agricultural Institute of Canada

Canadian Plowing Organization (1955)
43 Ewen Dr., Uxbridge, ON L9P 1L5
905/852-6221, Fax: 905/852-6221
Secretary, Robert Timbers
President, Lars Skjaveland
Vice-President, James Sache
Affiliates: World Ploughing Organization

Canadian Seed Growers' Association/Association canadienne des producteurs de semences (1904)
PO Box 8455, Ottawa, ON K1G 3T1
613/236-0497, Fax: 613/563-7855
Executive Director, W.K. Robertson

Canadian Seed Trade Association/Association canadienne du commerce des semences (CSTA) (1923)
#302, 39 Robertson Rd., Ottawa, ON K2H 8R2
613/829-9527, Fax: 613/829-3530, Email: csta@hookup.net
Executive Vice-President, W.C. Leask

Canadian Society of Agricultural Engineering/Société canadienne de génie rural (CSAE) (1958)
PO Box 381, RPO University, Saskatoon, SK S7N 4J8
306/966-5335, Fax: 306/966-5334
URL: http://www.engr.usask.ca/societies/csae/
Manager, D.I. Norum, 306/966-5319, Email: norum@sask.usask.ca
Publications: Canadian Agricultural Engineering
Affiliates: American Society of Agricultural Engineers

Canadian Society of Agronomy
#907, 151 Slater St., Ottawa, ON K1P 5H4
613/232-9459, Fax: 613/594-5190
Secretary, B.G. Rossnagel

Canadian Society of Extension (CSE)
14815 - 119 Ave., Edmonton, AB T5L 2N9
403/451-5959, Fax: 403/452-5385
President, Rob McNabb
Secretary, John Melicher
Publications: Extension Information Bulletin

Canadian Sphagnum Peat Moss Association (CSPMA) (1988)
4 Wycliff Pl., St Albert, AB T8N 3Y8
403/460-8280, Fax: 403/459-0939, Toll Free: 1-888-873-7328
URL: http://www.peatmoss.com
President, Gerry Hood, Email: ghood@peatmoss.com
Publications: Bale Mail; CSPMA Retailer Newsletter, s-a.

Canola Council of Canada
#400, 167 Lombard Ave., Winnipeg, MB R3B 0T6
204/982-2100, Fax: 204/942-1841
President, Dale Adolphe
Information Services Manager, Dave Wilkins

Christian Farmers Federation of Ontario/Fédération des agriculteurs chrétiens de l'Ontario (CFFO) (1954)
115 Woolwich St., Guelph, ON N1H 3V1
519/837-1620, Fax: 519/824-1835
Contact, Elbert van Donkersgoed
Affiliates: AG Care; Christian Farmers Federation of Alberta; Christian Environmental Council; Rural Development Advisory Committee

Co-op Atlantic/Co-op Atlantique (1927)
PO Box 750, Moncton, NB E1C 8N5
506/858-6000, Fax: 506/858-6477
General Manager, Eric Dean
Publications: Connections; The Director/L'Administrateur, m.

Conseil de l'industrie laitière du Québec inc./Québec Dairy Council Inc. (CILQ) (1963)
#310, 8585, boul St-Laurent, Montréal, PQ H2P 2M9
514/381-5331, Téléc: 514/381-6677
Président exécutif, Claude Lambert
Président du conseil d'administration, Camil Genesse
Adjointe administrative, Yolaine Villeneuve
Publications: Mise à Jour

Cooperative of Maple Syrup Producers of New Brunswick Inc./Cooperative des producteurs de sirop d'érable du Nouveau-Brunswick inc. (1988)
9 Industrielle St., PO Box 951, Saint-Quentin, NB E0K 1J0
506/235-3438, Fax: 506/235-3529
President, Denis Cote
Marketing Director, J.L. Paul Ouellet
Affiliates: International Maple Syrup Institute; Conseil acadien de la coopération; Canadian Federation of Chefs & Cooks

Crop Protection Institute of Canada/Institut canadien pour la protection des cultures (CPIC) (1953)
#627, 21 Four Seasons Pl., Etobicoke, ON M9B 6J8
416/622-9771, Fax: 416/622-6764, Email: rosew@cropro.org
URL: http://www.cropro.org
President, J.S. King
Communication Manager, Wendy Rose
Publications: Newsletter

Dairy Farmers of Ontario (DFO)
6780 Campobello Rd., Mississauga, ON L5N 2L8
905/821-8970, Fax: 905/821-3160
URL: http://www.milk.org/

Dairy Nutrition Council of Alberta (DNCA) (1988)
14904 - 121A Ave., Edmonton, AB T5V 1A3
403/453-5942, Fax: 403/455-2196, Toll Free: 1-800-252-7530
Manager, C. Thorvaldson
Publications: Fast Facts
Affiliates: Dairy Farmers of Canada

Dairyworld Foods (1992)
Agrifoods International Cooperative Ltd.
425 Winnipeg St., Regina, SK S4P 3A5
306/924-1300
Wendy Kelly
Publications: Dairyworld Digest; Agrifoods Milkline

Earthkeeping: Food & Agriculture in Christian Perspective (1978)
#205, 10711 - 107 Ave., Edmonton, AB T5H 0W6
403/428-6981, Fax: 403/428-1581,
    Email: earthkeeping@enabel.ccinet.ab.ca
President, Herman Bulten
Administrative Assistant, Rita Anema
Coordinator, Research & Policy, Kathryn W. Olson

Publications: Earthkeeping Alberta
Affiliates: Alberta Environment Network

Fédération des agricultrices du Québec
555, boul Roland-Therrien, Longueuil, PQ J4H 3Y9
514/679-0530, Téléc: 514/679-2652
Secrétaire, Lise Dufort

Fédération d'agriculture biologique du Québec
555, boul Roland-Therrien, Longueuil, PQ J4H 3Y9
514/679-0530, Téléc: 514/679-5436
Secrétaire, Alyne Savary

Fédération des producteurs de lait du Québec (FPLQ) (1983)
555, boul Roland-Therrien, Longueuil, PQ J4H 3Y9
514/679-0530, Téléc: 514/679-5899
Directeur général, Henri Dorval
Publications: Le Producteur de lait québécois
Organisation(s) affiliée(s): Union des producteurs agricoles

Fédération des producteurs de porc du Québec (FPPQ)
555, boul Roland-Thérrien, Longueuil, PQ J4H 3Y9
514/679-0530, Téléc: 514/679-0102, Courrier électronique: fppq@netaxis.qc.ca
Secrétaire, Benoît Desilet
Publications: Porc Québec
Organisation(s) affiliée(s): Union des producteurs agricoles du Québec

Flax Council of Canada (1985)
#465, 167 Lombard Ave., Winnipeg, MB R3B 0T6
204/982-2115, Fax: 204/942-1841
President, Donald H. Frith
Chairman, Garvin Hanley
Publications: Flax Focus

Flax Growers Western Canada
PO Box 832, Regina, SK S4P 3B1
306/781-7475, Fax: 306/525-4173
Contact, Donald R. Jaques

International Flying Farmers - Canadian Branch
910 Crescent Ave., High River, AB T1V 1H2
403/652-7373
Secretary, Lenora Jones

Jubilee Centre for Agricultural Research (1983)
115 Woolwich St., Guelph, ON N1H 3V1
519/837-1620, Fax: 519/824-1835
Research Director, Elbert van Donkersgoed
Chair, Tom Oegema
Publications: Earthkeeping Ontario
Affiliates: Christian Farmers Federation of Ontario

Milk Nova Scotia
Burnside Industrial Park, 202 Brownlow Ave., Unit F, Dartmouth, NS B3B 1T5
902/468-2122, Fax: 902/465-7757

National Dairy Council of Canada/Conseil national de l'industrie laitière du Canada
221 Laurier Ave. East, Ottawa, ON K1N 6P1
613/238-4116, Fax: 613/238-6247, Telex: 053-3952
President & CEO, Kempton L. Matte

National Farmers Union/Syndicat national des cultivateurs (NFU) (1969)
250C - 2 Ave. South, Saskatoon, SK S7K 2M1
306/652-9465, Fax: 306/664-6226
URL: http://www.wbm.ca/users/farmers
President, Nettie Wiebe, 306/493-2569
Vice-President, Chris Tait, 204/252-2773
Women's President, Karen Fyfe, 902/886-2993
Youth President, Karen Pedersen, 306/398-2795
Executive Secretary, Darrin Qualman, 306/652-9465, Email: farmers@eagle.wbm.ca
Publications: Union Farmer; Union Farmer Quarterly
Affiliates: Action Canada Network

Northern Ontario Dairymen's Association (1948)
PO Box 445, Kirkland Lake, ON P2N 3J1
705/567-3377
President, Michael Holland
Sec.-Treas., Dean Archer

Nova Scotia Beekeepers Association
RR#2, Berwick, NS B0P 1E0
902/538-7527
Manager, Joanne Moran

Nova Scotia Fruit Growers' Association (NSFGA) (1863)
Kentville Agricultural Centre, 32 Main St., Kentville, NS B4N 1J5
902/678-1093, Fax: 902/679-1567
Secretary Manager, Janice Lutz
Affiliates: Nova Scotia Federation of Agriculture

Nova Scotia Milk Producers Association
347 Willow St., PO Box 784, Truro, NS B2N 5E8
902/893-2293, Fax: 902/893-7063
Sec.-Treas., Donna Langille

Ontario Beekeepers' Association (OBA) (1881)
RR#3, Bayfield, ON N0M 1G0
519/565-2622, Fax: 519/565-5452
President, Henry Hiemstra
Business Administrator, Patricia A. Westlake
Publications: The Sting

Ontario Creamerymen's Association (1935)
26 Dominion St., Alliston, ON L9R 1L5
705/435-6751
President, Lloyd Kennedy
Publications: Newsletter

Ontario Dairy Council (ODC) (1971)
6533D Mississauga Rd., Mississauga, ON L5N 1A6
905/542-3620, Fax: 905/542-3624
President, Tom Kane
Chairman, Nick Quickert
Publications: News & Views
Affiliates: National Dairy Council; International Dairy Federation

Ontario Fruit & Vegetable Growers' Association/ L'Association des fruitculteurs et des maraîchers de l'Ontario (OFVGA) (1859)
#103, 355 Elmira Rd. North, Guelph, ON N1K 1S5
519/763-6160, Fax: 519/763-6604
Executive Secretary, Michael Mazur
Publications: The Grower

Ontario Grain & Feed Association (1965)
#106, 1400 Bishop St., Cambridge, ON N1R 6W8
519/622-3800, Fax: 519/622-3590
Executive Vice-President, D.O. Buttenham
Publications: Bulletin; Trade Directory, a.

Ontario Plowmen's Association (1913)
367 Woodlawn Rd. West, Guelph, ON N1H 7K9
519/767-1967, Fax: 519/661-7569, Toll Free: 1-800-661-7569
General Manager, John Fennell

Ordre des agronomes du Québec/Order of Agrologists of Québec (OAQ) (1974)
#710, 1259, rue Berri, Montréal, PQ H2L 4C7
514/844-3833, Téléc: 514/844-7462
Directeur général adjoint, Robert LeMay
Chargée de projets, Chantal Paul
Publications: Agro-Nouvelles

PEI Dairy Producers Association (1976)
PO Box 335, Charlottetown, PE C1A 7K7
902/892-5331, Fax: 902/566-2755
Chairman, Casey Van Diepen

Preservation of Agricultural Lands Society (PALS) (1977)
PO Box 1090, St Catharines, ON L2R 7A3
905/468-2841, Fax: 905/468-7614
Contact, Gracia Janes
President, John Bacher
Vice-President, Joan Ashcroft
Publications: Pals Newsletter
Affiliates: Ontario Environmental Network Land Use Caucus

Prince Edward Island Soil & Crop Improvement Association (1971)
PO Box 1600, Charlottetown, PE C1A 7N3
902/628-6997, Fax: 902/628-6998
President, Ronnie Gallant
Secretary, Marilyn Haslam

Prince Edward Island Vegetable Growers Co-op Association
81 Sherwood Rd., PO Box 1494, Charlottetown, PE C1A 7N1
902/892-5361, Fax: 902/566-2383
Manager, Don Read

Québec Farmers' Association (QFA) (1957)
PO Box 80, Ste-Anne-de-Bellevue, PQ H9X 3L4
514/457-2010, Fax: 514/398-7972
Executive Director, Hugh Maynard
President, Douglas Mackinnon
Publications: Québec Farmers' Advocate

Québec Young Farmers (1969)
PO Box 80, Ste-Anne-de-Bellevue, PQ H9X 3L4
514/457-2010, Fax: 514/398-7972
President, Amber Heatlie
Publications: News Spreader

Saskatchewan Association of Agricultural Societies & Exhibitions (SAASE) (1987)
PO Box 7602, Saskatoon, SK S7K 4R4
306/664-6654, Fax: 306/664-6654
Secretary Manager, Judy Reimer
Affiliates: Canadian Association of Fairs & Exhibitions

Saskatchewan Beekeepers Association
PO Box 154, Stn Main, Saskatoon, SK S7K 3K4
306/374-0581
President, Christopher Warriner
Sec.-Treas., Leo Monseler
Publications: Saskatchewan Beekeepers' Association Newsletter

Saskatchewan Canola Growers Association (1969)
#210, 111 Research Dr., Saskatoon, SK S7N 3R2
306/668-2380, Fax: 306/975-1126
President, Ken Mannle
Executive Director, Holly Rask
Administrative Assistant, Shelley Braun
Publications: Canola Country

Saskatchewan Dairy Foundation (SDF) (1981)
445 Winnipeg St., PO Box 1294, Regina, SK S4P 3B8
306/949-6999, Fax: 306/924-1352
President, M. Pearson
Vice-President, C. Baerg
Publications: Milk & More

Saskatchewan Game Farmers Association
2341 Robin Pl., North Battleford, SK S9A 3T6
306/445-7412, Fax: 306/445-4007

Canadian Almanac & Directory 1997

Executive Director, Terri Harris
Affiliates: Saskatchewan Stock Growers Association

SeCan Association/Association SeCan (1976)
#200, 57 Auriga Dr., Nepean, ON K2E 8B2
613/225-6891, Fax: 613/225-6422, Email: secanott@hook.up.net
General Manager, L.R. White
President, Robert Thom
Publications: SeCan News

Society of Ontario Nut Growers (SONG) (1972)
RR#2, 1540 Concession 6 Rd., Niagara on the Lake, ON L0S 1J0
905/682-4966
Secretary, G. Robert Hambleton
Publications: SONG News

Sustainable Agriculture Association (SAA) (1985)
PO Box 1181, Stn M, Calgary, AB T2P 2K9
403/686-3310
President, Raphael Thierrin
Publications: SAA Newsletter

Union des producteurs agricoles (UPA) (1924)
555, boul Roland-Therrien, Longueuil, PQ J4H 3Y9
514/679-0530; 4943, Téléc: 514/679-5436
URL: http://www.upa.qc.ca/
Directeur général, Claude Lafleur
Publications: La Terre de chéz-nous

Vegetable Growers' Association of Manitoba
808 Muriel St., Winnipeg, MB R2Y 0Y3
204/888-8989, Fax: 204/888-0944
Executive Secretary, Evelyn MacKenzie-Reid

Vegetable & Potato Producers' Association of Nova Scotia
Kentville Agricultural Centre, 32 Main St., Kentville, NS B4N 1J5
902/678-9335
Secretary Manager, Tammy Hall

Western Barley Growers Association (WBGA) (1973)
#232, 2116 - 27 Ave. NE, Calgary, AB T2E 7A6
403/291-3630, Fax: 403/291-9841
President, Wayne Kriz
Vice-President, Buck Spencer
Alberta Vice-President, Doug Robertson
Saskatchewan Vice-President, Darwin Kells
Treasurer, Eugene Boyko
Publications: The Barley Grower

Western Canadian Wheat Growers Association (WCWGA) (1970)
1836 Victoria Ave. East, Regina, SK S4N 7K1
306/586-5866, Fax: 306/586-2707
Executive Director, Alanna Koch
President, Larry Maguire
Publications: The Wheatgrower; Pro-Farm, bi-m.

Western Grains Research Foundation (WGRF) (1981)
118 Veterinary Rd., Saskatoon, SK S7N 2R4
306/975-0060, Fax: 306/975-3766
Chairman, Cam Henry
Executive Director, Dr. H.M. Austenson
Affiliates: United Grain Growers; Western Canadian Wheat Growers Association; Western Barley Growers Association; Flax Growers Western Canada; Canadian Canola Growers Association; Unifarm; Keystone Agricultural Producers; Oat Producers of Alberta; Canadian Seed Growers Association; Alberta Wheat Pool; Saskatchewan Wheat Pool; Manitoba Pool Elevators; National Farmers Union; Alberta Winter Wheat Commission

AIDS

The AIDS Foundation of Canada Inc. (1986)
#1000, 885 Dunsmuir, Vancouver, BC V6C 1N5
604/688-7294, Fax: 604/689-4888
President, Nathan S. Ganapathi

Canadian AIDS Society/Société canadienne du sida (CAS) (1985)
#400, 100 Sparks St., Ottawa, ON K1P 5B7
613/230-3580, Fax: 613/563-4998
Executive Director, Russell Armstrong
Manager of Finance, Kelly James Masterson
Development Officer, Susan Macintosh
Affiliates: International Council of AIDS Service Organizations

AFRICANS IN PARTNERSHIP AGAINST AIDS
#105, 15A Elm St., Toronto, ON M5G 1H1
416/340-9943, Fax: 416/340-1219
Program Coordinator, Morley Nakyonyi

AIDS ACTION NOW/LE GROUPE D'ACTION SIDA (1989)
#321, 517 College St., Toronto, ON M6G 1A8
416/928-2206, Fax: 416/928-2185
Co-Chair, Brian Farlinga
Co-Chair, Mark Freamo
Publications: AIDS Action News

AIDS CALGARY AWARENESS ASSOCIATION (1985)
#300, 1021 - 10 Ave. SW, Calgary, AB T2R 0B7
403/228-0198, Fax: 403/229-2077, Info Line: 403/228-0155
Executive Director, Daniel Holinda

AIDS COALITION OF CAPE BRETON
PO Box 177, Sydney, NS B1P 6H1
902/567-1766, Fax: 902/539-2526

AIDS COALITION OF NOVA SCOTIA (ACNS) (1985)
#300, 5675 Spring Garden Rd., Halifax, NS B3J 1H1
902/425-4882, Fax: 902/422-6200
Chair, Wilson Hudder
Publications: Thinking Positive

AIDS COMMITTEE OF CAMBRIDGE, KITCHENER/WATERLOO & AREA (ACCKWA) (1985)
123 Duke St., Kitchener, ON N2A 1A4
519/570-3687, Fax: 519/570-4034
Executive Director, Lorie Fioze
Publications: Advance
Affiliates: Ontario AIDS Network

AIDS COMMITTEE OF DURHAM REGION (1992)
#305, 209 Dundas St. East, Whitby, ON L1N 7H8
905/665-0051, Fax: 905/665-0056
Executive Director, Trudie Reid
President, Jennifer Stones
Publications: Positively Speaking

AIDS COMMITTEE OF GUELPH & WELLINGTON COUNTY (ACGWC) (1987)
#204, 85 Norfolk St., Guelph, ON N1H 4J4
519/763-2255, Fax: 519/763-8125
Executive Director, J. Tresidder
Publications: Between the Lines

AIDS COMMITTEE OF LONDON (ACOL) (1989)
#301, 343 Richmond St., London, ON N6A 3C2
519/434-1601, Fax: 519/434-1843, Info Line: 519/434-8160
Executive Director, Betty Anne Thomas
Education Coordinator, Clarence Crossman
Publications: ACOLade
Affiliates: Ontario AIDS Network

AIDS COMMITTEE OF NORTH BAY & AREA/COMITÉ DU SIDA DE NORTH BAY ET DE LA RÉGION (ACNBA) (1990)
#202, 240 Algonquin Ave., North Bay, ON P1B 4V9
705/497-3560, Fax: 705/497-7850
Executive Director, Steve Cripwell
Publications: Faces

AIDS COMMITTEE OF OTTAWA/COMITÉ DU SIDA D'OTTAWA
207 Queen St., 4th Fl., Ottawa, ON K1P 6E5
613/238-5014, Fax: 613/238-3425, Info Line: 613/238-4111
Interim Executive Director, Danl Loewen

AIDS COMMITTEE OF SIMCOE COUNTY (ACSC)
#20B, 80 Bradford St., PO Box 744, Barrie, ON L4M 4Y5
705/722-6778, Fax: 705/722-6560
Publications: The Link

AIDS COMMITTEE OF SUDBURY/COMITÉ DU SIDA DE SUDBURY
Access AIDS Committee
#203, 111 Elm St., Sudbury, ON P3C 1T3
705/688-0505, Fax: 705/688-0423

AIDS COMMITTEE OF THUNDER BAY (ACT-B) (1986)
PO Box 24025, RPO Downtown North, Thunder Bay, ON P7A 4T0
807/345-1516, Fax: 807/345-2505, Info Line: 807/345-7233
Executive Director, M. Sobota
Publications: ReACT-Believe
Affiliates: Ontario AIDS Network

AIDS COMMITTEE OF TORONTO (ACT) (1983)
399 Church St., 4th Fl., PO Box 55, Stn F, Toronto, ON M4Y 2L4
416/340-2437, Fax: 416/340-8224, Info Line: 416/340-8844, TDD: 416/340-8122
Executive Director, Charles Roy

AIDS COMMITTEE OF WINDSOR (ACW) (1985)
PO Box 2233, Stn Main, Windsor, ON N8Y 4R8
519/973-0222, Fax: 519/973-7389, Info Line: 519/256-2437
Information Coordinator, Donna Milito
Publications: ACW Newsletter
Affiliates: Ontario AIDS Network

AIDS COMMUNITY CARE MONTRÉAL/SIDA BÉNÉVOLES MONTRÉAL (ACCM) (1988)
#500, 231, St-Jacques ouest, Montréal, PQ H2Y 1M6
514/287-3551, Fax: 514/287-9475
Contact, Lynn Perkins
Publications: Vivace

AIDS HOUSING GROUP OF OTTAWA (AHGO) (1989)
#205, 200 Isabella, Ottawa, ON K1R 1V7
613/235-8815, Fax: 613/235-3897
Administrative Assistant, Marilyn Alkenbrack
Chair, Marc Gervais
Vice-Chair, Kevin Gibbs
Executive Director, Dr. Bruce Mills
Treasurer, Dr. Dona Bowers
Publications: AHGO Newsletter

AIDS NETWORK OF EDMONTON SOCIETY
Ross Armstrong Office, #201, 11456 Jasper Ave., Edmonton, AB T5K 0M1
403/488-5742, Fax: 403/488-3735, Info Line: 403/488-5816

AIDS NEW BRUNSWICK/SIDA NOUVEAU BRUNSWICK (1987)
65 Brunswick St., Fredericton, NB E3B 1G5
506/459-7518, 506/450-2620, Fax: 506/459-5782, Info Line: 1-800-561-4009
President, Barry Wanamaker
Secretary, Suzanne Webster
Publications: The Ribbon/Le Ruban
Affiliates: Atlantic AIDS Network

AIDS NIAGARA (1987)
#200, 50 William St., St Catharines, ON L2R 5J2
905/984-8684, Fax: 905/988-1921

Community Relations, Joan Blanchard
Publications: AIDS Niagara News
Affiliates: Ontario AIDS Network

AIDS PEI (1990)
#103, 199 Grafton St., PO Box 2762, Charlottetown, PE C1A 8C4
902/566-2437, Fax: 902/566-2437, Info Line: 902/894-3980, Toll Free: 1-800-314-2437
Executive Director, Andrea Scott

AIDS REGINA, INC. (1985)
1852 Angus St., Regina, SK S4T 1Z4
306/924-8420, Fax: 306/525-0904, Info Line: 306/525-0905
Executive Director, Christine Smith
Publications: AIDS Regina Newsletter

AIDS SAINT JOHN (ASJ) (1987)
115 Hazen St., Saint John, NB E2L 3L3
506/652-2437, Fax: 506/652-2438
Executive Director, Patti Daley
President, James Noble

AIDS SASKATOON
PO Box 4062, Saskatoon, SK S7K 4E3
306/242-5005, Fax: 306/244-2134, Toll Free: 1-800-667-6878
Administrator, Cheryl Loadman
Publications: AIDS Saskatoon Connection

AIDS SHELTER COALITION OF MANITOBA (1989)
#202, 222 Furby St., Winnipeg, MB R3C 2A7
204/775-9173, Fax: 204/774-8895, Toll Free: 1-800-670-6880
Co-Chair, Jim Stuart
Co-Chair, Beth Jackson

AIDS SOCIETY OF JASPER: A POSITIVE CO-ORDINATED COMMUNITY RESPONSE
AIDS Jasper
Jasper Activity Centre, 303 Pyramid Ave., PO Box 1090, Jasper, AB T0E 1E0
403/852-5274, Fax: 403/852-5274
Executive Director, K. Exchange

AIDS VANCOUVER (1983)
Vancouver AIDS Society
c/o Pacific AIDS Resource Centre, 1107 Seymour St., Vancouver, BC V6B 5S8
604/681-2122, Fax: 604/893-2211, Info Line: 604/687-2437, TDD: 604/893-2215
Executive Director, Rick Marchand
Chair, Ed Lee

AIDS VANCOUVER ISLAND (AVI) (1985)
Vancouver Island AIDS Society
#304, 733 Johnston St., Victoria, BC V8W 3C7
250/384-2366, Fax: 250/380-9411, Info Line: 384-4554, Toll Free: 1-800-665-2437
Publications: Update

AIDS YELLOWKNIFE (1993)
PO Box 864, Yellowknife, NT X1A 2L8
403/873-2626, Fax: 403/873-2626
President, Pansy Hamilton
Publications: AIDS Yellowknife

AIDS YUKON ALLIANCE (1989)
Yukon AIDS Program
7221 - 7th Ave., Whitehorse, YT Y1A 1R8
403/633-2437, Fax: 403/633-2447
Executive Director, Lois Rudd
Publications: SeroNorth

ALGOMA AIDS NETWORK
12 Herrick St., PO Box 23035, RPO Station Mall, Sault Ste Marie, ON P6A 6W6
705/256-2437, Fax: 705/254-5551

ALLIANCE FOR SOUTH ASIAN AIDS PREVENTION (ASAP) (1989)
#126, 20 Carlton St.., Toronto, ON M5B 2H5
416/599-2727
Executive Director, Anthony Mohamed

ASSOCIATION DES BÉNÉVOLES ACCOMPAGNATEURS-ACCOMPAGNATRICES DE PERSONNES ATTEINTES DU SIDA (1990)
ABAAPAS
1000, rue Sherbrooke est, Montréal, PQ H2L 1L5
514/281-2093, Téléc: 514/281-8004, Infoligne: 281-6629
Directrice générale, Hélène Arsenault
Publications: Bulletin de l'ABAAPAS
Organisation(s) affiliée(s): Coalition des organismes communautaires québécois de lutte contre le sida

ATLANTIC FIRST NATIONS AIDS TASK FORCE
2164 Gottingen St., PO Box 47049, Halifax, NS B3K 2B0
902/492-4255, Fax: 902/492-0500, Toll Free: 1-800-565-4255, Email: afnatf95@fox.nstn.ca
Project Coordinator, Kevin Barlow

BANFF REGIONAL AIDS COMMITTEE (BRAC) (1990)
PO Box 219, Banff, AB T0L 0C0
403/762-0690, Fax: 403/760-3007
Program Coordinator, Patricia Stutz

BLACK COALITION FOR AIDS PREVENTION (1987)
BLACK CAP
#103, 597 Parliament St., Toronto, ON M4X 1W3
416/926-0122, Fax: 416/926-0281, Email: blackcap@web.apc.org
Executive Director, Dionne A. Falconer
Publications: Black CAP Links

BODY POSITIVE COALITION OF MANITOBA
#460, 222 Furby St., Winnipeg, MB R3C 2A7
204/783-5848
Kurt McGifford

BRANDON AIDS SUPPORT INC. (BAS) (1989)
PO Box 32, Brandon, MB R7A 6Y2
204/763-4443
Contact, Maureen Keddie

BUREAU LOCAL D'INTERVENTION TRAITANT DU SIDA (BLITS) (1989)
#110, 59, rue Monfette, Victoriaville, PQ G6P 1J8
819/758-2662, Téléc: 819/758-8270
Coordonnateur général, Andre Beaudry

BUREAU RÉGIONAL D'ACTION SIDA (OUTAOUAIS) (BRAS) (1991)
#103, 110 rue de la Savane, Gatineau, PQ J8T 5B9
819/568-2727, Téléc: 819/568-8765
Directrice générale, Josceline Levesque

CANADIAN HIV/AIDS LEGAL NETWORK/RÉSEAU JURIDIQUE CANADIEN SUR LE VIH/SIDA
4007, rue de Mentana, Montréal, PQ H2L 3R9
514/526-1796, Fax: 514/526-5543
URL: http://www.odyssee.net/~jujube
Sarah Wilson
Publications: HIV/AIDS Policy & Law Newsletter

CASEY HOUSE HOSPICE INC.
9 Huntley St., Toronto, ON M4Y 2K8
416/962-7600, Fax: 416/962-5147
Administrative Services Coordinator, Saundra Millington

CENTRAL ALBERTA AIDS NETWORK SOCIETY (CAANS) (1986)
4935 - 51 St., Red Deer, AB T4N 2A8
403/346-8858, Fax: 403/346-2352
Executive Director, Jacquelin Green
Affiliates: Alberta Community Council on AIDS

CENTRE D'ACTION SIDA MONTRÉAL (FEMMES)/CENTRE FOR AIDS SERVICES OF MONTRÉAL (WOMEN) (CASMF) (1990)
1831, boul René-Lévesque ouest, Montréal, PQ H3H 1R4
514/989-7997, Téléc: 514/989-7811
Directrice générale, Daniella R. Boulay
Publications: Between Us/Entre Nous

CENTRE PIERRE HÉNAULT INC.
744, boul St-Joseph est, Montréal, PQ H2J 1K2
514/522-3339, Téléc: 514/522-6665
Coordonnateur général, Louis Richard

CENTRE DES R.O.S.É.S DE L'ABITIBI-TÉMISCAMINGUE (1991)
CP 581, Rouyn-Noranda, PQ J9X 5C6
819/764-9111
Présidente, Guylaine Boisvert
Publications: Info-SIDAction

CENTRE DES SERVICES SIDA SECOURS DU QUÉBEC
3736, rue St-Hubert, Montréal, PQ H2L 4A2
514/282-7777, Téléc: 514/842-2991
Directrice générale, Hélène Légaré

CENTRE SIDA AMITIÉ
705, boul des Laurentides, St-Antoine-des-Laurentides, PQ J7Z 4M6
514/431-7432
Président, Louis Aird

CHEZ MA COUSINE
CP 325, Succ Place-du-Parc, Montréal, PQ H2W 2N8
514/288-7244, Téléc: 514/288-3727
Secrétaire, Roger Le Clerc
Organisation(s) affiliée(s): Coalition des organismes communautaires québécois de lutte contre le sida

COALITION DES ORGANISMES COMMUNAUTAIRES QUÉBÉCOIS DE LUTTE CONTRE LE SIDA (COCQ-SIDA) (1990)
#320, 4205, rue St-Denis, Montréal, PQ H2J 2K9
514/844-2477, Téléc: 514/844-2498
Directrice générale, Lyse Pinault
Président, Jacques Gélinas
Publications: iti

COALITION SIDA DES SOURDS DU QUÉBEC (CSSQ) (1992)
Edifice Lafontaine, 1301, rue Sherbrooke est, Montréal, PQ H2L 1M8
514/521-1780, Téléc: 514/521-1137, Ligne sans frais: 1-800-363-6600
Directeur général, Michel Turgeon
Organisation(s) affiliée(s): Coalition des organismes communautaires québécois de lutte contre le sida

COMITÉ DES PERSONNES ATTEINTES DU VIH/COMMITTEE OF PERSONS LIVING WITH HIV (CPAVIH)
3600, av Hôtel-de-Ville, Montréal, PQ H2X 3B6
514/522-6673, Téléc: 514/281-8004
Coordonnateur général, Claude Lachapelle
Publications: Point de VIH Positif

COMITÉ SIDA AIDE MONTRÉAL (CSAM) (1985)
3600, av Hôtel-de-Ville, Montréal, PQ H2X 3B6
514/282-9888, Téléc: 514/282-0072, Infoligne: 514/282-9991, Ligne sans frais: 1-800-463-5656
Directrice générale, Sylvie Charbonneau
Président, Jean-Bernard Faucher
Responsable des communications, Patrice Allard
Publications: Vies à VIH; One Voice, bi-m.

COMMUNITY AIDS TREATMENT INFORMATION EXCHANGE/RÉSEAU COMMUNAUTAIRE D'INFO-TRAITEMENT SIDA (CATIE) (1989)
#420, 517 College St., Toronto, ON M6G 4A2
416/944-1916, Fax: 416/928-2185, Toll Free: 1-800-263-1638, Email: info@catie.ca
URL: http://www.catie.ca
Director, Paul Kenney
Director, Glen Brown
Co-Chair, L. Gardner
Co-Chair, A. DiLeonardo
Publications: Treatment Update; Traitement SIDA, 10 pa

Canadian Almanac & Directory 1997

ORGANIZATIONS — AIDS

COMMUNITY RESEARCH INITIATIVE OF TORONTO/INITIATIVE DE RECHERCHE COMMUNAUTAIRE DE TORONTO (CRIT) (1989)
#617, 2 Carlton St., Toronto, ON M5B 1J3
416/408-1041, Fax: 416/408-1044, Email: comm-res.crit@sympatico.ca
Executive Director, Jeff Toledano, MSW
Publications: Initiatives
Affiliates: Community-Based Clinical Trials Network; Canadian HIV Trials Network

EDMONTON PERSONS LIVING WITH HIV SOCIETY
c/o AIDS Network of Edmonton Society, #201, 11456 Jasper Ave., Edmonton, AB T5K 0M1
403/488-5768, Fax: 403/488-3735

FEATHER OF HOPE ABORIGINAL AIDS PREVENTION SOCIETY (FOHAAPS) (1990)
#201, 11456 Jasper Ave., Edmonton, AB T5K 0M1
403/488-5773, Fax: 403/488-3735, Toll Free: 1-800-256-0459

FIFE HOUSE FOUNDATION (1988)
#206, 72 Carlton St., Toronto, ON M5B 1L6
416/963-8218, Fax: 416/963-8204
Executive Director, Judith Tansley

FOOTHILLS AIDS AWARENESS ASSOCIATION
PO Box 758, Okotoks, AB T0L 1T0
403/938-4911

GAY ASIAN AIDS PROJECT (GAAP) (1990)
#214, 17 Saint Joseph St., Toronto, ON M4Y 1J8
416/963-4300, Fax: 416/963-4300 (Call first)
Contact, Dr. Alan Li

GAY & LESBIAN HEALTH SERVICES OF SASKATOON (1991)
PO Box 8581, Saskatoon, SK S7K 6K7
306/665-1224, Fax: 306/244-2134, Toll Free: 1-800-358-1833
Executive Director, Gens Hellquist
Publications: Perceptions

GROUPE D'ACTION POUR LA PRÉVENTION DU SIDA (1987)
GAP - SIDA
#101, 2577A, rue Jean Talon est, Montréal, PQ H2A 1T8
514/722-5655, Téléc: 514/722-0063
Directeur général, Dr. Jean Merveille

HAMILTON AIDS NETWORK FOR DIALOGUE & SUPPORT (HAN) (1986)
512 James St. North, Hamilton, ON L8P 3A1
905/528-0854, Fax: 905/528-6311, Toll Free: 1-800-563-6919
Acting Executive Director, Rui Pires
Publications: Network News

HEALING OUR SPIRIT (1992)
BC First Nations AIDS Society
415B West Esplanade, North Vancouver, BC V7M 1A6
604/983-8774, Fax: 604/983-2667
Elmer Starr
Rod Cunningham

JOHN GORDON HOME (1991)
London Regional AIDS Hospice
414 Dufferin Ave., London, ON N6B 1Z6
519/433-3951, Fax: 519/433-1314
Executive Director, Sam Conti
Publications: A Home with Heart

KALI-SHIVA AIDS SERVICES (1988)
#10, 222 Osborne St., Winnipeg, MB R3L 1Z3
204/477-9506, Fax: 204/477-9099
Publications: Kali-Shiva Volunteer Newsletter

KELOWNA & AREA AIDS RESOURCES, EDUCATION & SUPPORT SOCIETY (1992)
KARES
#3, 1404 Hunter Ct., Kelowna, BC V1X 6E6
250/862-2437, Fax: 250/868-8662, Toll Free: 1-800-616-2437
President, Ron Van Der Meer

KINGSTON AIDS PROJECT (KAP) (1986)
113 Johnson St., PO Box 120, Kingston, ON K7L 4V6
613/545-3698, Fax: 613/546-0981, Info Line: 613/545-1414
President, Maggie Lopes
Publications: KAP Newsletter
Affiliates: Ontario AIDS Network

LETHBRIDGE AIDS CONNECTION SOCIETY (LAC) (1987)
#421, 515 - 7 St. South, Lethbridge, AB T1J 2G8
403/328-8186, Fax: 403/328-8564
Program Coordinator, Jacqueline Preyde
Publications: Person to Person
Affiliates: Alberta Community Council on AIDS

MAISON AMARYLLIS
1462, rue Panet, Montréal, PQ H2L 2Z3
514/526-3635, Téléc: 514/521-9209
Directeur, Jean Martel
Organisation(s) affiliée(s): Coalition des organismes communautaires québécois de lutte contre le sida

MAISON D'HÉRELLE
3738, rue St-Hubert, Montréal, PQ H2L 4A2
514/842-7747, 844-4874, Téléc: 514/842-2991
Directrice générale, Michèle Blanchard

MAISON LUDOVIC (1990)
2555, rue Holt, Montréal, PQ H1Y 1N4
514/722-8523, Téléc: 514/722-2354
Directeur général, Stéphane Richard

MAISON DU PARC
1287, rue Rachel est, Montréal, PQ H2J 2J9
514/523-6467, Téléc: 514/523-7420
Coordonnatrice générale, Pauline Dumoulin

MOUVEMENT D'INFORMATION, D'ÉDUCATION ET D'ENTRAIDE DANS LA LUTTE CONTRE LE SIDA (MIENS) (1988)
387B, rue Racine est, CP 723, Chicoutimi, PQ G7H 5E1
418/693-8983, Téléc: 418/693-0409, Infoligne: 418/693-8983, Ligne sans frais: 1-800-463-3764
Directeur général, Sylvain Gauthier
Président, Ginette Desmeules
Agente de support psychosociale, Lisi Sauvard
Agente administrative, Nicole Boulet
Publications: L'Élan
Organisation(s) affiliée(s): Coalition des organismes québécois de lutte contre le sida

MOUVEMENT D'INFORMATION ET D'ENTRAIDE DANS LA LUTTE CONTRE LE SIDA À QUÉBEC (1986)
MIELS Québec
#200, 175, rue St-Jean, Québec, PQ G1R 1N4
418/649-1720, Téléc: 418/649-1256, Infoligne: 418/649-0788
Directeur général, Jocelyn Châteauneuf
Publications: Sidus

NEWFOUNDLAND & LABRADOR AIDS COMMITTEE (NLAC) (1988)
PO Box 626, Stn C, St. John's, NF A1C 5K8
709/579-8656, Fax: 709/579-0559, Toll Free: 1-800-563-1575
Executive Director, Gerard Yetman
Publications: Reaching Out

NOVA SCOTIA PWA COALITION (1988)
#300, 5675 Spring Garden Rd., Halifax, NS B3J 1H1
902/429-7922, Fax: 902/422-6200
Administrative Coordinator, Robert J. Allan
Chairperson, Wilson Hodder
Publications: News & Views
Affiliates: National Association of PWA Groups

ONTARIO AIDS NETWORK
#701, 100 Sparks St., Ottawa, ON K1P 5B7
613/230-3580, Fax: 613/563-4998

PERSONS LIVING WITH AIDS NETWORK OF SASKATCHEWAN INC. (1987)
PLWA Network of Saskatchewan
PO Box 7123, Saskatoon, SK S7K 4J1
306/373-7766, Fax: 306/374-7743
President, Rita DeGagne
Vice-President, Ron Gendron
Publications: PLWA Newsletter; Our Lives, 9 pa

PERSONS WITH AIDS SOCIETY OF BRITISH COLUMBIA (1987)
Vancouver People With AIDS Society
c/o Pacific AIDS Resource Centre, 1107 Seymour St., Vancouver, BC V6B 5S8
604/681-2122, Fax: 604/893-2251, Crisis-Line: 604/893-2253
Managing Director, Chris P. Sabean
Publications: PWA Newsletter
Affiliates: United Way of Lower Mainland

PETERBOROUGH AIDS RESOURCE NETWORK (PARN) (1990)
PO Box 1582, Peterborough, ON K9J 7H7
705/749-9110, Fax: 705/749-6310, Toll Free: 1-800-361-2895
Executive Director, Joanne Lush
Chairperson, Michelle McLean
Publications: Parn News

PICTOU COUNTY AIDS COALITION
169 Provost St., PO Box 964, New Glasgow, NS B2H 5K7
902/755-4647, Fax: 902/755-6775

POSITIVE WOMEN'S NETWORK (1989)
c/o Pacific AIDS Resource Centre, 1107 Seymour St., Vancouver, BC V6B 5S8
604/681-2122, ext.200, Fax: 604/893-2256
Executive Director, Marcie Summers
Publications: Positive Women's Network Newsletter

POSITIVE YOUTH OUTREACH (PYO)
399 Church St., 2nd Fl., Toronto, ON M5B 2J6
416/506-1400, Fax: 416/506-1404

PRINCE GEORGE AIDS SOCIETY
1371 - 4th Ave., Prince George, BC V2L 3J6
250/562-1172, Fax: 250/565-2284
Donita Kuzma

PROSTITUTE'S SAFER SEX PROJECT (PSSP) (1991)
Maggie's
PO Box 1143, Stn F, Toronto, ON M4Y 2T8
416/964-0150, Fax: 416/964-9653
Staff Administrator, Julien Francisco
Publications: Maggiezine

REGROUPEMENT DES PERSONNES ATTEINTES DU VIH (SIDA) DE QUÉBEC ET DE LA RÉGION (1990)
#201, 175, rue Saint-Jean, Québec, PQ G1R 1N4
418/529-1942, Téléc: 418/649-1256
Coordonnateur, Mario Lapointe

SERVICE SPÉCIALISÉ SIDA QUÉBEC
#200, 226, rue des Alpes, Laval, PQ H7G 3W2
514/668-1230, Téléc: 514/668-6860
Directeur général, Alain Gariépy

SIDA-AIDS MONCTON (SAM) (1989)
368 Cameron St., Moncton, NB E1C 5Z6
506/859-9616, Fax: 506/855-4726
Executive Director, Marc-André LeBlanc

SIDA INTERVENTION PRÉVENTION ÉCOUTE
331, rue St-Viateur, Joliette, PQ J6E 3A8
514/752-4004

SIDA/AIDS INFORMATION ET RESSOURCES SUD-OUEST
2044 Third Concession, Athelstan, PQ J0S 1A0
514/264-3379
Contact, Rev. Neil Wallace

SIDACTION TROIS-RIVIÈRES
952, rue Ste-Geneviève, CP 1142, Trois-Rivières, PQ G9A 5K8
819/374-5740, Téléc: 819/374-5740
Présidente, Martine Petitgrew

S.I.P.E. LANAUDIÈRE (1991)
Sida Information Prévention Écoute Lanaudière
#432, 260, Lavaltrie sud, Joliette, PQ J6E 5X7
514/752-4004
Directeur général, Michel Richard
Organisation(s) affiliée(s): Coalition des organismes communautaires québécois de lutte contre le sida

SOCIETY HOUSING AIDS RESTRICTED PERSONS
SHARP Foundation
223 - 12th Ave. SW, Calgary, AB T2R 0E9
403/263-8084, Fax: 403/265-3572

SOCIETY OF THE SOUTH PEACE AIDS COUNCIL (SPAC) (1987)
South Peace AIDS Council
PO Box 902, Grande Prairie, AB T8V 3Y1
403/538-3388, Fax: 403/532-3368, Email: spak@agt.net
President, Gordon Pellerin

THE TERESA GROUP (1990)
#308, 77 Gerrard St. West, Toronto, ON M5G 2A1
416/596-7703, Fax: 416/596-7910
Penelope Holeton
Publications: Teresa Group in Touch

TORONTO PWA FOUNDATION (TPWAF)
Toronto People With AIDS Foundation
399 Church St., 2nd Fl., Toronto, ON M5B 2J6
416/506-1400, Fax: 416/506-1404, Toll Free: 1-800-558-7923
URL: http://www.io.org/~pwa
Publications: Newsletter

VICTORIA AIDS RESPITE CARE SOCIETY (1991)
611 Superior St., Victoria, BC V8V 1V1
250/388-6220, Fax: 250/388-0711, Email: varcs@cyberstore.ca
Executive Director, Gary R. Murphy

VICTORIA PERSONS WITH AIDS SOCIETY (1994)
613 Superior St., Victoria, BC V8V 1V1
250/383-7494, Fax: 250/383-1617, Toll Free: 1-800-434-2959, Email: pwa@horizon.bc.ca
Office Manager, Jim Wilton
Publications: Living Proof
Affiliates: Wings Housing Society

VILLAGE CLINIC INC. (1990)
668 Corydon Ave., Winnipeg, MB R3M 0X7
204/453-0045, Fax: 204/453-5214, Info Line: 204/945-2437, Toll Free: 1-800-782-2437
President, William E. Crawford
Affiliates: Manitoba Association of Community Health Centres

VOICES OF POSITIVE WOMEN (1991)
PO Box 471, Stn C, Toronto, ON M6J 3P5
416/324-8703, Fax: 416/324-9701
Office Administrator, Vivian Keels
Chair, Louise Binder
Publications: Voices

WEST KOOTENAY/BOUNDRY AIDS NETWORK, OUTREACH & SUPPORT SOCIETY (1992)
ANKORS
903 - 4th St., Castlegar, BC V1N 3P3
Info Line: 604/365-2437, Toll Free: 1-800-421-2737
Executive Director, Karen Muirhead
President, Jim Belsham
Publications: Ankors Advocate: Care Team News
Affiliates: Nelson & District Hospice Society; Castlegar Hospice Society

WINGS HOUSING SOCIETY
#515, 1027 Davie St., Vancouver, BC V6E 4L2
604/682-0909, Fax: 604/893-2251
J. Hegadorn

Canadian Foundation for AIDS Research/ Fondation canadienne de recherche sur le SIDA (CanFar) (1987)
#800, 165 University Ave., Toronto, ON M5H 3B8
416/361-6281, Fax: 416/361-5736
General Manager, Roger C. Bullock

Hébergement de l'envol
6984, rue Fabre, Montréal, PQ H2E 2B2
514/593-6614
Directeur, Édouard Bolduc
Organisation(s) affiliée(s): Coalition des organisme communautaires québécois de lutte contre le sida

Intervention régionale et information sur le sida en Estrie (1988)
IRIS/Estrie
#204, 6, rue Wellington sud, Sherbrooke, PQ J1H 5C7
819/823-6704, Téléc: 819/823-5537
Directeur général, Roger Malenfant
Président, Ginette Therrien
Publications: IRIS Estrie
Organisation(s) affiliée(s): Coalition québécoise des organismes communautaires de lutte contre le sida

AIR CONDITIONING *see* **HEATING, AIR CONDITIONING, PLUMBING**

AIR SHOWS *see* **EVENTS**

ANIMAL BREEDING
see also Fur Trade

The Animal Health Trust of Canada/La Fondation canadienne de la santé animale (1972)
#1801, One Yonge St., Toronto, ON M5E 1W7
416/368-7914, Fax: 416/369-0515, Toll Free: 1-800-565-5235
Executive Director, Marcia Darling
Publications: Insight
Affiliates: Canadian Veterinary Medical Association (founding body)

Appaloosa Horse Club of Canada (ApHCC) (1954)
PO Box 940, Claresholm, AB T0L 0T0
403/625-3326, Fax: 403/625-3326
Executive Secretary, Suzanne Fjordbotten
Publications: ApHCC Annual Report; The Appaloosa, q.

Ayrshire Breeders Association of Canada (ABAC)
Ayrshire Canada
Glenaladale House, 21711 Lakeshore Rd., PO Box 188, Ste-Anne-de-Bellevue, PQ H9X 3V9
514/398-7970, Fax: 514/398-7972
General Manager, Alain Trudeau
Publications: Canadian Ayrshire Review

Canada Fox Breeder's Association
286 Fitzroy St., Summerside, PE C1N 1J2

902/436-9547, Fax: 902/436-1994
Sec.-Treas., Robynn Quinn
Affiliates: 9 provincial affiliates

Canada Mink Breeders Association/Association des éleveurs de visons du Canada (CMBA) (1953)
65B Skyway Ave., Etobicoke, ON M9W 6C7
416/675-9400, Fax: 416/675-9401
Executive Secretary, Karlene Hart
Publications: Newsletter

Canada Sheep Council
10 Campbell Cres., North York, ON M2P 1P2
416/489-4487
Executive Director, D.J. Sloan

Canadian Angus Association (1906)
Canada Centre Building, Exhibition Park, PO Box 3209, Regina, SK S4P 3H1
306/757-6885, Fax: 306/347-3323
Account Manager, Michelle Potapinski

Canadian Arabian Horse Registry (1958)
300 Terrace Plaza, 4445 Calgary Trail South, Edmonton, AB T6H 5R7
403/436-4244, Fax: 403/438-2971
Registrar/Administrator, Phyllis Kinsella
Publications: Canadian Arabian News
Affiliates: World Arabian Horse Registry; Canadian Equestrian Federation

Canadian Association of Animal Breeders/ Association canadienne des éleveurs de bétail (CAAB) (1984)
PO Box 817, Woodstock, ON N4S 8A3
519/539-0662, Fax: 519/537-5391
Executive Director, R.J. McDonald

Canadian Belgian Horse Association
RR#3, Schomberg, ON L0G 1T0
905/939-7497
Secretary, Barb Meyers

Canadian Bison Association/Association canadienne du bison (CBA) (1984)
PO Box 1387, Morden, MB R0G 1J0
204/822-3219, Fax: 204/822-4328
President, Len Ross
Show/Sale Chairman, Don Scott
Executive Secretary, Gail Reichert
Publications: Smoke Signals
Affiliates: American Bison Association - USA; National Bison Association - USA; Peace River Bison Association

Canadian Blonde d'Aquitaine Association (1972)
1608A Centre St. North, Calgary, AB T2E 2R9
403/276-5771, Fax: 403/276-7577
President, Lyle Hamann
Publications: Blonde Advantage

Canadian Brown Swiss Association (1914)
#9, 350 Speedvale Ave. West, Guelph, ON N1H 7M7
519/821-2811, Fax: 519/821-2723
Sec.-Manager, Bill Prins
Publications: The Bell/La Cloche

Canadian Cattle Breeders' Association/Société des éleveurs de bovins canadiens (CCBA) (1895)
468, rue Dolbeau, Sherbrooke, PQ J1G 2Z7
819/346-1258, Fax: 819/346-1258
Secretary, Jean-Guy Bernier
Publications: Entre-Nous

Canadian Cattlemen's Association (1932)
#215, 6715 - 8 St. NE, Calgary, AB T2E 7H7
403/275-8558, Fax: 403/274-5686
Executive Vice-President, Dennis Laycraft

Canadian Almanac & Directory 1997

Animal Health & Meat Inspection Committee, Heidi Grogan
Environmental Coordinator, Peggy Strankman
Ottawa Office: Assistant General Manager, Jim Caldwell, #602, 150 Metcalf St., Ottawa, ON K2P 1P1, 613/233-9375, Fax: 613/233-2860

Canadian Charolais Association
2320 - 41 Ave. NE, Calgary, AB T2E 6W8
403/250-9242, Fax: 403/291-9324
General Manager, Dale Kelly, P.Ag.
Publications: Charolais Banner

Canadian Co-operative Wool Growers Ltd. (1918)
PO Box 130, Carleton Place, ON K7C 3P3
613/257-2714, Fax: 613/257-8896
General Manager, Eric Bjergso
Publications: Canadian Wool Grower

Canadian Cutting Horse Association (CCHA) (1953)
540 McIntosh Rd. NE, Calgary, AB T2E 5Z3
403/276-6448, Fax: 403/276-6452
Dave Whittal
Publications: The Canadian Cutter

Canadian Dexter Cattle Association (CDCA) (1986)
2417 Holly Lane, Ottawa, ON K1V 0M7
613/731-7110, Fax: 613/731-0704
Secretary, Ron Black
Publications: CDCA Newsletter
Affiliates: Canadian Livestock Records Corporation

Canadian Donkey & Mule Association (CDMA)
RR#10, Brampton, ON L6V 3N2
519/455-8439
Sec.-Treas., Jan Sterritt
Publications: CDMA News
Affiliates: American Donkey & Mule Society; British Donkey Breed Society; Breed Societies of Britain, Australia, Sweden, Holland, Germany, New Zealand

Canadian Fjord Horse Association
PO Box 1, Site 203, RR#2, Tofield, AB T0B 4J0
403/922-6231
President, Keith Kemp

Canadian Galloway Association (1882)
1 Hallstone Rd., Brampton, ON L6V 3N2
905/459-0650, Fax: 905/459-0650
Sec.-Treas., Brigitte Morris
Publications: Newsletter; Canadian Galloway Advance, a.

Canadian Gelbvieh Association (1972)
#A123, 2116 - 27 Ave. NE, Calgary, AB T2E 7A6
403/250-8640, Fax: 403/291-5624
Secretary Manager, Wendy Belcher
Publications: Gelbvieh Guide

Canadian Goat Society/La Société canadienne des éleveurs de chèvres (CGS) (1917)
368 Woolwich St., Guelph, ON N1H 3W6
519/824-8738, Fax: 519/824-9250
Sec.-Treas., Suzanne Bishop
Publications: Canadian Goat Society Quarterly q.

Canadian Guernsey Association (1905)
368 Woolwich St., Guelph, ON N1H 3W6
519/836-2141, Fax: 519/824-9250
Secretary Manager, Vivianne Macdonald
Publications: Canadian Guernsey Journal
Affiliates: Canadian Dairy Breeds; Canadian Livestock Records Corporation; Joint Classification Board; Agriculture & Agri-Food Canada

Canadian Hays Converter Association (1976)
#450, 1207 - 11 Ave. SW, Calgary, AB T3C 0M5
403/245-6923, Fax: 403/244-3128
Office Manager, Terri Worms
Publications: Newsletter
Affiliates: Beef Improvement Federation; Canadian Beef Breeds Council; Saskatchewan Livestock Centre

Canadian Hereford Association (1890)
5160 Skyline Way NE, Calgary, AB T2E 6V1
403/275-2662, Fax: 403/295-1333
General Manager, Duncan J. Porteous
Publications: Canadian Hereford Digest

Canadian Highland Cattle Society/Société canadienne des éleveurs de bovins Highland (CHCS) (1964)
Maple Lea Farm, 58 Bailey Rd., RR#1, Knowlton, PQ J0E 1V0
514/243-5543, Fax: 514/243-5543
Secretary-Manager, Margaret Badger
Publications: The Kyloe Cry

Canadian Icelandic Horse Federation (CIHF) (1979)
5435 Rochdell Rd., Vernon, BC V1B 3E8
250/545-2336, Fax: 250/549-9116, Toll Free: 1-800-255-2336, Email: rhood@junction.net
Secretary, Christine Schwartz
Publications: CIHF Newsletter

Canadian Landrace Swine Breeders Association/Club des porcs Landrace (1990)
PO Box 34, Beebe, PQ J0B 1E0
819/876-5103, Fax: 819/876-7986
Secretary, Allan Smith
Affiliates: Purebred Swine Breeders Association of Canada

Canadian Limousin Association (1970)
5663 Burleigh Cres. SE, Calgary, AB T2H 1Z7
403/253-7309, Fax: 403/253-1704
Executive Manager, Beverly J. Leavitt
Publications: Limousin Leader

Canadian Livestock Records Corporation/Société canadienne d'enregistrement des animaux (CLRC) (1905)
2417 Holly Lane, Ottawa, ON K1V 0M7
613/731-7110, Fax: 613/731-0704
General Manager, Bruce E. Hunt
Publications: CLRC Newsletter

Canadian Maine-Anjou Association (CMAA) (1970)
#110, 3016 - 19 St. NE, Calgary, AB T2E 6Y9
403/291-7077, Fax: 403/291-0274
General Manager, Rod McLeod
Publications: Maine-Anjou International

Canadian Milking Shorthorn Society
RR#1, 3071 Range Allan, Kinnear's Mills, PQ G0N 1K0
418/424-3246, Fax: 418/424-3528
President, Dale Nugent
Secretary, Patricia Knott
Publications: The Improver

Canadian Morgan Horse Association Inc./Association des chevaux Morgan canadien inc. (CMHA) (1968)
PO Box 286, Port Perry, ON L9L 1A3
905/985-1691, Fax: 905/985-3385, Email: cmha@osha.igs.net
URL: http://www.osha.igs.net/~cmha/index.htm
Office Administrator, Nancy Kavanagh
President, Ivan Mackenzie

Publications: The Canadian Morgan
Affiliates: American Morgan Horse Association

Canadian Murray Grey Association (1970)
PO Box 605, Red Deer, AB T4N 5G6
403/343-1355, Fax: 403/346-4910
President, Kevin E. Willis
1st Vice-President, Harley Herman
2nd Vice-President, Doug Holtby
Sec.-Treas., Doris Burrington
Publications: MG National

Canadian Palomino Horse Breeders Association (1942)
631 Hendershott Rd., RR#1, Hannon, ON L0R 1P0
905/692-4328
President, Cliff Wismer
Secretary, Lorraine Holdaway
Publications: Gold Horse News; Palomino Horse Breeders, q.

Canadian Percheron Association
PO Bag 200, Crossfield, AB T0M 0S0
403/946-5426
Sec.-Treas., Cathie James

Canadian Pinto Horse Association
RR#1, Andrew, AB T0B 0C0
403/895-7399
Secretary, Georgina Campbell
Publications: Canadian Pinto Review

Canadian Pinzgauer Association (CPA) (1974)
PO Box 248, Nanton, AB T0L 1R0
403/646-2193, Fax: 403/646-2193
Executive Secretary, Terry A. Place
Publications: CPA News
Affiliates: Alberta Pinzaguer Association

Canadian Pork Council/Conseil canadien du porc (CPC) (1966)
75 Albert St., Ottawa, ON K1P 5E7
613/236-9239, Fax: 613/236-6658
Executive Secretary, Martin Rice

Canadian Quarter Horse Association
PO Box 1258, Stony Plain, AB T0E 2G0
403/963-3612, Fax: 403/963-8612
President, Peter Rice

Canadian Red Poll Cattle Association (1906)
RR#3, Ponoka, AB T4J 1R3
403/783-5951, Fax: 403/783-6722
President, Carl Blach
Secretary, Jackie Fleming
Publications: Canadian Red Poll Cattle Association Newsletter; Breeders List
Affiliates: Canadian Livestock Records Corporation

Canadian Romagnola-Marchigiana Association
Romark
PO Box 37, Priddis, AB T0L 1W0
403/931-2415, Fax: 403/931-2415
Secretary Manager, Janet Carscallen

Canadian Sheep Breeders Association/La Société Canadienne des Éleveurs de Moutons
c/o Francis Winger, RR#4, Mount Forest, ON N0G 2L0
519/323-0360, Fax: 519/323-0468
President, D.E. Acres, 613/623-5260

Canadian Shorthorn Association
Gummer Bldg., 5 Douglas St., Guelph, ON N1H 2S8
519/822-6841, Fax: 519/822-9753
Sec.-Treas., Patricia Coulson
Publications: Shorthorn News Magazine

Canadian Simmental Association (1969)
#13, 4101 - 19 St. NE, Calgary, AB T2E 7C4
403/250-7979, Fax: 403/250-5121
General Manager, Barry Bennett

Canadian Standardbred Horse Society/Société canadienne du cheval Standardbred (CSHS) (1909)
2150 Meadowvale Blvd., Mississauga, ON L5N 6R6
905/858-3060, Fax: 905/858-8047, Email: cantrot@io.org
URL: http://home.ican.net/~troton
General Manager, Ted Smith
Publications: Trot

Canadian Swine Breeders' Association (1889)
#215, 2435 Holly Lane, Ottawa, ON K1V 7P2
613/731-5531, Fax: 613/731-6655
Manager, Ron James
Publications: Canadian Swine

Canadian Tarentaise Association (1974)
PO Box 5097, Airdrie, AB T4B 2B2
306/948-1212
President, Paulette Martin
Sec.-Treas., Jan Petterson
Publications: Tarentaise Roundup
Affiliates: American Tarentaise Association; SOPEXA - Cambery, France

Canadian Thoroughbred Horse Society/Société canadienne du cheval thoroughbred (CTHS)
PO Box 172, Etobicoke, ON M9W 5L1
416/675-1370, Fax: 416/675-9525
National Executive Secretary, Fran Okihiro

Canadian Trakehner Horse Society (CTHS) (1974)
PO Box 1270, New Hamburg, ON N0B 2G0
519/662-3209, Fax: 519/662-3209, Email: cantrakivh@golden.net
President, Desmond Leeper
Registrar/Secretary, Ingrid Von Hausen
Publications: CTHS Newsletter

Canadian Welsh Black Cattle Society
PO Box 147, Hanna, AB T0J 1P0
403/579-2409
Secretary, Marlene Wallace

La Fédération des producteurs de bovins du Québec/Federation of Québec Beef Producers (FPBQ) (1974)
555, boul Roland-Therrien, Longueuil, PQ J4H 3Y9
514/679-0530, Téléc: 514/442-9348
Secrétaire-trésorier, Gaetan Bélanger
Publications: La Minute Bovine
Organisation(s) affiliée(s): Union des producteurs agricoles

Holstein Association of Canada/Association Holstein du Canada (HAC) (1884)
Holstein Canada
171 Colborne St., PO Box 610, Brantford, ON N3T 5R4
519/756-8300, Fax: 519/756-5878, Email: general@holstein.ca
URL: http://www.holstein.ca/index.htm
Secretary Manager, Keith Flaman
Publications: Info Holstein; Who's Who; Better Breeding Directory

Jersey Canada (1901)
Jersey Cattle Association of Canada
#9, 350 Speedvale Ave. West, Guelph, ON N1H 7M7
519/821-1020, Fax: 519/821-2723
Executive Sec.-Treas., Russell G. Gammon
President, Joan Westwick, 604/746-7076
Publications: Canadian Jersey Breeder
Affiliates: World Jersey Cattle Bureau

National Chinchilla Breeders of Canada (NCBC) (1946)
RR#10, Brampton, ON L6V 3N2
905/451-8736, Fax: 905/457-5326
Sec.-Treas., Betty Stone
Publications: Canada Chinchilla, The Bulletin
Affiliates: Agriculture Canada

Nova Scotia Mink Breeders' Association (1938)
RR#2, Weymouth, NS B0W 3T0
902/837-5565
Secretary, Austin Mullen

The Ontario Farm Animal Council (OFAC) (1988)
7195 Millcreek Dr., Mississauga, ON L5N 4H1
905/821-3880, Fax: 905/858-1589
Executive Director, Leslie Ballentine
Chairman, Mike Cooper
Publications: FAC's

Salers Association of Canada
#228, 2116 - 27 Ave. NE, Calgary, AB T2E 7A6
403/291-2620, Fax: 403/291-2176
Publications: Salers Magazine

Saskatchewan Stock Growers Association (1913)
PO Box 4752, Regina, SK S4P 3Y4
306/757-8523, Fax: 306/569-8799
President, Wilfred Campbell
Manager, Pamela Mitchell
Publications: Saskatchewan Stockgrower
Affiliates: Saskatchewan Angus Association; Saskatchewan Cattle Breeders Association; Saskatchewan Game Farmers Association; Saskatchewan Hereford Association; Saskatchewan Limousin Association; Saskatchewan Maine-Anjou Association; Saskatchewan Shorthorn Association; Saskatchewan Simmental Association; Saskatchewan Swine Breeders Association

Western Ontario Breeders Inc. (WOBI) (1969)
PO Box 457, Woodstock, ON N4S 7Y7
519/539-9831, Fax: 519/537-5391
General Manager, Paul Larmar
Publications: WOBI News

Western Stock Growers' Association (WSGA) (1896)
Stockmen's Centre, #101, 2116 - 27 Ave. NE, Calgary, AB T2E 7A6
403/250-9121, Fax: 403/250-9122
Manager, Pam Miller
Publications: Western Stock Growers Newsletter

World Jersey Cattle Bureau (Canadian Office)
PO Box 90, Richmond Hill, ON L4C 4X9
905/832-2229, Fax: 905/832-2229
Member, F. Redelmeier
Affiliates: Jersey Cattle Association of Canada

ANIMALS & ANIMAL SCIENCE

Animal Alliance of Canada
#101, 221 Broadview Ave., Toronto, ON M4M 2G3
416/462-9541, Fax: 416/462-9647
Director, Legislation & Media Relations, Liz White, 416/921-5256
Publications: Take Action

Animal Defence League of Canada (ADLC) (1958)
PO Box 3880, Stn C, Ottawa, ON K1Y 4M5
613/233-6117
Office Manager, J. Bélair
Publications: News Bulletin

ARK II
Canadian Animal Rights Network
PO Box 687, Stn Q, Toronto, ON M4T 2N5
416/223-4141, Fax: 416/730-8550, Info Line: 416/730-8552
President, Susan Hargreaves
Executive Consultant, Don Reobuck
Publications: The Ark II Activist

Canadian Animal Health Institute/Institut canadien de la santé animale (CAHI) (1968)
27 Cork St., Guelph, ON N1H 2W9
519/763-7777, Fax: 519/763-7407
Executive Director, Jean Szkotnicki
Executive Assistant, Jean Wood
Publications: Communiqué; CAHI Directory

Canadian Association of Animal Health Technologists & Technicians/Association canadienne des techniciens et technologistes en santé animale (CAAHTT) (1989)
PO Box 91, Grandora, SK S0K 1V0
306/329-8660, Fax: 306/283-4829
President, Sandy Hass
Publications: Newsletter

Canadian Association for Laboratory Animal Science (CALAS)
Biosciences Animal Service, University of Alberta, CW 401, Biological Science Bldg., Edmonton, AB T6G 2E9
403/492-5193, Fax: 403/492-7257
Executive Sec.-Treas., Donald G. McKay
Affiliates: International Council for Laboratory Animal Science

Canadian Association of Zoological Parks & Aquariums (CAZPA) (1975)
c/o Calgary Zoo, PO Box 3036, Stn B, Calgary, AB T2M 4R8
President, David R. Banks, 403/232-9300
Publications: CAZPA Newsletter; CAZPA Roster, a.

Canadian Council on Animal Care/Conseil canadien de protection des animaux (1968)
Constitution Square, Tower II, #315, 350 Albert St., Ottawa, ON K1R 1B1
613/238-4031, Fax: 613/238-2837, Email: lroach@bart.ccac.ca
Executive Director, Donald Boisvert, M.D., Ph.D.
Information Officer, Dr. Gillian Griffin
Publications: Resource

Canadian Federation of Humane Societies/ Fédération des sociétés canadiennes d'assistance aux animaux (CFHS) (1957)
#102, 30 Concourse Gate, Nepean, ON K2E 7V7
613/224-8072, Fax: 613/723-0252, Email: cfhs@magi.com
Executive Director, Frances Rodenburg
President, Eleanor Dawson
Publications: Animal Welfare in Focus; Farm Animal Welfare in Focus; Caring for Animals; Whalekind; Humane Education
Affiliates: American Humane Association; World Society for the Protection of Animals; Canadian Nature Federation; Delta Society
Alberta Society for the Prevention of Cruelty to Animals: Executive Director, Neil McDonald; President, Joy Ripley, 10806 - 124 St., Edmonton, AB T5M 0H3, 403/447-3600; Animal Abuse Line: 403/451-2273, Fax: 403/447-4748
Brandon Humane Society: PO Box 922, Brandon, MB R7A 5Z9, 204/728-1333
British Columbia Society for the Prevention of Cruelty to Animals: CEO, Al D. Hickey; President, Dr. Alan Longair, #322, 470 Granville St., Vancouver, BC V6C 1V5, 604/681-7271, Fax: 604/681-7022

Calgary Humane Society: President, Nancy Golding, 1323 - 36 Ave. NE, Calgary, AB T2E 6T6, 403/250-7722, Fax: 403/291-9818

Carleton County Animal Shelter Inc.: Dan Dobbelsteyn, RR#5, Debec, NB E0J 1J0, 506/277-1104

Fort McMurray Society for the Prevention of Cruelty to Animals: Treasurer, Sabrina Qureshi, PO Box 5604, Fort McMurray, AB T9H 3G5, 403/791-4444

Gloucester County Society for the Prevention of Cruelty to Animals: RR#1, Site 37, PO Box 4, Bathurst, NB E2A 3Y5, 506/548-8537

Humane Society Yukon: President, Andrea Lemphers; Secretary, Sandra Richardson, PO Box 5564, Whitehorse, YT Y1A 4Z2, 403/633-4337

London Humane Society; 624 Clarke Rd., London, ON N5V 3K5, 519/451-0630

Montréal SPCA: Executive Director, Tom Knott, 5215, rue Jean Talon ouest, Montréal, PQ H4P 1X4, 514/735-2711, Fax: 514/735-7448

New Brunswick Society for the Prevention of Cruelty to Animals: Executive Director, Raymond Ward; President, Ken Machin, PO Box 23100, Moncton, NB E1A 6S8, 506/857-8698, Fax: 506/383-8000

Newfoundland Society for the Prevention of Cruelty to Animals: President, David G.L. Buffett, LL.B.; Honorary Secretary, Hilda Smith, PO Box 1533, St. John's, NF A1C 5N8, 709/726-0301, Fax: 709/576-7333

Northwest Territories Society for the Prevention of Cruelty to Animals: Treasurer, Sabrina A. Port; President, Colin E.H. Port, PO Box 2278, Yellowknife, NT X1A 2P7, 403/920-4255, Fax: 403/920-4258

Nova Scotia Society for the Prevention of Cruelty: President, William Caudle, #422, 1600 Bedford Hwy., Bedford, NS B4A 1E8, 902/835-4798, Fax: 902/835-7885

Ontario Society for the Prevention of Cruelty to Animals: CEO, Victoria E.R. Earle; Chairman, Donald Cobb, 16640 Yonge St., Newmarket, ON L3Y 4V8, 905/898-7122, Fax: 905/853-8643

Parkland Society for the Prevention of Cruelty to Animals: President, James Glass, PO Box 931, Red Deer, AB T4N 5H3, 403/342-7722, Fax: 403/341-3147

Prince Edward Island Humane Society: President, James Schurman; Executive Director, Janice MacWilliam, PO Box 20022, Sherwood, PE C1A 9E3, 902/892-1190, Fax: 902/892-1191, Toll Free: 1-800-892-1191

Saskatchewan Society for the Prevention of Cruelty to Animals: President, Dr. Ernest Olfert; Secretary, Arlene Eberhardt, PO Box 37, Saskatoon, SK S4P 3G7, 306/382-7722

Société protectrice des animaux de Québec: Présidente, Ginette Garon; Secrétaire, M. George Thompson, 1130, de Galilée, Québec, PQ G1P 4B7, 418/527-9104, Téléc: 418/527-6685

Société québécoise pour la défense des animaux: Directeur général, Hélène Laferrière; Présidente, Johanne Fortin, #401, 1645, boul de Maisonneuve ouest, Montréal, PQ H3H 2N3, 514/932-4260, Téléc: 514/939-0919

Toronto Humane Society: COO, Kathleen Hunter, 11 River St., Toronto, ON M5A 4C2, 416/392-2273, Fax: 416/392-9978

Canadian Kennel Club/Club Canin Canadien (CKC) (1888)
#100, 89 Skyway Ave., Etobicoke, ON M9W 6R4
416/675-5511, Fax: 416/675-6506
URL: http://www.ncf.carleton.ca/freeport/community.associations/kennel-club/menu
CEO, Bryan Hocking
Publications: Dogs in Canada

Canadian Police Canine Association/Association canadienne de chiens policiers
8004 - 4A St. NE, Calgary, AB T2K 5W8
403/274-7401
President, A.B. Amm

Canadian Shire Horse Society
#1882, Concession 10, RR#2, Blackstock, ON L0B 1B0
905/263-8629
Secretary, Peggy Chapman

Canadian Society of Animal Science/Société canadienne de zootechnie (CSAS) (1951)
#907, 151 Slater St., Ottawa, ON K1P 5H4
613/232-9459, Fax: 613/594-5190
President, Mick Price
Sec.-Treas., Dr. Roland Rotter
Publications: Canadian Journal of Animal Science; CSAS Newsletter, q.
Affiliates: World Association for Animal Production

Canadian Society of Zoologists/Société canadienne de zoologie (CSZ) (1961)
Université du Québec à Rimouski, Dép. d'Océanographie, 300, allée des Ursulines, Québec, PQ G5L 3A1
418/724-1704, Fax: 418/724-1842,
Email: jocelyne_pellerin@uqar.uquebec.ca
Président, Dr. Andrew Spencer
Secrétaire, Dr. Jocelyne Pellerin-Massicotte
Publications: Bulletin
Affiliates: Canadian Council on Animal Care

Canadian Vegans for Animal Rights (C-VAR) (1986)
Hudson Bay Centre, 20 Bloor St. East, PO Box 75054, Toronto, ON M4W 3T3
416/924-1377
Director, Michael Schwab

Canadian Veterinary Medical Association/ Association canadienne des vétérinaires (CVMA) (1948)
339 Booth St., Ottawa, ON K1R 7K1
613/236-1162, Fax: 613/236-9681
Executive Director, Claude Paul Boivin
Publications: Canadian Veterinary Journal; Canadian Journal of Veterinary Research, q.

ALBERTA VETERINARY MEDICAL ASSOCIATION (AVMA) (1905)
#100, 8615 - 149 St., Edmonton, AB T5R 1B3
403/489-5007, Fax: 403/484-8311
President, Dr. Brent Jackson
Registrar, Dr. Malcolm Gray
Publications: AVMA Newsletter

BRITISH COLUMBIA VETERINARY MEDICAL ASSOCIATION (BCVMA) (1907)
#155, 1200 West 73 St., Vancouver, BC V6P 6G5
604/266-3441, Fax: 604/266-8447
Director of Member Services, Ilona Rule
Registrar, Dominic Leung
President, Dr. Robert Ashburner
Publications: The Bulletin

MANITOBA VETERINARY MEDICINE ASSOCIATION
#203, 2989 Pembina Hwy., Winnipeg, MB R3T 2H5
204/269-0625, Fax: 204/269-1129
President, Dr. Ron Mentz
Registrar, Sandra McKinnon

NEW BRUNSWICK VETERINARY MEDICAL ASSOCIATION (1919)
PO Box 1065, Moncton, NB E1C 8P2
506/851-7654, Fax: 506/851-2524
President, Dr. Josepha Delay
Executive Director, Dr. R. Pattie
Publications: NBVMA Newsletter

NEWFOUNDLAND & LABRADOR VETERINARY MEDICAL ASSOCIATION (NLVMA)
PO Box 818, Mount Pearl, NF A1N 3C8
709/576-2131, Fax: 709/576-6046
President, Darya Campbell
Sec.-Treas., Helene Van Doninck
Publications: NALVMA Newsletter

NOVA SCOTIA VETERINARY MEDICAL ASSOCIATION
15 Cobequid Rd., Lower Sackville, NS B4C 2M9
902/865-1876, Fax: 902/865-3759
President, Dr. Brian Manuel
Secretary Registrar, Dr. Frank Richardson
Publications: NSVMA Newsletter

ONTARIO VETERINARY MEDICAL ASSOCIATION
245 Commercial St., Milton, ON L9T 2J3
905/875-0756, Fax: 905/875-0958
Executive Director, Martha Smart-Wilder, CAE

PRINCE EDWARD ISLAND VETERINARY MEDICAL ASSOCIATION (1920)
PO Box 100, Montague, PE C0A 1R0
902/838-2281, Fax: 902/838-5077
Sec.-Treas., Dr. David Lister

SASKATCHEWAN VETERINARY MEDICAL ASSOCIATION
#104, 112 Research Dr., Saskatoon, SK S7N 3R3
306/955-7862
President, Dr. Don Wilson
Registrar, K. Ron Presnell
Publications: SVMA Directory

Canadians for Ethical Treatment of Food Animals (CETFA)
2225 West 41st Ave., PO Box 18024, Vancouver, BC V6M 4L3
604/261-3801, Fax: 604/261-3801
National Coordinator, Tina Harrison

College of Veterinarians of Ontario (CVO) (1872)
2106 Gordon St., Guelph, ON N1L 1G6
519/824-5600, Fax: 519/824-6497
Registrar, Dr. John L. Henry
Publications: Update
Affiliates: American Veterinary Medical Association; American Animal Hospital Association

Horse Council of BC (HCBC) (1980)
5746B - 176A St., Cloverdale, BC V3S 4C7
604/576-2722, Fax: 604/576-0401, Toll Free: 1-800-345-8055, Email: hcbc@thebarn.ca
Executive Director, Laurel Morrison
Publications: Horse Industry Directory

Jardin zoologique du Québec (JZQ) (1931)
8173, av du Zoo, Charlesbourg, PQ G1G 4G4
418/622-0313, Téléc: 418/646-9239
Directeur, Jean-Paul Bédard

National Retriever Club of Canada
RR#2, 1348 Mills Rd., Sidney, BC V8L 3S1
250/656-5987
Sec.-Treas., Jane Schmidt

Ordre des médecins vétérinaires du Québec (OMVQ) (1902)
#200, 795, av du Palais, Saint-Hyacinthe, PQ J2S 5C6
514/774-1427, Téléc: 514/774-7635, Ligne sans frais: 1-800-267-1427
Directeur général/Secrétaire, Dr. Marcel Bouvier
Présidente, Dr. Christiane Gagnon
Publications: Vétérinarius; Le Médecine vétérinaire du Québec, trimestriel

PIJAC Canada
Pet Industry Joint Advisory Council
#1001, 4 King St. West, Toronto, ON M5H 1B6

Canadian Almanac & Directory 1997

416/364-9317, Fax: 416/364-9118, Toll Free: 1-800-667-7452
Executive Director, Louis McCann
Secretary, David E. Hill

Regina Humane Society Inc. (1965)
PO Box 3143, Regina, SK S4P 3G7
306/543-6363, Fax: 306/545-7661
President, Jerry Kraus
General Manager, Cathy Costron
Publications: The Voice of the Animals

Société zoologique de Québec inc. (1932)
9141, av du Zoo, Charlesbourg, PQ G1G 4G4
418/627-3072, Téléc: 418/627-2062
Président, Gabriel Filteau
Publications: Ecozoo

Western Federation of Individuals & Dog Organizations (1973)
FIDO
8160 Railway Ave., Richmond, BC V7C 3K2
604/681-1929, Fax: 604/277-4285
President, Frances Clark

World Society for the Protection of Animals/ Société mondiale pour la protection des animaux (WSPA) (1953)
#1310, 44 Victoria St., Toronto, ON M5C 1Y2
416/369-0044, Fax: 416/369-0147, Toll Free: 1-800-363-9772, Email: 102232.3627@compuserve.com
Director, Canadian Operations, Silia Coiro-Smith
Publications: WSPA News

ZOOCHECK Canada Inc.
#1729, 3266 Yonge St., Toronto, ON M4N 3P6
416/696-0241, Fax: 416/696-0370, Email: zoocheck@idirect.com
Rob Laidlaw
Holly Penfound
Barry MacKay
Julie Woodyer
Lesli Bisgould
Andrea Villiers
Publications: Newsletter
Affiliates: American Association of Zookeepers; Canadian Association of Zoological Parks & Aquariums; Canadian Federation of Humane Societies

Zoological Society of Metropolitan Toronto (1969)
PO Box 370, Scarborough, ON M1E 4Y9
416/392-9100, Fax: 416/392-9115
President, Calvin White
Chair, David LaFayette
Publications: News Prints; Collections
Affiliates: Canadian Association of Zoos, Parks & Aquariums; American Association of Zoos, Parks & Aquariums; Canadian Centre for Philanthropy

Zoological Society of Montréal/Société zoologique de Montréal (1964)
2055 Peel, Montréal, PQ H3A 1V4
514/845-8317
Contact, Marlene Harris
Contact, George E. Midgley
Publications: The Zoological Society Newsletter

ANTIQUES

Antiquarian Booksellers' Association of Canada/ Association de la librairie ancienne du Canada (ABAC) (1966)
145 Main St. West, Port Colborne, ON L3K 3V3
905/834-5323, Fax: 905/834-5323, Email: alphabet@iaw.com
URL: http://206.217.21.64/ca/index.html
President, Richard Shuh, 905/834-5323
Secretary, Cameron Treleaven, 403/282-5832
Publications: ABAC/ALAC National Newsletter

Antique Automobile Club of America
501 West Governor Rd., Hershey, PA 17033 USA
717/534-1910
Executive Director, William H. Smith
Publications: Antique Automobile
Lord Selkirk Region: Contact, S. Jerry McCreery, #709, 595 River Ave., Winnipeg, MB R3L 0E6
Maple Leaf Region: Contact, David J. Gurney, PO Box 809, Richmond Hill, ON K0A 2Z0
Ontario Region: Contact, Bob Kelly, RR#2, Peterborough, ON K9J 6X3
St. Lawrence Valley Region: Contact, Steven J. Latimer, RR#4, Brockville, ON K6V 5T4

Antique & Classic Boat Society Inc. (Toronto) (1980)
PO Box 305, Islington, ON M9A 4X3
416/299-3311
President, Andrew Dyment
Publications: Classic Boat

Antique & Classic Car Club of Canada
41 Summer Dr., Scarborough, ON M1K 3E4
416/261-5571
Contact, Bud Murray
Publications: The Reflector

Canadian Antique Dealers Association (CADA)
250 Eglinton Ave. East, PO Box 89544, Toronto, ON M4P 3E1
416/961-6211
President, Robert Dirstein

Historic Vehicle Society of Ontario (HVSO) (1959)
PO Box 221, Harrow, ON N0R 1G0
519/776-6909, Fax: 519/776-8321
Administrator, Georgia Klym Skeates
Publications: HVSO Newsletter

Manitoba Antique Association
PO Box 2881, Winnipeg, MB R3C 4B4
Secretary, Gae Burns, 204/885-2781

Vintage Automobile Racing Association of Canada
2467 Yonge St., Toronto, ON M4P 2H6
416/487-8166; 416/482-4017, Fax: 416/488-9013
President, Mike Rosen

Vintage Locomotive Society Inc. (1968)
PO Box 33021, RPO Polo Park, Winnipeg, MB R3G 3N4
204/832-5259
Sec.-Treas., K. Gordon Younger
Publications: The Journal Box

ARBITRATION *see* **LABOUR RELATIONS**

ARCHAEOLOGY

Archaeological Society of British Columbia (ASBC) (1966)
PO Box 520, Stn A, Vancouver, BC V6C 2N3
604/822-2567, Fax: 604/822-6161
President, Joyce Johnson
Publications: The Midden
Affiliates: Society of American Archaeology

Canadian Archaeological Association/ Association d'archéologie canadienne (1968)
Space 162 - Box 127, 3170 Tillicum Rd., Victoria, BC V9A 7H7
250/478-1147, Fax: 250/388-7373
Executive Secretary, Bjorn O. Simonsen
Publications: Canadian Journal of Archaeology/ Journal canadien d'archéologie; Canadian Archaeological Association Newsletter, s-a.
Affiliates: Society of American Archaeology

ARCHAEOLOGICAL SOCIETY OF ALBERTA (ASA) (1975)
1202 Lansdowne Ave. SW, Calgary, AB T2S 1A6
403/243-4340
Executive Sec.-Treas., Jeanne Cody
Publications: Alberta Archaeological Review

ASSOCIATION DES ARCHÉOLOGUES DU QUÉBEC (AAQ) (1979)
CP 322, Succ Haute-Ville, Montréal, PQ G1R 4P8
514/525-7071, Téléc: 514/525-7071
Président, Jean-Yves Pintal

NOVA SCOTIA ARCHAEOLOGY SOCIETY
PO Box 36090, Halifax, NS B3J 3S9
902/823-1879
President, Dr. David Keenleyside
Treasurer, Lynne Schwarz

SASKATCHEWAN ARCHAEOLOGICAL SOCIETY (SAS) (1963)
#5, 816 - 1 Ave. North, Saskatoon, SK S7K 1Y3
306/664-4124, Fax: 306/665-1928, Email: ad583@sfn.saskatoon.sk.ca
Executive Director, Tim Jones
Business Administrator, Linda Drever
Publications: Saskatchewan Archaeological Society Newsletter; Saskatchewan Archaeology, a.

Manitoba Archaeological Society Inc. (MAS) (1961)
PO Box 1171, Winnipeg, MB R3C 2Y4
204/942-7243, Fax: 204/942-3749
President, A.P. Buchner
Vice-President, Leslie Burns
Publications: Manitoba Archaeological Journal

Newfoundland & Labrador Association of Amateur Archaeologists
108 New Cove Rd., St. John's, NF A1A 2C2
709/753-0665
President, Bruce Ryan

The Ontario Archaeological Society Inc. (1950)
126 Willowdale Ave., North York, ON M2N 4Y2
416/730-0797, Fax: 416/730-0797, Email: oas@io.org
Executive Director, Ellen Blaubergs
President, Henry van Lieshout
Publications: Arch Notes; Ontario Archaeology, a.

Ontario Society of Industrial Archaeology (OSIA) (1982)
88 Upper Canada Dr., North York, ON M2P 1S4
416/207-5872, Fax: 416/207-5911
President, Ian Livsey
Publications: OSIA Bulletin
Affiliates: The International Committee for the Conservation of the Industrial Heritage

Save Ontario Shipwrecks (SOS) (1981)
#310, 2175 Sheppard Ave. East, North York, ON M2J 1W8
416/491-2373, Fax: 416/491-1670
URL: http://yoda.sscl.uwo.ca/assoc/sos/
President, Barry Lyons
Publications: S.O.S. News
Affiliates: Underwater Council

Canadian Almanac & Directory 1997

Underwater Archaeological Society of British Columbia (1975)
c/o Vancouver Maritime Museum, 1905 Ogden Ave., Vancouver, BC V6J 1A3
604/257-8303, Fax: 604/737-2621
Executive Director, David Stone
President, Robyn Woodward
Publications: The FogHorn

ARCHITECTURE

Alberta Association of Architects (AAA) (1906)
Duggan House, 10515 Saskatchewan Dr., Edmonton, AB T6E 4S1
403/432-0224, Fax: 403/439-1431
Executive Director, Penny A. Cairns
President, Fraser Brinsmead, MRAIC
Publications: Columns: the Newsletter of the Alberta, Saskatchewan & Manitoba Associations of Architects

Architects Association of New Brunswick/ Association des architectes du Nouveau-Brunswick (AANB) (1933)
73 Duke St., Saint John, NB E2L 1N4
506/658-6116
Executive Director, N. Lynn Cornfield
Publications: Searching for Context

Architects Association of Prince Edward Island (AAPEI)
PO Box 1766, Charlottetown, PE C1A 7N4
902/892-8908, Fax: 902/368-7403
President, Larry Jones

The Architectural Conservancy of Ontario Inc.
Ontario Heritage Centre, #204, 10 Adelaide St. East, Toronto, ON M5C 1J3
416/367-8075, Fax: 416/947-1066
President, Alice King Sculthorpe
Publications: Acorn

Architectural Institute of British Columbia (AIBC) (1914)
#103, 131 Water St., Vancouver, BC V6B 4M3
604/683-8588, Fax: 604/683-8568, Toll Free: 1-800-667-0753, Email: aibc@aibc.bc.ca
URL: http://www.aibc.bc.ca/home.html
Executive Director, Cheryl Williams
President, B. Maples
Publications: AIBC Newsletter

Association des Architectes en pratique privée du Québec/Association of Architects in Private Practice of Québec (AAPPQ) (1977)
#600, 417, rue Saint-Pierre, Montréal, PQ H2Y 2M4
514/985-5371, Téléc: 514/985-5375
Directeur général, Claude Letarte
Publications: Nouvelles brèves

Association of Architectural Technologists of Ontario (AATO) (1969)
#407, 150 Consumers Rd., North York, ON M2J 1P9
416/493-6758, Fax: 416/493-6758 (voice req.), Toll Free: 1-800-563-2286
URL: http://aecinfo.com/assoc/aato/index.htm
Administrative Secretary, Rita Staniforth
Publications: AATO News

Design Exchange (DX) (1987)
The Group for the Creation of a Design Centre in Toronto
Toronto Dominion Centre, 234 Bay St., PO Box 18, Toronto, ON M5K 1B2
416/363-6121, Fax: 416/368-0684
President, Howard Cohen

Manitoba Association of Architects (MAA)
137 Bannatyne Ave., 2nd Fl., Winnipeg, MB R3B 0R3
204/925-4620, Fax: 204/925-4624
URL: http://cad9.cadlab.umanitoba.ca/MAA.html
Executive Director, Judy Pestrak
President, Andrew K. Wach
Publications: Columns: the Newsletter of the Alberta, Saskatchewan & Manitoba Associations of Architects

Newfoundland Association of Architects
PO Box 5204, St. John's, NF A1C 5V5
709/726-8550, Fax: 709/726-1549
President, Paul Blackwood
Administrative Assistant, Lynda Hayward

Northwest Territories Architectural Society
PO Box 1394, Yellowknife, NT X1A 2P1
403/920-2609, Fax: 403/920-4261
Contact, Darrell Vikse

Nova Scotia Association of Architects (NSAA) (1932)
1361 Barrington St., Halifax, NS B3J 1Y9
902/423-7607, Fax: 902/425-7024
Executive Director, Diane Scott-Stewart
President, John Emmett, MRAIC

Ontario Association of Architects (OAA) (1889)
111 Moatfield Dr., North York, ON M3B 3L6
416/449-6898, Fax: 416/449-5756, Toll Free: 1-800-565-2724
Executive Director, Brian Watkinson
President, Anthony J. Griffiths
Director of Communications, Phyllis Clasby
Publications: Directory of Architects; Perspectives

Ordre des architectes du Québec (OAQ) (1890)
1825, boul René-Lévesque ouest, Montréal, PQ H3H 1R4
514/937-6168, Téléc: 514/933-0242
Directrice générale, Beatrice Kowaliczko
Publications: Esquisses

Royal Architectural Institute of Canada/Institut royal d'architecture du Canada (RAIC) (1907)
#330, 55 Murray St., Ottawa, ON K1N 5M3
613/241-3600, Fax: 613/241-5750
URL: http://www.aecinfo.com/raic/index.html
Executive Director, Timothy Kehoe
President, Paul-André Tétreault, FIRAC
Director of Services, Alexandra Fitzgerald
Publications: RAIC Update; En Bref; Canadian Architectural Directory; RAIC Directory of Scholarships & Awards for Architecture; Advanced Buildings, bi-m.

Saskatchewan Association of Architects (SAA) (1911)
#200, 642 Broadway Ave., Saskatoon, SK S7N 1A9
306/242-0733, Fax: 306/664-2598
Executive Director, Margaret Topping
Publications: Columns: the Newsletter of the Alberta, Saskatchewan & Manitoba Associations of Architects

Society for the Study of Architecture in Canada/ Société pour l'étude de l'architecture au Canada (SSAC) (1974)
PO Box 2302, Stn D, Ottawa, ON K1P 5W5
President, Dorothy Field
Vice-President, Rhodri Windsor-Liscombe
Publications: Society for the Study of Architecture in Canada Bulletin/Bulletin de la Société pour l'étude de l'architecture au Canada
Affiliates: Society of Architectural Historians

ARCHIVES see **LIBRARIES & ARCHIVES**

ARMED FORCES see **MILITARY & VETERANS**

ARMS CONTROL see **INTERNATIONAL COOPERATION/INTERNATIONAL RELATIONS**

ART FESTIVALS see **EVENTS**

ARTS
see also Visual Art, Crafts, Folk Arts

Alberta Foundation for the Arts (1991)
Beaver House, 10158 - 103 St., 5th Fl., Edmonton, AB T5J 0X6
403/427-9968, Fax: 403/422-1162
Executive Director, Clive Padfield

Arts Foundation of Greater Toronto
#402, 151 John St., Toronto, ON M5V 2T2
416/597-8223, Fax: 416/597-6956
Executive Director, Julia Howell
President, Richard Ouzounian
Publications: Arts Foundation News

Assembly of BC Arts Councils
#201, 3737 Oak St., Vancouver, BC V6H 2M4
604/738-0749, Fax: 604/738-5161
Executive Director, Deborah Meyers

Association of National Non-Profit Artists' Centres/Regroupement des artistes des centres alternatifs (ANNPAC) (1976)
183 Bathurst St., Main Fl., Toronto, ON M5T 2R7
416/869-1275, 3854, Fax: 416/360-0781
President, Roger Lee
Publications: Parallélogramme
Affiliates: National Association of Artists' Organizations; Canadian Artists Representation; Canadian Conference of the Arts

Canadian Artists' Representation/Le Front des artistes canadiens (CARFAC) (1968)
100 Gloucester St., #B1, Ottawa, ON K2P 0A4
613/231-6277, Fax: 613/231-6315
National Director, Greg Graham
National Representative, Glen MacKinnon
Communications Officer, Flora Kallies
Publications: CARNET
Affiliates: International Association of Art; Canadian Conference of the Arts

Canadian Arts Presenting Association/ l'Association canadienne des organismes artistiques (CAPACOA) (1985)
189 Laurier Ave. East, Ottawa, ON K1N 6P1
613/567-8323, Fax: 613/567-5688, Email: capacoa@magi.com
URL: http://www.ffa.ucalgary.ca/capacoa/
Executive Director, Peter Feldman
Publications: CAPACOA Newsletter

Canadian Association of Artists Managers/ Association canadienne de direction d'artistes (CAAM)
c/o Renée Simmons Artists Management, 117 Ava Rd., Toronto, ON M6C 1W2
416/782-7712, Fax: 416/256-7657

Canadian Celtic Arts Association
University of Toronto, St. Michael's College, 81 St. Mary St., Toronto, ON M5S 1J4
416/926-7145, Fax: 416/926-7276
Membership Secretary, Jean Talman
Publications: CCAA Newsletter; Garm Lu, s-a.

Canadian Conference of the Arts/Conférence canadienne des arts (CCA) (1945)
189 Laurier Ave. West, Ottawa, ON K1N 6P1
613/238-3561, Fax: 613/238-4849, Toll Free: 1-800-463-3561, Email: ccarts@globalx.net
National Director, Keith Kelly
President, Mireille Gagné
Publications: Directory of the Arts/l'Annuaire des arts

Canadian Institute of the Arts for Young Audiences/Institut canadien des arts pour jeunes publics
#302, 601 Cambie St., Vancouver, BC V6B 2P1
604/687-7697, Fax: 604/669-3613, Email: kidsfest@youngarts.ca
URL: http://www.wimsey.com/Youngarts/
Executive Director, Marjorie MacLean

Conseil des arts et des lettres du Québec
#1500, 500, Place d'Armes, Montréal, PQ H2Y 2W2
514/864-3350, Téléc: 514/864-4160, Ligne sans frais: 1-800-608-3350

Council for Business & the Arts in Canada/Conseil pour le monde des affaires et des arts du Canada (CBAC) (1974)
#1507, 401 Bay St., PO Box 7, Toronto, ON M5H 2Y4
416/869-3016, Fax: 416/869-0435
President & CEO, Sarah Iley
Publications: CBAC News; CBAC Survey of Performing Arts Organizations, a.; CBAC Survey of Public Museums & Arts Galleries; CBAC Survey of Corporate Donations

Federation of Canadian Artists (FCA) (1989)
1241 Cartwright St., Vancouver, BC V6H 4B7
604/681-8534, Fax: 604/681-2740
President, Joyce Kamikura
Gallery Manager, Katie Reid
Publications: FCA News

Governor General's Performing Arts Foundation (1992)
PO Box 1534, Stn B, Ottawa, ON K1P 5W1
613/947-0631, Fax: 613/996-2828
Co-Chair, Peter Herrndorf
Co-Chair, Monique Mercure

Manitoba Arts Council/Conseil des Arts du Manitoba (MAC)
#525, 93 Lombard Ave., Winnipeg, MB R3B 3B1
204/945-2237, Fax: 204/945-5925
Executive Director, Victor Jerrett Enns
Publications: ArtVentures Newsletter

New Brunswick Arts Council Inc. (NBAC) (1979)
Brunswick Sq., 3rd Level, 39 King St., Saint John, NB E2L 4W3
506/635-8019, Fax: 506/635-8603
Coordinator, Sandra Donnelly
President, Jill Smith
Publications: Newsletter

Newfoundland & Labrador Arts Council (NLAC) (1980)
PO Box 98, Stn C, St. John's, NF A1C 5H5
709/726-2212, Fax: 709/726-0619
Chairman, Ronald Rompkey

Northwest Territories Arts Council
c/o NWT Education, Culture & Employment, PO Box 1320, Stn Main, Yellowknife, NT X1A 2L9
403/920-3103, Fax: 403/873-0487
Arts Liaison Coordinator, Tom Hudson

Ontario Arts Council/Conseil des arts de l'Ontario (OAC)
#600, 151 Bloor St. West, Toronto, ON M5S 1T6
416/961-1660, Fax: 416/961-7796, Toll Free: 1-800-387-0058, Email: oac@gov.on.ca
Executive Director, Gwenlyn Setterfield

Organization of Saskatchewan Arts Councils (OSAC) (1968)
1102 - 8 Ave., Regina, SK S4R 1C9
306/586-1250, Fax: 306/586-1550
Executive Director, Dennis Garreck
Communications Coordinator, Michelle Lavallee
Publications: OSAC News

PEI Council of the Arts (1974)
151 Richmond St., Charlottetown, PE C1A 1H7
902/368-4410, Fax: 902/368-4418
Executive Director, Judy MacDonald
Publications: PEI Council of Arts
Affiliates: West Prince Arts Council; East Kings Arts Council; Conseil des arts evangeline; Southern Kings Arts Council; South Shore Arts Council; Malpak Arts Council

Performing Arts Publicists Association Manitoba
#1B, 1 Roslyn Rd., Winnipeg, MB R3L 0G1
204/477-4191, Fax: 204/284-1842
Chairman, Norman Elson

Performing Arts Publicists Association Nova Scotia
PAPA Nova Scotia
#201, 5475 Spring Garden Rd., Halifax, NS B3J 1G2
902/426-6000, Fax: 902/426-8901
Marketing Officer, Amy Stewart

Performing Arts Publicists Association of Ontario (PAPA) (1976)
PAPA Ontario
c/o Ontario Arts Council, #600, 151 Bloor St. West, Toronto, ON M5S 1T6
416/698-0607, Fax: 416/698-0607
Chairman, Teri MacFarlane
Publications: PAPA Press

Performing Arts Publicists Association/Edmonton & Northern Alberta (1988)
PAPA Edmonton
PO Box 1704, Edmonton, AB T5J 2P1
President, James Morrissey

Professional Arts Publicists Association/Calgary & Southern Alberta (1987)
PAPA Calgary
PO Box 1240, Stn M, Calgary, AB T2P 2L2
403/228-9388, Fax: 403/229-3598, Telex: 038-27873
President, Edmund A. Oliverio
Publications: PAPA News
Affiliates: Canadian Film Celebration Society of Calgary

Saskatchewan Arts Alliance Corp. (SAA) (1984)
PO Box 3765, Regina, SK S4P 3N8
306/652-6122, Fax: 306/652-6628
President, Terry Schwalm
Treasurer, Karen Haggman
Administrator, Mark Rudoff

Vancouver Cultural Alliance (VCA) (1986)
#100, 938 Howe St., Vancouver, BC V6Z 1N9
604/681-3535, Fax: 604/681-7848, Info Line: 604/684-2787, Email: arts_yvr@cyberstore.net
URL: http://www.culturenet.ca/vca
Executive Director, Lori Baxter
Communications Manager, Doti Niedermayer

Yukon Arts Council (YAC) (1971)
PO Box 5120, Whitehorse, YT Y1A 4S3
403/668-6284, Info Line: 403/667-7787
Resource Administrator, Lilyan Grubach
Publications: Yukon Arts Council Newsletter

AUDITING see **ACCOUNTING**

AUTOMOTIVE
see also Transportation & Shipping

Association des propriétaires d'autobus du Québec/Québec Bus Owners Association (APAQ) (1927)
#107, 225, boul Charest est, Québec, PQ G1K 3G9
418/522-7131, Téléc: 418/522-6455, Courrier électronique: apaq@apaq.qc.ca
URL: http://www.apaq.qc.ca
Vice-président exécutif/Directeur général, Jacques Guay
Publications: Le Billet du bus; La Revue du bus, 10 fois par an

Association des spécialistes du pneu du Québec inc./Québec Tire Specialists Association Inc. (ASPQ) (1969)
#201, 407, boul Saint-Laurent, Montréal, PQ H2Y 2Y5
514/874-3716, Téléc: 514/866-5580
Directrice exécutive, Linda Carbone
Publications: INFOPNEUS

Automobile Dealers Association of Newfoundland
81 Smallwood Dr., Mount Pearl, NF A1N 1B2
709/364-9474, Fax: 709/364-9474
Business Manager, Fred J. Marshall

Automobile Journalists Association of Canada/Association des journalistes automobile du Canada (AJAC)
77 Wembley Dr., Toronto, ON M4L 3C9
416/463-2658, Fax: 416/463-0866
Administrator, Bert Coates
President, Alex Law
Publications: Express; Directory, s-a.

Automobile Protection Association/Association pour la protection automobile (APA)
292, boul St. Joseph ouest, Montréal, PQ H2V 2N7
514/272-5555, Fax: 514/273-0797
Président - directeur général, George Iny
Coordinateur administrative, Dany Duchemin
Publications: Roulez sans vous faire rouler Lemon Aid

Automotive Aftermarket Retailers of Ontario
#10, 5100 South Service Rd., Burlington, ON L7L 6A5
905/634-4040, Fax: 905/634-6274, Toll Free: 1-800-268-5400
Executive Director, William Burkimsher

Automotive Industries Association of Canada/Association des industries de l'automobile (AIA Canada)
1272 Wellington St., Ottawa, ON K1Y 3A7
613/728-5821, Fax: 613/728-6021, Email: aia@aia-canada.com
URL: http://www.aftmkt.com
President, Dean Wilson
Vice-President, Yaroslaw Zajac
Vice-President, Administration, Beverly Cook
Manager, Communications Services, Denise Faguy
Manager, Marc Brazeau
Publications: Aftermarket Update; Aftermarket Watch

Automotive Parts Manufacturers' Association/Association des fabricants de pièces d'automobile (APMA) (1952)
#516, 195 The West Mall, Etobicoke, ON M9C 5K1

Canadian Almanac & Directory 1997

416/620-4220, Fax: 416/620-9730
President, Pete Mateja
Publications: APMA Bulletin

Automotive Retailers Association of British Columbia (1951)
#1, 8980 Fraserwood Ct., Burnaby, BC V5J 5H7
604/432-7987, Fax: 604/432-1756
Executive Director, D. Robert Clarke
Publications: Automotive Retailer;

Automotive Trades Association (Manitoba) Inc. (ATA) (1937)
#105, 1200 Pembina Hwy., Winnipeg, MB R3T 2A6
204/475-3235, Fax: 204/453-5743
President, Herb Wittenberg
Business Manager, J. Henry Brodersen
Publications: Newsletter
Affiliates: Society of Collision Repair Specialists

Canadian All-Terrain Vehicle Distributors Council/Conseil canadien des distributeurs de véhicules tout terrain (CATV) (1984)
#235, 7181 Woodbine Ave., Markham, ON L3R 1A3
905/470-9406, Fax: 905/470-9407
Executive Director, Robert Ramsay

Canadian Association of Japanese Automobile Dealers (CAJAD) (1982)
#101, One Eva Rd., Etobicoke, ON M9C 4Z5
416/620-9717, Fax: 416/620-0392, Toll Free: 1-800-263-4340
Executive Director, Brian B. Caldwell
Director, Public Affairs, Michael Edmonds
Publications: Connections/Connexions

Canadian Automobile Association/Association canadienne des automobilistes (CAA) (1913)
#200, 1145 Hunt Club Rd., Ottawa, ON K1V 0Y3
613/247-0117, Fax: 613/247-0118
URL: http://www.caa.ca
President & CEO, Brian A. Hunt
Chairman, Raymond A. Cadieux, C.A.
Publications: Autopinion; The Motorist's Advocate
Affiliates: Alliance internationale de tourisme; Fédération internationale de l'automobile; Federacion interamericana de touring y automovil-clubes; Commonwealth Motoring Conference; American Automobile Association

ALBERTA MOTOR ASSOCIATION
10310 G.A. MacDonald Ave., Edmonton, AB T6J 6R7
403/430-5555, Fax: 403/430-5676, Toll Free: 1-800-642-3810
Contact, David Barr

BRITISH COLUMBIA AUTOMOBILE ASSOCIATION (BCAA) (1906)
4567 Canada Way, Burnaby, BC V5G 4T1
604/268-5000, Fax: 604/268-5560, Toll Free: 1-800-663-1956
URL: http://www.bcaa.bc.ca
President & CEO, William G. Bullis
Director, Public Affairs, Ellen Chesney, 604/268-5340
Publications: Westworld

CAA MANITOBA MOTOR LEAGUE
870 Empress St., Winnipeg, MB R3C 2Z3
204/987-6161, Fax: 204/775-9989
Contact, Donna Wankling

CANADIAN AUTOMOBILE ASSOCIATION MARITIMES
CAA Maritimes
737 Rothesay Ave., Saint John, NB E2H 2H6
506/634-1400, Fax: 506/653-9500, Toll Free: 1-800-561-8807
President, Steve McCall

CANADIAN AUTOMOBILE ASSOCIATION QUÉBEC (1904)
CAA Québec
444, rue Bouvier, Québec, PQ G2J 1E3
418/624-2424, Téléc: 418/624-3297, Ligne sans frais: 1-800-463-7232
Contact, Paul A. Pelletier
Publications: Touring; Vacances pour tous, trimestriel

CANADIAN AUTOMOBILE ASSOCIATION SASKATCHEWAN
CAA Saskatchewan
200 Albert St. North, Regina, SK S4R 5E2
306/791-4321, Fax: 306/791-4321
Contact, Gerald Butler

CANADIAN AUTOMOBILE ASSOCIATION CENTRAL ONTARIO (1903)
CAA Central Ontario
60 Commerce Valley Dr. East, Thornhill, ON L3T 7P9
905/771-3000, Fax: 905/771-3101
President, Stephen A. Wilgar
Publications: LeisureWays

CANADIAN AUTOMOBILE ASSOCIATION ELGIN NORFOLK
CAA Elgin Norfolk
1091 Talbot St., St Thomas, ON N5P 1G4
519/631-6490, Fax: 519/631-6578, Toll Free: 1-800-265-4343
Contact, Ms. Pat Jackson

CANADIAN AUTOMOBILE ASSOCIATION MID-WESTERN ONTARIO (1915)
CAA Mid-Western Ontario
PO Box 9030, Stn C, Kitchener, ON N2G 4W8
519/894-2582, Fax: 519/893-5512, Toll Free: 1-800-265-8975
President, Grady Liddle
Publications: Leisure World

CANADIAN AUTOMOBILE ASSOCIATION NIAGARA
CAA Niagara
3271 Schmon Pkwy., Thorold, ON L2V 4Y6
905/984-8585, Fax: 905/688-0289, Toll Free: 1-800-263-7272
Contact, Robert J. Spence

CANADIAN AUTOMOBILE ASSOCIATION NORTHEASTERN ONTARIO (1964)
CAA Northeastern Ontario
The Oaks Mall, 2140 Regent St., Sudbury, ON P3E 5S8
705/522-0000, Fax: 705/522-5202, Toll Free: 1-800-461-7111
President & CEO, R.J. Smith

CANADIAN AUTOMOBILE ASSOCIATION OTTAWA
CAA Ottawa
2525 Carling Ave., Ottawa, ON K2B 7Z2
613/820-1890, Fax: 613/820-4646
President, Brian A. Hunt

CANADIAN AUTOMOBILE ASSOCIATION PETERBOROUGH
CAA Peterborough
680 The Queensway, PO Box 1957, Peterborough, ON K9J 7X7
705/743-4343, Fax: 705/743-9740

CANADIAN AUTOMOBILE ASSOCIATION THUNDER BAY
CAA Thunder Bay
585 Memorial Ave., Thunder Bay, ON P7B 3Z1
807/345-1261, Fax: 807/345-8944
Contact, Greg Fayrik

CANADIAN AUTOMOBILE ASSOCIATION WINDSOR
CAA Windsor
1215 Ouellette Ave., Windsor, ON N8X 1J3
519/255-1212, Fax: 519/255-7379, Toll Free: 1-800-265-5681
Contact, Keith Robinson

Canadian Automobile Dealers Association (CADA) (1941)
85 Renfrew Dr., Markham, ON L3R 0N9
905/940-4959, Fax: 905/940-6870, Toll Free: 1-800-463-5289
President, Kenneth R. Graydon
Chairman, Douglas Leggat
Publications: Newsline

Canadian Automobile Sport Clubs - Ontario Region Inc. (CASC-OR) (1964)
703 Petrolia Rd., Downsview, ON M3J 2N6
416/667-9500, Fax: 416/667-9555
Business Manager, R.M. Varey
President, Martin Chenhall

Canadian Automotive Repair & Service Council (1991)
CARS Council
#230, 440 Laurier Ave. West, Ottawa, ON K1R 7X6
613/782-2402, Fax: 613/782-2362
President, Daniel Bell
Chairman, Norman Clark
Secretary, Kenneth R. Graydon
Treasurer, William Burkimsher
Publications: CARS Insider; L'Autoscope CARS, trimestriel
Affiliates: CARS Institute

Canadian Automotive Repair & Service Institute/ Institut du service d'entretien et de reparation automobiles du Canada (1991)
CARS Institute
#230, 440 Laurier Ave. West, Ottawa, ON K1R 7X6
613/782-2402, Fax: 613/782-2362, Toll Free: 1-800-661-2277
Executive Director, Keith Lancastle
Affiliates: CARS Council

Canadian Tire Dealers Association
#1707, 2200 Yonge St., Toronto, ON M4S 2C6
416/486-8032, Fax: 416/484-6902
Executive Director, Terry Connoy

Canadian Towing Society/Société canadienne de remorquage (1985)
PO Box 128, Bancroft, ON K0L 1C0
613/332-1666, Fax: 613/332-0623
Administrator, Brent Anderson

Corporation des concessionnaires d'automobiles du Québec inc. (CCAQ) (1945)
#750, 140, Grande-Allée est, Québec, PQ G1R 5M8
418/523-2991, Téléc: 418/523-3725
Président-directeur général, Jacques Béchard
Secrétaire, Suzanne Gauthier
Relationiste, Jean Cadoret
Publications: Bref; Contact, trimestriel
Organisation(s) affiliée(s): Eastern Townships Automobile Dealers Association; Eastern Québec Automobile Dealers Association; Laurentian Automobile Dealers Association; Mauricie Automobile Dealers Association; Montréal Automobile Dealers Association; North-Western Québec Automobile Dealers Association; Outaouais Automobile Dealers Association; Québec Automobile Dealers Association; Richelieu Automobile Dealers Association; Saguenay-Lac-St-Jean Automobile Dealers Association

Japan Automobile Manufacturers Association of Canada (JAMA Canada) (1984)
#1406, 2 Sheppard Ave. East, Toronto, ON M2N 5Y7
416/222-9515, Fax: 416/226-6774
Executive Director, David Worts

Manitoba Motor Dealers Association (1944)
#203, 2281 Portage Ave., Winnipeg, MB R3J 0M1
204/889-4924, Fax: 204/885-6552
Executive Director, Shirley Canty

Motor Dealers' Association of Alberta (1950)
9249 - 48 St., Edmonton, AB T6B 2R9
403/468-9552, Fax: 403/465-6201
URL: http://www.compusmart.ab.ca/mdaalta
President, Bill Watkin
Publications: Driveline

Motor Dealers' Association of BC (1943)
MDA of BC
3657 Wayburne Dr., Burnaby, BC V5G 3L1
604/294-8330, Fax: 604/298-8726
Executive Vice-President, Marion Keys
Publications: Signals
Affiliates: Automobile Dealers' Association of Greater Vancouver (same address & contact)

Motor Vehicle Manufacturers' Association/ Association des fabricants de véhicules à moteur (MVMA) (1926)
#1602, 25 Adelaide St. East, Toronto, ON M5C 1Y7
416/364-9333, Fax: 416/367-3221
President, Mark A. Nantais
Chairman, G. Yves Landry

National Auto League
248 Pall Mall St., PO Box 5845, London, ON N6A 4T4
519/434-3221, Fax: 519/434-5220
President, Glen Bessey
Affiliates: National Truck League
Regional Offices
Hull Regional Office: #303, 655, boul St-Joseph, Hull, PQ J8Y 4B3, 819/777-0086, Fax: 819/777-9066
Kitchener Regional Office: Manager, Link Bourne, #9, 279 Weber St. North, Waterloo, ON N2J 3H8, 519/746-5533, Fax: 519/746-6201
London Office: Manager, Glenn Caldwell, #110, 379 Dundas St., London, ON N6B 1S4, 519/439-0446, Fax: 519/439-4727
Ottawa Regional Office: Chateau Royale Professional Building, 1390 Prince of Wales, Ottawa, ON K2C 3N6, 613/225-6221, Fax: 613/596-2207
Québec Regional Office: Manager, Michel Lacasse, #108, 6955 Taschereau Blvd., Brossard, PQ J4Z 1A7, 514/462-3413, Fax: 514/462-2093
St Catharines Regional Office: Manager, Rene McKenzie, 33 Lakeshore Rd., St Catharines, ON L2R 2E1, 905/938-1331
Sudbury Regional Office: Montrose Mall, 788 Lasalle Blvd., Sudbury, ON P3A 4V4, 705/566-0278, Fax: 705/566-4192
Toronto Regional Office: Manager, Peter Hornung, #223, 1750 Steeles Ave. West, Concord, ON L4K 2L7, 905/798-7009, Fax: 905/738-6323
Windsor Regional Office: Manager, Bill Baker, #207, 1541 Ouellette Ave., Windsor, ON N8X 1K6, 519/971-7474, Fax: 519/971-0894

National Automotive Equipment Association (NAEA) (1989)
#11-12, 1520 Trinity Dr., Mississauga, ON L5T 1N9
905/564-7373, Fax: 905/564-7408
President, David Clarke
Secretary, Robert McVey

New Brunswick Automobile Dealers' Association
202 Pleasant St., PO Box 294, Newcastle, NB E1V 3M4
506/622-1422, Fax: 506/622-4498
Manager, George E. Irlam

Nova Scotia Automobile Dealers' Association
PO Box 9410, Stn A, Halifax, NS B3K 5S3
902/425-2445, Fax: 902/425-2441, Email: pathfndr@fox.nstn.ca
Executive Vice-President, John K. Sutherland
Publications: Klaxon

Ontario Automobile Dealer Association
85 Renfrew Dr., 2nd Fl., Markham, ON L3R 0N9
905/940-6232, Fax: 905/940-6235
Director General, Bill Davis
Publications: Automobile Journal

Organization of Registered Automobile Dealers in Ontario (ORADIO)
97 Guildwood Pkwy., PO Box 11021, Scarborough, ON M1E 5G5
416/283-1937
Managing Director, Clint McCormack

PEI Automobile Dealers Association
PO Box 22004, Parkdale, PE C1A 7J0
902/368-7116, Fax: 902/368-7116
Secretary, Norma Proud

Recreation Vehicle Dealers Association of Canada/Association des commerçants de véhicules récréatifs du Canada (RVDA) (1981)
#209, 20353 - 64 Ave., Langley, BC V2Y 1N5
604/533-4010, Fax: 604/533-0795
Executive Vice-President, Ernie Hamm
Executive Assistant, Eléonore Hamm
Affiliates: Recreation Vehicle Dealers of America

ONTARIO RECREATION VEHICLE DEALERS ASSOCIATION (ORVDA) (1979)
PO Box 270, Brechin, ON L0K 1B0
705/484-0295, Fax: 705/484-5740
Exeutive Director, William A. Mallatratt
Publications: ORVDA News

RECREATION VEHICLE DEALERS ASSOCIATION OF ALBERTA (1978)
11217 - 143 St., Edmonton, AB T5M 3P8
403/455-8562, Fax: 403/453-3927
Executive Vice-President, John Milligan
Publications: RVViewpoints

RECREATION VEHICLE DEALERS ASSOCIATION OF BRITISH COLUMBIA (1974)
#201, 19623 - 56 Ave., Langley, BC V3A 3X7
604/533-4200, Fax: 604/533-0795
Executive Director, Craig Lavido
Publications: Newsletter

RECREATION VEHICLE DEALERS ASSOCIATION OF MANITOBA
58 Leger Cres., Winnipeg, MB R3X 1J4
204/256-6119, Fax: 204/256-6119
Manager, Susan Andree

RECREATION VEHICLE DEALERS ASSOCIATION OF NOVA SCOTIA
140 Pinewood Cr., Dartmouth, NS B2V 2P9
902/462-4747, Fax: 902/435-9058
Executive Director, Ed Robillard

RECREATION VEHICLE DEALERS ASSOCIATION OF QUÉBEC
Service Caravane R.P. Inc., 8900, ch Chambly, Saint-Hubert, PQ J3Y 5K2
514/676-6667, Téléc: 514/676-6667
President, Pierre Jutras

RECREATION VEHICLE DEALERS ASSOCIATION OF SASKATCHEWAN
PO Box 1983, Regina, SK S4P 3E1
306/525-5666, Fax: 306/757-3670
President, Bill Ortman

Saskatchewan Automobile Dealers Association (SADA)
#330, 3303 Hillsdale St., Regina, SK S4S 6W9
306/721-2208, Fax: 306/721-2200
Executive Vice-President, Ben R. Holden, BSP

Société de l'assurance automobile du Québec (1978)
333, boul Jean-Lesage, CP 19 600, Québec, PQ G1K 8J6
418/528-4290, Téléc: 418/644-0339

Used Car Dealers Association of Ontario (UCDA) (1984)
#205, 4174 Dundas St. West, Toronto, ON M8X 1X3
416/231-2600, Fax: 416/232-0775, Toll Free: 1-800-268-2598
Executive Director, Robert G. Beattie
Publications: Members' Briefs

Vehicle Information Centre of Canada/Centre d'information sur les véhicules du Canada (VICC) (1989)
#220, 175 Commerce Valley Dr. West, Markham, ON L3T 7P6
905/764-5560, Fax: 905/764-6846
President, Henning M. Norup
Vice-President, Roch Lacroix
Publications: How Cars Measure Up; Choosing Your Car; Auto Insurance Rate Group Tables; Car Theft

AVIATION & AEROSPACE
see also Aerospace Industry

Aerospace Industries Association of Canada/ Association des industries aérospatiales du Canada (AIAC) (1962)
#1200, 60 Queen St., Ottawa, ON K1P 5Y7
613/232-4297, Fax: 613/232-1142, Email: aiac@fox.nstn.ca
URL: http://www.aiac.ca
President, Peter R. Smith
Publications: Aerospace News

Air Transport Association of Canada/Association du transport aérien du Canada (ATAC) (1934)
#1100, 255 Albert St., Ottawa, ON K1P 6A9
613/233-7727, Fax: 613/230-8648, Email: atac@pop.infoshare
URL: http://www.atac.ca
President/CEO, John W. Crichton
Affiliates: Alberta Aviation Council; BC Aviation Council; Canadian Business Aircraft Association; Helicopter Association International; National Air Transporation Association; Northern Air Transport Association; Saskatchewan Aviation Council; Federation of Canadian Municipalities

Aircraft Engineers Association (Atlantic) Inc. (AEA) (1980)
837 Charlotte St., Fredericton, NB E3B 1M7
506/452-1809, Fax: 506/452-8251
President, Ben L. McCarty
Secretary, Dario Mazzorana
Publications: AEA Newsletter

Airport Management Conference of Ontario
PO Box 179, Perkins Field, ON L0L 2J0
705/526-8086, Fax: 705/526-1769
President, Don Timlin
Secretary Manager, John O'Hara

Alberta Aviation Council (AAC) (1962)
67 Airport Rd., Edmonton, AB T5G 0W6
403/451-5289, Fax: 403/454-9474
Association Manager, Monika Burckhardt
Publications: Flight Times
Affiliates: Civil Air Rescue Emergency Services

British Columbia Aviation Council
#303, 5360 Airport Rd. South, Richmond, BC V7B 1B4
604/278-9330, Fax: 604/278-8210
Chairman, Jack Cameron

Canadian Aeronautical Preservation Association (CAPA)
PO Box 75057, Stn Cambrain, Calgary, AB T2K 6J8
403/289-1532

Canadian Almanac & Directory 1997

ORGANIZATIONS — BROADCASTING

Canadian Aeronautics & Space Institute/Institut aéronautique et spatial du Canada (CASI) (1954)
#818, 130 Slater St., Ottawa, ON K1P 6E2
613/234-0191, Fax: 613/234-9039, Email: ab144@freenet.carleton.ca
URL: http://www.ncf.carleton.ca/freeport/prof.assoc/casi/menu
Executive Director, Ian M. Ross
Publications: The Canadian Aeronautics & Space Journal; CASI Log, q.
Affiliates: International Congress of Aeronautical Sciences; International Astronautical Federation

Canadian Airports Council/Conseil des aéroports du Canada (CAC) (1991)
#2100, 1100, boul René-Lévesque ouest, Montréal, PQ H3B 4X8
514/394-7200, Fax: 514/394-7356
Contact, J.G. Auger, FCIT

Canadian Aviation Historical Society (CAHS) (1963)
PO Box 224, Stn A, North York, ON M2N 5S8
416/488-2247, Fax: 416/488-2247
President, Jack Gow
Treasurer, Terry Judge
Secretary, Ed Rice
Publications: Outbound; CAHS Journal, q.

Canadian Aviation Maintenance Council/Conseil canadien de l'entretien des aéronefs (CAMC) (1992)
#330, 955 Green Valley Cres., Ottawa, ON K2C 3V4
613/727-8272, Fax: 613/727-7018, Toll Free: 1-800-448-9715
Executive Director, Bill St. Jean
Publications: Update

Canadian Federation of AME Associations
Aircraft Maintenance Engineers Association
55 Archer Cres., Elmvale, ON L0L 1P0
705/322-9637, Fax: 705/322-8337
Chairperson, D. Snedden

Canadian Owners & Pilots Association (COPA)
#1001, 75 Albert St., Ottawa, ON K1P 5E7
613/236-4901, Fax: 613/236-8646
General Manager, W.N. Peppler
Publications: Canadian Flight News; Canadian Ultralight News, m.; Canadian Homebuilt Aircraft News, m.; Canadian Plane Trade, m.; Canadian Warplane Heritage News/Flightlines, bi-m.; Canadian Flight Annual

Canadian Seaplane Pilots Association
RR#6, Orillia, ON L3V 6H6
705/325-6153, Fax: 705/325-6377
President, R. Vodarek

The De Havilland Moth Club of Canada (1981)
305 Old Homestead Rd., Keswick, ON L4P 1E6
905/476-4225
Founder/Director, R. de H. "Ted" Leonard
Publications: DH Moth Newsletter

Institute for Aerospace Studies (UTIAS) (1949)
University of Toronto, 4925 Dufferin St., North York, ON M3H 5T6
416/667-7701, Fax: 416/667-7799, Email: info@utias.utoronto.ca
URL: http://www.utias.utoronto.ca/
Director, Dr. A.A. Haasz
Publications: Annual Progress Report

International Air Transport Association (IATA) (1945)
2000, rue Peel, Montréal, PQ H3A 2R4
514/844-6311, Fax: 514/844-5286
Director General, Pierre Jeanniot
General Counsel/Corporate Secretary, Lorne Clark
Manager, Public Relations, Wanda Potrykus
Affiliates: International Civil Aviation Organization

International Airline Passengers Association of Canada/Association canadienne des passagers de lignes aériennes internationales
12 Inglewood Cres., Kirkland, PQ H9J 2M6
Contact, Terry A. Evans
Contact, Martin Castonguay

International Civil Aviation Organization/Organisation de l'aviation civile internationale (ICAO - OACI) (1947)
1000, rue Sherbrooke ouest, Montréal, PQ H3A 2R2
514/285-8219, Fax: 514/288-4772, Telex: 05 24513
President, Dr. Assad Kotaite
Secretary General, Dr. Philippe Rochat
Publications: ICAO Journal

International Industry Working Group (IIWG) (1970)
International Air Transport Association, 2000, rue Peel, Montréal, PQ H3A 2R4
514/844-6311, Fax: 514/844-6727
Secretary, J. Durante
Chairman, Boeing Commercial Airplane Group, Seattle WA, USA, Edward L. Gervais

The Ninety-Nines Inc./International Women Pilots
7100 Terminal Drive, PO Box 965, Oklahoma City, OK 73159 USA
405/685-7969
President, Joyce Wells
Publications: The Ninety-Nines
East Canada Section: Governor, Joy Parker Blackwood, 221 Whitehall Dr., Markham, ON L3R 9T1, 905/841-7930, Fax: 905/475-7212
West Canada Section: Governor, Sonja Wilford, 725 Franklin Rd., Kamloops, BC V2B 6G5, 250/579-8584, Fax: 250/372-0330

Northern Air Transport Association (NATA) (1977)
PO Box 2457, Yellowknife, NT X1A 2P8
403/920-2985, Fax: 403/873-8077
Executive Director, Stu Grant
President, Al Kapty

Recreational Aircraft Association Canada (RAAC) (1983)
152 Harwood Ave. South, Ajax, ON L1S 2H6
905/683-3517, Fax: 905/428-2415, Toll Free: 1-800-387-1028
President, Barry Miller
Publications: Recreational Flyer

SEDS - Canada (1980)
Students for the Exploration & Development of Space
York University, Student Centre Building, Rm. 333, 4700 Keele St., North York, ON M3J 1P3
Email: seds@seds.ca
URL: http://www.seds.ca
Chair, H. Peter White, 416/650-9890, Email: white@eol.ists.ca
Secretary, Christine Marton, 416/699-0591, Email: cmarton.@epas.utoronto.ca
Publications: Ylem

Ultralight Pilots Association of Canada/Association Canadienne des Pilots d'Avions Ultra-Legers (UPAC)
Hunters Gate Plaza, #6, 14845 Yonge St., Aurora, ON L4G 6H8
905/833-3467

President, Chuck Kiernan
Vice-President, Membership & Administration, Peter Henshall

BANKING see FINANCE

BARS see RESTAURANTS, BARS, FOOD SERVICES

BETTER BUSINESS BUREAUX see BUSINESS

BEVERAGE INDUSTRY see FOOD & BEVERAGE INDUSTRY

BIRTH see CHILDBIRTH

BOOK TRADE see PUBLISHING

BOOKKEEPING see ACCOUNTING

BREEDERS see ANIMAL BREEDING

BROADCASTING
see also Film & Video; Telecommunications

The Alliance for Children & Television/Alliance pour l'enfant et la télévision (ACT) (1974)
#205, 344 Dupont St., Toronto, ON M5R 1V9
416/515-0466, Fax: 416/515-0467, Email: acttv@interlog.com
Executive Director, Kealy Wilkinson
Operations Manager, Judith Pyke
Chairman, Alan Mirabelli
Publications: Alliance Info
Montréal Office: #102, 3774, rue Saint-Denis, Montréal, PQ H2W 2M1, 514/844-6513, Téléc: 514/284-0168

Association for the Study of Canadian Radio & Television/Association pour les études sur la radio-télévision canadienne (ASCRT) (1978)
c/o Centre for Broadcasting Studies, Concordia University, 1455, boul de Maisonneuve ouest, Montréal, PQ H3G 1M8
514/848-2385, Fax: 514/848-4501
President, Prof. Howard Fink
Publications: ASCRT/AERTC Bulletin; Frequency/Fréquence

Audio Engineering Society
Box 292, #200, 131 Bloor St. West, Toronto, ON M5S 1R8
416/863-0898, Fax: 416/863-1047
Chair, D. Tremblay
Treasurer, R. Lynch
Communications, A. Reynolds

BBM Bureau of Measurement/Sondages BBM (1944)
#305, 1500 Don Mills Rd., North York, ON M3B 3L7
416/445-9800, Fax: 416/445-8644, Telex: 06-986-198
URL: http://www.bbm.ca/
President, Owen Charlebois
Publications: In Sync

Broadcast Educators Association of Canada/Association canadienne des éducateurs en radiodiffusion (BEAC) (1977)
741 Colborne St., Brantford, ON N3S 3R9
519/753-1058, Fax: 519/753-1682, Email: bradfoj@operatns.mohawkc.on.ca
Executive Director, John Bradford
President, Jane Bonisteel
Vice-President, Donna Leon-Millen
Publications: Communiqué
Affiliates: Canadian Association of Broadcasters

Broadcast Executives Society (BES) (1961)
#700, 890 Yonge St., Toronto, ON M4W 3P4
416/961-3201
Administrator, Deanna Toshack

Broadcast Research Council of Canada (BRC)
Box 409, #100, 2 Bloor St. West, Toronto, ON M4W 3E2
Fax: 416/929-2529
President, Daphne Hubble, 416/596-2489

Canadian Association of Broadcast Consultants
500 Van Buren St., PO Box 550, Kemptville, ON K0G 1J0
613/258-5928, Fax: 613/258-7418
President, Pierre Labarre
Sec.-Treas., M.A. Tilston

Canadian Association of Broadcasters/ Association canadienne des radiodiffuseurs (CAB) (1926)
#306, 350 Sparks St., PO Box 627, Stn B, Ottawa, ON K1P 5S2
613/233-4035, Fax: 613/233-6961
URL: http://www.cab-acr.ca
President & CEO, Michael McCabe
Executive Vice-President, Michel Tremblay
Communications Coordinator, Michael Buzzell
Senior Vice-President, Peter Miller
Publications: Radio Plus; TV Plus, m.; Info Plus, m.

ALBERTA BROADCASTERS ASSOCIATION
c/o CFRN-TV, PO Box 5030, Stn E, Edmonton, AB T5P 4C2
403/483-3311, Fax: 403/484-4426
President, Fred Filthaut

ASSOCIATION CANADIENNE DE LA RADIO ET TÉLÉVISION DE LANGUE FRANÇAISE (ACRTF)
CP 127, Longueuil, PQ J4P 3N4
514/923-5455, Téléc: 514/923-5525
Président, Michel Arpin
Vice-président Télévision, Michel Chamberland
Vice-Président Radio, Claude Beaudoin
Secrétaire-trésorier, Charles Bélanger

ATLANTIC ASSOCIATION OF BROADCASTERS (AAB)
c/o CFSX Radio, 30 Oregon Dr., Stephenville, NF A2N 2X9
709/643-2191, Fax: 709/643-5025
President, G. Murphy

BRITISH COLUMBIA ASSOCIATION OF BROADCASTERS (BCAB) (1946)
c/o Okanagan Radio Ltd., 2419 Hwy. 97 North, Kelowna, BC V1X 4J2
250/868-4713, Fax: 250/860-8856, Email: petrie@osgltd.com
URL: http://www.bcab.org
President, E. Petrie

BROADCASTERS ASSOCIATION OF MANITOBA
c/o CKY TV, Polo Park, Winnipeg, MB R3G 0L7
204/788-3300, Fax: 204/788-3399
President, Vaughan Tozer
Central Canada Broadcasters' Association: President, A. MacKay, c/o CJOH-TV, 1500 Merivale Rd., Ottawa, ON K2E 6Z5, 613/224-1313, Fax: 613/224-7998

ONTARIO ASSOCIATION OF BROADCASTERS
57 Cherrywood Dr., Nepean, ON K2H 6H1
613/829-0284
Executive Director, Gerry Acton

SASKATCHEWAN ASSOCIATION OF BROADCASTERS
c/o CJYM, 208 Hwy. 4, PO Box 490, Rosetown, SK S0L 2V0
306/882-2686, Fax: 306/882-3037
Sec.-Treas., Wax Williams

WESTERN ASSOCIATION OF BROADCASTERS (WAB) (1934)
c/o Alberta Hospitality, 22 Estate Cres., St Albert, AB T8N 5X2
403/460-7207, Fax: 403/460-4699
President, Ron Kizney
Sec.-Treas., J. Douglas, 403/460-7207

Canadian Association of Captioning Consumers/ Association canadienne pour le sous-titrage (CACC) (1993)
#203, 627 Lyons Lane, Oakville, ON L6J 5Z7
905/338-1246, Fax: 905/338-7483
President, Ellen Rusi
Publications: Captioning Today

ONTARIO CLOSED CAPTIONING CONSUMERS
#302, 190 Colin Ave., Toronto, ON M5P 2C6
Representative, Adrianne Cairns

PACIFIC CAPTIONING ASSISTANCE SOCIETY
#403, 41 Alexander St., Vancouver, BC V6A 1B2
Representative, Diana Hill

REGROUPEMENT QUÉBÉCOIS POUR LE SOUS-TITRAGE INC. (RQST) (1992)
65B, rue De Castelnau ouest, Montréal, PQ H2R 2W3
514/278-8722, Téléc: 514/278-8704, Ligne sans frais: 1-800-742-0529
URL: http://www.surdite.org/
Directeur général, Richard McNicoll
Publications: Bulletin RQST

Canadian Association of Ethnic (Radio) Broadcasters/Association canadienne des radiodiffuseurs éthniques (CAEB) (1981)
622 College St., Toronto, ON M6G 1B6
416/531-9991, Fax: 416/531-5274
URL: http://www.chinradio.com
Executive Director, Johnny Lombardi

Canadian Cable Television Association/ Association canadienne de télévision par cable (CCTA) (1957)
#1010, 360 Albert St., Ottawa, ON K1R 7X7
613/232-2631, Fax: 613/232-2137
President, Richard Stursberg
Sr. Vice-President, Public Affairs, Elizabeth Roscoe
Publications: Cable Communiqué

Canadian Satellite Users Association
#1105, 191 The West Mall, Etobicoke, ON M9C 5K8
416/620-4332, Fax: 416/620-5392, Email: bbande@enterprise.ca
URL: http://www.bbande.com
Executive Director, Don Braden
Chair, John Riley

Conseil international des radios-télévisions d'expression française (CIRTEF)
a/s Société Radio-Canada, 1400, boul René-Lévesque est, Montréal, PQ H2L 2M2
514/597-4700, Téléc: 514/597-4599
Président, Paul Saint-Pierre

Fédération professionnelle des réalisateurs de télévision et de cinéma
#1231, rue Panet, CP 870, Succ. C, Montréal, PQ H2L 4L6
514/525-8599, Téléc: 514/526-4124
Président, Jean Gagne

Friends of Canadian Broadcasting
29 Prince Arthur Ave., Toronto, ON M5R 1B2
416/964-0559, Fax: 416/964-9226
Spokesperson, Ian Morrison

ITVA CANADA (1989)
PO Box 1156, Stn Adelaide, Toronto, ON M5C 2K5
416/733-3757, Fax: 416/733-1741, Email: itvacda@informap.net
General Manager, Tosca Gazer
National President, Mark Arlett
Publications: Videosync

National Campus/Community Radio Association/ Association nationale des radio étudiantes & communautaires (NCRA) (1986)
c/o CFRU-FM, #273, University Centre, Guelph, ON N1G 2W1
President, Alka Sharma, 519/824-4120
Vice-President, Internal, Susan Kennard, 403/271-6477
Publications: Voices; NCRA Directory, a.; National Music Chart, a.; NCRN, q.
Affiliates: World Association of Community Broadcasters (AMAC)

Radio Advisory Board of Canada/Conseil consultatif canadien de la radio (RABC) (1944)
#201, 880 Lady Ellen Pl., Ottawa, ON K1Z 5L9
613/728-8692, Fax: 613/728-3278
General Manager, P.G. Bowie
President, R.B. Poirier

Radio Amateurs of Canada/Radio amateurs du Canada (RAC) (1993)
#6, 614 Norris Ct., Kingston, ON K7P 2R9
613/634-4184, Fax: 613/634-7118
URL: http://www.rac.ca/
General Manager, Deborah F. Norman
President, J. Farrell Hopwood
Publications: The Canadian Amateur

Radio Television News Directors' Association (Canada)/Association canadienne des directeurs de l'information en radio-télévision (RTNDA) (1961)
#310, 2175 Sheppard Ave. East, North York, ON M2J 1W8
416/756-2213, Fax: 416/491-1670
URL: http://www.vvv.com/~rtnda
President, Hudson Mack
Administrator, Diane Gaunt
Publications:
Affiliates: Radio-Television News Directors Association International

Society of Television Lighting Directors Canada/ Société des directeurs d'eclairage de télévision (STLDC) (1978)
46 Ladysbridge Dr., Scarborough, ON M1G 3H7
416/439-2875, Fax: 416/424-4682
Chair, Bruce Whitehead, 416/424-4284, Fax: 416/424-4682
Treasurer, Alf Hunter
Publications: Television Lighting; STLDC Newsletter
Affiliates: Society of Television Lighting Directors - United Kingdom

Telecaster Committee of Canada Inc./Le Comité des Télédiffuseurs du Canada inc. (1972)
#604, 890 Yonge St., Toronto, ON M4W 3P4
416/928-6046, Fax: 416/924-7644
President, P.A. Beatty

Television Bureau of Canada, Inc./Bureau de la télévision du Canada, inc. (1961)
TVB of Canada Inc.
#700, 890 Yonge St., Toronto, ON M4W 3P4
416/923-8813, Fax: 416/923-8739
President, Cameron Fellman
Senior Vice-President, Wendy Miles
Publications: TV Basics
Affiliates: Television Bureau of Advertising - New York, USA

Canadian Almanac & Directory 1997

2-30 ORGANIZATIONS —BUILDING & CONSTRUCTION

Montréal Branch Office: Vice-President, J.R. Genin, #980, 550, rue Sherbrooke ouest, Montréal, PQ H3A 1B9, 514/284-0425, Fax: 514/284-0698

Western Association of Broadcast Engineers
CFCN Radio-Broadcast House, PO Box 7060, Stn E, Calgary, AB T3C 3L9
403/240-5769, Fax: 403/240-5883
President, J. Bruins

Women in Film & Television - Toronto (1984)
WIFT-T
#902, 20 Eglinton St. West, PO Box 2009, Toronto, ON M4R 1K8
416/322-3430; Hotline: 416/322-3648, Fax: 416/322-3703, Email: wift-admin@goodmedia.com
URL: http://www.goodmedia.com/witt
Executive Director, Tracey Wood
Publications: Changing Focus

BUILDING & CONSTRUCTION
see also Equipment & Machinery; Housing

Aggregate Producers Association of Ontario (APAO) (1956)
#2, 365 Brunel Rd., Mississauga, ON L4Z 1Z5
905/507-0711, Fax: 905/507-0717
Executive Director, Robert Cook
Executive Assistant, Sonja Hamilton

Architectural Metal Association
#200, 670 Bloor St. West, Toronto, ON M6G 1L2
416/533-7800, Fax: 416/533-4795
Executive Director, Don Mockford

Architectural Woodwork Manufacturers Association of Canada (AWMAC) (1967)
925 - 5 St. West, High River, AB T1V 1A7
250/652-3666, Fax: 250/652-7384
President, Casey Beyers Bergen
Secretary/Manager, Frank Van Donzel

Association béton Québec (ABQ)
#107, 85, rue St-Charles ouest, Longueuil, PQ J4H 1C5
514/463-3569, Téléc: 514/463-1704
Directeur général, J. Gaétan Trudeau
Publications: L'Ere du béton

Builders Hardware Manufacturers Association of Canada/Association canadienne des fabricants de quincaillerie de bâtiment (BHMAC)
#1801, One Yonge St., Toronto, ON M5E 1W7
416/363-7845, Fax: 416/369-0515
Manager, Lois Marsh

Building Maintenance Contractors Association
#1219, 1644 Bayview Ave., Toronto, ON M4G 4E9
416/421-1598, Fax: 416/421-1598
Executive Director, Carla Kelman

Canadian Cement Council/Conseil canadien du ciment (1992)
Box 74, #1600, 350 Albert St., Ottawa, ON K1R 1A4
613/238-3348, Fax: 613/238-6594
Executive Director, Kenneth G. Whiting

Canadian Concrete Masonry Producers Association/Association canadienne des manufacturiers de maçonnerie en béton (CCMPA) (1949)
#101, 1013 Wilson Ave., Downsview, ON M3K 1G1
416/635-7179, Fax: 416/630-1916
Executive Director, M.A. Patamia
Publications: Update
Affiliates: National Concrete Masonry Association (U.S.)

Canadian Concrete Pipe Association/Association canadienne des fabricants de tuyaux de béton (CCPA) (1992)
#508, 6299 Airport Rd., Mississauga, ON L4V 1N6
905/677-1010, Fax: 905/677-1007, Toll Free: 1-800-435-0116
Chair, Edwin Kling
Vice-Chair, Bill Dunn
Manager, Grant Lee
Sec.-Treas., Ed McMenamin
Publications: Concrete Pipe Journal
Affiliates: Ontario Concrete Pipe Association; Tubecon; American Concrete Pipe Association

Canadian Construction Association/Association canadienne de la construction (CCA) (1918)
85 Albert St., 10th Fl., Ottawa, ON K1P 6A4
613/236-9455, Fax: 613/236-9526
President/CEO, Michael Atkinson
Chairman, Brian Scroggs

ALBERTA CONSTRUCTION ASSOCIATION (ACA) (1958)
10949 - 120 St., Edmonton, AB T5H 3R2
403/455-1122, Fax: 403/451-2152
Executive Director, Merv Ellis
Publications: Alberta Construction
Affiliates: Alberta Construction Safety Association; Alberta Construction Tendering System

ALBERTA ROADBUILDERS & HEAVY CONSTRUCTION ASSOCIATION (1954)
#201, 9333 - 45 Ave., Edmonton, AB T6E 5Z7
403/436-9860, Fax: 403/436-4910
Executive Director, Barrie McPhalen
Publications: Roadrunner; Directory, a.
Affiliates: Western Canada Roadbuilders Association; Alberta Construction Safety Association; Roads & Transportation Association Canada

ASSOCIATION DES CONSTRUCTEURS DE ROUTES ET GRANDS TRAVAUX DU QUÉBEC/QUÉBEC ROAD BUILDERS & HEAVY CONSTRUCTION ASSOCIATION (ACRGTQ) (1944)
435, av Grande-Allée est, Québec, PQ G1R 2J5
418/529-2949, Téléc: 418/529-5139, Ligne sans frais: 1-800-463-4672
Directrice générale par intérim, Maître Gisèle Bourque
Publications: Dossiers

ASSOCIATION DE LA CONSTRUCTION DU QUÉBEC/CONSTRUCTION ASSOCIATION OF QUÉBEC (ACQ) (1989)
#300, 4970, Place de la Savane, Montréal, PQ H4P 1Z6
514/739-2381, Téléc: 514/739-8933, Ligne sans frais: 1-800-361-7701
Président, Réjean Tardif
Secrétaire général, Michel Paré
Publications: Construire

ASSOCIATION DES ENTREPRENEURS EN CONSTRUCTION DU QUÉBEC/ASSOCIATION OF BUILDING CONTRACTORS OF QUÉBEC (AECQ)
#300, 7905, boul Louis-H-Lafontaine, Anjou, PQ H1K 4E4
514/353-5151, Téléc: 514/353-6689, Ligne sans frais: 1-800-361-4304
Directeur général, Pierre Dion

BRITISH COLUMBIA CONSTRUCTION ASSOCIATION (BCCA) (1969)
#400, 3795 Carey Rd., Victoria, BC V8Z 6T8
250/475-1077, Fax: 250/475-1078, Email: dmr@is-landnet.com
President, David Robertson
Executive Assistant, Kim Haakonson
Publications: Membership Directory & Buyer's Guide; The Bulletin, m.

BRITISH COLUMBIA ROAD BUILDERS & HEAVY CONSTRUCTION ASSOCIATION (1965)
#165, 10711 Cambie Rd., Richmond, BC V6X 3G5

604/276-0202, Fax: 604/276-2647
President, S. Anthony Toth

CONSTRUCTION ASSOCIATION OF NEW BRUNSWICK INC. (CANB)
190 Brunswick St., Fredericton, NB E3B 1G6
506/459-5770, Fax: 506/457-1913, Email: canb@nbnet.nb.ca
Executive Secretary, Margaret A. Wilby

CONSTRUCTION ASSOCIATION OF NOVA SCOTIA
PO Box 47040, Halifax, NS B3K 5Y2
902/429-6760, Fax: 902/429-3965
President, Carol MacCulloch

CONSTRUCTION ASSOCIATION OF PEI
Holland College Royalty Centre, 40 Enman Cres., PO Box 728, Charlottetown, PE C1A 7L3
902/368-3303, Fax: 902/894-9757
General Manager, Francis Reid
Affiliates: Canadian Electrical Contractors Association

CONSTRUCTION ASSOCIATION OF THUNDER BAY
857 North May St., Thunder Bay, ON P7C 3S2
807/622-9645, Fax: 807/623-2296
Administrator, Susan Hyndman
General Manager, Murray MacLeay
Publications: Construction North West

EDMONTON CONSTRUCTION ASSOCIATION (ECA) (1931)
10215 - 176 St., Edmonton, AB T5S 1M1
403/483-1130, Fax: 403/484-0299, Email: tonto@mail.planet.eon.net
URL: http://www.planet.eon.net/~tonto/eca.html
Executive Vice-President, G.L. MacPherson
Publications: Bulletin Board
Affiliates: Alberta Construction Association

GRAND VALLEY CONSTRUCTION ASSOCIATION
25 Sheldon Dr., Cambridge, ON N1R 6R8
519/622-4822, Fax: 519/621-3289
General Manager, John Bradbury

GRANDE PRAIRIE CONSTRUCTION ASSOCIATION
9809 - 116 Ave., Grande Prairie, AB T8V 4B4
403/532-4548, Fax: 403/539-4100
Secretary/Manager, F. Commet

HAMILTON CONSTRUCTION ASSOCIATION (HCA) (1921)
#100, 370 York Blvd., Hamilton, ON L8R 3L1
905/522-5220, Fax: 905/572-9166, Email: hca@netaccess.on.ca
Executive Director, J. Cameron Nolan, BA
Publications: In-Site
Affiliates: Council of Ontario Construction Associations

KINGSTON CONSTRUCTION ASSOCIATION
575 Counter St., PO Box 625, Kingston, ON K7L 4X1
613/542-9431, Fax: 613/542-2417
Secretary Manager, R. Bruce Warmington

LETHBRIDGE CONSTRUCTION ASSOCIATION
2918 - 7 Ave. North, Lethbridge, AB T1H 5C6
403/328-2474, Fax: 403/329-0971
Office Manager, Lorrie Vos

LLOYDMINSTER CONSTRUCTION ASSOCIATION
4420 - 50 Ave., Lloydminster, SK T9V 0W2
403/875-8875, Fax: 403/875-8874
Secretary/Manager, Caroline Helmeczi

LONDON & DISTRICT CONSTRUCTION ASSOCIATION
331 Aberdeen Dr., London, ON N5V 4S4
519/453-5322, Fax: 519/453-5335
General Manager, Tom Dool

MANITOBA HEAVY CONSTRUCTION ASSOCIATION INC.
1236 Ellice, Winnipeg, MB R3G 0E7

Canadian Almanac & Directory 1997

204/947-1379, Fax: 204/943-2279
Executive Director, Chirs Lorenc

MEDICINE HAT CONSTRUCTION ASSOCIATION
928A - 18 St. SW, Medicine Hat, AB T1A 7T4
403/527-9700, Fax: 403/526-0520
Manager, Val Perini

MONCTON NORTHEAST CONSTRUCTION ASSOCIATION
PO Box 628, Moncton, NB E1C 8M7
506/857-4038, Fax: 506/857-8861
Executive Director, Arnold Ogden

MOOSE JAW CONSTRUCTION ASSOCIATION
610 - 1 Ave. NW, Moose Jaw, SK S6H 4P4
306/693-1232, Fax: 306/694-1766
Manager, Bob Church

NEWFOUNDLAND & LABRADOR CONSTRUCTION ASSOCIATION
78 O'Leary Ave., PO Box 8008, St. John's, NF A1B 3M7
709/753-8920, Fax: 709/754-3968
President, Lawrence J. Rossiter

NEWFOUNDLAND & LABRADOR ROAD BUILDERS ASSOCIATION (1968)
26 Rostellan Pl., St. John's, NF A1B 2T9
709/722-2446
Manager, Rudy Wasmeier
President, Dave Burnell
Vice-President, Len Knox

NIAGARA CONSTRUCTION ASSOCIATION
34 Scott St., St Catharines, ON L2R 1C9
905/682-6661, Fax: 905/688-5029
Manager, Catharine Tribble

NORTHERN BRITISH COLUMBIA CONSTRUCTION ASSOCIATION
3851 - 18 Ave., Prince George, BC V2N 1B1
250/563-1744, Fax: 250/563-1107
President, Rosalind Thorn

NORTHWEST TERRITORIES CONSTRUCTION ASSOCIATION (1976)
#201, 4817 - 49 St., Yellowknife, NT X1A 3S7
403/873-3949, Fax: 403/873-8366
Executive Director, Richard Bushey
Office Manager, Rosemarie Laine
Publications: Weekly Bulletin; Construction North of 60, a.

NOVA SCOTIA ROAD BUILDERS ASSOCIATION (1948)
PO Box 29064, RPO Halifax Shopping Centre, Halifax, NS B3L 4T8
902/477-3481, Fax: 902/477-1543
Managing Director, Malcolm G. Williams

ONTARIO GENERAL CONTRACTORS ASSOCIATION (OGCA) (1939)
#703, 6299 Airport Rd., Mississauga, ON L4V 1N3
905/671-3969, Fax: 905/671-8212
President, Don J. Cameron
Publications: OGCA News
Affiliates: Council of Ontario Construction Associations

ONTARIO ROAD BUILDERS' ASSOCIATION
#1, 365 Brunel Rd., Mississauga, ON L4Z 1Z5
905/507-1107, Fax: 905/890-8122
Executive Director, Rob Bradford

ORILLIA & DISTRICT CONSTRUCTION ASSOCIATION (1959)
PO Box 235, Orillia, ON L3V 5J6
705/326-1844, Fax: 705/326-0774
President, Ralph McFadden
Executive Secretary, Keith Allen

OTTAWA CONSTRUCTION ASSOCIATION (1889)
196 Bronson Ave., Ottawa, ON K1R 6H4
613/236-0488, Fax: 613/238-6124
Executive Director/General Manager, Stephen D. Sulpher

PEACE RIVER CONSTRUCTION ASSOCIATION
PO Box 6599, Peace River, AB T8S 1S4
403/624-5351, Fax: 403/624-4663
Secretary/Manager, Tommy O'Neale

PEI ROADBUILDERS & HEAVY CONSTRUCTION ASSOCIATION (1962)
Holland College Royalty Centre, 40 Enman Cres., PO Box 1901, Charlottetown, PE C1A 7N5
902/894-9514, Fax: 902/894-9514
Manager, Roger Perry

PRINCE ALBERT CONSTRUCTION ASSOCIATION
3700 - 2 Ave. West, Prince Albert, SK S6W 1A2
306/764-2789, Fax: 306/922-4727
General Manager, Jerry J. Paskaruk

RED DEER CONSTRUCTION ASSOCIATION
#205, 7803 - 50 Ave., Red Deer, AB T4P 1M8
403/346-4846, Fax: 403/343-3280
Manager, Norma McCartney

REGINA CONSTRUCTION ASSOCIATION INC.
1935 Elphinstone St., Regina, SK S4T 3N3
306/791-7422, Fax: 306/565-2840
Executive Director, Marlene McLarty

ROAD BUILDERS ASSOCIATION OF NEW BRUNSWICK (1958)
606 Queen St., PO Box 1061, Fredericton, NB E3B 5C2
506/454-5079, Fax: 506/452-7646
Secretary Manager, J.C. Hoyt
President, Michael Washburn

ROADBUILDERS & HEAVY CONSTRUCTION ASSOCIATION OF SASKATCHEWAN (1956)
3026 Kings Rd., Regina, SK S4S 2H6
306/586-1805, Fax: 306/585-3750
Executive Administrator, Val Jakubowski
Affiliates: Western Canada Roadbuilders & Heavy Construction Association

SAINT JOHN CONSTRUCTION ASSOCIATION
263 Germain St., PO Box 2144, Stn C, Saint John, NB E2L 3T5
506/634-1747, Fax: 506/658-0651
Executive Director, Patrick Darrah

SARNIA CONSTRUCTION ASSOCIATION
954 Upper Canada Dr., PO Box 545, Sarnia, ON N7T 7J4
519/344-7441, Fax: 519/344-7501
General Manager, Andrew J. Pilat

SASKATCHEWAN CONSTRUCTION SAFETY ASSOCIATION INC. (1995)
1939 Elphinstone St., Regina, SK S4T 3N3
306/525-0171, Fax: 306/347-8595, Email: 1-800-817-2079
Executive Director, Art Brochu
President, James E. Chase
Publications: Advocate

SASKATOON CONSTRUCTION ASSOCIATION
532 - 2 Ave. North, Saskatoon, SK S7K 2C5
306/653-1771, Fax: 306/653-3515
Office Manager, Deb Labersweiler

SOUTHERN INTERIOR CONSTRUCTION ASSOCIATION (SICA) (1969)
710 Laval Cres., Kamloops, BC V2C 5P3
250/372-3364, Fax: 250/828-6634, Email: sica@net-shop.net
President, Debra Hicks
Publications: SICA Bulletin

SUDBURY CONSTRUCTION ASSOCIATION
257 Beatty St., Sudbury, ON P3C 4G1
705/673-5619, Fax: 705/673-7910
Executive Director, Ron Martin

SWIFT CURRENT CONSTRUCTION ASSOCIATION
PO Box 1358, Swift Current, SK S9H 3X5

TORONTO CONSTRUCTION ASSOCIATION
1 Sparks Ave., North York, ON M2H 2W1
416/499-4101, Fax: 416/499-5890
Executive Vice-President, Temple W. Harris
Director, Labour Relations, Brian M. Foote
Affiliates: International Council for Building Research Studies and Documentation

VANCOUVER ISLAND CONSTRUCTION ASSOCIATION
1075 Alston St., Victoria, BC V9A 3S6
250/388-6471, Fax: 250/388-5183, Email: cav@cav.com
President, Allan Graham

WESTERN CANADA ROADBUILDERS ASSOCIATION (1975)
1236 Ellice Ave., Winnipeg, MB R3G 0E7
403/947-1379, Fax: 403/943-2279
Executive Director, Chris Lorenc
President, Colleen Munro
Affiliates: Roads & Transportation Association of Canada

WINNIPEG CONSTRUCTION ASSOCIATION
290 Burnell St., PO Box 737, Winnipeg, MB R3G 2L4
204/775-8664, Fax: 204/783-6446
Executive Vice-President, Gervin L. Greasley

Canadian Masonry Contractors' Association (CMCA) (1972)
360 Superior Blvd., Mississauga, ON L5T 2N7
905/564-6622, Fax: 905/564-5744
Executive Administrator, Carol S. Elford
Publications: On the Level; Annual Masonry Magazine
Affiliates: Ontario Masonry Contractors' Association; Metro Mason Contractors Association; Canada Masonry Centre

Canadian Paint & Coatings Association/ L'Association canadienne de l'industrie de la peinture et du revêtement (CPCA) (1913)
#103, 9900, boul Cavendish, Saint Laurent, PQ H4M 2V2
514/745-2611, Fax: 514/745-2031
President, Dick Murry
Publications: Associ-Action

Canadian Portland Cement Association/ Association canadienne du ciment Portland (CPCA)
#206, 60 Queen St., Ottawa, ON K1P 5Y7
613/236-9471, Fax: 613/563-4498
Director, National Operations, Norman F. Macleod

Canadian Prestressed Concrete Institute/Institut canadien du béton précontraint (CPCI) (1961)
#100, 196 Bronson Ave., Ottawa, ON K1R 6H4
613/232-2619, Fax: 613/567-3064, Email: cpci@fox.nstn.ca
URL: http://www.buildingweb.com/cpci/
President, J.R. Fowler
Executive Secretary, Donna White
Publications: Update

Canadian Ready Mix Concrete Association
365 Brunel Rd., Mississauga, ON L4Z 1Z5
905/507-1122, Fax: 905/890-8122
Sec.-Treas., John Hull

ALBERTA READY-MIXED CONCRETE ASSOCIATION
#201, 9333 - 45 Ave., Edmonton, AB T6E 5Z7
403/436-5645, Fax: 403/436-4910
Executive Administrator, Ed Kalis

ATLANTIC PROVINCES READY-MIXED CONCRETE ASSOCIATION (1966)
PO Box 99, Lakeside, NS B3T 1M6

902/454-0139, Fax: 902/454-0164
Marketing Director, John M. Connely

MANITOBA READY-MIXED CONCRETE ASSOCIATION INC.
14 Mitchelson Way, Winnipeg, MB R2G 4E1
204/667-8539
President, Gary Kurz
Secretary, Angie Both

READY MIXED CONCRETE ASSOCIATION OF ONTARIO (RMCAO) (1959)
365 Brunel Rd., Mississauga, ON L4Z 1Z5
905/507-1122, Fax: 905/890-8122
Executive Director, John D. Hull
Publications: Flash; Directory of Members & Reference Manual, s-a.

SASKATCHEWAN READY-MIXED CONCRETE ASSOCIATION INC.
1024 Winnipeg St., Regina, SK S4R 8P8
306/757-2788, Fax: 306/757-5410
Executive Director, Garth Sanders

Canadian Renovators' Council
c/o A.B. Cameron, #850, 10201 Southport Rd. SW, Calgary, AB T2W 4X9
403/531-2700, Fax: 403/531-2707
Secretary, Alexander B. Cameron

Canadian Retail Building Supply Council
#1004, 213 Notre Dame Ave., Winnipeg, MB R3B 1N3
204/957-1077, Fax: 204/947-5195
President, Judy Huston

ASSOCIATION DES DÉTAILLANTS DE MATÉRIAUX DE CONSTRUCTION DU QUÉBEC/QUÉBEC BUILDING MATERIALS DEALERS ASSOCIATION (ADMACQ) (1940)
474, Place Trans-Canada, Longueuil, PQ J4G 1N8
514/646-5842, Téléc: 514/646-6171
Vice-président exécutif, Gabriel Pollender
Président, Renelle Anctil
Secrétaire-administrative, Lisette Leduc
Publications: Quart de Rond; Répertoire annuel
Organisation(s) affiliée(s): Conseil québécois du commerce de détail

ATLANTIC BUILDING SUPPLY DEALERS ASSOCIATION (ABSDA) (1954)
#203, 95 Foundry St., Moncton, NB E1C 5H7
506/858-0700, Fax: 506/859-0064, Toll Free: 1-800-561-7114
Executive Director, John J. Ward
President, Hal Winter
Publications: Atlantic Building Supply News

BUILDING SUPPLY DEALERS ASSOCIATION OF BRITISH COLUMBIA (1938)
#101, 630 Columbia St., New Westminster, BC V3M 1A5
604/524-8658, Fax: 604/524-6070
Executive Director, George R. Tracy
Publications: BSDA News Magazine; Annual Directory

LUMBER & BUILDING MATERIALS ASSOCIATION OF ONTARIO (LBMAO) (1917)
4500 Sheppard Ave. East, Unit F, Scarborough, ON M1S 3R6
416/298-1731, Fax: 416/298-4865, Toll Free: 1-800-465-5270
Executive Director, Stephen J. Johns
Publications: Directory of Ontario Lumber & Building; LBMAO Reporter
Affiliates: Retail Council of Canada

WESTERN RETAIL LUMBERMEN'S ASSOCIATION INC. (WRLA) (1890)
#1004, 213 Notre Dame Ave., Winnipeg, MB R3B 1N3
204/957-1077, Fax: 204/947-5195, Toll Free: 1-800-661-0253
Executive Director, Judy Huston
President, Chuck Fischer
Publications: Yardstick; WRLA Directory, a.

Canadian Roofing Contractors' Association/Association canadienne des entrepreneurs en couverture (CRCA) (1960)
#1300, 155 Queen St., Ottawa, ON K1P 6L1
613/232-6724, Fax: 613/232-2893
Executive Director, John E. Hill
Publications: Roofing Canada
Affiliates: Construction Specifications Canada

ALBERTA ROOFING CONTRACTORS ASSOCIATION LTD. (ARCA) (1961)
2725 - 12 St. NE, Calgary, AB T2E 7J2
403/250-7055, Fax: 403/250-1702, Toll Free: 1-800-382-8515
Executive Manager, Dennis Looten
Affiliates: National Roofing Contractors Association USA

ASSOCIATION DES MAÎTRES COUVREURS DU QUÉBEC/QUÉBEC MASTER ROOFERS ASSOCIATION (AMCQ) (1967)
#210, 3224, av Jean-Beraud, Laval, PQ H7T 2S4
514/973-2322, Téléc: 514/973-2321
Directrice administrative, Micheline Bonnaud
Publications: Nouvelles AMCQ; Membres, annuel

NEW BRUNSWICK ROOFING CONTRACTORS ASSOCIATION, INC.
PO Box 7242, Saint John, NB E2L 4S6
506/652-7003, Fax: 506/634-8765
Manager, Sean Darrah

ONTARIO INDUSTRIAL ROOFING CONTRACTORS' ASSOCIATION (OIRCA) (1964)
#207, 5233 Dundas St. West, Islington, ON M9B 1A6
416/239-9655, Fax: 416/239-6693
General Manager, Robert A. Hubbs
Publications: Roof Talk

ROOFING CONTRACTORS ASSOCIATION OF BRITISH COLUMBIA (RCABC) (1958)
RCABC Roofing Institute
9734 - 201st St., Langley, BC V1M 3E8
604/882-9734, Fax: 604/882-1744, Email: roofing@rcabc.org
URL: http://www.rcabc.org
Executive Vice-President, Klaus H. Thiel, CAE
Publications: RCABC on Top
Affiliates: International Federation of Roofing Contractors

ROOFING CONTRACTORS ASSOCIATION OF MANITOBA INC. (RCAM) (1966)
290 Burnell St., Winnipeg, MB R3G 2A7
204/783-6365, Fax: 204/783-6446
Secretary Manager, R.M. Stefanick

ROOFING CONTRACTORS' ASSOCIATION OF NOVA SCOTIA
112 Blue Water Rd., Bedford, NS B4B 1G7
902/835-0113, Fax: 902/835-4888
Secretary, Marg Woodworth

SASKATCHEWAN ROOFING CONTRACTORS ASSOCIATION
1935 Elphinstone St., Regina, SK S4T 3N3
306/721-8020, Fax: 306/565-2840
Manager, Marlene McLarty

Canadian Welding Bureau (1947)
7250 West Credit Ave., Mississauga, ON L5N 5N1
905/542-1312, Fax: 905/542-1318
President/CEO, D.E.H. Reynolds
Affiliates: Canadian Standards Association

Clay Brick Association of Canada/Association canadienne de brique d'argile cuite (CBAC) (1973)
#105, 5409 Eglinton Ave., Etobicoke, ON M9C 5K6
416/695-8388, Fax: 416/695-8399
National Accounts Executive, Peter Quigley
Office Manager, Michelle Hoby

Concrete Canada/Béton Canada (1990)
Dépt. de génie civil, Université de Sherbrooke, Sherbrooke, PQ J1K 2R1
819/821-8061, Fax: 819/821-6949, Email: concrete@andrew.sca.usherb.ca
Network Manager, Yves Delagrave

Conseil provincial du Québec des métiers de la construction (CPQMC)
#228, 4881, rue Jarry est, Montréal, PQ H1R 1Y1
514/323-9770, Téléc: 514/323-5042
Directeur général, Maurice Pouliot

Construction Safety Association of Ontario
74 Victoria St., Toronto, ON M5C 2A5
416/366-1501, Fax: 416/366-0232
Information & Systems Supervisor, Cyrelle Shoub
Reference Librarian, Patricia Dean

Construction Specifications Canada/Devis de construction Canada (CSC) (1954)
#200, 100 Lombard St., Toronto, ON M5C 1M3
416/777-2198, Fax: 416/777-2197
Executive Director, H. James Duncan, CAE
President, Dinshaw Kanga
Publications: Construction Canada; The Specifier, m.
Affiliates: Construction Specification Foundation; Construction Specifications Canada/Alberta Section Training Trust Fund; Construction Specifications Institute; Canadian Standards Association; Mechanical Contractors Association of Canada; Ontario Bid Depository Council; Alberta Building Envelope Council; Alberta Roofing Contractor's Association; Canadian Institute of Plumbing & Heating; Association of Professional Engineers of Canada; Royal Architectural Institute of Canada; Canadian Contruction Association; Toronto Constuction Association; Society of the Plastics Industry of Canada; Thermal Insulation Association of Canada

Council of Ontario Construction Associations (COCA) (1974)
#602, 920 Yonge St., Toronto, ON M4W 3C7
416/968-7200, Fax: 416/968-0362
Executive Vice-President, David Frame
President, David Surplis

Master Insulators' Association of Ontario Inc.
The Airway Centre, #525, 5915 Airport Rd., Mississauga, ON L4V 1T1
905/673-0004
Manager, Peter Woloszanskyj
Affiliates: Chapter of Thermal Insulation Association of Canada

Master Painters & Decorators Association of British Columbia (1911)
4090 Graveley St., Burnaby, BC V5C 3T6
604/298-7578, Fax: 604/298-5183
President, Alan Kelly
Manager, Barry G. Law

Mechanical Contractors Association of Canada/Association des entrepreneurs en mécanique du Canada
#408, 116 Albert St., Ottawa, ON K1P 5G3
613/232-0492, Fax: 613/235-2793
President, Richard McKeagan
Affiliates: Council of Construction Trade Associations

MECHANICAL CONTRACTORS ASSOCIATION OF ALBERTA
2725 - 12 St. NE, Calgary, AB T2E 7J2

403/250-7237, Fax: 403/291-0551
Contact, D. McCorquindale

MECHANICAL CONTRACTORS ASSOCIATION OF BRITISH COLUMBIA (MCA-BC) (1902)
3210 Lake City Way, Burnaby, BC V5A 3A4
604/420-9714, Fax: 604/420-0127
Executive Vice-President, Dana M. Taylor
President, Keith Hodgson
Manager, Membership Services, Aryeh Meir
Publications: Report to Members; Mechanical Contractor, q.

MECHANICAL CONTRACTORS ASSOCIATION OF MANITOBA (MCAM) (1970)
860 Bradford St., Winnipeg, MB R3H 0N5
204/774-2404, Fax: 204/772-0233
Executive Director, Don Shannon
Publications: MCAM Newsletter

MECHANICAL CONTRACTORS ASSOCIATION OF NEW BRUNSWICK/ ASSOCIATION DES ENTREPRENEURS EN MÉCHANIQUE DU N.-B. (1976)
105 Prospect St., Fredericton, NB E3B 2T7
506/452-0150, Fax: 506/450-8106, Email: bdixon@nbnet.nb.ca
President, Bill Dixon
Publications: Mechanical News & Views

MECHANICAL CONTRACTORS ASSOCIATION OF NEWFOUNDLAND & LABRADOR
PO Box 22, Pouch Cove, NF A0A 3L0
709/335-2875
Contact, Mary O'Keefe

MECHANICAL CONTRACTORS ASSOCIATION OF NOVA SCOTIA
c/o Constuction Association of Nova Scotia, PO Box 47040, Halifax, NS B3K 5Y2
902/429-6760, Fax: 902/429-3965
Manager, Donna Lewis

MECHANICAL CONTRACTORS ASSOCIATION OF ONTARIO
#105, 7 Director Ct., Woodbridge, ON L4L 4S5
905/856-0342, Fax: 905/856-0385
Executive Vice-President, Steve Coleman

MECHANICAL CONTRACTORS ASSOCIATION OF PRINCE EDWARD ISLAND
c/o Construction Association of PEI, PO Box 728, Charlottetown, PE C1A 7L3
902/368-3303, Fax: 902/894-9757
Manager, Francis Reid

MECHANICAL CONTRACTORS ASSOCIATION OF SASKATCHEWAN INC.
#32, 1736 Quebec Ave., Saskatoon, SK S7K 1V9
306/664-2154, Fax: 306/653-7233
Executive Director, Judy Nagus

National Building Envelope Council
18 Crispin Private, Ottawa, ON K1K 2T8
613/747-0251
Executive Director, Rick Quirouette

National Elevator & Escalator Association (NEEA) (1977)
#708, 6299 Airport Rd., Mississauga, ON L4V 1N3
905/678-9940, Fax: 905/677-7634
Executive Director, Andrew Reistetter

Ontario Carpentry Contractors Association
#305, One Greensboro Dr., Etobicoke, ON M9W 1C8
416/248-6213
Executive Director, Mauro Angeloni

Ontario Concrete Block Association (OCBA) (1962)
#101, 1013 Wilson Ave., Downsview, ON M3K 1G1
416/630-9944, Fax: 416/630-1916
Executive Director, M.A. Patamia
Publications: Block Focus; Design Focus, s-a.

Ontario Concrete & Drain Contractors Association (1981)
#6, 400 Creditstone Rd., Concord, ON L4K 3Z3
905/660-7676, Fax: 905/660-7611
Managing Director, P. Celsi

Ontario Concrete Pipe Association (OCPA) (1957)
#508, 6299 Airport Rd., Mississauga, ON L4V 1N6
905/677-1010, Fax: 905/677-1007, Toll Free: 1-800-435-0116
Contact, A. Grant Lee
Manager, Sue Tanenbaum
Sec.-Treas., Ed McMenamin
Affiliates: Municipal Engineers Association; Canadian Concrete Pipe Association; Tubecon; American Concrete Pipe Association; Canadian Portland Cement Association; Water Environment Association of Ontario; Canadian Public Works Association; Ontario Sewer & Watermain Construction Association

Ontario Erectors Association
#701, 6299 Airport Rd., Mississauga, ON L4V 1N3
905/677-5503, Fax: 905/677-7634
President, William Jemison

Ontario Painting Contractors Association (OPCA) (1976)
#305, 211 Consumers Rd., North York, ON M2J 4G8
416/498-1897, Fax: 416/498-6757, Toll Free: 1-800-461-3630
Executive Director, Maureen Marquardt, CAE
Publications: Brush Strokes
Affiliates: Federation of Painting and Decorating Contractors of Toronto

Ontario Sewer & Watermain Construction Association (OSWCA) (1970)
#300, 5045 Orbitor Dr., Unit 12, Mississauga, ON L4W 4Y4
905/629-7766, Fax: 905/629-0587
Executive Director, Sam Morra
Assistant Executive Director, J. Flannigan
Publications: The Undergrounder

Pipe Line Contractors Association of Canada (PLCAC) (1954)
#720, 5915 Airport Rd., Mississauga, ON L4V 1T1
905/673-0544, Fax: 905/673-0546
Executive Director, Barry L. Brown
Publications: Pipeline

Sealant & Waterproofing Association (SWA) (1989)
70 Leek Cres., Richmond Hill, ON L4B 1H1
416/499-4000, Fax: 416/499-8752
Secretary, Mary Thorburn

Structural Board Association/Association du panneaux structural (SBA) (1976)
#412, 45 Sheppard Ave. East, North York, ON M2N 5W9
416/730-9090, Fax: 416/730-9013
URL: http://www.sba_osb.ca
President, John D. Lowood, P.Eng

Terrazzo Tile & Marble Association of Canada
#5, 30 Capstan Gate, Concord, ON L4K 3E8
905/660-9640, Fax: 905/660-5706
Executive Director, Bob Sanelli

ORGANIZATIONS — BUSINESS   2-33

BUSINESS
see also Consumers; Management & Administration; Retail Trade; Trade

Association de la qualité
#L600, 455, rue Saint-Antoine ouest, Montréal, PQ H2Z 1J1
514/866-6696, Téléc: 514/866-6724
Directrice, Services administratifs, Johanne Cholette
Publications: Forum Qualité; Qualité totale, trimestriel

Business Council of British Columbia (1966)
#810, 1050 Pender St. West, Vancouver, BC V6E 3S7
604/684-3384, Fax: 604/684-7957
President/CEO, Jerry L. Lampert
Vice-President, Finance & Administration, Barbara Seymour-Gray
Chairman, Brian A. Canfield
Publications: Industrial Relations Bulletin; Government Directory, a.; Policy Perspectives; President's Report

Business Council on National Issues/Conseil canadien des chefs d'entreprise (BCNI) (1976)
Royal Bank Centre, #806, 90 Sparks St., Ottawa, ON K1P 5B4
613/238-3727, Fax: 613/236-8679
President/Chief Executive, Thomas d'Aquino
Vice-President, Policy & Research, George F. Skinner
Vice-President, Finance & Administration, Patricia A. Longino

Calmeadow (1983)
#600, 365 Bay St., Toronto, ON M5H 2V1
416/362-9670, Fax: 416/362-0769, Email: calmed@inforamp.net
Executive Director, Mary Coyle
President, Martin P. Connell

Canadian Association for Corporate Growth (CACG) (1973)
c/o ABN AMRO Bank Canada, 15th Fl., Aetna Tower, T-D Centre, PO Box 114, Stn Toronto Dominion, Toronto, ON M5K 1G8
416/365-2932, Fax: 416/367-1485
President, Mark Borkowski
Administrator, Barbara Corder

Canadian Association of Family Enterprise/ Association canadienne des enterprises familiales (CAFE) (1983)
#310, 7100 Woodbine Ave., Markham, ON L3R 5J2
905/940-9646, Fax: 905/940-8141
Executive Director, Stan Mandarich
Publications: The Family Enterpriser

The Canadian Centre for Business in the Community/Le Centre Canadien des Relations Entre L'Enterprise et la Collectivité (IDPAR)
255 Smyth Rd., Ottawa, ON K1H 8M7
613/526-3280, Fax: 613/526-4857
Director, George M. Khoury
Publications: Campaigns Outlook; Corporate Community Investment in Canada; The IDPAR Newsletter, 3 pa

Canadian Council of Better Business Bureaus/ Conseil canadien des bureaux d'éthique commerciale (CCBBB) (1972)
#209, 115 Apple Creek Blvd., Markham, ON L3R 6C9
905/415-1750, Fax: 905/415-1752, Email: ccbbb@inforamp.net
President, Wayne Lovely
Chairman, Raymond Whalen

Canadian Almanac & Directory 1997

2-34 ORGANIZATIONS — BUSINESS

BETTER BUSINESS BUREAU OF CENTRAL & NORTHERN ALBERTA (1957)
Capitol Place, #514, 9707 - 110 St., Edmonton, AB T5K 2L9
403/482-2341, Fax: 403/482-1150
President, P. Ross Bradford

BETTER BUSINESS BUREAU OF MAINLAND BC (1939)
#404, 788 Beatty St., Vancouver, BC V6B 2M1
604/682-2711, Fax: 604/681-1544, Email: bbbmail@bbbmbc.com
Executive Vice-President, Carol E. Tulk
Publications: Newsletter; Business Advisor, a.; Buyers' Guide

BETTER BUSINESS BUREAU OF MID-WESTERN ONTARIO
354 Charles St., Kitchener, ON N2G 4L5
519/579-3080, Fax: 519/570-0072
President, Patricia J. Tallman

BETTER BUSINESS BUREAU OF NEWFOUNDLAND
360 Topsail Rd., PO Box 516, St. John's, NF A1E 2B6
709/364-2222, Fax: 709/364-2255
Manager, Betty Mulrooney

BETTER BUSINESS BUREAU OF NOVA SCOTIA (1949)
#601, 1888 Brunswick St., Halifax, NS B3J 3J8
902/422-6581, Fax: 902/429-6457
General Manager, Marlene A. Moore

BETTER BUSINESS BUREAU OF OTTAWA & HULL (1937)
#603, 130 Albert St., Ottawa, ON K1P 5G4
613/237-4856, 233-3562, Fax: 613/237-4878
Executive Director, Leslie King
Publications: Capital Comment

BETTER BUSINESS BUREAU OF SASKATCHEWAN
#302, 2080 Broad St., Regina, SK S4P 1Y3
306/352-7601, Fax: 306/565-6236
Executive Director, Eileen McLeod

BETTER BUSINESS BUREAU OF SOUTH CENTRAL ONTARIO (1973)
100 King St. East, Hamilton, ON L8N 1A8
905/526-1111, Fax: 905/526-1225, Toll Free: 1-800-451-3815

BETTER BUSINESS BUREAU OF SOUTHERN ALBERTA (1955)
#350, 7330 Fisher St. SE, Calgary, AB T2H 2H8
403/531-8784
President, Norman Haines
General Manager, V.A. Briggs
Publications: Examiner

BETTER BUSINESS BUREAU OF VANCOUVER ISLAND (1962)
#201, 1005 Langley St., Victoria, BC V8W 1V7
250/386-6348, Fax: 250/386-2367
Contact, Susan Brice, 250/386-1416, Fax: 250/386-2367
Publications: The Better Business Bureau of Vancouver Island Membership Directory/Consumer Guide

BETTER BUSINESS BUREAU OF WESTERN ONTARIO (1983)
#616, 200 Queens Ave., London, ON N6A 1J3
519/673-3222, Fax: 519/673-5966
President, Janet B. Delaney
Publications: Membership Directory & Information Guide

BETTER BUSINESS BUREAU OF WINDSOR & SOUTHERN ONTARIO
500 Riverside Dr. West, Windsor, ON N9A 5K6
519/258-7222, Fax: 519/258-1198, Email: wbbb@wincom.net
URL: http://www.wincom.net/wbbb/
President, Joseph L. Amort

BETTER BUSINESS BUREAU OF WINNIPEG & MANITOBA (1930)
#301, 365 Hargrave St., Winnipeg, MB R3B 2K3
204/943-1486, Fax: 204/943-1489
Manager, T.S. Durham
Publications: Dateline Winnipeg

BUREAU D'ÉTHIQUE COMMERCIALE DE MONTRÉAL INC./BETTER BUSINESS BUREAU OF MONTRÉAL INC. (1928)
#460, 2055, rue Peel, Montréal, PQ H3A 1V4
514/286-1236, Téléc: 514/286-2658
Président/Directeur général, Robert Tremblay
Publications: Annuaire de la Confiance

BUREAU D'ÉTHIQUE COMMERCIALE DE QUÉBEC INC./BETTER BUSINESS BUREAU OF QUÉBEC INC. (1947)
485, rue Richelieu, Québec, PQ G1R 1K2
418/523-2555, Téléc: 418/523-2444
Vice-président executif, Jules Martineau

Canadian Council for International Business/Conseil canadien pour le commerce international (CCIB) (1990)
Canadian Secretariat ICC/BIAC
#1160, 55 Metcalfe St., Ottawa, ON K1P 6L2
613/230-5462, Fax: 613/230-7087
President/CEO, Timothy I. Page
Publications: CCIB Newsletter
Affiliates: International Chamber of Commerce; Business & Industry Advisory Committee to the OECD

Canadian Council for Public-Private Partnerships/Le conseil canadien des sociétés publiques-privées (1993)
#4700, Toronto Dominion Bank Tower, PO Box 48, Stn Toronto Dominion, Toronto, ON M5K 1E6
416/601-8333, Fax: 416/868-0673
URL: http://www.inforamp.net/~partners
Executive Administrator, Anne Dudman
President, Terry Stephen
Chair, The Hon. Donald S. Macdonald
Vice-President, Blair Cowper-Smith
Publications: Public-Private Review

Canadian Federation of Independent Business/Fédération canadienne de l'entreprise indépendante (CFIB) (1972)
#401, 4141 Yonge St., North York, ON M2P 2A6
416/222-8022, Fax: 416/222-4337, Email: cfib@cfib.ca
URL: http://www.cfib.ca
Chairman & CEO, John Bulloch
President, Catherine Swift
Senior Vice-President, Communications, Brien Gray
Alberta & Northwest Territories: Brad Wright, #940, 10123 - 99 St., Edmonton, AB T5J 3H1, 403/421-4253, Fax: 403/429-9619
British Columbia & the Yukon: Suromitra Sanatani, #525, 625 Howe St., Vancouver, BC V6C 2T6, 604/684-5325, Fax: 604/684-0529
Manitoba: Associate Director, Provincial Affairs, Dan Kelly, Holiday Towers, #607, 428 Portage Ave., Winnipeg, MB R3C 0E2, 204/947-0817, Fax: 204/957-5176
Prairie Region: Executive Director, Dale Botting, #101, 2400 College Ave., Regina, SK S4P IC8, 306/757-0000, Fax: 306/359-7623
Québec: Vice-Président, Pierre Cleroux, #900, 500, boul René-Lévesque ouest, Montréal, PQ H2Z 1W7, 514/861-3234

Canadian Franchise Association/Association canadienne de la franchise (1989)
#201, 5045 Orbitor Dr., Bldg. 12, Mississauga, ON L4W 4Y4
905/625-2896, Fax: 905/625-9076
President, Richard Cunningham
Publications: Franchising in Canada

Canadian Institute of Chartered Business Valuators (CICBV) (1971)
277 Wellington St. West, Toronto, ON M5V 3H2
416/204-3396, Fax: 416/977-8585
Executive Director, Denis R.T. White
Administrator, Kitty Jones
President, Linda Y. Brent, CBV

Vice-President, D. Jeffrey Harder, CBV
Sec.-Treas., Donald Spence
Publications: The Business Valuator; Journal of Business Valuation, a.

Canadian International Institute of Applied Negotiation/L'Institut international canadien de la négociation pratique (CIIAN) (1992)
#1422, 50 O'Connor St., Ottawa, ON K1P 6L2
613/237-9050, Fax: 613/230-1651
Executive Director, Flaurie M. Storie
Senior Associate & Director International Conflict Resolution, Senior Associate & Director International Conflict Resolutio, Benjamin Hoffman
Chair, Hon. Jus. M. MacGuigan

Canadian Labour Market & Productivity Centre/Centre canadien du marché du travail et de la productivité (CLMPC) (1984)
55 Metcalfe St., 15th Fl., Ottawa, ON K1P 6L5
613/234-0505, Fax: 613/234-2482, Email: clmpc@magi.com
CEO, Shirley Seward
Publications: Working Together

Canadian Organization of Small Business Inc. (COSBI) (1979)
The Voice of Business
PO Box 11246, Stn Main, Edmonton, AB T5H 3J5
403/423-2672, Fax: 403/423-2751
Managing Director, Donald Richard Eastcott
Chairman, Roy E. Shannon, C.A.
Publications: The Voice of Business
Eastern Office: Manager, Leonard Domino, Skymark Place, 3555 Don Mills Rd., Unit 6-105, North York, ON M2H 3N3, 416/539-7324, Fax: 416/537-7324

Canadian Professional Sales Association/Association canadienne des professionnels de la vente (CPSA) (1874)
#310, 145 Wellington St. West, Toronto, ON M5J 1H8
416/408-2685, Fax: 416/408-2684, Toll Free: 1-800-268-3794, Email: membership@cpsa.com
URL: http://www.cpsa.com
President, Terry J. Ruffell
Director, Sharon Armstrong
Publications: Contact; Travel Services, a.; Professional Development Services; Business Travel Survey; Guide to Car Costs & Policies; Canadian Sales Management Manual

Canadian Quality Council
1229 Meadow Brook Dr., Airdrie, AB T4A 1W7
403/948-3959, Fax: 403/948-3959
President, Kenneth Kivenko
Managing Director, Dirk Bannister
Event Manager, Sarah Kennedy
Publications: Canada Quality Journal

Canadian Society of Customs Brokers/Société canadienne des courtiers en douane (CSCB) (1991)
111 York St., Ottawa, ON K1N 5T4
613/562-3543, Fax: 613/562-3548
President, Carol West
Senior Policy Officer, M. Janice McBride
Publications: CSCB Bulletin
Affiliates: International Federation of Customs Brokers Associations

Canadian Turnaround Management Association/Association canadienne de redressement d'entreprises (CTMA) (1983)
1980, rue Sherbrooke ouest, 10e étage, Montréal, PQ H3H 1E5
514/937-6392, Fax: 514/933-9710
National Chairman, Harry H. Feldman, FCA
Vice-President, Bob Coffey

Secretary, Alan Mass
Treasurer, Stuart Mitchell
Publications: Journal of Corporate Renewal
Affiliates: Turnaround Management Association of America (TMA)

Conseil du patronat du Québec (CPQ) (1969)
#606, 2075 rue Université, Montréal, PQ H3A 2L1
514/288-5161, Téléc: 514/288-5165
Président, Ghislain Dufour
Publications: Bulletin d'information

Foundation for the Advancement of Canadian Entrepreneurship (FACE)
49 Wellington St. East, Toronto, ON M5E 1C9
416/363-9182

The Group for Design in Business (GDB)
275 King St. East, PO Box 119, Toronto, ON M5A 1K2
416/368-3626, Fax: 416/367-9743
President, Peter Francey
Vice-President, Peter Heywood
Secretary, Joseph Ruddy

International Association of Business Communicators
#1007, 950 Yonge St., Toronto, ON M4W 2J4
416/968-0264, Fax: 416/968-6818
Management Representative, Eden Spodek

Meeting Professionals International (MPI) (1972)
#5018, 1950 Stemmons Freeway, Dallas, TX 75207-3109 USA
214/712-7750, Fax: 214/746-7770, Telex: 535109 MPL
CEO, Edwin L. Griffin, Jr., CAE
Director of Marketing, Gary E. Boyler
Publications: The Meeting Manager; Membership Directory, a.; MPI Express
Toronto Chapter: Executive Director, Leslie Wright; President, Marsha Jones, CMP, 6519B Mississauga Rd., Mississauga, ON L5N 1A6, 905/567-9591, Fax: 905/567-9961

The National Citizens' Coalition (1967)
#907, 100 Adelaide St. West, Toronto, ON M5H 1S3
416/869-3838, Fax: 416/869-1891
President, David E.T. Somerville
Chairman, Colin T. Brown

National Quality Institute/Institut national de la qualité (NQI) (1992)
#1540, 360 Albert St., Ottawa, ON K1R 7X7
613/237-4111, Fax: 613/237-7171, Toll Free: 1-800-263-9648, Email: info@nqionline.com
URL: http://www.nqi.com
Executive Director, John Perry
Publications: NQI Newsletter

Ontario Public Buyers Association, Inc. (OPBA) (1952)
PO Box 608, Maple, ON L6A 1S5
905/682-3788, Fax: 905/682-3788
URL: http://vaxxine.com/opba
Executive Director, Carol Bott
President, James Goudreau
Vice-President, Kathryn Davey
Secretary, Patricia Baird
Treasurer, David Farrar
Publications: Caveat Emptor; Purchasing Manual
Affiliates: National Institute of Governmental Purchasing, Inc.; Institute of Purchasing & Supply of Great Britain; International Federation of Purchasing & Materials Management

Pacific Corridor Enterprise Council (PACE) (1990)
#1300, 720 Olive Way, Seattle, WA 98101-1812 USA
206/626-5474, Fax: 206/223-8984, Toll Free: 1-800-800-PACE

Chairman, Warren Wheeler
President, P. J. Fraser
Publications: Keeping PACE

CARGO HANDLING see TRANSPORTATION & SHIPPING

CASH MANAGEMENT see FINANCE

CENTRAIDE see SOCIAL RESPONSE/SOCIAL SERVICES

CHEMICAL INDUSTRY

Canadian Association of Chemical Distributors/ Association canadienne des distributeurs de produits chimiques (CACD) (1986)
627 Lyons Lane, Oakville, ON L6J 5Z7
905/844-9140, Fax: 905/844-5706
Executive Director, Aud Harlow

Canadian Chemical Producers' Association/ Association canadienne des fabricants de produits chimiques (CCPA) (1962)
#805, 350 Sparks St., Ottawa, ON K1R 7S8
613/237-6215, Fax: 613/237-4061, Toll Free: 1-800-267-6666, Email: info@ccpa.ca
URL: http://www.ccpa.ca
President, Richard Paton
Vice-President, Business Development/Sec.-Treas., D.W. Goffin
Vice-President, Technical Affairs, G.E. Lloyd
Director of Public Affairs, E.E. Alexander
Vice-President, Responsible Care, B.R. Wastle
Executive Assistant, Charlaine Gendron
Publications: Reducing Emissions Report

Canadian Explosives Distributors Association/ Association des distributeurs d'explosifs du Canada
CEDEC
35 Phylis St., Nepean, ON K2J 1W5
613/825-2989, Fax: 613/723-0013
Manager, René A. Morin
Manager, Doris Morin

Canadian Fertilizer Institute/L'Institut Canadien des Engrais (CFI)
#1540, 222 Queen St., Ottawa, ON K1P 5V9
613/230-2600, Fax: 613/230-5142
Managing Director, Roger L. Larson

ASSOCIATION DES FABRICANTS D'ENGRAIS DU QUÉBEC/QUÉBEC FERTILIZER MANUFACTURERS ASSOCIATION (AFEQ) (1956)
8075, rue Jobert, CP 218, Succ. Jean-Talon, Montréal, PQ H1S 2Z2
514/324-5081, Téléc: 514/324-6166
Directeur administratif, Donald Côté

THE ATLANTIC FERTILIZER INSTITUTE (AFI)
3 Birchwood St., Charlottetown, PE C1A 5B4
902/894-9361
Sec.-Treas., Jack Cutcliffe

CANADIAN ASSOCIATION OF AGRI-RETAILERS (1978)
#107, 1090 Waverley St., Winnipeg, MB R3T 0P4
204/989-9300, Fax: 204/989-9306
Executive Director, Jacqueline Ryrie
Publications: Input; Communicator, q.

WESTERN CANADA FERTILIZER ASSOCIATION (WCFA) (1963)
#101, 9250 - 120 St., Surrey, BC V3V 4B7
604/584-2270, Fax: 604/589-3977
Executive Secretary, D.C. McLean

Publications: WCFA Newsletter; WCFA Membership Directory, a.; Environmental Update, q.
Affiliates: Western Fertilizer & Chemical Dealers Association, Canadian Fertilizer Institute

Canadian Manufacturers of Chemical Specialties Association/Association canadienne des manufacturiers de spécialités chimiques (CMCS) (1958)
#702, 56 Sparks St., Ottawa, ON K1P 5A9
613/232-6616, Fax: 613/233-6350
President, Dr. David Halton
Publications: Mircogram

Canadian National Asbestos Council/Conseil National Canadien de l'Amiante (CANNAC) (1988)
70 Leek Cres., Richmond Hill, ON L4B 1H1
416/499-4000, Fax: 416/499-8752
Secretary/Manager, Mary Thorburn
Publications: Newsletter

The Chemical Institute of Canada/Institut de chimie du Canada (CIC) (1945)
#550, 130 Slater St., Ottawa, ON K1P 6E2
613/232-6252, Fax: 613/232-5862, Email: cscxt@acadvm1.uottawa.ca; cic_adm@fox.nstn.ca
URL: http://fox.nstn.ca/~cic_adm/
Executive Director, Anne E. Alper
President, J.R. Grace
Publications: Canadian Chemical News/L'Actualité chimique canadienne

CANADIAN SOCIETY FOR CHEMICAL ENGINEERING/SOCIÉTÉ CANADIENNE DU GÉNIE CHIMIQUE (CSCE) (1966)
#550, 130 Slater St., Ottawa, ON K1P 6E2
613/232-6252, Fax: 613/232-5862, Email: cscxt@acadvm1.uottawa.ca
URL: http://fox.nstn.ca/~cic_adm/csche.html
President, Lois Cramer
Executive Secretary, Anne E. Alper
Publications: Canadian Journal of Chemical Engineering; Canadian Chemical News, 10 pa

CANADIAN SOCIETY FOR CHEMICAL TECHNOLOGY/SOCIÉTÉ CANADIENNE DE TECHNOLOGIE CHIMIQUE (CSCT) (1971)
#550, 130 Slater St., Ottawa, ON K1P 6E2
613/232-6252, Fax: 613/232-5862, Email: cscxt@acadvm1.uottawa.ca
URL: http://fox.nstn.ca/~cic_adm/csct.html
Executive Secretary, Anne E. Alper
President, Paul Walsh

CANADIAN SOCIETY FOR CHEMISTRY/SOCIÉTÉ CANADIENNE DE CHIMIE (CSC) (1985)
#550, 130 Slater St., Ottawa, ON K1P 6E2
613/232-6252, Fax: 613/232-5862, Email: cic.adm@fox.nstn.ca
URL: http://fox.nstn.ca/~cic_adm/csc.html
Executive Secretary, Anne E. Alper
President, V. Smith

Institute for Chemical Science & Technology (ICST) (1985)
PO Box 2717, Sarnia, ON N7T 7V9
519/339-4053, Fax: 519/339-4436
Director, Dr. John Pasternak
Director, Dr. Don Murray

Oil & Colour Chemists' Organization of Ontario (OCCO) (1975)
125 Jeffcoat Dr., Etobicoke, ON M9W 3B9
416/247-6681, Fax: 416/247-7432
Secretary, John F. Ambury
Chair, David R. Hammett
Education Officer, M. Miller
Affiliates: Oil & Colour Chemists' Association (UK)

Potash & Phosphate Institute of Canada/Institut potasse et phosphate de Canada (PPIC) (1971)
CN Tower, Midtown Plaza, Saskatoon, SK S7K 1J5
306/652-3535, Fax: 306/664-8941
President, Dr. Mark D. Stauffer
Publications: Better Crops

Society of the Chemical Industry - Canadian Section (1881)
c/o Praxair Canada Inc., One City Centre Dr., Mississauga, ON L5B 1M2
905/803-1600, Fax: 905/803-1690
Honourary Secretary, Don Kirkwood

CHILD & FAMILY SERVICES see **SOCIAL RESPONSE/SOCIAL SERVICES**

CHILDBIRTH

Alberta Association of Midwives (AAM)
PO Box 1705, Edmonton, AB T5J 2P1
403/289-8334
Joy West
Affiliates: International Confederation of Midwives

Alliance québécoise des sages-femmes practiciennes/Québec Midwives Alliance (1986)
CP 246, Succ. E, Montréal, PQ H2T 3A7
514/278-8650, Téléc: 514/278-8650
Personne ressource, Michèle Champagne

Association of Ontario Midwives/Association des sages-femmes de l'Ontario (AOM) (1985)
#205, 2050 Sheppard Ave. East, North York, ON M2J 5B3
416/494-4819, Fax: 416/494-9002
President, Carol Cameron
Publications: AOM Journal

Infant Feeding Action Coalition
INFACT Canada
10 Trinity Sq., Toronto, ON M5G 1B1
416/595-9819; 488-3368, Fax: 416/598-0292,
    Email: infact@ftn.net
URL: http://www.io.org/~infacto
National Coordinator, Elisabeth Sterken
Publications: INFACT Canada Newsletter

International Society for the Study of Hypertension in Pregnancy (Canada) Inc./Société internationale pour l'étude de l'hypertension en frossesse (Canada) inc. (ISSHP) (1986)
Hôpital St-François D'Assise, Dept. OB-GYN, 10, rue de l'Espinay, Québec, PQ G1L 3L5
418/525-4461, Fax: 418/525-4481
President, Jean-Marie Moutquin

La Leche League Canada (LLLC) (1961)
18C Industrial Dr., Chesterville, ON K0C 1H0
613/448-1842, Fax: 613/448-1845
Executive Director, Carol Luck
Publications: New Beginnings
Affiliates: La Leche League International

Midwifery Task Force of British Columbia
PO Box 65343, Stn F, Vancouver, BC V5N 5P3
604/251-5976
Coordinator, Stan Howard

Midwives Association of British Columbia (MABC) (1981)
#55, 2147 Commercial Dr., Vancouver, BC V5N 5A3
604/436-6007, Fax: 604/255-1076, Info Line: 604/254-0744
Secretary, Sandy Anthony

Publications: MABC Newsletter
Affiliates: International Confederation of Midwives

Ontario Midwifery Consumer Network (OMCN) (1983)
260 Adelaide St. East, PO Box 64, Toronto, ON M5A 1N0
416/767-0427
Co-Director, Dena Zimbel
Co-Director, Beth Golden
President, Jackie Scott
Publications: Issue; Bulletin, m.
Affiliates: Association of Ontario Midwives

Parents of Multiple Births Association of Canada Inc./Association de parents de naissances multiples du Canada inc. (POMBA) (1978)
240 Graff Ave., PO Box 22005, Stratford, ON N5A 7V6
905/272-2203, Fax: 905/272-1926
President, Liz Boily
Business Services Director, Anita Grant
Publications: Double Feature; POMBA Reporter, q.

Serena Canada
151 Holland Ave., Ottawa, ON K1Y 0Y2
613/728-6536
Executive Director, Marie-Paule Doyle
Affiliates: International Federation for Family Life Promotion

Vaginal Birth After Caesarean Canada/ Accouchement vaginal après césarienne du Canada (1990)
VBAC/AVAC Canada
291 Glencairn Ave., Toronto, ON M5N 1T8
416/489-7710
Coordinator, Caroline Sufrin-Disler
Publications: VBAC/AVAC Canada Newsletter
Alberta: Contact, Bev Yadlowski, 8403 - 77 St., Edmonton, AB T6C 2L7, 403/465-2822
British Columbia: Contact, Laurie Brant, 4006 Nithsdale St., Burnaby, BC V5G 1P6, 604/433-5827

CHILDREN & YOUTH
see also Social Response/Social Services

Alberta Associations for Bright Children (AABC) (1981)
The Bright Site, #1280, 6240 - 113 St., Edmonton, AB T6H 3L2
403/413-1630, Fax: 403/413-1631, Email: aabc@freenet.edmonton.ab.ca
President, Debra Chinchilla
Publications: News Notes

Association for Bright Children (Ontario)/Société pour enfants doués et surdoués (Ontario) (ABC) (1975)
#100, 2 Bloor St. West, PO Box 156, Toronto, ON M4W 2G7
416/925-6136, Info Line: 416/925-6136
President, Margaret Tofflemire
Publications: ABC Newsmagazine

B'nai Brith Youth Organization Canada (BBYO)
BBYO Canada
4600 Bathurst St., North York, ON M2R 3V3
416/631-5724, Fax: 416/631-5718
Director, Elizabeth Sokolsky

Boys & Girls Clubs of Canada/Clubs garçons et filles du Canada (1947)
#703, 7030 Woodbine Ave., Markham, ON L3R 6G2
905/477-7272, Fax: 905/477-2056
National Executive Director, Robert Duck

National President, William R. Turner
Director, Resource Development, Michael Meadows
Publications: Canada's Kids

Canadian Association for Young Children/ L'Association canadienne pour les jeunes enfants (CAYC) (1974)
5417 Rannock Ave., Winnipeg, MB R3R 0N3
204/831-1658
President, Gayle Karen Robertson
Publications: Canadian Children

Canadian Child Care Federation/Fédération canadienne des services de garde à l'enfance (CCCF) (1987)
#306, 120 Holland Ave., Ottawa, ON K1Y 0X6
613/729-5289, Fax: 613/729-3159
Executive Director, Dianne Bascombe
President, Cathy McCormack
Publications: Interaction; Directory of Canadian Child Care Organizations, biennial

The Canadian Council for Exceptional Children/ Le Conseil canadien de l'enfance exceptionnelle
#36, 101 Polytek Ct., Gloucester, ON K1J 9J2
613/747-9226, Fax: 613/745-9282
Director, Bill Gowling
Publications: Keeping-in-Touch

Canadian Young Judaea
#205, 788 Marlee Ave., Toronto, ON M6B 3K1
416/781-5156, Fax: 416/787-3100
National Executive Director, Risa Epstein-Gamliel
Publications: The Judaean

Canadian Youth Foundation/La Fondation canadienne de la jeunesse (CYF) (1992)
215 Cooper St., 3rd Fl., Ottawa, ON K2P 0G2
613/231-6474, Fax: 613/231-6497, Email: au720@freenet.carleton.ca
Executive Director, Lucie Bohac Konrad
Executive Assistant/Project Coordinator, Elizabeth McJanet
President, David McGown
Publications: Directory of Youth Organizations in Canada

Child Find Canada Inc. (1983)
#404, 710 Dorval Dr., Oakville, ON L6K 3V7
905/845-3463, Fax: 905/845-9621, Toll Free: 1-800-387-7962
URL: http://www.discribe.ca/childfind/cfhome.htm
President, Bob Morris
Publications: Missing

CHILD FIND ALBERTA (CFA) (1983)
#101, 424 - 10 St. NW, Calgary, AB T2N 1V9
403/270-3463, Fax: 403/270-8355, Toll Free: 1-800-561-1733
Executive Director, Eric R. Sommerfeldt
Affiliates: Reseau Enfants Retour

CHILD FIND BRITISH COLUMBIA
#202, 724 Powell St., Vancouver, BC V6A 1H6
604/251-3463, Fax: 604/255-9968
President, Richard Achtem
Administrative Secretary, Connie Rauh

CHILD FIND MANITOBA (1985)
#204, 1181 Portage Ave., Winnipeg, MB R3G OT3
204/945-5735, Fax: 204/948-2461
Executive Director, Myrna Driedger
Administrative Assistant, Jennifer McFadyen
Publications: Newsletter

CHILD FIND NEW BRUNSWICK
210 Brunswick St., Fredericton, NB E3B 1G9

506/459-7250, Fax: 506/459-8742
Contact, Keith Ross

CHILD FIND NEWFOUNDLAND/LABRADOR
44 Cedar Brae Cres., St. John's, NF A1B 4R1
709/726-7735, Fax: 709/722-8404

CHILD FIND ONTARIO (1983)
#210, 710 Dorval Dr., Oakville, ON L6K 3V7
905/842-5353, Fax: 905/842-5383, Toll Free: 1-800-387-7962, Email: childfind@spectranet.ca
Executive Director, Jackie Cutmore
President, Bev Kennedy

CHILD FIND PEI INC. (CFPEI) (1988)
PO Box 1092, Charlottetown, PE C1A 7M4
902/368-1678, Fax: 902/368-1389, Toll Free: 1-800-387-7962
President, Mary Scott

CHILD FIND SASKATCHEWAN INC. (1984)
#41, 1002 Arlington Ave., Saskatoon, SK S7H 2X7
306/955-0070, Fax: 306/373-1311, Toll Free: 1-800-513-3463, Email: childfind@sasknet.sk.ca
President, Phyllis Hallatt
Child Find Yukon: Karen Routhier, PO Box 40, Watson Lake, YT Y0A 1C0, 403/536-2239

The Children's Wish Foundation of Canada/ Fondation canadienne rêves d'enfants (1984)
#8C, 1735 Bayly St., Pickering, ON L1W 3G7
905/420-4055, Fax: 905/831-9733, Toll Free: 1-800-267-9474
Executive Director, Laura Cole
National President, James Travers
Vice-President, Ciro Cucciniello
National Chairman, Lloyd Matthews
Director, PR & Communications, Wendy A. Murray
Publications: Chapters/Chapitres

Gifted Children's Association of BC (GCA/ BC) (1983)
PO Box 56589, RPO Lougheed Mall, Burnaby, BC V3J 7W2
604/534-6343, Fax: 604/534-9143
President, Cathy Martyn
Vice-President, Rae Desaulniers
Publications: Bright Connections
Affiliates: Coalition for Students with Special Needs

Giftedness Québec
École secondaire Lemoyne d'Iberville, 560, boul Lemoyne, Longueuil, PQ J4H 1X3
514/463-2900, Téléc: 514/463-3954
Personne resource, Anna-Maria F. Dumont

Girl Guides of Canada/Guides du Canada (1910)
50 Merton St., Toronto, ON M4S 1A3
416/487-5281, Fax: 416/487-5570
Chief Commissioner, Marsha Ross
Executive Director, Christine A. Featherstone
President, Rosalyn Schmidt
Communications Manager, Barbara Crocker
Publications: Canadian Guider
Affiliates: National Youth Serving Agencies; National Voluntary Organizations; Coalition on Rights of the Child; National Council of Women of Canada; Canadian Centre for Philanthropy; Canadian Camping Association; Canadian Council for Adult Education

Guides francophones du Canada (1962)
3827, rue St. Hubert, Montréal, PQ H2L 4A4
514/524-3753, Téléc: 514/524-3755
Présidente, Gilberte Gougeon
Directrice générale, Rita L. Lévesque
Commissaire nationale, Odette Lepage
Publications: Revue

Heritage of Children of Canada (1984)
73-1/2 Day Ave., Toronto, ON M6E 3W1
416/656-5408
Founder, Sylvia Lusher
Affiliates: Queens Park Legislature, all parties

Junior Achievement of Canada/Jeunes entreprises du Canada (JACAN) (1967)
One Westside Dr., Toronto, ON M9C 1B2
416/622-4602, Fax: 416/622-6861, Toll Free: 1-800-265-0699
President/CEO, Colin P. Campbell
Chairman, George E. Harvey
Publications: Revue

Kids Help Foundation/La fondation Jeunesse (1981)
#410, 60 Bloor St. West, Toronto, ON M4W 1A1
416/920-5437, Fax: 416/920-0651, Toll Free: 1-800-268-3062
National Executive Director, Heather Sproule
President, Stephen Graham
Manager of Development, Sylvia Kadlick

Manitoba Association for Bright Children (1993)
307 Country Club Blvd., Winnipeg, MB R3K 1X4
204/831-9622
President, Judith Newman
Publications: Exceptional Times

Manitoba Child Care Association (1974)
364 McGregor St., Winnipeg, MB R2W 4X3
204/586-8587, Fax: 204/589-5613
Executive Director, Dorothy Dudek
Publications: Child Care Focus

National CGIT Association (CGIT) (1915)
Canadian Girls in Training
#414, 195 The West Mall, Etobicoke, ON M9C 5k1
416/622-3979, Fax: 416/622-8356
National Co-ordinator, Susan Rogers
Publications: Torch; Carrying the Torch, a.; Creating Great Ideas Together, 3 pa
Affiliates: Canadian Baptist Federation; Christian Church (Disciples of Christ) in Canada; The Presbyterian Church in Canada; The United Church of Canada

Newfoundland & Labrador Association for Gifted Children (NLAGC)
PO Box 21364, St. John's, NF A1A 5G6
President, Susan Duffett
Publications: Newsletter

Réseau enfants retour Canada/Missing Children's Network Canada (1985)
#406, 231, rue Saint-Jacques, Montréal, PQ H2Y 1M6
514/843-4333, Téléc: 514/843-8211
Directrice générale, Susan Armstrong
Organisation(s) affiliée(s): Plaidoyer victimes - Montréal; Défense des droits des enfants internationale

SAFE KIDS Canada/Enfants en Sécurité (1993)
#1300, 180 Dundas St. West, Toronto, ON M5G 1Z8
416/813-6766, Fax: 416/813-4986
Executive Director, Dianne Merrick
Communications Coordinator, Christine Hudson
Publications: Snapshots

Saskatchewan Council on Children & Youth
PO Box 570, Pilot Butte, SK S0G 3Z0
306/352-1694
Sec.-Treas., Eunice M. Halen

Scouts Canada (1914)
Boy Scouts of Canada
1345 Baseline Rd., PO Box 5151, LCD Merivale, Ottawa, ON K2C 3G7
613/224-5131, Fax: 613/224-3571
URL: http://www.scouts.ca
Chief Executive, John C. Pettifer
President, William Forbes
Executive Director, Operations, Bob Hallett
Director, Sponsor Relations, Bryon Milliere
Executive Director, Communication & Revenue Development, John Rietveld
Director, Communications, Andy McLaughlin
Executive Director, Program Services, Robert J. Stewart
Executive Director, Supply Services, Ben Kruser
Director, Sales & Marketing, John P.J. Brugmans
Director, Purchasing, John Sharp
Executive Director, International Relations/Special Events, Robert C. Butcher
National Commissioner, Herbert C. Pitts
Information Systems Management, W. Thomas Obright
Publications: Canadian Leader
Affiliates: World Scout Bureau

CITIZENSHIP & IMMIGRATION

Canadian Citizenship Federation/Fédération canadienne du civisme (1968)
#402, 396 Cooper St., Ottawa, ON K2P 2H7
613/235-1467, Fax: 613/235-3233
Executive Secretary, Read E. Brook
President, Yaroslaw Markiza
Treasurer, Pearl Dobson
Publications: Views & News/Nouvelles et idées
Edmonton Chapter: President, Rajendra S. Chopra, 11233 - 34A Ave., Edmonton, AB T6J 3M4
Saint John Chapter: Secretary, Eric L. Teed, O.C., Q.C., PO Box 6446, Stn A, Saint John, NB E2L 4R8, 506/672-6856
Calgary Canadian Citizenship Council: Gita Boyd, #204, 4202 - 17 Ave. SE, Calgary, AB T2A 0T2, 403/272-9455
Greater Victoria Citizenship Council: President, Gladys Swityk, 1113 Fairfield Rd., Victoria, BC V8V 3A8, 250/382-0553
Montréal Citizenship Council: Menelaos Pavlides, 11227, James Morrice, Montréal, PQ H3M 2E6, 514/331-5318
Thompson Citizenship Council: Executive Director, Sukh D.H. Khokhar, 97 McGill Pl., Thompson, MB R8N 0H9, 204/677-3981, Fax: 204/778-5145
Vancouver Citizenship Council: President, Rudyard Spence, 7067 Ramsay Ave., Burnaby, BC V5E 3L3, 604/521-8793, Fax: 604/521-8793, Email: rspence@bcit.bc.ca

Chinese Information & Community Services of Metro Toronto (1968)
#310, 3852 Finch Ave. East, Toronto, ON M5T 1N6
416/292-7510, Fax: 416/292-9120, Info Line: 292-7244
Executive Director, Eliot Yip

Citizenship BC Society (1991)
268 - 59th Ave. West, Vancouver, BC V5X 1X2
604/321-5223, Fax: 604/321-5283
President, Susan French
Publications: Citizenship BC Newsletter

Citizenship Council of Manitoba Inc./Conseil Manitobain de la citoyenneté inc. (1948)
International Centre of Winnipeg
406 Edmonton St., Winnipeg, MB R3B 2M2
204/943-9158, Fax: 204/949-0734, Email: miicwpg@web.net
Executive Director, Tom R. Denton
President, R. Kaval Chohan
Publications: Daily
Affiliates: Canadian Council for Refugees

Canadian Almanac & Directory 1997

Cross Cultural Communication Centre (CCCC) (1971)
2909 Dundas St. West, Toronto, ON M6P 1Z1
416/760-7855, Fax: 416/767-4352
Chairperson, Angela Robertson
Publications: Cross Cultural Communication Centre Newsletter; Toronto Immigrant Services Directory, biennial

National Organization of Immigrant & Visible Minority Women of Canada/Organisation nationale des femmes immigrantes et des femmes appartenant à une minorité visible du Canada (NOIVMWC) (1986)
#504, 251 Bank St., Ottawa, ON K2P 1X3
613/232-0689, Fax: 613/232-0988
Executive Director, Shelley Das
Publications: NOIVMWC News

Ontario Council of Agencies Serving Immigrants (OCASI) (1977)
110 Eglinton Ave. West, 2nd Fl., Toronto, ON M4R 1A3
416/322-4950, Fax: 416/322-8082, Email: ocasi1@web.apc.org
Executive Director, Sharmini Peries
President, Kay Blair
Publications: OCASI Newsletter

Organization of Professional Immigration Consultants (OPIC) (1991)
Scotia Plaza, #6200, 40 King St. West, Toronto, ON M5H 3Z7
416/495-7965, Fax: 416/495-6373
President, Harry Goslett
Publications: Topic

Ottawa-Carleton Immigrant Services Organization/Organisation des services aux immigrants d'Ottawa-Carleton (OCISO) (1976)
959 Wellington St., Ottawa, ON K1Y 4W1
613/725-0202, Fax: 613/725-9054
URL: http://www.ncf.carleton.ca/freeport/social.services/cis/ociso/menu
Executive Director, Moy C. Tam
Publications: Newcomers' Guide to Education in Ottawa-Carleton

Portuguese Social Service Centre (PSSC) (1969)
1115 College St., Toronto, ON M6H 1B5
416/533-5507, Fax: 416/533-7175
Executive Director, Vasco Cabral

CIVIL LIBERTIES see **HUMAN RIGHTS & CIVIL LIBERTIES**

COLLEGES see **EDUCATION**

COMMUNICATIONS see **TELECOMMUNICATIONS**

COMMUNITY LIVING ASSOCIATIONS see **DISABLED PERSONS**

COMMUNITY PLANNING see **PLANNING & DEVELOPMENT**

COMPUTERS see **INFORMATION TECHNOLOGY**

CONSERVATION see **ENVIRONMENTAL**

CONSTRUCTION see **BUILDING & CONSTRUCTION**

CONSUMERS
see also Standards & Testing

Association des conseillers en consommation du Québec/Association of Consumer Consultants of Québec (ACECQ) (1978)
CP 9994, Ste-Foy, PQ G1V 4C6
418/622-1294
Personne ressource, Mary-Claude Tremblay
Publications: Info-Consom

Association des consommateurs du Québec (ACQ)
7383, rue de la Roche, Montréal, PQ H2R 2T4
514/278-5514, Téléc: 514/278-5515
Président, Alain Paquet

Canadian Society of Consumer Affairs Professionals
64 Mortimer Ave., Toronto, ON M4K 2A1
416/422-4049
Administrator, Constance Puotinen

Consumers' Association of Canada/Association des consommateurs du Canada (CAC) (1947)
#307, 267 O'Connor St., PO Box 9300, Ottawa, ON K1G 3T9
613/238-2533, Fax: 613/563-2254, Email: aa156@cfn.cs.dal.ca
URL: http://www.cfn.cs.dal.ca/Commerce/CAC/cac-script.html
Executive Director, Rosalie Daly Todd
Publications: Canadian Consumer
Affiliates: International Organization of Consumers Unions; Consumers Union - UK, USA
CAC Alberta: President, Wendy Armstrong, #304, 10136 - 100 St., Edmonton, AB T5J 0P1, 403/426-3270, Fax: 403/425-9578
CAC British Columbia: President, Evelyn Fox, #306, 198 West Hastings St., Vancouver, BC V6B 1H2, 604/682-3535, Fax: 604/682-2920
CAC Manitoba: President, Jackey Wasney, #21, 222 Osborne St. South, Winnipeg, MB R3L 1Z3, 204/452-2572, Fax: 204/284-1876
CAC New Brunswick: President, Mary Wood, PO Box 704, Rothesay, NB E2E 5A8, 506/849-1807
CAC Newfoundland: President, Dr. Robert W. Sexty, 92 Old Topsail Rd., St. John's, NF A1E 2A8, 709/737-4514, Fax: 709/737-7680
CAC Northwest Territories: President, Ruth Spence, 5007 - 50 St., PO Box 995, Yellowknife, NT X1A 2N7, 403/920-8845, Fax: 403/873-4058
CAC Nova Scotia: President, Hanson Dowell, QC, 250 Main St., PO Box 910, Middleton, NS B0S 1P0, 902/825-3059
CAC Québec: Président, Jean Carouzet, #225, 4823, rue Sherbrooke ouest, Montréal, PQ H3Z 1G7, 514/931-8556, Téléc: 514/938-1311
CAC Saskatchewan: President, Gales Barnes, 116 - 103 St. East, Saskatoon, SK S7N 1Y7, 306/242-4909, Fax: 306/373-5810
CAC Yukon: President, John Willson, c/o 11 Fiesta Lane, Etobicoke, ON M8Y 1V3, 416/255-1486, Fax: 416/255-0514

Fédération nationale des associations de consommateurs du Québec (FNACQ) (1978)
#301, 1212, rue Panet, Montréal, PQ H2L 2Y7
514/521-6820, Téléc: 514/521-0736
Personne ressource, Francesca Dalio
Secrétaire, Linda Mainville
Organisation(s) affiliée(s): International Organization of Consumers Unions

CONTRACEPTION see **REPRODUCTIVE ISSUES**

COOPERATIVE HOUSING see **HOUSING**

COPYRIGHT see **PATENTS & COPYRIGHT**

CORRECTIONAL SERVICES see **LAW**

COURTS see **LAW**

CRAFTS see **VISUAL ART, CRAFTS, FOLK ARTS**

CREDIT MANAGEMENT see **FINANCE**

CRISIS INTERVENTION see **SOCIAL RESPONSE/SOCIAL SERVICES**

CULTURE
see also Multiculturalism

Alliance for the Preservation of English in Canada (APEC) (1977)
#5068, 3080 Yonge St., Toronto, ON M4N 3N1
416/482-2732, Fax: 416/482-2732
President, Ronald P. Leitch
Publications: APEC Newsletter

Alliance Québec (1982)
#930, 630, boul René-Lévesque ouest, Montréal, PQ H3B 1S6
514/875-2771, Fax: 514/875-7507
Executive Director, David Birnbaum
President, Michael Hamelin
Director of Communications, Rob Bull
Publications: The Québecer

Assemblée internationale des parlementaires de langue française (AIPLF) (1992)
Région Amérique, 1025, rue St-Augustin, Bur. RC-13, Québec, PQ G1A 1A3
418/643-7391, Téléc: 418/643-1865
Secrétaire administrative régionale, Marie-Hélène Bergeron
Publications: Amérique

Association of Canadian Clubs/Association des cercles canadiens (1909)
237 Nepean St., Ottawa, ON K2P 0B7
613/236-8288, Fax: 613/236-8299
National Director, Barbara E. Crowder
President, The Hon. Lincoln Alexander
Publications: Association of Canadian Clubs

Association culturelle franco-manitobaine (ACFM) (1986)
340 Provencher Blvd., Winnipeg, MB R2H 0G7
204/233-8972, Téléc: 204/233-3324

Chateauguay Valley English-Speaking Peoples' Association (CVESPA) (1983)
27 Prince St., PO Box 1597, Huntingdon, PQ J0S 1H0
514/264-5386, Fax: 514/264-5387, Toll Free: 1-800-665-9841
President, Maurice J. King
Executive Director, Janet Hicks
Publications: CVESPA Newsletter

Compagnie des cent-associés francophones (1980)
182 Tanguay Ave., Sudbury, ON P3C 5G5
705/674-0281
Président, Rhéal Perron

Congrès mondial acadien (CMA)
CP 4530, Dieppe, NB E1A 6G1
506/859-1994, Téléc: 506/857-2252
Directeur général, Wilfred Roussel

ORGANIZATIONS — DENTAL 2-39

Conseil des organismes francophones du Toronto Métropolitain (COFTM) (1977)
Centre Francophone
20 Lower Spadina Ave., Toronto, ON M5V 2Z1
416/203-1220, Téléc: 416/203-1165
Directeur, Rosanna Bravar
Publications: Annuaire des ressources francophones du Grand Toronto
Organisation(s) affiliée(s): Assemblée des centres culturels de l'Ontario; Centraide

Conseil de la vie française en Amérique (CVFA) (1937)
56, rue Saint-Pierre, 1er étage, Québec, PQ G1K 4A1
418/692-1150, Téléc: 418/692-4578
Directeur général, Yvan Forest
Président, Gérard Lévesque
Secrétaire général, Roland G. La Flèche
Publications: Répertoire de la vie française en Amérique; Le Franc-Contact, trimestriel

The Council of Canadians/Le Conseil des Canadiens (COC) (1985)
#904, 251 Laurier Ave. West, Ottawa, ON K1P 5J6
613/233-2773, Fax: 613/233-6776, Toll Free: 1-800-387-7177, Email: coc@web.apc.org
Executive Director, Peter Bleyer
Chairperson, Maude Barlow
Calgary Contact, Barbara Thompson, 403/289-5006
Edmonton Contact, Jim Musson, 403/477-5341
Kingston Contact, Alan Nicholls, 613/389-4026
London Contact, Marion Brown, 519/471-8476
Regina Contact, Norm Bray, 306/586-5401
Vancouver Contact, Jim Macfarlan, 604/871-2155
North Shore Vancouver Contact, Fardad Moayeri, 604/986-5517
Victoria Contact, Beth Hill, 604/525-4765
Publications: Canadian Perspectives; ActionLink, irregular

English-Speaking Union of Canada (ESU)
#101, 485 Eglinton Ave. East, Toronto, ON M4P 1N2
416/481-8648, Fax: 416/485-5562
National President, Jean Horsey
Canadian National Secretary, Marion Owston
President, H.R.H. Prince Philip Duke of Edinburgh, KG, KT
Publications: Canadian Concord

Fédération des communautés francophones et acadienne du Canada (FCFAC)
#1404, One Nicholas St., Ottawa, ON K1N 7B7
613/241-7600, Téléc: 613/241-6046
Directeur général, Yvon Samson
Président, Jacques Michaud
Québec: #416, 2, Place Québec, Québec, PQ G1R 2B5, 418/523-8471, Téléc: 418/522-6449

ASSOCIATION CANADIENNE-FRANÇAISE DE L'ALBERTA (ACFA) (1926)
#200, 8923 - 82 Ave., Edmonton, AB T6C 1Z2
403/466-1680, Téléc: 403/465-6773
Directeur, Georges Arès
Président, Paul Denis
Publications: Le Franco

ASSOCIATION CANADIENNE-FRANÇAISE DE L'ONTARIO (ACFO) (1910)
#2005, 777 Bay St., Toronto, ON M5G 2C8
416/595-5585, Téléc: 416/595-0202
Président général, André J. Lalonde

ASSOCIATION CULTURELLE FRANCO-CANADIENNE DE LA SASKATCHEWAN (1912)
2132 Broad St., Regina, SK S4P 1Y5
306/569-1912, Téléc: 306/781-7916
Directeur général, Florent Bilodeau

ASSOCIATION FRANCO-YUKONNAISE (AFY) (1982)
CP 5205, Whitehorse, YT Y4A 4Z1
403/668-2663, Téléc: 403/663-3511
Directeur général, Pierre Bourbeau
Secrétaire, Martine Caron
Publications: L'Aurore boréale

FÉDÉRATION ACADIENNE DE LA NOUVELLE-ECOSSE/ACADIAN FEDERATION OF NOVA SCOTIA (FANE) (1968)
1106 South Park St., Halifax, NS B3H 2W7
902/421-1772, Téléc: 902/422-3942
Directrice de l'information, Joëlle Désy
Directeur général, Paul Comeau

FÉDÉRATION DES FRANCOPHONES DE TERRE-NEUVE ET DU LABRADOR (FFTNL) (1973)
265 Duckworth St., St. John's, NF A1C 1G9
709/722-0627, Téléc: 709/722-7904, Ligne sans frais: 1-800-563-9898
Directrice générale, Francine Labrie
Publications: Le Gaboteur

FÉDÉRATION DE LA JEUNESSE CANADIENNE-FRANÇAISE INC. (FJCF) (1974)
#440, 325 Dalhousie, Ottawa, ON K1N 7G2
613/562-4624, Téléc: 613/562-3995, Courrier électronique: fjcf@franco.ca
URL: http://franco.ca/fjcf/index
Directeur général, Gilles Vienneau
Présidente, Mona Fortier
Publications: Nouvelles en bref

SOCIÉTÉ DES ACADIENS ET ACADIENNES DU NOUVEAU-BRUNSWICK (SAANB)
CP 670, Petit-Rocher, NB E0B 2E0
506/783-4205, Téléc: 506/783-0629, Courrier électronique: saanbpro@nbnet.nb.ca
URL: http://www.rbmulti.nb.ca/saanb/saanb.htm
Directrice générale, Michèle Doiron
Présidente, Lise Ouellette

SOCIÉTÉ FRANCO-MANITOBAINE (SFM) (1969)
#212, 383 Provencher Blvd., Winnipeg, MB R2H 0G9
204/233-4915, Téléc: 204/233-1017, Ligne sans frais: 1-800-665-4443, Courrier électronique: sfm@franco-manitobain.org
URL: http://www.franco-manitobain.org
Directeur général, Daniel Boucher
Publications: Annuaire des services en français au Manitoba

The Royal Commonwealth Society of Canada/La Société Royale du Commonwealth du Canada (RCS)
PO Box 691, Stn Adelaide, Toronto, ON M5C 2J8
905/372-8323, Fax: 905/372-8323
Chairman, Sir Arthur Chetwynd, Bt
Publications: Commonwealth Notes

Servas Canada/To Serve Canada (1960)
229 Hillcrest Ave., North York, ON M2N 3P3
Coordinator, Michael Al Johnson
Publications: Bulletin, Servas International
Affiliates: Servas International

Société de développement des entreprises culturelles (SODEC) (1984)
#200, 1755, boul René-Lévesque est, Montréal, PQ H2K 4P6
514/873-7768, Téléc: 514/873-4388
Directrice de la planification, Martine-Andrée Racine

Société nationale de l'Acadie (SNA) (1881)
415, rue Notre-Dame, Dieppe, NB E1A 2A8
506/853-0404, Téléc: 506/853-0400
Présidente, Liane Roy
Secrétaire général, René Légère

La Société Saint-Jean-Baptiste de Montréal (SSJBM) (1834)
82, rue Sherbrooke ouest, Montréal, PQ H2X 1X3
514/843-8851, Téléc: 514/844-6369
Président général, François Lemieux
Publications: Bulletin

Townshippers' Association/Association des townshippers (TA) (1979)
#204, 1945, rue Belvedere sud, Ascot, PQ J1H 5Y3
819/566-5717, Fax: 819/566-0271
President, David Morgan
Executive Director, Susan C. Mastine
Publications: Crossroads
Affiliates: Alliance Québec; Châteauguay Valley English Speaking People's Association; Coasters Association; Committee for Anglophone Social Action; Outaouais Alliance; Voice of English Québec

Union culturelle des franco-ontariennes (UCFO) (1936)
#212, 435 St-Laurent Blvd., Ottawa, ON K1K 2Z8
613/741-1334, Téléc: 613/741-8577
Directrice générale, Guylaine Leclerc
Présidente, Madeleine Paquette
Publications: Communiqué
Organisation(s) affiliée(s): Fédération nationale des femmes canadiennes françaises; Match International; Réseau national d'action education femmes; Regroupement des organismes du patrimoine franco-ontarien; Table féministe francophone de concertation provinciale de l'Ontario

DATA PROCESSING see INFORMATION TECHNOLOGY

DEFENCE see MILITARY & VETERANS

DENTAL

Association des denturologistes du Québec (ADQ) (1971)
Complexe Raycom, #400, 5100, rue Sherbrooke est, Montréal, PQ H2K 1C8
514/252-0270, Téléc: 514/252-0392
Directrice générale, Johanne Nadeau
Publications: Le Denturo

Canadian Academy of Endodontics/L'Académie canadienne d'endodontie (1964)
#1250, 10665 Jasper Ave., Edmonton, AB T5J 3S9
403/425-8930, Fax: 403/420-1744
Executive Director, Dr. Carl Hawrish
Publications: Newsletter of the C.A.E.
Affiliates: Canadian Dental Association

Canadian Academy of Oral Pathology/Académie canadienne de pathologie buccale (CAOP)
University of Western Ontario, Dept. of Oral Pathology, London, ON N6A 5C1
519/679-2111, Fax: 519/661-3370
President, Dr. T.D. Dailey

Canadian Academy of Oral Radiology/Académie canadienne de radiologie buccale (CAOR)
University of Toronto, Faculty of Dentistry, 124 Edward St., Toronto, ON M5G 1G6
416/979-4932, ext.4365, Fax: 416/979-4936
President, Dr. P.A. Sikorski
Sec.-Treas., Dr. G. Petrikowski

Canadian Association for Dental Research/Association canadienne de recherches dentaires
University of Alberta, Faculty of Dentistry, #3036, 46 University Campus NW, Edmonton, AB T6G 2N8

Canadian Almanac & Directory 1997

403/492-3631, Fax: 403/491-1624
Sec.-Treas., Dr. Carl Osadetz

Canadian Association of Orthodontists/ Association canadienne des orthodontists (CAO) (1949)
#310, 2175 Sheppard Ave. East, North York, ON M2J 1W8
416/491-3186, Fax: 416/491-1670
Administrator, Diane Gaunt
Publications: CAO Newsletter

Canadian Association of Public Health Dentistry (CAPHD)
c/o Alberta Dental Association, #101, 8230 - 105th St., Edmonton, AB T6E 5H9
403/432-1012, Fax: 403/432-4864
President, G. Thompson
Secretary, E.C.S. Swan
Publications: Journal of Community Dentistry
Affiliates: Canadian Dental Association

Canadian Dental Assistants Association (CDAA) (1945)
#105, 1785 Alta Vista Dr., Ottawa, ON K1G 3Y6
613/521-5495, Fax: 613/521-5572
Executive Director, Dawn Roach
Executive Assistant, Jill Ramsey
Publications: CDAA Journal

Canadian Dental Association/L'Association dentaire canadienne (CDA) (1902)
1815 Alta Vista Dr., Ottawa, ON K1G 3Y6
613/523-1770, Fax: 613/523-7736
Executive Director, Jardine Neilson
President, Dr. James Brookfield
Manager, Information Services, Lisa Burke
Publications: Journal of Canadian Dental Association
Affiliates: Fédération dentaire internationale

ALBERTA DENTAL ASSOCIATION
#101, 8230 - 105 St., Edmonton, AB T6E 5H9
403/432-1012, Fax: 403/433-4864
Registrar, Dr. B.E. Leroy

ASSOCIATION DES CHIRURGIENS DENTISTES DU QUÉBEC
#1425, 425, boul de Maisonneuve ouest, Montréal, PQ H3A 3G5
514/282-1425, Téléc: 514/282-0255
Directeur général, Claude Chicoine

COLLEGE OF DENTAL SURGEONS OF BRITISH COLUMBIA (1908)
#500, 1765 - 8th Ave. West, Vancouver, BC V6J 5C6
604/736-3621, Fax: 604/734-9448
Registrar/CEO, Dr. G.R. Thordarson
Publications: Bulletin

COLLEGE OF DENTAL SURGEONS OF SASKATCHEWAN (1906)
#202, 728 Spadina Cres. East, Saskatoon, SK S7K 4H7
306/244-5072, Fax: 306/244-2476
Registrar, Dr. G.H. Peacock

DENTAL ASSOCIATION OF PRINCE EDWARD ISLAND
184 Belvedere Ave., Charlottetown, PE C1A 2Z1
902/566-5199, Fax: 902/892-4470
Secretary, Dr. B.D. Barrett

MANITOBA DENTAL ASSOCIATION (MDA) (1983)
#103, 698 Corydon Ave., Winnipeg, MB R3M 0X9
204/453-0055, Fax: 204/453-0108
Registrar, Dr. M.A. Lasko
Publications: The Bulletin

NEW BRUNSWICK DENTAL SOCIETY/SOCIÉTÉ DENTAIRE DU NOUVEAU-BRUNSWICK (1890)
Carleton Place, #820, 520 King St., PO Box 488, Stn A, Fredericton, NB E3B 4Z9
506/452-8575, Fax: 506/452-1872
Registrar, Dr. Philip Cyr

NEWFOUNDLAND DENTAL ASSOCIATION
139 Water St., 9th Fl., St. John's, NF A1C 1B2
709/579-2362, Fax: 709/579-1250
Executive Director, Dr. Gary MacDonald

NOVA SCOTIA DENTAL ASSOCIATION (NSDA) (1891)
#604, 5991 Spring Garden Rd., Halifax, NS B3H 1Y6
902/420-0088, Fax: 902/423-6537
Executive Director, D.V. Pamenter
Publications: Dispatch; NS Dentist, bi-m.

ONTARIO DENTAL ASSOCIATION (ODA)
4 New St., Toronto, ON M5R 1P6
416/922-3900, Fax: 416/922-9005
Executive Director, John C. Gillies, CAE
President, Dr. Elizabeth MacSween

Canadian Dental Hygienists' Association/ Association canadienne des hygiènistes denteurs (CDHA) (1963)
96 Centrepointe Dr., Nepean, ON K2G 6B1
613/224-5515, Fax: 613/224-7283
Executive Director, Carol Matheson Worobey
Publications: Probe; Explorer, bi-m.

College of Dental Technologists of Ontario
#321, 2100 Ellesmere Rd., Scarborough, ON M1H 3B7
416/438-5003, Fax: 416/438-5004
Registrar, E. Cheung
Chairman, Joseph B. Nagy, RDT
Publications: RDT Lists

Commercial Dental Laboratory Conference
PO Box 272, Kingston, ON K7L 4V8
613/531-8336, Fax: 613/548-8188
Treasurer, Rick King

CUMBA (1944)
562 Eglinton Ave. East, Toronto, ON M4P 1B9
416/487-5451, Fax: 416/487-3379
President/CEO, C.J. McCrodan

Dentistry Canada Fund/Fonds dentaire canadien (DCF) (1994)
1815 Alta Vista Dr., Ottawa, ON K1G 3Y6
613/523-1770, Fax: 613/523-7736, Email: dcfsjw@magi.com
Executive Vice-President, James Wegg
Chairman, Dr. Gordon Thompson
Affiliates: Canadian Dental Association

Denturist Association of Canada/Association des denturologistes du Canada (DAC) (1971)
PO Box 46114, RPO Westdale, Winnipeg, MB R3R 3S3
204/897-1087, Fax: 204/895-9595, Toll Free: 1-800-773-0099
Executive Director, William D. Buxton
President, Austin J. Carbone
Executive Secretary, Gerry Hansen
Publications: Canadian Denturist

ALBERTA DENTURIST SOCIETY (1980)
#1240, 10060 Jasper Ave., Edmonton, AB T5J 3R8
403/429-2330 (Edmonton & area), Fax: 403/429-2336, Toll Free: 1-800-260-2742
Administrator, Lorrie Rees
Affiliates: National Council of Denturist Governing Bodies; National Council of Denturist Educators

DENTURIST ASSOCIATION OF MANITOBA (1970)
PO Box 46105, RPO Westdale, Winnipeg, MB R3R 3S3
204/897-1087, Fax: 204/895-9595
Administrator, Gerry Hansen

DENTURIST ASSOCIATION OF NEWFOUNDLAND & LABRADOR
9 Bay Bulls Rd., St. John's, NF A1G 1A2
709/368-1332, Fax: 709/364-4813
President, John P. Browne

DENTURIST ASSOCIATION OF ONTARIO (DAO)
#200, 5925 Airport Rd., Mississauga, ON L4V 1W1
905/405-6258, Fax: 905/405-6259
Executive Director, Clifford Muzylowsky
Publications: The Denturist

DENTURIST SOCIETY OF BRITISH COLUMBIA
#C312, 9801 King George Hwy., Surrey, BC V3T 5H5
604/582-6823, Fax: 604/582-6823
Sec.-Treas., Dorothy MacArthur

DENTURIST SOCIETY OF NOVA SCOTIA
209 High St., Bridgewater, NS B4V 1W2
902/543-6228, Fax: 902/543-6278
President, Ken Edwards

DENTURIST SOCIETY OF PRINCE EDWARD ISLAND
151 Hanover St., Summerside, PE C1N 1E5
902/436-3295
President, Boyd P. Bernard

DENTURIST SOCIETY OF SASKATCHEWAN
231 - 23 St. East, Saskatoon, SK S7K 0J3
306/242-5088, Fax: 306/343-9361
President, Brent Rempel

NEW BRUNSWICK DENTURISTS SOCIETY/SOCIÉTÉ DES DENTUROLOGISTES DU NOUVEAU-BRUNSWICK (1973)
PO Box 954, Woodstock, NB E0J 2B0
506/450-4900
Executive Director, William D. Buxton

National Dental Examining Board of Canada
#203, 100 Bronson Ave., Ottawa, ON K1R 6G8
613/236-5912, Fax: 613/236-8386
Registrar & Executive Director, Dr. Jack D. Gerrow

Newfoundland Dental Board
139 Water St., 6th Fl., St. John's, NF A1C 1B2
709/579-2391, Fax: 709/579-2392
Secretary Registrar, Dr. Charles P. Daly

Ontario Dental Nurses & Assistants Association
869 Dundas St., London, ON N5W 2Z8
519/679-2566, Fax: 519/679-8494
CEO, Ian Tripp

Ordre des dentistes du Québec (ODQ) (1973)
625, boul René-Lévesque ouest, 15e étage, Montréal, PQ H3B 1R2
514/875-8511, Téléc: 514/393-9248, Ligne sans frais: 1-800-361-4888
URL: http://odq.qc.ca
Directeur général et secrétaire, Paul J. Thériault
Publications: Journal dentaire du Québec
Organisation(s) affiliée(s): Association dentaire canadienne

Ordre des denturologistes du Québec (ODQ) (1973)
#106, 45, Place Charles Lemoyne, Longueuil, PQ J4K 5G5
514/646-7922, Téléc: 514/646-2509, Ligne sans frais: 1-800-567-2251
Directrice générale et secrétaire, Monique Bouchard
Publications: Le Périodique

Provincial Dental Board of Nova Scotia
#602, 5991 Spring Garden Rd., Halifax, NS B3H 1Y6
902/420-0083, Fax: 902/492-0301
Registrar, Dr. D.M.J. Bonang

Provincial Dental Council of Prince Edward Island
184 Belvedere Ave., Charlottetown, PE C1A 2Z1
902/566-5199
Registrar, Dr. Ray Wenn

Royal College of Dental Surgeons of Ontario (1868)
RCDS of Ontario
6 Crescent Rd., 5th Fl., Toronto, ON M4W 1T1
416/961-6555, Fax: 416/961-5814, Toll Free: 1-800-565-4591
Registrar, Dr. Roger L. Ellis
Publications: Dispatch

Royal College of Dentists of Canada
#1706, 365 Bloor St. East, Toronto, ON M4W 3L4
416/929-2722, Fax: 416/929-5924
Executive Director, Kay Montgomery

DEVELOPING COUNTRIES see **INTERNATIONAL COOPERATION/INTERNATIONAL RELATIONS**

DEVELOPMENT EDUCATION RELATIONS see **INTERNATIONAL COOPERATION/INTERNATIONAL RELATIONS**

DISABLED PERSONS

AboutFace (1985)
99 Crowns Lane, 4th Fl., Toronto, ON M5R 3P4
416/944-3223, Fax: 416/944-2488, Email: aface@io.org
Executive Director, Anna Pileggi
Office Manager, Consuelo McQueen
Communications & Marketing Manager, Lorna Renooy
Community Outreach Coordinator, Linda Walters
Publications: Aboutfigure

Advocacy Resource Centre for the Handicapped/ Centre de la Défense des Droits des Handicapés (ARCH)
#255, 40 Orchard View Blvd., Toronto, ON M4R 1B9
416/482-8255, Fax: 416/482-2981, TDD: 416/482-1254
Executive Director, David Baker
President, Ron McInnes
Publications: ARCH-TYPE

Alberta Association of Rehabilitation Centres (AARC) (1972)
Box 105, 2725 - 12 St. NE, Calgary, AB T2E 7J2
403/250-9495, Fax: 403/291-9864
Executive Director, Gail Roberson
President, Rita Thompson
Publications: Network

Alberta Committee of Citizens with Disabilities (ACCD) (1973)
Princeton Place, #707, 10339 - 124 St., Edmonton, AB T5N 3W1
403/488-0988, Fax: 403/488-3757, TDD: 403/488-9090, Toll Free: 1-800-387-2514, Email: accd@oanet.com
Executive Director, Beverley D. Matthiessen
Publications: The Alberta Citizen; Action News
Affiliates: Council of Canadians with Disabilities

Association for the Neurologically Disabled of Canada (AND)
59 Clement Rd., Etobicoke, ON M9R 1Y5
416/244-1992, Fax: 416/244-4099, Toll Free: 1-800-561-1497
Executive Director, Kathleen Haswell
President, Robert S. Nelson
Publications: A.N.D. - NOW

Association du Québec pour enfants avec problèmes auditifs (AQEPA) (1969)
#427, 3700, rue Berri, Montréal, PQ H2L 4G9
514/842-8706, Téléc: 514/842-8706
Directrice générale, Pauline Lazure
Publications: Entendre

Association québécoise de loisir pour personnes handicapées/Québec Leisure Association for Handicapped Persons (AQLPH) (1979)
4545, av Pierre de Coubertin, CP 1000, Succ. M, Montréal, PQ H1V 3R2
514/252-3144, Téléc: 514/252-3164
Directrice générale, Madeleine Cruvelier
Publications: Habilités loisirs; Centre de doc., annuel
Organisation(s) affiliée(s): Regroupement loisir Québec; Confédération des organismes provinciaux de personnes handicapées du Québec

Association for Vaccine Damaged Children (1986)
56 Brisco St., Brampton, ON L6V 1W8
905/454-2237
Contact, Nancy Howes

BALANCE (1986)
#302, 4920 Dundas St. West, Etobicoke, ON M9A 1B7
416/236-1796, Fax: 416/236-4280, Email: balkh@terraport.net
Executive Director, Susan Archibald
Chairperson, Kevin Perry

Bob Rumball Centre for the Deaf (BRCD) (1979)
2395 Bayview Ave., North York, ON M2L 1A2
416/449-9651 (Voice & TDD), Fax: 416/449-8881, Toll Free: 1-800-841-9663
Interim Executive Director, Rev. Robert Rumball
Chairman, Alistair M. Fraser
Supervisor of Centre Programs, Shirley Cassel
Manager of Finance, James Pennock

Canadian Association for Community Living/ Association canadienne pour l'intégration communautaire (CACL) (1958)
Kinsmen Building, York University Campus, 4700 Keele St., North York, ON M3J 1P3
416/661-9611, Fax: 416/661-5701
President, Julia Stone
Executive Vice-President, Diane Richler
Publications: Entourage

ALBERTA ASSOCIATION FOR COMMUNITY LIVING (AACL) (1954)
11724 Kingsway Ave., Edmonton, AB T5G 0X5
403/451-3055, Fax: 403/453-5779, Toll Free: 1-800-252-7556, Email: aacl@ccinet.ab.ca
URL: http://www.ccinet.ab.ca//aacl/
Executive Director, Bruce Uditsky
President, Zuhy Sayeed
Publications: Bulletin; Connections, q.
Affiliates: Alberta Community Living Foundation

ASSOCIATION FOR COMMUNITY LIVING - MANITOBA
#1, 90 Market Ave., Winnipeg, MB R3B 0P3
204/947-1118, Fax: 204/949-1464
Executive Director, Dale Kendel
President, Moira Grahame

ASSOCIATION DU QUÉBEC POUR L'INTÉGRATION SOCIALE/ QUÉBEC ASSOCIATION FOR COMMUNITY LIVING (AQIS) (1951)
3958, rue Dandurand, Montréal, PQ H1X 1P7
514/725-7245, Téléc: 514/725-2976
Directrice générale, Diane Milliard
Présidente, Diane Roy
Conseillère aux communications, Nadia Lagha
Publications: L'Ebruiteur

BRITISH COLUMBIA ASSOCIATION FOR COMMUNITY LIVING (BCACL) (1955)
#300, 30 - 6th Ave. East, Vancouver, BC V5T 4P4
604/875-1119, Fax: 604/875-6744
Executive Director, Judy Carter-Smith
President, Dick Calkins
Publications: BCACL Chapter Information List; Community Living News, q.

NEW BRUNSWICK ASSOCIATION FOR COMMUNITY LIVING/ ASSOCIATION DU NOUVEAU-BRUNSWICK POUR L'INTÉGRATION COMMUNAUTAIRE (1957)
86 York St., 2nd Fl., Fredericton, NB E3B 3N5
506/458-8866, Fax: 506/452-9791
Executive Director, Lorraine Silliphant
President, Joanne Kraftcheck

NEWFOUNDLAND ASSOCIATION FOR COMMUNITY LIVING (NACL) (1976)
Prudential Bldg., 49 Elizabeth Ave., PO Box 5453, Stn C, St. John's, NF A1C 5W4
709/722-0790, Fax: 709/722-1325
Executive Director, Michele T. Neary
President, Florence Paul
Publications: Gateway

NOVA SCOTIA ASSOCIATION FOR COMMUNITY LIVING
10 Portland St., Dartmouth, NS B2Y 1G9
902/469-1174, Fax: 902/461-0196
Executive Director, Mary Rothman
President, Tim Boulton

THE ONTARIO ASSOCIATION FOR COMMUNITY LIVING/ ASSOCIATION POUR L'INTÉGRATION COMMUNAUTAIRE DE L'ONTARIO (OACL) (1953)
#403, 240 Duncan Mill Rd., North York, ON M3B 1Z4
416/447-4348, Fax: 416/447-8974
URL: http://www.acl.on.ca
Executive Director, Barbara A. Thornber
President, Nancy Stone
Publications: Directions; OACL Directory, bi-a.

PRINCE EDWARD ISLAND ASSOCIATION FOR COMMUNITY LIVING (1986)
1 Rochforn Ave., PO Box 280, Charlottetown, PE C1A 7K4
902/566-4844, Fax: 902/368-8057
Executive Director, Madonna Fradsham
President, Mary McPhee
Publications: Connections

SASKATCHEWAN ASSOCIATION FOR COMMUNITY LIVING (SACL) (1955)
3031 Louise St., Saskatoon, SK S7J 3L1
306/955-3344, Fax: 306/373-3070
Executive Director, Karen Rongve
President, Greg Plosz
Publications: Dialect

YELLOWKNIFE ASSOCIATION FOR COMMUNITY LIVING
4912 - 53 St., PO Box 981, Yellowknife, NT X1A 2N7
403/920-2644, Fax: 403/920-2348
Executive Director, Lanny Cooke
President, Don Clunie

YUKON ASSOCIATION FOR COMMUNITY LIVING (1964)
PO Box 4853, Whitehorse, YT Y1A 4N6
403/667-4606, Fax: 403/667-4606
President, Kathleen Curtis
Program Coordinator, Vicki Wilson
Publications: Visions

Canadian Association of the Deaf/Association des sourds du Canada (CAD) (1940)
#205, 2435 Holly Lane, Ottawa, ON K1V 7P2
613/526-4785, Fax: 613/526-4718
Executive Director, James D. Roots
Publications: Deaf Canada/CAD Chat
Affiliates: World Federation of the Deaf; Council of Canadians with Disabilities

Canadian Association of Independent Living Centres/Association canadienne des centres de vie autonome (CAILC) (1985)
#1004, 350 Sparks St., Ottawa, ON K1R 7S8
613/563-2581, Fax: 613/235-4497
National Director, Traci Walters
Publications: CAILC Communique

Canadian Almanac & Directory 1997

ORGANIZATIONS —DISABLED PERSONS

Canadian Brain Injury Coalition/La coalition canadienne des traumatisés craniens (CBIC) (1989)
29 Pearce Ave., Winnipeg, MB R2V 2K3
204/334-0471, Fax: 204/339-1034
Executive Director, Diane Bastiaansson

The Canadian Council of the Blind/Le Conseil canadien des aveugles (CCB) (1945)
#405, 396 Cooper St., Ottawa, ON K2P 2H7
613/567-0311, Fax: 613/567-2728
Executive Director, M.L. Moran
Affiliates: World Blind Union

Canadian Council on Rehabilitation & Work/Le Conseil canadien de la réadaptation et du travail (CCRW) (1976)
20 King St. West, 9th Fl., Toronto, ON M5H 1C4
204/974-5575; TTY/ATS: 416/974-3646, Fax: 204/974-5577, Email: info@ccrw.org
URL: http://www.ccrw.org
Executive Director, David Pollock
Publications: Ability & Enterprise

Canadian Cultural Society of The Deaf, Inc. (1973)
11337 - 61 Ave, House 144, Edmonton, AB T6H 1M3
403/436-2599, Fax: 403/430-9489
Contact, Carolyn Anne Fritz
Publications: CCSD Newsletter

Canadian Deafened Persons Association (CDPA) (1987)
310 Elmgrove Rd., Ottawa, ON K1A 3L1
613/729-6274, Fax: 613/729-5265
Publications: CDPA Newsletter
Affiliates: Canadian Association of Captioning Consumers

Canadian Deafness Research & Training Institute/Institut canadien de recherche et de formation sur la surdité (CDRTI) (1988)
2300, boul René-Lévesque ouest, Québec, PQ H3H 2R5
514/937-2191, Fax: 514/937-2284
President, Dr. J.C. MacDougall

Canadian Disability Rights Council/Conseil canadien des droits des personnes handicapées (CDRC) (1988)
#208, 428 Portage Ave., Winnipeg, MB R3C 0E2
204/943-4787, Fax: 204/949-1223
Executive Director, Sue Williams
Staff Lawyer, Priti Shaw
Publications: Update

Canadian Foundation for Physically Disabled Persons (1984)
731 Runnymede Rd., Toronto, ON M6N 3V7
416/760-7351, Fax: 416/760-9405
Administrator, Barbara Logan
Chairman, Vim Kochhar
Publications: WhyNot

Canadian Guide Dogs for the Blind (CGDB) (1984)
4120 Rideau Valley Dr. North, PO Box 280, Manotick, ON K4M 1A3
613/692-7777, Fax: 613/692-0650
Vice-President, Jane Thornton

Canadian Hard of Hearing Association/ Association des malentendants canadiens (CHHA) (1982)
#205, 2435 Holly Lane, Ottawa, ON K1V 7P2
613/526-1584; TTY 613/526-2692, Fax: 613/526-4718, Toll Free: 1-800-263-8068, Email: chhanational@cyberus.ca
National Coordinator, Janice McNamaro

Canadian Almanac & Directory 1997

President, Fred Clark
Publications: Listen/Écoute

Canadian Hearing Society (CHS) (1940)
271 Spadina Rd., Toronto, ON M5R 2V3
416/964-9595; TTY: 416/964-0023, Fax: 416/928-2525, Toll Free: 1-800-465-4327, Email: info@chs.ca
URL: http://www.chs.ca
Executive Director, David A. Allen
President, Keith Golem
Executive Assistant, Angela Palmer
Assistant Executive Director, Iris Boshes
Director, Social Services Development, Gary Malkowski
Director, Hearing Health Care, Joanne Deluzio
Director, Finance & Support Services, Tom McNeil
Director, Human Resources, Edna Soostar
Director, Information & Public Relations, Susan Main
Publications: Vibes
Affiliates: Canadian Hearing Society Foundation

The Canadian National Institute for the Blind/ L'Institut national canadien pour les aveugles (CNIB) (1918)
1929 Bayview Ave., Toronto, ON M4G 3E8
416/480-7580, Fax: 416/480-7677
National Director, Communications & Human Resources, Robert Elton
President/CEO, Euclid J. Herie
Chairman, National Council, F. Garrick Homer
Publications: CNIB National Annual Review
Affiliates: World Blind Union
Division du Québec: Interim Executive Director, Jim Sanders, 3622, rue Hochelaga, Montréal, PQ H1W 1J1, 514/529-2040, Téléc: 514/529-4662, Ligne sans frais: 1-800-465-4622

Canadian Speech Communicators Association
c/o Lethbridge Community College, 3000 South College Dr., Lethbridge, AB T1K 1L6
403/320-3344, Fax: 403/320-1461
Contact, Yvonne Holm
Publications: Spectrum

Christian Record Services Inc. (1899)
National Camps for the Blind
#119, 1300 King St. East, Oshawa, ON L1H 8N9
905/436-6938, Fax: 905/436-7102
Executive Director, Patricia L. Page
Publications: Christian Record; Christian Record Talking Magazine, bi-m.; Young & Alive, q.; Lifeglow, q.

Consumer Organization of Disabled People of Newfoundland & Labrador (COD) (1980)
PO Box 422, Stn C, St. John's, NF A1C 5K4
709/722-7011, Fax: 709/722-4424
Executive Director, Mary Ennis
Publications: COD-E-BATE
Affiliates: Council of Canadians with Disabilities

Council of Canadians with Disabilities/Conseil des Canadiens avec déficiences (CCD) (1976)
#926, 294 Portage Ave., Winnipeg, MB R3C 0B9
204/947-0303, Fax: 204/942-4625, Telex: 23 7601197, Email: ccd@pcs.mb.ca
National Coordinator, Laurie Beachell
Research Analyst, April D'Aufin
Publications: A Voice of Our Own
Affiliates: Consumer Organization of Disabled People of Newfoundland & Labrador; PEI Council of the Disabled; Nova Scotia League for Equal Opportunities; PUSH-Ontario; Manitoba League of the Physically Handicapped; Saskatchewan Voice of the Handicapped; Alberta Committee of Disabled Citizens; British Columbia Coalition of the Disabled; Association canadienne des sourds; DAWN Canada; National Network on Mental Health; Thalidomide Victims of Canada; National Education Association of Disabled Students; People First of Canada

Deaf Youth Canada/Jeunesse sourde canadienne (1975)
c/o Alberta School for the Deaf, 6240 - 113 St., Edmonton, AB T6H 3L2
403/422-0244, Fax: 403/422-2036
President, Joe McLaughlin
Affiliates: Canadian Association of the Deaf

Easter Seal Research Institute (1976)
#200, 250 Ferrand Dr., North York, ON M3C 3P2
416/421-8377, Fax: 416/696-1035, Toll Free: 1-800-668-6252, Email: info@easterseals.org
President, Roger Lee
Administrator, Anne Michie
Publications: PediaRehab

Easter Seals/March of Dimes National Council/ Conseil National des Timbres de Pâques et de la Parade des dix sous (1962)
Canadian Rehabilitation Council for the Disabled
#511, 90 Eglinton Ave. East, Toronto, ON M4P 2Y3
416/932-8382, Fax: 416/932-9844, TDD: 416/250-7490
National Executive Director, Heather Stonehouse
Publications: Rehabilitation Digest; The Lily Tree
Affiliates: Canadian Life & Health Insurance Association; Insurance Bureau of Canada; National Voluntary Organizations Committee; National Voluntary Health Agencies Committee; Canadian Council on Health Services Accreditation; Canadian Standards Association; National Institute for Disability Management & Research

ABILITIES FOUNDATION OF NOVA SCOTIA (1985)
Easter Seals
3670 Kempt Rd., Halifax, NS B3K 4X8
902/429-3420, Fax: 902/454-6121
President & CEO, Thomas G. Merriam
Publications: Abilities Foundation

ALBERTA REHABILITATION COUNCIL FOR THE DISABLED
Easter Seal Ability Council
#400, 10909 Jasper Ave., Edmonton, AB T5J 3L9
403/429-0137, Fax: 403/429-1937, TDD: 403/429-2065
Executive Director, Jim Killick
Provincial Administrator, Karon Shaw

CENTRE DE RÉADAPTATION CONSTANCE-LETHBRIDGE/ CONSTANCE LETHBRIDGE REHABILITATION CENTRE (CRCL) (1945)
7005, boul de Maisonneuve ouest, Montréal, PQ H4B 1T3
514/487-1770, Téléc: 514/487-2745
Directeur exécutif par intérim, Pierre G. Bourgeau
Organisation(s) affiliée(s): Association des centres d'accueil du Québec

THE EASTER SEAL SOCIETY (ONTARIO)/SOCIÉTÉ DU TIMBRE DE PÂQUES DE L'ONTARIO (TESS) (1922)
Ontario Society for Crippled Children
#200, 250 Ferrand Dr., North York, ON M3C 3P2
416/421-8377, Fax: 416/696-1035, Toll Free: 1-800-668-6252
Executive Director, Peter Ely
President, H. Richard C. Pedlar
Vice-President & Secretary, Steward D. Davidson
Treasurer, Nicholas E. O'Nians
Publications: Horizons
Barrie District Office: District Nurse, Donna Schwan, #25B, 80 Bradford St., PO Box 65, Barrie, ON L4N 6S7, 705/737-2621
Hamilton District Office: District Nurse, Angela Conlin, Chedoke-McMaster Hospitals, Chedoke Division, PO Box 2000, Stn A, Hamilton, ON L8N 3Z5, 905/385-5389, 5380

ORGANIZATIONS — DISABLED PERSONS

Hugh MacMillan Rehabilitation Centre: District Nurse, Carolyn Hitchinson, 350 Rumsey Rd., Toronto, ON M4G 1R8, 416/424-3853
Kingston District Office: District Nurse, N. Wiskin, #205, 797 Princess St., Kingston, ON K7L 1G1, 613/542-2408
Kitchener District Office: District Nurse, Raye Elmslie, 828 King St. West, Kitchener, ON N2G 1E8, 519/742-5489
London District Office: District Nurse, Marion Barnes, 779 Baseline Rd. East, London, ON N6C 5Y6, 519/685-8694, Fax: 519/685-8678
Mississauga District Office: District Nurse, Sandra Onyschuk, #205, 3415 Dixie Rd., Mississauga, ON L4Y 2B1, 905/625-3373
North Bay District: District Nurse, Carol Thorn, #307, 222 McIntyre St. West, North Bay, ON P1B 2Y8, 705/472-4320, 4812
Ottawa District Office: Contact, Joan Archibald, #603, 880 Wellington St., Ottawa, ON K1R 6K7, 613/238-6133
Peterborough District Office: District Nurse, Joan Moyer, #07B, 223 Aylmer St. North., Peterborough, ON K9J 3K3, 705/742-6435
Sault Ste. Marie District Office: District Nurse, Maria Vardy, #307, 369 Queen St. East, Sault Ste Marie, ON P6A 1Z4, 705/256-6112
Sudbury District Office: District Nurse, Catherine Rousell, #310, 51 Elm St., Sudbury, ON P3C 1S3, 705/673-7513, 7528
Thunder Bay District Office: Contact, Sheleigh McMillan, R.N., Chapple Building, #312, 101 Syndicate Ave. North, Thunder Bay, ON P7C 3V4, 807/622-1401, 7354
Timmins District Office: District Nurse, Aline Bouillon, The 101 Mall, #121, 38 Pine St. North, Timmins, ON P4N 6K6, 705/264-3005, 7909
Toronto Area District Office: 250 Ferrand Dr., Lower Concourse, North York, ON M3C 3P2, 416/421-8585
Windsor District Office: District Nurse, Nancy Shank, #701, 500 Ouellette Ave., Windsor, ON N9A 1B3, 519/252-5769

KINSMEN REHABILITATION FOUNDATION OF BRITISH COLUMBIA (KRF) (1952)
#300, 999 West Broadway, Vancouver, BC V5Z 4R1
604/736-8841, Fax: 604/738-0015, TDD: 604/738-0603
URL: http://mindlink.net/kinsmen_rehab/
CEO, Andy Danyliu
Manager, Client Support & Information Services, Kathy Ellis, Email: kathy@kinsmen.mlnet.com
Publications: Know No Limits

NEWFOUNDLAND SOCIETY FOR THE PHYSICALLY DISABLED
Building 567, St. John's Place, PO Box 1403, Stn C, Pleasantville, NF A1C 5N5
709/754-1970, Fax: 709/754-3116
Executive Director, Samuel Tibbo
President, Ed Stratton
Vice-President, Fraser Edison
Honorable Treasurer, Frank Kelly
Honorable Secretary, William Day

ONTARIO MARCH OF DIMES/MARCHE DES DIX SOUS DE L'ONTARIO (OMOD) (1951)
Rehabilitation Foundation for the Disabled
10 Overlea Blvd., Toronto, ON M4H 1A4
416/425-3463, Fax: 416/425-1920, Toll Free: 1-800-263-3463, Email: omod@inforamp.net
URL: http://www.omod.org
Executive Director, Andria Spindel
Publications: The Dime Planner; Dimensions; PoliOntario Newsletter; C.E. Bulletin
Affiliates: Stroke Recovery Association of Ontario; Positive Action for Conductive Education

Hamilton Regional Office: Regional Director, Pearl Wolfe, 20 Jarvis St., Hamilton, ON L8R 1M2, 905/528-9432
Kingston/Ottawa Regional Office: Regional Director, Jane Szilvassy, 324 Patrick St., Kingston, ON K7K 6R6, 613/549-4141, Fax: 613/549-6321
London Regional Office: Regional Director, Jean Knight, #8, 1940 Oxford St. East, London, ON N5V 2Z7, 519/457-3070
Niagara Regional Office: Regional Director, Jocelyne Ivanovskis, Brock Business & Industrial Park, 3300 Merrittville Hwy., PO Box 128, Thorold, ON L2V 3Y7, 905/687-8484, Toll Free: 1-800-263-4742
Peel/Waterloo Regional Office: Regional Director, Marsha Stephen, #300, 3034 Palston Rd., Mississauga, ON L4Y 2Z6, 905/276-6252
Post-Polio Program: Provincial Coordinator, Judith Lytle, 10 Overlea Blvd., Toronto, ON M4H 1A4, 416/425-3463, ext.213, Fax: 416/425-1920
Sudbury/Sault Ste Marie Regional Office: Regional Director, Elizabeth Violin, #510, 51 Elm St., Sudbury, ON P3C 1S3, 705/674-3377
Thunder Bay Regional Office: Regional Director, Terry Bellavance, 237 Camelot St., Thunder Bay, ON P7A 4B2, 807/345-6595, Fax: 807/345-7086
Toronto Regional Office: Regional Director, Sybille Hahn, 10 Overlea Blvd., Toronto, ON M4H 1A4, 416/425-3463, ext.206

QUÉBEC EASTER SEAL SOCIETY/SOCIÉTÉ DES TIMBRES DE PÂQUES DU QUÉBEC (1949)
Sun Life Building, #919, 1155, rue Metcalfe, Montréal, PQ H3B 2V6
514/866-1969, Fax: 514/866-6124, Toll Free: 1-800-263-1969
Executive Director, Robert C. Bédard

QUÉBEC MARCH OF DIMES FOR THE DISABLED/PARADES DES DIX SOUS POUR LES HANDICAPÉS DU QUÉBEC (1956)
#410, 1000, rue Saint-Antoine ouest, Montréal, PQ H3C 3R7
514/866-3689, Fax: 514/866-6303

THE REHABILITATION CENTRE/LE CENTRE DE RÉADAPTATION (1981)
Royal Ottawa Health Care Group
505 Smyth Rd., Ottawa, ON K1H 8M2
613/737-7350, Fax: 613/737-7056
Executive Director, George Langill
Associate Executive Director, Irene Giustini
Publications: Perspective
Affiliates: University of Ottawa

SASKATCHEWAN ABILITIES COUNCIL (1950)
2310 Louise Ave., Saskatoon, SK S7J 2C7
306/374-4448, Fax: 306/373-2665
Executive Director, Kirsti Clarke
Director of Central Services, Ian Wilkinson
Publications: SAC Bulletin; Handi Farmer, q.

SOCIÉTÉ POUR LES ENFANTS HANDICAPÉS DU QUÉBEC/QUÉBEC SOCIETY FOR DISABLED CHILDREN (1930)
2300, boul René-Lévesque ouest, Montréal, PQ H3H 2R5
514/937-6171, Téléc: 514/937-0082
Directeur général, Diane Tétreault
Président, Jacques Elie
Directeur, Communication, Michel Gailloux
Contrôleur, Richard Rioux
Publications: Bulletin Papillon
Organisation(s) affiliée(s): Centre canadien de philanthropie; Conseil québécois pour l'enfance et la jeunesse

SOCIETY FOR MANITOBANS WITH DISABILITIES INC. (SMD) (1946)
825 Sherbrook St., Winnipeg, MB R3A 1M5
204/786-5601, Fax: 204/783-2919, TDD: 204/784-3710, Toll Free: 1-800-282-8041
Communications Manager, Katherine Murdock

Executive Director, David L. Steen
President, David Hargrave
Publications: Annual Report; Communiqué, s-a.

John Milton Society for the Blind in Canada/Société John Milton pour les aveugles du Canada (JMS) (1970)
#202, 40 St. Clair Ave. East, Toronto, ON M4T 1M9
416/960-3953
President, James MacMillan
Publications: JMS Newsletter; Intouch; Insound, q.; Insight, bi-m.

Low Vision Association of Ontario
#101, 263 Russell Hill Rd., Toronto, ON M4V 2T4
416/921-6609
Contact, Karen Skead
Managing Director, Bill Carroll
Publications: Eye Trumpets; Cornets Visuels

Ontario Federation for Cerebral Palsy
#104, 1630 Lawrence Ave. West, Toronto, ON M6A 1C8
416/244-9686
Executive Director, Clarence Meyers
President, Fred Gardner

Ontario Rehabilitation & Work Council
700 Caledonia Rd., North York, ON M6B 4H9
416/789-7925, Fax: 416/789-3499
Manager, Dorothy Solate

People First Society of Alberta
11720 Kingsway Ave., Edmonton, AB T5G 0X5
403/453-3047, Fax: 403/453-5779
Publications: The Question Mark
Affiliates: National People First

Prince Edward Island Council of the Disabled (1975)
#302, 134 Kent St., PO Box 2128, Charlottetown, PE C1A 7N7
902/892-9149, Fax: 902/566-1919, Toll Free: 1-800-653-5999
Information & Development Coordinator, Teresa MacKinnon
Publications: PEI Council of the Disabled Newsletter

The Roeher Institute/L'Institut Roeher (1970)
Kinsmen Building, York University, 4700 Keele St., North York, ON M3J 1P3
416/661-9611, Fax: 416/661-5701, Toll Free: 1-800-856-2207, Email: rward@orion.yorku.ca
Executive Director, Marcia H. Rioux, Ph.D.
Publications: Entourage
Affiliates: International Association for Scientific Study of Intellectual Deficiency; Canadian Association for Community Living

Silent Voice Canada Inc.
699 Coxwell Ave., Toronto, ON M4C 3C1
416/463-1105, TDD: 416/463-3928
Executive Director, Beverly Pageau
Publications: Silent Echo

Speech Foundation of Ontario (SFO) (1977)
10 Buchan Ct., North York, ON M2J 1V2
416/491-7771, Fax: 416/491-7215
Program Director, Margit Pukonen
Chairman, Gerald Brown

Speech & Hearing Association of Nova Scotia
PO Box 775, Halifax Central CRO, Halifax, NS B3J 2V2
902/423-9331, Fax: 902/423-0981
President, Rachael Tabor
Publications: Reverberations

Canadian Almanac & Directory 1997

Speech Language Hearing Association of Alberta (SHAA)
#2210, 10060 Jasper Ave., Edmonton, AB T5J 3R8
403/944-1609, Fax: 403/426-6882
Contact, Christine Seskus
Publications: The SHAA Journal
Affiliates: Canadian Association of Speech-Language Pathologists & Audiologists

Vision Institute of Canada (VIC) (1981)
York Mills Centre, #110, 16 York Mills Rd., North York, ON M2P 2E5
416/224-2273, Fax: 416/224-9234
Chief of Clinical Services, Dr. Catherine Chiarelli
Executive Director, Dr. Mitchell Samek
Publications: Vision Institute

Vocational & Rehabilitation Research Institute (VRRI) (1966)
3304 - 33 St. NW, Calgary, AB T2L 2A6
403/284-1121, Fax: 403/289-6427
Executive Director, Gerrit Groeneweg
Chairman, Geri Price
Publications: Journal of Practical Approaches to Developmental Handicap; Bridges, s-a.

DISARMAMENT see INTERNATIONAL COOPERATION/INTERNATIONAL RELATIONS

DRILLING

Canadian Association of Drilling Engineers (CADE) (1974)
#800, 540 - 5 Ave. SW, Calgary, AB T2P 0M2
403/264-4311, Fax: 403/263-3796
URL: http://www.lexicom.ab.ca/~cade
President, Fred Yurkiw
Vice-President, Doug Long
Publications: CADEnews
Affiliates: Canadian Association of Oilwell Drilling Contractors

Canadian Association of Oilwell Drilling Contractors (CAODC) (1949)
#800, 540 - 5 Ave. SW, Calgary, AB T2P 0M2
403/264-4311, Fax: 403/263-3796
Managing Director, Don Herring
Publications: CAODC Membership Directory; Cost Study, a.; CAODC Newsletter, m.

Canadian Drilling Association (CDA) (1938)
#306, 222 McIntyre St. West, North Bay, ON P1B 2Y8
705/476-6992, Fax: 705/476-9494
Secretary Manager, Richard Niels
Publications: Drill Press; Directory of Goods & Services for the Drilling Industry

Canadian Ground Water Association/Association canadienne des eaux souterraines (CGWA) (1976)
PO Box 60, Lousana, AB T0M 1K0
403/749-2331, Fax: 403/749-2958
President, Martin Hammond
1st Vice-President, Jamie McDonald
2nd Vice-President, Guy Rohne
Secretary-Manager, Maurice Lewis
Publications: CGWA Newsletter
Affiliates: Canadian Earth Energy Association

ALBERTA WATER WELL DRILLING ASSOCIATION (AWWDA) (1958)
PO Box 130, Lougheed, AB T0B 2V0
403/386-2335, Fax: 403/386-2344
Sec.-Treas., Carol Larson
Publications: AWWDA Newsletter

ASSOCIATION DES EAUX SOUTERRAINES DU QUÉBEC
5930, boul Louis-H. Lafontaine, Anjou, PQ H1M 1S7
514/353-9960, Téléc: 514/353-4825
Directeur général, Gilles Doyon

BRITISH COLUMBIA GROUND WATER ASSOCIATION
1708 - 197A St., Langley, BC V2Z 1K2
604/530-8934
Secretary, Joan Perry

MANITOBA WATER WELL ASSOCIATION
PO Box 1648, Winnipeg, MB R3C 2Z6
204/231-3728
Secretary Manager, Judy Stevens

NEW BRUNSWICK GROUND WATER ASSOCIATION INC.
30 Blair St., Fredericton, NB E3B 5X3
506/455-8913, Fax: 506/454-9834
Executive Director, T. Roly Mockler

NEWFOUNDLAND & LABRADOR WATER WELL CORPORATION
PO Box 249, Clarkes Beach, NF A0A 1W0
709/786-3561, Fax: 709/786-7386
Contact, Martin B. Hammond

NOVA SCOTIA WELL DRILLERS' ASSOCIATION
20 Glencoe Dr., Dartmouth, NS B2X 1J1
902/435-6636, Fax: 902/434-7827
Sec-Treas., Patti Josey

ONTARIO GROUND WATER ASSOCIATION (OGWA) (1951)
2995 Delia Cres., Brights Grove, ON N0N 1C0
519/869-8933, Fax: 519/869-8940
Sec.-Treas., Judy Lethbridge
Publications: The Source

PRINCE EDWARD ISLAND GROUND WATER ASSOCIATION
RR#2, PO Box 857, Cornwall, PE C0A 1H0
902/675-2360, Fax: 902/675-2360
Contact, E. Watson MacDonald

SASKATCHEWAN GROUND WATER ASSOCIATION (SGWA)
PO Box 9434, Saskatoon, SK S7K 7E9
306/244-7551, Fax: 306/343-0001
Executive Secretary, Kathleen Watson
Publications: The Groundwater Journal

ECONOMICS

Association des économistes québécois (ASDÉQ)
CP 869, Succ. C, Montréal, PQ H2L 4L6
514/523-8872, Téléc: 514/523-8872
Directeur exécutif, Gilles Beausoleil

Association des professionnels en développement économique du Québec/ Economic Development Professionals Association of Québec (APDEQ) (1994)
#1000, 625, av du Président Kennedy, Montréal, PQ H3A 1K2
514/845-8275, Téléc: 514/845-4071, Ligne sans frais: 1-800-361-8470
Président, Guy Néron
Vice-Président, Laurent Thauvette
Secrétaire-trésorier, Howard R. Silverman
Publications: Apdéquat

Atlantic Association of Applied Economists
c/o Nova Scotia Economic Renewal Agency, #708, 1800 Argyle St., PO Box 519, Halifax, NS B3J 2R7
902/424-5617, Fax: 902/424-0505
President, Fred Morley

Atlantic Provinces Economic Council (APEC) (1954)
#500, 5121 Sackville St., Halifax, NS B3J 1K1
902/422-6516, Fax: 902/429-6803
Chairman, Ronald B. Smith
Publications: APEC Newsletter; Atlantic Report, q.

Canada West Foundation
#810, 400 - 3 Ave. SW, Calgary, AB T2P 4H2
403/264-9535, Email: cwf@freenet.calgary.ab.ca
URL: http://www.freenet.calgary.ab.ca/populati/communit/cwf/cwf.html
President, David K. Elton

Canadian Agricultural Economics & Farm Management Society/Société canadienne d'économie rurale et de gestion agricole
#1112, 141 Laurier Ave. West, Ottawa, ON K1P 5J3
613/232-9459, Fax: 613/594-5190
Secretary, Jeff Corman
Publications: Revue canadienne d'économie rurale; Canadian Journal of Agricultural Economics, 5 pa
Affiliates: Agricultural Institute of Canada

Canadian Association for Business Economics, Inc./Association canadienne de science économique des affaires, inc. (CABE)
130 Slater St., 11th Fl., Ottawa, ON K1P 6E2
613/238-4831, Fax: 613/238-7698
President, George Pedersson
Affiliates: International Federation of Associations of Business Economists

Canadian Economics Association/Association canadienne d'economique (1967)
Dept. of Economics, University of Toronto, 150 Saint George St., Toronto, ON M5S 3G7
416/978-6295, Fax: 416/978-6713
Sec.-Treas., Prof. Michael Denny
Publications: The Canadian Journal of Economics/La Revue canadienne d'économique; Canadian Public Policy/Analyse de politique; CEA Newsletter, s-a.

C.D. Howe Institute/Institut C.D. Howe (1973)
125 Adelaide St. East, Toronto, ON M5C 1L7
416/865-1904, Fax: 416/865-1866, Email: cdhowe@cd-howe.org
URL: http://www.cdhowe.org
Executive Vice-President, Angela Ferrante
President & CEO, Tom Kierans
Secretary, Joyce Vaz
Director of Publications, Barry A. Norris

Centre de recherche et développement en économique (CRDE) (1970)
Pavillon Lionel-Groulx, Université de Montréal, CP 6128, Succ Centre-Ville, Montréal, PQ H3C 3J7
514/343-6557, Téléc: 514/343-5831, Courrier électronique: crde@ere.umontreal.ca
Directeur, Jean-Marie Dufour
Secrétaire administrative, Josée Vignola

Community Economic Development Institute (1986)
University College of Cape Breton, PO Box 5300, Sydney, NS B1P 6L2
902/564-1366, Fax: 902/564-1366
CEO, Dr. Gerth MacIntyre
Publications: Centre for Community Economic Development

The Conference Board of Canada (1954)
255 Smyth Rd., Ottawa, ON K1N 6C3
613/526-3280, Fax: 613/526-4857, Telex: 053-3343
President, James R. Nininger
Senior Vice-President, Charles Barrett

Economic Developers Association of Canada/ Association canadienne de développement économique (EDAC) (1968)
#7, 714 Lakeshore Rd. East, Mississauga, ON L5G 1J6
905/891-8771, Fax: 905/891-8411

Executive Director, Penny A. Gardiner
Publications: Communiqué; Economic Development Papers, a.

Economic Developers Council of Ontario Inc. (EDCO) (1962)
PO Box 269, Cannington, ON L0E 1E0
705/432-3215, Fax: 705/432-3332
Executive Director, Gladys M. Schmidt
President, Reinold Kosciuw
Publications: EDCO Journal; EDCO News, m.; Ontario - Canada's Business Centre, a.

The Fraser Institute (1974)
626 Bute St., 2nd Fl., Vancouver, BC V6E 3M1
604/688-0221, Fax: 604/688-8539, Toll Free: 1-800-665-3558, Email: info@fraserinstitute.ca
URL: http://www.fraserinstitute.ca/
Executive Director, Dr. Michael A. Walker
Director, Events & Conferences, Lorena Baran
Director, David Hanley
Director, Brian April
Director, V. Waese
Publications: Fraser Forum; On Balance, 10 pa
Toronto Office: T-D Centre, #2550, 55 King St. West, Toronto, ON M5K 1E7, 416/363-6575, Fax: 416/601-7322

Institute for Policy Analysis (IPA) (1967)
University of Toronto, #707, 140 Saint George St., Toronto, ON M5S 1A1
416/978-4854, Fax: 416/978-5519
Contact, Prof. James E. Pesando

The North-South Institute/Institut Nord-Sud (NSI) (1976)
#200, 55 Murray St., Ottawa, ON K1N 5M3
613/241-3535, Fax: 613/241-7435, Telex: 053-3300, Email: nsi@web.apc.org
President, Dr. Roy Culpeper
Publications: Review

EDITORS see **WRITERS & EDITORS**

EDUCATION
see also Research & Scholarship

Agence francophone pour l'enseignement supérieur et la recherche (AUPELF-UREF) (1961)
Direction générale-Rectorat, CP 400, Succ Côte des Neiges, Montréal, PQ H3C 2S7
514/343-6630, Téléc: 514/343-2107, Télex: 055-60955, Courrier électronique: syfed@refer.qc.ca
URL: http://www.refer.qc.ca
Directeur général-Recteur, Michel Guillou
Documentaliste, Céline Brunel
Publications: Universités

Alberta Catholic School Trustees Association
#107, 17704 - 103 Ave., Edmonton, AB T5S 1J9
403/484-6209, Fax: 403/484-6248
Executive Director, J. Kevin McKinney
Affiliates: Canadian Catholic School Trustees Association

Alliance canadienne des responsables et enseignants en français (Langue maternelle)/Canadian Association for the Teachers of French as a First Language (ACREF) (1989)
Faculté d'éducation, Université d'Ottawa, 145, rue Jean-Jacques Lussier, CP 415, Succ. A, Ottawa, ON K1N 6N5
613/562-5800, ext.4144, Téléc: 613/562-5146
Président, Benoît Cazabon
Publications: Le Trait d'Union

Association for Baha'i Studies/Association d'études Baha'ies (ABS) (1975)
34 Copernicus St., Ottawa, ON K1N 7K4
613/233-1903, Fax: 613/233-3644, Email: as929@freenet.carleton.ca
Executive Secretary, Christine Zerbinis
Academic Director, Pierre-Yves Mocquais
Publications: Journal of Baha'i Studies; Baha'i Studies, irreg.; ABS Bulletin, s-a.; Campus Association, s-a.
Affiliates: International Fraternal Association for Baha'i Studies

Association of British Columbia Teachers of English as an Additional Language (BC TEAL) (1967)
#177, 4664 Lougheed Hwy., Burnaby, BC V5C 5T5
604/294-8325, Fax: 604/294-8355, Email: bcteal@unixg.ubc.ca
President, Christine Stechishin
Publications: TEAL Newsletter
Affiliates: Affiliation of Multicultural Societies & Service Agencies of B.C.

Association of Business Teacher Educators of Canada
Faculty of Education, University of Regina, Regina, SK S4S 0A2
306/585-4610, Fax: 306/585-4880
President, Prof. Nancy Hicks

Association des cadres scolaires du Québec
#170, 1195, rue de Lavigerie, Ste-Foy, PQ G1V 4N3
418/654-0014, Téléc: 418/654-1719
Directeur général, Jacques Fortin
Publications: Réussir; En Bloc, tous les 2 mois

Association of Canadian Bible Colleges (ACBC)
PO Box 4311, Three Hills, AB T0M 2N0
403/443-5511, Fax: 403/443-5540
President, Dr. Larry McKinney
Vice-President, Dr. James Richards
Sec.-Treas., Peter Doell
Publications: Association of Canadian Bible Colleges Directory

Association of Canadian Community Colleges/Association des collèges communautaires du Canada (ACCC) (1972)
#200, 1223 Michael St. North, Ottawa, ON K1J 7T2
613/746-2222, Fax: 613/746-6721
URL: http://www.accc.ca/index.html
President, Tom Norton
Vice-President, International Services, Jean-Robert Vaillancourt
Vice President, National Services, Terry Anne Boyles
Publications: ACCC Community; The National Advocate/Le Porte-Parole, bi-m.; ACCC International, q.; International Update, bi-m.

Association for Canadian Studies/Association d'études canadiennes (ACS) (1973)
c/o UQAM, V-5130, CP 8888, Succ Centre-Ville, Montréal, PQ H3C 3P8
514/987-7784, Fax: 514/987-8210, Email: c1015@er.uqam.ca
Administrative Director, Vincent Masciotra
President, John Dickinson
Treasurer, Christopher Dunn
Publications: ACS Bulletin AEC; Directory to Canadian Studies in Canada; Canadian Issues, a.

Association canadienne d'éducation de langue française (ACELF) (1947)
268, rue Marie-de-l'Incarnation, Québec, PQ G1N 3G4
418/681-4661, Téléc: 418/681-3389, Courrier électronique: informat@acelf.ca
URL: http://www.acelf.ca

Président, Louis-Gabriel Bordeleau
Secrétaire général par intérim, Fernand Langlais
Publications: Éducation et francophonie; Au fil des jours, 5 fois par an
Organisation(s) affiliée(s): UNESCO

Association canadienne française pour l'avancement des sciences (ACFAS) (1923)
425, rue de la Gauchetière est, Montréal, PQ H2L 2M7
514/849-0045, Téléc: 514/849-5558
Directeur général, Germain Godbout
Présidente, Jennifer Stoddart
Chargée de programmes, Patricia Legault
Publications: Interface

Association canadienne des professeurs d'immersion/Canadian Association of Immersion Teachers (ACPI) (1977)
72 Robertson Rd., CP 26148, Nepean, ON K2H 5Y8
613/727-6933, Téléc: 613/721-1588
Présidente, Greta Murtagh
Secrétaire, Nicole Sangemino
Publications: Le Journal de l'Immersion

Association of Colleges of Applied Arts & Technology of Ontario/Association des collèges d'arts appliquées et de technologie de l'Ontario (ACAATO)
#1010, 655 Bay St., Toronto, ON M5G 2K4
416/596-0744, Fax: 416/596-2364
URL: gopher://info.senecac.on.ca:2000/
Executive Director, Joan S. Homer
Publications: Ontario College News

Association des collèges privés du Québec (1968)
1940, boul Henri-Bourassa est, Montréal, PQ H2B 1S2
514/381-8891, Téléc: 514/381-4086
Secrétaire général, Jacques N. Tremblay
Président, Benoit Lauzière
Tech. administration, Francine Bisson
Publications: Annuaire administratif

Association des conseillers et conseillères scolaires francophones du Nouveau-Brunswick (ACCSFNB) (1980)
27, rue John, Moncton, NB E1C 2G7
506/857-2263, Téléc: 506/857-3070
Directeur général, Léon Richard
Présidente, Claudette Duclos
Agent d'information, Hugues Chiasson
Publications: Trait d'Union

Association des directeurs généraux des commissions scolaires du Québec (ADIGECS)
50, boul Taschereau, La Prairie, PQ J5R 4V3
514/444-4484, Téléc: 514/659-7131
Président, Gilles Taillon

Association of Early Childhood Educators, Ontario (AECEO) (1950)
#211, 40 Orchard View Blvd., Toronto, ON M4R 1B9
416/487-3157, Fax: 416/487-3758, Toll Free: 1-800-463-3391
Executive Director, Robyn Gallimore
Publications: The ECE Link

Association of Educational Research Officers of Ontario/Association ontarienne des agents de recherche en éducation (AERO) (1972)
Board of Education, 5050 Yonge St., North York, ON M2N 5N8
416/395-8147, Fax: 416/395-8346
President, Sylvia Larter
President Elect, Sandra Sangster
Publications: AERO Newsletter
Affiliates: American Educational Research Association

Canadian Almanac & Directory 1997

Association des enseignantes et des enseignants franco-ontariens/Franco-Ontarian Teachers' Association (AEFO) (1939)
681 Belfast Rd., Ottawa, ON K1G 0Z4
613/244-2336, Téléc: 613/563-7718
Directeur général, Guy Matte
Publications: En bref; Réseau, 5 fois par an
Organisation(s) affiliée(s): Ontario Teachers' Federation

Association française des conseils scolaires de l'Ontario
#211, 435 St. Laurent Blvd., Ottawa, ON K1K 2Z8
613/745-3195
Directeur général, J. Ladouceur

Association francophone internationale des directeurs d'établissements scolaires (AFIDES) (1983)
500, boul Crémazie est, Montréal, PQ H2P 1E7
514/383-7335, Téléc: 514/384-2139, Courrier électronique: afides@grics.qc.ca
URL: http://grics.qc.ca/afides
Secrétaire général, Richard Charron
Présidente du C.A., Khadidjatou Ka Sarr
Publications: La Revue des échanges

Association des institutions d'enseignement secondaire (AIES) (1968)
1940, boul Henri-Bourassa est, Montréal, PQ H2B 1S2
514/381-8891, Téléc: 514/381-4086, Ligne sans frais: 1-888-381-8891, Courrier électronique: cadre@cam.org
Directrice générale, Micheline Lavallée

Association des institutions de niveaux préscolaire et élémentaire du Québec (AIPÉQ)
1940, boul Henri-Bourassa est, Montréal, PQ H2B 1S2
514/381-1577, 8891, Téléc: 514/381-8126
Président, Jacques About

Association for Media & Technology in Education in Canada/Association des média et de la technologie en éducation au Canada (AMTEC) (1970)
#1318, 3-1750 The Queensway, Etobicoke, ON M9C 5H5
604/323-5627; Fax: 604/323-5577
URL: http://www.camosun.bc.ca/~amtec/
President, Dr. Richard Schwier
Publications: Canadian Journal of Educational Communication; Media News, q.
Affiliates: Canadian School Library Association; Canadian Association for Distance Education; Canadian Education Association; Pacific Instructional Media Association; Association for Educational Communications & Technology; Society for Instructional Technology/Edmonton

Association of New Brunswick Professional Educators/Association des éducateurs professionnels du Nouveau-Brunswick
91 Carlisle Rd., Fredericton, NB E3B 7X5
506/444-5331, Fax: 506/453-3325
President, Onil Dumont
Sec.-Treas., Mike Logue

Association québécoise du personnel de direction des écoles (AQPDE) (1967)
2965, boul Rive Sud, St-Romuald-d'Etchemin, PQ G6W 6N6
418/838-1088, Téléc: 418/838-1091
Président, Liliane Marcoux
Publications: Le Lien

Association québécoise des professeures et professeurs de français (AQPF) (1967)
#222, 2095, boul Charest ouest, Ste-Foy, PQ G1N 4L8
418/683-0947, Téléc: 418/527-4765, Ligne sans frais: 1-800-267-0947
Présidente, Huguette Lachapelle
Publications: Québec français
Organisation(s) affiliée(s): Fédération internationale des professeurs de français

Association of Universities & Colleges of Canada/Association des universités et collèges du Canada (AUCC) (1911)
#600, 350 Albert St., Ottawa, ON K1R 1B1
613/563-1236, Fax: 613/563-9745, Telex: 053-3329
URL: http://www.aucc.ca/
Vice-President, International & Canadian Programs, Eva Egron-Polak
Vice-President, External Relations, Sally Brown
Publications: Canadian University Distance Education Directory; Commonwealth Universities Yearbook, a.; Directory of Canadian Universities, a.; University Affairs, 10 pa (not in May & July); Financial Statistics of Universities & Colleges, a.; Universities Telephone Directory, a.; Uniworld, biennial

ASSOCIATION OF ATLANTIC UNIVERSITIES/ASSOCIATION DES UNIVERSITÉS DE L'ATLANTIQUE (AAU) (1964)
#403, 5657 Spring Garden Rd., Halifax, NS B3J 3R4
902/425-4230, Fax: 902/425-4233
Executive Director, Anne Marie MacKinnon
Publications: Association of Atlantic Universities Calendar

ASSOCIATION OF CANADIAN FACULTIES OF DENTISTRY/ASSOCIATION DES FACULTÉS DENTAIRES DU CANADA (ACFD)
#109, 1815 Alta Vista Dr., Ottawa, ON K1G 3Y6
613/738-7732, Fax: 613/738-2107
Executive Sec.-Treas., Lorraine Emmerson
Publications: Forum

ASSOCIATION OF CANADIAN MEDICAL COLLEGES/L'ASSOCIATION DES FACULTÉS DE MÉDECINE DU CANADA (ACMC) (1943)
774 Echo Dr., Ottawa, ON K1S 5P2
613/730-0687, Fax: 613/730-1196, Email: acmc@rcpsc.edu
Executive Director, Dr. David Hawkins
President, Dr. Arnold Aberman
Director, Administration, Janet Watt-Lafleur
Publications: ACMC Forum; Admission Requirements to Canadian Faculties of Medicine & their Selection Policies, biennial; Canadian Medical Education Statistics, a.
Affiliates: Canadian Medical Association; Association of Universities & Colleges of Canada

ASSOCIATION OF CANADIAN UNIVERSITIES FOR NORTHERN STUDIES/ASSOCIATION UNIVERSITAIRE CANADIENNE D'ÉTUDES NORDIQUES (ACUNS) (1977)
#405, 17 York St., Ottawa, ON K1N 9J6
613/562-0515, Fax: 613/562-0533
President, Dr. Roger H. King
Vice-President, Dr. Jill Oakes
Sec.-Treas., Frank Duerden
Publications: Northline/Point nord

ASSOCIATION OF CANADIAN UNIVERSITY PLANNING PROGRAMS (ACUPP)
Dept. of City Planning, University of Manitoba, Winnipeg, MB R3T 2N2
204/474-8761, Fax: 204/275-7198
President, Dr. Christine McKee
Sec.-Treas., Peter Boothroyd
Affiliates: Canadian Institute of Planners

ASSOCIATION OF DEANS OF PHARMACY OF CANADA (ADPC)
Faculty of Pharmacy, University of Montréal, Montréal, PQ H3C 3J7
514/343-6440, Fax: 514/343-7377, Email: goyerr@ere.umontreal.ca
President, Robert Goyer

ASSOCIATION OF DIRECTORS OF JOURNALISM PROGRAMS IN CANADIAN UNIVERSITIES/ASSOCIATION DES DIRECTEURS ET COORDONNATEURS DE PROGRAMMES DE JOURNALISME DES UNIVERSITÉS CANADIENNES (1982)
Director's Office, School of Journalism & Communication, Carleton U., Ottawa, ON K1S 5B6
613/520-7404, Fax: 613/520-6690
Dean, Peter Johansen

ASSOCIATION DES ÉCOLES D'OPTOMÉTRIE DU CANADA/ASSOCIATION OF SCHOOLS OF OPTOMETRY OF CANADA (1972)
École d'optométrie, Université de Montréal, CP 6128, Succ. A, Montréal, PQ H3C 3J7
514/343-7537, Téléc: 514/343-2382
Président, Dr. Roland Giroux
Organisation(s) affiliée(s): Association of Schools & Colleges of Optometry

ASSOCIATION OF REGISTRARS OF THE UNIVERSITIES & COLLEGES OF CANADA/ASSOCIATION DES REGISTRAIRES DES UNIVERSITÉS ET COLLÈGES DU CANADA (ARUCC) (1964)
Bishop's University, Lennoxville, PQ J1M 1Z7
819/822-9675, Fax: 819/822-9616, Email: amontgom@admin.ubishops.ca
President, Ann Montgomery
Publications: Contact; ARUCC Directory, a.

ASSOCIATION OF UNIVERSITY FORESTRY SCHOOLS OF CANADA/ASSOCIATION DES ÉCOLES FORESTIÈRES UNIVERSITAIRES DU CANADA (AUFSC)
Faculté de foresterie et de géomatique, Université Laval, CP 2208, Succ Terminus, Ste-Foy, PQ G1K 7P4
418/656-2116, Fax: 418/656-3177
Sec.-Treas., Prof. Claude Godbout

CANADIAN ASSOCIATION OF COLLEGE & UNIVERSITY STUDENT SERVICES/ASSOCIATION DES SERVICES AUX ÉTUDIANTS DES UNIVERSITÉS ET COLLÈGES DU CANADA (CACUSS) (1977)
Dept. of Residences, Maritime Hall, University of Guelph, #158, 50 Stone Rd. East, Guelph, ON N1G 2W1
519/824-4120, ext.3052, Fax: 519/767-1670, Email: Binet: adrcapes@vm.uoguelph.ca
Assistant Director of Residences, Blair Capes
Publications: CACUSS Communiqué; Membership Directory, a.

CANADIAN ASSOCIATION FOR GRADUATE STUDIES/ASSOCIATION CANADIENNE DES ÉTUDES AVANCÉES (CAGS) (1962)
University of Ottawa, Hagen Hall, Room 205, Ottawa, ON K1N 6N5
613/562-5291; Fax: 613/562-5292; Email: cags@uottawa.ca
Publications: CAGS Statistical Report

CANADIAN ASSOCIATION OF SCHOOLS OF SOCIAL WORK/ASSOCIATION DES ÉCOLES DE SERVICE SOCIAL (CASSW)
#100-B, 30 Rosemount Ave., Ottawa, ON K1Y 1P4
613/722-2974, Fax: 613/722-5661
Executive Director, Ann D. Sharp, MSW
Publications: Canadian Social Work Review

CANADIAN ASSOCIATION OF UNIVERSITY BUSINESS OFFICERS/ASSOCIATION CANADIENNE DE PERSONNEL ADMINISTRATIF UNIVERSITAIRE (CAUBO) (1937)
#320, 350 Albert St., Ottawa, ON K1R 1B1
613/563-1236, ext.268, Fax: 613/563-7739, Email: kclements@aucc.ca
Executive Director, Kenneth Clements
President, Carole Langlois
Publications: University Manager; Financial Statistics

CANADIAN ASSOCIATION FOR UNIVERSITY CONTINUING EDUCATION/ASSOCIATION POUR L'ÉDUCATION PERMANENTE DANS LES UNIVERSITÉS DU CANADA (CAUCE) (1974)
#320, 350 Albert St., Ottawa, ON K1R 1B1
613/563-1236, Fax: 613/563-7739, Email: kclements@aucc.ca
URL: http://www.tile.net/tile/listserv/caucel.html

Executive Director, Kenneth Clements
President, Ramona Lumpkin
Publications: Bulletin; Canadian Journal of University Continuing Education, s-a.; Yearbook of Exemplary Practice, a.

CANADIAN ASSOCIATION OF UNIVERSITY RESEARCH ADMINISTRATORS/ASSOCIATION CANADIENNE D'ADMINISTRATEURS DE RECHERCHE UNIVERSITAIRE (CAURA) (1972)
McMaster University, Gilmour Hall, #110B, 1280 Main St. West, Hamilton, ON L8S 4S8
905/529-7070, ext.24519, Fax: 905/540-8019
President, Kevin Keough
Vice-President, Noli Swatman
Sec.-Treas., Emmi Morwald
Publications: CAURA Bulletin

CANADIAN ASSOCIATION OF UNIVERSITY SCHOOLS OF NURSING/ ASSOCIATION CANADIENNE DES ÉCOLES UNIVERSITAIRES DE NURSING (CAUSN) (1942)
#325, 350 Albert St., Ottawa, ON K1R 1B1
613/563-1236, ext.280, Fax: 613/563-7739
Executive Director, Wendy McBride
Publications: CAUSN Newsletter/Bulletin d'information

CANADIAN COUNCIL OF UNIVERSITY BIOLOGY CHAIRS/CONSEIL UNIVERSITAIRE DES DIRECTEURS DE BIOLOGIE DU CANADA (CCUBC)
c/o Dept. of Botany, Axelrod Bldg., Univ. of Guelph, Guelph, ON N1G 2W1
519/824-4120, ext.6000, Fax: 519/767-1991, Email: lpeterso@uoguelph.ca
Sec.-Treas., John Vierula
Publications: CCUBC Newsletter

CANADIAN INTERUNIVERSITY ATHLETIC UNION/UNION SPORTIVE INTERUNIVERSITAIRE CANADIENNE (CIAU)
Place R. Tait McKenzie, 1600 James Naismith Dr., 7th Fl., Gloucester, ON K1B 5N4
613/748-5619, Fax: 613/748-5764, Telex: 053-3660
President, Dr. Robert Philip
Executive Vice-President, Mark Lowry
Affiliates: Fédération internationale du sport universitaire (CIAU is official Canadian representative); Atlantic Universities Athletic Association; Fédération québécoise du sport étudiant; Ontario Universities Athletic Association; Ontario Women's Intercollegiate Athletic Association; The Great Plains Athletic Conference; Canada West Universities Athletic Association

CONFEDERATION OF CANADIAN FACULTIES OF AGRICULTURE & VETERINARY MEDICINE/CONFÉDÉRATION DES FACULTÉS D'AGRICULTURE ET DE MÉDECINE VÉTÉRINAIRE DU CANADA (CCFAVM) (1990)
Ontario Agricultural College, Univ. of Guelph, Dean's Office, 50 Stone Rd. East, Guelph, ON N1G 2W1
519/763-5350, Fax: 519/763-5350
Executive Director, Dr. C.M. Switzer

COUNCIL OF CANADIAN LAW DEANS/CONSEIL DES DOYENS ET DES DOYENNES DES FACULTÉS DE DROIT DU CANADA (CCLD)
Faculty of Law, University of Ottawa, 57 Louis Pasteur, PO Box 415, Stn A, Ottawa, ON K1N 6N5
613/562-5889, Fax: 613/562-5121
Executive Director, Mistrale Goudreau

COUNCIL OF WESTERN CANADIAN UNIVERSITY PRESIDENTS (COWCUP)
University of Regina, #100, 3737 Wascana Pkwy., Regina, SK S4S 0A2
306/585-4382, Fax: 306/585-5200
Chair, Donald O. Wells, B.Sc., M.Sc., Ph.D.

DEANS & DIRECTORS OF HOME ECONOMICS & RELATED AREAS IN CANADIAN UNIVERSITIES (1942)
Université de Montréal, Fac. of Medicine, Dept. of Nutrition, CP 6128, Succ Centre Ville, Montréal, PQ H3C 3J7
514/343-6401, Fax: 514/343-7395
Suzanne Simard Mavrikakis

Atlantic Provinces Education Foundation
PO Box 2044, Halifax, NS B3J 2Z1
902/424-5352, Fax: 902/424-8976, Email: premiers@fox.nstn.ns.ca
Information Officer, Kim Thomson

Canadian Alliance of Student Associations/ Alliance canadienne des associations étudiantes (CASA)
PO Box 3408, Stn D, Ottawa, ON K1P 6H8
613/236-3457, Fax: 613/236-2386, Email: casa1@magi.com
National Director, Alex Usher

Canadian Asian Studies Association/Association canadienne des études asiatiques (CASA) (1968)
Centre d'Études de l'Asie de l'Est, Université de Montréal, PO Box 6128, Stn A, Montréal, PQ H3C 3J7
514/343-6569, Fax: 514/343-7716
Contact, Loy Denis
Publications: Contact
Affiliates: International Association of Sanskrit Studies

Canadian Association for Adult Education
29 Prince Arthur Ave., Toronto, ON M5R 1B2
416/964-0559, Fax: 416/964-9226
Executive Director, Ian Morrison
President, Teresa MacNeil
Contact, Daniel Benedict

Canadian Association for the Advancement of Netherlandic Studies (CAANS)
Dept. of Classics, Acadia University, Wolfville, NS B0P 1X0
902/542-2200, ext.1267, Fax: 902/542-4727
President, Beert Verstraete

Canadian Association of African Studies/ Association canadienne des études africaines (CAAS) (1971)
855, rue Sherbrooke ouest, Montréal, PQ H3A 2T7
514/398-4800, Fax: 514/398-1770
Contact, Prof. Frank Kanz
Publications: Canadian Journal of African Studies; Canadian Association of African Studies Newsletter

Canadian Association for American Studies/ Association d'études américaines au Canada (CAAS) (1964)
Dept. of English, University of Guelph, MacKinnon Bldg., Guelph, ON N1G 2W1
519/824-4120, Fax: 519/766-0844
President, Christine Bold
Publications: Canadian Review of American Studies
Affiliates: American Studies Association; British Association of American Studies; European Studies of American Studies

Canadian Association of Business Education Teachers/Association canadienne du personnel enseignant en commerce (1967)
c/o The Halton Board of Education, 2050 Guelph Line, PO Box 5005, Burlington, ON L7R 3Z2
905/335-3663, Fax: 905/335-9802
Executive Director, Lily Kretchman
President, Al Renner

Publications: The Canadian Journal of Business Education
Affiliates: National Business Educators Association; International Society of Business Educators

Canadian Association for Co-operative Education/Association canadienne de l'enseignement coopératif (CACE) (1973)
55 Eglinton Ave. East, Toronto, ON M4P 1G8
416/483-3311, Fax: 416/483-3365
Richard Murphy
Carol Cox
Publications: CAFCE News; Co-op Education, a.; CAFCE Co-op Program Directory

Canadian Association for Distance Education/ Association canadienne de l'éducation à distance (CADE) (1984)
#205, One Stewart St., Ottawa, ON K1N 6H7
613/230-3630, Fax: 613/230-2746, Email: csse@acadvm1.uottawa.ca
President, Barbara Spronk
Executive Secretary, Tim Howard
Publications: Journal of Distance Education; Communiqué, q.

Canadian Association of Foundations of Education/Association canadienne des fondements de l'éducation (CAFE) (1971)
c/o Dept. of Educational Studies, University of British Columbia, 2125 Main Mall, Vancouver, BC V6T 1Z4
604/822-5295, Fax: 604/822-4244, Email: donald.fisher@ubc.ca
President, Dr. Donald Fisher, Ph.D.
Publications: CAFE Newsletter
Affiliates: Canadian Philosophy of Education Society; Canadian History of Education Society

Canadian Association of Geographers/ Association canadienne des géographes (CAG) (1951)
Burnside Hall, McGill University, 805, rue Sherbrooke ouest, Montréal, PQ H3A 2K6
514/398-4946, Fax: 514/398-7437
President, Dr. John C. Everitt
Sec.-Treas., Mark Rosenberg
Publications: The Canadian Geographer; CAG Newsletter, bi-m.
Affiliates: Represented on the Canadian Commission for UNESCO, the Social Science Federation of Canada, & the Canadian Committee of the International Geographical Union

Canadian Association of Hispanists
Dept. of Modern Languages, University of Ottawa, PO Box 450, Stn A, Ottawa, ON K1N 6N5
613/564-2305, Fax: 613/564-9527
President, Nigel Dennis
Sec.-Treas., Marian G.R. Coope

Canadian Association of Independent Schools (CAIS) (1979)
PO Box 1502, St Catharines, ON L2R 7J9
905/688-4866, Fax: 905/688-5778, Email: cais@ridley.on.ca
Executive Secretary, Janet M. Lewis

Canadian Association for Pastoral Practice & Education/Association canadienne pour la pratique et l'éducation pastorales (CAPPE) (1965)
47 Queen's Park Cres., Toronto, ON M5C 2C3
416/977-3700, Fax: 416/978-7821, Email: jkraus@enterprise.ca
Executive Director, Rev. Jan K. Kraus

Canadian Almanac & Directory 1997

Publications: Newsletter/Nouvelles
Affiliates: American Association of Pastoral Counselling; Association for Clinical Pastoral Education

Canadian Association of Principals (CAP) (1977)
#36B, 1010 Polytek Ct., Gloucester, ON K1J 9J2
613/745-8472, Fax: 613/745-6325
General Secretary, Harvey Kingdon
Publications: CAP INFO; CAP Journal, a.

Canadian Association of School Social Workers & Attendance Counsellors (CASSWAC) (1982)
c/o London Board of Education, 1250 Dundas St. East, London, ON N6A 5L1
519/452-2125, Fax: 519/455-3545
President, Edward James
Treasurer, Gayle Stewart
Publications: CASSWAC News

Canadian Association for Scottish Studies (CASS) (1971)
Dept. of History, University of Guelph, Guelph, ON N1G 2W1
519/824-4120, ext.3888
General Editor, Scott McLean
Review Editor, Andrew Nicholls
Publications: Scottish Tradition
Affiliates: Scottish Studies Foundation

Canadian Association of Second Language Teachers/Association canadienne des professeurs de langue seconde (CASLT) (1970)
375 Jefferson Ave., Winnipeg, MB R2V 0N3
204/582-2457, Fax: 204/582-2469, Email: caslt@mts.net
URL: http://www2.tvo.org/education/caslt
Office Manager, Nancy Sametz
President, Bev Anderson
Publications: Second Language Bulletin

Canadian Association of Slavists/Association canadienne des slavistes (CAS) (1956)
Dept. of Modern Langs. & Comparative Studies, University of Alberta, Edmonton, AB T6G 2E6
403/492-2566, Fax: 403/492-2715
Sec.-Treas., Maxim Tarnawsky
President, Joan DeBardeleben
Publications: CAS Newsletter; Canadian Slavonic Papers, q.
Affiliates: International Conference of Slavic & East European Studies

Canadian Association for Teacher Education/Association canadienne pour la formation des enseignants (CATE) (1978)
c/o Faculty of Education, University of Windsor, Windsor, ON N9B 3P4
519/253-4232, ext.3828, Fax: 519/971-3612, Email: cball@server.uwindsor.ca
President, Colin Ball
Vice-President, Dr. Thérèse Laserriere
Sec.-Treas., Dr. Roger Neil
Affiliates: Canadian Association for Research in Early Childhood/Association canadienne pour la recherche préscolaire; Association of Business Teacher Educators of Canada/Association des professeurs en enseignement commercial au Canada

Canadian Association of Teachers of Community Health/Association canadienne des professeurs de santé communautaire (CATCH) (1967)
Dept. of Epidemiology & Community Medicine, University of Ottawa, 451 Smyth Rd., Ottawa, ON K1H 8M5
613/787-6458, Fax: 613/787-6472
President., Dr. J. Segovia, M.D.
Sec.-Treas., Dr. W. Thurston, Ph.D.
Publications: CATCH Newsletter
Affiliates: Canadian Public Health Association

Canadian Association of Teachers of Technical Writing
Dept. of English & Communications, Douglas College, PO Box 2503, New Westminster, BC V3L 5B2
604/527-5400
President, Diana Wagner

Canadian Association of University Teachers/Association canadienne des professeures et professeurs d'université (CAUT) (1951)
2675 Queensview Dr., Ottawa, ON K2B 8K2
613/820-2270, Fax: 613/820-7244, Email: acppu@caut.ca
URL: http://www.caut.ca
Executive Director, Dr. Donald C. Savage
Associate Executive Director, Gordon Piché
Director, Member Services, Rosalind Riseborough
Publications: CAUT Bulletin

CONFEDERATION OF ALBERTA FACULTY ASSOCIATIONS
University of Alberta, 115 Assiniboia Hall, Edmonton, AB T6G 2E7
403/492-5630, Fax: 403/492-6145
President, James Marino

CONFEDERATION OF UNIVERSITY FACULTY ASSOCIATIONS OF BRITISH COLUMBIA (CUFA/BC)
515 West Hastings St., Vancouver, BC V6B 5K3
604/291-5201, Fax: 604/291-5202
Executive Director, Robert Clift

FEDERATION OF NEW BRUNSWICK FACULTY ASSOCIATIONS/FÉDÉRATION DES ASSOCIATIONS DE PROFESSEURS D'UNIVERSITÉ DU NOUVEAU-BRUNSWICK
#297, 65 Brunswick St., Fredericton, NB E3B 1G5
506/458-8977, Fax: 506/458-5620
Executive Director, Desmond A. Morley
Secretary, Patricia Lewington

FÉDÉRATION QUÉBÉCOISE DES PROFESSEURES ET PROFESSEURS D'UNIVERSITÉ/QUÉBEC FEDERATION OF UNIVERSITY PROFESSORS (FQPPU)
#405, 4446, boul St-Laurent, Montréal, PQ H2W 1Z5
514/843-5953, Téléc: 514/843-6928
Président, Roch Denis

MANITOBA ORGANIZATION OF FACULTY ASSOCIATIONS (MOFA)
Collège Universitaire de St-Boniface, 200 Cathedral Ave., Winnipeg, MB R2H 0H7
204/235-4486, Fax: 204/237-3240
President, Luc Cote

NOVA SCOTIA CONFEDERATION OF UNIVERSITY FACULTY ASSOCIATIONS/CONFÉDERATION DES ASSOCIATIONS DE PROFESSEURS DES UNIVERSITÉS DE LA NOUVELLE-ÉCOSSE (NSCUFA) (1975)
#404, 1646 Barrington St., Halifax, NS B3J 2A3
902/422-1204, Fax: 902/422-1204
Executive Director, John D'Orsay
Administrator, Rose Norman
Publications: NSCUFA Bulletin

ONTARIO CONFEDERATION OF UNIVERSITY FACULTY ASSOCIATIONS/UNION DES ASSOCIATIONS DES PROFESSEURS DES UNIVERSITÉS DE L'ONTARIO (OCUFA) (1964)
#400, 27 Carlton St., Toronto, ON M5B 1L2
416/979-2117, Fax: 416/593-5607, Email: ocufa@ocufa.on.ca
Executive Director, Marion Perrin
Secretary, Lisa Alexis
Publications: Forum

Canadian Bureau for International Education/Bureau canadien de l'éducation internationale (CBIE) (1966)
#1100, 220 Laurier Ave. West, Ottawa, ON K1P 5Z9
613/237-4820, Fax: 613/237-1073, Telex: 053-3255, Email: jfox@cbic.ca
President, James W. Fox

Publications: Synthesis/Synthèse
Affiliates: UNESCO Canada; National Consortium of Scientific & Educational Societies

Canadian Catholic School Trustees' Association/Association canadienne des commissaires d'écoles catholique (CCSTA) (1960)
80 Sheppard Ave. East, North York, ON M2N 6E8
416/229-5326, Fax: 416/229-5345
President, Dorothy Fortier
Executive Secretary, Dr. John J. Flynn
Publications: Catholic Schools in Toronto; Reading for Catholic Teachers; CCSTA Newsletter, 3 pa

Canadian College of Teachers/Collège canadien des enseignants (1958)
201A Sherwood Dr., PO Box 57157, RPO Eastgate, Sherwood Park, AB T8A 5L7
403/922-6668, Fax: 403/922-2885
Sec.-Treas., Ronald E. Johnston

Canadian Council for the Advancement of Education/Le Conseil canadien pour l'avancement de l'education (CCAE) (1993)
PO Box 507, Stn Q, Toronto, ON M4T 2M5
416/483-7282, Fax: 416/489-1713
President, Capilano College, Randi Duke
Publications: Ensemble

Canadian Council for Multicultural & Intercultural Education/Conseil canadien pour l'éducation multiculturelle et interculturelle (CCMIE) (1983)
#200, 144 O'Connor St., Ottawa, ON K1P 5M9
613/233-4916, Fax: 613/233-4735
National Office & Resource Manager, Kamal Eddine Firdaous
President, Dr. Leticia Marques de Sa Messier
Publications: Multiculturalism/Multiculturalisme
Affiliates: International Association for Intercultural Education

Canadian Council of Teachers of English Language Arts (CCTELA) (1967)
c/o Association Management Centre, PO Box 4143, Stn C, Calgary, AB T2R 5M9
204/474-8564, Fax: 204/275-5962
Executive Director, Marita Watson
Publications: English Quarterly; CCTE Newsletter, q.
Affiliates: International Federation of Teachers of English; NCTE

Canadian Education Association/Association canadienne d'éducation (CEA) (1891)
#8-200, 252 Bloor St. West, Toronto, ON M5S 1V5
416/924-7721, Fax: 416/924-3188, Email: acea@hookup.net
Executive Director, Penny Milton
Publications: Education Canada; Newsletter/le bulletin, 9 pa

Canadian Ethnic Studies Association/Société canadienne d'études ethniques (CESA) (1977)
a/s Centre d'études ethniques, Université de Montréal, PO Box 6128, Stn Centre-Ville, Montréal, PQ H3C 3J7
President, Dr. Natalia Aponiuk
Sec.-Treas., Denis Hlynka
Publications: Canadian Ethnic Studies; CESA Bulletin, s-a.

Canadian Federation of Business School Deans/Fédération canadienne des doyens des écoles d'administration (1979)
#1005, 116 Albert St., Ottawa, ON K1P 5G3
613/564-3301, Fax: 613/564-7695
Director of Operations, Karen Fleming
Publications: Bulletin

Canadian Federation for the Humanities/ Fédération canadienne des études humaines (CFH) (1943)
#407, 151 Slater St., Ottawa, ON K1P 5H3
613/236-4686, Fax: 613/236-4853, Email: cfhxt@acadvm1.uottawa.ca
URL: http://137.122.12.15/HumCanada.html
Executive Director, J. Craig McNaughton
Publications: CFH Bulletin
Affiliates: Union académique internationale

Canadian Federation of Students/Fédération canadienne des étudiantes et étudiants (CFS) (1981)
#500, 170 Metcalfe St., Ottawa, ON K2P 1P3
613/232-7394, Fax: 613/232-0276
URL: http://www.cfs-fcee.ca
National Chairperson, Brad Lavigne
Publications: Student Advocate; Student Association Directory, a.
British Columbia Component: Chairperson, Michael Johal, 2344 Spruce St., Vancouver, BC V6H 2P2, 604/733-1880, Fax: 604/733-1852, Email: CFSnet id.:bcc.cfs
Manitoba: Chairperson, Jennifer Howard, c/o Collège de Saint Boniface, Association des Étudiants/es, 200, av de la Cathédrale, Winnipeg, MB R2H 0H7, 204/237-5094, Fax: 204/237-3240
New Brunswick: Chair, Paul Ward, University of New Brunswick, Student Union Bldg., PO Box 4400, Fredericton, NB E3B 5A3, 506/453-5081, Fax: 506/453-4958, Email: CFSnet id.: cfs-fce.nb
Ontario: Chairperson, Jason Hunt; Vice-Chairman, Scott Humphrey, 643 Yonge St., 2nd Fl., Toronto, ON M4Y 1Z9, 416/925-3825, Fax: 416/925-6774, Email: CFSnet id.: ofs.feo/ofs.chair
Prince Edward Island: Chair, Todd King, c/o UPEI Student Union, 550 University Ave., Charlottetown, PE C1A 4P3, 902/566-0398, Fax: 902/566-0648
Saskatchewan: Contact, Jason Stolz, Students' Union Building, University of Regina, #100, 3737 Wascana Pkwy., Regina, SK S4S 0A2

Canadian Federation of Students Services/ Fédération canadienne des étudiantes et étudiants services (1982)
CFS-Services
243 College St., Toronto, ON M5T 2Y1
416/977-3703, Fax: 416/977-4796, Telex: 06-22436
Executive Director, David A. Jones
Publications: The Student Traveller; The Student Association Directory, a.

Canadian Federation of University Women/ Fédération canadienne des femmes diplômées des universités (CFUW) (1919)
#308, 297 Dupuis St., Ottawa, ON K1L 7H8
613/747-7339, Fax: 613/747-8358
Executive Director, Sheila Givens
President, Phyllis Scott
Publications: CFUW/FCFDU Journal
Affiliates: International Federation of University Women

Canadian Foundation for Economic Education/ Fondation d'éducation économique (CFEE) (1974)
#501, 2 St. Clair Ave. West, Toronto, ON M4V 1L5
416/968-2236, Fax: 416/968-0488
President, Gary Rabbior

Canadian Home Economics Association/ Association canadienne d'économie familiale (CHEA) (1939)
#901, 151 Slater St., Ottawa, ON K1P 5H3
613/238-8817, Fax: 613/238-1677
Executive Director, Ellen Boynton
President, Nancy Cook
International Development Program Manager, Nicole Pelletier
Development Education Officer, Pat Ulrich
Publications: ID Connections; Canadian Home Economics Journal, q.; Rapport; Membership Directory
Affiliates: Canadian Council on Social Development; World Food Day Association; International Federation for Home Economics; Canadian Council for International Cooperation; National Council of Women of Canada; Vanier Institute of the Family

Canadian Home Economics Association Foundation/Fondation de l'association canadienne d'économie familiale (CHEAF) (1980)
303 Ashland Ave., Winnipeg, MB R3L 1L6
204/475-1508
Secretary, Dr. Margaret I. Morton
Chairperson, Dr. Elizabeth Feniak
Affiliates: Canadian Home Economics Association

Canadian Home & School Federation/Fédération canadienne des associations foyer-école (CHSF) (1927)
#104, 858 Bank St., Ottawa, ON K1S 3W3
613/234-7292, Fax: 613/234-3913, Email: chspft@cyberus.ca
URL: http://cnet.unb.ca/cap/partners/chsptf/
Acting Executive Director, G.T. Durkin
Publications: Newsletter

ALBERTA HOME & SCHOOL COUNCILS' ASSOCIATION
#102, 12310 - 105 Ave., Edmonton, AB T5N 0Y4
403/454-9867, Fax: 403/455-0167, Toll Free: 1-800-661-3470
President, Elizabeth Dobrovolsky
Publications: Newsletter

BRITISH COLUMBIA CONFEDERATION OF PARENT ADVISORY COUNCILS (BCCPAC)
#1540, 1185 Georgia St. West, Vancouver, BC V6E 4E6
604/687-4433, Fax: 604/687-4488, Email: hcameron@direct.ca
President, Silvia Dyck
Executive Director, Hélène Cameron
Publications: BCCPAC Bulletin; BCCPAC Newsletter, 4-5 pa

MANITOBA ASSOCIATION OF PARENT COUNCILS
#309, 1181 Portage Ave., Winnipeg, MB R3G 0T3
204/786-4722, Fax: 204/774-8553

NEW BRUNSWICK FEDERATION OF HOME & SCHOOL ASSOCIATIONS (NBFHSA) (1938)
RR#1, PO Box 367, Scoudouc, NB E0A 1N0
506/532-6775
Executive Director, Sharon Hurd
President, Anna LeBlanc
Publications: News & Views

NEWFOUNDLAND & LABRADOR HOME & SCHOOL FEDERATION
5 Merrymeeting Rd., PO Box 23140, St. John's, NF A1B 4J9
709/739-4830, Fax: 709/739-4833

NOVA SCOTIA FEDERATION OF HOME & SCHOOL ASSOCIATIONS
PO Box 91, LeHave, NS B0R 1C0
902/688-2463
Director, Anne White
President, Sandra Himmelman

ONTARIO FEDERATION OF HOME & SCHOOL ASSOCIATIONS INC. (1916)
#12-200, 252 Bloor St. West, Toronto, ON M5S 1V5
416/924-7491, Fax: 416/924-5354
Executive Secretary, Beth McGuire
President, Ann Smith
Publications: OFHSA Bulletin

PRINCE EDWARD ISLAND HOME & SCHOOL FEDERATION (1953)
3 Queen St., PO Box 1012, Charlottetown, PE C1A 7M4
902/892-0664, Fax: 902/628-1844, Toll Free: 1-800-916-0664
Executive Director, Shirley Jay
President, Audrey Newcombe

QUÉBEC FEDERATION OF HOME & SCHOOL ASSOCIATIONS/ FÉDÉRATION DES ASSOCIATIONS FOYER-ÉCOLE DU QUÉBEC (QFHSA) (1944)
#562, 3285, boul Cavendish, Montréal, PQ H4B 2L9
514/481-5619, Fax: 514/481-5619
President, Patricia Waters
Executive Secretary, Donna Sauriol
Publications: Québec Home & Safety School News

SASKATCHEWAN ASSOCIATION OF SCHOOL COUNCILS (SASC) (1938)
221 Cumberland Ave. North, Saskatoon, SK S7N 1M3
306/955-5723, Fax: 306/955-5723
Executive Director, Joy Bastness
President, Deborah Agema
Publications: What's New for Saskatchewan Home & School?

Canadian Industrial Arts Association
#45333, Faculty of Education BS, University of New Brunswick, Fredericton, NB E3B 6E3
506/453-3508, Fax: 506/453-3569
President, Alfred T. Steeves

Canadian School Boards Association/ Association canadienne des commissions/ conseils scolaires (CSBA) (1923)
#600, 130 Slater St., Ottawa, ON K1P 6E2
613/235-3724, Fax: 613/238-8434
President, Donna Cansfield
Executive Director, Marie Pierce
First Vice-President, Eric Jonasson
Second Vice-President, Roy Wilson
Publications: CSBAction

ALBERTA SCHOOL BOARDS ASSOCIATION (ASBA) (1907)
12310 - 105 Ave., Edmonton, AB T5N 0Y4
403/482-7311, Fax: 403/482-5659
Executive Director, David Anderson
President, Dr. Roy Wilson
Publications: Spectrum

MANITOBA ASSOCIATION OF SCHOOL TRUSTEES
191 Provencher Blvd., Winnipeg, MB R2H 0G4
204/233-1595, Fax: 204/231-1356
Executive Director, Dr. J.B. MacNeil

NEW BRUNSWICK SCHOOL TRUSTEES' ASSOCIATION
701 Churchill Row, Fredericton, NB E3B 1P7
506/450-4066, Fax: 506/450-8204
Executive Director, Marven Betts

NEWFOUNDLAND & LABRADOR SCHOOL BOARDS' ASSOCIATION (NLSTA) (1969)
#117, 19 Crosbie Pl., St. John's, NF A1B 3W9
709/722-7171, Fax: 709/722-8214
Executive Director, Myrle Vokey
Publications: Tidbits

NOVA SCOTIA SCHOOL BOARDS ASSOCIATION (NSSBA) (1954)
PO Box 605, Stn M, Halifax, NS B3J 2R7
902/420-9191, Fax: 902/429-7405, Email: nssba@fox.nstn.ca
Executive Director, Lloyd Gillis
Publications: NSSBA Newsletter

QUÉBEC SCHOOL BOARD ASSOCIATION/ASSOCIATION DES COMMISSIONS SCOLAIRES PROTESTANTES DU QUÉBEC (1929)
#520, 4999, rue Ste-Catherine ouest, Montréal, PQ H3Z 1T3

514/482-7522, Fax: 514/482-9399
Executive Director, Jeff Polenz

SASKATCHEWAN SCHOOL TRUSTEES ASSOCIATION (SSTA) (1915)
#400, 2222 - 13 Ave., Regina, SK S4P 3M7
306/569-0750, Fax: 306/352-9633
Executive Director, J.C. Melvin
Publications: School Trustee

Canadian Society of Biblical Studies/Société canadienne des études bibliques (CSBS) (1933)

Dept. of Religious Studies, Memorial University, PO Box 4200, Stn C, St. John's, NF A1C 5S7
709/737-8166, Fax: 709/737-4569
Executive Secretary, Prof. David J. Hawkin
Publications: Studies in Religion/Sciences religieuses; Bulletin, a.
Affiliates: Canadian Corporation for the Study of Religion; Canadian Federation of Humanities

Canadian Society for Education through Art/ Société canadienne d'éducation par l'art (CSEA) (1955)

675, Samuel de Champlain, Boucherville, PQ J4B 6C4
514/655-2435, Fax: 514/655-4379
President, Judy Freedman
Secretary, Louise Filion
Publications: CSEA/SCEA Newsletter; Canadian Review of Art Education; Research Review, s-a.
Affiliates: British Columbia Art Teachers' Association; Fine Arts Council, Alberta Teachers' Association; Saskatchewan Society for Education through Art; Manitoba Association of Art Educators; Ontario Society for Education through Art; Provincial Association of Art Teachers; Association québécoise des éducateurs spécialisés en arts plastiques; New Brunswick Arts Education Council; Nova Scotia Art Teachers' Association; PEI Art Teachers' Association; Art Council of the Newfoundland Teachers' Association; Canadian Art Gallery Educators

Canadian Society for the Study of Education/ Société canadienne pour l'étude de l'éducation (CSSE) (1972)

#205, One Stewart St., Ottawa, ON K1N 6H7
613/230-3532, Fax: 613/230-2746, Email: csse@acadvm1.uottawa.ca
Administrator, Tim Howard
President, Phil Nagy, Ph.D.
Publications: CSSE News/Nouvelles SCÉÉ; Canadian Journal of Education, q.; Yearbook

Canadian Society for the Study of Higher Education/Société canadienne pour l'étude de l'enseignement supérieur (CSSHE) (1970)

#320, 350 Albert St., Ottawa, ON K1R 1B1
613/563-1236, Fax: 613/563-7739, Email: kclements@aucc.ca
President, Glen Jones
Executive Secretary, Kenneth Clements
Publications: Canadian Journal of Higher Education; CSSHE Bulletin, 5 pa; CSSHE Directory, a.; Professional File, 3 pa

Canadian Teachers' Federation/Fédération canadienne des enseignantes et enseignants (CTF) (1920)

110 Argyle Ave., Ottawa, ON K2P 1B4
613/232-1505, Fax: 613/232-1886, Email: info@ctf-fce.ca
URL: http://www.ctf-fce.ca
President, Maureen Morris
Secretary-General, Jacques Schryburt

ALBERTA TEACHERS' ASSOCIATION (ATA) (1918)
Barnett House, 11010 - 142 St., Edmonton, AB T5N 2R1
403/453-2411, Fax: 403/455-6481
Executive Secretary, Julius S. Buski
Publications: ATA News; The ATA Magazine, q.; ATA Directory & Information Guide, a.

ASSOCIATION DES ENSEIGNANTES ET DES ENSEIGNANTS FRANCOPHONES DU NOUVEAU-BRUNSWICK (AEFNB) (1970)
CP 712, Fredericton, NB E3B 5B4
506/452-8921, Téléc: 506/453-9795
Directeur général, Ronald LeBreton
Publications: Nouvelles

BRITISH COLUMBIA TEACHERS' FEDERATION/FÉDÉRATION DES ENSEIGNANTS DE LA COLOMBIE-BRITANNIQUE (BCTF) (1916)
#100, 550 - 6th Ave. West, Vancouver, BC V5Z 4P2
604/871-2283, Fax: 604/871-2294
URL: http://www.bctf.bc.ca
Executive Director, Elsie McMurphy
President, Alice McQuade
Publications: Teacher

MANITOBA TEACHERS' SOCIETY/ASSOCIATION DES ENSEIGNANTS DU MANITOBA (MTS) (1919)
191 Harcourt St., Winnipeg, MB R3J 3H2
204/888-7961, Fax: 204/831-0877, Toll Free: 1-800-262-8803
President, Linda York
General Secretary, Jean Gisiger
Publications: The Manitoba Teacher

NEW BRUNSWICK TEACHERS' ASSOCIATION (1902)
PO Box 752, Fredericton, NB E3B 5R6
506/452-8921, Fax: 506/453-9795
Executive Director, Bob Fitzpatrick
Publications: NBTA News

NEWFOUNDLAND & LABRADOR TEACHERS' ASSOCIATION/ ASSOCIATION DES ENSEIGNANTS DE TERRE-NEUVE (NTA) (1890)
3 Kenmount Rd., St. John's, NF A1B 1W1
709/726-3223, Fax: 709/726-4302, Toll Free: 1-800-563-3599
Executive Director, Wayne Russell
Publications: NTA Bulletin

NORTHWEST TERRITORIES TEACHERS' ASSOCIATION/ ASSOCIATION DES ENSEIGNANTS DES TERRITOIRES DU NORD-OUEST
5018 - 48 St., PO Box 2340, Yellowknife, NT X1A 2P7
403/873-8501, Fax: 403/873-2366
Executive Director, Blake W. Lyons
Publications: Communicate; Professional Development & Teacher Welfare Bulletins

NOVA SCOTIA TEACHERS UNION/SYNDICAT DES ENSEIGNANTS DE LA NOUVELLE-ÉCOSSE (NSTU) (1895)
3106 Dutch Village Rd., Armdale, NS B3L 4L7
902/477-5621, Fax: 902/477-3517, Toll Free: 1-800-565-6788
URL: http://fox.nstn.ca/~nstu/
Executive Director, Ronald Morrison
Publications: The Teacher; Aviso, 3 pa

ONTARIO TEACHERS' FEDERATION/FÉDÉRATION DES ENSEIGNANTES ET DES ENSEIGNANTS DE L'ONTARIO (OTF) (1944)
#700, 1260 Bay St., Toronto, ON M5R 2B5
416/966-3424, Fax: 416/966-5450
President, Bill Martin
Sec.-Treas., Susan Langley
Publications: Interaction

PRINCE EDWARD ISLAND TEACHERS' FEDERATION/FÉDÉRATION DES ENSEIGNANTS DE L'ÎLE-DU-PRINCE-EDOUARD (PEITF) (1880)
PO Box 6000, Charlottetown, PE C1A 8B4
902/569-4157, Fax: 902/569-3682
President, Leo Broderick
Executive Assistant, Bob MacRae

Executive Assistant, Allan Murphy
General Secretary, James L. Blanchard
Publications: PEITF Newsletter

PROVINCIAL ASSOCIATION OF PROTESTANT TEACHERS OF QUÉBEC/ASSOCIATION PROVINCIALE DES ENSEIGNANTS PROTESTANTS DU QUÉBEC (PAPT) (1864)
#1, 17035 Brunswick Blvd., Kirkland, PQ H9H 5G6
514/694-9777, Fax: 514/694-0189
Executive Director, Alan Lombard
Publications: Sentinel/Sentinelle

SASKATCHEWAN TEACHERS' FEDERATION/FÉDÉRATION DES ENSEIGNANTS ET DES ENSEIGNANTES DE LA SASKATCHEWAN (STF)
2317 Arlington Ave., PO Box 1108, Saskatoon, SK S7K 3N3
306/373-1660, Fax: 306/374-1122
President, George Georget
Publications: Saskatchewan Bulletin

YUKON TEACHERS' ASSOCIATION/ASSOCIATION DES ENSEIGNANTS DU YUKON (YTA) (1955)
2064 - 2 Ave., Whitehorse, YT Y1A 1A9
403/668-6777, Fax: 403/667-4324
President, Terry Price
Publications: YTA Note

Canadian Test Centre Inc./Services d'évaluation pédagogique (CTC) (1990)

#7, 85 Citizen Court, Markham, ON L6G 1A8
905/513-6636, Fax: 905/513-6639, Toll Free: 1-800-668-1006, Email: echeng@ctestc.com
Managing Director, Ernest W. Cheng
Director, S. Shiu, CPA, CGA

Canadian University & College Conference Officers Association/Association des coordonnateurs de congrès des universités et des collèges du Canada (CUCCOA)

c/o Ryerson Polytechnic University, 160 Mutual St., Toronto, ON M5B 2M2
416/979-5284, Fax: 416/979-5212
Publications: CUCCOA Clips

Canadian University & College Counselling Association/Association canadienne de counselling universitaire et collégial (CUCCA) (1963)

Centre for Student Development, McMaster University, 409 Hamilton Hall, Hamilton, ON L8S 4K1
905/525-9140, ext.24711, Fax: 905/529-8972, Email: nifakis@mcmaster.ca
President, Dr. Debbie Nifakis
Publications: Coast to Coast with CUCCA
Affiliates: Canadian Association of College & University Student Services (CACUSS)

Canadian Vocational Association/Association canadienne de la formation professionelle (CVA) (1960)

PO Box 3435, Stn D, Ottawa, ON K1P 6L4
613/722-7696, Fax: 613/722-7696, Email: cva_acfp@magi.com
URL: http://www.cva.ca
President, Anna Kae Todd
Office Manager, P. McMahon
Publications: Canadian Vocational Journal

Centre d'animation de développement et de recherche en éducation (CADRÉ) (1968)

1940, boul Henri-Bourassa est, Montréal, PQ H2B 1S2
514/381-8891, Téléc: 514/381-4086, Ligne sans frais: 1-888-381-8891, Courrier électronique: cadre@cam.org
Directrice générale, Micheline Lavallée

ORGANIZATIONS — EDUCATION

Centre franco-ontarien de ressources pédagogiques (CFORP) (1974)
290 Dupuis St., Vanier, ON K1L 1A2
613/747-8000, Téléc: 613/747-2808
Directrice générale, Bernadette LaRochelle
Publications: Ressources

Co-operative, Career & Work Education Association of Canada/Association canadienne pour l'alternance travail-études (CCWEAC) (1983)
National Co-operative Education Centre
2 King St. West, Hamilton, ON L8P 1A1
905/523-6682, Fax: 905/523-7753
President, Hilda Pollard
Publications: CCWEAC Newsletter

Coalition for Education Reform
65 Parkway Ave., Markham, ON L3P 2G8
Affiliates: Organization for Quality Education; Quality Education Network; Educators' Association for Quality Education

College Institute Educators' Association of BC (CIEA) (1980)
#301, 555 - 8 Ave. West, Vancouver, BC V5Z 1C6
604/873-8988, Fax: 604/873-8865, Email: admin@ciea.bc.ca
President, Ed Lavalle
Publications: Profile
Affiliates: BC Federation of Labour; Canadian Association of University Teachers

The Commonwealth of Learning (COL) (1988)
Pacific Centre, Box 10428, #1700, 777 Dunsmuir St., PO Box 10428, Vancouver, BC V7Y 1K4
604/775-8200; Telex: 04507508 COMLEARN, Fax: 604/775-8210, Email: info@col.org
URL: http://www.col.org
Chairman, Dr. H. Ian Macdonald
President, Dato' Prof. Gajaraj Dhanarajan
Public Affairs Officer, Dave Wilson, CAE, Email: dwilson@col.org
Publications: Connections

Comparative & International Education Society of Canada/Société canadienne d'éducation comparée et internationale (CIESC/SCECI) (1967)
Faculty of Education, Queen's University, Kingston, ON K7L 3N6
613/545-6000, ext.7410, Fax: 613/545-6584
President, Dr. Eva Krugley-Smolska
Secretary, Iain Munro
Publications: CIESC Newsletter; Canadian & International Education, s-a.

Conférence des recteurs et des principaux des universités du Québec/Conference of Rectors & Principals of Quebec Universities (CREPUQ) (1963)
#1200, 300, Léo Pariseau, CP 952, Succ Place du Parc, Montréal, PQ H2W 2N1
514/288-8524, Téléc: 514/288-0554, Courrier électronique: crepuq@crepuq.qc.ca
URL: http://www.crepuq.qc.ca
Directeur général, Jacques Bordeleau
Publications: Répertoire des regroupements de recherche des établissements universitaires du Québec; CREPUQ en Bref; Répertoire des bibliothèques universitaires québécoises

Conseil des écoles françaises de la communauté urbaine de Toronto/Metro Toronto French-Language School Council (CEFCUT) (1988)
#207, One Concorde Gate, North York, ON M3C 3N6
416/391-1264, Téléc: 416/391-3892
Présidente, Daniel Joly
Directrice de l'éducation, Alice Ducharme

Responsable/Communications, Florence Giuly-Davis
Publications: Contact

Corporate-Higher Education Forum/Forum entreprises-universités (C-HEF) (1983)
#2501, 1155, boul René-Lévesque ouest, Montréal, PQ H3B 2K4
514/876-1356, Fax: 514/876-1498
President, John H. Dinsmore
Vice-President, Patricia Roman
Chairman, John Redfern
Publications: Rapport

Council of Ontario Universities/Conseil des universités de l'Ontario (COU) (1971)
#203, 444 Yonge St., Toronto, ON M5B 2H4
416/979-2165, Fax: 416/979-8635
URL: http://www.cou.on.ca
President, Bonnie M. Patterson
Chairperson, Dr. James Downey
Publications: COU Newsletter
Affiliates: Ontario Universities' Council on Admissions; Ontario Council on Graduate Studies; Ontario Council of University Libraries; Council of Ontario Faculties of Medicine; Ontario Council for University Continuing Education; Ontario University Registrars' Association; Ontario Council of Library Schools; Ontario Council of University Health Sciences; Association of Deans of Education in Ontario Universities; Association of Computer Services Directors; Council of Senior Administrative Officers; Ontario University Purchasing Management Association; Operations Planning & Analysis Group

Council of Outdoor Educators of Ontario (COEO) (1969)
#403, 1185 Eglinton Ave. East, North York, ON M3C 3C6
416/426-7276
Publications: Pathways; Directory of Programs Personnel

Council for Second Languages Programs in Canada/Conseil des programmes de langues secondes au Canada
#320, 350 Albert St., Ottawa, ON K1R 1B1
613/563-1236, Fax: 613/563-7739
President, Adrien Roy
Contact, Kenneth Clements

Educational Media Producers & Distributors Association of Canada/Association des producteurs et distributeurs du media d'education (1967)
3 Wellesley Ave., Toronto, ON M4X 1V2
416/923-7252, Fax: 416/929-2051
Executive Director, Jarvis Stoddart
Chairperson, Jennifer Baird

Fédération des associations de parents francophones de l'Ontario (FAPFO) (1954)
#302, 1173 Cyrville, Gloucester, ON K1J 7S6
613/741-8846, Téléc: 613/741-7322
Présidente, Francesca Piredda
Publications: APriorI

Federation of Catholic Parent-Teacher Associations of Ontario (FCPTAO) (1940)
#1216, 383 Richmond St., London, ON N6A 3C4
519/432-5573, Fax: 519/432-0126
President, Mary Ann Cuderman
Executive Director, Patrick Smith
Publications: FCPTAO Newsletter

Fédération des cégeps (1969)
500, boul Crémazie est, Montréal, PQ H2P 1E7
514/381-8631, Téléc: 514/381-2263

Directeur général, Gaëtan Boucher
Publications: Annuaire des cégeps; Cégepropos, trimestriel

Fédération des comités de parents de la Province de Québec inc.
389, boul Rochette, Beauport, PQ G1C 1A4
418/667-2432, Téléc: 418/667-6713
Directeur général, Jean-Pierre Jobidon
Publications: Veux-tu savoir?

Fédération des commissions scolaires du Québec (FCSQ) (1947)
1001, av Bégon, CP 490, Ste-Foy, PQ G1V 4C7
418/651-3220, Fax: 418/651-2574
URL: http://grics.qc.ca/fcsq/accueil.htm
Directeur général, Fernand Paradis
Présidente, Diane Drouin
Publications: Commissaires d'écoles

Federation of Independent Schools in Canada/Fédération canadienne des écoles privées (FISC) (1980)
9125 - 50 St., Edmonton, AB T6B 2H3
403/469-9868, Fax: 403/469-9880
Executive Director, Gary Duthler

ASSOCIATION OF INDEPENDENT SCHOOLS & COLLEGES IN ALBERTA (AISCA) (1965)
9125 - 50 St., Edmonton, AB T6B 2H3
403/469-9868, Fax: 403/469-9880
Executive Director, Gary Duthler
Publications: AISCA Directory of Independent Schools in Alberta

CONFERENCE OF INDEPENDENT SCHOOLS (ONTARIO) (CIS)
PO Box 1502, St Catharines, ON L2R 7J9
905/688-4866, Fax: 905/688-5778
Executive Director, Janet Lewis

FÉDÉRATION DES ASSOCIATIONS DE L'ENSEIGNEMENT PRIVÉS (FAEP) (1991)
1940, boul Henri-Bourassa est, Montréal, PQ H2B 1S2
514/381-8891, Téléc: 514/381-4086
Directeur exécutif, Auguste Servant

FEDERATION OF INDEPENDENT SCHOOL ASSOCIATIONS OF BC (FISA) (1966)
150 Robson St., Vancouver, BC V6B 2A7
604/684-6023, Fax: 604/684-3163
Executive Director, Fred Herfst
President, A. Blesch
Vice-President, Dr. L. Hollaar
Secretary, G. Baldwin
Treasurer, P. Vanderpol
Publications: Independent Schools Directory; Newsletter

MANITOBA FEDERATION OF INDEPENDENT SCHOOLS INC. (MFIS) (1974)
23 Pinecrest Bay, Winnipeg, MB R2G 1W2
204/339-5512, Fax: 204/339-3280
Executive Administrator, John Doornbos
President, Bill Gortemaker
Publications: MFIS Newsletter

ONTARIO ALLIANCE OF CHRISTIAN SCHOOLS (OACS) (1952)
617 Hwy. 53 East, Ancaster, ON L9G 3K9
905/648-2100, Fax: 905/648-2110, Email: oacs@netaccess.on.ca
Executive Director, Adrian Guldemond
Publications: The Communicator; The Digest
Affiliates: Christian Schools International

ONTARIO FEDERATION OF INDEPENDENT SCHOOLS (OFIS) (1974)
2199 Regency Terrace, Ottawa, ON K2C 1H2
905/596-4013, Fax: 905/596-4971
Acting Executive Director, Elaine Hopkins
Publications: OFIS News

Canadian Almanac & Directory 1997

SASKATCHEWAN ASSOCIATION OF HISTORICAL HIGH SCHOOLS (SAHHS)
c/o Lutheran College Bible Institute, PO Box 459, Outlook, SK S0L 2N0
306/867-8344, Fax: 306/867-9947
President, Daniel A. Haugen

SASKATCHEWAN ASSOCIATION OF INDEPENDENT CHURCH SCHOOLS
c/o Saskatoon Christian Centre, 102 Pinehouse Dr., Saskatoon, SK S7K 5H7
306/242-7141
President, Lou Brunelle

Fédération nationale des enseignants et des enseignantes du Québec/National Federation of Québec Teachers (FNEEQ) (1969)
1601, av de Lorimier, Montréal, PQ H2K 4M5
514/598-2241, Téléc: 514/598-2190, Télex: 055-60905
Président, Denis Choinière
Secrétaire général, Jean Salmon
Publications: FNEEQ-Actualité

Fédération des parents francophones de l'Alberta/Federation of Francophone Parents of Alberta (FPFA) (1986)
#205, 8925 - 82 Ave., Edmonton, AB T6C 0Z2
403/468-6934, Téléc: 403/469-4799, Courrier électronique: fpfa@portal.connect.ab.ca
Directrice générale, Mariette Rainville
Publications: Le Chaînon

Fédération provinciale des comités de parents du Manitoba (FPCP) (1976)
531 Marion St., Winnipeg, MB R2J 0J9
204/237-9666, Téléc: 204/231-1436
Directrice générale, Hélène d'Auteuil
Publications: Entre parents

Fédération québécoise des directeurs et directrices d'établissements d'enseignement (FQDE) (1961)
#100, 7855, boul Louis-H-Lafontaine, Anjou, PQ H1K 4E4
514/353-7511, Ligne sans frais: 1-800-361-4258
Président, Guy Lessard

Federation of Women Teachers' Associations of Ontario/Fédération des associations des enseignantes de l'Ontario (FWTAO/FAEO) (1918)
1260 Bay St., Toronto, ON M5R 2B8
416/964-1232, Fax: 416/964-0512
Executive Director, Joan Westcott
Publications: FWTAO Newsletter
Affiliates: Ontario Teachers' Federation

Foundation for Educational Exchange Between Canada & the United States (1990)
The Fulbright Program
#2015, 350 Albert St., Ottawa, ON K1R 1A4
613/237-5366, Fax: 613/237-2029, Email: av551@freenet.carleton.ca
URL: http://www.usis.canada.usia.gov/fulbrigh.htm
Executive Director, Dr. Victor Konrad
Publications: The Canada-US Fulbright Program

Humanities & Social Science Federation of Canada (1940)
#415, 151 Slater St., Ottawa, ON K1P 5H3
613/238-6112, Fax: 613/238-6114, Email: fedcan@hssfc.ca
Executive Director, Marcel Lauzière
Publications: SSFC Update

Institut canadien d'éducation des adultes
#300, 5225, rue Berri, Montréal, PQ H2J 2S4
514/948-2044, Téléc: 514/948-2040
Directrice général, Diane Laberge

International Association for Better Basic Education (1975)
34 Broadway Ave., Ottawa, ON K1S 2V6
613/232-3014
Secretary, F.D. Richardson

International Association of Master Penmen & Teachers of Handwriting (1950)
34 Broadway Ave., Ottawa, ON K1S 2V6
613/232-3014
Secretary, F.D. Richardson
Publications: Penmens Newsletter
Affiliates: International Association for Better Basic Education

International Council for Adult Education/Conseil international d'éducation des adultes (ICAE) (1973)
#500, 720 Bathurst St., Toronto, ON M5S 2R4
416/588-1211, Fax: 416/588-5725, Email: icae@web.apc.org
Executive Director, Raymond Desrochers
President, Lalita Ramdas
Publications: Convergence; ICAE News/Nouvelles du CIEA, q.

International Federation of Institutes for Advanced Study/Fédération internationale des instituts des hautes études (IFIAS) (1972)
39 Spadina Rd., Toronto, ON M5R 2S9
416/926-7570, Fax: 416/926-9481, Email: ifiastor@vm.utcs.toronto.ca
URL: http://www.ifias.ca/
Director, Robert I.G. McLean
Associate Director/Secretary, Peter Main
Chairman, Sir Hermann Bondi
Publications: IFIAS News; Member Institute Directory, a.; Latin American Scientists on Global Change (HDGC Program), a.

Learning Disabilities Association of Canada/ Troubles d'apprentissage - Association canadienne (LDAC) (1971)
#200, 323 Chapel St., Ottawa, ON K1N 7Z2
613/238-5721, Fax: 613/235-5391
President, Linda Jeppesen
Publications: National
Affiliates: Canadian Coalition for Prevention of Developmental Disabilities

ASSOCIATION QUÉBÉCOISE POUR LES TROUBLES D'APPRENTISSAGE/LEARNING DISABILITIES ASSOCIATION OF QUÉBEC (AQETA) (1966)
#300, 284, rue Notre-Dame ouest, Montréal, PQ H2Y 1T7
514/847-1324, Téléc: 514/281-5187
Directrice générale, Denise D. Marquez
Publications: Rendez-vous

LEARNING DISABILITIES ASSOCIATION OF ALBERTA/TROUBLES D'APPRENTISSAGE - ASSOCIATION DE L'ALBERTA (LDAA) (1968)
#145, 11343 - 61 Ave., Edmonton, AB T6H 1M3
403/448-0360, Fax: 403/438-0665, Info Line: 403/988-3349
Provincial Coordinator, Bill Lockhart
Publications: Agenda

LEARNING DISABILITIES ASSOCIATION OF BRITISH COLUMBIA/ TROUBLES D'APPRENTISSAGE - ASSOCIATION DE LA COLOMBIE-BRITANNIQUE (LDABC) (1974)
#203, 15463 - 104 St., Surrey, BC V3R 1N9
604/588-6322, Fax: 604/588-6344
Executive Director, Marny Ryan
Publications: The Advocate

LEARNING DISABILITIES ASSOCIATION OF MANITOBA/TROUBLES D'APPRENTISSAGE - ASSOCIATION DE MANITOBA (1966)
60 Maryland St., 2nd Fl., Winnipeg, MB R3G 1K7
204/774-1821, Fax: 204/788-4090

Executive Director, Jan Thiessen
Office Manager, Jan Kaludjer
Publications: LDAM Newsletter

LEARNING DISABILITIES ASSOCIATION OF NEW BRUNSWICK/ TROUBLES D'APPRENTISSAGE - ASSOCIATION DU NOUVEAU-BRUNSWICK (LDANB) (1980)
88 Prospect St. West, Fredericton, NB E3B 2T8
506/450-4944, Fax: 506/458-1352
President, Jan Greer
Publications: Reflections

LEARNING DISABILITIES ASSOCIATION OF NEWFOUNDLAND/ TROUBLES D'APPRENTISSAGE - ASSOCIATION DE TERRE-NEUVE (1981)
PO Box 26036, St. John's, NF A1E 5T9
709/754-3665, Fax: 709/754-3665
President, Patrick Daniels
Vice-President, Dianne Reddy
Publications: Newsletter

LEARNING DISABILITIES ASSOCIATION OF THE NORTHWEST TERRITORIES
PO Box 242, Yellowknife, NT X1A 2N2
403/873-6378, Fax: 403/873-6378
Contact, Irene Birin

LEARNING DISABILITIES ASSOCIATION OF NOVA SCOTIA/ TROUBLES D'APPRENTISSAGE - ASSOCIATION DE LA NOUVELLE ÉCOSSE (LDANS) (1988)
55 Ochterloney St., Dartmouth, NS B2Y 1C3
902/464-9751, Fax: 902/464-9167
Coordinator, Lori Steeves
President, Peter Woods
Publications: News & Events

LEARNING DISABILITIES ASSOCIATION OF ONTARIO/TROUBLES D'APPRENTISSAGE - ASSOCIATION DE L'ONTARIO (LDAO) (1964)
Box 39, #1004, 365 Bloor St. East, Toronto, ON M4W 3L4
416/929-4311, Fax: 416/929-3905
Executive Director, Sharon Bell-Wilson
Publications: Communiqué

LEARNING DISABILITIES ASSOCIATION OF PRINCE EDWARD ISLAND
PO Box 1081, Charlottetown, PE C1A 7M4
902/892-9664, Fax: 902/368-4548
Executive Director, Mike Howatt

LEARNING DISABILITIES ASSOCIATION OF SASKATCHEWAN/ TROUBLES D'APPRENTISSAGE - ASSOCIATION DE LA SASKATCHEWAN
Albert Community Centre, #26, 610 Clarence Ave. South, Saskatoon, SK S7H 2E2
306/652-4114, Fax: 306/652-3220
Executive Director, Laurie Garcea
Publications: The Provincial

LEARNING DISABILITIES ASSOCIATION OF YUKON TERRITORY (LDAY) (1973)
#205, 4133 - 4 Ave., PO Box 4853, Stn Main, Whitehorse, YT Y1A 4N6
403/668-5167, Fax: 403/668-5167
Executive Director, George Green
Publications: LDAY News; Learning Disabilities in the Classroom
Affiliates: Yukon Association for Community Living; Special Olympics; Yukon Literacy Council

Learning Enrichment Foundation (LEF) (1979)
116 Industry St., Toronto, ON M6M 4L8
416/769-0830, Fax: 416/769-9912
Executive Director, Eunice Grayson
Publications: In Touch; LEF Update

Manitoba Association for Bilingual Education
1574 Main St., Winnipeg, MB R2W 5J8

Canadian Almanac & Directory 1997

204/338-0395
Albert Christ
Betty Ann Watts

Manitoba Association of School Business Officials Inc.
19 Trowbridge Bay, St Vital, MB R2N 2V9
204/254-7570, Fax: 204/254-3606
Executive Director, Ede Fast

Manitoba Association of School Superintendents (MASS)
200 St. Mary's Rd., Winnipeg, MB R2H 1H9
204/231-1241, Fax: 204/231-1912, Email: sups@mbnet.mb.ca
Executive Director, Strini Reddy
Publications: MASS Communications
Affiliates: Canadian Association of School Administrators

Manitoba Parents for German Education Inc. (MPGE) (1981)
#15, 1110 Henderson Hwy., Winnipeg, MB R2G 1L1
204/338-7405
President, Leona Rew
Administrative Secretary, Anita Riedl
Publications: MPGE Newsletter
Affiliates: Manitoba Association for Bilingual Education

Mensa Canada Society (1967)
The High IQ Society
PO Box 1025, Stn O, Toronto, ON M4A 2V4
416/431-4314, Email: bn628@freenet.toronto.on.ca
URL: http://www.rohcg.on.ca/mensa/mensa.html
Executive Director, Lorraine MacNevin
President, Eric Matto
Publications: mc2

National Association of Career Colleges/ Association nationale des collèges carrières (NACC)
PO Box 340, Brantford, ON N3T 5N3
519/753-8689, Fax: 519/753-4712
Chief Administration Officer, Anne Burns
President, Addie Jason
Publications: Careers for the 90's; NACC National News, q.

National Educational Association of Disabled Students/Association nationale des étudiants handicapés au niveau post-secondaire (NEADS) (1986)
Carleton University, 4th Level Unicentre, 1125 Colonel By Dr., Ottawa, ON K1S 5B6
613/526-8008, Fax: 613/520-3704
Coordinator, Frank Smith
Publications: NEADS Newsletter
Affiliates: British Columbia Educational Association of Disabled Students; Nova Scotia Disability Action Committee; Association québécoise des étudiant(e)s handicapé(e)s au post-secondaire

North American Jewish Students' Network
#707, 40 Sheppard Ave. West, North York, ON M2N 6K9
416/512-0814, Fax: 416/512-9816, Email: jsnet@io.org
National Director, Howard Katz
National Chair, Talia Klein
Publications: Future Tense

Ontario Association of Career Colleges (OACC) (1972)
PO Box 340, Brantford, ON N3T 5N3
519/752-2124, Fax: 519/753-4712
Executive Director, Paul Kitchin
Administrative Assistant, Lorna Hillis

Ontario Association for Curriculum Development (OACD) (1950)
PO Box 931, London, ON N6A 5K1
519/438-8390, Fax: 519/679-6855
Executive Director, Jack D. Little
Publications: Curriculum Connections

Ontario Association of Deans of Education (OADE)
Faculty of Education, York University, 4700 Keele St., North York, ON M3J 1P3
416/736-5667, Fax: 416/736-5609
Contact, Dean Stan M. Shapson
Affiliates: Council of Ontario Universities

Ontario Association of School Business Officials (OASBO) (1945)
#5-110, 252 Bloor St. West, Toronto, ON M5S 1V5
416/923-3107, Fax: 416/923-3490
Executive Director, R.G. Jenkins
Administrative Assistant, S. Fernandes
Publications: The Advocate

Ontario Cooperative Education Association (OCEA) (1976)
939 Progress Ave., Scarborough, ON M1G 3T8
416/396-6329, Fax: 416/396-6739, Email: bmisener@interhop.net
President, Judi Misener
Publications: OCEA Exchange
Affiliates: Cooperative, Career, Work Education Association of Canada

Ontario Council on Graduate Studies
#203, 444 Yonge St., Toronto, ON M5B 2H4
416/979-2165, Fax: 416/979-8635

Ontario Council for Leadership in Educational Administration
#115, 252 Bloor St. West, Toronto, ON M5S 1V5
416/944-2652, Fax: 416/944-3822
Executive Director, Peter E. Angelini

Ontario Council for University Lifelong Learning
Div. of Continuing Education, University of Windsor, 401 Sunset Ave., Windsor, ON N9B 3P4
519/253-4232, Fax: 519/973-7038
President, Ramona Lumpkin

Ontario Educational Research Council/Conseil ontarien de recherches pédagogiques (OERC) (1959)
#8-200, 252 Bloor St. West, Toronto, ON M5S 1V6
416/924-6982, Fax: 416/924-3188
President, Dr. David Ireland
Publications: Reporting Classroom Research; Math 4 Girls; Aspects of/de l'immersion; Faîtes qu'ils ne décrochent pas/Give Them a Reason To Stay; Coming of Age: Co-operative Education

Ontario English Catholic Teachers' Association/ Association des enseignants catholiques de langue anglaise de l'Ontario (OECTA) (1944)
#400, 65 St. Clair Ave. East, Toronto, ON M4T 2Y8
416/925-2493, Fax: 416/925-7764, Toll Free: 1-800-268-7230
General Secretary, James J. Carey
Publications: The Reporter; Agenda, m.
Affiliates: Ontario Teachers' Federation

Ontario Principals' Association
#12-115, 252 Bloor St. West, Toronto, ON M5S 1V5
905/274-3601
President, William N. Bone
Publications: Ontario Principal

Ontario Public School Boards Association
Phoenix House, 439 University Ave., 18th Fl., Toronto, ON M5G 1Y8
416/340-2540, Fax: 416/340-7571
Executive Director, Mike Benson
President, Donna Cansfield
Executive Vice-President, Lynn Peterson
Publications: Fast Reports; Education Today, 5 pa

Ontario Public School Teachers' Federation/ Fédération des enseignants des écoles publiques de l'Ontario (OPSTF) (1921)
5160 Orbitor Dr., Mississauga, ON L4W 5H2
905/238-0200, Fax: 905/238-0201, Toll Free: 1-800-268-7221
President, R. Ferland
Publications: OPSTF News; NewsToday, 10 pa
Affiliates: Ontario Teachers' Federation

Ontario School Trustees' Council/Conseil ontarien des conseillers scolaires (OSTC)
#1804, 20 Eglinton Ave. West, Toronto, ON M4R 1K8
Fax: 416/932-9458
President, Mary Hendriks

Ontario Secondary School Teachers' Federation/ Fédération des enseignants des écoles secondaires de l'Ontario (OSSTF) (1919)
60 Mobile Dr., Toronto, ON M4A 2P3
416/751-8300, Fax: 416/751-3394
President, Earl Manners
General Secretary, Malcolm Buchanan
Publications: Forum

Ontario Separate School Trustees' Association
#1804, 20 Eglinton Ave. West, Toronto, ON M4R 1K8
416/932-9460, Fax: 416/932-9459
Executive Director, P. Slack
Publications: The Catholic Trustee
Affiliates: Canadian Catholic School Trustees Association

Parent Co-operative Preschools International (PCPI) (1962)
3767 Northwood Dr., Niagara Falls, ON L2H 2Y5
905/374-6605
President, Marika Townsend
Publications: Co-operatively Speaking

Provincial Association of Catholic Teachers/ Association provinciale des enseignants catholiques (PACT) (1969)
#330, 5800, boul Metropolitain est, Montréal, PQ H1S 1A7
514/252-7946, Fax: 514/252-9003
President, Michael Palumbo
Publications: PACT

Québec Association of Independent Schools/ Association des écoles privées du Québec (QAIS) (1965)
#206, 410, rue Gratton, Saint-Laurent, PQ H4M 2E2
514/744-6711, Fax: 514/744-6523
Executive Director, Soryl Naymark
President, Elizabeth Scanlan

Québec Council of Parent Participation Preschools/Conseil québécois des pre-maternelles coopératives (QCPPP)
20551, rue Lakeshore, Baie d'Urfé, PQ H9X 1R3
514/457-3291
President, Sandra Kingsland
Publications: QCPPP Communiqué

Le Réseau d'enseignement francophone à distance du Canada (REFAD) (1988)
CP 670, Succ. C, Montréal, PQ H2L 4L5

Canadian Almanac & Directory 1997

514/523-3143, Téléc: 514/525-7763, Courrier électronique: refad@village.ca
Directrice générale, Dominique Gervais
Président, Pierre Pelletier
Publications: Connexion; Répertoire de l'enseignement à distance en français, annuel; Actes du Colloque de REFAD, annuel

Rural Learning Association of Ontario (RLA) (1965)
PO Box 1588, Guelph, ON N1H 6R7
519/821-0926
Sec.-Treas., Sharon Smith
Publications: Rural Routes

Saskatchewan Association for Multicultural Education (SAME) (1984)
#201, 2205 Victoria Ave., Regina, SK S4P 0S4
306/780-9428, Fax: 306/525-4009, Email: same@sasknet.sk.ca
President, Marge Nainaar
Secretary, John Willms
Program Coordinator, Rhonda Rosenberg
Publications: S.A.M.E. Newsletter
Affiliates: Canadian Council for Multicultural & Intercultural Education

Société pour la promotion de l'enseignement de l'anglais (langue seconde) au Québec/Society for the Promotion of the Teaching of English as a Second Language in Québec (SPEAQ) (1976)
#530, 7400, boul Saint-Laurent, 5e étage, Montréal, PQ H2R 2Y1
514/271-3700, Téléc: 514/948-1231
URL: http://cyberscol.qc.ca/partenaires/speaq/speaq.htm
President, Jacquelyne Lord, Courrier électronique: gelyne@mercure.net
Administrative Assistant, Louis Lagrois
Publications: SPEAQ Out
Organisation(s) affiliée(s): TESOL

Society for Educational Visits & Exchanges in Canada/Société éducative de visites et d'échanges au Canada (SEVEC) (1981)
#201, 57 Auriga Dr., Nepean, ON K2E 8B2
613/998-3760, Fax: 613/998-7094, Toll Free: 1-800-387-3832, Email: sevec@hookup.net
Executive Director, A.D.S. MacKay
Coordinator of Communications, Marc Bourgeois
Publications: infoSEVEC
Québec Regional Office: Coordonnatrice, Nathalie Bouchard, 51, rue des Jardins, Québec, PQ G1R 4L6, 418/648-3588, Téléc: 418/648-4288

Students' Union of Nova Scotia/Association étudiante de la Nouvelle-Écosse (SUNS) (1978)
958 Barrington St., Halifax, NS B3H 2P7
902/494-6655, Fax: 902/494-6682, Email: suns@ac.dal.ca
Executive Officer, Suzanne Drapeau
Chairperson, Hal Maclean
Publications: Notes & News; SUNS Lobby Guide

Superannuated Teachers of Ontario/Enseignants et enseignantes retraités de l'Ontario (STO) (1968)
#200, 1260 Bay St., Toronto, ON M5R 2B1
416/962-9463, Fax: 416/962-1061, Toll Free: 1-800-361-9888

TeleLearning Research Network/Réseau de recherche en télé-apprentissage et formation (TL-RN) (1995)
Room 9701, Applied Science Bldg., Simon Fraser University, Burnaby, BC V5A 1S6
604/291-5396, Fax: 604/291-3439
URL: http://fas.sfu.ca/telelearn

Executive Director, Joanne Curry, Email: joanne@telelearn.ca
Dr. Linda Harasim
Dr. Tom Calvert

TESL Canada Federation (1978)
Teaching English as a Second Language Canada Federation
PO Box 44105, Burnaby, BC V5B 4Y2
604/298-4210, Fax: 604/298-4210, Toll Free: 1-800-393-9199, Email: teslcan@unixg.ubc.ca
URL: http://raven.ritslab.ubc.ca/teslcanada.html
Administrative Director, Carol May
President, William McMichael, Email: mcmichael@ritslab.ubc.ca
Vice-President, Silvia Begin, Email: gsabegin@oanet.com
Secretary, Linda Curtis, Email: 73322.2750@compuserve.com
Treasurer, Catherine Eddy, Email: ceddy@vsb.bc.ca
Publications: TESL Canada Journal/Revue TESL du Canada
Affiliates: Teachers of English to Speakers of Other Languages (TESOL); Société pour la promotion de l'enseignement de l'anglais (langue seconde) au Québec

United World Colleges (UWC) (1974)
Lester B. Pearson College of the Pacific, RR#1, Victoria, BC V9B 5T7
250/478-5591, Fax: 250/478-6421
Director, Dr. Peter D. Bovinton
Publications: Pearson Times

EGGS see POULTRY & EGGS

ELECTRONICS & ELECTRICITY

Association québécoise des consommateurs industriels d'électricité (AQCIE) (1984)
#904, 1080, Côte du Beaver Hall, Montréal, PQ H2Z 1S8
514/866-7774, Téléc: 514/866-8669, Ligne sans frais: 1-800-363-0226
Directrice générale, Lili Hayes
Organisation(s) affiliée(s): Association des manufacturiers du Québec

Canadian Electrical Contractors Association
#207, 23 Lesmill Rd., North York, ON M3B 3P6
416/391-3226, Fax: 416/391-3926
Executive Secretary, Eryl M. Roberts

CORPORATION DES MAÎTRES ÉLECTRICIENS DU QUÉBEC/ CORPORATION OF MASTER ELECTRICIANS OF QUÉBEC (CMEQ) (1950)
#100, 5925, boul Décarie, Montréal, PQ H3W 3C9
514/738-2184, Téléc: 514/738-2192, Ligne sans frais: 1-800-361-9061
Directeur général et secrétaire executif, Yvon Guilbault
Publications: Electricité Québec

ELECTRICAL CONTRACTORS ASSOCIATION OF ALBERTA (ECA ALBERTA)
11302 - 119 St., Edmonton, AB T5G 2X4
403/451-2412, Fax: 403/455-9815
Area Manager, Sheri McLean

ELECTRICAL CONTRACTORS ASSOCIATION OF BC (ECA-BC) (1952)
#510, 5050 Kingsway, Burnaby, BC V5H 4C2
604/435-4186, Fax: 604/439-1194
Executive Director, Clifford L. Pilkey, CAE
Director of Communications, Rick Stewart
Line Trade Director, Paddy Hatca
Publications: Relay; Membership List, a.
Affiliates: National Electrical Contractors Association

ELECTRICAL CONTRACTORS ASSOCIATION OF NEW BRUNSWICK INC. (ECANB) (1964)
PO Box 322, Fredericton, NB E3B 4Y9
506/452-7627, Fax: 506/452-1786
Executive Director, David Ellis
Publications: ECANB Today
Affiliates: Construction Association of New Brunswick Inc.; Canadian Construction Association

ELECTRICAL CONTRACTORS ASSOCIATION OF ONTARIO (ECA ONTARIO)
#207, 23 Lesmill Rd., North York, ON M3B 3P6
416/391-3226, Fax: 416/391-3926
Executive Vice-President, Eryl M. Roberts
Executive Assistant, Jo-Anne Jackson-Thorne
Affiliates: Council of Ontario Construction Associations

ELECTRICAL CONTRACTORS ASSOCIATION OF SASKATCHEWAN
Construction House, 1939 Elphinstone St., Regina, SK S4T 3N3
306/525-0171, Fax: 306/347-8595
Executive Director, Manley McLachlan

Canadian Electrical Manufacturers Representatives Association
#200, 670 Bloor St. West, Toronto, ON M6G 1L2
416/533-7800, Fax: 416/533-4795
Executive Director, Don Mockford

Canadian Electricity Association/Association canadienne de l'électricité (CEA) (1891)
#1600, One Westmount Square, Montréal, PQ H3Z 2P9
514/937-6181, Fax: 514/937-6498
President & CEO, Hans R. Konow
Secretary, I. Murray Phillips
Publications: Connections/Connexions

Canadian Electronic & Appliance Service Association/Organisation canadienne de service d'appareils domestique (CEASA) (1977)
#115, 10 Wynford Heights Cres., North York, ON M3C 1K8
416/447-7469, Fax: 416/447-2511
Executive Director, S. Rubicini
Publications: Service Contacts

Comité canadien des éléctrotechnologies/ Canadian Committee on Electrotechnologies
#2075, 630, boul René-Lévesque ouest, Montréal, PQ H3B 1S6
514/875-2341, Téléc: 514/875-9139
Directeur général, Bernard Houde

Consumer Electronics Marketers of Canada (CEMC)
#210, 10 Carlson Ct., Etobicoke, ON M9W 6L2
416/674-7410, Fax: 416/674-7412
Vice-President, Alda M. Murphy

Electrical Power Systems Construction Association (EPSCA)
c/o Ontario Hydro, #H2, 700 University Ave., Toronto, ON M5G 1X6
416/592-2547, Fax: 416/592-4229
Sec.-Treas., N.A. Donnelly

Electro-Federation Canada Inc. (1995)
#210, 10 Carlson Ct., Etobicoke, ON M9W 6L2
416/674-7410, Fax: 416/674-7412
President, Jim McCarthy

Electronic Industry Association of Alberta (1981)
9924 - 45 Ave., Edmonton, AB T6E 5J1
403/436-9750, Fax: 403/437-1240
Publications: Crosscurrents

Electronics & Information Association of Manitoba (EIAM) (1983)
#68, 1313 Border St., Winnipeg, MB R3H 0X4
204/697-6020, Fax: 204/697-6025, Email: eiam@mbnet.mb.ca
Publications: Networks

Institute of Electrical & Electronics Engineers Canada (1884)
IEEE Canada
86 Main St., PO Box 830, Dundas, ON L9H 2R1
905/628-9554, Fax: 905/628-9554,
    Email: member.services@ieee.ca
URL: http://www.ieee.ca
President, Linda Weaver
Publications: Canadian Review
Affiliates: The Engineering Institute of Canada

Manitoba Electrical League (1957)
#14, 395 Berry St., Winnipeg, MB R3J 1N6
204/885-3668, Fax: 204/885-3678
Executive Director, Larry McLennan
Publications: Feedback

Ontario Electrical League (1966)
#1000, 2 Lansing Sq., North York, ON M2J 4P8
416/495-0052, Fax: 416/495-1804
General Manager, R.S. McCarten
Publications: Dialogue

EMERGENCY RESPONSE
see also Safety & Accident Prevention

Canadian Avalanche Association (CAA) (1982)
Canadian Avalanche Centre
PO Box 2759, Revelstoke, BC V0E 2S0
250/837-2435, Fax: 250/837-4624, Toll Free: 1-800-667-1105, Email: canav@mindlink.bc.ca
URL: http://www.avalanche.ca/snow
President, Jack Bennetto
Manager, Alan Dennis
Publications: Avalanche News
Affiliates: Alpine Club of Canada; Canadian West Ski Areas; Association of Canadian Mountain Guides

Canadian Lifeboat Institution Inc. (CLI) (1981)
One Passage Island, West Vancouver, BC V7W 1V7
604/290-2701
President, P. Matty
Affiliates: International Lifeboat Federation

The Canadian Red Cross Society/La Société canadienne de la Croix-Rouge (1885)
1800 Alta Vista Dr., Ottawa, ON K1G 4J5
613/739-3000, Fax: 613/731-1411, Telex: 05-33784
Secretary General, Doug Lindores
President, Myrle Vokey
National Director, Blood Services, Dr. Maung T. Aye
Affiliates: International Committee of the Red Cross; International of Red Cross & Red Crescent Societies (Geneva)

Civil Air Search & Rescue Association (CASARA) (1984)
1180 Graham St., Kelowna, BC V1Y 9P5
250/861-7328, Fax: 250/861-7585
National President, Charles Pachal

Corporation des services d'ambulance du Québec
535, av des Oblats, Québec, PQ G1N 1V5
418/522-3456, Téléc: 418/522-3337
Directeur général, Gilles Ricard

Occupational First Aid Attendants Association of British Columbia
#204, 3855 Henning Dr., Burnaby, BC V5C 6N3
604/294-0244, Fax: 604/294-0289, Toll Free: 1-800-667-4566, Email: osaaa@lionsgate.com
President, Susan Hyde

REACT Canada Inc. (1962)
Radio Emergency Associated Communications Teams
32 The Queensway North, Keswick, ON L4P 1E3
905/476-5556
Director, Ronald W. McCracken
Publications: The REACTivist; The REACTer, bi-m.; Team Topics; REACT Team Directory
Affiliates: REACT International Inc.; Salvation Army; Red Cross

Royal Life Saving Society Canada/Société royale de sauvetage Canada (RLSSC) (1908)
287 McArthur Ave., Ottawa, ON K1L 6P3
613/746-5694, Fax: 613/746-9929
URL: http://www.interlog.com/~jlogan/rlss/rlssc.html
Executive Director, Rick Haga
Publications: The Communiqué
Affiliates: Royal Life International World Life Saving Association
Alberta & NWT Branch: Contact, Larry Patterson, 11759 Groat Rd., Edmonton, AB T5M 3K6, 403/453-8638, Fax: 403/453-8632
BC & Yukon Branch: Executive Director, Dale Miller, 1235 West Pender St., Vancouver, BC V6E 2V1, 604/684-6368, Fax: 604/685-6802
Manitoba Branch: Contact, Karine Levasseur, #504, 138 Portage Ave. East, Winnipeg, MB R3C 9Z9, 204/956-2124, Fax: 204/944-8546
New Brunswick Branch: Executive Director, Roger Dumont, Maritime Opportunities Centre, 1216 Sand Cove Rd., Saint John, NB E2M 4Z8, 506/635-1552, Fax: 506/635-0988
Newfoundland & Labrador Branch: Branch Administrator, Jeanette Jobson, PO Box 8065, Stn A, St. John's, NF A1B 3M9, 709/576-1953, Fax: 709/576-1953
Nova Scotia Branch: Executive Director, Pat Mombourquette, 5516 Spring Garden Rd., PO Box 3010, Halifax, NS B3J 3G6, 902/425-5450, Fax: 902/425-5606
Ontario Branch: Executive Director, Doug Ferguson, 322 Consumers Rd., North York, ON M2J 1P8, 416/490-8844, Fax: 416/490-8766
PEI Branch: President, Chrissy Costello, 30 MacMillan Cres., Sherwood, PE C1A 8G2, 902/368-1059, Fax: 902/894-7283
Québec Branch: Directeur général, Raynald Hawkins, 4545, av Pierre-de-Coubertin, CP 1000, Succ. M, Montréal, PQ H1V 3R2, 514/252-3100, Téléc: 514/252-3232
Saskatchewan Branch: Programme Director & CEO, Suzanne Gorman, 2205 Victoria Ave., Regina, SK S4P 0S4, 306/780-9254, Fax: 306/525-4009

St. John Ambulance/Ambulance Saint-Jean (1883)
The Priory of Canada of the Most Venerable Order of the Hospital of St. John of Jerusalem
312 Laurier Ave. East, Ottawa, ON K1N 6P6
613/236-7461, Fax: 613/236-2425
Secretary/CEO, D.J. Phillips
Chancellor, Dr. Eric L. Barry
Publications: St. John Canada Today/Saint-Jean Canada aujourd'hui
Federal District Council (Ottawa Area): Executive Director, D.A.F. Spry, 30 The Driveway, Ottawa, ON K2P 1C9, 613/236-3626, Fax: 613/233-0672
Alberta Council: Executive Director, D. Hook, 10975 - 124 St., Edmonton, AB T5M 0H9, 403/452-6565, Fax: 403/452-2835

BC Council: Executive Director, S.G. Hodgins, 6111 Cambie St., Vancouver, BC V5Z 3B2, 604/321-2651, Fax: 604/321-5316
Manitoba Council: Executive Director, C. Brent Thomas; President, L. Gander, St. John House, 535 Doreen St., Winnipeg, MB R3G 3H5, 204/784-7000, Fax: 204/786-2295
New Brunswick Council: Executive Director, John Yauss, PO Box 3599, Stn B, Fredericton, NB E3A 5J8, 506/458-9129, Fax: 506/452-8699
Newfoundland Council: Executive Director, J. O'Brien, PO Box 5489, St. John's, NF A1C 5W4, 709/726-4200, Fax: 709/726-4117
Nova Scotia Council: Executive Director, J. Ross, St. John House, 88 Slayter St., Dartmouth, NS B3A 2A6, 902/464-1314, Fax: 902/469-9609
NWT Council: Executive Director, D. Irwin, 5023 - 51 St., Yellowknife, NT X1A 1S5, 403/873-5658, Fax: 403/920-4458
Ontario Council: Executive Director, J.P. Pepin, 48 Wellesley St. East, Toronto, ON M4Y 1G5, 416/923-8411, Fax: 416/923-8456
PEI Council: Executive Director, C.S. Crockett, PO Box 1235, Charlottetown, PE C1A 7M8, 902/569-1234, Fax: 902/368-3231
Québec Council: Directeur exécutif, L. Farmer, 1407, rue de la Montagne, Montréal, PQ H3G 1Z3, 514/842-4801, Téléc: 514/842-4807
Saskatchewan Council: Executive Director, R.L. Rowlatt, 2625 - 3 Ave., Regina, SK S4T 0C8, 306/522-7226, Fax: 306/525-4177

EMPLOYMENT & HUMAN RESOURCES
see also Labour Relations

Action Group Against Harassment & Discrimination in the Workplace/Groupe d'action contre le harcèlement et discrimination au travail (AGAHD) (1991)
Action Against Harassment
49 Montpetit St., L'Orignal, ON K0B 1K0
613/632-9828, Fax: 613/632-9828
President, Bronwen Williams
Affiliates: Ontario Anti-Harassment Coalition

Association of Professional Placement Agencies & Consultants/Association de placement en personnel agences et conseillers (APPAC) (1962)
#L-109, 114 Richmond St. East, Toronto, ON M5C 1P1
416/362-0983, Fax: 416/360-5478
Executive Director, Jacqueline Carter
Publications: Dialogue
Affiliates: International Federation of Personnel Services Association

Association des professionnels en ressources humaines du Québec/Association of Human Resources Professionals of the Province of Québec (APRHQ) (1934)
#820, av 1253 McGill Collège, Montréal, PQ H3B 2Y5
514/879-1636, Téléc: 514/879-1722
Directrice générale, Chantal Décarie
Publications: Info Ressources Humaines

Association of Self Employment Developers of Ontario (ASEDO) (1994)
#200, 7 Innovation Dr., Flamborough, ON L9H 7H9
905/689-2920, Fax: 905/689-2889, Email: asedo@bigwave.ca
President, Sandie Heirwegh
Vice-President, Barbara Okanik
Sec.-Treas., David Jackson
Publications: Smart Starts

Canadian Almanac & Directory 1997

2-56 ORGANIZATIONS — ENERGY

Canadian Association of Career Educators & Employers/Association canadienne des spécialistes en emploi et des employeurs (CACEE) (1946)
#205, 1209 King St. West, Toronto, ON M6K 1G2
416/535-8126, Fax: 416/532-0934, Email: cacee@inforamp.net
URL: http://www.cacee.com/workweb
Executive Director, Graham B.F. Donald
Publications: Career Options

Canadian Career Information Association/Association canadienne de documentation professionnelle (CCIA) (1975)
PO Box 84, Stn P, Toronto, ON M5S 2S6
416/736-5351
Co-Facilitator, Cathy Clarke
Co-Facilitator, Marlis Hubbard
Publications: Career INFOcus

Canadian Recruiters Guild
2 Walton Ct., Ottawa, ON K1V 9T1
613/523-5957

Corporation professionnelle des conseilliers et conseillières d'orientation du Québec (CPCCOQ) (1963)
#520, 1100, rue Beaumont, Montréal, PQ H3P 3H5
514/737-4717, Téléc: 514/737-6431, Ligne sans frais: 1-800-363-2643
Secrétaire générale, Martine Lacharite
Présidente, Louise Landry
Publications: L'Orientation; Orientation Nouvelles, mensuel

Employment & Staffing Services Association of Canada/Association des entreprises en placement et gestion de personnel (FTHS) (1968)
#1105, 191 The West Mall, Etobicoke, ON M9C 5K8
416/626-7130, Fax: 416/620-5392, Email: bbandc@enterprise.ca
Executive Director, Amanda Curtis, CAE
Publications: Legislative Watch

Human Resources Professionals Association of Ontario (HRPAO) (1954)
#1902, 2 Bloor St. West, Toronto, ON M4W 3E2
416/923-2324 (Office & Resource Line), Fax: 416/923-7264, Toll Free: 1-800-387-1311
Executive Director, Christine A. Featherstone
Chair, Brian R. Gatien, C.H.R.P.
President, Yvonne Blaszczyk, C.H.R.P.
Publications: Human Resources Professional

Institute of Equality & Employment/Institut d'égalité et d'emploi
#2500, 1250 boul René Lévesque ouest, Montréal, PQ H3B 4Y1
514/846-1212, Fax: 514/846-3427
President, Roy L. Heenan

International Association for Human Resource Information Systems/L'Association canadienne des professionnels en systèmes de ressources humaines (IHRIM) (1985)
c/o Base Service Canada Inc., #301, 250 Consumers Rd., North York, ON M2J 4V6
416/490-6566, Fax: 416/495-8723, Toll Free: 1-800-780-6566, Email: ihrim@onramp.ca
Director, Canada, Brian L.G. Lechem
Associate Director, Canada, Ruth Abrahamson
Publications: IHRIMLink
Affiliates: American Association of Human Resource Systems Professionals

The Professional Development Institute Inc./Institut supérieur de gestion (PDI) (1973)
Proactive Management Group
79 Fentiman Ave., Ottawa, ON K1S 0T7
613/730-7777, Fax: 613/235-1115
President, A.P. Martin
Publications: The Harvard Planner; Think Proactive/La Gestion proactive; Essence of a Proactive Life; Bringing Time to Life

ENERGY
see also **Environmental**

Association of Major Power Consumers in Ontario (AMPCO) (1975)
#500, 10 Lower Spadina Ave., Toronto, ON M5V 2Z2
416/260-0225, Fax: 416/260-0442
Executive Director, Arthur Dickinson
Chairman, Michael G. Ford, P.Eng.
Publications: The AMPCO Report

Canadian Association of Energy Service Companies (CAESCO) (1987)
#404, 1235 Bay St., Toronto, ON M5R 3K4
416/927-9098, Fax: 416/560-5839
President, Tom Tamblyn
Executive Director, Marion Fraser
Information Contact, Michelle Dixon-Parent
Publications: CAESCO News; Directory, a.

Canadian Coalition for Nuclear Responsibility/Regroupement pour la surveillance du nucléaire (1975)
PO Box 236, Stn Snowdon, Montréal, PQ H3X 3T4
514/489-5118, Fax: 514/489-5118
President, Gordon Edwards
Sec.-Treas., Marc Chénier
Affiliates: Environment Liaison Centre - International; Friends of the Earth - Canada

Canadian Energy Research Institute (CERI) (1975)
#150, 3512 - 33 St. NW, Calgary, AB T2L 2A6
403/282-1231, Fax: 403/284-4181
President, Dr. Gerry E. Angevine
Director, Conferences & Communications, R.J. Buchanan
Publications: CERI Insight

Canadian Fluid Power Association/Association canadienne d'énergie fluide (CFPA) (1974)
c/o Trade Association Management Group, 208 Brimorton Dr., Scarborough, ON M1H 2C6
416/431-1330, Fax: 416/764-7463
Manager, John Martin
President, Al Trudelle
Publications: Fluid Power News

Canadian Gas Association/Association canadienne du gaz (CGA) (1907)
#1200, 243 Consumers Rd., North York, ON M2J 5E3
416/498-1994, Fax: 416/498-7465, Email: cga@cga.ca
URL: http://iplace.com/cga
President/CEO, Gerald Doucet
Publications: CGA Domestic Demand Forecast; Canadian Gas Facts, a.; Natural Gas Industry Data Tables, a.; Natural Gas Utility Directory, a.; Canadian Residential Heating Survey, a.; Gas Cogeneration Database, a.; Gas Cooling Database, a.; Canadian Gas Rates, a.; Areas Served by Natural Gas in Canada, biennial
Affiliates: International Gas Union; Canadian Gas Research Institute; Gas Technology Canada; International Approval Services

Canadian Gas Research Institute/Institut canadien des recherches gazières (CGRI) (1974)
55 Scarsdale Rd., North York, ON M3B 2R3
416/447-6661, Fax: 416/447-6757, Email: cgri@hookup.net
URL: http://www.hookup.net/~cgri/
General Manager, Roger Barker
Publications: CGRI Monitor

Canadian Institute of Energy (CIE) (1979)
#229, 640 - 5 Ave. SW, Calgary, AB T2P 0M6
403/262-6969, Fax: 403/269-2787
National President, Peter D. Faloon, 403/221-9011, Fax: 403/221-9010
Director, Eric Smith, 519/337-0511, Fax: 519/337-0519
Director, Julian Taylor, 604/691-5789, Fax: 604/691-5773
Treasurer, Sandy Constable, 604/688-1773, Fax: 604/669-4311
Publications: CIE National News
Affiliates: The Institute of Energy (UK); Canadian Institute of Fluidized Bed Technology; Canadian National Committee of the World Energy Congress

Canadian Nuclear Association/Association nucléaire canadienne (CNA) (1960)
#475, 144 Front St. West, Toronto, ON M5J 2L7
416/977-6152, Fax: 416/979-8356, Toll Free: 1-800-387-4477
President, Jack Richman
Publications: Nuclear Canada/Canada nucléaire

Canadian Nuclear Society/Société nucléaire canadienne (CNS)
#475, 144 Front St. West, Toronto, ON M5J 2L7
416/977-6152, Fax: 416/979-8356, Toll Free: 1-800-387-4477
President, Jerry Cuttler
Publications: Canadian Nuclear Society Bulletin

Canadian Renewable Fuels Association/Association canadienne des carburants renouvelables (CRFA)
90 Woodlawn Rd. West, Guelph, ON N1H 1B2
519/767-0431, Fax: 519/837-1674, Email: crfa@greenfuels.org
URL: http://www.greenfuels.org
President, Jim Johnson
Vice-President, Doug MacKenzie
Public Affairs Advisor, Terry Boland
Publications: Green Fuels Today

Canadian Solar Industries Association Inc./Association des industries solaires du Canada inc. (CanSIA) (1978)
#250, 2415 Holly Lane, Ottawa, ON K1V 7P2
613/736-9077, Fax: 613/736-8938, Email: solar@worldlink.ca
URL: http://www.newenergy.org/newenergy/sesci.html
Contact, Sheila McKirdy
Publications: CanSIA Newsletter

Canadian Wind Energy Association Inc./Association canadienne d'énergie éolienne (CANWEA) (1984)
#100, 3553 - 31 St. NW, Calgary, AB T2L 2K7
403/289-7713, Fax: 403/282-1238, Toll Free: 1-800-922-6932, Email: canwea@aol.com
Executive Coordinator, Cindy Bourns
Publications: Windsight
Affiliates: Solar Energy Society of Canada

Energy Council of Canada (1924)
#400, 30 Colonnade Rd., Nepean, ON K2E 7J6
613/727-1881, 952-6469, Fax: 613/952-6470

Canadian Almanac & Directory 1997

Executive Director, E. Philip Cockshutt
Publications: Proceedings: Canadian National Energy Forum

Energy Pathways Inc. (EPI) (1979)
#500, 251 Laurier Ave. West, Ottawa, ON K1P 5J6
613/235-7976, Fax: 613/235-2190, Email: epi@epi.ca
URL: http://www.epi.ca/home.htm
President, Bill Armstrong
Vice-President, Consulting, Charles Hodgson
Publications: On-Site

Energy Probe Research Foundation (EPRF) (1980)
225 Brunswick Ave., Toronto, ON M5S 2M6
416/964-9223, Fax: 416/964-8239, Toll Free: 1-800-263-2784
Chairman, Walter Pitman
President, Patricia Adams
Sec.-Treas., Annetta Turner
Research Coordinator, Lawrence Solomon
Director of Nuclear Research & Senior Policy Advisor, Norman Rubin
Utility Analyst, Tom Adams
Publications: EnergyFutures; Probe Alert; The Next City, q.

Nuclear Awareness Project
PO Box 104, Uxbridge, ON L9P 1M6
905/852-0571, Fax: 905/852-0571, Email: nucaware@web.net
Contact, David Martin
Publications: Nuclear Awareness News; The Facts About Food Irradiation
Affiliates: Nuclear Information & Resource Service; Canadian Environment Network

Planetary Association for Clean Energy, Inc./Société planétaire pour l'assainissement de l'énergie (PACE) (1975)
#1001, 100 Bronson Ave., Ottawa, ON K1R 6G8
613/236-6265, Fax: 613/235-5876
President, Andrew Michrowski
Publications: Newsletter

Solar Energy Society of Canada Inc./Société d'énergie solaire du Canada inc. (SESCI) (1974)
#250, 2415 Holly Lane, Ottawa, ON K1V 7P2
613/523-0974, Fax: 613/736-8938, Email: solar@worldlink.ca
URL: http://www.newenergy.org/newenergy/sesci.html
Managing Director, Sheila McKirdy
Publications: SOL-A Voice of Conservation & Renewable Energy in Canada; Canadian Renewable Energy Guide
Affiliates: International Solar Energy Society

Wood Energy Technology Transfer Inc. (WETT) (1993)
#1105, 191 The West Mall, Etobicoke, ON M9C 5K8
416/695-1676, Fax: 416/620-5392, Email: bbandc@onterprise.ca
Manager, Amanda Curtis, CAE
Publications: WETT Ink

ENGINEERING & TECHNOLOGY

American Society of Mechanical Engineers (ASME) (1880)
345 East 47 St., New York, NY 10017 USA
212/705-7722, Fax: 212/705-7674, Toll Free: 1-800-843-2763
Executive Director, David L. Belden
Publications: ASME News; Mechanical Engineering, m.; CIME (Computers in Mechanical Engineering), m.; Manufacturing Review, q.; Applied Mechanics Reviews
Ontario Section: Chairman/Secretary, John W. White; Chairman, Ernest F. Amor, Howden Canada, 1510 Birchmount Rd., Scarborough, ON M1P 2G6, 416/752-7310, Fax: 416/752-0147

Association of Consulting Engineers of Canada/Association des ingénieurs-conseils du Canada (ACEC) (1925)
#616, 130 Albert St., Ottawa, ON K1P 5G4
613/236-0569, Fax: 613/236-6193, Email: comm@acec.ca
URL: http://buildingweb.com/acec
Chairman & CEO, Kenneth A. Hyde, P.Eng.
President & COO, Pierre Franche
Communications Officer, J. Daniel Matko
Publications: Communiqué; Export Action, q.; ACEC Directory of Canadian Consulting Engineers, a.

ASSOCIATION OF CONSULTING ENGINEERS OF ALBERTA (CEA) (1978)
#1709 Toronto Dominion Tower, Edmonton, AB T5J 2Z1
403/420-6066, Fax: 403/420-6392, Telex: 037-2966
Executive Director, Allan C. Oliver
Executive Assistant, Elizabeth Hrushka
Publications: Newsletter
Affiliates: Alberta Construction Association; Alberta Chamber of Resources; Alberta Economic Development & Trade; Canadian Manufacturers' Association; International Federation of Consulting Engineers; Western Economic Diversification Canada; Alberta Association of Architects; Association of Professional Engineers, Geologists, & Geophysicists of Alberta; Alberta Society of Engineering Technologists; Alberta Research Council; Engineering Institute of Canada; Industry Canada

ASSOCIATION OF CONSULTING ENGINEERS OF MANITOBA INC. (ACEM) (1978)
4 Donald St. South, Winnipeg, MB R3L 2T7
204/475-7774, Fax: 204/475-7774
URL: http://www.tetres.ca/acem/index.html
Executive Director, Elaine P. Madison
President, K.G. Bolton, P.Eng.
Publications: ACEM Newsletter; ACEM Directory of Member Firms, biennial
Affiliates: Association of Professional Engineers of Manitoba; International Federation of Consulting Engineers; Manitoba Association of Architects

ASSOCIATION OF CONSULTING ENGINEERS OF ONTARIO (CEO) (1975)
#300, 86 Overlea Blvd., Toronto, ON M4H 1C6
416/425-8027, Fax: 416/425-8035
President, Donald Ingram
Publications: CEO Newsletter; Association of Consulting Engineers of Ontario Directory

ASSOCIATION OF CONSULTING ENGINEERS OF SASKATCHEWAN (ACES) (1977)
2123 Broad St., Regina, SK S4P 1Y6
306/359-3338, Fax: 306/522-5325
Executive Director, Ted Rey
Publications: ACES Newsletter

ASSOCIATION OF CONSULTING ENGINEERS OF THE YUKON (CEY) (1983)
c/o EBA Engineering Consultants Ltd., #6, 151 Industrial Rd., Whitehorse, YT Y1A 2V3
403/668-3068, Fax: 403/668-4349, Email: whitehorse@eba.ca
Executive Director, Richard Trimble

ASSOCIATION DES INGÉNIEURS-CONSEILS DU QUÉBEC/CONSULTING ENGINEERS OF QUÉBEC (AICQ) (1974)
#1200, 2050, rue Mansfield, Montréal, PQ H3A 1Y9
514/288-2032, Téléc: 514/288-2306
Vice-Présidente exécutive, Johanne Desrochers, BAA
Publications: Bulletin

CONSULTING ENGINEERS OF BRITISH COLUMBIA (CEBC) (1976)
#514, 409 Granville St., Vancouver, BC V6C 1T2
604/687-2811, Fax: 604/688-7110,
    Email: consulting_engineers@cebc.org
Executive Director, John Wilkins, B.Sc., DIC
Publications: Commentary; Directory of Member Firms; Industry Profile; Awards Magazine

CONSULTING ENGINEERS OF NEW BRUNSWICK/LES INGENIEURS-CONSEILS DU NOUVEAU-BRUNSWICK (CENB) (1983)
#105, 535 Beaverbrook Ct., Fredericton, NB E3B 1X6
506/458-8455, Fax: 506/452-2729
President, Andrew Steeves

CONSULTING ENGINEERS OF NEWFOUNDLAND & LABRADOR
140 University Ave., St. John's, NF A1B 1Z5
709/753-1014, Fax: 709/753-3466
Executive Director, Eric Mercer

CONSULTING ENGINEERS OF NWT (CENT) (1990)
c/o NAPEGG, #5, 4807 - 49 St., Yellowknife, NT X1A 3T5
403/920-4055, Fax: 403/873-4058
President, Gary Craig, P.Eng.

NOVA SCOTIA CONSULTING ENGINEERS ASSOCIATION (1973)
45 Hastings Dr., Dartmouth, NS B2Y 2C7
902/461-1325, Fax: 902/461-1321
Executive Director, P.S. Ferguson, P.Eng
Publications: Update; Newton, q.

Association des ingénieurs municipaux du Québec/Association of Québec Municipal Engineers (AIMQ) (1963)
2020, rue Université, 18e étage, Montréal, PQ H3A 2A5
514/649-7060, Téléc: 514/932-7149
Secrétaire, Alain Dulude
Publications: Contact Plus

British Columbia Technology Industries Association (1994)
#450, 1122 Mainland St., Vancouver, BC V6B 5L1
604/683-6159, Fax: 604/683-3879, Email: tia@mindlink.bc.ca
URL: http://technet.org
General Manager, Kathleen Troupe
Publications: TIA Monitor

Canadian Acoustical Association/Association canadienne d'acoustique
PO Box 1351, Stn F, Toronto, ON M4Y 2V9
President, Raymond Hétu
Executive Secretary, Trevor Nightingale
Publications: Canadian Acoustics

Canadian Advanced Technology Association/Association canadienne de technologie de pointe (CATA) (1978)
388 Albert St., 2nd Fl., Ottawa, ON K1P 5H9
613/236-6550, Fax: 613/236-8189, Toll Free: 1-800-387-2282
URL: http://www.cata.ca/
President, John Reid
Publications: CATAlist

Canadian Air Cushion Technology Society (CACTS)
#818, 130 Slater St., Ottawa, ON K1P 6E2
613/234-0191, Fax: 613/234-9039
Executive Director, Ian M. Ross

2-58 ORGANIZATIONS — ENGINEERING & TECHNOLOGY

Canadian Association for Composite Structures & Materials/Association canadienne pour les structures et matériaux composites (CACSMA) (1988)
75, boul de Mortagne, Boucherville, PQ J4B 6Y4
514/641-5139, Fax: 514/641-5117
Président, Germain Bélanger
Publications: CACSMA Bulletin

Canadian Automated Buildings Association/Association canadienne pour l'automatisation des bâtiments (CABA) (1988)
1500 Montréal Rd., Ottawa, ON K1A 0R6
613/990-7407, Fax: 613/954-5984, Email: caba@irc.lan.nrc.ca
Executive Director, Alan D. McKinley, P.Eng.
President, Jack Fraser
Publications: Home & Building Automation Quarterly; Information Series

Canadian Centre for Creative Technology/Centre canadien de technologie créative (CCCT) (1981)
8 Young St. East, Waterloo, ON N2J 2L3
519/884-8844, Fax: 519/884-8191, Email: info@ccct.ca
URL: http://www.ccct.ca
Vice-President, Shad Valley, Ron Champion
Vice-President, National Institute, Arthur Coren, 604/888-3030, Fax: 604/888-3010
Publications: Aurora

Canadian Council of Professional Engineers/Conseil canadien des ingénieurs professionnels (CCPE) (1936)
#401, 116 Albert St., Ottawa, ON K1P 5G3
613/232-2474, Fax: 613/230-5759, Email: lmacdon@fox.nstn.ns.ca
President, Daniel Verreault, P.Eng, M.P.A.
Chairman, John Bate
Publications: Canadian Professional Engineer
Affiliates: World Federation of Engineering Organizations

ASSOCIATION OF PROFESSIONAL ENGINEERS, GEOLOGISTS & GEOPHYSICISTS OF ALBERTA (APEGGA) (1920)
Scotia Place, Tower One, 10060 Jasper Ave, 15th Fl., Edmonton, AB T5J 4A2
403/426-3990, Fax: 403/426-1877, Toll Free: 1-800-661-7020, Email: email@apegga.com
URL: http://www.apegga.com
Executive Director & Registrar, Robert Ross, P.Eng.
Director, Professional Practice, Stewart McIntosh, P.Eng.
Director, Enforcement, Dave Todd, P.Eng.
Director, Registration, Al Schuld, P.Eng.
Director, Professional Affairs, Ray Chopiuk, P.Eng.
Director, Communications, Trevor Maine, P.Eng.
Public Affairs Officer, Kimberly Nishikaze
Publications Editor, Nordahl Flakstad
Career Development Administrator, Jeanne Keaschuk
Manager, Administration, Neil Little
Asst. Director, Registration, Len Shrimpton
Publications: The PEGG

ASSOCIATION OF PROFESSIONAL ENGINEERS, GEOLOGISTS & GEOPHYSICISTS OF THE NORTHWEST TERRITORIES (NAPEGG) (1979)
#5, 4807 - 49 St., Yellowknife, NT X1A 3T5
403/920-4055, Fax: 403/873-4058, Email: napegg@tamerac.nt.ca
Executive Director, Robert W. Spence, P.Eng.
Office Manager, Leigh Wells
Publications: NAPEGG Newsletter; NAPEGG Membership Directory, a.

ASSOCIATION OF PROFESSIONAL ENGINEERS & GEOSCIENTISTS OF BRITISH COLUMBIA (APEG BC) (1920)
#200, 4010 Regent St., Burnaby, BC V5C 6N2
604/430-8035, Fax: 604/430-8085

Executive Director & Registrar, H.N. Gray, P.Eng.
Director, Registration, G.M. Pichler, P.Eng.
President, L.E. Thorstad, P.Geo.
Publications: The BC Professional Engineer
Affiliates: BC Environmental Network

ASSOCIATION OF PROFESSIONAL ENGINEERS & GEOSCIENTISTS OF NEWFOUNDLAND (APEGN) (1952)
PO Box 21207, St. John's, NF A1A 5B2
709/753-7714, Fax: 709/753-6131
Executive Director, Allen L. Steeves, P.Eng.
President, Sam Banfield, P.Eng.
Publications: Dialogue for Engineers & Geoscientists

ASSOCIATION OF PROFESSIONAL ENGINEERS OF MANITOBA (APEM) (1920)
#530, 330 St. Mary Ave., Winnipeg, MB R3C 3Z5
204/942-6481, Fax: 204/942-3718
Executive Director, David A. Ennis, P.Eng.
Director of Admissions, S. Matile, P.Eng.

ASSOCIATION OF PROFESSIONAL ENGINEERS OF NEW BRUNSWICK (APENB)
#105, 535 Beaverbrook Ct., Fredericton, NB E3B 1X6
506/458-8083, Fax: 506/451-9629
Executive Director, Eddie Kinley, P.Eng.

ASSOCIATION OF PROFESSIONAL ENGINEERS OF NOVA SCOTIA (APENS) (1920)
PO Box 129, RPO Central, Halifax, NS B3J 2M4
902/429-2250, Fax: 902/423-9769
URL: www.cfn.cs.dal.ca/technology/apens/apenspg.html
Executive Director, C.E. Tupper, P.Eng., Email: etupper@apns.ns.ca
Director of Prof. Practice, Peter Mitchell, P.Eng.
Publications: The Engineer

ASSOCIATION OF PROFESSIONAL ENGINEERS OF PRINCE EDWARD ISLAND (APEPEI) (1955)
549 North River Rd., Charlottetown, PE C1E 1J6
902/566-1268, Fax: 902/566-5551, Email: apepei@peinet.pe.ca
Executive Director/Registrar, Graeme A. Linkletter, P.Eng.
President, Robert Sear, P.Eng.
Publications: APEPEI Newsletter

ASSOCIATION OF PROFESSIONAL ENGINEERS OF SASKATCHEWAN (APES) (1930)
#104, 2255 - 13 Ave., Regina, SK S4P 0V6
306/525-9547, Fax: 306/525-0851
Executive Director/Registrar, Dennis Paddock, P.Eng.
Publications: The Professional Edge

ASSOCIATION OF PROFESSIONAL ENGINEERS OF THE YUKON TERRITORY (1955)
PO Box 4125, Whitehorse, YT Y1A 3S9
403/667-6727, Fax: 403/667-6727
Sec.-Treas., Niels Jacobsen, P.Eng.
Publications: The Association Newsletter

ORDRE DES INGÉNIEURS DU QUÉBEC (OIQ) (1920)
2020, rue University, 18e étage, Montréal, PQ H3A 2A5
514/845-6141, Téléc: 514/845-1833, Ligne sans frais: 1-800-461-6141
Secrétaire/Directeur général, Hubert Stéphenne, ing.
Publications: Plan; Méga Plan, annuel
Organisation(s) affiliée(s): Corporation Interprofessionnelle du Québec

PROFESSIONAL ENGINEERS ONTARIO/ORDRE DES INGÉNIEURS DE L'ONTARIO (PEO) (1922)
#1000, 25 Sheppard Ave. West, North York, ON M2N 6S9
416/224-1100, Fax: 416/224-8168
URL: http://www.peo.on.ca
Executive Director, Peter Large, P.Eng.
President, David R. Anderson, P.Eng.

Manager, Public Relations, Virginia M. Brown
Publications: Engineering Dimensions; WE ACT (Women in Engineering Advisory Committee Tribune)

Canadian Council of Technicians & Technologists/Conseil canadien des techniciens et technologues (CCTT)
285 McLeod St., 2nd Fl., Ottawa, ON K2R 1A1
613/238-8123, Fax: 613/238-8822
URL: http://www.cabot.nf.ca/CCTT/index.html
Executive Director, C. Charles Brimley, C.E.T.

ALBERTA SOCIETY OF ENGINEERING TECHNOLOGISTS (ASET) (1963)
Canada Trust Tower, #2100, 10104 - 103 Ave. NW, Edmonton, AB T5J 0H8
403/425-0626, Fax: 403/424-5053, Toll Free: 1-800-272-5619
Executive Director, Brian McCormack, CAE
Registrar, Don Byers
Director, Communications, Jay Fisher
Publications: Technology Alberta

APPLIED SCIENCE TECHNOLOGISTS & TECHNICIANS OF BRITISH COLUMBIA (ASTTBC) (1958)
10767 - 148 St., Surrey, BC V3R 0S4
604/585-2788, Fax: 604/585-2790
URL: http://www.imaginet.ca/asttbc/
Executive Director, John E. Leech, A.Sc.T., CAE
Publications: ASTT Newsletter; Applied Science Technologists & Technicians of BC Membership Directory, a.; News for BC MLAs & BC MPs, q.; News for BC Municipalities, q.; Careers in Technology; Career Manager

ASSOCIATION OF ENGINEERING TECHNICIANS & TECHNOLOGISTS OF NEWFOUNDLAND (AETTN) (1968)
PO Box 790, Mount Pearl, NF A1N 2Y2
709/747-2868, Fax: 709/747-2869
URL: http://www.cabot.nf.ca/CCTT/aettn/index.html
Contact, Austin Sheppard
Publications: Technology Newfoundland & Labrador

CERTIFIED TECHNICIANS & TECHNOLOGISTS ASSOCIATION OF MANITOBA (CTTAM) (1965)
#602, 1661 Portage Ave., Winnipeg, MB R3J 3T7
204/783-0088, Fax: 204/783-6284, Email: cttam@mts.net
URL: http://www.rots.net/~cttam
Executive Director, Kenneth G. Campbell, C.E.T.
Administrative Coordinator, Anne Sawatzky
Publications: MB Technologist & Techlink

NEW BRUNSWICK SOCIETY OF CERTIFIED ENGINEERING TECHNICIANS & TECHNOLOGISTS/SOCIÉTÉ DES TECHNICIENS ET DES TECHNOLOGUES AGRÉÉS DU GÉNIE DU NOUVEAU-BRUNSWICK (NBSCETT) (1968)
#115, 535 Beaverbrook Ct., Fredericton, NB E3B 1X6
506/454-6124, Fax: 506/452-7076
Executive Director, Edward F. Leslie, CAE
Registrar, Ken C. Brown, CET
Administrative Assistant, Marie Colwell
Publications: NBSCETT Technologist; NBSCETT News

ONTARIO ASSOCIATION OF CERTIFIED ENGINEERING TECHNICIANS & TECHNOLOGISTS (OACETT) (1957)
#404, 10 Four Seasons Pl., Etobicoke, ON M9B 6H7
416/621-9621, Fax: 416/621-8694
URL: http://www.onramp.ca/business/oacett/
Executive Director, Bruce G. Wells
President, Fred Lougheed
Registrar, J.D. Holmes
Publications: The Ontario Technologist

ORDRE DES TECHNOLOGUES PROFESSIONNELS DU QUÉBEC (OTPQ) (1927)
#720, 1265, rue Berri, Montréal, PQ H2L 4X4

Canadian Almanac & Directory 1997

514/845-3247, Téléc: 514/845-3643, Ligne sans frais: 1-800-561-3459
Directeur général, Denis Daigneault
Publications: TP Express; Le Technologue, tous les 2 mois

PRINCE EDWARD ISLAND SOCIETY OF CERTIFIED ENGINEERING TECHNOLOGISTS (PEISCET)
PO Box 1436, Charlottetown, PE C1A 7N1
902/892-3085, Fax: 902/892-3085
President, Allan Lapp

SASKATCHEWAN APPLIED SCIENCE TECHNOLOGISTS & TECHNICIANS (SASTT) (1965)
363 Park St., Regina, SK S4N 5B2
306/721-6633, Fax: 306/721-0112, Email: sastt@sasknet.sk.ca
URL: http://www.siast.sk.ca/~wasect/sastt.html
Executive Director/Registrar, Jaime Briltz, A.Sc.T.
President, Brian Cobbledick, A.Sc.T
Publications: SASTT Journal; Annual Salary Survey

SOCIETY OF CERTIFIED ENGINEERING TECHNICIANS & TECHNOLOGISTS OF NOVA SCOTIA (SCETTNS)
PO Box 159, Stn Main, Dartmouth, NS B2Y 3Y3
902/463-3236, Fax: 902/465-7567
President, Gabe Gallant
Publications: Technology Nova Scotia

Canadian Institute of Marine Engineering
3530 Griffith St., Saint Laurent, PQ H4T 1A7
514/735-1775, Fax: 514/735-0035
Executive Secretary, Gernot Seebacher
Publications: Marine Engineering Digest

Canadian Remote Sensing Society/Société canadienne de télédétection (CRSS)
#818, 130 Slater St., Ottawa, ON K1P 6E2
613/234-0191, Fax: 613/234-9039
Executive Director, Ian M. Ross
Publications: Canadian Journal of Remote Sensing

Canadian Society for Color in Art, Industry & Science/Société canadienne pour la couleur (CSC) (1972)
NRC Institute for National Measurement Standards, Bldg. M36, Rm. 1119, Montréal Rd., Ottawa, ON K1A 0R6
613/993-9347, Fax: 613/952-1394
Contact, Dr. A.R. Robertson

Canadian Society for Industrial Engineering/Société canadienne de génie industriel
c/o KPMG Management Consulting, 2300 Yonge St, 18th Fl., Toronto, ON M4P 1G2
Brian Bush

Canadian Society for Professional Engineers (CSPE) (1979)
#303, 203 College St., Toronto, ON M5T 1P9
416/598-0520, Fax: 416/598-3679
President, Michael Robertson, P.Eng.
Communications Officer, E.K. Christian, P.Eng.
Publications: The CSPEaker

Canadian Technical Asphalt Association/Association canadienne des techniques de l'asphalte (CTAA) (1955)
825 Fort St., 2nd Fl., Victoria, BC V8W 1H6
250/361-9187, Fax: 250/361-9187
Sec.-Treas., Robert Noble, P.Eng.
Publications: Newsletter; Journal, a.

The Engineering Institute of Canada/Institut canadien des ingénieurs (EIC) (1887)
1980 Ogilvie Rd., PO Box 27078, RPO Gloucester Ctr, Gloucester, ON K1J 9L9
613/742-5185, Fax: 613/742-5189, Email: eic@nrc.ca

Executive Director, Michael Bozozuk
President, John Plant
Publications: President's Letter

CANADIAN GEOTECHNICAL SOCIETY/SOCIÉTÉ CANADIENNE DE GÉOTECHNIQUE (CGS) (1972)
#501, 170 Attwell Dr., Etobicoke, ON M9W 6A3
514/674-0366, Fax: 514/674-9507
Director General, A.G. Stermac
President, Jim Laing
Publications: Canadian Geotechnical Journal; Geotechnical News, q.
Affiliates: National Research Council, Institute for Research in Construction (IRC-NRC); Canadian Rock Mechanics Association; Tunnelling Association of Canada; Canadian Geoscience Council; International Society for Soil Mechanics & Foundation Engineering; International Society for Rock Mechanics; International Association of Engineering Geology; International Permafrost Association; International Geotextile Society; International Association of Hydrogeologists

CANADIAN SOCIETY FOR CIVIL ENGINEERING/SOCIÉTÉ CANADIENNE DE GÉNIE CIVIL (CSCE) (1972)
Tour Guy, #840, 2155, rue Guy, Montréal, PQ H3H 2R9
514/933-2634, Fax: 514/933-3504, Email: csc@musica.mcgill.ca
Director of Administration, Leslie C. West
Publications: Canadian Journal of Civil Engineering; Canadian Civil Engineer, 10 pa

CANADIAN SOCIETY FOR ENGINEERING MANAGEMENT/SOCIÉTÉ CANADIENNE DE GESTION EN INGÉNIERE (CSEM) (1981)
c/o Base Service Canada Inc., #301, 250 Consumers Rd., North York, ON M2J 4V6
416/494-1440, Fax: 416/495-8723, Email: base@on-ramp.ca
Sec.-Treas., J. Gordon Thomson
Chairman, John Dinsmore
Publications: Engineers Club

CANADIAN SOCIETY FOR MECHANICAL ENGINEERING/SOCIÉTÉ CANADIENNE DE GÉNIE MÉCANIQUE (CSME) (1887)
#307, 151 Slater St., Ottawa, ON K1P 5H3
613/232-8811, Fax: 613/230-9607
Executive Director, T.C. Arnold
President, Dr. R. Seshadri
Publications: The Bulletin; Transactions, q.

Industrial Research & Development Institute (IRDI) (1991)
355 Cranston Cres., PO Box 518, Midland, ON L4R 4L3
705/526-2163, Fax: 705/526-2701
President/CEO, C.M. Harper
Director, Research & Development, Paul Marmion
Director, Knowledge Centre, Steve Colbert
Director, Marketing, Laurence Whitby
Publications: IRDI Update

Institute of Power Engineers (IPE) (1940)
3532 Commerce Ct., Burlington, ON L7N 3L7
905/333-3348, Fax: 905/333-9258
National President, R.C. Wennerstrom
1st National Vice-President, Alain Fournier
National Secretary, J.J. Kolibash
Publications: Canadian Power Engineer Magazine

Intelligent Sensing for Innovative Structure/Systèmes intelligents pour structures innovatrices (ISIS)
Dept. of Civil & Geological Engineering, University of Manitoba, Winnipeg, MB R3T 5V6
204/474-8506, Fax: 204/261-5465, Email: rizkall@cc.umanitoba.ca
Network Manager, Christopher W. Lorenc

Municipal Engineers Association
#2, 530 Otto Rd., Mississauga, ON L5T 2L5
905/795-2555, Fax: 905/795-2660
Secretary, Mario Iatonna, P.Eng.
President, Bill Beveridge, P.Eng.
Publications: Municipal Engineers Association Newsletter

NACE - International (1943)
National Society of Corrosion Engineers
1440 South Creek Dr., PO Box 218340, Houston, TX 77218-8340 USA
713/492-0535, Fax: 713/492-8254
President, Joe Bowles
Treasurer, Elaine Bowman
Publications: Materials Performance
Toronto Region: c/o Gaberial Ogundele, Ontario Hydro Technologies, 800 Kipling Ave. (KR 178), Toronto, ON M8Z 5S4, 416/207-6842

National Optics Institute/Institut national d'Optique (1985)
369, rue Franquet, Ste-Foy, PQ G1P 4N8
418/657-7006, Fax: 418/657-7009
Jean-Guy Paquet
Pierre Lavigne
Russell Boulay
Publications: NOI Bulletin

Plant Engineering & Maintenance Association of Canada (PEMAC)
#18, 170 Wilkinson Rd., Brampton, ON L6T 4Z5
905/874-1154, Fax: 905/459-3690
Executive Director, Steve Galbauer
President, Brian Hurting
Publications: PEMACTION

Society of Motion Picture & Television Engineers (SMPTE) (1916)
595 West Hartsdale Ave., White Plains, NY 10607-1824 USA
914/761-1100, Fax: 914/761-3115, Telex: 4995348, Email: 71263.335@compuserve.com
Publications: SMPTE Journal

Society of Tribologists & Lubrication Engineers/Société des tribologistes et ingénieurs en lubrification (1987)
840 Busse Hwy., Park Ridge, IL 60068-2376 USA
708/825-5536, Fax: 708/825-1456
Executive Director, Maxine E. Hensley
President, Curtis L. Gordon
Publications: Lubrication Engineering

ENVIRONMENTAL
see also Naturalists

Air & Waste Management Association/Association pour la Prévention de la Contamination de l'Air et du Sol (A&WMA) (1907)
One Gateway Center, 3rd Fl., Pittsburgh, PA 15222 USA
412/232-3444, Fax: 412/232-3450, Email: info@awma.org
Executive Director, John Thorner
Deputy Director, Technical Programs, Steve Stasko
Canadian Office Director, Jane Meyboom
Chair, Atlantic Canada Section, Scott MacKnight, 902/463-0114, Fax: 902/466-5743
Chair, British Columbia & Yukon Section, Joffre Berry, 604/432-8401, Fax: 604/431-9258
Chair, Canadian Prairie & Northern Section, Lawrence Strachan, 204/945-7071, Fax: 204/945-5229
Chair, Ontario Section, Helle Tosine, 416/314-3920, Fax: 416/314-3225

Chair, Québec Section, Pierre Lupien, 514/499-4536, Fax: 514/499-4515
Chair, Vancouver Island Section, Michael Williams, 604/360-3092, Fax: 604/360-3079
Publications: The Journal of the Air & Waste Management Association; Directory & Resource Book; Environmental Manager
National Office: Director, Jane Meyboom, #1202, 155 Queen St., Ottawa, ON K1P 6L1, 613/233-2006, Fax: 613/233-8096

Alberta Wilderness Association (AWA) (1969)
455 - 12 St. NW, PO Box 6398, Stn D, Calgary, AB T2P 2E1
403/492-2311, Fax: 403/492-2364
President, Glenda Hanna
1st Vice-President, Peter Sherrington
2nd Vice-President, Jennifer Klimek
Publications: Wild Lands Advocate; Eastern Slopes Wildlands: Our Living Heritage; Rivers on Borrowed Time; Action Alert - Wise Use Newsletter, q.
Affiliates: Environmental Resource Centre

Association of Conservation Authorities of Ontario (ACAO)
418A Sheridan St., Peterborough, ON K9H 3J9
705/749-9131, Fax: 705/749-9345
General Manager, J. Anderson

Association of Municipal Recycling Coordinators (AMRC) (1987)
25 Douglas St., Guelph, ON N1H 2S7
519/823-1990, Fax: 519/823-0084
Executive Director, Linda Varangu
Chairperson, Jake Westerhof
Publications: For R Information

Association québécoise des techniques de l'eau (AQTE) (1962)
#220, 911, rue Jean-Talon est, Montréal, PQ H2R 1V5
514/270-7110, Téléc: 514/270-7154, Courrier électronique: assqenv@login.net
Directeur général, Eric Bouchard
Présidente, Johnny Izzi
Publications: Sciences et techniques de l'eau; Répertoire de produits et services dans le domaine de l'eau, annuel; Effluent, 10 fois par an
Organisation(s) affiliée(s): Association romande pour la protection des eaux et de l'air (ARPEA)

Association des récupérateurs du Québec, inc.
422, rue Caron, CP 2115, Succ. Québec, Québec, PQ G1K 7M9
418/529-6001

British Columbia Water & Wastewater Association (BCWWA) (1964)
1777 Harbour Dr., Coquitlam, BC V3J 5W4
604/936-4982, Fax: 604/931-3880
President, Prad Khare
Executive Director, Catherine Gibson
Secretary, Chester Merchant
Publications: Watermark; BCWWA Membership Directory
Affiliates: American Water & Waste Association; Water Pollution Control Federation; Lower Mainland Water & Sewer Supervisors Association; American Society of Plumbing Engineers - BC Chapter

Canadian Association for Environmental Analytical Laboratories/Association canadienne des laboratoires d'analyse environnementale (CAEAL) (1989)
#300, 265 Carling Ave., Ottawa, ON K1S 2E1
613/233-5300, Fax: 613/233-5501
Executive Director, Rick Wilson
Publications: CAEAL/ACLAE Newsletter

Canadian Association of Recycling Industries (CARI)
#502, 50 Gervais Dr., North York, ON M3C 1Z3
416/510-1244, Fax: 416/510-1248
Associate Manager, Donna Turner
Publications: CARI

Canadian Association on Water Quality/Association canadienne sur la qualité de l'eau (CAWQ) (1966)
Canadian National Committee of the International Association on Water Quality
Technology Development Branch, Environment Canada, 425, boul St-Joseph, 4e étage, Hull, PQ K1A 0H3
819/953-9365, Fax: 819/953-9029
Executive Officer, Dr. H.R. Eisenhauer
President, Dr. J.D. Norman
Secretary, Dr. Y. Comeau
Publications: Water Quality Research Journal of Canada; R & D News in Environmental Science & Engineering, bi-m.

Canadian Coalition for Ecology, Ethics & Religion (CCEER) (1991)
22 Carriage Bay, Winnipeg, MB R2Y 0M5
204/832-1882, Fax: 204/885-6105
Director, Dr. Freda Rajotte
Director, Peter Timmerman
Publications: Sacred Spaces
Affiliates: International Consultancy on Religion, Education & Culture; International Coordinating Committee on Religion & the Earth; North American Conference on Religion & Ecology; International Federation of Institutes for Advanced Study

Canadian Conservation Institute/Institut canadien de conservation (CCI) (1972)
1030 Innes Rd., Ottawa, ON K1A 0M5
613/998-3721, Fax: 613/998-4721
Director General, C.G. Gruchy
Publications: CCI Newsletter/Bulletin de l'ICC

Canadian Council for Human Resources in the Environment Industry/Le conseil canadien des ressources humaines de l'industrie de l'Environnement (CCHREI) (1993)
#700, 700 - 4th Ave. SW, Calgary, AB T2P 3J4
403/233-0748, Fax: 403/269-9544, Email: cchrei@netway.ab.ca
URL: http://www.chatsubo.com/cchrei
Executive Director & CEO, Grant Trump
Chair, Paul West
Publications: Changing Times Newsletter; Compendium of Environmental Training Courses; Definition of Environmental Employment; Classification of Environmental Occupations; Skill Set Documentation
Affiliates: Canadian Environment Industry Association; Association of Universities & Colleges of Canada; Association of Canadian Community Colleges; Canadian Council of Professional Engineers; Association Québécois des Techniques de L'Eau; Chemical Institute of Canada; Industry Canada; Environment Canada; Human Resources Development Canada; Canadian Standards Association; Canadian Council of Technicians & Technologists

Canadian Council of Ministers of the Environment
#400, 326 Broadway, Winnipeg, MB R3C 0S5
204/948-2090, Fax: 204/948-2125
Executive Director, Lise Forand

Canadian Earth Energy Association/Association canadienne de l'énergie du sol (CEEA) (1987)
#605, 130 Slater St., Ottawa, ON K1P 6E2
613/230-2332, Fax: 613/237-1480, Email: doitrite@magi.com
URL: http://www.earthenergy.org
Executive Director, Bill Eggertson
Publications: CEEA
Affiliates: International Ground Source Heat Pump Association

Canadian Ecophilosophy Network (1983)
PO Box 5853, Stn B, Victoria, BC V8R 6S8
250/598-7004, Fax: 250/598-9901
Publications Editor, Alan R. Drengson
Publications: The Trumpeter: Journal of Ecosophy

Canadian Environment Industry Association/Association canadienne des industries de l'environnement (CEIA) (1988)
#208, 350 Sparks St., Ottawa, ON K1R 7S8
613/236-6222, Fax: 613/236-6850, Email: ceia@capitalnet.com
URL: http://www.ceia.org
President, G. Steve Hart
Publications: CEIA Communiqué

L'ASSOCIATION DES ENTREPRENEURS DE SERVICES EN ENVIRONNEMENT DU QUÉBEC (AESEQ) (1959)
#220, 911, Jean Talon est, Montréal, PQ H2R 1V5
514/270-7110, Téléc: 514/270-7154, Courrier électronique: assqenv@login.net
Directeur général, Eric Bouchard

CANADIAN ENVIRONMENT INDUSTRY ASSOCIATION - BRITISH COLUMBIA
CEIA-BC
World Trade Centre, #504, 999 Canada Pl., Vancouver, BC V6C 3E1
604/775-7266, Fax: 604/775-5168, Email: ceiabc@cyberstore.ca
URL: http://www.ceia-bc.com/
Administrator, Steve Greentree

CANADIAN ENVIRONMENT INDUSTRY ASSOCIATION - ONTARIO
CEIA-Ontario
63 Polson St., 2nd Fl., Toronto, ON M5A 1A4
416/778-6590, Fax: 416/778-5702, Email: ceiaon@web.apc.org

ENVIRONMENTAL SERVICES ASSOCIATION OF ALBERTA (ESAA) (1988)
#250, 10508 - 82 Ave., Edmonton, AB T6E 2A4
403/439-6363, Fax: 403/439-4249, Toll Free: 1-800-661-9278, Email: info@esaa.ccinet.ab.ca
URL: http://www.ccinet.ab.ca/esaa/home.html
Executive Director, Tim Schultz, Email: schultz@esaa.ccinet.ab.ca
Publications: The Insider; Directory & Buyer's Guide, a.

MANITOBA ENVIRONMENTAL INDUSTRIES ASSOCIATION INC. (MEIA)
895A Century St., Winnipeg, MB R3H 0M3
204/987-8505, Fax: 204/772-6705, Email: meia@canpay.com
Executive Director, Monique Grabowski
President, Michael G. Van Wallenghem, BSA, B.Comm., 204/778-4969, Fax: 204/775-9381
Publications: MEIA Update

NEW BRUNSWICK ENVIRONMENT INDUSTRY ASSOCIATION
PO Box 637, Stn A, Fredericton, NB E3B 5B3
506/451-1991, Fax: 506/457-2100, Email: geobacnb@nbnet.nb.ca
President, Victor Nowicki

NEWFOUNDLAND ENVIRONMENTAL INDUSTRY ASSOCIATION (NEIA)
Atlantic Place, Box 43, #602, 215 Water St., St. John's, NF A1C 6C9
709/722-3333, Fax: 709/722-3879, Email: neia@newcomm.net
URL: http://enterprise.newcomm.net/webpage/neia

Executive Director, Nancy Creighton
President, Bevin LeDrew, 709/576-1458, Fax: 709/576-2126
Director, Public Relations, Jane Brewer

NOVA SCOTIA ENVIRONMENTAL INDUSTRY ASSOCIATION (NSEIA)
PO Box 563, Dartmouth, NS B2Y 3Y8
902/466-8421, Fax: 902/466-8421, Email: vision@ra.isisnet.com
URL: http://www.nseia.ns.ca/nseia
Contact, David Harrison

SASKATCHEWAN ENVIRONMENTAL MANAGERS' ASSOCIATION (SEMA)
PO Box 834, Regina, SK S4P 3B1
306/543-3831, Fax: 306/757-5410
Administrator, Robert Schultz

Canadian Environmental Law Association/Association canadienne du droit de l'environnement (CELA) (1970)
#401, 517 College St., Toronto, ON M6G 4A2
416/960-2284, Fax: 416/960-9392
Executive Director, Michelle Swenerchuk
Publications: Intervenor

Canadian Environmental Network/Réseau canadien de l'environnement (CEN) (1977)
#1004, 251 Laurier Ave. West, Ottawa, ON K1R 5J6
613/563-2078, Fax: 613/563-7236, Email: cen@web.apc.org
Executive Director, Eva Shacherl
Information Coordinator, Lesley Cassidy
Publications: CEN Bulletin; The Green List
Affiliates: Environment Liaison Centre - International

ALBERTA ENVIRONMENTAL NETWORK (AEN) (1987)
10511 Saskatchewan Dr., Edmonton, AB T6E 4S1
403/433-9302, Fax: 403/433-9305
Office Manager, Sam Gunsch
Publications: Environment Network News

BC ENVIRONMENTAL NETWORK (BCEN) (1979)
1672 - 10th Ave. East, Vancouver, BC V5N 1X5
604/879-2279, Fax: 604/879-2272, Email: bcen@alter-natives.com
URL: http://www.earthcare.org/bcen/bcen.html
Executive Director, Anne-Marie Sleeman
Administrative Coordinator, Sherry Reid
Publications: British Columbia Environmental Directory; The British Columbia Environmental Report, q.

MANITOBA ECO-NETWORK INC./RÉSEAU ÉCOLOGIQUE DU MANITOBA INC. (1988)
Manitoba Environmental Network
116 Sherbrook St., PO Box 26007, Winnipeg, MB R3G 4K9
204/772-7542, Fax: 204/772-7563
Executive Director, Anne Lindsey
President, Steering Committee, Jack Dubois
Director, Communications, Toby Maloney
Publications: Eco-Journal; Springtide, a.; Due Process, a.; Our Common Future - A Public Forum on Environment & Development, a.; Green Guide to Winnipeg

NEW BRUNSWICK ENVIRONMENTAL NETWORK/RÉSEAU ENVIRONNEMENTAL DU NOUVEAU-BRUNSWICK (NBEN) (1990)
RR#4, Sussex, NB E0E 1P0
506/433-6101, Fax: 506/433-6101
Contact, Mary Ann Coleman
Publications: Network Update/Mise à jour

NEWFOUNDLAND & LABRADOR ENVIRONMENTAL NETWORK (NLEN)
PO Box 944, Corner Brook, NF A2H 6J2
709/634-2520, Fax: 709/634-2520
Coordinator, Lori March
Publications: Environment Network News

NORTHERN ENVIRONMENTAL NETWORK
NORNET
PO Box 3932, Whitehorse, YT Y1A 3S7
403/668-2482, Fax: 403/668-6637
Coordinator, J. Hicklin

NOVA SCOTIA ENVIRONMENTAL NETWORK
RR#5, New Glasgow, NS B2H 5C8
902/922-3314, Fax: 902/922-2283
Coordinator, Ishbel Munro
Publications: Atlantic Resource Directory

ONTARIO ENVIRONMENTAL NETWORK (OEN) (1981)
25 Douglas St., Guelph, ON N1H 2S7
519/837-2565, Fax: 519/837-8113, Email: oen@web.net
URL: http://www.web.net/~oen
Coordinator, Cecilia Fernandez
Publications: Network News; Environmental Resource Book

PRINCE EDWARD ISLAND ENVIRONMENTAL NETWORK (PEIEN) (1990)
126 Richmond St., Charlottetown, PE C1A 1H9
902/566-4170, Fax: 902/566-4037
Co-Chair, Sharon Labchuk
Co-Chair, Gary Schneider
Office Coordinator, Susan Stephenson
Publications: The Networker

SASKATCHEWAN ECO-NETWORK (SEN) (1980)
#203, 115 - 2 Ave. North, Saskatoon, SK S7K 2B1
306/652-1275, Fax: 306/665-2128, Email: sen@link.ca
Office Administrator, Bernadette Richards
Working Group Coordinator, Phillip Penna
Publications: Network News

Canadian Environmental Technology Advancement Corporation - West (CETAC - WEST)
Alberta Regional Office, #420, 715 - 5 Ave. SW, Calgary, AB T2P 2X6
403/777-9595, Fax: 403/777-9599
President & CEO, Joe Lukacs

The Canadian Institute for Environmental Investigations (CIEI) (1993)
#202, 70 Fulton Way, Richmond Hill, ON L4B 1J5
905/731-7788, Fax: 905/731-7870
Director of Education, D. James Hawkins
Executive Vice-President, Elaine Konstan, 905/731-7387
Affiliates: International Investigations Agency Inc.

Canadian Institute for Environmental Law & Policy/Institut canadien du droit et de la politique de l'environnement (CIELAP) (1970)
#400, 517 College St., Toronto, ON M6G 4A2
416/923-3529, Fax: 416/923-5949, Email: cielap@web.net
URL: http://www.web.net/cielap
Executive Director, Anne Mitchell
Publications: Canadian Environmental Law Reports
Affiliates: Environmental Liaison Centre International; Canadian Environmental Network; Ontario Environmental Network, Great Lakes United

Canadian Institute of Resources Law/Institut canadien du droit des ressources (CIRL) (1979)
PF-B 3330, University of Calgary, 2500 University Dr. NW, Calgary, AB T2N 1N4
403/220-3200, Fax: 403/282-6182, Email: cirl@acs.ucalgary.ca
URL: http://www.ucalgary.ca/~cirl/
Executive Director, J. Owen Saunders
Publications: Resources

Affiliates: Australian Mining & Petroleum Law Association; The Canadian Petroleum Law Foundation; Centre for Natural Resources Law - University of Melbourne - Australia; Centre for Petroleum & Mineral Law Studies, University of Dundee - Scotland; Dalhousie Ocean Studies Program - Halifax; Energy Law Center - Salt Lake City; International Bar Association (Section of Energy & Natural Resources Law); International Institute for Energy Law - Leiden; Japan Energy Law Research Institute - Tokyo; Rocky Mountain Mineral Law Foundation - Denver; Scandinavian Institute of Marine Law, University of Oslo - Norway; Westwater Research Center - Vancouver

Canadian Land Reclamation Association/Association canadienne de réhabilitation des sites dégradés (CLRA)
PO Box 61047, RPO Kensington, Calgary, AB T2N 4S6
403/289-9435, Fax: 403/289-9435
Sec.-Treas., Linda Jones
Publications: CLRA-ASSMR Newsletter
Affiliates: American Society for Surface Mining & Reclamation

The Canadian Network for Environmental Education & Communication/Réseau canadien d'éducation et de communication relatives à l'environnement (EECOM) (1993)
PO Box 948, Stn B, Ottawa, ON K1P 5P9
902/863-5984, Fax: 902/863-9481
Chairperson, Anne Camozzi
Publications: The EECOM Newsletter; The Canadian Environmental Educators Guide to the Internet
Affiliates: North American Association for Environmental Education

Canadian Parks Partnership/Partenaires des parcs canadiens (CPP) (1986)
#360, 1414 - 8th St., Calgary, AB T2R 1J6
403/244-6067, Fax: 403/244-1842
Executive Director, Jocelyne Daw
Publications: Partners

Canadian Polystyrene Recycling Association/Association de recyclage du polystyréne du Canada (CPRA) (1989)
7595 Tranmere Dr., Mississauga, ON L5S 1L4
905/612-8290, Fax: 905/612-8024
President, Michael G. Scott
Publications: CPRA News

Canadian Society of Environmental Biologists/La Société canadienne des biologistes de l'environnement (CSEB) (1943)
PO Box 962, Stn F, Toronto, ON M4Y 2N9
President, Sean Sharpe
Sec.-Treas., Gerry Leering, 705/743-5780, Fax: 705/743-9592
Publications: CSEB Newsletter

Canadian Society for Peat & Peatlands/Société canadienne de la tourbe et des tourbières (1989)
RR#3, PO Box 4, Parrsboro, NS B0M 1S0
902/348-2304
President, Jean-Yves Daigle
Publications: CNC-IPS Newsletter
Affiliates: International Peat Society

Canadian Steel Can Recycling - Sponsored by Dofasco (CSCR) (1983)
1330 Burlington St. East, PO Box 2460, Hamilton, ON L8N 3J5
905/548-4253, Fax: 905/545-3236
Manager, John Paulowich
Affiliates: Steel Recycling Institute - Pittsburgh, PA

Canadian Almanac & Directory 1997

ORGANIZATIONS — ENVIRONMENTAL

Canadian Steel Environmental Association/ Association environnementale de la sidérurgie canadienne (CSEA) (1974)
#1425, 50 O'Connor St., Ottawa, ON K1P 6L2
613/238-6049, Fax: 613/238-1832
Chairperson, A. Schuldt

Canadian Water Quality Association/Association canadienne pour la qualité de l'eau (CWQA) (1960)
#201A, 151 Frobisher Dr., Waterloo, ON N2V 2C9
519/885-3854, Fax: 519/747-9124, Info Line: 519/885-3854
Executive Director, Lou J. Smith
Publications: Communique

Canadian Water Resources Association/ Association canadienne des ressources hydriques (CWRA) (1948)
c/o Membership Office, PO Box 1329, Cambridge, ON N1R 7G6
519/622-4764, Email: cwranat@genie.geis.com
URL: http://www.cwra.org/cwra
President, F.A. Ross, 403/327-3302
Publications: Water News; Canadian Water Resources Journal, q.

Canadian Water & Wastewater Association/ Association canadienne des eaux potables et usées (CWWA) (1986)
#402, 45 Rideau St., Ottawa, ON K1N 5W8
613/241-5692, Fax: 613/241-5193, Email: 102504.2443@compuserve.com
Executive Director, T. Duncan Ellison
Publications: CWWA/ACEPU Bulletin
Affiliates: Water Environment Association of Ontario; Western Canada Water & Wastewater Association; Association québécoise des techniques de l'eau; American Water Works Association - Atlantic & Ontario Sections

Canadian Wildlife Federation/Fédération canadienne de la faune (CWF) (1961)
2740 Queensview Dr., Ottawa, ON K2B 1A2
613/721-2286, Fax: 613/721-2902, Toll Free: 1-800-563-9453
General Manager, Richard Leitch
Executive Vice-President, Colin Maxwell
Manager, Communications & Programs, Sandy Baumgartner
Publications: Your Big Backyard; Canadian Wildlife, a.; Biosphère; Wild

ALBERTA FISH & GAME ASSOCIATION
6924 - 104 St., Edmonton, AB T6H 2L7
403/437-2342, Fax: 403/438-6872
Executive Vice-President, Ron Houser
Publications: The Outdoor Edge

BRITISH COLUMBIA WILDLIFE FEDERATION
#303, 19292 - 60 Ave., Surrey, BC V3S 8E5
604/533-2293, Fax: 604/533-1592
President, Bob Morris
Publications: The Outdoorsman

FÉDÉRATION QUÉBÉCOISE DE LA FAUNE/QUÉBEC WILDLIFE FEDERATION (1946)
319, rue St-Zotique est, Montréal, PQ H2S 1L5
514/271-2487, Téléc: 514/271-9262
Président, Claude Lamoureux
Publications: Info FQF

MANITOBA WILDLIFE FEDERATION (1944)
70 Stevenson Rd., Winnipeg, MB R3H 0W7
204/633-5967, Fax: 204/632-5200
President, Larry Thiessen
Publications: Outdoor Edge/Wildlife Crusader

NEW BRUNSWICK WILDLIFE FEDERATION/FÉDÉRATION DE LA FAUNE DU NOUVEAU-BRUNSWICK (NBWF) (1924)
PO Box 20211, Fredericton, NB E3B 7A2
506/457-7468, Fax: 506/451-0618
President, Dale Stickles

NEWFOUNDLAND & LABRADOR WILDLIFE FEDERATION (1963)
PO Box 13399, Stn A, St. John's, NF A1B 4B7
709/364-8415
Executive Director, Richard Bouzanne

NORTHWEST TERRITORIES WILDLIFE FEDERATION (1985)
5134 Forrest Dr. North, Yellowknife, NT X1A 2W4
403/873-3853
President, Lorne Schollar
Publications: Northwest Territories Wildlife Newsletter; Canadian Hunting & Fishing Annual

NOVA SCOTIA WILDLIFE FEDERATION (1930)
PO Box 654, Halifax, NS B3J 2T3
902/423-6793, Fax: 902/423-6793
Executive Director, Tony Rodgers

PEI WILDLIFE FEDERATION
PO Box 753, Charlottetown, PE C1A 7L3
902/687-3131, Fax: 902/687-2350
President, Steve Cheverie

SASKATCHEWAN WILDLIFE FEDERATION (SWF) (1929)
444 River St. West, PO Box 788, Moose Jaw, SK S6H 4P5
306/692-7772, Fax: 306/692-4370
Executive Director, Ed Begin
Publications: Outdoor Edge

YUKON FISH & GAME ASSOCIATION (YFGA) (1945)
PO Box 4095, Whitehorse, YT Y1A 3S9
403/667-4263, Fax: 403/667-4237
President, Joni MacKinnon
Publications: Outdoor Edge

Canadian Wildlife Foundation (1976)
2740 Queensview Dr., Ottawa, ON K2B 1A2
613/721-2286, Fax: 613/721-2902
Executive Secretary, Colin Maxwell
Affiliates: Canadian Wildlife Federation

Canadians for a Clean Environment
5017 Victoria Ave., Niagara Falls, ON L2E 4C9
905/356-1160
Contact, Al Oleksiuk
Publications: Clean Scene

Citizens Network on Waste Management (CNWM) (1981)
17 Major St., Kitchener, ON N2H 4R1
519/744-7503, Fax: 519/744-1546
Coordinator, John Jackson

Citizens' Clearinghouse on Waste Management (CCWM) (1989)
RR#2, Cameron, ON K0M 1G0
705/887-1553, Fax: 705/887-4401
Co-Director, Barbara Wallace
Co-Director, Milton Wallace

The Clean Nova Scotia Foundation (CNSF) (1987)
1675 Bedford Row, PO Box 2528, Stn Central, Halifax, NS B3J 3N5
902/420-3474, Fax: 902/424-5334, Toll Free: 1-800-665-5377, Email: cnsf@fox.nstn.ca
Executive Director, Martin W. Janowitz
Project Officer, Randy Miller
Project Officer, Rochelle Owen
Publications: Nova Scotia RENEWS
Affiliates: Pitch-In Canada; Centre for Marine Conservation - Washington DC, USA

The Composting Council of Canada/Le Conseil canadien du compostage (1991)
#300, 200 MacLaren St., Ottawa, ON K2P 0L6
613/238-4014, Fax: 613/238-7559
URL: http://www.compost.org/
Executive Director, Dr. Peter Meyboom
Publications: Communiqué; Decision-Makers Technology Guide

Conseil des Bio-Industries du Québec/Québec Bio-Industry Council (1991)
1555, boul Chomedy, Laval, PQ H7V 3Z1
514/978-5973, Téléc: 514/978-5970
Directeur général, Renaud Levesque
Président, Dupuis Angers

Conservation Council of New Brunswick/Conseil de la conservation du Nouveau-Brunswick (CCNB) (1969)
180 St. John St., Fredericton, NB E3B 4A9
506/458-8747, Fax: 506/458-1047, Email: ccnb@web.apc.org
Executive Director, Meredith Brewer
President, Janice Harvey
Honorary President, Dr. Reg E. Balch
Policy Director, David Coon
Publications: EcoAlert
Affiliates: Friends of the Earth Canada; linkage projects with Arbofilia in Costa Rica & MAN in Nicaragua

Conservation Council of Ontario/Le Conseil de conservation de l'Ontario (CCO) (1952)
#506, 489 College St., Toronto, ON M6G 1A5
416/969-9637, Fax: 416/960-8053, Email: cco@web.apc.org
Executive Director, Chris Winter
President, Dr. Kenneth H. MacKay
Publications: Ontario Conservation News

Ducks Unlimited Canada/Canards Illimités Canada (DUC) (1937)
DU Canada
Oak Hammock Marsh Conservation Centre, 1 Mallard Bay at Hwy. 220, PO Box 1160, Oak Hammock Marsh, MB R0C 2Z0
204/467-3000, Fax: 204/467-9028, Toll Free: 1-800-665-3825
Chairman of the Board, Claude H. Wilson
President, W.G. Turnbull
Executive Vice-President & COO, Don A. Young
Manager, Habitat Programs, Rod Fowler
Chief Biologist, Dr. Terry Neraasen
Communications Manager, Bob Kindrachuk
Publications: Conservator; Conservationniste, 3 fois par an
Affiliates: Ducks Unlimited organizations in Australia, Europe, Mexico, New Zealand, the UK & the US; North American Waterfowl Management Plan

Earth Day Canada/Jour de la terre Canada (EDC) (1991)
#250, 144 Front St. West, Toronto, ON M5J 2L7
416/599-1991, Fax: 416/599-3100, Toll Free: 1-900-561-3300
Executive Director, Robyn Jones-Martin
President, Jed Goldberg
Publications: Solutions

Ecology Action Centre (EAC) (1971)
#31, 1568 Argyle St., Halifax, NS B3J 2B3
902/429-2202, Fax: 902/422-6410
Co-Director, Wendy MacGregor
Co-Director, Amanda Lavers
Publications: Between the Issues

Elsa Wild Animal Appeal of Canada (1971)
2482 Yonge St., PO Box 45051, Toronto, ON M4P 3E3

416/489-8862, Fax: 416/489-4769
Contact, D.E. Henderson
Publications: Elsa Newsletter

Enviro-Accès Inc. (1993)
Centre pour l'avancement des technologies environnementales
#310, 855, rue Pepin, Sherbrooke, PQ J1L 2P8
819/823-2230, Téléc: 819/823-6632
URL: http://www.enviroaccess.ca
Présidente - directrice générale, Manon Laporte
Directeur exécutif, Philippe Morel, Courrier électronique: pmorel@enviroaccess.ca
Publications: Biomasse-environnement; Répertoire de l'expertise de recherche en l'environnement; Répertoire des programmes d'aide; Fiches technologiques; Guide Fiscal

Environment & Plastics Institute of Canada (EPIC) (1989)
#500, 5925 Airport Rd., Mississauga, ON L4V 1W1
905/678-7748, Fax: 905/678-0774
President, Sandra Birkenmayer
Vice-President, Dr. Fred Edgecombe
Director of Communications, Bob Hamp

Environment Probe (1988)
225 Brunswick Ave., Toronto, ON M5S 2M6
416/964-9223, Fax: 416/964-8239
Executive Director, Elizabeth Brubaker

The Environmental Coalition of PEI (1988)
126 Richmond St., Charlottetown, PE C1A 1H9
902/566-4696, Fax: 902/566-4037
Contact, Sharon Labchuk

Environmental Compensation Corporation/ Société d'indemnisation environnementale (ECC) (1985)
#1203, 2300 Yonge St., PO Box 2382, Toronto, ON M4P 1E4
416/484-7831, Fax: 416/484-7822
Executive Officer, Peter Fischer
Counsel, Mario D. Faieta

The Environmental Law Centre (Alberta) Society (ELC) (1981)
#204, 10709 Jasper Ave., Edmonton, AB T5J 3N3
403/482-4891, Fax: 403/488-6779, Toll Free: 1-800-661-4238, Email: elc@web.apc.org
Executive Director, Donna Tingley
Office Manager, Marjorie Hartfelder
Publications: Journal of Environmental Law & Practice; Environmental Law Centre News Brief, q.

Environmental Youth Alliance (EYA) (1989)
PO Box 34097, Stn D, Vancouver, BC V6J 3L1
604/873-0616, Email: dragon@wimsey.com
Contact, Doug Ragan
Publications: SCREAM

Environnement jeunesse (1979)
ENJEU
4545, av Pierre-de-Coubertin, CP 1000, Succ. M, Montréal, PQ H1V 3R2
514/252-3016, Téléc: 514/254-5873
Directrice générale, Christiane Dinelle
Publications: L'ENJEU
Organisation(s) affiliée(s): Réseau international jeunesse, environnement et développement de la Francophonie (RIJEDF); North American Association for Environmental Education (NAAEE); Réseau québécois des groupes écologistes (RQGE); Association québécoise pour la promotion de l'éducation relative à l'environnement (AQPERE)

The Evergreen Foundation/Fondation Evergreen (1991)
#500, 355 Adelaide St. West, Toronto, ON M5V 1S2
416/596-1495, Fax: 416/596-1443, Email: 74744.2403@compuserve.com
URL: http://www.evergreen.ca/
Executive Director, Geoff Cape
Publications: Evergreen Foundation News; Evergreen World; Outdoor Classroom News, s-a.

Fédération des associations pour la protection de l'environnement des lacs inc. (FAPEL) (1976)
CP 51128, Succ. Centre, Montréal, PQ H1N 3T8
514/256-6822, Téléc: 514/256-7005
Directrice générale, Lucie McNeil
Secrétaire, Lyne Vigneault

Fondation de la faune du Québec (FFQ) (1985)
#860, 140, av Grande-Allée est, Québec, PQ G1R 5M8
418/644-7926, Téléc: 418/643-7655
Président/directeur général, Gilles Barras
Publications: Nature

Forest Alliance of British Columbia (FABC) (1991)
1055 Dunsmuir St., PO Box 49312, Vancouver, BC V7X 1L3
604/685-7507, Fax: 604/685-5373, Toll Free: 1-800-567-8733, Email: fabc@mindlink.bc.ca
URL: http://www.forest.org
Executive Director, Tom Tevlin
Chairman, Jack Munro
Community Relations Manager, Donna Freeman
Publications: The Forest & the People; Choices - Issues & Options for BC Forests, q.

Fort Whyte Centre for Environmental Education (1966)
1961 McCreary Rd., PO Box 124, Winnipeg, MB R3Y 1G5
204/989-8355, Fax: 204/895-4700
President/CEO, Bill Elliott
Publications: Branta

Friends of the Earth/Ami(e)s de la Terre (FoE) (1978)
#701, 251 Laurier Ave. West, Ottawa, ON K1P 5J6
613/230-3352, Fax: 613/232-4354, Email: foe@web.apc.org
Executive Director, Susan Tanner
Director of Communication & Administration, Blaine Marchand
Publications: Earth Words
Affiliates: Canadian Environmental Network; Canadian Participatory Committee for UNCED

The Gaia Group (1985)
2108 Reynolds St., Regina, SK S4N 3N1
306/352-4804
President, Jim Elliott
Publications: Whisper in the Woods

GreenLEAP (1991)
The Independent Association of Legal, Engineering & Accounting Professionals for the Environment
#400, 70 Richmond St. East, Toronto, ON M5C 1N8
416/363-5577, Fax: 416/367-2653
Chief Administrative Officer, Glenna Ford
Publications: GreenLEAP; GreenNews, s-a.

Greenpeace Canada (1971)
#600, 185 Spadina Ave., Toronto, ON M5T 2C6
416/597-8408, Fax: 416/597-8422, Toll Free: 1-800-320-7183
URL: http://rs560.cl.msu.edu/weather/interactiv.html
Executive Director, Jeanne Moffat
Publications: Greenlink

Harmony Foundation of Canada/Fondation Harmonie du Canada (1985)
1183 Fort St., Victoria, BC V8V 3L1
250/380-3001, Fax: 250/380-0887, Email: harmony@island.net.com
Executive Director, Michael Bloomfield
Institute Coordinator, Katharine Ratcliffe
Publications: Workplace Guide: Practical Action for the Environment/Guide pour le milieu de travail vers la santé environnementale; Home & Family Guide: Practical Action for the Environment/Guide pour la famille et la maison: la protection de l'environnement au quotidien; Community Workshops for the Environment/Ateliers communautaires au sujet de l'environnement; Our Common Future: A Canadian Response to the Challenge of Sustainable Development; Earthworms, Nature's Recyclers
Affiliates: Centre for our Common Future; Canadian Environmental Network
Ottawa Office: #202A, 145 Spruce St., Ottawa, ON K1R 6P1, 613/230-5399, Fax: 613/238-6470

Institut de recherche en biologie végétale
4101, rue Sherbrooke est, Montréal, PQ H1X 2B2
514/872-0272, Téléc: 514/872-9406
Director, J. André Fortin

Institute for Environmental Policy & Stewardship/Institut de politique et environnementales d'intendance (IEPS) (1989)
Faculty of Environmental Sciences, Blackwood Hall, University of Guelph, Guelph, ON N1G 2W1
519/824-4120, ext.3798, 3072, Fax: 519/763-4686
Director, Isabel Hethcoate
Publications: The Green Web

International Environmental Liability Management Association (IELMA)
#2200, 181 University Ave., Toronto, ON M5H 3M7
416/601-6758, Fax: 416/863-1036, Email: actuarius@aol.com
URL: http://www.magic.ca/ielma/IELMA.html

International Institute for Sustainable Development/Institut international du développement durable (IISD) (1990)
161 Portage Ave. East, 6th Fl., Winnipeg, MB R3B 0Y4
204/958-7700, Fax: 204/958-7710, Email: reception@iisdpost.iisd.ca
URL: http://www.iisd.ca/linkages/; http://iisd1.iisd.ca/
President/CEO, Arthur J. Hanson
Sec.-Treas., Ian R. Seymour, CA
Project Officer, Marlene Roy
Publications: Developing Ideas

International Society of Indoor Air Quality & Climate (ISIAQ) (1992)
PO Box 22038, Sub 32, Ottawa, ON K1V 0W2
613/731-2559, Fax: 613/733-9394, Email: ae977@freenet.carleton.ca
URL: http://www.cyberus.ca/~dsw/
Contact, D.S. Walkinshaw
President, Olli Seppanen
Publications: Indoor Air: International Journal of Indoor Air Quality & Climate

National Energy Conservation Association/ Association nationale pour la conservation de l'énergie (NECA) (1983)
PO Box 3214, Winnipeg, MB R3C 4E7
204/783-1273, Fax: 204/774-6702, Toll Free: 1-800-263-5974
CEO/Sec.-Treas., Laverne Dalgleish
Manager, Trevor Anderson
Training Administrator, Kari Mackinnon
Chairman, Peter Etherington
Director, Len Wall
Publications: Visions

ORGANIZATIONS — ENVIRONMENTAL

The Nature Conservancy of Canada/Société canadienne pour la conservation de la nature (NCC) (1963)
#400, 110 Eglinton Ave. West, Toronto, ON M4R 2G5
416/932-3202, Fax: 416/932-3208, Toll Free: 1-800-465-0029
Executive Director, John Eisenhauer
Publications: The Ark

Newfoundland & Labrador Environmental Association
#603, 140 Water St., St. John's, NF A1C 6H6
709/722-1740, Fax: 709/726-1813
President, Stan Tobin

North American Recycled Rubber Association (NARRA) (1994)
160 Baseline Rd., Bowmanville, ON L1C 1A2
905/623-8919, Fax: 905/623-1791, Email: narra@oix.com
Secretary & Director of Research, Philip E. Coulter, P.Eng.
Office Manager, Margaret Carter
Publications: NARRA News

Nova Scotia Business Council on the Environment (NSBCE) (1992)
12 Portland St., Dartmouth, NS B2Y 1G9
902/469-7110, Fax: 902/464-0365
Project Manager, David W. Harrison
Project Coordinator, Joanne Hurshman
Publications: Environmental Management

Nova Scotia Centre for Environmentally Sustainable Economic Development (CESED) (1992)
1334 Barrington St., PO Box 1000, Halifax, NS B3J 2X4
902/420-7936, Fax: 902/429-4866
Affiliates: Council of Centres for Sustainable Development; International Institute for Sustainable Development (IISD); UK Centre for Economic & Environmental Development; Centre for Our Common Future

Ocean Voice International, Inc./Echo de l'océan, inc. (OVI) (1987)
PO Box 37026, Ottawa, ON K1V 0W0
613/264-8986, Fax: 613/521-4205, Email: mcall@superaje.com
URL: http://www.ovi.ca
President, Don E. McAllister
Treasurer, Phyllis Kofmel
Secretary, Katjo Rodriguez
Publications: Sea Wind
Affiliates: Global Coral Reef Alliance

OMMRI: Corporations in Support of Recycling
Ontario Multi-Material Recycling Inc.
#601, 26 Wellington St. East, Toronto, ON M5E 1S2
416/594-3456, Fax: 416/594-3463, Email: info@ommri.org
President/CEO, Robert A. Flemington, P.Eng.
Executive Director, Joseph P. Hruska
Publications: The Recycler
Affiliates: Ontario Newspaper Publishers; Grocery Products Manufacturers of Canada; Ontario Soft Drink Association; Canadian Council of Grocery Distributors; Society of Plastics Industry of Canada; Packaging Association of Canada

Ontario Centre for Environmental Technology Advancement (OCETA) (1994)
63 Polson St., 2nd Fl., Toronto, ON M5A 1A4
416/778-5624, Fax: 416/778-5624, Email: oceta@hookup.net
URL: http://www.oceta.on.ca
President & CEO, Ed Mallett
Chairman of the Board, Jane Pagel

Vice-President, Business Services, Brian Wanless, 416/778-5288
Vice-President, Technology & Research, Adele Buckley, 416/778-5281
Vice-President, Finance & Investment, Keith Lue, 416/778-5283
Publications: CEIA/OCETA Fax Newsletter
Affiliates: Ontario Environmental Training Consortium; Canadian Environmental Industry Association; Waste Technology International; Canadian Institute of Technology for the Environment

Ontario Pollution Control Equipment Association (OPCEA) (1970)
PO Box 137, Midhurst, ON L0L 1X0
705/725-0917, Fax: 705/725-1068
President, John Coomey
Publications: Product & Service Directory
Affiliates: Pollution Control Association of Ontario

Ontario Toxic Waste Research Coalition (OTWRC) (1986)
PO Box 35, Vineland Station, ON L0R 2E0
519/744-7503, Fax: 519/744-1546
CEO, John Jackson
Secretary, Ruth Burton, 905/563-8571
Affiliates: Concerned Citizens Group; Echo Site Study Committee; Niagara Citizens for Modern Waste Management; Niagara North Federation of Agriculture; Niagara Peninsula Fruit & Vegetable Growers; Niagara Residents for Safe Toxic Waste Disposal; Preservation of Agricultural Lands Society

Ontario Waste Management Association/Société ontarienne de gestion des déchets (OWMA) (1977)
#320, 4195 Dundas St. West, Etobicoke, ON M8X 1Y4
416/236-0172, Fax: 416/236-0174
Executive Director, Terry E. Taylor, CAE
General Manager, Nancy Crawford
Affiliates: National Solid Wastes Management Association

Osgoode Hall Environmental Law Society (1991)
Legal & Literary Society, Osgoode Hall Law School, York University, 4700 Keele St., North York, ON M3J 1P3
416/736-5027, Fax: 416/736-5736
Director, Colin Piercey
Director, Cheryl Sheruit
Director, Paul McCulloch
Director, Lara Edwards

The Pembina Institute for Appropriate Development (PIAD) (1985)
PO Box 7558, Drayton Valley, AB T7A 1S7
403/542-6272, Fax: 403/542-6464, Email: piad@ccinet.ab.ca
Executive Director, Thomas Marr-Laing
President, Wally Heinrichs
Publications: The Alberta Environmental Directory; Canadian Environmental Education Catalogue; Environmental Network News, bi-m.

Pitch-In Canada/Passons à l'action Canada (PIC) (1967)
PO Box 45011, RPO Ocean Park, White Rock, BC V4A 9L1
604/290-0498, Fax: 604/535-4653
President, Allard W. van Veen
Chairman, Bette Ballhorn
Publications: Pitch-In News
Affiliates: Clean World International - London, UK

Pollution Probe Foundation (PPF) (1969)
12 Madison Ave., Toronto, ON M5R 2S1
416/926-1907, Fax: 416/926-1601, Email: pprobe@web.net

Executive Director, Ken Ogilvie
Publications: ProbeAbilities
Affiliates: Clean Air Network

Prairie Association for Water Management (PAWM) (1983)
PO Box 1949, Hanna, AB T0J 1P0
403/854-2509
Coordinator, Candis Preston
President, Harry Gordon
Publications: PAWM

Recycling Council of Alberta (RCA) (1987)
PO Box 40552, RPO Highfield, Calgary, AB T2G 5G8
403/287-1477, Fax: 403/287-1942, Email: rca@cadvision.com; cseide@agt.net
Executive Director, Christina Seidel
Publications: The Connector

Recycling Council of British Columbia (RCBC) (1974)
#201, 225 Smithe St., Vancouver, BC V6B 4X7
604/683-6009, Fax: 604/683-7255, Toll Free: 1-800-667-4321
Executive Director, Renie D'Aquila
Publications: Reiterate; Update, bi-m.

Recycling Council of Manitoba (RCM) (1985)
Powers Bldg., #501, 428 Portage Ave., Winnipeg, MB R3C 1N7
204/925-3777, Fax: 204/942-4207
Executive Director, Glen Koroluk
Publications: The R Report

Recycling Council of Ontario/Conseil du recyclage de l'Ontario (RCO) (1978)
#504, 489 College St., Toronto, ON M6G 1A5
416/960-1025, Fax: 416/960-8053, Toll Free: 1-800-263-2849, Email: rco@web.apc.org
URL: http://www.web.apc.org/rco
Executive Director, John Hanson
Chair, Glenda Gies
Vice-Chair, Anne Mathewson
Sec.-Treas., John Lackie
Publications: RCO Update; RCO Policy Bulletin

Resource Efficient Agricultural Production Canada (REAP-Canada) (1988)
Sustainable Farming
Glenaladale House, Macdonald College, 21111 ch Lakeshore, PO Box 125, Ste-Anne-de-Bellevue, PQ H9X 3V9
514/398-7743, Fax: 514/398-7972
President, Roger Samson
Publications: Sustainable Farming; Weed Management in Sustainable Agriculture; Priorities in Sustainable Agriculture Research
Affiliates: Canadian Organic Growers; Ecological Farmers Association of Ontario

Saskatchewan Environmental Society (SES) (1970)
PO Box 1372, Saskatoon, SK S7K 3N9
306/665-1915, Fax: 306/665-2128
Program Coordinator, Ann Coxworth
President, Lynn Brown
Publications: SES Newsletter; SES Backgrounders, irreg.
Affiliates: Canadian Coalition for Nuclear Responsibility; Canadian Environmental Network; Saskatchewan Eco-Network

Saskatchewan Soil Conservation Association Inc. (SSCA) (1987)
PO Box 1360, Indian Head, SK S0G 2K0
306/695-4235, Fax: 306/695-4236
President, Dean Smith, 306/773-9029
Executive Manager, Doug McKell, P.Ag.

Office Manager, Clair Neill
Publications: Prairie Steward

Saskatchewan Waste Reduction Council (SWRC) (1991)
#203, 115 - 2nd Ave. North, Saskatoon, SK S7K 0G4
306/931-3242, Fax: 306/665-2128, Email: swrc@link.ca
Executive Director, Joanne Fedyk
Vice-Chair, Clayton Sampson
Chair, Bert Weichel
Publications: WasteWatch

Sea Shepherd Conservation Society (SSCS) (1977)
PO Box 48446, Vancouver, BC V7X 1A2
604/688-7325
International Director, Lisa Distefano
Director, Paul Watson
Publications: The Sea Shepherd Log

SEEDS Foundation (SEEDS) (1976)
Society, Environment & Energy Development Studies Foundation
#440, 10169 - 104 St., Edmonton, AB T5J 1A5
403/424-0971, Fax: 403/424-2444, Toll Free: 1-800-661-8751, Email: stokerm@pschools.st-albert.ab.ca
Executive Director, Dan Stoker
Publications: PAGES

Sierra Club of British Columbia (SCBC) (1969)
1525 Amelia St., Victoria, BC V8W 2K1
250/386-5255, Fax: 250/386-4453, Email: scbcgis@cyberstore.ca
Contact, Vicky Husband
Publications: Sierra Report

Sierra Club of Canada (1892)
#620, One Nicholas St., Ottawa, ON K1N 7B7
613/241-4611, Fax: 613/233-2292
Executive Director, Elizabeth May
Affiliates: Canadian Coalition for Biodiversity

Sierra Club of Eastern Canada (1972)
#204, 517 College St., Toronto, ON M6G 4A2
416/960-9606, Fax: 416/960-9020, Email: sierraec@interlog.com
Contact, Kerry Wilkins
Publications: Sanctuary
Affiliates: Sierra Club of Western Canada; Sierra Club - USA

Société québécoise d'assainissement des eaux (SQAE) (1980)
1055, boul René-Lévesque est, 10e étage, Montréal, PQ H2L 4S5
514/873-7411, Téléc: 514/873-7879
Président-directeur général, Guy Leclerc
Vice-Président, Administration & finance, Jean Genest
Vice-président, Gestion des projets, François Rochette
Secrétaire général, Marc Pinsonnault

Society Promoting Environmental Conservation (SPEC) (1968)
2150 Maple St., Vancouver, BC V6J 3T3
604/736-7732, Fax: 604/736-7115
President, Paul Hundal
Publications: SPECtrum

Soil Conservation Canada/Conservation des sols Canada (SCC) (1987)
#907, 151 Slater St., Ottawa, ON K1P 5H4
613/521-5444, Fax: 613/521-5444
Executive Director, Bryan James
President, Tom G. Sawyer
Publications: The Protector

Solid Waste Association of North America (SWANA) (1961)
PO Box 7219, Silver Spring, MD 20907 USA
301/585-2898, Fax: 301/589-7068
Executive Director, H. Lanier Hickman, Jr.
Chief of Staff, Lori Swain
Publications: Municipal Solid Waste News
BC Chapter: President, Dave Ellis, Environment Canada, 224 West Esplanade, North Vancouver, BC V7M 3H7, 604/666-2690
Canadian Prairie Chapter: Sec.-Treas., Murray Ashton, c/o City of Saskatoon, City Hall, Saskatoon, SK S7K 0J5, 306/975-2487
Ontario Chapter: Sec.-Treas., P. Wong, 2069 Elderwood Dr., Sudbury, ON P3B 2A7, 705/566-5147

STOP (1970)
716, rue St-Ferdinand, Montréal, PQ H4C 2T2
514/393-9559, Fax: 514/932-7267
Office Manager, Bruce Walker
Publications: STOP Press

United Nations Environment Program - Regional Office for North America (UNEP) (1972)
Two United Nations Plaza, Rm. DC2-0803, New York, NY 10017 USA
212/963-8138, Fax: 212/963-7341, Telex: 422311 UN UI, Email: collinst@un.org
Senior Information Officer, T. Collins
Affiliates: Canadian Committee for UNEP

Water Environment Association of Ontario (WEAO) (1971)
63 Hollyberry Trail, North York, ON M2H 2N9
416/502-1440, Fax: 416/502-1786
President, D.C. Edwardson
Executive Administrator, Sandy M. Pickett, 416/502-1440
Publications: WEAO Newsletter
Affiliates: Water Environment Federation; Canadian Water & Wastewater Association

Western Canada Water Environment Association (WCWEA) (1973)
PO Box 6168, Stn A, Calgary, AB T2H 2L4
403/259-4041, Fax: 403/258-1631
Manager, M.M. Janice Taylor
Chairman, Steve Blonsky

Western Canada Water & Wastewater Association (WCWWA) (1948)
PO Box 6168, Stn A, Calgary, AB T2H 2L4
403/259-4041, Fax: 403/258-1631
Manager, M.M. Janice Taylor
President, Steve Blonsky
Publications: WCWWA Bulletin; Who's Who, a.
Affiliates: Canadian Water & Wastewater Association

Western Canada Wilderness Committee (WCWC) (1980)
20 Water St., Vancouver, BC V6B 1A4
604/683-8220, Fax: 604/683-8229, Toll Free: 1-800-661-9453
URL: http://www.web.apc.org/wcwild/welcome.htm
Founder & Executive Director, Paul George
Executive Director, National Campaigns, Joe Foy
Executive Director, International Campaigns, Adriane Carr
Publications: Western Canada Wilderness Committee Reports

Wildlife Habitat Canada/Habitat faunique Canada (1984)
#200, 7 Hinton Ave. North, Ottawa, ON K1Y 4P1
613/722-2090, Fax: 613/722-3318, Email: jladd@whc.org
Executive Director, David J. Neave
Chairperson, John C. Perlin

Wildlife Preservation Trust Canada/Fiducie pour la faune au Canada (WPTC) (1985)
Greey Bldg., #205, 56 The Esplanade, Toronto, ON M5E 1A7
416/368-3550, Fax: 416/368-0272, Email: wptc@inforamp.net
Executive Director, Elaine Williams
President, Graham F. Hallward
Treasurer, Eleanor Clitheroe
Publications: On the Edge
Affiliates: Jersey Wildlife Preservation Trust; Wildlife Preservation Trust International; International Union for Conservation & Nature

World Wildlife Fund - Canada/Fonds mondial pour la nature (WWF) (1967)
#504, 90 Eglinton Ave. East, Toronto, ON M4P 2Z7
416/489-8800, Fax: 416/489-3611, Toll Free: 1-800-267-2632
President, Monte Hummel
Chairman, Dr. Donald A. Chant, O.C.
Publications: Working for Wildlife; Schools for Wildlife
Affiliates: World Wide Fund for Nature (International)

Yukon Conservation Society (YCS) (1968)
302 Hawkins St., PO Box 4163, Whitehorse, YT Y1A 3T3
403/668-5678, Fax: 403/668-6637
Coordinator, Shelley Gerber
Director, Bob Van Dijken
Publications: Walk Softly
Affiliates: Canadian Environmental Network; Tatshenshini International; Canadian Nature Federation

EQUIPMENT & MACHINERY
see also Building & Construction

Association des marchands de machines aratoires de la Province de Québec
CP 590, Bedford, PQ J0J 1A0
514/248-7946, Téléc: 514/248-3264
Directeur, René Maurice

Association des professionnels à l'outillage municipal
26, rue St-Raphael, Saint-Luc, PQ J2W 1T1
514/348-6139, Téléc: 514/348-5889
Secrétaire, Robert Marjanek

Association des propriétaires de machinerie lourde du Québec inc. (APMLQ) (1966)
#220, 365, rue Normand, St-Jean-sur-Richelieu, PQ J3A 1T6
514/348-7318, Téléc: 514/359-4894
Directeur général, André Daoust
Publications: APMLQ-Info

Canadian Association of Equipment Distributors
#300, 1272 Wellington St., Ottawa, ON K1Y 3A7
613/722-4711, Fax: 613/722-0099
Executive Director, Nancy Leu

Canadian Conveyor Manufacturers' Association
#701, 116 Albert St., Ottawa, ON K1P 5G3
613/232-7213, Fax: 613/232-7381
President, Arnold W.D. Garlick

Canadian Crane Manufacturers' Association
#701, 116 Albert St., Ottawa, ON K1P 5G3
613/232-7213, Fax: 613/232-7381
President, Arnold W.D. Garlick

Canadian Almanac & Directory 1997

ORGANIZATIONS — EVENTS

Canadian Custom Engineered Machinery Manufacturers' Association
#701, 116 Albert St., Ottawa, ON K1P 5G3
613/232-7213, Fax: 613/232-7381
President, Arnold W.D. Garlick

Canadian Environmental Equipment Manufacturers' Association
#701, 116 Albert St., Ottawa, ON K1P 5G3
613/232-7213, Fax: 613/232-7381
President, Arnold W.D. Garlick

Canadian Farm & Industrial Equipment Institute
#307, 720 Guelph Line, Burlington, ON L7R 4E2
905/632-8483, Fax: 905/632-7138
President, Brent M. Hamre

Canadian Machine Tool Distributors' Association (CMTDA)
208 Brimorton Dr., Toronto, ON M1H 2C6
416/431-1330, Fax: 416/431-5223
Sec.-Treas., John Martin

Canadian Mining Equipment Manufacturers' Association
#701, 116 Albert St., Ottawa, ON K1P 5G3
613/232-7213, Fax: 613/232-7381
President, Arnold W.D. Garlick

Canadian Outdoor Power Equipment Association
208 Brimorton Dr., Toronto, ON M1H 2C6
416/431-1330, Fax: 416/431-5223
Manager, John Martin

Canadian Packaging & Printing Machinery Manufacturers' Association
#701, 116 Albert St., Ottawa, ON K1P 5G3
613/232-7213, Fax: 613/232-7381
President, Arnold W.D. Garlick

Canadian Petroleum Equipment Manufacturers' Association
#701, 116 Albert St., Ottawa, ON K1P 5G3
613/232-7213, Fax: 613/232-7381
President, Arnold W.D. Garlick

Canadian Process Control Association (CPCA)
4 St. Thomas St., Toronto, ON M5S 2B8
416/595-0103, Fax: 416/595-9880
Manager, Bruce G. Lawson

Canadian Pulp & Paper Machinery Manufacturers' Association
#701, 116 Albert St., Ottawa, ON K1P 5G3
613/232-7213, Fax: 613/232-7381
President, Arnold W.D. Garlick

Compressed Air & Gas Machinery Manufacturers' Association
#701, 116 Albert St., Ottawa, ON K1P 5G3
613/232-7213, Fax: 613/232-7381
President, Arnold W.D. Garlick

Machinery & Equipment Manufacturers' Association of Canada/Association des manufacturiers de machines et d'équipement du Canada (MEMAC) (1955)
#701, 116 Albert St., Ottawa, ON K1P 5G3
613/232-7213, Fax: 613/232-7381
President, Arnold W.D. Garlick
Chairman, Thomas Krieser
Western Office: Vice-President, J. Stashuk, 1056 - 47th Ave. West, Vancouver, BC V6M 2L4, 604/266-3080

Municipal Equipment & Operations Association (Ontario)
City of Waterloo, PO Box 337, Waterloo, ON N2J 4A8

519/747-8619, Fax: 519/886-5788
President, Paul Udit

Ontario Retail Farm Equipment Dealers' Association (ORFEDA) (1945)
64 Temperance St., PO Box 430, Aurora, ON L4G 3L5
905/841-6888, Fax: 905/841-1214
Executive Vice-President, Glen E. Peart
Publications: ORFEDA Dealer Bulletin
Affiliates: North American Equipment Dealers Association

Prairie Implement Manufacturers Association (PIMA) (1970)
2152 Scarth St., Regina, SK S4P 2H6
306/522-2710, Fax: 306/781-7293
URL: http://www.pima.ca
General Manager, Larry Schneider
Publications: PIMA Pulse

ETHNIC GROUPS see MULTICULTURALISM

EVENTS

Association des professionnels en exposition du Québec (APEQ) (1990)
6940, rue Barry, Brossard, PQ J4Z 1V1
514/443-1570, Téléc: 514/443-8415
Directeur général, Yves Barré
Présidente, Francine Bois
Publications: L'Exposé

The BC Association of Festivals & Events (1976)
Festivals BC
PO Box 538, Squamish, BC V0N 3G0
604/892-5977, Fax: 604/892-5978, Toll Free: 1-800-661-2295
Executive Director, Garth McCreedy
President, Bryan Pasch
Publications: Newsletter
Affiliates: Northwest Festivals Association; International Festival Association

Canadian Association of Exposition Managers/ Association canadienne des directeurs d'expositions (CAEM) (1983)
Box 82, #239A, 6900 Airport Rd., Mississauga, ON L4V 1E8
905/678-9377, Fax: 905/678-9578
Executive Director, Carol Ann Burrell
Publications: Communiqué; Expresse; CAGM Buyers Guide and Directory

Canadian Association of Fairs & Exhibitions/ Association canadienne des foires et expositions (1926)
PO Box 1172, Stn Main, Edmonton, AB T5J 2M4
403/474-1902, Fax: 403/471-4981
Executive Director, Elwood F. Hart
President, Ed Sikorski
Publications: Fair Scope; Directory of Canadian Fairs & Exhibitions Industry, a.
Affiliates: International Association of Fairs & Exhibitions; Provincial Associations of Agricultural Societies; Outdoor Amusement Business Association; Showmens League of Canada

Carnaval de Québec/Québec Winter Carnival (1954)
290, rue Joly, Québec, PQ G1L 1N8
418/626-3716, Téléc: 418/626-7252
Directeur général, Denis Rhéaume
Directeur des commandités, Jean Pelletier
Directeur du marketing et des communications, Gabriel Béron

Edmonton Klondike Days Association (1965)
#1660, 10020 - 101A Ave., Edmonton, AB T5J 3G2
403/426-4055, Fax: 403/424-0418
General Manager, Don Gray
Affiliates: Northwest Festivals Association; International Festivals Association; Canadian Society of Association Executives; National Tour Association

The Exhibit & Display Association of Canada (EDAC)
#309, 2175 Sheppard Ave. East, North York, ON M2J 1W8
416/491-0308, Fax: 416/502-2115
Executive Director, Leona Crock
President, Sam Kohn

Exhibition Association of Nova Scotia
RR#2, Hubbards, NS B0J 1T0
902/857-3874
Administrator, D.C. Bishop

Federation of Canadian Music Festivals/ Fédération des festivals de musique du Canada (FCMF) (1949)
1034 Chestnut Ave., Moose Jaw, SK S6H 1A6
306/693-7087, Fax: 306/693-7087
Executive Director, Sharon L. Penner
President, J. Alexander Clark
Publications: Piu Mosso; Digest Report, a.
Affiliates: Canadian Conference of the Arts

ALBERTA MUSIC FESTIVAL ASSOCIATION (1963)
4408 - 63 St., Camrose, AB T4V 2J4
403/672-5709
Executive Director, Sue Reesor
Publications: Alberta Music Festival Association Provincial Syllabus

ASSOCIATED MANITOBA ARTS FESTIVALS, INC. (AMAF) (1977)
#424, 100 Arthur St., Winnipeg, MB R3B 1H3
204/945-4578, Fax: 204/948-2073
Executive Director, Karen Oliver
Publications: Focus on Festivals

BC ASSOCIATION OF PERFORMING ARTS FESTIVALS
#300, 764 Yates St., Victoria, BC V8W 1L4
250/920-7064, Fax: 250/920-7084
Coordinator, Helen Tuele

FEDERATION OF MUSIC FESTIVALS OF NOVA SCOTIA
RR#4, PO Box 4016, Armdale, NS B3L 4J4
902/852-3385
Secretary, Frances Tyrrell

NEW BRUNSWICK FEDERATION OF MUSIC FESTIVALS INC./LA FÉDÉRATION DES FESTIVALS DE MUSIQUE DU NOUVEAU-BRUNSWICK INC. (NBFMF) (1973)
801 Mitchell St., Fredericton, NB E3B 6E8
506/452-1132, Fax: 506/444-5207
Executive Secretary, Gerald Goguen

NEWFOUNDLAND FEDERATION OF MUSIC FESTIVALS (1969)
101 LeMarchant Rd., St. John's, NF A1C 2H1
709/726-2831
Sec.-Treas., Dr. David K. Peters

ONTARIO MUSIC FESTIVALS ASSOCIATION INC. (OMFA)
#501, 100 Adelaide St. West, Toronto, ON M5H 1S2
416/363-3238, Fax: 416/363-2657
Executive Secretary, Mary Ann Ross

PEI MUSIC FESTIVAL ASSOCIATION
17 MacMillan Cres., Charlottetown, PE C1A 8G3
902/368-1202, Fax: 902/892-1059
Provincial Secretary, Angela Matheson

QUÉBEC COMPETITIVE MUSIC FESTIVAL
364, av Olivier, Westmount, PQ H3Z 2C9

514/935-9074, Téléc: 514/935-4909
Secretary, Jan Simons

SASKATCHEWAN MUSIC FESTIVAL ASSOCIATION INC. (1908)
#201, 1819 Cornwall St., Regina, SK S4P 2K4
306/757-1722, Fax: 306/347-7789
URL: http://www.ffa.ucalgary.ca/scco/smea.html
Executive Director, Doris Lazecki
Assistant to Executive Director, Sandra Donisen

Festivals Ontario (1986)
PO Box 423, Orillia, ON L3V 6J8
705/325-0619, Fax: 705/325-7399
President, Jaye Robinson
Publications: Network/Réseau

Greater Vancouver International Film Festival Society (VIFF) (1982)
#410, 1008 Homer St., Vancouver, BC V6B 2X1
604/685-0260, Fax: 604/688-8221, Email: viff@viff.org
URL: http://viff.org/viff/
Festival Director, Alan Franey

International Special Events Society - Toronto Chapter
84 Seventh St., Toronto, ON M8V 3B4
416/252-9229, Fax: 416/252-7071, Toll Free: 1-800-688-4737
URL: http://www.ndgphoenix.com/ises.html
President, Anna McCusker
Vice-President, Education, Georgina DeCarlo
Vice-President, Membership, Larry Cuthbertson
Association Manager, Shelley Macdonald
Publications: Toronto Chapter Newsletter

Provincial Exhibition of Manitoba (1882)
Royal Manitoba Winter Fair
#3, 1175 - 18th St., Brandon, MB R7A 7C5
204/726-3590, Fax: 204/725-0202, Info Line: 204/728-7769
General Manager, Dave Wowchuk

Royal Agricultural Winter Fair Association/Foire agricole royale d'hiver (1922)
Coliseum, Exhibition Place, Toronto, ON M6K 3C3
416/393-6400, Fax: 416/393-6488, Email: rwfair@io.org
URL: http://www.royalfair.org
CEO, David E. Garrick
Marketing Manager, Sue Bundy
Publications: Around the Royal; Royal Horse Show Magazine, a.; Prize Lists, a.; RAWF Catalogue, a.

Société des fêtes et festivals du Québec (SFFQ) (1976)
4545, av Pierre-de-Coubertin, CP 1000, Succ. M, Montréal, PQ H1V 3R2
514/252-3037, Téléc: 514/254-1617, Ligne sans frais: 1-800-361-7688
Directeur Général, Pierre-Paul Leduc
Publications: Festivals et Attractions; Le Bottin de l'industrie des festivals et attractions, annuel; Le Guide des festivals et attractions, annuel
Organisation(s) affiliée(s): International Festivals Association

Toronto International Film Festival/Festival international du film de Toronto (1976)
Cinematheque Ontario
2 Carlton St., 16th Fl., Toronto, ON M5B 1J3
416/967-7371, Fax: 416/967-9477, Info Line: 416/923-3456
URL: http://www.bell.ca/toronto/filmfest
Director, Piers Handling
Managing Director, Suzanne Weiss
Director, Marketing & Communications, Michèle Maheux
Publications: Programme Guide; Programme Book, a.

Western Association of Exposition Managers (WAEM)
#523, 409 Granville St., Vancouver, BC V6C 1T2
604/669-3177, Fax: 604/604-669-5343
Executive Director, Tom Abbott

Westerner Exposition Association (1891)
The Westerner
4847A - 19 St., Red Deer, AB T4R 2N7
403/343-7800, Fax: 403/341-4699
General Manager, Larry Johnstone
Marketing & Events Manager, Noreen Stuart
Publications: The Westernews
Affiliates: International Association of Fairs & Exhibitions; International Association of Auditorium Management; Canadian Association of Fairs & Exhibitions

EXECUTIVES see **MANAGEMENT & ADMINISTRATION**

EXHIBITIONS see **EVENTS**

EXPORT TRADE see **TRADE**

FAIRS see **EVENTS**

FARMING see **AGRICULTURE & FARMING**

FASHION & TEXTILES

Allied Beauty Association (ABA) (1934)
#1001, 2 Sheppard Ave. East, PO Box 42, North York, ON M2N 5Y7
416/225-2359, Fax: 416/223-3610
Executive Director, Marc Speir

Apparel Manufacturers Association of Ontario
#605, 130 Slater St., Ottawa, ON K1P 6E2
613/565-3047, Fax: 613/231-2305, Toll Free: 1-800-661-1187
Executive Director, Stephen Beatty

Association of Nova Scotia Hairdressers (ANSH) (1962)
#9, 75 MacDonald Ave., Dartmouth, NS B3B 1S5
902/468-6477, Fax: 902/468-7147
Business Manager, Kimberly Carter
President, Larry MacDonald
Publications: Newsletter

Barbers Association of British Columbia (1924)
#411, 207 Hastings St. West, Vancouver, BC V6B 1H7
604/688-9731
Secretary, L.D. Carmichael

Canadian Apparel Federation/Fédération canadienne du vêtement (CAF)
#603, 130 Slater St., Ottawa, ON K1P 6E2
613/231-3220, Fax: 613/231-2305
Executive Director, Stephen Beatty
President, Jack Kivenko
Design Division: #112, 372 Richmond St. West, Toronto, ON M5V 1X6, 416/977-3620, Fax: 416/977-2637

Canadian Association of Textile Colourists & Chemists/Association canadienne des coloristes et chimistes du textile
269 MacDonald St., Woodstock, ON N4S 8C9
519/621-5722, Fax: 519/621-2420
Executive Director, Carl Webster
Publications: Canadian Textile Journal
Affiliates: Textile Federation of Canada

Canadian Association of Wholesale Sales Representatives/Association canadienne des représentants de ventes en gros
#336, 370 King St. West, PO Box 2, Toronto, ON M5V 1J9
416/593-6500, Fax: 416/593-5145
Executive Director, Karyn O'Neill
President, Julian Ernest
Administrator, S. Martineau
Publications: CAWS News

ALBERTA FASHION MARKET
#300L, 10403 - 172 St., Edmonton, AB T5S 1K9
403/484-7541
Administrator, Susan Brochu

APPAREL SALESMEN'S MARKET
3625, av Park, Montréal, PQ H2X 3P8
514/849-9497, Fax: 514/849-9498
Marketing Manager, Susan Trudeau

PRAIRIE APPAREL MARKET
#77, 81 Garry St., Winnipeg, MB R3C 4J9
204/947-0561
Administrator, Pat Herzog

WESTERN APPAREL MARKETS BC
#28, 910 Mainland St., Vancouver, BC V6B 1A9
604/682-5719, Fax: 604/682-3892
Executive Director, Wayne Abrams

WESTERN CANADA CHILDREN'S WEAR MARKETS
#407, 910 Mainland St., Vancouver, BC V6B 1A9
604/687-2778, Fax: 604/687-2779
President, John Knapton

Canadian Laundry & Linen Institute (CLLI) (1981)
PO Box 2277, Stn A, London, ON N6A 4E9
519/434-6261, Fax: 519/434-6261
Secretary, Ruth Baker

Canadian Sewing & Needlecraft Association/Association canadienne des travaux d'aiguilles (CSNA) (1972)
#204, 224 Merton St., Toronto, ON M4S 1A1
416/482-7724, Fax: 416/482-2862
General Manager, Elizabeth Kelembet
Publications: CSNA Trade News

Canadian Textiles Institute/Institut canadien des textiles (CTI) (1935)
#1720, 66 Slater St., Ottawa, ON K1P 5H1
613/232-7195, Fax: 613/232-8722
President, Eric L. Barry

Centre des technologies textiles/Textile Technology Centre (CTT) (1987)
3000, rue Boullé, Saint-Hyacinthe, PQ J2S 1H9
514/778-1870, Téléc: 514/778-3901
Président, Bernard Rose
Directeur, Technico-commercial, Ray-Marc Dumoulin
Secrétaire, Serge Cloutier
Publications: InfoTex-Info Sageos
Organisation(s) affiliée(s): Fédération canadienne du textile; Association canadienne des coloristes et chimistes du textile; Société des textiles du Canada; Association des textiles des Cantons de l'Est; Institut canadien du tapis; Institut canadien des textiles; Institut québécois des revêtements de sol; Société des diplômes en textile
Textile Technology Centre: Stephen Laramee, #202, 53 Village Centre Pl., Mississauga, ON L4Z 1V9, 905/897-1474, Fax: 905/566-0177

Children's Apparel Manufacturers Association/Association des Manufacturiers de Mode Enfantine (CAMA)
#101, 8270 Mountain Sights, Montréal, PQ H4P 2B7

Canadian Almanac & Directory 1997

514/731-7774, Fax: 514/731-7459
Executive Director, Murray W. Schwartz

Footwear Council of Canada
PO Box 644, Stn Don Mills, North York, ON M3C 2T6
Secretary, Sharon Maloney

Garment Manufacturers Association of Western Canada
#114, 85 Adelaide St., Winnipeg, MB R3A 0V9
204/943-2228
Executive Director, Allan Finkel

Hairdressers' Association of British Columbia (HABC) (1929)
#210, 1755 West Broadway, Vancouver, BC V6J 4S5
604/736-9891, Fax: 604/736-0720
Sec.-Treas., George D. Hutchison
Publications: Snippets; Essentials, q.

Institut des Manufacturiers du Vêtement du Québec/Apparel Manufacturers Institute of Québec (IMVQ) (1974)
#801, 555, rue Chabanel ouest, Montréal, PQ H2N 2H8
514/382-3846, Téléc: 514/383-1689
Directrice, Jane C. Binder
Publications: AMIQ Journal; AMIQ Apparel Directory; Internal AMIQ Newsletters, bi-m.; AMIQ Associate Directory

Luggage, Leathergoods, Handbags & Accessories Association of Canada
LLHA Association
#2112, 2330 Bridletowne Circle, Scarborough, ON M1W 3P6
416/491-5844, Fax: 416/496-9329
President, Sally MacGillivray
General Manager, Joyce Scobie

Manitoba Fashion Institute
#114, 85 Adelaide St., Winnipeg, MB R3A 0V9
204/942-7314, Fax: 204/943-2228
Executive Director, Allan Finkel

Men's Clothing Manufacturers Association Inc./ Association des manufacturiers de vêtements pour hommes inc. (MCMA)
#801, 555, rue Chabanel ouest, Montréal, PQ H2N 2H8
514/382-3846, Fax: 514/383-1689
Executive Director, Sydney J. Cohen
Publications: On the Button
Affiliates: Associated Clothing Manufacturers of the Province of Quebec Inc./Les Manufacturiers associés du vêtement de la Province de Québec inc; Canadian Trimmers Manufacturing Association; Montreal Clothing Contractors Association Inc./ L'Association entrepreneurs en confection de Montréal inc; Quebec Council of Odd Pants Employers Inc./Conseil du patronat des fabricants de pantalons du Québec inc; Rainwear & Sportswear Manufacturers Association/L'Association des fabricants de vêtements imperméables et vêtements sports

New Brunswick Hairdressers Association
440 Brunswick St., Fredericton, NB E3B 1H3
506/458-8087
Registrar, Gaye Cail

Ontario Fashion Exhibitors Inc. (OFE) (1955)
#219, 111 Peter St., Toronto, ON M5V 2H1
416/596-2401, Fax: 416/596-1808
Executive Director, Serge S. Micheli, CAE
President, Ronnie Kantor
Publications: OFE Buyers Guide
Affiliates: Canadian Association of Wholesale Sales Representatives

Québec Fashion Apparel Manufacturers' Guild/ Guilde des manufacturiers de vêtement de mode du Québec (1938)
#300, 9250, av du Parc, Montréal, PQ H2N 1Z2
514/384-3800, Fax: 514/383-5411
Executive Director, S. Purcell
Office Manager, Francine Paquette

Shoe Industry Suppliers' Association of Canada/ Association des fournisseurs à l'industrie de la chaussure du Canada (SISAC) (1953)
4101, rue Sherbrooke ouest, Montréal, PQ H3Z 1A8
514/937-8118, Fax: 514/937-7066
President, Shirley Laliberté
Sec.-Treas., Diane Cappella

Shoe Manufacturers' Association of Canada/ Association des manufacturiers de chaussures du Canada (SMAC) (1919)
4101, rue Sherbrooke ouest, Montréal, PQ H3Z 1A8
514/937-8118, Fax: 514/937-7066
President, Nathan Finkelstein
Executive Secretary, Diane Cappella
Publications: Update/Au point

Textile Federation of Canada/La Fédération canadienne du textile
1 Pacifique, Ste-Anne-de-Bellevue, PQ H9X 1C5
514/457-2347, Fax: 514/457-2147
Chairman, Ben Staving
Publications: Canadian Textile Journal

Wool Bureau of Canada
#820, 33 Yonge St., Toronto, ON M5E 1G4
416/361-1440, Fax: 416/361-3179, Toll Free: 1-800-986-9665, Email: woolmark@woolmark
URL: http://www.woolmark.com

FESTIVALS see **EVENTS**

FILM & VIDEO
see also Broadcasting

Academy of Canadian Cinema & Television/ Académie canadienne du cinéma et de la télévision (ACCT) (1979)
158 Pearl St., Toronto, ON M5H 1L3
416/591-2040, Fax: 416/591-2157, Toll Free: 1-800-644-5194
URL: http://www.academy.ca
CEO, Maria Topalovich
Chair, Ann Medina
National Vice-Chairman, David Cronenberg
Treasurer, John Vandervelde
Publications: Infocus; Who's Who in Canadian Film & TV

Alberta Motion Picture Industries Association (AMPIA) (1973)
606 Midland Walwyn Tower, Edmonton Centre, Edmonton, AB T5J 2Z2
403/944-0707, Fax: 403/426-3057
Executive Director, Deborah Braun
President, Andy Thomson, 403/482-2022
Executive Assistant, Catherine Morrison
Communications Officer, J. Margolis
Publications: AMPIA Directory; Moving Pictures, bi-m.

Association des producteurs de films et de télévision du Québec (APFTQ)
#201, 740, rue St-Maurice, Montréal, PQ H3C 1L5
514/397-8600, Téléc: 514/392-0232
Présidente-directrice générale, Louise Baillargeon
Organisation(s) affiliée(s): Canadian Association of Film Distributors & Exporters

Association québécoise des réalisateurs et réalisatrices de cinéma et de télévision (AQRRCT) (1973)
#122, 1600, rue de Lorimier, Montréal, PQ H2K 3W5
514/521-1984, postes 436, 437; 514/527-2197, Téléc: 514/527-7699
Président, François Côté
Directrice, Martine Maltais
Publications: Action
Organisation(s) affiliée(s): Coalition des créateurs et titulaires de droits d'auteur; Association littéraire et artistique internationale

Atlantic Filmmakers' Co-operative (AFCOOP) (1973)
PO Box 2043, Stn M, Halifax, NS B3J 2Z1
902/423-8833, Fax: 902/425-7339
Lynda Rossborough
Publications: AFCOOP News
Affiliates: Independent Film & Video Alliance; Academy of Canadian Cinema & TV; Linda Joy Busby Media Arts Foundation; Atlantic Independent Media; Atlantic Film Festival

British Columbia Motion Picture Association (BCMPA) (1965)
#305, 1622 West 7th Ave., Vancouver, BC V6J 1S5
604/736-8794, Fax: 604/736-4627
Administrative Director, Brenda D. Collins
Publications: BCMPA Newsletter

Canadian Animation Producers Association (CAPA)
c/o Nelvana Ltd., 32 Atlantic Ave., Toronto, ON M6K 1X9
416/588-5571, Fax: 416/588-5588
President, Michael Hirsh

Canadian Association of Video Distributors (1985)
4222 Manor St., Burnaby, BC V5G 1B2
604/433-3331, Fax: 604/433-4815
Executive Director, William McCartney

Canadian Film Centre/Centre canadien du film (CFC) (1988)
2489 Bayview Ave., North York, ON M2L 1A8
416/445-1446, Fax: 416/445-9481
URL: http://www.hype.com/cfc/home.htm
Executive Director, S. Wayne Clarkson
Chair, Barbara Barde
Founder & Chair Emeritus, Norman Jewison
Publications: at the centre

Canadian Film Institute/Institut canadien du film (CFI) (1935)
2 Daly Ave., Ottawa, ON K1N 6E2
613/232-8769, Fax: 613/232-6727, Info Line: 232-7662
President, Serge Losique
Director of Programming, Tom McSorley
Affiliates: Cinémathèque Canada

Canadian Film & Television Production Association/Association canadienne de production de film et télévision (CFTPA) (1948)
#806, 175 Bloor St. East, Toronto, ON M4W 3R8
416/927-8942, Fax: 416/922-4038
President, Elizabeth McDonald
Vice-President, Industrial Relations & Training, Mireille Watson
Publications: ACTION; CFTPA Directory of Members; The Guide, a.

Canadian Filmmakers Distribution Centre (CFMDC) (1967)
#220, 37 Hanna Ave., Toronto, ON M6K 1W8
416/588-0725, Fax: 416/588-7956, Email: cfmdc@gold.interlog.com

ORGANIZATIONS — FINANCE 2-69

Alan McNairn
Publications: The Independent Eye; Film Catalogue, a.
Affiliates: Canadian Filmmakers Distribution West

Canadian Motion Picture Distributors Association/Association canadienne des distributeurs de film (CMPDA) (1920)
#1603, 22 St. Clair Ave. East, Toronto, ON M4T 2S3
416/961-1888, Fax: 416/968-1016
Vice-President & Acting Director, Susan Peacock
Affiliates: Motion Picture Association of America, Inc.

Canadian Picture Pioneers (CPP) (1940)
#906, 21 Dundas Sq., Toronto, ON M5B 1B7
416/368-1139, Fax: 416/368-1130
President, Philip R. Carlton
Executive Assistant, Barry Chapman
Publications: CPP Newsletter

Canadian Society of Cinematographers (CSC)
#602, 235 Carlaw Ave., Toronto, ON M4M 2S1
416/466-5013
Contact, Jennifer Hietala
Publications: CSC Directory; CSC Newsletter, 10 pa

La Cinémathèque québécoise (1963)
Musée au cinéma
335, boul de Maisonneuve est, Montréal, PQ H2X 1K1
514/842-9763, Téléc: 514/842-1816
Directeur à la conservation, Robert Daudelin
Directeur à la gestion, Charles-Mathieu Brunelle
Directeur des communications, Jean Hamel
Directeur des Services Techniques, François Auger
Publications: Revue de la Cinémathèque

Directors Guild of Canada/La Guilde canadienne des réalisateurs (DGC) (1962)
#401, 387 Bloor St. East, Toronto, ON M4W 1H7
416/972-0098, Fax: 416/972-6058
President, Allan King
National Executive Secretary, Pamela Brand
Publications: DGC National News
Affiliates: ACTRA; Directors' Guild of America

Dreamspeakers Festival Society (1991)
9914 - 76 Ave., Edmonton, AB T6E 1K7
403/439-3456, Fax: 403/439-2066
Executive Director, Sharon Shirt

Festival international du court métrage de Montréal/Montréal International Short Film Festival (FICMM) (1993)
#326, 4205, rue St-Denis, Montréal, PQ H2J 2K9
514/285-4515, Téléc: 514/285-2886, Télex: 05-829647
Directeur général, Bernard Boulad
Directeur administratif, Paul-Jacques Hulot
Publications: Programme du festival

Independent Film & Video Alliance/Alliance de la vidéo et du cinéma indépendant (IFVA) (1980)
#3000, 5505, boul St-Laurent, Montréal, PQ H2T 1S6
514/277-0328, Fax: 514/277-0419, Toll Free: 1-800-567-0328, Email: ifva@cam.org
URL: http://www.ffa.ucalgary.ca/
National Coordinator, Peter Sandmark
President, Jean Claude Bustros
Publications: Alliance Bulletin/Le Bulletin de l'Alliance

Motion Picture Theatre Associations of Canada/ Les associations des propriétaires des cinémas du Canada (MPTAC) (1967)
1303 Yonge St., Toronto, ON M4T 2Y9
416/323-7214, Fax: 416/232-6633
Executive Director, Dina Lebo

The Moving Pictures Travelling Canadian Film Festival Society (1993)
#410, 1008 Homer St., Vancouver, BC V6B 2X1
604/685-8952, Fax: 604/688-8221
Festival Director, John Dippong
Publications: Newsletter

National Screen Institute - Canada/Institute national des arts de l'écran - Canada (NSI) (1985)
10022 - 103 St., 3rd Fl., Edmonton, AB T5J 0X2
403/421-4084, Fax: 403/425-8098, Toll Free: 1-800-480-4084
Executive Director, Jan Miller
Office Manager, Karen Cameron
Publications: Screen Sheet

Ontario Film Association, Inc. (OFA) (1949)
Association for the Advancement of Visual Media
#1341, 3-1750 The Queensway, Etobicoke, ON M9C 5H5
416/761-6056
Executive Director, Margaret Nix, Fax: 905/820-7397
Publications: Visual Media/Medias visuels

Saskatchewan Motion Picture Association (SMPIA) (1989)
2431 - 8th Ave., Regina, SK S4R 5J7
306/525- 9899, Fax: 306/569-1818, Email: smpia@uni-base.com
URL: http://midxpress.com/midxpress/smpia/main.htm
Executive Director, Elizabeth Verrall
Communications Officer, Colleen Mahoney
Publications: Storyboard; Saskatchewan Motion Picture Industry Directory, s-a.

FILM FESTIVALS see EVENTS

FINANCE
see also Taxation

Association des cadres financiers municipaux du Québec
#690, 1265 rue Berri, Montréal, PQ H2L 4X4
514/499-1130, Téléc: 514/499-1737, Télex: 051-3898
Diane Toupin

Association of Canadian Financial Corporations/ Association des compagnies financières canadiennes (ACFC) (1944)
Sussex Centre, #401, 50 Burnhamthorpe Rd. West, Mississauga, ON L5B 3C2
905/949-4920, Fax: 905/896-9380
President, John Bohdan Gregorovich

Association of Canadian Pension Management (ACPM) (1976)
#1103, 60 Bloor St. West, Toronto, ON M4W 3B8
416/964-1260, Fax: 416/964-0567
Executive Director, Marcia Barrett
President, Andrea Vincent
Vice-President, Patricia Cox
Publications: ACPM Reporter; Supplement, q.; Penfacts: A Guide to Pensions in Canada, a.

Association of Canadian Venture Capital Companies (ACVCC)
#1000, 120 Eglinton Ave. East, Toronto, ON M4P 1E2
416/487-0519, Fax: 416/483-9241
Executive Director, Deborah Cummings

Association de planification fiscale et financière (APFF) (1976)
#300, 445, boul Saint-Laurent, Montréal, PQ H2Y 2Y7
514/866-2733, Téléc: 514/866-0113
Président et directeur général, Yvon L. Caron

Publications: Flash Fiscal; Livre du congrès, annuel; Revue de planification fiscale et successorale, trimestrielle

The Canadian Association of Financial Planners (CAFP)
#1710, 439 University Ave., Toronto, ON M5G 1Y8
416/593-6592, Fax: 416/593-8459, Toll Free: 1-800-346-2237
Executive Director, Farida Karim
National Chairman, Fred Smith, RFP
President, Gary R. Duncan, CA, RFP
Publications: The Canadian Financial Planner

Canadian Association of Pension Supervisory Authorities/Association canadienne des organismes de contrôle des régimes de retraite (CAPSA)
250 Yonge St., 29th Fl., Toronto, ON M5B 2N7
416/314-0660, Fax: 416/314-0650
Susan Ellis

Canadian Association of Student Financial Aid Administrators
Queens University, Student Awards Office, 110 Alfred St., Kingston, ON K7L 3N6
613/545-2216, Fax: 613/545-6409
Director, P. Bogstad

Canadian Bankers Association/Association des banquiers canadiens (CBA) (1893)
Commerce Court West, 30th Fl., PO Box 348, Stn Commerce Court, Toronto, ON M5L 1G2
416/362-6092, Fax: 416/362-7705, Toll Free: 1-800-263-0231, Email: inform@cba.ca
URL: http://www.cba.ca/
President & CEO, Raymond J. Protti
Publications: Canadian Banker

Canadian Corporate Shareholder Services Association/Association canadienne des services aux actionnaires (CCSSA) (1985)
Royal Trust Tower, Toronto Dominion Centre, PO Box 110, Stn Toronto Dominion, Toronto, ON M5K 1G8
President, Francoise Bureau, 514/394-6081
Publications: Newsletter

Canadian Council of Financial Analysts
#1702, 390 Bay St., Toronto, ON M5H 2Y2
416/366-5755, Fax: 416/366-6716
Director, Deborah Kent

Canadian Finance & Leasing Association/ Association canadienne de financement et de location (CFLA) (1973)
Box 7, #1210, 151 Yonge St., Toronto, ON M5C 2W7
416/860-1133, Fax: 416/860-1140
URL: http://www.inforamp.net/~mreid/cfla.html
President & COO, David Powell
Chairman, Tim Hammill
Publications: Voicebox
Affiliates: Equipment Lessors Association of America

Canadian Insolvency Practitioners Association/ Association canadienne des professionnels de l'insolvabilité (CIPA) (1979)
277 Wellington St. West, Toronto, ON M5V 3H2
416/204-3242, Fax: 416/204-3410
Executive Director, Norman H. Kondo
President, Ralph W. Peterson, CA, CIP
Affiliates: The Canadian Institute of Chartered Accountants

Canadian Institute of Financial Planning (CIFP)
#503, 151 Yonge St., Toronto, ON M5C 2W7
416/865-1237, Fax: 416/861-9937
Executive Director, John W. Murray

Canadian Almanac & Directory 1997

Vice-President, Donald Johnston
Affiliates: Investment Funds Institute of Canada; Canadian Association of Financial Planners; Life Underwriters Association of Canada

Canadian Payments Association/Association canadienne des paiements (CPA) (1980)
#1212, 50 O'Connor St., Ottawa, ON K1P 6L2
613/238-4173, Fax: 613/233-3385
General Manager, Robert M. Hammond
Chairman, Serge Vachon
Director, Communications & Education, Wendy P. Hope
Publications: Forum; Review

The Canadian Payroll Association/L'Association canadienne de la paie (CPA) (1979)
#801, 1867 Yonge St., Toronto, ON M4S 1Y5
416/487-3380, Fax: 416/487-3384, Info Line: 416/487-3620, Toll Free: 1-800-387-4693, Email: bill@payroll.ca
URL: http://www.payroll.ca/
Chair & CEO, Ann Turner-Murphy
Vice-President & COO, Bill Williams
Publications: Dialogue Magazine

Canadian Pension & Benefits Institute/Institut canadien de la retraite et des avantages sociaux (1960)
#305, 2035, rue Victoria, Saint-Lambert, PQ J4S 1H1
514/465-4400, Fax: 514/465-1921
Executive Director, Louis-Joseph Reginbal
President, John J. Goodwin
Sec.-Treas., Pierre Laqueux
Publications: Forum

The Canadian Securities Institute/Institut canadien des valeurs mobilières (CSI) (1970)
#1550, 121 King St. West, PO Box 113, Toronto, ON M5H 3T9
416/364-9130, Fax: 416/359-0486
President, Dr. Roberta Wilton
Affiliates: Investment Dealers Association of Canada; Montreal Exchange; Toronto, Alberta, & Vancouver Stock Exchanges

Confédération des caisses populaires et d'économie desjardins du Québec (CCPÉDQ)
100, av des Commandeurs, Lévis, PQ G6V 7N5
418/835-2661, Téléc: 418/833-4769, Télex: 051-3533, Ligne sans frais: 1-800-463-4810
1er Président, Michel Doray
Chef du cabinet du président, Daniel Roussel
Directeur, Affairs Publiques et Communications Institutionnelles, Dominique De Pasquale

Credit Association of Canada/Association des directeurs de crédit du Canada (CAC) (1944)
St. Mary's Credit Union, 1515 - 20th St, Saskatoon, SK S7M 0Z5
306/382-1177, Fax: 306/382-7600
President, A. Musey
Publications: Credit Canada
Affiliates: International Credit Association

Credit Institute of Canada/L'Institut canadien du crédit (CIC) (1928)
#501, 5090 Explorer Dr., Mississauga, ON L4W 3T9
905/629-9805, Fax: 905/629-9809
President & Dean, Jim Tolton, CD, ACI
Corporate Secretary, Brenda Cornell
Publications: The Credit & Financial Journal

Credit Union Central of Canada/La Centrale des caisses de crédit du Canada (1953)
300 The East Mall, 5th Fl., Toronto, ON M9B 6B7
416/232-1262, Fax: 416/232-9196
URL: http://www.cucentral.ca

President/CEO, William G. Knight
Director, Communications, Veronica Feldcamp
Publications: Briefs
Affiliates: World Council of Credit Unions

Credit Union Institute of Canada (CUIC) (1972)
#400, 275 Bank St., Ottawa, ON K2P 2L6
613/238-4940, Fax: 613/567-0658

CREDITEL Division of Equifax Canada Inc.
110 Sheppard Ave. East, North York, ON M2N 6S1
416/590-8500
President/General Manager, Marcel A. Desautels
Sec.-Treas., A.D. Stirling

Fédération des associations coopérative d'économie familiale du Québec/Federation of Family Economics Cooperative Associations of Québec (FACEF) (1970)
#305, 5225, rue Berri, Montréal, PQ H2J 2S4
514/271-7004
Présidente, Louise Blain
Publications: Changements
Organisation(s) affiliée(s): International Organization of Consumers Unions

Fédération des caisses d'économie Desjardins du Québec (1962)
7755, boul Louis H. Lafontaine, Anjou, PQ H1L 4R5
514/353-4960, Téléc: 514/353-0588
Directeur général, Gilles Lafleur
Publications: Journal d'entreprise

Fédération des caisses populaires du Manitoba inc.
#200, 605, rue Des Meurons, CP 68, Winnipeg, MB R2H 3B4
204/237-8988, Téléc: 204/233-6405
Directeur général, Fernand Vermette

Fédération des caisses populaires de l'Ontario (FCPO) (1946)
450 Rideau St., Ottawa, ON K1N 5Z4
613/789-7777, Téléc: 613/789-3763
Directeur général, Pierre Lacasse
Administration et finance, Alain Boucher
Crédit et gestion réseau, Daniel Brault
Ressources humaines, Alain Kervran
Systèmes et marketing, Jean-Guy Laflèche
Publications: Info-Fédé
Organisation(s) affiliée(s): Mouvement Desjardins

Financial Executives Institute Canada
#1701, 141 Adelaide St. West, Toronto, ON M5H 3L5
416/366-3007, Fax: 416/366-3008
Director, Professional Affairs, Stan Udaskin
Publications: Newsletter

Institute of Canadian Bankers/Institut des banquiers canadiens
Tour Scotia, #1000, 1002, rue Sherbrooke ouest, 10e étage, Montréal, PQ H3A 3M5
514/282-9480, Fax: 514/282-8881
Executive Director, Dr. Rosaire Couturier
Atlantic Regional Office: Queen's Court, #501, 5475 Spring Garden Rd., Halifax, NS B3J 1G2, 902/429-0440, Fax: 902/429-5478
Ontario Regional Office: Regional Director, Anne Wettlaufer, #3000, 199 Bay St., PO Box 348, Stn Commerce Court, Toronto, ON M5L 1G2, 416/362-6092, Fax: 416/362-2939
Québec Regional Office: #1000, 1002, rue Sherbrooke ouest, 10th Fl., Montréal, PQ H3A 3M5, 514/282-9480, Téléc: 514/282-8881
Western Regional Office: #805, 550 - 6 Ave. SW, Calgary, AB T2P 0S2, 403/262-3422, Fax: 403/233-7698

International Association of State Lotteries/Association internationale des loteries d'état (AILE) (1958)
500, rue Sherbrooke ouest, Montréal, PQ H3A 3G6
514/282-0273, Fax: 514/873-8999, Telex: 055-60178, Email: aile@cam.ort
President, Guy Simonis
General Secretary, Marguerite Bourgeois
Publications: AILE Directory; AILE Review, q.

International Organization of Securities Commissions/Organisation internationale des commissions de valeurs (IOSCO) (1983)
Stock Exchange Tower, 800 Square Victoria, 42th Fl., PO Box 171, Montréal, PQ H4Z 1C8
514/875-8278, Fax: 514/875-2669, Telex: 05-26 8761
Secretary General, Eudald Canadell
Publications: Annual Report

Investment Counsel Association of Ontario (ICAO) (1952)
61 Shaw St., Toronto, ON M6J 2W3
416/504-1118, Fax: 416/504-1117
President, Kenneth E. Rae
Vice-President, William E. Rogan
Secretary, Robert R. McInnes
Treasurer, David Pennycook
Executive Director, Keith A. Douglas
Publications: Member Letter

Investment Dealers Association of Canada/Association canadienne des courtiers en valeurs mobilières (IDA) (1916)
#1600, 121 King St. West, Toronto, ON M5H 3T9
416/364-6133, Fax: 416/364-0753
President & CEO, Joseph J. Oliver
Chairman, John A. MacNaughton
Vice-President, Capital Markets, Ian Russell
Corporate Secretary & Vice-President, Operations, Eileen M. Andrews
Vice-President, Member Regulation, Gregory M. Clarke
Vice-President, Government & Member Relations, D.W. Grant
Publications: IDA Report; Provincial Economic Outlooks, a.; Capital Markets Update/Structural Trends in Canada Markets, s-a.; Economic Indicator Card, 3 pa; Statistical Bulletin, bi-m.; Fiscal Report Card; Bulletins
Affiliates: National Association of Securities Dealers; Securities Industry Association; Public Securities Association; Securities & Exchange Commission
Calgary Office: #2330, 355 - 4 Ave. SW, Calgary, AB T2P 0J1, 403/262-6393, Fax: 403/265-4603
Montréal Office: #2802, 1, Place Ville Marie, Montréal, PQ H3B 4R4, 514/878-2854, Téléc: 514/878-3860
Vancouver Office: Bentall Four, #944, 1055 Dunsmuir St., PO Box 49151, Vancouver, BC V7X 1J1, 604/683-6222, Fax: 604/683-6050

Investment Funds Institute of Canada/L'Institut des fonds d'investissement du Canada (IFIC) (1962)
#503, 151 Yonge St., Toronto, ON M5C 2W7
416/363-2158, Fax: 416/861-9937, Email: ific@mutfunds.com
URL: http://www.mutfunds.com/ific
President & CEO, The Honourable Thomas A. Hockin
Chairman, Andrew Scipio del Campo
Publications: IFIC Update Newsletter

Investors Association of Canada (IAC) (1986)
#380, 26 Soho St., Toronto, ON M5T 1Z7
416/340-1722, Fax: 416/340-9202
Chairman, Chuck Chakrapani
Publications: Money Digest

Municipal Finance Officers Association of Ontario
121 John St., Toronto, ON M5V 2E2
416/979-1414, Fax: 416/979-1060
Executive Director, Heather Bell

Ontario Association of Credit Counselling Services (OACCS) (1975)
PO Box 278, Grimsby, ON L3M 4G5
905/945-5644, Fax: 905/945-4680, Toll Free: 1-800-263-0260
Executive Director, Patricia White
Board President, John Curran
Publications: Connections

Ontario Mortgage Brokers Association (OMBA) (1960)
#8, 951 Wilson Ave., Downsview, ON M3K 2A7
416/631-0320, Fax: 416/631-8165
Executive Director, Lorne H. Collis

Ontario Society of Collection Agencies
77 Samuel Cres., Georgetown, ON L7G 5J3
905/873-2920
Executive Director, Don Sinclair

Pension Investment Association of Canada/ Association Canadienne des Gestionnaires de Fonds de Retraite (PIAC) (1977)
61 Shaw St., Toronto, ON M6J 2W3
416/504-1116, Fax: 416/504-1117
General Manager, Keith A. Douglas, CAE
Publications: Communique

Social Investment Organization (SIO) (1989)
#443, 366 Adelaide St. East, Toronto, ON M5A 3X9
416/360-6047, Fax: 416/861-0123, Email: 810@web.apc.org
Executive Director, Marc de Sousa-Shields
Director, Marketing & Membership Services, Darrell Ross
Publications: The SIO Forum; The SIO Forum Back Issues; Social Investment Groups & Activities, a.

Treasury Management Association of Canada/ Association de gestion de trésorerie du Canada (TMAC) (1982)
#1010, 8 King St. East, Toronto, ON M5C 1B5
416/367-8500, Fax: 416/367-3240, Email: tmac@inforamp.net
URL: http://www.tmac.ca./
Executive Vice-President, John Bumister
President, Keith Briggeman
Manager of Administration, Patricia Wood
Publications: The Canadian Treasurer
Affiliates: Canadian Institute of Chartered Accountants; Society of Management Accountants; Certified General Accountants; Financial Management Institute of Canada; Canadian Securities Lending Association
Insurance Companies TMA: Barbara Hryniewicz, c/o TMAC National Office, #1010, 8 King St. East, Toronto, ON M5C 1B5
Markham/York Region TMA: Director, Treasury, Johanne Bouchard, c/o AIMCO, 10 Allstate Pkwy., Markham, ON L3R 5P8
TMAC - Atlantic Canada: Manager, Banking & Debt Services, Thomas Collins, c/o Province of Nova Scotia, PO Box 187, Stn Central, Halifax, NS B3J 2N3, 902/424-5772, Fax: 902/429-0257
TMAC - B.C.: Coordinator, Cash Management, Anne Murdock, c/o Cominco Ltd., 200 Burrard St., Vancouver, BC V6C 3L7, 604/685-3096, Fax: 604/685-3089
TMAC - Calgary: Assistant Supervisor, Operations, Tracy Gerlitz, c/o TransCanada Pipelines, PO Box 1000, Stn M, Calgary, AB T2P 4K5, 403/267-6275, Fax: 403/267-8548

TMAC - Edmonton: Pam McCorkle, c/o Bank of Montréal, 10199 - 101 St., 2nd Fl., Edmonton, AB T5J 3Y4, 403/428-7319, Fax: 403/428-7305
TMAC - Manitoba: Financial Administration Officer, Marleen Church, c/o Manitoba Hydro, 820 Taylor, PO Box 815, Stn Main, Winnipeg, MB R3C 2P4, 204/474-4510, Fax: 204/474-3769
TMAC - Montréal: Associate Vice-President & Regional Director, Sean Sirois, c/o Toronto Dominion Bank, 500, rue Saint-Jacques, 5e étage, Montréal, PQ H2Y 1S1, 514/289-0152, Téléc: 514/289-0173
TMAC - Ottawa: Chief, Funds Acct. & Borrowing Admin., Chandra De Silva, c/o Canada Mortgage & Housing Corp., 700 Montréal Rd., Ottawa, ON K1A 0P7, 613/748-4010, Fax: 613/748-4849
TMAC - Regina: Treasurer, Bill Edwards, c/o Sask Tel, 2121 Saskatchewan Dr., 6th Fl., Regina, SK S4P 3Y2, 306/777-4772, Fax: 306/777-5539
TMAC - Toronto: General Manager, Cash Management, Susan Frostad, c/o CIBC, 7th Fl., CCW, Commerce Court, Toronto, ON M5L 1A2, 416/980-7060, Fax: 416/363-7982
Toronto Cash Management Society: Assistant Treasurer, Randy Brown, c/o Phillips Cables Limited, #200, 300 Consilium Place, Scarborough, ON M1H 3G2, 416/296-0250, Fax: 416/296-0755
Waterloo Wellington Cash & TMA: Treasury Manager, Joan Planta, c/o The Mutual Group, 227 King St. South, Waterloo, ON N2G 4C5, 519/888-3547, Fax: 519/888-3882

The Trust Companies Association of Canada/ L'Association des compagnies de fiducie du Canada (1952)
One Financial Place, #1002, 1 Adelaide St. East, PO Box 137, Toronto, ON M5C 2V9
416/866-8842, Fax: 416/866-2122
Corporate Secretary, Christine Kniehl

FIRST AID & SAFETY *see* **EMERGENCY RESPONSE**

FISHERIES & FISHING INDUSTRY
see also Marine Trades

Alliance des pêcheurs professionnels du Québec
#100, 56, rue St-Pierre, Québec, PQ G1K 4A1
418/692-1148, Téléc: 418/692-1854
Directeur général, François Poulin

Association québécoise de l'industrie de la pêche/Québec Fish Processor Association (AQIP) (1978)
1458, av Maguire, Sillery, PQ G1T 1Z4
418/527-3252, Téléc: 418/527-3360
Président, Jean-Paul Gagné
Publications: AQIP-Action

Atlantic Salmon Federation/Fédération du saumon atlantique (ASF) (1948)
PO Box 429, St. Andrews, NB E0G 2X0
506/529-4581, Fax: 506/529-4438, Email: atlsal@nbnet.nb.ca
URL: http://www.flyfishing.com/asf/
President, Bill Taylor
Director, Communications, Sue Scott
Publications: The Atlantic Salmon Journal; Salar; On The Rise, q.
Affiliates: Federation of Fly Fishers; Theodore Gordon Flyfishers; Trout Unlimited; Canadian Wildlife Federation

BC Salmon Farmers Association (BCSFA) (1984)
#506, 1200 Pender St. West, Vancouver, BC V6E 2S9
604/682-3077, Fax: 604/669-6974, Toll Free: 1-800-661-7256

Executive Director, Greg D'Avignon
Publications: Newsletter

BC Shellfish Growers Association (BCSGA) (1964)
647A Bunting Place, Comox, BC V9M 3R1
250/339-7419, Fax: 250/339-7463
President, Dave Mitchell
Vice-President, Judith Reid
Office Manager, Dave Conley
Publications: BC Shellfish Growers Association

BC Trout Farmers Association
24831 - 80 Ave., Langley, BC V3A 4P9
604/888-0660
President, Juanita Bouwmeester
Affiliates: Canadian Aquaculture Producers' Council

Canadian Aquaculture Industry Alliance/Alliance de l'industrie canadienne de l'aquiculture (CAIA) (1995)
45 O'Connor St., 20th Fl., Ottawa, ON K1P 1A4
613/788-6851, Fax: 613/235-7012, Email: sford.caia@eworld.com
Executive Director, Sharon Ford
President, William Thompson
Vice-President, Greg D'Avignon
Sec.-Treas., Gary Chapman

Canadian Association of Fish Exporters (CAFE) (1978)
#212, 1770 Woodward Dr., Ottawa, ON K2C 0P8
613/228-9220, Fax: 613/228-9223
President, Jane Barnett, Ph.D.
Operations Manager, Cynthia Smith
Publications: Seafood Canada; CAFE Seafood Market Report, m.

Canadian Centre for Fisheries Innovation/Centre canadien d'innovations des pêches (CCFI) (1989)
Ridge Rd., PO Box 4920, Stn C, St. John's, NF A1C 5R3
709/778-0517, Fax: 709/778-0516, Email: ccfi@gill.ifmt.nf.ca
Managing Director, Alastair O'Rielly
Chairman, Ian J. Reid
Affiliates: Memorial University of Newfoundland; Marine Institute

Fisheries Council of Canada/Conseil canadien des pêches (FCC) (1945)
#806, 141 Laurier Ave. West, Ottawa, ON K1P 5J3
613/238-7751, Fax: 613/238-3542
President, Ronald W. Bulmer
Vice-President, P.J. McGuinness
Chairman, Henry Demone
Publications: Fish & Seafood Products & Services Directory
Affiliates: International Coalition of Fisheries Associations; North Atlantic Seafood Association

FISH & SEAFOOD ASSOCIATION OF ONTARIO
c/o National Sea Products Ltd., #410, 295 The West Mall, Etobicoke, ON M9C 4Z4
416/622-9855, Fax: 416/622-7615
President, Gini Norris

FISHERIES ASSOCIATION OF NEWFOUNDLAND & LABRADOR LTD. (1945)
90 O'Leary Ave., PO Box 8900, Stn A, St. John's, NF A1B 3R9
709/726-7223, Fax: 709/754-3339
President, Bruce W. Chapman
Chairman, Bill Wells

FISHERIES COUNCIL OF BRITISH COLUMBIA
#1400, 1188 Georgia St. East, Vancouver, BC V6E 4A2

Canadian Almanac & Directory 1997

2-72 ORGANIZATIONS — FOOD & BEVERAGE INDUSTRY

604/684-6454, Fax: 604/684-5109
President, Michael Hunter

NEW BRUNSWICK FISH PACKERS' ASSOCIATION/L'ASSOCIATION DES EMPAQUETEURS DE POISSON DU NOUVEAU-BRUNSWICK (NBFPA) (1946)
#104, 1133 St. George Blvd., Moncton, NB E1E 4E1
506/857-3056, Fax: 506/857-3059
Executive Director, Peter A. Dysart
Affiliates: Canadian Manufacturers Association

PRINCE EDWARD ISLAND SEAFOOD PROCESSORS ASSOCIATION
c/o Atlantic Fish Specialties Ltd., 17 Walker Dr., Parkdale, PE C1A 8S5
902/894-7005, Fax: 902/566-3546
President, Jim Dunphy

SEAFOOD PRODUCERS ASSOCIATION OF NOVA SCOTIA
Queen Square, #1801, 45 Alderney Dr., PO Box 991, Dartmouth, NS B2Y 3Z6
902/463-7790, Fax: 902/469-8294
President, Roger C. Stirling

New Brunswick Salmon Growers Association (1987)
Lime Kiln Rd., RR#4, St. George, NB E0G 2Y0
506/755-3526, Fax: 506/755-6237
General Manager, William Thompson

Nova Scotia Salmon Association (NSSA) (1965)
#611, 5959 Spring Garden Rd., Halifax, NS B3H 1Y5
902/423-0077, Fax: 902/422-1415
Contact, K. Rice
Publications: Upstream

Ontario Aquaculture Association
PO Box 324, Elmira, ON N3B 2Z6
519/669-3400, Fax: 519/669 2864
Administrator, Laurie Taylor

Prince Edward Island Fishermen's Association
53 Queen St., PO Box 2224, Charlottetown, PE C1A 8B9
902/566-4050, Fax: 902/368-3748
Managing Director, Rory McLellan

FOLK ARTS see VISUAL ART, CRAFTS, FOLK ARTS

FOOD & BEVERAGE INDUSTRY

Association des brasseurs du Québec/Québec Brewers Association
Tour Laurentienne, #475, 1981, av McGill College, Montréal, PQ H3A 2W9
514/284-9199, Téléc: 514/284-0817
Directeur général, Yvon Millette

Association of Canadian Biscuit Manufacturers/ Association canadienne des manufacturiers de biscuits (ACBM) (1965)
885 Don Mills Rd., North York, ON M3C 1V9
416/510-8036
Executive Director, Carol A. Findlay
President, Gary MacLeod

Association of Canadian Distillers/Association des distallateurs canadiens (ACD) (1947)
#1100, 90 Sparks St., Ottawa, ON K1P 5T8
613/238-8444, Fax: 613/238-3411, Telex: 0533783
President, Ronald Veilleux
Chairman, Richard Fitzgerald
Vice-President, Communications, Françoise Parent

Association des distributeurs aux services alimentaires du Québec (ADSAQ) (1979)
#210, 8585, boul St-Laurent, Montréal, PQ H2P 2M9

Canadian Almanac & Directory 1997

514/385-5312
Personne ressource, Suzie Mousseau

Association des manufacturiers de produits alimentaires du Québec/Québec Food Processors Association (AMPAQ) (1954)
Édifice De Bleury, #102, 200, rue MacDonald, St-Jean-sur-Richelieu, PQ J3B 8J6
514/349-1521, Téléc: 514/349-6923
Directeur général, André Latour, caé
Publications: Courrier

Bakery Council of Canada/Conseil canadien de la boulangerie (BCC) (1947)
#301, 885 Don Mills Rd., Toronto, ON M3C 1V9
416/510-8041, Fax: 416/510-8043
President, Paul Hetherington
Affiliates: Grocery Products Manufacturers of Canada

Breakfast Cereal Manufacturers of Canada (1983)
#301, 885 Don Mills Rd., North York, ON M3C 1V9
416/510-8036, Fax: 416/510-8043
Manager, Shelly Girvan
Affiliates: Grocery Products Manufacturers of Canada

Brewers Association of Canada/Association des brasseurs du Canada (1943)
Heritage Place, #1200, 155 Queen St., Ottawa, ON K1P 6L1
613/232-9601, Fax: 613/232-2283
President & CEO, R.A. (Sandy) Morrison
Executive Assistant, M.E. Murphy
Publications: International Survey; Alcohol Taxation & Control Policies

Brewing & Malting Barley Research Institute/ Institut de recherche - brassage et orge de maltage (BMBRI) (1948)
#206, 167 Lombard Ave., Winnipeg, MB R3B 0T6
204/942-1407, Fax: 204/947-5960
Managing Director, N.T. Kendall, Ph.D.
President, J.T. Steer
Publications: Barley Briefs

Canadian Association of Specialty Foods/ L'Association canadienne des aliments fins (CASF) (1985)
19 Burlingame Rd., Etobicoke, ON M8W 1Y7
416/255-7071, Fax: 416/253-6571
Executive Director, Loraine Longo
Publications: Communiqué

Canadian Bottled Water Federation/Fédération canadienne des eaux embouteillées (CBWF) (1987)
#203-1, 70 East Beaver Creek Rd., Richmond Hill, ON L4B 3B2
905/886-6928, Fax: 905/886-9531, Email: ecgriswood@all.adl.com
Executive Director, Elisabeth Griswold-Woodworth
Publications: Water Power
Affiliates: Canadian Bottled Water Federation

Canadian Coalition to Stop Food Irradiation (1986)
#202, 5262 Rumble St., Burnaby, BC V5J 2B6
604/435-0512, Fax: 604/435-1561
Director, Lila Parker

Canadian College & University Food Service Association
National Office, Drew Hall, University of Guelph, Guelph, ON N1G 2W1
519/824-4120, Fax: 519/837-9302, Email: dboeckne@uoguelph.ca
Executive Director, David Boeckner
Publications: CCUFSA

Canadian Council of Grocery Distributors/Conseil canadien de la distribution alimentaire (CCGD) (1987)
CP 1082, Succ Place-du-Parc, Montréal, PQ H2W 2P4
514/982-0267, Fax: 514/849-3021
President/CEO, John F. Geci
Secretary, Francine Chevrier
Vice-President, Communications & Development, Monika Simon
Secretary, France Bessette
Publications: Precis; Bulletin; Communiqué
Affiliates: Retail Council of Canada

Canadian Dairy & Food Industries Supply Association/Association canadienne des fournisseurs des industries laitière & de l'alimentation (CDFISA) (1943)
1148 Vanier Dr., Mississauga, ON L5H 3X1
905/278-6496, Fax: 905/278-6496
Executive Secretary, Henry A. Dagorne
Publications: The Window
Affiliates: Dairy & Food Industries Supply Association (USA)

Canadian Federation of Independent Grocers/ Fédération canadienne des épiciers indépendants (CFIG) (1962)
#902, 2235 Sheppard Ave. East, North York, ON M2J 5B5
416/492-2311, Fax: 416/492-2347, Toll Free: 1-800-661-2344
President, John F.T. Scott
Executive Assistant, Leslie Johnston
Publications: The Independent Grocer; The Practical Grocer, q.

Canadian Food Brokers Association/Association canadienne des courtiers en alimentation (CFBA) (1943)
70 Aitken Circle, Unionville, ON L3R 7L1
905/477-4644, Fax: 905/477-9580, Email: bcraigon@idirect.com
URL: http://web.idirect.com/~cfba
Contact, Blair Craigon
Publications: CFBA News

Canadian Food Service Executives Association (CFSEA)
#3529, 1531 Bayview Ave., North York, ON M4G 4G8
416/421-5045, Fax: 416/421-5045
Business Manager, Carla Kelman

Canadian Food Supervisors' Association
#2G, 57 Simcoe St. South, Oshawa, ON L1H 7N1
905/436-0145, Fax: 905/436-2969

Canadian Health Food Association/Association canadienne des aliments de santé (CHFA) (1964)
370 Steelcase Rd. East, Markham, ON L3R 1G2
905/479-6939, Fax: 905/479-1516
Executive Director, Bill Reynolds

Canadian Hospitality Foundation (1962)
#213, 300 Adelaide St. East, Toronto, ON M5A 1N1
416/363-3401, Fax: 416/363-3403
Executive Director, Rigzin Dolkar

Canadian Industrial Sweetener Users (CISU) (1970)
#301, 885 Don Mills Rd., North York, ON M3C 1V9
416/510-8036, Fax: 416/510-8044, Info Line: 510-8044
Executive Director, David L. Armstrong
Affiliates: Grocery Products Manufacturers of Canada

Canadian Meat Council/Conseil des viandes du Canada (CMC) (1919)
Dow's Lake Court, #410, 875 Carling Ave., Ottawa, ON K1S 5P1

613/729-3911, Fax: 613/729-4997
General Manager, Robert Weaver

Canadian Meat Science Association
c/o Canadian Meat Council, #410, 875 Carling Ave., Ottawa, ON K1S 5P1
416/729-3911, Fax: 416/729-4997

Canadian National Millers Association (CNMA)
#1127, 90 Sparks St., Ottawa, ON K1P 5B4
613/238-2293, Fax: 613/235-5866
President, Gordon Harrison

Canadian Nut Council/Conseil canadien des noix (CNC) (1984)
#301, 885 Don Mills Rd., North York, ON M3C 1V9
416/510-8036, Fax: 416/510-8044
Manager, Linda N. Reid

Canadian Potato Chip/Snack Food Association/ Association canadienne des fabricants de chips/ grignotines (CPC) (1956)
#301, 885 Don Mills Rd., Toronto, ON M3C 1V9
416/510-8036, Fax: 416/510-8044
President, John Frostad
Manager, Linda N. Reid
Publications: CSFA Roster; Information Letter; Statistical Material
Affiliates: Canadian Horticultural Council

Canadian Produce Marketing Association/ Association canadienne de la distribution de fruits et légumes (CPMA) (1924)
#310, 1101 Prince of Wales Dr., Ottawa, ON K2C 3W7
613/226-4187, Fax: 613/226-2984
Executive Vice-President, Dan Dempster
Publications: Communiqué
Affiliates: Fresh for Flavour Foundation; Canadian Horticultural Council

Canadian Soft Drink Association/Association canadienne de l'industrie des boissons gazeuses (CSDA) (1942)
#330, 55 York St., Toronto, ON M5J 1R7
416/362-2424, Fax: 416/362-3229, Email: 102005.1662@compuserve.com
URL: http://www.softdrink.ca
President & CEO, Paulette Vinette, CAE
Publications: Perspectives; Packaging Stewardship Annual Report
Association des embouteilleurs des boissons gazeuses du Québec inc.: Vice-présidente régionale, Nycol Pageau-Goyette, #900, 500, rue Sherbrooke ouest, Montréal, PQ H3A 3C6, 514/282-3804, Téléc: 514/844-7556
Atlantic Region: Regional Vice-President, Calla Farn, #310, 1657 Barrington St., Halifax, NS B3J 2A1, 902/492-0910, Fax: 902/492-0090
Ontario Region: Regional Vice-President, Stuart Hartley, 32nd Floor, South Tower, Royal Bank Plaza, Box 32, Toronto, ON M5J 2J8, 416/369-3059, Fax: 416/865-0887
Western Region: Regional Vice-President, John Nixon, #130, 10691 Shellbridge Way., Richmond, BC V6X 3P3, 604/244-2920, Fax: 604/244-2945

Canadian Spice Association (CSA) (1942)
Halford-Lewis Ltd., #606, 465, rue St-Jean, Montréal, PQ H2Y 2R6
514/842-7857, Fax: 514/842-6312
Treasurer, Herbert S. Lewis

Canadian Sugar Institute/Institut canadien du sucre (CSI) (1966)
Water Park Place, #620, 10 Bay St., Toronto, ON M5J 2R8
416/368-8091, Fax: 416/368-6426

President, Sandra Marsden
Publications: Sugar in Perspective/Parlons sucre

Canadian Wine Institute/Institut du vin canadien (CWI) (1948)
#401, 50 Burnhamthorpe Rd. West, Mississauga, ON L5B 3C2
905/949-8463, Fax: 905/949-8465
President, Roger Randolph
Affiliates: Wine Council of Ontario; British Columbia Wine Institute

Coffee Association of Canada/Association du café du Canada (CAC) (1991)
#301, 885 Don Mills Rd., North York, ON M3C 1V9
416/510-8032, Fax: 416/510-8044, Email: info@coffee-assoc.com
President, David Wilkes
Affiliates: Grocery Products Manufacturers of Canada

Confectionery Manufacturers Association of Canada/Association canadienne des fabricants de confiseries (CMAC) (1919)
#301, 885 Don Mills Rd., North York, ON M3C 1V9
416/510-8034, Fax: 416/510-8044, Email: carolh@fcpmc.com
President, Carol L. Hochu
Chairman, Michael McKean
Publications: ; CMAC News Clips, m.

Conseil de la Boulangerie du Québec/Québec Bakery Council (CBQ) (1938)
Édifice de Bleury, #102, 200, rue MacDonald, St-Jean-sur-Richelieu, PQ J3B 8J6
514/349-0107, Téléc: 514/349-6923
Directeur général, André Latour, caé
Publications: La Fournée
Organisation(s) affiliée(s): Conseil canadien de la boulangerie

Consumers United to Stop Food Irradiation (CUSFI) (1986)
RR#1, Ilderton, ON N0M 2A0
519/666-2072
President, Anne Marie Brown

Flavour Manufacturers Association of Canada
#301, 885 Don Mills Rd., North York, ON M3C 1V9
416/510-8036, Fax: 416/510-8043
Technical Chairman, Robert J. Gordon

Food Institute of Canada/Institut des aliments du Canada (FIC) (1989)
#415, 1600 Scott St., Ottawa, ON K1Y 4N7
613/722-1000, Fax: 613/722-1404, Email: fic@foodnet.fic.ca
URL: http://foodnet.fic.ca
Executive Director, Christopher J. Kyte
Publications: Technical Communiqué; Executive Summary, m.; Frozen Food, bi-m.; Quarterly

Fresh for Flavour Foundation/Fondation fraîcheur égale saveur (FFFF) (1972)
#310, 1101 Prince of Wales Dr., Ottawa, ON K2C 3W7
613/226-4187, Fax: 613/226-2984, Toll Free: 1-800-668-7763, Email: question@cpma.ca
Chairman, Wayne McKnight
National Director of Promotions, Susan Sutherland
Publications: Fresh News/Nouvelles fraîches

German Wine Society
415 Yonge St., 10th Fl., Toronto, ON M5B 2E7
416/598-5528, Fax: 416/598-3584
Executive Director, Ron Fiorelli
Publications: German Wine in Canada

Grocery Products Manufacturers of Canada/ Fabricants canadiens de produits alimentaires (GPMC) (1959)
#301, 885 Don Mills Rd., North York, ON M3C 1V9
416/510-8024, Fax: 416/510-8043
President/CEO, George Fleischmann
Senior Vice-President, Governmental Affairs, Sandra Banks
Vice-President, Corporate & Communications, Christina Bisanz
Senior Vice-President, Trade Relations, Nick Jennery
Publications: GPMC Newsletter

Institute of Edible Oil Foods (IEOF) (1954)
#301, 885 Don Mills Rd., North York, ON M3C 1V9
416/510-8036, Fax: 416/510-8044
Manager, Linda N. Reid
Secretary, Paige Entwistle

International Maple Syrup Institute/Institut international du sirop d'érable (1975)
643, rue Grosvenor, Montréal, PQ H3Y 2S9
514/842-9471, Fax: 514/842-3541
President, Lynn Reynolds
Director, Claude Tardif

Master Brewers Association of The Americas (MBAA) (1887)
#310, 2421 North Mayfair Rd., Wauwatosa, WI 53226 USA
414/774-8558, Fax: 414/774-8556
Administrator, Catherine Beug

Ontario Coffee & Vending Service Association
#301, 885 Don Mills Rd., North York, ON M3C 1V9
905/510-8036, Fax: 905/510-8044
President, Ed Loveys

Ontario Flour Millers Association (1935)
40 George St. North, Cambridge, ON N1S 2M8
519/621-4060, Fax: 519/740-3490
Secretary, R.L. Lovell
Affiliates: Canadian National Millers' Association

Ontario Food Processors Association (OFPA) (1935)
6533C Mississauga Rd., Mississauga, ON L5N 1A6
905/821-2321, Fax: 905/821-9702
Executive Vice-President, Jane Graham

Ontario Independent Meat Packers & Processors Society (OIMPP) (1979)
PO Box 162, Port Perry, ON L9L 1A3
905/985-9858, Fax: 905/985-3002, Toll Free: 1-800-263-3797
President, Gerry Houtzager
Administrator, Laurie Murdock
Publications: Block Talk
Affiliates: American Association of Meat Processors

Ontario Maple Syrup Producers' Association (OMSPA) (1966)
RR#6, Strathroy, ON N7G 3H7
519/232-4596, Fax: 519/232-9166
Sec.-Treas., Kenneth McGregor
Publications: Maple Mainline

Ontario Tender Fruit Institute
6533C Mississauga Rd., Mississauga, ON L5N 1A6
905/821-2321, Fax: 905/821-8702
Secretary, Jane Graham

Organic Trade Association (OTA) (1985)
PO Box 1078, Greenfield, MA 01302 USA
413/774-7511, Fax: 413/774-6432, Email: ota@igc.apc.org
Executive Director, Katherine Dimatteo
Publications: The Organic Report

2-74 ORGANIZATIONS — FORESTRY & FOREST PRODUCTS

Pet Food Association of Canada/Association des fabricants d'aliments pour animaux familiers du Canada (PFAC) (1967)
1435 Goldthorpe Ave., Mississauga, ON L5G 3R2
905/891-2921, Fax: 905/278-4778
Manager, J. David Mitchell
President, Shelley Martin

Saskatchewan Brewers Association Limited
380 Dewdney Ave. East, PO Box 3057, Regina, SK S4P 3G7
306/525-0376
Director of Brewery Operations, Larry Kitz

Tea Association of Canada/Association du thé du Canada (TAC) (1991)
#301, 885 Don Mills Rd., North York, ON M3C 1V9
416/510-8649, Fax: 416/510-8044
President, Danielle J. O'Rourke
Executive Assistant, Nancy O'Rourke

Tea Council of Canada/Conseil canadien du thé (TCC)
#301, 855 Don Mills Rd., North York, ON M3C 1V9
416/510-8647, Fax: 416/510-8044
President, Danielle J. O'Rourke
Executive Assistant, Nancy Ritchie

Wine Council of Ontario (1974)
#8205, 110 Hannover Dr., St Catharines, ON L2W 1A4
905/684-8070, Fax: 905/684-2993
Executive Director, Linda Franklin
Publications: Ontario Wine News

FOOD SERVICES *see* **RESTAURANTS, BARS, FOOD SERVICES**

FORESTRY & FOREST PRODUCTS

Alberta Forest Products Association (AFPA) (1960)
#200, 11738 Kingsway Ave., Edmonton, AB T5G 0X5
403/452-2841, Fax: 403/455-0505
Executive Director, Garry Leithead
Affiliates: Alberta Forestry Association; Canadian Lumber Standards; Canadian Wood Council; Forintek Canada; National Lumber Grade Authority

Association of British Columbia Professional Foresters (ABCPF) (1947)
#1201, 1130 West Pender St., Vancouver, BC V6E 4A4
604/687-8027, Fax: 604/687-3264, Email: guest@rpf-bc.org
President, Greg Templeman, R.P.F.
Executive Director, E.V. Scoffield, R.P.F.
Registrar, Jerome Marburg, LL.B.
Publications: Forum

Association des industries forestières du Québec ltée/Québec Forest Industries Association Ltd. (AIFQ) (1924)
#102, 1200, av Germain-des-Prés, Ste-Foy, PQ G1V 3M7
418/651-9352, Téléc: 418/651-4622
Président/Directeur général, André Duchesne
Président du conseil d'administration, L. Olivier
Secrétaire, Julien Michaud
Publications: Le papetier

Association des manufacturiers de bois de sciage du Québec/Québec Lumber Manufacturers Association (AMBSQ) (1953)
#200, 5055, boul Hamel ouest, Québec, PQ G2E 2G6
418/872-5610, Téléc: 418/872-3062, Courrier électronique: ambsq@riq.qc.ca

Président/Directeur général, Gaston Déry
Publications: Pribec; Asso-Scié, trimestriel

Association of Registered Professional Foresters of New Brunswick/Association des forestiers agréés du Nouveau-Brunswick (ARPFNB) (1937)
c/o John Hugh Flemming Forestry Centre, RR#10, Fredericton, NB E3B 6H6
506/452-6933, Fax: 506/450-3128
President, Gilles Couturier, R.P.F.
Executive Director, T.E. Sifton, R.P.F.
Publications: Newsletter
Affiliates: Canadian Forestry Institute; Canadian Forestry Association; New Brunswick Forest Products Association

Canadian Forest Industries Council/Conseil canadien des industries forestières
#1200, 555 Burrard St., Vancouver, BC V7X 1S7
604/684-0211, Fax: 604/687-4930
President, Mike Apsey
Co-chairman, Jake Kerr

Canadian Forestry Association/Association forestière canadienne (CFA) (1900)
#203, 185 Somerset St. West, Ottawa, ON K2P 0J2
613/232-1815, Fax: 613/232-4210
Executive Director, Glen Blouin
Publications: Forest Forum

ALBERTA FORESTRY ASSOCIATION (1970)
101 Alberta Block, 10526 Jasper Ave., Edmonton, AB T5J 1Z7
403/428-7582, Fax: 403/428-7557
Executive Director, Audrey Ruff
Publications: News & Views Newsletter

BRITISH COLUMBIA FORESTRY ASSOCIATION (BCFA) (1925)
Forestry Education BC
9800A - 140 St., Surrey, BC V3T 4M5
604/582-0100, Fax: 604/582-0101
President, Victor Godin
Vice-President, Finance, Don Gladwin
Manager, Dave Campbell
Publications: Landscapes

CANADIAN FORESTRY ASSOCIATION OF NEW BRUNSWICK/ ASSOCIATION FORESTIÈRE CANADIENNE DU NOUVEAU-BRUNSWICK (1939)
The Tree House, 124 St. John St., Fredericton, NB E3B 4A7
506/452-1339, Fax: 506/452-7950
Secretary Manager, David Folster
President, Robert Spurway
Publications: The Arbor Day Planter

MANITOBA FORESTRY ASSOCIATION INC. (1972)
900 Corydon Ave., Winnipeg, MB R3M 0Y4
204/453-3182, Fax: 204/477-5765
Executive Director, Dianne J. Beaven
President, Michael S. Allen
Publications: Adventuring in Conservation

NEWFOUNDLAND FOREST PROTECTION ASSOCIATION (1910)
c/o Corner Brook Pulp & Paper Ltd., PO Box 2001, Corner Brook, NF A2H 6J4
President, S.R. Weldon
Chairman, Education Committee, George VanDusen

NOVA SCOTIA FORESTRY ASSOCIATION (NSFA) (1959)
PO Box 1113, Truro, NS B2N 5G9
902/893-4653, Fax: 902/895-1197
Executive Director, Jeff Vroom

ONTARIO FORESTRY ASSOCIATION/ASSOCIATION FORESTIÈRE DE L'ONTARIO (OFA) (1949)
#502, 150 Consumers Rd., North York, ON M2J 1P9
416/493-4565, Fax: 416/493-4608, Email: oforest@interlog.com

Executive Director, Richard M. Monzon
Publications: OFA Newsletter

PEI FOREST IMPROVEMENT ASSOCIATION
Covehead Rd., RR#1, York, PE C0A 1P0
General Manager/Coordinator, Wanson Hemphill

SASKATCHEWAN FORESTRY ASSOCIATION (SFA) (1977)
PO Box 400, Prince Albert, SK S6V 5R7
306/763-2189, Fax: 306/764-7463
Manager, Marie Grono
President, Dwayne Dye
Publications: Tree Lines

Canadian Hardwood Plywood Association/Association canadienne du contreplaqué de bois dur (CHPA)
27 Goulburn Ave., Ottawa, ON K1N 8C7
613/233-6205, Fax: 613/233-1929
Executive Vice-President, Richard Lipman
President, Wm. Caine, Jr.
Publications: CHPA Membership & Product Directory/Répertoire des membres et produits de l'ACCBD

Canadian Institute of Forestry/Institut forestier du Canada (CIF) (1908)
#606, 151 Slater St., Ottawa, ON K1P 5H3
613/234-2242, Fax: 613/234-6181, Email: 103741.553@compuserve.com
URL: http://www.episet/cif
Executive Director, Roxanne Comeau, R.P.F.
President, Hap Oldham
Publications: The Forestry Chronicle

Canadian Institute of Treated Wood/Institut canadien des bois traités (CITW) (1955)
#200, 2430 Don Reid Dr., Ottawa, ON K1H 8P5
613/737-4337, Fax: 613/247-0540
Executive Director, Henry Walthert
President, Lawrence Prendiville
Affiliates: Canadian Wood Council

Canadian Lumber Standards Accreditation Board (CLSAB) (1960)
#103, 4400 Dominion St., Burnaby, BC V5G 4G3
604/451-7313, Fax: 604/451-7343
Executive Director, Nils Larsson

Canadian Lumbermen's Association/Association canadienne de l'industrie du bois (CLA) (1908)
27 Goulburn Ave., Ottawa, ON K1N 8C7
613/233-6205, Fax: 613/233-1929
Executive Director, R.H. Rivard
President, Ross Staples
Assistant Executive Director, Richard Lipman
Publications: Hardwood Bureau Membership & Product Directory/Répertoire des membres et services du bureau du bois dur de l'ACIB

Canadian Pallet Council/Conseil des palettes du Canada (1977)
208C Division St., Cobourg, ON K9A 3P7
905/372-1871, Fax: 905/373-0230, Email: http://www.cpcpallet.com
General Manager, Belinda Junkin
Publications: Newsletter

Canadian Paper Trade Association (CPTA) (1922)
#200, 670 Bloor St. West, Toronto, ON M6G 1L2
416/533-7800, Fax: 416/533-4795
Secretary, Don Mockford

Canadian Particleboard Association/Association canadienne des fabricants de panneaux de particules (CPA)
4612, rue Sainte-Catherine ouest, Westmount, PQ H3Z 1S3

Canadian Almanac & Directory 1997

ORGANIZATIONS — FRATERNAL

514/989-1002, Fax: 514/989-9318
President, Kelly Shotbolt
Executive Vice-President, Michel G. Tremblay, CAE

Canadian Pulp & Paper Association/Association canadienne des de pâtes et papier (CPPA) (1913)
Sun Life Building, 1155, rue Metcalfe, 19e étage, Montréal, PQ H3B 4T6
514/866-6621, Fax: 514/866-3035
President & CEO, Lise Lachapelle
Chairman, Arild S. Nielssen
President, Forest Products Ltd., E.B. Eddy
Publications: CPPA Trade Directory; CPPA Monthly Statistical Report
Affiliates: Pulp & Paper Research Institute of Canada

Canadian Well Logging Society (CWLS) (1957)
#1600, 734 - 7th Ave. SW, Calgary, AB T2P 3P8
403/269-9366, Fax: 403/269-2787
URL: http://www.canpic.ca/CWLS
President, Al Lye, 403/262-6306
Publications: CWLS Journal; Symposium Transactions, biennial

Canadian Wood Council/Conseil canadien du bois (CWC) (1959)
#350, 1730 St. Laurent Blvd., Ottawa, ON K1G 5L1
613/247-7077, Fax: 613/247-7856
URL: http://www.cwc.metrics.com/
President, Kelly McCloskey
Chairman, David McElroy
Publications: Wood le Bois; Wood Leader, m.; CWC Directory, s-a.

Canadian Wood Pallet & Container Association/Association canadienne des manufacturiers de palettes et contenants (CWPCA) (1967)
PO Box 640, Pickering, ON L1V 3T3
905/831-3477, Fax: 905/831-3477
Executive General Manager, Gordon R. Hughes
Publications: CWPCA Newsletter/Bulletin; Pallet Enterprise, bi-m.; CWPCA Membership Guide, a.
Affiliates: National Wooden Pallet & Container Association; Western Pallet Association

Canadian Wood Preservers Bureau/Bureau canadien de la préservation du bois (CWPB) (1988)
#200, 2430 Don Reid Dr., Ottawa, ON K1H 8P5
613/737-4337, Fax: 613/247-0540
General Manager, Henry Walthert
President, Craig Wilson

Canadian Woodwork Manufacturers Association
33 Atomic Ave., Toronto, ON M8Z 5K8
416/259-5446, Fax: 416/259-5614
Contact, W. Len Goldson

Cariboo Lumber Manufacturers' Association (CLMA) (1959)
#205, 197 North Second Ave., Williams Lake, BC V2G 1Z5
250/392-7778, Fax: 250/392-4692, Email: peterson@clma.cofi.org
President, J. Dave Peterson
Public Affairs, Astrid Gagnier
Forestry, Gord Rattray
Chief Quality Control Supervisor, Bob Onofrechuk
Aboriginal Affairs, Duncan Barnett
Publications: Member Mill Directory

Christmas Tree Growers' Association of Ontario Inc. (1950)
RR#1, Lynden, ON L0R 1T0
519/647-3530, Fax: 519/647-3515
URL: http://www.christmastree.on.ca
Manager, Hubert A. Will
Publications: OCT News

Consulting Foresters of British Columbia
#600, 890 West Pender St., Vancouver, BC V6C 1J9
604/687-5500, Fax: 604/687-1327
Sec.-Treas., P.W. Appleby

Council of Forest Industries (COFI)
#203, 197 Second Ave. North, Williams Lake, BC V2G 1Z5
250/392-7770, Fax: 250/392-4692
Vice President, Aboriginal Affairs, Marlie Beets

La Fédération des producteurs de bois du Québec (FPBQ) (1970)
555, boul Roland-Therrien, Longueuil, PQ J4H 3Y9
514/679-0530, Téléc: 514/679-5682
Directeur général, Victor Brunette, ing.f.
Publications: Forêt de Chez Nous
Organisation(s) affiliée(s): Union des producteurs agricoles

Junior Forest Wardens Association of Canada
9920 - 108 St., 10th Fl., Edmonton, AB T5K 2M4
403/422-8474, Fax: 403/427-0292
Chief Warden, W.F. Myring

Maritime Lumber Bureau/Bureau de bois de sciage des Maritimes
PO Box 459, Amherst, NS B4H 4A1
902/667-3889, Fax: 902/667-0401
Executive Director, Diana L. Blenkhorn

Mechanical Wood-Pulps Network/Réseau des pâtes de bois mécaniques (1990)
Wood-Pulps Network
570, boul Saint-Jean, Pointe-Claire, PQ H9R 3J9
514/630-4100, Fax: 514/630-4107, Email: nce@paprican.ca

Millwork Manufacturers Association
#174, 4664 Lougheed Hwy., Burnaby, BC V5C 5R7
604/298-3555, Fax: 604/298-3558
Secretary-Manager, Edward Wheatley
Publications: Architectural Woodwork Digest

National Aboriginal Forestry Association (NAFA) (1989)
Head Office, PO Box 200, Golden Lake, ON K0J 1X0
613/625-2245, Email: nafa@web.net
Executive Director, Harry M. Bombay
Senior Advisor, Peggy Smith, RPF
Office Manager, Sheila Wolynski
Branch Office: Office Manager, S. Wolynski, 875 Bank St., Ottawa, ON K1S 3W4, 613/233-5563, Fax: 613/233-4329

New Brunswick Forest Products Association Inc.
Hugh John Flemming Forestry Centre, RR#10, Fredericton, NB E3B 6H6
506/452-6930, Fax: 506/450-3128
Executive Director, M.R. Cater

Nova Scotia Forest Products Association
PO Box 696, Truro, NS B2N 5E5
902/895-1179, Fax: 902/893-1197
Executive Director, Steve Talbot

Nova Scotia Forestry Exhibition Committee (NSFE) (1984)
PO Box 1149, Middleton, NS B0S 1P0
902/825-4344, Fax: 902/825-4634
Executive Manager, Dianne Hankinson LeGard
Publications: AVABT Action

Ontario Forest Industries Association/l'Industrie forestière de l'Ontario (OFIA) (1943)
#1700, 130 Adelaide St. West, Toronto, ON M5H 3P5
416/368-6188, Fax: 416/368-5445, Email: 73573.2032@compuserve.com
President/CEO, R. Marie Rauter
Publications: Code of Forest Practices; Principes directeurs et code de pratiques forestières, annuel

Ontario Lumber Manufacturers' Association/Association des manufacturiers de bois de sciage de l'Ontario (OLMA) (1966)
#1105, 55 University Ave., PO Box 8, Toronto, ON M5J 2H7
416/367-9717, Fax: 416/367-3415
President, David G. Milton, RPF
Manager, Eleanor Siegel
Chairman, Jules Fournier
Publications: OLMA Newsletter
Affiliates: Bureau de promotion des industries du bois; Canadian Forest Industry Council; Canadian Wood Council

Ontario Professional Foresters Association (OPFA) (1957)
#102, 27 Beaver Creek Rd. West, Richmond Hill, ON L4B 1M8
905/764-2921, Fax: 905/764-2921
Executive Director, John W. Ebbs, R.P.F.
Publications: The Professional Forester

Ontario Shade Tree Council (OSTC) (1964)
2842 Bloor St. West, Etobicoke, ON M8X 1B1
416/231-4181, Fax: 416/231-3863
President, Patricia Thomson
Treasurer, Mark Procunier
Publications: OSTC Yearbook; OSTC News, bi-m.

Ordre des ingénieurs forestiers du Québec (OIFQ) (1921)
#380, 2750, rue Einstein, Québec, PQ G1P 4R1
418/650-2411, Téléc: 418/650-2168
Président/Directeur général, Magella Morasse
Directeur des communications, Pierre Breton
Publications: L'Aubelle
Organisation(s) affiliée(s): Canadian Forestry Association/Fédération canadienne des associations d'ingénieurs forestiers

Sustainable Forest Management Network of Centres of Excellence/Réseau de Centres d'Excellence sur la Gestion Durable des Forêts (SFM) (1995)
208G Biological Sciences Bldg., University of Alberta, Edmonton, AB T6G 2E9
403/492-3316, Fax: 403/492-8160
Dr. Ellie Prepas
Network Manager, Dr. Bruce MacLock

Wholesale Lumber Dealers Association Inc. (1918)
#806, 5075 Yonge St., North York, ON M2N 6C6
416/222-7030, Fax: 416/222-7402, Toll Free: 1-800-363-2091
President, Ted Rowe

FRANCOPHONES IN CANADA see **CULTURE**

FRATERNAL
see also **Service Clubs**

Benevolent & Protective Order of Elks of Canada (1913)
BPO Elks of Canada
#100, 2629 - 29 Ave., Regina, SK S4G 2N9
306/359-9010, Fax: 306/565-2860, Toll Free: 1-888-843-3557
National Executive Director, William J. Blake, CAE
Publications: The Canadian Elk

Canadian Almanac & Directory 1997

Canadian Association, Sovereign Military Order of Malta (1952)
Knights of Malta
1247 Kilborn Ave., Ottawa, ON K1H 6K9
613/731-8897, Fax: 613/731-1312
President, F. Vincent Regan, KM, Q.C.
Publications: Knights of Malta Newsletter

Canadian Woman's Christian Temperance Union (1884)
Charles Promenade Building, #203, 730 Yonge St., Toronto, ON M4Y 2B7
416/921-4909
National Secretary, Wendy Harker

Empire Club of Canada
Royal York Hotel, 100 Front St. West, Toronto, ON M5J 1E3
416/364-2878

Grand Orange Lodge of Canada (1830)
Loyal Orange Association
94 Sheppard Ave. West, North York, ON M2N 1M5
416/223-1690, Fax: 416/223-1324, Toll Free: 1-800-565-6248
Grand Secretary, Norman R. Ritchie
Publications: The Sentinel
Grand Lodge of Alberta: Grand Secretary, Doug Robbins, 11116 - 36A Ave., Edmonton, AB T6J 0E5, 403/434-2943
Grand Lodge of British Columbia: Grand Secretary, Dave Johnson, 13581 - 88A Ave., Surrey, BC V3V 1A3, 604/596-0998
Grand Lodge of Manitoba: Grand Secretary, J. Cox, 11 Ascot Bay, Winnipeg, MB R3A 0X5, 204/832-1094
Grand Lodge of New Brunswick: Grand Secretary, Allan Hasson, RR#1, Hampstead, NB E0G 1Y0, 506/425-2474
Grand Lodge of Newfoundland: Grand Secretary, Moses Herald, PO Box 13, Glovertown, NF A0G 2L0, 709/533-2213
Grand Lodge of Nova Scotia: Grand Secretary, Howard Harris, RR#1, Stellarton, NS B0K 1S0, 902/923-2608
Grand Lodge of Ontario East: Grand Secretary, Richard Lowery, #502, 2 Meadow Glen Pl., Scarborough, ON M1G 2V6, 416/289-0964
Grand Lodge of Ontario West: Grand Secretary, Gerry Darroch, 85 Yorkminster Rd., North York, ON M2P 1M4, 416/222-5889
Grand Lodge of Prince Edward Island: Grand Secretary, James Moore, Crapaud, PE C0A 1J0, 902/658-2875
Grand Lodge of Québec: Grand Secretary, James Allan, 3080 Allan Rg., Kinnear's Mills, PQ G0N 1K0, 418/424-3252
Grand Lodge of Saskatchewan: Grand Secretary, Harold K. Morrow, Site 6, Box 18, RR#1, Melfort, SK S0E 1A0, 306/752-3682

LADIES' ORANGE BENEVOLENT ASSOCIATION OF CANADA
RR#6, Owen Sound, ON N4K 5N8
519/376-9964
Grand Secretary, Velma Hart

The Independent Order of Foresters
Forester House, 789 Don Mills Rd., Don Mills, ON M3C 1T9
416/429-3000
Executive Secretary, J. Robert Heatley

Knights of Columbus/Chevaliers de Colomb (1882)
PO Box 1670, New Haven, CT 06507 USA
203/772-2130, Fax: 203/865-2310
Supreme Knight, Virgil C. Knight
Chief Agent & Assistant to Supreme Knight, Canadian Affairs, Edward J. Buckley

Canadian Almanac & Directory 1997

Supreme Secretary, Charles P. Reisbeck, Jr.
Publications: Columbia; Knightline
Alberta Chapter: David D. Kolasa, 20 MacLeod Close, Red Deer, AB T4N 0K4, 403/347-2771
British Columbia Chapter: James Watson, 304 - 10th St. South, Cranbrook, BC V1C 1S2, 250/426-4047
Conseil d'État du Québec: Jean-Claude LaForest, 1031, Champs Fleuris, CP 33, St-Jean-Chrysostome-de-Lévis, PQ G6Z 2L3, 418/839-0169
Manitoba Chapter: Roger Degagne, 141 Harrowby Ave., Winnipeg, MB R2M 0H1, 204/237-1990
New Brunswick Chapter: Dennis A. Savoie, 34 Reading St., Fredericton, NB E3B 6B2, 506/357-9509
Newfoundland Chapter: Hubert Power, PO Box 552, Kelligrews, NF A0A 2T0, 709/834-4238
Nova Scotia Chapter: Paul G. Perry, 3 Rodan St., Sydney Mines, NS B1V 3E6, 902/736-2479
Ontario Chapter: Raymond Braun, 1727 Rodin Way, Orleans, ON K1C 4Y9, 613/830-9554
Prince Edward Island Chapter: Reginald Hooper, PO Box 935, Charlottetown, PE C1A 7M4, 902/368-7317
Saskatchewan Chapter: Mervyn Welter, 2512 Eagle Rise, North Battleford, SK S9A 3Z1, 306/445-5958

Knights of Pythias - Domain of British Columbia (1880)
447 Penticton Ave., Penticton, BC V2A 2M5
250/492-6520, Fax: 250/492-6520
Grand Secretary, Marv Wilson
Affiliates: Supreme Lodge Knights of Pythias

The National Chapter of Canada IODE (IODE) (1900)
#254, 40 Orchard View Blvd., Toronto, ON M4R 1B9
416/487-4416, Fax: 416/487-4417
President, Valerie P. Willard
Publications: Echoes
Affiliates: IODE Bahamas; IODE Bermuda

Order of The Eastern Star (Grand Chapter of Ontario)
18 Central Park Blvd. North, Oshawa, ON L1G 5Y2
905/728-8901
Grand Secretary, M. Ruth Wales

Order of Sons of Italy in Canada
505, rue Jean Talon est, Montréal, PQ H2R 1T6
514/271-2281
Secretary, F. Pantaleo

Royal Arch Masons of Canada
361 King St. West, Hamilton, ON L8P 1B4
905/522-5775, Fax: 905/522-5099
Grand Scribe E., Ezra-Melvyn J. Duke

Society of Kabalarians of Canada
Kabalarian Philosophy
5912 Oak St., Vancouver, BC V6M 2W2
604/263-9551, Fax: 604/263-5514; Email: admin@kabalarians.com; URL: http://www.kabalarians.com
President, Lorenda Bardell
Office Manager, Garrett Hennigan

Sons of Scotland Benevolent Association
#411, 90 Eglinton Ave. East, Toronto, ON M4P 2Y3
416/482-1250, Fax: 416/482-9576
Sec.-Treas., Effie MacFie

Sovereign Order of St. John of Jerusalem, Knights of Malta, Grand Priory of Canada (OSJ) (1048)
Knights Hospitallers of Cyprus, Rhodes, Malta & Russia
Grand Chancery Canada, 52 Kingswood Dr., Bowmanville, ON L1E 1Z3
905/579-0326, Fax: 905/723-5392

Grand Chancellor, H.E. Marquis & Count Joseph Frendo Cumbo
Secretary General, Chev. Raymond Borg
Treasurer General, Chev. Alfred Bonello
Publications: OSJ News

United Commercial Travelers of America (UCT)
#300, 901 Centre St. North, Calgary, AB T2E 2P6
403/277-0745, Fax: 403/277-6662, Toll Free: 1-800-267-2371
Chief Agent for Canada, Lindsay Maxwell
Grand Council, Atlantic Provinces: Grand Secretary, Clifford E. Boucher, 692 St. Simon St., Bathurst, NB E2A 3L9, 506/546-2441, Fax: 506/546-2441
Grand Council, Manitoba, Saskatchewan, Alberta: Grand Secretary, Phyllis M. Poets, 3 Broda Bay, Brandon, MB R7A 6L8
Grand Council, Ontario & Québec: Grand Secretary, Albert Powers, 16 Romney Rd., Chatham, ON N7L 3S3
Grand Council, Oregon-Washington-BC: Grand Secretary, Justine L. Mays, 8640 Foster Grove Court NE, Bremerton, WA 98310-9269 USA

FREIGHT FORWARDING *see* **TRANSPORTATION & SHIPPING**

FUNERAL SERVICES

Alberta Funeral Service Association (1931)
#130, 6715 - 8 St. NE, Calgary, AB T2E 7H7
403/274-1922, Fax: 403/274-8191, Toll Free: 1-800-803-8809
Executive Administrator, Gail Paget
Publications: AFSA
Affiliates: Funeral Service Association of Canada

Cemetery & Crematorium Association of British Columbia (CCABC) (1970)
15800 - 32 Ave., Surrey, BC V4P 2J9
604/531-2141, Fax: 604/536-8828
Sec.-Treas., Nunzio J. Defoe
Publications: Cemetery Dispatch

Corporation des thanatologues du Québec (CTQ) (1958)
945, rue Paradis, Roberval, PQ G8H 2J9
418/275-4875, Téléc: 418/275-7496
Directeur général, Ghislain Harvey
Publications: Le Bulletin

Funeral Advisory & Memorial Society (1956)
55 St. Phillips Rd., Etobicoke, ON M9P 2N8
416/241-6274
Executive Director, Sylvia Hill

Funeral Service Association of BC
1551 Pandora Ave., Victoria, BC V8R 6P9
250/388-7055, Fax: 250/388-6134
Contact, Janet Ricciuti
Affiliates: Funeral Service Association of Canada

Funeral Service Association of Canada/ L'Association des services funéraires du Canada
#201, 206 Harwood Ave. South, Ajax, ON L1S 2H6
905/619-0982, Fax: 905/619-0983
Executive Director, Susan MacKinnon

Manitoba Funeral Service Association (1964)
PO Box 243, Winnipeg, MB R3C 2G9
204/947-0927, Fax: 204/269-7148
Executive Secretary, Lorrie Waugh
Publications: Newsletter

New Brunswick Funeral Directors & Embalmers Association
343 Main St., PO Box 31, Hampton, NB E0G 1Z0
506/832-5541, Fax: 506/832-3082

Newfoundland & Labrador Funeral Services Association
PO Box 138, Winterton, NF A0B 3M0
709/583-2700
Secretary, Don Green
Affiliates: Funeral Service Association of Canada

Nova Scotia Licensed Embalmers & Funeral Directors Association
172 Main St., Kentville, NS B4N 1J8
902/678-1999, Fax: 902/679-2226
President, Wayne Eiffin
Affiliates: Funeral Service Association of Canada

Ontario Association of Cemeteries
PO Box 1156, Stn F, Toronto, ON M4Y 2T8
416/920-4823, Fax: 416/920-4135
Publications: The Journal

Ontario Funeral Service Association Inc. (OFSA) (1922)
#130, 320 North Queen St., Etobicoke, ON M9C 5K4
416/695-3434, Fax: 416/695-3583, Toll Free: 1-800-268-2727
Executive Director, Sheelah H. Brodie
Publications: OFSA Newsletter
Affiliates: Funeral Service Association of Canada

Prince Edward Island Funeral Directors & Embalmers Association
RR#6, Kensington, PE C0B 1M0
902/836-3313, Fax: 902/886-4461
Treasurer, John MacIsaac
Affiliates: Funeral Service Association of Canada

Saskatchewan Funeral Service Association
#12, 2700 Montague St., Regina, SK S4S 0J9
306/584-1575, Fax: 306/584-9259
Contact, Gerri Monsees
Affiliates: Funeral Service Association of Canada

FUR TRADE
see also Animal Breeding

Aboriginal Trappers Federation of Canada (ATFC) (1984)
PO Box 1869, Cornwall, ON K6H 6N6
613/932-1258
Executive Director, Bob Stevenson

Association for the Protection of Fur-Bearing Animals (1953)
The Fur Bearers
2235 Commercial Dr., Vancouver, BC V5N 4B6
604/255-0411, Fax: 604/255-1491
Executive Director, Michelle Clausius
Publications: The Furbearers

Canadian Association for Humane Trapping (CAHT) (1954)
#1202, 390 Bay St., Toronto, ON M5H 2Y2
416/363-2614, Fax: 416/363-8451
President, Robert Gardiner
Publications: CAHT Bulletin

The Fur Council of Canada/Conseil canadien de la fourrure
#1270, 1435, rue Saint-Alexandre, Montréal, PQ H3A 2G4
514/844-1945, Fax: 514/844-8593

Executive Director, Del Haylock
Secretary, Angela Gurley

Fur Institute of Canada/Institut de la fourrure du Canada (FIC) (1983)
#804, 255 Albert St., Ottawa, ON K1P 6A9
613/231-7099, Fax: 613/231-7940
Executive Director, Alison Beal
Chairman, Bruce Williams
Affiliates: International Union for Nature & Natural Resources

Fur Trade Association of Canada (Québec) Inc./Association canadienne du commerce de la fourrure (Québec) inc.
#1270, 1435, rue Saint-Alexandre, Montréal, PQ H3A 2G4
514/844-1945, Fax: 514/844-8593
Executive Director, Del Haylock

Furriers Guild of Canada
#300, 461 King St. West, Toronto, ON M5V 1K4
416/593-0324, Fax: 416/593-1546
Executive Director, Linda Jagros-May

Retail Fur Council of Canada/Conseil des détaillants en fourrures
#1270, 1435, rue Saint-Alexandre, Montréal, PQ H3A 2G4
514/844-1945, Fax: 514/844-8593
Contact, Del Haylock

GALLERIES & MUSEUMS
see also Visual Art, Crafts, Folk Arts

Atlantic Provinces Art Gallery Association (APAGA) (1975)
Acadia University Art Gallery, Wolfville, NS B0P 1X0
902/542-2201, ext.1166, Fax: 902/542-4727
President, Franziska Kruschen
Affiliates: Canadian Museums Association

Canadian Art Museum Directors Organization/Organisation des directeurs des musées d'art canadiens (CAMDO)
c/o The Nickle Arts Museum, University of Calgary, 2500 University Dr. NW, Calgary, AB T2N 1N4
Email: nickle@acs.ucalgary.ca
President, Ann Davis
Affiliates: Canadian Conference of Arts

Canadian Federation of Friends of Museums/Fédération canadienne des amis de musées (CFFM)
c/o Art Gallery of Ontario, 317 Dundas St. West, Toronto, ON M5T 1G4
416/979-6650, Fax: 416/979-6666
President, Dr. Sean B. Murphy
National Director, Carol Sprachman
Publications: Communiqué
Affiliates: World Federation of Friends of Museums - Brussels; Canadian Museums Association

Canadian Museums Association/Association des musées canadiens (1947)
280 Metcalfe St., Ottawa, ON K2P 1R7
613/567-0099, Fax: 613/233-5438
Executive Director, John G. McAvity
Business Manager, Robert Levesque
Publications: ND Reports; Muséogramme, m.; Muse, q.; Directory of Canadian Museums & Related Institutions, biennial

ALBERTA MUSEUMS ASSOCIATION (AMA) (1971)
Rosedale House, 9829 - 103 St., Edmonton, AB T5J 0X9

403/424-2626, Fax: 403/425-1679, Email: can-ama@immedia.ca
Executive Director, Adriana A. Davies
Publications: Alberta Museums Review; The Directory of Alberta Museums & Related Institutions, bi-a.

ASSOCIATION OF MANITOBA MUSEUMS (AMM) (1972)
#422, 167 Lombard Ave., Winnipeg, MB R3B 0T6
204/947-1782, Fax: 204/942-1555
Executive Director, Marilyn de von Flindt
President, Philippe Mailhot
Publications: AMM Newsletter; Dawson & Hind, irreg.

ASSOCIATION MUSEUMS NEW BRUNSWICK/ASSOCIATION DES MUSÉES DU NOUVEAU-BRUNSWICK (AMNB) (1974)
503 Queen St., PO Box 116, Stn A, Fredericton, NB E3B 4Y2
506/452-2908, Fax: 506/459-0481, Email: muse@nbnet.nb.ca
Publications: AMNB Bulletin; Directory of NB Museums & Related Institutions

BRITISH COLUMBIA MUSEUMS ASSOCIATION (1957)
514 Government St., Victoria, BC V8V 4X4
250/387-3315, Fax: 250/387-1251
URL: http://www.MuseumsAssn.bc.ca/~bcma/
Executive Director, Gregory Evans
Professional Development Coordinator, Lee Boyko
Dogwood Regional Network Coordinator, Cliff Quinn
Publications: Museum Round-Up

COMMUNITY MUSEUMS ASSOCIATION OF PRINCE EDWARD ISLAND (1983)
2 Kent St., Charlottetown, PE C1A 1M6
902/892-8837
President, Dr. C.W.J. Eliat
Training Coordinator, Barry King
Publications: CMA PEI Newsletter

ONTARIO MUSEUM ASSOCIATION/ASSOCIATION DES MUSÉES DE L'ONTARIO (OMA) (1972)
George Brown House, 50 Baldwin St., Toronto, ON M5T 1L4
416/348-8672, Fax: 416/348-0438, Email: can-oma@immedia.ca
URL: http://www.museum.assn.on.ca
Managing Director, Dr. Barbara Efrat
Publications: Currently; Ontario Museum Annual/L'Annuaire des musées de l'Ontario, a.
Affiliates: Ontario Heritage Alliance

ICOM Museums Canada/ICOM Musées Canada (1946)
International Council of Museums
#400, 280 Metcalfe St., Ottawa, ON K2P 1R7
613/567-0099, Fax: 613/233-5438
President, Michel Côté
Publications: ICOM Canada Newsletter; UNESCO Museum Quarterly

Museum Association of Newfoundland & Labrador (MANL)
One Springdale St., PO Box 5785, St. John's, NF A1C 5X3
709/722-9034, Fax: 709/722-9035, Email: can_manl@immedia.ca
Executive Director, Ute Okshevsky, MMST
President, Marilyn Dawe
Publications: MANL Newsletter
Affiliates: Heritage Canada

Museums Association of Saskatchewan (MAS) (1967)
1808 Smith St., Regina, SK S4P 2N4
306/780-9279, Fax: 306/359-6758, Email: can-mas@immedia.ca
Executive Director, Gayl Hipperson

Canadian Almanac & Directory 1997

Communications Manager, Teresa Quilty
Publications: Bulletin

Ontario Association of Art Galleries (OAAG) (1968)
#306, 489 King St. West, Toronto, ON M5V 1K4
416/598-0714, Fax: 416/598-4128, Email: oaag@interlog.com
URL: http://www.culturenet.ca/oaag/
Executive Director, Anne Kolisnyk
Publications: Context

Organization of Military Museums of Canada, Inc./L'Organisation des musées militaires du Canada inc. (OMMC Inc.) (1967)
72 Robertson Rd., PO Box 26106, Nepean, ON K2H 9R6
613/829-0280, Fax: 613/829-0280
Executive Director, Major R.K. Malott, MSc, BA, CD, Ret'd
Publications: The Bulletin
Affiliates: Friends of the Canadian War Museum; Directorate of Military Traditions & Heritage; Military Collectors Club of Canada

La Société des musées québécois (SMQ) (1958)
CP 8888, Succ Centre-Ville, Montréal, PQ H3C 3P8
514/987-3264, Téléc: 514/987-3379
URL: http://www.uqam.ca/musees/
Directrice générale, Sylvie Gagnon
Publications: SMQ Bulletin; Musées, 3 fois par an

GAMES see **RECREATION, HOBBIES & GAMES**

GARDENING see **HORTICULTURE, GARDENING, LANDSCAPE ARCHITECTURE**

GAS & OIL

Canadian Association of Petroleum Producers/ Association canadienne des producteurs pétroliers (CAPP) (1992)
#2100, 350 - 7 Ave. SW, Calgary, AB T2P 3N9
403/267-1100, Fax: 403/261-4622,
Email: communication@capp.ca
URL: http://www.capp.ca
President, David J. Manning, Q.C.
Vice-President, Strategic Planning, Chris Peirce
Vice-President, Environment & Operations, Bill Harlan
Vice-President, Fiscal Policy & Corporate Services, Len Landry
Vice-President, Markets & Transporation, Richard Woodward
General Counsel, Nick Schultz
Publications: Crude Oil Report; Natural Gas Report, m.; ReCAPP, m.; Canada's Upstream Petroleum Industry, a.; CAPP Statistical Handbook, a.; Petrographs, a.; CAPP Perspective, 3 pa
Affiliates: Natural Gas Council

Canadian Energy Pipeline Association (CEPA) (1993)
#1650, 801 - 6 Ave. SW, Calgary, AB T2P 3W2
403/221-8777, Fax: 403/221-8760
URL: http://www.cepa.com
President, Myron F. Kanik

Canadian Gas Processors Association (CGPA) (1960)
#1600, 700 - 4 Ave. SW, Calgary, AB T2P 3J4
403/263-6881, Fax: 403/263-6886
President, Bob Draper
Secretary, Heather Douglas
Publications: News in Brief

Canadian Gas Processors Suppliers Association
#1600, 700 - 4 Ave. SW, Calgary, AB T2P 3J4
403/263-5388
President, Karsten Pedersen
Publications: The Downstream Review

Canadian Petroleum Products Institute/Institut canadien des produits pétroliers (CPPI) (1989)
#1000, 275 Slater St., Ottawa, ON K1P 5H9
613/232-3709, Fax: 613/236-4280, 4345
President, Alain Perez
Vice-President, Public Affairs, Brendan P. Hawley
Vice-President, External Relations, T.R. Clapp
Chairman, Brian Fischer

Canadian Society of Petroleum Geologists (CSPG) (1928)
#505, 206 - 7 Ave. SW, Calgary, AB T2P 0W7
403/264-5610, Fax: 403/264-5898, Email: cspg@cspg.org
URL: http://www.cspg.org
President, Gerry Reinson
Vice-President, Ric Sebastian
Publications: Bulletin of Canadian Petroluem Geology; The Reservoir, m.
Affiliates: Association of Professional Engineers, Geologists & Geophysicists of Alberta; Canadian Institute of Mining, Metallurgy & Petroleum; Geological Association of Canada; Petroleum Communications Foundation

Compressed Gas Association - Canada (CGA-Canada)
44 Revcoe Dr., North York, ON M2M 2B8
905/278-2456
Executive Secretary, Lloyd R. Jacobson, Fax: 416/223-5747

Industrial Gas Users Association/Association des consommateurs industriels de gaz (IGUA) (1973)
#900, 170 Laurier Ave. West, Ottawa, ON K1P 5V5
613/236-8021, Fax: 613/230-9531
Executive Director, Ted Bjerkelund, CAE
Administrative Assistant, Margaret Blair
Publications: Executive Update

Ontario Natural Gas Association
#1104, 77 Bloor St. West, Toronto, ON M5S 1M2
416/961-2339, Fax: 416/961-1173
President, Paul E. Pinnington

Petroleum Communication Foundation/ Fondation des communications sur les ressources pétrolières (PCF) (1975)
#214, 311 - 6th Ave. SW, Calgary, AB T2P 3H2
403/264-6064, Fax: 403/237-6286, Email: pcomm@pcf.ab.ca
URL: http://www.pcf.ab.ca
Executive Director, Leonard F. Bradley
President, Rick L. Harrop
Publications: Connections

Petroleum Recovery Institute (PRI) (1966)
#100, 3512 - 33 St. NW, Calgary, AB T2L 2A6
403/282-1211, Fax: 403/289-1988
Executive Director, Dr. Conrad Ayasse
Manager, Technology Development, B. Hawkins
Publications: Partners

Petroleum Services Association of Canada (PSAC) (1981)
Aquitaine Tower, #1800, 540 - 5 Ave. SW, Calgary, AB T2P 0M2
403/264-4195, Fax: 403/263-7174, Email: info@psac.ca
URL: http://www.psac.ca
President, Roger Soucy
Publications: On Stream; Fastline, 9 pa

Propane Gas Association of Canada Inc./ Association canadienne du gaz propane inc. (PGAC) (1967)
#1800, 300 - 5 Ave. SW, Calgary, AB T2P 3C4
403/543-6508, Fax: 403/543-6500
Chairman, John Bechtold
Managing Director, Bill Curtze
Publications: The Propane Letter; PGAC Directory, a.
Eastern Office: Director, Government Affairs, René Chartier, 1155 North Service Rd. West, Oakville, ON L6M 1J8, 905/827-8505, Fax: 905/827-0690

GEMS & JEWELLERY

Alberta Federation of Rock Clubs
47 Garland Cres., Sherwood Park, AB T8A 2P7
403/467-0520
President, Dave Engberg
Affiliates: Gem & Mineral Federation of Canada

Canadian Gemmological Association (1958)
1767 Avenue Rd., Toronto, ON M5M 3Y8
416/785-0962, Fax: 416/785-9043
President, Zia Hasan
Publications: The Canadian Gemmologist
Affiliates: Gemmological Association & Gem Testing Laboratory of Great Britain

Canadian Institute of Gemmology/Institut canadien de gemmologie (CIG) (1983)
Pacific Institute of Gemmology
PO Box 57010, Vancouver, BC V5K 5G6
604/530-8569, Fax: 604/530-8569, Toll Free: 1-800-294-2211, Email: wolf@kwantlen.bc.ca
URL: http://deepcove.com/cig
Executive Director, Wolf Kuehn
Publications: Gemmology Canada
Affiliates: Allied Teaching Centre of the Gemmological Association; Gem Trading Lab of Great Britain

Canadian Jewellers Association (CJA) (1922)
Box 2021, #1108, 20 Eglinton Ave. West, Toronto, ON M4R 1K8
416/480-1424, Fax: 416/480-2342
General Manager, Karen Bassels
Publications: Jewellery World

Corporation des bijoutiers du Québec/Québec Jewellers' Corporation (CBQ) (1952)
#0.1, 7585, rue Lacordaire, St-Léonard, PQ H1S 2A6
514/251-2410, Téléc: 514/251-1702
Directrice générale, Lise Petitpas
Publications: Bijouterie

Gem & Mineral Federation of Canada/Fédération canadienne des gemmes et des minéraux (GMFC) (1977)
#202, 237 Wellington Cres., Winnipeg, MB R3M 0A1
204/452-1035
President, Marjorie Reynolds
Membership Chair, Alice Clarke
Treasurer, Jack Wrightson
Historian, Margaret Lowe
Publications: GMFC Newsletter; GMFC Membership Directory

Jewellers Vigilance Canada Inc. (JVC) (1987)
20 Eglinton Ave. West, PO Box 2021, Toronto, ON M4R 1K8
416/480-1452, Fax: 416/480-2342, Toll Free: 1-800-636-9536, Email: jvc@maple.net
Executive Coordinator, Carla J. Adams
Publications: Action Update

Jewellery Appraisers Association of Canada (1988)
#13, 5501 - 204 St., PO Box 26003, Langley, BC V3A 5N0
604/530-6807, Fax: 604/530-6807
President, Geoffrey Dominy
Director, Anna Miller

GENEALOGY *see* **HISTORY, HERITAGE, GENEALOGY**

GOVERNMENT & PUBLIC ADMINISTRATION
see also Politics

Alberta Association of Municipal Districts & Counties (1909)
4504 - 101 St., Edmonton, AB T6E 5G9
403/436-9375, Fax: 403/437-5993
Executive Director, Larry Goodhope
President, Roelof Heinen

Alberta Rural Municipal Administrators Association (1922)
c/o County of Grande Prairie, 8611 - 108 St., Grande Prairie, AB T8V 4C5
403/532-9722, Fax: 403/532-4234
President, Ron Pfau

Alberta Urban Municipalities Association (AUMA) (1905)
8712 - 105 St., Edmonton, AB T6E 5V9
403/433-4431, Fax: 403/433-4454, Toll Free: 1-800-661-2862, Email: main@auma.ab.ca
URL: http://www.auma.ab.ca
Executive Director, John E. Maddison, CAE
Publications: Urban Perspective

Association of Clerks-At-The-Table in Canada/Association des greffiers parlementaires du Canada (1969)
Legislative Assembly of Alberta, Legislature Annex, #801, 9718 - 107th St., Edmonton, AB T5K 1E4
403/427-2580, Fax: 403/427-5688
President, Camille Montpetit
Vice-President, Lori Sonier
Secretary, Robert Vaive

Association des communicateurs municipaux du Québec (ACMQ) (1975)
144, boul de l'Hôpital, Gatineau, PQ J8T 7S7
819/243-2331, Téléc: 819/243-2338, Ligne sans frais: 1-800-668-8383
Président, Jean Boileau
Publications: Le Triangle
Organisation(s) affiliée(s): Sociétés des relationistes du Québec

Association des directeurs généraux des municipalités du Québec (1973)
51, rue Auteuil, Québec, PQ G1R 4C2
418/694-2163, Téléc: 418/694-9462
Président, Michel-C. Gagnon
Secrétaire, Roger Noël
Publications: Bulletin éclair; Le Sablier, trimestriel

Association internationale des maires francophones - Bureau à Québec (AIMF)
51, rue d'Auteuil, Québec, PQ G1R 4C2
418/694-1973, Téléc: 418/694-4649
Conseiller technique, Jean Lenoir

Association of Municipal Administrators of New Brunswick/Association des administrateurs municipaux du Nouveau-Brunswick (1977)
#402, 200 Prospect St. West, Fredericton, NB E3B 2T8
506/453-4229, Fax: 506/453-7954

Executive Director, Eva Turnbull
Publications: President's Newsletter

Association of Municipal Administrators, Nova Scotia (AMANS) (1970)
#1106, 1809 Barrington St., Halifax, NS B3J 3K8
902/423-2215, Fax: 902/425-5592
Administrative Director, Janice Wentzell
Publications: AMA Newsletter

Association of Municipal Clerks & Treasurers of Ontario/Association des secrétaires et trésoriers municipaux de l'Ontario (AMCTO) (1937)
#520, 2810 Matheson Blvd. East, Mississauga, ON L4W 4X7
905/602-4294, Fax: 905/602-4295
Executive Director, Kenneth S. Cousineau, CAE
President, Larry Simons, CMO
Publications: Municipal Monitor
Affiliates: Association of Municipalities of Ontario; International Institute of Municipal Clerks; Municipal Information Systems Association

Association des municipalités du Nouveau-Brunswick (AMNB) (1989)
702, rue Principale, CP 849, Petit-Rocher, NB E0B 2E0
506/783-4211, Téléc: 506/783-0808
Directeur général, Léopold Chiasson
Président, Maire Jacques Martin
Publications: L'Elue
Organisation(s) affiliée(s): Association internationale des maires et responsables des capitales et métropoles partiellement ou entièrement francophones (AIMF); Fédération canadienne des municipalités (FCM); Union des municipalités régionales de comté et des municipalités locales du Québec (UMRCQ)

Association of Municipalities of Ontario (AMO) (1889)
#701, 250 Bloor St. East, Toronto, ON M4W 1E6
416/929-7573, Fax: 416/929-7574
Executive Director, Douglas Raven
President, Terry Mundell
Information Manager, Renata Kulpa
Director of Policy, Deborah Dubinofsky
Publications: Updates

Association des urbanistes et des aménagistes municipaux du Québec
295, boul Charest est, Québec, PQ G1K 3G8
418/691-6855, Téléc: 418/691-3942
Présidente, Nathalie Prud'homme
Publications: URB-INFO

Association of Yukon Communities (AYC) (1974)
3128 3rd Ave., Whitehorse, YT Y1A 1E7
403/668-4388, Fax: 403/665-7574
Executive Director, Larry Bagnell
President, Kathy Watson
Affiliates: Federation of Canadian Municipalities

Canadian Association of Municipal Administrators (CAMA)
24 Clarence St., 2nd Fl., Ottawa, ON K1N 5P3
613/241-8444, Fax: 613/241-7440 Executive Director, Maria Hughes

Canadian Council on Social Development/Conseil canadien de développement social (CCSD) (1920)
441 MacLaren St., 4th Fl., Ottawa, ON K2P 2H3
613/236-8977, Fax: 613/236-2750, Email: council@achilles.net
URL: http://www.achilles.net/~council/; http://www.ncf.carleton.ca/freeport/social.services/ccsd/menu
Executive Director, David Ross
President, Sharon Manson Singer

Communications Officer, Nancy Perkins
Publications: Vis-a-Vis; Perception, q.

Cities of New Brunswick Association
#404, 200 Prospect St., Fredericton, NB E3B 2T8
506/457-7297, Fax: 506/453-7954
Executive Director, Frederick Martin
President, Mayor Thomas Higgins

City Clerks & Election Officers Association (1975)
City of St. Albert, 5 St. Anne St., St Albert, AB T8N 3Z9
403/459-1633, Fax: 403/460-2394
Secretary, Adele Cordell
Publications: Minute Talk

Corporation des officiers municipaux agréés du Québec/Corporation of Chartered Municipal Officers of Québec (COMAQ) (1968)
#210, 1135, ch St-Louis, Sillery, PQ G1S 1E7
418/527-1231, Téléc: 418/527-4462
Secrétaire général, Erick Parent
Publications: Le Carrefour; Répertoire des membres, annuel

Corporation des secrétaires municipaux du Québec inc. (CSMQ) (1939)
#500, 580, av Grande-Allée est, Québec, PQ G1R 2K2
418/647-4518, Téléc: 418/647-4115
Directeur général, Marie-Andrée Levasseur
Publications: Le Scribe

Federal Superannuates National Association/Association nationale des retraités fédéraux (FSNA) (1963)
#401, 233 Gilmour St., Ottawa, ON K2P 0P2
613/234-9663, Fax: 613/234-2314, Email: postmaster@fsna.com
National President, Claude A. Edwards
Executive Director, Jean-Guy Soulière
Publications: On Guard/En Garde

Federation of Canadian Municipalities/Fédération canadienne des municipalités (FCM) (1937)
24 Clarence St., 2nd Fl., Ottawa, ON K1N 5P3
613/241-5221, Fax: 613/241-7440, Telex: 053-4451
Executive Director, James W. Knight
President, Mayor John Les
Communication Director, Sheila Keating
Director, Corporate Services, Ron Zimmer, CAE
Publications: Forum; Communiqué, irreg.

Federation of Northern Ontario Municipalities (FONOM) (1960)
81 St. Brendon St., Sudbury, ON P3E 1K4
705/669-0135, Fax: 705/669-0135
Executive Director, Phyllis Floyd

Federation of Prince Edward Island Municipalities Inc. (FPEIM) (1957)
1 Kirkdale Rd., Charlottetown, PE C1E 1R3
902/566-1493, Fax: 902/368-1239, Email: macbain@peinet.pe.ca
Executive Director, Lisa B. Doyle-MacBain
President, Doug Doncaster
Publications: FPEIM Municipal Directory; Information Update, m.
Affiliates: Association of Municipal Administrators, PEI; Maritime Municipal Training & Development Board

Foreign Service Community Association/Association de la communauté du service extérieur (FSCA) (1976)
c/o Dept. of External Affairs, 125 Sussex Dr., Ottawa, ON K1A 0G2
613/944-5729

Canadian Almanac & Directory 1997

Office Coordinator, Diane Villeneuve
Publications: Bulletin

Government Finance Officers Association of the US & Canada
#800, 180 North Michigan Ave., Chicago, IL 60601 USA
312/977-9700, Fax: 312/977-4806
Executive Director, Jeffrey L. Esser
President, Bonnie Ridley Kraft

Institute on Governance/Institut sur la gouvernance (IOG) (1990)
122 Clarence St., Ottawa, ON K1N 5P6
613/562-0090, Fax: 613/562-0097
Managing Director, Tim Plumptre
Director, Kathleen Lauder
Director, Claire McQuillan
Director, Maureen O'Neil

Institute of Public Administration of Canada/ Institut d'administration publique du Canada (IPAC) (1947)
#305, 150 Eglinton Ave. East, Toronto, ON M4P 1E8
416/932-3666, Fax: 416/923-3667
Executive Director, Joseph M. Galimberti
Publications: Canadian Public Administration/Administration publique du Canada; Public Sector Management, q.

Local Government Administrators of Alberta
4233 - 53 Ave., Red Deer, AB T4N 2E1
403/347-4782
Sec.-Treas., Lois Hyland

Manitoba Association of Urban Municipalities (MAUM) (1950)
#200, 611 Corydon Ave., Winnipeg, MB R3L 0P3
204/982-6286; Purchasing 1-800-563-6286, Fax: 204/478-1005
Executive Director, Rochelle Zimberg
Publications: Mirror on Urban Scene

Manitoba Municipal Administrators Association Inc.
PO Box 220, Rorketon, MB R0L 1R0
204/732-2333, Fax: 204/732-2557
Secretary, Elizabeth Tymchuk

Municipal Officers' Association of British Columbia (1919)
#200, 880 Douglas St., Victoria, BC V8W 2B7
250/383-7032, Fax: 250/384-3000
Executive Director, Lillian Whittier
Sec.-Treas., M. Phelan
President, West Kootenay Chapter, Rae Sawyer
President, East Kootenay Chapter, Mike Cave
President, Okanagan Chapter, Hillary Hettinga
President, Lower Mainland, Chad Turpin
President, Vancouver Island Chapter, Patrick Durban
President, North Central Chapter, Doug Ruttan
Publications: Chapter 290

Newfoundland & Labrador Federation of Municipalities (NLFM) (1951)
PO Box 5756, St. John's, NF A1C 5X3
709/753-6820, Fax: 709/738-0071
Chief Administrator, Patricia Hempstead
President, Sam Synard
Publications: Municipal News

Northeastern Ontario Municipal Association
PO Box 249, Smooth Rock Falls, ON P0L 2B0
705/338-2717, Fax: 705/338-2584
Sec.-Treas., P. Cyr

Northwest Territories Association of Municipalities
Northwest Tower, #904, 5201 - 50 Ave., Yellowknife, NT X1A 3S9
403/873-8359, Fax: 403/873-5801
Executive Director, Yvette Gonzalez
President, Dennis Bevington

Northwestern Ontario Municipal Association (1946)
161 East Brock St., Thunder Bay, ON P7E 4H1
807/626-0155, Fax: 807/626-8163
Executive Director, Ken Taniwa
Affiliates: Association of Municipalities of Ontario

Ontario Municipal Administrators' Association
#101, 49 Emma St., Guelph, ON N1E 6X1
519/837-3369, Fax: 519/837-0729
Sec.-Treas., M.R. Sather

Ontario Municipal Human Resources Association
PO Box 400, Waterloo, ON N2J 4A9
519/886-0844, Fax: 519/886-1197
Administrative Officer, Terry Hallman

Ontario Municipal Management Institute (OMMI) (1979)
PO Box 58009, Oshawa, ON L1J 8L6
905/434-8885, Fax: 905/434-7381
Executive Director, Bill McKim
President, Mario Belvedere
Publications: You & Your Local Government; OMMI Quarterly Report; Network

Organization of Small Urban Municipalities (Ontario)
55 King St. West, Cobourg, ON K9A 2M2
905/372-4301, Fax: 905/372-1533
Executive Secretary, B.W. Baxter

The Public Affairs Association of Canada/ Association des affaires publiques du Canada (PAAC) (1988)
#1105, 191 The West Mall, Etobicoke, ON M9C 5K8
416/620-5055, Fax: 416/626-5392
Association Manager, Brenda Looyenga
Publications: Public Affairs

Rural & Improvement Districts Association of Alberta (RIDAA) (1976)
Site 206, RR#2, PO Box 36, St Albert, AB T8N 1M9
403/973-6762, Fax: 403/973-6864
Executive Director, Shirley Mercier

Rural Municipal Administrators' Association of Saskatchewan (RMAAS)
PO Box 146, Harris, SK S0L 1K0
306/656-2072, Fax: 306/656-2151
Executive Director, Jim Angus
President, Audrey Trombley
Publications: Newsletter

Saskatchewan Association of Rural Municipalities (SARM) (1905)
2075 Hamilton St., Regina, SK S4P 2E1
306/757-3577, Fax: 306/565-2141, Toll Free: 1-800-667-3604
Executive Director, Ken Engel
Publications: The Rural Councillor

Saskatchewan Urban Municipalities Association (SUMA) (1906)
#200, 1819 Cornwall St., Regina, SK S4P 2K4
306/525-3727, Fax: 306/565-3552
Executive Director, Keith Schneider
Publications: The Urban Voice

Society of Local Government Managers of Alberta
4629 - 54 Ave., PO Box 308, Bruderheim, AB T0B 0S0
403/796-3836, Fax: 403/796-2081
Sec.-Treas., Linda M. Davies

Union of BC Municipalities (1904)
#15, 10551 Shellbridge Way, Richmond, BC V6X 2W9
604/270-8226, Fax: 604/660-2271, Email: ubcm@civ-icnet.gov.bc.ca
Executive Director, Richard Taylor
President, Joanne Monaghan
Publications: UBCM News

Union of Manitoba Municipalities (UMM) (1903)
PO Box 397, Portage La Prairie, MB R1N 3B7
204/857-8666, Fax: 204/239-5050
Executive Director, Jerome Mauws
Secretary, Connie Krawec
Publications: Keystone Municipal News

Union des municipalités du Québec (UMQ) (1919)
#680, 680, rue Sherbrooke ouest, Montréal, PQ H3A 2M7
514/282-7700, Téléc: 514/282-7711
Directeur général, Raymond L'Italien
Président, Gilles Vaillancourt
Publications: Partenaires; Urba, 10 fois par an
Organisation(s) affiliée(s): Conseil du patronat du Québec; Fédération canadienne des municipalités;

Union des municipalités régionales de comté et des municipalités locales du Québec (UMRCQ) (1944)
#560, 2954, boul Laurier, Ste-Foy, PQ G1V 4T2
418/651-3343, Téléc: 418/651-1127
Directeur général, Michel Fernet
Publications: Quorum; L'Union, 5 fois par an

Union of Municipalities of New Brunswick/Union des Municipalités du Nouveau-Brunswick (UMNB) (1995)
115 Allan-a-dale Lane, Rothesay, NB E2E 1H2
506/849-6997, Fax: 506/849-6994
Executive Director, Yvonne Gibb
President, Ronald Long
Publications: Newsletter

Union of Nova Scotia Municipalities (1905)
#1106, 1809 Barrington St., Halifax, NS B3J 3K8
902/423-8331, Fax: 902/425-5592
Executive Director, Kenneth Simpson
Administrative Assistant, Judy Webber
Publications: Municipal Open Line

Urban Municipal Administrators' Association of Saskatchewan (UMAAS) (1974)
PO Box 730, Hudson Bay, SK S0E 0Y0
306/865-2261, Fax: 306/865-2800
Executive Director, Richard Dolezsar
President, John Wade
Publications: UMAAS Update

GRAPHIC ARTS see **PRINTING INDUSTRY & GRAPHIC ARTS**

GROCERY TRADE see **FOOD & BEVERAGE INDUSTRY**

HEALTH & MEDICAL
see also AIDS; Dental; Disabled Persons; Hospitals; Mental Health; Nursing; Research & Scholarship;

Academy of Medicine, Ottawa (1931)
#1, 1867 Alta Vista Dr., PO Box 8223, Ottawa, ON K1G 3H7

613/733-2604, Fax: 613/731-1779
Executive Secretary, Gayle Desserud
President, Dr. Byron Lemmex
Publications: Newsletter
Affiliates: Ontario Medical Association

Academy of Medicine, Toronto (1907)
704 Spadina Rd., PO Box 549, Stn P, Toronto, ON M5S 2T1
President, Dr. John H. Fowler, M.D., 416/465-2800
Publications: The Bulletin

Acoustic Neuroma Association of Canada/Association pour les Neurinomes acoustiques du Canada (ANAC) (1984)
PO Box 369, Edmonton, AB T5J 2J6
403/428-3384, Toll Free: 1-800-561-2622, Email: anac@compusmart.ab.ca
President, Shirley Entis
Office Manager, Linda Gray
Publications: The Connection

Acupuncture Foundation of Canada Institute/Institut de la Fondation d'Acupuncture du Canada (AFCI) (1995)
3003 Danforth Ave., PO Box 93688, RPO Shoppers World, Toronto, ON M4C 5R5
416/752-3988, Fax: 416/752-4398, Email: info@afcinstitute.com
URL: http://www.afcinstitute.com/afc.html
Executive Director, Cheryll A. Kwok
Executive President, Linda Rapson, MD
Publications: Acupuncture Canada
Affiliates: World Federation of Acupuncture Societies; Pan Pacific Medical Acupuncture Forum; NAFTA Acupuncture Commission

Addictions Foundation of Manitoba
1031 Portage Ave., Winnipeg, MB R3G 0R8
204/944-6200, Fax: 204/772-0225
Publications: Wings; Directions, 3 pa

African Medical & Research Foundation Canada (AMREF Canada) (1973)
59 Front St. East, Toronto, ON M5E 1B3
416/601-6981, Fax: 416/601-6984
Executive Director, Gillian Evans
Treasurer/Secretary, Bill Crawford
Chairman, Arthur S. Labatt
Publications: News Update
Affiliates: African Medical & Research Foundations Nairobi; Ontario Africa Working Group

Alberta Association of Naturopathic Practitioners
921 - 17 Ave. SW, Calgary, AB T2T 0A4
403/244-4989, Fax: 403/228-6750
Executive Sec.-Treas., Dr. Karen Jansen

Alberta Heritage Foundation for Medical Research
Manulife Place, #3125, 10180 - 101 St., Edmonton, AB T5J 3S4
403/423-5727, Fax: 403/429-3509
President, Matthew Spence
Contact, Public Relations, Lois Hammond

Allergy Asthma Information Association/Association de l'information sur l'allergie et l'asthme (AAIA) (1964)
30 Eglinton Ave. West, Mississauga, ON L5R 3E7
905/712-2242, Fax: 905/712-2245
Executive Director, Susan Daglish
Operations Manager, Tom J. Christie
Publications: Newsletter
Affiliates: Canadian Society of Allergy & Clinical Immunology

Atlantic Regional Office: Coordinator, Gloria J. Shanks, 20 South Rd., Doaktown, NB E0C 1G0, 506/365-4501
BC/Yukon Regional Office: Mairee Gandera, #303, 1212 West Broadway, Vancouver, BC V6H 3V1, 604/731-9884
Ontario Regional Office: Ontario Regional Coordinator, Megan Boyes, 27 Griselda Cres., Scarborough, ON M1G 3P5, 416/439-8616
Prairies/NWT Regional Office: Coordinator, Lilly Byrtus, 16531 - 114 St., Edmonton, AB T5X 3V4, 403/456-6651
Québec Regional Office: Regional Coordinator, Mary L. Allen, 172, rue Andover, Beaconsfield, PQ H9W 2Z8, 514/694-0679, Fax: 514/694-0679

Allergy Foundation of Canada/Fondation du Canada des allergies (1974)
PO Box 1904, Saskatoon, SK S7K 3S5
306/373-7591, Email: swoynars@eagle.wbm.ca
President, Sandy Woynarski
Publications: Allergy Alert

Alliance of Physiotherapy Regulatory Boards/Alliance des corporations professionnelles de physiothérapeutes (1987)
230 Richmond St. West, 10th Fl., Toronto, ON M4V 1V6
416/591-3828, Fax: 416/591-3834
Executive Director, Susan G. Takahashi
Chair, Brenda Hudson
Publications: The Alliance Newsletter

Alzheimer Society of Canada/Société Alzheimer du Canada (ASC) (1977)
#201, 1320 Yonge St., Toronto, ON M4T 1X2
416/925-3552, Fax: 416/925-1649
Executive Director, Stephen E. Rudin, M.Ed.
Director, Communications & Public Relations, Lisa Dower
Publications: Alzheimer Report
Affiliates: HealthPartners

ALZHEIMER ASSOCIATION OF ALBERTA (1988)
#218A, 2323 - 32 Ave. NE, Calgary, AB T2E 6Z3
403/250-1303, Fax: 403/250-8241, Toll Free: 1-888-233-0332, Email: alzhab@agt.net
Publications: Alberta Perspective
Affiliates: Canadian Association on Gerontology; Alberta Association on Gerontology; Canadian Centre for Philanthropy

ALZHEIMER ASSOCIATION OF ONTARIO/ASSOCIATION ALZHEIMER D'ONTARIO (1983)
Alzheimer Ontario
#202, 1200 Bay St., Toronto, ON M5R 2A5
416/967-5900, Fax: 416/967-3826
Executive Director, John Ellis
President, Shelley McEachern
Publications: Alzheimer Journal

ALZHEIMER ASSOCIATION OF SASKATCHEWAN INC. (1982)
#301, 2550 - 12th Ave., Regina, SK S4P 3X1
306/949-4141, Fax: 306/949-3069, Toll Free: 1-800-263-3367
Executive Director, Joan Kortje
Office Coordinator, Linda Orell
President, Barbara Wilson
Publications: Alzheimer Newsletter

ALZHEIMER MANITOBA (1982)
205 Edmonton St., Winnipeg, MB R3C 1R4
204/943-6622, Fax: 204/942-5408, Toll Free: 1-800-378-6699
Executive Director, Sylvia Rothney
Publications: Reflects

ALZHEIMER SOCIETY OF BC (1981)
#20, 601 West Cordova St., Vancouver, BC V6B 1G1

604/681-6530, Fax: 604/669-6907, Toll Free: 1-800-667-3742
Executive Director, Ian Ross
Publications: Contact; In Touch, bi-m.

ALZHEIMER SOCIETY OF NEW BRUNSWICK/SOCIÉTÉ ALZHEIMER DU NOUVEAU BRUNSWICK (1987)
PO Box 1553, Stn A, Fredericton, NB E3A 5G2
506/459-4280, Fax: 506/452-0313, Toll Free: 1-800-664-8411
Executive Director, Gloria McIlveen
President, Exelda Gaston
Secretary, Joan McKell
Publications: The Beacon

ALZHEIMER SOCIETY OF NOVA SCOTIA (1983)
5954 Spring Garden Rd., Halifax, NS B3H 1Y7
902/422-7961, Fax: 902/422-7971
Executive Director, Penny Doherty
Publications: Alzheimers Nova Scotia

ALZHEIMER SOCIETY OF PEI
166 Fitzroy St., Charlottetown, PE C1A 1S1
902/628-2257, Fax: 902/368-2715
Executive Director, Judy McCann-Beranger

FÉDÉRATION QUÉBÉCOISE DES SOCIÉTÉS ALZHEIMER (FQSA) (1985)
1474, rue Fleury est, Montréal, PQ H2C 1S1
514/388-3148, Téléc: 514/381-3462, Ligne sans frais: 1-800-636-6473, Courrier électronique: alzqc@generation.net
Directrice générale, Dr. Lise Hébert

NEWFOUNDLAND ALZHEIMER ASSOCIATION INC. (1988)
Southcott Hall, #328-329, 100 Forest Rd., 3rd Fl., St. John's, NF A1A 1E5
709/576-0608, Fax: 709/576-0608
President, Margaret Adey
Publications: Newsletter

Amyotrophic Lateral Sclerosis Society of Canada/Société canadienne de la sclérose latérale amyotrophique (ALS) (1977)
ALS Society of Canada
#220, 6 Adelaide St. East, Toronto, ON M5C 1H6
416/362-0269, Fax: 416/362-0414, Toll Free: 1-800-267-4257, Email: alssoc@inforamp.net
URL: http://www.als.ca
President, W. Brian Smith
Director of Marketing & Communications, Geoff Dewar
Publications: ALS Outlook
Affiliates: Amyotrophic Lateral Sclerosis Association (USA)

Aplastic Anemia Association of Canada (AAAC)
22 Aikenhead Rd., Etobicoke, ON M9R 2Z3
416/235-0468, Fax: 416/576-7400, Toll Free: 1-800-668-3683
Chairperson, Don McIntyre
Publications: Newsletter

The Arthritis Society/Société d'arthrite (1948)
#901, 250 Bloor St. East, Toronto, ON M4W 3P2
416/967-1414, Fax: 416/967-7171
Chairperson, Douglas S. Price
President/CEO, Denis Morrice
Vice-President/Communications, Sharon McConnell
Publications: Intercom; Arthritis News/ArthroExpress, q.

Association Canadienne de l'Ataxie de Friedreich/Canadian Association of Friedreich's Ataxia (ACAF) (1972)
Fondation Claude St-Jean
5620, rue C.A. Jobin, St-Léonard, PQ H1P 1H8
514/321-8684
Président, Claude St-Jean

Canadian Almanac & Directory 1997

Publications: Eldorado
Bureau des Services sociaux: Personne ressource, Gina Tourigny, 3800, rue Radisson, Montréal, PQ H1M 1X6, 514/899-1586, Téléc: 514/899-1586

Association des chirurgiens généraux du Québec
#3000, 2, Complexe Desjardins, Montréal, PQ
H5B 1G8
514/350-5107, Téléc: 514/350-5157
Président, Michel Talbot
Secrétaire, Grégoire Bégin
Secrétariat, Marcelle Rousseau

Association des conseils des médecins, dentistes et pharmaciens du Québec/Association of Councils of Physicians, Dentists & Pharmacists of Québec (1947)
308, boul St-Joseph est, Montréal, PQ H2T 1J2
514/842-5059, Téléc: 514/842-5356
Directrice générale, Françoise Cloutier
Ajointe administrative, Nicole Du Rand, 514/842-5050
Publications: Bulletin

Association des dermatologistes du Québec/ Association of Dermatologists of Québec (ADQ)
#3000, 2, Complexe Desjardins, Montréal, PQ
H5B 1G8
514/350-5111, Téléc: 514/350-5161
Président, Pierre Ricard, m.d.
Vice-président, David Gratton, m.d.
Secrétaire, Jacques Tanguay, m.d.
Trésorier, Normand Doré, m.d.
Personne ressource, Louise Papillon

Association Diabète Québec/Québec Diabetes Association (ADQ)
5635, rue Sherbrooke est, Montréal, PQ H1N 1A2
514/259-3422, Téléc: 514/259-9286, Ligne sans frais: 1-800-361-3504
Président-Directeur General, Serge Langlois
Présidente, CPADQ, Jana Havrankova
Publications: Plein Soleil; Info-Diàbete; Info-ADQ
Organisation(s) affiliée(s): Canadian Diabetes Association

Association of District Health Councils of Ontario/ Association des conseils régionaux de santé de l'Ontario (ADHCO)
#201, 4141 Yonge St., North York, ON M2P 2A8
416/222-1445, Fax: 416/222-3229
Executive Director, Gordon E. Gunning, CAE

Association of Local Official Health Agencies (ALOHA) (1986)
#1618, 415 Yonge St., Toronto, ON M5B 2E7
416/595-0006, Fax: 416/595-0030
Executive Director, Gordon White
Coordinator of Associations Services, Susan Lee

Association des médecins de langue française du Canada (1902)
8355, boul Saint-Laurent, Montréal, PQ H2P 2Z6
514/388-2228, Téléc: 514/388-5335
Directeur général, André de Sève

Association des médecins ophtalmologistes du Québec
#3000, 2, Complexe Desjardins, Montréal, PQ
H5B 1G8
514/350-5124
Président, Jean Deschênes
Secrétaire, Pierre Turcotte

Association des médecins du travail du Québec/ Québec Occupational Medical Association
#505, 1100, av Beaumont, Mount Royal, PQ H3P 3E5
514/344-1662, Téléc: 514/737-6431

Directrice administrative, Jocelyne Lessard
Président, Alain Gagnon

Association des néphrologues du Québec
#3000, 2, Complexe Desjardins, Montréal, PQ
H5B 1G8
514/350-5134, Téléc: 514/350-5151
Président, Dr. Raymond Dandavino
Secrétaire, Robert Charbonneau
Secrétariat, Raymonde Dionne

Association des neurochirurgiens du Québec
#3000, 2, Complexe Desjardins, Montréal, PQ
H5B 1G8
514/350-5120, Téléc: 514/350-5100
Président, Jacques Boucher
Secrétaire, Georges L'Espérance
Secrétariat, Raymonde Dionne

Association des neurologues du Québec
#3000, 2, Complexe Desjardins, Montréal, PQ
H5B 1G8
514/350-5122, Téléc: 514/350-5100
Président, Yves Lapierre
Secrétaire, Michel Lebel

Association des obstétriciens et gynécologues du Québec
#3000, 2, Complexe Desjardins, Montréal, PQ
H5B 1G8
514/849-4969, Téléc: 514/350-5100
Présidente, Vyta M. Senikas
Secrétaire, Luc Saint-Pierre
Secrétariat, Francine Charlebois

Association d'orthopédie du Québec
#3000, 2, Complexe Desjardins, Montréal, PQ
H5B 1G8
514/844-0803 ou 350-5000, Téléc: 514/350-5100
Président, Gaétan Langlois
Secrétaire-trésorier, Charles Hilaire Rivard
Secrétariat, Louise Leclaire

Association d'oto-rhino-laryngologie et de chirurgie cervico-faciale du Québec
#3000, 2, Complexe Desjardins, Montréal, PQ
H5B 1G8
514/350-5125
Président, Michel Rouleau
Secrétaire, Ted Tewfik

Association des pathologistes du Québec
#3000, 2, Complexe Desjardins, Montréal, PQ
H5B 1G8
514/350-5102, Téléc: 514/350-5100
Président, Rénald Morency
Secrétaire, Pierre Russo

Association des pédiatres du Québec
#3000, 2, Complexe Desjardins, Montréal, PQ
H5B 1G8
514/350-5127, Téléc: 514/350-5100
Président, Claude Lemoine
Secrétaire, Pierre Gaudreault

Association des pharmaciens des établissements de santé du Québec (APES) (1963)
4874, av Grosvenor, Montréal, PQ H3W 2M1
514/487-8912, Téléc: 514/381-2781
Directeur général, Jean-Claude Martin
Publications: Pharmactuel

Association des physiâtres du Québec
#3000, 2, Complexe Desjardins, Montréal, PQ
H5B 1G8
514/350-5119, Téléc: 514/350-5100

Président, Marcel Morand
Secrétaire-trésorier, Denis Raymond

Association professionnelle des technologues diplômés en electrophysiologie médicale (APTDEPM) (1989)
1063A, av Larivière, Rouyn-Noranda, PQ J9X 4K9
819/762-2376, Téléc: 819/762-2376
Président, Steve Girard
Secrétaire-trésorière, Isabelle Charbonneau
Administratrice, Marléne Galarneau
Directrice des comités, Annie Dubois
Publications: Le Potentiel

Association québécoise de la fibrose kystique/ Québec Cystic Fibrosis Association (AQFK) (1981)
#2260, 800, boul René-Lévesque ouest, Montréal, PQ
H3B 1X9
514/877-6161, Téléc: 514/877-6116, Ligne sans frais: 1-800-363-7711
Directrice générale, Denise Ménard
Publications: Commentaires; À Propos, trimestriel; Santé vous bien, trimestriel; Info FK

Association des radiologistes du Québec
#3000, 2, Complexe Desjardins, Montréal, PQ
H5B 1G8
514/350-5129, Téléc: 514/350-5100
Président, Guy Breton
Secrétaire, Jacques Lévesque

Asthma Society of Canada/Société canadienne de l'asthme (ASC) (1974)
#425, 130 Bridgeland Ave., Toronto, ON M6A 1Z4
416/787-4050, Fax: 416/787-5807, Toll Free: 1-800-787-3880
Executive Director, Elizabeth Kovac
Publications: Attack on Asthma

Autism Society Canada/Société canadienne d'autisme (ASC) (1976)
#202, 129 Yorkville Ave., Toronto, ON M5R 1C4
416/922-0302, Fax: 416/922-1032
Executive Director, David White
Publications: Rendezvous

AUTISM SOCIETY ALBERTA (ASA) (1972)
#101, 11720 Kingsway Ave., Edmonton, AB T5G 0X5
403/453-3971, Fax: 403/447-4948
Contact, Barbara Stewart

AUTISM SOCIETY OF BRITISH COLUMBIA
1584 Rand Ave., Vancouver, BC V6P 3G2
604/261-8888, Fax: 604/261-7898
Executive Director, Natalia Bouvier
Autism Support Network Director, S. Janssen
Publications: PAAC Newsletter

AUTISM SOCIETY MANITOBA
825 Sherbrook St., 2nd Fl., Winnipeg, MB R3A 1M5
204/772-6979, Fax: 204/786-0860
President, Tony Schweitzer
Publications: Newsletter

AUTISM SOCIETY NEW BRUNSWICK
PO Box 635, Fredericton, NB E3B 5B4
506/363-3200, Fax: 506/363-4106
President, Karen Cunningham

AUTISM SOCIETY NEWFOUNDLAND & LABRADOR (1987)
#407, 156 Portugal Cove Rd., St. John's, NF A1B 4H9
709/737-2073, Fax: 709/753-3801
President, Barbara Hopkins

AUTISM SOCIETY NOVA SCOTIA (ASNS) (1977)
PO Box 392, Sydney, NS B1P 6H2
902/539-8323
President, Phyllis Frost

ORGANIZATIONS — HEALTH & MEDICAL 2-83

Publications: Newsletter
Affiliates: Society for Treatment of Autism

AUTISM SOCIETY ONTARIO (1973)
#302, 300 Sheppard Ave. West, North York, ON M2N 1N5
416/512-9880, Fax: 416/512-8026
Executive Director, Jane Vinet
Publications: Newslink

AUTISM SOCIETY PEI
PO Box 75, York, PE C0A 1P0
902/368-2685
President, Carolyn Bateman

SASKATCHEWAN SOCIETY FOR THE AUTISTIC INC. (1976)
3510 - 25 Ave., Regina, SK S4S 1L8
306/586-4615
President, Dennis Nestegard
Affiliates: Saskatoon Society for Autism; Regina District Society for the Autistic

SOCIÉTÉ QUÉBÉCOISE DE L'AUTISME/QUÉBEC SOCIETY FOR AUTISM (1976)
2300, boul René-Lévesque ouest, Montréal, PQ H3H 2R5
514/931-2215, Téléc: 514/931-2397
Directrice générale, Manon Carle Dagenais
Publications: Express

Autism Treatment Services of Canada
404 - 94 Ave. SE, Calgary, AB T2J 0E8
403/253-6961, Fax: 403/253-6974
Executive Director, Dr. Dave Mikkelson

Breast Cancer Society of Canada/Société du cancer du sein du Canada
401 St. Clair St., Point Edward, ON N7V 1P2
519/336-6846
Contact, L.M. Greenaway

British Columbia Cancer Foundation (BCCF) (1935)
601 - 10th Ave. West., Vancouver, BC V5Z 1L3
604/877-6010, Fax: 604/872-4596
President, Anna Linsley
Affiliates: British Columbia Cancer Research Centre

British Columbia Ear Bank (1973)
Burrard Bldg., St. Paul's Hospital, #1353, 1081 Burrard St., Vancouver, BC V6Z 1Y6
604/631-5636, Fax: 604/631-5705
Manager, Dr. Leo Yang
Director, Chee N. Thong

British Columbia Health Association (BCHA) (1917)
#600, 1333 Broadway West, Vancouver, BC V6H 4C7
604/734-2423, Fax: 604/734-7202, Telex: 04-54300
President/CEO, Mary Collins
Chairman, Paul Chapin
Publications: BCHA News; BC Health Care: Facts & Views; BC Health Management Review, s-a.; From the President, m.; Figuring Health Care

British Columbia Medical Services Foundation (1968)
230, One Bentall Centre, 505 Burrard St., Vancouver, BC V7X 1M3
604/688-2204, Fax: 604/688-4170
Program Director, Barbara Oates

British Columbia Paraplegic Association (BCPA) (1957)
780 Marine Dr. SW, Vancouver, BC V6P 5Y7
604/324-3611, Fax: 604/324-3671
Executive Director, Norman Haw
Executive Assistant, M. Brownlee

Publications: Paragraphic
Affiliates: BC Injury Prevention Centre

British Columbia Parkinson's Disease Association (BCPDA)
411 Dunsmuir St., 3rd Fl., Vancouver, BC V6B 1X4
604/662-3240, Fax: 604/662-3241, Toll Free: 1-800-668-3330
Executive Director, Lois Raphael
Publications: BCPDA Newletter

British Columbia Transplant Society (BCTS) (1985)
East Tower, 555 West 12th Ave., 4th Fl., Vancouver, BC V5Z 3X7
604/877-2100, Fax: 604/877-2111, Toll Free: 1-800-663-6189
Director/CEO, Bill Barrable

Canadian Academy of Facial Plastic & Reconstructive Surgery/Académie canadienne de chirurgie plastique et reconstructive faciale (CAFPRS) (1981)
#401, 600 University Ave., Toronto, ON M5G 1X5
905/569-6965, Toll Free: 1-800-545-8864
President, Dr. Steven Cohen
Executive Director, Marcy Binsky

Canadian Anaesthetists' Society/Société canadienne des anesthésistes (CAS) (1943)
#208, One Eglinton Ave. East, Toronto, ON M4P 3A1
416/480-0602, Fax: 416/480-0320, Email: cas@multinet.org
Executive Director, Ann Andrews
President, Dr. Pierre Limoges
Meeting & Congress Coordinator, Annette Schilz
Publications: Canadian Journal of Anaesthesia; CAS Newsletter, triennial
Affiliates: World Federation of Societies of Anaesthesiologists; Royal College of Physicians & Surgeons of Canada; Canadian Medical Association; Canadian Standards Association; Society for Education in Anesthesia

Canadian Association of Cardio-Pulmonary Technologists (CACPT) (1970)
PO Box 848, Stn A, Toronto, ON M5W 1G3
416/243-3600, ext.2201
President, John Fedirko
Treasurer, Lori Davis
Publications: C-P Update

Canadian Association of Centres for the Management of Hereditary Metabolic Diseases
GARROD Association
c/o Winnipeg Children's Hospital, 840 Sherbrook St., FE229, Winnipeg, MB R3A 1S1
204/787-4591, Fax: 204/787-1419
Contact, Dr. Cheryl R. Greenberg

Canadian Association of Child Neurology Corporation/Corporation de l'association canadienne de neurologie pédiatrique (1991)
Hospital for Sick Children, 555 University Ave., Toronto, ON M5G 1X8
416/813-6332, Fax: 416/813-6334
President, Dr. William J. Logan

Canadian Association for Clinical Microbiology & Infectious Diseases/Association canadienne de microbiologie clinique et des maladies contagieuses (CACMID) (1980)
20045, Montée Sainte-Marie, Montréal, PQ H9X 3R5
514/457-2070, Fax: 514/457-6346
Director, Head of Infectious Diseases, Dr. I. Salit
Sec.-Treas., Dr. Wayne C. Bradbury
Publications: CACMID Newsletter; Directory of Specialists in Microbiology & Infectious Disease, a.

Affiliates: Canadian Association of Medical Microbiologists; Canadian Infectious Diseases Society; Canadian Society of Microbiologists; Association des microbiologistes du Québec; Pan-American Group for Rapid Viral Diagnosis; Biological Implications of Pathogenicity Group; Canadian Society for International Health

The Canadian Association of Emergency Physicians/L'Association canadienne des médecins d'urgence (CAEP)
#102, 1785 Alta Vista Dr., Ottawa, ON K1G 3Y6
613/523-3343, Fax: 613/521-4314
URL: http://unixg.ubc.ca:780/~grunfeld/caep.html
President, Dr. Garth Dickinson
Treasurer, Dr. Garnet Cummings
Secretary, Dr. John Talon
Publications: Communiqué; Journal of Emergency Medicine, bi-m.
Affiliates: Canadian Medical Association; Royal College of Physicians & Surgeons of Canada; International Federation of Emergency Medicine; American College of Emergency Physicians

Canadian Association of Gastroenterology/Association canadienne de gastroentérologie
University of Calgary, Dept. of GI Research, #1709, 3330 Hospital Dr. NW, Calgary, AB T2N 4N1
403/220-4539, Fax: 403/283-3028
Executive Director, Dr. John L. Wallace
Affiliates: Canadian Medical Association; World Organization of Gastroenterology

Canadian Association of General Surgeons/Association canadienne des chirurgiens généraux
Health Sciences Centre, 300 Prince Phillip Dr., St. John's, NF A1B 3V6
902/737-6558
President, Dr. Christopher Heughan
Secretary, Dr. Roger Keith
Affiliates: Canadian Medical Association

Canadian Association of Internes & Residents/Association canadienne des internes et résidents
#500, 505 University Ave., Toronto, ON M5G 1X4
416/979-1182, Fax: 416/595-9778
Executive Director, Lois Ross

Canadian Association of Medical Biochemists/Association des médecins biochimistes du Canada (CAMB) (1975)
Hôtel-Dieu de Québec, 11, Côte du Palais, Québec, PQ G1R 2J6
418/691-5135, Fax: 418/691-5383
Sec.-Treas., Dr. Pierre Douville
Affiliates: Royal College of Physicians & Surgeons of Canada

Canadian Association of Medical Microbiologists/Association canadienne des médecins microbiologistes (CAMM) (1961)
c/o Victoria General Hospital, 35 Helmken Rd., Victoria, BC V8Z 6R5
250/727-4494; Fax: 250/727-4480
President, Dr. David Colby, 519/663-3396
Affiliates: Canadian Medical Association; International Congress of Chemotherapy

Canadian Association of Medical Oncologists/Association des oncologues médicaux du Canada
Cross Cancer Institute, 11560 University Ave., Edmonton, AB T6G 1Z2
403/492-8763, Fax: 403/432-7359
President, Dr. Anthony. Fields
Sec.-Treas., Dr. Glenwood Goss

Canadian Almanac & Directory 1997

Canadian Association of Medical Radiation Technologists/Association canadienne des technologues en radiation médicale (CAMRT)
#601, 294 Albert St., Ottawa, ON K1P 6E6
613/234-0012, Fax: 613/234-1097
Executive Director, Dr. Richard Lauzon,
  Email: rlauzon@camrt.ca
President, Bill Brodie, Email: wbrodie@
  neuro_rad.lan.mcgill.ca
Director of Communications, Steven Brasier,
  Email: az972@freenet.carleton.ca
Registrar, Norma Saunders
Director of Education, Susan Ward
Publications: The Canadian Journal of Medical Radiation Technology; CAMRT News, 5 pa

Canadian Association of Neuropathologists/Association canadienne de neuropathologistes (1960)
London Health Services Centre - Victoria Campus, 375 South St., London, ON N6A 4G5
519/667-6756, Fax: 519/667-6749, Email: davidr@lhsc.on.ca
President, Dr. S. Ludwin
Sec.-Treas., Dr. D.A. Ramsay
Affiliates: International Society of Neuropathology

Canadian Association of Nuclear Medicine Inc./Association canadienne de médecine nucléaire
774 Echo Dr., Ottawa, ON K1S 5N8
613/730-6254, Fax: 613/730-1116
President, Dr. Karen Gulchyn
Publications: Photon
Affiliates: Canadian Medical Association; Society of Nuclear Medicine - USA; Canadian Association of Radiation Protection

Canadian Association of Occupational Therapists/Association canadienne des ergothérapeutes (CAOT) (1926)
Carleton Technology & Training Centre, #3400, 1125 Colonel By Dr., Ottawa, ON K1S 5R1
613/523-2268, Fax: 613/523-2552, Toll Free: 1-800-434-2268
President, Heather Chilton
Executive Director, Anne Strickland
Publications: National; The Canadian Journal of Occupational Therapy, bi-m.

Canadian Association of Optometrists/Association canadienne des optométristes (CAO) (1948)
#301, 1785 Alta Vista Dr., Ottawa, ON K1G 3Y6
613/738-4412, Fax: 613/738-7161
URL: http://fox.nstn.ca/~eyedocs/caoorg.html
CEO, Michael J. DiCola
Director of Administration, Chantale Wall
Publications: Canadian Journal of Optometry
Affiliates: American Optometric Association; International Federation of Asian & Pacific Associations of Optometrists; World Council of Optometry

ALBERTA ASSOCIATION OF OPTOMETRISTS
#902, 11830 Kingsway Ave., Edmonton, AB T5G 0X5
403/451-6824, Fax: 403/452-9918
Executive Director, R. Glenn Campbell
President, Dr. Dorrie Morrow

ASSOCIATION DES OPTOMÉTRISTES DU QUÉBEC (AOQ)
133, rue de la Commune ouest, 4e étage, Montréal, PQ H2Y 2C7
514/849-8051, Téléc: 514/849-7201
Directeur général, François Charbonneau
Président, Dr. Claude Neilson

BRITISH COLUMBIA ASSOCIATION OF OPTOMETRISTS (BCAO) (1921)
#125, 10451 Shellbridge Way, Richmond, BC V6X 2W8
604/270-9909
Executive Director, Thomas J. Little
President, Dr. Joan Hansen
Publications: The Optometrist

MANITOBA ASSOCIATION OF OPTOMETRISTS (MAO) (1909)
#878, 167 Lombard Ave., Winnipeg, MB R3B 0V3
204/943-9811, Fax: 204/943-1208
Executive Director, Carol Loyd
President, Dr. Jane Thrall

NEW BRUNSWICK ASSOCIATION OF OPTOMETRISTS/ASSOCIATION DES OPTOMÉTRISTES DU NOUVEAU-BRUNSWICK
20 Woodstock Rd., Fredericton, NB E3B 2H3
506/458-8759, Fax: 506/450-1271
Executive Director, Denise Roy
President, Dr. Lillian Linton

NEWFOUNDLAND ASSOCIATION OF OPTOMETRISTS
PO Box 2284, Stn C, St. John's, NF A1C 6E6
709/368-0380, Fax: 709/368-4139
Executive Director, Nap Dupuis
President, Dr. Ian Henderson

NOVA SCOTIA ASSOCIATION OF OPTOMETRISTS
Comp 83, Caribou Wilds, RR#4, Lower Sackville, NS B4C 3B1
902/835-9318, Fax: 902/928-0933
President, Dr. Ray Wagg
Sec.-Treas., Dr. Carl Davis

ONTARIO ASSOCIATION OF OPTOMETRISTS (1909)
290 Lawrence Ave. West, Toronto, ON M5M 1B3
416/256-4411, Fax: 416/256-9881
Executive Director, Dennis E. Souder, CAE
President, Dr. Richard Kniaziew
Publications: Insight

PRINCE EDWARD ISLAND ASSOCIATION OF OPTOMETRISTS
111 Pownal St., PO Box 2847, Charlottetown, PE C1A 3W4
902/566-4418, Fax: 902/566-4694
President, Dr. Jane Toombs
Secretary, Dr. David McKenna

SASKATCHEWAN ASSOCIATION OF OPTOMETRISTS (SAO) (1909)
125 - 3 Ave. South, Saskatoon, SK S7K 1L6
306/652-2069, Fax: 306/652-2642
Executive Director, Donald D. Sauer
President, Dr. W. Bruce Robinson
Publications: SAO Newsletter

Canadian Association of Oral & Maxillofacial Surgeons/Association canadienne de spécialistes en chirurgie buccale et maxillo-faciale (1953)
#304, 333 Wethersfield Dr., Vancouver, BC V5X 4M9
604/322-3025, Fax: 604/322-3025, Email: caoms@portal.ca
President, Dr. Sam Kucey
Publications: The Voice

Canadian Association of Paediatric Surgeons/Association de la chirurgie infantile canadienne
Regina General Hospital, 1440 - 14th Ave., Regina, SK S4P 0W5
306/359-4542, Fax: 306/359-4723
President, Dr. Angus Juckes
Publications: Journal of Paediatric Surgery

Canadian Association of Pathologists
Toronto General Hospital, #EC4-316, 200 Elizabeth St., Toronto, ON M5G 2C4
416/340-3008, Fax: 416/340-4706
Sec.-Treas., Joan Sweet
Secrétaire-trésorier, Dr. Vincent Bernier
Publications: Newsletter

Canadian Association of Physical Medicine & Rehabilitation/Association canadienne de médecine physique et de réadaptation (CAPMR)
774 Echo Dr., Ottawa, ON K1S 5N8
613/730-6240, Fax: 613/730-1116
President, Dr. Ron Bowie
Publications: CAPM&R News
Affiliates: Canadian Medical Association

Canadian Association of Prosthetists & Orthotists/Association canadienne des prosthesistes et orthesistes (CAPO) (1955)
#401, 225 Vaughan St., Winnipeg, MB R3C 1T7
204/949-4970, Fax: 204/947-3627
President, Allan O'Neill
Publications: CAPO Yearbook
Affiliates: Canadian Board for Certification of Prosthetists & Orthotists

Canadian Association for Quality in Health Care/Association canadienne pour la qualité dans les services de santé (CAQHC) (1981)
8 Astley Ave., Toronto, ON M4W 3B4
416/975-0204, Fax: 416/972-1366,
  Email: caqhc_admin@hpb.hwc.ca
URL: http://www.hwc.ca:8080/caqhc/
President, MaryLou Harrigan
Publications: QA Link; The Canadian Journal of Quality in Health Care

Canadian Association of Radiologists/L'Association canadienne des radiologistes (CAR) (1937)
#510, 5101, rue Buchan, Montréal, PQ H4P 2R9
514/738-3111, Fax: 514/738-5199
Executive Director, Suzanne Charette
Publications: Canadian Association of Radiologists' Journal; Illuminator, bi-m.

Canadian Association of Speech-Language Pathologists & Audiologists/Association canadienne des orthophonistes et audiologistes (CASLPA) (1965)
#2006, 130 Albert St., Ottawa, ON K1P 5G4
613/567-9968, Fax: 613/567-2859
Executive Director, Keith Christopher
President, Randall Murphy
Manager, Publications & Communications, Carole Saidon
Publications: Communiqué; Journal of Speech-Language Pathology & Audiology, q.
Affiliates: International Association of Logopedics & Phoniatrics

Canadian Athletic Therapists Association/Association canadienne des thérapeutes du sport (CATA) (1965)
Place R. Tait McKenzie, #507, 1600 James Naismith Dr., Gloucester, ON K1B 5N4
613/748-5876, Fax: 613/748-5850
President, Dale Butterwick
Program Coordinator, Laurel McDonald
Publications: CATA Newsletter; Journal of the Canadian Athletic Therapists' Association, a.

Canadian Brain Tissue Bank
Banting Institute, #127, 100 College St., Toronto, ON M5G 1L5
416/977-3398, Fax: 416/964-2165
Coordinator, Administration, R.D. Brown
Tissue Coordinator, M. Pataki
Medical Director, T.P. Morley

Canadian Cancer Society/Société canadienne du cancer (1938)
#200, 10 Alcorn Ave., Toronto, ON M4V 3B1
416/961-7223, Fax: 416/961-4189; Toll-Free: 1-800-939-3333

CEO, Dorothy J. Lamont
Executive Director, Programs & Planning, Maaike Asselbergs
President, Dr. Ronald J. Potter
Director of Public Relations, Michael McFarland
Publications: National News; Progress Against Cancer, q.; Canadian Cancer Statistics, a.
Affiliates: International Union Against Cancer

Canadian Cardiovascular Society/Societé canadienne de cardiologie (CCS) (1962)
#401, 360, av Victoria, Westmount, PQ H3Z 2N4
514/482-3407, Fax: 514/482-6574
Executive Director, Linda Theriault
Affiliates: International Society & Federation of Cardiology; Inter-American Society of Cardiology; Canadian Society of Clinical Perfusionists; Canadian Society of Cardiology Technologists; Canadian Association of Cardiopulmonary Technologists; Canadian Medical Association; Canadian Coalition for High Blood Pressure Prevention & Control

Canadian Celiac Association/Association canadienne de la maladie coéliaque (CCA) (1976)
Celiac Canada
6519B Mississauga Rd., Mississauga, ON L5N 1A6
905/567-7195, Fax: 905/567-0710, Toll Free: 1-800-363-7296
Executive Director, Judi Sennett
President, Gwen Shaver
Publications: Celiac News

Canadian Centre for Occupational Health & Safety/Centre canadien d'hygiène et de sécurité au travail (CCOHS) (1978)
250 Main St. East, Hamilton, ON L8N 1H6
905/570-8094, Fax: 905/572-2206, Toll Free: 1-800-668-4284, Email: custserv@ccohs.ca
URL: http://www.ccohs.ca/
President/CEO, J. Arthur St-Aubin
Vice-President, P.K. Abeytunga
Manager, Inquiries Service, Roger Cockerline
Manager, Operations Support, Eleanor Irwin
Comptroller, Brian Hutchings
Manager, Health & Safety Products, Anne Gravereaux
Manager, Computer Systems, Ashok Setty
Publications: Operations; Materials; Working Environments; Work Related Diseases; Programs; Physical Agents; Statistics; Occupational Health & Safety Issues; Liaison, q.

Canadian Chiropractic Association/Association chiropratique canadienne (CCA) (1943)
1396 Eglinton Ave. West, Toronto, ON M6C 2E4
416/781-5656, Fax: 416/781-7344
Executive Director, Edward Barisa
Publications: Journal of the Canadian Chiropractic Association; CCA News, bi-m.
Affiliates: Canadian Chiropractic Examining Board; Canadian Chiropractic Historical Association; Canadian Chiropractic Protective Association; Canadian Chiropractic Supply Division; Canadian Federation of Chiropractic Regulatory Boards; Canadian Memorial Chiropractic College; Chiropractic Foundation for Spinal Research; Council on Chiropractic Education (Canada); Module de chiropratique - L'UQTR

ASSOCIATION DES CHIROPRATICIENS DU QUÉBEC
7960, boul Metropolitain est, Anjou, PQ H1K 1A1
514/355-0557, Téléc: 514/355-0070
Secrétaire exécutive, M. Marois
Président, Dr. C. Gelinas, 418/835-6064

BRITISH COLUMBIA CHIROPRACTIC ASSOCIATION (BCCC) (1934)
#102, 7031 Westminster Hwy., Richmond, BC V6X 1A3
604/270-1332, Fax: 604/278-0093
Executive Director, Dr. D. Nixdorf

COLLEGE OF CHIROPRACTORS OF ALBERTA (1986)
Manulife Place, #1870, 10180 - 101 St., Edmonton, AB T5J 3S4
403/420-0932, Fax: 403/425-6583
Executive Director, Debbie Manz
Publications: Portfolio; Bargain Finder, m.

MANITOBA CHIROPRACTORS' ASSOCIATION (MCA) (1945)
#2706, 83 Garry St., Winnipeg, MB R3C 4J9
204/942-3000, Fax: 204/942-3010
Executive Director, G.L. Clement

NEW BRUNSWICK CHIROPRACTORS' ASSOCIATION (1958)
PO Box 21046, Oromocto, NB E2V 2R9
506/450-0600
President, Dr. M.L. Blanchette, 506/548-9595
Secretary, Dr. C.J. Levere

NEWFOUNDLAND & LABRADOR CHIROPRACTIC ASSOCIATION
724 Water St., St. John's, NF A1E 1C2
709/726-4076
President, Dr. K. Beatty
President, Dr. L. Goyeche, 709/726-4076, Fax: 709/739-7762

NOVA SCOTIA CHIROPRACTIC ASSOCIATION
PO Box 1041, Port Hawkesbury, NS B0E 2V0
902/625-0005, Fax: 902/625-1441
President, Dr. M.I. Parker, 902/667-1236
Sec.-Treas., Dr. D. MacNeil

ONTARIO CHIROPRACTIC ASSOCIATION (OCA) (1929)
#30, 5160 Explorer Dr., Mississauga, ON L4W 4T7
905/629-8211, Fax: 905/629-8214
Executive Director, Peter Waite, CAE

PRINCE EDWARD ISLAND CHIROPRACTIC ASSOCIATION
266 Read Dr., Summerside, PE C1N 5A9
902/436-7183
Sec.-Treas., Dr. Vincent Adams
President, Dr. R.J. Belyea, 902/892-6432

Canadian Coalition for High Blood Pressure Prevention & Control/Coalition canadienne pour la prévention et le contrôle de l'hypertension artérielle (CCHBPPC) (1985)
#200, 160 George St., Ottawa, ON K1N 9M2
613/241-4361, ext.317, Fax: 613/241-3278
President, Dr. Arun Chockalingam
Secretary, Sherron Elliot
Publications: Message
Affiliates: World Hypertension League

Canadian College of Health Service Executives/Collège canadien des directeurs de services de santé (CCHSE) (1970)
#402, 350 Sparks St., Ottawa, ON K1R 7S8
613/235-7218, Fax: 613/235-5451, Email: cchse@hph.hwc.ca
Acting President, Don Schurman
Publications: Contact; Healthcare Management Forum, q.

Canadian College of Legal Medicine
#605, 190 St. George St., Toronto, ON M5R 2N4
416/968-2808
Vice-President, Richard Isaac

Canadian College of Medical Geneticists/Collège canadien de généticiens médicaux (CCMG) (1975)
774 Echo Dr., Ottawa, ON K1S 5N8
613/730-6250, Fax: 613/730-1116, Email: ccmg@rcpsc.edu
Secretary, Dr. Alessandra Duncan
Publications: CCMG Newsletter
Affiliates: Royal College of Physicians & Surgeons of Canada

Canadian Coordinating Office for Health Technology Assessment/Office canadien de coordination de l'évaluation des technolgies de la Santé (CCOHTA) (1989)
#110, 955 Green Valley Cres., Ottawa, ON K2C 3V4
613/226-2553, Fax: 613/226-5392
URL: http://www.ccohta.ca
Executive Director, Dr. Dev Menon
Publications: CCOHTA Update/Nouvelles de l'OC-CETS

The Canadian Council for Accreditation of Pharmacy Programs/Le Conseil canadien de l'agrément des programmes de pharmacie (CCAPP) (1993)
Univ. of Sask. Campus, Thorvaldson Bldg., #123, 110 Science Place, Saskatoon, SK S7N 5C9
306/966-6388, Fax: 306/966-6377
Executive Director, Dr. Bruce R. Schnell
Publications: CCAPP Directory & Annual Report

Canadian Council on Smoking & Health/Conseil canadien sur le tabagisme et la santé (CCSH) (1974)
#1000, 170 Laurier Ave. West, Ottawa, ON K1P 5V5
613/567-3050, Fax: 613/567-2730
Executive Director, Janice Forsythe
President, David H. Hill
Associate Director, David Mair
Publications: Smoking or Health Update

Canadian Critical Care Society/Société canadienne de soins intensifs (CCCS)
700 William Ave., Room GH 723, Winnipeg, MB R3E 0Z3
416/787-3112, Fax: 416/787-2823
Sec.-Treas., Dr. Hugh Devitt
Publications: CCCS Newsletter
Affiliates: Canadian Medical Association; World Federation of Societies of Intensive & Critical Care Medicine

Canadian Cystic Fibrosis Foundation/Fondation canadienne de la fibrose kystique (CCFF) (1960)
#601, 2221 Yonge St., Toronto, ON M4S 2B4
416/485-9149, Fax: 416/485-0960, Email: http://www.ccff.ca/~cfwww/index.html
Executive Director, Cathleen Morrison
Assistant Executive Director, Rod Morrison
President, Raye Jerrard
Vice-President, Denis Mouton
Vice-President, Gord Thow
Publications: Candid Facts/A Propos
Affiliates: International Cystic Fibrosis (Mucoviscidosis) Association

Canadian Deafblind & Rubella Association/Association canadienne de la surdi-cécité et de la rubéole (CDBRA) (1976)
#4, 747 - 2 Ave. East, Owen Sound, ON N4K 2G9
519/372-1333, Fax: 519/372-1334
National Executive Director, Sandra Maitland
President, Stan Munroe
Secretary, Wendy Taylor
Publications: Intervention

Canadian Dermatology Association/Association canadienne de dermatologie
#521, 774 Echo Dr., Ottawa, ON K1S 5N8
613/730-6262, Fax: 613/730-1116
Sec.-Treas., Paul Brisson
Publications: Canadian Dermatology Association Journal

Affiliates: Canadian Medical Association; American Academy of Dermatology

Canadian Diabetes Association/Association canadienne du diabète (CDA) (1953)
#800, 15 Toronto St., Toronto, ON M5C 2E3
416/363-3373, Fax: 416/363-3393, Toll Free: 1-800-226-8464, Email: info@cda-nat.org
URL: http://www.diabetes.ca/
Executive Director, Jim O'Brien
Publications: Canadian Diabetes; Canadian Journal of Diabetes Care; Diabetes Dialogue, q.
Affiliates: Association du diabète du Québec

Canadian Dietetic Association/Association canadienne des diététistes (CDA) (1935)
#601, 480 University Ave., Toronto, ON M5G 1V2
416/596-0857, Fax: 416/596-0603
CEO, Marsha Sharp
President, Kathy Morpurgo
Publications: Communiqué; Journal of the Canadian Dietetic Association, q.
Affiliates: 10 provincial dietetic associations

ALBERTA REGISTERED DIETITIANS ASSOCIATION (ARDA) (1959)
18104 - 102 Ave., Edmonton, AB T5S 1S7
403/448-0059, Fax: 403/489-7759
Office Manager, L. Cannataro, R.D.
Publications: The A.R.D.A Advocate

BRITISH COLUMBIA DIETITIANS' & NUTRITIONISTS' ASSOCIATION (BCDNA) (1956)
#402, 1755 West Broadway, Vancouver, BC V6J 4S5
604/736-3790, Fax: 604/736-5606
Executive Director, Janice Macdonald
Publications: BCDNA News

MANITOBA ASSOCIATION OF REGISTERED DIETITIANS
#700, 360 Broadway, Winnipeg, MB R3C 4G6
204/235-1792, Fax: 204/235-1792
Executive Director, Corinne Eisenbraun
Publications: MARD Matters

NEW BRUNSWICK ASSOCIATION OF DIETITIANS/ASSOCIATION DES DIÉTÉTISTES DU NOUVEAU-BRUNSWICK (NBAD)
165 Regent St., Fredericton, NB E3B 3W5
506/459-2830
Publications: Diascope

NEWFOUNDLAND DIETETIC ASSOCIATION (NDA)
PO Box 1756, Stn C, St. John's, NF A1C 5P5
709/729-4424, Fax: 709/729-5824
President, Maureen Loat
Publications: Digest
Affiliates: HEAL (Health Action Lobby)

NOVA SCOTIA DIETETIC ASSOCIATION (NSDA) (1953)
PO Box 36104, RPO Spring Garden, Halifax, NS B3J 3S9
902/835-9706
President, Kimberlee A. Mitchell
Publications: NSDA Newsletter; Membership Directory, a.

ONTARIO DIETETIC ASSOCIATION/ASSOCIATION DES DIÉTÉTISTES DE L'ONTARIO (1929)
#604, 480 University Ave., Toronto, ON M5G 1V2
416/599-7289, Fax: 416/596-0603
Executive Director, Mary Ann Rangam
Administrative Coordinator, Robert Fraser
Publications: UPDATE

ORDRE PROFESSIONNEL DES DIÉTÉTISTES DU QUÉBEC (OPDQ) (1956)
#703, 1425, boul René-Lévesque ouest, Montréal, PQ H3G 1T7
514/393-3733, Téléc: 514/393-3582, Courrier électronique: opdq@opdq.org
URL: http://www.opdq.org

Directrice générale, Arlette Marcotte
Présidente, Micheline Seguin Bernier
Conseillère aux communications, Annie Langlois, Dt.P.
Publications: Diététique en action; Contact

PRINCE EDWARD ISLAND DIETETIC ASSOCIATION
PO Box 2575, Charlottetown, PE C1A 8C2
902/892-6004
Provincial Representative, Betty McNab
President, Margie Kays
Publications: Prince Edward Dietetic Association Newsletter

SASKATCHEWAN DIETETIC ASSOCIATION (SDA) (1958)
PO Box 3894, Regina, SK S4P 3R8
306/359-3040, Fax: 306/757-8161
Provincial President, Michael Chan
Administration, Teressa Isaac
Publications: SDA Newsletter 3-4 pa

Canadian Down Syndrome Society/Société canadienne de syndrome de Down (CDSS) (1987)
#811 - 14 St. NW, Calgary, AB T2N 2A4
604/270-8500, Fax: 604/270-8291, Toll Free: 1-800-883-5608
Executive Director, Dianna Jossa
Publications: CDSS News

Canadian Dyslexia Association/Association canadienne de la dyslexie (1991)
25, rue St-Médard, Aylmer, PQ J9H 1Z4
819/684-0542, Fax: 819/684-6157
Director, Louise Ward
Publications: Dyslexia Concerns Us

Canadian Federation of Medical Students
#500, 505 University Ave., Toronto, ON M5G 1X4
416/595-9778, Fax: 416/595-9778
President, Natasha Leighl
Vice-President, Education, Bridget Fernandez
Vice-President, Communications, Stephen Brown

Canadian Foundation of Homeopathic Research & Development
4624 - 99th St., Edmonton, AB T6E 5H5
403/438-4465
Executive Director, Anne MacFerlene

Canadian Foundation for Pharmacy/Fondation canadienne pour la pharmacie (CFP) (1945)
9 Hawthorn Cres., Brampton, ON L6S 1A9
905/454-4818, Fax: 905/454-4860
Executive Director, Dr. Stuart Ryan
Publications: Board Bulletin; Your Foundation News, s-a.
Affiliates: Canadian Pharmaceutical Association

Canadian Foundation for the Study of Infant Deaths/Fondation canadienne sur l'étude de la mortalité infantile (CFSID) (1973)
SIDS Foundation
#308, 586 Eglinton Ave. East, Toronto, ON M4P 1P2
416/488-3260, Fax: 416/488-3864, Toll Free: 1-800-363-7437, Email: sidscanada@inforamp.net
URL: http://www.sidscanada.org/sids.html
Executive Director, Beverley De Bruyn
Publications: The Baby's Breath
Affiliates: SIDS International

Canadian Health Coalition/Coalition canadienne de la santé (1979)
2841 Riverside Dr., Ottawa, ON K1V 8X7
613/521-3400, Fax: 613/521-4655
Coordinator, Pam Fitzgerald
Publications: Medicare Monitor

Canadian Health Economics Research Association/Association canadienne pour la recherche en économie de la santé (CHERA) (1982)
Abramsky Hall, 3rd Fl., Queen's University, Kingston, ON K7L 3N6
613/545-6000, ext.4871, Fax: 613/545-6353, Email: chera@post.queensu.ca
Executive Coordinator, Bill Swan
President, Raisa Deber
Publications: CHERAction

Canadian Healthy Communities Network/Réseau canadien des communautés en santé
541 Sussex Dr., 2nd Fl., Ottawa, ON K1N 5T5
613/562-4646, Fax: 613/562-4648
Chairman, Stephen Jewczyk
Publications: Challenge/Change; Transform/Action

Canadian Hematology Society/Societe Canadienne d'Hematologie (1971)
Ottawa General Hospital, 501 Smyth Rd., Ottawa, ON K1H 8L6
613/737-8178, Fax: 613/737-8141
Sec.-Treas., Jeanne Drouin, M.D.
Publications: Canadian Hematology Newsletter

Canadian Hemochromatosis Society/Société canadienne de l'hémochromatose (CHS) (1982)
#272, 7000 Minoru Blvd., Richmond, BC V6Y 3Z5
604/279-7135, Fax: 604/279-7138
National Vice-President, Eugene Boyko
National President, Charm Cottingham
Publications: Among Ourselves
Affiliates: Haemochromatosis Society of Great Britain; Haemochromatosis Society of Southern Africa; Haemochromatosis Research Foundation (Albany) New York; Association hémochromatose France; Haemochromatosis Information & Support Service, Australia

Canadian Hemophilia Society/Société canadienne de l'hémophilie (CHS) (1953)
#1210, 625, av President Kennedy, Montréal, PQ H3A 1K2
514/848-0503, Fax: 514/848-9661
Executive Director, Lindee David
Finance Manager, Pierre Latreille
Publications: Hemophilia Today
Affiliates: World Federation of Hemophilia

Canadian Implant Association/L'Association canadienne des implantes intraoculaires (CIA) (1975)
5591, Côte des Neiges, Montréal, PQ H3T 1Y8
514/735-1133, Fax: 514/731-0657
President, Dr. Marvin L. Kwitko
Affiliates: International Intraocular Implant Council

Canadian Infectious Disease Society/Société canadienne de maladies infectieuses (CIDS) (1978)
774 Echo Dr., Ottawa, ON K1S 5N8
613/730-6251, Fax: 613/730-1116
President, Dr. Gary Garber
Secretary, Dr. Anne-Marie Bourgault
Publications: CIDS Newsletter

Canadian Institute of Academic Medicine/Institut canadien de médecine académique (CIAM) (1990)
774 Echo Dr., Ottawa, ON K1S 5P2
613/730-0687, Fax: 613/730-1196
Contact, Dr. James C. Hogg

ORGANIZATIONS — HEALTH & MEDICAL 2-87

Canadian Institute of Child Health/Institut canadien de la santé infantile (CICH) (1977)
#512, 885 Meadowlands Dr. East, Ottawa, ON K2C 3N2
613/224-4144, Fax: 613/224-4145, Email: cich@igs.net
Executive Director, Denise Avard
Publications: Child Health
Affiliates: Canadian Coalition for the Prevention of Developmental Disabilities

Canadian Institute of Health Care
1851 Eglinton Ave. West, Toronto, ON M6E 2J6
416/785-5572
Executive Director, M. Lapuente

Canadian Institute of Hypnotism (CIH) (1953)
110, rue Greystone, Montréal, PQ H9R 5T6
514/426-1010, Fax: 514/426-4680
Executive Director, Maurice Kershaw
Publications: Newsletter of CIH

Canadian Institute of Public Health Inspectors/Institut canadien des inspecteurs en hygiène publique (CIPHI) (1934)
#201, 38 Auriga Dr., Nepean, ON K2E 8A5
613/224-7568, Fax: 613/224-6055
Executive Director, James D. Bradley
Publications: Environmental Health Review

Canadian Liver Foundation/Fondation canadienne du foie (CLF) (1969)
#301, 1320 Yonge St., Toronto, ON M4T 1X2
416/964-1953, Fax: 416/964-0024, Toll Free: 1-800-563-5483
Executive Director, Ron McClory
National Coordinator of Communications Materials, Nancy Zorzi
Publications: Communique; LiverLetter, s-a.; Annual Research Report

Canadian Lung Association/Association pulmonaire du Canada (CLA) (1900)
#508, 1900 City Park Dr., Gloucester, ON K1J 1A3
613/747-6776, Fax: 613/747-7430
Executive Director, Margo Craig Garrison
Affiliates: Canadian Nurses' Respiratory Society; Canadian Thoracic Society; Canadian Physiotherapy Cardio-Respiratory Society

ALBERTA LUNG ASSOCIATION
PO Box 4500, Edmonton, AB T6E 6K2
403/492-0354, Fax: 403/492-0362, Toll Free: 1-800-661-5864
Executive Director, Gary Lathan
Yellowknife Branch Office: PO Box 121, Yellowknife, NT X1A 2N1, 403/920-2929

ASSOCIATION PULMONAIRE DU QUÉBEC/QUÉBEC LUNG ASSOCIATION
#100, 4837, rue Boyer, Montréal, PQ H2J 3E6
514/596-0805, Téléc: 514/596-1883
Directeur général, Claude Robillard

BC LUNG ASSOCIATION (BCLA) (1903)
2675 Oak St., Vancouver, BC V6H 2K2
604/731-5864, Fax: 604/731-5810
Executive Director, Scott McDonald
President, Richard Gage
Publications: Your Health

CANADIAN THORACIC SOCIETY/SOCIÉTÉ CANADIENNE DE THORACOLOGIE (CTS) (1958)
c/o Canadian Lung Association, #508, 1900 City Park Dr., Gloucester, ON K1J 1A3
613/747-6776, Fax: 613/747-7430
Sections Coordinator, Michelle Gaudreau
Publications: Airwaves
Affiliates: American Thoracic Society

THE LUNG ASSOCIATION OF NOVA SCOTIA
17 Alma Cres., Halifax, NS B3N 3E6
902/443-8141, Fax: 902/445-2573, Toll Free: 1-800-465-5864
Executive Director, Bill VanGorder

MANITOBA LUNG ASSOCIATION
629 McDermot Ave., 2nd Fl., Winnipeg, MB R3A 1P6
204/774-5501, Fax: 204/772-5083
Executive Director, Arlene Gibson

NEW BRUNSWICK LUNG ASSOCIATION/ASSOCIATION PULMONAIRE DU NOUVEAU-BRUNSWICK
Victoria Health Centre, #257, 65 Brunswick St., Fredericton, NB E3B 1G5
506/455-8961, Fax: 506/462-0939, Toll Free: 1-800-565-5864
Executive Director, Ken Maybee

NEWFOUNDLAND LUNG ASSOCIATION (NLA) (1944)
1 Campbell Ave., PO Box 5250, Stn C, St. John's, NF A1C 5W1
709/726-4664, Fax: 709/726-2550
Executive Director, Peggy Johnson

ONTARIO LUNG ASSOCIATION (OLA) (1945)
#201, 573 King St. East, Toronto, ON M5A 4L3
416/864-9911, Fax: 416/864-9916, Toll Free: 1-800-668-7682
URL: http://www.on.lung.ca; http://www.web.net/cando/
President & CEO, R. Ross Reid
Director/Public Relations, Jill Palmer
Publications: LungLine; Ontario Respiratory Care Society Update, 3 pa; Ontario Thoracic Reviews, 3 pa
Affiliates: Ontario Thoracic Society; Ontario Respiratory Care Society

PRINCE EDWARD ISLAND LUNG ASSOCIATION (1936)
#2, 1 Rochford St., Charlottetown, PE C1A 9L2
902/892-5957, Fax: 902/368-7281
Executive Director, Vicki Bryanton
Executive Assistant, Bernadette Flood

SASKATCHEWAN LUNG ASSOCIATION (SLA) (1911)
Saskatchewan Anti-Tuberculosis League
1231 - 8 St. East, Saskatoon, SK S7H 0S5
306/343-9511, Fax: 306/343-7007
Executive Director, Brian Graham
Publications: Life & Breath

YUKON LUNG ASSOCIATION
PO Box 4754, Whitehorse, YT Y1A 4N6
403/668-6974
President, Marian Bakica

Canadian Marfan Association/Association du syndrome de Marfan (1986)
PO Box 42257, RPO Central Plaza, Mississauga, ON L5L 2B9
905/826-3223
Executive Director, Laura Libralesso
President, Anne Bakewell

Canadian Massage Therapist Alliance/Alliance canadienne de massothérapeutes (CMTA) (1991)
#1807, 365 Bloor St. East, Toronto, ON M4W 3L4
416/968-2149, Fax: 416/968-6818
Association Administrator, Peggy Ball
Chair, Doug Benson
Publications: Hand in Hand

Canadian Medical Association/Association médicale canadienne (CMA) (1867)
1867 Alta Vista Dr., Ottawa, ON K1G 3Y6
613/731-9331, Fax: 613/731-9013, Toll Free: 1-800-267-9703
President, Dr. Judith Kazimirski
Secretary General, L.P. Landry
Publications: Canadian Medical Association Journal; Canadian Journal of Surgery; Humane Medicine; Canadian Journal of Respiratory Therapy; CMA News; Strategy
Affiliates: Association of Canadian Medical Colleges; Association of Canadian Pharmaceutical Physicians; Canadian Academy of Sport Medicine; Canadian Anaesthetists Society; Canadian Association of Emergency Physicians; Canadian Association of Gastroenterology; Canadian Association of General Surgeons; Canadian Association of Internes & Residents; Canadian Association of Medical Microbiologists; Canadian Association of Nuclear Medicine; Canadian Association of Pathologists; Canadian Association of Physical Medicine & Rehabilitation; Canadian Association of Radiologists; Canadian Cardiovascular Society; Canadian Critical Care Society; Canadian Dermatology Association; Canadian Life Insurance Medical Officers Association; Canadian Medical Protective Association; College of Family Physicians of Canada; Royal College of Physicians & Surgeons of Canada; Society of Obstetricians & Gynaecologists of Canada

ALBERTA MEDICAL ASSOCIATION
#400, 12230 - 106 Ave. NW, Edmonton, AB T5N 3Z1
403/482-2626, Fax: 403/482-5445
Executive Director, Dr. Robert A. Burns
Communications Officer, Ron Kustra

ASSOCIATION MÉDICALE DU QUÉBEC/QUÉBEC MEDICAL ASSOCIATION (AMQ) (1929)
#660, 1000, rue de La Gauchetière ouest, Montréal, PQ H3B 4W5
514/866-0660, Téléc: 514/866-0670, Ligne sans frais: 1-800-363-3932
Directeur administratif, Gilles Bellefeuille
Agente de communication, Michelle Hébert
Publications: AMQ Express/QMA Express

BRITISH COLUMBIA MEDICAL ASSOCIATION (BCMA) (1900)
#115, 1665 Broadway West, Vancouver, BC V6J 5A4
604/736-5551, Fax: 604/733-7317
Executive Director, Dr. Norman D. Finlayson
President, Dr. Derryck Smith
Communications Officer, David McPhee
Publications: The British Columbia Medical Journal

MANITOBA MEDICAL ASSOCIATION/ASSOCIATION MÉDICALE DU MANITOBA (MMA)
125 Sherbrook St., Winnipeg, MB R3C 2B5
204/786-7565, Fax: 204/775-9696
Executive Director, John A. Laplume
Communications Officer, Debbie Bride
Publications: Inter-Com

MEDICAL SOCIETY OF NOVA SCOTIA (MSNS)
City of Lakes Business Park, 5 Spectacle Lake Dr., Dartmouth, NS B3B 1X7
902/468-1866, Fax: 902/468-6578
Executive Director, Richard Dyke, MBA, CMA
President, Dr. Rob Kimball, MD, FCFP
Communications Officer, Camille Finlay
Publications: News

MEDICAL SOCIETY OF PRINCE EDWARD ISLAND (MSPEI) (1855)
559 North River Rd., Charlottetown, PE C1E 1J7
902/368-7303, Fax: 902/566-3934
Executive Director, Marilyn Lowther

NEW BRUNSWICK MEDICAL SOCIETY/SOCIÉTÉ MÉDICALE DU NOUVEAU-BRUNSWICK (NBMS) (1867)
176 York St., Fredericton, NB E3B 3N7
506/458-8860, Fax: 506/458-9853, Toll Free: 1-800-661-2001
Executive Director, David H. Balmain, CAE
Communications Officer, Janet Maston
Publications: NBMS Newsletter; President's Letter, bi-m.

Canadian Almanac & Directory 1997

ORGANIZATIONS — HEALTH & MEDICAL

NEWFOUNDLAND & LABRADOR MEDICAL ASSOCIATION (NLMA) (1924)
164 MacDonald Dr., St. John's, NF A1A 4B3
709/726-7424, Fax: 709/726-7525
Executive Director, Bruce Squires
Communications Officer, Lana Collins
Publications: Communiqué

NORTHWEST TERRITORIES MEDICAL ASSOCIATION
4920 - 47th St., 3rd Fl., PO Box 1709, Yellowknife, NT X1A 2P3
403/873-9253, Fax: 403/873-9254
CEO, Paula Lessard

ONTARIO MEDICAL ASSOCIATION (OMA) (1880)
#300, 525 University Ave., Toronto, ON M5G 2K7
416/599-2580, Fax: 416/599-9309
Chief Administrative Officer, David Pattenden
General Director, Administration, Tom Magyarody
President, Gerry Rowland
Publications: Ontario Medical Review; The Medical Times

SASKATCHEWAN MEDICAL ASSOCIATION (1906)
#200, 211 - 4th Ave. South, Saskatoon, SK S7K 1N1
306/244-2196, Fax: 306/653-1631
Executive Director, Dr. Brian Scharfstein
Communications Officer, Donna Hjertaas

YUKON MEDICAL ASSOCIATION
406 Lambert St., Whitehorse, YT Y1A 1Z7
403/667-4421, Fax: 403/668-3736
President, Dr. Roger Mitchell
Vice-President, Dr. Cindy Breitkreitz
Treasurer, Dr. Bruce Beaton
Affiliates: British Columbia Medical Association

Canadian Medical Foundation
1867 Alta Vista Dr., Ottawa, ON K1G 3Y6
613/731-9331, Fax: 613/731-1779
Manager, Darlene Brown

Canadian Medical Malpractice Prevention Association (CMMPA) (1987)
#41653, 1711 McCowan Rd., Scarborough, ON M1S 5G8
416/969-1587
President, Sharon Roberts
Vice-President, Suzanne Christie

Canadian MedicAlert Foundation, Inc./Fondation canadienne MedicAlert, inc. (1961)
MedicAlert
#301, 250 Ferrand Dr., PO Box 9800, Stn Don Mills, North York, ON M3C 2T9
416/696-0267, 0142, Fax: 416/696-0156, Toll Free: 1-800-668-1507
President, Shelagh Tippet-Fagyas
Chairman, Ivan C. Juul-Hansen
Affiliates: MedicAlert Foundation International

Canadian Natural Health Association (1960)
#5, 439 Wellington St. West, Toronto, ON M5V 1E7
416/977-2642, Fax: 416/977-1536
Office Manager, Hélène Roussel
Publications: Living Naturally
Affiliates: American Natural Hygiene Society

Canadian Naturopathic Association/Association canadienne de naturopathie (CNA) (1930)
PO Box 4520, Stn C, Calgary, AB T2T 5N3
403/244-4487, Fax: 403/244-2340, Info Line: 403/245-0633
Executive Director, Marjorie Zingle, CAE
President, Kelly Farnsworth
Publications: Journal of Naturopathic Medicine; Canadian Naturopathic Association Newsletter

Canadian Network of Toxicology Centres/Réseau canadien des centres de toxicologie (CNTC) (1988)
620 Gordon St., Guelph, ON N1G 1Y4
519/837-3320, Fax: 519/837-3861
Executive Director, Dr. L. Ritter
Program Coordinator, Donna Warner
Affiliates: Centre for Toxicology

Canadian Neurological Society/Société canadienne de neurologie (CNS)
#810, 906 - 12th Ave., Calgary, AB T2R 1K7
403/229-9544, Fax: 403/229-1661
President, Dr. O. Suchowersky
Executive Director, Lucile Edwards
Affiliates: Canadian Medical Association

Canadian Occupational Therapy Foundation
#308, 55 Eglinton Ave. East, Toronto, ON M4P 1G3
416/487-5438
Executive Assistant, Charmaine Francis

Canadian Ophthalmological Society/Société canadienne d'opthalmologie (COS/SCO) (1937)
#610, 1525 Carling Ave., Ottawa, ON K1Z 8R9
613/729-6779, Fax: 613/729-7209, Toll Free: 1-800-267-5763
Executive Director, Hubert Drouin
Publications: Canadian Journal of Opthalmology
Affiliates: Canadian Medical Association; Concilium Ophthalmological Universale

Canadian Orthopaedic Association/Association canadienne d'orthopédie (COA) (1945)
#421, 1440, rue Sainte-Catherine ouest, Montréal, PQ H3G 1R8
514/874-9003, Fax: 514/874-0464
Executive Secretary, K. DeCruz
President, Michael A. Simurda
Secretary, Dr. Robert Hollinshead
Treasurer, Dr. Hubert Labelle
Publications: Bulletin
Affiliates: World Orthopaedic Concern; Canadian Medical Association

Canadian Orthoptic Council
c/o University Hospital, Dept. of Ophthalmology, Saskatoon, SK S7N 0X0
306/966-8045
Contact, Dr. K. Romanchuk

The Canadian Orthoptic Society (TCOS) (1967)
I.W.K. Children's Hospital, Orthoptic Clinic, 5850 University Ave., PO Box 3070, Halifax, NS B3J 3G9
902/428-8021, Fax: 902/428-3207
President, Brenda Hum-Boutilier

Canadian Osteogenesis Imperfecta Society
128 Thornhill Cres., Chatham, ON N7L 4M3
Contact, Mary Lou Kearney
Publications: Connect

Canadian Osteopathic Aid Society (COAS) (1960)
575 Waterloo St., London, ON N6B 2R2
519/439-5521
Executive Secretary, Marguerite Torney

Canadian Osteopathic Association (1926)
575 Waterloo St., London, ON N6B 2R2
519/439-5521
Administrative Secretary, Marguerite Torney

Canadian Paediatric Society/Société canadienne de pédiatrie (CPS) (1951)
Children's Hospital of Eastern Ontario, 401 Smyth Rd., Ottawa, ON K1H 8L1
613/737-2728, Fax: 613/737-2794
President, Dr. Pierre Beaudry

Vice-President, Dr. T. Emmett Francoeur
Executive Vice-President, Dr. Victor Marchessault
Publications: CPS News; Gazette SCP; Paediatrics & Child Health

Canadian Pain Society/Société canadienne pour le traitement de la douleur (1982)
University of Vancouver, Dept. of Psychology, Vancouver, BC V6T 1Z4
604/822-3948, Fax: 604/822-6923
President, Kenneth Craig
Publications: Pain Research & Management
Affiliates: International Association for the Study of Pain

Canadian Palliative Care Association/Association canadienne des soins palliatifs (CPCA) (1991)
5 Blackburn Ave., Ottawa, ON K1N 8A2
Toll Free: 1-800-668-2785
Executive Director, Linda Lysne
Publications: AVISO; Directory of Services

Canadian Paraplegic Association/Association canadienne des paraplégiques (CPA) (1945)
#320, 1101 Prince of Wales Dr., Ottawa, ON K2C 3W7
613/723-1033, Fax: 613/723-1060, Email: eboyd@cyberplus.ca
President, Marie Trudeau
Managing Director, Eric Boyd
Publications: Caliper

Canadian Paraplegic Association (Ontario)
CPA Ontario
520 Sutherland Dr., Toronto, ON M4G 3V9
416/422-5644, Fax: 416/422-5943
Executive Director, William Adair
Publications: Outspoken

Canadian Pediatric Foundation/La fondation canadienne de pédiatrie (CPF) (1985)
401 Smyth Rd., Ottawa, ON K1H 8L1
613/738-3940, Fax: 613/737-2794, Toll Free: 1-800-580-0940
President, Barrett A. Adams, Dr.

Canadian Pelvic Inflammatory Disease Society/ La Société canadienne AIP (1985)
Canadian P.I.D. Society
PO Box 33804, Stn D, Vancouver, BC V6J 4L6
604/684-5704, Info Line: 604/684-5704
Coordinator, Jill Weiss

Canadian Peptic Ulcer Research Foundation
Manulife Centre, #3200, 10180 - 101 St., Edmonton, AB T5J 3W8
403/425-9510, Fax: 403/429-3044, Telex: 037-2073
Contact, Dr. Alan B. Thomson

Canadian Physiotherapy Association/ L'Association canadienne de physiothérapie (CPA) (1920)
890 Yonge St., 9th Fl., Toronto, ON M4W 3P4
416/924-5312, Fax: 416/924-7335, Toll Free: 1-800-387-8679
Director, Katrina Schmitz
Acting Co-CEO, Dianne Parker-Taillon
Acting Co-CEO, Elizabeth Di Chiara
Director, Melanie Galyin
Director, Liliane Asseraf Pasin
Publications: Physiotherapy Canada; Contact, 10 pa
Affiliates: World Confederation for Physical Therapy

Canadian Post-MD Education Registry/Système informatisé sur les stagiaires post-MD en formation clinique (CAPER) (1986)
774 Echo Dr., Ottawa, ON K1S 5P2
613/730-1204, Fax: 613/730-1196
Director, A.D. Thurber

Office Manager, K. Edmonds
Publications: The CAPER Annual Census of Post-M.D. Trainees
Affiliates: Association of Canadian Medical Colleges

Canadian Psoriasis Foundation/Fondation canadienne du psoriasis (CPF) (1983)
#500A, 1306 Wellington St., Ottawa, ON K1Y 3B2
613/728-4000, Fax: 613/728-8913, Toll Free: 1-800-265-0926
National Coordinator, Patricia Normandeau
President, Raymond L. du Plessis
Executive Director, Carolyn Karpoff
Publications: Canadian Psoriasis Foundation; Understanding Psoriasis
Affiliates: US National Psoriasis Foundation; Psoriasis Association of Great Britain

Canadian Public Health Association/Association canadienne de santé publique (CPHA) (1912)
#400, 1565 Carling Ave., Ottawa, ON K1Z 8R1
613/725-3769, Fax: 613/725-9826
Executive Director, Gerald Dafoe
President, Dr. John Hastings
Assistant Executive Director, National Programs, Janet MacLachlan
Publications: Canadian Journal of Public Health; CPHA Health Digest, q.
Affiliates: Canadian Association of Teachers of Social & Preventive Medicine; The Canadian Society for International Health; Canadian Coalition for High Blood Pressure Prevention & Control; Society for the Study of Pathophysiology of Pregnancy

ALBERTA PUBLIC HEALTH ASSOCIATION (APHA) (1943)
11715 - 101 St., Peace River, AB T8S 1L8
403/624-7120, Fax: 403/624-7122
President, H. Campsall
Publications: The Promoter

ASSOCIATION POUR LA SANTÉ PUBLIQUE DU QUÉBEC/QUÉBEC PUBLIC HEALTH ASSOCIATION (ASPQ) (1943)
3958, rue Dandurand, Montréal, PQ H1X 1P7
514/593-9939, Téléc: 514/593-4554
Directrice générale, Janine Dalaire
Président, Françoise Bouchard
Publications: Le périscoop; Bulletin de santé publique, trimestriel

BRITISH COLUMBIA PUBLIC HEALTH ASSOCIATION (BCPHA)
#101, 2182 - 12th St. West, Vancouver, BC V6K 2N4
604/731-4970, Fax: 604/731-5965
Executive Director, Kaela Jubas
President, Ann Geddes
Publications: The Public's Health

MANITOBA PUBLIC HEALTH ASSOCIATION (MPHA) (1940)
PO Box 22002, RPO Broadway, Winnipeg, MB R3C 4K6
204/477-6336
President, Brian Peel
Publications: MPHA Newsletter

NEWFOUNDLAND PUBLIC HEALTH ASSOCIATION
OXFAM Resource Centre, 382 Duckworth St., St. John's, NF A1C 1H8
709/753-2202, Fax: 709/753-4110
President, Linda Ross

ONTARIO PUBLIC HEALTH ASSOCIATION/ASSOCIATION POUR LA SANTÉ PUBLIQUE DE L'ONTARIO (OPHA) (1949)
#202, 468 Queen St. East, Toronto, ON M5A 1T7
416/367-3313, Fax: 416/367-2844, Toll Free: 1-800-267-6817
Executive Director, Peter R. Elson
President, Winston Miller
Publications: Health Beat; OPHA News
Affiliates: ANDSOOHA - Public Health Nursing Management; Association of Ontario Public Health Business Administrators; Association of Supervisory Public Health Inspectors; Canadian Institute of Public Health Inspectors (Ontario Branch); Ontario Society of Nutritionists in Public Health; RNAO (Community Health Nurses Interest Group); Ontario Society of Public Health Dentists; Ontario Association of Health Promotion Specialists in Public Health

PUBLIC HEALTH ASSOCIATION OF NOVA SCOTIA (PHANS)
PO Box 20129, RPO Spryfield, Halifax, NS B3R 2K9
902/477-6102, Fax: 902/479-1177
President, Marjorie Willison

SASKATCHEWAN PUBLIC HEALTH ASSOCIATION INC.
159 McKee Cres., Regina, SK S4S 5N7
President, Sandra Craig, 306/787-3180

Canadian Rett Syndrome Association (CRSA)
#301, 555 Fairway Rd., Kitchener, ON N2C 1X4
416/494-1954, Fax: 519/893-1169
President, Eugene Bradley

Canadian Rheumatism Association/Société canadienne de rhumatologie
2705, boul Laurier, Ste-Foy, PQ G1V 4G2
418/654-2242, Fax: 418/654-2798
President, Dr. Simon Carette
Affiliates: Canadian Medical Association, Royal College of Physicians & Surgeons of Canada

Canadian Sickle Cell Society/La société de l'anemie falciforme du Canada (1978)
#33, 6999, Côte des Neiges, Montréal, PQ H3S 2B8
514/735-5109
Regional Director, Rosetta Cadogan

Canadian Sleep Society/Société canadienne du sommeil (CSS) (1986)
#5055, 3080 Yonge St., Toronto, ON M4N 3N1
416/483-6260, Fax: 416/483-7081
President, C.F.P. George, M.D., Email: cgeorge@julian.uwo.ca
Sec.-Treas., R.L. Morehouse, M.D., Email: morehour@is.dal.ca
Publications: Vigilance
Affiliates: Association of Professional Sleep Societies; World Federation of Sleep Research

Canadian Society of Aerospace Medicine/Société médicale aéronautique du Canada (CSAM)
c/o Canadian Aeronautics & Space Institute, 818, 130 Slater St., Ottawa, ON K1P 6E2
613/234-0191, Fax: 613/234-9039
Executive Director, Ian M. Ross
President, Dr. C. Thibeault
Publications: CASI Log
Affiliates: Canadian Medical Association; Aerospace Medical Association

Canadian Society of Allergy & Clinical Immunology/Société canadienne d'allergie et d'immunologie clinique (CSACI) (1962)
202 St. Clair Ave. West, Toronto, ON M4V 1R2
416/923-4348, Fax: 416/944-1582
President, Dr. Gordon L. Sussman
Secretary, Dr. A.B. Becker
Publications: CSACI Newsletter

Canadian Society of Cardiology Technologists/Société canadienne des technologues en cardiologie
#2200, 201 Portage Ave., Winnipeg, MB R3B 3L3
President, Ruth Scott
Publications: Atrium

Canadian Society of Cardiovascular & Thoracic Surgeons/Société des chirurgiens cardiovasculaires et thoraciques
Ottawa Heart Institute, Civic Hospital, #211, 1053 Carling Ave., Ottawa, ON K1Y 4E9
613/761-4233, Fax: 613/761-5367
Secretary, Dr. Roy Masters
Publications: Newsletter
Affiliates: Royal College of Physicians & Surgeons of Canada

Canadian Society for Clinical Investigation/Société canadienne de recherches cliniques (CSCI) (1951)
774 Echo Dr., Ottawa, ON K1S 5N8
613/730-6240, Fax: 613/730-8194
Sec.-Treas., Dr. J.H. Matthews
President, Dr. Paul M. Walker
Executive Administrator, Caroline Frewer
Publications: Clinical & Investigative Medicine; CSCI News Bulletin, s-a.

Canadian Society of Clinical Neurophysiologists/Société canadienne de neurophysiologistes cliniques (CSCN)
PO Box 4220, Stn C, Calgary, AB T2T 5N1
403/229-9544, Fax: 403/229-1661
Executive Director, Lucile Edwards
President, Dr. G.B. Young
Publications: Canadian Journal of Neurological Sciences
Affiliates: Canadian Medical Association; Canadian Association for Neuroscience; Canadian Association of Neuroscience Nurses; Canadian Stroke Society; Canadian League Against Epilepsy; Canadian Headache Society; Movement Disorders Group; Multiple Sclerosis Society of Canada; Amyotrophic Lateral Sclerosis Society of Canada; Canadian Peripheral Nerve Group

Canadian Society for Clinical Pharmacology/Société canadienne de pharmacologie clinique (CSCP)
c/o Ms. C. Van Der Giessen, 33 Russell St., Toronto, ON M5S 2S1
416/595-6119, Fax: 416/595-6619
President, Dr. Robert E. Rangno
Sec.-Treas., Dr. Jake Onrot
Publications: The Canadian Journal of Clinical Pharmacology
Affiliates: Royal College of Physicians & Surgeons of Canada; Canadian Society for Clinical Investigation

Canadian Society of Cytology/Société canadienne de cytologie (CSC) (1961)
Dept. of Pathology, H.S.C., 820 Sherbrook St., Winnipeg, MB R3A 1R9
204/787-1657, Fax: 204/787-4942
Sec.-Treas., Dr. M. Auger
Chairman, Dr. M. Duggan
Publications: CSC Bulletin
Affiliates: Canadian Association of Pathologists

Canadian Society of Diagnostic Medical Sonographers (CSDMS) (1981)
PO Box 5395, Fort McMurray, AB T9H 3G4
403/743-2962, Fax: 403/743-2962, Email: csdms@ccinet.ab.ca
Executive Director, Sandra Mayer
Publications: Interface

Canadian Society of Endocrinology & Metabolism/Société canadienne d'endocrinologie et métabolisme (CSEM) (1972)
The Montreal Children's Hospital, 2300 Tupper St., #C1238, Montréal, PQ H3H 1P3
514/934-4400, Fax: 514/934-4494
President, Dr. Otto Rorstad

Canadian Almanac & Directory 1997

Sec.-Treas., Dr. Cindy Goodyer
Publications: Newsletter; Membership Directory
Affiliates: Canadian Society of Clinical Investigation

Canadian Society for the History of Medicine
Memorial University of Newfoundland, Faculty of Medicine, St. John's, NF A1B 3V6
709/737-6592, Fax: 709/737-6400
Dr. John Crellin

Canadian Society of Internal Medicine/Société canadienne de médecine interne (CSIM) (1984)
774 Echo Dr., Ottawa, ON K1S 5N8
613/730-6244, Fax: 613/730-1116, Email: csim@rcpsc.edu
Head, M. Dallimore
Publications: CSIM Bulletin
Affiliates: Canadian Medical Association

Canadian Society for International Health/Société canadienne de la santé internationale (CSIH) (1977)
#902, 170 Laurier Ave. West, Ottawa, ON K1P 5V5
613/230-2654, Fax: 613/230-8401, Email: csih@fox.nstn.ca
URL: http://hpb1.hwc.ca:8500/default.html
Executive Director, Charles A. Shields Jr., CAE
Publications: Synergy
Affiliates: Pan American Health Organization

Canadian Society of Laboratory Technologists/Société canadienne des technologistes de laboratoire (CSLT) (1937)
PO Box 2830, Stn A, Hamilton, ON L8N 3N8
905/528-8642, Fax: 905/528-4968
URL: http://cslt.com/
Executive Director, E. Valerie Booth
Director of Communications, Kurt Davis, FCSLT, CAE
Publications: CSLT Bulletin; Canadian Journal of Medical Technology, q.; Annual Roster
Affiliates: International Association of Medical Laboratory Technologists; Intersociety Council of Laboratory Medicine; Conjoint Council on Accreditation of Allied Programs in Health Care

Canadian Society for Medical Mycology/Société canadienne de mycologie médicale (CSMM) (1987)
Université de Montréal, Dept. of Microbiology & Immunology, PO Box 6128, Stn A, Montréal, PQ H3C 3J7
514/343-7184, Fax: 514/343-5701
President, Dr. Louis de Repentigny
Publications: CSMM Newsletter
Affiliates: International Society for Human & Animal Mycology

Canadian Society of Nephrology/Société canadienne de néphrologie (CSN) (1967)
c/o Victoria General Hospital, Div. of Nephrology, #5076, 5820 University Ave., Halifax, NS B3H 1V8
902/428-4023, Fax: 902/428-2675
President, Dr. M.L. West, M.D.
Publications: ; Scientific Meeting Abstract, a.

Canadian Society of Nutrition Management/Société canadienne de gestion de la nutrition
#2M, 57 Simcoe St., PO Box 948, Oshawa, ON L1H 7N1
905/436-0145, Fax: 905/436-2969
Executive Director, Janet Milner

Canadian Society of Orthopaedic Technologists/Société canadienne des technologistes en orthopédie (CSOT) (1972)
#200, 4433 Sheppard Ave. East, Agincourt, ON M1S 1V3

416/292-0687, Fax: 416/292-1038, Email: cinascot@idirect.com
URL: http://web.idirect.com/~scotcina
Registrar/Office Manager, Pamela Smith
Publications: BodyCast; Newscast, q.

Canadian Society of Otolaryngology - Head & Neck Surgery/Société canadienne d'otolaryngologie et de chirurgie cervico-faciale (CSO-HNS) (1947)
55 MacGregor Ave., Toronto, ON M6S 2A1
519/439-1850, Fax: 519/672-4602
Administrator, Donna Humphrey
President, Dr. Murray Morrison
Publications: Journal of Otolaryngology
Affiliates: International Federation of Oto-Rhino-Laryngological Societies; Canadian Medical Association; Canadian Deaf & Hard of Hearing Forum

Canadian Society of Plastic Surgeons/Société canadienne des chirurgiens plasticiens (CSPS) (1947)
#520, 30, boul Saint-Joseph est, Montréal, PQ H2T 1G9
514/843-5415, Fax: 514/843-5415, Toll Free: 1-800-665-5413
President, Dr. Carolyn Kerrigan
Vice-President, Dr. John Taylor
Sec.-Treas., Dr. D. Kimit Rai
Publications: CSPS News
Affiliates: Canadian Medical Association

Canadian Society of Respiratory Therapists/La Société canadienne des thérapeutes respiratoires (CSRT) (1964)
#102, 1785 Alta Vista Dr., Ottawa, ON K1G 3Y6
613/731-3164, Fax: 613/521-4314, Toll Free: 1-800-267-3422
Executive Director, Cheryl Homuth
Publications: RRT

Canadian Society of Surgical Oncology/Société canadienne d'oncologie chirurgicale (CSSO)
502 Burton Hall, 60 Grosvenor St., Toronto, ON M5S 1B6
416/323-7747, Fax: 416/323-6535
Sec.-Treas., Dr. David McCready

Canadian Society for Transfusion Medicine/Société canadienne de médecine transfusionnelle (CSTM) (1989)
#306, 2311 McEown Ave., Saskatoon, SK S7J 2H3
306/655-2189, Fax: 306/655-1044
Director, Edna Blum
Publications: CSTM Bulletin

Canadian Society for Vascular Surgery/Société canadienne de chirurgie vasculaire
#100, 215 Bloor St. West, Toronto, ON M6S 1M8
416/763-3797, Fax: 416/763-3797
Secretary, Dr. Douglas Woostor

Canadian Spinal Research Organization (CSRO) (1984)
#1, 120 Newkirk Rd., Richmond Hill, ON L4C 9S7
905/508-4000, Fax: 905/508-4002, Toll Free: 1-800-361-4004, Email: csro@inforamp.net
President, Ray Wickson
Vice-President, Barry Munro
Publications: CSRO Quarterly

Canadian Urological Association/Association canadienne d'urologie (1945)
Health Sciences Centre, Rm. GE446, 820 Sherbrook St., Winnipeg, MB R3A 1R9
204/787-3677, Fax: 204/787-3040
President, Dr. Normand Sullivan
Secretary, Denis H. Hosking

Publications: Newsletter
Affiliates: Canadian Medical Association

Canadians for Health Research/Canadiens pour la recherche médicale (1976)
PO Box 126, Westmount, PQ H3Z 2T1
514/398-7478, Fax: 514/398-8361
National President, Patricia Guyda
Secretary, Linda Bazinet
Publications: The Diary; Future Health/Perspectives santé, q.

Candlelighters Childhood Cancer Foundation Canada/Fondation des éclaireurs pour le cancer dans l'enfance Canada (CCCFC) (1987)
Candlelighters Canada
#401, 55 Eglinton Ave. East, Toronto, ON M4P 1G8
416/489-6440, Fax: 416/489-9812, Toll Free: 1-800-363-1062, Email: staff@candlelighters.ca
URL: http://www.candlelighters.ca
Executive Director, Eleanor G. Pask, RN, MScN, Ed.D.
President, Bill Buchanan, Email: buchanan@voyager.newcomm.net
Secretary, Richard A.B. Devenney
Treasurer, Winston Marcellin
Director, Fundraising, Jo Anne Wilson
Director, Alberta, Valerie Figliuzzi, 403/460-8590
Director, BC, Ruth Morley, 604/372-3222
Director, Manitoba, Leslie Sneyd, 204/983-1067
Director, New Brunswick, Judy Allen, 506/847-9627
Director, Newfoundland, Bill Buchanan, 709/739-2009
Director, Nova Scotia, Greg Tanner, 902/434-9095
Director, Ontario, Dr. Helen Pastoric, Email: pastoric@enterprise.ca
Director, Québec, Camille de Varennes, 514/471-7498, Email: tulipe@accent.net
Director, PEI, Janet MacQuarrie, 902/628-8195
Director, Saskatchewan, Janis Miller, 306/545-6766
Publications: Contact; Resource Catalogue, a.

Catholic Health Association of Canada/Association catholique canadienne de la santé (CHAC) (1939)
1247 Kilborn Pl., Ottawa, ON K1H 6K9
613/731-7148, Fax: 613/731-7797
President, Richard M. Haughian
Director of Programs & Communications, Maryse Blouin
Chairperson, Leo Steven
Publications: CHAC Info/Info ACCS; CHAC Review/Revue ACCS, q.

Centre for Toxicology/Réseau canadien des centres de toxicologie (1983)
Bovey Bldg., 2nd Fl., Gordon St., Guelph, ON N1G 2W1
519/837-3320, Fax: 519/837-3861, Email: dwarner@tox.uoguelph.ca
URL: http://www.uoguelph.ca/cntc/
Director, Dr. Keith R. Solomon
Program Coordinator, Donna Warner
Controller, J.W. Cooper
Publications: CNTC News
Affiliates: Administrative office for the Canadian Network of Toxicology Centres

Children's Oncology Care of Ontario Inc. (COCO) (1981)
Ronald McDonald House
26 Gerrard St. East, Toronto, ON M5B 1G3
416/977-0458, Fax: 416/977-8807
Executive Director, C. Kimpton
President, Betsy Wright
Publications: Ronald McDonald House Newsletter

Children's Rehabilitation & Cerebral Palsy Association
The Neurological Centre, 2805 Kingsway, Vancouver, BC V5R 5H9
604/451-5511, Fax: 604/451-5651
Executive Director, Dot Ewen
Affiliates: International Cerebral Palsy Society

Chinese Medicine & Acupuncture Association of Canada/L'Association de médecine chinoise et d'acupuncture du Canada (CMAAC)
154 Wellington St., London, ON N6B 2K8
519/642-1970, Fax: 519/642-2932
Director General, Hsi Ping Lin, Dr. Ac.

Chronic Fatigue Syndrome/Myalgic Encephalomyelitis Group
M.E. Association of Ontario
PO Box 322, Stn K, Toronto, ON M4P 2G7
416/763-9025
Contact, Alan Stern

College of Chiropractic Science
#235, 1333 Neilson Rd., Scarborough, ON M1B 4Y9
416/281-0640, Fax: 416/281-9519
President, Dr. Michael Willes
Affiliates: Canadian Chiropractic Association

College of Dieticians of Ontario/L'Ordre des diététistes de l'Ontario (CDO)
700 Bay St., 14th Fl., Toronto, ON M5G 1Z6
416/327-8224, Fax: 416/327-0867
Registrar, Carol J. Shapiro
Publications: Resumé

College of Family Physicians of Canada/Collège des médecins de famille du Canada (CFPC) (1954)
2630 Skymark Ave., Mississauga, ON L4W 5A4
905/629-0900, Fax: 905/629-0893
Executive Director, Dr. Calvin Gutkin
President, Dr. Cheri Bethune
Communications Officer, Leslie Challis
Director of Professional Affairs, Dr. Claude Renaud
Publications: Canadian Family Physician
Alberta Chapter: Executive Secretary, Elaine R. Taschuk, #203, 12230 - 106 Ave., Edmonton, AB T5N 3Z1, 403/488-2395, Fax: 403/488-2396
British Columbia College of Family Physicians: Executive Director, Bev Kulyk, #350, 1665 West Broadway, Vancouver, BC V6J 1X1, 604/736-6400, Fax: 604/736-4675
Manitoba Chapter: Administrative Secretary, Susan Patek, #101, 1390 Taylor Ave., Winnipeg, MB R3M 3V8, 204/488-3188, Fax: 204/488-3188
New Brunswick Chapter: Secrétaire administrative, Mavis Alain, 2, rue Veinot, Fredericton, NB E3B 6T3, 506/455-6051, Fax: 506/455-6051
Newfoundland Chapter: Administrator, Linda Kirby, Health Sciences Centre, Memorial University, 300 Prince Philip Dr., St. John's, NF A1B 3V6, 709/753-9041, Fax: 709/753-7867
Nova Scotia College of Family Physicians: Administrator, Beth MacPherson, RR#1, PO Box 925, Bedford, NS B0J 3J0, 902/823-1021, Fax: 902/823-1021
Ontario College of Family Physicians: Executive Director, L. Cheryl Katz, 2630 Skylark Ave., Mississauga, ON L4W 5A4, 905/629-1600, Fax: 905/629-4810
Prince Edward Island Chapter: Chapter Secretary, Elaine Caseley, RR#4, Kensington, PE C0B 1M0, 902/836-4638, Fax: 902/836-4638
Saskatchewan Chapter: Administrator, Lois Hislop, PO Box 7111, Saskatoon, SK S7K 4J1, 306/665-7714, Fax: 306/665-7714
Section du Québec: Secrétaire administrative, Micheline Guilbault, #101, 310 av Victoria, Westmount, PQ H3Z 2M9, 514/481-5962, Téléc: 514/481-6948

College of Medical Laboratory Technologists of Ontario/Ordre des technologistes de laboratoire médical de l'Ontario (CMLTO) (1993)
#330, 10 Bay St., Toronto, ON M5J 2R8
416/861-9605, Fax: 416/861-0934, Toll Free: 1-800-323-9672
Registrar, Sheila Woodcock
Publications: Focus

Community & Hospital Infection Control Association Canada/Association pour la prévention des infections à l'hôpital et dans la communauté - Canada (1976)
CHICA-Canada
PO Box 46125, RPO Westdale, Winnipeg, MB R3R 3S3
250/897-5990, Fax: 250/895-9595
President, Clare E. Barry
Executive Secretary, Gerry Hansen
Treasurer, Ilana Warner
Publications: Canadian Journal of Infection Control
Affiliates: International Federation of Infection Control

Consumer Health Organization of Canada (CHOC) (1975)
#205, 250 Sheppard Ave. East, North York, ON M2N 6M9
416/222-6517, Fax: 416/225-1243
President, Libby Gardon
Publications: Consumer Health Newsletter
Affiliates: National Health Federation in US

Corporation professionnelle des acupuncteurs du Québec
6731, rue St-Denis, Montréal, PQ H2S 2S3
514/464-0805
Président, Claude B. Prevost

Corporation professionnelle des physiothérapeutes du Québec (CPPQ) (1973)
#530, 1100, av Beaumont, Montréal, PQ H3P 3H5
514/737-2770, Téléc: 514/737-6431, Ligne sans frais: 1-800-361-2001
Présidente, France Hétu, pht, MBA
Publications: Physio-Québec

Council on Chiropractic Education (Canada) (CCE(C))
#440, 6091 Gilbert Rd., Richmond, BC V7C 5L9
604/278-3505
President, Dr. D. Nixdorf

Crohn's & Colitis Foundation of Canada/Fondation canadienne des maladies inflammatoires de l'intestin (CCFC) (1974)
#301, 21 St. Clair Ave. East, Toronto, ON M4T 1L9
416/920-5035, Fax: 416/929-0364
National Executive Director, Michael J. Howorth
Director of Communications, Barbara Victor

DES Action Canada (1982)
PO Box 233, Stn Snowdon, Montréal, PQ H3X 3T4
514/482-3204, Fax: 514/482-1445, Toll Free: 1-800-482-1337
Executive Director, Dawn Kiddell
President, Shirley Simand
Publications: DES Action Newsletter
Affiliates: DES Action Australia; DES Action Britain; DES Action Italy; DES Action Germany; DES Action The Netherlands; DES Action USA; DES Action Ireland; Info DES France

Dystonia Medical Research Foundation/Fondation de recherches médicales sur la dystonie (1976)
#2430, 1 East Wacker Dr., Chicago, IL 60601-2001 USA
312/755-0198
President, Dennis Kessler
Publications: Dystonia Dialogue

Endometriosis Association, Inc./Association de l'endometriose inc. (1980)
International Headquarters, 8585 North 76th Place, Milwaukee, WI 53223 USA
414/355-2200, Fax: 414/355-6065, Toll Free: 1-800-426-2363
Executive Director, Mary Lou Ballweg
Publications: Endometriosis Association Newsletter

Epilepsy Canada/Epilepsie Canada (EC) (1966)
#745, 1470, rue Peel, Montréal, PQ H3A 1T1
514/845-7855, Fax: 514/845-7866
National Executive Director, Denise Crépin
President, Dr. Madelane Riley-Reidy
Vice-President, James LaMartina
Vice-President, Patrick S. Kinnear
National Director of Programs, Rebecca Rupp
Publications: Lumina

ASSOCIATION QUÉBÉCOISE DE L'ÉPILEPSIE
#111, 1015, Côte du Beaver Hall, Montréal, PQ H2Z 1S1
514/875-5595, Téléc: 514/875-6734
Directrice générale, France Picard

Epilepsy Ontario/Epilepsie Ontario (1956)
#308, 1 Promenade Circle, Thornhill, ON L4J 4P8
905/764-5099, Fax: 905/764-1231, Toll Free: 1-800-463-1119, Email: epilepsy@epilepsy.org
URL: http://www.epilepsy.org
Chief Executive Director, Dianne Findlay
Publications: Sharing
Affiliates: Epilepsy Association of Metropolitan Toronto

Eye Bank of BC (EBBC) (1983)
Eye Care Centre, 2550 Willow St., Vancouver, BC V5Z 3N9
604/875-4567, Fax: 604/875-5316, Toll Free: 1-800-667-2060
Coordinator, Debbie Chow
Medical Director, Dr. J.S.F. Richards
Affiliates: Canadian National Institute for the Blind; Eye Bank Association of America; Canadian Ophthalmological Society

Eye Bank of Canada - Ontario Division (1955)
Ontario Eye Bank
One Spadina Cres., Toronto, ON M5S 2J5
416/480-7465, 978-7355, Fax: 416/978-1522
Administrator, Dr. Marilyn Schneider
Affiliates: Canadian National Institute for the Blind; University of Toronto

Federation of Canadian Naturists (1985)
PO Box 186, Islington, ON M9A 4X2
416/267-2283, Email: naturist@torfree.net
President, David Basford, Fax: 905/627-9935
Publications: Going Natural
Affiliates: International Naturist Federation

Fédération des médecins omnipraticiens du Québec/Québec Federation of General Practitioners (FMOQ) (1963)
#1000, 1440, rue Ste-Catherine ouest, Montréal, PQ H3G 1R8
514/878-1911, Téléc: 514/878-4455, Ligne sans frais: 1-800-361-8499, Courrier électronique: directi@fmoq.org
Président, Dr. Renald Dutil
Publications: Le Médecin du Québec

Canadian Almanac & Directory 1997

Fédération des médecins spécialistes du Québec (FMSQ) (1965)
#3000, 2, Complexe Desjardins, Montréal, PQ H5B 1G8
514/350-5000, Téléc: 514/350-5100

Federation of Medical Licensing Authorities of Canada/Fédération des ordres des médecins du Canada (FMLAC) (1968)
PO Box 8234, Ottawa, ON K1G 3H7
613/738-0372, Fax: 613/738-8977
President, Dr. L.R. Ohlhauser
Executive Secretary, Sylvia Smith
Publications: Communiqué

COLLÈGE DES MÉDECINS DU QUÉBEC (CMQ) (1847)
Corporation des médecins du Québec
2170, boul René-Lévesque ouest, Montréal, PQ H3H 2T8
514/933-4441, Téléc: 514/933-3112, Courrier électronique: cdoccmq@interlink.net
Président, Dr. Roch Bernier
Publications: Le Collège; Annuaire médical

COLLEGE OF PHYSICIANS & SURGEONS OF ALBERTA
#900, 10180 - 101 St., Edmonton, AB T5J 4P8
403/423-4764, Fax: 403/420-0651
Registrar, L. Ohlhauser

COLLEGE OF PHYSICIANS & SURGEONS OF BRITISH COLUMBIA
1383 - 8th Ave. West, Vancouver, BC V6H 4C4
604/733-6671, Fax: 604/737-8582, Email: leinblau@wimsey.com
Registrar, T.F. Handley

COLLEGE OF PHYSICIANS & SURGEONS OF MANITOBA (CPS MANITOBA) (1871)
494 St. James St., Winnipeg, MB R3G 3J4
204/774-4344, Fax: 204/774-0750
Registrar, K. Brown
Publications: From the College

COLLEGE OF PHYSICIANS & SURGEONS OF NEW BRUNSWICK/COLLÈGE DES MÉDECINS ET CHIRURGIENS DU NOUVEAU-BRUNSWICK
One Hampton Rd., PO Box 628, Rothesay, NB E2E 5A7
506/658-0959, Fax: 506/849-5069, Toll Free: 1-800-667-4641, Email: cpsnb@nbnet.nb.ca
Registrar, Ed Schollenberg, MD, LLB, FRCPC

COLLEGE OF PHYSICIANS & SURGEONS OF NOVA SCOTIA
5248 Morris St., Halifax, NS B3J 1B4
902/422-5823, Fax: 902/422-5035
Registrar, Dr. Cameron Little
Publications: Newsletter

COLLEGE OF PHYSICIANS & SURGEONS OF ONTARIO (1866)
80 College St., Toronto, ON M5G 2E2
416/967-2600
Registrar, Dr. Michael E. Dixon
Publications: Members' Dialogue

COLLEGE OF PHYSICIANS & SURGEONS OF PRINCE EDWARD ISLAND (1988)
199 Grafton St., Charlottetown, PE C1A 1L2
902/566-3861, Fax: 902/566-3861
President, Dr. Cyril Moyse
Office Secretary, Ruth Stavert
Registrar, H.E. Ross

COLLEGE OF PHYSICIANS & SURGEONS OF SASKATCHEWAN (CPSS) (1905)
211 - 4th Ave. South, Saskatoon, SK S7K 1N1
306/244-7355, Fax: 306/244-0090
Registrar, D.A. Kendel, M.D.
Executive Secretary, Jeannette Heinen
Publications: The College Newsletter; Bulletin, q.

NEWFOUNDLAND MEDICAL BOARD (1893)
#6, 139 Water St., St. John's, NF A1C 1B2
709/726-8546, Fax: 709/726-4725
Registrar, R.W. Young
Publications: Newsletter

Fédération québécoise des masseurs et massothérapeutes (FQMM) (1979)
#204, 1265, Mont-Royal est, Montréal, PQ H2J 1Y4
514/597-0505, Téléc: 514/597-0141, Ligne sans frais: 1-800-363-9609
Directeur général, Daniel Bouffard
Publications: Le Massager

Fondation de la banque d'yeux du Québec inc./Québec Eye Bank Foundation (1976)
5689, boul Rosemont, Montréal, PQ H1T 2H1
514/252-3886, Téléc: 514/252-3821
Directrice administrative, Maryse Senécal
Publications: Les Amis de la banque d'yeux

Fondation québécoise du cancer (1979)
2075, rue de Champlain, Montréal, PQ H2L 2T1
514/527-2194, Téléc: 514/527-1943, Infoligne: 514/522-6237, Ligne sans frais: 1-800-361-4212
Directeur, Guy Germain

Health Action Network Society (HANS) (1984)
#202, 5262 Rumble St., Burnaby, BC V5J 2B6
604/435-0512, Fax: 604/435-1561, Email: info@hans.org
URL: http://www.hans.org/
President, Lorna Hancock
Executive Administrator, Cathrine Gabriel
Publications: Health Action

Health Care Public Relations Association of Canada/L'Association des relations publiques des organismes de la santé, Canada (HCPRA) (1973)
253 College St., PO Box 166, Toronto, ON M5T 1R5
416/699-6353, Fax: 416/699-6353
Executive Director, Judy Hodgson
Publications: Impressions
Affiliates: Canadian Healthcare Association

Health Evidence Application & Linkage Network/Réseau de liaison et d'application de l'information sur la santé (HEALNet) (1995)
Dept. of Clinical Epidemiology & Biostatistics, McMaster University, 1200 Main St. West, Hamilton, ON L8N 3Z5
905/525-9140, ext.22282, Fax: 905/577-0017
Network Manager, Corey Wentzell, Email: wentzell@fhs.mcmaster.ca

Health Sciences Centre Foundation (1981)
MS7, 820 Sherbrook St., Winnipeg, MB R3A 1R9
204/787-2022, Fax: 204/787-4547, Info Line: 204/787-1900
Executive Director, Janet Walker
Chairman, James A. Ferguson
Publications: Foundation Newsletter; Magazine, a.
Affiliates: Health Sciences Centre; Foundations for Health

Heart & Stroke Foundation of Alberta (1957)
1825 Park Rd. SE, Calgary, AB T2G 3Y6
403/264-5549, Fax: 403/237-0803
Executive Director, John Paquet
Publications: Heart & Stroke Foundation of Alberta Lifelines

Heart & Stroke Foundation of Canada/Fondation des maladies du coeur du Canada (HSFC) (1983)
#200, 160 George St., Ottawa, ON K1N 9M2
613/241-4361, Fax: 613/241-3278
National Executive Director, William G. Tholl
President, Gary M. Sutherland
Affiliates: International Society & Federation of Cardiology; Canadian Coalition for High Blood Pressure Prevention & Control

Hemophilia Ontario (1988)
#308, 60 St. Clair Ave. East, Toronto, ON M4T 1N5
416/972-0641, Fax: 416/972-0307
President, David Mitchell
Publications: Hemophilia Ontario
Affiliates: Ontario AIDS Network

Huntington Society of Canada/Société Huntington du Canada (1973)
13 Water St. North, PO Box 1269, Cambridge, ON N1R 7G6
519/622-1002, Fax: 519/622-7370
Executive Director, Ralph M. Walker
President, Carol Ellis
Director of Communications, Isla Horvath
Publications: Horizon
Affiliates: Canadian Neurological Coalition; International Huntington Association

Huntington Society of Québec/Société Huntington du Québec (1986)
4841, rue Rivard, Montréal, PQ H2J 2N7
514/842-5740, Fax: 514/842-5961
Social Worker, Diane Guertin
Publications: Horizon

Interior Alzheimer Foundation (1981)
2020 Springfield Rd., Kelowna, BC V1Y 7V8
250/762-3312
President, Marjorie Chermishnuk
Publications: Sensor

International Association for Medical Assistance to Travellers (IAMAT) (1960)
40 Regal Rd., Guelph, ON N1K 1B5
519/836-0102, Fax: 519/836-3412, Info Line: 416/652-0137, Email: iamat@sentex.net
URL: http://www.sentex.net/~iamat
President, M.A. Uffer-Marcolongo
Toronto Office: Contact, Nadia Sallese, #1, 1287 St. Clair Ave. West, Toronto, ON M6E 1B8, 416/652-0137

Interstitial Cystitis Association of Canada/Association canadienne pour la cystite interstitielle (ICA) (1987)
PO Box 5814, Stn A, Toronto, ON M5W 1P2
416/920-8986, Fax: 416/968-9081
President, Helen Klukach
Vice-President & Treasurer, Sheila Holmes, 905/434-6858, Fax: 905/432-3847
Publications: National Report; Helpline, q.
Affiliates: Interstitial Cystitis Association - USA Head Office

Juvenile Diabetes Foundation Canada/Fondation du diabète juvénile Canada (JDF) (1974)
JDF Canada
89 Granton Dr., Richmond Hill, ON L4B 2N5
905/889-4171, Fax: 905/889-4209, Toll Free: 1-800-668-0274
Executive Director, Tim Feher
President/CEO, Terry A. Jackson
Publications: Countdown; Tielines
Affiliates: Juvenile Diabetes Foundation International; Diabetes Canada

The Kidney Foundation of Canada/La Fondation canadienne du rein (KFOC) (1964)
#780, 5160, boul Décarie, Montréal, PQ H3X 2H9
514/369-4806, Fax: 514/369-2472, Toll Free: 1-800-361-7494
National President, Owen Brown

ORGANIZATIONS — HEALTH & MEDICAL   2-93

National Executive Director, Gavin Turley
Publications: Let's Talk Research; Kidney Heart Watch

Leprosy Mission Canada/La Mission évangélique contre la lèpre (Canada) (1892)
TLM Canada
#216, 40 Wynford Dr., North York, ON M3C 1J5
416/441-3618, Fax: 416/441-0203
Executive Director, Peter Derrick
President, Dr. John Clement
Publications: The Leprosy Mission in Action
Affiliates: The Leprosy Mission International

Lupus Canada (1989)
5512 - 4 St. NW, PO Box 64034, Calgary, AB T2K 6J1
403/274-5599, Fax: 403/274-5599, Toll Free: 1-800-661-1468, Email: lupuscan@cadvision.com
President, Mae Boa, 306/787-6066, Email: mboa@sasked.gov.sk.ca
National Office Coordinator, P.K. O'Brien
Publications: Lupus Canada Bulletin
Affiliates: Lupus Foundation of America

Manitoba Cancer Treatment & Research Foundation
100 Olivia St., Winnipeg, MB R3E 0V9
204/787-2136, Fax: 204/783-6875
Donna Pacholok

Manitoba Medical Service Foundation Inc.
100A Polo Park Centre, 1485 Portage Ave., Winnipeg, MB R3G 0W4
204/788-6801, Fax: 204/774-1761
Executive Director, John Wade

Manitoba Paraplegia Foundation Inc. (1980)
825 Sherbrook St., Winnipeg, MB R3A 1M5
204/786-4753, Fax: 204/786-1140
President, Doug Finkbeiner, QC
Publications: Paratracks

M.E. Association of Canada/Association E.M. du Canada (1988)
Myalgic Encephalomyelitis/Chronic Fatigue Syndrome Association of Canada
#400, 246 Queen St., Ottawa, ON K1P 5E4
613/563-1565, Fax: 613/567-0614, Info Line: 613/563-1565, Email: tharvey@hookup.net
Chairperson, Rod Blaker
Director, Membership & Support Group Services, Peter Bates
Publications: Messenger

The Medical Council of Canada/Le Conseil médical du Canada (1912)
#300, 2283 St. Laurent Blvd., PO Box 8234, Stn T, Ottawa, ON K1G 3H7
613/521-8787, Fax: 613/521-9417
Executive Director/CEO, Dr. W. Dale Dauphinee
Publications: Echo

Medical Devices Canada (MEDEC) (1972)
MEDEC
#510, 401 The West Mall, Etobicoke, ON M9C 5J5
416/620-1915, Fax: 416/620-1595
President, Dennis W. Bryant
Publications: Canadian Assistive Devices Directory; Medec Pulse, 10 pa; Medical Devices Industry Directory; Medec Membership Directory; Annual MEDCOMP Survey; Annual Survey of Industry Trends

Medical Reform Group (1979)
PO Box 158, Stn D, Toronto, ON M6P 3J8
416/588-9167, Email: udiemer@sources.copy
Contact, Ulli Diemer

Publications: Medical Reform
Affiliates: International Organization of Consumers Unions

The Michener Institute for Applied Health Sciences
222 St. Patrick St., Toronto, ON M5T 1V4
416/596-3101, ext.3123; Fax: 416/596-3156; Email: cdandary@staff.michener.on.ca; URL: http://www.michener.on.ca
President & CEO, Renate Krakauer

The Migraine Association of Canada (1974)
#1912, 365 Bloor St. East, Toronto, ON M4V 3L4
416/920-4916, Fax: 416/920-3677, Info Line: 416/920-4917, Toll Free: 1-800-663-3557
Executive Director, Anne Kerr
President, Bill Ross
Fund Development Manager, Cindy Stanleigh
Communications Coordinator, Shaaron McDonald
Publications: Headlines

Multiple Organ Retrieval & Exchange Program of Ontario/Programme de récupération et d'échange de multiples organes de l'Ontario (MORE) (1988)
#503, 984 Bay St., Toronto, ON M5S 2A5
416/921-1130, Fax: 416/921-7313, Toll Free: 1-800-263-2833
Executive Director, Gary Cooper
Acting Executive Secretary, Catherine Gilboord

Multiple Sclerosis Society of Canada/Société canadienne de la sclérose en plaques (1948)
MS Society
#1000, 250 Bloor St. East, Toronto, ON M4W 3P9
416/922-6065, Fax: 416/922-7538, Toll Free: 1-800-268-7582, Email: info@mssoc.ca
URL: http://www.mssoc.ca
National Executive Director, Alistair M. Fraser
President, Bruce R. Richmond, C.A.
National Communications Director, Deanna Groetzinger
Publications: MS/SP Canada
Affiliates: Canadian Medical Association

Muscular Dystrophy Association of Canada/Association canadienne de la dystrophie musculaire (MDAC) (1954)
#900, 2345 Yonge St., Toronto, ON M4P 2E5
416/488-0030, Fax: 416/488-7523, Toll Free: 1-800-567-2873
URL: http://www.trends.ca/MDAC
Acting Executive Director, Patricia Parker
Executive Assistant, Rosanne Portelance
Publications: Connections/Connexions

Myasthenia Gravis Foundation of British Columbia (1955)
2805 Kingsway Ave., Vancouver, BC V5R 5H9
604/451-5511, Fax: 604/451-5651
President, Brenda Kelsey

National Cancer Institute of Canada/Institut national du cancer du Canada (NCIC)
#200, 10 Alcorn Ave., Toronto, ON M4V 3B1
416/961-7223, Fax: 416/961-4189
CEO, Dorothy J. Lamont
Executive Director, Dr. D.J. Beatty
Publications: Journal of the National Cancer Institute

National Clearinghouse on Tobacco & Health/Centre national de documentation sur le tabac et la santé (NCTH) (1988)
#1000, 170 Laurier Ave. West, Ottawa, ON K1P 5V5
613/567-3050, Fax: 613/567-2730
Director, John Hamilton
Affiliates: Canadian Council on Smoking & Health

National Eating Disorder Information Centre (NEDIC) (1985)
College Wing 1-211, 200 Elizabeth St., Toronto, ON M5G 2C4
416/340-4156, Fax: 416/340-4736
Programme Coordinator, Merryl Bear
Publications: Bulletin

National Institute of Nutrition/Institut national de la nutrition (NIN) (1983)
#302, 265 Carling Ave., Ottawa, ON K1S 2E1
613/235-3355, Fax: 613/235-7032, Email: nin@hpb.hwca.ca
URL: http://www.hwc.ca:8080/nin
President, Suzanne Hendricks
Chairman, Dr. George Ivany
Publications: Rapport; NIN Review/Le Point INN, q.
Affiliates: Agricultural Institute of Canada; Canadian Dental Association; Canadian Dental Hygienists' Association; Canadian Dietetic Association; Canadian Home Economics Association; Canadian Institute of Food Science & Technology; Canadian Medical Association; Canadian Nurses Association; Canadian Paediatric Society; Canadian Pharmaceutical Association; Canadian Public Health Association; Canadian Society for Nutritional Sciences; Canadian Society of Allergy & Clinical Immunology; College of Family Physicians of Canada; Organization for Nutrition Education; Sport Medicine Council of Canada

North American Chronic Pain Association of Canada (NACPAC) (1986)
#105, 150 Central Park Dr., Brampton, ON L6T 2T9
905/793-5230, Fax: 905/793-8781, Toll Free: 1-800-616-7246
President, Dr. Ric Edwards
Publications: ACPA Chronicle; The NacPac Track, q.
Affiliates: American Chronic Pain Association

Occupational & Environmental Medical Association of Canada/Association canadienne de la médecine du travail et de l'environnement (OEMAC) (1983)
54 Forward Ave., London, ON N6H 5C8
519/439-7970
OEMAC Secretariat, Lise Jamieson
President, Dr. Bernard Gascon
Publications: Liaison; OMAC Membership Directory, a.
Affiliates: Canadian Medical Association; Canadian Board of Occupational Medicine

Ontario Cancer Institute
Princess Margaret Hospital, 500 Sherbourne St., Toronto, ON M4X 1K9
416/926-4482, Fax: 416/926-6566
Chief Librarian, Carol Morrison, 416/413-2000
Reference Librarian, Carole Tullis, 416/413-2002

Ontario Council on Community Health Accreditation
#1618, 415 Yonge St., Toronto, ON M5B 2E7
416/595-0321, Fax: 416/595-0294

Ontario Naturopathic Association (ONA) (1950)
Lambton Business Centre, #304, 4174 Dundas St. West, Etobicoke, ON M8X 1X3
416/233-2001, Fax: 416/233-2924
President, Pamela Milroy, ND
Office Coordinator, Heather Fleck
Publications: ONA Pulse

Ontario Podiatry Association
#900, 2 Sheppard Ave. East, North York, ON M2N 5Y7
416/927-9111, Fax: 416/733-2491
Executive Secretary, Gloria Patterson

Canadian Almanac & Directory 1997

Ontario Society of Clinical Hypnosis (OSCH) (1970)
#402, 200 St. Clair Ave. West, Toronto, ON M4V 1R1
416/251-2442
Executive Secretary, Patricia Derraugh
Publications: OSCH News

Ordre des ergothérapeutes du Québec (OEQ) (1974)
#710, 1259, rue Berri, Montréal, PQ H2L 4C7
514/844-5778, Téléc: 514/844-0478, Ligne sans frais: 1-800-265-5778
Directeur général, Réjean Pedneault
Publications: Revue Québécoise d'Ergothérapie

Ordre des orthophonistes et audiologistes du Québec (OOAQ) (1973)
#730, 1265, rue Berri, Montréal, PQ H2L 4X4
514/282-9123, Téléc: 514/282-9541
Présidente, Renée Boisclair-Papillon
Secrétaire, Jean-Philippe Legault
Trésorière, Carmen Phénix
Publications: Bulletin de l'OOAQ

Ordre professionnel des technologistes médicaux du Québec (OPTMQ) (1973)
#300, 1150, boul Saint-Joseph est, Montréal, PQ H2J 1L5
514/527-9811, Téléc: 514/527-7314, Ligne sans frais: 1-800-567-7763
Directeur général, Alain Collette
Président, Richard Charette
Coordonnatrice des services professionnels, Marie France Gionet
Publications: Sommaire

Organ Donors Canada/Donneurs d'organes du Canada (1974)
5326 Ada Blvd., Edmonton, AB T5W 4N7
403/474-9363
Executive Director, Mae Cox

Osteoporosis Society of Canada/La Société de l'Ostéoporose du Canada (1982)
33 Laird Dr., Toronto, ON M4G 3S9
416/696-2663, Fax: 416/696-2673, Toll Free: 1-800-463-6842
Executive Director, Joyce Gordon
Office Manager, Maxine Smith
Publications: Osteoporosis Bulletin for Physicians; News & Views, q.
Affiliates: Osteoporosis Canada Walk Foundation

Parkinson Foundation of Canada/La fondation canadienne du parkinson (1965)
#710, 390 Bay St., Toronto, ON M5H 2Y2
416/366-0099, Fax: 416/366-9190, Toll Free: 1-800-565-3000
CEO, Trevor Williams
National Director, Finance, Carol Giannone
Publications: Network

Post-Polio Awareness & Support Society of BC (PPASS) (1986)
Depot#1, PO Box 6579, Victoria, BC V8P 5N7
250/477-8244, 6546, Fax: 250/477-8287
President, Alf Foxgord
Publications: PPASS News

Post-Polio Network (Manitoba)
Manitoba Clearing House, 825 Sherbrook St., Winnipeg, MB R3A 1M5
Publications: Newsletter

Psoriasis Society of Canada/Société Psoriasis du Canada (1983)
National Office, PO Box 25015, Halifax, NS B3M 4H4
902/443-8680, Fax: 902/457-1664

President, Judy Misner
Vice-President, John Merlini
Sec.-Treas., Diane Drake
Director, Robert Kotler
Publications: National Psoriasis Newsletter
Affiliates: International Federation of Psoriasis Associations

Respiratory Health Network of Centres of Excellence/Réseau de centres d'excellence en santé respiratoire (1990)
Inspiraplex
Institut thoracique de Montréal, 3650, rue Saint-Urbain, Montréal, PQ H2X 2P4
514/843-2096, Fax: 514/843-2098
Network Manager, Anne Vézina, Email: annev@nixtor.sni.ca

The Royal College of Physicians & Surgeons of Canada/Le Collège royal des médecins et chirurgiens du Canada (RCPSC) (1929)
774 Echo Dr., Ottawa, ON K1S 5N8
613/730-8177, Fax: 613/730-8833, Toll Free: 1-800-668-3740
Executive Director, Gilles D. Hurteau
President Elect, Dr. Henry B. Dinsdale
Head, Communications Section, Pierrette Leonard
Publications: RCPSC Bulletin; Annals RCPSC, 8 pa
Affiliates: Canadian Medical Association; College of Family Physicians of Canada

RP Research Foundation/Fondation RP pour la recherche (1974)
#704, 366 Adelaide St. West, Toronto, ON M5V 1R9
416/360-4200, Fax: 416/360-0060, Toll Free: 1-800-461-3331
National Executive Director, Sharon Colle
President, John Dryden
Publications: Vision
Affiliates: US RP Foundation

Saint Elizabeth Health Care (1908)
#320, 10 Gateway Blvd., North York, ON M3C 3A1
416/429-1234, Fax: 416/429-8244
President, Shirlee Sharkey
Publications: Elizabethan Times

Sleep/Wake Disorders Canada/Affections du Sommeil/Eveil Canada (SWDC) (1975)
#5055, 3080 Yonge St., Toronto, ON M4N 3N1
416/483-9654, Fax: 416/483-7081, Toll Free: 1-800-387-9253
Ontario Coordinator, Wendy Stratton
National Coordinator, Bev Devins
Publications: Good Night Good Day
Affiliates: Canadian Neurological Coalition

Society of Obstetricians & Gynaecologists of Canada/Société des obstétriciens et gynécologues du Canada (SOGC) (1944)
774 Echo Dr., Ottawa, ON K1S 5N8
613/730-4192, Fax: 613/730-4314, Toll Free: 1-800-561-2416
URL: http://www.medical.org/sogc_docs/SOGC.html
Executive Vice-President, Dr André Lalonde
Director, Finance, Brenda Dashney
Publications: SOGC News; SOGC Journal, m.

Spina Bifida Association of Canada/Association spina-bifida du Canada (SBAC) (1981)
#220, 388 Donald St., Winnipeg, MB R3B 2J4
204/957-1784, Fax: 204/957-1794, Toll Free: 1-800-565-9488, Email: spinab@mts.net
President, Wally Sagansky
Publications: Podium
Affiliates: International Federation for Hydrocephalus & Spina Bifida

L'ASSOCIATION DE SPINA-BIFIDA ET D'HYDROCÉPHALIE DU QUÉBEC (ASBHQ) (1975)
#425, 5757, rue Decelles, Montréal, PQ H3S 2C3
514/340-9019, Téléc: 514/340-9109, Ligne sans frais: 1-800-567-1788
Directrice générale, Tina Marie Lalonde
Publications: Contact

Stroke Recovery Association of Ontario (SRAO) (1975)
#292, 10 Overlea Blvd., Toronto, ON M4H 1A4
416/425-4209, Fax: 416/425-1920
Provincial Coordinator, Cheryl L. Denomy
Publications: The Phoenix

Thyroid Foundation of Canada/Fondation du Canada pour les maladies thyroidiennes (1980)
1040 Gardiners Rd., Kingston, ON K7P 1R7
613/634-3426, Fax: 613/634-3483, Email: thyroid@io.org
URL: http://www.io.org/~thyroid/canada.html
Founder, Diana Meltzer Abramsky, C.M., B.A.
President, Don McKelvie, C.A.
National Office Coordinator, Katherine Keen
Publications: Thyrobulletin

Tourette Syndrome Foundation of Canada/La Foundation Canadienne du Syndrome de la Tourette (TSFC) (1976)
#203, 3675 Keele St., North York, ON M3J 1M6
416/636-2800, Fax: 416/636-1688, Toll Free: 1-800-361-3120
Executive Director, Rosie Wartecker
President, Barry Berenstein
Publications: The Greenleaflet

Turner's Syndrome Society/Association du syndrome de Turner (TSS) (1982)
7777 Keele St., 2nd Fl., Concord, ON L4K 1Y7
905/660-7766, Fax: 905/660-7450, Toll Free: 1-800-465-6744
Executive Director, Sandi Hofbauer
Publications: The Turner Syndrome News; The X's & O's of Turner's Syndrome; Across the Lifespan

United Ostomy Association, Canada (1987)
UOA Canada
5 Hamilton Ave., Hamilton, ON L8V 2S3
905/389-8822
President, Allan Porter
Publications: UOA Canada Talks
Affiliates: United Ostomy Association - USA

World Federation of Occupational Therapists (WFOT) (1952)
104 Hardy Rd., Glen Forest 6071 Western Australia
011/61-09-274-1228, Fax: 011/61-09-426-9380
Honorary Secretary, Prof. Carolyn Webster
Publications: WFOT Bulletin
Affiliates: Committee of Occupational Therapists of the European Community

HEART & STROKE ASSOCIATIONS *see* **HEALTH & MEDICAL**

HEATING, AIR CONDITIONING, PLUMBING

American Society of Heating, Refrigerating & Air Conditioning Engineers - Toronto Chapter (ASHRAE)
Bldg. 11, #300, 5045 Orbitor Dr., Mississauga, ON L4W 4Y4
905/602-4714, Fax: 905/602-1197
President, D. Taylor
Publications: Toronto Chapter Gazette

American Society of Plumbing Engineers (ASPE) (1964)
#210, 3617 Thousand Oaks Blvd., Westlake, CA 91362 USA
805/495-7120
British Columbia Chapter: President, Graham Aspinal, PO Box 2201, Stn Terminal, Vancouver, BC V6B 3W2, 604/688-8671
Montréal Chapter: Président, André Lavallée, c/o Cosertec, 5070, av des Sorbiers, Montréal, PQ H1T 2H5, 514/382-1556
Québec City Chapter: President, Marcel Fortier, T.Sc.A., CIPE, 1937, rue Delisle, Bernières, PQ G7A 2A3, 418/623-7013

British Columbia Insulation Contractors Association (BCICA) (1958)
#242, 4299 Canada Way, Burnaby, BC V5G 1H3
604/438-6616, Fax: 604/438-6525
Administrator, Debbie Hoover
Affiliates: Thermal Insulation Association of Canada

Canadian Institute of Plumbing & Heating/ L'Institut canadien de plomberie et de chauffage (CIPH) (1933)
#330, 295 The West Mall, Etobicoke, ON M9C 4Z4
416/695-0447, Fax: 416/695-0450
President/General Manager, Edward R. Hardison
Program Manager, Ralph P. Suppa
Show Manager, Elizabeth McCullough
Publications: Pipeline; Canadian Institute of Plumbing & Heating Directory; Canadian Institute of Plumbing & Heating Statistics

Canadian Refrigeration & Air Conditioning Contractors Association (CRACCA) (1972)
Bldg. 11, #300, 5045 Orbitor Dr., Mississauga, ON L4W 4Y4
905/602-4700, Fax: 905/602-1197
Secretary, Warren J. Heeley

Heating, Refrigerating & Air Conditioning Institute of Canada/Institut canadien du chauffage, de la climatisation et de la réfrigération (HRAI) (1969)
Bldg. 11, #300, 5045 Orbitor Dr., Mississauga, ON L4W 4Y4
905/602-4700, Fax: 905/602-1197
President, Warren J. Heeley
Communications Manager, Gerald J. Smith
Manager, Government Relations & Chapter Development, Fred Chorley
Manager, Marketing Education & Delivery, Joanne Campbell
Publications: HRAI News; HRAI Membership Directory; The HRAI Catalogue
Affiliates: Air Conditioning & Refrigeration Wholesalers Canada; North American Heating & Air Conditioning Wholesalers, Heating & Air Conditioning Contractors Section; Ontario Building Officials

Independent Plumbing & Heating Contractors' Association (IPHCA) (1980)
#305, 1 Greensboro Dr., North York, ON M9W 1C8
416/248-6213, Fax: 416/248-6214
Manager, Mauro Angeloni

Ontario Plumbing Inspectors Association (OPIA) (1920)
1677 Gregory Rd., RR#3, St Catharines, ON L2R 6P9
905/685-9402, Fax: 905/685-0640
Secretary, F. Penfold
Publications: OPIA Bulletin

Ontario Refrigeration & Air Conditioning Contractors Association (ORAC)
Office Mall II, #7A, 1400 Bayly St., Pickering, ON L1W 3R2
905/420-7272, Fax: 905/420-7288
President, Marv Lindgren
Secretary, Barry Eon
Affiliates: Heating, Refrigerating & Air Conditioning Institute of Canada

Refrigeration Service Engineers Society (Canada) (RSES Canada) (1952)
PO Box 1400, Stn A, North York, ON M2N 5T5
416/221-3538, Fax: 416/222-3927
President, Gary Struhar, CMS
First Vice-President, Wesley Maxfield, CM
Second Vice-President, Garry MacKenzie, CM
Secretary, Eglal Homsy
Treasurer, Stephen Manson
Executive Assistant, Norman B. Fraser
Publications: RSES Canada Bulletin

Thermal Insulation Association of Canada/ Association canadienne de l'isolation thermique (TIAC) (1964)
#210, 44 Byward Market Sq., Ottawa, ON K1N 7A2
613/562-1012, Fax: 613/562-1014
Executive Vice-President, Alison Bowick, MBA, CAE
Office Manager, Heather McIntosh
Publications: TIAC Times

HERALDRY *see* **HISTORY, HERITAGE, GENEALOGY**

HERITAGE *see* **HISTORY, HERITAGE, GENEALOGY**

HISTORY, HERITAGE, GENEALOGY
see also Culture; Multiculturalism

Alberta Family History Society (AFHS) (1980)
PO Box 30270, Stn B, Calgary, AB T2M 4P1
URL: http://www.freenet.calgary.ab.ca/science/afhs.html
Chair, Noreen Chambers
Queries Coordinator, Myrna Waldroff, Fax: 403/252-2957
Publications: Chinook
Affiliates: Federation of Family History Societies (England)

Alberta Historical Resources Foundation (AHRF) (1976)
Old St. Stephen's College, 8820 - 112 St., Edmonton, AB T6G 2P8
403/431-2300, Fax: 403/432-1376
Director, Mark Rasmussen

Alberta Pioneer Railway Association (1968)
PO Box 70014, Londonderry, AB T5C 3R6
403/472-6229
Contact, Herb Dickson
Publications: The Marker
Affiliates: Heritage Canada

Association québécoise d'interprétation du patrimoine (AQIP) (1977)
82, Grande Allée ouest, Québec, PQ G1R 2G6
418/647-1927, Téléc: 418/647-6483
Directeur général, Patrice Groulx
Publications: Bulletin de Liaison

Association québécoise pour le patrimoine industriel (AQPI) (1988)
CP 905, Succ. C, Montréal, PQ H2L 4V2
514/598-8185, Téléc: 514/598-8185
Présidente, Marie-Claude Robert
Publications: Bulletin
Organisation(s) affiliée(s): The International Committee for the Conservation of the Industrial Heritage

British Columbia Genealogical Society (BCGS) (1971)
PO Box 88054, Lansdowne Mall, Richmond, BC V6X 3T6
604/988-6075
President, Peter S.N. Claydon
Corresponding Secretary, Marian Elder, 604/522-6453
Publications: The British Columbia Genealogist

British Columbia Historical Federation (1922)
PO Box 746, Grand Forks, BC V0H 1H0
250/442-3865
President, Alice Glanville
Publications: BC Historical News

British Columbia Railway Historical Association (BCRHA) (1961)
PO Box 8114, VCPO, Victoria, BC V8W 3R8
250/389-0584, Email: uah46@freenet.victoria.bc.ca
President, Paul J. Smith
Publications: Callboard

Bus History Association, Inc. (BHA) (1963)
965 MacEwan, Windsor, ON N9B 2G1
519/977-0664
Chair, Paul Leger
Publications: Bus Industry; News

Canada's National History Society/Société d'historie nationale du Canada (CNHS)
#478, 167 Lombard Ave., Winnipeg, MB R3C 0E7
204/988-9309, Fax: 204/988-9300, Email: beaver@cyberspc.mb.ca
URL: http://www.cyberspc.mb.ca/~otmw/cnhs/cnhs-ind.html
Vice-President, Laird Rankin

Canadian Association of Professional Heritage Consultants/Association canadienne des consultants patrimoine (CAPHC) (1987)
PO Box 1023, Stn F, Toronto, ON M5A 2T7
President, Susan Maltby, B.A., M.A.C., 416/537-3446, Fax: 416/537-3446
Secretary, David Nasby
Treasurer, Bob Mitchell
Vice-President, Robert Shipley
Publications: The Heritage Consultants' Forum; Membership Directory, a.
Affiliates: ICOMOS International (International Council on Monuments & Sites); ICOMOS Canada - English-Speaking Committee

Canadian Canal Society/Société des canaux du Canada (CCS) (1982)
80 King St., PO Box 24102, St Catharines, ON L2R 7P7
905/688-5550, ext.3264, Fax: 905/988-5490
President, Robert Sparks
Secretary, Doris Bates
Treasurer, Carol Gaspari
Publications: Canals Canada/Canaux du Canada

Canadian Catholic Historical Association - English Section/Société canadienne d'histoire de l'église catholique - Section anglaise (CCHA) (1933)
1155 Yonge St., Toronto, ON M4T 1W2
416/934-3400, ext.504, Fax: 416/934-3444
Secretary General, Rev. Edward Jackman
Publications: Canadian Catholic Historical Studies; Bulletin, s-a.

Canadian Federation of Genealogical & Family History Societies Inc. (1984)
CanFed
227 Parkville Bay, Winnipeg, MB R2M 2J6
204/256-6176
Acting President, Harry Skene

Canadian Almanac & Directory 1997

Secretary, Cécile Skene
Publications: CANFED Newsletter

Canadian Friends Historical Association (CFHA) (1972)
60 Lowther Ave., Toronto, ON M5R 1C7
416/969-9675
Chairperson, Kyle Jolliffe
Publications: Canadian Quaker History Journal; Directory of Canadian Biography; Index of Quaker Records
Affiliates: Friends Historical Society

Canadian Heritage Information Network/Réseau canadien d'information sur le patrimoine (CHIN)
15, rue Eddy, 4e étage, Hull, ON K1A 0M5
819/994-1200, Fax: 819/994-9555
URL: http://www.chin.gc.ca
Director General, Lynn Elliott-Sherwood
Director, Systems Development, Gail Eagen
Publications: CHIN Update

Canadian Historical Association/Société historique du Canada (CHA) (1922)
395 Wellington St., Ottawa, ON K1A 0N3
613/233-7885, Fax: 613/567-3110, Email: 74143.1061@compuserve.com
Administrative Assistant, Joanne Mineault
President, Nadia Fahmyeid
Publications: Register of Dissertations; CHA Bulletin, q.; Journal of the CHA, a.

Canadian Institute for Historical Microreproductions/Institut canadien de microreproductions historiques (CIHM) (1978)
PO Box 2428, Stn D, Ottawa, ON K1P 5W5
613/235-2628, Fax: 613/235-9752, Email: cihmicmh@nlo.nlc.bnc.ca
URL: http://www.nlc-bnc.ca/cihm/cihm.html
Executive Director, Pam Bjornson
Publications: Facsimile

Canadian Oral History Association/Société canadienne d'histoire orale (COHA) (1974)
PO Box 2064, Stn D, Ottawa, ON K1P 5W3
613/996-6996, Fax: 613/995-6575
President, Janet Trimble
Vice-President, Joan Fairweather
Sec.-Treas., Carolyn Vachon
Publications: Canadian Oral History Association Journal; Canadian Oral History Association Newsletter

Canadian Railroad Historical Association/Association canadienne d'histoire ferroviaire (CRHA) (1932)
120 rue St-Pierre, Saint-Constant, PQ J5A 2G9
514/632-2410
President, Walter J. Bedbrook
Vice-President, Robert V.V. Nicholls
Treasurer, Robert Carlson
Publications: Canadian Rail

Canadian Society of Church History/Société canadienne d'histoire de l'église (1960)
Dept. of History, University of Maine, Orono, ME 04469-5774 USA
207/581-1908, Fax: 207/581-1817
President, William Katerberg
Publications: Canadian Society of Church History Papers

Canadian Society for Industrial Heritage/Société canadienne de l'héritage industriel (CSIH) (1991)
240 Sparks St., PO Box 55122, Ottawa, ON K1P 1A1
613/991-6705, Fax: 613/990-3636
Chairperson, Louise Trottier
Publications: Machines

Canadian Almanac & Directory 1997

Canadian Society of Mayflower Descendants (1980)
#802, 500 Duplex Ave., Toronto, ON M4R 1V6
Governor, Robert M. Cruikshank
Publications: Canadian Pilgrim
Affiliates: General Society of Mayflower Descendants - USA

Canadian Society for the Study of Names/Société canadienne d'onomastique (CSSN) (1951)
c/o Geographical Names, 615 Booth St., Ottawa, ON K1A 0E9
Email: hkerfoot@emr1.emr.ca
President, Helen Kerfoot
Vice-President, Jean-Yves Dugas
Publications: Onomastica Canadiana; The Name Gleaner, q.

Canadian Steam Preservation & Industrial Archaeological Association
13541 - 62 Ave., Surrey, BC V3X 2J3
604/594-1970, Fax: 604/594-1820
Sec.-Treas., David Jackson
Publications: Industrial Age
Affiliates: The International Committee for the Conservation of the Industrial Heritage

Canadian Warplane Heritage (CWH) (1971)
#300, 9300 Airport Rd., Mount Hope, ON L0R 1W0
905/679-4183, Fax: 905/679-4186
President, Dennis Bradley
Publications: Flightlines

Conseil des monuments et sites du Québec (CMSQ) (1975)
82, Grande-Allée ouest, Québec, PQ G1R 2G6
418/647-4347, Téléc: 418/647-6483, Ligne sans frais: 1-800-494-4347
Présidente, France Gagnon Pratte
Directrice, Marie Nolet
Publications: Continuité
Succursale de Montréal: 5695, rue Waverley, Montréal, PQ H2T 2Y2, 514/270-8645, Téléc: 514/270-8355

The Family History Association of Canada/Association canadienne de l'histoire des familles (1976)
#301, 2245 West Broadway, Vancouver, BC V6K 2E4
250/223-2112
National Chairman, Gretha M. Warren

Federation of Nova Scotian Heritage (FNSH) (1976)
#901, 1809 Barrington St., Halifax, NS B3J 3K8
902/423-4677, Fax: 902/422-0881, Toll Free: 1-800-355-6873, Email: fnsh@fox.nstn.ca
Executive Director, Susan Charles
Publications: Federation News
Affiliates: Heritage Canada; Canadian Museums Association; Association for State & Local History

Fédération québécoise des sociétés de généalogie (1984)
CP 9454, Ste-Foy, PQ G1V 4B8
418/653-3940
Présidente, Esther Taillon
Publications: Info-Généalogie

Fédération des sociétés d'histoire du Québec (1965)
4545, av Pierre-De-Coubertin, CP 1000, Succ. M, Montréal, PQ H1V 3R2
514/252-3031, Téléc: 514/251-8038
Directeur général, Mario Boucher
Publications: Actualités Histoire Québec; Histoire Québec, semi-annuel

Genealogical Association of Nova Scotia/Association généalogique de la Nouvelle-Écosse (1982)
PO Box 641, Stn M, Halifax, NS B3J 2T3
President, Vernon Spurr, 902/434-2945
Publications: Nova Scotia Genealogist

Genealogical Institute of The Maritimes/Institut généalogique des Provinces Maritimes (GIM) (1983)
PO Box 3142, Stn Halifax South, Halifax, NS B3J 3H5
902/424-6065
Registrar, Virginia Clark
President, Lois Yorke

Heraldry Society of Canada/Société héraldique du Canada (1966)
PO Box 8128, Stn T, Gloucester, ON K1G 3H9
613/231-0867
President, Jean Matheson
Secretary, Howard Heck
International Correspondent, James Taylor
Publications: Heraldry in Canada
Affiliates: Commonwealth Heraldry Board

Heritage Canada (1973)
Heritage Canada Foundation
412 MacLaren St., PO Box 1358, Stn B, Ottawa, ON K1P 5R4
613/237-1066, Fax: 613/237-5987, Email: hercanot@interserv.com
Executive Director, Jacques Dalibard
Director, Government & Public Relations, Douglas Franklin
Atlantic Office Contact, Peter Hyndman, 902/421-1889
Central Office Contact, Stephen Lauer, 519/622-3036
Québec Office Contact, Hélène Deslauriers, 418/694-9944
Western Office Contact, Cecile Allard, 306/934-3622
Publications: The Heritage Directory; Heritage Canada, 5 pa; Press Review, bi-weekly
Affiliates: Canadian Heritage Network

L'Héritage canadien du Québec/The Canadian Heritage of Québec (HCQ) (1960)
1181, rue de la Montagne, Montréal, PQ H3G 1Z2
514/393-1417, 481-5796, Fax: 514/393-9444
Executive Director, Arnold Sharp
Président, C. Robin Molson
Publications: Le Bulletin de l'Héritage canadien du Québec/The Canadian Heritage of Québec Newsletter

Heritage Council of British Columbia (1988)
c/o BC Museums Association, 514 Government St., Victoria, BC V8V 4X4
250/387-3315, Fax: 250/387-1251
Chair, Greg Evans
Affiliates: Archaeological Society of BC; Archives Association of BC; BC Museums Association; BC Historical Federation; Heritage Society of BC; Underwater Archaeological Society of BC

Heritage Foundation of Newfoundland & Labrador (1984)
PO Box 5171, St. John's, NF A1C 5V5
709/739-1892, Fax: 709/739-5413
Executive Secretary, George Chalker
Chairperson, Victoria Collins

Historic Theatres' Trust/Société des salles historiques (1989)
PO Box 387, Stn Victoria, Montréal, PQ H3Z 2V8
514/933-8077
President, Janet MacKinnon
Vice-President, Jean-Marc Larrue
Secretary, Claude Fortin

Treasurer, Philip Dombowsky
Publications: Bulletin

Historical Society of Alberta (1907)
PO Box 4035, Stn C, Calgary, AB T2T 5M9
403/261-3662, Fax: 403/269-6029
President, Kathryn Ivany
Publications: Alberta History; Chinook Country Newsletter; Lethbridge Historical Society Newsletter; Edmonton Historical Newsletter; Edmonton & District Historical Society Newsletter; Central Alberta Historical Society Newsletter
Affiliates: Heritage Canada

Huguenot Society of Canada/Société Huguenote du Canada (1966)
#105, 4936 Yonge St., North York, ON M2N 6S3
President, Richard W. Pogson
Publications: Huguenot Trails
Affiliates: Ontario Historical Society

International Council on Monuments & Sites Canada (ICOMOS Canada) (1975)
PO Box 737, Stn B, Ottawa, ON K1P 5R4
613/749-0971, Fax: 613/749-0971, Email: icomosca@ottawa.icomos.org
URL: http://www.icomos.org/canada
President, François Leblanc
Président, Comité francophone, Michel Bonnette
President, English Committee, Alistair Kerr
Executive Assistant, Renée Leblanc
Publications: ICOMOS Canada
Affiliates: UNESCO; International Centre for the Study of the Preservation & Restoration of Cultural Property (ICCROM)

J. Douglas Ferguson Historical Research Foundation (1971)
654 Hiawatha Blvd., Ancaster, ON L9G 3A5
905/648-4041
Sec.-Treas., Dorte Brace
Chairperson, William H. McDonald

Jewish Genealogical Society of Canada (JGSC) (1985)
PO Box 446, Stn A, North York, ON M2N 2T1
416/638-3280
President, Henry Wellisch
Publications: Shem Tov
Affiliates: Jewish Federation of Greater Toronto

Literary & Historical Society of Québec (1824)
44 St-Stanislas, Québec, PQ G1R 4H3
418/694-9147
Librarian, Cynthia Dooley

Manitoba Genealogical Society Inc. (1976)
PO Box 2066, Winnipeg, MB R3C 3R4
204/944-1153
Library Chair, Louisa Shermerhorn
Publications: Generations

Manitoba Heritage Federation Inc. (1985)
21 - 2nd Ave. NW, 2nd Fl., Dauphin, MB R7N 1H1
204/638-9154, Fax: 204/638-0683, Email: 76766.35@compuserve.com
President, Norm Black
Vice-President, Joan Whiston
Treasurer, Jack Watts, CMA, FCMA
Secretary, Patricia Bourbonnais
Administrator, Karin Overgaard
Publications: Heritage Now

Manitoba Historical Society (1879)
#470, 167 Lombard Ave., Winnipeg, MB R3B 0T6
204/947-0559
Executive Director, Celine M. Kean
Publications: Manitoba History; Manitoba Historical Society Newsletter; Manitoba Historical Atlas
Affiliates: Heritage Canada

Monarchist League of Canada/Ligue Monarchiste du Canada (MLC) (1970)
PO Box 1057, Oakville, ON L6J 5E9
905/855-7262, Fax: 905/972-9179, Toll Free: 1-800-465-6925
Chairman, John Aimers
Dominion Vice-Chairman & Editor, Arthur Bousfield
Dominion Vice-Chairman, Public Relations, Paul Benoit
Publications: Canadian Monarchist News; Monarchy Canada, q.
Affiliates: Canadian Royal Heritage Trust

New Brunswick Genealogical Society (1979)
PO Box 3235, Stn B, Fredericton, NB E3A 5G9
President, Joan Pearce
Publications: Generations

New Brunswick Historical Society (1874)
120 Union St., Saint John, NB E2L 1A3
506/672-4056
President, Doreen Hamilton
Vice-President, Denis Knibb
Secretary, Carolyn Johnson
Treasurer, George F. Teed
Publications: New Brunswick H.S. Newsletter

Newfoundland Historical Society (1881)
Colonial Building, Rm #15, St. John's, NF A1C 2C9
709/722-3191, Fax: 709/729-0578
Office Manager, Mary Bridson
President, Dr. Pat O'Brien
Publications: Newfoundland Quarterly; Newfoundland Historical Society Newsletter
Affiliates: Heritage Canada

Newfoundland & Labrador Genealogical Society Inc. (NLGS) (1984)
Colonial Building, Military Rd., St. John's, NF A1C 2C9
709/754-9525
President, Dianne Jackman
Publications: The Newfoundland Ancestor

North-West Mounted Police Commemorative Association
PO Box 876, Cochrane, AB T0L 0W0
403/932-4167
Contact, Cliff Christian

Ontario Black History Society (OBHS) (1978)
Ontario Heritage Centre, #202, 10 Adelaide St. East, Toronto, ON M5C 1J3
416/867-9420, Fax: 416/867-8691
President, Rosemary J. Sadlier
Publications: Ontario Black History News
Affiliates: Ontario Historical Society

Ontario Electric Railway Historical Association (1953)
Halton County Radial Railway
PO Box 578, Milton, ON L9T 5A2
519/856-9802
Contact, Garry Gladden
Publications: Radial Report
Affiliates: Association of Railroad Museums; Ontario Museum Association; Canadian Museums Association

Ontario Genealogical Society/Société de généalogie de l'Ontario (OGS) (1961)
#102, 40 Orchard View Blvd., Toronto, ON M4R 1B9
416/489-0734, Fax: 416/489-9803
URL: htpp://www.interlog.com/~dreed/ogs_home.htm
President, Ann Ward
Publications: Newsleaf; Families, q.; Newsline
Affiliates: Ontario Heritage Alliance

Ontario Heritage Foundation (OHF) (1967)
10 Adelaide St. East, Toronto, ON M5C 1J3
416/325-5000, Fax: 416/314-4930
Chair, Joanna Bedard
Executive Director, Lesley Lewis
Director, Heritage Programs, Richard Moorhouse
Manager, Heritage Community Services, Brian Rogers
Manager, Marketing, John Ecker, 416/325-5013
Natural Heritage Consultant, James Duncan
Natural Heritage Consultant, Patti Priestman
Publications: Heritage Dimensions

Ontario Historical Society/La Société historique de l'Ontario (OHS) (1888)
34 Parkview Ave., North York, ON M2N 3Y2
416/226-9011, Fax: 416/226-2740
Executive Director, Dorothy Duncan
Communications Coordinator, Meribeth Clow
Publications: Ontario History; OHS Bulletin, bi-m.

Postal History Society of Canada (PHSC) (1972)
216 Mailey Dr., Carleton Place, ON K7C 3X9
613/257-5453
President, Eugene Labiuk
Vice-President, Dr. Robert C. Smith
Secretary, R.F. Narbonne
Treasurer, Geoffrey R. Newman
Publications: PHSC Journal
Affiliates: American Philatelic Society; British North America Philatelic Society

Prince Edward Island Genealogical Society Inc. (PEIGS)
PO Box 9066, Charlottetown, PE C1A 8C4
President, Elizabeth Glen

Prince Edward Island Museum & Heritage Foundation (PEIMHF) (1983)
2 Kent St., Charlottetown, PE C1A 1M6
902/368-6600, Fax: 902/368-6608
Executive Director, Chris Severance
Publications: The Island Magazine

Québec Family History Society/Société de l'histoire des familles du Québec (QFHS) (1977)
PO Box 1026, Pointe Claire, PQ H9S 4H9
514/695-1502
URL: http://www.cam.org/~qfhs/index.html
President, G. Schroder
Publications: Connections
Affiliates: International Federation of Family History Societies

Regroupement des organismes du patrimoine franco-ontarien (ROPFO) (1989)
50 Maple Lane, Ottawa, ON K1M 1G8
613/744-6728, Téléc: 613/744-6508
Présidente, Huguette Parent
Publications: Fleur de trille

Richard III Society of Canada (1966)
331 Rose Park Dr., Toronto, ON M4T 1R8
416/486-0031
Secretary, Noreen Armstrong
Publications: Newsletter

The Royal Nova Scotia Historical Society (RNSHS) (1878)
PO Box 2097, Dartmouth, NS B2W 3X8
902/422-4610, Fax: 902/422-4610
President, Donald F. Maclean

Canadian Almanac & Directory 1997

Secretary, Rosemary Barbour
Publications: Collections of the RNSHS

Saskatchewan Architectural Heritage Society (SAHS) (1987)
Historic Strathdee Mall, #311, 2066 Dewdney Ave., Regina, SK S4R 1H3
306/359-0933, Fax: 306/359-3899
Executive Director, Michael Phelps
President, Kent Smith-Windsor
Publications: Facade; Saskatchewan Architectural Heritage Directory; Heritage Artisans Directory

Saskatchewan Council of Cultural Organizations (SCCO) (1979)
#210, 438 Victoria Ave. East, Regina, SK S4N 0N7
306/780-9284, Fax: 306/780-9252, Email: scco.general@sasknet.sk.ca
URL: http://www.sasknet.sk.ca/scco/
General Manager, Mary Mahon Jones
Communications Coordinator, Olivia Shumski, Email: olivia.shumski@sasknet.sk.ca
Publications: Cultural Report
Affiliates: Canadian Society of Association Executives

Saskatchewan Cultural Exchange Society (SCES) (1979)
2431 - 8 Ave., Regina, SK S4R 5J7
306/569-8966, Fax: 306/757-4422
Executive Director, Margaret Fry
President, Ross Taylor
Publications: The Exchange; Bulletin, m.

Saskatchewan Genealogical Society (SGS) (1969)
1870 Lorne St., Regina, SK S4P 2L7
306/780-9207, Fax: 306/781-6021,
    Email: margethomas.sgs@cabler.cableregina.com
URL: http://www.regina.ism.ca/orgs/sgs/index.htm
Executive Director, Marge Thomas
Publications: Bulletin
Affiliates: Saskatchewan Heritage Committee

Société canadienne d'histoire de l'Église Catholique - Section française/Canadian Catholic Historical Association - French Section (SCHEC) (1933)
175 Main St., Ottawa, ON K1S 1C3
613/237-0580, Téléc: 613/232-4064
Secrétaire trésorier, Romuald Boucher, O.M.I.
Publications: Études d'histoire religieuse; Bulletin de liaison, semi-annuel

Société franco-ontarienne d'histoire et de généalogie (SFOHG) (1981)
CP 1363, Succ. B, Sudbury, ON P3E 5K4
705/853-4849
Président, Richard Pelland
Publications: Le Chaînon

Société généalogique canadiénne-française (1943)
CP 335, Succ. Place-d'Armes, Montréal, PQ H2Y 3H1
514/729-8366, Téléc: 514/729-1180
Président, Normand Robert
Publications: Memoires de la Société généalogique canadienne-française

La Société historique acadienne (1960)
CP 632, Moncton, NB E1C 8M7
506/855-5918
Président, Léone Boudreau-Nelson
Secrétaire, E. Roy
Publications: Les Cahiers de la Société historique acadienne

Société historique de Québec (1937)
171, rue Grande-Allée ouest, Québec, PQ G1R 2H1

418/649-0085, Téléc: 418/649-0085
Gilles Mathieu
Publications: Quebecensia

United Empire Loyalists' Association of Canada (1914)
UEL Association
Dominion Office, The George Brown House, 50 Baldwin St., Toronto, ON M5T 1L4
416/591-1783, Fax: 416/591-1783
Executive Director, Dorothy Chisholm
Publications: The Loyalist Gazette

West Coast Railway Association (WCRA) (1961)
PO Box 2790, Vancouver, BC V6B 3X2
604/524-1011, Fax: 604/522-1293, Toll Free: 1-800-722-1233
President, Don Evans, 604/520-2243
Publications: WCRA News

Western Heritage Centre Society
105 River Ave., PO Box 1477, Cochrane, AB T0L 0W0
403/932-3514, Fax: 403/932-3515
General Manager, Norm Haines

Yukon Historical & Museums Association (1977)
3126 - 3 Ave., PO Box 4357, Whitehorse, YT Y1A 3T5
403/667-4704
President, Brent Slobodin
Coordinator, Marjorie Copp
Publications: Yukon Historical & Museums Association Newsletter
Affiliates: Heritage Canada; BC Heritage Trust

HOBBIES see **RECREATION, HOBBIES & GAMES**

HOME & SCHOOL ASSOCIATIONS see **EDUCATION**

HOME BUILDERS see **HOUSING**

HOMOSEXUALITY

Canadian Lesbian & Gay Archives (CLGA) (1973)
#201, 56 Temperance St., PO Box 639, Stn A, Toronto, ON M5W 1G2
416/777-2755, Email: queeries@clga.ca
URL: http://www.clga.ca/archives
President, Ray Brillinger
Publications: Lesbian & Gay Archivist
Affiliates: Association of Canadian Archivists; Ontario Association of Archives

Coalition for Lesbian & Gay Rights in Ontario/Coalition pour les droits des lesbiennes et personnes gaies en Ontario (CLGRO) (1975)
PO Box 822, Stn A, Toronto, ON M5W 1G3
416/533-6824
Publications: CLGRO Newsletter
Affiliates: International Lesbian & Gay Association

Council on Homosexuality & Religion/Conseil de l'homosexualité et la religion (CHR) (1976)
PO Box 1912, Winnipeg, MB R3C 3R2
204/474-0212, Fax: 204/478-1160, Info Line: 204/284-5208
President, Rev. A.E. Millward
Sec.-Treas., Chris Vogel

Equality for Gays & Lesbians Everywhere/Égalité pour les gais et lesbiennes (EGALE) (1986)
Arts Court, 2 Daly Ave., Ottawa, ON K1N 6E2
613/230-1043, Fax: 613/237-6651, Email: egale@netfinder.com
URL: http://www.netfinder.com/egale/
President, Denis LeBlanc

Integrity/Vancouver
PO Box 2797, Stn Main, Vancouver, BC V6B 3X2
604/874-3428
President, Lynette Ley
Affiliates: Integrity Inc. - USA

HORTICULTURE, GARDENING, LANDSCAPE ARCHITECTURE

Alberta Association of Landscape Architects (AALA) (1970)
#2, 9804 - 47 Ave., Edmonton, AB T6E 5P3
403/435-9902, Fax: 403/435-7503
President, Brian Baker
Publications: AALA

Alberta Horticultural Association
1 Fenwick Cres., St Albert, AB T8N 1N5
403/460-1578
Sec.-Treas., Donna Dawson

Les Amis du Jardin botanique de Montréal/Friends of the Montréal Botanical Garden (1975)
4101, rue Sherbrooke est, Montréal, PQ H1X 2B2
514/872-1493, Téléc: 514/872-3765
Directrice générale, Karen Grislis
Président, Michel Labrecque
Secrétaire, Paule Lamontagne
Publications: Le Quatre-Temps

Association des architectes paysagistes du Québec (AAPQ)
#811, 3575, boul St-Laurent, Montréal, PQ H2X 2T7
514/990-7731
President, Vincent Guamis

Association des jardiniers maraîchers du Québec
#102, 805, rue du Marché Central, Montréal, PQ H4N 1K2
514/387-8319, Téléc: 514/387-1406
Directeur général, Alin Gravel

Atlantic Provinces Association of Landscape Architects (APALA)
PO Box 3415, Stn South, Halifax, NS B3J 3J1
902/422-6514, Fax: 902/425-0402
President, Cary Vollick
Publications: APALA Newsletter

British Columbia Society of Landscape Architects (BCSLA) (1964)
#110, 355 Burrard St., Vancouver, BC V6C 2G8
604/682-5610, Email: bcsla@mindlink.bc.ca
Secretary, Claudia Brhlick
Publications: Sitelines

Canadian Association of Pesticide Control Officials/Association canadienne des responsables du contrôle des pesticides
c/o Pest Management Regulatory Agency, Health Canada, 59 Camelot Dr., Ottawa, ON K1A 0Y9
613/952-5330, Fax: 613/990-0605
President, Madeline Waring
Secretary, Ginette Robert

Canadian Horticultural Council/Conseil canadien de l'horticulture (CHC) (1922)
#310, 1101 Prince of Wales Dr., Ottawa, ON K2C 3W7
613/226-4187, Fax: 613/226-2984
Executive Vice-President, Dan Dempster
Assistant Executive Vice-President, Steven Whitney
Publications: Rapporteur
Affiliates: Canadian Federation of Agriculture

Canadian Iris Society (CIS) (1946)
199 Florence Ave., North York, ON M2N 1G5

416/225-1088
Secretary, Verna Laurin
President, Ed Jowett
Publications: CIS Newsletter

Canadian Nursery Trades Association (CNTA) (1968)
Landscape Canada
RR#4, Stn Main, 7856 Fifth Line South, Milton, ON L9T 2X8
905/875-1399, Fax: 905/875-1840
Executive Director, Chris D. Andrews
Publications: CNTA Newsbrief; CNTA Membership Directory, a.; Canadian Standards for Nursery Stock, biennial
Affiliates: Flowers Canada

BRITISH COLUMBIA NURSERY TRADES ASSOCIATION (BCNTA) (1964)
#101, 5830 - 176A St., Surrey, BC V3S 4E3
604/574-7772, Fax: 604/574-7773
Executive Director, Jane Stock
Program & Technology Coordinator, Bill Hardy
Publications: Dig This; Hortwest

LANDSCAPE ALBERTA NURSERY TRADES ASSOCIATION (LANTA) (1957)
10215 - 176 St., Edmonton, AB T5S 1M1
403/489-1991, Fax: 403/444-2152, Toll Free: 1-800-378-3198, Email: lanta@planet.eon.net
Executive Director, Nigel Bowles
Publications: Prairie Landscape; Clippings, m.

LANDSCAPE NEW BRUNSWICK
c/o Price Contractors Ltd., PO Box 433, Moncton, NB E1C 8L4
506/858-7800, Fax: 506/859-6919
Executive Secretary, Ellen Ruddick

LANDSCAPE NOVA SCOTIA
Kentville Agricultural Centre, Blair House, Kentville, NS B4N 1J5
902/768-0533, Fax: 902/679-1074
Executive Secretary, Sonya MacKillop

LANDSCAPE ONTARIO HORTICULTURAL TRADES ASSOCIATION (LOHTA) (1973)
7856 Fifth Line South, RR#4, Milton, ON L9T 2X8
905/875-1805, Fax: 905/875-3942
Executive Director, Tony DiGiovanni
Publications: Landscape Trades; Horticulture Review

MANITOBA NURSERY & LANDSCAPE ASSOCIATION (MNLA) (1958)
Landscape Manitoba
808 Muriel St., Winnipeg, MB R2Y 0Y3
204/889-5981, Fax: 204/888-0944
Executive Secretary, Evelyn MacKenzie-Reid
Publications: Green Scene Gazette

SASKATCHEWAN NURSERY TRADES ASSOCIATION (SNTA)
c/o Keon Garden Centre Ltd., 1102 Caribou St. West, Moose Jaw, SK S6H 2L9
306/693-6771, Fax: 306/691-0558
Ron Johnson

Canadian Ornamental Plant Foundation/ Fondation canadienne des plantes ornementales (COPF) (1964)
PO Box 21083, North Bay, ON P1B 7N8
705/495-2563, Fax: 705/495-1449
Managing Director, Peggy Walsh Craig
Publications: COPF News

Canadian Rose Society (CRS) (1955)
10 Fairfax Cres., Scarborough, ON M1L 1Z8
416/757-8809, Fax: 416/757-4796
Secretary, Anne Graber
Publications: The Rosarian; The Canadian Rose πAnnual
Affiliates: World Federation of Rose Societies

Canadian Society for Horticultural Science (CSHS)
c/o Plant Science Dept., McDonald Campus, McGill University, Montréal, PQ H9X 1C0
514/398-7756, Fax: 514/398-7955
Contact, Dr. David Wees

Canadian Society of Landscape Architects/ Association des architectes paysagistes du Canada (CSLA) (1934)
Box 7, Site 5, RR#1, Okotoks, AB T0L 1T0
403/938-2476, Fax: 403/938-2476, Email: csla@agt.net
URL: http://www.clr.utoronto.ca/ORG/CSLA/
Executive Director, Larry Paterson
Secretary, Linda LeGeyt
Publications: CSLA Bulletin
Affiliates: International Federation of Landscape Architects; Landscape Alliance

Canadian Wildflower Society
#228, 4981 Hwy. 7, Markham, ON L3R 1N1
Contact, Robert K. Lounsbury
Publications: Wildflower

City Farmer - Canada's Office of Urban Agriculture (1978)
#801, 318 Homer St., Vancouver, BC V6B 2V3
604/685-5832, Fax: 604/685-0431, Email: cityfarm@unixg.ubc.ca
URL: http://www.cityfarmer.org
Executive Director, Michael Levenston
Publications: Gardening with People with Disabilities; Urban Home Composting; Urban Agriculture Notes

Fédération interdisciplinaire de l'horticulture ornementale du Québec (FIHOQ) (1976)
Pavillon Envirotron, Cité Universitaire, CP 2208, Succ. Terminus, Ste-Foy, PQ G1K 7P4
418/659-3562, Téléc: 418/651-7439
Directrice administrative, Aline Munger
Publications: L'Actuel horticole
Organisation(s) affiliée(s): Association internationale des producteurs en horticulture; Conseil canadien de l'horticulture; Chambre de commerce du Québec; Conseil québécois de l'Horticulture

Fédération des sociétés d'horticulture et d'écologie du Québec (FSHÉQ)
4545, av Pierre-de-Coubertin, CP 1000, Succ. M, Montréal, PQ H1V 3R2
514/252-3010, Téléc: 514/251-8038
Président, René Paquet

Flowers Canada Inc./Fleurs Canada inc. (FC) (1967)
7856 Fifth Line South, RR#4, Milton, ON L9T 2X8
519/875-0707, Fax: 519/875-3494, Email: flowers@spectranet.ca
Executive Director, Garry R. Watson
Publications: News Vine

Manitoba Association of Landscape Architects (MALA) (1973)
635 Bardal Bay, Winnipeg, MB R2G 0J1
204/663-4863, Fax: 204/663-4863
Executive Director, Gunter A. Schoch
Publications: MALA News

Ontario Association of Landscape Architects (OALA) (1968)
#101, 2842 Bloor St. West, Etobicoke, ON M8X 1B1
416/231-4181, Fax: 416/231-2679, Email: oala@interlog.com
URL: http://www.clr.utoronto.ca/org/oala
Executive Director, Arthur M. Timms, B.Sc., Ph.D., CAE
President, David Anselmi
Publications: OALA News
Affiliates: Conservation Council of Ontario

Ontario Horticultural Association (1951)
PO Box 842, Sutton, ON L0E 1R0
URL: http://www.interlog.com/~onthort
President, Jim Anderson

Prince Edward Island Horticultural Association, Inc. (1984)
PO Box 2232, Charlottetown, PE C1A 8B9
902/566-2733, Fax: 902/566-2383
President, Ralph Yeo
Treasurer, Gerald Dykerman
Agrologist, Joanne Driscoll
Affiliates: PEI Vegetable Growers Cooperative; PEI Cole Crop Growers Co-op Ltd.; PEI Greenhouse Growers Association; PEI Federation of Agriculture; PEI Strawberry Growers Association; Canadian Horticulture Council

Rhododendron Society of Canada (1971)
RR#2, St George Brant, ON N0E 1N0
519/448-1537
Contact, Dr. H.G. Hedges

Royal Botanical Gardens/Les jardins botaniques royaux (RBG) (1932)
PO Box 399, Hamilton, ON L8N 3H8
905/527-1158, Fax: 905/577-0375
Publications: Pappus

Saskatchewan Association of Landscape Architects (SALA) (1979)
#200, 642 Broadway Ave., Saskatoon, SK S7N 1A9
306/975-3238, Fax: 306/975-3034
President, Heather Edwards
Secretary, Michael Beresnak
Publications: SALA Digest
Affiliates: International Federation of Landscape Architects

Saskatchewan Horticultural Association
PO Box 68, Parkside, SK S0J 2A0
306/747-3296
President, Helen Buchanan
Secretary, Alan Daku
Treasurer, Jean Procknow

Seeds of Diversity Canada (1984)
PO Box 36, Stn Q, Toronto, ON M4T 2L7
905/623-0353
President, Garrett Pittenger
Publications: Seeds of Diversity; Seed Listing, a.; Resource List of Seeds Companies & Nurseries Selling Heirloom Varieties

Southern Ontario Orchid Society
45 Stamford Sq. South, Scarborough, ON M1L 1X2
416/759-1439
Contact, Walter Norman

HOSPITALS
see also Health & Medical; Nursing

Association of Canadian Teaching Hospitals (ACTH)
#E408, 4500 Oak St., Vancouver, BC V6H 3N1
604/875-3468, Fax: 604/872-3290
Executive Director, James B. Flett

Association des centres hospitaliers et centres d'accueil privés du Québec (ACHAP) (1979)
#200, 204, rue Notre-Dame ouest, Montréal, PQ H2Y 1T3
514/499-3630, Téléc: 514/873-7063
Directeur général, Jacques Renaud

Association of Ontario Health Centres/ Association des centres de santé de l'Ontario (AOHC) (1982)
#102, 5233 Dundas St. West, Etobicoke, ON M9B 1A6
416/236-2539, Fax: 416/236-0431, Email: mail@aohc.com
URL: http://www.aohc.org
Executive Director, Ms. Sonny Arrojado
Publications: Healthlink; CHC News for CHC People, q.
Affiliates: Healthy Communities; Broader Health Sector Task Force

British Columbia Association of Community Care (BCACC) (1991)
#101, 1700 - 75th Ave. West, Vancouver, BC V6P 6G2
604/734-1464, Fax: 604/263-1458, Email: bcacc@mindlink.bc.ca
Executive Director, Leslie Arnold
Publications: The Communicator

British Columbia Association of Private Care (1978)
BC Pricare
#101, 1700 - 75th Ave. West, Vancouver, BC V6P 6G2
604/263-4223, Fax: 604/263-4229
Chief Executive Officer, Ed Helfrich
Coordinator, Board & Member Services, Pat Christie
Publications: BC Pricare News
Affiliates: Canadian College of Health Services Executives; Canadian & BC Gerontology Associations; Canadian Home Care Association; Canadian Association for Community Care; Quality Council of BC

Canadian Administrative Housekeepers Association/L'Association Canadienne des Intendants Administratif (CAHA) (1972)
c/o Property Management Services, BC Buildings Corp., 500 Lougheed Hwy., Port Coquitlam, BC V3C 4J2
604/528-3868, Fax: 604/528-3871
President, Bonnie Suni, CAH
Director of Membership, Gordon Sisco, CAH
Sec.-Treas., Gillian Profitt, CAH
Publications: Magazine

Canadian Association for Community Care/ Association canadienne de soins et services communautaires (CLS) (1977)
#701, 45 Rideau St., Ottawa, ON K1N 5W8
613/241-7510, Fax: 613/241-5923
Co-Executive Director, Dawn Walker
Co-Executive Director, Sharon Sholzberg-Gray
Publications: National Bulletin

ALBERTA LONG TERM CARE ASSOCIATION
CN Tower, #910, 10004 - 104 Ave., Edmonton, AB T5J 0K1
403/421-1137, Fax: 403/426-0479
Executive Director, Claire Mills

ASSOCIATED HOMES FOR SPECIAL CARE, NOVA SCOTIA (1964)
#260, 33 Ochterloney St., Dartmouth, NS B2Y 4P5
902/469-1730, Fax: 902/464-3791
Executive Director, Brian Vandervaart

CONFÉDÉRATION QUÉBÉCOISE DES CENTRES D'HÉBERGEMENT ET DE RÉADAPTATION (CQCHR) (1974)
#1100, 1001, boul de Maisonneuve est, Montréal, PQ H2L 4P9
514/597-1007, Téléc: 514/873-5411

Vice-président exécutif, Louis Champoux
Agente d'information, Nancy Leggett-Bachand
Publications: L'Accueil

NEW BRUNSWICK ASSOCIATION OF NURSING HOMES, INC./ ASSOCIATION DES FOYERS DE SOINS DU NOUVEAU-BRUNSWICK, INC. (1972)
197 Main St., Fredericton, NB E3A 1E1
506/458-9466, Fax: 506/458-9206
Executive Director, Michel Desjardins
Publications: Intercom

NEWFOUNDLAND & LABRADOR ASSOCIATION OF HOMES FOR SPECIAL CARE
PO Box 95, Holyrood, NF A0A 2R0
709/229-7053
Sec.-Treas., Tom Power

NEWFOUNDLAND & LABRADOR HEALTH CARE ASSOCIATION
Beclin Building, Topsail Rd., PO Box 8234, Stn A, St. John's, NF A1B 3N4
709/364-7701, Fax: 709/364-6460
Executive Director, John S. Peddle

NURSING HOME ASSOCIATION OF MANITOBA (NHAM) (1974)
#700, 360 Broadway, Winnipeg, MB R3C 4G8
204/956-1819, Fax: 204/943-5370
Executive Director, Isabel Rourke
President, R. Bazinet

ONTARIO ASSOCIATION OF NON-PROFIT HOMES & SERVICES FOR SENIORS (OANHSS) (1919)
#700, 7050 Weston Rd., Woodbridge, ON L4L 8G7
905/851-8821, Fax: 905/851-0744
Executive Director, Michael Klejman
Publications: Action Update

Canadian Association of Health-Care Auxiliaries/ Association des auxiliaires bénévoles des établissements de santé du Canada (CAHA) (1951)
#100, 17 York St., Ottawa, ON K1N 9J6
613/241-8005, Fax: 613/241-5055
President, Carol Clemenhagen
Vice-President, Finance, Tim Julien
Publications: Volunteering for Health/Bénévole de la Santé
Affiliates: Canadian Hospital Association

ALBERTA HEALTH CARE AUXILIARIES ASSOCIATION (AHAA) (1948)
#334, 1480 Southview, Medicine Hat, AB T1B 3I3
403/527-6442, Fax: 403/529-5859
President, Mary Kundert
Publications: Around Alberta

ASSOCIATION DES AUXILIAIRES BÉNÉVOLES DES ÉTABLISSEMENTS DE SANTÉ DU QUÉBEC/ASSOCIATION OF HOSPITAL AUXILIARIES OF THE PROVINCE OF QUÉBEC (ABESQ) (1952)
#400, 505, boul de Maisonneuve ouest, Montréal, PQ H3A 3C2
514/282-4264, Téléc: 514/282-4289
Présidente, Monique C. Boulanger
Secrétaire, Andrée Quinn
Trésorière, Suzanne Gagnon
Publications: Servo

BRITISH COLUMBIA ASSOCIATION OF HEALTH CARE AUXILIARIES (BCAHA)
#600, 1333 West Broadway, Vancouver, BC V6H 4C7
604/734-2423, Fax: 604/734-7202
President, Lorraine Grant, 604/964-6574
Administrative Secretary, Irene Popil
Director, Communications, Elena Tighe, 604/758-0415
Publications: Auxiliary Action
Affiliates: BC Health Association; Canadian Association of Health Care Auxiliaries; Canadian Hospital Association

HOSPITAL AUXILIARIES ASSOCIATION OF ONTARIO (HAAO) (1910)
52 Karen Cres., Hamilton, ON L9L 5M6
705/574-0020, Fax: 705/574-1025
President, Diane Jackson
Publications: The Volunteer

MANITOBA HEALTH AUXILIARIES ASSOCIATION
#8A, 2366 Portage Ave., Winnipeg, MB R3J 0N4
204/889-6150
President, Jessie Wright

NEW BRUNSWICK ASSOCIATION OF HEALTHCARE AUXILIARIES
770 Reid St., Fredericton, NB E3B 3V9
506/455-7359
Secretary/Archivist, R. John Booker
President, Helen MacTavish

NEWFOUNDLAND/LABRADOR ASSOCIATION OF HEALTH CARE AUXILIARIES
PO Box 29, Grand Bag East, Port Aux Basques, NF A0N 1K0
709/645-2480
President, Roslyn Tucker

NOVA SCOTIA ASSOCIATION OF HEALTH AUXILIARIES
PO Box 156, Hantsport, NS B0P 1P0
902/684-9448
President, Elizabeth Caldwell

SASKATCHEWAN HEALTH CARE AUXILIARIES ASSOCIATION (1941)
PO Box 85, Eyebrow, SK S0H 1L0
306/759-2132
Contact, Jean Gurney

Canadian Association of Medical Clinics
The Raxlen Clinic, 500 Parliament St., Toronto, ON M4X 1P4
416/966-3641, Fax: 416/944-8662
Executive Director, Derek Evelyn

Canadian Association of Paediatric Hospitals/ Association canadienne des hôpitaux pédiatriques (1968)
#430, 1730 St. Laurent Blvd., Ottawa, ON K1G 5L1
613/738-7706, Fax: 613/738-7941
Executive Director, Diane C. Barei

Canadian Association of Social Work Administrators in Health Facilities/Association canadienne des administrateurs de services sociaux en milieu de santé (CASWAHF) (1973)
Social Work Department, Kingston General Hospital, 76 Stuart St., Kingston, ON K7L 2V7
613/549-6666, ext.4443, Fax: 613/548-2354
President, Patrick F. Whalen-Browne
Publications: Connections

Canadian Council on Health Services Accreditation/Conseil canadien d'agrément des services de santé (CCHSA) (1958)
#430, 1730 St. Laurent Blvd., Ottawa, ON K1G 5L1
613/738-3800, Fax: 613/738-3755
Executive Director, Elma Heidemann

Canadian Healthcare Association/Association canadienne des soins de santé (1953)
#100, 17 York St., Ottawa, ON K1N 9J6
613/241-8005, Fax: 613/241-5055
President, Carol Clemenhagen
Vice-President, Tim Julien
Chairman, Gaston Levac
Publications: Leadership in Health Services
Affiliates: International Hospital Federation; American Hospital Association

ASSOCIATION DES HÔPITAUX DU QUÉBEC/QUÉBEC HOSPITAL ASSOCIATION (AHQ)
#400, 505, boul de Maisonneuve ouest, Montréal, PQ H3A 3C2
514/842-4861, Téléc: 514/282-4271
Vice-président exécutif, Jacques A. Nadeau
Président, Serge Bélisle
Publications: Artére

HEALTH ASSOCIATION OF PEI (HAPEI) (1961)
10 Pownal St., PO Box 490, Charlottetown, PE C1A 7L1
902/368-3901, Fax: 902/368-3231
Executive Director, Carol Gabanna
Group Tendering Coordinator, Donna Butler

MANITOBA HEALTH ORGANIZATIONS (MHO) (1921)
#600, 360 Broadway, Winnipeg, MB R3C 4G6
204/942-6591, Fax: 204/956-1373
President, Ronald G. Birt
Chairman, Edwin H. Klassen
Communications Officer, Wendy Fox
Publications: Healthbeat

NEW BRUNSWICK HEALTHCARE ASSOCIATION/ASSOCIATION DES SOINS DE SANTÉ DU NOUVEAU-BRUNSWICK (NBHA) (1962)
861 Woodstock Rd., RR#3, Fredericton, NB E3B 4X4
506/451-0750, Fax: 506/451-0760
Executive Director, Michel J. Poirier
Director, Corporate Affairs, Dr. Karon Croll
Publications: Telescope

NORTHWEST TERRITORIES HEALTH CARE ASSOCIATION (NWTHCA) (1965)
4920 - 47 St., 3rd Fl., PO Box 1709, Yellowknife, NT X1A 2P3
403/873-9253, Fax: 403/873-9254
Executive Director, Persa Kovich
Publications: NWTHCA Newsletter

NOVA SCOTIA ASSOCIATION OF HEALTH ORGANIZATIONS (NSAHO) (1960)
Bedford Professional Centre, 2 Dartmouth Rd., Halifax, NS B4A 2K7
902/832-8500, Fax: 902/832-8505
Acting CEO, Robert Cook
Publications: Newsletter; Your Association this Week, w.; Clipboard, bi-weekly

ONTARIO HOSPITAL ASSOCIATION (OHA) (1924)
#2800, 200 Front St. West, Toronto, ON M5V 3L1
416/205-1300, Fax: 416/205-1301
President & CEO, David C. MacKinnon
Chair, Robert K. Muir
Corporate Secretary, M. Murray
Publications: Executive Report; Hospital Perspectives, q.

PROVINCIAL HEALTH AUTHORITIES OF ALBERTA (1919)
44 Capital Blvd., #200, 10044 - 108 St. NW, Edmonton, AB T5J 3S7
403/426-8502, Fax: 403/424-4309
Executive Director, Mike Higgins

SASKATCHEWAN ASSOCIATION OF HEALTH ORGANIZATIONS (SAHO) (1993)
1445 Park St., Regina, SK S4N 4C5
306/347-5500, Fax: 306/525-1960
President, Arliss Wright
Publications: SAHO News; Materials Manager

Canadian Home Care Association/Association canadienne de soins et services à domicile (CHCA) (1990)
#1005, 350 Sparks St., Ottawa, ON K1R 7F8
613/569-1585, Fax: 613/569-1604
Executive Director, Lesley Larsen
President, Michael Sorochan
Publications: At Home/Chez Nous

Hospital Engineers Association of Alberta
2007 - 14th St. SW, Calgary, AB T2V 1P9
403/541-3291
President, Allan Potter

National Sanitarium Association
PO Box 100, Stn Commerce Court, Toronto, ON M5L 1B9
416/980-4457, Fax: 416/980-7012
Sec.-Treas., J.G. Barraclough

Ontario Association of Directors of Volunteer Services in Healthcare (OADHVS) (1970)
#1437, 1011 Upper Middle Rd., Oakville, ON L6H 5Z9
416/926-4823, Fax: 416/926-4992
President, Carol Dixon
Publications: Directions
Affiliates: Volunteer Ontario

Ontario Association of Medical Laboratories (OAML) (1974)
#206, 4120 Yonge St., North York, ON M2P 2B8
416/250-8555, Fax: 416/250-8464
President, Paul J. Gould

Ontario Nursing Home Association (ONHA) (1959)
#202, 345 Renfrew Dr., Markham, ON L3R 9S9
905/470-8995, Fax: 905/470-9595
Executive Director, Shelly Jamieson
President, Dianne Anderson
Publications: Long Term Care

HOUSING
see also Real Estate

Association of Condominium Managers of Ontario (ACMO) (1977)
#1105, 191 The West Mall, Etobicoke, ON M9C 5K8
416/626-7895, Fax: 416/620-5392, Toll Free: 1-800-265-3263
Executive Director, Don Braden
Publications: The Condominium Manager

Canadian Association of Home Inspectors (CAHI) (1992)
PO Box 22010, RPO Capri Centre, Kelowna, BC V1Y 9N9
Fax: /1-800-610-5665, Toll Free: 1-800-610-5665
URL: http://www.bconnex.net/~jmlueck/cahi.html
Co-Chairman, Jeff Clarke
Affiliates: American Society of Home Inspectors; Canadian Council of Building Officials Associations; Interprovincial Building Codes Education Association

Canadian Condominium Institute - National Chapter (CCI) (1982)
#310, 2175 Sheppard Ave. East, North York, ON M2J 1W8
416/491-6216, Fax: 416/491-1670
President, Janice Payne
Chairman, Mark Freedman
National Executive Director, Diane Gaunt
Publications: CCI Review

Canadian Home Builders' Association/Association canadienne des constructeurs d'habitations (CHBA) (1943)
#200, 150 Laurier Ave. West, Ottawa, ON K1P 6M7
613/230-3060, Fax: 613/232-8214, Email: chba@chba.ca
URL: http://www.chba.ca
Chief Operating Officer, John K. Kenward
President, Gerhard Ruehr

ASSOCIATION PROVINCIALE DES CONSTRUCTEURS D'HABITATIONS QUÉBEC/PROVINCIAL HOME BUILDERS ASSOCIATION OF QUÉBEC (APCHQ)
2825, boul Wilfrid-Hamel, Québec, PQ G1P 2H9
418/682-3353, Téléc: 418/682-3851
Directeur général, Jean-Pierre Sirard

Canadian Housing & Renewal Association/Association canadienne d'habitation et de rénovation urbaine (CHRA) (1968)
#401, 251 Laurier Ave. West, Ottawa, ON K1P 5J6
613/594-3007, Fax: 613/594-9596
Executive Director, Sharon Chisholm
Office Manager, Elisa Ruiz
Publications: Canadian Housing/Habitation canadienne

Canadian Manufactured Housing Institute
#200, 150 Laurier Ave. West, Ottawa, ON K1P 5J4
613/563-3520, Fax: 613/232-8600
General Manager, Hank Starno

Canadian Shareowners Association (1987)
#202, 1090 University Ave. West, PO Box 7337, Windsor, ON N9C 4E9
519/252-1555, Fax: 519/252-9570
President, John Bart
Publications: Canadian Shareowner

Co-operative Housing Federation of BC (CHF-BC) (1982)
133 East 8th Ave., Vancouver, BC V5T 1R8
604/879-5111, Fax: 604/879-4611, Info Line: 604/879-5112
Executive Director, Mary Flynn
Publications: SCOOP

Cooperative Housing Association of Newfoundland & Labrador
PO Box 453, Mount Pearl, NF A1N 2C4
709/747-5615, Fax: 709/747-5606
Financial Services Officer, Dave Adams

Cooperative Housing Federation of Canada/Fédération de l'habitation coopérative du Canada (CHF) (1968)
#311, 225 Metcalfe St., Ottawa, ON K2P 1P9
613/230-2201, Fax: 613/230-2231, Toll Free: 1-800-465-2752
Executive Director, Alexandra Wilson
Coordinator/Communications, Suzan Schmekel
Publications: Coopservations
Ontario Region: Managing Director, Dale Reagan, #207, 2 Berkeley St., Toronto, ON M5A 2W3, 416/366-1711, Fax: 416/366-3876

Cooperative Housing Federation of Nova Scotia (CHFNS) (1981)
#609, 5251 Duke St., Halifax, NS B3J 1P3
902/492-3881, Fax: 902/429-1329
Coordinator, Sheila Mackenzie
Publications: Co-op Housing News
Affiliates: Affordable Housing Association of Nova Scotia

Federation of Metro Toronto Tenants' Associations (FMTA) (1974)
#403, 344 Bloor St. West, Toronto, ON M5S 3A7
416/921-9494, Fax: 416/921-4177
Administrator, Charlene Baker
Chairperson, Kenn Hale
Vice-Chairperson, Henk Mulder
Policy Coordinator, Deborah Wandal
Publications: Tenants Bulletin
Affiliates: United Tenants of Ontario; Tenant Non-Profit Redevelopment Company; Metro Tenants Legal Service

Canadian Almanac & Directory 1997

Federation of Ottawa-Carleton Tenants' Associations/Fédération des associations de locataires d'Ottawa-Carleton
780 Somerset St. West, 2nd Fl., Ottawa, ON K1R 6R2
613/594-5429, Fax: 613/594-5804
Executive Director, D. McIntyre

Institute of Municipal Assessors of Ontario
#303, 109 Railside Rd., North York, ON M3A 1B2
416/447-7213, Fax: 416/447-3452
Executive Director, W.J. Lettner
Publications: Assessors Review

Manitoba Landlords Association
738 Elgin Ave., Winnipeg, MB R3E 1B2
204/775-1726
Contact, L. Holubowich

Manufactured Housing Association - Alberta & Saskatchewan (1976)
#201, 4921 - 49 St., Red Deer, AB T4N 1V2
403/347-8925, Fax: 403/347-2505, Toll Free: 1-800-661-7444
Executive Director, Vi Tkachuk
Publications: Newsletter

Multiple Dwelling Standards Association (MDSA) (1970)
163 Beechwood Ave., North York, ON M2L 1J9
416/449-7700
President/General Manager, Jan Schwartz

Nova Scotia Institute of Assessors (1967)
PO Box 706, Sydney, NS B1P 6H7
902/563-2150
Secretary, Mora Smith

Ontario Association of Property Standards Officers Inc.
148 Braemar Rd., Kingston, ON K7M 4B8
613/544-7222
Secretary, P. Clark
Publications: The Property Standard

Ontario Non-Profit Housing Association (ONPHA) (1988)
#400, 489 College St., Toronto, ON M6G 1A5
416/927-9144, Fax: 416/927-8401
Executive Director, Robin Campbell
Publications: Connections

Rental Housing Council of British Columbia
#1011, 470 Granville St., Vancouver, BC V6C 1V5
604/681-0045, Fax: 604/681-4261
Executive Director, Edward N. Whitlock

HUMAN RESOURCES see EMPLOYMENT & HUMAN RESOURCES

HUMAN RIGHTS & CIVIL LIBERTIES

Amnesty International, Canadian Section (English Speaking)
214 Montréal Rd., 4th Fl., Vanier, ON K1L 1A4
613/744-7667, Fax: 613/746-2411, Email: aiamnest@web.apc.org
President, Donna Thiessen
Secretary General, Roger Clark
Communications, John Tackaberry
Documentalist, Lillibeth Ackbarali
Publications: The Activist
Affiliates: Formal relations with the United Nations Economic & Social Council (ECOSOC), UNESCO, the Council of Europe; the Organization of American States, the Organization of African Unity & the Inter-Parliamentary Union

Pacific Regional Office: #4, 3664 Hastings St. West, Vancouver, BC V5K 2A9, 604/294-5160, Fax: 604/294-5130
Toronto Regional Office: 400 Bloor St. West, 2nd Fl., Toronto, ON M5S 1X5, 416/929-9477, Fax: 416/929-0539

Amnistie internationale, Section canadienne (Francophone) (1971)
6250, boul Monk, Montréal, PQ H4E 3H7
514/766-9766, Téléc: 514/766-2088, Courrier électronique: aimtl@cam.org
URL: http://www.amnistie.qc.ca
Directeur général, Michel Frenette
Responsable, Communications, Anne Sainte-Marie
Publications: Agir

Canada Council on Human Rights & Race Relations (1988)
Human Rights & Race Relations Centre
#1506, 141 Adelaide St. West, Toronto, ON M5H 3L5
416/440-1971, Fax: 416/481-7793, Toll Free: 1-888-667-5877
President, Hasanat Ahmad Syed
Secretary, Ismat Pasha
Publications: New Canada

The Canadian Centre/International P.E.N. (PEN) (1926)
PEN Canada
24 Ryerson Ave., Toronto, ON M5T 2P3
416/703-8448, Fax: 416/703-3870, Email: pencan@web.apc.org
President, Nino Ricci
Policy Director, Isabel Harry
Administrative Director, Margaret Purcell
Publications: Canadian PEN Newsletter

Canadian Civil Liberties Association/Association canadienne des libertés civiles (CCLA) (1964)
#403, 229 Yonge St., Toronto, ON M5B 1N9
416/363-0321, Fax: 416/861-1291
President, Sybil Shack
General Counsel, A. Alan Borovoy
Publications: CCLA Newsnotes

ALBERTA CIVIL LIBERTIES ASSOCIATION
#310, 1167 Kensington Ave. NW, Calgary, AB T2N 1X7
403/283-3643, Fax: 403/283-1489
President, Rick Bennett

MANITOBA ASSOCIATION FOR RIGHTS & LIBERTIES (1970)
#502, 177 Lombard Ave., Winnipeg, MB R3B 0W5
204/947-0213, Fax: 204/946-0403
Executive Director, Valerie Price
Publications: MARL Newsletter
Affiliates: Manitoba Coalition of Organizations Against Apartheid

SAINT JOHN CHARTER RIGHTS & CIVIL LIBERTIES ASSOCIATION (1971)
PO Box 6446, Stn A, Saint John, NB E2L 4R8
506/632-0096, Fax: 506/634-7423
President, Fred D. Hodges, CM, LLD
Secretary, Eric L. Teed, OC, Q.C.

The Canadian Free Speech League
810 Courtney St., Victoria, BC V8W 1C4
250/385-1022, Fax: 250/479-3294
General Counsel, Douglas Christie
Publications: Friends of Freedom

Canadian Human Rights Foundation/Fondation canadienne des droits humains
#304, 1425, rue René-Levesque, Montréal, PQ H3G 1T7
514/954-0382, Fax: 514/954-0659

Executive Director, Ruth Selwyn
President, Pearl Eliadis
Publications: Newsletter/Bulletin

Canadian Tribute to Human Rights/Monument canadien pour les droits de la personne (1984)
PO Box 510, Stn B, Ottawa, ON K1P 5P6
President, Stephen Naor
Sec.-Treas., George Wilkes

Citizens for Public Justice (CPJ) (1963)
#311, 229 College St., Toronto, ON M5T 1R4
416/979-2443, Email: cpj@web.apc.org
Executive Director, Harry J. Kits
Chairman, Brian Walsh
Publications: The Catalyst

Human Rights Institute of Canada/Institut canadien des droits humains (HRIC) (1974)
#303, 246 Queen St., Ottawa, ON K1P 5E4
613/232-2920, Fax: 613/232-3735
President, Dr. Marguerite E. Ritchie
Publications: Research Studies & Submissions to Parliamentary Committees

International Centre for Human Rights & Democratic Development/Centre international des droits de la personne et du développement démocratique (ICHRDD) (1988)
#100, 63, rue de Bresoles, Montréal, PQ H2Y 1V7
514/283-6073, Fax: 514/283-3792
President, Ed Broadbent
Chair, Gisèle Côté-Harper
Publications: Libertas

League for Human Rights of B'nai Brith Canada/Ligue des droits de la personne de B'nai Brith Canada (1965)
15 Hove St., Downsview, ON M3H 4Y8
416/633-6227, Fax: 416/630-2159
National Director, Dr. Karen Mock
Publications: Review of Anti-Semitism in Canada; Research Reports on Hate Groups in Canada

Macedonian Human Rights Movement of Canada/Mouvement canadien de défense des droits de la personne dans la communauté macédonienne (MHRMC) (1986)
2376 Eglinton Ave. East, PO Box 44532, Toronto, ON M1K 5K3
416/236-6952, Fax: 416/412-3385
President, Dragi Stojkovski
Secretary, Cary Zalba
Treasurer, Dr. Andy Plukov
Vice-President, John Markov
Publications: Annual Report

Network on International Human Rights/Réseau des droits de la personne au plan international (NIHR) (1986)
c/o CCIC, #300, One Nicholas St., Ottawa, ON K1N 7B7
613/241-7007, ext.361, Fax: 613/241-5302
Coordinator, Myriam de Feyter

Patients' Rights Association
170 Merton St., Toronto, ON M4S 1A1
416/487-6287, Fax: 416/489-7533
Executive Director, Mary Margaret Steckle
Publications: The Patients' Advocate

South Okanagan Civil Liberties Society
#103, 304 Martin St., Penticton, BC V2A 5K4
250/493-0210
Chairperson, Cheryl Saxon

Vancouver Island Human Rights Coalition (1982)
#418, 620 View St., Victoria, BC V8W 1J6

250/382-3012
President, Ron MacIsaac
Director, Tom Loring
Publications: Newsletter

Victoria Civil Liberties Association (VCLA) (1983)
PO Box 5207, Stn B, Victoria, BC V8R 6N4
250/592-1544, Email: togo@uvvm.uvic.ca
President, Allan Grove, Res: 604/477-0279
Publications: VCLA News

HUMANE SOCIETIES see **ANIMALS & ANIMAL SCIENCE**

ILLUSTRATION see **VISUAL ART, CRAFTS, FOLK ARTS**

IMMIGRATION see **CITIZENSHIP & IMMIGRATION**

IMPLEMENT MANUFACTURING see **EQUIPMENT & MACHINERY**

IMPORT TRADE see **TRADE**

INDUSTRIAL RELATIONS see **LABOUR RELATIONS**

INDUSTRY see **MANUFACTURING & INDUSTRY**

INFORMATION CENTRES see **SOCIAL RESPONSE/SOCIAL SERVICES**

INFORMATION TECHNOLOGY

ASM International (1947)
Association for Systems Management
1433 West Bagley Rd., Berea, OH 44017 USA
216/243-6900, Fax: 216/234-2930
Managing Director, Susan Goodrich
President, Montréal Chapter, Lise Trudel, 514/481-4632
Contact, Ottawa Valley Chapter, Robert Elliott, 613/748-2816
Contact, London Chapter, Patricia White, 519/971-2908
Contact, Calgary Chapter, Eric Pattrie, 403/266-2266
Contact, Edmonton Chapter, Eddie Nealon, 403/420-8938
Contact, Vancouver Chapter, Sandra Cunningham, 604/986-6468
Publications: Journal of Systems Management

Association for Computer Operations Management (AFCOM) (1980)
742 East Chapman Ave., Orange, CA 92666 USA
714/997-7966, Fax: 714/997-9743
President, Leonard Eckhaus
Publications: The Computer Operations Manager; Communiqué

Association of Professional Computer Consultants - Canada (1992)
#310, 2175 Sheppard Ave. East, North York, ON M2J 1W8
416/491-2886, Fax: 416/491-1670
President, Frank McCrea
Administrator, Diane Gaunt
Publications: News & Information

BC Advanced Systems Institute (ASI)
#450, 1122 Mainland St., Vancouver, BC V6B 5L1
604/689-0551, Fax: 604/689-4198, Toll Free: 1-800-501-3388, Email: asi@asi.bc.ca
URL: http://www.asi.bc.ca/asi/
Executive Director, Brent Sauder, Email: bsauder@asi.bc.ca

Operations Manager, Carol M. Hassell, Email: hassell@asi.bc.ca
Industry Programs Manager, Vince Lum, Email: vincelum@asi.bc.ca

Canada's Coalition for Public Information (CPI) (1993)
200 Adelaide St. West, 3rd Fl., Toronto, ON M5H 1W7
416/977-6018, Fax: 416/597-1617, Email: cpi@web.net
CEO, Stan Skrzeszewski
Chair, Liz Hoffman

Canadian Alliance Against Software Theft/Alliance canadienne contre le vol de logiciels (CAAST) (1990)
c/o Strategic Ampersand Inc., #1440, 250 Bloor St. East, Toronto, ON M4W 1E6
416/961-5595, Fax: 416/961-7955
Chief Counsel, Michael Eisen

Canadian Association of SAS Users/Association canadienne des utilisateurs SAS (CASU) (1991)
BCE Place, #2220, 181 Bay St., PO Box 819, Toronto, ON M5J 2T3
416/363-4424, Fax: 416/363-5399
Contact, Jeff Read

Canadian Children's Multimedia Foundation (CCMF) (1994)
#404, 1080 Broughton St., Vancouver, BC V6G 2A8
604/662-3805
President, Sharon Lipovsky

Canadian Community of Computer Educators (CCCE)
15 Lone Oak Ave., Brampton, ON L6S 5V4
905/796-9311
President, Alania Baldwin
Consortium Training Director, Gord McDougall
Membership/Public Relations Director, Joyce Holland
Program Director, Annetta Wange

Canadian Computer Dealer Association (CCDA) (1981)
PO Box 21547, RPO Upper Canada Mall, Newmarket, ON L3Y 8J1
General Manager, Bruce Hampson, 416/229-4206
Publications: Connections

Canadian Human-Computer Communications Society
#106, 430 King St. West, Toronto, ON M5V 1L5
416/593-4040, Fax: 416/593-5184
Chair, Dr. Wayne Davis

Canadian Image Processing & Pattern Recognition Society/Association canadienne de traitement d'images et reconnaissance des formes (CIPPRS) (1984)
Campus de l'Universite de Montreal, 2900, boul Édouard-Montpetit, Montréal, PQ H3C 3A7
President, Prof. Réjean Plamondon, 514-340-4539, Fax: 514/340-4147, Email: ha03@music.mus.polymtl.ca
Affiliates: Canadian Information Processing Society

Canadian Information & Image Management Society/Société canadienne de la gestion de l'information et des images (CIIMS) (1967)
86 Wilson St., Oakville, ON L6K 3G5
905/842-6067, Fax: 905/842-2646
Executive Director, Donald Donahue
Secretary, Joan Donahue
Publications: Imaging Canada

Canadian Information Processing Security SIG/Sécurité informatique canadienne
Security SIG
#106, 430 King St. West., Toronto, ON M5V 1L5
416/593-4040, Fax: 416/593-5184
Chair, Peter Kingston

Canadian Information Processing Society/Association Canadienne de L'Informatique (CIPS) (1958)
#106, 430 King St. West, Toronto, ON M5V 1L5
416/593-4040, Fax: 416/593-5184, Email: info@cips.ca
URL: http://cips.ca
President, Kevin Brown
Vice-President, Dorothy Josephson
Publications: Canadian Computer Census
Affiliates: British Computer Society; Australian Computer Society; Association for Computing Machinery

Canadian Organization for Advancement of Computers in Health (COACH) (1975)
#216, 10458 Mayfield Rd., Edmonton, AB T5P 4P4
403/489-4553, Fax: 403/489-3290, Email: coachorg@agt.net
URL: http://www.agt.net/public/coachorg
Executive Director, Steven A. Huesing
Publications: Healthcare Computing & Communications Canada

Canadian Society for Computational Studies of Intelligence/Société canadienne pour l'étude d'intelligence par ordinateur (CSCSI) (1973)
c/o Dept. of Computer Science, University of Ottawa, Ottawa, ON K1N 6B5
613/564-5069, Fax: 613/564-9486
URL: http://ai.iit.nrc.ca/cscsi_point.html
President, Clare Cremer, I.S.P.
Secretary, Dr. F. Popowich, Email: popowich@cs.sfu.ca
Publications: Canadian AI Magazine

CANARIE Inc. (1993)
Canadian Network for the Advancement of Research, Industry & Education
#470, 410 Laurier Ave. West, Ottawa, ON K1P 6H5
613/660-3634, Fax: 613/660-3806, Email: info@canarie.ca
URL: http://www.canarie.ca/
President & CEO, Andrew K. Bjerring, Email: Andrew.K.Bjerring@canarie.ca
Office Manager, Susy Carrière, Email: Susy.Carriere@canarie.ca
Communications Officer, Phil Sampson, Email: Phil.Sampson@canarie.ca

Chinese Canadian Information Processing Professionals (1981)
CIPro
PO Box 361, North York, ON M3C 2S7
416/286-6584, Fax: 416/250-6873, Email: cipro@idirect.com
President, Auck Siu
Publications: CIPro News

Electronic Commerce Council of Canada/Conseil canadien de l'échange électronique de données (EDI) (1985)
Electronic Data Interchange Council of Canada
#203, 5401 Eglinton Ave. West, Etobicoke, ON M9C 5K6
416/621-7160, Fax: 416/620-9175, Email: edicc@idirect.com
URL: http://www.edicc.ca/edicc
President, Marshall A. Spence
Publications: EDIFact Trade Data Elements Directory; Interchange, bi-m.; Membership Directory

Atlantic Region Office: Executive Director, Dan De-Matteis, PO Box 962, Wolfville, NS B0P 1X0, 902/542-1113, Fax: 902/542-1714, Email: ddematte@fox.nstn.ns.ca

EDI Institute of Québec: President, André Vallerand; Director, Communications, Philip van Leeuwen; Senior Project Officer, Douglas Beeson, World Trade Centre, #3280, 380, rue Saint-Antoine ouest, Montréal, PQ H2Y 3X7, 514/288-6346, Fax: 514/288-4199, Email: institute@ecworld.org

Western Regional Office: Executive Director, Jeff Connie, #450, 1122 Mainland St., Vancouver, BC V6B 5L1, 604/689-8220, Fax: 604/689-0141, Email: jconnie@cyberstore.ca

Electronic Frontier Canada Inc.
20 Richmond Ave., Kitchener, ON N2G 1Y7
Email: efc@efc.ca
URL: http://insight.mcmaster.ca/org/efc/efc.html

Groupe interuniversitaire de recherche en informatique cognitive des organisations/Cognitive & Computer Science Interuniversity Research Group (GIRICO) (1986)
#912, 276, rue St-Jacques, Montréal, PQ H2Y 1N3
514/985-5459, Téléc: 514/985-2720
Président/Directeur général, Ghislain Lévesque
Publications: ICO Québec

Information Resource Management Association of Canada (IRMAC)
Database Association of Ontario
PO Box 5639, Stn A, Toronto, ON M5W 1N8
Email: irmac@io.org
URL: http://www.io.org/~irmac/
President, Jim Sullivan, 905/837-3227, Email: jsullivan@clearnet.com
Secretary, Craig Lloyd, 416/228-5817
Treasurer, Ray Hensel, 416/365-3858
Publications: Primary Key

Information Technology Association of Canada/Association canadienne de la technologie de l'information (ITAC) (1987)
#402, 2800 Skymark Ave., Mississauga, ON L4W 5A6
905/602-8345, Fax: 905/602-8346, Email: info@itac.ca
URL: http://www.itac.ca/ITAC.home
President/CEO, Gaylen Duncan
Vice-President, Membership, Winston Kinch
Vice-President, Policy, Robert Crow
Vice-President, Government Relations, Peter Broadmore
Publications: Fax Flash
Affiliates: Software Industry Association of Nova Scotia (SIANS); Technologies Industry Association of British Columbia (TIA BC); ITAC Ontario; Québec Software Promotion Centre; New Brunswick Information Technology Alliance; Software Technology Centre Saskatchewan; Newfoundland & Labrador Alliance of Technical Industries (NATI)

Information Technology Research Centre (ITRC)
D.L. Pratt Building, #286, 6 King's College Rd., Toronto, ON M5S 1A1
416/978-7203, Fax: 416/978-7207
URL: http://www.itrc.on.ca/
Vice-President, Vic DiCiccio, 519/747-1510
Director, Industry Support, Anne Tyrie, 613/599-3028
Publications: Bulletin

Instrument Society of America (ISA) (1945)
67 Alexander Dr., PO Box 12277, Research Triangle Park, NC 27709 USA
919/549-8411, Fax: 919/549-8288, Telex: 802-540 ISA DURM
Executive Director, Glenn F. Harvey

Contact, Montréal Section, James Bouchard, 514/251-5148
Contact, Vancouver Section, Roger Nordom, 604/663-3141
Contact, Winnipeg Section, Leonard Berube
Publications: Intech; Industrial Computing, m.
Affiliates: American Association for the Advancement of Science; American Institute of Physics; International Measurement Confederation; National Institute for Certification in Engineering Technologies; National Inventors Hall of Fame; American National Standards Institute; American Society of Mechanical Engineers; Fluid Controls Institute; Institute of Electrical & Electronic Engineers;
Calgary Section: #200, 1100 - 8th Ave. SW, Calgary, AB T2P 3T9, 403/299-0866, Fax: 403/299-0949, Email: milnei@cadvision.com
Edmonton Section: Contact, Paul Pritchard, 8525 Davies Rd., Edmonton, AB T6E 4N3, 403/468-5463, Fax: 403/465-1220
Toronto Section: Contact, J. Kavanaugh, #210, 605 Royal York Rd., Toronto, ON M8Y 4G5, 416/454-0777

Interactive Multimedia Arts & Technologies Association/Association des arts et des technologies de l'interactivité et du multimedia (IMAT) (1995)
#6, 37 Kodiak Cres., Downsview, ON M3J 3E5
416/636-9684, Fax: 416/636-4454, Email: imat@goodmedia.com
URL: http://www.goodmedia.com/imat/
President, Adam Froman, Email: adam_froman@goodmedia.com
Operations, Jeffery Murphy
Publications: Wave

National Capital FreeNet/Libertel de la Capitale Nationale (NCF) (1993)
c/o Carleton University, 1125 Colonel By Dr., Ottawa, ON K1S 5B6
613/520-9001, Fax: 613/520-3524, Email: office@freenet.carleton.ca; telnet: telnet.ncf.carleton.ca
URL: http://www.ncf.carleton.ca/
Executive Director, Lisa K. Donnelly, Email: lkd@freenet.carleton.ca
Chairman, David Sutherland
Publications: The Official FreeNet Survival Guide

Newfoundland & Labrador Alliance of Technical Industries (NATI)
Atlantic Place, #602, 215 Water St., PO Box 41, St. John's, NF A1C 6C9
709/722-3069, Fax: 709/722-3879, Email: acollins@public.compusult.nf.ca
Executive Director, Andrew Collins
Affiliates: Canadian Advanced Technology Association; Information Technology Association of Canada

Ontario Software Development Association
150 York St., 7th Fl., PO Box 710, Toronto, ON M5H 3A9
Chairman, Joseph Koenig

reBOOT Canada
#6, 37 Hanna Ave., Toronto, ON M6K 1W9
416/534-6017, Fax: 416/534-6083, Email: info@reboot.on.ca
URL: http://www.reboot.on.ca
Director of Operations, Ron Piovesan

Software Human Resource Council (Canada) Inc./Conseil des ressources humaines du logiciel (Canada) Inc. (SHRC)
#608, 155 Queen St., Ottawa, ON K1P 6L1
613/237-8551, Fax: 613/230-3490
President & CEO, Paul Swinwood

Software Industry Association of Nova Scotia (SIANS)
#101, 1046 Barrington St., Halifax, NS B3J 2N7
902/423-5332, Fax: 902/423-9400
John MacCulloch
Affiliates: Information Technology Association of Canada

Technologies Industry Association of British Columbia
#108, 4800 Kingsway, Burnaby, BC V6E 3W1
604/878-0393, Fax: 604/438-6564
Nancy Moser

INSURANCE INDUSTRY

Association of Canadian Insurers/Association des Assureurs Canadiens (ACI) (1990)
181 University Ave., 13th Fl., Toronto, ON M5H 3M7
416/362-9729, Fax: 416/361-5952
Sue White

Association des courtiers d'annuités
1155, rue Metcalfe, 5e étage, Montréal, PQ H3B 4S9
514/284-0606, Téléc: 514/879-2353
Président, André Matte

Association des intermédiaires en assurance de personnes du Québec/Life Intermediaries Association of Québec (AIAPQ) (1989)
#500, 1, Westmount Sq., Montréal, PQ H3Z 2P9
514/932-4277, Téléc: 514/932-6400
Executive Director, Lucie Granger
Publications: Prospective

Association of Marine Underwriters of British Columbia (AMUBC)
c/o Johnson & Higgins Ltd., #1700, 200 Granville St., Vancouver, BC V6C 2S2
604/681-6141, Fax: 604/681-9846
Secretary, Marilyn M. Randle

Canadian Association of Blue Cross Plans
c/o Alberta Blue Cross, 10009 - 108 St., Edmonton, AB T5J 3C5
403/498-8297, Fax: 403/498-8532
President, V. George Ward

Canadian Association of Mutual Insurance Companies (CAMIC) (1980)
#907, 325 Dalhousie St., PO Box 117, Stn B, Ottawa, ON K1P 6C3
613/789-6851, Fax: 613/789-6854
Executive Director, Mel McIntyre, FIIC
President, Normand Lafrenière
Publications: CAMIC Newsletter

Canadian Board of Marine Underwriters (CBMU) (1917)
#1105, 191 The West Mall, Etobicoke, ON M9C 5K8
416/626-7380, Fax: 416/620-5392, Email: cbmu@webcom.com
URL: http://www.webcom.com/cbmu
Sec.-Treas., Amanda Curtis
Publications: The Log

Canadian Boiler & Machinery Underwriters' Association/Association canadienne des assureurs en bris des machines (1925)
#1804, 33 Elmhurst Ave., North York, ON M2N 6G8
416/221-9755
Sec.-Treas., Margaret Wansbrough

Canadian Council of Insurance Regulators
Ontario Insurance, 5160 Yonge St., PO Box 85, Toronto, ON M2N 6L9

416/590-7272
Superintendent, Laurie Savage

Canadian Foresters Life Insurance Society (1879)
Canadian Foresters
PO Box 850, Brantford, ON N3T 5S3
905/525-9559
CEO, Donald G. Payne
President, William J. Taggart
Publications: Fraternal Newsletter; The Canadian Forester, a.

Canadian Independent Adjusters' Association/Association canadienne des experts indépendants (CIAA) (1953)
#1305, 55 Queen St. East, Toronto, ON M5C 1R6
416/362-7466, Fax: 416/362-8251
Executive Director, Ann M. Wolochatiuk
Publications: The Canadian Independent Adjuster
Affiliates: National Association of Independent Insurance Adjusters (USA); Chartered Institute of Loss Adjustors (UK)

Canadian Industrial Risks Insurers (CIRI) (1973)
#1906, 180 Dundas St. West, Toronto, ON M5G 1Z8
416/595-0155, Fax: 416/595-0948
Manager, Henry D. Ulozas
Publications: Inside IRI; Sentinel
Affiliates: International Risks Insurers

Canadian Institute of Actuaries/Institut canadien des actuaires
#820, 360 Albert St., Ottawa, ON K1R 7X7
613/236-8196, Fax: 613/233-4552
URL: http://www.actuaries.ca/CIA/CIA.html
Executive Director, Rick Neugebauer
President, Neville S. Henderson, FCIA, FSA
Affiliates: International Actuarial Association; American Academy of Actuaries; Society of Actuaries; Casualty Actuarial Society; Conference of Consulting Actuaries

Canadian Life & Health Insurance Association Inc./Association canadienne des compagnies d'assurances de personnes inc. (CLHIA) (1894)
#1700, One Queen St. East, Toronto, ON M5C 2X9
416/777-2221, Fax: 416/777-1895, Info Line: 416/777-2344, Toll Free: 1-800-268-8099
URL: http://www.inforamp.net/~clhia/
Chairman, David A. Nield
President, Mark R. Daniels
Vice-President, Administrative & Member Services, Judy E. Barrie
Executive Vice-President, Policy Development, Gregory R. Traversy
Vice-President & Corporate Secretary, Charles C. Black
Vice-President, Communications, Isabel Wegg
Vice-President & General Counsel, J-P Bernier
Senior Vice-President, Quebec Affairs, Yves Millette
Vice-President, Taxation & Research, James S. Witol
Montréal Office: #630, 1001, boul de Maisonneuve ouest, Montréal, PQ H3A 3C8, 514/845-6173
Ottawa Office: Andrew Casey, #710, 60 Queen St., Ottawa, ON K1P 5Y7, 613/230-0031

Canadian Life Insurance Medical Officers Association/Association canadienne des directeurs médicaux en assurance-vie (CLIMOA)
142 Cassandra Blvd., North York, ON M3A 1S9
416/449-6791
Secretary, Dr. A.E. Wallace
Publications: Annual Proceedings
Affiliates: Canadian Medical Association

Centre for Study of Insurance Operations (CSIO)
#402, 480 University Ave., Toronto, ON M5G 1V2
416/591-1773, Fax: 416/591-1482

President, Len W. Ashby, CMC
Director of Communications, Terrie Dionne
Publications: Connections

Conseil des assurances de dommages (CAD) (1991)
#1919, 2020, rue University, Montréal, PQ H3A 2A5
514/282-8765, Téléc: 514/282-7466, Ligne sans frais: 1-800-667-7089, Courrier électronique: conseil@montrealnet.ca
URL: http://wure.montrealnet.ca/conseilad
Directrice générale, Diane Paradis
Publications: Intermède; Intermède Plus

Groupement des assureurs automobiles (GAA) (1978)
#900, 425, boul de Maisonneuve ouest, Montréal, PQ H3A 3G5
514/288-1537, Téléc: 514/288-0753
Directeur général, Raymond Medza
Publications: Contact Info

Insurance Brokers Association of Canada/Association des courtiers d'assurances du Canada (IBAC) (1921)
#1902, 181 University Ave., Toronto, ON M5H 3M7
416/367-1831, Fax: 416/367-3687
Executive Director, Joanne Brown

ASSOCIATION DES COURTIERS D'ASSURANCES DE LA PROVINCE DE QUÉBEC/INSURANCE BROKERS ASSOCIATION OF QUÉBEC (ACAPQ)
#801, 300, rue Léo-Pariseau, CP 985, Succ. Place du Parc, Montréal, PQ H2W 2N1
514/842-2591, Téléc: 514/842-3138
Directeur général, Serge Lavoie

INSURANCE BROKERS ASSOCIATION OF ALBERTA (1925)
#701, 10109 - 106 St., Edmonton, AB T5J 3L7
403/424-3320, Fax: 403/424-7418, Toll Free: 1-800-318-0197
Executive Director, Harold Baker
Publications: Alberta Broker

INSURANCE BROKERS ASSOCIATION OF BRITISH COLUMBIA (1920)
#1601, 409 Granville St., Vancouver, BC V6C 1T2
604/683-8471, Fax: 604/683-7831
General Manager, J.F. Hamilton
Publications: BC Broker

INSURANCE BROKERS ASSOCIATION OF MANITOBA (IBAM) (1951)
#205, 530 Kenaston Blvd., Winnipeg, MB R3N 1Z4
204/488-1857, Fax: 204/489-0316, Toll Free: 1-800-204-5649
Executive Director, William T. O'Brien
Publications: The Manitoba Broker

INSURANCE BROKERS ASSOCIATION OF NEW BRUNSWICK/ASSOCIATION DES COURTIERS D'ASSURANCES DU NOUVEAU-BRUNSWICK
PO Box 1523, Stn A, Fredericton, NB E3B 5G2
506/450-2898, Fax: 506/450-1494
Executive Director, Linda M. Dawe

INSURANCE BROKERS ASSOCIATION OF NEWFOUNDLAND
Cabot Place, #900, 100 New Gower Pl., St. John's, NF A1C 6K3
709/737-1625, Fax: 709/737-1550
Secretary, Keith Goodyear

INSURANCE BROKERS ASSOCIATION OF NOVA SCOTIA
14 Dufferin St., Bridgewater, NS B4V 2E8
902/543-5569, Fax: 902/543-8508
Executive Director, Heather A. Winters, AIIC, CAIB, CCIB, CRM

INSURANCE BROKERS ASSOCIATION OF ONTARIO
90 Eglinton Ave. East, 2nd Fl., Toronto, ON M4P 2Y3

416/488-7422, Fax: 416/488-7526
Executive Director, Robert J. Carter

INSURANCE BROKERS ASSOCIATION OF PRINCE EDWARD ISLAND
c/o J. Leroy Gallant Insurance Ltd., 125 Ryan St., PO Box 1360, Summerside, PE C1N 4K2
902/436-9237, Fax: 902/436-1513
President, Blake Craig

INSURANCE BROKERS ASSOCIATION OF SASKATCHEWAN (IBAS)
#310, 2631 - 28th Ave., Regina, SK S4S 6X3
306/525-5900, Fax: 306/569-3018
General Manager, Ernie Gaschler
Publications: IBAS Newsletter; Saskatchewan Insurance Directory, a.

REGROUPEMENT DES CABINETS DE COURTAGE D'ASSURANCE DU QUÉBEC/INSURANCE BROKERS' ASSOCIATION OF QUÉBEC - ASSEMBLY
#139, 955, rue D'Assigny, Longueuil, PQ J4K 5C3
514/674-6258, Téléc: 514/674-3609
Directrice générale, Claudette Carrier

TORONTO INSURANCE CONFERENCE (TIC) (1918)
c/o Base Service Canada Inc., #301, 250 Consumers Rd., North York, ON M2J 4V6
416/498-7722, Fax: 416/495-8723, Email: base@on-ramp.ca
Executive Secretary, Ruth Abrahamson

Insurance Bureau of Canada/Bureau d'assurance du Canada (IBC) (1964)
181 University Ave., 13th Fl., Toronto, ON M5H 3M7
416/362-2031, Fax: 416/361-5952, Toll Free: 1-800-387-2880
URL: http://www.ibc.ca
President, George D. Anderson
Vice-President, Policy Development, Paul Kovacs
Vice-President, Legel Counsel, Alex Kennedy
Vice-President, Public Affairs, Marc-André Charlebois
Publications: Facts of the General Insurance Industry in Canada; Perspective, q.; Between the Lines, q.
Affiliates: Canadian Coalition Against Insurance Fraud
Atlantic Canada Office: Regional Vice-President, Don Forgeron, Purdy's Wharf, Tower II, #1706, 1969 Upper Water St., PO Box 13, Halifax, NS B3J 3R7, 902/429-2730, Fax: 902/420-0157, Toll Free: 1-800-565-7189
British Columbia & Yukon Office: Regional Vice-President, Brian E. Stanhope, #550, 409 Granville St., Vancouver, BC V6C 1W9, 604/684-3635, Fax: 604/684-6235
Ottawa Office: Director, Government Relations, Mark Yakabuski, #1208, 155 Queen St., Ottawa, ON K1P 6L1, 613/236-5043, Fax: 613/236-5208
Prairies & Northwest Territories Office: Regional Vice-President, Alan D. Wood, #1105, 10080 Jasper Ave., Edmonton, AB T5J 1V9, 403/423-2212, Fax: 403/423-4796, Toll Free: 1-800-232-7275
Québec Office: Administrateur général, Raymond Medza, #900, 425, boul de Maisonneuve ouest, Montréal, PQ H3A 3G5, 514/288-1563, Téléc: 514/288-0753, Ligne sans frais: 1-800-361-5131

Insurance Council of British Columbia (1930)
Box 7, #300, 1040 West Georgia St., Vancouver, BC V6E 4H1
604/688-0321, Fax: 604/662-7767
General Manager, Jerry Matier

Insurance Crime Prevention Bureau/Service anti-crime des assureurs (ICPB) (1923)
PO Box 919, Stn U, Toronto, ON M8Z 5P9
416/252-5215, Fax: 416/252-5226
President, J.C. Cloutier
Vice-President, Canada East, G.R. Garand
Publications: Communique

2-106 ORGANIZATIONS — INTERIOR DESIGN

Insurance Institute of Canada/Institut d'assurance du Canada (IIC) (1952)
18 King St. East, 6th Fl., Toronto, ON M5C 1C4
416/362-8586, Fax: 416/362-4239, Email: iican@ibm.net
URL: http://insurance-canada.ca/iic/
CEO/President, J.C. Rhind
Publications: Perspectives; The Graduate, biennial; Exam Statistics, a.; Eduquorum, a.
Affiliates: Insurance Institute of America; Chartered Insurance Institute; Australian Insurance Institute; Insurance Institute of New Zealand; Insurance Institute of India; Insurance Institute of Malaysia

L'INSTITUT D'ASSURANCE DE DOMMAGES DU QUÉBEC - BUREAU RÉGIONAL DE L'EST DU QUÉBEC
#305, 5400 boul des Galeries, Québec, PQ G2K 2B5
418/623-3688, Fax: 418/623-6935
Christine Dufour
Carole Forcier

L'INSTITUT D'ASSURANCE DE DOMMAGES DU QUÉBEC - BUREAU RÉGIONAL DE L'OUEST DU QUÉBEC (1927)
#2230, 1200, av McGill College, Montréal, PQ H3B 4G7
514/393-8156, Téléc: 514/393-9222
Directrice générale, Diane Laflamme
Publications: Bulletin

INSURANCE INSTITUTE OF BRITISH COLUMBIA (IIBC)
#410, 800 Pender St. West, Vancouver, BC V6C 2V6
604/681-5491, Fax: 604/681-5479
Manager, Malcolm C. Simpson
Publications: Newsletter

INSURANCE INSTITUTE OF MANITOBA (IIM) (1923)
#533, 167 Lombard Ave., Winnipeg, MB R3B 0T6
204/956-1702, Fax: 204/956-0758
Manager, Marjorie J. Peabody
Publications: Insurance Omnibus

INSURANCE INSTITUTE OF NEW BRUNSWICK (IINB) (1952)
Parrtown Place, 32 King St., 6th Fl., Saint John, NB E2L 1G3
506/658-0331, Fax: 506/658-0977
Manager, Janet Kyle

INSURANCE INSTITUTE OF NEWFOUNDLAND INC. (IIN) (1956)
PO Box 576, Mount Pearl, NF A1N 2W4
709/754-4398, Fax: 709/754-4399
Manager, Bernadette Hughes

INSURANCE INSTITUTE OF NORTHERN ALBERTA (IINA)
Oxford Tower, #602, 10235 - 101 St., Edmonton, AB T5J 3E8
403/424-1268, Fax: 403/420-1940
Education Co-ordinator, Christine J. Chaston
Education Co-ordinator, Donna McEwen
Publications: IINA Newsletter

INSURANCE INSTITUTE OF NOVA SCOTIA (IINS) (1953)
414 Duke Tower, Scotia Square, PO Box 1561, RPO Central, Halifax, NS B3J 2Y3
902/422-4112, Fax: 902/423-9307
Manager, Jennifer Simpson
Publications: Calendar of Events

INSURANCE INSTITUTE OF ONTARIO (1899)
18 King St. East, 6th Fl., Toronto, ON M5C 1C4
416/362-8586, Fax: 416/362-1126
General Manager, J.C. Rhind
Publications: In Ontario

INSURANCE INSTITUTE OF PRINCE EDWARD ISLAND (IIPEI) (1960)
57 Queen St., 2nd Fl., Charlottetown, PE C1A 7L9
902/892-1692, Fax: 902/368-2936
Manager, Violet L. MacDonald

INSURANCE INSTITUTE OF SASKATCHEWAN (IIS)
1424 Broad St., Regina, SK S4R 1Y9
306/525-9799, Fax: 306/569-3018

Canadian Almanac & Directory 1997

Manager, Donna Dunn
Publications: Newsletter

INSURANCE INSTITUTE OF SOUTHERN ALBERTA (IISA) (1954)
#801, 1015 - 4 St. SW, Calgary, AB T2R 1J4
403/266-3427, Fax: 403/269-3199
General Manager, Frances A. Lang
President, Jackie L. Tatebe
Publications: IISA Newsletter

Insurers' Advisory Organization (1989) Inc. (IAO) (1883)
IAO Commercial & Residential Risk Services
#700, 18 King St. East, Toronto, ON M5C 1C4
416/368-1801, Fax: 416/368-0333, Info Line: 416/601-4532, Toll Free: 1-800-268-8080
President & CEO, Barry L. Wilson, BBA
Environmental Engineer, Ian D. Greason, P.Eng.
Environmental Services, Elizabeth M. Trolio
Alberta Branch: Branch Manager, Gilles Proulx, #1505, 700 - 6 Ave. SW, Calgary, AB T2P 0T8, 403/262-7283, Fax: 403/262-8068
Atlantic Branch: Branch Manager, Frank Sabo, #810, 1660 Hollis St., Halifax, NS B3J 1V7, 902/429-4333, Fax: 902/423-7376
British Columbia Branch: Branch Manager, Cindy Guyatt, #708, 595 Howe St., PO Box 21, Vancouver, BC V6C 2T5, 604/681-3113, Fax: 604/688-6986
Edmonton Customer Service Centre: Branch Manager, Steve Coolidge, #906, 10004 - 104 Ave., Edmonton, AB T5J 0K1, 403/425-8561, Fax: 403/425-8224
Québec Branch: Branch Manager, Sam Hasbani, #2600, 300, rue Léo Pariseau, CP 990, Montréal, PQ H2W 2N1, 514/285-1201, Téléc: 514/844-0777
Winnipeg Customer Service Centre: Branch Manager, Tino Brambilla, #200, 428 Portage Ave., Winnipeg, MB R3C 0E2, 204/944-9756, Fax: 204/944-9550

Life Insurance Institute of Canada/Institut d'assurance-vie du Canada (LIIC) (1936)
#1600, One Queen St. East, Toronto, ON M5C 2X9
416/359-2020, Fax: 416/359-9173
Executive Director, Debbie Cole-Gauer
Publications: LIIC News

The Life Insurance Managers Association of Canada/Association des directeurs d'agence-vie du Canada (LIMAC) (1974)
#1700, One Queen St. East, Toronto, ON M5C 2X9
416/359-2000, Fax: 416/359-9173
Executive Vice-President, Gordon A. Dunn, 416/359-2005
Publications: LIMAC Newsletter

Life Underwriters Association of Canada/ L'Association des assureurs-vie du Canada (LUAC) (1906)
41 Lesmill Rd., North York, ON M3B 2T3
416/444-5251, Fax: 416/444-8031
President, David J. Thibaudeau
Executive Assistant, Shirley Fingler
Chair & CEO, John Dean
Publications: Forum

CANADIAN INSTITUTE OF CHARTERED LIFE UNDERWRITERS & CHARTERED FINANCIAL CONSULTANTS
41 Lesmill Rd., North York, ON M3B 2T3
416/444-5251, Fax: 416/444-8031
Vice-President/Manager, Clifford Sadgrove

Nuclear Insurance Association of Canada (NIAC)
18 King St. East, Toronto, ON M5C 1C4
416/368-1801, Fax: 416/368-0333
Manager, E. Collier
Assistant Manager, T. Soutar

Ontario Insurance Adjusters Association
132 Bonham Blvd., Mississauga, ON L5M 1C7

905/542-0576, Fax: 905/542-1301
Business Manager, Jackie Johnston-Schnurr
Publications: Without Prejudice

Ontario Mutual Insurance Association
PO Box 3055, Cambridge, ON N3H 4S1
519/622-9220, Fax: 519/622-9227
President, Glen Johnson, CAE
Treasurer, Sarah Underwood

Reinsurance Research Council/Conseil de recherche en réassurance (1973)
#800, 18 King St. East, Toronto, ON M5C 1C4
416/601-4651, Fax: 416/368-0333
Chairman, David Wilmot

Risk & Insurance Management Society Inc. (RIMS) (1962)
1310 Ingledene Dr., Oakville, ON L6H 2G4
905/845-8226, Fax: 905/845-9578
Canadian Director, Risk Management, Legislative & Public Affairs, Lloyd Hackett
Publications: RIMSCAN; RIMSCOPE, q.; Risk Management, m.

Saskatchewan Municipal Hail Association
2100 Cornwall St., Regina, SK S4P 2K7
306/569-1852
Secretary, Murray Otterson

Society of Public Insurance Administrators of Ontario (1977)
2 Wellington St. West, Brampton, ON L6Y 4R2
905/874-2143, Fax: 905/874-2149
President, Deborah Tracogna

Underwriters' Laboratories of Canada/ Laboratoires des assureurs du Canada (ULC) (1920)
7 Crouse Rd., Scarborough, ON M1R 3A9
416/757-3611, Fax: 416/757-8915
President, Peter Higginson
Publications: ULC News
Montréal: #503, 650 - 32e av, Lachine, PQ H8T 3K5, 514/639-5343, Téléc: 514/639-5313
Vancouver: #201, 3540 West 41st Ave., Vancouver, BC V6N 3E6, 604/264-1355, Fax: 604/264-1306

INTERIOR DESIGN

Associated Designers of Canada (ADC) (1965)
#220, 35 McCaul St., Toronto, ON M5T 1V7
416/351-0148, Fax: 416/977-3553
URL: http://www.ffa.ucalgary.ca/adc/indexadc.htm
Executive Director, Chuck Homewood
Publications: ADC Newsletter; ADC Standards & Working Procedures

Association of Canadian Industrial Designers/ Association des designers industriels du Canada (ACID) (1948)
315, rue du St-Sacrement, 3e étage, Montréal, PQ H2Y 1Y1
514/287-6531, Fax: 514/287-6532
President, Philippe Lalonde
Publications: ACID Leaf
Affiliates: International Council of Societies of Industrial Design - Helsinki, Finland

ASSOCIATION OF CHARTERED INDUSTRIAL DESIGNERS OF ONTARIO (ACIDO) (1984)
c/o Axis Group Inc., 65 Bellwoods Ave., Toronto, ON M6J 3N4
416/364-3388, Fax: 416/364-1530
President, Harry Mahler
Publications: ACIDO News

ASSOCIATION DES DESIGNERS INDUSTRIELS DU QUÉBEC (ADIQ)
CP 1122, Succ Place Bonaventure, Montréal, PQ
H5A 1G4
514/397-8775, Téléc: 514/397-9601
Directrice générale, Florence Lebeau

BRITISH COLUMBIA INDUSTRIAL DESIGNERS
1050 Homer St., Vancouver, BC V6B 2W9
604/684-9890, Fax: 604/684-5447
President, Peter Busby

Association of Registered Interior Designers of Ontario (ARIDO) (1984)
717 Church St., Toronto, ON M4W 2M5
416/921-2127, Fax: 416/921-3660, Toll Free: 1-800-334-1180
Contact, Cathy Clark
Publications: ARIDO Newsletter
Affiliates: Interior Designers Educators Council; National Council for Interior Design Education; American Society of Interior Designers; Foundation for Interior Design Education; International Federation of Interior Designers

Interior Designers of Canada/Designers d'intérieur du Canada (IDC)
Ontario Design Centre, #414, 260 King St. East, Toronto, ON M5A 1K3
416/594-9310, Fax: 416/594-9313
Office Manager, Kymberley Krause
Affiliates: International Federation of Interior Architects/Interior Designers

ASSOCIATION OF REGISTERED INTERIOR DESIGNERS OF NEW BRUNSWICK/ASSOCIATION DES DESIGNERS D'INTÉRIEUR IMMATRICULÉS DU NOUVEAU-BRUNSWICK (IDNB)
PO Box 121, Stanley, NB E0H 1T0
506/459-3014
Sara Dunton
Publications: Perspective

INTERIOR DESIGNERS OF ALBERTA (IDA)
5512 - 4 St. NW, PO Box 64024, Calgary, AB T2K 6J0
403/274-9290, Fax: 403/274-9388
Association Manager, Sandra Morrow
Publications: Dimensions

INTERIOR DESIGNERS INSTITUTE OF BRITISH COLUMBIA (IDI OF BC) (1950)
#523, 409 Granville St., Vancouver, BC V5C 1T2
604/251-5343, Fax: 604/251-5347, Email: assn@portal.ca
URL: http://www.designsource.bc.ca
President, Ellen Collison
Association Manager, Sue Osterman
Publications: Dimensions
Affiliates: Design Resource Association

INTERIOR DESIGNERS OF NOVA SCOTIA (IDNS)
PO Box 2042, Stn M, Halifax, NS B3J 3B4
902/425-5397, Fax: 902/425-5606
President, Linda Rodie

PROFESSIONAL INTERIOR DESIGNERS INSTITUTE OF MANITOBA
137 Bannatyne Ave. East, 2nd Fl., Winnipeg, MB R3B 0R3
204/925-4625, Fax: 204/925-4624
Executive Secretary, Joyce Sandall

SOCIÉTÉ DES DECORATEURS-ENSEMBLIERS DU QUÉBEC
20 Elmira, étage E, Place Bonaventure, CP 1122, Montréal, PQ H5A 1G4
514/397-1770, Téléc: 514/397-9601
Directeur exécutif, Louise Clément
Publications: Bulletin Image

INTERNATIONAL COOPERATION/ INTERNATIONAL RELATIONS

Act for Disarmament Coalition (1982)
602 Markham St., Toronto, ON M6G 2L8
416/849-5501
Contact, John Bacher
Publications: The ACTivist
Affiliates: International Peace Bureau; Helsinki Citizens' Assembly; Ontario Peace Network; Ontario Environment Network; Toronto Environment Alliance

AFS Interculture Canada (1978)
Interculture Canada
#505, 1231, rue Ste-Catherine ouest, Montréal, PQ H3G 1P5
514/288-3282, Fax: 514/843-9119, Toll Free: 1-800-361-7248
National Director, Claude Roberge
National Chair, Paul Van Houtte
Publications: The Link/Le Lien
Affiliates: Scouts International

Association canadienne des clubs UNESCO/ Canadian Association of UNESCO Clubs
2448, rue Sicotte, Saint-Hyacinthe, PQ J2S 2K8
Contacte, Brigitte Parent

Atlantic Council of Canada/Conseil atlantique du Canada (ACC) (1966)
Trinity College, 6 Hoskin Ave., Toronto, ON M5S 1H8
416/979-1875, Fax: 416/979-0825, Email: atlantic@idirect.com
President, Prof. Robert Spencer
Publications: The Atlantic Council Letter
Affiliates: NATO; Atlantic Treaty Association - Paris, France

Bridgehead Inc. (1981)
20 James St., Ottawa, ON K2P 0T6
613/567-1455, Fax: 613/567-1468, Toll Free: 1-800-565-8563
Managing Director, Howard Esbin
Publications: Food for Thought

Canada-Caribbean-Central American Policy Alternatives (CAPA)
947 Queen St. East, Toronto, ON M4M 1J9
416/469-1123, Fax: 416/469-3579
Executive Secretary, Joe Gunn
Publications: CAPA Newsletter
Affiliates: CRIES Coordinadora Regional de Investigacioues Economicas

Canada-Latin America Resource Centre (CLARC) (1987)
603 1/2 Parliament St., Toronto, ON M4X 1P9
416/960-0604, Fax: 416/921-0071
Librarian, Aida Morris

Canada-Taiwan Friendship Association (CTFA) (1984)
PO Box 346, Iqaluit, NT X0A 0H0
819/979-2235, Fax: 819/979-2235
Secretary General, Gabriel Fritzen
President, David J. Speer
Publications: CTFA Newsletter

Canada World Youth/Jeunesse Canada Monde (CWY) (1971)
2330, rue Notre-Dame Ouest, 3e étage., Montréal, PQ H3J 1N4
514/931-3526, Fax: 514/939-2621, Telex: 055-60979, Email: jcmcwy@web.apc.org
Executive Director, Paul Shay
Communications Coordinator, Suzanne Hamel

Publications: Bulletin
Affiliates: World Assembly of Youth
Atlantic Regional Office: Regional Director, Matthew Pearce, #125, 1657 Barrington St., Halifax, NS B3J 2A1, 902/422-1782, Fax: 902/429-1274
British Columbia Regional Office: Regional Director, Gary Henkelmann, #201, 1894 West Broadway, Vancouver, BC V6J 1Y9, 604/732-5113, Fax: 604/732-9141
Ontario Regional Office: Regional Director, Anne Game, 386 Bloor St. West, 2nd Fl., Toronto, ON M5S 1X4, 416/922-0776, Fax: 416/922-3721
Prairies Regional Office: #205, 10816A - 82 Ave., Edmonton, AB T5H 2P2, 403/432-1877, Fax: 403/433-4489
Québec Regional Office: Directrice régionale, Joanne Bourgeois, 2330, rue Notre Dame ouest, 4e étage, Montréal, PQ H3J 1N4, 514/931-3933, Téléc: 514/935-4580, Télex: 055-60979

Canadian Action for Nicaragua (CAN) (1979)
PO Box 398, Stn E, Toronto, ON M6H 4E3
416/534-1766
Collective Member, Peter Bruer
Publications: Membership Mailing

Canadian Association for the Study of International Development/L'Association canadienne d'études du développement international (CASID)
c/o The North-South Institute, #200, 55 Murray St., Ottawa, ON K1N 5M3
613/241-3535, Fax: 613/241-7435, Email: nsi@web.apc.org
President, Patricia Paton
Vice-President, Arpi Hamalian
Sec.-Treas., Rosalind Boyd, 514/398-3508, Fax: 514/398-8432
Publications: Canadian Journal of Development Studies

Canadian Commission for UNESCO/Commission canadienne pour l'UNESCO (1957)
350 Albert St., PO Box 1047, Ottawa, ON K1P 5V8
613/566-4414, Fax: 613/566-4405, Toll Free: 1-800-263-5588
Secretary-General, Viviane F. Launay

Canadian Council for International Co-operation/ Conseil canadien pour la coopération internationale (CCIC) (1968)
#300, One Nicholas St., Ottawa, ON K1N 7B7
613/241-7007, Fax: 613/241-5302, Email: ccic@web.apc.org
President/CEO, Betty Plewes
Commuications Officer, Denise Fournier
Publications: Au Courant; Who's Who in International Development
Affiliates: International Coalition for Voluntary Agencies; International Coalition for Development Action; World Bank NGO Consultative Committee; Steering Committee of the UN Program of Action for African Economic Recovery & Development; Canadian Council for International Development; International Organization of Consumers Unions; African Medical & Research Foundation

Canadian Foundation for the Americas/Fondation canadienne pour les Amériques (FOCAL) (1990)
#230, 55 Murray St., Ottawa, ON K1N 5M3
613/562-0005, Fax: 613/562-2525, Email: focal@focal.ca
URL: http://www.focal.ca
Executive Director, Dean J. Browne
Director of Programs, Juanita Montalvo
Director of Communications, Michelle Hibler
Publications: FOCAL Update/Le point FOCAL; The FOCAL Papers/Les cahiers de FOCAL, 5 pa

Canadian Almanac & Directory 1997

Canadian Foundation for World Development (CFWD) (1977)
2441 Bayview Ave., North York, ON M2L 1A5
416/445-4740, Fax: 416/441-4025
President, Kenneth G. Davis
Secretary, R. Davis
Publications: Grassroots

Canadian Friends of Burma/Les Amis Canadiens de la Birmanie (CFOB) (1991)
#206, 145 Spruce St., Ottawa, ON K1R 6P1
613/237-8056, Fax: 613/563-0017, Email: cfob@web.apc.org
Coordinator, Christine Harmston
Advisor, Executive Committee, Penny Sanger
Advisor, Executive Committee, Murray Thomson
Financial Officer, Khine Thinn
Publications: Burma Links
Affiliates: World University Service of Canada; Canadian Asia Pacific Working Group

Canadian Friends of Soviet People (1918)
280 Queen St. West, Toronto, ON M5V 2A1
416/977-5819, Fax: 416/593-0781
President, Michael Lukas
Publications: Northstar Compass

Canadian Hunger Foundation/Fondation canadienne contre la faim (CHF) (1961)
323 Chapel St., Ottawa, ON K1N 7Z2
613/237-0180, Fax: 613/237-5969, Email: chfott@web.apc.org
Executive Director, Bruce Moore
Deputy Director, Tom Taylor
Director, Finance & Administration, Marion Lacelle
Publications: Global Link

Canadian Institute for Conflict Resolution/ Institute canadien pour la résolution des conflits (CICR) (1988)
St. Paul University, 223 Main St., Ottawa, ON K1S 1C4
613/235-5800, Fax: 613/782-3005
President, Robert P. Birt

Canadian Institute of Cultural Affairs/Institut canadien des affaires culturelles (1976)
ICA Canada
579 Kingston Rd., Toronto, ON M4E 1R3
416/691-2316, Fax: 416/691-2491
Executive Director, T. Duncan Holmes
Publications: Edges: New Planetary Patterns
Affiliates: Part of a network of nationally autonomous ICAs in 29 countries; through ICA International in Brussels, ICA Canada has consultative status with the UN, UNICEF, the World Health Organization & the Food & Agricultural Organization

Canadian Institute of International Affairs/ Institut canadien des affaires internationales (CIIA) (1928)
5 Devonshire Pl., Toronto, ON M5S 2C8
416/979-1851, Fax: 416/979-8575
URL: http://www.trinity.utoronto.ca/ciia/intro.html
President/CEO, Alan Sullivan
Chairman, Peter White
Publications: Behind the Headlines; International Journal, q.

Canadian Peace Alliance/Alliance canadienne pour la paix (CPA) (1985)
#5, 555 Bloor St. West, Toronto, ON M5S 1Y6
416/588-5555, Fax: 416/588-5556, Email: cpa@web.apc.org
Coordinator, Tryna Booth
Affiliates: Action Canada Network; International Peace Bureau

Canadian Peace Congress
873 Jane St., PO Box 98516, Toronto, ON M6N 5A6
416/762-3874
President, Larri Prokop

Canadian Physicians for Aid & Relief (CPAR) (1983)
#202, 111 Queen St. East, Toronto, ON M5C 1S2
416/369-0865, Fax: 416/369-0294, Toll Free: 1-800-263-2727
URL: cpar@web.net
Executive Director, Joy Woolfrey
President, Mark Doidge
Publications: CPAReport
Affiliates: Canadian Environmental Network; Canadian Centre for Philanthropy

CARE Canada (1946)
6 Antares Dr., PO Box 9000, Ottawa, ON K1G 4X6
613/228-5600, Fax: 613/226-5777, Telex: 053-4513, Toll Free: 1-800-267-5232, Email: info@care.ca
Executive Director, A. John Watson
Chairman, Peter Crossgrove
Media Relations, Angela Mackay
Affiliates: CARE International; Canadian Council for International Cooperation

Carrefour de solidarité internationale inc. (1976)
CSI - Sherbrooke
555, rue Short, Sherbrooke, PQ J1H 2E6
819/566-8595, Téléc: 819/566-8076
Coordonnateur général, François Faucher
Publications: CSI - Informe

Centre canadien d'étude et de coopération internationale/Canadian Centre for International Studies & Cooperation (CECI) (1958)
180, rue Sainte-Catherine est, Montréal, PQ H2X 1K9
514/875-9911, Téléc: 514/875-6469, Courrier électronique: ceci@web.apc.org
Directrice des communications, Lise Londei
Directeur général, Yves Pétillon
Publications: CECI Dit...
Bureau de Québec: 160, rue St-Joseph est, Québec, PQ G1K 3A7, 418/523-6552, Téléc: 418/523-7525

Child Haven international/Accueil international pour l'enfance (1985)
RR#1, Maxville, ON K0C 1T0
613/527-2829, Fax: 613/527-1118
Director, Bonnie Cappuccino
Director, Fred Cappuccino
Publications: Child Haven International/Accueil international pour l'enfance
Affiliates: Child Haven International - USA, India, Nepal

Children's International Summer Villages (Canada) Inc.
5 Dunvegan St., Ottawa, ON K1K 3E7
613/749-9680, Fax: 613/749-9680
National Secretary, Coreen Blackburn

Citizens for Foreign Aid Reform Inc. (C-FAR)
PO Box 392, Etobicoke, ON M9W 5L3
905/897-7221, Fax: 905/897-3914
Director, Paul Fromm

CNEC - Partners International
#48, 8500 Torbram Rd., Brampton, ON L6T 5C6
905/458-1202, Fax: 905/458-4339
President, Rev. Grover Crosby
Publications: Partners

CODE (1959)
Canadian Organization for Development through Education
321 Chapel St., Ottawa, ON K1N 7Z2
613/232-3569, Fax: 613/232-7435, Toll Free: 1-800-661-2633
National Director, Robert Dyck
President, Ray Fast
Publications: NGOMA (Talking Drum)
Affiliates: International Book Bank; CODE Europe; CODE Inc.; CODE Foundation

CoDevelopment Canada (CODEV) (1985)
#205, 2929 Commercial Dr., Vancouver, BC V5N 4C8
604/708-1495, Fax: 604/708-1497, Email: codev@web.apc.org
President, Bill Brassington

Compassion Canada (1963)
PO Box 5591, London, ON N6A 5G8
519/668-0224, Fax: 519/685-1107, Telex: Cable: COMPASSI, Toll Free: 1-800-563-5437,
Email: compcan@web.apc.org
President, Barry Slauenwhite
Publications: Compassion Today

Conseil de la Coopération de l'Ontario (CCO) (1964)
450 Rideau St., Ottawa, ON K1N 5Z4
613/789-7777, Téléc: 613/789-3763
Directrice générale, Ethel Côté
Publications: Le Coopère-action
Organisation(s) affiliée(s): Association canadienne française de l'Ontario

Conseil de la coopération du Québec (CCQ) (1939)
#304, 4950, boul de la Rive Sud, Lévis, PQ G6V 4Z6
418/835-3710, Téléc: 418/835-6322
Président, Majella St-Pierre
Publications: Réseau Coop
Organisation(s) affiliée(s): Conseil canadien de la coopération; Alliance coopérative internationale

Counterpoint: A Resource Centre for Global Analyses (1993)
603 1/2 Parliament St., Toronto, ON M4X 1P9
416/921-4424, Fax: 416/921-0071, Email: cpoint@web.apc.org
President, Linda Levo
Affiliates: Founded by a pooling of three resouce centres - The Development Education Centre (DEC), The Canada Latin America Resource Centre (CLARC) & The Southern Africa Resource Centre (SARC)

CUSO (1961)
2255 Carling Ave., Ottawa, ON K2B 1A6
613/829-7445, Fax: 613/829-7996, Email: cusoppu@web.net
Executive Director, Melanie Macdonald
Chair, François Faucher
Publications: Forum
Calgary Office: Regional Coordinator, Rebekah Seidel, 233 - 10th St. NW, Calgary, AB T2N 1V5, 403/283-2871, Fax: 403/283-2902, Email: cusoalbt@web.net
Halifax Office: Regional Coordinator, Linda Snyder, #508, 1657 Barrington St., Halifax, NS B3J 2A1, 902/423-6709, Fax: 902/423-9736, Email: cusoatl@web.net
Manitoba & Western Ontario Office: Regional Coordinator, George Harris, 60 Maryland St., Winnipeg, MB R3G 1K7, 204/774-8489, Fax: 204/786-3012, Email: cusoman@web.net
Québec Regional Office: Regional Coordinator, Francine Néméh, #380, 1600, av de Lorimier, Montréal, PQ H2K 3W5, 514/528-8465, Fax: 514/528-1750, Email: cusoque@web.net
Saskatoon Office: Regional Coordinator, Don Kossick, 614B - 10th St. East, Saskatoon, SK S7H 0G9, 306/933-4141, Fax: 306/933-4346, Email: cusosask@web.net
Toronto Office: Regional Coordinator, Steve Seaborn, #200, 133 Richmond St. West, Toronto, ON

M5H 2L3, 416/363-2191, Fax: 416/363-6041,
Email: cusoont@web.net
Vancouver Office: Regional Coordinator, Brenda
Kuecks, #914, 207 West Hastings St., Vancouver, BC
V6B 1H6, 604/683-2099, Fax: 604/683-8536,
Email: cusobc@web.net

Four Arrows/Las Cuatro Flechas (1968)
PO Box 1332, Ottawa, ON K1P 5R4
613/234-5887, Fax: 613/234-5887
Coordinator, R. Rarihokwats

Group of 78/Groupe des 78 (1980)
#206, 145 Spruce St., Ottawa, ON K1R 6P1
613/ 230-0860, Fax: 613/563-0017
Chairperson, Geoffrey Pearson

HOPE International Development Agency (1985)
214 - 6 St., New Westminster, BC V3L 3A2
604/525-5481, Fax: 604/525-3471, Email: hope@
web.apc.org
Executive Director, David S. McKenzie
Communications Director, John King
Chairman, Girve Fretz
Publications: HOPE Newsletter; Concern, q.

Horizons of Friendship (HOF) (1973)
50 Covert St., PO Box 402, Stn Main, Cobourg, ON
K9A 4L1
905/372-5483, Fax: 905/372-7095, Email: horizons@
web.apc.org
Executive Director, Rick Arnold
Publications: Newsletter
Affiliates: Inter Agency Working Group on Latin
America

Inter Pares/Among Equals
58 Arthur St., Ottawa, ON K1R 7B9
613/563-4801, Fax: 613/594-4704
Director, Lise Latrémouille
Publications: Inter Pares Bulletin

**International Child Care (Canada)
Inc. (ICC) (1973)**
#103, 195 King St., PO Box 2125, Stn B, St Catharines,
ON L2M 6P5
905/688-0632, Fax: 905/688-6069
Administrative Manager, Lorna Rogalski
Publications: Grace Notes

**International Development Education Resource
Association (IDERA) (1974)**
#200, 2678 Broadway Ave. West, Vancouver, BC
V6K 2G3
604/732-1496; Film Line: 604/739-8815, Fax: 604/738-
8400, Email: idera@web.apc.org
URL: http://www.vcn.bc.ca/idera
Executive Director, Stuart Black
Film Programmer, David Pettigrew
Publications: IDERA Newsletter; Press Relief, a.
Affiliates: Independent Film & Video Alliance

International Relief Agency Inc. (IRA) (1979)
95 Wood St., Toronto, ON M4Y 2Z3
416/922-7120, Fax: 416/928-0901
Director General, Adam A. Budzanowski
Office Manager, Eileen Brown
Chairman, Olivia Aquino
Publications: The Global Forum Magazine
Affiliates: Best of 7 Continents Inc.; International
Hippocrates Foundation; Council of First Nations

JCI - Global Strategists (CCGS) (1995)
Global Strategists
#704, 153 Nepean St., Ottawa, ON K2P 0B5
613/231-2428, Fax: 613/231-2428
President, Joanne Charnetski

Vice-President, Tariq Rauf
Publications: Policy Forum Notes

**Mahatma Gandhi Canadian Foundation for World
Peace (1986)**
PO Box 60002, RPO U of Alberta, Edmonton, AB
T6G 2S4
403/492-5504
Vijay Bhardwaj

**Manitoba Council for International Cooperation/
Conseil du Manitoba pour la coopération
internationale (MCIC) (1974)**
#202, 583 Ellice Ave., Winnipeg, MB R3B 1Z7
204/786-2106, Fax: 204/772-7179
Executive Director, Darlene Henderson
Publications: MCIC News; Bridging the Gap

The Marquis Project, Inc. (1979)
#200, 107 - 7 St., Brandon, MB R7A 3S5
204/727-5675, Fax: 204/727-5683, Email: marquis@
docker.com
Executive Director, Zack Gross
Publications: Newsletter
Affiliates: Canadian Council for International Cooperation; Manitoba Council for International Cooperation; Partnership Africa-Canada; Canadian Peace
Alliance; Manitoba Eco-Network

Mercy International Canada (1993)
#2400, 180 Dundas St. West, PO Box 44, Toronto, ON
M5G 1Z8
416/971-9200, Fax: 416/971-5613, Toll Free: 1-800-465-
0088
Executive Director, Janis Kazaks
Business Manager, Elizabeth Lin
Publications: Bringing Hope to Life
Mercy International Ottawa: Director, International
Programs, Janis Kazaks, 629 Highland Ave., Ot-
tawa, ON K2A 2K2, 613/728-7170, Fax: 613/728-
0033

**Ontario Council for International Cooperation/
Conseil de l'Ontario pour la coopération
internationale (OCIC)**
80 Gerrard St. East, Toronto, ON M5B 1G6
416/597-2799, Fax: 416/597-2798
Executive Director, Tonia de Sousa-Shields
President, Linda Slavin
Publications: OCIC Newsletter

Operation Eyesight Universal (OEU) (1963)
4 Parkdale Cres. NW, Calgary, AB T2N 3T8
403/283-6323, Fax: 403/270-1899, Toll Free: 1-800-585-
8265, Email: oeuca@cadvision.com
Director, Community Relations, Barry Boyack
Publications: Gift of Sight
Affiliates: Royal Commonwealth Society for the Blind;
Kenya Society for the Blind; International Agency
for the Prevention of Blindness
Central Canada Regional Office: Manager, Commu-
nity Relations, Stephen Faul, #323, 2100 Ellesmere
Rd., Scarborough, ON M1H 3B7, 416/438-3555,
Fax: 416/438-6132

Oxfam-Canada (1963)
#300, 294 Albert St., Ottawa, ON K1P 6E6
613/237-5236, Fax: 613/237-0524
National Secretary, John W. Foster
Affiliates: Oxfam - United Kingdom & Ireland

**Peace Brigades International
(Canada) (PBI) (1981)**
Central American Projects Office/Peace Brigades
International (Canada)
#304, 192 Spadina Ave., Toronto, ON M5T 2C2
416/504-4429, Fax: 416/504-4430

Coordinator, Louise Palmer
Publications: Project Bulletin

**Peacefund Canada/Fonds canadien pour la
paix (PFC) (1986)**
#206, 145 Spruce St., Ottawa, ON K1R 6P1
613/230-0860, Fax: 613/563-0017
Executive Secretary, Murray Thomson
Publications: Peacefund Canada
Affiliates: International Council for Adult Education;
Canadian Association for Adult Education

**Physicians for Global Survival (Canada)/
Association des Médecins pour la Survie
Mondiale (Canada) (PGS) (1980)**
#208, 145 Spruce St., Ottawa, ON K1R 6P1
613/233-1982, Fax: 613/233-9028, Email: pgs@
web.apc.org
URL: http://www.web.apc.org/~pgs/
Executive Director, Debbie Grisdale
President, Dr. Warren Bell
Publications: Turning Point; Position Papers
Affiliates: International Physicians for the Prevention
of Nuclear War (IPPNW)

Project Peacemakers (1982)
745 Westminster Ave., Winnipeg, MB R3G 1A5
204/775-8178, Fax: 204/775-8178
Karen Schlichting-Enns
Publications: Peace Projections
Affiliates: Canadian Peace Alliance; Canadian Centre
for Arms Control & Disarmament; Winnipeg Coor-
dinating Committee for Disarmament; Project
Ploughshares; Manitoba Environmental Network;
Coalition of Organizations Against Apartheid; The
IDEA Centre; Project Ploughshares

Project Ploughshares (1976)
Institute of Peace & Conflict Studies, Conrad Grebel
College, Waterloo, ON N2L 3G6
519/888-6541, Fax: 519/885-0806, Email: plough@wat-
servl.uwaterloo.ca
URL: http://watserv1.uwaterloo.ca/~plough/
Policy & Public Affairs Director, Ernie Regehr
Program Coordinator, Ken Epps
Director of Development & Administration, Nancy
Regehr
Publications: Ploughshares Monitor; Peace Resource
Catalogue; Armed Conflicts Report, a.
Affiliates: Canadian Council of Churches

**Saskatchewan Council for International Co-
operation/Conseil de la Saskatchewan pour la
co-opération internationale (SCIC) (1974)**
2138 McIntyre St., Regina, SK S4P 2R7
306/757-4669, Fax: 306/757-3226
Publications: Earthbeat; Development Education Directory; Environment & Development Directory;
One World, q.

**Save the Children - Canada/Aide à l'enfance -
Canada (1946)**
#6020, 3080 Yonge St., Toronto, ON M4N 3P4
416/488-0306, Fax: 416/483-4430, Toll Free: 1-800-668-
5036, Email: sccan@web.apc.org
National Director, René De Grâce

Save a Family Plan (SAFP) (1965)
1040 Waterloo St., PO Box 3622, London, ON
N6A 4L4
519/672-1115, Fax: 519/672-6379
Executive Director, Fr. Sebastian Adayanthrath
President, Rev. Dr. Michael Ryan

Science for Peace/Science et Paix (SfP) (1981)
University of Toronto, University College, Toronto,
ON M5S 3H8
416/978-3606, Email: sfp@physics.utoronto.ca

Canadian Almanac & Directory 1997

URL: http://www.math.yorku.ca/sfp/
President, Prof. Peter Nicholls, 905/682-2343
Vice-President, Eric Fawcett, 416/485-0990
Secretary, Helmut Burkhardt, 416/694-8385
Treasurer, Ian Russell, 416/769-2630
Publications: SfP Bulletin
Affiliates: Canadian Peace Research & Education Association

Ten Days for Global Justice/Dix jours pour le justice global (1973)
Inter-Church Committee for World Development Education
85 St. Clair Ave. East, Toronto, ON M4T 1M8
416/922-0591, Fax: 416/922-1419, Email: tendays@web.net
National Coordinator, Dennis Howlett
Publications: Ten Days Update; Freedom From Debt, a.; Reexamining Development; Development Demands Democracy

United Nations Association in Canada/Association canadienne pour les Nations-Unies (UNAC) (1946)
#900, 130 Slater St., Ottawa, ON K1P 6E2
613/232-5751, Fax: 613/563-2455, Email: unac@magi.com
Executive Director, Harry Qualman
Information Officer, Joan Broughton
Publications: UNAC Bulletin
Affiliates: World Federation of United Nations Associations
Estrie Office: Président, Patrick Morin, a/s Carrefour de Solidarité Intle, 555, rue Short, Sherbrooke, PQ J1H 2E6, 819/566-8595, Fax: 819/655-8076
Montréal Office: President, Joel Bonn, 1055, Côte du Beaver Hall, 2e étage, Montréal, PQ H2Z 1S5, 514/395-1646, Fax: 514/395-1608
Québec Office: Présidente, Marie-Thérèse Wéra, 913, av Painchaud, Québec, PQ G1S 4L7, 418/681-2991, Téléc: 418/681-9235, Courrier électronique: mtwera@web.apc.org
Toronto Office: President, Bill Staples, #116, 2 College St., Toronto, ON M6G 1K3, 416/929-0990, Fax: 416/691-2491
Vancouver Office: President, Gulzar Samji, #101, 1956 Broadway West, Vancouver, BC V6J 1Z2, 604/732-0448, Fax: 604/736-8963, Email: unacvan@web.apc.org
Victoria Office: President, Mike Sproule, #217, 620 View St., Victoria, BC V8W 1J6, 250/383-4635, Fax: 250/383-4635, Email: unacvic@web.apc.org
Winnipeg Office: President, Glenn Nicholls, #2, 340 Cockburn St., Winnipeg, MB R3N 2P5, 204/475-0513, Email: ywgunac@web.apc.org

World Federalists of Canada/Mouvement canadien pour une fédération mondiale (WFC) (1948)
#207, 145 Spruce St., Ottawa, ON K1R 6P1
613/232-0647, Fax: 613/562-0017
Executive Director, Fergus Watt
President, Allan Blakeney
Administrative Officer, D. Welch
Publications: Canadian World Federalist
Affiliates: World Federalist Movement

World University Service of Canada/Entraide universitaire mondiale du Canada (WUSC) (1939)
PO Box 3000, Stn C, Ottawa, ON K1Y 4M8
613/798-7477, Fax: 613/798-0990, Email: wusc@wusc.ca
URL: http://www.wusc.ca
Executive Director, Marc Dolgin
Deputy Executive Director, Ravi Gupta
Publications: Communiqué
Affiliates: Canadian Council for International Cooperation

World Vision Canada/Vision Mondiale (WVC) (1950)
6630 Turner Valley Rd., Mississauga, ON L5N 2S4
905/821-3030, Fax: 905/821-1354, Telex: 06-23112, Toll Free: 1-800-268-5863
President, J. Donald Scott
COO, Dave Toycen
Publications: Childview; Vision mondiale, trimestriel; Caring Together, 3 pa; Context, q.; Voices, q.; Prospects, q.

INTERNATIONAL TRADE see **TRADE**

INTERPRETERS see **LANGUAGE, LINGUISTICS, LITERATURE**

INVESTMENT see **FINANCE**

JEWELLRY see **GEMS & JEWELLERY**

JUDGES see **LAW**

LABOUR RELATIONS
see also Employment & Human Resources

Arbitration & Mediation Institute of Canada Inc./Institut d'arbitrage et de médiation du Canada inc. (AMIC) (1974)
#204, 315 Lakeshore Rd. East, Oakville, ON L6J 1J3
905/849-8993, Fax: 905/849-7312
Executive Director, F.G. (Jerry) Fox
Publications: Canadian Arbitration & Mediation/Journal 'd Arbitrage et de Médiation Canadien

ALBERTA ARBITRATION & MEDIATION SOCIETY (AAMS) (1982)
#408, McLeod Building, 10136 - 100 St., Edmonton, AB T5J 0P1
403/426-0650, Fax: 403/425-4556, Toll Free: 1-800-232-7214
Executive Director, Peter Portlock
President, Rick Solkowski
Publications: AAMS Newsletter; AAMS Directory, a.

ARBITRATION & MEDIATION INSTITUTE OF MANITOBA INC.
PO Box 737, Winnipeg, MB R3C 2L4
204/775-8664, Fax: 204/783-7805

ARBITRATION & MEDIATION INSTITUTE OF ONTARIO INC.
#602, 234 Eglinton Ave. East, Toronto, ON M4P 1K5
416/487-4447, Fax: 416/487-4429
Office Manager, Mena Peckan
President, David McCutcheon

ARBITRATION & MEDIATION INSTITUTE OF SASKATCHEWAN INC. (AMIS) (1987)
152 Rupert Dr., Saskatoon, SK S7K 1B5
306/244-4508, Fax: 306/955-1239, Info Line: 306/975-1245
President, Robert C. Graham, C.Arb.
Secretary, James N. Perry, C.Arb.

ATLANTIC PROVINCES ARBITRATION & MEDIATION INSTITUTE
PO Box 247, Halifax, NS B3J 2N9
902/492-2000, Fax: 902/429-5215
President, A. Douglas Tupper

BRITISH COLUMBIA ARBITRATION & MEDIATION INSTITUTE (1980)
1628 - 7 Ave. West, Vancouver, BC V6J 1S5
604/736-6614, Fax: 604/736-6225
Administrator, Reva Lander

INSTITUT D'ARBITRAGE DU QUÉBEC
#100, 4444, rue Ste-Catherine ouest, Montréal, PQ H3Z 1R2

514/939-3849, Téléc: 514/939-0828
Président, Pierre Lefort

Association canadienne des relations industrielles/Canadian Industrial Relations Association (ACRI) (1963)
Département des relations industrielles, Université Laval, Pavillon J.-A.-deSève, Québec, PQ G1K 7P4
418/656-2468, Téléc: 418/656-3175
Secrétaire-trésorier, Anthony Giles
Organisation(s) affiliée(s): International Industrial Relations Association; Industrial Relations Research Association; La Fédération canadienne des sciences sociales

Association of Workers' Compensation Boards of Canada/Association des commissions des accidents du travail du Canada (1919)
#1350, 10665 Jasper Ave., Edmonton, AB T5J 3S9
403/425-5462, Fax: 403/427-2385
Executive Director, John Wisocky
Publications: Workers' Compensation Benefit Summaries

Canadian Association of Administrators of Labour Legislation/Association canadienne des administrateurs de la législation ouvrière
c/o Federal-Provincial Relations Branch, Department of Labour, 165, rue Hôtel de Ville, Hull, PQ K1A 0J2
819/997-1333, Fax: 819/997-0126
Secretary, Monique Poitras
Sec.-Treas., Louise Guertin

Canadian Association of Labour Media
c/o Canadian Labour Congress, 2841 Riverside Dr., Ottawa, ON K1V 8X7
613/521-3400, Fax: 613/521-4655

Canadian Committee on Labour History/Comité canadien sur l'histoire du travail (CCLH) (1971)
History Dept., Memorial University of Newfoundland, PO Box 4200, Stn C, St. John's, NF A1C 5S7
709/737-2144, Fax: 709/737-4342, Email: joanb@plato.ucs.mun.ca
Editor, Dr. G.S. Kealey
Publications: Labour/Le Travail
Affiliates: International Association of Labour History Institutions; Canadian Historical Association; Canadian Association of Labour Media; Conference of Historical Journals; Council of Editors of Learned Journals

Canadian Compensation Association/Association canadienne de rémuneration (1985)
10435 Islington Ave., PO Box 294, Kleinburg, ON L0J 1C0
905/893-1689, Fax: 905/893-2392
Manager, Canadian Operations, Wayne Glover, CAE
Affiliates: American Compensation Association

Canadian Injured Workers Alliance/L'Alliance canadienne des victimes d'accidents et de maladies du travail (CIWA) (1990)
PO Box 3678, Thunder Bay, ON P7E 6E3
807/345-3429, Fax: 807/345-7086
Coordinator, Ursula Tannert
Publications: Highlights

Centre d'arbitrage commercial national et international du Québec/Québec National & International Commercial Arbitration Centre (CACNIQ) (1986)
Édifice la Fabrique, #090, 295, boul Charest est, Québec, PQ G1K 3G8
418/649-1374; Montréal: 519/393-3774, Téléc: 418/649-0845

Directeur général, Jean Gauthier
Président, Nabil Antaki

Construction Labour Relations - An Alberta Association (CLRA) (1971)
#207, 2725 - 12 St. NE, Calgary, AB T2E 7J2
403/250-7390, Fax: 403/250-5516, Toll Free: 1-800-308-9466
President, R. Neil Tidsbury
Publications: Newsletter

Construction Labour Relations Association of British Columbia (1969)
97 - 6 St., PO Box 820, New Westminster, BC V3L 4Z8
604/524-4911, Fax: 604/524-3925
President, C.C. McVeigh
Office Manager, W. Mazur

Construction Labour Relations Association of Manitoba
290 Burnell St., Winnipeg, MB R3G 2A7
204/775-0441, Fax: 204/783-7270
Director of Labour Relations, Kam Gajdosik

Construction Management Bureau Ltd.
#200, 5450 Cornwallis St., Halifax, NS B3K 1A9
902/429-6763, Fax: 902/422-5303
President, Hugh A.R. Simpson

Inter-American Commercial Arbitration Commission - Canadian Section
Canadian Arbitration Centre & Amicable Composition Centre, Inc., Faculty of Law, University of Ottawa, PO Box 450, Stn A, Ottawa, ON K1N 6N5
613/564-5939, Fax: 613/564-9800, Telex: 0533338
Contact, Prof. Paul J. Davidson

International Federation of Commercial Arbitration Institutions/Fédération internationale des institutions d'arbitrage commercial (IFCAI) (1985)
140 West 51 St., 9th Fl., New York, NY 10023 USA
212/484-4110, Fax: 212/765-4874
President, Michael F. Hoellering
Sec.-Treas., Prof. Paul J. Davidson
Publications: International Federation of Commercial Arbitration Institutions Newsletter
Inter-American Commercial Arbitration Commission: Director General, Charles R. Norberg; President, Julio Gonzales Soria, OAS Administrative Building, Rm. 211, 19th & Constitution Ave. NW, Washington, DC 20006 USA, 202/458-3249, Telex: 64128 ANSWERBAC

Newfoundland Construction Labour Relations Association (NCLRA)
15 Hallett Cres., PO Box 28065, RPO Avalon Mall, St. John's, NF A1B 4J8
709/753-5770, Fax: 709/753-5771
Chairman, Craig Power
Publications: NCLRA Newsletter

L'Ordre professionnel des conseillers en relations industrielles du Québec (OPCRIQ) (1971)
#503, 1100, av Beaumont, Mount Royal, PQ H3P 3E5
514/344-1609, Téléc: 514/344-1610, Courrier électronique: opcriq@opcriq.qc.ca
URL: http://www.opcriq.qc.ca
Directeur général, Florent Francoeur
Publications: Ecriteau

Provincial Building & Construction Trades Council of Ontario (1959)
Provincial Building Trades Council
#604, 15 Gervais Dr., North York, ON M3C 1Y8
416/449-4830, Fax: 416/449-5713
Business Manager/Sec.-Treas., Joseph Duffy

Publications: Naylor Communications
Affiliates: International Foundation of Employee Benefit Plans - Building Trades Department

Pulp & Paper Employee Relations Forum
#800, 505 Burrard St., Vancouver, BC V7X 1M4
604/683-8571, Fax: 604/683-4259
President, E.Y. Mitterndorfer

Union of Injured Workers of Ontario, Inc.
#1, 1474 St. Clair Ave. West, Toronto, ON M6E 1C6
416/657-1215, Fax: 416/657-8122
Executive Director, Philip Biggin
Publications: Injured Workers' Voice

Western Employers Labour Relations Association
#507, 4190 Lougheed Hwy., Burnaby, BC V5C 6A8
604/291-2871, Fax: 604/291-0538
Executive Vice-President, Jim Galbraith

LANDSCAPE ARCHITECTURE see HORTICULTURE, GARDENING, LANDSCAPE ARCHITECTURE

LANGUAGE, LINGUISTICS, LITERATURE

ABC CANADA (1990)
ABC CANADA Literacy Foundation
1450 Don Mills Rd., North York, ON M3B 2X7
416/442-2292, Fax: 416/442-2293, Toll Free: 1-800-303-1004, Email: abccanada@southam.ca
URL: http://www.abc-canada.org
Executive Director, Colleen Albiston
Chair, Peter Gilchrist
Publications: Literacy at Work

Association canadienne de traductologie/ Canadian Association for Translation Studies
École de traducteurs et d'interprètes, Université d'Ottawa, CP 415, Succ. A, Ottawa, ON K1N 6N5
613/564-9046; 819/770-0571
Secrétaire-trésorier, Geneviève Mareschal
Président, Jean Delisle
Vice-présidente, Christel Gallant
Directeur de la revue, Jean-Marc Govanvic
Publications: TTR

Association of Visual Language Interpreters of Canada, Inc./Association des interprètes en langage visuel du Canada
c/o Canadian Hearing Society, #502, 2197 Riverside Dr., Ottawa, ON K1H 7X3
613/521-0509, Fax: 613/521-0838
President, Susan Margaret
Affiliates: International Association of Logopedics & Phoniatrics

The Brontë Society - Canada (1893)
142 Glenforest Rd., Toronto, ON M4N 1Z9
416/488-0888
Canadian Representative, Judith Watkins-Kapsa

Canadian Association for Commonwealth Literature & Language Studies/Association canadienne pour l'étude des langues et de la littérature du Commonwealth (CACLALS) (1973)
Dept. of English, University of Calgary, 2500 University Dr. NW, Calgary, AB T2N 1N4
403/220-5470, Fax: 403/289-1123
President, Victor J. Ramraj
Sec.-Treas., Kelly Hewson
Publications: Chimo
Affiliates: Association for Commonwealth Literature & Language Studies (ACLALS)

Canadian Comparative Literature Association/ Association canadienne de littérature comparée (1969)
Dept. of English, University of Victoria, Victoria, BC V8W 1W3
250/721-7240, Fax: 250/721-6498
President, Prof. Evelyn Cobley
Secretary, Hilary Clark
Treasurer, Richard Cavell
Publications: Canadian Review of Comparative Literature

Canadian Give the Gift of Literacy Foundation (CGGLF) (1986)
35 Spadina Rd., Toronto, ON M5R 2S9
416/975-9366, Fax: 416/975-1839
Chairperson, Susan Froud
Coordinator, Anne Goldspink
Publications: Literacy Letter

Canadian Linguistic Association/Association canadienne de linguistique
Dept. of Linguistics, Memorial University, St. John's, NF A1B 3X9
709/737-8134, Fax: 709/737-4000
Sec.-Treas., James Black
Publications: The Canadian Journal of Linguistics/La Revue canadienne de linguistique; Bulletin, a.

Canadian Literary & Artistic Association/ Association littéraire et artistique canadienne inc.
ALAI Canada
c/o Ogivy Renault, #1000, 1981, av McGill College, Montréal, PQ H3A 3C1
514/847-4512, Fax: 514/658-5993
President, Ghislain Roussel
Publications: ALAI Canada Newsletter

Canadian Parents for French (CPF) (1977)
#210, 309 Cooper St., Ottawa, ON K2P 0G5
613/235-1481, Fax: 613/230-5940, Email: cpf@vli.ca
Executive Director, J. Elmer Hynes
National Vice-President, Kate Merry
Interim Treasurer, Wendy Green
Publications: CPF Immersion Registry; CPF National News, 3 pa
Affiliates: Fédération des communautés francophones et acadienne du Canada; Association canadienne des professeurs d'immersion; Canadian Association of Second Language Teachers

Canadian Translators & Interpreters Council/ Conseil des traducteurs et interprètes du Canada (1956)
#1402, One Nicholas St., Ottawa, ON K1N 7B7
613/562-0379, Fax: 613/241-4098
President, Diane Blais-Ialenti
Executive Asssistant, Béatrice Dugué
Publications: Action CTIC

ASSOCIATION DES TRADUCTEURS ET INTERPRÈTES DU MANITOBA/ASSOCIATION OF TRANSLATORS & INTERPRETERS OF MANITOBA
200, av de la Cathédrale, CP 83, Winnipeg, MB R2H 0H7
204/233-1757

ASSOCIATION OF TRANSLATORS & INTERPRETERS OF ALBERTA/ ASSOCIATION DES TRADUCTEURS ET INTERPRÈTES DE L'ALBERTA (ATIA) (1979)
PO Box 2635, Stn M, Calgary, AB T2P 3C1
403/243-3477
President, Valerie Henitiuk
Publications: Transforum

Canadian Almanac & Directory 1997

ASSOCIATION OF TRANSLATORS & INTERPRETERS OF ONTARIO/ ASSOCIATION DES TRADUCTEURS ET INTERPRÈTES DE L'ONTARIO (ATIO) (1921)
#1202, One Nicholas St., Ottawa, ON K1N 7B7
613/241-2846, Fax: 613/241-4098
Executive Director, Marc Beaulieu
President, Joël Larrue
Sec.-Treas., Michel Trahan
Publications: informatio; Directory

ASSOCIATION OF TRANSLATORS & INTERPRETERS OF SASKATCHEWAN/ASSOCIATION DES TRADUCTEURS ET INTERPRÈTES DE LA SASKATCHEWAN (ATIS) (1981)
2341 Broad St., Regina, SK S4P 1Y9
306/522-2847
President, Catherine Laratte
Vice-President, Joan Boyer
Publications: ATIS Bulletin
Affiliates: Canadian Translators & Interpreters Council Regional North - American Centre (USA, Canada, Mexico); Fédération internationale des traducteurs

CORPORATION DES TRADUCTEURS, TRADUCTRICES, TERMINOLOGUES ET INTERPRÈTES DU NOUVEAU-BRUNSWICK/ CORPORATION OF TRANSLATORS, TERMINOLOGISTS & INTERPRETERS OF NEW BRUNSWICK (CTINB) (1970)
CP 427, Fredericton, NB E3B 4Z9
506/458-1519
Présidente, Nicole Vienneau
Publications: Bulletin de la CTINB/CTINB Bulletin; Répertoire/Directory, au deux ans
Organisation(s) affiliée(s): Fédération internationale des traducteurs

INTERPRETERS/TRANSLATORS SOCIETY OF NORTHWEST TERRITORIES (1989)
PO Box 995, Yellowknife, NT X1A 2N7
403/873-9715
President, Violet Hardisty

ORDRE DES TRADUCTEURS ET INTERPRÈTES AGRÉÉS DU QUÉBEC (OTIAQ) (1949)
#1108, 2021, rue Union, Montréal, PQ H3A 2S9
514/845-4411, Téléc: 514/845-9903, Ligne sans frais: 1-800-265-4815
Directrice générale, Lise Gauthier
Présidente, Michel Lemay
Relations publiques, Josette Martel
Publications: Antenne; Circuit, trimestriel; Répertoire annuel de tous les membres

SOCIETY OF TRANSLATORS & INTERPRETERS OF BRITISH COLUMBIA/SOCIÉTÉ DES TRADUCTEURS ET INTERPRÈTES DE COLOMBIE-BRITANNIQUE (1981)
#400, 905 Pender St. West, Vancouver, BC V6C 1L6
604/684-9371, Fax: 604/687-6130
President, Yolanda Hobrough
Publications: The Transletter; Directory, a.

Centre international de recherche en aménagement linguistique/International Center for Research on Language Planning (CIRAL) (1967)
Pavillon Charles-de-Koninck, Université Laval, Ste-Foy, PQ G1K 7P4
418/656-3232, Téléc: 418/656-7144, Courrier électronique: cirdoc@vmi.ulaval.ca
Directrice, Denise Deshaies

Dhe Internasional Union for Kanadan (IUK) (1987)
92 Glenholm Ave., Toronto, ON M6H 3B1
Internasional Prezident, Jonathan Kates/Keets
Publications: Dhe Times uv Toronto; The Kanadan Nuuzletter, 3 pa

Esperanto Association of Canada/Association canadienne d'esperanto (KEA) (1958)
Kanada Esperanto-Asocio
PO Box 2159, Sidney, BC V8L 3S6
URL: http://www.engcorp.com/kea/
President, Ciprian Jauca
Publications: Lumo; Esperanto Update, q.
Affiliates: Universal Esperanto Association - Rotterdam

AKADEMIO DE ESPERANTO - SEKCIO FAKAJ TERMINAROJ/ ACADEMY OF ESPERANTO - SECTION DICTIONARIES FOR SPECIAL FIELDS (1978)
54 Scriven Rd., RR#1, Bailieboro, ON K0L 1B0
705/939-6088
Director, R. Eichholz
Publications: Akademiaj Studoj
Affiliates: Akademio de Esperanto

CANADIAN ESPERANTO YOUTH/JEUNESSE ESPERANTISTE CANADIENNE (1976)
Junularo Esperantista Kanada
PO Box 2159, Sidney, BC V8L 3S6
250/474-3137, Email: phopkins@sol.uvic.ca
Secretary, Bruce Arthur
Publications: Juna Alumeto
Affiliates: World Esperanto Youth Organization

SOCIÉTÉ QUÉBÉCOISE D'ESPÉRANTO/ESPERANTO SOCIETY OF QUÉBEC (SQE) (1983)
6358A, rue de Bordeaux, Montréal, PQ H2G 2R8
514/272-0151, Téléc: 514/495-8442, Infoligne: 514/272-0151, Courrier électronique: normand.fleury@sympatico.ca
Président, Normand Fleury
Secrétaire-trésorier, Marco Maertens
Publications: La Riverego; Catalogue du service de librairie, annuel
Organisation(s) affiliée(s): Universala Esperanto-Asocio; Tutmonda Esperantista Junulara Organizo

WORLD ESPERANTO ASSOCIATION (UEA) (1908)
Universala Esperanto Associo
765 Braemar Ave., Sidney, BC V8L 5G5
250/656-1767, Email: uea@intern.nl.net
Canadian Representative, Olga du Temple

Fédération canadienne pour l'alphabétisation en français (FCAF) (1991)
235, ch Montréal, Vanier, ON K1L 6C7
613/749-5333, Téléc: 613/749-6660
Directrice générale, Luce Lapierre
Publications: de A à Z

International Reading Association (IRA) (1956)
800 Barksdale Rd., PO Box 8139, Newark, DE 19714-8139 USA
302/731-1600, ext.220, Fax: 302/731-1057
Executive Director, Alan E. Farstrup
Public Information Coordinator, Janet Butler
Publications: Reading Today; The Reading Teacher; Journal of Adolescent & Adult Literacy; Reading Research Quarterly; Lecturay Vida
Alberta - Northwest Territories: Coordinator, J. Stickle, 38 - 5 St. SW, Medicine Hat, AB T1A 4G4, 403/650-3001
Manitoba Branch: Coordinator, Betty Stewart, 204/726-5687, 1915 Braecrest Dr., Brandon, MB R7C 1A3
Nova Scotia Branch: Coordinator, Jane Baskwill, RR#1, Lawrencetown, NS B0S 1M0
Ontario Branch: Coordinator, Paul O'Brien, #1306, 260 Heath St., Toronto, ON M5P 3L6
Quebec Branch: Coordinator, Charlotte Colson, 5952, Ferncroft, Montréal, PQ H3X 1C7
Saskatchewan Branch: 82 - 4 Ave. North, Yorkton, SK S3N 1A5

Jane Austen Society of North America (JASNA) (1979)
200 Kingsmount Blvd., Sudbury, ON P3E 1K9
705/670-1357
Canadian Membership Secretary, Nancy Thurston
President, G. Bass
Publications: Persuasions; JASNA News, s-a.

Laubach Literacy Canada/Alphabétisation Laubach du Canada (1981)
#225, 70 Crown St., Saint John, NB E2L 2X6
506/634-1980, Fax: 506/634-0944
President, James B. Morrow
Publications: Literacy Connections
Affiliates: Laubach Literacy International

Literary Translators' Association of Canada/ Association des traducteurs et traductrices littéraires du Canada (LTCA) (1975)
3492, rue Laval, Montréal, PQ H2X 3C8
514/849-8540
President, Beatriz Zeller
Publications: Transmission; Répertoire/Directory, biennial

Manitoba Association for the Promotion of Ancestral Languages (MAPAL) (1983)
1574 Main St., Winnipeg, MB R2W 5J8
204/338-7951, Fax: 204/334-8277
Acting President, Laura Shabaga
Publications: Manitoba Heritage Review; Reaching Out

Movement for Canadian Literacy/ Rassemblement canadien pour l'alphabétisation (MCL) (1977)
458 MacLaren St., Ottawa, ON K1R 5K6
613/563-2464, Fax: 613/563-2504
Executive Director, Nancy Jennings
President, Susan Sussman
Publications: Hot Fax; Literacy Bin, 10 pa

Québec Society for the Promotion of English Language Literature/Société québécoise pour la promotion de la littérature de la langue anglaise (QSPELL)
1200 Atwater Ave., Montréal, PQ H3Z 1X6
514/933-0878, Fax: 514/933-0878
President, John Pepper
Secretary, Jeanne Randle

Saskatchewan Elocution & Debate Association/ Association d'élocution et des débats de la Saskatchewan (SEDA) (1974)
1860 Lorne St., Regina, SK S4P 2L7
306/780-9243, Fax: 306/781-6021
Executive Director, Doug Chase
Program Assistant, Tanya Sturgeon
Publications: Voice
Affiliates: Canadian Student Debating Federation

Saskatchewan Organization for Heritage Languages Inc. (SOHL) (1985)
2144 Cornwall St., Regina, SK S4P 2K7
306/780-9275, Fax: 306/780-9407, Toll Free: 1-800-780-9460, Email: schladmin@sasknet.sk.ca
Executive Director, Joan Kanigan-Fairen
President, Betty McDougall
Publications: SOHL Newsletter
Affiliates: Saskatchewan Council of Cultural Organizations

Sweetgrass First Nations Language Council (1989)
184 Mohawk St., PO Box 22019, Brantford, ON N3S 7B1
519/759-2650, Fax: 519/759-8912

Speaker, Dorothy Lazore
Publications: Sweetgrass News

World Literacy of Canada/Alphabétisation mondiale Canada (WLC) (1955)
59 Front St. East, Toronto, ON M5E 1B3
416/863-6262, Fax: 416/601-6984
Executive Director, Mamta Mishra
Canadian Program Officer, Stephanie Garrow
Publications: Worldlit

LAW
see also Prisoners & Ex-Offenders

The Advocates' Society (1963)
Campbell House, 160 Queen St. West, Toronto, ON M5H 3H3
416/597-0243, Fax: 416/597-1588
Executive Director, Alexandra Chyczij
Publications: The Advocates' Journal; The Advocates' Brief, 10 pa

Alberta Civil Trial Lawyers' Association (ACTLA) (1986)
#550, 10055 - 106 St., Edmonton, AB T5J 2Y2
403/429-1133, Fax: 403/429-1199, Toll Free: 1-800-665-7248
Executive Director, Lyn Bromilow
President, Gary J. Bigg
Publications: The Barrister
Affiliates: Association of Trial Lawyers of America

Alberta Federation of Police Associations (AFPA)
9636 - 102 Ave., Edmonton, AB T5H 0G5
403/429-0557, Fax: 403/428-0374
President, Darryl da Costa
Affiliates: Canadian Police Association

Alberta Government Civil Lawyers Association (AGCLA) (1976)
Alberta Justice, Civil Law Division, Bowker Building, 9833 - 109 St., 5th Fl., Edmonton, AB T5K 2E8
403/408-3311, Fax: 403/425-0307, Info Line: 403/498-3300
President, Herb Schlotter

Alberta Law Foundation (ALF) (1973)
#300, 407 - 8 Ave. SW, Calgary, AB T2P 1E5
403/264-4701
Executive Director, Owen G. Snider
Affiliates: Association of Canadian Law Foundations

Association of Canadian Courts Administrators (ACCA) (1975)
Court Services, Dept. of Justice, 9833 - 109 St., Edmonton, AB T5K 2E8
403/427-9620, Fax: 403/422-9639
President, Rod Wacewich
Vice-President, Thelma Costello
Secretary, Barbara Hookenson
Treasurer, William Wendt
Publications: Canadian Court Forum

Association des directeurs de polices et pompiers du Québec
1701, rue Parthenais, bur. C-1.12, Montréal, PQ H2K 3S7
514/521-2311, Téléc: 514/521-2311
Secrétaire-trésorier, Pierre-André Duchesneau

Association des juristes d'expression française de l'Ontario (AJEFO) (1980)
17 Copernicus St., Ottawa, ON K1N 6N5
613/564-6563, Téléc: 613/564-9878
Directeur général, Gérard Lévesque
Président, Guy Pratte

Directeur adjoint, Christian Hyde
Publications: L'Expression

Association des juristes d'expression française de la Saskatchewan/French Jurists Association of Saskatchewan (AJEFS) (1989)
2132 Broad St., Regina, SK S4P 1Y5
306/565-2507, Téléc: 306/781-7916
Présidente, Suzanne B. Stradecki
Publications: Bulletin des juristes

Association of Legal Court Interpreters & Translators/Association des interprètes et des traducteurs judiciares (1972)
2114, boul Saint-Laurent, Montréal, PQ H2X 2T2
514/845-3111, Fax: 514/845-3006
President, Henri Keleny
Translations Manager, Betty Farkas

Atlantic Association of Chiefs of Police
c/o Fredericton Police Department, 311 Queen St., Fredericton, NB E3B 1B1
506/452-9701, Fax: 506/450-2102
Sec.-Treas., R.M. Cronkhite
Publications: Atlantic News

Barreau de Montréal/Bar of Montréal (1849)
Palais de Justice, #980, 1, rue Notre Dame est, Montréal, PQ H2Y 1B6
514/866-9392, Téléc: 514/866-1488
Directeur général, Maurice Boileau

Barreau du Québec/Québec Bar Association (1849)
Maison du Barreau, 445, boul Saint-Laurent, Montréal, PQ H2Y 3T8
514/954-3400, Téléc: 514/954-3407
Directeur général, Pierre Gauthier
Publications: Journal du Barreau; Revue de Barreau; Rapport Annuel; Cours de formation permanente
Organisation(s) affiliée(s): Fédération des professions juridiques du Canada

Canadian Association of Chiefs of Police/ Association canadienne des chefs de police (CACP) (1905)
#1908, 112 Kent St., Ottawa, ON K1P 5P2
613/233-1106, Fax: 613/233-6960
Executive Director, Fred Schultz
President, Thomas O'Grady
Administrative Assistant & Office Manager, Catherine Toner
Publications: Canadian Police Chief Newsletter

Canadian Association on Competition Law/ Association canadienne d'étude du droit de la concurrence
55, rue Saint-Jacques, Montréal, PQ H2Y 3X2
514/987-6242, Fax: 514/845-7874, Telex: 05-268656 ROBIC
President, Jacques A. Léger
Affiliates: International League of Unfair Competition - Paris, France

Canadian Association of Crown Counsel
55 Munsee St., Cayuga, ON N0A 1E0
905/772-5043, Fax: 905/772-3494
President, Jean-Pierre Major

Canadian Association of Law Teachers/ Association canadienne des professeurs de droit (CALT)
c/o Canadian Bar Association, #902, 50 O'Connor St., Ottawa, ON K1P 6L2
URL: http://www.droit.umontreal.ca/acpd/liste/
President, Dr. Anne Stalker
Publications: CALT/ACPD Bulletin

Canadian Association of Legal Support Staff (CALSS) (1978)
PO Box 3186, Winnipeg, MB R3C 4E7
President, Sheila Down
Publications: Connection

Canadian Association of Police Boards (CAPB) (1989)
10 Peel Centre Dr., Brampton, ON L6T 4B9
905/458-1342, Fax: 905/458-7278
Executive Director, Frederick Biro, CAE
Publications: Police Board News; CAPB News, 10 pa

Canadian Association of Provincial Court Judges/Association Canadienne des Juges des Cours Provinciales (CAPCJ) (1973)
#207, 444 Yonge St., 2nd Fl., Toronto, ON M5B 2H4
416/325-8920, Fax: 416/325-8944
President, Judge James G. McNamee, 506/658-2568
Sec.-Treas., Judge Pamela Thomson, 416/325-8922
Publications: Provincial Judges Journal

Canadian Bar Association/Association du barreau canadien (CBA) (1921)
#902, 50 O'Connor St., Ottawa, ON K1P 6L2
613/237-2925, Fax: 613/237-0185, Toll Free: 1-800-267-8860, Email: info@cba.org
URL: http://cba.org/abc
Acting Executive Director, Steve Bresolin
President, Gordon Proudfoot
Publications: National; Canadian Bar Review, q.; Ottawa Report, q.; Canadian Bar Association Directory, a.
Affiliates: Canadian Association of Law Teachers; Canadian Law Information Council; Commonwealth Bar Association; Inter-American Bar Association; International Bar Association; Union internationale des avocats

Canadian Bar Foundation/Fondation du barreau canadien (1978)
#902, 50 O'Connor St., Ottawa, ON K1P 6L2
613/237-2925, Fax: 613/237-0185
President, Gordon Proudfoot
Publications: Canadian Bar Review; National, m.

Canadian Bar Insurance Association/Association d'assurance du barreau canadien (CBIA) (1966)
#5070, 3080 Yonge St., Toronto, ON M4N 3R2
416/488-0702, Fax: 416/488-2254
Contact, Barry Reynolds

Canadian Canon Law Society/Société canadienne de droit canonique (CCLS) (1966)
223 Main St., Ottawa, ON K1S 1C4
613/236-1393, ext.2215, Fax: 613/782-3005
Sec.-Treas., Lucy Gorman-McCoy
Publications: Newsletter of the Canadian Canon Law Society/Bulletin de nouvelles de La Société canadienne de droit canonique

Canadian Council on International Law/Conseil canadien de droit international (CCIL) (1972)
#215, 236 Metcalfe St., Ottawa, ON K2P 1R3
613/235-0442
Executive Director, Madeleine Renaud
Publications: Newsletter
Affiliates: Société québécoise de droit international; American Society of International Law; Japanese Association of International Law

Canadian Criminal Justice Association/ Association canadienne de justice pénale (CCJA) (1919)
#304, 383 Parkdale Ave., Ottawa, ON K1Y 4R4
613/725-3715, Fax: 613/725-3720, Email: ccja@istar.ca
Executive Director, Gaston St-Jean

Canadian Almanac & Directory 1997

Publications: The Bulletin; Canadian Journal of Criminology, q.; Justice Report, 3 pa; Directory of Justice Services; Directory of Services to Victims of Crime
Affiliates: Alberta Criminal Justice Association; British Columbia Criminal Justice Association; Manitoba Criminal Justice Association; New Brunswick Chapter, Canadian Criminal Justice Association; Newfoundland & Labrador Criminology & Corrections Association; Nova Scotia Criminology & Corrections Association; Ontario Association of Corrections & Criminology; Saskatchewan Criminal Justice Association

Canadian Institute for the Administration of Justice/Institut canadien d'administration de la justice (CIAJ) (1974)
Faculté de droit, Université de Montréal, CP 6128, Stn Centre-Ville, Montréal, PQ H3C 3J7
514/343-6157, Fax: 514/343-6296, Email: ciaj@umontreal.ca
Executive Director, Christine Robertson
Publications: CIAJ Newsletter

Canadian Law & Society Association/Association canadienne de droit et société (CLSA) (1985)
318 Osgoode, 4700 Keele St., Toronto, ON M3G 1P3
416/736-5037, Fax: 416/736-5615, Email: fzemans@yorku.ca
President, Wes Pue
Sec.-Treas., Fred Zemans
Publications: Canadian Journal of Law & Society/Revue canadienne de droit et société; ACDS/CLSA Bulletin

Canadian Maritime Law Association/Association canadienne de droit maritime (1951)
#2000, 360, rue Saint-Jacques, Montréal, PQ H2Y 1P5
514/849-4161, Fax: 514/849-4167
Sec.-Treas., J.A. Cantello
Publications: Membres/Members

Canadian Petroleum Law Foundation (1963)
c/o Canadian Occidental Petroleum Ltd., #1500, 635 - 8 Ave. SW, Calgary, AB T2P 3Z1
403/234-6700, Fax: 403/234-6971
Secretary, John B. McWilliams
Publications: Petroleum Law Supplement of Alberta Law Review

Canadian Police Association/L'Association canadienne des policiers (CPA) (1953)
141 Catherine St., Ottawa, ON K2P 1C3
613/231-4168, Fax: 613/231-3254, Email: cpa@igs.net
Executive Officer, Scott Newark
Publications: Yearbook; CPANews, m.; Express, q.

Canadian Society for the Advancement of Legal Technology/Association canadienne pour l'avancement de l'informatique juridique (CSALT)
#200, 20 Toronto St., Toronto, ON M5C 2B8
416/663-5290, Fax: 416/663-6502
URL: http://www.io.org/~csalt/csalt.htm
Administrator, Carolynn R. Parke, 416/420-2208, Fax: 416/420-3542
Publications: CSALT News; CSALT Review

Chambre des notaires du Québec (1847)
Ordre des notaires du Québec
#1700, 630, boul René-Lévesque ouest, Montréal, PQ H3B 1T6
514/879-1793, Téléc: 514/879-1923
Directeur général, Richard Gagnon

Publications: Revue du notariat; Cours de perfectionnement du notariat, semi-annuel; Entracte, 18 fois par an
Organisation(s) affiliée(s): Fédération des professions juridiques

Church Council on Justice & Corrections/Conseil des églises pour la justice et la criminologie (CCJC) (1974)
507 Bank St., 2nd Fl., Ottawa, ON K2P 1Z5
613/563-1688, Fax: 613/237-6129
Communication Coordinator, Rick Prashaw
Publications: Update/À Jour

Community Legal Education Association (Manitoba) Inc./Association d'éducation juridique communautaire (Manitoba) inc. (CLEA) (1985)
#304, 283 Bannatyne Ave., Winnipeg, MB R3B 3B2
204/943-2382; 943-2305(legal info./lawyer ref.), Fax: 204/943-3600, Toll Free: 1-800-262-8800, Email: clea@web.apc.org.
Executive Director, Alan Diduck
President, Don Lofendale
Publications: Manitoba Directory of Legal Services
Affiliates: Public Legal Education Association of Canada

Community Legal Education Ontario (CLEO) (1975)
#600, 119 Spadina Ave., Toronto, ON M5V 2L1
416/408-4420, Fax: 416/408-4424
Executive Director, Mary Marrone

Community Legal Information Association of Prince Edward Island (1985)
Sullivan Building, #158, 20 Fitzroy, PO Box 1207, Stn Central, Charlottetown, PE C1A 7M8
902/892-0853, Email: cliapei@web.apc.org
Executive Director, Ann Sherman
Publications: CLIA Newsletter

Continuing Legal Education Society of BC (1965)
#300, 845 Cambie St., Vancouver, BC V6B 5T2
250/699-3544, Fax: 250/669-9260, Toll Free: 1-800-663-0437
Executive Director, Jack J. Huberman, Q.C.

Corporation de service des notaires du Québec (1988)
#1660, 630, boul René-Lévesque ouest, Montréal, PQ H3B 1S6
514/861-6588, Téléc: 514/879-1093
Directrice générale, Danielle Godbout
Publications: Maître-usager
Organisation(s) affiliée(s): Chambre des notaires du Québec

County of York Law Association (1885)
361 University Ave., Toronto, ON M5G 1T3
416/327-5700, Fax: 416/947-9148, Email: matthea@gov.on.ca
Administrator, A. Matthewman
Publications: Vox

Court Interpreters Association of Ontario
#D, 1396A Yonge St., Toronto, ON M4T 1Y5
416/975-9564, Fax: 416/967-5281
President, Rajeshwar Singh

Criminal Lawyers' Association of Ontario (1971)
#700, 480 University Ave., Toronto, ON M5G 1V2
416/351-0853, Fax: 416/351-8131
Executive Director, Stephanie Mealing
Publications: Newsletter
Affiliates: Canadian Council of Criminal Defence Lawyers; National Association of Criminal Defense Lawyers - USA

Federation of Law Reform Agencies of Canada
c/o Manitoba Law Reform Commission, 405 Broadway, 12th Fl., Winnipeg, MB R3C 3L6
204/945-2900, Fax: 204/948-2184
President, Jeffrey A. Schnoor, Q.C., Email: jschnoor@jus.gov.mb.ca

Federation of Law Societies of Canada/Fédération des professions juridiques du Canada (1972)
#480, 445, boul Saint-Laurent, Montréal, PQ H2Y 2Y7
514/875-6350, Fax: 514/875-6115
Executive Director, Diane Bourque
Sec.-Treas., Patricia-Ann Foley

Fondation du barreau du Québec
#404, 445, boul Saint-Laurent, Montréal, PQ H2Y 3T8
514/954-3461, Téléc: 514/954-3449
Président, Henri Grondin
Président du conseil d'administration, Guy Gilbert

Foundation for Legal Research in Canada
c/o Canadian Bar Association, #902, 50 O'Connor St., Ottawa, ON K1P 6L2
613/237-2925, Fax: 613/237-0185
Treasurer, Stephen Bresolin

Institute of Law Clerks of Ontario (ILCO) (1968)
#1150, 36 Toronto St., Toronto, ON M5C 2C5
416/214-6252; Employment Hotline: 416/214-6256
President, Lynn Sweeney
Secretary, Carolyn Keates
Publications: Law Clerks Review

International Commission of Jurists (Canadian Section)/La Commission Internationale de Juristes (Section canadienne) (ICJ)
#902, 50 O'Connor St., Ottawa, ON K1P 6L2
613/237-2925 (Wed. only), Fax: 613/237-0185
Executive Secretary, Patricia Whiting

Law Foundation of British Columbia
#1340, 605 Robson St., Vancouver, BC V6B 5J3
604/688-2337, Fax: 604/688-4586
Executive Director, Jane MacFadgen

Law Foundation of Newfoundland
PO Box 5907, Stn C, St. John's, NF A1C 5X4
709/754-4424, Fax: 709/754-4320
Chairman, P.D. Lewis, Q.C.

Law Foundation of Nova Scotia
PO Box 325, Halifax, NS B3J 2N7
902/422-8335, Fax: 902/492-0424
Executive Director, Mary Helleiner

Law Foundation of Ontario/La fondation du droit de l'Ontario
#2210, 20 Queen St. West, Toronto, ON M5H 3R3
416/598-1550, Fax: 416/598-1526
Controller & Secretary, Mary Shannon Brown
Chair, Roger D. Yachetti, QC

Law Foundation of Prince Edward Island (1972)
49 Water St., Charlottetown, PE C1A 7K2
902/566-1666, Fax: 902/368-7557
Executive Director, Kathy Stuart
Chair, John Mitchell, LLB
Affiliates: Association of Canadian Bar Foundations

Law Foundation of Saskatchewan
#620, 2220 - 12 Ave., Regina, SK S4P 0M8
306/352-1121, Fax: 306/522-3499
Chairman, H. Harry Dahlem, Q.C.

Law Society of Alberta (1907)
#600, 919 - 11 Ave. SW, Calgary, AB T2R 1P3
403/229-4700, Fax: 403/228-1728

URL: http://www.law.ualberta.ca/lawsociety
Secretary, Peter L. Freeman, Q.C.
Publications: The Benchers' Advisory
Affiliates: Federation of Law Societies of Canada

Law Society of British Columbia (1884)
845 Cambie St., 8th Fl., Vancouver, BC V6B 4Z9
604/669-2533, Fax: 604/669-5232
Secretary, Bryan F. Ralph, Q.C.
Publications: Benchers' Bulletin
Affiliates: Federation of Law Societies of Canada

Law Society of Manitoba
219 Kennedy St., Winnipeg, MB R3C 1S8
204/942-5571, Fax: 204/956-0624
CEO, Deborah J. McCawley, Q.C.
Publications: Communique
Affiliates: Federation of Law Societies of Canada

Law Society of New Brunswick/Barreau du Nouveau-Brunswick
#206, 1133 Regent St., Fredericton, NB E3B 3Z2
506/458-8540, Fax: 506/451-1421
President, Sherron J.L. Hughes, QC
Vice-President, Peter Zed
Treasurer, Gilles Godbout
Secretary, Michel Carrier
Affiliates: Federation of Law Societies of Canada

Law Society of Newfoundland
Atlantic Place, 5th Fl., PO Box 1028, Stn C, St. John's, NF A1C 5M3
709/722-4740, Fax: 709/722-8902
Executive Director, Peter G. Ringrose
Affiliates: Federation of Law Societies of Canada

Law Society of the Northwest Territories/Le Barreau des Territoires du Nord-Ouest (1978)
4916 - 47 St., PO Box 1298, Yellowknife, NT X1A 2N9
403/873-3828, Fax: 403/873-6344
Executive Director, Becky McCaffrey
Publications: Northwest Territories Reports
Affiliates: Federation of Law Societies of Canada

Law Society of Prince Edward Island (1876)
49 Water St., PO Box 128, Charlottetown, PE C1A 7K2
902/566-1666, Fax: 902/368-7557
Sec.-Treas., Beverly Mills Stetson, LLB
Director of Administration, Kathy Stuart
Affiliates: Federation of Law Societies of Canada

Law Society of Saskatchewan (LSS) (1907)
#1100, 2500 Victoria Ave., Regina, SK S4P 3X2
306/569-8242, Fax: 306/352-2989
Secretary & Director of Administration, A. Kirsten Logan
General Counsel & Co-Director of Administration, Allan T. Snell
Senior Counsel, Iain A. Mentiply
Publications: LSS Newsletter
Affiliates: Federation of Law Societies of Canada

Law Society of Upper Canada (LSUC) (1797)
Osgoode Hall, 130 Queen St. West, Toronto, ON M5H 2N6
416/947-3300, Fax: 416/947-5967
Secretary, Richard F. Tinsley
Publications: Benchers' Bulletin
Affiliates: Federation of Law Societies of Canada

Law Society of Yukon (YLS) (1985)
Yukon Law Society
#201, 302 Steele St., Whitehorse, YT Y1A 2C5
403/668-4231, Fax: 403/667-7556
President, Kenneth A. Dyler
1st Vice-President, Terrence W. Boylan
2nd Vice-President, Malcolm E.J. Campbell
Secretary, Rodney G. Garson

Treasurer, Geraldine J. Hutchings
Publications: LSY Newsletter
Affiliates: Federation of Law Societies of Canada

Legal Education Society of Alberta (LESA) (1975)
Canada Trust Tower, #2610, 10104 - 103 Ave., Edmonton, AB T5J 0H8
403/420-1987, Fax: 403/425-0885, Toll Free: 1-800-282-3900, Email: lesa@lesa.org
URL: http://www.law.ualberta.ca/lesa/
Executive Director, Hugh A. Robertson, Q.C.

Manitoba Association of Crown Attorneys/Association des avocats de la couronne du Manitoba (1974)
405 Broadway Ave., Winnipeg, MB R3C 3L6
204/945-0242, Fax: 204/948-2041
President, Gord Hannon

The Manitoba Law Foundation/La Fondation manitobaine du droit
412 McDermot Ave., Winnipeg, MB R3A 0A9
204/947-3142, Fax: 204/942-3221
Executive Director, W.K. Greenaway, Ph.D., LL.B.

Municipal Law Enforcement Officers' Association (Ontario) Inc. (1979)
PO Box 247, Wasaga Beach, ON L0L 2P0
705/429-2511
President, B. Russell
Vice-President, D.H. Kemp
Publications: The Summit

National Judicial Institute
#202, 100 Metcalfe St., Ottawa, ON K1P 5M1
613/237-1118
Executive Director, Judge Dolores Hansen

New Brunswick Law Foundation/Fondation pour l'avancement du droit au Nouveau-Brunswick (1975)
#204, 1133 Regent St., Fredericton, NB E3B 3Z2
506/453-7776, Fax: 506/451-1421
Chairman, Harry H. Williamson

New Brunswick Probation Officers Association Inc.
Justice Bldg., Rm. 110, Queen St., Fredericton, NB E3B 5E2
506/453-2367
President, K. Douglas Pitts

Northwest Territories Association of Provincial Court Judges
Court House, PO Box 297, Iqaluit, NT X0A 0H0
403/979-5450, Fax: 403/979-6384
Judge Beverley. Browne
Publications: Newsletter

Northwest Territories Law Foundation
PO Box 2594, Yellowknife, NT X1A 2P9
403/873-8275, Fax: 403/873-6064
Executive Manager, Wendy Carter

Nova Scotia Barristers' Society (1857)
#1101, 1645 Granville St., Halifax, NS B3J 1X3
902/422-1491, Fax: 902/429-4869
Executive Director, Darrel I. Pink
Administration Director, Victoria Rees
Publications: Society Record; Law News, bi-m.; Current Law, m.
Affiliates: Continuing Legal Education Society; Public Legal Education Society; Law Foundation; Canadian Bar Association

Ontario Association of Chiefs of Police (OACP) (1952)
PO Box 193, Sault Ste Marie, ON P6A 5L6

705/946-6389, Fax: 705/942-2093
Executive Director, William M. Malpass

Ontario Association of Police Services Boards (OAPSB) (1962)
#601, 920 Yonge St., Toronto, ON M4W 3C7
416/323-9343, Fax: 416/323-3955
Executive Director, Sandi L. Humphrey, CAE
Publications: PSB News

Ontario Crown Attorneys Association (OCAA) (1946)
#1420, 439 University Ave., Toronto, ON M5G 1Y8
416/599-4499, Fax: 416/599-4609
President, Paul Vesa

Ontario Family Law Judges' Association/Association des juges de la cour de famille de l'Ontario
80 Dundas St. East, PO Box 5600, Stn A, London, ON N6A 2P3
519/660-3045
Secretary, Judge Eleanor Schnall

Ontario Judges Association/Association des juges provinciaux des tribunaux criminels de l'Ontario (1952)
c/o Ontario Court (Provincial Division), #1000, 200 Frederick St., Kitchener, ON N2H 6P1
519/741-3366, Fax: 519/741-3399
Judge Donald C. Downie
Affiliates: Canadian Association of Provincial Court Judges

People's Law School
#150, 900 Howe St., Vancouver, BC V6Z 2M4
604/331-5400, Fax: 604/331-5401
Executive Director, Gordon Hardy

Police Association of Ontario/Association des policiers de l'Ontario (PAO) (1944)
#1, 6730 Davand Dr., Mississauga, ON L5T 2K8
905/670-9770, Fax: 905/670-9755
Administrator, David Griffin
President, John Moor
Publications: News Bulletin

Prince Edward Island Association of Chiefs of Police (PEIACP)
c/o Borden-Carleton Community Police, PO Box 69, Borden-Carleton, PE C0B 1X0
902/437-2228, Fax: 902/437-6049
Contact, Chief Jamie Fox

Probation Officers Association of Ontario
PO Box 582, Cobourg, ON K9A 4C3
613/523-4985, Fax: 613/523-1096
President, Penny Arp

Provincial Judges Association of Manitoba
Provincial Court, 408 York Ave., 5th Fl., Winnipeg, MB R3C 0P9
204/945-8005, Fax: 204/945-0552
Judge Ronald J. Meyers

Provincial Prosecutors Association
c/o Court House, 155 Elm St. West, Sudbury, ON P3C 1T9
705/671-5900, Fax: 705/675-4146
President, Wayne Gervais

The Public Interest Advocacy Centre/Centre pour la défense de l'intérêt public (PIAC) (1976)
#1204, One Nicholas St., Ottawa, ON K1N 7B7
613/562-4002, Fax: 613/562-0007
Executive Director, Michael Janigan
Publications: Consumer Advocacy Manual

Public Legal Education Association of Saskatchewan, Inc. (PLEA Sask.) (1980)
#115, 701 Cynthia St., Saskatoon, SK S7L 6B7
306/653-1868, Fax: 306/653-1869, Email: pleasask@web.apc.org
URL: http://www.sfn.saskatoon.sk.ca/education/pleasask/index.html
Co-Director, Doug Surtees
Co-Director, Joel Janow
President, Lucille Lamb
Publications: PLEA

Public Legal Education Society of Nova Scotia (PLENS) (1982)
#911, 6080 Young St., Halifax, NS B3K 5L2
902/454-2198, Fax: 902/455-3105, Info Line: 902/455-3135, Toll Free: 1-800-665-9779
Executive Director, Maria G. Franks
President, Carmen Moir
Publications: PLE News

Public Legal Information Association of Newfoundland (PLIAN) (1984)
PO Box 1064, Stn C, St. John's, NF A1C 5M5
709/722-2643, Fax: 709/722-8902, Email: plian@web.apc.org
Executive Director, Heidi A. Wells, LL.B.

Société de criminologie du Québec
#620, 425, rue Viger ouest, Montréal, PQ H2Z 1X2
514/873-4239, Téléc: 514/873-6460
Secrétaire général, Samir Rizkalla, Ph.D.
Publications: Ressources-et-vous

The Society of Notaries Public of British Columbia (1926)
#621, 736 Granville St., Vancouver, BC V6Z 1G3
604/681-4516, Fax: 604/681-7258
Secretary, Stanley J. Nicol

Yukon Law Foundation
PO Box 5330, Whitehorse, YT Y1A 4Z2
403/668-4231, Fax: 403/667-7556
Executive Secretary, Jan Graham

Yukon Public Legal Education Association (YPLEA) (1984)
Yukon College, PO Box 2799, Whitehorse, YT Y1A 5K4
403/668-5297, Fax: 403/668-5541, Toll Free: 1-800-668-5297
Contact, Susan Dennehy

LIBRARIES & ARCHIVES

Administrators of Medium Public Libraries of Ontario (AMPLO)
Whitby Public Library, 405 Dundas St., Whitby, ON L1N 6A1
905/668-6541, Fax: 905/668-7445
Chair, Ken Roberts

Alberta Association of College Librarians (AACL)
Grant MacEwan Community College, Learning Resources Centre, 10700 - 104 Ave., Edmonton, AB T5J 4S2
403/497-5894, Fax: 403/497-5895, Email: aaclserv@acd.mhc.ab.ca
Contact, Patricia Lloyd
Publications: AACL Newsletter

Alberta Association of Library Technicians (AALT) (1974)
PO Box 700, Edmonton, AB T5J 2L4
403/422-8243
President, Kim Varey
Publications: AALT Technician

Alberta Government Libraries' Council (AGLC) (1975)
Cooperative Government Library Services Section, 902 Legislature Annex, 9718 - 107 St., Edmonton, AB T5K 1E4
403/427-3837, Fax: 403/427-1623
Coordinator, Karen Powell

American Society for Information Science - Western Canada Chapter
WesCan ASIS
c/o University of Lethbridge Library, 4401 University Dr., Lethbridge, AB T1K 3M4
403/329-2008, Fax: 403/329-2022
Chair, Leona Jacobs

Art Libraries Society of North America (ARLIS/NA)
#201, 4101 Lake Boone Trail, Raleigh, NC 27607 USA
919/787-5181, Fax: 919/787-4916, Toll Free: 1-800-892-7547, Email: arlisna@mercury.interpath.com
URL: http://caroline.eastlib.ufl.edu/arlis/
Executive Director, Penney De Pas, CAE

Association des bibliothécaires professionel(le)s du Nouveau-Brunswick/Association of Professional Librarians of New Brunswick (ABPNB) (1992)
Oromocto Public Library, 54 Miramichi Rd., Oromocto, NB E2V 1S2
506/357-3329, Téléc: 506/357-2266
Présidente, Muriel Morton, 506/357-3329, Téléc: 506/357-2266
Vice-présidente, Sylvie Nadeau, 506/632-2807, Téléc: 506/632-2235
Trésorier, Jean-Claude Arcand
Secrétaire, Marilynn Rudi
Publications: Biblio-Net

Association des bibliothécaires du Québec/ Québec Library Association (ABQ) (1932)
CP 1095, Pointe Claire, PQ H9S 4H9
514/630-4875
Secrétaire exécutive, Marie Eberlin
Publications: Bulletin; Read: A Guide to Excellent Books for Children & Young Adults; Lire

Association des bibliothèques de droit de Montréal/Montréal Association of Law Libraries (ABDM) (1987)
#900, 1000, rue de la Gauchetière, Montréal, PQ H3B 4W5
514/954-3159, Téléc: 514/393-1919, Courrier électronique: charest@cam.org
Bibliothécaire, Ronald Charest
Publications: Info

Association des bibliothèques publiques de l'Estrie (ABIPE) (1990)
5086, rue Frontenac, Lac Mégantic, PQ G6B 1H3
819/583-0876, Téléc: 819/583-0878
Président, Yves Tanguay

Association des bibliothèques de la région Mauricie-Bois-Francs (1985)
Bibli-o-Coeur
Bibliothèque de Shawinigan, 550, de l'Hôtel de Ville, CP 400, Shawinigan, PQ G9N 6V3
819/536-7218, Téléc: 819/536-7255
Présidente, Charlotte Lecours-Picard

Association of Canadian Archivists (ACA) (1975)
PO Box 2596, Stn D, Ottawa, ON K1P 5W6
613/443-0251, Fax: 613/443-0261, Email: ltardif@magmacom.com
President, Terry Thompson
Sec.-Treas., Patrick Burden
Office Manager, Lyne St-Hilaire-Tardif
Publications: Archivaria; ACA Bulletin, bi-m.
Affiliates: Bureau of Canadian Archivists

ARCHIVES ASSOCIATION OF ONTARIO/L'ASSOCIATION DES ARCHIVES DE L'ONTARIO (AAO) (1993)
PO Box 46009, Stn College Park, Toronto, ON M5B 2L8
416/792-1173, Fax: 416/792-2530
President, Stephen Posner
Executive Assistant, Barbara Schon
Publications: Archives Grants Guide; Off the Record, bi-m.; Directory of Ontario Archives 1995
Affiliates: Ontario Heritage Foundation

ASSOCIATION DES ARCHIVISTES DU QUÉBEC (AAQ) (1967)
CP 423, Sillery, PQ G1T 2R8
418/652-2357, Téléc: 418/646-0868, Courrier électronique: aaq@libertel.montreal.qc.ca
URL: http://www.libertel.montreal.qc.ca/info/aaq
Secrétaire administrative, Sylvie Parent
Publications: La Chronique; Archives, trimestriel

ASSOCIATION OF NEWFOUNDLAND & LABRADOR ARCHIVES (ANLA) (1982)
Colonial Building, Military Rd., St. John's, NF A1C 2C9
709/726-2867, Fax: 709/729-0578
President, Larry Dohey
Vice-President, Joan Ritcey
Secretary, Iris Power
Treasurer, Howard Brown
Publications: ANLA Bulletin; Directory of Archival Holdings in Newfoundland & Labrador

SASKATCHEWAN ARCHIVISTS SOCIETY (SAS) (1988)
#120, 3303 Hillsdale, Regina, SK S4S 6W9
306/787-4741, Fax: 306/787-1975
President, Lenora Toth
Vice-President, Eric Anderson
Secretary, Paula Rein
Publications: Checklist

Association of Canadian Map Libraries & Archives/Association des cartothèques et archives cartographiques du Canada (ACMLA) (1967)
Visual & Sound Archives Division, National Archives of Canada, 344 Wellington St., Ottawa, ON K1A 0N3
613/996-6009; 7611, Fax: 613/995-6575
Membership Chairperson, Bruce Weedmark
President, Auringer Wood
Publications: ACMLA Bulletin; Directory of Canadian Map Collections; University Map Libraries in Canada: A Folio of Selected Plans; Guide for a Small Map Collection; Canadian Fire Insurance Plans in Ontario

Association des directeurs de bibliothèques publiques du Québec
Bibliothèque Gabrielle-Roy, 350, rue Saint-Joseph est, Québec, PQ G1K 3B2
418/529-0924, Téléc: 418/529-1588
Présidente, Jean Payer
Publications: DEFI

Association of Parliamentary Librarians in Canada/Association des bibliothécaires parlementaires au Canada (ABPAC)
c/o Library of Parliament, 111 Wellington St., Ottawa, ON K1A 0A9
613/996-4934, Fax: 613/996-7092
Contact, François Le May
Publications: APLIC Bulletin

Association pour l'avancement des sciences et des techniques de la documentation (ASTED) (1973)
202, 3414, av du Parc, Montréal, PQ H2X 2H5
514/281-5012, Téléc: 514/281-8219, Courrier électronique: info@asted.org
URL: http://www.asted.org
Directeur général, Louis Cabral
Président, Joanne Cournoyer
Publications: Nouvelles ASTED; Documentation et bibliothèques, trimestriel
Organisation(s) affiliée(s): Fédération internationale des bibliothécaires (IFLA); Fédération internationale de documentation (FID); Fédération des associations de bibliothécaires, archivistes et documentalistes des états francophones (FABADEF)

Association des responsables des bibliothèques/centres de documentation universitaires et recherche d'expression française au Canada (ABCDEF-Canada) (1991)
CP 400, Succ. Côte des Neiges, Montréal, PQ H3S 2S7
Président, Claude Bonnelly
Vice-président, Albert Lévesque
Publications: Répertoire des Journaux et périodiques de langue française

Association of Small Public Libraries of Ontario (ASPLO) (1981)
St. Marys Public Library, 15 Church St. North, St Marys, ON N4X 1B4
519/284-3346, Fax: 519/284-2630
Chairman, Barb Taylor

Atlantic Provinces Library Association (APLA) (1957)
School of Library & Information Studies, Dalhousie University, 6225 University Ave., Halifax, NS B3H 4H8
902/494-3656, Fax: 902/494-2319
President, Susan Libby
Publications: APLA Bulletin

BC Courthouse Library Society
800 Smithe St., Vancouver, BC V6Z 2E1
604/660-2910, Fax: 604/660-9418, Toll Free: 1-800-665-2570, Email: bccls@bccls.bc.ca
Chief Librarian & Executive Officer, Maureen B. McCormick

Bibliographical Society of Canada/Société bibliographique du Canada (BSC) (1946)
PO Box 575, Stn P, Toronto, ON M5S 2T1
Email: dondertman@library.utoronto.ca
URL: http://www.library.utoronto.ca/~bsc
President, Thomas Vincent
Secretary, Anne Dondertman
Publications: BSC Bulletin; Papers/Cahiers, s-a.

Les Bibliothèques publics du Québec - Montérégie (1981)
Bibliothèque Municipale de Beloeil, 620, rue Richelieu, Beloeil, PQ J3G 5E8
514/467-7872, Téléc: 514/467-3257
Présidente, Sylvie Provost
Vice-Présidente, Johanne Guevremont
Secrétaire, Alain Larouche

Bibliothèques publiques du Bas-Saint-Laurent
CRSBP du Bas-St-Laurent, 465, rue St-Pierre, Rivière-du-Loup, PQ G5R 4T6
418/867-1682
Présidente, Nicole Gagnon
Secrétaire-trésorier, Yves Savard

Les bibliothèques publiques des régions de Québec et Chaudière-Appalaches (1989)
3189, rue Albert-Demers, Charny, PQ G6X 3A1
418/832-6166, Téléc: 418/832-6168
Présidente, Lucie Gobeil
Trésorière, Claire Sénéclauze
Secrétaire, Claudette Auger

British Columbia Library Association (BCLA) (1911)
#110, 6545 Bonsor Ave., Burnaby, BC V5H 1H3
604/430-9633, Fax: 604/430-8595, Email: bcla@unixg.ubc.ca
URL: http://www.interchg.ubc.ca/bcla
President, Ron Clancy
Publications: BCLA Reporter

British Columbia Library Trustees Association (BCLTA) (1978)
#110, 6545 Bonsor Ave., Burnaby, BC V5H 1H3
604/430-9626, Fax: 604/430-8595, Email: bclta@mind-link.bc.ca
President, Daniel Greene
Publications: Open Door

Bureau canadien des archivistes/Bureau of Canadian Archivists
CP 2485, Succ. D, Ottawa, ON K1P 5W6
613/996-7778, Téléc: 613/995-6226
Secrétaire générale, Sylvie Gervais

Canadian Association of Children's Librarians (CACL)
c/o Canadian Library Association, #602, 200 Elgin St., Ottawa, ON K2P 1L5
613/232-9625, Fax: 613/563-9895, Email: ai077@freenet.carleton.ca
President, Joanne Grierer

Canadian Association of College & University Libraries (CACUL) (1963)
c/o Canadian Library Association, #602, 200 Elgin St., Ottawa, ON K2P 1L5
613/232-9625, Fax: 613/563-9895
President, Frank Winter, 306/966-5942, Email: winter@sklib.usask.ca

The Canadian Association of Family Resource Programs/L'Association canadienne des programmes de ressources pour la famille (1975)
FRP Canada
#205, 120 Holland Ave., Ottawa, ON K1Y 0X6
613/728-3307, Fax: 613/729-5421
Executive Director, Alla Ivask
Publications: Play & Parenting Connections; FRP Canada Directory, a.

Canadian Association for Information Science/Association canadienne des sciences de l'information (CAIS) (1974)
CAIS Secretariat, FIS, University of Toronto, 140 Saint George St., Toronto, ON M5S 1A1
416/978-8876, Fax: 416/971-1399
President, Kent Weaver
Ottawa Chapter President, Pat Johnston, 613/737-2207
West Chapter President, Jocelyn Godolphin, 604/228-2499
Publications: The Canadian Journal of Information & Library Science/Revue canadienne des sciences de l'information et de bibliotechéconomie

Canadian Association of Law Libraries/Association canadienne des bibliothèques de droit (CALL) (1961)
190 Railway St., PO Box 1570, Kingston, ON K7L 5C8
613/531-9338, Fax: 613/531-0626, Email: call@adan.kingston.net
URL: http://www.kingston.net/iknet/call
Administrative Officer, Elizabeth Hooper
Publications: Canadian Law Libraries

Canadian Association of Music Libraries, Archives & Documentation Centres Inc./Association canadienne des bibliothèques, archives et centres de documentation musicaux inc. (CAML) (1973)
National Library of Canada, Music Division, 395 Wellington St., Ottawa, ON K1A 0N4
613/996-2300, Fax: 613/952-2895, Email: stm@psb.nlc-bnc.ca
URL: http://www.caml.yorku.ca/
President, Dr. S. Timothy Maloney
Publications: CAML Newsletter/Les Nouvelle de l'ACBM
Affiliates: International Association of Music Libraries, Archives & Documentation Centres

Canadian Association of Public Libraries (CAPL) (1972)
c/o Brentwood Branch, Etobicoke Public Library, 36 Brentwood Rd. North, Etobicoke, ON M8X 2B5
416/394-5245, Fax: 416/394-5257
President, Virginia Van Vliet

Canadian Association of Research Libraries/Association des bibliothèques de recherche du Canada (CARL) (1976)
Morisset Hall, University of Ottawa, #602, 65 University St., Ottawa, ON K1N 9A5
613/562-5800, ext.3652, Fax: 613/562-5195
Interim Executive Director, Timothy Mark
President, Carolynne Presser

Canadian Association of Special Libraries & Information Services (CASLIS) (1969)
#29, 3 Greystone Walk, Scarborough, ON M1K 5J4
403/261-1263
President, Mary-Lu Brennan
Publications: Special Issues

Canadian Council of Archives/Conseil canadien des archives (CCA) (1985)
West Memorial Bldg., #1109, 344 Wellington St., Ottawa, ON K1A 0N3
613/995-2373, Fax: 613/947-6662, Email: mhoude@archives.ca
Executive Director, Michel Houde
Chairperson, Christopher Hives
Publications: Directory of Canadian Archives; Institutional Guidelines for Small Archives

ARCHIVES ASSOCIATION OF BRITISH COLUMBIA (AABC) (1990)
PO Box 78530, RPO University, Vancouver, BC V6T 1Z4
URL: http://www.harbour.com/AABC/
President, Joni Mitchell, 604/360-2577
Publications: AABC Newsletter

ARCHIVES COUNCIL OF PRINCE EDWARD ISLAND (1987)
Public Archives, George Coles Bldg., PO Box 1000, Charlottetown, PE C1A 7M4
902/368-4351, Fax: 902/368-5544
President, Marilyn Bell

ARCHIVES SOCIETY OF ALBERTA (ASA) (1993)
PO Box 21080, RPO Dominion, Calgary, AB T2P 4H5
President, Bryan Corbett
Publications: ASA Newsletter

ASSOCIATION FOR MANITOBA ARCHIVES (1992)
PO Box 26005, RPO Westminster, Winnipeg, MB R3C 4K9
204/477-8086
Program Coordinator, Diane Haglund
Publications: Communique
Affiliates: Association of Canadian Archivists

COUNCIL OF ARCHIVES NEW BRUNSWICK/CONSEIL DES ARCHIVES DU NOUVEAU-BRUNSWICK (CANB) (1985)
c/o Provincial Archives of New Brunswick, PO Box 6000, Fredericton, NB E3B 5H1
506/453-2122, Fax: 506/453-3288
Contact, Fred Farrell
Publications: CANB Gazette

COUNCIL OF NOVA SCOTIA ARCHIVES (CNSA) (1983)
c/o Public Archives of Nova Scotia, 6016 University Ave., Halifax, NS B3H 1W4
902/424-7093, Fax: 902/424-0628, Email: cnsa@fox.nstn.ca
President, Carolyn Gimian
Education & Outreach Archivist, Johanna Smith
Publications: Council of Nova Scotia Archives Newsletter
Affiliates: Federation of NS Heritage; Society of American Archivists; Association of Canadian Archivists

NORTHWEST TERRITORIES ARCHIVES COUNCIL (NWTAC) (1985)
c/o Northwest Territories Archives, Government of the Northwest Territories, PO Box 1320, Yellowknife, NT X1A 2L9
403/873-7698, Fax: 403/873-0205
President, Dr. Richard Valpy

RÉSEAU DES ARCHIVES DU QUÉBEC (RAQ) (1987)
CP 160, Succ. D, Montréal, PQ H3K 3B9
514/954-3400, Téléc: 514/954-3463
Présidente, Thérèse Perreault
Secrétaire-trésorier, Agathe Dunan
Publications: Bulletin du RAQ

SASKATCHEWAN COUNCIL OF ARCHIVES (1987)
PO Box 22041, Regina, SK S4S 7G7
306/787-4066, Fax: 306/787-1975
President, Trevor Powell

YUKON COUNCIL OF ARCHIVES (YCA) (1986)
PO Box 6053, Whitehorse, YT Y1A 5L7
403/667-5321, Fax: 403/393-6253, Email: lbuchan@gov.yk.ca
President, Lesley Buchan
Publications: YCA Newsletter

Canadian Council of Library Schools/Conseil canadien des écoles de bibliothéconomie (CCLS)
École de Bibliothéconomie et des Sciences de l'Information, CP 6128, Succ. A, Montréal, PQ H3C 3J7
514/343-7400, Téléc: 514/343-5753
Président, Prof. Gilles Deschatelets

Canadian Health Libraries Association/ Association des bibliothèques de la santé du Canada (CHLA) (1976)
3332 Yonge St., PO Box 94038, Toronto, ON M4N 3R1
416/485-0377, Fax: 416/485-0377, Email: Envoy 100: chla
President, Lea Starr
Office of Secretariat, Dorothy Davey
Publications: Bibliotheca Medica Canadiana; Directory, a.
Affiliates: Ontario Hospital Libraries Association

ASSOCIATION DES BIBLIOTHÈQUES DE LA SANTÉ DE MONTRÉAL/MONTRÉAL HEALTH LIBRARIES ASSOCIATION
Centre de documentation, Centre hospitalier Côte-des-Neiges, 4565, ch de la Reine-Marie, Montréal, PQ H3W 1W5
514/340-1424, ext.3266, Téléc: 514/340-3500
Présidente, Louise Bourbonnais

CENTRAL ONTARIO HEALTH LIBRARIES ASSOCIATION
Library, Oshawa General Hospital, 24 Alma St., Oshawa, ON L1G 2B9
905/576-8711, ext.3567, Fax: 905/433-2859, Email: library@hospital.oshawa.on.ca
President, Susan Hendricks

HEALTH LIBRARIES ASSOCIATION OF BRITISH COLUMBIA (HLABC) (1980)
BC Cancer Agency, 600 - 10th Ave. West., Vancouver, BC V5Z 4E6
604/877-6000, ext.2692, Fax: 604/872-4596, Email: bccalib@wimsey.com
President, Beth Morrison
Publications: HLABC Forum

KINGSTON AREA HEALTH LIBRARIES ASSOCIATION (KAHLA)
Staff Library, Kingston Psychiatric Hospital, PO Box 603, Kingston, ON K7L 4X3
613/546-1101, ext.5745, Fax: 613/548-5588, Email: Envoy:ill.okph
President, Karen Gagnon

LONDON AREA HEALTH LIBRARIES ASSOCIATION (LAHLA)
Medical Library, London Psychiatric Hospital, PO Box 2532, Terminal A, London, ON N6A 4H1
519/455-5110, ext.2167, Fax: 519/455-9986, Email: mwhy@julian.uwo.ca
President, Mai Why

MANITOBA HEALTH LIBRARIES ASSOCIATION (MHLA) (1979)
Medical Library, Univ. of Manitoba, 770 Bannatyne Ave., Winnipeg, MB R3E 0W3
204/237-2808, Fax: 204/235-3339, Email: poluha@bldghsc.lan1.umanitoba.ca
President, David Colborne
Secretary, Mark Rabnett
Publications: MHLA News

MARITIMES HEALTH LIBRARIES ASSOCIATION/ASSOCIATION DES BIBLIOTHÈQUES DE LA SANTÉ DES MARITIMES (MHLA)
Dr. Everett Chalmers Hospital, 700 Priestman St., PO Box 9000, Fredericton, NB E3B 5N5
506/452-5432, Fax: 506/452-5571, Email: dlibrary@nbnet.nb.ca
President, Paul E. Clark
Publications: MHLA/ABSM Bulletin

NEWFOUNDLAND & LABRADOR HEALTH LIBRARIES ASSOCIATION (NLHLA) (1978)
School of Nursing Library, Salvation Army Grace General Hospital, 241 LeMarchant Rd., St. John's, NF A1E 1P9
709/778-6645, Fax: 709/722-0449, Email: doreilly@cabot.fac.nf.ca
President, Debbie O'Reilly

NORTHERN ALBERTA HEALTH LIBRARIES ASSOCIATION
6 Longview Cres., St. Albert, AB T8N 2W2
403/459-4084
President, Georgia Makowski

NORTHWESTERN ONTARIO HEALTH LIBRARIES ASSOCIATION
Hargan Medical Library, Thunder Bay Regional Cancer Centre, 290 Munroe St., Thunder Bay, ON P7A 7T1
807/343-6732, Fax: 807/343-2630, Email: cwalsh@smtp-gate.octrf.on.ca
President, Catherine Walsh

OTTAWA VALLEY HEALTH LIBRARIES GROUP
Library, Canadian Nurses Association, 50 The Driveway, Ottawa, ON K2P 1E2
613/237-2133, ext.223, Fax: 613/237-3520, Email: cna@hookup.net
President, Elizabeth Hawkins Brady

SASKATCHEWAN HEALTH LIBRARIES ASSOCIATION (SHLA) (1988)
Health Sciences Library, Wascana Rehabilitation Centre, 2180 - 23rd Ave., Regina, SK S4S 0A5
306/766-5650, Fax: 306/766-5554
President, Lily Walter-Smith

SOUTHERN ALBERTA HEALTH LIBRARIES ASSOCIATION
c/o Medical Library, University of Calgary, 3330 Hospital Dr. NW, Calgary, AB T2N 4N1
403/220-3752, Fax: 403/282-7992
President, Alix Hayden

TORONTO HEALTH LIBRARIES ASSOCIATION (THLA) (1965)
Science & Medicine Library, University of Toronto, 7 King's College Circle, Toronto, ON M5S 1A5
416/978-1331, Fax: 416/978-7666, Email: wright@library.utoronto.ca
President, Elaine Wright, y
Publications: THLA News
Affiliates: Ontario Hospital Libraries Association

WELLINGTON/WATERLOO/DUFFERIN HEALTH LIBRARY NETWORK
Groves Memorial Community Hospital, 235 Union St. East, Fergus, ON N1M 2W3
519/843-2010, ext.228, Fax: 519/843-7420
Co-chair, Elizabeth Andrushko

WINDSOR AREA HEALTH LIBRARIES ASSOCIATION
Medical Library, Hôtel Dieu Hospital, 1030 Ouellette Ave., Windsor, ON N9A 1E1
519/973-4411, ext.3178, Fax: 519/973-0642, Email: library@netcore.ca
President, Toni Janik

Canadian Health Record Association/Association canadienne interprofessionnelle des dossiers de santé (CHRA) (1942)
Canadian College of Health Record Administrators
#501, 1090 Don Mills Rd., North York, ON M3C 3R6
416/447-4900, Fax: 416/447-4598
Executive Director, Deborah Del Duca
Publications: Progress Notes; The Legislative Page, q.; Canadian Health Record Association Position Statements; Principles & Guidelines to Access & Release Health Information
Affiliates: International Federation of Health Records Organizations

Canadian Libraries in Occupational Safety & Health (1975)
c/o Alberta Labour Library, 10808 - 99 Ave, 3rd Fl., Edmonton, AB T5K 0G5
403/427-8533, Fax: 403/422-0084
Librarian, Debbie Hunter
Publications: Health & Safety on the Job

Canadian Library Association (CLA) (1946)
#602, 200 Elgin St., Ottawa, ON K2P 1L5
613/232-9625, Fax: 613/563-9895, Email: ai077@freenet.carleton.ca
Executive Director, Karen Adams
President, Karen Harrison, 807/684-6802, Email: kharriso@flash.lakehead.ca
Vice-President, President-Elect, Paul Whitney, Email: pwhitnea@sfu.ca
Treasurer, Rowena Lunn, 403/934-5334, Email: rlunn@freenet.calgary.ab.ca
Publications: Feliciter; CLA Directory of Members
Affiliates: Canadian Association of Public Libraries; Canadian Association of College & University Libraries; Canadian Library Trustees Association; Canadian School Library Association; Canadian Association of Special Libraries & Information Services

Canadian Library Trustees Association (CLTA)
c/o Canadian Library Association, #602, 200 Elgin St., Ottawa, ON K2P 1L5
613/232-9625, Fax: 613/563-9895
President, Barrie Lynch, 604/944-9655, Email: aa072@freenet.victoria.bc.ca

ORGANIZATIONS — LIBRARIES & ARCHIVES

Canadian School Library Association (CSLA)
c/o Canadian Library Association, #602, 200 Elgin St., Ottawa, ON K2P 1L5
613/232-9625, Fax: 613/563-9895
President, Judith Kootte, 604/668-6056, Email: jkootte@cln.etc.bc.ca
Vice-President, Jean Ludlam
Sec.-Treas., Jean McCarthy
Publications: School Libraries in Canada

Chief Executives of Large Public Libraries of Ontario (CELPLO)
Etobicoke Public Libraries, PO Box 501, Toronto, ON M9C 5G1
416/394-5005, Fax: 416/394-5050
Chairperson, Jennifer Milne

Church Library Association of Ontario (1969)
13 Tallwood Dr., West Montrose, ON N0B 2V0
519/669-4789
President, Elsie Riva
Publications: Library Lines
Affiliates: Church & Synagogue Library Association (USA)

Comité des bibliothèques de la région du Nord de Montréal (COBREN) (1977)
a/s Bibiothèque municipale de Saint-Jérôme, 185, rue du Palais, St-Jérôme, PQ J7Z 1X6
514/436-1511
Présidente, Renée Chalifoux-Massé

Conférence des directeurs des bibliothèques publiques de l'Île de Montréal/Conference of Public Library Directors of the Island of Montréal (CDPIM)
a/s Bibliothèque de Verdun, 5955, av Bannantyne, Montréal, PQ H4H 1H6
514/765-7167
Présidente, Lois Ann Clouthier

Corporation des bibliothécaires professionnels du Québec/Corporation of Professional Librarians of Québec (CBPQ) (1969)
#320, 307, rue Ste-Catherine ouest, Montréal, PQ H2X 2A3
514/845-3327, Téléc: 514/845-1618, Courrier électronique: cbpq@interlink.net
Directrice générale, Régine Horinstein
Président, Florian Dubois
Publications: Argus

Council of Administrators of Large Urban Public Libraries (CALUPL) (1978)
6100 Willingdon Ave., Burnaby, BC V5H 4N5
Chairman, Paul Whitney

Council of Federal Libraries/Conseil des bibliothèques du gouvernement fédéral (CFL) (1976)
National & International Programs, National Library of Canada, 395 Wellington St., Ottawa, ON K1A 0N4
613/943-8571, Fax: 613/947-2916, Email: jan.bryenton@nlc-bnc.ca
Chairperson, Marianne Scott
Publications: Liaison

Council of Head Librarians of New Brunswick/Conseil des directeurs de bibliothèques de Nouveau-Brunswick
Saint John Regional Library, 1 Market Sq., Saint John, NB E2L 4Z6
506/648-1191, Fax: 506/658-2903
President, Eileen Travis

Council of Prairie & Pacific University Libraries (COPPUL) (1991)
2500 University Dr. NW, #MLB325, Calgary, AB T2N 1N4
403/249-8626, Fax: 403/246-6976, Email: hafry@acs.ucalgary.ca
URL: http://library.usask.ca/coppul
Executive Director, Hazel Fry
Chair, Director of Library & Information Services, U. of Regina, William Maes

County & Regional Municipality Librarians of Ontario (CARML)
c/o Frontenac County Library, Frontenac County Court House, Court St., Kingston, ON K7L 2N4
613/548-8657, Fax: 613/548-8193, Email: mwatkins@frontenac.county.library.on.ca
Chair, Marion Watkins

Golden Horseshoe Health Libraries Association
Health Sciences Library, 1200 Main St. West, Hamilton, ON L8N 3Z5
905/525-9140, ext.22545, Fax: 905/528-3733, Email: bayley1@fhs.mcmaster.ca
President, Liz Bayley

Government Libraries Association of British Columbia (GLABC) (1976)
794 Fort St., PO Box 38044, Victoria, BC V8W 3N2
250/387-9745
President, Del Rosario
Vice-President, Antje Helmut
Secretary, Anne Speer
Treasurer, Bonnie Brugger
Publications: GLABC Newsletter; GLABC Directory, a.

Groupe biblio-santé de la région de Québec (1982)
L'Hotel-Dieu de Québec, 11, Côte du Palais, Québec, PQ G1R 2J6
418/691-5073, Téléc: 418/691-5468
Présidente, Lisette Germain
Publications: Catalogue collectif des périodiques dans les bibliothèques de santé de la région de Québec

Indexing & Abstracting Society of Canada/Société canadienne pour l'analyse des documents (IASC) (1977)
PO Box 744, Stn F, Toronto, ON M4Y 2N6
416/496-5025, Fax: 416/496-5068
President, Christine Jacobs, Email: incj@musicb.mcgill.ca
Vice-President, James Turner
Sec.-Treas., Noelina Bridge
Central Canada Representative, Jin Tan
Publications: IASC/SCAD Bulletin; Register of Indexers/Répertoire des indexeurs
Affiliates: Society of Indexers; American Society of Indexers; Australian Society of Indexers

Library Association of Alberta (LAA) (1939)
80 Baker Cres. NW, Calgary, AB T2L 1R4
403/284-5818, Fax: 403/282-6646, Email: laa@freenet.calgary.ab.ca
President/Provincial Representative, Peg Hofmann
Executive Director, Christine Sheppard
Treasurer, Clive Maishment
Publications: Letter of the LAA

Library Boards Association of Nova Scotia (LBANS) (1976)
c/o Eastern Counties Regional Library, PO Box 2500, Mulgrave, NS B0E 2G0
902/747-2597, Fax: 902/747-2500, Email: mfrost@nsme.library.ns.ca
Secretary, Mary Frost

Manitoba Association of Library Technicians (MALT) (1971)
PO Box 1872, Winnipeg, MB R3C 3R1
President, Kris Rytter, 204/945-3360
Publications: MALT Newsletter

Manitoba Government Libraries Council
c/o Manitoba Energy & Mines Library, #360, 1395 Ellice Ave., Winnipeg, MB R3G 3P2
204/945-6569, Fax: 204/945-8427, Email: mlavergne@em.gov.mb.ca
Chairperson, Monique Lavergne

Manitoba Library Association (MLA) (1936)
#208, 100 Arthur St., Winnipeg, MB R3B 1H3
204/943-4567, Fax: 204/942-1555
URL: http://www.mbnet.mb.ca/cm
President, Karen Hunt
Publications: Newsline
Affiliates: Manitoba School Library Audio Visual Association; Manitoba Association of Library Technicians

Manitoba Library Trustees Association
PO Box 1168, Gimli, MB R0C 1B0
204/642-8860
President, Shirley Bergen

Manitoba School Library Association (MSLA)
c/o The Manitoba Teachers' Society, 191 Harcourt St., Winnipeg, MB R3J 3H2
204/888-7961, Fax: 204/831-0872
President, Barb Poustie
President-Elect, Michelle Larose-Kuzenko
Publications: MSLA Journal
Affiliates: Manitoba Teachers' Society

National Archival Appraisal Board/Conseil national d'évaluation des archives (NAAB) (1983)
PO Box 69016, Stn Place de Ville, Ottawa, ON K1R 1A9
613/996-7604, Fax: 613/995-2267, Email: lpilon@archives.ca
Administrator, Louise Pilon

New Brunswick Library Trustees' Association/Association des commissaires de bibliothèque du Nouveau-Brunswick, inc. (NBLTA) (1979)
105 Scarlet Dr., Rothsay, NB E2E 1S3
506/847-7208
Chairman, Judy Heron
Publications: NBLTA Newsletter

Northwest Territories Library Association
PO Box 2276, Yellowknife, NT X1A 2P7
403/920-8617, Fax: 403/873-0368, Email: nwt.court.lib
President, Susan Baer
Publications: Snowshoe; NWTLA Directory, biennial

Nova Scotia Government Libraries Council (NSGLC)
c/o Dept. of Natural Resources, PO Box 698, Halifax, NS B3J 2T9
Chairperson, Valerie Brisco, 902/424-8633

Nova Scotia Library Association (NSLA) (1973)
c/o Nova Scotia Provincial Library, 3770 Kempt Rd., Halifax, NS B3K 4X8
902/453-2810, Fax: 902/422-0633
President, Frances Newman, 902/667-1767
Publications: NSLA Newsletter

Ontario Association of Library Technicians/Association des bibliotechniciens de l'Ontario (OALT) (1973)
Abbey Market, 1500 Upper Middle Rd. West, PO Box 76010, Oakville, ON L6M 3H5

President, Penni Lee
Publications: Newsletter/Nouvelles

Ontario College & University Library Association (OCULA) (1969)
#303, 100 Lombard St., Toronto, ON M5C 1M3
416/363-3388, Fax: 416/941-9581, Email: jgilbert@interlog.com
Executive Director, Larry Moore
President, Martha Wolfe
Publications: Inside OCULA
Affiliates: Ontario Library Association

Ontario Council of University Libraries (OCUL)
University of Ottawa, 65 University, Ottawa, ON K1N 9A5
613/562-5883, Fax: 613/562-5195
Chief Librarian, Richard Greene

Ontario Government Libraries Council (OGLC)
Ferguson Block, 4th Fl., 77 Wellesley St. West, Toronto, ON M7A 1N3
416/327-2535, Fax: 416/327-2530
Chair, Maria Cece
Publications: Exchange

Ontario Hospital Libraries Association (OHLA) (1985)
#2800, 200 Front St. West, Toronto, ON M5V 3J1
613/737-8529, Fax: 613/737-8521
President, Jessie McGowan
Publications: OHLA Newsline
Affiliates: Canadian Hospital Libraries Association

Ontario Library Association/Association des bibliothèques de l'Ontario (OLA) (1900)
#303, 100 Lombard St., Toronto, ON M5C 1M3
416/363-3388, Fax: 416/941-9581, Email: jgilbert@interlog.com
Executive Director, Larry Moore
President, Jane Horrocks
Publications: Inside OLA; Access, 3 pa
Affiliates: Divisions at same address: Ontario College & University Library Association; Ontario Library Trustees' Association; Ontario Public Library Association; Ontario School Library Association; Ontario Library & Information Technology Association

Ontario Library & Information Technology Association (OLITA) (1992)
#300, 100 Lombard St., Toronto, ON M5C 1M3
416/363-3388, Fax: 416/941-9581, Email: jgilbert@interlog.com
President, Bill Oldfield

Ontario Library Trustees Association (OLTA)
#300, 100 Lombard St., Toronto, ON M5C 1M3
416/363-3388, Fax: 416/941-9581
President, Maureen Rudaik
Publications: Inside OLTA
Affiliates: Ontario Library Association

Ontario Public Library Association (OPLA)
#303, 100 Lombard St., Toronto, ON M5C 1M3
416/363-3388, Fax: 416/941-9581, Email: jgilbert@interlog.com
President, Lynne Jordan
Vice-President, Ann Mckenzie
Publications: Inside OPLA

Ontario School Library Association (OSLA) (1972)
#303, 100 Lombard St., Toronto, ON M5C 1M3
416/363-3388, Fax: 416/941-9581, Email: jgilbert@interlog.com
President, Elizabeth Kerr
Publications: Inside OSLA

Prince Edward Island Professional Librarians Association (1982)
c/o Robertson Library Reference Dept., 550 University Ave., Charlottetown, PE C1A 4P3
902/368-4637
President, Brenda Brady
Vice-President, Barrie Stanfield

Rassemblement des bibliothèques publiques du Lac-Saint-Jean et Saguenay (RABLES) (1988)
1058, boul Sacré-coeur, St-Félicien, PQ G8K 245
418/679-5334
Présidente, Joanne Laprise

Regroupement des bibliothèques publiques de l'Abitibi-Témiscamingue (RBPAT) (1985)
Bibliothèque municipale de Rouyn-Noranda, 201, av Dallaire, Rouyn-Noranda, PQ J9X 4T5
819/762-0944, Téléc: 819/797-7136
Président, Luc Sigouin

Regroupement des bibliothèques publiques de la Côte-Nord
Bibliothèque centrale de prêt de la Côte-Nord, 59, rue Napoléon, Sept-Îles, PQ G4R 5C5
418/962-1020
Président, Yvon Grondin

Saskatchewan Association of Library Technicians (SALT)
PO Box 9388, Saskatoon, SK S7K 7E9
306/477-2743, Fax: 306/975-7521
President, Louise Hajlasz
Membership Secretary, Elisabeth Eilingen
Publications: SALT Newsletter

Saskatchewan Government Libraries Council
c/o Saskatchewan Agriculture & Food Library, 3085 Albert St., #B5, Regina, SK S4S 0B1
306/787-5151, Fax: 306/787-0216
Contact, Helene Stewart

Saskatchewan Library Association (SLA) (1942)
PO Box 3388, Regina, SK S4P 3H1
306/780-9413, Fax: 306/780-9447, Email: sla@pleis.lib.sk.ca
Executive Director, Andrea Wagner
Publications: Forum

Saskatchewan Library Trustees Association (SLTA) (1942)
PO Box 67, Vanguard, SK S0N 2V0
306/582-2026, Fax: 306/582-4811
President, Dorothy Saunderson
Affiliates: Canadian Library Association

Special Libraries Association
1700 - 18 St. NW, Washington, DC 20009 USA
204/234-4700, Fax: 204/265-9317, Email: sla1@capcon.net
Executive Director, David R. Bender, Ph.D.
Associate Executive Director, Lois Schoenbrun, CAE
President, Eastern Canada Chapter, Claire B. Kelly, 514/695-7920
President, Toronto Chapter, Juanita Richardson, 416/601-6150
President, Western Canada Chapter, Grace Makarewicz, 604/661-6960

Ukrainian Librarians Association of Canada
St. Vladimir Institute Library, 620 Spadina Ave., Toronto, ON M5S 2H4
416/480-2440, Fax: 416/480-1247
President, Andrew Gregorovich

Yukon Teacher-Librarians' Association (YTLA)
2064 - 2nd Ave., Whitehorse, YT Y1A 1A9
403/668-2426, Fax: 403/667-4324

Affiliates: Association of Teacher Librarians in Canada; Canadian Special Library Association

LIFESAVING see **EMERGENCY RESPONSE**

LINGUISTICS see **LANGUAGE, LINGUISTICS, LITERATURE**

LITERACY see **LANGUAGE, LINGUISTICS, LITERATURE**

LITERARY ARTS see **WRITERS & EDITORS**

LITERATURE see **LANGUAGE, LINGUISTICS, LITERATURE**

LIVESTOCK see **ANIMAL BREEDING**

LONG-TERM CARE see **HOSPITALS**

MACHINERY see **EQUIPMENT & MACHINERY**

MANAGEMENT & ADMINISTRATION

Administrative Sciences Association of Canada/Association des sciences administratives du Canada (ASAC) (1982)
Dept. of Administrative Sciences, UQAM, PO Box 6192, Stn A, Montréal, PQ H3C 4R2
514/987-3697, Fax: 514/987-3343
Secretary, Iréne Lepine
President, P. Andiappan
Publications: Canadian Journal of Administrative Sciences/Revue canadienne des sciences administratives; ASAC Bulletin, s-a.

Association of Administrative Assistants/Association des adjoints administratifs (AAA) (1951)
PO Box 5107, Stn A, Toronto, ON M5W 1N4
416/760-6907
President, Linda Varsava, Q.A.A.
Publications: Communique

Association of Cultural Executives/Association des cadres d'institutions culturelles (ACE) (1976)
133 Barton Ave., Toronto, ON M6G 1R1
416/633-6663, Fax: 416/633-2340, Email: ace@inforamp.net
President, Jeremy Morgan
Administration, Anthony Schatzky
Publications: ACE News; Management Matters, q.

Association des MBA du Québec (AMBAQ)
#500, 407, boul Saint-Laurent, Montréal, PQ H2Y 2Y5
514/874-3710, Téléc: 514/866-4020
Directeur général, Laurent Vezina
Publications: Ratio

Association of Professional Executives of the Public Service of Canada/L'Association professionnelle des cadres de la fonction publique du Canada (APEX) (1984)
LaSalle Academy Bldg., 65 Guigues St., PO Box 420, Stn A, Ottawa, ON K1N 8V4
613/995-6252, Fax: 613/943-8919
Executive Director, Pierre de Blois
Publications: Bulletin

Association of Records Managers & Administrators
ARMA International
#215, 4200 Somerset Dr., Prairie Village, KA 66208 USA

913/341-3808, Fax: 913/341-3742, Toll Free: 1-800-422-2762
Halifax Chapter: President, Christina Corkett, Email: corkett@gov.ns.ca; PO Box 2381, Stn M, Halifax, NS B3J 3E4
Vancouver Chapter: #300, 3665 Kingsway, Vancouver, BC V5R 5W2, 604/435-2897; Fax: 604/435-8181

Atlantic Canada Plus Association (1977)
Metropolitan Place, #601, 6009 Quinpool Rd., PO Box 9410, Stn A, Halifax, NS B3K 5S3
902/492-3807, Fax: 902/425-2441
Executive Director, John Sutherland
Chairman, Don MacVey

Canadian Association of School Administrators/ Association canadienne des administrateurs et des administratrices scolaires (CASA) (1975)
#1133 - 160A St., White Rock, BC V4A 7G9
604/535-6330, Fax: 604/531-6454
Director, Programs & Services, Douglas S. McCall
Publications: The President Reports
Affiliates: Association of British Columbia Superintendents; Conference of Alberta School Superintendents; Saskatchewan League of Educational Administrators, Directors & Superintendents; Manitoba Association of School Superintendents; Ontario Catholic Supervisory Officers' Association; Québec Association of School Administrators; Association of Directors General of Protestant School Boards of Québec; New Brunswick School Superintendents Association; Association des directions générales scolaires du Nouveau-Brunswick; Association of Nova Scotia Educational Administrators; School Administrators of Prince Edward Island; Newfoundland & Labrador Association of Superintendents of Education

Canadian Executive Service Organization/Service administratif canadien aux organismes (CESO) (1967)
South Tower, #400, 175 Bloor St. East, Toronto, ON M4W 3R8
416/961-2376, Fax: 416/961-1096, Telex: 06-23583, Toll Free: 1-800-268-9052, Email: toronto@ceso-saco.com
CEO/President, Daniel W. Haggerty
Senior Vice-President, Andrew M. Salkeld
Sec.-Treas., Terry Brackenridge
Regional Manager, Québec, Jean-Louis Castonguay
Publications: Focus; Dreamcatcher - Aboriginal Services Newsletter
Alberta & Western Arctic Office: Regional Manager, George Ferrand; Secretary/Receptionist, Debra Racicot, Edmonton Centre, 1724 Royal Trust Tower, Edmonton, AB T5J 2Z2, 403/421-4740, Fax: 403/429-3186, Email: alberta@ceso-saco.com
Atlantic Region Office: Regional Manager, Paddy Moran, #305, 802 Prince St., Truro, NS B2N 1H1, 902/893-2477, Fax: 902/893-1159
Manitoba & Northwestern Ontario Office: Regional Manager, Gwen La Frenière; Administrative Assistant, Yvonne Dubois, #1000, 191 Lombard Ave., Winnipeg, MB R3B 0X1, 204/949-0177, Fax: 204/942-1647, Email: manitoba@ceso-saco.com
National Capital Region: Contact, Andrew M. Salkeld, 323 Chapel St., 2nd Fl., Ottawa, ON K1N 7Z2, 613/236-7763, Fax: 613/237-5969, Email: ottawa@ceso-saco.com
Ontario & Eastern Arctic Office/Operations Centre: Regional Manager, Laurie Blachford; Administrative Assistant, Sonya Mergler, #400, 175 Bloor St. East, Toronto, ON M4W 3R8, 416/961-2376, Fax: 416/961-1096, Email: toronto.centre@ceso-saco.com
Saskatchewan Office: Regional Manager, Murray McConnell; Administrative Assistant, Velma Krahenbil, #1050, 2002 Victoria Ave., Regina, SK S4P 0R7, 306/757-0651, Fax: 306/565-8741, Email: saskatchewan@ceso-saco.com

Canadian Institute of Certified Administrative Managers (CICAM) (1979)
#700, 2 Bloor St. West, Toronto, ON M4W 3R1
416/921-7962, Fax: 416/923-2071
Executive Director, Dr. Albert E. Ballantyne, DHL, M.Phil., FCAM
President, John E.G. Stone
Alberta: Alberta Director, Rose M. Bradley, DTM, FCAM, 906 Cottonwood Ave., Sherwood Park, AB T8A 1Z4, 403/467-5214
British Columbia: President, R. John Duff Stuart, B.Comm., CGA, FCAM, 527 Cleek Close, Qualicum Beach, BC V9K 1E5, 250/752-3038
Manitoba/Saskatchewan: Manitoba/Saskatchewan Director, Howard W. Morrow, FCAM, 65 St. Michael Rd., Winnipeg, MB R2M 2K7, 204/253-7710
Maritimes: Maritimes Coordinator, Gary A. Slauenwhite, BBA, CAM, FBA, MBA, PO Box 1043, Liverpool, NS B0T 1K0, 902/354-7228
Ottawa/Hull Region: Ottawa/Hull Region Director, David H. Jones-Delcorde, Ph.D., FCEA, FCAM, 25 Ridgefield Cres., Nepean, ON K2H 6S3, 613/721-6127
Québec: Quebec Coordinator, Peter Tsasis, B.Sc., DIA, MBA, FCAM, 3012, rue Noorduyn, Montréal, PQ H4R 1A2, 514/334-2017

Canadian Institute of Management/Institut canadien de gestion (CIM) (1942)
#110, 2175 Sheppard Ave. East, North York, ON M2J 1W8
416/493-0155, Fax: 416/491-1670, Toll Free: 1-800-387-5774
URL: http://www.interlog.com/~consult/cimhp1.html
Executive Director, Joan L. Milne, P.Mgr., RMP
National President, Jim Peacock
Administrator, Carolyn Vigon
Publications: The Canadian Manager

Canadian Institute for Organization Management (CIOM)
#1160, 55 Metcalfe St., Ottawa, ON K1P 6N4
613/238-4000, Fax: 613/238-7643
Director, Roger Stanion
Administrator, Linda Robert
Affiliates: Canadian Chamber of Commerce

Canadian Management Centre of AMA (American Management Association) International
150 York St., 5th Fl., Toronto, ON M5H 3S5
416/214-5678, Fax: 416/214-1453
Managing Director, William P. Sutton
Marketing Manager, Deborah Spencer
Affiliates: American Management Association International

Canadian Public Personnel Management Association
5 Tournament Dr., North York, ON M2P 1K1
416/362-2805
Director of Professional Development, Joseph Fernandes

The Canadian Public Relations Society, Inc./La Société canadienne des relations publiques, inc. (CPRS) (1948)
#720, 220 Laurier Ave. West, Ottawa, ON K1P 5Z9
613/232-1222, Fax: 613/232-0565
Executive Director, Arbo A. Mattila, APR, CAE
Contact, A.M. St. Amour
Affiliates: International Public Relations Association; Public Relations Society of America

Canadian Society of Association Executives/ Société canadienne des directeurs d'association (CSAE) (1951)
#1104, 40 University Ave., Toronto, ON M5J 1T1
416/596-6433, Fax: 416/596-7994
President, Judith Wiley
Chairperson, John Leech, CAE
Executive Vice-President, Wayne Amundson, CAE
Vice-President, Michel G. Tremblay, c.a.é.
Publications: CSAE News; Association, bi-m.; CSAE Membership Directory, a.; CSAE Salary Surveys, a.; The Association Agenda; Association Contact
Affiliates: European Society of Association Executives; American Society of Association Executives; Australian Society of Association Executives

Canadian Society of Corporate Secretaries (CSCS) (1994)
#255, 55 St. Clair Ave. West, Toronto, ON M4V 2Y7
416/921-5449, Toll Free: 1-800-774-2850
Executive Director, Jacqueline Tilford
President, Larry Sikorski
Publications: Professional Administrator

Centre pour l'avancement des associations du Québec (CEPAQ)
CP 188, Succ. Outremont, Montréal, PQ H2V 4M8
514/523-7636, Téléc: 514/528-4353
Directrice générale, Michele Cyr
Publications: Inter-Action

Confédération nationale des cadres du Québec (CNCQ) (1992)
a/s Association des cadres des collèges du Québec, 6365, boul Hamel, L'Ancienne-Lorette, PQ G2E 5W2
418/877-1500, Téléc: 418/877-4469
Président, Jean Perron
Organisation(s) affiliée(s): Confédération internationale des cadres

Couchiching Institute on Public Affairs (CIPA) (1931)
c/o Base Service Canada Inc., #301, 250 Consumers Rd., North York, ON M2J 4V6
416/494-1440, Fax: 416/495-8723, Email: base@on-ramp.ca
Executive Director, Ruth Abrahamson
Publications: Couchiching News

Fédération des secrétaires professionnelles du Québec (FSPQ)
#300, 1173, boul Charest ouest, Québec, PQ G1N 2C9
418/527-5041, Téléc: 418/682-3430
Présidente, Louise M. Gosselin

Foundation for Association Research & Education (FARE) (1991)
c/o Canadian Society of Association Executives, #1104, 40 University Ave., Toronto, ON M5J 1T1
416/596-6433, Fax: 416/596-7994
Foundation Administrator, Andrea Sametz

Institute of Certified Management Consultants of Canada/Institut des conseillers en management du Canada (ICMCC)
Heritage Bldg., BCE Place, PO Box 835, 181 Bay St., Toronto, ON M5J 2T3
416/869-3001, Fax: 416/860-1535, Email: icmcc@cmc-consult.org
URL: http://www.cmc-consult.org
Executive Director, Heather Osler, CAE
Publications: Common Body of Knowledge; Management Practices in Information Technology
Affiliates: International Council of Management Consulting Institutes

Canadian Almanac & Directory 1997

ORGANIZATIONS — MANUFACTURING & INDUSTRY

INSTITUT DES CONSEILLERS EN MANAGEMENT DU QUÉBEC (ICMQ) (1966)
#306, 455, rue Saint-Antoine est, Montréal, PQ H2Z 1J1
514/395-2313, Téléc: 514/395-8835
Directrice générale, Nicole Giroux
President, J.-Pierre Naud
Vice-President, Administration, Jean Klein
Publications: Le Consultant

INSTITUTE OF CERTIFIED MANAGEMENT CONSULTANTS OF ALBERTA (ICMCA) (1977)
582 Manulife Place, 10180 - 101 St., Edmonton, AB T5J 3S4
403/424-2056, Fax: 403/425-8766, Toll Free: 1-800-565-0902
Executive Director, Linda Wood, CAE
Publications: Perspective; Member Directory

INSTITUTE OF CERTIFIED MANAGEMENT CONSULTANTS OF ATLANTIC CANADA (ICMCAC) (1982)
PO Box 1440, Sackville, NB E0A 3C0
Toll Free: 1-800-565-5314
Publications: Atlantic Update

INSTITUTE OF CERTIFIED MANAGEMENT CONSULTANTS OF BRITISH COLUMBIA (1973)
#1501, 650 Georgia St. West, PO Box 11606, Vancouver, BC V6B 4N9
604/681-1419, Fax: 604/687-6688
Executive Director, Jennie Ambrose
Publications: CMC Report

INSTITUTE OF CERTIFIED MANAGEMENT CONSULTANTS OF MANITOBA/INSTITUT MANITOBAIN DES CONSEILLERS EN ADMINISTRATION AGRÉÉS (ICMCM) (1977)
1315 Pembina Hwy., PO Box 23041, Winnipeg, MB R3T 5S3
204/488-4507, Fax: 204/489-1749
Executive Director, Barbara Campbell, CMC
Publications: Consulting Perspectives; Membership Directory, a.

INSTITUTE OF CERTIFIED MANAGEMENT CONSULTANTS OF ONTARIO (ICMCO) (1966)
Heritage Bldg., BCE Place, PO Box 835, 181 Bay St., Toronto, ON M5J 2T3
416/860-1515, Fax: 416/860-1535, Toll Free: 1-800-268-1148, Email: icmco@cmc-consult.org
Executive Director, Heather Osler, CAE
President, Wayne Atkinson, FCMC
Membership/Board Secretary, Marina Melrinho
Publications: Straight Forward

INSTITUTE OF CERTIFIED MANAGEMENT CONSULTANTS OF SASKATCHEWAN (ICMCS) (1990)
901 - 3rd Ave. North, 2nd Fl., Saskatoon, SK S7K 2K4
306/244-6061, Fax: 306/242-7844
President, Gilbert Ackerman

Institute of Chartered Secretaries & Administrators in Canada/Institut des secrétaires et administrateurs agréés au Canada (ICSA) (1920)
#255, 55 St. Clair Ave. West, Toronto, ON M4V 2Y7
416/944-9727, Fax: 416/967-6320
Executive Director, Lezlie Oler
Publications: Professional Administrator; Directory of Members, a.
Affiliates: International Institute of Chartered Secretaries & Administrators

Institute of Corporate Directors/Institut des administrateurs des corporations (IOCD) (1980)
#255, 55 St. Clair Ave. West, Toronto, ON M4V 2Y7
416/944-8282, Fax: 416/967-6320
President, Andre J. Galipeault
Publications: Director
Affiliates: Institute of Directors

Institute of Professional Management
2 Walton Ct., Ottawa, ON K1V 9T1
613/523-5957, Fax: 613/523-8505
Executive Director, Peggy Winstan

International Federation of Project Management Organizations/Fédération internationale des organisations de gestion de projets (1980)
79 Fentiman Ave., Ottawa, ON K1S 0T7
613/730-4446
Contact, Roger Lewis Ford

National Society of Fund Raising Executives
#700, 1101 King St., Alexandria, VA 22314-2967 USA
703/684-0410, Fax: 703/684-0540, Toll Free: 1-800-666-3863
President, Patricia F. Lewis
Executive Assistant, Sandra J. Bond
Greater Toronto Chapter: President, Douglas McLaren, c/o CFRE, 15 Clarence Sq., Toronto, ON M5V 1H1, 416/596-6642

Ontario Medical Secretaries' Association (OMSA) (1959)
#300, 525 University Ave., Toronto, ON M5G 2K7
416/599-2580, Fax: 416/599-9309, Toll Free: 1-800-268-7215
Administrator, Katharine Brown

Ordre des administrateurs agréés du Québec (1973)
#640, 680, rue Sherbrooke ouest, Montréal, PQ H3A 2M7
514/499-0880, Téléc: 514/499-0892, Ligne sans frais: 1-800-465-0880
Directeur général et vice-président exécutif, Richard Gagnon, Adm.A.
Directrice aux communications et au recrutement, Francine Labelle
Coordonnatrice, Lysane Martel
Publications: Dimensions
Organisation(s) affiliée(s): Institut des conseillers en management du Québec; Institut des planificateurs financiers du Canada

The Presidents Association Canada
The Chief Executive Officers Division of the AMA International, 150 York St., 5th Fl., Toronto, ON M5H 3S5
416/214-5678, Fax: 416/214-1453
Executive Director, Dodie Teplinsky

Professional Secretaries International - Canada District
Waterford Hospital, St. John's, NF A1E 4J8
Director, Dianne Clements, CPS
Publications: The Secretary
Eastern Canada Division: President, Patricia Mombourquette, CPS, 20 Joffre St., Dartmouth, NS B2Y 3C8
Ontario Division: President, Susan L. Martin, CPS, CAM, 233 Cheltonwood Cres., Waterloo, ON N2V 1X5
Western Canada Division: President, Cindy Caton, 435 Aldine St., Winnipeg, MB R3J 3B5

Project Management Institute (PMI) (1969)
130 South State Rd., Upper Darby, PA 19082 USA
610/734-3330, Fax: 610/734-3266
URL: http://www.pmi.org
Executive Director, Deborah Bigelow
Manager, Membership & Marketing, Karen Alfons
Publications: PMI; PM Network, m.

Purchasing Management Association of Canada/ Association canadienne de gestion des achats (PMAC) (1919)
#1414, 2 Carlton St., Toronto, ON M5B 1J3
416/977-7111 (English); 514/255-8618 (Français), Fax: 416/977-8886
President, Leon Harder, CPP
Executive Vice-President, David S. Cameron
Director, Membership Services, Bill Kirkwood
Publications: Progressive Purchasing

Société des relationnistes du Québec inc.
#500, 407, boul St-Laurent, Montréal, PQ H2Y 2Y5
514/874-3705, Téléc: 514/866-4020
Responsable, Irène Langis

MANUFACTURING & INDUSTRY

Alliance of Manufacturers & Exporters Canada/ Alliance des manufacturiers et des exportateurs du Canada (1996)
75 International Blvd., 4th Fl., Toronto, ON M9W 6L9
416/798-8000, Fax: 416/798-8050, Email: national@the-alliance.com
President, Stephen Van Houten
Senior Vice-President, Mark Drake
Controller, Dorothy Featherstone
Publications: In Focus; Export News, 15 pa
Ottawa Office: #250, 99 Bank St., Ottawa, ON K1P 6B9, 613/238-8888, Fax: 613/563-9218, Email: ottawa@the-alliance.com
Alberta Division: #1531, 10060 Jasper Ave., Edmonton, AB T5J 3R8, 403/426-6622, Fax: 403/426-1509, Email: alberta@the-alliance.com
Alliance of Manufacturers & Exporters Newfoundland: Parsons Bldg., 90 O'Leary Ave., 1st Fl., St. John's, NF A1B 2C7, 709/772-3682, Fax: 709/772-3213, Email: nfld@the-alliance.com
Association des manufacturiers du Québec: #904, 1080, côte du Beaver Hall, Montréal, PQ H2Z 1S8, 514/866-7774, Téléc: 514/866-3779, Courrier électronique: quebec@the-alliance.com
BC Manufacturers' Association: #1330, 1100 Melville St., Vancouver, BC V6E 4A6, 604/685-8131, Fax: 604/685-9623, Email: bc@the-alliance.com
Manitoba Division: Century Plaza, #100, One Wesley Ave., Winnipeg, MB R3C 4C6, 204/949-1454, Fax: 204/943-3476, Email: manitoba@the-alliance.com
New Brunswick Division: #104, 1133 St. George Blvd., Moncton, NB E1E 4E1, 506/857-3056, Fax: 506/857-3059, Email: nb@the-alliance.com
Nova Scotia Division: #1020, 1801 Hollis St., Halifax, NS B3J 3N4, 902/422-4477, Fax: 902/422-9563, Email: ns@the-alliance.com
Ontario Division: #400, 75 International Blvd., Toronto, ON M9W 6L9, 416/798-8000, Fax: 416/798-8050, Email: ontario@the-alliance.com
Ontario Division: Hearst Block, #539A, 900 Bay St., Toronto, ON M7A 2E1, 416/325-6396, Fax: 416/325-6509
Saskatchewan Division: 1024 Winnipeg St., Regina, SK S4R 8P8, 306/522-2773, Fax: 306/757-5410, Email: sask@the-alliance.com

American Electroplaters & Surface Finishers Society/Association des galvanoplastes d'Amérique (AESF) (1909)
12644 Research Pkwy., Orlando, FL 32826 USA
407/281-6441, Fax: 407/281-6446, Telex: 5106016246
Executive Director, Ted Witt
Publications: Plating & Surface Finishing
Canadian Branches
Montréal Branch: President, Gerald Loh, CEF, #715, 717 av Lajoie, Dorval, PQ H0P 1G7, 514/631-3730
Ottawa Branch: President, John Cody, c/o British American Bank Note Inc., PO Box 399, Stn A, Ottawa, ON K1N 8V4, 613/728-5854

Toronto Branch: Treasurer, Walter Nikaruk, 68 Burnamthorpe Cres., Islington, ON M9A 1G7, 416/237-1400
Western Ontario Branch: President, Paul Starr, 70 Book St., Wallaceburg, ON N8A 2T6, 519/627-1691

American Foundrymen's Society (AFS) (1896)
505 State St., Des Plaines, IL 60016-8399 USA
708/824-0181, Fax: 708/824-7848, Toll Free: 1-800-537-4237
Executive Vice-President, Charles H. Jones
Publications: Modern Casting
Canadian Chapters
British Columbia Chapter: Chairman, Mike Johnston, Inproheat Industries Ltd., 680 Raymur Ave., Vancouver, BC V6A 2R1, 604/254-0461
Eastern Canada Chapter: Chairman, Yves Marchand, Sefford Foundry, 480 Robinson St., Granby, PQ J2G 7N4, 514/777-1075
Manitoba Chapter: Chairman, Graham A. Corlett, PO Box 1090, Winkler, MB R6W 4B2, 204/325-4393
Ontario Chapter: Chairman, John E. Parr, c/o Dofasco, Inc., PO Box 2460, Hamilton, ON L8N 3J5, 905/544-3761

Association of Independent Corrugated Converters (1975)
AICC Canada - Region Eleven
PO Box 10569, Winona, ON L8E 5R1
905/643-4550, Fax: 905/643-4550
Executive Director, Donald H. Lumb

Association de manutention du Québec/Material Handling Association of Québec (AMQ) (1986)
62A, Labelle, Laval, PQ H7N 2S3
514/662-3717, Téléc: 514/662-6096
Vice-président exécutif, Victor Vonka
Business Manager, Stephanie Vonka

Association de la recherche industrielle du Québec (ADRIQ)
#100, 425, rue de la Gauchetière est, Montréal, PQ H2L 2M7
514/847-7570, Téléc: 514/849-5558
Directeur général, Claude Demers

Canadian Appliance Manufacturers Association (CAMA)
#210, 10 Carlson Ct., Etobicoke, ON M9W 6L2
416/674-7410, Fax: 416/674-7412
Vice-President, Alda M. Murphy

Canadian Association of Moldmakers (CAMM) (1991)
424 Tecumseh Rd. East, Windsor, ON N8Y 2R6
519/255-7863, Fax: 519/255-9446, Toll Free: 1-800-567-2266
Treasurer, C. Butcher
Publications: CAMM News

Canadian Association for Production & Inventory Control/Association canadienne pour la gestion de la production et les stocks (CAPIC) (1962)
APICS Region VIII
#604, 3 Church St., Toronto, ON M5E 1M2
416/364-5007, Fax: 416/862-0315, Info Line: 364-5007, Toll Free: 1-800-567-8207
Administrator, Marilyn Ryder
Publications: APICS - The Performance Advantage; Production & Inventory Management, q.
Affiliates: American Production & Inventory Control Society

Canadian Battery Association (CBA)
#1801, One Yonge St., Toronto, ON M5E 1W7
416/363-7845, Fax: 416/369-0515
Executive Director, Lois Marsh

Canadian Boiler Society/Société canadienne de manufacturiers chaudières (CBS)
3266 Douglas St., Burlington, ON L7N 1G9
905/681-9886, Fax: 905/681-1533
Executive Director, J.R. Cassidy

Canadian Brush, Broom & Mop Manufacturers Association/Association canadienne des fabricants de brosses, balais et vadrouilles (CBBMMA) (1944)
#200, 670 Bloor St. West, Toronto, ON M6G 1L2
416/533-7800, Fax: 416/533-4795
Executive Director, Don Mockford

Canadian Carpet Institute
#605, 130 Slater St., Ottawa, ON K1P 6E2
613/232-7183, Fax: 613/232-3072
Executive Director, Michael B. Kronick

Canadian Cosmetic, Toiletry & Fragrance Association/Association canadienne des cosmétiques, produit de toilette et parfums (CCTFA) (1928)
#510, 5090 Explorer Dr., Mississauga, ON L4W 4T9
905/629-0111, Fax: 905/629-0112
President, C.A. Low
Vice-President, Administration & Meetings, S. Wissler

Canadian Council of Furniture Manufacturers/ Conseil canadien des fabricants de meubles (CCFM)
1873 Inkster Blvd., Winnipeg, MB R2R 2A6
204/694-5872, Fax: 204/694-1281
Acting President, Terry Clark

Canadian Decorating Products Association/ Association canadienne de l'industrie de décoration (CDPA) (1949)
#5, 7895 Tranmere Dr., Mississauga, ON L5S 1V9
905/678-0331, Fax: 905/678-0335
Office Manager, Rosemary Schooley
Publications: Decorating Centre; Members Update, s-a.
Affiliates: National Decorating Products Association

Canadian Die Casters Association/Association canadienne des mouleurs sous pressions
#307, 151 Slater St., Ottawa, ON K1P 5H3
613/232-8663, Fax: 613/230-9607
Executive Director, Donald P. Kennedy

Canadian Fibreboard Manufacturers' Association/Association canadienne des manufacturiers d'isolant de fibre de bois (CFMA) (1958)
#200, 670 Bloor St. West, Toronto, ON M6G 1L2
416/533-7800, Fax: 416/533-4795
Executive Director, Don Mockford
President, Paul St. Louis

Canadian Flexible Foam Manufacturers' Association (CFFMA) (1981)
#200, 6900 Airport Rd., PO Box 85, Mississauga, ON L4V 1E8
905/677-6594, Fax: 905/677-5212
Secretary, George D. Sinclair

Canadian Gear Products Manufacturers' Association
#701, 116 Albert St., Ottawa, ON K1P 5G3
613/232-7213, Fax: 613/232-7381
President, Arnold W.D. Garlick

Canadian Hardware & Housewares Manufacturers' Association/Association canadienne des fabricants en quincaillerie et articles ménagers (CHHMA) (1966)
#101, 1335 Morningside Ave., Scarborough, ON M1B 5M4
416/282-0022, Fax: 416/282-0027
President, Vaughn Crofford
Publications: CHHMA Newsletter

Canadian Heat Exchange & Vessel Manufacturers Association (CHEVMA) (1976)
#310, 2175 Sheppard Ave. East, North York, ON M2J 1W8
416/491-2886, Fax: 416/491-1670
Administrator, Diane Gaunt
Publications: CHEVMA Members Directory; Bulletin, q.

Canadian Industrial Innovation Centre (CIIC/W) (1981)
156 Columbia St. West, Waterloo, ON N2L 3L3
519/885-5870, Fax: 519/885-5729, Toll Free: 1-800-265-4559, Email: info@innovationcentre.ca
URL: http://www.innovationcentre.ca
Manager, Marketing Services Group, Gary Svoboda
Publications: Eureka The Canadian Investors Newsletter; The Innovation Showcase

Canadian Juvenile Products Association
PO Box 294, Kleinburg, ON L0J 1C0
905/893-1689, Fax: 905/893-2392
Executive Director, Wayne Glover, CAE

Canadian Kitchen Cabinet Association/ Association canadienne de fabricants d'armoires de cuisine (CKCA)
27 Goulburn Ave., Ottawa, ON K1N 8C7
613/233-6205, Fax: 613/233-1929
President, James Deslaurier
Executive Vice-President, R.H. Rivard
Executive Secretary, Suzanne Cardinal

Canadian Laboratory Suppliers Association/ Association canadienne de fournisseurs de laboratoire
94 Torrance Rd., Scarborough, ON M1J 2J4
416/431-4301, Fax: 416/431-5889
Administrator, Lorraine MacNevin

Canadian Lamp & Fixture Manufacturers Association Inc. (CLFMA)
30 Dovedale Crt., Scarborough, ON M1S 5A7
416/754-3377, Fax: 416/754-8077
Frank Delorey

Canadian Plastics Institute/Institut canadien du plastique (CPI) (1983)
#515, 5925 Airport Rd., Mississauga, ON L4V 1W1
905/612-9997, Fax: 905/612-8664
Executive Director, Nabil Mustafa
Director, Communications, Karen Wolfe
Manager, Seminars, Paul Waller
Administrative Assistant, Liliane M.R. Veilleux
Publications: The Communique
Affiliates: SPI Canada

Canadian Pump Manufacturers' Association
#701, 116 Albert St., Ottawa, ON K1P 5G3
613/232-7213, Fax: 613/232-7381
President, Arnold W.D. Garlick

Canadian Sanitation Supply Association/ Association canadienne des fournisseurs de produits sanitaires (CSSA) (1957)
#G10, 300 Mill Rd., Etobicoke, ON M9C 4W7
416/620-9320, Fax: 416/620-7199, Email: cssa@the_wire.com

Canadian Almanac & Directory 1997

Executive Director, Diane Gosling
President, Denis Goulet
Publications: Update; Bulletin; CSSA Roster, a.

Canadian Tobacco Manufacturers' Council/ Conseil canadien des fabricants des produits de tabac (CTMC) (1963)
#701, 99 Bank St., Ottawa, ON K1P 6B9
613/238-2799, Fax: 613/238-4463
President, Robert Parker
Director, Communications, Marie Josée Lapointe
Publications: Tobacco File

Canadian Tooling & Machining Association (CTMA) (1963)
Gatewood Office Centre, 1425 Bishop St., Cambridge, ON N1R 6J9
519/622-4302, Fax: 519/740-8350
General Manager, Leslie Payne
Publications: CTMA View
Affiliates: Auto Parts; Canadian Foundry Association; Canadian Plastics Institute; GTMA England; PMPTB - Ohio, USA; SPI - Toronto; CAMM - Windsor

Canadian Toy Association/L'Association Canadienne du Jouet (1932)
PO Box 294, Kleinburg, ON L0J 1C0
905/893-1689, Fax: 905/893-2392
Executive Director, Sheila Edmondson
Chairman, Ian Bradley
Publications: The Insider; Canadian Toy & Decoration Fair

Canadian Urethane Manufacturers Association (CUMA) (1974)
32 Baleberry Cr., Weston, ON M9P 3L2
416/244-9859
Manager, Rodger G. Davis

Canadian Valve Manufacturers' Association
#701, 116 Albert St., Ottawa, ON K1P 5G3
613/232-7213, Fax: 613/232-7381
President, Arnold W.D. Garlick

Canadian Window & Door Manufacturers Association/Association canadienne des manufacturiers de portes et de fenêtres (CWDMA) (1967)
27 Goulburn Ave., Ottawa, ON K1N 8C7
613/233-9804, Fax: 613/233-1929
Executive Director, Richard Lipman
Executive Vice-President, R.H. Rivard
Publications: Membership & Product Directory

Cellulose Insulation Manufacturers Association of Canada (CIMAC)
PO Box 245, Stn Mont-Royal, Montréal, PQ H3P 3C5
514/737-6482, Fax: 514/737-6929
Executive Director, Harry Hencher
President, Norman Carbonneau

Door & Hardware Institute (1975)
Canadian Headquarters, 208 Evans Ave., Toronto, ON M8Z 1J7
416/251-0702, Fax: 416/252-4064
Canadian Administrator, Les Groves
Publications: Doors & Hardware

Institut québécois des revêtements de sol inc./ Québec Institute of Floor Covering (1972)
9420, rue Pascal Gagnon, St-Léonard, PQ H1P 1Z7
514/323-8480, Téléc: 514/323-1511
Directeur général, Richard P. Bolduc
Administrateur délégué, Huguette Rémillard
Publications: Surface

Insulating Glass Manufacturers Association of Canada/Association canadienne des manufacturiers de vitrage isolant (IGMAC) (1967)
PO Box 25013, Brantford, ON N3T 6K5
519/449-2487, Fax: 519/449-2887
General Manager, Susan Macivor

National Floor Covering Association
#605, 130 Slater St., Ottawa, ON K1P 6E2
613/232-7845, Fax: 613/232-3072
Executive Director, Michael B. Kronick

The National Marine Manufacturers Association (NMMA)
#810, 310 Front St. West, Toronto, ON M5V 3B5
416/591-6772, Fax: 416/591-3582
Manager, Carol Bell

Office Products Manufacturers Association of Canada
#240, 4600 Highway #7, Woodbridge, ON L4L 4Y7
905/850-3892, Fax: 905/850-3895
Executive Assistant, Jo Anne Falkenburger

Organization of CANDU Industries/Association des industries CANDU (OCI) (1979)
#1801, One Yonge St., Toronto, ON M5E 1W7
416/363-7845, Fax: 416/369-0515
General Manager, Jack R. Howett
Administrator, Lois Marsh
Affiliates: Atomic Energy of Canada

Portable Appliance Manufacturers Association of Canada (PAMA)
#210, 10 Carlson Ct., Etobicoke, ON M9W 6L2
416/674-7410, Fax: 416/674-7412
Vice-President, Alda M. Murphy

The Rubber Association of Canada/Association canadienne de l'industrie du caoutchouc (RAC) (1920)
#308, 89 The Queensway West, Mississauga, ON L5B 2V2
905/270-8322, Fax: 905/270-2640, Email: rac@inforamp.net
President, Brian E. James
Chairman, Dan Patrick
Office Manager, Glenn Maidment
Publications: RAC News

Soap & Detergent Association of Canada/ Association des savonniers canadiens (SDAC) (1969)
#301, 885 Don Mills Rd., North York, ON M3C 1V9
416/510-8036, Fax: 416/510-8044
Manager, Linda N. Reid
Affiliates: Grocery Products Manufacturers of Canada

Society of the Plastics Industry of Canada/ Société des industries du plastique du Canada (SPI Canada)
#500, 5925 Airport Rd., Mississauga, ON L4V 1W1
905/678-7748, Fax: 905/678-0774
President, Pierre Dubois
Québec Regional Office: Directrice, Odette Mercier, Place du Parc, #2210, 300, rue Léo Pariseau, Montréal, PQ H2W 2N1, 514/499-0500, Téléc: 514/499-9258

Tanners Association of Canada
122 Curzon St., Toronto, ON M4M 3B5
416/463-3118, Fax: 416/466-1277
Executive Vice-President, Ian C. Kennedy

MAPPING see SURVEYING & MAPPING

MARINE TRADES
see also Fisheries & Fishing Industry; Transportation & Shipping

Atlantic Marine Trades Association (1988)
PO Box 2705, Stn Central, Halifax, NS B3J 3P7
902/453-4761, Fax: 902/453-0012
Coordinator, Ed Robillard

British Columbia Marine Trades Association
#270, 1075 West Georgia St., Vancouver, BC V6E 3C9
604/683-5191, Fax: 604/688-3105
President, Bill Falk
Publications: Newsletter

British Columbia Maritime Employers Association
#500, 349 Railway St., Vancouver, BC V6A 1A4
604/688-1155, Fax: 604/684-2397
CEO/President, R.V. Wilds
Director, Labour Relations, M.H. Cahan

Canadian Centre for Marine Communications
PO Box 8454, St. John's, NF A1B 3N9
709/579-4872, Fax: 709/579-0492, Email: wayneb@ccm-post.ifmt.f.ca
President & CEO, Wayne Buffey

Canadian Navigation Society (CNS)
#818, 130 Slater St., Ottawa, ON K1P 6E2
613/234-0191, Fax: 613/234-9039
Executive Director, Ian M. Ross

Canadian Port & Harbour Association/ Association des ports et havres du Canada (CPHA) (1959)
8 Parmalea Cres., Toronto, ON M9R 2X7
416/245-1742, Fax: 416/245-1250
URL: http://www.newswire.ca/cpha.
Executive Director, John Jursa
Publications: CPHA Newsletter; CPHA Monitor, s-a.
Affiliates: American Association of Port Authorities

International Association of Great Lakes Ports (IAGLP) (1960)
c/o Chamber of Maritime Commerce, #704A, 350 Sparks St., Ottawa, ON K1R 7S8
613/233-8779, Fax: 613/232-6211
Sec.-Treas., Genevieve Rickman

Mid-Canada Marine Dealers Association
23 Sage Cres., Winnipeg, MB R2Y 0X8
204/831-5438, Fax: 204/831-5438
President, Rene St. Onge
Executive Secretary, Brian Ans

Shipbuilding Association of Canada/Association de la construction navale du Canada (1989)
#1502, 222 Queen St., Ottawa, ON K1P 5V9
613/232-7127, Fax: 613/238-5519
President, André Lafond
Publications: CMIA Summary; CMIA Directory, a.; CMIA Annual Statistical Report; CMIA Quarterly Reports

MARKETING see ADVERTISING & MARKETING

MASONIC ORDERS see FRATERNAL

MEDIATION see LABOUR RELATIONS

MEDICAL see HEALTH & MEDICAL

MENTAL HEALTH

Agoraphobic Foundation of Canada Inc./ Fondation canadienne pour les agoraphobes inc. (AFC) (1982)
PO Box 132, Laval, PQ H7W 4K2
514/628-5215
President, F. Rosen, 514/688-4726
Publications: AFC Newsletter

Association des Psychologues du Québec/ Québec Psychological Association (APQ) (1989)
#208, 1150 boul St-Joseph est, Montréal, PQ H2J 1L5
514/528-7498, Téléc: 514/528-6020
Président, Daniel-Laurent Frégeau
Vice-Président, Richard Gauthier
Trésorier, Jean Grégoire
Publications: Bulletin

Association des sexologues du Québec (ASQ) (1978)
#300, 6915, rue St-Denis, Montréal, PQ H2S 2S3
514/270-9289, Téléc: 514/270-9289
Directrice générale, Sylviane Larose
Présidente, Normande Couture
Publications: Sexologie Actuelle; Repertoire des sexologues, annuel; Les sexologues peuvent vous aider

Canadian Association of Psychoanalytic Child Therapists (CAPCT)
42 Brookmount Rd., Toronto, ON M4L 3N2
416/690-5464, Fax: 416/690-2746
President, Janet Morrison, 416/925-2831

Canadian Association for Suicide Prevention/ L'Association canadienne pour la prévention du suicide (CASP) (1985)
#201, 1615 - 10th Ave. SW, Calgary, AB T3C 0J7
403/245-3900
President, Joan Wright, 403/482-0198
Publications: CASP/ACPS News; Directory of Crisis Centres

Canadian Centre for Stress & Well-Being (1982)
Stress Management Centre
#1506, 141 Adelaide St. West, Toronto, ON M5H 3L5
416/363-6204, Fax: 416/367-1014
Director, Dr. Lucille C. Peszat, Ed.D.

Canadian Group Psychotherapy Association (CGPA)
11 Millstone Cres., Whitby, ON L1R 1T4
905/666-0555, Fax: 905/666-0000
Executive Secretary, Anne Eberle
President, Dr. Kent Mahoney
Publications: CGPA Chronicle

Canadian Hypertension Society/Société canadienne d'hypertension artérielle (CHS) (1979)
Dept. of Pharmacology, Chown Bldg., Univ. of Manitoba, #A329, 753 McDermot Ave., Winnipeg, MB R3E 0T6
204/789-3356, Fax: 204/783-6915
President, Dr. R.M.K.W. Lee, 905/521-2100, Fax: 905/523-1224
Sec.-Treas., Dr. Donald D. Smyth
Publications: Hypertension Canada
Affiliates: Canadian Society for Clinical Investigation; Royal College of Physicians & Surgeons of Canada

Canadian Institute of Stress
#500, 1235 Bay St., Toronto, ON M5R 3K4
416/961-8575, Fax: 416/237-1828
Contact, Dr. Richard Earle

Canadian Mental Health Association/Association canadienne pour la santé mentale (CMHA) (1918)
2160 Yonge St., Toronto, ON M4S 2Z3
416/484-7750, Fax: 416/484-4617
URL: http://www.io.org/~cmhator/
General Director, Edward J. Pennington
National President, Sharon Barnes
Director of Administration, Jeannine Hurd
Publications: Mental Health Matters

Canadian Play Therapy Institute (CPTI) (1985)
PO Box 2153, Kingston, ON K7L 5J9
613/384-2795, Fax: 613/634-0866, Email: cplayti@limestone.kosone.com
URL: http://www.playtherapy.org/
Executive Director, Mark Barnes, Ph.D.
Publications: Canadian Play Therapy Newsletter
Affiliates: Play Therapy International

Canadian Psychiatric Association/Association des psychiatres du Canada (CPA) (1951)
#200, 237 Argyle Dr., Ottawa, ON K2P 1B8
613/234-2815, ext.26, Fax: 613/234-9857, Toll Free: 1-800-267-1555, Email: cpa@medical.org
URL: http://medical.org
Chief Executive Officer, Alex Saunders
Manager, Communications, Sharon Petrie
Publications: Journal of Psychiatry & Neuroscience; Bulletin, bi-m.; The Canadian Journal of Psychiatry, 10 pa
Affiliates: Canadian Medical Association; World Psychiatric Association

ALBERTA PSYCHIATRIC ASSOCIATION (APA)
Holy Cross Hospital, Calgary, AB T5J 2J7
403/247-9507
President, Dr. Ron Aldons

MANITOBA PSYCHIATRIC ASSOCIATION
Room P2433, Dept. of Psychiatry, Health Sciences Centre, 771 Bannatyne Ave., Winnipeg, MB R3E 3N4
204/787-7056, Fax: 204/787-4879
President, Dr. Samia Barakat

NEW BRUNSWICK PSYCHIATRIC ASSOCIATION
PO Box 3220, Stn B, Saint John, NB E2M 4H7
506/672-7871, Fax: 506/635-1614
President, Dr. Roger. Guzman
Secretary, Jeanette Logan

NEWFOUNDLAND PSYCHIATRIC ASSOCIATION
Terrace Clinic, #8, 10 Rowan St., PO Box 15, St. John's, NF A1B 2X3
709/579-0138
Dr. John Angel
Nova Scotia Psychiatric Association: President, Dr. Simon Brooks, PO Box 280, Tatamagouche, NS B0K 1V0, 902/657-2009

ONTARIO PSYCHIATRIC ASSOCIATION (OPA) (1920)
Queen Street Mental Health Centre, 1001 Queen St. West, Toronto, ON M6J 1H4
416/535-8501, Fax: 416/583-4307
Executive Director, Allison Stuart
President, Clive Chamberlain
Publications: Dialogue

PEI PSYCHIATRIC ASSOCIATION
#10, 1 Rochford St., Charlottetown, PE C1A 3T1
902/628-6258, Fax: 902/628-2383
President, Dr. Ben Stears

SASKATCHEWAN PSYCHIATRIC ASSOCIATION
222 Ave. P South, Saskatoon, SK S7M 2W2
306/652-8777, Fax: 306/665-3304
President, Dr. Annu Thakur

Canadian Psychiatric Research Foundation
#307, 60 Bloor St. West, Toronto, ON M4W 3B8
416/975-9891
Executive Director, Ron Rea

Canadian Psychoanalytic Society/Institut canadien de psychanalyse
7000, ch Côte-des-Neiges, Montréal, PQ H3S 2C1
514/738-6105, Fax: 514/738-6393
Administrative Director, Nadia Gargour

Canadian Psychological Association/Société canadienne de psychologie (CPA) (1939)
#205, 151 Slater St., Ottawa, ON K1P 5H3
613/237-2144, Fax: 613/237-1674, Email: cpa@psychologyassoc.ca
URL: http://www.phoenix.ca/cpa/
Executive Director, Dr. John C. Service
President, Dr. David R. Evans
Publications: Psynopsis; Canadian Psychology; Canadian Journal of Experimental Psychology; Canadian Journal of Behavioural Science
Affiliates: Canadian Register of Health Service Providers in Psychology; Social Science Federation of Canada; Correctional Services Canada; Council of Provincial Associations of Psychologists; International Union of Psychological Science; National Associations Active in Criminal Justice; Youth Science Foundation

Canadian Schizophrenia Foundation (CSF) (1969)
16 Florence Ave., North York, ON M2N 1E9
416/733-2117, Fax: 416/733-2352
Executive Director, Steven Carter
Publications: Journal of Orthomolecular Medicine; Health Counsellor & Nutrition, q.; Mental Health

Children's Psychiatric Research Institute
600 Sanitorium Rd., London, ON N6H 3W7
519/471-2540, Fax: 519/847-8268
Administrator, E. Sorin

Depressive & Manic Depressive Association of Ontario/L'Association ontarienne de la dépression et de la psychose maniaco-dépressive (DMDAO) (1989)
#101, 214 Merton St., Toronto, ON M4S 1A6
416/481-5413, Fax: 416/481-5545
Executive Director, Sue Trevor, C.A.
President, Allan Strong
Publications: The Link

Fédération des familles et amis de la personne atteinte de maladie mentale/Federation of Families & Friends of Persons with a Mental Illness (FFAPAMM)
#203, 1990, boul Charest ouest, Ste-Foy, PQ G1N 4K8
418/687-0474, Téléc: 418/687-0123, Ligne sans frais: 1-800-323-0474
Directrice générale, Hélène Fradette
Publications: Le Porte Parole

Manic Depressive Association of Metropolitan Toronto (MDAMT) (1984)
#252, 40 Orchard View Blvd., Toronto, ON M4R 1B9
416/486-8046
Executive Director, Neasa Martin
President, Jack Norris
Publications: MDAMT Newsletter

National Mental Health Fund (NMHF) (1986)
#307, 60 Bloor St. West, Toronto, ON M4W 3B8
416/975-9891
Executive Director, Ron Rea
President, Timothy R. Price

Canadian Almanac & Directory 1997

ORGANIZATIONS —MILITARY & VETERANS

Publications: NMHF Newsletter; Campaigner Update, q.

Affiliates: Canadian Mental Health Association; Canadian Psychiatric Research Foundation

Ontario Association of Children's Mental Health Centres
#309, 40 St. Clair Ave. East, Toronto, ON M4T 1M9
416/921-2109
Executive Director, Sheila Weinstock

Ontario Psychological Association (OPA) (1946)
#221, 730 Yonge St., Toronto, ON M4Y 2B7
416/961-5552, Fax: 416/961-5516
Executive Director, Dr. Ruth Berman
Administrative Officer, C. Mardoner
Publications: The Ontario Psychologist

L'Ordre des psychologues du Québec (OPQ) (1962)
#510, 1100, av Beaumont, Montréal, PQ H3P 3H5
514/738-1881, Téléc: 514/737-6431, Infoligne: 514/738-1223, Ligne sans frais: 1-800-561-1223
Directeur général, René Corriveau
Publications: Psychologie-Québec
Organisation(s) affiliée(s): American Psychological Association

Schizophrenia Society of Canada/Société canadienne de schizophrénie (SSC) (1979)
#814, 75 The Donway West, North York, ON M3C 2E9
416/445-8204, Fax: 416/445-2270
Executive Director, Penelope Marrett
President, Ann Braden
Publications: The Bulletin
Affiliates: Canadian Alliance for Research on Schizophrenia; World Schizophrenia Fellowship

Society for the Treatment & Study of Stress/ Société de traitement et d'étude sur le stress
125, av Pagnuelo, Montréal, PQ H2V 3C3
514/277-8696
President, J. Pierre Hogue

Survivors of Suicide Support Program (1989)
#301, 349A George St. North, Peterborough, ON K9H 3P9
705/748-6711, Fax: 705/748-2577
Executive Director, Mark Graham

World Federation for Mental Health/Fédération mondiale pour la santé mentale (WFMH) (1948)
1021 Prince St., Alexandria, VA 22314-2971 USA
703/838-7543, Fax: 703/519-7648
Secretary General, Dr. Eugene Brody
Deputy Secretary General, Richard Hunter
Publications: The WFMH Newsletter
North American Regional Council: PO Box 185, Lethbridge, AB T1J 3T5, 403/329-1008, Fax: 403/329-0264

MENTALLY CHALLENGED PERSONS see DISABLED PERSONS

METAL INDUSTRIES see STEEL & METAL INDUSTRIES

METALLURGY see MINES & MINERAL RESOURCES

MIDWIFERY see CHILDBIRTH

MILITARY & VETERANS

Air Cadet League of Canada/Ligue des cadets de l'air du Canada (1941)
Constitution Bldg., 313 Rideau St., Ottawa, ON K1N 5Y4
613/991-4349, Fax: 613/991-4347
URL: http://www.isisnet.com/smacdouga/rcac.html
Executive Director, Richard Logan
President, W.C.F. Beattie
Publications: In-Formation

Air Force Association of Canada/L'Association des forces aériennes du Canada (1948)
PO Box 2460, Stn D, Ottawa, ON K1P 5W6
613/992-7482, Fax: 613/995-2196
Executive Director, Robert Tracy
Publications: Airforce
Affiliates: Air Force Association of United States; Alliance of Air Force Associations; Royal Air Forces Association

The Army Cadet League of Canada/Ligue des cadets de l'armée du Canada (1971)
Constitution Bldg., 305 Rideau St., Ottawa, ON K1N 9E5
613/991-4348, Fax: 613/990-8701
Executive Director, C.J. Devaney
President, L.K. Deane
Publications: Journal
Affiliates: Army Cadet Force Association; Deutscher-Bundeswehr-Verband

Army, Navy & Air Force Veterans in Canada/Les Anciens combattants de l'armée, de la marine et des forces aeriennes au Canada (ANAVETS) (1917)
#2, 6 Beechwood Ave., Vanier, ON K1L 8B4
613/744-0222, Fax: 613/744-0208
Sec.-Treas., I.D. Inrig

Canadian Battle of Normandy Foundation/ Fondation canadienne de la Bataille de Normandie (CBNF) (1992)
1650 Featherston Dr., Ottawa, ON K1H 6P2
613/731-7767, Fax: 613/731-6577
President, Cdr. W.A.B. Douglas, Ph.D., RCN (Ret'd)
Honorary Patron, Col. the Hon. Brian Dickson, PC, CC, CD
General Manager, Lawrence E. Davies, CD
Publications: Normandy Newsletter

Canadian Corps Association (1934)
201 Niagara St., Toronto, ON M5V 1C9
416/504-6694
Dominion Secretary, Shirley Wood Heesaker

The Canadian Corps of Commissionaires/Les Corps canadien des commissionnaires (1925)
The Commissionaires
#201, 100 Gloucester St., Ottawa, ON K2P 0A4
613/236-4936, Fax: 613/563-8508
Chairman, Lt.Col. R.G. Smellie, CD, QC
Executive Secretary, Lt.Gen. J.A.R. Gutknecht, CMM, OStJ, CD

Canadian Council of War Veterans' Associations
60 Morrow St., Peterborough, ON K9J 1X3
705/742-2901
President, John E. Denniston
Vice-President, Frank Caldwell
Treasurer, Bill Hughes

Canadian Infantry Association/Association canadienne de l'infanterie (CIA) (1912)
PO Box 158, Anjou, PQ H1K 4G6
514/355-2211, Fax: 514/355-2211
Sec.-Treas., LCol P. Caron, CD (Ret'd)

Canadian Naval Association
14 Hayden St., Toronto, ON M4Y 1V8
416/924-2811
Executive Director, Jean Brodie

Commission canadienne d'histoire militaire/ Canadian Commission of Military History (CCHM) (1973)
Quartier général de la défense nationale, Ottawa, ON K1A 0K2
613/998-7063, Téléc: 613/990-8579
Secrétaire général, René Chartrand
Président, Dr. Serge Bernier
Trésorière, Jean Morin
Publications: Revue internationale d'historie militaire
Organisation(s) affiliée(s): Commission internationale d'histoire militaire

Commonwealth War Graves Commission - Canadian Agency/Commission des sépultures de guerre du Commonwealth (CWGC) (1921)
#1707, 66 Slater St., Ottawa, ON K1A 0P4
613/992-3224, Fax: 613/952-6826
Secretary General, Daniel F. Wheeldon
Publications: Commonwealth War Graves Commission Annual Report
Affiliates: Commonwealth War Graves Commission

Conference of Defence Associations Institute/ Institut du congrès des associations de la défense (CDAI) (1987)
#500, 100 Gloucester, Ottawa, ON K2P 0A4
613/563-1387, Fax: 613/235-0784, Email: cdai@magi.com
President, Col. B. Shapiro
Executive Director, D.E. Code
Publications: CDAI Newsline; Vanguard, q.

Defence Associations National Network/Réseau des associations de la défense nationale (DANN) (1989)
PO Box 17, Stn B, Ottawa, ON K1P 6C3
613/727-0199, Fax: 613/727-5141
Chairman, J.C. O'Brien
National Secretary, William G. Hillaby
Publications: National Network News
Affiliates: The Royal Canadian Legion; The Navy League of Canada; The Federation of Military & United Services Institutes of Canada; The Air Force Officers Advisory Group; The Business Council on National Issues; Aerospace Industries Association of Canada; Canadian Defence Preparedness Association; The Naval Officers Association of Canada; Canadian Maritime Industries Association; The Conference of Defence Associations

Defence Research & Education Centre (DREC) (1985)
Site 4, Box 3B8, RR#1, Tantallon, NS B0J 3J0
902/823-2770, Fax: 902/823-3057
President, Commodore R.W. Crocks, Ret'd.
Executive Director, Mary Kitley
Publications: Next Steps in Canadian Foreign Policy; The Defence Debate in Canada; DREC Reports
Affiliates: Veterans Against Nuclear Arms

Dominion Civil Service War Veterans Association
1403 Gerrard St. East, Toronto, ON M4L 1Z5
416/465-0477
President, John Murray

Federation of Military & United Services Institutes of Canada/Fédération des instituts

militaires et des instituts des services unis du Canada (FMUSIC) (1973)
Fort Frontenac, Kingston, ON K7K 5L0
613/544-7307, Fax: 613/541-5944
Executive Vice-Chair, Col. W.B. MacLeod
Publications: FMUSIC Newsletter; Bulletin FIMIC

Jewish War Veterans of Canada
#353, 1111 Finch Ave., Downsview, ON M3J 2E5
416/663-8387
Post Commander, Jack Cahan

Korea Veterans Association of Canada Inc./ Association canadienne des vétérans de la Corée (1974)
8 Moorside Dr., Ottawa, ON K2C 3P4
613/225-0443, Fax: 613/225-9935
President, H. St. Laurent
Secretary, Les Peate
Publications: National Report
Affiliates: International Federation of Korea War Veterans Associations

Liaison Association of War Veterans/Association liaison des anciens combattants (1987)
CP 21, Succ Sainte-Anne-de-Bellevue, Montréal, PQ H9X 3L4
514/457-3440, Fax: 514/457-2143
Secretary, Ivette Glimont

Military Collectors Club of Canada (MCCC) (1963)
525 London St., PO Box 64009, Winnipeg, MB R2K 2Z0
204/669-0871
Sec.-Treas., John Zabarylo
Publications: Journal of the MCC of C

National Council of Veteran Associations
2827 Riverside Dr., Ottawa, ON K1V 0C4
613/731-3821, Fax: 613/731-3234
Chair, H. Clifford Chadderton
Director of Administration, Claire Roy

The Naval Officers Association of Canada/ L'Association des officiers de la marine du Canada (NOAC) (1946)
72 Robertson Rd., PO Box 26083, Nepean, ON K2H 9R6
613/832-3045, Fax: 613/832-3917
Executive Director, R.N. Duncan Mathieson, Email: duncan.mathieson@sympatico.ca
President, F.W. Crickard, 902/423-4251
Director, Maritime Affairs, P.T. Haydon, 902/835-5994
Publications: Starshell; Niobe Papers, a.

Navy League of Canada/Ligue navale du Canada (1895)
305 Rideau St., Ottawa, ON K1N 9E5
613/993-5415, Fax: 613/990-8701, Toll Free: 1-800-375-6289
Executive Director & National Secretary, Douglas J. Thomas, 613/998-0447
Publications: Info-clips
Affiliates: Conference of Defence Associates

Princess Patricia's Canadian Light Infantry Association
Regimental Headquarters, 4520 Crowchild Trail SW, Calgary, AB T3E 1T8
403/974-2862, Fax: 403/974-2864
National President, Doug Bedford
Sec.-Treas., Capt. William Lewis
Publications: Newsletter

Royal Canadian Air Force Benevolent Fund/La Caisse de Bienfaisance de l'Aviation Royale du Canada (1944)
Berger Building, 100 Metcalfe St., Ottawa, ON K1A 0K2
613/992-6082
Secretary-Manager, J.G. Allen
Publications: Benevolent Fund News

Royal Canadian Legion/Légion royale canadienne (RCL) (1926)
Dominion Secretary, Legion House, 359 Kent St., Ottawa, ON K2P 0R7
613/235-4391, Fax: 613/563-1670
Public Relations Manager, Robert J. Butt
Dominion President, Joe Kobolak
1st Vice-President, Chuck Murphy
Dominion Secretary, Duane Daly
Director of Administration, Jacques Coté
Publications: Legion
Affiliates: British Commonwealth Ex-Services League; National Council of Veterans Associations
Provincial Commands
Alberta & NWT Command: PO Box 3067, Stn B, Calgary, AB T2M 4L6, 403/284-1161, Fax: 403/284-9899
Manitoba Command: 563 St. Mary's Rd., Winnipeg, MB R2M 3L6, 204/233-3405, Fax: 204/237-1775
New Brunswick Command: PO Box 3426, Stn B, Saint John, NB E2M 4X9, 506/634-8850, Fax: 506/633-4836
Newfoundland & Labrador Command: PO Box 5745, St. John's, NF A1E 5X3, 709/753-6290, Fax: 709/753-5514
Nova Scotia Command: PO Box 9075, Stn A, Halifax, NS B3K 5M7, 902/429-6425, Fax: 902/429-7481
Ontario Command: 218 Richmond St. West, Toronto, ON M5V 1V8, 416/598-4466, Fax: 416/598-4256
Pacific Command: 3026 Arbutus St., Vancouver, BC V6J 4P7, 604/736-8166, Fax: 604/736-1635
PEI Command: Provincial Secretary, Betty Maclachlan, PO Box 20132, RPO Sherwood, Charlottetown, PE C1A 9E3, 902/892-2161, Fax: 902/368-8853
Québec Command: #410, 1000, rue Saint-Antoine ouest, Montréal, PQ H3C 3R7, 514/866-7491, Téléc: 514/866-6303
Saskatchewan Command: Provincial Secretary, Brent G. Burns, 3079 - 5 Ave., Regina, SK S4T 0L6, 306/525-8739, Fax: 306/525-5023

Royal Canadian Military Institute (RCMI) (1890)
426 University Ave., Toronto, ON M5G 1S9
416/597-0286, Fax: 416/597-6919
President, LCol. J.D. Gibson
Vice-President, Capt. Nicholas Stethem
Vice-President, LCol. E.B. Pinnington
General Manager, Norbert Luth
Publications: SITREP

Royal Canadian Mounted Police Veterans' Association/Gendarmerie royale du Canada association des ancien (1924)
Dominion HQ Secretariat, 1200 Vanier Pkwy., Ottawa, ON K1A 0R2
613/993-6497, Fax: 613/993-4353
President, Keith Trail
Secretary, Frank Korycan
Treasurer, J.H. MacLaughlan
Chief Administrative Officer, K.E. Koch
Publications: Keeping in Touch

Royal Canadian Naval Benevolent Fund (RCNBF) (1945)
PO Box 505, Stn B, Ottawa, ON K1P 5P6
613/996-5087, Fax: 613/236-8830
Sec.-Treas., L.F. Harrison

Eastern Committee: Secretary, René Cloutier, Canadian Forces Base Halifax, FMO Halifax, Halifax, NS B3K 2X0, 902/427-7825, Fax: 902/427-7824
Western Committee: Secretary, Don Ross, Canadian Forces Base Esquimalt, FMO Victoria, Victoria, BC V0S 1B0, 250/383-6264

MINES & MINERAL RESOURCES

The Asbestos Institute/Institut de l'amiante (1984)
#1750, 1002, rue Sherbrooke ouest, Montréal, PQ H3A 3L6
514/844-3956, Fax: 514/844-1381
Director General, Scott Houston
Publications: The Asbestos Institute

Association of Exploration Geochemists (AEG) (1970)
72 Robertson Rd., PO Box 26099, Nepean, ON K2H 9R0
613/828-0199, Fax: 613/828-9288, Email: aeg@synapse.net
URL: http://aeg.org./aeg/aeghome.htm/
President, William B. Coker
Business Manager, Betty Arseneault
Publications: Journal of Geochemical Exploration

Association des Mines d'Amiante du Québec/ Québec Asbestos Mining Association (AMAQ)
a/s Byers Casgrain, #3900, 1, Place Ville-Marie, Montréal, PQ H3B 4M7
514/878-3711, Téléc: 514/866-2241
Directeur général, David McAuslad
Division Protection de l'Environnement: 4125, rue Garlock, Sherbrooke, PQ J1L 1W9, 819/821-7633, Téléc: 819/821-7824

Association of Mining Municipalities of Ontario
c/o Town of Kirkland Lake, PO Bag 1757, Kirkland Lake, ON P2N 3P4
705/567-9361, Fax: 705/567-3535
President, Ernest Massicotte

Association des prospecteurs du Québec/Québec Prospectors Association (APQ) (1975)
#108, 640, 3e av, Val-d'Or, PQ J9P 1S5
819/825-4335, Téléc: 819/825-2265
Directeur général, Gratien Gélinas
Publications: Bulletin

Canadian Copper & Brass Development Association (1958)
#375, 10 Gateway Blvd., North York, ON M3C 3A1
416/421-0788, Fax: 416/421-8092
Executive Director, A. Arnold Knapp
President, J.D. Coulton
Publications: Canadian Copper/Cuivre canadien
Affiliates: International Copper Association

Canadian Institute of Mining, Metallurgy & Petroleum/Institut canadien des mines, de la métallurgie et du pétrole (CIM) (1898)
#1210, 3400, boul de Maisonneuve ouest, Montréal, PQ H3Z 3B8
514/939-2710, Fax: 514/939-2714
Executive Director, Yvan Jacques
Director of Communications, Toby King
Publications: CIM Bulletin; Journal of Canadian Petroleum Technology, 10 pa; CIM Reporter, 3 pa; CIM Directory, a.; Canadian Metallurgical Quarterly

Canadian Mineral Analysts/Analystes des minéraux canadiens (CMA) (1969)
PO Box 894, Lynn Lake, MB R0B 0W0
204/356-2902, Fax: 204/356-2902

Canadian Almanac & Directory 1997

URL: http://www.info-mine.com/assoc-inst/cma/
Managing Secretary, Sigrid Fast
Treasurer, Bill Clifford
Conference Chair, Ross Calow
Publications: Alchemist's Digest

Canadian Mining Contractors Association/ Association des entrepreneurs miniers du Canada (1991)
1088 Staghoru Ct., Mississauga, ON L5C 3R2
905/279-0104, Fax: 905/279-1646
President, Bruce Campbell

The Coal Association of Canada (CAC) (1973)
#502, 205 - 9 Ave. SE, Calgary, AB T2G 0R3
403/262-1544, Fax: 403/265-7604, Toll Free: 1-800-910-2625, Email: showes@agt.net
President, D.O. Downing
Director, Communications, W.J. Wood
Publications: Coal Forum

International Council for Applied Mineralogy (ICAM) (1980)
c/o CANMET, 555 Booth St., Ottawa, ON K1A 0G1
613/992-1376, Fax: 613/996-9673
Canadian Representative, William Petruk
Chairman, S.A. de Waal
Publications: Proceedings Volume
Affiliates: National Mineralogical Association - USA, Australia, South Africa, Europe, Brazil, South America, Poland; International Mineralogical Association

Mineralogical Association of Canada/Association minéralogique du Canada (MAC) (1957)
1460 Merivale Rd., PO Box 78087, RPO Merivale, Ottawa, ON K2E 1B1
613/226-4651, Fax: 613/226-4651
President, Dr. Roger Mitchell
Secretary, G.M. LeCheminant
Publications: MAC Newsletter; The Canadian Mineralogist, q.
Affiliates: International Mineralogical Association

Mining Association of Canada/Association minière du Canada (MAC)
#1105, 350 Sparks St., Ottawa, ON K1R 7S8
613/233-9391, Fax: 613/233-8897
URL: http://www.mining.ca
President, Dr. C. George Miller

ASSOCIATION MINIÈRE DU QUÉBEC/QUÉBEC MINING ASSOCIATION (AMQ) (1936)
Place la Cité, #942, 2600, boul Laurier, Ste-Foy, PQ G1V 4W2
418/657-2016, Téléc: 418/657-2154
Directeur général, Dan Tolgyesi
Secrétaire de direction, Lise Belisle
Publications: Filon de l'Association minière du Québec inc.

MINING ASSOCIATION OF BRITISH COLUMBIA (MABC)
840 West Hastings St., Vancouver, BC V6E 1C8
604/681-4321, Fax: 604/681-5305
President, Gary Livingstone

MINING ASSOCIATION OF MANITOBA INC. (1940)
#700, 305 Broadway Ave., Winnipeg, MB R3C 3J7
204/942-2789, Fax: 204/943-4371
Executive Vice-President, Ed Huebert

MINING ASSOCIATION OF NEWFOUNDLAND
c/o Iron Ore Company of Canada, PO Box 1000, Labrador City, NF A2V 2L8
709/944-8486, Fax: 709/944-8343
President, Reg Gagnon

MINING SOCIETY OF NOVA SCOTIA (1887)
88 Leeside Dr., Sydney, NS B1R 1S6

902/567-2147, Fax: 902/567-2147
Sec.-Treas., George Sigut
Affiliates: Canadian Institute of Mining, Metallurgy & Petroleum

NEW BRUNSWICK MINING ASSOCIATION/L'ASSOCIATION MINIÈRE DU NOUVEAU-BRUNSWICK
#104, 1133 St. George Blvd., Moncton, NB E1E 4E1
506/857-3056, Fax: 506/857-3059, Telex: 014-2126
Manager, Gerald R. Cluney

ONTARIO MINING ASSOCIATION (OMA)
#1501, 110 Yonge St., Toronto, ON M5C 1T4
416/364-9301, Fax: 416/364-5986
President, Patrick Reid
Publications: Mining in Ontario; Mining Matters, m.

SASKATCHEWAN MINING ASSOCIATION (1965)
1740 Avord Tower, 2002 Victoria Ave., Regina, SK S4P 0R7
306/757-9505, Fax: 306/569-1085
Executive Director, Robert M. Cunningham
President, Lorne Repka
Publications: Mining Issues; Mineral Scene, q.

New Brunswick Prospectors & Developers Association
PO Box 1195, Bathurst, NB E2A 4H9
506/546-4779, Fax: 506/546-4088
President, Earnest Brooks, 506/548-2156
Secretary, Don Hoy, 506/548-2772, Fax: 506/546-2332
Affiliates: Prospectors & Developers Association of Canada

Newfoundland & Labrador Explorationists (NALE) (1989)
PO Box 23013, St. John's, NF A1B 4J9
709/747-4425, Fax: 709/747-4491
President, Peter Tallman
Affiliates: Canadian Mineral Industries Federation; Prospectors & Developers Association of Canada

Petroleum Society of CIM (1949)
#320, 101 - 6 Ave. SW, Calgary, AB T2P 3P4
403/237-5112, Fax: 403/262-4792, Email: petsoc@canpic.ca
URL: http://www.canpic.ca/PETSOC/
Office Manager, Catherine Buchanan
Publications: JCPT

Prospectors & Developers Association of Canada/Association canadienne des prospecteurs & entrepreneurs (PDAC) (1932)
34 King St. East, 9th Fl., Toronto, ON M5C 2X8
416/362-1969, Fax: 416/362-0101
Managing Director, Dr. Anthony Andrews
President, Dr. John A. Hansuld
Publications: PDAC Digest; Exploration & Development Highlights, a.; PDAC in Brief, bi-m.
Affiliates: Mining Association of Canada

MONUMENTS & SITES see HISTORY, HERITAGE, GENEALOGY

MOTOR LEAGUES see AUTOMOTIVE

MULTICULTURALISM
see also Culture

Affiliation of Multicultural Societies & Service Agencies of B.C. (AMSSA) (1977)
385 Boundary Rd., Vancouver, BC V5K 4S1
604/298-5949, Fax: 604/298-0747
Executive Director, Beverly Nann
President, Alix James
Publications: Cultures West; Update Bulletin, q.

Armenian National Committee of Canada (ANC)
3401, rue Olivar-Asselin, Montréal, PQ H4J 1L5
514/334-1299, Fax: 514/334-6853
Executive Director, Asbed Azedissian
President, Dr. Girair Basmadjian
Publications: The Armenian Cause
Affiliates: Armenian National Federation

Armenian National Federation (ANF)
3401, rue Olivar-Asselin, Montréal, PQ H4J 1L5
514/334-1299, Fax: 514/334-6853
President, Stepan Nadjarian
Affiliates: Armenian National Committee of Canada

Association France-Canada Inc. (1948)
CP 195, Succ. A, Toronto, ON M5W 1B2
416/469-0097
Président, Essy A. Erfani
Vice-présidente, Nadia Gagnon
Publications: Bulletin de France-Canada
Organisation(s) affiliée(s): La Fédération canadienne France-Canada

Association of Soviet Jewry in Canada (1980)
#6, 5987 Bathurst St., North York, ON M2R 1Z3
416/229-6057, Fax: 416/229-2592
Coordinator, Ella Ceurevicm
President, Rudy Favelyukis

Association of United Ukrainian Canadians (AUUC) (1918)
1604 Bloor St. West, Toronto, ON M6P 1A7
Fax: 416/535-1546, Info Line: 416/535-1063
National President, George Moskal

Australia-New Zealand Association (ANZA) (1935)
The ANZA Club
3 - 8th Ave. West, Vancouver, BC V5Y 1M8
604/876-7128, Fax: 604/872-0421
Manager, Paul Woodley
Publications: ANZA News

B'nai Brith Canada (BBC)
Children of the Covenant
15 Hove St., North York, ON M3H 4Y8
416/633-6224, Fax: 416/630-2159, Email: bnai_brith@uarr.org
URL: http://www.canada.ibm.net/bnaibrith
President, Lyle Smordin
Executive Vice-President, Frank Dimant
National Director, Field Services, Pearl Gladman
Publications: The Jewish Tribune; Annual Audit of Anti-Semitism, a.
Affiliates: B'nai Brith International
Midwestern Region: Regional Director, Sophie Tapper, 370 Hargrave St., Winnipeg, MB R3B 2K1, 204/942-2597, Fax: 204/956-2819
National Capital Region: Director, Government Relations, Ian J. Kagedan, 151 Chapel St., Ottawa, ON K1N 7Y2, 613/789-4922, Fax: 613/789-1325
Québec Region: Regional Director, Yechiel Glustein, #219, 6900, boul Decarie, Montréal, PQ H3X 2T8, 514/733-5377, Fax: 514/342-9632
Western Region: 1607 - 90 Ave. SW, Calgary, AB T2V 4V7, 403/255-6554

Baltic Federation in Canada
4 Credit Union Dr., Toronto, ON M4A 2N8
416/755-2353, Fax: 416/755-1244
President, Viesturs Zarins

ESTONIAN CENTRAL COUNCIL IN CANADA (1952)
#308, 958 Broadview Ave., Toronto, ON M4K 2R6
416/465-2219, Fax: 416/461-0488
Secretary General, Peter P. Aruvald

President, Laas Leiviat
Publications: Estonian Central Council in Canada Newsletter

LATVIAN NATIONAL FEDERATION IN CANADA
4 Credit Union Dr., Toronto, ON M4A 2N8
416/755-2353, Fax: 416/755-1244
President, Ted Kronbertes

THE LITHUANIAN CANADIAN COMMUNITY
1011 College St., Toronto, ON M6H 1A8
416/533-3292, Fax: 416/533-2282
Executive Director, Darija Powell
President, Al Pacevious

Bangladesh Awami League of Canada (1992)
Parkview Towers, #1514, 2777 Kipling Ave., Etobicoke, ON M9V 4M2
416/742-3469, Fax: 416/742-9530, Email: fkhan@interlog.com
URL: http://www.interlog.com/~fkhan/; http://www.ica.net/pages/fkhan420
President, Farook H. Khan
Publications: Joy Bangla

Belarusian Canadian Alliance (BCA) (1948)
524 Clarens Ave., Toronto, ON M6H 3W7
416/530-1025, Fax: 416/267-0798
President, Mykolaj Ganko, 416/267-0798
Secretary, George Repetski, 905/564-3578
Publications: Info-BCA

Belgo-Canadian Association (BCA) (1948)
121 Chillery Ave., Scarborough, ON M1K 4T5
416/261-4603; 705/877-3072
President, Yvonne Kennedy
Publications: Newsletter

Black Cultural Centre for Nova Scotia (1977)
Society for the Protection & Preservation of Black Culture in Nova Scotia
1149 Main St., Dartmouth, NS B2Z 1A8
902/434-6223
President, Alma Johnston

The Black Secretariat (1984)
#202, 394A Euclid Ave., Toronto, ON M6G 2S9
416/924-1104, Fax: 416/924-3406
Chairperson, Enid Lee
Publications: Black Voices; The Black Directory, a.

Canada-Israel Foundation for Academic Exchanges/Fondation Canada-Israel pour les échanges universitaires (CIFAE)
255 Wychwood Park, London, ON N6A 3K7
519/661-3820
Academic Director, Alain Goldschlager, Email: agold@bosshog.arts.uwo.ca

Canadian Arab Federation/Fédération Canado-Arabe (CAF) (1967)
5298 Dundas St. West, Etobicoke, ON M9B 1B2
416/231-7524, Fax: 416/231-6850
Executive Director, Dr. Nada El-Yassir
President, Dr. Nassib El-Husseini
Publications: Arab Canadian

Canadian Centre for Jewish Community Studies/Centre canadien pour l'étude de la communauté juive (1980)
Jerusalem Centre for Public Affairs
#414, 855, rue Sherbrooke ouest, Montréal, PQ H3A 2T7
514/398-4806, Fax: 514/398-1770
Director, Harold M. Waller

The Canadian Doukhobor Society (CDS)
RR#1, Site 2, CB4, Castlegar, BC V1N 3H7
250/365-5327, Fax: 250/365-5327
Sec.-Treas., Larry A.. Ewashen
Co-Chair, Alex A. Wishlow
Co-Chair, Ken P. Bonderoff
Publications: The Canadian Doukhobor Newsletter

Canadian Ethnocultural Council/Conseil ethnoculturel du Canada (1980)
#1100, 251 Laurier Ave. West, Ottawa, ON K1P 5J6
613/230-3867, Fax: 613/230-8051
Executive Director, Irene Kamchen
Publications: Ethno Canada

Canadian Hispanic Congress
#200, 1829 - 54 St. SE, Calgary, AB T2B 1N5
403/248-3457, Fax: 403/273-5100
Contact, Felix Mora

Canadian Institute for Jewish Research/Institut canadien de recherche sur le Judaisme
#550, 5250, boul Decarie, Montréal, PQ H3X 2H9
514/486-5544, Fax: 514/488 3064
Director, Prof. Frederick Krantz
Publications: Israfax

Canadian Jewish Congress/Congrès juif canadien (CJC) (1919)
1590, av Docteur Penfield, Montréal, PQ H3G 1C5
514/931-7531, Fax: 514/931-0548
National Executive Director, Jack Silverstone
President, Goldie Hershon
Communications, Michael Beigleman
Publications: National Archives Newsletter; National Small Communities Newsletter, q.; Intercom, q.
Atlantic Jewish Community Council: Program Coordinator, John Goldberg, Lord Nelson Hotel, #305, 1515 South Park St., Halifax, NS B3J 2L2, 902/422-7491, Fax: 902/425-3722
Calgary Jewish Community Council: Executive Director, Joel Miller, 1607 - 90 Ave. SW, Calgary, AB T2V 4V7, 403/253-8600, Fax: 403/253-7915
Jewish Community Council of Ottawa: Executive Director, Stanley A. Urman, 151 Chapel St., Ottawa, ON K1N 7Y2, 613/789-7306, Fax: 613/789-4593
Jewish Federation of Edmonton: Chief Administrative Officer, Miriam Cooper, 7200 - 156 St., Edmonton, AB T5R 1X3, 403/487-0585, Fax: 403/481-1854
Ontario Region: Executive Director, Manuel Prutschi, 4600 Bathurst St., North York, ON M2R 3V2, 416/635-2883, ext.123, Fax: 416/635-1408
Pacific Region: Executive Director, Erwin Nest, 950 - 41st Ave. West, Vancouver, BC V5Z 2N7, 604/257-5101, Fax: 604/257-5131
Saskatchewan Region - Regina: Community Development Officer, Eileen Curtis, 4715 McTavish St., Regina, SK S4S 6H2, 306/569-8166, Fax: 306/352-3499
Saskatchewan Region - Saskatoon: Community Development Officer, Walter Gumprich, c/o Congregation Agudas Israel, 715 McKinnon Ave., Saskatoon, SK S7H 2G2, 306/343-7023, Fax: 306/374-7715
Winnipeg Jewish Community Council: Executive Director, Robert Freedman, #200, 370 Hargrave St., Winnipeg, MB R3B 2K1, 204/943-0406, Fax: 204/956-0609

Canadian Latvian Business & Professional Association (CLBPA)
123 Overland Dr., North York, ON M3C 2C7
416/444-5201, Fax: 416/444-5208
President, Alexander Budrevics
Publications: CLBPA Newsletter

Canadian Polish Congress (CPC) (1944)
Kongres Polonii Kanadyjskiej, 288 Roncesvalles Ave., Toronto, ON M6R 2M4
416/532-2876; 7197, Fax: 416/532-5730
Secretary General, Andrew Guzkowski
President, Marek Malicki
Executive Vice-President, Jan Kaszuba
Publications: Newsletter
Affiliates: Polonia of the Free World; Canadian Polish Research Institute; Adam Mickiewicz Foundation; Polish Combattants Association; Polish National Union

Canadian Polish Society
43 Facer St., St Catharines, ON L2M 5H4
905/937-1413
Financial Secretary, Teresa Spera

Canadian Serbian National Committee (1965)
One Secroft Cres., North York, ON M3N 1R5
416/663-3409; 769-7181, Fax: 416/604-8565
Contact, William Dyrovic
Publications: Fraternity Review

Canadian Slavonic Association
3431 av Mont-Royal est, Montréal, PQ H1X 3H2
514/527-3720; 672-5262
National President, Gregoire Maksymiuk
Executive Director, Jean-Pierre Olinick

Canadian Slovak League
1736 Dundas St. West, Toronto, ON M6K 1V5
416/533-6924, Fax: 416/533-6924
Secretary, Helen Danko

Canadian Tibetan Association of Ontario
19 Collingwood St., Scarborough, ON M1S 1A4
416/298-0464, Fax: 416/240-2083
President, Rinchen Takpa

Canadian Turkish Islamic Heritage Association
336 Pape Ave., Toronto, ON M4M 2W7
416/469-2610

Canadian Ukrainian Immigrant Aid Society (CUIAS) (1977)
#96, 2150 Bloor St. West, Toronto, ON M6S 1M8
416/767-4595, Fax: 416/767-2658
Executive Director, Eugen Duvalko
Affiliates: Ukrainian Canadian Congress

Canadian Zionist Federation/La fédération sioniste canadienne (CZF) (1967)
#550, 5250, boul Decarie, Montréal, PQ H3X 2H9
514/486-9526, Fax: 514/483-6392
National President, Kurt Rothschild
Affiliates: World Zionist Organization; Jewish Agency

Caribbean Cultural Committee
Caribana
#300, 474 Bathurst St., Toronto, ON M5J 2S6
416/925-5435, Fax: 416/925-1108
Contact, Rodney Davis

Central Organization of Sudeten-German Clubs in Canada (1957)
20 Banff Rd., Toronto, ON M4S 2V5
416/483-8240
President, Rolf Lorenz
Publications: Freund Schaft/Friendship

Chinese Canadian Intercultural Association (1980)
112 Huron St., Toronto, ON M5T 2B2
416/591-6347, Fax: 416/591-6347
Executive Director, Yiu-Kuen Chan
President, Mr. On-Po Sze

Chinese Canadian National Council/Conseil national des canadiens chinois (CCNC) (1980)
Chinese Canadian National Council for Equality
#605, 119 Spadina Ave., Toronto, ON M5V 2L1
416/977-9871, Fax: 416/977-1630

Executive Director, John Tang
Publications: Newsletter

Clans & Scottish Societies of Canada (CASSOC) (1976)
St. Andrews Church, 73 Simcoe St., Toronto, ON M5J 1W9
416/593-0518, Toll Free: 1-800-593-0518
Chairman, John H. MacDonald
Sec.-Treas., W. Neil Fraser
Publications: An Drochaid

Congrès Hellenique du Québec
a/s Centre Communautaire Grec, #211, 5777, rue Wilderton, Westmount, PQ H3S 2V7
514/738-2421, Téléc: 514/340-3586
Directrice générale, Kalioki Hagiepepros

Cypriot Federation of Canada
1430 Ellice Ave., Winnipeg, MB R3G 0G4
204/774-4444, Fax: 204/774-2002
President, Costas Ataliotis

Czech & Slovak Association of Canada (1939)
740 Spadina Ave., Toronto, ON M5S 2J2
416/925-2241, Fax: 416/925-1940
Executive Director, Anna Otypka
President, Blanca Rohn
Publications: Vestnik

Fédération des associations lao du Canada/Federation of Lao Associations of Canada (FALC) (1987)
833, rue Murdoch, Chicoutimi, PQ G7H 3Z6
418/543-9960, Téléc: 418/545-5012
Président, Khamlay Mounivongs

Federation of Cambodian Associations of Canada/Fédération des associations cambodgiennes du Canada
PO Box 389, Stn Jean-Talon, Montréal, PQ H1S 2G3
514/327-9129, Fax: 514/327-4940
Secretary General, Simon Yim

Federation of Canada-China Friendship Associations
2948 Scott St., Victoria, BC V8R 4J6
250/598-5962, Fax: 250/598-5962
President, Barbara Chen

Federation of Canadian Turkish Associations (1985)
660 Eglinton Ave. East, PO Box 50029, Toronto, ON M4G 4G1
416/480-0954, Fax: 416/480-0682
President, Demir Delen

Federation of Chinese Canadian Professionals (Ontario)
Market Village, Box 127, #A203, 4350 Steeles Ave. East, Markham, ON L3R 9V4
905/940-3227

Federation of Chinese Canadian Professionals (Québec)/Fédération des professionnels chinois canadiens (Québec)
1111, rue St-Urbain, #R16, Montréal, PQ H2Z 1Y6
514/393-1071, Fax: 514/393-9709
President, Arthur C.F. Lau

Federation of Danish Associations in Canada/Fédération des associations danoises du Canada (1981)
The Danish Federation
679 Eastvale Ct., Gloucester, ON K1J 6Z7
613/238-6464; 747-9764
President, Rolf Buschardt Christensen
Publications: Conference Book

Federation of Italian Canadian Seniors Clubs
Casa del Zotto, 3010 Dufferin St., Toronto, ON M6B 4J5
416/787-4340, Fax: 416/787-3745
Executive Director, Antonietta Gulli

Federation of Russian Canadians (FRC) (1930)
799 College St., Toronto, ON M6G 1C7
416/536-7330, Fax: 416/535-3265
Vice-President, Nita Miskevich
Secretary, Nicole Tichnovich
Treasurer, Emily Bradshaw
Publications: Vestnik
Affiliates: Association of Canadians of Russian Descent

Federation of Scottish Clans in Nova Scotia
6079 Compton Ave., Halifax, NS B3K 1E8
President, Fran Sutherland, 902/423-3095
Vice-President, Jean Watson, 902/864-8335

Federation of Sikh Societies of Canada/Fédération des sociétés Sikhs du Canada
PO Box 91, Stn B, Ottawa, ON K1P 6C3
613/737-7296, Fax: 613/739-7153
President, Mohinder Singh Gosal

Finnish Canadian Cultural Federation/Fédération culturelle finno-canadienne (1971)
Kanadan Suomalainen Kultturriliitto, #1001, 470 Cambridge St. South, Ottawa, ON K1S 4H8
613/235-4216
President, Mauri A. Jalava
Affiliates: Finland Society, R.Y.; Finn Fest USA, Inc.

Finnish Organization of Canada
PO Box 65070, Toronto, ON M4K 3Z2
416/465-8981
Executive Secretary, Eric Junnila
Publications: KAIKU/ECHO

Fondation de l'amitié libano-canadienne/Libano-Canadian Friendship Foundation (1988)
82, rue de Paris, Dollard-des-Ormeaux, PQ H9B 3E3
514/875-2033, Téléc: 514/685-5743
Président, Ayad Karkouti

German-Canadian Congress/Congrès germano-canadien (GCC) (1985)
DeutschKanadischer Kongress, 965 Richmond Rd., Ottawa, ON K2B 6R1
613/728-6850, Fax: 613/728-2875
Executive Director, Irene Kamchen
Publications: Kongressnachrichten; News...nouvelles...nachrichten, q.

Goethe-Institut (Montréal)
418, rue Sherbrooke est, Montréal, PQ H2L 1J6
514/499-0159, Fax: 514/499-0905
Contact, Uwe Förster

Goethe-Institut Toronto (1962)
German Cultural Centre
1067 Yonge St., Toronto, ON M4W 2L2
416/924-3327, Fax: 416/924-0589, Info Line: 416/924-7953, Email: goethetoront@cis.compuserve.com
URL: http://www.goethe.de/uk/tor
Director, Wilfried Scheffler
Administrator, Brigitte Furch

Goethe-Institut/German Cultural Centre (Vancouver)
944 - 8th Ave. West, Vancouver, BC V5Z 1E5
604/732-3966, Fax: 604/732-5062
Contact, Werner Wolf

Hebrew Culture Organization of Canada (HCOC) (1949)
#550, 5250, boul Décarie, Montréal, PQ H3X 2H9
514/486-9526, Fax: 514/483-6392

Holocaust Education & Memorial Centre of Toronto (HEMC) (1985)
4600 Bathurst St., North York, ON M2R 3V2
416/635-2883, ext.144, Fax: 416/635-0925
Director, Pnina Zilberman
Publications: HEMC Newsletter

Hungarian Canadian Federation
840 St. Clair Ave. West, Toronto, ON M6C 1C1
416/654-4926

Icelandic National League (INL)
699 Carter Ave., Winnipeg, MB R3M 2C3
204/284-3402, Fax: 204/284-3870
URL: http://www.helix.net/~rasgeirs/
President, Laurence Johnson
Affiliates: INL USA; Icelandic International League

Institut interculturel de Montréal/Intercultural Institute of Montréal (IIM) (1963)
4917, rue St-Urbain, Montréal, PQ H2T 2W1
514/288-7229, Téléc: 514/844-6800, Courrier électronique: andre_giguere@fcmm.login.qc.ca
Présidente/Directrice générale, Kalpana Das
Président du C.A., Carlo Sterlin
Publications: Interculture; Babillard interculturel, mensuel

Irish Canadian Cultural Association of New Brunswick (1983)
109 Roy Ave., Miramichi, NB E1V 3N8
506/622-4007, Fax: 506/773-5997
President, Farrell McCarthy
Publications: The Shamrock Leaf

Irish Freedom Association (IFA) (1981)
PO Box 171, Stn F, Toronto, ON M4Y 2L5
416/778-7821
Secretary, Farha'd O'Neill
Chair, Rita Adams
Secretary, Michelle M'Sherry
Publications: The Harp
Affiliates: Québec Irlande (Montréal)

Islamic Foundation of Toronto, Inc.
441 Nugget Ave., Scarborough, ON M1S 5E1
416/321-0909, Fax: 416/321-1995

Islamic Information Foundation (IIF) (1981)
8 Laurel Lane, Halifax, NS B3M 2P6
902/445-2494, Fax: 902/445-2494
Chairperson, Jamal Badawi

Italian Cultural Institute (1976)
496 Huron St., Toronto, ON M5R 2R3
416/921-3802, Fax: 416/962-2503
Director, Francesca Valente
Assistant Director, Martin Stiglio
Publications: News

Jamaican Canadian Association (JCA)
995 Arrow Rd., North York, ON M9M 2Z5
416/746-5772, Fax: 416/746-5772
Executive Director, Akwatu Khenti
Publications: In Focus
Affiliates: The Black Secretariat

Japanese Canadian Citizens Association
58 Northbrook Rd., Toronto, ON M4J 4G3
416/461-5765
President, Edward R. Ide

Jewish Association for Development - Canada/ Juifs associés pour le développement - Canada (JAD/Canada) (1987)
151 Chapel St., Ottawa, ON K1N 7Y2
613/789-7306
President, Elaine Sigler
Vice-President, Dr. K. Hoffman
Sec.-Treas., Seymour Dubrow
Publications: JAD Report
Affiliates: American Jewish World Service

The Jewish Federation of Greater Toronto (JFGT) (1917)
4600 Bathurst St., North York, ON M2R 3V2
416/635-2883, Fax: 416/631-5715
Executive Director, Dr. Allan Reitzes
President, Sandra Brown

Jewish Immigrant Aid Services of Canada/ Services canadiens d'assistance aux immigrants juifs (JIAS) (1922)
#325, 4600 Bathurst St., North York, ON M2R 3V3
416/630-6481, Fax: 416/630-1376
Director, Perry Romberg

Jewish National Fund of Canada
#500, 1980, rue Sherbrooke ouest, Montréal, PQ H3H 1E8
514/934-0313, Fax: 514/934-0382
Executive Vice-President, Avner Regev
Affiliates: World Zionist Organization

Labor Zionist Alliance of Canada
Labor Zionist Movement of Canada
#10, 7005, rue Kildare, Montréal, PQ H4W 1C1
514/342-9710
Chairman, David Kofsky
Affiliates: World Labor Zionist Movement & Israel Labor Party
Central Region Office: Director, Hy Fogelman, 272 Codsell Ave., North York, ON M3H 3X2, 416/630-9444
Western Region Office: 1727 Main St., Winnipeg, MB R2V 1Z4

Latin American Working Group (LAWG) (1966)
603 1/2 Parliament St., Toronto, ON M5S 2T2
416/966-4773, Fax: 416/921-0071
George Cram
Eduardo Geray
Victoria Bay
Publications: Americas Update
Affiliates: Canada-Latin America Resource Centre; Canadian Information Network on Development Issues

Lithuanian Canadian R.C. Cultural Society (1949)
Ziburiai - Lights of Homeland
2185 Stavebank Rd., Mississauga, ON L5C 1T3
905/275-4672, Fax: 905/275-1336
President, Ramune Jonaitis
Editor, P. Gaida
Publications: The Lights of Homeland

Maltese Canadian Society of Toronto, Inc. (1922)
3084 Dundas St. West, Toronto, ON M6P 1Z8
416/767-3645
Publications: Information Letter
Affiliates: Maltese-Canadian Federation Inc.

Manitoba Intercultural Council Inc.
#500, 283 Bannatyne Ave., Winnipeg, MB R3B 3B2
204/943-9196, Fax: 204/956-1137
President, Terry Prychitko
Administrative Secretary, Maria Bansee

Manitoba Multicultural Resources Centre Inc. (MMRC) (1984)
1910 Portage Ave., 2nd Fl., Winnipeg, MB R3J 0J2
204/831-6672, Fax: 204/986-3798, Email: mmrc@freenet.mb.ca
Chairperson, Dr. Fred Stambrook
Vice-Chair, Betty Ann Watts
Treasurer, Daman Johnston
Secretary, Ragini Dayal
Publications: Ethnobank
Affiliates: Coalition for Human Equity

Mizrachi-Hapoel Hamizrachi Organization of Canada
#503, 3101 Bathurst St., Toronto, ON M6A 2A6
416/789-7576, Fax: 416/789-7733
National Executive Vice-President, Rabbi Menachem Gopin
Publications: Or Hamizrach
Montréal Regional Office: Director, Peter Berkovitch, #216, 5250, boul Decarie, Montréal, PQ H3X 2H9, 514/483-3660, Fax: 514/483-6392

Multicultural Association of Northwestern Ontario (MANWO) (1980)
711 Victoria Ave. East, Thunder Bay, ON P7C 5X9
807/622-4666, Fax: 807/622-7271
Executive Director, Moffat S. Makuto
Resource Development Officer, Erika Rebernik
Publications: Regional Youth Council Newsletter; NWO Resource Directory, biennial

Multicultural Association of Nova Scotia (MANS) (1975)
#901, 1809 Barrington St., Halifax, NS B3J 3K8
902/423-6534, Fax: 902/422-0881
Executive Director, Barbara Campbell
President, Kulvinder Dhillon
Publications: Share
Affiliates: Cultural Federations of Nova Scotia; Atlantic Multicultural Council

Multicultural Council of Saskatchewan (MCoS) (1975)
369 Park St., Regina, SK S4N 5B2
306/721-2767, Fax: 306/721-3342
General Manager, Wade F. Luzny
Publications: News Circular; Saskatchewan Multicultural Magazine, q.; Our Multicultural Wish, biennial
Affiliates: Saskatchewan Council of Cultural Organizations

Multicultural History Society of Ontario (1976)
43 Queen's Park Cres. East, Toronto, ON M5S 2C3
416/979-2973, Fax: 416/979-7947
Director & CEO, Prof. Paul R. Magocsi
Associate Director, Finances, Carl Thorpe
Publications: Polyphony; Multicultural History Society of Ontario Newsletter

Muslim Education & Welfare Foundation of Canada (MEWFC) (1987)
2580 McGill St., Vancouver, BC V5K 1H1
604/255-9941, Fax: 604/255-9941
President, Shamim Ahmad Sambhali
Secretary, Syed E. Rehman
Treasurer, Basil Ahmad

Muslim World League (1962)
#1018, 191 The West Mall, Etobicoke, ON M9C 5K8
416/622-2184, Fax: 416/622-2618
Director, Dr. Arafat El-Ashi

National Association of Canadians of Origin in India (NACOI) (1976)
PO Box 2308, Stn D, Ottawa, ON K1P 5W5
613/235-7343, Fax: 613/567-0655
Executive Director, Harbans Singh
Publications: Forum

National Association of Japanese Canadians (NAJC) (1947)
404 Webb Pl., Winnipeg, MB R3B 3J4
204/943-2910, Fax: 204/947-3145
Executive Director, Caroline Yamashita
President, Roy Inouye
Publications: Nikkei Voice
Affiliates: Canadian Ethnocultural Council; Canadian Council for Refugees; National Capital Alliance on Race Relations

National Congress of Italian Canadians/Congrès national des italo-canadiens (NCIC) (1974)
#300, 427 Preston St., Ottawa, ON K1S 4N3
613/232-7321, Fax: 613/232-8286
Executive Director, Laura Del Bosco, 514/279-6357
President, Renzo Orsi
Publications: Il Nazionale

National Council of Ghanaian-Canadians (NCGC)
925 Albion Rd., Etobicoke, ON M9V 1A5
416/740-5554
President, Charles Agyei-Amoama

National Council of Trinidad & Tobago Organizations in Canada (NCTTOC) (1983)
#1, 66 Oakmeadow Blvd., Scarborough, ON M1E 4G5
416/283-9672, Fax: 416/393-0834
President, Emmanuel J. Dick, 416/393-0190
Publications: NCTTOC News

National Federation of Pakistani Canadians Inc. (NFPC) (1982)
#1100, 251 Laurier Ave. West, Ottawa, ON K1P 5J6
613/232-5346, Fax: 613/232-6607
Executive Director, Talat Ali
President, Ali Khan
Treasurer, Naki Chaudhary
Publications: NFPC Newsletter

New Brunswick Multicultural Council/Conseil Multiculturel du Nouveau-Brunswick (NBMC) (1983)
374 St. George St., Moncton, NB E1C 1X2
506/853-0013, Fax: 506/857-9430
Executive Director, Cynthia Black
Publications: NBMC Newsletter
Affiliates: Atlantic Multicultural Council; Canadian Federation of Multicultural Councils

Ontario Korean Businessmen's Association (1973)
One Mobile Dr., North York, ON M4A 1H5
416/285-1100, Fax: 416/285-1103
Administrator, Sam Chung
Publications: KBA News
Affiliates: Ontario Korean Businessmen's Association Cooperative

Ontario Multicultural Association (OMAMO) (1983)
#0116, 65 Front St. West, PO Box 137, Toronto, ON M5J 1E6
416/696-9071, Fax: 416/696-8706
President, Dr. Keith Lowe
Affiliates: Canadian Council for Multicultural & Intercultural Education

ORT Canada (1944)
Organization for Educational Resources & Technological Training
#208, 5165, rue Sherbrooke ouest, Montréal, PQ H4A 1T6
514/481-2787, Fax: 514/481-4119
National President, Dr. Mel Schwartz
Publications: ORT Reporter

Affiliates: World ORT Union
Toronto: National Executive Director, Diane Uslaner; National Administrative Coordinator, Sandy Stern, #604, 3101 Bathurst St., Toronto, ON M6A 2A6, 416/787-0339, Fax: 416/787-9420

Pan-Macedonian Association (1960)
406 Danforth Ave., Toronto, ON M4K 1P3
416/297-9530
President, Dr. Basil Solkaridis
Secretary, Alec Kalasatis

Polish Alliance of Canada
1640 Bloor St. West, Toronto, ON M6P 4A8
416/531-4826

Progressive Pakistan Canadian Friendship Society (1992)
4944 Joyce St., Vancouver, BC V5R 4G6
604/433-1859, Fax: 604/433-1859
President, M.Z. Khan
Affiliates: Vancouver Multicultural Society

Romanian World Congress
170 Garden Ave., Richmond Hill, ON L4C 6M2
905/889-8228, Fax: 905/881-8552
President, Tudor Bompa, Ph.D.
Publications: Stindardul Romanilor

Russian Canadian Cultural Aid Society
91 Kersdale Ave., Toronto, ON M6M 1E4
416/653-1361
President, Victor Popov

Slavic Congress of Canada (1989)
9 Helene St. South, Mississauga, ON L5G 3A8
905/278-3996, Fax: 905/278-3996
President, W. Strok

Slovak Canadian National Council/Conseil national des slovaques canadiens
#210, 50 MacIntosh Dr., Markham, ON L3R 9T3
905/513-1215, Fax: 905/513-1215
President, Margaret A. Dvorsky

Slovak Heritage & Cultural Society of British Columbia (1990)
3804 Yale St., Burnaby, BC V5C 1P6
604/291-8065, Fax: 604/291-1966, Email: vlinder@direct.ca
Chairperson, Vladimir Linder
Publications: Slovak Heritage Live

Slovenian Christian Democratic Association of Canada (1965)
251 Golfdale Rd., Toronto, ON M4N 2C2
416/488-3381, Fax: 416/486-2320
President, Peter Klopchic
Affiliates: International Union of Christian Democratic Parties; European Union of Christian Democratic Parties

Somali Immigrant Aid Organization (1992)
#21, 698 Weston Rd., Toronto, ON M6N 3R3
416/766-7326, Fax: 416/769-9217
Executive Director, Dr. Mohammed H. Ali

South Pacific Peoples Foundation of Canada (SPPF) (1975)
#415, 620 View St., Victoria, BC V8W 1J6
250/381-4131, Fax: 250/388-5258, Email: sppf@web.apc.org
Executive Director, Stuart Wulff
Publications: Tok Blong Pasifik
Affiliates: Nuclear Free & Independent Pacific Movement

Toronto Jewish Historical Society (1948)
402 Richview Ave., Toronto, ON M5P 3G6
416/486-7856
President, Dr. Gordon Kerbel

Ukrainian Canadian Congress/Congrès des ukrainiens-canadiens (UCC) (1940)
456 Main St., Winnipeg, MB R3B 1B6
204/942-4627, Fax: 204/947-3882, Email: ucc_hg@mbnet.mb.ca
Executive Director, Lydia Hawryshkiw
President, W. Oleh Romaniw, QC
Director of Public Relations, Ihor Shawarsky
Publications: The Bulletin; Congress Report, triennial
Affiliates: Ukrainian Catholic Brotherhood; Ukrainian Self-Reliance Association (Orthodox); Ukrainian National Federation; League of Ukrainian Canadians; Ukrainian Canadian Professional & Business Federation

Ukrainian Canadian Research Foundation (1965)
4 Island View Blvd., Toronto, ON M8V 2P4
416/255-9090
President, S.T. Pawluk

Ukrainian National Aid Association
140 Bathurst St., Toronto, ON M5V 2R3
416/703-0687, Fax: 416/703-0687
Contact, Walter Okipniuk

Ukrainian National Association
Canadian Office, 18 Leland Ave., Toronto, ON M8Z 2X5
416/231-4685
Chief Agent, Yaroslava Zorych

United Israel Appeal of Canada (1967)
UIA of Canada
#315, 4600 Bathurst St., North York, ON M2R 3V2
416/636-7655, Fax: 416/636-9897, Email: uiacan@cjf.noli.com
Executive Vice-President, Steven Ain

Urban Alliance on Race Relations (UARR) (1975)
#202, 675 King St. West, Toronto, ON M5V 1M9
416/703-6607, Fax: 416/363-0415
Executive Director, Antoni Shelton
Publications: Currents

Vietnamese Canadian Federation/Fédération vietnamienne du Canada (1980)
249 Rochester St., Ottawa, ON K1R 7M9
613/230-8282, Fax: 613/230-8282
Executive Director, Cham Ho
President, An X. Vu
Treasurer, Hoa Luong
Publications: Lien Hoi; Vietnamese Associations in Canada, a.; Bulletin, bi-m.
Affiliates: Canadian Ethnocultural Council

MUSEUMS see **GALLERIES & MUSEUMS**

MUSIC FESTIVALS see **EVENTS**

NATIVE PEOPLES

2-Spirited People of the First Nations (TPFN) (1989)
#1419, 2 Carlton St., Toronto, ON M5B 1J3
416/944-9300, Fax: 416/944-8381
President, Board of Directors, Sue Lamure
Publications: The Sacred Fire

Aboriginal Nurses Association of Canada/Association des infirmières et infirmiers autochtones du Canada (ANAC) (1974)
#133, 1785 Alta Vista Dr., Ottawa, ON K1G 3Y6
613/733-1555, Fax: 613/733-1137
Executive Director, Ruth Ann Cyr
President, Lea Bill
Vice-President, Leanne Kelly
Sec.-Treas., Marsha Forrest, 604/559-8466
Publications: The Aboriginal Nurse
Affiliates: Health Canada; Canadian Nurses Association

Aboriginal People's Business Association (APBA) (1985)
Centre for Native Small Business, #680, 1155 Georgia St. West, Vancouver, BC V6E 3H4
604/687-7166, Fax: 604/687-5519
Executive Director, David Anderson
Publications: The Native Entrepreneur

Aboriginal Urban Alliance of Ontario (1990)
College Park, 444 Yonge St., PO Box 46035, Toronto, ON M5B 2L8
416/923-6453
Vice-President, Michael Cheena

Assembly of First Nations/Assemblée des Premières Nations (AFN)
#1002, 1 Nicholas St., Ottawa, ON K1N 7B7
613/241-6789, Fax: 613/241-5808
National Chief, Ovide Mercredi
Head Office: Territory of Akwesasne, Hamilton's Island, Summerstown, ON K0C 2E0, 613/241-6789, Fax: 613/241-5808

Assembly of Manitoba Chiefs
260 St. Mary Ave., 2nd Fl., Winnipeg, MB R3C 0M6
204/956-0610, Fax: 204/956-2109
Grand Chief, Phil Fontaine
Affiliates: Assembly of First Nations

Association of Iroquois & Allied Indians
Onyota'A:Ka, RR#2, Southwold, ON N0L 2G0
519/652-3251, Fax: 519/652-9287
Chief Doug Maracle

Association for Native Development in the Performing & Visual Arts (ANDPVA) (1974)
39 Spadina Rd., 2nd Fl., Toronto, ON M5R 2S9
416/972-0871, Fax: 416/972-0892
Executive Director, Shelley Charles
Publications: Newsletter

Canadian Aboriginal Science & Engineering Association (1993)
22 College St., 2nd Fl., Toronto, ON M5G 1K2
416/972-0212, Fax: 416/972-0217
Contact, M. Dewasha

Canadian Alliance in Solidarity with the Native Peoples (CASNP) (1960)
39 Spadina Rd., PO Box 574, Stn P, Toronto, ON M5R 2S9
416/972-1573, Fax: 416/972-6232
National Coordinator, Jay Mason
Office Manager, Kay Murphy
Publications: The Phoenix

Canadian Council for Aboriginal Business/Conseil canadien pour le commerce autochtone (CCAB) (1984)
204 Saint George St., 2nd Fl., Toronto, ON M5R 2N5
416/961-8663, Fax: 416/961-3995, Toll Free: 1-800-465-7078
Executive Director, Brenda Maracle-O'Toole
National Director, Internship, Jason Thibault

Canadian Almanac & Directory 1997

Publications: Contact
Affiliates: Foundation for the Advancement of Aboriginal Youth

Canadian Native Arts Foundation/Fondation canadienne des arts autochtones (CNAF) (1985)
#508, 77 Mowat Ave., Toronto, ON M6K 3E3
416/588-3328, Fax: 416/588-9198
Founder/President, John Kim Bell

Canadian Native Friendship Centre (CNFC) (1962)
11205 - 101 St. NW, Edmonton, AB T5G 2A4
403/479-1999, Fax: 403/479-0043
Executive Director, Donna Woodward
Publications: Edmonton Native News

Chiefs of Ontario
22 College St., 2nd Fl., Toronto, ON M5G 1K2
416/972-0212, Fax: 416/972-0217
Ontario Regional Chief, Gordon B. Peters
Affiliates: Assembly of First Nations

Congress of Aboriginal Peoples
65 Bank St., 4th Fl., Ottawa, ON K1P 5N2
613/238-3511, Fax: 613/230-6273, Telex: 053-3301
Executive Director, Daniel R. Ryan

ABORIGINAL COUNCIL OF BRITISH COLUMBIA (1978)
#207,1999 Marine Dr., Vancouver, BC V7R 3J3
604/990-9939, Fax: 604/990-9949

ALLIANCE AUTOCHTONE DU QUÉBEC INC./NATIVE ALLIANCE OF QUÉBEC INC.
21, rue Brodeur, Hull, PQ J8Y 2P6
819/770-7763, Téléc: 819/770-7764
Président, Rheal Boudrias
Trésorier, Suzanne Dufour

CONGRESS OF ABORIGINAL PEOPLES - ALBERTA (1984)
#45, 10350 - 124 St., Edmonton, AB T5N 1R6
403/429-6003, Fax: 403/428-6964
Executive Director, Richard Long
President, Doris Ronnenberg
Publications: Aboriginal Women
Affiliates: Aboriginal Trappers Federation of Canada

COUNCIL FOR YUKON INDIANS (CYI)
11 Nisutlin Dr., Whitehorse, YT Y1A 3S4
403/667-7631, Fax: 403/668-6577
Secretary, Tina Dickson

FEDERATION OF NEWFOUNDLAND INDIANS
PO Box 375, St Georges, NF A0N 1Z0
709/882-2303, Fax: 709/882-2292
President, Gerrard Webb
Vice-President, Calvin Francis

INDIAN COUNCIL OF FIRST NATIONS OF MANITOBA, INC.
Otineka Mall, PO Box 2857, The Pas, MB R9A 1M6
204/623-7227, Fax: 204/623-4041
Grand Chief, Andrew Kirkness

LABRADOR METIS ASSOCIATION
PO Box 599, Stn B, Happy Valley-Goose Bay, NF A0P 1E0
709/896-0592, Fax: 709/896-0594
President, Todd Russell
Vice-President, Richard Learning
Treasurer, Herman Bird
Secretary, James Learning

METIS NATION-NWT
PO Box 1375, Yellowknife, NT X1A 2P1
403/873-3505, Fax: 403/873-3395
President, Gary Bohnet
Vice-President, Michael Paulette
Environmental Director, William Carpenter

NATIVE COUNCIL OF NOVA SCOTIA (NCNS) (1975)
Abenaki Rd., PO Box 1320, Truro, NS B2N 5N2
902/895-1524, 1525, Fax: 902/895-0024, Toll Free: 1-800-565-4372
Executive Director, Roger Hunka
President, Dwight A. Dorey
Micmac Language Coordinator, Lee Paul
Outreach Coordinator, Paul Marr
Education Coordinator, Spencer Wilmot
Social Counsellor, Charlene MacCallum
Rural & Native Housing Coordinator, Sidney Peters
Financial Comptroller, Heather Joudrie
Publications: NCNS Newsletter

NATIVE COUNCIL OF PEI
33 Allen St., Charlottetown, PE C1A 2V6
902/892-5314, Fax: 902/368-7464
President, Graham Tuplin
Publications: Our People/Gigmanag

NATIVE COUNCIL OF SASKATCHEWAN
PO Box 132, Green Lake, SK S0M 1B0
306/288-2125, Fax: 306/288-4622
President, Harvey Young

NEW BRUNSWICK ABORIGINAL PEOPLES COUNCIL (NBAPC) (1972)
320 St. Mary's St., Fredericton, NB E3A 2S4
506/458-8422, 8423, Fax: 506/450-3749, Email: nbapc@nbnet.ca
President, Frank Palmater
Vice-President, Alfred Sock
Publications: Mal-I-Mic News

ONTARIO METIS & ABORIGINAL ASSOCIATION (OMAA) (1971)
452 Albert St. East, 2nd Fl., Sault Ste Marie, ON P6B 4T6
705/949-8220, Fax: 705/946-1161, Toll Free: 1-800-461-5112
President, Michael McGuire
1st Vice-President, Henry Wetelainen
2nd Vice-President, Lorraine Gisborn
Publications: Aboriginal Voice

UNITED NATIVE NATIONS
Regional Head Office, 736 Granville St., 8th Fl., Vancouver, BC V6Z 1G3
604/688-1821, Fax: 604/688-1823
President, Ron George
Vice-President, Ernie Crey

Dene Nation
Dene National Office, 4701 Franklin Ave., PO Box 2338, Yellowknife, NT X1A 2P7
403/873-3301, Fax: 403/920-2254
Affiliates: Assembly of First Nations

Federation of Saskatchewan Indians
Executive Office, 109 Hodsman Rd., Regina, SK S4N 5W5
306/721-2822, Fax: 306/775-2994
Secretary/Receptionist, Sherry Andrews

First Nations Confederacy Inc.
#203, 286 Smith St., Winnipeg, MB R3C 1K4
204/943-3203, Fax: 204/956-1032

Grand Council of the Crees/Grand Conseil des Cris
2, rue Lakeshore, Nemaska, Némiscau, PQ J0Y 3B0
819/673-2600, Fax: 819/673-2606
Grand Chief, Matthew Coon-Come

Indian Association of Alberta
Head Office, Stoney Plain Reserve, PO Box 516, Winterburn, AB T0E 2N0
403/470-5751, Fax: 403/470-3077

International Native Arts Festivals Association (INAF) (1989)
PO Box 502, Stn M, Calgary, AB T2P 2J1
403/233-0022, Fax: 403/233-7681
Executive Director, Maria Donato

Inuit Art Foundation/Fondation d'Art Inuit (IAF) (1985)
2081 Merivale Rd., Nepean, ON K2G 1G9
613/224-8189, Fax: 613/224-2907
Executive Director, Marybelle Mitchell
President, John Terriak
Publications: Inuit Art Quarterly

Inuit Tapirisat of Canada
#510, 170 Laurier Ave. West, Ottawa, ON K1P 5V5
613/238-8181, Fax: 613/234-1991, Telex: 053-3517, Email: itc@magi.com
President, Rosemarie Kuptana

Labrador Inuit Association
PO Box 70, Nain, NF A0P 1L0
709/922-2942, Fax: 709/922-2931
President, William Barber

Makivik Corporation/Société Makivik (1978)
PO Box 179, Kuujjuaq, PQ J0M 1C0
819/964-2925; Fax: 819/964-2613; URL: http://www.accent.net/adst/MakWeb/Index.html
President, Zebedee Nungak
Treasurer, Pita Aatami
Secretary, Sheila Watt-Cloot
Publications: Makivik News

Manitoba Indian Cultural Education Centre
119 Sutherland Ave., Winnipeg, MB R2W 3C9
204/942-0228, Fax: 204/947-6564
Executive Director, Dennis Daniels

Manitoba Métis Federation/Fédération des Métis du Manitoba
Head Office, 408 McGregor St., Winnipeg, MB R2W 4X5
204/586-8474, Téléc: 204/947-1816
President, Billyjo DeLaRonde
Publications: Le Métis

Metis Nation of Alberta
13140 St. Albert Trail, Edmonton, AB T5L 4R8
403/455-2200, Fax: 403/452-8946
Acting President, Lyle Donald

Métis Nation in BC
126 Braelyn Cres., Penticton, BC V2A 6V3
250/493-8090, Fax: 250/493-3082
Spokesperson, Rick Poitras
Affiliates: Métis National Council

Métis Nation of Ontario
193 Holland Ave., Ottawa, ON K1Y 0Y3
613/798-1488, Fax: 613/722-4225
President, Tony Belcourt
Affiliates: Métis National Council

Métis Nation of Saskatchewan
219 Robin Cres., 2nd Fl., Saskatoon, SK S7L 6M8
306/343-8285, Fax: 306/343-0171
President, Jim Durocher
Affiliates: Métis National Council

Métis National Council/Ralliement National des Métis (MNC) (1983)
#310, 50 O'Connor St., Ottawa, ON K1P 6L2
613/232-3216, Fax: 613/232-4262
CEO, Gerald Morin

Métis National Council of Women (MNCW) (1992)
#600, 99 Bank St., Ottawa, ON K1P 6B9

Canadian Almanac & Directory 1997

613/566-7022, Fax: 613/233-9527
President, Shelia Genaille

Metis Settlements General Council
Alberta Federation of Metis Settlement Associations
Mayfield Business Centre, 10525 - 170 St., Edmonton, AB T5P 4W2
403/427-1122, Fax: 403/489-9558
Executive Director, Thomas Droege

National Association of Friendship Centres/ Association nationale des centres d'amitié (NAFC) (1971)
#204, 396 Cooper St., Ottawa, ON K2P 2H7
613/563-4844, Fax: 613/594-3428
Executive Director, Terry Doxtator
Office Manager, Gary Peters

ABORIGINAL FRIENDSHIP CENTRES OF SASKATCHEWAN
1440 Scarth St., Regina, SK S4R 2E9
306/525-5469, Fax: 306/525-3005
President, Sharon Ironstar

ALBERTA NATIVE FRIENDSHIP CENTRES ASSOCIATION
#1102, 10025 - 106 St., Edmonton, AB T5M 1R1
403/423-3138, Fax: 403/425-6227
Coordinator, Raymond Chambers
President, Berv Martin

BRITISH COLUMBIA ASSOCIATION OF INDIAN FRIENDSHIP CENTRES
#3, 2475 Mount Newton, Saanichton, BC V0S 1M0
250/652-0210, Fax: 250/652-3102
Coordinator, Florence Wylie
President, Marie Anderson

FREDERICTON NATIVE FRIENDSHIP CENTRE (FNFC) (1986)
266 Douglas Ave., Fredericton, NB E3A 2N7
506/459-5283, Fax: 506/459-1756
Executive Director, Phil Fraser
President, Duane Pluss
Publications: Mocassin Telegraph

MANITOBA ASSOCIATION OF FRIENDSHIP CENTRES
PO Box 716, Winnipeg, MB R3C 2K3
204/256-7443, Fax: 204/254-3834
Coordinator, Grace Buhr
President, David Chartrand

MICMAC NATIVE FRIENDSHIP CENTRE (1973)
2158 Gottingen St., Halifax, NS B3K 3B4
902/420-1576, Fax: 902/423-6130
Executive Director, Gordon King

NORTHWEST TERRITORIES COUNCIL OF FRIENDSHIP CENTRES
PO Box 470, Fort Simpson, NT X0E 0N0
403/695-2577, Fax: 403/695-2141
Secretary, Hilda Antoine

ONTARIO FEDERATION OF INDIAN FRIENDSHIP CENTRES
290 Shuter St., Toronto, ON M5A 1W7
416/956-7575, Fax: 416/956-7577
Executive Director, Sylvia Maracle
President, Vera Pawis-Tabobondung

REGROUPEMENT DES CENTRES D'AMITIÉ AUTOCHTONES DU QUÉBEC (RCAAQ) (1976)
30, rue de l'Ours, Village-des-Hurons, PQ G0A 4V0
418/842-6354, Téléc: 418/842-9795
Directeur, Raymond Picard
Présidente, Edith Cloutier

Native Alcoholism Council of Manitoba
160 Salter St., Winnipeg, MB R2W 4K1
204/586-8395, Fax: 204/589-3921
Executive Director, Bertha Fontaine
Supervisor/Outreach, Berry Fontaine
Supervisor/Rehab, Elizabeth Fontaine

Native Business Institute of Canada (NBI)
#101, 2055 Carling Ave., Ottawa, ON K2A 1G6
613/761-9734, Fax: 613/725-9031
Executive Director, Frank Craddock
Program Manager, Dorothy McCue

Native Counselling Services of Alberta (NCSA) (1970)
#208, 324 - 7 St. South, Lethbridge, AB T1J 2G2
403/423-2141, Fax: 403/380-2562
Executive Director, Allen Benson

Native Investment & Trade Association (NITA) (1989)
Box 10, #150, 1111 Melville St., Vancouver, BC V6E 3V6
604/684-0880, Fax: 604/684-0881
President, Calvin Helin

Native Women's Association of Canada (NWAC)
9 Melrose Ave., Ottawa, ON K1Y 1T8
613/722-3033, Fax: 613/722-7687

ABORIGINAL WOMEN'S COUNCIL OF SASKATCHEWAN (1972)
#101, 118 - 12th St. East, Prince Albert, SK S6V 1B6
306/763-6005, Fax: 306/922-6034
Provincial Coordinator, Julie Pitzel
Accountant, Gail Lamb

FEMMES AUTOCHTONES DU QUÉBEC INC./QUÉBEC NATIVE WOMEN'S ASSOCIATION INC.
#204, 1450, rue City Councillors, Montréal, PQ H3A 2E5
514/844-9618, Téléc: 514/844-2108
Directrice générale, Beverly Sabourin

INDIGENOUS WOMEN'S COLLECTIVE OF MANITOBA
#120, 388 Donald St., Winnipeg, MB R3B 2J4
204/944-8709, Fax: 204/949-1336

LABRADOR NATIVE WOMEN'S ASSOCIATION
PO Box 516, Stn B, Happy Valley-Goose Bay, NF A0P 1E0
709/896-2125

NATIVE WOMEN'S ASSOCIATION OF THE NWT
PO Box 2321, Yellowknife, NT X1A 2P7
403/873-5509, Fax: 403/873-3152

NEW BRUNSWICK NATIVE INDIAN WOMEN'S COUNCIL
Victoria Health Centre, 65 Brunswick St., Fredericton, NB E3B 1G5
506/458-1114, Fax: 506/451-9386

NOVA SCOTIA NATIVE WOMEN'S ASSOCIATION
PO Box 805, Truro, NS B2N 5E8
902/893-7402
President, Clara Gloade

ONTARIO NATIVE WOMEN'S ASSOCIATION (1972)
RR#4, Site 7, Comp. 144, Thunder Bay, ON P7C 4Z2
807/623-3442, Fax: 807/623-1104
Executive Director, Madeline Beardy
President, Shirley Salt

YUKON INDIAN WOMEN'S ASSOCIATION
11 Nisutlin Dr., Whitehorse, YT Y1A 3S4
403/667-6162, Fax: 403/668-7539
President, Linda MacDonald

Ontario Native Council on Justice (ONCJ)
#1004, 2 Carleton St., Toronto, ON M5B 1J3
416/592-1393, Fax: 416/592-1394
Executive Director, Carol Montagnes
Publications: Council News

The Pacific Metis Federation
225 Vancouver Ave., Nanaimo, BC V9S 4E9
250/753-6616, Fax: 250/753-8671

Saskatchewan Indian Cultural Centre
120 - 33rd St. East, Saskatoon, SK S7K 0S2
306/244-1146, Fax: 306/665-6520, Email: sicc@sasknet.sk.ca
Director, Jim Bruce

Tecumseh Community Development Corporation
RR#1, Muncey, ON N0L 1Y0
519/289-2122, Fax: 519/289-5550
Affiliates: London District Chiefs Council

Union of British Columbia Indian Chiefs (1969)
342 Water St., 5th Fl., Vancouver, BC V6B 1B6
604/684-0231, Fax: 604/684-5726
President/Chief, Saul Terry
Publications: Union of BC Indian Chiefs Newsletter

Union of New Brunswick Indians
#105, 565 Priestman St., Fredericton, NB E3B 5X8
506/458-9444, Fax: 506/458-2850
Chief, Roger Augustine

Union of Nova Scotia Indians
111 Membertou St., PO Box 961, Sydney, NS B1P 6J4
902/539-4107, Fax: 902/564-2137
Sec.-Treas., Carl Gould

Union of Ontario Indians (UOI)
Anishinabek
Nipissing First Nation, PO Box 711, North Bay, ON P1B 8J8
705/497-9127, Fax: 705/497-9135
Grand Council Chief, Joe Hare
Deputy Grand Chief, Vernon Roote
Publications: Anishinabek News

Woodland Cultural Centre (WCC) (1972)
184 Mohawk St., PO Box 1506, Brantford, ON N3T 5V6
519/759-2650, Fax: 519/759-8912
Executive Director, Joanna Bedard

NATURALISTS
see also Environmental

Avicultural Advancement Council of Canada (AACC) (1972)
PO Box 5126, Stn B, Victoria, BC V8R 6N4
250/477-9982, Fax: 250/477-9935, Email: aacc@islandnet.com
URL: http://www.islandnet.com/~aacc
Executive Director, Doreen E. Albion
President, Dunstan H. Browne, Email: browne@islandnet.com
Editor & Membership, Mark S. Curtis, Email: chemmark@islandnet.com
Publications: The Avicultural Journal
Affiliates: American Singer Canary Club of Canada; Association des amateurs d'oiseaux de la Maurice; Association des éléveurs d'oiseaux de Montréal; BC Avicultural Society; BC Exotic Bird Society; Budgerigar & Foreign Bird Society; Cage Bird Society of Hamilton; Calgary Canary Club; Canadian Dove Association; Canadian Gloster Club; Cowichan Valley & Upper Island Cage Bird Club; Durham Avicultural Society; Edmonton Avicultural Association; Essex-Kent Cage Bird Society; Feather Fanciers Club; Golden Triangle Parrot Club; Kamloops Aviculturalist Society; London & District Cage Bird Society; Manitoba Canary & Finch Club; Mid Island Exotic Bird Club; Montréal Cage Bird Society; Northern Alberta Cage Bird Society; Okanagan Bird Club; Ontario Cage Bird Society; Ottawa Cage Bird Society; Ottawa Parrot Club; PACAF/Calgary Parrot Club; Southern Alberta Cage Bird Society; Tri County Cage Bird Club; Vancouver Canary

Club; Vancouver Island Cage Bird Society; Zebra Finch Society of Canada

British Columbia Waterfowl Society (1961)
Reifel Bird Sanctuary
5191 Robertson Rd., RR#1, Delta, BC V4K 3N2
604/946-6980, Fax: 604/946-6980
Manager, John Ireland
President, George Reifel
Publications: Marshnotes

Canadian Nature Federation/Fédération canadienne de la nature (CNF) (1971)
#520, One Nicholas St., Ottawa, ON K1N 7B7
613/562-3447, Fax: 613/562-3371, Toll Free: 1-800-267-4088, Email: cnf@web.apc.org
URL: http://www.web.apc.org~cnf
President, Robert Ballantyne
Vice-President, Letha MacLachlan
Regional Director (Atlantic), Brenda Penak
Regional Director (Québec), Francine Hone
Regional Director (Ontario), John Cartwright
Regional Director (Prairies), Lloyd Saul
Regional Director (Western), Cliff Wallis
Publications: Nature Canada; Nature Alert, q.
Affiliates: International Union for the Conservation of Nature; Committee on the Status of Endangered Wildlife in Canada; International Council for Bird Preservation; Canadian Council on Ecological Areas

Les Cercles des jeunes naturalistes (CJN) (1931)
a/s Jardin Botanique de Montréal, #124, 4101, rue Sherbrooke est, Montréal, PQ H1X 2B2
514/252-3023, Téléc: 514/252-3023
Directeur général, Claude Ouellet
Publications: Les Feuillets du naturaliste

Federation of Alberta Naturalists (FAN) (1970)
PO Box 1472, Edmonton, AB T5J 2N5
403/453-8629, Fax: 403/453-8553
Executive Director, Glen Semenchuk
President, Jorden Johnston
Publications: Alberta Naturalist

Federation of BC Naturalists (1970)
#321, 1367 Broadway West, Vancouver, BC V6H 4A7
604/737-3057, Fax: 604/738-7175
URL: http://edie.cprost.sfu.ca/~jacsen7/land4nature.html
Office Manager, Leslie-Ann Drummond
Publications: BC Naturalist; Cordillera

Federation of Nova Scotia Naturalists (FNSN) (1990)
c/o Nova Scotia Museum, 1747 Summer St., Halifax, NS B3H 3A6
902/467-3380
URL: http://ccn.cs.dal.ca/Environment/FNSN/hp-fnsn.html
President, Alice L. White
Publications: FNSN News

Federation of Ontario Naturalists (FON) (1931)
355 Lesmill Rd., North York, ON M3B 2W8
416/444-8419, Fax: 416/444-9866, Email: fon@web.apc.org
URL: http://www.web.net/fon
Executive Director, John Lounds
President, Jane Allen
Chief Administrative Officer, Jean Labreque
Director, Conservation & Environment, John Riley
Manager, Conservation & Stewardship Programs, Judy Eising
Manager, Education & Interpretive Programs, Nancy Croome Makowski
Coordinator, Club & Region Support Services, Sandy Symmes

Publications: Seasons
Affiliates: Coalition on the Niagara Escarpment; Conservation Council of Ontario; Great Lakes United; International Union for Conservation of Nature & Natural Resources; International Committee for Bird Preservation

Jack Miner Migratory Bird Foundation, Inc.
PO Box 39, Kingsville, ON N9Y 2E8
519/733-4034
Executive Director, Kirk W. Miner

Manitoba Naturalists' Society (MNS) (1920)
#401, 63 Albert St., Winnipeg, MB R3B 1G4
204/943-9029, Fax: 204/943-9029
Executive Director, Herta Gudauskas
President, Ron Clay
Publications: MNS Bulletin

Natural History Society of Newfoundland & Labrador (1963)
PO Box 1013, Stn C, St. John's, NF A1C 5M3
President, John McConnel, 506/459-8685
Publications: Osprey

Natural History Society of Prince Edward Island (NHSPEI) (1969)
PO Box 2346, Charlottetown, PE C1A 1Y6
902/894-9297
President, Ray Cooke
Publications: Island Naturalist
Affiliates: Island Nature Trust; Canadian Nature Federation

Nature Saskatchewan (1949)
Saskatchewan Natural History Society
#206, 1860 Lorne St., Regina, SK S4P 2L7
306/780-9273, Fax: 306/780-9263, Toll Free: 1-800-667-4668, Email: Nature.Sask@vcomnet.unibase.com
URL: http://www.unibase.com/~naturesk
Executive Director, Curt Schroeder
President, Paul James
Publications: Blue Jay; Nature Views, q.; The Eskimo Curlew

New Brunswick Federation of Naturalists/ Fédération des naturalistes du Nouveau-Brunswick
277 Douglas Ave., Saint John, NB E2K 1E5
President, Jim Goltz, 506/489-8683
Publications: NB Naturalist/Le Naturalist du NB

Society of Canadian Ornithologists/Société des ornithologistes du Canada (SCO) (1983)
c/o Canadian Museum of Nature, PO Box 3443, Stn D, Ottawa, ON K1P 6P4
President, Henri Ouellet
Secretary, Dr. Nancy Ford, 604/828-5436
Membership Secretary, Nancy Flood
Publications: Picoides

Union québécoise pour la conservation de la nature/Québec Union for Nature Conservation (UQCN) (1981)
690, Grande Allée est, 4e étage, Québec, PQ G1R 2K5
418/648-2104, Téléc: 418/648-0991
Président, Harvey Mead
Publications: Franc-Vert

NEWSPAPERS *see* **PUBLISHING**

NURSERY TRADE *see* **HORTICULTURE, GARDENING, LANDSCAPE ARCHITECTURE**

ORGANIZATIONS — NURSING 2-135

NURSING
see also Health & Medical; Hospitals

Academy of Canadian Executive Nurses (ACEN) (1982)
1650, av Cedar, Montréal, PQ H3G 1A4
514/934-8088, Fax: 514/934-8200
President, Valerie Shannon
Publications: Canadian Journal of Nursing Administration

British Columbia Nurses' Union/Syndicat des infirmières de la Colombie-Britannique (BCNU) (1981)
#100, 4259 Canada Way, Burnaby, BC V5G 1H1
604/433-2268, Fax: 604/433-7945, Toll Free: 1-800-663-9991
COO, Anne Harvey
President, Ivory Warner
Publications: BCNU Update

Canadian Association of Burn Nurses/ Association canadienne des infirmières et infirmiers en soins aux brûlés (CABN)
Ross Tilley Regional Burn Centre, The Wellesley Hospital, 160 Wellesley St. East, Toronto, ON M4Y 1J3
416/926-7021, Fax: 416/926-4858
President, Joy Kramarich
Publications: Newsletter
Affiliates: Canadian Nurses Association

Canadian Association of Critical Care Nurses/ Association canadienne des infirmières et infirmiers en soins de phase aiguë (CACCN) (1985)
PO Box 22006, London, ON N6C 5Y3
519/649-5284, Fax: 519/668-2499
President, Sandra Matheson
Vice-President, Colleen Shelton
Secretary, Karen Palmer
Publications: Official Journal of CACCN

Canadian Association for the History of Nursing (CAHN)
130 Caruthers Ave., Kingston, ON K7L 1M7
613/545-2668, ext.4757, Fax: 613/545-6770
President, Lynn Kirkwood
Affiliates: Canadian Nurses Association

Canadian Association of Nephrology Nurses & Technicians/Association canadienne des infirmières/iers et techniciens/iennes de néphrologie (CANNT) (1968)
PO Box 4091, Stn C, Calgary, AB T2T 5M9
403/244-4487, Fax: 403/244-2340
President, Dawn Evans
Publications: CANNT Journal
Affiliates: Canadian Nurses Association

Canadian Association of Neuroscience Nurses/ Association canadienne des infirmières et infirmiers en soins neurologiques (CANN) (1969)
71 Inch Bay, Winnipeg, MB R2Y 0X2
204/787-3577, Fax: 204/831-0888
President, Kathy Doerksen
Publications: Axon
Affiliates: Canadian Congress of Neurological Sciences

Canadian Association of Nurse Administrators (CANA)
PO Box 3272, Prince Albert, ON L9L 1C3
President, Bonnie Lynn Wright, Res: 905/985-1918
Affiliates: Canadian Nurses Association

Canadian Almanac & Directory 1997

ORGANIZATIONS —NURSING

Canadian Association of Nurses in AIDS Care/ Association canadienne des infirmières et infirmiers en sidologie (CANAC) (1991)
c/o Casey House Hospice, 9 Huntley St., Toronto, ON M4Y 2K8
416/962-7600, Fax: 416/962-5147
President, John S. Flannery
Publications: CANAC/ACIIS Newsletter
Affiliates: Canadian Nurses Association

Canadian Association of Nurses in Independent Practice/Association canadienne des infirmiers/ères autorisés en service privé (CANIP)
RR#5, Lucknow, ON N0G 2H0
519/395-3515, Fax: 519/395-3515
President, Nancy Elliott-Greenwood
Vice-President, Mary Ratensperger
Treasurer, Jean Millar
Secretary, Kelly Doran
Publications: Visions

Canadian Association of Nurses in Oncology/ Association canadienne des infirmières en oncologie (CANO) (1983)
#219, 111 Peter St., Toronto, ON M5V 2H1
416/596-6565, Fax: 416/596-1808
President, Doris Howell
Publications: Canadian Oncology Nursing Journal
Affiliates: Canadian Nurses Association; International Society of Cancer Nurses

Canadian Association of Pediatric Nurses/ Association canadienne des infirmières et infirmiers en pédiatrie (CAPN) (1988)
c/o Montréal Children's Hospital, 2300, rue Tupper, Montréal, PQ H3H 1P3
514/934-4400, ext.2855, Fax: 514/934-4355
President, Franco Carnevale
Publications: Newsletter

Canadian Association of Practical Nurses & Nursing Assistants/Association des infirmières et infirmiers auxiliaires du Canada (CAPNA) (1975)
#200, 440 Laurier Ave. West, Ottawa, ON K1R 7X6
613/782-3104; Fax: 905/432-7604
National President, Shiela Arsenault
Secretary, Sally Hurley
Publications: Across the Nation
Affiliates: The Health Action Lobby; Canadian Council on Health Facilities Accreditation

ASSOCIATION OF NEW BRUNSWICK REGISTERED NURSING ASSISTANTS/ASSOCIATION DES INFIRMIERS ET INFIRMIÈRES AUXILIAIRES IMMATRICULÉES DU NOUVEAU-BRUNSWICK (1965)
384 Smythe St., Fredericton, NB E3B 3E4
506/454-0747, Fax: 506/459-0503
President, Dianne Parent
Publications: The Blue Band

LICENSED NURSING ASSISTANTS ASSOCIATION OF PRINCE EDWARD ISLAND
PO Box 1254, Charlottetown, PE C1A 7M8
902/566-1512, Fax: 902/892-6315
President, Brenda Coles

LICENSED PRACTICAL NURSES ASSOCIATION OF BRITISH COLUMBIA (LPNA) (1965)
RR#1, S-17B, C-A5, Peachland, BC V0H 1X0
250/767-3384, Fax: 250/767-3384
President, Jan J. van Doorn
Publications: Dogwood News

MANITOBA ASSOCIATION OF LICENSED PRACTICAL NURSES (1945)
615 Kernaghan Ave., Winnipeg, MB R2C 2Z4
204/222-6743, Fax: 204/224-0166
Executive Director, Verna Holgate
Publications: Current Affairs
Affiliates: Manitoba Health Organization

NEWFOUNDLAND COUNCIL FOR NURSING ASSISTANTS
Lemarchant Road Medical Centre, 195 LeMarchant Rd., St. John's, NF A1C 2H5
709/579-3843, Fax: 709/579-8268
Executive Director, Anne Keough

NOVA SCOTIA CERTIFIED NURSING ASSISTANTS ASSOCIATION (1956)
Sunnyside Place, #212, 1600 Bedford Hwy., Bedford, NS B4A 3E4
902/835-9510, Fax: 902/835-9510, Toll Free: 1-800-565-9510
Executive Director, Albert MacIntyre
Publications: CNA News

ORDRE DES INFIRMIÈRES ET INFIRMIERS AUXILIAIRES DU QUÉBEC (OIIAQ) (1974)
531, rue Sherbrooke est, Montréal, PQ H2L 1K2
514/282-9511, Téléc: 514/282-0631, Ligne sans frais: 1-800-283-9511
Directrice générale, Dominique Aubertin
Publications: Santé Québec; L'infirmière auxiliaire, 3 fois par an

PROFESSIONAL COUNCIL OF LICENSED PRACTICAL NURSES (1985)
10604 - 170 Ave., Edmonton, AB T5S 1P3
403/484-8886, Fax: 403/484-9069, Toll Free: 1-800-661-5877
President, Sally Hurley
Publications: News & Views

REGISTERED PRACTICAL NURSES ASSOCIATION OF ONTARIO (1958)
#200, Building 4, 5025 Orbitor Dr., Mississauga, ON L4W 4Y5
905/602-4664, Fax: 905/602-4666
Executive Director, Verna Steffler
President, Jean Bennett
Publications: RPNAO Update; The Care Connection, q.
Affiliates: Gerontological Nurses Association

SASKATCHEWAN ASSOCIATION OF LICENSED PRACTICAL NURSES (SALPN) (1957)
2310 Smith St., Regina, SK S4P 2P6
306/525-1436, Fax: 306/347-7784
President, Heather Cagnet
Publications: Hand in Hand
Affiliates: Alzheimers Association

Canadian Clinical Nurse Specialist Interest Group (CCNSIG)
RR#2, Halifax County, NS B0J 1N0
902/827-4437, Fax: 902/496-2119, Email: martinm@fhs.mcmaster.ca
President, Deborah McLeod
Publications: The Canadian CNS
Affiliates: Canadian Nurses Association

Canadian Council of Cardiovascular Nurses/ Conseil canadien des infirmières(iers) en nursing cardiovasculaire (CCCN) (1973)
#200, 160 George St., Ottawa, ON K1N 9M2
613/241-4361, Fax: 613/241-3278
President, Lynne Maxwell
Publications: Canadian Journal of Cardiovascular Nursing
Affiliates: Heart & Stroke Foundation of Canada; Canadian Coalition for High Blood Pressure Prevention & Control

Canadian Federation of Mental Health Nurses/ Fédération canadienne des infirmières et infirmiers en santé mentale (CFMHN)
10820 - 58 Ave., Edmonton, AB T6H 1C2
403/492-5250, Fax: 403/492-2551, Email: waustin@ua.nursing.ualberta.ca
President, Wendy Austin, 403/492-5250
Publications: CFMHN Newsletter
Affiliates: Canadian Nurses Association

Canadian Gerontological Nursing Association/ Association canadienne des infirmières et infirmiers en gérontologie (CGNA) (1984)
3223 Kenmore Cr. SW, Calgary, AB T3E 6K4
403/240-6882, Fax: 403/240-6203
President, Jean Miller
Publications: The Canadian Gerontological Nurse
Affiliates: Canadian Nurses Association

Canadian Holistic Nurses Association/ Association canadienne des infirmières en approches holistiques de soins (CHNA) (1986)
7535 Hunterview Dr. NW, Calgary, AB T2K 4P7
403/275-6288, Fax: 403/275-2527
President, Betty Petersen
Publications: Insight
Affiliates: Canadian Nurses Association

Canadian Intravenous Nurses Association/ Association canadienne des infirmiers(ères) en soins intraveineux (CINA) (1975)
#200, 4433 Sheppard Ave. East, Agincourt, ON M1S 1V3
416/292-0687, Fax: 416/292-1038, Email: cinacsot@idirect.com
URL: http://web.idirect.com/~csotcina
President, Elaine Walker
Publications: CINA Journal & Mainliner Newsletter; I.V. Therapy Guidelines

Canadian Nurse Educators Association/ Association des infirmières enseignantes (CNEA) (1990)
400 Waterloo St., Winnipeg, MB R3N 0F6
204/889-2986, Fax: 204/888-1805
President, Dorothy Froman
Publications: Canadian Nurse Educators Association Newsletter
Affiliates: Canadian Nurses Association

Canadian Nurses Association/Association des infirmières et infirmiers du Canada (CNA) (1908)
50 Driveway, Ottawa, ON K2P 1E2
613/237-2133, Fax: 613/237-3520
Executive Director, Dr. Mary Ellen Jeans
President, Rachel Bard
Director of Communications, Maureen Farrington
Publications: The Canadian Nurse/L'infirmière canadienne

ALBERTA ASSOCIATION OF REGISTERED NURSES (AARN) (1916)
11620 - 168 St., Edmonton, AB T5M 4A6
403/451-0043, Fax: 403/452-3276, Toll Free: 1-800-252-9392
Executive Director, Elizabeth Turnbull
Information Officer, Evelyn Henderson
Publications: AARN Newsletter

ASSOCIATION OF NURSES OF PRINCE EDWARD ISLAND (ANPEI) (1922)
17 Pownal St., Charlottetown, PE C1A 3V7
902/368-3767, Fax: 902/628-1430
Executive Director/Registrar, Becky Gosbee
Publications: ANPEI Update

ASSOCIATION OF REGISTERED NURSES OF NEWFOUNDLAND (ARNN) (1953)
55 Military Rd., PO Box 6116, Stn C, St. John's, NF A1C 5X8
709/753-6040, Fax: 709/753-4940
Executive Director, Elizabeth Adey
Publications: ARNN Access

ORGANIZATIONS — NURSING

MANITOBA ASSOCIATION OF REGISTERED NURSES (1913)
647 Broadway, Winnipeg, MB R3C 0X2
204/774-3477, Fax: 204/775-6052, Toll Free: 1-800-665-2027
Executive Director, Diana Davidson-Dick
Publications: Nurscene

NORTHWEST TERRITORIES REGISTERED NURSES ASSOCIATION (NWTRNA)
PO Box 2757, Yellowknife, NT X1A 2R1
403/873-2745, Fax: 403/873-2336
Executive Director/Registrar, Karen Hilliard
Publications: Northwest Territories Registered Nurses Association Newsletter

NURSES ASSOCIATION OF NEW BRUNSWICK/ASSOCIATION DES INFIRMIÈRES ET INFIRMIERS DU NOUVEAU-BRUNSWICK (1916)
165 Regent St., Fredericton, NB E3B 3W5
506/458-8731, Fax: 506/459-2838
Executive Director, Lucille Auffrey
Publications: Info Nursing

REGISTERED NURSES ASSOCIATION OF BRITISH COLUMBIA (1912)
2855 Arbutus St., Vancouver, BC V6J 3Y8
604/736-7331, Fax: 604/738-2272
Executive Director, Pat Cutshall
Publications: Nursing BC

REGISTERED NURSES ASSOCIATION OF NOVA SCOTIA (RNANS)
#104, 120 Eileen Stubbs Ave., Dartmouth, NS B3H 1Y1
902/468-9744, Fax: 902/468-9510
Executive Director, Carolyn Moore
Publications: Nurse to Nurse

REGISTERED NURSES ASSOCIATION OF ONTARIO/L'ASSOCIATION DES INFIRMIÈRES ET INFIRMIERS AUTORISES DE L'ONTARIO (RNAO) (1925)
#1600, 438 University Ave., Toronto, ON M5G 2K8
416/599-1925, Fax: 416/599-1926
Executive Director, Doris Grinspun
Publications: Registered Nurse Journal

SASKATCHEWAN REGISTERED NURSES ASSOCIATION (SRNA) (1917)
2066 Retallack St., Regina, SK S4T 7X5
306/757-4643, Fax: 306/525-0849, Toll Free: 1-800-667-9945
Executive Director, Marianne Hodgson
Publications: Concern

YUKON REGISTERED NURSES ASSOCIATION (YRNA) (1993)
#14, 1114 - 1 Ave., Whitehorse, YT Y1A 1A3
403/667-4062, Fax: 403/668-5123
Executive Director, Patricia McGarr
President, Colleen Wirth
Publications: Nurses Notes

Canadian Nurses Foundation/Fondation des infirmières et infirmiers du Canada (CNF) (1962)
50 Driveway, Ottawa, ON K2P 1E2
613/237-2133, Fax: 613/237-3520
Executive Director, Beverly A. Campbell
Publications: In Touch with the Foundation; Foundation Focus, a.

Canadian Nurses Protective Society/Société de protection des infirmières et infirmiers du Canada (CNPS) (1988)
50 The Driveway, Ottawa, ON K2P 1E2
613/237-2133, Fax: 613/237-3520, Toll Free: 1-800-267-3390
Managing Director, Patricia McLean
Publications: Infolaw

Canadian Nurses Respiratory Society/Société canadienne des infirmières en santé respiratoire (CNRS)
10 Cowan Ave., St. John's, NF A1E 3N5
709/737-4253, Fax: 709/737-6795
President, Pamela Baker
Publications: CNRS/SCISR Newsletter
Affiliates: Canadian Lung Association; Canadian Nurses Association; International Council of Nurses

Canadian Obstetric, Gynecologic & Neonatal Nurses (COGNN)
315 Oakwood Ave., Winnipeg, MB R3L 1E8
204/774-6581, Fax: 204/774-7834
President, Vera Rosolwich
Affiliates: Canadian Nurses Association

Canadian Occupational Health Nurses Association/Association canadienne des infirmières et infirmièrs en santé du travail (COHNA) (1986)
c/o BC Telephone, #5, 3777 Kingsway, Burnaby, BC V5H 3Z7
604/432-4012, Fax: 604/432-9456
President, Sharon Blaney
Affiliates: Canadian Nurses Association

Canadian Orthopaedic Nurses Association/Association canadienne des infirmiéres et infirmiers en orthopédie (CONA) (1978)
Ottawa General Hospital, Nurse Clinical Rm. 4232, 501 Smythe Rd., Ottawa, ON K1H 8L6
613/737-8303, Fax: 613/737-8470
President, Hélène Rairville
Publications: CONA Newsletter
Affiliates: Canadian Nurses Association

College of Nurses of Ontario/Ordre des infirmières et infirmiers de l'Ontario (CNO) (1963)
101 Davenport Rd., Toronto, ON M5R 3P1
416/928-0900, Fax: 416/928-6507, Toll Free: 1-800-387-5526
Executive Director, Margaret Risk
Publications: College Communiqué

Community Health Nurses Association of Canada/Association canadienne des infirmières et infirmiers en santé communautaire (CHNAC) (1987)
1329 Spadina Cres. East, Saskatoon, SK S7K 3J2
306/966-6237, Fax: 306/966-6703
President-Elect, Barbara Mathur, Fax: 306/966-7603
President, Ann Finigan
Affiliates: Canadian Nurses Association

Community Mental Health Nurses' Association (1975)
#1600, 438 University Ave., Toronto, ON M5W 2K8
416/599-1925, Fax: 416/599-1926, Toll Free: 1-800-668-7626
President, Florence Bentley, 416/535-8501
Treasurer, Joan Scott, 416/923-1112, 1113

Fédération des infirmières et infirmiers auxiliaires du Québec/Québec Federation of Nurses' Aids (FIIAQ)
5385 - 1e av, Charlesbourg, PQ G1H 2V5
418/622-8077, Téléc: 418/622-8471, Ligne sans frais: 1-800-463-5664
Présidente, Johanne Morin
Publications: ECHO-FIIAQ

Fédération des infirmières et infirmiers du Québec (FIIQ) (1987)
2050, rue de Bleury, 4e étage, Montréal, PQ H3A 2J5
514/987-1141, Téléc: 514/987-7273
Présidente, Jennie Skene
Secrétaire directrice, Danielle Y. Mailhot
Publications: FIIQ; Le Pouls, semi-annuel
Bureau régional: #300, 1260, boul Lebourgneuf, Québec, PQ G2K 2G2, 418/626-2226

Gerontological Nursing Association of Ontario (1974)
PO Box 368, Stn K, Toronto, ON M4P 2G7
Publications: Perspectives
Affiliates: Registered Nurses Association of Ontario

Manitoba Nurses' Union/Syndicat des infirmières du Manitoba (MNU) (1975)
#502, 275 Broadway, Winnipeg, MB R3C 4M6
204/942-1320, Fax: 204/942-0958
Executive Director, Irene Giesbrecht
President, Vera Chernecki
Publications: Pulse

National Emergency Nurses Affiliation/Affiliation des infirmières et infirmiers d'urgence (NENA)
20 Jasper St., St. John's, NF A1A 4E2
709/737-7238, Fax: 709/737-6770
President, Louanne Kinsella
Affiliates: Canadian Nurses Association

New Brunswick Nurses' Union/Syndicat des infirmières du Nouveau-Brunswick
750 Brunswick St., Fredericton, NB E3B 1H9
506/453-0820, 0822, Fax: 506/453-0828
Executive Director, Thomas Mann
President, Linda Silas Martin
Publications: The Parasol

Newfoundland & Labrador Nurses' Union/Syndicat des infirmières de Terre-Neuve et du Labrador
59A Le Marchant Rd., PO Box 416, Stn C, St. John's, NF A1C 5J9
709/753-9961, Fax: 709/753-1210
President, Joan Marie Aylward
Publications: In Touch

Nova Scotia Nurses' Union/Syndicat des infirmières de la Nouvelle-Écosse (NSNU)
65 Queen St., Dartmouth, NS B2Y 1G4
902/469-1474, Fax: 902/466-6935
Executive Director, Tom Patterson
Publications: NSNU Newsletter

Ontario Nurses' Association/Association des infirmières de l'Ontario (ONA) (1973)
#600, 85 Grenville St., Toronto, ON M5S 3A2
416/964-8833, Fax: 416/964-8864, Toll Free: 1-800-387-5580
CEO, Lesley M. Bell
Chief Operating Officer, Heather Dolan
Publications: ONA News

Operating Room Nurses Association of Canada/Association des infirmières et infirmiers de sales d'opération du Canada (ORNAC) (1983)
Queensway Carleton Hospital, 3045 Baseline Rd., Nepean, ON K2H 8P4
613/721-2000, ext.2901, Fax: 613/721-4774
President, Vija Hay
Publications: Canadian Operating Room Nurses Journal; Communiqué

Ordre des infirmières et infirmiers du Québec (OIIQ) (1920)
Corporation professionnelle des infirmières et infirmiers du Québec
4200, boul Dorchester ouest, Westmount, PQ H3Z 1V4
514/935-2501, Téléc: 514/935-1799, Ligne sans frais: 1-800-363-6048
Directrice générale/Secrétaire, Hélène Rajotte
Secrétaire adjointe, Pierette Lange-Sondack
Publications: L'infirmière du Québec; Le journal de l'OIIQ, tous les 2 mois

ORGANIZATIONS — PACKAGING

Practical Nurses Federation of Ontario (Ind.)
Bldg. 4, #200, 5025 Orbitor Dr., Mississauga, ON
L4W 4Y5
905/602-6705, Fax: 905/602-4666
President, Ruth Cartwright
Director of Labour Relations, Bill Sly
Publications: PNFO Newsletter

Prince Edward Island Nurses' Union/Syndicat des infirmières de l'Île-du-Prince-Edouard (PEINU) (1987)
25 Kensington Ct., Charlottetown, PE C1A 8K4
902/892-7152, Fax: 902/368-2974
Executive Director, Elizabeth MacFadyen
President, Beryl Chandler
Publications: Concerns
Affiliates: National Federation of Nurses' Unions

Psychiatric Nurses Association of Canada (PNAC) (1951)
509 Pandora Ave. West, Winnipeg, MB R2C 1M8
204/222-6984, Fax: 204/222-6984
President, Gary Thronberg
Executive Assistant, Beverley Hill

REGISTERED PSYCHIATRIC NURSES ASSOCIATION OF ALBERTA
#201, 9711 - 45 Ave., Edmonton, AB T6E 5V8
403/434-7666, Fax: 403/436-4165
Executive Director, Janice Trylinski
President, Judy Dahl

REGISTERED PSYCHIATRIC NURSES ASSOCIATION OF BRITISH COLUMBIA (1974)
#251, 3041 Anson Ave., Coquitlam, BC V3B 2H6
604/944-4941, Fax: 604/944-4945
Executive Director, Keith Best
President, Dorothy Jennings
Publications: Intercom

REGISTERED PSYCHIATRIC NURSES ASSOCIATION OF MANITOBA (RPNAM) (1960)
1854 Portage Ave., Winnipeg, MB R3J 0G9
204/888-4841, Fax: 204/888-8638
Executive Director, Annette D. Osted
President, Ellen Ledieu
Publications: R.P.N.A.M. Update; IBID, q.

REGISTERED PSYCHIATRIC NURSES ASSOCIATION OF SASKATCHEWAN (RPNAS) (1948)
#101, 2631 - 28th Ave., Regina, SK S4S 6X3
306/586-4617, Fax: 306/586-6000
Executive Director, Marion Rieger
President, Roger Bitschy
Publications: RP News

St. Elizabeth Visiting Nurses Association (1921)
698 King St. West, Hamilton, ON L8P 1C7
905/522-6887, Fax: 905/529-6646
President & CEO, Rita M. Soluk

Saskatchewan Union of Nurses/Syndicat des infirmières de la Saskatchewan (SUN)
2330 - 2 Ave., Regina, SK S4R 1A6
306/525-1666, Fax: 306/522-4612
President, Judy Junor
Publications: Sunspots

Staff Nurses Associations of Alberta/Association du personnel infirmier de l'Alberta (SNAP)
#303, 10328 - 81 Ave., Edmonton, AB T6E 1X2
403/439-3788, Fax: 403/439-1036, Toll Free: 1-800-461-8612
President, Linda Sloan
Publications: SNAP

Union of Psychiatric Nurses/Syndicat des infirmières psychiatriques (1966)
#200, 508 Clarke Rd., Coquitlam, BC V3J 3X2
604/931-2471, Fax: 604/931-1070

President, Stew Johnson
Publications: Spotlite
Affiliates: B.C. Government Employees Union; B.C. Federation of Labour

Union québécoise des infirmières et infirmiers/Québec Union of Nurses (UQII) (1988)
9405, rue Sherbrooke est, Montréal, PQ H1L 6P3
514/356-8888, Téléc: 514/356-9999
Présidente, Louise Chabot
Publications: L'Union

United Nurses of Alberta/Infirmières unies de l'Alberta (UNA) (1977)
Park Plaza, 10611 - 98 Ave., 9th Fl., Edmonton, AB T5K 2P7
403/425-1025, Fax: 403/426-2093
President, Heather Smith
Publications: UNA News Bulletin; UNA Stat, bi-weekly; UNA Frontline, bi-m.

Victorian Order of Nurses for Canada/Infirmières de l'Ordre de Victoria du Canada (VON Canada) (1897)
5 Blackburn Ave., Ottawa, ON K1N 8A2
613/233-5694, Fax: 613/230-4376
Chief Executive Officer, Donna Roe
Chair, Brian Barrington
Publications: National Network; VON Canada Report, q.; Annual Report

NUTRITION see **HEALTH & MEDICAL**

OIL see **GAS & OIL**

PACKAGING

Canadian Corrugated Case Association/Association canadienne des fabricants de carton ondulé
#402, 701 Evans Ave., Etobicoke, ON M9C 1A3
416/695-1062, Fax: 416/695-0693
Executive Director, Steve Purwitsky
Administrator, Donna W. Mehta

Canadian Paper Box Manufacturers' Association Inc./Association canadienne des fabricants de boîtes en cartons (CPBMA) (1921)
#400, 701 Evans Ave., Etobicoke, ON M9C 1A3
416/626-7056, Fax: 416/626-7054
Executive Director, R.G. McCaw

Canadian Seniors Packaging Advisory Council/Conseil consultatif canadien pour l'adaptation de l'emballage aux besoins des aînés (CASPAC) (1991)
#407, 2255 Sheppard Ave. East, Toronto, ON M2J 4Y1
416/497-7511, Fax: 416/496-6160
Chairperson, Marina Kovrig
Project Manager, Karen Cuggy-Murphy

Environmentally-Sound Packaging Coalition of Canada (1987)
#404, 198 West Hastings St., Vancouver, BC V6B 1H2
604/689-3770, Fax: 604/689-3779
President, Ruth Lotzkar
Publications: ESP Newsletter

Packaging Association of Canada/Association canadienne de l'emballage (PAC) (1949)
#330, 2255 Sheppard Ave. East, North York, ON M2J 4Y1
416/490-7860, Fax: 416/490-7844
President/CEO, Alan M. Robinson
Chairman, John O'Niell

Paper & Paperboard Packaging Environmental Council/Conseil de l'environnement des emballages de papier et de carton (PPEC) (1990)
#400, 701 Evans Ave., Etobicoke, ON M9C 1A3
416/626-0350, Fax: 416/626-7054
Executive Director, John Mullinder
Chairman, Cam Gentile
Publications: PPEC News
Affiliates: Recycling Council of Ontario; Recycling Council of BC; Recycling Council of Manitoba

PATENTS & COPYRIGHT

Canadian Copyright Institute (CCI) (1965)
35 Spadina Rd., Toronto, ON M5R 2S9
416/975-1756, Fax: 416/975-1839
Chairman, Ron B. Thomson
Publications: CCI Newsletter
Affiliates: Canadian Conference of the Arts; Book & Periodical Council

Canadian Copyright Licensing Agency (1988)
CANCOPY
#900, 6 Adelaide St. East, Toronto, ON M5C 1H6
416/868-1620, Fax: 416/868-1621, Toll Free: 1-800-893-5777
URL: http://cancopy.com/
Executive Director, Andrew Martin, Email: amartin@cancopy.com
Associate Director, Lucy White, Email: lwhite@can-copy.com
Communications Manager, Alexandra Soiseth, Email: soiseth@cancopy.com
Publications: CANCOPY News; CANCOPY Update, m.
Affiliates: International Federation of Reproduction Rights Organization

Canadian Musical Reproduction Rights Agency/Agence canadienne des droits de production musicaux limitée (CMRRA) (1976)
#320, 56 Wellesley St. West, Toronto, ON M5S 2S3
416/926-1966, Fax: 416/926-7521
President, David A. Basskin
Sec.-Treas., C.C. Devereux

Canadian Society of Copyright Consumers/Societé canadienne des consommaters copyright (CSCC) (1927)
2160 New St., Burlington, ON L7R 1H8
905/632-8404, Fax: 905/632-6520
Executive Vice-President, J. Lyman Potts, CM
President, John Riley
Publications: CSCC/SCCC Newsletter

Copyright Collective of Canada/Société de perception de droit d'auteur du Canada (CCC) (1989)
#1603, 22 St. Clair Ave. East, Toronto, ON M4T 2S4
416/961-1888, Fax: 416/968-1016
General Manager, Susan Peacock

Inventors Association of Canada
PO Box 281, Swift Current, SK S9H 3V6
306/773-7762
General Manager, Phyllis Tengum

Patent & Trademark Institute of Canada/Institut canadien des brevets et marques (1957)
PO Box 1298, Stn B, Ottawa, ON K1P 5R3
613/234-0516
Executive Director, Jane Donaldson
Publications: Bulletin; Canadian Intellectual Property Review, s-a.; Centennial Index III - Index of Learned Papers on Intellectual Property Subjects
Affiliates: Industry Canada

Society of Composers, Authors & Music Publishers of Canada/Société canadienne des auteurs, compositeurs et éditeurs de musique (SOCAN) (1990)
41 Valleybrook Dr., North York, ON M3B 2S6
416/445-8700, Fax: 416/445-7108, Toll Free: 1-800-557-6226
General Manager, Michael R. Rock
Publications: Words & Music; Paroles et musique

PEACE see INTERNATIONAL COOPERATION/INTERNATIONAL RELATIONS

PENSION MANAGEMENT see FINANCE

PENSIONERS see SENIOR CITIZENS

PHARMACEUTICAL

Association of Faculties of Pharmacy of Canada/Association des facultés de pharmacie du Canada (AFPC) (1969)
425 Adelaide St., Saskatoon, SK S7J 0H9
306/653-3513, Fax: 306/665-1916
Executive Director, Kenneth A. Ready
Publications: AFPC Communications; Directory of Pharmaceutical Research in Canadian Faculties of Pharmacy, biennial
Affiliates: Canadian Pharmaceutical Association

Association professionnelle des pharmaciens salariés du Québec (APPSQ)
CP 102, Succ. M, Montréal, PQ H2X 3M6
514/899-0879
René Dubois, p.d.g.
Publications: Activox

Association québécoise des pharmaciens propriétaires/Québec Association of Pharmacy Owners (AQPP) (1970)
4378, av Pierre-de-Coubertin, Montréal, PQ H1V 1A6
514/254-0676, Téléc: 514/254-1288, Ligne sans frais: 1-800-361-7765
Directeur général, Normand Cadieux
Publications: Québec Pharmacie

Atlantic Provinces Pharmacy Council
1526 Dresden Rd., PO Box 3363, Halifax, NS B3J 3J1
902/422-8528, Fax: 902/422-2619
Registrar, Susan Wedlake

British Columbia Pharmacy Association
#150, 3751 Shell Rd., Richmond, BC V6X 2W2
604/279-2053, Fax: 604/279-2065
Executive Director, Frank M. Archer

Canadian Association of Pharmacy Students & Interns/Association canadienne des étudiants et internes en pharmacie (CAPSI) (1968)
50 Nanaimo Dr., Nepean, ON K2H 6Y3
613/820-3371, Email: ay043@freenet.carleton.ca
President, Sean Hopkins
Publications: CAPSIL
Affiliates: International Pharmacy Student Foundation; Canadian Pharmaceutical Association; Academy of Students; Canadian Society of Hospital Pharmacists

Canadian Drug Manufacturers Association (CDMA) (1984)
#606, 4120 Yonge St., Toronto, ON M2P 2B8
416/223-2333, Fax: 416/223-2425
President, Brenda Drinkwalter
Chairman, Jack Kay

Director, Professional & Scientific Affairs, James J. Keon
Publications: Drug News & Views

Canadian Pharmaceutical Association/Association pharmaceutique canadienne (CPhA) (1907)
1785 Alta Vista Dr., 2nd Fl., Ottawa, ON K1G 3Y6
613/523-7877, Fax: 613/523-0445, Toll Free: 1-800-917-9489
Executive Director, L.C. Fevang
President, Bill Wilson
Publications: Compendium of Pharmaceuticals & Specialities; Self-Medication
Affiliates: Commonwealth Pharmaceutical Association; Fédération internationale pharmaceutique

ALBERTA PHARMACEUTICAL ASSOCIATION (APHA) (1911)
10130 - 112 St., 7th Fl., Edmonton, AB T5K 2K4
403/990-0321, Fax: 403/990-0328
Registrar, Greg Eberhart
Publications: APhA Newsletter

COLLEGE OF PHARMACISTS OF BRITISH COLUMBIA (1891)
#200, 1765 - 8th Ave. West, Vancouver, BC V6J 1V8
604/733-2440, Fax: 604/733-2493, Toll Free: 1-800-663-1940, Email: copbc@axionet.com
Registrar, Linda J. Lytle
Publications: The Bulletin

MANITOBA PHARMACEUTICAL ASSOCIATION
187 St. Mary's Rd., Winnipeg, MB R2H 1J2
204/233-1411, Fax: 204/237-3468
Registrar, S.G. Wilcox

NEW BRUNSWICK PHARMACEUTICAL SOCIETY
#204, 95 Foundry St., Moncton, NB E1C 5H7
506/857-8957, Fax: 506/857-8838
Registrar, J.V. Robichaud

NEWFOUNDLAND PHARMACEUTICAL ASSOCIATION (NPHA) (1954)
Apothecary Hall, 488 Water St., St. John's, NF A1E 1B3
709/753-5877, Fax: 709/753-8615
Secretary Registrar, Donald F. Rowe
Publications: The Apothecary

NOVA SCOTIA PHARMACEUTICAL SOCIETY (1876)
1526 Dresden Row, PO Box 3363, Halifax, NS B3J 3J1
902/422-8528, Fax: 902/422-2619
Registrar, Susan Wedlake

ONTARIO COLLEGE OF PHARMACISTS
31 Governers Rd., Toronto, ON M4W 2E9
416/962-4861, Fax: 416/962-1619
Manager, Patient Relations Program, Christina M. Langlois

ORDRE DES PHARMACIENS DU QUÉBEC (1974)
#301, 266, rue Notre Dame ouest, Montréal, PQ H2Y 1T5
514/284-9588, Téléc: 514/284-3420, Ligne sans frais: 1-800-363-0324
Directeur général/Secrétaire, Alain Boisvert
Publications: L'Ordonnance

SASKATCHEWAN PHARMACEUTICAL ASSOCIATION (1911)
#301, 2631 - 28 Ave., Regina, SK S4S 6X3
306/584-2292, Fax: 306/584-9695
Registrar, R.J. Joubert

Canadian Society of Hospital Pharmacists/Société canadienne des pharmaciens d'hôpitaux (CSHP) (1947)
#350, 1145 Hunt Club Rd., Ottawa, ON K1V 0Y3
613/736-9733, Fax: 613/736-5660, Email: bleslie@worldlink.ca
URL: http://www.cshp.ca/~cshp

Executive Director, William J. Leslie
Publications: Pharmascope; Canadian Journal of Hospital Pharmacy, bi-m.; The Employment Opportunities Bulletin, s-m.

Canadian Wholesale Drug Association/Association des grossistes en médicaments du Canada (CWDA) (1964)
#2206, 1110, rue Sherbrooke ouest, Montréal, PQ H3A 1G8
514/842-8627, Fax: 514/842-3061
Executive Director, John A. Stante
President & CEO, Theresa S. Firestone
Publications: CWDA Newsletter

Conference of Pharmacy Registrars of Canada/Association canadienne des secrétaires généraux de pharmacie
c/o Ordre des Pharmaciens du Québec, 266, rue Notre Dame ouest, Montréal, PQ H2Y 1T6
514/284-9588, Fax: 514/284-3420
Chairman, S.G. Wilcox

Council for the Accreditation of Pharmaceutical Manufacturers Representatives of Canada
3489, rue Ashby, Saint Laurent, PQ H4R 2K3
514/333-8362, Fax: 514/333-1119
Executive Director, Gilles Lachance

Manitoba Society of Pharmacists Inc. (MSP) (1973)
187 St. Mary's Rd., Winnipeg, MB R2H 1J2
204/233-6227, Fax: 204/237-3468
Executive Director, Doug Nanton
President, Ross Forsyth
Publications: Communication; MSP Newsletter, bi-m.

National Association of Pharmacy Regulatory Authorities
#305, 116 Albert St., Ottawa, ON K1P 5G3
613/569-9658, Fax: 613/569-9659
Executive Director, Barbara Wells

New Brunswick Pharmacists' Association/Association des Pharmaciens du Nouveau-Brunswick (1981)
410, 212 Queen St., Fredericton, NB E3B 1A8
506/459-6008, Fax: 506/453-0736
Executive Director, George L. Bastin
Publications: Pharmacy NB; Activities Update, every 6 weeks

Nonprescription Drug Manufacturers Association of Canada/Association canadienne des fabricants de médicaments sans ordonnance (NDMAC) (1896)
#406, 1111 Prince of Wales Dr., Ottawa, ON K2C 3T2
613/723-0777, Fax: 613/723-0779, Email: ndmac@ndmac.ca
President, David S. Skinner
Communications Officer, Mary Wyllie
Publications: Self-Medication Digest

Ontario Pharmacists' Association (OPA)
#301, 23 Lesmill Rd., North York, ON M3B 3P6
416/441-0788, Fax: 416/441-0791
CEO, Barbara Stuart
President, Wayne Marigold

Ordre des chimistes du Québec (1926)
#1010, 300, rue Léo-Pariseau, CP 1089, Succ Place-du-Parc, Montréal, PQ H2W 2P4
514/844-3644, Téléc: 514/844-9601
Directeur général, Gilles Leduc
Présidente, Éveline de Médicis
Publications: Chimiste

ORGANIZATIONS —PHOTOGRAPHY

Pharmaceutical Manufacturers Association of Canada/Association canadienne de l'industrie du médicament (PMAC)
#302, 1111 Prince of Wales Dr., Ottawa, ON K2C 3T2
613/727-1380, Fax: 613/727-1407
President, Judy Erola
Chairman, Ger van Amersfoort

Pharmacy Association of Nova Scotia
PO Box 3214, Stn South, Halifax, NS B3J 3H5
902/422-9583, Fax: 902/422-2619
Executive Director, J. Patrick King
Publications: The Pharmacist

The Pharmacy Examining Board of Canada/Le Bureau des examinateurs en pharmacie du Canada (1963)
#603, 123 Edward St., Toronto, ON M5G 1E2
416/979-2431, Fax: 416/599-9244
President, Byron Sarson
Director of Administration, Lori Horley
Registrar/Treasurer, Dr. John Pugsley

Prince Edward Island Pharmacy Board (1983)
PO Box 89, Charlottetown, PE C0A 1J0
902/658-2780, Fax: 902/658-2198
Registrar, Neila I. Auld
Chairman, Allan Greene
Publications: Newsletter

PHOTOGRAPHY

Canadian Association of Photographers & Illustrators in Communications/Association canadienne de photographes et illustrateurs de publicité (CAPIC) (1978)
#322, 100 Broadview Ave., Toronto, ON M4M 2E8
416/462-3700, Fax: 416/462-3678
President, Stephen Quinlan
Secretary, David Nichols
Publications: CAPIC Journal

Canadian Imaging Trade Association (1955)
145 Upper Canada Dr., North York, ON M2P 1S9
416/226-2750, Fax: 416/226-3347
General Manager, Dori Gospodaric
Publications: Image Line

National Association for Photographic Art/Association nationale d'art photographique (NAPA) (1969)
31858 Hopedale Ave., Clearbrook, BC V2T 2G7
604/855-4848, Fax: 604/859-6288
President, Rosemarie Culver
Publications: Foto Flash
Affiliates: Fédération internationale de l'art photographique

Photo Marketing Association International - Canada (PMAI) (1924)
78 Lytton Blvd., Toronto, ON M4R 1L3
416/489-5614, Fax: 416/489-5780, Email: 102077.1464@compuserve.com
URL: http://www.pmai.org
Director/Canadian Activities, Lynn McGregor
Publications: Newsline Canada; Photo Marketing Magazine, m.

Photographers Gallery Society Inc. (PGS) (1971)
12 - 23 St. East, 2nd Fl., Saskatoon, SK S7K 0H5
306/244-8018, Fax: 306/665-6568
Director, Monte Greenshields
Publications: Newsletter

Photographical Historical Society of Canada (PHSOC) (1974)
1512 Avenue Rd., PO Box 54620, Toronto, ON M5M 4N5
416/691-1555, Fax: 416/693-0018, Email: phsc@onramp.ca
URL: http://web.onramp.ca/phsc
President, Les Jones
Publications: Photographic Canadiana

Professional Photographers of Canada/Photographes professionnelles du Canada (PPOC)
PO Box 337, Gatineau, PQ J8P 6J3
819/643-5177, Fax: 819/643-7177, Email: ppoc@magi.com
Directrice générale, Suzanne Despatie

ALBERTA PROFESSIONAL PHOTOGRAPHERS ASSOCIATION
16136 - 110B Ave, Edmonton, AB T5P 4E6
403/483-4275, Fax: 403/489-7724
Executive Secretary, Pat Eisenbarth

CORPORATION DES MAÎTRES PHOTOGRAPHES DU QUÉBEC INC./QUÉBEC CORPORATION OF MASTER PHOTOGRAPHERS INC. (CMPQ) (1950)
#202, 650, boul de Grande Prairie, St-Léonard, PQ H1P 1A2
514/328-1071
URL: http://www.intertower.com/rimage/cmpq.html
Publications: Bulletin Image

MARITIME PROFESSIONAL PHOTOGRAPHERS ASSOCIATION
19 Hill St., Edmundston, NB E3V 1H7
506/735-8186
Michael Jessop

PROFESSIONAL PHOTOGRAPHERS ASSOCIATION OF BRITISH COLUMBIA (PPABC) (1945)
1215 Penticton Ave., Penticton, BC V2A 2N3
250/492-0202
Sec.-Treas., Eleanor R. McDonald
Publications: In Focus

PROFESSIONAL PHOTOGRAPHERS ASSOCIATION OF MANITOBA INC.
PO Box 1575, Winnipeg, MB R3C 2Z4
204/482-4425
President, Thomas Podruchny
Publications: PPAM News

PROFESSIONAL PHOTOGRAPHERS OF ONTARIO INC. (PPO) (1884)
RR#4, Kemptville, ON K0G 1J0
613/258-5432, Fax: 613/258-5432
Executive Assistant, Eileen K. Gilbert
Publications: Exposure Ontario

PHYSICALLY CHALLENGED PERSONS see **DISABLED PERSONS**

PLANNING & DEVELOPMENT

Canadian Association of Certified Planning Technicians (CACPT) (1979)
PO Box 3844, Stn C, Hamilton, ON L8H 7R6
905/578-4681, Fax: 905/578-4681
Executive Director, Donna Madden
Publications: Tech Talk

Canadian Institute for Development Management (CIDM) (1991)
#202, 1900 Merivale Rd., Nepean, ON K2G 4N4
613/723-8698, Fax: 613/723-7333
Contact, Keith A.J. Hay

Canadian Institute of Planners/Institut canadien des urbanistes (CIP) (1919)
541 Sussex Dr., 2nd Fl., Ottawa, ON K1N 6Z6
613/562-4646, Fax: 613/562-4648, Toll Free: 1-800-207-2138
URL: http://infoweb.magi.com/~cip/cip.html
Executive Director, Rachael Corbett, MCIP
President Elect, Barbara Dembek, MCIP
President, Gerry Couture, MCIP
Publications: Plan Canada; Reflections on Sustainable Planning
Affiliates: International Federation for Housing & Planning; Commonwealth Association of Planners

ALBERTA ASSOCIATION, CANADIAN INSTITUTE OF PLANNERS (AACIP) (1963)
#100, 4246 - 97 St., PO Box 596, Edmonton, AB T5J 2K8
403/435-8716, Fax: 403/435-7503, Email: b.holtby@ccinet.ab.ca
President, Barb Koch
Publications: Newsletter

ATLANTIC PLANNING INSTITUTE/INSTITUT DES URBANISTES DE L'ATLANTIQUE
PO Box 2012, RPO Central, Halifax, NS B3J 2Z1
506/577-4391, Email: ncollins@fox.nstn.ca
Representative, Armand Robichaud, MCIP
Publications: Planners Pen

MANITOBA ASSOCIATION OF THE CANADIAN INSTITUTE OF PLANNERS
137 Bannatyne Ave., Winnipeg, MB R3B 0K3
204/943-3637
President, D.J. Kalcsics, MCIP
Treasurer, A.P. Regiec, MCIP

ONTARIO PROFESSIONAL PLANNERS INSTITUTE/INSTITUT DES PLANIFICATEURS PROFESSIONNELS DE L'ONTARIO (OPPI) (1986)
#201, 234 Eglinton Ave. East, Toronto, ON M4P 1K5
416/483-1873, Fax: 416/483-7830, Toll Free: 1-800-668-1448, Email: oppi@interlog.com
URL: http://www.interlog.com/~oppi
Executive Director, Susan Smith
President, P. Wong
Publications: Ontario Planning Journal

ORDRE DES URBANISTES DU QUÉBEC (OUQ) (1963)
85, rue St-Paul ouest, 4e étage, #B5, Montréal, PQ H2Y 3V4
514/849-1177, Téléc: 514/849-7176
Directrice générale, Gisèle Floch Rousselle
Publications: En Bref

PLANNING INSTITUTE OF BRITISH COLUMBIA (PIBC)
#20, 10551 Shellbridge Way, Richmond, BC V6X 2W9
604/270-2061, Fax: 604/660-2271
President, Linda Allen
Secretary, Gary Holisko
Publications: PIBC News

Canadian Urban Institute/Institut urbain du Canada (CUI) (1991)
30 St. Patrick St., 6th Fl., Toronto, ON M5T 3A3
416/598-1606, Fax: 416/598-5145
President, John Farrow

Intergovernmental Committee on Urban & Regional Research/Comité intergouvernemental de recherches urbaines et régionales (ICURR) (1967)
#301, 150 Eglinton Ave. East, Toronto, ON M4P 1E8
416/973-5629, Fax: 416/973-1375, Email: mafar@icurr.org
URL: http://www.icurr.org/icurr/
Executive Director, André Lanteigne
Chairman, Ken MacLeod
Research Coordinator, Claude Marchand
Information Officer, John Slatcher, 416/973-9408

Senior Information Officer, Victoria Gregor, 416/973-1339
Information Officer, Michael Afar, 416/973-1331
Publications: Liaison

Rural Dignity of Canada/Dignité rurale du Canada (1986)
PO Box 70, Barachois-de-Malbaie, PQ G0C 1A0
418/645-3766, Fax: 418/645-3835
National Coordinator, Cynthia Patterson
Assistant to National Coordinator, Sandra LeMieux
Publications: Newsletter
Affiliates: Transport 2000 Canada

Strategic Leadership Forum, The International Society for Strategic Management/Toronto Chapter (1950)
26 Rose Park Dr., Toronto, ON M4T 1R1
416/481-7228, Fax: 416/489-3304, Email: mstreet@inforamp.net
President, Gay Gooderham
Publications: Focus; Strategy of Leadership, bi-m.

Urban Development Institute of Canada/Institut de développement urbain du Canada (UDI)
717 Pender St. West, 3rd Fl., Vancouver, BC V6C 1G9
604/669-9585, Fax: 604/689-8691
URL: http://www.udi.bc.ca
Executive Director, Maureen Enser
National President, F. Bucci
Manager, Information Services, David Helem

PLUMBING see HEATING, AIR CONDITIONING, PLUMBING

POLICE see LAW

POLITICS
see also Government & Public Administration

Association Canado-Américaine (ACA) (1896)
898, rue Ste-Julie, Trois-Rivières, PQ G9A 1Y2
819/376-2111, Téléc: 819/376-2662
Chief Agent, Henri Lemay
Président Général, Eugene A. Lemieux, 603/625-8977
Publications: Le Canado-Americain
Organisation(s) affiliée(s): Canadian Fraternal Association

BC Social Credit Party
PO Box 26088, Richmond, BC V6Y 3V3
604/270-4040, Fax: 604/270-4726
President, Jane Sorko

Bloc québécois (BQ) (1991)
#1475, 425, rue de Maisonneuve ouest, Montréal, PQ H3A 3G5
514/499-3000, Téléc: 514/499-3638
Directeur général, Yves Dufour

Canadian Political Science Association/Association canadienne de science politique (CPSA) (1913)
#205, One Stewart St., Ottawa, ON K1N 6H7
613/564-4026, Fax: 613/230-2746, Email: cpscc@acadvm1.uottawa.ca
Executive Secretary, Michelle Hopkins
Publications: The Canadian Journal of Political Science/La Revue canadienne de science politique; The Bulletin; The Directory of Political Scientists in Canada

Christian Heritage Party of Canada/Parti d'héritage du Canada (CHP) (1986)
800 Niagara St., PO Box 23033, RPO Seaway Mall, Welland, ON L3C 7E7

905/788-2238, Fax: 905/788-2943
National Leader, Ron Gray
Party President, Carol Speelmah
Party Secretary, Betty Schaap
Party Treasurer, Gerald Tot
Executive Director, Margaret Purcell
Publications: Ambassador
Affiliates: CHP New Zealand

Comité Québécois pour le Canada/Québec Committee for Canada
#3040, 6900, boul Décarie, Montréal, PQ H3X 2T8
514/344-2410, Fax: 514/344-2760

The Confederation of Regions Party of New Brunswick (1983)
CoR Party of New Brunswick
PO Box 25001, RPO York Plaza, Fredericton, NB E3A 5V7
506/444-4040, Fax: 506/444-4053

Family Coalition Party of Ontario/Parti de la Coalition des Familles de l'Ontario (FCP) (1987)
#19, 117 Ringwood Dr., Stouffville, ON L4A 8C1
416/640-6702, Fax: 416/640-8102
Party Leader, Don Pennell
Chief Financial Officer, Henri Cloudt
Publications: Impact

Green Party of Canada/Parti vert du Canada (GPC) (1983)
Canadian Greens/Canadiens Verts
#5, 3147 Kingsway, Vancouver, BC V5R 5K2
604/436-1437, Fax: 604/436-1438
Leader, Wendy Priesnitz
Executive Secretary, Annie Humphries-Loutit
Treasurer, Eileen Stevens
Fundraising Coordinator, Eric Saumur
Publications Coordinator, Peggy Robinson
Membership Secretary, John Beverley
Publications Coordinator, Dylan Maxwell
Membership Secretary, Jutta Keylwerth
Chief Agent, Richard Bidwell

GREEN PARTY POLITICAL ASSOCIATION OF BRITISH COLUMBIA (1983)
Green Party of Canada in BC
#5, 3147 Kingsway., Vancouver, BC V5R 5K2
604/436-1437, Fax: 604/436-1438, Email: bcgreens@alternatives.com
URL: http://www.islandnet.com/~bcgreens/
Chair, David G. Cursons
Provincial Party Leader, Stuart Parker
Secretary, Annie Humphries-Loutit
Provincial Treasurer, Eileen Stevens
Membership Chair, David Walters
Publications: BC Green Party News

THE ONTARIO GREENS
Green Party of Ontario/Green Party of Canada - Ontario Wing
PO Box 35101, Ottawa, ON K1Z 1A2
613/724-6061, Fax: 613/232-3081, Email: greenpty@freenet.toronto.on.ca
Information Officer, Sharon Tivers, Res: 416/283-4303
Publications: Ontario Greenhouse; Ontario Green News

PARTI VERT DU CANADA (QUÉBEC)/GREEN PARTY OF CANADA (QUÉBEC) (1984)
Les verts/The Greens
CP 262, Succ. Jean-Talon, Montréal, PQ H1S 2Z2
514/259-3580, Téléc: 514/843-3757
Coordonateur, Rolf Bramann
Secrétaire général, Jean Guérnon

PARTI VERT DU QUÉBEC/QUÉBEC GREEN PARTY (PVQ) (1985)
196, ch de la Côte St-Antoine, Montréal, PQ H3Y 2J2
514/937-9399
Victor Martel

Bernard Cooper
Publications: Verus

The Liberal Party of Canada/Le Parti Libéral du Canada (1848)
#200, 200 Laurier Ave. West, Ottawa, ON K1P 6M8
613/237-0740, Fax: 613/235-7208
URL: http://www.liberal.ca/
Leader, Right Honourable Jean Chrétien
President, Senator Dan Hays
Vice-President, English, Mobina Jaffer
Vice-President, French, Jean-Paul Boily
Sec.-Treas., Joe Thornley
Publications: The Liberal Times

ALBERTA LIBERAL PARTY
#100, 10045 - 111 St., Edmonton, AB T5K 2M5
403/482-3994, Fax: 403/488-7513
Executive Director, Rob Van Walleghem

THE LIBERAL PARTY OF CANADA (BC) (LPC)
1447 Hornby St., Vancouver, BC V6Z 1W8
604/689-9776, Fax: 604/689-9788, Email: admin@bc.liberal.ca
President, Norman Morrison

THE LIBERAL PARTY OF CANADA (ONTARIO)
PO Box 1108, Stn F, Toronto, ON M4Y 2T8
416/921-2844, Fax: 416/921-3880, Toll Free: 1-800-361-3881
President, Stephen LeDrew

THE LIBERAL PARTY OF CANADA IN ALBERTA
#520 - 10303 Jasper Ave. NW, Edmonton, AB T5J 3N6
403/424-1984, Fax: 403/424-1966
President, Kathy O'Neill

THE LIBERAL PARTY IN MANITOBA
#2, 140 Roslyn Rd., Winnipeg, MB R3L 0G8
204/453-7343, Fax: 204/284-1492
President, Jean-Paul Boily

THE LIBERAL PARTY OF NEWFOUNDLAND & LABRADOR
PO Box 998, Stn C, St. John's, NF A1C 5M3
709/754-1813, Fax: 709/754-0820
President, Gerry Glavine

THE LIBERAL PARTY OF PRINCE EDWARD ISLAND
129 Kent St., 2nd Fl., PO Box 2559, Charlottetown, PE C1A 8C2
902/368-3449, Fax: 902/368-3687
President, Brendan Curley

NEW BRUNSWICK LIBERAL ASSOCIATION
715 Brunswick St., Fredericton, NB E3B 1H8
506/453-3950, Fax: 506/453-2476, Toll Free: 1-800-442-4902
President, Réginald Léger

NORTHWEST TERRITORIES LIBERAL ASSOCIATION
104 Dagenais Dr., Yellowknife, NT X1A 3B6
President, Pat Thomas

NOVA SCOTIA LIBERAL ASSOCIATION
#911, 1660 Hollis St., PO Box 723, Halifax, NS B3J 2T3
902/429-1993, Fax: 902/423-1624
President, Lloyd Campbell
Publications: Newsletter

PARTI LIBÉRAL DU CANADA (QUÉBEC)
#106, 640, rue St-Paul ouest, Montréal, PQ H3C 1L9
514/866-6391, Téléc: 514/866-8182
Président, Martial Guay

PARTI LIBERAL DU QUÉBEC/QUÉBEC LIBERAL PARTY
4364, rue Saint-Denis, Montréal, PQ H2J 2L1
514/288-4364, Téléc: 514/288-9455
Directeur général, Stéphane Bertrand

Canadian Almanac & Directory 1997

ORGANIZATIONS — POULTRY & EGGS

SASKATCHEWAN LIBERAL ASSOCIATION
2060 Broad St., PO Box 4401, Regina, SK S4P 1Y3
306/522-8507, Fax: 306/569-9271
President, Dennis Barnett

YUKON LIBERAL ASSOCIATION
70 Teslin Rd., Whitehorse, YT Y1A 3M6
President, Lesley Cabott

The Libertarian Party of Canada
#301, One St. John's Rd., Toronto, ON M6P 1T7
416/763-3688, Fax: 416/763-5306
President, Chris Blatchly
Contact, D. Kublas

BRITISH COLUMBIA LIBERTARIAN PARTY (1986)
922 Cloverley St., North Vancouver, BC V7L 1N3
604/980-7370, Fax: 604/980-6690
President, Bill Tomlinson
Affiliates: Foundation for Research on Economics & the Environment

GREATER VANCOUVER LIBERTARIAN ASSOCIATION (1973)
922 Cloverley St., North Vancouver, BC V7L 1N3
604/980-7370, Fax: 604/980-6690
Director, Bill Tomlinson
President, Kerry Pearson
Publications: West Coast Libertarian
Affiliates: Foundation for Research on Economics & the Environment - USA

MANITOBA LIBERTARIAN ASSOCIATION
PO Box 245, Winnipeg, MB R3C 3R3
204/474-1056
Contact, C. Smith

New Democratic Party/Nouveau Parti Démocratique (NDP)
Federal Headquarters, #900, 81 Metcalfe St., Ottawa, ON K1P 6K7
613/236-3613, Fax: 613/230-9950
URL: http://www.ncf.carleton.ca/freeport/government/fedelect/nat/ndp/menu
Leader, Alexa McDonough
Director of Policy, Judy Randall
Federal President, Iain Angus
Treasurer, Armand Roy

Parti communiste du Québec (1965)
CP 29, Succ. C, Montréal, PQ H2L 4J7
514/273-6577
André Cloutier
Panagiotis Vamvakaris
Publications: L'Alternative; Le Communiste
Organisation(s) affiliée(s): Solidarité populaire Québec; Ligue des droits et libertés

Parti québécois (PQ) (1968)
#150, 1200, av Papineau, Montréal, PQ H2K 4R5
514/526-0020, Téléc: 514/526-0272, Ligne sans frais: 1-800-363-9531, Courrier électronique: pqnatio@cam.org
Directeur général, Yves Dufour
Président, Lucien Bouchard
2e Vice-président, Denis Ménard
Directeur des communications, Daniel Bussières
Publications: La Lettre du Parti

Parti des travailleurs du Québec
1221, rue Marie-Anne est, Montréal, PQ J2J 2B9
514/277-7794
Representant Officiel, Serge Turmel
Publications: Le Journal choc

Progressive Conservative Party of Canada/Parti Progressiste-Conservateur du Canada
#501, 275 Slater St., Ottawa, ON K1P 5H9
613/238-6111, Fax: 613/238-7429, Email: pcinfo@pcparty.ca
URL: http://www.pcparty.ca/
Leader, Honourable Jean Charest, PC, MP
National President, Pierre W. Fortier
National Director, Michael Allen
Secretary, Dr. Kellie Leitch
Treasurer, Rick Perkins
BC Regional Office: Manager, Matt Burns, 1917 West 4th Ave., PO Box 360, Vancouver, BC V6J 1M7, 604/730-8451, Fax: 604/730-8471
Montreal Office: Contact, Sylvia English,Tour de la Bourse, #1225, 800, Place Victoria, CP 55, Montréal, PQ H4Z 1A8, 506/875-5464, Téléc: 506/875-5981
Ontario Regional Office: Ontario Organizer, Suzanne Warren, 21 Howland Ave., Toronto, ON M4K 2Z4, 416/469-5525, Fax: 416/469-2671

MANITOBA PROGRESSIVE CONSERVATIVE PARTY
23 Kennedy St., Winnipeg, MB R3C 1S5
204/942-8283, Fax: 204/943-1706
Executive Director, Val Hueging

NOVA SCOTIA PROGRESSIVE CONSERVATIVE ASSOCIATION
PC Party of Nova Scotia
#401, 1660 Hollis St., Halifax, NS B3J 1V7
902/429-9470, Fax: 902/423-2465
Provincial Director, Jim David
President, Jim White
Publications: Grassroots

PROGRESSIVE CONSERVATIVE ASSOCIATION OF ALBERTA
9919 - 106 St., Edmonton, AB T5K 1E2
403/423-1624, Fax: 403/423-1634, Email: altapc@supernet.ab.ca
URL: http://www.albertapc.ab.ca
Executive Director, Peter Elzinga

PROGRESSIVE CONSERVATIVE ASSOCIATION OF NEWFOUNDLAND & LABRADOR
General Delivery, Holyrood, NF A0A 1Z0
709/229-4421, Fax: 709/229-3307
Organizer, Mary Hayes

PROGRESSIVE CONSERVATIVE YOUTH FEDERATION/FÉDÉRATION DES JEUNES PROGRESSISTES-CONSERVATEURS (PCYF)
#501, 275 Slater St., Ottawa, ON K1P 5H9
613/238-6111, Fax: 613/238-7429
National President, Tasha Kheiriddin

Reform Party of Canada/Parti reformiste du Canada (REF) (1987)
#600, 833 - 4 Ave. SW, Calgary, AB T2P 0K5
403/269-1990, Fax: 403/269-4077
Executive Director, Glenn McMurray
Leader, Preston Manning
Publications: Reformer

Socialist Party of Canada/Parti socialiste du Canada (SPC) (1931)
PO Box 4280, Victoria, BC V8X 3X8
250/595-2144, Email: 72607.2404@compuserve.com
General Secretary, Steve Szalai
Publications: Socialist Standard; World Socialist Review, q.
Affiliates: World Socialist Movement

POLLUTION see ENVIRONMENTAL

POULTRY & EGGS

Alberta Egg Producers' Board
#15, 1915 - 32 Ave. NE, Calgary, AB T2E 7C8
403/250-1197, Fax: 403/291-9216
General Manager, Warren Chorney

Atlantic Provinces Hatchery Federation
Agriculture Centre, #B122, 32 Main St., Kentville, NS B4N 1J5
902/679-5333, Fax: 902/679-6062
Sec.-Treas., Herbert N. Jansen

British Columbia Broiler Hatching Egg Producers' Association (1980)
PO Box 667, Abbotsford, BC V2S 6R7
604/850-1854, Fax: 604/850-1683
President, Rob Guliker
Affiliates: BC Broiler Hatching Egg Commission

Canadian Broiler Hatching Egg Marketing Agency
#705, 200 Elgin St., Ottawa, ON K2P 1L5
613/232-3023, Fax: 613/232-5241
Secretary, Paul Jelley

Canadian Chicken Marketing Agency/Office canadien de commercialisation des poulets (CCMA) (1978)
#300, 377 Dalhousie St., Ottawa, ON K1N 9N8
613/241-2800, Fax: 613/241-5999, Telex: 053-4518
General Manager, Cynthia Currie
Policy Manager, Albert Chambers
Communications Manager, Nicole Beauchamp
Publications: Chicken Forum

Canadian Egg Marketing Agency/Office canadien de commercialisation des oeufs (CEMA)
#1900, 320 Queen St., Ottawa, ON K1R 5A3
613/238-2514, Fax: 613/238-1967
Chief Executive, Neil Currie
Publications: Today's Egg Producer

Canadian Egg Producers Council
#1101, 75 Albert St., Ottawa, ON K1P 5E7
613/236-3633, Fax: 613/236-5749
Executive Secretary, Sally Rutherford

Canadian Poultry & Egg Processors Council/Conseil canadien des transformateurs d'oeufs et de volailles (CPEPC) (1975)
#600, 2 Gurdwara Rd., Ottawa, ON K2E 1A2
613/224-0001, Fax: 613/224-2023
Chairman, Pieter Vanderpol
Publications: Newsletter

Canadian Turkey Marketing Agency/Office canadien de commercialisation du dindon (CTMA) (1974)
#102, 969 Derry Rd. East., Mississauga, ON L5T 2J7
905/564-3100, Fax: 905/792-7535, Email: ctma@idirect.com
URL: http://www.canturk.ca
Executive Director, Kenneth E. Crawford
Publications: Plume

Fédération des producteurs d'oeufs de consommation du Québec (1965)
555, boul Roland-Therrien, Longueuil, PQ J4H 3Y9
514/679-0530, Téléc: 514/679-0855
Président, Jacques Bouchard

Fédération des producteurs de volailles du Québec/Federation of Quebec Poultry Producers
555, boul Roland-Therrien, Longueuil, PQ J4H 3Y9
514/679-0530, Fax: 514/679-5375
Président, Luc Lamy
Publications: PROVOQUE

New Brunswick Poultry Council
#103, 1115 Regent St., Fredericton, NB E3B 3Z2
506/452-8085, Fax: 506/451-2121

Ontario Hatcheries Association
#101, 49 Emma St., Guelph, ON N1E 6X1
519/763-6360, Fax: 519/837-0729

PRINTING INDUSTRY & GRAPHIC ARTS

Association des arts graphiques du Québec, inc. (AAGQ) (1983)
#101, 65, rue de Castelnau ouest, Montréal, PQ H2R 2W3
514/274-7446, Téléc: 514/274-7482, Ligne sans frais: 1-800-607-7446
Directrice générale, Hélène Lagadec
Président, Pierre Audet
Publications: Le Maître imprimeur
Organisation(s) affiliée(s): Association canadienne de l'imprimerie; Printing Industries of America

Canadian Business Forms Association
#906, 75 Albert St., Ottawa, ON K1P 5E7
613/236-7208, Fax: 613/236-8169
Executive Director, Albert Lacroix

Canadian Printing Industries Association/ Association canadienne de l'imprimerie (CPIA) (1958)
#906, 75 Albert St., Ottawa, ON K1P 5E7
613/236-7208, Fax: 613/236-8169
President, Michael Makin
Publications: CPIA Membership Directory; National Communiqué, m.; National Impressions, m.
Affiliates: Graphic Arts Council of North America; Printing Industries of America

Canadian Printing Ink Manufacturers Association (CPIMA) (1936)
1532 Greenridge Circle, Oakville, ON L6M 2J4
905/847-2838, Fax: 905/847-2838
Sec.-Treas., John A. Nace
President, Ralph Marshall

Council of Printing Industries of Canada
#208, 510 Front St. West, Toronto, ON M5V 3H3
416/599-1931, Fax: 416/408-4704
General Manager, Jean-Marc Metthé

Forms & Manuals Management Association
PO Box 5338, Stn A, Toronto, ON M5W 1N6
416/285-2854, Fax: 416/285-2955
President, Carol MacDonald
Publications: Platform

GraphComm Training Centre (1969)
#109, 80 Park Lawn Rd., Toronto, ON M8Y 3H8
416/593-4018
Mike Zajac
John Marc-Metthé

Printing Equipment & Supply Dealers' Association of Canada (PESDA) (1975)
#320, 304 East Mall, Etobicoke, ON M9B 6E2
416/236-3733, Fax: 416/236-2171
Contact, Jennifer Rogers

Printing & Graphics Industries Association of Alberta (1987)
PO Box 21006, RPO Dominion, Calgary, AB T2P 4H5
403/281-1421, Fax: 403/251-6702
President, Steve Cropper
Executive Sec.-Treas., Joan Kumlin
Publications: Impressions

Saskatchewan Graphic Arts Industries Association Inc. (SGAIA)
c/o PrintWest, PO Box 2500, Saskatoon, SK S7K 2C4
306/665-3549, Fax: 306/653-1255
Contact, Don Breher

Society of Graphic Designers of Canada/Société des graphistes du Canada
Arts Court, 2 Daly Ave., Ottawa, ON K1N 6E2
613/567-5400
URL: http://www.swifty.com/gdc/
President, Mary Ann Maruska
Publications: Axis; Graphic Design Journal; The National
Affiliates: International Council of Graphic Design Associations

PRISONERS & EX-OFFENDERS
see also Law

British Columbia Borstal Association
#202, 2425 Quebec St., Vancouver, BC V5T 4L6
604/879-3224
Executive Director, John A. Cooper

Canadian Association of Elizabeth Fry Societies/ Association canadienne des sociétés Elizabeth Fry (CAEFS) (1978)
#600, 251 Bank St., Ottawa, ON K2P 1X3
613/238-2422, Fax: 613/232-7130
URL: http://www.web.apc.org/~kpate
Executive Director, Kim Pate
President, Susan Hendricks
Affiliates: National Associations Active in Criminal Justice; National Action Committee on the Status of Women; National Association of Women & the Law; National Voluntary Organizations; Canadian Criminal Justice Association; Women's Legal & Education & Action Fund; National Council of Women of Canada; United Way National Agencies Committee

The John Howard Society of Canada/Société John Howard du Canada
#404, 383 Parkdale Ave., Ottawa, ON K1Y 4R4
613/761-7678, Fax: 613/729-7715
Executive Director, James M. MacLatchie
President, Doug Wright

Operation Springboard (1974)
Springboard
230 Richmond St. East, Toronto, ON M5A 1P4
416/367-4288, Fax: 416/367-4291
Executive Director, Diane Nicholls
Publications: Perspectives

Prisoners' Rights Group (PRG) (1975)
3570 Dease Lane, Vancouver, BC V5S 1M6
604/432-6132, Fax: 604/430-2019
Coordinator, Claire Culhane

Quaker Committee on Jails & Justice (QCJJ) (1975)
60 Lowther Ave., Toronto, ON M5R 1C7
416/920-5213
Program Associate, Marc Forget
Clerk, Marianne Ostopovich
Publications: QCJJ Newsletter
Affiliates: Alternatives to Violence Project - Canada

St. Leonard's Society of Canada
#205, 122 Saint Patrick St., Toronto, ON M5T 2X8
416/598-4446, Fax: 416/977-6698
Executive Director, Elizabeth White

Seventh Step Society of Canada
10620 Waneta Cres. SE, Calgary, AB T2J 1J6
403/271-2278, Fax: 403/271-8907
Executive Director, Patrick Graham
Affiliates: Seventh Step Society International

PRO-LIFE ORGANIZATIONS see **REPRODUCTIVE ISSUES**

PROFESSIONAL DEVELOPMENT see **EMPLOYMENT & HUMAN RESOURCES**

PROFIT SHARING see **FINANCE**

PSYCHIATRY see **MENTAL HEALTH**

PSYCHOLOGY see **MENTAL HEALTH**

PUBLIC ADMINISTRATION see **GOVERNMENT & PUBLIC ADMINISTRATION**

PUBLIC HEALTH see **HEALTH & MEDICAL**

PUBLIC UTILITIES

Canadian Association of Members of Public Utility Tribunals (CAMPUT)
PO Box 21040, St. John's, NF A1A 5B2
709/726-1133, Fax: 709/726-9604
Sec.-Treas., Carol Horwood
Chair, Leslie E. Galway
Affiliates: National Association of Regulatory Utility Commissioners

Canadian Council of Electrical Leagues (1984)
#1000, 2 Lansing Sq., North York, ON M2J 4P8
416/495-0052, Fax: 416/495-1804
Secretary, Richard McCarten

Canadian Public Works Association (CPWA)
3370 South Service Rd., Garden Level, Burlington, ON L7N 3M6
905/634-7736, Fax: 905/634-1304

Electrical Utilities Safety Association of Ontario (EUSA) (1915)
220 Traders Blvd. East, Mississauga, ON L4Z 1W7
905/890-1011, Fax: 905/890-9249
General Manager, C.J. Tallon
Publications: Safe-T-Line; Safety Topics, m.

Municipal Electric Association (MEA) (1986)
#500, 20 Eglinton Ave. West, PO Box 2004, Toronto, ON M4R 1K8
416/483-7739, Fax: 416/483-9039
CEO, I.H. Jennings

Ontario Municipal Water Association (OMWA)
#69, 225 Benjamin Rd., Waterloo, ON N2J 3Z4
519/888-6402, Fax: 519/725-5987
Executive Director, D.J. Black
Publications: OMWA Newsletter; Pipeline, q.
Affiliates: America Water Works Association

Utility Contractors' Association of Ontario Inc. (UCA)
#720, 5915 Airport Rd., Mississauga, ON L4V 1T1
905/673-0548, Fax: 905/673-0546
General Manager, Barry L. Brown

PUBLISHING
see also Printing Industry & Graphic Arts; Writers & Editors

Alcuin Society (1965)
PO Box 3216, Vancouver, BC V6B 3X8

604/872-2326, Fax: 604/872-4235
Secretary, Doreen E. Eddy, 604/888-9049
Publications: Amphora

Alternative Newspapers Association
NOW Communications, 150 Danforth Ave., Toronto, ON M4K 1N1
416/461-0871, Fax: 416/461-2886
Contact, Alice Klein

Association of Canadian Publishers/Association des éditeurs canadiens (ACP) (1972)
#301, 2 Gloucester St., Toronto, ON M4Y 1L5
416/413-4929, Fax: 416/413-4920
URL: http://www.can.net/marketplace/pub/acp/acp.htm
Executive Director, Paul Davidson
President, Jack Stoddart
Vice-President, Lois Pike
Treasurer, Peter Milroy
Secretary, Robert Davies
Publications: Just the Fax; ACP Directory, a.
Affiliates: Association of Book Publishers of British Columbia; Book Publishers Association of Alberta; Saskatchewan Publishers Group; Association of Manitoba Book Publishers; Ontario Publishers Group; Association des editeurs anglophones du Québec; Atlantic Publishers Association

ASSOCIATION OF BOOK PUBLISHERS OF BRITISH COLUMBIA (ABPBC) (1974)
#107, 100 West Pender St., Vancouver, BC V6B 1R8
604/684-0228, Fax: 604/684-5788
Executive Director, Margaret Reynolds
President, Bob Tyrrell
Publications: ABPBC Directory; General Industry Survey, a.

ASSOCIATION DES ÉDITEURS ANGLOPHONES DU QUÉBEC/QUÉBEC ENGLISH LANGUAGE PUBLISHERS ASSOCIATION (1990)
#3, 1200, av Atwater, Montréal, PQ H3Z 1X4
514/932-5633, Téléc: 514/932-5456
Président, Robert Davies

ASSOCIATION OF MANITOBA BOOK PUBLISHERS
#404, 100 Arthur St., Winnipeg, MB R3B 1H3
204/947-3335, Fax: 204/942-1555
Executive Director, Maureen Devanik

ATLANTIC PUBLISHERS ASSOCIATION (APA)
Lord Nelson Arcade, #202, 5675 Spring Garden Rd., Halifax, NS B3J 1H1
902/420-0711, Fax: 902/423-4302
Executive Director, Paulette Soloman

BOOK PUBLISHERS ASSOCIATION OF ALBERTA (BPA) (1975)
#123, 10523 - 100 Ave., Edmonton, AB T5J 0A8
403/424-5060, Fax: 403/424-7343 ; Email: bpaa@planet.eon.net
Executive Director, Katherine Shute
Publications: Newsletter

Association of Canadian Publishers - Ottawa
2 Daly Ave., Ottawa, ON K1N 6E2
613/567-1159, Fax: 613/567-5276

Association of Canadian University Presses/Association des presses universitaires canadiennes (ACUP)
c/o University of Toronto Press, #700, 10 Saint Mary St., Toronto, ON M4Y 2W8
416/978-5850, Fax: 416/978-4738
Secretary, Kathryn Bennett
Publications: Directory of Members

Association for the Export of Canadian Books/Association pour l'exportation du livre canadien (AECB) (1972)
#504, One Nicholas St., Ottawa, ON K1N 7B7

613/562-2324, Fax: 613/562-2329, Email: aecb@magi.com
URL: http://infoweb.magi.com/~aecb/
Executive Director, Luc Jutras
Publications: Biblio Export; Books on Canada; Rights Canada/Droits du Canada, biennial
Affiliates: Association of Canadian Publishers; Canadian Book Publishers Council; Association of Canadian University Publishers; Association nationale des éditeurs de livres

Association des libraires du Québec (ALQ) (1969)
1306, rue Logan, Montréal, PQ H2L 1X1
514/526-3349, Téléc: 514/526-3340
Directrice générale, Lucie Lachapelle
Président, Guy Beaulieu
Vice-président, Robert Leroux
Trésorier, Jacques Boutin
Secrétaire, Lynne Magnan
Recherchiste et rédactrice, Francine Déry
Publications: Bulletin de nouvelles; Répertoire des éditeurs et de leurs distributeurs, trimestriel; Annuaire des membres, annuel

Association nationale des éditeurs de livres (ANEL) (1991)
2514, boul Rosemont, Montréal, PQ H1Y 1K4
514/273-8130, Téléc: 514/273-9657
Directeur général, Michel Gay
Directrice générale adjointe, Jocelyne Daze

Association québécoise des presses universitaires (AQPU)
a/s Presses de l'Université Laval, CP 2208, Succ. Terminus, Québec, PQ G1K 7R4
418/656-3001, Téléc: 418/656-3305
Denis Vaugeois

Association québécoise des salons du livre (1978)
#200, 480, rue St-Laurent, Montréal, PQ H2Y 3Y7
514/845-2365, Téléc: 514/845-7119
Président, Francine Bois
Secrétaire, Denis LeBrun

Book & Periodical Council (BPC) (1975)
35 Spadina Rd., Toronto, ON M5R 2S9
416/975-9366, Fax: 416/975-1839
Executive Director, Nancy Fleming
Chair, Richard Lee

Book Promoters' Association of Canada (BPAC)
c/o Random House of Canada, #210, 33 Yonge St., Toronto, ON M5E 1G4
President, Sheila Kay, 416/777-9841
Publications: BPAC Newsletter

Canadian Book Manufacturers Association (CBMA)
#906, 75 Albert, Mississauga, ON L4Z 2J1
613/236-7941, Fax: 613/236-7084
Executive Director, Albert Lacroix

Canadian Bookbinders & Book Artists Guild/Guilde canadienne des relieurs et des artisans du livre (CBBAG) (1983)
Chalmers Building, #221, 35 McCaul St., Toronto, ON M5T 1V7
416/581-1071
URL: http://knet.flemingc.on.ca/~rmiller/cbbag/CBBAGhome.html
President, Ann Douglas
Publications: The CBBAG Newsletter
Affiliates: Ontario Crafts Council

Canadian Booksellers Association (CBA) (1952)
301 Donlands Ave., Toronto, ON M4J 3R8

416/467-7883, Fax: 416/467-7886, Email: enquiries@cbabook.org
URL: http://www.cbabook.org
Executive Director, John Finlay, CAE
President, Jane Conney
First Vice-President, Ron Johnson
Second Vice-President, Gailmarie Anderson
Treasurer, Wayne Oakley
Publications: The Canadian Bookseller

The Canadian Children's Book Centre (CCBC) (1976)
35 Spadina Rd., Toronto, ON M5R 2S9
416/975-0010, Fax: 416/975-1839, Email: ccbc@lglobal.com
URL: http://www.lglobal.com/~ccbc/
Executive Director, Charlotte Teeple
Program Coordinator, Jeffrey Canton
Publications: Children's Book News

Canadian Circulation Management Association/Association canadienne des chefs de tirage (CCMA) (1933)
298 Highfield St., Moncton, NB E1C 5R6
506/854-7091, Fax: 506/855-1334
Secretary, Dave Dorman
Publications: CCMA Newsletter
Affiliates: Newspaper Association of America

Canadian Circulations Audit Board Inc./Office canadien de vérification de la diffusion (CCAB) (1937)
#304, 188 Eglinton Ave. East, Toronto, ON M4P 2X7
416/487-2418, Fax: 416/487-6405
General Manager/President, Patrick Sweeney
Publications: Circulate

Canadian Community Newspapers Association (CCNA) (1919)
#206, 90 Eglinton Ave. East, Toronto, ON M4P 2Y3
416/482-1090, Fax: 416/482-1908, Email: ccna@sentex.net
URL: http://www.sentex.net/~ccna
Executive Director, Michael Anderson

ALBERTA WEEKLY NEWSPAPERS ASSOCIATION (AWNA)
Terrace Plaza, #360, 4445 Calgary Trail South, Edmonton, AB T6H 5R7
403/434-8746, Fax: 403/438-8356
Executive Director, Dennis Merrell, CAE

ATLANTIC COMMUNITY NEWSPAPERS ASSOCIATION (ACNA)
224 Queen St., Charlottetown, PE C1A 4B6
902/628-6012, Fax: 902/628-8671
Publications: Canada Catch

BRITISH COLUMBIA & YUKON COMMUNITY NEWSPAPERS ASSOCIATION (1916)
#230, 1380 Burrard St., Vancouver, BC V6Z 2B7
604/669-9222, Fax: 604/684-4713
Executive Director, Allen L. Treleaven
Publications: Communicator; Publishers' Update, biweekly

MANITOBA COMMUNITY NEWSPAPERS ASSOCIATION (MCNA) (1919)
#310, 275 Portage Ave., Winnipeg, MB R3B 2B3
204/947-1691, Fax: 204/947-1919
Executive Director, Emily Boitson-Murray
Publications: Reaching the Manitoba Market

ONTARIO COMMUNITY NEWSPAPERS ASSOCIATION (OCNA) (1950)
1184 Speers Rd., Oakville, ON L6J 5A8
905/844-0184, Fax: 905/844-2769, Email: info@ocna.org
URL: http://www.ocna.org
Executive Director, Don Lamont
Publications: Newsclips

QUÉBEC COMMUNITY NEWSPAPER ASSOCIATION/ASSOCIATION DES JOURNAUX RÉGIONAUX DU QUÉBEC (QCNA) (1980)
Glenaladale House, MacDonald College, 21111, rue Lakeshore, Ste-Anne-de-Bellevue, PQ H9X 3V9
514/398-7706, Fax: 514/398-7972
Executive Director, Allan S. Davis, CAE
Publications: Intermedia; Québec Community Newspapers Databook, a.
Affiliates: Conseil du presse du Québec; Literacy Partners of Québec; Canadian Daily Newspapers Association

SASKATCHEWAN WEEKLY NEWSPAPERS ASSOCIATION (1913)
#4, 2155 Airport Dr., Saskatoon, SK S7G 6M5
306/382-9683, Fax: 306/382-9421
Sec.-Treas., Linda Bobowski
Publications: SWNA Publisher

Canadian Newspaper Association/Association canadienne des journaux (CNA) (1919)
#1100, 890 Yonge St., Toronto, ON M4W 3P4
416/923-3567, Fax: 416/923-7206, Email: bcantley@fox.nstn.ca
URL: http://fox.nstn.ca/~bcantley/cdna.html
President & CEO, Richard Dicerni

Canadian Magazine Publishers Association (CMPA) (1973)
#202, 130 Spadina Ave., Toronto, ON M5V 2L4
416/504-0274, Fax: 416/504-0437, Email: cmpainfo@cmpa.ca
URL: http://www.cmpa.ca/
President, Catherine Keachie
Media Coordinator, Cindy Goldrick, Email: cindyg@cmpa.ca
Publications: CMPA Newsletter; Ad Exchange/Subscription List Exchange, a.; Magazines for Everyone, a.
Affiliates: Book & Periodical Development Council; Canadian Copyright Institute; Periodical Writers' Association of Canada; Annual Magazines Conference

Canadian Multilingual Press Federation
PO Bag 9033, Surrey, BC V3T 4X3
604/532-1733
President, A.A. Van Der Heide

Canadian Music Publishers Association/Association canadienne des éditeurs de musique (CMPA) (1949)
#320, 56 Wellesley St. West, Toronto, ON M5S 2S3
416/926-1966, Fax: 416/926-7521
President, David A. Basskin
Secretary, Cyril Devereux
Publications: CMPA Newsletter
Affiliates: International Federation of Serious Music Publishers; International Federation of Popular Music Publishers; Canadian Conference of the Arts; Coalition of Canadian Copyright Owners & Creators; Music Copyright Action Group

The Canadian Press/La Presse canadienne (1917)
36 King St. East, Toronto, ON M5C 2L9
416/364-0321; Broadcast News: 364-3172, Fax: 416/364-0207, Telex: 06-217715; 06-2
URL: http://www.xe.com/canpress/
Acting General Manager, Jim Poling
Office Manager, Lee White
Calgary Bureau: Steve Ewart, #507, 200 - 4th Ave. SW, Calgary, AB T2P 3N1, 403/233-7004, Fax: 403/262-7520
Edmonton Bureau: Chris Vaughan-Johnston, Cornerpoint Bldg., #305, 10179 - 105 St., Edmonton, AB T5J 3N1, 403/428-6107, Fax: 403/428-0663
Fredericton Bureau: Judy Monchuk, c/o Press Gallery, Box 6000, Queen St., Fredericton, NB E3B 5H1, 506/455-9493, Fax: 506/457-9708
Halifax Bureau: Trade Mart Bldg., #400, 2021 Brunswick St., Halifax, NS B3K 2Y5, 902/422-8496, Fax: 902/425-2675
Montréal Bureau: Denis Tremblay, Place d'Armes, 245, rue St-Jacques ouest, CP 998, Montréal, PQ H2Y 3J6, 514/849-3212, Téléc: 514/282-6915 (Editorial)
Ottawa Bureau: Bureau Chief, Gerry Arnold, 140 Wellington St., PO Box 595, Stn B, Ottawa, ON K1P 5P7, 613/238-4142, Fax: 613/238-4452
Regina Bureau: Sandra Cordon, #335, Press Gallery, Legislative Bldg., Regina, SK S4S 0B3, 306/585-1011, Fax: 306/585-1027
St. John's Bureau: Ian Bailey, Battery Hotel Media Centre, PO Box 5951, St. John's, NF A1C 5X4, 709/576-0687, Fax: 709/576-0049
Vancouver Bureau: Stephen Ward, #250, 840 Howe St., Vancouver, BC V6Z 2L2, 604/731-3191, Fax: 604/687-5040
Victoria Bureau: Michael Smyth, #350, Press Gallery, Legislative Building, Victoria, BC V8V 1X4, 250/384-4912, Fax: 250/356-8217
Winnipeg Bureau: Nelle Oosterom, #101, 386 Broadway, Winnipeg, MB R3C 3R6, 204/942-8188, Fax: 204/942-4788
London (England) Bureau: Helen Branswell, Associated Press House, 12 Norwich St., London EC4 1EJ UK, 011/44-171-353-6355, Fax: 011/44-171-583-4238
Washington Bureau: Christine Morris, #615, 1825 K St. NW, Washington, DC 20006-1253 USA, 202/828-9669, Fax: 202/778-0348

Canadian Publishers' Council (CPC) (1910)
#203, 250 Merton St., Toronto, ON M4S 1B1
416/322-7011, Fax: 416/322-6999
URL: http://www.pubcouncil.ca
Executive Director, Jacqueline Hushion, Email: jhushion@pubcouncil.ca
President, Gary Rodrigues
Publications: A View from the Inside; This Week..., w.
Affiliates: International Publishers Association

Canadian Telebook Agency (1981)
#301, 2 Gloucester St., Toronto, ON M4Y 1K5
416/929-7332, Fax: 416/929-3015
General Manager, Elizabeth Bryant

Canadian University Press/Presse universitaire canadienne (CUP) (1938)
#404, 73 Richmond St., Toronto, ON M5H 1Z4
416/364-0258, Fax: 416/364-6512, Email: cup@io.org
President, Joanna Shepherd
Bureau Chief/Vice-President, Stu Clark
National Conference Coordinator, Calinda Brown
Publications: CUP News Exchange; Canadian Student Press Styleguide

The Christian Booksellers Association
679 Southgate Dr., Guelph, ON N1G 4S2
519/766-1683, Fax: 519/763-8184, Telex: Telebook 119-60
Executive Director, Bonnie Pioveson

Commonwealth Press Union - Canadian Section
c/o Southam Newspapers, 1450 Don Mills Rd., North York, ON M3B 2X7
416/445-6641, Fax: 416/442-3386
Chairman, Bill Ardell

Connexions Information Sharing Services (1975)
PO Box 158, Stn D, Toronto, ON M6P 3J8
416/537-3949, Email: connex@sources.com
Coordinator, Ulli Diemer
Publications: Connexions Digest; Connexions Annual; Media Guide

Conseil de presse du Québec/Québec Press Council (CPQ) (1973)
55 1/2, rue Saint-Louis, Québec, PQ G1R 3Z2
418/692-3008, Téléc: 418/692-5148
Secrétaire général, Jean-Paul Sabourin
Publications: Rapport annuel

Les Hebdos du Québec Inc. (1932)
#1410, 625, boul René-Lévesque ouest, Montréal, PQ H3B 2R2
514/861-2088, Téléc: 514/861-1966
Vice-présidente et directrice générale, Francine Bouchard
Publications: L'Éditeur Nouveau
Organisation(s) affiliée(s): Publicité Club de Montréal; Société des relationnistes du Québec

International Association for Publishing Education
c/o Canadian Centre for Studies in Publishing, SFU at Harbour Centre, 515 Hastings St. West, Vancouver, BC V6B 5K3
604/291-5074
Anne Cowan

International Board on Books for Young People - Canadian Section/Union internationale pour les livres de jeunesse (IBBY - Canada) (1980)
c/o Canadian Children's Book Centre, 35 Spadina Rd., Toronto, ON M5R 2S9
416/975-0010, Fax: 416/975-1839
President, Theo Hersh
Publications: IBBY - Canada Newsletter

The Literary Press Group of Canada (LPG) (1976)
#301, 2 Gloucester St., Toronto, ON M4Y 1L5
416/413-4929, Fax: 416/413-4920,
Email: craig_laudrum@canbook.org
General Manager, Craig Laudrum
Publications: Surface Noise; The Little Prints, bi-m.; Extra Static, bi-m.
Affiliates: Association of Canadian Publishers

Magazines Canada (1968)
The Magazine Association of Canada
777 Bay St., 7th Fl., Toronto, ON M5W 1A7
416/596-5382, Fax: 416/596-6043, Email: magscan@hookup.net
President, Maureen Werner
Chairman, Brian Segal

Manitoba Press Council Inc. (1984)
#103, 2015 Portage Ave., Winnipeg, MB R3J 0K3
204/831-6359, Fax: 204/889-0021, Email: masw@magic.mb.ca
Executive Secretary, Diane Cullen

Newsletter Publishers Association (1977)
#207, 1401 Wilson Blvd., Arlington, VA 22209 USA
703/527-2333, Fax: 703/841-0629, Toll Free: 1-800-356-9302
Acting Executive Director, Patricia M. Wysocki
Office Manager, Janine Lee
Publications: Hotline

Ontario Press Council/Conseil de presse de l'Ontario (1972)
#206, 80 Gould St., Toronto, ON M5B 2M7
416/340-1981
Executive Secretary, Mel Sufrin
Chairman, Hon. Willard Z. Estey

Periodical Marketers of Canada (PMC) (1942)
South Tower, #1007, 175 Bloor St. East, Toronto, ON M4W 3R8
416/968-7218, Fax: 416/968-6182
Executive Director, Ray Argyle
Asst. Executive Director, Janette Hatcher

Saskatchewan Publishers Group (SPG) (1989)
1925 - 7th Ave., Regina, SK S4R 1C1
306/359-7466, Fax: 306/352-0991
Executive Director, Brenda Niskala
President, Darlene Speidel
Publications: SPG PaperCuts; Best of the West; Prairie Books Now
Affiliates: Association of Canadian Publishers

Société de développement des périodiques culturels québécois (SODEP) (1978)
Périodiques culturels québécois
CP 786, Succ. Place d'Armes, Montréal, PQ H2Y 3J2
514/523-7724, Téléc: 514/523-9401
Directrice générale, Francine Bergeron
Président, Robert Legendre
Publications: Le Québec en revue

Toronto Press Club (1944)
276 King St. West, Toronto, ON M5V 1H9
416/408-3550
Past President, Ed Patrick, 416/964-8180
Publications: Quote

PULP & PAPER see FORESTRY & FOREST PRODUCTS

RADIO BROADCASTING see BROADCASTING

REAL ESTATE
see also Housing

Alberta Real Estate Association (AREA) (1947)
828 - 12 Ave. SW, Calgary, AB T2R 0J3
403/264-5581, Fax: 403/266-1597, Toll Free: 1-800-661-0231
Executive Vice-President, Dan Russell
Brooks Real Estate Co-operative Ltd.: President, Karen Hazell, PO Box 997, Brooks, AB T1R 1B8, 403/362-0123, Fax: 403/362-8543
Calgary Real Estate Board Co-op Ltd.: Executive Vice-President, Ron Esch, FRI, 805 - 5 Ave. SW, Calgary, AB T2P 0N6, 403/263-0530, Fax: 403/262-4432
Edmonton Real Estate Board Co-operative Listing Bureau Ltd.: Executive Vice-President, Ronald Hutchinson, 14220 - 112 Ave., Edmonton, AB T5M 2T8, 403/451-6666, Fax: 403/452-1135
Fort McMurray Real Estate Board Co-operative Listing Bureau Ltd.: Executive Officer, Chris Moskolyk, 9912 Manning Ave., Fort McMurray, AB T9H 2B9, 403/791-1124, Fax: 403/743-4724
Grande Prairie Real Estate Board: Executive Officer, Norma Christie, #102, 9905 - 101 Ave., Grande Prairie, AB T8V 0X7, 403/532-4508, Fax: 403/539-3515
Lethbridge Real Estate Board: Executive Officer, Marilyn Baxter-Brown, 522 - 6 St. South, Lethbridge, AB T1J 2E2, 403/328-8838, Fax: 403/328-8906
Lloydminster Real Estate Board Association: Executive Officer, Karyn Ranger, #9, 5009 - 48th St., Lloydminster, AB T9V 0H7, 403/875-6939, Fax: 403/875-5560
Medicine Hat Real Estate Board Co-operative Ltd.: Executive Officer, Joan McKenna, 403 - 4 St. SE, Medicine Hat, AB T1A 0K5, 403/526-2879, Fax: 403/526-0307
Northeastern Alberta Real Estate Board Co-op Ltd.: Executive Officer, Mary Clarke, Lakecentre Plaza, PO Box 1678, Grand Centre, AB T0A 1T0, 403/594-5958, Fax: 403/594-3181
Red Deer & District Real Estate Board Co-op Ltd.: Executive Officer, Nick Medwid, 4922 - 45 St., Red Deer, AB T4N 1K6, 403/343-0881, Fax: 403/347-9080
West Central Real Estate Association: Executive Officer, Valerie Gregg, PO Box 2386, Hinton, AB T7V 1Y2, 403/865-7511, Fax: 403/865-7517

Appraisal Institute of Canada/Institut canadien des évaluateurs (AIC) (1938)
1111 Portage Ave., Winnipeg, MB R3G 0S8
204/783-2224, Fax: 204/783-5575
Executive Vice-President, Terrence J. Gifford, CAE
President, D. Allan Beatty, AACI
Executive Secretary, Darlene Brown
Publications: The Digest; The Canadian Appraiser, q.

ALBERTA ASSOCIATION OF THE APPRAISAL INSTITUTE OF CANADA (AA-AIC)
#740, 540 - 5 Ave. SW, Calgary, AB T2P 0M2
403/263-7722, Fax: 403/290-0899, Email: abaaic@agt.net
URL: http://www.cyberpage.com/appraisal/alberta/appraisal.html
President, Dallas Maynard
Executive Director, Suzanne E. Teal
Publications: Newsletter

BRITISH COLUMBIA ASSOCIATION OF THE APPRAISAL INSTITUTE OF CANADA
#590, 789 Pender St. West, Vancouver, BC V6C 1H2
604/685-4018, Fax: 604/685-7592
President, Keith Goodwin
Executive Director, Janice P. O'Brien
Publications: West Coast Appraiser

MANITOBA ASSOCIATION OF THE APPRAISAL INSTITUTE OF CANADA
23 Rosewood Pl., Winnipeg, MB R2H 1M5
204/986-6405, Fax: 204/944-8476
Secretary, Wendy Sigmar
President, Susan Gifford, AACI

NEW BRUNSWICK ASSOCIATION OF REAL ESTATE APPRAISERS/ASSOCIATION DES ÉVALUATEURS IMMOBILIERS DU NOUVEAU-BRUNSWICK (1995)
Assumption Place, #110, 740 Main St., Moncton, NB E1C 1E6
506/450-2016, Fax: 506/450-3010
Executive Director, Susan Keirstead
President, Les Smith, AACI
Secretary, Louis Poirier

NEWFOUNDLAND ASSOCIATION OF THE APPRAISAL INSTITUTE OF CANADA
718 Water St., St. John's, NF A1E 1C1
709/753-7644, Fax: 709/753-7469
Executive Assistant, Gina Goodyear
President, Gordon A. Brewer

NOVA SCOTIA ASSOCIATION OF THE APPRAISAL INSTITUTE OF CANADA
PO Box 3093, Stn South, Halifax, NS B3J 3G6
902/422-5481, Fax: 902/429-7566
Administrative Secretary, Davida Mackay
President, Lorraine Porter, AACI, 902/453-7091
Vice-President, Keith Conrod, AACI, 902/426-8435

ONTARIO ASSOCIATION OF THE APPRAISAL INSTITUTE OF CANADA (OA-AIC)
#505, 295 The West Mall, Etobicoke, ON M9C 424
416/695-9333, Fax: 416/695-9321
President, Roly Mayr, AACI
Executive Director, Eileen Richmond
Publications: Quarterly

PRINCE EDWARD ISLAND ASSOCIATION OF THE APPRAISAL INSTITUTE OF CANADA
25 Westhill Dr., Charlottetown, PE C1E 1N9
902/368-6395, Fax: 902/368-6164
Secretary, D.B. Sinclair

SASKATCHEWAN ASSOCIATION OF THE APPRAISAL INSTITUTE OF CANADA
1935 Elphinstone St., Regina, SK S4T 3N3
306/352-4195, Fax: 306/565-2840
Executive Director, Marlene McLarty
President, Guy Carbonneau

Association des propriétaires du Québec inc. (APQ)
#520, 50, place Crémazie ouest, Montréal, PQ H2P 2T2
514/382-9670, Téléc: 514/382-9676
Directeur général, Jacques Couture

British Columbia Real Estate Association (BCREA) (1967)
#309, 1155 Pender St. West, Vancouver, BC V6E 2P4
604/683-7702, Fax: 604/683-8601, Email: bcrea@helix.net
URL: http://www.bcrea.bc.ca
Executive Officer, Robin Hill
Communications Director, Fred Morley
Education Director, June Piry
Publications: Bulletin; Legally Speaking, 18 pa; MLA Real Estate Industry News, q.; Regional Advisory Committee on Land Claims Newsletter
Affiliates: National Association of Realtors - USA
Cariboo Real Estate Association: Executive Officer, Dorothy D. Friesen, 2609 Queensway, Prince George, BC V2L 1N3, 250/563-1236, Fax: 250/563-3637
Chilliwack & District Real Estate Board: Executive Officer, Sharon J. Labiuk, #201, 9319 Nowell St., PO Box 339, Chilliwack, BC V2P 4V8, 604/792-0912, Fax: 604/792-6795
Fraser Valley Real Estate Board: Executive Officer, Kenneth E. MacKenzie, 15463 - 104 Ave., PO Box 99, Surrey, BC V3R 1N9, 604/588-6555, Fax: 604/588-0325
Kamloops & District Real Estate Association: Executive Officer, Patrick J. Lindsay; Financial Officer, Cathy Boer, Email: boer@netshop.net, #101, 418 St. Paul St., Kamloops, BC V2C 2J6, 250/372-9411, Fax: 250/828-1986
Kootenay Real Estate Board: Office Manager, Irene Cook, #208, 402 Baker St., PO Box 590, Nelson, BC V1L 5R4, 250/352-5477, Fax: 250/352-7184
Northern Lights Real Estate Board: Executive Officer, Marie Chilton, 1101 - 103 Ave., Dawson Creek, BC V1G 2G8, 250/782-2412
Northwest Real Estate Board: Executive Officer, Myrna Rolfsen, #117, 4546 Park Ave., Terrace, BC V8G 1V4, 250/638-8491, Fax: 250/638-1837
Okanagan-Mainline Real Estate Board: Executive Officer, Roger I. Cottle, 1889 Spall Rd., Kelowna, BC V1Y 4R2, 250/860-6292, Fax: 250/860-7704
Powell River Sunshine Coast Real Estate Board: Executive Officer, Linda Shillito, 4699 Marine Ave., Powell River, BC V8A 2L2, 604/485-6944, Fax: 604/485-6974
Real Estate Board of Greater Vancouver: Executive Officer, Larry A. Buttress, 1101 West Broadway, Vancouver, BC V6H 1G2, 604/736-4551, Fax: 604/734-1778
South Okanagan Real Estate Board: Executive Officer, Margaret Van, #3, 212 Main St., Penticton, BC V2A 5B2, 250/492-0626, Fax: 250/493-0832
Vancouver Island Real Estate Board: Executive Officer, Donn Gardner, 6374 Metral Dr., PO Box 719, Nanaimo, BC V9R 5M2, 250/390-4212, Fax: 250/390-5014
Victoria Real Estate Board: Executive Officer, Anthony C. Quarless, 3035 Nanaimo St., Victoria, BC V8T 4W2, 250/385-7766, Fax: 250/385-8773, Email: vreb@islandnet.com

Building Inspectors Association of Nova Scotia
2343 Barrington St., Halifax, NS B3K 2X2
902/422-8316

President, Rick Fraser
Treasurer, Ed Thornhill

Building Owners & Managers Association of Canada
BOMA Canada
#2012, 20 Queen St. W, Toronto, ON M5H 3R3
416/596-8065, Fax: 416/596-1085
Executive Director, Lynn Johnston

Canadian Institute of Professional Home Inspectors Inc.
535 - 55th Ave. East, Vancouver, BC V5X 1N6
604/327-0262, Fax: 604/738-4080
President, Ed R.R. Witzke, B.A., B.Arch., MCHBA
Publications: The Complete Canadian Home Inspection Guide

Canadian Institute of Public Real Estate Companies
#1210, 123 Edward St., Toronto, ON M5G 1E2
416/598-0694, Fax: 416/598-0779
Executive Director, Ronald A. Daniel

The Canadian Real Estate Association/ Association canadienne de l'immeuble (CREA) (1943)
Minto Place, The Canada Bldg., #1600, 344 Slater St., Ottawa, ON K1R 7Y3
613/237-7111, Fax: 613/234-2567, Email: info@crea.ca
URL: http://www.mls.ca/crea.ca
CEO, Pierre J. Beauchamp, FRI (E)
President, Thomas W. Bosley
Publications: Realtor News
Affiliates: National Association of Realtors; International Real Estate Federation

Fédération des chambres immobilières du Québec
990, av Holland, Québec, PQ G1S 3T1
418/682-6102, Téléc: 418/682-8107
Directeur général, Louis Renaud
Publications: Contact
Chambre d'immeuble du Bas St-Laurent Inc.: Directrice générale, Brigitte Parent; Président, Raymond Bock, 14, rue St-Germain est, Rimouski, PQ G5L 1A2, 418/723-5393, Téléc: 418/723-3553
Chambre d'immeubles de Québec: Directrice générale, Louise Clément, 990, av Holland, Québec, PQ G1S 3T1, 418/688-3362, Téléc: 418/688-3577
Chambre immobilière de l'Abitibi-Témiscamingue Inc.: Président, Luc Lemayes, 209 - 9e rue, Rouyn-Noranda, PQ J9X 2C1, 819/797-6666, Téléc: 819/797-9214
Chambre immobilière Centre du Québec Inc.: Secrétaire, Mariette Proulx, #101, 925 boul St-Joseph, Drummondville, PQ J2C 2C4, 819/477-1033, Téléc: 819/474-7913
Chambre immobilière de l'Estrie inc.: Présidente, Jocelyne Fontaine, a/s Le Permanent Sherbrooke inc., #300, 65, rue Belvedère nord, Sherbrooke, PQ J1H 4A7, 819/563-3000
Chambre immobilière du Grand Montréal: Vice-président/Directeur général, Louis Cherrier, 600, ch du Golf, Île-des-Soeurs, PQ H3E 1A8, 514/762-2440, Téléc: 514/762-1854
Chambre immobilière de la Haute Yamaska Inc.: Secrétaire exécutive, Carole Corbeil, #32, 1, Carrier, Granby, PQ J2G 8C8, 514/378-6702, Téléc: 514/375-5268
Chambre immobilière de Lanaudière Inc.: Secrétaire exécutive, Sylvie Payette, #207, 37, Place Bourget sud, Joliette, PQ J6E 5G1, 514/759-8511, Téléc: 514/759-6557
Chambre immobilière des Laurentides: Directrice, Rose Girard, 555, boul Sainte-Adèle, CP 1615, Sainte-Adèle, PQ J0R 1L0, 514/229-3511, Téléc: 514/229-3812

Chambre immobilière de la Mauricie Inc.: Secrétaire exécutif, Josée Charland, #102, 1640 - 6e rue, Trois-Rivières, PQ G8Y 5B8, 819/379-9081, Téléc: 819/379-9262
Chambre immobilière de l'Outaouais: Directrice générale, Lise Guillemette, 197, boul St-Joseph, Hull, PQ J8Y 3X2, 819/771-5221, Téléc: 819/771-8715
Chambre immobilière du Saguenay-Lac St-Jean Inc.: Directrice générale, Ginette Gaudreault, #106, 735, boul Barrette, Chicoutimi, PQ G7J 4C4, 418/545-8187, Téléc: 418/545-6305
Chambre immobilière de St-Hyacinthe Inc.: Secrétaire, Monique Plaberge, CP 667, Saint-Hyacinthe, PQ J2S 7P5, 514/771-0343

International Institute of Public Appraisers Ltd. (1977)
404 Queen St., PO Box 3132, Stn B, Fredericton, NB E3A 5G9
506/458-9179, Fax: 506/453-0088
President, Beverly E. Doyle
Executive Secretary, Wanda L. Scott
Publications: International Estates

Manitoba Building Officials Association
56 Wascana Dr., Brandon, MB R7B 3B4
204/729-2110
President, Richard Nicholas

Manitoba Real Estate Association (1949)
1240 Portage Ave., 2nd Fl., Winnipeg, MB R3G 0T6
204/772-0405, Fax: 204/775-3781, Email: realest@magic.mb.ca
Executive Director, Brian M. Collie
Publications: Real Estate Manitoba; MREAction, m.
Brandon Real Estate Board: Executive Officer, Bill Madder, 907 Princess Ave., Brandon, MB R7A 6E3, 204/727-4672, Fax: 204/727-8331
Portage La Prairie Real Estate Board: Executive Officer, Jo-Anne Knox, 19 Royal Rd. North, Portage La Prairie, MB R1N 1T9, 204/857-4111, Fax: 204/857-7207
Thompson Real Estate Board: Treasurer, Larry Reid, c/o GJ Sherry & Associates (1987) Ltd., 1B City Centre Mall, Thompson, MB R8N 0M2, 204/677-4538, Fax: 204/677-4530
Winnipeg Real Estate Board: Executive Director, Gary Simonsen, 1240 Portage Ave., Winnipeg, MB R3G 0T6, 204/786-8854, Fax: 204/783-9447
URL: http://www.mls.ca

New Brunswick Building Officials Association
c/o City of Saint John, Bldg. Inspectors Office, PO Box 1971, Saint John, NB E2L 4L1
506/658-2911, Fax: 506/632-6199
Secretary, Rick Armstrong

New Brunswick Real Estate Association/ Association des agents des immeubles du Nouveau-Brunswick (NBREA) (1958)
PO Box 774, Stn A, Fredericton, NB E3B 5B4
506/459-8055, Fax: 506/459-8057
Executive Officer, Karen Small
Greater Moncton Real Estate Board Inc.: Executive Officer, Faye Andersen, 107 Cameron St., Moncton, NB E1C 5Y7, 506/857-8200, Fax: 506/857-1760
Northern New Brunswick Real Estate Board Inc.: Executive Officer, Carmelle F. Mallet, #5, 360 Parkside Dr., PO Box 185, Bathurst, NB E2A 3Z2, 506/548-3045, Fax: 506/548-4002
Real Estate Board of the Fredericton Area Inc.: Executive Officer, Louise E. Mazerall, 544 Brunswick St., PO Box 1295, Fredericton, NB E3B 5C8, 506/458-8163, Fax: 506/459-8922
Saint John Real Estate Board Inc.: Executive Officer, Linda Rector, #P100, Place 400, 400 Main St., Saint John, NB E2K 4N5, 506/634-8772, Fax: 506/634-8775
Valley Real Estate Board Inc.: President, Nicole Lévesque, PO Box 1809, Grand Falls, NB E3Z 1E1, 506/473-4999, Fax: 506/473-6368

Newfoundland Real Estate Association
251 Empire Ave., 2nd Fl., St. John's, NF A1C 3H9
709/739-8600, Fax: 709/726-4221
Executive Secretary, Dorothy V. Saunders
Central Newfoundland Real Estate Board: President, Owen Grimes, PO Box 733, Grand Falls-Windsor, NF A2A 2K2, 709/489-7000, Fax: 709/489-5601
Humber Valley Real Estate Board: President, Alan Robinson; Secretary, Melva Sims, PO Box 553, Corner Brook, NF A2H 6E6, 709/634-9400, Fax: 709/634-3251
St. John's Real Estate Board: Executive Officer, Dorothy V. Saunders, 77 Portugal Cove Rd., St. John's, NF A1B 2M4, 709/726-5110, Fax: 709/726-4221

Nova Scotia Real Estate Association (NSREA) (1960)
7 Scarfe Ct., Dartmouth, NS B3B 1W4
902/468-2515, Fax: 902/468-2533
Executive Officer, Douglas Dixon
Annapolis Valley Real Estate Board: Executive Officer, Cathy Simpson, PO Box 117, Auburn, NS B0P 1A0, 902/847-9336, Fax: 902/847-9869
Cape Breton Real Estate Board: Executive Secretary, Carol Williston, 329 George St., Sydney, NS B1P 1J7, 902/562-8199, Fax: 902/564-2007
Halifax-Dartmouth Real Estate Board: Executive Officer, Al Demings, 7 Scarfe Ct., Dartmouth, NS B3B 1W4, 902/468-7681, Fax: 902/468-7684
Highland Real Estate Board: President, Valerie Chugg, c/o The Prudential Highland Properties, #104, 219 Main St., Antigonish, NS B2G 2C1, 902/863-1878, Fax: 902/863-1933
Northern Nova Scotia Real Estate Board: Executive Assistant, Carol Burgess, PO Box 1185, Truro, NS B2N 5H1, 902/895-5586, Fax: 902/893-4533
South Shore Real Estate Board: President, Mary MacDonald; Sec.-Treas., Jon Walker, PO Box 81, Bridgewater, NS B4V 2W6, 902/354-5775, Fax: 902/354-2735
Yarmouth Real Estate Board: President, Ray Nelson, c/o Vaughne Realty, #2000, 255 Main St., Yarmouth, NS B5A 1E2, 902/742-4545, Fax: 902/742-1067

Ontario Building Officials Association Inc./ Association de l'Ontario des officers en bâtiment inc. (OBOA) (1956)
PO Box 70, Stn E, Etobicoke, ON M9C 4X9
416/255-8057, Fax: 416/253-8374
Administrator, Tracey Preston
President, Garry Davis
Publications: OBOA Journal

Ontario Real Estate Association (OREA) (1922)
99 Duncan Mill Rd., North York, ON M3B 1Z2
416/445-9910, Fax: 416/445-2644
Executive Director, Don Richardson
President, Rose E. Leroux
Board & Member Services Coordinator, Lynn Buck
Conference & Meeting Coordinator, Dina Sibellino
Publications: News & Views
Bancroft District Real Estate Board: Executive Officer, Dana Yonemitsu, PO Box 1522, Bancroft, ON K0L 1C0, 613/332-3842, Fax: 613/332-3842
Barrie & District Real Estate Board Inc.: Executive Officer, Frances Clarke, 85 Ellis Dr., Barrie, ON L4M 6E7, 705/739-4650, Fax: 705/721-9101
Brampton Real Estate Board: Executive Director, Bruce S. Lupton, 119 West Dr., Brampton, ON L6T 2J6, 905/451-1515, Fax: 905/451-8034
Brantford Regional Real Estate Association Inc.: Executive Manager, Louise Sharland, 59 Roy Blvd.,

2-148 ORGANIZATIONS — REAL ESTATE

Brantford, ON N3R 7K1, 519/753-0308, Fax: 519/753-8638

Chatham-Kent Real Estate Board: Executive Officer, Dorothy Ritchie, 188 St. Clair St., PO Box 384, Chatham, ON N7M 5K5, 519/352-4351, Fax: 519/352-6938

Cobourg-Port Hope District Real Estate Board: Executive Officer, Donna Causton, Victoria Place, #23, 1011 William St., Cobourg, ON K9A 5J4, 905/372-8630, Fax: 905/372-1443

Cornwall & District Real Estate Board: Executive Officer, Johanna Murray, 25 Cumberland St., Cornwall, ON K6J 4G8, 613/932-6457, Fax: 613/932-1687

Durham Region Real Estate Board: Executive Officer, Barbara Cail Maclean, #14, 50 Richmond St. East, Oshawa, ON L1H 7L1, 905/723-8184, Fax: 905/723-7531

Golden Triangle Real Estate Board: Executive Officer, Yvonne Klysen, 54 Third St., Collingwood, ON L9Y 1K3, 705/445-7295, Fax: 705/445-7253

Grey Bruce Real Estate Board: Executive Officer, Chris Ransome, 504 - 10th St., Hanover, ON N4N 1R1, 519/364-3827, Fax: 519/364-6800

Guelph & District Real Estate Board: Executive Officer, Janet Ceolin, 400 Woolwich St., Guelph, ON N1H 3X1, 519/824-7270, Fax: 519/824-5510

Haliburton District Real Estate Board: Executive Officer, Susan Schell, PO Box 99, Haliburton, ON K0M 1S0, 705/457-9093, Fax: 705/457-9094

Huron Real Estate Board: Executive Officer, Patricia Spence, 60 East St., Goderich, ON N7A 1N3, 519/524-4191, Fax: 519/524-5093

Kingston & Area Real Estate Association: Executive Officer, Susan Swann, 720 Arlington Park Pl., Kingston, ON K7M 8H9, 613/384-0880, Fax: 613/384-0863

Kitchener-Waterloo Real Estate Board Inc.: Executive Officer, Valerie Feick, 540 Riverbend Dr., Kitchener, ON N2K 3S2, 519/576-1400, Fax: 519/741-5364

Lindsay & District Real Estate Board: Executive Officer, Muriel Trowsdale, 31 Kent St. East, Lindsay, ON K9V 2C3, 705/324-4515, Fax: 705/324-3916

London & St. Thomas Real Estate Board: Executive Director, Elizabeth Doré, 342 Commissioners Rd. West, London, ON N2J 1Y3, 519/641-1400, Fax: 519/641-1419

Metropolitan Hamilton Real Estate Board: Executive Officer, Karan Mechar, 505 York Blvd., Hamilton, ON L8R 3K4, 905/529-8101, Fax: 905/529-4349

Midland-Penetang District Real Estate Board Inc.: Executive Officer, Neil Grant, #2, 578 King St., PO Box 805, Midland, ON L4R 4P4, 705/526-8706, Fax: 705/526-0701

Mississauga Real Estate Board: Executive Director, Deborah Doyle, #29, 3355 The Collegeway, Mississauga, ON L5L 5T3, 905/608-6732, Fax: 905/608-0045

Muskoka Real Estate Board: Executive Officer, Susan Glassford, 18 Chaffey St., Huntsville, ON P1H 1K7, 705/788-1504, Fax: 705/788-2040

Niagara Falls-Fort Erie Real Estate Association: Executive Officer, Joan Swartz; President, Josephine C. DeLazzari, 4411 Portage Rd., PO Box 456, Niagara Falls, ON L2E 6V2, 905/356-7593

North Bay Real Estate Board: Executive Officer, Evelyn A. Reid, 926 Castle St., PO Box 774, North Bay, ON P1B 4A8, 705/472-6812, Fax: 705/472-0529

The Oakville, Milton & District Real Estate Board: General Manager, May Barrett, FRI, 125 Navy St., Oakville, ON L6J 2Z5, 905/844-6491, Fax: 905/844-6699

Orangeville & District Real Estate Board: Executive Officer, June Moir, 228 Broadway Ave., Orangeville, ON L9W 1K5, 519/941-4547, Fax: 519/941-8482

Orillia & District Real Estate Board: Executive Officer, Dorothy Young, 100 Coldwater St. East, PO Box 551, Orillia, ON L3V 6K2, 705/325-9958, Fax: 705/325-0605

Owen Sound & District Real Estate Board: Executive Officer, Joanne Green, 653 - 2nd Ave. East, Owen Sound, ON N4K 2G7, 519/371-1922, Fax: 519/376-8465

Parry Sound Real Estate Board: Executive Officer, Margaret Hammel, 33 James St., Parry Sound, ON P2A 1T6, 705/746-4020, Fax: 705/746-2955

Peterborough Real Estate Board Inc.: Executive Officer, Carolyn J. Mills, 273 Charlotte St., PO Box 1330, Peterborough, ON K9J 7H5, 705/745-5724, Fax: 705/745-9377

Quinte & District Real Estate Board: Executive Officer, Elizabeth Palmateer, General Delivery, Cannifton, ON K0K 1K0, 613/969-7873, Fax: 613/962-1851

Real Estate Board of Cambridge: Executive Officer, Shirley Highfield, 75 Ainslie St. North, PO Box 693, Cambridge, ON N1R 5W6, 519/623-3660, Fax: 519/623-8253

Real Estate Board of Ottawa-Carleton: Executive Director, Carol Mallett, 1826 Woodward Dr., Ottawa, ON K2C 0P7, 613/225-2240, Fax: 613/225-6420
URL: http://www.ottawarealestate.org

Renfrew County Real Estate Board: Executive Officer, Ann Anderson, 377 Isabella St., Pembroke, ON K8A 5T4, 613/735-5840, Fax: 613/735-0405

Rideau-St. Lawrence Real Estate Board: Executive Officer, Wilda Brown, #12, 1275 Kensington Pkwy., Brockville, ON K6V 6C3, 613/342-3103

St. Catharines District Real Estate Board: Executive Officer, Nancy Dingman, 116 Niagara St., St Catharines, ON L2R 4L4, 905/684-9459, Fax: 905/687-7010

Sarnia-Lambton Real Estate Board: Executive Director, Tom Woods, 555 Exmouth St., Sarnia, ON N7T 5P6, 519/336-6871, Fax: 519/344-1928

Sault Ste. Marie Real Estate Board: Secretary Manager, Geri White, #1, 498 Queen St. East, Sault Ste Marie, ON P6A 1Z8, 705/949-4560, Fax: 705/949-5935

Simcoe & District Real Estate Board: Executive Officer, Yvonne Stewart, 44 Young St., Simcoe, ON N3Y 1Y5, 519/426-4454, Fax: 519/426-9330

Stratford & District Real Estate Board: Executive Officer, Gwen Kirkpatrick, 91 Brunswick St., Stratford, ON N5A 3L9, 519/271-6870, Fax: 519/271-3040

Sudbury Real Estate Board: Executive Officer, Myra Lahti, 190 Elm St., Sudbury, ON P3C 1V3, 705/673-3388, Fax: 705/673-3197

Thunder Bay Real Estate Board: Executive Officer, Irene Holowka, 1135 Barton St., Thunder Bay, ON P7B 5N3, 807/623-8422, Fax: 807/623-0375

Tillsonburg District Real Estate Board: Secretary Manager, Sharon Smith, 1 Library Lane, PO Box 35, Tillsonburg, ON N4G 4H3, 519/842-9361, Fax: 519/688-6850

Timmins Real Estate Board: Executive Officer, Margot Hamel, 7 Balsam St. South, Timmins, ON P4N 2C7, 705/268-5451, Fax: 705/264-6420

Toronto Real Estate Board: President, John England; Executive Vice-President, Brian Smith, 1400 Don Mills Rd., North York, ON M3B 3N1, 416/443-8100, 8142, Fax: 416/443-0028, 1495

Welland District Real Estate Board: Executive Officer, Tammy Smith; President, John Fletcher, 706 East Main St., Welland, ON L3B 3Y4, 905/735-3624, Fax: 905/735-8722

Windsor-Essex County Real Estate Board: Executive Director, Leona MacIntyre, CAE, 3005 Marentette Ave., Windsor, ON N8X 4G1, 519/966-6432, Fax: 519/966-4469

Woodstock-Ingersoll & District Real Estate Board: Executive Officer, Carol Smith-Gee, #6, 65 Springbank Ave., Woodstock, ON N4S 8V8, 519/539-3616, Fax: 519/539-1975

York Region Real Estate Board: Executive Director, David S. Brown, CAE, Fax: 905/841-2778, 16441 Yonge St., Newmarket, ON L3Y 4V8, 416/969-8271

Prince Edward Island Real Estate Association
75 St. Peter's Rd., Charlottetown, PE C1A 5N7
902/368-8451, Fax: 902/894-9487
Executive Officer, J. Earle Arsenault

Real Estate Institute of Canada/Institut canadien de l'immeuble (REIC) (1955)
#208, 5407 Eglinton Ave. West, Toronto, ON M9C 5K6
416/695-9000, Fax: 416/695-7230
Executive Vice-President, E. Peter Jacobs, CAE
Communications Officer, Susan Arnold
Publications: Contact - The Official Publication of the Real Estate Institute of Canada

Saskatchewan Building Officials Association
PO Box 1671, Prince Albert, SK S6V 5T2
306/975-3235, Fax: 306/975-7212
President, Terry Roulston
Sec.-Treas., LeRoy Evanson

Saskatchewan Real Estate Association (SREA) (1949)
231 Robin Cres., Saskatoon, SK S7L 6M8
306/373-3350, Fax: 306/373-5377
Executive Vice-President, Kirk Bacon
Publications: Sequence

Association of Battlefords Realtors: Executive Officer, Nancy Wappel, #501, 1101 - 101 St., PO Box 611, North Battleford, SK S9A 2Y7, 306/445-6300, Fax: 306/445-9020

Association of Regina Realtors Inc.: Executive Officer, Gord Archibald, 1854 McIntyre St., Regina, SK S4P 2P9, 306/791-2700, Fax: 306/781-7940

Estevan Real Estate Board: Executive Officer, J. Fomwald, PO Box 445, Estevan, SK S4A 2A4, 306/634-7885, Fax: 306/634-8610

Melfort Real Estate Board: Executive Officer, Debby McAlister, 606 Bemister Ave. East, PO Box 3157, Melfort, SK S0E 1A0, 306/752-4994, Fax: 306/752-4994

Moose Jaw Real Estate Board: Executive Officer, Trudy Rees, 79 Hochelaga St. West, Moose Jaw, SK S6H 2E9, 306/693-9544, Fax: 306/692-4463

Prince Albert Real Estate Board: Executive Officer, Charlene Welch-Leachman, 218B South Industrial Dr., Prince Albert, SK S6V 7L8, 306/764-8755, Fax: 306/763-0555

Saskatoon Real Estate Board: Executive Officer, Bill Benoit, 1149 - 8th St. East., Saskatoon, SK S7H 0S3, 306/244-4453, Fax: 306/343-1420, Email: bbenoit@sreb.com

Swift Current Real Estate Board: Executive Officer, Nancy Hunter, #211, 12 Cheadle St. West, Swift Current, SK S9H 0A9, 306/773-4326, Fax: 306/773-3917

Weyburn Real Estate Board: Executive Officer, Eric Douglas, 140 First St. NE, Weyburn, SK S4H 0T2, 306/842-0300, Fax: 306/842-5520

Yorkton Real Estate Association Inc.: Executive Officer, Marlene Gloster, #040, 41 Broadway West, Yorkton, SK S3N 0L6, 306/783-3067, Fax: 306/786-3231

Yellowknife Real Estate Board
#2, 5201 - 50 Ave., Yellowknife, NT X1A 3S9
403/920-4624, Fax: 403/873-6387
President, Dale Vance
Executive Officer/Sec.-Treas., Julia Mott

Yukon Real Estate Association (1977)
PO Box 5292, Whitehorse, YT Y1A 4Z2
403/668-2070, Fax: 403/668-2070
Executive Officer, Nicholas Smart
President, Dan Lang

RECREATION, HOBBIES & GAMES

Alberta Snowmobile Association (ASA) (1972)
Percy Page Centre, 11759 Groat Rd., Edmonton, AB T5M 3K6
403/453-8668, Fax: 403/453-8553
Executive Director, Louise A. Sherren
Publications: The Alberta Snowmobiler
Affiliates: Canadian Council of Snowmobile Organizations; International Snowmobile Council

Alberta Whitewater Canoe Association
Percy Page Centre, 11759 Groat Rd., Edmonton, AB T5M 3K6
403/453-8585, Fax: 403/892-4920
President, Jean Leduc
Technical Director, Bruce Lord

Amusement Machine Operators of Canada/ Opérateurs d'appareils d'amusement du Canada
2684 Fenton Rd., Gloucester, ON K1T 3T7
613/822-6808, Fax: 613/822-2721
Coordinator, Gus Ragland

Association des camps du Québec inc./Québec Camping Association (ACQ) (1961)
4545, av Pierre-de-Coubertin, CP 1000, Succ. M, Montréal, PQ H1V 3R2
514/252-3113, Téléc: 514/252-1650, Ligne sans frais: 1-800-361-3586
Directeur général, Louis Jean
Président, Claude Jette
Publications: L'Express; Répertoire des camps de vacances, annuel
Organisation(s) affiliée(s): Regroupement loisir Québec

Association of Canadian Mountain Guides/ Association des guides de montagne canadiens (ACMG) (1963)
PO Box 1537, Banff, AB T0L 0C0
403/678-2885, Fax: 403/678-6464, Email: acmg@cariboo.bc.ca
President, Hans Gmoser
Sec.-Treas., George Field
Technical Director, Colin Zacharias
Publications: ACMG Newsletter
Affiliates: Canada Avalanche Association; Alpine Club of Canada; World Wildlife Fund

Association canadienne de la raquette inc./ Canadian Snowshoe Association Inc. (ACR) (1907)
9, rue Bériault, Hull, PQ J8X 1A1
613/741-7874
Secretary, Audette LeBel
President, Maurice Pichette
Publications: Info-Raquette

Association canadienne de saut de barils inc./ Canadian Barrel Jumping Association Inc. (1963)
a/s Service récréatif, 1585, rue Montarville, Saint-Bruno, PQ J3V 3T8
514/653-9460
Président, Gilles Leclerc

Backpackers International Association (Canada)
Backpackers Resorts Canada
168 Maryland St., Winnipeg, MB R3G 1L3
204/772-1272, Fax: 204/772-4117, Email: BMacdonald@msn.com
President, Bill Macdonald
Affiliates: American Association of International Hostels

BC Fishing Resorts & Outfitters Association
PO Box 3301, Kamloops, BC V2C 6B9
250/374-6836, Fax: 250/374-6640
Executive Director, J.R. McMaster

BC Sailing
BC Sailing Association
#304, 1367 West Broadway, Vancouver, BC V6H 4A7
604/737-3126, Fax: 604/737-0677
Executive Director, Stephen Tupper
Publications: Yearbook; Commodore's Newsletter, q.

BC Snowmobile Federation (BCSF) (1965)
PO Box 849, Valemount, BC V0E 2Z0
250/566-4627, Fax: 250/566-4622
President, Debbie Paynton
Publications: Sno-Scene
Affiliates: International Snowmobile Council; Canadian Council of Snowmobile Organizations

The Bruce Trail Association (BTA) (1963)
PO Box 857, Hamilton, ON L8N 3N9
905/529-6821, Fax: 905/529-6823, Toll Free: 1-800-665-4453, Email: Bruce.Trail@freenet.Hamilton.on.ca
URL: http://www.brucetrail.org/
Executive Director, Jacqueline Winters
Publications: Bruce Trail News
Affiliates: Ontario Trails Council; National Trail Council

Canadian Aerophilatelic Society/La société canadienne d'aérophatélie (CAS) (1986)
16 Harwick Cres., Nepean, ON K2H 6R1
613/829-0280, Fax: 613/829-0280
President, Major R.K. Malott, MSc, BA, CD, FRPSC, Ret'd
Treasurer, Ivan W. MacKenzie, Res: 613/235-8361
Secretary, Ronald Miyanishi, Res: 416/421-5846
Publications: The Canadian Aerophilatelist
Affiliates: American Air Mail Society; Royal Philatelic Society of Canada; American Philatelic Society

Canadian Association of Numismatic Dealers (CAND)
PO Box 10272, Stoney Creek, ON L8E 5R1
613/643-4988, Fax: 613/643-6329
Richard Simpson

Canadian Association of Wooden Money Collectors (CAWMC)
592 Sheppard Ave. West, PO Box 77575, North York, ON M3H 6A7
416/633-8390
Membership Secretary, Don Robb
Publications: Timber Talk

Canadian Baton Twirling Federation/Fédération baton canadienne
35 Traynor Bay, Winnipeg, MB R2M 4H7
204/257-2206, Fax: 204/253-6738
President, Gladys Peteleski
First Vice-President, Joyce Ormshaw

Canadian Boating Federation
50, rue Jacques Cartier, Salaberry-de-Valleyfield, PQ J6T 4R3
514/377-4122, Fax: 514/377-5282

Canadian Body Building Federation/Fédération canadienne de culturisme amateur
1520 Brookmill Lane, Gloucester, ON R1B 5G4
613/746-2223
President, Syd Pukalo
General Secretary, Winston Roberts

Canadian Bridge Federation
2719 East Jolly Place, Regina, SK S4V 0X8
306/761-1677, Fax: 306/761-1697
URL: http://www.cbf.ca/query/CBFHome.html
Executive Secretary, J. Anderson

Canadian Camping Association/Association des camps du Canada (CCA) (1936)
#303, 1810 Avenue Rd., Toronto, ON M5M 3Z2
416/781-4717, Fax: 416/781-7875
President, Margaret Steel
Publications: Camps Canada

ALBERTA CAMPING ASSOCIATION (ACA) (1949)
Percy Page Centre, 11759 Groat Rd., Edmonton, AB T5M 3K6
403/453-8570, Fax: 403/453-8553
President, Michael Nelson
Office Manager, Barb Lambert
Treasurer, Gordon Matchett
Publications: Camping News; Directory of Camps, a.; Camping Standards of the ACA

BRITISH COLUMBIA CAMPING ASSOCIATION
c/o Sasamat Outdoor Centre, 3302 Senkler Rd., Belcarra, BC V3H 4S3
604/875-6760, Fax: 604/875-6760
President, Carol Voorhoeve

CAMPING ASSOCIATION OF NOVA SCOTIA
PO Box 3243, Stn South, Halifax, NS B3J 3H5
902/865-3523, Fax: 902/425-0155
President, Norma Lloyd

MANITOBA CAMPING ASSOCIATION (1937)
194A Sherbrook St., Winnipeg, MB R3C 2B6
204/784-1134, Fax: 204/784-1133
President, Steve Schwartz
Publications: Manitoba Camping Scene
Affiliates: Christian Camping International

NEWFOUNDLAND & LABRADOR CAMPING ASSOCIATION
c/o Circle Square Ranch, PO Box 1120, Manuels, NF A1W 1N6
709/781-5330, Fax: 709/781-5430
President, Cal Sparkes

ONTARIO CAMPING ASSOCIATION (OCA) (1933)
#302, 1810 Avenue Rd., Toronto, ON M5M 3Z2
416/781-0525, Fax: 416/781-7875, Email: oca@ont-camp.on.ca
URL: http://www.ontcamp.on.ca
President, John Jorgenson
Administrative Secretary, Bobsie Ebbs
Publications: OCAsional News; The Camping Guide, a.

RECREATION & PARKS ASSOCIATION OF NEW BRUNSWICK INC. (RPANB) (1987)
#105, 440 Wilsey Rd., Fredericton, NB E3B 7G5
506/459-1929, Fax: 506/450-6066
Executive Director, Art Murphy
Administrative Assistant, Susan Hebert
Publications: RECorder

SASKATCHEWAN CAMPING ASSOCIATION (SCA) (1974)
c/o Saskatoon YMCA, 25 - 22 St. East, Saskatoon, SK S7K 0C7
306/652-7515, Fax: 306/652-2828
President, Felix Tillmanns
Publications: SCAN

Canadian Canoe Association/Association canadienne de canotage (CCA) (1900)
Place R. Tait McKenzie, 1600 James Naismith Dr., Gloucester, ON K1B 5N4
613/748-5623, Fax: 613/748-5700, Telex: 053-3660 SPORTR
URL: http://www.openface.ca/paddle/
Director General, Anne Merklinger
Commodore, Sharon Mousseau
Publications: Paddles Up

ALBERTA FLATWATER CANOE ASSOCIATION
48 Redwood Meadows, Redwood Meadows, AB T3Z 1A3
403/949-2873, Fax: 403/249-5277
President, Janet Davies

ASSOCIATION QUÉBÉCOISE DE CANOË-KAYAK DE VITESSE (AQCKV) (1979)
4545, av Pierre-de-Coubertin, CP 1000, Succ. M, Montréal, PQ H1V 3R2
514/252-3086, Téléc: 514/252-3094
Président, Jean-Guy Lahaie
Publications: La Pagaie

MANITOBA PADDLING ASSOCIATION INC. (MPA) (1982)
200 Main St., Winnipeg, MB R3C 4M2
204/985-4103, Fax: 204/985-4223
Executive Director, Denis Van Laeken
Publications: MPA Newsletter

NEWFOUNDLAND & LABRADOR CANOE ASSOCIATION
PO Box 5961, Stn C, St. John's, NF A1C 5X4
Director, Phil Powers, 709/724-1134

SASKATCHEWAN CANOE ASSOCIATION
PO Box 6064, Saskatoon, SK S7K 4E5
306/653-5568
Contact, Margery McDougall, 306/653-5568

Canadian Casting Federation (1978)
c/o Toronto Sportsmen's Association, 17 Mill St., North York, ON M2P 1B3
416/487-4477, Fax: 416/487-4478
Executive Director, Peter Edwards

Canadian Correspondence Chess Association
1669 Front Rd. West, L'Orignal, ON K0B 1K0
613/632-3166
General Secretary, Manny Migicovsky
Publications: Check

Canadian Council of Snowmobile Organizations/ Conseil canadien des organismes de motoneige (CCSO) (1974)
#12, 106 Saunders Rd., Barrie, ON L4M 6E7
705/725-1121, Fax: 705/739-5005, Email: ccso@transdata.ca
President, Don Lumley
Executive Director, Marc Lacroix
Publications: Canadian Snowmobiler
Affiliates: International Snowmobile Manufacturers Association

Canadian Fitness & Lifestyle Research Institute/ Institut canadien de la recherche sur la condition physique et le mode de vie (CFLRI) (1985)
#201, 185 Somerset St. West, Ottawa, ON K2P 0J2
613/233-5528, Fax: 613/233-5536, Email: cflri@hookup.net
URL: http://activeliving.ca/activeliving/cflri.html
President, Cora Lynn Craig
Chair, Lise Gauvin
Communications Officer, Angèle Beaulieu
Publications: The Research File; Progress in Prevention

Canadian Flag Association/Association canadienne de vexillologie (CFA) (1985)
50 Heathfield Dr., Scarborough, ON M1M 3B1
416/267-9618, Fax: 416/267-9618
President, Kevin Harrington
Publications: Flagscan
Affiliates: North American Vexillological Association

Canadian Go Kart Track Owners' Association
#1, 234 Clements Rd. West, Ajax, ON L1S 3K5
905/683-9700, Fax: 905/683-9828
Office Manager, Wendy Calhoun-Clark

Canadian International Checkers Federation (1985)
6 Wellington St., Lindsay, ON K9V 3N1
705/324-3476
Vice-President, M. Jerry Van Halteren
Affiliates: Fédération mondiale du jeu de dames

Canadian International DX Radio Club (CIDX) (1962)
79, rue Kipps, Greenfield-Park, PQ J4V 3B1
514/462-1459, Fax: 514/671-3775
President, Sheldon Harvey
Publications: Messenger

Canadian Intramural Recreation Association/ Association canadienne de loisirs intramuros (CIRA) (1977)
Place R. Tait McKenzie, 1600 James Naismith Dr., Gloucester, ON K1B 5N4
613/748-5639, Fax: 613/748-5706, Telex: 053-3660
URL: http://www.cdnsport.ca/activeliving/cira.html
President, Lynn Dyck
President-Elect, Rob Stinson
Executive Vice-President, Rick Turnbull
Publications: CIRA Bulletin

Canadian Long Distance Riding Association (CaLDRA) (1985)
RR#2, Flesherton, ON N0C 1E0
905/473-3688
President, Nancy Beacon

Canadian Mariners Association (1979)
376 Orenda Dr., Brampton, ON L6T 1G1
905/790-0440, Fax: 905/790-0455
Contact, W.A. Milne
Publications: Newsletter

Canadian Motorcycle Association/Association motocycliste canadienne (CMA) (1946)
PO Box 448, Stn LCD 1, Hamilton, ON L8L 8C4
905/522-5705, Fax: 905/522-5716
General Manager, Marilyn Bastedo
President, Joseph Godsall
Publications: The Link/Le Lien
Affiliates: Fédération internationale motocycliste

Canadian Numismatic Association/Association canadienne de numismatique (CNA) (1950)
PO Box 226, Barrie, ON L4M 4T2
705/737-0845, Fax: 705/737-0293
President, Yvon Marquis
Publications: Canadian Numismatic Journal

Canadian Orienteering Federation/Fédération canadienne de course d'orientation (COF) (1967)
#408, 1600 James Naismith Dr., Gloucester, ON K1B 5N4
613/748-5649, Fax: 613/748-5402, Telex: 053-3660 SPORTR
Executive Director, Colin Kirk
President, Jack Forsyth
Publications: Orienteering Canada
Affiliates: International Orienteering Federation

Canadian Outrigger Racing Association (CORA) (1992)
PO Box 216, Pemberton, BC V0N 2L0
604/894-5684, Fax: 604/894-6918
Contact, Hugh Fisher
Affiliates: Canadian Canoe Association

Canadian Paper Money Society (CPMS) (1965)
PO Box 562, Pickering, ON L1V 2R7
905/509-1146
Sec.-Treas., Dick Dunn
Publications: The Canadian Paper Money Journal

Canadian Parks & Wilderness Society/Société pour la protection des parcs et des sites naturales du Canada (CPAWS) (1963)
#380, 401 Richmond St. West, Toronto, ON M5V 3A8
416/979-2720, Fax: 416/979-3155, Email: cpaws@web.net
URL: http://web.idirect.com/~wildland
President, Harvey Locke
Executive Director, Mary Granskou
Publications: The Wilderness Activist

Canadian Parks/Recreation Association/ Association canadienne des loisirs/parcs (CP/RA) (1945)
#306, 1600 James Naismith Dr., Gloucester, ON K1B 5N4
613/748-5651, Fax: 613/748-5854, Telex: 053-3660, Email: cpra@cdnsport.ca
URL: http://www.cdnsport.ca/activeliving/cpra.html
Executive Director, Geraldine Hebert
President, Herb Pirk
Publications: Recreation Canada

ALBERTA RECREATION & PARKS ASSOCIATION
Percy Page Centre, 11759 Groat Rd. NW, Edmonton, AB T5M 3K6
403/453-8631, Fax: 403/453-8553
Executive Director, Paul Servos
President, Roger Smolnicky
Publications: Recreation Alberta

BRITISH COLUMBIA RECREATION & PARKS ASSOCIATION (BCRPA) (1954)
#30, 10551 Shellbridge Way, Richmond, BC V6X 2W9
604/273-8055, Fax: 604/273-8059
Executive Director, Gordon J. Stewart
Publications: Recreation BC Magazine

NEWFOUNDLAND & LABRADOR PARKS & RECREATION ASSOCIATION (NLPRA) (1971)
PO Box 8700, Stn A, St. John's, NF A1B 4J6
709/729-3892, Fax: 709/729-3814
Executive Director, Gary Milley
Program Officer, Joanne Bennett
Publications: Recreation Quarterly; NLPRA Membership Directory

NORTHWEST TERRITORIES RECREATION & PARKS ASSOCIATION (1989)
PO Box 841, Yellowknife, NT X1A 2N6
403/669-9129, Fax: 403/669-9129
Executive Director, Adrienne Forest
Publications: The Energizer
Affiliates: Sport North

PARKS & RECREATION ONTARIO/PARCS ET LOISIRS DE L'ONTARIO (PRO) (1984)
#406, 1185 Eglinton Ave. East, North York, ON M3C 3C6
416/426-7142, Fax: 416/426-7371
Executive Director, Barbara Bridle
Publications: Pro Job Mart; PROfile

RECREATION ASSOCIATION OF NOVA SCOTIA (RANS) (1973)
PO Box 3010, Stn South, Halifax, NS B3J 3G6
902/425-1128, Fax: 902/425-5606
Executive Director, Jean Robinson-Dexter
Publications: Recreation Matters

SASKATCHEWAN PARKS & RECREATION ASSOCIATION (SPRA) (1962)
#210, 3303 Hillsdale St., Regina, SK S4S 6W9
306/780-9214, Fax: 306/780-9257
General Manager, Carol E. Brasok
Publications: Recreation Saskatchewan
Affiliates: Canadian Parks & Recreation Association

Canadian Power & Sail Squadrons (Canadian Headquarters)/Escadrilles canadiennes de plaisance (1938)
26 Golden Gate Ct., Scarborough, ON M1P 3A5
416/293-2438, Fax: 416/293-2445, Toll Free: 1-800-268-3579
President/Executive Director, Brian Burch
Chief Commander, A.H. Mitton
Publications: The Port Hole

Canadian Racing Pigeon Union (1929)
4500 Blakie Rd., London, ON N6L 1G5
519/652-5704, Fax: 519/652-6406
President, Bill Badgerow
Sec.-Treas., Dorothy Deveau
Affiliates: Fédération colombophile internationale

Canadian Recreational Canoeing Association/ Association canadienne de canotage récréatif (CRCA) (1971)
446 Main St. West, PO Box 5000, Merrickville, ON K0G 1N0
613/269-2910, Fax: 613/269-2908, Email: staff@crca.ca
URL: http://www.crca.ca/
Executive Director, Joseph Agnew
Publications: KANAWA - Canada's Canoeing & Kayaking Magazine
Affiliates: American Rivers Conservation Council; Canadian Camping Association; Canadian Marathon Racing Canoe Association; Canadian Red Cross; National Council Boy Scouts of Canada; Canadian White Water Association; Royal Life Saving Society of Canada; Girl Guides of Canada; Canoe Canada; American Canoe Association; Canadian Heritage River System; Canadian Parks Service

ALBERTA RECREATIONAL CANOE ASSOCIATION
c/o Calgary Outdoor Area Council, 1111 Memorial Dr. NW, Calgary, AB T2N 3E4
403/270-2262, Fax: 403/270-3654
Director, Gordon Harris

CANOE NEW BRUNSWICK
PO Box 243, Moncton, NB E1C 8K9
506/859-3548, Fax: 506/859-3697
President, George W. Geldart

CANOE NOVA SCOTIA
5516 Spring Garden Rd., PO Box 3010, Stn South, Halifax, NS B3J 3G6
902/425-5450, Fax: 902/425-5606
Executive Director, Ike Whitehead

FÉDÉRATION QUÉBÉCOISE DU CANOT CAMPING INC. (1976)
4545, av Pierre-de-Coubertin, CP 1000, Succ. M, Montréal, PQ H1V 3R2
514/252-3001, Téléc: 514/252-3091
Directeur général, Pierre Trudel
Président, Benoît Chartrand
Publications: Le Courant

MANITOBA RECREATIONAL CANOEING ASSOCIATION
PO Box 2663, Winnipeg, MB R3C 4B3
204/925-5681, Fax: 204/985-4223
URL: http://kohlrabi.cs.umanitoba.ca/mrca/mrca.html
Publications: MRCA Newsletter
Affiliates: Manitoba Paddling Association

NORTHWEST TERRITORIES CANOEING ASSOCIATION
PO Box 2763, Yellowknife, NT X1A 2R1
403/873-2339, Fax: 403/920-7809, Toll Free: 1-800-661-0797
President, Hillary Pounsett
Treasurer, Gordon Stewart

ONTARIO RECREATIONAL CANOEING ASSOCIATION
Canoe Ontario
#104, 1185 Eglinton Ave. East, North York, ON M3C 3C6
416/426-7170, Fax: 416/426-7363
Executive Director, John Pugsley, 416/426-7172
Publications: Canews
Affiliates: Canoe Ontario

PEI RECREATIONAL CANOEING ASSOCIATION
RR#5, PO Box 5604, Charlottetown, PE C1A 7J8
902/368-6355, Fax: 902/368-6186
Chairman, Shawn Shea

RECREATIONAL CANOEING ASSOCIATION BC
1367 West Broadway, Vancouver, BC V6H 4A7
604/275-6651
President, Carey Robson, 604/437-1140

YUKON CANOE & KAYAK CLUB
PO Box 5546, Whitehorse, YT Y1A 5H4
Contact, Ingrid Wilcox, 403/668-6562, Fax: 403/633-5625

Canadian Sport Parachuting Association/ Association canadienne de parachutisme sportive (CSPA) (1956)
4185 Dunning Rd., RR#3, Navan, ON K4B 1J1
613/835-3731, Fax: 613/835-3731, Email: cspa@travel-net.com
URL: http://www.islandnet.com/~murrays/cspa.html
President, Aiden Walters
Office Manager, Cathy Johnson
Publications: CanPara

Canadian Stamp Dealers' Association (CSDA)
PO Box 1123, Stn Adelaide, Toronto, ON M5C 2K5
416/653-9885
President, John Sheffield, 519/681-3420, Fax: 519/668-6872
Vice-President, Roy Houtby
Secretary, Rick Day
Treasurer, Emil Talacko
Publications: CSDA Directory; CSDA Newsletter, 4-6 pa

Canadian Table Tennis Association/Association canadienne de tennis de table (CTTA) (1937)
Table Tennis Canada
Place R. Tait McKenzie, 1600 James Naismith Dr., Gloucester, ON K1B 5N4
613/748-5675, Fax: 613/746-5705, Telex: 053-3660 SPORTR
Director General, Mr. Adham Sharara
President, Bruce Burton
Publications: 20/20
Affiliates: Sports Council of Canada

Canadian Toy Collectors' Society Inc. (CTCS)
#245, 91 Rylander Blvd., Unit 7, Toronto, ON M1B 5M5
President, Ed Barclay
Treasurer, Roger J. Pride, 905/383-5719
Publications: Canadian Toy Collector

Canadian Trapshooting Association (1966)
17 Stirling Close, Red Deer, AB T4N 0A9
403/347-5284, Fax: 403/347-5284
President, Bob Brown

Canadian Yachting Association/Association canadienne de yachting (CYA) (1931)
#504, 1600 James Naismith Dr., Gloucester, ON K1B 5N4
613/748-5687, Fax: 613/748-5688, Telex: 053-3660
URL: http://www.cdnsport.ca/~smorrow
Executive Director, Brian Lane
President, Chris Campbell
Publications: Canadian Sailing Review; Annual Directory
Affiliates: International Yacht Racing Union; International Sailing Schools Association

Chess Federation of Canada/Fédération canadienne des échecs
2212 Gladwin Cr., #E1, Ottawa, ON K1B 5N1
613/733-2844, Fax: 613/733-2844
URL: http://www.globalx.net/cfc/
Executive Director, Hal Bond
President, Nathan Davinski
Publications: En Passant
Affiliates: Fédération internationale des échecs

Classical & Medieval Numismatic Society (CMNS) (1991)
PO Box 956, Stn B, North York, ON M2K 2T6
416/490-8659, Fax: 416/490-6452, Email: billmcdo@idirect.com
Executive Sec.-Treas., W.H. McDonald
Publications: The Anvil; The Picus, a.

Council of BC Yacht Clubs
1367 West Broadway, Vancouver, BC V6H 4E9
604/929-3235
President, Peter Lissett

Dominion of Canada Rifle Association (1868)
PO Box 11160, Stn H, Nepean, ON K2H 7T9
613/829-8281, Fax: 613/990-0434
Executive Director, LCol (ret'd) T.J. Kaulbach
Executive Vice-President, S.E. Frost
Publications: The Canadian Marksman

Elvis in Canada Fan Club (EIC) (1980)
PO Box 20236, RPO Upper James, Hamilton, ON L9C 7M8
President, Frances M. Roberts
Affiliates: National Association of Fan Clubs

Fantasy Balloon Owners & Pilots Association (1989)
205 Bridge St., New Dundee, ON N0B 2E0
519/696-2414, Fax: 519/696-2414
Director, Karen Rosenthal

Fédération des clubs de motoneigistes du Québec (FCMQ) (1974)
4545, av Pierre-de-Coubertin, CP 1000, Succ. M, Montréal, PQ H1V 3R2
514/252-3076, Téléc: 514/254-2066
Président, Mario Gareau
Agent d'Administration, Danielle Poirier
Publications: Motoneige Québec

Federation of Mountain Clubs of British Columbia (1980)
#336, 1367 West Broadway, Vancouver, BC V6H 4A9
604/737-3053, Fax: 604/738-7175, Email: fmcbc@sport.bc.ca
Executive Director, Linda Coss

Federation of Ontario Cottagers' Associations Inc. (FOCA) (1964)
#101, 215 Morrish Rd., Scarborough, ON M1C 1E9
416/284-2305, Fax: 416/284-7108
Executive Director, J.G. Strickland
President, John Carter
Vice-President, Finance, Barb MacLeod
Secretary, John Hough
Contact, Environment Committee, Shannon McCorquodale
Publications: Lake Stewards Newsletter

Fédération de pétanque du Québec
4545, av Pierre-de-Coubertin, CP 1000, Succ. M, Montréal, PQ H1V 3R2
514/252-3077, Téléc: 514/252-3169
Secrétaire administrative, Line M. Dalard

Canadian Almanac & Directory 1997

Fédération québécoise de camping et de caravaning inc. (FQCC) (1967)
4545, av Pierre-de-Coubertin, CP 1000, Succ. M, Montréal, PQ H1V 3R2
514/252-3003, Téléc: 514/254-0694
Directeur général, Irman Bolduc
Directrice, Services aux membres et du développement régional, Francine Langevin
Publications: Camping Caravaning

Fédération québécoise de canoë kayak d'eau vive
4545, av Pierre-de-Coubertin, CP 1000, Succ. M, Montréal, PQ H1V 3R2
514/252-3099, Téléc: 514/252-3232
Président, Jean Obry

La Fédération québécoise des échecs/Québec Chess Federation (FQE) (1967)
CP 640, Succ. C, Montréal, PQ H2L 4L5
514/252-3034, Téléc: 514/251-8038
Directeur général, Robert Finta
Président, Luc Nolet
Publications: Échec+

Fédération québécoise des jeux récréatifs (1975)
4545, av Pierre-de-Coubertin, CP 1000, Succ. M, Montréal, PQ H1V 3R2
514/252-3032, Téléc: 514/251-8038
Directeur général, André Leclerc
Publications: Récréation Québec

Fédération québécoise de la marche/Walking & Hiking Federation of Québec (1982)
4545, av Pierre-de-Coubertin, CP 1000, Succ. M, Montréal, PQ H1V 3R2
514/252-3157, Téléc: 514/254-1363
Publications: Marche

Fly Fishing Canada (FFC) (1987)
#50, 7171 Torbram Rd., Mississauga, ON L4T 3W4
905/678-0422, Fax: 905/678-0424
Executive Director, Jack Simpson

Guide Outfitters Association of British Columbia (GOABC) (1966)
PO Box 94675, Richmond, BC V6Y 4A4
604/278-2688, Fax: 604/278-3440
General Manager, Dale Drown
Publications: BC Hunter

Hang Gliding & Paragliding Association of Canada/Association canadienne de vol libre (HPAC) (1977)
21593 - 94A Ave., Langley, BC V1M 2A5
604/882-5090
URL: http://www.cadvision.com/Home_Pages/accounts/midtoad/hpac.html
Administrator, Barry Bateman
Publications: AIR

Hike Ontario (1974)
Federation of Ontario Hiking Trail Associations
#411, 1185 Eglinton Ave. East, North York, ON M3C 3C6
416/426-7362, Fax: 416/426-7362, Toll Free: 1-800-422-0552, Email: AY625@torfree.net
URL: http://www.freenet.durham.org/hikeon/
President, Jeff Hemming
Publications: Outlook
Affiliates: Ontario Trails Council; National Trail Association of Canada

Horseshoe Canada Association/Association canadienne de fer à cheval
PO Box 548, Raymore, SK S0A 3J0
306/746-2041, Fax: 306/746-5811
President, Sharon Ellison

Treasurer, Jack E. Adams
Publications: Canadian Horseshoe Pitchers Year Book

International Computer Chess Association (Canada) (ICCA) (1977)
Dept. of Computing Science, University of Alberta, Edmonton, AB T6G 2H1
403/492-3971, Fax: 403/492-1071, Email: tony@cs.UAlberta.ca
President, Prof. T.A. Marsland
Vice-President, David N.L. Levy
Sec.-Treas, D.F. Beal
Publications: Journal of the International Computer Chess Association

International Laser Class Association (North American Region)
#328, 8466 North Lockwood Ridge Rd., Sarasota, FL 34243 USA
813/359-1384, Fax: 813/359-1384, Telex: 05-839600 LASER
General Manager, Allan Broadribb

Lawn Bowls Canada/Boulingrin Canada
Place R. Tait McKenzie, #708, 1600 James Naismith Dr., Gloucester, ON K1B 5N4
613/748-5643, Fax: 613/748-5796, Telex: 053-3660 SPORT
Executive Director, Margot Clayton Jones
President, Jim Keeling

Lionel Collectors Association of Canada (LCAC) (1978)
PO Box 976, Oshawa, ON L1H 7N2
905/728-5025
President, George Spall
Vice-President, Hans Hudsonroder
Publications: LCAC Switch List

Lottery Collectors Society (LCS) (1987)
10760 Shellbridge Way, Richmond, BC V6X 3H1
Sec.-Treas., Richard Bertrand
Publications: Lotologist

Maritime Boating Association
Martins Brook, PO Box 448, Lunenburg, NS B0J 2C0
902/634-3173
Contact, Weldon W. Allen

Model Aeronautics Association of Canada Inc. (MAAC) (1949)
#9, 5100 South Service Rd., Burlington, ON L7L 6A5
905/632-9808, Fax: 905/632-3304
URL: http://www.maac.ca
Sec.-Treas., Linda Patrick
Publications: Model Aviation Canada
Affiliates: Aero Club of Canada; Fédération aeronautique internationale

National Association of Watch & Clock Collectors (NAWCC)
514 Poplar St., Columbia, PA 17512-2124 USA
717/684-8261, Fax: 717/684-0878
Executive Director, Thomas Bartels

National Firearms Association (NFA) (1984)
PO Box 1779, Edmonton, AB T5J 2P1
403/439-1394, Fax: 403/439-4091
National President, David A. Tomlinson
Publications: Pointblank

New Brunswick Camping Committee
Park Office Centre, #105, 440 Wilsey Rd., Fredericton, NB E3B 7G5
506/459-1929, Fax: 506/450-6066
CCA Liaison, Dana Welner

Ontario Federation of Anglers & Hunters (OFAH) (1928)
PO Box 2800, Peterborough, ON K9J 8L5
705/748-6324, Fax: 705/748-9577, Email: ofah@oncomdis.on.ca
Executive Vice-President, Rick Morgan
President, Gerry Courtemanche
Communications Officer, Mark Holmes
Publications: Call of the Loon; Hotline, m.; Hunter Education News, q.; Canadian Fishing & Hunting Trade News
Affiliates: Canadian Wildlife Federation

Ontario Federation of Snowmobile Clubs (OFSC) (1966)
PO Box 94, Barrie, ON L4M 4S9
705/739-7669, Fax: 705/739-5005, Email: ofsc@mail.transdata.ca
URL: http://www.transdata.ca/ofsc/index.html
President, Bert Grant
Manager, Ron Purchase
Publications: Main Trail

Ontario Marina Operators Association (OMOA) (1967)
#211, 4 Cataraqui St., Kingston, ON K7K 1Z7
613/547-6662, Fax: 613/547-6813
Executive Director, Michael S. Shaw
Publications: Marina News
Affiliates: Canadian Marine Trades Federation

Ontario Municipal Recreation Association (OMRA)
#404, 1185 Eglinton Ave. East, North York, ON M3C 3C6
416/426-7151
Contact, Trish Donnelly

Ontario Numismatic Association (ONA) (1962)
PO Box 40033, Stn Waterloo Square, Waterloo, ON N2J 4V1
519/745-3104
Membership Chairman, Bruce Raszmann
Publications: The Ontario Numismatic

Ontario Parks Association (OPA) (1936)
1185 Eglinton Ave. East, North York, ON M3C 3C7
416/426-7157, Fax: 416/426-7366, Email: opa@hookup.net
URL: http://www.hookup.net/~opa
Executive Director, Denyse A. Morrissey
Publications: Green Sward
Affiliates: Landscape Ontario; Ontario Association of Landscape Architects

Ontario Recreation Facilities Association (ORFA) (1947)
1185 Eglinton Ave. East, North York, ON M3C 3C7
416/426-7062, Fax: 416/426-7385, Toll Free: 1-800-661-6732
Executive Director, John Milton
Publications: Facility Forum

Ontario Research Council on Leisure (ORCOL) (1975)
School of Rural Planning & Development, University of Guelph, #158, 50 Stone Rd. E., Guelph, ON N1G 2W1
519/824-4120, Fax: 519/767-1690
Vice-President, Don Reid
Publications: Applied Leisure Research

Ontario Sport Fishing Guides' Association (OSGA) (1980)
40 Sherwood Rd. East, Ajax, ON L1T 2Y9
905/683-3214, Fax: 905/683-2872
President, Hugh Caulfield

Secretary, Doug Kettle
Publications: Charter Chatter

Ontario Vintage Radio Association (OVRA) (1980)
197 Humberside Ave., Toronto, ON M6P 1K7
416/769-9627
President, Ted Catton
Publications: OVRA Newsletter

Outdoor Recreation Council of British Columbia (ORC) (1976)
#334, 1367 Broadway West, Vancouver, BC V6H 4A7
604/737-3058, Fax: 604/737-3666,
    Email: outrec_council@sport.bc.ca
URL: http://mindlink.net/outrec_council/outrec.htm
Executive Director, Norma Wilson
Publications: The Outdoor Report

Outward Bound Ontario (COBWS) (1976)
Canadian Outward Bound Wilderness School
#302, 150 Laird Dr., Toronto, ON M4G 3V7
416/421-8111, Fax: 416/421-9062, Toll Free: 1-800-268-7329
Executive Director, Philip Blackford
Publications: Alumni News

Outward Bound Western Canada (1969)
#109, 1367 Broadway West, Vancouver, BC V6H 4A9
604/737-3093, Fax: 604/738-7175
Executive Director, Andrew Orr
Marketing Manager, Anne Marie Barrett

Paddle Sport BC
c/o Sport BC, 1367 Broadway West, Vancouver, BC V6H 4A9
604/275-6651, Fax: 604/275-6651
Treasurer, Brian Creer
Publications: Canews; Paddle Post

Racetracks of Canada, Inc./Hippodromes du Canada inc. (ROC) (1965)
2150 Meadowvale Blvd., Mississauga, ON L5N 6R6
905/821-7795, Fax: 905/858-3111
President, Bill Taylor
Executive Vice-President, Roly Roberts
Publications: Track Talk
Affiliates: Canadian Horse Racing Hall of Fame

Recreation Facilities Association of British Columbia (RFABC) (1948)
8550 Young Rd. South, Chilliwack, BC V2P 4P1
604/793-2904, Fax: 604/792-2583, Email: mulligan@chilliwack.com
Sec.-Treas., Ryan Mulligan
President, Bruce Tilbury
Publications: Facility to Facility

Regroupement loisir Québec
4545, av Pierre-de-Coubertin, CP 1000, Succ. M, Montréal, PQ H1V 3R2
514/252-3000, Téléc: 514/251-8038, Télex: 05829647
Directeur général, François Hamel

Roller Sports Canada/Sports à roulettes du Canada
c/o Roller Sports Manitoba, 200 Main St., Winnipeg, MB R3C 4M2
204/925-5699, Fax: 204/925-5703
Executive Director, Rick Bochinski
President, Norm Dawkin

The Royal Philatelic Society of Canada/Société royale de philatélie du Canada (1887)
PO Box 929, Stn Q, Toronto, ON M4T 2P1
President, William G. Robinson
Publications: The Canadian Philatelist

The RPSC Philatelic Research Foundation/Fondation de recherche philatélique de la SRPC (1986)
PO Box 5320, Stn F, Ottawa, ON K2C 3J1
613/224-4189
President, James E. Kraemer, F.R.P.S.C.
Secretary, Harry Sutherland, Q.C., R.D.P., F.R.P.S.C.
Publications: The Opusculum

SALTS Sail & Life Training Society (1974)
PO Box 5014, Stn B, Victoria, BC V8R 6N3
250/383-6811, Fax: 250/383-7781
Executive Director, Martyn Clark
Business Manager, Ron Howatson
Publications: Saltings

Saskatchewan Recreation Society (SRS) (1969)
2205 Victoria Ave., Regina, SK S4P 0S4
306/780-9267, Fax: 306/525-4009, Toll Free: 1-800-667-7780
Executive Director, Bob Phillips
Publications: Update
Affiliates: Saskatchewan Parks & Recreation Association

Saskatchewan Snowmobile Association Inc. (1971)
#210, 438 Victoria Ave. East, Regina, SK S4N 0N7
306/780-9404, Fax: 306/780-9422
President, Chris Brewer
Manager, John Prebushewsky
Publications: Saskatchewan Snowmobiler

Sea Kayak Association of BC
7955 - 161 St., Surrey, BC V3S 7H9
604/597-1122
President, Mercia Sixta

Shooting Federation of Canada/Fédération de tir du Canada (1932)
45 Shirley Blvd., Nepean, ON K2K 2W6
613/828-7338, Fax: 613/828-7333
President, David Hitchcock
Publications: Aim

Sky Line Hikers of the Canadian Rockies (1933)
PO Box 75055, Stn Cambrian, Calgary, AB T2K 6J8
403/240-4016
Sec.-Treas., Irene Garvin
Publications: Skyliner

Snowmobilers Association of Nova Scotia (SANS) (1976)
5516 Spring Garden Rd., PO Box 3010, Stn Parklane Centre, Halifax, NS B3J 3G6
902/425-5450, Fax: 902/425-5606
Executive Director, Robert Semple
Publications: Sno' Trails-SANS

Soaring Association of Canada/Association canadienne de vol à voile (SAC) (1945)
#101, 1090 Ambleside Dr., Ottawa, ON K2B 8G7
613/829-0536, Fax: 613/829-9497, Email: 6x271@freenet.carleton.ca
President, Pierre Pepin
Director, James F. McCullum
Publications: Free Flight
Affiliates: Aero Club of Canada

Taoist Tai Chi Society of Canada (1970)
1376 Bathurst St., Toronto, ON M5R 3J1
416/656-2110, Fax: 416/654-3937
President, Albert Chan
Founder, Moy Lin-shin

Trail Riders of the Canadian Rockies (1923)
PO Box 6742, Stn D, Calgary, AB T2P 2E6
403/264-8656, Fax: 403/264-8657, Email: trcr@canuck.com
URL: http://www.canuck.com/~trcr
President, Gordon Thomson
Executive Director, Barbara Rostron
Secretary, Penny Egeland
Publications: Ridin' High

Tunnelling Association of Canada (TAC)
Dept. of Civil Engineering, University of Toronto, Toronto, ON M5S 1A4
416/978-3115
President, Prof. A.M. Crawford
Publications: Canadian Tunnelling

Whitewater Kayaking Association of BC (1974)
1367 West Broadway, Vancouver, BC V6H 4A9
604/275-6651, Fax: 604/275-6651
Treasurer, Brian Creer
Publications: Paddle Post
Affiliates: Canadian Whitewater Association

Wilderness Canoe Association (WCA)
1881 Yonge St., PO Box 48022, Stn Davisville, Toronto, ON M4S 3C6
905/831-3554
Contact, Brian Buttigieg
Publications: Nastawgan

YMCA Canada (1851)
The National Council of Young Men's Christian Associations of Canada
#200, 2160 Yonge St., Toronto, ON M4S 2A9
416/485-9447, Fax: 416/485-8228
CEO, Sol Kasimer
Chair, Edward G. Robinson
Director of Communications, Dianne LeBreton
Publications: Between the Lines; Entre les lignes, trimestriel
Affiliates: Canadian Centre for Philanthropy; Canadian Child Care Federation; Canadian Coalition for the Rights of Children; Canadian Council for International Cooperation; Canadian Council on Children & Youth; Canadian Learning Consortium; Canadian Recreational Canoeing Association; Canadian Society of Association Executives; Coalition on National Voluntary Organizations; Conference Board of Canada; Huronia Tourism Association; National Fitness Leadership Advisory Committee; National Life Guard Service; National Voluntary Health Agencies; National Youth Serving Agencies; Partnership Africa Canada; Resorts Ontario; Royal Life Saving Society

YWCA of/du Canada (1893)
Young Women's Christian Association of Canada
80 Gerrard St. East, Toronto, ON M5B 1G6
416/593-9886, Fax: 416/971-8084, Email: ywcajw@web.apc.org
President, Ann Mowatt
CEO, Judith Wiley
Director, Organizational & Community Development, Judi Anne Osborne
Publications: Journal
Affiliates: Selective: Canadian Association for the Advancement of Women in Sports; Canadian Congress for Learning Opportunities for Women; Canadian Coalition for the Rights of the Child; Canadian Daycare Advocacy; Canadian Research Institute for the Advancement of Women; Federated Women's Institutes of Canada; National Action Committee on the Status of Women

RECYCLING see **ENVIRONMENTAL**

RED CROSS see **EMERGENCY RESPONSE**

RENEWABLE FUELS see **ENERGY**

Canadian Almanac & Directory 1997

REPRODUCTIVE ISSUES

Alliance for Life/Alliance pour la vie (1972)
#B1, 90 Garry St., Winnipeg, MB R3C 4H1
204/942-4772, Fax: 204/943-9283, Crisis-Line: 1-800-665-0570, Email: ikrueger@infobahn.mb.ca
Executive Director, Anna M. Desilets
Affiliates: Alliance Action Inc.

Birthright/Accueil Grossesse (1968)
777 Coxwell Ave., Toronto, ON M4C 3C6
416/469-1111, Fax: 416/469-1772, Toll Free: 1-800-550-4900
Co-President, Stephenie Fox
Co-President, Mary Berney
Co-President, Louise R. Summerhill
Publications: Life Guardian

Canadian Abortion Rights Action League/Association canadienne pour le droit à l'avortement (CARAL) (1974)
#306, 344 Bloor St. West, Toronto, ON M5S 3A7
416/961-1507, Fax: 416/961-5771, Email: caral@interlog.com
URL: http://www.io.org/~caral
Executive Coordinator, Marcy Gilbert
President, Amanda LeRougetel
Vice-President, Pauline Raven
Vice-President, Dee Pearson
Treasurer, Rhonda Hendel
Publications: Pro-choice News

Canadian Fertility & Andrology Society/Société canadienne de fertilité et d'andrologie (CFAS) (1954)
#409, 2065, rue Alexandre Desève, Montréal, PQ H2L 2W5
514/524-9009, Fax: 514/524-2163
Executive Director, Susan Orr-Mongeau
Publications: Directory

Childbirth By Choice Trust (1982)
#306, 344 Bloor St. West, Toronto, ON M5S 3A7
416/961-1507, Fax: 416/961-5771
Administrator, Robin Rowe

Coalition for Reproductive Choice (1982)
PO Box 51, Stn L, Winnipeg, MB R3H 0Z4
204/946-5018
Director, Amanda Le Rougetel
Administrative Coordinator, Susan Riley
Publications: Manitoba Pro Choice News
Affiliates: Manitoba Federation of Labour; Women's Health Clinic; Canadian Abortion Rights Action League; National Council of Jewish Women; YWCA

Fédération du Québec pour le planning des naissances (FQPN) (1972)
#302, 4428, boul St-Laurent, Montréal, PQ H2W 1Z5
514/844-3721, Téléc: 514/844-8736
Coordonnatrice, Anne St-Cerny
Publications: Cahier femmes et sexualité

Infertility Awareness Association of Canada/Association canadienne de sensibilisation à l'infertilité (IAAC) (1990)
#523, 774 Echo Dr., Ottawa, ON K1S 5N8
613/730-1322, Fax: 613/730-1323, Toll Free: 1-800-263-2929, Email: ax626@freenet.carleton.ca
Executive Director, Trish Maynard
Publications: Infertility Awareness
Affiliates: Canadian Fertility & Andrology Society; Society of Obstetricians & Gynaecologists of Canada

League for Life in Manitoba/Ligue pour la vie au Manitoba (1970)
579 Des Meurons St., Winnipeg, MB R2H 2P6
204/233-8047, 7283, Fax: 204/233-0523, Toll Free: 1-800-665-0570
Executive Director, Patricia Soenen
President, Laverne Hudson
Publications: League for Life News

Natural Family Planning Association
#205, 3050 Yonge St., Toronto, ON M4N 2K4
416/481-5465
Executive Director, M. Isabel Graham
President, Merrilyn Currie

Ontario Coalition for Abortion Clinics (OCAC)
PO Box 753, Stn P, Toronto, ON M5S 2Z1
416/969-8463
Coordinating Committee, Miriam Jones

Planned Parenthood Federation of Canada/Fédération pour le planning des naissances du Canada (PPFC) (1964)
#430, One Nicholas St., Ottawa, ON K1N 7B7
613/241-4474, Fax: 613/241-7550, Email: ppfed@web.apc.org
Executive Director, Bonnie Johnson
Director, Resource Development, Sharon Bradford
Publications: PPFC Bulletin

PLANNED PARENTHOOD ALBERTA (PPA) (1973)
#301, 1220 Kensington Rd. NW, Calgary, AB T2N 3P5
403/283-8591, Fax: 403/270-3209
Executive Director, Melanie Anderson
Publications: The Voice of Alberta's Pro-Choice Majority
Affiliates: Calgary Birth Control Association; Planned Parenthood Association of Edmonton; Planned Parenthood Banff

PLANNED PARENTHOOD ASSOCIATION OF BRITISH COLUMBIA (1963)
#201, 1001 West Broadway, Vancouver, BC V6K 2G8
604/731-4252, Fax: 604/731-4698, Toll Free: 1-800-739-7367
Executive Director, Marcena S. Croy
President, Dr. Dorothy Shaw
Publications: Facts of Life

PLANNED PARENTHOOD MANITOBA (1966)
#206, 819 Sargent Ave., Winnipeg, MB R3E 0B9
204/982-7800, Fax: 204/982-7819
Executive Director, Miriam Baron
President, Roberta Ellis

PLANNED PARENTHOOD NEWFOUNDLAND/LABRADOR
203 Merrymeeting Rd., St. John's, NF A1C 2W6
709/579-1009, Fax: 709/726-2308
President, Alison Earle
Clinic Coordinator, Nancy Stokes

PLANNED PARENTHOOD NOVA SCOTIA
Quinpool Medical Centre, #100, 6156 Quinpool Rd., Halifax, NS B3L 1A3
902/492-0444, Fax: 902/492-7155
Executive Director, Cari Patterson

PLANNED PARENTHOOD ONTARIO (1975)
790 Bay St., 8th Fl., Toronto, ON M5S 2Z2
416/595-9989, Fax: 416/595-9984, Toll Free: 1-800-463-6739
Executive Director, Cheryll Corness
President, Joan Toogood
Publications: Choice Words

PLANNED PARENTHOOD SASKATCHEWAN
2006 York Ave., Saskatoon, SK S7J 1H6
306/343-9343
President, Linda Holmes

Pro-Life Society of British Columbia
#204, 1755 Springfield Rd., Kelowna, BC V1Y 5V5
250/862-3731, Email: egerk@awinc.com
President, Ted Gerk

Right to Life Association of Newfoundland
PO Box 5427, St. John's, NF A1C 5W2
709/579-1500, Fax: 709/579-3818
President, Philomena Rogers

Right to Life Association of Toronto (1972)
#700, 120 Eglinton Ave. East, Toronto, ON M4P 1E2
416/483-7869, Fax: 416/483-7052
President, June Scandiffio
Publications: Newsletter

World Organization Ovulation Method Billings Inc.
WOOMB Canada Inc.
1506 Dansey Ave., Coquitlam, BC V3K 3J1
604/936-4472, Fax: 604/936-5690
President, Lou Specken
Vice-President, Sheila J. Howard
Affiliates: WOOMB International - Australia

RESEARCH & SCHOLARSHIP
see also Education; Health & Medical; Scientific

APRO - The Canadian Technology Network (1984)
Association of Provincial Research Organizations
#1004, 280 Albert St., Ottawa, ON K1P 5G8
613/567-2993, Fax: 613/567-4562
Chairman, Brian Barge
President & CEO, Graham Taylor
Office Manager, Deborah Pelletier

Canadian Association for HIV Research
c/o Jewish General Hospital, 3755, ch Côte-Ste-Catherine, Montréal, PQ H3T 1E2
514/340-8260, Fax: 514/340-7537
President, Dr. Mark A. Wainberg
Publications: The Clarion

Canadian Association for Research in Nondestructive Evaluation/Association canadienne de recherche en évaluation nondestructifs (CARNDE) (1987)
75, boul de Montagne, Boucherville, PQ J4B 6Y4
514/641-5252, Fax: 514/641-5104
Contact, Dr. Jean Bussière
Publications: Canadian Association for Research
Affiliates: Canadian Society for Nondestructive Testing, Inc.

Canadian Bacterial Diseases Network/Réseau canadien de recherche sur les bactérioses (CBDN) (1990)
University of British Columbia, #351, 2125 East Mall, Vancouver, BC V6T 1Z4
604/822-4040, Fax: 604/822-6938
URL: http://www.cbdn.ca/
Network Manager, Helen Becker, Email: becker@cbdn.ca

Canadian Carbonization Research Association (CCRA) (1965)
PO Box 85291, RPO Brant Plaza, Burlington, ON L7R 4K4
905/637-0666
Treasurer, G.A. Chapman
Chairman, Wayne Jonasson

Canadian Centre for Policy Alternatives/Centre canadien de politique alternatives (CCPA) (1980)
#804, 251 Laurier Ave. West, Ottawa, ON K1P 5J6
613/563-1341, Fax: 613/233-1458

Executive Director, Bruce Campbell
President, Duncan Cameron

Canadian Committee of Byzantinists
University of Waterloo, 200 University Ave. West, Waterloo, ON N2L 3G1
519/885-1211, ext.3565, Fax: 519/746-3097,
    Email: dsahas@uwaterloo.waterloo.ca
President, Daniel Sahas
Publications: Canadio-Byzantina
Affiliates: Association internationale des études byzantines

Canadian Genetic Diseases Network/Réseau canadien sur les maladies génétiques (CGDN) (1990)
University of British Columbia, #349, 2125 East Mall, Vancouver, BC V6T 1Z4
604/822-7217, Fax: 604/822-7945
URL: http://www.bc.irap.nrc.ca/ctn/cgdn/cgdn-e.html
Managing Director, Dr. David Shindler
Network Manager, Carol J. Smith
Commercial Director, Margaret Moore

Canadian Institute for Advanced Research/La fondation de l'institut canadien de recherches avancées
#701, 179 John St., Toronto, ON M5T 1X4
416/971-4252, Fax: 416/971-6169
President, Dr. J. Fraser Mustard
Vice-President, L. Douglas Todgham

Canadian Institute of Strategic Studies/Institut canadien d'études stratégiques (CISS) (1976)
Box 2321, #402, 2300 Yonge St., Toronto, ON M4P 1E4
416/322-8128, Fax: 416/322-8129, Toll Free: 1-800-831-5695, Email: ciss@inforamp.net
URL: http://www.ciss.ca
Executive Director, Alex Morrison
Director, Finance & Administration, Mark Larsen
Director, Media Relations, Jim Hanson
Director, Publications, Susan McNish
Publications: CISS Bulletin; McNaughton Papers
The Lester B. Pearson Canadian International Peacekeeping Training Centre: President, Alex Morrison; Vice-President, Tim Sparling, Cornwallis Park, PO Box 100, Clementsport, NS B0S 1E0, 902/638-8611, Fax: 902/638-8888

Canadian Institute for the Study of the Soviet Union & East European Countries (1982)
72 Elise Terrace, North York, ON M2R 2X1
416/250-0269, Fax: 416/250-0269
President, Dr. Roman Fin

Canadian Institute of Ukrainian Studies/Institut canadien d'études ukrainiennes (CIUS) (1976)
352 Athabasca Hall, University of Alberta, Edmonton, AB T6G 2E8
403/492-2972, Fax: 403/492-4967, Telex: 037-2979
Director, Dr. Zenon E. Kohut, Ph.D.
Publications: Journal of Ukrainian Studies; CIUS Newsletter, a.

Canadian Mathematical Society/Société mathématique du Canada (CMS) (1945)
#109, 577 King Edward St., PO Box 415, Stn A, Ottawa, ON K1N 6N5
613/562-5702, Fax: 613/565-1539, Email: exsmc@acadvm1.uottawa.ca
URL: http://camel.cecm.sfu.ca/index.html
Executive Director/Secretary, G.P. Wright
Publications: Canadian Journal of Mathematics; Canadian Mathematical Bulletin; Crux Mathematicorum; C.M.S. Notes

Canadian Mediterranean Institute/Institut canadien de la Méditerranée (CMI) (1980)
113 Osgoode St., Ottawa, ON K1N 6S1
613/238-2207, Fax: 613/238-6115
President, Dr. David Anido
Assistant to President, Anouk Guillaume
Publications: Bulletin
Affiliates: Canadian Institute in Egypt; Canadian Archaeological Institute at Athens; Canadian Academic Centre in Italy

Canadian Mining Industry Research Organization (CMIRO)
c/o Iron Ore Company of Canada, 100, rue Retty, Sept-Îles, PQ G4R 3E1
418/968-7502, Fax: 418/968-7108
Chairman, Derek Rance

Canadian Nautical Research Society/Société canadienne pour la recherche nautique (CNRS) (1982)
151A Second Ave., PO Box 21076, Ottawa, ON K1S 5N1
President, Faye Kert
Secretary, Prof. Lewis Fischer, 709/737-8424, Fax: 709/737-4569, Email: lfisher@kean.ucs.mun.ca
Publications: Argonauta; The Northern Mariner/Le Marin du Nord, m.
Affiliates: International Commission for Maritime History

Canadian Numismatic Research Society (CNRS) (1963)
PO Box 1351, Victoria, BC V8W 2W7
250/385-9703, Fax: 250/598-5539
Secretary, R. Greene
Publications: Transactions

Canadian Operational Research Society/Société canadienne de recherche opérationelle (CORS)
PO Box 2225, Stn D, Ottawa, ON K1P 5W4
URL: http://www.ncf.carleton.ca/freeport/prof.assoc/cors/menu
Secretary, Dr. Sia Kahkeshan
Publications: INFOR - Information Systems & Operational Research

Canadian Philosophical Association/Association canadienne de philosophie (1962)
Dept. of Philosophy, UQAM, 400, rue Ste-Catherine est, Montréal, PQ H2X 3J8
514/987-3253, Fax: 514/987-8721
URL: http://www.uwindsor.ca/cpa
Présidente, Josiane Boulad Ayoub
Publications: Dialogue
Affiliates: Fédération internationale des sociétés de philosophie

Canadian Quaternary Association
NBDNR Geological Surv., PO Box 6000, Fredericton, NB E3B 5H1
506/453-7947, Fax: 506/444-4176
Sec.-Treas., Toon Pronk
Publications: Newsletter/Bulletin; Géographie physique et quaternaire, 3 pa

Canadian Research Institute for the Advancement of Women/Institut canadien de recherches sur les femmes (CRIAW) (1976)
#408, 151 Slater St., Ottawa, ON K1P 5H3
613/563-0681, Fax: 613/563-0682, Email: ak976@freenet.carleton.ca
Executive Director, Linda Clippingdale
Publications: CRIAW Newsletter; The CRIAW Papers; Feminist Perspectives; Resources for Research & Action
Affiliates: National Action Committee on the Status of Women

Canadian Research Management Association/Association canadienne de la gestion de la recherche (CRMA) (1963)
#1004, 130 Albert St., Ottawa, ON K1P 5G4
613/567-9049, Fax: 613/567-4562
Executive Director, Dr. Clem W. Bowman, 519/869-8610, Fax: 519/869-6840
Secretary, Debbie Pelletier
Publications: CRMA Newsletter

Canadian Society for Aesthetics/Société canadienne d'esthétique (CSA) (1984)
Dept. of Theatre & Drama, University of Winnipeg, 515 Portage Ave., Winnipeg, MB R3B 2E9
204/786-9292, Fax: 204/453-5680
Co-President, Douglas Arrell
Co-President, Manon Regimbald

Canadian Society for Eighteenth-Century Studies/Société canadienne d'étude du dix-huitième siècle (CSECS) (1969)
Dept. of English, Wilfred Laurier University, Waterloo, ON N2L 3C5
519/884-0710, ext.3581, Fax: 519/884-8854
President, Peter Sabor
Sec.-Treas., Eleanor Ty
Publications: Bulletin; Man & Nature/L'Homme et la Nature, a.
Affiliates: International Society for Eighteenth-Century Studies

The Canadian Society for Mesopotamian Studies/La Société canadienne des études mésopotamiennes (CSMS) (1980)
4 Bancroft Ave., 4th Fl., Toronto, ON M5S 1A1
416/978-4531, Fax: 416/978-5294
Administrator, Linda Wilding
President, T. Cuyler Young, Jr.
Sec.-Treas., Ralph E. Warren
Publications: Bulletin of the CSMS
Affiliates: Canadian Mediterranean Institute; Royal Inscriptions of Mesopotamia Project

Canadian Society of Patristic Studies/Association canadienne des études patristiques (CSPS) (1975)
Vancouver School of Theology, 6000 Long Dr., Vancouver, BC V6T 1L4
604/228-9031, Fax: 604/228-0189
President, Prof. Harry O. Maier
Secretary, Patrick T.R. Gray
Treasurer, Andrius Valecius
Publications: The Bulletin; Sciences Religieuses/Studies in Religion
Affiliates: Canadian Corporation for the Study of Religion

Canadian Sociology & Anthropology Association/Société canadienne de sociologie et d'anthropologie (CSAA) (1966)
1455, boul de Maisonneuve ouest, Montréal, PQ H3G 1M8
514/848-8780, Fax: 514/848-4539, Email: csaa@vax2.concordia.ca
Sec.-Treas., Suzanne Dubé
Publications: The Canadian Review of Sociology & Anthropology/La Revue canadienne de sociologie et d'anthropologie; Society/Société, 3 pa

Canadian Steel Industry Research Association/Association pour la recherche dans l'industrie sidérurgique canadienne (CSIRA) (1978)
#1425, 50 O'Connor St., Ottawa, ON K1P 6L2
613/238-6049, Fax: 613/238-1832
Chairman, M. Kostic

Canadian Technion Society (1945)
Technion - Israel Institute of Technology
#206, 970 Lawrence Ave. West, Toronto, ON M6A 3B6
416/789-4545, Fax: 416/789-0255, Toll Free: 1-800-935-8864
National Executive Director, Jerry Enchin
Executive Director, Cheryl Koperwas

Cancer Research Society Inc./Société de recherche sur le cancer inc. (CRS) (1945)
#2332, 1, Place Ville Marie, Montréal, PQ H3B 3M5
514/861-9227, Fax: 514/861-9220
Executive Director, Ivy Steinberg
President/CEO, Flora Caplan
Vice-President, Jean-Jacques Gagnon
Treasurer, William Epstein, CA
Secretary, Jack Engels
Publications: The Recorder

Centre for Research-Action on Race Relations (CRARR)
#801, 3465, Côte-des-Neiges, Montréal, PQ H3H 1T7
514/939-3342, Fax: 514/939-9763
Executive Director, Fo Niemi
Publications: Newsletter

Centre for Research on Latin America & The Caribbean (CERLAC) (1978)
240 York Lanes, York University, 4700 Keele St., North York, ON M3J 1P3
416/736-5237, Fax: 416/736-5737, Email: cerlac@yorku.ca
Director, Prof. Ricardo Grinsdun
Deputy Director, Prof. Patrick Taylor
Publications: CERLAC News
Affiliates: Canadian Association for Latin American & Caribbean Studies; Counterpoint: A Resource Centre for Global Analyses; Canada-Caribbean-Central America Policy Alternatives; Development Education Centre; International Council for Adult Education; Jesuit Centre for Social Faith & Justice; Latin American Working Group; OXFAM-Canada; Inter-Church Committee on Human Rights in Latin America; Centre for Caribbean Dialogue; Centre for Spanish Speaking People

Classical Association of Canada/Société canadienne des études classiques (1946)
Dept. of Classics, University of Winnipeg, Winnipeg, MB R3B 2E9
204/786-9343
URL: http://137.122.12.15/Docs/Societies/ClassAc/Classic.Assoc.html
President, Andre Daviault
Secretary, Ivan Cohen
Treasurer, Craig Cooper
Publications: Phoenix; Classical Views, 3 pa
Affiliates: Canadian Federation for the Humanities

Commission canadienne pour la théorie des machines et des mécanismes/Canadian Committee for the Theory of Machines & Mechanisms (CCToMM) (1993)
Université Laval, Génie Mécanique, Ste-Foy, PQ G1K 7P4
418/656-3474, Téléc: 418/656-7415, Courrier électronique: cctomm@gmc.ulaval.ca
Secrétaire Général, Clément Gosselin
Président, Louis Cloutier
Publications: Bulletin de la CCToMM

Forest Engineering Research Institute of Canada/Institut canadien de recherches en génie forestier (FERIC) (1974)
580, boul Saint-Jean, Pointe Claire, PQ H9R 3J9
514/694-1140, Fax: 514/694-4351
President/CEO, Pierre Y. Bourdages
Sec.-Treas., Pierre Giguère

Affiliates: International Union of Forest Research Organizations; Canadian Pulp & Paper Association; Pulp & Paper Research Institute of Canada
Eastern Division: Manager, D.Y. Guimier, 580, boul Saint-Jean, Pointe Claire, PQ H9R 3J9, 514/694-1140, Téléc: 514/694-4351
Western Division: Manager, Western Division, Alex W.J. Sinclair, 2601 East Mall, Vancouver, BC V6T 1Z4, 604/228-1555, Fax: 604/228-0999

Great Lakes Institute for Environmental Research (GLIER) (1981)
University of Windsor, 304 Sunset Ave., Windsor, ON N9B 3P4
519/253-4232, Fax: 519/971-3616
Director, G.D. Haffner

Humanist Association of Canada/Association humaniste du Canada (HAC) (1968)
PO Box 3736, Stn C, Ottawa, ON K1Y 4J8
613/739-9569, Fax: 613/738-1462, Email: hac@magi.com
URL: http://magi.com/~hac/hac.html
President, H. Ernie Schreiber
Publications: HAC Newsletter
Affiliates: International Humanist & Ethical Union (Netherlands)

Humanities Association of Canada/Association canadienne des humanités (1951)
Faculty of Philosophy, F.A. Savard Pavillion, Laval University, CP 2208, Succ Terminus, Québec, PQ G1K 7P4
418/656-2244, Fax: 418/656-7267
President, Henri-Paul Cunningham
Sec.-Treas., Thomas Reisner

Institut national de la recherche scientifique/National Scientific Research Institute (INRS)
#640, 2600, boul Laurier, CP 7500, Ste-Foy, PQ G1V 4C7
418/654-2500, Téléc: 418/654-2525
Directeur général, Alain Soucy
Information et relations publiques, Diane Lespérance
Publications: INRS - Nouvelles

Institute for Research on Public Policy/Institut de recherches politiques (1972)
#200, 1470, rue Peel, Montréal, PQ H3A 1T1
514/985-2461, Fax: 514/985-2559
President/CEO, Monique Jérome-Forget
Executive Director, Marye Bos
Publications: Policy Options

Institute for Robotics & Intelligent Systems/Institut de robotique et d'intelligence des systèmes (IRIS) (1990)
PRECARN Associates Inc., #300, 30 Colonnade Rd., Nepean, ON K2E 7J6
613/727-9576, Fax: 613/727-5672, Email: johnston@precarn.ca
URL: http://www.precarn.ca
Network Manager, Paul Johnston
Publications: Intellinet
Affiliates: PRECARN Associates

Institute of Speculative Philosophy (1988)
PO Box 913, Stn B, Ottawa, ON K1P 5P9
613/594-5881, Fax: 613/594-3952
President, Dr. Francis K. Peddle
Publications: Eleutheria

Institute for Stuttering Treatment & Research (ISTAR) (1986)
8220 - 114 St., 3rd Fl., Edmonton, AB T6G 2P4
403/492-2619, Fax: 403/492-8457
Acting Executive Director, Dr. Lois Stanford
Chairman, Helen Ilott

Office Manager, Shirley Vanaelst
Publications: Institute News; The Other Side of the Block; Stuttering: Current Status of Theory & Therapy; A Retrospective Look at Stuttering Therapy; Long-Term Results of an Intensive Therapy Program for Adult & Adolescent Stutterers
Affiliates: Alberta Stutterers Association; The University of Alberta; Canadian Association of Speech & Language Pathology & Audiology; American Speech & Hearing Association

Institute of Urban Studies (IUS) (1969)
University of Winnipeg, 346 Portage Ave., Winnipeg, MB R3C 0C3
204/982-1140, Fax: 204/943-4695, Email: ius@coned.uwinnipeg.ca
Director, Tom Carter
Administrative Officer, Mary Ann Beavis
Publications: Canadian Journal of Urban Research

International Council for Canadian Studies/Conseil international d'études canadiennes (ICCS) (1981)
2 Daly Ave., Ottawa, ON K1N 6E2
613/789-7834, Fax: 613/232-2495, Telex: 053-3906
Executive Director, Alain Guimont
President, Daniel Ben-Natan
Communications Officer, Louise Poulin
Librarian, Linda Jones
Publications Officer, Guy Leclair
Director of Administration & Programs, Gaëtan Vallières
Program Officer, Diane Cyr
Publications: ICCS Contact; International Journal of Canadian Studies, s-a.; The International Canadianist, bi-m.; Canada: A Reader's Guide; Foreign Publications & Theses
Affiliates: Association for Canadian Studies in Australia & New Zealand; Association for Canadian Studies in China; Association for Canadian Studies in German-Speaking Countries; Association for Canadian Studies in Ireland; Association for Canadian Studies in The Netherlands; Association for Canadian Studies in the US; British Association for Canadian Studies; French Association for Canadian Studies; Indian Association for Canadian Studies; Israel Association for Canadian Studies; Italian Association for Canadian Studies; Japanese Association for Canadian Studies; Nordic Association for Canadian Studies; Soviet Association for Canadian Studies; Spanish Association for Canadian Studies; American Council for Québec Studies; Centre d'études canadiennes in Belgium; Association for Canadian Studies in Venezuela; Brazilian Association for Canadian Studies; Korean Association for Canadian Studies; Mexican Association for Canadian Studies

International Council for Central & East European Studies (Canada)/Conseil international d'études centrales et est-européennes (Canada) (ICCEES) (1974)
Dept. of Political Science, Glendon College, York University, 2275 Bayview Ave., Toronto, ON M4N 3M6
416/736-2100, ext.88327, Fax: 416/487-6728, Email: gl250114@venus.yorku.ca
Secretary, Prof. Stanislav J. Kirschbaum
President, Prof. Ferdinand J.M. Fledbrugge
Publications: International Newsletter
Affiliates: American Association for the Advancement of Slavic Studies; Association hellénique d'études Slaves; Associazione Italiana degli Slavisti; Australasian Association for the Study of the Socialist Countries; Australia & New Zealand Slavists' Association; British Association for Soviet, Slavonic & East European Studies; Canadian Association of Slavists; Centre Belge D'Études Slaves; Deutsche

Gesellschaft für Osteuropakunde; Dutch Slavists' Association; Finnish Institute for Russian & East European Studies; Institut d'études slaves; Irish Slavists' Association; Israeli Association of Slavic & East European Studies; Japan Institute of International Affairs; Korean Association for Slavic Studies; Korean Institute of International Studies; Nordic Committee for Soviet & East European Studies

International Geographical Union - Canadian Committee
Dept. of Geography, University of Victoria, PO Box 3050, Victoria, BC V8W 3P5
506/721-7340
Secretary, Larry McCann

Leukemia Research Fund of Canada (LRF) (1955)
#220, 1110 Finch Ave. West, Toronto, ON M3J 2T2
416/661-9541, Fax: 416/661-7799, Toll Free: 1-800-268-2144
Executive Director, Mona Forrest
National Spokesperson, Bob Rae
Affiliates: Canadian Centre for Philanthropy

Microelectronic Devices, Circuits & Systems for Ultra Large Scale Integration (ULSI) (1990)
Micronet
University of Toronto, 10 King's College Circle, Toronto, ON M5S 1A4
416/978-1638, Fax: 416/978-4516
URL: http://www.utoronto.ca/micronet
Program Leader, Dr. C.A.T. Salama
Network Manager, Dr. Zahir Parpia, 416/978-6998, Email: zahir@vrg.utoronto.ca
Publications: Micronet News

The M.S.I. Foundation (1971)
Medical Services Incorporated
#1220, 10405 Jasper Ave., Edmonton, AB T5J 3N4
403/421-7532, Fax: 403/425-4467
Chairperson, Dr. L.H. Le Riche
Associate Secretary, M. Yates
Publications: The M.S.I. Foundation Annual Report

NeuroScience Network/Réseau NeuroSciences (1990)
Room L7-132, 1650, av Cedar, Montréal, PQ H3G 1A4
514/934-8290, Fax: 514/934-8216, Email: mc93@musica.mcgill.ca
URL: http://www.cns.ucalgary.ca/nce
Network Manager, Warren Bull

Ontario Centres of Excellence
2938 Dundas St. West, PO Box 70681, Toronto, ON M6P 4E7
416/767-3389, Email: oce@itrc.on.ca

Ontario Public Interest Research Group/Groupe de recherche d'intérêt public de l'Ontario (OPIRG)
#201, 455 Spadina Ave., Toronto, ON M5S 2G8
416/978-7770
Provincial Coordinator, Andrea Calver

Protein Engineering Network of Centres of Excellence/Réseau des centres d'excellence en génie protéique (PENCE) (1990)
University of Alberta, 750 Heritage Medical Research Centre, Edmonton, AB T6G 2S2
250/492-8851, Fax: 250/492-6995
URL: http://diadem.biochem.ualberta.ca/pence.html
Network Manager, Stephen Herst, Email: stephen.herst@ualberta.ca
Manager, Business Development, James Chivers-Wilson, Email: james.chivers-wilson@ualberta.ca

Pulp & Paper Research Institute of Canada/Institut canadien de recherches sur les pâtes et papiers (PAPRICAN) (1925)
570, boul St-Jean, Pointe Claire, PQ H9R 3J9
514/630-4100, Fax: 514/630-4105
President/CEO, Dr. Joseph D. Wright
Affiliates: Canadian Pulp & Paper Association

The Royal Canadian Geographical Society/Société géographique royale du Canada (RCGS) (1929)
39 McArthur Ave., Vanier, ON K1L 8L7
613/745-4629, Fax: 613/744-0947
Executive Director, Louise Maffett
President, Dr. Denis St-Onge
Publications: Canadian Geographic

Royal Canadian Institute (RCI) (1849)
196 Carleton St., Toronto, ON M5A 2K8
416/928-2096
URL: http://www.psych.utoronto.ca/people/vislab/rci.html
President, Veronika Huta

The Royal Society of Canada/La Société royale du Canada (RSC) (1882)
National Academy of Canada
#308, 225 Metcalfe St., Ottawa, ON K2P 1P9
613/991-6990, Fax: 613/991-6996, Email: adminrsc@rsc.ca
URL: http://library.utoronto.ca/www/rsc/
President, Robert H. Haynes
Publications: Présentations; Transactions/Mémoires; Delta, q.; Proceedings/Délibérations, a.; Profile/Profil; ACTION: Newsletter of the Canadian National Committee, s-a.

The Royal Society for the Encouragement of Arts, Manufactures & Commerce (RSA) (1754)
8 John Adam St., London WC2N 6EZ UK
011/44-71-930-5115, Fax: 011/44-71-839-5805
Director, Peter Cowling
President, H.R.H. The Prince Philip, Duke of Edinburgh, KG, KT
Publications: RSA Journal
Atlantic Provinces Chapter: President, Prof. Ronald C. Gilkie, 1146 Studley Ave., Halifax, NS B3H 3R7

Society of Applied Anthropology in Canada/Société d'anthropologie appliquée du Canada
Département d'Anthropologie, Université de Montréal, CP 6128, Succ A, Montréal, PQ H3C 3J7
President, Gilles Bibeau

Society for the Study of Egyptian Antiquities (SSEA) (1969)
PO Box 578, Stn P, Toronto, ON M5S 2T1
416/978-6838, Fax: 416/978-5294
President, Taber M. James
Secretary, Patricia Paice
Publications: SSEA Newsletter; SSEA Journal, a.
Affiliates: Canadian Institute in Egypt; Canadian Mediterranean Institute

Theosophical Society in Canada (1919)
RR#3, Burks Falls, ON P0A 1C0
705/382-6012
General Secretary, Dr. David Gardner
Publications: The Canadian Theosophist

Traffic Injury Research Foundation of Canada/Fondation de recherches sur les blessures de la route au Canada (TIRF) (1963)
#200, 171 Nepean St., Ottawa, ON K2P 0B4
613/238-5235, Fax: 613/238-5292, Email: tirf@sonetis.com
Executive Director, Dr. Herbert M. Simpson
President, S.H. Van Houten

Director, Information & Communication, D.J. Beirness

RESOURCE MANAGEMENT see ENVIRONMENTAL

RESTAURANTS & FOOD SERVICES

Association des fournisseurs d'hôtels et restaurants inc./Hotel & Restaurant Suppliers Association Inc. (AFHR) (1936)
2435, rue Guénette, Saint Laurent, PQ H4R 2E9
514/334-5161, Téléc: 514/334-1279, Ligne sans frais: 1-800-567-2347
Directeur administratif, Jean Cyr
Président, Guy Lussier
Secrétaire, Jean-Pierre Verreault
Trésorier, Raymond Mayrand
Publications: Le Fournisseur

Association des restaurateurs du Québec/Québec Restaurant Association (ARQ) (1938)
2485, rue Sherbrooke est, Montréal, PQ H2K 1E8
514/527-9801, Téléc: 514/527-3066, Ligne sans frais: 1-800-463-9801
Vice-président directeur général, Bernard Fortin
Publications: ARQ Info

Canadian Culinary Institute (CCI)
#202, 738A Bank St., Ottawa, ON K1S 3V4
613/563-2433, Fax: 613/563-2317, Email: essence@ottawa.net
Chairman, Fred Malley, CCC
Affiliates: The educational arm of the Canadian Federation of Chefs & Cooks

Canadian Federation of Chefs & Cooks/La Fédération canadienne des chefs et cuisiniers (CFCC) (1963)
#202, 738A Bank St., Ottawa, ON K1S 3V4
613/563-2433, Fax: 613/563-2317, Email: essence@ottawa.net
President, Guy Ethier
Coordinator, National Office, Claire Forster
Publications: Essence; Chefs Directory, biennial
Affiliates: Canadian Culinary Institute; World Association of Cooks Societies

Canadian Restaurant & Foodservices Association/Association canadienne des restaurateurs et des services alimentaires (CRFA) (1944)
316 Bloor St. West, Toronto, ON M5S 1W5
416/923-8416, Fax: 416/923-1450, Toll Free: 1-800-387-5649, Email: 102447.3104@compuserve.com
President, Douglas C. Needham
Senior Vice-President, David Harris
Vice-President, Government Affairs, Michael Ferrabee
Chairman, Paul Hollands
Publications: CRFA News; Membership Directory, a.; Foodservice Facts Magazine
Affiliates: Canadian Hospitality Foundation

ALBERTA RESTAURANT & FOODSERVICES ASSOCIATION (ARFA) (1977)
10085 - 166 St., Edmonton, AB T5P 4Y1
403/444-9494, Fax: 403/481-8727, Toll Free: 1-800-461-9762
President, Elizabeth Kuhnel
Publications: Provincial ARFA News; Alberta Restaurant News, q.; ARFA Membership Directory, a.

MANITOBA RESTAURANT & FOODSERVICES ASSOCIATION (MRFA)
#201, 698 Corydon Ave., Winnipeg, MB R3M 0X9
204/475-6660, Fax: 204/475-6661
Executive Director, Michael Moore

ORGANIZATIONS — RETAIL TRADE

NEWFOUNDLAND RESTAURANT & FOODSERVICES ASSOCIATION
PO Box 402, Mount Pearl, NF A1N 2C4
709/753-2380
President, Brenda Power

NOVA SCOTIA RESTAURANT & FOODSERVICES ASSOCIATION
5411 Spring Garden Rd., Halifax, NS B3J 1G1
902/429-5343, Fax: 902/425-1025
Managing Director, Denise Burns

ONTARIO RESTAURANT ASSOCIATION (ORA) (1931)
#1201, 121 Richmond St. West, Toronto, ON M5H 2K1
416/359-0533, Fax: 416/359-0531, Toll Free: 1-800-668-8906
President, Paul Oliver
Publications: Buyers Guide Directory; Maincourse

PRINCE EDWARD ISLAND RESTAURANT & FOODSERVICES ASSOCIATION
PO Box 742, Charlottetown, PE C1A 7L3
902/963-2382, Fax: 902/963-2382
President, Dale Larkin

QUICK SERVICE RESTAURANT COUNCIL/CONSEIL DES RESTAURANTS À SERVICE RAPIDE (QSRC) (1991)
316 Bloor St. West, Toronto, ON M5S 1W5
416/923-8416, Fax: 416/923-1450, Toll Free: 1-800-387-5649

RESTAURANT & FOODSERVICES ASSOCIATION OF BRITISH COLUMBIA & THE YUKON (RFABCY) (1977)
#140, 475 West Georgia St., Vancouver, BC V6B 4H9
604/669-2239, Fax: 604/669-6175, Toll Free: 1-800-663-4482
URL: http://www.yes.net/RFABCY/
Executive Director, Earl Manning, CAE
Publications: Newsletter

SASKATCHEWAN RESTAURANT & FOODSERVICES ASSOCIATION (SRFA) (1979)
PO Box 1545, Saskatoon, SK S7K 3R5
306/665-1444, Fax: 306/665-1444
Executive Director, Michael van Grondelle
Publications: The Association Reporter

Institute of Culinary Art & Technology
3 Kitsilano Cres., Richmond Hill, ON L4C 5A4
905/884-9380
Chancellor, Maurice Prior

Société des chefs, cuisiniers et patissiers du Québec (SCCPQ) (1953)
3577, rue Ste-Catherine est, Montréal, PQ H1W 2E6
514/528-1083, Téléc: 514/528-1037
Président, Denis Paquin, 514/463-3139
Secrétaire, Normand Corriveau
Agent Permanent, Mario Gringras
Publications: Le Pot-au-feu

RETAIL TRADE

Association des détaillants en alimentation du Québec/Québec Food Retailers' Association (ADA) (1955)
CP 455, Succ Place-du-Parc, Montréal, PQ H2W 2N9
514/982-0104, Téléc: 514/849-3021, Ligne sans frais: 1-800-363-3923
Président/Directeur général, Michel Gadbois
Directeur, Affaires publiques et Communications, Jacques Robert Blanchette
Publications: Bulletin Express; Info-Stats, 10 fois par an

Association nationale des distributeurs de tabac et de confiserie/National Association of Tobacco & Confectionery Distributors (ANDTC) (1955)
#504, 3090, boul le Carrefour, Laval, PQ H7T 2J7
514/682-6556, Téléc: 514/682-6732, Ligne sans frais: 1-888-686-2823, Courrier électronique: natcd@atmail.com
Vice-président exécutif, Luc A. Dumulong
Publications: Contact

Canadian Association of Chain Drug Stores (CACDS) (1995)
#600, 210 Dundas St. West, Toronto, ON M5G 2E8
416/348-8595, Fax: 416/977-8020
President & CEO, Sherry E. Porter

Canadian Gift & Tableware Association/Association canadienne de cadeaux et d'accessoires de table (1976)
#301, 265 Yorkland Blvd., North York, ON M2J 1S5
416/497-5771, Fax: 416/497-8487, Toll Free: 1-800-750-1967
President, Jack Shand
Publications: CGTA Retail News

Canadian Office Machine Dealers Association/Association canadienne des distributeurs de machine de bureau (COMDA) (1942)
#204, 3464 Kingston Rd., Scarborough, ON M1M 1R5
416/261-1607, Fax: 416/261-1679
Executive Director, Don Vickery
Publications: COMDA Key
Affiliates: National Office Machine Dealers Association

Canadian Office Products Association/Association canadienne des produits de bureau (COPA) (1933)
#911, 1243 Islington Ave., Toronto, ON M8X 1Y9
416/239-2737, Fax: 416/239-1553
President, James Preece
Publications: COPA Conversation
Affiliates: Retail Council of Canada; Canadian Association of Exposition Managers; International Federation of Office Stationary Associations; International Stationary Press Association

Canadian Retail Hardware Association/Association canadienne des détaillants en quincaillerie (CRHA) (1954)
6800 Campobello Rd., Mississauga, ON L5N 2L8
905/821-3470, Fax: 905/821-8946, Toll Free: 1-800-268-3965, Email: crha@crha.com
Executive Director, Thomas M. Ross
Director, Administration, Maura Bella
Director, Membership Services & Legislative Affairs, Linda Nolet
Publications: Reporter; Journaliste, 10 pa; Wage & Benefit Survey
Affiliates: International Federation of Ironmongers Association - Zurich; National Retail Hardware Association - USA

Canadian Sporting Goods Association/Association canadienne d'articles de sport (CSGA) (1945)
#510, 455, rue Saint-Antoine ouest, Montréal, PQ H2Z 1J1
514/393-1132, Fax: 514/393-9513
President & CEO, Yves Paquette
Publications: Action
Affiliates: World Federation of the Sporting Goods Industry

Conseil québécois du commerce de détail (CQCD)
#1000, 550, rue Sherbrooke ouest, Montréal, PQ H3A 1B9
514/842-6681, Téléc: 514/842-7627
Directeur général, Gaston Lafleur

Direct Sellers Association
#3, 100 West Beaver Creek Rd., Richmond Hill, ON L4B 1H4
905/886-8555, Fax: 905/885-8102
Contact, Ross Creber

Gift Packaging & Greeting Card Association of Canada/Association canadienne du papier cadeau et de la carte de voeux (GPGCA)
1407 Military Trail, Scarborough, ON M1C 1A7
416/281-8147
Chairman, Don Bichard
Vice-Chairman, M. Dionne
Office Manager, Clancy Delbarre

Independent Toy Store Association of Canada
c/o Retail Council of Canada, #600, 210 Dundas St. West, Toronto, ON M5G 2E8
416/598-4684
Director, Marketing & Communications, Judy Johnson

National Spa & Pool Institute of Canada (NSPI) (1958)
#5, 7370 Bramalea Rd., Mississauga, ON L5S 1N6
905/676-1591, Fax: 905/676-1598, Toll Free: 1-800-879-7066
Executive Director, Nancy Lumb
Publications: NSPI of Canada Report

Retail Council of Canada/Le Conseil canadien du commerce de détail (RCC) (1963)
#1210, 121 Bloor St. West, Toronto, ON M4W 3M5
416/922-6678, Fax: 416/922-8011
President/CEO, Diane J. Brisebois, CAE
Senior Vice-President, Peter Woolford
Senior Vice-President, Jill Birch
Publications: Canadian Retailer

Retail Merchants Association of Canada (Alberta) Inc. (RMA) (1896)
#205, 11125 - 107 Ave. NW, Edmonton, AB T5H 0X9
403/428-6781, Fax: 403/428-6785
Executive Director, Linda S. Gagnon
Publications: RMA News
Affiliates: Retail Council of Canada

Retail Merchants Association of Canada, Inc. (RMA) (1910)
1780 Birchmount Rd., Scarborough, ON M1P 2H8
416/291-7903, Fax: 416/291-5635
President, Sean McMahon
Publications: Retail Merchants News

Retail Merchants' Association of BC (1911)
1758 - 8th Ave. West, Vancouver, BC V6J 1V6
604/736-0368, Fax: 604/736-3154
President, Mark Startup, CAE
Publications: BC Retailer

RETIREES see SENIOR CITIZENS

SAFETY & ACCIDENT PREVENTION
see also Emergency Response

Alberta Safety Council (1946)
#201, 10526 Jasper Ave., Edmonton, AB T5J 1Z7
403/428-7555, Fax: 403/428-7557
Executive Director, Eya Zariwny
Program Director, Mel Mottram
Publications: Safety Counsellor
Affiliates: Canada Safety Council; National Safety Council

Association of Canadian Fire Marshals & Fire Commissioners/L'Association canadienne des directeurs et commissaires des incendies (ACFM/FC) (1919)
2425 Don Reid Dr., Ottawa, ON K1H 1A4
613/736-6600, Fax: 613/736-0684
Sec.-Treas., Robert Kearney
Publications: Fire Losses in Canada

Association for Canadian Registered Safety Professionals/Association des professionnels en securité agréés du Canada (ACRSP) (1976)
6519B Mississauga Rd., Mississauga, ON L5N 1A6
905/567-7198, Fax: 905/567-7191
Chairman, Renzo Dalla Via
Executive Secretary, Peter Fletcher
Publications: Governor's Table

Association des chefs de service d'incendie du Québec/Québec Fire Chief Association (ACSIQ) (1968)
327, rue de Rouville, Beloeil, PQ J3G 1X1
514/464-6413, Téléc: 514/467-6297
Secrétaire administrative, Nicole Aubin
Publications: L'Étincelle

Association paritaire pour la santé et la sécurité du travail - Administration provinciale
#10, 1220, boul Lebourgneuf, Québec, PQ G2K 2G4
418/624-4801, Téléc: 418/624-4858
Directrice générale, Collette Trudel

Association paritaire pour la santé et la sécurité du travail - Affaires municipales (APSAM) (1985)
#710, 715, carré Victoria, Montréal, PQ H2Y 2H7
514/849-8373, Téléc: 514/849-8873, Ligne sans frais: 1-800-465-1754
Directeur général, Alain Langlois
Publications: APSAM

Association paritaire pour la santé et la sécurité du travail - Affaires sociales
#950, 5100, rue Sherbrooke est, Montréal, PQ H1V 3R9
514/253-6871, Téléc: 514/253-1443, Ligne sans frais: 1-800-361-4528
Directeur général, Gilles Le Beau

Association paritaire pour la santé et la sécurité du travail - Construction (1985)
ASP Construction
#460, 7450, boul Les Galeries d'Anjou, Anjou, PQ H1M 3M3
514/355-6190, Téléc: 514/355-7861, Ligne sans frais: 1-800-361-2061
Directeur général, Paul Héroux
Publications: Prévenir aussi

Association paritaire pour la santé et la sécurité du travail - Habillement
#1060, 9310, boul Saint-Laurent, Montréal, PQ H2N 1N4
514/383-8317, Téléc: 514/383-7938
Directeur général, Christian Millet

Association paritaire pour la santé et la sécurité du travail - Imprimerie et activités connexes
#300, 405, rue de la Concorde, Montréal, PQ H3A 1J3
514/284-3318, Téléc: 514/284-9255
Directeur général, Claude Payette

Association paritaire pour la santé et la sécurité du travail - Industrie chimique/caoutchouc-plastique/pétrole
801, rue Sherbrooke est, 2e étage, Montréal, PQ H2L 4X9
514/524-6871
Directeur général, Laurent Gratton

Association paritaire pour la santé et la sécurité du travail - Mines (APSM) (1986)
#570, 979, av de Bourgogne, Ste-Foy, PQ G1W 2L4
418/653-1933, Téléc: 418/653-7726
Directeur général, Pierre Lapointe
Publications: Vi.Ta.Mine

Association paritaire pour la santé et la sécurité du travail - Produits en métal et électriques
#201, 6705, rue Jean-Talon est, St-Léonard, PQ H1S 1N2
514/253-5549, Téléc: 514/253-8193
Directeur général, Alain Langlois

Association paritaire pour la santé et la sécurité du travail - Services automobiles
#608, 455, rue Saint-Antoine ouest, Montréal, PQ H2Z 1J1
514/876-2886, Téléc: 514/876-4452
Directrice générale, Louis Lapres

Association paritaire pour la santé et la sécurité du travail - Textiles primaires
Préventex
#200, 2035, av Victoria, Saint-Lambert, PQ J4S 1H1
514/671-6925, Téléc: 514/671-9267
Directeur général, Jean-Marc Champoux

Association québécoise des pompiers volontaires et permanents (1978)
9401, rue St-Jean-Baptiste, CP 206, Ste-Scholastique, PQ J0N 1S0
514/478-8634
Président, André Ouellette
Publications: Info-Pompier

Association de santé et sécurité des industries de la forêt du Québec inc./Québec Logging Health & Safety Association Inc. (ASSIFQ) (1969)
#102, 1200, av Germain-des-Prés, Ste-Foy, PQ G1V 3M7
418/657-2268, Téléc: 418/651-4622
Président - directeur général, J. Aurèle St-Pierre
Secrétaire, Suzanne Lavoie
Publications: Action Prévention
Organisation(s) affiliée(s): Association canadienne des producteurs de pâtes et papiers; Association des industries de la forêt du Québec ltée; Canadian Safety Council; Conseil du patronat du Québec; Canadian Society of Safety Engineering

Association de santé et sécurité des pâtes et papiers du Québec inc./Québec Pulp & Paper Health & Safety Association Inc. (ASSPPQ) (1932)
#102, 1200, av Germain-des-Prés, Ste-Foy, PQ G1V 3M7
418/657-2267, Téléc: 418/651-4622
Président - directeur général, J. Aurèle St-Pierre
Secrétaire, Suzanne Lavoie
Publications: Action-Prévention
Organisation(s) affiliée(s): Association canadienne des producteurs de pâtes et papiers; Association des industries de la forêt du Québec ltée; Canadian Safety Council; Conseil du Patronat de Québec; Canadian Society of Safety Engineering

Association sectorielle - Fabrication d'équipement de transport et machines/Sectorial Association - Transportation Equipment & Machinery Manufacturing (ASFETM) (1983)
#202, 3565, rue Jarry est, Montréal, PQ H1Z 4K6
514/729-6961, Téléc: 514/729-8628, Ligne sans frais: 1-888-527-3386
Directeur général, J. Adolphe Roy, c.r.
Responsable des communications, Suzanne Ready
Publications: Santé Sécurité +

Association sectorielle transport entreposage (ASTE) (1983)
#401, 6555, boul Métropolitain est, St-Léonard, PQ H1P 3H3
514/955-0454, Téléc: 514/955-0449
Directeur général, Nicholas Lapierre

British Columbia Safety Council (1945)
8589 Baxter Place, Burnaby, BC V5A 4V7
604/420-4110, Fax: 604/420-9043
Executive Director, Bryan Lowes
President, Martin Pochurko
Publications: Safety First
Affiliates: Canada Safety Council; National Safety Council

Canada Safety Council/Conseil canadien de la sécurité (CSC) (1968)
1020 Thomas Spratt Place, Ottawa, ON K1G 5L5
613/739-1535, Fax: 613/739-1566
President, Émile-J. Thérien
General Manager, Programs, Jack A. Smith
Publications: Living Safety; Safety Canada, q.
Affiliates: Canadian Standards Association; Environment Canada; Operation Lifesaver National Committee; Advisory Committee on International Driver Improvement - USA; Motorcycle & Moped Industry Council; Transport Canada; Canadian General Standards Board; National Research Council of Canada; Transportation Research Council of Canada; Transportation Research Board - USA; Canadian Association of Chiefs of Police; Institute of Transportation Engineers; Urban Transportation Engineers Council; Council of Uniform Traffic Control Devices for Canada; Selective Traffic Enforcement Committee; Canadian Automobile Association; Canadian Cycling Association; International Occupational Safety & Health Information Centre

Canadian Alarm & Security Association/Association canadienne de l'alarme et de la sécurité (CANASA) (1977)
#201, 610 Alden Rd., Markham, ON L3R 9Z1
905/513-0622, Fax: 905/513-0624, Email: staff@canasa.com
URL: http://www.canasa.com
Communication Manager, Shayla Gunter
Publications: Show Buyer's Guide & Directory; Security Pulse, q..

Canadian Association of Fire Chiefs/Association canadienne des chefs de pompiers
#1, 2425 Don Reid Dr., Ottawa, ON K1H 1A4
613/736-0576, Fax: 613/736-0684
Executive Director, Marcel Ethier

Canadian Association of Poison Control Centres
Children's Hospital, 840 Sherbrook St., Winnipeg, MB R3A 1S1
204/787-2591, Fax: 204/787-4807
Contact, Milton Tenenbein
Affiliates: World Federation of Associations of Clinical Toxicology & Poison Control Centres

Canadian Automatic Sprinkler Association (CASA) (1961)
#302, 335 Renfrew Dr., Markham, ON L3R 9S9
905/477-2270, Fax: 905/477-3611
President, John Galt
Administrator, Lisa Miles
Publications: CASA Notes

Canadian Fire Safety Association (CFSA) (1971)
#310, 2175 Sheppard Ave. East, North York, ON M2J 1W8
416/492-9417, Fax: 416/491-1670, Email: taylor@interlog.com

Canadian Almanac & Directory 1997

2-160 ORGANIZATIONS — SAFETY & ACCIDENT PREVENTION

President, Alan Speed
1st Vice-President, Brian Murphy
Administrator, Diane Gaunt
Publications: CFSA Newsletter

Canadian Institute for Radiation Safety/Institut canadien de radioprotection (CAIRS) (1981)
#1106, 555 Richmond St. West, Toronto, ON M5V 3B1
416/504-6565, Fax: 416/504-3531, Email: cairs.info@cairs.ca
President/CEO, Dr. Fergal Nolan
Director, Science & Technology, Science & Technology, Dr. R. Moridi
National Laboratory & Centre for Public Education: Program Coordinator, Science & Technology, Brian Bjorndal, #102, 110 Research Dr., Saskatoon, SK S7N 3R3, 306/975-0566, Fax: 306/975-0494

Canadian Society for Industrial Security Inc./La société canadienne de la sûreté industrielle inc. (CSIS Inc.) (1957)
51 Lake Ave. West, Carleton Place, ON K7C 1L3
613/257-7203, Fax: 613/257-5383, Toll Free: 1-800-461-7748
National Sec.-Treas., L. Surrett
Publications: Forum

Canadian Society of Safety Engineering, Inc./ Société canadienne de la santé et de la sécurité, inc. (CSSE) (1972)
#602, 330 Bay St., Toronto, ON M5H 2S8
416/368-2230, Fax: 416/368-8429
URL: http://www.csse.org
Executive Manager, John H. Murphy
Publications: CSSE Contact
Affiliates: American Society of Safety Engineers

Centre patronal de santé et sécurité du travail du Québec (CPSSTQ) (1982)
#401, 666, rue Sherbrooke ouest, Montréal, PQ H3A 1E7
514/842-8401, Téléc: 514/842-9375
Présidente-directrice générale, Denise Turenne, p.d.g.
Directeur des communications, Denis Michaud
Publications: Convergence

Conseil des agences de sécurité et d'investigation du Québec inc. (CASIQ) (1966)
#400, 5115, av de Gaspé, Montréal, PQ H2T 3B7
514/273-8578, Téléc: 514/277-1922
Président, Louis J. Joron
Secrétaire-trésorier, Paul Guay, 514/935-2533, Téléc: 514/935-2996

Council of Private Investigators
#8, 130 Melford Dr., Scarborough, ON M1B 2X4
416/293-1479, Fax: 416/293-2390
President, Bud Davis
Publications: The Journal

Farm Safety Association Inc.
#22, 340 Woodlawn Rd. West, Guelph, ON N1H 1G8
519/823-5600, Fax: 519/823-8880
General Manager/Sec.-Treas., Jane Reed
Publications: Farmsafe

Federal Association of Security Officials/ Association fédérale des représentants de la sécurité (FASO) (1992)
PO Box 2384, Stn D, Ottawa, ON K1P 5W5
613/990-2615, Fax: 613/990-9077
Contact, Eva Plunkett
Publications: News & Views

Fire Prevention Canada Association
FIPRECAN
#1, 2425 Don Reid Dr., Ottawa, ON K1H 1A4

613/736-8131, Fax: 613/736-0684
Sec.-Treas., Marcel Ethier

Heavy Construction Association of Saskatchewan
1939 Elphinstone St., Regina, SK S4T 3N3
306/757-2646, Fax: 306/757-2798
Safety Director, Steve Wallace

Industrial Accident Prevention Association Ontario/Association pour la prévention des accidents industriels - Ontario (IAPA) (1917)
Eaton Tower, 250 Yonge St., 28th Fl., Toronto, ON M5B 2N4
416/506-8888, Fax: 416/506-8880, Toll Free: 1-800-669-4939
Executive Vice-President & General Manager, Maureen C. Shaw
Director, Field Operations, J.A. Pirie
Director, Sales & Marketing, D.J. Pedley
Director, Administration, M.J. Nichols
Volunteer Services Coordinator, Carolynn J. George
Publications: Accident Prevention; Update Releases; Impact, q.
Affiliates: Amalgamated Industry Groups - Ceramics & Stone Accident Prevention Association; Chemical Industries Accident Prevention Association; Food Products Accident Prevention Association; Grain, Feed & Fertilizer Accident Prevention Association; Leather, Rubber & Tanners Accident Prevention Association; Metal Trades Accident Prevention Association; Ontario Retail Accident Prevention Association; Printing Trades Accident Prevention Association; Textile & Allied Industries Accident Prevention Association; Woodworkers' Accident Prevention Association

Industrial Accident Victims Group of Ontario (IAVGO) (1975)
#203, 489 College St., Toronto, ON M6G 1A5
416/924-6477, Fax: 416/924-2472
Coordinator, Valerie Verah
Publications: Newsletter

Institut de recherche en santé et en sécurité de travail - Québec/Québec Occupational Health & Safety Research Institute (IRSST) (1980)
505, boul de Maisonneuve ouest, Montréal, PQ H3A 3C2
514/288-1551, Téléc: 514/288-0998, Télex: 055 61348
Directeur général, Jean Yves Savoie
Directeur des opérations, Alain Lajoie
Directrice des communications, Françoise Cloutier
Publications: Prévention au travail
Organisation(s) affiliée(s): International Occupational Safety & Health Information Centre

International Radiation Protection Association - Canadian Office/Association internationale de radioprotection - Bureau canadienne (IRPA)
#820, 2155, rue Guy, Montréal, PQ H3H 2R9
514/932-9552, Fax: 514/932-9419
President, Jean-Pierre Gauvin

Ligue de sécurité du Québec/Québec Safety League (1923)
2536, rue Lapierre, Lasalle, PQ J4B 6E6
514/641-9867, Téléc: 514/595-9110
Publications: Signal

Major Industrial Accidents Council of Canada/ Conseil canadien des accidents industriels majeurs (MIACC) (1987)
#600, 265 Carling Ave., Ottawa, ON K1S 2E1
613/232-4435, Fax: 613/232-4915, Email: miacc@globalx.net
Executive Director & CEO, Michael Salib, CAE
Chair, Allan G. Jones

Secretary, Paul A. Brazeau
Treasurer, David Egar
Director, Technical Programs, Roland Andersson
Publications: MIACC News; Life Cycle Management of Hazardous Substances

Manitoba Safety Council (1920)
#700, 213 Notre Dame Ave., Winnipeg, MB R3B 1N3
204/949-1085, Fax: 204/956-2897
Executive Director, Rita L. Roeland
Publications: Spotlight Safety

Mines Accident Prevention Association of Manitoba (1962)
#700, 305 Broadway, Winnipeg, MB R3C 3J7
204/942-2789, Fax: 204/943-4371
Executive Vice-President, Ed Huebert
Safety Director, B.D. Simoneau
Office Administrator, Sharon Schaubroeck

New Brunswick Safety Council Inc./Conseil de sécurité du Nouveau-Brunswick inc. (NBSC) (1967)
#204, 440 Wilsey Rd., Fredericton, NB E3B 7G5
506/458-8034, Fax: 506/444-0177
Business & Promotions Manager, Heather J. Wilson
President, Ron Carr
Affiliates: Canada Safety Council

Newfoundland Safety Council
354 Water St., PO Box 5123, St. John's, NF A1C 5V5
709/754-0210, Fax: 709/754-0010
President, Ray O'Neill
Affiliates: Canada Safety Council

Nova Scotia Safety Council (1958)
Bloomfield Centre, #207, 2786 Agricola St., Halifax, NS B3K 4E1
902/454-9621, Fax: 902/454-6027
Executive Director, Lloyd A. Mitchell
Publications: Safety Lines
Affiliates: Canada Safety Council

Ontario Association of Fire Chiefs (OAFC) (1973)
#502, 1530 Markham Rd., Scarborough, ON M1B 3G4
416/396-7786, Fax: 416/396-7665, Info Line: 416/396-7775
President, Chief Harold Tulk
Publications: OAFC Newsletter

Ontario Industrial Fire Protection Association (OIFPA) (1981)
193 James St. South, Hamilton, ON L8P 3A8
905/527-0700, Fax: 905/527-6254
President, J. David Wallace
Publications: OIPFA Newsletter

Ontario Natural Resources Safety Association/ Association ontarienne de sécurité au travail - ressources naturelles (ONRSA) (1994)
690 McKeown Ave., PO Box 2050, North Bay, ON P1B 9P1
705/474-7233, Fax: 705/472-5800, Toll Free: 1-800-850-5519, Email: onrsa@onlink.net
Executive Director, John J.G. Connors
Publications: Health & Safety Resource
Affiliates: Workplace Health & Safety Agency

Ontario Safety League/Ligue de sécurité du Ontario (1913)
#100, 21 Four Seasons Pl., Etobicoke, ON M9B 6J8
416/620-1720, Fax: 416/620-5977
President/General Manager, John L. Sharpe
Publications: Safety Update; Fleet Safety & Health, m.; In the Drivers Seat, m.; Let's Talk Safety, m.; Catalogue of Safety Material; Film & Video Catalogue
Affiliates: Canada Safety Council; Provincial Safety Leagues/Councils

Canadian Almanac & Directory 1997

Saskatchewan Professional Driver's Safety Council (SPDSC) (1947)
1335 Wallace St., Regina, SK S4N 3Z5
306/569-9696, Fax: 306/781-7066, Toll Free: 1-800-563-7623
Affiliates: Canadian Trucking Association; Saskatchewan Trucking Association

Saskatchewan Safety Council
445 Hoffer Dr., Regina, SK S4N 6E2
306/757-3197, Fax: 306/569-1907
Executive Director, Harley P. Toupin

Transportation Safety Association of Ontario/ Association de sécurité dans les transports de l'Ontario (TSAO) (1942)
#101, 555 Dixon Rd., Etobicoke, ON M9W 1H8
416/242-4771, Fax: 416/242-4714, Toll Free: 1-800-263-5016
Executive Director, William R. Boyle
Publications: Drivers' Newsletter; Bulletin, q.

SAFETY & FIRST AID see EMERGENCY RESPONSE

SCHOLARLY see EDUCATION

SCHOOLS see EDUCATION

SCIENTIFIC
see also Education; Health & Medical; Research & Scholarship

Alberta Society of Professional Biologists (ASPB) (1973)
#100, 4246 - 97 St., Edmonton, AB T6E 5Z9
403/434-5765, Fax: 403/435-7503, Email: aspb@ccinet.ab.ca
URL: http://www.ccinet.ab.ca/aspb
Executive Director, Bonnie Holtby
Publications: ASPB Newsletter

Arctic Institute of North America (AINA) (1945)
University of Calgary, 2500 University Dr. NW, Calgary, AB T2N 1N4
403/220-7515, Fax: 403/282-4609
Executive Director, Michael P. Robinson
Publications: Arctic; Information North, q.

Association de biodynamie du Québec inc./Bio-Dynamic Association of Québec Inc. (1979)
416, rang 4 ouest, Baie-des-Sables, PQ G0J 1C0
418/772-6574
Personne Ressource, Lise Beaulieu
Publications: Le Dynamot; Le Germe, trimestriel

Association des biologistes du Québec (ABQ) (1973)
#102, 1208, rue Beaubien est, Montréal, PQ H2S 1T7
514/279-7115
Coordonnatrice, Nadège Marion
Président, Robert Hamelin
Publications: In Vivo

Association des microbiologistes du Québec (AMQ)
#102, 1208, rue Beaubien est, Montréal, PQ H2S 1T7
514/279-7115, Téléc: 514/279-7115
Président, Pierre Ward

Association of Professional Biologists of British Columbia (APB) (1980)
#205, 733 Johnson St., Victoria, BC V8W 3C7
250/383-3306, Fax: 250/383-3306, Email: apbbc@tnet.net
Office Manager, Pat McLellan
Registrar, Linda Stordeur, R.P.Bio., 250/727-7612
President, Christopher J. Clement, R.P.Bio., A.Sc.T., R.P.F., 250/361-3979
Publications: BioLine; BioNews, bi-m.
Affiliates: BC Institute of Agrologists; Canadian Society of Professional Biologists; Professional Pest Management Association of BC; Association of BC Professional Foresters; Alberta Society of Professional Biologists; Association des biologistes du Québec; Association of Professional Engineers & Geoscientists; Applied Science Technologists & Technicians of BC

Association for the Promotion & Advancement of Science Education (APASE) (1983)
#200, 1111 Homer St., Vancouver, BC V6B 2Y1
604/687-8712, Fax: 604/687-8715, Email: cyoung@pinc.com
URL: http://www.swifty.com/apase/charlotte/apase!.html
Executive Director, Caroline Young
Environmental Education Projects, Jane McRae
New Media Projects, Nicholas Beatty
Project & Volunteer Manager, Interactive & Educator Workshops, Rani McInnes
Finance & Administration, Joan Powell
Publications: Diverse; Prism
Affiliates: Architectural Institute of BC; Association of Professional Engineers & Geoscientists; BC Teachers' Federation; Sierra Club Vancouver; CC West; SCWIST; BC Science Council

Atlantic Provinces Council on the Sciences/ Conseil des provinces atlantiques pour les sciences (APCS)
Memorial University of Newfoundland, PO Box 4200, St. John's, NF A1B 3X7
709/737-8918, Fax: 709/737-4569
Executive Director, Joan Atkinson

Canadian Association of Geoscience Companies (1990)
#643, 7305 Woodbine Ave., Markham, ON L3R 3V7
905/513-1444, Fax: 905/475-8616
Managing Director, Frank Bottos

Canadian Association of Palynologists/ Association canadienne des palynologues (CAP) (1978)
Dept. of Geology, Earth Sciences Centre, University of Toronto, 22 Russell St., Toronto, ON M5S 3B1
613/954-0355, Fax: 613/954-4724
URL: http://gpu.srv.ualberta.ca/~abeaudoi/cap/cap.html
President, Dr. Ian Campbell
President Elect, Dr. Rob Fensome
Sec.-Treas., Dr. Martin Head
CAP Councillor to IFPS, Dr. Julian Szeicz
Publications: CAP Newsletter
Affiliates: International Federation of Palynological Societies

Canadian Association of Physicists/Association canadienne des physiciens et physiciennes (CAP) (1945)
#903, 151 Slater St., Ottawa, ON K1P 5H3
613/237-3392, Fax: 613/238-1677, Email: cap@physics.carleton.ca
President, Dr. Paul Vincett
Executive Director, Francine M. Ford
Publications: Physics in Canada; Directory of Employers of Physicists; Careers in Physics
Affiliates: Chemical Institute of Canada; Canadian Organization of Medical Physicists; American Physical Society

Canadian Astronomical Society/Société canadienne d'astronomie (CASCA) (1971)
Département de Physique, Université de Montréal, Montréal, PQ H3C 3J7
514/343-2364, Fax: 514/343-2071, Email: casca@astro.umontreal.ca
Secretary, Serge Demers
Publications: Cassiopeia

Canadian Botanical Association/Association botanique du Canada (CBA) (1965)
Dept. of Botany, University of Guelph, #158, 50 Stone Rd. East, Guelph, ON N1G 2W1
519/824-4120, ext.2745, Fax: 519/767-1991
Past President, Dr. U. Posluszny
Publications: The Bulletin of CBA/ABC

Canadian College of Microbiologists
100 Richmond St. West, Toronto, ON M5H 3K6
416/777-0407

Canadian College of Physicists in Medicine/ Collège canadien des physiciens en médecine (CCPM) (1979)
11328 - 88 St., Edmonton, AB T5B 3P8
403/479-1110, Fax: 403/474-5894
Registrar, Alistair Baillie
Sec.-Treas., Karen Breitman
Publications: Canadian Medical Physics Newsletter
Affiliates: Canadian Organization of Medical Physicists

Canadian Committee of Scientists & Scholars/ Comité canadien des savants et scientifiques (CCSS) (1980)
Dept. of Physics, University of Toronto, 60 Saint George St., Toronto, ON M5S 1A7
416/978-5217, Fax: 416/978-7606, Email: fawcett@physics.utoronto.ca
Secretary, Eric Fawcett
President, John C. Polanyi
Vice-President, Ashok Vijh
Treasurer, Anton Kuerti

Canadian Congress of Neurological Sciences/ Congrès canadien des sciences neurologiques (CCNS)
906 - 12 Ave. SW, PO Box 4220, Stn C, Calgary, AB T2R 1K7
403/229-9544, Fax: 403/229-1661
Executive Director, Lucile Edwards
Publications: Canadian Journal of Neurological Sciences

Canadian Federation of Biological Societies/ Fédération canadienne des sociétés de biologie (CFBS) (1957)
#104, 1750 Courtwood Cres., Ottawa, ON K2C 2B5
613/225-8889, Fax: 613/225-9621, Email: cfbs@hpb.hwc.ca
Executive Director, Dr. Paul Hough
President, Dr. Judy Anderson
Publications: CFBS Newsletter

BIOPHYSICAL SOCIETY OF CANADA/LA SOCIÉTÉ DE BIOPHYSIQUE DU CANADA (BSC) (1985)
c/o Institute of Biodiagnostics, National Research Council, 435 Ellice Ave., Winnipeg, MB R3B 1Y6
204/984-5146, Fax: 204/984-6978
Secretary, Dr. Roxanne Deslauriers, 204/984-5146
President, Peter B. Canham, 519/661-3053
Publications: Biophysical Society of Canada Newsletter

Canadian Almanac & Directory 1997

ORGANIZATIONS — SCIENTIFIC

CANADIAN ASSOCIATION FOR ANATOMY, NEUROBIOLOGY & CELL BIOLOGY/ASSOCIATION CANADIENNE D'ANATOMIE, DE NEUROBIOLOGIE ET DE BIOLOGIE CELLULAIRE (CAANCB) (1956)
Dept. of Anatomy, University of Manitoba, 730 William Ave., Winnipeg, MB R3E 0W3
204/789-3796, Fax: 204/772-0622, Email: bruni@bldghsc.lanl.umanitoba.ca
President, Peter Haase
Publications: CAANCB/ACANBC Bulletin

CANADIAN PHYSIOLOGICAL SOCIETY/SOCIÉTÉ CANADIENNE DE PHYSIOLOGIE (CPS) (1935)
Dept. of Physiology, Medical Sciences Bldg., Univ. of Alberta, Edmonton, AB T6G 2H7
403/492-2620, Fax: 403/492-8915, Email: cheese@dean.med.ualberta.ca
Secretary, C.I. Cheeseman
Publications: Physiology Canada
Affiliates: International Union of Physiological Sciences; Canadian Journal of Physiology & Pharmacology

THE CANADIAN SOCIETY OF BIOCHEMISTRY & MOLECULAR BIOLOGY/LA SOCIÉTÉ CANADIENNE DE BIOCHIMIE ET BIOLOGIE MOLÉCULAIRE (1958)
Dept. of Biochemistry, University of Western Ontario, London, ON N6A 5C1
519/661-3060, Fax: 519/661-3175
Secretary, Dr. Eugene Reno Tustanoff
Publications: Biochemistry & Cell Biology; The Bulletin of the Canadian Biochemical Society, s-a.

CANADIAN SOCIETY FOR NUTRITIONAL SCIENCES/SOCIÉTÉ CANADIENNE DES SCIENCES DE LA NUTRITION
Dept. of Home Economics, Mount St. Vincent University, 166 Bedford Hwy., Halifax, NS B3M 2J6
902/443-4450, ext.248
Contact, Theresa Glanville

PHARMACOLOGICAL SOCIETY OF CANADA/SOCIÉTÉ DE PHARMACOLOGIE DU CANADA (PSC)
Dept. of Pharmacology, Faculty of Medecine, Dalhousie University, Halifax, NS B3H 4H7
902/494-2596, Fax: 902/494-1388, Email: sawydalu@ac.dal.ca
Secretary, Dr. Jana Sawynok
Publications: Canadian Journal of Physiology & Pharmacology

Canadian Geoscience Council/Conseil géoscientifique canadien (CGC) (1972)
Dept. of Earth Sciences, University of Waterloo, 200 University Ave. West, Waterloo, ON N2L 3G1
519/885-1211, ext.3029, Fax: 519/746-0183, Email: avmorgan@sciborg.uwaterloo.ca
URL: http://www.science.uwaterloo.ca/earth/cgc/cgc.html
Administrative Director, Alan V. Morgan
Financial Director, Ron McMillan

Canadian Hydrographic Association/Association canadienne d'hydrographie (CHA)
162 Cleopatra Dr., Ottawa, ON K2G 5X2
613/224-9851, Fax: 613/224-9577
URL: http://www.cciw.ca/dfo/chs/cha/cha-home.html
President, Ken McMillan
Publications: Lighthouse
Affiliates: Canadian Institute of Surveying

Canadian Institute of Biotechnology/Institut canadien de la biotechnologie (CIB) (1989)
#420, 130 Albert St., Ottawa, ON K1P 5G4
613/563-8849, Fax: 613/563-8850, Email: cib@biotech.ca
URL: http://www.biotech.ca/
Executive Director, Rick Walter
Operations Manager, Michelle Campbell

Canadian Institute of Food Science & Technology/Institut canadien de science et technologie alimentaires (1951)
#1105, 191 The West Mall, Etobicoke, ON M9C 5K8
416/626-3140, Fax: 416/620-5392
Publications: Food Research International

Canadian Institute for Research in Atmospheric Chemistry/Institut canadien de la recherche en chimie atmosphérique (CIRAC) (1988)
#006, Steacie Building, York University, 4700 Keele St., North York, ON M3J 1P3
416/736-5586, Fax: 416/736-5690, Email: cirac@turing.sci.yorku.ca
Executive Director, Dr. David M. Halton
Publications: The Right Atmosphere

Canadian Medical & Biological Engineering Society Inc./Société canadienne de génie biomédical inc. (CMBES) (1965)
National Research Council of Canada, Rm. 393, Bldg. M55, 1500 Montreal Rd., Ottawa, ON K1A 0R8
613/993-1686, Fax: 613/954-2216
National Executive Secretary, Sally Chapman, Email: sally.chapman@nrc.ca
Publications: Newsletter
Affiliates: International Federation for Medical & Biological Engineering

Canadian Meteorological & Oceanographic Society/Société canadienne de météorologie et d'océanographie (CMOS) (1967)
#903, 151 Slater St., Ottawa, ON K1P 5H3
613/990-0300, Fax: 613/990-5510, Email: cmos@ottmed.meds.dfo.ca
Executive Director, Dr. Neil J. Campbell
President, Dr. Michel Beland
Publications: Atmosphere-Ocean; CMOS Bulletin SCMO, bi-m.

Canadian Phytopathological Society/Société canadienne de phytopathologie (CPS) (1929)
MAPAQ Centre de Recherche, PO Box 455, Les Buissons, PQ G0H 1H0
418/567-2235, Fax: 418/567-8791
Secretary, Dr. B. Otrysko
Treasurer, Dr. R. Utkhede
Publications: CPS News; Canadian Journal of Plant Pathology, q.
Affiliates: International Society for Plant Pathology

Canadian Science & Technology Historical Association/Association pour l'histoire de la science et de la technologie au Canada (CSTHA) (1980)
758 Holt Cres., Ottawa, ON K1G 2Y7
613/733-3188, Email: ae267@freenet.carleton.ca
URL: http://www.physics.uoguelph.ca/hist/CSTHA.html
President, Marianne Ainley
Sec.-Treas., Philip Enros
Publications: Scientia Canadensis; Dialogues, 3 pa

Canadian Society of Exploration Geophysicists (CSEG) (1949)
#406, 206 - 7 Ave. SW, Calgary, AB T2P 0W7
403/262-0015, Fax: 403/262-7383, Email: cseg@cadvision.com
URL: http://www.geo.ucalgary.ca:80/cseg
Office Manager, Heather Payne
Publications: Recorder; Canadian Journal of Exploration Geophysics, bi-a.
Affiliates: Society of Exploration Geophysicists - USA; European Association of Geoscientists & Engineers - Netherlands

Canadian Society of Forensic Science (CSFS) (1953)
#215, 2660 Southvale Cres., Ottawa, ON K1B 4W5
613/738-0001, Fax: 613/738-0001
Executive Secretary, Fredricka Monti
Publications: Canadian Society of Forensic Science - Journal

Canadian Society for the History & Philosophy of Science/Société canadienne d'histoire et philosophie des sciences (1959)
Department of History, Simon Fraser University, Burnaby, BC V5A 1S6
604/291-3521, Fax: 604/291-5837, Email: hgay@sfu.ca
Sec.-Treas., Prof. Hannah Gay
President, Maurice Gagnon, 819/821-7954, Fax: 819/821-7238
Publications: Communiqué
Affiliates: International Union for History & Philosophy of Science

Canadian Society of Microbiologists/Société canadienne des microbiologistes (CSM) (1958)
1200 Prince of Wales Dr., East, Ottawa, ON K2C 1M9
613/723-7233, Fax: 613/723-8792
President, T. Trust
Secretariat, Lynn Anderson
Publications: CSM Newsletter
Affiliates: Youth Science Foundation; International Union of Microbiological Societies

Canadian Society of Plant Physiologists/Société canadienne de physiologie végétale (CSPP) (1958)
Dept. of Biological Sciences, University of Alberta, Edmonton, AB T6G 2E9
613/492-5463, Fax: 613/492-9234
President, Dr. Ronald Poole
Secretary, Dr. David Gifford
Publications: Bulletin of/de CSPP/SCPV

Canadian Society of Soil Science/Société canadienne de la science du sol (CSSS)
PO Box 21018, RPO West End, Brandon, MB R7B 3W8
204/725-4336, Fax: 204/725-0624
President, Al Fedkenheuer
Publications: Canadian Journal of Soil Science; Newsletter, q.
Affiliates: International Society of Soil Science

Canadian Society for the Weizmann Institute of Science
#218, 45 Sheppard Ave. East, North York, ON M2N 5W9
416/733-9220, Fax: 416/733-9430
Contact, Edie Bayer

Entomological Society of Canada/Société d'entomologie du Canada (ENTSOC) (1863)
393 Winston Ave., Ottawa, ON K2A 1Y8
613/725-2619, Fax: 613/725-9349
President, Hugh Danks
Treasurer, Gary Gibson
Office Manager, A. Devine
Publications: ESC Bulletin; The Canadian Entomologist, bi-m.; Memoirs, irreg.

Genetics Society of Canada/Société de génétique du Canada (GSC) (1956)
#907, 151 Slater St., Ottawa, ON K1P 5H4
613/232-9459, Fax: 613/594-5190
Coordinator, Joanne Lechuk
President, Phyllis McAlpine
Publications: Bulletin of the GSC; Genome, q.
Affiliates: Canadian Federation of Biological Sciences; International Genetics Federation

Geological Association of Canada/Association géologique du Canada (GAC) (1947)
Dept. of Earth Sciences, Memorial University, 240 Prince Philip Dr., St. John's, NF A1B 3X5
709/737-8394, Fax: 709/737-2532, Email: gac@sparky2.esd.mun.ca
Sec.-Treas., R.N. Hiscott
Publications: Geoscience Canada; Geolog, q.
Affiliates: Canadian Society of Petroleum Geologists; Toronto Geological Discussion Group; Atlantic Geoscience Society; Canadian Quaternary Association; Canadian Geophysical Union

Human Factors Association of Canada/Association canadienne d'ergonomie (HFAC) (1968)
6519B Mississauga Rd., Mississauga, ON L5N 1A6
905/567-7193, Fax: 905/567-7191
Executive Manager, Peter Fletcher
President, Dr. Leslie Buck
Publications: Communiqué

Industrial Biotechnology Association of Canada/Association canadienne de l'industrie de la biotechnologie (IBAC) (1987)
#420, 130 Albert St., Ottawa, ON K1P 5G4
613/230-5585, Fax: 613/233-7541, Email: IBAC@biotech.ca
URL: http://www.biotech.ca/members/ibac.htm
President, Roger A. Perrault, M.D.
Chairman, Dr. Jack Wearing
Sec.-Treas., Dennis Lawson
Publications: Industry Directory; IBAC Focus

Institute for Space & Terrestrial Science/Institut de science terrestre et spatiale (ISTS) (1988)
4850 Keele St., 2nd Fl., North York, ON M3J 3K1
416/665-3311, Fax: 416/665-2032, Email: inquiries@ists.ca
URL: http://www.ists.ca/
Executive Director, Dr. Ian Rowe
Communications Officer, Ian A. Thomson, Email: thomson@ists.ists.ca
Publications: Waves

Institute of Textile Science/Institut des sciences textiles (ITS) (1956)
1, rue Pacifique, Ste-Anne-de-Bellevue, PQ H9X 1C5
514/457-2347
Secretary, Carmen Morosan

International Association of Science & Technology for Development (IASTED) (1977)
#80, 4500 - 16 Ave. NW, Calgary, AB T3B 0M6
403/288-1195, Fax: 403/247-6851, Toll Free: 1-800-995-2161, Email: iasted@cadvision.com
URL: http://www.curg.ab.ca:8001/~warwodad/iasted.html
Conference Manager, Nadia Hamza
Publications: Control & Computers; Power & Energy Systems, 3 pa; International Journal of Modelling & Simulation, q.; Robotics & Automation, q.

Microscopical Society of Canada (MSC) (1973)
c/o Dept. of Pathology, McMaster University, 1200 Main St. West, Hamilton, ON L8N 3Z5
905/525-9140, ext.22496, Fax: 905/577-0198
Executive Secretary, Marie Colbert
Publications: Bulletin of the Microscopical Society of Canada

Nova Scotian Institute of Science (NSIS) (1862)
Dalhousie University, Science Services University Library, Halifax, NS B4H 4H8
902/494-2384, Fax: 902/494-2062
President, R.P. Gupta
Publications: Proceedings of the Nova Scotia Institute of Science

Oceans Institute of Canada/Institut canadien des océans (OIC) (1976)
1226 LeMarchant St., Halifax, NS B3H 3P7
902/494-3879, Fax: 902/494-1334
Chairman, Management Committee, Board of Directors, Peter Duthil

Ontario Herpetological Society (OHS)
PO Box 244, Mississauga, ON L5G 4L8
416/285-6646, Fax: 416/285-9669
President, Grant Ankenman
Publications: The Ontario Herpetological Society News

Ontario Kinesiology Association (OKA) (1982)
6519B Mississauga Rd., Mississauga, ON L5N 1A6
905/567-7194, Fax: 905/567-7191
Executive Manager, Leslie Wright
Publications: Kinnection

Royal Astronomical Society of Canada/Société royale d'astronomie du Canada (RASC) (1903)
136 Dupont St., Toronto, ON M5R 1V2
416/924-7973, Fax: 416/924-7973
National Secretary, R.C. Brooks
Executive Secretary, Rosemary Freeman
National Treasurer, R. Gupta
Publications: RASC Journal

Science Alberta Foundation (1990)
#2100, 700 - 6 Ave. SW, Calgary, AB T2P 0T8
403/260-1996, Fax: 403/260-1165, Email: saf@freenet.calgary.ab.ca
URL: http://www.FreeNet.Calgary.ab.ca/science/sciencab.html
Executive Director, Anne Tingle
Publications: Between Friends

Society of Toxicology of Canada/Société de toxicologie du Canada (STC) (1964)
PO Box 517, Beaconsfield, PQ H9W 5V1
514/428-2676, Fax: 514/428-2685
Executive Director, Gordon Krip
Secretary, B. Virgo
Publications: Canadian Journal of Physiology & Pharmacology; STC News/Nouvelles, 3 pa
Affiliates: Canadian Federation of Biological Societies; International Union of Toxicology

Spectroscopy Society of Canada/Société de spectroscopie du Canada (SSC) (1957)
PO Box 332, Stn A, Ottawa, ON K1N 8V3
613/597-1067
President, Dr. Ralph M. Paroli
Publications: Canadian Journal of Analytical Sciences & Spectroscopy; Canadian Spectroscopic News
Affiliates: Society for Applied Spectroscopy - USA; Colloquium Spectroscopicum Internationale; Chemical Institute of Canada; Canadian Society of Forensic Science

Statistical Society of Canada/Société statistique du Canada (1977)
Rm. 4356 HP, Carleton University, 1125 Colonel By Dr., London, ON K1S 5B6
613/788-3988, Fax: 613/788-3822, Telex: 064-7134
URL: http://www.mast.queensu.ca/~ssc
Publications: Canadian Journal of Statistics; Liaison, q.; Directory of Statistics Programs in Canadian Universities, biennial
Affiliates: Committee of Presidents of Statistical Societies; International Statistical Institute

Youth Science Foundation
#904, 151 Slater St., Ottawa, ON K1P 5H3
613/238-1671, Fax: 613/238-1677

SEARCH & RESCUE see **EMERGENCY RESPONSE**

SECURITIES see **FINANCE**

SENIOR CITIZENS

Alberta Council on Aging (ACA)
#1740, 10130 - 103 St., Edmonton, AB T5J 3N9
403/423-7781, Fax: 403/425-9246, Email: acaging@compusmart.ab.ca
Executive Director, Christine Lawrence
Publications: ACA News

Alberta Provincial Pensioners & Senior Citizens Organization
PO Box 266, Fort MacLeod, AB T0L 0Z0
President, Rulon Hirsche

Alberta Senior Citizens Sport & Recreation Association (ASCSRA) (1980)
#203, 2616 - 18 St. NE, Calgary, AB T2E 7R1
403/297-2703, Fax: 403/297-2702
Executive Director, Ruth Becker
Publications: SeniorAction
Affiliates: Alberta Sport Council; Alberta Recreation, Parks & Wildlife Foundation

L'Assemblée des Aînées at Aînés Francophones du Canada (1992)
#1404, 1 Nicholas, Ottawa, ON K1N 7B7
613/241-7600, Téléc: 613/241-6046
Président, André Lécuyer

L'Association internationale francophone des aînés (AIFA) (1981)
150, boul René-Lévesque est, 7e étage, Québec, PQ G1R 4Y1
418/646-9117, Téléc: 418/646-1305
Secrétaire général, Guy Desrosiers
Publications: Maturité
Section Montréal: Présidente, Ruth T. Mendes, 1474, rue Fleury est, Montréal, PQ H2C 1S1, 514/383-6019, Téléc: 514/383-3462

Canadian Association on Gerontology/Association canadienne de gérontologie (CAG) (1971)
#500, 1306 Wellington St., Ottawa, ON K1Y 3B2
613/728-9347, Fax: 613/728-8913
Executive Director, Linda O'Rourke, M.S.W., 613/728-8913
President, Colette Tracyk
Publications: Canadian Journal on Aging

Canadian Association of Retired Persons/Association canadienne des individus retraités (CARP) (1976)
#1304, 27 Queen St. East, Toronto, ON M5C 2M6
416/363-8748, Fax: 416/363-8747
Executive Director, Murray Morgenthau
President, Lillian Morgenthau
Publications: CARP News

The Canadian Grey Panthers Advocacy Network
#20, 5225 Orbitor Dr., Mississauga, ON L4W 4Y8
905/624-1616, Fax: 905/624-0015, Toll Free: 1-800-561-4739, Email: panthers@io.org
URL: http://www.panthers.net
Executive Director & Founder, Joe Moniz
Communications Director, Isobel Warren
President, Frank Oliver

Canadian Institute of Senior Centres
Northwood Multipurpose Centre, 2515 Northwood Terrace, Halifax, NS B3K 3S5
902/258-3264, Fax: 902/454-3352

Canadian Pensioners Concerned Inc./ Corporation canadienne des retraités concernés
#24, 830 McLean St., Halifax, NS B3H 2T8
902/455-7684
National President, M. Doreen E. Fraser

Elderhostel Canada/Séjours culturels des aînés du Canada (1980)
308 Wellington St., Kingston, ON K7K 7A7
613/530-2222, Fax: 613/530-2096, Email: ehcpgmdp@limestone.kosone.com
Executive Director, Dr. Robert H. Williston
Director, Atlantic Region, Joyce Kennedy, 902/457-6327, Fax: 902/445-3960
Director, BC Region, Loretta Krauter, 604/494-4469
Director, Doug Thompson, 613/530-2095, Fax: 613/530-2096
Director, Prairies Region, Diane Osberg, 403/949-2165
Director, Québec Region, Judy Swedburg, 514/848-3313
Directeur des programmes français, Daniel Lavoie, 819/376-5124, Fax: 819/376-5166
Publications: Elderhostel Canada Catalogue

Fédération de l'âge d'or du Québec/Québec Federation of Senior Citizens (FADOQ) (1970)
4545, av Pierre-de-Couberin, CP 1000, Succ. M, Montréal, PQ H1V 3R2
514/252-3017, 3145, Téléc: 514/252-3154
Directrice générale, Nicole T. Moir
Publications: Magazine FADOQ
Organisation(s) affiliée(s): Association québécoise de gérontologie; Conseil canadien de développement social; Réseau canadien des aînés (One Voice); l'Assemblée des aîné(e)s francophones du Canada

Help the Aged (Canada)/Aide aux aînés (Canada) (HTA) (1975)
99 - 5 Ave., Ottawa, ON K1S 5K4
613/232-0727, Fax: 613/232-7625, Toll Free: 1-800-263-5463
Executive Director, Pierre Barbeau
Publications: Agecare/Secours aux Aînés
Affiliates: HelpAge International

Manitoba Association on Gerontology (1980)
PO Box 1833, Winnipeg, MB R3C 3R1
204/783-8389, Fax: 204/948-2511, Info Line: 204/945-5165
President, Sharon Wilford
Vice-President, Patti Chiappetta
Publications: MAG Quarterly

Manitoba Society of Seniors (MSOS) (1979)
#803, 294 Portage Ave., Winnipeg, MB R3C 0B9
204/942-3147, Fax: 204/943-1290, Toll Free: 1-800-561-6767
Acting Executive Director, Laura Mikuska
Editor, Irv Kroeker
Publications: MSOS Journal

National Pensioners & Senior Citizens Federation (NPSCF) (1945)
3033 Lake Shore Blvd. West, Toronto, ON M8V 1K5
416/251-7042, Fax: 416/252-5770
President, Ted Azevedo
Secretary, Edith M. Johnston
Publications: The National News
Affiliates: International Senior Citizens Association

New Brunswick Senior Citizens Federation Inc./ Fédération des Citoyens Aînés (1968)
#100E, 236 St. George St., Moncton, NB E1C 1W1
506/857-8242, Fax: 506/857-0315
Executive Director, Steven J. Boyce
Publications: Horizons

Older Adult Centres' Association of Ontario/ Association des centres pour aînés de l'Ontario (OACAO) (1972)
#401, 1185 Eglinton Ave. East, North York, ON M3C 3C6
416/426-7038, Fax: 416/426-7388
President, Anita Machin
Treasurer, Marilyn Latham
Fundraising & Secretary, Karen Bentham
Publications: OACAO MEMO; The Centre Member

One Voice - The Canadian Seniors Network/La Voix - Le Réseau canadien des aîné(e)s (1987)
#1005, 350 Sparks St., Ottawa, ON K1R 7S8
613/238-7624, Fax: 613/235-4497, Email: onevoice@magi.com
National Secretary, Ivan Hale
Publications: One Voice/La Voix

Ontario Coalition of Senior Citizens' Organizations (OCSCO) (1985)
25 Cecil St., 3rd Fl., Toronto, ON M5T 1N1
416/979-7057, Fax: 416/979-5826
Executive Director, Morris Jesion
Publications: OCSCO Newsletter

Prince Edward Island Senior Citizens Federation
420 Queen St., PO Box 152, Charlottetown, PE C1A 7K4
902/628-8388, Fax: 902/892-1843
President, Ron McKinnon
Coordinator, Olive Bryington

Society for the Retired & Semi-Retired
15 Sir Winston Churchill Sq., Edmonton, AB T5J 2E5
403/423-5510, Fax: 403/426-5175
Executive Director, Walter Coombs
Publications: News for Seniors

United Senior Citizens of Ontario Inc. (USCO) (1961)
3033 Lakeshore Blvd. West, Toronto, ON M8V 1K5
416/252-2021, Fax: 416/252-5770
President, Jack Dyce
Publications: The Voice USCO

SERVICE CLUBS
see also Fraternal

Association des Grands Frères/Grandes Soeurs du Québec/Big Brothers/Big Sisters of Québec (1981)
2300, boul René-Lévesque ouest, Montréal, PQ H3H 2R5
514/935-4252, Téléc: 514/935-6518, Ligne sans frais: 1-800-661-4252
Directrice générale, Lise Bouchard

Big Brothers of British Columbia & Affiliated Big Sisters (1953)
#800, 15355 - 24th Ave., Unit 371, Surrey, BC V4A 2H9
604/878-1037, Fax: 604/536-5717
Executive Director, George Alliston

Big Brothers of Canada/Les Grands Frères du Canada (BBSC) (1964)
Big Brothers & Sisters of Canada
5230 South Service Rd., Burlington, ON L7L 5K2
905/639-0461, Fax: 905/639-0124, Toll Free: 1-800-263-9133, Email: bbsc@bbsc.ca
URL: http://www.bbsc.ca
National Executive Director, Michael McKnight
President, Rich Bassett
Director of Marketing, Bruce MacDonald
Publications: Rapport

Atlantic Regional Office: Resource Coordinator, Betty Hitchcox, 29 Bedell Ave., Saint John, NB E2K 2C1, 506/648-9794, Fax: 506/633-7781
BC/Alberta Regional Office: Executive Director, George Alliston, Unit 371, #800, 15355 - 24 Ave., Surrey, BC V4A 2H9, 604/878-1037, Fax: 604/536-5717
Québec Regional Office: Directrice générale, Lise Bouchard, 2300, boul René-Lévesque ouest, Montréal, PQ H3H 2R5, 514/935-4252, Téléc: 514/935-6518, Ligne sans frais: 1-800-661-4252

Big Sisters Association of Ontario (BSAO) (1981)
2750 Dufferin St., Toronto, ON M6B 3R4
416/789-7859, Fax: 416/789-7850
Executive Director, Madeline Bergin

British Columbia Lions Society for Children with Disabilities (1952)
#300, 177 - 7th Ave. West, Vancouver, BC V5Y 1K5
604/873-1865, Fax: 604/873-0166
Executive Director, William J. Townsend
Associate Executive Director, A.W. Connell
Assistant Executive Director, Linda Wells
Comptroller, William Simpson
Publications: Main Event
Affiliates: BC Lions Foundation; Custom Service Transit Society

Canadian Progress Club/Club progrès du Canada (1922)
2395 Bayview Ave., North York, ON M2L 1A2
416/446-1830, Fax: 416/446-6857
Executive Director, Lee Irwin
National President, Carlos Pardo
National Sec.-Treas., Mary Kutarna
Publications: Progression

Federation of Junior Leagues of Canada/ Fédération des jeunes ligues du Canada
#2, 442 Pearl St., Burlington, ON L7R 2N1
905/632-5579

Kinsmen & Kinette Clubs of Canada/Les clubs Kin du Canada (1920)
1920 Hal Rogers Dr., PO Box KIN, Cambridge, ON N3H 5C6
519/653-1920, Fax: 519/650-1091
Executive Director, Robert W. Elliott
Publications: Contact; Kin Magazine, q.

Kiwanis International/Eastern Canada & Caribbean District
330 Walmer Rd., Toronto, ON M5R 2Y4
416/921-1297, Fax: 416/921-9054
Sec.-Treas., Ted Sievert
District Administrative Secretary, Jacqueline Ashcroft

Kiwanis International/Western Canada District
125 Sheep River Bay, Okotoks, AB T0L 1T4
403/938-5985, Fax: 403/938-2703
Sec.-Treas., Walter P. Voth

Last Post Fund/Fonds du souvenir (LPF) (1909)
#916, 685, rue Cathcart, Montréal, PQ H3B 1M7
514/866-2727, Fax: 514/866-2147, Toll Free: 1-800-465-7113
Executive Director, Lt. Col. P. Ranger
Alberta North Branch: Sec.-Treas., J.W. Ritchie, PO Box 335, Edmonton, AB T5J 2J6, 403/495-3766, Fax: 403/495-6960
Alberta South Branch: #209, 1235 - 17 Ave. SW, Calgary, AB T2T OC2, 403/244-6821, Fax: 403/228-6825
British Columbia Branch: Capt. Ronald D. Rowdon, #520, 510 Hastings St. West, Vancouver, BC V6B 1L8, 604/685-8833, Fax: 604/685-4521

Manitoba Branch: Robert W. Rollings, 51 St. Anne's Rd., Winnipeg, MB R2M 1Y4, 204/233-3073, Fax: 204/237-1169
New Brunswick & Prince Edward Island Branch: Ida DeGrâce, PO Box 2054, Saint John, NB E2L 3T5, 506/658-9707, Fax: 506/658-9623
Newfoundland Branch: Sec.-Treas., Hugh R. Peden, Prudential Bldg., 49 Elizabeth Ave., St. John's, NF A1A 1W9, 709/579-4288, Fax: 709/579-0966
Nova Scotia Branch: Lois Townsend, #1003, 6080 Young St., Halifax, NS B3K 5L2, 902/455-5283, Fax: 902/455-4058, Toll Free: 1-800-565-4777
Ontario Branch: Sec.-Treas., Richard Noble, #624, 55 St. Clair Ave. East, Toronto, ON M4T 1M2, 416/923-1608, Fax: 416/923-3695, Toll Free: 1-800-563-2508
Québec Branch: Sec.-Treas., René Pothier, #921, 685, rue Cathcart, Montréal, PQ H3B 1M7, 514/866-2888, Fax: 514/866-1471, Toll Free: 1-800-866-5229
Saskatchewan Branch: Major Gerry Barr, 506 Federal Bldg., 101 - 22 St. East, Saskatoon, SK S7K 0E6, 306/975-6045, Fax: 306/975-4306
California Branch: #104, 929 East Foothill Blvd., Upland, CA 91786 USA, 909/946-7876
Florida Representative: 3695 Ridgemount Ct., Palm Harbour, FL 34684 USA, 813/784-9745
United Kingdom Representative: MacDonald House, 1 Grosvenor Sq., London W1X 0AB UK, /011-441-71-258-6339, Fax: /011-441-71-258-6645

Lions Clubs International - District A
#9, 155 Beaver Creek Rd., Richmond Hill, ON L4B 2N1
416/771-6400, Fax: 416/771-6692
Secretary, Roger L. Lacroix

Rotary Clubs in Canada (1905)
1 Rotary Center, Evanston, IL 60201 USA
312/866-3000, Fax: 312/328-8554, Telex: 724-465
General Secretary, Herbert Pigman
Promotional Services Dept., Hank Ottery
Publications: The Rotarian

Soroptimist Foundation of Canada (1963)
#22, 185 Woodridge Dr. SW, Calgary, AB T2W 3X7
403/249-9191, Fax: 403/249-9199
Sec.-Treas., Marguerite Duguid
Affiliates: Soroptimist International of the Americas

Variety - The Children's Charity (Ontario) (1945)
#300, 37 King St. East, Toronto, ON M5C 1E9
416/367-2828, Fax: 416/367-0028
Director, Finance & Administration, Mary Anne Beatty
Chief Barker, Bruce Raymond
Publications: Tent Topics
Affiliates: Variety Village; Variety Ability Systems Inc.

Variety Club of British Columbia, Tent 47 (1965)
Variety Club
1250 Homer St., Vancouver, BC V6B 2Y5
604/669-2313, 7770, Fax: 604/683-1025, Toll Free: 1-800-381-2040
Chief Barker/President, Bob Stewart
Publications: Voice of Variety

Variety Club of Manitoba, Tent 58 Inc. (1979)
611 Wellington Cres., Winnipeg, MB R3M 0A7
204/982-1058, Fax: 204/475-3198
Executive Director, Shirley Seidel
Publications: Variety Views

Variety Club of Southern Alberta, Tent 61 (1982)
#202, 110 -11 Ave. SE, Calgary, AB T2G 0X5
403/261-0061, Fax: 403/264-9041
Chief Officer, Audreu Cunneyworth
Publications: Variety Voice

SHIPPING see TRANSPORTATION & SHIPPING

SOCIAL CLUBS see FRATERNAL

SOCIAL RESPONSE/SOCIAL SERVICES

Alberta Association for Marriage & Family Therapy (AAMFT) (1978)
PO Box 52053, Edmonton, AB T6G 2T5
403/448-9497
Affiliates: American Association for Marriage & Family Therapy

Alberta Association of Services for Children & Families (AASCF) (1967)
#54, 9912 - 106 St., Edmonton, AB T5K 1C5
403/424-4498, Fax: 403/425-4828
Executive Director, Leslie McCallum
Publications: Post-It

Alberta Association of Social Workers/ Association des travailleurs sociaux de l'Alberta (AASW)
#52, 9912 - 106 St., Edmonton, AB T5K 1C5
403/421-1167, Fax: 403/421-1168
Executive Director, Rod Adachi
Publications: The Advocate

Association of Community Information Centres in Ontario (ACICO) (1980)
#205, 5233 Dundas St. West, Etobicoke, ON M9B 1A6
416/237-0405, Fax: 416/237-1395
URL: http://www.web.apc.org/acico/
Executive Director, Serge Lavoie
President, Rosanna Thoms
Publications: A CICO Online; Profiles, a.

Association of Food Banks & C.V.A.'s for New Brunswick (1989)
378 McKenna Ave., Miramichi, NB E1V 1A8
506/622-7787, Fax: 506/622-2094
Contact, Jim Hayter

Association of Human Services in Alberta (AHSA) (1980)
#205, 10426 - 81 Ave., Edmonton, AB T6E 1X5
403/431-0626, Fax: 403/431-0626, Email: ahsa@agt.net
Executive Director, Walter Walchuk
President, Gerrit Groeneweg
Publications: Human Services

Association québécoise des personnes de petite taille (AQPPT) (1976)
1251, rue Robin, Montréal, PQ H2L 1W8
514/521-9671
Directrice générale, Louiselle St-Pierre
Publications: Des nouvelles de notre association; Grandis ensemble, annuel

Association québécoise Plaidoyer-Victimes (PV) (1984)
Plaidoyer-Victimes
#300, 2570, rue Nicolet, Montréal, PQ H1W 3L5
514/526-9037, Téléc: 514/523-8637
Coordonnatrice, Josée Coiteux
Publications: Info PV

Association des services de réhabilitation sociale du Québec inc./Association of Social Rehabilitation Agencies of Québec Inc. (ASRSQ) (1962)
1657, boul St-Joseph est, Montréal, PQ H2G 1N1
514/521-3733, Téléc: 514/521-3753
Directrice générale, Johanne Vallée
Publications: Porte Ouverte

L'Autre Parole (1976)
CP 393, Succ. C, Montréal, PQ H2L 4K3
Responsable, Relations publiques, Yvette Laprise
Publications: L'Autre Parole

BC Council for the Family (BCCF) (1977)
#204, 2590 Granville St., Vancouver, BC V6H 3H1
604/660-0675, Fax: 604/732-4813, Toll Free: 1-800-663-5638, Email: bccf_vancouver@mindlink.bc
URL: http://familyforum.com/
President, Gwenn Cutler
Executive Director, Dr. Carol Matusicky
Publications: BCCF Newsletter; Family Connections, q.

BC Parents in Crisis Society (BCPIC) (1974)
#620, 1155 West Pender St., Vancouver, BC V6E 2P4
604/669-1616, Fax: 604/669-1636, Toll Free: 1-800-665-6880
Executive Director, Julie Norton
Publications: BC Parents in Crisis Society
Victoria Office: 941 Kings Rd., Victoria, BC V8T 1W7, 250/384-8042, Fax: 250/388-4391

Bereaved Families of Ontario (BFO) (1978)
#204, 214 Merton St., Toronto, ON M4S 1A6
Toll Free: 1-800-236-6364, Email: bfo@inforamp.net
URL: http://www.inforamp.net/~bfo
Executive Director, Margaret McGovern

Birthparent & Relative Group Society (BRGS) (1983)
PO Box 20089, RPO Beverly, Edmonton, AB T2W 5E6
403/473-1912
President, Louise McLean
Publications: BRGS Newsletter

Block Parent Program of Canada Inc./ Programme parents-secours du Canada inc. (BPPCI) (1968)
12206 - 86 Ave., Surrey, BC V3W 3H7
604/594-6788, Fax: 604/594-6788, Toll Free: 1-800-663-1134
President, Rose Marie Brien
Secretary, Martha McArthur
Finance Manager, Judy Vizbar
Vice-Chairperson, Debbie Stewart
Publicity & Promotion Manager, Joan Barnhill
Publications: National Voice of Block Parents

British Columbia Association of Social Workers/ Association des travailleurs sociaux de la Colombie-Britannique (BCASW) (1956)
#402, 1755 West Broadway, Vancouver, BC V6J 4S5
604/730-9111, Fax: 604/730-9112, Toll Free: 1-800-665-4747
Executive Director, Margaret Duncan
Publications: Perspectives; The Social Worker, q.
Affiliates: End Legislated Poverty; End the Arms Race Coalition; BC Human Rights Coalition

British Columbia Block Parent Program
12070 - 96 Ave., Surrey, BC V3W 1W2
604/581-0678, Fax: 604/581-8633
Contact, Sheila Knox

British Columbia Federation of Foster Parent Associations (BCFFPA) (1967)
#206, 3680 East Hastings St., Vancouver, BC V5K 2A9
604/660-7696, Fax: 604/775-1183, Toll Free: 1-800-663-9999
Executive Director, Joan Wenstob
President, Doug Anderson
Publications: BCFFPA Newsletter

Campaign 2000 (1991)
22 Wellesley St. East, Toronto, ON M4Y 1G3

Canadian Almanac & Directory 1997

416/922-3126, Fax: 416/922-9235
Coordinator, Rosemarie Popham
Publications: Campaign 200 Countdown
Affiliates: Canadian Academy of Child Psychiatry; Canadian Association of Social Workers; Canadian Association of Food Banks; Canadian Association of Toy Libraries & Parent Resource Centres; Canadian Council for Reform Judaism; Canadian Council on Social Development; Canadian Housing & Renewal Association; Canadian Institute of Child Health; Canadian Mental Health Association; Canadian Teachers' Federation; Catholic Health Association of Canada; Child Care Advocacy Association of Canada; Child Poverty Action Group; Child Welfare League of Canada; Family Service Canada; National Anti-Poverty Organization; National Organization of Immigrant & Visible Minority Women; Save the Children, Canada; YWCA of/du Canada

Canadian Association Against Sexual Harassment in Higher Education/Association canadienne contre le harcèlement sexuel en milieu d'enseignement supérieur (CAASHHE) (1985)
University of Victoria, School of Social Work, PO Box 1700, Victoria, BC V8W 2Y2
250/721-8044, Fax: 250/721-7067
President, Prof. Barbara Whittington

Canadian Association of Food Banks/Association canadienne des banques alimentaires (CAFB) (1987)
530 Lakeshore Blvd. West, Toronto, ON M5V 1A5
416/203-9241, Fax: 416/203-9244
Executive Director, Julia Bass
National Coordinator, Barry Davidson
Chairperson, Dianne Swinemar
Publications: Provisions
Affiliates: Campaign 2000

Canadian Association of Neighbourhood Services (CANS) (1978)
#203, 3102 Main St., Vancouver, BC V5T 3G7
604/875-9111, Fax: 604/875-1256
Executive Director, Doug Sabourin
Publications: Viewpoint
Affiliates: Association of Neighbourhood Houses of Greater Vancouver; Toronto Association of Neighbourhood Services; International Federation of Settlements

Canadian Association of Sexual Assault Centres/Association canadienne des centres contre le viol (CASAC) (1977)
77 - 20th Ave. East, Vancouver, BC V5V 1L7
604/872-8212, Fax: 604/876-8450
Contact, Lee Lakeman
Affiliates: United Way

Canadian Association of Social Workers/Association canadienne des travailleurs sociaux (CASW) (1926)
#402, 383 Parkdale Ave., Ottawa, ON K1Y 4R4
613/729-6668, Fax: 613/729-9608, Email: casw@casw-acts.ca
Executive Director, Eugenia Repeteur Moreno
Publications: The Social Worker/Le Travailleur social
Affiliates: International Federation of Social Workers

Canadian Career Development Foundation/Fondation canadienne pour l'avancement de la carrière (CCDF) (1979)
#202, 411 Roosevelt Ave., Ottawa, ON K2A 3X9
613/729-6164, Fax: 613/729-3515, Email: ccdffcac@magi.com
URL: http://infoweb.magi.com/~ccdffcac
Executive Director, M. Lynne Bezanson

Consultant, K. Sareena Hopkins
Publications: The Career Counsellor/Regard sur l'orientation professionnelle
Affiliates: International Association for Educational & Vocational Guidance

Canadian Centre for Philanthropy/Centre canadien de philanthropie (1980)
IMAGINE
1329 Bay St., 2nd Fl., Toronto, ON M5R 2C4
416/515-0764, Fax: 416/515-0773, Toll Free: 1-800-263-1178
President/CEO, Patrick Johnston
IMAGINE Program Director, Chris Pinney
Publications: The Canadian Directory to Foundations; Front & Centre

Canadian Centre for Victims of Torture (CCVT) (1983)
25 Merton St., Toronto, ON M4S 1A7
416/480-0489, Fax: 416/480-1984
Executive Director, Mulugeta Abai
Publications: CCVT Newsletter

Canadian Charitable Assistance Organization
778 Haig Rd., Ancaster, ON L9G 3G9

Canadian Council for Refugees/Conseil canadien pour les réfugiés (CCR) (1978)
#302, 6839, rue Drolet, Montréal, PQ H2S 2T1
514/277-7223, Fax: 514/277-1447, Email: ccr@web.apc.org
Executive Director, Nancy Worsfold
President, David Matas
Publications: Contact

Canadian Counselling & Guidance Association/Société canadienne d'orientation et de consultation (CCGA) (1965)
#600, 220 Laurier Ave. West, Ottawa, ON K1P 5Z9
613/230-4236, Fax: 613/230-5884
President, Chris Cooper
Publications: Canadian Journal of Counselling
Affiliates: International Round Table for the Advancement of Counselling

Canadian Crossroads International/Carrefour canadien international (CCI) (1958)
31 Madison Ave., Toronto, ON M5R 2S2
416/967-0801, Fax: 416/967-9078, Telex: 06-217-661 CCI
Executive Director, John Patterson
Publications: Echo; Baobab, q.; Virage, bi-m.
Affiliates: Canadian Centre for Philanthropy
Atlantic Office: Wayne McGill, #525, 1657 Barrington St., Halifax, NS B3J 2A1, 902/422-2933, Fax: 902/423-0579
Bureau du centre: Frédéric Gordeau, 715, rue Richelieu, Québec, PQ G1R 1K8, 418/525-9943, Téléc: 418/525-5283
Group Program Office: 912, rue Sherbrooke est, Montréal, PQ H2L 1L2, 514/528-5363, Téléc: 514/528-5367
Western Office: Helen Rusich, #101, 10920 - 88 Ave., Edmonton, AB T6G 0Z1, 403/433-8015, Fax: 403/439-9677
Western Office: 1830 Cultra Ave., Saanichton, BC V0S 1M0, 250/544-1366

Canadian Feed the Children (CFTC) (1986)
174 Bartley Dr., Toronto, ON M4A 1E1
416/757-1220, Fax: 416/757-3318, Toll Free: 1-800-387-1221
Acting President, John Irwin
Publications: Newsletter

Canadian Fellowship for Romanian Orphans
112 Peevers Cres., Newmarket, ON L3Y 7T2

905/898-2564
President, Mary-Lee Conte

Canadian Foundation on Compulsive Gambling (Ontario) (CFCG) (1983)
#605, 505 Consumers Rd., North York, ON M2J 4V8
416/499-9800, Fax: 416/493-2653
Executive Director, Tibor I. Barsony
Secretary, K. Raic

Canadian Social Work Foundation/Fondation canadienne du service social
1620 Scott St., PO Box 64177, Ottawa, ON K1Y 4V2
President, Julie Foley

Canadian Society for the Prevention of Cruelty to Children (CSPCC)
356 First St., PO Box 700, Midland, ON L4R 4P4
705/526-5647, Fax: 705/526-0214
President, E.T. Barker, M.D.
Publications: Empathic Parenting
Affiliates: The Robertson Centre, England; The Infant-Parent Institute, USA; Attachment Parenting International

Canadians Concerned About Violence in Entertainment (C-CAVE) (1983)
167 Glen Rd., Toronto, ON M4W 2W8
416/961-0853, Fax: 416/929-2720, Email: rdyson@oise.utoronto.ca
Chairperson, Dr. Rose Anne Dyson, Ed.D.
Publications: C-CAVE News

Canadians for Decency (CFD) (1974)
PO Box 637, Stn B, North York, ON M2K 2P9
416/438-2374, Fax: 416/438-2723
President, Dolina Smith
Publications: CFD Newsletter

Catholic Charities of The Archdiocese of Toronto (1913)
#400, 1155 Yonge St., Toronto, ON M4T 1W2
416/934-3401, Fax: 416/934-3402
Executive Director, Michael J. Fullan
Publications: Catholic Charities
Affiliates: Catholic Family Services of Toronto & 26 member agencies

Child Abuse Research & Education Productions Association of British Columbia
CARE Productions
#112, 10070 King George Hwy., PO Box 183, Surrey, BC V3T 4W8
604/581-5116, Fax: 604/581-3307

Child Care Advocacy Association of Canada/Association canadienne pour la promotion des services de garde à l'enfance (CCAAC) (1982)
323 Chapel St., Ottawa, ON K1N 7Z2
613/594-3196, Fax: 613/594-9375
Publications: Vision; Bulletin
Affiliates: Canadian Labour Congress; Public Service Alliance; Canadian Union of Public Employees

Child Welfare League of Canada/La Ligue pour la protection de l'énfance du Canada (CWLC) (1994)
#312, 180 Argyle Ave., Ottawa, ON K2P 1B7
613/235-4412, Fax: 613/788-5075, Email: cwlc@magi.com
Executive Director, Sandra Scarth
Publications: In Brief; Canada's Children, q.
Affiliates: Child Welfare League of America

Coalition of National Voluntary Organizations/Regroupement des organisations nationales bénévoles (NVO) (1973)
National Voluntary Organizations
#420, 396 Cooper St., Ottawa, ON K2P 2H7

613/238-1591, Fax: 613/238-5257
Executive Director, Al Halton
Chair, Joan Howell
Publications: Bulletin; Fact Sheet; Consultation Reports, s-a.

Confédération des organismes familiaux du Québec inc. (COFAQ) (1972)
4098, rue St-Hubert, Montréal, PQ H2L 4A8
514/521-4777, Téléc: 514/521-6272, Courrier électronique: cofaq3ci@odyssee.net
URL: http://www.odyssee.net/~cofaq3ci/cofaq
Secrétaire général, Denis Perreault
Publications: Info-COFAQ

COSTI (1981)
1710 Dufferin St., Toronto, ON M6E 3P2
416/658-1600, Fax: 416/658-8537
Executive Director, Mario J. Calla
Publications: The Newsletter
Affiliates: United Way

Dying with Dignity/Mourir dans la dignité (DWD) (1980)
#706, 188 Eglinton Ave. East, Toronto, ON M4P 2X7
416/486-3998, Fax: 416/489-9010, Email: dwdca@web.apc.org
URL: http://www.web.apc.org/dwd
Executive Director, Marilynne Seguin
President, Douglas Campbell
Publications: Dying with Dignity Newsletter
Affiliates: World Federation of Right to Die Societies

Eastman Crisis Centre (1985)
Agape House
PO Box 3130, Steinbach, MB R0A 2A0
204/326-6062, Fax: 204/326-2359, Crisis-Line: 1-800-326-3431
Executive Director, Debby Anderson
Publications: Agape House Newsletter

Edmonton Social Planning Council (ESPC) (1940)
#41, 9912 - 106 St., Edmonton, AB T5K 1C5
403/423-2031, Fax: 403/425-6244
Executive Director, Jonathan Murphy
Publications: First Reading; Alberta Facts, q.

Education Wife Assault (EWA) (1978)
427 Bloor St. West, Toronto, ON M5S 1X7
416/968-3422, Fax: 416/968-2026
Contact Person, Marsha Sfeir
Publications: EWA
Affiliates: The Black Secretariat; The National Action Committee on the Status of Women; MATCH International; Ontario Association of Interval & Transition Houses

End Physical Punishment of Children - Canada
EPOCH - Canada
c/o The Canadian Society for the Prevention of Cruelty to Children, PO Box 700, Midland, ON L4R 4P4
National Co-ordinator, James Lindfield, Bus: 604/255-5443, Res: 534-9884

Equal Justice for All (EJA) (1984)
230 - R Ave. South, Saskatoon, SK S7M 2Z1
306/653-6260, Fax: 306/655-5895
Co-Chair, Mildred Kerr
Co-Chair, Earle Mireau
Publications: News for Youse

Family & Community Support Services Association of Alberta (FCSSAA) (1981)
City Hall, PO Box 5008, Red Deer, AB T4N 3T4
403/342-8101, Fax: 403/347-4636
Secretary, Colleen Jensen
Publications: FCSS Community Connections

Family Mediation Canada/Médiation familiale du Canada (FMC) (1985)
123 Woolwich St., 2nd Fl., Guelph, ON N1H 3V1
519/836-7750, Fax: 519/836-7204, Email: fmcpyoung@web.net
Executive Director, Paul Young
Publications: Resolve

Family Service Association of Metropolitan Toronto (FSA) (1914)
22 Wellesley St. East, Toronto, ON M4Y 1G3
416/922-3126, Fax: 416/922-9235
Executive Director, Paul Zarnke
Communications Manager, Michele Fisher
Publications: On Record; Impact
Affiliates: Family Service Canada

Family Service Canada/Services à la famille - Canada (1982)
#600, 220 Laurier Ave. West, Ottawa, ON K1P 5Z9
613/230-9960, Fax: 613/230-5884
CEO/President, Trevor C. Williams
Executive Assistant, Joanne Rivet

Family Service Ontario/Services à la famille - Ontario (1973)
#802, 1243 Islington Ave., Toronto, ON M8X 1Y9
416/231-6003
Executive Director, Dr. Hugh Drouin
Publications: Family Times
Affiliates: Ontario Association of Credit Counselling Services; Family Services Canada; Catholic Charities; United Way; Canadian Council of Social Development

Fédération des associations de familles monoparentales du Québec/Federation of Single-Parent Family Associations of Québec (FAFMRQ) (1974)
8059, boul St-Michel, Montréal, PQ H1Z 3C9
514/729-6666, Téléc: 514/729-6746
Directrice générale, Sylvie Lévesque
Publications: Bulletin de liaison

Fédération des centres d'action bénévole du Québec (FCABQ) (1972)
1246, rue Bishop, Montréal, PQ H3G 2E3
514/866-6312, Téléc: 514/866-6315
Directrice générale, Daniele Feredj
Publications: Info éclair
Organisation(s) affiliée(s): International Association for Volunteer Effort

Frontiers Foundation/Fondation frontière (1968)
Operation Beaver
#203, 2615 Danforth Ave., Toronto, ON M4C 1L6
416/690-3930, Fax: 416/698-9846, Toll Free: 1-800-668-4130
Executive Director, Charles R. Catto
President, Herb Nabigon
Publications: Program Report
Affiliates: Native Council of Canada

Goodwill Rehabilitation Services of Alberta
PO Box 1680, Edmonton, AB T5J 2N9
403/462-1666, Fax: 403/463-7396, Email: goodwill@ccinet.ab.ca
President, Kenneth W. Delooze
Affiliates: Alberta Easter Seal Ability Council; Canadian Council on Rehabilitation & Work; United Way of The Alberta Capital Region

Goodwill Toronto (1935)
234 Adelaide St. East, Toronto, ON M5A 1M9
416/362-4711, Fax: 416/362-0720
President, Jim Dreiling
Chairman, Brian Fetherstonaugh
Public Relations Manager, Jill Kehoe
Publications: Goodwill UPDATE; Goodwill Works

GRAND Society (1983)
Grandparents Requesting Access & Dignity
219 Browning Ave., Toronto, ON M4K 3J5
416/469-5471
President, Joan Brooks
Publications: Newsletter

International Social Service Canada/Service Social International Canada (ISS Canada) (1979)
#714, 151 Slater St., Ottawa, ON K1P 5H3
613/236-6161, Fax: 613/233-7306
Director of Services, L. Agnes Casselman
Publications: ISS Canada Newsletter
Affiliates: International Social Service - Geneva, Switzerland

Kids First Parent Association of Canada (1987)
PO Box 5256, Airdrie, AB T4B 2B3
403/289-1440
President, Cathy Perri
Vice-President, Cheryl Stewart
National Secretary, Catherine Buchanan
Treasurer, Debbie Kusturin
Publications: Kids First Newsletter

Kids Help Phone/Jeunesse j'écoute (KHP) (1989)
439 University Ave., Toronto, ON M5G 1Y8
416/586-0100, Fax: 416/586-1880, Toll Free: 1-800-668-6868
National Executive Director, Heather Sproule
Publications: Phone Link

Lawyers for Social Responsibility/Avocats en faveur d'une conscience sociale (LSR) (1984)
5120 Carney Rd. NW, Calgary, AB T2L 1T2
403/282-8260, Fax: 403/289-4272, Email: bdelong@web.apc.org
President, Beverley Delong
Publications: Newsletter
Affiliates: International Association of Laws Against Nuclear Arms; Mines Action Canada; Canadian Network for the Abolition of Nuclear Weapons

Manitoba Anti-Poverty Organization Inc. (MAPO) (1982)
#102, 365 McGee St., Winnipeg, MB R3G 3M5
204/786-3323
Organizational Coordinator, Diane Sovie
President, Gail Allard
Publications: The MAPO Memo; Know Your Welfare Rights; Who We Are?; The MAPO Cookbook for Low Income Families
Affiliates: National Anti-Poverty Organization

Manitoba Association of Social Workers/Association des travailleurs sociaux du Manitoba (MASW) (1961)
#103, 2015 Portage Ave., Winnipeg, MB R3J 0K3
204/888-9477, Fax: 204/889-0021, Email: masw@magic.mb.ca
Administrative Coordinator, Diane Cullen
President, Brenda Douglas
Publications: The Manitoba Social Worker
Affiliates: Manitoba Institute of Registered Social Workers

Manitoba Institute of Registered Social Workers (MIRSW) (1963)
#103, 2015 Portage Ave., Winnipeg, MB R3J 0K3
204/888-9477, Fax: 204/889-0021, Email: masw@magic.mb.ca
Administrative Coordinator, Diane Cullen

Canadian Almanac & Directory 1997

Missing Children Society of Canada (MCSC) (1986)
#219, 3501 - 23rd St. NE, Calgary, AB T2E 6V8
403/291-0705, Fax: 403/291-9728, Toll Free: 1-800-661-6160
URL: http://www.childcybersearch.org
Chairman, Rhonda M. Morgan
Publications: The Missing Link
Affiliates: RCMP Missing Children's Registry, Ottawa
Eastern Canada Office: Case Director, Barb Snider, #814, 99 Bronte Rd., Oakville, ON L6K 3B7, 905/469-8826, Fax: 905/469-8828, Toll Free: 1-800-661-6160

Mouvement québécois pour combattre le racisme
9405, rue Sherbrooke est, Montréal, PQ H1L 6P3
514/356-8888, Téléc: 514/356-9999
Présidente, Lise Saint-Jean

National Anti-Poverty Organization/Organisation nationale anti-pauvreté (NAPO) (1971)
#316, 256 King Edward Ave., Ottawa, ON K1N 7M1
613/789-0096, Fax: 613/789-0141, Email: napo@web.apc.org
Executive Director, Lynne Toupin
Assistant Director, François Dumaine
Publications: NAPO News

New Brunswick Association of Social Workers/Association des travailleurs sociaux du Nouveau-Brunswick
PO Box 1533, Stn A, Fredericton, NB E3B 5G2
506/459-5595, Fax: 506/457-1421

Newfoundland & Labrador Association of Social Workers/Association des travailleurs sociaux de Terre-Neuve et Labrador (NLASW) (1970)
PO Box 5244, St. John's, NF A1C 5W1
709/753-0200, Fax: 709/753-0120, Email: NLASW@newcomm.net
Executive Director/Registrar, Bruce Cooper
President, Beverley Clarke
Publications: NLASW Newsletter
Affiliates: Canadian Association of Social Workers

Non-Smokers' Rights Association/Association pour les droits des non-fumeurs (NSRA) (1975)
#221, 720 Spadina Ave., Toronto, ON M5S 2T9
416/928-2900, Fax: 416/928-1860, Email: nsra@io.org
Executive Director, Garfield Mahood
General Manager, Dr. C.F. Folz
Legal Counsel, David Sweanor
Publications: Indorair
Affiliates: Canadian Society of Association Executives; Canadian Centre of Philanthropy

Nova Scotia Association of Social Workers/Association des travailleurs sociaux de la Nouvelle-Écosse (NSASW) (1963)
#106, 1891 Brunswick St., Halifax, NS B3J 2G8
902/429-7799, Fax: 902/429-7650
Executive Director, Harold Beals
Publications: Connections

One Parent Families Association of Canada (1973)
#203, 6979 Yonge St., North York, ON M2M 3X9
416/226-0062, Fax: 416/226-3089
President, Christopher Wren

Ontario Association of Children's Aid Societies/Association ontarienne des sociétés de l'aide à l'enfance (OACAS) (1912)
75 Front St. East, 2nd Fl., Toronto, ON M5E 1V9
416/366-8115, Fax: 416/366-8317
Executive Director, Mary McConville
Executive Assistant, Andrea Mills

Publications: OACAS Journal; Municipal Directory for CAS Referrals, a.; Child Welfare Contacts in Canada, a.

Ontario Association of Distress Centres (OADC) (1971)
Distress Centres Ontario
#418, 99 Atlantic Ave., Toronto, ON M6K 3J8
416/537-7373, Fax: 416/537-6739
Executive Director, Neville Twine
Publications: Focus on Listening
Affiliates: Canadian Association of Distress Centres

Ontario Association of Interval & Transition Houses (OAITH) (1977)
#1404, 2 Carleton St., Toronto, ON M5B 1J3
416/977-6619, Fax: 416/977-1227, Email: oaith@web.net
Lobby Coordinator, Eileen Morrow

Ontario Association for Marriage & Family Therapy (OAMFT) (1974)
660 Eglinton Ave. West, PO Box 50055, Toronto, ON M4G 4G1
Toll Free: 1-800-267-2638
URL: http://www.inforamp.net/~mbehar/index.htm
President, Prof. Ed Bader
Publications: The Bond

Ontario Association of Volunteer Bureaux/Centres/L'Association des centres d'action bénévole de L'Ontario (1979)
Volunteer Ontario
#203, 2 Dunbloor Rd., Etobicoke, ON M9A 2E4
416/236-0588, Fax: 416/236-0590
Executive Director, Lorraine Street
Publications: Volunteer Ontario Newsletter; Volunteer Ontario Bulletin, m.

Ontario Block Parent Program Inc. (OBPPI) (1977)
83 Sherwood Forest Dr., Markham, ON L3P 1P9
905/294-7173, Fax: 905/294-7173, Toll Free: 1-800-563-2771
Chairman, Marianne MacBride
Publications: Newsletter

Ontario Coalition for Better Child Care (OCBCC) (1981)
Better Child Care Ontario, Inc.
500A Bloor St. West, 2nd Fl., Toronto, ON M5S 1Y3
416/538-0628, Fax: 416/538-6737
Executive Director, Kerry McCuaig
Publications: Network News
Affiliates: Canadian Child Care Advocacy Association

Ontario Coalition of Rape Crisis Centres/Coalition des centres anti-viol de l'Ontario (OCRCC) (1980)
8 Essa Rd., Barrie, ON L4N 3K3
705/737-0464, Fax: 705/739-7268
Executive Director, Anne Marie Aikins

Ontario Community Support Association/Association ontarienne de soutien communautaire (OCSA) (1992)
#104, 970 Lawrence Ave. West, Toronto, ON M6A 3B6
416/256-3010, Fax: 416/256-3021, Toll Free: 1-800-267-6272
Executive Director, Dan Stapleton
Publications: OCSA News

Ontario Municipal Social Services Association/Association des services sociaux des municipalités de l'Ontario (OMSSA) (1950)
#100, 5720 Timberlea Blvd., Mississauga, ON L4W 4W2
905/629-3115, Fax: 905/629-1633
Chief Administrative Officer, Pauline Carter
Publications: OMSSA Connection

Affiliates: Association of Municipal Employment Services; Association of Municipalities of Ontario

Ontario Social Development Council
#402, 130 Spadina Ave., Toronto, ON M5V 2L4
416/703-5351, Fax: 416/203-0552
Executive Director, Malcolm Shookner

Ordre professionnelle des travailleurs sociaux du Québec (OPTSQ) (1960)
#335, 5757, av Decelles, Montréal, PQ H3S 2C3
514/731-3925, Téléc: 514/731-6785
Directeur général, René Pagé, T.S.
Publications: Intervention
Organisation(s) affiliée(s): Conseil interprofessionnel du Québec

Parent Finders of Canada (1974)
Canadian Adoption Reunion Register
3998 Bayridge Ave., Vancouver, BC V7V 3J5
604/980-6005, Fax: 604/926-2037
National Director, Joan E. Vanstone
Affiliates: American Adoption Congress; International Soundex Reunion Register

Parents of the Environmentally Sensitive (1982)
PO Box 434, Stn R, Toronto, ON M4G 4C3
416/424-1611
Founder/President, Marge Nikiforuk

Pen-Parents of Canada (1993)
PO Box 52548, RPO Coquitlam Centre, Coquitlam, BC V3B 7J4
604/469-1272
Director, Patty Lou Bryant
Publications: The Pen-Parents of Canada Newsletter

People, Words & Change/Monde des mots (PWC) (1979)
211 Bronson Ave., Ottawa, ON K1R 6H5
613/234-2494
Senior Counsellor, Kae Bee
Publications: The Reader; This Is It, a.

PLAN International Canada (1968)
Foster Parents Plan
#1001, 95 St. Clair Ave. West, Toronto, ON M4V 3B5
416/920-1654, Fax: 416/920-9942, Telex: 06-367-00847, Info Line: 416/920-1654, Toll Free: 1-800-268-7174
National Director, Paula M. McTavish
Marketing Manager, Linda Antonacci
Communications, Kim Campbell
Publications: Plan News
Vancouver Office: Catherine Sloot, #305, 675 West Hastings St., Vancouver, BC V6B 1N2, 604/682-3717, Fax: 604/681-6406

PRIDE Canada Inc. (1984)
Parent Resources Institute for Drug Education
College of Pharmacy, University of Saskatchewan, Saskatoon, SK S7N 0W0
306/975-3755, 931-9690, Fax: 306/975-0503, Toll Free: 1-800-667-3747
Executive Director, Eloise Opheim
Program Director/Parent Development Coordinator, Shelly Porter
Youth Coordinator, Michelle Basket
Office Administrator/Resource Coordinator, Marie Boechler
Volunteer Coordinator, Mary Snatinsky
Conference Coordinator, Diane Romanuck
Publications: Survival Tactics for Drug-Free Youth
Affiliates: PRIDE International

Prince Edward Island Block Parent Program
PO Box 531, Alberton, PE C0B 1B0
902/853-4324
Chairperson, Pierre Legresley

Regroupement québécois des CALACS
Centres d'aide et de lutte contre les agressions à caractère sexuel
CP 605, Sherbrooke, PQ J1H 5K5
819/563-9940, Téléc: 819/563-9944
Coordonnatrice, Diane Lemieux

The Right to Die Society of Canada (RTDSC) (1991)
PO Box 39018, Victoria, BC V8V 4X8
250/380-1112, Fax: 250/386-3800, Email: rights@islandnet.com
URL: http://www.islandnet.com/~deathnet
Executive Director, John Hofsess
Head, Toronto Chapter, Ruth von Fuchs, 416/535-1323
Publications: Last Rights
Affiliates: World Federation of Right to Die Societies

Ronald McDonald Children's Charities of Canada/ Oeuvres de bienfaisance pour enfants Ronald McDonald du Canada (1982)
McDonald's Restaurants of Canada, McDonald's Place, Toronto, ON M3C 3L4
416/443-1000, Fax: 416/446-3415, Toll Free: 1-800-387-8808
Director, Heather Clark

Royal Canadian Humane Association (1894)
PO Box 3948, Stn C, Hamilton, ON L8H 7P2
905/662-2800
President, Dr. Mary Keyes
Sec.-Treas., Jean Best

Samaritan's Purse - Canada (1973)
Operation Christmas Child
PO Box 20100, RPO Calgary Place, Calgary, AB T2P 4J2
403/250-6565, Fax: 403/250-6567, Toll Free: 1-800-663-6500
Executive Director, Sean P. Campbell
President, Franklin Graham
Publications: Samaritan's Purse

Saskatchewan Block Parent Advisory Committee Inc.
135 Brown Cres., Saskatoon, SK S7J 2R9
306/373-2559
President, Daphne Bahnmann

Secours aux lépreux (Canada) inc./Leprosy Relief (Canada) Inc. (SLC) (1961)
#125, 1275, rue Hodge, Montréal, PQ H4N 3H4
514/744-3199, Téléc: 514/744-9095
Président, P.E. Legault
Publications: Le secours aux lèpreux/Leprosy Relief

Sex Information & Education Council of Canada/ Conseil du Canada d'information et éducation sexuelles (SIECCAN) (1964)
850 Coxwell Ave., East York, ON M4C 5R1
416/466-5304, Fax: 416/778-0785
Chairperson, Michael Barrett
Publications: SIECCAN Newsletter; Canadian Journal of Human Sexuality, q.

Sharelife (1976)
1155 Yonge St., Toronto, ON M4T 1W2
416/934-3411, Fax: 416/934-3412, Toll Free: 1-800-263-2595
Executive Director, Terry Thompson
Communications Director, Marilyn Burns
Publications: LifeLines; ShareLife at Work
Affiliates: Canadian Centre for Philanthropy

Social Planning Council of Metropolitan Toronto
#1001, 2 Carleton St., Toronto, ON M5B 1J3
416/351-0095, Fax: 416/351-0107
Executive Director, Peter Clutterbuck

Social Planning Council of Ottawa-Carleton (1928)
#317, 256 King Edward Ave., Ottawa, ON K1N 7M1
613/789-3658, Fax: 613/789-6680
Interim Executive Director, Terry Gilhen
President, Ron Caza
Affiliates: District Health Council; Ontario Social Development Council

Social Planning Council of Winnipeg
412 McDermot Ave., Winnipeg, MB R3A 0A9
204/943-2561, Fax: 204/942-3221
Executive Director, Wayne Helgason

Social Planning & Research Council of BC (SPARC) (1966)
#106, 2182 - 12th Ave. West, Vancouver, BC V6K 2N4
604/736-8118, Fax: 604/736-8697
Executive Director, Eva Cheung Robinson
President, Dorothy Argent
Publications: SPARC News: Community Affairs in British Columbia

Société de St-Vincent de Paul
2010, Mathias Tellier, Québec, PQ G1J 1G6
418/661-8600, Téléc: 418/661-9548
Présidente, Ellen Schryburt

Society of Transition Houses - BC & Yukon
#1112, 409 Granville St., Vancouver, BC V6C 1T2
604/669-6943, Fax: 604/689-6962
Coordinator, Greta Smith

SOS Children's Village British Columbia Society (SOS-BC) (1986)
14851 - 66A Ave., Surrey, BC V3S 2A3
604/599-0887, Fax: 604/599-0854
Office Manager, Alana Hicik
Publications: SOS Newsletter
Affiliates: SOS - Kinderdorf International - Vienna, Austria

SOS Children's Villages Canada/Villages d'enfants SOS Canada (1969)
SOS - Canada
#203, 396 Cooper St., Ottawa, ON K2P 2H7
613/232-3309, Fax: 613/232-6764
National Director, Carol Faulkner
Publications: SOS-Messenger
Affiliates: SOS-Kinderdorf International

Streetkids' Foundation (1987)
First Global Place, #201, 7 Concorde Pk., North York, ON M3C 3N4
416/391-1801
President, J.H. Vowles
Affiliates: Childhope Foundation Canada; Street Kids International

Suicide Information & Education Centre (SIEC) (1982)
#201, 1615 - 10 Ave. SW, Calgary, AB T3C 0J7
403/245-3900, Fax: 403/245-0299, Email: siec@nucleus.com
URL: http://www.siec.ca
Director, Gerry Harrington
Publications: Current Awareness Bulletin; SIEC Clipping Service, m.
Affiliates: Canadian Mental Health Associaton - Alberta Division

Thalidomide Victims Association of Canada (TVAC)
#607, 1105 Jalna Blvd., London, ON N6E 2S9
519/681-0357, Fax: 519/685-1518
CEO, R. Warren
Founder, H. Clifford Chadderton

Thompson Crisis Centre (1977)
PO Box 1226, Thompson, MB R8N 1P1
204/677-9668; Crisis: 204/778-7273, Fax: 204/677-9042, Toll Free: 1-800-446-0613
Executive Director, Michelle Lacroix
Publications: Newsletter

The TRIAD Society for Truth in Adoption of Canada (1986)
TRIAD
PO Box 5922, Stn B, Victoria, BC V8R 6S8
250/598-9887, Fax: 250/388-9423
President, Wayne Schultz, 403/229-0268
Vice-President, Audrey Scammell, 250/598-9887
Sec.-Treas., Brian Ritchie, 250/385-7884
Publications: TRIAD Tribune; Chapter Newsletter, q.
Affiliates: Canadian Adoption Reunion Registry; International Soundex Reunion Registry (assists with international searches)

UNICEF Canada/Comité UNICEF Canada (1955)
Canadian UNICEF Committee
443 Mt. Pleasant Rd., Toronto, ON M4S 2L8
416/482-4444, Fax: 416/482-8035, Toll Free: 1-800-567-4483
Executive Director, Harry S. Black
Publications: Project's Communique

United Way Canada/Centraide Canada
#404, 56 Sparks St., Ottawa, ON K1P 5A9
613/236-7041, Fax: 613/236-3087, Toll Free: 1-800-267-8221
President, David Armour
Chair, Ethne Cullen
Affiliates: United Way International
Affiliated United Way/Centraide Offices
Battlefords United Way Inc.: Administrator, Fran Sawula; President, Edna Logan; Treasurer, Rob Rongve, PO Box 904, North Battleford, SK S9A 2Z3, 306/445-1717
Brandon & District United Way: Executive Director, Debbie Arsenault; Campaign Director, Donna August, 638 Princess Ave., Brandon, MB R7A 0P3, 204/727-5923, Fax: 204/727-8939
Brant United Way: Executive Director, Dawn Grainger; Campaign Manager, Karina Poplar; Finance/Systems Coordinator, Rassam Flsaad, 82 Charlotte St., Brantford, ON N3T 2X1, 519/752-7848, Fax: 519/752-7913
Campbell River & District United Way: Executive Director, Carol Marshall; Board Chair, Brenda Matthews, 1253 Ironwood Rd., PO Box 135, Campbell River, BC V9W 5A7, 250/287-3213
Castlegar District United Way: Administrator, Nona Paulson; President, Ann Pollock, 1995 - 6 Ave., Castlegar, BC V1N 4B7, 250/365-7331, Fax: 250/365-5778
Centraide Abitibi-Témiscamingue-Ungava: Directrice générale, Pierrette Theberge; Président, Claude Girard, 175, ch Sullivan, CP 607, Val-d'Or, PQ J9P 4P6, 819/825-7139, Téléc: 819/825-7155
Centraide Bas St-Laurent: Directeur général, François Poulin; Présidente, Carole Duval; Secrétaire, Micheline Beaulieu, 103, rue de l'Evêché ouest, CP 636, Rimouski, PQ G5L 7C7, 418/723-1258, 1250, Téléc: 418/722-6128
Centraide Coeur du Québec: Directeur général, Pierre Métivier, #200, 154, rue Dunkin, Drummondville, PQ J2B 5V1, 819/477-0505, Téléc: 819/477-6719
Centraide Côte-Nord/Secteur est: Directeur, Denis Auray, 410A, rue Évangéline, Sept-Îles, PQ G4R 2N5, 418/962-2011, Téléc: 418/968-2923
Centraide Côte-Nord/Secteur ouest: Responsable administratrice, Muriel Phaneuf, #301, 858, rue de Puyjalon, Baie-Comeau, PQ G5C 1N1, 418/589-5567
Centraide Estrie: Directeur général, Claude Forgues, 1150, rue Belvédère sud, Sherbrooke, PQ J1H 4C7, 819/569-9281, Téléc: 819/569-5195

2-170 ORGANIZATIONS —SOCIAL RESPONSE/SOCIAL SERVICES

Centraide Gaspésie Îles-de-la-Madeleine: Directeur général, Jean Martel; Présidente, Christiane Brinck, Pavillon de la Montagne, 230, route du Parc, CP 596, Ste-Anne-des-Monts, PQ G0E 2G0, 418/763-2171, Téléc: 418/763-5631

Centraide Gatineau-Labelle-Hautes-Laurentides: Directeur général, Jean-Claude LeBel, 671, rue de la Madone, CP 154, Mont-Laurier, PQ J9L 3G9, 819/623-4090, Téléc: 819/623-7646

Centraide du Grand Montréal: Présidente et Directrice générale, Michèle Thibodeau-DeGuire; Directeur, Allocation et analyse sociale, Jean-Guy Bissonnette; Directeur, Services administratifs, Jean Camerlain; Directeur de la campagne, Pierre-Marie Cotte; Secrétaire exécutive de la corporation, Solange Vincent; Directrice, Communications, Lucie Rémillard; Président du conseil d'administration, Jean-François de Grandpré, 493, rue Sherbrooke ouest, Montréal, PQ H3A 1B6, 514/288-1261, Téléc: 514/844-9900

Centraide Lanaudière: Directrice générale, Simone Éthier, 54, Place Bourget nord, Joliette, PQ J6E 5E4, 514/753-7571, Téléc: 514/752-2603

Centraide Laurentides: Directeur général, André Aubert; Président, Réjean Kingsbury; Directrice de la campagne, Suzanne Piché; Agente de communications, Violette Gingras, 281, rue Brière, CP 335, St-Jérôme, PQ J7Z 5T9, 514/436-1584, Téléc: 514/436-3025

Centraide Mauricie: Président, Denise Tremblay; Trésorier, Denis Gervais; Secrétaire, Lisette Dionne; Directeur général, Faby N. Dresdell; Agente de communication, Carole Ebacher; Secrétaire, Sylvie Denis; Coordonnateur de la campagne de financement, Jean Yves Perron, 880, Place Boland, Trois-Rivières, PQ G8Z 4H2, 819/374-6207, Téléc: 819/374-6857

Centraide Outaouais: Directeur général, Marie-France Gosselin; Directrice de la campagne, Sylvie Moisan; Directrice, Allocations et relations avec les organismes, Nathalie LeBlanc; Responsable du programme des déléguées et délégués sociaux, Michel Renaud, 74, boul Montclair, Hull, PQ J8Y 2E7, 819/771-7751, Téléc: 819/771-0301

Centraide Portage-Taché: Directrice générale, Renée Lajeunesse, Collège de Ste-Anne, #100, 4e av, CP 520, La Pocatière, PQ G0R 1Z0, 418/856-3012

Centraide Québec: Directeur général, Pierre Métivier; Directrice de la campagne, Sylvie Simard; Directrice des communications, Andrée Lafleur, #101, 3100, av Bourg-Royal, Beauport, PQ G1C 5S7, 418/660-2100, Téléc: 418/660-2111

Centraide Richelieu-Yamaska: Directeur général, Laurent Nantel; Président, Claude Marchesseault, #4, 600, boul Casavant ouest, Saint-Hyacinthe, PQ J2S 7S3, 514/773-6679, Téléc: 514/773-4734

Centraide Saguenay-Lac St-Jean: Directeur général, Martin St-Pierre, 2876, Place Davis, Jonquière, PQ G7S 2C5, 418/548-4686, Téléc: 418/548-9715

Centraide sud-ouest du Québec: Directrice générale, Francine Bourdeau; Président, Normand O'Brien; Agente de bureau, Murielle Couture; Coordonnatrice de la campagne, Lise Dumont, 98, rue Champlain, CP 427, Salaberry-de-Valleyfield, PQ J6S 4V7, 514/371-2061, Téléc: 514/377-2309

Central Okanagan United Way: Executive Director, Len Lifahus; President, Terry Rolfo, 480 Leon Ave., Kelowna, BC V1Y 6J3, 250/860-2356, Fax: 250/868-3206

Comox District United Way: Executive Director, Marie Gordon; President, Pamela Jolin, PO Box 3097, Courtenay, BC V9N 5N3, 250/338-1151, Fax: 250/338-0609

Cowichan United Way: President, J. Bodard; Executive Secretary, Barbara Ziraldo, PO Box 11, Duncan, BC V9L 3X1, 250/748-1312, Fax: 250/748-7652

Deep River District United Way: President, John H. Ormrod; Secretary, Charlotte McWilliam; Treasurer, Bill Hunter; Campaign Chair, Al Bancroft, PO Box 188, Deep River, ON K0J 1P0

Elgin-St.Thomas United Way Services: Executive Director, Betty Want; President, Richard Haddow, 120 Centre St., St Thomas, ON N5R 2Z9, 519/631-3171, Fax: 519/631-9253, Toll Free: 1-800-233-9420

Elrose & District United Appeal: President, Jack Elliot; Secretary, Elizabeth Knorr, PO Box 591, Elrose, SK S0L 0Z0, 306/378-2927

Eston United Way: President, Sharon McNichol; Sec.-Treas., Marjorie Ryland, PO Box 561, Eston, SK S0L 1A0, 306/962-4363

Grande Prairie & District United Way: President, Patricia G. Reid, 9902 - 101 St., Grande Prairie, AB T8V 2P5, 403/532-1105, Fax: 403/532-3532

Guelph & Wellington United Way Social Planning Council: Executive Director, Morris Twist; Campaign Director, Allison Haskin-Brown, 161 Waterloo Ave., Guelph, ON N1H 3H9, 519/821-0571, Fax: 519/821-7847

Huron United Way: Office Administrator, Carol Randle, RR#5, Clinton, ON N0M 1L0, 519/482-7643

Kimberley & District United Way: President, Desiree McKay; Sec.-Treas., Bonnie Kreutz, 280 Spokane St., Kimberley, BC V1A 2E4, 250/427-2566

Kindersley & District United Appeal: President, Stan Humeny, 306/463-4131; Sec.-Treas., Sandy Grocholski, PO Box 489, Kindersley, SK S0L 1S0, 306/875-3743

Kirkland & District United Way: President, Bertha Boisvert; Secretary, Judy MacLeod, PO Box 313, Kirkland Lake, ON P2N 3H7, 705/567-6926

Lakeland United Way: President, Earla Burqe, #104, 311 - 10 St., Cold Lake, AB T0A 0V2, 403/639-2699, Fax: 403/594-2750

Lloydminster & District United Way: President, Ken Gillis; Secretary/Manager, M. Ellen Meldrum, PO Box 391, Lloydminster, SK S9V 0Y4, 403/875-3743

Metro United Way (Halifax-Dartmouth): President, Joanne Linzey; Director, Finance & Administration, Evelyn M. Barkhouse; Campaign Director, Linda Crockett; Director, Agency & Community Services, Peter Mortimer; Manager, Marketing & Development, Sharon Heading; Campaign Coordinator, Marlene Hopkins; Chairperson, John Mullowney, Cogswell Tower, #506, 2000 Barrington St., Halifax, NS B3J 3K1, 902/422-1501, Fax: 902/423-6837

Neepawa & District United Way: Chairman, Susan Hall, PO Box 1545, Neepawa, MB R0J 1H0, 204/476-2371

Nelson & District United Way: President, Joan Reichardt; Secretary, Leslie Bow, PO Box 89, Nelson, BC V1L 1P5, 250/352-7207

North Okanagan United Way: Executive Director, Ken Buchanan, #103, 3307 - 32 Ave., PO Box 533, Vernon, BC V1T 6M4, 250/549-1346

Northumberland United Way: Executive Director, Lynda Kay, 19 King St. East, PO Box 476, Cobourg, ON K9A 4L1, 905/372-6955, Fax: 905/372-4417

Porcupine United Way: Executive Director, Joanne Krakana; President, Joseph Ferrari, 98 Pine St. South, PO Box 984, Timmins, ON P4N 7H6, 705/268-9696, Fax: 705/268-9700

Portage Plains United Way: Executive Director, Angela Fooks; President, Stan Lee, PO Box 810, Portage La Prairie, MB R1N 3C3, 204/857-4440, Fax: 204/239-1543

Powell River & District United Way: President, Terry Kruger, 604/485-3070, PO Box 370, Powell River, BC V8A 5C2

Prince George United Way: Executive Director, David Coflin; President, Ole Sorensen, 1306 - 7 Ave., Prince George, BC V2L 4S6, 250/561-1040, Fax: 250/562-8102, Email: pgunited@netbistro.com; URL: http://www.pgonline.com/unitedway

Rossland United Way: President, Don Thompson, 604/362-5533, PO Box 154, Rossland, BC V0G 1Y0

Swift Current United Way: President, Archie Green; Executive Secretary, Marlene Arndt, 306/773-4828, c/o Swift Current Chamber of Commerce, Route 35, Mobile Delivery, Swift Current, SK S9H 3X6, Fax: 306/773-5686

The Pas & District United Way Inc.: President, Fletcher Stewart, 204/623-3311, PO Box 2998, The Pas, MB R9A 1R7

United Way of Ajax-Pickering: Executive Director, Peter Beattey; Executive Assistant, Susan Frudd, #407, 95 Bayly St. West, Ajax, ON L1S 7K8, 905/686-0606, Fax: 905/686-0609

United Way of the Alberta Capital Region: President, Anne Smith; Chair, Kerry Bjarnason; Vice-President, Agency & Community Services, Don Taylor; Vice-President, Marketing, Anne Smith; Vice-President, Resource Development, George Smith; Labour Coordinator, Gordon Steele; Controller, Joe Lavorato, 10020 - 108 St., Edmonton, AB T5J 1K6, 403/990-1000, Fax: 403/990-1919

United Way of Barrie/South Simcoe: Director, John McCullough, 150 Bayfield St., Barrie, ON L4M 3B1, 705/726-2301, Fax: 705/726-4897, Email: uwbss@bconnex.net; URL: http://www.bconnex.net/~uwbss

United Way of Burlington, Hamilton-Wentworth: CEO, Jody Orr, 177 Rebecca St., Hamilton, ON L8R 1B9, 905/527-4543, Fax: 905/527-5152

United Way of Calgary & Area: Chairman, Alan Tamaki; President, Dr. Ed Johnston; Community Services Director, Patricia Bond; Director, Finance, Lorne Hutchison, 120 - 13 Ave. SE, Calgary, AB T2G 1B3, 403/231-6265, Fax: 403/266-1271

United Way of Cambridge & North Dumfries: Executive Director, Brenda Peters; President, David Mogg; Campaign Director, Mary Park; VLD Coordinator, Diana Drackley; Labour Representative, Sandi Ellis, Old Fire Hall, Dickson St., PO Box 22053, Cambridge, ON N1R 8E3, 519/621-1030, Fax: 519/621-6220

United Way of Cape Breton: Executive Director, Ken Willingston; President, David Reynolds, Cabot House, 500 Kings Rd., 2nd Fl., PO Box 1929, Sydney, NS B1P 6W4, 902/562-5226, Fax: 902/562-5721

United Way of Central Alberta: Executive Director, Delta A. Rempel, 4322 - 52 Ave., PO Box 97, Red Deer, AB T4N 5E7, 403/343-3900, Fax: 403/346-0280

United Way of Colchester County: Executive Assistant, Shelly Andrews, 30 Esplanade, PO Box 32, Truro, NS B2N 5B6, 902/895-9313, Fax: 902/895-5003

United Way of Cornwall & District: Administrator, Keith E. Jodoin; President, Glen Grant; Executive Secretary, Elaine Myers, 331 Water St. East, PO Box 441, Cornwall, ON K6H 5T2, 613/932-2051, Fax: 613/932-7534

United Way of County Kent: Executive Director, Karen S. Kirkwood-Whyte; President, Tom McCarthy; Secretary, Helen McNaughton; Fundraising/Labour Services, Elaine Unsworth; VLD Coordinator, Janice Kominek, 177 King St. East, PO Box 606, Chatham, ON N7M 5K8, 519/354-0430, Fax: 519/354-9511

United Way of Cranbrook: Executive Secretary, Sharen Malone; President, Joe Oviatt, PO Box 657, Cranbrook, BC V1C 4J2, 250/426-8833

United Way of Cumberland County: Executive Director, Marilyn Mitchell; President, James Black, 43 Prince Arthur St., PO Box 535, Amherst, NS B4H 4A1, 902/667-2203, Fax: 902/667-3819

United Way of Estevan: President, Debbie Gress; Sec.-Treas., Debra Salaway, 621 Henry St., PO Box 611, Estevan, SK S4A 2A5, 306/634-9484 (after 5:00 pm), Fax: 306/634-8922

Canadian Almanac & Directory 1997

United Way of Fort McMurray: Executive Director, Ruby Olson, PO Box 4011, Fort McMurray, AB T9H 3L3, 403/791-0077, Fax: 403/791-0088

United Way of the Fraser Valley: Executive Director, Ken Becotte, 2445B West Railway St., Abbotsford, BC V2S 2E3, 604/852-1234 (Abbotsford); 792-2979(Chilliwack), Fax: 604/852-1234

United Way of Greater Fort Erie: Executive Director, Colleen Hardie; President, Peter Collee, 427 Garrison Rd., Fort Erie, ON L2A 6E6, 905/871-5454, Fax: 905/871-2064

United Way of Greater Saint John Inc.: Executive Director, Ann-Marie Tingley; Labour Liaison Representative, Ron Oldfield, 69 King St., Saint John, NB E2L 1G5, 506/658-1212, Fax: 506/633-7724

United Way of Greater Toronto: President, Dr. Anne Golden; Chair, Bahadur Madhani, 26 Wellington St. East, 11th Fl., Toronto, ON M5E 1W9, 416/777-2001, Fax: 416/777-0962

United Way of Greater Victoria: Executive Director, Maureen Duncan; President, Dick Cavaye; Labour Director, André Pel; Associate Director, Marketing & Communications, Marilyn Francis; Associate Director, Agency & Community Service, Chris Poirier-Skelton; Director, Finance & Administration, Alexander Giguere; Campaign Director, Sid Larsen, 1144 Fort St., Victoria, BC V8V 3K8, 250/385-6708, Fax: 250/385-6712, Email: Uway@tnet.net

United Way of Haldimand-Norfolk: Executive Director, Vincent Taylor; President, Ron Roberts, PO Box 472, Simcoe, ON N3Y 4L5, 519/426-5660, Fax: 519/426-0017

United Way of Halton Hills: Executive Director, Kathleen Hayward; President, Jim Lindsay, 115 Main St. South., PO Box 286, Halton Hills, ON L7G 4Y5, 905/877-3066, Fax: 905/877-3067

United Way of Kamloops & Region: Executive Director, Ingrid Caines, #14, 219 Victoria St., Kamloops, BC V2C 2A1, 250/372-9933, Fax: 250/372-5926

United Way of Kingston & District: Executive Director, Jack Butt; President, Robert Boucher; Finance Manager, Louise Adam; Administrative Assistant, Maria Smedes, #102, 16 Bath Rd., Kingston, ON K7L 1C4, 613/542-2674, Fax: 613/542-1379

United Way of Kitchener-Waterloo & Area: Executive Director, John Thompson; Administration Director, Janet Lawrence; Campaign Director, Diana Borowski, #1100, 20 Erb St. West, Waterloo, ON N2L 1T2, 519/888-6100, Fax: 519/888-7737

United Way of Lanark County: Executive Director, Elizabeth Clarke, PO Box 3, Carleton Place, ON K7C 3P3, 613/624-5658, Fax: 613/624-5579

United Way of Leeds & Grenville: Executive Director, Judith Baril, #103, 187 King St. West, PO Box 576, Brockville, ON K6V 5V7, 613/342-8889, Fax: 613/342-8850

United Way of Lethbridge & District: Executive Director, Audrey Porter, Bill Kergan Centre, #230, 207 - 13 St. North, Lethbridge, AB T1H 2R6, 403/327-1700, Fax: 403/320-2046

United Way of London & Middlesex: Chair, Peter Polischuk; Executive Director, Peter Lea, 409 King St., London, ON N6B 1S5, 519/438-1721, Fax: 519/438-9938

United Way of the Lower Mainland: Executive Director, Gary McCarthy; President, Marguerite Ford; Campaign Director, Kim Fenlon; Director, Agency & Community Services, Gil Martin; Labour Staff Representative, Ken Isomura; Labour Participation Director, Mervyn Van Steinburg; Finance Director, Kim Lockhart; VLD Coordinator, Cheryl Milton; Communications Director, Rhoda MacKillop, 4543 Canada Way, Burnaby, BC V5G 4T4, 604/294-8929, Fax: 604/293-0220

United Way of Medicine Hat, Redcliffe & District: Executive Director, Garth Vallely; President, Clarence Heringer, 457 - 3 St. SE, PO Box 783, Medicine Hat, AB T1A 7G7, 403/526-5544, Fax: 403/526-5244

United Way of Milton: Executive Director, Ann Eadie, PO Box 212, Milton, ON L9T 4N9, 905/875-2550, Fax: 905/875-2402

United Way of Moose Jaw: Chair, David Jukes, PO Box 1510, Moose Jaw, SK S6H 7A8, 306/693-0414

United Way of Morden & District Inc.: President, Lorne Stelmach, #2, 801 Stephen St., Morden, MB R6M 1G2, 204/822-4421, Fax: 204/822-4079

United Way of Nanaimo & District: Executive Director, Ron Walker, PO Box 1088, Nanaimo, BC V9R 5Z2, 250/753-8929, Fax: 250/753-7227

United Way of Niagara Falls: Executive Director, Janie Palmer; Campaign Manager, Carole Porter, 5017 Victoria Ave., Niagara Falls, ON L2E 4C9, 905/354-9342, Fax: 905/354-2717

United Way of Oakville: Executive Director, Julia Dumanian; President, Fran Richardson, #200, 466 Speers Rd., Oakville, ON L6K 3G1, 905/845-5571, Fax: 905/845-0166, Email: uwo_postoffice@msn.com

United Way of Oshawa-Whitby-Newcastle: Executive Director, Cindy J. Murray; President, Marianne Zakarow; Campaign Director, Robert Howard, 419 King St. West, Oshawa, ON L1J 2K5, 905/436-7377, Fax: 905/436-6414

United Way of Oxford: Executive Director, Marilyn Mann, 943 Dundas St., PO Box 354, Woodstock, ON N4S 7X6, 519/539-3851, Fax: 519/539-3209

United Way of Peel Region: CEO, Roy Spooner; Division Manager, Cathy Davis, #800, 151 City Centre Dr., Mississauga, ON L5B 1M7, 905/896-7335, Fax: 905/896-7338

United Way of Peterborough & District: Executive Director, Casey L. Ready, 277 Stewart St., Peterborough, ON K9J 3M8, 705/742-8839, Fax: 705/742-9186

United Way of Pictou County: Executive Director, Rae Foshay-Langille, PO Box 75, New Glasgow, NS B2H 5E1, 902/755-1754

United Way of Prince Albert: Administrator, Ivy Rue; President, Lawrence Joseph, #102, 1100 - 1 Ave East, PO Box 818, Prince Albert, SK S6V 5S4, 306/763-3686

United Way of Prince Edward Island: Executive Director, Anthony Sosnkowski, 129 Queen St., PO Box 247, Charlottetown, PE C1A 7K4, 902/894-8202

United Way of Quinte: Executive Director, Lillian Duffy; President, Donald Cook, 240 William St., Belleville, ON K8N 3K3, 613/962-9531, Fax: 613/962-4165

United Way of Regina: Executive Director, Wayne Hellquist; President, Paul Fudge; Director, Agency & Community Services, Karen Rowan; Director, Labour Community Services, Allen Lefebvre, 2022 Halifax St., Regina, SK S4P 1T7, 306/757-5671, Fax: 306/522-7199

United Way of St. Catharines & District: Executive Director, Larry Gemmel; Director, Julie Darney; Director, Labour Community Services, Mariea McNelis; Director, Finance & Administration, Bhavana Varma; VLD Coordinator, Janet Rouse, 55 St. Paul St., PO Box 816, St Catharines, ON L2R 6Y3, 905/688-5050, Fax: 905/688-2997

United Way of Sarnia-Lambton: Executive Director, Dave Brown; Campaign Coordinator, Pamela Vanroboys; Planning/Allocations & Government Relations, Heather Sherlock, 507 Louisa St., PO Box 548, Sarnia, ON N7T 7J4, 519/336-5452, Fax: 519/383-6032, Info Line: 519/336-2422

United Way of Saskatoon: Executive Director, Arla Gustafson; President, Shelley Brown; Campaign Director, Bernie Sutton, 345A - 3 Ave. South, Saskatoon, SK S7K 1M6, 306/975-7700, Fax: 306/244-0583

United Way of Sault Ste. Marie: Executive Director, Carmen J. Borghese, 8 Albert St. East, Sault Ste Marie, ON P6A 2H6, 705/256-7476, Fax: 705/759-5899

United Way of Slave Lake Society: President, Tyler Bray, 403/849-3999, PO Box 1985, Slave Lake, AB T0G 2A0

United Way of South Georgian Bay: President, Peter Webb, 127 Hurontario St., Collingwood, ON L9Y 2L9, 705/444-1141, Fax: 705/444-1141

United Way of South Niagara: Executive Director, Gary W. Clement, CAE, Seaway Mall, 800 Niagara St., Welland, ON L3C 5Z4, 905/735-0490, Fax: 905/735-5432

United Way of Stratford-Perth: Executive Director, Judith Spicer; President, Ted Radke, 38 Albert St., PO Box 21100, Stratford, ON N5A 7V4, 519/271-7730, Fax: 519/273-9350

United Way of Thompson Inc.: President, Manisha Pandya; Coordinator, Leah Passler, PO Box 202, Thompson, MB R8N 1N1, 204/778-5564, Fax: 204/778-5564

United Way of Thunder Bay: Executive Director, Joanne Kembel; Campaign Director, Debbie Escott, #102, 130 South Brodie St., PO Box 876, Thunder Bay, ON P7C 4X7, 807/623-6420, Fax: 807/623-6180

United Way of Trail: President, Jim Nelson; Executive Secretary, Joyce Demore-Powell, 1145 Cedar Ave., Trail, BC V1R 4B8, 250/364-0999, Fax: 250/364-1564

United Way of Victoria County: Executive Director, Mike Puffer; President, Chuck Piercy; Office Manager, Barbara Rose, #209, 189 Kent St. West, Lindsay, ON K9V 5G6, 705/878-5081, Fax: 705/878-5081

United Way of Windsor-Essex County: Executive Director, Hilary Payne, 1695 University Ave. West, Unit A, Windsor, ON N9B 1C3, 519/258-3033, Fax: 519/258-2346

United Way of Winnipeg: Executive Director, Susan Lewis; President, Bill Bowles; Director, Communications, Marg Wedlake; Comptroller, Bev Passey, 5 Donald St, 3rd Fl., Winnipeg, MB R3L 2T4, 204/477-5360, Fax: 204/453-6198

United Way of York Region: Executive Director, Vacant, #201, 3950 - 14th Ave., Markham, ON L3R 0A9, 905/474-9974; 416/324-3331, Fax: 905/474-0051

United Way/Centraide (Central NB) Inc.: CEO, Clair F. Smith; President, Graham Fraser, Park Office Centre, #201, 440 Wilsey Rd., Fredericton, NB E3B 6E9, 506/459-7773, Fax: 506/451-1104

United Way/Centraide of the Moncton Region: Executive Director, Kim Halliday; Campaign Coordinator, Julie Arsenault, PO Box 768, Moncton, NB E1C 8M9, 506/858-8600, Fax: 506/858-0584

United Way/Centraide Ottawa-Carleton: Executive Director, Claude Léost; President, W.E.R. Little, 106 Colonnade Rd., Nepean, ON K2E 7P4, 613/228-6700, Fax: 613/228-6730, Email: unitedwy@in-asec.ca

United Way/Centraide Sudbury & District: Executive Director, Monique Doolittle; President, Ted Keehn; Campaign Director, Michele Liebrock, #3, 764 Notre Dame, Sudbury, ON P3A 2T4, 705/560-3330, Fax: 705/560-3331

United Way/Centraide of the Upper Ottawa Valley: President, John Hempstead; Administrative Secretary, Catherine Dick, 214 Church St., PO Box 727, Pembroke, ON K8A 6X9, 613/735-0436, Fax: 613/735-0436

Weyburn & District United Way: President, Dennis Pilon, 306/848-3240; Sec.-Treas, Hannah Bell, 306/842-7529, PO Box 608, Weyburn, SK S4H 2K7

Winkler & District United Way: President, Shirley Banman; Treasurer, Mary Froese, PO Box 1528, Winkler, MB R6W 4B4, 204/325-6448

Yorkton & District United Way Inc.: President, Tom Seeley; Secretary, Carol Bobowski, 306/783-6566,

PO Box 44, Yorkton, SK S3N 2V6, 306/783-9409,
Fax: 306/786-7116

Vanier Institute of The Family/Institut Vanier de la famille (VIF) (1965)
#300, 120 Holland Ave., Ottawa, ON K1Y 0X6
613/722-4007, Fax: 613/729-5249
President, Jerome Berthelette
Executive Director, Administration, Alan Mirabelli
Publications: Transition

Volunteer Grandparents Society of British Columbia (VGPS) (1974)
1734 Broadway West, Vancouver, BC V6J 1Y1
604/736-8271, Fax: 604/736-8279
Executive Director, Hinda Simkin
Publications: Getting Started

The War Amputations of Canada
2827 Riverside Dr., Ottawa, ON K1V 0C4
613/731-3821, Fax: 613/731-3234, Toll Free: 1-800-465-2677
URL: http://www.waramps.ca
CEO, H. Clifford Chadderton
National President, B. Alan Russell
Director of Administration, Claire Roy
Publications: The Fragment; Champ; Les Vainqueurs

Yukon Block Parent Association (1989)
PO Box 5553, Whitehorse, YT Y1A 5H4
403/668-5840
Sec.-Treas., Jennifer Maura
Contact, Jan Hooper

SOFT DRINK INDUSTRY *see* **FOOD & BEVERAGE INDUSTRY**

SPCAS *see* **ANIMALS & ANIMAL SCIENCE**

SPORTS

Active Living Alliance for Canadians with a Disability/Alliance de vie active pour les canadiens/canadiennes ayant un handicap
#707A, 1600 James Naismith Dr., Gloucester, ON K1B 5N4
613/748-5747, Fax: 613/748-5782, Email: alc@rtm.activeliving.ca
URL: http://www.activeliving.ca/activeliving/alliance/alliance.html
Director, Jane Arkell
Chair, Dr. Don Hunter

Alberta Schools Athletic Association (ASAA) (1956)
Percy Page Centre, 11759 Groat Rd., Edmonton, AB T5M 3K6
403/453-8670, Fax: 403/453-8672
Executive Director, John F. Paton
Administrative Assistant, Judy Sware
Publications: ASAA Newsletter
Affiliates: National Federation of State High School Associations

Alpine Club of Canada/Club national canadien d'alpinisme (ACC) (1906)
PO Box 2040, Canmore, AB T0L 0M0
403/678-3200, Fax: 403/678-3224
URL: http://www.culturenet.ucalgary.ca/acc/
Provincial Coordinator, Leslie DeMarsh
Publications: The Gazette; Canadian Alpine Journal, a.
Affiliates: International Union of Alpinist Associations

American & Canadian Underwater Certification Inc.
ACUC International
1264 Osprey Dr., Ancaster, ON L9G 3L2
905/648-5500, Fax: 905/648-5440
President, R.W. Cronkwright
Executive Secretary, Marg Cronkwright
Publications: Contact
Affiliates: World Diving Federation; Undersea Hyperbaric Medical Society

Aquatic Federation of Canada/Fédération canadienne des sports aquatiques (1964)
c/o Synchro Canada, #310, 1600 James Naismith Dr., Gloucester, ON K1B 5N4
613/748-5674, Fax: 613/748-5724
President, Rob Campbell
Affiliates: Synchro Canada; Canadian Amateur Diving Association Inc.; Water Polo Canada; Swimming Canada

Arctic Winter Games International Committee (AWGIC) (1968)
c/o Sport & Recreation Division, Municipal & Community Affairs, #600, 5201 - 50th Ave., Yellowknife, NT X1A 3S9
403/873-7245, Fax: 403/920-6467, Email: ilegaree@maca.gov.nt.ca
President, Gerry Thick, Email: gthick@hyper-tech.yknet.yk.ca
Secretary, Wendell Shiffler
Treasurer, Peter Milner
Technical Director, Ian D. Legaree

Association of Ontario Sport Administrators
1185 Eglinton Ave. East, Toronto, ON M3C 3C6
416/426-7000, Fax: 416/426-7381
President, Sterling Ivany
Publications: The Insider

Athletics Canada/Athlétisme Canada
#805, 1600 James Naismith Dr., Gloucester, ON K1B 5N4
613/748-5678, Fax: 613/748-5645, Telex: 053-3660 SPORTR
President/CEO, Paul Dupré
Président du conseil, Brian Langley
Publications: Athletics Canada; Track & Field Journal, q.
Affiliates: International Amateur Athletic Federation

Badminton Canada
#603A, 1600 James Naismith Dr., Gloucester, ON K1B 5N4
613/748-5605, Fax: 613/748-5695
CEO, Roy Roberts
President, Wayne Macdonnell
Affiliates: International Badminton Federation

BADMINTON BC (1925)
#328, 1367 West Broadway, Vancouver, BC V6H 4A7
604/737-3030, Fax: 604/737-3130, Toll Free: 1-800-483-2473
Executive Director, Denise Coutts
Office Manager, Judy Cowan
Publications: Courtlines

BADMINTON NEW BRUNSWICK
PO Box 149, RR#1, Scoudouc, NB E0A 1N0
President, Bob Lee
Provincial Secretary, Rheal Chiasson

BADMINTON NEWFOUNDLAND & LABRADOR INC.
PO Box 21248, St. John's, NF A1A 5B2
709/576-7606, Fax: 709/579-3355
President, Wayne Somers

FÉDÉRATION QUÉBÉCOISE DE BADMINTON INC. (1929)
Badminton Québec
#100, 5648, rue Hochelaga, Montréal, PQ H1N 3L7
514/252-3066, Téléc: 514/252-3175
Directeur général, Gaetan Jean
Publications: Entrefilet/Badmintonien

Baseball Canada/Fédération canadienne de baseball amateur (CFAB) (1962)
Canadian Federation of Amateur Baseball
#712, 1600 James Naismith Dr., Gloucester, ON K1B 5N4
613/748-5606, Fax: 613/748-5767, Info Line: 613/748-5754
URL: http://www.cdnsport.ca/baseball
President, Richard Bélec
Publications: Executive Director's Report; Directory, a.; RBI Newsletter
Affiliates: Canadian Olympic Association

BASEBALL ALBERTA
Percy Page Centre, 11759 Groat Rd., Edmonton, AB T5M 3K6
403/453-8601, Fax: 403/453-8603
President, Doug Jones
Publications: Hits, Runs & Errors

BASEBALL BC
#200, 1367 West Broadway, Vancouver, BC V6H 4A9
604/737-3031, 3037, Fax: 604/737-6043
Executive Director, Rob Arnold

BASEBALL NEW BRUNSWICK
80 St. Roch St., Fredericton, NB E3C 1A9
506/450-1891, Fax: 506/444-9889
Contact, Donna Whalen

BASEBALL NOVA SCOTIA
PO Box 3010, Stn South, Halifax, NS B3J 3G6
902/425-5450, ext.355, Fax: 902/425-5606
Contact, Grant McDonald

BASEBALL QUÉBEC
4545, av Pierre-de-Coubertin, CP 1000, Succ. M, Montréal, PQ H1V 3R2
514/252-3075; 3000, Téléc: 514/252-3134
Directeur général, Leonard Pelland

MANITOBA BASEBALL ASSOCIATION
200 Main St., Winnipeg, MB R3C 4M2
204/985-4121, Fax: 204/640-6311
Contact, Guy Constant

NEWFOUNDLAND AMATEUR BASEBALL ASSOCIATION (1947)
PO Box 8700, St. John's, NF A1B 4J6
709/576-4935, Fax: 709/576-7493, Email: sad1024@infonet.st_johns.nf.ca
Executive Director, Ken Dawe, 709/576-4932
Publications: Baseball Scoop

ONTARIO BASEBALL ASSOCIATION (OBA) (1918)
Baseball Ontario
#16, 1425 Bishop St., Cambridge, ON N1R 6J9
519/740-3900, Fax: 519/740-6311
Contact, Jillian Graves
Affiliates: Little League Ontario

PEI AMATEUR BASEBALL ASSOCIATION (1967)
PO Box 92, Morell, PE C0A 1S0
902/961-2420, Fax: 902/961-3040
President & Secretary, George Morrison
Vice-President, Walter MacEwen

SASKATCHEWAN BASEBALL ASSOCIATION (SBA) (1953)
1870 Lorne St., Regina, SK S4P 2L7
306/780-9200, Fax: 306/352-3669
Executive Assistant, Sharon Bergerman
Publications: Reading the Pitch

ORGANIZATIONS — SPORTS

Basketball Canada (1972)
1600 James Naismith Dr., Gloucester, ON K1B 5N4
613/748-5607, Fax: 613/748-5741,
Email: basketball.canada@cdnsport.ca
URL: http://www.cdnsport.ca/basketball/
Executive Director, Rick Traer
President, Tony Wakeham
Coordinator, Marketing/Communications, Brenda MacFee
Affiliates: 10 provincial + 2 territorial associations; Canadian Interuniversity Athletic Union; Canadian Colleges Athletic Association; Canadian School Sports Federation; Toronto Raptors; Vancouver Grizzlies; Canadian Wheelchair Basketball Association; Canadian Association of Basketball Officials; National Association of Basketball Coaches of Canada; Women's Basketball Coaches Association

BASKETBALL ALBERTA
Percy Page Centre, 11759 Groat Rd., Edmonton, AB T5M 3K6
403/453-8649, Fax: 403/453-8553
Executive Director, Don Warren

BASKETBALL BC
#410, 1367 West Broadway, Vancouver, BC V6H 4A7
604/737-3032, Fax: 604/738-7173, Telex: 04-51588
Executive Director, Michael Hind
Publications: The Baseline

BASKETBALL MANITOBA
200 Main St., Winnipeg, MB R3C 4M2
204/985-4119, Fax: 204/985-4028
Executive Director, Gail Kenoall

BASKETBALL NEW BRUNSWICK/BASKETBALL NOUVEAU-BRUNSWICK (BNB) (1973)
53D Clark Rd., Fairvale, NB E2E 2K9
506/849-4667, Fax: 506/849-4668
Executive Director, Cindy Floyd
President, Chuck Beyea
Publications: Pivot
Affiliates: New Brunswick Association of Approved Basketball Officials; New Brunswick Interscholastic Athletic Association

BASKETBALL NOVA SCOTIA
PO Box 3010, Stn Parklane Centre, Halifax, NS B3J 3G6
902/425-5450, Fax: 902/425-5606
Executive Director, Patti Dow

BASKETBALL PEI
112 Heron Ave., Summerside, PE C1N 5R9
902/436-1943
President, Doug Dexter, Res: 902/894-7604
Sec.-Treas., Dana Barron

BASKETBALL SASKATCHEWAN INC. (BSI) (1976)
2205 Victoria Ave., Regina, SK S4P 0S4
306/780-9290, Fax: 306/525-4009
Executive Director, Bryan Nicurity
Publications: Tip-Off
Affiliates: Saskatchewan Sport

FÉDÉRATION DE BASKET-BALL DU QUÉBEC/QUÉBEC BASKETBALL FEDERATION (FBBQ) (1970)
Basketball Québec
4545, av Pierre-de-Coubertin, CP 1000, Succ. M, Montréal, PQ H1V 3R2
514/252-3057, Téléc: 514/252-3357
Directeur des programmes, Louis McNulty

NEWFOUNDLAND & LABRADOR BASKETBALL ASSOCIATION (1988)
PO Box 21029, St. John's, NF A1A 5B2
709/576-2047, Fax: 709/576-8787
President, Glenn Normore
Treasurer, Kathy Bolger

Secretary, Jamie Jennings
Technical Director, Bill Murphy
Publications: Key Points

ONTARIO BASKETBALL ASSOCIATION (1977)
#704, 1185 Eglinton Ave. East, North York, ON M3E 3C6
416/426-7200, Fax: 416/426-7360
Executive Director, Leslie Dal Cin
Publications: Time Out

Biathlon Canada (1985)
#509, 1600 James Naismith Dr., Gloucester, ON K1B 5N4
613/748-5608, Fax: 613/748-5762, Telex: 053-3660
Executive Director, Terrence Sheahan
President, Ray Kokkonen
Publications: Biathlon Broadcast
Affiliates: International Biathlon Union; Canadian Olympic Association

Bobsleigh Canada
#308, 1600 James Naismith Dr., Gloucester, ON K1B 5N4
613/748-5610, Fax: 613/748-5773, Telex: 053-3660 SPORTR
URL: http://www.cdnsport.ca/bobcan
Executive Director, Benoit Morin
President, Robert Storey
Affiliates: Fédération internationale de bobsleigh et de tobogganing

Bowling Federation of Canada/Fédération des quilles du Canada
#3, 1475 Star Top Rd., Gloucester, ON K1B 3W5
613/744-5090, Fax: 613/744-2217
Executive Director, Kevin Jepson
President, John Hoffman
Program Coordinator, Sheila Carr

Bowling Proprietors' Association of Canada
#10A, 250 Shields Ct., Markham, ON L3R 9W7
905/479-1560, Fax: 905/479-8613
Executive Director, Inge Malcolmson

Canada Games Council/Conseil des jeux du Canada (1969)
#409, 1600 James Naismith Dr., Gloucester, ON K1B 5N4
905/746-5799, Fax: 905/748-5759
President/CEO, Lane MacAdam
Chairman, Jack Pelech

Canadian 5 Pin Bowlers' Association/Association canadienne des cinq quilles (C5PBA) (1978)
#3, 1475 Star Top Rd., Gloucester, ON K1B 3W5
613/744-5090, Fax: 613/744-2217
Executive Director, Kevin Jepson
President, John Hoffman
Publications: Semi Annual & Annual Meetings; The Canadian Bowler, 3 pa
Affiliates: International Bowling Association

Canadian Academy of Sport Medicine/Académie canadienne de médecine sportive (CASM) (1970)
1600 James Naismith Dr., Gloucester, ON K1B 5N4
613/748-5851, Fax: 613/748-5850
President, Dr. Nicholas Montadi
Programme Coordinator, Jacqueline Burke
Publications: Clinical Journal of Sport Medicine; Nouvelles/News, q.
Affiliates: Canadian Medical Association

Canadian Adult Recreational Hockey Association
1600 James Naismith Dr., Gloucester, ON K1B 5N4
613/748-5646, Fax: 613/748-5714
Executive Director, Mike Peski
President, Larry Regan

Canadian Amateur Boxing Association/Association canadienne de boxe amateur
#711, 1600 James Naismith Dr., Gloucester, ON K1B 5N4
613/748-5611, Fax: 613/748-5740
Executive Director, Stuart Charbula
President, Jimmy MacInnis
Affiliates: International Amateur Boxing Association

Canadian Amateur Diving Association Inc./Association canadienne du plongeon amateur inc. (CADA) (1968)
#705, 1600 James Naismith Dr., Gloucester, ON K1B 5N4
613/748-5631, Fax: 613/748-5766, Telex: SPORTREC OTT 05
URL: http://www.diving.ca/diving/cada.html
Executive Director, Don Adams, CAE,
Email: dadams@rtm.cdnsport.ca
President, Gordon Peterson
Publications: Bulletin
Affiliates: Aquatic Federation of Canada; Sport Federation of Canada

Canadian Amateur Netball Association/Association canadienne de netball amateur
4948, rue Grey, Pierrefonds, PQ H8Z 2T4
416/248-5884
President, Helen Norman
Affiliates: International Federation of Netball Associations

Canadian Amateur Speed Skating Association/Association canadienne de patinage de vitesse amateur (CASSA) (1960)
#312, 1600 James Naismith Dr., Gloucester, ON K1B 5N4
613/748-5669, Fax: 613/748-5600, Telex: 053-3660
Executive Director, Guy Leclair
President, Henrietta Goplen
Publications: The Racer
Affiliates: International Skating Union

Canadian Amateur Wrestling Association/Association canadienne de lutte amateur (CAWA) (1970)
Place R. Tait McKenzie, #505, 1600 James Naismith Dr., Gloucester, ON K1B 5N4
613/748-5686, Fax: 613/748-5722, Telex: 053 3660
URL: http://www.cdnsport.ca/~kellyd
Executive Director, Greg Mathieu
President, Hank Lyth
Publications: Canadian Wrestler
Affiliates: International Amateur Wrestling Association

Canadian Amputee Sports Association/Association canadienne des sports pour amputés (CASA) (1977)
428 Lake Bonavista Dr. SE, Calgary, AB T2J 0M1
403/278-8772, Fax: 403/271-1920
President, Robert Wade
Publications: Ampscan
Affiliates: Canadian Paralympic Committee; International Sports Organization for the Disabled

Canadian Association for Disabled Skiing/Association canadienne des sports pour skieurs handicapés (CADS) (1976)
2860 Rotary Dr., PO Box 307, Kimberley, BC V1A 1E9
250/427-7712, Fax: 250/427-7715
Executive Director, Jerry Johnston
President, Henry Wohler
Publications: CADS Newsletter
Affiliates: International Paralympic Committee; Canadian Paralympic Committee; Canadian Ski Association

CANADIAN ASSOCIATION FOR DISABLED SKIING - NEWFOUNDLAND DIVISION
6 Albany Pl., St. John's, NF A1E 1Y2
709/753-3625
Contact, Marg Tibbo

CANADIAN ASSOCIATION FOR DISABLED SKIING NEW BRUNSWICK
CADS New Brunswick
PO Box 359, Saint-Jacques, NB E0L 1K0
506/735-3924, Fax: 506/735-4209
Contact, Elaine Corriveau

CANADIAN ASSOCIATION FOR DISABLED SKIING NOVA SCOTIA
CADS Nova Scotia
RR#2, Mahone Bay, NS B0J 2E0
902/624-8051, Fax: 902/624-8118

DISABLED SKIERS ALBERTA
Percy Page Centre, 11759 Groat Rd., Edmonton, AB T5M 3K6
403/453-8691, Fax: 403/453-8553
President, Greg McAndrews
Executive Coordinator, Allyson Holgate
Publications: Newsletter

DISABLED SKIERS ASSOCIATION OF BC (DSABC) (1973)
#324, 1367 West Broadway, Vancouver, BC V6H 4A9
604/737-3042, Fax: 604/738-7175
Executive Director, Diane Urquhart
President, Martin Grundy
Publications: Snowdrift

DISABLED SKIING ASSOCIATION OF MANITOBA (DSAM) (1974)
130 Cree Cres., Winnipeg, MB R3J 3W1
204/889-9202, Fax: 204/831-6650

ONTARIO ASSOCIATION FOR SKIERS WITH DISABILITIES
1185 Eglinton Ave. East, North York, ON M3C 3C6
416/426-7263, Fax: 416/426-7346

SASKATCHEWAN SKI ASSOCIATION - DISABLED DIVISION
17 Clark Cres., Saskatoon, SK S7H 3L8
306/374-7745

SKI QUÉBEC
165, Place Lilac, Pincourt, PQ J7V 5B6
514/453-6351, Téléc: 514/453-6353
Contact, Henry Wohler, Numéro á la maison: 514/453-3956

Canadian Association for Health, Physical Education, Recreation & Dance/Association canadienne pour la santé, l'éducation physique, le loisir et la danse (CAHPERD) (1933)
#809, 1600 James Naismith Dr., Gloucester, ON K1B 5N4
613/748-5622, Fax: 613/748-5737
URL: http://www.cdnsport.ca/activeliving/cahperd/index.html
Executive Director, Sue Cousineau
President, Mo MacKendrick
President-Elect, Dr. Rick Bell
Vice-President, Programs & BC Representative, John O'Flynn
Vice-President, Programs & NB Representative, Gordon Hopkins
Vice-President, Membership & Alberta Representative, Merri-Ann Ford
Vice-President, Networking & Saskatchewan Representative, Ken Loehndorf
Vice-President, Health & Manitoba Representative, Ernie Wilson
Vice-Président, Faculty & Francophone Affairs, Hugues Leblanc
Vice-President, Advocacy & Student Affairs, & NS Representative, Farida Blacklock
Vice-President, Human Resources Development & PEI Representative, Garth Turtle

Vice-President, Communications & Newfoundland Representative, Greg Wood
Vice-President, Special Interest Groups & Ontario Representative, Harrold Sawchuk
Publications: CAHPERD Journal; AVANTE; In Touch

Canadian Association of Nordic Ski Instructors (CANSI) (1976)
#409, 1185 Eglinton Ave. East, North York, ON M3C 3C6
416/426-7262, Fax: 416/426-7346
President, Kelly-Anne Rover
Publications: Snow News

Canadian Association for Sport Heritage/Association canadienne pour l'heritage sportif (CASH) (1979)
Canada's Sport Hall of Fame, Exhibition Place, Toronto, ON M6K 3C3
416/260-6789, Fax: 416/260-9347
President, Cheryl Rielly
Publications: Communique

Canadian Ball Hockey Association/Association canadienne de hockey-balle
Box 223, 21 - 10405 Jasper Ave., Edmonton, AB T5J 3S2
403/413-3474, Fax: 403/481-4619
President, Steve Posavec

Canadian Blind Sports Association Inc./Association canadienne des sports pour aveugles inc. (1976)
#606A, 1600 James Naismith Dr., Gloucester, ON K1B 5N4
613/748-5609, Fax: 613/748-5899
Executive Director, Ross Bales
President, Gerry York
Publications: Beyond Sight; Plein la Vue, q.
Affiliates: International Blind Sports Association; Canadian Paralympic Committee

ALBERTA SPORTS & RECREATION ASSOCIATION FOR THE BLIND (ASRAB) (1975)
PO Box 85056, RPO Albert Park, Calgary, AB T2A 7R7
403/262-5332, Fax: 403/265-7221
Executive Director, Shelley Allen
President, Darlene Murphy
Publications: ASRAB in Action

ASSOCIATION SPORTIVE DES AVEUGLES DU QUÉBEC INC.
4545, av Pierre-de-Coubertin, CP 1000, Succ. M, Montréal, PQ H1V 3R2
514/252-3178, Téléc: 514/254-1303
Directrice, Marie-Josée Bélanger

BC BLIND SPORTS & RECREATION ASSOCIATION (BCBSRA) (1978)
#317, 1367 Broadway West, Vancouver, BC V6H 4A7
604/325-1638, 8638, Fax: 604/325-1638, Email: bcbs@express.ca
Executive Director, Jane Blaine
Program Coordinator, Michael York
Publications: BCBSRA Newsletter
Affiliates: International Blind Sports Association

MANITOBA BLIND SPORTS ASSOCIATION
200 Main St., Winnipeg, MB R3C 4M2
204/925-5694, Fax: 204/925-5703
Executive Director, Michelle Wort
President, Wayne Peters
Publications: MSRAB in Motion

NEW BRUNSWICK RECREATION & SPORT ASSOCIATION FOR THE VISUALLY IMPAIRED INC./ASSOCIATION DES LOISIRS ET DU SPORT POUR LES PERSONNES HANDICAPÉES DE LA VUE DU NOUVEAU-BRUNSWICK (NBRSAVI) (1976)
80 Riverside Dr., Fredericton, NB E3A 3Y1

506/472-5941
President, Bill Turney
Publications: Bulletin
Affiliates: Active Living Alliance; Sport New Brunswick

NOVA SCOTIA BLIND SPORTS ASSOCIATION
c/o CNIB, 6136 Almond St., Halifax, NS B3K 1T8
902/454-2002
President, Alfredo Abdo

ONTARIO BLIND SPORT ASSOCIATION (1976)
1185 Eglinton Ave. East, North York, ON M3C 3C6
416/426-7187, Fax: 416/426-7361
Director, Douglas J. Wilton

SASKATCHEWAN BLIND SPORTS ASSOCIATION INC.
#210, 438 Victoria Ave. East, Regina, SK S4N 0N7
306/780-9425, Fax: 306/347-7500
Executive Director, Brian Fedler
President, Gerry Nelson

Canadian Centre for Drug-Free Sport/Centre canadien sur le dopage sportif (CCDS) (1991)
#702, 1600 James Naismith Dr., Gloucester, ON K1B 5N4
613/748-5755, Fax: 613/748-5746
Chairperson, Dr. Andrew Pipe
CEO, Victor Lachance

Canadian Cerebral Palsy Sports Association/Association canadienne des sports de paralysie cérébrale (CCPSA)
#606A, 1600 James Naismith Dr., Gloucester, ON K1B 5N4
613/748-5725, Fax: 613/748-5899
Executive Director, Christopher Hill
Affiliates: Canadian Paralympic Committee; Cerebral Palsy International Sport & Recreation Association

Canadian Colleges Athletic Association/Association canadienne du sport collégial (1979)
1600 James Naismith Dr., Gloucester, ON K1B 5N4
613/748-5626, Fax: 613/748-5757
Executive Director, Sandra Murray-MacDonell
President, Allan Ferchuk
Affiliates: Nova Scotia Colleges Athletic Association; Fédération québécoise du sport étudiant; Ontario Colleges Athletic Association; Prairie Athletic Conference; Alberta Colleges Athletic Conference; British Columbia Colleges Athletic Association

Canadian Council of Provincial/Territorial Sport Federations
PO Box 3010 South, Halifax, NS B3J 2G6
902/425-5450, Fax: 902/425-5606
Chairperson, Jim Newman
Sec.-Treas., David J. MacLean

Canadian Cricket Association/Association canadienne de cricket (1892)
1650 Abbey Rd., Ottawa, ON K1G 0H3
613/526-0173, Fax: 613/526-0173
President, Capt. S. James Siew
Publications: The Canadian Cricketer
Affiliates: International Cricket Council; Kanga Ball Canada

Canadian Curling Association/Association canadienne de curling
#803, 1600 James Naismith Dr., Gloucester, ON K1B 5N4
613/748-5628, Fax: 613/748-5713, Email: cdn.curling@rtm.cdnsport.ca
URL: http://www.cdnsport.ca/curling
General Manager, Dave W. Parkes
Affiliates: International Curling Federation

Canadian Cycling Association/Association cycliste canadienne
#212A, 1600 James Naismith Dr., Gloucester, ON
  K1B 5N4
613/748-5629, Fax: 613/748-5692, Telex: 053-3660
President, Richard Camirand
Director General, Andre Robitaille

Canadian Deaf Sports Association/Association des sports des sourds du Canada (CDSA) (1965)
#218, 1367 West Broadway, Vancouver, BC V6H 4A9
604/737-3041, Fax: 604/738-7175
President, Ron Fee
Treasurer, Derek Sweeting
Program/Technical Director, D.A. Shirton
Publications: Competitor
Affiliates: International Committee of Sports for the Deaf

ALBERTA DEAF SPORTS ASSOCIATION (ADSA) (1974)
Federation of Silent Sports of Alberta
PO Box 11741, Edmonton, AB T5J 3K8
403/438-8079, Fax: 403/438-9114
President, Jo-Anne Robinson
Publications: Alberta Deaf Sports Association

BC DEAF SPORTS FEDERATION (BCDSF) (1975)
Deaf Sports Office, #218, 1367 Broadway West, Vancouver, BC V6H 4A7
604/737-3041, Fax: 604/737-6043, TDD: 604/783-7122
President, Bradford Bentley
Office Administrator, Derek Sweeting
Publications: Newsletter

DEAF SPORTS NOVA SCOTIA
PO Box 20030, Halifax, NS B3R 2K9
President, Garfield Fisher

FÉDÉRATION SPORTIVE DES SOURDS DU QUÉBEC
4545, av Pierre-de-Coubertin, CP 1000, Succ. M, Montréal, PQ H1V 3R2
418/252-3069
Présidente, Ghyslaine Fiset

MANITOBA DEAF SPORTS ASSOCIATION
#322, 285 Pembina Hwy., Winnipeg, MB R3L 2E1
204/222-6025
President, Lawrence Prokopchuk

NEWFOUNDLAND DEAF SPORTS ASSOCIATION (NDSA) (1987)
PO Box 21313, St. John's, NF A1A 5G6
709/576-4592, Fax: 709/576-7501
President, Judy Shea
Affiliates: Sport Newfoundland & Labrador

SASKATCHEWAN DEAF SPORTS ASSOCIATION
1816 Lorne St., Regina, SK S4P 3N8
TDD: 306/787-3432
Contact, Dale Birley

Canadian Equestrian Federation/Fédération équestre canadienne (CEF) (1977)
#501, 1600 James Naismith Dr., Gloucester, ON
  K1B 5N4
613/748-5632, Fax: 613/747-2920
Executive Director, Basil Collett
President, Don Martz
Publications: The Bulletin
Affiliates: Fédération équestre internationale

Canadian Fencing Federation/Fédération canadienne d'escrime (CFF) (1971)
#305, 1600 James Naismith Dr., Gloucester, ON
  K1B 5N4
613/748-5633, BBS: 613/748-5881, Fax: 613/748-5742,
  Telex: 053-3660
URL: http://www.fencing.ca/
Executive Director, Jan Meyer
President, Gilles Chatel

Publications: Fencing Forum/L'Écho de l'escrime
Affiliates: Fédération internationale d'escrime

Canadian Figure Skating Association/Association canadienne de patinage artistique (CFSA)
#403, 1600 James Naismith Dr., Gloucester, ON
  K1B 5N4
613/748-5635, Fax: 613/748-5718, Telex: 053-3660,
  Email: cfsa@cfsa.ca
URL: http://www.cfsa.ca/
President, Jean MacLellan
Director General, David M. Dore

Canadian Football League/Ligue canadienne de football (CFL) (1958)
110 Eglinton Ave. West, 5th Fl., Toronto, ON
  M4R 1A3
416/322-9650, Fax: 416/322-9651
URL: http://www.cfl.ca/
Commissioner, Larry W. Smith
Sec.-Treas., Gregory B. Fulton
Events Manager, Sandra Taylor
Communications Manager, Jim Neish
Publications: CFL Facts, Figures & Records; CFL Rules & Regulations Handbook, a.; Weekly Statistics Package

Canadian Freestyle Ski Association
Canadian Ski Association - Freestyle
1600 James Naismith Dr., Gloucester, ON K1B 5N4
613/748-5663, Fax: 613/748-5710
Executive Director, Tom McIllfaterick
President, Chris Robinson

Canadian Golf Foundation/Fondation du Golf du Canada (CGF) (1979)
1333 Dorval Dr., Oakville, ON L6J 4Z3
905/849-9700, Fax: 905/845-7040
General Manager, Paul MacDonald
Publications: Winning Shots

Canadian Golf Industry Association/Association canadienne de l'industrie du golf
54 Haileybury Dr., Scarborough, ON M1K 4X5
416/267-3802, Fax: 416/267-4959
Secretary, Carl Banks

Canadian Golf Superintendents Association/Association canadienne des surintendants de golf (CGSA) (1966)
#509, 5580 Explorer Dr., Mississauga, ON L4W 4Y1
905/602-8873, Fax: 905/602-1958, Toll Free: 1-800-387-1056
Executive Director, R. Vince Gillis, CAE
Publications: GreenMaster

Canadian Gymnastics Federation/Fédération canadienne de gymnastique
#510, 1600 James Naismith Dr., Gloucester, ON
  K1B 5N4
613/748-5637, Fax: 613/748-5691, Telex: 053-3660
President, Slava Corn
Director General, Bill Houldsworth
Publications: Gymnastics Canada
Affiliates: Fédération internationale de gymnastique

Canadian Handball Association/Fédération de balle au mur du Canada (CHA)
3 Milburn Pl., Sherwood Park, AB T8A 0T8
403/467-6829
Contact, Pat Brennan

Canadian Hearing Impaired Hockey Association
1650 Lewes Way, Cooksville, ON L4W 3L2
705/624-7494
Executive Director, Roy Hysen

Canadian Highland Games Council/Conseil canadien des jeux de Highland
87 Woodlawn Ave., Brantford, ON N3Y 1A6
519/753-5027
President, Eric Davidson

Canadian Hockey (1969)
2424 University Dr. NW, Calgary, AB T2N 3Y9
403/777-3636, Fax: 403/777-3635
Director, Finance & Administration, Earl T. Young

Canadian Hockey Association/Association canadienne de Hockey (CHA) (1914)
#607, 1600 James Naismith Dr., Gloucester, ON
  K1B 5N4
613/748-5613, Fax: 613/748-5709
URL: http://www.cadnsport.ca/hockey
Chairman, Bill MacGillivary
President, Murray Costello
Publications: Hockey Today
Affiliates: International Ice Hockey Federation

ALBERTA AMATEUR HOCKEY ASSOCIATION/ASSOCIATION DE HOCKEY AMATEUR DE L'ALBERTA
#1, 7875 - 48 Ave., Red Deer, AB T4P 2K1
403/342-6777, Fax: 403/346-4277
Executive Director, Howard Wurban
President, Marv Bird

BRITISH COLUMBIA AMATEUR HOCKEY ASSOCIATION/ ASSOCIATION DE HOCKEY AMATEUR DE LA COLOMBIE-BRITANNIQUE (1919)
6671 Oldfield Rd., Saanichton, BC V8M 2A1
250/652-2978, Fax: 250/652-4536
Executive Director, Donald Freer
President, Florence Remple

FÉDÉRATION QUÉBÉCOISE DE HOCKEY SUR GLACE/QUÉBEC ICE HOCKEY FEDERATION (FQHG) (1976)
4545, av Pierre-de-Coubertin, CP 1000, Succ. M, Montréal, PQ H1V 3R2
514/252-3079, Téléc: 514/252-3158
Président, René Marcil
Directeur Général, Guy Blondeau

MANITOBA AMATEUR HOCKEY ASSOCIATION/ASSOCIATION DE HOCKEY AMATEUR DU MANITOBA
200 Main St., Winnipeg, MB R3C 4M2
204/985-4240, Fax: 204/985-4246
President, Jeff Hnatiuk

NEW BRUNSWICK AMATEUR HOCKEY ASSOCIATION/ ASSOCIATION DE HOCKEY DU NOUVEAU-BRUNSWICK (1968)
#4, 165 Regent St., PO Box 456, Fredericton, NB
  E3B 4Z9
506/453-0089, Fax: 506/452-8088
President, Scott Smith
Chairman, Harold Post

NEWFOUNDLAND AMATEUR HOCKEY ASSOCIATION/ASSOCIATION DE HOCKEY AMATEUR DE TERRE-NEUVE (1935)
15A High St., PO Box 176, Grand Falls-Windsor, NF
  A2A 2J4
709/489-5512, Fax: 709/489-2273
Executive Director, Barbara Power
Publications: Minor Hockey Directory; Minor Hockey News, a.

NOVA SCOTIA HOCKEY ASSOCIATION/ASSOCIATION DE HOCKEY DE LA NOUVELLE-ÉCOSSE
#910, 6080 Young St., Halifax, NS B3K 2A2
902/454-9400, Fax: 902/454-3883
Executive Director, Patricia MacDougall

ONTARIO HOCKEY ASSOCIATION/ASSOCIATION DE HOCKEY DE L'ONTARIO (1890)
#6, 1425 Bishop St., Cambridge, ON N1R 6J9
519/622-2402, Fax: 519/622-3550
President, Brent Ladds
Affiliates: International Ice Hockey Federation

PEI HOCKEY ASSOCIATION/ASSOCIATION DE HOCKEY DE L'ÎLE-DU-PRINCE-EDOUARD
20 Falconwood Rd., Sherwood, PE C1A 6B5
902/566-5171, Fax: 902/894-8412
Secretary/Manager, Gordie Lund

SASKATCHEWAN AMATEUR HOCKEY ASSOCIATION/ASSOCIATION DE HOCKEY AMATEUR DE LA SASKATCHEWAN (SAHA) (1912)
1844 Victoria Ave. East, Regina, SK S4N 7K3
306/789-5101, Fax: 306/759-6112
Executive Director, Kelly McClintock
Publications: Newsletter

Canadian In-Line & Roller Skating Association (CIRSA) (1994)
#117, 679 Queens Quay West, Toronto, ON M5V 3A9
416/260-5959, Fax: 416/260-0798, Toll Free: 1-800-958-0000, Email: cirsa@io.org
URL: http://www.io.org/~cirsa/cirsa.html
Acting Managing Director, Sandy Nimmo
Publications: Freewheel'n
Affiliates: Canadian Amateur Speed Skating Association; Canadian Hockey Association

Canadian Kendo Federation/Fédération canadienne de kendo
205 Riviera Dr., Markham, ON L3R 5J8
416/445-1481, Fax: 416/445-0519
President, Roy T. Asa
Secretary, Kiyoski Hao

Canadian Lacrosse Association/Association canadienne de crosse (CLA) (1867)
#508, 1600 James Naismith Dr., Gloucester, ON K1B 5N4
613/748-5641, Fax: 613/748-5698, Telex: 053-3660
Executive Director, Wes Clark
Chairman, William Hutton
Publications: Canadian Lacrosse News
Affiliates: International Lacrosse Federation; International Federation of Women's Lacrosse Associations; Fédération internationale d'Inter-crosse; Canadian Lacrosse Foundation; Sport Canada; Coaching Association of Canada; Canadian Sport & Fitness Administration Centre

Canadian Ladies' Golf Association/Association canadienne des golfeuses (CLGA) (1913)
Golf House, Glen Abbey, 1333 Dorval Dr., Oakville, ON L6J 4Z3
905/849-2542, Fax: 905/849-0188, Toll Free: 1-800-455-2542
National Executive Director, Peggy Brown
President, Mary Drummie
Publications: CLGA Yearbook
Affiliates: World Amateur Golf Council; United States Golf Association; Royal & Ancient Golf Association

Canadian Luge Association/Association canadienne de luge (1990)
#308, 1600 James Naismith Dr., Gloucester, ON K1B 5N4
613/748-5610, Fax: 613/748-5773, Telex: 053-3660
Executive Director, Terrence J. Sheahan
President, Don Vierboom
Technical Director, Wally Rauf
Publications: Luge News
Affiliates: Canadian Olympic Association; Fédération internationale de luge de course

Canadian Master Athlete Federation (CMAF) (1988)
#8, 100 West Beaver Creek Rd., Richmond Hill, ON L4B 1H4
905/707-8464, Fax: 905/707-8464, Toll Free: 1-800-363-9709, Email: sports@passport.ca
President, Liz Roach

Vice-President, Jim Walker
Sec.-Treas., Iain Douglas

Canadian Masters Cross-Country Ski Association/Association canadienne des maîtres en ski de fond (CMCSA) (1980)
5770 Seaview Rd., West Vancouver, BC V7W 1P8
604/921-0742, Fax: 604/921-0752
President, Alena Branda
Publications: CMCSA Newsletter
Affiliates: World Masters Cross-Country Ski Association; Cross-Country Canada

Canadian Masters Track & Field Association
1185 Eglinton Ave. East, North York, ON M3C 3C6
416/426-7310, Fax: 416/426-7326

Canadian Olympic Association/Association olympique canadienne (COA) (1907)
#900, 21 St. Clair Ave. East, Toronto, ON M4T 1L9
416/962-0262, Fax: 416/967-4902
CEO/Secretary General, Carol Anne Letheren
Executive Director, Marketing, Paul Shugart
Montréal: Director, Corporate Affairs, Kathleen Giguère, 2380, av Pierre Dupuy, Montréal, PQ H3C 3R4, 514/861-3371, Fax: 514/861-2896
Ottawa: Executive Director, Sports, Paul Dupré, #309, 1600 James Naismith Dr., Gloucester, ON K1B 5N4, 613/748-5647, Fax: 613/747-9483

Canadian Paralympic Committee/Comité paralympique du Canada (CPC) (1982)
#707A, 1600 James Naismith Dr., Gloucester, ON K1B 5N4
613/748-5630, Fax: 613/748-5731, Telex: 053-3660
Managing Director, Linda Hancock
President, Helen Manning
Publications: Resource Index for the Physically Disabled
Affiliates: International Paralympic Committee

Canadian Polo Association (1985)
Polo Canada
c/o Armadale Co. Ltd. Toronto Buttonville Airport, Markham, ON L3P 3J9
905/477-8000, Fax: 905/477-6897
Contact, Michael C. Sifton
Publications: The Corinthian Horse Sport

Canadian Pony Club (1934)
RR#1, King City, ON L7B 1A3
905/727-5224, Fax: 905/727-5224
Administrative Assistant, Barbara Grimm
Publications: The Pony Express

Canadian Professional Boxing Federation
RR#2, Site 16A, PO Box 187, Halifax, NS B3L 4J2
902/424-4560
Sec.-Treas., Ken Weston

Canadian Professional Golfers' Association/Association canadienne des golfeurs professionels (CPGA) (1911)
13450 Dublin Line, RR#1, Acton, ON L7J 2W7
519/853-5449, Fax: 519/853-5449
Executive Director, David J. Colling
Publications: CPGA Bulletin

Canadian Professional Rodeo Association
#223, 2116 - 27 Ave. NE, Calgary, AB T2E 7A6
403/250-7440, Fax: 403/250-6926
General Manager, Ralph Murray

Canadian Racing Drivers Association
#116, 295 The Westway, Etobicoke, ON M9C 4Z4
Vice-President, Paul Anderson

Canadian Racquetball Association/Association canadienne de racquetball (CRA) (1972)
Racquetball Canada
#303, 1600 James Naismith Dr., Gloucester, ON K1B 5N4
613/748-5653, Fax: 613/748-5644
Executive Director, Tom MacWilliam
President, David Bell
1st Vice-President, David Arsenault
Publications: First Service; Premier Service, q.
Affiliates: Canadian Sport Council; Canadian Olympic Association; Coaching Association of Canada

Canadian Rhythmic Sportive Gymnastic Federation/Fédération canadienne de gymnastique rythmique sportive (CRSGF) (1970)
Place R. Tait McKenzie, 1600 James Naismith Dr., Ottawa, ON K1B 5N4
613/748-5654, Fax: 613/748-5761, Telex: SPORTREC OTT 05
President, John Biggs
Publications: Techtalk

Canadian School Sports Federation/Fédération canadienne du sport scolaire
#218, 11 Victoria St., Barrie, ON L4N 6T3
705/739-7888, Fax: 705/739-7176
President, Colin Hood

Canadian Ski Association/Association canadienne de ski
#410, 1600 James Naismith Dr., Gloucester, ON K1B 5N4
613/748-5660, Fax: 613/748-5730
Executive Director, Neil MacDonald
President, Jim Gardner

Canadian Ski Council/Conseil canadien du ski (CSC) (1977)
#36, 7035 Fir Tree Dr., Mississauga, ON L5S 1V6
905/677-0020, Fax: 905/677-2055, Email: canski@interlog.com
URL: http://www.skican.org
President, Colin S. Chedore
Publications: Ski Focus
Affiliates: Canadian Association for Disabled Skiing; Canadian Association of Nordic Ski Instructors; Canadian Ski Area Operators' Association; Canadian Ski Association; Canadian Ski Instructors' Alliance; Canadian Ski Marathon; Canadian Ski Patrol System; Professional Ski Retailers of Canada; National Ski Industries Association

Canadian Ski Instructors' Alliance (CSIA) (1938)
#310, 774, boul Décarie, Montréal, PQ H4L 3L5
514/748-2648, Fax: 514/748-2476
Executive Director, André Derome
Publications: Ski-Pro
Affiliates: International Ski Instructors Association

Canadian Ski Marathon/Marathon canadien de ski (CSM) (1967)
CP 400, Gatineau, PQ J8P 6T9
819/669-7383, Fax: 819/722-0666
President, Christopher Busby
Publications: Entry Brochure; Essential Information Bulletin; Results Brochure

Canadian Ski Media Association/Association canadienne des journalistes de ski
7 Macleod St., Ottawa, ON K2P 0Z4
613/230-4126
Guy Thibaudeau, 514/226-7258

Canadian Ski Patrol System/Organisation de la patrouille canadienne de ski (CSPS) (1941)
4531 Southclark Pl., RR#5, PO Box 921, Ottawa, ON K1G 3N3

613/822-2245, Fax: 613/822-1088
Executive Director, John Leu
National President, Ron Gathercole
Manager, Renée Thivierge
Publications: Sweep

Canadian Soccer Association/Association canadienne de soccer (1912)
c/o Place Soccer Canada, 237 Metcalfe St., Ottawa, ON K2P 1R2
613/237-7678, Fax: 613/237-1516
COO, Kevan Pipe
President, Terry Quinn

ALBERTA SOCCER ASSOCIATION
Commonwealth Stadium, 1100 Stadium Rd., Edmonton, AB T5H 4E2
403/474-2200, Fax: 403/474-6300, Telex: 037-41708
Executive Director, Gary Sampley
Publications: Soccer Express

BRITISH COLUMBIA SOCCER ASSOCIATION
1126 Douglas Rd., Burnaby, BC V5C 4Z6
604/299-6401, Fax: 604/299-9610
Contact, Alex Kemp

FÉDÉRATION QUÉBÉCOISE DE SOCCER FOOTBALL (FQSF) (1911)
Soccer Québec
4545, av Pierre-de-Coubertin, CP 1000, Succ. M, Montréal, PQ H1V 3R2
514/252-3068, Téléc: 514/252-3162
Secrétaire général, Jean Gandubert
Publications: Québec Soccer

MANITOBA SOCCER ASSOCIATION
200 Main St., Winnipeg, MB R3C 4M2
204/985-4139, Fax: 204/985-4028
Executive Director, David Kerr

NEWFOUNDLAND SOCCER ASSOCIATION
PO Box 21029, St. John's, NF A1A 5B2
709/576-0601, Fax: 709/576-0588
Executive Director, Andrew Cameron
Publications: Kickoff

ONTARIO SOCCER ASSOCIATION
#606, 1185 Eglinton Ave. East, North York, ON M3C 3C6
416/426-7300, Fax: 416/426-7313, Telex: 06-986157
Executive Director, Brian Avey

PEI SOCCER ASSOCIATION (PEISA)
Confederation Court Mall, Lower Level, PO Box 1863, Charlottetown, PE C1A 7N5
902/368-6251, Fax: 902/368-6251
President, John Diamond
Secretary/Registrar, Daphne Andrews
Treasurer, Wendy Ripley
Office Manager, Anne Matheson

SASKATCHEWAN SOCCER ASSOCIATION INC.
1870 Lorne St., Regina, SK S4P 2L7
306/780-9225, Fax: 306/781-6021

SOCCER NEW BRUNSWICK
79 Hazen Ave., Renforth, NB E2H 1N9
506/849-4183, Fax: 506/849-4895
President, Alex Savoie

SOCCER NOVA SCOTIA
5516 Spring Garden Rd., 4th Fl., Halifax, NS B3J 3G6
902/425-5606
President, Peter Rogers
Publications: Spotlight on Soccer

Canadian Society for Exercise Physiology/ Société canadienne de physiologie de l'exercice (CSEP) (1967)
#311, 1600 James Naismith Dr., Gloucester, ON K1B 5N4
613/748-5768, Fax: 613/748-5763
Executive Director, William Hearst
President, Hélène Perrault, Ph.D.
Publications: Canadian Journal of Applied Physiology
Affiliates: Canadian Fitness & Lifestyle Research Institute; Canadian Physiotherapy Association - Cardio-Respiratory Division; Canadian Association of Cardiac Rehabilitation; American College of Sports Medicine

Canadian Society for Psychomotor Learning & Sport Psychology/Société canadienne de apprentissage psycho-motrice et psychologie du sport (SCAPPS) (1970)
Faculty of Kinesiology, University of Calgary, Calgary, AB T2N 1N4
403/220-3428, Fax: 403/289-9117
Sec.-Treas., Dr. T. Gabriele
President, Dr. J. Deakin
Publications: Newsletter
Affiliates: International Society of Sport Psychology

Canadian Special Olympics Inc./Jeux olympiques spéciaux du Canada inc. (1969)
#209, 40 St. Clair Ave. West, Toronto, ON M4V 1M2
416/927-9050, Fax: 416/927-8475, Email: solympic@inforamp.net
URL: http://www.incontext.ca/cso/index.html
President, Jim Jordan
Executive Vice-President, Frank Selke
Chairman of the Board, Brian Etherington
Publications: National Office Bulletin
Affiliates: Special Olympics International

ALBERTA SPECIAL OLYMPICS INC. (1980)
Percy Page Centre, 11759 Groat Rd., Edmonton, AB T5M 3K6
403/453-8520, Fax: 403/453-8553
Executive Director, Dave Keating
President, Hans Tiedemann

BRITISH COLUMBIA SPECIAL OLYMPICS (BCSO) (1980)
#226, 1367 West Broadway, Vancouver, BC V6H 4A7
604/737-3078, Fax: 604/737-6043
Executive Director, Dan Howe
Publications: Newsletter

MANITOBA SPECIAL OLYMPICS
200 Main St., 4th Fl., Winnipeg, MB R3C 4M2
204/925-5628, Fax: 204/925-5635
Executive Director, Maureen Dowds

NEW BRUNSWICK SPECIAL OLYMPICS
#207, 390 King St., Fredericton, NB E3B 1E3
506/459-3999
Program Director, Jennifer Bent

NEWFOUNDLAND & LABRADOR SPECIAL OLYMPICS (1986)
#201, 102 - 104 LeMarchant Rd., St. John's, NF A1C 2H2
709/738-1923, Fax: 709/238-0119
Executive Director, Michael J. Walsh

NOVA SCOTIA SPECIAL OLYMPICS
5516 Spring Garden Rd., PO Box 3010, Stn Parklane Cntr, Halifax, NS B3J 3G6
902/425-5450, Fax: 902/425-5606
Executive Director, Geraldine Dowling

ONTARIO SPECIAL OLYMPICS (OSO) (1980)
#503, 1185 Eglinton Ave. East, North York, ON M3C 3C6
416/426-7277, Fax: 416/426-7341, Toll Free: 1-888-333-5515

Executive Director, Glenn MacDonell
President, Don Pagnutti
Publications: Torch

PEI SPECIAL OLYMPICS (1987)
PO Box 841, Charlottetown, PE C1A 7L9
902/368-4543, Fax: 902/368-4542
Executive Director, Angela Marchbank
President, Elmer Williams
Secretary, Florence Birch

SASKATCHEWAN SPECIAL OLYMPICS SOCIETY
353 Broad St., Regina, SK S4R 1X2
306/780-9247, Fax: 306/780-9441
Executive Director, Pat Stellek

YUKON SPECIAL OLYMPICS (1981)
PO Box 4007, Whitehorse, YT Y1A 3S9
403/668-6511, Fax: 403/667-4237
Executive Director, Renée Hartling
Publications: Rendezvous; Special Olympic News, 3 pa
Affiliates: Special Olympics International

Canadian Sport Council/Conseil canadien du sport (1951)
#301A, 1600 James Naismith Dr., Gloucester, ON K1B 5N4
613/748-5670, Fax: 613/748-5732, Telex: 053-3660
URL: http://cansport.magi.com/cansport
Managing Partner, Deborah Evans
Managing Partner, Sandy Johnson
Publications: Sports Directory/Répertoire des sports; Coast to Coast, 4-6 pa

SASK SPORT INC.
1870 Lorne St., Regina, SK S4P 2L7
306/780-9302, Fax: 306/781-6021
President, Dorothy Josephson
Program Manager, John Lee

SPORT BC (1966)
#509, 1367 Broadway West, Vancouver, BC V6H 4A9
604/737-3005, Fax: 604/737-3097, Info Line: 604/737-3000
URL: http://www.sport.bc.ca/SportBC/
Executive Director, John Mills, Email: john_mills@sport.bc.ca
Chair, Tricia Smith

SPORT MANITOBA (MSF) (1970)
200 Main St., Winnipeg, MB R3C 4M2
204/925-5605, Fax: 204/925-5624
Executive Director, David Kilfoyle
President, Dennis Davis
Marketing Director, Debbie Guenette Lavigne
Publications: Sport Report

SPORT NEW BRUNSWICK/SPORT NOUVEAU-BRUNSWICK (SNB) (1968)
#103, 565 Priestman St., Fredericton, NB E3B 5X8
506/451-1320, Fax: 506/451-1325
President, Harold Nicholson
Contact, Kathleen MacFarlane
Publications: Initiatives

SPORT NEWFOUNDLAND & LABRADOR (1972)
PO Box 8700, Stn A, St. John's, NF A1B 4J6
709/576-4932, Fax: 709/576-7493
President, Bill Halfyard
Administrative Officer, Lynn Hindy

SPORT NORTH FEDERATION
PO Box 336, Yellowknife, NT X1A 2N3
403/873-3032, Fax: 403/920-4047
Executive Director, David Hurley
President, Jean Hinton

SPORT NOVA SCOTIA
PO Box 3010, Stn Parklane Centre, Halifax, NS B3J 3G6
902/425-5450, Fax: 902/425-5606
Executive Director, David J. MacLean
President, Carol Miller

SPORT ONTARIO (1969)
1185 Eglinton Ave. East, North York, ON M3C 3C6
416/426-7310
Chairperson, Dr. Susan Vial
Publications: For the Love of Sport

SPORT PEI INC. (1973)
PO Box 302, Charlottetown, PE C1A 7K7
902/368-4110, Fax: 902/368-4548
Executive Director, David MacNeill
President, Mike Conroy, Res: 902/569-5501
Public Relations Coordinator, Cy Yard
Sports Marketing & Development Officer, Kim Griffin
Publications: The Communicator; Island Sport Scene, q.; The Island Sport Directory, a.

SPORT YUKON
4061 - 4th Ave., Whitehorse, YT Y1A 1H1
403/668-4236, Fax: 403/667-4237
Executive Director, Vern Haggard
President, George Arcand

SPORTS QUÉBEC
Société de sports du Québec
4545, av Pierre-du-Coubertin, CP 1000, Succ. M, Montréal, PQ H1V 3R2
514/252-3114, Téléc: 514/254-9621
Directeur général, Luc Gélineau

Canadian Sport & Fitness Administration Centre/ Centre canadien d'administration du sport et de la condition physique (CSFAC) (1970)
#203, 1600 James Naismith Dr., Gloucester, ON K1B 5N4
613/747-2900, Fax: 613/748-5706
URL: http://www.cdnsport.ca/
President, Wilf Wedmann
Chief Operating Officer, Sue Killam
Vice-President, Business Affairs, John Restivo

Canadian Sporting Arms & Ammunition Association (CSAAA) (1973)
PO Box 235, Cobourg, ON K9A 4K5
905/373-1623, Fax: 905/373-1706, Email: showgun@eagle.ca
URL: http://www.eagle.ca/showgun
Executive Director, René J.J. Roberge
Publications: Shooting Sports Today; Canadian Hunting & Shooting Sport Trade Magazine, a.

Canadian Swimming Coaches Association (1991)
1950 Cedar Cres., Vancouver, BC V6J 2R6
Paul McKinnon

Canadian Team Handball Federation/Fédération canadienne de handball olympique (1956)
#304, 1600 James Naismith Dr., Gloucester, ON K1B 5N4
613/748-5676, Fax: 613/748-5783, Telex: 053-3660 SPORT
President, Ron Gorgichuk
Administrative Coordinator, Sylvie Guibert
Affiliates: International Handball Federation; Pan American Team Handball Federation; Commonwealth Handball Federation

Canadian Tennis Association/Association canadienne de tennis (1890)
Tennis Canada
3111 Steeles Ave. West, Downsview, ON M3J 3H2
416/665-9777, Fax: 416/665-9017, Email: commnctn@tenniscanada.com
URL: http://www.tenniscanada.com
Chair, Jacqueline Boutet
President & CEO, Robert H. Moffatt

ALBERTA TENNIS ASSOCIATION
Tennis Alberta
Percy Page Centre, 11759 Groat Rd., Edmonton, AB T5M 3K6
403/453-8611, Fax: 403/453-8553
Program Director, Gail Kawecki

FÉDÉRATION QUÉBÉCOISE DE TENNIS/QUÉBEC TENNIS FEDERATION (1899)
4545, av Pierre-de-Coubertin, CP 1000, Succ. M, Montréal, PQ H1V 3R2
514/252-3072, Téléc: 514/252-3164
Directeur général, Jean François Manibal
Président, Réjean Genois
Publications: L'Écriteau

NATIONAL CAPITAL TENNIS ASSOCIATION
1 Donald St., Ottawa, ON K1K 4E6
613/742-7559
Office Manager, Beverley Verney
Publications: NCTA News

NEWFOUNDLAND & LABRADOR TENNIS ASSOCIATION
Provincial Recreation Centre, PO Box 8700, St. John's, NF A1B 4J6
709/576-0902, Fax: 709/576-7493
Executive Director, Rick Kirby

NOVA SCOTIA TENNIS ASSOCIATION
5516 Spring Garden Rd., Halifax, NS B3J 1G6
902/425-5450, Fax: 902/423-0574
Executive Director, Kevin Reidy

ONTARIO TENNIS ASSOCIATION (OTA) (1918)
#412, 1185 Eglinton Ave. East, North York, ON M3C 3C6
416/426-7135, Fax: 416/426-7353, Toll Free: 1-800-387-5066
Executive Director, Peter Budreo
President, Pam Olley
Publications: Ontario Tennis; Ontario Tennis Yearbook & Tournament Schedule, s-a.
Affiliates: International Tennis Federation

PEI TENNIS ASSOCIATION
5 Wyndwood Cres., Charlottetown, PE C1A 8S2
902/566-5051, Fax: 902/628-1514
Executive Director, Linda Durling

SASKATCHEWAN TENNIS ASSOCIATION
Tennis Saskatchewan
2205 Victoria Ave., Regina, SK S4P 0S4
306/780-9410, Fax: 306/525-4009
Executive Director, Rory Park
Publications: Court Talk
Affiliates: Sasksport

TENNIS BC
#204, 1367 Broadway West, Vancouver, BC V6H 4A7
604/737-3086, Fax: 604/737-6043
Executive Director, Tom Fawsitt

TENNIS MANITOBA (1881)
Manitoba Tennis Association
#303, 200 Main St., Winnipeg, MB R3C 4M2
204/925-5660, Fax: 204/925-5663
Executive Director, Mark Farand
Publications: Toba Tennis News

TENNIS NEW BRUNSWICK
PO Box 549, Moncton, NB E1C 8L9
506/853-7578, Fax: 506/857-8240
Program Director, Phyllis Cairns

Canadian Tenpin Federation Inc./Fédération canadienne des dix quilles Inc.
530 Home St., Winnipeg, MB R3G 1X7
204/783-7453, Fax: 204/786-4856
President, Paul Foster
Sec.-Treas., Adrianne Bride
Affiliates: Fédération internationale des quilleurs

Canadian Therapeutic Riding Association/ Association canadienne d'équitation thérapeutique (1981)
CanTRA
PO Box 1055, Guelph, ON N1H 6J6
519/767-0700, Fax: 519/767-0435
President, Ann Caine
Publications: CANTRA Caller; CANTRA Communique

Canadian Trotting Association
2150 Meadowvale Blvd., Mississauga, ON L5N 6R6
905/858-3060, Fax: 905/858-3111
Executive Director, Tom Gorman
Publications: Trot

Canadian Weightlifting Federation/Fédération haltérophile canadienne
755, Croissant Savard, Longueuil, PQ J4X 1X9
514/466-4476, Fax: 514/931-6868
President, Philippe Saint-Cyr
General Manager, Dan Steinwald
Affiliates: International Weightlifting Federation

FÉDÉRATION D'HALTÉROPHILIE DU QUÉBEC/QUÉBEC WEIGHTLIFTING FEDERATION (FHQ) (1969)
4545, av Pierre-de-Coubertin, CP 1000, Succ. M, Montréal, PQ H1V 3R2
514/252-3046, Téléc: 514/254-4545
Directeur technique, Augustin Brassard
Publications: Coup d'oeil sur l'halterophilie

Canadian Wheelchair Basketball Association/ Association Canadienne de Basketball en Fauteuil Roulant (CWBA) (1994)
#715, 1600 James Naismith Dr., Gloucester, ON K1B 5N4
613/748-5888, Fax: 613/748-5889
URL: http://www.cwba.ca/
Executive Director, Reg McClellan
President, Maureen Orchard
Publications: Communiqué; Give & Go/Passe et Va, bi-weekly

Canadian Wheelchair Sports Association/ Association canadienne des sports en fauteuil roulant (CWSA) (1967)
#212A, 1600 James Naismith Dr., Gloucester, ON K1B 5N4
613/748-5685, Fax: 613/748-5722
Director General, Clare Gillespie
President, Laurel Crosby
Affiliates: International Stoke Mandeville Wheelchair Sports Federation

Canadian Women's Field Hockey Association/ Association canadienne féminine de hockey sur gazon (1962)
1600 James Naismith Dr., Gloucester, ON K1B 5N4
613/748-5634, Fax: 613/748-5790, Telex: 053-3660
Executive Director, Catherine Cadieux
Publications: Bulletin; Counter Attack, 3 pa; Handbook & Directory, a.
Affiliates: Canadian Olympic Association; Fédération internationale de hockey; Pan American Hockey Federation; Sport Federation of Canada

Coaching Association of Canada/Association canadienne des entraîneurs (CAC) (1971)
#604, 1600 James Naismith Dr., Gloucester, ON K1B 5N4
613/748-5624, Fax: 613/748-5707, Email: coach@coach.ca
URL: http://www.coach.ca/
President, Dr. Geoff R. Gowan
Vice-President, Technical, John Bales
Chairman, Ken Bellemare
Communications Director, Carole Slight
Affiliates: Professional Arm: Canadian Professional Coaches Association

The Commonwealth Games Association of Canada Inc./Association canadienne des jeux du Commonwealth inc. (CGAC) (1977)
#105, 1600 James Naismith Dr., Gloucester, ON K1B 5N4
613/748-5625, Fax: 613/748-5781
President, Judy Kent
Affiliates: Commonwealth Games Federation - London, England

Cross Country Canada/Ski de fond Canada
#407, 1600 James Naismith Dr., Gloucester, ON K1B 5N4
613/748-5662, Fax: 613/748-5703
Executive Director, Neil MacDonald
President, Guy Laviolette
Affiliates: Canadian Ski Association

Dr. James Naismith Basketball Foundation/La Fondation du Basket-Ball Dr James Naismith
1 James Naismith Way, PO Box 1991, Almonte, ON K0A 1A0
613/256-0492, Fax: 613/256-0492
Honourary President, Jack Donahue

Equestrian Association for the Disabled (TEAD)
6095 Dickenson Rd., RR#2, Hannon, ON L0R 1P0
905/679-8323, Fax: 905/679-1705
Program Director/Instructor, Hilary Webb
Publications: Rocking Horse Review
Affiliates: Ontario Therapeutic Riding Association

Federation of Canadian Archers Inc./Fédération canadienne des archers inc. (FCA) (1927)
#209, 1600 James Naismith Dr., Gloucester, ON K1B 5N4
613/748-5604, Fax: 613/748-5785, Telex: 053-3660, Email: brian.macpherson@cdnsport.ca
Executive Director, Brian MacPherson
President, Al Wills
Technical Director, Pascal Colmaire
Publications: The Canadian Archer
Affiliates: Federation internationale de tir à l'arc; Canadian Olympic Association; Sports Federation of Canada

Fédération de patinage artistique du Québec (FPAQ)
4545, av Pierre-de-Coubertin, CP 1000, Succ. M, Montréal, PQ H1V 3R2
514/252-3073, Téléc: 514/252-3170
Directrice executive, Anita Choquet

Fédération du plongeon amateur du Québec (FPAQ) (1971)
4545, av Pierre-de-Coubertin, CP 1000, Succ. M, Montréal, PQ H1V 3R2
514/252-3096, Téléc: 514/252-3094, Courrier électronique: plongeon@mlink.ca
URL: http://www.cigp.com/atlanta/federati/plongeon/
Directeur exécutif, Donald Normand
Publications: La Vrille

Fédération québécoise du sport étudiant (FQSE) (1988)
4545, av Pierre-De Coubertin, CP 1000, Succ. M, Montréal, PQ H1V 3R2
514/252-3300, Téléc: 514/254-3292
Directeur général, Jean Hamel
Président, Michel Carrières

Fédération de rugby du Québec
4545, av Pierre-de-Coubertin, CP 1000, Succ. M, Montréal, PQ H1V 3R2
514/341-6780, Téléc: 514/341-7699
Secrétaire, Simon Davies

Field Hockey Canada/Hockey sur gazon Canada
#206, 1600 James Naismith Dr., Gloucester, ON K1B 5N4
613/748-5634, Fax: 613/748-5790, Email: field.hockey@cdnsport.ca
URL: http://www.cdnsport.ca/~snichols/1fhc.html
President, Janet Ellis
Senior Manager, Suzzanne Nicholson
Affiliates: Fédération internationale de hockey

Football Canada (CAFA) (1882)
Canadian Amateur Football Association
Lansdowne Park Civic Centre, 1015 Bank St., Ottawa, ON K1S 3W7
613/564-2675, Fax: 613/564-6309
Executive Director, Jack Jordan
President, Joe Pistilli

Horse Trials Canada/Concours Complet Canada
RR#1, Dwight, ON P0A 1H0
705/635-1569
Secretary, Nancy Tapley
Publications: The Eventer

Jockey Club of Canada
PO Box 156, Etobicoke, ON M9W 5L2
416/675-7756, Fax: 416/675-6378
Executive Director, Gary Loschke

Judo Canada (1956)
Canadian Kodokan Black Belt Association
#401, 1600 James Naismith Dr., Ottawa, ON K1B 5N4
613/748-5640, Fax: 613/748-5697, Telex: 053-3660, Email: judo@cdnsport.ca
Executive Director, Gary Gardiner
President, Luc Larocque
Publications: Yudansha Journal
Affiliates: International Judo Federation

Manitoba High Schools Athletic Association (1962)
200 Main St., Winnipeg, MB R3C 4M2
204/925-5640, Fax: 204/925-5624
Dr. Ron Buzahora
Publications: Pacer
Affiliates: National Federation of State Associations

National Karate Association of Canada/Association nationale de karaté (1974)
#230, 2616 - 18 St. NE, Calgary, AB T2E 7R1
250/297-2720, Fax: 250/297-2702
President, Peter Brown

National Ski Industries Association/Association nationale de l'industrie du ski (NSIA) (1962)
#340, 8250, boul Decarie, Montréal, PQ H4P 2P5
514/737-1672, Fax: 514/737-0724
Executive Director, Carol Hopper

National Youth Bowling Council
#10A, 250 Shields Ct., Markham, ON L3R 9W7
905/479-1560, Fax: 905/479-8610
National Administrator, Inge Malcolmson

Newfoundland & Labrador Curling Association
PO Box 21238, St. John's, NF A1A 5B2
709/722-1156, Fax: 709/722-1156
Secretary, Eugene Trickett

Newfoundland & Labrador High School Athletic Federation (NFHSAF) (1969)
Torbay Airport, Bldg. 25, St. John's, NF A1B 4J6
709/729-2795, Fax: 709/576-7493
Executive Director, Karen Richard

Nordic Combined Ski Canada
#407, 1600 James Naismith Dr., Gloucester, ON K1B 5N4
613/748-5664, Fax: 613/748-5765
Executive & Marketing Director, Jean R. Dupré
Chairman, Bruce Keith

Nova Scotia School Athletic Federation
5516 Spring Garden Rd., PO Box 3010, Stn South, Halifax, NS B3J 3G6
902/425-5450, Fax: 902/425-5606
Executive Director, Ron O'Flaherty

Olympic Trust of Canada/Trust Olympique du Canada (1970)
#606, 2 St Clair Ave. West, Toronto, ON M4V 1L5
Chairman, Bob McGavin
President, Julia Foster

Ontario Federation of School Athletic Associations (OFSAA) (1948)
11 Victoria St., Barrie, ON L4N 6T3
705/739-7888, Fax: 705/739-7176
Executive Director, Colin Hood
Publications: OFSAA Bulletin
Affiliates: International School Sport Federation; Canadian School Sport Federation; Ontario Physical & Health Education Association; Ontario Coalition of Women in Educational Athletics; National Federation of State High School Associations

The Ontario Jockey Club
PO Box 156, Etobicoke, ON M9W 5L2
416/675-6110, Fax: 416/213-2126

Ontario Ladies' Golf Association (OLGA) (1926)
#304, 1185 Eglinton Ave. East, North York, ON M3C 3C6
416/426-7090, Fax: 416/426-7379
Executive Director, Honey Crossley

Ontario Minor Hockey Association
#43, 40 Vogell Rd., Richmond Hill, ON L4B 3N6
905/780-6642, Fax: 905/780-0344
President, Mike Hammond
Secretary Manager, Michael McCauley

Ontario Sports & Recreation Centre Inc./Centre ontarien des sports et des loisirs inc.
1185 Eglinton Ave. East, North York, ON M3C 3C6
416/426-7000, Fax: 416/426-7381
General Manager, Guy Bradbury

PEI Men's Golf Association (PEIGA) (1971)
PO Box 51, Charlottetown, PE C1A 7K2
902/894-8462, Fax: 902/628-1759
Executive Director, Fred Coady, 902/368-1177
Publications: PEI Golf Record

PEI Recreation & Sports Association for the Physically Challenged (PEIRSAPC)
PO Box 841, Charlottetown, PE C1A 7L9
902/368-4540, Fax: 902/368-4542
Recreation & Sport Consultant, Frank MacIntyre, 902/368-4540

Canadian Almanac & Directory 1997

PEI School Athletic Association
c/o Dept. of Education, PO Box 2000, Charlottetown, PE C1A 7N8
President, Walter MacEwan
Sec.-Treas., Clem Gallant
Executive Secretary, Lyall Huggan, 902/368-4672

Régie de la sécurité dans les sports du Québec (RSSQ) (1980)
#302, 100, rue Laviolette, Trois-Rivières, PQ G9A 5S9
819/371-6033, Téléc: 819/371-6992
URL: http://www.rssq.gouv.qc.ca
Président, Roger Landry
Publications: Le Sécuritaire

Ringette Canada/Ringuette Canada (1975)
#806, 1600 James Naismith Dr., Gloucester, ON K1B 5N4
613/748-5655, Fax: 613/748-5860, Telex: 053-3660 SPORTR
URL: http://www.cdnsport.ca/~anikd
Executive Director, Carolyne Hudson
President, Audra Antoniuk
Publications: Ringette Review

FÉDÉRATION SPORTIVE DE RINGUETTE DU QUÉBEC (1973)
4545, av Pierre-de-Coubertin, CP 1000, Succ. M, Montréal, PQ H1V 3R2
514/252-3085, Téléc: 514/254-1069
Directeur administratif, Daniel Dussault
Présidente, Francine Lussier

Rowing Canada Aviron (RCA)
Canadian Amateur Rowing Association
#716, 1600 James Naismith Dr., Gloucester, ON K1B 5N4
613/748-5656, Fax: 613/748-5712
Executive Director, Alan Roof
President, Joe Grey
Publications: Rowing Canada Aviron
Affiliates: Fédération Internationale des Sociétés d'Aviron

Royal Canadian Golf Association/Association royale de golf du Canada (RCGA) (1895)
Golf House, 1333 Dorval Dr., Oakville, ON L6J 4Z3
905/849-9700, Fax: 905/845-7040, Email: golfhous@rcga.org
URL: http://www.rcga.org
Executive Director, Stephen D. Ross
Publications: Golf Canada
Affiliates: World Amateur Golf Council

ALBERTA GOLF ASSOCIATION (1912)
#104, 4116 - 64 Ave. SE, Calgary, AB T2B 2C3
403/236-4616, Fax: 403/236-2915
Executive Director, Brent Ellenton
Publications: The AGA Director; The Alberta Golfer, a.

ASSOCIATION DE GOLF DU QUÉBEC/QUÉBEC GOLF ASSOCIATION (AGQ) (1920)
CP 399, Pierrefonds, PQ H9H 4L1
514/620-6565, Téléc: 514/620-3413
Directeur général, Phil Gribbin

BRITISH COLUMBIA GOLF ASSOCIATION
Sperling Plaza 2, #185, 6450 Roberts St., Burnaby, BC V5G 4E1
604/294-1818, Fax: 604/294-1819
Executive Director, Don Gardner
Administrative Manager, Betty MacDonald

MANITOBA GOLF ASSOCIATION INC.
#211, 200 Main St., Winnipeg, MB R3C 4M2
204/925-5730
Executive Director, Don Craig

NEW BRUNSWICK GOLF ASSOCIATION/ASSOCIATION DE GOLF DU NOUVEAU BRUNSWICK
#103, 565 Priestman St., Fredericton, NB E3B 5X8
506/451-1324, Fax: 506/451-1325
Acting Executive Director, Larry Marshall

NEWFOUNDLAND/LABRADOR GOLF ASSOCIATION
PO Box 5361, St. John's, NF A1C 5W2
709/754-1090
Contact, Charles Cook

NOVA SCOTIA GOLF ASSOCIATION (NSGA) (1931)
14 Limardo Dr., Dartmouth, NS B3A 3X4
902/465-7306, Fax: 902/465-7306
Executive Director, Warren MacDonald

ONTARIO GOLF ASSOCIATION (OGA) (1923)
RR#3, Newmarket, ON L3Y 4W1
905/853-8511, Fax: 905/853-0803
Executive Director, John Gordon
Publications: Ontario Golf News

PRINCE EDWARD ISLAND GOLF ASSOCIATION
PO Box 2245, Charlottetown, PE C1A 8B9
902/894-8462
Executive Director, Fred Coady

SASKATCHEWAN GOLF ASSOCIATION (1914)
510 Cynthia St., Saskatoon, SK S7L 7K7
306/975-0834, Fax: 306/242-8007
Executive Director, Bill Taylor
Publications: SGA Newsletter

Ski Jumping Canada/Saut en ski Canada
#407, 1600 James Naismith Dr., Gloucester, ON K1B 5N4
613/748-5665, Fax: 613/748-5765
URL: http://www.cdnsport.ca/jump
Chairman, Rob McCormack
Executive & Marketing Director, Jean R. Dupré

Société des jeux d'hiver de Québec 2002/Québec 2002 Winter Games Corporation (1992)
#500, 525, boul René-Lévesque est, Québec, PQ G1R 5R2
418/529-2002, Téléc: 418/529-2606
Documentaliste, Danièle Desmeules

Softball Canada (1967)
Canadian Amateur Softball Association
#802, 1600 James Naismith Dr., Gloucester, ON K1B 5N4
613/748-5668, Fax: 613/748-5760, Email: softball@rtm.cdnsport.ca
URL: http://www.cdnsport.ca/softball/
CEO, Rick Johnson
President, Dale McMann

Sport for Disabled - Ontario (SDO)
1185 Eglinton Ave. East, North York, ON M3C 3C7
416/426-7187, Fax: 416/426-7361
Acting Executive Director, Faye Blackwood
Affiliates: Ontario Amputee Sports Association; Ontario Blind Sports Association; Ontario Cerebral Palsy Sports Association; Ontario Wheelchair Sports Association

Sport Medicine & Science Council of Canada/Conseil canadien de la médecine sportive (SMCC) (1978)
1600 James Naismith Dr., Gloucester, ON K1B 5N4
613/748-5671, Fax: 613/748-5729
Executive Director, Rick Nickelchok
President, Mike Plyley
Publications: Sport Med Connection; Sport Med Info, q.; SMSCC Directory, a.
Affiliates: Fédération internationale de médecine sportive

Sports Physiotherapy Division of the Canadian Physiotherapy Association/Groupe de physiothérapie sportive d'Association canadienne de physiothérapie (SPD)
#507, 1600 James Naismith Dr., Gloucester, ON K1B 5N4
613/748-5794, Fax: 613/748-5850
Program Coordinator, Gary Leslie

Squash Canada (1914)
#603, 1600 James Naismith Dr., Gloucester, ON K1B 5N4
613/748-5672, Fax: 613/748-5861, Telex: 053-3660
URL: http://symphony.eecg.toronto.edu:8888/danv/
Executive Director, Susan Dodge
President, Anne Smith
Technical Director, Nancy Cranbury
Publications: Canadian Squash

Swimming/Natation Canada
#503, 1600 James Naismith Dr., Gloucester, ON K1B 5N4
613/748-5673, Fax: 613/748-5715
CEO, Harold Cliff
Corporate Communications Director, Penny Joyce
Affiliates: Aquatic Federation of Canada

Synchro Canada/Association canadienne de nage synchronisée amateur
Canadian Amateur Synchronized Swimming Association
1600 James Naismith Dr., Gloucester, ON K1B 5N4
613/748-5674, 746-0060, Fax: 613/748-5724
Executive Director, Jost am Rhyn
President, Joan Roberts

Vélo-Québec
1251, rue Rachel est, Montréal, PQ H2J 2J9
514/521-8356, Téléc: 514/521-5711
Directeur général, Jean-François Pronovost

Volleyball Canada (1973)
Canadian Volleyball Association
#811, 1600 James Naismith Dr., Gloucester, ON K1B 5N4
613/748-5681, Fax: 613/748-5727, Toll Free: 1-800-461-0124, Email: volleyball.canada@cdnsport.ca
Director General, Sylvie Bigras
President, Alan Ahac
Affiliates: International Volleyball Association; Canadian Olympic Association; Coaching Association of Canada

ALBERTA VOLLEYBALL ASSOCIATION (AVA) (1957)
Percy Page Centre, 11759 Groat Rd., Edmonton, AB T5M 3K6
403/453-8530, Fax: 403/453-8532
President, Bruce Kirkland
Executive Director, Terry Archer
Publications: Volleyball Today; Volley Notes, q.
Affiliates: Federation of Outdoor Volleyball Associations

BRITISH COLUMBIA VOLLEYBALL ASSOCIATION (1965)
#405, 1367 Broadway West, Vancouver, BC V6H 4A9
604/737-3087, Fax: 604/738-7175, Email: bcvolleyball@sport.bc.ca
Executive Director, Tom Caverly

FÉDÉRATION DE VOLLEY-BALL DU QUÉBEC (FVBQ) (1968)
4545, av Pierre-de-Coubertin, CP 1000, Succ. M, Montréal, PQ H1V 3R2
514/252-3065, Téléc: 514/252-3176
Directrice générale, Elaine Lauzon
Président, Raymond Côté
Publications: Smash
Organisation(s) affiliée(s): Sports Québec; Regroupement loisirs Québec

MANITOBA VOLLEYBALL ASSOCIATION
200 Main St., Winnipeg, MB R3C 4M2
204/925-5783, Fax: 204/925-5786
Executive Director, Greg Guenther
President, Kolleen Picklyk

NEWFOUNDLAND & LABRADOR VOLLEYBALL ASSOCIATION
PO Box 21248, St. John's, NF A1A 5B2
709/576-0817, Fax: 709/576-7493
Program Coordinator, Craig Neil
President, Todd Martin

NORTHWEST TERRITORIES VOLLEYBALL ASSOCIATION
c/o Sport North, PO Box 336, Yellowknife, NT X1A 2N3
403/873-3032, Fax: 403/920-4047, Toll Free: 1-800-661-0797
President, Rob Meckling

ONTARIO VOLLEYBALL ASSOCIATION
#507, 1185 Eglinton Ave. East, North York, ON M3C 3C6
416/426-7316, Fax: 416/426-7386, Toll Free: 1-800-563-5938
Executive Director, Diane Wood

PRINCE EDWARD ISLAND VOLLEYBALL ASSOCIATION
150 Gardiner St., Summerside, PE C1N 5J2
902/436-3933, Fax: 902/436-0133
President, Freddy Martin
Publications: Tip Off the Block
Affiliates: Sport PEI

SASKATCHEWAN VOLLEYBALL ASSOCIATION
1870 Lorne St., Regina, SK S4P 2L7
306/780-9250, Fax: 306/780-9288
Executive Director, Tim Bjornson
Publications: The Scoop

VOLLEYBALL NEW BRUNSWICK
PO Box 638, Stn A, Fredericton, NB E3B 5A6
506/458-1386, Fax: 506/452-0986
Director, Judy Hogan

VOLLEYBALL NOVA SCOTIA
5516 Spring Garden Rd., Halifax, NS B3J 1G6
902/425-5450, Fax: 902/425-5606
Director, June Lumsden

VOLLEYBALL YUKON
4061 - 4th Ave., Whitehorse, YT Y1A 1H1
403/633-4599, Fax: 403/667-4237
Sport Coordinator, Darlene Ries

Water Polo Canada
#708, 1600 James Naismith Dr., Gloucester, ON K1B 5N4
613/748-5682, Fax: 613/748-5777
Executive Director, Michel Langelier
President, Victor Tetreault
Publications: Inside 4 Metres
Affiliates: Aquatic Federation of Canada

Water Ski Canada/Ski nautique Canada
#606B, 1600 James Naismith Dr., Gloucester, ON K1B 5N4
613/748-5683, Fax: 613/748-5867, Telex: 53-3660
Executive Director, Hugh Mitchener
President, Peter Person
Publications: Ski Nautique News

World University Games/Jeux mondiaux universitaires
c/o Canadian Intervuniversity Athletic Union, #302, 1600 James Naismith Dr., Gloucester, ON K1B 5N4
613/748-5619, Fax: 613/748-5764
Director, Promotions & Communications, Jennifer Brenning

STANDARDS & TESTING
see also Consumers

Cable Television Standards Foundation/Fondation des normes de télévision par câble (1988)
Standards Foundation
#560, 220 Laurier Ave. West, Ottawa, ON K1P 5Z9
613/230-5442, Fax: 613/230-5679, Toll Free: 1-800-426-4170
President & CEO, Gérald Lavallée
Affiliates: Canadian Cable Television Association

Canadian Educational Standards Institute (CESI) (1986)
3 Elm Ave., Toronto, ON M4W 1M8
416/488-2244, Fax: 416/488-1773
Director, Solette N. Gelberg
Publications: CESI Newsletter

Canadian Evaluation Society/Société canadienne l'évaluation (CES) (1981)
582 Somerset St. West, Ottawa, ON K1R 5K2
613/230-1007, Fax: 613/237-9900
Executive Secretary, Kathy Jones
President, Linda E. Lee
Publications: CES Newsletter; Canadian Journal of Program Evaluation, s-a.
Affiliates: American Evaluation Society; Australasian Evaluation Society

Canadian General Standards Board/Office des normes générales du Canada (CGSB) (1934)
#1402, 222 Queen St., Ottawa, ON K1A 1G6
613/941-8709, 8703 (Sales Centre), Fax: 613/941-8706, Toll Free: 1-800-665-2472
Director General, B. Geiger
Chief of Sales Centre, Debra Imre
Publications: Calibre
Affiliates: Canadian Society for Nondestructive Testing, Inc.

Canadian Society for Nondestructive Testing, Inc./Société canadienne pour essais nondestructifs, inc. (CSNDT) (1964)
#7, 966 Pantera Dr., Mississauga, ON L4W 2S1
905/238-4846, Fax: 905/238-0689
President, Peter Brady
Administrator, Angie Giglio
Publications: CSNDT Journal

Canadian Standards Association/Association canadienne de normalisation (CSA) (1919)
178 Rexdale Blvd., Etobicoke, ON M9W 1R3
416/747-4007, Fax: 416/747-2475, Telex: 06-989344, Toll Free: 1-800-463-6727
URL: http://www.csa.ca/isotes
President/CEO, John E. Kean
Chairman, Roland J. Thompson
Vice-President, Human Resources & Communications, Pat Keindel
Vice-President, Certification & Testing, Nick Maalouf
Vice-Chairman, Robert T.E. Gillespie
Vice-Chairman, David C. Colville
Vice-President, Standards Development, Pat Paladino
Publications: CSA Plus The Consumer; Information Update; Guideline on Environmental Labelling; Design for the Environment; Guidelines for Environmental Auditing: Statement of Principles & General Practices; Guideline for Pollution Prevention; Environmentally Responsible Procurement; A Voluntary Environmental Management System; Sustainable Forest Management
Central Region: 178 Rexdale Blvd., Etobicoke, ON M9W 1R3, 416/747-4044, Fax: 416/747-2475

Eastern Region: Manager, Terry Drew, 865, rue Ellingham, Pointe Claire, PQ H9R 5E8, 514/694-8110, Fax: 514/694-5001
Western Region: Operations Manager, James M. Brown, 403/490-2007, 1707 - 94 St., Edmonton, AB T6N 1E6, 403/450-2111, Fax: 403/461-5322
Pacific Region: T. Nagy, 13799 Commerce Pkwy., Richmond, BC V6V 2N9, 604/273-4581, Fax: 604/273-5815

Canadian Toy Testing Council/Conseil canadien d'évaluation des jouets (CTTC) (1952)
22 Hamilton St. North, 2nd Fl., Ottawa, ON K1Y 1B6
613/729-7101, Fax: 613/729-7185
Executive Director, Leigh A. Poirier
Chairperson, Maxine Whelan
Communications/Program Manager, Marie C. Levine
Publications: Toy Report

Société québécoise d'évaluation de programmes/Québec Society of Program Evaluation (SQEP) (1988)
199, boul Val Cartier, Loretteville, PQ G2A 2M8
418/847-9850, Téléc: 418/847-9850
Président, Jean-René Bibeau
Publications: Bulletin de la SQEP

STEEL & METAL INDUSTRIES

Association de l'industrie de l'aluminium du Québec (AIAQ)
#1509, 1010, rue Sherbrooke ouest, Montréal, PQ H3A 2R7
514/288-4842, Téléc: 514/288-0944
Directeur général, Christian L. Van Houtte

Canadian Foundry Association/Association des fonderies canadiennes (CFA) (1975)
#405A, 130 Slater St., Ottawa, ON K1P 6E2
613/232-2645, Fax: 613/230-9607
Director, Operations, Judith Arbour, CAE
Publications: Report to Members

Canadian Institute of Steel Construction/Institut canadien de la construction en acier (CISC) (1942)
#300, 201 Consumers Rd., North York, ON M2J 4G8
416/491-4552, Fax: 416/491-6461, Email: 76331.1001@compuserve.com
President, Hugh A. Krentz
Affiliates: Canadian Steel Construction Council; Steel Structures Education Foundation

Canadian Sheet Steel Building Institute/Institut canadien de la tôle d'acier pour le bâtiment (CSSBI) (1961)
#2A, 652 Bishop St. North, Cambridge, ON N3H 4V6
519/650-1285, Fax: 519/650-8081
General Manager, Steven R. Fox

Canadian Steel Construction Council/Conseil canadien de la construction en acier (CSCC) (1960)
#300, 201 Consumers Rd., North York, ON M2J 4G8
416/491-9898, Fax: 416/491-6461, Email: 76331.1001@compuserve.com
Chairman, H.A. Krentz
Affiliates: Canadian Institute of Steel Construction; Steel Structures Education Foundation

Canadian Steel Producers Association/L'Association canadienne des producteurs d'acier (CSPA) (1986)
#1425, 50 O'Connor St., Ottawa, ON K1P 6L2
613/238-6049, Fax: 613/238-1832

Executive Director, Jean Van Loon
Chairman, John Mayberry

Canadian Steel Service Centre Institute/Institut canadien des centres de service des produits métallurgiques (CSSCI) (1957)
#104, 370 York Blvd., Hamilton, ON L8R 3L1
905/524-1100, Fax: 905/524-5600
President, David R. Roland
Vice-President, Robert J. Miller

Canadian Steel Trade & Employment Congress
#501, 234 Eglinton Ave. East, Toronto, ON M4P 1K7
416/480-1797, Fax: 416/480-2986
Executive Director, George Nakitsas
Publications: Steel Trade Between the USA & Canada; Newsletter, 3 pa

Corrugated Steel Pipe Institute/Institut pour tuyaux de tôle ondulée
#2A, 652 Bishop St. North, Cambridge, ON N3H 4V6
519/650-8080, Fax: 519/650-8081
Manager, Steven Fox
Publications: Railways Renew with Corrugated Steel; Timber Resource Roads Save with 'Soil-Steel' Engineering; CSP Void Forms Fill Bridge Overpass Design Requirements; Fully Perforated CSP Key To Disposal of Storm-Water Runoff; Perforated CSP for 'Recharge to Ground' of Storm Water Runoff; Quality Control Guidelines for CSP & SPCSP Products

Nickel Development Institute (NiDI) (1984)
#510, 214 King St. West, Toronto, ON M5H 3S6
416/591-7999, Fax: 416/591-7987, Telex: 06-218565
Executive Director, Michael O. Pearce
President, Johannes P. Schade
Publications: Nickel; Communiqué

Ontario Sheet Metal & Air Handling Group (1967)
#310, 1110 Sheppard Ave. East, North York, ON M2K 2W2
416/226-5533, Fax: 416/226-9277
Executive Director, William H. Gardner
Publications: Crossflow
Affiliates: Sheet Metal & Air Conditioning Contractors' National Association

Reinforcing Steel Institute of Canada/Institut d'acier d'armature du Canada (RSIC) (1976)
70 Leek Cres., Richmond Hill, ON L4B 1H1
416/499-4000, ext.28, Fax: 416/707-0610
Executive Vice-President, J. Warren Webster, P.Eng., Fax: 905/707-0610
Publications: Reinforcing Steel Manual of Standard Practice

INSTITUT D'ACIER D'ARMATURE DU QUÉBEC
4970, place de la Savane, Montréal, PQ H4P 1Z6
514/345-1655
Contact, André Morin

WESTERN REINFORCING CONTRACTORS ASSOCIATION
3636 - 4 Ave. East, Vancouver, BC V5N 1M3
604/294-3766

Sheet Metal & Air Conditioning Contractors' National Association (SMACNA) (1943)
4201 Lafayette Center Dr., Chantilly, VA 22021-1209 USA
703/803-2989, Fax: 703/803-3732
Executive Vice-President, John W. Sroka
Publications: SMACNews; Technical Manuals & Standards

SURVEYING & MAPPING

Association of Ontario Land Economists
#650, 144 Front St. West, Toronto, ON M5J 1G2
416/340-7818, Fax: 416/979-9159
Office Manager, Mary Sargent
Publications: The Land Economist

Association québécoise de cartographie (1981)
CP 8684, Ste-Foy, PQ G1V 4N6
418/776-2624
Président, Alain Laliberté
Secrétaire trésorier, Michel Dufault
Publications: Revue de carto Québec

Canadian Cartographic Association/Association canadienne de cartographie (CCA) (1975)
Geography Dept., University of Calgary, 2500 University Dr. NW, Calgary, AB T2N 1N4
403/278-5069, Fax: 403/282-6561, Email: mkrieger@acs.ucalgary.ca
President, Dr. Janet Mersey
Publications: Cartouche; Cartographica, q.
Affiliates: International Cartographic Association

Canadian Council of Land Surveyors/Conseil canadien des arpenteurs-géomètres (CCLS)
PO Box 5378, Stn Merivale, Ottawa, ON K2C 3J1
613/228-8519, Fax: 613/224-9577
Office Manager, Diane Sims
Sec.-Treas., Gerry Hawryluk
Publications: Focus; Bulletin, q.

ALBERTA LAND SURVEYORS' ASSOCIATION (ALSA) (1910)
#2501, 10004 - 104 Ave., Edmonton, AB T5J 0K1
403/428-8805, Fax: 403/429-3374, Toll Free: 1-800-665-2572
Executive Director, Brenwyn Mary Cooley
Publications: ALS News

ASSOCIATION OF MANITOBA LAND SURVEYORS (1881)
#202, 83 Garry St., Winnipeg, MB R3C 4J9
204/943-6972, Fax: 204/957-7602
Sec.-Treas., Selwyn L. Sanderson
Administrative Assistant, Carol Lee
Publications: Association of Manitoba Land Surveyors Newsletter; The Quarter Post
Affiliates: Canadian Institute of Surveying & Mapping; Western Canadian Board of Examiners for Land Surveyors

ASSOCIATION OF NEW BRUNSWICK LAND SURVEYORS/ ASSOCIATION DES ARPENTEURS-GÉOMÈTRES DU NOUVEAU-BRUNSWICK (ANBLS) (1954)
#120, 535 Beaverbrook Ct., Fredericton, NB E3B 1X6
506/458-8266, Fax: 506/458-8267, Email: abbls@m1.net
Sec.-Treas., Douglas E. Morgan
President, Paul E. Ingraham
Publications: Annual Report

ASSOCIATION OF NEWFOUNDLAND LAND SURVEYORS (1953)
78 O'Leary Ave., St. John's, NF A1B 2C7
709/722-2031, Fax: 709/722-4104
Sec.-Treas., Dominic J. Howard

ASSOCIATION OF NOVA SCOTIA LAND SURVEYORS (1951)
#301, 159 Portland St., Dartmouth, NS B2Y 1H9
902/469-7962, Fax: 902/469-7963
Executive Director, Robert Daniels
Publications: Nova Scotia Surveyor

ASSOCIATION OF ONTARIO LAND SURVEYORS
1043 McNicoll Ave., Scarborough, ON M1W 3W6
416/491-9020, Fax: 416/491-2576
Executive Director, Carl J. Rooth

ASSOCIATION OF PRINCE EDWARD ISLAND LAND SURVEYORS
PO Box 818, Charlottetown, PE C1A 7L9
902/894-5531, Fax: 902/566-4134
Sec.-Treas., Derek French

CORPORATION OF LAND SURVEYORS OF THE PROVINCE OF BRITISH COLUMBIA (BCLS) (1905)
BC Land Surveyors
#306, 895 Fort St., Victoria, BC V8W 1H7
250/382-4323, Fax: 250/382-5092, Email: corpbcls@islandnet.com
Sec.-Treas./Registrar, Gordon McKay Thomson, BCLS
President, Richard T. Hargraves
Publications: The Link; Circular Letters, m.
Affiliates: Canadian Institute of Geomatics

ORDRE DES ARPENTEURS-GÉOMÈTRES DU QUÉBEC/QUÉBEC LAND SURVEYORS ASSOCIATION (OAGQ) (1882)
#350, 2954, boul Laurier, Ste-Foy, PQ G1V 4T2
418/656-0730, Téléc: 418/656-6352
Président, Jean-Luc Léger
Publications: Arpenteur-Géometre; La Source
Organisation(s) affiliée(s): Fédération des arpenteurs-géometres du Québec

SASKATCHEWAN LAND SURVEYORS' ASSOCIATION (SLSA) (1910)
2402 - 2nd Ave., 2nd Fl., Regina, SK S4R 1A6
306/352-8999, Fax: 306/352-8366, Email: slsa@sknet.sk.ca
Executive Director, A. Carl Shiels
Publications: Newsletter

Canadian Geophysical Union/Union géophysique canadienne (CGU) (1973)
Geological Survey of Canada, 7 Observatory Cres., Ottawa, ON K1A 0Y3
613/947-2783, Fax: 613/992-8836, Email: eaton@cg.emr.ca
URL: http://www.cg.nrcan.gc.ca/cgu/cgu.html
Secretary, David Eaton
President, Roy Hyndman
Treasurer, Ron Kurtz
Publications: Elements

Canadian Institute of Geomatics/Association canadienne des sciences géomatiques (CIG) (1882)
#120, 162 Cleopatra Dr., Ottawa, ON K2G 5X2
613/224-9851, Fax: 613/224-9577, Email: cig-acsg@inasec.ca
Executive Manager, Susan Pugh
President, Sue Nichols, 506/453-4698
Publications: Geomatica; NAD '83 Redefinition & Impact on Users
Affiliates: International Federation of Surveyors; International Society for Photogrammetry & Remote Sensing; International Cartographic Association; Commonwealth Association of Canada Lands Surveyors; Canadian Council of Land Surveyors; Canadian Hydrographic Association

Canadian Institute of Quantity Surveyors
PO Box 124, Stn R, Toronto, ON M4G 3Z3
416/471-0882, Fax: 416/471-7545
Executive Director, Lois Metcalfe
Affiliates: Commonwealth Association of Surveying & Land Economy

Geomatics Industry Association of Canada/ Association canadienne des entreprises de géomatique (GIAC) (1961)
#1204, 170 Laurier Ave. West, Ottawa, ON K1P 5V5
613/232-8770, Fax: 613/232-4908, Email: giac@globalx.net
President, Ed Kennedy
Chairman, Clark Beattie
Publications: Canadian GIS Source Book

SUSTAINABLE DEVELOPMENT *see* **ENVIRONMENTAL**

TAXATION
see also Finanace

Association of Municipal Tax Collectors of Ontario
PO Box 69, Stn A, Toronto, ON M5W 1A2
905/725-0019
President, Jackie Turbitt
Publications: Tax Collectors Journal

Canadian Federation of Tax Consultants
#502, 161 Eglinton Ave. East, Toronto, ON M4P 1J5
416/488-5404
Jack Poolc

Canadian Institute of Taxation
Boughton, Peterson, Yang, Anderson, #2500, 1055 Dunsmuir St., PO Box 49290, Vancouver, BC V7X 1S8
604/687-6789, Fax: 604/683-5317

Canadian Petroleum Tax Society
PO Box 2562, Stn M, Calgary, AB T2P 3K8
Fax: 403/261-6355
Secretary, Marvin Lamb
Publications: Canadian Petroleum Tax Journal

Canadian Property Tax Association, Inc. (1967)
#225, 6 Lansing Sq., North York, ON M2J 1T5
416/493-3276, Fax: 416/493-3905
National Office Coordinator, Carole Munn
Publications: Communication Update

Canadian Tax Foundation/Association canadienne d'études fiscales (CTF) (1945)
#1800, One Queen St. East, Toronto, ON M5C 2Y2
416/863-9784, Fax: 416/863-9785
Director, Robin J. MacKnight
Secretary, Patricia Hillmer
Treasurer, Norman H. Witherell
Publications: Canadian Tax Journal; Tax Papers; The National Finances; Canadian Tax Highlights, m.; Tax Memos
Affiliates: Canadian Bar Association; Canadian Institute of Chartered Accountants

Canadian Taxpayers Federation (CTF) (1989)
#105, 438 Victoria Ave. East, Regina, SK S4N 0N7
Toll Free: 1-800-667-7933
Chairman, Bob Matheson
National Director, Jason Kenney
Publications: The Taxpayer
Affiliates: Alberta Taxpayers Association; British Columbia Taxpayers Association; Manitoba Taxpayers Association; Ontario Taxpayers Federation; Saskatchewan Taxpayers Association

Ontario Taxpayers Federation
Manulife Centre, 55 Bloor St. West, PO Box 19518, Toronto, ON M4W 3T9
Toll Free: 1-800-265-0442
Executive Director, Paul Pagnuelo
Affiliates: Canadian Taxpayers Federation

Taxpayers Coalition - Niagara (TCN) (1990)
70 St. Paul St. West, PO Box 86, St Catharines, ON L2R 6R4
905/688-3713, Fax: 905/688-6454
Contact, Frank Sheehan

TEACHING *see* **EDUCATION**

TECHNOLOGY *see* **ENGINEERING & TECHNOLOGY**

TELECOMMUNICATIONS
see also Broadcasting

Air Force Telecom Association (AFTA) (1985)
PO Box 2058, Kingston, ON K7L 5J8
613/549-3582, Fax: 613/549-4557
Chairman, Capt. H.F. Huggins
Sec.-Treas., Sgt. R.A. Koopman
Publications: Newsletter

Association des câblodistributeurs du Québec inc. (ACQ) (1974)
#002, 1755, boul René-Lévesque est, Montréal, PQ H2K 4P6
514/525-1083, Téléc: 514/525-1186
Directrice générale, Lysline Parenteau
Publications: Tête de ligne

Association of Competitive Telecommunications Suppliers (ACTS)
#1105, 191 The West Mall, Etobicoke, ON M9C 5K8
416/620-5393, Fax: 416/620-5392, Email: bbande@enterprise.ca
URL: http://www.bbande.com
President, Don Braden

Canadian Association of Message Exchanges, Inc./Association canadienne d'échange de messages, inc. (CAM-X) (1964)
37 Park Rd. South, PO Box 373, Grimsby, ON L3M 4H8
905/309-0224, Fax: 905/309-0225
Manager, Barbara Clausen
Publications: Cam-X Communiqué

Canadian Business Telecommunications Alliance/L'Alliance canadienne des télécommunications de l'entreprise (CBTA) (1962)
Canada Trust Tower, Box 705, #3650, 161 Bay St., Toronto, ON M5J 2S1
416/865-9993, Fax: 416/865-0859, Toll Free: 1-800-668-2282, Email: cbta@inforamp.net
URL: http://www.telecon.ca
Executive Director, Patrick M. Daly
Chairman/CEO, Majid Shahidi
President, Douglas Robson
General Manager & Controller, Alan E. Gaffen, B.Sc., CGA
Publications: Contact; Direct Line, m.; Making the Connections; Canadian Telecom Alert

Canadian Independent Telephone Association/Association canadienne du téléphone indépendant (CITA) (1938)
c/o CEM, 55 Vansco Rd., Toronto, ON M8Z 5Z8
416/259-7308, Fax: 416/259-2053
General Manager, Margi Taylor
Publications: CITA Communicator

Canadian Institute for Telecommunications Research/Institut canadien de recherches en télécommunications (CITR) (1990)
Department of Electrical Engineering, McGill University, #633, 3480 University St., Montréal, PQ H3A 2A7
514/398-7475, Fax: 514/398-3127
URL: http://www.citr.ee.mcgill.ca
President, Dr. Maier Blostein
Network Manager, Lynn-Marie Holland, Email: lynn@citr.ee.mcgill.ca

Canadian Telecommunications Consultants Association (CTCA) (1985)
#604, 3 Church St., Toronto, ON M5E 1M2
416/860-1774, Fax: 416/862-0315, Toll Free: 1-800-463-2569, Email: office@ctca.ca
URL: http://www.ctca.ca
President, Betty Hodkinson, 416/594-2015

Canadian Wireless Telecommunications Association/Association canadienne des télécommunications sans fil (CWTA) (1970)
#2004, 275 Slater St., Ottawa, ON K1P 5H9
613/233-4888, Fax: 613/233-2032
URL: http://www.cwta.ca
President/CEO, Roger Poirier
Chairman, Frank Maw
Publications: Wireless Telecom

Frequency Co-ordination System Association/Association pour la coordination des fréquences (FCSA) (1983)
#700, One Nicholas St., Ottawa, ON K1N 7B7
613/241-3080, Fax: 613/241-9632
General Manager/Sec.-Treas., J. Burns
President, D.W. Varey
Vice-President, S.A. Baker
Publications: Microwave Radio Catalog

International Interactive Communications Society - Toronto Chapter (IICS) (1986)
c/o Tayson Information Technology Inc., 275 Comstock, Scarborough, ON M1L 2H2
416/288-0550, Fax: 416/285-4395, Email: peterr@hookup.com
URL: http://toronto.ark.com/~iics
President, Peter Richardson
Publications: IICS Reporter; IICS Journal, 3 pa; Informedia, q.

Ontario Cable Telecommunications Association
#1304, 2025 Sheppard Ave. East, North York, ON M2J 1V6
416/498-1515, Fax: 416/498-1559
Executive Director, Roy O'Brien
Publications: CableOntario

Telecommunications Research Institute of Ontario (TRIO) (1988)
#400, 340 March Rd., Kanata, ON K2K 2E4
613/592-9211, Fax: 613/592-8163
URL: http://www.trio.ca/trio/
Contact, Peter Leach
Publications: TRIO Network

TELEVISION *see* **BROADCASTING**

TENANTS & LANDLORDS *see* **HOUSING**

TESTING *see* **STANDARDS & TESTING**

TEXTILES *see* **FASHION & TEXTILES**

THIRD WORLD *see* **INTERNATIONAL COOPERATION/INTERNATIONAL RELATIONS**

TOURISM & TRAVEL

Accommodation Motel Ontario Association (AMOA) (1949)
Motels Ontario
347 Pido Rd., RR#6, Peterborough, ON K9J 6X7
705/745-4982, Fax: 705/745-4983, Toll Free: 1-800-461-1972, Email: motels@oncomdis.on.ca
President, Bruce M. Gravel
Publications: Newsline; Accommodator, q.; Buyers Guide/Member Directory, a.

Affiliates: Accommodation Canada; Canadian Federation of Independent Business; Canadian Tourism Research Institute; Ontario Tourism Education; Tourism Federation of Ontario

Alberta League for Environmentally Responsible Tourism (ALERT) (1979)
PO Box 1288, Rocky Mountain House, AB T0M 1T0
403/845-4667, Fax: 403/845-5377
Contact, Martha Kostuch

Alberta Tourism Partnership Corporation (ATPC) (1995)
#500, 999 - 8 St. SW, Calgary, AB T2R 1J5
403/297-2957, Fax: 403/297-5068
URL: http://www.atp.ab.ca/
President & CEO, Tom McCabe
Executive Assistant, Joanna Suehwold
Calgary Convention & Visitors Bureau: President & CEO, Henry Kutarna, 237 - 8 Ave. SE, Calgary, AB T2G 0K8, 403/263-8510, Fax: 403/262-3809, Toll Free: 1-800-661-1678
URL: http://www.visitor.calgary.ab.ca/
Greater Edmonton Visitor & Convention Association: General Manager, Cindy Béland, 9797 Jasper Ave., Edmonton, AB T5J 1N9, 403/429-9915, Fax: 403/425-0725
Red Deer Visitor & Convention Bureau: Manager, Wendy Martindale; Chairperson, Merv Phillips, PO Box 5008, Red Deer, AB T4N 3T4, 403/346-0180, Fax: 403/346-5081, Toll Free: 1-800-215-8946

Alliance of Canadian Travel Associations/ Alliance canadienne des associations touristiques (ACTA) (1977)
#201, 1729 Bank St., Ottawa, ON K1V 7Z5
613/521-0474, Fax: 613/521-0805
Executive Director, Terry Ohman
President, Hugh Campbell
Affiliates: Universal Federation of Travel Agency Associations

ALLIANCE OF CANADIAN TRAVEL ASSOCIATIONS - ALBERTA (ACTA - ALBERTA) (1977)
625 - 25 Ave. NE, Calgary, AB T2E 1Y6
403/277-9445, Email: waym@cia.com
Contact, Jona Way
Publications: ACTA Advisor

ALLIANCE OF CANADIAN TRAVEL ASSOCIATIONS - ATLANTIC (ACTA - ATLANTIC) (1976)
#423, 1800 Argyle St., PO Box 3131, Stn Halifax South, Halifax, NS B3J 3N8
902/422-7311, Fax: 902/492-5657, Email: andread@fox.nstn.ca
Contact, Andrea Davidson
Publications: News & Views

ALLIANCE OF CANADIAN TRAVEL ASSOCIATIONS - BRITISH COLUMBIA (ACTA - BC)
#905, 850 West Hastings St., Vancouver, BC V6C 1E1
604/688-0516, Fax: 604/688-6056
Executive Director, Glen Steeves
Publications: ACTA BC Communicates

ALLIANCE OF CANADIAN TRAVEL ASSOCIATIONS - MANITOBA (1978)
#17, 399 Berry St., Winnipeg, MB R3J 1N6
204/831-0831, Fax: 204/885-3764
Contact, Veronica Lopez
Publications: Travel Talk

ALLIANCE OF CANADIAN TRAVEL ASSOCIATIONS - ONTARIO (OTIC)
#4020, 3080 Yonge St., Toronto, ON M4N 3N1
416/488-2282, Fax: 416/488-2686
Executive Director, Marion Graber

ALLIANCE OF CANADIAN TRAVEL ASSOCIATIONS - QUÉBEC/ ASSOCIATION DES AGENTS DE VOYAGES DU QUÉBEC (ACTA-QUÉBEC)
#6600, 515, rue Ste-Catherine ouest, CP 8000, Succ. Centre Ville, Montréal, PQ H3C 3L4
514/987-8733, Téléc: 514/987-3571
Contact, Louise Hodder

ALLIANCE OF CANADIAN TRAVEL ASSOCIATIONS - SASKATCHEWAN (SATA)
122 Wood Cres., PO Box 1149, Assiniboia, SK S0H 0B0
306/642-5500, Fax: 306/642-4700
Contact, Judy Silzer
Publications: Saskatchewan

Associated Canadian Travellers
116 - 16th Ave. NE., Calgary, AB T2E 1J5
403/277-0745, Fax: 403/277-6662
General Manager, Yvette Stewart

Association of National Tourist Organization Representatives - Canada
c/o Irish Tourist Bureau, #934, 160 Bloor St., Toronto, ON M4W 1B9
416/929-2777, Fax: 416/929-6783
President, Joe Kennedy

Association des terrains de camping du Québec
#700, 2001, rue de la Metropole, Longueuil, PQ J4G 1S9
514/651-7396, Téléc: 514/651-7397
Vice-président executif, Maryse Catellier

Associations touristiques régionales associées du Québec/Québec Regional Tourist Associations Inc. (ATRAQ) (1981)
2900, boul St-Martin ouest, Chomedey, Laval, PQ H7T 2J2
514/686-8358, Téléc: 514/686-9630
Directrice générale, Louise Nadeau
Président, Jean Thiffault
Association touristique de l'Abitibi-Témiscamingue: Directeur général, Louis Laliberte, #103, 170, av Principale, Rouyn-Noranda, PQ J9X 4P7, 819/762-8181, Téléc: 819/762-5212, Ligne sans frais: 1-800-808-0706
Association touristique du Bas-Saint-Laurent: 189, rue Hôtel-de-Ville, Rivière-du-Loup, PQ G5R 5C4, 418/867-3015, Téléc: 418/867-3245, Ligne sans frais: 1-800-563-5268
Association touristique de Charlevoix: 630, boul de Comporté, CP 275, La Malbaie, PQ G5A 1T8, 418/665-4454, Téléc: 418/665-3811, Ligne sans frais: 1-800-667-2276
Association touristique de Chaudière-Appalaches: 800, autoroute Jean-Lesage, Bernières, PQ G7A 1C9, 418/831-4411, Téléc: 418/831-8442
Association touristique du Coeur-du-Québec: 1180, rue Royale, 2e étage, Trois-Rivières, PQ G9A 4J1, 819/375-1222, Téléc: 819/375-0301, Ligne sans frais: 1-800-567-7603
Association touristique de Duplessis: 865, boul Laure, Sept-Îles, PQ G4R 1Y6, 418/962-0808, Téléc: 418/962-6518
Association touristique de l'Estrie: Directeur général, Alain Larouche; Président, Jacques Robidas, 25, rue Bocage, Sherbrooke, PQ J1L 2J4, 819/820-2020, Téléc: 819/566-4445, Ligne sans frais: 1-800-355-5755
Association touristique de la Gaspésie: Secrétaire, Dorothée Renaud, 357, route de la Mer, Ste-Flavie, PQ G0J 2L0, 418/775-2223, Téléc: 418/775-2234, Ligne sans frais: 1-800-463-0323
Association touristique des Îles-de-la-Madeleine: 128, rue Principale, CP 1028, Cap-aux-Meules, PQ G0B 1B0, 418/986-2245, Téléc: 418/986-2327

Association touristique de Lanaudière: 3643, rue Queen, CP 1210, Rawdon, PQ J0K 1S0, 514/834-2535, Téléc: 514/834-8100, Ligne sans frais: 1-800-363-2788
Association touristique des Laurentides: 14142, rue de Lachapelle, RR#1, St-Jérôme, PQ J7Z 5T4, 514/436-8532, Téléc: 514/436-5309
Association touristique de Manicouagan: 847, rue de Puyjalon, CP 2366, Baie-Comeau, PQ G5C 2T1, 418/589-5319, Téléc: 418/589-9546
Association touristique de l'Outaouais: Agente d'information, Lyne Voyer, 103, rue Laurier, Hull, PQ J8X 3V8, 819/778-2222, Téléc: 819/778-7758, Ligne sans frais: 1-800-265-7822, Courrier électronique: ato@achilles.net
URL: http://www.achilles.net/~ato/
Association touristique régionale de la Montérégie: Directeur général, Denis Brisebois, #989, rue Pierre-Dupuy, Longueuil, PQ J4K 1A1, 514/674-5555, Téléc: 514/463-2876
Association touristique du Saguenay-Lac-Saint-Jean: #210, 198, rue Racine est, Chicoutimi, PQ G7H 1R9, 418/543-9778, Téléc: 418/543-1805
Office des congrès et du tourisme du Grand Montréal: Vice-President, Marketing, Claude Zalloni, #600, 1555, rue Peel, Montréal, PQ H3A 1X6, 514/844-5400, Téléc: 514/844-5757; URL: http://www.cum.qc.ca/octgm/Welcome.html
Office du tourisme et des congrès de la communauté urbaine de Québec: Directeur, Pierre Fabrie; Director, Sales & Marketing, Claire Verreault; Director, Advertising, Communication & Membership, Daniel Gagnon, Communauté urbaine de Québec, 399, rue St-Joseph est, Québec, PQ G1K 8E2, 418/522-3511, Téléc: 418/529-3121, Télex: CUQ QBC 051-230

BC Motels, Campgrounds, Resorts Association (1944)
#209, 3003 St. John's St., Port Moody, BC V3H 2C4
604/945-7676, Fax: 604/945-7606
Executive Director, Patricia Cashin
Publications: The Dogwood Express; Super Camping BC

Canadian Association of Retail Travel Agents (CARTA)
765 Barton St. East, Hamilton, ON L8L 3A9
905/547-1324, Fax: 905/522-1752
President, Caesar Tam

Canadian Business Travel Association/ Association canadienne des chargés de voyages (CBTA) (1983)
Deloitte & Touche, #2000, 1055 Dunsmuir St., PO Box 49279, Vancouver, BC V7X 1P4
604/669-4466, Fax: 604/684-0458
President, Pat Haygarth
CBTA Vancouver: Contact, Pat Haygarth, 604/669-4466
CBTA Calgary: Contact, Peggy Orchard, 403/233-6000
CBTA Winnipeg: Contact, Helen Mitchell, 204/942-5466
CBTA Toronto: Contact, Michele Butt, 416/920-8100
CBTA Ottawa: Contact, Lisa O'Driscoll, 613/232-2000
CBTA Montreal: Contact, Bryan Williams, 514/428-3260
Publications: Connector
Affiliates: National Business Travel Association, USA; International Business Travel Association

Canadian Business Travel Association - Montréal/Association canadienne des chargés de voyages - Montréal (CBTA) (1968)
29, Hazelwood, Dollard-des-Ormeaux, PQ H9A 2N7
514/990-2228, Fax: 514/637-1880
President, Andi La Rivière
Vice-President, Maria Cacchione

Secretary, Diane Chan
Treasurer, A. Leblanc
Publications: The Connector

Canadian Hotel Marketing & Sales Executives, BC Chapter
#100, 951 - 16th St., West Vancouver, BC V7V 3S4
604/926-2056, Fax: 604/926-4115
Executive Director, Mary Hiscox

Canadian Hotel Marketing & Sales Executives, Ontario Chapter (CHMSE) (1982)
84 Seventh St., Toronto, ON M8V 3B4
416/252-9800, Fax: 416/252-7071
President, Karan Kerber
Vice-President, Georgia Salaverri
Vice-President, Cathy Wallbank
Association Manager, Shelley Macdonald
Publications: Hospitality Update

Canadian Institute of Travel Counsellors/Institut canadien des conseillers en voyages (CITC) (1979)
#209, 55 Eglinton Ave. East, Toronto, ON M4P 1G8
416/484-4450, Fax: 416/484-4140
Executive Director, Mary Notley
President, Debbie Redmond, CTC
Publications: The Professional Travel Counsellor; CITC National Update, q.
CITC - Alberta: President, Kim Killoran, CTC, 625 - 25 Ave. NE, Calgary, AB T2E 1Y6, 403/276-2118, Fax: 403/230-5247
CITC - Atlantic: Contact, Chess Chard, CTC; President, Joan Kingham, CTC, c/o Intra Travel, 141 Torbay Rd., St. John's, NF A1A 2H1, 902/722-5800, Fax: 902/722-5803
CITC - BC & Yukon: President, Roxanne Ang, CTC, #905, 850 Hastings St. West, Vancouver, BC V6E 1E1, 604/687-2482, Fax: 604/688-6056
CITC - Manitoba: President, Roland Hoffman, CTC, PO Box 38, Group 355, RR#3, Winnipeg, MB R3C 2E7, 204/667-6285, Fax: 204/667-6285
CITC - Québec: Contact, John Lupien, CTC; President, Diane Brooks, c/o CAA Travel, 1180, rue Drummond, Montréal, PQ H3G 2R7, 514/861-5111, Téléc: 514/861-7259
CITC - Saskatchewan: President, Marie Kent, CTC, PO Box 22012, RPO Wildwood, Saskatoon, SK S7H 5P1, 306/665-5577, Fax: 306/653-1808

Canadian National Aboriginal Tourism Association/Association canadienne nationale des autochtones pour le tourisme (CNATA)
875 Bank St., Ottawa, ON K1S 3W4
613/567-7566, Fax: 613/233-4329
URL: http://www.v1i.ca/clients/abc/cnata/cnata3.htm
President, Barry Parker
Head Office: Wahpeton Dakota Nation, PO Box 128, Prince Albert, SK S9V 5R4

Canadian Recreational Vehicle Association (CRVA) (1975)
#200, 670 Bloor St. West, Toronto, ON M6G 1L2
416/533-7800, Fax: 416/533-4795
Executive Vice-President, Don Mockford

Canadian Resort Development Association (CRDA) (1980)
48 Hayden St., Toronto, ON M4Y 1V8
416/960-4930, Fax: 416/923-8348
Director/President, Gloria A. Collinson
Publications: CRDA Newsletter
Affiliates: American Resort & Residential Development Association - Washington DC

Canadian Tourism Research Institute
255 Smyth Rd., Ottawa, ON K1H 8M7
613/526-4306, Fax: 613/526-4857, Telex: 053-3333
Director, Harry French

Council of Tourism Associations of British Columbia (COTA) (1991)
PO Box 28005, RPO Harbour Centre, Vancouver, BC V6B 5L8
604/685-5956, Fax: 604/730-4801, Email: jimmann@uniserve.com
President, Pat Corbett
Publications: COTA News
Cariboo Tourism Association: Managing Director, G.R. Drew, 190 Yorsten St., PO Box 4900, Williams Lake, BC V2G 2V8, 250/392-2226, Fax: 250/392-2838, Toll Free: 1-800-663-5885, Email: cariboo@netshop.ca
High Country Tourism Association: General Manager, Lee Morris, #2, 1490 Pearson Pl., Kamloops, BC V1S 1J9, 250/372-7770, Fax: 250/828-4656
Kootenay Country Tourist Association: Executive Director, Geoff Sturgeon, 610 Railway St., Nelson, BC V1L 1H4, 250/352-6033, Fax: 250/352-1656, Toll Free: 1-800-661-6603, Email: kcta@worldtel.com; URL: http://travel.bc.ca.kootenay
North by Northwest Tourism Association of BC: General Manager, Marilyn Quilley, 3736 - 16th Ave., PO Box 1030, Smithers, BC V0J 2N0, 250/847-5227, Fax: 250/847-7585
Okanagan Similkameen Tourism Association: Executive Director, Deanna Rainey; President, Allen Tozer, 1332 Water St., Kelowna, BC V1Y 9P4, 250/860-5999, Fax: 250/861-7493, Email: osta@awinc.com
Peace River Alaska Highway Tourism Association: Manager, Ella Fraser, 10631 - 100th St., PO Box 6850, Stn Main, Fort St. John, BC V1J 4J3, 250/785-2544, Fax: 250/785-4424
Rocky Mountain Visitor's Association: Managing Director, Chris Dadson; President, Mike Smith, 495 Wallinger Ave., PO Box 10, Kimberley, BC V1A 2Y5, 250/427-4838, Fax: 250/427-3344
Tourism Association of Vancouver Island: Managing Director, Joyce Brookbank, #302, 45 Bastion Sq., Victoria, BC V8W 1J1, 250/382-3551, Fax: 250/382-3523
Tourism Vancouver/Greater Vancouver Convention & Visitors Bureau: President & CEO, Rick Antonson, Two Bentall Centre, #210, 200 Burrard St., Vancouver, BC V6C 3L6, 604/682-2222, Fax: 604/682-1717
Tourism Victoria/Greater Victoria Visitors & Convention Bureau: CEO, Lorne Whyte, #710, 1175 Douglas St., Victoria, BC V8W 2E1, 250/382-2160, Fax: 250/361-9733, Info Line: 250/953-2033, Toll Free: 1-800-663-3883; URL: http://travel.victoria.bc.ca/
Vancouver Coast & Mountains Tourism Region: Executive Director, Kevan Ridgway, #204, 1755 Broadway West, Vancouver, BC V6J 4S5, 604/739-9011, Fax: 604/739-0153, Toll Free: 1-800-667-3306, Email: vcm.tourism@mindlink.bc.ca; URL: http://travel.bc.ca

Hostelling International - Canada (HI-C) (1933)
Canadian Hostelling Association
#400, 205 Catherine St., Ottawa, ON K2P 1C3
613/237-7884, Fax: 613/237-7868, Telex: 053-3660
Executive Director, Richard McCarron
President, François Vidal
Affiliates: International Youth Hostel Federation

Hotel Association of Canada Inc./Association des hôtels du Canada (HAC) (1913)
#1016, 130 Albert St., Ottawa, ON K1P 5G4
613/237-7149, Fax: 613/238-3878
President, Anthony P. Pollard, 613/237-7149, Fax: 613/238-3878
Chairman, David McMillan
Sec.-Treas., John D. Read, 204/942-0671, Fax: 204/942-6719
Publications: HAC Newsletter
Affiliates: American Hotel & Motel Association

ALBERTA HOTEL ASSOCIATION (1920)
#401, 5241 Calgary Trail South, Edmonton, AB T6H 5G8
403/436-6112, Fax: 403/436-5404, Email: aha@alberta-hotels.ab.ca
URL: http://www.albertahotels.ab.ca
Executive Vice-President, James P. Hansen

L'ASSOCIATION DES HÔTELIERS DU QUÉBEC/QUÉBEC HOTEL ASSOCIATION (AHDQ) (1949)
Pavillon Le Rigaud, #0.04, 425, rue Sherbrooke est, Montréal, PQ H2L 1J9
514/282-5135, Téléc: 514/849-1157
Directeur général, André P. Jean-Richard
Publications: L'Hôtelier

BRITISH COLUMBIA & YUKON HOTELS ASSOCIATION
948 Howe St., 2nd Fl., Vancouver, BC V6Z 1N9
604/681-7164, Fax: 604/681-7649, Toll Free: 1-800-663-3153
URL: http://www.fleethouse.com/fhcanada/bc-acco.htm
Executive Vice-President, James C. Chase, C.M.A., DMATP
Publications: Inn Touch; Inn Focus, q.

HOTEL ASSOCIATION OF NOVA SCOTIA
PO Box 473, Stn M, Halifax, NS B3J 2P8
902/443-3635, Fax: 902/457-3304
Administrator, Jose Cabrita

HOTEL/MOTEL ASSOCIATION OF PRINCE EDWARD ISLAND
455 University Ave., Charlottetown, PE C1A 4NA
902/566-3137, Fax: 902/368-3806
President, Kevin Murphy

HOTELS ASSOCIATION OF SASKATCHEWAN
1054 Winnipeg St., Regina, SK S4R 8P8
306/522-1664, Fax: 306/525-1944
Executive Director, Bill Nelson

MANITOBA HOTEL ASSOCIATION (MHA) (1927)
#1505, 155 Carlton St., Winnipeg, MB R3C 3H8
204/942-0671, Fax: 204/942-6719
Executive Vice-President, John D. Read
Affiliates: Manitoba Chamber of Commerce; Tourism Association of Manitoba

NORTHWEST TERRITORIES HOTELS' ASSOCIATION
Yellowknife Inn, PO Box 490, Yellowknife, NT X1A 2N4
403/873-2601, Fax: 403/873-2602
Acting President, Jack Walker

ONTARIO HOTEL & MOTEL ASSOCIATION (OH&MA) (1924)
#8-201, 2600 Skymark Ave., Mississauga, ON L4W 5B2
905/602-9650, Fax: 905/602-9654, Toll Free: 1-800-387-0010
Executive Director, Diane Stefaniak, CAE
President, Mary Lapaine
Membership Coordinator, Pat Cara
Publications: InnTouch; Ontario Innkeeper Magazine, q.; OH & MA Directory
Affiliates: American Hotel & Motel Association

Institut de tourisme et d'hôtellerie du Québec (ITHQ) (1968)
401, rue de Rigaud, Montréal, PQ H2L 4P3
514/282-5108, Téléc: 514/864-3183, Ligne sans frais: 1-800-361-5111
Directeur général, Pierre D. Brodeur
Secrétaire général, René-Luc Blaquière
Publications: Une formation en première classe

Motel Association of Alberta (MAA)
#202, 10335 - 178 St., Edmonton, AB T5S 1R5
403/944-1199, Fax: 403/455-6675
Operations Manager, Wendy J. Schrader
President, Don Serediak
Publications: Western Innkeeper

North West Commercial Travellers' Association of Canada (NWCTA) (1882)
28 Main St. South, Winnipeg, MB R3L 2R1
204/284-8900, Fax: 204/284-8909, Toll Free: 1-800-665-6928
General Manager, Terry D. Carruthers
Publications: The Travellers; Hotel/Motel Directory, a.
Affiliates: Maritime Commercial Travellers Association; Canadian Professional Sales Association; The Order of United Commercial Travellers of America

Nunavut Tourism (1995)
PO Box 1450, Iqaluit, NT X0A 0H0
819/979-6551, Fax: 819/979-1261, Toll Free: 1-800-491-7910, Email: nunatour@nunanet.com
URL: http://nunanet.com/~nunanet.com
President, Paul Landry
Sec.-Treas., Tracy Beeman
Publications: Tourism Bulletin; Arctic Travellers, biennial

Ontario Convention & Visitors Association (OCVA) (1979)
c/o Base Service Canada Inc., #301, 250 Consumers Rd., North York, ON M2J 4V6
416/494-1440, Fax: 416/495-8723, Email: base@on-ramp.ca
Algoma Kinniwabi Travel Association: President, Ian McMillan, #1, 553 Queen St. East, Sault Ste Marie, ON P6A 2M3, 705/254-4293, Fax: 705/254-4892, Email: 1-800-263-2541
Almaguin-Nipissing Travel Association: Executive Director, Ted Day, PO Box 351, North Bay, ON P1B 8H5, 705/474-6634, Fax: 705/474-9271, Toll Free: 1-800-387-0516
Burlington Visitor & Convention Bureau: General Manager, Penny MacKenzie, 1340 Lakeshore Rd., Burlington, ON L7S 1Y2, 905/634-5948, Fax: 905/634-7220
Cambridge Visitor & Convention Bureau: Coordinator, Debbie Yantzi, 531 King St. East, Cambridge, ON N3H 3N4, 519/653-1424, Fax: 519/653-1734, Toll Free: 1-800-749-7560
Cochrane Timiskaming Travel Association: Manager, Guy Lamarche; Executive Secretary, April Tremblay, 76 McIntyre Rd., PO Box 920, Schumacher, ON P0N 1G0, 705/360-1989, Fax: 705/268-5526, Toll Free: 1-800-461-3766
Convention & Visitors Bureau of Windsor: General Manager, Elizabeth Hamel, City Centre, #103, 333 Riverside Dr. West, Windsor, ON N9A 5K4, 519/255-6530, Fax: 519/255-6192, Toll Free: 1-800-265-3633
Cornwall & Seaway Valley Tourism: Executive Manager, Dawn Murray, 231 Augustus St., Cornwall, ON K6J 3W2, 613/938-4748, Fax: 613/938-4751, Toll Free: 1-800-937-4748, Email: dmurray@cnwl.igs.net; URL: http://www.visit.cornwall.on.ca
The Georgian Triangle Tourist Association & Convention Bureau: Executive Director, Sheila Metras; President, D.J. McNichol, 601 First St., Collingwood, ON L9Y 4L2, 705/445-7722, Fax: 705/444-6082
Greater Hamilton Tourism & Convention Services: Manager, Joseph Fardell, One James St. South, 3rd Fl., Hamilton, ON L8P 4R5, 905/546-4222, Fax: 905/546-4107, Toll Free: 1-800-263-8590
Huronia Tourism Association: President, Julian H. Huffer, 705/726-8502; Chair, Michael J. Stewart; Vice-Chair, Josephine Martensson, Simcoe County Bldg., Midhurst, ON L0L 1X0, 705/726-9300, Fax: 705/726-3991
Kitchener-Waterloo Area Visitor & Convention Bureau: General Manager, Jane Falconer, 2848 King St. East, Kitchener, ON N2A 1A5, 519/748-0800, Fax: 519/748-6411, Toll Free: 1-800-265-6959
London Visitors & Convention Bureau: Manager, Michael Harris, 300 Dufferin Ave., London, ON N6B 1Z2, 519/661-5000, Fax: 519/661-6160
Metropolitan Toronto Convention & Visitors Association: President, Kirk Shearer, Queen's Quay Terminal at Harbourfront, #590, 207 Queen's Quay West, PO Box 126, Toronto, ON M5J 1A7, 416/203-2600, Fax: 416/203-6753, Info Line: 416/203-2500, Toll Free: 1-800/363-1990
Muskoka Tourism: General Manager, Dave Thomas, RR#2, Kilworthy, ON P0E 1G0, 705/689-0660, Fax: 705/689-7118, Toll Free: 1-800-267-9700
Niagara Falls Canada Visitor & Convention Bureau: 5433 Victoria Ave., Niagara Falls, ON L2G 3L1, 905/356-6061, Fax: 905/356-5567, Toll Free: 1-800-563-2557, Email: nfcvcb@niagara.com
North of Superior Tourism Association: Executive Director, Bruce C. Hole, 1119 East Victoria Ave., Thunder Bay, ON P7C 1B7, 807/626-9420, Fax: 807/626-9421, Toll Free: 1-800-265-3951, Email: nosta@lakeheadu.ca
Northern Ontario Tourist Outfitters Association: Executive Director, Jim Grayston, #408, 269 Main St. West, North Bay, ON P1B 2T8, 705/472-5552, Fax: 705/472-0621, Email: noto@onlink.net; URL: http://virtualnorth.com/noto/
Ontario's Sunset Country Travel Association: Executive Director, Neil McInnis, PO Box 647, Kenora, ON P9N 3X6, 807/468-5853, Fax: 807/468-5484, Info Line: 1-800-665-7567
Ottawa Tourism & Convention Authority: President, Ken Lambert; Director of Sales, Andrée Steel, #1800, 130 Albert St., Ottawa, ON K1P 5G4, 613/237-5150, Fax: 613/237-7339, Info Line: 613/237-5158, Toll Free: 1-800-363-4465
Peterborough Kawartha Tourism & Convention Bureau: General Manager, Glenda Hunter; Chairperson, Anne Marshall, 175 George St. North, Peterborough, ON K9J 3G6, 705/742-2201, Fax: 705/742-2494, Toll Free: 1-800-461-6424
Rainbow Country Travel Association: Executive Director, Erin Downey, Cedar Point Mall, 1984 Regent St. South, Sudbury, ON P3E 5S1, 705/522-0104, Fax: 705/522-3132, Toll Free: 1-800-465-6655
Sarnia/Lambton Visitor & Convention Bureau: Manager, Pat Laframboise, 224 North Vidal St., Sarnia, ON N7T 5Y3, 519/336-3232, Fax: 519/336-3278, Toll Free: 1-800-265-0316
Sault Ste. Marie Hospitality & Travel: President, David Saunders; Managing Director, Suzanne J. Curran, 99 Foster Dr., 3rd Fl., Sault Ste Marie, ON P6A 5X6, 705/759-5432, Fax: 705/759-2185, Toll Free: 1-800-461-6020
Sudbury Convention & Visitors Services: Manager, Paul Brokenshire, PO Box 5000, Stn A, Sudbury, ON P3A 5P3, 705/674-3141, Fax: 705/671-8145
Tourism Brantford: Coordinator, Valerie Wilson, 3 Sherwood Dr., Brantford, ON N3T 1N3, 519/751-9900, Fax: 519/759-5975, Toll Free: 1-800-265-6299
Tourism Stratford: Tourism Manager, Barbara Quarry, 88 Wellington St., PO Box 818, Stratford, ON N5A 6W1, 519/271-5140, Fax: 519/273-1818, Toll Free: 1-800-561-7926
Tourism Thunder Bay: Manager, Patricia Forrest, 807/625-2565, 500 Donald St. East, Thunder Bay, ON P7E 5V3, 807/625-2149, Fax: 807/623-3768, Info Line: 807/346-4636, Toll Free: 1-800-667-8386

Ontario East Tourism Association (OETA) (1974)
RR#1, Lansdowne, ON K0E 1L0
613/659-4300, Fax: 613/659-4306, Toll Free: 1-800-567-3278
Executive Director, Rose Wakim
President, Ronald Huck
Publications: Ontario East Discovery Map

Ontario Hostelry Institute (OHI)
#213, 300 Adelaide St. East, Toronto, ON M5A 1N1
416/363-3401, Fax: 416/363-3403
Executive Director, Rigzin Dolkar

Ontario Private Campground Association (OPCA) (1969)
RR#5, Owen Sound, ON N4K 5N7
519/371-3393, Fax: 519/371-5315, Email: opca@bmts.com
Managing Director, Marcel Gobeil
Publications: Update; Camping in Ontario, a.

Ontario Ski Resorts Association (OSRA)
#22, 850 Tapscott Rd., Scarborough, ON M1X 1N4
416/321-2252, Fax: 416/321-2336
President, Donald K. McIlveen

Ottawa Hoteliers Inc.
PO Box 53206, Ottawa, ON K1N 1C5
613/778-3999, Fax: 613/778-3999
President, Michel Garnier

Pacific Asia Travel Association (PATA) (1951)
Telesis Tower, #1000, 1 Montgomery St., San Francisco, CA 94104 USA
415/986-4646, Fax: 415/986-3458
President & CEO, Lakshman Ratnapala
Publications: PATA Travel News; Membership Directory

Regroupement tourisme jeunesse (1989)
Tourisme jeunesse
4545, av Pierre-de-Coubertin, Montréal, PQ H1V 3R2
514/252-3117, Téléc: 514/252-3119, Ligne sans frais: 1-800-461-8585
Directeur général, Joël Marier
Présidente, Claude Moreau
Publications: Temps libre; Les Auberges au Québec, annuel
Organisation(s) affiliée(s): Fédération internationale des auberges de jeunesse; Regroupment loisir Québec; Bureau canadien de l'éducation internationale

Resorts Ontario (1942)
Association of Tourist Resorts of Ontario
10 Peter St. North, PO Box 214, Orillia, ON L3V 6S1
705/325-9115, Fax: 705/325-7999, Toll Free: 1-800-363-7227
Managing Director, Grace Cerniuk, CAE
Publications: Resort News

Sahtu Tourism Association
PO Box 115, Norman Wells, NT X0E 0V0
403/587-2054, Fax: 403/587-2935

Société de développement économique de la région sherbrookoise - Tourisme/Greater Sherbooke Economic Development Corporation - Tourism
SDERS - Tourisme
1308, boul Portland, CP 426, Sherbrooke, PQ J1H 5J7
819/822-6195, Téléc: 819/822-6074
Directeur, Alain Deschâtelets

Tourism Industry Association of Canada/ Association de l'industrie touristique du Canada (TIAC) (1931)
#1016, 130 Albert St., Ottawa, ON K1P 5G4
613/238-3883, Fax: 613/238-3878, Email: tiac@achilles.net
URL: http://www.achilles.net/~tiac/homepage.html
President, Debra Sara Ward

Chairman, John Gow
Publications: Update
Affiliates: Heritage Canada

Tourism Industry Association of New Brunswick Inc./Association de l'industrie touristique du Nouveau-Brunswick inc. (TIANB) (1978)
Prospect Place, #206, 191 Prospect St., Fredericton, NB E3B 2T7
506/458-5646, Fax: 506/459-3634
President, Patrick Valardo
General Manager, Graham McOuat
Publications: The Open Door
Fredericton Visitor & Convention Bureau: Manager, Nancy Lockerbie, PO Box 130, Fredericton, NB E3B 4Y7, 506/452-9508, Fax: 506/452-9509, Email: tourism@darwin.nbnet.nb.ca
Saint John Visitor & Convention Bureau: #360, 560 Main St., Saint John, NB E2K 1J5, 506/658-2990, Fax: 506/658-2879

Tourism Industry Association of Newfoundland & Labrador (1983)
Hospitality Newfoundland & Labrador
107 LeMarchant Rd., PO Box 13516, St. John's, NF A1B 4B8
709/722-2000, Fax: 709/722-8104, Toll Free: 1-800-563-0700, Email: dlough@bridges.entnet.nf.ca
Executive Director, Dave Lough
Publications: Tourism Times

Tourism Industry Association of Nova Scotia (TIANS) (1977)
The World Trade & Convention Centre, #402, 1800 Argyle St., Halifax, NS B3J 3N8
902/423-4480, Fax: 902/422-0184
Managing Director, J.B. Cabrita
Cape Breton Tourist Association: Executive Director, Don Blackwood, 10 Keltic Dr., Sydney, NS B1S 1P5, 902/539-9876, Fax: 902/539-8430
Central Nova Tourist Association: Executive Director, Sally Anderson; Office Manager, Suzanne Waeelock, PO Box 1761, Truro, NS B2N 5Z5, 902/893-8782, Fax: 902/897-6641
Evangeline Trail Tourism Association: Executive Director, Donna Thomas; Administrative Assistant, Sandra Lyons, 5518 Prospect Rd., New Minas, NS B4N 3K8, 902/681-1645, Fax: 902/681-2747
Tourism Halifax: Director, Lewis M. Rogers, PO Box 1749, Halifax, NS B3J 3A5, 902/421-6448, Fax: 902/421-2842, Telex: 019-22641

Tourism Industry Association of the NWT
#2, 4807 - 49th St., Yellowknife, NT X1A 3T5
403/873-2122, Fax: 403/873-3654
Executive Director, Jackie Coulter
President, Yvonne Quick
Arctic Coast Tourism Association: PO Box 91, Cambridge Bay, NT X0C 0C0, 403/983-2224, Fax: 403/983-2302
Baffin Tourism Association: PO Box 1450, Iqaluit, NT X0A 0H0, 819/979-6551, Fax: 819/979-1261
Big River Tourism Association: PO Box 185, Hay River, NT X0E 0R0, 403/874-2422, Fax: 403/874-2027
Nahanni-Ram Tourism Association: PO Box 177, Fort Simpson, NT X0E 0N0, 403/695-3182, Fax: 403/695-2511
Northern Frontier Visitors Association: Manager, Melissa Daoust; President, Ron McCuaig, #4, 4807 - 49th St., Yellowknife, NT X1A 3T5, 403/873-4262, Fax: 403/873-3654, Email: nfva@netnorth.com
Travel Keewatin: PO Box 328, Rankin Inlet, NT X0C 0G0, 819/645-2618, Fax: 819/645-2320

Tourism Industry Association of PEI (TIAPEI)
64 Great George St., PO Box 2050, Charlottetown, PE C1A 7N7
902/566-5008, Fax: 902/368-3605
URL: http://www.gov.pe.ca/conv/tiapei.html
General Manager, Don Cudmore
President, Alfred Groom
Publications: Tourism Tides

Tourism Industry Association of Saskatchewan
TISASK
2154 Airport Dr., Saskatoon, SK S7L 6M6
306/343-3610, Fax: 306/664-1971
Executive Director, Stephen McLellan
Hugh Vassos
Tourism Regina/Regina Convention & Visitors Bureau: Marketing Manager, Gayle E. Zimmerman, Hwy. 1 East, PO Box 3355, Regina, SK S4P 3H1, 306/789-8166, Fax: 306/789-3171, Toll Free: 1-800-661-5099
Tourism Saskatoon: Executive Director, Susan Lamb; Director of Marketing, Marnie McNiven, #6, 305 Idylwyld Dr. North, Saskatoon, SK S7L 0Z1, 306/242-1206, Fax: 306/242-1955, Toll Free: 1-800-567-2444

Tourism Industry Association of the Yukon (1972)
TIA Yukon
1109 - 1st Ave., Whitehorse, YT Y1A 2A9
403/668-3331, Fax: 403/667-7379, Email: tiayukon@yknet.yk.ca
Executive Director, Lowry Toombs
Publications: TIA Yukon Newsletter
Klondike Visitors Association: Executive Director, Denny Kobayashi, PO Box 389, Dawson, YT Y0B 1G0, 403/993-5575, Fax: 403/993-6415

Tourism Industry of Manitoba Inc. (TIM) (1969)
c/o Viscount Gort Hotel, #104, 1670 Portage Ave., Winnipeg, MB R3C 0C9
204/774-8406, Fax: 204/774-8420, Email: tourism@solutions.mb.ca
President, Lilian Tankard
Publications: Tourism Journal of Manitoba
Tourism Winnipeg: President, M. Kulba; Executive Director, P. McMillan, #320, 25 Forks Market Rd., Winnipeg, MB R3C 4S8, 204/943-1970, Fax: 204/942-4043, Toll Free: 1-800-665-0204, Email: wpginfo@tourism.winnipeg.mb.ca
URL: http://www.tourism.winnipeg.mb.ca/tourismw/

Travellers' Aid Society of Metropolitain Toronto
Room B23, Union Station, Toronto, ON M5J 1E6
416/366-7788, Fax: 416/366-0829
Executive Director, Helen Heffernan
Publications: Newsletter

Vacances familles inc. (1971)
#120, 1291, boul Charest ouest, Québec, PQ G1N 2C9
418/682-5464, Téléc: 418/682-0746, Télex: 051-31619
Directeur général, Pierre Tremblay
Publications: Vacances pour tous

WorldHomes Holiday Exchange (WHE) (1986)
HomeLink International Canada
1707 Platt Cres., North Vancouver, BC V7J 1X9
604/987-3262, Fax: 604/987-3262, Email: jgraber@direct.ca
Director, Jack Graber
Publications: Holiday Exchange Book

TRADE
see also Retail Trade

Action Canada Network/Réseau canadien d'action (ACN) (1987)
#804, 251 Laurier Ave. West, Ottawa, ON K1P 5J6
613/233-1764, Fax: 613/233-1458, Email: actcan@web.apc.org
Administrative Coordinator, Mandy Rocks
National Co-Chair, Jean Claude Parrot
Communications Coordinator, Marcella Munro
Publications: Action Dossier; Action Bulletin

Asia Pacific Foundation of Canada/Fondation Asie Pacifique du Canada (APFC) (1984)
#666, 999 Canada Pl., Vancouver, BC V6C 3E1
604/684-5986, Fax: 604/681-1370
President/CEO, Dr. William Saywell
Executive Vice-President, Dr. John D. Wiebe
Information Resources Coordinator, Rachel Charron
Publications: Dialogue

Canada Beef Export Federation
#235, 6715 - 8 St. NE, Calgary, AB T2E 7H7
403/274-0005, Fax: 403/274-7275
Executive Director, Ted Haney

Canadian Association of Regulated Importers/Association canadienne des importateurs réglementés (CARI) (1986)
#203, 2525 St. Laurent Blvd., Ottawa, ON K1H 8P5
613/738-1729, Fax: 613/733-9501
General Manager, Robert De Valk
Publications: Importers Edge

Canadian Courier Association
555 Dixon Rd., Etobicoke, ON M9W 1H8
905/242-2570, Fax: 905/242-9874
Executive Director, Douglas Moffatt
President, Kal Tobias

Canadian Importers Association Inc./Association des importateurs canadiens inc.
#700, 210 Dundas St. West, Toronto, ON M5G 2E8
416/595-5333, Fax: 416/595-8226, Email: info@importers.ca
URL: http://www.importers.ca
President, Donald McArthur, CAE
Publications: Importweek; Importfile
Affiliates: National Trade Committees - Association of International Automobile Manufacturers of Canada; Canadian Meat Importers Committee; Canadian Association of Footwear Importers, Inc., Customs & Legislation Committee; Electronics Import Committee; International Cheese Council of Canada

ASSOCIATION OF INTERNATIONAL AUTOMOBILE MANUFACTURERS OF CANADA/ASSOCIATION DES FABRICANTS INTERNATIONAUX D'AUTOMOBILES DU CANADA (AIAMC) (1973)
#700, 210 Dundas St. West, Toronto, ON M5G 2E8
416/595-5333, Fax: 416/595-8226
President, Donald R. McArthur
Associate Executive Director, Adrian Bradford, CAE
Publications: International Automobile Manufacturers Update

CANADIAN ASSOCIATION OF FOOTWEAR IMPORTERS INC. (CAFI)
#700, 210 Dundas St. West, Toronto, ON M5G 2E8
416/595-5333, Fax: 416/595-8226
Chair, Claude Church
Corporate Secretary, Catherine McPherson

CANADIAN MEAT IMPORTERS COMMITTEE (CMIC) (1969)
#700, 210 Dundas St. West, Toronto, ON M5G 2E8
416/595-5333, Fax: 416/595-8226, Email: info@importers.ca
URL: http://www.importers.ca
Executive Director, Fée Kiessling
Chairman, William Fenton

CUSTOMS & LEGISLATION COMMITTEE
#700, 210 Dundas St. West, Toronto, ON M5G 2E8
416/595-5333, Fax: 416/595-8226

Chair, Bud Hollings
Corporate Secretary, Catherine McPherson

ELECTRONICS IMPORT COMMITTEE (EIC)
#700, 210 Dundas St. West, Toronto, ON M5G 2E8
416/595-5333, Fax: 416/595-8226
Chair, Trent Cosgrove
Corporate Secretary, Catherine McPherson
Publications: Importweek

INTERNATIONAL CHEESE COUNCIL OF CANADA/CONSEIL CANADIEN DES FROMAGES INTERNATIONAUX (ICCC) (1975)
#700, 210 Dundas St. West, Toronto, ON M5G 2E8
416/595-5333, Fax: 416/595-8226
Chair, Peter Couture
Vice-Chair, Doug Smith
Treasurer, Walter Pelley
Secretary, Donald R. McArthur

Canadian International Trade Association (CITA) (1988)
#611, 2 Carlton St., Toronto, ON M5B 1J3
416/351-9728, Fax: 416/351-9911
President, Sydney King
Vice-President, Lee Meister
Publications: World Trade Showguide

Citizens Concerned About Free Trade (CCAFT)
PO Box 8052, Saskatoon, SK S7K 4R7
306/244-5757, Fax: 306/244-3790
National Chairman, David Orchard
National Organizer/Editor, Marjaleena Repo
Publications: True North: The Voice of Canadian Independence

Club export agro-alimentaire du Québec/Québec Agri-Food Export Club (1990)
Édifice de Bleury, #102, 200, rue MacDonald, St-Jean-sur-Richelieu, PQ J3B 8J6
514/349-1521, Téléc: 514/349-6923, Ligne sans frais: 1-800-563-9767
Secrétaire général, André Latour, caé
Publications: Exportise

Federation of Export Clubs Canada (1980)
Export Club
#1402, 67 Yonge St., Toronto, ON M5E 1J8
416/364-4112, Fax: 416/364-4074
Chairman, H.J. Janthur

France Technology Press Agency/Bureau de Presse France Technologies (1984)
FRANTECH
#2004, 20 Queen St. West, Toronto, ON M5H 3R3
416/977-2587, Fax: 416/977-9671, Email: 76001.2110@compuserve.com
Executive Director, Alexandra Sutton
Affiliates: French Trade Commission

Hong Kong Trade Development Council
Office Tower, Convention Plaza, 1 Harbour Rd., 38th Fl., Wanchai Hong Kong
852/2584 4333, Fax: 852/2824 0249
Toronto Office: Director, Andrew Yui; Trade Enquiry Officer, Lily Kam, #1100, 347 Bay St., Toronto, ON M5H 2R7, 416/366-3594, Fax: 416/366-1569, Telex: 06218056 HKTDC
Vancouver Office: 1500 West Georgia St., 11th Fl., Vancouver, BC V6G 2Z6, 604/685-0883, Fax: 604/681-0093

Institute for Canadian Studies (ICS) (1992)
298 Garry St., Winnipeg, MB R3C 1H3
204/925-8781, Fax: 204/943-2261, Email: lisashaw@instcanstudies.mb.ca
URL: http://www.instcanstudies.mb.ca
Director, W.H. Loewen
Researcher, Lisa Shaw

Latin American Canadian Business Association
PO Box 16076, Vancouver, BC V7J 3S9
604/986-3147, Fax: 604/988-5559
President, Antonio Arreaga-Valdes

Offshore Trade Association of Nova Scotia (OTANS) (1982)
#813, 1800 Argyle St., Halifax, NS B3J 3N8
902/425-4774, Fax: 902/422-2332
Executive Director, Karen Monnon

The Parliamentary Centre/Le Centre parlementaire (1968)
250 Albert St., 4th Fl., Ottawa, ON K1P 6M1
613/237-0143, Fax: 613/235-8237
Director, Peter C. Dobell

World Trade Centre - Inforum Montréal (1984)
#2100, 380, rue Saint-Antoine ouest, Montréal, PQ H2Y 3X7
514/849-1999, Fax: 514/847-8343, Email: wtc.mtl@lanternette.com
Executive Director, Baxter D. Laporte
Administrative Assistant, Marie Claude Morin
Affiliates: UNCTAD Trade Point

TRANSLATION see **LANGUAGE, LINGUISTICS, LITERATURE**

TRANSPORTATION & SHIPPING
see also Marine Trades

American Bureau of Shipping - Canadian Division (ABS-Can)
1577 Thompson St., Mississauga, ON L5C 1B4
905/897-9110, Fax: 905/897-9110
Canadian Representative, G.H. Mason

Association québécoise du transport et des routes inc. (AQTR) (1965)
#100, 1595, rue Saint-Hubert, Montréal, PQ H2L 3Z2
514/523-6444, Téléc: 514/523-2666, Infoligne: 514/523-0413
Directrice générale, Catherine Hirou
Président, Claude Beaupré
Publications: Information; Revue routes et transports, trimestriel

Atlantic Provinces Transportation Commission
#330, 1133 St. George Blvd., Moncton, NB E1E 4E1
506/857-2820, Fax: 506/857-2835
General Manager, Ramsay Armitage
Staff Secretary, Cathy Peters

Canadian Bus Association/Association canadienne de l'autobus (CBA) (1935)
#600, 99 Bank St., Ottawa, ON K1P 6B9
613/238-1800, Fax: 613/233-9656
Executive Director, David Long
Association Manager, S.M. Beaudin

Canadian Business Aircraft Association Inc. (CBAA) (1962)
#1317, 50 O'Connor St., Ottawa, ON K1P 6L2
613/236-5611, Fax: 613/236-2361
CEO/President, J.D. Lyon
Chairman, Doug Thierman
Publications: CBAA Newsbrief; CBAA Bulletin; Membership Directory, a.; Leading Edge, s-a.
Affiliates: National Business Aircraft Association; International Business Aircraft Council; European Business Aircraft Association

Canadian Council of Motor Transport Administrators/Conseil canadien des administrateurs en transport motorisé (CCMTA) (1940)
2323 St. Laurent Blvd., Ottawa, ON K1G 4K6
613/736-1003, Fax: 613/736-1395
Executive Director, Louise Pelletier, CAE
Publications: CCMTA News

Canadian Industrial Transportation League
#602, 1090 Don Mills Rd., North York, ON M3C 3R6
416/447-7766, Fax: 416/447-7312
President, Maria Rehner

Canadian Institute of Traffic & Transportation/Institute canadien du trafic et du transport (CITT) (1958)
#710, 33 Yonge St., Toronto, ON M5E 1G4
416/363-5696, Fax: 416/363-5698
President & COO, P.E. Cullen

Canadian International Freight Forwarders Association, Inc./Association des transitaires internationaux canadiens, inc. (CIFFA) (1948)
PO Box 929, Streetsville, ON L5M 2C5
905/567-4633, Fax: 905/542-2716, Email: massoud.m@ciffa
URL: http://www.webcom.com.ciffa/
President, William M. Gottlieb
Secretary Manager, Marilyn Massoud
Publications: CIFFA Newsletter; Membership Directory, a.
Affiliates: International Federation of Freight Forwarders Associations

Canadian Professional Logistics Institute/Institut Canadien des Professionnels de la Logistique (1990)
The Logistics Institute
#710, 33 Yonge St., Toronto, ON M5E 1G4
416/363-3005, Fax: 416/363-5598
President, Victor S. Deyglio
Publications: Canadian Logistics Journal
Affiliates: Canadian Institute of Traffic & Transportation; Canadian International Freight Forwarders Association

Canadian Shipowners Association/Association des armateurs canadiens (CSA) (1903)
#705, 350 Sparks St., Ottawa, ON K1R 7S8
613/232-3539, Fax: 613/232-6211
President, T. Norman Hall
Manager, Marine Operations, Neil C. Hunter
Sec.-Treas., Silvie Dagenais
Publications: Seaports

Canadian Shippers' Council
48 Balsam Dr., Baie-d'Urfé, PQ H9X 3K5
514/457-7268, Fax: 514/457-7269
Secretary, Walter Mueller

Canadian Transportation Research Forum/Le Groupe de recherches sur les transports au Canada (CTRF) (1967)
#209, 15 Innovation Blvd., Saskatoon, SK S7N 2X8
306/668-2828, Fax: 306/668-7603
President, Roger Roy
Secretary, Gail Sparks
Publications: Going the Distance; Forumation, 5 pa

Canadian Trucking Association/L'Association canadienne du camionnage (CTA) (1937)
#1025, 130 Slater St., Ottawa, ON K1P 6E2
613/236-9426, Fax: 613/563-2701, Email: cta@magi.com
President, Gilles J. Bélanger
Publications: CTA Bulletin; CTA Magazine, q.

ORGANIZATIONS — TRANSPORTATION & SHIPPING

ALBERTA TRUCKING ASSOCIATION
#240, 6025 - 12 St. SE, PO Box 5520, Stn A, Calgary, AB T2H 1X9
403/253-8401, Fax: 403/255-2724
General Manager, Collin Heath

ASSOCIATION DU CAMIONNAGE DU QUÉBEC INC./QUÉBEC TRUCKING ASSOCIATION INC. (ACQ) (1951)
#200, 6450, rue Notre Dame ouest, Montréal, PQ H4C 1C4
514/932-0377, Téléc: 514/932-1358, Ligne sans frais: 1-800-361-5813
Président, Serge Leclerc
Vice-président exécutif, Claude Pigeon
Publications: ACQ-Plus
Organisation(s) affiliée(s): Union Internationale des Transports Routiers - Genève; American Trucking Association - Washington, DC

ATLANTIC PROVINCES TRUCKING ASSOCIATION (APTA) (1950)
Executive Building, #14, One Trites Rd., Riverview, NB E1B 2V5
506/387-4413, Fax: 506/387-7424
Executive Director, Ralph Boyd
Publications: APTA Newsletter; Atlantic Trucking, q.

BRITISH COLUMBIA TRUCKING ASSOCIATION (BCTA) (1913)
PO Box 381, Port Coquitlam, BC V3C 4K6
604/942-3200, Fax: 604/942-3191, Toll Free: 1-800-565-2282
Manager, Administration & Member Services, Karen Westerby
President, Paul Landry
Publications: News & Views; BC Motor Transport Directory, a.; BCTA Membership Roster, a.

MANITOBA TRUCKING ASSOCIATION
25 Bunting St., Winnipeg, MB R2X 2P5
204/632-6600, Fax: 204/694-7134
General Manager, Al Harris
Publications: Manitoba Highway News & Manitoba Ship-by-Truck Directory

NORTHWEST TERRITORIES MOTOR TRANSPORT ASSOCIATION (NWTMTA) (1971)
PO Box 574, Yellowknife, NT X1A 2N4
403/873-2831, Fax: 403/255-2724
President, Charlie Fair
Director, Public Affairs, Keith Mundy
Publications: NWTMTA Newsletter

ONTARIO TRUCKING ASSOCIATION (1926)
555 Dixon Rd., Etobicoke, ON M9W 1H8
416/249-7401, Fax: 416/245-6152, Email: info@ontruck.org
URL: http://www.ontruck.org
President, David H. Bradley
Manager, Safety & Operations, Barrie Montague
Manager, Membership & Accounting, Barbara P. Cole
Communications Manager, Rebecka Torn
Publications: Update; Ship By Truck, s-m.

SASKATCHEWAN TRUCKING ASSOCIATION (STA) (1937)
1335 Wallace St., Regina, SK S4N 3Z5
306/569-9696, Fax: 306/781-7066, Toll Free: 1-800-563-7623
General Manager, Warren Smith

Canadian Urban Transit Association/Association canadienne du transport urbain (CUTA) (1904)
#901, 55 York St., Toronto, ON M5J 1R7
416/365-9800, Fax: 416/365-1295
Executive Vice-President, Al Cormier, CAE
Affiliates: Ontario Urban Transit Association

Chartered Institute of Transport in North America/Institut agrée des transports Amérique du Nord (CIT) (1919)
CIT in North America
#600, 99 Bank St., Ottawa, ON K1P 6B9
613/566-7033, Fax: 613/233-9656, Email: cit@worldlink.ca
URL: http://www.worldlink.ca/~cit
Executive Director, Sheilagh Beaudin
Publications: CIT Newsletter; North American Transit, a.

Electric Vehicle Association of Canada/Association canadienne du véhicule électrique (1978)
#11, 21 Concourse Gate, Nepean, ON K2E 7S4
613/723-3127, Fax: 613/723-8275
Executive Director, Tom Lewinson
Publications: Electric Propulsion
Affiliates: Association européenne des véhicules électriques routiers; World Electric Vehicle Association; Electric Vehicle Association of Americas

Freight Carriers Association of Canada (FCA) (1939)
660 Garrison Rd., Fort Erie, ON L2A 5M9
905/994-0560, Fax: 905/994-0117
Executive Vice-President, Micheline S. Tansey
Publications: News
Affiliates: Niagara Frontier Tariff Bureau

Industrial Truck Association of Canada (1967)
c/o Trade Association Management Group, 208 Brimorton Dr., Scarborough, ON M1H 2C6
416/431-1330, Fax: 416/431-5223
Manager, John Martin

Motorcycle & Moped Industry Council/Le Conseil de l'industrie de la motocyclette et du cyclomoteur (MMIC) (1971)
#235, 7181 Woodbine Ave., Markham, ON L3R 1A3
905/470-6123, Fax: 905/470-9407
Executive Director, Robert Ramsay
Publications: MMIC Bulletin

Ontario Good Roads Association (OGRA) (1894)
#2, 530 Otto Rd., Mississauga, ON L5T 2L5
905/795-2555, Fax: 905/795-2660
Executive Director, Sheila Richardson
Office Manager, Cathy Houston
Publications: Municipal Routes

Ontario Movers Association (OMA)
555 Dixon Rd., Etobicoke, ON M9W 1H8
416/249-7401, Fax: 416/245-6152
Publications: OMA Newsletter

Ontario Traffic Council (OTC)
#121, 20 Carlton St., Toronto, ON M5B 2H5
416/598-4138, Fax: 416/598-0449
Administrative Assistant, Judy Woodley

Ontario Urban Transit Association
#901, 55 York St., Toronto, ON M5J 1R7
416/365-9800, Fax: 416/365-1295
Executive Director, Dave Roberts

Private Motor Truck Council of Canada/Association canadienne du camionnage d'entreprise (PMTC) (1977)
1275 Ingledene Dr., Oakville, ON L6H 2J1
905/844-0587, Fax: 905/844-4255
President, Bruce J. Richards
Chairman, G. Dennis
Vice-Chairman, R. Miskelly
Publications: News Briefs; The Counsellor, q.
Affiliates: National Private Truck Council

The Railway Association of Canada/L'Association des chemins de fer du Canada (RAC) (1919)
#1105, 800, boul René-Lévesque ouest, Montréal, PQ H3B 1X9
514/879-8558, Fax: 514/879-1522
President, R.H. Ballantyne
Affiliates: Association of American Railroads

The Shipping Federation of Canada/La Fédération maritime du Canada (1903)
#326, 300, rue St-Sacrement, Montréal, PQ H2Y 1X4
514/849-2325, Fax: 514/849-6992, Telex: 055-61042
President, Francis C. Nicol
Publications: Maritime Perspective

Transport 2000 Canada (1977)
#102, 111 Metcalfe St., PO Box 858, Stn B, Ottawa, ON K1P 5P9
613/594-3290, Fax: 613/594-3271, Info Line: 613/594-3291
National Office Manager, Dirk Partridge
President, David W. Glastonbury
Vice-President, Harry Gow
Secretary, Anton Turrittin
Membership Secretary, John deWit
Publications: Transport Action
Affiliates: Transport 2000 International
Transport 2000 Alberta: President, John Bakker; Treasurer, Frank J. Testin, Res: 403/426-6567, PO Box 4385, Edmonton, AB T6E 4T5, 403/458-2225
Transport 2000 Atlantic: President, John Pearce; Treasurer, William T. McIntyre, Res: 506/459-8726, 40 Lorne Ave., Dartmouth, NS B2Y 3E7, 902/469-3474, Fax: 902/466-8832
Transport 2000 British Columbia: President, Ian Fisher, #213, 1728 Alberni St., Vancouver, BC V6G 1B2, 604/687-6219
Transport 2000 Ontario: President, Elizabeth Hill; Secretary, David G. Scott, 28 Vradenberg Dr., Scarborough, ON M1T 1M6, 416/497-6090
Transport 2000 Québec: Président, Luc Côté, 2520, rue Lionel-Groulx, 2e étage, Montréal, PQ H3J 1J8, 514/932-8008, Téléc: 514/932-2024
Transport 2000 Saskatchewan: President, Jim Richards, PO Box 2134, Melfort, SK S0E 1A0, 306/752-2603

Transportation Association of Canada/Association des transports du Canada (1970)
2323 St. Laurent Blvd., Ottawa, ON K1G 4K6
613/736-1350, Fax: 613/736-1395
Executive Director, Louise Pelletier, CAE
Publications: RTAC News/Nouvelles de L'ARTC; Transportation Forum, irreg.

Western Canada Motor Coach Association (WCMCA) (1961)
PO Box 4520, Stn C, Calgary, AB T2T 5N3
403/244-4487, Fax: 403/244-2340
Executive Director, Marjorie Zingle, CAE
President, Rick Colborne
Publications: Headlights

Western Transportation Advisory Council (WESTAC) (1973)
#1140, 800 Pender St. West, Vancouver, BC V6C 2V6
604/687-8691, Fax: 604/687-8751
President, B. Maureen Melville
Vice-President/Corporate Secretary, Paul Ovimet
Transportation Analyst, Amanda Levey

TRAVEL see TOURISM & TRAVEL

TREASURY MANAGEMENT see FINANCE

TRUCKING see TRANSPORTATION & SHIPPING

Canadian Almanac & Directory 1997

UNDERWATER ARCHAEOLOGY see ARCHAEOLOGY

UNDERWRITERS see INSURANCE INDUSTRY

UNITED WAY see SOCIAL RESPONSE/SOCIAL SERVICES

UNIVERSITIES see EDUCATION

URBAN DEVELOPMENT see PLANNING & DEVELOPMENT

USER GROUPS see INFORMATION TECHNOLOGY

VACATION INDUSTRY see TOURISM & TRAVEL

VENTURE CAPITAL see FINANCE

VETERANS see MILITARY & VETERANS

VETERINARY MEDICINE see ANIMALS & ANIMAL SCIENCE

VIDEO see FILM & VIDEO

VISUAL ART, CRAFTS, FOLK ARTS
see also The Arts; Galleries & Museums

Alberta Craft Council (ACC) (1980)
10106 - 124 St., Edmonton, AB T5N 1P6
403/488-6611, Fax: 403/488-8855
President, Arne Handley
Publications: Alberta Craft Magazine

Artists in Stained Glass (AISG)
c/o Ontario Crafts Council, 35 McCaul St., Toronto, ON M5T 1V7
416/977-3551, Fax: 416/977-3552
Co-Chair, Sue Obata
Co-Chair, Robert Brown
Publications: A Flat Glass Journal

Association of Canadian Editorial Cartoonists/ Association canadienne des dessinateurs éditoriaux (ACEC) (1986)
180 Elgin St., 12th Fl., Ottawa, ON K2P 6K7
President, Guy Badeaux
Publications: Portfolio: The Year in Canadian Caricature

Association des collections d'entreprises/ Corporate Art Collectors Association (1990)
Secrétariat: Banque nationale du Canada, 600, rue de la Gauchetière ouest, 8e étage, Montréal, PQ H3B 4L2
514/394-8533, Téléc: 514/394-6258
Président, Maurice Forget
Secrétaire, Francine Paul

The Canadian Art Foundation (1991)
6 Church St., 2nd Fl., Toronto, ON M5E 1M1
416/368-8854, Fax: 416/368-6135
Contact, Richard Rhodes
Publications: Canadian Art

Canadian Art Therapy Association - Eastern Chapter (CATA) (1977)
#601, 6-2400 Dundas St. West, Mississauga, ON L5K 2R8
905/858-9642, Fax: 905/542-7199
President, Lois Woolf
Publications: Journal of the Canadian Art Therapy Association

Canadian Art Therapy Association - Western Chapter
#350, 1425 Marine Dr., West Vancouver, BC V7T 1B9
604/926-9381, Fax: 604/926-5729
Contact, Lois Woolf

Canadian Association of Film Distributors & Exporters/Association canadienne des distributeurs et exportateurs de films
62 Humewood Dr., Toronto, ON M6C 2W4
416/658-2929, Fax: 416/658-3176
President & CEO, Dan Johnson
Co-Chair, Victor Loewy
Co-Chair, Stephen Greenberg
Vice-Chair, Québec, Andre Link
Vice-Chair, Ontario, Bryan Gliserman
Affiliates: Association des producteurs de films et de television du Québec

Canadian Association of Professional Conservators/Association canadienne des restaurateurs professionnels (1971)
#400, 280 Metcalfe St., Ottawa, ON K2P 1R7
613/998-4971, Fax: 613/993-3412
Chairman, Karen Colby-Stothart
Secretary, Carole Dignard
Publications: Directory

Canadian Ceramic Society (CCS) (1901)
#310, 2175 Sheppard Ave. East, North York, ON M2J 1W8
416/491-2886, Fax: 416/491-1670, Email: taylor@interlog.com
President, Al Matthews
Vice-President, Brian Sellars
Administrator, Diane Gaunt
Publications: Canadian Ceramics Quarterly; The Journal of the Canadian Ceramic Society

Canadian Craft & Hobby Association (CCHA) (1978)
4404 - 12 St. NE, PO Box 44, Calgary, AB T2E 6K9
403/291-0559, Fax: 403/291-0675, Email: parentp@cadvision.com
Executive Director, Patrice Baron-Parent
Publications: Canadian Craft Trade; Craft & Needlework Age; Canadian Florist, Greenhouse & Nursery

Canadian Crafts Council/Conseil canadien des métiers d'art (CCC) (1974)
189 Laurier Ave. East, Ottawa, ON K1N 6P1
613/235-8200, Fax: 613/235-7425
Executive Director, Peter Weinrich
Publications: CCC Bulletin

Canadian Folk Arts Council/Conseil canadien des arts populaires
263 Adelaide St. West, 5th Fl., Toronto, ON M5H 1Y2
416/977-7456
Director General, Leon Kossar

Canadian Guild of Crafts Québec/Guild canadienne des métiers d'art Québec (1906)
2025, rue Peel, Montréal, PQ H3A 1T6
514/849-6091
Managing Director, Nairy Kalemkerian

Canadian Quilters Association/Association canadienne de la courtepointe (CQA)
PO Box 22010, RPO Herongate, Ottawa, ON K1V 0C2
URL: http://www.nt.net/~giselef/cqaacc1.htm
President, Virginia Newey, 705/969-8720, Email: newey@cyberbeach.net
Vice-President, Jackie Philpott, 709/686-5007, Email: jphilptt@atcon.com
Publicity, Elena Keen, 613/523-2633, Email: elena@sce.carleton.ca

Treasurer, Carol Galloway, 204/269-9566, Email: cgallow@MTS.Net
Publications: CQA/ACC Newsletter

Canadian Society of Decorative Arts/Cercle canadien des arts décoratifs (CSDA) (1981)
PO Box 4, Stn B, Toronto, ON M5T 2T2
Email: mbradley@chin.gc.ca
President, Merridy Bradley, 613/992-3333
Publications: Bulletin

Canadian Society of Painters in Water Color/ Société canadienne de peintres en aquarelle (CSPWC) (1926)
#102, 258 Wallace Ave., Toronto, ON M6P 3M9
416/533-5100
Administrator, Shirley Barrie
Publications: Watercolour Newsletter; Aquarelle: A History of CSPWC

Conseil des arts textiles du Québec (CATQ) (1980)
811A, rue Ontario est, Montréal, PQ H2L 1P1
514/524-6645, Téléc: 514/525-2621
Présidente, Micheline Couture
Coordonnatrice, Jocelyne Gaudreau
Publications: Textile

Conseil des métiers d'art du Québec/Québec Crafts Council (1985)
378, rue St-Paul ouest, Montréal, PQ H2Y 2A6
514/287-7555, Téléc: 514/287-9923
Directeur général, Yvan Gauthier
Présidente, Louise Lemieux Bérubé

Conseil de la Peinture du Québec (CPQ) (1966)
#913, 460, rue Sainte-Catherine ouest, Montréal, PQ H3B 1A7
514/279-5600, Téléc: 514/279-7795
Présidente, Monic Thouin-Perrault
Directrice, Sylvie Rousseau
Publications: Bulletin
Organisation(s) affiliée(s): International Association of Art

Conseil de la Sculpture du Québec (CSQ) (1962)
#306, 911, rue Jean-Talon est, Montréal, PQ H2R 1V5
514/270-7209, Téléc: 514/270-4623
Président, Pierre Tessier
Publications: Infosculpture

Crafts Association of British Columbia
Granville Island, 1386 Cartwright St., Vancouver, BC V6H 3R8
604/687-6511
Ann Wray
Publications: Craft Contacts

Crafts Guild of Manitoba Inc. (1928)
183 Kennedy St., Winnipeg, MB R3C 1S6
204/943-1190, Fax: 204/942-6069
Manager, S. Sulkers
Publications: Newsletter

Embroiderers' Association of Canada, Inc. (EAC) (1973)
1311 Salisbury Rd., RR#1, Moncton, NB E1C 8J5
506/852-8816, Fax: 506/478-2879
URL: http://www.antibe.com/westview/eac.html
President, Sheila Horseman
Past President, Barbara Gilbert
Secretary, Leslie Burrows
Vice-President, Joan Mills
Publications: Embroidery Canada

Folklore Canada International (FCI) (1986)
PO Box 9, Stn DeLorimier, Montréal, PQ H2H 2N6
514/524-8552, Fax: 514/524-0269

Director General, Guy Landry
Publications: Folklore Canada Express; Directory of Living Heritage Festivals & Events in Canada

Fondation d'art nationale du Canada
#2500, 1155, boul René-Lévesque ouest, Montréal, PQ H3B 2K4
514/876-1632, Téléc: 514/875-8967
Directeur général, Pierre Lorrain

Fusion: The Ontario Clay & Glass Association
The Gardener's Cottage, 225 Confederation Dr., Scarborough, ON M19 1B2
416/438-8946, Fax: 416/438-0192
Contact, Elizabeth Dingman
Publications: Fusion Magazine

International Association of Art Critics (Canada) Inc./Association internationale des critiques d'art (Canada) inc.
#706, 15 McMurrich St., Toronto, ON M5R 3M6
416/925-5564, Fax: 416/925-2972
President, Normand Biron
Treasurer, Pat Fleisher

Manitoba Crafts Council (1978)
Council of Manitoba Artisans Inc.
#003, 100 Arthur St., Winnipeg, MB R3B 1H3
204/942-1816, Fax: 204/942-1555
President, Ron Mark
Administrator, Mary Krieger
Publications: The Bulletin

The Metal Arts Guild (MAG) (1946)
#303, 80 Spadina Ave., Toronto, ON M5S 2J3
416/504-8453
President, Louise Jarvis
Administrator, Camille Anderson
Publications: MAGazine

Newfoundland & Labrador Crafts Development Association (NLCDA) (1972)
Devon House, 59 Duckworth St., St. John's, NF A1C 1E6
709/753-2749, Fax: 709/753-2766,
    Email: anne_manuel@porthole.entnet.nf.ca
Executive Director, Anne Manuel
Chairperson, Ray Will
Publications: NLCDA Newsletter
Affiliates: Canadian Crafts Council

Nova Scotia Designer Crafts Council (NSDCC) (1973)
#901, 1809 Barrington St., Halifax, NS B3J 3K8
902/423-3837, Fax: 902/422-0881
Executive Director, Carol Oliver
Publications: Nova Scotia Craft News

Ontario Crafts Council (1976)
Chalmer's Building, 35 McCaul St., Toronto, ON M5T 1V7
416/977-3551, Fax: 416/977-3552
Executive Director, Sarah Lupmanis
Publications: Ontario Craft

Ontario Folk Arts Multicultural Council (1966)
Ontario Heritage Centre, #101G, 10 Adelaide St. East, Toronto, ON M5C 1J3
416/367-8027, Fax: 416/367-8027
Executive Director, Bryn Lloyd
Publications: News & Views

Ontario Society for Education Through Art
345 Balliol St., Toronto, ON M4S 1E1
416/487-0705
President, Susan Brown

Ontario Woodcarvers Association (OWCA)
14 Rintella Ct., Scarborough, ON M1P 3V5
Contact, Donald Swenor
Publications: Ontario Woodcarver

Prince Edward Island Crafts Council (PEICC) (1965)
156 Richmond St., Charlottetown, PE C1A 1H9
902/892-5152, Fax: 902/628-8740
URL: http://www.crafts-council.pe.ca/index.html
Publications: Craft News

Professional Art Dealers Association of Canada Inc./Association Professionnelle des Galeries d'Art du Canada inc. (PADAC) (1966)
#307, 80 Spadina Ave., Toronto, ON M5V 2J3
416/703-0061, Fax: 416/703-0063
Executive Administrator, Louise Durham
Publications: Membership Directory

Royal Canadian Academy of Arts/Académie royale des arts du Canada (1880)
Office of the Secretary, 163 Queen St. East, PO Box 2, Toronto, ON M5A 1S1
416/363-9612, Fax: 416/363-9612
President, Ernest Annau, RCA
Sec.-Treas., Vello Hubel, RCA
Publications: RCA Newsletter
Affiliates: National Gallery of Canada (founded by RCA in 1880); Royal Academy, England

Saskatchewan Crafts Council (SCC) (1975)
813 Broadway Ave., Saskatoon, SK S7N 1B5
306/653-3616, Fax: 306/244-2711
URL: http://www.ffa.ucalgary.ca/scco/scc.html; http://www.sasknet.sk.ca/SCCO/SCC.html
Executive Director, Terry Schwalm
Publications: The Bulletin; The Craft Factor, 3 pa
Affiliates: Canadian Craft Council

Sculptor's Society of Canada/Société sculpteurs du Canada (SSC) (1928)
Exchange Tower, First Canadian Place, 130 King St. West, PO Box 40, Stn 1st Canadian Place, Toronto, ON M5X 1B5
416/214-0389
President, Desmond Scott
Publications: SSC Newsletter; Sculpture for the City Catalogue

SIAS International Art Society (1986)
PO Box 3039, Sherwood Park, AB T8A 2A6
403/922-5463, Fax: 403/922-5463
Managing Director/President, Klaus Bous
Associate Director, Horatio Venancio

Society of Canadian Artists/Société des artistes canadiens (SCA) (1957)
1435 Woodbine Ave., Toronto, ON M4C 4G8
President, George Sanders
Treasurer, Marg Nurse
Corresponding Secretary, Joy Orzy
Publications: Newsletter

Visual Arts Nova Scotia (VANS) (1976)
#901, 1809 Barrington St., Halifax, NS B3J 3K8
902/423-4694, Fax: 902/422-0881
Executive Director, Andrew Terris
Publications: Visual Arts News

Visual Arts Ontario (VAO) (1974)
439 Wellington St. West, 3rd Fl., Toronto, ON M5V 1E7
416/591-8883, Fax: 416/591-2432, Email: vao@castlecom.net
URL: http://vao.on.ca
Executive Director, Hennie L. Wolff
Publications: Agenda

Western Canada Art Association (WCAA) (1970)
Kelowna Art Gallery, 470 Queensway, Kelowna, BC V1Y 6S7
250/762-2226
Sec.-Treas., Gerald Jessop
Publications: Wagon

WATER & WASTEWATER see **ENVIRONMENTAL**

WATER RESOURCES see **ENVIRONMENTAL**

WILDLIFE see **ENVIRONMENTAL**

WOMEN

Association of Canadian Women Composers/Association des femmes compositrices canadiennes (ACWC) (1980)
20 St. Joseph St., Toronto, ON M4Y 1J9
416/239-5195
Chairperson, Jana Skarecky
Publications: ACWC Newsletter; Directory of Canadian Women Composers

Association féminine d'éducation et d'action sociale/Feminine Association for Education & Social Action (AFEAS) (1966)
5999, rue de Marseille, Montréal, PQ H1N 1K6
514/251-1636, Téléc: 514/251-9023
Secrétaire générale, Lise Girard
Publications: Femmes d'ici
Organisation(s) affiliée(s): Union mondiale des organisations féminines catholiques (UMOFC)

Association des femmes d'affaires du Québec (AFAQ)
3702, rue St-Denis, Montréal, PQ H2X 3L7
514/845-4281, Téléc: 514/845-3365
Présidente, Henriette Lanctot

Breast Cancer Action/Sensibilisation au cancer du sein
PO Box 39041, RPO Billings Bridge Plaza, Ottawa, ON K1H 1A1
613/736-5921, Fax: 613/736-8422, Email: bcanet@magi.com
URL: http://infoweb.magi.com/~bcanet/

Canadian Association for the Advancement of Women & Sport & Physical Activity/Association canadienne pour l'avancement des femmes du sport et de l'activité physique (CAAWS) (1981)
#308A, 1600 James Naismith Dr., Gloucester, ON K1B 5N4
613/748-5793, Fax: 613/748-5775
URL: http://infoweb.magi.com/~wmnsport/index.html
Executive Director, Marg McGregor
Publications: Action Bulletin
Affiliates: National Action Committee on the Status of Women

Canadian Association of Women Executives & Entrepreneurs/Association canadienne des femmes cadres et entrepreneurs (CAWEE) (1976)
#300, 595 Bay St., Toronto, ON M5G 2C2
416/482-2933, Fax: 416/596-7894
President, Dianna Rhodes
Manager, Linda Hatfield
Publications: Newsletter

Canadian Congress for Learning Opportunities for Women/Congrès canadien pour la promotion des études chez la femme (CCLOW) (1979)
47 Main St., Toronto, ON M4E 2V6
416/699-1909, Fax: 416/699-2145, Email: cclow@web.apc.org

Executive Director, Aisla Thomson
President, Pamela Dos Ramos
Publications: Women's Education des femmes

Canadian Federation of Business & Professional Women's Clubs/Fédération canadienne des clubs de femmes de carrières commerciales et professionnelles (CFBPWC) (1930)
#308, 56 Sparks St., Ottawa, ON K1P 5A9
613/234-7619, Fax: 613/234-7619
President, Sharon Selkirk
General Secretary, Shirley Côté
Publications: The Business & Professional Woman

Canadian Women in Communications/Association canadienne des femmes en communication (CWC) (1991)
#804, 372 Bay St., Toronto, ON M5H 2W9
416/363-1880, Fax: 416/363-1882, Toll Free: 1-800-361-2978
Executive Director, Stephanie MacKendrick
Publications: CWC Newsletter

Canadian Women's Foundation/Fondation des femmes canadiennes
#208, 214 Merton St., Toronto, ON M4S 1A6
416/484-8268, Fax: 416/486-8604
Executive Director, Beverley Wybrow

Catholic Women's League of Canada
#1, 160 Murray Park Rd., Winnipeg, MB R3J 3X5
204/885-4856, Fax: 204/831-9507
Executive Director, Carrie Ehman

Congress of Black Women of Canada
590 Jarvis St., Toronto, ON M4Y 2J4
416/961-2427, Fax: 416/961-8842
President, Cloe Calendar
Affiliates: The Black Secretariat

Federated Women's Institutes of Canada/Fédération des instituts féminins du Canada (FWIC) (1919)
#606, 251 Bank St., Ottawa, ON K2P 1X3
613/234-1090, Fax: 613/234-1090
Executive Director, Arlene Strugnell
President, Charlotte Johnson
Publications: Federated News
Affiliates: Associated Country Women of the World

ALBERTA WOMEN'S INSTITUTES (AWI) (1909)
6604 - 82 Ave., Edmonton, AB T6B 0E7
403/469-1254, Fax: 403/469-1254
Acting Executive Secretary, Janet Halberg

BRITISH COLUMBIA WOMEN'S INSTITUTES (1909)
20510 Fraser Hwy., Langley, BC V3A 4G2
604/533-6564, Fax: 604/533-6564
Office Administrator, Jan Marshall
President, Muriel Washington
Publications: Network News
Affiliates: BC Federation of Agriculture

FEDERATED WOMEN'S INSTITUTES OF ONTARIO (FWIO) (1897)
7382 Wellington Rd. 30, RR#5, Guelph, ON N1H 6J2
519/836-3078, Fax: 519/836-9456
President, Arthena Hecker
Public Relations Officer, Mary Janes
Publications: Home & Country

MANITOBA WOMEN'S INSTITUTES (1910)
Norquay Bldg., #908, 401 York Ave., Winnipeg, MB R3C 0P8
204/945-8976, Fax: 204/945-6134
Executive Organizator, Shirley Bell
Publications: Institute News
Affiliates: Associated Country Women of the World; Provincial Council of Women

NEW BRUNSWICK WOMEN'S INSTITUTE (NBWI) (1911)
Victoria Health Centre, #251, 65 Brunswick St., Fredericton, NB E3B 1G5
506/454-0798, Fax: 506/453-1723
Administrative Officer, Stella Quartermain
Publications: For Home & Country

NEWFOUNDLAND & LABRADOR WOMEN'S INSTITUTES (NLWI) (1935)
Arts & Culture Centre, PO Box 1854, Stn C, St. John's, NF A1C 5P9
709/753-8780, Fax: 709/753-8780
Executive Administrator, Sylvia O. Manning
Publications: The Newfoundland & Labrador Women's Institutes Newsletter
Affiliates: Associated County Women of the World

PRINCE EDWARD ISLAND WOMEN'S INSTITUTE
Department of Agriculture, PO Box 2000, Charlottetown, PE C1A 7N8
902/368-4860, Fax: 902/368-5651
Liaison, Karen Lee Craig

QUÉBEC WOMEN'S INSTITUTES (QWI) (1911)
Macdonald Campus, McGill University, 21111 ch Lakeshore, PO Box 58, Montréal, PQ H9X 3V9
514/398-7705, Fax: 514/398-7955
Publications: Québec Women's Institutes Newsletter
Affiliates: Associated Country Women of the World

SASKATCHEWAN WOMEN'S INSTITUTES
#137, Kirk Hall, University of Saskatchewan, 117 Science Pl., Saskatoon, SK S7N 0W0
306/966-5566, Fax: 306/966-8717
President, Alison Wilson, 306/264-3864
Administrative Coordinator, Beth Ratzlaff
Publications: The Second Penny
Affiliates: Saskatchewan Council of Women; Saskatchewan Safety Council; Saskatchewan Federation of Agriculture; Saskatchewan Farm Vacation Association; Saskatchewan Action Committee, Status of Women; Saskatchewan Agricultural Hall of Fame; Saskatchewan Committee on Rural Area Development

WOMEN'S INSTITUTES OF NOVA SCOTIA (WINS) (1913)
NSAC, PO Box 550, Truro, NS B2N 5E3
902/893-6520, Fax: 902/893-6393
Executive Director, Sandy Savage
President, Isabel Archibald
Publications: Home & Country; Nova Scotia Farm Women, q.
Affiliates: Associated Country Women of the World

Fédération des femmes du Québec (FFQ) (1966)
#100, 5225, rue Berri, Montréal, PQ H2J 2S4
514/948-3262, Téléc: 514/948-3264
Directrice générale, Céline Signori

Federation of Medical Women of Canada/Fédération des femmes médecins du Canada (FMWC) (1924)
#107, 1815 Alta Vista Dr., Ottawa, ON K1G 3Y6
613/731-1026, Fax: 613/731-8748
Executive Coordinator, Kay Moffatt
Publications: FMWC Newsletter
Affiliates: Canadian Medical Association; Medical Women's International Association

Fédération nationale des femmes canadiennes-françaises (FNFCF) (1914)
#525, 325 Dalhousie St., Ottawa, ON K1N 7G2
613/241-3500, Téléc: 613/241-6679
Directrice générale, Diane Vachon
Présidente, Ghislaine Foulem
Ressource de l'information, Micheline Piché
Publications: Concert action

Organisation(s) affiliée(s): Fédération des communautés francophones et acadienne du Canada; Comité canadien d'action sur le statut de la femme

Hadassah-WIZO Organization of Canada (1917)
#900, 1310, av Greene, Montréal, PQ H3Z 2B8
514/937-9431, Fax: 514/933-6483
Executive Vice-President, Lily Frank
National President, Judy Mandleman
Publications: Orah
Affiliates: Canadian Jewish Congress; Canadian Zionist Federation; National Council of Women of Canada; United Nations Association; Women's International Zionist Organization

Immigrant & Visible Minority Women Against Abuse (IVMWAA) (1989)
PO Box 67041, Ottawa, ON K2A 0E0
613/729-3145, Fax: 613/729-9308
Executive Director, Lucya Spencer

Jewish Women International of Canada (JWIC)
#210, 638A Sheppard Ave. West, Downsview, ON M3H 2S1
416/630-9313, Fax: 416/630-9319
Executive Director, Penny Krowitz, CAE
Affiliates: Jewish Women International

MATCH International Centre/Centre international Match (1977)
#1102, 200 Elgin St., Ottawa, ON K2P 1L5
613/238-1312, Fax: 613/238-6867, Email: matchint@web.apc.org
Executive Director, Madonna Larbi
Accounting Officer, Yim-Chu Kwong
Publications: Match News

Na'amat Canada Inc. (1924)
#6, 7005, rue Kildare, Montréal, PQ H4W 1C1
514/488-0792, Fax: 514/487-6727
National Executive Director, Vivian Reisler
Publications: Na'amat Canada
Affiliates: Canadian Jewish Congress; National Action Committee on the Status of Women

National Action Committee on the Status of Women/Comité canadien d'action sur le statut de la femme (NAC) (1971)
#203, 234 Eglinton Ave. East, Toronto, ON M4P 1K5
416/932-1718, Fax: 416/932-0646, Toll Free: 1-800-665-5124
President, Sunera Thobani
Executive Coordinator, Beverly Bain
Treasurer, Maureen Leyland
Secretary, Laura Sky
Publications: Action Now

National Association of Women in Construction (NAWIC) (1955)
327 South Adams St., Fort Worth, TX 76104 USA
817/877-5551, Fax: 817/877-0324, Toll Free: 1-800-552-3506
Executive Vice-President, Rachel R.R. Searson
Publications: The NAWIC Image

National Association of Women & the Law/Association nationale de la femme et du droit (NAWL) (1974)
#604, 1 Nicholas St., Ottawa, ON K1N 7B7
613/241-7570, Fax: 613/241-4657
Executive Director, Cheryl Boon
Coordinator, National Steering Committee, Darlene Jamieson
Publications: Jurisfemme

National Council of Jewish Women of Canada
#118, 1588 Main St., Winnipeg, MB R2V 1Y3
204/339-9700, Fax: 204/334-3779

The National Council of Women of Canada/Le conseil national des femmes du Canada (NCWC) (1893)
#33, 270 MacLaren St., Ottawa, ON K2P 0M3
613/232-5025, Fax: 613/232-8419, Email: ncwc@intranet.ca
President, Win Whitfield
Publications: NCWC News

Prince Edward Island Women's Network
PO Box 233, Charlottetown, PE C1A 7K4
902/368-5040, Fax: 902/368-5039
Contact, Anne McCallum
Publications: Common Ground

Réseau d'action et d'information pour les femmes (RAIF) (1973)
CP 36088, CSP Place Ste-Foy, Ste-Foy, PQ G1V 1C0
418/658-1973
Coordonnatrice, Marcelle Dolment
Publications: RAIF

Réseau national d'action-éducation des femmes (1983)
#208, 435 boul St-Laurent, Ottawa, ON K1K 2Z8
613/741-9978, Téléc: 613/741-3805
Présidente nationale, Monique Hébert
Directrice générale, Monique Roy

Society for Canadian Women in Science & Technology/Société des canadiennes dans la science et la technologie (SCWIST) (1981)
#410, 515 Hastings St. West, Vancouver, BC V6B 5K3
604/291-5163, Fax: 604/291-5236, Email: scwist@sfu.ca
President, Maria Issa
Publications: SCWIST News
Affiliates: BC Ministry of Advanced Education, Training & Technology; Industry, Science & Technology Canada; BC Ministry of Education; Canada Employment & Immigration Council; Secretary of State Canada, Women's Program; University of BC, Faculty of Science; Simon Fraser University; BC Institute of Technology; Capilano College; Vancouver School Board; Knowledge Network; Vancouver Foundation; Immigrant Women in Science Program; Douglas College

Voice of Women/La Voix des femmes (VOW) (1960)
Canadian Voice of Women for Peace
#215, 736 Bathurst St., Toronto, ON M5S 2R4
416/537-9343, Fax: 416/531-6214
Chair, Joy Warner
Publications: Voices
Affiliates: NGO status at the United Nations

Western Businesswomen's Association (WBA)
#302, 1107 Homer St., Vancouver, BC V6B 2Y1
604/688-0951, Fax: 604/681-4545
Administrator, Teena Keizer
Publications: WBA Newsletter

Womanpower Inc. (1974)
#2, 73 King St., London, ON N6A 1C1
519/438-1782, Fax: 519/438-7904
Coordinator, Darlene Labadie

Women Entrepreneurs of Canada/Les Femmes Chefs d'Entreprises du Canada (WEC) (1992)
#1200, 390 Bay St., Toronto, ON M5H 2Y2
416/860-1125, Fax: 416/860-1188
President, Andrina Lever
Vice-President, Administration, Liz Nash
Publications: WECan

The Women & Environments Education & Development Foundation (1987)
WEED Foundation
736 Bathurst St., Toronto, ON M5S 2R4
416/516-2600, Fax: 416/531-6214, Email: weed@apc.org
Coordinator, S. Inward
Publications: Women & Environments

Women in Music (WIM) (1991)
Society for Women in Music
#1212, 207 West Hastings St., Vancouver, BC V6B 1H7
604/684-9461, Fax: 604/684-1543, Email: marian rose@mindlink.bc.ca
President, Gayle Webster
Publications: Brava

Women in Science & Engineering Corporation/ Corporation des femmes en sciences et en génie (WISE) (1977)
6519B Mississauga Rd., Mississauga, ON L5N 1A6
905/567-7190, Fax: 905/567-7191
National President, Elza Seregelyi, 613/763-5994, Fax: 709/729-5878
Publications: WISE/CFSG National Newsletter

Women of Unifarm (1970)
14815 - 119 Ave., Edmonton, AB T5L 4W2
403/451-5912, Fax: 403/453-2669

Women's Art Association of Canada (WAA) (1887)
Lyceum Club & Women's Art Association of Canada
23 Prince Arthur Ave., Toronto, ON M5R 1B2
416/922-2060
President, A.L. Cumine
Publications: Bulletin
Affiliates: Lyceum Club (International)

Women's Art Resource Centre (WARC) (1984)
#506, 80 Spadina Ave., Toronto, ON M5V 2J3
416/703-0074, Fax: 416/703-0441, Email: warc@intacc.web.net
Director, Z. Packer
Director, L. Abrahams
Publications: Matriart: A Canadian Visual Art Journal

Women's Counselling & Referral & Education Centre (WCREC) (1975)
525 Bloor St. West, Toronto, ON M5S 1Y4
416/534-7501, TTY: 416/534-5078, Fax: 416/534-1704
Annette Clough
Publications: WCREC Newsletter

Women's Enterprise Bureau (1990)
30 Harvey Rd., St. John's, NF A1C 2G1
709/754-5555, Fax: 709/754-0079
Executive Director, Susan J. Adams, CAE
Chairperson, Ann Bell
Publications: Women Business Owners Directory
Affiliates: Provincial Advisory Council on the Status of Women

Women's Inter-Church Council of Canada/ Conseil oecumenique des chrétiennes du Canada (WICC) (1918)
#402, 815 Danforth Ave., Toronto, ON M4J 1L2
416/462-2528, Fax: 416/462-3915
Executive Director, Karen Hincke
President, Ann Austin-Cardwell
Publications: The Wick
Affiliates: International Committee for World Day of Prayer; International Committee for the Fellowship of the Least Coin

Women's International League for Peace & Freedom (WILPF) (1915)
PO Box 4781, Stn E, Ottawa, ON K1S 5H9

Fax: 613/567-2384
President, Marcelene Holyk, Res: 613/544-1226
Publications: WILPF News

Women's Legal Education & Action Fund/Fonds d'action et d'éducation juridiques pour les femmes (LEAF) (1985)
#1800, 415 Yonge St., Toronto, ON M5B 2E7
416/595-7170, Fax: 416/595-7191
Chair, Joyce Burpee
Publications: LEAF Lines
West Coast LEAF: Coordinator, Janet Kee, #905, 207 Hastings St. West, Vancouver, BC V6B 1H7, 604/684-8772
Alberta: Contact, Linda Taylor, PO BOX 82006, RPO Glenmore Landing, Calgary, AB T2V 5H9, Toll Free: 1-800-661-5323
Manitoba: Representative, Kimberley Gilson, 400 St. Mary Ave., 9th Fl., Winnipeg, MB R3P 0B9, 204/988-0336, Fax: 204/957-0945
New Brunswick: Contact, Lisa Murphy, #2, McKenzie House, University of New Brunswick, PO Box 4400, Stn A, Fredericton, NB E3B 5A3, 506/453-4800, Fax: 506/453-3585
Newfoundland: Contact, Kathryn Crosbie, PO Box 8700, St. John's, NF A1B 4J6, 709/576-2601
Northwest Territories: Contact, Wendy A. Hutchinson, PO Box 939, Yellowknife, NT X1A 2N7, 403/873-6543
Nova Scotia: Contact, Joan Jones, 2830 Agricola St., Halifax, NS B3K 4E4, 902/420-3452, Fax: 902/423-3544
Ontario: Contact, Mary Lue Hinds, 477 Ramsey Rd., Sudbury, ON P3E 2Z8, 705/675-5400, Fax: 705/674-4916
Prince Edward Island: Representative, Frances Piercey, 3 Sunset Dr., Charlottetown, PE C1A 3J6, 902/368-5574, Fax: 902/368-5526
Saskatchewan: Contact, Leslie Belloc-Pinder, #601, 402 - 21 St. East, Saskatoon, SK S7K 0C3, 306/653-5150
Yukon: Contact, M. Lynn Gaudet, 409 Lowe St., Whitehorse, YT Y1A 1W7, 403/668-6576

Women's Research Centre (1973)
#101, 2245 Broadway West, Vancouver, BC V6K 2E4
604/734-0485, Fax: 604/734-0484
Research Associate, Andrée Buchanan

WRITERS & EDITORS
see also Publishing

Association canadienne des rédacteurs agricoles de langue française (ACRA) (1956)
1001, boul de Maisonneuve ouest, 10e étage, Montréal, PQ H3A 3E1
514/843-2112, Téléc: 514/845-6261
Secrétaire-trésorière, Sylvie Bouchard, agr.
Publications: ARADITION

Association de la presse francophone (APF) (1976)
#702, 325, rue Dalhousie, Ottawa, ON K1N 7G2
613/241-1017, Téléc: 613/241-6193, Courrier électronique: pressapf@globalx.net
Président, Roger Duplantie
Directeur, Yves Chartrand
Vice-Président, Jean Mongenais
Vice-Président, François Pageau
Trésorier, François Bélair
Secrétaire, Jacinthe LaFrance

Canadian Association of Journalists/ L'Association canadienne des journalistes (CAJ) (1978)
St. Patrick's Building, Carleton University, 1125 Colonel By Dr., Ottawa, ON K1S 5B6

Canadian Almanac & Directory 1997

613/526-8061, Fax: 613/521-3904, Email: cf408@freenet.carleton.ca
URL: http://freenet.carleton.ca/freeport/prof.assoc/caj/menu; http://www.ncf.carleton.ca/freeport/prof.assoc/caj/menu
Executive Director, Rob Henderson
Publications: Media

Canadian Authors Association (CAA) (1921)
27 Doxsee Ave. North, Campbellford, ON K0L 1L0
705/653-0323, Fax: 705/653-0593
Administrator, Alec McEachern
National President, Cora Taylor
National Vice-President, Dr. Kathleen Bradford
Sec.-Treas., Roger Tulk
Membership Chairman, Anna Marie Kowalski
Awards Chairman, Nancy Gibson
Publications Chairman, Welwyn Wilton Katz
Publications: Canadian Author; The Canadian Writer's Guide; National Newsline, q.
Affiliates: La Société des écrivains canadiens

Canadian Farm Writers' Federation (1955)
c/o Office of Research, University of Guelph, Guelph, ON N1G 2W1
519/824-4120, ext.8278, Fax: 519/821-5236
URL: http://www.uoguelph.ca/Research/cfwf
President, Owen Roberts, Email: owen@ornet.or.uoguelph.ca
Affiliates: British Columbia Farm Writers' Association; Alberta Farm Writers' Association; Saskatchewan Farm Writers' Association; Manitoba Farm Writers' & Broadcasters' Association; Eastern Canada Farm Writers' Association

Canadian Journalism Foundation/La Fondation pour le journalisme canadien (CJF) (1990)
TD Bank Tower, #546, 66 Wellington St. West, PO Box 166, Toronto, ON M5K 1H6
416/366-8573, Fax: 416/367-2339
Chair, Knowlton Nash
Executive Director, William Wilton
Sec.-Treas., Donald J. Crawford

Canadian Science Writers' Association/Association canadienne des rédacteurs scientifiques (CSWA) (1971)
PO Box 75, Stn A, Toronto, ON M5W 1A2
416/928-9624, Fax: 416/960-0528, Email: cswa@interlog.com
URL: http://www.interlog.com/~cswa
Administrative Director, Andy F. Visser-deVries
Publications: Science Link; CSWA Directory, a.

Canadian Society of Children's Authors, Illustrators & Performers/La société canadienne des auteurs, illustrateurs et artistes pour enfants (CANSCAIP) (1977)
35 Spadina Rd., Toronto, ON M5R 2S9
416/515-1559, Fax: 416/515-7022, Email: canscaip@interlog.com
President, Paul Kropp
Publications: CANSCAIP News

Canadian Society of Magazine Editors (CSME) (1990)
c/o Canadian Living, #100, 25 Sheppard Ave. West, North York, ON M2N 6S7
416/596-5177
President, Brian Banks, 416/596-5177
Membership Director, Christine Langlois, 416/733-7600

The Crime Writers of Canada (CWC) (1981)
3007 Kingston Rd., PO Box 113, Scarborough, ON M1M 1P1
416/782-3116, Fax: 416/789-4680, Email: ap113@torfree.net
URL: http://www.swifty.com/cwc/cwchome.htm
President, Peter Robinson
Sec.-Treas., Rick Blechta
Publications: Fingerprints; In Cold Blood

Editors' Association of Canada/Association canadienne des rédacteurs-réviseurs (EAC) (1979)
35 Spadina Rd., Toronto, ON M5R 2S9
416/975-1379, Fax: 416/975-1839, Email: editors@web.net
URL: http://www.web.net/eac-acr
President, Rosemary Tanner
Secretary, Jane Broderick
Treasurer, Susan Wilson
Publications: Active Voice/Voix active; Members' Handbook, a.; Directory of Members, a.
Affiliates: Book & Periodical Council; Canadian Conference of the Arts

Federation of British Columbia Writers (FBCW) (1976)
#600, 890 West Pender St., PO Box 2206, Stn Main, Vancouver, BC V6B 3W2
604/683-2057, Fax: 604/683-8269, Email: fedbcwrt@pinc.com
Executive Director, Corey Van't Haaff
President, D.C. Reid
Publications: Wordworks; Literary Arts Directory II

Fédération internationale des écrivains de langue française (FIDELF)
3492, rue Laval, Montréal, PQ H2X 3C8
514/849-8540, Téléc: 514/849-6239
Secrétaire général, Ronald Fornerod

The League of Canadian Poets (LCP) (1966)
The Writers' Centre, 54 Wolseley St., 3rd Fl., Toronto, ON M5T 1A5
416/504-1657, Fax: 416/703-0059, Email: league@io.org
Executive Director, Edita Petrauskaite
Executive Assistant, Sandra Drzewiecki
Publications: LCP Newsletter; Museletter, s-a.; Members Directory
Affiliates: Book & Periodical Council

Loisir littéraire du Québec (LLQ) (1961)
Fédération québécoise du loisir littéraire
4545, av Pierre-de-Coubertin, CP 1000, Succ. M, Montréal, PQ H1V 3R2
514/252-3033, Téléc: 514/251-8038
Directrice générale, Ghislaine Lacasse
Président du conseil, François Rajotte
Publications: Le Courlis

Manitoba Writers' Guild (MWG) (1981)
#206, 100 Arthur St., Winnipeg, MB R3B 1H3
204/942-6134, Fax: 204/942-5754
Executive Director, Robyn Maharaj
Publications: Wordwrap

Periodical Writers Association of Canada (PWAC) (1976)
#203, 54 Wolseley St., Toronto, ON M5T 1A5
416/504-1645, Fax: 416/703-0059
Executive Director, Ruth Biderman
President, Mark Zuehlke
Publications: PWAContact; Who Pays What; Words for Sale; Directory of Members

Saskatchewan Writers Guild Inc. (SWG) (1969)
PO Box 3986, Regina, SK S4P 3R9
306/757-6310, Fax: 306/565-8554
URL: http://bailey2.unibase.com/~grain/SWG_Homepage.html
Executive Director, Mary Drover
Publications: FreeLance; Grain, q.; Readings & Workshops Guide, a.; WindScript, s-a.

Société des écrivains canadiens (SEC) (1936)
a/s Fondation Macdonald-Stewart, 1195, rue Sherbrooke ouest, Montréal, PQ H3A 1H9
514/733-0754, Téléc: 514/342-3866
Secrétaire général, Jacques Constantin
Président général, Jacques G. Ruelland
Publications: Parléecrit; L'Écritoire, trimestriel

Société professionelle des auteurs et des compositeurs du Québec (SPACQ) (1981)
#420, 759, Square Victoria, Montréal, PQ H2Y 2J7
514/845-3739, Téléc: 514/845-1903
Directrice générale, Francine Bertrand-Venne
Organisation(s) affiliée(s): Coalition des créateurs et titulaires de droits d'auteurs; Groupe action musique pour le droit d'auteur (GAMDA)

Society of American Travel Writers - Canadian Chapter (SATW) (1964)
5 Runnymede Rd., Toronto, ON M6S 2Y1
416/766-6522
Chairman, Joanna Ebbutt
Publications: Maple Leaf Rag

Union des écrivaines et écrivains québécois (UNEEQ) (1977)
La Maison des écrivains, 3492, av Laval, Montréal, PQ H2X 3C8
514/849-8540, Téléc: 514/849-6239, Courrier électronique: UNEQ@login.net
Directeur, Pierre Lavoie
Président, Bruno Roy
Directrice des communications, Nicole Blouin
Publications: Bulletin UNEQ

Writers Association for Romance & Mainstream (WARM) (1983)
#7, 436 Terrasse Talbot, Longueuil, PQ J4L 1T5
514/468-5410
President, Jeanette Paul
Vice-President, Brian Selwood
Treasurer, Kenneth Gee
Publications: Warm Times

Writers Guild of Alberta (WGA) (1980)
Percy Page Centre, 11759 Groat Rd., 3rd Fl., Edmonton, AB T5M 3K6
403/422-8174, Fax: 403/422-2663, Toll Free: 1-800-665-5354
Executive Director, Miki Andrejevic
Assistant Director, Darlene Diver
President, Darlene Quaife
Publications: Directory of AB Writers; WestWord, bi-m.
Affiliates: Manitoba Writers' Guild; Federation of BC Writers; Saskatchewan Writers' Guild; Writers' Union of Canada; Newfoundland & Labrador Guilds; Periodical Writers' Association of Canada; League of Canadian Poets

Writers Guild of Canada (WGC) (1991)
35 McCaul St., Toronto, ON M5T 1V7
416/979-7907, Fax: 416/979-9273, Toll Free: 1-800-567-9974
President, Pete White
Manager, Member & Information Services, Sarah Dearing
Publications: WGC News

Writers' Alliance of Newfoundland & Labrador (WANL) (1987)
PO Box 2681, St. John's, NF A1C 5M5
709/739-5215, Fax: 709/739-5215
Executive Director, Patricia Warren

The Writers' Development Trust
The Writers' Centre, #201, 24 Ryerson Ave., Toronto, ON M5T 2P3

416/504-8222, Fax: 416/504-9090
Executive Director, Nancy Kroeker

Writers' Federation of New Brunswick (1983)
PO Box 37, Stn A, Fredericton, NB E3B 4Y2
506/459-7228
President, Michael Thorpe
Treasurer, Sylvia Morice
Secretary, Gary Langguth
Publications: New Brunswick ink

Writers' Federation of Nova Scotia (WFNS) (1975)
#901, 1809 Barrington St., Halifax, NS B3J 3K8
902/423-8116, Fax: 902/422-0881
Executive Director, Jane Buss
Executive Assistant, Claudette Hammock
Publications: EastWord
Affiliates: Cultural Federation of Nova Scotia; Writers' Development Trust; Coalition of Copyright Owners; Canadian Copyright Institute; Metro Council on Continuing Education; Canadian Children's Book Centre

The Writers' Union of Canada (TWUC) (1972)
24 Ryerson Ave., Toronto, ON M5T 2P3
416/703-8982, Fax: 416/703-0826, Email: twuc@the_wire.com
URL: http://www.swifty.com/twuc
Executive Director, Penny Dickens
Chair, Paul Quarrington
Publications: Who's Who in the Writers' Union of Canada: A Directory of Members; The Writers' Union of Canada Newsletter, m.; Anthology Rates & Contracts; Authors & Archives; Author & Editor; Awards, Competitions & Prizes; Help Yourself to a Better Contract; Income Tax Guide for Writers; Libel Handbook; Trade Book Contract; Writer's Guide to Canadian Publishers; Writer & Literary Agent; Ghost Writing; Writers' Guide to Electronic Publishing Rights; Writers' Guide to Grants; Workshops, Courses & Retreats
Affiliates: Canadian Copyright Institute; Canadian Conference of the Arts; Canadian Reprography Collective; Writers Development Trust; Give the Gift of Literacy

TRADE UNIONS

CENTRAL LABOUR

American Federation of Labor & Congress of Industrial Organizations (AFL-CIO)/Fédération Américaine du travail et congrès des organisations industrielles (FAT-COI) (AFL-CIO)
AFL-CIO Building, 815 - Sixteenth St. NW, Washington, DC 20006 USA
202/637-5000, Fax: 202/637-5058
President, John Sweeney
Sec.-Treas., Richard Trumka
Executive Vice-President, Linda Chavez-Thomson

AMERICAN FEDERATION OF LABOR & CONGRESS OF INDUSTRIAL ORGANIZATIONS (AFL-CIO)
#910, 350 Sparks St., Ottawa, ON K1R 7S8
613/236-0653, Fax: 613/230-5138
Executive Secretary, Guy Dumoulin

Canadian Federation of Labour/Fédération canadienne du travail (CFL) (1982)
CF of L
#300, 107 Sparks St., Ottawa, ON K1P 5B5
613/234-4141, Fax: 613/234-5188
President, James A. McCambly
Sec.-Treas., Terry D. Boudreau
Publications: Federation Update

Affiliates: American Federation of Labor & Congress of Industrial Organizations
Provincial Councils of Labour with Presidents
Alberta & Northwest Territories (District of MacKenzie) Council of Labour: President, John Lester, 5649 Burbank Rd. SE, Calgary, AB T2H 1Z5, 403/252-1166
British Columbia & Yukon Territory: President, Harry Cossey, #290, 2885 Boys Rd., Duncan, BC V9L 4Y9, 250/748-8491
Conseil du Québec: Président, Mario Di Pesa, #201, 9203, boul St-Laurent, Montréal, PQ H2N 1N2, 514/385-0131
Manitoba Council: President, Ron McLean, #26B, 1313 Border St., Winnipeg, MB R3H 0X4, 204/697-3277, Fax: 204/697-3278
New Brunswick Council: President, Larry Calhoun, 138 Neill St., Fredericton, NB E3A 2Z6, 506/450-8888
Newfoundland & Labrador Council: President, Mike Power, 25 Nelder Dr., Mount Pearl, NF A1N 4M2, 709/747-4239
Nova Scotia Council: President, Charles Weir Jr., PO Box 419, Lower Sackville, NS B4C 2T2, 902/865-8811, Fax: 902/865-7317
Ontario Council: President, Reg Conrad, 30 Greendowns Dr., Scarborough, ON M1M 2G7, 416/266-3825, Fax: 416/266-0377
Prince Edward Island Council: President, Ted Crockett, 25 Kensington Ct., Charlottetown, PE C1A 8K4, 902/566-3255
Saskatchewan Council: President, Brian Woznesensky, 1402 Rose St., Regina, SK S4N 6C4, 306/569-8787

Canadian Labour Congress/Congrès du travail du Canada (CLC) (1956)
2841 Riverside Dr., Ottawa, ON K1V 8X7
613/521-3400, Fax: 613/521-4655, Telex: 053-4750
President, Robert White
Sec.-Treas., Richard Martin
Executive Vice-President, Jean-Claude Parrot
Executive Vice-President, Nancy Riche
Financial Advisor/Controller, Pierre Ouimet
National Director, Environment, Dave Bennett
Canadian Health Coalition, Michael McBane
National Representative, Health & Safety, Amber Hockin
National Director, International Affairs, Stephen Benedict
National Director, Organization & Education Services, Martin J. Hanratty
National Director, Technical Services, Bob Baldwin
Director, Political Action, Patrick Kerwin
National Director, Women & Human Rights, Penni Richmond
Regions
Atlantic Regional Office: Regional Director, Linda Gallant, 2282 Mountain Rd., Moncton, NB E1G 1B4, 506/858-9350
Ontario Regional Office: Regional Director, Michael MacIssac, #305, 15 Gervais Dr., North York, ON M3C 1Y8, 416/441-3710, Fax: 416/441-4073
Pacific Regional Office: Regional Director, Rick Byrne, 1888 Angus St., Regina, SK S4T 1Z4, 604/525-6137
Prairie Regional Office: Regional Director, David Rice, 7621 Kingsway, Burnaby, BC V3N 3C7, 604/524-0391
Provincial Federations of Labour

ALBERTA FEDERATION OF LABOUR/FÉDÉRATION DU TRAVAIL DE L'ALBERTA (AFL) (1912)
#350, 10451 - 170 St., Edmonton, AB T5P 4T2
403/483-3021, Fax: 403/484-5928
President, Linda Karpowich
Sec.-Treas., Audrey M. Cormack
Publications: Labour News

BRITISH COLUMBIA FEDERATION OF LABOUR/FÉDÉRATION DU TRAVAIL DE LA COLOMBIE-BRITANNIQUE (BCFL) (1956)
4279 Canada Way, Burnaby, BC V5G 4P1
604/430-1421, Fax: 604/430-5917
President, Ken Georgetti
Director of Communications, Bill Tieleman
Sec.-Treas., Angela Schira
Publications: The Bulletin
Affiliates: Canadian Centre for Policy Alternatives; Canadian Association of Labour Media

FÉDÉRATION DES TRAVAILLEURS ET TRAVAILLEUSES DU QUÉBEC/QUÉBEC FEDERATION OF LABOUR (FTQ) (1957)
545, boul Crémazie est, 17e étage, Montréal, PQ H2M 2V1
514/383-8000, Télec: 514/383-8001, Courrier électronique: ftq@montrealnet.ca
Président, Clément Godbout
Secrétaire général, Henri Massé
Directeur des communications, Louis Fournier
Publications: Le Monde ouvrier

MANITOBA FEDERATION OF LABOUR/FÉDÉRATION DU TRAVAIL DU MANITOBA (1956)
#101, 275 Broadway, Winnipeg, MB R3C 4M6
204/947-1400, Fax: 204/943-4276
President, Susan Hart-Kulbaba
Publications: News & Views

NEW BRUNSWICK FEDERATION OF LABOUR/FÉDÉRATION DU TRAVAIL DU NOUVEAU-BRUNSWICK (NBFL) (1914)
96 Norwood Ave., Moncton, NB E1C 6L9
506/857-2125, Fax: 506/383-1597
President, John McEwen
Publications: Newsletter

NEWFOUNDLAND & LABRADOR FEDERATION OF LABOUR/FÉDÉRATION DU TRAVAIL DE TERRE-NEUVE ET DU LABRADOR (NLFL) (1936)
PO Box 6114, Stn C, St. John's, NF A1C 5X8
709/754-1660, Fax: 709/754-1220
President, Elaine Price
Sec.-Treas., Marie St. Aubin

NORTHWEST TERRITORIES FEDERATION OF LABOUR/FÉDÉRATION DU TRAVAIL DES TERRITOIRES DU NORD-OUEST (NWTFL) (1980)
PO Box 2787, Yellowknife, NT X1A 2R1
403/873-3695
President, James Evoy
Sec.-Treas., Sharon Burns

NOVA SCOTIA FEDERATION OF LABOUR/FÉDÉRATION DU TRAVAIL DE LA NOUVELLE-ECOSSE
#218, 3700 Kempt Rd., Halifax, NS B3K 4X8
902/892-7331
President, Rick Clarke
Executive Secretary, Alex MacDonald

ONTARIO FEDERATION OF LABOUR/FÉDÉRATION DU TRAVAIL DE L'ONTARIO (OFL) (1957)
#202, 15 Gervais Dr., North York, ON M3C 1Y8
416/441-2731, Fax: 416/441-0722
President, Gordon F. Wilson
Executive Vice-President, Ken Signoretti
Sec.-Treas., Ethel Lavalley
Publications: Focus; The Advocate, q.; Women's Bulletin, q.

PRINCE EDWARD ISLAND FEDERATION OF LABOUR/FÉDÉRATION DU TRAVAIL DU L'ÎLE-DU-PRINCE-EDOUARD
184 Belvedere Ave., Charlottetown, PE C1A 2Z1
902/368-3068, Fax: 902/368-3192
President, Sandy MacKay
Treasurer, Heath Ellis

SASKATCHEWAN FEDERATION OF LABOUR/FÉDÉRATION DU TRAVAIL DE LA SASKATCHEWAN
#103, 2709 - 12 Ave., Regina, SK S4T 1J3
306/525-0197, Fax: 306/525-8960
President, Barbara Byers

Canadian Almanac & Directory 1997

Treasurer, Larry Hubich
Publications: Labour Report

YUKON FEDERATION OF LABOUR/FÉDÉRATION DU TRAVAIL DU YUKON (1980)
106 Strickland St., Whitehorse, YT Y1A 2J5
403/667-6676, Fax: 403/633-5558
President, Michael Miller

Canadian National Federation of Independent Unions/Fédération canadienne nationale des syndicats indépendants (CNFIU) (1980)
136 East Main St., Welland, ON L3B 3W6
905/735-0531, Fax: 905/788-9700
President, Vince Vocal
Sec.-Treas., Bryan Harris

Centrale de l'enseignement du Québec/Québec Teaching Congress (CEQ) (1946)
#300, 1170, boul Lebourgneuf, Québec, PQ G2K 2G1
418/627-8888, Téléc: 418/627-9999
Directeur général, Michel Dagenais
Directeur des Communications, Guy Brouillette
Attaché administrative, Lisette Gaulin
Publications: Nouvelles CEQ

ALLIANCE DES PROFESSEURES ET PROFESSEURS DE MONTRÉAL (APPM) (1919)
8225, boul Saint-Laurent, Montréal, PQ H2P 2M1
514/383-4880, Téléc: 514/384-5756
Directeur général, Fernand Gauvreau
Publications: L'Alliance

FÉDÉRATION DES ENSEIGNANTES ET ENSEIGNANTS DE CÉGEPS
9405, rue Sherbrooke est, Montréal, PQ H1L 6P3
514/356-8888, Téléc: 514/354-8535
Président, Réal Trottier
Publications: L'Enjeu

FÉDÉRATION DES ENSEIGNANTES ET ENSEIGNANTS DE COMMISSIONS SCOLAIRES (CEQ) (1988)
#300, 1170, boul Lebourgneuf, Québec, PQ G2K 2G1
418/627-8888, Téléc: 418/627-9999
Directrice générale, Diane Fortin

FÉDÉRATION DU PERSONNEL DES ÉTABLISSEMENTS DE LOISIR/ FEDERATION OF RECREATION CENTRES' STAFF (FPEL)
9405, rue Sherbrooke est, Montréal, PQ H1L 6P3
514/356-8888, Téléc: 514/356-9999
Président, Martin Plourde

FÉDÉRATION DU PERSONNEL DES ÉTABLISSEMENTS PRIVÉS D'ENSEIGNEMENT/FEDERATION OF PRIVATE TEACHING INSTITUTIONS STAFF (FPEPE) (1986)
9405, rue Sherbrooke est, Montréal, PQ H1L 6P3
514/356-8888, Téléc: 514/356-1866
Présidente, Francine Lamoureux
Publications: Le Bulletin

FÉDÉRATION DU PERSONNEL PROFESSIONNEL DES UNIVERSITÉS (CEQ) (FPPU) (1993)
9405, rue Sherbrooke est, Montréal, PQ H1L 6P3
514/356-8888, Téléc: 514/356-9999
Présidente, Carole Demers

FÉDÉRATION DU PERSONNEL DE LA SANTÉ ET DES SERVICES SOCIAUX/FEDERATION OF HEALTH & SOCIAL SERVICES STAFF (FPSSS)
9405, rue Sherbrooke est, Montréal, PQ H1L 6P3
514/356-8888, Téléc: 514/356-2845
Président, André Rodrigue
Publications: La Jazette Officielle

FÉDÉRATION DU PERSONNEL DE SOUTIEN/FEDERATION OF SUPPORT STAFF
9405, rue Sherbrooke est, 4e étage, Montréal, PQ H1L 6P3
514/356-8888, Téléc: 514/493-3697
Présidente, Christiane Bigras
Publications: Le Relais

FÉDÉRATION DES PROFESSEUR(E)S ET CHARGÉ(E)S DE COURS DES UNIVERSITÉS/FEDERATION OF UNIVERSITY PROFESSORS & LECTURERS (1974)
555, boul de l'Université, local 4-602, Chicoutimi, PQ G7H 2B1
418/545-5378, Téléc: 418/545-6659
Président, André Leblond

FÉDÉRATION DES PROFESSIONNELLES ET PROFESSIONNELS DE L'ÉDUCATION DU QUÉBEC/QUÉBEC FEDERATION OF PROFESSIONAL EMPLOYEES IN EDUCATION (FPPE) (1985)
9405, rue Sherbrooke est, Montréal, PQ H1L 6P3
514/356-0505, Téléc: 514/356-1324
Président, Pierre Tellier
1er Vice-président, Yves Lanctôt
Vice-président aux affaires administratives, François Ferland
3e Vice-présidente, Francine Paquin
4e Vice-président, Richard Gardner
Publications: Le Passerelle

SYNDICAT DES EMPLOYÉS EN RADIO-TÉLÉDIFFUSION DE RADIO-QUÉBEC/RADIO-QUÉBEC TELEVISION BROADCAST EMPLOYEES' UNION
2480, rue Sainte-Catherine est, Montréal, PQ H2K 4N7
514/525-2922, Téléc: 514/525-6375
Président, Jacques Poulin

SYNDICAT DES PROFESSIONNELS ET DES TECHNICIENS DE LA SANTÉ DU QUÉBEC/QUÉBEC UNION OF HEALTH PROFESSIONALS & TECHNICIANS (SPTSQ)
#850, 1001, rue Sherbrooke est, Montréal, PQ H2L 1L3
514/526-1214, Téléc: 514/521-0086
Présidente, Carolle Dubé

Centrale des syndicats démocratiques/Congress of Democratic Unions (CSD) (1972)
801, 4e rue, 3e étage, Québec, PQ G1J 2T7
418/529-2956, Téléc: 418/529-6323
Président, Claude Gingras
Vice-président, François Vaudreuil
Trésorier, Serge Tremblay
Secrétaire, Robert Légaré
Publications: La Base
Organisation(s) affiliée(s): Fédération démocratique de la métallurgie, des mines et des produits chimiques; Fédération des syndicats du textile et du vêtement (CSD) inc.
Bureau de Montréal: #600, 1259, rue Berri, Montréal, PQ H2L 4C7, 514/842-3801, Téléc: 514/842-0518

Confederation of Canadian Unions/Confédération des syndicats canadiens (CCU) (1969)
PO Box 1159, Gold River, BC V0P 1G0
250/283-7111, Fax: 250/283-2451
President, Garry Gifford
Sec.-Treas., Karen Cooling
Publications: CCU Bulletin

Confédération des syndicats nationaux/ Confederation of National Trade Unions (CSN) (1921)
1601, av de Lorimier, Montréal, PQ H2K 4M5
514/598-2121, Téléc: 514/598-2089
Secrétaire général, Pierre Paquette
Président, Gérald Larose
Trésorier, Léopold Beaulieu
Publications: Nouvelles CSN

Congress of Union Retirees Canada (CLC)/ Association des syndicalistes retraités du Canada (CURC) (1993)
2841 Riverside Dr., Ottawa, ON K1V 8X7
613/521-3400, Fax: 613/521-0423
President, Edith M. Johnston
Publications: Union Retiree
Affiliates: Canadian Labour Congress

Fédération du personnel professionnel des collèges (CEQ)
9405, rue Sherbrooke est, Montréal, PQ H1L 6P3
514/356-8888, Téléc: 514/356-3377
Président, Jacques Legault
Publications: Chronique

Independent Canadian Extrusion Workers Union (CNFIU)
PO Box 752, Midland, ON L4R 4P4
705/526-6783
Director, Steve Miller
President, Steve Bonnett

International Union of Bricklayers & Allied Craftsmen (AFL-CIO/CFL)
3 Forwell Rd., Kitchener, ON N2B 1W3
519/576-4610, Fax: 519/576-7382
Director, Canadian Operation, Brian Strickland

LABOUR UNIONS

Aircraft Operations Group Association (Ind.)/ Association du groupe des opérations d'aéronefs (ind.) (AOGA)
#330, 130 Slater St., Ottawa, ON K1P 6E2
613/230-5476, 5758, Fax: 613/230-2668
Chairman, Wayne C. Foy
Vice-Chairman, G. Dewar
Sec.-Treas., R. Walker
Publications: AOGA Bulletin

Alberta Dairy Employees & Driver Salesmen (Ind.)/Employés laitiers et des chauffeur-vendeurs de l'Alberta (ind.)
10515 Princess Elizabeth Ave., Edmonton, AB T5G 0Y5
403/474-3255, Fax: 403/479-5722
President, Robert Paquin
Publications: Bread & Butter Gazette

Alliance of Canadian Cinema, Television & Radio Artists (CLC)/Alliance des artistes canadiens du cinéma, de la télévision et de la radio (ACTRA) (1963)
2239 Yonge St., Toronto, ON M4S 2B5
416/489-1311, Fax: 416/489-1435
National President, Alexander (Sandy) Crawley
National Vice-President, Mitch O'Connor
National Treasurer, Brian Gromoff
President, Performers Guild, Dan MacDonald
Chair, Media Guild (Broadcast Journalists), Mitch O'Connor
Chair, Media Guild (ACTRA Writers Guild), Mark O'Neill
National Executive Director, Performers Guild, Stephen Waddell
National Executive Director, Media Guild, Christine Jacobs
Director, Communications & Research, Catherine Allman
Director, Management Information Services, Bernie Metzner
Executive Director, Writers Guild of Canada, Margaret Collier
President, Writers Guild, Jack Gray
Publications: Actrascope; Face to Face with Talent, biennial; Writers Directory, biennial
British Columbia Office: Branch Representative, Louise Chwin, #301, 1622 West 7 Ave., Vancouver, BC V6J 1S5, 604/734-1414, Fax: 604/734-1417
Calgary Office: Branch Representative, Joan Frank, Mount Royal Place, #260, 1414 - 8 St. SW, Calgary, AB T2R 1J6, 403/228-3123, Fax: 403/228-3299
Edmonton Office: Branch Representative, Sharon Killey, #201, 10816A - 82 Ave., Edmonton, AB T6E 2B3, 403/433-4090, Fax: 403/433-4099

Maritimes Office: Branch Representative, Ed J. Frenette, 5510 Spring Garden Rd., Halifax, NS B3J 1G5, 902/420-1404, Fax: 902/422-0589
Montréal Office: Branch Representative, Arden Ryshpan, #530, 1450, rue City Councillors, Montréal, PQ H3A 2E6, 514/844-3318, 3319, Fax: 514/844-2068
Newfoundland Office: Branch Representative, Marlene Cahill, 210 Water St., PO Box 575, St. John's, NF A1C 5K8, 709/722-0430, Fax: 709/722-2113
Ottawa Office: Branch Representative, Betty Hackett, #808, 130 Slater St., Ottawa, ON K1P 6E2, 613/230-0327, 0328, Fax: 613/230-2473
Saskatchewan Office: Branch Representative, Bill Siggins, #212, 1808 Smith St., Regina, SK S4P 2N4, 306/757-0885, Fax: 306/359-0044
Toronto Office: 2239 Yonge St., Toronto, ON M4S 2B5, 416/489-1311, Fax: 416/489-1435
Winnipeg Office: Branch Representative, Susan Robinson, Phoenix Building, #110, 388 Donald St., Winnipeg, MB R3B 2J4, 204/943-1307, 2365, Fax: 204/947-5664

Alliance professionnelle des infirmières et infirmiers auxiliaires du Québec (ind.)
3868, boul Sainte-Rose, Fabreville, PQ H7P 1C9
514/963-5400, Téléc: 514/963-5231
Directrice générale, Monique Leroux
Vice-président, Luc Séguin
Secrétaire, Heather L'Heureux
Publications: L'Envoi

Aluminum, Brick & Glass Workers International Union (AFL-CIO/CLC)/Syndicat international des ouvriers de l'aluminum, de la brique et du verre (FAT-COI/CTC) (ABGWIU)
3362 Hollenberg Dr., Bridgeton, MO 63044 USA
314/739-6142, Fax: 314/739-1216
President, Ernest J. LaBaff
Sec.-Treas., Harvey Martin
Canadian Office: Canadian Director, Rodney Bezo, #2, 406 North Service Rd. East, Oakville, ON K6G 5R2, 905/842-9710, Fax: 905/842-9713

Amalgamated Clothing & Textile Workers Unions (AFL-CIO/CLC)/Travailleurs amalgamés du vêtement et du textile (FAT-COI/CTC) (1914)
15 Union Sq., New York, NY 10003 USA
212/242-0700, Fax: 212/255-8169
General President, Jack Sheinkman
General Sec.-Treas., Arthur Loevy
Publications: ABG Light
Canadian Office: Canadian Director, John Alleruzzo, #700, 15 Gervais Dr., North York, ON M3C 1Y8, 416/441-1806, Fax: 416/441-9680

Amalgamated Transit Union (AFL-CIO/CLC)/Syndicat uni du transport (FAT-COI/CTC)
5025 Wisconsin Ave. NW, Washington, DC 20016 USA
202/537-1645, Fax: 202/244-7824
President, James LaSala
Sec.-Treas., Oliver Green
Canadian Office: Canadian Director, Ken Foster, #603, 15 Gervais Dr., Don Mills, ON M3C 1Y8, 416/445-6204, Fax: 416/445-6208

American Federation of Grain Millers (AFL-CIO/CLC)/Fédération américaine des meuniers (FAT-COI/CTC) (AFGM) (1936)
4949 Olson Memorial Hwy., Minneapolis, MN 55422 USA
612/545-0211, Fax: 612/545-5489
General President, Larry R. Jackson
General Sec.-Treas., Larry Barber
Canadian Office: Trustee, D. Maldeis, 287 Second St., Midland, ON L4R 3R2, 705/526-8342

American Federation of Musicians of the United States & Canada (AFL-CIO/CLC)/Fédération des musiciens des États-Unis et du Canada (FAT-COI/CTC) (AFM)
Paramount Building, #600, 1501 Broadway, New York, NY 10036 USA
212/869-1330, Fax: 212/764-6134
President, Mark Tully Massagli
Secretary, Stephen R. Sprague
Publications: International Musician
Canadian Office: Canadian Vice-President, Ray Patch, #1010, 75 The Donway West, North York, ON M3C 2E9, 416/391-5161, Fax: 416/391-5165, Toll Free: 1-800-463-6333

American Federation of Television & Radio Artists (AFL/CIO)
260 Madison Ave., New York, NY 10016 USA
National Executive Director, Bruce York
President, Reed Farrell
Canadian Office: Shop Steward, Lyn Martin; Shop Steward, Lorna McCormick, 1640 Ouellette Ave., Windsor, ON N8X 1K9, 519/258-8888, Fax: 519/966-1090

American Guild of Variety Artists (AFL-CIO)/Guilde américaine des artistes de variétés (FAT-COI) (AGVA) (1939)
184 Fifth Ave., New York, NY 10010 USA
212/675-1003, Fax: 212/633-0097
President, Rod McKuen
Executive Vice-President, Eileen Collins
Sec.-Treas., Frances Gaar

Association of Allied Health Professionals: Newfoundland & Labrador (Ind.)/Association des professionnels unis de la santé: Terre-Neuve et Labrador (ind.) (AAHP) (1975)
538 Water St., St. John's, NF A1E 1B7
709/722-3353, Fax: 709/722-3353
President, Nena Sandoval
Secretary, Noel Browne
Publications: News & Views

Association of Allied Health Professionals, Ontario (Ind.)/Association des professionnels unis de la santé, Ontario (ind.) (AAHP-O) (1975)
#305, 234 Eglinton Ave. East, Toronto, ON M4P 1K5
416/484-9685, Fax: 416/484-9959
Executive Director, Catherine E. Bowman
Publications: AAHPO - Update

Association of Canadian Film Craftspeople (Ind.)/Association des artisans du film canadien (ind.) (ACFC)
#105, 65 Heward Ave., Toronto, ON M4M 2T5
416/462-0211, Fax: 416/462-3248
President, Jane Manchee
General Secretary, Donato L. Baldassarra
Publications: Newsletter
BC Office: Contact, Brenda Collins, #140C, 555 Brooksbank Ave., North Vancouver, BC V7J 3S5, 604/983-5450, Fax: 604/983-5451
Manitoba Office: Office Manager, Darrell Varga, #302, 63 Albert St., Winnipeg, MB R3B 1G4, 204/943-1866, Fax: 204/943-1860

Association canadienne des métiers de la truelle, section locale 100 (CTC)/Trowel Trades Canadian Association, Local 100 (CLC)
9083, boul Saint-Michel, Montréal, PQ H1Z 3G6
514/326-3691, Téléc: 514/326-5562
Président, Luc Chalifoux
Secrétaire, Christian Thomassin
Publications: L'Éclaireur
Organisation(s) affiliée(s): 2 000 + sections locales

Association des employés en service social de la Province du Québec (ind.)/Association of Social Service Employees of the Province of Québec (1972)
#850, 1001, rue Sherbrooke est, Westmount, PQ H2L 1L3
514/521-2514, Téléc: 514/521-0086
Président, Daniel Citrome
Publications: Action notes
Organisation(s) affiliée(s): Centrale des Profesionnel en Santé

Association des manoeuvres interprovinciaux (CTC)/Interprovincial Labourers Association (CLC) (AMI)
#910, 545, boul Crémazie est, Montréal, PQ H2M 2V1
514/374-8780, Téléc: 514/381-4614
Directeur général, Ludger Synnett
Publications: Journal AMI

Association nationale des ferblantiers et couvreurs, section locale 2020 (CTC)/National Association of Tinsmiths & Tilers, Local 2020 (CLC) (ANFC) (1982)
#203, 3730, boul Crémazie est, Montréal, PQ H2A 1B4
514/374-1515, Téléc: 514/374-2282
Président, Pierre Lavoie
Publications: L'Informateur 2020

Association nationale des mécaniciens industriels, section local 1981 (CTC)/National Association of Industrial Mechanics, Local 1981 (CLC)
#307, 3750, boul Crémazie est, Montréal, PQ H2A 1B6
514/374-4527, Téléc: 514/374-2140, Ligne sans frais: 1-800-361-6585
Président, Gilles Pichette
Publications: L'Indicateur

Association nationale des peintres et métiers connexes, section locale 99 (CTC)/National Association of Painters & Allied Trades, Local 99 (CLC)
#1401, 3637, boul Crémazie est, Montréal, PQ H1Z 2J9
514/593-5413
Directeur, Marc Lirette

Association nationale des travailleurs en réfrigération, climatisation et protection-incendie, section locale 3 (CTC)/National Association of Refrigeration, Air-Conditioning & Fire Protection Workers, Local 3 (CLC)
#340, 5800, boul Métroplitain est, Montréal, PQ H1S 1A7
514/253-7475, Téléc: 514/253-7028
Directeur général, Jules Bergeron

Association nationale des travailleurs en tuyauterie et calorifugeurs, section locale 618 (CTC)/National Association of Plumbers, Pipe Fitters & Insulators, Local 618 (CLC)
#206, 3730, boul Crémazie est, Montréal, PQ H2A 1B4
514/723-0618, Téléc: 514/721-6204
Directeur général, Claude Allard
Publications: Le 618

Association des perfusionnistes du Québec/Association of Perfusionnistes of Quebec
31, rue Leroy, Repentigny, PQ J6A 1P7
514/934-4400, Téléc: 514/934-4368
Président, David Edgell

Association des policiers provinciaux du Québec (ind.)/Québec Provincial Police Association (Ind.) (APPQ) (1966)
1981, Léonard-de-Vinci, Sainte-Julie, PQ J3E 1Y9
514/922-5414, Téléc: 514/922-5417
Président, Jocelyn Turcotte

Canadian Almanac & Directory 1997

Secrétaire général, Luc Lebel
Trésorier, Régent Larochelle
Vice-président, Discipline et déontologie, André K. Malouf
Vice-président, Griefs et formation, Réjean Corriveau
Vice-président, Aide au personnel, Réjean Veilleux, Téléc:
Publications: Au Devoir

Association of Postal Officials of Canada (Ind.)/Association des officiers des postes du Canada (ind.) (APOC) (1966)
#201, 28 Concourse Gate, Nepean, ON K2E 7T7
613/727-1310, Fax: 613/727-5354
National President, Ronald Goodwin
Sec.-Treas., Michel Taddeo
Publications: APOC Bulletin

Association of Professional Student Services Personnel (Ind.)/Association du personnel professionnel des services aux étudiants (ind.) (APSSP) (1975)
#168, 615 Mount Pleasant Rd., Toronto, ON M4S 3C5
416/367-5267, Fax: 416/367-5267
President, Richard Waugh
Publications: APSSP Newsletter; APSSP Directory, a.

Association professionnelle des gardes du corps du gouvernement du Québec (ind.)/Professional Association of Body Guards of the Government of Quebec (Ind.)
#15, 5350, boul Henri-Bourassa, Charlesbourg, PQ G1H 6Y8
418/628-7856, Téléc: 418/628-3122
Président, Réal Lizotte

Association professionnelle des ingénieurs du gouvernement du Québec (ind.)/Association of Professional Engineers of the Government of Québec (Ind.) (APIGQ) (1986)
#201, 455, rue Marais, Vanier, PQ G1M 3A2
418/683-3633, Téléc: 418/683-6878
Président, Gaétan Lefebvre, ing.
Publications: L'Info

Association professionnelle des inhalothérapeutes du Québec (ind.)/Professional Association of Inhalation Therapists of Québec (Ind.)
#201, 3925, rue Rachel est, Montréal, PQ H1X 3G8
514/251-8050, Téléc: 514/259-8084
Président, Michel Talbot
Publications: L'Informapiq

Association professionnelle des technologistes médicaux du Québec (ind.)/Québec Professional Association of Medical Technologists (Ind.) (1955)
1595, rue St-Hubert, 3e étage, Montréal, PQ H2L 3Z2
514/524-3734, Téléc: 514/524-7863, Ligne sans frais: 1-800-361-4306
Présidente, Francine Genest
Publications: L'Express; Point d'interrogation, au deux ans; Rapport Annuel

Association of Public Service Financial Administrators (Ind.)/Association des gestionnaires financiers de la Fonction publique (ind.) (APSFA) (1989)
#302, 666 Kirkwood Ave., Ottawa, ON K1Z 5X9
613/728-0695, Fax: 613/761-9568
President, Merdon Hosking
Publications: FI Newsletter

Association for Residential Treatment Concepts (CNFIU)/Association pour concept de traitement résidentiel (FCNSI)
256 King St. North, PO Box 38012, Waterloo, ON N2J 4T9
519/740-1338, Fax: 519/622-7241
President, Mary Withers

Association des techniciennes et techniciens en diététique du Québec (ind.)/Québec Association of Dietary Technicians (Ind.) (ATDQ) (1975)
#850, 1001, rue Sherbrooke est, Montréal, PQ H2L 1L3
514/522-1153, Téléc: 514/521-0086
Présidente, Luce Leblanc
Vice-présidente, Christiane Bénard
Publications: Bulletin
Organisation(s) affiliée(s): Centrale des professionnelles et professionels de la santé (CPS)

Atlantic Communication & Technical Workers' Union (Ind.)/Syndicat des travailleurs de l'Atlantique (ind.) (AC & TWU) (1984)
6148 Quinpool Rd., Halifax, NS B3L 1A2
902/425-2440, Fax: 902/422-4647, Toll Free: 1-800-565-2289
Business Manager, Carl E. Simpson
Publications: Info Update

Atlantic Oil Workers (CCU)/Travailleurs du pétrole de l'Atlantique (CSC)
PO Box 3138, Dartmouth, NS B2W 4Y3
902/365-6340
President, Michael Williams

Bakery, Confectionery & Tobacco Workers International Union (AFL-CIO/CLC)/Syndicat international des travailleurs et travailleuses de la boulangerie, de la confiserie et du tabac (FAT-COI/CTC)
10401 Connecticut Ave., Kensington, MD 20895-3961 USA
301/933-8600
President, Frank Hurt
Sec.-Treas., Gene McDonald
Canadian Office: International Vice-President, Alphonse De Césaré; Executive Vice-President & Director or Organization, David B. Durkee, 3329, rue Ontario est, Montréal, PQ H1W 1P8, 514/527-9371, Fax: 514/527-8105

Bricklayers, Masons Independent Union of Canada (CLC)/Syndicat indépendant des briqueteurs et des maçons du Canada (CTC)
#105, 1263 Wilson Ave., North York, ON M3M 3G2
416/247-9841, Fax: 416/247-7346
President, Giuseppe Bellotto
Secretary, John Meiorin

British Columbia Federation of Police Officers (Ind.)/Fédération des agents de police de la Colombie-Britannique (ind.)
#603, 190 Alexander St., Vancouver, BC V6A 1B5
250/383-6182
President, Daryl Tottenhan

British Columbia Ferry & Marine Workers' Union (CLC)/Syndicat des travailleurs marins et de bacs de la Colombie-Britannique (CTC) (BCFMWU) (1977)
Ferry Workers' Union
#301, 710 Redbrick St., Victoria, BC V8T 5J3
250/382-2119, Fax: 250/385-9042
President, Ken Michael
Executive Assistant, P. Crawford
Affiliates: BC Federation of Labour; National Union of Public & General Employees (NUPGE)

British Columbia Government & Service Employees' Union/Syndicat des fonctionnaires provinciaux et de service de la Colombie-Britannique
4911 Canada Way, Burnaby, BC V5G 3W3
604/291-9611, Fax: 604/291-6030
President, John Shields
Sec.-Treas., Diane Wood
Affiliates: BC Federation of Labour; Canadian Labour Congress; National Union of Public & General Employees

Brotherhood of Maintenance of Way Employees (AFL-CIO/CLC)/Fraternité des préposés à l'entretien des voies (FAT-COI/CTC)
#200, 26555 Evergreen Rd., Southfield, MI 48076-4225 USA
313/948-1010, Fax: 313/948-7150
International President, Mac A. Fleming
Sec.-Treas., William E. LaRue
Canadian Office: Vice-President, Gary D. Housch; Vice-President, Ken Deptuck; Director of Communications, Martine Bouchard, #1, 2775 Lancaster Rd., Ottawa, ON K1B 4V8, 613/731-7356, Fax: 613/733-3158

Canadian Actors' Equity Association (CLC)/Association canadienne des artistes de la scène (CTC) (CAEA) (1976)
Actors' Equity
260 Richmond St. East, 2nd Fl., Toronto, ON M5A 1P4
416/867-9165, Fax: 416/867-9246, Email: caea@passport.ca
Executive Director, Susan Wallace
President, Terry Tweed
Communications & Special Projects Coordinator, David Caron
Publications: The News
Western Office: Business Representative, Colleen A. Fee, 505 Hudson House, 321 Water St., Vancouver, BC V6B 1B8, 604/682-6173, Fax: 604/682-6174

Canadian Air Line Dispatchers Association (CLC)/Association canadienne des régulateurs de vols (CTC)
35 Devonshire Dr., Brampton, ON L6T 3G5
905/791-4680
President, D. Michael McLeod

Canadian Air Line Pilots Association (Ind.)/Association canadienne des pilotes de ligne aérienne (ind.) (CALPA) (1937)
1300 Steeles Ave. East, Brampton, ON L6T 1A2
905/453-8210, Fax: 905/453-8757
President, Capt. D. Johnny
First Vice-President, Capt. J.R. Saunders
Vice-President, Finance, Capt. K. Freeman
Publications: Pilot; CALPA Newsletter, m.
Affiliates: International Federation of Air Line Pilots' Associations

Canadian Air Traffic Control Association (Ind.)/Association canadienne du contrôle du trafic aérien (ind.) (CATCA) (1959)
Camelot Business Park, 162 Cleopatra Dr., Nepean, ON K2G 5X2
613/225-3553, Fax: 613/225-8448
Managing Director, Joanne St-Gelais, CAE
President, Dave Lewis
Publications: CATCA News
Affiliates: International Federation of Air Traffic Control Associations

Canadian Association of Communications & Allied Workers (CCU)/Association canadienne des employés de communications et travailleurs connexes (CSC) (CACAW) (1981)
#204, 215, rue St. Laurent, St-Eustache, PQ J7P 4W4

514/491-5738, 6222, Fax: 514/491-5738
National Chairman, G. Coguet
National Sec.-Treas., Dave Halikowski
Publications: CACAW Newsletter

Canadian Association of Firefighters (Ind.)/ Association canadienne des pompiers (ind.) (CAFF) (1979)
11J Rayborn Cres., St Albert, AB T8N 5C3
403/458-2503, Fax: 403/458-2503, Toll Free: 1-800-661-4924
President, Maurice Sandford
Sec.-Treas., Tom Burton
Publications: The Canadian Association of Fire Fighters

Canadian Association of Professional Radio Operators (Ind.)/Association canadienne des professionnels de l'exploitation radio (ind.) (CAPRO)
#402, 120 Holland Ave., Ottawa, ON K1Y 0X6
613/761-7711, Fax: 613/761-7712
National President, Gary Wilson
Publications: ROCOM

Canadian Association of Simulator Technologists (Ind.) (1990)
c/o Canadian Airlines International, 6001 Grant McConachie Way, Richmond, BC V7B 1K3
604/270-5090, Fax: 604/276-3620
Chairman, Bruce Fingarson

Canadian Association of Smelter & Allied Workers (CCU)/Association canadienne des travailleurs de fonderie et ouvriers assimilés (CSC) (CASAW) (1972)
235 Enterprise Ave., Kitimat, BC V8C 2C8
250/632-2602, Fax: 250/632-2627
President, Ross Slezak
Publications: Hotline

Canadian Council of Railway Shopcraft Unions/ Conseil canadien des syndicats de métiers d'ateliers ferroviaires
#409, 1000, St-Antoine ouest, Montréal, PQ H3C 3R7
514/878-2601, Fax: 514/878-3995
President, Loukas Biniaris
Executive Secretary, Abe Rosner

Canadian Farmworkers Union (CLC)/Syndicat canadien des travailleurs agricoles (CTC) (CFU) (1980)
#1, 10667 - 135 A St., Surrey, BC V3T 4E3
604/583-9334, Fax: 604/583-9334
President, Jawala Singh Grewal
Publications: The Farmworker

Canadian Football League Players' Association (Ind.)/Association des joueurs de la ligue de football canadienne (ind.) (CFLPA)
#700, 10104 - 103 Ave., Edmonton, AB T5J 0H8
403/426-4535
President, Dan Ferrone
Publications: CFLPA Newsletter

Canadian Guard Association (Ind.)/Association canadienne des gardiens (ind.) (CGA) (1957)
#305, 2841 Riverside Dr., Ottawa, ON K1V 8X7
613/737-4417, Fax: 613/737-5248
President, Stuart Deans

Canadian Health Care Guild (Ind.)/Guilde canadienne des soins de la santé (ind.)
#200, 17410 - 107 Ave., Edmonton, AB T5S 1E9
403/483-8126, Fax: 403/484-3341, Toll Free: 1-800-252-7984
President, Robert Metheral

Vice-President, Myrna Wright
Publications: Pulse

Canadian Iron, Steel & Industrial Workers' Union (Ind.)/Syndicat canadien des travailleurs du fer, des métallurgistes et des travailleurs industriels (ind.)
17 East Broadway, Vancouver, BC V5T 1V4
604/879-8137, Fax: 604/873-9112
President, Frank Nolan
Publications: The Canadian Unionist

Canadian Marine Officers' Union (AFL-CIO/CLC)/ Syndicat canadien des officiers de la marine marchande (FAT-COI/CTC)
9670, rue Notre-Dame est, Montréal, PQ H1L 3P8
514/354-8321, Fax: 514/354-8368
President/Sec.-Treas., Richard Vézina
Vice-President, Non-Maritime, Jean Brisebois
Vice-President, Robert Ford
Affiliates: Seafarers International Union of North America/Syndicat international des marins de l'Amérique du Nord

Canadian Media Guild/La Guilde canadienne des médias (CMG) (1950)
#300, 144 Front St. West, Toronto, ON M5J 2L7
416/591-5333, Fax: 416/591-7278
President, Ray Aboud
Administrative Officer, Kathy Viner
Publications: SCAN

Canadian Merchant Service Guild (CLC)/Guilde de la marine marchande du Canada (CTC)
1150 Morrison Dr., Ottawa, ON K2H 8S9
613/829-9531, Fax: 613/596-6079
National President, Maury R. Sjoquist
National Sec.-Treas., Larry Dempsey
Publications: CMSG News
Eastern Branch: Sec.-Treas., Earle Simpson, 3235, av Granby, Montréal, PQ H1N 2Z8, 514/254-4571, Fax: 514/254-2141
Western Branch: Sec.-Treas., Leo M. Gray, 230 West Broadway, Vancouver, BC V5Y 1P7, 604/872-7811, Fax: 604/872-5323

CANADIAN ASSOCIATION OF MASTERS & CHIEF ENGINEERS (CLC)/ ASSOCIATION DES CAPITAINES ET CHEFS INGÉNIEURS DU CANADA (CTC)
22 Cabot St., St Anthony, NF A0K 4S0
President, Capt. Herb Murrin

CANADIAN MARINE PILOTS' ASSOCIATION (CLC)/ASSOCIATION DES PILOTES DE LA MARINE CANADIENNE (CTC)
1311, av Allard, Ste-Foy, PQ G1W 3G3
President, Capt. Michel Pouliot

Canadian National Railways Police Association (Ind.)/Association des policiers des chemins de fer nationaux du Canada (ind.)
6479 Miller's Grove, Mississauga, ON L5N 3E5
905/824-0856, Fax: 905/824-4584
National President, Frank Morgan

Canadian Overseas Telecommunications Union (CCU)/Syndicat canadien des télécommunications transmarines (CSC)
#200, 440, boul René-Lévesque ouest, Montréal, PQ H2Z 1V7
514/866-9015, Fax: 514/868-8364
President, Carlos Saldanha
Vice-President, Daniel McDuff
Treasurer, Daniel Séguin

Canadian Pacific Police Association (Ind.)/ Association des policiers du Canadien Pacifique (ind.) (CPPA) (1972)
1237, Vallée, Chambly, PQ J3L 5K4

514/678-4906, Fax: 514/658-6212
National President, François Dubuc

Canadian Postmasters & Assistants Association (CLC)/Association canadienne des maîtres de poste et adjoints (CTC) (CPAA) (1902)
281 Queen Mary St., Ottawa, ON K1K 1X1
613/745-2095, Fax: 613/745-5559
National President, Ernie Blois
Senior National Vice-President, L.K. Kuan
National Sec.-Treas., S. Duguay
Publications: The Canadian Postmaster/Le Maître de poste canadien; CPAA/ACMPA Bulletin, m.

Canadian Red Cross Blood Transfusion Service Employees Association (Ind.)/Association des employés des services de transfusion sanguine de la Croix-Rouge (ind.)
850 Commissioners Rd. East, London, ON N6C 2V5
519/681-6781
President, Bea Dykeman

Canadian Staff Union (Ind.)/Syndicat canadien du personnel (ind.)
2100, av Papineau, Montréal, PQ H2K 4J4
514/527-9681
President, André Lamoureux

Canadian Telephone Employees' Association (Ind.)/Association canadienne des employés de téléphone (ind.)
#360, Place du Canada, Montréal, PQ H3B 2N2
514/861-9963
President, Judith King
Publications: Teleforum/Téléforum

Canadian Transport Workers Union (Ind.)/ Syndicat canadien des travailleurs du transport (ind.) (CTWU)
266 Livingstone Ave. North, Listowel, ON N4W 1P9
519/886-1603
President, Bill Johnston
Vice-President, Don Spence
General Secretary, Bev Strachan
Publications: News Letter

Canadian Union of Educational Workers (Ind.)/ Syndicat canadien des travailleuses et travailleurs en éducation (ind.)
#304, 385 Yonge St., Toronto, ON M5B 1S1
416/979-7394, Fax: 416/979-0678
Chair/National Affairs, Vanessa Kelly
Communications Officer, Thérèse Brabant
Publications: Connexions; En Masse, q.
Affiliates: International Federation of Workers' Educational Associations

Canadian Union of Operating Engineers & General Workers (Ind.)/Syndicat canadien des techniciens de chaufferies et des manoeuvres (ind.)
#106, 2087 Dundas St. East, Mississauga, ON L4X 2V7
905/238-8823
President, Bob Souliere
Vice-President, Douglas Draycott
Sec.-Treas., Allen Nesbitt

Canadian Union of Postal Workers (CLC)/ Syndicat des travailleurs et travailleuses des postes (CUPW)
377 Bank St., Ottawa, ON K2P 1Y3
613/236-7238, Fax: 613/563-7861
National President, Darrell Tingley
National Sec.-Treas., George Kuehnbaum
Publications: CUPW/SPC

Canadian Almanac & Directory 1997

Canadian Union of Professional & Technical Employees (Ind.)/Syndicat canadien des employés professionnels et techniques (ind.) (CUPTE)
#1610, 85 Albert St., Ottawa, ON K1P 6A4
613/230-4747, Fax: 613/230-6399
President, Line Niquet
Publications: TR Newsletter; CUPTE News, q.

Canadian Union of Public Employees (CLC)/Syndicat canadien de la Fonction publique (CTC) (CUPE) (1963)
21 Florence St., Ottawa, ON K2P 0W6
613/237-1590, Fax: 613/237-5508
National President, Judy Darcy
National Sec.-Treas., Geraldine McGuire
Publications: Organize
Affiliates: Canadian Labour Congress
Airline Division Office: President, Donna Hendrick, #600, 180 Attwell Dr., Etobicoke, ON M9W 6A9, 416/798-3399, Fax: 416/798-3411
Canadian Broadcast Employees Union: President, Glenn Gray, #413, 1840 Victoria Park Ave., Scarborough, ON M1R 1S9
Regions
Alberta Division: Recording Secretary, Richard Scarfe, #210, 534 - 17 Ave. SW, Calgary, AB T2S 0B1
BC Division: Sec.-Treas., Colleen Jordan, #500, 4940 Canada Way, Burnaby, BC V5G 4T3, 604/291-1940, Fax: 604/291-1194
Division du Québec: Secrétaire archiviste, Henri Massé, 545, boul Crémazie, 12e étage, Montréal, PQ H2M 2V1
Manitoba Division: Recording Secretary, Bernice Bryan, 743 McPhillips St., Winnipeg, MB R2X 2J1
New Brunswick Division: Sec.-Treas., Claire Doiron, #222, 96 Norwood Ave., Moncton, NB E1C 6L9
Newfoundland & Labrador Division: Recording Secretary, Dawn Lahey, 205 New Pennywell Rd., St. John's, NF A1B 1C5
Nova Scotia Division: Sec.-Treas., Betty Warrell, 12 Smith Ave., Dartmouth, NS B2V 1M4
Ontario Division: President, Sid Ryan; Sec.-Treas., Terry O'Connor, 156 Shorting Rd., Scarborough, ON M1S 3S6
Prince Edward Island Division: Recording Secretary, Rosalie Wade, 106 York Point Rd., RR#4, Cornwall, PE C0A 1H0
Saskatchewan Divison: Recording Secretary, Judy Henley, 26 Matheson Cres., Yorkton, SK S3N 3M3

Canadian Union of Restaurant & Related Employees (Ind.)/Syndicat canadien des employé(e)s restaurantation et des employé(e)s relié(e)s (ind.)
94 Kenhar Dr., Weston, ON M9L 1N2
416/665-3842
President, James Whyte

Canadian Union of Transportation Employees (CCU)/Syndicat canadien des employés du transport (CSC)
1615B - 6 Ave., Prince George, BC V2L 3N5
250/562-4272, Fax: 250/562-4279
President, Ron Stavast

Cariboo Woodworkers Association (Ind.)/Association des travailleurs du bois de Cariboo (ind.)
PO Box 1798, 100 Mile House, BC V0K 2E0
250/395-5332
Secretary, Paul Klassen

Centrale des professionnelles et professionnels de la santé (CPS) (1988)
#850, 1001, rue Sherbrooke est, Montréal, PQ H2L 1L3
514/521-4469, Téléc: 514/521-0086
Directrice générale, Huguette Côté

Président, Jacques Paradis
Publications: Proposyndical

Christian Labour Association of Canada (Ind.)/Association chrétienne du travail du Canada (ind.) (CLAC) (1952)
5920 Atlantic Dr., Mississauga, ON L4W 1N6
905/670-7383, Fax: 905/670-8416
Executive Director, Ed Grootenboer
President, Stan Baker
Director of Research & Education, Harry Antonides
Publicity Director, Ray Pennings
Publications: The Guide

Communications, Energy & Paperworkers Union of Canada (CLC)/Syndicat canadien des communications, de l'énergie et du papier (CTC) (CEP) (1992)
350 Sparks St., 19th Fl., Ottawa, ON K1R 1A4
613/230-5200, Fax: 613/230-5801, Email: info@cep.ca
URL: http://www.cep.ca/cep/
President, Fred W. Pomeroy
Executive Vice-President, John McInnes
Executive Vice-President, Reg Basken
Publications: CEP Journal/Journal SCEP
Affiliates: Canadian Labour Congress; Ontario Federation of Labour
Section locale 145: Président, Gilles Leblanc, #201, 4555, boul Metropolitain est, St-Léonard, PQ H1R 1Z4, 514/593-5323

Communications Workers of America (AFL-CIO/CLC)/Travailleurs en communication d'Amérique (FAT-COI/CTC)
501 Third St. NW, Washington, DC 20001-2797 USA
202/434-1100, Fax: 202/434-1279
President, Morton Bahr
President, Printing, Publishing & Media Workers Sector, William J. Boarman
Canadian Office: Representative, David Esposti, #B, 288 Dalhousie St., Ottawa, ON K1N 7E6, 613/234-9159, Fax: 613/241-4120

Compensation Employees' Union (Ind.)/Syndicat des employés d'indemnisation (ind.)
#241, 7080 River Rd., Richmond, BC V6X 1X5
604/278-4050, Fax: 604/278-5002
President, Bill Hawkins
Publications: Newsletter; Newspaper, q.; Newsletter/Womens' Issues, q.

Conseil des syndicats hospitaliers de Montréal inc. (Ind.)/Montréal Council of Hospital Syndicates Inc. (Ind.) (CSHM)
#1610, 2050, rue Mansfield, Montréal, PQ H3A 1Y9
514/844-9569, Téléc: 514/844-9560
Présidente, Mary Ann Korabel
Secrétaire administrative, Guylaine Guay

Custodial & Maintenance Association (CNFIU)/Association du personnel de conciergerie et d'entretien (FCNSI) (CAMA) (1968)
c/o Rockway Public School, 70 Vanier Dr., Kitchener, ON N2C 1J5
519/745-5266
President, David Weiler
Publications: CAMA News

Distillery, Wine & Allied Workers' International Union (AFL-CIO/CLC)/Union internationale des employés de distilleries, vins et industries connexes (FAT-COI/CTC) (DWAW)
66 Grand Ave., PO Box 567, Englewood, NJ 07631 USA
President, George J. Orlando
Publications: DWAW Journal; News Letter/Lettre d'information, q.

Canadian Office: Vice-President/Canadian Director, Raymond Bisson, 11, rue Monette, Delson, PQ J0L 1G0, 514/632-4700

Engineers & Scientists Association (Marconi) (Ind.)/Association des ingénieurs et des scientifiques (Marconi) (ind.)
600, boul Frederick Phillips, St-Laurent, PQ H4M 2S9
514/748-3150, Fax: 514/748-3136
President, Henri Noory

ESSA/AESS (1915)
#700, 220 Laurier Ave. West, Ottawa, ON K1P 5Z9
613/236-9181, Fax: 613/236-6017, Toll Free: 1-800-265-9181
Executive Director, Marvin Gandall
President, W.E. Krause
Publications: ESSA Bulletin/Bulletin AESS
Affiliates: International Labour Organization

Federal Government Dockyard Chargehands Association (Ind.)/Association des chefs d'équipe des chantiers maritimes du gouvernement (ind.) (FGDCA) (1988)
C.F.B. Halifax, F.M.O., Halifax, NS B3K 2X0
902/429-9426, Fax: 902/421-1095
President, Darryl Roode
Vice-President, Tom Hillier
Treasurer, Bill Johnson
Secretary, Willie Courtney

Fédération des affaires sociales inc. (CSN)/Social Affairs Federation Inc. (CNTU)
1601, av de Lorimier, Montréal, PQ H2K 4M5
514/598-2210, Téléc: 514/598-2223
Président, Sylvio Robinson
Secrétaire générale, Cécile Côté
Trésorière, Lucille Poirier
Publications: Fas aux défis

Fédération autonome du collégial (ind.)/Autonomous Federation of Collegial Staff (Ind.) (FAC) (1988)
1067, rue St-Denis, Montréal, PQ H2X 3J3
514/848-9977, Téléc: 514/848-0166
Président, Michel Duffy
Publications: FACsimilé; FACtuel, 3 fois par an

Fédération du commerce inc. (CSN)/Commerce Federation Inc. (CNTU)
#122, 1601, av de Lorimier, Montréal, PQ H2K 4M5
514/598-2353, Téléc: 514/598-2304
Présidente, Lise Poulin
Publications: Info-Commerce

Fédération CSN - Construction (CSN)/CNTU Federation - Construction (CNTU)
1594, av de Lorimier, Montréal, PQ H2K 3W5
514/598-2044, Téléc: 514/598-2040
Président, Olivier Lemieux
Publications: Batisseur

Fédération démocratique de la métallurgie, des mines et des produits chimiques (CSD)/Metal Trades, Mines & Chemical Products Democratic Federation (CSD)
801, 4e rue, Québec, PQ G1J 2T7
418/529-2956, Téléc: 418/529-0483
Directeur, Richard Beaulieu
Président, Jean Roy
Secrétaire, Gilles Goulet

Fédération des employées et employés de services publics inc. (CSN)/Federation of Public Service Employees Inc. (CNTU) (FEESP)
1601, av de Lorimier, Montréal, PQ H2K 4M5
514/598-2231, Téléc: 514/598-2398
Président, Ginette Guérin

Vice-président, Denis Marcoux
Secrétaire, François Juneau
Publications: Nouvelles CSN
Organisation(s) affiliée(s): Confederation des syndicats nationaux

Federation of Engineering & Scientific Associations/Fédération d'associations d'ingénieurs et de scientifiques (FESA)
#206, 3199 Bathurst St., Toronto, ON M6A 2B2
416/784-1284, Fax: 416/784-1366
President, Leo J. Kok
Administrative Officer, Gordon Flowers
Publications: Information Digest
Affiliates: Association of Northern Telecom Engineers & Scientists; Canadian Standards Association Professional Engineers Association; Northern Electric London Professional Association; Salaried Employees Alliance, Computing Devices Company; Society of Ontario Hydro Professional & Administrative Employees; Society of Professional Engineers & Associates - CANDU Operations, Atomic Energy of Canada Limited; SPAR Engineers & Scientists Association; SPAR Professional & Allied Technical Employees Association
Montréal Office: Personne ressource, Suzanne Béliveau, #500, 7575, rte. Transcanadienne, Saint Laurent, PQ H4T 1V6, 514/331-1403

Fédération indépendante des syndicats affiliés (ind.)/Independent Federation of Affiliated Unions (Ind.) (FISA)
1250 - 3e av, Québec, PQ G1L 2X7
418/529-4571, 4572, Téléc: 418/529-4695
Directeur, Claude Roy
Président, Paul Talbot
Publications: Info-FISA

Fédération des intervenantes en garderie (CEQ)
9405, rue Sherbrooke est, Montréal, PQ H1L 6P3
514/356-8888, Téléc: 514/356-0202
Présidente, Denise Dextraze

Fédération des médecins résidents du Québec inc. (ind.)/Québec Federation of Residents (Ind.) (FMRQ) (1970)
445, rue Sherbrooke ouest, Montréal, PQ H3A 1B6
514/282-0256, Téléc: 514/282-0471, Ligne sans frais: 1-800-465-0215
Président, Denis Soulières
Trésorier, Vacant
Secrétaire, Dr. Pierre Lacaille-Bélanger
Publications: Le Bulletin

Fédération de la métallurgie (CSN)/Federation of Metal Trades (CNTU) (1944)
#204, 2100, boul de Maisonneuve est, Montréal, PQ H2K 4S1
514/529-4937, Téléc: 514/529-4935
Président, Alain Lampron
Publications: Fer de Lance

Fédération nationale des communications (CSN)/National Federation of Communication Workers (CNTU) (FNC) (1972)
1601, av de Lorimier, Montréal, PQ H2K 4M5
514/598-2132, Téléc: 514/598-2431
Présidente, Chantale Larouche
Publications: La Dépêche

Fédération nationale des travailleurs de l'industrie vêtement inc. (CSD)/National Federation of Clothing Workers Inc. (CSD)
#301, 2235, rue Sherbrooke est, Montréal, PQ H2K 1E2
514/527-2115, Téléc: 514/527-2310
Président, Jacques Morin

Fédération des policiers du Québec (ind.)/Québec Federation of Policemen (Ind.)
7955, boul. Louis-H. Lafontaine, Anjou, PQ H1K 4E4
514/356-3321, Téléc: 514/356-1158
Président, Jean-Guy Roch
Directeur exécutif, Guy Marcil

Fédération des professionnels et professionnelles salarié(e)s et des cadres de Québec (CSN)/Quebec Federation of Managers & Professional Salaried Workers (CNTU) (FPPEQ)
1601, av de Lorimier, Montréal, PQ H2K 4M5
514/598-2143, Téléc: 514/598-2089
Président, Michel Kane

Fédération des syndicats du secteur de l'aluminium inc. (ind.)/Federation of Aluminum Unions Inc. (Ind.) (FSSA) (1972)
1924, boul Mellon, Jonquière, PQ G7S 3H3
418/548-4667, Téléc: 418/548-7992
Président, Raymond Labonté
Secrétaire exécutif, Marcien Bisson
Publications: Contact

Fédération des syndicats du textile et du vêtement (C.S.D.) inc. (CSD) (1993)
#300, 1259, rue Berri, Montréal, PQ H2L 4C7
514/842-6941, Téléc: 514/842-6385
Directeur professionnel, Yvon Jacques
Président, François Hamel
Secrétaire, Daniel Rodier

Fédération des travailleurs forestiers du Québec (ind.)/Québec Woodworkers Federation (Ind.) (FTFQ) (1965)
422, rue Racine est, Chicoutimi, PQ G7H 1T3
418/549-7353, Téléc: 418/543-4873
Président, Serge Théberge

Fédération des travailleuses et travailleurs du papier et de la forêt (CSN)/Federation of Paper & Forest Workers (CNTU) (FTPF) (1937)
155, boul Charest est, Québec, PQ G1K 3G6
418/647-5775, Téléc: 418/647-5884
Président, Claude Plamondon
Coordonnateur, Claude Rioux
Publications: Le Travailleur
Organisation(s) affiliée(s): Fédération internationale des syndicats des travailleurs à la chimie, de l'énergie, des mines et des industries diverses (ICEM)

Fraternité des constables du contrôle routier de la Sûreté du Québec (ind.)/Brotherhood of Constables of Highway Traffic Controllers of the Québec Provincial Police (Ind.)
4165, rue Chauveau, Sherbrooke, PQ J1L 1R9
819/567-9784
Président, Guy Lalumière
Publications: Le Fraternel

Fraternité des constables spéciaux d'Hydro-Québec (ind.)/Brotherhood of Special Constables of Hydro-Québec (Ind.)
2713, rue Lupien, Saint-Hubert, PQ J3Y 6C4
514/462-1653
Président, Richard Seyer

Fraternité interprovinciale des ouvriers en électricité (CTC)/Interprovincial Brotherhood of Electrical Workers (CLC) (FIPOÉ)
#1600, 545, boul Crémazie est, Montréal, PQ H2M 2V1
514/385-3476, Téléc: 514/385-9298
President, André Farley
Publications: Journal FIPOE

Fraternité nationale des charpentiers-menuisiers, forestiers et travailleurs d'usine (CTC)/National Brotherhood of Carpenters, Joiners, Foresters & Industrial Workers (CLC) (1981)
#205, 3730, boul Crémazie est, Montréal, PQ H2A 1B4
514/374-0952, Téléc: 514/374-8800, Ligne sans frais: 1-800-465-9791
Président, Gaston Pageau
Secrétaire, Diane Lanthier
Publications: La Fraternité
Organisation(s) affiliée(s): Congrès du travail du Canada; Fédération des travailleurs et travailleuses de Quebec

Fraternité nationale des monteurs d'acier de structure, serruriers de bâtiments et chaudronniers, section locale 737 (CTC)/National Brotherhood of Structural Steel Erectors, Building Locksmiths & Boilermakers, Local 737 (CLC)
#301, 3730, boul Crémazie est, Montréal, PQ H2A 1B4
514/374-2326, Téléc: 514/374-2140
Président, Gérald Ducharme

General Workers Union of Canada - Local 1 (Ind.)/Syndicat des travailleurs généraux du Canada - section locale 1 (ind.)
#102, 5512 East Hastings St., Burnaby, BC V5B 1R3
604/291-6310, Fax: 604/291-6290
President, Rocco Salituro

Glass, Molders, Pottery, Plastic & Allied Workers International Union (AFL-CIO/CLC)/Union internationale des travailleurs du verre, mouleurs, poterie, plastique et autres (FAT-COI/CTC)
GMP International Union
608 East Baltimore Pike, PO Box 607, Media, PA 19063-0607 USA
610/565-5051, Fax: 610/565-0983
Director, Joseph Galvin, Jr.
International President, James E. Hatfield
Sec.-Treas., Frank W. Carter
Publications: Horizons
Canadian Office: Canadian Vice-President, Ross L. Armstrong, #103, 61 International Blvd., Etobicoke, ON M9W 6K4, 416/674-4690, Fax: 416/674-1690

Grain Services Union (CLC)/Syndicat des services du grain (CTC) (GSU)
2334 McIntyre St., Regina, SK S4P 2S2
306/522-6686, Fax: 306/565-3430
President, Garnet Lee
Secretary-Manager, Hugh J. Wagner
Publications: GSU News

Graphic Communications International Union (AFL-CIO/CLC)/Syndicat international des communications graphiques (FAT-COI/CTC) (GCIU)
1900 L St. NW, Washington, DC 20036 USA
212/462-1400, Fax: 212/331-9516
International President, James J. Norton
Canadian Office: Canadian Vice-President, James Cowan, #600, 1110 Finch Ave. West, North York, ON M3J 2T2, 416/661-9761

Health Care Employees Union of Alberta (Ind.)/Syndicat des employés des soins de la santé de l'Alberta (ind.)
10540 - 106 St., Edmonton, AB T5H 2X6
403/420-6600, Fax: 403/424-1230
President, Benjamin P. Horvath
Executive Sec.-Treas., Ken Archer

Health Sciences Association of Alberta (Ind.)/ Association des sciences de la santé de l'Alberta (ind.)
10340 - 124 St., Edmonton, AB T5N 1R2
403/488-0168, Fax: 403/488-0534
President, Patricia Ennis
Publications: The Bulletin

Health Sciences Association of Saskatchewan (Ind.)/Association des sciences de la santé de la Saskatchewan (ind.) (HSAS)
#2, 3002 Louise St., Saskatoon, SK S7J 3L8
306/955-3399, Fax: 306/955-3399
Executive Director, Tim Slattery
President, Roberta Ekberg
Publications: Dispatches

Hospital Employees Union (CLC)/Syndicat des employés d'hôpitaux (CTC) (1944)
2006 - 10 Ave. West, Vancouver, BC V6J 4P5
604/734-3431, Fax: 604/734-3163
Provincial President, Julie Eckert
Publications: The Hospital Guardian

Hotel Employees & Restaurant Employees' International Union (AFL-CIO/CLC)/Union internationale des employés d'hôtels et de restaurants (FAT-COI/CTC)
1219 - 28 St. NW, Washington, DC 20007 USA
202/393-4373, Fax: 202/333-0468
General President, Edward T. Hanley
General Sec.-Treas., Herman Leavitt
Canadian Regional Office: International Representative, Paul Clifford, 20 Austin Cres., Toronto, ON M5R 3E3

Independent Canadian Transit Union (CCU)/ Syndicat canadien indépendant du transport (CSC)
#206, 5050 Kingsway, Burnaby, BC V5H 4H2
604/433-1892, Fax: 604/435-0160
National President, Hunter Wallace
Eastern Vice-President, Dan Carriere
Western Vice-President, Joe Elworthy
National Sec.-Treas., Neal Barreca
Publications: Progress

Independent Paperworkers of Canada (Ind.) (IPC) (1992)
#D412, 1450 Glen Abbey Gate, Oakville, ON L6M 2V7
905/825-2593, Fax: 905/825-2593
General Administrator, Gary Buccella
Publications: The Independent

Independent Union of Precision Diecasters (CNFIU)/Syndicat indépendant de Precision Diecasters (FCNSI)
PO Box 1295, Peterborough, ON K9J 5T2
705/745-6428
President, Jon Lunt

International Alliance of Theatrical Stage Employees & Moving Picture Machine Operators of the United States & Canada (AFL-CIO/CLC)/ Alliance internationale des employés de la scène et des projectionnistes des États-Unis et du Canada (FAT-COI/CTC) (IATSE)
#601, 1515 Broadway, New York, NY 10036 USA
212/730-1770, Fax: 212/921-7699
President, Alfred W. Ditolla
Canadian Office: Canadian Vice-President, Alan L. Cowley, 416/281-5054, Fax: 416/441-4073; International Representative, East Coast, Robert Thomson, 902/883-8346; International Representative, West Coast, Gus Bottas, 403/456-7156, 6 Havilland Dr., West Hill, ON M1C 2T6, 416/441-3710, Fax: 416/441-4073

International Allied Printing Trades Association/ Association internationale des métiers alliés de l'imprimerie
501 - 3 St. NW, Washington, DC 20001-2797 USA
202/434-1238, Fax: 202/434-1245
President, William J. Boarman
Sec.-Treas., Guy De Vito

International Association of Bridge, Structural & Ornamental Iron Workers (AFL-CIO)/Association internationale des travailleurs de ponts, de fer structural et ornemental (FAT-COI)
#400, 1750 New York Ave. NW, Washington, DC 20006 USA
202/383-4800
President, Jacob West
General Secretary, Leroy Worley
Publications: The Ironworker
Canadian Office: General Vice-President, James Phair, 1350 L'Heritage Dr., Sarnia, ON N7S 6H8, 519/542-1413, Fax: 519/542-3790

International Association of Fire Fighters (AFL-CIO/CLC)/Association internationale des pompiers (FAT-COI/CTC)
1750 New York Ave. NW, Washington, DC 20006 USA
202/737-8484
General President, Alfred K. Whitehead
Canadian Office: Canadian Director, Doug Coupar, #350, 130 Slater St., Ottawa, ON K1P 6E2, 613/567-8988, Fax: 613/567-8986

International Association of Heat & Frost Insulators & Asbestos Workers (AFL-CIO/CLC)/ Association internationale des isolateurs en amiante (FAT-COI/FCT)
#301, 1776 Massachusetts Ave. NW, Washington, DC 20036-1989 USA
202/785-2388, Fax: 202/429-0568
General President, William G. Bernard
Publications: The Asbestos Worker
Canadian Office: Canadian Vice-President, André Chartrand, 3585, av Diane, Terrebonne, PQ J6Y 1A2, 514/433-2926, Fax: 514/353-8653

International Association of Machinists & Aerospace Workers (AFL-CIO/CLC)/Association internationale des machinistes et des travailleurs de l'aérospatiale (FAT-COI/CTC)
Machinists Bldg., 9000 Machinists Place, Upper Marlborg, MD 20772 USA
301/967-4500, Fax: 301/967-4588
President, George J. Kourpias
Canadian Office: General Vice-President, Valérie E. Bourgeois, #300, 100 Metcalfe St., Ottawa, ON K1P 5M1, 613/236-9761, Fax: 613/563-7830

International Brotherhood of Boilermakers, Iron Ship Builders, Blacksmiths, Forgers & Helpers (AFL-CIO/CLC)/Fraternité internationale des chaudronniers, constructeurs de navires en fer, forgerons, forgeurs et aides (FAT-COI/ FCT) (IBB) (1880)
Boilermakers
New Brotherhood Bldg., #570, 753 State Ave., Kansas City, KS 66101 USA
913/371-2640, Fax: 913/281-8101
International President, Charles W. Jones
International Sec.-Treas., Jerry Z. Willburn
Publications: The Boilermaker Reporter
Eastern Canada Office: International Vice-President, Eastern Canada, Alexander C. MacDonald, #139, 1216 Sandcove Rd., PO Box 3279, Stn B, Saint John, NB E2M 4X8, 506/634-8203, Fax: 506/634-0307
Western Canada Office: International Vice-President, Western Canada, Richard C. Albright, #206, 17205 - 106 A Ave., Edmonton, AB T5S 1M7, 403/483-0823, Fax: 403/489-3043

International Brotherhood of Electrical Workers (AFL-CIO/CFL)/Fraternité internationale des ouvriers en électricité (FAT-COI/ FCT) (IBEW) (1891)
1125 - 15th St. NW, Washington, DC 20005 USA
202/833-7000, Fax: 202/467-6316
International President, John J. Barry
International Secretary, Jack F. Moore
International Representative, Lawrence Liles, 202/728-6107
Publications: IBEW Journal
Canadian Office: International Vice-President, Ken J. Woods, #401, 45 Sheppard Ave. East, North York, ON M2N 5Y1, 416/226-5155, Fax: 416/226-1492

International Brotherhood of Firemen & Oilers (AFL-CIO/CLC)/Fraternité internationale des chauffeurs et huileurs (FAT-COI/ CTC) (IBF&O) (1898)
1100 Circle, 75 Pkwy., #350, Atlanta, GA 30339 USA
404/933-9104, Fax: 404/933-0361
President, Jimmy L. Walker
Canadian Office: Canadian International Vice-President, Domenic Mancini, #6, 648 Finch Ave. East, North York, ON M2K 2E6, 416/221-5200, Fax: 416/221-5207

International Brotherhood of Locomotive Engineers/Fraternité internationale des ingénieurs de locomotives (BLE) (1863)
Standard Building, Mezzanine, 1370 Ontario St., Cleveland, OH 44113-1702 USA
216/241-2630, Fax: 216/861-0932
International President, Ronald P. McLaughlin
Public Relations Director, Stephen W. FitzGerald
Publications: Locomotive Engineers Journal; Locomotive Engineers Magazine, q.
Canadian Office: Vice-President/Director, Gilles Hallé, #1401, 150 Metcalfe St., Ottawa, ON K2P 1P1, 613/235-1828, Fax: 613/235-1069

International Brotherhood of Painters & Allied Trades (AFL-CIO/CFL)/Fraternité internationale des peintres et métiers connexes (FAT-COI/FCT)
1750 New York Ave. NW, Washington, DC 20006 USA
202/637-0700, Fax: 202/637-0771
President, A.L. (Mike) Monroe
Canadian Office: General Vice-President, 8th District, Armando Colafranceschi, 12 Morgan Ave., Thornhill, ON L3T 1R1, 905/882-6490, Fax: 905/882-9604

International Brotherhood of Teamsters (AFL-CIO/CLC)/Fraternité internationale des teamsters (FAT-COI/CTC)
25 Louisiana Ave. NW, Washington, DC 20001 USA
202/624-6800
General President, Ron Carey

International Federation of Professional & Technical Engineers (AFL-CIO/CLC)/Fédération internationale des ingénieurs et techniciens (FAT-COI/CTC)
#701, 8701 Georgia Ave., Silver Springs, MD 20910 USA
301/565-9016
President, James E. Sommerhauser
Canadian Office: Canadian International Representative Vice-President, Desmond Cupid, 24 Port Royal Trail, Scarborough, ON M1V 2G5

International Longshoremen's Association (AFL-CIO/CLC)/Association internationale des débardeurs (FAT-COI/CTC) (ILA)
#1530, 17 Battery Pl., New York, NY 10004 USA
212/425-1200, Fax: 212/809-6826
President, John Bowers
Publications: ILA News

Canadian Division: Canadian Vice-President, David W. Quinn, 1 Seaview Ave., Halifax, NS B3P 2A6, 902/479-1732

International Longshoremen's & Warehousemen's Union (CLC)/Syndicat international des débardeurs et magasiniers (CTC)
1188 Franklin St., San Francisco, CA 94109 USA
President, David Arian
Canadian Office: President, Gordie Westrand, #020, 1880 Triumph St., Vancouver, BC V5L 1K3, 604/254-8141, Fax: 604/254-8183

International Plate Printers, Die Stampers, & Engravers Union of North America (AFL-CIO/CLC)/Syndicat international des graveurs et matriceurs de l'Amérique du Nord (FAT-COI/CTC)
906 Dennis Ave., Silver Springs, MD 20901 USA
International President, Daniel Bradley
Canadian Contact: Secretary, Glen Bull, #26A, 778 St. Andre Dr., Orleans, ON K1C 4R6, 613/824-8568

International Union of Allied Novelty & Production Workers (AFL-CIO/CLC)/Syndicat international des employés de la production de la nouveauté et autres travailleurs assimilés (FAT-COI/CTC)
25 Rosalyn Rd., Mineola, NY 11501 USA
212/889-1212
President, Julius Isaacson
Canadian Office: Canadian Representative, Frank Johnston, 34 Madison Ave., Toronto, ON M5R 3N6, 416/960-5523, Fax: 416/960-1093

International Union of Bricklayers & Allied Craftsmen (AFL-CIO/CFL)/Union internationale des briqueteurs et métiers connexes (FAT-COI/FCT)
Bowen Bldg., 815 - 15 St. NW, Washington, DC 20005 USA
202/783-3788, Fax: 202/393-0219
President, John T. Joyce

International Union of Electronic, Electrical, Salaried, Machine & Furniture Workers (AFL-CIO)/Syndicat international des travailleurs de l'électricité, salariés, de machines et de meubles (FAT-COI)
1126 - 16 St. NW, Washington, DC 20036 USA
202/296-1200
President, William H. Bywater
Canadian Office: President, Earl Staples, 55 Columbia St. East, Waterloo, ON N2J 4N7, 519/746-8140, Fax: 519/746-5414

International Union of Elevator Constructors (AFL-CIO/CFL)/Union internationale des constructeurs d'ascenseurs (FAT-COI/FCT) (IUEC) (1901)
#310, 5565 Sterrett Pl., Columbia, MD 21044 USA
410/997-9000, Fax: 410/997-0243
General President, John N. Russell
General Sec.-Treas., Richard W. Scariot
Canadian Office: Canadian Vice-President & Director, J. Warner Baxter, 108 Teal Ave., Stoney Creek, ON L8E 3B4, 416/849-6288, Fax: 416/849-7342

International Union of Operating Engineers (AFL-CIO/CFL)/Union internationale des opérateurs de machines lourdes (FAT-COI/FCT)
1125 - 17 St. NW, Washington, DC 20036 USA
202/429-9100
President, Frank Hanley
Publications: The International Operating Engineer
Canadian Office: Canadian Regional Director, J.V. Biddle, #401, 4211 Kingsway, Burnaby, BC V5H 1Z6, 403/438-1616, Fax: 403/439-2459

International Union, United Automobile, Aerospace & Agricultural Implement Workers of America, Local 251 (CLC)/Syndicat international des travailleurs unis de l'automobile, de l'aérospatiale et de l'outillage agricole d'Amérique (CTC)
8000 East Jefferson Ave., Detroit, MI 48214 USA
313/926-5000
President, Owen Bieber
Canadian Office: President, Jim Lee, PO Box 22024, Wallaceburg, ON N8A 5G4, 519/627-1629, Fax: 519/627-2055

International Union, United Plant Guard Workers of America (Ind.)/Syndicat international des gardiens d'usine d'Amérique (ind.) (UPGWA)
25510 Kelly Rd., Roseville, MI 48066 USA
313/772-7250, Fax: 313/772-9644
President, Eugene P. McConville
Publications: The Security Link
Region 12 - Canada: Director/Region 12, Watson E. Cook, #204, 5468 Dundas St. West, Toronto, ON M9B 6E3, 416/236-7523, Fax: 416/234-1564

IWA - Canada (CLC) (1985)
#500, 1285 West Pender St., Vancouver, BC V6E 4B2
604/683-1117, Fax: 604/688-6416
President, G.A. Stoney
Publications: IWA Canada Lumber Worker
Affiliates: British Columbia Federation of Labour

Laborers' International Union of North America (AFL-CIO/CLC)/Union internationale des journaliers d'Amérique (FAT-COI/CTC) (LIUNA) (1903)
905 - 16 St. NW, Washington, DC 20006 USA
202/737-8320, Fax: 202/737-2754
President, Arthur A. Coia
General Sec.-Treas., James J. Norwood
Publications: The Laborer
Affiliates: American Federation of Labour & Congress of Industrial Organizations; Canadian Labour Congress
Canadian Office: Canadian Director & Vice-President, Enrico H. Mancinelli; Sub-Regional Manager, Eastern Canada, Nello Scipioni; Sub-Regional Manager, Central Canada, Joseph S. Mancinelli; Sub-Regional Manager, Western Canada, Victor Morden, #44 Hughson St. South, Hamilton, ON L8N 2A7, 905/522-7177, Fax: 905/522-9310

Major League Baseball Players' Association (Ind.)/Association des joueurs de la Ligue majeure de baseball (ind.)
12 East 49th St., New York, NY 10002 USA
212/826-0808, Fax: 212/752-3649
Executive Director, Donald M. Fehr

Management & Professional Employees Society (Ind.)/Société des employés professionnels et administratifs (ind.) (MAPES)
#523, 409 Granville St., Vancouver, BC V6C 1T2
604/669-3177, Fax: 604/669-5343
Executive Director, Thomas Abbott, CAE
Publications: MAPES Newsletter

Manitoba Association of Health Care Professionals (CFL)/Association des professionnels de la santé du Manitoba (FCT) (MAHCP)
#216, 819 Sargent Ave., Winnipeg, MB R3E 0B9
204/772-0425, Fax: 204/775-6829
President, C. Mark
Executive Director, Ron Wally
Publications: MAHCP Newsletter

Marine Workers' Federation (CLC)/Fédération des travailleurs de construction navale (CTC) (1945)
#200, 3700 Kempt Rd., Halifax, NS B3K 4X8
902/455-7279, Fax: 902/455-4716
President, Gary Marr

Maritime Fishermen's Union (CLC)/Union des pêcheurs des Maritimes (CTC)
1200 Main St., PO Box 1418, Shediac, NB E0A 3G0
506/532-2485, Fax: 506/532-2487
President, Guy Cormier
Sec.-Treas., Léo-Paul Guimond

Metal Polishers, Buffers, Platers & Allied Workers International Union (AFL-CIO/CLC)/Syndicat international des polisseurs de métal, plaqueurs et travailleurs assimilés (FAT-COI/CTC)
5578 Montgomery Rd., Cincinnati, OH 45212 USA
President/Sec.-Treas., Glenn Holt
Canadian Representation: Recording & Financial Sec.-Treas., Maud Doyle; President, Local 19, Bernice Baker, 39 Beachall St., Scarborough, ON M1S 3B3, 416/759-2211, Fax: 416/752-2854

Miramichi Trades & Labour Union (Ind.)/Syndicat des métiers et du travail de la Miramichi (ind.)
PO Box 684, Newcastle, NB E1V 3M5
506/622-1792
President, Greg Sullivan

National Automobile, Aerospace, Transportation & General Workers Union of Canada (CLC)/Syndicat national de l'automobile, de l'aérospatiale, du transport et des autres travailleurs et travailleuses du Canada (CTC) (CAW-Canada) (1985)
Canadian Auto Workers Union
205 Placer Ct., North York, ON M2H 3H9
416/497-4110, Fax: 416/495-6559
National President, Basil "Buzz" Hargrove
National Sec.-Treas., Jim O'Neil
Quebec Director, Claude Ducharme
Publications: Contact; Union, bi-m.

National Federation of Nurses' Unions/Fédération nationale des syndicats d'infirmières et d'infirmiers (1981)
377 Bank St., Ottawa, ON K2P 1Y3
613/233-1018, Fax: 613/233-3892
President, Kathleen Connors
Sec.-Treas., D. Bragg
Publications: Front Lines

National Hockey League Players' Association (Ind.)/Association des joueurs de la Ligue nationale de hockey (ind.) (NHLPA) (1967)
#2300, One Dundas St. West, Toronto, ON M5G 1Z3
416/408-4040, Fax: 416/408-3685
URL: http://www.nhlpa.com
Executive Director, Robert W. Goodenow
President, Mike Gartner
Publications: Goals

National Union of Public & General Employees/Syndicat national des employés généraux et du secteur public (NUPGE) (1976)
#204, 2841 Riverside Dr., Ottawa, ON K1V 8N4
613/526-1663, Fax: 613/526-0477
National President, James Clancy
National Sec.-Treas., Larry Brown
Publications: National News; Economic Indicators, s-m.; Bagdad Café, q.
Affiliates: Public Services International; Canadian Labour Congress
Member Unions

Canadian Almanac & Directory 1997

ALBERTA UNION OF PROVINCIAL EMPLOYEES/SYNDICAT DE LA FONCTION PUBLIQUE DE L'ALBERTA
10451 - 170 St., Edmonton, AB T5P 4S7
403/930-3300, Fax: 403/930-3392
President, Carol Anne Dean
Contact, Public Relations, Don McMann
Publications: Impact

BREWERY, GENERAL & PROFESSIONAL WORKERS UNION
238 Jane St., Toronto, ON M6S 3Z1
416/762-7477, Fax: 416/762-0182
President, Cam Nelson
Business Agent, George Redmond
Publications: Local 304 News

CANADIAN UNION OF BREWERY & GENERAL WORKERS, LOCAL 325/SYNDICAT CANADIEN DES TRAVAILLEURS DE BRASSERIES ET TRAVAILLEURS EN GÉNÉRAL, SECTION LOCALE 325
One Carlingview Dr., Etobicoke, ON M9W 5E5
416/675-2648, Fax: 416/675-6694
President, Greg Greco

HEALTH SCIENCES ASSOCIATION OF BRITISH COLUMBIA/ ASSOCIATION DES SCIENCES DE LA SANTÉ DE LA COLOMBIE-BRITANNIQUE (HSA) (1971)
#600, 4710 Kingsway, Vancouver, BC V5H 4M6
604/299-2707, Fax: 604/299-0306, Toll Free: 1-800-663-2017
Executive Co-Director, Maureen Whelan
Executive Co-Director, Lisa Hansen
Publications: HSA Newsletter
Affiliates: BC Federation of Labour; Canadian Labour Congress; National Union of Public & General Employees

MANITOBA GOVERNMENT EMPLOYEES' UNION/ASSOCIATION DE LA FONCTION PUBLIQUE DU MANITOBA (MGEU)
#601, 275 Broadway, Winnipeg, MB R3C 4M6
204/982-6432, Fax: 204/942-2146, Toll Free: 1-800-262-8891
President, Peter Olfert
Publications: Contact

NEW BRUNSWICK GOVERNMENT EMPLOYEES UNION/SYNDICAT DES EMPLOYÉS DU GOUVERNEMENT DU NOUVEAU-BRUNSWICK (NBGEU)
500 Beaverbrook Ct., Ground Fl., Fredericton, NB E3B 5X4
506/453-9929, Fax: 506/458-9358
President, Alfred Watson
Director, Jerry Dunnett
Publications: NBGEU Bulletin

NEWFOUNDLAND ASSOCIATION OF PUBLIC EMPLOYEES/ ASSOCIATION DE LA FONCTION PUBLIQUE DE TERRE-NEUVE (NAPE)
PO Box 8100, St. John's, NF A1B 3M9
709/754-0700, Fax: 709/754-0726, Toll Free: 1-800-563-4442
President, Dave Curtis
Sec.-Treas., Allan Carter
Public Relations/Communications/Research, Trudi Brake
Publications: The Communicator
Affiliates: Newfoundland Federation of Labour

NOVA SCOTIA GOVERNMENT EMPLOYEES UNION/SYNDICAT DE LA FONCTION PUBLIQUE DE LA NOUVELLE-ÉCOSSE (NSGEU)
100 Eileen Stubbs Ave., Dartmouth, NS B3B 1Y6
902/424-4063, Fax: 902/455-2749
President, Dave Peters
Publications: NSGEU Newsletter

ONTARIO LIQUOR BOARD EMPLOYEES' UNION/SYNDICAT DES EMPLOYÉS DE LA RÉGIE DES ALCOOLS DE L'ONTARIO
5757 Coopers Ave., Mississauga, ON L4Z 1R9
905/712-2912, Fax: 905/712-2916
President, John Coones
Executive Officer, Sharon McTamaney
Publications: Echo

ONTARIO PUBLIC SERVICE EMPLOYEES UNION/SYNDICAT DES EMPLOYÉES ET EMPLOYÉS DE LA FONCTION PUBLIQUE DE L'ONTARIO (OPSEU) (1911)
100 Lesmill Rd., North York, ON M3B 3P8
416/443-8888, Fax: 416/443-9670, Toll Free: 1-800-268-7376
President, Leah Casselman
Publications: OPSEU News Update; Voices, q.
Affiliates: Canadian Labour Council; Ontario Federation of Labour

PRINCE EDWARD ISLAND UNION OF PUBLIC SECTOR EMPLOYEES/ SYNDICAT DE LA FONCTION PUBLIQUE DE L'ÎLE-DU-PRINCE-EDOUARD
PO Box 1116, Charlottetown, PE C1A 7M8
902/892-5335, Fax: 902/892-0978
President, Mike Butler
Publications: Accent; The Advocate, q.

SASKATCHEWAN GOVERNMENT EMPLOYEES' UNION/SYNDICAT DE LA FONCTION PUBLIQUE DE LA SASKATCHEWAN (SGEU)
1440 Broadway Ave., Regina, SK S4P 1E2
306/522-8571, Fax: 306/352-1969
CEO, Pat Gallagher
President, Barry Nowoselsky
Publications: Common Ground

Native Brotherhood of British Columbia (Ind.)/ Fraternité des Indiens de la Colombie-Britannique (ind.)
#200, 1755 East Hastings St., Vancouver, BC V5L 1T1
604/255-3137, Fax: 604/251-7107, Telex: 04-51439
President, Cecil Hill
Publications: Native Voice

New Brunswick Public Employees Association (Ind.)/Association des employés de la Fonction publique du Nouveau-Brunswick (ind.)
238 King St., PO Box 95, Fredericton, NB E3B 4Y2
506/458-8440, Fax: 506/450-8481
President, Ian MacMichael
Publications: Newsline/Bulletin

New Brunswick School Business Employees' Association (Ind.)/Association des employés de l'administration des écoles du Nouveau-Brunswick (ind.)
PO Box 190, Chipman, NB E0E 1C0
506/339-7000, Fax: 506/339-7001
President, Wesley Miller

New Brunswick School Supervisor's Organization (Ind.)/Association des conseillers en pédagogie du Nouveau-Brunswick (ind.) (NPSSO)
c/o School District 15, 1077 St. George Blvd., PO Box 1058, Moncton, NB E2A 4H8
506/547-2777, Fax: 506/547-2783
President, Kathy Baldwin
Publications: NBSSO Newsletter/ACPNB Bulletin de nouvelles

The Newspaper Guild (AFL-CIO/CLC)/La Guilde des journalistes (FAT-COI/CTC) (TNG) (1933)
8611 Second Ave., Silver Spring, MD 20907 USA
301/585-2990, Fax: 301/585-0668
President, Charles Dale
Publications: The Guild Reporter
Affiliates: International Federation of Journalists
Canadian Region: Canadian Director, Mike Bocking, #103, 30 Concourse Gate, Nepean, ON K2E 7V7, 613/727-0990, Fax: 613/723-9236

Nova Scotia Union of Public Employees (Ind.)/ Syndicat des employés du secteur public de la Nouvelle-Écosse (ind.)
6309 Chebucto Rd., Halifax, NS B3L 1K9
902/429-7655, Fax: 902/422-6055

Business Agent, R.A. Stockton
President, Cathie Osborne

Office & Professional Employees International Union (AFL-CIO/CLC)/Union internationale des employés professionnels et de bureau (FAT-COI/CTC)
#606, 815 - 16 St. NW, Washington, DC 20006 USA
President, John Kelly
Canadian Office: Canadian Director & International Vice-President, Michel Lajeunesse, #630, 1265, rue Berri, Montréal, PQ H2L 4C6, 514/288-6511, Fax: 514/288-6540

Ontario Hospital Association/Blue Cross Employees Association (CNFIU)/Association des employés de la Croix-Bleue/Association des hôpitaux de l'Ontario (FCNSI)
150 Ferrand Dr., North York, ON M3C 1H6
416/429-2661, Fax: 416/429-2773
President, Marie Samuel-Andrew

Ontario Professional Fire Fighters Association (Ind.)/Association des pompiers professionnels de l'Ontario (ind.) (OPFFA) (1970)
#7, 871 Equestrian Ct., Oakville, ON L6L 6L7
905/847-1060, Fax: 905/847-9725
Executive Sec.-Treas., Wayne De Mille
Affiliates: Canadian Association of Fire Fighters

Ontario Provincial Police Association (Ind.)/ Association de la Sûreté provinciale de l'Ontario (ind.) (OPPA) (1954)
119 Ferris Lane, Barrie, ON L4M 2Y1
705/728-6161, Fax: 705/721-4867, Toll Free: 1-800-461-4282
Administrator, Jim Drennan
Publications: OPPA Newsletter

Operative Plasterers' & Cement Masons' International Association of the US & Canada (AFL-CIO/CFL)/Association internationale des plâtiers et des finisseurs en ciment des États-Unis et du Canada (FAT-COI/FCT)
1125 - 17 St. NW, Washington, DC 20036 USA
202/393-6569, Fax: 202/393-2514
General President, Dominic A. Martell
Canadian Office: Vice-President, Canadian Consultant, Director of Jurisdiction, Michael J. Gannon, 1413 Hayes St., Orleans, ON K1E 3M8, 613/824-5973, Fax: 613/837-7156

Police Association of Nova Scotia (Ind.)/ Association des policiers de la Nouvelle-Écosse (ind.) (PANS)
PO Box 1557, RPO Central, Halifax, NS B3J 2Y3
902/468-7555, Fax: 902/468-2202
Executive Director, Joe Ross
Publications: Police Review Magazine

Police Brotherhood of the Royal Newfoundland Constabulary Association (Ind.)/Fraternité des policiers de la Gendarmerie royale de Terre-Neuve (ind.)
PO Box 7444, Stn C, St. John's, NF A1E 3Y4
709/739-5946, Fax: 709/739-6276
President, J. Gullage

Professional Association of Foreign Service Officers (Ind.)/L'Association professionnelle des agents du Service extérieur (ind.) (PAFSO)
#600, 45 Rideau St., Ottawa, ON K1N 5W8
613/241-1391, Fax: 613/241-5911
Executive Director, Peter Cenne
Director of Administration, Debra Hulley
President, Colin Robertson
Publications: Bout de papier

Professional Association of Internes & Residents of Alberta (Ind.)/Association professionnelle des internes et résidents de l'Alberta (ind.) (PAIRA) (1975)
#460, 8409 - 112 St., Edmonton, AB T6G 1K6
403/432-1749, Fax: 403/432-1778, Email: paira@planet.eon.net
Executive Director, Connie Becker
Publications: PAIRAphrase

Professional Association of Internes & Residents of Newfoundland (Ind.)/Association professionnelle des internes et résidents de Terre-Neuve (ind.) (PAIRN)
c/o Faculty of Medicine, Student Affairs, Memorial University, 300 Prince Philip Dr., St. John's, NF A1B 3V6
709/737-7118, Fax: 709/737-6968
President, Michael Green, M.D.

Professional Association of Internes & Residents of Ontario (Ind.)/Association professionnelle des internes et résidents de l'Ontario (ind.)
505 University Ave., Toronto, ON M5G 1X4
416/979-1182
President, Steven Tishler

Professional Association of Internes & Residents of Saskatchewan (Ind.)/Association professionnelle des internes et résidents de la Saskatchewan (ind.) (PAIRS) (1976)
Royal University Hospital, Box 23, 103 Hospital Dr., Saskatoon, SK S7N 0W8
306/655-2134, Email: pairs@link.ca
President, Dr. Steve Kraus
Publications: Pairscript

Professional Association of Residents & Internes of British Columbia (Ind.)/Association professionnelle des résidents et internes de la Colombie-Britannique (ind.)
#305, 828 - 8 Ave. West, Vancouver, BC V5Z 1E2
604/876-7636, Fax: 604/876-7690
President, Dr. Eric Webber
Publications: PARI Scope

Professional Association of Residents & Internes of Manitoba (Ind.)/Association professionnelle des résidents et internes du Manitoba (ind.) (PARIM) (1976)
PARI Manitoba
#AD107, 720 McDermot Ave., Winnipeg, MB R3E 0T3
204/787-3673, Fax: 204/787-2692
President, Dr. Kurt Skakum
Vice-President, Dr. Phil Neilsen
Publications: PARIM News

Professional Association of Residents & Interns of the Maritime Provinces (Ind.)/Association professionnelle des résidents et internes des provinces maritimes (ind.)
Room 564, Bethune Building, Victoria General Hospital, 1278 Tower Rd., Halifax, NS B3H 2Y9
902/428-4091
President, E. Mackay

Professional Employees Association (Ind.)/Association des employés professionnels (ind.) (1974)
#201, 1001 Wharf St., Victoria, BC V8W 1T6
250/385-8791, Fax: 250/385-6629
Executive Director, Alan MacLeod
Publications: The Professional
Vancouver Office: Senior Staff Officer, Doug Hensby, #390, 6450 Roberts St., Burnaby, BC V5G 4E1, 604/299-6677, Fax: 604/299-2717

Professional Institute of The Public Service of Canada/Institut professionnel de la Fonction publique du Canada (PIPSC) (1920)
53 Auriga Dr., Nepean, ON K2E 8C3
613/228-6310, Fax: 613/228-9048, Toll Free: 1-800-267-0446
President, Steve Hindle
Executive Secretary, Lorraine Neville
Publications: Communications; Dialogue with Parliament/Dialogue parlementaire, a.
Regional Offices
Atlantic Regional Office - Fredericton:Regional Representative, Yvette G. Michaud; #211, 1133 Regent St., Fredericton, NB E3B 3Z2, 506/459-3471, Fax: 506/450-3271, Toll Free: 1-800-561-0027
Atlantic Regional Office - Halifax: Regional Representative, Wayne Rogers, #1081, 5161 George St., Halifax, NS B3J 1M7, 902/420-1519, Fax: 902/422-8516, Toll Free: 1-800-565-0727
BC/Yukon/Inuvik Regional Office: Regional Representative, Dave Riffel; Labour Relations Officer, Evan Heidinger, #1385, 200 Granville St., Vancouver, BC V6C 1S4, 604/688-8238, Fax: 604/688-8290, Toll Free: 1-800-663-0485
Edmonton Regional Office: Regional Representative, Joe Ahren; Labour Relations Officer, Ed Gilles, #955, 10020 - 101A Ave., Edmonton, AB T5J 3G2, 403/428-1347, Fax: 403/426-5962, Toll Free: 1-800-661-3939
Ontario Regional Office: Regional Representative, Dan Rafferty; Labour Relations Officer, Marija Dolenc, #253, 40 Orchard View Blvd., Toronto, ON M4R 1B9, 416/487-1114, Fax: 416/487-7268, Toll Free: 1-800-668-3943
Québec Regional Office: Représentant régional, Pierrette Gosselin; Agente des relations du travail, Suzelle Brosseau, #1920, 1200, av McGill College, Montréal, PQ H3B 4G7, 514/878-1159, Téléc: 514/878-4650, Ligne sans frais: 1-800-363-0622
Winnipeg Regional Office: Regional Representative, George Smith; Office Administrator, D'Arcy Brown, #570, 125 Garry St., Winnipeg, MB R3C 3P2, 204/942-1304, Fax: 204/942-4348, Toll Free: 1-800-665-0094

Provincial Federation of Ontario Firefighters (PFOFF)
#310, 2630 Skymark Ave., Mississauga, ON L4W 5A3
905/602-9501, Fax: 905/602-9504
President, Bruce Carpenter
Vice-President, Jim Simmons
Sec.-Treas., Larry Staples
Affiliates: International Association of Fire Fighters; Ontario Federation of Labour; Canadian Labour Congress

Public Service Alliance of Canada (CLC)/Alliance de la Fonction publique du Canada (CTC) (PSAC)
233 Gilmour St., Ottawa, ON K2P 0P1
613/560-4200, Fax: 613/563-3492
URL: http://www.psac.com/
National President, Daryl T. Bean
First Executive Vice-President, Nycole Turmel
Second Executive Vice-President, Susan Giampietri
Third Executive Vice-President, John Baglow
Vice-présidente exécutive régionale/Québec, Joane Hurens
Publications: Alliance; PSAC Union Update/AFPC Parlons Syndicat, w.
Affiliates: Canadian Labour Congress
Components of PSAC
Agriculture Union: National President, Larry Leng, #1000, 233 Gilmour St., Ottawa, ON K2P 0P2, 613/560-4306
National Component/Elément national: National President, Doug Chalk, #301, 233 Gilmour St., Ottawa, ON K2P 0P2, 613/560-4364

Canada Employment & Immigration Union/Syndicat de l'emploi et de l'immigration du Canada: National President, Cres Pascucci, #1004, 233 Gilmour St., Ottawa, ON K2P 0P2, 613/236-9634, Fax: 613/236-7871
Customs Excise Union/Douanes Accise: National President, Mansel Legacy, 1741 Woodward Dr., Ottawa, ON K2C 0P9, 613/723-8008
Environment Component/Elément de l'environnement: National President, Joe Pacholik, 2181 Thurston Dr., Ottawa, ON K1G 4Z2, 613/736-5533
National Health & Welfare Union/Syndicat de la Santé nationale et du Bien-être social: National President, Al MacIntyre, #1202, 233 Gilmour St., Ottawa, ON K2P 0P2, 613/237-2732
SECO Component/Elément SECO: National President, John Carter, #1001, 233 Gilmour St., Ottawa, ON K2P 0P2, 613/560-4334
Supply & Services Union/Syndicat des approvisionnements et services: National President, Valerie Denesiuk; Administrative Officer, Laura J. Griffin, #400, 233 Gilmour St., Ottawa, ON K2P 0P2, 613/560-4282, Fax: 613/569-2669
Union of Canadian Transport Employees/Union canadienne des employés des transports: National President, Robert Desfonds, #302, 275 Bank St., Ottawa, ON K2P 2L6, 613/238-4003
Union of Energy, Mines & Resources Employees/Syndicat des employés de l'Energie, Mines et Ressources: National President, Bernice Miller, #803, 233 Gilmour St., Ottawa, ON K2P 0P1, 613/560-4378
Union of National Defence Employees/Union des employés de la Défense nationale: National President, Paul Millette, 330 McLeod St., Ottawa, ON K2P 2C5, 613/594-4505
Union of Northern Workers/Syndicat des travailleurs du Nord: President, Darm Crook, #200, 5112 - 52 St., Yellowknife, NT X1A 1T6, 403/873-5668, Fax: 403/920-4448
Union of Postal Communications Employees/Syndicat des employés des postes et des communications: National President, Stephen White, #701, 233 Gilmour St., Ottawa, ON K2P 0P2, 613/560-4342
Union of Public Works Employees/Syndicat des employés des travaux publics: National President, John Gordon, #705, 233 Gilmour St., Ottawa, ON K2P 0P2, 613/560-4393
Union of Solicitor General Employees/Syndicat des employés du Solliciteur général: National President, Lynn Ray, #603, 233 Gilmour St., Ottawa, ON K2P 0P2, 613/232-4821
Union of Taxation Employees/Syndicat des employé(e)s de l'impôt: National President, David Flinn, #602, 233 Gilmour St., Ottawa, ON K2P 0P2, 613/235-6704
Union of Veterans' Affairs Employees/Syndicat des employé(e)s des Affaires des anciens combattants: National President, Sandra L. Messer, #703, 233 Gilmour St., Ottawa, ON K2P 0P2, 613/560-5460
Yukon Employees Union/Syndicat des employés du Yukon: National President, David Hobbis, 208 Strickland St., Whitehorse, YT Y1A 2J8, 403/667-2332, Fax: 403/667-6521

Pulp, Paper & Woodworkers of Canada (CCU) (PPWC) (1963)
#201, 1184 - 6 Ave. West, Vancouver, BC V6H 1A4
604/731-1909, Fax: 604/731-6448
President, Stan J. Shewaga
Publications: The Leaflet
Affiliates: Confederation of Canadian Unions

Research Council Employees' Association (Ind.)/Association des employés du Conseil de recherches (ind.) (RCEA) (1967)
PO Box 8256, Ottawa, ON K1G 3H7
613/746-9341, Fax: 613/745-7868

President, Wayne J. Findlay
Publications: RCEA Newsletter/AECR Bulletin

Retail, Wholesale & Department Store Union (AFL-CIO/CLC)/Union des employés de gros, de détail et de magasins à rayons (FAT-COI/CTC) (1937)
30 East 29 St., New York, NY 10016 USA
212/684-5300, Fax: 212/779-2809
President, Lenore Miller
Publications: The Record

Retail Wholesale Union (CLC)/Syndicat des employés de gros et de détail (CTC)
4371 Fraser St., Vancouver, BC V5V 4G4
604/879-2996, Fax: 604/879-2456
President, Darrell Craig
Publications: The Target

Saskatchewan Joint Board, Retail, Wholesale & Department Store Union (CLC)/Conseil mixte du Syndicat des employés de gros, de détail et de magasins à rayons de la Saskatchewan (CTC)
1233 Winnipeg St., Regina, SK S4R 1K1
306/569-9311, Fax: 306/569-9521
President, Dennis Hicks

Seafarers' International Union of Canada (AFL-CIO/CLC)/Syndicat international des marins canadiens (FAT-COI/CTC)
1333, rue Saint-Jacques, Montréal, PQ H3C 4K2
514/931-7859, Fax: 514/931-3667
President, Roman Gralewicz
Publications: Canadian Sailor/Le Marin canadien
Affiliates: Seafarers' International Union of North America (AFL-CIO); International Transport Workers' Federation

Service Employees International Union (AFL-CIO/CLC)/Union internationale des employés des services (FAT-COI/CTC)
1313 L St. NW, Washington, DC 20005 USA
International President, John J. Sweeney
Canadian Office: Vice-President in Canada, S.E. (Ted) Roscoe; Vice-President in Canada, Louis Duvall, 1 Credit Union Dr., Toronto, ON M4A 2S6, 416/752-4073, Fax: 416/752-1966

Sheet Metal Workers' International Association (AFL-CIO/CFL)/Association internationale des travailleurs du métal en feuilles (FAT-COI/FCT)
1750 New York Ave. NW, Washington, DC 20006-5386 USA
202/662-0842, Fax: 202/662-0894
General President, Arthur R. Moore
Canadian Office: Director of Canadian Affairs, Robert Belleville, #204, 2742 Saint Joseph Blvd., Orleans, ON K1C 1G4, 613/834-1816, Fax: 613/834-0501

CANADIAN COUNCIL OF SHEET METAL WORKERS
#4, 724 Bath Rd., Kingston, ON K7M 4Y2
613/384-2269, Fax: 613/384-7682
President, Leo Lavalle

Shipyard General Workers' Federation of British Columbia (CLC)/Fédération des ouvriers des chantiers navals de la Colombie-Britannique (CTC)
#130, 111 Victoria Dr., Vancouver, BC V5L 4C4
604/254-8204, Fax: 604/254-7447
President, George MacPherson
General Secretary, Joe Hrgovic
Publications: Ship & Shop
Affiliates: Machinists, Fitters & Helpers Industrial Union #3, Marine Workers & Boilerworkers' Industrial Union #1, Shipwrights, Joiners & Caulkers' Industrial Union #9

Société des auteurs, recherchistes, documentalistes et compositeurs (Ind.)/Society of Writers, Researchers & Composers (Ind.) (SARDEC) (1949)
1229, rue Panet, Montréal, PQ H2L 2Y6
514/526-9196, Téléc: 514/526-4124
Directeur général, Yves Légaré
Présidente, Louise Pelletier
Publications: Info-SARDEC

Society of Ontario Hydro Professional & Administrative Employees (Ind.)/Société des employés professionnels et administratifs de l'Hydro-Ontario (ind.) (1944)
#630, 525 University Ave., Toronto, ON M5G 2L3
416/979-2709, Fax: 416/979-5794
President, Chris Cragg
Publications: Society News

Syndicat des agents de conservation de la faune du Québec (ind.)/Québec Wildlife Conservation Employees' Union (Ind.) (SACFQ) (1982)
6953, boul St-Michel, Montréal, PQ H2A 2Z3
514/722-0492, Téléc: 514/722-4569
Président, Paul Legault
Publications: Faune-éthique

Syndicat des agents de maîtrise de Québec-Téléphone (ind.)/Québec-Telephone Professional Employees Union (Ind.) (SAQT) (1980)
216, rue de la Cathédrale, CP 126, Rimouski, PQ G5L 7B7
418/722-6144
Présidente, Madeleine B. Hudon
Secrétaire, Lynda Fortin
Publications: Bulletin d'information

Syndicat des agents de la paix en services correctionnels du Québec (ind.)/Union of Prison Guards of Québec (Ind.) (1982)
4906, boul Gouin est, Montréal, PQ H1G 1A4
514/528-7774, Téléc: 514/328-0889, Ligne sans frais: 1-800-361-3559
Président provincial, Escola Jorge
Secrétaire général, Roberge Gaétan
Secrétaire administrative, Huguette Desbiens-Lafontaine
Publications: L'Horizon

Syndicat canadien des employés de bureau (FCT)/Canadian Office Employees Union (CFL) (1977)
#203, 5584, ch Côte de Liesse, Mount Royal, PQ H4P 1A9
905/737-6717, Téléc: 905/855-4149
Président, Wilfred Harrigan
Publications: Bulletin

Syndicat des constables spéciaux du gouvernement du Québec (ind.)/Union of Special Constables for the Government of Québec (Ind.)
#201, 650, rue Graham Bell, Ste-Foy, PQ G1N 4H5
418/527-2512, Téléc: 418/527-2513, Ligne sans frais: 1-800-665-7880
Président, Gilles Tremblay
Publications: Assemblée nationale du Québec

Syndicat construction Côte-Nord (ind.)/North Shore Construction Union Inc. (Ind.) (SCCN) (1975)
1045, av Boulle, CP 760, Saint-Hyacinthe, PQ J2S 7P5
514/773-8833, Téléc: 514/773-2232
Président, Marcel Gendron

Syndicat des employé(e)s de magasins et de bureau de la Société des alcools du Québec (ind.)/Québec Liquor Board Store & Office Employees Union (Ind.)
1065, rue St-Denis, Montréal, PQ H2X 3J3
514/849-7754, Téléc: 514/849-7914
Président, Ronald Asselin
Publications: Le Pionnier

Syndicat des employés de production du Québec et de l'Acadie (ind.) (SEPQA)
1250, rue de la Visitation, Montréal, PQ H2L 3B4
514/527-9869, Téléc: 514/527-6941
Présidente, Lillian Campbell

Syndicat de la fonction publique du Québec inc. (ind.)/Québec Government Employees' Union (Ind.) (SFPQ) (1962)
5100, boul des Gradins, Québec, PQ G2J 1N4
418/623-2424, Téléc: 418/623-6109
Présidente, Danielle-Maude Gosselin
Publications: Le Journal SFPQ

Syndicat général du cinéma et de la télévision - Section Office national du film (ind.) (SGCT) (1968)
#5-6A, 2360, ch Lucerne, Mont-Royal, PQ H3R 2J8
514/344-9399, Téléc: 514/283-9509
Présidente, Camille Laperrière

Syndicat du personnel technique et professionel de la Société des alcools du Québec (ind.)/Québec Liquor Board's Union of Technical & Professional Employees (Ind.)
905, rue de Lorimier, Montréal, PQ H2K 3V9
514/873-5878
Président, Jacques Paquette
Publications: Bulletin-Communiqué

Syndicat des physiothérapeutes et des thérapeutes en réadaptation physique du Québec (SPTRPQ) (1971)
#850, 1001, rue Sherbrooke est, Montréal, PQ H2L 1L3
514/526-3719, Téléc: 514/521-0086
Présidente, Marie Hélène Boudreau
Publications: Vie-SPTRPQ

Syndicat des pompiers du Québec (CTC)/Québec Union of Firefighters (CLC) (SPQ) (1989)
#430, 110, boul Crémazie ouest, Montréal, PQ H2P 1B9
514/383-4698, Téléc: 514/383-6782
Président, Gilles Raymond
Publications: Pompier 90

Syndicat des professeurs de l'État du Québec (ind.)/Union of Professors for the Government of Québec (Ind.) (SPEQ) (1965)
#513, 801, rue Sherbrooke est, Montréal, PQ H2L 1K7
514/525-7979, Téléc: 514/525-4655
Président, Luc Perron
Publications: L'Autre Dimension

Syndicat professionnel des diététistes du Québec (ind.)/Québec Professional Union of Dieticians (Ind.) (SPDQ)
#2, 6321, rue Marquette, Montréal, PQ H2G 2Y3
514/274-5353, Téléc: 514/274-6114
Présidente, Claudette Péloquin
Publications: Informel

Syndicat professionnel des ingénieurs d'Hydro-Québec (ind.)/Hydro-Québec Professional Engineers Union (Ind.) (SPIHQ) (1964)
#200, 600, rue Sherbrooke est, Montréal, PQ H2L 1K1
514/845-4239, Téléc: 514/845-0082, Ligne sans frais: 1-800-567-1260, Courrier électronique: spihq@mtl.net
Président, Louis Champagne

Adjointe administrative, Michèle Côté
Publications: Echo

Syndicat professionnel des médecins du gouvernement du Québec (ind.)/Professional Union of Government of Québec Physicians (Ind.)
3691, boul Neilson, Ste-Foy, PQ G1W 1T3
418/656-1910; 682-5150
Président, Dr. Roland Leblanc

Syndicat des professionnelles et professionnels du gouvernement du Québec (ind.)/Union of Professional Employees of the Québec Government (Ind.) (SPGA) (1966)
7, rue Vallière, Québec, PQ G1K 6S9
418/692-0022, Téléc: 418/692-1338, Ligne sans frais: 1-800-463-5079
Président, Robert Caron
Publications: Info-express

Syndicat des techniciens du réseau français de Radio-Canada (ind.)/CBC French Network Technicians' Union (Ind.)
1250, rue de la Visitation, Montréal, PQ H2L 3B4
514/524-1109, Téléc: 514/524-6023
Président national, Jean-Paul Rouillard

Syndicat des technologues en radiologie du Québec (ind.)/Québec Professional Union of Medical Radiological Technicians (STRQ) (1965)
#850, 1001, rue Sherbrooke est, Montréal, PQ H2L 1L3
514/521-3999, Téléc: 514/521-0086
Président, Jacques Paradis

Syndicat des travailleurs et travailleuses de produits manufacturés et de services (ind.)/Manufactured Goods & Services Employees Union (Ind.) (STTPM)
#210, 1010, rue Sherbrooke ouest, Montréal, PQ H3A 2R7
514/843-8041, Téléc: 514/844-9330
Président, Pierre Collin

Syndicat des travailleurs et travailleuses unis du Québec (ind.)/United Workers Union of Québec (Ind.)
875, rue Coudret, Beauport, PQ G1C 6A2
418/624-4012
Président, Paul Ringuette

Teaching Support Staff Union
Simon Fraser University, AQ 5129/30, Burnaby, BC V5A 1S6
604/291-4735, Fax: 604/291-5369, Email: tssu@sfu.ca
President, Tonio Sadik
Publications: TSSU Newsletter

Teamsters Canada (CLC) (CCT) (1976)
#804, 2540, boul Daniel Johnson, Laval, PQ H7T 2S3
514/682-5521, Téléc: 514/681-2244
Directeur, Louis Lacroix
Directeur, Affaires gouvernmentales et relations publiques, François Laporte
Organisation(s) affiliée(s): International Brotherhood of Teamsters
Central Region: 1194 Matheson Blvd., Mississauga, ON L4W 1Y2, 905/629-4144
Eastern Region: 19 Alma Cres., Halifax, NS B3N 2C4, 902/445-5301
Western Region: 899 West 8 Ave., Vancouver, BC V5Z 1E3, 604/875-9321

Telecommunications Employees Association of Manitoba (Ind.)/Association des employés en télécommunications du Manitoba (ind.) (TEAM)
#216, 666 St. James St., Winnipeg, MB R3G 3J6
204/784-2370

President, Arlene Verbrugghe
Business Manager, Bill Hales

Telecommunications Workers' Union (CLC)/Syndicat des travailleurs en télécommunications (CTC) (TWU) (1980)
5261 Lane St., Burnaby, BC V5H 4A6
604/437-8601, Fax: 604/435-7760, Info Line: 604/435-2224
President, Rod Hiebert
Sec.-Treas., Carol Nagy
Director of Communications, Myron Johnson
Publications: Transmitter
Affiliates: BC Federation of Labour; Post, Telegraph & Telecommunications International

Textile Processors, Service Trades, Health Care, Professional & Technical Employees International Union (Ind.)/Syndicat international des employés professionnels et techniques des soins de la santé, des métiers, des services, textiles (ind.)
#905, 360 North Michigan Ave., Chicago, IL 60601 USA
General President, Frank A. Scalish
Canadian Office: International Vice-President, Thomas W. Corrigan, 34 Madison Ave., Toronto, ON M5R 3N6, 416/960-3359, Fax: 416/960-1093

Transportation Communications International Union (AFL-CIO/CLC)/Syndicat international du transports communication (FAT-COI/CTC) (1899)
3 Research Pl., Rockville, MD 20850 USA
301/948-4910, Fax: 301/330-7661
International President, Robert A.. Scardelletti
Canadian Office: National President, Jack Boyce, #2285D, 11 St. Laurent Blvd., Ottawa, ON K1G 4Z7, 613/731-6315, Fax: 613/731-0233

Travailleurs unis du pétrole du Canada (CSC)/United Oil Workers of Canada (CCU)
11975, rue Victoria, CP 47, Succ. PAT, Pointe-aux-Trembles, PQ H1B 2R2
514/645-8111, Téléc: 514/645-1332
Président, Brian Rius

Union des artistes (FIA)/Artists' Union (UDA) (1937)
1290, rue St-Denis, 6e étage, Montréal, PQ H2X 3J7
514/288-6682, Téléc: 514/288-7150
Directeur général, Serge Demers
Président, Serge Turgeon
Publications: Union express

Union canadienne des travailleurs en communication (ind.)/Canadian Union of Communication Workers (Ind.)
3983, rue Wellington, Verdun, PQ H4G 1V6
514/768-6667, Téléc: 514/768-6121
Président, Giuseppe Giarrusso
Publications: Le Transmetteur/The Transmitter

Union des carreleurs et métiers connexes, section locale 1 (CTC)/Union of Tile Workers & Allied Trades, Local 1 (CLC)
#1401, 3637, boul Crémazie est, Montréal, PQ H1Z 2J9
514/727-2950, Téléc: 514/727-8331
Gérant d'affaires, Claude Labbé
Président, Mario Basilico

Union nationale des poseurs de systèmes intérieurs, de revêtements souples et travailleurs d'usine, section locale 2366 (CTC)/National Union of Interior Systems, Resilient Floor Layers, & Plant Workers, Local 2366 (CLC)
#202, 3730, boul Crémazie est, Montréal, PQ H2A 1B4
514/723-2366, Téléc: 514/723-4130
Directeur, Leo Annett

Union of Needletrades, Industrial & Textile Employees/Syndicat du vêtement, textile et autres industries (UNITE) (1995)
1710 Broadway, New York, NY 10019 USA
212/265-7000, Fax: 212/265-3415
International President, Jay Mazur
Canadian Manager/Vice-President, International, Gérald Roy
Canadian Office: Canadian Director (ACTWU), John Alleruzzo, 15 Gervais Dr., North York, ON M3C 1Y8, 416/441-1806, Téléc: 416/441-9680

Union des opérateurs de machinerie lourde, section locale 791 (CTC)
8350, boul St-Michel, Montréal, PQ H1Z 4G3
514/374-0300, Téléc: 514/374-9725
Président, Michel Paquet

Union of Rail Canada Traffic Controllers (CCU)/Syndicat des contrôleurs de circulation ferroviaire du Canada (CSC) (RCTC)
1002 Pembina Hwy., Winnipeg, MB R3T 1Z5
204/477-0260, Fax: 204/477-0998
National President/Secretary, Darrell H. Arnold
Publications: RCTC Newsletter

United Association of Journeymen & Apprentices of the Plumbing & Pipe Fitting Industry of the U.S. & Canada (AFL-CIO/CFL)/Association unie des compagnons et apprentis de l'industrie de la plomberie et de la tuyauterie des Etats-Unis et du Canada (FAT/COI/FCT)
901 Massachusetts Ave. NW, PO Box 37800, Washington, DC 20013 USA
202/628-5823, Fax: 202/628-5024
President, Marvin J. Boede
General Sec.-Treas., Marion A. Lee
Canadian Office: Vice-President & Canadian Director, George Meservier, #316, 1959 - 152 St., Surrey, BC V4A 9E3, 604/531-0516, Fax: 604/531-0547

United Brotherhood of Carpenters & Joiners of America (AFL-CIO/CLC)/Fraternité unie des charpentiers et menuisiers d'Amérique (FAT-COI/CTC)
101 Constitution Ave. NW, Washington, DC 20001 USA
202/546-6206, Fax: 202/543-5724
General President, Sigurd Lucassen
Canadian Office: Research Director, Derrick Manson, #807, 5799 Yonge St., North York, ON M2M 3V3, 416/225-8885, Fax: 416/225-5390

United Fishermen & Allied Workers' Union (CLC)/Syndicat des pêcheurs et travailleurs assimilés (CTC) (1945)
#160, 111 Victoria Dr., Vancouver, BC V5L 4C4
604/255-1336, Fax: 604/255-3162
President, John Radosevic
Publications: The Fisherman

United Food & Commercial Workers' International Union (AFL-CIO/CLC)/Union internationale des travailleurs et travailleuses unis de l'alimentation et du commerce (FAT-COI/CTC)
1775 K St. NW, Washington, DC 20006 USA
202/223-3111, Fax: 202/466-1562
International President, Douglas H. Dority
Canadian Region: Canadian Director, Tom Kukovica, #300, 61 International Blvd., Etobicoke, ON M9W 6K4, 416/675-1104, Fax: 416/675-6919

United Garment Workers of America (AFL-CIO/CLC)/Travailleurs unis du vêtement d'Amérique (FAT-COI/CTC)
4207 Lebanon Rd., Hermitage, TN 37076 USA
615/889-9221, Fax: 615/885-3102

Canadian Almanac & Directory 1997

President, David Johnson
Canadian Office: Representative, Eastern Canada, Nancy Depinto, 416/368-9841; Representative, Western Canada, Frank Dicesare, #103, 111 West Broadway, Vancouver, BC V5J 1P4, 604/875-0070, Fax: 604/875-0070

United Mine Workers of America (CLC)/Mineurs unis d'Amérique (CTC)
900 - 15 St. NW, Washington, DC 20005 USA
202/842-7200
President, Richard Trumka
Canadian Office: Executive Board Member, District No. 18 (AB, SK & BC), Robin Campbell; Executive Board Member, District No. 26 (NS & NB), Don MacRae, 4718 - 1 St. SW, Calgary, AB T2G 0A2, 403/287-2155, Fax: 403/243-8006

United Paperworkers International Union (AFL-CIO/CLC)/Syndicat international des travailleurs unis du papier (FAT-COI/CTC)
3340 Perimeter Hill Dr., PO Box 1475, Nashville, TN 37211 USA
615/834-8590, Fax: 615/834-7741
President, Wayne Glenn
Canadian Office: International Representative, Gary Talarico, 807/468-1898, 227 Otto St., Thunder Bay, ON P7A 2T4, 807/344-0844, Fax: 807/345-0375

United Rubber, Cork, Linoleum & Plastic Workers of America (AFL-CIO/CLC)/Union des ouvriers unis du caoutchouc, liège, linoléum et plastique d'Amérique (FAT-COI/CTC)
570 White Pond Dr., Akron, OH 44320-1156 USA
216/869-0320, Fax: 216/869-5627
President, Kenneth L. Coss
Canadian Office: Canadian Director, Reginald Duguay, #202, 61 International Blvd., Rexdale, ON M9W 6K4, 416/674-2011, Fax: 416/674-6736

United Steelworkers of America (AFL-CIO/CLC)/Métallurgistes unis d'Amérique (FAT-COI/CTC)
5 Gateway Center, Pittsburgh, PA 15222 USA
President, George Becker
Canadian Office: National Director in Canada, Lawrence McBrearty, 234 Eglinton Ave. East, 7th Fl., Toronto, ON M4P 1K7, 416/487-1571, Fax: 416/482-5548
Retail Wholesale Canada/Canadian Service Sector Division: Canadian Director/Vice-President, Thomas E. Collins, Bldg. 11, #200, 5045 Orbitor Dr., Mississauga, ON L4W 4Y4, 905/624-8800, Fax: 905/624-2314

United Textile Workers of America (AFL-CIO/CLC)/Ouvriers unis des textiles d'Amérique (FAT-COI/CTC)
#200, 2 Echelon Plaza, Laurel Rd., Voorhees, NJ 08043 USA
609/772-9699, Fax: 609/772-6177
International President, Ron Myslowka
Canadian Office: President & Regional Director, Stanley Condie, #6, 4377, rue Notre Dame ouest, Montréal, PQ H4C 1R9, 514/935-5213, Fax: 514/936-5214

United Transportation Union - Canada (AFL-CIO/CLC)/Travailleurs unis des transports - Canada (FAT-CIO/CTC) (UTU)
#750, 1595 Telesat Ct., Gloucester, ON K1B 5R3
613/747-7979, Fax: 613/747-2815
National President, Larry H. Olson
Publications: UTU News Canada

CANADIAN FOUNDATIONS

Abe & Sophie Bronfman Foundation, 4333, av Westmount, Montréal PQ H3Y 1W2 – Chairperson, Mildred Lande, CM

Abe Stern Family Foundation, #1001, 9310, boul St-Laurent, Montréal PQ H2N 1N4 – President, Abraham Stern

Abraham & Malka Green Charitable Foundation, c/o Greenwin Developments, #1600, 20 Eglinton Ave. West, Toronto ON M4R 2H1 – President, Abraham J. Green

A.D. Penner Family Foundation, PO Box 909, Steinbach MB R0A 2A0 – President, A.D. Penner

Aga Khan Foundation Canada, Constitution Square, #1820, 350 Albert St., Ottawa ON K1R 1A4 – 613/237-2532; Fax: 613/567-2532 – CEO, Nazeer Aziz Ladhani

The Albert & Nancy Friedberg Foundation, 347 Bay St., 2nd Fl., Toronto ON M5H 2R7 – President, Albert D. Friedberg

Albert & Temmy Latner Family Foundation, 69 Old Forest Hill Rd., Toronto ON M5P 2R3 – President, Albert J. Latner

Alberta Orange Foundation for Children, RR#3, Red Deer AB T4N 5E3 – 403/340-0077 – Secretary, L. Tiihonen

Alexandra Marine & General Hospital Foundation, 120 Napier St., Goderich ON N7A 1W5 – 519/524-8323; Fax: 519/524-5579 – Administrator, Ken Engelstad

The Allan & Susan Seidenfeld Charitable Foundation, 227 Bridgeland Ave., Toronto ON M6A 1Y7 – Director, Dr. Allan Seidenfeld

Allard Foundation Ltd., #210, 5324 Calgary Trail, Edmonton AB T6H 4J8 – Vice-President, Shirley C. Allard

Allen & Milli Gould Family Foundation, 310 Main St. West, Hamilton ON L8P 1J8 – 905/527-1531; Fax: 905/527-3624 – President, Allen H. Gould

Allstate Foundation of Canada, 10 Allstate Pkwy., Markham ON L3R 5P8 – 905/477-6900; Fax: 905/475-4488 – Executive Vice-President, Eric Pickering

Alva Foundation, 199 Albertus Ave., Toronto ON M4R 1J6 – ; Fax: 416/481-3014 – President, John P. Fisher

The Alvin & Mona Libin Foundation, Bow Valley Square III, #3200, 255 - 5 Ave. SW, Calgary AB T2P 3G6 – President, Mona Libin

D'Ancona Charitable Trust, 122 Barse St., Toronto ON M5M 4L4 – Trustee, David D'Ancona

Anglican Foundation of Canada, Anglican Church House, 600 Jarvis St., Toronto ON M4Y 2J6 – 416/924-9192; Fax: 416/968-7983 – Secretary, Rev. Canon A.G. Baker

Animal Welfare Foundation of Canada, 1205 - 7th Ave. East, Vancouver BC V5T 1R1 – 604/879-7011; Fax: 604/879-7099 – Sec.-Treas., Michael H. Weeks

Anna & Edward C. Churchill Foundation, c/o National Trust Co., 168 Wellington St., Kingston ON K7L 3E4 – 613/544-3033; Fax: 613/544-6060 – Sec.-Treas., Brenda Pearce

Anvil Foundation Inc., 273 Germain St., Saint John NB E2L 2G8 – Contact, Judith Meinert

The Arcangelo Rea Family Foundation, #5, 320 Ferndale Ave., London ON N6C 5P7 – Director, Juliann Good

Arthur & Margaret Weisz Family Foundation, c/o Weisz & Associates, #200, 242 Main St. East, Hamilton ON L8N 1H5 – President, Thomas J. Weisz

Atkinson Charitable Foundation, One Yonge St., 5th Fl., Toronto ON M5E 1E5 – 416/368-5152; Fax: 416/865-3619 – President, Catherine Atkinson-Murray

Audrey S. Hellyer Charitable Foundation, #50, 1262 Don Mills Rd., North York ON M3B 2W7 – 416/445-1121 – Treasurer, Geoffrey Hobsbawn

Austrian Society Trust Fund, 2255, rue Dudemaine, Montréal PQ H3M 1R4 – 514/335-5906 – Chairperson, Elfi Valenta

AWB Charitable Foundation, #4700, TD Bank Tower, Toronto ON M5K 1E6 – 416/601-7500; Fax: 416/868-1793 – Secretary, A.W. Baillie

Azrieli Foundation, 1155, rue Sherbrooke ouest, Montréal PQ H3A 2N3

Banting Research Foundation, c/o Faculty of Medicine, McMurrich Building, University of Toronto, Toronto ON M5S 1A8 – 416/978-4952 – Chair, Dorothy M. Hellebust

Beaverbrook Canadian Foundation, #1506, 1260 Marlborough Ct., Oakville ON L6H 3H5 – 905/337-0215; Fax: 905/337-0215 – Sec.-Treas., Alfred Lang Madley

Bechtel Foundation of Canada, #200, 12 Concorde Pl., North York ON M3C 3T1 – 416/441-4900; Fax: 416/441-4941 – Secretary, Manuel T. Estima

Benjamin Family Foundation, 2401 Steeles Ave. West, Downsview ON M3J 2P1 – President, Michael C. Benjamin

Bennett Family Foundation, #902, 481 University Ave., Toronto ON M5G 2E9 – Director, Avram J. Bennett

Berman Family Foundation, #1207, 211 Queen's Quay West, Toronto ON M5J 2M6 – President, Joseph Berman

Bessin Family Foundation, 68 Hillmount Ave., Toronto ON M6B 1X4 – Vice-President, Berl Bessin

The B.I. Ghert Family Foundation, 5 Junewood Cres., North York ON M2L 2C3 – President, Bernard I. Ghert

Bill & Judith Rubinstein Charitable Foundation, #503, 3625 Dufferin St., North York ON M5K 1N4 – President, Bill Rubinstein

Birks Family Foundation, 1240 Phillips Square, Montréal PQ H3B 3H4 – 514/397-2566; Fax: 514/397-2578 – Chairman & Executive Director, G. Drummond Birks

Black Family Foundation, 10 Toronto St., Toronto ON M5C 2B7 – 416/363-8721 – Sec.-Treas., Cecelia Black

The Block Charitable Foundation, #800, 1030 West Georgia St., Vancouver BC V6E 3B9 – President, Henry J. Block

The Body Shop Charitable Foundation, 33 Kern Rd., North York ON M3B 1S9 – 416/441-4189, ext.296; Fax: 416/441-0712 – President, Margot Franssen

Boland Foundation, 161 Glenrose Ave., Toronto ON M4T 1K7 – Lawrence Hynes

Brandon Area Foundation, PO Box 216, Brandon MB R7A 58Y – Sec.-Treas., Zella Mills

Branscombe Family Foundation, 6746 Morrison St., PO Box 576, Niagara Falls ON L2E 6V2 – Vice-President, Frank A. Branscombe

Brawn Foundation, #500, 505 - 3rd St. SW, Calgary AB T2P 3E6 – 403/261-9010; Fax: 403/262-6977 – Managing Director, Kelley A. Buckley

The Brooke Foundation, #3106, 99 Harbour Sq., Toronto ON M5J 2H2 – Trustee, Barrie D. Rose

Bumper Foundation, #1501, 300 - 5 Ave. SW, Calgary AB T2P 3C4 – 403/266-9700; Fax: 403/265-8155

Burns Memorial Fund, Rocky Mountain Plaza, #1109, 615 MacLeod Trail SE, Calgary AB T2G 4T8 – 403/234-9396; Fax: 403/233-0513 – Executive Director, Pamela Burke

The Burton Charitable Foundation, 26 Swanhurst Blvd., Mississauga ON L5N 1B7 – 905/826-3952 – Sec.-Treas., Myrna R. Wagner

Butters Foundation, 109 William St., Cowansville PQ J2K 1K9 – 514/263-4123 – Vice-Chairman, William D. Duke

Calgary Foundation, #1850, 540 - 5 Ave. SW, Calgary AB T2P 0M2 – 403/264-1662; Fax: 403/265-0152 – Executive Director, Sam W. Aylesworth

Canada Europe Foundation, #600, 99 Bank St., Ottawa ON K1P 6B9 – 613/748-3511; Fax: 613/749-1556 – CEO, Donald G. Mitchell

Canada Iceland Foundation, 54 Siddall Cres., Winnipeg MB R2K 3W6 – Treasurer, D. Olafson

Canada-Israel Cultural Foundation, #503, 2221 Yonge St., Toronto ON M4S 2B4 – 416/932-2260; Fax: 416/482-8281 – National President, S. Bresler

Canadian Aldeburgh Foundation, 34 Glenallan Rd., Toronto ON M4N 1G8 – 416/481-1964 – President, M.B. Sutton

Canadian Foundation for Masorti Judaism, #112, 1520 Steeles Ave. West, Concord ON L3K 3B9 – 905/738-1717; Fax: 905/738-1331 – President, Ron Hoffman

Canadian Friends of the American Israel Medical Foundation, #656, 600 University Ave., Toronto ON M5G 1X5 – 416/596-4473 – Contact, Noe Zamel, MD, Email: noe@io.org

Canadian Pacific Charitable Foundation, One Palliser Square, #2300, 125 - 9th Ave. SE, Calgary AB T2G 0P6

Canadian Progress Charitable Foundation, 2395 Bayview Ave., North York ON M2L 1A2 – 905/852-5300; Fax: 905/852-5301 – Chairman, Al Gordon

Canadian-Scandinavian Foundation, Geography Dept., McGill University, 805, rue Sherbrooke ouest, Montréal PQ H3A 2K6 – 514/398-4304; Fax: 514/398-7437 – Contact, Dr. Jan Lundgren

Canadian Scholarship Trust Foundation, #200, 240 Duncan Mills Rd., North York ON M3B 3P1 – 416/445-7377; Fax: 416/445-1708; Toll Free: 1-800-387-4622 – Chair, David Baird

Canadian Television Series Development Foundation, 777 Bay St., 7th Fl., Toronto ON M5W 1A7 – 416/596-5878; Fax: 416/596-2650; Email: ipf@inforamp.net – Executive Director, Andra Sheffer

Carol & Morton Rapp Foundation, c/o Harold L. Wilson, #330, 100 Cowdray Ct., Scarborough ON M1S 5C8 – President, Morton Rapp

Carolyn Sifton Foundation, #1700, One Lombard Pl., Winnipeg MB R3B 0X2 – 204/942-7884; Fax: 204/943-8060 – President, Graeme D. Sifton

Carthy Foundation, #200, 707 - 7 Ave. SW, Calgary AB T2P 3H6 – President, Paul S. Christensen

Catherine & Maxwell Meighen Foundation, #1702, 110 Yonge St., Toronto ON M5C 1T4 – 416/366-2931 – President, Col. Maxwell C.G. Meighen

Catholic Education Foundation of Ontario, 80 Sheppard Ave. East, Toronto ON M2N 6E8 – 416/229-5326; Fax: 416/229-5345 – Executive Secretary, Dr. John J. Flynn

Central Okanagan Foundation, PO Box 1233, Stn A, Kelowna BC V1Y 7V8 – 250/861-6160; Fax: 250/861-6156 – Executive Secretary, Janice Henry

C.G. Jung Foundation of the Ontario Association of Jungian Analysts, 223 St. Clair Ave. West, 3rd Fl., Toronto ON M4V 1R3 – 416/961-9767

Chalmers Fund, c/o Ontario Arts Council, 151 Bloor St. West, 6th Fl., Toronto ON M5S 1T6 – 416/961-1660; 969-7450; Fax: 416/961-7796; Toll Free: 1-800-387-0058 – Grant Coordinator, Linda Brown

Charles H. Ivey Foundation, #105, 201 Consumers Rd., North York ON M2J 4G8 – 416/498-1555 – Sec.-Treas., Mary D. Megson

The Charles Johnson Charitable Fund, #428, 1, carré Westmount, Montréal PQ H3Z 2P9 – Chairman, Charles Johnson

The Charles Wilson Charitable Foundation, PO Box 1410, Saint John NB E2L 4J9 – Vice-President, Keith M. Wilson

Chastell Foundation, 1170, rue Peel, 8e étage, Montréal PQ H3B 4P2 – Executive Director, Thomas X. Axeworthy

The Chawkers Foundation, 41 Union St., Ottawa ON K1M 1R5 – 613/741-1440 – President, Charles S. Alexander

Cheshire Homes Foundation Canada Inc., #215, 40 Orchard View Blvd., Toronto ON M4R 1B9 – 416/487-0443; Fax: 416/487-0624 – Chairman, John Brown

Chris Spencer Foundation, c/o Douglas, Symes & Brissenden, 2100, One Bentall Centre, 505 Burrard St., Vancouver BC V7X 1R4 – 604/683-6911; Fax: 604/669-1337 – Secretary, William S. Armstrong

CHUM Charitable Foundation, 1331 Yonge St., Toronto ON M4T 1Y1 – 416/925-6666; Fax: 416/926-4095; Telex: 06-22063 – Contact, Taylor Baiden

Citadel Charity Foundation, 12, rue des Grisons, Québec PQ G1R 4M7 – Sec.-Treas., J. Michael McCormack

Clifford E. Lee Foundation, Metropolitan Place, #1668, 10303 Jasper Ave., Edmonton AB T5J 3N6 – 403/423-4674; Fax: 403/424-1797 – Executive Director, Judith K. Padua

Clifford & Mabel Beckett Foundation, 10977 - 74 Ave., Edmonton AB T6G 0E5 – President, James M. Murland

Cole Foundation, #3050, 600, boul de Maisonneuve ouest, Montréal PQ H3A 3J2 – President, John N. Cole

Columbus Charity Foundation, #12, 31255 Upper Maclure Rd., Abbotsford BC V2T 5N4 – Secretary, Lawrence A. King

Community Foundation for Greater Toronto, 1 Dundas St. West, 15th Fl., PO Box 78, Toronto ON M5G 1Z3 – President & CEO, Marjorie J. Sharpe

Community Foundation of Ottawa-Carleton, #320, 150 Laurier Ave. West, Ottawa ON K1P 5J4 – 613/236-1616; Fax: 613/236-1621; Email: csocbm@ibm.net – President, Grete Hale

Conn Smythe Foundation, c/o Fraser & Beatty, PO Box 100, Stn 1st Canadian Place, Toronto ON M5X 1B2 – President, Dr. Hugh Arthur Smythe

Counselling Foundation of Canada, #410, 1 Toronto St., Toronto ON M5C 2W3

C.P. Loewen Family Foundation, PO Box 2260, Steinbach MB R0A 2A0 – Sec.-Treas., C.N. Loewen

Crake Foundation Inc., 791 Brunswick St., Fredericton NB E3B 1H8 – Sec.-Treas., Bishop George Lemmon

The CRB Foundation, 1170, rue Peel, 8e étage, Montréal PQ H3B 4P2 – 514/878-5263; Fax: 514/878-5299 – Administrative Director, Ann Dadson

DAAT Charitable Foundation, 37 Main St. South, Georgetown ON L7G 3G2 – Secretary, Martin Vaughan

DAC Foundation for People with Special Needs, c/o National Trust Company, One Adelaide St. East, Toronto ON M5C 2W8 – 416/361-4096; Fax: 416/361-3717 – Senior Foundations Officer, David R. Windeyer

Dakamagaro Charitable Foundation, 9 Ava Rd., Toronto ON M5P 1X8 – Sec.-Treas., Gary Goldberg

Danbe Foundation Inc., c/o Minto Construction Ltd., PO Box 5152, Stn F, Ottawa ON K2C 3H8 – Sec.-Treas., Daniel Greenberg

Daryl K. Seaman Foundation, #1850, 540 - 5th Ave. SW, Calgary AB T2P 0M2 – 403/264-1662; Fax: 403/265-0152 – Daryl K. Seaman

The David Bloomfield Family Foundation, 80 Boundary Rd., Cornwall ON K6H 5V3

David & Dorothy Lam Foundation, #400, 576 Seymour St., Vancouver BC V6B 3K1 – President, David Lam

The Davies Charitable Foundation, Landmark Centre, 165 Ontario St., Kingston ON K7L 2Y6 – 613/546-4000; Fax: 613/546-9130 – Executive Director, Eileen Bruce

DeFehr Foundation Inc., 55 Vulcan Ave., Winnipeg MB R2G 1B9 – President, A.A. DeFehr

D.E.K.E. Charitable Foundation, 47 Auckland Lane, RR#4, King City ON L0G 1K0 – Contact, Philip J. Wolfenden

Deloitte, Touche Foundation Canada, 800 Sun Life Tower, Box 40, 150 King St. West, Toronto ON M5H 1J9 – 416/351-3988; Fax: 416/599-2399 – Director, R.G. Harris

Devonian Foundation, #770, 999 - 8 St. SW, Calgary AB T2R 1J5 – Sec.-Treas., A.T. Bosovich

Diamond Foundation, 105 North Commercial Dr., Vancouver BC V5L 4V7 – President, G. Diamond

The Dominion Group Foundation, 165 University Ave., Toronto ON M5H 3B9 – President, George Cooke

Dominion Textile Foundation, 1950, rue Sherbrooke ouest, Montréal PQ H3H 1E7 – 514/989-6468; Fax: 514/989-6331 – Director, Colleen Smith

Donald F. Hunter Charitable Foundation, Aldermines Corp., #2603, 130 Adelaide St. West, Toronto ON M3H 3P5

Donner Canadian Foundation, #402, 212 King St. West, Toronto ON M5H 1K5 – 416/593-5125 – President, Devon Gaffney Cross

Dr. Baxter Temple Carmichael Foundation, c/o Valin, Innes, #405, 96 Larch St., Sudbury ON P3E 1C1 – 705/673-3655; Fax: 705/673-8758

The Dr. David Friesen Family Corporation, #711, 213 Notre Dame Ave., Winnipeg MB R3B 1N3 – President, Dr. David Friesen

Dr. Helen Creighton Memorial Foundation, 6350 Cobourg Rd., Halifax NS B3H 2A1 – 902/422-1271, ext. 174; Fax: 902/423-3357 – President, Dr. Alan Wilson

E. & G. Odette Charitable Foundation, #410, 4120 Yonge St., North York ON M2P 2C8 – Director, Edmond G. Odette

E.A. Baker Foundation for the Prevention of Blindness, 1929 Bayview Ave., Toronto ON M4G 3E8 – 416/480-7587; Fax: 416/480-7000 – Administrative Secretary, Glacia d'Cambre

Eaton Foundation, 250 Yonge St., 11th Fl., Toronto ON M5B 1C8 – 416/343-3423; Fax: 416/343-3526 – Chairman, Patrick J. Wilson

Ed Mirvish Family Charitable Foundation, 581 Bloor St. West, Toronto ON M6G 1K3 – President, Eleanor Gene Misener

The Edith & Bernard Ennis Foundation, 177 Parkway Dr., Welland ON L3C 4C5 – President., Bernard Ennis

Edith H. Turner Foundation, #400, 21 King St. West, PO Box 990, Hamilton ON L8N 3R1 – 905/528-8411; Fax: 905/528-9008 – President, J. Benjamin Simpson

Edmonton Community Foundation, #601, 10117 Jasper Ave., Edmonton AB T5J 1W8 – President, Jean Forest

Educational & Charitable Fund of The Prince Edward Island Medical Society, 557 North River Rd., Charlottetown PE C1E 1J7 – 902/368-7303; Fax: 902/566-3934 – Executive Director, Marilyn Lowther

The Edward Bronfman Family Foundation, BCE Place, Box 778, 181 Bay St., PO Box 778, Toronto ON M5J 2T3 – Director, Dayle Rakowsky

Edward J. Freeland Foundation, 4741 Queen St., Niagara Falls ON L2E 2M2 – President, Edward James Freeland

Edwards Charitable Foundation, 9 Anewen Dr., Toronto ON M4A 1R9 – President, John Bruce McLellan

The EJLB Foundation, #1050, 1350, rue Sherbrooke ouest, Montréal PQ H3G 1J1 – 514/843-5112; Fax: 514/843-4080 – Executive Director, Robert Alain

Eldee Foundation, #1720, 1080, Côte du Beaver Hall, Montréal PQ H2Z 1S8 – 514/871-9261; Fax: 514/397-0816 – President, Neri J. Bloomfield

Elizabeth Greenshields Foundation, #1, 1814, rue Sherbrooke ouest, Montréal PQ H3H 1E4 – 514/937-9225 – Secretary, Micheline Leduc

Emes Charitable Foundation, 32 Stormont Ave., Toronto ON M5N 2B9 – President, Leslie Z. Gerendasi

Emil Skarin Fund, c/o The Senate, 150 Athabasca Hall, University of Alberta, Edmonton AB T6G 2E8 – 403/492-2268; Fax: 403/492-2448 – Executive Officer, Sandra Kereliuk

E.P. Taylor Equine Research Fund, c/o Ontario Jockey Club, PO Box 156, Etobicoke ON M9W 5L2 – 416/675-6110; Fax: 416/674-1958 – Sec.-Treas., Robert J. Careless

Eugene & Eva Kohn Family Foundation, 102 Caribou Rd., Toronto ON M5N 2A9 – Secretary-Treasurer, Eva Kohn

CANADIAN FOUNDATIONS

Evelyn Steinberg Alexander Family Foundation, #250, 5601, rue Paré, Montréal PQ H4P 1P7 – Co-Chairperson, James Alexander

E.W. Bickle Foundation, Scotia Plaza, PO Box 105, Toronto ON M5H 3Y2 – 416/367-9003; Fax: 416/367-9004 – President, W.P. Wilder

The Farha Foundation, 7080, av du Parc, Montréal PQ H3N 1X6 – 514/270-4900; Fax: 514/270-5363 – Executive Director, Gail Small

Fast Foundation, #600, 4150, rue Ste-Catherine ouest, Montréal PQ H3Z 2Y5 – President, Simone Fast

Federation of Chinese Canadian Professionals (Ontario) Education Foundation, 150 Heath St. West, PO Box 6402, Stn A, Toronto ON M4V 2Y4 – 416/635-2550 – President, Dr. John Chiu

F.K. Morrow Foundation, #402, 357 Bay St., Toronto ON M5H 2T7 – 416/364-4124 – President, Sr. M. Walters

Fleming Foundation, 223 Ontario St., Beamsville ON L0R 1B0 – President, Arthur DeWitt Fleming

Fondation Alfred Dallaire, 1115, rue Laurier ouest, Outremont PQ H2V 2L3

Fondation Caldwell, 5151, côte Ste-Catherine, Montréal PQ H3W 1M6 – Trésorier, Howard Gilmour

Fondation Caritas-Sherbrooke inc., 636, rue Québec, Sherbrooke PQ J1H 3M2 – 819/566-6345 – Directeur, Abbé Desève Cormier

Fondation Caroline Durand, #2300, 630, boul René-Lévesque ouest, Montréal PQ H3B 4T8 – Responsable, Pierre Venne

Fondation Charles Cusson, a/s Montreal Trust Company, CP 1900, Succ B, Montréal PQ H3B 3L6 – 514/982-7000; Fax: 514/982-7069 – Secrétaire, Marcel Brochu

Fondation Charles LeMoyne, 3120, boul Taschereau, Greenfield-Park PQ J4V 2H1 – 514/466-5487; Fax: 514/672-1716 – Directrice générale, Denis Jacob

Fondation Charles O. Monat, 630, boul René-Lévesque ouest, Montréal PQ H3B 4H7 – 514/876-7779 – Trésorier, Paul G. Côté

Fondation Desjardins, Complexe Desjardins Tour Sud, 40e étage, CP 7, Montréal PQ H5B 1B2 – 514/281-7171; Fax: 514/281-0652 – Directeur exécutif/Président, Gérard Chabot

Fondation Edward Assh, 842, rue St-Joseph est, CP 2036, Québec PQ G1K 7N4 – 418/522-6458; Fax: 418/522-5414 – President, Maurice Assh

Fondation Felix Goyer, 1940, boul Henri-Bourassa est, Montréal PQ H2B 1J1 – President, Jean-Claude Leclerc

Fondation Fournier-Ethier, a/s Trust Général du Canada, 1100, rue Université, Montréal PQ H3B 2G7 – Trustee, Pierre Favreau

Fondation Guadeloupe, 9, rue Cayer, Hull PQ J8Y 1K2 – 819/776-3877; Fax: 819/776-6358 – Responsable, Jacques Beaucage

Fondation Guy Vanier, 1981, av McGill College, Montréal PQ H3A 2Y2 – Trustee, Therese Nguyen

Fondation J. Armand Bombardier, 1000, rue J.A. Bombardier, CP 370, Valcourt PQ J0E 2L0 – 514/532-2258; Fax: 514/532-5499 – Directrice générale, France Bissonnette

La Fondation J. Raymond Pepin, #783, 3, de Longpré, Ste-Foy PQ G1V 2S2 – Président, J.R. Pepin

Fondation J.A. De Seve, #2402, 505, rue Sherbrooke ouest, Montréal PQ H2L 4N3 – Secrétaire, Thérèse de Grandpré

Fondation Jacques Francoeur, #1350, 1130, rue Sherbrooke ouest, Montréal PQ H3A 2M8 – Coordonnateur des projets, Josée Francoeur

La Fondation Jean Beliveau, 2313, rue Ste-Catherine ouest, Montréal PQ H3H 1N2 – Président, Jean Beliveau

Fondation Jean-Louis Lévesque, #2340, 2000, av McGill College, Montréal PQ H3A 3H3 – President, Suzanne Lévesque

La Fondation Julius Richardson Inc., 5425, av Bessborough, Montréal PQ H4V 2S7 – 514/483-1380; Fax: 514/483-4596 – Executive Director, Jean Michaud

Fondation des maladies mentales, 212, boul Saint-Joseph ouest, Montréal PQ H2T 2P8 – 514/270-5354; Fax: 514/270-6382 – Directrice générale, Lina Dessureault

Fondation Marcel Leger, 60, rue Saint-Jacques, 9e étage, Montréal PQ H2Y 1L5 – 514/982-2464; Fax: 514/987-1960 – Jean Marc Léger

La Fondation Marcelle et Jean Coutu, #101, 1374, Mont-Royal est, Montréal PQ H2V 4P3 – Présidente, Marie-Josée Coutu

Fondation Ménopause Ostéoporose, 2100, av Marlowe, Montréal PQ H4A 3L6 – 514/482-7422; Fax: 514/482-7939; Toll Free: 1-800-977-1778 – Présidente, Lucille Rouleau-Ross

Fondation Monseigneur Victor Tremblay inc., 930, rue Jacques Cartier est, CP 456, Chicoutimi PQ G7H 5C8 – 418/549-2805 – Secrétaire, Roland Bélanger

La Fondation Peladeau inc., 612, rue St-Jacques ouest, 13e étage, Montréal PQ H3C 1C8 – Président, Pierre Peladeau

Fondation Père-Eusèbe-Ménard, 65, rue de Castelnau ouest, Montréal PQ H2R 2W3 – 514/274-7645; Fax: 514/274-7647 – Directeur général, André Franche

Fondation Richelieu International, #200, 1173, ch Cyrville, Ottawa ON K1J 7S6 – 613/742-6911; Fax: 613/742-6916 – Directeur général, G. Mathias Pagé

Fondation Richmond du Canada, inc., 6885, av 16e, Montréal PQ H1X 2T5 – 514/593-4885; Fax: 514/593-7714 – Vice-présidente, Jeannine Guindon

Fondation Tex-Scope inc., 3000, rue Boulle, Saint-Hyacinthe PQ J2S 1H9 – 514/773-6800 – Secrétaire-trésorier, Pierre Comtois

Fondation Yvon Boulanger, 2325, rue Deschamps, Repentigny PQ J6A 2X9 – Trustee, Gaston Boulanger

Foster Hewitt Foundation, c/o Dixon Management Services, 34 Weatherstone Ct., PO Box 1090, Niagara on the Lake ON L0S 1J0 – Vice-President, Frederick E. Dixon

Foundation to Underwrite New Drama for Pay Television, BCE Place, Box 787, #100, 181 Bay St., Toronto ON M5J 2T3 – 416/956-5431; Fax: 416/956-2087 – Chairperson, Wendy MacKeigan

Francofonds inc., #242, 340, boul Provencher, Winnipeg MB R2H 0G9 – 204/237-5852; Fax: 204/233-3324 – Directrice générale, Maria Chaput

Frank Gerstein Charitable Foundation, c/o National Trust Co., National Trust Tower, One Financial Pl., One Adelaide St. East, Toronto ON M5C 2W8 – 416/361-4096 – Senior Foundations Officer, David R. Windeyer

The Frankel Family Foundation, 9 Dorchester Dr., North York ON M3H 3J2 – President, Aaron Frankel

Fraser Elliott Foundation, #5300, Commerce Court West, Toronto ON M5L 1B9 – President, Roy Fraser Elliott

Fredericton Foundation Inc., PO Box 130, Fredericton NB E3B 4Y7 – 506/455-8329 – Executive Director, Jack J. Kimm

Friends of the Environment Foundation, PO Box 5703, London ON N6A 4S4 – ; Toll Free: 1-800-361-5333; URL: http://www.fef.ca/ – Vice-President, Corporate Affairs, Dianne Smith-Sanderson

The Gairdner Foundation, #220, 255 Yorkland Blvd., North York ON M2J 1S3 – 416/493-3101; Fax: 416/493-8158 – Executive Director, Sally-Anne Hrica

Gamma-Rho Foundation Ltd., #630, 1980, rue Sherbrooke ouest, Montréal PQ H3H 1G1 – President, James D. Raymond

Gelmont Foundation, #1901, 1, Place Ville-Marie, Montréal PQ H3B 2C3 – President, Nahum Gelber

Genesis Research Foundation, 92 College St., Toronto ON M5G 1L4 – 416/978-2667; Fax: 416/978-8350 – Executive Director, Kathy Green

Geoffrey H. Wood Foundation, #750, 304 The East Mall, Etobicoke ON M9B 6E2 – 416/234-0240; Fax: 416/234-5140 – President & Executive Director, Samuel Tughan

George Cedric Metcalf Charitable Foundation, 105 Pears Ave., Toronto ON M5R 1S9 – 416/926-0366 – President, George Metcalf

George Hogg Family Foundation, 1205, rue Lucien l'Allier, Montréal PQ H3G 2C4 – Secretary, Thomas S. Gillespie

George Lunan Foundation, c/o National Trust Company, National Trust Tower, One Financial Place, One Adelaide St. East, Toronto ON M5C 2W8 – 416/361-4095; Fax: 416/361-3717 – Senior Foundation Officer, David R. Windeyer

Georgina Foundation, 39 Maple Ave., Toronto ON M4W 2T8 – 416/921-7496 – Vice-President, Margaret Opekar

Gestetner Bros. Memorial Fund, 9101, Montée Louis H. Lafontaine, Anjou PQ H1J 1Z1 – President, Alfred Gestetner

Good Foundation Inc., RR#1, Breslau ON N0B 1M0 – 519/648-2823 – Secretary, James M. Good

The Great Lakes Marine Heritage Foundation, 55 Ontario St., Kingston ON K7L 2Y2 – 613/542-2261; Fax: 613/542-0043 – Contact, Marie Smith

Greey-Lennox Charitable Foundation, c/o National Trust Company, National Trust Tower, One Financial Place, One Adelaide St. East, Toronto ON M5C 2W8 – 416/361-4096; Fax: 416/361-3717 – Treasurer, David R. Windeyer

Griffith Laboratories Foundation, 757 Pharmacy Ave., Scarborough ON M1L 3J8 – 416/288-3050; Fax: 416/288-3481

Grocery Industry Foundation...Together, #500, 1240 Bay St., Toronto ON M5R 2A7 – 416/975-8488; Fax: 416/922-8469 – Executive Director, John P. McNeil

Grotto Cerebral Palsy Foundation Inc., 324 Scarborough Rd., Toronto ON M4E 3M8 – 416/699-6297 – Executive Secretary, Charles M. Sinclair

Gustav Levinschi Foundation, #110, 1820, av Docteur Penfield, Montréal PQ H3H 1B4 – Sec.-Treas., Anita David

Halifax Children's Foundation, PO Box 788, Halifax NS B3J 2V2 – 902/455-3846 – Chairperson, Ron MacDonald

Halton Region Conservation Foundation, 2596 Britannica Rd. West, RR#2, Milton ON L9T 2X6 – 905/336-1158; Fax: 905/336-7014

The Hamber Foundation, 1055 Dunsmuir St., PO Box 49390, Stn Bentall Centre, Vancouver BC V7X 1P3 – Chairman, G.W. MacLaren

Hamilton Community Foundation, Standard Life Centre, #205, 120 King St. West, Hamilton ON L8P 4V2 – 905/523-5600; Fax: 905/523-0741 – Executive Director, Judith McCulloch

Hans Klinkenberg Memorial Scholarship Fund, c/o The Canadian Institute of Surveying & Mapping, PO Box 5378, Stn F, Ottawa ON K2C 3J1 – 613/224-9851; Fax: 613/224-9577 – Executive Director, Susan Pugh

Harold Crabtree Foundation, Varette Building, #2005, 130 Albert St., Ottawa ON K1P 5G4 – 613/563-4589 – President, Sandra Crabtree

The Harry Bronfman Family Foundation, #1525, 1245, rue Sherbrooke ouest, Montréal PQ H3G 1H4 – Contact, Charles R. Bronfman, PC, CC

Harry E. Foster Foundation, #209, 40 St. Clair Ave. West, Toronto ON M4V 1M2 – 416/927-9077; Fax: 416/927-8475 – Executive Assistant, Carol Davis-Kerr

The Harry & Max Korolnek Family Foundation, c/o Consolidated Bottle Co., PO Box 369, Stn D, Toronto ON M6P 3J9 – 416/656-7777; Fax: 416/656-6394 – President, Harry Korolnek

Harry A. Newman Memorial Foundation, 1268 Royal York Rd., Etobicoke ON M9A 4C5 – Chairman, William DeLaurentis

Canadian Almanac & Directory 1997

Harry P. Ward Foundation, c/o Royal Trust Co., 55 Metcalfe St., Ottawa ON K1P 6L5 – Assistant Secretary, David W. Schiller

The Harweg Foundation, 23 Bedford Rd., Toronto ON M5R 2J9 – 416/925-3557 – Secretary, Jerome S. Cooper

Helen McCrea Peacock Foundation, PO Box 132, Midhurst ON L0L 1X0 – Sec.-Treas., Martha Tovee

Help Fill a Dream Foundation of Canada, 902 Hillside Ave., Victoria BC V8T 1Z8 – 250/382-3135; Fax: 250/382-2711 – President, Barry George

The Henry & Berenice Kaufmann Foundation, #210, 4670, rue Ste-Catherine ouest, Montréal PQ H3Z 1S5 – Executive Vice-President, Marion Greenwood

The Henry N.R. Jackman Foundation, 165 University Ave., 10th Fl., Toronto ON M5H 3B8 – President, Henry N.R. Jackman

The Henry White Kinnear Foundation, #4700, Toronto Dominion Bank Tower, PO Box 48, Stn Toronto Dominion, Toronto ON M5K 1E6 – 416/601-7500; Fax: 416/868-1793 – President, A.R.A. Scace, Q.C.

Herbert Marshall McLuhan Foundation, 122 St. Ninian St., Antigonish NS B2G 1Y9 – 902/863-2360; URL: http://www.mcluhan.ca/mcluhan/foundation.html – Director, George Sanderson

The Herschel Victor Foundation, 1250, rue Saint-Alexandre, Montréal PQ H3B 3H6 – 514/866-4891 – President, Herschel Victor

H.G. Bertram Foundation, c.o Royal Trust Corp. of Canada, PO Box 7500, Stn A, Toronto ON M5W 1P9 – Trust Officer, Henri F. Ashley

Hofstedter Family Charitable Foundation, #503, 3625 Dufferin St., North York ON M3K 1N4 – President, S. Hofstedter

Hope Charitable Foundation, c/o National Trust Company, National Trust Tower, One Financial Pl., One Adelaide St. East, Toronto ON M5C 2W8 – 416/361-4096; Fax: 416/361-3717 – Senior Foundations Officer, David R. Windeyer

Hospital for Sick Children Foundation, 555 University Ave., Toronto ON M5G 1X8 – 416/813-6166; Fax: 416/813-5024 – Director, Communications, Natalie Jascott

Hospitals of Regina Foundation, PO Box 1697, Regina SK S4P 3Z6 – 306/766-7500; Fax: 306/766-7504; Toll Free: 1-800-766-7500 – Executive Director, Bruce C. Anderson, CAE

HUME Foundation, #1, 125 Traders Blvd. East, Mississauga ON L4Z 2E5 – 905/568-8111 – Secretary, Barbara M. Humeniuk

Hylcan Foundation, #103, 4920, boul de Maisonneuve ouest, Montréal PQ H3Z 1N1 – Secretary, Joan F. Sutherland

I.C.C. Foundation, #504, 170 Laurier Ave. W., Ottawa ON K1P 5V5 – 613/563-2642; Fax: 613/565-3089 – Executive Director, Corinne Gray

Ignat Kaneff Charitable Foundation, 1290 Central Pkwy. West, Mississauga ON L5C 4R3 – President, Dimitrina Kaneff

Imperial Oil Charitable Foundation, 111 St Clair Ave. West, Toronto ON M5W 1K3 – ; Fax: 416/968-4272; Toll Free: 1-800-668-3776 – Treasurer, Susan Young

Inter-Church Fund for International Development, #404, 77 Charles St. West, Toronto ON M5S 1K5 – 416/944-8182; Fax: 416/922-1419; Email: icfid@web.net – Executive Director, Bob Fugere

Ionic Lodge Foundation for Human Welfare, #245, 5180, rue Queen Mary, Montréal PQ H3W 3E7 – 514/481-7761 – Chairperson, Stanley Litwin

Ireland Fund of Canada, 51 Front St. East, 2nd Fl., Toronto ON M5E 1B3 – 416/367-8311; Fax: 416/367-5931 – Executive Director, Paul Farrelly

Israel Cancer Research Fund, #1111, 20 Eglinton Ave. West, Toronto ON M4R 1K8 – 416/487-5246; Fax: 416/489-8932 – Executive Director, Pearl Greenbaum

Israel Koschitzky Family Charitable Foundation, c/o Laven & Pittman, Western Canada Pl., #2200, 700 - 8 Ave. SW, Calgary AB T2P 3V4 – Secretary, David L. Laven

Jack Cooper Family Foundation, #206, 1 Eglinton Ave. East, Toronto ON M4P 3A1 – Director, Jack Cooper

Jackman Foundation, #1300, 44 Victoria St., Toronto ON M5C 1Y2 – 416/366-8567; Fax: 416/367-2339 – Secretary, Donald J. Crawford

Jacob & Dorothy Hendeles Foundation, c/o Robins, Appleny & Taub, #2500, 130 Adelaide St. West, PO Box 102, Toronto ON M5E 2M2 – President, Dorothy H. Hendeles

James Wallace McCutcheon Foundation, Toronto Dominion Centre, Box 35, Toronto ON M5K 1A1 – President & Chairman, J.W. McCutcheon

The Japan Foundation, Toronto, #213, 131 Bloor St. West, Toronto ON M5S 1R1 – 416/966-1600; Fax: 416/966-9773; Email: jftor@interlog.com – Director, Masamichi Sugihara

Jarislowsky Foundation, #2609, 1110, rue Sherbrooke ouest, Montréal PQ H3A 1G8 – President, S.A. Jarislowsky

Jean Cameron Palliative Care Foundation, #777, 1130, rue Sherbrooke ouest, Montréal PQ H3A 2M8 – 514/842-1714; Fax: 514/842-1718 – Vice-President, Gordon L. McGilton

Jewish Community Foundation of Greater Montréal, 5151, ch Côte-Sainte-Catherine, Montréal PQ H3W 1M6 – 514/735-3541; Fax: 514/735-8972 – Executive Director, Robert Kleinman

Jewish Foundation of Manitoba, #204, 370 Hargrave St., Winnipeg MB R3B 2K1 – 204/958-4499; Fax: 204/958-4497 – Executive Director, David Cohen

The Jim Pattison Foundation, #1600, 1055 West Hastings St., Vancouver BC V6E 2H2 – Treasurer, M. Chant

The Joan & Clifford Hatch Foundation, 7130 Riverside Dr. East, Windsor ON N85 1C3 – President, H. Clifford Hatch

The Joe Brain Foundation, PO Box 24061, RPO Kenaston, Winnipeg MB R3N 2B1 – 204/897-3513; Fax: 204/897-3513 – President, Walter Dubowec, FCA

John Deere Foundation of Canada, PO Box 1000, Grimsby ON L3M 4H5 – President, G.J. Clark

The John Dobson Foundation, #1409, 1010, rue Sherbrooke ouest, Montréal PQ H3A 2R7 – President, John W. Dobson

John Hardie Mitchell Family Foundation, 777 Dunsmuir St., PO Box 10426, Vancouver BC V7Y 1K3 – Secretary, Duncan Bell-Irving

John Hart Hunter Educational Foundation of Canada, c/o Scotia Plaza, #4400, 40 King St. West, Toronto ON M5H 3Y4

John Labatt Foundation, 150 Simcoe St. North, London ON N6A 4M3 – Administrator, Carol Bober

John McKellar Charitable Foundation, #1600, 2 First Canadian Place, PO Box 480, Toronto ON M5X 1J5 – President, John D. McKellar

The John A. Sanderson & Family Trust, c/o Canada Trust., 70 Market St., Brantford ON N3T 2Z7 – Paul Read, QC

The Johnson Family Foundation, 95 Elizabeth Ave., PO Box 12049, St. John's NF A1B 1R7 – President, Paul J. Johnson

Joseph C. Edwards Foundation, Place Montréal Trust, 1900, av McGill College, Montréal PQ H3A 3K9 – 514/982-7196; Fax: 514/982-7069 – Executive Vice-President, Dan J. Sullivan

Joseph Kerzner Charitable Foundation, #701, 1500 Don Mills Rd., North York ON M3B 3K4 – Director, Joseph Kerzner

The Joseph Louis Rotman Charitable Foundation, #1701, 22 St. Clair Ave. East, Toronto ON M4T 2J3 – President, Isaac Silverstein

The Joseph Segal Family Foundation, #520, 701 West Georgia St., Vancouver BC V7Y 1A1 – President, Joseph Segal

Joseph Tanenbaum Charitable Foundation, 1051 Tapscott Rd., Scarborough ON M1X 1A1 – President, Kurt Rothschild

The Joseph & Wolfe Lebovic Foundation, PO Box 1240, Stouffville ON L4A 8A2 – President, Joseph Lebovic

J.P. Bickell Foundation, c/o National Trust Company, National Trust Tower, One Financial Place, One Adelaide St. East, Toronto ON M5C 2W8 – 416/361-4096; Fax: 416/361-3717 – Secretary, David R. Windeyer

J.W. McConnell Family Foundation, #1800, 1002, rue Sherbrooke ouest, Montréal PQ H3A 3L6 – 514/288-2133; Fax: 514/288-1479 – President & CEO, Tim Brodhead

J.W. Smith Foundation, 5657 Harold St., Vancouver BC V5R 5V6 – Vice-President, J.A. Gowans

Kahanoff Foundation, #4206, 400 - 3 Ave. SW, Calgary AB T2P 4H2 – 403/237-7896; Fax: 403/261-9614 – President, James B. Hume

Kaiser Youth Foundation, 1500 Georgia St. West, 19th Fl., Vancouver BC V6G 2Z8 – 604/681-9211; Fax: 604/685-9046; Email: kyf@wimsey.com; URL: http://www.tether.com/KYF – Executive Director, Diane Champion-Smith

Kamloops Foundation, PO Box 15, Kamloops BC V2C 5K3 – Sec.-Treas., Michael Black

Kathleen M. Richardson Foundation, Richardson Bldg., 1 Lombard Pl., 30th Fl., Winnipeg MB R3B 0Y1 – Secretary, Sheila A. Berthon

The Kitchener & Waterloo Community Foundation, Marsland Centre, 20 Erb St. West, 11th Fl., Waterloo ON N2L 1T2 – 519/725-1806; Fax: 519/888-7737 – Executive Director, Jane Humphries

The Klemke Foundation, #1703, 9923 - 103 St., Edmonton AB T5K 2J3 – John Klemke

K.M. Hunter Charitable Foundation, #266, 171 Rink St. A, Peterborough ON K9J 2J6 – President, William T. Hunter

KPMG Charitable Foundation, Scotia Plaza, 20 King St. West, PO Box 122, Toronto ON M5H 3Z2 – 416/777-8500; Fax: 416/777-3969 – Sec.-Treas., Wayne Brownlee

Kroeker Foundation, Inc., PO Box 1450, Winkler MB R0G 2X0 – 204/325-4333 – Chairman, Walter E. Kroeker

Laidlaw Foundation, #2000, 365 Bloor St. East, Toronto ON M4W 3L4 – 416/964-3614; Fax: 416/975-1428 – Executive Director, Nathan Gilbert

Laura & B. Aaron Foundation, PO Box 984, Montréal PQ H4L 4W3 – President, Arnold Aaron

Law for the Future Fund, c/o Canadian Bar Association, #902, 50 O'Connor St., Ottawa ON K1P 6L2 – Director, George Boros, LLM

The Lawson Foundation, #100, 248 Pall Mall St., London ON N6A 5P6 – Executive Director, Joan A. Francolini

Leon & Evelyn Kahn Family Charitable Foundation, #800, 1030 West Georgia St., Vancouver BC V6E 3B9 – Director, Leon Kahn

Leon & Thea Koerner Foundation, PO Box 39209, RPO Point Grey, Vancouver BC V6R 4P1 – 604/224-2611; Fax: 604/224-1059 – Executive Secretary, Alice Macaulay

Leonard Ellen Family Foundation, #1430, 5 Place Ville Marie, Montréal PQ H3B 2G2 – 514/861-9666 – President, Leonard Ellen

Lethbridge Community Foundation, #200, 220 - 3rd Ave. South, Lethbridge AB T1J 0G9 – 403/328-5297; Fax: 403/328-9534 – Executive Director, Neil H. Manning

Lewis C. Smith Foundation, c/o Bessner, Gallay, Schapira, Kreisman, #812, 5250, rue Ferrier, Montréal PQ H4P 1L4 – 514/341-5551; Fax: 514/341-2947 – Vice-President, Lawrence Bessner, F.C.A.

Canadian Almanac & Directory 1997

Lifeforce Foundation, PO Box 3117, Vancouver BC V6B 3X6 – 604/669-4673; Fax: 604/299-2822 – Director, Peter Hamilton

Lillian & Leroy Page Foundation, c/o National Trust Co., PO Box 2290, Hamilton ON L8N 3B5 – 905/526-1200 – Secretary, David G. Hartfield

Lithuanian Canadian Foundation, c/o Lithuanian Community Hall, 1573 Bloor St. West, Toronto ON M6P 1A6 – 416/532-3311 – President, J. Storvkus

Lloyd & Gladys Fogler Foundation, c/o Fogler, Rubinoff, #1400, 150 York St., Toronto ON M5H 3S5 – Director, Lloyd S.D. Fogler

Lloydminster Foundation, 5503 - 50 St., Lloydminster AB T9V 0Y4 – Sec.-Treas., Jean White

Lockwood Foundation, c/o National Trust Company, National Trust Tower, One Financial Pl., One Adelaide St. East, Toronto ON M5C 2W8 – 416/361-4096; Fax: 416/361-3717 – President, H.S. Lockwood

London Community Foundation, #100, 248 Pall Mall St., London ON N6A 5P6 – Executive Director, Terry Campbell

Lorne & Evelyn Johnson Foundation, 2400 - 13 Ave., Regina SK S4P 0V9 – 306/586-0944 – Executive Director, Douglas A. Lee, C.M.

Lovelight International Foundation, Inc., 4334, rue Fullum, Montréal PQ H2H 2J5 – 514/931-9237; Telex: 524371

MacDonald Stewart Foundation, 1195, rue Sherbrooke ouest, Montréal PQ H3A 1H9 – Executive Director, James P. Carroll

MAGFRAT Foundation (Magnus Fratres), c/o Big Brothers of Sarnia-Lambton, 193 George St., Sarnia ON N7T 4N6 – 519/336-0460 – President, Adrian Verstraaten

Malloch Foundation, c/o Lazier Hickey Langs O'Neal, 25 Main St. West, 17th Fl., Hamilton ON L8P 1H1 – 905/525-3652; Fax: 905/525-6278 – Sec.-Treas., Colin G. Lazier

The Manuel & Eva Kimel Foundation, 76 Miranda Ave., Toronto ON M6E 5A1 – Director, Manuel Kimel

Maple Leaf Foundation, 1055 Talbot St., St Thomas ON N5P 1G5 – Sec.-Treas., W.D. Husband

Maranatha Foundation, #201, 41 Valleybrook Dr., North York ON M3B 2S6 – Chairman, Donald Miller

Marion Ferguson Foundation, PO Box 752, Stn Adelaide, Toronto ON M5C 2K1

Maritime Provinces Education Foundation, #1006, 5161 George St., PO Box 2044, Halifax NS B3J 2Z1 – 902/424-5352; Fax: 902/424-8976 – Secretary, Barbara Murray

The Marjorie & Gerald Bronfman Foundation, #1525, 1245, rue Sherbrooke ouest, Montréal PQ H3G 1H4 – President, Marjorie Bronfman

Marnie McDiarmid Foundation Inc., 1455 Buffalo Pl., Winnipeg MB R3T 1L8 – 204/453-4343; Fax: 204/475-7964; Telex: 07-57879 – Treasurer, Richard Andison

The Martin Foundation, c/o National Trust Co., 120 King St. West, PO Box 2290, Hamilton ON L8N 3B5 – 905/526-1200 – Sec.-Treas., David G. Hartfield

The Martin Wise Goodman Trust, c/o Dian Kesler-Corneil, One Yonge St., Toronto ON M5E 1D9 – 416/869-4545; Fax: 416/869-4183

Masonic Foundation of Manitoba Inc., 420 Corydon, Winnipeg MB R3L 0N8 – 204/453-7410; Fax: 204/284-3527 – Sec.-Treas., Robert T. Crossley

Masonic Foundation of Ontario, 361 King St. West, Hamilton ON L8P 1B4 – Administrator, C. Moore

Masonic Foundation of Québec, 2295, rue Saint-Marc, Montréal PQ H3H 2G9 – Treasurer, D. Drury

Matinée Ltd. Fashion Foundation, 3820, rue Saint-Antoine ouest, Montréal PQ H4C 1B5

Maurice Joseph & Louis Weisfeld Charitable Foundation, 11 Chiltern Hill Rd., Toronto ON M6C 3B4 – Trustee, Louis Weisfeld

The Maurice Pollack Foundation, #801, 1 Westmount Sq., Montréal PQ H3Z 2P9 – President, Florence P. Pedvis

Maurice & Tillie Wolfe Family Foundation, 302 The East Mall, Etobicoke ON M9B 6B8 – President, Rose Wolfe

Max Bell Foundation, #3516, Aetna Tower, Toronto-Dominion Centre, 79 Wellington St. West, PO Box 105, Stn Toronto Dominion, Toronto ON M5K 1G8 – 416/601-4770; Fax: 416/601-1630 – President, Donald S. Rickerd

The Max Clarkson Foundation, 23 Dunloe Rd., Toronto ON M4V 2W4 – President, Max B.E. Clarkson

Maxwell Cummings Family Foundation, 4115, rue Sherbrooke ouest, 6e étage, Montréal PQ H3Z 1K1 – President, Robert M. Cummings

Maytree Foundation, #804, 170 Bloor St. West, Toronto ON M5S 1T9 – 416/944-2627; Fax: 416/944-8915 – President, Judy Broadbent

McGeachy Charitable Foundation, RR#3, Chatham ON N7M 5J3 – President, Neil Wallace McGeachy

McLean Foundation, #1008, 2 St. Clair Ave. West, Toronto ON M4V 1L5 – 416/964-6802; Fax: 416/926-2218 – Secretary, Muriel Alvares

McPherson Playhouse Foundation, 3 Centennial Square, Victoria BC V8W 1P5

Mennonite Foundation of Canada, #4, 117 Victor Lewis Dr., Winnipeg MB R3P 1J6 – 204/488-1985; Fax: 204/488-1986 – National Manager, Edgar Rempel

Milan Ilich Foundation, #201, 5631 No. 3 Rd., Richmond BC V6X 2C7 – Director, Milan Ilich

Mimi & Sam Pollock Foundation, #404, 625 Avenue Rd., Toronto ON M4V 2K7 – President, Samuel P.S. Pollock

Minerva Foundation, Edmonton House, #340, 10205 - 100 Ave., PO Box 3160, Edmonton AB T5J 2G7 – President, Douglas O. Goss

Minto Foundation, PO Box 5152, Stn F, Ottawa ON K2C 3H8 – President, Daniel Greenberg

The Miriam & Harold Green Family Foundation, #1600, 20 Eglinton Ave. West, Toronto ON M4R 2H1 – President, Harold Green

Mitzi & Mel Dobrin Family foundation, #400, 4150, rue Ste-Catherine ouest, Montréal PQ H3Z 2Y5 – President, Melvyn A. Dobrin

M.M. Webb Foundation, PO Box 6521, Stn A, Toronto ON M5W 1X4 – President, Mary Margaret Webb

Moe Levin Family Foundation, 15, av Windsor, Westmount PQ H3Y 2L7 – President, Moe Levin

Mohawk College Foundation, PO Box 2034, Hamilton ON L8N 3T2 – 905/575-2066; Fax: 905/575-2443 – Executive Director, Richard Court

Molly Towell Perinatal Research Foundation, 1750 West 36th Ave., Vancouver BC V6M 1K2 – 604/261-4818 – Contact, J. Bryans

Molson Companies Donations Fund, Scotia Plaza, #3600, 40 King St. West, Toronto ON M5H 3Z5 – 416/860-6462 – Secretary & National Coordinator & Supt., Judy McClelland

The Molson Foundation, 1555, rue Notre Dame est, Montréal PQ H2L 2R5 – 514/521-1786; Fax: 514/598-6866 – Secretary, Stephen T. Molson

Mon Sheong Foundation, 36 D'Arcy St., Toronto ON M5T 1J7 – 416/977-3762; Fax: 416/977-3231 – Executive Director, K.W. Cheng

Morley & Rita Cohen Foundation, c/o Ritaley Investments Inc., #1705, 1155, boul René-Lévesque ouest, Montréal PQ H3B 4S5 – President, Morley M. Cohen

The Morrison Foundation, #1008, 341 Bloor St. West, Toronto ON M5S 1W8 – Treasurer, Tom Falls

Mr. and Mrs. P.A. Woodward's Foundation, c/o Medical Advisor, #305, 1155 Pender St. West, Vancouver BC V6E 2P4 – 604/682-8116; Fax: 604/682-8153 – Contact & Medical Advisor, Dr. Craig R. Arnold

Murphy Foundation Inc., #919, 167 Lombard Ave., Winnipeg MB R3B 0V3 – 204/942-5281 – Secretary, E.C. Fenton

Muttart Foundation, #530, 9919 - 105 St., Edmonton AB T5K 1B1 – 403/425-9616; Fax: 403/425-0282 – Executive Director, Robert S. Wyatt

Nancy's Very Own Foundation, 184 Roxborough Dr., Toronto ON M4W 1X8 – 416/961-7744; Fax: 416/961-7104 – President, Nancy Jackman

The Nat Christie Foundation, #1850, 540 - 5 Ave. SW, Calgary AB T2P 0M2 – 403/264-1662; Fax: 403/265-0152 – President, C. Peter Valentine

Nathan & Lily Silver Family Foundation, #510, 1 Yorkdale Rd., North York ON M6A 3A1 – President, Shoel Silver

Nathan Steinberg Family Foundation, 94 Forest Heights Blvd., North York ON M2L 2K8 – Secretary, H. Arnold Steinberg

National Magazine Awards Foundation, #207, 109 Vanderhoof Ave., Toronto ON M4G 2H7 – 416/422-1358; Fax: 416/422-3762 – Contact, Sandra Eikins

N.E. Peters Foundation, #3000, 1 Place Ville Marie, Montréal PQ H3B 4T9 – Sec.-Treas., Robert M. Rennie

Nelson Arthur Hyland Foundation, #601, 45 St. Clair Ave. West, Toronto ON M4V 1K9 – 416/920-6010 – President, Gerald F. Hayden, Q.C.

Nelson Lumber Foundation, PO Box 620, Lloydminster AB S9V 0Y8 – President, Raymond J. Nelson

Newman Foundation of Toronto, 89 St. George St., Toronto ON M5S 2E8 – 416/979-2468; Fax: 416/596-6920 – Administrative Coordinator, Pat Hayward

Nickle Family Foundation, Highstreet House, #401, 933 - 17 Ave. SW, Calgary AB T2T 5R6 – 403/244-4237; Fax: 403/244-3269; Email: peeverd@cadvision.com – Executive Director, David F. Peever

Noranda Foundation, BCE Place, Box 755, #4100, 181 Bay St., Toronto ON M5J 2T3 – 416/982-7431; Fax: 416/982-7446 – Sec.-Treas., Janet Greaves

Norman & Margaret Jewison Charitable Foundation, 18 Gloucester Lane, 4th Fl., Toronto ON M4Y 1L5 – 416/923-2787; Fax: 416/923-8580 – Director, Ralph Brown, QC

Norwood Community Scholarship Foundation, #201, 65 Swindon Way, Winnipeg MB R3P 0T8 – 204/837-1830 – Secretary, B.V. Angus

Old Strathcona Foundation, #401, 10324 White Ave., Edmonton AB T6E 1Z8 – 403/433-5866; Fax: 403/431-1938 – Executive Director, Liz Iggulden

Ole Evinrude Foundation Canada Inc., 910 Monaghan Rd., Peterborough ON K9J 7B6 – 705/876-2699 – Sec.-Treas., C.F. Eagleson

Ontario Mental Health Foundation, #1708, 365 Bloor St. East, Toronto ON M4W 3L4 – 416/920-7721; Fax: 416/920-0026 – Executive Director, Dr. Howard Cappell

Ontario Trucking Association Education Foundation Inc., 555 Dixon Rd., Etobicoke ON M9W 1H8 – 416/249-7401; Fax: 416/245-6152 – Executive Director, Ana Ideias

The Oscar Ascher Schmidt Charitable Foundation, 3638 Bathurst St., Toronto ON M6A 2E5 – President, S. Schmidt

Oswald, Smith Foundation Society, #441, 1755 Robson St., Vancouver BC V6G 3B7 – President, K.O. Smith

Otnim Foundation Inc., PO Box 5152, Stn F, Ottawa ON K2C 3H8 – Vice-President, Robert Greenberg

Our Lady of The Prairies Foundation, 620 Spadina Cres. East, Saskatoon SK S7K 3G5 – 306/652-6767 – Chair, Joseph B. Leier

The P. Schwartz Family Foundation, #701, 2 St. Clair Ave. East, Toronto ON M4T 2T5 – President, Phineas Schwartz

Pfeiffer Family Charitable Trust, #400, 1085, rue Saint-Alexandre, Montréal PQ H2Z 1P4 – 514/393-8122; Fax: 514/393-8120 – President, Dr. Julius Pfeiffer

Phillip Smith Foundation, c/o Montreal Trust, 15 King St. West, Toronto ON M5H 1B4 – 416/860-5555 – Sec.-Treas., Bruce Smith

Phoenix Community Works Foundation, 316 Dupont St., Toronto ON M5R 1V9 – 416/964-7919; Fax: 416/964-6941 – Executive Director, Larry Rooney

Physicians Services Inc. Foundation, #1006, 5160 Yonge St., North York ON M2N 6L9 – 416/226-6277; Fax: 416/226-6080 – Executive Director, Sandra Bennett

The Posluns Family Foundation, 637 Lakeshore Blvd. West, Toronto ON M5V 1A8 – President, Wilfred Posluns

Québec-Labrador Foundation (Canada) Inc., #680, 1253 av McGill College, Montréal PQ H7L 3W3 – 514/395-6020; Fax: 514/395-4505 – Program Manager, Helen Meredith

Québec & Ontario Paper Company Foundation, 80 King St., 7th Fl., St Catharines ON L2R 7G2 – 905/688-5030 – Celine G. Arsenault

Quetico Foundation, #610, 48 Yonge St., Toronto ON M5E 1G6 – 416/941-9388; Fax: 416/941-9236 – Contact, Dave Taylor

QUNO Foundation, 80 King St., 7th Fl., St Catharines ON L2R 7G1 – Celine G. Arsenault

R. Howard Webster Foundation, #2912, 1155, boul René-Lévesque ouest, Montréal PQ H3B 2L5 – Treasurer, Howard W. Davidson

R. Howard Webster Foundation, #2912, 1155, boul René-Lévesque ouest, Montréal PQ H3B 2L5 – 514/866-2424; Fax: 514/866-9918 – Treasurer, Howard W. Davidson

R. Samuel McLaughlin Foundation, c/o National Trust Company, National Trust Tower, One Financial Pl., One Adelaide St. East, Toronto ON M5C 2W8 – 416/361-4096; Fax: 416/361-3717 – Secretary, David R. Windeyer

Rappaport Family Charitable Foundation, c/o Mintz & Partners, #100, 1446 Don Mills Rd., North York ON M3B 3N6 – Director, Abraham Rappaport

RBC Dominion Securities Foundation, PO Box 21, Stn Commerce Court, Toronto ON M5L 1A7 – Chairman, Derek Brown

Reader's Digest Foundation of Canada, 215, av Redfern, Montréal PQ H3Z 2V9 – 514/934-0751; Fax: 514/932-3637 – President, Joe Beauduin

Recreation, Parks & Wildlife Foundation, Harley Court Bldg., 10045 - 111 St., 7th Fl., Edmonton AB T5K 1K4 – 403/482-6467; Fax: 403/488-9755 – Executive Director, Chuck Moser

The Red Deer Community Foundation, #503, 4808 Ross St., Red Deer AB T4N 1X5 – 403/341-6911; Fax: 403/341-4177 – Chairperson, Monica Bast

Reena Foundation, #200, 75 Dufflaw Rd., Toronto ON M6A 2W4 – 416/787-0131; Fax: 416/787-8052; Email: skeshen@reena.org – Executive Director, Sandy Keshen

Reichmann Charitable Trust, 2 First Canadian Place, 28th Fl., Toronto ON M5X 1B5 – Administrator, Lionel Weber

The Reimer Express Foundation Inc., 1400 Inkster Blvd., Winnipeg MB R2X 1R1 – Vice-President, Delbert J. Reimer

Rhodes Scholarship Trust, c/o McCarthy Tetrault, TD Centre, #4700, TD Bank Tower, Toronto ON M5K 1E6 – 416/362-1812; Fax: 416/868-1793 – Secretary, A.R.A. Scace, Q.C.

Richard & Edith Strauss Canada Foundation, #400, 1303, av Greene, Montréal PQ H3Z 2A7 – President, Richard Strauss

Richard Ivey Foundation, 630 Richmond St., London ON N6A 3G6 – 519/673-1280; Fax: 519/672-4790; Email: 102704.353@compuserve.com – Executive Director, Ms. Marvi Ricker

Richard & Jean Ivey Fund, #508, 380 Wellington St., London ON N6A 5B5 – 519/679-0870 – Sec.-Treas., Keith L. Sumner

Richardson Century Fund, Richardson Bldg., 1 Lombard Pl., 30th Fl., Winnipeg MB R3B 0Y1 – Secretary, Sheila A. Berthon

Rita Steinberg Goldfarb Foundation, c/o Spiegel Sohmer, #1203, 5, Place Ville Marie, Montréal PQ H3B 2G2 – President, Eileen Pelletier

Robert Campeau Family Foundation, 64 The Bridle Path, North York ON M3B 2B1 – Vice-President, Roland Villemarie

Rockwell International Canadian Trust, c/o Royal Trust Corp., PO Box 7500, Stn A, Toronto ON M5W 1P9 – 416/981-6243 – E. Leslie Frederick

Rona & Irving Levitt Family Foundation, c/o Forden Investments Inc., #1055, Place du Canada, Montréal PQ H3B 2N2 – President, Irving Levitt

Rotary Club of Toronto Charitable Foundation, c/o Royal York Hotel, 100 Front St. West, Toronto ON M5J 1E4 – 416/363-8321 – Secretary, Eunice J. Doucette

Roy C. Hill Charitable Foundation, 147 McClure Dr., RR#4, King City ON L0G 1K0 – 905/833-0189 – Executive Director, Alan Coulter

Royal Bank of Canada Charitable Foundation, Royal Bank Plaza, South Tower, 9th Fl., Toronto ON M5J 2J5 – 416/974-3113; Fax: 416/974-0624 – Executive Director, Blair McRobie

Royal LePage Charitable Foundation, #400, 39 Wynford Dr., Toronto ON M5E 1S9 – President, George J. Cormack

The S. Schulich Foundation, 24 Junewood Cres., North York ON M2L 2C3 – President, Seymour Schulich

St. Andrew's Charitable Foundation, 51 Rosedale Rd., Toronto ON M4W 2P5 – Treasurer, C.B. Paterson

The Saint John Foundation, c/o Touche Ross & Co., PO Box 6549, Stn A, Saint John NB E2L 4R9 – Treasurer, John F. McCrossin

Sam Yakubowicz Family Foundation, 14 Banton Rd., North York ON M3H 3H1 – President, Sam Yakubowicz

Samuel & Bessie Orfus Family Foundation, 108 Vesta Dr., Toronto ON M5P 2Z9 – President, Howard Orfus

The Samuel H. Cohen Family Foundation, 5 Clarence Sq., Toronto ON M5V 1H1 – President, Samuel H. Cohen

Samuel Lunenfeld Charitable Foundation, #1609, 8 King St. East, Toronto ON M5C 1B5 – 416/363-9191 – Executive Director, Mitchell Kunin

Samuel & Saidye Bronfman Family Foundation, 1170, rue Peel, Montréal PQ H3B 4P2 – 514/878-5270; Fax: 514/878-5293 – Executive Director, John Hobday

Samuel W. Stedman Foundation, 70 Market St., PO Box 751, Brantford ON N3T 2Z7 – Sec.-Treas., Vyrtle H. Sisson

Sandford Fleming Foundation, Room 4300, Carl Pollock Hall, University of Waterloo, Waterloo ON N2L 3G1 – 519/888-4008; Fax: 519/746-1457 – Executive Director, Jeff Weller

The Sandra & Leo Kolber Foundation, 1170, rue Peel, 8e étage, Montréal PQ H3B 4P2 – President, Sandra Kolber

Saskatchewan K of C Charitable Foundation, PO Box 73, Cupar SK S0G 0Y0 – 306/723-4484 – Executive Director, Lloyd Macknak

The Saskatoon Foundation, #101, 308 - 4 Ave. North, Saskatoon SK S7K 2L7 – 306/665-1766 – Executive Director, Moira R. Birney

Saul A. Silverman Family Foundation, 76 St. Clair Ave. West, 4th Fl., Toronto ON M4V 1N2 – President, Peter A. Silverman, QC

Savoy Foundation Inc., CP 69, St-Jean-sur-Richelieu PQ J3B 6Z3 – 514/358-9779 – Directrice, Caroline Savoy

Scottish Rite Charitable Foundation of Canada, 152 George St., Hamilton ON L8P 1E5 – 905/522-0033 – Assistant Secretary, John I. Carrick

Scottish Studies Foundation Inc., 2482 Yonge St., PO Box 45069, Toronto ON M4P 3E3 – 416/359-8012 – Chairman, Alan McKenzie, FSA Scot

Seagull Foundation, PO Box 370, Pugwash NS B0K 1L0 – Executive Director, Heather Scott

Seamont Foundation, #2600, 600, rue de la Gauchetière ouest, Montréal PQ H3B 4M3 – President, Constance V. Pathy

Senator Norman M. Paterson Foundation, 1918 Yonge St., PO Box 664, Thunder Bay ON P7C 4W6 – 807/577-8421; Fax: 807/475-3493 – President & Sec.-Treas., Donald C. Paterson

Shaw Family Foundation, 4190 Marblethorne Ct., Mississauga ON L4W 2H9 – Secretary, Dianne Rowett

Shawbridge Foundation for Youth, #520, 5250, rue Ferrier, Montréal PQ H4P 1L4 – 514/731-3419; Fax: 514/731-4999 – Executive Director, Peter L. Clement

Shiff Family Charitable Foundation, #412, 1867 Yonge St., Toronto ON M4S 1Y5 – Executive Director, Howard Driman

The Sikh Foundation, #4900, 40 King St. West, Toronto ON M5H 4A2 – 416/777-6697; Fax: 416/484-9656 – Contact, Kawal Kohli

Sir Ernest MacMillan Memorial Foundation, c/o McCarthy Tétrault, Toronto Dominion Centre, PO Box 48, Stn Toronto Dominion, Toronto ON M5K 1E6 – 416/601-7588; Fax: 416/868-1891 – President, John B. Lawson

Sir James Dunn Foundation, PO Box 6549, Stn A, Saint John NB E2L 3W8 – Vice-President, H.H. Stikeman

Sir Joseph Flavelle Foundation, c/o National Trust Company, National Trust Tower, One Financial Pl., One Adelaide St. East, Toronto ON M5C 2W8 – 416/361-4096; Fax: 416/361-3717 – Sec.-Treas., David R. Windeyer

Sky Works Charitable Foundation, 566 Palmerston Ave., Toronto ON M6G 2P7 – 416/536-6581; Fax: 416/536-7728 – Managing Director, Laura Sky

S.M. Blair Family Foundation, c/o National Trust Company, National Trust Tower, 21 King St. East, Toronto ON M5C 1B3 – 416/361-4096; Fax: 416/361-3717 – Assistant Sec.-Treas., David R. Windeyer

SMARTRISK Foundation, #301, 658 Danforth Ave., Toronto ON M4J 5B9 – 416/463-9878; Fax: 416/463-0137; Email: choose@smartrisk.ca – Executive Director, Dr. Robert Conn

The Sobey Foundation, 115 King St., Stellarton NS B0K 1S0 – President, D.F. Sobey

The Sonor Foundation, Toronto ON – 416/369-1499 – President, Michael R. Gardiner

Sons of Norway Foundation in Canada, 1020 Glenayre Dr., Port Moody BC V3H 1J6 – 604/937-7247 – Sec.-Treas., Ron Stubbings

South Saskatchewan Community Foundation, PO Box 277, Assiniboia SK S0H 0B0 – 306/642-4515 – Executive Director, Dianne Kessler

Steve Atanas Stavro Foundation, #202, 1900 Eglinton Ave. East, Scarborough ON M1L 2L9 – 416/751-4600; Fax: 416/751-3095 – President, Steve Stavro

Strathcona Trust, c/o Director General Reserves & Cadets, Dept. of National Trust, 101 Colonel By Dr., Ottawa ON K1A 0K2 – 613/992-3390 – Secretary, L.Col. W.J. Molnar

Stupp/Cohen Families Foundation, #1, 30 St. Clair Ave. West, Toronto ON M4V 3A1 – President, Jack Stupp

SUS Foundation of Canada, 620 Spadina Ave., Toronto ON M5S 2H4 – 416/923-3318; Fax: 416/923-8266 – Treasurer, William Kereliuk

Sydney & Florence Cooper Foundation, c/o TRL Investments Ltd., #1000, 920 Yonge St., Toronto ON M4W 3C7 – President, Sydney C. Cooper

T. Donald Miller Foundation, #801, 45 St. Clair Ave. West, Toronto ON M4V 1K9 – 416/920-6010; Fax: 416/920-6089 – President, Gerald F. Hayden, Q.C.

Tabachnick Foundation, c/o Rosenswig, Carere, McRae, #1134, 20 Dundas St. West, PO Box 134, Toronto ON M5G 2C2 – 416/977-6600; Fax: 416/927-5874 – Contact, Michael Rosenswig

TEAL Charitable Foundation, #177, 4664 Lougheed Hwy., Burnaby BC V5C 5T5 – 604/294-8325; Fax: 604/294-8355

tecNICA Foundation of Canada, 2060 Queen St. East, PO Box 51528, Toronto ON M4E 3V7 – 416/691-1529; Fax: 416/964-9226 – Chairperson, Juan Miranda

The Tecolote Foundation, Office of the President, 166 Pearl St., Toronto ON M5H 1L3 – Secretary, J. Ian Whitcomb

The Terry Fox Foundation, #605, 60 St Clair Ave. East, Toronto ON M4T 1N5 – 416/962-7866; Fax: 416/962-5677 – Breeda McClew

Themadel Foundation, #2, 260 Water St., PO Box 79, St. Andrews NB E0G 2X0 – 506/529-4882; Fax: 506/529-4882 – Manager, Ardeth Holmes

Thomas Beck Family Foundation, #502, 4100 Yonge St., North York ON M2P 2B5 – President, H. Thomas Beck

Thomas Sill Foundation Inc., #600, 175 Hargrave St., Winnipeg MB R3C 3R8 – Executive Director, C. Hugh Arklie

Tippet Foundation, #300, 95 Barber Greene Rd., North York ON M3C 3E9 – Sec.-Treas., John A.R. McCleery, CA

Tom & Annie Kohn Charitable Foundation, 103 Laurelcrest Ave., North York ON M3H 2B2 – President, Thomas Kohn

Toronto Hospital Foundation, Thomas J. Bell Wing, Rm.#614, 585 University Ave., Toronto ON M5G 2C4

TREE Foundation for Youth Development, #520, 5250, rue Ferrier, Montréal PQ H4P 1L4 – Executive Director, Peter L. Clement

Trillium Foundation, 21 Bedford Rd., 3rd Fl., Toronto ON M5R 2J9 – 416/961-0194; Fax: 416/961-9599 – Executive Director, Julie White

Two/Ten Charity Trust of Canada Inc., PO Box 4219, Stn Westmount, Montréal PQ H3Z 3B6 – 514/671-3604; Fax: 514/671-3604 – Sec.-Treas., Diane Cappella

Ukranian Canadian Foundation of Taras Shevchenko, 456 Main St., Winnipeg MB R3B 1B6 – 204/942-4627; Fax: 204/947-3882 – Executive Director, Lydia Hawryshkiw

United Ukrainian Charitable Trust, 2445 Bloor St. West, Toronto ON M6S 1P7 – 416/763-4982; Fax: 416/766-5812 – President, Wasyl Bybyk

Vancouver Foundation, #1200, 555 West Hastings St., PO Box 12132, Vancouver BC V6B 4N6 – 604/688-2204; Fax: 604/688-4170 – President/CEO, Richard Mulcaster

Vancouver Ski Foundation, #306, 1367 West Broadway, Vancouver BC V6H 4A9 – 604/878-0754; Fax: 604/878-0754

Verda & Weldon Bateman Foundation, 4123 Whitemud Rd., Edmonton AB T6H 5R5 – President, Mary A. Radostits

The Vered Foundation, 1801 Woodward Dr., Ottawa ON K2C 0R3 – President, Zeev Vered

The Vicbir Family Foundation, #609, 55 Water St. East, Brockville ON K6V 1A3 – President, Robert W.M. Birks

The Victoria Foundation, #118, 645 Fort St., Victoria BC V8W 1G2 – Executive Director, Sheila Henley

VideoFACT, A Foundation to Assist Canadian Talent, #501, 151 John St., Toronto ON M5V 2T2 – 416/596-8696; Fax: 416/596-6861 – Program Director, Julie Thorburn

The Viliam Frankel Family Charitable Foundation, #510, 333, rue Chabanel ouest, Montréal PQ H2N 2E7 – President, Viliam Frankel

Virginia Parker Moore Foundation, Canada Trust, 45 O'Connor St., 6th Fl., Ottawa ON K1P 1A4 – President, Martha C. Price

The Vivian & David Campbell Foundation, #706, 95 Wellington St. West, Toronto ON M5J 2N7 – Contact, Henry Campbell

W. Garfield Weston Foundation, #2001, 22 St. Clair Ave. East, Toronto ON M4T 2S3 – Secretary, Roger A. Lindsay

W. Maurice Young Foundation, PO Box 10053, Vancouver BC V7Y 1B6 – Chairman & President, W. Maurice Young

Walker Lynch Foundation, 72 Railside Rd., North York ON M3A 1A3 – 416/449-5464; Fax: 416/449-9165 – Director, Karl E.G. McIntyre

Walter C. Sumner Foundation, c/o Montreal Trust Co., 1690 Hollis St., Halifax NS B3J 3C5 – Vice-President, Susan G. Byrne

Walter & Duncan Gordon Charitable Foundation, #307, 11 Church St., Toronto ON M5E 1W1 – 416/601-4776; Fax: 416/601-1689 – Executive Director, Christine Lee

The Walter J. Blackburn Federation, 369 York St., PO Box 2280, London ON N6A 4G1 – Administrator, Linda A. Callaghan

The Werner Family Foundation, 1191 Bathurst St., Toronto ON M5R 3H4 – President, Ernest Webster

West Vancouver Foundation, PO Box 91447, West Vancouver BC V7V 3P1 – 604/925-8153 – Chairman, J. Cowan McKinney

Weston Canada Foundation, #2001, 22 St. Clair Ave. East, Toronto ON M4T 2S3 – 416/922-2500; Fax: 416/922-4394 – Secretary, Roger A. Lindsay

Wild Rose Foundation, Edmonton Centre, #2007, Toronto Dominion Tower, Edmonton AB T5J 2Z1 – 403/422-9305; Fax: 403/427-4155 – Executive Director, Stan C. Fisher

Windsor Foundation, c/o Montreal Trust Company of Canada, 1690 Hollis St., Halifax NS B3J 3C5 – Sec.-Treas., Paul Dyer

Winnipeg Foundation, #301, 161 Portage Ave. East, Winnipeg MB R3B 0Y4 – 204/944-9474 – Executive Director, Dan H. Kraayeveld, CA

Winspear Foundation, PO Box 1740, Stn Main, Edmonton AB T5J 2P1 – 403/425-0121; Fax: 403/425-0121 – Honorary Secretary, Judge Peter M. Caffaro

The Wood Gundy Charitable Foundation, PO Box 500, Stn BCE Place, Toronto ON M5J 2S8 – Executive Assistant, C. Ferron

A!World of Dreams Foundation Canada, #708, 465, rue St-Jean, Montréal PQ H2Y 2R6 – 514/843-7254; Fax: 514/843-3822; Toll Free: 1-800-567-7254 – Executive Director/President, Deborah Sims

W.P. Scott Charitable Foundation, PO Box 26, Stn Toronto Dominion, Toronto ON M5K 1A1 – Sec.-Treas., Pamela J. Roumeliotis

Yukon Foundation, #200, 2131 Second Ave., Whitehorse YT Y1A 1C3 – Chair, R. Hougen

Zeller Family Foundation, c/o National Trust Company, #600, 2000, av McGill College, Montréal PQ H3A 3H4 – Sec.-Treas., Gail Belanger, 514/985-5657

The Zoltan Freeman Family Foundation, 369 Ferrie St. East, Hamilton ON L8N 3G9 – President, Zoltan Freeman

Zukerman Charitable Foundation, 33 Prince Arthur Ave., 2nd Fl., Toronto ON M5R 1B2 – Trustee, Helen Zukerman

SECTION 3

GOVERNMENT DIRECTORY

QUICK REFERENCE	1	NORTHWEST TERRITORIES	150
GOVERNMENTS:		NOVA SCOTIA	154
CANADA	43	ONTARIO	164
ALBERTA	92	PRINCE EDWARD ISLAND	187
BRITISH COLUMBIA	105	QUÉBEC	193
MANITOBA	120	SASKATCHEWAN	210
NEW BRUNSWICK	131	YUKON TERRITORY	221
NEWFOUNDLAND & LABRADOR	140		

FOREIGN GOVERNMENTS	226
THE QUEEN & ROYAL FAMILY	245
THE COMMONWEALTH	246
INTERNATIONAL ORGANIZATIONS IN CANADA	247
FOREIGN DIPLOMATS IN CANADA	248
CANADIAN DIPLOMATS ABROAD	259

See ADDENDA at the back of this book for late changes & additional information.

GOVERNMENT QUICK REFERENCE

Editor's Note: Following are government agencies listed alphabetically under topics of frequent need or interest. Under each topic, federal agencies are listed first followed by provincial agencies. Applied titles are used. Only head office addresses are given. Refer to the in-depth government listings in this book for regional offices of the federal government.

If no government branch or division is given, address inquiries to Information/Communication Services.

See GOVERNMENT, alphabetically following, for the main source of information in each province and for the federal government departments.

Suggestions, corrections or additions to this table are welcome. Contact: The Editor, Section 3, Copp Clark Professional, 200 Adelaide St. West, 3rd Fl., Toronto ON M5H 1W7.

ABORIGINAL AFFAIRS

Fisheries & Oceans Canada, Aboriginal Affairs, 200 Kent St., Ottawa ON K1A 0E6, 613/991-0181; Fax: 613/993-7651

Health Canada, First Nations & Inuit Health Program, Ottawa ON K1A 0L3, 613/952-7177; Fax: 613/941-5366

Indian & Northern Affairs Canada, Claims & Indian Government Sector, Tour Nord, Les Terrasses de la Chaudière, 10 Wellington St., Hull PQ K1A 0H4, 819/997-0380; Fax: 819/953-3017

    Lands & Trusts Services Sector, Tour Nord, Les Terrasses de la Chaudière, 10 Wellington St., Hull PQ K1A 0H4, 819/997-0380; Fax: 819/953-3017

    Northern Affairs Sector, Tour Nord, Les Terrasses de la Chaudière, 10 Wellington St., Hull PQ K1A 0H4, 819/997-0380; Fax: 819/953-3017

Industry Canada, Aboriginal Business Canada, 235 Queen St., Ottawa ON K1A 0H5, 613/954-2788; Fax: 613/954-2303

National Aboriginal Management Board, Portage IV, #4F00, 140, Promenade du Portage, Hull PQ K1A 0J9, 819/994-2274

Alta: Alberta Family & Social Services, Aboriginal Affairs, Seventh St. Plaza, 10030 - 107 St., Edmonton AB T5J 3E4, 403/427-2734; Fax: 403/427-4019

Alberta Federal & Intergovernmental Affairs, Aboriginal Affairs, AGT Tower II, #2200, 10025 Jasper Ave., Edmonton AB T5J 1S6, 403/427-6706; Fax: 403/427-0939

Alberta Justice, Aboriginal Justice Initiatives, J.E. Brownlee Bldg., 10365 - 97th St., Edmonton AB T5J 3W7, 403/422-2779; Fax: 403/427-4670

B.C.: Ministry of Aboriginal Affairs, 908 Pandora Ave., Victoria BC V8V 1X4, 250/356-8281; Fax: 250/387-1785

Ministry of Education, Skills & Training, Aboriginal Education Branch (K-12), PO Box 9150, Stn Prov Govt, Victoria BC V8W 9H1, 250/387-1544; Fax: 250/387-1470

Ministry of Social Services, Aboriginal Services, Parliament Bldgs., 614 Humboldt St., 7th Fl., Victoria BC V8V 1X4, 250/387-7091; Fax: 250/387-7914

Man.: Manitoba Northern Affairs, Native Affairs Secretariat, 59 Elizabeth Dr., Thompson MB R8N 1X4, 204/677-6607; Fax: 204/677-6753

N.B.: Department of Intergovernmental & Aboriginal Affairs, Aboriginal Affairs, PO Box 6000, Fredericton NB E3B 5H1, 506/453-2671; Fax: 506/453-2995

NWT: Ministry of Intergovernmental & Aboriginal Affairs, Precambrian Bldg., 7th Fl., PO Box 1320, Yellowknife NT X1A 2L9, 403/873-7143; Fax: 403/873-0233

N.S.: Nova Scotia Priorities & Planning Secretariat, Aboriginal Affairs, PO Box 1617, Halifax NS B3J 2Y3, 902/424-8910; Fax: 902/424-7638

Ont.: Ministry of Citizenship, Culture & Recreation, Native Community Branch, 77 Bloor St. West, 6th Fl., Toronto ON M7A 2R9, 416/314-7265

Ministry of Community & Social Services, Aboriginal Healing & Wellness, Hepburn Block, 80 Grosvenor St., 6th Fl., Toronto ON M7A 1E9, 416/325-5666; Fax: 416/325-5172, 5171

Ontario Native Affairs Secretariat, #1009, 595 Bay St., Toronto ON M5G 2C2, 416/326-4740; Fax: 416/326-4017

Qué.: Ministère de l'Environnement et de la Faune, Affaires intergouvernementales et relations avec les autochtones, Édifice Marie-Guyart, 675, boul René-Lévesque est, Québec PQ G1R 5V7, 418/643-8209; Toll Free: 1-800-561-1616; Fax: 418/644-4598

Ministère des Affaires Municipales, Bureau de coordination des Affaires autochones/Native Affairs, Édifice Cook-Chauveau, 20, rue Chauveau, Québec PQ G1R 4J3, 418/691-2031; Fax: 418/643-8611

Secrétariat aux affaires autochtones, Edifice H, 875, Grande-Allée est, 2e étage, Québec PQ G1R 4Y8, 419/644-5848; Fax: 419/644-9659

Sask.: Saskatchewan Indian & Metis Affairs Secretariat, 1870 Albert St., 3rd Fl., Regina SK S4P 3V7, 306/787-6250; Fax: 306/787-6336

Yuk.: Executive Council, Aboriginal Language Services, PO Box 2703, Whitehorse YT Y1A 2C6, 403/667-3737; Fax: 403/393-6229

    Bureau of Management Improvement, PO Box 2703, Whitehorse YT Y1A 2C6, 403/667-5740; Fax: 403/393-6202

    Land Claims, Self Government & Devolution, PO Box 2703, Whitehorse YT Y1A 2C6, 403/667-5908; Fax: 403/393-6214

ADOPTION *See* **CHILD WELFARE**

AGRICULTURE

See Also **Land Resources**

Agriculture & Agri-Food Canada, Sir John Carling Bldg., 930 Carling Ave., Ottawa ON K1A 0C5, 613/759-1000; Fax: 613/759-6726

    Prairie Farm Rehabilitation Administration, CIBC Tower, #603, 1800 Hamilton St., Regina SK S4P 4L2, 306/780-6545; Fax: 306/780-5018

Canadian Grain Commission, #600, 303 Main St., Winnipeg MB R3C 3G8, 204/983-2734; Fax: 204/983-2751

Canadian Almanac & Directory 1997

Canadian Wheat Board, 423 Main St., PO Box 816, Winnipeg MB R3C 2P5, 204/983-0239, 3416; Fax: 204/983-3841

National Farm Products Council, Martel Bldg., 270 Albert, 13th Fl., PO Box 3430, Stn D, Ottawa ON K1P 6L4, 613/952-6752; Fax: 613/995-2097

Alta: Agriculture Financial Service Corporation, 4910 - 52 St., PO Box 5000, Camrose AB T4V 4E8, 403/679-1311 (Lending); Fax: 403/679-1308

Alberta Agricultural Research Institute, J.G. O'Donoghue Bldg., #300, 7000 - 113 St., Edmonton AB T6H 5T6, 403/422-5384; Fax: 403/427-1835

Alberta Agriculture, Food & Rural Development, 7000 - 113 St., Edmonton AB T6H 5T6, 403/427-2727; Fax: 403/427-2861

B.C.: Ministry of Agriculture, Fisheries & Food, 808 Douglas St., Victoria BC V8W 2Z7, 250/387-5121; Fax: 250/387-5130

Farm Income & Crop Insurance, 808 Douglas St., Victoria BC V8W 2Z7, 250/356-1615; Fax: 250/387-5130

Ministry of Health, Regional Programs, 1515 Blanshard St., 7th Fl., Victoria BC V8W 3C8, 250/952-3456

Provincial Agricultural Land Commission, #133, 4940 Canada Way, Burnaby BC V5G 4K6, 604/660-7000; Fax: 604/660-7033

Man.: Manitoba Agricultural Credit Corporation, #100, 1525 - 1 St., Brandon MB R7A 7A1, 204/726-6850; Fax: 204/726-6849

Manitoba Crop Insurance Corporation, #400, 50 - 24 St. NW, Portage la Prairie MB R1N 3V9, 204/239-3246; Fax: 204/239-3401

Manitoba Agriculture, Norquay Bldg., #809, 401 York Ave., Winnipeg MB R3C 0P8, 204/945-3433 (Administration); Fax: 204/945-5024

N.B.: Agricultural Development Board, c/o Department of Agriculture & Rural Development, PO Box 6000, Fredericton NB E3B 5H1, 506/453-2185; Fax: 506/453-7406

Department of Agriculture & Rural Development, PO Box 6000, Fredericton NB E3B 5H1, 506/453-2666; Fax: 506/453-7978

Nfld.: Department of Forest Resources & Agrifoods, Agrifoods Branch, Provincial Agriculture Bldg., Brookfield Rd., PO Box 8700, St. John's NF A1B 4J6, 709/729-4716

NWT: Department of Resources, Wildlife & Economic Development, #600, Scotia Centre, Bldg. Box 21, 5102 - 50 Ave., Yellowknife NT X1A 3S8, 403/873-7420, 7134; Fax: 403/873-0114

N.S.: Department of Agriculture & Marketing, Joseph Howe Bldg., 1690 Hollis St., 7th Fl., PO Box 190, Halifax NS B3J 2M4, 902/424-6734; Fax: 902/424-3948

Nova Scotia Farm Loan Board, PO Box 550, Truro NS B2N 5E3, 902/893-6506; Fax: 902/895-7693

Ont.: Agricultural Research Institute of Ontario, 801 Bay St., 6th Fl., Toronto ON M7A 1A3, 416/326-3396; Fax: 416/326-3394

PEI: Agricultural Development Corporation, PO Box 2000, Charlottetown PE C1A 7N8, 902/368-4830; Fax: 902/368-5743

Department of Agriculture, Fisheries & Forestry, Jones Bldg., 11 Kent St., PO Box 2000, Charlottetown PE C1A 7N8, 902/368-4880; Fax: 902/368-4857

Qué.: Ministère de l'Agriculture, des Pêcheries et de l'Alimentation, 200, ch Sainte-Foy, Québec PQ G1R 4X6, 418/643-2673; Fax: 418/646-0829

Société québécoise d'initiatives agro-alimentaires, #284, 1275, ch Ste-Foy, Québec PQ G1S 4S5, 418/643-2238; Fax: 418/643-2553

Sask.: Saskatchewan Agriculture & Food, Walter Scott Bldg., 3085 Albert St., Regina SK S4S 0B1, 306/787-5140; Fax: 306/787-0600

AIDS
See Also **Health Services; Sexually Transmitted Disease Control**

Health Canada, HIV/Aids Policy Coordination & Program Division, Brooke Claxton Bldg., Tunney's Pasture, Ottawa ON K1A 0K9, 613/952-5258; Fax: 613/941-5366

Laboratory Centre for Disease Control, Ottawa ON K1A 0L2, 613/957-0315; Fax: 613/941-5366

Alta: Alberta Health, Centre for Disease Control, PO Box 222, Edmonton AB T5J 2P4, 403/427-7687

NWT: Department of Health & Social Services, Community Programs & Services, Centre Square Tower, 8th Fl., PO Box 1320, Yellowknife NT X1A 2L9, 403/920-6173; Fax: 403/873-0266

N.S.: Nova Scotia Advisory Commission on AIDS, 1740 Granville St., 6th Fl., Halifax NS B3J 1X5, 902/424-5730; Fax: 902/424-0558

Ont.: Ministry of Health, Community Health Division, Hepburn Block, 8th Fl., Queen's Park, Toronto ON M7A 1S2, 416/327-7225; Toll Free: 1-800-668-2437 (AIDS Bureau); Fax: 416/327-7230

PEI: Department of Health & Social Services, Jones Bldg., 11 Kent St., 2nd Fl., PO Box 2000, Charlottetown PE C1A 7N8, 902/368-4985; Fax: 902/368-4969

Sask.: Saskatchewan Health, Strategic Services Division, 3475 Albert St., Regina SK S4S 6X6, 306/787-8332; Fax: 306/787-8310

AIR POLLUTION *See* AIR RESOURCES; ENVIRONMENT

AIR RESOURCES
See Also **Environment**

Environment Canada, Air Pollution Prevention Directorate, Place Vincent-Massey, 351, boul St-Joseph, Hull PQ K1A 0H3, 819/997-1298; Fax: 819/953-9547

Atmospheric Environment Service, 4905 Dufferin St., Downsview ON M3H 5T4, 416/739-4521; Fax: 819/953-2225

International Joint Commission, 100 Metcalfe St., Ottawa ON K1P 5M1, 613/995-2984; Fax: 613/993-5583

Alta: Alberta Environmental Protection, Air & Water Approvals Division, 9915 - 108 St., Edmonton AB T5K 2G8, 403/427-5883

B.C.: Ministry of Environment, Lands & Parks, Air Resources Branch, 777 Broughton St., Victoria BC V8V 1X4, 250/387-9987; Fax: 250/356-9836

Man.: Manitoba Environment, Bldg. 2, 139 Tuxedo Ave., Winnipeg MB R3N 0H6, 204/945-7100

N.B.: Department of the Environment, Air Quality Program Section, 364 Argyle St., PO Box 6000, Fredericton NB E3B 5H1, 506/457-4848; Fax: 506/453-2265

Nfld.: Department of Environment & Labour, Environment Branch, Confederation Bldg., PO Box 8700, St. John's NF A1B 4J6, 709/729-1930; Fax: 709/729-1930

NWT: Department of Resources, Wildlife & Economic Development, Air Quality, #600, Scotia Centre, Bldg. Box 21, 5102 - 50 Ave., Yellowknife NT X1A 3S8, 403/920-6396; Fax: 403/873-0114

N.S.: Department of the Environment, Air Quality Branch, PO Box 2107, Halifax NS B3J 3B7, 902/424-2550; Fax: 902/424-0503

PEI: Department of Environmental Resources, Air Quality & Hazardous Materials Section, Jones Bldg., 11 Kent St., 4th Fl., PO Box 2000, Charlottetown PE C1A 7N8, 902/368-5037; Fax: 902/368-5830

Qué.: Ministère de l'Environnement et de la Faune, Milieu atmosphérique, Édifice Marie-Guyart, 675, boul René-Lévesque est, Québec PQ G1R 5V7, 418/644-3460; Fax: 418/643-9591

AIRPORTS & AVIATION
See Also **Transportation**

Canadian Transportation Agency, Ottawa ON K1A 0N9, 819/997-0344 (Communications); Fax: 819/953-8353

Air & Accessible Transportation Branch, Ottawa ON K1A 0N9, 819/997-0344 (Communications); Fax: 819/953-8353

Civil Aviation Tribunal, 333 Laurier Ave. West, 12th Fl., Ottawa ON K1A 0N5, 613/998-1275; Fax: 613/990-9153

Industry Canada, Aerospace & Defence, C.D. Howe Bldg., 235 Queen St., Ottawa ON K1A 0H5, 613/954-3343; Fax: 613/941-2379

Institute for Aerospace Research, 1500 Montreal Rd., Ottawa ON K1A 0R6, 613/993-0141; Fax: 613/952-7214

National Defence (Canada), MGen. George R. Pearkes Bldg., 101 Colonel By Dr., Ottawa ON K1A 0K2, 613/992-4581

Air Command, MGen. George R. Pearkes Bldg., 101 Colonel By Dr., Ottawa ON K1A 0K2, 613/992-4581

Natural Resources Canada, Mapping & Services Branch, 615 Booth St., Ottawa ON K1A 0E9, 613/995-4945; Fax: 613/995-8737

Transport Canada, Airports Group, Transport Canada Building, 330 Sparks St., Ottawa ON K1A 0N5, 613/990-2309; Fax: 613/995-0351

Safety & Security Group, Transport Canada Building, 330 Sparks St., Ottawa ON K1A 0N5, 613/990-2309; Fax: 613/995-0351

Alta: Alberta Public Works, Supply & Services, Air Transportation Services, 11940 - 109th St., Edmonton AB T5G 2T8, 403/427-7341; Fax: 403/422-1232

Man.: Manitoba Highways & Transportation, Northern Airports & Marine, 215 Garry St., 14th Fl., Winnipeg MB R3C 3Z1, 204/945-3421; Fax: 204/945-5539

Nfld.: Department of Works, Services & Transportation, Transportation Branch, Confederation Bldg., PO Box 8700, St. John's NF A1B 4J6, 709/729-3283; Fax: 709/729-0703

NWT: Department of Transportation, Arctic Airports Division, Lahm Ridge Bldg., PO Box 1320, Yellowknife NT X1A 2L9, 403/873-7725; Fax: 403/873-0363

Ont.: Ministry of Natural Resources, Aviation, Flood & Fire Management, #400, 70 Foster Dr., Sault Ste. Marie ON P6A 6V5, 705/945-5937; Fax: 807/475-1503

Qué.: Conseil du trésor, Services aériens et postaux, Édifice Lomer-Gouin, 575, rue St-Amable, Québec PQ G1R 5N9, 418/643-1529; Fax: 418/643-9226

Sask.: Saskatchewan Highways & Transportation, Logistics, Planning & Compliance Division, 1855 Victoria Ave., Regina SK S4P 3V5, 306/787-4804; Fax: 306/787-9777

Yuk.: Yukon Community & Transportation Services, Aviation & Marine Branch, PO Box 2129, Haines Junction YT Y0B 1L0, 403/634-2035; Fax: 403/634-2131

ALCOHOL & ALCOHOLISM *See* DRUGS & ALCOHOL; LIQUOR CONTROL

ALL-TERRAIN VEHICLES *See* LEISURE CRAFT & VEHICLE REGULATIONS

APPRENTICESHIP PROGRAMS

Alta: Alberta Advanced Education & Career Development, Apprenticeship & Industry Training Division, Commerce Place, 10155 - 102 St., 7th Fl., Edmonton AB T5J 4L5, 403/422-4488; Fax: 403/422-7376

B.C.: British Columbia Labour Force Development Board, #221, 560 Johnson St., Victoria BC V8V 1X4, 250/356-5360; Fax: 250/356-9444

Ministry of Labour, Apprenticeship Initatives Division, 825 Fort St., Victoria BC V8W 9K1, 250/387-0172; Fax: 250/356-1653

Man.: Manitoba Education & Training, Apprenticeship, 185 Carlton St., 4th Fl., Winnipeg MB R3C 3J1, 204/945-3339; Fax: 204/948-2346

N.B.: Apprenticeship & Occupational Certification Board, PO Box 6000, Fredericton NB E3B 5H1, 506/453-2260; Fax: 506/453-3806

Department of Advanced Education & Labour, Collège Communautaire du NB, Edmundston, Chestnut Complex, 470 York St., PO Box 6000, Fredericton NB E3B 5H1, 506/735-2500; Fax: 506/735-1108

NWT: Department of Education, Culture & Employment, Career Development, PO Box 1320, Yellowknife NT X1A 2L9, 403/873-7146; Fax: 403/873-0155

Northwest Territories Apprenticeship & Trade Certification Board, PO Box 1192, Yellowknife NT X1A 2N8, 403/873-7357

N.S.: Department of Education & Culture, Apprenticeship Training Division, 2021 Brunswick St., PO Box 578, Halifax NS B3J 2S9, 902/424-8903; Fax: 902/424-0717

Nova Scotia Provincial Apprenticeship Board, PO Box 578, Halifax NS B3J 2S9, 902/424-0872; Fax: 902/424-0717

Ont.: Ministry of Education & Training, Apprenticeship Reform Project, Mowat Block, 900 Bay St., Toronto ON M7A 1L2, 416/314-5166; Fax: 416/325-2934

PEI: Office of Higher Education, Training & Adult Learning, Apprenticeship & Industrial Training, Shaw Bldg., 105 Rochford St., 3rd Fl., PO Box 2000, Charlottetown PE C1A 7N8, 902/368-4465; Fax: 902/368-6144

Qué.: Conseil consultatif du travail & de la main d'oeuvre, #2026, 800, Tour de la Place Victoria, CP 87, Montréal PQ H4Z 1B7, 514/873-2880; Fax: 514/873-1129

Ministère de l'Éducation, Formation continue, 1035, rue De La Chevrotière, 15e étage, Québec PQ G1R 5A5, 418/646-1562; Fax: 418/646-6561

Société québécoise de développement de la main-d'oeuvre, 425, rue St-Amable, Québec PQ G1R 2C5, 418/643-1892; Fax: 418/643-1714

Sask.: Saskatchewan Post-Secondary Education & Skills Training, Training Programs Branch, 2220 College Ave., Regina SK S4P 3V7, 306/787-2093

Yuk.: Yukon Education, Training Services, PO Box 2703, Whitehorse YT Y1A 2C6, 403/667-5141; Fax: 403/667-4754

AQUACULTURE See **FISHERIES**

ARBITRATION See **LABOUR**

ARCHIVES See **HISTORY & ARCHIVES**

ARCTIC & NORTHERN AFFAIRS

Canadian Polar Commission, Constitution Square, #1710, 360 Albert St., Ottawa ON K1R 7X7, 613/943-8605; Fax: 613/943-8607

Indian & Northern Affairs Canada, Tour Nord, Les Terrasses de la Chaudière, 10 Wellington St., Hull PQ K1A 0H4, 819/997-0380; Fax: 819/953-3017

Northern Affairs Sector, Tour Nord, Les Terrasses de la Chaudière, 10 Wellington St., Hull PQ K1A 0H4, 819/997-0380; Fax: 819/953-3017

Institute for Marine Biosciences, 1411 Oxford St., Halifax NS B3H 3Z1, 902/426-8332; Fax: 902/426-9413

Office of the Nunavut Environmental Scientist, PO Box 1500, Yellowknife NT X1A 2R3, 403/920-8200; Fax: 403/920-7809

Alta: Northern Alberta Development Council, #206, Provincial Bldg., 9621 - 96 Ave., PO Bag 900-14, Peace River AB T8S 1T4, 403/624-6274; Fax: 403/624-6184

Man.: Manitoba Northern Affairs, 59 Elizabeth Dr., Thompson MB R8N 1X4, 204/677-6607; Fax: 204/677-6753

NWT: Department of Resources, Wildlife & Economic Development, Trade & Investment Division, #600, Scotia Centre, Bldg. Box 21, 5102 - 50 Ave., Yellowknife NT X1A 3S8, 403/873-7420, 7134; Fax: 403/873-0114

Northwest Territories Development Corporation, Tower 7, PO Box 1437, Yellowknife NT X1A 2P1, 403/920-7700; Fax: 403/920-7701

Ont.: Ministry of Northern Development & Mines, Northern Development Division, #200, 70 Foster Dr., Sault Ste. Marie ON P6A 6V8, 705/945-5900; Fax: 705/945-5931

Sask.: Saskatchewan Northern Affairs, PO Box 5000, La Ronge SK S0J 1L0, 306/425-4200

Yuk.: Yukon Economic Development, 211 Main St., PO Box 2703, Whitehorse YT Y1A 2C6, 403/667-5466; Fax: 403/668-8601

ARTS & CULTURE

Canadian Artists & Producers Professional Relations Tribunal, C.D. Howe Bldg., 240 Sparks St., 8th Fl. West, Ottawa ON K1A 1A1, 613/996-4052; Toll Free: 1-800-263-ARTS (2787); Fax: 613/947-4125

Canadian Broadcasting Corporation, 1500 Bronson Ave., PO Box 8478, Ottawa ON K1G 3J5, 613/724-1200; TDD: 613/738-6686

Canadian Heritage, Jules Léger Bldg., 25 Eddy St., Hull PQ K1A 1K5, 819/997-0055; TDD: 819/997-8776; Fax: 819/953-5382

National Archives of Canada, 395 Wellington St., Ottawa ON K1A 0N3, 613/995-5138; Fax: 613/995-6274

National Arts Centre, 53 Elgin St., PO Box 1534, Stn B, Ottawa ON K1P 5W1, 613/996-5051, 947-7000; Fax: 613/996-9578

National Film Board of Canada, 3155, rue Côte de Liesse, St-Laurent PQ H4N 2N4, 514/283-9000; Fax: 514/283-8971

Natural Resources Canada, Mapping & Services Branch, 615 Booth St., Ottawa ON K1A 0E9, 613/995-4945; Fax: 613/995-8737

Telefilm Canada, Tour de la Banque Nationale, 600, De La Gauchetière ouest, 14e étage, Montréal PQ H3B 4L8, 514/283-6363; Fax: 514/283-8212

The Canada Council, 350 Albert St., PO Box 1047, Ottawa ON K1P 5V8, 613/566-4365; Toll Free: 1-800-263-5588; Fax: 613/566-4390

Alta: Alberta Community Development, Arts, Recreation & Libraries Branch, Beaver House, 10158 - 103 St., 3rd Fl., Edmonton AB T5J 0X6, 403/427-6315; Fax: 403/422-9132

Cultural Facilities & Historical Resources Division, Old St. Stephen's College, 8820 - 112 St., Edmonton AB T6G 2P8, 403/431-2300; Fax: 403/432-1376

B.C.: British Columbia Arts Council, 800 Johnson St., 5th Fl., Victoria BC V8V 1X4, 250/356-1718

British Columbia Festival of the Arts Society, 3577 Douglas St., Victoria BC V8Z 3L6, 250/383-4214

Ministry of Small Business, Tourism & Culture, Culture Division, 1117 Wharf St., Victoria BC V8W 2Z2, 250/356-6363 (Tourism); Fax: 250/356-8248

Man.: Manitoba Arts Council, #525, 93 Lombard Ave., Winnipeg MB R3B 3B1, 204/945-2237

Manitoba Culture, Heritage & Citizenship, Culture, Heritage & Recreation Programs Division, 213 Notre Dame., Winnipeg MB R3B 1N3, 204/945-3729

N.B.: Department of Municipalities, Culture & Housing, Arts Branch, Marysville Place, 20 McGloin St., PO Box 6000, Fredericton NB E3B 5H1, 506/453-3610; Fax: 506/453-2416

Nfld.: Department of Tourism, Culture & Recreation, Confederation Bldg., PO Box 8700, St. John's NF A1B 4J6, 709/729-0928; Fax: 709/729-0662

Cultural Affairs, Historic Resources & Provincial Archives, Confederation Bldg., PO Box 8700, St. John's NF A1B 4J6, 709/729-0928; Fax: 709/729-0662

NWT: Department of Education, Culture & Employment, Culture & Heritage, PO Box 1320, Yellowknife NT X1A 2L9, 403/873-7551; Fax: 403/873-0155

Northwest Territories Arts Council, PO Box 1320, Stn Main, Yellowknife NT X1A 2L9

N.S.: Department of Education & Culture, Acadian & French Language Services Branch, 2021 Brunswick St., PO Box 578, Halifax NS B3J 2S9, 902/424-5168; Fax: 902/424-0511

Heritage & Culture Branch (Nova Scotia Museum), 2021 Brunswick St., PO Box 578, Halifax NS B3J 2S9, 902/424-5168; Fax: 902/424-0511

Ont.: Ministry of Citizenship, Culture & Recreation, Heritage, Arts & Cultural Industries Policy Branch, 77 Bloor St. West, 6th Fl., Toronto ON M7A 2R9, 416/314-7115

Ontario Arts Council, 151 Bloor St. West, 5th Fl., Toronto ON M5S 1T6, 416/961-1660; Fax: 416/969-7447

Royal Ontario Museum, 100 Queen's Park Cres., Toronto ON M5S 2C6, 416/586-5549; Fax: 416/586-5863

TV Ontario, 2180 Yonge St., 5th Fl., Toronto ON M4S 2C1, 416/484-2600; Fax: 416/484-4234

PEI: Department of Education, Culture, Heritage & Recreation, Sullivan Bldg., 16 Fitzroy St., PO Box 2000, Charlottetown PE C1A 7N8, 902/368-4789; Fax: 902/368-4663

Qué.: Conseil des arts et des lettres du Québec, 79, boul René-Lévesque est, Québec PQ G1R 5N5, 418/643-1707; Toll Free: 1-800-897-1707; Fax: 418/643-4558

Conseil des communautés culturelles & de l'immigration, #418. Tour de la Place-Victoria, CP 158, Montréal PQ H4Z 1C3, 514/873-8501; Fax: 514/873-3469

Ministère de la Culture et des Communications, 225, Grand-Allée est, Québec PQ G1R 5G5, 418/643-2183; Fax: 418/643-4457

Sask.: Saskatchewan Arts Board, T.C. Douglas Bldg., 3475 Albert St., 3rd Fl., Regina SK S4S 6X6, 306/787-4056; Toll Free: 1-800-667-7526 (Saskatchewan); Fax: 306/787-4199

Saskatchewan Municipal Government, Arts, Cultural Industries & Multiculturalism, 1855 Victoria Ave., Regina SK S4P 3V7, 306/787-4753; Fax: 306/787-8560

Yuk.: Yukon Tourism, Arts Branch, PO Box 2703, Whitehorse YT Y1A 2C6, 403/667-8592; Fax: 403/667-3546

ASTRONOMY See **SPACE & ASTRONOMY**

ATOMIC ENERGY See **NUCLEAR ENERGY**

ATTORNEYS-GENERAL See **JUSTICE DEPARTMENTS**

AUDITORS-GENERAL

Auditor General of Canada, 240 Sparks St., Ottawa ON K1A 0G6, 613/995-3708; Fax: 613/957-4023

Alta: Alberta Office of the Auditor General, 9925 - 109 St., 8th Fl., Edmonton AB T5K 2J8, 403/427-4222; Fax: 403/422-9555

B.C.: Office of the Auditor General, 8 Bastion Sq., Victoria BC V8V 1X4, 250/387-6803; Fax: 250/387-1230

Canadian Almanac & Directory 1997

Man.: Office of the Provincial Auditor, 405 Broadway, 12th Fl., Winnipeg MB R3C 3L6, 204/945-3790; Fax: 204/945-2169

N.B.: Office of the Auditor General, PO Box 758, Fredericton NB E3B 5B4, 506/453-2243; Fax: 506/453-3067

Nfld.: Office of the Auditor General, Confederation Bldg., PO Box 8700, St. John's NF A1B 4J6, 709/729-2700; Fax: 709/729-5970

NWT: Executive Council, Audit Bureau, PO Box 1320, Yellowknife NT X1A 2L9, 403/873-7106; Fax: 403/873-0209

Financial Management Board Secretariat, PO Box 1320, Yellowknife NT X1A 2L9

N.S.: Office of the Auditor General, #302, 1888 Brunswick St., Halifax NS B3J 3J8, 902/424-5907; Fax: 902/424-4350

Ont.: Office of the Provincial Auditor, #1530, 20 Dundas St. West, PO Box 105, Toronto ON M5G 2C2, 416/327-2381; Fax: 416/327-9862

PEI: Office of the Auditor General, PO Box 2000, Charlottetown PE C1A 7N8, 902/368-4520; Fax: 902/368-4598

Sask.: Provincial Auditor Saskatchewan, #1500, 1920 Broad St., Regina SK S4P 3V7, 306/787-6398; Fax: 306/787-6383

AUTOMOBILE INSURANCE
See Also **Insurance (Life, Fire, Property)**
Alta: Automobile Insurance Board, #407, Terrace Bldg., 9515 - 107 St., Edmonton AB T5K 2C3, 403/427-5428; Fax: 403/422-2175

B.C.: Insurance Corporation of BC (Autoplan), 151 West Esplanade, North Vancouver BC V7M 3H9, 604/661-2800; Fax: 604/661-6647

Man.: Manitoba Public Insurance, 234 Donald St., 9th Fl., PO Box 6300, Winnipeg MB R3C 1M8, 204/985-7000; Fax: 204/943-9851

N.B.: Board of Commissioners of Public Utilities, 110 Charlotte St., PO Box 5001, Saint John NB E2L 4Y9, 506/658-2504; Fax: 506/633-0163

Nfld.: Department of Government Services & Lands, Commercial Relations, PO Box 8700, St. John's NF A1B 4J6, 709/729-2594

NWT: Department of Safety & Public Services, Panda 2 Mall, 3rd Fl., PO Box 1320, Yellowknife NT X1A 2L9, 403/873-7619; Fax: 403/873-0260

Ont.: Ontario Insurance Commission, 5160 Yonge St., PO Box 85, Toronto ON M2N 6L9, 416/250-7250; Toll Free: 1-800-668-0128; Fax: 416/590-7070

PEI: Department of Provincial Affairs & Attorney General, Insurance & Real Estate Division, PO Box 2000, Charlottetown PE C1A 7N8, 902/368-4564; Fax: 902/368-5283; 5355

Qué.: Société de l'assurance automobile du Québec, 333, boul Jean-Lesage, CP 19600, Québec PQ G1K 8J6, 418/528-3100; Fax: 418/644-0339

Sask.: Saskatchewan Government Insurance, 2260 - 11th Ave., Regina SK S4P 0J9, 306/751-1200; Fax: 306/787-7477

BANKING & FINANCIAL INSTITUTIONS
Auditor General of Canada, 240 Sparks St., Ottawa ON K1A 0G6, 613/995-3708; Fax: 613/957-4023

Bank of Canada, 234 Wellington St., Ottawa ON K1A 0G9, 613/782-8111; Fax: 613/782-8655

Business Development Bank of Canada, Tour de la Place-Victoria, #800, Place Victoria, CP 335, Montréal PQ H4Z 1L4, 514/283-5904; Toll Free: 1-888-463-6232; Fax: 514/283-0617

Canada Deposit Insurance Corporation, 50 O'Connor St., 17th Fl., PO Box 2340, Stn D, Ottawa ON K1P 5W5, 613/996-2081; Toll Free: 1-800-461-2342; Fax: 613/996-6095

Finance Canada, Financial Institutions Division, Esplanade Laurier, 140 O'Connor St., Ottawa ON K1A 0G5, 613/992-9214; Fax: 613/996-8404

Office of the Superintendent of Financial Institutions, Kent Square, 255 Albert St., Ottawa ON K1A 0H2, 613/990-7788; Toll Free: 1-800-385-8647; Fax: 613/952-8219

Revenue Canada, 875 Heron Rd., Ottawa ON K1A 0L8, 613/957-0275

Treasury Board of Canada, 140 O'Connor St., Ottawa ON K1A 0R5, 613/957-2400; Fax: 613/952-3658

Alta: Alberta Treasury, Banking & Cash Management, Terrace Bldg., 9515 - 107 St., Edmonton AB T5K 2C3, 403/427-3035; Fax: 403/422-2463

Financial Institutions, Terrace Bldg., 9515 - 107 St., Edmonton AB T5K 2C3, 403/427-3035; Fax: 403/422-2463

B.C.: Financial Institutions Commission, #1900, 1050 West Pender St., Vancouver BC V6E 3S7, 604/660-2947; Fax: 604/660-3170

International Finance Centre - Vancouver Society, World Trade Centre, #658, 999 Canada Place, Vancouver BC V6C 3E1, 604/683-6626; Fax: 604/683-6646

Ministry of Finance & Corporate Relations, 617 Government St., Victoria BC V8V 1X4, 250/387-9278

Man.: Manitoba Agricultural Credit Corporation, #100, 1525 - 1 St., Brandon MB R7A 7A1, 204/726-6850; Fax: 204/726-6849

Manitoba Finance, #109, Legislative Bldg., Winnipeg MB R3C 0V8, 204/945-3754; Fax: 204/945-8316

Manitoba Treasury Board, 333 Broadway, 3rd Fl., Winnipeg MB R3C 0S9, 204/945-1101; Fax: 204/945-4878

N.B.: Department of Justice, Corporate Affairs, #412, Centennial Bldg., PO Box 6000, Fredericton NB E3B 5H1, 506/453-3860; Fax: 506/453-2613

Credit Unions, Cooperatives & Trust Companies, #412, Centennial Bldg., PO Box 6000, Fredericton NB E3B 5H1, 506/457-4850; Fax: 506/453-7474

Nfld.: Department of Finance & Treasury Board, Confederation Bldg., PO Box 8700, St. John's NF A1B 4J6, 709/729-2858; Fax: 709/729-2856

NWT: Department of Finance, PO Box 1320, Yellowknife NT X1A 2L9

Northwest Territories Business Credit Corporation, Northern United Place, 5004 - 54 St., PO Box 1320, Yellowknife NT X1A 2L9, 403/920-6454; Fax: 403/873-0101

Northwest Territories Development Corporation, Tower 7, PO Box 1437, Yellowknife NT X1A 2P1, 403/920-7700; Fax: 403/920-7701

N.S.: Department of Finance, PO Box 187, Halifax NS B3J 2N3, 902/424-5554; Fax: 902/424-0635

Ont.: Ministry of Finance, Deposit Institutions, Frost Bldg. South, 7 Queen's Park Cres., Toronto ON M7A 1Y7, 416/325-0333 (Communications & Corporate Affairs); Fax: 416/325-0339

Fiscal & Financial Policy Division, Frost Bldg. South, 7 Queen's Park Cres., Toronto ON M7A 1Y7, 416/325-0333 (Communications & Corporate Affairs); Fax: 416/325-0339

Ontario Financing Authority, #1400, 1 Dundas St. West, Toronto ON M7A 1Y7

PEI: Department of Provincial Affairs & Attorney General, Securities, PO Box 2000, Charlottetown PE C1A 7N8, 902/368-4552; Fax: 902/368-5283; 5355

Department of the Provincial Treasury, PO Box 2000, Charlottetown PE C1A 7N8, 902/368-4000; Fax: 902/368-5544

Qué.: Caisse de dépôt et placement du Québec, 1981, av McGill College, Montréal PQ H3A 3C7, 514/842-3261; Fax: 514/842-4833

Commission des valeurs mobilières du Québec, Tour de la Bourse, 800, Place Victoria, 17e étage, Montréal PQ H4Z 1G3, 514/873-5326; Fax: 514/873-0711

L'Inspecteur général des Institutions financières, 800, place D'Youville, Québec PQ G1R 4Y5, 418/694-5016 (Communications); Fax: 418/643-3336

Ministère des Finances, Politiques-Institutions Financières, 12, rue St-Louis, Québec PQ G1R 5L3, 418/691-2233; Fax: 418/646-5643, 1631

Sask.: Saskatchewan Securities Commission, Toronto Dominion Bank Bldg., #850, 1914 Hamilton St., Regina SK S4P 3V7, 306/787-5645; Fax: 306/787-5899

Saskatchewan Finance, 2350 Albert St., Regina SK S4P 4A6, 306/787-6768; Fax: 306/787-6544

Saskatchewan Justice, Insurance, 1874 Scarth St., Regina SK S4P 3V7, 306/787-7881; Fax: 306/787-9779

Yuk.: Yukon Finance, PO Box 2703, Whitehorse YT Y1A 2C6, 403/667-5343; Fax: 403/393-6217

Yukon Justice, Corporate Affairs & Registrar of Securities, PO Box 2703, Whitehorse YT Y1A 2C6, 403/667-5225; Fax: 403/393-6272

BANKRUPTCY
Industry Canada, Office of the Superintendent of Bankruptcy, Journal Tower South, 365 Laurier St. West, 8th Fl., Ottawa ON K1A 0C8, 613/941-1000; Fax: 613/941-2862

BIBLIOGRAPHIC SERVICES
Library of Parliament, 111 Wellington St., Ottawa ON K1A 0A9, 613/995-1166; Fax: 613/992-1269

National Archives of Canada, 395 Wellington St., Ottawa ON K1A 0N3, 613/995-5138; Fax: 613/995-6274

National Research Council (Canada), Canadian Institute for Scientific & Technical Information, Bldg. M-58, 1200 Montreal Rd., Ottawa ON K1A 0R6, 613/993-9101; Fax: 613/952-7928

Alta: Alberta Community Development, Arts, Recreation & Libraries Branch, Beaver House, 10158 - 103 St., 3rd Fl., Edmonton AB T5J 0X6, 403/427-6315; Fax: 403/422-9132

Provincial Archives, 12845 - 102 Ave., Edmonton AB T5N 0H6, 403/427-1750; Fax: 403/427-4646

Alberta Justice, Law Libraries, Law Courts Bldg., 5th Fl., North, 1A Sir Winston Churchill Square, 2nd Fl. South, Edmonton AB T5J 0R2, 403/427-5579, 5580; Fax: 403/427-0481

B.C.: Ministry of Municipal Affairs & Housing, Library Services, Municipal Affairs, PO Box 9490, Victoria BC V8W 9N7, 250/356-1795; Fax: 250/387-4048

Man.: Manitoba Culture, Heritage & Citizenship, Public Library Services, #200, 1595 - 1 St., Brandon MB R7A 7A1, 204/726-6864; Fax: 204/726-6868

N.B.: Department of Municipalities, Culture & Housing, Libraries, Marysville Place, 20 McGloin St., PO Box 6000, Fredericton NB E3B 5H1, 506/453-2354; Fax: 506/457-4991

Nfld.: Department of Tourism, Culture & Recreation, Provincial Archives, Confederation Bldg., PO Box 8700, St. John's NF A1B 4J6, 709/729-3065; Fax: 709/729-0578

NWT: Department of Education, Culture & Employment, NWT Public Library Services, PO Box 1100, Hay River NT X0E 0R0, 403/874-6531; Fax: 403/873-0155

N.S.: Department of Education & Culture, Provincial Library, 2021 Brunswick St., PO Box 578, Halifax NS B3J 2S9, 902/424-2457; Fax: 902/424-0633

Ont.: Ministry of Citizenship, Culture & Recreation, Libraries & Community Information Branch, 77 Bloor St. West, 6th Fl., Toronto ON M7A 2R9, 416/314-7265

Northern Ontario Library Service, 334 Regent St., Sudbury ON P3C 4E2, 705/675-6467; Fax: 705/675-6108

Southern Ontario Library Service, #50, 55 West Beaver Creek, Richmond Hill ON L4B 1K5, 905/771-1522; Fax: 905/771-1526

PEI: Department of Education, Provincial Libraries & Archives, Sullivan Bldg., 16 Fitzroy St., PO Box 2000, Charlottetown PE C1A 7N8, 902/368-4227; Fax: 902/961-3203
Qué.: Ministère de la Culture et des Communications, Archives nationales et centre de conservation du Québec, Pavillon Louis-Jacques Casault, 1210 av du Séminaire, Ste-Foy PQ G1N 4V1, 418/643-4376; Fax: 418/646-0868
Sask.: Saskatchewan Archives Board, University of Regina, 3737 Wascana Pkwy., Regina SK S4S 0A2, 306/787-4068; Fax: 306/787-1975
Yuk.: Yukon Education, Libraries & Archives, PO Box 2703, Whitehorse YT Y1A 2C6, 403/667-5309; Fax: 403/667-4253

BILINGUALISM

Canadian Heritage, Official Languages, Jules Léger Bldg., 25 Eddy St., Hull PQ K1A 1K5, 819/994-0943; Fax: 819/953-9353
Office of the Commissioner of Official Languages, 110 O'Connor St., Ottawa ON K1A 0T8, 613/996-6368; Fax: 613/993-5082
Treasury Board of Canada, Official Languages & Employment Equity Branch, 140 O'Connor St., Ottawa ON K1A 0R5, 613/952-2852; Fax: 613/941-4262
Alta: Alberta Education, Language Services, Devonian Bldg., 11160 Jasper Ave., Edmonton AB T5K 0L2, 403/427-2940; Fax: 403/422-1947
B.C.: Ministry of Education, Skills & Training, Policy, Planning & Special Programs Division, PO Box 9150, Stn Prov Govt, Victoria BC V8W 9H1, 250/356-2500; Fax: 250/356-5945
Man.: Le Centre Culturel Franco-Manitobain, 340, boul Provencher, St. Boniface MB R2H 0G7, 204/233-8972; Fax: 204/233-3324
Manitoba Culture, Heritage & Citizenship, Translation Services, 213 Notre Dame Ave., 2nd Fl., Winnipeg MB R3B 1N3, 204/945-3095; Fax: 204/945-5879
Manitoba Education & Training, Bureau de l'Education Française, #509. 1181 Portage Ave., Winnipeg MB R3C 0T3, 204/945-4325; Fax: 204/945-1291
N.B.: Department of Education, Educational Services Division (Anglophone), PO Box 6000, Fredericton NB E3B 5H1, 506/453-3678; Fax: 506/453-3325
Secteur des services Francophones d'éducation, PO Box 6000, Fredericton NB E3B 5H1, 506/453-3678; Fax: 506/453-3325
Department of Finance, Official Languages, PO Box 6000, Fredericton NB E3B 5H1, 506/453-2059; Fax: 506/457-4989
NWT: Department of Education, Culture & Employment, Language Bureau, PO Box 1320, Yellowknife NT X1A 2L9, 403/920-6484; Fax: 403/873-0155
Executive Council, Office of Official Languages, PO Box 1320, Yellowknife NT X1A 2L9, 403/920-6960
Legislative Assembly, Office of the Languages Commissioner, PO Box 1320, Yellowknife NT X1A 2L9, 403/873-7034; Fax: 403/920-4735
N.S.: Department of Education & Culture, Acadian & French Language Services Branch, 2021 Brunswick St., PO Box 578, Halifax NS B3J 2S9, 902/424-5168; Fax: 902/424-0511
Ont.: Languages of Instruction Commission of Ontario, 56 Wellesley St. West, 11th Fl., Toronto ON M7A 2B7, 416/314-3500; Fax: 416/314-3502
Ministry of Education & Training, French-Language Education Policy & Programs, Mowat Block, 900 Bay St., Toronto ON M7A 1L2, 416/325-2127; Fax: 416/325-2934
Ministry of Municipal Affairs & Housing, Office of Francophone Municipal Relations, 777 Bay St., 17th Fl., Toronto ON M5G 2E5, 416/585-7556; Fax: 416/585-6227

Office of Francophone Affairs, Mowat Block, 900 Bay St., 4th Fl., Toronto ON M7A 1C2, 416/325-4949; Toll Free: 1-800-268-7507; Fax: 416/325-4980
PEI: Department of Education, French Programs & Services, Sullivan Bldg., 16 Fitzroy St., PO Box 2000, Charlottetown PE C1A 7N8, 902/368-4671; Fax: 902/368-4622
Department of Provincial Affairs & Attorney General, Francophone Affairs Secretariat, PO Box 2000, Charlottetown PE C1A 7N8, 902/368-4509; Fax: 902/368-5283; 5355
Qué.: Ministère de l'Éducation, Communauté anglophone, 600, rue Fullum, Montréal PQ H2K 4L1, 514/873-4630; Fax: 514/873-1082
Secrétariat aux affaires intergouvernementales canadiennes, Bureaux coopération et francophonie, Edifice H, 3e étage, 875, Grande Allée est, Québec PQ G1R 4Y8, 418/643-4011; Fax: 418/643-8730
Sask.: Saskatchewan Education, Official Minority Language Office Branch, 2220 College Ave., Regina SK S4P 3V7, 306/787-6089; Fax: 306/787-2280
Saskatchewan Intergovernmental Affairs, Office of French Language Coordination, 1919 Saskatchewan Dr., Regina SK S4P 3V7, 306/787-2028; Fax: 306/787-6352
Yuk.: Executive Council, Bureau of French Language Services, PO Box 2703, Whitehorse YT Y1A 2C6, 403/667-3775; Fax: 403/393-6226
Yukon Education, French Programs, PO Box 2703, Whitehorse YT Y1A 2C6, 403/667-5141; Fax: 403/667-4754

BIOTECHNOLOGY

Biotechnology Research Centre, 6100, av Royalmount, Montréal PQ H4P 2R2, 514/496-6100; Fax: 514/496-6388
Industry Canada, Chemicals & Bio-Industries, C.D. Howe Bldg., 235 Queen St., Ottawa ON K1A 0H5, 613/954-3071; Fax: 613/952-4209
Institute for Biological Sciences, 1500 Montreal Rd., Ottawa ON K1A 0R6, 613/993-5998; Fax: 613/957-7867
Plant Biotechnology Institute, 110 Gymnasium Rd., Saskatoon SK S7N 0W9, 306/975-5248; Fax: 306/975-4839
Alta: Alberta Research Council, Biotechnology, 250 Karl Clark Rd., PO Box 8330, Edmonton AB T6H 5X2, 403/450-5319; Fax: 403/461-2651
B.C.: Science Council of British Columbia, #800, 4710 Kingsway, Burnaby BC V5H 4M2, 604/438-2752; Toll Free: 1-800-665-7222; Fax: 604/438-6564
N.B.: New Brunswick Research & Productivity Council, Chemical & Biotechnical Services, 921 College Hill Rd., Fredericton NB E3B 6Z9, 506/452-1369; Fax: 506/452-1395
NWT: Aurora Research Institute, c/o Aurora College, PO Box 1430, Inuvik NT X0E 0T0
Nunavut Research Institute, Aeroplex Bldg., PO Box 160, Iqualuit NT X0A 0H0, 819/979-4114; Fax: 819/979-4119
N.S.: Innovation Corporation (InNOVAcorp), Woodside Industrial Park, 101 Research Dr., PO Box 790, Dartmouth NS B2Y 3Z7, 902/424-8670; Toll Free: 1-800-565-7051; Fax: 902/424-4679
Ont.: Ministry of Agriculture, Food & Rural Affairs, Education, Research & Laboratories Division, 95 Stone Rd. West, PO Box 3650, Guelph ON N1H 8J7, 519/767-3603; Fax: 519/767-3635
PEI: Department of Agriculture, Fisheries & Forestry, Research, Resources & Laboratories, PO Box 306, Kensington PE C0B 1M0, 902/368-5646; Fax: 902/368-5661
Qué.: Centre québécois de valorisation des biomasses et des biotechnologies, #620, 2875, boul Laurier, Ste-Foy PQ G1V 2M2, 418/657-3853; Fax: 418/657-7934

Sask.: Saskatchewan Research Council, 15 Innovation Blvd., Saskatoon SK S7N 2X8, 306/933-5400; Fax: 306/933-7896

BIRDS *See* **WILDLIFE RESOURCES**

BIRTH CERTIFICATES *See* **VITAL STATISTICS**

BOARDS OF REVIEW

Alta: Alberta Board of Review, J.E. Brownlee Bldg., 10365 - 97 St., 5th Fl., Edmonton AB T5J 3W7, 403/422-5994; Fax: 403/427-1762
B.C.: British Columbia Review Board, #310, 435 Columbia St., New Westminster BC V3L 5N8, 604/669-8789; Fax: 604/660-8809
Man.: Board of Review, 408 York St., 2nd Fl., Winnipeg MB R3C 3L6, 204/945-4438; Fax: 204/945-1260
NWT: Territorial Board of Revision, PO Box 1320, Yellowknife NT X1A 2L9, 403/873-7997; Fax: 403/920-3159
N.S.: Nova Scotia Utility & Review Board, #300, 1601 Lower Water St., PO Box 1692, Stn M, Halifax NS B3J 3S3, 902/424-4448; Fax: 902/424-3919
Qué.: Bureau de révision de l'évaluation foncière du Québec, #RC10, 575, rue St-Amable, Québec PQ G1R 5R4, 418/643-3355; Fax: 418/646-0846
Bureau de révision en immigration, 2055, rue Peel, Montréal PQ H3A 1V4, 514/864-3010; Fax: 514/864-3181

BOATS *See* **LEISURE CRAFT & VEHICLE REGULATIONS**

BROADCASTING

Canadian Broadcasting Corporation, 1500 Bronson Ave., PO Box 8478, Ottawa ON K1G 3J5, 613/724-1200; TDD: 613/738-6686
Canadian Heritage, Broadcasting, Jules Léger Bldg., 25 Eddy St., Hull PQ K1A 1K5, 613/990-7937; Fax: 613/952-5109
Canadian Radio-Television & Telecommunications Commission, 1, du Portage Promenade, Terrasses de la Chaudière, Hull PQ J8X 4B1, 819/997-0313 (Public Affairs); Fax: 819/994-0218
House of Commons, Canada, Broadcasting Service, House of Commons, 111 Wellington St., PO Box 1103, Ottawa ON K1A 0A9, 613/995-3490
Industry Canada, Radio Communications & Broadcast Research, 3701 Carling Ave., PO Box 11490, Stn H, Ottawa ON K2H 8S2, 613/998-2332; Fax: 613/990-7986
Ont.: TV Ontario, 2180 Yonge St., 5th Fl., Toronto ON M4S 2C1, 416/484-2600; Fax: 416/484-4234
Qué.: Ministère de la Culture et des Communications, Arts, médias et technologies de l'information, 225, Grand-Allée est, Québec PQ G1R 5G5, 418/643-1887; Fax: 418/643-7853
Inforoutes et communications, 225, Grand-Allée est, Québec PQ G1R 5G5, 418/643-8096; Fax: 418/528-0874
Régie des télécommunications du Québec, #5.00, 900 place d'Youville, Québec PQ G1R 3P7, 418/643-5560; Fax: 418/643-2960
Société de radio-télévision du Québec, 1000, rue Fullum, Montréal PQ H2K 3L7, 514/521-2424; Toll Free: 1-800-361-4301; Fax: 514/873-7739
Sask.: Legislative Assembly, Broadcast Services, c/o Clerk's Office, #239, Legislative Bldg., Regina SK S4S 0B3, 306/787-2181; Fax: 306/787-0408
Saskatchewan Communications Network, North Block, 2440 Broad St., Regina SK S4P 3V7, 306/787-0490; Fax: 306/787-0496

Canadian Almanac & Directory 1997

BUSINESS ASSISTANCE PROGRAMS *See* **INDUSTRY**

BUSINESS DEVELOPMENT
See Also **Industry; Science, Technology Development**

Agriculture & Agri-Food Canada, Market & Industry Services Branch, Sir John Carling Bldg., 930 Carling Ave., 5th Fl., Ottawa ON K1A 0C5, 613/759-7561; Fax: 613/759-7497

Atlantic Canada Opportunities Agency, 644 Main St., 3rd Fl., PO Box 6051, Moncton NB E1C 9J8, 506/851-2271; Toll Free: 1-800-561-7862, TDD: 506/851-3540; Fax: 506/851-7403

Business Development Bank of Canada, Tour de la Place-Victoria, #800, Place Victoria, CP 335, Montréal PQ H4Z 1L4, 514/283-5904; Toll Free: 1-888-463-6232; Fax: 514/283-0617

Canadian Commercial Corporation, Metropolitan Centre, #1100, 50 O'Connor St., Ottawa ON K1A 0S6, 613/996-0034; Fax: 613/995-2121

Export Development Corporation, 151 O'Connor St., Ottawa ON K1A 1K3, 613/598-2500; Fax: 613/237-2690

Federal Office of Regional Development (Québec), Tour de la Bourse, #3800, 800, Place Victoria, CP 247, Montréal PQ H4Z 1E8, 514/283-6412, 4843; Toll Free: 1-800-263-4689; Fax: 514/283-7778

Industry Canada, C.D. Howe Bldg., 235 Queen St., Ottawa ON K1A 0H5, 613/954-2788; Fax: 613/954-2303
Aboriginal Business Canada, 235 Queen St., Ottawa ON K1A 0H5, 613/954-2788; Fax: 613/954-2303

Public Works & Government Services Canada, Supply Operations Service Branch, Place du Portage, Phase III, 11, rue Laurier, Hull PQ K1A 0S5, 819/956-0921; Fax: 819/953-1058

Statistics Canada, Business & Trade Statistics, R.H. Coats Bldg., Tunney's Pasture, 120 Parkdale Ave., Ottawa ON K1A 0T6, 613/951-8116; Fax: 613/951-0581

Treasury Board of Canada, Office of Infrastructure, West Tower, 300 Laurier Ave. West, 3rd Fl., Ottawa ON K1A 0R5, 613/952-3171; Fax: 613/952-7979

Western Economic Diversification Canada, Canada Place, #1500, 9700 Jasper Ave., Edmonton AB T5J 4H7, 403/495-4164; Fax: 403/495-6876

Alta: Alberta Economic Development Authority, Commerce Place, 10155 - 102nd St., 6th Fl., Edmonton AB T5J 4L6, 403/427-2251; Fax: 403/427-5922

Alberta Opportunity Company, 5110 - 49 Ave., PO Box 4040, Ponoka AB T4J 1R5, 403/783-7011; Toll Free: 1-800-661-3811; Fax: 403/783-7032

Alberta Economic Development & Tourism, Commerce Place, 10155 - 102 St., Edmonton AB T5J 4L6, 403/427-2280
Tourism, Trade & Investment, Commerce Place, 10155 - 102 St., Edmonton AB T5J 4L6, 403/427-2280; Fax: 403/427-1700

Northern Alberta Development Council, #206, Provincial Bldg., 9621 - 96 Ave., PO Bag 900-14, Peace River AB T8S 1T4, 403/624-6274; Fax: 403/624-6184

Sustainable Development Coordinating Council, South Petroleum Plaza, 9915 - 108 St., 10th Floor, Edmonton AB T5K 2G8, 403/427-6236; Fax: 403/422-6305

B.C.: Ministry of Employment & Investment, British Columbia Trade & Investment Office, 712 Yates St., Victoria BC V8V 1X4, 250/953-4701; Fax: 250/387-7969
Science, Technology & Capital Development Division, 712 Yates St., Victoria BC V8V 1X4, 250/356-5478; Fax: 250/387-4410

Ministry of Small Business, Tourism & Culture, Business Equity Branch, 1405 Douglas St., 4th Fl., Victoria BC V8W 3C1, 250/387-0225, 844-1823 (Vancouver); Fax: 250/387-1080

Premiers' Advisory Council on Science & Technology, #501, 168 Chadwick Ct., North Vancouver BC V7M 3L4, 604/987-8477; Fax: 604/987-5617

Man.: Economic Development Board, #648, 155 Carlton St., Winnipeg MB R3C 3H8, 204/945-8221; Fax: 204/945-8229

Manitoba Development Corporation, #555, 155 Carlton St., Winnipeg MB R3C 3H8, 204/945-7626; Fax: 204/957-1793

Manitoba Industry, Trade & Tourism, 155 Carlton St., 6th Fl., Winnipeg MB R3C 3H8, 204/945-2066; Fax: 204/945-1354

N.B.: Department of Economic Development & Tourism, Centennial Bldg., 670 King St., 5th Fl., PO Box 6000, Fredericton NB E3B 5H1, 506/453-2850 (Communications & Promotion); Fax: 506/444-4586
Small Business Directorate, Centennial Bldg., 670 King St., 5th Fl., PO Box 6000, Fredericton NB E3B 5H1, 506/453-3890; Fax: 506/457-4845

New Brunswick Industrial Development Board, PO Box 6000, Fredericton NB E3B 5H1, 506/453-2474; Fax: 506/453-7904

Regional Development Corporation, 836 Churchill Row, PO Box 428, Fredericton NB E3B 5R4, 506/453-2277; Fax: 506/453-7988

Nfld.: Enterprise Newfoundland & Labrador, 136 Crosbie Rd., St. John's NF A1B 3K3, 709/729-7000; Toll Free: 1-800-563-9179; Fax: 709/729-7135

NWT: Department of Resources, Wildlife & Economic Development, Trade & Investment Division, #600, Scotia Centre, Bldg. Box 21, 5102 - 50 Ave., Yellowknife NT X1A 3S8, 403/873-7420, 7134; Fax: 403/873-0114

Northwest Territories Business Credit Corporation, Northern United Place, 5004 - 54 St., PO Box 1320, Yellowknife NT X1A 2L9, 403/920-6454; Fax: 403/873-0101

Northwest Territories Development Corporation, Tower 7, PO Box 1437, Yellowknife NT X1A 2P1, 403/920-7700; Fax: 403/920-7701

N.S.: Department of Business & Consumer Services, Joseph Howe Bldg., 1681 Granville St., PO Box 1003, Halifax NS B3J 2X1, 902/424-7777; Fax: 902/424-7434

Innovation Corporation (InNOVAcorp), Woodside Industrial Park, 101 Research Dr., PO Box 790, Dartmouth NS B2Y 3Z7, 902/424-8670; Toll Free: 1-800-565-7051; Fax: 902/424-4679

Nova Scotia Business Development Corporation, World Trade & Convention Centre, 1800 Argyle St., 6th Fl., Halifax NS B3J 2R7, 902/424-6488; Fax: 902/424-6823

Nova Scotia Economic Renewal Agency, 1800 Argyle St., PO Box 519, Halifax NS B3J 2R7, 902/424-8920; Fax: 902/424-0582

Ont.: Ministry of Agriculture, Food & Rural Affairs, Farm Business Management & Western Region, Information Centre, 801 Bay St., 1st Fl., Toronto ON M7A 2B2, 416/767-3151; Fax: 416/837-3049

Ministry of Economic Development, Trade & Tourism, Hearst Block, 900 Bay St., Toronto ON M7A 2E1, 416/325-6666; Fax: 416/325-6688

Ontario Development Corporation, 56 Wellesley St. West, 6th Fl., Toronto ON M7A 2E7, 416/326-1070; Fax: 416/326-1073

PEI: Department of Economic Development & Tourism, Business Support Programs, Annex 2, West Royalty Park, 2 First Ave., Charlottetown PE C1E 1B0, 902/368-6300; Fax: 902/368-6301

Qué.: Ministère de l'Industrie, du commerce, de la Science et de la technologie, 710, Place d'Youville, 9e étage, Québec PQ G1R 4Y4, 418/691-5950 (Renseignements); Fax: 418/644-0118

Sask.: Saskatchewan Development Fund Corporation, #300, 2400 College Ave., Regina SK S4P 1C8, 306/787-1645; Fax: 306/787-8125

Saskatchewan Economic Development, 1919 Saskatchewan Dr., Regina SK S4P 3V7, 306/787-2232
Industry Development Programs, 1919 Saskatchewan Dr., Regina SK S4P 3V7, 306/787-9215

Yuk.: Business Development Advisory Board, PO Box 2703, Whitehorse YT Y1A 2C6, 403/667-5470

Yukon Economic Development, Rural Business/Community Development Office, Dawson City, 211 Main St., PO Box 2703, Whitehorse YT Y1A 2C6, 403/667-5466; Fax: 403/668-8601

Whitehorse Business/Community Development Office, 211 Main St., PO Box 2703, Whitehorse YT Y1A 2C6, 403/667-5466; Fax: 403/668-8601

BUSINESS REGULATIONS

Industry Canada, C.D. Howe Bldg., 235 Queen St., Ottawa ON K1A 0H5, 613/954-2788; Fax: 613/954-2303

Revenue Canada, 875 Heron Rd., Ottawa ON K1A 0L8, 613/957-0275

Alta: Alberta Economic Development & Tourism, Business Finance, Commerce Place, 10155 - 102 St., Edmonton AB T5J 4L6, 403/427-3300; Fax: 403/422-9319

Alberta Municipal Affairs, Registries Division, John E. Brownlee Bldg., 10365 - 97 St., Edmonton AB T5J 3W7, 403/422-2362 (Edmonton), 297-8980 (Calgary); Toll Free: 1-800-465-5009 (in Alberta); Fax: 403/422-9105

B.C.: Ministry of Finance & Corporate Relations, Registries & Ministry Support Services, 617 Government St., Victoria BC V8V 1X4, 250/387-9278

Man.: Manitoba Consumer & Corporate Affairs, Companies Office, #317, 450 Broadway, Winnipeg MB R3C 0V8, 204/945-4206

N.B.: Department of Justice, Consumer Affairs & Chief Rentalsman, #412, Centennial Bldg., PO Box 6000, Fredericton NB E3B 5H1, 506/453-2682; Fax: 506/444-4494
Corporate Affairs, #412, Centennial Bldg., PO Box 6000, Fredericton NB E3B 5H1, 506/453-3860; Fax: 506/453-2613

Nfld.: Department of Government Services & Lands, Commercial & Corporate Affairs, PO Box 8700, St. John's NF A1B 4J6

NWT: Northwest Territories Business Credit Corporation, Northern United Place, 5004 - 54 St., PO Box 1320, Yellowknife NT X1A 2L9, 403/920-6454; Fax: 403/873-0101

Northwest Territories Development Corporation, Tower 7, PO Box 1437, Yellowknife NT X1A 2P1, 403/920-7700; Fax: 403/920-7701

Ont.: Ministry of Consumer & Commercial Relations, Companies Branch, 393 University Ave., 2nd Fl., Toronto ON M7A 2H6, 416/596-3725; Fax: 416/596-0438

PEI: Department of Provincial Affairs & Attorney General, PO Box 2000, Charlottetown PE C1A 7N8, 902/368-4551; Fax: 902/368-5283
Securities, PO Box 2000, Charlottetown PE C1A 7N8, 902/368-4552; Fax: 902/368-5283; 5355

Qué.: L'Inspecteur général des Institutions financières, 800, place D'Youville, Québec PQ G1R 4Y5, 418/694-5016 (Communications); Fax: 418/643-3336

Ministère de l'Industrie, du commerce, de la Science et de la technologie, 710, Place d'Youville, 9e étage, Québec PQ G1R 4Y4, 418/691-5950 (Renseignements); Fax: 418/644-0118

Sask.: Saskatchewan Justice, Consumer Protection Branch, 1874 Scarth St., Regina SK S4P 3V7, 306/787-2952; Fax: 306/787-5550

Yuk.: Yukon Economic Development, Economic Policy, Planning & Research Branch, 211 Main St., PO Box 2703, Whitehorse YT Y1A 2C6, 403/667-5466; Fax: 403/668-8601

Yukon Justice, Consumer Services, PO Box 2703, Whitehorse YT Y1A 2C6, 403/667-5257; Fax: 403/393-6272

CABINETS & EXECUTIVE COUNCILS
See Also Government (General Information); Parliament

The Canadian Ministry, House of Commons, 111 Wellington St., Ottawa ON K1A 0A6

Alta: Executive Council, Legislature Bldg., 10800 - 97 Ave., Edmonton AB T5K 2B6, 403/427-2251; Fax: 403/427-1349

B.C.: Executive Council, #156, Parliament Bldgs., Victoria BC V8V 1X4

Man.: Executive Council, Legislative Bldg., Winnipeg MB R3C 0V8

N.B.: Executive Council, Centennial Bldg., PO Box 6000, Fredericton NB E3B 5H1

Nfld.: Executive Council, Confederation Bldg., PO Box 8700, St. John's NF A1B 4J6, 709/729-5645

NWT: Executive Council, PO Box 1320, Yellowknife NT X1A 2L9

N.S.: Executive Council, One Government Place, PO Box 2125, Halifax NS B3J 3B7, 902/424-5970; Fax: 902/424-0667

Ont.: Executive Council, #4340, Whitney Block, Queen's Park, 99 Wellesley St. West, Toronto ON M7A 1A1, 416/325-7641

PEI: Executive Council, Shaw Bldg., PO Box 2000, Charlottetown PE C1A 7N8

Qué.: Conseil exécutif, Hôtel du Parlement, Québec PQ G1A 1A4

Sask.: Executive Council, Legislative Bldg., Regina SK S4S 0B3

Yuk.: , PO Box 2703, Whitehorse YT Y1A 2C6, 403/667-5812; Fax: 403/393-6202

CANADA PENSION PLAN *See* PENSIONS

CAREER PLANNING
Human Resources Development Canada, Occupational & Career Information, Place du Portage, Phase IV, 140, Promenade du Portage, Hull PQ K1A 0J9, 819/953-7434; Fax: 819/997-5851

Alta: Alberta Advanced Education & Career Development, System Funding & Accountability Division, Commerce Place, 10155 - 102 St., 11th Fl., Edmonton AB T5J 4L5, 403/422-4488; Fax: 403/422-5126

B.C.: Ministry of Education, Skills & Training, Career Programs Branch, PO Box 9150, Stn Prov Govt, Victoria BC V8W 9H1, 250/387-7044; Fax: 250/387-1418

Skills Development Division, PO Box 9150, Stn Prov Govt, Victoria BC V8W 9H1, 250/356-2500; Fax: 250/356-5945

Man.: Manitoba Education & Training, Workforce 2000 & Youth Programs, 185 Carlton St., 4th Fl., Winnipeg MB R3C 3J1, 204/945-6195; Fax: 204/945-1792

N.B.: Department of Advanced Education & Labour, Learning in the Workplace Initiative, Chestnut Complex, 470 York St., PO Box 6000, Fredericton NB E3B 5H1, 506/444-4331; Fax: 506/453-3300

Student Services, Chestnut Complex, 470 York St., PO Box 6000, Fredericton NB E3B 5H1, 506/453-3358; Fax: 506/444-4333

Nfld.: Department of Education, Advanced Studies Branch, Confederation Bldg., PO Box 8700, St. John's NF A1B 4J6, 709/729-5097; Fax: 709/729-5896

Department of Environment & Labour, Youth Strategy & Career Support, Confederation Bldg., PO Box 8700, St. John's NF A1B 4J6, 709/729-2314; Fax: 709/729-6639

NWT: Department of Education, Culture & Employment, Career Development, PO Box 1320, Yellowknife NT X1A 2L9, 403/873-7146; Fax: 403/873-0155

N.S.: Department of Education & Culture, Student Services Division, 2021 Brunswick St., PO Box 578, Halifax NS B3J 2S9, 902/424-7454; Fax: 902/424-0749

Ont.: Ministry of Education & Training, Training Division, Mowat Block, 900 Bay St., Toronto ON M7A 1L2, 416/325-2929; Fax: 416/325-2934

PEI: Department of Economic Development & Tourism, Special Projects Division, Shaw Bldg., 105 Rochford St., 4th Fl., Charlottetown PE C1A 7N8, 902/368-4240; Fax: 902/368-4224

Office of Higher Education, Training & Adult Learning, Shaw Bldg., 105 Rochford St., 3rd Fl., PO Box 2000, Charlottetown PE C1A 7N8, 902/368-5988; Fax: 902/368-6144

Qué.: Ministère de l'Éducation, 1035, rue De La Chevrotière, 15e étage, Québec PQ G1R 5A5, 418/643-3810; Fax: 418/646-6561

Service de placement étudiant, 2700, boul Laurier, 3e étage, Sainte-Foy PQ G1V 2L8, 418/643-6965; Fax: 418/643-7901

Sask.: Saskatchewan Post-Secondary Education & Skills Training, 2220 College Ave., Regina SK S4P 3V7, 306/787-1002

Yuk.: Yukon Education, Training Services, PO Box 2703, Whitehorse YT Y1A 2C6, 403/667-5141; Fax: 403/667-4754

CENSORSHIP (MEDIA)
Canadian Heritage, Arts Policy, Jules Léger Bldg., 25 Eddy St., Hull PQ K1A 1K5, 613/991-5727; Fax: 613/952-3632

Alta: Alberta Community Development, Film Classification Board, Standard Life Centre, 10405 Jasper Ave., 7th Fl., Edmonton AB T5J 4R7, 403/427-2006; Fax: 403/427-1496

B.C.: Motion Picture Appeal Board, #310, 435 Columbia St., New Westminster BC V3L 5N8, 604/660-8789; Fax: 604/660-8809

Man.: Film Classification Board (& Film Classification Appeal Board), #216, 301 Weston St., Winnipeg MB R3E 3H4, 204/945-8962; Fax: 204/945-0890

N.B.: New Brunswick Film Classification Board, c/o Dept. of Municipalities, Culture & Housing, 20 McGloin St., PO Box 6000, Fredericton NB E3B 5H1, 506/453-2553

N.S.: Nova Scotia Amusements Regulation Board, PO Box 607, Halifax NS B3J 2R7, 902/424-4690

Ont.: Ministry of Consumer & Commercial Relations, Entertainment Standards, 1075 Millwood Rd., Toronto ON M4G 1X6, 416/314-3626; Fax: 416/314-3632

Ontario Film Review Board, 1075 Millwood Rd., Toronto ON M4G 1X6, 416/314-3626

Qué.: Régie du Cinéma, 455, rue Ste-Hélène, Montréal PQ H2Y 2L3, 514/873-2491; Fax: 514/873-8874

Sask.: Saskatchewan Film Classification Appeal Commission, 1871 Smith St., Regina SK S4P 3V7, 306/787-5884; Fax: 306/787-9779

Saskatchewan Film Classification Board, 1871 Smith St., Regina SK S4P 3V7, 306/787-5884; Fax: 306/787-9779

CHEMICAL RELEASES *See* EMERGENCY RESPONSE

CHEMICALS
Environment Canada, Toxics Pollution Prevention Directorate, Place Vincent-Massey, 351, boul St-Joseph, Hull PQ K1A 0H3, 819/953-1114; Fax: 819/953-5371

Fisheries & Oceans Canada, Science, 200 Kent St., Ottawa ON K1A 0E6, 613/993-0999

Industrial Materials Institute, 75, boul de Montagne, Boucherville PQ J4B 6Y4, 514/641-5050; Fax: 514/641-5101

Industry Canada, Chemicals & Bio-Industries, C.D. Howe Bldg., 235 Queen St., Ottawa ON K1A 0H5, 613/954-3071; Fax: 613/952-4209

Institute for Chemical Process & Environmental Technology, 1500 Montreal Rd., Ottawa ON K1A 0R6, 613/990-6618

Steacie Institute for Molecular Sciences, 100 Sussex Dr., Ottawa ON K1A 0R6, 613/993-1053; Fax: 613/954-5242

Alta: Alberta Environmental Protection, Chemical Assessment Management Division, 9915 - 108 St., Edmonton AB T5K 2G8, 403/427-5855

B.C.: Ministry of Environment, Lands & Parks, Industrial Waste & Hazardous Contaminants Branch, 777 Broughton St., Victoria BC V8V 1X4, 250/387-9992; Fax: 250/387-9935

Man.: Manitoba Industry, Trade & Tourism, Industry Development, 155 Carlton St., 6th Fl., Winnipeg MB R3C 3H8, 204/945-2066; Fax: 204/945-1354

N.B.: New Brunswick Pesticides Advisory Council, c/o Department of the Environment, PO Box 6000, Fredericton NB E3B 5H1, 506/457-4848; Fax: 506/453-2893

New Brunswick Research & Productivity Council, Chemical & Biotechnical Services, 921 College Hill Rd., Fredericton NB E3B 6Z9, 506/452-1369; Fax: 506/452-1395

Nfld.: Department of Environment & Labour, Environment Branch, Confederation Bldg., PO Box 8700, St. John's NF A1B 4J6, 709/729-1930; Fax: 709/729-1930

NWT: Department of Resources, Wildlife & Economic Development, Hazardous Substances, #600, Scotia Centre, Bldg. Box 21, 5102 - 50 Ave., Yellowknife NT X1A 3S8, 403/920-6476; Fax: 403/873-0114

N.S.: Department of the Environment, Industrial Pollution Control Branch, PO Box 2107, Halifax NS B3J 3B7, 902/424-2284; Fax: 902/424-0503

Pesticide Management Branch, PO Box 2107, Halifax NS B3J 3B7, 902/424-2541; Fax: 902/424-0503

Ont.: Ministry of Environment & Energy, Environmental Sciences & Standards Division, 135 St. Clair Ave. West, Toronto ON M4V 1P5, 416/325-4000 (Public Information Centre); Fax: 416/323-4396

PEI: Department of Environmental Resources, Environmental Protection Division, Jones Bldg., 11 Kent St., 4th Fl., PO Box 2000, Charlottetown PE CIA 7N8, 902/368-5024; Fax: 902/368-5830

Qué.: Ministère de l'Environnement et de la Faune, Édifice Marie-Guyart, 675, boul René-Lévesque est, Québec PQ G1R 5V7, 418/643-3127; Toll Free: 1-800-561-1616; Fax: 418/646-5974

Ministère de l'Industrie, du commerce, de la Science et de la technologie, Chimie, matériaux, santé, mode et textiles, 710, Place d'Youville, 9e étage, Québec PQ G1R 4Y4, 418/691-5950 (Renseignements); Fax: 418/644-0118

CHILD WELFARE
See Also Day Care Services

Justice Canada, Family & Youth Law Policy Section, Justice Bldg., 239 Wellington St., Ottawa ON K1A 0H8, 613/941-2339; Fax: 613/954-0811

Alta: Alberta Family & Social Services, Children's Services, Seventh St. Plaza, 10030 - 107 St., Edmonton AB T5J 3E4, 403/427-2734; Fax: 403/422-9044

Children's Services Division, Seventh St. Plaza, 10030 - 107 St., Edmonton AB T5J 3E4, 403/427-2734; Fax: 403/422-9044

Office of the Commissioner of Services for Children & Families, c/o Alberta Family & Social Services, Seventh St. Plaza, 10030 - 107 St., Edmonton AB T5J 3E4, 403/422-5011; Fax: 403/422-5036

Canadian Almanac & Directory 1997

B.C.: Ministry of Social Services, Child, Family & Community Service, Parliament Bldgs., 614 Humboldt St., 7th Fl., Victoria BC V8V 1X4, 250/387-6485; Fax: 250/356-7801

Children with Special Needs, Parliament Bldgs., 614 Humboldt St., 7th Fl., Victoria BC V8V 1X4, 250/387-1275; Fax: 250/356-6534

Man.: Manitoba Family Services, #219, 114 Garry St., Winnipeg MB R3C 4V6, 204/945-2324 (Policy & Planning); Fax: 204/945-2156

Children's Special Services, #219, 114 Garry St., Winnipeg MB R3C 4V6, 204/945-3251; Fax: 204/945-2669

N.B.: Department of Health & Community Services, Family & Community Social Services Division, PO Box 5100, Fredericton NB E3B 5G8, 506/453-2536; Fax: 506/444-4697

Youth Council of New Brunswick, 736 King St., PO Box 6000, Fredericton NB E3B 5H1, 506/453-3271; Fax: 506/444-4413

Nfld: Child Welfare Board, Confederation Bldg., PO Box 8700, St. John's NF A1B 4J6

Department of Social Services, Child Welfare, Confederation Bldg., PO Box 8700, St. John's NF A1B 4J6, 709/729-2668; Fax: 709/729-6996

NWT: Department of Health & Social Services, Family Support & Child Protection, Centre Square Tower, 8th Fl., PO Box 1320, Yellowknife NT X1A 2L9, 403/920-6255; Fax: 403/873-0444

N.S.: Department of Community Services, Family & Children's Services, Johnston Bldg., 5182 Prince St., 5th Fl., PO Box 696, Halifax NS B3J 2T7, 902/424-4326; Fax: 902/424-0502

Ont.: Ministry of Community & Social Services, Adoption Operational Services, 2 Bloor St. West, 24th Fl., Toronto ON M7A 1E9, 416/327-4930; Fax: 416/325-5172, 5171

Child Care Branch, Hepburn Block, 4th Fl., Toronto ON M7A 1E9, 416/327-4865; Fax: 416/327-0563

Ministry of the Attorney General, 393 University Ave., 14th Fl., Toronto ON M5G 1W9, 416/314-8011; Fax: 416/314-8000

PEI: Health & Community Services Agency, 4 Sydney St., PO Box 2000, Charlottetown PE C1A 7N8, 902/368-6130; Fax: 902/368-6136

Qué.: Ministère de la Justice, Direction du droit de la jeunesse, 1200, rte de l'Église, Ste-Foy PQ G1V 4M1, 418/643-5140 (Communications); Fax: 418/646-4449

Ministère de la Santé et des services sociaux, 1075, ch Ste-Foy, Québec PQ G1S 2M1

Secrétariat à la famille, #3.300, 875, Grande-Allée est, Québec PQ G1R 4Y8, 418/643-6414; Fax: 418/528-2009

Sask.: Saskatchewan Social Services, Child Day Care Division, 1920 Broad St., Regina SK S4P 3V6, 306/787-3855; Fax: 306/787-3441

Family & Youth Services Division, 1920 Broad St., Regina SK S4P 3V6, 306/787-7010; Fax: 306/787-0925

Protection & Children's Services, 2240 Albert St., Regina SK S4P 3V7, 306/787-2928; Fax: 306/694-3842

Saskatoon Child Centre, c/o Saskatchewan Justice, 1874 Scarth St., Regina SK S4P 3V7, 306/975-8250

Yuk.: Yukon Health & Social Services, Family/Children's Services, PO Box 2703, Whitehorse YT Y1A 2C6, 403/667-8117; Fax: 403/668-4613

Yukon Justice, Family Violence Prevention Unit, PO Box 2703, Whitehorse YT Y1A 2C6, 403/667-3581; Fax: 403/393-6272

Official Guardian's Office, PO Box 2703, Whitehorse YT Y1A 2C6, 403/667-5366; Fax: 403/393-6272

CITIZENSHIP

Citizenship & Immigration Canada, Journal Tower South, 365 Laurier Ave. West, Hull PQ K1A 1L1, 613/954-9019; Fax: 613/954-2221

Citizenship Services, Journal Tower South, 365 Laurier Ave. West, Hull PQ K1A 1L1, 613/941-8405; Fax: 613/941-0061

Immigration & Refugee Board, 240 Bank St., Ottawa ON K1A 0K1, 613/995-6486; Fax: 613/996-0270

Alta: Alberta Community Development, Community & Citizenship Services Division, Standard Life Centre, 10405 Jasper Ave., 7th Fl., Edmonton AB T5J 4R7, 403/427-6530; Fax: 403/427-1496

Alberta Human Rights & Citizenship Commission, Standard Life Centre, #1600, 10405 Jasper Ave., Edmonton AB T5J 4R7, 403/427-3116, 427-7661; Fax: 403/422-3563, 427-6013

B.C.: Ministry of the Attorney General, Multiculturalism & Immigration Branch, #309, 703 Broughton St., Victoria BC V8W 1E2, 250/387-7970; Fax: 250/356-5316

Man.: Manitoba Culture, Heritage & Citizenship, Citizenship Division, 213 Notre Dame., Winnipeg MB R3B 1N3, 204/945-3729

Ont.: Ministry of Citizenship, Culture & Recreation, Communications Branch (Citizenship), 77 Bloor St. West, 6th Fl., Toronto ON M7A 2R9, 416/325-7725; Fax: 416/314-4965

Ontario Advisory Council on Multiculturalism & Citizenship, 35 McCaul St., 3rd Fl., Toronto ON M5T 1V7, 416/314-6650 (Voice & TDD); Fax: 416/314-6658

Qué.: Ministère des Relations avec les citoyens et de l'Immigration, 360, rue McGill, 4e étage, Montréal PQ H2Y 2E9, 514/873-9940; Fax: 514/864-2899

CLIMATE & WEATHER

Environment Canada, Atmospheric Environment Service, 4905 Dufferin St., Downsview ON M3H 5T4, 416/739-4521; Fax: 819/953-2225

Canadian Meteorological Centre (Montréal), 4905 Dufferin St., Downsview ON M3H 5T4, 514/421-4601; Fax: 514/421-4600

Climate & Atmospheric Research Directorate, 4905 Dufferin St., Downsview ON M3H 5T4, 416/739-4995; Fax: 416/739-4265

Qué.: Ministère de l'Environnement et de la Faune, Milieu atmosphérique, Édifice Marie-Guyart, 675, boul René-Lévesque est, Québec PQ G1R 5V7, 418/644-3460; Fax: 418/643-9591

COAL

See Also Energy

Natural Resources Canada, Coal, Ferrous & Industrial Minerals Division, 580 Booth St., Ottawa ON K1A 0E4, 613/992-2018; Fax: 613/996-9094

Earth Sciences Sector, 601 Booth St., Ottawa ON K1A 0E8, 613/995-0947; Fax: 613/996-9094

Minerals & Metals Sector, 580 Booth St., Ottawa ON K1A 0E4, 613/995-0947; Fax: 613/996-9094

Nfld.: Department of Mines & Energy, Energy Branch, PO Box 8700, St. John's NF A1B 4J6, 709/729-2301

N.S.: Department of Natural Resources, Minerals & Energy Branch, Founder's Square, 1701 Hollis St., PO Box 698, Halifax NS B3J 2T9, 902/424-5346; Fax: 902/424-7735

COMMUNICATIONS See TELECOMMUNICATIONS

COMMUNITY HEALTH See HEALTH SERVICES; PUBLIC SAFETY

COMMUNITY SERVICES

Canadian Heritage, Citizenship & Canadian Identity Sector, Jules Léger Bldg., 25 Eddy St., Hull PQ K1A 1K5, 819/997-0055; Fax: 819/953-5382

Human Resources Development Canada, Social Development, Place du Portage, Phase IV, 140, Promenade du Portage, Hull PQ K1A 0J9, 613/957-8672; Fax: 613/941-8274

Alta: Alberta Municipal Financing Corporation, Terrace Bldg., #403, 9515 - 107 St., Edmonton AB T5K 2C3, 403/427-9711; Fax: 403/422-2175

Alberta Community Development, Standard Life Centre, 10405 Jasper Ave., 7th Fl., Edmonton AB T5J 4R7, 403/427-6530; Fax: 403/427-1496

Alberta Municipal Affairs, Housing & Consumer Affairs Division, Commerce Place, 10155 - 102 St., Edmonton AB T5J 4L4, 403/427-3917; Fax: 403/427-0418

Northern Alberta Development Council, #206, Provincial Bldg., 9621 - 96 Ave., PO Bag 900-14, Peace River AB T8S 1T4, 403/624-6274; Fax: 403/624-6184

B.C.: Ministry of Social Services, Child, Family & Community Service, Parliament Bldgs., 614 Humboldt St., 7th Fl., Victoria BC V8V 1X4, 250/387-6485; Fax: 250/356-7801

Community Support Services, Parliament Bldgs., 614 Humboldt St., 7th Fl., Victoria BC V8V 1X4, 250/387-6485; Fax: 250/356-7801

Man.: Manitoba Family Services, Community Living Division, #219, 114 Garry St., Winnipeg MB R3C 4V6, 204/945-2324 (Policy & Planning); Fax: 204/945-2156

N.B.: Department of Health & Community Services, Family & Community Social Services Division, PO Box 5100, Fredericton NB E3B 5G8, 506/453-2536; Fax: 506/444-4697

Department of Municipalities, Culture & Housing, Local Government Administration Branch, Marysville Place, 20 McGloin St., PO Box 6000, Fredericton NB E3B 5H1, 506/453-2434; Fax: 506/457-4991

Nfld.: Department of Health, Community Health, West Block, Confederation Bldg., PO Box 8700, St. John's NF A1B 4J6, 709/729-5021; Fax: 709/729-5824

Department of Social Services, Confederation Bldg., PO Box 8700, St. John's NF A1B 4J6, 709/729-2478; Fax: 709/729-6996

NWT: Department of Health & Social Services, Community Programs & Services, Centre Square Tower, 8th Fl., PO Box 1320, Yellowknife NT X1A 2L9, 403/920-6173; Fax: 403/873-0266

Department of Municipal & Community Affairs, #600, 5201 - 50th Ave., PO Box 1310, Yellowknife NT X1A 2L9, 403/873-7118; Fax: 403/873-0309

N.S.: Department of Community Services, Johnston Bldg., 5182 Prince St., 5th Fl., PO Box 696, Halifax NS B3J 2T7, 902/424-4326; Fax: 902/424-0502

Ont.: Ministry of Community & Social Services, Hepburn Block, 80 Grosvenor St., 6th Fl., Toronto ON M7A 1E9, 416/325-5666; Fax: 416/325-5172, 5171

Ministry of Health, Population Health & Community Services System Group, Hepburn Block, 8th Fl., Queen's Park, Toronto ON M7A 1S2, ; Toll Free: 1-800-668-2437 (AIDS Bureau); Fax: 416/327-8781

PEI: Council on Health & Community Services Policy, Jones Bldg., 2nd Fl., PO Box 2000, Charlottetown PE C1A 7N8, 902/368-4985; Fax: 902/368-4969

Health & Community Services Agency, 4 Sydney St., PO Box 2000, Charlottetown PE C1A 7N8, 902/368-6130; Fax: 902/368-6136

Sask.: Saskatchewan Municipal Government, Municipal Services Division, 1855 Victoria Ave., Regina SK S4P 3V7, 306/787-8282; Fax: 306/787-4181

Sport, Recreation & Lotteries, 1855 Victoria Ave., Regina SK S4P 3V7, 306/787-5737; Fax: 306/787-8560

Saskatchewan Social Services, 1920 Broad St., Regina SK S4P 3V6, 306/787-3494; Fax: 306/787-1032

Yuk.: Yukon Community & Transportation Services, Community Services Branch, PO Box 2703, Whitehorse YT Y1A 2C6, 403/667-5299; Fax: 403/667-7056

COMPENSATION *See* **CRIMES COMPENSATION; WORKERS' COMPENSATION**

CONFLICT OF INTEREST
Industry Canada, Office of the Ethics Counsellor, 66 Slater St., 22nd Fl., Ottawa ON K1A 0C9, 416/995-0721; Fax: 416/995-7308
Alta: Alberta Office of the Ethics Commissioner, #410, 9925 - 109 St., Edmonton AB T5K 2J8, 403/422-2273; Fax: 403/422-2261
B.C.: Office of the Conflict of Interest Commissioner, #101, 431 Menzies St., Victoria BC V8V 1X4, 250/356-9283; Fax: 250/356-6580
Ont.: Commission on Integrity, 101 Bloor St. West, 4th Fl., Toronto ON M5S 2Z7, 416/314-8983; Fax: 416/314-8987

CONSERVATION
See Also **Heritage Resources; Natural Resources**
Canadian Heritage, Canadian Conservation Institute, 1030 Innes Rd., Ottawa ON K1A 0C8, 613/998-3721; Fax: 613/998-4721
Environment Canada, Environmental Conservation Service, Place Vincent-Massey, 351, boul St-Joseph, Hull PQ K1A 0H3, 819/997-2800; Fax: 819/953-2225
Fisheries & Oceans Canada, Conservation & Protection, 200 Kent St., Ottawa ON K1A 0E6, 613/990-6012
Fisheries Resource Conservation Council, PO Box 2001, Stn D, Ottawa ON K1A 5W3
North American Wetlands Conservation Council (Canada), #200, 1750 Courtwood Cres., Ottawa ON K2C 2B5, 613/228-2601; Fax: 613/228-0206
Alta: Alberta Agriculture, Food & Rural Development, Irrigation & Resource Management Division, 7000 - 113 St., Edmonton AB T6H 5T6, 403/422-4596; Fax: 403/422-0474
Alberta Community Development, Cultural Facilities & Historical Resources Division, Old St. Stephen's College, 8820 - 112 St., Edmonton AB T6G 2P8, 403/431-2300; Fax: 403/432-1376
Alberta Environmental Protection, Land & Forest Service, 9915 - 108 St., Edmonton AB T5K 2G8, 403/427-2739, 944-0313 (Information Centre)
Natural Resources Service, 9915 - 108 St., Edmonton AB T5K 2G8, 403/427-2739, 944-0313 (Information Centre)
Natural Resources Conservation Board, Pacific Plaza, 10909 Jasper Ave., Edmonton AB T5J 2L9, 403/422-1977
Sustainable Development Coordinating Council, South Petroleum Plaza, 9915 - 108 St., 10th Floor, Edmonton AB T5K 2G8, 403/427-6236; Fax: 403/422-6305
B.C.: Ministry of Environment, Lands & Parks, 810 Blanshard St., Victoria BC V8V 1X5, 250/387-9419; Fax: 250/356-6464
Ministry of Forests, PO Box 9517, Stn Prov Govt, Victoria BC V8W 9C2, 250/387-5255; Fax: 250/387-8485
Man.: Ecological Reserves Advisory Committee, PO Box 355, Stn St. Vital, Winnipeg MB R2M 5C8, 204/942-6617
Endangered Species Advisory Committee, 200 Saulteaux Cr., PO Box 80, Winnipeg MB R3J 3W3, 204/945-6829
Manitoba Natural Resources, Resources Division, #327, Legislative Bldg., Winnipeg MB R3C 0V8, 204/945-3730; Fax: 204/945-3586
Manitoba Rural Development, Manitoba Conservation Districts Commission, Legislative Bldg., #309, 450 Broadway Ave., Winnipeg MB R3C 0V8, 204/945-7496; Fax: 204/945-5059
N.B.: Department of Natural Resources & Energy, Conservation Services, PO Box 6000, Fredericton NB E3B 5H1, 506/453-2440; Fax: 506/453-6699
Nfld.: Department of Fisheries & Aquaculture, Resource Analysis, Fisheries Bldg., 30 Strawberry Marsh Rd., PO Box 8700, St. John's NF A1B 4J6, 709/729-3735; Fax: 709/729-0360
NWT: Department of Resources, Wildlife & Economic Development, Conservation Education, #600, Scotia Centre, Bldg. Box 21, 5102 - 50 Ave., Yellowknife NT X1A 3S8, 403/873-7134; Fax: 403/873-0114
N.S.: Department of Natural Resources, Renewable Resources Branch, Founder's Square, 1701 Hollis St., PO Box 698, Halifax NS B3J 2T9, 902/424-5935; Fax: 902/424-7735
Ont.: Conservation Review Board, 77 Bloor St. West, 2nd Fl., Toronto ON M7A 2R9, 416/314-7125; Fax: 416/314-7175
Ministry of Environment & Energy, Conservation & Prevention Division, 135 St. Clair Ave. West, Toronto ON M4V 1P5, 416/323-4320; Fax: 416/323-4481
Ministry of Natural Resources, Water Management & Conservation Authorities, Whitney Block, #6540, 99 Wellesley St. West, Toronto ON M7A 1W3, 416/314-1977; Fax: 416/314-1995
PEI: Department of Environmental Resources, Jones Bldg., 11 Kent St., 4th Fl., PO Box 2000, Charlottetown PE C1A 7N8, 902/368-4808; Fax: 902/368-5830
Sask.: Conservation Data Centre, #422, 3211 Albert St., Regina SK S4S 5W6, 306/787-7197; Fax: 306/787-7196
Saskatchewan Wetland Conservation Corporation, 3211 Albert St., 2nd Fl., Regina SK S4S 5W6, 306/787-5419; Fax: 306/787-2847

CONSTITUTION
See Also **Federal-Provincial Affairs**
Justice Canada, Communications & Executive Services Branch, Justice Bldg., 239 Wellington St., Ottawa ON K1A 0H8, 613/957-4222; Fax: 613/954-0811
National Archives of Canada, 395 Wellington St., Ottawa ON K1A 0N3, 613/995-5138; Fax: 613/995-6274
Alta: Alberta Federal & Intergovernmental Affairs, Constitution/Planning, AGT Tower II, #2200, 10025 Jasper Ave., Edmonton AB T5J 1S6, 403/427-6706; Fax: 403/427-0939
Ont.: Ministry of Intergovernmental Affairs, 900 Bay St., 6th Fl., Toronto ON M7A 1C2, 416/325-4760 (Communications); Fax: 416/325-4759
Sask.: Saskatchewan Intergovernmental Affairs, Constitutional Relations, 1919 Saskatchewan Dr., Regina SK S4P 3V7, 306/787-8006; Fax: 306/787-1987
Saskatchewan Justice, Constitutional Branch, 1874 Scarth St., Regina SK S4P 3V7, 306/787-8385; Fax: 306/787-3874

CONSTRUCTION
Canada Mortgage & Housing Corporation, 700 Montreal Rd., Ottawa ON K1A 0P7, 613/748-2000; Fax: 613/748-2098
Defence Construction Canada, Sir Charles Tupper Bldg., "A" Wing, Riverside Dr., 3rd Fl., Ottawa ON K1A 0K3, 613/998-9548; Fax: 613/998-1061
Industry Canada, Service Industries & Capital Projects, C.D. Howe Bldg., 235 Queen St., Ottawa ON K1A 0H5, 613/954-2990; Fax: 613/954-2303
Institute for Research in Construction, 1500 Montreal Rd., Ottawa ON K1A 0R6, 613/993-3772; Fax: 613/941-0822
Treasury Board of Canada, Office of Infrastructure, West Tower, 300 Laurier Ave. West, 3rd Fl., Ottawa ON K1A 0R5, 613/952-3171; Fax: 613/952-7979
Alta: Alberta Municipal Affairs, Housing & Consumer Affairs Division, Commerce Place, 10155 - 102 St., Edmonton AB T5J 4L4, 403/427-3917; Fax: 403/427-0418
Alberta Transportation & Utilities, Contracts & Infrastructure Management, Twin Atria, 4999 - 98 Ave., Edmonton AB T6B 2X3, 403/427-2731; Fax: 403/422-6515
Safety & Technical Services, Twin Atria, 4999 - 98 Ave., Edmonton AB T6B 2X3, 403/427-2731; Fax: 403/422-6515
B.C.: Ministry of Municipal Affairs & Housing, Safety & Standards Department, Municipal Affairs, PO Box 9490, Victoria BC V8W 9N7, 250/387-4089; Fax: 250/356-1070
Ministry of Transportation & Highways, Planning & Major Projects Department, 940 Blanshard St., Victoria BC V8W 3E6, 250/387-7788 (Public Affairs); Fax: 250/356-7706
Man.: Manitoba Highways & Transportation, Construction & Maintenance Division, 215 Garry St., 16th Fl., Winnipeg MB R3C 3Z1, 204/945-3888; Fax: 204/945-3841
Manitoba Rural Development, Infrastructure Services (Manitoba Water Services Board), 2022 Currie Blvd., PO Box 22080, Brandon MB R7A 6Y9, 204/726-6073; Fax: 204/726-6290
N.B.: Department of Transportation, Construction, King Tower, Kings Pl., 2nd Fl., PO Box 6000, Fredericton NB E3B 5H1, 506/453-2673
New Brunswick, Buildings Division, Central Purchasing Branch, #205, Marysville Place, PO Box 6000, Fredericton NB E3B 5H1, 506/453-2245; Fax: 506/444-4400
Nfld.: Department of Works, Services & Transportation, Confederation Bldg., PO Box 8700, St. John's NF A1B 4J6, 709/729-3283; Fax: 709/729-0703
Highway Design & Construction, Confederation Bldg., PO Box 8700, St. John's NF A1B 4J6, 709/729-3796; Fax: 709/729-0703
NWT: Department of Transportation, Lahm Ridge Bldg., PO Box 1320, Yellowknife NT X1A 2L9, 403/920-3460; Fax: 403/873-0363
Northwest Territories Housing Corporation, Construction Services, Scotia Centre, 5102 - 50th Ave., 10th Fl., PO Box 2100, Yellowknife NT X1A 2P6, 403/873-7876; Fax: 403/870-8024
N.S.: Construction Industry Panel, PO Box 697, Halifax NS B3J 2T8, 902/424-6730; Fax: 902/424-3239
Department of Transportation & Public Works, Capital Development & Environmental Engineering, 1969 Upper Water St., PO Box 186, Halifax NS B3J 2N2, 902/424-5837
Ont.: Ministry of Municipal Affairs & Housing, Municipal Operations Divsion, 777 Bay St., 17th Fl., Toronto ON M5G 2E5, 416/585-7041 (Communications Branch); Fax: 416/585-6227
Ministry of Transportation, Quality & Standards Division, 1201 Wilson Ave., Downsview ON M3M 1J8
PEI: Department of Provincial Affairs & Attorney General, Inspection Services, PO Box 2000, Charlottetown PE C1A 7N8, 902/368-4884; Fax: 902/368-5544
Department of Transportation & Public Works, Buildings Division, Jones Bldg., PO Box 2000, Charlottetown PE C1A 7N8, 902/368-5100; Fax: 902/368-5395
Qué.: Ministère des Transports, Planification et technologie, 700, boul René-Lévesque est, Québec PQ G1R 5H1, 418/528-0808
Régie du bâtiment du Québec, 545, boul Crémazie est, Montréal PQ H2M 2V2, 514/873-0976; Toll Free: 1-800-361-0761; Fax: 514/873-7667

Sask.: Saskatchewan Municipal Government, Building Standards Branch, 1855 Victoria Ave., Regina SK S4P 3V7, 306/787-4517; Fax: 306/787-9273

Yuk.: Yukon Community & Transportation Services, Engineering & Development, PO Box 2703, Whitehorse YT Y1A 2C6, 403/667-5707; Fax: 403/667-6109 Transportation Engineering, PO Box 2703, Whitehorse YT Y1A 2C6, 403/633-7928; Fax: 403/677-2647

Yukon Housing Corporation, Construction & Maintenance, 410A Jarvis St., PO Box 2703, Whitehorse YT Y1A 2C6, 403/667-3549; Fax: 403/667-3664

CONSUMER PROTECTION
See Also **Public Safety**

Health Canada, Health Protection Branch, Ottawa ON K1A 0L2, 613/957-2991; Fax: 613/941-5366

Alta: Alberta Municipal Affairs, Housing & Consumer Affairs Division, Commerce Place, 10155 - 102 St., Edmonton AB T5J 4L4, 403/427-3917; Fax: 403/427-0418

B.C.: Ministry of the Attorney General, Consumer Services Division, 1019 Wharf St., Victoria BC V8V 1X4, 250/356-9596 (Policy & Education); Fax: 604/356-1092

Man.: Manitoba Consumer & Corporate Affairs, Consumers' Bureau, #302, 258 Portage Ave., Winnipeg MB R3C 0B6, 204/945-3800; Fax: 204/945-0728

N.B.: Department of Justice, Consumer Affairs & Chief Rentalsman, #412, Centennial Bldg., PO Box 6000, Fredericton NB E3B 5H1, 506/453-2682; Fax: 506/444-4494

Nfld.: Department of Government Services & Lands, Commercial & Corporate Affairs, PO Box 8700, St. John's NF A1B 4J6

NWT: Department of Safety & Public Services, Consumer Services, Panda 2 Mall, 3rd Fl., PO Box 1320, Yellowknife NT X1A 2L9, 403/920-8054; Tenant Hotline: 403/920-8047; Consumer Complaints: 403/873-7125; Fax: 403/873-0260

N.S.: Department of Business & Consumer Services, Consumer & Commercial Relations, Alderney Gate, 40 Alderney Dr., PO Box 815, Dartmouth NS B2Y 3Z3, 902/424-5602; 5552; Toll Free: 1-800-774-5130; Fax: 902/424-8652

Ont.: Ministry of Consumer & Commercial Relations, Consumer Affairs Branch, 250 Yonge St., 35th Fl., Toronto ON M5B 2N5, 416/326-8600; Fax: 416/326-8665

PEI: Department of Provincial Affairs & Attorney General, Consumer Services, PO Box 2000, Charlottetown PE C1A 7N8, 902/368-4580; Fax: 902/368-5355

Sask.: Saskatchewan Justice, Consumer Protection Branch, 1874 Scarth St., Regina SK S4P 3V7, 306/787-2952; Fax: 306/787-5550

Yuk.: Yukon Justice, Consumer Services, PO Box 2703, Whitehorse YT Y1A 2C6, 403/667-5257; Fax: 403/393-6272

CONVENTION FACILITIES *See* **TOURISM & TOURIST INFORMATION**

COPYRIGHT *See* **PATENTS & COPYRIGHT**

CORONERS

Alta: Alberta Justice, 7007 - 116th St. NW, Edmonton AB T6H 5R8, 403/427-4987; Fax: 403/422-1265

B.C.: British Columbia Coroner's Service, 4595 Canada Way, 2nd Fl., Burnaby BC V5G 4L9, 604/660-7739; Fax: 604/660-7776

Man.: Manitoba Justice, Office of the Chief Medical Examiner, #607, 330 Graham Ave., Winnipeg MB R3C 4A5, 204/945-0571

N.B.: Department of the Solicitor General, Sheriff/Coroner's Office, Barker House, 4th Fl., PO Box 6000, Fredericton NB E3B 5H1, 506/453-3604; Fax: 506/453-3870

Nfld.: Department of Justice & Attorney General, Forensic Pathology, Health Sciences Complex, 300 Prince Philip Dr., St. John's NF A1B 3V6, 709/737-6402; Fax: 709/729-2129

NWT: Department of Justice, Coroner's Office, PO Box 1320, Yellowknife NT X1A 2L9, 403/873-7460

N.S.: Department of Justice, Office of the Chief Medical Examiner, 5788 University Ave., Halifax NS B3H 1V8, 902/428-4052; Fax: 902/424-0607

Ont.: Ministry of the Solicitor General & Correctional Services, Office of the Chief Coroner, 26 Grenville St., 2nd Fl., Toronto ON M7A 2G9, 416/314-4000; Fax: 416/314-4030

PEI: Department of Provincial Affairs & Attorney General, Office of the Chief Coroner, PO Box 2000, Charlottetown PE C1A 7N8, 902/566-4100; Fax: 902/368-5283; 5355

Qué.: Bureau du coroner, Tour Belle Cour, #2350, 2600 boul Laurier, 3e étage, Ste Foy PQ G1V 4M6, 418/643-1845; Fax: 418/643-6174

Sask.: Saskatchewan Justice, Coroner's Branch, 1874 Scarth St., Regina SK S4P 3V7, 306/787-5541; Fax: 306/787-3874

Yuk.: Yukon Justice, Coroner's Service, PO Box 2703, Whitehorse YT Y1A 2C6, 403/667-5317; Fax: 403/393-6272

CORRECTIONAL SERVICES

Correctional Service Canada, c/o Solicitor General Canada, 340 Laurier Ave. West, Ottawa ON K1A 0P9, 613/992-8423 (Communications); Fax: 613/947-0091

Office of the Correctional Investigator, #402, 275 Slater St., Ottawa ON K1P 5H9, 613/990-2695; Toll Free: 1-800-267-5982; Fax: 613/990-9091

Solicitor General Canada, Sir Wilfrid Laurier Bldg., 340 Laurier Ave. West, Ottawa ON K1A 0P8, 613/990-2733; Fax: 613/993-7062

Alta: Alberta Justice, Correctional Services Division, 9833 - 109th St., Edmonton AB T5K 2E8, 403/427-2745; Fax: 403/427-5905

B.C.: Ministry of the Attorney General, Corrections Branch, 910 Government St., 5th Fl., Victoria BC V8V 1X4, 250/387-5059; Fax: 250/387-5698

Man.: Manitoba Justice, Adult Correctional Services, 405 Broadway, 8th Fl., Winnipeg MB R3C 3L6, 204/945-7307

N.B.: Department of the Solicitor General, Correctional Services, Barker House, 4th Fl., PO Box 6000, Fredericton NB E3B 5H1, 506/453-7414; Fax: 506/453-3870

Nfld.: Department of Justice & Attorney General, Adult Corrections Division, Confederation Bldg., PO Box 8700, St. John's NF A1B 4J6, 709/729-3880; Fax: 709/729-0416

NWT: Department of Justice, Corrections, PO Box 1320, Yellowknife NT X1A 2L9, 403/920-8922

N.S.: Department of Justice, Correctional Services Division, PO Box 968, Stn M, Halifax NS, 902/424-6290; Fax: 902/424-0692

Ont.: Ministry of the Solicitor General & Correctional Services, Correctional Services Division, 101 Bloor St. West, 7th Fl., Toronto ON M5S 2Z7, 705/497-9500

PEI: Health & Community Services Agency, 4 Sydney St., PO Box 2000, Charlottetown PE C1A 7N8, 902/368-6130; Fax: 902/368-6136

Qué.: Ministère de la Sécurité publique, Services Correctionnels, Tour des Laurentides, 2525, boul Laurier, 5e étage, Ste-Foy PQ G1V 2L2, 418/643-3500; Fax: 418/643-0275

Sask.: Saskatchewan Justice, Corrections Division, 1874 Scarth St., Regina SK S4P 3V7, 306/787-7872 (Communications); Fax: 306/787-8084

Yuk.: Yukon Justice, Corrections & Community Programs Branch, PO Box 2703, Whitehorse YT Y1A 2C6, 403/667-8292 (Communications); Fax: 403/393-6272

COURTS & JUDGES *See* **JUSTICE DEPARTMENTS**

CREDIT COUNSELLING *See* **DEBTORS' ASSISTANCE**

CRIMES COMPENSATION

Justice Canada, Communications & Executive Services Branch, Justice Bldg., 239 Wellington St., Ottawa ON K1A 0H8, 613/957-4222; Fax: 613/954-0811

Alta: Crimes Compensation Board, J.E. Brownlee Bldg., 10365 - 97 St., 7th Fl., Edmonton AB T5J 3W7, 403/427-7217; Fax: 403/422-4213

B.C.: Ministry of the Attorney General, Victim Services, 910 Government St., 5th Fl., Victoria BC V8V 1X4, 250/387-6848; Fax: 604/356-1092

Man.: Criminal Injuries Compensation Board, 763 Portage Ave., Winnipeg MB R3G 3N2, 204/775-7821; Fax: 204/784-1452

N.B.: Department of the Solicitor General, Victim & Community Services, Barker House, 4th Fl., PO Box 6000, Fredericton NB E3B 5H1, 506/453-2846; Fax: 506/453-3870

Nfld.: Department of Justice & Attorney General, Victim Services, Confederation Bldg., PO Box 8700, St. John's NF A1B 4J6, 709/729-0885; Fax: 709/729-2129

NWT: Department of Justice, Victims Services, PO Box 1320, Yellowknife NT X1A 2L9, 403/920-6911

Victims Assistance Committee, c/o Community Justice Division, PO Box 1320, Yellowknife NT X1A 2L9, 403/920-6911; Fax: 403/873-0299

N.S.: Department of Justice, Victims' Services Division, 5151 Terminal Rd., PO Box 7, Halifax NS B3J 2L6, 902/424-8785; Fax: 902/424-0252

Ont.: Criminal Injuries Compensation Board, 439 University Ave., 4th Fl., Toronto ON M5G 1Y8, 416/326-2900; Fax: 416/326-2883

Qué.: Ministère de la Justice, Bureau d'aide aux victimes d'actes criminels, 1200, rte de l'Église, Ste-Foy PQ G1V 4M1, 418/643-5140 (Communications); Fax: 418/646-4449

Sask.: Saskatchewan Justice, Victims Services, 1874 Scarth St., Regina SK S4P 3V7, 306/787-0418; Fax: 306/787-3874

Yuk.: Yukon Justice, Justice Services Branch, PO Box 2703, Whitehorse YT Y1A 2C6, 403/667-8292 (Communications); Fax: 403/393-6272

CROP MANAGEMENT *See* **AGRICULTURE**

CROWN LAND *See* **LAND RESOURCES**

CULTURE *See* **ARTS & CULTURE**

CURRENCY

Bank of Canada, 234 Wellington St., Ottawa ON K1A 0G9, 613/782-8111; Fax: 613/782-8655

Royal Canadian Mint, 320 Sussex Dr., Ottawa ON K1A 0G8, 613/993-3500

CUSTOMS

Revenue Canada, Commercial Services Directorate, 875 Heron Rd., Ottawa ON K1A 0L8, 613/954-7190

Customs Border Services, 875 Heron Rd., Ottawa ON K1A 0L8, 613/957-0275

Travellers Directorate, 875 Heron Rd., Ottawa ON K1A 0L8, 613/954-6368

DAIRYING

Agriculture & Agri-Food Canada, Animal & Plant Health Directorate, 59 Camelot Dr., Nepean ON K1A 0Y9, 613/952-8000; Fax: 613/952-0677

Dairy Section, 2200 Walkley Rd., 1st Fl., Ottawa ON K1A 0C5, 613/957-7078; Fax: 613/957-1527

Dairy, Fruit & Vegetable Division, 59 Camelot Dr., Nepean ON K1A 0Y9, 613/952-8000; Fax: 613/990-0607

Canadian Dairy Commission, Carling Executive Park, 1525 Carling Ave., Ottawa ON K1A 0Z2, 613/998-9490; Fax: 613/998-4492

Alta: Alberta Dairy Control Board, 5201 - 50 Ave., Wetaskiwin AB T9A 0S7, 403/361-1231; Fax: 403/361-1236

B.C.: British Columbia Milk Marketing Board, #105, 4664 Lougheed Hwy., Burnaby BC V5C 5T5, 604/294-6454; Fax: 604/294-4566

Man.: Manitoba Milk Producers' Marketing Board, 36 Scurfield Blvd., Winnipeg MB R3T 3N5, 204/488-6455; Fax: 204/488-4772

N.B.: New Brunswick Milk Marketing Board, Rochville Rd., PO Box 490, Sussex NB E0E 1P0, 506/432-9120; Fax: 506/432-9130

Nfld.: Newfoundland Milk Marketing Board, 655 Topsail Rd., St. John's NF A1E 2E3, 709/364-6634; Fax: 709/364-8364

N.S.: Nova Scotia Dairy Commission, PO Box 782, Truro NS B2N 5E8, 902/893-6379; Fax: 902/897-9768

Ont.: Ministry of Agriculture, Food & Rural Affairs, Dairy, Fruit & Vegetable Industry Inspection Branch, Information Centre, 801 Bay St., 1st Fl., Toronto ON M7A 2B2, 519/837-5045; Fax: 519/767-0336

Ontario Milk Marketing Board, 6780 Campobello Rd., Mississauga ON L5N 2L8, 905/821-8970; Fax: 905/821-3160

PEI: Department of Agriculture, Fisheries & Forestry, Dairy Lab, 16 Walker Dr., Charolottetown PE C1A 8S6, 902/368-4480; Fax: 902/368-4486

Qué.: L'Union des Producteurs Agricoles, 555, boul Roland-Therrien, Longueuil PQ J4H 3Y9, 514/679-0530; Fax: 514/679-5436

Sask.: Milk Control Board, #1210, 2500 Victoria Ave., Regina SK S4P 3X2, 306/787-5319; Fax: 306/787-1988

DANGEROUS GOODS & HAZARDOUS MATERIALS

See Also Occupational Safety; Waste Management

Environment Canada, Toxics Pollution Prevention Directorate, Place Vincent-Massey, 351, boul St-Joseph, Hull PQ K1A 0H3, 819/953-1114; Fax: 819/953-5371

Health Canada, Environmental Health Directorate, Ottawa ON K1A 0L2, 613/954-0291; Fax: 613/941-5366

Transport Canada, Transport Dangerous Goods, Transport Canada Building, 330 Sparks St., Ottawa ON K1A 0N5, 613/990-1147; Fax: 613/993-5925

Alta: Alberta Special Waste Management Corporation, #600, 10909 Jasper Ave., Edmonton AB T5J 3L9, 403/422-5029; Fax: 403/428-9627

Alberta Environmental Protection, Chemical Assessment Management Division, 9915 - 108 St., Edmonton AB T5K 2G8, 403/427-5855

Alberta Transportation & Utilities, Dangerous Goods Control, Twin Atria, 4999 - 98 Ave., Edmonton AB T6B 2X3, 403/427-8901; Fax: 403/422-6515

B.C.: Ministry of Environment, Lands & Parks, Industrial Waste & Hazardous Contaminants Branch, 777 Broughton St., Victoria BC V8V 1X4, 250/387-9992; Fax: 250/387-9935

Man.: Manitoba Environment, Transportation & Handling of Dangerous Goods, Bldg. 2, 139 Tuxedo Ave., Winnipeg MB R3N 0H6, 208/945-7039; Fax: 204/945-5229

N.B.: Department of the Environment, Hazardous Materials Section, 364 Argyle St., PO Box 6000, Fredericton NB E3B 5H1, 506/457-4848; Fax: 506/453-2265

New Brunswick Pesticides Advisory Council, c/o Department of the Environment, PO Box 6000, Fredericton NB E3B 5H1, 506/457-4848; Fax: 506/453-2893

Nfld.: Department of Environment & Labour, Environment Branch, Confederation Bldg., PO Box 8700, St. John's NF A1B 4J6, 709/729-1930; Fax: 709/729-1930

Department of Government Services & Lands, Motor Vehicles & Coordinator, Transportation of Dangerous Goods, PO Box 8710, St. John's NF A1B 4J5, 709/729-2958; Fax: 709/729-6955

NWT: Department of Resources, Wildlife & Economic Development, Hazardous Substances, #600, Scotia Centre, Bldg. Box 21, 5102 - 50 Ave., Yellowknife NT X1A 3S8, 403/920-6476; Fax: 403/873-0114

Ont.: Ministry of Transportation, Compliance Branch, 1201 Wilson Ave., Downsview ON M3M 1J8, 416/235-5147

PEI: Department of Environmental Resources, Air Quality & Hazardous Materials Section, Jones Bldg., 11 Kent St., 4th Fl., PO Box 2000, Charlottetown PE CIA 7N8, 902/368-5037; Fax: 902/368-5830

Qué.: Ministère de l'Environnement et de la Faune, Direction générale des opérations, Édifice Marie-Guyart, 675, boul René-Lévesque est, Québec PQ G1R 5V7, 418/643-3127; Fax: 418/643-4747

Sask.: Saskatchewan Environment & Resource Management, Environmental Protection Branch, 3211 Albert St., Regina SK S4S 5W6, 306/787-6178; Fax: 306/787-5623

DAY CARE SERVICES

See Also Child Welfare

Alta: Alberta Family & Social Services, Day Care Programs, Seventh St. Plaza, 10030 - 107 St., Edmonton AB T5J 3E4, 403/427-4477; Fax: 403/422-9044

B.C.: Ministry of Social Services, Day Care Subsidies/Community Projects, Parliament Bldgs., 614 Humboldt St., 7th Fl., Victoria BC V8V 1X4, 250/387-1275; Fax: 250/356-6534

Man.: Economic Innovation & Technology Council, #648, 155 Carlton St., Winnipeg MB R3C 3H8, 204/945-5940; Fax: 204/945-8229

Manitoba Family Services, Child Day Care, #219, 114 Garry St., Winnipeg MB R3C 4V6, 204/945-2668; Fax: 204/948-2143

N.B.: Department of Health & Community Services, Family & Community Social Services Division, PO Box 5100, Fredericton NB E3B 5G8, 506/453-2536; Fax: 506/444-4697

Nfld.: Day Care & Homemaker Services Licensing Board, Confederation Bldg., PO Box 8700, St. John's NF A1B 4J6

Department of Social Services, Program Development, Confederation Bldg., PO Box 8700, St. John's NF A1B 4J6, 709/729-2478; Fax: 709/729-6996

NWT: Department of Health & Social Services, Family Support & Child Protection, Centre Square Tower, 8th Fl., PO Box 1320, Yellowknife NT X1A 2L9, 403/920-6255; Fax: 403/873-0444

Ont.: Ministry of Community & Social Services, Child Care Branch, Hepburn Block, 4th Fl., Toronto ON M7A 1E9, 416/327-4865; Fax: 416/327-0563

Children, Family & Community Services Division, Hepburn Block, 80 Grosvenor St., 6th Fl., Toronto ON M7A 1E9, 416/325-5666; Fax: 416/325-5172, 5171

PEI: Department of Health & Social Services, Jones Bldg., 11 Kent St., 2nd Fl., PO Box 2000, Charlottetown PE C1A 7N8, 902/368-4900; Fax: 902/368-4969

Health & Community Services Agency, 4 Sydney St., PO Box 2000, Charlottetown PE C1A 7N8, 902/368-6130; Fax: 902/368-6136

Sask.: Saskatchewan Social Services, Child Day Care Division, 1920 Broad St., Regina SK S4P 3V6, 306/787-3855; Fax: 306/787-3441

Child Day Care Subsidy Unit, 1920 Broad St., Regina SK S4P 3V6, 306/787-3885; Fax: 306/787-1032

Yuk.: Yukon Health & Social Services, Family/Children's Services, PO Box 2703, Whitehorse YT Y1A 2C6, 403/667-8117; Fax: 403/668-4613

DEATH CERTIFICATES *See* VITAL STATISTICS

DEBTORS' ASSISTANCE

Alta: Alberta Municipal Affairs, Commerce Place, 10155 - 102 St., Edmonton AB T5J 4L4, 403/427-2732; Fax: 403/422-9105

B.C.: Ministry of the Attorney General, Debtor Assistance Branch, 1019 Wharf St., Victoria BC V8V 1X4, 250/387-1747; Fax: 250/353-4782

Man.: Manitoba Consumer & Corporate Affairs, Cooperative & Credit Union Regulations, #317, 450 Broadway, Winnipeg MB R3C 0V8, 204/945-2771

N.B.: Department of Justice, Consumer Affairs & Chief Rentalsman, #412, Centennial Bldg., PO Box 6000, Fredericton NB E3B 5H1, 506/453-2682; Fax: 506/444-4494

Nfld.: Department of Finance & Treasury Board, Debt Management & Pensions, Confederation Bldg., PO Box 8700, St. John's NF A1B 4J6, 709/729-2949; Fax: 709/729-2856

PEI: Department of Provincial Affairs & Attorney General, PO Box 2000, Charlottetown PE C1A 7N8, 902/368-4551; Fax: 902/368-5283

Sask.: Saskatchewan Finance, Cash & Debt Management Branch, 2350 Albert St., Regina SK S4P 4A6, 306/787-3923; Fax: 306/787-6544

Yuk.: Yukon Finance, Investments & Debt Services, PO Box 2703, Whitehorse YT Y1A 2C6, 403/667-5346; Fax: 403/393-6217

DEFENCE

See Also Emergency Response; Public Safety

Foreign Affairs & International Trade Canada, Political & International Security Affairs Branch, Lester B. Pearson Bldg., 125 Sussex Dr., Ottawa ON K1A 0G2, 613/996-9134; Fax: 613/952-3904

National Defence (Canada), MGen. George R. Pearkes Bldg., 101 Colonel By Dr., Ottawa ON K1A 0K2, 613/992-4581

Defence Science Advisory Board, MGen. George R. Pearkes Bldg., 101 Colonel By Dr., Ottawa ON K1A 0K2, 613/992-4073

Emergency Preparedness Canada, Jackson Bldg., 122 Bank St., 2nd Fl., Ottawa ON K1A 0W6, 613/991-7077; Fax: 613/998-9589

DELINQUENCY *See* YOUNG OFFENDERS

DIPLOMATIC REPRESENTATIVES
See Also **International Affairs**
Foreign Affairs & International Trade Canada, Diplomatic Corps Services, Lester B. Pearson Bldg., 125 Sussex Dr., Ottawa ON K1A 0G2, 613/995-5185; Fax: 613/952-3904

DISABLED PERSONS SERVICES
Human Resources Development Canada, Coordination Group on Persons with Disabilities & SSR, Place du Portage, Phase IV, 140, Promenade du Portage, Hull PQ K1A 0J9, 613/954-3854; Fax: 613/957-4404
 Status of Disabled Persons, Place du Portage, Phase IV, 140, Promenade du Portage, Hull PQ K1A 0J9, 819/994-5692; Fax: 819/994-1346
Alta: Alberta Family & Social Services, Services to Persons with Disabilities, Seventh St. Plaza, 10030 - 107 St., Edmonton AB T5J 3E4, 403/422-0305; Fax: 403/422-9044
Premier's Council on the Status of Persons with Disabilities, #250, 11044 - 82 Ave., Edmonton AB T6G 0T2, 403/422-1095; Fax: 403/422-9691
B.C.: Ministry of Education, Skills & Training, Office for Disability Issues, PO Box 9150, Stn Prov Govt, Victoria BC V8W 9H1, 250/387-3813; Fax: 250/387-3114
Man.: Manitoba Family Services, Administration & Finance, #219, 114 Garry St., Winnipeg MB R3C 4V6, 204/945-5600; Fax: 204/948-2153
 Vulnerable Persons' Commission Office, #219, 114 Garry St., Winnipeg MB R3C 4V6, 204/945-5039; Fax: 204/948-2603
N.B.: Premier's Council on the Status of Disabled Persons, #648, 440 King St., Fredericton NB E3B 5H8, 506/452-1112; Fax: 506/450-2747
Nfld.: Department of Social Services, Family & Rehabilitative Services, Confederation Bldg., PO Box 8700, St. John's NF A1B 4J6, 709/729-2436; Fax: 709/729-6996
Rehabilitation Appeal Board, Confederation Bldg., PO Box 8700, St. John's NF A1B 4J6
NWT: Department of Health & Social Services, Centre Square Tower, 8th Fl., PO Box 1320, Yellowknife NT X1A 2L9, 403/920-6173; Fax: 403/873-0266
N.S.: Department of Community Services, Transitional Planning & Supply Services, Johnston Bldg., 5182 Prince St., 5th Fl., PO Box 696, Halifax NS B3J 2T7, 902/424-5863; Fax: 902/424-0502
Nova Scotia Disabled Persons Commission, #203, 2695 Dutch Village Rd., Halifax NS B3L 4T9, 902/424-8280; Toll Free: 1-800-565-8280 (within Nova Scotia); Fax: 902/424-0592
Ont.: Ministry of Citizenship, Culture & Recreation, Disability Issues Group, 700 Bay St., 3rd Fl., Toronto ON M5G 1Z6, 416/326-0201; Disability Issues Inquiry/Voice & TDD: 1-800-387-4456; 416/326-0111; Fax: 416/327-4080
Ontario Advisory Council on Disability Issues, 35 McCaul St., 3rd Fl., Toronto ON M5T 1V7, 416/314-6650 (Voice & TDD); Fax: 416/314-6658
PEI: Council on Health & Community Services Policy, Jones Bldg., 2nd Fl., PO Box 2000, Charlottetown PE C1A 7N8, 902/368-4985; Fax: 902/368-4969
Health & Community Services Agency, 4 Sydney St., PO Box 2000, Charlottetown PE C1A 7N8, 902/368-6130; Fax: 902/368-6136
Qué.: Bureau des personnes handicapées du Québec, 309, rue Brock, CP 820, Drummondville PQ J2B 6X1, 819/477-7100; Fax: 819/477-8493
Sask.: Saskatchewan Health, 3475 Albert St., Regina SK S4S 6X6, 306/787-8332; Fax: 306/787-8310
Yuk.: Yukon Health & Social Services, PO Box 2703, Whitehorse YT Y1A 2C6, 403/667-3673 (Communications); Fax: 403/667-3096

DISCRIMINATION & EMPLOYMENT EQUITY
Canadian Human Rights Commission, Place de Ville, Tower A, #1300, 320 Queen St., Ottawa ON K1A 1E1, 613/995-1151; TDD: 613/996-5211; Fax: 613/996-9661
Alta: Labour Relations Board/Public Service Employee Relations Board, #503, 10808 - 99 Ave., Edmonton AB T5K 0G5, 403/427-8547; Toll Free: 1-800-463-2572; Fax: 403/422-0970
B.C.: British Columbia Council of Human Rights, 844 Courtney St., 2nd. Fl., Victoria BC V8V 1X4, 250/387-3710; Fax: 250/387-3643
Ministry of the Attorney General, Employment Equity & Women's Programs, 910 Government St., 5th Fl., Victoria BC V8V 1X4, 250/387-3247; Fax: 250/356-5368
Man.: Human Rights Commission, #301, 259 Portage Ave., Winnipeg MB R3B 2A9, 204/945-3007; TDD: 945-3442; Fax: 204/945-1292
N.B.: New Brunswick Human Rights Commission, 751 Brunswick St., PO Box 6000, Fredericton NB E3B 5H1, 506/453-2301; Fax: 506/453-2653
Nfld.: Newfoundland & Labrador Human Rights Commission, PO Box 8700, St. John's NF A1B 4J6, 709/729-2709; Fax: 709/729-0790
N.S.: Pay Equity Commission, PO Box 697, Halifax NS B3J 1T8, 902/424-8595; Fax: 902/424-3239
Ont.: Management Board of Cabinet, Employment Equity Division, #393, 595 Bay St., PO Box 51, Toronto ON M5G 2C2, 416/325-1300; Fax: 416/325-1313
Ontario Human Rights Commission, 400 University Ave., 12th Fl., Toronto ON M7A 2R9, 416/314-4500; Fax: 416/314-4533
PEI: Prince Edward Island Human Rights Commission, 3 Queen St., PO Box 2000, Charlottetown PE C1A 7N8, 902/368-4180; Fax: 902/368-4236
Sask.: Saskatchewan Human Rights Commission, 122 - 3 Ave. North, 8th Fl., Saskatoon SK S7K 2H6, 306/933-5952; Fax: 306/933-7863
Saskatchewan Public Service Commission, Employee Relations, 2103 - 11th Ave., Regina SK S4P 3V7, 306/787-7606; Fax: 306/787-7533
Yuk.: Yukon Human Rights Commission, 205 Rogers St., Whitehorse YT Y1A 1X1, 403/667-6226
Yukon Public Service Commission, Staffing Relations Branch, PO Box 2703, Whitehorse YT Y1A 2C6, 403/667-5201; Fax: 403/667-6705

DIVORCE
Justice Canada, Justice Bldg., 239 Wellington St., Ottawa ON K1A 0H8, 613/957-4222; Fax: 613/954-0811
Alta: Alberta Justice, Civil & Family Legal Services, 9833 - 109th St., Edmonton AB T5K 2E8, 403/498-3390; Fax: 403/425-0307
B.C.: Ministry of the Attorney General, 910 Government St., 5th Fl., Victoria BC V8V 1X4, 250/356-9596 (Policy & Education); Fax: 250/356-9037
Man.: Manitoba Justice, 405 Broadway, 5th Fl., Winnipeg MB R3C 3L6, 204/945-2852
N.B.: Department of Justice, #412, Centennial Bldg., PO Box 6000, Fredericton NB E3B 5H1, 506/453-2719 (Administration); Fax: 506/453-8718
Nfld.: Department of Justice & Attorney General, Confederation Bldg., PO Box 8700, St. John's NF A1B 4J6, 709/729-5942; Fax: 709/729-2129
NWT: Department of Justice, PO Box 1320, Yellowknife NT X1A 2L9, 403/873-7453
N.S.: Department of Justice, Civil Litigation, 5151 Terminal Rd., PO Box 7, Halifax NS B3J 2L6, 902/424-4024; Fax: 902/424-0252
Ont.: Ministry of the Attorney General, Civil Law Division, 720 Bay St., 11th Fl., Toronto ON M5G 2K1, 416/326-2607; Fax: 416/326-4014
PEI: Department of Provincial Affairs & Attorney General, PO Box 2000, Charlottetown PE C1A 7N8, 902/368-4594; Fax: 902/368-4563
Qué.: Ministère de la Justice, 1200, rte de l'Église, Ste-Foy PQ G1V 4M1, 418/643-5140 (Communications); Fax: 418/646-4449
Sask.: Saskatchewan Justice, Civil Law Division, 1874 Scarth St., Regina SK S4P 3V7, 306/787-7872 (Communications); Fax: 306/787-3874
Yuk.: Yukon Justice, PO Box 2703, Whitehorse YT Y1A 2C6, 403/667-8292 (Communications); Fax: 403/393-6272

DRINKING DRIVING COUNTERMEASURES
Justice Canada, Policy Sector, Justice Bldg., 239 Wellington St., Ottawa ON K1A 0H8, 613/957-4222; Fax: 613/954-0811
Alta: Alberta Justice, Public Security Division, 10365 - 97th St., Edmonton AB T5J 3W7, 403/427-2745; Fax: 403/427-1194
Nfld.: Department of Health, Drug Dependency Services, West Block, Confederation Bldg., PO Box 8700, St. John's NF A1B 4J6, 709/729-0623; Fax: 709/729-5824
N.S.: Alcohol & Driving Countermeasures Office, 1690 Hollis St., PO Box 217, Stn M, Halifax NS B3J 2M4, 902/424-4673; Fax: 902/424-0700
Ont.: Ministry of the Attorney General, Drinking/Driving Countermeasures, 720 Bay St., 3rd Fl., Toronto ON M5G 2K1, 416/326-4408; Fax: 416/326-4007
PEI: Department of Transportation & Public Works, Safety, 17 Haviland St., 1st Fl., Charlottetown PE C1A 3S7, 902/368-5100; Fax: 902/368-5395
Qué.: Société de l'assurance automobile du Québec, 333, boul Jean-Lesage, CP 19600, Québec PQ G1K 8J6, 418/528-3100; Fax: 418/644-0339
Sask.: Saskatchewan Justice, Public Law & Policy Division, 1874 Scarth St., Regina SK S4P 3V7, 306/787-7872 (Communications); Fax: 306/787-3874

DRIVERS' LICENCES
Alta: Alberta Municipal Affairs, Registries Division, John E. Brownlee Bldg., 10365 - 97 St., Edmonton AB T5J 3W7, 403/422-2362 (Edmonton), 297-8980 (Calgary); Toll Free: 1-800-465-5009 (in Alberta); Fax: 403/422-9105
B.C.: Ministry of Transportation & Highways, Motor Vehicle Branch, 2631 Douglas St., Victoria BC V8T 5A3, 250/387-3140; Fax: 250/387-1169
Man.: Manitoba Highways & Transportation, Driver & Vehicle Licensing Division, 1075 Portage Ave., Winnipeg MB R3G 0S1, 204/945-3888; Fax: 204/948-2018
N.B.: Department of Transportation, Motor Vehicles & Policy, King Tower, Kings Pl., 2nd Fl., PO Box 6000, Fredericton NB E3B 5H1, 506/453-2552
Nfld.: Department of Government Services & Lands, Motor Vehicles Registration, PO Box 8710, St. John's NF A1B 4J5, 709/729-2518; Fax: 709/729-6955
NWT: Department of Transportation, Registration & Licensing, Lahm Ridge Bldg., PO Box 1320, Yellowknife NT X1A 2L9, 403/873-7418; Fax: 403/873-0363
N.S.: Department of Business & Consumer Services, Registry of Motor Vehicles, #215, 6061 Young St., PO Box 1652, Halifax NS B3J 2Z3, 902/424-5851; Toll Free: 1-800-898-7668; Fax: 902/424-0544
Ont.: Licence Suspension Appeal Board, 700 Bay St., 24th Fl., PO Box 329, Toronto ON M5G 1Z6, 416/325-0209
Ministry of Transportation, Licensing & Control Branch, 1201 Wilson Ave., Downsview ON M3M 1J8, 416/235-4793

Canadian Almanac & Directory 1997

PEI: Department of Transportation & Public Works, Motor Vehicles, 17 Haviland St., 1st Fl., Charlottetown PE C1A 3S7, 902/368-5200; Fax: 902/368-5236

Qué.: Société de l'assurance automobile du Québec, 333, boul Jean-Lesage, CP 19600, Québec PQ G1K 8J6, 418/528-3100; Fax: 418/644-0339

Sask.: Saskatchewan Government Insurance, Driver Licensing, 2260 - 11th Ave., Regina SK S4P 0J9, 306/751-1200; Fax: 306/787-7477

Yuk.: Yukon Driver Control Board, PO Box 2703, Whitehorse YT Y1A 2C6, 403/667-5313

Yukon Community & Transportation Services, Motor Vehicles, PO Box 2703, Whitehorse YT Y1A 2C6, 403/667-5315; Fax: 403/667-7056

DRUGS & ALCOHOL
See Also **Liquor Control**

Canadian Centre on Substance Abuse, #300, 75 Albert St., Ottawa ON K1P 5E7, 613/235-4048; Fax: 613/235-8101

Health Canada, National Pharmaceutical Strategy/Drugs Directorate, Ottawa ON K1A 0L2, 613/957-0369; Fax: 613/941-5366

Justice Canada, National Strategy for Drug Prosecutions, Justice Bldg., 239 Wellington St., Ottawa ON K1A 0H8, 613/952-7553; Fax: 613/954-0811

Patented Medicine Prices Review Board, Standard Life Centre, #1400, 333 Laurier Ave. West, PO Box L40, Ottawa ON K1P 1C1, 613/952-7360

Alta: AADAC Recovery Centre, 10302 - 107 St., Edmonton AB T5J 1K2, 403/427-4291; Fax: 403/422-2881

Alberta Alcohol & Drug Abuse Commission, Pacific Plaza Bldg., 10909 Jasper Ave., 6th Fl., Edmonton AB T5J 3M9, 403/427-2837; Fax: 403/423-1419

B.C.: Ministry of Health, 1515 Blanshard St., 7th Fl., Victoria BC V8W 3C8, 250/952-3456; Toll Free: AIDS Hotline 1-800-661-3886~

Ministry of the Attorney General, Liquor Control & Licensing Branch, 1019 Wharf St., Victoria BC V8V 1X4, 250/387-1254; Fax: 250/387-9184

   Liquor Distribution Branch, 2625 Rupert St., Vancouver BC V5M 3T5, 604/252-3021; Fax: 604/252-3026

Man.: Drug Standards/Therapeutics Committee, #128, 599 Empress St., PO Box 925, Winnipeg MB R3C 2T6, 204/786-7233; Fax: 204/783-2171

Manitoba Health, Program Development, 599 Empress St., Winnipeg MB R3G 3H2, 204/786-7312; Fax: 204/774-1325

N.B.: Department of Health & Community Services, PO Box 5100, Fredericton NB E3B 5G8, 506/453-3092; Fax: 506/444-4697

   Prescription Drug Program, PO Box 5100, Fredericton NB E3B 5G8, 506/453-2415; Fax: 506/444-4697

Nfld.: Department of Health, Drug Dependency Services, West Block, Confederation Bldg., PO Box 8700, St. John's NF A1B 4J6, 709/729-0623; Fax: 709/729-5824

PEI: Health & Community Services Agency, 4 Sydney St., PO Box 2000, Charlottetown PE C1A 7N8, 902/368-6130; Fax: 902/368-6136

Qué.: Ministère de la Santé et des services sociaux, 1075, ch Ste-Foy, Québec PQ G1S 2M1

Sask.: Saskatchewan Health, Prescription Drug Services Branch, 3475 Albert St., Regina SK S4S 6X6, 306/787-3301; Fax: 306/787-8679

Saskatchewan Liquor & Gaming Authority, 2500 Victoria Ave., PO Box 5054, Regina SK S4P 3M3, 306/787-4213; Fax: 306/787-8468

ECONOMIC DEVELOPMENT *See* BUSINESS DEVELOPMENT

EDUCATION

Human Resources Development Canada, Student Assistance Branch/Education Support Branch, Place du Portage, Phase IV, 140, Promenade du Portage, Hull PQ K1A 0J9, 819/994-2377; Fax: 819/953-4226

Alta: Alberta Advanced Education & Career Development, Commerce Place, 10155 - 102 St., 7th Fl., Edmonton AB T5J 4L5, 403/422-4488; Fax: 403/422-5126

Alberta Education, Devonian Bldg., 11160 Jasper Ave., Edmonton AB T5K 0L2, 403/427-7219; Fax: 403/427-0591

B.C.: British Columbia School Districts Capital Financing Authority, c/o Provincial Treasury, 620 Superior St., Victoria BC V8V 1X4, 250/387-7132; Fax: 250/387-3024

Ministry of Education, Skills & Training, PO Box 9150, Stn Prov Govt, Victoria BC V8W 9H1, 250/356-2500; Fax: 250/356-5945

Man.: Manitoba Education & Training, #168, Legislative Bldg., Winnipeg MB R3C 0P8, 204/945-4325; Fax: 204/945-1291

N.B.: Department of Advanced Education & Labour, Chestnut Complex, 470 York St., PO Box 6000, Fredericton NB E3B 5H1; Fax: 506/453-3806

Department of Education, PO Box 6000, Fredericton NB E3B 5H1, 506/453-3678; Fax: 506/453-3325

Nfld.: Department of Education, Confederation Bldg., PO Box 8700, St. John's NF A1B 4J6, 709/729-5097; Fax: 709/729-5896

NWT: Department of Education, Culture & Employment, Educational Development Branch, PO Box 1320, Yellowknife NT X1A 2L9, 403/920-8061; Fax: 403/873-0155

N.S.: Department of Education & Culture, 2021 Brunswick St., PO Box 578, Halifax NS B3J 2S9, 902/424-5168; Fax: 902/424-0511

Nova Scotia Council on Higher Education, 2021 Brunswick St., PO Box 2086, Stn M, Halifax NS B3J 3B7, 902/424-6992; Fax: 902/424-0651

Ont.: Conseil de l'Education Franco-Ontarienne, #203, 880 Bay St., Toronto ON M7A 1L2, 416/325-4626; Fax: 416/325-4627

Ministry of Education & Training, Organization Development & Services Division, Mowat Block, 900 Bay St., Toronto ON M7A 1L2, 416/325-2772; Fax: 416/325-2778

PEI: Department of Education, Sullivan Bldg., 16 Fitzroy St., PO Box 2000, Charlottetown PE C1A 7N8, 902/368-4600; Fax: 902/368-4663

Office of Higher Education, Training & Adult Learning, Shaw Bldg., 105 Rochford St., 3rd Fl., PO Box 2000, Charlottetown PE C1A 7N8, 902/368-5988; Fax: 902/368-6144

Qué.: Ministère de l'Éducation, 1035, rue De La Chevrotière, 15e étage, Québec PQ G1R 5A5, 418/643-7095; Fax: 418/646-6561

Sask.: Saskatchewan Education, 2220 College Ave., Regina SK S4P 3V7, 306/787-2010; Fax: 306/787-2280

Yuk.: Yukon Education, PO Box 2703, Whitehorse YT Y1A 2C6, 403/667-5141; Fax: 403/667-4754

ELECTIONS

Elections Canada, The Jackson Bldg., 257 Slater St., Ottawa ON K1A 0M6, 613/993-2975; Toll Free: 1-800-463-6868, TDD: 1-800-361-8935; Fax: 613/954-8584

National Archives of Canada, 395 Wellington St., Ottawa ON K1A 0N3, 613/995-5138; Fax: 613/995-6274

Alta: Alberta Office of the Chief Electoral Officer, #100, 11510 Kingsway Ave., Edmonton AB T5G 2Y5, 403/427-7191; Fax: 403/422-2900

B.C.: Elections British Columbia, 1075 Pendergast St., Victoria BC V8V 1X4, 250/387-5305; Fax: 250/387-3578

Man.: Elections Manitoba, #302, 379 Broadway, Winnipeg MB R3C 0T9, 204/945-3225; Fax: 204/945-6011

N.B.: Office of the Chief Electoral Officer, PO Box 6000, Fredericton NB E3B 5H1, 506/453-2218; Toll Free: 1-800-308-2922; Fax: 506/457-4926

Nfld.: Office of the Chief Electoral Officer, 39 Hallett Cr., St. John's NF A1B 4C4, 709/729-0712; Fax: 709/729-0679

NWT: Legislative Assembly, Elections NWT/Plebiscite Office, PO Box 1320, Yellowknife NT X1A 2L9, 403/920-6999; Fax: 403/920-4735

N.S.: Nova Scotia Elections Office, Joseph Howe Bldg., 9th Fl., PO Box 2246, Halifax NS B3J 3C8, 902/424-8584; Fax: 902/424-6622

Ont.: Elections Ontario, 51 Rolark Dr., Scarborough ON M1R 3B1, 416/321-3000; Toll Free: 1-800-668-2727; Fax: 416/321-6853

PEI: Elections Prince Edward Island, 180 Richmond St., 2nd Fl., PO Box 2000, Charlottetown PE C1A 7N8, 902/368-5895; Fax: 902/368-6500

Qué.: Élections du Québec, 3460, rue de La Pérade, Ste-Foy PQ G1X 3Y5, 418/643-5380; Fax: 418/643-7291

Secrétariat à la réforme électorale et parlementaire, 875, Grande Allée est, Québec PQ G1R 4Y8, 418/643-2483; Fax: 418/643-5612

Sask.: Office of the Chief Electoral Officer, 1702 Park St., Regina SK S4N 6B2, 306/787-4000; Fax: 306/787-4052

Yuk.: Legislative Assembly, c/o Clerk's Office, PO Box 2703, Whitehorse YT Y1A 2C6, 403/667-5498; Fax: 403/667-4180

EMERGENCY RESPONSE

Environment Canada, Terrasses de la Chaudière, 10 Wellington St., Hull PQ K1A 0H3, 819/997-2800; Toll Free: 1-800-668-6767; Fax: 819/953-2225

Fisheries & Oceans Canada, Rescue & Environmental Response, Canada Bldg., 344 Slater St., Ottawa ON K1A 0N7, 613/990-3110; Fax: 613/990-2780

National Defence (Canada), Emergency Preparedness Canada, Jackson Bldg., 122 Bank St., 2nd Fl., Ottawa ON K1A 0W6, 613/991-7077; Fax: 613/998-9589

National Search & Rescue Secretariat, Standard Life Bldg., 275 Slater St., 4th Fl., Ottawa ON K1A 0K2, ; Toll Free: 1-800-727-9414; Fax: 613/996-3746

Solicitor General Canada, National Security, Sir Wilfrid Laurier Bldg., 340 Laurier Ave. West, Ottawa ON K1A 0P8, 613/993-4136; Fax: 613/990-3632

Transport Canada, Security & Emergency Planning, Transport Canada Building, 330 Sparks St., Ottawa ON K1A 0N5, 613/990-3651; Fax: 613/996-6381

Transportation Safety Board of Canada, 200 Promenade du Portage, 4e étage, Hull PQ K1A 1K8, 819/994-3741; Fax: 819/997-2239

Alta: Alberta Environmental Protection, Alberta Environmental Centre, PO Box 4000, Vegreville AB T0B 4L0, 403/427-2739, 944-0313 (Information Centre); Fax: 403/632-8385

Alberta Health, Emergency Health Services, PO Box 222, Edmonton AB T5J 2P4, 403/427-4105

Alberta Transportation & Utilities, Disaster & Emergency Programs, Twin Atria, 4999 - 98 Ave., Edmonton AB T6B 2X3, 403/422-9000; Fax: 403/422-6515

B.C.: British Columbia Provincial Emergency Program, 455 Boleskine Rd., Victoria BC V8Z 1E7, 250/387-5956; Fax: 250/952-4888

Ministry of Environment, Lands & Parks, Enforcement & Environmental Emergencies Branch, 810 Blan-

shard St., 4th Fl., Victoria BC V8V 1X4, 250/387-9401; Fax: 250/387-1041
Man.: Manitoba Disaster Assistance Board, #101, 800 Portage Ave., Winnipeg MB R3G 0N4, 204/945-3050; Fax: 204/945-4929
Manitoba Emergency Measures Organization, 405 Broadway, 15th Fl., Winnipeg MB R3C 3L6, 204/945-4772; Fax: 204/945-4620
Manitoba Environment, Environmental Operations Division, Bldg. 2, 139 Tuxedo Ave., Winnipeg MB R3N 0H6, 204/945-7008; Fax: 204/945-5229
Nfld.: Department of Municipal & Provincial Affairs, Emergency Measures Division, West Block, Confederation Bldg., PO Box 8700, St. John's NF A1B 4J6, 709/729-3703; 24-hour Emergencies: 709/722-7107; Fax: 709/729-3857
NWT: Department of Resources, Wildlife & Economic Development, Environmental Protection Division, #600, Scotia Centre, Bldg. Box 21, 5102 - 50 Ave., Yellowknife NT X1A 3S8, 403/873-7420, 7134; Fax: 403/873-0114
Northwest Territories Emergency Measures Organization, Northwest Tower, #600, 5201 - 50 Ave., Yellowknife NT X1A 3S9, 403/873-7554; Fax: 403/873-8193
N.S.: Nova Scotia Emergency Measures Organization, PO Box 2107, Halifax NS B3J 3B7, 902/424-5620; Fax: 902/424-5376
Ont.: Ministry of Environment & Energy, Spills Action Centre, 5775 Yonge St., 10th Fl., Toronto ON M2M 4S1, 416/325-3000; Fax: 416/325-3011
Ministry of the Solicitor General & Correctional Services, Emergency Measures Ontario, 25 Grosvenor St., 19th Fl., Toronto ON M7A 1Y6, 416/314-3723; Fax: 416/314-3758
PEI: Prince Edward Island Emergency Measures Organization, East Prince Regional Service Centre, PO Box 2063, Summerside PE C1N 5L2, 902/888-8050; Fax: 902/888-8054
Sask.: Saskatchewan Environment & Resource Management, 3211 Albert St., Regina SK S4S 5W6, 306/787-2700; Toll Free: 1-800-667-2757; Fax: 306/787-3941
Saskatchewan Municipal Government, Emergency Planning, 1855 Victoria Ave., Regina SK S4P 3V7, 306/787-9567; Fax: 306/787-1694

EMPLOYMENT

Human Resources Development Canada, Communications, Place du Portage, Phase IV, 140, Promenade du Portage, Hull PQ K1A 0J9, 819/994-6013
Employment, Place du Portage, Phase IV, 140, Promenade du Portage, Hull PQ K1A 0J9, 819/953-3729; Fax: 819/994-2085
National Defence (Canada), Canadian Forces Recruiting, Education & Training System, MGen. George R. Pearkes Bldg., 101 Colonel By Dr., Ottawa ON K1A 0K2, 613/992-4581
Alta: Alberta Advanced Education & Career Development, Learner Assistance Division, Commerce Place, 10155 - 102 St., 7th Fl., Edmonton AB T5J 4L5, 403/422-4488; Fax: 403/422-5126
Alberta Family & Social Services, Income & Employment Programs, Seventh St. Plaza, 10030 - 107 St., Edmonton AB T5J 3E4, 403/427-2635; Fax: 403/422-9044
Alberta Labour, Work Standards, 10808 - 99 Ave., Edmonton AB T5K 0G5, 403/427-8541; Fax: 403/422-3562
B.C.: Environmental Appeal Board, #125, 911 Yates St., Victoria BC V8V 1X5, 250/387-3464; Fax: 250/356-9923
Ministry of Education, Skills & Training, PO Box 9150, Stn Prov Govt, Victoria BC V8W 9H1, 250/356-2500; Fax: 250/356-5945

Ministry of Employment & Investment, 712 Yates St., Victoria BC V8V 1X4, 250/356-8702
Policy Division, 712 Yates St., Victoria BC V8V 1X4, 250/356-8702
Ministry of Labour, 825 Fort St., Victoria BC V8W 9K1, 250/387-0172; Fax: 250/356-1653
Man.: Manitoba Education & Training, Workforce 2000 & Youth Programs, 185 Carlton St., 4th Fl., Winnipeg MB R3C 3J1, 204/945-6195; Fax: 204/945-1792
Manitoba Labour, Labour Services Division, #611, Norquay Bldg., 401 York Ave., Winnipeg MB R3C 0P8, 204/945-8190 (Management Services); Fax: 204/948-2085
N.B.: Department of Advanced Education & Labour, Labour & Employment Division, Chestnut Complex, 470 York St., PO Box 6000, Fredericton NB E3B 5H1; Fax: 506/453-3806
Department of Human Resources Development, PO Box 6000, Fredericton NB E3B 5H1, 506/453-2001; Fax: 506/453-7478
New Brunswick Labour & Employment Board, 191 Prospect St., PO Box 908, Fredericton NB E3B 1B0, 506/453-2881; Fax: 506/453-3892
Nfld.: Department of Mines & Energy, PO Box 8700, St. John's NF A1B 4J6, 709/729-2301
NWT: Department of Education, Culture & Employment, Career Development, PO Box 1320, Yellowknife NT X1A 2L9, 403/873-7146; Fax: 403/873-0155
Culture & Careers Branch, PO Box 1320, Yellowknife NT X1A 2L9, 403/873-7252; Fax: 403/873-0155
N.S.: Department of Community Services, Income & Employment Support, Johnston Bldg., 5182 Prince St., 5th Fl., PO Box 696, Halifax NS B3J 2T7, 902/424-4326; Fax: 902/424-0502
Department of Human Resources, One Government Place, 1700 Granville St., PO Box 943, Halifax NS B3J 2V9, 902/424-7660; TDD: 424-3966; Fax: 902/424-0611
Ont.: Ministry of Community & Social Services, Social Assistance & Employment Opportunities Division, Hepburn Block, 80 Grosvenor St., 6th Fl., Toronto ON M7A 1E9, 416/325-5666; Fax: 416/325-5172, 5171
Ministry of Labour, Employment Practices Branch, 400 University Ave., 14th Fl., Toronto ON M7A 1T7, 416/326-7000; Fax: 416/326-7061
PEI: Department of Provincial Affairs & Attorney General, Labour & Industrial Relations Division, PO Box 2000, Charlottetown PE C1A 7N8, 902/368-5250; Fax: 902/368-5283; 5355
Qué.: Ministère du Travail, 200, ch Ste-Foy, 6e étage, Québec PQ G1R 5S1, 418/643-4817; Fax: 418/644-6969
Sask.: Saskatchewan Post-Secondary Education & Skills Training, 2220 College Ave., Regina SK S4P 3V7, 306/787-1002
Yuk.: Employment Standards Board, PO Box 2703, Whitehorse YT Y1A 2C6

EMPLOYMENT EQUITY See DISCRIMINATION & EMPLOYMENT EQUITY

ENERGY
See Also **Natural Resources**

Atomic Energy of Canada Limited, 2251 Speakman Dr., Mississauga ON L5K 1B2, 905/823-9040; Fax: 905/823-8006
Energy Supplies Allocation Board, 580 Booth St., 17th Fl., Ottawa ON K1A 0E4, 613/995-5594; Fax: 613/992-8738
Indian Oil & Gas Canada, #100, 9911 Chula Blvd., Tsuu T'ina (Sarcee) AB T2W 6H6, 403/292-5625; Fax: 403/292-5618

National Energy Board, 311 - 6th Ave. SW, Calgary AB T2P 3H2, 403/292-4800; Fax: 403/292-5503
Natural Resources Canada, Canada Centre for Mineral & Energy Technology, 580 Booth St., Ottawa ON K1A 0E4, 613/995-0947; Fax: 613/996-9094
Energy Sector, 580 Booth St., Ottawa ON K1A 0E4, 613/996-7432; Fax: 613/992-1405
Alta: Alberta Energy, Petroleum Plaza, North Tower, 9945 - 108 St., Edmonton AB T5K 2G6, 403/427-7425; Fax: 403/427-3198
Alberta Research Council, Energy Technologies, 250 Karl Clark Rd., PO Box 8330, Edmonton AB T6H 5X2, 403/987-8119; Fax: 403/461-2651
B.C.: Ministry of Employment & Investment, Energy & Minerals Division, 1810 Blanshard St., 8th Fl., Victoria BC V8W 9N3, 250/356-8702
Man.: Manitoba Energy & Mines, #360, 1395 Ellice Ave., Winnipeg MB R3G 3P2, 204/945-4154; Fax: 204/945-0586, 1406
Petroleum & Energy Branch, 360 - 1395 Ellice Ave., Winnipeg MB R3G 3P2, 204/945-6577; Toll Free: 1-800-282-8069 (Energy); Fax: 204/945-0586
N.B.: Department of Natural Resources & Energy, Mineral Resources & Energy, PO Box 6000, Fredericton NB E3B 5H1, 506/453-2614; Fax: 506/453-3322
Nfld.: Canada-Newfoundland Offshore Petroleum Board, TD Place, #500, 140 Water St., St. John's NF A1C 6H6, 709/778-1400; Fax: 709/778-1473
Department of Mines & Energy, Energy Branch, PO Box 8700, St. John's NF A1B 4J6, 709/729-2301
NWT: Department of Resources, Wildlife & Economic Development, Energy Policy & Programs, #600, Scotia Centre, Bldg. Box 21, 5102 - 50 Ave., Yellowknife NT X1A 3S8, 403/920-8944; Fax: 403/873-0114
Resource Policy, #600, Scotia Centre, Bldg. Box 21, 5102 - 50 Ave., Yellowknife NT X1A 3S8, 403/873-7420, 7134; Fax: 403/873-0114
N.S.: Canada-Nova Scotia Offshore Petroleum Board, TD Centre, 1791 Barrington St., 6th Fl., Halifax NS B3J 3K9, 902/422-5588; Fax: 902/422-1799
Department of Natural Resources, Minerals & Energy Branch, Founder's Square, 1701 Hollis St., PO Box 698, Halifax NS B3J 2T9, 902/424-5346; Fax: 902/424-7735
Petroleum Development Agency, Founder's Square, 1701 Hollis St., PO Box 698, Halifax NS B3J 2T9, 902/424-5935; Fax: 902/424-7735
Ont.: Ministry of Environment & Energy, 135 St. Clair Ave. West, Toronto ON M4V 1P5, 416/325-4000 (Public Information Centre); Toll Free: 1-800-565-4923; Fax: 416/323-4564
Energy Conservation & Liaison, 135 St. Clair Ave. West, Toronto ON M4V 1P5, 416/323-5626; Fax: 416/323-5636
Ontario Energy Board, 2300 Yonge St., 23rd Fl., PO Box 2382, Toronto ON M4P 1E4, 416/481-1967; Fax: 416/440-7656
Ontario Energy Corporation, South Tower, #905, 175 Bloor St. East, Toronto ON M4W 3R8, 416/926-4200; Fax: 416/926-9641
Ontario Hydro, 700 University Ave., Toronto ON M5G 1X6, 416/592-5111; Toll Free: 1-800-263-9000
PEI: Prince Edward Island Energy Corporation, 11 Kent St., PO Box 2000, Charlottetown PE C1A 7N8, 902/368-4220; Fax: 902/368-5982
Qué.: Ministère des Ressources Naturelles, Énergie, #B-302, 5700 - 4 av ouest, 3e étage, Charlesbourg PQ G1H 6R1, 418/646-2727 (Renseignements); Fax: 418/643-8337
Sask.: Saskatchewan Energy & Mines, 1914 Hamilton St., Regina SK S4P 4V4, 306/787-2526; Fax: 306/787-7338
Yuk.: Yukon Economic Development, Energy & Mines Branch, 211 Main St., PO Box 2703, Whitehorse YT Y1A 2C6, 403/667-5466; Fax: 403/668-8601

ENVIRONMENT

Auditor General of Canada, Environment & Sustainable Development, 240 Sparks St., Ottawa ON K1A 0G6, 613/995-3708; Fax: 613/957-4023

Environment Canada, Terrasses de la Chaudière, 10 Wellington St., Hull PQ K1A 0H3, 819/997-2800; Toll Free: 1-800-668-6767; Fax: 819/953-2225

Foreign Affairs & International Trade Canada, Environment & Sustainable Development, Lester B. Pearson Bldg., 125 Sussex Dr., Ottawa ON K1A 0G2, 613/944-0886; Fax: 613/952-3904

Indian & Northern Affairs Canada, Natural Resources & Environment Branch, Tour Nord, Les Terrasses de la Chaudière, 10 Wellington St., Hull PQ K1A 0H4, 819/997-9381; Fax: 819/953-8766

Industry Canada, Environmental Affairs, C.D. Howe Bldg., 235 Queen St., Ottawa ON K1A 0H5, 613/954-3080; Fax: 613/952-9564

National Round Table on the Environment & Economy, #1500, 1 Nicholas St, Ottawa ON K1N 7B7, 613/992-7189; Fax: 613/992-7385

Natural Resources Canada, 580 Booth St., Ottawa ON K1A 0E4, 613/995-0947; Fax: 613/996-9094

Alta: Alberta Environmental Protection, 9915 - 108 St., Edmonton AB T5K 2G8, 403/427-2739, 944-0313 (Information Centre)

Alberta Environmental Centre, PO Box 4000, Vegreville AB T0B 4L0, 403/427-2739, 944-0313 (Information Centre); Fax: 403/632-8385

B.C.: Ministry of Environment, Lands & Parks, 810 Blanshard St., Victoria BC V8V 1X5, 250/387-9419; Fax: 250/356-6464

Man.: Manitoba Environment, Bldg. 2, 139 Tuxedo Ave., Winnipeg MB R3N 0H6, 204/945-7100

N.B.: Department of the Environment, 364 Argyle St., PO Box 6000, Fredericton NB E3B 5H1, 506/453-3700; Fax: 506/453-3843

Communications & Environmental Education, 364 Argyle St., PO Box 6000, Fredericton NB E3B 5H1, 506/453-3700; Fax: 506/453-3843

Nfld.: Department of Environment & Labour, Confederation Bldg., PO Box 8700, St. John's NF A1B 4J6, 709/729-1930; Fax: 709/729-1930

NWT: Department of Resources, Wildlife & Economic Development, #600, Scotia Centre, Bldg. Box 21, 5102 - 50 Ave., Yellowknife NT X1A 3S8, 403/873-7420, 7134; Fax: 403/873-0114

N.S.: Department of the Environment, PO Box 2107, Halifax NS B3J 3B7, 902/424-5300; Fax: 902/424-0644

Ont.: Environmental Commissioner of Ontario, #605, 1075 Bay St., Toronto ON M5S 2B1, 416/325-3377; Toll Free: 1-800-701-6454; Fax: 416/325-3370

Ministry of Environment & Energy, 135 St. Clair Ave. West, Toronto ON M4V 1P5, 416/325-4000 (Public Information Centre); Toll Free: 1-800-565-4923; Fax: 416/323-4564

PEI: Department of Environmental Resources, Jones Bldg., 11 Kent St., 4th Fl., PO Box 2000, Charlottetown PE C1A 7N8, 902/368-5000; Fax: 902/368-5830

Qué.: Ministère de l'Environnement et de la Faune, Édifice Marie-Guyart, 675, boul René-Lévesque est, Québec PQ G1R 5V7, 418/643-3127; Toll Free: 1-800-561-1616; Fax: 418/646-5974

Sask.: Saskatchewan Environment & Resource Management, #422, 3211 Albert St., Regina SK S4S 5W6, 306/787-7197; Fax: 306/787-7196

Yuk.: Yukon Council on the Economy & the Environment, A-8E, PO Box 2703, Whitehorse YT Y1A 2C6, 403/667-5939; Fax: 403/668-4936

Yukon Renewable Resources, Environment Protection & Assessment Branch, PO Box 2703, Whitehorse YT Y1A 2C6, 403/667-5237; Fax: 403/393-6213

ENVIRONMENTAL HEALTH See OCCUPATIONAL SAFETY

EXPORTS See TRADE

EXPROPRIATION

Canada Lands Company, #1500, 200 King St. West, Toronto ON M5H 3T4, 416/974-9700; Fax: 416/974-9661

Justice Canada, Justice Bldg., 239 Wellington St., Ottawa ON K1A 0H8, 613/957-4222; Fax: 613/954-0811

National Defence (Canada), MGen. George R. Pearkes Bldg., 101 Colonel By Dr., Ottawa ON K1A 0K2, 613/992-4581

Public Works & Government Services Canada, Real Property Services Branch, Place du Portage, Phase III, 11, rue Laurier, Hull PQ K1A 0S5, 819/956-3115

Alta: Alberta Public Works, Supply & Services, Land Acquisition Branch, 6950 - 113th St., 3rd Fl., Edmonton AB T6H 5V7, 403/422-1384; Fax: 403/422-5419

Land Compensation Board, Phipps-McKinnon Bldg., 10020 - 101A Ave., 18th Fl., Edmonton AB T5J 3G2, 403/422-2988; Fax: 403/427-5798

B.C.: Expropriation Compensation Board, 514 Government St., Victoria BC V8V 2L7, 250/387-4321; Fax: 250/387-0711

Man.: Manitoba Government Services, Land Acquisition, 25 Tupper St. North, Portage la Prairie MB R1N 3K1, 204/945-3001

N.B.: Expropriations Advisory Office, 295 boul St-Pierre ouest, CP 297, Caraquet NB E0B 1K0, 506/727-3481; Fax: 506/727-4162

Nfld.: Department of Government Services & Lands, Lands Branch, PO Box 8700, St. John's NF A1B 4J6

Department of Works, Services & Transportation, Realty Services, Confederation Bldg., PO Box 8700, St. John's NF A1B 4J6, 709/729-3356; Fax: 709/729-0703

NWT: Department of Municipal & Community Affairs, Community Planning & Lands, #600, 5201 - 50th Ave., PO Box 1310, Yellowknife NT X1A 2L9, 403/920-8916; Fax: 403/920-6343

N.S.: Expropriations Compensation Board, 1601 Lower Water St., PO Box 1692, Stn M, Halifax NS B3J 3S3, 902/424-4448; Fax: 902/424-3919

Ont.: Ontario Municipal Board, 655 Bay St., 15th Fl., Toronto ON M5G 1E5, 416/326-6800

PEI: Department of Transportation & Public Works, Properties & Surveys Section, Jones Bldg., PO Box 2000, Charlottetown PE C1A 7N8, 902/368-5131; Fax: 902/368-5395

Qué.: Ministère de la Justice, 1200, rte de l'Église, Ste-Foy PQ G1V 4M1, 418/643-5140 (Communications); Fax: 418/646-4449

Ministère des Transports, 700, boul René-Lévesque est, Québec PQ G1R 5H1, 418/643-6740

Société immobilière du Québec, 475, rue St-Amable, Québec PQ G1R 4X9, 418/646-1766 poste 3470; Fax: 418/643-7932

Sask.: Public & Private Rights Board, 2151 Scarth St., Regina SK S4P 3V7, 306/787-4071; Fax: 306/787-0088

Saskatchewan Property Management Corporation, 1840 Lorne St., Regina SK S4P 3V7, 306/787-6911; Fax: 306/787-1061

EXTERNAL AFFAIRS See INTERNATIONAL AFFAIRS

FAMILY BENEFITS

See Also Income Security; Social Services

Human Resources Development Canada, Income Security Program, Place Vanier, 120 Parkdale Ave., Ottawa ON K1A 0L1, 819/994-6013

Veterans Affairs Canada, Benefits, Daniel J. MacDonald Bldg., 161 Grafton St., PO Box 7700, Charlottetown PE C1A 8M9, 613/566-8808; Fax: 613/566-8073

Alta: Alberta Family & Social Services, Seventh St. Plaza, 10030 - 107 St., Edmonton AB T5J 3E4, 403/427-2734; Fax: 403/422-9044

Office of the Commissioner of Services for Children & Families, c/o Alberta Family & Social Services, Seventh St. Plaza, 10030 - 107 St., Edmonton AB T5J 3E4, 403/422-5011; Fax: 403/422-5036

Man.: Manitoba Family Services, #219, 114 Garry St., Winnipeg MB R3C 4V6, 204/945-2324 (Policy & Planning); Fax: 204/945-2156

N.B.: Department of Health & Community Services, Family & Community Social Services Division, PO Box 5100, Fredericton NB E3B 5G8, 506/453-2536; Fax: 506/444-4697

Nfld.: Department of Social Services, Family & Rehabilitative Services, Confederation Bldg., PO Box 8700, St. John's NF A1B 4J6, 709/729-2436; Fax: 709/729-6996

NWT: Department of Health & Social Services, Family Support & Child Protection, Centre Square Tower, 8th Fl., PO Box 1320, Yellowknife NT X1A 2L9, 403/920-6255; Fax: 403/873-0444

N.S.: Department of Community Services, Family & Children's Services, Johnston Bldg., 5182 Prince St., 5th Fl., PO Box 696, Halifax NS B3J 2T7, 902/424-4326; Fax: 902/424-0502

PEI: Department of Health & Social Services, Jones Bldg., 11 Kent St., 2nd Fl., PO Box 2000, Charlottetown PE C1A 7N8, 902/368-4900; Fax: 902/368-4969

Health & Community Services Agency, 4 Sydney St., PO Box 2000, Charlottetown PE C1A 7N8, 902/368-6130; Fax: 902/368-6136

Qué.: Ministère de la Sécurité du revenu, 425, rue St-Amable, 1er étage, Québec PQ G1R 4Z1, 418/643-9818; Toll Free: 1-800-361-4743; Fax: 418/646-5426

Sask.: Saskatchewan Social Services, Income Security Programs Division, 1920 Broad St., Regina SK S4P 3V6, 306/787-7469; Fax: 306/787-1032

Yuk.: Yukon Health & Social Services, Social Services Branch, PO Box 2703, Whitehorse YT Y1A 2C6, 403/667-3673 (Communications); Fax: 403/667-3096

FEDERAL-PROVINCIAL AFFAIRS

Canadian Intergovernmental Conference Secretariat, 110 O'Connor St., PO Box 488, Stn A, Ottawa ON K1N 8V5, 613/995-2341; Fax: 613/996-6091

Citizenship & Immigration Canada, Federal-Provincial Partnerships & Projects, Journal Tower South, 365 Laurier Ave. West, Hull PQ K1A 1L1, 613/957-4166; Fax: 613/957-5955

Federal Office of Regional Development (Québec), Tour de la Bourse, #3800, 800, Place Victoria, CP 247, Montréal PQ H4Z 1E8, 514/283-6412, 4843; Toll Free: 1-800-263-4689; Fax: 514/283-7778

Finance Canada, Federal Provincial Relations & Social Policy Branch, Esplanade Laurier, 140 O'Connor St., Ottawa ON K1A 0G5, 613/992-1573; Fax: 613/996-8404

Human Resources Development Canada, Federal-Provincial Relations, Place du Portage, Phase IV, 140, Promenade du Portage, Hull PQ K1A 0J9, 819/997-0519; Fax: 819/997-7329

Industry Canada, Internal Trade, Consultations & Federal-Provincial Relations, C.D. Howe Bldg., 235 Queen St., Ottawa ON K1A 0H5, 613/954-9633; Fax: 613/954-2303

Office of Intergovernmental Affairs, c/o Privy Council Office, Langevin Block, 80 Wellington St., Ottawa ON K1A 0A3

Privy Council Office, Intergovernmental Affairs, Langevin Block, 80 Wellington St., Ottawa ON K1A 0A3, 613/957-5153; Fax: 613/995-0101

Canadian Almanac & Directory 1997

Treasury Board of Canada, Office of Infrastructure, West Tower, 300 Laurier Ave. West, 3rd Fl., Ottawa ON K1A 0R5, 613/952-3171; Fax: 613/952-7979

Alta: Alberta Federal & Intergovernmental Affairs, #2200, 10025 Jasper Ave., Edmonton AB T5J 1S6, 403/427-2611; Fax: 403/423-6654

B.C.: Executive Council, Intergovernmental Relations, #272, West Annex, Legislative Bldgs., Victoria BC V8V 1X4, 250/387-0752; Fax: 250/387-1920

Ministry of Employment & Investment, International Branch, 712 Yates St., Victoria BC V8V 1X4, 250/387-0249; Fax: 250/356-8109

Ministry of Finance & Corporate Relations, Federal-Provincial Relations & Research, 617 Government St., Victoria BC V8V 1X4, 250/387-9018

Man.: Manitoba Finance, Federal-Provincial Relations & Research Division, #203, 333 Broadway Ave., Winnipeg MB R3C 0S9, 204/945-3754; Fax: 204/945-8316

N.B.: Department of Intergovernmental & Aboriginal Affairs, PO Box 6000, Fredericton NB E3B 5H1, 506/453-2384; Fax: 506/453-2995

Federal-Provincial Affairs, PO Box 6000, Fredericton NB E3B 5H1, 506/457-7275; Fax: 506/453-2995

Nfld.: Department of Municipal & Provincial Affairs, Canada/Newfoundland Infrastructure Program, West Block, Confederation Bldg., PO Box 8700, St. John's NF A1B 4J6, 709/729-5411

Executive Council, Intergovernmental Affairs Secretariat, Confederation Bldg., PO Box 8700, St. John's NF A1B 4J6, 709/729-5038

NWT: Ministry of Intergovernmental & Aboriginal Affairs, Precambrian Bldg., 7th Fl., PO Box 1320, Yellowknife NT X1A 2L9, 403/873-7143; Fax: 403/873-0233

N.S.: Executive Council, Intergovernmental Affairs, One Government Place, PO Box 2125, Halifax NS B3J 3B7, 902/424-4899; Fax: 902/424-0728

Ont.: Ministry of Finance, Intergovernmental Finance Policy Branch, Frost Bldg. South, 7 Queen's Park Cres., Toronto ON M7A 1Y7, 416/327-0140; Fax: 416/327-0160

Ministry of Intergovernmental Affairs, Constitutional Affairs, 900 Bay St., 6th Fl., Toronto ON M7A 1C2, 416/325-4804; Fax: 416/325-4759

PEI: Department of Health & Social Services, Jones Bldg., 11 Kent St., 2nd Fl., PO Box 2000, Charlottetown PE C1A 7N8, 902/368-4926; Fax: 902/368-4969

Qué.: Secrétariat aux affaires intergouvernementales canadiennes, Edifice H, 3e étage, 875, Grande Allée est, Québec PQ G1R 4Y8, 418/643-4011; Fax: 418/643-8730

Sask.: Saskatchewan Finance, Taxation & Intergovernmental Affairs Branch, 2350 Albert St., Regina SK S4P 4A6, 306/787-6731; Fax: 306/787-6544

Saskatchewan Intergovernmental Affairs, 1919 Saskatchewan Dr., Regina SK S4P 3V7, 306/787-1643; Fax: 306/787-1987

Yuk.: Executive Council, Federal Relations Office, #707, 350 Sparks St., Ottawa ON K1R 7S8, 613/234-3206; Fax: 613/563-9602

Policy & Communications, PO Box 2703, Whitehorse YT Y1A 2C6, 403/667-5854, 5393, 5939; Fax: 403/393-6202

FILM CLASSIFICATION See CENSORSHIP (MEDIA)

FILM PRODUCTION & COLLECTIONS

Canadian Broadcasting Corporation, 1500 Bronson Ave., PO Box 8478, Ottawa ON K1G 3J5, 613/724-1200; TDD: 613/738-6686

National Film Board of Canada, 3155, rue Côte de Liesse, St-Laurent PQ H4N 2N4, 514/283-9000; Fax: 514/283-8971

Telefilm Canada, Tour de la Banque Nationale, 600, De La Gauchetière ouest, 14e étage, Montréal PQ H3B 4L8, 514/283-6363; Fax: 514/283-8212

Alta: Alberta Motion Picture Development Corporation, #690, 10020 - 101A Ave., Edmonton AB T5J 3G2, 403/424-8855; Fax: 403/424-7669

B.C.: Ministry of Small Business, Tourism & Culture, BC Film Commission, 1117 Wharf St., Victoria BC V8W 2Z2, 604/660-2732; Fax: 604/660-4790

Man.: Manitoba Culture, Heritage & Citizenship, Arts Branch, 213 Notre Dame., Winnipeg MB R3B 1N3, 204/945-4579; Fax: 204/945-1684

N.B.: Department of Education, Instructional Resources, PO Box 6000, Fredericton NB E3B 5H1, 505/453-2319; Fax: 506/453-3325

N.S.: Department of Education & Culture, Education Media Services, 2021 Brunswick St., PO Box 578, Halifax NS B3J 2S9, 902/424-2462; Fax: 902/424-0633

Nova Scotia Film Development Corporation, 1724 Granville St., Halifax NS B3J 1X5, 902/424-7177, 7185

Ont.: Ontario Film Development Corporation, North Tower, #300, 175 Bloor St. East, Toronto ON M4W 3R8, 416/314-6858; Fax: 416/314-6876

PEI: Department of Education, Provincial Libraries & Archives, Sullivan Bldg., 16 Fitzroy St., PO Box 2000, Charlottetown PE C1A 7N8, 902/368-4227; Fax: 902/961-3203

Qué.: Ministère de la Culture et des Communications, Archives nationales et centre de conservation du Québec, Pavillon Louis-Jacques Casault, 1210 av du Séminaire, Ste-Foy PQ G1N 4V1, 418/643-4376; Fax: 418/646-0868

Sask.: Saskatchewan Government Media Services, #3, Legislative Bldg., Regina SK S4S 0B3, 306/787-6281

Yuk.: Yukon Education, Libraries & Archives, PO Box 2703, Whitehorse YT Y1A 2C6, 403/667-5309; Fax: 403/667-4253

Yukon Tourism, Heritage Branch, PO Box 2703, Whitehorse YT Y1A 2C6, 403/667-5363; Fax: 403/667-3546

FINANCE
See Also Banking & Financial Institutions

Auditor General of Canada, 240 Sparks St., Ottawa ON K1A 0G6, 613/995-3708; Fax: 613/957-4023

Bank of Canada, 234 Wellington St., Ottawa ON K1A 0G9, 613/782-8111; Fax: 613/782-8655

Business Development Bank of Canada, Tour de la Place-Victoria, #800, Place Victoria, CP 335, Montréal PQ H4Z 1L4, 514/283-5904; Toll Free: 1-888-463-6232; Fax: 514/283-0617

Canada Deposit Insurance Corporation, 50 O'Connor St., 17th Fl., PO Box 2340, Stn D, Ottawa ON K1P 5W5, 613/996-2081; Toll Free: 1-800-461-2342; Fax: 613/996-6095

Finance Canada, Esplanade Laurier, 140 O'Connor St., Ottawa ON K1A 0G5, 613/992-1573; TDD: 613/996-0035; Fax: 613/996-8404

Office of the Superintendent of Financial Institutions, Kent Square, 255 Albert St., Ottawa ON K1A 0H2, 613/990-7788; Toll Free: 1-800-385-8647; Fax: 613/952-8219

Treasury Board of Canada, 140 O'Connor St., Ottawa ON K1A 0R5, 613/957-2400; Fax: 613/952-3658

Alta: Alberta Economic Development & Tourism, Business Finance, Commerce Place, 10155 - 102 St., Edmonton AB T5J 4L6, 403/427-3300; Fax: 403/422-9319

Alberta Treasury, Terrace Bldg., 9515 - 107 St., Edmonton AB T5K 2C3, 403/427-3035; Fax: 403/422-2463

Banking & Cash Management, Terrace Bldg., 9515 - 107 St., Edmonton AB T5K 2C3, 403/427-3035; Fax: 403/422-2463

B.C.: Financial Institutions Commission, #1900, 1050 West Pender St., Vancouver BC V6E 3S7, 604/660-2947; Fax: 604/660-3170

Ministry of Finance & Corporate Relations, 617 Government St., Victoria BC V8V 1X4, 250/387-9278

Man.: Manitoba Finance, #109, Legislative Bldg., Winnipeg MB R3C 0V8, 204/945-3754; Fax: 204/945-8316

N.B.: Department of Finance, PO Box 6000, Fredericton NB E3B 5H1, 506/453-2286; Fax: 506/457-4989

New Brunswick Investment Management Corporation, PO Box 6000, Fredericton NB E3B 5H1, 506/444-5800

Nfld.: Department of Finance & Treasury Board, Confederation Bldg., PO Box 8700, St. John's NF A1B 4J6, 709/729-2858; Fax: 709/729-2856

NWT: Department of Finance, PO Box 1320, Yellowknife NT X1A 2L9

N.S.: Department of Finance, PO Box 187, Halifax NS B3J 2N3, 902/424-5554; Fax: 902/424-0635

Ont.: Ministry of Finance, Frost Bldg. South, 7 Queen's Park Cres., Toronto ON M7A 1Y7, 416/325-0333 (Communications & Corporate Affairs); Fax: 416/325-0339

Ontario Financing Authority, #1400, 1 Dundas St. West, Toronto ON M7A 1Y7

PEI: Department of the Provincial Treasury, PO Box 2000, Charlottetown PE C1A 7N8, 902/368-4000; Fax: 902/368-5544

Qué.: Ministère des Finances, 12, rue St-Louis, Québec PQ G1R 5L3, 418/691-2233; Fax: 418/646-5643, 1631

Sask.: Saskatchewan Finance, 2350 Albert St., Regina SK S4P 4A6, 306/787-6768; Fax: 306/787-6544

Yuk.: Yukon Finance, PO Box 2703, Whitehorse YT Y1A 2C6, 403/667-5343; Fax: 403/393-6217

FINANCIAL INSTITUTIONS See BANKING & FINANCIAL INSTITUTIONS

FIRE PREVENTION

Human Resources Development Canada, Office of the Fire Commissioner of Canada, Place du Portage, Phase II, 165, rue Hôtel de Ville, Hull PQ K1A 0J2, 819/997-1748; TDD: 819/953-8000

Institute for Research in Construction, 1500 Montreal Rd., Ottawa ON K1A 0R6, 613/993-3772; Fax: 613/941-0822

Natural Resources Canada, 580 Booth St., Ottawa ON K1A 0E4, 613/995-0947; Fax: 613/996-9094

Alta: Alberta Labour, Office of the Provincial Fire Commissioner, 10808 - 99 Ave., Edmonton AB T5K 0G5, 403/427-8392; Fax: 403/422-3562

B.C.: Ministry of Municipal Affairs & Housing, Office of the Fire Commissioner, Municipal Affairs, PO Box 9490, Victoria BC V8W 9N7, 250/356-9000; Fax: 250/356-9019

Man.: Manitoba Labour, Office of the Fire Commissioner, #611, Norquay Bldg., 401 York Ave., Winnipeg MB R3C 0P8, 204/945-3328; Fax: 204/948-2089

N.B.: Department of Municipalities, Culture & Housing, Office of the Fire Marshall, PO Box 6000, Fredericton NB E3B 5H1, 506/453-2004; Fax: 506/457-4899

Department of Natural Resources & Energy, Forest Fire Management, PO Box 6000, Fredericton NB E3B 5H1, 506/453-2530; Fax: 506/453-3322

Nfld.: Office of the Fire Commissioner, Bldg. 9001, Pleasantville, PO Box 8700, St. John's NF A1B 4J6, 709/726-1050; Fax: 709/729-2524

NWT: Department of Resources, Wildlife & Economic Development, Fire Operations, #600, Scotia Centre, Bldg. Box 21, 5102 - 50 Ave., Yellowknife NT X1A 3S8, 403/873-7420, 7134; Fax: 403/873-0114

Department of Safety & Public Services, Office of the Fire Marshal, Panda 2 Mall, 3rd Fl., PO Box 1320,

Yellowknife NT X1A 2L9, 403/873-7472; Fax: 403/873-0260
N.S.: Department of Labour, 5151 Terminal Rd., PO Box 697, Halifax NS B3J 2T8, 902/424-4553; Fax: 902/424-3239
Ont.: Ministry of Natural Resources, Aviation, Flood & Fire Management, #400, 70 Foster Dr., Sault Ste. Marie ON P6A 6V5, 705/945-5937; Fax: 807/475-1503
Ministry of the Solicitor General & Correctional Services, Office of the Fire Marshal, 7 Overlea Blvd., 3rd Fl., Toronto ON M7H 1A8, 416/325-3100; Fax: 416/325-3119
Ontario Fire College, PO Box 850, Gravenhurst ON P0C 1G0, 705/687-2294; Fax: 705/687-7911
PEI: Department of Agriculture, Fisheries & Forestry, Forestry Division, J. Frank Gaudet Tree Nursery, Upton Rd., West Royalty, PO Box 2000, Charlottetown PE C1A 7N8, 902/368-4700; Fax: 902/368-4713
Department of Provincial Affairs & Attorney General, Office of the Fire Marshal, PO Box 2000, Charlottetown PE C1A 7N8, 902/368-4869; Fax: 902/368-5526
Qué.: Commissariat aux incendies, 455, rue Dupont, Québec PQ G1K 6N2, 418/529-5706; Fax: 418/529-9922
Ministère de la Sécurité publique, Direction des affaires policières et de la sécurité incendie, 2525, boul Laurier, 2e étage, Ste-Foy PQ G1V 2L2, 418/644-9774; Fax: 418/646-3564
Sask.: Saskatchewan Environment & Resource Management, Forest Fire Management, 3211 Albert St., Regina SK S4S 5W6, 306/953-2206; Fax: 306/953-2530
Saskatchewan Municipal Government, Municipal Boundary & Planning & Fire Prevention Appeals Committees, 2151 Scarth St., 4th Fl., Regina SK S4P 3V7, 306/787-6244; Fax: 306/787-1610
Office of the Fire Commissioner, 1855 Victoria Ave., Regina SK S4P 3V7, 306/787-4516; Fax: 306/787-9273
Yuk.: Yukon Community & Transportation Services, Office of the Fire Marshal, PO Box 2703, Whitehorse YT Y1A 2C6, 403/667-5217; Fax: 403/667-7056

FIREARMS
Justice Canada, Firearms Control Task Group, Justice Bldg., 239 Wellington St., Ottawa ON K1A 0H8, 613/941-3586; Fax: 613/954-0811
Alta: Alberta Justice, Provincial Firearms, 10365 - 97th St., Edmonton AB T5J 3W7, 403/427-0437; Fax: 403/427-1100
B.C.: Ministry of the Attorney General, 910 Government St., 5th Fl., Victoria BC V8V 1X4, 250/356-9596 (Policy & Education); Fax: 250/356-9037
N.B.: Department of the Solicitor General, Provincial Firearms Office, Barker House, 4th Fl., PO Box 6000, Fredericton NB E3B 5H1, 506/453-3775; Fax: 506/453-3870
NWT: Department of Justice, Firearms Office, PO Box 1320, Yellowknife NT X1A 2L9, 403/920-8714
N.S.: Department of Justice, Licensing & Gun Control, 5151 Terminal Rd., PO Box 7, Halifax NS B3J 2L6, 902/424-6689; Fax: 902/424-0700
Sask.: Saskatchewan Justice, Provincial Firearms Office, 1874 Scarth St., Regina SK S4P 3V7, 306/787-7872 (Communications); Fax: 306/787-3874

FISHERIES
Fisheries & Oceans Canada, 200 Kent St., Ottawa ON K1A 0E6, 613/993-0999; TDD: 1-800-668-5228
Fisheries Prices Support Board, 200 Kent St., Ottawa ON K1A 0E6, 613/990-0012; Fax: 613/941-2717
Fisheries Resource Conservation Council, PO Box 2001, Stn D, Ottawa ON K1A 5W3
Foreign Affairs & International Trade Canada, Fisheries Conservation, Lester B. Pearson Bldg., 125 Sussex Dr., Ottawa ON K1A 0G2, 613/995-6907; Fax: 613/952-3904
Freshwater Fish Marketing Corporation, 1199 Plessis Rd., Winnipeg MB R2C 3L4, 204/983-6483; Fax: 204/983-6497
Gulf Fisheries Centre, PO Box 5030, Moncton NB E1C 9B6, 506/851-6227; Fax: 506/851-7732
Halifax Fisheries Research Laboratory, 1707 Lower Water St., PO Box 550, Halifax NS B3J 2S7, 902/426-7444; Fax: 902/426-2698
Northern Cod Research Program, PO Box 5667, St. John's NF A1C 5X1, 709/772-2051; Fax: 709/772-6100
Northwest Atlantic Fisheries Centre, PO Box 5667, St. John's NF A1C 5X1, 709/772-2020; Fax: 709/772-2156
B.C.: Ministry of Environment, Lands & Parks, Fisheries Branch, 780 Blanshard St., 2nd Fl., Victoria BC V8V 1X4, 250/387-9711; Fax: 250/387-9750
Man.: Manitoba Industry, Trade & Tourism, Master Angler Program, 155 Carlton St., 6th Fl., Winnipeg MB R3C 3H8, 204/945-4254; Toll Free: 1-800-665-0040, ext.TH6; Fax: 204/945-1354
Manitoba Natural Resources, Fisheries Branch, 200 Saulteaux Cr., PO Box 20, Winnipeg MB R3J 3W3, 204/945-7814; Fax: 204/945-2308
N.B.: Department of Natural Resources & Energy, Fish & Wildlife, PO Box 6000, Fredericton NB E3B 5H1, 506/453-2440; Fax: 506/453-6699
Nfld.: Department of Fisheries & Aquaculture, Fisheries Bldg., 30 Strawberry Marsh Rd., PO Box 8700, St. John's NF A1B 4J6, 709/729-3707; Fax: 709/729-6082
NWT: Department of Resources, Wildlife & Economic Development, Wildlife & Fisheries Division, #600, Scotia Centre, Bldg. Box 21, 5102 - 50 Ave., Yellowknife NT X1A 3S8, 403/873-7420, 7134; Fax: 403/873-0114
N.S.: Department of Fisheries, Bank of Montreal Bldg., 5151 George St., 7th Fl., PO Box 2223, Halifax NS B3J 3C4, 902/424-4560; Fax: 902/424-4671
Ont.: Ministry of Natural Resources, Fish & Wildlife Branch, Whitney Block, #6540, 99 Wellesley St. West, Toronto ON M7A 1W3, 416/314-6132; Fax: 416/314-1994
PEI: Department of Agriculture, Fisheries & Forestry, Fisheries & Aquaculture Division, Jones Bldg., 11 Kent St., PO Box 2000, Charlottetown PE C1A 7N8, 902/368-5251; Fax: 902/368-5542
Department of Environmental Resources, Fish & Wildlife Division, Jones Bldg., 11 Kent St., 4th Fl., PO Box 2000, Charlottetown PE CIA 7N8, 902/368-4683; Fax: 902/368-5830
Qué.: Ministère de l'Agriculture, des Pêcheries et de l'Alimentation, Pêches et aquiculture commerciales, 200, ch Sainte-Foy, Québec PQ G1R 4X6, 418/643-2673; Fax: 418/646-0829
Sask.: Saskatchewan Environment & Resource Management, Fisheries Branch, 3211 Albert St., Regina SK S4S 5W6, 306/787-2884; Fax: 306/787-0737
Yuk.: Yukon Renewable Resources, Fisheries, PO Box 2703, Whitehorse YT Y1A 2C6, 403/667-5117; Fax: 403/393-6213

FITNESS See RECREATION

FLOODS See EMERGENCY RESPONSE

FOOD See AGRICULTURE; NUTRITION

FOREIGN AFFAIRS See INTERNATIONAL AFFAIRS (

FOREIGN INVESTMENT See INVESTMENT

FOREST RESOURCES
Industry Canada, Forest Industries & Building Products, C.D. Howe Bldg., 235 Queen St., Ottawa ON K1A 0H5, 613/954-3082; Fax: 613/952-8988
Alta: Alberta Economic Development & Tourism, Forestry Industry Development, Commerce Place, 10155 - 102 St., Edmonton AB T5J 4L6, 403/422-7011; Fax: 403/427-5299
Alberta Environmental Protection, Forest Management Division, 9915 - 108 St., Edmonton AB T5K 2G8, 403/427-8474
Alberta Research Council, Pulp & Paper Research, 250 Karl Clark Rd., PO Box 8330, Edmonton AB T6H 5X2, 403/472-4253; Fax: 403/461-2651
B.C.: Forest Renewal BC, 727 Fisgard St., Victoria BC V8V 1X4, 250/387-2500
Ministry of Environment, Lands & Parks, Forest Practices Code, 965 Broughton St., 6th Fl., Victoria BC V8V 1X4, 250/387-6989; Fax: 250/953-5170
Ministry of Forests, PO Box 9517, Stn Prov Govt, Victoria BC V8W 9C2, 250/387-5255; Fax: 250/387-8485
Man.: Manitoba Natural Resources, Forestry Branch, 200 Saulteaux Crescent, PO Box 70, Winnipeg MB R3J 3W3, 204/945-7998; Fax: 204/948-2671
N.B.: Department of Natural Resources & Energy, Timber Management, PO Box 6000, Fredericton NB E3B 5H1, 506/453-2432; Fax: 506/453-6689
Forest Protection Limited, Comp 5, Site 24, RR#1, Fredericton NB E3B 4X2, 506/446-6930; Fax: 506/446-6934
New Brunswick Forest Products Commission, PO Box 6000, Fredericton NB E3B 5H1, 506/453-2196; Fax: 506/457-4966
Nfld.: Department of Forest Resources & Agrifoods, Forestry & Wildlife Branch, Confederation Complex, PO Box 8700, St. John's NF A1B 4J6, 709/729-4716
NWT: Department of Resources, Wildlife & Economic Development, Forest Management Division, #600, Scotia Centre, Bldg. Box 21, 5102 - 50 Ave., Yellowknife NT X1A 3S8, 403/873-7420, 7134; Fax: 403/873-0114
N.S.: Department of Natural Resources, Forestry, Founder's Square, 1701 Hollis St., PO Box 698, Halifax NS B3J 2T9, 902/893-5749; Fax: 902/893-6102
Ont.: Algonquin Forestry Authority - Huntsville, 222 Main St. West, PO Box 1198, Huntsville ON P0A 1K0, 705/789-9647; Fax: 705/789-3353
Algonquin Forestry Authority - Pembroke, #84, 6 Isabella St., Pembroke ON K8A 5S5, 613/735-0173; Fax: 613/735-4192
Ministry of Natural Resources, Forest Management Branch, Whitney Block, #6540, 99 Wellesley St. West, Toronto ON M7A 1W3, 705/945-6660; Fax: 416/314-1994
PEI: Department of Agriculture, Fisheries & Forestry, Forestry Division, J. Frank Gaudet Tree Nursery, Upton Rd., West Royalty, PO Box 2000, Charlottetown PE C1A 7N8, 902/368-4700; Fax: 902/368-4713
Qué.: Ministère des Ressources Naturelles, Forêts, 880, ch Ste-Foy, Québec PQ G1S 4X4, 418/646-2727 (Renseignements); Fax: 418/644-7160
Société de récupération, d'exploitation et de développement forestier, 1195, ave de Lavigerie, Ste-Foy PQ G1V 4N3, 418/659-4530; Fax: 418/643-4037
Sask.: Saskatchewan Environment & Resource Management, Forestry Branch, 3211 Albert St., Regina SK S4S 5W6, 306/953-2486; Fax: 306/953-2360
Yuk.: Yukon Renewable Resources, PO Box 2703, Whitehorse YT Y1A 2C6, 403/667-5237; Toll Free: 1-800-661-0408 (Yukon)

FUEL See NUCLEAR ENERGY; OIL & NATURAL GAS RESOURCES

GARBAGE See WASTE MANAGEMENT

Canadian Almanac & Directory 1997

GAS *See* **OIL & NATURAL GAS RESOURCES**

GEOGRAPHY *See* **MAPS, CHARTS & AERIAL PHOTOGRAPHS**

GEOLOGICAL SERVICES

Natural Resources Canada, Geological Survey of Canada, 601 Booth St., Ottawa ON K1A 0E8, 613/996-3919; Fax: 613/996-9990

Geomatics Canada, 580 Booth St., Ottawa ON K1A 0E4, 613/995-4321; Fax: 613/996-9094

Alta: Alberta Energy, Mineral Access, Geology & Mapping, Petroleum Plaza, North Tower, 9945 - 108 St., Edmonton AB T5K 2G6, 403/422-9466; Fax: 403/427-3198

Alberta Research Council, Alberta Geological Survey, 250 Karl Clark Rd., PO Box 8330, Edmonton AB T6H 5X2, 403/438-7615; Fax: 403/461-2651

B.C.: Ministry of Employment & Investment, Energy & Minerals Division, 1810 Blanshard St., 8th Fl., Victoria BC V8W 9N3, 250/356-8702

Man.: Manitoba Energy & Mines, Geological Services Branch, #360, 1395 Ellice Ave., Winnipeg MB R3G 3P2, 204/945-6567; Fax: 204/945-0586, 1406

N.B.: Department of Natural Resources & Energy, Geological Surveys Branch, PO Box 6000, Fredericton NB E3B 5H1, 506/453-2206; Fax: 506/453-3671

Nfld.: Department of Mines & Energy, Geological Survey, PO Box 8700, St. John's NF A1B 4J6, 709/729-2301; Fax: 709/729-3493

NWT: Department of Resources, Wildlife & Economic Development, #600, Scotia Centre, Bldg. Box 21, 5102 - 50 Ave., Yellowknife NT X1A 3S8, 403/920-3344; Fax: 403/873-0114

Mineral Initiatives Office, #600, Scotia Centre, Bldg. Box 21, 5102 - 50 Ave., Yellowknife NT X1A 3S8, 403/873-7420, 7134; Fax: 403/873-0114

N.S.: Department of Natural Resources, Surveys Division, Founder's Square, 1701 Hollis St., PO Box 698, Halifax NS B3J 2T9, 902/424-3145; Fax: 902/424-7735

Ont.: Ministry of Northern Development & Mines, Ontario Geological Survey, 933 Ramsey Lake Rd., Sudbury ON P3E 6B5, 705/670-7044; Fax: 705/670-7046

PEI: Department of the Provincial Treasury, Geomatics Information Centre, PO Box 2000, Charlottetown PE C1A 7N8, 902/368-5165; Fax: 902/368-4399

Qué.: Ministère des Ressources Naturelles, Géologie, #B-302, 5700 - 4 av ouest, 3e étage, Charlesbourg PQ G1H 6R1, 418/643-5159; Fax: 418/644-7160

Sask.: Saskatchewan Energy & Mines, Exploration & Geological Services Division, 1914 Hamilton St., Regina SK S4P 4V4, 306/787-2526; Fax: 306/787-7338

Geology & Petroleum Lands Branch, 1914 Hamilton St., Regina SK S4P 4V4, 306/787-2606; Fax: 306/787-2478

Yuk.: Yukon Economic Development, Geological Surveys, 211 Main St., PO Box 2703, Whitehorse YT Y1A 2C6, 403/667-5466; Fax: 403/668-8601

GOVERNMENT (GENERAL INFORMATION)

Agriculture & Agri-Food Canada, Communications Branch, Sir John Carling Bldg., 930 Carling Ave., Ottawa ON K1A 0C5, 613/759-7976; Fax: 613/759-7969

Auditor General of Canada, 240 Sparks St., Ottawa ON K1A 0G6, 613/995-3708; Fax: 613/957-4023

Canadian Heritage, Communications Branch, Jules Léger Bldg., 25 Eddy St., Hull PQ K1A 1K5, 819/997-0055; Fax: 819/953-5382

Citizenship & Immigration Canada, Journal Tower South, 365 Laurier Ave. West, Hull PQ K1A 1L1, 613/954-9019; Fax: 613/954-2221

Correctional Service Canada, c/o Solicitor General Canada, 340 Laurier Ave. West, Ottawa ON K1A 0P9, 613/992-8423 (Communications); Fax: 613/947-0091

Environment Canada, Terrasses de la Chaudière, 10 Wellington St., Hull PQ K1A 0H3, 819/997-2800; Toll Free: 1-800-668-6767; Fax: 819/953-2225

Finance Canada, Consultations & Communications Branch, Esplanade Laurier, 140 O'Connor St., Ottawa ON K1A 0G5, 613/992-1573; Fax: 613/996-8404

Fisheries & Oceans Canada, 200 Kent St., Ottawa ON K1A 0E6, 613/993-0999; TDD: 1-800-668-5228

Foreign Affairs & International Trade Canada, Lester B. Pearson Bldg., 125 Sussex Dr., Ottawa ON K1A 0G2, 613/996-9134; Fax: 613/952-3904

Health Canada, Brooke Claxton Bldg., Tunney's Pasture, Ottawa ON K1A 0K9, 613/957-2991; Fax: 613/941-5366

House of Commons, Canada, House of Commons, 111 Wellington St., PO Box 1103, Ottawa ON K1A 0A9

Human Resources Development Canada, Place du Portage, Phase IV, 140, Promenade du Portage, Hull PQ K1A 0J9, 819/994-6013

Indian & Northern Affairs Canada, Tour Nord, Les Terrasses de la Chaudière, 10 Wellington St., Hull PQ K1A 0H4, 819/997-0380; Fax: 819/953-3017

Industry Canada, C.D. Howe Bldg., 235 Queen St., Ottawa ON K1A 0H5, 613/954-2788; Fax: 613/954-2303

Justice Canada, Communications & Executive Services Branch, Justice Bldg., 239 Wellington St., Ottawa ON K1A 0H8, 613/957-4222; Fax: 613/954-0811

National Defence (Canada), MGen. George R. Pearkes Bldg., 101 Colonel By Dr., Ottawa ON K1A 0K2, 613/992-4581

Natural Resources Canada, Communications Branch, 580 Booth St., Ottawa ON K1A 0E4, 613/992-0267; Fax: 613/996-9094

Office of the Prime Minister, Langevin Block, 80 Wellington St., Ottawa ON K1A 0A2, 613/992-4211; Fax: 613/941-6900

Public Works & Government Services Canada, Communications, Place du Portage, Phase III, 11, rue Laurier, Hull PQ K1A 0S5, 819/956-2304; TDD: 819/994-5389; Fax: 819/994-8404

Revenue Canada, Customs Border Services, 875 Heron Rd., Ottawa ON K1A 0L8, 613/957-0275

Solicitor General Canada, Communications Group, Sir Wilfrid Laurier Bldg., 340 Laurier Ave. West, Ottawa ON K1A 0P8, 613/991-2799; Fax: 613/993-7062

Statistics Canada, R.H. Coats Bldg., Tunney's Pasture, 120 Parkdale Ave., Ottawa ON K1A 0T6, 613/951-8116; Toll Free: 1-800-263-1136, TDD: 1-800-363-7629; Fax: 613/951-0581

Transport Canada, Transport Canada Building, 330 Sparks St., Ottawa ON K1A 0N5, 613/990-2309; Fax: 613/995-0351

Treasury Board of Canada, 140 O'Connor St., Ottawa ON K1A 0R5, 613/957-2400; Fax: 613/952-3658

Veterans Affairs Canada, Daniel J. MacDonald Bldg., 161 Grafton St., PO Box 7700, Charlottetown PE C1A 8M9, 902/566-8195; Fax: 902/566-8508

Alta: Alberta Public Affairs Bureau, Park Plaza, 10611 - 98 Ave., 6th Fl., Edmonton AB T5K 2P7, 403/427-2754; Fax: 403/422-9704

B.C.: British Columbia Government Communications Office, 612 Government St., Victoria BC V8V 1X4, 250/387-1337; Fax: 250/387-3534

Ministry of Finance & Corporate Relations, Enquiry BC, 525 Superior St., 1st Fl., Victoria BC V8V 1X4, 250/387-9273; Fax: 250/953-4302

Man.: Manitoba Information Services, Citizens' Inquiry Service, #511, 401 York Ave., Winnipeg MB R3C 0P8, 204/945-3744; Toll Free: 1-800-282-8060, TDD: 204/945-4796; Fax: 204/945-4261

N.B.: Communications New Brunswick, 225 King St., PO Box 6000, Fredericton NB E3B 5H1, 506/453-2240; Fax: 506/453-5329

Nfld.: Newfoundland Information Service, Confederation Bldg., PO Box 8700, St. John's NF A1B 4J6, 709/729-4164; Fax: 709/729-0584

NWT: Northwest Territories Government Inquiries Service, PO Box 1320, Yellowknife NT X1A 2L9, 403/873-7110; Fax: 403/920-4218

N.S.: Department of Business & Consumer Services, Access Nova Scotia, Joseph Howe Bldg., 1681 Granville St., Granville Level, PO Box 519, Halifax NS B3J 2X1, 902/424-7009; Toll Free: 1-800-225-8227; Fax: 902/424-2633

Communications Services/Public Inquiries Office, One Government Place, 1700 Granville St., Ground Fl., PO Box 608, Halifax NS B3J 2R7, 902/424-5200; Toll Free: 1-800-670-4357; Fax: 902/425-3026

Ont.: Management Board of Cabinet, Citizens' Inquiry Bureau, 77 Wellesley St. West, 12th Fl., Toronto ON M7A 1N3, 416/326-1234 (Ontario collect); TDD: 416/325-3408; Fax: 416/327-3517

Communications Services Branch, Ferguson Block, 77 Wellesley St. West, 12th Fl., Toronto ON M7A 1N3, 416/327-2789; Fax: 416/327-2817

PEI: Department of the Provincial Treasury, Island Information Service, 11 Kent St., PO Box 2000, Charlottetown PE C1A 7N8, 902/368-4000; Fax: 902/368-5544

Qué.: Conseil du trésor, Communication-Québec, 1500-C, boul Charest Ouest, 1er étage, Ste-Foy PQ G1N 2E5, 418/643-1430; Fax: 418/643-5190

Sask.: Saskatchewan Government Media Services, #3, Legislative Bldg., Regina SK S4S 0B3, 306/787-6281

Yuk.: Executive Council, Policy & Communications, PO Box 2703, Whitehorse YT Y1A 2C6, 403/667-5854, 5393, 5939; Fax: 403/393-6202

Yukon Government Services, Information Services, PO Box 2703, Whitehorse YT Y1A 2C6, 403/667-5436; Fax: 403/667-5304

GOVERNMENT PURCHASING

Public Works & Government Services Canada, Open Bidding Service, c/o Information Systems Management Corporation, PO Box 22011, Ottawa ON K1V 0W2, 613/737-3374; Toll Free: 1-800-361-4637; Fax: 613/737-3643

Supply Operations Service Branch, Place du Portage, Phase III, 11, rue Laurier, Hull PQ K1A 0S5, 819/956-0921; Fax: 819/953-1058

Alta: Alberta Public Works, Supply & Services, Purchasing Branch, 6950 - 113th St., 3rd Fl., Edmonton AB T6H 5V7, 403/427-3222; Fax: 403/427-0812

B.C.: Ministry of Finance & Corporate Relations, British Columbia Purchasing Commission, 617 Government St., Victoria BC V8V 1X4, 250/655-2400; Fax: 250/356-5851

Man.: Manitoba Government Services, Supply & Services Division, Woodsworth Bldg., 405 Broadway, 15th Fl., Winnipeg MB R3C 3L6, 204/945-3001

N.B.: Department of Supply & Services, Central Purchasing Branch, #205, Marysville Place, PO Box 6000, Fredericton NB E3B 5H1, 506/453-2245

Nfld.: Department of Works, Services & Transportation, Government Purchasing Agency, Confederation Bldg., PO Box 8700, St. John's NF A1B 4J6, 709/729-3343; Fax: 709/729-0703

NWT: Department of Public Works & Services, Bldg. YK-7, PO Box 1320, Yellowknife NT X1A 2L9, 403/873-7114; Fax: 403/873-0264

N.S.: Department of Finance, Government Purchasing Agency/Public Tenders Office, Central Services Bldg., 6176 Young St., Suite 120, Halifax NS B3K 2A6, 902/424-5520; Fax: 902/463-5732

Ont.: Management Board of Cabinet, Supply & Service Division, 77 Wellesley St. West, 12th Fl., Toronto ON M7A 1N3, 416/327-3515; Fax: 416/327-3517

PEI: Department of the Provincial Treasury, Procurement Services, PO Box 2000, Charlottetown PE C1A 7N8, 902/368-4040; Fax: 902/368-5171

Qué.: Conseil du trésor, Approvisionnements, Édifice Cyrille-Duquette, 1500 H, boul Charest ouest, Ste-Foy PQ G1N 4T5, 418/643-1529; Fax: 418/643-9226

GRANTS & SUBSIDIES
See Also **Student Aid**

Atlantic Canada Opportunities Agency, 644 Main St., 3rd Fl., PO Box 6051, Moncton NB E1C 9J8, 506/851-2271; Toll Free: 1-800-561-7862, TDD: 506/851-3540; Fax: 506/851-7403

Business Development Bank of Canada, Tour de la Place-Victoria, #800, Place Victoria, CP 335, Montréal PQ H4Z 1L4, 514/283-5904; Toll Free: 1-888-463-6232; Fax: 514/283-0617

Canada Mortgage & Housing Corporation, 700 Montreal Rd., Ottawa ON K1A 0P7, 613/748-2000; Fax: 613/748-2098

Farm Credit Corporation Canada, 1800 Hamilton St., PO Box 4320, Regina SK S4P 4L3, 306/780-8100; Fax: 306/780-5703

Federal Office of Regional Development (Québec), Tour de la Bourse, #3800, 800, Place Victoria, CP 247, Montréal PQ H4Z 1E8, 514/283-6412, 4843; Toll Free: 1-800-263-4689; Fax: 514/283-7778

Human Resources Development Canada, Employment, Social Development & Education Group, Place du Portage, Phase IV, 140, Promenade du Portage, Hull PQ K1A 0J9, 819/994-6013

Indian & Northern Affairs Canada, Indian Program & Funding Allocation Directorate, Tour Nord, Les Terrasses de la Chaudière, 10 Wellington St., Hull PQ K1A 0H4, 819/953-9540; Fax: 819/953-3017

Industry Canada, Industry Sector, C.D. Howe Bldg., 235 Queen St., Ottawa ON K1A 0H5, 613/954-2788; Fax: 613/954-2303

International Development Research Centre, PO Box 8500, Ottawa ON K1G 3H9, 613/236-6163; Fax: 613/238-7230

Medical Research Council of Canada, Tower B, Holland Cross, 1600 Scott St., 5th Fl., Ottawa ON K1A 0W9, 613/954-1809; Fax: 613/954-1800

National Film Board of Canada, 3155, rue Côte de Liesse, St-Laurent PQ H4N 2N4, 514/283-9000; Fax: 514/283-8971

Natural Sciences & Engineering Research Council of Canada, Constitution Square, 350 Albert St., Ottawa ON K1A 1H5, 613/996-7235; Fax: 613/992-5337

Task Force on Incomes & Adjustment in the Atlantic Fishery, 200 Kent St., Ottawa ON K1A 0E6, 613/941-6502

The Canada Council, 350 Albert St., PO Box 1047, Ottawa ON K1P 5V8, 613/566-4365; Toll Free: 1-800-263-5588; Fax: 613/566-4390

Western Economic Diversification Canada, Canada Place, #1500, 9700 Jasper Ave., Edmonton AB T5J 4H7, 403/495-4164; Fax: 403/495-6876

Alta: Alberta Municipal Affairs, Grants, Subsidies & Recoveries, Commerce Place, 10155 - 102 St., Edmonton AB T5J 4L4, 403/427-6897; Fax: 403/427-4315

Local Government Services Division, Commerce Place, 10155 - 102 St., Edmonton AB T5J 4L4, 403/427-2732; Fax: 403/422-9105

B.C.: Ministry of Small Business, Tourism & Culture, Community & Regional Development Division, 1405 Douglas St., 4th Fl., Victoria BC V8W 3C1, 250/356-7363; Fax: 250/387-5633

Man.: Manitoba Agricultural Credit Corporation, #100, 1525 - 1 St., Brandon MB R7A 7A1, 204/726-6850; Fax: 204/726-6849

Manitoba Culture, Heritage & Citizenship, Grants Administration, 213 Notre Dame., Winnipeg MB R3B 1N3, 204/945-4580; Fax: 204/945-5760

Multicultural Grants Advisory Council, 213 Notre Dame Ave., 4th Fl., Winnipeg MB R3B 1N3, 204/945-4458; Fax: 204/945-1675

N.B.: Department of Justice, Financial Services, #412, Centennial Bldg., PO Box 6000, Fredericton NB E3B 5H1, 506/453-2719; Fax: 506/453-7483

New Brunswick Research & Productivity Council, IRAP, 921 College Hill Rd., Fredericton NB E3B 6Z9, 506/452-1385; Fax: 506/452-1395

Nfld.: Department of Municipal & Provincial Affairs, Canada/Newfoundland Infrastructure Program, West Block, Confederation Bldg., PO Box 8700, St. John's NF A1B 4J6, 709/729-5411

Department of Tourism, Culture & Recreation, Tourism & Craft Development, Confederation Bldg., PO Box 8700, St. John's NF A1B 4J6, 709/729-0928; Fax: 709/729-0662

Newfoundland Municipal Financing Corporation, Confederation Bldg., PO Box 8700, St. John's NF A1B 4J6, 709/729-6686; Fax: 709/729-2070

N.S.: Department of Education & Culture, Grants & Audit Division, 2021 Brunswick St., PO Box 578, Halifax NS B3J 2S9, 902/424-3956; Fax: 902/424-0511

Department of Finance, PO Box 187, Halifax NS B3J 2N3, 902/424-5554; Fax: 902/424-0635

Ont.: Management Board of Cabinet, Communications Services Branch, Ferguson Block, 77 Wellesley St. West, 12th Fl., Toronto ON M7A 1N3, 416/327-2789; Fax: 416/327-2817

Northern Ontario Heritage Fund Corporation, Roberta Bondar Place, #150, 70 Foster Dr., Sault Ste. Marie ON P6A 6V8, 705/945-6700; Fax: 705/945-6701

PEI: Department of the Provincial Treasury, PO Box 2000, Charlottetown PE C1A 7N8, 902/368-4000; Fax: 902/368-5544

Qué.: Société de développement industriel du Québec, Place Sillery, 1126, ch St-Louis, 5e étage, Québec PQ G1S 1E5, 418/643-5172

Sask.: Saskatchewan Arts Board, T.C. Douglas Bldg., 3475 Albert St., 3rd Fl., Regina SK S4S 6X6, 306/787-4056; Toll Free: 1-800-667-7526 (Saskatchewan); Fax: 306/787-4199

Saskatchewan Economic Development, 1919 Saskatchewan Dr., Regina SK S4P 3V7, 306/787-2232

Yuk.: Yukon Community & Transportation Services, Sport & Recreation Branch, PO Box 2703, Whitehorse YT Y1A 2C6, 403/667-5608; Fax: 403/393-6416

Yukon Tourism, Arts Branch, PO Box 2703, Whitehorse YT Y1A 2C6, 403/667-8592; Fax: 403/667-3546

GUARANTEED INCOME *See* INCOME SECURITY

GUN CONTROL *See* FIREARMS

HANDICAPPED SERVICES *See* DISABLED PERSONS SERVICES

HEALTH CARE INSURANCE

Citizenship & Immigration Canada, Immigration Health Service, Journal Tower South, 365 Laurier Ave. West, Hull PQ K1A 1L1, 613/954-4470; Fax: 613/941-2179

Health Canada, Health Promotions & Programs Branch, Brooke Claxton Bldg., Tunney's Pasture, Ottawa ON K1A 0K9, 613/957-2991; Fax: 613/941-5366

Alta: Alberta Health, Population Health Division, PO Box 222, Edmonton AB T5J 2P4, 403/427-7164

B.C.: Ministry of Health, Medical Services Plan Operations, 1515 Blanshard St., 7th Fl., Victoria BC V8W 3C8, 250/952-3187; Fax: 250/952-3131

Pharmacare, 1515 Blanshard St., 7th Fl., Victoria BC V8W 3C8, 250/952-1706; Fax: 250/952-2235

Man.: Manitoba Health, 599 Empress St., PO Box 925, Winnipeg MB R3C 2T6, 204/786-7191 (Finance & Administration Branch); Fax: 204/774-1325

Health Services Insurance Fund, 447 Portage Ave., 12th Fl., Winnipeg MB R3B 3H5, 204/786-7191 (Finance & Administration Branch); Fax: 204/774-1325

N.B.: Department of Health & Community Services, Medicare/Prescription Drug Program, PO Box 5100, Fredericton NB E3B 5G8, 506/453-2415; Fax: 506/444-4697

Nfld.: Department of Health, West Block, Confederation Bldg., PO Box 8700, St. John's NF A1B 4J6, 709/729-3127; Fax: 709/729-5824

Newfoundland Medical Care Commission, Elizabeth Towers, 100 Elizabeth Ave., St. John's NF A1C 5J3, 709/722-6980; Fax: 709/722-0718

NWT: Department of Health & Social Services, Health Services Administration, Centre Square Tower, 8th Fl., PO Box 1320, Yellowknife NT X1A 2L9, 403/873-7714; Fax: 403/873-0280

N.S.: Department of Health, Insured Programs Management, Joseph Howe Bldg., 1690 Hollis St., 12th Fl., PO Box 488, Halifax NS B3J 2R8, 902/424-4310; Fax: 902/424-0559

Ont.: Ministry of Health, Health Insurance & Related Programs, Hepburn Block, 8th Fl., Queen's Park, Toronto ON M7A 1S2, 416/327-4327 (Health Information Centre); Fax: 416/327-8781

PEI: Health & Community Services Agency, 4 Sydney St., PO Box 2000, Charlottetown PE C1A 7N8, 902/368-6130; Fax: 902/368-6136

Qué.: Régie de l'Assurance-maladie du Québec, 1125, ch St-Louis, Québec PQ G1K 7T3, 418/682-5111

Sask.: Saskatchewan Health, Insured Services Division, 3475 Albert St., Regina SK S4S 6X6, 306/787-8332; Fax: 306/787-8310

Yuk.: Yukon Health & Social Services, Health Care Insurance Services, PO Box 2703, Whitehorse YT Y1A 2C6, 403/667-5202; Fax: 403/668-3786

HEALTH SERVICES

See Also **Health Care Insurance; Occupational Safety**

Citizenship & Immigration Canada, Immigration Health Service, Journal Tower South, 365 Laurier Ave. West, Hull PQ K1A 1L1, 613/954-4470; Fax: 613/941-2179

Correctional Service Canada, Health Care, c/o Solicitor General Canada, 340 Laurier Ave. West, Ottawa ON K1A 0P9, 613/992-5713; Fax: 613/947-0091

Health Canada, Brooke Claxton Bldg., Tunney's Pasture, Ottawa ON K1A 0K9, 613/957-2991; Fax: 613/941-5366

Industry Canada, Health Industries, C.D. Howe Bldg., 235 Queen St., Ottawa ON K1A 0H5, 613/954-5258; Fax: 613/954-2303

Veterans Affairs Canada, Daniel J. MacDonald Bldg., 161 Grafton St., PO Box 7700, Charlottetown PE C1A 8M9, 902/566-8195; Fax: 902/566-8508

B.C.: Ministry of Health, 1515 Blanshard St., 7th Fl., Victoria BC V8W 3C8, 250/952-3456; Toll Free: AIDS Hotline 1-800-661-3886~

Man.: Manitoba Health, 599 Empress St., PO Box 925, Winnipeg MB R3C 2T6, 204/786-7191 (Finance & Administration Branch); Fax: 204/774-1325

N.B.: Department of Health & Community Services, Communications, PO Box 5100, Fredericton NB E3B 5G8, 506/453-2536; Fax: 506/444-4697

Canadian Almanac & Directory 1997

Nfld.: Department of Health, West Block, Confederation Bldg., PO Box 8700, St. John's NF A1B 4J6, 709/729-5021; Fax: 709/729-5824

NWT: Department of Health & Social Services, Health Services Development, Centre Square Tower, 8th Fl., PO Box 1320, Yellowknife NT X1A 2L9, 403/920-6173; Fax: 403/873-0266

N.S.: Department of Health, Joseph Howe Bldg., 1690 Hollis St., 12th Fl., PO Box 488, Halifax NS B3J 2R8, 902/424-4310; Fax: 902/424-0559

Emergency Health Services Nova Scotia, c/o Dept. of Health, PO Box 488, Halifax NS B3J 2R8, 902/424-3928

Ont.: Ministry of Health, Communications & Information Branch, Hepburn Block, 8th Fl., Queen's Park, Toronto ON M7A 1S2, 416/327-8501; Toll Free: 1-800-268-1153; Fax: 416/327-8791

PEI: Department of Health & Social Services, Jones Bldg., 11 Kent St., 2nd Fl., PO Box 2000, Charlottetown PE C1A 7N8, 902/368-4900; Fax: 902/368-4969

Qué.: Ministère de la Santé et des services sociaux, 1075, ch Ste-Foy, Québec PQ G1S 2M1

Sask.: Saskatchewan Health, 3475 Albert St., Regina SK S4S 6X6, 306/787-8332; Fax: 306/787-8310

Yuk.: Yukon Health & Social Services, Health Services Branch, PO Box 2703, Whitehorse YT Y1A 2C6, 403/667-3673 (Communications); Fax: 403/667-3096

HERITAGE RESOURCES
See Also **Land Resources; Parks**

Canadian Heritage, Jules Léger Bldg., 25 Eddy St., Hull PQ K1A 1K5, 819/997-0055; TDD: 819/997-8776; Fax: 819/953-5382

Canadian Heritage Information Network, 365 Laurier Ave. West, 12th Fl., Ottawa ON K1A 0C8, 613/992-3333; URL://www.chin.gc.ca/; Fax: 613/952-2318

National Archives of Canada, 395 Wellington St., Ottawa ON K1A 0N3, 613/995-5138; Fax: 613/995-6274

National Battlefields Commission, 390, av de Bernières, Québec PQ G1R 2L7, 418/648-3506; Fax: 418/648-3638

Alta: Alberta Community Development, Cultural Facilities & Historical Resources Division, Old St. Stephen's College, 8820 - 112 St., Edmonton AB T6G 2P8, 403/431-2300; Fax: 403/432-1376

B.C.: Ministry of Small Business, Tourism & Culture, Heritage Conservation Branch, 1117 Wharf St., Victoria BC V8W 2Z2, 250/356-1434; Fax: 250/356-7796

Man.: Heritage Grants Advisory Council, 213 Notre Dame Ave., Winnipeg MB R3B 1N3, 204/945-4580; Fax: 204/945-5760

Manitoba Heritage Council, 213 Notre Dame Ave., Main Fl., Winnipeg MB R3B 1N3, 204/945-4389; Fax: 204/948-2384

Manitoba Culture, Heritage & Citizenship, Culture, Heritage & Recreation Programs Division, 213 Notre Dame., Winnipeg MB R3B 1N3, 204/945-3729

N.B.: Department of Municipalities, Culture & Housing, Heritage Branch, Marysville Place, 20 McGloin St., PO Box 6000, Fredericton NB E3B 5H1, 506/453-2324; Fax: 506/453-2416

Nfld.: Department of Tourism, Culture & Recreation, Cultural Affairs, Historic Resources & Provincial Archives, Confederation Bldg., PO Box 8700, St. John's NF A1B 4J6, 709/729-0928; Fax: 709/729-0662

NWT: Department of Education, Culture & Employment, Culture & Heritage, PO Box 1320, Yellowknife NT X1A 2L9, 403/873-7551; Fax: 403/873-0155

N.S.: Department of Education & Culture, Heritage & Culture Branch (Nova Scotia Museum), 2021 Brunswick St., PO Box 578, Halifax NS B3J 2S9, 902/424-5168; Fax: 902/424-0511

Ont.: Ministry of Citizenship, Culture & Recreation, Heritage, Arts & Cultural Industries Policy Branch, 77 Bloor St. West, 6th Fl., Toronto ON M7A 2R9, 416/314-7115

Ontario Heritage Foundation, 10 Adelaide St. East, Toronto ON M5C 1J3, 416/325-5000; Fax: 416/325-5071

PEI: Department of Education, Culture, Heritage & Recreation, Sullivan Bldg., 16 Fitzroy St., PO Box 2000, Charlottetown PE C1A 7N8, 902/368-4789; Fax: 902/368-4663

Qué.: Commission des biens culturels du Québec, 12, rue Ste-Anne, 2e étage, Québec PQ G1R 3X2, 418/643-8378; Fax: 418/643-8591

Ministère de la Culture et des Communications, Archives nationales et centre de conservation du Québec, Pavillon Louis-Jacques Casault, 1210 av du Séminaire, Ste-Foy PQ G1N 4V1, 418/643-4376; Fax: 418/646-0868

Centre de conservation du Québec, 1825, rue Semple, Québec PQ G1N 4B7, 418/643-7001; Fax: 418/646-5419

Sask.: Saskatchewan Municipal Government, Culture & Recreation Division, 1855 Victoria Ave., Regina SK S4P 3V7, 306/787-8282; Fax: 306/787-4181

Yuk.: Yukon Tourism, Heritage Branch, PO Box 2703, Whitehorse YT Y1A 2C6, 403/667-5363; Fax: 403/667-3546

HISTORY & ARCHIVES

Library of Parliament, 111 Wellington St., Ottawa ON K1A 0A9, 613/995-1166; Fax: 613/992-1269

National Archives of Canada, 395 Wellington St., Ottawa ON K1A 0N3, 613/995-5138; Fax: 613/995-6274

The Canada Council, 350 Albert St., PO Box 1047, Ottawa ON K1P 5V8, 613/566-4365; Toll Free: 1-800-263-5588; Fax: 613/566-4390

Alta: Alberta Community Development, Historic Sites Service, Old St. Stephen's College, 8820 - 112 St., Edmonton AB T6G 2P8, 403/431-2310; Fax: 403/432-1376

Provincial Archives, 12845 - 102 Ave., Edmonton AB T5N 0H6, 403/427-1750; Fax: 403/427-4646

B.C.: Ministry of Finance & Corporate Relations, BC Archives & Records Services, 655 Belleville St., Victoria BC V8V 1X4, 250/387-5885; Fax: 250/387-2072

Man.: Manitoba Culture, Heritage & Citizenship, Historic Resources, 213 Notre Dame., Winnipeg MB R3B 1N3, 204/945-4389; Fax: 204/948-2384

Provincial Archives, 200 Vaughan St., Winnipeg MB R3C 1T5, 204/945-4233; Fax: 204/948-2008

Nfld.: Department of Tourism, Culture & Recreation, Cultural Affairs, Historic Resources & Provincial Archives, Confederation Bldg., PO Box 8700, St. John's NF A1B 4J6, 709/729-0928; Fax: 709/729-0662

Historic Resources, Confederation Bldg., PO Box 8700, St. John's NF A1B 4J6, 709/729-2460; Fax: 709/729-0870

NWT: Department of Education, Culture & Employment, PO Box 1320, Yellowknife NT X1A 2L9, 403/873-7657; Fax: 403/873-0155

Culture & Heritage, PO Box 1320, Yellowknife NT X1A 2L9, 403/873-7551; Fax: 403/873-0155

N.S.: Department of Education & Culture, Nova Scotia Museum of Natural History, 2021 Brunswick St., PO Box 578, Halifax NS B3J 2S9, 902/424-7353; Fax: 902/424-0560

Provincial Library, 2021 Brunswick St., PO Box 578, Halifax NS B3J 2S9, 902/424-2457; Fax: 902/424-0633

Ont.: Archives of Ontario, 77 Grenville St., Toronto ON M5S 1B3, 416/327-1600; Toll Free: 1-800-668-9933; Fax: 416/327-1999

PEI: Department of Education, Culture, Heritage & Recreation, Sullivan Bldg., 16 Fitzroy St., PO Box 2000, Charlottetown PE C1A 7N8, 902/368-4789; Fax: 902/368-4663

Provincial Libraries & Archives, Sullivan Bldg., 16 Fitzroy St., PO Box 2000, Charlottetown PE C1A 7N8, 902/368-4227; Fax: 902/961-3203

Qué.: Ministère de la Culture et des Communications, Archives nationales et centre de conservation du Québec, Pavillon Louis-Jacques Casault, 1210 av du Séminaire, Ste-Foy PQ G1N 4V1, 418/643-4376; Fax: 418/646-0868

Sask.: Saskatchewan Archives Board, University of Regina, 3737 Wascana Pkwy., Regina SK S4S 0A2, 306/787-4068; Fax: 306/787-1975

Saskatchewan Municipal Government, Heritage Branch, 1855 Victoria Ave., Regina SK S4P 3V7, 306/787-2809; Fax: 306/787-0069

Yuk.: Yukon Education, Libraries & Archives, PO Box 2703, Whitehorse YT Y1A 2C6, 403/667-5309; Fax: 403/667-4253

Yukon Tourism, Historic Sites, PO Box 2703, Whitehorse YT Y1A 2C6, 403/667-5295; Fax: 403/667-3546

HOSPITALS
See Also **Health Care Insurance**

Health Canada, Medical Services Branch, Ottawa ON K1A 0L3, 613/957-2991; Fax: 613/941-5366

Alta: Alberta Health, Area Services Division, PO Box 222, Edmonton AB T5J 2P4, 403/427-7164

B.C.: Ministry of Health, Medical Services Commission, 1515 Blanshard St., 7th Fl., Victoria BC V8W 3C8, 250/952-3465; Fax: 250/952-3131

Strategic Services, 1515 Blanshard St., 7th Fl., Victoria BC V8W 3C8, 250/952-3456

Man.: Manitoba Health, Health Services Insurance Fund, 447 Portage Ave., 12th Fl., Winnipeg MB R3B 3H5, 204/786-7191 (Finance & Administration Branch); Fax: 204/774-1325

Urban Hospital Services, 599 Empress St., Winnipeg MB R3G 3H2, 204/786-7138; Fax: 204/774-1325

N.B.: Department of Health & Community Services, Hospital Services, PO Box 5100, Fredericton NB E3B 5G8, 506/453-2283; Fax: 506/444-4697

Nfld.: Department of Health, Institutions, West Block, Confederation Bldg., PO Box 8700, St. John's NF A1B 4J6, 709/729-5021; Fax: 709/729-5824

Newfoundland Medical Care Commission, Elizabeth Towers, 100 Elizabeth Ave., St. John's NF A1C 5J3, 709/722-6980; Fax: 709/722-0718

NWT: Department of Health & Social Services, Health Services Development, Centre Square Tower, 8th Fl., PO Box 1320, Yellowknife NT X1A 2L9, 403/920-6173; Fax: 403/873-0266

N.S.: Department of Health, Regional Support, Joseph Howe Bldg., 1690 Hollis St., 12th Fl., PO Box 488, Halifax NS B3J 2R8, 902/424-4310; Fax: 902/424-0559

Ont.: Ministry of Health, Institutional Health, Hepburn Block, 8th Fl., Queen's Park, Toronto ON M7A 1S2, 416/327-4327 (Health Information Centre); Fax: 416/327-8781

PEI: Council on Health & Community Services Policy, Jones Bldg., 2nd Fl., PO Box 2000, Charlottetown PE C1A 7N8, 902/368-4985; Fax: 902/368-4969

Department of Health & Social Services, Medical Services, 4 Sydney St., PO Box 2000, Charlottetown PE C1A 7N8, 902/368-6143; Fax: 902/368-6136

Qué.: Ministère de la Santé et des services sociaux, 1075, ch Ste-Foy, Québec PQ G1S 2M1

HOUSE OF COMMONS *See* **PARLIAMENT**

HOUSING

Canada Mortgage & Housing Corporation, 700 Montreal Rd., Ottawa ON K1A 0P7, 613/748-2000; Fax: 613/748-2098

Alta: Alberta Social Housing Corporation, 10155 - 102 St., 14th Fl., Edmonton AB T5J 4L4, 403/422-9222; Fax: 403/427-0961

Alberta Municipal Affairs, Housing & Consumer Affairs Division, Commerce Place, 10155 - 102 St., Edmonton AB T5J 4L4, 403/427-3917; Fax: 403/427-0418

B.C.: British Columbia Housing Management Commission/BC Housing, #1701, 4330 Kingsway, Burnaby BC V5H 4G7, 604/433-1711; Fax: 604/439-4722

Ministry of Municipal Affairs & Housing, Municipal Affairs, PO Box 9490, Victoria BC V8W 9N7, 250/387-4089; Fax: 250/356-1070

Man.: Manitoba Housing Authority, 280 Broadway Ave., 2nd Fl., Winnipeg MB R3C 0R8

Manitoba Housing, 280 Broadway Ave., Winnipeg MB R3C 0R8, 204/945-4109

N.B.: Department of Municipalities, Culture & Housing, Marysville Place, 20 McGloin St., PO Box 6000, Fredericton NB E3B 5H1, 506/453-2690; Fax: 506/457-4991

Housing & Public Safety Services Division, Marysville Place, 20 McGloin St., PO Box 6000, Fredericton NB E3B 5H1, 506/453-4991; Fax: 506/457-4991

Nfld.: Newfoundland & Labrador Housing Corporation, 2 Canada Dr., PO Box 220, St. John's NF A1C 5J2, 709/724-3000; Fax: 709/724-3250

NWT: Northwest Territories Housing Corporation, Scotia Centre, 5102 - 50th Ave., 10th Fl., PO Box 2100, Yellowknife NT X1A 2P6, 403/873-7850; Fax: 403/870-8024

N.S.: Department of Housing & Municipal Affairs, PO Box 216, Halifax NS B3J 2M4, 902/424-4141; Fax: 902/424-0531

Ont.: Ministry of Municipal Affairs & Housing, Housing Operations Division, 777 Bay St., 17th Fl., Toronto ON M5G 2E5, 416/585-7041 (Communications Branch); Fax: 416/585-6227

Ontario New Home Warranty Program, North East Tower, 6th Fl., 5160 Yonge St., Toronto ON M2N 6L9, 416/229-9200; Fax: 416/229-3800

Qué.: Société d'habitation du Québec, Bloc 2, 1054, Conroy, 4e étage, Québec PQ G1R 5E7, 418/643-7676; Fax: 418/643-2166

Sask.: Saskatchewan Municipal Government, Housing Division, 1855 Victoria Ave., Regina SK S4P 3V7, ; Toll Free: 1-800-667-7567 (Saskatchewan); Fax: 306/787-4181

Yuk.: Yukon Housing Corporation, 410A Jarvis St., PO Box 2703, Whitehorse YT Y1A 2C6, 403/667-5759; Fax: 403/667-3664

HUMAN RIGHTS
See Also Boards of Review

Canadian Human Rights Commission, Place de Ville, Tower A, #1300, 320 Queen St., Ottawa ON K1A 1E1, 613/995-1151; TDD: 613/996-5211; Fax: 613/996-9661

Citizenship & Immigration Canada, Refugees, Journal Tower South, 365 Laurier Ave. West, Hull PQ K1A 1L1, 613/957-5873; Fax: 613/957-5869

Alta: Alberta Community Development, Human Rights Secretariat, Standard Life Centre, 10405 Jasper Ave., 7th Fl., Edmonton AB T5J 4R7, 403/427-3116; Fax: 403/422-3563

Alberta Human Rights & Citizenship Commission, Standard Life Centre, #1600, 10405 Jasper Ave., Edmonton AB T5J 4R7, 403/427-3116, 427-7661; Fax: 403/422-3563, 427-6013

B.C.: British Columbia Council of Human Rights, 844 Courtney St., 2nd. Fl., Victoria BC V8V 1X4, 250/387-3710; Fax: 250/387-3643

Man.: Human Rights Commission, #301, 259 Portage Ave., Winnipeg MB R3B 2A9, 204/945-3007; TDD: 945-3442; Fax: 204/945-1292

N.B.: New Brunswick Human Rights Commission, 751 Brunswick St., PO Box 6000, Fredericton NB E3B 5H1, 506/453-2301; Fax: 506/453-2653

Nfld.: Newfoundland & Labrador Human Rights Commission, PO Box 8700, St. John's NF A1B 4J6, 709/729-2709; Fax: 709/729-0790

N.S.: Nova Scotia Human Rights Commission, Lord Nelson Arcade, 5675 Spring Garden Rd., 7th Fl., PO Box 2221, Halifax NS B3J 3C4, 902/424-4111; Fax: 902/424-0596

Ont.: Ontario Human Rights Commission, 400 University Ave., 12th Fl., Toronto ON M7A 2R9, 416/314-4500; Fax: 416/314-4533

PEI: Prince Edward Island Human Rights Commission, 3 Queen St., PO Box 2000, Charlottetown PE C1A 7N8, 902/368-4180; Fax: 902/368-4236

Sask.: Saskatchewan Human Rights Commission, 122 - 3 Ave. North, 8th Fl., Saskatoon SK S7K 2H6, 306/933-5952; Fax: 306/933-7863

Yuk.: Yukon Human Rights Commission, 205 Rogers St., Whitehorse YT Y1A 1X1, 403/667-6226

Yukon Human Rights Panel of Adjudicators, #202, 208 Main St., Whitehorse YT Y1A 2B2, 403/667-7667

IMMIGRATION
See Also Citizenship

Citizenship & Immigration Canada, Journal Tower South, 365 Laurier Ave. West, Hull PQ K1A 1L1, 613/954-9019; Fax: 613/954-2221

Immigration Services, Journal Tower South, 365 Laurier Ave. West, Hull PQ K1A 1L1, 613/941-1550; Fax: 613/941-0061

Refugees, Journal Tower South, 365 Laurier Ave. West, Hull PQ K1A 1L1, 613/957-5873; Fax: 613/957-5869

Foreign Affairs & International Trade Canada, Passport Office, Place du Centre, 200, Promenade du Portage, 6e étage, Hull PQ K1A 0G3, 819/994-3500; Toll Free: 1-800-567-6868, TDD: 613/994-3560; Fax: 819/992-6587

Immigration & Refugee Board, 240 Bank St., Ottawa ON K1A 0K1, 613/995-6486; Fax: 613/996-0270

Alta: Alberta Human Rights & Citizenship Commission, Standard Life Centre, #1600, 10405 Jasper Ave., Edmonton AB T5J 4R7, 403/427-3116, 427-7661; Fax: 403/422-3563, 427-6013

B.C.: Ministry of the Attorney General, Multiculturalism & Immigration Branch, #309, 703 Broughton St., Victoria BC V8W 1E2, 250/387-7970; Fax: 250/356-5316

Man.: Manitoba Culture, Heritage & Citizenship, Immigration/Settlement Policy & Planning Branch, 213 Notre Dame., Winnipeg MB R3B 1N3, 204/945-2802; Fax: 204/948-2148

N.B.: Department of Advanced Education & Labour, Multiculturalism & Immigration, Chestnut Complex, 470 York St., PO Box 6000, Fredericton NB E3B 5H1, 506/444-4331; Fax: 506/453-3300

PEI: Department of Economic Development & Tourism, Immigration & Procurement, Annex 2, West Royalty Park, 2 First Ave., Charlottetown PE C1E 1B0, 902/368-4265; Fax: 902/368-6301

IMPORTS
See Also Trade

Canadian International Trade Tribunal, Standard Life Centre, 333 Laurier Ave. West, Ottawa ON K1A 0G7, 613/990-2452; Fax: 613/990-2439

Finance Canada, Tariffs Division, Esplanade Laurier, 140 O'Connor St., Ottawa ON K1A 0G5, 613/992-6881; Fax: 613/996-8404

Foreign Affairs & International Trade Canada, Lester B. Pearson Bldg., 125 Sussex Dr., Ottawa ON K1A 0G2, 613/996-9134; Fax: 613/952-3904

Trade & Economic Policy Branch, Lester B. Pearson Bldg., 125 Sussex Dr., Ottawa ON K1A 0G2, 613/996-9134; Fax: 613/952-3904

North American Free Trade Agreement (NAFTA) Secretariat, Canadian Section, #705, 90 Sparks St., Ottawa ON K1P 5B4, 613/992-9388; Fax: 613/992-9392

Alta: Alberta Federal & Intergovernmental Affairs, Trade Policy Team, AGT Tower II, 10025 Jasper Ave., 23rd Fl., Edmonton AB T5J 1S6, 403/427-2611; Fax: 403/427-0939

Man.: Manitoba Trading Corporation, 155 Carlton St., 4th Fl., Winnipeg MB R3C 3H8, 204/945-2420

INCOME SECURITY
See Also Social Services

Human Resources Development Canada, Income Support Programs Communications, Place du Portage, Phase IV, 140, Promenade du Portage, Hull PQ K1A 0J9, 613/957-2807

Veterans Affairs Canada, Veterans Services, Daniel J. MacDonald Bldg., 161 Grafton St., PO Box 7700, Charlottetown PE C1A 8M9, 902/566-8195; Fax: 902/566-8508

Alta: Alberta Family & Social Services, Income & Employment Programs, Seventh St. Plaza, 10030 - 107 St., Edmonton AB T5J 3E4, 403/427-2635; Fax: 403/422-9044

B.C.: Ministry of Social Services, Income Support, Parliament Bldgs., 614 Humboldt St., 7th Fl., Victoria BC V8V 1X4, 250/387-6485; Fax: 250/356-7801

Man.: Manitoba Family Services, Employment & Income Assistance Division, #219, 114 Garry St., Winnipeg MB R3C 4V6, 204/945-2324 (Policy & Planning); Fax: 204/945-2156

N.B.: Department of Human Resources Development, PO Box 6000, Fredericton NB E3B 5H1, 506/453-2379; Fax: 506/453-7478

Social Welfare Appeals Board, PO Box 12999, Fredericton NB E3B 6C2, 506/444-5182

Nfld.: Department of Social Services, Income Support, Confederation Bldg., PO Box 8700, St. John's NF A1B 4J6, 709/729-3243; Fax: 709/729-6996

NWT: Department of Education, Culture & Employment, Income Security Branch, PO Box 1320, Yellowknife NT X1A 2L9, 403/920-6160; Fax: 403/920-0443

N.S.: Department of Community Services, Income & Employment Support, Johnston Bldg., 5182 Prince St., 5th Fl., PO Box 696, Halifax NS B3J 2T7, 902/424-4326; Fax: 902/424-0502

Ont.: Ministry of Community & Social Services, Social Assistance & Employment Opportunities Division, Hepburn Block, 80 Grosvenor St., 6th Fl., Toronto ON M7A 1E9, 416/325-5666; Fax: 416/325-5172, 5171

PEI: Health & Community Services Agency, 4 Sydney St., PO Box 2000, Charlottetown PE C1A 7N8, 902/368-6130; Fax: 902/368-6136

Qué.: Ministère de la Sécurité du revenu, 425, rue St-Amable, 1er étage, Québec PQ G1R 4Z1, 418/643-9818; Toll Free: 1-800-361-4743; Fax: 418/646-5426

Sask.: Saskatchewan Social Services, Income Security, 2151 Scarth St., 1st Fl., Regina SK S4P 3V7, 307/787-3536; Fax: 306/694-3842

Income Security Programs Division, 1920 Broad St., Regina SK S4P 3V6, 306/787-7469; Fax: 306/787-1032

Canadian Almanac & Directory 1997

Saskatchewan Income Plan (SIP), 1920 Broad St., Regina SK S4P 3V6, 306/787-3389; Fax: 306/787-1032

Yuk.: Yukon Health & Social Services, PO Box 2703, Whitehorse YT Y1A 2C6, 403/667-3673 (Communications); Fax: 403/667-3096

INCOME TAX *See* TAXATION

INCORPORATION OF COMPANIES & ASSOCIATIONS

Industry Canada, C.D. Howe Bldg., 235 Queen St., Ottawa ON K1A 0H5, 613/954-2788; Fax: 613/954-2303

Office of the Corporate Secretary, C.D. Howe Bldg., 235 Queen St., Ottawa ON K1A 0H5, 613/943-7039; Fax: 613/952-0273

B.C.: Ministry of Finance & Corporate Relations, Registries & Ministry Support Services, 617 Government St., Victoria BC V8V 1X4, 250/387-9278

Man.: Manitoba Consumer & Corporate Affairs, Companies Office, #317, 450 Broadway, Winnipeg MB R3C 0V8, 204/945-4206

N.B.: Department of Justice, Corporate Affairs, #412, Centennial Bldg., PO Box 6000, Fredericton NB E3B 5H1, 506/453-3860; Fax: 506/453-2613

Nfld.: Department of Government Services & Lands, Commercial Relations, PO Box 8700, St. John's NF A1B 4J6, 709/729-2594

NWT: Department of Justice, PO Box 1320, Yellowknife NT X1A 2L9, 403/873-7453

N.S.: Department of Business & Consumer Services, Registry of Joint Stock Companies, Centennial Bldg., 1670 Hollis St., PO Box 1529, Halifax NS B3J 2Y4, 902/424-7742; Fax: 902/424-4633

Ont.: Ministry of Consumer & Commercial Relations, Companies Branch, 393 University Ave., 2nd Fl., Toronto ON M7A 2H6, 416/596-3725; Fax: 416/596-0438

PEI: Department of Provincial Affairs & Attorney General, Securities, PO Box 2000, Charlottetown PE C1A 7N8, 902/368-4552; Fax: 902/368-5283; 5355

Qué.: L'Inspecteur général des Institutions financières, 800, place D'Youville, Québec PQ G1R 4Y5, 418/694-5016 (Communications); Fax: 418/643-3336

Sask.: Saskatchewan Justice, Registry Services Division, 1874 Scarth St., Regina SK S4P 3V7, 306/787-7872 (Communications); Fax: 306/787-3874

Yuk.: Yukon Justice, Corporate Affairs & Registrar of Securities, PO Box 2703, Whitehorse YT Y1A 2C6, 403/667-5225; Fax: 403/393-6272

INDIANS *See* ABORIGINAL AFFAIRS

INDUSTRIAL DESIGN & INTELLECTUAL PROPERTY

Industry Canada, Canadian Intellectual Property Office, Place du Portage, Tour I, 50, rue Victoria, Hull PQ K1A 0C9, 613/954-2788; Fax: 613/954-2303

Institute for Advanced Manufacturing Technology, 1500 Montréal Rd., Ottawa ON K1A 0R6, 613/993-5802; Fax: 613/952-6081

Institute for Information Technology, 1500 Montreal Rd., Ottawa ON K1A 0R6, 613/993-2491; Fax: 613/952-0074

B.C.: Ministry of Finance & Corporate Relations, Corporate & Personal Property, 617 Government St., Victoria BC V8V 1X4, 250/356-8658; Corporate Registry Hotline: 604/387-7848; Fax: 604/356-0206

N.B.: New Brunswick Research & Productivity Council, Product Innovation, 921 College Hill Rd., Fredericton NB E3B 6Z9, 506/452-0590; Fax: 506/452-1395

INDUSTRIAL RELATIONS *See* LABOUR

INDUSTRIAL SAFETY *See* OCCUPATIONAL SAFETY

INDUSTRY
See Also **Business Development**

Agriculture & Agri-Food Canada, Agricultural Industry Services Directorate, 2200 Walkley Rd., 1st Fl., Ottawa ON K1A 0C5, 613/957-7078; Fax: 613/957-1527

Business Development Bank of Canada, Tour de la Place-Victoria, #800, Place Victoria, CP 335, Montréal PQ H4Z 1L4, 514/283-5904; Toll Free: 1-888-463-6232; Fax: 514/283-0617

Industry Canada, C.D. Howe Bldg., 235 Queen St., Ottawa ON K1A 0H5, 613/954-2788; Fax: 613/954-2303

Statistics Canada, Large Enterprise Statistics, R.H. Coats Bldg., Tunney's Pasture, 120 Parkdale Ave., Ottawa ON K1A 0T6, 613/951-4055; Fax: 613/951-0581

Alta: Alberta Economic Development Authority, Commerce Place, 10155 - 102nd St., 6th Fl., Edmonton AB T5J 4L6, 403/427-2251; Fax: 403/427-5922

Alberta Economic Development & Tourism, Commerce Place, 10155 - 102 St., Edmonton AB T5J 4L6, 403/427-2280

Industry Technology & Forestry Development, Commerce Place, 10155 - 102 St., Edmonton AB T5J 4L6, 403/427-2280

B.C.: Ministry of Employment & Investment, 712 Yates St., Victoria BC V8V 1X4, 250/356-8702

British Columbia Trade & Investment Office, 712 Yates St., Victoria BC V8V 1X4, 250/953-4701; Fax: 250/387-7969

Man.: Economic Development Board, #648, 155 Carlton St., Winnipeg MB R3C 3H8, 204/945-8221; Fax: 204/945-8229

Manitoba Industry, Trade & Tourism, Industry Development, 155 Carlton St., 6th Fl., Winnipeg MB R3C 3H8, 204/945-2066; Fax: 204/945-1354

N.B.: Department of Economic Development & Tourism, Corporate Services, Centennial Bldg., 670 King St., 5th Fl., PO Box 6000, Fredericton NB E3B 5H1, 506/453-2482; Fax: 506/453-5428

Small Business Directorate, Centennial Bldg., 670 King St., 5th Fl., PO Box 6000, Fredericton NB E3B 5H1, 506/453-3890; Fax: 506/457-4845

New Brunswick Industrial Development Board, PO Box 6000, Fredericton NB E3B 5H1, 506/453-2474; Fax: 506/453-7904

Nfld.: Department of Industry, Trade & Technology, Confederation Annex, 4th Fl., PO Box 8700, St. John's NF A1B 4J6, 709/729-5600; Toll Free: 1-800-563-2299; Fax: 709/729-5936

NWT: Department of Resources, Wildlife & Economic Development, Industrial Benefits, #600, Scotia Centre, Bldg. Box 21, 5102 - 50 Ave., Yellowknife NT X1A 3S8, 403/920-0333; Fax: 403/873-0114

Northwest Territories Development Corporation, Tower 7, PO Box 1437, Yellowknife NT X1A 2P1, 403/920-7700; Fax: 403/920-7701

N.S.: Innovation Corporation (InNOVAcorp), Woodside Industrial Park, 101 Research Dr., PO Box 790, Dartmouth NS B2Y 3Z7, 902/424-8670; Toll Free: 1-800-565-7051; Fax: 902/424-4679

Nova Scotia Economic Renewal Agency, 1800 Argyle St., PO Box 519, Halifax NS B3J 2R7, 902/424-8920; Fax: 902/424-0582

Ont.: Innovation Ontario Corporation, 56 Wellesley St. West, 7th Fl., Toronto ON M7A 2E7, 416/326-1025; Fax: 416/326-1109

Ministry of Economic Development, Trade & Tourism, Hearst Block, 900 Bay St., Toronto ON M7A 2E1, 416/325-6666; Fax: 416/325-6688

Ministry of Environment & Energy, Green Industry Office, 135 St. Clair Ave. West, Toronto ON M4V 1P5, 416/323-4578; Fax: 416/323-4436

PEI: Department of Economic Development & Tourism, Shaw Bldg., 95 Rochford St., 5th Fl., PO Box 2000, Charlottetown PE C1A 7N8, 902/368-4240; Fax: 902/368-4224

Qué.: Ministère de l'Industrie, du commerce, de la Science et de la technologie, 710, Place d'Youville, 9e étage, Québec PQ G1R 4Y4, 418/691-5950 (Renseignements); Fax: 418/644-0118

Société de développement industriel du Québec, Place Sillery, 1126, ch St-Louis, 5e étage, Québec PQ G1S 1E5, 418/643-5172

Sask.: Saskatchewan Crown Investments Corporation, #400, 2400 College Ave., Regina SK S4P 1C8, 306/787-6851; Fax: 306/787-8125

Saskatchewan Economic Development, 1919 Saskatchewan Dr., Regina SK S4P 3V7, 306/787-2232

Yuk.: Yukon Economic Development, 211 Main St., PO Box 2703, Whitehorse YT Y1A 2C6, 403/667-5466; Fax: 403/668-8601

INSURANCE (LIFE, FIRE, PROPERTY)
See Also **Automobile Insurance; Health Care Insurance**

Canada Deposit Insurance Corporation, 50 O'Connor St., 17th Fl., PO Box 2340, Stn D, Ottawa ON K1P 5W5, 613/996-2081; Toll Free: 1-800-461-2342; Fax: 613/996-6095

Human Resources Development Canada, Insurance, Place du Portage, Phase IV, 140, Promenade du Portage, Hull PQ K1A 0J9, 819/997-8662

Office of the Superintendent of Financial Institutions, Kent Square, 255 Albert St., Ottawa ON K1A 0H2, 613/990-7788; Toll Free: 1-800-385-8647; Fax: 613/952-8219

Insurance, Kent Square, 255 Albert St., Ottawa ON K1A 0H2, 613/990-7788; Toll Free: 1-800-385-8647; Fax: 613/952-8219

Alta: Alberta Treasury, Insurance, Terrace Bldg., 9515 - 107 St., Edmonton AB T5K 2C3, 403/427-3035; Fax: 403/422-2463

B.C.: Insurance Council of BC, #300, 1040 West Georgia St., PO Box 7, Vancouver BC V6E 4H1, 604/688-0321; Fax: 604/662-7767

Ministry of Finance & Corporate Relations, Insurance & IFBs, #1900, 1050 West Pender St., Vancouver BC V6E 3S7, 604/660-4825; Fax: 604/660-3170

Man.: Manitoba Public Insurance, 234 Donald St., 9th Fl., PO Box 6300, Winnipeg MB R3C 1M8, 204/985-7000; Fax: 204/943-9851

Manitoba Consumer & Corporate Affairs, Insurance, #1142, 405 Broadway, Winnipeg MB R3C 3L6, 204/945-2542

N.B.: Department of Justice, Insurance, #412, Centennial Bldg., PO Box 6000, Fredericton NB E3B 5H1, 506/453-2512; Fax: 506/453-2613

Nfld.: Department of Government Services & Lands, Commercial Relations, PO Box 8700, St. John's NF A1B 4J6, 709/729-2594

NWT: Department of Safety & Public Services, Panda 2 Mall, 3rd Fl., PO Box 1320, Yellowknife NT X1A 2L9, 403/873-7619; Fax: 403/873-0260

N.S.: Department of Business & Consumer Services, Consumer & Commercial Relations, Alderney Gate, 40 Alderney Dr., PO Box 815, Dartmouth NS B2Y 3Z3, 902/424-5602; 5552; Toll Free: 1-800-774-5130; Fax: 902/424-8652

Ont.: Ontario Deposit Insurance Corporation, #700, 4711 Yonge St., Toronto ON M2N 6K8

Ontario Insurance Commission, 5160 Yonge St., PO Box 85, Toronto ON M2N 6L9, 416/250-7250; Toll Free: 1-800-668-0128; Fax: 416/590-7070

PEI: Department of Provincial Affairs & Attorney General, Insurance & Real Estate Division, PO Box 2000, Charlottetown PE C1A 7N8, 902/368-4564; Fax: 902/368-5283; 5355

Qué.: L'Inspecteur général des Institutions financières, Assurances, 800, place D'Youville, Québec PQ G1R 4Y5, 418/694-5011; Fax: 418/528-0835

Sask.: Saskatchewan Crop Insurance Corporation, 484 Prince William Dr., PO Box 3000, Melville SK S0A 2P0; Fax: 306/728-7260

Saskatchewan Government Insurance, 2260 - 11th Ave., Regina SK S4P 0J9, 306/751-1200; Fax: 306/787-7477

Yuk.: Yukon Justice, Consumer Services, PO Box 2703, Whitehorse YT Y1A 2C6, 403/667-5257; Fax: 403/393-6272

INTERGOVERNMENTAL AFFAIRS *See* **FEDERAL-PROVINCIAL AFFAIRS; INTERNATIONAL AFFAIRS**

INTERNATIONAL AFFAIRS
See Also **Diplomatic Representatives; Trade**

Canadian International Development Agency, Communications, Place du Centre, 200, Promenade du Portage, Hull PQ K1A 0G4, 819/953-6535; TDD: 819/953-5023; Fax: 819/953-6088

Canadian International Trade Tribunal, Standard Life Centre, 333 Laurier Ave. West, Ottawa ON K1A 0G7, 613/990-2452; Fax: 613/990-2439

Environment Canada, Policy, Program & International Affairs, 4905 Dufferin St., Downsview ON M3H 5T4, 416/739-4344; Ottawa: 613/997-0142; Fax: 613/994-8854; Fax: 819/953-2225

Finance Canada, International Trade & Finance Branch, Esplanade Laurier, 140 O'Connor St., Ottawa ON K1A 0G5, 613/992-1573; Fax: 613/996-8404

Foreign Affairs & International Trade Canada, Lester B. Pearson Bldg., 125 Sussex Dr., Ottawa ON K1A 0G2, 613/996-9134; Fax: 613/952-3904

    Diplomatic Corps Services, Lester B. Pearson Bldg., 125 Sussex Dr., Ottawa ON K1A 0G2, 613/995-5185; Fax: 613/952-3904

    Political & International Security Affairs Branch, Lester B. Pearson Bldg., 125 Sussex Dr., Ottawa ON K1A 0G2, 613/996-9134; Fax: 613/952-3904

Industry Canada, International Business, C.D. Howe Bldg., 235 Queen St., Ottawa ON K1A 0H5, 613/954-3508; Fax: 613/952-0540

International Development Research Centre, PO Box 8500, Ottawa ON K1G 3H9, 613/236-6163; Fax: 613/238-7230

National Defence (Canada), MGen. George R. Pearkes Bldg., 101 Colonel By Dr., Ottawa ON K1A 0K2, 613/992-4581

Revenue Canada, Customs Border Services, 875 Heron Rd., Ottawa ON K1A 0L8, 613/957-0275

B.C.: International Finance Centre - Vancouver Society, World Trade Centre, #658, 999 Canada Place, Vancouver BC V6C 3E1, 604/683-6626; Fax: 604/683-6646

Qué.: Ministère des Relations Internationales, Édifice Hector-Fabre, 525, boul Réne-Levesque est, Québec PQ G1R 5R9, 418/649-2300; Fax: 418/649-2656

Sask.: Saskatchewan Intergovernmental Affairs, International Relations & Protocol, 1919 Saskatchewan Dr., Regina SK S4P 3V7, 306/787-6322; Fax: 306/787-7317

INTERNATIONAL AID

Canadian International Development Agency, Place du Centre, 200, Promenade du Portage, Hull PQ K1A 0G4, 819/997-5456; TDD: 819/953-5023; Fax: 819/953-6088

International Development Research Centre, PO Box 8500, Ottawa ON K1G 3H9, 613/236-6163; Fax: 613/238-7230

INUIT *See* **ABORIGINAL AFFAIRS**

INVESTMENT
See Also **Business Development ; Industry (**

Business Development Bank of Canada, Tour de la Place-Victoria, #800, Place Victoria, CP 335, Montréal PQ H4Z 1L4, 514/283-5904; Toll Free: 1-888-463-6232; Fax: 514/283-0617

Federal Office of Regional Development (Québec), Tour de la Bourse, #3800, 800, Place Victoria, CP 247, Montréal PQ H4Z 1E8, 514/283-6412, 4843; Toll Free: 1-800-263-4689; Fax: 514/283-7778

Foreign Affairs & International Trade Canada, International Business Development Branch, Lester B. Pearson Bldg., 125 Sussex Dr., Ottawa ON K1A 0G2, 613/995-4128; Fax: 613/995-9604

    Investment & Technology Bureau, Lester B. Pearson Bldg., 125 Sussex Dr., Ottawa ON K1A 0G2, 613/995-2224; Fax: 613/995-9604

Industry Canada, C.D. Howe Bldg., 235 Queen St., Ottawa ON K1A 0H5, 613/954-2788; Fax: 613/954-2303

Alta: Alberta Treasury, Investment Management, Terrace Bldg., 9515 - 107 St., Edmonton AB T5K 2C3, 403/427-3035; Fax: 403/422-2463

B.C.: Ministry of Employment & Investment, 712 Yates St., Victoria BC V8V 1X4, 250/356-8702

    British Columbia Trade & Investment Office, 712 Yates St., Victoria BC V8V 1X4, 250/953-4701; Fax: 250/387-7969

Man.: Manitoba Industry, Trade & Tourism, Co-op Development, 155 Carlton St., 6th Fl., Winnipeg MB R3C 3H8, 204/945-3748; Fax: 204/945-1354

N.B.: Department of Economic Development & Tourism, Centennial Bldg., 670 King St., 5th Fl., PO Box 6000, Fredericton NB E3B 5H1, 506/453-2850 (Communications & Promotion); Fax: 506/444-4586

    Trade & Investment, Centennial Bldg., 670 King St., 5th Fl., PO Box 6000, Fredericton NB E3B 5H1, 506/453-2876; Fax: 506/453-3783

New Brunswick Investment Management Corporation, PO Box 6000, Fredericton NB E3B 5H1, 506/444-5800

Nfld.: Department of Industry, Trade & Technology, Marketing, Confederation Annex, 4th Fl., PO Box 8700, St. John's NF A1B 4J6, 709/729-5600; Fax: 709/729-5936

NWT: Department of Resources, Wildlife & Economic Development, Investments, Tower 7, PO Box 1437, Yellowknife NT X1A 2P1, 403/920-7700; Fax: 403/920-7701

N.S.: Department of Finance, Investments, Pensions & Treasury Services Branch, PO Box 187, Halifax NS B3J 2N3, 902/424-5554; Fax: 902/424-0635

Nova Scotia Economic Renewal Agency, Investment & Trade, 1800 Argyle St., PO Box 519, Halifax NS B3J 2R7, 902/424-8920; Fax: 902/424-0582

Ont.: Ministry of Finance, Corporate Services Division, Frost Bldg. South, 7 Queen's Park Cres., Toronto ON M7A 1Y7, 416/325-0333 (Communications & Corporate Affairs); Fax: 416/325-0339

PEI: Department of Economic Development & Tourism, Enterprise PEI, Holman Bldg., 3rd Fl., 25 University Ave., PO Box 910, Charlottetown PE C1A 7L9, 902/368-6300; Toll Free: 1-800-563-3734; Fax: 902/368-6301

    Investments, Annex 2, West Royalty Park, 2 First Ave., Charlottetown PE C1E 1B0, 902/368-5957; Fax: 902/368-6301

Qué.: Le Groupe Société générale de financement, #1700, 600, rue de la Gauchetière ouest, Montréal PQ H3B 4L8, 514/876-9290; Fax: 514/395-8055

Ministère de l'Industrie, du commerce, de la Science et de la technologie, 710, Place d'Youville, 9e étage, Québec PQ G1R 4Y4, 418/691-5950 (Renseignements); Fax: 418/644-0118

Investissements étrangers et sociétés d'état, 710, Place d'Youville, 9e étage, Québec PQ G1R 4Y4, 418/691-5950 (Renseignements); Fax: 418/644-0118

Sask.: Saskatchewan Economic Development, Diversification Division, 1919 Saskatchewan Dr., Regina SK S4P 3V7, 306/787-2232

    Investment Programs, 1919 Saskatchewan Dr., Regina SK S4P 3V7, 306/787-3524

Saskatchewan Finance, Investment & Liability Management Branch, 2350 Albert St., Regina SK S4P 4A6, 306/787-9474; Fax: 306/787-6544

Yuk.: Yukon Economic Development, 211 Main St., PO Box 2703, Whitehorse YT Y1A 2C6, 403/667-5466; Fax: 403/668-8601

JUSTICE DEPARTMENTS

Canadian Judicial Council, #450, 112 Kent St., Ottawa ON K1A 0W8, 613/998-5182; Fax: 613/998-8889

Justice Canada, Justice Bldg., 239 Wellington St., Ottawa ON K1A 0H8, 613/957-4222; Fax: 613/954-0811

Solicitor General Canada, Sir Wilfrid Laurier Bldg., 340 Laurier Ave. West, Ottawa ON K1A 0P8, 613/990-2733; Fax: 613/993-7062

Alta: Alberta Justice, 9833 - 109th St., Edmonton AB T5K 2E8, 403/427-2745; Fax: 403/427-6821

B.C.: Ministry of the Attorney General, 910 Government St., 5th Fl., Victoria BC V8V 1X4, 250/356-9596 (Policy & Education); Fax: 250/356-9037

Man.: Manitoba Justice, 405 Broadway, 5th Fl., Winnipeg MB R3C 3L6, 204/945-2852

N.B.: Department of Justice, #412, Centennial Bldg., PO Box 6000, Fredericton NB E3B 5H1, 506/453-2719 (Administration); Fax: 506/453-8718

Nfld.: Department of Justice & Attorney General, Confederation Bldg., PO Box 8700, St. John's NF A1B 4J6, 709/729-5942; Fax: 709/729-2129

NWT: Department of Justice, PO Box 1320, Yellowknife NT X1A 2L9, 403/873-7453

N.S.: Department of Justice, 5151 Terminal Rd., PO Box 7, Halifax NS B3J 2L6, 902/424-7125; Fax: 902/424-0510

Ont.: Ministry of the Attorney General, 720 Bay St., 11th Fl., Toronto ON M5G 2K1, 416/326-2220; Fax: 416/326-4088

PEI: Department of Provincial Affairs & Attorney General, PO Box 2000, Charlottetown PE C1A 7N8, 902/368-5250; Fax: 902/368-5283; 5355

Qué.: Ministère de la Justice, 1200, rte de l'Église, Ste-Foy PQ G1V 4M1, 418/643-5140 (Communications); Fax: 418/646-4449

Sask.: Saskatchewan Justice, 1874 Scarth St., Regina SK S4P 3V7, 306/787-7872 (Communications); Fax: 306/787-3874

Yuk.: Yukon Justice, PO Box 2703, Whitehorse YT Y1A 2C6, 403/667-8292 (Communications); Fax: 403/393-6272

JUVENILES *See* **YOUNG OFFENDERS; YOUTH SERVICES**

LABOUR

Canada Labour Relations Board, 240 Sparks St., 4th Fl., Ottawa ON K1A 0X8, 613/996-9466; Fax: 613/947-5407

Human Resources Development Canada, Communications, Place du Portage, Phase IV, 140, Promenade du Portage, Hull PQ K1A 0J9, 819/994-6013

Statistics Canada, National Accounts & Analytical Studies, R.H. Coats Bldg., Tunney's Pasture, 120 Parkdale Ave., Ottawa ON K1A 0T6, 613/951-8116; Fax: 613/951-0581

Alta: Alberta Labour, 10808 - 99 Ave., Edmonton AB T5K 0G5, 403/427-2723

Canadian Almanac & Directory 1997

Labour Relations Board/Public Service Employee Relations Board, #503, 10808 - 99 Ave., Edmonton AB T5K 0G5, 403/427-8547; Toll Free: 1-800-463-2572; Fax: 403/422-0970
B.C.: British Columbia Labour Force Development Board, #221, 560 Johnson St., Victoria BC V8V 1X4, 250/356-5360; Fax: 250/356-9444
Labour Relations Board, 1125 Howe St., Vancouver BC V6Z 2K8, 604/660-1300; Fax: 604/660-1892
Ministry of Finance & Corporate Relations, Labour & Social Statistics, 617 Government St., Victoria BC V8V 1X4, 250/387-0374; Fax: 250/387-0380
Ministry of Labour, 825 Fort St., Victoria BC V8W 9K1, 250/387-0172; Fax: 250/356-1653
Man.: Manitoba Labour Board, A.A. Heaps Bldg., #402, 254-258 Portage Ave., Winnipeg MB R3C 0B6, 204/945-5873; Fax: 204/945-1296
Manitoba Labour, #611, Norquay Bldg., 401 York Ave., Winnipeg MB R3C 0P8, 204/945-8190 (Management Services); Fax: 204/948-2085
N.B.: Department of Advanced Education & Labour, Chestnut Complex, 470 York St., PO Box 6000, Fredericton NB E3B 5H1; Fax: 506/453-3806
New Brunswick Labour & Employment Board, 191 Prospect St., PO Box 908, Fredericton NB E3B 1B0, 506/453-2881; Fax: 506/453-3892
Nfld.: Department of Environment & Labour, Labour Relations Branch, Confederation Bldg., PO Box 8700, St. John's NF A1B 4J6, 709/729-1930; Fax: 709/729-1930
Department of Mines & Energy, PO Box 8700, St. John's NF A1B 4J6, 709/729-2301
Labour Relations Board, Metro Place, 261 Kenmount Rd., PO Box 8700, St. John's NF A1B 4J6, 709/729-2707; Fax: 709/729-5736
Labour Standards Board, Confederation Bldg., West Block, PO Box 8700, St. John's NF A1B 4J6, 709/729-2742; Fax: 709/729-6639
NWT: Department of Education, Culture & Employment, PO Box 1320, Yellowknife NT X1A 2L9, 403/920-6222 (Policy & Planning)
Northwest Territories Labour Standards Board, PO Box 2804, Yellowknife NT X1A 2R1, 403/873-7924; Fax: 403/873-0302
N.S.: Department of Labour, 5151 Terminal Rd., PO Box 697, Halifax NS B3J 2T8, 902/424-4125; Fax: 902/424-3239
Labour Relations Board, PO Box 697, Halifax NS B3J 2T8, 902/424-6730; Fax: 902/424-3239
Labour Standards Tribunal, PO Box 697, Halifax NS B3J 2T8, 902/424-6730; Fax: 902/424-3239
Ont.: Ministry of Labour, Communications & Marketing Branch, 400 University Ave., 14th Fl., Toronto ON M7A 1T7, 416/326-7400; Toll Free: 1-800-267-9517; Fax: 416/326-7406
Ontario Labour Relations Board, 400 University Ave., 4th Fl., Toronto ON M7A 1T7, 416/326-7500; Fax: 416/326-7531
PEI: Department of Provincial Affairs & Attorney General, Labour & Industrial Relations Division, PO Box 2000, Charlottetown PE C1A 7N8, 902/368-5250; Fax: 902/368-5283; 5355
Labour Relations Board, PO Box 2000, Charlottetown PE C1A 7N8, 902/368-5550; Fax: 902/368-5526
Qué.: Commission des normes du travail, 400, boul Jean-Lesage, Québec PQ G1K 8W1, ; Toll Free: 1-800-265-1414; Fax: 514/864-4711
Conseil consultatif du travail & de la main d'oeuvre, #2026, 800, Tour de la Place Victoria, CP 87, Montréal PQ H4Z 1B7, 514/873-2880; Fax: 514/873-1129
Ministère du Travail, 200, ch Ste-Foy, 6e étage, Québec PQ G1R 5S1, 418/643-4817; Fax: 418/644-6969
Société québécoise de développement de la main-d'oeuvre, 425, rue St-Amable, Québec PQ G1R 2C5, 418/643-1892; Fax: 418/643-1714
Sask.: Labour Relations Board, 1914 Hamilton St., Regina SK S4P 4V4, 306/787-2406; Fax: 306/787-2664

Office of the Worker's Advocate, 1870 Albert St., Regina SK S4P 3V7, 306/787-2456
Saskatchewan Labour, 1870 Albert St., Regina SK S4P 3V7, 306/787-4496; TDD: 306/787-2429; Fax: 306/787-2208
Yuk.: Yukon Justice, Labour Services, PO Box 2703, Whitehorse YT Y1A 2C6, 403/667-5944; Fax: 403/393-6272

LAND RESOURCES
See Also Agriculture; Forest Resources; Parks
Canada Lands Company, #1500, 200 King St. West, Toronto ON M5H 3T4, 416/974-9700; Fax: 416/974-9661
Canadian Heritage, Parks Canada Sector, Jules Léger Bldg., 25 Eddy St., Hull PQ K1A 1K5, 819/997-0055; Fax: 819/953-5382
Indian & Northern Affairs Canada, Lands & Trusts Services Sector, Tour Nord, Les Terrasses de la Chaudière, 10 Wellington St., Hull PQ K1A 0H4, 819/997-0380; Fax: 819/953-3017
Natural Resources Canada, 580 Booth St., Ottawa ON K1A 0E4, 613/995-0947; Fax: 613/996-9094
Nunavut Planning Commission, #1902, 130 Albert St., Ottawa ON K1P 5G4, 613/238-1155; Fax: 613/238-5724
Alta: Alberta Environmental Protection, Land & Forest Service, 9915 - 108 St., Edmonton AB T5K 2G8, 403/427-2739, 944-0313 (Information Centre)
B.C.: Ministry of Environment, Lands & Parks, Lands & Water Management Department, 810 Blanshard St., 4th Fl., Victoria BC V8V 1X4, 250/387-1288; Fax: 250/387-5669
Man.: Farm Lands Ownership Board, #915 Norquay Bldg., 401 York Ave., Winnipeg MB R3C 0P8, 204/945-3149; Fax: 204/945-6134
Manitoba Land Value Appraisal Commission, Norquay Bldg., #408, 900 Portage Ave., Winnipeg MB R3G 0P4, 204/945-3087; Fax: 204/945-3087
Manitoba Natural Resources, Land Information Centre, 1007 Century St., Winnipeg MB R3H 0W4, 204/945-3730; Fax: 204/945-3586
N.B.: Department of Municipalities, Culture & Housing, Land Use Planning Branch, Marysville Place, 20 McGloin St., PO Box 6000, Fredericton NB E3B 5H1, 506/453-2171; Fax: 506/457-4991
Department of Natural Resources & Energy, Crown Lands, PO Box 6000, Fredericton NB E3B 5H1, 506/453-2513; Fax: 506/453-3322
Department of the Environment, Land & Water Planning Section, 364 Argyle St., PO Box 6000, Fredericton NB E3B 5H1, 506/457-4846; Fax: 506/453-3843
New Brunswick Geographic Information Corporation, 985 College Hill Rd., PO Box 6000, Fredericton NB E3B 5H1, 506/457-3581; Fax: 506/453-3898
Nfld.: Department of Forest Resources & Agrifoods, Soil & Land Management Division, Provincial Agriculture Bldg., Brookfield Rd., PO Box 8700, St. John's NF A1B 4J6, 709/729-6587
NWT: Department of Municipal & Community Affairs, Community Planning & Lands, #600, 5201 - 50th Ave., PO Box 1310, Yellowknife NT X1A 2L9, 403/920-8916; Fax: 403/920-6343
Department of Resources, Wildlife & Economic Development, Land Protection, #600, Scotia Centre, Bldg. Box 21, 5102 - 50 Ave., Yellowknife NT X1A 3S8, 403/873-7178; Fax: 403/873-0114
Ont.: Mining & Lands Commissioner, 700 Bay St., 24th Fl., PO Box 330, Toronto ON M5G 1Z6, 416/314-2320; Fax: 416/314-2327
Ministry of Agriculture, Food & Rural Affairs, Land Use Planning Branch, Information Centre, 801 Bay St., 1st Fl., Toronto ON M7A 2B2, 416/326-3126; Fax: 416/326-3065
Ministry of Natural Resources, Land Use Planning Branch, Whitney Block, #6540, 99 Wellesley St.

West, Toronto ON M7A 1W3, 705/789-9611; Fax: 416/314-1994
Lands & Natural Heritage Branch, Whitney Block, #6540, 99 Wellesley St. West, Toronto ON M7A 1W3, 705/755-1212; Fax: 416/314-1994
Ontario Land Corporation, Ferguson Block, 77 Wellesley St. West, 13th Fl., Toronto ON M7A 1N3, 416/327-3937
Qué.: Commission de protection du territoire agricole, 200, ch Ste-Foy, 2e étage, Québec PQ G1R 4X6, 418/643-3314; Fax: 418/643-2261
Ministère des Ressources Naturelles, Terres, #B-302, 5700 - 4 av ouest, 3e étage, Charlesbourg PQ G1H 6R1, 418/646-2727 (Renseignements); Fax: 418/644-7160
Sask.: Saskatchewan Land Allocations Appeal Board, #302, 3085 Albert St., Regina SK S4S 0B1, 306/787-5955; Fax: 306/787-5134
Saskatchewan Agriculture & Food, Lands Branch, Walter Scott Bldg., 3085 Albert St., Regina SK S4S 0B1, 306/787-5140; Fax: 306/787-0600
Saskatchewan Environment & Resource Management, Sustainable Land Management Branch, 3211 Albert St., Regina SK S4S 5W6, 306/787-7024; Fax: 306/787-1349
Saskatchewan Property Management Corporation, 1840 Lorne St., Regina SK S4P 3V7, 306/787-6911; Fax: 306/787-1061
Yuk.: Executive Council, Land Claims, Self Government & Devolution, PO Box 2703, Whitehorse YT Y1A 2C6, 403/667-5908; Fax: 403/393-6214
Yukon Community & Transportation Services, Lands Branch, PO Box 2703, Whitehorse YT Y1A 2C6, 403/667-5218; Fax: 403/667-2167

LAND TITLES
See Also Real Estate
British Columbia Treaty Commission, #203, 1155 West Pender St., Vancouver BC V6E 2P4, 604/775-2075; Toll Free: 1-800-665-8330
Canada Lands Company, #1500, 200 King St. West, Toronto ON M5H 3T4, 416/974-9700; Fax: 416/974-9661
Alta: Alberta Municipal Affairs, Inspector, Land Titles, John E. Brownlee Bldg., 10365 - 97 St., Edmonton AB T5J 3W7, 403/427-4095; Toll Free: 1-800-465-5009 (in Alberta); Fax: 403/422-0818
B.C.: Ministry of the Attorney General, Land Title Branch, 910 Government St., 1st Fl., Victoria BC V8V 1X4, 250/387-1903; Fax: 250/387-1763
Man.: Manitoba Justice, Land Titles, 405 Broadway, 14th Fl., Winnipeg MB R3C 3L6, 204/945-2852
Property Rights Division, 405 Broadway, 14th Fl., Winnipeg MB R3C 3L6, 204/945-2852
N.B.: New Brunswick Geographic Information Corporation, Legal, & Chief Registrar of Deeds, 985 College Hill Rd., PO Box 6000, Fredericton NB E3B 5H1, 506/453-2963; Fax: 506/453-3898
Nfld.: Department of Government Services & Lands, Lands Branch, PO Box 8700, St. John's NF A1B 4J6
NWT: Department of Justice, Legal Registries/Land Titles, PO Box 1320, Yellowknife NT X1A 2L9, 403/873-7490
N.S.: Department of Housing & Municipal Affairs, Land Information Management Services, PO Box 216, Halifax NS B3J 2M4, 902/424-7136; Fax: 902/424-0531
Ont.: Ministry of Consumer & Commercial Relations, Real Property Registration, 393 University Ave., 4th Fl., Toronto ON M7A 2H6, 416/596-3643; Fax: 416/596-3802
Ministry of the Attorney General, Assessment Review Board, 121 Bloor St. East, 3rd Fl., Toronto ON M4W 3H5, 416/314-6900; Toll Free: 1-800-263-3237; Fax: 416/314-6906

PEI: Department of the Provincial Treasury, Deeds, PO Box 2000, Charlottetown PE C1A 7N8, 902/368-4591; Fax: 902/368-4399

Yuk.: Yukon Justice, Land Titles, PO Box 2703, Whitehorse YT Y1A 2C6, 403/667-5612; Fax: 403/393-6272

LANDLORD & TENANT REGULATIONS
Justice Canada, Regulations Section, Justice Bldg., 239 Wellington St., Ottawa ON K1A 0H8, 613/957-0065; Fax: 613/954-0811

Alta: Alberta Justice, 9833 - 109th St., Edmonton AB T5K 2E8, 403/427-2745; Fax: 403/427-6821

B.C.: Ministry of Municipal Affairs & Housing, Shelter Aid for Elderly Renters, 1175 Douglas St., 4th Fl., Victoria BC V8W 2E1, 250/387-3461; Fax: 250/387-4264

Ministry of the Attorney General, Residential Tenancy Branch, 1019 Wharf St., Victoria BC V8V 1X4, 250/356-3413; Fax: 250/387-0271

Man.: Manitoba Consumer & Corporate Affairs, Residential Tenancies Branch, #317, 450 Broadway, Winnipeg MB R3C 0V8, 204/945-4069

N.B.: Department of Justice, Consumer Affairs & Chief Rentalsman, #412, Centennial Bldg., PO Box 6000, Fredericton NB E3B 5H1, 506/453-2682; Fax: 506/444-4494

Nfld.: Department of Government Services & Lands, Real Estate & Landlord-Tenant Relations, PO Box 8700, St. John's NF A1B 4J6, 709/729-2608

Residential Tenancies Boards, PO Box 8700, St. John's NF A1B 4J6

NWT: Department of Safety & Public Services, Panda 2 Mall, 3rd Fl., PO Box 1320, Yellowknife NT X1A 2L9, 403/873-7619; Fax: 403/873-0260

Ont.: Ministry of Municipal Affairs & Housing, Rent Registry, 415 Yonge St., 19th Fl., Toronto ON M5B 2E7, 416/326-0923; Fax: 416/326-0930

Rent Review Hearings Board, 77 Bloor St. West, 10th Fl., Toronto ON M5S 1M2, 416/314-0051; Fax: 416/314-0061

PEI: Department of Provincial Affairs & Attorney General, Consumer Services, PO Box 2000, Charlottetown PE C1A 7N8, 902/368-4580; Fax: 902/368-5355

Qué.: Régie du logement, #11.65, 1, rue Notre-Dame est, Montréal PQ H2Y 1B6, 514/873-6575; Fax: 514/873-6805

Sask.: Provincial Mediation Board/Office of the Rentalsman, 2103 - 11 Ave., 5th Fl., Regina SK S4P 3V7, 306/787-2699; Fax: 306/787-5574

Yuk.: Yukon Justice, Consumer Services, PO Box 2703, Whitehorse YT Y1A 2C6, 403/667-5257; Fax: 403/393-6272

LANGUAGE (OFFICIAL) See BILINGUALISM

LEGAL AID SERVICES
Alta: Alberta Legal Aid Society, Revlon Bldg., #300, 10320 - 102 Ave., Edmonton AB T5J 4A1, 403/427-7575; Fax: 403/427-5909

B.C.: Legal Services Society, #300, 1140 West Pender St., PO Box 3, Vancouver BC V6E 4G1, 604/660-4661; Fax: 604/660-9578

Man.: Legal Aid Manitoba, #402, 294 Portage Ave., Winnipeg MB R3C 0B9, 204/985-8505; Fax: 204/944-8582

N.B.: Department of Justice, Legal Aid New Brunswick, #412, Centennial Bldg., PO Box 6000, Fredericton NB E3B 5H1, 506/451-1424; Fax: 506/451-1429

Nfld.: Newfoundland Legal Aid Commission, Centre Bldg., 21 Church Hill St., St. John's NF A1C 3Z8, 709/753-7860; Fax: 709/753-6226

NWT: Legal Services Board of the Northwest Territories, PO Box 1320, Yellowknife NT X1A 2L9, 403/873-7450; Fax: 403/873-5320

N.S.: Nova Scotia Legal Aid Commission, #401, 5475 Spring Garden Rd., Halifax NS B3J 3T2, 902/420-6584; Fax: 902/420-3471

Ont.: Ministry of the Attorney General, Legislative Counsel, Whitney Block, #3600, 99 Wellesley St. West, Toronto ON M7A 1A2, 416/326-2841; Fax: 416/326-2806

PEI: Department of Provincial Affairs & Attorney General, Legal Aid, PO Box 2000, Charlottetown PE C1A 7N8, 902/368-6042; Fax: 902/368-5283; 5355

Qué.: Fonds d'Aide aux Recours Collectifs, #1201, 360, rue St-Jacques ouest, Montréal PQ H2Y 1P5, 514/864-2750; Fax: 514/864-2998

Ministère de la Justice, 1200, rte de l'Église, Ste-Foy PQ G1V 4M1, 418/643-5140 (Communications); Fax: 418/646-4449

Sask.: Saskatchewan Legal Aid Commission, #820, 410 - 22 St. East, Saskatoon SK S7K 2H6, 306/933-5300; Fax: 306/933-6764

Yuk.: Yukon Legal Services Society, #167, 2134 - 2 Ave., Whitehorse YT Y1A 5H6, 403/667-5210

Yukon Justice, Legal Aid, PO Box 2703, Whitehorse YT Y1A 2C6, 403/667-5210; Fax: 403/393-6272

LEGISLATURES See PARLIAMENT

LEISURE CRAFT & VEHICLE REGULATIONS
Canadian Heritage, Parks Canada Sector, Jules Léger Bldg., 25 Eddy St., Hull PQ K1A 1K5, 819/997-0055; Fax: 819/953-5382

Fisheries & Oceans Canada, Canadian Coast Guard, Canada Bldg., 344 Slater St., Ottawa ON K1A 0N7, 613/998-1574; Fax: 613/990-2780

Small Craft Harbours, 200 Kent St., Ottawa ON K1A 0E6, 613/993-3012; Fax: 613/952-6788

Transport Canada, Communications, Transport Canada Building, 330 Sparks St., Ottawa ON K1A 0N5, 613/990-6138; Fax: 613/995-0351

Alta: Alberta Municipal Affairs, Registries Division, John E. Brownlee Bldg., 10365 - 97 St., Edmonton AB T5J 3W7, 403/422-2362 (Edmonton), 297-8980 (Calgary); Toll Free: 1-800-465-5009 (in Alberta); Fax: 403/422-9105

B.C.: Ministry of Transportation & Highways, Motor Vehicle Branch, 2631 Douglas St., Victoria BC V8T 5A3, 250/387-3140; Fax: 250/387-1169

Man.: Manitoba Highways & Transportation, Driver & Vehicle Licensing Division, 1075 Portage Ave., Winnipeg MB R3G 0S1, 204/945-3888; Fax: 204/948-2018

N.B.: Department of Transportation, Motor Vehicles & Policy, King Tower, Kings Pl., 2nd Fl., PO Box 6000, Fredericton NB E3B 5H1, 506/453-2552

NWT: Department of Transportation, Motor Vehicles, Lahm Ridge Bldg., PO Box 1320, Yellowknife NT X1A 2L9, 403/920-8915; Fax: 403/873-0363

N.S.: Department of Business & Consumer Services, Registry of Motor Vehicles, #215, 6061 Young St., PO Box 1652, Halifax NS B3J 2Z3, 902/424-5851; Toll Free: 1-800-898-7668; Fax: 902/424-0544

Ont.: Ministry of Transportation, Licensing & Control Branch, 1201 Wilson Ave., Downsview ON M3M 1J8, 416/235-4793

PEI: Department of Transportation & Public Works, Motor Vehicles, 17 Haviland St., 1st Fl., Charlottetown PE C1A 3S7, 902/368-5200; Fax: 902/368-5236

Qué.: Ministère des Transports, 700, boul René-Lévesque est, Québec PQ G1R 5H1, 418/643-6740

Sask.: Saskatchewan Government Insurance, Vehicle Standards & Inspection, 2260 - 11th Ave., Regina SK S4P 0J9, 306/751-1200; Fax: 306/787-7477

Yuk.: Yukon Community & Transportation Services, Motor Vehicles, PO Box 2703, Whitehorse YT Y1A 2C6, 403/667-5315; Fax: 403/667-7056

LIBRARIES See BIBLIOGRAPHIC SERVICES

LIQUOR CONTROL
See Also Drugs & Alcohol

Canadian Centre on Substance Abuse, #300, 75 Albert St., Ottawa ON K1P 5E7, 613/235-4048; Fax: 613/235-8101

Alta: Alberta Gaming & Liquor Commission, 50 Corriveau Ave., St. Albert AB T8N 3T5, 403/447-8600; Fax: 403/447-8916

B.C.: Liquor Appeal Board, #1304, 865 Hornby St., Vancouver BC V6Z 2H4, 604/660-2987; Fax: 604/660-3372

Ministry of the Attorney General, Liquor Control & Licensing Branch, 1019 Wharf St., Victoria BC V8V 1X4, 250/387-1254; Fax: 250/387-9184

Liquor Distribution Branch, 2625 Rupert St., Vancouver BC V5M 3T5, 604/252-3021; Fax: 604/252-3026

Man.: Manitoba Liquor Control Commission, 1555 Buffalo Place, PO Box 1023, Winnipeg MB R3C 2X1, 204/284-2501

N.B.: New Brunswick Liquor Corporation, PO Box 20787, Fredericton NB E3B 5B8, 506/452-6826; Fax: 506/452-9890

Liquor Licensing Branch, PO Box 3000, Fredericton NB E3B 5G5, 506/453-3732; Fax: 506/457-7335

Nfld.: Newfoundland Liquor Corporation, Kenmount Rd., PO Box 8750, Stn A, St. John's NF A1B 3V1, 709/754-1100; Fax: 709/754-0321

NWT: Northwest Territories Liquor Commission, Hay River NT X0E 0R0, 403/874-2100; Fax: 403/874-2180

Northwest Territories Liquor Licensing Board, Hay River NT X0E 0R0, 403/874-2906; Fax: 403/873-0302

N.S.: Nova Scotia Liquor Commission, 93 Chainlake Dr., PO Box 8720, Stn A, Halifax NS B3K 5M4, 902/454-5841; Fax: 902/453-1153

Nova Scotia Liquor Licence Board, PO Box 545, Dartmouth NS B2Y 3Y8, 902/424-3660; Fax: 902/424-8987

Ont.: Liquor Control Board of Ontario, 55 Lake Shore Blvd. East, Toronto ON M7A 2H6, 416/864-2400; Fax: 416/864-2476

Liquor Licence Board of Ontario, 55 Lake Shore Blvd. East, Toronto ON M5E 1A4; Fax: 416/326-0308

PEI: Prince Edward Island Liquor Control Commission, PO Box 967, Charlottetown PE C1A 7M4, 902/368-5710; Fax: 902/368-5735

Qué.: La Société des alcools du Québec, 905, rue de Lorimier, Montréal PQ H2K 3V9, 514/873-2020; Fax: 514/873-6788

Sask.: Saskatchewan Liquor & Gaming Authority, 2500 Victoria Ave., PO Box 5054, Regina SK S4P 3M3, 306/787-4213; Fax: 306/787-8468

Yuk.: Yukon Liquor Corporation, PO Box 2703, Whitehorse YT Y1A 2C6, 403/667-5245; Fax: 403/668-7806

LOTTERIES & GAMING
Atlantic Lottery Corporation

Alta: Alberta Gaming & Liquor Commission, 50 Corriveau Ave., St. Albert AB T8N 3T5, 403/447-8600; Fax: 403/447-8916

B.C.: British Columbia Lottery Corporation, 74 West Seymour St., Kamloops BC V2C 1E2, 604/270-0649; Fax: 604/828-5637

N.B.: Atlantic Lottery Corporation, 770 St. George Blvd., PO Box 5500, Moncton NB E1C 8W6, 506/867-5800; Fax: 506/388-4246

N.S.: Nova Scotia Gaming Control Commission, Metropolitan Place, 99 Wyse Rd., PO Box 545, Dartmouth NS B2Y 3Y8, 902/424-7711; Fax: 902/424-3356

Ont.: Gaming Control Commission, 1099 Bay St., 2nd Fl., Toronto ON M5S 2B3, 416/326-8880; Fax: 416/326-8711

Ontario Lottery Corporation, #800, 70 Foster Dr., Sault Ste. Marie ON P6A 6V2, 705/946-6400; Fax: 705/946-6846

Ontario Racing Commission, #1400, 180 Dundas St. West, Toronto ON M5G 1Z8, 416/327-0520; Fax: 416/325-3478

Qué.: Société des loteries du Québec, #2000, 500, rue Sherbrooke ouest, Montréal PQ H3A 3G6, 514/282-8000; Fax: 514/873-8999

Sask.: Saskatchewan Liquor & Gaming Authority, 2500 Victoria Ave., PO Box 5054, Regina SK S4P 3M3, 306/787-4213; Fax: 306/787-8468

Yuk.: Yukon Lottery Appeal Board, c/o Consumer Services, PO Box 2703, Whitehorse YT Y1A 2C6, 403/667-5257

Yukon Lottery Corporation, PO Box 2703, Whitehorse YT Y1A 2C6, 403/667-3749

MANPOWER CENTRES See EMPLOYMENT; UNEMPLOYMENT INSURANCE

MANUFACTURING See INDUSTRY

MAPS, CHARTS & AERIAL PHOTOGRAPHS
Northwest Territories Centre for Remote Sensing; Fax: 403/873-0221

Fisheries & Oceans Canada, Canadian Hydrographic Service, 200 Kent St., Ottawa ON K1A 0E6, 613/995-4413; Chart Distribution: 613/998-4931; Fax: 613/996-9053

Natural Resources Canada, Canada Centre for Remote Sensing, 588 Booth St., Ottawa ON K1A 0Y7, 613/947-1216; Fax: 613/947-3125

Centre for Topographic Information, #010, 2144, rue King ouest, Sherbrooke PQ J1J 2E8, 819/564-5600; Fax: 819/564-5698

Legal Surveys Division, 601 Booth St., Ottawa ON K1A 0E8, 613/996-3919; Fax: 613/996-9990

Mapping & Services Branch, 615 Booth St., Ottawa ON K1A 0E9, 613/995-4945; Fax: 613/995-8737

Alta: Alberta Energy, Mineral Access, Geology & Mapping, Petroleum Plaza, North Tower, 9945 - 108 St., Edmonton AB T5K 2G6, 403/422-9466; Fax: 403/427-3198

Alberta Environmental Protection, Resource Data Division, 9915 - 108 St., Edmonton AB T5K 2G8, 403/427-3131

B.C.: Ministry of Environment, Lands & Parks, Geographic Data BC, 810 Blanshard St., 4th Fl., Victoria BC V8V 1X4, 250/387-6316; Fax: 250/356-7831

Man.: Manitoba Energy & Mines, Maps, Reports & Publications, 360 - 1395 Ellice Ave, Winnipeg MB R3G 3P2, 204/748-1557; Toll Free: 1-800-282-8069 (Energy); Fax: 204/945-0586

N.B.: Department of Natural Resources & Energy, Geological Surveys Branch, PO Box 6000, Fredericton NB E3B 5H1, 506/453-2206; Fax: 506/453-3671

N.S.: Department of Natural Resources, Surveys Division, Founder's Square, 1701 Hollis St., PO Box 698, Halifax NS B3J 2T9, 902/424-3145; Fax: 902/424-7735

Ont.: Office of the Surveyor General, 90 Sheppard Ave. East, 4th Fl., North York ON M2N 3A1, 416/314-1286; Fax: 416/223-6215

PEI: Department of Transportation & Public Works, Properties & Surveys Section, Jones Bldg., PO Box 2000, Charlottetown PE C1A 7N8, 902/368-5131; Fax: 902/368-5395

Department of the Provincial Treasury, Geomatics Information Centre, PO Box 2000, Charlottetown PE C1A 7N8, 902/368-5165; Fax: 902/368-4399

Qué.: Ministère des Ressources Naturelles, Direction Générale du cadastre, #B-302, 5700 - 4 av ouest, 3e étage, Charlesbourg PQ G1H 6R1, 418/644-6224; Fax: 418/644-7160

Sask.: Saskatchewan Geographical Names Board, 2045 Broad St., Main Fl., Regina SK S4P 3V7, 306/787-2800

Saskatchewan Energy & Mines, Northern Survey Branch, 1914 Hamilton St., Regina SK S4P 4V4, 306/787-2568; Fax: 306/787-2488

Saskatchewan Highways & Transportation, Geographic Information Services, 1855 Victoria Ave., Regina SK S4P 3V5, 306/787-4857; Fax: 306/787-9777

Yuk.: Yukon Renewable Resources, Geographic Information Section, PO Box 2703, Whitehorse YT Y1A 2C6, 403/667-8137; Fax: 403/667-3641

Geographic Information Section, PO Box 2703, Whitehorse YT Y1A 2C6, 403/667-8137; Fax: 403/667-3641

MARINE NAVIGATION
Atlantic Pilotage Authority Canada, Purdy's Wharf, Tower 1, #1402, 1959 Upper Water St., Halifax NS B3J 3N2, 902/426-2550; Fax: 902/426-4004

Fisheries & Oceans Canada, Canadian Hydrographic Service, 200 Kent St., Ottawa ON K1A 0E6, 613/995-4413; Chart Distribution: 613/998-4931; Fax: 613/996-9053

Great Lakes Pilotage Authority Ltd., PO Box 95, Cornwall ON K6H 5R9, 613/933-2995; Fax: 613/932-3793

Pacific Pilotage Authority Canada, #300, 1199 West Hastings St., Vancouver BC V6E 4G9, 604/666-6771; Fax: 604/666-6093

St. Lawrence Seaway Authority, #1400, 360 Albert St., Ottawa ON K1R 7X7, 613/598-4600; Fax: 613/598-4620

MARRIAGE LICENCES See VITAL STATISTICS

MEDICAL EXAMINERS See CORONERS

MENTAL HEALTH See HEALTH SERVICES

MERCHANDISING See TRADE

METALS
See also MINERALS & MINING
Natural Resources Canada, Minerals & Metals Sector, 580 Booth St., Ottawa ON K1A 0E4, 613/995-0947; Fax: 613/996-9094

NWT: Department of Resources, Wildlife & Economic Development, Mineral Initiatives Office, #600, Scotia Centre, Bldg. Box 21, 5102 - 50 Ave., Yellowknife NT X1A 3S8, 403/873-7420, 7134; Fax: 403/873-0114

METEOROLOGY See CLIMATE & WEATHER

METRIC SYSTEM See WEIGHTS & MEASURES

MILK PRODUCTION See DAIRYING

MINERALS & MINING
Industry Canada, Metals & Minerals Processing, C.D. Howe Bldg., 235 Queen St., Ottawa ON K1A 0H5, 613/954-3176; Fax: 613/954-2303

Natural Resources Canada, Canada Centre for Mineral & Energy Technology, 580 Booth St., Ottawa ON K1A 0E4, 613/995-0947; Fax: 613/996-9094

Earth Sciences Sector, 601 Booth St., Ottawa ON K1A 0E8, 613/995-0947; Fax: 613/996-9094

Geological Survey of Canada, 601 Booth St., Ottawa ON K1A 0E8, 613/996-3919; Fax: 613/996-9990

Alta: Alberta Energy, Mineral Operations Division, Petroleum Plaza, North Tower, 9945 - 108 St., Edmonton AB T5K 2G6, 403/427-7425; Fax: 403/427-3198

B.C.: British Columbia Advisory Council on Mining, 1810 Blanshard St., Victoria BC V8V 1X4, 250/952-0152

Mine Accident Reporting System, 1810 Blanshard St., Victoria BC V8V 1X4, 250/952-0494; Fax: 250/952-0491

Ministry of Employment & Investment, Energy & Minerals Division, 1810 Blanshard St., 8th Fl., Victoria BC V8W 9N3, 250/356-8702

Man.: Manitoba Mining Board, #360, 1395 Ellice Ave., Winnipeg MB R3G 3P2, 204/943-6740

Manitoba Energy & Mines, #360, 1395 Ellice Ave., Winnipeg MB R3G 3P2, 204/945-4154; Fax: 204/945-0586, 1406

N.B.: Department of Natural Resources & Energy, Mineral Resources & Energy, PO Box 6000, Fredericton NB E3B 5H1, 506/453-2614; Fax: 506/453-3322

Nfld.: Department of Mines & Energy, Mines Branch, PO Box 8700, St. John's NF A1B 4J6, 709/729-2301; Fax: 709/729-6782

NWT: Department of Resources, Wildlife & Economic Development, Mineral Resources, #600, Scotia Centre, Bldg. Box 21, 5102 - 50 Ave., Yellowknife NT X1A 3S8, 403/920-3222; Fax: 403/873-0114

Minerals, Oil & Gas Division, #600, Scotia Centre, Bldg. Box 21, 5102 - 50 Ave., Yellowknife NT X1A 3S8, 403/873-7420, 7134; Fax: 403/873-0114

N.S.: Department of Natural Resources, Minerals & Energy Branch, Founder's Square, 1701 Hollis St., PO Box 698, Halifax NS B3J 2T9, 902/424-5346; Fax: 902/424-7735

Ont.: Mining & Lands Commissioner, 700 Bay St., 24th Fl., PO Box 330, Toronto ON M5G 1Z6, 416/314-2320; Fax: 416/314-2327

Ministry of Northern Development & Mines, Mines & Minerals Division, 159 Cedar St., 7th Fl., Sudbury ON P3E 6A5, 705/670-7188; Fax: 705/670-7046

Qué.: Ministère des Ressources Naturelles, Mines, #B-302, 5700 - 4 av ouest, 3e étage, Charlesbourg PQ G1H 6R1, 418/646-2727 (Renseignements); Fax: 418/644-7160

Société québécoise d'exploration minière, Place Belle Cour, #2500, 2600, boul Laurier, Ste-Foy PQ G1V 4M6, 418/658-5400; Fax: 418/658-5459

Sask.: Saskatchewan Energy & Mines, 1914 Hamilton St., Regina SK S4P 4V4, 306/787-2526; Fax: 306/787-7338

Yuk.: Yukon Economic Development, Mineral Resources Development, 211 Main St., PO Box 2703, Whitehorse YT Y1A 2C6, 403/667-5466; Fax: 403/668-8601

MINIMUM WAGES
See Also Labour
Human Resources Development Canada, Labour Program, Place du Portage, Phase II, 165, rue Hôtel de Ville, Hull PQ K1A 0J2, 819/997-2617; TDD: 819/953-8000

Alta: Alberta Labour, Work Standards, 10808 - 99 Ave., Edmonton AB T5K 0G5, 403/427-8541; Fax: 403/422-3562

B.C.: Ministry of Labour, Employment Standards Headquarters, 825 Fort St., 2nd Fl., Victoria BC V8W 9K1, 250/387-3300; Fax: 250/356-1886

Man.: Manitoba Labour, Employment Standards Division, #611, Norquay Bldg., 401 York Ave., Winnipeg MB R3C 0P8, 204/945-8190 (Management Services); Fax: 204/948-2085

N.B.: Department of Advanced Education & Labour, Employment Standards Branch, Chestnut Complex, 470 York St., PO Box 6000, Fredericton NB E3B 5H1, 506/453-3902; Fax: 506/453-3806

Nfld.: Labour Standards Board, Confederation Bldg., West Block, PO Box 8700, St. John's NF A1B 4J6, 709/729-2742; Fax: 709/729-6639

NWT: Northwest Territories Labour Standards Board, PO Box 2804, Yellowknife NT X1A 2R1, 403/873-7924; Fax: 403/873-0302

N.S.: Department of Labour, Labour Standards, 5151 Terminal Rd., PO Box 697, Halifax NS B3J 2T8, 902/424-4311; Fax: 902/424-0648

Ont.: Ministry of Labour, Labour Policy Division, 400 University Ave., 14th Fl., Toronto ON M7A 1T7, 416/326-7558; Fax: 416/326-7599

PEI: Department of Provincial Affairs & Attorney General, Employment Standards, PO Box 2000, Charlottetown PE C1A 7N8, 902/368-5550; Fax: 902/368-5283; 5355

Qué.: Commission des normes du travail, 400, boul Jean-Lesage, Québec PQ G1K 8W1, ; Toll Free: 1-800-265-1414; Fax: 514/864-4711

Sask.: Minimum Wage Board, 1870 Albert St., Regina SK S4P 3V7, 306/787-2474; Fax: 306/787-4780

Yuk.: Employment Standards Board, PO Box 2703, Whitehorse YT Y1A 2C6

MOTION PICTURES See FILM PRODUCTION & COLLECTIONS

MOTOR VEHICLES See DRIVERS' LICENCES

MULTICULTURALISM

Canadian Heritage, Citizens' Participation & Multiculturalism, Jules Léger Bldg., 25 Eddy St., Hull PQ K1A 1K5, 819/994-2994; Fax: 819/953-8720

Citizenship & Canadian Identity Sector, Jules Léger Bldg., 25 Eddy St., Hull PQ K1A 1K5, 819/997-0055; Fax: 819/953-5382

Alta: Alberta Community Development, Citizenship & Services Branch, Standard Life Centre, 10405 Jasper Ave., 7th Fl., Edmonton AB T5J 4R7, 403/422-4927; Fax: 403/422-1105

Alberta Human Rights & Citizenship Commission, Standard Life Centre, #1600, 10405 Jasper Ave., Edmonton AB T5J 4R7, 403/427-3116, 427-7661; Fax: 403/422-3563, 427-6013

B.C.: Ministry of the Attorney General, Multiculturalism BC, #309, 703 Broughton St., Victoria BC V8W 1E2, 250/660-2395; Fax: 250/660-1150

Man.: Multicultural Grants Advisory Council, 213 Notre Dame Ave., 4th Fl., Winnipeg MB R3B 1N3, 204/945-4458; Fax: 204/945-1675

Multiculturalism Secretariat, 794 Sargent Ave., Winnipeg MB R3E 0B7, 204/945-1287; Fax: 204/948-2006

N.B.: Department of Advanced Education & Labour, Multiculturalism & Immigration, Chestnut Complex, 470 York St., PO Box 6000, Fredericton NB E3B 5H1, 506/444-4331; Fax: 506/453-3300

Ministerial Advisory Committee on Multiculturalism, PO Box 6000, Fredericton NB E3B 5H1, 506/444-4331; Fax: 506/453-3300

Nfld.: Department of Tourism, Culture & Recreation, Cultural Affairs, Confederation Bldg., PO Box 8700, St. John's NF A1B 4J6, 709/729-3650; Fax: 709/729-5952

NWT: Department of Education, Culture & Employment, Culture & Heritage, PO Box 1320, Yellowknife NT X1A 2L9, 403/873-7551; Fax: 403/873-0155

Ont.: Ministry of Citizenship, Culture & Recreation, Culture Division, 77 Bloor St. West, 6th Fl., Toronto ON M7A 2R9, 416/314-7265

Ontario Advisory Council on Multiculturalism & Citizenship, 35 McCaul St., 3rd Fl., Toronto ON M5T 1V7, 416/314-6650 (Voice & TDD); Fax: 416/314-6658

Qué.: Ministère des Relations avec les citoyens et de l'Immigration, Secteur immigration et communautés culturelles, 360, rue McGill, 4e étage, Montréal PQ H2Y 2E9, 514/499-2199; Fax: 514/873-1810

Sask.: Saskatchewan Municipal Government, Arts, Cultural Industries & Multiculturalism, 1855 Victoria Ave., Regina SK S4P 3V7, 306/787-4753; Fax: 306/787-8560

MUNICIPAL AFFAIRS

Environment Canada, Municipal Pollution Prevention, 25 St. Clair Ave. East, 6th Fl., Toronto ON M4T 1M2, 416/973-1162; Fax: 416/973-7438

Treasury Board of Canada, Office of Infrastructure, West Tower, 300 Laurier Ave. West, 3rd Fl., Ottawa ON K1A 0R5, 613/952-3171; Fax: 613/952-7979

Alta: Alberta Municipal Affairs, Commerce Place, 10155 - 102 St., Edmonton AB T5J 4L4, 403/427-2732; Fax: 403/422-9105

B.C.: Ministry of Employment & Investment, Community Development Unit, 1810 Blanshard St., 8th Fl., Victoria BC V8W 9N3, 604/775-1695; Fax: 604/775-1184

Infrastructure & Program Management Branch, 712 Yates St., Victoria BC V8V 1X4, 250/387-0686; Fax: 250/387-4410

Ministry of Municipal Affairs & Housing, Municipal Affairs, PO Box 9490, Victoria BC V8W 9N7, 250/387-4089; Fax: 250/356-1070

Man.: Manitoba Municipal Board, #408, 800 Portage Ave., Winnipeg MB R3G 0N4, 204/945-1789; Fax: 204/948-2235

Manitoba Northern Affairs, Local Government Development Division, 59 Elizabeth Dr., Thompson MB R8N 1X4, 204/677-6607; Fax: 204/677-6753

Manitoba Rural Development, Community Economic Development Branch, #600, 800 Portage Ave., Winnipeg MB R3G 0N4, 204/945-2192; Fax: 204/945-5059

Local Government Services Division, #609, 800 Portage Ave., Winnipeg MB R3G ON4; Fax: 204/945-1383

N.B.: Department of Municipalities, Culture & Housing, Marysville Place, 20 McGloin St., PO Box 6000, Fredericton NB E3B 5H1, 506/453-2690; Fax: 506/457-4991

Nfld.: Department of Municipal & Provincial Affairs, West Block, Confederation Bldg., PO Box 8700, St. John's NF A1B 4J6, 709/729-3053

Newfoundland Municipal Financing Corporation, Confederation Bldg., PO Box 8700, St. John's NF A1B 4J6, 709/729-6686; Fax: 709/729-2070

NWT: Department of Municipal & Community Affairs, #600, 5201 - 50th Ave., PO Box 1310, Yellowknife NT X1A 2L9, 403/873-7118; Fax: 403/873-0309

N.S.: Department of Housing & Municipal Affairs, PO Box 216, Halifax NS B3J 2M4, 902/424-4141; Fax: 902/424-0531

Nova Scotia Municipal Finance Corporation, Founders Square, #602, 1701 Hollis St., PO Box 850, Stn M, Halifax NS B3J 2V2, 902/424-4590; Fax: 902/424-0525

Ont.: Ministry of Municipal Affairs & Housing, Communications Branch, 777 Bay St., 17th Fl., Toronto ON M5G 2E5, 416/585-6900; Fax: 416/585-6227

Municipal Finance Branch, 777 Bay St., 17th Fl., Toronto ON M5G 2E5, 416/585-6951; Fax: 416/585-6227

Ontario Municipal Board, 655 Bay St., 15th Fl., Toronto ON M5G 1E5, 416/326-6800

PEI: Department of Provincial Affairs & Attorney General, PO Box 2000, Charlottetown PE C1A 7N8, 902/368-5250; Fax: 902/368-5283; 5355

Qué.: Ministère des Affaires Municipales, Édifice Cook-Chauveau, 20, rue Chauveau, Québec PQ G1R 4J3, 418/691-2015; Fax: 418/643-7385

Sask.: Saskatchewan Municipal Board, 2151 Scarth St., 4th Fl., Regina SK S4P 3V7, 306/787-6221; Fax: 306/787-1610

Saskatchewan Municipal Government, Municipal Services Division, 1855 Victoria Ave., Regina SK S4P 3V7, 306/787-8282; Fax: 306/787-4181

Yuk.: Yukon Community & Transportation Services, Municipal & Community Affairs Division, PO Box 2703, Whitehorse YT Y1A 2C6, 403/667-5431; Fax: 403/667-7056

MUSEUMS

Canadian Heritage, Cultural Development & Heritage Sector, Jules Léger Bldg., 25 Eddy St., Hull PQ K1A 1K5, 819/997-0055; Fax: 819/953-5382

Alta: Alberta Community Development, Cultural Facilities & Historical Resources Division, Old St. Stephen's College, 8820 - 112 St., Edmonton AB T6G 2P8, 403/431-2300; Fax: 403/432-1376

B.C.: Ministry of Small Business, Tourism & Culture, Culture Division, 1117 Wharf St., Victoria BC V8W 2Z2, 250/356-6363 (Tourism); Fax: 250/356-8248

Man.: Manitoba Culture, Heritage & Citizenship, Culture, Heritage & Recreation Programs Division, 213 Notre Dame., Winnipeg MB R3B 1N3, 204/945-3729

N.B.: Department of Municipalities, Culture & Housing, Cultural Affairs Division, Marysville Place, 20 McGloin St., PO Box 6000, Fredericton NB E3B 5H1, 506/453-2690; Fax: 506/453-2416

Nfld.: Department of Tourism, Culture & Recreation, Cultural Affairs, Historic Resources & Provincial Archives, Confederation Bldg., PO Box 8700, St. John's NF A1B 4J6, 709/729-0928; Fax: 709/729-0662

Historic Resources, Confederation Bldg., PO Box 8700, St. John's NF A1B 4J6, 709/729-2460; Fax: 709/729-0870

NWT: Department of Education, Culture & Employment, Culture & Heritage, PO Box 1320, Yellowknife NT X1A 2L9, 403/873-7551; Fax: 403/873-0155

N.S.: Department of Education & Culture, Heritage & Culture Branch (Nova Scotia Museum), 2021 Brunswick St., PO Box 578, Halifax NS B3J 2S9, 902/424-5168; Fax: 902/424-0511

Ont.: Ministry of Citizenship, Culture & Recreation, Culture Division, 77 Bloor St. West, 6th Fl., Toronto ON M7A 2R9, 416/314-7265

Royal Ontario Museum, 100 Queen's Park Cres., Toronto ON M5S 2C6, 416/586-5549; Fax: 416/586-5863

PEI: Department of Education, Sullivan Bldg., 16 Fitzroy St., PO Box 2000, Charlottetown PE C1A 7N8, 902/368-4600; Fax: 902/368-4663

Sask.: Saskatchewan Municipal Government, Culture & Recreation Division, 1855 Victoria Ave., Regina SK S4P 3V7, 306/787-8282; Fax: 306/787-4181

Heritage Branch, 1855 Victoria Ave., Regina SK S4P 3V7, 306/787-2809; Fax: 306/787-0069

Heritage Foundation, 1855 Victoria Ave., Regina SK S4P 3V7, 306/787-4188; Fax: 306/787-4181

Royal Saskatchewan Museum, College Ave. & Albert St., Regina SK S4P 3V7, 306/787-2813; Fax: 306/787-2820

Yuk.: Yukon Tourism, Heritage Branch, PO Box 2703, Whitehorse YT Y1A 2C6, 403/667-5363; Fax: 403/667-3546

NARCOTICS See DRUGS & ALCOHOL

Canadian Almanac & Directory 1997

NATIONAL DEFENCE *See* **DEFENCE**

NATIVE AFFAIRS *See* **ABORIGINAL AFFAIRS**

NATURAL GAS *See* **OIL & NATURAL GAS RESOURCES**

NATURAL RESOURCES

Canadian Heritage, Parks Canada Sector, Jules Léger Bldg., 25 Eddy St., Hull PQ K1A 1K5, 819/997-0055; Fax: 819/953-5382

Environment Canada, Terrasses de la Chaudière, 10 Wellington St., Hull PQ K1A 0H3, 819/997-2800; Toll Free: 1-800-668-6767; Fax: 819/953-2225

Fisheries & Oceans Canada, 200 Kent St., Ottawa ON K1A 0E6, 613/993-0999; TDD: 1-800-668-5228

Natural Resources Canada, Communications Branch, 580 Booth St., Ottawa ON K1A 0E4, 613/992-0267; Fax: 613/996-9094

Alta: Alberta Energy, Petroleum Plaza, North Tower, 9945 - 108 St., Edmonton AB T5K 2G6, 403/427-7425; Fax: 403/427-3198

Alberta Environmental Protection, Natural Resources Service, 9915 - 108 St., Edmonton AB T5K 2G8, 403/427-2739, 944-0313 (Information Centre)

B.C.: Ministry of Employment & Investment, Energy & Minerals Division, 1810 Blanshard St., 8th Fl., Victoria BC V8W 9N3, 250/356-8702

Ministry of Environment, Lands & Parks, 810 Blanshard St., Victoria BC V8V 1X5, 250/387-9419; Fax: 250/356-6464

  Lands & Water Management Department, 810 Blanshard St., 4th Fl., Victoria BC V8V 1X4, 250/387-1288; Fax: 250/387-5669

Man.: Manitoba Natural Resources, Management Services Division, 1577 Dublin Ave., Winnipeg MB R3E 3J5, 204/945-3730; Fax: 204/945-3586

N.B.: Department of Natural Resources & Energy, PO Box 6000, Fredericton NB E3B 5H1, 506/453-2614; Fax: 506/453-3322

Nfld.: Department of Forest Resources & Agrifoods, PO Box 8700, St. John's NF A1B 4J6, 709/729-4716

Department of Government Services & Lands, Lands Branch, PO Box 8700, St. John's NF A1B 4J6

Department of Mines & Energy, PO Box 8700, St. John's NF A1B 4J6, 709/729-2301

NWT: Department of Resources, Wildlife & Economic Development, #600, Scotia Centre, Bldg. Box 21, 5102 - 50 Ave., Yellowknife NT X1A 3S8, 403/873-7420, 7134; Fax: 403/873-0114

  Resource Policy, #600, Scotia Centre, Bldg. Box 21, 5102 - 50 Ave., Yellowknife NT X1A 3S8, 403/873-7420, 7134; Fax: 403/873-0114

N.S.: Department of Natural Resources, Founder's Square, 1701 Hollis St., PO Box 698, Halifax NS B3J 2T9, 902/424-5935; Fax: 902/424-7735

Ont.: Ministry of Natural Resources, Communications Services Branch, Whitney Block, 99 Wellesley St. West, Toronto ON M7A 1W3, 416/314-2119; Fax: 416/314-2051

PEI: Department of Environmental Resources, Jones Bldg., 11 Kent St., 4th Fl., PO Box 2000, Charlottetown PE C1A 7N8, 902/368-5000; Fax: 902/368-5830

Qué.: Ministère des Ressources Naturelles, #B-302, 5700 - 4 av ouest, 3e étage, Charlesbourg PQ G1H 6R1, 418/646-2727 (Renseignements); Toll Free: 1-800-463-4558; Fax: 418/644-7160

Sask.: Saskatchewan Environment & Resource Management, 3211 Albert St., Regina SK S4S 5W6, 306/787-2700; Toll Free: 1-800-667-2757; Fax: 306/787-3941

Saskatchewan Northern Affairs, Resource Development Division, 1919 Saskatchewan Dr., Regina SK S4P 3V7, 306/787-2908

Saskatchewan Water Corporation (Sask Water), Water Resources Management, Victoria Place, 111 Fairford St. East, Moose Jaw SK S6H 7X9, 306/694-3950; Fax: 306/694-3944

Yuk.: Yukon Renewable Resources, PO Box 2703, Whitehorse YT Y1A 2C6, 403/667-5237; Toll Free: 1-800-661-0408 (Yukon)

NUCLEAR ENERGY

Atomic Energy Control Board, 280 Slater St., PO Box 1046, Stn B, Ottawa ON K1P 5S9, 613/995-5894; Toll Free: 1-800-668-5284; Fax: 613/995-5086

Atomic Energy of Canada Limited, 2251 Speakman Dr., Mississauga ON L5K 1B2, 905/823-9040; Fax: 905/823-8006

Natural Resources Canada, Uranium & Nuclear Energy Branch, 580 Booth St., Ottawa ON K1A 0E4, 613/996-7432; Fax: 613/992-1405

Ont.: Ontario Hydro, Nuclear, 700 University Ave., Toronto ON M5G 1X6, 416/592-2151; Fax: 416/592-3924

Qué.: Hydro-Québec, 75, boul René-Lévesque ouest, Montréal PQ H2Z 1A4, 514/289-2211; Fax: 514/843-3163

NUTRITION

Agriculture & Agri-Food Canada, Food Bureau, Sir John Carling Bldg., 930 Carling Ave., 5th Fl., Ottawa ON K1A 0C5, 613/759-7557; Fax: 613/759-7496

  Research Branch, Sir John Carling Bldg., 930 Carling Ave., Ottawa ON K1A 0C5, 613/759-7794; Fax: 613/759-7772

Health Canada, Health Promotions & Programs Branch, Brooke Claxton Bldg., Tunney's Pasture, Ottawa ON K1A 0K9, 613/957-2991; Fax: 613/941-5366

Alta: Alberta Health, Population Health Division, PO Box 222, Edmonton AB T5J 2P4, 403/427-7164

B.C.: Ministry of Health, Health Protection & Safety, 1515 Blanshard St., 7th Fl., Victoria BC V8W 3C8, 250/952-1731; Fax: 250/952-1486

Man.: Manitoba Health, Community & Mental Health Services Division, 599 Empress St., Winnipeg MB R3G 3H2, 204/786-7191 (Finance & Administration Branch); Fax: 204/774-1325

N.B.: Department of Health & Community Services, Public Health & Medical Services Division, PO Box 5100, Fredericton NB E3B 5G8, 506/453-2536; Fax: 506/444-4697

Nfld.: Department of Health, Health Promotion, West Block, Confederation Bldg., PO Box 8700, St. John's NF A1B 4J6, 709/729-3940; Fax: 709/729-5824

NWT: Department of Health & Social Services, Health Services Development, Centre Square Tower, 8th Fl., PO Box 1320, Yellowknife NT X1A 2L9, 403/920-6173; Fax: 403/873-0266

N.S.: Department of Health, Policy & Planning, Joseph Howe Bldg., 1690 Hollis St., 12th Fl., PO Box 488, Halifax NS B3J 2R8, 902/424-4310; Fax: 902/424-0559

Ont.: Ministry of Health, Community Health Branch, Hepburn Block, 8th Fl., Queen's Park, Toronto ON M7A 1S2, 416/327-7535; Toll Free: 1-800-668-2437 (AIDS Bureau); Fax: 416/327-8781

PEI: Department of Health & Social Services, Jones Bldg., 11 Kent St., 2nd Fl., PO Box 2000, Charlottetown PE C1A 7N8, 902/368-4900; Fax: 902/368-4969

Qué.: Ministère de la Santé et des services sociaux, 1075, ch Ste-Foy, Québec PQ G1S 2M1

Sask.: Saskatchewan Health, Wellness & Health Promotion Branch, 3475 Albert St., Regina SK S4S 6X6, 306/787-3083; Fax: 306/787-8310

Yuk.: Yukon Health & Social Services, Health Services Branch, PO Box 2703, Whitehorse YT Y1A 2C6, 403/667-3673 (Communications); Fax: 403/667-3096

OCCUPATIONAL SAFETY

See Also **Dangerous Goods & Hazardous Materials**

Canadian Centre for Occupational Health & Safety, 250 Main St. East, Hamilton ON L8N 1H6, 905/572-2981; Toll Free: 1-800-263-8466; Fax: 905/572-2206

Health Canada, Occupational & Environmental Health Services, Ottawa ON K1A 0L3, 613/957-7699; Fax: 613/941-5366

Alta: Alberta Health, Environmental Health, PO Box 222, Edmonton AB T5J 2P4, 403/427-2643

Alberta Labour, Occupational Health & Safety Services, 10011 - 109 St., 5th Fl., Edmonton AB T5J 3S8, 403/427-2655; Fax: 403/427-5698

Occupational Health & Safety Council, 10808 - 99 Ave., 9th Fl., Edmonton AB T5K 0G5, 403/427-6971; Fax: 403/427-5698

B.C.: Employment Standards Tribunal, #504, 815 Hornby St., Vancouver BC V6Z 2E6, 604/775-3512; Fax: 604/775-3372

Workers' Compensation Board, 6951 Westminster Hwy., Richmond BC V7C 1C6, 604/273-2266; Fax: 604/276-3151

Man.: Advisory Council on Workplace Safety & Health, #200, 401 York Ave., Winnipeg MB R3C 0P8, 204/945-4153; Fax: 204/945-4556

Manitoba Highways & Transportation, Occupational Health & Safety, 215 Garry St., 17th Fl., Winnipeg MB R3C 3Z1, 204/945-5819; Fax: 204/945-5115

Manitoba Labour, Workplace Safety & Health Division, #200, 401 York Ave., Winnipeg MB R3C 0P8, 204/945-3446; Fax: 204/945-4556

N.B.: Workplace Health, Safety & Compensation Commission of New Brunswick, 1 Portland St., PO Box 160, Saint John NB E2L 3X9, 506/632-2200; Toll Free: 1-800-222-9775; Fax: 506/632-2226

Nfld.: Department of Environment & Labour, Occupational Health & Safety Services, Confederation Bldg., PO Box 8700, St. John's NF A1B 4J6, 709/729-5548; Fax: 709/729-1930

N.S.: Department of Labour, Occupational Health & Safety, 5151 Terminal Rd., PO Box 697, Halifax NS B3J 2T8, 902/424-4328; Toll Free: 1-800-952-2687; Fax: 902/424-3239

Ont.: Ministry of Labour, Occupational Health & Safety Branch, 400 University Ave., 14th Fl., Toronto ON M7A 1T7, 416/326-1359; Fax: 416/326-7761

Workplace Health & Safety Agency, #900, 121 Bloor St. East, Toronto ON M4W 3M5, 416/975-9728; Fax: 416/975-9775

PEI: Department of the Provincial Treasury, Occupational Health & Safety, PO Box 2000, Charlottetown PE C1A 7N8, 902/368-4200; Fax: 902/368-6622

Qué.: Commission de la santé et de la sécurité du travail du Québec, 1199, rue de Bleury, CP 6056, Succ Centre-Ville, Montréal PQ H3C 4E1, 514/873-7183; Fax: 514/873-7007

Sask.: Office of the Worker's Advocate, 1870 Albert St., Regina SK S4P 3V7, 306/787-2456

Saskatchewan Labour, Occupational Health & Safety Division, 1870 Albert St., Regina SK S4P 3V7, 306/787-4496; Toll Free: 1-800-567-7233 (Saskatchewan); Fax: 306/787-2208

Yuk.: Yukon Workers' Compensation Board, Occupational Health & Safety, 401 Strickland St., Whitehorse YT Y1A 5N8, 403/667-8616; Fax: 403/668-2079

OCCUPATIONAL TRAINING
Canadian Centre for Management Development, PO Box 420, Stn A, Ottawa ON K1N 8V4, 613/997-4163; Fax: 613/953-6240
Human Resources Development Canada, Communications, Place du Portage, Phase IV, 140, Promenade du Portage, Hull PQ K1A 0J9, 819/994-6013
Public Service Commission of Canada, Training Programs Branch, Ottawa ON K1A 0M7, 613/992-9562; Fax: 613/954-7561
Alta: Alberta Apprenticeship & Industry Training Board, 10155 - 102 St., 10th Fl., Edmonton AB T5J 4L5, 403/427-4601
Alberta Advanced Education & Career Development, Apprenticeship & Industry Training Division, Commerce Place, 10155 - 102 St., 7th Fl., Edmonton AB T5J 4L5, 403/422-4488; Fax: 403/422-7376
B.C.: British Columbia Labour Force Development Board, #221, 560 Johnson St., Victoria BC V8V 1X4, 250/356-5360; Fax: 250/356-9444
Ministry of Education, Skills & Training, Skills Development Division, PO Box 9150, Stn Prov Govt, Victoria BC V8W 9H1, 250/356-2500; Fax: 250/356-5945
Man.: Manitoba Education & Training, Training & Advanced Education, 185 Carlton St., 4th Fl., Winnipeg MB R3C 3J1, 204/945-4325; Fax: 204/945-1291
N.B.: Department of Advanced Education & Labour, Chestnut Complex, 470 York St., PO Box 6000, Fredericton NB E3B 5H1; Fax: 506/453-3806
Nfld.: Department of Environment & Labour, Youth Strategy & Career Support, Confederation Bldg., PO Box 8700, St. John's NF A1B 4J6, 709/729-2314; Fax: 709/729-6639
NWT: Department of Education, Culture & Employment, Career Development, PO Box 1320, Yellowknife NT X1A 2L9, 403/873-7146; Fax: 403/873-0155
N.S.: Department of Labour, Occupational Health, 5151 Terminal Rd., PO Box 697, Halifax NS B3J 2T8, 902/424-8055; Toll Free: 1-800-952-2687; Fax: 902/424-3239
Ont.: Ministry of Education & Training, Training Division, Mowat Block, 900 Bay St., Toronto ON M7A 1L2, 416/325-2929; Fax: 416/325-2934
PEI: Office of Higher Education, Training & Adult Learning, Training & Adult Learning, Shaw Bldg., 105 Rochford St., 3rd Fl., PO Box 2000, Charlottetown PE C1A 7N8, 902/368-5988; Fax: 902/368-6144
Qué.: Ministère de l'Éducation, Formation professionnelle et technique, 1035, rue De La Chevrotière, 15e étage, Québec PQ G1R 5A5, 418/643-7095; Fax: 418/646-6561
Société québécoise de développement de la main-d'oeuvre, 425, rue St-Amable, Québec PQ G1R 2C5, 418/643-1892; Fax: 418/643-1714
Sask.: Saskatchewan Post-Secondary Education & Skills Training, Training Programs Branch, 2220 College Ave., Regina SK S4P 3V7, 306/787-2093
Yuk.: Yukon Education, Training Services, PO Box 2703, Whitehorse YT Y1A 2C6, 403/667-5141; Fax: 403/667-4754

OCEANOGRAPHY
Bayfield Institute for Marine Science & Surveys, 867 Lakeshore Rd., PO Box 5050, Burlington ON L7R 4A6, 905/336-4871; Fax: 905/336-6637
Bedford Institute of Oceanography, PO Box 1006, Dartmouth NS B2Y 4A2, 902/426-2373; Fax: 902/426-7827
Fisheries & Oceans Canada, Canadian Hydrographic Service, 200 Kent St., Ottawa ON K1A 0E6, 613/995-4413; Chart Distribution: 613/998-4931; Fax: 613/996-9053
Institute for Marine Biosciences, 1411 Oxford St., Halifax NS B3H 3Z1, 902/426-8332; Fax: 902/426-9413
Institute for Marine Dynamics, Memorial University, Kerwin Pl. & Arctic Ave., PO Box 12093, Stn A, St. John's NF A1B 3T5, 709/772-4939; Fax: 709/772-3101
Institute of Ocean Sciences, 9860 West Saanich Rd., PO Box 6000, Sidney BC V8L 4B2, 250/363-6517; Fax: 250/353-6807
Maurice Lamontagne Institute, 850, Rte de le Mer, CP 1000, Mont-Joli PQ G5H 3Z4, 418/775-6553; Fax: 418/775-0542
Qué.: Ministère de l'Agriculture, des Pêcheries et de l'Alimentation, Innovation et des technologies, 96, montée Sandy Beach, CP 1070, Gaspé PQ G0C 1R0, 418/368-7637; Fax: 418/368-1275
Ministère de l'Environnement et de la Faune, Écosystèmes aquatiques, Édifice Marie-Guyart, 675, boul René-Lévesque est, Québec PQ G1R 5V7, 418/644-3678; Fax: 418/646-8483

OIL & NATURAL GAS RESOURCES
See Also **Energy; Natural Resources**
Indian Oil & Gas Canada, #100, 9911 Chula Blvd., Tsuu T'ina (Sarcee) AB T2W 6H6, 403/292-5625; Fax: 403/292-5618
National Energy Board, 311 - 6th Ave. SW, Calgary AB T2P 3H2, 403/292-4800; Fax: 403/292-5503
Natural Resources Canada, Canada Centre for Mineral & Energy Technology, 580 Booth St., Ottawa ON K1A 0E4, 613/995-0947; Fax: 613/996-9094
Energy Resources Branch, 580 Booth St., Ottawa ON K1A 0E4, 613/996-7432; Fax: 613/992-1405
Alta: Alberta Energy, Petroleum Plaza, North Tower, 9945 - 108 St., Edmonton AB T5K 2G6, 403/427-7425; Fax: 403/427-3198
B.C.: Ministry of Employment & Investment, Energy & Minerals Division, 1810 Blanshard St., 8th Fl., Victoria BC V8W 9N3, 250/356-8702
Man.: Manitoba Energy & Mines, Petroleum & Energy Branch, 360 - 1395 Ellice Ave, Winnipeg MB R3G 3P2, 204/945-6577; Toll Free: 1-800-282-8069 (Energy); Fax: 204/945-0586
N.B.: Department of Natural Resources & Energy, Mineral Resources & Energy, PO Box 6000, Fredericton NB E3B 5H1, 506/453-2614; Fax: 506/453-3322
Nfld.: Canada-Newfoundland Offshore Petroleum Board, TD Place, #500, 140 Water St., St. John's NF A1C 6H6, 709/778-1400; Fax: 709/778-1473
Department of Mines & Energy, Energy Branch, PO Box 8700, St. John's NF A1B 4J6, 709/729-2301
Hibernia Project, PO Box 8700, St. John's NF A1B 4J6, 709/729-2848
Petroleum & Energy Resources Development, PO Box 8700, St. John's NF A1B 4J6, 709/729-2323
NWT: Department of Public Works & Services, Petroleum Products Division, Bldg. YK-7, PO Box 1320, Yellowknife NT X1A 2L9, 819/645-5165; Fax: 819/945-3554
Department of Resources, Wildlife & Economic Development, Minerals, Oil & Gas Division, #600, Scotia Centre, Bldg. Box 21, 5102 - 50 Ave., Yellowknife NT X1A 3S8, 403/873-7420, 7134; Fax: 403/873-0114
N.S.: Canada-Nova Scotia Offshore Petroleum Board, TD Centre, 1791 Barrington St., 6th Fl., Halifax NS B3J 3K9, 902/422-5588; Fax: 902/422-1799
Department of Natural Resources, Petroleum Development Agency, Founder's Square, 1701 Hollis St., PO Box 698, Halifax NS B3J 2T9, 902/424-5935; Fax: 902/424-7735
Qué.: Ministère des Ressources Naturelles, Gaz et pétrole, #B-302, 5700 - 4 av ouest, 3e étage, Charlesbourg PQ G1H 6R1, 418/644-6711; Fax: 418/643-8337
Société québécoise d'initiatives pétrolières, #180, 1175, ave de Lavigerie, Ste-Foy PQ G1V 4P1, 418/651-9543; Fax: 418/651-2292
Sask.: Saskatchewan Energy & Mines, Petroleum & Natural Gas Division, 1914 Hamilton St., Regina SK S4P 4V4, 306/787-2526; Fax: 306/787-2478
Yuk.: Yukon Economic Development, Energy & Mines Branch, 211 Main St., PO Box 2703, Whitehorse YT Y1A 2C6, 403/667-5466; Fax: 403/668-8601

OLD AGE ASSISTANCE *See* SENIOR CITIZENS SERVICES

OMBUDSMEN
Information Commissioner of Canada, Tower B, Place de Ville, 112 Kent St., 3rd Fl., Ottawa ON K1A 1H3, 613/995-2410; Toll Free: 1-800-267-0441; Fax: 613/995-1501
Office of the Correctional Investigator, #402, 275 Slater St., Ottawa ON K1P 5H9, 613/990-2695; Toll Free: 1-800-267-5982; Fax: 613/990-9091
Privacy Commissioner of Canada, Tower B, Place de Ville, 112 Kent St., Ottawa ON K1A 1H3, 613/995-2410; Toll Free: 1-800-267-0441; TDD: 613/992-9190; Fax: 613/995-1501
Alta: Alberta Office of the Ombudsman, Phipps-McKinnon Bldg., #1630, 10020 - 101A Ave., Edmonton AB T5J 3G2, 403/427-2756; Fax: 403/427-2759
B.C.: Office of the Ombudsman, 931 Fort St., Victoria BC V8V 3K3, 250/387-5855; Toll Free: 1-800-567-3247; Fax: 250/387-0198
Man.: Manitoba Office of the Ombudsman, #750, 500 Portage Ave., Winnipeg MB R3C 3X1, 204/786-6483; Toll Free: 1-800-665-0531; Fax: 204/942-7803
N.B.: Office of the Ombudsman, 767 Brunswick St., PO Box 6000, Fredericton NB E3B 5H1, 506/453-2789; Fax: 506/453-5599
N.S.: Office of the Ombudsman, Lord Nelson Arcade, #300, 5675 Spring Garden Rd., PO Box 2152, Halifax NS B3J 3B7, 902/424-6780; Toll Free: 1-800-670-1111; Fax: 902/424-6675
Ont.: Commission on Integrity, 101 Bloor St. West, 4th Fl., Toronto ON M5S 2Z7, 416/314-8983; Fax: 416/314-8987
Office of the Ombudsman, 125 Queen's Park, Toronto ON M5S 2C7, 416/586-3300; Toll Free: 1-800-263-1830 (English); TDD: 416/586-3510; Fax: 416/586-3485
Qué.: Protecteur du Citoyen, 2875, boul Laurier, 4e étage, Ste-Foy PQ G1V 2M2, 418/643-2688; Fax: 418/643-8759
Sask.: Saskatchewan Ombudsman, #150, 2401 Saskatchewan Dr., Regina SK S4P 3V7, 306/787-6211; Fax: 306/787-9090

PARKS
See Also **Land Resources**
Canadian Heritage, Parks Canada Sector, Jules Léger Bldg., 25 Eddy St., Hull PQ K1A 1K5, 819/997-0055; Fax: 819/953-5382
Citizenship & Immigration Canada, Canada Immigration Centres & Citizenship Offices, Journal Tower South, 365 Laurier Ave. West, Hull PQ K1A 1L1, 613/954-9019; Fax: 613/954-2221
National Battlefields Commission, 390, av de Bernières, Québec PQ G1R 2L7, 418/648-3506; Fax: 418/648-3638
Roosevelt Campobello International Park Commission, Campobello Island, Campobello Is. NB E0G 3H0, 506/752-2922; Fax: 506/752-2052
Alta: Alberta Sport, Recreation, Parks & Wildlife Foundation, Percy Page Centre, 11759 Groat Rd., Edmonton AB T5M 3K9, 403/427-1976; Fax: 403/488-9755

Canadian Almanac & Directory 1997

Alberta Environmental Protection, Parks, 9915 - 108 St., Edmonton AB T5K 2G8, 403/427-2739, 944-0313 (Information Centre)

B.C.: Ministry of Environment, Lands & Parks, Parks Department, 800 Johnson St., 2nd Fl., Victoria BC V8V 1X4, 250/387-5002; Fax: 250/387-5757

Man.: Ecological Reserves Advisory Committee, PO Box 355, Stn St. Vital, Winnipeg MB R2M 5C8, 204/942-6617

Manitoba Natural Resources, Parks & Natural Areas Branch, 200 Saulteaux Cr., PO Box 50, Winnipeg MB R3J 3W3, 204/945-4362; Fax: 204/945-0012

N.B.: Department of Natural Resources & Energy, Parks, PO Box 6000, Fredericton NB E3B 5H1, 506/453-2730; Fax: 506/453-6630

Nfld.: Department of Tourism, Culture & Recreation, Parks & Recreation, Confederation Bldg., PO Box 8700, St. John's NF A1B 4J6, 709/729-0928; Fax: 709/729-0662

NWT: Department of Resources, Wildlife & Economic Development, Parks & Tourism Division, #600, Scotia Centre, Bldg. Box 21, 5102 - 50 Ave., Yellowknife NT X1A 3S8, 403/873-7420, 7134; Fax: 403/873-0114

N.S.: Department of Natural Resources, Parks & Recreation (Belmont), Founder's Square, 1701 Hollis St., PO Box 698, Halifax NS B3J 2T9, 902/662-3030; Fax: 902/662-2160

Ont.: Ministry of Natural Resources, Ontario Parks, Whitney Block, #6540, 99 Wellesley St. West, Toronto ON M7A 1W3, 705/740-1224; Fax: 416/314-1994

Provincial Parks Council, 2450 McDougall St., Windsor ON N8X 3N6, 519/255-6731; Fax: 519/255-7990

PEI: Department of Economic Development & Tourism, Tourism PEI, Annex 1, West Royalty Industrial Park, 1 First Ave., Charlottetown PE C1E 1B0, 902/368-5540; Fax: 902/368-4438

Qué.: Ministère de l'Environnement et de la Faune, Direction générale de la ressource faunique et des parcs, Édifice Marie-Guyart, 675, boul René-Lévesque est, Québec PQ G1R 5V7, 418/643-3127; Fax: 418/643-3619

Sask.: Saskatchewan Environment & Resource Management, Parks & Facilities Branch, 3211 Albert St., Regina SK S4S 5W6, 306/787-2846; Fax: 306/787-7000

Yuk.: Yukon Renewable Resources, Parks & Outdoor Recreation Branch, PO Box 2703, Whitehorse YT Y1A 2C6, 403/667-5237; Fax: 403/668-7823

PARLIAMENT
See Also **Government (General Information); Protocol (State)**

House of Commons, Canada, House of Commons, 111 Wellington St., PO Box 1103, Ottawa ON K1A 0A9, 613/992-2986

Library of Parliament, 111 Wellington St., Ottawa ON K1A 0A9, 613/995-1166; Fax: 613/992-1269

Office of the Prime Minister, Langevin Block, 80 Wellington St., Ottawa ON K1A 0A2, 613/992-4211; Fax: 613/941-6900

Privy Council Office, Langevin Block, 80 Wellington St., Ottawa ON K1A 0A3, 613/957-5153; Fax: 613/995-0101

Senate of Canada, Senate Bldg., 111 Wellington St., Ottawa ON K1A 0A4, 613/992-2493; Toll Free: 1-800-267-7362; Fax: 613/995-4998

Alta: Legislative Assembly, c/o Clerk's Office, #801, Legislature Annex, 9718 - 107 St., Edmonton AB T5K 1E4, 403/427-2478; Fax: 403/427-5688

B.C.: Legislative Assembly, c/o Clerk's Office, #221 Parliament Bldgs., Victoria BC V8V 1X4, 250/387-3785; Fax: 250/387-0942

Man.: Legislative Assembly, c/o Clerk's Office, Legislative Bldg., #237, 450 Broadway Ave., Winnipeg MB R3C 0V8, 204/945-3707; Fax: 204/948-2507

N.B.: Legislative Assembly, c/o Clerk's Office, Legislative Bldg., PO Box 6000, Fredericton NB E3B 5H1, 506/453-2506; Fax: 506/453-7154

Nfld.: House of Assembly, c/o Clerk's Office, Confederation Bldg., PO Box 8700, St.John's NF A1B 4J6, 709/729-3405; Fax: 709/729-4820

NWT: Legislative Assembly, c/o Clerk's Office, PO Box 1320, Yellowknife NT X1A 2L9, 403/669-2299, 669-2200; Toll Free: 1-800-661-0784; Fax: 403/920-4735

N.S.: Legislative House of Assembly, c/o Clerk's Office, Province House, 2nd Fl., Halifax NS B3J 2Y3, 902/424-5978; Fax: 902/424-0574

Ont.: Legislative Assembly, c/o Clerk's Office, #104, Legislative Bldg., Queen's Park, Toronto ON M7A 1A2, 416/325-7340; Fax: 416/325-7344

PEI: Legislative Assembly, c/o Clerk's Office, Province House, PO Box 2000, Charlottetown PE C1A 7N8, 902/368-5970; Fax: 902/368-5175

Qué.: Assemblée nationale, c/o Secrétariat général, Édifice Honoré-Mercier, #3.57, 1025, rue St-Augustin, Québec PQ G1A 1A3, 418/643-2724; Fax: 418/643-5062

Sask.: Legislative Assembly, c/o Clerk's Office, #239, Legislative Bldg., Regina SK S4S 0B3, 306/787-2279; Fax: 306/787-0408

Yuk.: Legislative Assembly, c/o Clerk's Office, PO Box 2703, Whitehorse YT Y1A 2C6, 403/667-5498; Fax: 403/667-4180

PAROLE BOARDS
See Also **Correctional Services**

National Parole Board, 340 Laurier Ave. West, Ottawa ON K1A 0R1, 613/954-7474; Fax: 613/995-4380

Solicitor General Canada, Sir Wilfrid Laurier Bldg., 340 Laurier Ave. West, Ottawa ON K1A 0P8, 613/990-2733; Fax: 613/993-7062

Alta: Alberta Justice, Community Corrections & Release Programs Branch, J.E. Brownlee Bldg., 10365 - 97 St., Edmonton AB T5J 3W7, 403/422-5757; Fax: 403/427-1904

Criminal Justice Division, 9833 - 109th St., Edmonton AB T5K 2E8, 403/427-2745; Fax: 403/422-9639

B.C.: British Columbia Board of Parole, #301, 10090 - 152nd St., Surrey BC V3R 8X8, 604/660-8846; Fax: 604/660-8877

Man.: Manitoba Justice, Corrections Division, 405 Broadway, 8th Fl., Winnipeg MB R3C 3L6, 204/945-2852

N.B.: Department of the Solicitor General, Barker House, 4th Fl., PO Box 6000, Fredericton NB E3B 5H1, 506/453-7414; Fax: 506/453-3870

Nfld.: Department of Justice & Attorney General, Adult Corrections Division, Confederation Bldg., PO Box 8700, St. John's NF A1B 4J6, 709/729-3880; Fax: 709/729-0416

NWT: Department of Justice, Solicitor General Branch, PO Box 1320, Yellowknife NT X1A 2L9, 403/873-7005

N.S.: Department of Justice, Probate, 5151 Terminal Rd., PO Box 7, Halifax NS B3J 2L6, 902/424-7421; Fax: 902/424-0595

Ont.: Ontario Board of Parole, #201, 2195 Yonge St., Toronto ON M4S 2B1, 416/325-4480; Fax: 416/325-4485

Qué.: Commission québécoise des libérations conditionnelles, #200, 2055, rue Peel, Montréal PQ H3A 1V4, 514/873-2230; Fax: 514/873-7580

Sask.: Saskatchewan Justice, Corrections Division, 1874 Scarth St., Regina SK S4P 3V7, 306/787-7872 (Communications); Fax: 306/787-8084

Yuk.: Yukon Justice, Adult Probation Services, PO Box 2703, Whitehorse YT Y1A 2C6, 403/667-5231; Fax: 403/393-6272

PASSPORT INFORMATION
See Also **Citizenship; Immigration**

Foreign Affairs & International Trade Canada, Passport Office, Place du Centre, 200, Promenade du Portage, 6e étage, Hull PQ K1A 0G3, 819/994-3500; Toll Free: 1-800-567-6868, TDD: 613/994-3560; Fax: 819/992-6587

PATENTS & COPYRIGHT

Industry Canada, Canadian Intellectual Property Office, Place du Portage, Tour I, 50, rue Victoria, Hull PQ K1A 0C9, 613/954-2788; Fax: 613/954-2303

Copyright & Industrial Design, Place du Portage, Tour I, 50, rue Victoria, Hull PQ K1A 0C9, 819/997-1657; Fax: 819/953-6977

Patent, Place du Portage, Tour I, 50, rue Victoria, Hull PQ K1A 0C9, 819/953-5864; Fax: 819/994-1989

Trade-Marks, Place du Portage, Tour I, 50, rue Victoria, Hull PQ K1A 0C9, 819/997-2423; Fax: 819/997-1421

PAY EQUITY

Human Resources Development Canada, Place du Portage, Phase IV, 140, Promenade du Portage, Hull PQ K1A 0J9, 819/994-6013

Treasury Board of Canada, Official Languages & Employment Equity Branch, 140 O'Connor St., Ottawa ON K1A 0R5, 613/952-2852; Fax: 613/941-4262

Alta: Alberta Labour, Work Standards, 10808 - 99 Ave., Edmonton AB T5K 0G5, 403/427-8541; Fax: 403/422-3562

B.C.: Ministry of the Attorney General, Employment Equity & Women's Programs, 910 Government St., 5th Fl., Victoria BC V8V 1X4, 250/387-3247; Fax: 250/356-5368

Man.: Manitoba Labour, Employment Standards Division, #611, Norquay Bldg., 401 York Ave., Winnipeg MB R3C 0P8, 204/945-8190 (Management Services); Fax: 204/948-2085

N.B.: Department of Finance, Compensation Policy, PO Box 6000, Fredericton NB E3B 5H1, 506/453-5359; Fax: 506/457-4989

N.S.: Pay Equity Commission, PO Box 697, Halifax NS B3J 1T8, 902/424-8595; Fax: 902/424-3239

Ont.: Management Board of Cabinet, Employment Equity Division, #393, 595 Bay St., PO Box 51, Toronto ON M5G 2C2, 416/325-1300; Fax: 416/325-1313

Pay Equity Commission, 150 Eglinton Ave. East, 5th Fl., Toronto ON M4P 1E8, 416/481-4464; Fax: 416/314-8741

PEI: Labour Relations Board, PO Box 2000, Charlottetown PE C1A 7N8, 902/368-5550; Fax: 902/368-5526

Sask.: Saskatchewan Public Service Commission, Employee Relations, 2103 - 11th Ave., Regina SK S4P 3V7, 306/787-7606; Fax: 306/787-7533

PENSIONS

Bureau of Pension Advocates, J. MacDonald Bldg., 2nd Fl., PO Box 7700, Charlottetown PE C1A 8M9, 902/566-8640; Fax: 902/566-7804

Finance Canada, Esplanade Laurier, 140 O'Connor St., Ottawa ON K1A 0G5, 613/992-1573; TDD: 613/996-0035; Fax: 613/996-8404

Human Resources Development Canada, Income Security Program, Place Vanier, 120 Parkdale Ave., Ottawa ON K1A 0L1, 819/994-6013
Revenue Canada, CPP/UI Division, 875 Heron Rd., Ottawa ON K1A 0L8, 613/957-2237
Veterans Review & Appeal Board, Daniel J. MacDonald Bldg., Ground Fl., PO Box 7700, Charlottetown PE C1A 8M9, 902/566-8636; Fax: 902/566-7371
Alta: Alberta Pensions Administration, Park Plaza, 3rd Fl., 10611 - 98 Ave., Edmonton AB T5K 2P7, 403/427-2782; Fax: 403/427-1621
Alberta Labour, Pensions, 10808 - 99 Ave., Edmonton AB T5K 0G5, 403/427-8322; Fax: 403/422-4283
B.C.: Ministry of Labour, Pension Benefits Standards, #210, 4946 Canada Way, Burnaby BC V5G 4J6, 604/775-1349; Fax: 604/660-6517
Ministry of Social Services, Income Support, Parliament Bldgs., 614 Humboldt St., 7th Fl., Victoria BC V8V 1X4, 250/387-6485; Fax: 250/356-7801
Man.: Manitoba Labour, Pension Commission, #611, Norquay Bldg., 401 York Ave., Winnipeg MB R3C 0P8, 204/945-2742; Fax: 204/945-1990
N.B.: Department of Advanced Education & Labour, Pensions Branch, Chestnut Complex, 470 York St., PO Box 6000, Fredericton NB E3B 5H1, 506/453-2055; Fax: 506/453-3806
Nfld.: Department of Finance & Treasury Board, Pensions Administration, Confederation Bldg., PO Box 8700, St. John's NF A1B 4J6, 709/729-6093; Fax: 709/729-2856
N.S.: Department of Finance, Pensions, PO Box 187, Halifax NS B3J 2N3, 902/424-5911; Fax: 902/424-0635
Ont.: Ontario Pension Board, #1200, 1 Adelaide St. East, Toronto ON M5C 2X6, 416/364-8558; Toll Free: 1-800-668-6203; Fax: 416/364-7578
Pension Commission of Ontario, 101 Bloor St. West, 9th Fl., Toronto ON M7A 2K2, 416/314-0660; Fax: 416/314-0620
PEI: Department of Education, Teacher Certification & Pensions, Sullivan Bldg., 16 Fitzroy St., PO Box 2000, Charlottetown PE C1A 7N8, 902/368-4650; Fax: 902/368-4663
Department of Provincial Affairs & Attorney General, PO Box 2000, Charlottetown PE C1A 7N8, 902/368-5250; Fax: 902/368-5283; 5355
Qué.: Ministère de la Sécurité du revenu, 425, rue St-Amable, 1er étage, Québec PQ G1R 4Z1, 418/643-9818; Toll Free: 1-800-361-4743; Fax: 418/646-5426
Régie des rentes, 2600, boul Laurier, Ste-Foy PQ G1V 4T3, 418/643-8302; Fax: 418/643-9586
Sask.: Saskatchewan Crown Investments Corporation, #400, 2400 College Ave., Regina SK S4P 1C8, 306/787-6851; Fax: 306/787-8125
Saskatchewan Finance, Saskatchewan Pension Plan, 2350 Albert St., Regina SK S4P 4A6, 306/463-5412; Fax: 306/463-3500
Saskatchewan Justice, 1874 Scarth St., Regina SK S4P 3V7, 306/787-2458; Fax: 306/787-9779

PERFORMING ARTS See ARTS & CULTURE

PIPELINES
National Energy Board, 311 - 6th Ave. SW, Calgary AB T2P 3H2, 403/292-4800; Fax: 403/292-5503
Northern Pipeline Agency Canada, Lester B. Pearson Bldg., 125 Sussex Dr., Ottawa ON K1A 0G2, 613/993-7466; Fax: 613/998-8787
Transportation Safety Board of Canada, 200 Promenade du Portage, 4e étage, Hull PQ K1A 1K8, 819/994-3741; Fax: 819/997-2239
Alta: Alberta Energy, Petroleum Plaza, North Tower, 9945 - 108 St., Edmonton AB T5K 2G6, 403/427-7425; Fax: 403/427-3198
Man.: Manitoba Energy & Mines, Pipelines & Surface Rights, 360 - 1395 Ellice Ave, Winnipeg MB R3G 3P2, 204/945-6574; Toll Free: 1-800-282-8069 (Energy); Fax: 204/945-0586
Qué.: Régie du gaz naturel, Tour de la Bourse, #255, 800, Place Victoria, CP 001, Montréal PQ H4Z 1A2, 514/873-2452; Fax: 514/873-2070
Sask.: Saskatchewan Energy & Mines, Engineering Services Branch, 1914 Hamilton St., Regina SK S4P 4V4, 306/787-2318; Fax: 306/787-2478

POLICING SERVICES
Justice Canada, Legal Operations Sector, Justice Bldg., 239 Wellington St., Ottawa ON K1A 0H8, 613/957-4222; Fax: 613/954-0811
Royal Canadian Mounted Police, 1200 Vanier Pkwy., Ottawa ON K1A OR2, 613/993-1085; Fax: 613/993-5894
Solicitor General Canada, Policing & Law Enforcement, Sir Wilfrid Laurier Bldg., 340 Laurier Ave. West, Ottawa ON K1A 0P8, 613/990-2703; Fax: 613/993-5252
Alta: Alberta Justice, Public Security Division, 10365 - 97th St., Edmonton AB T5J 3W7, 403/427-2745; Fax: 403/427-1194
B.C.: British Columbia Police Commission, #405, 815 Hornby St., Vancouver BC V6Z 2E6, 604/660-2385; Fax: 604/660-1223
Ministry of the Attorney General, Police Services, 910 Government St., 5th Fl., Victoria BC V8V 1X4, 250/356-5483; Fax: 250/356-7747
Man.: Law Enforcement Review Agency, 405 Broadway, 12th Fl., Winnipeg MB R3C 3L6, 204/945-8667; Fax: 204/945-6692
Manitoba Justice, 405 Broadway, 5th Fl., Winnipeg MB R3C 3L6, 204/945-2852
N.B.: Department of the Solicitor General, Barker House, 4th Fl., PO Box 6000, Fredericton NB E3B 5H1, 506/453-3603; Fax: 506/457-4957
New Brunswick Police Commission, #103, 191 Prospect St. West, Fredericton NB E3B 2T7, 506/453-2069; Fax: 506/457-3542
Nfld.: Department of Justice & Attorney General, Royal Newfoundland Constabulary, Confederation Bldg., PO Box 8700, St. John's NF A1B 4J6, 709/729-8151; Inquiries: 709/729-8000; Fax: 709/729-2129
Royal Newfoundland Constabulary Public Complaints Commission, PO Box 21128, St. John's NF A1A 5B2, 709/729-0950
NWT: Department of Justice, Law Enforcement, PO Box 1320, Yellowknife NT X1A 2L9, 403/873-7002
N.S.: Department of Justice, Policing Services Division, 5151 Terminal Rd., PO Box 7, Halifax NS B3J 2L6, 902/424-2504; Fax: 902/424-0700
Nova Scotia Police Commission, #300, 1601 Lower Water St., Halifax NS B3J 2Y3, 902/424-3246; Fax: 902/424-3919
Ont.: Ministry of the Solicitor General & Correctional Services, Ontario Provincial Police, 50 Andrew St. South, 3rd Fl., Orillia ON L3V 7T5, 705/497-9500
Policing Services Division, 25 Grosvenor St., 9th Fl., Toronto ON M7A 2H3, 705/497-9500
PEI: Department of Provincial Affairs & Attorney General, PO Box 2000, Charlottetown PE C1A 7N8, 902/368-5250; Fax: 902/368-5283; 5355
Qué.: Ministère de la Sécurité publique, Sécurité et Prévention, Tour des Laurentides, 2525, boul Laurier, 5e étage, Ste-Foy PQ G1V 2L2, 418/643-3500; Fax: 418/643-0275
Sask.: Saskatchewan Police Commission, 1874 Scarth St., 7th Fl., Regina SK S4P 3V7, 306/787-6534
Saskatchewan Police Complaints Investigator, 2151 Scarth St., 3rd Fl., Regina SK S4P 3V7, 306/787-6519; Fax: 306/787-6528

Saskatchewan Justice, Law Enforcement Services, 1874 Scarth St., Regina SK S4P 3V7, 306/787-0400; Fax: 306/787-3874
Saskatchewan Municipal Government, Protection Services Branch, 1855 Victoria Ave., Regina SK S4P 3V7, 306/787-4509; Fax: 306/787-9273
Yuk.: Yukon Community & Transportation Services, Public Safety Branch, PO Box 2703, Whitehorse YT Y1A 2C6, 403/667-5707; Fax: 403/393-6249

POLLUTION See AIR RESOURCES ; WATER RESOURCES

POPULATION
See Also Statistics
National Archives of Canada, 395 Wellington St., Ottawa ON K1A 0N3, 613/995-5138; Fax: 613/995-6274
Statistics Canada, R.H. Coats Bldg., Tunney's Pasture, 120 Parkdale Ave., Ottawa ON K1A 0T6, 613/951-8116; Toll Free: 1-800-263-1136, TDD: 1-800-363-7629; Fax: 613/951-0581
Alta: Alberta Municipal Affairs, Registries Division, John E. Brownlee Bldg., 10365 - 97 St., Edmonton AB T5J 3W7, 403/422-2362 (Edmonton), 297-8980 (Calgary); Toll Free: 1-800-465-5009 (in Alberta); Fax: 403/422-9105
B.C.: Ministry of Finance & Corporate Relations, Population Statistics, 617 Government St., Victoria BC V8V 1X4, 250/387-0337; Fax: 250/387-0380
Man.: Manitoba Bureau of Statistics, #333, 260 St. Mary Ave., Winnipeg MB R3C 0M6, 204/945-2982
N.B.: Department of Finance, New Brunswick Statistics Agency, PO Box 6000, Fredericton NB E3B 5H1, 506/453-7970; Fax: 506/453-2381
Nfld.: Department of Government Services & Lands, Vital Statistics, PO Box 8700, St. John's NF A1B 4J6, 709/729-3311
NWT: Department of Finance, Statistics Office, PO Box 1320, Yellowknife NT X1A 2L9, 403/873-7147; Fax: 403/873-0275

POSTAL SERVICE
Canada Post Corporation, 2701 Riverside Dr., Ottawa ON K1A 0B1, 613/734-8440; Toll Free: 1-800-267-1177

PREMIERS & LEADERS
See Also Cabinets & Executive Councils; Government (General Information)
Office of the Prime Minister, Langevin Block, 80 Wellington St., Ottawa ON K1A 0A2, 613/992-4211; Fax: 613/941-6900
Alta: Office of the Premier, Legislature Bldg., #307, 10800 - 97 Ave., Edmonton AB T5K 2B6, 403/427-2251; Fax: 403/427-1349
B.C.: Office of the Premier, #156, West Annex, Legislative Bldgs., Victoria BC V8V 1X4, 250/387-1715; Fax: 250/387-0087
Man.: Office of the Premier, Legislative Bldg., #204, 450 Broadway, Winnipeg MB R3C 0V8, 204/945-3714; Fax: 204/949-1484
N.B.: Office of the Premier, Centennial Bldg., 670 King St., PO Box 6000, Fredericton NB E3B 5H1, 506/453-2144; Fax: 506/453-7407
Nfld.: Office of the Premier, Confederation Bldg., 8th Fl., PO Box 8700, St. John's NF A1B 4J6; Fax: 709/729-5875
NWT: Office of the Premier, Lang Bldg., 5003 - 49 St., PO Box 1320, Yellowknife NT X1A 2L9, 403/873-7112; Fax: 403/873-0385

N.S.: Office of the Premier, One Government Place, 1700 Granville St., PO Box 726, Halifax NS B3J 1X5, 902/424-6600; Fax: 902/424-7648

Ont.: Office of the Premier, Legislative Bldg., #281, 1 Queen's Park Cres. South, Toronto ON M7A 1A1, 416/325-1941; TDD: 416/325-7702; Fax: 416/325-3745

PEI: Office of the Premier, Shaw Bldg., 95 Rochford St., 5th Fl. South, PO Box 2000, Charlottetown PE C1A 7N8, 902/368-4400; Fax: 902/368-4416

Qué.: Cabinet du premier ministre, Édifice J, 885, Grande-Allée est, 3e étage, Québec PQ G1A 1A2, 418/643-5321; Fax: 418/643-3924

Sask.: Office of the Premier, 2405 Legislative Dr., Regina SK S4S 0B3, 306/787-9433; Fax: 306/787-0885

Yuk.: Office of the Government Leader, PO Box 2703, Whitehorse YT Y1A 2C6, 403/667-5885; Fax: 403/667-3035

PRISONS See **CORRECTIONAL SERVICES**

PROPERTY See **REAL ESTATE**

PROTOCOL (STATE)
See Also **Parliament**

Canadian Heritage, Citizenship & Canadian Identity Sector, Jules Léger Bldg., 25 Eddy St., Hull PQ K1A 1K5, 819/997-0055; Fax: 819/953-5382

Foreign Affairs & International Trade Canada, Office of Protocol, Lester B. Pearson Bldg., 125 Sussex Dr., Ottawa ON K1A 0G2, 613/996-9134; Fax: 613/952-3904

Governor General & Commander-in-Chief of Canada, Rideau Hall, 1 Sussex Dr., Ottawa ON K1A 0A1, 613/993-8200; Fax: 613/990-7636

House of Commons, Canada, Parliamentary Exchanges & Protocol, House of Commons, 111 Wellington St., PO Box 1103, Ottawa ON K1A 0A9, 613/996-1102

Alta: Alberta Federal & Intergovernmental Affairs, Protocol Office, #2200, 10025 Jasper Ave., Edmonton AB T5J 1S6, 403/427-2611; Fax: 403/422-0786

B.C.: Ministry of Finance & Corporate Relations, Protocol & Events Branch, 617 Government St., Victoria BC V8V 1X4, 250/387-4304; Fax: 250/356-2814

N.B.: Department of Intergovernmental & Aboriginal Affairs, Office of Protocol, PO Box 6000, Fredericton NB E3B 5H1, 506/453-2671; Fax: 506/453-2995

NWT: Office of the Premier, Protocol Office, Lang Bldg., 5003 - 49 St., PO Box 1320, Yellowknife NT X1A 2L9, 403/873-7153; Fax: 403/873-0385

N.S.: Executive Council, One Government Place, PO Box 2125, Halifax NS B3J 3B7, 902/424-4463; Fax: 902/424-4309

Ont.: Ministry of Economic Development, Trade & Tourism, International Relations & Protocol Branch, Hearst Block, 900 Bay St., Toronto ON M7A 2E1, 416/325-8545; Fax: 416/325-8550

PEI: Office of the Premier, Protocol, Shaw Bldg., 95 Rochford St., 5th Fl. South, PO Box 2000, Charlottetown PE C1A 7N8, 902/368-4400; Fax: 902/368-4416

Qué.: Ministère des Relations Internationales, Protocole, Édifice Hector-Fabre, 525, boul Réne-Levesque est, Québec PQ G1R 5R9, 418/649-2346; Fax: 418/649-2657

Sask.: Saskatchewan Intergovernmental Affairs, Protocol Office, 1919 Saskatchewan Dr., Regina SK S4P 3V7, 306/787-3109; Fax: 306/787-1269

PUBLIC HEALTH See **HEALTH SERVICES**

PUBLIC SAFETY
See Also **Occupational Safety**

Atomic Energy Control Board, Reactor Regulation Directorate, 280 Slater St., PO Box 1046, Stn B, Ottawa ON K1P 5S9, 613/995-5894; Toll Free: 1-800-668-5284; Fax: 613/995-5086

Canadian Centre for Occupational Health & Safety, 250 Main St. East, Hamilton ON L8N 1H6, 905/572-2981; Toll Free: 1-800-263-8466; Fax: 905/572-2206

Canadian Transportation Agency, Ottawa ON K1A 0N9, 819/997-0344 (Communications); Fax: 819/953-8353

Fisheries & Oceans Canada, Canadian Coast Guard, Canada Bldg., 344 Slater St., Ottawa ON K1A 0N7, 613/998-1574; Fax: 613/990-2780

Foreign Affairs & International Trade Canada, International Security Bureau, Arms Control & CSCE Affairs, Lester B. Pearson Bldg., 125 Sussex Dr., Ottawa ON K1A 0G2, 613/992-3402; Fax: 613/952-3904

Health Canada, Health Protection Branch, Ottawa ON K1A 0L2, 613/957-2991; Fax: 613/941-5366

Industry Canada, Office of Consumer Affairs, 235 Queen St., Ottawa ON K1A 0H5, 613/954-2788; Fax: 613/954-2303

National Defence (Canada), MGen. George R. Pearkes Bldg., 101 Colonel By Dr., Ottawa ON K1A 0K2, 613/992-4581

Royal Canadian Mounted Police, 1200 Vanier Pkwy., Ottawa ON K1A 0R2, 613/993-1085; Fax: 613/993-5894

Solicitor General Canada, Canadian Security Intelligence Service, PO Box 9732, Ottawa ON K1G 4G4, 613/993-9620; Fax: 613/993-7062

National Security, Sir Wilfrid Laurier Bldg., 340 Laurier Ave. West, Ottawa ON K1A 0P8, 613/993-4136; Fax: 613/990-3632

Transport Canada, Safety & Security Group, Transport Canada Building, 330 Sparks St., Ottawa ON K1A 0N5, 613/990-2309; Fax: 613/995-0351

Alta: Alberta Health, Area Services Division, PO Box 222, Edmonton AB T5J 2P4, 403/427-7164

Alberta Justice, Public Security Division, 10365 - 97th St., Edmonton AB T5J 3W7, 403/427-2745; Fax: 403/427-1194

Alberta Transportation & Utilities, Disaster & Emergency Programs, Twin Atria, 4999 - 98 Ave., Edmonton AB T6B 2X3, 403/422-9000; Fax: 403/422-6515

B.C.: Ministry of the Attorney General, Public Safety & Regulatory Branch, 910 Government St., 5th Fl., Victoria BC V8V 1X4, 250/356-9596 (Policy & Education); Fax: 250/356-9037

Man.: Manitoba Health, Community & Mental Health Services Division, 599 Empress St., Winnipeg MB R3G 3H2, 204/786-7191 (Finance & Administration Branch); Fax: 204/774-1325

N.B.: Department of Municipalities, Culture & Housing, Housing & Public Safety Services Division, Marysville Place, 20 McGloin St., PO Box 6000, Fredericton NB E3B 5H1, 506/453-4991; Fax: 506/457-4991

Nfld.: Department of Justice & Attorney General, Public Protection & Support Services, Confederation Bldg., PO Box 8700, St. John's NF A1B 4J6, 709/729-5942; Fax: 709/729-2129

NWT: Department of Justice, Law Enforcement, PO Box 1320, Yellowknife NT X1A 2L9, 403/873-7002

Northwest Territories Emergency Measures Organization, Northwest Tower, #600, 5201 - 50 Ave., Yellowknife NT X1A 3S9, 403/873-7554; Fax: 403/873-8193

N.S.: Department of Labour, Public Safety, 5151 Terminal Rd., PO Box 697, Halifax NS B3J 2T8, 902/424-4125; Fax: 902/424-3239

Ont.: Ministry of the Solicitor General & Correctional Services, Public Safety Division, 200 - 1 Ave. West, North Bay ON P1B 9M3, 416/314-3382; Fax: 416/314-3388

PUBLIC TRUSTEE

Alta: Alberta Justice, Office of the Public Trustee, #400S, 10365 - 97th St., Edmonton AB T5J 3Z8, 403/427-2744; Fax: 403/422-9136

B.C.: Office of the Public Trustee, #600, 808 West Hastings St., Vancouver BC V6C 3L3, 604/660-4444; Fax: 604/660-4456

Man.: Manitoba Justice, Office of the Public Trustee, 405 Broadway, 7th Fl., Winnipeg MB R3C 3L6, 204/945-2703

NWT: Department of Justice, Public Trustee's Office, PO Box 1320, Yellowknife NT X1A 2L9, 403/873-7464

Ont.: Ministry of the Attorney General, Office of the Public Trustee, 720 Bay St., 11th Fl., Toronto ON M5G 2K1, 416/314-2690; General Inquiry: 416/314-2800; Fax: 416/314-2716

Qué.: Curateur public du Québec, #500, 600, boul René-Lévesque ouest, Montréal PQ H3B 4W9, 514/873-4074; Fax: 514/873-4972

Sask.: Saskatchewan Justice, Public Trustees' Office, 1874 Scarth St., Regina SK S4P 3V7, 306/787-5427; Fax: 306/787-3874

Yuk.: Yukon Justice, Official Guardian's Office, PO Box 2703, Whitehorse YT Y1A 2C6, 403/667-5366; Fax: 403/393-6272

PUBLIC UTILITIES

Alta: Alberta Energy & Utilities Board, 640 - 5 Ave. SW, Calgary AB T2P 3G4, 403/297-8311; Fax: 403/297-8398

Alberta Transportation & Utilities, Twin Atria, 4999 - 98 Ave., Edmonton AB T6B 2X3, 403/427-2731

B.C.: British Columbia Hydro & Power Authority, 6911 Southpoint Dr., Burnaby BC V3N 4X8, 604/528-1600; Fax: 604/623-3901

Man.: Public Utilities Board, 280 Smith St., 2nd Fl., Winnipeg MB R3C 1K2, 204/945-2638; Fax: 204/945-2643

N.B.: Board of Commissioners of Public Utilities, 110 Charlotte St., PO Box 5001, Saint John NB E2L 4Y9, 506/658-2504; Fax: 506/633-0163

Nfld.: Newfoundland & Labrador Hydro, PO Box 12400, St. John's NF A1B 4K7, 709/737-1400; Fax: 709/737-1231

Newfoundland & Labrador Public Utilities Commission, PO Box 21040, St. John's NF A1A 5B2, 709/726-0955; Fax: 709/726-9604

NWT: Northwest Territories Power Corporation, 4 Capital Drive, Hay River NT X0E 1G2, 403/874-5200; Fax: 403/874-5251

Northwest Territories Water Board, PO Box 1500, Yellowknife NT X1A 2R3, 403/920-8191; Fax: 403/873-9572

Public Utilities Board of the Northwest Territories, PO Bag 5006, Hay River NT X0E 0R0, 403/874-3944

N.S.: Department of the Environment, Utilities Division, PO Box 2107, Halifax NS B3J 3B7, 902/424-5300; Fax: 902/424-0503

Nova Scotia Utility & Review Board, #300, 1601 Lower Water St., PO Box 1692, Stn M, Halifax NS B3J 3S3, 902/424-4448; Fax: 902/424-3919

Ont.: Ontario Energy Board, 2300 Yonge St., 23rd Fl., PO Box 2382, Toronto ON M4P 1E4, 416/481-1967; Fax: 416/440-7656

Ontario Hydro, 700 University Ave., Toronto ON M5G 1X6, 416/592-5111; Toll Free: 1-800-263-9000

PEI: Island Regulatory & Appeals Commission, 134 Kent St., PO Box 577, Charlottetown PE C1A 7L1, 902/892-3501; Fax: 902/566-4076

Prince Edward Island Energy Corporation, 11 Kent St., PO Box 2000, Charlottetown PE C1A 7N8, 902/368-4220; Fax: 902/368-5982

Qué.: Hydro-Québec, 75, boul René-Lévesque ouest, Montréal PQ H2Z 1A4, 514/289-2211; Fax: 514/843-3163

Sask.: SaskEnergy Incorporated, #1100, 1945 Hamilton St., Regina SK S4P 2C7, 306/777-9426; Fax: 306/777-9889

Saskatchewan Water Corporation (Sask Water), Victoria Place, 111 Fairford St. East, Moose Jaw SK S6H 7X9, 306/694-3900; Fax: 306/694-3944

Yuk.: Yukon Utilities Board, PO Box 6070, Whitehorse YT Y1A 5L7, 403/667-5058

Yukon Energy Corporation, #304, 204 Lambert St., Whitehorse YT Y1A 1Z4, 403/667-5028; Fax: 403/393-6327

PUBLIC WORKS & SERVICES

Canada Lands Company, #1500, 200 King St. West, Toronto ON M5H 3T4, 416/974-9700; Fax: 416/974-9661

Defence Construction Canada, Sir Charles Tupper Bldg., "A" Wing, Riverside Dr., 3rd Fl., Ottawa ON K1A 0K3, 613/998-9548; Fax: 613/998-1061

Public Works & Government Services Canada, Place du Portage, Phase III, 11, rue Laurier, Hull PQ K1A 0S5, 819/956-3115; TDD: 819/994-5389

Alta: Alberta Public Works, Supply & Services, 6950 - 113th St., 3rd Fl., Edmonton AB T6H 5V7, 403/422-0326; Fax: 403/427-0812

B.C.: Ministry of Transportation & Highways, Planning & Major Projects Department, 940 Blanshard St., Victoria BC V8W 3E6, 250/387-7788 (Public Affairs); Fax: 250/356-7706

Man.: Manitoba Government Services, Administration & Finance Division, Woodsworth Bldg., 405 Broadway, 15th Fl., Winnipeg MB R3C 3L6, 204/945-3001

N.B.: New Brunswick, Services Division, Central Purchasing Branch, #205, Marysville Place, PO Box 6000, Fredericton NB E3B 5H1, 506/453-2245

Nfld.: Department of Works, Services & Transportation, Confederation Bldg., PO Box 8700, St. John's NF A1B 4J6, 709/729-3283; Fax: 709/729-0703

Works Branch, Confederation Bldg., PO Box 8700, St. John's NF A1B 4J6, 709/729-3283; Fax: 709/729-0703

NWT: Department of Public Works & Services, Bldg. YK-7, PO Box 1320, Yellowknife NT X1A 2L9, 403/873-7114; Fax: 403/873-0264

N.S.: Department of Transportation & Public Works, 1969 Upper Water St., PO Box 186, Halifax NS B3J 2N2, 902/424-5837

Ont.: Management Board of Cabinet, Communications, Ferguson Block, 77 Wellesley St. West, 12th Fl., Toronto ON M7A 1N3, 416/326-9091; Fax: 416/327-3790

PEI: Department of Transportation & Public Works, Jones Bldg., PO Box 2000, Charlottetown PE C1A 7N8, 902/368-5100; Fax: 902/368-5395

Qué.: Ministère des Affaires Municipales, Infrastructures et financement municipal, Édifice Cook-Chauveau, 20, rue Chauveau, Québec PQ G1R 4J3, 418/691-2007; Fax: 418/646-9149

Société immobilière du Québec, 475, rue St-Amable, Québec PQ G1R 4X9, 418/646-1766 poste 3470; Fax: 418/643-7932

Sask.: Saskatchewan Highways & Transportation, Engineering Services Division, 1855 Victoria Ave., Regina SK S4P 3V5, 306/787-4804; Fax: 306/787-9777

Saskatchewan Municipal Government, Saskatchewan Infrastructure Program, 1855 Victoria Ave., Regina SK S4P 3V7, 306/787-8887; Fax: 306/787-3641

Saskatchewan Property Management Corporation, 1840 Lorne St., Regina SK S4P 3V7, 306/787-6911; Fax: 306/787-1061

Yuk.: Yukon Community & Transportation Services, Engineering & Development, PO Box 2703, Whitehorse YT Y1A 2C6, 403/667-5707; Fax: 403/667-6109

Yukon Government Services, Building Development, PO Box 2703, Whitehorse YT Y1A 2C6, 403/667-3064; Fax: 403/393-6218

PUBLICATIONS

Canadian Heritage, Publishing Policy & Programs, Jules Léger Bldg., 25 Eddy St., Hull PQ K1A 1K5, 613/990-4897; Fax: 613/941-8975

Public Works & Government Services Canada, Canada Communication Group, 45, boul Sacré-Coeur, Hull PQ K1A 0S7, 819/956-3115

Communications, Place du Portage, Phase III, 11, rue Laurier, Hull PQ K1A 0S5, 819/956-2304; TDD: 819/994-5389; Fax: 819/994-8404

Alta: Alberta Public Affairs Bureau, Publication Services, 11510 Kingsway Ave., 2nd Fl., Edmonton AB T5G 2Y5, 403/422-2787; Fax: 403/452-0668

B.C.: Ministry of Finance & Corporate Relations, Queen's Printer & Product Sales & Services, 617 Government St., Victoria BC V8V 1X4, 250/356-5849; Fax: 250/356-5851

Queen's Printer Financial & Administrative Services, 617 Government St., Victoria BC V8V 1X4, 250/387-4180; Fax: 250/387-0388

Man.: Manitoba Culture, Heritage & Citizenship, Provincial Services Division, 200 Vaughan St., Winnipeg MB R3C 1T5, 204/945-3729

Statutory Publications, 155 Carlton St., 10th Fl., Winnipeg MB R3C 3H8, 204/945-3101; Fax: 204/945-7172

N.B.: Department of Justice, Office of the Queen's Printer, PO Box 6000, Fredericton NB E3B 5H1, 506/453-2520; Fax: 506/453-7408

Nfld.: Department of Works, Services & Transportation, Printing Services & Queen's Printer, Confederation Bldg., PO Box 8700, St. John's NF A1B 4J6, 709/729-3210; Fax: 709/729-0703

Ont.: Management Board of Cabinet, Publishing Inc., Ferguson Block, 77 Wellesley St. West, 12th Fl., Toronto ON M7A 1N3, 416/325-1353; Fax: 416/325-1367

Queen's Printer (Publications Ontario), 77 Wellesley St. West, 12th Fl., Toronto ON M7A 1N3, 416/326-5316; Fax: 416/327-3517

PEI: Department of the Provincial Treasury, PO Box 2000, Charlottetown PE C1A 7N8, 902/368-5190, 5084; Fax: 902/368-5544

Qué.: Ministère de la Culture et des Communications, Communications, 225, Grand-Allée est, Québec PQ G1R 5G5, 418/643-6300; Fax: 418/643-4457

Sask.: Saskatchewan Justice, Queen's Printer, 1874 Scarth St., Regina SK S4P 3V7, 306/787-9345; Fax: 306/787-9111

Yuk.: Yukon Government Services, Queen's Printer, PO Box 2703, Whitehorse YT Y1A 2C6, 403/667-3585; Fax: 403/668-3585

RADIO & TELEVISION See BROADCASTING

RAIL TRANSPORTATION
See Also Transportation

Canadian National Railway Company, PO Box 8100, Montréal PQ H3C 3N4, 514/399-5430; Fax: 514/399-5586, 5479

Transport Canada, Railway Legislation, Transport Canada Building, 330 Sparks St., Ottawa ON K1A 0N5, 613/993-7392; Fax: 613/990-7767

Transportation Safety Board of Canada, 200 Promenade du Portage, 4e étage, Hull PQ K1A 1K8, 819/994-3741; Fax: 819/997-2239

Via Rail Canada Inc., 2, Place Ville-Marie, CP 8116, Succ A, Montréal PQ H3C 3N3, 514/871-6000; Fax: 514/861-6463

Alta: Alberta Resources Railway, #501, 10130 - 103 St., Edmonton AB T5J 3N9, 403/427-3165

B.C.: British Columbia Rail Ltd., PO Box 8770, Vancouver BC V6B 4X6, 604/984-5001; Fax: 604/984-5201

Ont.: GO Transit, 1120 Finch Ave. West, Toronto ON M3J 3J8, 416/869-3600; Fax: 416/869-1755

Ministry of Transportation, Freight Transportation Policy, 1201 Wilson Ave., Downsview ON M3M 1J8, 416/235-4039

Ontario Northland, 555 Oak St. East, North Bay ON P1B 8L3, 705/472-4500; Fax: 705/476-5598

Qué.: Ministère des Transports, 700, boul René-Lévesque est, Québec PQ G1R 5H1, 418/643-6740

Sask.: Saskatchewan Highways & Transportation, Grain & Rail Logistics, 1855 Victoria Ave., Regina SK S4P 3V5, 306/787-5311; Fax: 306/787-9777

REAL ESTATE
See Also Land Titles

Canada Mortgage & Housing Corporation, 700 Montreal Rd., Ottawa ON K1A 0P7, 613/748-2000; Fax: 613/748-2098

Justice Canada, Civil Litigation & Real Property Law (Québec) Section, Justice Bldg., 239 Wellington St., Ottawa ON K1A 0H8, 613/957-4670; Fax: 613/954-0811

Alta: Alberta Municipal Affairs, Registries Division, John E. Brownlee Bldg., 10365 - 97 St., Edmonton AB T5J 3W7, 403/422-2362 (Edmonton), 297-8980 (Calgary); Toll Free: 1-800-465-5009 (in Alberta); Fax: 403/422-9105

B.C.: Ministry of Environment, Lands & Parks, Lands & Water Management Department, 810 Blanshard St., 4th Fl., Victoria BC V8V 1X4, 250/387-1288; Fax: 250/387-5669

Real Estate Services Branch, 810 Blanshard St., 4th Fl., Victoria BC V8V 1X4, 250/387-1934; Fax: 250/387-5669

Real Estate Council of BC, 750 West Pender St., 9th Fl., Vancouver BC V6C 2T8, 604/683-9664; Fax: 604/683-9017

Man.: Manitoba Justice, Property Rights Division, 405 Broadway, 14th Fl., Winnipeg MB R3C 3L6, 204/945-2852

N.B.: Department of Justice, Consumer Affairs & Chief Rentalsman, #412, Centennial Bldg., PO Box 6000, Fredericton NB E3B 5H1, 506/453-2682; Fax: 506/444-4494

New Brunswick Real Estate Council, PO Box 785, Fredericton NB E3B 5B4, 506/455-9733; Fax: 506/450-8719

Nfld.: Department of Government Services & Lands, Real Estate & Landlord-Tenant Relations, PO Box 8700, St. John's NF A1B 4J6, 709/729-2608

Department of Works, Services & Transportation, Realty Services, Confederation Bldg., PO Box 8700, St. John's NF A1B 4J6, 709/729-3356; Fax: 709/729-0703

NWT: Department of Justice, PO Box 1320, Yellowknife NT X1A 2L9, 403/873-7453

Legal Registries/Land Titles, PO Box 1320, Yellowknife NT X1A 2L9, 403/873-7490

Ont.: Management Board of Cabinet, Real Estate Services Division, 777 Bay St., 16th Fl., Toronto ON M5G 2E5, 416/585-6777; Fax: 416/585-7577

Ministry of Consumer & Commercial Relations, Real Estate & Business Brokers, 250 Yonge St., 35th Fl., Toronto ON M5B 2N5, 416/326-8679; Fax: 416/326-8859

GOVERNMENT QUICK REFERENCE — RECREATION

Ministry of Finance, Property Assessment Division, Frost Bldg. South, 7 Queen's Park Cres., Toronto ON M7A 1Y7, 416/325-0333 (Communications & Corporate Affairs); Fax: 416/325-0339

PEI: Department of Provincial Affairs & Attorney General, Insurance & Real Estate Division, PO Box 2000, Charlottetown PE C1A 7N8, 902/368-4564; Fax: 902/368-5283; 5355

Qué.: Ministère des Ressources Naturelles, Terres, #B-302, 5700 - 4 av ouest, 3e étage, Charlesbourg PQ G1H 6R1, 418/646-2727 (Renseignements); Fax: 418/644-7160

Sask.: Saskatchewan Justice, Consumer Protection Branch, 1874 Scarth St., Regina SK S4P 3V7, 306/787-2952; Fax: 306/787-5550

Yuk.: Yukon Government Services, Property Management, PO Box 2703, Whitehorse YT Y1A 2C6, 403/667-5436; Fax: 403/393-6218

Yukon Justice, Land Titles, PO Box 2703, Whitehorse YT Y1A 2C6, 403/667-5612; Fax: 403/393-6272

RECREATION
See Also **Tourism & Tourist Information**

Canadian Heritage, Parks Canada Sector, Jules Léger Bldg., 25 Eddy St., Hull PQ K1A 1K5, 819/997-0055; Fax: 819/953-5382

Sport Canada, Jules Léger Bldg., 25 Eddy St., Hull PQ K1A 1K5, 819/956-8151; Fax: 819/956-8006

Industry Canada, C.D. Howe Bldg., 235 Queen St., Ottawa ON K1A 0H5, 613/957-4200; Fax: 613/954-2303

Alta: Alberta Sport, Recreation, Parks & Wildlife Foundation, Percy Page Centre, 11759 Groat Rd., Edmonton AB T5M 3K9, 403/427-1976; Fax: 403/488-9755

Alberta Community Development, Community & Citizenship Services Division, Standard Life Centre, 10405 Jasper Ave., 7th Fl., Edmonton AB T5J 4R7, 403/427-6530; Fax: 403/427-1496

B.C.: Ministry of Small Business, Tourism & Culture, Recreation Branch, 1117 Wharf St., Victoria BC V8W 2Z2, 250/356-1160; Fax: 250/387-4253

Man.: Manitoba Culture, Heritage & Citizenship, Recreation & Wellness Promotion, 213 Notre Dame., Winnipeg MB R3B 1N3, 204/945-0487; Fax: 204/945-1684

N.B.: Department of Municipalities, Culture & Housing, Sports, Recreation & Libraries Division, Marysville Place, 20 McGloin St., PO Box 6000, Fredericton NB E3B 5H1, 506/453-2690; Fax: 506/457-4991

NWT: Department of Municipal & Community Affairs, Sport & Recreation, #600, 5201 - 50th Ave., PO Box 1310, Yellowknife NT X1A 2L9, 403/873-7245; Fax: 403/920-6467

N.S.: Department of Natural Resources, Parks & Recreation (Belmont), Founder's Square, 1701 Hollis St., PO Box 698, Halifax NS B3J 2T9, 902/662-3030; Fax: 902/662-2160

Ont.: Ministry of Citizenship, Culture & Recreation, Recreation Division, 77 Bloor St. West, 6th Fl., Toronto ON M7A 2R9, 416/314-6200

Ministry of Consumer & Commercial Relations, Office of the Athletic Commissioner, 1075 Millwood Rd., Toronto ON M4G 1X6, 416/314-3630; Fax: 416/314-3623

PEI: Department of Economic Development & Tourism, Tourism PEI, Annex 1, West Royalty Industrial Park, 1 First Ave., Charlottetown PE C1E 1B0, 902/368-5540; Fax: 902/368-4438

Department of Education, Culture, Heritage & Recreation, Sullivan Bldg., 16 Fitzroy St., PO Box 2000, Charlottetown PE C1A 7N8, 902/368-4789; Fax: 902/368-4663

Qué.: Ministère des Affaires Municipales, Loisir et sports, Édifice Cook-Chauveau, 20, rue Chauveau, Québec PQ G1R 4J3, 418/691-2040; Fax: 418/643-7385

Tourisme Québec, #329, 2, Place Québec, Québec PQ G1R 2B5, 418/643-5959; Toll Free: 1-800-363-7777 (Tourism Information); Fax: 418/646-8723

Sask.: Saskatchewan Municipal Government, Sport, Recreation & Lotteries, 1855 Victoria Ave., Regina SK S4P 3V7, 306/787-5737; Fax: 306/787-8560

Yuk.: Yukon Community & Transportation Services, Sport & Recreation Branch, PO Box 2703, Whitehorse YT Y1A 2C6, 403/667-5608; Fax: 403/393-6416

REHABILITATION *See* DISABLED PERSONS SERVICES

RENT CONTROL *See* LANDLORD & TENANT REGULATIONS

RESOURCE DEVELOPMENT *See* NATURAL RESOURCES

SALES TAX

Revenue Canada, GST Rulings & Interpretations, Tower C, Vanier Towers, 25 McArthur Rd., Ottawa ON K1A 0L5, 613/952-9198

Alta: Alberta Treasury, Tax & Revenue Administration, Terrace Bldg., 9515 - 107 St., Edmonton AB T5K 2C3, 403/427-3035; Fax: 403/422-2463

B.C.: Ministry of Finance & Corporate Relations, Revenue Division, 617 Government St., Victoria BC V8V 1X4, 250/387-9278

Man.: Manitoba Finance, Taxation Division, 401 York Ave., 4th Fl., Winnipeg MB R3C 0P8, 204/945-3754; Fax: 204/945-8316

N.B.: Department of Finance, Revenue Division, PO Box 6000, Fredericton NB E3B 5H1, 506/453-2286; Fax: 506/457-7335

Nfld.: Department of Finance & Treasury Board, Tax Administration, Confederation Bldg., PO Box 8700, St. John's NF A1B 4J6, 709/729-2966; Fax: 709/729-2856

NWT: Department of Finance, PO Box 1320, Yellowknife NT X1A 2L9

N.S.: Department of Business & Consumer Services, Provincial Tax Commission, 1723 Hollis St., PO Box 755, Halifax NS B3J 2V4, 902/424-4411; Toll Free: 1-800-565-2336; Fax: 902/424-0523

Ont.: Ministry of Finance, Retail Sales Tax Branch, Frost Bldg. South, 7 Queen's Park Cres., Toronto ON M7A 1Y7, 905/433-6156; Fax: 416/325-0339

PEI: Department of the Provincial Treasury, Tax Administration, PO Box 2000, Charlottetown PE C1A 7N8, 902/368-4146; Fax: 902/368-6164

Qué.: Ministère du Revenu, 3800, rue De Marly, Ste-Foy PQ G1X 4A5

Sask.: Saskatchewan Finance, Revenue Division, 2350 Albert St., Regina SK S4P 4A6, 306/787-6768; Fax: 306/787-6544

Taxation & Intergovernmental Affairs Branch, 2350 Albert St., Regina SK S4P 4A6, 306/787-6731; Fax: 306/787-6544

SCHOOL BOARDS (383) *See* EDUCATION (245)

SCIENCE, TECHNOLOGY DEVELOPMENT
See Also **Business Development**

Agriculture & Agri-Food Canada, Central Experimental Farm, Sir John Carling Bldg., 930 Carling Ave., Ottawa ON K1A 0C5, 613/759-7865; Fax: 613/759-1970

Bayfield Institute for Marine Science & Surveys, 867 Lakeshore Rd., PO Box 5050, Burlington ON L7R 4A6, 905/336-4871; Fax: 905/336-6637

Canadian Space Agency, 6767, rte de l'Aéroport, Saint-Hubert PQ J3Y 8Y9, 514/926-4351; Fax: 514/926-4352

Industry Canada, National Advisory Council on Science & Technology Secretariat, C.D. Howe Bldg., 235 Queen St., Ottawa ON K1A 0H5, 613/998-1306; Fax: 613/990-2007

Spectrum, Information Technologies & Telecommunications, Journal Tower North, 300 Slater St., 20th Fl., Ottawa ON K1A 0C8, 613/954-2788; Fax: 613/954-2303

Institute of Ocean Sciences, 9860 West Saanich Rd., PO Box 6000, Sidney BC V8L 4B2, 250/363-6517; Fax: 250/353-6807

Medical Research Council of Canada, Tower B, Holland Cross, 1600 Scott St., 5th Fl., Ottawa ON K1A 0W9, 613/954-1809; Fax: 613/954-1800

National Research Council (Canada), Bldg. M-58, 1200 Montreal Rd., Ottawa ON K1A 0R6, 613/993-9101; Fax: 613/952-7928

Natural Sciences & Engineering Research Council of Canada, Constitution Square, 350 Albert St., Ottawa ON K1A 1H5, 613/996-7235; Fax: 613/992-5337

Office of the Nunavut Environmental Scientist, PO Box 1500, Yellowknife NT X1A 2R3, 403/920-8200; Fax: 403/920-7809

Alta: Alberta Economic Development & Tourism, Technology Development, Commerce Place, 10155 - 102 St., Edmonton AB T5J 4L6, 403/422-0626

Alberta Research Council, 250 Karl Clark Rd., PO Box 8330, Edmonton AB T6H 5X2, 403/450-5111; Fax: 403/461-2651

B.C.: Premiers' Advisory Council on Science & Technology, #501, 168 Chadwick Ct., North Vancouver BC V7M 3L4, 604/987-8477; Fax: 604/987-5617

Science Council of British Columbia, #800, 4710 Kingsway, Burnaby BC V5H 4M2, 604/438-2752; Toll Free: 1-800-665-7222; Fax: 604/438-6564

Man.: Economic Innovation & Technology Council, #648, 155 Carlton St., Winnipeg MB R3C 3H8, 204/945-5940; Fax: 204/945-8229

N.B.: Department of Economic Development & Tourism, Information Highway Secretariat, Centennial Bldg., 670 King St., 5th Fl., PO Box 6000, Fredericton NB E3B 5H1, 506/453-2850 (Communications & Promotion); Fax: 506/444-4586

New Brunswick Research & Productivity Council, 921 College Hill Rd., Fredericton NB E3B 6Z9, 506/452-8994; Fax: 506/452-1395

Nfld.: Department of Industry, Trade & Technology, Strategic Technologies, Confederation Annex, 4th Fl., PO Box 8700, St. John's NF A1B 4J6, 709/729-5652; Fax: 709/729-5936

Operation ONLINE, PO Box 8700, St. John's NF A1B 4J6, 709/729-0050

NWT: Aurora Research Institute, c/o Aurora College, PO Box 1430, Inuvik NT X0E 0T0

Nunavut Research Institute, Aeroplex Bldg., PO Box 160, Iqaluit NT X0A 0H0, 819/979-4114; Fax: 819/979-4119

N.S.: Nova Scotia Research Foundation Corporation, Woodside Industrial Park, 101 Research Dr., PO Box 790, Dartmouth NS B2Y 3Z7, 902/424-8670; Fax: 902/424-4679

Nova Scotia Technology & Science Secretariat, Maritime Centre, 1505 Barrington St., 14th Fl., PO Box 2311, Halifax NS B3J 3C8, 902/424-0377; Fax: 902/424-0129

Ont.: Ontario Science Centre, 770 Don Mills Rd., Toronto ON M3C 1T3, 416/696-2000; Fax: 416/696-3135

Science North, 100 Ramsey Lake Rd., Sudbury ON P3E 5S9, 705/522-3701; Fax: 705/522-4954

Qué.: Ministère de l'Industrie, du commerce, de la Science et de la technologie, Industrie et développement technologique, 710, Place d'Youville, 9e étage, Québec PQ G1R 4Y4, 418/691-5950 (Renseignements); Fax: 418/644-0118

Canadian Almanac & Directory 1997

Sask.: Saskatchewan Research Council, 15 Innovation Blvd., Saskatoon SK S7N 2X8, 306/933-5400; Fax: 306/933-7896

SECURITIES ADMINISTRATION
See Also Finance
Bank of Canada, Securities Department, 234 Wellington St., Ottawa ON K1A 0G9, 613/782-8111; Fax: 613/782-8655

Alta: Alberta Securities Commission, 10025 Jasper Ave., 19th Fl., Edmonton AB T5J 3Z5, 403/422-5201; Fax: 403/427-0777

B.C.: British Columbia Securities Commission, #1100, 865 Hornby St., Vancouver BC V6Z 2H4, 604/660-4800; Toll Free: 1-800-373-6393 (outside Vancouver area); Fax: 604/660-2688

Man.: Manitoba Securities Commission, #1128, 405 Broadway, Winnipeg MB R3C 3L6, 204/945-2548; Fax: 204/945-0330

N.B.: Department of Justice, Securities Administration, #412, Centennial Bldg., PO Box 6000, Fredericton NB E3B 5H1, 506/658-3060; Fax: 506/658-3059

Nfld.: Department of Government Services & Lands, Commercial & Corporate Affairs, PO Box 8700, St. John's NF A1B 4J6

NWT: Department of Justice, Legal Securities, PO Box 1320, Yellowknife NT X1A 2L9, 403/920-8987

N.S.: Nova Scotia Securities Commission, PO Box 458, Halifax NS B3J 2P8, 902/424-7768; Fax: 902/424-4625

Ont.: Ontario Securities Commission, #1800, 20 Queen St. West, Toronto ON M5H 3S8, 416/597-0681; Fax: 416/593-8240

Qué.: Commission des valeurs mobilières du Québec, Tour de la Bourse, 800, Place Victoria, 17e étage, Montréal PQ H4Z 1G3, 514/873-5326; Fax: 514/873-0711

Sask.: Saskatchewan Securities Commission, Toronto Dominion Bank Bldg., #850, 1914 Hamilton St., Regina SK S4P 3V7, 306/787-5645; Fax: 306/787-5899

SENIOR CITIZENS SERVICES
Human Resources Development Canada, Income Security Program, Place Vanier, 120 Parkdale Ave., Ottawa ON K1A 0L1, 819/994-6013

National Advisory Council on Aging, Postal Locator 4203A, Ottawa ON K1A 0K9, 613/957-1968; Fax: 613/957-7627

Alta: Seniors' Advisory Council for Alberta, 10025 Jasper Ave., Main Fl., Edmonton AB T5J 2N3, 403/422-2321; Fax: 403/422-3207

B.C.: Ministry of Health, Office for Seniors, 1515 Blanshard St., 7th Fl., Victoria BC V8W 3C8, 250/952-1238; Fax: 250/952-1159

Ministry of Social Services, Adult Residential Care, Parliament Bldgs., 614 Humboldt St., 7th Fl., Victoria BC V8V 1X4, 250/387-1275; Fax: 250/356-6534

Man.: Manitoba Council on Aging, #204, 800 Portage Ave., Winnipeg MB R3G 0W5, 204/945-1997

Manitoba Seniors Directorate, #822, 155 Carlton St., Winnipeg MB R3C 3H8, 204/945-2127; Fax: 204/948-2514

N.B.: Department of Health & Community Services, Seniors' Office, PO Box 5100, Fredericton NB E3B 5G8, 506/453-2480; Fax: 506/453-2082

Nfld.: Department of Health, Personal Care Home Program, West Block, Confederation Bldg., PO Box 8700, St. John's NF A1B 4J6, 709/772-3553; Fax: 709/729-5824

NWT: Department of Health & Social Services, Family Support & Child Protection, Centre Square Tower, 8th Fl., PO Box 1320, Yellowknife NT X1A 2L9, 403/920-6255; Fax: 403/873-0444

N.S.: Senior Citizens Secretariat, 1740 Granville St., 4th Fl., PO Box 2065, Halifax NS B3J 2Z1, 902/424-6322; Fax: 902/424-0561

Ont.: Ministry of Citizenship, Culture & Recreation, Seniors' Issues Group, 76 College St., 6th Fl., Toronto ON M7A 1N3, 416/327-2441; Fax: 416/327-2425

Ministry of Health, In-Home Services Branch, Hepburn Block, 8th Fl., Queen's Park, Toronto ON M7A 1S2, 416/326-9750; Toll Free: 1-800-668-2437 (AIDS Bureau); Fax: 416/327-8781

Ontario Advisory Council on Senior Citizens, 35 McCaul St., 3rd Fl., Toronto ON M5T 1V7, 416/314-6650 (Voice & TDD); Fax: 416/314-6658

PEI: Department of Health & Social Services, Jones Bldg., 11 Kent St., 2nd Fl., PO Box 2000, Charlottetown PE C1A 7N8, 902/368-4900; Fax: 902/368-4969

Health & Community Services Agency, 4 Sydney St., PO Box 2000, Charlottetown PE C1A 7N8, 902/368-6130; Fax: 902/368-6136

Qué.: Conseil des aînes, 1005, ch Ste-Foy, Québec PQ G1S 4N4, 418/643-6720; Fax: 418/646-9895

Ministère de la Santé et des services sociaux, 1075, ch Ste-Foy, Québec PQ G1S 2M1

Sask.: Saskatchewan Social Services, Community Living Division, Central Office, #216, 110 Ominica St. West, Moose Jaw SK S6H 6V2, 306/787-694-3800; Fax: 306/694-3842

Income Security Programs Division, 1920 Broad St., Regina SK S4P 3V6, 306/787-7469; Fax: 306/787-1032

Yuk.: Yukon Health & Social Services, PO Box 2703, Whitehorse YT Y1A 2C6, 403/667-3673 (Communications); Fax: 403/667-3096

SEXUALLY TRANSMITTED DISEASE CONTROL
See Also AIDS
Health Canada, Laboratory Centre for Disease Control, Ottawa ON K1A 0L2, 613/957-0315; Fax: 613/941-5366

Alta: Alberta Health, Centre for Disease Control, PO Box 222, Edmonton AB T5J 2P4, 403/427-7687

B.C.: Ministry of Health, Community Health Programs, 1515 Blanshard St., 7th Fl., Victoria BC V8W 3C8, 250/952-1544; Fax: 250/952-1426

Man.: Manitoba Health, Public Health & Epidemiology Branch, #301, 800 Portage Ave., Winnipeg MB R3G 0N4, 204/945-6720; Fax: 204/948-2190

N.B.: Department of Health & Community Services, PO Box 5100, Fredericton NB E3B 5G8, 506/453-3092; Fax: 506/444-4697

Nfld.: Department of Health, Disease Control & Epidemiology, West Block, Confederation Bldg., PO Box 8700, St. John's NF A1B 4J6, 709/729-3430; Fax: 709/729-5824

NWT: Department of Health & Social Services, Health Services Development, Centre Square Tower, 8th Fl., PO Box 1320, Yellowknife NT X1A 2L9, 403/920-6173; Fax: 403/873-0266

N.S.: Department of Health, Policy & Planning, Joseph Howe Bldg., 1690 Hollis St., 12th Fl., PO Box 488, Halifax NS B3J 2R8, 902/424-4310; Fax: 902/424-0559

Ont.: Ministry of Health, Health Information Centre, Hepburn Block, 8th Fl., Queen's Park, Toronto ON M7A 1S2, 416/314-8337; Toll Free: 1-800-268-1153; Fax: 416/314-8721

PEI: Department of Health & Social Services, Jones Bldg., 11 Kent St., 2nd Fl., PO Box 2000, Charlottetown PE C1A 7N8, 902/368-4996; Fax: 902/368-4969

Health & Community Services Agency, 4 Sydney St., PO Box 2000, Charlottetown PE C1A 7N8, 902/368-6130; Fax: 902/368-6136

Qué.: Ministère de la Santé et des services sociaux, Santé publique, 1075, ch Ste-Foy, Québec PQ G1S 2M1, 418/646-3487; Fax: 418/528-2651

Sask.: Saskatchewan Health, 3475 Albert St., Regina SK S4S 6X6, 306/787-1580; Fax: 306/787-8310
, 3475 Albert St., Regina SK S4S 6X6, 306/787-8332; Fax: 306/787-8310

Wellness & Health Promotion Branch, 3475 Albert St., Regina SK S4S 6X6, 306/787-3083; Fax: 306/787-8310

Yuk.: Yukon Health & Social Services, Health Services Branch, PO Box 2703, Whitehorse YT Y1A 2C6, 403/667-3673 (Communications); Fax: 403/667-3096

SMALL BUSINESS DEVELOPMENT See BUSINESS DEVELOPMENT; INDUSTRY

SNOWMOBILES See LEISURE CRAFT & VEHICLE REGULATIONS

SOCIAL SERVICES
See Also Community Services
Citizenship & Immigration Canada, Social Policy, Journal Tower South, 365 Laurier Ave. West, Hull PQ K1A 1L1, 613/957-5915; Fax: 613/957-5955

Human Resources Development Canada, Employment, Social Development & Education Group, Place du Portage, Phase IV, 140, Promenade du Portage, Hull PQ K1A 0J9, 819/994-6013

Veterans Affairs Canada, Veterans Services, Daniel J. MacDonald Bldg., 161 Grafton St., PO Box 7700, Charlottetown PE C1A 8M9, 902/566-8195; Fax: 902/566-8508

Alta: Alberta Family & Social Services, Seventh St. Plaza, 10030 - 107 St., Edmonton AB T5J 3E4, 403/427-2734; Fax: 403/422-9044

B.C.: Ministry of Social Services, Parliament Bldgs., 614 Humboldt St., 7th Fl., Victoria BC V8V 1X4, 250/387-6485; Fax: 250/356-7801

Man.: Manitoba Family Services, Finance & Administration, #219, 114 Garry St., Winnipeg MB R3C 4V6, 204/945-3080; Fax: 204/945-2760

N.B.: Department of Health & Community Services, Family & Community Social Services Division, PO Box 5100, Fredericton NB E3B 5G8, 506/453-2536; Fax: 506/444-4697

Department of Human Resources Development, PO Box 6000, Fredericton NB E3B 5H1, 506/453-2001; Fax: 506/453-7478

Nfld.: Department of Social Services, Confederation Bldg., PO Box 8700, St. John's NF A1B 4J6, 709/729-2478; Fax: 709/729-6996

Social Services Appeal Board, Confederation Bldg., PO Box 8700, St. John's NF A1B 4J6

NWT: Department of Health & Social Services, Community Programs & Services, Centre Square Tower, 8th Fl., PO Box 1320, Yellowknife NT X1A 2L9, 403/920-6173; Fax: 403/873-0266

N.S.: Department of Community Services, Family & Children's Services, Johnston Bldg., 5182 Prince St., 5th Fl., PO Box 696, Halifax NS B3J 2T7, 902/424-4326; Fax: 902/424-0502

Ont.: Ministry of Community & Social Services, Program Management Division, Hepburn Block, 80 Grosvenor St., 6th Fl., Toronto ON M7A 1E9, 416/325-5666; Fax: 416/325-5172, 5171

Social Assistance Review Board, 1075 Bay St., 7th Fl., Toronto ON M5S 2B1, 416/326-5104; Toll Free: 1-800-387-5655; Fax: 416/326-5135

PEI: Department of Health & Social Services, Jones Bldg., 11 Kent St., 2nd Fl., PO Box 2000, Charlottetown PE C1A 7N8, 902/368-4900; Fax: 902/368-4969

Health & Community Services Agency, 4 Sydney St., PO Box 2000, Charlottetown PE C1A 7N8, 902/368-6130; Fax: 902/368-6136

Canadian Almanac & Directory 1997

Qué.: Ministère de la Santé et des services sociaux, 1075, ch Ste-Foy, Québec PQ G1S 2M1
Sask.: Saskatchewan Social Services, 1920 Broad St., Regina SK S4P 3V6, 306/787-3494; Fax: 306/787-1032
Yuk.: Yukon Health & Social Services, Social Services Branch, PO Box 2703, Whitehorse YT Y1A 2C6, 403/667-3673 (Communications); Fax: 403/667-3096

SOLICITORS GENERAL
Solicitor General Canada, Sir Wilfrid Laurier Bldg., 340 Laurier Ave. West, Ottawa ON K1A 0P8, 613/990-2733; Fax: 613/993-7062
Man.: Manitoba Justice, 405 Broadway, 5th Fl., Winnipeg MB R3C 3L6, 204/945-2852
N.B.: Department of the Solicitor General, Barker House, 4th Fl., PO Box 6000, Fredericton NB E3B 5H1, 506/453-7414; Fax: 506/453-3870
NWT Department of Justice, Solicitor General Branch, PO Box 1320, Yellowknife NT X1A 2L9, 403/873-7005
Ont.: Ministry of the Solicitor General & Correctional Services, Communications Branch, 200 - 1 Ave. West, North Bay ON P1B 9M3, 416/326-5010
Qué.: Ministère de la Sécurité publique, Tour des Laurentides, 2525, boul Laurier, 5e étage, Ste-Foy PQ G1V 2L2, 418/643-3500; Fax: 418/643-0275

SPACE & ASTRONOMY
Canadian Space Agency, 6767, rte de l'Aéroport, Saint-Hubert PQ J3Y 8Y9, 514/926-4351; Fax: 514/926-4352
Environment Canada, Canadian Meteorological Centre (Montréal), 4905 Dufferin St., Downsview ON M3H 5T4, 514/421-4601; Fax: 514/421-4600
Herzberg Institute of Astrophysics, 100 Sussex Dr., Ottawa ON K1A 0R6, 613/990-0907; Fax: 613/952-6602
Industry Canada, Aerospace & Defence, C.D. Howe Bldg., 235 Queen St., Ottawa ON K1A 0H5, 613/954-3343; Fax: 613/941-2379
Institute for Aerospace Research, 1500 Montreal Rd., Ottawa ON K1A 0R6, 613/993-0141; Fax: 613/952-7214
Natural Resources Canada, Canada Centre for Remote Sensing, 588 Booth St., Ottawa ON K1A 0Y7, 613/947-1216; Fax: 613/947-3125

SPILLS *See* **EMERGENCY RESPONSE**

SPORTS *See* **RECREATION**

STANDARDS
Canadian Transportation Agency, Ottawa ON K1A 0N9, 819/997-0344 (Communications); Fax: 819/953-8353
Environment Canada, Environmental Protection Service, Place Vincent-Massey, 351, boul St-Joseph, Hull PQ K1A 0H3, 819/997-2800; Fax: 819/953-2225
Institute for National Measurement Standards, 1500 Montreal Rd., Ottawa ON K1A 0R6, 613/990-8750; Fax: 613/952-5113
National Research Council (Canada), 1500 Montreal Rd., Ottawa ON K1A 0R6, 613/990-8750; Fax: 613/952-5113
Public Works & Government Services Canada, Canadian General Standards Board, 222 Queen St., Ottawa ON K1A 1G6, 613/941-8709; Fax: 819/953-1058
Standards Council of Canada, #1200, 45 O'Connor St., Ottawa ON K1P 6N7, 613/238-3222; Fax: 613/995-4564
Transport Canada, Safety & Security Group, Transport Canada Building, 330 Sparks St., Ottawa ON K1A 0N5, 613/990-2309; Fax: 613/995-0351

Transportation Safety Board of Canada, 200 Promenade du Portage, 4e étage, Hull PQ K1A 1K8, 819/994-3741; Fax: 819/997-2239
Ont.: Ministry of Consumer & Commercial Relations, Entertainment Standards, 1075 Millwood Rd., Toronto ON M4G 1X6, 416/314-3626; Fax: 416/314-3632
 Technical Standards Division, West Tower, 3300 Bloor St. West, 4th Fl., Toronto ON M8X 2X4, 416/326-8555; Fax: 416/325-2000

STATISTICS
See Also **Vital Statistics**
Human Resources Development Canada, Workplace Information, Place du Portage, Phase II, 165, rue Hôtel de Ville, Hull PQ K1A 0J2, 819/994-6119; TDD: 819/953-8000
Statistics Canada, R.H. Coats Bldg., Tunney's Pasture, 120 Parkdale Ave., Ottawa ON K1A 0T6, 613/951-8116; Toll Free: 1-800-263-1136, TDD: 1-800-363-7629; Fax: 613/951-0581
 Statistics Canada Regional Reference Centres, R.H. Coats Bldg., Tunney's Pasture, 120 Parkdale Ave., Ottawa ON K1A 0T6, ; Toll Free: 1-800-263-1136, TDD: 1-800-363-7629; Fax: 613/951-0581
Alta: Alberta Municipal Affairs, Registries Division, John E. Brownlee Bldg., 10365 - 97 St., Edmonton AB T5J 3W7, 403/422-2362 (Edmonton), 297-8980 (Calgary); Toll Free: 1-800-465-5009 (in Alberta); Fax: 403/422-9105
Man.: Manitoba Bureau of Statistics, #333, 260 St. Mary Ave., Winnipeg MB R3C 0M6, 204/945-2982
N.B.: Department of Finance, New Brunswick Statistics Agency, PO Box 6000, Fredericton NB E3B 5H1, 506/453-7970; Fax: 506/453-2381
NWT: Department of Finance, Statistics Office, PO Box 1320, Yellowknife NT X1A 2L9, 403/873-7147; Fax: 403/873-0275
N.S.: Department of Finance, Statistics Division, PO Box 187, Halifax NS B3J 2N3, 902/424-5691; Fax: 902/424-0714
Ont.: Ministry of Consumer & Commercial Relations, Registrar General Branch, 189 Red River Rd., PO Box 4600, Thunder Bay ON P7B 6L8, 807/343-7414; Toll Free: 1-800-461-2156; Fax: 807/343-7411
Qué.: Bureau de la statistique du Québec, 200, ch Ste-Foy, 5e étage, Québec PQ G1R 5T4, 418/691-2401; Toll Free: 1-800-463-4090; Fax: 418/643-4129
Sask.: Saskatchewan Finance, Bureau of Statistics, 2350 Albert St., Regina SK S4P 4A6, 306/787-6328; Fax: 306/787-6544
Yuk.: Executive Council, Bureau of Statistics, PO Box 2703, Whitehorse YT Y1A 2C6, 403/667-5640; Fax: 403/393-6203

STUDENT AID
Human Resources Development Canada, Student Assistance Branch/Education Support Branch, Place du Portage, Phase IV, 140, Promenade du Portage, Hull PQ K1A 0J9, 819/994-2377; Fax: 819/953-4226
Indian & Northern Affairs Canada, Indian Program & Funding Allocation Directorate, Tour Nord, Les Terrasses de la Chaudière, 10 Wellington St., Hull PQ K1A 0H4, 819/953-9540; Fax: 819/953-3017
Alta: Students Finance Board, Baker Centre, 10025 - 106 St., 10th Fl., Edmonton AB T5J 1G7, 403/427-2740; Fax: 403/422-4516
B.C.: Ministry of Education, Skills & Training, Policy, Planning & Special Programs Division, PO Box 9150, Stn Prov Govt, Victoria BC V8W 9H1, 250/356-2500; Fax: 250/356-5945
Man.: Manitoba Education & Training, Student Financial Assistance Program, Box 6, 693 Taylor Ave.,

Winnipeg MB R3M 3T9, 204/945-8729; Fax: 204/477-5596
N.B.: Department of Advanced Education & Labour, Student Services, Chestnut Complex, 470 York St., PO Box 6000, Fredericton NB E3B 5H1, 506/453-3358; Fax: 506/444-4333
Nfld.: Department of Education, Student Aid Division, Confederation Bldg., PO Box 8700, St. John's NF A1B 4J6, 709/729-5849; Fax: 709/729-5896
NWT: Department of Education, Culture & Employment, Early Childhood & School Services, PO Box 1320, Yellowknife NT X1A 2L9, 403/920-3491; Fax: 403/873-0155
N.S.: Department of Education & Culture, Student Assistance Office, 2021 Brunswick St., PO Box 578, Halifax NS B3J 2S9, 902/424-8433; Fax: 902/424-0540
Ont.: Ministry of Education & Training, Postsecondary Education Division, Mowat Block, 900 Bay St., Toronto ON M7A 1L2, 416/325-2929; Fax: 416/325-2934
PEI: Office of Higher Education, Training & Adult Learning, Student Aid, Shaw Bldg., 105 Rochford St., 3rd Fl., PO Box 2000, Charlottetown PE C1A 7N8, 902/368-4640; Fax: 902/368-6144
Qué.: Ministère de l'Éducation, Aide financière aux étudiants, 1035, rue De La Chevrotière, 15e étage, Québec PQ G1R 5A5, 418/646-5315; Fax: 418/646-6561
Sask.: Saskatchewan Post-Secondary Education & Skills Training, Student Support & Employment Services Branch, 2220 College Ave., Regina SK S4P 3V7, 306/787-5896
Yuk.: Yukon Education, Student Financial Assistance, PO Box 2703, Whitehorse YT Y1A 2C6, 403/667-5141; Fax: 403/667-4754

TAXATION
See Also **Sales Tax**
Finance Canada, Tax Policy Branch, Esplanade Laurier, 140 O'Connor St., Ottawa ON K1A 0G5, 613/992-1573; Fax: 613/996-8404
Indian Taxation Advisory Board, 90 Elgin St., 2nd Fl., Ottawa ON K1A 0H4, 613/954-9769; Fax: 613/954-2073
Revenue Canada, 875 Heron Rd., Ottawa ON K1A 0L8, 613/957-0275
Alta: Alberta Treasury, Tax & Revenue Administration, Terrace Bldg., 9515 - 107 St., Edmonton AB T5K 2C3, 403/427-3035; Fax: 403/422-2463
B.C.: Ministry of Finance & Corporate Relations, Revenue Division, 617 Government St., Victoria BC V8V 1X4, 250/387-9278
Man.: Manitoba Finance, Taxation Division, 401 York Ave., 4th Fl., Winnipeg MB R3C 0P8, 204/945-3754; Fax: 204/945-8316
N.B.: Department of Finance, Revenue Division, PO Box 6000, Fredericton NB E3B 5H1, 506/453-2286; Fax: 506/457-7335
 Taxation & Fiscal Policy, PO Box 6000, Fredericton NB E3B 5H1, 506/453-2286; Fax: 506/457-4989
Nfld.: Department of Finance & Treasury Board, Tax Administration, Confederation Bldg., PO Box 8700, St. John's NF A1B 4J6, 709/729-2966; Fax: 709/729-2856
NWT: Department of Finance, Tax Administration, PO Box 1320, Yellowknife NT X1A 2L9, 403/920-3470; Fax: 403/873-0325
N.S.: Department of Business & Consumer Services, Provincial Tax Commission, 1723 Hollis St., PO Box 755, Halifax NS B3J 2V4, 902/424-4411; Toll Free: 1-800-565-2336; Fax: 902/424-0523
Ont.: Ministry of Finance, Office of the Budget & Taxation, Frost Bldg. South, 7 Queen's Park Cres., Toronto ON M7A 1Y7, 416/325-0333 (Communications & Corporate Affairs); Fax: 416/325-0339

Tax Division, Frost Bldg. South, 7 Queen's Park Cres., Toronto ON M7A 1Y7, 416/325-0333 (Communications & Corporate Affairs); Fax: 416/325-0339
PEI: Department of the Provincial Treasury, Tax Administration, PO Box 2000, Charlottetown PE C1A 7N8, 902/368-4146; Fax: 902/368-6164
Qué.: Ministère du Revenu, 3800, rue De Marly, Ste-Foy PQ G1X 4A5
Sask.: Saskatchewan Finance, Revenue Division, 2350 Albert St., Regina SK S4P 4A6, 306/787-6768; Fax: 306/787-6544
Taxation & Intergovernmental Affairs Branch, 2350 Albert St., Regina SK S4P 4A6, 306/787-6731; Fax: 306/787-6544
Yuk.: Yukon Finance, Revenue Services, PO Box 2703, Whitehorse YT Y1A 2C6, 403/667-3074; Fax: 403/393-6217

TELECOMMUNICATIONS
See Also Broadcasting
Canadian Broadcasting Corporation, 1500 Bronson Ave., PO Box 8478, Ottawa ON K1G 3J5, 613/724-1200; TDD: 613/738-6686
Canadian Radio-Television & Telecommunications Commission, 1, du Portage Promenade, Terrasses de la Chaudière, Hull PQ J8X 4B1, 819/997-0313 (Public Affairs); Fax: 819/994-0218
Industry Canada, Communications Research Centre & Centre for Information Technologies Innovation, 3701 Carling Ave., PO Box 11490, Stn H, Ottawa ON K2H 8S2, 613/998-2264; Fax: 613/954-2303
Spectrum, Information Technologies & Telecommunications, Journal Tower North, 300 Slater St., 20th Fl., Ottawa ON K1A 0C8, 613/954-2788; Fax: 613/954-2303
Telecommunications Policy, Journal Tower North, 300 Slater St., 20th Fl., Ottawa ON K1A 0C8, 613/998-4241; Fax: 613/998-1256
Alta: Alberta Public Works, Supply & Services, Telecommunications Division, 6950 - 113th St., 3rd Fl., Edmonton AB T6H 5V7, 403/422-1140; Fax: 403/427-0238
B.C.: Ministry of Employment & Investment, Science, Technology & Capital Development Division, 712 Yates St., Victoria BC V8V 1X4, 250/356-5478; Fax: 250/387-4410
Man.: Manitoba Government Services, Telecommunications, 401 York Ave., Winnipeg MB R3C 0P8, 204/945-3001
Manitoba Industry, Trade & Tourism, Information & Telecommunications Initiative, 155 Carlton St., 6th Fl., Winnipeg MB R3C 3H8, 204/945-4287; Fax: 204/945-1354
Manitoba Telephone System, 489 Empress St., Winnipeg MB R3C 3V6, 204/941-4111; Fax: 204/956-0836
Nfld.: Department of Industry, Trade & Technology, Advanced Technology, Confederation Annex, 4th Fl., PO Box 8700, St. John's NF A1B 4J6, 709/729-5600; Fax: 709/729-5936
Ont.: Ministry of Economic Development, Trade & Tourism, Capital Goods & Technology Sectors Branch, Hearst Block, 900 Bay St., Toronto ON M7A 2E1, 416/326-9627; Fax: 416/325-6688
Qué.: Ministère de la Culture et des Communications, 225, Grand-Allée est, Québec PQ G1R 5G5, 418/643-2183; Fax: 418/643-4457
Régie des télécommunications du Québec, #5.00, 900 place d'Youville, Québec PQ G1R 3P7, 418/643-5560; Fax: 418/643-2960
Sask.: Saskatchewan Telecommunications (SaskTel), 2121 Saskatchewan Dr., Regina SK S4P 3Y2, 306/777-3737; Fax: 306/565-8717

TELEPHONES *See* **TELECOMMUNICATIONS**

TELEVISION *See* **BROADCASTING**

THIRD WORLD ASSISTANCE *See* **INTERNATIONAL AID**

TIMBER MANAGEMENT *See* **FOREST RESOURCES**

TOURISM & TOURIST INFORMATION
Canadian Heritage, Parks Canada Sector, Jules Léger Bldg., 25 Eddy St., Hull PQ K1A 1K5, 819/997-0055; Fax: 819/953-5382
Foreign Affairs & International Trade Canada, USA Trade, Tourism & Investment Bureau, Lester B. Pearson Bldg., 125 Sussex Dr., Ottawa ON K1A 0G2, 613/944-5725; Fax: 613/952-3904
Industry Canada, Tourism Canada, C.D. Howe Bldg., 235 Queen St., Ottawa ON K1A 0H5, 613/954-2788; Fax: 613/954-2303
Alta: Alberta Economic Development & Tourism, Tourism, Trade & Investment, Commerce Place, 10155 - 102 St., Edmonton AB T5J 4L6, 403/427-2280; Fax: 403/427-1700
B.C.: Ministry of Small Business, Tourism & Culture, Tourism Division, 1117 Wharf St., Victoria BC V8W 2Z2, 250/356-6363 (Tourism); Fax: 250/356-8248
Man.: Manitoba Industry, Trade & Tourism, Tourism Initiative, 155 Carlton St., 6th Fl., Winnipeg MB R3C 3H8, 204/945-3796; Toll Free: 1-800-665-0040, ext.TH6; Fax: 204/945-1354
N.B.: Department of Economic Development & Tourism, Tourism Directorate, Centennial Bldg., 670 King St., 5th Fl., PO Box 6000, Fredericton NB E3B 5H1, 506/453-4283; URL: http://www.gov.nb.ca/tourism/index.htm; Fax: 506/453-7127
Nfld.: Department of Tourism, Culture & Recreation, Confederation Bldg., PO Box 8700, St. John's NF A1B 4J6, 709/729-0928; Fax: 709/729-0662
Tourism & Craft Development, Confederation Bldg., PO Box 8700, St. John's NF A1B 4J6, 709/729-0928; Fax: 709/729-0662
NWT: Department of Resources, Wildlife & Economic Development, Parks & Tourism Division, #600, Scotia Centre, Bldg. Box 21, 5102 - 50 Ave., Yellowknife NT X1A 3S8, 403/873-7420, 7134; Fax: 403/873-0114
N.S.: Nova Scotia Economic Renewal Agency, Tourism Nova Scotia, 1800 Argyle St., PO Box 519, Halifax NS B3J 2R7, 902/424-8920; Fax: 902/424-0582
Ont.: Alberta Tourism Partnership, c/o Alberta Economic Development & Tourism, 10155 - 102 St., Edmonton ON T5J 4L6, 403/531-4671
Ministry of Economic Development, Trade & Tourism, Business Development & Tourism Division, Hearst Block, 900 Bay St., Toronto ON M7A 2E1, 416/325-6666; Fax: 416/325-6688
PEI: Department of Economic Development & Tourism, Tourism PEI, Annex 1, West Royalty Industrial Park, 1 First Ave., Charlottetown PE C1E 1B0, 902/368-5540; Fax: 902/368-4438
Qué.: Tourisme Québec, #329, 2, Place Québec, Québec PQ G1R 2B5, 418/643-5959; Toll Free: 1-800-363-7777 (Tourism Information); Fax: 418/646-8723
Sask.: Saskatchewan Tourism Authority, #500, 1900 Albert St., Regina SK S4P 4L9, 306/787-9600; Toll Free: 1-800-667-7191; Fax: 306/787-0715
Yuk.: Yukon Tourism, PO Box 2703, Whitehorse YT Y1A 2C6, 403/667-5430; Fax: 403/667-3546

TRADE
See Also Business Development; Imports
Agriculture & Agri-Food Canada, Market & Industry Services Branch, Sir John Carling Bldg., 930 Carling Ave., 5th Fl., Ottawa ON K1A 0C5, 613/759-7561; Fax: 613/759-7497
Business Development Bank of Canada, Tour de la Place-Victoria, #800, Place Victoria, CP 335, Montréal PQ H4Z 1L4, 514/283-5904; Toll Free: 1-888-463-6232; Fax: 514/283-0617
Canadian International Grains Institute, #1000, 303 Main St., Winnipeg MB R3C 3G7, 204/983-5344; Fax: 204/983-2642
Canadian International Trade Tribunal, Standard Life Centre, 333 Laurier Ave. West, Ottawa ON K1A 0G7, 613/990-2452; Fax: 613/990-2439
Canadian Wheat Board, 423 Main St., PO Box 816, Winnipeg MB R3C 2P5, 204/983-0239, 3416; Fax: 204/983-3841
Export Development Corporation, 151 O'Connor St., Ottawa ON K1A 1K3, 613/598-2500; Fax: 613/237-2690
Finance Canada, International Trade & Finance Branch, Esplanade Laurier, 140 O'Connor St., Ottawa ON K1A 0G5, 613/992-1573; Fax: 613/996-8404
Foreign Affairs & International Trade Canada, International Business Development Branch, Lester B. Pearson Bldg., 125 Sussex Dr., Ottawa ON K1A 0G2, 613/995-4128; Fax: 613/995-9604
Industry Canada, International Business, C.D. Howe Bldg., 235 Queen St., Ottawa ON K1A 0H5, 613/954-3508; Fax: 613/952-0540
North American Free Trade Agreement (NAFTA) Secretariat, Canadian Section, #705, 90 Sparks St., Ottawa ON K1P 5B4, 613/992-9388; Fax: 613/992-9392
Revenue Canada, Customs Border Services, 875 Heron Rd., Ottawa ON K1A 0L8, 613/957-0275
Trade Administration Branch, 875 Heron Rd., Ottawa ON K1A 0L8, 613/957-0275
Statistics Canada, Business & Trade Statistics, R.H. Coats Bldg., Tunney's Pasture, 120 Parkdale Ave., Ottawa ON K1A 0T6, 613/951-8116; Fax: 613/951-0581
Statistics Canada Regional Reference Centres, R.H. Coats Bldg., Tunney's Pasture, 120 Parkdale Ave., Ottawa ON K1A 0T6, ; Toll Free: 1-800-263-1136, TDD: 1-800-363-7629; Fax: 613/951-0581
Alta: Alberta Economic Development & Tourism, Tourism, Trade & Investment, Commerce Place, 10155 - 102 St., Edmonton AB T5J 4L6, 403/427-2280; Fax: 403/427-1700
Alberta Federal & Intergovernmental Affairs, Trade Policy Team, AGT Tower II, 10025 Jasper Ave., 23rd Fl., Edmonton AB T5J 1S6, 403/427-2611; Fax: 403/427-0939
B.C.: Ministry of Employment & Investment, British Columbia Trade & Investment Office, 712 Yates St., Victoria BC V8V 1X4, 250/953-4701; Fax: 250/387-7969
Office of the Premier, British Columbia Trade Development Corporation, #730, 999 Canada Place, Vancouver BC V6C 3E1, 604/844-1900; Fax: 604/660-2457
Man.: Manitoba Trading Corporation, 155 Carlton St., 4th Fl., Winnipeg MB R3C 3H8, 204/945-2420
Manitoba Development Corporation, #555, 155 Carlton St., Winnipeg MB R3C 3H8, 204/945-7626; Fax: 204/957-1793
Manitoba Industry, Trade & Tourism, 155 Carlton St., 6th Fl., Winnipeg MB R3C 3H8, 204/945-2066; Fax: 204/945-1354
N.B.: Department of Economic Development & Tourism, Centennial Bldg., 670 King St., 5th Fl., PO Box 6000, Fredericton NB E3B 5H1, 506/453-2850 (Communications & Promotion); Fax: 506/444-4586

Nfld.: Department of Industry, Trade & Technology, Confederation Annex, 4th Fl., PO Box 8700, St. John's NF A1B 4J6, 709/729-5600; Toll Free: 1-800-563-2299; Fax: 709/729-5936

NWT: Department of Resources, Wildlife & Economic Development, Strategic Planning Division, #600, Scotia Centre, Bldg. Box 21, 5102 - 50 Ave., Yellowknife NT X1A 3S8, 403/873-7420, 7134; Fax: 403/873-0114

Trade & Investment Division, #600, Scotia Centre, Bldg. Box 21, 5102 - 50 Ave., Yellowknife NT X1A 3S8, 403/873-7420, 7134; Fax: 403/873-0114

N.S.: Nova Scotia Economic Renewal Agency, Investment & Trade, 1800 Argyle St., PO Box 519, Halifax NS B3J 2R7, 902/424-8920; Fax: 902/424-0582

Ont.: Ministry of Economic Development, Trade & Tourism, Marketing & Trade Division, Hearst Block, 900 Bay St., Toronto ON M7A 2E1, 416/325-6666; Fax: 416/325-6688

Trade Policy Branch, Hearst Block, 900 Bay St., Toronto ON M7A 2E1, 416/325-6930; Fax: 416/325-6949

PEI: Department of Agriculture, Fisheries & Forestry, Trade Relations, Jones Bldg., 11 Kent St., PO Box 2000, Charlottetown PE C1A 7N8, 902/368-5087; Fax: 902/368-4857

Department of Economic Development & Tourism, Trade Development, Annex 2, West Royalty Park, 2 First Ave., Charlottetown PE C1E 1B0, 902/368-5954; Fax: 902/368-6301

Trade Development, Annex 2, West Royalty Park, 2 First Ave., Charlottetown PE C1E 1B0, 902/368-6307; Fax: 902/368-6301

Qué.: Ministère de l'Industrie, du commerce, de la Science et de la technologie, Commerce extérieur, 710, Place d'Youville, 9e étage, Québec PQ G1R 4Y4, 418/691-5950 (Renseignements); Fax: 418/644-0118

Ministère des Relations Internationales, Secteur affaires internationales, Édifice Hector-Fabre, 525, boul Réne-Levesque est, Québec PQ G1R 5R9, 418/649-2300; Fax: 418/649-2656

Sask.: Saskatchewan Trade & Export Partnership, 1919 Saskatchewan Dr., Regina SK S4P 3V7, 306/787-9210; Fax: 306/787-6666

Saskatchewan Economic Development, Market Development, 1919 Saskatchewan Dr., Regina SK S4P 3V7, 306/787-0927

Yuk.: Yukon Economic Development, Economic Programs Branch, 211 Main St., PO Box 2703, Whitehorse YT Y1A 2C6, 403/667-5466; Fax: 403/668-8601

TRADE-MARKS See PATENTS & COPYRIGHT

TRAINING See APPRENTICESHIP PROGRAMS; OCCUPATIONAL TRAINING

TRANSPORTATION

Centre for Surface Transportation Technology, U-89,, 1500 Montreal Rd., Ottawa ON K1A 0R6, 613/998-9639; Fax: 613/957-0831

Natural Resources Canada, Transportation Energy Use Division, 580 Booth St., Ottawa ON K1A 0E4, 613/996-7432; Fax: 613/992-1405

Transport Canada, Transport Canada Building, 330 Sparks St., Ottawa ON K1A 0N5, 613/990-2309; Fax: 613/995-0351

Transportation Safety Board of Canada, 200 Promenade du Portage, 4e étage, Hull PQ K1A 1K8, 819/994-3741; Fax: 819/997-2239

Alta: Alberta Public Works, Supply & Services, Transportation Utility Corridor Management, 6950 - 113th St., 3rd Fl., Edmonton AB T6H 5V7, 403/427-3881; Fax: 403/422-2661

Alberta Transportation & Utilities, Twin Atria, 4999 - 98 Ave., Edmonton AB T6B 2X3, 403/427-2731

Traffic Safety Board, Twin Atria Bldg., 4999 - 98 Ave., 1st Fl., Edmonton AB T6B 2X3, 403/427-7178; Fax: 403/427-1740

B.C.: British Columbia Transportation Financing Authority, 2250 Granville Square, Vancouver BC V6C 1S4, 604/775-1174; Fax: 604/775-2792

Ministry of Transportation & Highways, 940 Blanshard St., Victoria BC V8W 3E6, 250/387-7788 (Public Affairs); Fax: 250/356-7706

Man.: Manitoba Highways & Transportation, 215 Garry St., Winnipeg MB R3C 3Z1, 204/945-3888; Fax: 204/945-7610

N.B.: Department of Transportation, King Tower, Kings Pl., 2nd Fl., PO Box 6000, Fredericton NB E3B 5H1, 506/453-3626

New Brunswick Transportation Agency, Kings Place, PO Box 6000, Fredericton NB E3B 5H1, 506/453-2802; Fax: 506/453-2900

Nfld.: Department of Works, Services & Transportation, Transportation Branch, Confederation Bldg., PO Box 8700, St. John's NF A1B 4J6, 709/729-3283; Fax: 709/729-0703

NWT: Department of Transportation, Lahm Ridge Bldg., PO Box 1320, Yellowknife NT X1A 2L9, 403/920-3460; Fax: 403/873-0363

Transportation Planning, Lahm Ridge Bldg., PO Box 1320, Yellowknife NT X1A 2L9, 403/873-7666; Fax: 403/920-2565

N.S.: Department of Transportation & Public Works, Transportation Planning & Policy, 1969 Upper Water St., PO Box 186, Halifax NS B3J 2N2, 902/424-6726; Fax: 902/424-0517

Ont.: Ministry of Transportation, 1201 Wilson Ave., Downsview ON M3M 1J8, ; Toll Free: 1-800-268-4686

Ontario Highway Transport Board, 151 Bloor St. West, 10th Fl., Toronto ON M5S 2T5, 416/326-6739; Fax: 416/326-6728

PEI: Department of Transportation & Public Works, Buildings Division, Jones Bldg., PO Box 2000, Charlottetown PE C1A 7N8, 902/368-5100; Fax: 902/368-5395

Highway Operations Division, Jones Bldg., PO Box 2000, Charlottetown PE C1A 7N8, 902/368-5100; Fax: 902/368-5395

Qué.: Conseil de la Recherche et du développement en transport, #300, 6455, av Christophe-Colomb, Montréal PQ H2S 2G5, 514/274-3573; Fax: 514/274-9608

Ministère des Affaires Municipales, Infrastructures et financement municipal, Édifice Cook-Chauveau, 20, rue Chauveau, Québec PQ G1R 4J3, 418/691-2007; Fax: 418/646-9149

Ministère des Transports, Planification et technologie, 700, boul René-Lévesque est, Québec PQ G1R 5H1, 418/528-0808

Sask.: Saskatchewan Highways & Transportation, Logistics, Planning & Compliance Division, 1855 Victoria Ave., Regina SK S4P 3V5, 306/787-4804; Fax: 306/787-9777

Planning & Research, 1855 Victoria Ave., Regina SK S4P 3V5, 306/787-4838; Fax: 306/787-9777

Saskatchewan Municipal Government, Saskatchewan Infrastructure Program, 1855 Victoria Ave., Regina SK S4P 3V7, 306/787-8887; Fax: 306/787-3641

Yuk.: Yukon Community & Transportation Services, Transportation Engineering, PO Box 2703, Whitehorse YT Y1A 2C6, 403/633-7928; Fax: 403/677-2647

TRAPPING & FUR INDUSTRY

Environment Canada, Canadian Wildlife Service, Place Vincent-Massey, 351, boul St-Joseph, Hull PQ K1A 0H3, 819/997-1301; Fax: 819/953-7177

B.C.: Ministry of Environment, Lands & Parks, Wildlife Branch, 780 Blanshard St., Victoria BC V8V 1X4, 250/387-9731; Fax: 250/356-9145

N.B.: Department of Natural Resources & Energy, Fish & Wildlife, PO Box 6000, Fredericton NB E3B 5H1, 506/453-2440; Fax: 506/453-6699

NWT: Department of Resources, Wildlife & Economic Development, Fur Management, #600, Scotia Centre, Bldg. Box 21, 5102 - 50 Ave., Yellowknife NT X1A 3S8, 403/873-7771; Fax: 403/873-0114

N.S.: Department of Natural Resources, Enforcement & Hunter Safety, Founder's Square, 1701 Hollis St., PO Box 698, Halifax NS B3J 2T9, 902/424-5254; Fax: 902/424-7735

PEI: Department of Environmental Resources, Waterfowl & Furbearers Section, Jones Bldg., 11 Kent St., 4th Fl., PO Box 2000, Charlottetown PE C1A 7N8, 902/368-4666; Fax: 902/368-5830

Sask.: Saskatchewan Environment & Resource Management, Wildlife Branch, 3211 Albert St., Regina SK S4S 5W6, 306/787-2309; Email: dennis.sherratt.erm@govmail.gov.sk.ca; Fax: 306/787-9544

Yuk.: Yukon Renewable Resources, Wildlife Management, PO Box 2703, Whitehorse YT Y1A 2C6, 403/667-5177; Fax: 403/393-6213

UNEMPLOYMENT INSURANCE

Human Resources Development Canada, Insurance, Place du Portage, Phase IV, 140, Promenade du Portage, Hull PQ K1A 0J9, 819/997-8662

Unemployment Insurance Communications, Place du Portage, Phase IV, 140, Promenade du Portage, Hull PQ K1A 0J9, 819/953-7250

B.C.: Ministry of Social Services, Income Support, Parliament Bldgs., 614 Humboldt St., 7th Fl., Victoria BC V8V 1X4, 250/387-6485; Fax: 250/356-7801

Man.: Manitoba Family Services, Employment & Income Assistance Division, #219, 114 Garry St., Winnipeg MB R3C 4V6, 204/945-2324 (Policy & Planning); Fax: 204/945-2156

N.B.: Department of Human Resources Development, Income Security Division, PO Box 6000, Fredericton NB E3B 5H1, 506/453-2001; Fax: 506/453-7478

Nfld.: Department of Social Services, Income Support, Confederation Bldg., PO Box 8700, St. John's NF A1B 4J6, 709/729-3243; Fax: 709/729-6996

NWT: Department of Education, Culture & Employment, Income Security Branch, PO Box 1320, Yellowknife NT X1A 2L9, 403/920-6160; Fax: 403/920-0443

N.S.: Department of Community Services, Income & Employment Support, Johnston Bldg., 5182 Prince St., 5th Fl., PO Box 696, Halifax NS B3J 2T7, 902/424-4326; Fax: 902/424-0502

URBAN RENEWAL & DESIGN
See Also **Municipal Affairs**

Canada Mortgage & Housing Corporation, 700 Montreal Rd., Ottawa ON K1A 0P7, 613/748-2000; Fax: 613/748-2098

Treasury Board of Canada, Office of Infrastructure, West Tower, 300 Laurier Ave. West, 3rd Fl., Ottawa ON K1A 0R5, 613/952-3171; Fax: 613/952-7979

Alta: Alberta Municipal Affairs, Local Government Services Division, Commerce Place, 10155 - 102 St., Edmonton AB T5J 4L4, 403/427-2732; Fax: 403/422-9105

B.C.: Ministry of Municipal Affairs & Housing, Local Government Services, Municipal Affairs, PO Box 9490, Victoria BC V8W 9N7, 250/387-4089; Fax: 250/356-1070

Ministry of Transportation & Highways, Planning & Major Projects Department, 940 Blanshard St., Victoria BC V8W 3E6, 250/387-7788 (Public Affairs); Fax: 250/356-7706

Man.: Manitoba Urban Affairs, #203, 280 Broadway Ave., Winnipeg MB R3C 0R8; Fax: 204/945-1249

N.B.: Department of Municipalities, Culture & Housing, Downtown Development Branch, Marysville Place, 20 McGloin St., PO Box 6000, Fredericton NB E3B 5H1, 506/457-4947; Fax: 506/458-9369

Nfld.: Department of Municipal & Provincial Affairs, Urban & Rural Planning, West Block, Confederation Bldg., PO Box 8700, St. John's NF A1B 4J6, 709/729-3090

Newfoundland & Labrador Housing Corporation, 2 Canada Dr., PO Box 220, St. John's NF A1C 5J2, 709/724-3000; Fax: 709/724-3250

NWT: Department of Municipal & Community Affairs, Community Planning & Lands, #600, 5201 - 50th Ave., PO Box 1310, Yellowknife NT X1A 2L9, 403/920-8916; Fax: 403/920-6343

Ont.: Ministry of Municipal Affairs & Housing, Municipal Operations Division, 777 Bay St., 17th Fl., Toronto ON M5G 2E5, 416/585-7041 (Communications Branch); Fax: 416/585-6227

Office for the Greater Toronto Area, Waterpark Pl., #300, 10 Bay St., Toronto ON M5J 2R8, 416/314-6400; Fax: 416/314-6440

Urban Economic Development, 777 Bay St., 17th Fl., Toronto ON M5G 2E5, 416/585-7474; Fax: 416/585-6227

PEI: Department of Economic Development & Tourism, Community Development Section, Shaw Bldg., 105 Rochford St., 4th Fl., Charlottetown PE C1A 7N8, 902/368-4240; Fax: 902/368-4224

Qué.: Ministère de la Métropole, Édifice H, #2.600, 875, Grande Allée Est, Québec PQ G1R 4Y8, 418/646-3018; Fax: 418/643-6377

Société d'habitation du Québec, Bloc 2, 1054, Conroy, 4e étage, Québec PQ G1R 5E7, 418/643-7676; Fax: 418/643-2166

Sask.: Saskatchewan Municipal Government, Municipal Development, 1855 Victoria Ave., Regina SK S4P 3V7, 306/787-2710; Fax: 306/787-4181

Yuk.: Yukon Economic Development, Whitehorse Business/Community Development Office, 211 Main St., PO Box 2703, Whitehorse YT Y1A 2C6, 403/667-5466; Fax: 403/668-8601

VETERANS AFFAIRS
Veterans Affairs Canada, Daniel J. MacDonald Bldg., 161 Grafton St., PO Box 7700, Charlottetown PE C1A 8M9, 902/566-8195; Fax: 902/566-8508

Ont.: Soldiers Aid Commission, 2 Bloor St. West, 24th Fl., Toronto ON M7A 1E9, 416/327-4674

VICTIM ASSISTANCE *See* **CRIMES COMPENSATION; JUSTICE DEPARTMENTS**

VIOLENCE
See Also Policing Services
Correctional Service Canada, Sex Offender Programming, c/o Solicitor General Canada, 340 Laurier Ave. West, Ottawa ON K1A 0P9, 613/545-8248; Fax: 613/947-0091

Alta: Alberta Family & Social Services, Family Violence Prevention, Seventh St. Plaza, 10030 - 107 St., Edmonton AB T5J 3E4, 403/422-5916; Fax: 403/422-9044

Alberta Justice, Serious & Violent Crime Initiatives, Bowker Bldg., 9833 - 109 St., Edmonton AB T5K 2E8, 403/427-9030; Fax: 403/422-1330

Man.: Manitoba Family Services, Family Dispute Services, #219, 114 Garry St., Winnipeg MB R3C 4V6, 204/945-7259; Fax: 204/945-2156

N.B.: Department of Health & Community Services, Access/Assessment, Protection & Post Adoption Services, PO Box 5100, Fredericton NB E3B 5G8, 506/453-2040; Fax: 506/444-4697

Ont.: Ministry of Citizenship, Culture & Recreation, Ontario Anti-Racism Secretariat, 77 Bloor St. West, 6th Fl., Toronto ON M7A 2R9, 416/314-6200

Ministry of Community & Social Services, Children, Family & Community Services Division, Hepburn Block, 80 Grosvenor St., 6th Fl., Toronto ON M7A 1E9, 416/325-5666; Fax: 416/325-5172, 5171

PEI: Department of Provincial Affairs & Attorney General, Legal & Judicial Services Division, PO Box 2000, Charlottetown PE C1A 7N8, 902/368-5250; Fax: 902/368-5283; 5355

Qué.: Ministère de la Justice, Bureau d'aide aux victimes d'actes criminels, 1200, rte de l'Église, Ste-Foy PQ G1V 4M1, 418/643-5140 (Communications); Fax: 418/646-4449

Ministère de la Sécurité publique, Direction Générale de la Sécurité et de la prévention, 2525, boul Laurier, 2e étage, Ste-Foy PQ G1V 2L2, 418/646-8523; Fax: 418/646-5427

Sask.: Saskatchewan Justice, Victims Services, 1874 Scarth St., Regina SK S4P 3V7, 306/787-0418; Fax: 306/787-3874

Saskatchewan Social Services, Family & Youth Services Division, 1920 Broad St., Regina SK S4P 3V6, 306/787-7010; Fax: 306/787-0925

Protection & Children's Services, 2240 Albert St., Regina SK S4P 3V7, 306/787-2928; Fax: 306/694-3842

Yuk.: Yukon Justice, Family Violence Prevention Unit, PO Box 2703, Whitehorse YT Y1A 2C6, 403/667-3581; Fax: 403/393-6272

VITAL STATISTICS
Statistics Canada, R.H. Coats Bldg., Tunney's Pasture, 120 Parkdale Ave., Ottawa ON K1A 0T6, 613/951-8116; Toll Free: 1-800-263-1136, TDD: 1-800-363-7629; Fax: 613/951-0581

Census & Demographic Statistics, R.H. Coats Bldg., Tunney's Pasture, 120 Parkdale Ave., Ottawa ON K1A 0T6, 613/951-6537; Fax: 613/951-0581

Alta: Alberta Municipal Affairs, Registries Division, John E. Brownlee Bldg., 10365 - 97 St., Edmonton AB T5J 3W7, 403/422-2362 (Edmonton), 297-8980 (Calgary); Toll Free: 1-800-465-5009 (in Alberta); Fax: 403/422-9105

B.C.: Ministry of Health, Vital Statistics, 818 Fort St., Victoria BC V8W 1H8, 250/952-2681; Fax: 250/952-2576

Man.: Manitoba Consumer & Corporate Affairs, 254 Portage Ave., Winnipeg MB R3C 0B8, 204/945-3701; Toll Free: Fax Certificate Requests: 204/948-3128; Fax: 204/945-0777

N.B.: Department of Health & Community Services, Vital Statistics, PO Box 5100, Fredericton NB E3B 5G8, 506/453-2536; Fax: 506/453-3245

Nfld.: Department of Government Services & Lands, Vital Statistics, PO Box 8700, St. John's NF A1B 4J6, 709/729-3311

NWT: Department of Safety & Public Services, Vital Statistics Office, Panda 2 Mall, 3rd Fl., PO Box 1320, Yellowknife NT X1A 2L9, 403/920-3143; Fax: 403/873-0260

N.S.: Department of Business & Consumer Services, Vital Statistics, Provincial Bldg., 1723 Hollis St., 1st Fl., Halifax NS B3J 2M9, 902/424-8907; Fax: 902/424-0678

Ont.: Ministry of Consumer & Commercial Relations, Registrar General Branch, 189 Red River Rd., PO Box 4600, Thunder Bay ON P7B 6L8, 807/343-7414; Toll Free: 1-800-461-2156; Fax: 807/343-7411

PEI: Department of Health & Social Services, Vital Statistics, 4 Sydney St., PO Box 2000, Charlottetown PE C1A 7N8, 902/368-4420; Fax: 902/368-6136

Sask.: Saskatchewan Health, Vital Statistics & Health Insurance Registration Branch, 1919 Rose St., Regina SK S4P 3V7, 306/787-1167; Fax: 306/787-8310

Yuk.: Yukon Health & Social Services, Vital Statistics, PO Box 2703, Whitehorse YT Y1A 2C6, 403/667-5207; Fax: 403/667-3096

WAGES *See* **LABOUR**

WASTE MANAGEMENT
See Also Dangerous Goods & Hazardous Materials
Natural Resources Canada, Radioactive Waste Division, 580 Booth St., Ottawa ON K1A 0E4, 613/996-7432; Fax: 613/992-1405

Alta: Alberta Racing Commission, Sloane Square, #507, 5920 - 1A St. SW, Calgary AB T2H 0G3, 403/297-6551; Fax: 403/255-4078

Alberta Environmental Protection, Action on Waste Division, 9915 - 108 St., Edmonton AB T5K 2G8, 403/422-8466; Fax: 403/427-1594

Tire Recycling Management Board, 10060 Jasper Ave., 10th Fl., Edmonton AB T5J 3N4, 403/990-1111; Fax: 403/990-1122

B.C.: Ministry of Environment, Lands & Parks, Industrial Waste & Hazardous Contaminants Branch, 777 Broughton St., Victoria BC V8V 1X4, 250/387-9992; Fax: 250/387-9935

Municipal Waste Reduction Branch, 777 Broughton St., Victoria BC V8V 1X4, 250/387-9974; Fax: 250/356-9974

Man.: Manitoba Rural Development, Municipal Services, #609, 800 Portage Ave., Winnipeg MB R3G ON4, 204/945-2570; Fax: 204/945-1383

N.B.: Department of the Environment, Solid Waste & Recycling Section, 364 Argyle St., PO Box 6000, Fredericton NB E3B 5H1, 506/457-4848; Fax: 506/453-2265

Nfld.: Department of Environment & Labour, Civil & Sanitary Environmental Engineering, Confederation Bldg., PO Box 8700, St. John's NF A1B 4J6, 709/729-2556; Fax: 709/729-1930

NWT: Department of Municipal & Community Affairs, #600, 5201 - 50th Ave., PO Box 1310, Yellowknife NT X1A 2L9, 403/873-7118; Fax: 403/873-0309

Department of Resources, Wildlife & Economic Development, Industrial Waste, #600, Scotia Centre, Bldg. Box 21, 5102 - 50 Ave., Yellowknife NT X1A 3S8, 403/873-7178; Fax: 403/873-0114

N.S.: Department of Housing & Municipal Affairs, Municipal Services Division, PO Box 216, Halifax NS B3J 2M4, 902/424-7415; Fax: 902/424-0531

Nova Scotia Resource Recovery Fund Board, PO Box 2107, Halifax NS B3J 3B7, 902/424-2577; Fax: 902/424-0503

Ont.: Ministry of Environment & Energy, Waste Reduction Branch, 40 St. Clair Ave. West, 7th Fl., Toronto ON M4V 1M2, 416/325-4440; Fax: 416/323-4481

PEI: Department of Environmental Resources, Solid Waste Section, Jones Bldg., 11 Kent St., 4th Fl., PO Box 2000, Charlottetown PE CIA 7N8, 902/368-5029; Fax: 902/368-5830

Qué.: Société québécoise de récupération et de recyclage, #500, 7171 rue Jean-Talon est, Anjou PQ H1M 3N2, 514/352-5002; Fax: 514/864-2484

Sask.: Saskatchewan Environment & Resource Management, Environmental Protection Branch, 3211 Albert St., Regina SK S4S 5W6, 306/787-6178; Fax: 306/787-5623

Saskatchewan Municipal Government, Municipal Services Division, 1855 Victoria Ave., Regina SK S4P 3V7, 306/787-8282; Fax: 306/787-4181

Yuk.: Yukon Community & Transportation Services, Community Services Branch, PO Box 2703, Whitehorse YT Y1A 2C6, 403/667-5299; Fax: 403/667-7056

WATER POLLUTION See **ENVIRONMENT; WATER RESOURCES**

WATER RESOURCES
See Also Oceanography

Environment Canada, Environmental Protection Service, Place Vincent-Massey, 351, boul St-Joseph, Hull PQ K1A 0H3, 819/997-2800; Fax: 819/953-2225

Federal Water Policy Office, Place Vincent-Massey, 351, boul St-Joseph, Hull PQ K1A 0H3, 819/953-1513; Fax: 819/944-0237

Freshwater Institute, 501 University Cr., Winnipeg MB R3T 2N6, 204/983-5000; Fax: 204/983-6285

Great Lakes Pollution Prevention Centre, #112, 265 North Front St., Sarnia ON N7T 7X1, 519/337-3423; Toll Free: 1-800-667-9790; Fax: 519/337-3486

International Joint Commission, 100 Metcalfe St., Ottawa ON K1P 5M1, 613/995-2984; Fax: 613/993-5583

National Water Research Institute, 867 Lakeshore Rd., PO Box 5050, Burlington ON L7R 4A6, 905/336-4625; Fax: 905/336-4989

Nunavut Water Board, Gjoa Haven NT X0E 1J0

Alta: Alberta Agriculture, Food & Rural Development, Irrigation & Resource Management Division, 7000 - 113 St., Edmonton AB T6H 5T6, 403/422-4596; Fax: 403/422-0474

Alberta Environmental Protection, Air & Water Approvals Division, 9915 - 108 St., Edmonton AB T5K 2G8, 403/427-5883

Water Resources, 9915 - 108 St., Edmonton AB T5K 2G8, 403/427-2739, 944-0313 (Information Centre)

B.C.: Ministry of Environment, Lands & Parks, Water Resources Branch, 810 Blanshard St., 4th Fl., Victoria BC V8V 1X4, 250/387-6945; Fax: 250/356-8298

Man.: Manitoba Water Services Board, 2022 Currie Blvd., PO Box 1059, Brandon MB R7A 6A3, 204/726-6076; Fax: 204/726-6290

Manitoba Natural Resources, Water Resources Branch, 1577 Dublin Ave., Winnipeg MB R3E 3J5, 204/945-7488; Fax: 204/945-7419

N.B.: Department of the Environment, Water & Wastewater Section, 364 Argyle St., PO Box 6000, Fredericton NB E3B 5H1, 506/457-4848; Fax: 506/453-2265

Water Resource Monitoring Section, 364 Argyle St., PO Box 6000, Fredericton NB E3B 5H1, 506/457-4844; Fax: 506/453-3843

Nfld.: Department of Environment & Labour, Water Resource Division, Confederation Bldg., PO Box 8700, St. John's NF A1B 4J6, 709/729-2563; Fax: 709/729-1930

NWT: Department of Resources, Wildlife & Economic Development, Environmental Protection Division, #600, Scotia Centre, Bldg. Box 21, 5102 - 50 Ave., Yellowknife NT X1A 3S8, 403/873-7420, 7134; Fax: 403/873-0114

Northwest Territories Water Board, PO Box 1500, Yellowknife NT X1A 2R3, 403/920-8191; Fax: 403/873-9572

N.S.: Department of the Environment, Water Resources Branch, PO Box 2107, Halifax NS B3J 3B7, 902/424-2554; Fax: 902/424-0503

Ont.: Ministry of Natural Resources, Water Management & Conservation Authorities, Whitney Block, #6540, 99 Wellesley St. West, Toronto ON M7A 1W3, 416/314-1977; Fax: 416/314-1995

Ontario Clean Water Agency, #700, 20 Bay St., Toronto ON M5J 2N8, 416/314-5600; Toll Free: 1-800-667-6292; Fax: 416/314-8300

PEI: Department of Environmental Resources, Water Resources Division, Jones Bldg., 11 Kent St., 4th Fl., PO Box 2000, Charlottetown PE CIA 7N8, 902/368-5028; Fax: 902/368-5830

Qué.: Ministère de l'Environnement et de la Faune, Écosystèmes aquatiques, Édifice Marie-Guyart, 675, boul René-Lévesque est, Québec PQ G1R 5V7, 418/644-3678; Fax: 418/646-8483

Société québécoise d'assainissement des eaux, 1055, boul René-Lévesque est, 10e étage, Montréal PQ H2L 4S5, 514/873-7411; Fax: 514/873-7879

Sask.: Saskatchewan Environment & Resource Management, 3211 Albert St., Regina SK S4S 5W6, 306/787-2700; Toll Free: 1-800-667-2757; Fax: 306/787-3941

Saskatchewan Water Corporation (Sask Water), Victoria Place, 111 Fairford St. East, Moose Jaw SK S6H 7X9, 306/694-3900; Fax: 306/694-3944

Yuk.: Yukon Renewable Resources, PO Box 2703, Whitehorse YT Y1A 2C6, 403/667-5237; Toll Free: 1-800-661-0408 (Yukon)

WEATHER

Environment Canada, Atmospheric Environment Service, 4905 Dufferin St., Downsview ON M3H 5T4, 416/739-4521; Fax: 819/953-2225

WEED CONTROL See AGRICULTURE

WEIGHTS & MEASURES

Industry Canada, Legal Metrology, C.D. Howe Bldg., 235 Queen St., Ottawa ON K1A 0H5, 613/952-0655; Fax: 613/954-2303

Standards Council of Canada, #1200, 45 O'Connor St., Ottawa ON K1P 6N7, 613/238-3222; Fax: 613/995-4564

WELFARE See INCOME SECURITY; SOCIAL SERVICES

WILDLIFE RESOURCES

Committee on the Status of Endangered Wildlife in Canada, 10 Wellington St., Hull PQ K1A 0H3, 819/997-4991; Fax: 819/953-6283

Environment Canada, Canadian Wildlife Service, Place Vincent-Massey, 351, boul St-Joseph, Hull PQ K1A 0H3, 819/997-1301; Fax: 819/953-7177

National Wildlife Research Centre, 100, boul Gamelin, Hull PQ K1A 0H3, 819/997-1092; Fax: 819/953-6612

North American Waterfowl Management Plan, c/o Canadian Wildlife Service, Place Vincent-Massey, 351, boul St-Joseph, 3e étage, Hull PQ K1A 0H3, 819/997-2392; Fax: 819/994-4445

Alta: Alberta Sport, Recreation, Parks & Wildlife Foundation, Percy Page Centre, 11759 Groat Rd., Edmonton AB T5M 3K9, 403/427-1976; Fax: 403/488-9755

Alberta Environmental Protection, Fish & Wildlife, 9915 - 108 St., Edmonton AB T5K 2G8, 403/427-2739, 944-0313 (Information Centre)

Man.: Endangered Species Advisory Committee, 200 Saulteaux Cr., PO Box 80, Winnipeg MB R3J 3W3, 204/945-6829

Manitoba Natural Resources, Wildlife Branch, 200 Saulteaux Cr., PO Box 24, Winnipeg MB R3J 3W3, 204/945-7761; Fax: 204/945-3077

Saskeram Wildlife Management Area Advisory Committee, PO Box 2550, The Pas MB R9A 1M4, 204/627-8266

N.B.: Department of Natural Resources & Energy, Fish & Wildlife, PO Box 6000, Fredericton NB E3B 5H1, 506/453-2440; Fax: 506/453-6699

Nfld.: Department of Forest Resources & Agrifoods, Forestry & Wildlife Branch, Confederation Complex, PO Box 8700, St. John's NF A1B 4J6, 709/729-4716

NWT: Department of Resources, Wildlife & Economic Development, Wildlife & Fisheries Division, #600, Scotia Centre, Bldg. Box 21, 5102 - 50 Ave., Yellowknife NT X1A 3S8, 403/873-7420, 7134; Fax: 403/873-0114

N.S.: Department of Natural Resources, Wildlife Division, PO Box 516, Kentville NS B4N 3X3, 902/678-6091; Fax: 902/679-6176

Ont.: Ministry of Natural Resources, Fish & Wildlife Branch, Whitney Block, #6540, 99 Wellesley St. West, Toronto ON M7A 1W3, 416/314-6132; Fax: 416/314-1994

PEI: Department of Environmental Resources, Fish & Wildlife Division, Jones Bldg., 11 Kent St., 4th Fl., PO Box 2000, Charlottetown PE CIA 7N8, 902/368-4683; Fax: 902/368-5830

Qué.: Ministère de l'Environnement et de la Faune, Direction générale de la ressource faunique et des parcs, Édifice Marie-Guyart, 675, boul René-Lévesque est, Québec PQ G1R 5V7, 418/643-3127; Fax: 418/643-3619

Sask.: Saskatchewan Environment & Resource Management, Wildlife Branch, 3211 Albert St., Regina SK S4S 5W6, 306/787-2309; Email: dennis.sherratt.erm@govmail.gov.sk.ca; Fax: 306/787-9544

Yuk.: Yukon Renewable Resources, Wildlife Management, PO Box 2703, Whitehorse YT Y1A 2C6, 403/667-5177; Fax: 403/393-6213

WOMEN'S ISSUES
See Also Pay Equity

Canadian Heritage, Multiculturalism & Status of Women, Jules Léger Bldg., 25 Eddy St., Hull PQ K1A 1K5, 819/997-9900; TDD: 819/997-8776; Fax: 819/953-8055

Industry Canada, Women's Bureau, C.D. Howe Bldg., 235 Queen St., Ottawa ON K1A 0H5, 613/954-3130; Fax: 613/954-4301

Status of Women Canada, #700, 360 Albert St., Ottawa ON K1A 1C3, 613/995-7835; Fax: 613/957-3359

B.C.: Ministry of Women's Equality, Parliament Bldgs., 756 Fort St., Victoria BC V8V 1X4, 250/387-3600; Fax: 250/356-1396

Ministry of the Attorney General, Employment Equity & Women's Programs, 910 Government St., 5th Fl., Victoria BC V8V 1X4, 250/387-3247; Fax: 250/356-5368

Man.: Executive Council, Justice & Attorney General, Legislative Bldg., Winnipeg MB R3C 0V8, 204/945-3728; Fax: 204/945-2517

Nfld.: Provincial Advisory Council on the Status of Women, 131 Le Marchant Rd., St. John's NF A1C 2H3, 709/753-7270; Fax: 709/753-2606

NWT: Executive Council, Status of Women, PO Box 1320, Yellowknife NT X1A 2L9, 403/920-3106; Fax: 403/873-0122

Status of Women of the Northwest Territories, PO Box 1320, Yellowknife NT X1A 2L9, 403/920-6177

N.S.: Nova Scotia Advisory Council on the Status of Women, #202, 6169 Quinpool Rd., PO Box 745, Halifax NS B3J 2T3, 902/424-8662; Fax: 902/424-0573

Ont.: Ontario Womens Directorate, 2 Carlton St., 12th Fl., Toronto ON M5B 2M9, 416/314-0270; Fax: 416/314-0253

PEI: Advisory Council on the Status of Women, PO Box 2000, Charlottetown PE C1A 7N8, 902/368-4510; Fax: 902/368-4516

Office of Higher Education, Training & Adult Learning, Shaw Bldg., 105 Rochford St., 3rd Fl., PO Box 2000, Charlottetown PE C1A 7N8, 902/368-4710; Fax: 902/368-6144

Qué.: Secrétariat à la Condition féminine, #2.700, 875, Grande-Allée est, Québec PQ G1R 5W5, 418/643-9052; Fax: 418/643-4991

Conseil du Statut de la Femme, #300, 8, rue Cook, Québec PQ G1R 5J7, 418/643-4326; Fax: 418/643-8926

Sask.: Saskatchewan Women's Secretariat, 1914 Hamilton St., 3rd Fl., Regina SK S4P 4V4, 306/787-2329; Fax: 306/787-2058

Yuk.: Yukon Women's Directorate, PO Box 2703, Whitehorse YT Y1A 2C6, 403/667-3030; Fax: 403/393-6270

WORKERS' COMPENSATION

Human Resources Development Canada, Place du Portage, Phase IV, 140, Promenade du Portage, Hull PQ K1A 0J9, 819/994-6013

Merchant Seamen Compensation Board, Portage II, Place du Portage, 165 Hotel-de-Ville St., Ottawa ON K1A 0J2, 819/997-2555; Fax: 819/997-1664

Alta: Alberta Workers' Compensation Board, 9912 - 107 St., PO Box 2415, Edmonton AB T5J 2S5, 403/498-4000; Fax: 403/422-0972

B.C.: Workers' Compensation Board, 6951 Westminster Hwy., Richmond BC V7C 1C6, 604/273-2266; Fax: 604/276-3151

Man.: Manitoba Workers' Compensation Board, 333 Maryland St., Winnipeg MB R3G 1M2, 204/786-5471; Toll Free: 1-800-362-3340 (Manitoba); Fax: 204/786-3704

N.B.: Workplace Health, Safety & Compensation Commission of New Brunswick, 1 Portland St., PO Box 160, Saint John NB E2L 3X9, 506/632-2200; Toll Free: 1-800-222-9775; Fax: 506/632-2226

Nfld.: Newfoundland & Labrador Workers' Compensation Commission, #146, 148 Forest Rd., PO Box 9000, St. John's NF A1A 3B8, 709/778-1000; Fax: 709/738-1714

NWT: Northwest Territories Workers' Compensation Board, PO Box 8888, Yellowknife NT X1A 2R3, 403/920-8686; Fax: 403/873-4596

N.S.: Workers' Compensation Board of Nova Scotia, 5668 South St., PO Box 1150, Halifax NS B3J 2Y2, 902/424-8440; Fax: 902/424-0509

Ont.: Workers' Compensation Board, 2 Bloor St. East, 20th Fl., Toronto ON M4W 3C3, 416/927-4135; Fax: 416/927-5141

PEI: Prince Edward Island Workers' Compensation Board, PO Box 757, Charlottetown PE C1A 7L7, 902/368-5680; Fax: 902/368-5696

Qué.: Commission de la santé et de la sécurité du travail du Québec, 1199, rue de Bleury, CP 6056, Succ Centre-Ville, Montréal PQ H3C 4E1, 514/873-7183; Fax: 514/873-7007

Sask.: Saskatchewan Workers' Compensation Board, #200, 1881 Scarth St., Regina SK S4P 4L1, 306/787-4370; Fax: 306/787-0213

Yuk.: Yukon Workers' Compensation Board, 401 Strickland St., Whitehorse YT Y1A 5N8, 403/667-5645; Fax: 403/668-2079

WORKPLACE HAZARDOUS MATERIALS INFORMATION SYSTEM (WHMIS) See OCCUPATIONAL SAFETY

YOUNG OFFENDERS

Justice Canada, Family & Youth Law Policy Section, Justice Bldg., 239 Wellington St., Ottawa ON K1A 0H8, 613/941-2339; Fax: 613/954-0811

Alta: Alberta Justice, Young Offender Branch, 10365 - 97th St., Edmonton AB T5J 3W7, 403/422-5019; Fax: 403/422-0732

B.C.: Ministry of the Attorney General, Family Justice Reform, 910 Government St., 5th Fl., Victoria BC V8V 1X4, 250/387-1111; Fax: 604/356-1092

Man.: Manitoba Justice, Community & Youth Correctional Services, 405 Broadway, 8th Fl., Winnipeg MB R3C 3L6, 204/945-8165; Fax: 204/948-2166

N.B.: Department of the Solicitor General, Institutional & Young Offender Services, Barker House, 4th Fl., PO Box 6000, Fredericton NB E3B 5H1, 506/453-2846; Fax: 506/453-2307

Nfld.: Department of Social Services, Youth Corrections, Confederation Bldg., PO Box 8700, St. John's NF A1B 4J6, 709/729-3540; Fax: 709/729-6996

NWT: Department of Justice, Young Offenders, PO Box 1320, Yellowknife NT X1A 2L9, 403/920-8823

Ont.: Ministry of the Solicitor General & Correctional Services, Operational Support & Coordination Branch, 101 Bloor St. West, 7th Fl., Toronto ON M5S 2Z7, 705/494-3339

PEI: Health & Community Services Agency, 4 Sydney St., PO Box 2000, Charlottetown PE C1A 7N8, 902/368-6130; Fax: 902/368-6136

Qué.: Chambre de la jeunesse, 410, rue Bellechasse est, Montréal PQ H2S 1X3, 514/495-5817; Fax: 514/873-8938

Ministère de la Justice, Direction du droit de la jeunesse, 1200, rte de l'Église, Ste-Foy PQ G1V 4M1, 418/643-5140 (Communications); Fax: 418/646-4449

Sask.: Saskatchewan Social Services, Young Offenders, Central Office, #216, 110 Ominica St. West, Moose Jaw SK S6H 6V2, 306/787-9165; Fax: 306/694-3842

Yuk.: Yukon Health & Social Services, Social Services Branch, PO Box 2703, Whitehorse YT Y1A 2C6, 403/667-3673 (Communications); Fax: 403/667-3096

YOUTH SERVICES

Human Resources Development Canada, Student Assistance Branch/Education Support Branch, Place du Portage, Phase IV, 140, Promenade du Portage, Hull PQ K1A 0J9, 819/994-2377; Fax: 819/953-4226

Training & Youth, Place du Portage, Phase IV, 140, Promenade du Portage, Hull PQ K1A 0J9, 613/953-8385; Fax: 613/953-0944

Justice Canada, Family & Youth Law Policy Section, Justice Bldg., 239 Wellington St., Ottawa ON K1A 0H8, 613/941-2339; Fax: 613/954-0811

Alta: Alberta Family & Social Services, Child Welfare, Seventh St. Plaza, 10030 - 107 St., Edmonton AB T5J 3E4, 403/422-5187; Fax: 403/422-9044

B.C.: Ministry of Social Services, Child, Family & Community Service, Parliament Bldgs., 614 Humboldt St., 7th Fl., Victoria BC V8V 1X4, 250/387-6485; Fax: 250/356-7801

Children with Special Needs, Parliament Bldgs., 614 Humboldt St., 7th Fl., Victoria BC V8V 1X4, 250/387-1275; Fax: 250/356-6534

Man.: Manitoba Education & Training, Workforce 2000 & Youth Programs, 185 Carlton St., 4th Fl., Winnipeg MB R3C 3J1, 204/945-6195; Fax: 204/945-1792

Manitoba Family Services, Child & Family Services Division, #219, 114 Garry St., Winnipeg MB R3C 4V6, 204/945-2324 (Policy & Planning); Fax: 204/945-2156

N.B.: Youth Council of New Brunswick, 736 King St., PO Box 6000, Fredericton NB E3B 5H1, 506/453-3271; Fax: 506/444-4413

Nfld.: Department of Education, Youth Services Division, Confederation Bldg., PO Box 8700, St. John's NF A1B 4J6, 709/729-3503; Fax: 709/729-3669

NWT: Department of Education, Culture & Employment, Early Childhood & School Services, PO Box 1320, Yellowknife NT X1A 2L9, 403/920-3491; Fax: 403/873-0155

N.S.: Nova Scotia Youth Secretariat, One Government Place, 1700 Granville St., 5th Fl., PO Box 1617, Halifax NS B3J 2Y3, 902/424-3780; Fax: 902/424-7638

Ont.: Ministry of Environment & Energy, Environmental Youth Corps, 135 St. Clair Ave. West, Toronto ON M4V 1P5, 416/314-9387; General Inquiry: 416/314-5906; Fax: 416/323-4645

PEI: Department of Health & Social Services, Jones Bldg., 11 Kent St., 2nd Fl., PO Box 2000, Charlottetown PE C1A 7N8, 902/368-4900; Fax: 902/368-4969

Health & Community Services Agency, 4 Sydney St., PO Box 2000, Charlottetown PE C1A 7N8, 902/368-6130; Fax: 902/368-6136

Qué.: Ministère de la Santé et des services sociaux, 1075, ch Ste-Foy, Québec PQ G1S 2M1

Sask.: Saskatchewan Social Services, Family & Youth Services Division, 1920 Broad St., Regina SK S4P 3V6, 306/787-7010; Fax: 306/787-0925

Yuk.: Yukon Health & Social Services, Social Services Branch, PO Box 2703, Whitehorse YT Y1A 2C6, 403/667-3673 (Communications); Fax: 403/667-3096

ZONING

Alta: Alberta Municipal Affairs, Local Government Services Division, Commerce Place, 10155 - 102 St., Edmonton AB T5J 4L4, 403/427-2732; Fax: 403/422-9105

B.C.: British Columbia Assessment Authority, 1537 Hillside Ave., Victoria BC V8T 4Y2, 250/595-6211; Fax: 250/595-6222

Ministry of the Attorney General, Land Title Branch, 910 Government St., 1st Fl., Victoria BC V8V 1X4, 250/387-1903; Fax: 250/387-1763

Man.: Manitoba Municipal Board, #408, 800 Portage Ave., Winnipeg MB R3G 0N4, 204/945-1789; Fax: 204/948-2235

Manitoba Natural Resources, Land Information Centre, 1007 Century St., Winnipeg MB R3H 0W4, 204/945-3730; Fax: 204/945-3586

Manitoba Rural Development, Assessment Branch, #609, 800 Portage Ave., Winnipeg MB R3G 0N4, 204/945-2605; Fax: 204/945-1994

Community Economic Development Branch, #600, 800 Portage Ave., Winnipeg MB R3G 0N4, 204/945-2192; Fax: 204/945-5059

N.B.: Department of Municipalities, Culture & Housing, Land Use Planning Branch, Marysville Place, 20 McGloin St., PO Box 6000, Fredericton NB E3B 5H1, 506/453-2171; Fax: 506/457-4991

Nfld.: Department of Municipal & Provincial Affairs, Urban & Rural Planning, West Block, Confederation Bldg., PO Box 8700, St. John's NF A1B 4J6, 709/729-3090

NWT: Department of Municipal & Community Affairs, Community Planning & Lands, #600, 5201 - 50th Ave., PO Box 1310, Yellowknife NT X1A 2L9, 403/920-8916; Fax: 403/920-6343

N.S.: Department of Housing & Municipal Affairs, Land Information Management Services, PO Box 216, Halifax NS B3J 2M4, 902/424-7136; Fax: 902/424-0531

Ont.: Ministry of Municipal Affairs & Housing, Plans Administration Branch (Central & Southwest), 777 Bay St., 17th Fl., Toronto ON M5G 2E5, 416/585-6025; Fax: 416/585-6227

Plans Administration Branch (North & East), 777 Bay St., 17th Fl., Toronto ON M5G 2E5, 416/585-6093; Fax: 416/585-6227

PEI: Department of Provincial Affairs & Attorney General, Inspection Services, PO Box 2000, Charlottetown PE C1A 7N8, 902/368-4884; Fax: 902/368-5544

Qué.: Commission municipale du Québec, 20, rue Chauveau, 5e étage, Québec PQ G1R 4J3, 418/691-2014; Fax: 418/644-4676

Sask.: Saskatchewan Municipal Government, Municipal Planning & Advisory Services, 1855 Victoria Ave., Regina SK S4P 3V7, 306/787-2656; Fax: 306/787-4181

Yuk.: Yukon Community & Transportation Services, Municipal & Community Affairs Division, PO Box 2703, Whitehorse YT Y1A 2C6, 403/667-5431; Fax: 403/667-7056

GOVERNMENT OF CANADA

Seat of Government: House of Commons, 111 Wellington St., PO Box 1103, Ottawa ON K1A 0A6
URL: http://canada.gc.ca
InfoCan URL: http://www.infocan.gc.ca/

All political authority in Canada is divided between the federal and provincial governments according to the provisions of the Constitution Act, 1867. Local municipalities are a concern of the provinces, and derive their authority from Acts of provincial legislation.

The Parliament of Canada consists of the Queen (represented in Canada by the Governor General), an Upper House called the Senate, and an elected House of Commons.

GOVERNOR GENERAL & COMMANDER-IN-CHIEF OF CANADA/Gouverneur général et Commandant en chef du Canada

Rideau Hall, 1 Sussex Dr., Ottawa ON K1A 0A1
613/993-8200; Fax: 613/990-7636; URL: http://canada.gc.ca/howgoc/govgen/ggind_e.html

Canada is a constitutional monarchy; under the terms of its Constitution, Her Majesty Queen Elizabeth II is the Head of State. The Queen is represented in Canada by the Governor General who is also Commander-in-Chief of the Canadian Forces, Chancellor & Principal Companion of the Order of Canada, Chancellor & Commander of the Order of Military Merit, & Head of the Canadian Heraldic Authority.

The office of the Governor General encompasses a number of responsibilities, both constitutional & traditional in nature. These fall into six categories: the Crown in Canada, Canadian Sovereignty, Recognition of Excellence, National Identity, National Unity & Moral Leadership.

Canada's twenty-fifth Governor General, His Excellency the Right Honourable Roméo LeBlanc, was sworn in on February 8, 1995.

Governor General, His Excellency the Right Honourable Roméo LeBlanc, P.C., C.C., C.M.M., C.D.
Personal Secretary, Kay Higgins
Executive Asst., Kevin Fram
Secretary to the Governor General, Judith A. LaRocque, C.V.O.

CHANCELLERY
Deputy Secretary, Lt.Gen. James C. Gervais, C.M.M., C.D.(Retired)
Director, Honours, Mary de Bellefeuille-Percy
Director, Heraldry, Robert Watt

POLICY, PROGRAM & PROTOCOL
Deputy Secretary, Anthony P. Smyth, L.V.O.
Director, Policy & Planning, Lise DesRosiers
Director, Program Implementation & Security, Lt.Col. Normand Jodoin, M.V.O., C.D.
Acting Director, Public Information, Kate McGregor
Senior Aide-de-Camp, Lt.(N) Philip Gothe
Aide-de-Camp, Capt. Jocelyn Paul
Aide-de-Camp, Capt. Gavin Menzies
Aide-de-Camp, Maj. Sylvain Bédard

PRIVY COUNCIL OFFICE (PCO)/ Bureau du Conseil privé (BCP)

Langevin Block, 80 Wellington St., Ottawa ON K1A 0A3
613/957-5153; Fax: 613/995-0101; URL: http://canada.gc.ca/depts/agencies/pcoind_e.html

The PCO is a public service department that provides advice to the Prime Minister with regard to the organization of the government and its relationships with Parliament, the Crown and other institutions; the delineation of responsibilities among Ministers; senior appointments; and matters for which the Prime Minister has a particular concern, such as national security. It supports the Prime Minister's power to organize Cabinet and the Cabinet decision-making process; and secretariat support to the Cabinet, its committees and their chairs. It also advises the Prime Minister regarding governmental issues; and government policies.

The Office has a special responsibility to ensure the continuity of government, which includes facilitating changes of government and briefing newly appointed Ministers. A member of the Privy Council is awarded the title "Honourable" for life. The Governor General, the Prime Minister and the Chief Justice of Canada are accorded the title "The Rt. Honourable" for life. The Canadian Transportation Accident & Safety Investigation Board and the Public Service Staff Relations Board report to Parliament through the President of the Privy Council.

Note: A list of Privy Council members may be obtained from: Orders-in-Council Division, #418, Blackburn Bldg., 85 Sparks St., Ottawa ON K1A 0A3, 613/957-5434; Fax: 613/957-5026

ACTS ADMINISTERED
Canadian Transportation Accident Investigation & Safety Board Act
Oaths of Allegiance Act
Parliamentary Employment & Staff Relations Act
Public Service Staff Relations Act
Representation Act

President of the Privy Council, Hon. Stéphane Dion, 613/943-1838, Fax: 613/943-8377
Parliamentary Secretary, Office of the President, Paul De Villiers, House of Commons, 80 Wellington St., Ottawa ON K1A 0A6, 613/992-6582
Executive Asst., Office of the President, Françoise Ducros, House of Commons, 80 Wellington St., Ottawa ON K1A 0A6, 613/943-1838
Clerk of the Privy Council & Secretary to the Cabinet, Jocelyne Bourgon, 613/957-5400, Fax: 613/957-5729
Executive Asst., Marc O'Sullivan, 613/967-5403
Executive Asst., Guylaine Roy, 613/957-5270
Assoc. Secretary to the Cabinet & Deputy Clerk, Privy Council, Vacant, 613/957-5390
Deputy Clerk & Associate Secretary to the Cabinet, Ronald Bilodeau, 613/947-5695, Fax: 613/943-1857
Deputy Clerk, Security & Intelligence & Counsel, Mario Dion, 613/957-5696
Deputy Minister to the Cabinet, Intergovernmental Affairs, George Anderson
Deputy Secretary to the Cabinet, Intergovernmental Policy, Michael Horgan, 613/957-5462
Deputy Secretary to the Cabinet, Operations, Morris Rosenberg, 613/957-5368
Deputy Secretary to the Cabinet, Plans & Consultation, Wayne Wouters, 613/957-5390
Asst. Clerk, Orders in Council, Michel Garneau, 613/957-5430
Asst. Deputy Minister, Corporate Services, Elizabeth Nadeau, 613/957-5151
Executive Director, Intelligence Assessment, Anthony Campbell, 613/957-5683
Asst. Secretary, Communications & Consultations, Ruth Cardinal, 85 Sparks St., Ottawa ON K1A 0A3, 613/957-5495
Asst. Secretary, Foreign & Defence Policy, Jim Bartleman, 613/957-5476
Asst. Secretary, Legislation & House Planning Counsel, Suzanne Poirier, 613/957-5792
Asst. Secretary, Liaison Secretariat for Macroeconomic Policy, Patrice Muller, 613/957-5473
Asst. Secretary, Machinery of Government, Nicole Jauvin, 613/957-5491
Asst. Secretary, Management Priorities & Senior Personnel, David Holdsworth, 613/957-5293
Asst. Secretary, Security & Intelligence, M. Purdy, 613/957-5275
Asst. Secretary, Social Development, Alex Himelfarb, 613/957-5446

Privy Council Members & Date When Sworn In:
Hon. Walter Edward Harris, Jan. 18, 1950
Rt. Hon. John Whitney Pickersgill, June 12, 1953
Hon. Paul Theodore Hellyer, Apr. 26, 1957
Hon. Edmund Davie Fulton, June 21, 1957
Hon. Douglas Scott Harkness, June 21, 1957
Rt. Hon. Ellen Louks Fairclough, June 21, 1957
Hon. John Angus MacLean, June 21, 1957
Hon. Michael Starr, June 21, 1957
Rt. Hon. Frances Alvin George Hamilton, Aug. 22, 1957
H.R.H. Prince Philip, The Duke of Edinburgh, Oct. 14, 1957
Hon. Joseph-Pierre-Albert Sévigny, Aug. 20, 1959
Hon. Jacques Flynn, Dec. 28, 1961
Hon. Paul Martineau, Aug. 9, 1962
Hon. Marcel-Joseph-Aimé Lambert, Feb. 12, 1963
Hon. J.H. Théogène Ricard, Mar. 18, 1963
Hon. Frank Charles McGee, Mar. 18, 1963
Rt. Hon. Martial Asselin, Mar. 18, 1963
Hon. Mitchell William Sharp, Apr. 22, 1963
Hon. Allan Joseph MacEachen, Apr. 22, 1963
Hon. Hédard Robichaud, Apr. 22, 1963
Hon. Roger Joseph Teillet, Apr. 22, 1963
Hon. Yvon Dupuis, Feb. 3, 1964
Hon. Edgar John Benson, June 29, 1964
Hon. Léo Alphonse Joseph Cadieux, Feb. 15, 1965
Hon. Lawrence T. Pennell, July 7, 1965
Hon. Alan Aylesworth Macnaughton, Oct. 25, 1965
Hon. Joseph Julien Jean-Pierre Côté, Dec. 18, 1965
Rt. Hon. John Napier Turner, Dec. 18, 1965
Rt. Hon. Pierre Elliott Trudeau, Apr. 4, 1967
Rt. Hon. Jean Chrétien, Apr. 4, 1967
Hon. Louis Joseph Robichaud, July 5, 1967
Hon. Dufferin Roblin, July 5, 1967
Hon. Alexander Bradshaw Campbell, July 5, 1967
Rt. Hon. Robert L. Stanfield, July 7, 1967
Hon. Bryce Stuart Mackasey, Feb. 9, 1968
Hon. Donald Stovel Macdonald, Apr. 20, 1968
Hon. John Carr Munro, Apr. 20, 1968
Hon. Gérard Pelletier, Apr. 20, 1968
Hon. Horace Andrew Olson, July 6, 1968
Hon. Jean-Eudes Dubé, July 6, 1968
Hon. Stanley Ronald Basford, July 6, 1968
Hon. Eric William Kierans, July 6, 1968
Hon. James Armstrong Richardson, July 6, 1968
Hon. Otto Emil Lang, July 6, 1968
Hon. Herbert Eser Gray, Oct. 20, 1969
Hon. Robert Douglas George Stanbury, Oct. 20, 1969
Hon. Jean-Pierre Goyer, Dec. 22, 1970
Hon. Alastair William Gillespie, Aug. 12, 1971
Hon. Martin Patrick O'Connell, Aug. 12, 1971
Hon. Patrick Morgan Mahoney, Jan. 28, 1972
Hon. Stanley Haidasz, Nov. 27, 1972
Hon. Eugene Francis Whelan, Nov. 27, 1972
Hon. W. Warren Allmand, Nov. 27, 1972
Hon. James Hugh Faulkner, Nov. 27, 1972
Hon. André Ouellet, Nov. 27, 1972
Hon. Marc Lalonde, Nov. 27, 1972
Hon. Lucien Lamoureux, June 10, 1974
Hon. Raymond Joseph Perrault, Aug. 8, 1974
Hon. Barnett Jerome Danson, Aug. 8, 1974
Hon. J. Judd Buchanan, Aug. 8, 1974
Hon. Roméo LeBlanc, Aug. 8, 1974
Hon. Muriel McQueen Ferguson, Nov. 7, 1974
Hon. Pierre Juneau, Aug. 29, 1975
Hon. Marcel Lessard, Sept. 26, 1975
Hon. Jack Sidney George Cullen, Sept. 26, 1975
Hon. Leonard Stephen Marchand, Sept. 15, 1976
Hon. John Roberts, Sept. 15, 1976
Hon. Monique Bégin, Sept. 15, 1976
Hon. Jean-Jacques Blais, Sept. 15, 1976
Hon. Francis Fox, Sept. 15, 1976

Canadian Almanac & Directory 1997

Hon. Anthony Chisholm Abbott, Sept. 15, 1976
Hon. Iona Campagnolo, Sept. 15, 1976
Hon. Joseph-Philippe Guay, Nov. 3, 1976
Hon. John Henry Horner, Apr. 21, 1977
Hon. Norman A. Cafik, Sept. 16, 1977
Hon. J. Gilles Lamontagne, Jan. 19, 1978
Hon. John M. Reid, Nov. 24, 1978
Hon. Pierre De Bané, Nov. 24, 1978
Rt. Hon. Charles Joseph Clark, June 4, 1979
Hon. Flora Isabel MacDonald, June 4, 1979
Hon. James Aloysius McGrath, June 4, 1979
Hon. Erik H. Nielsen, June 4, 1979
Hon. Allan Frederick Lawrence, June 4, 1979
Hon. John Carnell Crosbie, June 4, 1979
Hon. David Samuel Horne MacDonald, June 4, 1979
Hon. Lincoln MacCauley Alexander, June 4, 1979
Hon. Roch La Salle, June 4, 1979
Rt. Hon. Donald Frank Mazankowski, June 4, 1979
Hon. Elmer MacIntosh MacKay, June 4, 1979
Hon. Arthur Jacob Epp, June 4, 1979
Hon. John Allen Fraser, June 4, 1979
Hon. William H. Jarvis, June 4, 1979
Hon. Sinclair McKnight Stevens, June 4, 1979
Hon. John Wise, June 4, 1979
Hon. Ronald George Atkey, June 4, 1979
Rt. Hon. Ramon John Hnatyshyn, June 4, 1979
Hon. David Crombie, June 4, 1979
Hon. Robert René de Cotret, June 4, 1979
Hon. William Heward Grafftey, June 4, 1979
Hon. Perrin Beatty, June 4, 1979
Hon. J. Robert Howie, June 4, 1979
Hon. Arthur Ronald Huntington, June 4, 1979
Hon. Michael Holocombe Wilson, June 4, 1979
Hon. Renaude Lapointe, Nov. 30, 1979
Hon. Stanley Howard Knowles, Nov. 30, 1979
Hon. Gerald Regan, Mar. 3, 1980
Hon. Mark R. MacGuigan, Mar. 3, 1980
Hon. Robert Phillip Kaplan, Mar. 3, 1980
Hon. James Sydney Fleming, Mar. 3, 1980
Hon. William H. Rompkey, Mar. 3, 1980
Hon. Pierre Bussières, Mar. 3, 1980
Hon. Charles Lapointe, Mar. 3, 1980
Hon. Edward C. Lumley, Mar. 3, 1980
Hon. Yvon Pinard, Mar. 3, 1980
Hon. Donald James Johnston, Mar. 3, 1980
Hon. Lloyd Axworthy, Mar. 3, 1980
Hon. Paul James Cosgrove, Mar. 3, 1980
Hon. Judith A. Erola, Mar. 3, 1980
Hon. James A. Jerome, Feb. 16, 1981
Hon. Jacob Austin, Sept. 22, 1981
Hon. Charles L. Caccia, Sept. 22, 1981
Hon. Serge Joyal, Sept. 22, 1981
Hon. W. Bennett Campbell, Sept. 22, 1981
Hon. Robert Gordon Robertson, Mar. 2, 1982
Hon. John Edward Broadbent, Apr. 17, 1982
Hon. William Grenville Davis, Apr. 17, 1982
Hon. Allan Emrys Blakeney, Apr. 17, 1982
Hon. E. Peter Lougheed, Apr. 17, 1982
Hon. William Richards Bennett, Apr. 17, 1982
Hon. John MacLennan Buchanan, Apr. 17, 1982
Hon. Alfred Brian Peckford, Apr. 17, 1982
Hon. James Matthew Lee, Apr. 17, 1982
Hon. Howard Russell Pawley, Apr. 17, 1982
Hon. Sterling Rufus Lyon, Apr. 17, 1982
Hon. David Michael Collenette, Aug 12, 1983
Hon. Céline Hervieux-Payette, Aug. 12, 1983
Hon. Roger Simmons, Aug. 12, 1983
Hon. David Paul Smith, Aug. 12, 1983
Hon. Roy MacLaren, Aug. 17, 1983
Rt. Hon. Robert George Brian Dickson, Apr. 19, 1984
Hon. Robert B. Bryce, Apr. 19, 1984
Hon. Peter Michael Pitfield, Apr. 19, 1984
Rt. Hon. Martin Brian Mulroney, May 7, 1984
Rt. Hon. Edward Richard Schreyer, June 3, 1984
Hon. Herb Breau, June 30, 1984
Hon. Joseph Roger Rémi Bujold, June 30, 1984
Hon. Jean-C. Lapierre, June 30, 1984
Hon. Ralph Ferguson, June 30, 1984

Hon. Douglas Cockburn Firth, June 30, 1984
Hon. Robert Carman Coates, Sept. 17, 1984
Hon. Jack Burnett Murta, Sept. 17, 1984
Hon. Harvie Andre, Sept. 17, 1984
Hon. Otto John Jelinek, Sept. 17, 1984
Hon. Charles James Mayer, Sept. 17, 1984
Hon. Thomas Edward Siddon, Sept. 17, 1984
Hon. William Hunter McKnight, Sept. 17, 1984
Hon. Walter Franklin McLean, Sept. 17, 1984
Hon. Thomas Michael McMillan, Sept. 17, 1984
Hon. Patricia Carney, Sept. 17, 1984
Hon. André Bissonnette, Sept. 17, 1984
Hon. Suzanne Blais-Grenier, Sept. 17, 1984
Hon. Benoît Bouchard, Sept. 17, 1984
Hon. Andrée Champagne, Sept. 17, 1984
Hon. Michel Côté, Sept. 17, 1984
Hon. James Francis Kelleher, Sept 17, 1984
Hon. Robert E.J. Layton, Sept. 17, 1984
Hon. Marcel Masse, Sept. 17, 1984
Hon. Barbara Jean McDougall, Sept. 17, 1984
Hon. Gerald Stairs Merrithew, Sept. 17, 1984
Hon. Monique Vézina, Sept. 17, 1984
Hon. Maurice Riel, Nov. 30, 1984
Hon. Cyril Lloyd Francis, Nov. 30, 1984
Hon. Saul Mark Cherniack, Nov. 30, 1984
Hon. Paule Gauthier, P.C., Q.C., Nov. 30, 1984
Hon. Lloyd Roseville Crouse, June 10, 1985
Hon. Stewart Donald McInnes, Aug. 20, 1985
Hon. Frank Oberle, Nov. 20, 1985
Hon. Gordon Francis Joseph Osbaldeston, Feb. 13, 1986
Hon. Lowell Murray, June 30, 1986
Hon. Paul Wyatt Dick, June 30, 1986
Hon. Pierre H. Cadieux, June 30, 1986
Hon. Jean Charest, June 30, 1986
Hon. Thomas Hockin, June 30, 1986
Hon. Monique Landry, June 30, 1986
Hon. Bernard Valcourt, June 30, 1986
Hon. Gerry Weiner, June 30, 1986
Hon. John William Bosley, June 30, 1987
Hon. Douglas Grinslade Lewis, Aug. 27, 1987
Hon. Pierre Blais, Aug. 27, 1986
Hon. Lucien Bouchard, Mar. 31, 1988
Hon. Gerry St. Germain, Mar. 31, 1988
Hon. John H. McDermid, Sept. 15, 1988
Hon. Shirley Martin, Sept. 15, 1988
Hon. Mary Collins, Jan. 30, 1989
Hon. Alan Redway, Jan. 30, 1989
Hon. William Charles Winegard, Jan. 30, 1989
Rt. Hon. A. Kim Campbell, Jan. 30, 1989
Hon. Jean Corbeil, Jan. 30, 1989
Hon. Gilles Loiselle, Jan. 30, 1989
Hon. John White Hughes Bassett, Nov. 30, 1989
Hon. Marcel Danis, Feb. 23, 1990
Rt. Hon. Joseph Antonio Charles Lamer, July 3, 1990
Hon. Audrey McLaughlin, Jan. 10, 1991
Hon. Pauline Browes, Apr. 21, 1991
Hon. Edmond Jacques Courtois, Dec. 5, 1991
Hon. J.J. Michel Robert, Dec. 5, 1991
Hon. Marcel Prud'homme, July 1, 1992
Hon. William C. Scott, July 1, 1992
Hon. Lorne Edmund Nystrom, July 1, 1992
Hon. Gerhard Herzberg, July 1, 1992
Hon. Arthur Tremblay, July 1, 1992
Hon. David Alexander Colville, July 1, 1992
Hon. Paul Desmarais, July 1, 1992
Hon. John Charles Polanyi, July 1, 1992
Hon. Maurice F. Strong, July 1, 1992
Hon. Antonine Maillet, July 1, 1992
Hon. Rita Joe, July 1, 1992
Hon. James Bourque, July 1, 1992
Hon. Richard Cashin, July 1, 1992
Hon. Paul M. Tellier, July 1, 1992
Hon. Patricia Helen Rogers, July 1, 1992
Hon. David Robert Peterson, July 1, 1992
Hon. Conrad M. Black, July 1, 1992
Hon. Charles Rosner Bronfman, Oct. 21, 1992
Hon. Maurice Richard, Oct. 30, 1992

Hon. William Ormond Mitchell, Nov. 5, 1992
Hon. Edwin A. Goodman, Nov. 30, 1992
Hon. George W. Vari, Dec. 23, 1992
Hon. Pierre H. Vincent, Jan. 4, 1993
Hon. Rosemary Brown, Apr. 20, 1993
Hon. James Stewart Edwards, June 25, 1993
Hon. Robert Douglas Nicholson, June 25, 1993
Hon. Barbara Jane Sparrow, June 25, 1993
Hon. Peter L. McCreath, June 25, 1993
Hon. Ian Angus Ross Reid, June 25, 1993
Hon. Larry Schneider, June 25, 1993
Hon. Garth Turner, June 25, 1993
Hon. David Anderson, Nov. 4, 1993
Hon. Ralph Goodale, Nov. 4, 1993
Hon. David Charle Dingwall, Nov. 4, 1993
Hon. Ron Irwin, Nov. 4, 1993
Hon. Brian Tobin, Nov. 4, 1993
Hon. Joyce Fairbairn, Nov. 4, 1993
Hon. Sheila Maureen Copps, Nov. 4, 1993
Hon. Sergio Marchi, Nov. 4, 1993
Hon. John Manley, Nov. 4, 1993
Hon. Diane Marleau, Nov. 4, 1993
Hon. Paul Martin, Nov. 4, 1993
Hon. Douglas Young, Nov. 4, 1993
Hon. Michel Dupuy, Nov. 4, 1993
Hon. Art Eggleton, Nov. 4, 1993
Hon. Marcel Massé, Nov. 4, 1993
Hon. Anne McLellan, Nov. 4, 1993
Hon. Allan Rock, Q.C., Nov. 4, 1993
Hon. Sheila Finestone, Nov. 4, 1993
Hon. Fernand Robichaud, Nov. 4, 1993
Hon. Ethel Blondin-Andrew, Nov. 4, 1993
Hon. Lawrence MacAulay, Nov. 4, 1993
Hon. Christine Stewart, Nov. 4, 1993
Hon. Raymond Chan, Nov. 4, 1993
Hon. Jon Gerrard, Nov. 4, 1993
Hon. Doug Peters, Nov. 4, 1993
Hon. Alfonso Gagliano, Sept. 15, 1994
Hon. Lucienne Robillard, Feb. 22, 1995
Hon. Fred Mifflin, Jan. 25, 1996
Hon. Jane Stewart, Jan. 25, 1996
Hon. Stéphane Dion, Jan. 25, 1996
Hon. Pierre Pettigrew, Jan. 25, 1996
Hon. Martin Cauchon, Jan. 25, 1996
Hon. Hedy Fry, Jan. 25, 1996

SENATE OF CANADA/Le Sénat du Canada
Senate Bldg., 111 Wellington St., Ottawa ON K1A 0A4
613/992-1149; Fax: 613/995-4998; URL: http://www.parl.gc.ca/english/emember.html
Toll Free: 1-800-267-7362

Senators are appointed by the Governor General on the recommendation of the Prime Minister of Canada. Senators appointed prior to 2nd June 1965 hold their positions for life, but those appointed after that date hold their positions only until they attain the age of seventy-five years.

To be eligible for appointment, a senatorial candidate must be a Canadian citizen, or a British subject, and be at least thirty years of age. He must own real property worth a net of $4,000 in the province he represents and he must be worth at least $4,000 over and above all debts. He must be a resident of the province for which he was appointed or if he is appointed for Québec, he must either own his real property qualification or else be a resident in the electoral division for which he is appointed.

The Speaker of the Senate is appointed by the Governor General also on the recommendation of the Prime Minister.

The Senate can initiate any bills except those providing for expenditure of public money or imposing taxes. Although it can amend or reject any bill, it has seldom had to do either. No bill may become law unless it is passed by the Senate.

The main thrust of the Senate's work is carried out in committees, where bills are interpreted & reviewed clause by clause, & evidence is heard from groups & individuals who may be affected by the particular bill under review.

In recent decades, the Senate has begun examining major public concerns within Canada (including inflation, land use, international relations, unemployment, government efficiency). The Senate reports produced from such studies have proved to be valuable & less expensive than royal commissions or task forces, & have often led to changes in government policy or legislation. The Speaker of the Senate is appointed by the Governor General upon the recommendation of the Prime Minister. It is tradition to alternate between English-speaking & French-speaking selections as Speaker of the Senate.

The Senate as originally constituted at Confederation consisted of 72 members. Through the addition of new provinces and the general growth of Canada it now has 104 regular members.
By provinces, representation is as follows:
Alta. 6; B.C. 6; Man. 6; N.B. 10; N.S. 10; N.W.T. 1; Nfld. 6; Ont. 24; P.E.I. 4; Qué. 24; Sask. 6; Yukon 1; Total 104.
By party affiliation, representation is as follows (July 29, 1996):
PC 50; Lib. 49; Ind. 3; Vacant 2; Total 104

Speaker of the Senate, Hon. Gildas L. Molgat, 613/992-4416
Government Leader, Hon. Joyce Fairbairn, 613/996-4382
Opposition Leader, Hon. John Lynch-Staunton, 613/943-1481
Government Whip, Hon. Jacques Hébert, 613/992-3756
Opposition Whip, Hon. Noel Kinsella, 613/943-0753

Officers of the Senate
Clerk & Parliament Clerk, Paul Bélisle, 613/992-2493
Clerk's Assistant, Richard G. Greene, 613/996-0397
Acting Law Clerk & Parliamentary Counsel, Mark Audcent, 613/992-2416
Director, Committees, Gary O'Brien, 613/990-0088
Gentleman Usher of the Black Rod, Col. Jean Doré, 613/992-8483
Director, Human Resources, Suzanne Beaudoin, 613/996-1096
Director, Finance, Siroun Aghajanian, 613/992-7951
Senior Asst. Editor, Debates, Jeanie Morrison, 613/996-0854
Senior Legislative Clerk, Communications, André Reny, 613/992-1149

Senators, with appointment year, political affiliation & phone no.
Hon. Willie Adams, 1977, Lib., 613/992-2753
Hon. Doris Anderson, 1995, Lib., 613/942-7964
Hon. Raynell Andreychuk, 1993, PC, 613/947-2239
Hon. David W. Angus, 1993, PC, 613/947-3193
Hon. Norman K. Atkins, 1986, PC, 613/992-7172
Hon. Jack Austin, 1975, Lib., 613/992-1437
Hon. Lise Bacon, 1994, Lib., 613/995-6194
Hon. James Balfour, 1979, PC, 613/995-2864
Hon. Gérald Beaudoin, 1988, PC, 613/995-6128
Hon. Eric Arthur Berntson, 1990, PC, 613/743-1424
Hon. Roch Bolduc, 1988, PC, 613/995-6185
Hon. M. Lorne Bonnell, 1971, Lib., 613/996-0370
Hon. Peter Bosa, 1977, Lib., 613/995-7235
Hon. John Bryden, 1994, Lib., 613/947-7305
Hon. John Buchanan, 1990, PC, 613/943-1409
Hon. Patricia Carney, 1990, PC, 613/943-1433
Hon. Sharon Carstairs, 1994, Lib., 613/947-7123
Hon. Guy Charbonneau, 1979, PC, 613/992-4416
Hon. Ethel Cochrane, 1986, PC, 613/992-1577
Hon. Michel Cogger, 1986, PC, 613/992-2974
Hon. Erminie J. Cohen, 1993, PC, 613/947-3187
Hon. Gérald Joseph Comeau, 1990, PC, 613/934-1448
Hon. Anne C. Cools, 1984, Lib., 613/992-2808
Hon. Eymard Corbin, 1984, Lib., 613/996-8485
Hon. Pierre De Bané, 1984, Lib., 613/992-8289

Hon. Mabel Margaret DeWare, 1990, PC, 613/943-0759
Hon. Consiglio Di Nino, 1990, PC, 613/943-1454
Hon. C. William Doody, 1979, PC, 613/995-1144
Hon. Richard J. Doyle, 1985, PC, 613/995-7287
Hon. John Trevor Eyton, 1990, PC, 613/943-1460
Hon. Joyce Fairbairn, 1984, Lib., 613/996-4382
Hon. Jean B. Forest, 1996, Lib., 613/992-0648
Hon. J. Michael Forrestall, 1990, PC, 613/943-1442
Hon. Jean-Robert Gauthier, 1994, Lib., 613/947-7536
Hon. Ronald D. Ghitter, 1993, PC, 613/947-2220
Hon. Philippe D. Gigantès, 1984, Lib., 613/992-2852
Hon. Jerahmiel S. Grafstein, 1984, Lib., 613/992-2642
Hon. B. Alasdair Graham, 1972, Lib., 613/992-3770
Hon. Normand Grimard, 1990, PC, 613/943-1419
Hon. Leonard J. Gustafson, 1993, PC, 613/947-2233
Hon. Stanley Haidasz, 1978, Lib., 613/992-2713
Hon. Daniel Hays, 1984, Lib., 613/996-3485
Hon. Jacques Hébert, 1983, Lib., 613/992-3756
Hon. Céline Hervieux-Payette, 1995, Lib., 613/947-8008
Hon. Duncan J. Jessiman, 1993, PC, 613/947-2230
Hon. Janis Johnson, 1990, PC, 613/943-1430
Hon. James Kelleher, 1990, PC, 613/943-0762
Hon. William M. Kelly, 1982, PC, 613/992-0081
Hon. Colin Kenny, 1984, Lib., 613/996-2877
Hon. Wilbert Joseph Keon, 1990, PC, 613/943-1415
Hon. Noel Kinsella, 1990, PC, 613/943-0753
Hon. Michael Kirby, 1984, Lib., 613/992-2976
Hon. Leo Kolber, 1983, Lib., 613/992-2690
Hon. Joseph Landry, 1996, Lib., 613/942-0672
Hon. Thérèse Lavoie-Roux, 1990, PC, 613/943-1427
Hon. Edward M. Lawson, 1970, Ind., 613/996-5453
Hon. Marjory LeBreton, 1993, PC, 613/943-0756
Hon. P. Derek Lewis, 1978, Lib., 613/995-0765
Hon. Rose-Marie Losier-Cool, 1995, Lib., 613/947-8011
Hon. Paul Lucier, 1975, Lib., 613/992-2568
Hon. John Lynch-Staunton, 1990, PC, 613/943-1481
Hon. Finlay MacDonald, 1984, PC, 613/995-2150
Hon. John M. Macdonald, 1960, PC, 613/992-1448
Hon. Shirley Maheu, 1996, Lib., 613/947-2212
Hon. Len Marchand, 1984, Lib., 613/996-7282
Hon. Michael Arthur Meighen, 1990, PC, 613/943-1421
Hon. Leonce Mercier, 1996, Lib.
Hon. Lorne Milne, 1995, Lib., 613/947-7695
Hon. Gildas L. Molgat, 1970, Lib., 613/992-4416
Hon. Wilfrid P. Moore, 1996, Lib.
Hon. Lowell Murray, 1979, PC, 613/995-2407
Hon. Joan Neiman, 1972, Lib., 613/996-1916
Hon. Pierre-Claude Nolin, 1993, PC, 613/943-1451
Hon. Donald Oliver, 1990, PC, 613/943-1445
Hon. Gerald R. Ottenheimer, 1987, PC, 613/996-9389
Hon. Landon Pearson, 1994, Lib., 613/947-7134
Hon. Raymond J. Perrault, 1973, Lib., 613/992-2682
Hon. William J. Petten, 1968, Lib., 613/992-4294
Hon. Orville H. Phillips, 1963, PC, 613/992-5432
Hon. P.M. Pitfield, 1982, Ind., 613/992-2784
Hon. Marie-P. Poulin, 1995, Lib., 613/947-8005
Hon. Marcel Prud'homme, 1993, Ind., 613/947-2227
Hon. Maurice Riel, 1973, Lib., 613/996-9164
Hon. Jean-Claude Rivest, 1993, PC, 613/947-2236
Hon. Pietro Rizzuto, 1976, PC, 613/995-0698
Hon. Fernand Roberge, 1993, PC, 613/947-3250
Hon. Brenda M. Robertson, 1984, Lib., 613/998-5585
Hon. Louis J. Robichaud, l973, Lib., 613/996-4134
Hon. William Romkey, 1995, Lib., 613/947-9584
Hon. Eileen Rossiter, 1986, PC, 613/992-1650
Hon. Gerry St. Germain, 1993, PC, 613/947-2242
Hon. Jean-Maurice Simard, 1985, PC, 613/995-0925
Hon. Herbert O. Sparrow, 1968, Lib., 613/996-5994
Hon. Mira Spivak, 1986, PC, 613/995-1488
Hon. Richard J. Stanbury, 1968, Lib., 613/992-6981
Hon. John B. Stewart, 1984, Lib., 613/992-2751
Hon. Peter Stollery, 1981, Lib., 613/992-3012
Hon. Terrance R. Stratton, 1993, PC, 613/947-2224
Hon. Nicholas W. Taylor, 1996, Lib., 613/947-1605
Hon. Andrew Thompson, 1967, Lib., 613/992-1306
Hon. David Tkachuk, 1993, PC, 613/947-3196
Hon. W.P. Twinn, 1990, PC, 613/943-1457

Hon. Charlie Watt, 1984, Lib., 613/992-2981
Hon. Eugene Francis Whelan, 1996, Lib.
Hon. Dalia Wood, 1979, Lib., 613/992-3161

HOUSE OF COMMONS, CANADA/
Chambre des communes
House of Commons, 111 Wellington St., PO Box 1103, Ottawa ON K1A 0A9
URL: http://www.parl.gc.ca; gopher.parl.gc.ca/
Public Information Office: #377, East Block, 111 Wellington St., Ottawa ON K1A 0A6
613/992-4793, Fax: 613/992-1273
TDD: 613/995-2266

The House of Commons is the major law-making unit in Canada. The 295 members of the House represent each constituency, or riding, across Canada. Members are elected in general elections, held at least once every five years. During general elections one candidate per riding is elected, based on the largest number of seats, even if his or her vote is less than half the total. When a member resigns or dies between general elections, a by-election is held.

The party that wins the largest number of seats in the general election usually forms the government. The party with the second largest number of votes becomes the Official Opposition. If the government prior to a general election, comes out of the election without a clear majority, it has the right to meet the new House of Commons & determine whether it can develop enough support from the minor parties to give it a majority.

A minority government is created when one particular party holds no clear majority of seats in the House. In this case, the government is usually led by the party with the most seats in Parliament, providing it can sustain the support from other minor parties that enable it to pass legislation.

Any bills within federal jurisdiction must be passed by a majority of House members to become law. Members usually vote on proposed legislation according to party affiliation. They may vote against their party & may also leave their elected party to sit as an independent within the House.

The Speaker of the House of Commons is elected after each general election through a secret ballot process within the Commons Chamber. The person elected as Speaker must be a member of the House of Commons & is expected to be an impartial, nonpartisan & firm controller of all questions & procedures within it's confines. If the Speaker elected is an English-speaking member, it is customary that a French-speaking member be chosen as the Deputy Speaker.

Speaker of the House, Hon. Gilbert Parent, 613/992-5042
Deputy Speaker & Chair, Committees of the Whole House, David Kilgour
Deputy Chair, Committees of the Whole House, Bob Kilger
Asst. Deputy Chair, Committees of the Whole House, Pierrette Ringuette-Maltais
Government Whip, Vacant
Bloc Québécois Party Whip, Madeleine Dalphond-Guiral
Reform Party Whip, Chuck Strahl
NDP Party Whip, John Solomon
PC Party Whip, Vacant

House of Commons Staff
Clerk of the House, Robert Marleau, 613/992-2986

Administration Services
Deputy Clerk, Mary Anne Griffith, 613/996-0485
General Legal Counsel, Legal Services, Diane Davidson, 613/992-1511
Comptroller, John McCrae, 613/992-0100

Canadian Almanac & Directory 1997

3-46 GOVERNMENT OF CANADA

Director General, Human Resources, Jacques Sabourin, 613/992-9721
Director, Personnel Operations, Rose Bussière, 613/996-7883
Director General, Information Technologies, R.J. Desramaux, 613/992-1459
Director, Parliamentary Publications, A. Dambraskas, 613/992-2419
Director, Information Systems, Louis Bard, 613/992-7363
Director, Program Evaluation & Review, L. McRae, 613/995-0224
Chief, Broadcasting Service, Philippe Parent, 613/995-3490

Parliamentary Precinct Services
Sergeant-at-Arms, Maj.-Gen. M.G. Cloutier, 613/995-7521
Director, Building Services, K.R. Macquarrie, 613/995-1990
Director, Security Services, Denis Gagnon, 613/995-7020

Procedural Services
Clerk Asst., Camille Montpetit, 613/995-5990
Principal Clerk, House Proceedings & Parliamentary Exchanges, William Corbett, 613/996-3611
Acting Deputy Principal Clerk, Parliamentary Exchanges & Protocol, Carol Chafe, 613/996-1102
Director, Committees & Parliamentary Associations & General Legislative Counsel, R.R. Walsh, 613/992-3150

COMMITTEES OF THE HOUSE OF COMMONS
Following is a list of Standing Committees as set out in the Standing Orders. Each committee has between seven and 15 members except the Standing Committee on Procedure & House Affairs (formerly the Standing Committee on House Management) which consists of 14 members. The committee also acts as the Striking Committee.

There are also three Standing Joint Committees: Scrutiny of Regulations, Library of Parliament and Official Languages.

Committee members change frequently. Contact the Public Information Office listed above for an up-to-date list.

Standing Committees of the House
Aboriginal Affairs & Northern Development
Agriculture & Agri-Food
Canadian Heritage
Citizenship & Immigration
Environment & Sustainable Development
Finance
Fisheries & Oceans
Foreign Affairs & International Trade
Government Operations
Health
Human Resources Development
Human Rights & the Status of Persons with Disabilities
Industry
Justice & Legal Affairs
National Defence & Veterans Affairs
Natural Resources
Procedure & House Affairs
Public Accounts
Transport

OFFICE OF THE PRIME MINISTER (Lib.)/ Cabinet du Premier ministre
Langevin Block, 80 Wellington St., Ottawa ON K1A 0A2
613/992-4211; Fax: 613/941-6900; Email: pm@pm.gc.ca; URL: http://canada.gc.ca/english/pmo/index.htm

Correspondence Page URL: http://canada.gc.ca/english/pmo/e_co

The Prime Minister is the Head of Government in Canada & usually the leader of the party in power in the House of Commons. The Prime Minister recommends to the monarchy, the appointment of the Governor General & is responsible for selecting a team of ministers, who are then appointed by the Governor General to the Queen's Privy Council. In addition, he or she also controls the appointment of cabinet ministers, senators, judges & parliamentary secretaries. It is customary, that the Prime Minister is also appointed to the Imperial Privy Council & is thus titled "The Right Honourable". The Prime Minister has the right to dissolve parliament & can therefore control the timing of general elections.

Prime Minister/Premier ministre, Rt. Hon. Jean Chrétien, 613/992-4211, Email: pm@pm.gc.ca
Chief of Staff, Jean Pelletier, 613/957-5517
Senior Policy Advisor, Eddie Goldenberg, 613/957-5788
Executive Asst., Bruce Hartley, 613/957-5549
Legislative Asst., Graeme Clark, 613/957-5080
Director, Appointments, Penny Collenette, 613/957-5540
Director, Communications, Peter Donolo, 613/957-5555
Director, Operations, Jean Carle, 613/957-5520
Director, Policy & Research, Chaviva Hosek, 613/957-5566
Press Secretary, Patrick Parisot, 613/957-5555
Manager, Finance, Personnel & Administration, Ray Monnot, 613/957-5564
Manager, Correspondence, Mark Stokes, 613/957-5561
Chief House Leader, Hon. Herbert Eser Gray, 613/995-7548
Chief Party Whip, Vacant
Senior Deputy Whip, Marlene Catterall

OFFICE OF THE DEPUTY PRIME MINISTER
Langevin Block, 80 Wellington St., Ottawa ON K1A 0A3
613/997-1441
Deputy Prime Minister, Hon. Sheila Copps, Email: mincopps@am@ncrsv2.am.doe.ca

OFFICE OF THE LEADER, OPPOSITION (BQ)
#409-S, Centre Block, House of Commons, 111 Wellington St., Ottawa ON K1A 0A6
613/996-6740; Fax: 613/954-2121; URL: http://www.ncf.carleton.ca/freeport/government/fedelect/nat/bq/menu
Montréal Office: #1475, 425, de Maisonneuve ouest, Montréal PQ H3A 3G5, 514/499-3000, Fax: 514/499-3638
Toll Free: 1-800-267-2562
Leader of the Bloc Québécois, Michel Gauthier
Chief Party Whip, Pierrette Ringuette-Maltais
Deputy Leader, Vacant, 613/995-7398
Director, Cabinet & Chief of Staff, Gilbert Charland, 613/996-6740
Senior Policy Advisor, Pierre-Paul Roy, 613/996-6740

OFFICE OF THE LEADER, REFORM PARTY (Ref.)
Centre Block, House of Commons, #531-S, 111 Wellington St., Ottawa ON K1A 0A6
613/992-3602; Fax: 613/947-0310; Email: info@reform.ca; URL: http://www.reform.ca/english/
National Office Email: national-office@reform.ca
Reform Question Period Hotline Email: hotline@reform.ca
Membership Email: membership@reform.ca
Calgary Office: #600, 833 - 4 Ave. SW, Calgary AB T2P 0K5; 403/269-1990, Fax: 403/269-4077

Leader of the Reform Party, Preston Manning, Email: pmanning@reform.ca
Chair, Clifford Fryers
Chief of Staff, Stephen Greene
Executive Director (Calgary), Glenn McMurray
Chief Party Whip, Chuck Strahl
Deputy Caucus Coordinator, Stephen Harper, Email: harper@reform.ca
Caucus Chair, Deborah Grey, Email: grey@reform.ca
House Leader, Elwin Hermanson
Deputy House Leader, Ed Harper
Director, Communications, Lucille Hodgins

OFFICE OF THE LEADER, NEW DEMOCRATIC PARTY (NDP)
#900, 81 Metcalfe St., Ottawa ON K1P 6K7
613/236-3613; Fax: 613/230-9950; Email: ndpadmin@fed.ndp.ca; URL: http://www.fed.ndp.ca/fndp
Leader of the New Democratic Party, Alexa McDonough, Email: ndpadmin@fed.ndp.ca
New Democratic Party House Leader, William Blaikie, #214, West Block, House of Commons, Ottawa ON K1A 0A6, 613/995-6339, Fax: 613/995-6688, Email: blaikb@parl.gc.ca
New Democratic Party Whip, John Solomon, 724 Confederation Bldg., House of Commons, Ottawa ON K1A 0A6, 613/992-4573, Fax: 613/996-6885, Email: solomj@parl.gc.ca
Principal Secretary, Dan O'Connor

OFFICE OF THE LEADER, PROGRESSIVE CONSERVATIVE PARTY (PC)
#436-N, Centre Block, House of Commons, 111 Wellington St., Ottawa ON K1A 0A6
613/943-1106; Fax: 613/995-0364; URL: http://www.ncf.carleton.ca/freeport/government/fedelect/nat/pc/menu
Leader, Progressive Conservative Party, Hon. Jean Charest
National Director, Michael Allen
National President, Pierre Fortier
Director, Communications, Rita Mezzanotte
Chief of Staff, Albert Cooper
Legislative Asst., Chad Schella
Scheduling Asst., Anik Trépanier
Constituency Asst., Suzanne Poulin
Special Asst., Francine Carrier

THE CANADIAN MINISTRY/The Cabinet
House of Commons, 111 Wellington St., Ottawa ON K1A 0A6
URL: http://canada.gc.ca/howgoc/cab/cabind_e.html

The Canadian Ministry, or Cabinet, is the most significant of all federal government committees or councils. Cabinet members are selected & led by the Prime Minister, they must also be or become members of the Queen's Privy Council. Cabinet ministers determine specific policies & are responsible for them in the House of Commons. The Cabinet is responsible for initiating all public bills in the House of Commons, & in some instances can create regulations that have the strength of law, termed decisions of the "Governor-in-Council.

Cabinet meetings are usually closed to the public, allowing members to discuss their opinions on particular policy in secret. Once decided, members usually support all policy uniformly. If a minister is unable to support the Ministry, he or she is obligated to resign.

Prime Minister, Rt. Hon. Jean Chrétien, Langevin Block, 80 Wellington St., Ottawa ON K1A 0A2, 613/992-4211, Fax: 613/941-6900, Email: pm@pm.gc.ca
Minister, Transport, Hon. David Anderson, Connaught Mackin Bldg., Mackenzie Ave., 7th Fl.,

Canadian Almanac & Directory 1997

Ottawa ON K1A 0L5, 613/991-0700, Fax: 613/995-0327

Minister, Foreign Affairs, Hon. Lloyd Axworthy, 140 Promenade du Portage, Phase IV, 14th Fl., Hull PQ K1A 0J9, 819/994-2482, Fax: 819/994-0448

Secretary of State, Training & Youth, Hon. Ethel Blondin-Andrew, 140 Promenade du Portage, Phase IV, 12th Fl., Hull PQ K1A 0J9, 819/953-8385, Fax: 819/953-0944

Minister, International Cooperation & Minister Responsible, Francophonie, Hon. Don Boudria

Secretary of State, Federal Office of Regional Development - Québec, Hon. Martin Cauchon, 613/995-7691

Secretary of State, Asia-Pacific, Hon. Raymond Chan, Tower A, Lester B. Pearson Bldg., 125 Sussex Dr., 10th Fl., Ottawa ON K1A 0G2, 613/995-1851, Fax: 613/996-3443

Deputy Prime Minister & Minister, Canadian Heritage, Hon. Sheila Copps, Terrasses de la Chaudière, 10 Wellington St., 28th Fl., Hull PQ K1A 0H3, 613/995-2773

Minister, Health, Hon. David C. Dingwall, Phase III, Place du Portage, #18A1, 11 Laurier St., Hull PQ K1A 0S5, 819/996-1154

President, Privy Council & Minister Responsible, Intergovernmental Affairs, Hon. Stéphane Dion, Heritage Bldg., 155 Queen St., 5th Fl., Ottawa ON K1A 0A3, 613/943-1838, Fax: 613/943-1855

Minister, International Trade, Hon. Art Eggleton, East Tower, L'Esplanade Laurier, 140 O'Connor St., 9th Fl., Ottawa ON K1A 0R5, 613/992-7332, Fax: 613/996-8924

Leader of Government in the Senate & Minister Responsible, Literacy, Hon. Joyce Fairbairn, Centre Block, #275-S, Senate of Canada, Ottawa ON K1A 0A4, 613/996-4382, Fax: 613/995-3223

Secretary of State, Multiculturalism & Status of Women, Hon. Hedy Fry, 613/992-3213

Minister, Labour & Deputy House Leader, Hon. Alphonso Gagliano, #219-S, Centre Block, Ottawa ON K1A 0A6, 613/995-9414, Fax: 613/992-8523

Secretary of State, Science, Research & Development & Secretary of State, Western Economic Diversification, Hon. Jon Gerrard, 235 Queen St., 11th Fl. East, Ottawa ON K1A 0H5, 613/995-9001, Fax: 613/990-4056

Minister, Agriculture & Agri-Food, Hon. Ralph Goodale, Sir John A. Carling Bldg., 930 Carling Ave., Ottawa ON K1A 0C5, 613/996-2508, Fax: 613/996-9219

Solicitor General of Canada & Government House Leader, Hon. Herbert Eser Gray, Sir Wilfred Laurier Bldg., 340 Laurier Ave. West, 13th Fl., Ottawa ON K1A 0P8, 613/991-2924, Fax: 613/952-2240

Solicitor General of Canada & Government House Leader, Hon. Herbert Eser Gray, Sir Wilfred Laurier Bldg., 340 Laurier Ave. West, 13th Fl., Ottawa ON K1A 0P8, 613/991-2924, Fax: 613/952-2240

Minister, Indian Affairs & Northern Development, Hon. Ronald A. Irwin, C.M., Q.C., #2100, 10 Wellington St., Hull PQ K1A 0H4, 819/997-0002, Fax: 819/953-4941

Secretary of State, Veterans Affairs & Minister Responsible, Atlantic Canada Opportunities Agency, Hon. Lawrence MacAulay, 66 Slater St., 16th Fl., Ottawa ON K1A 0P4, 613/996-4649, Fax: 613/954-1054

Minister, Industry & Minister, Atlantic Canada Opportunities Agency, Western Economic Diversification, Federal Office of Regional Development - Québec, Hon. John Manley, 235 Queen St., 11th Fl. East, Ottawa ON K1A 0H5, 613/995-9001, Fax: 613/992-0302

Minister, Environment, Hon. Sergio Marchi, Place du Portage, Phase I, 50 Victoria St., 23rd Fl., Hull PQ K1A 1L1, 819/997-1843, Fax: 819/953-4930

Minister, Public Works & Government Services, Hon. Diane Marleau, Tunney's Pasture, #1603-A, Brooke Claxton Bldg., Ottawa ON K1A 0K9, 613/996-8963

Minister, Finance, Hon. Paul Martin, East Tower, 140 O'Connor St., 21st Fl., Ottawa ON K1A 0G5, 613/996-7861, Fax: 613/995-5176, Email: pmartin@fin.gc.ca

President, Treasury Board & Minster Responsible, Infrastructure, Hon. Marcel Massé, 155 Queen St., 5th Fl., Ottawa ON K1A 1K2, 613/943-1838, Fax: 613/943-1855

Minister, Natural Resources, Hon. Anne McLellan, 580 Booth St., 21st Fl., Ottawa ON K1A 0E4, 613/996-2007, Fax: 613/996-4516

Minister, Fisheries & Oceans, Hon. Fred Mifflin, 613/992-4133

Secretary of State, International Financial Institutions, Hon. Douglas Peters, East Tower, 140 O'Connor St., 21st Fl., Ottawa ON K1A 0C5, 613/996-3170, Fax: 613/995-2355

Minister, Human Resources Development, Hon. Pierre Pettigrew, Place du Centre, 200, promenade du Portage, 12e étage, Hull PQ K1A 0G4

Secretary of State, Agriculture & Agri-food & Fisheries & Oceans, Hon. Fernand Robichaud, House of Commons, #107, Confederation Bldg., Ottawa ON K1A 0A6, 613/947-4592, Fax: 613/947-4595

Minister, Citizenship & Immigration, Hon. Lucienne Robillard, 819/953-5646

Minister, Justice & Attorney General of Canada, Hon. Allan Rock, Q.C., Justice Bldg., 239 Wellington St., Ottawa ON K1A 0H8, 613/992-4621, Fax: 613/990-7255

Secretary of State, Latin America & Africa, Hon. Christine Stewart, Tower A, Lester B. Pearson Bldg., 125 Sussex Dr., 10th Fl., Ottawa ON K1A 0G2, 613/992-6560, Fax: 613/996-0461

Minister, National Revenue, Hon. Jane Stewart

Minister, National Defence & Minister, Vetrans Affairs, Hon. Douglas Young, Tower C, Place de Ville, 330 Sparks St., 29th Fl., Ottawa ON K1A 0N5, 613/991-0700, Fax: 613/995-0327

THIRTY-FIFTH PARLIAMENT - CANADA

House of Commons, 111 Wellington St., Ottawa ON K1A 0A9
613/992-4793; URL: http://www.parl.gc.ca/english/index.html

Members of the House of Commons are elected by the people. The legal limit of duration for each House is five years, sitting at least once a year. The Speaker is elected by the House.

By virtue of the Constitution Act, after each decennial census the representation in the House of Commons is readjusted. Pursuant to the Electoral Boundaries Readjustment Act, and rule laid down therein, a representation order is prepared which redraws the constituency boundaries in each province. Last General Election, October 25th, 1993.
Legal duration, 5 years from the day of the return of the writs.

Political Party Leaders

Liberal, Rt. Hon. Jean Chrétien, P.C., Q.C.
Bloc Québécois, Michel Gauthier
Reform Party, Preston Manning
New Democratic Party, Hon. Alexa McDonough
Progressive Conservative Party, Hon. Jean Charest, P.C.

Party Standings

By provinces, representation in the House of Commons is as follows: Alta. 26; B.C. 32; Man. 14; N.B. 10; Nfld. 7; N.W.T. 2; N.S. 11; Ont. 99; P.E.I. 4; Qué. 75; Sask. 14; Yukon 1; Total 295

By party affiliation, representation is as follows (June 17, 1996): Liberal (Lib.) 176; Bloc Québécois (BQ) 53; Reform Party (Ref.) 51; New Democratic Party (NDP) 9; Progressive Conservative Party (PC) 2; Independent (Ind.) 2; Independent Liberal (Ind. Lib.) 2; Total 295

Salaries & Allowances

At January, 1991 the sessional allowance of each Member of Parliament was $64,400 plus a tax-free expense allowance of $21,300. Members representing the larger Canadian ridings (those electoral districts listed in Schedule III of the Canada Elections Act) received a tax-free expense allowance of $26,200 per annum, while those from the Northwest Territories were entitled to $28,200.

In addition to the salary & expense allowance, Members occupying certain positions in the House of Commons received the following supplementary annual allowances:

Prime Minister: $69,920*
Speaker of the House; & Leader of the Official Opposition: $49,100
Cabinet Ministers: $46,645*
Leaders of Other Parties: $29,500
Deputy Speaker of the House: $25,700
House Leader of the Official Opposition: $23,800
Government Whip; Official Opposition Whip: $13,200
Deputy Chair, House Committees; Asst. Deputy Chair, House Committees; Parliamentary Secretaries: $10,500
House Leaders of Other Parties: $10,100
Party Whips; Deputy Government Whip; Deputy Official Opposition Whip: $7,500

Note: *According to the 1992 budget, the Prime Minister & Cabinet Ministers took a five percent cut in ministerial pay effective April 1, 1992 as per Chapter 12 (1993) The Budget Implementation (fiscal measures) Act, 1992.

MEMBERS BY CONSTITUENCY

See also alphabetical list following. Listed here are constituency (eligible voters in 1993), name of member, party affiliatation, Ottawa phone number.

Alberta

Athabasca (45,987) Dave Chatters, Ref., 613/996-1783
Beaver River (42,434) Deborah Grey, Ref., 613/996-9778
Calgary Centre (71,895) Jim Silye, Ref., 613/995-1127
Calgary North (76,602) Diane Ablonczy, Ref., 613/996-2756
Calgary Northeast (66,504) Art Hanger, Ref., 613/947-4487
Calgary Southeast (69,264) Jan Brown, Ind., 613/996-2791
Calgary Southwest (75,976) Preston Manning, Ref., 613/992-3602
Calgary West (67,784) Stephen Harper, Ref., 613/992-3066
Crowfoot (44,558) Jack Ramsay, Ref., 613/947-4608
Edmonton East (56,015) Judy Bethel, Lib., 613/992-3821
Edmonton North, John Loney, Lib., 613/947-4566
Edmonton Northwest (53,099) Hon. Anne McLellan, Lib., 613/992-4525
Edmonton Southeast (63,776) David Kilgour, Lib., 613/995-8695
Edmonton Southwest (69,333) Ian McClelland, Ref., 613/992-3594
Edmonton-Strathcona (65,848) Hugh Hanrahan, Ref., 613/995-7325
Elk Island (49,816) Ken Epp, Ref., 613/995-3611
Lethbridge (61,456) Ray Speaker, Ref., 613/996-0633
Macleod (43,333) Grant Hill, Ref., 613/995-8471

Canadian Almanac & Directory 1997

Medicine Hat (57,220) Monte Solberg, Ref., 613/992-4516
Peace River (60,031) Charlie Penson, Ref., 613/992-5685
Red Deer (61,261) Bob Mills, Ref., 613/995-0590
St. Albert (52,844) John Williams, Ref., 613/996-4722
Vegreville, Leon Benoit, Ref., 613/992-4171
Wetaskiwin (52,832) Dale Johnston, Ref., 613/995-8886
Wild Rose (52,020) Myron Thompson, Ref., 613/996-5152
Yellowhead, Cliff Breitkreuz, Ref., 613/992-1653

British Columbia
Burnaby-Kingsway (71,059) Svend J. Robinson, NDP, 613/996-5597
Capilano-Howe Sound (50,756) Herb Grubel, Ref., 613/947-4617
Cariboo-Chilcotin (40,836) Philip Mayfield, Ref., 613/996-2205
Comox-Alberni (59,533) Bill Gilmour, Ref., 613/992-5243
Delta (53,024) John Cummins, Ref., 613/992-2957
Esquimalt-Juan de Fuca (54,651) Keith Martin, Ref., 613/996-2625
Fraser Valley East (51,736) Chuck Strahl, Ref., 613/992-2940
Fraser Valley West (63,338) Randy White, Ref., 613/995-0183
Kamloops (50,976) Nelson A. Riis, NDP, 613/995-6931
Kootenay East (41,915) Jim Abbott, Ref., 613/995-7246
Kootenay West-Revelstoke (40,309) Jim Gouk, Ref., 613/996-8036
Mission-Coquitlam (59,990) Daphne Jennings, Ref., 613/947-4613
Nanaimo-Cowichan (66,810) Bob Ringma, Ref., 613/943-2180
New Westminster-Burnaby (71,462) Paul Forseth, Ref., 613/947-4455
North Island-Powell River (52,850) John Duncan, Ref., 613/992-2503
North Vancouver (58,864) Ted White, Ref., 613/995-1225
Okanagan Centre (64,860) Werner Schmidt, Ref., 613/992-7006
Okanagan-Shuswap (52,097) Darrel Stinson, Ref., 613/995-9095
Okanagan-Similkameen-Merritt (51,971) Jim Hart, Ref., 613/995-2581
Port Moody-Coquitlam (65,955) Sharon Hayes, Ref., 613/947-4482
Prince George-Bulkley Valley (47,164) Dick Harris, Ref., 613/995-6704
Prince George-Peace River (47,339) Jay Hill, Ref., 613/947-4524
Richmond (70,891) Hon. Raymond Chan, Lib., 613/996-1995
Saanich-Gulf Island (75,360) Jack Frazer, Ref., 613/996-1119
Skeena (39,977) Mike Scott, Ref., 613/993-6654
Surrey North (69,813) Margaret Bridgman, Ref., 613/992-2922
Surrey-White Rock-South Langley (74,076) Val Meredith, Ref., 613/947-4497
Vancouver Centre (77,445) Hon. Hedy Fry, Lib., 613/992-3213
Vancouver East (55,080) Anna Terrana, Lib., 613/992-6030
Vancouver Quadra, Ted McWhinney, Lib., 613/992-2430
Vancouver South (64,192) Herb Dhaliwal, Lib., 613/995-7052
Victoria (70,394) Hon. David Anderson, Lib., 613/996-2358

Manitoba
Brandon-Souris (50,427) Glen McKinnon, Lib., 613/995-9372
Churchill (39,710) Elijah Harper, Lib., 613/992-3018
Dauphin-Swan River (45,963) Marlene Cowling, Lib., 613/992-3176
Lisgar-Marquette (45,820) Jake Hoeppner, Ref., 613/995-9511
Portage-Interlake (47,672) Hon. Jon Gerrard, Lib., 613/947-4245
Provencher, David Iftody, Lib., 613/992-3128
Selkirk-Red River (57,452) Ron Fewchuk, Lib., 613/996-6426
St. Boniface (57,480) Ronald J. Duhamel, Lib., 613/995-0579
Winnipeg North (57,507) Rey Pagtakhan, Lib., 613/992-7148
Winnipeg North Centre (42,465) David Walker, Lib., 613/992-5308
Winnipeg South (59,974) Reg Alcock, Lib., 613/995-7517, Email: winnipeg_south@mbnet.mb.ca, URL: http://www.mbnet.mb.ca:80/wpgsth
Winnipeg South Centre (56,248) Hon. Lloyd Axworthy, Lib., 613/995-0153
Winnipeg St. James (50,606) John Harvard, Lib., 613/995-5609
Winnipeg Transcona (55,100) William Blaikie, NDP, 613/995-6339

New Brunswick
Acadie-Bathurst (50,206) Hon. Douglas Young, Lib., 613/992-5991
Beausejour, Hon. Fernand Robichaud, Lib., 613/947-4592
Carleton-Charlotte (45,026) Harold Culbert, Lib., 613/996-9726
Fredericton-York-Sunbury (61,381) Andy Scott, Lib., 613/992-1067
Fundy-Royal (58,215) Paul Zed, Lib., 613/996-2332
Madawaska-Victoria (40,185) Pierrette Ringuette-Maltais, Lib., 613/947-4431
Miramichi (38,388) Charles Hubbard, Lib., 613/992-5335
Moncton (63,793) George S. Rideout, Lib., 613/992-8072
Restigouche-Chaleur (37,729) Guy Arseneault, Lib., 613/995-0581
Saint John (54,649) Elsie Wayne, PC, 613/947-4571

Newfoundland
Bonavista-Trinity-Conception (61,321) Hon. Fred Mifflin, Lib., 613/992-4133
Burin-St. George's (53,569) Hon. Roger Simmons, Lib., 613/992-8655
Gander-Grand Falls (55,162) George S. Baker, Lib., 613/996-1541
Humber-St. Barbe-Baie Verte (53,109) Gerry Byrne, Lib., 613/996-5509
Labrador (16,931) Lawrence O'Brien, Lib., 613/996-4630
St. John's East (72,992) Bonnie Hickey, Lib., 613/995-3013
St. John's West, Jean Payne, Lib., 613/992-0927

Northwest Territories
Nunatsiaq (10,888) Jack Iyerak Anawak, Lib., 613/992-2848
Western Arctic (18,142) Hon. Ethel Blondin-Andrew, Lib., 613/992-4587

Nova Scotia
Annapolis Valley-Hants (64,708) John Murphy, Lib., 613/995-8231
Cape Breton Highlands-Canso (47,670) Francis G. LeBlanc, Lib., 613/992-5041
Cape Breton-East Richmond (42,446) Hon. David C. Dingwall, Lib., 613/996-4743
Cape Breton-The Sydneys (47,301) Russell MacLellan, Lib., 613/995-6459
Central Nova (52,184) Roseanne Skoke, Lib., 613/995-5822
Cumberland-Colchester (58,302) Dianne Brushett, Lib., 613/992-3366
Dartmouth (66,681) Ron MacDonald, Lib., 613/995-9378
Halifax (68,144) Mary Clancy, Lib., 613/995-9368
Halifax West (72,431) Geoff Regan, Lib., 613/992-1624
South Shore (56,419) Derek Wells, Lib., 613/996-0877
South West Nova (51,561) Harry Verran, Lib., 613/995-5711

Ontario
Algoma (43,688) Brent St. Denis, Lib., 613/996-5376
Beaches-Woodbine (57,838) Maria Minna, Lib., 613/992-2115
Bramalea-Gore-Milton (56,348) Gurbax Malhi, Lib., 613/992-9105
Brampton (80,678) Colleen Beaumier, Lib., 613/996-2878
Brant (65,336) Hon. Jane Stewart, Lib., 613/992-3118
Broadview-Greenwood (52,661) Dennis J. Mills, Ind.L, 613/992-7771
Bruce-Grey (66,746) Ovid Jackson, Lib., 613/996-5191
Burlington (63,577) Paddy Torsney, Lib., 613/995-0881
Cambridge (69,634) Janko Peric, Lib., 613/996-1307
Carleton-Gloucester (75,578) Eugène Bellemare, Lib., 613/995-6296
Cochrane-Superior (41,262) Réginald Bélair, Lib., 613/992-2919
Davenport (36,869) Charles Caccia, Lib., 613/992-2576
Don Valley East (54,706) Hon. David Collenette, Lib., 613/995-4988
Don Valley North (50,433) Sarkis Assadourian, Lib., 613/995-4843
Don Valley West (62,286) John Godfrey, Lib., 613/992-2855
Durham (68,790) Alex Shepherd, Lib., 613/996-4984
Eglinton-Lawrence (52,331) Joseph Volpe, Lib., 613/992-6361
Elgin-Norfolk (56,065) Gar Knutson, Lib., 613/990-7769
Erie (51,617) John Maloney, Lib., 613/995-0988
Essex-Kent (51,100) Jerry Pickard, Lib., 613/992-2612
Essex-Windsor (56,457) Susan Whelan, Lib., 613/992-1812
Etobicoke Centre, Hon. Allan Rock, Q.C., Lib., 613/947-5000
Etobicoke North (63,617) Roy Cullen, Lib.
Etobicoke-Lakeshore (60,279) Jean Augustine, Lib., 613/995-9364
Glengarry-Prescott-Russell (67,681) Hon. Don Boudria, Lib., 613/996-2907
Guelph-Wellington (76,618) Brenda Chamberlain, Lib., 613/996-4758
Haldimand-Norfolk (60,021) Bob Speller, Lib., 613/996-4974
Halton-Peel (67,417) Julian Reed, Lib., 613/996-7046
Hamilton East (52,117) Hon. Sheila Copps, Lib., 613/995-2773
Hamilton Mountain (64,576) Beth Phinney, Lib., 613/995-9389
Hamilton West (60,728) Stan Keyes, Lib., 613/995-1757
Hamilton-Wentworth (72,906) Hon. John Bryden, Lib., 613/995-8042
Hastings-Frontenac-Lennox and Addington (58,252) Larry McCormick, Lib., 613/992-3640
Huron-Bruce (60,955) Paul Steckle, Lib., 613/992-8234
Kenora-Rainy River (48,102) Robert D. Nault, Lib., 613/996-1161
Kent (54,943) Rex Crawford, Lib., 613/995-7784
Kingston and the Islands (73,775) Peter Milliken, Lib., 613/996-1955
Kitchener (70,875) John English, Lib., 613/995-8913
Lambton-Middlesex (52,210) Rose-Marie Ur, Lib., 613/947-4581
Lanark-Carleton (72,621) Ian Murray, Lib., 613/947-2277
Leeds-Grenville (59,819) Jim Jordan, Lib., 613/992-8756

Lincoln (65,699) Tony Valeri, Lib., 613/992-6535
London East (71,537) Joe Fontana, Lib., 613/992-0805
London West (76,807) Sue Barnes, Lib., 613/996-6674
London-Middlesex (64,749) Pat O'Brien, Lib., 613/995-2901
Markham-Whitchurch-Stouffville (89,270) Jag Bhaduria, Ind.L, 613/996-3374
Mississauga East (68,321) Albina Guarnieri, Lib., 613/996-0420
Mississauga South (61,134) Paul Szabo, Lib., 613/992-4848
Mississauga West (90,244) Carolyn Parrish, Lib., 613/995-7321
Nepean (67,383) Beryl Gaffney, Lib., 613/992-2772
Niagara Falls (59,547) Gary Pilliteri, Lib., 613/995-1547
Nickle Belt (50,182) Ray Bonin, Lib., 613/995-9107
Nipissing (49,699) Bob Wood, Lib., 613/995-6255
Northumberland (60,058) Hon. Christine Stewart, Lib., 613/992-8585
Oakville-Milton (92,495) Bonnie Brown, Lib., 613/995-4014
Ontario (92,772) Dan McTeague, Lib., 613/995-8082
Oshawa (62,540) Ivan Grose, Lib., 613/996-4756
Ottawa Centre (57,676) Mac Harb, Lib., 613/996-5322
Ottawa South (65,111) Hon. John Manley, Lib., 613/992-3269
Ottawa West (57,698) Marlene Catterall, Lib., 613/996-0984
Ottawa-Vanier (61,395) Mauril Bélanger, Lib., 613/992-4766
Oxford (63,866) John Finlay, Lib., 613/995-4432
Parkdale-High Park (55,383) Jesse Flis, Lib., 613/992-2936
Parry Sound-Muskoka (55,985) Andy Mitchell, Lib., 613/996-3434
Perth-Wellington-Waterloo (63,234) John Richardson, Lib., 613/992-6124
Peterborough (71,714) Peter Adams, Lib., 613/995-6411
Prince Edward-Hastings (63,637) Lyle Vanclief, Lib., 613/992-5321
Renfrew-Nipissing-Pembroke (59,236) Leonard Hopkins, Lib., 613/992-7712
Rosedale (68,521) Bill Graham, Lib., 613/992-5234
Sarnia-Lambton (56,106) Roger Gallaway, Lib., 613/957-2649
Sault Ste. Marie (52,681) Hon. Ronald A. Irwin, C.M., Q.C., Lib., 613/992-6418
Scarborough Centre (56,099) John Cannis, Lib., 613/992-6823
Scarborough East (54,705) Hon. Doug Peters, Lib., 613/947-4552
Scarborough West (55,112) Tom Wappel, Lib., 613/995-0284
Scarborough-Agincourt (56,996) Jim Karygiannis, Lib., 613/992-4501
Scarborough-Rouge River (66,294) Derek Lee, Lib., 613/996-9681
Simcoe Centre (71,264) Ed Harper, Ref., 613/992-3394
Simcoe North (67,552) Paul DeVillers, Lib., 613/992-6582
St. Catharines (63,404) Walt Lastewka, Lib., 613/992-3352
St. Paul's, Barry Campbell, Lib., 613/995-9666
Stormont-Dundas (57,993) Bob Kilger, Lib., 613/992-2521
Sudbury (57,071) Hon. Diane Marleau, Lib., 613/996-8963
Thunder Bay-Atikokan (47,817) Stan Dromisky, Lib., 613/992-3061
Thunder Bay-Nipigon (49,527) Joe Comuzzi, Lib., 613/996-4792
Timiskaming-French River (39,849) Ben Serré, Lib., 613/992-2792
Timmins-Chapleau (43,328) Peter Thalheimer, Lib., 613/992-3802
Trinity-Spadina (50,326) Tony Ianno, Lib., 613/992-2352
Victoria-Haliburton (64,658) John O'Reilly, Lib., 613/992-2474
Waterloo (78,497) Andrew Telegdi, Lib., 613/996-5928
Welland-St. Catharines-Thorold (62,458) Hon. Gilbert Parent, Lib., 613/995-9579
Wellington-Grey-Dufferin-Simcoe (68,043) Murray Calder, Lib., 613/995-7813
Willowdale (62,734) Jim Peterson, Lib., 613/992-4964
Windsor West (61,339) Hon. Herbert Eser Gray, Lib., 613/995-7548
Windsor-St. Clair (57,763) Shaughnessy Cohen, Lib., 613/947-3445
York Centre (54,776) Hon. Art Eggleton, Lib., 613/941-6339
York North (129,479) Maurizio Bevilacqua, Lib., 613/996-4971
York South-Weston (51,428) John Nunziata, Lib., 613/995-0777
York West (47,213) Hon. Sergio Marchi, Lib., 819/997-3530
York-Simcoe (75,898) Karen Kraft Sloan, Lib., 613/996-7752

Prince Edward Island
Cardigan (20,021) Hon. Lawrence MacAulay, Lib., 613/995-9325
Egmont (22,642) Joe McGuire, Lib., 613/992-9223
Hillsborough (23,694) George Proud, Lib., 613/996-4714
Malpeque (20,716) Wayne Easter, Lib., 613/992-2406

Québec
Abitibi (58,861) Bernard Deshaies, BQ, 613/992-3030
Ahuntsic (65,283) Michel Daviault, BQ, 613/995-9287
Anjou-Rivière-des-Prairies (71,398) Roger Pomerleau, BQ, 613/995-0580
Argenteuil-Papineau (53,693) Maurice Dumas, BQ, 613/992-0902
Beauce (67,578) Gilles Bernier, Ind., 613/992-8053
Beauharnois-Salaberry (64,011) Laurent Lavigne, BQ, 613/992-5036
Beauport-Montmorency-Orléans (67,686) Michel Guimond, BQ, 613/995-9732
Bellechasse (59,228) François Langlois, BQ, 613/992-2289
Berthier-Montcalm (71,176) Michel Bellehumeur, BQ, 613/992-0164
Blainville-Deux-Montagnes (85,847) Paul Mercier, BQ, 613/947-4788
Bonaventure-Îles-de-la-Madeleine (35,892) Patrick Gagnon, Lib., 613/992-1161
Bourassa (60,863) Osvaldo Nunez, BQ, 613/995-6108
Brome-Missisquoi (53,983) Denis Paradis, Lib., 613/947-8185
Châteauguay (69,660) Maurice Godin, BQ, 613/996-7265
Chambly (66,151) Ghislain Lebel, BQ, 613/992-6035
Champlain (61,141) Réjean Lefebvre, BQ, 613/995-4895
Charlesbourg (76,055) Jean-Marc Jacob, BQ, 613/995-8857
Charlevoix (55,066) Gérard Asselin, BQ, 613/992-2363
Chicoutimi (57,792) Gilbert Fillion, BQ, 613/995-8554
Drummond (56,841) Pauline Picard, BQ, 613/947-4550
Frontenac, Jean-Guy Chrétien, BQ, 613/995-1377
Gaspé (40,609) Yvan Bernier, BQ, 613/992-6188
Gatineau-La Lièvre (75,575) Mark Assad, Lib., 613/992-4351
Hochelaga-Maisonneuve (59,470) Réal Ménard, BQ, 613/947-4576
Hull Aylmer (61,134) Hon. Marcel Massé, Lib., 613/952-5555
Joliette (70,865) René Laurin, BQ, 613/996-6910
Jonquière (45,537) André Caron, BQ, 613/992-2617
Kamouraska-Rivière-du-Loup (50,569) Paul Crête, BQ, 613/995-0265
La Prairie (71,246) Richard Bélisle, BQ, 613/998-5961
Lac-Saint-Jean (46,267) Stéphan Tremblay, BQ, 613/947-2745
Lachine-Lac-Saint-Louis (67,931) Clifford Lincoln, Lib., 613/995-8281
LaSalle-Émard (65,920) Hon. Paul Martin, Lib., 613/992-4284
Laurentides (76,636) Monique Guay, BQ, 613/992-3257
Laurier-Sainte-Marie (57,939) Gilles Duceppe, BQ, 613/992-6779
Laval Centre (68,949) Madeleine Dalphond-Guiral, BQ, 613/995-7398
Laval-Est (69,581) Maud Debien, BQ, 613/992-0611
Laval-Ouest (69,215) Hon. Michel Dupuy, Lib., 613/992-2659
Lévis (76,123) Antoine Dubé, BQ, 613/992-7434
Longueuil (73,700) Nic Leblanc, BQ, 613/992-8514
Lotbinière (64,590) Jean Landry, BQ, 613/992-2639
Louis-Hébert (74,645) Phillipe Paré, BQ, 613/995-4996
Manicouagan (36,267) Bernard St-Laurent, BQ, 613/992-5681
Matapédia-Matane (45,406) René Canuel, BQ, 613/995-1013
Mégantic-Compton-Stanstead (51,855) Maurice Bernier, BQ, 613/995-2024
Mercier (76,343) Francine Lalonde, BQ, 613/995-6327
Mont-Royal (58,664) Hon. Sheila Finestone, Lib., 613/995-0121
Notre-Dame-de-Grâce (52,256) Warren Allmand, Lib., 613/995-2251
Outremont (57,971) Hon. Martin Cauchon, Lib., 613/995-7691
Papineau-Saint-Michel (56,328) Hon. Pierre Pettigrew, Lib., 613/995-8872
Pierrefonds-Dollard (67,802) Bernard Patry, Lib., 613/992-2689
Pontiac-Gatineau-Labelle (53,311) Robert Bertrand, Lib., 613/995-5516
Portneuf (54,841) Pierre de Savoye, BQ, 613/992-2798
Québec (71,630) Christiane Gagnon, BQ, 613/992-8865
Québec-Est (69,243) Jean-Paul Marchand, BQ, 613/996-4151
Richelieu (58,488) Louis Plamondon, BQ, 613/995-9241
Richmond-Wolfe (53,203) Gaston Leroux, BQ, 613/992-4473
Rimouski-Témiscouata (53,161) Suzanne Tremblay, BQ, 613/992-5302
Roberval, Michel Gauthier, BQ, 613/996-6740
Rosemont (65,899) Benoît Tremblay, BQ, 613/992-0423
Saint-Denis (55,070) Eleni Bakopanos, Lib., 613/992-0983
Saint-Henri-Westmount (49,667) Hon. Lucienne Robillard, Lib., 613/996-7267
Saint-Hubert (71,038) Pierrette Venne, BQ, 613/992-2416
Saint-Hyacinthe-Bagot (62,326) Yvan Loubier, BQ, 613/996-4585
Saint-Jean (61,038) Claude Bachand, BQ, 613/992-5296
Saint-Laurent-Cartierville (55,336) Hon. Stéphane Dion, Lib., 613/996-5789
Saint-Léonard (61,361) Hon. Alfonso Gagliano, Lib., 613/995-9414
Shefford (62,382) Jean Leroux, BQ, 613/992-5279
Sherbrooke (71,940) Hon. Jean Charest, PC, 613/943-1106
St. Maurice, Rt. Hon. Jean Chrétien, Lib., 613/992-4211
Témiscamingue (55,624) Pierre Brien, BQ, 613/996-3250
Terrebonne (86,760) Benoit Sauvageau, BQ, 613/992-5257
Trois-Rivières (58,356) Yves Rocheleau, BQ, 613/992-2349
Vaudreuil, Nick Discepola, Lib., 613/957-3744
Verchères (60,438) Stéphane Bergeron, BQ, 613/996-2998

Canadian Almanac & Directory 1997

3-50 GOVERNMENT OF CANADA

Verdun-Saint-Paul (59,774) Raymond Lavigne, Lib., 613/995-6403

Saskatchewan

Kindersley-Lloydminster, Elwin Hermanson, Ref., 613/996-0920

Mackenzie (42,875) Vic Althouse, NDP, 613/995-8321

Moose Jaw-Lake Centre (45,272) Allan Kerpan, Ref., 613/995-5653

Prince Albert-Churchill River (43,538) Gordon Kirkby, Lib., 613/995-3295

Regina-Lumsden (49,132) John Solomon, NDP, 613/992-4573

Regina-Qu'Appelle (44,262) Simon de Jong, NDP, 613/992-4593

Regina-Wascana (53,301) Hon. Ralph Goodale, Lib., 613/759-1059

Saskatoon-Clark's Crossing (54,490) Chris Axworthy, NDP, 613/995-1551

Saskatoon-Dundurn (54,996) Morris Bodnar, Lib., 613/996-3265

Saskatoon-Humboldt (49,294) Georgette Sheridan, Lib., 613/992-8052

Souris-Moose Mountain (46,285) Bernie Collins, Lib., 613/992-7685

Swift Current-Maple Creek-Assiniboia (44,077) Lee Morrison, Ref., 613/992-0657

The Battlefords-Meadow Lake (47,329) Len Taylor, NDP, 613/995-7080

Yorkton-Melville (44,576) Garry Breitkruz, Ref., 613/992-4394

Yukon

Yukon (15,680) Hon. Audrey McLaughlin, NDP, 613/995-7224

MEMBERS (ALPHABETICAL)

See also Constituency List, preceding. **Correspondence** to Members of the House of Commons should be addressed individually and may be sent postage free to the House of Commons, Ottawa, ON K1A 0A6. Listed here are: Name of member, constituency, (number of eligible voters in 1993 election), party affiliation, province, Ottawa office phone number.

Jim Abbott, Kootenay East (41,915)Ref., BC, 613/995-7246

Diane Ablonczy, Calgary North (76,602)Ref., Alta., 613/996-2756

Peter Adams, Peterborough (71,714)Lib., Ont., 613/995-6411

Reg Alcock, Winnipeg South (59,974)Lib., Man., 613/995-7517, Email: winnipeg_south@mbnet.mb.ca, URL: http://www.mbnet.mb.ca:80/wpgsth

Warren Allmand, Notre-Dame-de-Grâce (52,256)Lib., Qué., 613/995-2251

Vic Althouse, Mackenzie (42,875)NDP, Sask., 613/995-8321

Jack Iyerak Anawak, Nunatsiaq (10,888)Lib., NWT, 613/992-2848

Hon. David Anderson, Victoria (70,394)Lib., BC, 613/996-2358

Guy Arseneault, Restigouche-Chaleur (37,729)Lib., NB, 613/995-0581

Mark Assad, Gatineau-La Lièvre (75,575)Lib., Qué., 613/992-4351

Sarkis Assadourian, Don Valley North (50,433)Lib., Ont., 613/995-4843

Gérard Asselin, Charlevoix (55,066)BQ, Qué., 613/992-2363

Jean Augustine, Etobicoke-Lakeshore (60,279)Lib., Ont., 613/995-9364

Chris Axworthy, Saskatoon-Clark's Crossing (54,490)NDP, Sask., 613/995-1551

Hon. Lloyd Axworthy, Winnipeg South Centre (56,248)Lib., Man., 613/995-0153

Claude Bachand, Saint-Jean (61,038)BQ, Qué., 613/992-5296

George S. Baker, Gander-Grand Falls (55,162)Lib., Nfld., 613/996-1541

Eleni Bakopanos, Saint-Denis (55,070)Lib., Qué., 613/992-0983

Sue Barnes, London West (76,807)Lib., Ont., 613/996-6674

Colleen Beaumier, Brampton (80,678)Lib., Ont., 613/996-2878

Réginald Bélair, Cochrane-Superior (41,262)Lib., Ont., 613/992-2919

Mauril Bélanger, Ottawa-Vanier (61,395)Lib., Ont., 613/992-4766

Richard Bélisle, La Prairie (71,246)BQ, Qué., 613/998-5961

Michel Bellehumeur, Berthier-Montcalm (71,176)BQ, Qué., 613/992-0164

Eugène Bellemare, Carleton-Gloucester (75,578)Lib., Ont., 613/995-6296

Leon Benoit, VegrevilleRef., Alta., 613/992-4171

Stéphane Bergeron, Verchères (60,438)BQ, Qué., 613/996-2998

Gilles Bernier, Beauce (67,578)Ind., Qué., 613/992-8053

Maurice Bernier, Mégantic-Compton-Stanstead (51,855)BQ, Qué., 613/995-2024

Yvan Bernier, Gaspé (40,609)BQ, Qué., 613/992-6188

Robert Bertrand, Pontiac-Gatineau-Labelle (53,311)Lib., Qué., 613/992-5516

Judy Bethel, Edmonton East (56,015)Lib., Alta., 613/992-3821

Maurizio Bevilacqua, York North (129,479)Lib., Ont., 613/996-4971

Jag Bhaduria, Markham-Whitchurch-Stouffville (89,270)Ind.L, Ont., 613/996-3374

William Blaikie, Winnipeg Transcona (55,100)NDP, Man., 613/995-6339

Hon. Ethel Blondin-Andrew, Western Arctic (18,142)Lib., NWT, 613/992-4587

Morris Bodnar, Saskatoon-Dundurn (54,996)Lib., Sask., 613/996-3265

Ray Bonin, Nickle Belt (50,182)Lib., Ont., 613/995-9107

Hon. Don Boudria, Glengarry-Prescott-Russell (67,681)Lib., Ont., 613/996-2907

Cliff Breitkreuz, YellowheadRef., Alta., 613/992-1653

Garry Breitkruz, Yorkton-Melville (44,576)Ref., Sask., 613/992-4394

Margaret Bridgman, Surrey North (69,813)Ref., BC, 613/992-2922

Pierre Brien, Témiscamingue (55,624)BQ, Qué., 613/996-3250

Bonnie Brown, Oakville-Milton (92,495)Lib., Ont., 613/995-4014

Jan Brown, Calgary Southeast (69,264)Ind., Alta., 613/996-2791

Dianne Brushett, Cumberland-Colchester (58,302)Lib., NS, 613/992-3366

Hon. John Bryden, Hamilton-Wentworth (72,906)Lib., Ont., 613/995-8042

Gerry Byrne, Humber-St. Barbe-Baie Verte (53,109)Lib., Nfld., 613/996-5509

Charles Caccia, Davenport (36,869)Lib., Ont., 613/992-2576

Murray Calder, Wellington-Grey-Dufferin-Simcoe (68,043)Lib., Ont., 613/995-7813

Barry Campbell, St. Paul'sLib., Ont., 613/995-9666

John Cannis, Scarborough Centre (56,099)Lib., Ont., 613/992-6823

René Canuel, Matapédia-Matane (45,406)BQ, Qué., 613/995-1013

André Caron, Jonquière (45,537)BQ, Qué., 613/992-2617

Marlene Catterall, Ottawa West (57,698)Lib., Ont., 613/996-0984

Hon. Martin Cauchon, Outremont (57,971)Lib., Qué., 613/995-7691

Brenda Chamberlain, Guelph-Wellington (76,618)Lib., Ont., 613/996-4758

Hon. Raymond Chan, Richmond (70,891)Lib., BC, 613/996-1995

Hon. Jean Charest, Sherbrooke (71,940)PC, Qué., 613/943-1106

Dave Chatters, Athabasca (45,987)Ref., Alta., 613/996-1783

Rt. Hon. Jean Chrétien, St. MauriceLib., Qué., 613/992-4211

Jean-Guy Chrétien, FrontenacBQ, Qué., 613/995-1377

Mary Clancy, Halifax (68,144)Lib., NS, 613/995-9368

Shaughnessy Cohen, Windsor-St. Clair (57,763)Lib., Ont., 613/947-3445

Hon. David Collenette, Don Valley East (54,706)Lib., Ont., 613/995-4988

Bernie Collins, Souris-Moose Mountain (46,285)Lib., Sask., 613/992-7685

Joe Comuzzi, Thunder Bay-Nipigon (49,527)Lib., Ont., 613/996-4792

Hon. Sheila Copps, Hamilton East (52,117)Lib., Ont., 613/995-2773

Marlene Cowling, Dauphin-Swan River (45,963)Lib., Man., 613/992-3176

Rex Crawford, Kent (54,943)Lib., Ont., 613/995-7784

Paul Crête, Kamouraska-Rivière-du-Loup (50,569)BQ, Qué., 613/995-0265

Harold Culbert, Carleton-Charlotte (45,026)Lib., NB, 613/996-9726

Roy Cullen, Etobicoke North (63,617)Lib., Ont.

John Cummins, Delta (53,024)Ref., BC, 613/992-2957

Madeleine Dalphond-Guiral, Laval Centre (68,949)BQ, Qué., 613/995-7398

Michel Daviault, Ahuntsic (65,283)BQ, Qué., 613/995-9287

Simon de Jong, Regina-Qu'Appelle (44,262)NDP, Sask., 613/992-4593

Pierre de Savoye, Portneuf (54,841)BQ, Qué., 613/992-2798

Maud Debien, Laval-Est (69,581)BQ, Qué., 613/992-0611

Bernard Deshaies, Abitibi (58,861)BQ, Qué., 613/992-3030

Paul DeVillers, Simcoe North (67,552)Lib., Ont., 613/992-6582

Herb Dhaliwal, Vancouver South (64,192)Lib., BC, 613/995-7052

Hon. David C. Dingwall, Cape Breton-East Richmond (42,446)Lib., NS, 613/996-4743

Hon. Stéphane Dion, Saint-Laurent-Cartierville (55,336)Lib., Qué., 613/996-5789

Nick Discepola, VaudreuilLib., Qué., 613/957-3744

Stan Dromisky, Thunder Bay-Atikokan (47,817)Lib., Ont., 613/992-3061

Antoine Dubé, Lévis (76,123)BQ, Qué., 613/992-7434

Gilles Duceppe, Laurier-Sainte-Marie (57,939)BQ, Qué., 613/992-6779

Ronald J. Duhamel, St. Boniface (57,480)Lib., Man., 613/995-0579

Maurice Dumas, Argenteuil-Papineau (53,693)BQ, Qué., 613/992-0902

John Duncan, North Island-Powell River (52,850)Ref., BC, 613/992-2503

Hon. Michel Dupuy, Laval-Ouest (69,215)Lib., Qué., 613/992-2659

Wayne Easter, Malpeque (20,716)Lib., PEI, 613/992-2406

Hon. Art Eggleton, York Centre (54,776)Lib., Ont., 613/941-6339

John English, Kitchener (70,875)Lib., Ont., 613/995-8913

Ken Epp, Elk Island (49,816)Ref., Alta., 613/995-3611

Ron Fewchuk, Selkirk-Red River (57,452)Lib., Man., 613/996-6426

Gilbert Fillion, Chicoutimi (57,792)BQ, Qué., 613/995-8554

Hon. Sheila Finestone, Mont-Royal (58,664)Lib., Qué., 613/995-0121

John Finlay, Oxford (63,866)Lib., Ont., 613/995-4432

Jesse Flis, Parkdale-High Park (55,383)Lib., Ont., 613/992-2936
Joe Fontana, London East (71,537)Lib., Ont., 613/992-0805
Paul Forseth, New Westminster-Burnaby (71,462)Ref., BC, 613/947-4455
Jack Frazer, Saanich-Gulf Island (75,360)Ref., BC, 613/996-1119
Hon. Hedy Fry, Vancouver Centre (77,445)Lib., BC, 613/992-3213
Beryl Gaffney, Nepean (67,383)Lib., Ont., 613/992-2772
Hon. Alfonso Gagliano, Saint-Léonard (61,361)Lib., Qué., 613/995-9414
Christiane Gagnon, Québec (71,630)BQ, Qué., 613/992-8865
Patrick Gagnon, Bonaventure-Îles-de-la-Madeleine (35,892)Lib., Qué., 613/992-1161
Roger Gallaway, Sarnia-Lambton (56,106)Lib., Ont., 613/957-2649
Michel Gauthier, RobervalBQ, Qué., 613/996-6740
Hon. Jon Gerrard, Portage-Interlake (47,672)Lib., Man., 613/947-4245
Bill Gilmour, Comox-Alberni (59,533)Ref., BC, 613/992-5243
John Godfrey, Don Valley West (62,286)Lib., Ont., 613/992-2855
Maurice Godin, Châteauguay (69,660)BQ, Qué., 613/996-7265
Hon. Ralph Goodale, Regina-Wascana (53,301)Lib., Sask., 613/759-1059
Jim Gouk, Kootenay West-Revelstoke (40,309)Ref., BC, 613/996-8036
Bill Graham, Rosedale (68,521)Lib., Ont., 613/992-5234
Hon. Herbert Eser Gray, Windsor West (61,339)Lib., Ont., 613/995-7548
Deborah Grey, Beaver River (42,434)Ref., Alta., 613/996-9778
Ivan Grose, Oshawa (62,540)Lib., Ont., 613/996-4756
Herb Grubel, Capilano-Howe Sound (50,756)Ref., BC, 613/947-4617
Albina Guarnieri, Mississauga East (68,321)Lib., Ont., 613/996-0420
Monique Guay, Laurentides (76,636)BQ, Qué., 613/992-3257
Michel Guimond, Beauport-Montmorency-Orléans (67,686)BQ, Qué., 613/995-9732
Art Hanger, Calgary Northeast (66,504)Ref., Alta., 613/947-4487
Hugh Hanrahan, Edmonton-Strathcona (65,848)Ref., Alta., 613/995-7325
Mac Harb, Ottawa Centre (57,676)Lib., Ont., 613/996-5322
Ed Harper, Simcoe Centre (71,264)Ref., Ont., 613/992-3394
Elijah Harper, Churchill (39,710)Lib., Man., 613/992-3018
Stephen Harper, Calgary West (67,784)Ref., Alta., 613/992-3066
Dick Harris, Prince George-Bulkley Valley (47,164)Ref., BC, 613/995-6704
Jim Hart, Okanagan-Similkameen-Merritt (51,971)Ref., BC, 613/995-2581
John Harvard, Winnipeg St. James (50,606)Lib., Man., 613/995-5609
Sharon Hayes, Port Moody-Coquitlam (65,955)Ref., BC, 613/947-4482
Elwin Hermanson, Kindersley-LloydminsterRef., Sask., 613/996-0920
Bonnie Hickey, St. John's East (72,992)Lib., Nfld., 613/995-3013
Grant Hill, Macleod (43,333)Ref., Alta., 613/995-8471
Jay Hill, Prince George-Peace River (47,339)Ref., BC, 613/947-4524
Jake Hoeppner, Lisgar-Marquette (45,820)Ref., Man., 613/995-9511

Leonard Hopkins, Renfrew-Nipissing-Pembroke (59,236)Lib., Ont., 613/992-7712
Charles Hubbard, Miramichi (38,388)Lib., NB, 613/992-5335
Tony Ianno, Trinity-Spadina (50,326)Lib., Ont., 613/992-2352
David Iftody, ProvencherLib., Man., 613/992-3128
Hon. Ronald A. Irwin, C.M., Q.C., Sault Ste. Marie (52,681)Lib., Ont., 613/992-6418
Ovid Jackson, Bruce-Grey (66,746)Lib., Ont., 613/996-5191
Jean-Marc Jacob, Charlesbourg (76,055)BQ, Qué., 613/995-8857
Daphne Jennings, Mission-Coquitlam (59,990)Ref., BC, 613/947-4613
Dale Johnston, Wetaskiwin (52,832)Ref., Alta., 613/995-8886
Jim Jordan, Leeds-Grenville (59,819)Lib., Ont., 613/992-8756
Jim Karygiannis, Scarborough-Agincourt (56,996)Lib., Ont., 613/992-4501
Allan Kerpan, Moose Jaw-Lake Centre (45,272)Ref., Sask., 613/995-5653
Stan Keyes, Hamilton West (60,728)Lib., Ont., 613/995-1757
Bob Kilger, Stormont-Dundas (57,993)Lib., Ont., 613/992-2521
David Kilgour, Edmonton Southeast (63,776)Lib., Alta., 613/995-8695
Gordon Kirkby, Prince Albert-Churchill River (43,538)Lib., Sask., 613/995-3295
Gar Knutson, Elgin-Norfolk (56,065)Lib., Ont., 613/990-7769
Karen Kraft Sloan, York-Simcoe (75,898)Lib., Ont., 613/996-7752
Francine Lalonde, Mercier (76,343)BQ, Qué., 613/995-6327
Jean Landry, Lotbinière (64,590)BQ, Qué., 613/992-2639
François Langlois, Bellechasse (59,228)BQ, Qué., 613/992-2289
Walt Lastewka, St. Catharines (63,404)Lib., Ont., 613/992-3352
René Laurin, Joliette (70,865)BQ, Qué., 613/996-6910
Laurent Lavigne, Beauharnois-Salaberry (64,011)BQ, Qué., 613/992-5036
Raymond Lavigne, Verdun-Saint-Paul (59,774)Lib., Qué., 613/995-6403
Ghislain Lebel, Chambly (66,151)BQ, Qué., 613/992-6035
Francis G. LeBlanc, Cape Breton Highlands-Canso (47,670)Lib., NS, 613/992-5041
Nic Leblanc, Longueuil (73,700)BQ, Qué., 613/992-8514
Derek Lee, Scarborough-Rouge River (66,294)Lib., Ont., 613/996-9681
Réjean Lefebvre, Champlain (61,141)BQ, Qué., 613/995-4895
Gaston Leroux, Richmond-Wolfe (53,203)BQ, Qué., 613/992-4473
Jean Leroux, Shefford (62,382)BQ, Qué., 613/992-5279
Clifford Lincoln, Lachine-Lac-Saint-Louis (67,931)Lib., Qué., 613/995-8281
John Loney, Edmonton NorthLib., Alta., 613/947-4566
Yvan Loubier, Saint-Hyacinthe-Bagot (62,326)BQ, Qué., 613/996-4585
Hon. Lawrence MacAulay, Cardigan (20,021)Lib., PEI, 613/995-9325
Ron MacDonald, Dartmouth (66,681)Lib., NS, 613/995-9378
Russell MacLellan, Cape Breton-The Sydneys (47,301)Lib., NS, 613/995-6459
Gurbax Malhi, Bramalea-Gore-Milton (56,348)Lib., Ont., 613/992-9105
John Maloney, Erie (51,617)Lib., Ont., 613/995-0988
Hon. John Manley, Ottawa South (65,111)Lib., Ont., 613/992-3269

Preston Manning, Calgary Southwest (75,976)Ref., Alta., 613/992-3602
Jean-Paul Marchand, Québec-Est (69,243)BQ, Qué., 613/996-4151
Hon. Sergio Marchi, York West (47,213)Lib., Ont., 819/997-3530
Hon. Diane Marleau, Sudbury (57,071)Lib., Ont., 613/996-8963
Keith Martin, Esquimalt-Juan de Fuca (54,651)Ref., BC, 613/996-2625
Hon. Paul Martin, LaSalle-Émard (65,920)Lib., Qué., 613/992-4284
Hon. Marcel Massé, Hull Aylmer (61,134)Lib., Qué., 613/952-5555
Philip Mayfield, Cariboo-Chilcotin (40,836)Ref., BC, 613/996-2205
Ian McClelland, Edmonton Southwest (69,333)Ref., Alta., 613/992-3594
Larry McCormick, Hastings-Frontenac-Lennox and Addington (58,252)Lib., Ont., 613/992-3640
Joe McGuire, Egmont (22,642)Lib., PEI, 613/992-9223
Glen McKinnon, Brandon-Souris (50,427)Lib., Man., 613/995-9372
Hon. Audrey McLaughlin, Yukon (15,680)NDP, YT, 613/995-7224
Hon. Anne McLellan, Edmonton Northwest (53,099)Lib., Alta., 613/992-4525
Dan McTeague, Ontario (92,772)Lib., Ont., 613/995-8082
Ted McWhinney, Vancouver QuadraLib., BC, 613/992-2430
Réal Ménard, Hochelaga-Maisonneuve (59,470)BQ, Qué., 613/947-4576
Paul Mercier, Blainville-Deux-Montagnes (85,847)BQ, Qué., 613/947-4788
Val Meredith, Surrey-White Rock-South Langley (74,076)Ref., BC, 613/947-4497
Hon. Fred Mifflin, Bonavista-Trinity-Conception (61,321)Lib., Nfld., 613/992-4133
Peter Milliken, Kingston and the Islands (73,775)Lib., Ont., 613/996-1955
Bob Mills, Red Deer (61,261)Ref., Alta., 613/995-0590
Dennis J. Mills, Broadview-Greenwood (52,661)Ind.L, Ont., 613/992-7771
Maria Minna, Beaches-Woodbine (57,838)Lib., Ont., 613/992-2115
Andy Mitchell, Parry Sound-Muskoka (55,985)Lib., Ont., 613/996-3434
Lee Morrison, Swift Current-Maple Creek-Assiniboia (44,077)Ref., Sask., 613/992-0657
John Murphy, Annapolis Valley-Hants (64,708)Lib., NS, 613/995-8231
Ian Murray, Lanark-Carleton (72,621)Lib., Ont., 613/947-2277
Robert D. Nault, Kenora-Rainy River (48,102)Lib., Ont., 613/996-1161
Osvaldo Nunez, Bourassa (60,863)BQ, Qué., 613/995-6108
John Nunziata, York South-Weston (51,428)Lib., Ont., 613/995-0777
Lawrence O'Brien, Labrador (16,931)Lib., Nfld., 613/996-4630
Pat O'Brien, London-Middlesex (64,749)Lib., Ont., 613/995-2901
John O'Reilly, Victoria-Haliburton (64,658)Lib., Ont., 613/992-2474
Rey Pagtakhan, Winnipeg North (57,507)Lib., Man., 613/992-7148
Denis Paradis, Brome-Missisquoi (53,983)Lib., Qué., 613/947-8185
Phillipe Paré, Louis-Hébert (74,645)BQ, Qué., 613/995-4996
Hon. Gilbert Parent, Welland-St. Catharines-Thorold (62,458)Lib., Ont., 613/995-9579
Carolyn Parrish, Mississauga West (90,244)Lib., Ont., 613/995-7321
Bernard Patry, Pierrefonds-Dollard (67,802)Lib., Qué., 613/992-2689

Canadian Almanac & Directory 1997

Jean Payne, St. John's WestLib., Nfld., 613/992-0927
Charlie Penson, Peace River (60,031)Ref., Alta., 613/992-5685
Janko Peric, Cambridge (69,634)Lib., Ont., 613/996-1307
Hon. Doug Peters, Scarborough East (54,705)Lib., Ont., 613/947-4552
Jim Peterson, Willowdale (62,734)Lib., Ont., 613/992-4964
Hon. Pierre Pettigrew, Papineau-Saint-Michel (56,328)Lib., Qué., 613/995-8872
Beth Phinney, Hamilton Mountain (64,576)Lib., Ont., 613/995-9389
Pauline Picard, Drummond (56,841)BQ, Qué., 613/947-4550
Jerry Pickard, Essex-Kent (51,100)Lib., Ont., 613/992-2612
Gary Pilliteri, Niagara Falls (59,547)Lib., Ont., 613/995-1547
Louis Plamondon, Richelieu (58,488)BQ, Qué., 613/995-9241
Roger Pomerleau, Anjou-Rivière-des-Prairies (71,398)BQ, Qué., 613/995-0580
George Proud, Hillsborough (23,694)Lib., PEI, 613/996-4714
Jack Ramsay, Crowfoot (44,558)Ref., Alta., 613/947-4608
Julian Reed, Halton-Peel (67,417)Lib., Ont., 613/996-7046
Geoff Regan, Halifax West (72,431)Lib., NS, 613/992-1624
John Richardson, Perth-Wellington-Waterloo (63,234)Lib., Ont., 613/992-6124
George S. Rideout, Moncton (63,793)Lib., NB, 613/992-8072
Nelson A. Riis, Kamloops (50,976)NDP, BC, 613/995-6931
Bob Ringma, Nanaimo-Cowichan (66,810)Ref., BC, 613/943-2180
Pierrette Ringuette-Maltais, Madawaska-Victoria (40,185)Lib., NB, 613/947-4431
Hon. Fernand Robichaud, BeausejourLib., NB, 613/947-4592
Hon. Lucienne Robillard, Saint-Henri-Westmount (49,667)Lib., Qué., 613/996-7267
Svend J. Robinson, Burnaby-Kingsway (71,059)NDP, BC, 613/996-5597
Yves Rocheleau, Trois-Rivières (58,356)BQ, Qué., 613/992-2349
Hon. Allan Rock, Q.C., Etobicoke CentreLib., Ont., 613/947-5000
Benoit Sauvageau, Terrebonne (86,760)BQ, Qué., 613/992-5257
Werner Schmidt, Okanagan Centre (64,860)Ref., BC, 613/992-7006
Andy Scott, Fredericton-York-Sunbury (61,381)Lib., NB, 613/992-1067
Mike Scott, Skeena (39,977)Ref., BC, 613/993-6654
Ben Serré, Timiskaming-French River (39,849)Lib., Ont., 613/992-2792
Alex Shepherd, Durham (68,790)Lib., Ont., 613/996-4984
Georgette Sheridan, Saskatoon-Humboldt (49,294)Lib., Sask., 613/992-8052
Jim Silye, Calgary Centre (71,895)Ref., Alta., 613/995-1127
Hon. Roger Simmons, Burin-St. George's (53,569)Lib., Nfld., 613/992-8655
Roseanne Skoke, Central Nova (52,184)Lib., NS, 613/995-5822
Monte Solberg, Medicine Hat (57,220)Ref., Alta., 613/992-4516
John Solomon, Regina-Lumsden (49,132)NDP, Sask., 613/992-4573
Ray Speaker, Lethbridge (61,456)Ref., Alta., 613/996-0633
Bob Speller, Haldimand-Norfolk (60,021)Lib., Ont., 613/996-4974

Brent St. Denis, Algoma (43,688)Lib., Ont., 613/996-5376
Bernard St-Laurent, Manicouagan (36,267)BQ, Qué., 613/992-5681
Paul Steckle, Huron-Bruce (60,955)Lib., Ont., 613/992-8234
Hon. Christine Stewart, Northumberland (60,058)Lib., Ont., 613/992-8585
Hon. Jane Stewart, Brant (65,336)Lib., Ont., 613/992-3118
Darrel Stinson, Okanagan-Shuswap (52,097)Ref., BC, 613/995-9095
Chuck Strahl, Fraser Valley East (51,736)Ref., BC, 613/992-2940
Paul Szabo, Mississauga South (61,134)Lib., Ont., 613/992-4848
Len Taylor, The Battlefords-Meadow Lake (47,329)NDP, Sask., 613/995-7080
Andrew Telegdi, Waterloo (78,497)Lib., Ont., 613/996-5928
Anna Terrana, Vancouver East (55,080)Lib., BC, 613/992-6030
Peter Thalheimer, Timmins-Chapleau (43,328)Lib., Ont., 613/992-3802
Myron Thompson, Wild Rose (52,020)Ref., Alta., 613/996-5152
Paddy Torsney, Burlington (63,577)Lib., Ont., 613/995-0881
Benoît Tremblay, Rosemont (65,899)BQ, Qué., 613/992-0423
Stéphan Tremblay, Lac-Saint-Jean (46,267)BQ, Qué., 613/947-2745
Suzanne Tremblay, Rimouski-Témiscouata (53,161)BQ, Qué., 613/992-5302
Rose-Marie Ur, Lambton-Middlesex (52,210)Lib., Ont., 613/947-4581
Tony Valeri, Lincoln (65,699)Lib., Ont., 613/992-6535
Lyle Vanclief, Prince Edward-Hastings (63,637)Lib., Ont., 613/992-5321
Pierrette Venne, Saint-Hubert (71,038)BQ, Qué., 613/996-2416
Harry Verran, South West Nova (51,561)Lib., NS, 613/995-5711
Joseph Volpe, Eglinton-Lawrence (52,331)Lib., Ont., 613/992-6361
David Walker, Winnipeg North Centre (42,465)Lib., Man., 613/992-5308
Tom Wappel, Scarborough West (55,112)Lib., Ont., 613/995-0284
Elsie Wayne, Saint John (54,649)PC, NB, 613/947-4571
Derek Wells, South Shore (56,419)Lib., NS, 613/996-0877
Susan Whelan, Essex-Windsor (56,457)Lib., Ont., 613/992-1812
Randy White, Fraser Valley West (63,338)Ref., BC, 613/995-0183
Ted White, North Vancouver (58,864)Ref., BC, 613/995-1225
John Williams, St. Albert (52,844)Ref., Alta., 613/996-4722
Bob Wood, Nipissing (49,699)Lib., Ont., 613/995-6255
Hon. Douglas Young, Acadie-Bathurst (50,206)Lib., NB, 613/992-5991
Paul Zed, Fundy-Royal (58,215)Lib., NB, 613/996-2332

FEDERAL GOVERNMENT DEPARTMENTS & AGENCIES

Editor's Note: The entries listed below are entered alphabetically, using "applied titles" as registered by the Federal Identity Program. Cross references are used to help you to locate the entry quickly. The two departments that incorporate "Department of" as part of their applied titles (Department of Finance Canada; Department of Justice Canada) are nevertheless listed alphabetically under Finance and Justice.

AGRICULTURE & AGRI-FOOD CANADA/
Agriculture et Agro-alimentaire Canada

Sir John Carling Bldg., 930 Carling Ave., Ottawa ON K1A 0C5
613/759-1000; Fax: 613/759-6726; URL: http://aceis.agr.ca

ACTS ADMINISTERED
Advance Payments for Crops Act
Agricultural Products Board Act
Agricultural Products Co-operative Marketing Act
Agricultural Products Marketing Act
Animal Pedigree Act
Canada Agricultural Products Act
Canada Grain Act
Canadian Dairy Commission Act
Canadian Wheat Board Act
Canagrex Dissolution Act (Dormant)
Department of Agriculture & Agri-Food Act
Experimental Farm Stations Act
Farm Credit Corporation Act
Farm Debt Review Act
Farm Improvement & Marketing Cooperatives Loans Act
Farm Improvement Loans Act
Farm Income Protection Act
Farm Products Agencies Act
Feeds Act
Fertilizers Act
Grain Futures Act
Hay & Straw Inspection Act
Health of Animals Act
Livestock Feed Assistance Act
Meat Inspection Act
Plant Breeders' Rights Act
Plant Protection Act
Prairie Farm Rehabilitation Act
Prairie Grain Advance Payments Act
Prairie Grain Provisional Payments Act (Dormant)
Seeds Act

Acts Administered in Part by Agriculture & Agri-Food Canada
Consumer Packaging & Labelling Act (Industry)
Criminal Code (Justice & Attorney General)
Department of Foreign Affairs & International Trade Act
(Foreign Affairs & International Trade)
Food & Drugs Act (Health & Welfare)

The department is dedicated to the well-being of all Canadians through the advancement of the agriculture & food sectors by promoting the growth, stability & competitiveness of the agri-food sector, by making available policies, programs & services that are most appropriately provided by the federal government, so that the sector makes its maximum contribution to the economy.

Agriculture & Agri-Food Canada's responsibilities encompass most aspects of the production, processing & marketing of crops & livestock, ranging from the marketing of products, the conservation of soil & water, protection of crops & livestock from pests & disease, research & technology, crop insurance & stabilization programs & food processing, to the inspection of the food for consumption & export, & trade policies & programs to help industry be competitive in the international marketplace.

The Department meets its responsibilities through the Agri-Food Program which is implemented in cooperation with client groups (e.g. provincial governments, national & international organizations, universities, etc.). The objective of the program is to promote the development, adaptation & competitiveness of the agri-food sector to provide equitable returns to producers & processors & make maximum contributions to national economic & environmental objectives. Program activities include the following:
• agricultural research & development
• inspection & regulation
• farm income & adaptation

- policy
- market & industry services
- rural prairie rehabilitation, sustainability & development
- corporate management & services
- canadian grain commission operations

Minister, Hon. Ralph Goodale, 613/759-1059, Fax: 613/759-1081
Deputy Minister, Frank Claydon, 613/759-1101, Fax: 613/759-1040
Minister of State, Hon. Fernand Robichaud, 613/947-4592, Fax: 613/947-4595

Communications Branch
613/759-7976; Fax: 613/759-7969
Acting Director General, G. Shaw
Director, Policy & Planning, Susan Leah, 613/759-7933
Acting Director, Strategic Planning & Operations Division, Eric Mikkelbory, 613/759-7903

CORPORATE SERVICES BRANCH
613/995-5118; Fax: 613/943-8115
Acting Asst. Deputy Minister & Director General, Finance & Resource Management Services, Dennis Kam
Director General, Finance & Resource Management Services, D. Miller
Director General, Information Services, Jane Roszell, 613/759-6801, Fax: 613/759-6729

FOOD PRODUCTION & INSPECTION BRANCH
59 Camelot Dr., Nepean ON K1A 0Y9
613/952-8000; Fax: 613/991-1131
Asst. Deputy Minister, Dr. A.O. Olson
Director General, Canadian Pari-Mutuel Agency, E. Massey, 613/998-4922 ext.4516, Fax: 613/952-7466

Animal & Plant Health Directorate
613/952-8000; Fax: 613/952-0677
Director General, Dr. Norm G. Willis, 613/952-8000 ext.4192
Director, Animal Diseases Research Institute, Dr. P. Ide, 3851 Fallowfield Rd., Nepean ON K2H 8P9, 613/998-9320, Fax: 613/941-0891
Director, Animal Health Division, B. Stemshorn, 613/952-8000 ext.4601
Director, Central Issues & Strategies, Dr. R. Stevens, 613/952-8000 ext.4189
Director, Central Plant Health Laboratory, E. Singh, 613/998-9320 ext.5931, Fax: 613/996-2497
Director, Diagnostic Resource Centre, Dr. W. Sterritt, 613/998-9320 ext.4967, Fax: 613/991-6988
Director, Management Services, D. Buckland, 613/952-8000 ext.3854
Director, Plant Protection Division, Dr. Jean Hollebone, 613/952-8000 ext.4316

Food Inspection Directorate (FID)
Director General, Dr. A. MacKenzie, 613/952-8000 ext.4188, Fax: 613/998-5967
Director, Dairy, Fruit & Vegetable Division, P.J. Brackenridge, Fax: 613/990-0607
Acting Director, Food Division, Gerry Riasbeck, Fax: 613/993-8511
Director, Laboratory Services Division, Dr. W.P. Cochrane, 613/759-1207, Fax: 613/759-1277
Director, Meat & Poultry Products Division, Dr. M. Baker, Fax: 613/998-0958

Food Production & Inspection Regional Offices
Alberta: #654, 220 - 4 Ave. SE, PO Box 752, Stn M, Calgary AB T2G 4X3 – 403/292-4301; Fax: 403/292-6132, Director General, Dr. L. Anderson
Atlantic: 1081 Main St., 5th Fl., Moncton NB E1C 8R2 – 506/851-7670; Fax: 506/851-2911, Director General, Dr. A. Gravel

British Columbia: #202, 620 Royal Ave., PO Box 2523, New Westminster BC V3L 5A8 – 604/666-6513; Fax: 604/666-6130, Director General, A. Oliver
Mid West: #613, 269 Main St., Winnipeg MB R3C 1B2 – 204/983-2200; Fax: 204/983-8022, Director General, P. Amundson
Ontario: 174 Stone Rd. West, Guelph ON N1G 4S9 – 519/837-5802; Fax: 519/837-9766, Director General, L. Hillier
Québec: 2001, av Université, 7e étage, Montréal PQ H3A 3N2 – 514/283-8888; Fax: 514/283-3143, Director General, Dr. G. Roy

Human Resources Branch
613/759-7471; Fax: 613/759-1196
Director General, Jane Roszell
Director, Human Resources Management & Development Division, A. Ettinger, 613/759-1174
Director, Official Languages Division, C.R. Desrochers, 613/957-4028 ext.5660
Director, Management Services Division, W. Newby, 613/759-1121

MARKET & INDUSTRY SERVICES BRANCH (MISB)
Sir John Carling Bldg., 930 Carling Ave., 5th Fl., Ottawa ON K1A 0C5
613/759-7561; Fax: 613/759-7497
Asst. Deputy Minister, D. Vincent
Director General, International Markets Bureau, Victor Jarjour, Sir John Carling Bldg., 930 Carling Ave., 10th Fl., Ottawa ON K1A 0C5, 613/759-7684, Fax: 613/759-7499
Director General, International Trade Policy Directorate, Mike Gifford, Sir John Carling Bldg., 930 Carling Ave., 10th Fl., Ottawa ON K1A 0C5, 613/759-7675, Fax: 613/759-7503
Director, Management Services Division, B. Cameron, 613/759-7613
Acting Director General, National Marketing Programs Directorate, Gilles Lavoie, 2200 Walkley Rd., 1st Fl., Ottawa ON K1A 0C5, 613/957-7078, Fax: 613/957-1527
Acting Director General, Planning & Regional Operations Directorate, L. Keen, 613/759-7564

Agricultural Industry Services Directorate
2200 Walkley Rd., 1st Fl., Ottawa ON K1A 0C5
613/957-7078; Fax: 613/957-1527
Director General, Gilles Lavoie
Director, Animal Industry Division, B. Howard, 613/957-7078 ext.3044, Fax: 613/957-1527
Director, Horticulture & Special Crops Division, M. Pearson
Asst. Director, Dairy Section, P. Doyle
Asst. Director, Poultry Section, D. McGonnegal
Asst. Director, Red Meat Section, John Ross

Food Bureau
613/759-7557; Fax: 613/759-7496
Director General, Sharon McKay
Director, Industry Analysis Division, G.M. McGregor
Director, Industry Services, R. Cooper
Director, Seafood Division, A. Gauthier

Market & Industry Regional Offices
Alberta: Canada Place, #810, 9700 Jasper Ave., Edmonton AB T5J 4G5 – 403/495-5525; Fax: 403/495-3324, Regional Director, Ken McCready
Atlantic (Newfoundland): 354 Water St., 2nd Fl., PO Box 1878, St. John's NF A1C 5P9 – 709/772-4063; Fax: 709/772-4803, Asst. Director, Al McIssac
Atlantic (Prince Edward Island): 500 Queen St., PO Box 2949, Charlottetown PE C1A 8C5 – 902/566-7300; Fax: 902/566-7316, Atlantic Director, Dave Faulkner, 902/566-7033, Fax: 902/566-7316, Asst. Director, Rollin Andrew

Atlantic (Nova Scotia): #200, 35 Commercial St., PO Box 698, Truro NS B2N 5E5 – 902/893-0068; Fax: 902/893-6777, Asst. Director, Janet Steele
Atlantic (New Brunswick): #213, 633 Queen St., Fredericton NB E3B 1C3 – 506/452-3706; Fax: 506/452-3509, Asst. Director, Renald Cormier
British Columbia: #204, 620 Royal Ave., PO Box 2522, New Westminster BC V3L 5A8 – 604/666-6344; Fax: 604/666-7235, Regional Director, John Berry
Manitoba: #402, 303 Main St., Winnipeg MB R3C 3G7 – 204/983-3032; Fax: 204/983-4583, Regional Director, Bill Breckman
Ontario: 174 Stone Rd. West, Guelph ON N1G 4S9 – 519/837-9400; Fax: 519/837-9782, Regional Director, Conrad Paquette
Québec: Gare Maritime Champlain, #350-4, 901, Cap Diamant, Québec PQ G1K 4K1 – 418/648-4775; Fax: 418/648-7342, Acting Regional Director, Jean Lamoureux
Saskatchewan: #270, 1955 Broad St., PO Box 8035, Regina SK S4P 4C7 – 306/780-5545; Fax: 306/780-7360, Regional Director, Susie Miller

POLICY BRANCH
Sir John Carling Bldg., 930 Carling Ave., Ottawa ON K1A 0C5
613/759-7349; Fax: 613/759-7229
Asst. Deputy Minister, David Oulton
Director General, Strategic & Corporate Relations, G. O'Sullivan
Executive Director, Co-operatives Secretariat, M. Therrien, 613/759-7195

Adaptation & Grain Policy Directorate
#400, 200 Graham Ave., PO Box 6200, Winnipeg MB R3C 4N1
204/983-8371; Fax: 204/983-5300
Sir John Carling Bldg., 930 Carling Ave., Ottawa ON K1A 0C5
613/759-7315, Fax: 613/759-7315
Director General, H. Migie
Director, Environment Bureau, Christine Nymark, Sir John Carling Bldg., 930 Carling Ave., Ottawa ON K1A 0C5, 613/943-1611, Fax: 613/943-1612
Director, Market Analysis Division, M. Liu
Director, Policy Development Division, Bruce Kirk

Economic & Policy Analysis Directorate
Executive Director, Ken Ash
Director, Farm Economic Analysis & Regulatory Policy Division, B. Davey

Farm Income Policy & Programs Directorate
613/759-7269; Fax: 613/759-7235
Director General, Dr. T.G. Richardson
Director, Policy Development Division, R. Eyvindson
Director, Insurance Division, M. Ellis

Industry Performance & Analysis Directorate
613/759-7369; Fax: 613/759-7237
Director General, Dr. D. Hedley
Director, Industry Information Program, B. Huff
Director, Marketing Policy Division, R. Tudor-Price

Net Income Stabilization Administration
PO Box 6100, Winnipeg MB R3C 3A4
204/983-0761; Fax: 204/983-7557
Toll Free: 1-800-665-NISA
  A federal-provincial-farmer initiative designed to provide long-term income stabilization to farmers.
Executive Director, R. Charron

Rural Secretariat & Strategic Directorate
Director General, G. O'Sullivan
Director, Industry Consultations, P. Sheffin, 613/759-7263
Director, Strategic Directions Division, G. Pearson

RESEARCH BRANCH
Sir John Carling Bldg., 930 Carling Ave., Ottawa ON K1A 0C5
613/759-7794; Fax: 613/759-7772
Asst. Deputy Minister, Dr. J.B. Morrissey

Research Coordination Directorate
613/759-7855; Fax: 613/759-7769
Director General, Dr. Jean-Claude St-Pierre

Strategies & Planning Directorate
613/759-7851; Fax: 613/759-7768
Director General, J. Milne
Director, Financial & Administrative Services, D. Schmid
Director, Industry Relations Office, F. Yassa

Eastern Region Directorate
Research Stations at: St. John's Nfld., Charlottetown PEI, Fredericton NB, Kentville NS, Lennoxville Qué., Ste-Foy Qué., St-Hyacinthe Qué., St-Jean-sur-Richelieu Qué., London Ont., Harrow Ont.
Director General, Dr. Yvon Martel, 613/759-7636, Fax: 613/759-7771

Central Experimental Farm
613/759-7865; Fax: 613/759-1970
Director General, Dr. Gordon Dorell
Director, Centre for Food & Animal Research, Dr. A. Lachance, 613/759-1431
Acting Director, Centre for Land & Biological Resources Research, M. Feldman, 613/759-1847
Acting Director, Plant Research Centre, Dr. H. Voldeng, 613/759-1652

Western Region Directorate
Research Stations at: Vancouver BC, Agassiz BC, Summerland BC, Lethbridge Alta., Lacombe Alta., Beaverlodge Alta., Swift Current Sask., Saskatoon Sask., Brandon Man., Morden Man., Winnipeg Man.
Director General, Dr. R.G. Dorrell, 613/759-7864, Fax: 613/759-7770

Review Branch
613/759-6470; Fax: 613/759-6499
Director General, Elaine Lawson
Director, Planning & Coordination, Frank Brunette

PRAIRIE FARM REHABILITATION ADMINISTRATION (PFRA)
CIBC Tower, #603, 1800 Hamilton St., Regina SK S4P 4L2
306/780-6545; Fax: 306/780-5018
Shelterbelt Centre, Indian Head SK S0G 2K0
306/695-2284, Fax: 306/695-2568
Director General, Dr. H.M. Hill, 306/780-5081
Director, Ottawa Affairs, Jamshed Merchant, Sir John Carling Bldg., #4103, 930 Carling Ave., Ottawa ON K1A 0C5, 613/759-7225, Fax: 613/759-6623

PFRA Regional Offices
Manitoba Region: The Cargill Bldg., 238-240 Graham Ave., Winnipeg MB R3C 0J7 – 204/983-3116; Fax: 204/983-2178
Northern Alberta: Royal Lepage Bldg., #1200, 10130 - 103rd St., Edmonton AB T5J 3N9 – 403/495-4526; Fax: 403/495-4504, Regional Director, Fred Kraft
Northern Saskatchewan: Peterson Bldg., University of Saskatchewan, North Rd., PO Box 908, Saskatoon SK S7K 3M4 – 306/975-4663; Fax: 306/975-4594, Regional Director, Brian Abrahamson
Southern Alberta: Harry Hays Bldg., #832, 220 - 4th Ave. SE, PO Box 2906, Calgary AB T2G 4X3 – 403/292-5641; Fax: 403/292-5659, Regional Director, Andrew Cullen
Southern Saskatchewan: 1800 Hamilton St., Regina SK S4P 4L2 – 306/780-5142; Fax: 306/780-5018, Regional Director, Gerry Wetterstrand

ASSOCIATED AGENCIES, BOARDS & COMMISSIONS
Listed alphabetically in detail, this section.
Canadian Dairy Commission
Canadian Grain Commission
Canadian Wheat Board
Farm Credit Corporation
National Farm Products Council

ATLANTIC CANADA OPPORTUNITIES AGENCY (ACOA)/
Agence de promotion économique du Canada atlantique (APECA)
644 Main St., 3rd Fl., PO Box 6051, Moncton NB E1C 9J8
506/851-2271; Fax: 506/851-7403; URL: http://www.acoa.ca/
Toll Free: 1-800-561-7862, TDD: 506/851-3540

A federal government development agency providing support to entrepreneurs in the Atlantic Region. The goal of the ACOA is to improve the economy of Atlantic Canadian communities, through the successful development of businesses and job opportunities. The organization helps people set up new, and to expand existing businesses; market Atlantic Canada, nationally and internationally; works together with other federal departments, the provincial governments and private sector within the four Atlantic provinces to ensure maximum benefit for the region.

Minister Responsible, Hon. John Manley, 613/995-9001, Fax: 613/992-0302
Secretary of State, Hon. Lawrence MacAulay, 613/996-4649, Fax: 613/954-1054
President, J. David Nicholson
Vice-President, Regional Programming & Development Branch, Peter Estey, 506/851-3550
Director, Research & Policy Development, Christine Hewett, 506/851-3201
Vice-President, Major Projects, Leo Walsh, 506/851-2271
Asst. Director General, Policy, Planning & Research, F. Arsenault, 506/851-7731

Regional Offices
Cape Breton: ACOA Cape Breton, 15 Dorchester St., 4th Fl., PO Box 2001, Sydney NS B1P 6K7 – 902/564-3614; Fax: 902/564-3825
New Brunswick: 570 Queen St., PO Box 578, Fredericton NB E3B 5A6 – 506/452-3184; Fax: 506/452-3285, Toll Free: 1-800-561-4030
Newfoundland: Atlantic Place, #801, 215 Water St., PO Box 1060, Stn C, St. John's NF A1C 5M5 – 709/772-2751; Fax: 709/772-2712, Toll Free: 1-800-563-5766
Nova Scotia: #600, 1801 Hollis St., PO Box 2284, Stn M, Halifax NS B3J 3C8 – 902/426-6743; Fax: 902/426-2054, Toll Free: 1-800-565-1228
Ottawa: PO Box 1667, Stn B, Ottawa ON K1P 5R5 – 613/954-2422; Fax: 613/954-0429
Prince Edward Island: 75 Fitzroy St., PO Box 40, Charlottetown PE C1A 7K2 – 902/566-7492; Fax: 902/566-7098

ATLANTIC PILOTAGE AUTHORITY CANADA/
Administration de pilotage de l'Atlantique Canada
Purdy's Wharf, Tower 1, #1402, 1959 Upper Water St., Halifax NS B3J 3N2
902/426-2550; Fax: 902/426-4004; URL: http://canada.gc.ca/depts/agencies/apaind_e.html

The Authority operates a pilotage service within the Atlantic Region which includes all the compulsory pilotage waters of the four Atlantic provinces. Responsible for establishing, operating, maintaining and administering an efficient and economical pilotage service within the coastal waters of the Atlantic region. The authority prescribes tariffs of pilotage charges that are fair, reasonable and consistent with providing revenues allowing the Authority to operate on a self-sustaining financial basis. Reports to government through the Minister of Trasport.
Chair, R. Anthony McGuinness

ATOMIC ENERGY OF CANADA LIMITED (AECL)/
Énergie atomique du Canada ltée (EACL)
2251 Speakman Dr., Mississauga ON L5K 1B2
905/823-9040; Fax: 905/823-8006; Email: webmaster@crl.aecl.ca; URL: http://www.aecl.ca

AECL develops, markets & manages the construction of CANDU power reactors & MAPLE research reactors.
President & CEO, J.R. Morden

ATOMIC ENERGY CONTROL BOARD (AECB)/Commission de contrôle de l'énergie atomique (CCEA)
280 Slater St., PO Box 1046, Stn B, Ottawa ON K1P 5S9
613/995-5894; Fax: 613/995-5086; Email: info@atomcon.gc.ca; URL: http://www.gc.ca/aecb/
Toll Free: 1-800-668-5284

AECB derives authority from the Atomic Energy Control Act & is responsible for regulatory control of the health, safety, security & environmental aspects of the development, application & use of nuclear energy in Canada.
President & CEO, Dr. Agnes J. Bishop
Director General, Secretariat, J.P. Marchildon
Director General, Administration Directorate, G.C. Jack
Director General, Analysis & Assessment Directorate, J.G. Waddington
Director General, Fuel Cycle & Materials Regulation Directorate, R.M. Duncan
Director General, Reactor Regulation Directorate, J.D. Harvie
Legal Advisor, L.S. Holland
Chief, Office of Public Information, H.J.M. Spence

AUDITOR GENERAL OF CANADA/
Vérificateur Général du Canada
240 Sparks St., Ottawa ON K1A 0G6
613/995-3708; Fax: 613/957-4023; URL: http://www.oag-bvg.gc.ca

The Office of the Auditor General of Canada is responsible for examining the Public Accounts of Canada, including those relating to the Consolidated Revenue Fund, public property & various Crown Corporations, & also for conducting audits & studies involving the management of financial, physical & human resources of the federal government. The Auditor General must report annually to the House of Commons &, in addition, may report up to three times a year. He may also make a special report to the House on any matter that he feels should not be deferred.

Following amendments to the Auditor General Act made in December 1995, the Auditor General is also required to report to the House of Commons annually on all significant matters related to the environment & sustainable development. Reports to government through the Minister of Finance.
Auditor General, L. Denis Desautels, FCA.
Commissioner, Environment & Sustainable Development, Brian Emmett
Director, Public Affairs, John Zegers

Regional Offices
Edmonton: Manulife Place, #2460, 10180 - 101 St., Edmonton AB T5J 3S4 – 403/495-2028; Fax: 403/495-2031
Halifax: 1660 Hollis St., 4th Fl., Halifax NS B3J 1V7 – 902/426-7721; Fax: 902/426-8591

Montréal: #1005, rue 685 Cathcart, Montréal PQ
H3B 1M7 – 514/283-6086; Fax: 514/283-1715
Vancouver: #250, 757 West Hastings St.,
Vancouver BC V6C 1A1 – 604/666-3596; Fax: 604/666-6162
Winnipeg: #630, 240 Graham Ave., Winnipeg MB
R3C 0J7 – 204/983-2426; Fax: 204/983-0003

BANK OF CANADA/Banque du Canada
234 Wellington St., Ottawa ON K1A 0G9
613/782-8111; Fax: 613/782-8655; URL: http://www.bank-banque-canada.ca/english/intro-e.htm

The Bank is responsible for regulating "credit and currency in the best interests of the economic life of the nation". The Bank acts as fiscal agent for the Government of Canada in respect of the management of the public debt of Canada & the Exchange Fund Account. The sole right to issue paper money for circulation in Canada is vested in the Bank of Canada. Reports to government through the Minister of Finance.

Governor, Gordon Thiessen
Senior Deputy Governor, B. Bonin
Deputy Governor, C. Freedman
Deputy Governor, W. Paul Jenkins
Advisor, S. Vachon
Advisor, Janet Cosier
Advisor, Vaughn O'Regan
Advisor, Pierre Duguay
Secretary, L. Theodore Requard
Associate Advisor, Jacques Clément
Associate Advisor, D.R. Stephenson
Chief, Automation Services Department, D.W. MacDonald
Chief, Banking Operations Department, D.G.M. Bennett
Chief, International Department, J.D. Murray
Chief, Market Analysis & Open Market Operations, Pat Demerse
Chief, Monetary & Financial Analysis Department, D.J. Longworth
Chief, Personnel Department, G.M. Pike
Chief, Premises Management Department, C.J. Stephenson
Chief, Public Debt Department, B.J. Schwab
Chief, Research Department, S.S. Poloz
Chief, Securities Department, B. Mantador
Chief, Securities, Don Cameron, Toronto Office, 250 University Ave., Toronto ON M5H 3E5
Comptroller & Chief Accountant, J.-P. Aubry
Auditor, Carman L. Young

BUSINESS DEVELOPMENT BANK OF CANADA (BDBC)/Banque de développement du Canada (BDC)
Tour de la Place-Victoria, #800, Place Victoria, CP 335, Montréal PQ H4Z 1L4
514/283-5904; Fax: 514/283-0617; URL: http://www.bdc.ca/
Ligne sans frais: 1-888-463-6232

Promotes & assists in the establishment & development of business enterprises in Canada by providing, in the manner & to the extent authorized by its Act of Incorporation, financial assistance, management counselling & management training to small businesses. The BDC is dedicated to supporting the creation and development of small & medium-sized businesses by providing timely & relevant financial & management services.

President & CEO, François Beaudoin
Director & Chair, Patrick J. Lavelle
Director, Communications, Peter Stewart
Ombudsman, Jean-Pierre Houle
National Director, Aboriginal Banking, James A. Richardson

Regional Offices
Atlantic: 1400 Cogswell Tower, Scotia Sq., PO Box 1656, Halifax NS B3J 2Z7 – 902/426-7860; Fax: 902/426-9033
British Columbia & Yukon: #700, 601 West Hastings St., Vancouver BC V6B 5G9 – 604/666-7800; Fax: 604/666-5872
Ontario: #1101, 150 King St. West, Toronto ON M5H 1J9 – 416/973-1144; Fax: 416/973-0032
Prairie & Northern: #1200, 155 Carlton St., Winnipeg MB R3C 3H8 – 204/983-7811; Fax: 204/983-8522
Québec: #4600, 800 Place Victoria, Montréal PQ H4Z 1C8 – 514/283-3657; Fax: 514/283-5626

THE CANADA COUNCIL/Conseil des Arts du Canada
350 Albert St., PO Box 1047, Ottawa ON K1P 5V8
613/566-4365; Fax: 613/566-4390; URL: http://www.culturenet.ca/cc
Toll Free: 1-800-263-5588

An independent agency created by the Parliament of Canada in 1957 to foster & promote the arts. The Council provides a wide range of grants & services to professional Canadian artists & arts organizations in dance, media arts, music, theatre, writing, publishing & the visual arts. In addition to its primary role in the arts, the Council maintains the secretariat for the Canadian Commission for UNESCO & administers the Killam Program of Prizes & Fellowships to scholars of exceptional ability engaged in significant research projects. Reports to government through the Minister of Canadian Heritage.

Chair, Donna M. Scott
Vice-Chair, François Colbert
Director, Roch Carrier

CANADA DEPOSIT INSURANCE CORPORATION (CDIC)/Société d'assurance-dépôts du Canada
50 O'Connor St., 17th Fl., PO Box 2340, Stn D, Ottawa ON K1P 5W5
613/996-2081; Fax: 613/996-6095; URL: http://canada.gc.ca/depts/agencies/cdiind_e.html
Toll Free: 1-800-461-2342

CDIC was established in 1967 & membership is limited to banks, trust companies, & loan companies. Members may be either federally or provincially incorporated. Funding is provided by its members through premiums paid on insured deposits. Reports to government through the Minister of Finance.
CDIC responsibilities include:
• the provision of insurance against the loss of all or part of deposits;
• the promotion of sound business & financial practices for member institutions;
• to contribute to the stability of the Canadian financial system.

Chair, G.L. Reuber
President & CEO, J.P. Sabourin
Senior Vice-President, Field Operations, W. Acton
Senior Vice-President, Insurance & Risk Assessment, G. Saint-Pierre
Vice-President, Finance, J.R. Lanthier
Vice-President, Operations, B.C. Scheepers
Corporate Secretary & General Counsel, L.T. Lederman
Director, Communications & Public Affairs, M.A. Pearcy

CANADA LABOUR RELATIONS BOARD (CLRB)/Conseil canadien des Relations du Travail (CCRT)
240 Sparks St., 4th Fl., Ottawa ON K1A 0X8
613/996-9466; Fax: 613/947-5407

The Board is an independent, administrative, quasi-judicial tribunal which administers Part I & certain provisions of Part II of the Canada Labour Code. Its responsibilities include the granting or revoking of collective bargaining rights, the mediation & adjudication of unfair labour practice complaints, the determination of unlawful strikes & lockouts, the disposition of appeals of a safety officer's decision, & other matters.

Chair, Ted Weatherill
Vice-Chair, L. Doyon
Vice-Chair, J.L. Guilbeault
Vice-Chair, Suzanne Handman
Vice-Chair, R.I. Hornung
Vice-Chair, P. Morneault

CANADA LANDS COMPANY/Société Immobilière du Canada
#1500, 200 King St. West, Toronto ON M5H 3T4
416/974-9700; Fax: 416/974-9661; Email: clc@clc.ca; URL: http://www.clc.ca

The CLC is a Crown Corporation responsible for the management &/or disposal of certain surplus federal lands on behalf of the Government of Canada. The agency reports to government through the Minister of Public Works & Government Services.

President & CEO, Erhard Buchholz
Chair, Jon Grant
Secretary, Brian Way

OLD PORT OF MONTRÉAL CORPORATION INC.
333, rue de la Commune ouest, Montréal PQ H2Y 2E2
514/283-5256; Fax: 514/283-8423
President, Bernard Lamarre

CANADA MORTGAGE & HOUSING CORPORATION (CMHC)/Société canadienne d'hypothèques et de logement (SCHL)
700 Montreal Rd., Ottawa ON K1A 0P7
613/748-2000; Fax: 613/748-2098; URL: http://www.cmhc-schl.gc.ca
Public Affairs Centre: 613/748-4627
Canadian Housing Information Centre: 613/748-2367

CMHC insures loans so that first time homebuyers can purchase a home with a five or ten percent downpayment.

Over 660,000 social housing units are supported on behalf of the federal government. All types of housing-related research & designed projects are conducted &/or funded by CMHC to improve the quality of housing & residential environments. Through its offices, CMHC provides service & advice to the public, mortgage lenders, real estate agents and the housing construction industry. Reports to government through Public Works & Government Services.

ACTS ADMINISTERED
National Housing Act
Minister Responsible, Hon. Diane Marleau, 613/997-5421, Fax: 613/953-1908
Chair, Peter Smith, 613/748-2786
President, Marc Rochon, 613/748-2900
Senior Vice-President, Corporate Resources, P.C. Connolly, 613/748-2682
Vice-President, Finance, K.A. Kinsley, 613/748-2186
Vice-President, Land Management, J.T. Lynch, 613/748-2562
Vice-President, Policy, Research & Communications, D.A. Stewart, 613/748-2553
Vice-President, Programs & General Counsel & Corporate Secretary, C. Poirier-Defoy, 613/748-2221

CMHC Regional Offices
Atlantic: PO Box 7320, Stn A, Saint John NB E2L 4S7 – 506/636-4460; Fax: 506/636-4607, General Manager, J. Black

Canadian Almanac & Directory 1997

British Columbia & Yukon: #450, 999 Canada Pl., Vancouver BC V6C 3E1 – 604/666-2516; Fax: 604/666-3020, General Manager, P.D. Anderson

Ontario: Atria North, 100 Sheppard Ave. East, North York ON M2M 6N5 – 416/221-2642; Fax: 416/495-2004, General Manager, W.G. Mulvihill

Prairie & NWT: #200, 119 - 4th Ave. South, Saskatoon SK S7K 3N2 – 306/975-4900; Fax: 306/975-5134, General Manager, B. Dornan

Québec: Place du Canada, 1010, rue De La Gauchetière ouest, 11th Fl., Montréal PQ H3B 2N2 – 514/283-4464; Fax: 514/283-7595, General Manager, D. St-Onge

CANADA PLACE CORPORATION/ Corporation Place du Canada

#1001, 999 Canada Pl., Vancouver BC V6C 3C1
604/666-7200; Fax: 604/666-0695

The Corporation is in charge of property management at Canada Place in Vancouver, which includes a cruise ship facility, a trade & convention centre, a hotel, an IMAX theatre, restaurants & a food fair/retail area.

Chair, Farouk Verjee

Vice-President & General Manager, William J. Watson

CANADA PORTS CORPORATION (CPC)/ Société canadienne des ports (SCP)

99 Metcalfe St., Ottawa ON K1A 0N6
613/957-6787; Fax: 613/996-9629; URL: http://canada.gc.ca/depts/agencies/cpoind_e.html

A federal system of ports administered pursuant to the Canada Ports Corporation Act, which was proclaimed in 1983. Seven of these ports are autonomous local port corporations located in Halifax, Montréal, Prince Rupert, Québec, Saint John, St. John's & Vancouver. The other ports are directly administered by the Canada Ports Corporation & are located in Belledune, Churchill, Port Colborne, Port Saguenay/Baie des Ha!Ha!, Prescott, Sept-Îles & Trois-Rivières. In providing a public service, the ports are administered according to common commercial principles.

Acting Chair, Barney Powers, 613/957-6794

Local Port Corporations

Halifax: PO Box 366, Halifax NS B3J 2P6 – 902/426-3643, David Bellefontaine

Montréal: Port of Montréal Bldg., Wing #1, Cité du Havre, Montréal PQ H3C 3R5 – 514/283-7042; Fax: 514/283-0829, Dominic Taddeo

Prince Rupert: 110 Third Ave. West, Prince Rupert BC V8J 1K8 – 250/627-7545; Fax: 250/627-7101, Don Krusel

Québec: CP 2268, Québec PQ G1K 7P7 – 418/648-3558; Fax: 418/648-4160, Ross Gaudreault

Saint John: PO Box 6429, Stn A, Saint John NB E2L 4R8 – 506/636-4869; Fax: 506/636-4443, Capt. A.G. Scott

St. John's: PO Box 6178, St. John's NF A1C 5X8 – 709/772-4664; Fax: 709/772-4689, David Fox

Vancouver: #1900, 200 Granville St., Vancouver BC V6C 2P9 – 604/666-8978; Fax: 604/666-8916, N.C. Stark

Divisional Ports

Belledune: Port of Belledune, Belledune NB E0B 1G0 – 506/522-2859; Fax: 506/522-0803, Guy Desgagnes

Churchill: PO Box 217, Churchill MB R0B 0E0 – 204/675-8823; Fax: 204/675-2550, Ray Robusky, 613/957-6762 (Ottawa)

Port Colborne: PO Box 129, Port Colborne ON L3K 5V8 – 905/834-3644, Ray Robusky, 613/957-6762 (Ottawa)

Port Saguenay: CP 760, Chicoutimi PQ G7H 5E1 – 418/543-0263; Fax: 418/543-4633, Ghyslaine Collard

Prescott: PO Box 520, Prescott ON K0E 1T0 – 613/925-4228; Fax: 613/925-5022, Ray Robusky, 613/957-6762 (Ottawa)

Sept-Îles: #202, 421, av Arnaud, Sept-Îles PQ G4R 3B3 – 418/968-1231; Fax: 418/962-4445, Jean-Maurice Gaudreau

Trois-Rivières: CP 999, Trois-Rivières PQ G9A 5K2 – 418/378-3939; Fax: 418/378-2487, Capt. Serge Tremblay

CANADA POST CORPORATION/ Société canadienne des postes

2701 Riverside Dr., Ottawa ON K1A 0B1
613/734-8440; URL: http://www.canpost.ca/
Toll Free: 1-800-267-1177
Toll Free (French): 1-800-267-1155
Toll Free TDD: 1-800-267-2797

Federal government agency responsible for Canada's postal system. Reports to government through Public Works & Government Services. For postal rates, codes, abbreviations & other general information; see Postal Information in the main/global Index.

Chair, Hon. André Ouellet

President & CEO, Georges C. Clermont, Q.C.

Vice President & Chief Information Officer, Gilles Farley

Vice-President, Administration, Hank J. Klassen

Senior Vice-President & Chief Financial Officer, Ian A. Bourne

Senior Vice President, Electronic Products & Services, L. Philippe Lemay

Senior Vice President, Marketing & Product Management, C. Anne Joynt

Senior Vice-President, Operations, Léo Blanchette

President, Canada Post Systems Management Ltd., Elisabeth Kriegler

Director, Public Affairs, Marylyn Belch Venner

Canada Post Communications Offices

Atlantic Division: PO Box 1689, Halifax NS B3J 2B1 – 902/494-4076; Fax: 902/494-4328

Prairie Division: #1300, 10020 - 101A Ave., Edmonton AB T5J 4J4 – 403/944-3137; Fax: 403/944-3140

Winnipeg Office: #3M, 266 Graham Ave., Winnipeg MB R3C 0K0
204/987-5355, Fax: 204/987-5110

Huron Division: 955 Highbury Ave., London ON N5Y 1A3 – 519/457-5234; Fax: 519/453-2112

Pacific Division: (1010 Howe St.), PO Box 2110, Vancouver BC V6B 4Z3 – 604/662-1388; Fax: 604/662-1569

Québec Division: #100, 475, boul de l'Atrium, Charlesbourg PQ G1H 7K2 – 418/624-6424; Fax: 418/624-6422

Montréal Office: #346, 1000, rue De La Gauchetière ouest, Montréal PQ H3B 5B7
514/345-4569, Fax: 514/345-4307

York Division: #700, 1 Dundas St. West, Toronto ON M5G 2L5 – 416/204-4188; Fax: 416/204-4444

CANADIAN ARTISTS & PRODUCERS PROFESSIONAL RELATIONS TRIBUNAL/ Tribunal canadien des relations professionnelles artistes-producteurs

C.D. Howe Bldg., 240 Sparks St., 8th Fl. West, Ottawa ON K1A 1A1

613/996-4052; Fax: 613/947-4125;
Email: tribunal.artists@ic.gc.ca; URL: http://info.ic.gc.ca/opengov/capprt
Toll Free: 1-800-263-ARTS (2787)

ACTS ADMINISTERED

Status of the Artist Act

Acting Chair & CEO, Hon. André Fortier, 613/996-4052

Secretary General, Elizabeth MacPherson, 613/996-4052

CANADIAN BROADCASTING CORPORATION (CBC)/ Société Radio-Canada (SRC)

1500 Bronson Ave., PO Box 8478, Ottawa ON K1G 3J5
613/724-1200; URL: http://www.cbc.ca/
TDD: 613/738-6686

The Canadian Broadcasting Corporation (CBC) is a publicly owned corporation providing a national broadcasting service in Canada in two languages (English & French). The CBC was established by an Act of Parliament in 1936. The CBC reports to Parliament each year on its operations through the Minister of Canadian Heritage. The agency is governed by the 1991 Broadcasting Act & is subject to regulations of the Canadian Radio-television & Telecommunications Commission (CRTC).

President & Chief Executive Officer, Hon. Perrin Beatty

Chair, Board of Directors, Guylaine Saucier

Senior Vice-President, Media, Vacant

Senior Vice-President, Resources, Louise Tremblay

Senior Advisor to the President & CEO, Michael McEwen

Vice President, General Counsel & Corporate Secretary, Gerald Flaherty, Q.C.

Vice-President, Human Resources, George C.B. Smith

Vice-President, Internal Audit, Robert Hertzog

Senior Director, Corporate Communications & Public Affairs, Charlotte O'Dea

CBC OMBUDSMAN

Ombudsman, English Services, David Bazay, PO Box 500, Stn A, Toronto ON M5W 1E6

Ombudsman, French Services, Mario Cardinal, 1400, boul René-Lévesque est, CP 6000, Montréal PQ H3C 3A8

ENGLISH NETWORKS

PO Box 500, Stn A, Toronto ON M5W 1E6
416/205-3311
TDD: 416/205-6688

Vice-President, English Radio, Harold Redekopp

Vice-President, English Television Networks, Jim Byrd

Vice-President, News, Current Affairs & Newsworld, Television, Bob Culbert

Executive Director, Media Operations, Michael Harris

Head, CBC Newsworld, Slawko Klymkiw

Senior Director, Broadcast Communications, Diane Kenyon

Senior Director, Media & Public Relations, Tom Curzon

FRENCH NETWORKS

1400, boul René-Lévesque est, CP 6000, Montréal PQ H3C 3A8
514/597-5970
TDD: 514/597-6013

Vice-President, French Radio, Marcel Pépin

Vice-President, French Television, Michèle Fortin

Director General, Communications, Raymond Guay

Director, Public Relations, Micheline Savoie

Executive Director, RDI, Renaud Gilbert

General Manager, TV5 (Consortium Québec-Canada), Guy Gougeon

CBC ENGINEERING

7925, rue Côte St-Luc, Montréal PQ H4W 1R5
514/485-1301

Senior Director, Engineering, Brian D. Baldry

RADIO CANADA INTERNATIONAL
1055, boul René-Lévesque est, CP 6000, Montréal PQ H3C 3A8

514/597-7555

Executive Director, Terry Hargreaves

Program Director, Allan Familiant

CBC Regional Offices

Alberta (English & French): PO Box 555, Edmonton AB T5J 2P4 – 403/468-7500, Regional Director, Ron Smith, Regional Manager, Communications, Glenn Luff, Director, Radio, French Services, Denis Collette, Communications Manager, Radio & Television, Pierre Nöel

Atlantic (French): 250 Archibald St., PO Box 950, Moncton NB E1C 8N8 – 506/853-6666, Director, Radio, Jules Chiasson, Director, Television, Louise Imbeault, Regional Manager, Communications, Marc A. Leblanc

British Columbia (English & French): PO Box 4600, Vancouver BC V6B 4A2 – 604/662-6000, Regional Director, English Services, Donna Logan, Director, Radio, French Services, Robert Groulx, Regional Manager, Communications, Gilian Dusting, Regional Manager, Communications, Johanne Huard

Manitoba (English & French): 491 Portage Ave., PO Box 160, Winnipeg MB R3C 2H1 – 204/788-3222 (English) – 204/788-3141 (French), Acting Regional Director, English Services, Jane Chalmers, Senior Manager, Central Regional Communications, Bridget Hoffer, Director, Radio, René Fontaine, Regional Manager, Communications, Huguette Le Gall

Maritimes (English): 5600 Sackville St., PO Box 3000, Halifax NS B3J 3E9 – 902/420-8311, Acting Regional Director, Fred Mattocks, Senior Manager, Eastern Regional Communications, Jessie Clarey

Newfoundland (English): Ayre's Centre, Pippy Place, PO Box 12010, Stn A, St. John's NF A1B 3T8 – 709/576-5000, Regional Director, Ron Crocker, Regional Manager, Communications, John O'Mara

Ontario (English): Broadcast Centre, 250 Front St. West, PO Box 500, Stn A, Toronto ON M5W 1E6 – 416/205-3311, Acting Regional Director, (Windsor), Doug Ward, TV Publicist, (Ottawa), Jane Patterson, TV Publicist, (Toronto), Susan Grant

Ontario (French): 250 Lanark Ave., PO Box 3220, Stn C, Ottawa ON K1Y 1E4 – 613/724-1200, Director, Radio, Denis Pellerin, Director, Television, Christine Marais, Regional Manager, Communications, Maryse Lairot

Québec (English): 1400, boul René-Lévesque est, CP 6000, Montréal PQ H3C 3A8 – 514/ 597-5970; Fax: 514/597-5551, Regional Director, English Services, Nicole Bélanger, Acting Regional Manager, Communications, Jackie Moore

Québec City & Eastern Québec (French): 2475, boul Laurier, CP 10400, Ste-Foy PQ G1V 2X2 – 418/654-1341, Director, French Services, Jacques D. Landry, Manager, Communications, Ginette D'Aigle

Saskatchewan (English & French): 2440 Broad St., Regina SK S4P 4A1 – 306/347-9540, Regional Director, English Services, Brian Cousins, Acting Manager, Communications, Glenn Lemchuk, Director, Radio, French Services, Richard Marcotte, Director, Television for the Four Western Stations, French Services, Lionel Bonneville, Manager, Communications, Françoise Sigur-Cloutier

CBC North: 5129 - 49 St., PO Box 160, Yellowknife NT X1A 1P8 – 403/669-3500, Regional Director, & Director, Television, Marie Wilson, Regional Manager, Communications, Craig Yeo

CANADIAN CENTRE FOR MANAGEMENT DEVELOPMENT (CCMD)/
Centre canadien de gestion (CCG)
PO Box 420, Stn A, Ottawa ON K1N 8V4
613/997-4163; Fax: 613/953-6240; Email: CCMD@on.infoshare.ca; URL: http://www.infoshare.ca/ccmd/mainpage.html
Business Enquiries: 613/992-9045

Training and development programs for senior managers in the federal government. The institution is dedicated to providing public service executives with leading edge learning solutions through executive education and development.

Principal, Dr. Janet R. Smith, 613/992-8165, Fax: 613/943-1038

Director General, Business Centre/Communications & Marketing, D. Burke, 613/992-8059

Executive Director, Management Services, L. Durocher, 613/992-8171

Chief Operating Officer, E.P. Hossack, 613/947-4860

Vice-Principal, Executive Development Programs, B. Marson, 819/997-8735

Vice-Principal, Research, R. Heintzman, 613/995-5839

Head, Negotiation, Consultation & Conflict Management, Joseph Stanford, 613/943-2334

Campus Locations
Touraine Campus: 646, rue Principale, Touraine PQ J1N 8V4 – 819/997-4163; Fax: 819/953-7907
De La Salle Campus: 373 Sussex Dr., Ottawa ON K1N 8V4 – 819/997-4163

CANADIAN CENTRE FOR OCCUPATIONAL HEALTH & SAFETY (CCOHS)/
Centre canadien d'hygiène et de sécurité au travail (CCHST)
250 Main St. East, Hamilton ON L8N 1H6
905/572-2981; Fax: 905/572-2206; Email: custserv@ccohs.ca; URL: http://www.ccohs.ca
Toll Free: 1-800-263-8466
Inquiries: 905/572-4400; Fax: 905/572-4500

Provides occupational health & safety information in the form of publications, responses to inquiries & a computerized information service which is available both on-line & on CD-ROM. It is governed by a tripartite council representing employers, labour & governments. The Centre reports to Parliament through the Minister of Labour.

Minister, Hon. Alphonso Gagliano
President & CEO, J. Arthur St-Aubin, 905/572-4432
Chair of the Council, Nicole Senécal
Vice-President, Dr. P.K. Abeytunga, 905/572-4537
Comptroller, Brian Hutchings, 905/572-4401
Manager, Computer Systems & Services, Ashok Setty, 905/572-4498
Manager, Health & Safety Products & Services, Anne Gravereaux, 905/572-4487
Manager, Inquiries Service, Dr. Roger Cockerline, 905/572-4523
Manager, Operations Support, Eleanor Irwin, 905/572-4408

CANADIAN CENTRE ON SUBSTANCE ABUSE/
Centre canadien de lutte contre l'alcoolisme et les toxicomanies
#300, 75 Albert St., Ottawa ON K1P 5E7
613/235-4048; Fax: 613/235-8101; URL: http://www.ccsa.ca

Established in 1988 under Canada's Drug Strategy, to determine methods of treating & preventing substance abuse. Works to minimize the harm associated with the use of alcohol, tobacco and other drugs.

Chair, William G. Deeks
CEO, Jacques LeCavalier
Director, Communications, Richard Garlick

CANADIAN COMMERCIAL CORPORATION (CCC)/
Corporation commerciale canadienne
Metropolitan Centre, #1100, 50 O'Connor St., Ottawa ON K1A 0S6
613/996-0034; Fax: 613/995-2121; Email: info@ccc.ca; URL: http://www.ccc.ca

Federal Crown Corporation which reports to Parliament through the Minister of International Trade. By serving as prime contractor, the Corporation facilitates exports of a wide range of goods & services from Canadian sources to foreign governments & international agencies.

In response to requests from foreign customers for individual products or services, CCC identifies Canadian firms capable of meeting the customer's requirements, executes prime as well as back-to-back contracts, & follows through with contract management, inspection, acceptance, and payment.

Minister Responsible, Hon. Art Eggleton, 613/992-7332

Deputy Minister for International Trade & President of CCC, Robert G. Wright, 613/994-5000, Fax: 613/944-8493

Executive Vice-President & COO, Douglas Patriquin

Director, Business Development, Stephen Bigsby, 613/995-9116

Head, Communications & Awareness, M.V. Asfar, 613/995-0560

CANADIAN DAIRY COMMISSION (CDC)/
Commission canadienne du lait (CCL)
Carling Executive Park, 1525 Carling Ave., Ottawa ON K1A 0Z2
613/998-9490; Fax: 613/998-4492; URL: http://www.agr.ca/cdc

The Commission provides efficient producers of milk & cream with the opportunity of obtaining a fair return for their labour & investment. Also provides consumers of dairy products with a continuous & adequate supply of dairy products of high quality. Reports to government through the Minister of Agriculture & Agri-food.

Chair, Gilles Prégent
Vice-Chair, Louis Balcaen
Commissioner, Alvin Johnstone

CANADIAN GRAIN COMMISSION/
Commission canadienne des grains
#600, 303 Main St., Winnipeg MB R3C 3G8
204/983-2734; Fax: 204/983-2751

Regulates grain handling in Canada & establishes & maintains quality standards for Canadian grains. Responsibilities include official inspection & grading of grain, weighing of grain at terminal & transfer elevators, licensing of grain elevators & dealers, conducting & publishing statistical & economic studies, & conducting basic & applied research on Canadian grain. Reports to government through the Minister of Agriculture & Agri-food.

Chief Commissioner, M.E. Wakefield
Asst. Chief Commissioner, R.A. Groundwater
Asst. Chief Commissioner, Vacant
Executive Director, D. Wallace
Director, Corporate Services Division, D.N. Kennedy
Director, Grain Research Laboratory, K.H. Tipples, Ph.D.
Director, Industry Services Division, Elizabeth Larmond

Canadian Almanac & Directory 1997

CANADIAN HERITAGE/
Patrimoine canadien
Jules Léger Bldg., 25 Eddy St., Hull PQ K1A 1K5
819/997-0055; Fax: 819/953-5382; URL: http://www.pch.gc.ca/
TDD: 819/997-8776

Ensures the protection of Canada's natural heritage & historic sites, promotion of artistic development & Canadian heritage, & encourages full participation of all Canadians in our country's development.

Develops & administers policies & programs to promote Canadian values & identity. These policies & programs comprise the development of official languages minority communities & the recognition & use of English & French throughout Canadian society. Ensures the promotion of better understanding & respect among Canadians of all backgrounds & works to eliminate barriers to full integration of all Canadians (including the administration of the Canadian Multiculturalism Act).

Provides programming, largely managed by off-reserve Aboriginal people, to help them define & participate in solving social, cultural, political & economic issues affecting their lives. Coordinates Canada's international commitments on human rights & works to advance civic education & to provide young people greater opportunities to learn about Canada & to participate in their communities.

Promotes voluntaryism, Canadian symbols & the organization of events of national significance. Promotes amateur sport across the country, by providing policy leadership & financial cooperation to national sport organzations & athletes, as well as significant technical & financial support to major amateur sporting events, such as the Canada Games.

ACTS ADMINISTERED
An Act to Incorporate the Jules & Paul-Émile Léger Foundation
Broadcasting Act
Canada Council Act
Canadian Film Development Corporation Act
Canadian Heritage Languages Institute Act
Canadian Multiculturalism Act
Canadian Race Relations Foundation Act
Canadian Radio-television & Telecommunications Commission Act
Corrupt Practices Inquiries Act
Cultural Property Export & Import Act
Department of Communications Act
Department of Multiculturalism & Citizenship Act
Department of State Act
Department of Transport Act
Disfranchising Act
Dominion Controverted Elections Act
Dominion Water Power Act
Federal Real Property Act
Fitness & Amateur Sport Act
Heritage Railway Stations Protection Act
Historic Sites & Monuments Act
Holidays Act
Laurier House Act
Lieutenant Governors Superannuation Act
Mingan Archipelago National Park Act
Museums Act
National Anthem Act
National Archives of Canada Act
National Arts Centre Act
National Battlefields at Québec Act
National Film Act
National Flag of Canada Manufacturing Standards Act
National Library Act
National Parks Act
National Symbol of Canada Act
Official Languages Act
Persons of Japanese Ancestry Ex Gratia Payments Order
Public Service Employment Act
Salaries Act
Status of the Artist Act
Trade-marks Act

Minister, Hon. Sheila Copps, 613/997-7788, Fax: 613/994-5987
Deputy Minister, Suzanne Hurtubise, 819/994-1132, Fax: 819/997-0913
Secretary of State, Multiculturalism & Status of Women, Hon. Hedy Fry, 819/997-9900, Fax: 819/953-8055

CORPORATE SERVICES
Asst. Deputy Minister, Jane Roszell, 819/994-3046, Fax: 819/953-4796
Director General, Administrative Services Branch, Denis Thompson, 819/997-3717
Director, Access to Information & Privacy, Ernie Aumond, 819/997-2894, General Inquiries: 819/997-6874
Director General, Banque Internationale d'Information, sur les États Francophones, Suzanne Richer, 819/997-3857, Fax: 819/953-8439
Director General, Corporate & Intergovernmental Affairs, Erika Bruce, 819/994-2061, Fax: 819/997-7624
Director General, Financial Management, Alain Latourelle, 819/997-1923, Fax: 819/953-2156
Director General, Human Resources, Michel Desjardins, 819/997-1873, Fax: 819/953-1084
Director General, Information Management Branch, Peter Homulos, 819/994-4689, Fax: 819/994-3681
General Counsel, Beverly J. Wilton, 613/990-5339, Fax: 613/798-7920
Director, Central Correspondence & Documentation, Marie Bergeron, 819/994-3542, Fax: 819/997-4191

Communications Branch
Director General, Jean Chartier, 819/997-0231, Fax: 819/953-5382
Director, Citizenship & Canadian Identity Sector, Jodi Redmond, 819/953-6782, Fax: 819/994-7687
Director, Communications Services, Michael Holmes, 819/997-9700, Fax: 819/953-8770
Director, Cultural Development & Heritage Sector, Ghislaine Roy, 613/990-4839, Fax: 613/957-2203
Director, Ministerial Services, Gilles Déry, 819/994-5606, Fax: 819/953-5382
Director, Parks Canada Sector, Wayne Scott, 819/997-7392, Fax: 819/953-5523
Director, Strategic Communications Services, Denis Vezina, 819/953-6783, Fax: 819/953-5382

CITIZENSHIP & CANADIAN IDENTITY SECTOR
Asst. Deputy Minister, Roger Collet, 819/994-2164, Fax: 819/953-7067
Director General, Citizens' Participation & Multiculturalism, Susan Scotti, 819/994-2994, Fax: 819/953-8720
Director General, Official Languages, Hilaire Lemoine, 819/994-0943, Fax: 819/953-9353
Director General, Sport Canada, Adam Ostry, 819/956-8151, Fax: 819/956-8006
Director General, Policy, Coordination & Strategic Planning, Sean Berrigan, 819/994-5644, Fax: 819/997-0743

Regional Operations Coordination & Services
Director General, Anne Scotton, 819/994-7798, Fax: 819/997-0177

Regional Offices
Alberta: Canada Place, #552, 220 - 4th Ave. SE, Calgary AB T2P 3H8 – 403/292-4444; Fax: 403/292-8868, Regional Executive Director, Donna Petrachenko
Atlantic: Historic Properties, Upper Water St., Halifax NS B3J 1S9 – 902/426-4912; Fax: 902/426-1378, Regional Executive Director, Joe O'Brien
Ontario: North York City Centre, #500, 5160 Yonge St., Toronto ON M2N 6L9 – 416/954-0396; Fax: 416/954-2909, Regional Executive Director, Gilbert H. Scott
Pacific & Yukon: #300, 300 West Georgia St., Vancouver BC V6B 6C6 – 604/666-0146; Fax: 604/666-3508, Regional Executive Director, Orest Kruhlak
Prairies & Northwest Territories: #201, 303 Main St., Winnipeg MB R3C 4S3 – 204/983-2630; Fax: 204/984-6996, Regional Executive Director, Bill Balan
Québec: Complexe Guy-Favreau, Tour ouest, 200, boul René-Lévesque ouest, 6e étage, Montréal PQ H2Z 1X4 – 514/283-5797; Fax: 514/283-7727, Regional Executive Director, Élisabeth Châtillon

CULTURAL DEVELOPMENT & HERITAGE SECTOR
Asst. Deputy Minister, Victor Rabinovitch, 613/993-4393, Fax: 613/957-3557
Director General, Arts Policy, Denise Perrier, 613/991-5727, Fax: 613/952-3632
Director General, Broadcasting, Susan Baldwin, 613/990-7937, Fax: 613/952-5109
Director General, Canadian Conservation Institute, Charles Gruchy, 1030 Innes Rd., Ottawa ON K1A 0C8, 613/998-3721, Fax: 613/998-4721
Director General, Canadian Heritage Information Network, Lyn Elliott-Sherwood, 365 Laurier Ave. West, 12th Fl., Ottawa ON K1A 0C8, 613/992-3333, Fax: 613/952-2318, URL://www.chin.gc.ca/
Director General, Heritage, Bill Peters, 613/991-1690, Fax: 613/952-6894
Chair, Canadian Cultural Property Export Review Board, Ian Christie Clark, 613/990-4161, Fax: 613/954-8826

Cultural Industries
Acting Director General, Susan Katz, 613/990-4874, Fax: 613/952-9868
Acting Director, Copyright Policy & Economic Planning, Allan Clarke, 613/990-4222, Fax: 613/952-5312
Acting Director, Film, Video & Sound Recording Policy & Programs, J.-F. Bernier, 613/990-4145, Fax: 613/957-3558
Director, Publishing Policy & Programs, Susan Katz, 613/990-4897, Fax: 613/941-8975
Manager, Book Publishing Industry Development Program (BPIDP), E. Rosenberg, 613/990-4140

PARKS CANADA SECTOR
URL: http://parkscanada.pch.gc.ca/
Asst. Deputy Minister, Thomas E. Lee, 819/997-9525, Fax: 819/953-9745
Director General, National Historic Sites, Dr. Christina Cameron, 819/994-1808
Director General, National Parks, Michael Porter, 819/994-2657
Director General, Parks Canada Investments, Patrick Borbey, 819/953-4013

Canal Offices
Carillon: 1, rue du Barrage, Carillon PQ J0V 1C0 – 514/537-3534; Fax: 514/537-3733
Chambly: 1369, rue de Bourgogne, Chambly PQ J3L 1Y4 – 514/658-0681; Fax: 514/658-2428
Lachine: Complex Guy-Favreau, Montréal PQ H2Z 1X4 – 514/283-6054; Fax: 514/496-1263
Rideau: 34A Beckwith St. South, Smith Falls ON K7A 2A8 – 613/283-5170; Fax: 613/283-0677
St. Peters: PO Box 8, St. Peters NS B0E 3B0 – 902/535-2118 (seasonal), 733-2280 (year-round); Fax: 902/733-2362
Saint-Ours: Rte 133, CP 7, Saint-Ours PQ J0G 1P0 – 514/785-2212
Sainte-Anne-de-Bellevue: 170, rue Sainte-Anne, Sainte-Anne-de-Bellevue PQ H9X 1N1 – 514/457-5546; Fax: 514/457-0378

Sault: One Canal Dr., Sault Ste. Marie ON P6A 1P0 – 705/942-6262; Fax: 705/942-2101

Trent-Severn Waterway: Ashburnham Dr., PO Box 567, Peterborough ON K9J 6Z6 – 705/742-9267; Fax: 705/742-9644

Parks Canada Regional Information Centres

Alberta: #552, 220 - 4th Ave. SE, PO Box 2989, Stn M, Calgary AB T2P 3H8 – 403/292-4401; Fax: 403/292-4242, Executive Director, Donna Petrachenko

Atlantic: Historic Properties Bldg., 1869 Upper Water St., Halifax NS B3J 1S9 – 902/426-3436; Fax: 902/426-6881, Executive Director, J.J. O'Brien

Ontario: 111 Water St. East, Cornwall ON K6H 6S3 – 613/938-5866; Fax: 613/938-5785, Executive Director, Gilbert Scott

#500, 5160 Yonge St., Toronto ON M2N 6L9 416/954-9243, Fax: 416/973-6891

Pacific & Yukon: #300, 300 West Georgia St., Vancouver BC V6B 6C6 – 604/666-1280; Fax: 604/666-7957, Executive Director, Orest Kruhlak

Prairies & Northwest Territories: 45 Forks Market Rd., Winnipeg MB R3C 4T6 – 204/983-2290; Fax: 204/983-2221, Executive Director, Bill Balan

Québec: Tour Ouest, Guy-Favreau Complex, 200, boul René-Lévesque ouest, 6e étage, Montréal PQ H2Z 1X4 – 514/283-2332; Fax: 514/283-7727, Ligne sans frais: 1-800-463-6769, Executive Director, Elisabeth Châtillon

3, rue Buade, Québec PQ G1R 4V7 418/648-4177, Fax: 418/648-4234

Alberta National Parks/National Historic Sites

Banff National Park: PO Box 900, Banff AB T0L 0C0 – 403/762-1500; Fax: 403/762-3380

Elk Island National Park: RR#1, Site 4, Fort Saskatchewan AB T8L 2N7 – 403/992-6380; Fax: 403/998-3686

Jasper National Park: PO Box 10, Jasper AB T0E 1E0 – 403/852-6161; Fax: 403/852-5601

Rocky Mountain House National Historic Site: PO Box 2130, Rocky Mountain House AB T0M 1T0 – 403/845-3948; Fax: 403/845-5320

Waterton Lakes National Park: Waterton Park AB T0K 2M0 – 403/859-2224; Fax: 403/859-2650

Yoho National Park: PO Box 99, Field BC V0A 1G0 – 250/343-6324; Fax: 250/343-6330

Atlantic National Parks/National Historic Sites

Acadian Odyssey National Historic Site: #106, 1045 Main St., Moncton NB E1C 1H1 – 506/851-3063; Fax: 506/851-7079

Alexander Graham Bell Historic Site: PO Box 159, Baddeck NS B0E 1B0 – 902/295-2069; Fax: 902/295-3496

Ardgowan National Historic Site: 2 Palmers Lane, Charlottetown PE C1A 5V6 – 902/566-7050; Fax: 902/566-7226

L'Anse au Meadows National Historic Site: PO Box 70, St-Lunaire-Griquet NF A0K 2X0 – 709/623-2608; Fax: 709/623-2028

Bank Fishery National Heritage Exhibit: PO Box 9080, Stn A, Halifax NS B3K 5M7 – 902/426-5080; Fax: 902/426-4228

Cape Breton Highlands National Park: Ingonish Beach NS B0C 1L0 – 902/285-2270; Fax: 902/285-2866

Cape Spear National Historic Site: PO Box 1268, St. John's NF A1C 5M9 – 709/772-5367; Fax: 709/772-6302

Carleton Martello Tower National Historic Site: PO Box 850, Moncton NB E1C 8N6 – 506/851-3083; Fax: 506/851-7079

Castle Hill National Historic Site: PO Box 10, Jerseyside, Placentia Bay NF A0B 2G0 – 709/227-2401; Fax: 709/227-2452

Fort Amherst National Historic Site: 2 Palmers Lane, Charlottetown PE C1A 5VL – 902/566-6350; Fax: 902/566-7226

Fort Anne National Historic Site: PO Box 9, Annapolis Royal NS B0S 1A0 – 902/532-2397; Fax: 902/532-2232

Fort Beausejour National Historic Site: #106, 1045 Main St., Moncton NB E1C 1H1 – 506/851-3083; Fax: 506/851-7079

Fort Edward National Historic Site: PO Box 150, Grand Pré NS B0P 1M0 – 902/542-3631; Fax: 902/542-1619

Fortress of Louisbourg National Historic Site: PO Box 160, Louisbourg NS B0A 1M0 – 902/733-2280; Fax: 902/733-2362

Fundy National Park: PO Box 40, Alma NB E0A 1B0 – 506/887-6000; Fax: 506/887-2308

Grand Pré National Historic Site: Grand Pré NS B0P 1M0 – 902/542-3631; Fax: 902/542-1619

Grassy Island National Historic Site: PO Box 159, Baddeck NS B0E 1E0 – 902/295-2069; Fax: 902/295-3496

Gros Morne National Park: PO Box 130, Rocky Harbour NF A0K 4N0 – 709/458-2417; Fax: 709/458-2059

Halifax Citadel National Historic Site: PO Box 9080, Stn A, Halifax NS B3K 5M7 – 902/426-5080; Fax: 902/426-4228

Hawthorne Cottage National Historic Site: PO Box 5542, St. John's NF A1C 5X4 – 709/753-9262; Fax: 709/772-2940

Kejimkujik National Park: PO Box 236, Maitland Bridge NS B0T 1N0 – 902/682-2770; Fax: 902/682-3367

Kouchibouguac National Park: Kouchibouguac NB E0A 2A0 – 506/876-2443; Fax: 506/876-4802

Marconi National Historic Site: PO Box 159, Baddeck NS B0E 1B0 – 902/295-2069; Fax: 902/295-3496

New England Planters National Heritage Exhibit: PO Box 150, Grand Pré NS B0P 1M0 – 902/542-3631; Fax: 902/542-1619

Port aux Choix National Historic Site: PO Box 70, St-Lunaire-Griquet NF A0K 2X0 – 709/623-2608; Fax: 709/623-2028

Port Royal National Historic Site: PO Box 9, Annapolis Royal NS B0S 1A0 – 902/532-2397; Fax: 902/532-2232

Prince Edward Island National Park: 2 Palmer's Lane, Charlottetown PE C1A 5V6 – 902/566-7050; Fax: 902/566-7226

Prince of Wales Martello Tower National Historic Site: PO Box 9080, Stn A, Halifax NS B3K 5M7 – 902/426-5080; Fax: 902/426-4228

Province House National Historic Site: 2 Palmers Lane, Charlottetown PE C1A 5V6 – 902/566-7626; Fax: 902/566-7050

Red Bay National Historic Site: General Delivery, Red Bay NF A0X 4X0 – 709/920-2197

St. Andrews Blockhouse National Historic Site: #106, 1045 Main St., Moncton NB E1C 1H1 – 506/851-3083; Fax: 506/851-7079

St. Peter's Canal: PO Box 8, St. Peter's NS B0E 3B0 – 902/733-2280; Fax: 902/733-2362

Signal Hill National Historic Site: PO Box 1268, St. John's NF A1C 5M9 – 709/772-5367; Fax: 709/772-6302

Terra Nova National Park: Glovertown NF A0G 2L0 – 709/533-2801; Fax: 709/533-2706

York Redoubt National Historic Site: PO Box 9080, Stn A, Halifax NS B3K 5M7 – 902/426-5080; Fax: 902/426-4228

Ontario National Parks/National Historic Sites

Bellvue House National Historic Site: 35 Centre St., Kingston ON K7L 4E5 – 613/545-8666; Fax: 613/545-8721

Bethune Memorial House National Historic Site: 235 John St., Gravenhurst ON P0C 1G0 – 705/687-5443; Fax: 705/687-4935

Bruce Peninsula National Park: PO Box 189, Tobermory ON N0H 2R0 – 519/596-2233; Fax: 519/596-2298

Fathom Five National Marine Park: Tobermory ON – 519/596-2233; Fax: 519/596-2298

Fort George National Historic Site: 26 Queen St., PO Box 787, Niagara-on-the-Lake ON L0S 1J0 – 905/468-4257; Fax: 905/468-4638

Fort Malden National Historic Site: 100 Laird Ave., PO Box 38, Amherstburg ON N9V 2Z2 – 519/736-5416; Fax: 519/736-6603

Fort St. Joseph National Historic Site: PO Box 220, Richard's Landing ON P0R 1J0 – 705/942-6262; 705/246-2664

Fort Wellington National Historic Site: 370 Vankoughnet St., PO Box 479, Prescott ON K0E 1T0 – 613/925-2896; Fax: 613/925-1536

Georgian Bay Islands National Park: PO Box 28, Honey Harbour ON P0E 1E0 – 705/756-2415; Fax: 705/756-3886

Kingston Martello Towers: 35 Centre St., Kingston ON K7L 4E5 – 613/545-8666

Niagara National Historic Sites: 26 Queen St., PO Box 787, Niagara-on-the-Lake ON L0S 1J0 – 905/468-4258; Fax: 905/468-4638

Point Pelee National Park: RR#1, Leamington ON N8H 3V4 – 519/322-2365; Fax: 519/322-1277

Pukaskwa National Park: Hwy 627, Hattie Cove, PO Box 39, Heron Bay ON P0T 1R0 – 807/229-0801; Fax: 807/229-2097

Queenston Heights & Brock's Monument: c/o Fort George National Historic Site, 26 Queen St., PO Box 787, Niagara-on-the-Lake ON L0S 1J0 – 905/468-4257; Fax: 905/468-4638

St. Lawrence Islands National Park: 2 County Rd. 5, RR#3, Mallorytown Landing ON K0E 1R0 – 613/923-5261; Fax: 613/923-2224

Woodside National Historic Site: 528 Wellington St. North, Kitchener ON N2H 5L5 – 519/742-5273; Fax: 519/742-0561

Pacific & Yukon National Parks/National Historic Sites

Chilkoot Trail National Historic Site: #205, 300 Main St., Whitehorse YT Y1A 2B5 – 403/667-3910; Fax: 403/393-6701

Fisgard Lighthouse National Historic Site: 603 Fort Rodd Hill Rd., Victoria BC V9C 2W8 – Fax: 604/478-8415

Fort Langley National Historic Site: 23433 Mavis St., PO Box 129, Fort Langley BC V1M 2R5 – 604/888-4424; Fax: 604/888-2577

Fort Rodd Hill National Historic Site: 603 Fort Rodd Hill Rd., Victoria BC V9C 2W8 – 250/478-5849; Fax: 250/478-8415

Fort St. James National Historic Site: PO Box 1148, Fort St. James BC V0J 1P0 – 250/996-7191; Fax: 250/996-8566

Glacier National Park: PO Box 350, Revelstoke BC V0E 2S0 – 250/837-7500; Fax: 250/837-7536

Gulf of Georgia Cannery National Historic Site: 12138 - 4th Ave., Richmond BC V7E 3J1 – 604/664-9009; Fax: 604/664-9008

Gwaii Haanas National Park Reserve & Haida Heritage Site: PO Box 37, Queen Charlotte BC V0T 1S0 – 250/559-8818; Fax: 250/559-8366

Kitwanga National Historic Site: PO Box 1148, Fort St. James BC V0J 1P0 – 250/996-7191; Fax: 250/996-8566

Klondike National Historic Sites: PO Box 390, Dawson City YT Y0B 1G0 – 403/993-7200; Fax: 403/993-7299

Kluane National Park Reserve: Haines Junction YT Y0B 1L0 – 403/634-2251; Fax: 403/634-2686

Canadian Almanac & Directory 1997

3-60 GOVERNMENT OF CANADA

Kootenay National Park: PO Box 220, Radium Hot Springs BC V0A 1M0 – 250/347-7250; Fax: 250/347-7207

Mount Revelstoke National Park: PO Box 350, Revelstoke BC V0E 2S0 – 250/837-7500; Fax: 250/837-7536

Pacific Rim National Park: PO Box 280, Ucluelet BC V0R 3A0 – 250/726-7721; Fax: 250/726-4720

S.S. Klondide National Historic Site: #205, 300 Main St., PO Box 5540, Whitehorse YT Y1A 2B5 – 403/667-3910; Fax: 403/393-6701

Vuntut National Park: #200, 300 Main St., PO Box 390, Whitehorse YT Y1A 2B5 – 403/667-3910; Fax: 403/393-6701

Prairies & Northwest Territories National Parks/National Historic Sites

Aulavik National Park: General Delivery, Sachs Harbour NT X0E 0T0 – 403/560-3904; Fax: 403/690-48081

Auyuittuq National Park: PO Box 353, Pangnirtung NT X0A 0R0 – 819/473-8828; Fax: 819/473-5612

Batoche National Historic Site: PO Box 999, Rosthern SK S0K 3R0 – 306/423-6227; Fax: 306/423-5400

Ellesmere Island National Park: PO Box 343, Pangnirtung NT X0A 0R0 – 819/473-8828; Fax: 819/473-8612

Forks National Historic Site: 45 Forks Market Rd., Winnipeg MB R3C 4T6 – 204/983-5988; Fax: 204/983-2221

Fort Battleford National Historic Site: PO Box 70, Battleford SK S0M 0E0 – 306/937-2621; Fax: 306/937-3370

Fort Prince of Wales National Historic Site: PO Box 127, Churchill MB R0B 0E0 – 204/675-8863; Fax: 204/675-2026

Fort Walsh National Historic Site: PO Box 278, Maple Creek SK S0N 1N0 – 306/662-3590; Fax: 306/662-2711

Grasslands National Park: PO Box 150, Val Marie SK S0J 2Y0 – 306/298-2257; Fax: 306/298-2042

Ivvavik National Park: PO Box 1840, Inuvik NT X0E 0T0 – 403/979-3248; Fax: 403/949-4491

Lower Fort Garry National Historic Site: PO Box 37, Group 343, RR#3, Selkirk MB R1A 2A8 – 204/785-6050; Fax: 204/482-5887

Motherwell Homestead National Historic Site: PO Box 247, Abernethy SK S0A 0A0 – 306/333-2116; Fax: 306/333-2210

Nahanni National Park Reserve: PO Box 300, Fort Simpson NT X0E 0N0 – 403/695-2713; Fax: 403/695-2446

Prince Albert National Park: PO Box 100, Waskesiu SK S0J 2Y0 – 306/663-5322; Fax: 306/663-5424

Riding Mountain National Park: Wasagaming MB R0J 2H0 – 204/848-7275; Fax: 204/848-2596

Riel House National Historic Site: 330 River Rd., PO Box 37, Winnipeg MB R3M 4A5 – 204/257-1783

St. Andrews Rectory National Historic Site: RR#3, Grp. 343, PO Box 37, Selkirk MB R1A 2A8 – 204/785-6050; Fax: 204/482-5887

Wood Buffalo National Park: PO Box 750, Fort Smith NT X0E 0P0 – 403/872-2349; Fax: 403/872-3910

York Factory National Historic Site: PO Box 127, Churchill MB R0B 0E0 – 204/675-8863; Fax: 204/675-2026

Québec National Parks/National Historic Sites

Artillery Park National Historic Site: 2, rue d'Auteuil, CP 2474, Québec PQ G1K 7R3 – 418/648-4205; Fax: 418/648-4825

Cartier-Brébeuf Park: 175, rue de l'Espinay, CP 2474, Québec PQ G1K 7R3 – 418/648-4038; Fax: 418/648-4367

(Bataille de la) Chateauguay National Historic Site: RR#4, Alban's Corners, Ormstown PQ J0S 1K0 – 514/829-2003; Fax: 514/829-3325

Coteau-du-Lac National Historic Site: 308, ch du Pleuve, CP 550, Coteau-du-Lac PQ J0P 1B0 – 514/763-5631; Fax: 514/763-1654

(Les) Forges du Saint-Maurice: 10000, boul des Forges, Trois-Rivières PQ G9C 1B1 – 819/378-5116; Fax: 819/378-0887

Forillon National Park: CP 1220, Gaspé PQ G0C 1R0 – 418/368-5505; Fax: 418/368-6837

Fort Chambly National Historic Site: 2, rue Richelieu, Chambly PQ J3L 2B9 – 514/658-1585; Fax: 514/658-7216

Fort Lennox National Historic Site: 1 - 61e av, CP 90, St-Paul-de-l'Île-aux-Noix PQ J0J 1G0 – 514/291-5700

Fort Témiscamingue National Historic Site: CP 636, Ville Marie PQ J0Z 3W0 – 819/629-3222; Fax: 819/629-2977

Fortifications of Québec: 100, rue St-Louis, Québec PQ G1K 7R3 – 418/648-7016

Fur Trade in Lachine National Historic Site: 1255, boul Saint-Joseph, Lachine PQ H8S 2M2 – 514/637-7433

Grosse-Île National Historic Site: CP 2474, Terminus postal, Québec PQ G1K 7R3 – 418/563-4009; Fax: 418/563-1678

Lachine Canal: West Tower, 200, boul René-Lévesque ouest, 6e étage, Montréal PQ H2Z 1XY – 514/283-6054

Louis-S. St-Laurent National Historic Site: 6, rue Principale, Compton PQ J0B 1L0 – 819/835-5448; Fax: 819/835-9101

Maison Cartier National Historic Site: 458, rue Notre-Dame, Montréal PQ H2Y 1C8 – 514/283-2282; Fax: 514/283-5560

Maison Laurier National Historic Site: #205, 12, av Laurier, CP 70, Ville des Laurentides PQ J0R 1C0 – 514/439-3702

Manoir Papineau National Historic Site: 500, rue Notre-Dame, CP 444, Montebello PQ J0V 1L0 – 819/423-6965; Fax: 819/423-6455

La Mauricie National Park: 794, 5e rue, CP 758, Shawinigan PQ G9N 6V9 – 819/536-2638; Fax: 819/536-3661

Mingan National Park: 1303, rue de la Digue, CP 1180, Havre-St-Pierre PQ C0G 1P0 – 418/538-3331; Fax: 418/538-3595

National Battlefields Park: 390, av de Bernières, Québec PQ G1R 2L7 – 418/648-3506; Fax: 418/648-3638

Old Port of Québec National Historic Site: 100, rue Saint-André, CP 2474, Succ Terminus postal, Québec PQ G1K 7R3 – 418/648-3300; Fax: 418/648-3678

Le Phare de Pointe-au-Père: 1034, rue du Phare, Pointe-au-Père PQ G5M 1L8 – 418/724-6214; Fax: 418/724-6214

Point-de-Lévis Fort: #1, 41, ch du Gouvernement, CP 2474, Lévis-Lauzon PQ G1K 7R3 – 418/835-5182

Québec Historic Canals: 1899, boul Pe@rigny, Chambly PQ J3L 4C3 – 514/658-0681; Fax: 514/658-2428

(Bataille de la) Restigouche National Historic Site: CP 359, Pointe-à-la-Croix PQ G0C 1L0 – 418/788-5676; Fax: 418/778-5895

Saguenay Marine Park: 182, rte de l'Église, CP 220, Tadoussac PQ G0T 2A0 – 418/235-4703; Fax: 418/235-4686

Associated Agencies, Boards & Commissions

Listed alphabetically in detail, this section.

Canada Council/Conseil des Arts du Canada

Canadian Broadcasting Corporation/Société Radio-Canada (CBC)

Canadian Museum of Civilization/Musée canadien des civilisations
Listed in Section 6; see Index.

Canadian Museum of Nature/Musée canadien de la nature
Listed in Section 6; see Index.

Canadian Radio-television & Telecommunications Commission/Conseil de la radiodiffusion et des télécommunications (CRTC)

National Archives of Canada/Archives nationales du Canada

National Arts Centre/Centre national des Arts (NAC)

National Battlefields Commission/Commission des champs de bataille nationaux

National Capital Commission/Commission de la Capitale nationale

National Film Board of Canada/Office national du film

National Gallery of Canada/Musée des Beaux-Arts du Canada
Listed in Section 6; see Index.

National Library of Canada/Bibliothèque nationale du Canada
Listed in Section 5; see Index.

National Museum of Science & Technology/Musée national des sciences et de la technologie
Listed in Section 6; see Index.

Public Service Commission of Canada/Commission de la fonction publique du Canada

Telefilm Canada/Téléfilm Canada

CANADIAN HUMAN RIGHTS COMMISSION/ Commission canadienne des droits de la personne

Place de Ville, Tower A, #1300, 320 Queen St., Ottawa ON K1A 1E1
613/995-1151; Fax: 613/996-9661; Email: info@chrc.ca; URL: http://www.chrc.ca/chrc.html
TDD: 613/996-5211

The Commission administers the Canadian Human Rights Act which applies to federal government departments & agencies, & businesses under federal jurisdiction. The Commission accepts complaints of discrimination based on race, national or ethnic origin, colour, religion, age, sex, marital & family status, pardoned offence, disability & sexual orientation. Collect Calls accepted throughout Canada.

Chief Commissioner, Maxwell F. Yalden

Deputy Chief, Michelle Falardeau-Ramsay

Secretary General, John Hucker

Director, Corporate Services, Pierre Cousineau, 613/943-9031

Regional Offices

Alberta & Northwest Territories: Highfield Place, #308, 10010 - 106th St., Edmonton AB T5J 3L2 – 403/495-4040; Fax: 403/495-4044, TDD: 403/495-4108

Atlantic: 5657 Spring Garden Rd., 2nd Fl., PO Box 3545, Halifax NS B3J 3J2 – 902/426-8380; Fax: 902/426-2685, Toll Free: 1-800-565-1752, TDD: 902/426-9345

Ontario: #1002, 175 Bloor St. East, Toronto ON M4W 3R8 – 416/973-5527; Fax: 416/973-6184, TDD: 416/973-8912

Prairie: #242, 240 Graham St., Winnipeg MB R3C 0J8 – 204/983-2189; Fax: 204/983-6132, TDD: 204/983-2882

Québec: #470, 1253, av McGill College, Montréal PQ H3B 2Y5 – 514/283-5218; Fax: 514/283-5084, TDD: 514/283-1869

Western: 800 Burrard St., 13th Fl., Vancouver BC V6Z 1X9 – 604/666-2251; Fax: 604/666-2386, TDD: 604/666-3071

CANADIAN INTERGOVERNMENTAL CONFERENCE SECRETARIAT (CICS)/ Secrétariat des conférences intergouvernementales canadiennes
110 O'Connor St., PO Box 488, Stn A, Ottawa ON K1N 8V5
613/995-2341; Fax: 613/996-6091

CICS is a conference support body which provides the administrative services required for the planning & the conduct of federal-provincial & interprovincial conferences at the First Ministers, ministers & deputy ministers level. The agency is at the disposal of individual federal & provincial government departments which may be called upon to organize & chair such meetings.
Secretary, Stuart MacKinnon

CANADIAN INTERNATIONAL DEVELOPMENT AGENCY (CIDA)/ Agence canadienne de développement international (ACDI)
Place du Centre, 200, Promenade du Portage, Hull PQ K1A 0G4
819/997-5456; Fax: 819/953-6088; URL: http://www.acdi.cida.gc.ca
TDD: 819/953-5023
Public Inquiries: 819/997-5006

Supports the efforts of the peoples of developing countries to achieve sustainable economic & social development by cooperating with them in development activities & by providing humanitarian assistance. The Official Development Assistance Program contributes to Canada's political & economic interests abroad in promoting social justice, international stability & long-term economic relationships. Reports to government through the Department of Foreign Affairs & International Trade.
President, Huguette Labelle, 819/997-7951, Fax: 819/953-3352
Acting Vice-President, Corporate Management Branch, Claudia Roberts, 819/953-6596
Vice-President, Africa & Middle East Branch, Carolyn McAskie, 819/997-1643
Vice-President, Eastern & Central Europe Branch, Charles Bassett, 819/994-4787
Vice-President, Americas Branch, Pierre Racicot, 819/997-3291
Vice-President, Policy Branch, John Robinson, 819/997-6133
Acting Vice-President, Asia Branch, Jean-Marc Métivier, 819/997-1666
Acting Vice-President, Canadian Partnership Branch, Pierre David, 819/997-6057
Vice-President, Multilateral Programs Branch, Nicole Senécal, 819/997-7537
Vice-President, Personnel & Administration Branch, Nicole Charette, 819/997-6383
Director General, Communications, Theresa M. Keleher, 819/953-6535

CANADIAN INTERNATIONAL GRAINS INSTITUTE (CIGI)/Institut international du Canada pour le grain
#1000, 303 Main St., Winnipeg MB R3C 3G7
204/983-5344; Fax: 204/983-2642

The Institute is an instructional facility offering courses in grain handling, marketing & technology. It works in affiliation with the Canadian Wheat Board, the Canadian Grain Commission, & various departments of the federal government. It also works in cooperation with all segments of Canada's grain industry.
Executive Director, A.W. Tremere
Director, Feed Technology, D.R. Hickling
Director, Food Technology, A.R. Tweed
Director, Marketing, P.S. Westdal
Manager, Communications & Public Relations, V.S. Sloan
Manager, Finance & Administration, J.L. Peake
Executive Secretary, Mona Brisson

CANADIAN INTERNATIONAL TRADE TRIBUNAL/Tribunal canadien du commerce extérieur
Standard Life Centre, 333 Laurier Ave. West, Ottawa ON K1A 0G7
613/990-2452; Fax: 613/990-2439; URL: http://canada.gc.ca/depts/agencies/cttind_e.html

The Tribunal is an independent, quasi-judicial body, which carries out both judicial & advisory functions relating to trade remedies. On December 31, 1988, it took over all of the inquiry & appeal functions of the Tariff Board, the Canadian Import Tribunal, & the Textile & Clothing Board, all of which no longer exist. With the proclamation of the North American Free Trade Agreement Implementation Act set on January 1, 1994, the Tribunal has been designated as the bid challenge authority for Canada. In this capacity, the Tribunal succeeds the Procurement Review Board of Canada. The main legislation governing the Tribunal's work is the Canadian International Trade Tribunal Act, the Special Import Measures Act, the Customs Act & the Excise Tax Act. Reports to government through the Minister of Finance.
Chair, A.T. Eyton
Vice-Chair, A.B. Trudeau
Vice-Chair, R.A. Guay
Secretary, Michel P. Granger
Executive Director, Research, R.W. Erdmann
General Counsel, Gerry Stobo
Director, Procurement Division, Jean Archambault

CANADIAN JUDICIAL COUNCIL/Conseil canadien de la magistrature
#450, 112 Kent St., Ottawa ON K1A 0W8
613/998-5182; Fax: 613/998-8889

The members of the Council are the Chief Justice of Canada, who is the Chair, the Chief Justices & Associate Chief Justices of each Superior Court or Branch or Division thereof, the senior judges of the Supreme Court of the Yukon Territory & the Supreme Court of the Northwest Territories succeeding each other on the Council every two years, & the Chief Judge and Associate Chief Judge of the Tax Court of Canada.
Executive Director, Jeannie Thomas

CANADIAN MUSEUM OF CIVILIZATION/ Musée Canadien des Civilisations
Listed in Section 6; see Index.

CANADIAN MUSEUM OF NATURE/ Musée Canadien de la Nature
Listed in Section 6; see Index.

CANADIAN NATIONAL RAILWAY COMPANY (CNR)/Compagnie des chemins de fer nationaux du Canada
PO Box 8100, Montréal PQ H3C 3N4
514/399-5430; Fax: 514/399-5586, 5479

The Company, incorporated in 1919 as a federal Crown corporation, is administered by a Board of Directors appointed by the Cabinet. It reports to Parliament through the Minister of Transport. CN's mandate is to operate a rail-based transportation system, offering rail and intermodal freight services across Canada. Other business units operate a freight railway network in the US, run the CN Tower in Toronto, develop the real estate and natural resource potentials of railway lands, provide technical consulting services, & invest the corporation's pension funds.
Chair, David McLean
President & CEO, Paul M. Tellier
Executive Vice-President & Chief Financial Officer, Y.H. Masse
Senior Vice-President, Marketing, Gerald Davies
Senior Vice-President, Operations, J.T. McBain
Senior Vice-President, Western Canada, Rick Boyd
Treasurer & Principal Tax Counsel, Sean Finn

CANADIAN PERMANENT COMMITTEE ON GEOGRAPHICAL NAMES/ Comité permanent canadien des noms géographiques
#650, 615 Booth St., Ottawa ON K1A 0E9
613/992-3405; Fax: 613/943-8282; Email: geonames@NRCan.ca; URL: http://www-nais.com.NRCan.gc.ca/cgndb/
General Enquiries: 613/992-3892
Chair, E.A. Price
Executive Secretary, H. Kerfoot

CANADIAN POLAR COMMISSION (CPC)/ Commission canadienne des affaires polaires (CCAP)
Constitution Square, #1710, 360 Albert St., Ottawa ON K1R 7X7
613/943-8605; Fax: 613/943-8607; Email: mail@polarcom.gc.ca; URL: http://www.polarcom.gc.ca/

Canada's national advisory agency on polar affairs. The CPC monitors & promotes the development of knowledge in polar regions, with the view that social & scientific research involves all northern peoples & reflects their interests & concerns.
Executive Officer, Albert Haller
Coordinator, Communications & Information, Alan Saunders
Research Assistant, Elaine Aderson

Regional Offices
Kuujjuaq: PO Box 1031, Kuujjuaq PQ J0M 1C0 – 819/964-6344; Fax: 819/964-2462, Northern Science Officer, Sonia Bélanger
Yellowknife: #10, 4807 - 49th St., Yellowknife NT X1A 3TA – 403/920-7401; Fax: 403/920-7098, Northern Science Officer, Stephanie Irlbacher

CANADIAN RADIO-TELEVISION & TELECOMMUNICATIONS COMMISSION (CRTC)/Conseil de la radiodiffusion et des télécommunications
1, du Portage Promenade, Terrasses de la Chaudière, Hull PQ J8X 4B1
819/997-0313 (Public Affairs); Fax: 819/994-0218; URL: http://www.crtc.gc.ca/
TTY: 819/994-0423
Mailing Address: CRTC, Ottawa ON K1A 0N2

The Commission is responsible for regulating all federally chartered telecommunication carriers, & regulating & supervising all aspects of the Canadian broadcasting system. Reports to government through the Minister of Canadian Heritage.
Chair, Françoise Bertrand, 819/997-3430
Vice-Chair, Fernand Bélisle, 819/997-4126
Vice-Chair, David C. Colville, 819/997-8766
Secretary General, Allan Darling, 819/997-1027
Executive Director, Telecommunications, Stuart MacPherson, 819/997-4644
Director General, Broadcast Analysis, Diane Rhéaume, 819/997-5225
Director General, Broadcast Distribution & Technology, Wayne Charman, 819/997-5369
Director General, Broadcast Planning, Peter Fleming, 819/997-3643
Director General, Competition, Tariff & Convergence Policy, Malcolm Andrew, 819/997-2755

Director General, Decisions & Operations, Henry Pau, 819/994-0293
Director General, Finance & Management Services, Bill Weizenbach, 819/997-4009
Director General, Financial Services, Don Donovan, 819/997-4818
Director, Public Affairs, Stephen Boissonneault, 819/997-0313
Director General, Secretariat Operations & Licensing, Rosemary Chisholm, 819/997-4427
General Counsel, Avrum Cohen, 819/997-5533

CANADIAN SPACE AGENCY (CSA)/ Agence spatiale canadienne (ASC)
6767, rte de l'Aéroport, Saint-Hubert PQ J3Y 8Y9
514/926-4351; Fax: 514/926-4352; Email: webmaster@radarsat.space.gc.ca; URL: http://www.space.gc.ca/welcomee.html

In partnership with the United States, nine Canadian provinces & the private sector, the CSA operates the Canadian RADARSAT Program; involves the development & operation of a remote sensing satellite launched in 1995; officially opened the Western Canadian RADARSAT tracking station in Saskatoon in late 1994.

The Canadian RADARSAT satellite observes the earth using a Sythetic Aperture Radar (SAR) sensor capable of obtaining detailed images in darkness & through clouds; gathers essential data for more efficient resource management & environmental monitoring (including the survey of natural resources, & ice types & movementsd).

RADARSAT International Inc. (RSI) is a consortium of Canadian aerospace companies, incorporated to market & distribute RADARSAT data worldwide.
President, William MacDonald Evans
Executive Vice-President, Alain-F. Desfossés
Legal Counsel, Robert Lefebvre
Vice-President, Human Spaceflights, Karl Doetsch
Vice-President, Research & Applications, Garry Martin Lindberg
Acting Director General, Canadian Astronaut Program, Steven Glenwood MacLean
Director, Communications, Louis Fortier
Director General, David Florida Laboratory, Rolf Mamen
Director General, RADARSAT Program, Joseph L. McNally
Acting Director General, Space Science Program, Barry Wetter
Director General, Space Technology Program, Jack Chambers

CANADIAN TRANSPORTATION AGENCY (CTA)/ Office des transports du Canada (OTC)
Ottawa ON K1A 0N9
819/997-0344 (Communications); Fax: 819/953-8353; URL: http://www.cta-otc.gc.ca
Factsline: 819/997-5834; Air Complaints: 1-800-263-3027; Air & Accessible Complaints: 1-800-883-1813

Serves as economic regulator & decision-maker with respect to transportation services under federal jurisdiction. Responsibilities include issuing licences to air carriers & railways; dispute resolution over various air, rail & marine transportation rate & service matters; and determining the annual maximum rate scale for western grain movements. Also has powers to remove undue obstacles to the mobility of travellers with disabilities in the federally regulated transportation network. Reports to government through the Minister of Transport.

ACTS ADMINISTERED
Canada Transportation Act
Chair, Marian L. Robson

Vice-Chair, Jean Patenaude
Secretary & General Legal Counsel, Director General, Communications Branch, Marie-Paule Scott, Q.C., 819/953-6698
Director General, Air & Accessible Transportation Branch, Gavin Currie
Director General, Corporate Management Branch, Roger Roy, 819/997-6764
Director General, Rail & Marine Branch, Seymour Isenberg, 819/953-4657

Regional Office
Pacific: #250, 1095 West Pender St., Vancouver BC V6E 2M6 – 604/666-7513; Fax: 604/666-1267

Field Investigation Offices
Atlantic: Assumption Place Bldg., 770 Main St., 10th Fl., PO Box 6080, Moncton NB E1C 9L5 – 506/851-6950; Fax: 506/851-7105, Senior Investigator, Brian Mercer, 506/851-6950
Central: PO Box 27007, Stn Winnipeg Square RPO, Winnipeg MB R3C 4T3 – 204/984-6092; Fax: 204/984-6093, Senior Investigator, Mervyn Caldwell, 204/984-6092
Ontario: 7548 Bath Rd., Mississauga ON L4T 1L2 – 905/612-5792; Fax: 905/612-5794, Senior Investigator, Jeanette Anderson, 905/612-5792
Pacific: #250, 1095 West Pender St., Vancouver BC V6E 2M6 – 604/666-3034; Fax: 604/666-1267, Senior Investigator, Gordon King, 604/666-0620
Québec: #803.2, 101, boul Rolland-Therrien, Longueuil PQ J4H 4B9 – 514/928-4173; Fax: 514/928-4174, Senior Investigator, Richard Laliberté, 514/928-4173
Western: Edmonton AB – 403/495-6618; Fax: 403/495-5639, Senior Investigator, Linda Brooklyn, 403/495-6618

CANADIAN WHEAT BOARD (CWB)/ Commission canadienne du blé
423 Main St., PO Box 816, Winnipeg MB R3C 2P5
204/983-0239, 3416; Fax: 204/983-3841; URL: http://canada.gc.ca/depts/agencies/cwbind_e.html
Telex: 07-57801; Cable: Wheatboard

Crown agency responsible for marketing Prairie-grown wheat, durum & barley. With sales of over $4.5 billion per year, it markets grain to more than 70 countries. The Wheat Board's operations are funded by Prairie grain producers. Reports to government through the Minister of Agriculture & Agri-food.
Minister Responsible, Hon. Ralph Goodale
Chief Commissioner, Lorne F. Hehn
General Counsel & Corporate Secretary, Margaret Redmond
Executive Director, Finance & Treasurer, Donald E. Vernon
Executive Director, Human Resources, Patricia Wallace
Executive Director, Marketing, Adrian C. Measner
Executive Director, Planning, Brian T. Olsen

Overseas Offices
China: Tower B, Beijing COFCO Plaza, #708, 8 Jianguomen Nei St., Beijing 100005, China – /6526-3906; 6526-3908; Fax: /6526-3907
Japan: Kowa No. 9 Bldg., Annex 6-7, Akasaka 1-chome, 6th Fl., Tokyo 107, Japan – /81-33-583-4291; Fax: /81-33-587-1593

CITIZENSHIP & IMMIGRATION CANADA/ Citoyenetté et Immigration Canada
Journal Tower South, 365 Laurier Ave. West, Hull PQ K1A 1L1
613/954-9019; Fax: 613/954-2221; URL: http://cicnet.ingenia.com/english/index.html

The Department of Citizenship & Immigration administers both Canada's citizenship & immigration policies, procedures & service. The department is responsible for the following:
• examining immigrants, visitors & people claiming refugee status at land borders, seaports & airports;
• processing applications for permanent residence, extensions of visitor status requests & sponsorships for relatives & refugees overseas;
• admitting students, temporary workers & qualified business immigrants;
• investigating & removing people who are in Canada illegally;
• working with & helping fund a network of settlement agencies & services to help immigrants adapt to & participate in day-to-day Canadian life;
• promoting the acceptance of immigrants by Canadians;
• cooperating with various levels of government on enforcement, program development & the delivery of services;
• accepting applications & verifying the eligibility & documentation of applicants;
• granting citizenship & administration of the Oath of Citizenship at ceremonies in Citizenship Courts & numerous community facilities across Canada;
• confirming Canadian citizenship status &;
• issuing proofs of citizenship to Canadians.
The Immigration & Refugee Board reports to Parliament through the minister.

ACTS ADMINISTERED
Citizenship Act
Immigration Act
Minister, Hon. Lucienne Robillard, 613/996-7267
Deputy Minister, Janice Cochrane, 613/954-3501
Asst. Deputy Minister, Operations, R. Girard, 613/952-1770, Fax: 613/957-8887
Asst. Deputy Minister, Partnerships, George Tsai, 613/957-3338, Fax: 613/957-3196
Assoc. Deputy Minister, Marc Lafrenière
Director General, Finance & Administration, Jerry Robbins, 613/954-4443, Fax: 613/957-2775
Director General, Human Resources, Cathy Downes, 613/941-7788, Fax: 613/941-7798
Director, Legal Services, John Sims
Director General, Public Affairs, Colin Robertson, 613/941-7077, Fax: 613/941-7099

CASE MANAGEMENT
613/957-3940; Fax: 613/957-7235
Director General, Bill Sheppit, 613/957-3941
Director, Case Review, Theresa Harvey, 613/957-1167
Director, Litigation, Joanne DesLauriers, 613/954-2508, Fax: 613/954-5896
Director, Organized Crime, Michel Gagné, 613/957-3515, Fax: 613/952-6319
Director, Security Review, Ian Taylor, 613/952-6336, Fax: 613/952-6825

DEPARTMENTAL DELIVERY NETWORK
613/941-9291; Fax: 613/941-0061
Director General, Tom Ryan, 613/941-9291
Acting Director, Immigration Health Service, Dr. George Giovinazzo, 613/954-4470, Fax: 613/941-2179
Manager, Case Processing Centre, Frank Perriccioli, Mississauga ON, 905/803-7371, Fax: 905/803-7398
Manager, Case Processing Centre, Bill White, Sydney NS, 902/564-7825, Fax: 902/564-3567
Manager, Case Processing Centre, Phil Pirie, Vegreville AB, 403/632-8000, Fax: 403/632-8100
Manager, Citizenship Services, Danielle Charbonneau, 613/941-8405
Manager, Immigration Services, Brian Beaupré, 613/941-1550
Manager, Immigration Warrant Response Centre, Chris McDonell, 613/954-2816, Fax: 613/954-9291

Manager, Interim Federal Health, Dr. Roland Fuca, 613/954-8210
Manager, Project Services, Brian Hudson, 613/941-0998
Manager, Query Response Centre, Jean-Yves Prevost, 613/957-4418, Fax: 613/957-4660
Manager, Support Services, Jim Trussler, 613/957-1090

ENFORCEMENT
613/954-4159; Fax: 613/954-6765
Director General, Pierre Bourget, 613/954-6132
Director, Case Presentation, Neil Cochrane, 613/957-4333, Fax: 613/954-5896
Director, Intelligence & Interdiction, Gord Cheesman, 613/952-7291, Fax: 613/954-8571
Director, Investigation & Removal, Susan Leith, 613/954-5628, Fax: 613/954-5238
Director, Port of Entry Management, Brian McQuillan, 613/941-9026, Fax: 613/954-1673
Director, Program Development, Brian Grant, 613/954-2124, Fax: 613/952-9187

INFORMATION MANAGEMENT & TECHNOLOGIES
613/941-4873; Fax: 613/954-6209
Acting Director General, Peg Blair, 613/954-2700
Director, Architecture & Data, J.P. Lortie, 613/941-5160, Fax: 613/954-2263
Director, CIC Modernization Project Office, Al Bezanson, 613/941-4526, Fax: 613/954-2263
Director, Implementation & Roll-out, Paul-André Laurin, 613/954-5866, Fax: 613/941-2620
Director, Information Management, Rick Herringer, 613/957-9349, Fax: 613/954-4441
Director, International Region System, Christian Labelle, 613/952-7008, Fax: 613/954-2263
Acting Director, Operations, Vicky McAulay, 613/954-5017, Fax: 613/954-6510
Director, Systems Development, Program Departmental Delivery, Frank Brown, 613/954-5683, Fax: 613/954-2263
Director, Systems Development, Service Line & Departmental Support, Chris McGee, 613/954-8043, Fax: 613/954-6510

INTEGRATION
613/957-4483; Fax: 613/957-0594
Director General, Agnes Jaouich, 613/957-3257
Director, Citizenship, Normand Sabourin, 613/952-7173, Fax: 613/957-7479
Director, Education & Development, Ingrid Hauck, 613/952-2301, Fax: 613/957-4431
Director, Service Line Support, Helen Amundsen, 613/954-3355
Director, Settlement Operations, Marcia Shaw, 613/957-3433, Fax: 613/957-7673

INTERNATIONAL REGION
613/957-5892; Fax: 613/957-5802
Director General, Gerry Campbell, 613/957-5893
Director, Africa-Middle East, Claire Lavoie, 613/957-5891, Fax: 613/957-5802
Director, Asia-Pacific, Brian O'Connor, 613/957-5813, Fax: 613/957-6985
Director, Europe, Gerry VanKessel, 613/957-5890, Fax: 613/957-6988
Director, Overseas Medical Services, Dr. Brian Dobie, 613/954-6553, Fax: 613/957-6992
Director, Personnel, Vacant, 613/941-1372, Fax: 613/957-6909
Director, Resource Management, Frank Andrews, 613/957-6944, Fax: 613/957-6952
Director, Western Hemisphere, Rodney Fields, 613/957-5820, Fax: 613/957-6988

MINISTERIAL & EXECUTIVE SERVICES
613/952-5497; Fax: 613/952-5497
Acting Director General, Susan Gregson, 613/954-9004
Director, Briefings & Parliamentary Affairs, Kathleen O'Connor, 613/952-5567
Director, Ministerial Enquiries Unit, Carrie Hunter, 613/957-1476
Director, Public Rights Administration, Janet Brooks, 613/957-6512

STRATEGIC POLICY, PLANNING & RESEARCH
613/957-5953; Fax: 613/957-5955
Director General, Laura Chapman, 613/957-5956
Director, Collaboration, Paula Bennett, 613/957-5907
Director, Program Support, Elizabeth Ruddick, 613/957-5907, Fax: 613/957-5913
National Director, Settlement Renewal, David Neuman, 613/957-5910, Fax: 613/957-5913
Acting Director, Strategic Direction, Scott Heatherington, 613/957-5951
Manager, Federal-Provincial Partnerships & Projects, Danielle Racette, 613/957-4166
Manager, Legislation & Regulations, Don MacKay, 613/957-5934
Manager, Scanning & Intelligence, Sheila Gariepy, 613/957-9803, Fax: 613/957-5940
Manager, Social Policy, Colette Arnal, 613/957-5915

REFUGEES
613/957-5873; Fax: 613/957-5869
Director General, Jeff Lebane, 613/957-5874
Director, Asylum, Craig Goodes, 613/957-5867
Director, International Liaison, Anton Jrukovich, 613/957-5868
Acting Director, Resettlement, Holly Edward, 613/957-5837
Acting Director, Service Line, John Kent, 613/957-5831

SELECTION
613/941-8990; Fax: 613/941-9323
Director General, Doreen Steidle, 613/941-8990
Director, Business Immigration, John Martin, 613/941-9009
Director, Economic Policy, Dougall Aucoin, 613/954-4214
Director, Immigration Health Policy, Neil Heywood, 613/957-5939, Fax: 613/954-8653
Director, Service Line Support, Don Slack, 613/941-8991, Fax: 613/954-0850
Director, Social Policy, Nick Oosterveen, 613/941-8225

CANADA IMMIGRATION CENTRES & CITIZENSHIP OFFICES
Immigration visa offices are located in most Canadian Embassies and Consulates abroad, see Diplomats. Immigration centres are located at most ports of entry in Canada, and citizenship & immigration offices in major cities throughout the country. For specific addresses and other information contact the relevant regional Citizenship & Immigration Canada Communications Branch.

Regional Offices
British Columbia, Prairies & Territories: Royal Centre, 1055 Georgia St. West, PO Box 11145, Vancouver BC V6E 2P8 – 604/666-6301; Fax: 604/666-1927, Director, Chris Taylor
Ontario: 4900 Yonge St., Willowdale ON M2N 6A8 – 416/954-7800; Fax: 416/426-2905, Acting Director General, Pierre Gaulin
Québec & Atlantic: 1441, rue St-Urbain, CP 7500, Succ A, Montréal PQ H3C 3L4 – 514/283-4900; Fax: 514/496-2060, Director General, Richard Anderson

Office of the CORRECTIONAL INVESTIGATOR/
L'Enquêteur correctionnel Canada
#402, 275 Slater St., Ottawa ON K1P 5H9
613/990-2695; Fax: 613/990-9091; URL: http://canada.gc.ca/depts/agencies/ociind_e.html
Toll Free: 1-800-267-5982
Investigates complaints from inmates in Canadian institutions. Reports on problems inmates have that fall within the responsibility of the Solicitor General of Canada and meet the certain conditions. Reports to government through the Solicitor General of Canada.
Correctional Investigator, Ron L. Stewart

CORRECTIONAL SERVICE CANADA/
Service correctionnel Canada
c/o Solicitor General Canada, 340 Laurier Ave. West, Ottawa ON K1A 0P9
613/992-8423 (Communications); Fax: 613/947-0091; Email: agraham@magi.com; URL: http://www.csc-scc.gc.ca/csce.htm
An agency within the Department of the Solicitor General responsible for the administration of sentences with respect to convicted offenders sentenced to two or more years as decided by the federal courts, & certain provincial inmates who have been transferred to a federal institution. CSC is also responsible for the supervision of inmates who have been granted conditional release by the authority of the National Parole Board.
Commissioner, Ole Ingstrup, 613/995-5781, Fax: 613/995-3352
Senior Deputy Commissioner, Andrew Graham, 613/947-0643
Deputy Commissioner, Women, Nancy Stableforth
Asst. Commissioner, Accountability & Performance Measurement, Yvonne Latta, 613/995-8977
Asst. Commissioner, Communications & Executive Services, Karen Wiseman, 613/992-2973
Asst. Commissioner, Correctional Policy & Corporate Planning, Tom Epp, 613/995-4377
Asst. Commissioner, Correctional Research & Development, Arden Thurber, 613/992-8396
Asst. Commissioner, Information Management & Technical Services, Gerry Hooper, 613/992-2871
Senior Financial Officer, André Lepage, 613/992-0670
General Counsel, Legal Services, M. Zazulak, 613/995-2660
Corporate Advisor, Aboriginal Programming, Teresa Nahanee, 613/996-7715
Corporate Advisor, Chaplaincy, Pierre Allard, 613/996-0373
Corporate Advisor, Community Corrections, Gerry Minard, 613/992-4801
Corporate Advisor, Health Care, Robert Climie, 613/992-5713
Corporate Advisor, Human Resources, John Rama, 613/995-8899
Corporate Advisor, Intergovernmental Affairs, Brendan Reynolds, 613/995-2792
Corporate Advisor, Sex Offender Programming, Sharon Williams, 613/545-8248

Regional Headquarters
Atlantic: 1045 Main St., 2nd Fl., Moncton NB E1C 1H1 – 506/851-6313; Fax: 506/851-2418, Deputy Commissioner, Alphonse Cormier
Ontario: 440 King St. West, PO Box 1174, Kingston ON K7L 4Y8 – 613/545-8211; Fax: 613/545-8684, Deputy Commissioner, Irving Kulik
Pacific: 32560 Simon Ave., PO Box 4500, Clearbrook BC V2T 5L7 – 604/870-2501; Fax: 604/870-2430, Deputy Commissioner, Pieter De Vink
Prairies: 2313 Hanselman Pl., PO Box 9223, Saskatoon SK S7K 3X5 – 306/975-4850; Fax: 306/975-4435, Deputy Commissioner, Rémi Gobeil
Québec: 3 Pl. Laval, 2e étage, Laval PQ H7N 1A2 – 514/967-3333; Fax: 514/967-3326, Deputy Commissioner, Jean-Claude Perron

GOVERNMENT OF CANADA

District Parole Offices

Abbotsford-Fraser Valley: #200, 33119 South Fraser Way, Abbotsford BC V2S 2B1 – 604/853-7781; Fax: 604/854-8735, Director, P. Jacks

Calgary: #311, 510 - 12 Ave. SW, Calgary AB T2R 0H3 – 403/292-5505; Fax: 403/292-5510, Director, Bernard Pitre

Edmonton-Alberta North, NWT: 9530 - 101th Av., 2nd Fl., Edmonton AB T5H 0B3 – 403/495-4900; Fax: 403/495-4975, Director, Don Kynoch

Guelph-Western Ontario: 42 Wyndham St. North, Guelph ON N1H 4E6 – 519/826-2144; Fax: 519/826-2143, Director, Craig Townson

Halifax/Dartmouth: #605, 1888 Brunswick St., Halifax NS B3J 2G7 – 902/426-3408; Fax: 902/426-8000, Director, Ron Lawton

Hamilton: #411 - 150 Main St., Hamilton ON L8P 1H8 – 905/572-2695; Fax: 905/572-2072, Director, Derek Orr

Kingston-Eastern Ontario: #203, 920 Princess St., Kingston ON K7L 1H1 – 613/545-8734; Fax: 613/545-8079, Director, Dave Connor

Moncton-New Brunswick & PEI: #1 Factory Lane, 1st Fl., Moncton NB E1C 9M3 – 506/851-6350; Fax: 506/851-2057, Director, Don Leblanc

Montréal-Métropolitan: 200, boul René Lévesque ouest, 9e étage, Montréal PQ H2Z 1X4 – 514/283-1776; Fax: 514/283-1783, Directeur, Gilles Thibault

Ottawa: 207 Queen St., 1st Fl., Ottawa ON K1P 6E5 – 613/996-7011; Fax: 613/954-1687, Director, Rosemary O'Brien

Prince George-Northern Interior: #201, 280 Victoria St., Prince George BC V2L 4X3 – 250/561-5314; Fax: 250/561-5537, Director, B. Lang

Regina-Saskatchewan: #200, 2550 - 15 Ave., Regina SK S4P 1A5 – 306/780-5050; Fax: 306/780-6935, Director, A. Rollo

St-Jérome-East & West Québec: #300, 222, rue St-Georges, St-Jérôme PQ J7Z 4Z9 – 514/432-3737; Fax: 514/432-3221, Directeur, Normand Granger

Saint John-New Brunswick West: 61 Union St., 5th Fl., Saint John NB E2L 1A3 – 506/636-4795; Fax: 506/636-4870, Director, Marc Brideau

St. John's-Newfoundland & Area: 102 Churchill Ave., St. John's NF A1A 1N1 – 709/772-6308; Fax: 709/772-6415, Director, B. Devine

Toronto-Central Ontario: 330 Keele St., Toronto ON M6P 2K7 – 416/604-4390; Fax: 416/973-9723, Director, Peter White

Truro/Kentville/Sydney: 14 Court St., Truro NS B2N 3H7 – 902/893-6760; Fax: 902/893-4961, Director, David Cail

Vancouver: New Westminster Federal Bldg., #417, 549 Columbia, New Westminster BC V3L 1B3 – 604/666-3731; Fax: 604/666-2000, Director, Wayne Oster

Victoria-Vancouver Island: #323, 816 Government St., Victoria BC V8W 1W9 – 250/363-3267; Fax: 250/363-3969, Director, Bob Brown

Winnipeg-Manitoba/Northwestern Ontario: 470 Notre-Dame Ave., 2nd Fl., Winnipeg MB R3B 1R5 – 204/983-4306; Fax: 204/983-5869, Director, Gord Holloway

DEFENCE CONSTRUCTION CANADA/ Construction de Défense Canada

Sir Charles Tupper Bldg., "A" Wing, Riverside Dr., 3rd Fl., Ottawa ON K1A 0K3
613/998-9548; Fax: 613/998-1061; URL: http://canada.gc.ca/depts/agencies/dccind_e.html

The Crown company that administers the major construction, building repair, maintenance programs & contracts for engineering consultant & architectural services for the Department of National Defence. The Company's legal title is "Defence Construction (1951) Limited". Reports to goverment through the Minister of Public Works & Government Services.
President, Ross Nicholls, P.Eng.

Vice-President, Finance & Administration & Sec.-Treas., Trevor Heavens
Vice-President, Operations & Chief Engineer, Vacant, P.Eng.

DEPARTMENT OF

These are listed in this book alphabetically by applied titles as follows:
Department of Agriculture & Agri-Food: AGRICULTURE & AGRI-FOOD CANADA
Department of Canadian Heritage: CANADIAN HERITAGE
Department of Citizenship & Immigration: CITIZENSHIP & IMMIGRATION CANADA
Department of Environment: ENVIRONMENT CANADA
Department of Finance: FINANCE CANADA (Department of)*
Department of Fisheries & Oceans: FISHERIES & OCEANS CANADA
Department of Foreign Affairs & International Trade: FOREIGN AFFAIRS & INTERNATIONAL TRADE CANADA
Department of Health: HEALTH CANADA
Department of Human Resources Development: HUMAN RESOURCES DEVELOPMENT CANADA
Department of Indian & Northern Affairs: INDIAN & NORTHERN AFFAIRS CANADA
Department of Industry: INDUSTRY CANADA
Department of Justice: JUSTICE CANADA (Department of)*
Department of National Defence: NATIONAL DEFENCE
Department of Natural Resources: NATURAL RESOURCES CANADA
Department of Public Works & Government Services: PUBLIC WORKS & GOVERNMENT SERVICES CANADA
Department of National Revenue: REVENUE CANADA
Department of the Solicitor General: SOLICITOR GENERAL CANADA
Department of Transport: TRANSPORT CANADA
Department of Veterans Affairs: VETERANS AFFAIRS CANADA
Department of Western Economic Diversification: WESTERN ECONOMIC DIVERSIFICATION CANADA

*Note that there are two departments that actually incorporate the words "Department of" in their applied titles; nevertheless departments are listed alphabetically in similar style to the rest of the departments.

ELECTIONS CANADA/Élections Canada

The Jackson Bldg., 257 Slater St., Ottawa ON K1A 0M6
613/993-2975; Fax: 613/954-8584; Email: eleccan@magi.com; URL: http://www.elections.ca/
Toll Free: 1-800-463-6868, TDD: 1-800-361-8935

The Chief Electoral Officer of Canada is responsible for the conduct of federal elections & referendums in Canada & for ensuring that all provisions of the *Canada Elections Act* are complied with & enforced. Major activities include implementation of public education & information programs, the training of returning officers, the revision of polling division boundaries, the acquisition of election materials & supplies, the maintenance of a register of political parties, the compiling & publishing of statutory & statistical reports, the provision of advice & assistance to Parliament, as required, the production of lists of electors, & the certification of statutory payments to be made to auditors, political parties, & candidates under the election expenses provisions of the Act.

Following each decennial census, the Chief Electoral Officer must calculate the number of electoral districts to be assigned to each province according to rules contained in s. 51 of the *Constitution Act*, prepare population distribution maps for use by the eleven electoral boundaries commissions (ten provincial & one territorial) that are directly responsible for readjusting federal electoral district boundaries & publish their reports. Elections Canada also administers elections to the Legislative Assembly of the Northwest Territories, by agreement with the Commissioner of the Northwest Territories.

Chief Electoral Officer, Jean-Pierre Kingsley
Asst. Chief Electoral Officer, Ronald A. Gould
Commissioner of Canada Elections, Raymond Landry
Arbitrator, Broadcasting, Peter S. Grant
Director, Administration & Human Resources, Louise Gravel
Director, Communications, Marilyn Amondola
Director, Election Financing, Janice Vézina
Director, Information Technology, Wayne Donovan
Director, Legal Services & Registrar, Political Parties, Jacques Girard
Director, Operations, Jean-Claude Léger
Director, Strategic Planning, Judy Charles

ENERGY SUPPLIES ALLOCATION BOARD/ Office de répartition des approvisionnements d'énergie

580 Booth St., 17th Fl., Ottawa ON K1A 0E4
613/995-5594; Fax: 613/992-8738
Chair, Jean C. McCloskey
Board Secretary, R. Lyman

ENVIRONMENT CANADA (EC)/ Environnement Canada

Terrasses de la Chaudière, 10 Wellington St., Hull PQ K1A 0H3
819/997-2800; Fax: 819/953-2225; Email: enviroinfo@cpgsv1.am.doe.ca; URL: http://www.ec.gc.ca
Toll Free: 1-800-668-6767
Environmental Emergencies (24-hour): 819/997-3743

Fosters a national capacity for sustainable development in cooperation with other governments, departments of government & the private sector that will result in a safe & healthy environment & a sound & prosperous economy by:
• undertaking & promoting programs to augment understanding of the environment;
• supporting environmentally responsible public & private decision-making;
• warning Canadians of risks to & from the environment;
• engaging Canadians as partners in measurably beneficial action to conserve, protect & restore the integrity of Canada's environment for the benefit of present & future generations.

ACTS ADMINISTERED

Canada Water Act (Part III is repealed)
Canada Wildlife Act
Canadian Environment Week Act
Canadian Environmental Assessment Act
Canadian Environmental Protection Act
Department of the Environment Act
Game Export Act
International River Improvements Act
Lac Seul Conservation Act
Lake of the Woods Control Board Act
Migratory Birds Convention Act
National Round Table on the Environment & the Economy Act
National Wildlife Week Act
Weather Modification Information Act
Wild Animal & Plant Protection & Regulation of International & Interprovincial Trade Act

GOVERNMENT OF CANADA

Other Acts Administered by Environment Canada
(A) In Part:
Arctic Waters Pollution Prevention Act
Export & Import Permits Act
Fisheries Act
James Bay & Northern Québec Native Claims Settlement Act
Pest Control Products Act
Resources & Technical Surveys Act
Transportation of Dangerous Goods Act, 1992
(B) Assistance to other Departments
Aeronautics Act
Agriculture & Rural Development Act
Canada Shipping Act
Energy Supplies Emergency Act
Hazardous Products Act
Health of Animals Act
International Boundary Waters Treaty Act
Motor Vehicle Safety Act
National Energy Board Act
National Housing Act
Territorial Lands Act
(C) Major Legislation of General Application
Access to Information Act
Federal Real Property Act
Financial Administration Act
Privacy Act
Minister, Hon. Sergio Marchi, 819/997-1441, Fax: 819/953-3457
Deputy Minister, Ian Glen, 819/997-4203, Fax: 819/953-6897
Associate Deputy Minister, Vacant, 819/953-7137
President, Canadian Environmental Assessment Review Office, Michel Dorais, 200, boul Sacré-Coeur, Hull PQ K1A 0H3, 819/997-1000, Fax: 819/994-1469
Director General, Corporate Human Resources Directorate, Ginette Cloutier, 819/997-1845, Fax: 819/953-2757
Director General & Corporate Secretary, Corporate Secretariat, Jean-Claude Dumesnil, 819/953-9300, Fax: 819/953-0749
General Counsel, Legal Services, Ellen Fry, 819/953-1380, Fax: 819/953-9110

Environment Canada Regional Directors General
Atlantic: Queen Sq., 45 Alderney Dr., 5th Fl., Dartmouth NS B2Y 2N6 – 902/426-7475; Fax: 902/426-6348, Regional Director General, Garth Bangay
Ontario: Canada Centre for Inland Waters Bldg., 867 Lakeshore Rd., PO Box 5050, Burlington ON L7R 4A6 – 905/973-6540; Fax: 905/954-4963, Regional Director General, John Mills
Pacific & Yukon: 224 West Esplanade, North Vancouver BC V7T 1A2 – 604/666-5881; Fax: 604/666-4707, Regional Director General, Art Martell
Prairies & Northwest Territories: Twin Atria II, 4999 - 98 Ave., 2nd Fl., Edmonton AB T6B 2X3 – 403/951-8869, Regional Director General, Jim Vollmershausen
Québec: 1141, rte de l'Église, 6e étage, CP 10100, Ste-Foy PQ G1V 4H5 – 418/648-4077; Fax: 418/649-6213, Regional Director General, François Guimont

ATMOSPHERIC ENVIRONMENT SERVICE (AES)
4905 Dufferin St., Downsview ON M3H 5T4
416/739-4521
Asst. Deputy Minister, Dr. Gordon A. McBean, 416/739-4770, Fax: 416/739-4232, Hull: 819/997-2686
Director General, Policy, Program & International Affairs, David Grimes, 416/739-4344, Ottawa: 613/997-0142; Fax: 613/994-8854
Director General, Canadian Meteorological Centre (Montréal), Hubert Allard, 514/421-4601, Fax: 514/421-4600
Acting Director General, Canadian Forces Weather Services, Ted Koolwine, Place Vincent Massey, 351, boul St-Joseph, Hull PQ K1A 0H3, 613/995-4173, Fax: 613/995-4197
Director General, Climate & Atmospheric Research Directorate, Dr. Phil E. Merilees, 416/739-4995, Fax: 416/739-4265
Director General, National Weather Services Directorate, Nancy Cutler, 416/739-4938, Fax: 416/739-4967

CORPORATE SERVICES
Terrasses de la Chaudière, 10 Wellington St., Hull PQ K1A 0H3
Asst. Deputy Minister, Laura Talbot-Allan, 819/953-7026, Fax: 819/953-4064
Director General, Administration, Jean Bilodeau, 819/997-2991, Fax: 819/997-1781
Director General, Corporate Management & Review, Cynthia Wright, 819/953-2091, Fax: 819/953-3388
Director General, Finance, Luc Desroches, 819/997-1561, Fax: 819/953-2459
Director General, Systems & Informatics, Jim Alexander, 819/994-3634, Fax: 819/953-5995

ENVIRONMENTAL CONSERVATION SERVICE (ECS)
Place Vincent-Massey, 351, boul St-Joseph, Hull PQ K1A 0H3
Asst. Deputy Minister, Dr. Robert W. Slater, 819/997-2161, Fax: 819/997-1541
Director General, Biodiversity Directorate, Stephen McClellan, 819/994-2541, Fax: 819/997-1541
Director General, Canadian Wildlife Service, Dave B. Brackett, 819/997-1301, Fax: 819/953-7177
Director General, Ecosystem Conservation Directorate, Karen Brown, 819/953-9309, Fax: 819/953-0461
Director General, State of the Environment Reporting, Ian D. Rutherford, 613/994-9865, Fax: 613/994-6826

ECS Regional Offices
Atlantic: 63 East Main St., PO Box 1590, Sackville NB E0A 3C0, Director, Dr. George Finney, 506/364-5011, Fax: 506/364-5062
Ontario: 4905 Dufferin St., Downsview ON M3H 5T4, Director, Simon Llewellyn, 416/739-5839, Fax: 416/739-4408
Pacific & Yukon: 5421 Robertson Rd., Delta BC V4K 3N2, Director, Brian Wilson, 604/946-8546, Fax: 604/946-7022
Prairie & Northern: Twin Atria Bldg., 4999 - 98 Ave., 2nd Fl., Edmonton AB T6B 2X3, Director, Gerald McKeating, 403/951-8853, Fax: 403/495-2615
Québec: 1141, rte de l'Église, CP 10100, Ste-Foy PQ G1V 4H5, Directeur, Michel Lamontagne, 418/648-7808, Fax: 418/649-6591

ENVIRONMENTAL PROTECTION SERVICE (EPS)
Place Vincent-Massey, 351, boul St-Joseph, Hull PQ K1A 0H3
Asst. Deputy Minister, Tony Clarke, 819/997-1575, Fax: 819/953-9452
Director General, Air Pollution Prevention Directorate, Vic Buxton, 819/997-1298, Fax: 819/953-9547
Director General, Environmental Technology Advancement Directorate, Ed Norrena, 819/953-3090, Fax: 819/953-9029
Director General, National Programs Directorate, David Egar, 819/997-2019, Fax: 819/997-0086
Acting Director General, Regulatory Affairs & Program Integration Directorate, Jennifer Moore, 819/997-5674, Fax: 819/953-5916
Director General, Toxics Pollution Prevention Directorate, Vic Shantora, 819/953-1114, Fax: 819/953-5371

POLICY & COMMUNICATIONS (P&C)
Terrasses de la Chaudière, 10 Wellington St., Hull PQ K1A 0H3
Asst. Deputy Minister, Avrim Lazar, 819/997-4882, Fax: 819/953-5981
Director General, Communications & Consultations Directorate, Anne-Marie Smart, 819/997-6820, Fax: 819/953-6789
Director General, Planning & Coordination Directorate, Rick Smith, 819/953-7634, Fax: 819/953-7632
Director, Federal-Provincial Relations Branch, Christine Guay, 819/994-1659, Fax: 819/953-5975
Director, International Affairs Branch, Brigita Gravitis-Beck, 819/953-9461, Fax: 819/953-7025
Acting Director General, Policy & Economics Directorate, Mike Beale, 819/994-5208, Fax: 819/997-0709

Regional Communications Offices
Atlantic: Queen Sq., 45 Alderney Dr., 15th Fl., Dartmouth NS B2Y 2N6 – 902/426-1930; Fax: 902/426-5340, Manager, Wayne Eliuk
Ontario: 4905 Dufferin St., Toronto ON M3H 5T4 – 416/739-4848; Fax: 416/739-4776, Manager, Claire Scrivens
Pacific & Yukon: 224 West Esplanade, North Vancouver BC V7M 3H7 – 604/666-9733; Fax: 604/666-4810, Acting Manager, Sheila Ritchie
Prairie & North: #1000, 266 Graham Ave., Winnipeg MB R3C 0J7 – 204/983-2110; Fax: 204/983-0964, Manager, Tim Hibbard
Québec: 1141, rte de l'Église, 7e étage, CP 6060, Ste-Foy PQ G1V 4H5 – 418/648-5777; Fax: 418/648-3859, Manager, Pierre Normand

Associated Agencies, Boards & Commissions
•North American Wetlands Conservation Council (Canada) (NAWCC): #200, 1750 Courtwood Cres., Ottawa ON K2C 2B5 – 613/228-2601; Fax: 613/228-0206
Executive Secretary, Dr. Kenneth W. Cox
•Committee on the Status of Endangered Wildlife in Canada (COSEWIC): 10 Wellington St., Hull PQ K1A 0H3 – 819/997-4991; Fax: 819/953-6283
•Federal Water Policy Office: Place Vincent-Massey, 351, boul St-Joseph, Hull PQ K1A 0H3 – 819/953-1513; Fax: 819/944-0237
Analyst, Frank Quinn
•Great Lakes Pollution Prevention Branch: 25 St. Clair Ave. East, 6th Fl., Toronto ON M4T 1M2 – 416/973-1162; Fax: 416/973-7438 – GLAP Information: 416/336-4884
Coordinator, Municipal Pollution Prevention, Marcus Ginder
•Great Lakes Pollution Prevention Centre (GLPPC): #112, 265 North Front St., Sarnia ON N7T 7X1 – 519/337-3423; Fax: 519/337-3486; Email: sarnia@glppc.org, Toll Free: 1-800-667-9790
Executive Director, Stewart Forbes
Manager, Communications, Marianne Lines
•National Hydrology Research Institute (NHRI): 11 Innovation Blvd., Saskatoon SK S7N 3H5 – 306/975-5717; Fax: 306/975-5143
Director, Robert A. Halliday
•National Round Table on the Environment & Economy
Listed alphabetically in detail, this section.
•National Water Research Institute (NWRI): 867 Lakeshore Rd., PO Box 5050, Burlington ON L7R 4A6 – 905/336-4625; Fax: 905/336-4989
Executive Director, Dr. R.J. Daley
•National Wildlife Research Centre (NWRC): 100, boul Gamelin, Hull PQ K1A 0H3 – 819/997-1092; Fax: 819/953-6612
Director, J.A. Keith
•North American Waterfowl Management Plan (NAWMP): c/o Canadian Wildlife Service, Place Vincent-Massey, 351, boul St-Joseph, 3e étage, Hull PQ K1A 0H3 – 819/997-2392; Fax: 819/994-4445; Email: sagik@cpits1.am.doe.ca
Communications Contact, Kelly Sagi, 819/953-9414

Canadian Almanac & Directory 1997

• St. Lawrence Centre: #400, 105, rue McGill, Montréal PQ H2Y 2E7 – 514/283-7000; Fax: 514/283-1719
Director, Lynn Cleary, 514/283-5869

EXPORT DEVELOPMENT CORPORATION (EDC)/Société pour l'expansion des exportation (SEE)
151 O'Connor St., Ottawa ON K1A 1K3
613/598-2500; Fax: 613/237-2690; Email: export@edc4.edc.ca; URL: http://www.edc.ca

Financial services corporation dedicated to helping Canadian business succeed & compete in the global marketplace. The EDC provides a wide range of flexible & innovative financial solutions to exporters across Canada & their customers around the world. Provides risk management services, including export-credit insurance, sales financing & guarantees. Represents a financially self-sustaining Crown corporation & operates on commercial principles, charging fees & premiums for its products & interest on its loans.

EDC is governed by a board of directors composed of representatives from both the private & public sectors, & reports to the Canadian Parliament through the Minister of International Trade.

President & CEO, Paul Labbé
Chair, Alexander K. Stuart
Finance, Roger Pruneau
Market Management, Don Curtis
Medium- & Long-Term Financial Services, Eric Siegel
Risk Management & Corporate Performance, Ian Gillespie
Secretariat & Legal Services, Gilles Ross
Short Term Financial Services, Rolfe Cooke

EDC Regional Offices
Calgary: #1030, 510 - 5 St. SW, Calgary AB T2P 3S2 – 403/292-6898; Fax: 403/292-6902
Halifax: Purdy's Wharf Tower II, #1410, 1969 Upper Water St., Halifax NS B3J 3R7 – 902/429-0426; Fax: 902/423-0881
London: #1512, 148 Fullarton St., London ON N6A 5P3 – 519/645-5828; Fax: 519/645-5580
Montréal: #4520, Tour de la Bourse, 800, Carre Victoria, CP 124, Succ Tour de la Bourse, Montréal PQ H4Z 1C3 – 514/283-3013; Fax: 514/878-9891
Ottawa: 151 O'Connor St., Ottawa ON K1A 1K3 – 613/598-2992; Fax: 613/598-3098
Toronto: 150 York St., PO Box 810, Toronto ON M5H 3S5 – 416/973-6211; Fax: 416/862-1267
Vancouver: 1 Bentall Centre, #1030, 505 Burrard St., Vancouver BC V7X 1M5 – 604/666-6234; Fax: 604/666-7550
Winnipeg: 330 Portage Ave., 8th Fl., Winnipeg MB R3C 0C4 – 204/983-5114; Fax: 204/983-2187

FARM CREDIT CORPORATION CANADA/Société du crédit agricole Canada
1800 Hamilton St., PO Box 4320, Regina SK S4P 4L3
306/780-8100; Fax: 306/780-5703; URL: http://canada.gc.ca/depts/agencies/fccind_e.html

Provides Canadian farmers with a reliable source of long-term credit & personalized counselling services. Creates, administers & supervises farm loans, & carries out other duties required by the Governor in Council. Reports to government through the Minister of Agriculture & Agri-food.

President & CEO, Gerry Penney
Controller, Marie-José Bourassa

Regional Offices
Edmonton, AB: #1550, 10250 - 101 St., Edmonton AB T5J 3P4 – 403/495-4488; Fax: 403/495-5665
Guelph, ON: 450 Speedvale Ave. West, Unit 201, Guelph ON N1H 7G7 – 519/821-1330; Fax: 519/821-2066
Kelowna, BC: #200, 595 K.L.O. Rd., Kelowna BC V1Y 8E7 – 250/861-6018; Fax: 250/861-6031
Moncton, NB: 1133 St. George Blvd., Moncton NB E1E 4E1 – 506/851-6595; Fax: 506/851-6613
Québec (Ste-Foy), PQ: #2000, Édifice Champlain, 2700, boul Laurier, PO Box 3600, Ste-Foy PQ G1V 4C7 – 418/648-3993; Fax: 418/648-3996
Regina, SK: #900, 1801 Hamilton St., Regina SK S4P 4L5 – 306/780-5610; Fax: 306/780-6383
Winnipeg, MB: #400, 5 Donald St., Winnipeg MB R3L 2T4 – 204/963-4039; Fax: 204/983-6342

Office of the Commissioner for FEDERAL JUDICIAL AFFAIRS/Bureau du Commissaire à la magistrature fédérale
110 O'Connor St., 11th Fl., Ottawa ON K1A 1E3
613/992-9175; Fax: 613/995-5615
Commissioner, Guy Y. Goulard, 613/992-9175, Email: guy.goulard@fja-cmf.x400.gc.ca
Deputy Commissioner, Denis Guay, 613/995-7438, Email: denis.guay@fja-cmf.x400.gc.ca
Director General, Policy & Corporate Services, André Gareau, 613/992-2930, Email: andre.gareau@fja-cmf.x400.gc.ca
Executive Editor, Federal Court Reports, William Rankin, 613/995-2706, Email: william.rankin@fja-cmf.x400.gc.ca

FEDERAL OFFICE OF REGIONAL DEVELOPMENT (QUÉBEC)/Bureau fédéral de développement régional (Québec)
Tour de la Bourse, #3800, 800, Place Victoria, CP 247, Montréal PQ H4Z 1E8
514/283-6412, 4843; Fax: 514/283-7778; URL: http://canada.gc.ca/depts/agencies/frqind_e.html
Ligne sans frais: 1-800-263-4689
Hull: Place du Portage II, 165, rue Hôtel de Ville, CP 1110, Succ B, Hull PQ J8X 3X5

FORDQ defines federal objectives relating to development opportunities in Québec. The agency delivers business assistance programs to small & medium-sized businesses in Québec for innovation, entrepreneurial & market development purposes. Provides support to programs for industry sector initiatives & fosters alliances among industry stakeholders (including small & medium-sized enterprises & industrial associations). Also, strengthens new & existing partnerships, improves access to government programs, & provides support for research & development for technology, demonstration, marketing & transfer programs.

Minister Responsible, Hon. John Manley, 613/995-9001, Fax: 613/992-0302
Secretary of State, Hon. Martin Cauchon, 514/496-1282, Fax: 514/496-5096
Deputy Minister, Renaud Caron, 514/283-4843, Fax: 514/283-7778
Director General, Communications, Jacques Cloutier, 514/283-8817
Director General, Finance, Administration & Corporate Services, Daniel McCraw, 514/283-4276

OPERATIONS
Asst. Deputy Minister, Guy Mckenzie, 514/283-4766
Director General, Central Regions, Germain Simard, 514/283-3995, Fax: 514/283-3637
Director General, Montréal Region, Guy Bédard, 514/283-4766
Director General, Resources Regions, Robin D'Anjou, 514/283-6771, Fax: 514/283-3637

POLICY & LIAISON
Asst. Deputy Minister, Michel Cailloux, 819/997-7716
Director General, Liaison & Regional Advocacy, François Gauthier, 819/997-2476
Director General, Policy Analysis, Federal-Provincial Affairs, Micheline Côté, 514/283-2664

FINANCE CANADA/Finances Canada
Esplanade Laurier, 140 O'Connor St., Ottawa ON K1A 0G5
613/992-1573; Fax: 613/996-8404; URL: http://www.fin.gc.ca/fin-eng.html
TDD: 613/996-0035

Department responsible for providing the federal government with analysis & advice on financial & economic issues. Monitors & researches the performance of the Canadian economy's major factors (output, growth, employment, income, price stability, monetary policy, long-term change). Finance Canada interacts with various other federal departments to encourage coordination in all federal initiatives with an impact on the economy. The department places emphasis on consulting with the public regarding policy directions & options.

ACTS ADMINISTERED
Bank Act
Bank of Canada Act
Banks & Banking Law Revision Act
Bills of Exchange Act
Bretton Woods & Related Agreements Act
Canada Deposit Insurance Corporation Act
Canada Development Corporation Reorganization Act
Canada Mortgage & Housing Corporation Act
Canada-Newfoundland Atlantic Accord Implementation Act
Canada-Nova Scotia Offshore Petroleum Resources Accord Implementation Act
Canada Pension Plan Act
Canadian International Trade Tribunal Act
Canadian National Railways Capital Revision Act
Canadian National Railways Refunding Act
Canadian National Steamship (West Indies Service) Act
Co-operative Credit Association Act
Currency Act
Customs & Excise Offshore Application Act
Customs Tariff, Debt Servicing & Reduction Account Act
Diplomatic Service (Special) Superannuation Act
Excise Tax Act
Export Credit Insurance Act
Federal Provincial Fiscal Arrangements & Federal Post-Secondary Education & Health Contributions Act
Financial Administration Act
Garnishment Attachment & Pension Diversion Act
Governor General's Retiring Annuity Act
Halifax Relief Commission Pension Continuation Act
Income Tax Act
Income Tax Conventions Interpretation Act
Insurance Companies Canadian & British Act
Insurance Companies Foreign Act
Interest Act
International Development (Financial Institutions) Assistance Act
Investment Companies Act
Loan Companies Act
Members of Parliament Retiring Allowances Act
Newfoundland Additional Finance Assistance Act
Nova Scotia Offshore Retail Sales Tax Act
Office of the Superintendent of Financial Institutions Act
Oil Export Act
Pension Benefits Standards Act
Prairie Grain Loans Act
Prince Edward Island Subsidy Act
Provincial Subsidies Act
Public Service Superannuation Act
Québec Savings Bank Act

Residential Mortgage Financing Act
Small Business Loans Act
Special Import Measures Act
Tax Rental Agreements Act
Trust & Loans Companies Act
Winding Up Act
Minister, Hon. Paul Martin, 613/992-4284; 996-7861, Fax: 613/992-4291; 995-5176, Email: pmartin@fin.gc.ca
Secretary of State, International Financial Institutions, Hon. Doug Peters, 613/996-3170, Fax: 613/995-2355
Deputy Minister, David Dodge, 613/992-4925, Fax: 613/952-9569
Assoc. Deputy Minister, Ian E. Bennett
Assoc. Deputy Minister, C. Scott Clark, 613/996-1963, Fax: 613/952-9569
Chief of Staff, Terrie O'Leary
Departmental Secretary, Suzanne McKellips, 613/992-2580

CONSULTATIONS & COMMUNICATIONS BRANCH
Asst. Deputy Minister, C. Peter Daniel, 613/995-5683, Fax: 613/943-0938
Director General, Bruce Yemen, 613/992-9194
Acting Director, Communications Policy & Strategy Division, Amanda Maltby, 613/992-9195
Director, Public Affairs & Consultations Division, Vacant, 613/943-2340

CORPORATE SERVICES BRANCH
Provides joint services for the federal Treasury Board Secretariat & Finance Canada.
Asst. Deputy Minister, Joy Kane, 613/995-8487, Fax: 613/947-3643
Director, Administrative Services Division, Jim T. Eadie, 613/992-6650
Director, Financial Services Division, Larry Paquette, 613/992-0554
Director, Human Resources Division, Fran M. Leblanc, 613/992-1996
Director, Informatics Division, R. Brodeur, 613/992-4306
Director, Security Services Division, Reg C. Langille, 613/995-5660
Director, Systems Integration and Process Reengineering Division, Sue MacGowan, 613/995-1755

CROWN CORPORATIONS & PRIVATIZATION BRANCH
Provides joint services for the federal Treasury Board Secretariat & Finance Canada.
Asst. Secretary, David Watters, 613/957-0124, Fax: 613/957-0151
Senior Director, Privatization, Dean McLean, 613/957-2658, Fax: 613/995-2355

ECONOMIC DEVELOPMENT POLICY BRANCH
Fax: 613/992-0387
Asst. Deputy Minister, Mike E. Francino, 613/992-1527, Fax: 613/992-0387
Senior Director, Operations Division, Anne Park, 613/992-6403
Director, Policy Division, Rob Fonberg, 613/996-0808

FEDERAL PROVINCIAL RELATIONS & SOCIAL POLICY BRANCH
Asst. Deputy Minister, Susan Peterson, 613/996-0735, Fax: 613/992-7754
General Director, Guillaume Bissonnette, 613/996-1432
Acting Director, Federal Provincial Relations Division, Peter Gusen, 613/943-0916
Director, Social Policy Division, Joy Kane, 613/996-0533

FINANCIAL SECTOR POLICY BRANCH
Asst. Deputy Minister, Doug Smee, 613/992-6843, Fax: 613/952-1596
General Director, Bob Hamilton, 613/995-5798
Director, Financial Institutions Division, Ray Labrosse, 613/992-9214
Acting Director, Financial Sector Policy Division, F. Swedlove, 613/992-4679
Acting Director, Financial Markets, Bill Mitchell, 613/992-9032

FISCAL POLICY & ECONOMIC ANALYSIS BRANCH
Asst. Deputy Minister, Don Drummond, 613/995-6391, Fax: 613/992-5773
General Director, Paul-Henri Lapointe, 613/996-0321
Director, Economic Forecasting & Analysis Division, David Moloney, 613/992-0590
Director, Economic Studies & Policy Analysis Division, Munir Sheikh, 613/992-4910
Director, Fiscal Policy Division, Peter DeVries, 613/996-7397

INTERNATIONAL TRADE & FINANCE BRANCH
Asst. Deputy Minister & Acting G-7 Deputy, Thomas A. Bernes, 613/992-6985, Fax: 613/992-7347
General Director, Rick Egelton, 613/996-8927
Director, International Economic Relations Division, Terry Collins-Williams, 613/996-8650
Director, Economic Analysis Division, Alan Gill, 613/992-6765
Director, Tariffs Division, Patricia Close, 613/992-6881

LEGAL SERVICES BRANCH
Acting Asst. Deputy Minister (Justice) & Counsel, Ross Hornby, L.Q.C., 613/996-4667, Fax: 613/995-7223
General Counsel, General Legislative Services Division, Ross Hornby, Q.C., 613/995-8724
General Counsel, Tax Counsel Division, Gaston Jorré, 613/996-0941

TAX POLICY BRANCH
Asst. Deputy Minister, Michael E. Francino, 613/992-1630, Fax: 613/996-0660
General Director, Samy Watson, 613/992-2555
Chair, Legislative Committee, Alan Short, 613/992-1785
Acting Director, Business Income Tax Division, Paul Dick, 613/992-1008
Director, Sales & Personal Income Tax Division, Vacant, 613/996-8267
Director, Tax Legislation Division, Len Farber, 613/992-1916

Associated Agencies, Boards & Commissions
Listed alphabetically in detail, this Section.
Auditor General
Bank of Canada
Canada Deposit Insurance Corporation
Canadian International Trade Tribunal
Revenue Canada
Office of the Superintendent of Financial Institutions
Treasury Board Secretariat

Office of the Superintendent of FINANCIAL INSTITUTIONS (OSFI)/
Bureau du surintendant des institutions financières Canada
Kent Square, 255 Albert St., Ottawa ON K1A 0H2
613/990-7788; Fax: 613/952-8219; URL: http://www.osfi-bsif.gc.ca/english.htm
Toll Free: 1-800-385-8647

Regulates all financial institutions and pension plans under federal jurisdiction. Included under federal jurisdiction are: banks, insurance firms, trust companies, loan and investment companies, & cooperative credit associations and fraternal benefit societies. Provides actuarial services and advice to the Government of Canada. Reports to government through the Minister of Finance.
Superintendent, John Palmer

Deputy Superintendent, Operations, John R. Thompson
Deputy Superintendent, Policy, Nick LePan
Executive Director, Corporate Services, Edna MacKenzie
Director General, Deposit Taking Institutions, Jack Heyes
Director General, Insurance, Michael Hale
Chief Actuary, Actuarial Services, Bernard Dussault
Director, Communications & Public Affairs, Jackie Breithaupt, 613/993-0577, Fax: 613/990-5591

FISHERIES & OCEANS CANADA (DFO)/
Pêches et Océans Canada (POC)
200 Kent St., Ottawa ON K1A 0E6
613/993-0999; Email: info@www.ncr.dfo.ca; URL: http://www.ncr.dfo.ca/home_e.htm
TDD: 1-800-668-5228
Coastal & Information Network URL: http://192.139.141.30

The only federal department with resource management & safety services responsibilities primarily focusing on water & the resources within it. DFO is responsible for all matters respecting oceans not by law assigned to any other department. Parliament's jurisdiction over sea-coast & inland fisheries & public harbours is established by the Constitution Act. DFO's merger with the Canadian Coast Guard (CCG) on April 1, 1995, consolidated the government's main civilian marine organizations.

DFO's vision is to be a leader in ocean & marine resource management through the management of Canada's oceans & major waterways so that they are clean, safe, productive & accessible, to ensure sustainable use of fisheries resources & to facilitate marine trade & commerce.

ACTS ADMINISTERED
Atlantic Fisheries Restructuring Act
Coastal Fisheries Protection Act
Department of Fisheries & Oceans Act
Fish Inspection Act
Fisheries Act
Fisheries Development Act
Fisheries Improvement Loans Act
Fisheries Prices Support Act
Fisheries & Oceans Research Advisory Council Act
Fishing & Recreational Harbours Act
Freshwater Fish Marketing Act
Great Lakes Fisheries Convention Act
North Pacific Fisheries Convention Act
Northern Pacific Halibut Fisheries Convention Act
Saltfish Act
Territorial Sea & Fishing Zones Act
Minister, Hon. Fred Mifflin, 613/992-3474, Fax: 613/990-7292, Email: Min@www.ncr.dfo.ca
Deputy Minister, William A. Rowat, 613/993-2200, Fax: 613/993-2194
Secretary of State, Hon. Fernand Robichaud, 613/947-4592, Fax: 613/947-4595
Executive Asst. to Deputy Minister, Darlene Elie, 613/993-2200
General Counsel, C. Beckton, 613/993-0966, Fax: 613/990-9385

CANADIAN COAST GUARD (CCG)
Canada Bldg., 344 Slater St., Ottawa ON K1A 0N7
613/998-1574; Fax: 613/990-2780
Senior Asst. Deputy Minister & Commissioner, John F. Thomas, 613/993-0678
Deputy Commissioner, Michael A.H. Turner, 613/998-1570
Director General, Business Planning Development, Neil Tiessen, 613/993-5792
Director General, Marine Navigational Services, J. Lonquet, 613/990-5608

Director General, Marine Technical & Support Services, J. Clavelle, 613/998-1638

Director General, Program Planning & Coordination, J.R.F. Hodgson, 613/998-1439

Director General, Rescue & Environmental Response, J. Murray, 613/990-3110

COMMUNICATIONS DIRECTORATE
Director General, Vacant, 613/993-0989
Director, Communications Operations, John Camp, 613/990-0211
Manager, Public Affairs, Lynda Cameron, 613/993-0996

CORPORATE SERVICES
Fax: 613/990-9557
Asst. Deputy Minister, Martha Hynna, 613/993-0868
Director General, Finance & Administration Directorate, R. Ken Bond, 613/993-2670, Fax: 613/996-9055
Director General, Information Management & Technical Services, Bev Hopkins, 613/993-2051
Director General, Personnel Directorate, Pat Napoli, 613/990-0023, Fax: 613/990-0035

FISHERIES MANAGEMENT
Asst. Deputy Minister, Pat Chamut, 613/990-9864, Fax: 613/990-9557
Director General, Aboriginal Affairs, Gerald Yaremchuk, 613/991-0181, Fax: 613/993-7651
Director General, Conservation & Protection, David Bevan, 613/990-6012
Director General, International, Earl Wiseman, 613/998-2644, Fax: 613/993-5995
Director General, Program Planning & Coordination, David Balfour, 613/993-2574
Director General, Resource Management, Jacque Robichaud, 613/990-0189

INDUSTRY SERVICES
Acting Asst. Deputy Minister, John Emberley, 613/990-0144, Fax: 613/993-4220
Director General, Inspection, John Emberley, 613/990-0144, Fax: 613/993-4220
Director General, Small Craft Harbours, Mike Godin, 613/993-3012, Fax: 613/952-6788

POLICY
Asst. Deputy Minister, Cheryl Fraser, 613/993-1808, Fax: 613/993-6958
Acting Director General, Economic & Policy Analysis, Les Burke, 613/993-1914, Fax: 613/991-3254
Director General, Industry Renewal, Karl Laubstein, 613/990-0140, Fax: 613/952-6802
Director General, International Directorate, Earl Wiseman, 613/993-1873, Fax: 613/993-5995
Acting Director General, Strategic Planning & Liaison, Susan Schultz, 613/998-5739, Fax: 613/990-2811

SCIENCE
Asst. Deputy Minister, L. Scott Parsons, 613/993-0850, Fax: 613/990-2768
Director General, Canadian Hydrographic Service, S.B. MacPhee, 613/995-4413, Fax: 613/996-9053, Chart Distribution: 613/998-4931
Director General, Fisheries Science, Bill Doubleday, 613/990-0271, Fax: 613/954-0807
Director General, Habitat Management & Environmental Science, Gerry Swanson, 613/991-1280, Fax: 613/993-7493
Director General, Program Planning & Coordination, Mary Zamparo, 613/993-0802, Fax: 613/990-0313
Special Advisor to the ADM, Oceans Science, Geoff L. Holland, 613/990-0298, Fax: 613/990-5510

Regional Offices
Central & Arctic: 501 University Cr., Winnipeg MB R3T 2N6 – 204/983-5118; Fax: 204/984-2401, Regional Director General, Ray Pierce
Gulf: PO Box 5030, Moncton NB E1C 9B6 – 506/851-7750; Fax: 506/851-7732, Regional Director General, Bernard LeBlanc
Laurentian: CP 15500, Québec PQ G1K 7Y7 – 418/648-4158; Fax: 418/648-4470, Regional Director General, Pierre Boisvert
Newfoundland: PO Box 5667, St. John's NF A1C 5X1 – 709/772-5150; Fax: 709/772-2156, Regional Director General, Lorne Humpries
Pacific: 555 West Hastings St., Vancouver BC V6B 5G3 – 604/666-6098; Fax: 604/666-3450, Regional Director General, L. Tousignant
Scotia-Fundy: PO Box 550, Halifax NS B3J 2S7 – 902/426-2581; Fax: 902/426-2256, Regional Director General, Neil Bellefontaine

Research Facilities
Bayfield Institute for Marine Science & Surveys: 867 Lakeshore Rd., PO Box 5050, Burlington ON L7R 4A6 – 905/336-4871; Fax: 905/336-6637; URL: http://www.cciw.ca/dfo/dfo-home.html
Bedford Institute of Oceanography: PO Box 1006, Dartmouth NS B2Y 4A2 – 902/426-2373; Fax: 902/426-7827; URL: http://biome.bio.dfo.ca
Freshwater Institute: 501 University Cr., Winnipeg MB R3T 2N6 – 204/983-5000; Fax: 204/983-6285
Gulf Fisheries Centre: PO Box 5030, Moncton NB E1C 9B6 – 506/851-6227; Fax: 506/851-7732
Halifax Fisheries Research Laboratory: 1707 Lower Water St., PO Box 550, Halifax NS B3J 2S7 – 902/426-7444; Fax: 902/426-2698
Institute of Ocean Sciences: 9860 West Saanich Rd., PO Box 6000, Sidney BC V8L 4B2 – 250/363-6517; Fax: 250/353-6807; URL: http://www.ios.bc.ca/
Maurice Lamontagne Institute: 850, Rte de le Mer, CP 1000, Mont-Joli PQ G5H 3Z4 – 418/775-6553; Fax: 418/775-0542; URL: http://www.ncr.dfo.ca/communic/offices/iml/iml_e.htm
Northwest Atlantic Fisheries Centre: PO Box 5667, St. John's NF A1C 5X1 – 709/772-2020; Fax: 709/772-2156
Pacific Biological Station: Hammond Bay Rd., Nanaimo BC V9R 5K8 – 250/756-7000; Fax: 250/756-7053
Regional Fish Inspection Laboratory: 1721 Lower Water St., PO Box 550, Halifax NS B3J 2S7 – 902/426-2373
St. Andrews Biological Station: St. Andrews NB E0G 2X0 – 506/529-8854; Fax: 506/529-4274; URL: http://www.ncr.dro.ca/communic/office/st_andre/st_and-e.htm
West Vancouver Laboratory: 4160 Marine Dr., West Vancouver BC V7V 1N6 – 604/666-4813; Fax: 604/666-3497

Associated Agencies, Boards & Commissions
•Fisheries Prices Support Board
Listed alphabetically in detail, this Section.
•Fisheries Resource Conservation Council (FRCC)/Le Conseil pour la conservation des ressources halieutiques (CCRH): PO Box 2001, Stn D, Ottawa ON K1A 5W3
Created in 1993 to form a partnership between scientific & academic expertise, & all sectors of the fishing industry. Council members make public recommendations to the Minister of Fisheries & Oceans on such issues as total allowable catches (TACs) & other conservation measures for the Atlantic fishery. The Council also provides advice in the areas of scientific research & assessment priorities.
Executive Director, David Rideout, 613/998-0433
•Freshwater Fish Marketing Corporation
Listed alphabetically in detail, this Section.

•Task Force on Incomes & Adjustment in the Atlantic Fishery: 200 Kent St., Ottawa ON K1A 0E6 – 613/941-6502
Chair, R. Cashin
Executive Director, K. Laubstein
•Northern Cod Research Program: PO Box 5667, St. John's NF A1C 5X1 – 709/772-2051; Fax: 709/772-6100
Director, Dr. J.S. Campbell

FISHERIES PRICES SUPPORT BOARD/
Office des prix des produits de la pêches Canada
200 Kent St., Ottawa ON K1A 0E6
613/990-0012; Fax: 613/941-2717

The Board, subject to approval of the Governor-in-Council, is empowered to purchase fishery products at prescribed prices or to pay deficiency payments to producers of fishery products equal to the difference between a prescribed price & the average price at which such products were sold. Reports to government through the Minister of Fisheries & Oceans.
Minister Responsible, Hon. Fred Mifflin, 613/992-3474, Fax: 613/990-7292
Chair, Morrissey Johnson
Executive Director, Joe Fitzgibbon

FOREIGN AFFAIRS & INTERNATIONAL TRADE CANADA (DFAIT)/
Affaires étrangères et du Commerce international (MAECI)
Lester B. Pearson Bldg., 125 Sussex Dr., Ottawa ON K1A 0G2
613/996-9134; Fax: 613/952-3904; Email: canadian@shell.portal.com; URL: http://www.dfait-maeci.gc.ca
Info Centre: 613/944-4000; Toll Free: 1-800-267-8376
Media Relations: 613/995-1874
Technology Inflow Program: 613/996-0971
Travel Advisory: 1-800-267-6788
FaxLink Service: 613/944-4500
International FaxLink Service: 613/944-6500
Consular Inquiries: 613/996-4376; TDD: 613/996-9136
Export Permits: 613/996-2387
Export Trade Information: 613/944-4000
Foreign Policy Information & Publications: 613/944-4000
Free Trade: 613/991-2014
Trade Information: 613/944-4000; 1-800-267-8376
Import Permits: Agriculture: 613/995-7762; Clothing & Textiles: 613/996-3711; Steel/Coffee: 613/995-2744
Passport Office: 613/994-3500
Protocol: 613/996-8683

ACTS ADMINISTERED
Asia-Pacific Foundation of Canada Act
Bretton Woods Agreements Act
Canadian Commercial Corporation Act
Canadian Institute for International Peace & Security Act
Cultural Property Export & Import Act
Diplomatic & Consular Privileges & Immunities Act
Export Development Act
Exports & Import Permits Act
Food & Agriculture Organization of the United Nations Act
Forgiveness of Certain Official Development Assistance Debts Act
Fort-Falls Bridge Authority Act
Geneva Conventions Act
High Commissioner of the United Kingdom Act
International Boundary Waters Treaty Act
International Centre for Ocean Development Act
International Development (Financial Institutions) Continuing Assistance Act
International Development Research Centre Act

Meat Import Act
Privileges & Immunities (International Organizations) Act
Privileges & Immunities (North Atlantic Treaty Organization) Act
Prohibition of International Air Services Act
Rainy Lake Watershed Emergency Control Act
Roosevelt-Campobello International Park Commission Act
Skagit River Valley Treaty Implementation Act
Softwood Lumber Products Charge Act
State Immunity Act
Territorial Sea & Fishing Zone Act
United Nations Act

The Department of Foreign Affairs & International Trade advises the government on foreign policy matters & implements the policy decisions the government takes. It is responsible for the promotion & protection of Canada's interests abroad & the conduct of Canada's external relations by:
• conducting all diplomatic & consular relations on behalf of Canada including assisting distressed Canadians abroad & ensuring that they are treated fairly under the laws of foreign countries;
• promoting the achievement of international peace and a safer world for the security of Canadians & the safe pursuit of their interests in all regions of the world;
• fostering the development of international law in order to defend & promote Canadian interests;
• coordinating the pursuit of Canada's interests through its international, political & economic relations;
• assisting Canadian businesses in expanding their sales to export markets;
• promoting foreign investment & technology inflow into Canada;
• delivering the Official Development Assistance and Immigration & Refugee programs abroad;
• conducting all official communications between the Government of Canada & all other countries' governments or international organizations;
• providing advice to the government on economic, political or other developments abroad likely to affect Canada's interests;
• ensuring that all domestic policy developments of other government departments are consistent with Canada's international obligations & foreign affairs interests;
• managing the foreign service including Canada's missions & delegations abroad.

Complete listings of "Canadian Diplomatic Representatives Abroad" and "Diplomatic & Consular Representatives in Canada" may be found in this directory. Please consult the main/global Index.

Minister, Foreign Affairs, Hon. Lloyd Axworthy, 613/995-1851, Fax: 613/996-3443
Minister, International Trade, Hon. Art Eggleton, 613/992-7332, Fax: 613/996-8924
Secretary of State, Asia-Pacific, Hon. Raymond Chan, 613/995-1851, Fax: 613/996-3443
Secretary of State, Africa-Latin America, Hon. Christine Stewart, 613/992-6560, Fax: 613/996-3443
Deputy Minister, International Trade, R. Allen Kilpatrick, 613/944-5000
Deputy Minister, Foreign Affairs, Gordon F. Smith, 613/993-4911, Fax: 613/944-0856
Associate Deputy Minister, Gatéan Lavertu, 613/944-5764, Fax: 613/944-0856
Ambassador, Disarmament, Peggy Mason, 613/992-5071
Ambassador, Environment & Sustainable Development, Hon. John A. Fraser, P.C., Q.C., 613/944-0886
Ambassador, Fisheries Conservation, Randolph Gherson, 613/995-6907
Chief, Air Negotiator, Daniel Molgat, 613/993-4323
Head, Canadian Delegation to the Human Rights Commission, Anne Park
Advisor, Economics, John Curtis
Departmental Ombudsman, Saul Grey, 613/990-1524
Canadian Agent, Canada-France Maritime Boundary Arbitration, F.A. Mathys, 613/952-8653, Fax: 613/952-8663

AFRICA & MIDDLE EAST BRANCH
Asst. Deputy Minister, Marc Perron, 613/944-6288
Director General, Africa & Middle East Bureau, Wilfrid-Guy Licari, 613/944-5989

ASIA & PACIFIC BRANCH
Asst. Deputy Minister, Vacant, 613/996-5095
Director General, Asia Pacific Bureau, Roger Ferland, 613/995-1097
Director General, Asia Pacific Bureau, Gary Smith, 613/992-3372

COMMUNICATIONS BUREAU
Director General, Peter Lloyd, 613/996-2213
Director, Corporate Communications Division, Alan Dorisse, 613/992-7005
Director, Foreign Policy Communications Division, Colin Robertson, 613/992-0760
Director, Media Relations Office, Yves Gagnon, 613/992-0956
Director, Trade Communications Division, Paul Desbiens, 613/996-7415

Policy Staff
Head, George Haynal, 613/944-1144
Economic Summit Coordination, Peter Boehm, 613/992-1894
Director, Economic & Trade Policy, Keith Christie, 613/994-0367
Director, Government Policy, Christine Desloges, 613/944-0384
Director, Political & Security Policy, Gary Soroka, 613/944-6846

CORPORATE SERVICES BRANCH
Asst. Deputy Minister, William L. Clarke
Senior Full-Time Financial Advisor, Administrative Services Bureau, K.F. McCarthy, 613/992-6109
Acting Director General, Client Services Bureau, Michael Conway
Director General, Human Resources Development Bureau, Claude Laverdure
Director General, Information Resources Bureau, M. Hutton, 613/944-1227
Director General, Information Systems Bureau, Victor Lotto, 613/943-1125
Director General, Physical Resources Branch, Ian Dawson, 613/952-8732
Director General, Resource Planning & Management Secretariat, Hugh Stephen
Dean, Canadian Foreign Service Institute, Graham Mitchell

Office of the Inspector General
Tower A, Place Vanier, 333 River Rd., 18th Fl., Ottawa ON K1A 0G2
Inspector General, Vacant
Deputy Inspector General, James D. Leach, 613/941-6022
Deputy Director General, J. Bédard, 613/952-8656

UNITED STATES BRANCH
Senior Asst. Deputy Minister & Chief Negotiator (NAFTA), John M. Weekes, 613/944-6183
Director General, USA Relations Bureau, Paul Dingledine, 613/944-6900
Director General, USA Trade & Economic Policy Bureau, Tom A. MacDonald, 613/944-2002
Director General, USA Trade, Tourism & Investment Bureau, Vacant, 613/944-5725

EUROPE BRANCH
Asst. Deputy Minister, Vacant, 613/992-6149
Director General, Bureau of Assistance for Central/Eastern Europe, Nancy Stiles, 613/992-2099
Director General, Central & Eastern Europe Bureau, Vacant, 613/992-5303
Director General, Western Europe Bureau, Kathryn McCallion, 613/992-8333

INTERNATIONAL BUSINESS DEVELOPMENT BRANCH
613/995-4128; Fax: 613/995-9604
Asst. Deputy Minister & Chief Trade Commissioner, Brian Schumacher, 613/995-6871
Director General, Investment & Technology Bureau, John Church, 613/995-2224
Director General, Trade Planning & Operations Bureau, John Treleaven, 613/996-1745
Director General, International Business Programs Bureau, Vacant, 613/992-8785

LATIN AMERICA & CARIBBEAN BRANCH
Asst. Deputy Minister, Stanley E. Gooch, 613/996-7065
Director General, Latin America & Caribbean Bureau, Jack Whittleton, 613/996-8435

MULTILATERAL TRADE NEGOTIATIONS BRANCH
Asst. Deputy Minister, Vacant, 613/995-8041
Senior Coordinator, Market Access, Kevin Gore, 613/992-7259
Senior Coordinator, Services & Investment, David P. Lee, 613/992-6700

POLITICAL & INTERNATIONAL SECURITY AFFAIRS BRANCH
Asst. Deputy Minister, Michael Kergin, 613/944-4228
Acting Director General, Cultural Affairs & Higher Education Bureau, Derek Fraser, 613/996-0232
Director General, International Organizations Bureau, Vacant, 613/992-4341
Director General, International Security Bureau, Arms Control & CSCE Affairs, Vacant, 613/992-3402
Director General, Security & Intelligence Bureau, Vacant, 613/992-7400

OFFICE OF PROTOCOL
Chief, Lawrence David Lederman, 613/992-2344
Director, Administrative & Hospitality Services, J. Visutskie, 613/996-9862
Director, Diplomatic Corps Services, W.R. Bowden, 613/995-5185
Director, Visits & Conferences, Vaughan P. Martin, 613/996-9740

TRADE & ECONOMIC POLICY BRANCH
Asst. Deputy Minister, Vacant, 613/995-7759
Director General, Economic Policy Bureau, Philip Somerville, 613/992-7825
Director General, Export & Import Permits Bureau, Margaret Huber, 613/992-3386
Director General, Trade Policy Bureau, D.G. Waddell, 613/992-0293

LEGAL, CONSULAR & PASSPORT AFFAIRS BRANCH
Asst. Deputy Minister, Vacant, 613/995-8901
Senior Advisor, Federal-Provincial Relations, Dilys Buckley-Jones, 613/996-1025
Director General, Consular Affairs Bureau, Pierre Giguère, 613/996-0639
Director General, Bureau of Legal Affairs, Phillipe Kirsch, 613/992-2728
Coordinator, Access to Information & Privacy Protection, Vacant, 613/992-1487
Coordinator, Environmental Assessment & Stewardship, D'Arcy Thorpe, 613/944-0428

Passport Office
Place du Centre, 200, Promenade du Portage, 6e étage, Hull PQ K1A 0G3

819/994-3500; Fax: 819/992-6587; URL: http://www.dfait-maeci.gc.ca/passport/passport.htm
Ligne sans frais: 1-800-567-6868, TDD: 613/994-3560
Chief Executive Officer, R.J. MacPhee, 613/944-3530

Passport Information
Toll Free (Canada): 1-800-567-6868
Toronto: 416/973-3251
Montréal: 514/283-2152
Mailed in Applications: Passport Office, Department of Foreign Affairs & International Trade, Ottawa ON K1A 0G3

Passports:
Canadian passports are issued only to Canadian citizens. The total life of a Canadian passport is five years. The passport is a valuable document, the loss of which must be reported to the local police & either to the Passport Office, Ottawa, one of the regional offices listed below, or to the nearest Canadian diplomatic mission (Embassy, High Commissioner's Office) or Consular Office abroad.

Passport Requirements:
All applicants (including children whose names will appear in a parent's passport) must submit original documentary evidence of Canadian Citizenship (not photocopies): (a) (Applicants born in Canada) Certificate of Birth; or Certificate of Canadian Citizenship (includes miniature certificate); large certificates issued after Feb. 14, 1977 are not acceptable. Applicants born in Québec prior to January 1994 may submit an original certificate issued by religious, municipal or judicial authorities, showing place & date of birth if it was issued prior to January 1, 1994; for individuals born after this date, only provincial birth certificates are accepted; (b) (Applicants born outside Canada) Certificate of Canadian Citizenship, or Certificate of Naturalization in Canada, or Certificate of Registration of Birth Abroad, or Certificate of Retention of Canadian Citizenship.

Fee Schedule:
Canadian passport $35.00
    48-page Canadian Passport $37.00
    Name changes/additions to a passport $5.00

Application for passport:
Applications for a passport should be mailed to the Passport Office, Department of Foreign Affairs & International Trade Canada, Ottawa K1A 0G3, at least two weeks plus mailing time before the passport is required. Alternatively, they may be presented in person at any of the regional offices listed below, & persons who reside in a community where there is a passport office are requested to submit the applications in person. *Regional offices do not accept mailed-in applications.*

Canadian citizens residing abroad should complete Form A (abroad) or Form B (abroad), available at the Canadian mission in their country of residence. Canadians living in the United States requiring a Canadian passport shoud apply by mail directly to Passport Office headquarters in Ottawa. Application forms can be obtained from the Canadian Embassy in Washington DC, or at any consulate, or by calling 819/994-3500.

Regulations & instructions for persons applying for Canadian passports in Canada are contained in "Passport Application Form A (applicants 16 & over)", & "Passport Application Form B (for a child under 16)" which can be obtained from any post office in Canada, from the Passport Office, Ottawa, from the regional offices, or from most travel agencies.

Every application for a passport must be signed by a guarantor from one of the eligible categories listed on the form who must also certify the back of one of the applicant's photographs. In addition to being a member of one of the groups listed, the guarantor must be a Canadian citizen residing in Canada who has known the applicant personally for at least two years. If there is no person available within the group of eligible guarantors who has known the applicant for the required two years, appropriate instructions will be found in the application form.

Warning:
The attention of applicants & guarantors is drawn to Section 57(2) of the Criminal Code covering passport fraud whereby: "Every one who, while in or out of Canada, for the purpose of procuring a passport for himself or any other person or for the purpose of procuring any material alteration or addition to any such passport, makes a written or oral statement that he knows is false or misleading (a) is guilty of an indictable offence & liable to imprisonment for a term not exceeding two years or (b) is guilty of an offence punishable on summary conviction."

Children:
The name of a child under 16 years of age may be included in the passport of a parent. The child's name may be included in the passport of only one parent. Separate passports for children under 16 years may be obtained by using application Form B. A child's name may be added to a parent's existing passport by applying on Form B-1, which is available from any passport issuing office.

Visas:
A passport alone does not confer the right to enter any country. Travellers are advised to check with the embassy or consulate of the country they wish to visit to determine visa and entry/exit requirements, health certificates, customs, currency, etc., all of which are subject to change without notice.

Work Permits:
Most countries will not allow non-residents to accept gainful employment unless they have applied for & been granted work permits prior to their entry.

Regional Passport Offices
Brampton: Civic Centre, 150 Central Park Dr., 3rd Fl., Brampton ON – 905/791-3444; Fax: 905/791-3495
Calgary: #440, First St. Plaza, 138 - 4th Ave. SE, Calgary AB – 403/292-5173; Fax: 403/292-4885
Edmonton: #1630, Canada Place, 9700 Jasper Ave., Edmonton AB – 403/495-6187; Fax: 403/495-6536
Fredericton: Frederick Square, #470, 77 Westmorland St., Fredericton NB – 506/452-3901; Fax: 506/452-2411
Halifax: #608, Duke Tower, 5251 Duke St., Halifax NS – 902/426-2717; Fax: 902/426-4620
Hamilton: #330, 120 King St. West, Hamilton ON – 905/572-2791; Fax: 905/572-2895
Jonquière: #302, Place St-Michel, 3885, boul Harvey, Jonquière PQ – 418/542-8301; Fax: 418/542-4620
Kitchener: 55 King St. West, 5th Fl., Kitchener ON – 519/571-6823; Fax: 519/571-6827
Laval: #300, 2550, boul Daniel-Johnson, Laval PQ – 514/973-5601; Fax: 514/973-5609
London: 451 Talbot St., 8th Fl., London ON – 519/645-5104; Fax: 519/645-5446
Montréal: #215, Tour Ouest, 200, boul René-Lévesque ouest, Montréal PQ – 514/283-5133; Fax: 514/283-5698
North York: 5001 Yonge St., 4th Fl., North York ON – 416/954-4676; Fax: 416/954-4686
Ottawa: 1st Fl., West Tower, 240 Sparks St., Ottawa ON
Québec (Ste-Foy): #2410, 2600, boul Laurier, 4e étage, Ste-Foy PQ – 418/648-3069; Fax: 418/649-6195
Regina: #502, 1867 Hamilton St., Regina SK – 306/780-7522; Fax: 306/780-7573
St. Catharines: 43 Church St., 6th Fl., St. Catharines ON L2R 7E1 – 905/988-4119; Fax: 905/988-4118
St. John's: #702, 140 Water St., St. John's NF – 709/772-2073; Fax: 709/772-4679
St-Laurent: #112, 3300, ch Côte Vertu, St-Laurent PQ – 514/496-1343; Fax: 514/496-2260
Saskatoon: #605, 101 - 22 St. East, Saskatoon SK – 306/975-5107; Fax: 306/975-5740
Scarborough: #828, 200 Town Centre Crt., Scarborough ON – 416/973-4700; Fax: 416/973-7671
Surrey: #405, 15127 - 100 Ave., Surrey BC – 604/775-6255; Fax: 604/775-6248
Thunder Bay: #406, 28 North Cumberland St., Thunder Bay ON – 807/344-8660; Fax: 807/345-4836
Toronto: 438 University Ave., 11th Fl., Toronto ON – 416/954-5309; Fax: 416/973-1755
Vancouver: #240, 757 West Hastings St., Vancouver BC – 604/666-0942; Fax: 604/666-1691
Victoria: #228, 816 Government St., Victoria BC – 250/363-3243; Fax: 250/363-3184
Windsor: #504, 100 Ouellette Ave., Windsor ON – 519/257-6622; Fax: 519/257-6625
Winnipeg: #910, 200 Graham Ave., Winnipeg MB – 204/983-1294; Fax: 204/983-4025

Associated Agencies, Boards & Commissions
In addition to the Department, the Minister of Foreign Affairs is responsible to Parliament for the following agencies, which are listed separately among the federal government listings.
Canadian Commercial Corporation
Canadian International Development Agency
Canadian International Grains Institute
Export Development Research Centre
International Joint Commission (Canadian Section)
International Boundary Commission (Canadian Section)
Roosevelt-Campobello International Park Commission

FRESHWATER FISH MARKETING CORPORATION/
Office de commercialisation du poisson d'eau douce
1199 Plessis Rd., Winnipeg MB R2C 3L4
204/983-6483; Fax: 204/983-6497; URL: http://canada.gc.ca/depts/agencies/fwfind_e.html

The Corporation is empowered to market & trade in lake fish & fish by-products in Canada & abroad. Reports to government through the Minister of Fisheries & Oceans.
President, J.T. Dunn
Chair, Sam Murdock
Vice-President, Marketing, Gerald F. Malone

GREAT LAKES PILOTAGE AUTHORITY LTD./
Administration de pilotage des Grands Lacs ltée
PO Box 95, Cornwall ON K6H 5R9
613/933-2995; Fax: 613/932-3793; URL: http://canada.gc.ca/depts/agencies/glpind_e.html

The Authority provides pilotage services in the waters of the St. Lawrence River commencing at the northern entrance of St. Lambert Lock, the Great Lakes area & the Port of Churchill, Manitoba. Reports to government through the Minister of Transportation.
President, R.G. Armstrong, 613/933-2991
Sec.-Treas., R. Lemire, C.A.

Regional Offices
Eastern: 202 Pitt St., Cornwall ON – 613/933-2991
Western: 345 Lakeshore Blvd., St.Catharines ON – 905/934-2921

HEALTH CANADA/Santé Canada
Brooke Claxton Bldg., Tunney's Pasture, Ottawa ON K1A 0K9
613/957-2991; Fax: 613/941-5366; URL: http://www.hwc.ca/links/english.html
Pest Management Regulatory Agency (PMRA) URL: http://www.hwc.ca/pmra

Main federal government department focused on issues relating to the health & safety of Canadians. Provides the fundamental funding & policy in maintaining a high-quality, affordable health system in Canada. Responsibilities include:
- health protection & consumer product safety;
- delivery of health services to Indian bands & the Inuit;
- promotion of fitness;
- financial support to the provinces & territories for insured health care.

ACTS ADMINISTERED
Canada Health Act
Canada Medical Act
Canadian Centre on Substance Abuse Act
Canadian Environmental Protection Act
Controlled Drugs & Substances Act
Department of Health Act
Federal-Provincial Fiscal Arrangements & Federal Post-Secondary Education & Health Contributions Act
Financial Administration Act
Fitness & Amateur Sport Act
Food & Drugs Act
Hazardous Materials Information Review Act
Hazardous Products Act
Health Resources Fund Act
Medical Research Council Act
Narcotic Control Act
Patent Act
Quarantine Act
Queen Elizabeth II Canadian Research Fund Act
Radiation Emitting Devices Act
Sport Pool & Loto Canada Winding-Up Act
Tobacco Products Control Act
Tobacco Restraint Act
Tobacco Sales to Young Persons Act
Minister, Hon. David C. Dingwall, 613/957-0200, Fax: 613/952-1154
Deputy Minister, Michèle S. Jean, 613/957-0212, Fax: 613/952-8422
Assoc. Deputy Minister, Alan Nymark
Director General, Assets Management, M. Williams, 613/957-3375
Director General, Human Resources, R. Joubert, 613/957-3236

CORPORATE SERVICES BRANCH
Asst. Deputy Minister, R. Lafleur, 613/952-3984
Director General, Planning & Financial Administration, O. Marquardt, 613/957-7762
Director General, Informatics, F. Bull, 613/954-8713

HEALTH PROMOTIONS & PROGRAMS BRANCH
Asst. Deputy Minister, Kay Stanley, 613/957-2953
Director General, Population Health, Catherine Lane, 613/957-7792
Director General, Research & Program Policy, Jo Hauser, 613/954-8543
Director General, Systems for Health, Diane Kirkpatrick, 613/954-8602
Director, HIV/Aids Policy Coordination & Program Division, Gweneth Gowanlock, 613/952-5258

Regional Offices
Alberta & Northwest Territories: #815, 9700 Jasper Ave. NW, Edmonton AB T5J 4C3, Regional Director, Don Onischak
Atlantic: #709, 1557 Hollis St., Halifax NS B3J 3V4 – 902/426-3931, Acting Regional Director, Kathy Coffin
Manitoba & Saskatchewan: #603, 213 Notre Dame Ave., Winnipeg MB R3B 1N3 – 204/983-2557; Fax: 204/983-8674, Regional Director, Gary Ledoux
Ontario: 55 St. Clair Ave. East, Toronto ON M4T 1M2 – 416/973-1804; Fax: 416/973-6409, A/Regional Director, Pageen Walsh
Pacific: 750 Cambie St., 4th Fl., Vancouver BC V6B 4V5 – 604/666-7128; Fax: 604/666-8986, Acting Regional Director, Heather Fraser
Québec: #210, Tour Est, 200, boul René-Lévesque ouest, Montréal PQ H2Z 1X4 – 514/283-1043; Fax: 514/283-3309, Regional Director, Yvette Mongeon

HEALTH PROTECTION BRANCH
Ottawa ON K1A 0L2
Asst. Deputy Minister, Kent Foster, 613/957-1804
Director General, Environmental Health Directorate, J.R. Hickman, 613/954-0291
Director General, Foods Directorate, Dr. George Paterson, 613/957-1821
Director General, Laboratory Centre for Disease Control, Dr. J.Z. Losos, 613/957-0315
Director General, National Pharmaceutical Strategy/Drugs Directorate, Dann Michols, 613/957-0369
Director, Management & Program Services, W. Newton, 613/957-7984
Director, Policy & Scientific Affairs, J. Weiner, 613/952-3665

Regional Offices
Alberta/British Columbia/Yukon/NWT: 3155 Willingdon Green, Burnaby BC V5G 4P2 – 604/666-3359, Regional Director, Greg Smith
Atlantic: 1992 Baffin Blvd., PO Box 1060, Dartmouth NS B2Y 3Z7 – 902/426-2160, Acting Regional Director, Sharon Chard
Manitoba & Saskatchewan: 510 Lagimodière Blvd., Winnipeg MB R2J 3Y1 – 204/983-3004; Fax: 204/983-5547, Acting Regional Director, Donna-Mae Burgener
Ontario: 2301 Midland Ave., Scarborough ON M1P 4R7 – 416/973-1451; Fax: 416/291-1431, Regional Director, C. Broughton
Québec: 1001, rue St-Laurent ouest, Longueuil PQ J4K 1C7 – 514/238-5488; Fax: 514/283-5471, Regional Director, Jean Lambert

MEDICAL SERVICES BRANCH
Ottawa ON K1A 0L3
Acting Asst. Deputy Minister, Paul Cochrane, 613/957-7701
Acting Director General, First Nations & Inuit Health Program, Paul Glover, 613/952-7177
Acting Director General, Non-Insured Health Benefits, Dr. J. Wortman, 613/954-8825
Director General, Occupational & Environmental Health Services, Dr. G.I. Lynch, 613/957-7699
Director General, Program, Policy, Transfer Secretariat & Planning, Mavis Dellert, 613/957-3402

Regional Offices
Alberta: Canada Place, #730, 9700 Jasper Ave., Edmonton AB T5J 4C3 – 403/495-2690, Regional Director, G. Corrigall
Atlantic: Park Lane Terrace, #301, 5657 Spring Garden Rd., Halifax NS B3J 1V6 – 902/426-3646, Regional Director, A. Garman
Manitoba: #500, Commissioners Bldg., 303 Main St., Winnipeg MB R3C 0H4 – 204/983-4172, Regional Director, P. Bighetty
Ontario: 1547 Merivale Rd., Ottawa ON K1A 0L3 – 613/952-0087, Regional Director, R. Jock
Pacific: #540, 757 Hastings St. West, Vancouver BC V6C 3E6 – 604/666-3235, Regional Director, P. Kyba
Québec: #202, Tour Est, 200, boul René-Lévesque ouest, Montréal PQ H2Z 1X4 – 514/283-4774, Regional Director, C. Paradis
Saskatchewan: 1911 Broad St., Regina SK S4P 1Y1 – 306/780-5413, Regional Director, J. Roll
Yukon: Yukon Manor, No. 2 Hospital Rd., Whitehorse YT Y1A 3H8 – 403/668-6461, Regional Director, R. Dowdall

Federal Hospitals (of twenty beds or more)
Blood Indian Hospital: PO Box 490, Cardston AB T0K 0K0 – 403/653-3351
Fort Qu'Appelle Indian Hospital: Fort Qu'Appelle SK S0G 1S0 – 306/332-5611
Mayo General Hospital: Mayo YT Y0B 1M0 – 403/996-2345
Moose Factory General Hospital: Moose Factory ON P0L 1W0 – 705/658-4544
Percy E. Moore Hospital: Hodgson MB R0C 1N0 – 204/372-8444
Sioux Lookout Zone Hospital: Sioux Lookout ON P0V 2T0 – 807/737-3030
Whitehorse General Hospital: 5 Hospital Rd., Whitehorse YT Y1A 3H8 – 403/668-9444

POLICY & CONSULTATION BRANCH
Asst. Deputy Minister, A. Juneau, 613/957-3059
Director General, Health Policy & Information Directorate, J. Ferguson, 613/957-3066
Director General, Intergovernmental Affairs, G. Bujold, 613/957-3081
Director General, Strategic Planning & Review, Carmelita Boivin-Cole, 613/954-8072
Director General, Women's Health Bureau, Dr. A. Hoffman, 613/957-1940

Communications Directorate
Director General, Carla Gilders, 613/957-2979, Fax: 613/952-7266
Director, Communications Services, Carole Peacock, 613/957-2987
Director, Communications Strategy & Planning, Denis Schuthe, 613/957-2981

Regional Communications Offices
Alberta: Canada Place, #710, 9700 Jasper Ave., Edmonton AB T5J 4C3 – 403/495-2651; Fax: 403/495-5551, Director, Win Kennedy
Atlantic: #750, 1557 Hollis St., Halifax NS B3J 3V4 – 902/426-2038; Fax: 902/426-3768, Director, Pat Brownlow
British Columbia: #405, Sinclair Centre, 757 West Hastings St., Vancouver BC V6C 1A1 – 604/666-2083; Fax: 604/666-2258, Director, Blair Parkhurst
Manitoba: #205, Eaton Place, 330 Graham Ave., Winnipeg MB R3C 4C8 – 204/983-2508; Fax: 204/983-3912, Director, Morgan Fontaine
Ontario: 25 St. Clair Ave. East, 4th Fl., Toronto ON M4T 1M2 – 416/954-9021; Fax: 416/973-1423, Director, Darryl Perry
Québec: Tour Est, #218, 200, boul René-Lévesque ouest, Montréal PQ H2Z 1X4 – 514/283-2306; Fax: 514/283-6739, Director, Gaston Pelletier

Associated Agencies, Boards & Commissions
- Hazardous Materials Information Review Commission (HMIRC): #9000, 200 Kent St., Ottawa ON K1A 0M1 – 613/993-4331; Fax: 613/993-4686; URL: http://canada.gc.ca/depts/agencies/hmiind_e.html

Independent agency that examines applications from suppliers & employers seeking exemptions from WHMIS disclosure requirements. The agency reviews product labels & material safety data sheets related to the claim &, if satisfied, keeps the actual ingredients on file & issues confidential numbers to safeguard the formulas. Fees are charged for the screening process & for

administering appeals against the Commission's decisions.
President, Claude St-Pierre, 613/993-4441
Executive Assistant, M. Branch, 613/993-4429
• Pest Management Regulatory Agency: 59 Camelot Dr., Nepean ON K1A 0Y9 – 613/952-5330; Fax: 613/998-1312; Email: pminfoserv@em.agr.ca Pesticides Information: 1-800-267-6315
Director General, W. Ormrod, 613/736-3570, Fax: 613/736-3707
Associate Director, Compliance & Regional Operations, J.B. Reid, 613/736-3500
Director, Management & Information, G. Flores, 613/736-3570, Fax: 613/736-3666
Director, Product Sustainability & Coordination, J. Taylor, 613/736-3780, Fax: 613/736-3770
Director, Regulatory Affairs & Innovation Division, Dr. R. Taylor, 613/736-3675, Fax: 613/736-3699

HUMAN RESOURCES DEVELOPMENT CANADA (HRDC)/Développement des ressources humaines

Place du Portage, Phase IV, 140, Promenade du Portage, Hull PQ K1A 0J9
819/994-6013; URL: http://www.hrdc-drhc.gc.ca/hrdc/menu-en.html
Environmental Youth Internship Program: 403/233-0748; EYI Email: cchrei@netway.ab.ca

HRDC provides an integrated approach to Canada's national investment in people. It brings income programs supporting Canadians together with human resource programs linked to the requirements of the national economy & labour market. The department was created to develop & build a mobile, educated & skilled workforce to increase Canada's productivity & international competitiveness & the prosperity of its citizens. Main objectives of the HRDC are:
• develop, promote & implement social policies & programs that foster the development, participation & well-being of Canadians;
• promote & strengthen the income security of seniors, disabled persons, survivors, families with children & migrants;
• promote economic growth & flexibility by providing temporary income support of unemployed workers who qualify for benefits under the Unemployment Insurance Act;
• facilitate & sustain stable industrial relations & a safe, fair & equitable workplace;
• develop & support the use of Canada's human resources in order to promote economic growth & social well-being.

ACTS ADMINISTERED
Canada Assistance Plan
Canada Labour Code
Canada Pension Plan
Canada Student Loans Act
Canadian Centre for Occupational Health & Safety Act
Children Special Allowances Act
Department of Labour Act
Employment & Immigration Department & Commission Act
Employment & Equity Act
Fair Wages & Hours of Labour Act
Family Orders & Agreements Enforcement Assistance Act
Federal-Provincial Fiscal Arrangements & Federal Post-Secondary Education & Health Contributions Act
Government Annuities Act
Government Annuities Improvement Act
Government Employees Compensation Act
Hudson Bay Mining & Smelting Company Ltd.
Labour Adjustment Benefits Act
Merchant Seamen Compensation Act
National Training Act
Non-smokers' Health Act
Old Age Security Act
Status of the Artist Act
Unemployment Assistance Act
Unemployment Insurance Act
Vocational Rehabilitation of Disabled Persons Act
Wages Liability Act

Minister, Hon. Pierre Pettigrew
Minister, Labour, Hon. Alphonso Gagliano, 819/953-5646, Fax: 819/994-5168
Secretary of State, Training & Youth, Hon. Ethel Blondin-Andrew, 613/953-8385, Fax: 613/953-0944
Minister Responsible, Literacy, Hon. Joyce Fairbairn, 613/996-4382, Fax: 613/995-3223
Deputy Minister, Jean-Jacques Noreau, 819/994-4514, Fax: 819/953-5603
Associate Deputy Minister, Peter Harrison, 819/994-4520, Fax: 819/953-5603
Asst. Deputy Minister, Systems, D. McNaughton, 819/994-1592
Senior General Counsel, Legal Services, Kathie MacCormick, 819/953-8301
Director General, Corporate Secretariat, N. Gavignan, 819/994-2893

COMMUNICATIONS
Asst. Deputy Minister, H. Lacombe, 819/664-6013
Director, Communication Employment, Social Development & Education, J. Bélisle, 819/994-1651
Director, Communications Policy, F. Taylor, 819/994-6710
Director, Income Support Programs Communications, Richard Fixx, 613/957-2807
Director, Research & Planning, J. Bélisle, 819/994-1651
Acting Director, Unemployment Insurance Communications, G. Lavoie, 819/953-7250

EMPLOYMENT, SOCIAL DEVELOPMENT & EDUCATION GROUP
Asst. Deputy Minister/Executive Director, Ian C. Green, 819/953-7363, Fax: 819/953-7427
Acting Executive Director, Status of Disabled Persons, Bruce Clark, 819/994-5692, Fax: 819/994-1346
Senior Director General, Employment, Marcel Nouvet, 819/953-3729, Fax: 819/994-2085
Director General, Coordination Group on Persons with Disabilities & SSR, Nancy Lawand, 613/954-3854, Fax: 613/957-4404
Acting Director General, Cost Shared Programs Branch, Larry Doucet, 613/957-1537, Fax: 613/941-5799
Director General, Human Resource Investment Fund, Yves Poisson, 819/953-7405, Fax: 819/953-3134
Director General, Intergovernmental Administrative Arrangements Secretariat, Wayne Guthrie, 819/953-2337, Fax: 819/953-7568
Director General, Labour Market Services, J. McWhinnie, 819/994-3713, Fax: 819/953-3512
Director General, National Literacy Secretariat, James Page, 819/953-5460, Fax: 819/953-8076
Director General, Occupational & Career Information, Maeve Hancey, 819/953-7434, Fax: 819/997-5851
Director General, Older Worker Adjustment Branch, Elayne Van Snellenberg, 819/994-8146, Fax: 819/953-8804
Director General, Program Planning & Coordination, Virginia Miller, 819/997-9217, Fax: 819/953-3134
Director General, Social Development, Don Ogston, 613/957-8672, Fax: 613/941-8274
Special Advisor & Director General, Strategic Initiatives, Dean Moodie, 819/994-4509, Fax: 819/953-7427
Director General, Student Assistance Branch/Education Support Branch, Martha Nixon, 819/994-2377, Fax: 819/953-4226

FINANCIAL & ADMINISTRATIVE SERVICES
Fax: 819/997-2407
Asst. Deputy Minister, Debbie Good, 819/997-6481, Fax: 819/997-2407
Director General, Administrative Services, David A. Murray, 819/994-2580
Director General, Financial Services, G. Tremblay, 819/994-2576, Fax: 819/994-5813
Director General, Internal Audit Bureau, J. Jackson, 819/953-0821, Fax: 819/953-0831
Director General, Policy & Systems, R. Holland, 819/994-1714

HUMAN RESOURCES SERVICES
Asst. Deputy Minister, Monique Plante, 819/944-1791
Director, Executive Group Services, Sue Pettis, 819/953-1263
Director, Headquarters Human Resources Services, Jean-Pierre Lecours, 819/997-3168
Director, Planning & Coordination, Robert St-Jean, 819/994-5438
Director General, Strategy & Development, J. Bélanger, 819/994-2329, Fax: 819/953-9373

INCOME SECURITY PROGRAM
Place Vanier, 120 Parkdale Ave., Ottawa ON K1A 0L1
Asst. Deputy Minister, Serge Rainville, 613/957-3111
Director General, General Programs, Cathy Drummond, 613/957-2813
Project Manager, ISP Redresing, D. Kealy, 613/941-5076
Director General, Program Delivery Services, W. Ganim, 613/954-8401

INSURANCE PROGRAM
819/997-8662
Executive Director, H. Braiter, 819/994-1600, Fax: 819/997-8662
Chief Actuary, Actuarial Services, Michel Bedard, 819/994-4590
Acting Director General, Control Branch, R. Stewart, 819/994-6868
Director General, Insurance Policy, J.J. Verbruggen, 819/994-1880
Director General, Insurance Services, D. Matheson, 819/994-6299

LABOUR PROGRAM
Place du Portage, Phase II, 165, rue Hôtel de Ville, Hull PQ K1A 0J2
819/997-2617
TDD: 819/953-8000
Bureau of Labour Information: 819/997-3117
Women's Bureau: 819/997-1551
Asst. Deputy Manager, J. Lahey, 819/997-1493
Director General, Federal Mediation & Conciliation Service, Warren R. Edmondson, 819/997-3290
Director General, Legislation & Research, David Head, 613/954-3138
Director General, Operations, Renée Godmer, 819/997-2555
Director General, Workplace Information, Andrée Dubois, 819/994-6119
Commissioner, Office of the Fire Commissioner of Canada, Tom Dunfield, 819/997-1748
Chief, Fire Protection Services, E. Marotta, 819/997-1306

STRATEGIC POLICY
Fax: 819/997-7329
Senior Asst. Deputy Minister, Harvey Lazar, 819/994-4272
Director General, Applied Research Branch, Jean-Pierre Voyer, 819/994-1620
Director General, Federal-Provincial Relations, Guy McKenzie, 819/997-0519
Director General, Labour Market & Education Policy, Norine Smith, 819/994-4989

Director General, Labour Market Outlook & Sectoral Analysis, Judith Moses, 819/957-4700
Director General, Program Evaluation Branch, Ian Midgley, 819/957-2737
Director General, Strategic Planning & Information, Phil Fay, 819/941-1044
Director General, Working Time & Distribution of Work Task Group, Lynne Jamieson, 819/994-0167

Regional Offices
Alberta & Northwest Territories: Canada Place, #1440, 9700 Jasper Ave., Edmonton AB T5J 4C1 – 403/495-2414; Fax: 403/495-5609, Regional Manager, Communications, Anne Milne
British Columbia & Yukon: Royal Centre, 1055 West Georgia St., 8th Fl., PO Box 11345, Vancouver BC V6E 2P8 – 604/666-0075; Fax: 604/666-7328, Regional Manager, Communications, Gill Eston
Manitoba: Paris Bldg., #500, 259 Portage Ave., Winnipeg MB R3B 3L4 – 204/983-3781; Fax: 204/984-2113, Acting Regional Manager, Communications, Donna Burt
New Brunswick: 615 Prospect St. West, PO Box 2600, Fredericton NB E3B 5V6 – 506/452-3012; Fax: 506/452-3518, Regional Manager, Communications, Roch Rollin
Newfoundland: 167 Kenmount Rd., 2nd Fl., PO Box 12051, St. Johns NF A1B 3Z4 – 709/772-5346; Fax: 709/772-0444, Regional Manager, Communications, Bonnie Pope
Nova Scotia: Metropolitan Place, 99 Wyse Rd., PO Box 1350, Dartmouth NS B2Y 4B9 – 902/426-7859; Fax: 902/426-8724, Acting Regional Manager, Communications, Kathy Moggrtgi
Ontario: #900, 4900 Yonge St., Willowdale ON M2N 6A8 – 416/954-7604; Fax: 416/954-7822, Manager, Communications, Carole Gardner
Prince Edward Island: 85 Fitzroy St., PO Box 8000, Charlottetown PE C1A 8K1 – 902/566-7653; Fax: 902/566-7699, Communications Officer, Catherine McInnis
Québec: 1441, rue St. Urbain, Montréal PQ H3C 3L4 – 514/283-3180; Fax: 514/283-0123, Director, Communications, Léona Talbot
Saskatchewan: Financial Bldg., #814, 2101 Scarth St., Regina SK S4P 2H9 – 306/780-6249; Fax: 306/780-6221, Regional Manager, Communications, Brian Harris

Associated Agencies, Boards & Commissions
• Canadian Centre for Occupational Health & Safety
Listed alphabetically in detail, this section.
• Canadian Labour Force Development Board (CLFDB): 66 Slater St., 23rd Fl., Ottawa ON K1P 5H1 – 613/230-6264; Fax: 613/230-7681
Provides a unique partnership between business, labour, the four designated equality groups & the training & education community. Advises the government on a broad range of labour force development policies & programs. Provides development of a coordinated training system for Canada.
Co-Chair, Jean Andréa Bernard
Co-Chair, Jean-Claude Parrot
• Canada Labour Relations Board
Listed alphabetically in detail, this section.
• Labour Adjustment Review Board: Portage II, Place du Portage, 165 Hotel-de-ville St., Hull PQ K1A 0J2 – 819/997-2555; Fax: 819/997-1664
Chair, Renée Godmer
• Merchant Seamen Compensation Board: Portage II, Place du Portage, 165 Hotel-de-Ville St., Ottawa ON K1A 0J2 – 819/997-2555; Fax: 819/997-1664
Chair, Renée Godmer
Vice-Chair, Capt. Barry F. McKay
• National Aboriginal Management Board (NAMB): Portage IV, #4F00, 140, Promenade du Portage, Hull PQ K1A 0J9 – 819/994-2274

Determines human resouce development priorities regarding training & employment activities for aboriginal people.
Manager, Brian Chapman

IMMIGRATION & REFUGEE BOARD (IRB)/ Commission de l'immigration et du statut de réfugié
240 Bank St., Ottawa ON K1A 0K1
613/995-6486; Fax: 613/996-0270; URL: http://www.ncf.carleton.ca/freeport/government/federal/irb/menu

The IRB is responsible for immigration inquiries & detention reviews, immigration appeals &, refugee determination. It operates with a committment to providing both fair & efficient proceedings to all persons appearing before it. The Chair of the Board reports to government through the Minister of Citizenship and Immigration.

Chair, Nurjehan Mawani
Deputy Chair, John Frecker
Executive Director, Jean-Guy Fleury
Director General, Adjudication, Vacant
Director General, Documentation, Information & Research, Graham Howell
Director General, Finance & Administration, Alain Séguin
General Counsel, Legal Services, Philip Palmer
Director General, Programs, Policy & Standards Development Branch, Evelyn Lerine
Director, Communications, Robert Desperrier
Director, Information Services, Sam Ho
Director, Personnel, Sharon Fleming

INDIAN & NORTHERN AFFAIRS CANADA (INAC)/Affaires indiennes et du Nord Canada (AINC)
Tour Nord, Les Terrasses de la Chaudière, 10 Wellington St., Hull PQ K1A 0H4
819/997-0380; Fax: 819/953-3017; Email: InfoPubs@ inac.gc.ca; URL: http://www.inac.gc.ca/
Arctic Environmental Strategy: 819/994-7457
Environmental Action Program: 403/667-3180 (Yukon), 403/669-2589 (NWT)
Community Resource Mgmt. Programs: 403/669-2589
Indian Art Section: 819/994-1262
Inuit Art Section: 819/997-8307
Northern Information Network: 819/997-7281

The department fulfills the lawful obligations of the federal government to First nations & Inuit people arising from treaties, the Indian Act & other legislation. Has the primary federal mandate for providing basic services to registered Indians living on reserves, including the funding of First Nations for education, schools, housing, roads, water & sewage systems, & for the funding for social & family services. The Indian Act assigns specific trust responsibilities to the department with respect to Indian moneys, estates, & reserve lands, & creates responsibilities for elementary & secondary education & for band government. Negotiates & oversees the implementation of claims settlements, promotes economic development, & implements practical forms of self-government.

In the North, the department is responsible for assisting the development of political & economic institutions, managing sustainable development of natural resources, & protecting & rehabilitating the northern environment. INAC manages ongoing federal interests, including the administration of Crown land in the territories.

ACTS ADMINISTERED
Alberta Natural Resources Act
Arctic Waters Pollution Prevention Act
British Columbia Indian Cut-off Lands Settlement Act
British Columbia Indian Lands Settlement Act
British Columbia Indian Reserves Mineral Resources Act
British Columbia Treaty Commission Act
Canada Lands Surveys Act
Canada Oil & Gas Operations Act
Canada Petroleum Resources Act
Canadian Polar Commission Act
Caughnawaga Indian Reserve Act
Condominium Ordinance Validation Act
Cree-Naskapi (of Québec) Act
Department of Indian Affairs & Northern Development Act
Dominion Water Act
Fort Nelson Indian Reserve Minerals Revenue Sharing Act
Grassy Narrows & Islington Indian Bands Mercury Pollution Claims Settlement Act
Gwich'in Land Claim Settlement Act
Indian Act
Indian Lands Agreement (1986) Act
Indian Land Titles Act
Indian Land Titles Repeal Act
Indian Oil & Gas Act
Indian (Soldier Settlement) Act
James Bay & Northern Québec Native Claims Settlement Act
Manitoba Natural Resources Act
Manitoba Supplementary Provisions Act
Natural Resources Transfer (School Lands) Amendment Act
New Brunswick Indian Reserves Agreement Act
Northern Canada Power Commission (Share Issuance & Sale Authorization) Act
Northern Canada Power Commission Yukon Assets Disposal Authorization Act
Northwest Territories Act
Northwest Territories Waters Act
Nova Scotia Indian Reserves Agreement Act
Nunavut Act
Nunavut Land Claims Agreement Act
Pictou Landing Indian Band Agreement Act
Railway Belt Act
Railway Belt & Peace River Block Act
Railway Belt Water Act
St. Peters Indian Reserve Act
St. Regis Islands Act
Sahtu Dene & Metis Land Claim Settlement Act
Saskatchewan Natural Resources Act
Saskatchewan Treaty Land Entitlement Act
Sechelt Indian Band Self-Government Act
An Act for the settlement of certain questions between the Governments of Canada & Ontario respecting Indian Reserve Lands Act
Songhees Indian Reserve Act
Split Lake Cree First Nation Flooded Land Act
Territorial Lands Act
Western Arctic (Inuvialuit) Claims Settlement Act
Yukon Act
Yukon First Nations Land Claims Settlement Act
Yukon First Nations Self-Government Act
Yukon Placer Mining Act
Yukon Quartz Mining Act
Yukon Surface Rights Board Act
Yukon Waters Act

Minister, Hon. Ronald A. Irwin, C.M., Q.C., 819/997-0002, Fax: 819/953-4941
Deputy Minister, Scott Serson, 819/997-0133, Fax: 819/953-2251
Director, Indian Program & Funding Allocation Directorate, Al Horner, 819/953-9540

CLAIMS & INDIAN GOVERNMENT SECTOR
Asst. Deputy Minister, John Sinclair, 819/953-3180, Fax: 819/953-3246
Acting Director General, Claims Implementation Branch, Terry Henderson, 819/994-3434, Fax: 819/953-6430

Canadian Almanac & Directory 1997

3-74 GOVERNMENT OF CANADA

Director General, Comprehensive Claims Branch, Gordon Shanks, 819/997-8145, Fax: 819/953-4366

Director General, Specific Claims Branch, Rem Westland, 819/994-4924, Fax: 819/994-4924

Treaty Negotiation Offices

Vancouver: Comprehensive Claims Branch, #2700, 650 West Georgia St., PO Box 11576, Vancouver BC V6B 4N8 – 604/775-7114; Fax: 604/775-7149

Victoria: 535 Yates St., 2nd Fl., Victoria BC V8W 2Z6 – 250/363-6910; Fax: 250/363-6911

CORPORATE SERVICES SECTOR

Asst. Deputy Minister, Brent DiBartolo, 819/997-0020, Fax: 819/953-4094

Acting Director General, Departmental Audit & Evaluation Branch, Marie-France D'Auray-Boult, 819/994-1323

Director General, Finance Branch, Bill Austin, 819/997-0640, Fax: 819/953-8475

Director General, Human Resources Branch, James Dalzell, 819/997-9646, Fax: 819/953-1311

Director General, Information Management Branch, James Phillips, 819/994-3334

Director General, INAC Technical Services, Jim Davison, 819/994-6456, Fax: 819/953-9395

LANDS & TRUSTS SERVICES SECTOR

Acting Asst. Deputy Minister, John Graham, 819/953-5577

Director General, Lands & Environment Branch, John Graham, 819/994-7551, Fax: 819/953-3201

Director General, Registration, Revenues & Band Governance Branch, Gregor MacIntosh, 819/994-0951, Fax: 819/953-3371

NORTHERN AFFAIRS SECTOR

Asst. Deputy Minister, John Rayner, 819/953-3760, Fax: 819/953-6121

Director General, Sectoral Policy & Program Devolution Branch, John Berg, 819/997-9449, Fax: 819/997-0552

Director General, Natural Resources & Environment Branch, Hiram Beaubier, 819/997-9381, Fax: 819/953-8766

POLICY & STRATEGIC DIRECTION SECTOR

Asst. Deputy Minister, Jack Stagg, 819/994-7555, Fax: 819/953-9465

Director General, Communications Branch, Jean-Pierre Villeneuve, 819/997-9885, Fax: 819/953-9465

Director General, Government Relations Branch, George Da Pont, 819/953-4968, Fax: 819/953-9027

Director General, Legislation Branch, John Graham, 819/997-8212

Director General, Strategic Policy Branch, Ian Potter, 819/997-8359, Fax: 819/953-3320

Regional Offices

Alberta: #630, Canada Place, 9700 Jasper Ave., Edmonton AB T5J 4G2 – 403/495-2773; Fax: 403/495-4088, Regional Director General, Ken Kirby

Atlantic: 40 Havelock St., PO Box 160, Amherst NS B4H 3Z3 – 902/661-6200; Fax: 902/661-6237, Regional Director General, George Fotheringham

British Columbia: #340, 1550 Alberni St., Vancouver BC V6G 3C5 – 604/666-7891; Fax: 604/666-2546, Regional Director General, John Watson

Manitoba: #1100, 275 Portage Ave., Winnipeg MB R3B 3A3 – 204/983-4928; Fax: 204/983-7820, Regional Director General, Brenda Kustra

Northwest Territories: PO Box 1500, Yellowknife NT X1A 2R3 – 403/669-2500; Fax: 403/669-2709, Regional Director General, Warren Johnson

Ontario: 25 St. Clair Ave. East, 5th Fl., Toronto ON M4T 1M2 – 416/973-6234; Fax: 416/954-6329, Acting Regional Director General, John Donnelly

Québec: 320, rue St-Joseph est, CP 51127, Succ Comptoir postal, Québec PQ G1K 8Z7 – Fax: 418/648-4040, Ligne sans frais: 1-800-263-5592, Acting Regional Director General, Jérome Lapierre

Saskatchewan: 2221 Cornwall St., Regina SK S4P 4M2 – 306/780-5945; Fax: 306/780-5733, Regional Director General, Myler Savill

Yukon: #345, 300 Main St., Whitehorse YT Y1A 2B5 – 403/667-3100; Fax: 403/667-3196, Regional Director General, Mike Ivanski

Associated Agencies, Boards & Commissions

• Beverly & Qamanirjuaq Caribou Management Board: c/o 3565 Revelstoke Dr., Ottawa ON K1V 7B9 – 613/733-2007; Fax: 613/733-1304

Chairperson, Jerome Denechezhde

• British Columbia Treaty Commission: #203, 1155 West Pender St., Vancouver BC V6E 2P4 – 604/775-2075, Toll Free: 1-800-665-8330

Chief Commissioner, Alec Robertson, Q.C.

• Environmental Impact Review Board: PO Box 2120, Inuvik NT X0E 0T0 – 403/979-2828; Fax: 403/979-2610

• Environmental Impact Screening Committee Joint Secretariat: PO Box 2120, Inuvik NT X0E 0T0

• Indian Commission of Ontario: 14 Prince Arthur Ave., Toronto M5R 1A9 – 416/973-6390

Commissioner, Philip Goulet

• Indian Oil & Gas Canada (IOGC): #100, 9911 Chula Blvd., Tsuu T'ina (Sarcee) AB T2W 6H6 – 403/292-5625; Fax: 403/292-5618

CEO & Executive Director, W.J. Douglas, 403/292-5628, Fax: 403/292-4864

• Indian Taxation Advisory Board: 90 Elgin St., 2nd Fl., Ottawa ON K1A 0H4 – 613/954-9769; Fax: 613/954-2073; Email: admin-itab@itab.cactuscom.com; URL: http://itab.cactuscom.com/

• Nunavut Impact Review Board: PO Box 2264, Cambridge Bay NT X0E 0C0 – 403/983-2564; Fax: 403/983-2594

Contact, Larry Aknavigak

• Nunavut Implementation Commission: PO Box 1109, Iqaluit NT X0A 0H0 – 819/979-4199; Fax: 819/979-6862

Contact, John Amagoalik

• Nunavut Planning Commission: #1902, 130 Albert St., Ottawa ON K1P 5G4 – 613/238-1155; Fax: 613/238-5724

Contact, Bobby Lyall

• Nunavut Water Board: Gjoa Haven NT X0E 1J0

Contact, Thomas Kudlow

• Office of the Nunavut Environmental Scientist (NES): PO Box 1500, Yellowknife NT X1A 2R3 – 403/920-8200; Fax: 403/920-7809

Environmental Scientist, Lyn Hartley, 403/902-8238

• Porcupine Caribou Management Board: 35 Harbottle Rd., Whitehorse YT Y1A 5T2

Chairperson, Joe Tetlichi, 403/996-3930

Secretary Treasurer, Linda Hoffmann, 403/633-4780, Fax: 403/633-4780

INDUSTRY CANADA/Industrie Canada

C.D. Howe Bldg., 235 Queen St., Ottawa ON K1A 0H5 613/954-2788; Fax: 613/954-2303; URL: http://info.ic.gc.ca/ic-data/index.html; Strategis URL: http://strategis.ic.gc.ca

Publications: 613/954-5716; Fax: 613/952-9620

Access to Information & Privacy Rights Administration: 613/954-2752

Strategis Information: 1-800-328-6189

As Canada's flagship economic department, Industry Canada is now responsible for the majority of federal legislation & programs for business, science & consumer groups within a single federal department to better mobilize resources, merge complementary programs, & avoid duplication & overlap.

Responsible for national economic issues & provides policy advice, industry sector information & business services.

Industry Canada encourages international competitiveness & economic development, new technology development activities & formulates, integrates & coordinates regulations regarding industry & science. Provides strategic intelligence & helps industry develop & apply research & technology. Also provides reviews & updates of standards for the accurate measurement of products & services.

Nationally administers & enforces consumer legislation for identification & safe usage of products. Provides access to federal trade development services & programs & has developed the Canadian Technology Network to provide access for small & medium-sized companies to support services, data, information & strategic intelligence.

ACTS ADMINISTERED

Bankruptcy & Insolvency Act
Boards of Trade Act
Canadian Space Agency Act
Cape Breton Development Corporation Act
Communications Act, Department of
Companies' Creditors Arrangement Act
Competition Act
Competition Tribunal Act
Consumer & Corporate Affairs Act, Department of
Consumer Packaging & Labelling Act
Cooperative Associations Act, Canada
Copyright Act
Corporations Act, Canada
Corporations Act, Canada Business
Electricity & Gas Inspection Act
Farmers' Creditors Arrangement Act
Federal Business Development Bank Act
Government Companies Operation Act
Hazardous Products Act
Industrial Design Act
Industry, Science & Technology Act, Department of
Integrated Circuit Topography Act
Investment Canada Act
Lobbyists Registration Act
National Research Council Act
National Trade-mark & True Labelling Act
Natural Sciences & Engineering Research Council Act
"Parliament Hill" use of expression Act
Patent Act
Pawnbrokers Act
Pension Fund Societies Act
Precious Metals Marking Act
Public Documents Act
Public Officers Act
Public Servants Inventions Act
Radiocommunication Act
Seals Act
Small Business Loans Act
Social Sciences & Humanities Research Council Act
Standards Council of Canada Act
Statistics Act
Tax Rebate Discounting Act
Telecommunications Act
Textile Labelling Act
Timber Marking Act
Trade-marks Act
Trade Unions Act
Weights & Measures Act

The Department Also Participates in the Administration of the Following Statutes

Agricultural Products Standards Canada Act
Bills of Exchange Act
Broadcasting Act
Canada Agricultural Products Act
Canada Development Corporation Act
Cooperative Credit Associations Act
Corporations & Labour Unions Returns Act
Dairy Products Canada Act

Canadian Almanac & Directory 1997

Defence Prodution Act
Energy Supplies Emergency Act, 1979
Excise Act
Fish Inspection Act
Food & Drugs Act
Insurance Companies, Canadian & British, Act
Interest Act
Loan Companies Act
Maple Products Industry Act
National Transportation Act
Northern Pipeline Act
Publication of Statutes Act
Radiocommunications Act
Railway Act
Shipping Conferences Exemption Act, 1987
Teleglobe Canada Reorganization & Divestiture Act
Telesat Canada Reorganization & Divestiture Act
Trust Companies Act
Winding-up Act
Minister, Hon. John Manley, 613/995-9001, Fax: 613/954-4367
Secretary of State, Science, Research & Development, Hon. Jon Gerrard, 613/995-9001, Fax: 613/990-4056
Deputy, Minister, H. Swain, 613/992-4292
Assoc. Deputy Minister, Kevin Lynch, 613/954-0709
Assoc. Deputy Minister, Shirley Serafini
Special Advisor to the DM, Claire Monette, 613/954-2873
Special Advisor to the DM, Charles Stedman, 613/954-3589
Executive Director, Science & Technology Review Secretariat, Vacant, 613/943-7034
Director General, Audit & Evaluation Branch, Owen Taylor, 613/954-5084, Fax: 613/954-4070
Director General, Communications Branch, Francine Chabot-Plante, 613/943-2507, Fax: 613/952-9620
Director General, Finance Branch, George Willis, 613/957-9288, Fax: 613/998-6950
Director General, Human Resources Branch, Tom Wright, 613/954-5474

Legal Services
General Counsel, Commercial Law, Doug Lewis, 613/954-5340, Fax: 613/954-9536
General Counsel, Competition & Consumer Law Division, F. Côté, 613/953-3884

Office of Consumer Affairs
235 Queen St., Ottawa ON K1A 0H5
Director General, V. Watson, 613/954-3277
Director, Outreach Programs, A. Blauveldt, 613/952-8025
Director, Government Liaison & Policy Coordination, K. Ellis, 613/952-1971

Office of the Corporate Secretary
613/943-7039; Fax: 613/952-0273
Corporate Secretary, John MacKillop, 613/943-7038
Deputy Corporate Secretary, Philippe Bussy, 613/943-7040
Manager, Executive Correspondence & Records Centre, Cécile Langelier, 613/943-7072

Office of the Ethics Counsellor
66 Slater St., 22nd Fl., Ottawa ON K1A 0C9
416/995-0721; Fax: 416/995-7308
Ethics Counsellor, Howard Wilson, 613/995-6852
Director, Lobbyist Registration Branch, Corinne MacLaurin, Place du Portage, Phase I, 50 Victoria St., 4th Fl., Hull PQ K1A 0C9, 819/957-2760, Fax: 819/757-3078
Director, Operations, Robert F. Benson, 613/995-7374
Director, Policy, Planning & Procedures, Cornelius von Baeyer, 613/996-3920

Tourism Canada
Director General, Doug Fyfe, 613/957-4200

Director, Asia-Pacific Marketing, K. de Bellefeuille-Percy, 613/954-3975
Acting Director, Canada Marketing, L. Barber, 613/954-3961
Director, Europe Marketing, M. Tremblay, 613/954-3838
Director, Research & Information Management, B. Stevens, 613/954-3882
Acting Director, USA Marketing, T. Penny, 613/954-3874

BUREAU OF COMPETITION POLICY
Place du Portage, Tour I, 50, rue Victoria, 21e étage, Hull PQ K1A 0C9
613/994-0798; Fax: 613/953-5013
Director, Investigation & Research, George Addy, 819/997-3301
Director General, Compliance & Operations, Mary Zamparo, 819/953-7942
Director General, Consumer Products, Zane Brown, 613/953-3187, Fax: 613/953-2931
Director General, Economics & International Affairs, Val Traversy, 819/953-3318, Fax: 819/953-6400
Senior Deputy Director, Mergers, Francine Matte, 819/994-1860, Fax: 819/953-6169
Deputy Director, Civil Matters, Gilles Menard, 819/997-1209, Fax: 819/953-8546
Acting Deputy Director, Criminal Matters, D. Mercer, 613/997-1208
Deputy Director, Marketing Practices, Rachel Larabie-LeSieur, 819/997-1231, Fax: 819/953-2557
Head, Amendments, Harry S. Chandler, 819/997-7669

INDUSTRY & SCIENCE POLICY
Asst. Deputy Minister, Andrei Sulzenko, 613/995-9605, Fax: 613/995-2233
Director, Investments (Investment Canada Act), Andrei Sulzenko, 613/995-9605
Director General, Corporate Governance, David Tobin, 613/952-0211, Fax: 613/952-1980
Director General, Entrepreneurship & Small Business Office, P. Sager, 613/954-5489
Director General, Internal Trade, Consultations & Federal-Provincial Relations, T. Wallace, 613/954-9633
Director General, International Business, R. Watkins, 613/954-3508, Fax: 613/952-0540
Acting Director General, Micro-Economic Policy Analysis, D. Gauthier, 613/941-9224
Director General, Science Promotion & Academic Affairs, Doug Hull, 613/993-6857, Fax: 613/952-2307
Director General, Science Strategy, Ozzie Silverman, 613/991-9472, Fax: 613/996-7887
Director General, Strategic Policy, Jerry Beausoleil, 613/954-3558, Fax: 613/952-8761
Director, Operations, G. Dingledine, 613/941-0624
Asst. Secretary, National Advisory Council on Science & Technology Secretariat, Vacant, 613/998-1306, Fax: 613/990-2007

INDUSTRY SECTOR
Senior Asst. Deputy Minister, John Banigan, 613/954-3798, Fax: 613/941-1134
Director General, Advanced Materials & Plastics, John Mihalus, 613/954-3064
Director General, Aerospace & Defence, William Laycock, 613/954-3343, Fax: 613/941-2379
Director General, Automotive, Slawek Skorupinski, 613/954-3797, Fax: 613/952-8088
Director General, Coordination & Management Services, Bruce Deacon, 613/954-3801, Fax: 613/957-8912
Director General, Fashion Leisure & Household Products, Richard Pageau, 613/954-3585, Fax: 613/954-3107
Director General, Environmental Affairs, Lucien Bradet, 613/954-3080, Fax: 613/952-9564

Director General, Forest Industries & Building Products, Rocco Delvecchio, 613/954-3082, Fax: 613/952-8988
Director General, Manufacturing & Processing Technologies, M. McCuaig-Johnston, 613/954-3279, Fax: 613/941-2463
Director General, Service Industries & Capital Projects, D. DeMelto, 613/954-2990
Director, Chemicals & Bio-Industries, G. Michaliszyn, 613/954-3071, Fax: 613/952-4209
Director, Health Industries, D. Hoye, 613/954-5258
Director, Metals & Minerals Processing, C. Ethier, 613/954-3176
Director, Transportation Industries, G. Leclaire, 613/954-2949
Director, Women's Bureau, Johanne Roberge, 613/954-3130, Fax: 613/954-4301

OPERATIONS
Asst. Deputy Minister, Jean-François Martin, 613/954-3405, Fax: 613/954-4883
Associate Asst. Deputy Minister, Jacques Lyrette, 613/954-3406
Director General, Corporations, M. Walsh, 613/941-2837
Director General, Legal Metrology, Allan Johnston, 613/952-0655
Director General, Management Consulting, Norm Fraser, 613/954-5592, Fax: 613/954-0017
Director General, Management Services & Facilities Management, Y. Moisan, 613/954-3750
Director General, Strategic Planning & Corporate Development, Michael Jenkin, 613/952-8075
Administrator, Regional Development, Ontario (FEDNOR), Hal McGonigal, 705/942-1327, Fax: 705/942-5434
Correspondence Officer, L. Fournier, 613/954-2880
Director, Operations, R.A. Porter, 613/954-3449
Director, Programs & Services, Serge Croteau, 613/954-5533, Fax: 613/952-2635
Director, Small Business Loans Administration, M.-J. Thivierge, 613/954-5556
Director, Small Business Loans Re-engineering, C. Edlund, 613/954-4578

Aboriginal Business Canada
235 Queen St., Ottawa ON K1A 0H5
Executive Director, B. Dickson, 613/954-5430
Acting Director, Aboriginal Capital Corporation, D. McDougall, 904/666-0744
Director, East, D. Elgie, 416/-954-6870
Director, West, L. Gates, 604/666-8514

Canadian Intellectual Property Office (CIPO)
Place du Portage, Tour I, 50, rue Victoria, Hull PQ K1A 0C9
EMail: CIPO.CONTACT@ic.gc.ca; URL: http://info.ic.ca/opengov/cipo/inq/inq_e.html
Acting CEO & Commissioner, Patents & Registrar, Trademarks, Anthony McDonough
Executive Director, Jean Gariépy, 819/953-2990, Fax: 819/997-1890
Acting Chair, Patent Appeal Board, Peter Davies, 819/953-9067, Fax: 819/997-1890
Chair, Trade-Marks Opposition Board, Gary Partington, 819/994-4794, Fax: 819/997-1890
Director, Automated Systems, Ray Taylor, 819/997-2186, Fax: 819/953-5059
Director & Registrar, Copyright & Industrial Design, Linda Steingarten, 819/997-1657, Fax: 819/953-6977
Director, Finance & Administration, Brenda Snarr, 819/997-3024, Fax: 819/997-2987
Director, Human Resources, Élise Morin, 819/997-2673, Fax: 819/997-2987
Director, Information, Ed Rymek, 819/994-4775, Fax: 819/953-7620
Director, Marketing, C. McDermott, 819/953-6131

Director, Patent, Anthony McDonough, 819/953-5864, Fax: 819/994-1989
Director, Planning, International & Regulatory Affairs, Douglas Kuntze, 819/953-9090, Fax: 819/997-1890
Director, Trade-Marks, Barbara Bova, 819/997-2423, Fax: 819/997-1421

Communications Research Centre & Centre for Information Technologies Innovation
3701 Carling Ave., PO Box 11490, Stn H, Ottawa ON K2H 8S2
613/998-2264
President, Jacques Lyrette, 613/990-3929, Fax: 613/990-7983
Executive Vice-President, Stewart McCormick, 613/998-2768, Fax: 613/998-9875
President, CITI Board of Directors (Montreal), P. Lortie, 514/744-7950
President, CRC Board of Directors (Edmonton), W. Dunbar, 403/668-5355
Vice-President, Communications Systems Research, Robert Huck, 613/998-2329, Fax: 613/990-6339
Vice-President, Radio Communications & Broadcast Research, William Sawchuk, 613/998-2332, Fax: 613/990-7986
Director General, Centre for Information Technologies Innovation, Mario Drouin, 1575, boul Chomedey, Laval PQ H7V 2X2, 514/973-5702, Fax: 514/973-5858
Director, Pan Canadian Network of Research Centres, M. Century, 514/973-5737
Director, Technology & Society, G. DeCouvreur, 514/973-5790

Office of the Chief Information Officer
235 Queen St., Ottawa ON K1A 0H5
Chief Information Officer, Grant Westcott, 613/954-3574, Fax: 613/941-4615
Director General, Strategic Information, David Waung, 613/952-6368, Fax: 613/990-4848
Director General, Information Technology, Vacant
Acting Director, Computing & Telecommunications, M. Ozols, 613/954-2634
Acting Director, Customer Service, A. Bettinger, 613/954-2612
Director, Information Management, N. Charlebois, 613/952-5817
Director, National Secretariat, Canadian Business Service Centres, R. Smith, 613/954-3576
Director, Product Operations, Vacant, 613/954-4969
Director, Publishing & Product Development, Vacant, 613/952-5817
Director, Strategic Directions & Planning, S. Talbert, 613/954-2622

Office of the Superintendent of Bankruptcy
Journal Tower South, 365 Laurier St. West, 8th Fl., Ottawa ON K1A 0C8
613/941-1000; Fax: 613/941-2862
Superintendent, George Redling
Deputy Superintendent, Operations, J. Armstrong
Deputy Superintendent, Policy, Programs & Regulatory Affairs, Marc Mayrand
Manager, Revenue & Adminstration Services, Steve Simpson

Regional Offices
Atlantic: Central Guaranty Trust Tower, 1801 Hollis St., 5th Fl., PO Box 940, Stn M, Halifax NS B3J 2V9
Executive Director, Robert Russell
Senior Trade Commissioner, B. Giacomin, 902/426-9362
Director, Trade, D. Punter, 902/426-6125
Ontario: 1 Front St. West, 4th Fl., Toronto ON M5J 1A4

Executive Director & Executive Director, Canada-Ontario Infrastructure Works Program, William Cram, 416/973-5001
Senior Trade Commissioner, D. Valentine, 416/954-6326
Director, Consumer Products, S. Allan, 519/954-5453
Director, Canada/Ontario Business Service Centre, A. Anderson, 519/954-8593
Director, Industry, G. Cooper, 519/973-5173
Director, Infrastructure, S. Hertzberg, 519/973-5153
Pacific: #2000, 300 West Georgia St., Vancouver BC V6B 5E1
Executive Director, Barbara Fulton, 604/666-1400
Director, International Trade Centre, R. Pedersen, 604/666-8888
Director, Planning, Analysis & Sector Team Coordination, B. Andersen, 604/666-1414
Director, Spectrum & Consumer Operations, B. Drake, 604/666-5507
Acting Director, Corporate Services, H. Hickey, 604/666-4663
Prairies: Canada Place, #540, 9700 Jasper Ave., Edmonton AB T5J 4C3
Executive Director, G. Fields, 403/495-2951
Senior Trade Commissioner, J. Graham, 403/495-4415
Director, Consumer Products, D. McElheran, 204/983-2843
Director, Industry & Director, Alberta, D. Letilley, 403/495-3327
Director, Spectrum & Director, Manitoba, K. Paterson, 204/983-4395
Acting Director, Tourism, Small Business & Service Industries & Director, Saskatchewan, R. Morin, 306/975-4318
Québec: 5, Place Ville Marie, 7e étage, Montréal PQ H3B 2G2
Executive Director, D. Boudrias, 514/283-1885
Director, Consumer Products, J. Lambert, 514/283-2453
Director, Industrial Development, R. Noël, 514/283-7375
Director, International Trade Centre, B. Goulet, 514/283-4160
Director, Marketing Practices, R. Malo, 514/283-3970
Director, Tourism Industries, A. Samuelli, 514/283-4015
Manager, Aboriginal Business Canada, C. DeCroix, 514/283-1837

SPECTRUM, INFORMATION TECHNOLOGIES & TELECOMMUNICATIONS
Journal Tower North, 300 Slater St., 20th Fl., Ottawa ON K1A 0C8
Asst. Deputy Minister, Michael Binder, 613/998-0368, Fax: 613/952-1203
Director General, Community Development & Planning, David Mulcaster, 561/990-4294, Fax: 561/957-8839
Chair, Information Highway Advisory Council, D. Johnston, 613/993-3522
Executive Director, Information Highway Advisory Council, P. Liebel, 613/993-3085
Director General, Information Technologies Industry, Tim Garrard, 613/954-5599, Fax: 613/952-8419
Director General, Information Highway Advisory Council, Parke Davis, 613/990-4262, Fax: 613/941-1164
Director General, Radiocommunications & Broadcasting Regulatory, J. Skora, 613/990-4817, Fax: 613/993-4433
Director General, Spectrum Engineering, Ronald Begley, 613/990-4820, Fax: 613/954-6091
Director General, Telecommunications Policy, Michael Helm, 613/998-4241, Fax: 613/998-1256

Associated Agencies, Boards & Commissions
•Standards Council of Canada (SCC): #1200, 45 O'Connor St., Ottawa ON K1P 6N7 – 613/238-3222;
Fax: 613/995-4564; URL: http://www.scc.ca/indexe.html – Sales Department: 1-800-267-8220
A non-regulatory body which administers the National Standards System, a federation of Canadian governments & organizations that develop standards & test products to specific standards.
President, Richard Lafontaine
Executive Director, Michael McSweeney
•National Advisory Council on Science & Technology (ACST): 240 Sparks St., 8th Fl. West, Ottawa ON K1A 0H5 – 613/990-2007; Fax: 613/990-6260; Email: nabst@ic.gc.ca; URL: http://info.ic.gc.ca/opengov/nabst/nabst.html
Newly formed Council, created with the mandate to review the nation's performance in science & technology innovation, identify emerging issues & provide advice on future developments.
Chair, Hon. John Manley, 613/995-9001
Vice-Chair & Secretary of State, Science, Research & Development, Hon. Jon Gerrard

INFORMATION COMMISSIONER OF CANADA/
Commissaire à l'information du Canada
Tower B, Place de Ville, 112 Kent St., 3rd Fl., Ottawa ON K1A 1H3
613/995-2410; Fax: 613/995-1501; URL: http://infoweb.magi.com/ZXaccessca/oic.html
Toll Free: 1-800-267-0441
The Commissioner investigates complaints that Federal Government departments & agencies have not complied with the Access to Information Act.
Information Commissioner, John W. Grace
Deputy Information Commissioner, Alan Leadbeater
Director General, Investigations, Dan Dupuis
Legal Counsel, Paul Tetro

Office of INTERGOVERNMENTAL AFFAIRS/ Bureau des affaires intergouvernementales
c/o Privy Council Office, Langevin Block, 80 Wellington St., Ottawa ON K1A 0A3
URL: http://www.aia.gc.ca/
Federal government office responsible for the management of federal-provincial relations. The office supports the Prime Minister and the Minister of Intergovernmental Affairs & works closely with other federal and provincial departments & territorial governments to cover a variety of areas in which the federal government, the provinces & the territories are involved.
Operations of the office are divided into four secretariats: Policy and Research Secretariat, Intergovernmental Communications Secretariat, Federal-Provincial Relations Secretariat, Aboriginal Affairs Secretariat. The Office of Intergovernmental Affairs is a branch of the Privy Council Office.
Minsiter Responsible, Hon. Stéphane Dion, 613/943-1838, Fax: 613/943-8377
Deputy Minister, George Anderson, 613/947-7569, Fax: 613/947-7580
Information Contact, Gerard Simoneau, 613/957-5262, Fax: 613/957-5154

INTERNATIONAL BOUNDARY COMMISSION/
Commission de la frontière internationale
615 Booth St., Ottawa ON K1A 0E9
613/992-1294; Fax: 613/947-1337
This Commission has jurisdiction over regulation & maintenance of the Canada-US boundary in accordance with the Boundary Treaty of 1925, & the International Boundary Commission Act, RSC 1985, c. I-16.
Commissioner, Canadian Section, Mike O'Sullivan, 613/995-4341

Commissioner, United States Section, Thomas Baldini, 202/736-9007

INTERNATIONAL DEVELOPMENT RESEARCH CENTRE (IDRC)/Centre de recherches pour le développement international (CRDI)
PO Box 8500, Ottawa ON K1G 3H9
613/236-6163; Fax: 613/238-7230; Email: info@idrc.ca; URL: http://www.idrc.ca
Gopher: gopher.idrc.ca; Telnet: ddbs.idrc.ca
IDRC Report on the WWW: http:www.idrc.ca/books/reports
 Through support for research, IDRC assists scientists in developing countries to identify long-term, practical solutions to pressing developmental problems.
Chair, Flora MacDonald
President, Dr. Keith Bezanson
Vice-President, Corporate Services Branch, Pierre Beemans
Vice-President, Programs Branch, Caroline Pestieau
Information Officer, Public Information Program, Barbara Davidson, 613/236-6163, ext. 2460
Information Officer, Public Information Program, Pauline Dole
Vice-President & CEO, Finance & Administration, Ray Audet

Regional Offices
Southeast & East Asia: IDRC, Tanglin, PO Box 101, Singapore 9124, Republic of Singapore – (011-65) 235-1344; Fax: (011-65) 235-1849; Telex: RS 61061; Cable: IDRECENTRE SINGAPORE
East & South Asia: IDRC, PO Box 62084, Nairobi, Kenya – (011-254-2) 7131601; Fax: (011-254-2) 711063
Latin America & the Caribbean: Centro Internacional de Investigaciones para el Desarrollo, Casilla de Correos 6379, Montevideo, Uruguay – (011-598-2) 92-20-31/34; Fax: (011-598-2) 92-02-23
Middle East & North Africa: PO Box 14, Orman, Giza, Cairo, Egypt – (011-20-2) 336-7051; Fax: (011-20-2) 336-7056
South Africa: IDRC, Braamfontein Centre, 23 Jorissen St., 9th Fl., Braamfontein, Johannesburg 2001, South Africa – (011-27-11) 403-3952; Fax: (011-27-11) 403-1417
South Asia: IDRC, 17 Jor Bagh, New Delhi 110 003, India – (011-91-11) 461-9411; Fax: (011-91-11) 462-2707; Telex: 3161536 IDRC IN
West & Central Africa: CRDI, CD Annexe, CP 11007, Dakar, Sénégal – (011-221) 24-42-31; Fax: (011-221) 25-32-55; Telex: 21674 RECENTRE SG; Cable: RECENTRE DAKAR

INTERNATIONAL JOINT COMMISSION (IJC)/ Commission mixte internationale (CMI)
100 Metcalfe St., Ottawa ON K1P 5M1
613/995-2984; Fax: 613/993-5583
Great Lakes Water Quality Information: 519/257-6700
 Under the Boundary Waters Treaty, this Commission has jurisdiction over certain questions arising between Canada & the United States, involving the use & regulation of waters forming or crossing the common boundary; it also has certain advisory responsibilities relating to transboundary air quality.
Acting Chair, Dr. Pierre Béland
Commissioner, Francis Murphy, Q.C.
Acting Secretary, Dr. Murray Claymen

United States Section
#100, 1250 - 23 St. NW, Washington DC 20440
202/736-9000; Fax: 202/736-9015
Chair, Thomas L. Baldini
Commissioner, Susan B. Bayh

Commissioner, Alice B. Chamberlin
Secretary, Kathy Prosser

Canada/United States-Great Lakes Regional Water Quality Agreement
Information: 519/257-6700
Director, Great Lakes Regional Office, Doug McTavish

JUSTICE CANADA
Justice Bldg., 239 Wellington St., Ottawa ON K1A 0H8
613/957-4222; Fax: 613/954-0811; URL: http://canada.justice.gc.ca/
Toll Free Firearms Act Info: 1-800-731-4000
 Provides legal services to the Government of Canada, including its departments & agencies, & supervises the administration of justice in governmental affairs.

ACTS ADMINISTERED
Access to Information Act
Annulment of Marriages (Ontario) Act
Bills of Lading Act
 Canada Evidence Act
Canada Prize Act
Canada-United Kingdom Civil & Commercial Judgements Convention Act
Canadian Bill of Rights
Canadian Human Rights Act
Canadian Laws Offshore Application Act
Commercial Arbitration Act (2nd Supp.)
Contraventions Act
Criminal Code
Crown Liability Act & Proceedings
Department of Justice Act
Divorce Act (2nd Supp.)
Escheats Act
Expropriation Act
Extradition Act
Family Orders & Agreements Enforcement Assistance Act (2nd. Supp.)
Federal Court Act
Federal Real Property Act
Foreign Enlistment Act
Foreign Extraterritorial Measures Act
Fugitive Offenders Act
Garnishment, Attachment & Pension Diversion Act
Identification of Criminals Act
International Sale of Goods Contracts Convention Act
Interpretation Act
Judges Act
Marriage (Prohibited Degrees) Act
Mutual Legal Assistance in Criminal Matters Act (2nd Supp.)
Narcotic Control Act
Official Languages Act (4th Supp.)
Official Secrets Act
Permanent Court of International Justic Act
Postal Services Interruption Relief Act
Privacy Act
Revised Statutes of Canada Act (3rd Supp.)
Security Offenses Act
State Immunity Act
Statute Revision Act
Statutory Instruments Act
Supreme Court Act
Tax Court of Canada Act
Tobacco Restraint Act
United Nations Foreign Arbitral Awards Convention Act (2nd Supp.)
Young Offenders Act
Minister & Attorney General, Hon. Allan Rock, Q.C., 613/992-4621, Fax: 613/990-7255
Deputy Minister & Deputy Attorney General, George M. Thomson, Q.C., 613/957-4997, Fax: 613/941-2279
Assoc. Deputy Minister, Canadian Unity, Mary Elizabeth Dawson, 613/957-4898, Fax: 613/952-4279
Assoc. Deputy Minister, Richard Thompson

CIVIL LAW & CORPORATE MANAGEMENT SECTOR
Asst. Deputy Minister, Vacant, 613/941-4073
Acting Assoc. Deputy Minister, Lionel Levert, Q.C., 613/957-4660
Corporate Counsel, Deborah McNair, 613/952-1578
Director General, Corporate Management Policy, Systems & Services Directorate, Richard Asselin, 613/941-4095
Director General, Human Resources Directorate, Fiona Spencer, 613/941-1885
Director General, Information Management Directorate, Bob Wilson, 613/941-3444
Senior General Counsel, Civil Litigation & Real Property Law (Québec) Section, Jean-Claude Marcotte, 613/957-4670
General Counsel, Civil Code Section, Louise Sabourin-Hébert, 613/941-0375
Acting Senior Counsel, Legal Education Division, Marie-Claude Turgeon, 613/952-2271
Director, Renewal Secreatariat, Michel Valée, 613/991-8212

COMMUNICATIONS & EXECUTIVE SERVICES BRANCH
Director General, Dawn Nicholson-O'Brien, 613/957-4221, Fax: 613/941-2329
Director, Operations & Minsterial Services, Wendy Sailman, 613/957-4211
Director, Planning, Advice & Program Communications, Courtney Garneau, 613/957-4219
Director, Publishing & Corporate Communications, Marie-Claire Wallace, 613/957-4216
Head, Media Relations, Irène Arsenault, 613/957-4207
Coordinator, Firearms, Darryl Davies, 613/957-9419

LEGAL OPERATIONS SECTOR
Asst. Deputy Minister, Mark Jewett, 613/996-4667
Asst. Deputy Attorney General, Aboriginal Affairs, Kathie MacCormick, 613/957-4626
Asst. Deputy Minister, Business Law & Counsel to Industry Canada, Konrad von Finckenstein, Q.C., 613/954-3946
Asst. Deputy Attorney General, Citizenship & Immigration, John Sims, 613/994-2277
Asst. Deputy Attorney General, Civil Litigation Branch, Ted Thompson, Q.C., 613/957-4840
Asst. Deputy Attorney General, Criminal Law, Daniel Bellemare, Q.C., 613/957-4756
Asst. Deputy Attorney General, Tax Law Branch, Ian MacGregor, Q.C., 613/957-4811
Chief General Counsel, General Counsel Group, Ivan Whitehall, Q.C., 613/957-4801
Senior General Counsel, Native Law Sector, Fred Caron, 613/957-4972
General Counsel, Aboriginal Justice, David Arnot, 613/957-4717
Senior General Counsel, Admiralty & Maritime Law Sector, Alfred Popp, Q.C., 613/957-4666
Senior General Counsel & Director, Criminal Law Sector, William Corbett, Q.C., 613/957-4765
Senior General Counsel, Indian & Northern Affairs Canada, William Elliott, 613/994-4141
Senior General Counsel & Director, National Strategy for Drug Prosecutions, Paul Kennedy, 613/952-7553

LEGISLATIVE SERVICES BRANCH
Acting Director, Legislation Section, Don Maurais, 613/957-0011
Chief Legislative Editor, Legislative Editing & Publishing Services, Robert DuPerron, 613/957-0005
Senior General Counsel, Regulations Section, Ginette Williams, 613/957-0065

POLICY SECTOR
Asst. Deputy Minister, Criminal Policy, Richard Mosley, 613/957-4725
Executive Director, National Crime Prevention Council Secretariat, Elaine Scott, 613/957-9639

Director, Consultation Division, Nancy DeClerq, 613/957-4217
Director General, Programs Directorate, Mehat Ajit, 613/957-4344
Director General, Research, Statistics & Evaluation Directorate, Richard Berger, 613/957-8281
Director General, Social Policy Section, Susan Campbell, 613/957-1524
Coordinator, Conviction Review Group, Eugene Williams, 613/957-4784
Coordinator, Firearms Control Task Group, James Hayes, 613/941-3586
Coordinator, Sentencing Team, Gordon Parry, 613/957-4720
Senior General Counsel, Corporate Policy Group, David Paget, 613/952-8755
General Counsel, Criminal Law Policy Section, Yvan-Paul Roy, 613/957-4728
General Consel, Family & Youth Law Policy Section, Glenn Rivard, 613/941-2339

Regional Offices
Edmonton: Bank of Montreal Tower, #211, 10199 - 101 St., Edmonton AB T5J 3Y4 – 403/495-2970; Fax: 403/495-2970, General Counsel, David Gates
Halifax: 5161 George St., 4th Fl., Halifax NS B3J 1M7 – 902/426-7592; Fax: 902/426-2329, General Counsel, Ted K. Tax
Montréal: Complexe Guy-Favreau, Tour Est, 200, boul René-Lévesque ouest, 9e étage, Montréal PQ H2Z 1X4 – 514/283-4972; Fax: 514/283-3856, Senior General Counsel, Jacques Letellier, c.r.
Saskatoon: 229 - 4 Ave. South, 7th Fl., Saskatoon SK S7K 4K3 – 306/975-4761; Fax: 306/975-5013, General Counsel, Pat MacLean, Q.C.
Regina Sub Office: #603, 1800 Hamilton St., Regina SK S4P 4L2
306/780-5080
Toronto: #3400, First Canadian Place, PO Box 36, Stn First Canadian Place, Toronto ON M5X 1K6 – 416/973-3102; Fax: 416/983-3636, Senior General Counsel, Paul Evraire
Vancouver: #2800, Royal Centre, 1055 West Georgia St., PO Box 11118, Vancouver BC V6E 3P9 – 604/666-0131; Fax: 604/661-2760, General Counsel, J. Bissell, Q.C.
Whitehorse: #200, 300 Main St., Whitehorse YT Y1A 2B5 – 403/667-8103; Fax: 403/668-4809, General Counsel, Judith Bowers
Winnipeg: #301, Centennial House, 310 Broadway, Winnipeg MB R3C 0S6 – 204/983-2252; Fax: 204/983-3636, General Counsel, D.G. Frayer, Q.C.
Yellowknife: Joe Tobie Bldg., 5020 - 48th St., Yellowknife NT X1A 2N1 – 403/920-7711; Fax: 403/920-4022, General Counsel, Pierre Rousseau

Associated Agencies, Boards & Commissions
• Office of Conflict Resolution: 239 Wellington St., Ottawa ON K1A 0H8 – 613/941-1993; Fax: 613/952-8538

LAURENTIAN PILOTAGE AUTHORITY CANADA/Administration de pilotage de Laurentides Canada
Tour de la Bourse, 715, Sq. Victoria, 6e étage, CP 680, Montréal PQ H4Z 1J9
514/283-6320; Fax: 514/496-2409; URL: http://canada.gc.ca/depts/agencies/lpaind_e.html
The Authority provides pilotage services in the province of Québec, north of St. Lambert Lock. Reports to government through the Minister of Transport.
President, Jean-Claude Michaud
Director, Operations, Clément Deschênes
Secretary, Guy P. Major
Treasurer, Yvon Martel

LIBRARY OF PARLIAMENT/ Bibliothèque du Parlement
111 Wellington St., Ottawa ON K1A 0A9
613/995-1166; Fax: 613/992-1269
The Library of Parliament is administered by the Parliamentary Librarian appointed by the Crown. The library maintains a basic collection of 616,000 books, documents, periodicals, microfilm, video tapes & a diversity of automated information retrieval services. Staff provides information, reference & research services to Parliament, its officers & personnel, Parliamentary committees & Parliamentary associations. As of July 1995, the Library of Parliament has responsibility over the Public Information Office (PIO).
Parliamentary Librarian, Richard Paré
Associate Parliamentary Librarian, Vacant
Director General, Information & Technical Services Branch, François LeMay
Director General, Research Branch, Hugh Finsten
Director General, Administration & Personnel Branch, Jean-Jacques Cardinal

MARINE ATLANTIC INC.
100 Cameron St., Moncton NB E1C 5Y6
506/851-3600; Fax: 506/851-3615
Marine Atlantic Inc. operates passenger, auto & freight ferry services throughout Atlantic Canada under contract to the federal government. The company reports to the Minister of Transport.
President & CEO, R.J. Morrison
Executive Vice-President, J. Laurie Brean
Vice-President, Finance & Administration, D.J. Weaver
Vice-President, Human Resources, Bud Harbidge
Vice-President, Operations, M.O. Ryder
Vice-President, Public Affairs, Passenger Services & Marketing, D.G. Newman
Vice-President, Safety & Regulatory Affairs, Bud Streeter
Director, Public Relations, T.G. Bartlett

MEDICAL RESEARCH COUNCIL OF CANADA/Conseil de recherches médicales Canada
Tower B, Holland Cross, 1600 Scott St., 5th Fl., Ottawa ON K1A 0W9
613/954-1809; Fax: 613/954-1800; Email: mrcinfocrm@hpb.hwc.ca; URL: http://hpb1.hwc.ca:8100/
Queen Elizabeth II Canadian Research Fund: 613/954-1814
Promotes basic, applied & clinical research in the health sciences through funding assistance & manages a health-related centre of excellence network.
The primary function of the MRC is to assist & promote basic, applied, & clinical research in Canada in the health sciences. Research is carried out in universities, in the health sciences faculties, affiliated hospitals & institutions & other departments & faculties when the research projects are highly relevant to human health. University-Industry programs create the opportunity for collaboration between Canadian companies & researchers now conducting research in Canadian universities or affliated institutions. The Council also manages the health-related networks of centres of excellence.
President, Dr. Henry Friesen
Executive Director, Ian Shugart
Director, Business Development, Marc LePage
Director, Communications & Information Branch, Denis Saint-Jean, 613/954-1812
Director, Finance, Guy D'Aloisio
Director, Innovation Teams, Dr. F.S. Rolleston
Director, Programs, Dr. Elizabeth Dickson
Deputy Director, Public Affairs, Neil Morris, 613/954-1958
Director, University-Industry Programs, Vacant
Secretary to Council, Mary-Anne Lipke

NATIONAL ADVISORY COUNCIL ON AGING/ Conseil consultatif national sur le troisième âge
Postal Locator 4203A, Ottawa ON K1A 0K9
613/957-1968; Fax: 613/957-7627; Email: seniors@hpb.hwc.ca; URL: http://hpb1.hwc.ca/datahpsb/seniors/senpage.html
Physical Address: 473 Albert St., 3rd Fl., Ottawa ON K1A 0K9
The Council advises the Minister of Health on matters relating to the quality of Canada's aging population. It reviews the needs & problems of seniors & recommends remedial action; consults with institutions & groups involved in aging or representing seniors; publishes reports; disseminates information & stimulates public discussion on aging.
Minister Responsible, Hon. David C. Dingwall, 819/996-1154
Chair, John Edward MacDonell
Communications Officer, Renée Blanchet

NATIONAL ARCHIVES OF CANADA/ Archives nationales du Canada
395 Wellington St., Ottawa ON K1A 0N3
613/995-5138; Fax: 613/995-6274; URL: http://www.archives.ca/
Reference Desk: 613/995-5138
The National Archives of Canada is a research institution responsible for acquiring archival material "every kind, nature & description" concerning all aspects of Canadian life & the development of the country. It provides research services & facilities to make this material available to the public. In addition, as part of the federal government admininstration, it has broad responsibilities with regard to the promotion of efficiency & economy in the management of government records. The National Archives includes private papers, public records, machine-readable archives, maps, paintings, photographs, films, sound recordings & books on Canadian history & related subject fields. Reports to government through the Minister of Canadian Heritage.
National Archivist, J.-P. Wallot, 613/992-2473
Asst. National Archivist, M. Swift, 613/992-7445
Director General, Archives & Government Records Branch, L. McDonald, 613/995-3525
Director General, Public Programs Branch, F. Houle, 613/996-1241

Regional Offices
Edmonton Federal Records Centre: 8707 - 51 Ave., Edmonton AB T6H 5H1 – 403/420-3120; Fax: 403/495-2259, Chief, Brian Sloan
Halifax Federal Records Centre: 270 Bluewater Rd., Bedford NS B4B 1J6 – 902/426-5940; Fax: 902/426-8970, Chief, Cindi Palmer
Montréal Federal Records Centre: 665A, Montée de Liesse, St-Laurent PQ H4T 1P5 – 514/283-4044; Fax: 514/283-7347
Ottawa Federal Records Centre: Bldg. No. 15, Tunney's Pasture, Goldenrod St., Ottawa ON K1A 0N3 – 613/954-4175; Fax: 613/952-3972, Chief, Gilles Pommainville
Québec City Federal Records Centre: 75, de Hambourg, St-Augustin PQ G3A 1S6 – 418/878-2825; Fax: 418/878-3123, Chief, Guy Ricard
Toronto Federal Records Centre: 190 Carrier Dr., Toronto ON M9W 5R1 – 416/739-2546; Fax: 416/675-2862, Chief, Charles Dwarka
Vancouver Federal Records Centre: Lake City Industrial Park, 2751 Production Way, Burnaby BC V5A 3G7 – 604/666-6539; Fax: 604/666-4990, Chief, Gord Fryer

Winnipeg Federal Records Centre: 201 Weston St., Winnipeg MB R3E 3H4 – 204/983-8845; Fax: 204/983-4649, Chief, Rick Weinholdt

NATIONAL ARTS CENTRE (NAC)/ Centre national des Arts (CNA)
53 Elgin St., PO Box 1534, Stn B, Ottawa ON K1P 5W1
613/996-5051, 947-7000; Fax: 613/996-9578

Dedicated to the development of the performing arts, the NAC produces, co-produces & commissions a wide range of theatre, music & dance productions. Reports to government through the Minister of Canadian Heritage.

Minister Responsible, Hon. Sheila Copps, 613/995-2773
Chair, Jean Thérèse Riley
Executive Director, Vacant
Director, Communications, Ken Anderson
Director, Human Resources, Bernard Geneste
Chief Financial Officer, Cy Cook
Artistic Advisor, Trevor Pinnock

NATIONAL BATTLEFIELDS COMMISSION/ Commission des champs de bataille nationaux
390, av de Bernières, Québec PQ G1R 2L7
418/648-3506; Fax: 418/648-3638

Established to preserve, administer & enhance the Plains of Abraham battlefield park in Québec City. Reports to government through the Minister of Canadian Heritage.

Chair, André Juneau, Archit.
Secretary, Michel Leullier

NATIONAL CAPITAL COMMISSION (NCC)/ Commission de la Capitale nationale
#202, 40 Elgin St., Ottawa ON K1P 1C7
613/239-5555; Fax: 613/239-5063; URL: http://canada.gc.ca/depts/agencies/nccind_e.html

Responsible for the planning, development, preservation & improvement of the National Capital Region, & for the support, organization, & promotion of public activities & events which enrich the Capital as a place representative of all Canadians & which reflect its special role as the seat of the Government of Canada. Reports to government through the Minister of Canadian Heritage.

Minister Responsible, Hon. Sheila Copps
Chair, Marcel Beaudry
Executive Vice-President & General Manager, John D.V. Hoyles

NATIONAL DEFENCE (CANADA)/Défense nationale
MGen. George R. Pearkes Bldg., 101 Colonel By Dr., Ottawa ON K1A 0K2
613/992-4581; URL: http://www.debbs.ndhq.dnd.ca/dnd.htm

The control & management of the Canadian forces, & all matters relating to national defence establishments & works for the defence of Canada, fall under the authority of the Minister of National Defence, who is responsible for presenting before the Cabinet those matters of major defence policy for which Cabinet direction is required.

The Deputy Minister is the senior public servant & principal civilian advisor to the Minister on all departmental affairs. The Deputy Minister is responsible for ensuring that all policy direction emanating from the government is reflected in the administration of the department.

The Chief of Defence Staff, the senior military adviser to the Minister, is charged with the control & administration of the Canadian Forces. He is responsible for the effective conduct of military operations & the readiness of the Canadian Forces to meet the commitments assigned to the department by the government.

In National Defence Headquarters, the Vice Chief of the Defence Staff, the Deputy Chief of the Defence Staff, six Asst. Deputy Ministers, as well as the Judge Advocate General, report to the Deputy Minister & the Chief of the Defence Staff. The Vice chief of the Defence Staff is the principal assistant & adviser to the Deputy Minister & the Chief of Defence Staff, & acts for the latter during his absence. The Deputy Chief of the Defence Staff is responsible to the Chief of the Defence Staff for the effective & efficient performance of the operations of the Canadian Forces.

ACTS ADMINISTERED
Canadian Forces Superannuation Act
National Defence Act
Official Secrets Act
Supplementary Retirement Benefits Act
Visiting Forces Act
Minister, Hon. Douglas Young
Deputy Minister, Louise Fréchette, 613/992-4258, Fax: 613/995-2028
Acting Chief of Defence Staff, V.Adm. L.E. Murray, 613/992-6052
Vice-Chief of Defence Staff, V.Adm. L.E. Murray, 613/992-6052
Deputy Chief of the Defence Staff, L.Gen. J.A. Roy, 613/992-3355
Asst. Deputy Minister, Finance & Corporate Services, Robert M. Emond, 613/992-0359
Asst. Deputy Minister, Infrastructure & Environment, John L. Adams, 613/945-7545
Asst. Deputy Minister, Personnel, R.Adm. David N. Kinsman, 613/992-7582
Asst. Deputy Minister, Policy & Communication, Dr. Ken J. Calder, 613/992-3458
Asst. Deputy Minister, Matieriel, Pierre L. Legueux, 613/992-6622
Assoc. Asst. Deputy Minister, Policy & Communications, R.Adm. J.A. King, 613/992-2769
Assoc. Asst. Deputy Minister, Finance & Corporate Services, R.Adm. B.M. Keeler, 613/945-7362
Assoc. Asst. Deputy Minister, Defence Information Services, M.Gen. J.G. Leech, 613/995-2017
Assoc. Asst. Deputy Minister, Personnel, Douglas Lindley, 613/992-7443
Judge Advocate General, B.Gen. Pierre Boutet, 613/992-3019
Chief, Reserves & Cadets, M.Gen. E.W. Linden, 613/995-9802
Acting Director General, Public Affairs, Col. R.C. Coleman, 613/995-3427, Fax: 613/995-1158
Head, Defence Science Advisory Board, W.R. Bullock, 613/992-4073
Chief, Review Services, M.Gen. K.W. Penney, 613/992-7975

EMERGENCY PREPAREDNESS CANADA (EPC)/Protection civile Canada (PCC)
Jackson Bldg., 122 Bank St., 2nd Fl., Ottawa ON K1A 0W6
613/991-7077; Fax: 613/998-9589; Email: cominfo@x400.gc.ca; URL: http://hoshi.cic.sfu.ca/epc
Emergency Coordination Centre: 613/991-7000

Under the Emergency Preparedness Act, the Minister of Defence is also responsible for advancing civil emergency preparedness in Canada for emergencies of all types, including war & other armed conflict, by facilitating & coordinating among government institutions & in cooperation with provincial governments, foreign governments & international organizations, the development of civil emergency plans.

Executive Director, Dr. Eric L. Shipley, 613/991-7031
Director, Communications, André Lamalice, 613/991-7034
Senior Communications Officer, Sharleen Bannon, 613/991-7038
Senior Communications Officer, Joan Borsu, 613/991-7039

COMMANDS
Commander, Air Command, L.Gen. A.M. DeQuetteville, C.M.M., C.D.
Commander, Land Force Command, L.Gen. J.M. Baril, C.M.M., C.D.
Commander, Maritime Command, V.Adm. L.G. Mason, C.M.M., C.D.
Commander, Northern Area, Col. P. Leblanc, C.D.
Commander, Canadian Forces Recruiting, Education & Training System, M.Gen. M. Caines, C.D.

Operations Groups
10 Tactical Air Group Headquarters: St-Hubert PQ – 514/462-8777, ext7207, Commander, B.Gen. K.R. Pennie, 514/462-8777, ext7207
Air Transport Group: Trenton ON – 613/827-3509, Commander, B.Gen. J.R.B. Proulx, O.M.M., C.D.
Fighter Group Headquarters: North Bay ON – 705/494-4715, Commander, B.Gen. D.M. Jurkowski, O.M.M., C.D.
Land Force Atlantic Area Headquarters: Halifax NS – 902/427-7580, Commander, M.Gen. R. Crabbe, O.M.M., C.D.
Land Force Central Area Headquarters: Toronto ON – 416/733-4681, ext.5905, Commander, M.Gen. B.E. Stephenson, C.D.
Land Force Western Area Headquarters: Edmonton AB – 403/457-6007, Commander, M.Gen. N.B. Jeffries, C.D.
Maritime Air Group: Halifax NS – 902/427-2141, Commander, B.Gen. Brian Cameron, O.M.M., C.D.
Maritime Forces Atlantic Headquarters: Halifax NS – 902/427-6355, Commander, R.Adm. G.L. Garnett, O.M.M., C.D.
Maritime Forces Pacific Headquarters: Victoria BC – 250/363-2020, Commander, R.Adm. R.D. Moore, C.D.
Secteur du Québec de la Force terrestre: Montréal PQ – 514/846-4102, Commander, M.Gen. A.R. Forand, S.C., C.D.

Canadian Forces Bases (CFB) & Detachments
BFC Bagotville: Alouette PQ G0C 1A0
CFB Borden: Borden ON L0M 1C0
CFB Calgary: Calgary AB T3E 1T8
CFB Cold Lake: Medley AB T0A 2M0
CFB Comox: Lazo BC V0R 2K0
CFB Edmonton: PO Box 10500, Edmonton AB T5J 4J5
CFB Esquimalt: FMO, Victoria BC V0S 1B0
CFB Gagetown: Oromocto NB E0G 2P0
CFB Gander: PO Box 6000, Gander NF A1V 1X1
CFB Goose Bay: Goose Airport, Stn A, Goose Bay NF A0P 1S0
CFB Greenwood: Greenwood NS B0P 1N0
CFB Halifax: FMO Halifax NS B3K 2X0
CFB Kingston: Vimy Post Office, Kingston ON K0K 5L0
BFC Montréal: St-Hubert PQ J3Y 5T4
CFB Moose Jaw: PO Box 5000, Moose Jaw SK S6H 7Z8
CFB North Bay: Hornell Heights ON P0H 1P0
CFB Petawawa: Petawawa ON K8H 2X3
CFB Shearwater: Shearwater NS B0J 3A0
CFB Shilo: Shilo MB R0K 2A0
CFB Suffield: PO Box 6000, Medicine Hat AB T1A 8K8
CFB Trenton: Astra ON K0K 1B0
BFC Valcartier: Courcelette PQ G0A 1R0
CFB Winnipeg: Westwin MB R3J 0T0

Canadian Forces Stations
CFS Alert: Belleville ON K0K 3S0

CFS Debert: Debert NS B0M 1G0
CFS Flin Flon: PO Box 338, Flin Flon MB R8A 1N1
CFS Leitrim: Ottawa ON K1A 0K5
CFS Masset: PO Box 2000, Masset BC V0T 1M0
CFS St. John's: PO Box 2028, St. John's NF A1C 6B5

Canadian Service Colleges
Canadian Forces College: Toronto ON – 416/482-6800, ext.6822, Commandant, B.Gen. E.H. Gosden, C.D.
Canadian Land Forces Command & Staff College: Kingston ON – 613/451-5818, Commandant, B.Gen. M.K. Jeffrey, O.M.M., C.D.
Centre for National Security Studies: Kingston ON – 613/541-5010, ext.5840, Commanding Officer, Col. J. Roeterink, C.D.
Royal Military College: Kingston ON – 613/541-6000, Commandant, B.Gen. C. Emond, C.D.

Regional Public Affairs Office (National Defence)
Québec: Tour Ouest, Guy-Favreau Complex, #911, 200, boul René Lévesque, Montréal PQ H2Z 1X4 – 514/283-5272

NATIONAL ENERGY BOARD (NEB)/
Office national de l'énergie (ONE)
311 - 6th Ave. SW, Calgary AB T2P 3H2
403/292-4800; Fax: 403/292-5503; URL: http://canada.gc.ca/depts/agencies/nebind_e.html
The Board is a regulatory tribunal that reports to Parliament through the Minister of Natural Resources. It regulates specific areas of the oil, gas & electricity industries relating to: construction & operation of pipelines & international power lines; traffic, tolls & tariffs of pipelines; exports of natural gas, oil & electricity; imports of gas &; regulatory control of oil & gas resources on frontier lands, in all non-Accord areas.
Minister Responsible, Hon. Anne McLellan, 613/996-2007
Chair, Roland Priddle
Executive Director, Gaétan Caron
Director, Economics Branch, J. Hayward
Director, Energy Commodities Branch, R. Choy
Director, Energy Resources Branch, G.R. Campbell
Director, Engineering Branch, J.F. McCarthy
Director, Finance, Administration & Information Technology, B. Kenny
Director, Financial Regulation Branch, Terance Rochefort

NATIONAL FARM PRODUCTS COUNCIL (NFPC)/
Conseil national des produits agricoles
Martel Bldg., 270 Albert, 13th Fl., PO Box 3430, Stn D, Ottawa ON K1P 6L4
613/952-6752; Fax: 613/995-2097; URL: http://www.aceis.agr.ca/./nfpce.html
Operates closely with non-government marketing agencies established by federal legislation & financed through levies. Reports to government through the Minister of Agriculture & Agri-food.
Minister Responsible, Hon. Ralph Goodale, 613/996-2508
Chair, Dr. Cliff McIssac
Vice-Chair, Laurent Mercier
Executive Director, Larry F. Matheson
Director, Regulatory & Public Affairs, Carola McWade

Marketing Agencies
Canadian Egg Marketing Agency: #1900, 320 Queen St., Ottawa ON K1R 5A3 – 613/238-2514; Fax: 613/238-1967, CEO, Neil Currie
Canadian Turkey Marketing Agency: #102, 960 Derry Rd., Mississauga ON L5T 2J7 – 905/564-3100; Fax: 905/564-9356, Executive Director, K.E. Crawford
Canadian Chicken Marketing Agency: #300, 377 Dalhousie St., Ottawa ON K1N 9N8 – 613/241-2800; Fax: 613/241-5999, General Manager, Cynthia Currie
Canadian Broiler Hatching Egg Marketing Agency: #705, 200 Elgin St., Ottawa ON K2P 1L5 – 613/232-3023; Fax: 613/232-5241, General Manager, Paul Jelley

NATIONAL FILM BOARD OF CANADA (NFB)/
Office national du film
3155, rue Côte de Liesse, St-Laurent PQ H4N 2N4
514/283-9000; Fax: 514/283-8971; Email: L.Jones@nfb-onf.ca; URL: http://www.nfb.ca/
The Board is mandated to initiate & promote the production & distribution of films in the national interest, with the primary object of interpreting Canada to Canadians & to other nations. Reports to government through the Minister of Canadian Heritage.
Minister Responsible, Hon. Sheila Copps
Film Commissioner & Board Chair, Sandra Macdonald, 514/283-9244, 613/992-3615
Director General, English Program Branch, Barbara Janes, 514/283-9501
Director General, French Program Branch, Claude Bonin, 514/283-9285
Director General, Services & Technological Branch, Robert Forget, 514/283-9148
Director, Communications & Distribution, Laurie Jones, 514/283-9247, Fax: 514/283-8971
Director, Human Resources, Guy Gauthier, 514/283-9108

Regional Centres
Edmonton: #120, 9700 Jasper Ave., Edmonton AB T5J 4C3 – 403/495-3015; Fax: 403/495-6412, Chief, Graydon McCrea
Halifax: Queens Court, 5475 Spring Garden Rd., 2nd Fl., Halifax NS B3J 1G2 – 902/426-2000; Fax: 902/426-8901, Chief, Vacant
Moncton: 1222 Main St., Moncton NB E1C 1H6 – 506/851-6105; Fax: 506/851-2246, Producer, Pierre Bernier
Montreal: 1564, rue St-Denis, Montréal PQ H2X 3K2 – 514/496-6887; Fax: 514/283-0225
Toronto: 150 John St., Toronto ON M5V 3C3 – 416/973-2979; Fax: 416/973-7007, Chief, Louise Lore
Toronto (French Program): 150 John St., Toronto ON M5V 3C3 – 416/973-2226; Fax: 416/954-0775, Producer, Jacques Ménard
Vancouver: #100, 1045 Howe St., Vancouver BC V6Z 2B1 – 604/666-5410; Fax: 604/666-1569, Chief, Svend-Erik Eriksen
Winnipeg: 245 Main St., Winnipeg MB R3C 1A7 – 204/983-7996; Fax: 204/983-0742, Chief, Vacant

Offices Abroad
France: 5, rue de Constantine, Paris 75007, France – (011-33-1) 44-18-35-40; Fax: (011-33-1) 47-05-75-89
USA: 1251 Ave. of the Americas, 16th Fl., New York NY 10020, USA – 514/283-9441; Fax: 514/496-1895, Sales Manager, United States, Lynne Williams
UK: 1 Grosvenor Sq., London W1X 0AB, UK – (011-44-171) 258-6481; Fax: (011-44-171) 258-6532, Representative, Ann Vautier

NATIONAL GALLERY OF CANADA/
Musée des Beaux-Arts du Canada
Listed in Section 6; see Index.

NATIONAL JOINT COUNCIL (NJC)/
Conseil national mixte
C.D. Howe Bldg., 240 Sparks St. West, 7th Fl., PO Box 1525, Stn B, Ottawa ON K1P 5V2
613/990-1807

The NJC provides a forum for consultation on labour issues between the Government of Canada & the bargaining agents for it's employees.
Chair & Employer Side, c/o Human Resources Policy Branch, Treasury Board, 300 Laurier Ave. West, 4th Fl., Ottawa ON K1A 0R5, Jean-Claude Bouchard
Co-Chair & Bargaining Agent Side, G. Myers, c/o International Brotherhood of Electrical Workers, Local 2228, 1091 Wellington St., Ottawa ON K1Y 2Y4
General Secretary, F.M. Lalonde

NATIONAL LIBRARY OF CANADA/
Bibliothèque nationale du Canada
Listed in Section 5, see Index.

NATIONAL MUSEUM OF SCIENCE & TECHNOLOGY/Musée national des sciences et de la technologie
Listed in Section 6; see Index

NATIONAL PAROLE BOARD/Commission nationale des libérations conditionnelles
340 Laurier Ave. West, Ottawa ON K1A 0R1
613/954-7474; Fax: 613/995-4380; URL: http://canada.gc.ca/depts/agencies/npbind_e.html
The Board exercises authority for the conditional release of federal inmates & makes conditional release decisions on cases of those inmates in provinces & territories which do not have their own parole board. The Board also grants, issues, denies & revokes pardons & makes recommendations for the exercise of the royal prerogative of mercy.
Minister Responsible, Hon. Herbert Eser Gray, 613/991-2924
Chair, Willie Gibbs, 613/954-1150
Executive Vice-Chair, Vacant
Vice-Chair, Appeal Division (Headquarters), C. Ebbs-Lepage
Vice-Chair, Atlantic, J. Trevors
Vice-Chair, Ontario, F. Baines
Vice-Chair, Pacific, K. Louis
Vice-Chair, Prairies, G.R. Bellavance
Vice-Chair, Québec, K. Morgan

Regional Offices
Atlantic: 1045 Main St., 1st Fl., Moncton NB E1C 1H1 – 506/851-6345; Fax: 506/851-6926, Regional Director, H. Chevalier
Ontario: #100, 516 O'Connor Dr., Kingston ON K7P 1N3 – 613/634-3857; Fax: 613/634-3861, Regional Director, S. Ferguson
Pacific: #305, 32315 South Fraser Way, Abbotsford BC V2T 1W6 – 604/854-2468; Fax: 604/854-2498, Regional Director, F. Simmons
Prairies: PO Box 9210, Saskatoon SK S7K 3X5 – 306/975-4228; Fax: 306/975-5892, Regional Director, N. Fagnou
Québec: 200, boul René-Lévesque ouest, 2e étage, Montréal PQ H2Z 1X4 – 514/283-4584; Fax: 514/283-5484, Regional Director, Serge Lavallée

NATIONAL RESEARCH COUNCIL (NRC)/
Conseil national de recherches Canada (CNR)
Bldg. M-58, 1200 Montreal Rd., Ottawa ON K1A 0R6
613/993-9101; Fax: 613/952-7928; URL: http://www.nrc.ca/
IRAP Information: 613/993-1790
CISTI Information: 613/993-1800
Canada's leading science & technology agency with laboratories & facilities coast to coast. NRC helps Canadian firms increase their technical competence, improve productivity, develop new products & solve

technical problems in areas such as transportation, construction, biotechnology, manufacturing systems, & industrial materials.

NRC carries out R&D in collaboration with, & maintains national facilities for, universities, other government departments & private sector organizations in areas such as health care, public safety & national security.

The Canada Institute for Scientific & Technical Information (CISTI) is the largest service in the country & provides customized literature searches, & maintains highly specialized databanks. NRC's Industrial Research Assistance Program (IRAP) helps Canadian firms develop technology that they cannot afford on their own.

President, Dr. Arthur J. Carty, 613/993-2024
Vice-President, Research, Dr. C. Willis, 613/993-9244
Vice-President, Technology & Industry Support, Jacques Lyrette, 613/998-3664
Secretary General, Lucie Lapointe-Shaw
Director General, Canadian Institute for Scientific & Technical Information, Margot Montgomery
Director General, Industrial Research Assistance Program, David Ellis, 613/993-0695

Research & Technology Institutes

- Biotechnology Research Centre (BRC)/Institut de recherche en biotechnologie: 6100, av Royalmount, Montréal PQ H4P 2R2 – 514/496-6100; Fax: 514/496-6388
  Biochemical, genetic & protein engineering; pilot plant.
Director General, Dr. M. Desrochers
- Herzberg Institute of Astrophysics (HIA)/Institut Herzberg d'astrophisique: 100 Sussex Dr., Ottawa ON K1A 0R6 – 613/990-0907; Fax: 613/952-6602
Director General, Dr. D.C. Morton
- Industrial Materials Institute (IMI)/Institut des matériaux industriels: 75, boul de Montagne, Boucherville PQ J4B 6Y4 – 514/641-5050; Fax: 514/641-5101
  Instrumentation & sensors; metals & ceramics; industrial polymers; computer-integrated materials processing (CIMP).
Director General, Dr. J.G. Martel
- Institute for Advanced Manufacturing Technology (IME)/Institut des technologies de fabrication Intégrée: 1500 Montréal Rd., Ottawa ON K1A 0R6 – 613/993-5802; Fax: 613/952-6081
Director General, Dr. W.F. Petryschuk
- Institute for Aerospace Research (IAR)/Institut de recherche aérospatiale: 1500 Montreal Rd., Ottawa ON K1A 0R6 – 613/993-0141; Fax: 613/952-7214
  Research & development in support of the aerospace industry in design, manufacture, performance, use & safety of aircraft & related vehicles.
Acting Director General, Dr. T. LeFeuvre
- Institute for Biodiagnostics/Institut du biodiagnostic: 435 Ellice Ave., Winnipeg MB R3B 1Y6 – 204/983-7526; Fax: 204/984-4722
Director General, Dr. I.C.P. Smith
- Institute for Biological Sciences (IBS)/Institut des sciences biologiques: 1500 Montreal Rd., Ottawa ON K1A 0R6 – 613/993-5998; Fax: 613/957-7867
Director General, Dr. G. Adams
- Institute for Chemical Process & Environmental Technology (ICIPET)/Institut de technologie des procédés chimiques et de l'environnement: 1500 Montreal Rd., Ottawa ON K1A 0R6 – 613/990-6618
  Synthesis, chemical modification & evaluation of materials; environmental process technology; environmental measurement science.
Director General, Dr. J.B. Taylor
- Institute for Information Technology (IIT)/Institut de technologie de l'information: 1500 Montreal Rd., Ottawa ON K1A 0R6 – 613/993-2491; Fax: 613/952-0074

  Software engineering; sensor systems & sensor-based robotics; photonics; systems integration for manufacturing & resource sectors.
Director General, Vacant
- Institute for Marine Biosciences (IMB)/Institut des biosciences marines: 1411 Oxford St., Halifax NS B3H 3Z1 – 902/426-8332; Fax: 902/426-9413; URL: http://www.corpserv.nrc.ca/corpserv/imd.html
  Marine biology; biological chemistry; analytical chemistry.
Director General, Dr. R.A. Foxall
- Institute for Marine Dynamics (IMD)/Institut de dynamique marine: Memorial University, Kerwin Pl. & Arctic Ave., PO Box 12093, Stn A, St. John's NF A1B 3T5 – 709/772-4939; Fax: 709/772-3101; URL: http://www.corpserv.nrc.ca/corpserv/imd.html
  Arctic vessel research & ice science; ocean engineering; computational hydrodynamics.
Director General, N.E. Jeffrey
- Institute for Microstructural Sciences (IMS)/Institut des sciences des microstructures: 1500 Montreal Rd., Ottawa ON K1A 0R6 – 613/993-4583; Fax: 613/957-8734
Director General, Dr. P.H. Dawson
- Institute for National Measurement Standards/Institut des étalons nationaux de mesure: 1500 Montreal Rd., Ottawa ON K1A 0R6 – 613/990-8750; Fax: 613/952-5113
  Radiation standards & thermometry.
Director General, Dr. R. Van Koughnett
- Institute for Research in Construction (IRC)/Institut de recherche en construction: 1500 Montreal Rd., Ottawa ON K1A 0R6 – 613/993-3772; Fax: 613/941-0822
  Organic & inorganic construction materials; building envelope, indoor environment & energy conservation; acoustics & noise control; fire safety; cold climate infrastructure & roadways; development of national model building codes.
Director General, G. Seaden
- Institute for Sensor & Control Technology/Institut de technologie des capteurs et des systèmes de contrôle: 6620 North West Marine Dr., Vancouver BC V6T 1Z4 – 604/666-4456; Fax: 604/666-4449
  Scarping & diagnostics, modeling & control, surface technologies & tribology.
Director General, J. McBeth
- Plant Biotechnology Institute (PBI)/Institut de biotechnologie des plantes: 110 Gymnasium Rd., Saskatoon SK S7N 0W9 – 306/975-5248; Fax: 306/975-4839
Director General, Vacant
- Steacie Institute for Molecular Sciences/Institut Steacie des sciences moléculaires: 100 Sussex Dr., Ottawa ON K1A 0R6 – 613/993-1053; Fax: 613/954-5242
Director General, Dr. M.J. Laubitz

Technology Centres

- Canadian Hydraulics Centre/Centre canadien d'hydraulique: Bldg M-32, Montreal Rd., Ottawa ON K1A 0R6 – 613/993-2417; Fax: 613/952-7679
Director, Dr. B.D. Pratte, Email: bruce.pratte@nrc.ca
- Centre for Fluid Power Technology/Centre de technologie des fluides puissants: Ottawa ON – 613/993-2731; Fax: 613/952-1395
Director, Dr. Mohan Vijay, Fax: /mohan.vijay@nrc.ca
- Centre for Surface Transportation Technology/Centre de tehnologie des transports de surface: U-89, 1500 Montreal Rd., Ottawa ON K1A 0R6 – 613/998-9639; Fax: 613/957-0831
Director, John Coleman, 613/998-9638, Email: john.coleman@nrc.ca
- Thermal Technology Centre/Centre de technologie thermique: M-17, Montreal Rd., Ottawa ON K1A 0R6 – 613/993-4892; Fax: 613/954-1235
Director, Dr. Keith Snelson, Email: keith.snelson@nrc.ca

NATIONAL ROUND TABLE ON THE ENVIRONMENT & ECONOMY (NRTEE)/ Table ronde nationale sur l'environnement et l'économie (TRNEE)
#1500, 1 Nicholas St, Ottawa ON K1N 7B7
613/992-7189; Fax: 613/992-7385; Email: admin@nrtee-trnee.ca

NRTEE promotes the principles & practices of sustainable development in all sectors of Canadian society and in all regions of Canada. Reporting directly to the Prime Minister, the NRTEE is an independent forum composed of individuals from government, business, science, academia, environmental groups, labour unions and native peoples. It brings together traditionally competing interests & makes decisions by consensus.

Chair, Dr. Stuart Smith
Executive Director, David McGuinty
Director, Communications, Moira Forrest

NATIONAL SEARCH & RESCUE SECRETARIAT/Secrétariat national de recherches et sauvetage
Standard Life Bldg., 275 Slater St., 4th Fl., Ottawa ON K1A 0K2
Fax: 613/996-3746; URL: http://www.synapse.net/ZXnss/nss/nsshome.htm
Toll Free: 1-800-727-9414

The Secretariat provides a central managerial role in the overall coordination of search & rescue. It addresses program & policy issues related to the National Search & Rescue Program, & advises the lead minister for search & rescue.

Minister Responsible, Hon. Douglas Young
Executive Director, R. William Slaughter, 613/992-0054

NATURAL RESOURCES CANADA (NRCan)/ Ressources naturelles canada (RNCan)
580 Booth St., Ottawa ON K1A 0E4
613/995-0947; Fax: 613/996-9094; URL: http://www.NRCan.gc.ca/
Emergency Operations Centre: 613/995-5555, 943-0000

The Minister of Natural Resources is responsible for coordinating, promoting & recommending national policies concerning energy, mines, minerals & other non-renewable resources & formulating plans for their conservation, development & use. In addition the Department is authorized to conduct research & technical surveys to assess mineral & energy resources, including a full & scientific examination & survey of Canada's geological structure & legal boundaries. NRCan also Prepares & provides public maps, conducts scientific & economic research relating to the energy, mining, & metallurgical industries, & establishes & operates scientific laboratories required for the conduct of these duties.

ACTS ADMINISTERED

Atomic Energy Act
Canadian Exploration & Development Incentives Program Act
Canadian Exploration & Incentives Program Act
Canadian Home Insulation Program Act
Co-operative Energy Act
Department of Energy, Mines & Resources Act
Energy Monitoring Act
Energy Supplies Emergency Act (Environment & Health have a role
in respect of environmental considerations)
Explosives Act
Hibernia Development Project Act
Home Insulation (Nova Scotia & PEI) Program Act
International Boundary Act
Nuclear Liability Act
Oil Substitution & Conservation Act

Canadian Almanac & Directory 1997

Petro-Canada Act
Petroleum & Gas Revenue Tax Act
Petroleum Incentives Program Act
Administration of Acts re Changes in Provincial Boundaries
Alberta Act
Alberta/BC Boundary Act, 1974
Alberta/NWT Boundary Act, 1958
BC-Yukon-NWT Boundary Act, 1967
Manitoba Boundaries Extension Act, 1912
Manitoba-NWT Boundary Act, 1966
Manitoba/Saskatchewan Boundary Act, 1966
Ontario Boundaries Extension Act, 1912
Ontario-Manitoba Boundary Act
Québec Boundaries Extension Act, 1912
Saskatchewan/NWT Boundary Act, 1966
Acts Administered in Part by Minister of Natural Resources
Access to Information Act
Arctic Waters Pollution Prevention Act (Transport/Indian & Northern Affairs)
Canada Lands Survey Act (Indian & Northern Affairs)
Canada-Newfoundland Atlantic Accord Implementation Act (Finance/Revenue)
Canada-Nova Scotia Offshore Petroleum Resources Accord Implementation Act (Finance/Revenue)
Canada Oil & Gas Act (Indian & Northern Affairs)
Canada Petroleum Resources Act (Indian & Northern Affairs)
Canadian Ownership & Control Determination Act
Emergencies Act
Energy Administration Act (Environment/Fisheries & Oceans)
International Boundary Commission Act (Indian & Northern Affairs)
International Boundary Water Treatment Act
Motor Vehicle Fuel Consumption Standards Act (Transport)
National Energy Board Act (Transport)
Oil & Gas Production & Conservation Act (Indian & Northern Affairs)
Privacy Act
Resources & Technical Surveys Act (Fisheries & Oceans/Environment)
Transportation of Dangerous Goods Act
Minister, Hon. Anne McLellan, 613/996-2007, Fax: 613/996-4516
Deputy Minister, Jean C. McCloskey, 613/992-3458, Fax: 613/992-3828

Communications Branch
613/992-0267; Fax: 613/996-9094
Director General, Karen Laughlin, 613/996-3355
Director, Client Services Division, Pierre Sauvé, 613/996-8070
Director, Strategic Analysis & Research, Mary O'Rourke, 613/992-9323

Legal Services
613/992-7795; Fax: 613/995-2598
General Counsel, S.K. Fraser, 613/992-0039
Senior Counsel, C. Scullion, Q.C., 613/992-0432

Canada Centre for Mineral & Energy Technology (CANMET)
580 Booth St., Ottawa ON K1A 0E4
As a key research & technology development arm of NRCan, CANMET works with the minerals, metals & energy industries to find safer, cleaner & more efficient methods to develop & use Canada's mineral & energy resources. In partnership with clients, the agency performs & sponsors commercial & cost-shared research & development, & technology transfer. The Energy Technology Branch & Mineral Technology Branch have recently been joined with policy groups of Energy Sector & Minerals & Metals Sector to ensure that policies & regulations are based on sound science.
Asst. Deputy Minister, Minerals & Metals Sector, Ron R. Sully, 613/992-2490, Fax: 613/996-7425
Asst. Deputy Minister, Energy Sector, Michael Cleland, 613/996-7848, Fax: 613/992-1405

Mineral Technology Branch (CANMET)
568 Booth St., Ottawa ON K1A 0G1
Director, Mining & Mineral Sciences Laboratory, R. Sage, 613/995-8248, Fax: 613/992-8735
Director, Western Research Centre, T.D. Brown, 1 Oil Patch Dr., Devon AB T0C 1E0, 403/987-8214, Fax: 403/987-8690

Mining & Mineral Sciences Laboratory
555 Booth St., Ottawa ON K1A 0G1
Director, R. Hargreaves, 613/947-6604, Fax: 613/992-8928

Policy, Planning & Services Branch
555 Booth St., Ottawa ON K1A 0G1
613/992-0593; Fax: 613/995-6881
Director, Johanne Desjardins, 613/996-1700, Fax: 613/952-7501
Director, Administrative & Informatics Services Division, Louis Marmen, 613/943-0273, Fax: 613/995-6881
Director, Corporate Planning & Communications Division, Keith Belinko, 613/995-4267, Fax: 613/995-3192
Director, Engineering & Technical Services Division, R. Webster, 613/996-5679
Director, Library & Documentation Services Division, M. Laurin, 562 Booth St., Ottawa ON K1A 0G1, 613/995-4059, Fax: 613/952-2587

CANADIAN FOREST SERVICE (CFS)
Place Vincent-Massey, 580 Booth St., Ottawa ON K1A 0E4
613/947-7399; URL: http://mf.ncr.forestry.ca
Asst. Deputy Minister, Dr. Yvan Hardy, 819/947-7400

Industry, Economics & Programs Branch
Director General, Doug Ketcheson, 613/947-9052
Director, Economics & Statistics Division, D. Boulter, 613/947-9076
Director, Harvesting & Wood Products Division, M. Mes-Hartree, 613/947-9040
Director, Paper & Allied Industry Division, R. Glandon, 613/947-9051
Director, Programs Division, D. Welsh, 613/947-9053

Policy, Planning & International Affairs Branch
Director General, Jacques Carette, 613/947-9100
Director, International Affairs Division, D. Drake, 613/947-9078
Director, Policy Division, Vacant

Science Branch
Acting Director General, G. Miller, 819/947-8984
Director, Science Marketing & Business Opportunities Division, W. Cheliak, 613/947-9012
Director, Science Programs Division, G. Miller, 613/947-8984
Director, Science Relations Division, D. Winston, 613/947-8986

CFS Regional Offices
Edmonton: 5320 - 122nd St., Edmonton AB T6H 3S5 – 403/435-7210; Fax: 403/435-7359, Director General, B. Case
Fredericton: Regent St. South, PO Box 4000, Fredericton NB E3B 5P7 – 506/452-3500; Fax: 506/452-3525, Director General, Hap Oldham
Victoria: 506 West Burnside Rd., Victoria BC V8Z 1M5 – 250/363-0600; Fax: 250/363-0775; URL: http://www.fpc.forestry.ca/, Director General, Carl H. Winget
Québec: 1055, rue du PEPS, CP 3800, Ste-Foy PQ G1V 4C7 – 418/648-5850; Fax: 418/648-5849, Director General, Normand Lafrenière
Sault Ste. Marie: 1219 Queen St. East, PO Box 490, Sault Ste. Marie ON P6A 5M7 – 705/949-9461; Fax: 705/759-5700, Director General, E. Kondo

CORPORATE SERVICES SECTOR
613/995-4243; Fax: 613/922-8922
Asst. Deputy Minister, Richard B. Fadden, 613/995-4252
Director General, Assets Management, Administrative Services Branch, Neil MacLeod, 613/996-0981
Director General, Financial Management Branch, Dave Bickerton, 613/943-8763
Director General, Human Resources Services, M. Boudrias, 613/996-4008
Director, Accounting Policy & Systems Division, J. Klimczak
Director, Information Management Branch, A. Shaw, 613/996-8261
Director, Strategic Direction & Coordination Division, Vacant
Director, Technical Services Division, Vacant

EARTH SCIENCES SECTOR
601 Booth St., Ottawa ON K1A 0E8
URL: http://www.emr.ca/ess/esshp8.html
Asst. Deputy Minister, Dr. Marc Denis Everell, 613/992-9983, Fax: 613/992-8874
Chief Geoscientist, Dr. J.M. Franklin, 613/995-4482, Fax: 613/996-8059

Geological Survey of Canada (GSC)
601 Booth St., Ottawa ON K1A 0E8
613/996-3919; Fax: 613/996-9990; Email: gsc_bookstore@gsc.nrcan.gc.ca; URL: http://www.emr.ca/gsc/; NAISMap GIS URL: http://www-nais.ccm.NRCan.gc.ca/wnaismap/naismap.html
Bookstore Information: 613/995-4342
Geoscience information is used to find & develop natural resources & understand the impact natural resource exploitations can have on the environment. Through environment-related activities, provides industry with the knowledge required to face environmental challenges, particularly in dealing with various land use issues, & the influence of activities on the environment & provides Canadian governments, at all levels, with scientifically sound data on which to base their policies & regulations.

Minerals & Regional Geoscience Branch
Acting Director General, J.M. Duke, 613/995-4093, Fax: 613/995-7322
Director, Continental Geoscience Division, J.E. King, 613/995-4314, Fax: 613/995-7322
Director, GSC Calgary, Dr. Grant Mossop, 3303 - 33rd St. NW, Calgary AB T2L 2A7, 403/292-5376, Fax: 403/292-5377
Director, GSC Pacific, A.C. Colvine, 9860 West Saanich Rd., Sidney BC V8L 4B2, 250/363-6438, Fax: 250/363-6739
Acting Director, Mineral Resources Division, C. Jefferson, 613/996-9223, Fax: 613/992-5694

Sedimentary & Marine Geoscience Branch
This branch is also called the Geophysics & Marien Geoscience Branch.
Director General, Sedimentary & Marine Geoscience Branch, Dr. Richard T. Haworth, 613/995-2340, Fax: 613/996-6575
Director, Business Development, Dave Carney, 613/996-0441, Fax: 613/995-8737
Director, Centre Géoscientifique de Québec, Dr. A. Achab, 2700, rue Einstein, CP 7500, Ste-Foy PQ G1V 4C7, 418/654-2603, Fax: 418/654-2615
Acting Director, GSC Atlantic, D. McAlpine, c/o Bedford Institute of Oceanography, PO Box 1006, Dartmouth NS B2Y 4A2, 902/426-2367, Fax: 902/426-4266
Director, Terrain Sciences Division, Dr. Jean-Serge Vincent, 613/995-4938, Fax: 613/992-0190
•Canada Centre for Remote Sensing
588 Booth St., Ottawa ON K1A 0Y7

613/947-1216; Fax: 613/947-3125; URL: http://www.ccrs.nrcan.gc.ca/
Director General, Ed Shaw, 613/947-1222
Director, Applications Division, F.E. Guertin, 613/947-1356
Director, Data Acquisition Division, Dr. S. Till, 613/998-9060
Acting Director, Geographic Information Systems & Services, Dr. Mossad Allam
Director, Methods & Systems Division, Dr. R.A. O'Neil, 613/947-1245
Director, Technology Assessment Division, A.L. Whitney, 613/947-1211
•Centre for Topographic Information
#010, 2144, rue King ouest, Sherbrooke PQ J1J 2E8
819/564-5600; Fax: 819/564-5698
Director, Yves Belzile, 819/564-5602
Acting Asst. Director, Data Standardization Section, D. DeGagne
•Geodetic Survey Division
615 Booth St., Ottawa ON K1A 0E9
613/995-4443; Fax: 613/995-3215
Director, Mike Corey, 613/995-4282
Chief, Geodetic Networks, L.W. Nabe, 613/995-4341
•Legal Surveys Division
URL: http://www.geocan.NRCan.gc.ca/lsd/
Surveyor General & Director, M.J. O'Sullivan
Acting Asst. Surveyor General, P. Sauvé
Commissioner, International Boundary Commission, S. Jacques

Geomatics Canada
580 Booth St., Ottawa ON K1A 0E4
613/995-4321; URL: http://www.geocan.nrcan.gc.ca/
Surveys Canadian lands & waters; prepares & distributes topographic, geographic, electoral & aeronautical maps & digital products, surveys federal-provincial boundaries; manages a national program for acquiring & using remote sensing data.

Mapping & Services Branch
615 Booth St., Ottawa ON K1A 0E9
613/995-4945; Fax: 613/995-8737
Canada Map Office 1-800-465-6277 or 613/952-7009

Regional Offices/Surveys, Mapping & Remote Sensing
Alberta: #930, 9700 Jasper Ave., Edmonton AB T5J 4C3 – 403/420-2495; Fax: 403/495-4052, Regional Surveyor, G.E. Olsson
Atlantic: 136 Victoria St., Amherst NS B4H 1Y1 – 902/661-6766; Fax: 902/661-6769, Acting Regional Surveyor, G. Isaacs
British Columbia: #800, 1550 Alberni St., Vancouver BC V6G 3C6 – 604/666-5316; Fax: 604/666-0522, Regional Surveyor, D.K. Neilson
Manitoba: #501, 275 Portage Ave., Winnipeg MB R3B 2B3 – 204/983-4954; Fax: 204/983-0157, Regional Surveyor, G.W. Kitchen
Northwest Territories: Bellanca Bldg., 50th St., 8th Fl., PO Box 668, Yellowknife NT X1A 2N5 – 403/920-8295; Fax: 403/873-9949, Regional Surveyor, L. McNeice
Ontario: #606, 55 St. Clair Ave. East, Toronto ON M4T 1M2 – 416/973-7503; Fax: 416/973-6043, Regional Surveyor, Jim Hill
Québec: 2144, rue King ouest, Sherbrooke PQ J1J 2E8 – 819/564-5781; Fax: 819/564-5775, Regional Surveyor, Jacques Sasseville
Saskatchewan: #304, 2110 Hamilton St., Regina SK S4P 2E3 – 306/780-5401; Fax: 306/780-5191, Regional Surveyor, D.A. Bouck
Yukon: #225, 300 Main St., Whitehorse YT Y1A 2B5 – 403/667-3950; Fax: 403/668-2382, Regional Surveyor, S.A. Hutchinson

Polar Continental Shelf Project
#6146, 344 Wellington St., Ottawa ON K1A 0E4
613/990-6990; Fax: 613/990-1508
Resolute NWT Base: 403/252-3872; Fax: 403/252-3605
Tuktoyaktuk NWT Base: 403/997-2333; Fax: 403/977-2144
Director, Bonni Hrycyk, 613/990-1505

Policy, Planning & Information Services Branch
Director General, P. Fisher, 819/996-9551, Fax: 819/953-8296
Director, Coordination & Planning Division, G. Kendall, 613/992-5032, Fax: 613/996-9670
Director, Geoscience Information Division, A.E. Bourgeois, 613/995-4089, Fax: 613/996-8748
Director, Planning & Administration Division, N.J. Corbett, 613/995-3665, Fax: 613/996-9670
Special Advisor, Policy, Planning & Information Services Branch, Dr. A.G. Plant, 613/995-9495, Fax: 613/996-9670

ENERGY SECTOR
580 Booth St., Ottawa ON K1A 0E4
613/996-7432; Fax: 613/992-1405
Acting Asst. Deputy Minister, Michael Cleland, 613/996-7848
Secretary General, Deep River Disposal Project, Dr. V. Lafferty, 613/995-3539
Director, Management Services Division, L. Marmen, 613/943-0273
Director, Operations & Research, M. Rodrigue, 613/996-5914

Energy Efficiency Branch
Director General, Bill Jarvis, 613/995-0081,
Energy Efficiency Programs, 613/996-7512; Fax: 613/943-1590
Transportation Energy Division, 613/995-7300; Fax: 613/952-8169
Alternative Energy & Technology Division, 613/996-2873
Director, Demand Policy & Analysis Division, N.K. Marty
Director, Industrial, Commercial & Institutional Programs, R.A. McKenzie
Director, Residential, Regulatory & Information Programs Division, Vacant
Director, Transportation Energy Use Division, A.C. Taylor

Energy Policy Branch
Acting Director General, S. Kirby, 613/996-7669
Director, Economic & Fiscal Analysis Division, J.P. Campbell, 613/996-2663
Director, Energy Forecasting Division, N. McIlveen, 613/995-8762
Acting Director, Environment Division, B. Moore, 613/996-6474
Director, International Division, G. Winstanley, 613/996-2993
Director, Policy Analysis & Coordination Division, J.T. Lowe, 613/995-2821
Acting Director, Projects & Industrial Benefits Division, J.P. Campbell, 613/996-2663

Energy Resources Branch
Director General, D. Whelan
Director, Frontier Lands Management Division, D. Cioccio
Director, Natural Gas Division, J.S. Booth
Director, Oil Division, R. Lyman
Director, Renewable & Electrical Energy Division, D. Burpee

Energy Technology Branch (CANMET)
613/996-6220; Fax: 613/996-9416
Director General, B.D. Cook
Director, Energy Diversification Research Laboratory, Gilles Jean, Varennes PQ, 514/652-6639, Fax: 514/652-5177
Acting Director, Energy Efficiency Centre, F.R. Campbell, 613/996-5419

Office of Energy Research & Development (OERD)
613/995-8860; Fax: 613/995-6146
Director General, Dr. D.A. Reeve
Senior Advisor, Science Policy & Planning Division, K.M. Cliffe

Uranium & Nuclear Energy Branch
Director General, R.W. Morrison
Director, Nuclear Division, H.E. Thexton
Director, Radioactive Waste Division, P.A. Brown
Director, Uranium Division, R.W. Williams

MINERALS & METALS SECTOR
580 Booth St., Ottawa ON K1A 0E4
Asst. Deputy Minister, Ron R. Sully, 613/992-2490, Fax: 613/996-7425

Economic & Financial Analysis Branch
613/995-4577; Fax: 613/943-8453
Director General, Keith J. Brewer, 613/992-2662
Director, Economic Analysis Division, D.L. Hull, 613/995-5301
Director, Financial & Corporate Analysis Division, R.K. Jones, 613/995-3422
Director, Fiscal Analysis Divsion, W.D. Kitts, 613/995-6351
Director, Tax Legislation Interpretation Division, R. Clark, 613/996-3286

Mineral & Metal Policy Branch
Director General, Bill McCann, 613/995-7029, Fax: 613/996-7425
Senior Policy Advisor, A. Ignatow
Director, Coal, Ferrous & Industrial Minerals Division, D.M. Lagacé, 613/992-2018
Director, International Division, B. McKean, 613/995-2661
Director, Nonferrous Division, R. Telewiak, 613/992-4481
Director, Regional & Intergovernmental Affairs Division, A. Clark, 613/995-8839
Director, Resource Management Division, D.W. Pasho, 613/992-7958

STRATEGIC PLANNING & COORDINATION BRANCH
Coordinator, P. McLean
Director General, Audit & Evaluation Branch, Marcel Gibeault, 613/996-4940, Fax: 613/992-8799
Director General, Communications Branch, K. Laughlin, 613/996-3355
Director, Client Services Division, Pierre Sauvé, 613/996-8070
Director, Corporate Secretariat, M. Macies, 613/947-8235
Director, Policy Coordination & Planning Division, L. Ree, 613/995-9263
Director, Science & Technology Policy Division, Vacant
Director, Strategic Analysis & Research Division, M. O'Rourke, 613/992-9323
Director, Sustainable Development & Environment Division, J. Forster, 613/992-4451

SITING TASK FORCE SECRETARIAT
580 Booth St., 9th Fl., Ottawa ON K1A 0E4
613/995-5201; Fax: 613/996-6206
Secretary General, Dr. V. Lafferty, 613/995-3539
Chief, Technical Operations (North), Dr. D. Paktunc, 613/995-3236

Associated Agencies, Boards & Commissions
•Energy Council of Canada: #400, 30 Colonnade Rd., Ottawa ON K2E 7J6 – 613/952-6469; Fax: 613/952-6470
Executive Director, Dr. E.P. Cockshutt

Other Associated Agencies, Boards & Commissions
Listed alphabetically in detail, this section
Atomic Energy of Canada Ltd.
Atomic Energy Control Board
International Boundary Commission
National Energy Board

NATURAL SCIENCES & ENGINEERING RESEARCH COUNCIL OF CANADA (NSERC)/ Conseil de recherches en sciences naturelles et en génie du Canada
Constitution Square, 350 Albert St., Ottawa ON K1A 1H5
613/996-7235; Fax: 613/992-5337; Email: comm@nserc.ca; URL: http://www.nserc.ca

NSERC fosters the discovery & application of knowledge through the support of university research & the training of scientists & engineers. The Council promotes the use of this knowledge to build a strong national economy & improve the quality of life of all Canadians. NSERC fulfills its mission by awarding grants & scholarships through a competitive process & by building partnerships among universities, governments & the private sector.

President, Thomas A. Brzustowski, 613/995-5840
Secretary to Council, Marilyn Taylor, 613/995-5896
Director General, Common Administrative Services Directorate, Bruce Mitchell, 613/995-3914
Director General, Research Grants & Scholarships Directorate, Dr. Nigel Lloyd, 613/995-5833
Director General, Targeted Research Directorate, Leo Derikx, 613/996-1545
Director, Policy & International Relations, Steve Shugar, 613/995-6449

NORTH AMERICAN COMMISSION FOR ENVIRONMENTAL COOPERATION (NACEC)/ Commission Nord-Américaine de coopération environnementale
Secretariat, #200, 393, rue St-Jacques ouest, Montréal PQ H2Y 1N9
514/350-4300; Fax: 514/350-4314

Established to compliment the environmental aspects of the North American Free Trade Agreement (NAFTA). Comprises a council of ministers, secretariat & consultive committee with representatives from Canadian, American & Mexican governments. Promotes sustainable development, provides trinational forum for the fight against pollution & advocates the observance of laws & regulations.

Executive Director, Victor Lichtinger
Director, J. Ferretti
Manager, Communications, Rachel Vincent

NORTH AMERICAN FREE TRADE AGREEMENT (NAFTA) SECRETARIAT/ Secrétariat de l'ALENA
Canadian Section, #705, 90 Sparks St., Ottawa ON K1P 5B4
613/992-9388; Fax: 613/992-9392
Canadian Secretary, Cathy Beehan
Deputy Secretary, Michael Eastman, 613/992-9383

NORTHERN PIPELINE AGENCY CANADA (NPAC)/Administration du pipe-line du Nord Canada (APNC)
Lester B. Pearson Bldg., 125 Sussex Dr., Ottawa ON K1A 0G2
613/993-7466; Fax: 613/998-8787; URL: http://canada.gc.ca/depts/agencies/npaind_e.html

The Agency was established to oversee the planning & construction of the Canadian portion of the Alaska Highway Gas Pipeline to provide access to the Arctic natural gas reserves of both Canada & the United States.

Commissioner, Robert G. Wright
Special Advisor, Policy & Public Affairs, Bruce E. Macdonald

Office of the Commissioner of OFFICIAL LANGUAGES/Commissariat aux langues officielles
110 O'Connor St., Ottawa ON K1A 0T8
613/996-6368; Fax: 613/993-5082
Commissioner/Commissaire, Dr. Victor C. Goldbloom, O.C., O.Q.
Director General, Investigations Branch, Michel Robichaud
Director General, Policy Branch, Marc Thérien
Executive Director, Corporate Secretariat & Regional Operations Branch, Monique Matza
Director, Communications Branch, Marc Demers
Acting Director, Corporate Services Branch, Marc Thérien
Director, Legal Services Branch, Richard Tardif

PACIFIC PILOTAGE AUTHORITY CANADA/ Administration de Pilotage du Pacifique Canada
#300, 1199 West Hastings St., Vancouver BC V6E 4G9
604/666-6771; Fax: 604/666-6093

The Authority operates pilotage services in Canadian waters in & around British Columbia. Reports to government through the Minister of Transportation.

Chair, Dennis B. Mclennan
Corporate Secretary & Office Manager, Eileen M. Hall
Controller, Bruce D. Chadwick
Director, Marine Operations, Capt. R.P. Heath

PATENTED MEDICINE PRICES REVIEW BOARD/Conseil d'examen du prix des médicaments brevetés
Standard Life Centre, #1400, 333 Laurier Ave. West, PO Box L40, Ottawa ON K1P 1C1
613/952-7360
Chair, Dr. R.G. Elgie, 613/952-7625
Vice-Chair, R. Sureau, 613/954-0454
Executive Director, W.D. Critchley, 613/952-7622
Secretary to the Board, S. Dupont Kirby, 613/954-8299

PRIVACY COMMISSIONER OF CANADA/ Commissariat à la protection de la vie privée du Canada
Tower B, Place de Ville, 112 Kent St., Ottawa ON K1A 1H3
613/995-2410; Fax: 613/995-1501; URL: http://infoweb.magi.com/ZXprivcan/
Toll Free: 1-800-267-0441, TDD: 613/992-9190

The Privacy Commissioner investigates complaints from any persons present in Canada who consider that the federal government has wrongly denied them access to their personal records or refused to correct (or annotate) disputed information. The Commissioner may also investigate complaints the federal government is improperly collecting, using, disclosing or disposing of personal information which may be recorded in any form. The Commissioner may investigate government compliance with the Privacy Act on his own initiative.

Privacy Commissioner, Bruce Phillips
Executive Director, Julien Delisle
Legal Advisor, Holly Harris
Director, Policy, Planning & Compliance, Catherine Bastedo-Boileau
Director, Privacy Complaints, Gerald Neary
Director, Public Affairs, Sally Jackson

PUBLIC SERVICE COMMISSION OF CANADA/Commission de la fonction publique du Canada
Ottawa ON K1A 0M7
613/992-9562; Fax: 613/954-7561; URL: http://www.psc-cfp.gc.ca

The Commission is responsible for staffing the public service according to the merit principle. Delegates its authority wherever practical, though not its responsibility to Parliament. Provides training & development services (including language training, for public servants), hears appeals on appointments & investigates complaints of questionable staffing practices. Reports to government through the Minister of Canadian Heritage.

President, Ruth Hubbard, 613/992-2788, Fax: 613/996-4337
Commissioner, Ginette Stewart
Commissioner, Mary Gusella
Director General, Appeals & Investigations Branch, L.M. Lalonde
Director General, Audit & Review Branch, R. Jelking
Director General, Human Resources Management Branch, Jacques M. Pelletier
Director General, Strategic Planning & Communications Directorate, Carole Jolicoeur
Executive Director, Corporate Management Branch & Secretary General, A. Armit
Executive Director, Executive Programs Branch, Margaret Amoroso
Acting Executive Director, Staffing Programs Branch, Len Slivinski
Executive Director, Training Programs Branch, M.J. Murphy

Regional & District Staffing Offices
Charlottetown: #420, 119 Kent St., Charlottetown PE C1A 1N3 – 902/566-7030; Fax: 902/566-7036
Edmonton: #830, 9700 Jasper Ave., Edmonton AB T5J 4G3 – 403/495-3144; Fax: 403/495-3145
Halifax: 1557 Hollis St., Halifax NS B3J 3V3 – 902/426-2990; Fax: 902/426-7455
Moncton: 777 Main St., 7th Fl., Moncton NB E1C 1E9 – 506/851-6616; Fax: 506/851-6618
Montréal: 200, boul René-Lévesque ouest, 8e étage, Montréal PQ H2Z 1X4 – 514/283-5776; Fax: 514/283-6380
Ottawa: 66 Slater St., 3rd Fl., Ottawa ON K1A 0M7 – 613/996-8436; Fax: 613/996-8048
Regina: #400, 1975 Scarth St., Regina SK S4P 2H1 – 306/780-5720; Fax: 306/780-5723
St. John's: #302, 2 Steers Cove, St. John's NF A1C 5X8 – 709/772-4812; Fax: 709/772-4316
Sillery: 1126, ch St-Louis, 7e étage, Sillery PQ G1S 1E5 – 418/648-3230; Fax: 418/648-4575
Toronto: 1 Front St. West, 3rd Fl., Toronto ON M5J 2R5 – 416/973-3131; Fax: 416/973-1883
Vancouver: 757 West Hastings St., 2nd Fl., Vancouver BC V6C 3M2 – 604/666-4829; Fax: 604/666-6808
Whitehorse: #400, 300 Main St., Whitehorse YT Y1A 2B5 – 403/667-3900; Fax: 403/668-5033
Winnipeg: #200, 344 Edmonton St., Winnipeg MB R3B 2L4 – 204/983-2486; Fax: 204/983-8188
Yellowknife: 4922 - 52 St., PO Box 2730, Yellowknife NT X1A 2R1 – 403/873-3545; Fax: 403/873-3601

PUBLIC SERVICE STAFF RELATIONS BOARD (PSSRB)/ Commission des relations de travail dans la fonction publique
240 Sparks St., PO Box 1525, Stn B, Ottawa ON K1P 5V2
613/990-1800; Fax: 613/990-1849

PSSRB reports to Parliament through the President of the Privy Council.

Chair, Ian Deans, 613/990-1777
Vice-Chair, Y. Tarte, 613/990-1779

Secretary/General Counsel, J.E. McCormick, 613/990-1830
Director, Mediation Services, N. Berstein, 613/990-1836
Special Advisor, C. Greer, 613/990-1804

PUBLIC WORKS & GOVERNMENT SERVICES CANADA (PWGSC)/Travaux publics et services gouvernmentaux
Place du Portage, Phase III, 11, rue Laurier, Hull PQ K1A 0S5
819/956-3115; URL: http://www.pwgsc.gc.ca
TDD: 819/994-5389
Sir Charles Tupper Bldg., 2250 Riverside Dr., Ottawa ON K1A 0M2

The Department serves as the purchasing & accounting arm of the Federal Government. It provides a number of major common services in the areas of procurement, supply & printing & in the areas of accounting, payment, audit & management advisory services. It manages real property for the Government & provides planning, design, construction & realty services to government departments & agencies.

ACTS ADMINISTERED
Bridges Act
Currency Act
Defence Production Act
Department of Supply & Services Act
Dry Docks Subsidies Act
Expropriation Act
Federal-Provincial Fiscal Arrangements & Federal Post-secondary Education & Health Contributions Act
Garnishment Attachment & Pension Diversion Act
Government Property Traffic Act
Government Works Toils Act
Municipal Grants Act
National Film Act
Ottawa River Act
Public Lands Grants Act
Public Works Act
Public Works Health Act
Publication of Statutes Act
Royal Canadian Mint Act
Surplus Crown Assets Act
Trading with the Enemy Act
Trans-Canada Highway Act
Minister, Hon. Diane Marleau, 819/997-5421, Fax: 819/953-1908
Deputy Minister & Deputy Receiver General, Ranald A. Quail, 819/956-1706, Fax: 819/956-8280
General Counsel, Frank Brodie, 819/956-0993, Fax: 819/953-6705
Director General, Communications, Carol Rutherford, 819/956-2304, Fax: 819/994-8404
Asst. Deputy Minister, Human Resources, Michael Cardinal, 613/736-2455

Canadian Government Publications
Approximately 180 commercial & university bookstores in Canada are recognized by the Canadian Government Publishing Centre as Associated Bookstores for the sale of federal government priced publications.

CANADA COMMUNICATION GROUP (CCG)
45, boul Sacré-Coeur, Hull PQ K1A 0S7
URL: http://www.ccg-gcc.ca
Marketing Enquiries: 819/956-9111

Provides printing & publishing services & information management services to public sector agencies. Portions of this CCG's operations may be privatized in (or just prior to) 1997.
CEO (Queen's Printer for Canada), Lynne Pearson, 819/997-5321

Director General/Vice-President, Business Development, Kim McKinnon, 819/953-0991, Fax: 819/956-8794
Director General/Vice-President, Information Technology, Vacant, 819/994-7166
Director General/Vice-President, Operations Directorate, B.M. McLean, 819/956-8340
Director General/Vice-President, Professional Services, L. Saint-Pierre, 350 Albert St., Ottawa ON K1A 0S5, 613/990-8047

Enquiries Canada
47 Clarence St., 3rd Fl., Ottawa ON K1A 0S5
Toll Free: 1-800-667-3355
Director, Jean Brazeau, 613/941-3792
Asst. Director, 1-800 Services, Gerard Blais, 613/941-1826
Asst. Director, Reference Canada Program, Suzanne Beaudoin, 613/941-3382

CONSULTING & AUDIT CANADA
Tower B, Place de Ville, 112 Kent St., Ottawa ON K1A 0S5
613/996-0188
CEO, Jane Billings, 613/996-0231
Acting Director General, Audit, J. Shah, 613/995-6341
Director General, Client Services, N. McIntosh, 613/947-4972
Director General, Consulting, J. Kentz, 613/947-2010

GOVERNMENT OPERATIONAL SERVICE BRANCH (GOS)
Asst. Deputy Minister, Jim Stobbe, 819/956-2871, Fax: 819/956-7853
Director General, Banking & Cash Management Sector, Ralph Sprague, 819/956-2942, Fax: 819/956-7585
Director General, Central Accounting & Reporting Sector, Guy Beaudry, 819/956-2875, Fax: 819/956-7583
Director General, Compensation Sector, Phil Charko, 819/956-1936, Fax: 819/956-2098
Director General, Departmental Products Sector, Joan Catterson, 819/956-2877, Fax: 819/956-5599

GOVERNMENT TELECOMMUNICATIONS & INFORMATICS SERVICES (GTIS)
819/956-4444; Fax: 819/956-4627
CEO, Philip McLellan, 819/956-2632
COO, René Guindon, 819/956-2610
Vice-President, Application Management Services, John Riddle, 819/956-2354
Vice-President, Business & Departmental Support Services, Bruno Kierczak, 819/956-9492
Vice-President, Customer Services & Business Development Sector, Roger Bason, 819/956-9495
Vice-President, Network & Computer Services, Fred McCallum, 819/956-2348
Vice-President, Telecommunications, Paul Hayes, 613/990-2217, Fax: 613/998-9122

REAL PROPERTY SERVICES BRANCH
Asst. Deputy Minister, Michael G. Nurse, 613/736-2882
Director, Accommodation Management Directorate, M. Turcotte, 613/736-2162
Director, Asset & Investment Management - Capital Directorates, Laura Jackson, 613/736-2181
Director, Corporate Health & Safety, Robert Begin, 613/736-2520
Director, Federal Facilities Directorate, Sue Axam, 613/736-2238
Director, Holdings Management & Custodial Services, Marcia Carlyn, 613/736-2207
Director, Investment Management-Leasing Directorate, M. Ballantine, 613/736-3157
Director & Owner, Investor Office Accommodation Services, Hank van der Linde, 613/736-2179
Director, Maintenance Management, Richard Marleau, 613/736-2655

Director, Operations, D. Sinclaire-Chenier, 613/736-2824
Director, Technology & Environmental Services, Moe Cheung, 613/736-2121

SUPPLY OPERATIONS SERVICE BRANCH
819/956-0921; Fax: 819/953-1058
Open Bidding Info-line: 819/956-3440

Canada's largest purchasing organization, purchasing contracts on behalf of over 100 federal government agencies. Responsible for the organization of the Open Bidding System (OBS), an entirely electronic procurement process which awards most federal government (& some provincial government) contracts. The OBS is the official distribution channel for all open bidding procurement notices & documents issued by PWGSC. Requirements are listed on an electronic board & are printed three times per week in "Government Business Opportunities".
Asst. Deputy Minister, Alan Williams, 819/956-1727, Fax: 819/953-1058
Director, European Region, Graeme J. Brown, MacDonald House, #1, Grosvenor Square, London, / 011-44-71-258-6612, Fax: /011-44-71-258-6440
Director, Washington Region, Eleonor Lewicki, Canadian Embassy, 501 Pennsylvania Ave. NW, Washington DC 20001, 202/682-7604, Fax: 202/682-7613
Director General, Aerospace, Marine & Electronics Systems Sector, Harry T. Webster, 819/956-0010,
Aerospace & Electronics, 819/956-0236
Marine & Armament, 819/956-0684
Canadian Patrol Frigate Project, 613/996-6337
Canadian Airspace Systems Plan, 613/990-5755
Long Range Surveillance DRONE System Project, 819/952-9640
Director General, Industrial & Commercial Products Sector, Bob Spickett, 819/956-4056,
Food, Drug & Scientific Products, 819/956-3892
Special & Standard Vehicles, 819/956-3937
Security Safety & Industrial Products, 819/956-3553
Electronics, Electrical & Construction Products, 819/956-3940
Director General, Industrial & Commercial Products & Standardization Sector, Mel Skinner, 819/956-3539, Fax: 819/956-5145
Director General, Science, Informatics & Professional Services Sector, Noel Bhumgara, 819/956-1782
Director General, Supply Program Management Sector, Barry Lipsett, 819/956-0930
Chief, Open Bidding Business Management, Luci Dove, 819/956-3435

Canadian General Standards Board (CGSB)
222 Queen St., Ottawa ON K1A 1G6
613/941-8709

One of seven standards-writing organizations accredited by the Standards Council. A major portion of federal government purchasing is done by reference to CGSB standards & accreditations.
Contact, Mel Skinner, 613/956-0930

Open Bidding Service (OBS)
c/o Information Systems Management Corporation, PO Box 22011, Ottawa ON K1V 0W2
613/737-3374; Fax: 613/737-3643; URL: http://www.obs.ism.ca/eginfo.html
Toll Free: 1-800-361-4637

The OBS is now the official distribution channel for all open bidding procurement notices & documents issued by PWGSC. Requirements are listed on an electronic board & are printed three times per week in "Government Business Opportunities". Provides suppliers with instant access to purchasing information via a computer & modem either directly to the service or through the internet. All Canadian firms, whether or not they are on a source list, can use the open bidding method. The OBS makes new markets instantly available to all companies through an open, fair, & cost-effective service. The service has expanded to include notices of other federal government departments (ie. Defence Construction Canada, CIDA, Environment Canada, National Resources Canada, etc.), provincial/territorial government procurement agencies (Alberta, Manitoba, New Brunswick, Ontario, Québec, & Saskatchewan), crown corporations, academic institutions & other public sector institutions. Informs 27,000 subscribers of business opportunities.

TRANSLATION SERVICES BRANCH
Jules Léger Bldg., 15 Eddy St., Hull PQ K1A 0M5
Provides translation, interpretation & terminology services to federal departments, organizations & Parliament. Translation services are optional & are provided on a fee-for-Parliament.
CEO, Diana Monnet
Director General, Translation Operations Sector, Ginette Cloutier, 819/997-1719, Fax: 819/953-9585
Deputy Director General, Departmental Translation Services, Gabriel Huard, 819/997-7919, Fax: 819/953-5799
Director General, Management Services Sector, Christine O'Meara, 819/994-3653, Fax: 819/997-5686

Regional Offices
Atlantic: 1713 Bedford Row, 7th Fl., PO Box 2247, Stn M, Halifax NS B3J 3C9 – 902/496-5133; Fax: 902/426-5041, Acting Regional Director General, Greg Vaughan
Ontario: 4900 Yonge St., North York ON M2N 6A6 – 416/512-5710; Fax: 416/512-5615, Regional Director General, Susanne Borup
Pacific: #2300, 650 West Georgia, PO Box 11538, Vancouver BC V6B 4N7 – 604/666-1862; Fax: 604/666-0398, Regional Director General, Bonnie MacKenzie
Québec: Complexe Guy-Favreau, 200, boul René-Lévesque ouest, Montréal PQ H2Z 1X4 – 514/496-3739; Fax: 514/496-3744, Regional Director General, René Crête
Western: #1000, 9700 Jasper Ave., Edmonton AB T5J 4E2 – 403/497-3551; Fax: 403/497-3562, Regional Director General, Earl Bauckman

Associated Agencies, Boards & Commissions
Listed alphabetically in detail, this section.
Canada Lands Co. Ltd.
Canada Mortgage & Housing Corporation
Canada Post Corporation
Defence Construction Canada
Royal Canadian Mint

REVENUE CANADA/Revenu Canada
875 Heron Rd., Ottawa ON K1A 0L8
613/957-0275; URL: http://www.revcan.ca/menue.html
Customs Information: 613/993-0534
GST Information: 613/990-8584

ACTS ADMINISTERED
Canada Pension Plan Act, Part I
Customs Act
Customs & Excise Offshore Application Act
Customs Tariff Act
Department of National Revenue Act
Excise Act
Excise Tax Act
Exports & Imports Permits Act
Softwood Lumber Products Export Charge Act
Special Import Measures Act
Unemployment Insurance Act, Part III & VII
Minister, Hon. Jane Stewart, 613/995-2960, Fax: 613/952-6608
Deputy Minister, Pierre Gravelle, 613/957-3688, Fax: 613/952-1547
Senior General Counsel, Legal Services, Charles McNab, 613/957-2558

Asst. Deputy Minister, Human Resources Branch, Vacant, 613/954-8220
Director General, Communications Branch, Vacant
Director General, Corporate Affairs Branch, S. Rigby, 613/957-3708

APPEALS BRANCH
Interim Asst. Deputy Minister, R.M. Beith, 613/957-2179
Director, Appeals Division, B. McGivern, 613/954-4817
Director, CPP/UI Division, L. Levasseur, 613/957-2237
Director, Income Tax Appeals Division, L.C. Tremblay, 613/957-2189
Director, Policy & Programs Division, P. Meerburg, 613/957-2225

ASSESSMENT & COLLECTIONS BRANCH
Asst. Deputy Minister, K.M. Burpee, 613/954-6144
Director General, Business Returns & Payments Processing Directorate, Rod Quiney, 613/941-5007
Director General, Client Services Directorate, H. Beauchemin, 613/957-9362
Director General, Individual Returns & Payment Processing, G. Venner, 613/957-7497
Acting Director General, Revenue Collection Directorate, L. Gauvin, 613/954-1269
Director, Business Process Development Team, Marj Ogden, 613/952-9314

CUSTOMS BORDER SERVICES
Asst. Deputy Minister, Allan Cocksedge, 613/954-7220
Director General, Commercial Services Directorate, E.D. Warren, 613/954-7190
Director General, Enforcement Directorate, W.E. LeDrew, 613/954-6431
Acting Director General, Program Planning & Analysis Directorate, B. McCauley, 613/954-7820
Director General, Travellers Directorate, R. Tait, 613/954-6368
Director, Systems Operations, L. Bratina, 613/954-6844
Acting Director, Enforcement Operations, M. Connolly, 613/954-7620
Director, Inspection & Control, L. Noble, 613/954-7056
Director, Intelligence Services, F. Stefanelli, 613/954-7575
Director, Postal Courier & LVS, F. Light, 613/954-7130
Acting Director, Project Management, G. Goatbe, 613/954-7501
Director, Transportation Division, G. Rochon, 613/954-7191
Director, Travellers Assessment & Tax Policy Division, D. Cruikshank, 613/954-6360
Director, Travellers Services & Compliance, C. Collingridge, 613/954-7122
Acting Director, Operations & Policy, A. Lalonde, 613/952-6368
Director, Program Development, G. Gulas, 613/952-3907

TRADE ADMINISTRATION BRANCH
Interim Asst. Deputy Minister, A. Cocksedge, 613/954-7400
Director General, Anti-Dumping & Countervailing, B.W. Brimble, 613/954-7269
Director General, Tariff Programs, J. Shearer, 613/954-6990
Director, Adjudications, G. Greene, 613/954-7273
Acting Director, Management Systems & Services, P. Cork, 613/954-6970
Director, Valuation Division, M.R. Jordan, 613/954-7335

FINANCE & ADMINISTRATION BRANCH
Asst. Deputy Minister, William J. Crandall, 613/952-8668
Director General, Administration Directorate, R.C. Dudding, 613/957-9270

Director General, Finance Administration Directorate, William D. Boston, 613/954-6400
Director General, Laboratory & Scientific Services Directorate, Wayne Morris, 613/954-2200
Director General, Resource Management Directorate, John Kowalski, 613/952-3660
Director, Consolidation Administration, L. McElroy, 613/954-0248
Director, Facilites Management, S. Parent, 613/954-8330
Acitng Director, Publishing Services, R. Jones, 613/954-9302
Director, Security Directorate, Vacant, 613/957-2269

INFORMATION TECHNOLOGY BRANCH
Asst. Deputy Minister, Richard Manicom, 613/954-8983
Director General, Client Identification & Returns Processing, Al Landsberg, 613/954-8995
Director General, Compliance & Information Systems Directorate, J. Patrick Beynon, 613/954-9039
Director General, Development Support Directorate, Dick Sansom, 613/954-9405
Director General, Revenue & Accounting Systems Directorate, Susan Brown, 613/994-1233
Director General, Strategic Planning & Management Services Directorate, G.A. Peters, 613/941-3505
Director General, Technology Operations & Client Support Directorate, Jill Velenosi, 613/941-2870

POLICY & LEGISLATION BRANCH
123 Slater St., Ottawa ON K1A 0L8
Asst. Deputy Minister, Denis Lefebvre, 613/957-2041
Director General, Excise Act Review, R. O'Riordan, MacKenzie Ave., 7th Fl., Ottawa ON K1A 0L5, 613/941-3001
Deputy Director General, Excise Duties & Taxes, Jean-Francois Apgrall, Tower C, Vanier Towers, 25 McArthur Rd., Ottawa ON K1A 0L5, 613/954-0111
Director General, GST Rulings & Interpretations, W.K. McCloskey, Tower C, Vanier Towers, 25 McArthur Rd., Ottawa ON K1A 0L5, 613/952-9198
Acting Director General, Income Tax Rulings & Interpretations Directorate, Roy Shultis, 613/957-2132
Acting Associate Director General, GST Rulings & Interpretations Directorate, J. Daman, Tower C, Vanier Towers, 25 McArthur Rd., Ottawa ON K1A 0L5, 613/954-4291
Director General, Policy & Intergovernmental Affairs, W. Baker, 613/941-9964
Director, Business & General Division, Bryan Dath, 613/957-2089
Director, Charities Division, Ronald Davis, 613/954-0931
Director, Field Service & Administration Division, Keith Schinnour, Tower C, Vanier Towers, 25 McArthur Rd., Ottawa ON K1A 0L5, 613/952-9200
Director, Financial Industries Division, Brian Darling, 613/957-9767
Acting Director, Financial Institutions & Corporate Reorganizations Division, John Sitka, Tower C, Vanier Towers, 25 McArthur Rd., Ottawa ON K1A 0L5, 613/952-9248
Director, General Applications Division, L. Jones, Tower C, Vanier Towers, 25 McArthur Rd., Ottawa ON K1A 0L5, 613/954-7656
Director, International Relations Coordination Office, D. Meunier, 613/957-9776
Director, Legislative Policy Division, Robert D'Aurelio, 613/957-2061
Director, Manufacturing Industries, Partnerships & Trusts Division, Rick Biscaro, 613/957-8970
Director, Registered Plans Division, Stella Black, 613/954-0933
Director, Reorganization & Foreign Division, Michael Hiltz, 613/957-2113

Director, Special Sectors, A. Venne, Tower C, Vanier Towers, 25 McArthur Rd., Ottawa ON K1A 0L5, 613/954-7558

VERIFICATION, ENFORCEMENT & COMPLIANCE RESEARCH BRANCH
Asst. Deputy Minister, Barry Lacombe, 613/957-3709
Director General, Audit Directorate, Ed Gauthier, 613/957-3585
Director General, Compliance Research Directorate, Vacant, 613/941-4621
Director General, International Tax, Carole Gouin, 613/952-7472
Director General, Special Investigations Directorate, Jeanne Flemming, 613/957-7780
Director, Compliance Enhancement & Services, Jean-Pierre Lavigne, 613/957-9390
Director, Enforcement Technology Support, Frank Fingust, 613/957-3649
Director, Large Business Division, Vacant, 613/957-3585
Director, Planning Division, A. Potvin, 613/957-3665
Director, Small & Medium Enterprises Division, Dick Courneyea, 613/954-5725

ATLANTIC REGION
Cogswell Tower, #800, 2000 Barrington St., Halifax NS B3J 3K1
902/426-7994
Asst. Deputy Minister, Regional Operations, Dan Tucker, 902/426-6370

Customs/Border Services Office
Atlantic: 1809 Barrington St., PO Box 3080, Stn Park Lane Centre, Halifax NS B3J 3G6 – 902/426-2911, Interim Director, Dan Coffin, 902/426-2914

Trade Administration Services Office
Atlantic: Ralston Bldg., 1557 Hollis St., PO Box 3080, Stn Park Lane Centre, Halifax NS B3J 3G6 – 902/426-2911, Director, K. Larter, 902/426-6808

Tax Services Offices
Bathurst: 120 Harbourview Blvd., 4th Fl., PO Box 8888, Bathurst NB E2A 4L8 – 506/548-6744
Charlottetown: 94 Euston St., Charlottetown PE C1A 8L3 – 902/628-4200
Halifax: 1256 Barrington St., PO Box 638, Halifax NS B3J 2T5 – 902/426-2210
Moncton: #107, 1170 Main St., PO Box 1070, Moncton NB E1C 8P2 – 506/636-5999
Newfoundland & Labrador: Atlantic Place, 165 Duckworth St., PO Box 5968, St. John's NF A1C 5X6 – 709/772-2610
Saint John: 126 Prince William St., PO Box 6300, Saint John NB E2L 4H9 – 506/636-5999
St. John's: 290 Empire Ave., St. John's NF A1B 3Z1 – 709/772-2200
Summerside: 275 Pope Rd., Summerside PE C1N 5Z7 – 902/432-6000
Sydney: 47 Dorchester St., PO Box 1300, Sydney NS B1P 6K3 – 902/564-7080

NORTHERN ONTARIO REGION
2265 St. Laurent Blvd., 2nd Fl., Ottawa ON K1G 4K3
613/991-0549
Asst. Deputy Minister, Regional Operations, Robin Glass, 613/952-1676

Customs/Border Services Office
Northern Ontario: 2265 St. Laurent Blvd., Ottawa ON K1K 4K3 – 613/991-0534, Acting Interim Director, Gary Gustafson, 613/993-0534

Trade Administration Services Office
Northern Ontario: 2265 St. Laurent Blvd., Ottawa ON K1K 4K3 – 613/993-0537, Director, Arthur Lawrence, 613/598-3946

International Taxation Office
Northern Ontario: 2204 Walkey Rd., Ottawa ON K1A 1A8 – 613/952-3741

Tax Services Offices
Belleville: 11 Station St., Belleville ON K8N 2S3 – 613/962-2887
Kingston: 385 Princess St., Kingston ON K7L 1C1 – 613/541-3607
Kirkland Lake: 145 Government Rd. West, PO Box 4500, Kirkland Lake ON P2N 3R5 – 705/568-4222
Ottawa: #9088B, 875 Heron Rd., Ottawa ON K1A 1A2 – 613/941-3333
Ottawa: 333 Laurier Ave. West, Ottawa ON K1A 0L9 – 613/598-2275
Peterborough: 185 King St. West, 5th Fl., Peterborough ON K9J 8M3 – 705/876-6420
Sault Ste. Marie: #301, 205 McNabb St., Sault Ste. Marie ON P6B 1Y3 – 705/941-5218
Sudbury: 1050 Notre Dame Ave., Sudbury ON P3A 6C1 – 705/671-0582
Thunder Bay: 130 Syndicate Ave. South, Thunder Bay ON P7E 1C7 – 807/623-1774

PACIFIC REGION
#708, 333 Dunsmuir St., Vancouver BC V6B 5R4
604/666-0456
Asst. Deputy Minister, Regional Operations, Barbara Fulton

Customs/Border Services Office
Pacific: #709, 333 Dunsmuir St., Vancouver BC V6B 5R4 – 604/666-8633

Trade Administration Services Office
Pacific: #501, 333 Dunsmuir St., Vancouver BC V6B 5R4 – 604/666-0545, Interim Director, Rita Barill

Tax Services Offices
Burnaby: #201, 4664 Lougheed Hwy., PO Box 02110, Burnaby BC V5C 6C2 – 604/689-5411
Kelowna: #200, 1835 Gordon Dr., PO Box 5181, Stn A, Kelowna BC V1Y 3H5 – 604/470-6670
Prince George: 280 Victoria St., PO Box 7500, Prince George BC V2L 5N8 – 250/561-7800
Penticton: 277 Winnipeg St., Penticton BC V2A 1N6 – 250/492-9393
Surrey Taxation Centre: 9755 King George Hwy., Surrey BC V3T 5E1 – 604/585-5200
Vancouver: 1166 West Pender St., Vancouver BC V6E 3H8 – 604/669-8376
Victoria: 910 Government St., Victoria BC V8W 1X8 – 250/363-0121
Whitehorse: 120 - 300 Main St., Whitehorse YT Y1A 2B5 – 403/667-8154

PRAIRIE REGION
391 York Ave., 4th Ave., PO Box 1022, Winnipeg MB R3C 0P5
204/983-1845
Asst. Deputy Minister, Regional Operations, Rodney Monette

Customs/Border Services Office
Prairies: Federal Bldg., 269 Main St., Winnipeg MB R3C 1B3 – 204/983-6004, Director, Mike Styre

Trade Administration Services
Prairies: Federal Bldg., 269 Main St., Winnipeg MB R3C 1B3 – 204/983-0004, Director, Arlene White

Tax Services Offices
Brandon: 153 - 11th St., PO Box 99, Brandon MB R7A 7K6 – 204/726-7800
Calgary: 220 - 4 Ave. SE, Calgary AB T2G 0L1 – 403/221-8919
Edmonton: #10, 9700 Jasper Ave., Edmonton AB T5J 4C8 – 403/495-5400
Lethbridge: #301, 704 - 4th Ave. South, PO Box 3009, Lethbridge AB T1J 4A9 – 403/382-3010
Red Deer: 4996 - 49 Ave., PO Box 5013, Red Deer AB T4N 6X2 – 403/341-7006
Regina: 1955 Smith St., Regina SK S4P 2N9 – 306/780-6015
Saskatoon: 340 - 3rd Ave. North, Saskatoon SK S7K 0A8 – 306/975-4595
Winnipeg: 325 Broadway, Winnipeg MB R3C 4T4 – 204/983-3960
Winnipeg: 66 Stapon Rd., Winnipeg MB R3C 3M3 – 204/984-2470
Yellowknife: #902, 4920 - 52nd St., Yellowknife NT X1A 3T1 – 403/920-6650

QUÉBEC REGION
400, Place d'Youville, 8e étage, Montréal PQ H2Y 2C2
514/283-2464
Asst. Deputy Minister, Regional Operations, Danielle Vincent

Customs/Border Services Offices
Québec: 400, Place d'Youville, Montréal PQ H2Y 2C2 – 514/283-9900, Interim Director, Richard Watkins, 514/283-6201

Trade Administrtion Services Office
Québec: 400, Place d'Youville, Montréal PQ H2Y 2C2 – 514/-283-9900, Director, Jacques Monette, 514/283-6332

Tax Services Offices
Chicoutimi: #211, 100, rue Lafontaine, Chicoutimi PQ G7H 6X2 – 418/698-5580
Jonquière: 2251, boul Centrale, Jonquière PQ G7S 5J1 – 418/699-0450
Laval: 3131, boul St-Martin ouest, Laval PQ H7T 2A7 – 514/956-9101
Montérégie-Rive-Sud: 1000, rue de Serigny, Longueuil PQ J4K 5J7 – 514/283-5300
Montréal: 305, boul René-Lévesque ouest, Montréal PQ H2Z 1A6 – 514/283-5300
Outaoais: 15 Eddy St., Hull PQ K1A 1L4 – 819/994-1995
Québec: 165, rue de la Pointe-aux-Lievres sud, Québec PQ G1K 7L3 – 418/649-3180
Rimouski: 320, St-Germain est, Rimouski PQ G5L 1C2 – 418/722-3104
Rouyn-Noranda: 44, av du Lac, Rouyn-Noranda PQ J9X 6Z9 – 819/764-5171
Shawinigan-Sud: 4695, 12e av, Shawinigan-Sud PQ G9N 7S6 – 819/537-5192
Sherbrooke: 50, Place de la Cité, CP 1300, Sherbrooke PQ J1H 5L8 – 819/564-5888
Trois-Rivières: #111, 25, rue des Forges, Trois-Rivières PQ G9A 2G4 – 819/373-2723

SOUTHERN ONTARIO REGION
Ontario Regional Taxation Office, #909, 148 Fullarton St., London ON N6A 5P3
519/645-4360
Asst. Deputy Minister, Regional Operations, Ruby Howard

Customs/Border Services Offices
Mississauga: #604, 6725 Airport Rd., PO Box 6000, Mississauga ON L4V 1V2 – 905/676-3574, Director, Barbara Hébert
Windsor: 185 Ouellette Ave., 5th Fl., Stn Walkerville, Windsor ON N9A 5S8, Director, Dr. John Johnston

Trade Administration Services Office
Southern Ontario: Dominion Public Bldg., #2538, 1 Front St. West, Toronto ON M5J 1A5 – 416/954-5623, Director, Alice Shields

Canadian Almanac & Directory 1997

Tax Services Offices
Hamilton: 150 Main St. West, PO Box 2220, Hamilton ON L8N 3E1 – 905/570-7125
Kitchener: 166 Frederick St., Kitchener ON N2G 4N1 – 519/579-2230
London: 451 Talbot St., London ON N6A 5E5 – 519/645-4211
St. Catharines: 32 Church St., St. Catharines ON L2R 3B9 – 905/688-5996
Toronto East: 200 Town Centre Court, Scarborough ON M1P 4Y3 – 905/973-5150
Toronto Centre: 36 Adelaide St. East, Toronto ON M5C 1J7 – 416/954-3500
Toronto North: 5001 Yonge St., 7th Fl., North York ON M2N 6P6 – 416/954-9303
Toronto West: 77 City Centre Dr., Mississauga ON L5B 1M5 – 905/566-6700
Windsor: 185 Ouellette Ave., Windsor ON N9A 5S8 – 519/973-7188

ROOSEVELT CAMPOBELLO INTERNATIONAL PARK COMMISSION
Campobello Island, Campobello Is. NB E0G 3H0
506/752-2922; Fax: 506/752-2052

The Commission administers an international park on Campobello Island, New Brunswick, as a memorial to the late President of the United States, F.D. Roosevelt.

Chair (American), Hon. Christopher du Pont Roosevelt
Vice-Chair (Canadian), Roland C. Frazee
Acting Executive Secretary & Superintendent, Henry W. Stevens, Lubec ME

ROYAL CANADIAN MINT/ Monnaie royale canadienne
320 Sussex Dr., Ottawa ON K1A 0G8
613/993-3500; URL: http://www.rcmint.ca

The RCM has two plants located in Ottawa & Winnipeg. Foreign & domestic circulating coinage is manufactured in Winnipeg. The Ottawa facility is responsible for the production of foreign & domestic numismatic products, precious metals & the refining of gold. Reports to government through Public Works & Government Services.

Chair, Dr. Jose Blanco
Master, Danielle V. Wetherup
Vice-President, Manufacturing, Jean-Pierre Tremblay, 613/995-1975
Executive Director, Communications, Diane Plouffe Reardon, 613/993-2239, Fax: 613/998-5472

ROYAL CANADIAN MOUNTED POLICE (RCMP)/Gendarmerie royale du Canada
1200 Vanier Pkwy., Ottawa ON K1A OR2

613/993-1085; Fax: 613/993-5894; URL: http://www.rcmp-grc.gc.ca/html/rcmp2.htm

ACTS ADMINISTERED
RCMP Act
Commissioner, J.P.R. Murray
Honorary Commissioner, Her Majesty Queen Elizabeth II
Deputy Commissioner, National Transition, C.G. Allen
Deputy Commissioner, Atlantic Region, R.A. Bergman
Deputy Commissioner, Central Region, J.R.H. Beaulac
Deputy Commissioner, North Western Region, F.G. Palmer
Deputy Commissioner, Pacific Region, Deputy Commr. L.R. Proke

Public Affairs & Information Directorate, C/Supt. P.D.D. Hovey

RCMP Divisions & Commanding Officers
"A" Division: 155 McArthur Ave., Vanier ON K1A 0R4 – 613/993-8860; Fax: 613/995-4677, A/Commr. J.W.B. McConnell
"B" Division: PO Box 9700, Stn B, St. John's NF A1A 3T5 – 709/772-5437; Fax: 709/772-6392, C/Supt. L. Warren
"C" Division: 4225, boul Dorchester ouest, CP 559, Westmount PQ H3Z 1V5 – 514/939-8301; Fax: 514/939-8471, A/Commr. J.O.O. Edmond
"D" Division: 1091 Portage Ave., Winnipeg MB R3C 3K2 – 204/983-5414; Fax: 204/984-2342P, A/Commr. E.F. Moodie
"E" Division: 657 West 37 St., Vancouver BC V5Z 1K6 – 604/264-2000; Fax: 604/264-3547, Deputy Commr. L.R. Proke
"F" Division: PO Box 2500, Regina SK S4P 3K7 – 306/780-5477; Fax: 306/780-5410, A/Commr. B.G. Watt
"G" Division: PO Box 5000, Yellowknife NT X1A 2R3 – 403/920-8322; Fax: 403/873-3633, C/Supt.. R.A. Grimmer
"H" Division: 3139 Oxford St., PO Box 2286, Halifax NS B3J 3E1 – 902/426-3940; Fax: 902/426-8845, A/Commr. R.F. Falkingham
"J" Division: PO Box 3900, Fredericton NB E3B 4Z8 – 506/452-3419; Fax: 506/451-6053, C/Supt. R.V. Berlinquette
"K" Division: 11140 - 109 St., PO Box 1320, Edmonton AB T5J 2N1 – 403/945-5444; Fax: 403/945-5601, A/Commr. D. McDermid
"L" Division: 450 University Ave., PO Box 1360, Charlottetown PE C1A 7N1 – 902/566-7132; Fax: 902/368-0357, C/Supt. A.E. Crosby
"M" Division: 4100 - 4 Ave., Whitehorse YT Y1A 1H5 – 403/667-5584; Fax: 403/667-2621, C/Supt. T. Egglestone
"O" Division: PO Box 3240, Stn B, London ON N6A 4K3 – 519/640-7309, A/Commr. G. Zaccardelli

Training Facilities
Canadian Police College: St. Laurent Blvd. & Sandridge Rd., PO Box 8900, Ottawa ON K1G 3J2 – 613/998-0883; Fax: 613/990-9738, C/Supt. R. Goulet
RCMP Training Academy: PO Box 650, Regina SK S4P 3J7 – 306/780-5760; Fax: 306/780-6337, C/Supt. J.R.A. Gauthier

ROYAL CANADIAN MOUNTED POLICE EXTERNAL REVIEW COMMITTEE/ Comité externe d'examen de la Gendarmerie royale du Canada
PO Box 1159, Stn B, Ottawa ON K1P 5R2
613/998-2134; Fax: 613/990-8969; Email: cloutierb@sm+p.gc.ca; URL: http://canada.gc.ca/depts/agencies/ercind_e.html

Acting Chair, F. Jennifer Lynch, Q.C.
Executive Director, Bernard Cloutier

ROYAL CANADIAN MOUNTED POLICE PUBLIC COMPLAINTS COMMISSION/ Commission des plaintes du public contre la Gendarmerie royale
PO Box 3423, Stn D, Ottawa ON K1P 6L4
613/952-1471; Fax: 613/952-8045; URL: http://canada.gc.ca/depts/agencies/pccind_e.html
Toll Free: 1-800-267-6637

The Commission is responsible for the receipt of complaints from the public about the conduct of members of the RCMP. It is also responsible for the review of complaints when complainants are not satisfied with the disposition of their complaints by the RCMP. The Commission can inquire into complaints by means of public hearings & the chair of the Commission can investigate complaints. Annually, the chair reports to Parliament through the Solicitor General.

Chair, J.P. Beaulne
Executive Director, J.B. Giroux

Regional Offices
British Columbia & Yukon: #670, 840 Howe St., Vancouver BC V6Z 2L2 – 604/666-7363; Fax: 604/666-7362
Prairies & NWT: #1909, 10060 Jasper Avenue, PO Box 50, Edmonton AB T5J 3R8 – 403/495-4201; Fax: 403/495-4200

ROYAL SOCIETY OF CANADA/ Société royale du Canada
Listed in Section 2; *see* Index.

ST. LAWRENCE SEAWAY AUTHORITY (SLSA)/L'Administration de la voie maritime du Saint-Laurent
#1400, 360 Albert St., Ottawa ON K1R 7X7
613/598-4600; Fax: 613/598-4620; Email: marketing@seaway.ca; URL: http://www.seaway.ca/english/seaway/index.html

The SLSA is the federal government agency responsible for the safe and efficient movement of marine traffic through Canadian Seaway facilities. It shares operations with its American counterpart, the Saint Lawrence Seaway Development Corporation, in maintaining 13 locks between Montréal & Lake Erie. The authority reports to government through the Minister of Transportation.

President & CEO, G.R. Stewart, 613/598-4601
Vice-President, C. Côté
Vice President, M. Fournier
Corporate Secretary, V.C. Durant

Regional Offices
Maisonneuve: PO Box 97, St. Lambert PQ J4P 3N7, Vice-President, J.P. Patoine
Niagara: 508 Glendale Ave., St Catharines ON L2R 6V8, Vice-President, C.G. Trépanier

SECURITY INTELLIGENCE REVIEW COMMITTEE (SIRC)/ Surveillance des activités de renseignements de sécurité (CSARS)
PO Box 2430, Stn D, Ottawa ON K1P 5W5
613/990-8441; Fax: 613/990-5230; Email: sirc@synapse.net; URL: http://canada.gc.ca/depts/agencies/sirind_e.html

Has as its mandate, under the Canadian Security Intelligence Service Act, to carry out the independent & external review of the Canadian Security Intelligence Service (CSIS) & to investigate of complaints about CSIS activities. It is also required to investigate complaints from individuals who have had their employment prospects affected by the denial of a security clearance, & complaints referred to it by the Human Rights Commission. It is required to investigate reports made to it by, the Minister of Citizenship & Immigration, & the Solicitor General of Canada, which relate to national security or to an individual's involvement in organized crime. The Committee is required to report annually to Parliament through the Solicitor General on these matters.

Chair, Hon. Paule Gauthier, P.C., Q.C.

SOLICITOR GENERAL CANADA/ Solliciteur général Canada
Sir Wilfrid Laurier Bldg., 340 Laurier Ave. West, Ottawa ON K1A 0P8
613/990-2733; Fax: 613/993-7062; URL: http://www.sgc.gc.ca

The duties, powers & functions of the Solicitor General of Canada extend to & include all matters over which the Parliament of Canada has jurisdiction, not by law assigned to any other department, branch or agency of the Government of Canada, relating to (a) reformatories, prisons & penitentiaries; (b) parole & remissions; (c) The Royal Canadian Mounted Police; & (d) The Canadian Security Intelligence Service.

ACTS ADMINISTERED
Canadian Security Intelligence Act
Corrections & Conditional Release Act
Criminal Records Act
Department of the Solicitor General Act
Royal Canadian Mounted Police Act
Royal Canadian Mounted Police Pension Continuation Act
Royal Canadian Mounted Police Superannuation Act
Prisons & Reformatories Act
Security Offences Act
Transfer of Offenders Act

Solicitor General, Hon. Herbert Eser Gray, 613/991-2924, Fax: 613/996-2771
Deputy Solicitor General, Jean T. Fournier, 613/991-2895, Fax: 613/990-8312
Asst. Deputy Solicitor General, Horst Intscher, 613/991-2820, Fax: 613/990-8301
Director General, Aboriginal Policing, Christiane Ouimet, 613/993-4325, Fax: 613/991-0961
Director General, Communications Group, T.R.W. Farr, 613/991-2799, Fax: 613/993-7062
Acting Director General, Corporate Services, Eva Plunkett, 613/990-2669, Fax: 613/990-8297
Director General, Corrections, Richard Zubrycki, 613/991-2821, Fax: 613/990-8295
Director General, National Security, Paul Dubrule, 613/993-4136, Fax: 613/990-3632
Director General, Policing & Law Enforcement, Yvette Aloïsi, 613/990-2703, Fax: 613/993-5252
Acting Director General, Policy, Planning & Coordination, Jane Johnston, 613/998-3617
Director, External Relations (Regional Affairs), Jane Johnston, 613/991-2952, Fax: 613/990-7023

CANADIAN SECURITY INTELLIGENCE SERVICE (CSIS)
PO Box 9732, Ottawa ON K1G 4G4
613/993-9620; URL: http://www.csis-scrs.gc.ca/eng/menu/menue.html
Director, Ward Elcock, 613/231-0000
Director General, Communications Branch, Phil Gibson, 613/231-0100, Fax: 613/231-0612

CORRECTIONAL SERVICE OF CANADA
Listed alphabetically in detail, this section.

NATIONAL PAROLE BOARD
Listed alphabetically in detail, this section.

ROYAL CANADIAN MOUNTED POLICE (RCMP)
Listed alphabetically in detail, this section.

STATISTICS CANADA/Statistique Canada
R.H. Coats Bldg., Tunney's Pasture, 120 Parkdale Ave., Ottawa ON K1A 0T6
613/951-8116; Fax: 613/951-0581; Email: infostats@statcan.ca; URL: http://www.statcan.ca
Toll Free: 1-800-263-1136, TDD: 1-800-363-7629

ACTS ADMINISTERED
Statistics Act
Corporations & Labour Unions Returns Act

Agency of the federal government, headed by the Chief Statistician of Canada which reports to Parliament through the Minister of Industry. As Canada's central statistical agency, it has a mandate to "collect, compile, analyse, abstract and publish statistical information relating to the commercial, industrial, financial, social, economic and general activities and condition of the people of Canada".

Coordinates activities with its federal and provincial partners in the national statistical system to avoid duplication of effort and to ensure the consistency and usefulness of statistics. The Agency provides information to governments at every level, to business, labour, academic and social institutions, to professional associations, to the international statistical community, and to the general public.

The agency profiles and measures both social and economic changes in Canada. It presents a comprehensive picture of the national economy through statistics on manufacturing, agriculture, exports and imports, retail sales, services, prices, productivity changes, trade, transportation, employment and unemployment, and aggregate measures such as gross domestic product. It also presents a comprehensive picture of social conditions through statistics on demography, health, education, justice, culture, and household incomes and expenditures. This information is produced at the national and provincial levels and, in some cases, for major population centres and other sub-provincial or "small" areas.

Statistics Canada produces some 800 print publications, as well as computer tapes, printouts, microcomputer diskettes, CD-ROMs, microfilm and microfiche. All catalogued publications are distributed through the Depository Services Program, which includes some 700 libraries. The most popular titles are Canada Year Book; Canada: A Portrait; Canadian Economic Observer; Canadian Social Trends; Perspectives on Labour and Income; and Health Reports. The Statistics Canada Catalogue-available in print, on CD-ROM and on the Internet-contains information about the wide range of print and electronic information sources and services offered by Statistics Canada.

In addition, the Agency maintains an extensive online computerized database called CANSIM (Canadian Socio-economic Information Management System), which contains 700,000 time series collected from throughout Statistics Canada. Another important database is TIERS (Trade Information Enquiry and Retrieval System), which is a data and software package designed to facilitate the recovery of Canadian trade information.

Published electronically every working day, The Daily is Statistics Canada's official release bulletin; it contains summary findings of statistical programs and major conclusions of analytical studies. Infomat is a weekly analytical summary of articles that appeared in The Daily.

Online access to Statistics Canada information is available through StatsCan Online and the Internet. Currently available on StatsCan Online are CANSIM, The Daily, and extensive databases containing international trade information and horticulture information. Currently available on Statistics Canada's growing Internet site are Canadian Dimensions (tables presenting basic economic and social data about Canada), CANSIM and other databases, The Daily, research papers, the Statistics Canada Catalogue and ordering information, and links to the web servers of other Government of Canada departments and other national statistical agencies.

Statistics Canada's national role is manifested by its regional presence. Household surveys, census operations, and, increasingly, business surveys are conducted from the regional offices located across Canada. The nine regional offices handle sales of print and electronic products and provide reference and consultative services. Each provides a professional staff to assist clients in the access and use of statistical information and to carry out research and custom work.

Listings of Canadian Statistics may be found in this book. Please conusIt the main/global Index.
Chief Statistician of Canada, Dr. Ivan P. Fellegi, 613/951-9757, Fax: 613/951-4842

BUSINESS & TRADE STATISTICS
Asst. Chief Statistician, J. Ryten, 613/951-8096, Fax: 613/951-3231
Director General, Resources, Technology & Services Statistics, A. Meguerditchian, 613/951-3423, Includes Services; Science & Technology; Industrial Organization & Finance; Agriculture; Investment & Capital Stock; Small Business & Special Surveys.
Director General, Industry, Trade & Prices Statistics, R. Ryan, 613/951-9493, Includes Industry; Prices; International Trade & Transportation.
Manager, Large Enterprise Statistics, P. Demmons, 613/951-4055

COMMUNICATIONS & OPERATIONS
Asst. Chief Statistician, Y. Goulet, 613/951-6088, Fax: 613/951-0556
Director General, Marketing & Information Services, D.J. Desjardins, 613/951-7614, Includes Communications; Dissemination; Library Services; & Marketing.
Director General, Regional Operations, M. Levine, 613/951-9750, Includes Survey Operations; & Advisory Services.
Director General, Surveys Branch, J.-P. Trudel, 613/951-9660, Includes Operations & Integration; Operations Research & Development; & Administrative Support Services.

INFORMATICS & METHODOLOGY
Asst. Chief Statistician, G.J. Brackstone, 613/951-9908, Fax: 613/951-4842
Director General, Informatics, B. Slater, 613/951-9932, Includes Informatics User Services; Systems Development; & Main Computer Centre.
Director General, Classification Systems, R. Barnabé, 613/951-8096, Includes Business Register; Standards; & Geography.
Acting Director General, Methodology, G.J. Brackstone, 613/951-9908, Includes Social Survey Methods; Small Area & Administrative Data; Business Survey Methods, Household Survey Methods.
Director, International & Professional Relations, B. Prigly, 613/951-8917

MANAGEMENT SERVICES
Asst. Chief Statistician, Y. Fortin, 613/951-9866, Fax: 613/951-5290
Director General, Human Resources, J.P. McLaughlin, 613/951-9955
Director, Data Access & Control Services, L. Desramaux, 613/951-9349
Director, Finance, Planning, Audit & Evaluation, J.W. Coombs, 613/951-3730

NATIONAL ACCOUNTS & ANALYTICAL STUDIES
Asst. Chief Statistician, J.S. Wells, 613/951-9760, Fax: 613/951-5290
Acting Director General, Analytical Studies, J.S. Wells, 613/951-9760, Includes Social & Economic Studies; Current Economic Analysis; Business & Labour Market Analysis; Micro Economic Studies & Analysis; & Family & Community Support Systems.
Director General, System of National Accounts, K. Lal, 613/951-9157, Includes Input-Output; Industry Measures & Analysis; National Accounts & Environment; Balance of Payments; & Public Institutions.
Senior Social Scientist, P. Reed, 613/951-8217

SOCIAL, INSTITUTIONS & LABOUR STATISTICS
Asst. Chief Statistician, D.B. Petrie, 613/951-6155, Fax: 613/951-0556
Acting Director General, Census & Demographic Statistics, B. Laroche, 613/951-6537, Includes Census Management Office; Census Operations; Housing; Family & Social Statistics; & Demolinguistics.

Director General, Institutions & Social Statistics, M.C. Wolfson, 613/951-8216, Includes Education, Culture & Tourism; & Health Statistics.
Director General, Labour & Household Surveys, Vacant, 613/951-0053, Includes Household Surveys; Labour; Labour & Household Surveys Analysis; Post Censal Survey Program; & Special Surveys.
Executive Director, Canadian Centre for Justice Statistics, A. Kohut, 613/951-5858
Director, Integration & Development of Social Statistics, G.E. Priest, 613/951-9301

STATISTICS CANADA REGIONAL REFERENCE CENTRES
Toll Free: 1-800-263-1136, TDD: 1-800-363-7629
Toll Free Orders: 1-800-267-6677

Each centre provides a full range of the Agency's products and services. Each has a library and a sales counter where users can consult or purchase print and electronic publications, microcomputer diskettes, microfiche, maps and more. Each also has facilities to retrieve information from CANSIM and other databases, and most offer seminars and consultations.

Statistics Canada Regional Centres
Calgary: First Street Plaza, #401, 138 - 4 Ave. SE, Calgary AB T2G 4Z6 – 403/292-6717; Fax: 403/292-4958
Edmonton: Park Square, 10001 Bellamy Hill, 9th Fl., Edmonton AB T5J 3B6 – 403/495-3027; Fax: 403/495-5318
Halifax: North American Life Centre, 1770 Market St., Halifax NS B3J 3M3 – 902/426-5331; Fax: 902/426-9538
Montréal: Tour Est, Complexe Guy-Favreau, #412, 200, boul René-Lévesque ouest, Montréal PQ H2Z 1X4 – 514/283-5725; Fax: 514/283-9350
National Capital Region: R.H. Coats Bldg., Lobby, Tunney's Pasture, Ottawa ON K1A 0T6 – 613/951-8116; Fax: 613/951-0581
Regina: Avord Tower, 2002 Victoria Ave., 9th Fl., Regina SK S4P 0R7 – 306/780-5405; Fax: 306/780-5403
Toronto: Arthur Meighen Bldg., 25 St. Clair Ave. East, 10th Fl., Toronto ON M4T 1M4 – 416/973-6586; Fax: 416/973-7475
Vancouver: Library Square Tower, #600, 300 West Georgia St., Vancouver BC V6B 6C4 – 604/666-3691; Fax: 604/666-4863
Winnipeg: MacDonald Bldg., #300, 344 Edmonton St., Winnipeg MB R3B 3L9 – 204/983-4020; Fax: 204/983-7543

STATUS OF WOMEN CANADA (SWC)/ Condition féminine Canada
#700, 360 Albert St., Ottawa ON K1A 1C3
613/995-7835; Fax: 613/957-3359; URL: http://canada.gc.ca/depts/agencies/swcind_e.html

SWC is the federal government department dedicated to women's equality. It is responsible for policy coordination, research, funding & technical assistance, & communications activities related to the promotion of women's equality in all spheres of Canadian life. SWC was the lead government department involved in the coordination of Canadian preparations for the Fourth United Nations World Conference on Women in Bejing, China (September 1995).

The Agency ensures that women's equality is integrated into all federal government legislation, policies, programs & initiatives. It provides financial & technical assistance to women's groups & other voluntary organizations which promote public understanding of women's equality issues. SWC also encourages action by key institutions to incorporate women's equality into their decision-making structures, policies & programs, & enables women's organizations working on women's equality issues to improve & develop their planning & organizaitonal skills.
Secretary of State, Hon. Hedy Fry
Coordinator, Louise Bergeron-de Villiers

Canadian Almanac & Directory 1997

Director General, External Relations & Communications, Mary Glen
Director, Executive Secretariat, Donna McKeeby
Acting Director, Policy, Zeynep Karman
Director, Resource Management, Guylaine Metayer
Director, Women's Program, Jackie Claxton

TELEFILM CANADA/Téléfilm Canada
Tour de la Banque Nationale, 600, De La Gauchetière ouest, 14e étage, Montréal PQ H3B 4L8
514/283-6363; Fax: 514/283-8212

The Corporation supports & promotes private sector development of Canada's film, television & video industry. Reports to government through the Minister of Canadian Heritage.
Chair, Robert Dinan
Executive Director, François Macerola

Offices in Canada
Halifax: 5523 Spring Garden Rd., PO Box 27, Halifax NS B3J 3T1 – 902/426-8425; Fax: 902/426-4445
Toronto: 2 Bloor St. West, 22nd Fl., Toronto ON M4W 3E2 – 416/973-6436; Fax: 416/973-8606
Vancouver: #350, 375 Water St., Vancouver BC V6B 5C6 – 604/666-1566; Fax: 604/666-7754

International Offices
France: 91, rue du Faubourg, Saint-Honoré, Paris 75008, France – /011-33-1-44-18-35-30; Fax: /011-33-1-47-05-72-76
USA: #400, 9350 Wilshire Rd., Beverly Hills CA 90212, USA – 310/859-0268; Fax: 310/276-4741

TRANSPORT CANADA (TC)/ Transports Canada
Transport Canada Building, 330 Sparks St., Ottawa ON K1A 0N5
613/990-2309; Fax: 613/995-0351; URL: http://www.tc.gc.ca

Provides for a safe, environmentally sound national transportation system consistent with a competitive economy. Department consists of operational & support groups working at headquarters in Ottawa & sites across Canada.

ACTS ADMINISTERED
Aeronautics Act
Act respecting regulations made pursuant to section 5 of the Aeronautics Act
Airport Transfer Act
Arctic Waters Pollution Prevention Act
Canada Shipping Act
Canada Transportation Act
Coasting Trade Act
Department of Transport Act
Government Railways Act
Hamilton Harbour Commissioners Act
Harbour Commissions Act
Intercolonial & PEI Railways Employees' Provident Fund Act
Marine & Aviation War Risks Act
Marine Insurance Act
Marine Transportation Security Act
Maritime Code Act
Meaford Harbour Act
Montréal Port Wardens Act
Motor Vehicle Fuel Consumption Standards Act
Motor Vehicle Safety Act
Navigable Waters Protection Act
Ontario Harbours Agreement Act
Pilotage Act
Public Harbours & Port Facilities Act
Québec Port Wardens Act
Railway Act
Railway Safety Act
Safe Containers Convention Act

Toronto Harbour Commissioners Act
Toronto Harbour Commissioners Act
Transportation of Dangerous Goods Act
Acts Transport Canada is Responsible for, but does not Administer
Bills of Lading Act
Canada Ports Corporation Act
Canadian National Commercialization Act
Canadian National Montréal Terminals Act
Canadian National Railways Act
Canadian National Railways Financing & Guarantee Act
Canadian National Toronto Terminals Act
Carriage by Air Act
Carriage of Goods by Water Act
Civil Air Navigation Services Commercialization Act
International Rapids Power Development Act
Marine Atlantic Inc. Acquisition Authorization Act
Motor Vehicle Transport Act
National Transcontinental Railway Act
Northern Transportation Company Ltd., Disposal Authorization
Railway Relocation & Crossing Act
St. Lawrence Seaway Authority Act
Shipping Conferences Exemption Act
Winnipeg Terminals Act
Some Transport Implications
Blue Water Bridge Authority Act
Bridges Act
Buffalo & Fort Erie Public Bridge Act
Canadian Environmental Assessment Act
Canadian Environmental Protection Act
Canadian Transportation Accident Investigation & Safety Board Act
Excise Tax Act
Government Property Traffic Act
National Energy Board Act
Non-smoker's Health Act
Public Works Act
Ste-Foy-St-Nicholas Bridge Act
United States Wreckers Act
Minister, Hon. David Anderson, 613/991-0700
Deputy Minister, Nick Mulder, 613/990-7127, Fax: 613/991-0851
Associate Deputy Minister, Margaret Bloodworth
Senior Asst. Deputy Minister, Paul Gauvin, 613/991-3016, Fax: 613/990-8890
Executive Director, Transition Secretariat, David Bell, 613/993-4465, Fax: 613/954-1993
Director General, Communications, Rhoda Barrett, 613/990-6138, Fax: 613/995-0351
Director General, Financial Policy & Operations, Les Kom, 613/998-6522, Fax: 613/998-1337
Regional Director General, Atlantic, Gerry Berigan, 506/851-7315, Fax: 506/851-3099
Regional Director General, Ontario, Terence Gibson, 416/952-2170, Fax: 416/952-0170
Regional Director General, Pacific, Mark Duncan, 604/666-5849, Fax: 604/666-2961
Regional Director General, Prairie & Northern, J. Scott Broughton, 204/984-8105, Fax: 204/984-8119
Regional Director General, Québec, Suzanne Tining, 514/283-0084, Fax: 514/283-4661
Departmental General Counsel, R.J. Green, 613/990-5768, Fax: 613/990-5777
Deputy Chief Negotiator, ANS Negotiating Team, Glen J.D. McDougall, 613/990-3811, Fax: 613/990-3189

AIRPORTS GROUP
Responsible for implementing the National Airports Policy, under which the government retains ownership of the largest & busiest airports, turning their operation over to Canadian Airport Authorities, & withdraws from the ownership, opration & subsidization of other airports; operating airport facilities & services -- such as airfields & terminals, as well as emergency response services -- until the full implementation of the new policy, & continuing to run remote air-

ports; providing financial support for the operation of non-Transport Canada operated airports until the new policy is implemented; & administering an Airports Capital Assistance Program to provide financial assistance for safety-related airside capital projects, heavy airside mobile equipment purchases, safety-related groundside improvements, & refurbishing or protecting other assets anywhere on airport property.

Acting Asst.Deputy Minister, Iain Henderson, 613/990-3001, Fax: 613/998-5008

Director General, Airport Transfers, Michael Farquhar, 613/998-2956, Fax: 613/998-2960

Director General, Business Management, Rod Dean, 613/990-0510, Fax: 613/990-8889

Manager, National Airports Policy Implementation, Lorne Pennycook, 613/990-3725, Fax: 613/957-4261

CORPORATE SERVICES GROUP

Provides overall direction, management & services within the department in the areas of finance, human resources, information management & technology, audit & administration.

Asst. Deputy Minister, Micheline Desjardins, 613/991-6565, Fax: 613/991-0426

Director General, Executive Services, William J. McCullough, 613/993-7412, Fax: 613/991-2731

Director General, Financial Management, Jim Lynes, 613/993-5660, Fax: 613/991-4410

Director General, Finance Policy & Operations, Les kom, 613/998-6522, Fax: 613/998-1337

Director General, Human Resources, Antoinette Fracassi, 613/991-6315, Fax: 613/991-0722

Director General, Informatics & Administrative Services, André Morency, 613/993-4307, Fax: 613/990-2469

POLICY GROUP

Responsible for setting policies relating to rail, marine, highways, motor carrier & air transportation, as well as setting departmental strategic policy & coordinating intergovernmental relations. Also responsible for assessing the performance of the overall transportation systems & its components, & developing supporting information. Supports rail passenger services through payments to VIA Rail, ferry services through payments to Marine Atlantic & to provincial & private operators, & highway construction & improvement projects with the provinces.

Asst. Deputy Minister, Moya Greene, 613/998-1880, Fax: 613/991-1440

Director General, Air Policy & Programs, Robert Mayes, 613/993-0054

Director General, Corporate Relations, Ted Cherrett, 613/991-6500, Fax: 613/991-6422

Director General, Economic Analysis, Ted Rudback, 613/998-0684, Fax: 613/957-3280

Director General, Marine Policy & Programs, André Pageot, 613/998-1843, Fax: 613/998-1845

Director General, Surface Policy & Programs, Kristine Burr, 613/998-2689, Fax: 613/998-2686

PORTS & HARBOURS GROUP

Responsible for converting ports essential to international trade into Canada Port Authorities, as set out in the National Marine Policy announced in December 1995. The Group is divesting the more than 500 remaining public harbours & ports to other interests over the next six years under the new policy. Responsible for ensuring the safety & efficiency of the public ports system.

Executive Director, Neil MacNeil, 613/990-9885, Fax: 613/952-1356

Director General, Randy Morriss, 613/990-3014, Fax: 613/954-0838

Harbour Commissions

Fraser River: #505, 713 Columbia St., New Westminster BC V3M 1B2 – 604/597-9058; Fax: 604/524-1127, CEO, Rick Pearce, 604/524-6655

Hamilton: 605 James St. North, Hamilton ON L8L 1K1 – 905/383-9121; Fax: 905/528-6282, 525-7258, CEO, Bob Hennessy, 905/525-4330

Nanaimo: 104 Front St., PO Box 131, Nanaimo BC V9R 5K4 – 250/753-4146; Fax: 250/753-4899, CEO, William E. Mills

North Fraser: 2020 Airport Rd., Richmond BC V8B 1C6 – 604/530-9370; Fax: 604/530-6729, CEO, George Colquhoun, 604/273-1866

Oshawa: 1050 Farewell St., Ottawa ON L1H 6N6 – 905/576-0400; Fax: 905/576-3701, CEO, Donna Taylor

Port Alberni: 2750 Harbour Rd., PO Box 99, Port Alberni BC V9Y 7M6 – 250/723-3373; Fax: 250/723-1114, CEO, Denis White, 250/723-5312

Thunder Bay: 100 Main St., Thunder Bay ON P7B 6R9 – 807/345-0557; Fax: 807/345-9058, CEO, Denis Johnson, 807/345-6400

Toronto: 60 Harbour St., Toronto ON M5J 1B7 – 416/863-2020; Fax: 416/863-4830, CEO, Gary Reid, 416/863-2028

Windsor: 500 Riverside Dr. West, Windsor ON N9A 5K6 – 519/991-2001; Fax: 519/258-5905, CEO, David Cree, 519/258-5741

SAFETY & SECURITY GROUP

Responsible for establishing & administering regulations & standards necessary for the safe conduct of Canadian civil aviation. Develops & enforces marine regulaitons & the regulatory aspects of rail safety, transport of dangerous goods, motor vehicles & motor carrier safety, & motor vehicle emissions. Also responsible for developing & enforcing regulations & standards under federal jurisdiction to prevent unlawful interference with air, rail & marine transportation.

Asst. Deputy Minister, Ronald Jackson, 613/990-3838, Fax: 613/990-2947

Director General, Aircraft Services, Ronald D. Armstrong, 613/998-3316, Fax: 613/991-0365

Director General, Air Navigation System, G. Rodrigue, 613/990-3896

Director General, Civil Aviation, Don Spruston, 613/990-1322, Fax: 613/957-4208

Director General, Marine Safety, Vacant

Director General, Railway Legislation, Colin J. Churcher, 613/993-7392, Fax: 613/990-7767

Director General, Railway Safety, Terry Burtch, 613/998-2984, Fax: 613/990-2924

Director General, Research & Development, August E. Pokotylo, 613/991-6029, Fax: 613/991-6045

Director General, Road Safety & Motor Vehicle Regulation, Nicole Pageot, 613/993-6735, Fax: 613/990-2914

Acting Director General, Safety Programs, Strategies & Co-ordination, Gaétan Boucher, 613/990-3797, Fax: 613/990-5058

Acting Director General, Security & Emergency Planning, Hal Whiteman, 613/990-3651, Fax: 613/996-6381

Director General, Transport Dangerous Goods, Dr. John Read, 613/990-1147, Fax: 613/993-5925

Associated Agencies, Boards & Commissions
- Civil Aviation Tribunal: 333 Laurier Ave. West, 12th Fl., Ottawa ON K1A 0N5 – 613/998-1275; Fax: 613/990-9153

Chair, Faye Helen Smith

Other Associated Agencies, Boards & Commissions
Listed alphabetically in detail, this section.
Atlantic Pilotage Authority
Canadian Transportation Agency
Great Lakes Pilotage Authority
Laurentian Pilotage Authority
Marine Atlantic Inc.
Pacific Pilotage Authority
St. Lawrence Seaway Authority
Via Rail Canada

TRANSPORTATION SAFETY BOARD OF CANADA/Bureau de la sécurité des transports du Canada
200 Promenade du Portage, 4e étage, Hull PQ K1A 1K8

819/994-3741; Fax: 819/997-2239

The Board is an independent agency reporting to Parliament through the President of the Queen's Privy Council. The formal name for the Board is the Canadian Transportation Accident Investigation & Safety Board. Its sole aim is the advancement of transportation safety in the marine, rail, commodity pipeline & air modes of transport. It conducts investigations of occurrences, makes findings, identifies safety deficiencies, conducts safety studies, & makes recommendations designed to prevent further occurrences. Because the Board is independent, its transportation accident investigations are completely separate from the regulatory agencies responsible for transportation. In making findings & recommendations it is not the function of the Board to assign fault or determine civil or criminal liability.

Chair, Hon. Benoît Bouchard

Executive Director, Ken Johnson

Chief, Communications, Jacques Babin, 819/994-8051, Email: Jacques.Babin@bst-tsb.x400.gc.ca

TREASURY BOARD OF CANADA/Conseil du Trésor du Canada
140 O'Connor St., Ottawa ON K1A 0R5

613/957-2400; Fax: 613/952-3658; URL: http://www.tbs-sct.gc.ca

The Treasury Board is a Cabinet Committee of government headed by the President of the Treasury Board. The committee constituting the Treasury Board includes, in addition to the President, the Minister of Finance & four other ministers appointed by the Governor-in-Council. The main role of the Treasury Board is the management of the government's financial, personnel & administrative responsibilities. The Treasury Board derives its authority primarily from the Financial Administration Act & is supported by the Treasury Board Secretariat.

President & Minister Responsible, Infrastructure, Hon. Marcel Massé, 613/957-2666, Fax: 613/990-2806

Secretary & Comptroller General of Canada, V. Peter Harder, 613/952-1777, Fax: 613/952-6596

Deputy Minister, Corporate Services, Joy Kane, 613/995-8487, Fax: 613/947-3643

Deputy Secretary, Human Resources Policy Branch, Jean-Claude Bouchard, 613/952-3011, Fax: 613/954-1018

Deputy Secretary, Official Languages & Employment Equity Branch, Madeleine Ouellon, 613/952-2852, Fax: 613/941-4262

Acting Deputy Secretary, Program Branch, Paul Thibault, 613/957-0531, Fax: 613/957-0525

Special Advisor to the Secretary, John Edwards

OFFICE OF INFRASTRUCTURE
West Tower, 300 Laurier Ave. West, 3rd Fl., Ottawa ON K1A 0R5

613/952-3171; Fax: 613/952-7979; Email: infrastructure@tbs-sct.x400.gc.ca

Executive Director, Norman Moyer

Director General, Policy & Coordination, Len Endemann

Canadian Almanac & Directory 1997

VETERANS AFFAIRS CANADA/
Anciens combattants Canada
Daniel J. MacDonald Bldg., 161 Grafton St., PO Box 7700, Charlottetown PE C1A 8M9
902/566-8195; Fax: 902/566-8508
Ottawa: 66 Slater St., Ottawa ON K1A 0P4
613/992-7467, Fax: 613/996-9969

ACTS ADMINISTERED
Army Benevolent Fund Act
Children of Deceased Veterans Education Assistance Act
Department of Veterans Affairs Act
Merchant Navy Veterans & Civilian War-related Benefits Act
Pension Act
The Returned Soldiers' Insurance Act
Soldier Settlement Act
Special Operators War Service Benefits Act
Supervisors War Service Benefits Act
Veterans Review & Appeal Board Act
Veterans Benefits Act
Veterans Insurance Act
Veterans' Land Act
War Service Grants Act
War Veterans Allowance Act
Women's Royal Naval Services & the South African Military Nursing Service (Benefits) Act
Related Acts
Halifax Relief Commission Pension Continuation Act
Royal Canadian Mounted Police Pension Contrinuation Act (in Part)
Royal Canadian Mounted Police Superannuation Act (in Part)
Minister, Hon. Douglas Young
Secretary of State (Veterans Affairs), Hon. Lawrence MacAulay, 613/996-4649, Fax: 613/954-1054
Deputy Minister, J. David Nicholson, 902/566-8666, Fax: 902/566-7868, Ottawa: 613/996-6881; Fax: 613/952-7709
Director General, Audit, J.G. Harper, 902/566-8018
Director General, Portfolio Executive Services, B. Bowen, 613/992-3801
Director General, Communications, Sandra Lavigne, 902/566-8457
Director, Corporate Planning, Keith Hillier, 902/566-8150
Project Manager, Benefits Redesign Project, Ron Herbert, 902/368-0530

CORPORATE SERVICES
Asst. Deputy Minister, Brian Ferguson, 902/566-8047, Fax: 902/566-8521
Director General, Finance, Ray Bray, 902/566-8320, Fax: 902/368-0411
Director General, Human Resources, Ted Marks, 902/566-8408, Fax: 902/566-8781
Asst. Director General, Information Technology Division, Howard Williams, 902/566-8236

VETERANS SERVICES
Asst. Deputy Minister, Dennis Wallace, 902/947-4908, Fax: 902/947-4901
Director General, Benefits, Doris Boulet, 613/566-8808, Fax: 613/566-8073
Acting Executive Director, Ste. Annes Hospital, R. Gravel, 514/457-8400
Director General, Health Care, W.D. Mogan, 902/566-8302, Fax: 902/566-8039

Regional Offices
Atlantic: 45 Alderney Dr., PO Box 1002, Dartmouth NS B3Y 3Z7 – 902/426-6305; Fax: 902/426-7447, Director General, Ron Witt
Ontario: 6 Tweedsmuir Rd., Kirkland Lake ON P2N 3P4 – 705/566-4132; Fax: 705/567-7971, Director General, Giséle Toupin
Pacific: #400, 1185 West Georgia St., PO Box 5600, Vancouver BC V6E 4J5 – 604/666-3101; Fax: 604/666-2881, Director General, Bob Atkinson
Prairie: #610, 330 Graham Ave., PO Box 6050, Winnipeg MB R3C 4G1 – 204/983-5316; Fax: 204/983-2563, Director General, Elaine Heinicke
Québec: 4545, rue Queen Mary, Montréal PQ H3W 1W4 – 514/496-6412; Fax: 514/496-4339, Director General, Suzanne Lalonde

Associated Agencies, Boards & Commissions
•Army Benevolent Fund: Veterans Affairs Bldg., 66 Slater St., Ottawa ON K1A 0P4 – 613/996-6150
National Secretary, H. Graham Ball
•Bureau of Pension Advocates: J. MacDonald Bldg., 2nd Fl., PO Box 7700, Charlottetown PE C1A 8M9 – 902/566-8640; Fax: 902/566-7804
Chief Pensions Advocate, Simon Coakeley
•Veterans Review & Appeal Board: Daniel J. MacDonald Bldg., Ground Fl., PO Box 7700, Charlottetown PE C1A 8M9 – 902/566-8636; Fax: 902/566-7371
Chair, Brian Chambers

VIA RAIL CANADA INC.
2, Place Ville-Marie, CP 8116, Succ A, Montréal PQ H3C 3N3
514/871-6000; Fax: 514/861-6463

The corporation manages Canada's national passenger rail network. Reports to government through the Minister of Transport.

Chair, Marc LeFrançois
President, Terry Ivany, 514/871-6161
Executive Vice-President & COO, James Roche
Vice-President & Chief of Transportation, Robert J. Guiney
Vice-President, Equipment Maintenance, Réjean Béchamp
Vice-President, Planning & Finance, Roger Paquette
Vice-President, Customer Service, Roy Arnold
Senior Vice-President, Human Resources & Administration, Jean-Roch Boivin
Treasurer, Rashid Maqsood
Vice-President, Marketing, Christena Keon Sirsly
General Manager, Public Affairs, Marc-André Charlebois
General Counsel, Jean Patenaude

WESTERN ECONOMIC DIVERSIFICATION CANADA (WD)/Diversification de l'économie de l'Ouest Canada
Canada Place, #1500, 9700 Jasper Ave., Edmonton AB T5J 4H7
403/495-4164; Fax: 403/495-6876; URL: http://www.myriadgate.net/wd/

Promotes the development & diversification of the economy of Western Canada & advances the interests of Western Canada in national economic policy. Seeks new innovative partnerships with both the public & private sectors to address the information, business services & financing needs of small & medium-sized enterprises. By partnering with financial institutions, industry associations & the four western provinces, WD is satisfying the needs of small business by creating a positive business climate & by improving access to capital, information & business services. Resources are strategically targeted to industries having the greatest potential for growth in economic activity.

Minister, Hon. Jon Gerrard, 613/995-9001, Fax: 613/990-4056
Deputy Minister, John D. McLure, 613/952-9382, Fax: 613/954-1044
Director General, Public Affairs, Don Carlson, 403/495-4164, Fax: 403/495-6874

Regional Offices
Alberta: Canada Place, #1500, 9700 Jasper Ave., Edmonton AB T5J 4H7 – 403/495-4164, Director, Amin Visram
British Columbia: #1200, 1055 Dunsmuir St., PO Box 49276, Bentall Postal Stn, Vancouver BC V7X 1L3 – 604/666-6256, Toll Free: 1-800-663-2008, Director, Dan Genn
Manitoba: #712, 240 Graham Ave., PO Box 777, Winnipeg MB R3C 2L4 – 204/983-0697, Director, Dave Boldt
Ottawa: 200 Kent St., 8th Fl., PO Box 2128, Stn D, Ottawa ON K1P 5W3 – 613/952-9378, Director, Onno Kremers
Saskatchewan: #601, 119 - 4th Ave. South, PO Box 2025, Saskatoon SK S7K 3S7 – 306/975-4373, Director, Laura Small

GOVERNMENT OF ALBERTA
Seat of Government: Legislative Assembly, 9718 - 107 St., Edmonton AB T5K 1E4
URL: http://www.gov.ab.ca/

The Province of Alberta entered Confederation September 1, 1905. It has an area of 638,232.66 km2, and the StatsCan census population in 1991 was 2,454,553.

Office of the LIEUTENANT GOVERNOR
Legislature Bldg., 10800 - 97 Ave., 3rd Fl., Edmonton AB T5K 2B6
403/427-7243; Fax: 403/422-5134
Lieutenant Governor, Hon. Horace Andrew Olson
Secretary, Astrid Casavant

Office of the PREMIER
Legislature Bldg., #307, 10800 - 97 Ave., Edmonton AB T5K 2B6
403/427-2251; Fax: 403/427-1349; URL: http://www.gov.ab.ca/gov/prem/premier.html
Premier, Hon. Ralph Klein, Email: altatalk@censsw.gov.ab.ca
Deputy Minister, Executive Council, Vance MacNichol
Executive Director, Rod Love
Executive Asst., Sheryl Burns
Administrative Asst., Nargis Zaver
Director, Communications, Jim Dau, Fax: 403/422-3669
Director, Southern Alberta Office, Gordon Olsen, 403/297-6464, Fax: 403/297-4276

EXECUTIVE COUNCIL
Legislature Bldg., 10800 - 97 Ave., Edmonton AB T5K 2B6
403/427-2251; Fax: 403/427-1349

ACTS ADMINISTERED
Alberta Bill of Rights
Family Day Act
Northern Alberta Development Council Act
Public Service Act
Queen's Printer Act
Premier, President, Executive Council, Hon. Ralph Klein, 403/427-2251, Email: altatalk@censsw.gov.ab.ca
Minister, Advanced Education & Career Development, Hon. Jack W. Ady, 403/427-2291
Minister, Energy & Deputy Government House Leader, Hon. Patricia Black, 403/427-3740
Minister without Portfolio, Hon. Pearl Calahasen, 403/427-2180

Minister, Family & Social Services & Government House Leader, Hon. Stockwell Day, 403/427-2606
Provincial Treasurer, Hon. Jim Dinning, 403/427-8809
Minister, Justice & Attorney General & Deputy Government House Leader, Hon. Brian Evans, 403/427-3339
Minister, Transportation & Utilities, Hon. Robert Fischer, 403/427-2080
Minister, Health, Hon. Halvar Jonson, 403/427-3665
Minister, Environmental Protection, Hon. Ty Lund, 403/427-2391
Minister, Education, Hon. Gary G. Mar, 403/427-2025
Minister, Community Development, Hon. Shirley McClellan, 403/427-4928
Minister Responsible, Science & Research, Hon. Dianne Mirosh, 403/427-2294
Minister, Agriculture, Food & Rural Development, Hon. Walter Paszkowski, 403/427-2137
Minister, Federal & Intergovernmental Affairs, Hon. Ken Rostad, Q.C., 403/427-2585
Minister, Labour, Hon. Murray Smith, 403/427-3664
Minister, Municipal Affairs, Hon. Tom Thurber, 403/427-3744
Minister, Economic Development & Tourism, Hon. Dr. Steven West, 403/427-3162
Minister, Public Works, Supply & Services, Hon. Stan Woloshyn, 403/427-3162

Cabinet Office
Deputy Secretary, David Steeves
Director, Finance & Administration, Keray Henke, 403/427-1076
Coordinator, Cabinet Policy, Ivan Bernardo
Coordinator, Cabinet Policy, Doris Porter
Coordinator, Cabinet Policy, Wendy Rogers

Cabinet Standing Committees
Agenda & Priorities
Agriculture & Rural Development
Community Resources
Financial Planning
Health Restructuring
Natural Resources & Sustainable Development
Treasury Board

LEGISLATIVE ASSEMBLY
c/o Clerk's Office, #801, Legislature Annex, 9718 - 107 St., Edmonton AB T5K 1E4
403/427-2478; Fax: 403/427-5688; URL: http://www.assembly.ab.ca/

ACTS ADMINISTERED
Auditor General Act
Conflict of Interest Act
Election Act
Election Finances & Contributions Disclosure Act
Electoral Boundaries Commission Act
Electoral Divisions Act
Legislative Assembly Act
Ombudsman Act
Clerk: W.J. David McNeil
Speaker: Hon. Stanley Schumacher, 403/427-2464, Fax: 403/422-9553
Hansard: Gary Garrison, 403/427-2490, Fax: 403/427-1623
Librarian: Lorne Buhr, 403/422-5085, Fax: 403/427-6016
Clerk Asst., Louise Kamuchik
Speaker Asst., Moses Jung
Parliamentary Counsel, Rob Reynolds
Manager, Financial Management & Administrative Services, Jacquie Breault, 403/427-1359
Director, Human Resources, Cheryl Scarlett, 403/427-1364
Director, Public Information, Gary Garrison, 403/427-2490

Government Caucus Office (PC)
Legislature Annex, 9718 - 107 St., 7th Fl., Edmonton AB T5K 1E4
403/427-1800; Fax: 403/422-1671
Chief of Staff, Lisa Bowes, #402, Legislature Bldg., Edmonton AB T5K 2B6

Official Opposition Office (Lib.)
Legislature Annex, #204, 9718 - 107 St., Edmonton AB T5K 1E4
403/427-2292; Fax: 403/427-3697
Leader, Grant Mitchell
Chief of Staff, Kevin Stringer
Senior Researcher, Peter Taylor
Deputy Leader, Bettie Hewes

Standing Committees of the Legislature
Alberta Heritage Savings Trust Fund Act, Clerk, Diane Shumyla, 403/427-1350
Law & Regulations, Clerk, Corrine Dacyshyn, 403/427-1348
Legislative Offices, Clerk, Diane Shumyla, 403/427-1350
Members' Services, Clerk, David McNeil, 403/427-2478
Private Bills, Clerk, Florence Marston, 403/422-4837
Privileges & Election, Standing Orders & Printing, Clerk, Corinne Dacyshyn, 403/427-1348
Public Accounts, Clerk, Corrine Dacyshyn, 403/427-1348
Public Affairs, Clerk, Diane Shumlya, 403/427-1350

TWENTY-THIRD LEGISLATURE - ALBERTA
403/427-2478
Last General Election, June 15, 1993. Maximum Duration, 5 Years.
Party Standings (June 21, 1996):
Progressive Conservative (PC) 54
Liberal (Lib.) 29
Total 83
Salaries, Indemnities & Allowances: March 1, 1993 frozen - Members' sessional indemnity $36,420 plus $18,210 tax-free expense allowance. In addition to this are the following:
Premier $56,865
Ministers $44,700 (with portfolio); $19,869 (without portfolio)
Leader of the Official Opposition $44,700
Speaker $44,700
Deputy Speaker; Chair of Committees $22,350
Leader of a recognized Opposition $19,869
Following is: constituency (number of eligible voters at 1993 election) member, party affiliation, Edmonton telephone number. (Address for all is Legislature Bldg., 10800 - 97 Ave., Edmonton AB T5K 2B6.)

MEMBERS BY CONSTITUENCY
Athabasca-Wabasca (10,410) Mike Cardinal, PC, 403/427-8098
Banff-Cochrane (18,756) Hon. Brian Evans, PC, 403/427-2339
Barrhead-Westlock (15,900) Ken Kowalski, PC, 403/427-4557
Bonnyville (16,430) Leo Vasseur, Lib., 403/427-2292
Bow Valley (13,925) Dr. Lyle Oberg, PC, 403/427-1830
Calgary Bow (22,386) Bonny Laing, PC, 403/427-1811
Calgary Buffalo (21,606) Gary Dickson, Lib., 403/427-2293
Calgary Cross (20,889) Yvonne Fritz, PC, 403/422-5375
Calgary Currie (23,207) Jocelyn Burgener, PC, 403/427-1837
Calgary East (20,041) Moe Amery, PC, 403/422-5382
Calgary Egmont (27,858) Dennis Herard, PC, 403/422-5378
Calgary Elbow (24,727) Hon. Ralph Klein, PC, 403/427-2251
Calgary Fish Creek (22,079) Heather Forsyth, PC, 403/427-1851
Calgary Foothills (22,478) Hon. Patricia Black, PC, 403/427-3740
Calgary Glenmore (23,077) Hon. Dianne Mirosh, PC, 403/427-2294
Calgary Lougheed (20,053) Hon. Jim Dinning, PC, 403/427-8809
Calgary McCall (18,015) Shiraz Shariff, PC, 403/422-0685
Calgary Montrose (20,314) Hung Pham, PC, 403/427-1865
Calgary Mountain View (22,666) Mark Hlady, PC, 403/422-5380
Calgary North Hill (22,990) Richard Magnus, PC, 403/427-3018
Calgary North West (20,843) Frank Bruseker, Lib., 403/427-2293
Calgary Nose Creek (22,043) Hon. Gary G. Mar, PC, 403/427-2025
Calgary Shaw (23,485) Jon Havelock, PC, 403/422-5376
Calgary Varsity (26,888) Hon. Murray Smith, PC, 403/427-3664
Calgary West (22,250) Danny Dalla-Longa, Lib., 403/427-2292
Cardston-Chief Mountain (8,675) Hon. Jack W. Ady, PC, 403/427-2291
Chinook (10,128) Hon. Shirley McClellan, PC, 403/427-4928
Clover Bar-Fort Saskatchewan (20,543) Muriel Abdurahman, Lib., 403/427-2293
Cypress-Medicine Hat (13,288) Lorne Taylor, PC, 403/427-1822
Drayton Valley-Calmar (16,444) Hon. Tom Thurber, PC, 403/427-3744
Drumheller (16,990) Hon. Stanley Schumacher, PC, 403/427-2464
Dunvegan (15,926) Glen Clegg, PC, 403/427-1806
Edmonton Avonmore (21,282) Gene Zwozdesky, Lib., 403/427-2292
Edmonton Beverly-Belmont (18,397) Julius Yankowsky, PC, 403/422-1357
Edmonton Centre (20,761) Michael Henry, Lib., 403/427-2293
Edmonton Ellerslie (16,774) Debby Carlson, Lib., 403/427-2293
Edmonton Glengarry (19,388) Laurence Decore, Lib., 403/427-2292
Edmonton Glenora (23,653) Howard Sapers, Lib., 403/427-2292
Edmonton Gold Bar (26,462) Bettie Hewes, Lib., 403/427-2292
Edmonton Highlands-Beverly (19,421) Alice Hanson, Lib., 403/427-2293
Edmonton Manning (20,143) Peter Sekulic, Lib., 403/427-2293
Edmonton Mayfield (22,264) Lance White, Lib., 403/427-2293
Edmonton McClung (22,520) Grant Mitchell, Lib., 403/427-2292
Edmonton Meadowlark (21,339) Karen Liebovici, Lib., 403/427-2293
Edmonton Millwoods (16,263) Don Massey, Lib., 403/427-2293
Edmonton Norwood (21,997) Andrew Beniuk, PC, 403/422-3848
Edmonton Roper (18,257) Sine Chadi, Lib., 403/427-2292
Edmonton Rutherford (22,546) Percy Wickman, Lib., 403/427-2292
Edmonton Strathcona (24,721) Al Zariwny, Lib., 403/427-2293
Edmonton Whitemud (20,348) Mike Percy, Lib., 403/427-2292
Fort McMurray (20,344) Adam Germain, Lib., 403/427-2292
Grande Prairie-Smoky (15,622) Hon. Walter Paszkowski, PC, 403/427-2137
Grande Prairie-Wapiti (15,600) Wayne Jacques, PC, 403/427-1858

Canadian Almanac & Directory 1997

3-94 GOVERNMENT OF ALBERTA

Highwood (18,163) Don Tannas, PC, 403/427-1826
Innisfail-Sylvan Lake (16,014) Gary Severtson, PC, 403/427-1857
Lac La Biche-St. Paul (15,218) Paul Langevin, PC, 403/422-5843
Lacombe-Stettler (17,957) Judy Gordon, PC, 403/427-1807
Leduc (20,399) Terry Kirkland, Lib., 403/427-2293
Lesser Slave Lake (11,617) Hon. Pearl Calahasen, PC, 403/427-2180
Lethbridge East (21,759) Ken Nicol, Lib., 403/427-2293
Lethbridge West (19,446) Clint Dunford, PC, 403/427-1142
Little Bow (14,608) Barry McFarland, PC, 403/427-0879
Medicine Hat (22,019) Rob Renner, PC, 403/427-5381
Olds-Didsbury (19,585) Roy Brassard, PC, 403/427-1812
Peace River (14,100) Gary Friedel, PC, 403/422-5374
Pincher Creek-MacLeod (15,061) David Coutts, PC, 403/427-1828
Ponoka-Rimbey (13,847) Hon. Halvar Jonson, PC, 403/427-3665
Red Deer North (18,286) Hon. Stockwell Day, PC, 403/427-2606
Red Deer South (19,670) Victor Doerksen, PC, 403/427-1145
Redwater (18,999) Mary Anne Balsillie, Lib., 403/427-2292
Rocky Mountain House (14,307) Hon. Ty Lund, PC, 403/427-2391
Sherwood Park (24,425) Bruce Collingwood, Lib., 403/427-2293
Spruce Grove-Sturgeon-St. Albert (18,846) Colleen Soetaert, Lib., 403/427-2293
St. Albert (18,846) Len Bracko, Lib., 403/427-2293
Stony Plain (18,828) Hon. Stan Woloshyn, PC, 403/427-3666
Taber-Warner (17,406) Ron Hierath, PC, 403/427-1864
Three Hills-Airdrie (17,406) Carol Haley, PC, 403/427-3020
Vegreville-Viking (18,853) Ed Stelmach, PC, 403/427-1879
Vermillion-Lloydminster (17,201) Hon. Dr. Steven West, PC, 403/427-3162
Wainwright (15,600) Hon. Robert Fischer, PC, 403/427-2080
West Yellowhead (16,495) Duco Van Binsbergen, Lib., 403/427-2293
Wetaskiwin-Camrose (20,693) Hon. Ken Rostad, Q.C., PC, 403/427-2585
Whitecourt-St. Anne (17,367) Peter Trynchy, PC, 403/427-0495

MEMBERS (ALPHABETICAL)

Muriel Abdurahman, Clover Bar-Fort Saskatchewan (20,543)Lib., 403/427-2293
Hon. Jack W. Ady, Cardston-Chief Mountain (8,675)PC, 403/427-2291
Moe Amery, Calgary East (20,041)PC, 403/422-5382
Mary Anne Balsillie, Redwater (18,999)Lib., 403/427-2292
Andrew Beniuk, Edmonton Norwood (21,997)PC, 403/422-3848
Hon. Patricia Black, Calgary Foothills (22,478)PC, 403/427-3740
Len Bracko, St. Albert (18,846)Lib., 403/427-2293
Roy Brassard, Olds-Didsbury (19,585)PC, 403/427-1812
Frank Bruseker, Calgary North West (20,843)Lib., 403/427-2293
Jocelyn Burgener, Calgary Currie (23,207)PC, 403/427-1837
Hon. Pearl Calahasen, Lesser Slave Lake (11,617)PC, 403/427-2180
Mike Cardinal, Athabasca-Wabasca (10,410)PC, 403/427-8098

Debby Carlson, Edmonton Ellerslie (16,774)Lib., 403/427-2293
Sine Chadi, Edmonton Roper (18,257)Lib., 403/427-2292
Glen Clegg, Dunvegan (15,926)PC, 403/427-1806
Bruce Collingwood, Sherwood Park (24,425)Lib., 403/427-2293
David Coutts, Pincher Creek-MacLeod (15,061)PC, 403/427-1828
Danny Dalla-Longa, Calgary West (22,250)Lib., 403/427-2292
Hon. Stockwell Day, Red Deer North (18,286)PC, 403/427-2606
Laurence Decore, Edmonton Glengarry (19,388)Lib., 403/427-2292
Gary Dickson, Calgary Buffalo (21,606)Lib., 403/427-2293
Hon. Jim Dinning, Calgary Lougheed (20,053)PC, 403/427-8809
Victor Doerksen, Red Deer South (19,670)PC, 403/427-1145
Clint Dunford, Lethbridge West (19,446)PC, 403/427-1142
Hon. Brian Evans, Banff-Cochrane (18,756)PC, 403/427-2339
Hon. Robert Fischer, Wainwright (15,600)PC, 403/427-2080
Heather Forsyth, Calgary Fish Creek (22,079)PC, 403/427-1851
Gary Friedel, Peace River (14,100)PC, 403/422-5374
Yvonne Fritz, Calgary Cross (20,889)PC, 403/422-5375
Adam Germain, Fort McMurray (20,344)Lib., 403/427-2292
Judy Gordon, Lacombe-Stettler (17,957)PC, 403/427-1807
Carol Haley, Three Hills-Airdrie (17,406)PC, 403/427-3020
Alice Hanson, Edmonton Highlands-Beverly (19,421)Lib., 403/427-2293
Jon Havelock, Calgary Shaw (23,485)PC, 403/422-5376
Michael Henry, Edmonton Centre (20,761)Lib., 403/427-2293
Dennis Herard, Calgary Egmont (27,858)PC, 403/422-5378
Bettie Hewes, Edmonton Gold Bar (26,462)Lib., 403/427-2292
Ron Hierath, Taber-Warner (17,406)PC, 403/427-1864
Mark Hlady, Calgary Mountain View (22,666)PC, 403/422-5380
Wayne Jacques, Grande Prairie-Wapiti (15,600)PC, 403/427-1858
Hon. Halvar Jonson, Ponoka-Rimbey (13,847)PC, 403/427-3665
Terry Kirkland, Leduc (20,399)Lib., 403/427-2293
Hon. Ralph Klein, Calgary Elbow (24,727)PC, 403/427-2251
Ken Kowalski, Barrhead-Westlock (15,900)PC, 403/427-4557
Bonny Laing, Calgary Bow (22,386)PC, 403/427-1811
Paul Langevin, Lac La Biche-St. Paul (15,218)PC, 403/422-5843
Karen Liebovici, Edmonton Meadowlark (21,339)Lib., 403/427-2293
Hon. Ty Lund, Rocky Mountain House (14,307)PC, 403/427-2391
Richard Magnus, Calgary North Hill (22,990)PC, 403/427-3018
Hon. Gary G. Mar, Calgary Nose Creek (22,043)PC, 403/427-2025
Don Massey, Edmonton Millwoods (16,263)Lib., 403/427-2293
Hon. Shirley McClellan, Chinook (10,128)PC, 403/427-4928
Barry McFarland, Little Bow (14,608)PC, 403/427-0879
Hon. Dianne Mirosh, Calgary Glenmore (23,077)PC, 403/427-2294
Grant Mitchell, Edmonton McClung (22,520)Lib., 403/427-2292

Ken Nicol, Lethbridge East (21,759)Lib., 403/427-2293
Dr. Lyle Oberg, Bow Valley (13,925)PC, 403/427-1830
Hon. Walter Paszkowski, Grande Prairie-Smoky (15,622)PC, 403/427-2137
Mike Percy, Edmonton Whitemud (20,348)Lib., 403/427-2292
Hung Pham, Calgary Montrose (20,314)PC, 403/427-1865
Rob Renner, Medicine Hat (22,019)PC, 403/427-5381
Hon. Ken Rostad, Q.C., Wetaskiwin-Camrose (20,693)PC, 403/427-2585
Howard Sapers, Edmonton Glenora (23,653)Lib., 403/427-2292
Hon. Stanley Schumacher, Drumheller (16,990)PC, 403/427-2464
Peter Sekulic, Edmonton Manning (20,143)Lib., 403/427-2293
Gary Severtson, Innisfail-Sylvan Lake (16,014)PC, 403/427-1857
Shiraz Shariff, Calgary McCall (18,015)PC, 403/422-0685
Hon. Murray Smith, Calgary Varsity (26,888)PC, 403/427-3664
Colleen Soetaert, Spruce Grove-Sturgeon-St. Albert (18,846)Lib., 403/427-2293
Ed Stelmach, Vegreville-Viking (18,853)PC, 403/427-1879
Don Tannas, Highwood (18,163)PC, 403/427-1826
Lorne Taylor, Cypress-Medicine Hat (13,288)PC, 403/427-1822
Hon. Tom Thurber, Drayton Valley-Calmar (16,444)PC, 403/427-3744
Peter Trynchy, Whitecourt-St. Anne (17,367)PC, 403/427-0495
Duco Van Binsbergen, West Yellowhead (16,495)Lib., 403/427-2293
Leo Vasseur, Bonnyville (16,430)Lib., 403/427-2292
Hon. Dr. Steven West, Vermillion-Lloydminster (17,201)PC, 403/427-3162
Lance White, Edmonton Mayfield (22,264)Lib., 403/427-2293
Percy Wickman, Edmonton Rutherford (22,546)Lib., 403/427-2292
Hon. Stan Woloshyn, Stony Plain (18,828)PC, 403/427-3666
Julius Yankowsky, Edmonton Beverly-Belmont (18,397)PC, 403/422-1357
Al Zariwny, Edmonton Strathcona (24,721)Lib., 403/427-2293
Gene Zwozdesky, Edmonton Avonmore (21,282)Lib., 403/427-2292

ALBERTA GOVERNMENT DEPARTMENTS & AGENCIES

Alberta ADVANCED EDUCATION & CAREER DEVELOPMENT

Commerce Place, 10155 - 102 St., 7th Fl., Edmonton AB T5J 4L5
403/422-4488; Fax: 403/422-5126; URL: http://www.gov.ab.ca/dept/aecd.html

ACTS ADMINISTERED

Advanced Education Foundations Act
Alberta Heritage Scholarship Act
Banff Centre Act
Colleges Act
Department of Advanced Education Act
Department of Career Development & Employment Act
Education of Service Men's Children Act
Private Vocational Schools Act
Student & Temporary Employment Act
Students Finance Act
Students Loan Guarantee Act

GOVERNMENT OF ALBERTA 3-95

Technical Institutes Act
Universities Act
Minister, Hon. Jack W. Ady, 403/427-2291, Fax: 403/427-2610
Deputy Minister, Lynne Duncan, 403/427-3659, Fax: 403/427-1510
Director, Communications, Kathie Konarzewski, 403/422-4495, Fax: 403/422-1263
Director, Human Resources, John Bergin, 403/422-4493, Fax: 403/422-5362
Manager, Apprenticeship Operations, Tom Bodner, 403/427-6976

APPRENTICESHIP & INDUSTRY TRAINING DIVISION
Fax: 403/422-7376
Executive Director, Shirley Dul, 403/422-1185
Director, Apprenticeship & Industry Training Board Secretariat, Don Ogaranko, 403/427-8765
Director, Policy, Promotion & Certification, Susan Johnston, 403/427-8765
Director, Program Development & Trades Occupations, Mal Cook, 403/427-4601

FINANCE, ADMINISTRATION & AVC SUPPORT DIVISION
403/422-5126
Executive Director, Gerry Waisman, 403/427-5601
Director, Finance, Shubert Kwan, 403/427-5592

INFORMATION & POLICY SERVICES DIVISION
Fax: 403/422-0408
Asst. Deputy Minister, Lois Hawkins, 403/427-3663, Fax: 403/422-0408
Director, Evaluation, Bill Wong, 403/427-4746, Fax: 403/422-0897
Director, Federal/Provincial Activities, Thorsten Duebel, 403/422-5853, Fax: 403/422-0793
Director, Information Technology Services, Grant Chaney, 403/422-1255, Fax: 403/422-5126
Acting Director, Learner Issues, Michelle Kirshner, 403/422-1281, Fax: 403/422-0880
Director, Legislative Services, Linda Richardson, 403/427-3798, Fax: 403/427-5362
Director, Policy Development, Peter Hill, 403/422-4845, Fax: 403/422-0880
Director, Strategic Planning & Research, Archie Clark, 403/422-1281, Fax: 403/422-0880

LEARNER ASSISTANCE DIVISION
Asst. Deputy Minister, Fred Hemingway, 403/427-5557
Executive Director, Program Development & Evaluation, Ried Zittlau, 403/422-0010, Fax: 403/422-1651
Executive Director, Operations, Steve MacDonald, 403/427-5551
Director, Corporate Services, Jean Sprague, 403/427-7106

Regional Offices
North: Seventh Street Plaza South, 10030 - 107 St., 8th Fl., Edmonton AB T5J 4X7 – 403/422-6991, Director, Joe-Anne Priel
South: Century Park Place, 855 - 8 Ave. SW, Calgary AB T2P 3P1 – 403/297-5318; Fax: 403/297-5183, Director, Alan Edser

SYSTEM FUNDING & ACCOUNTABILITY DIVISION
Commerce Place, 10155 - 102 St., 11th Fl., Edmonton AB T5J 4L5
Asst. Deputy Minister, Neil Henry, 403/427-5607, Fax: 403/427-9430
Director, Adult Development, John Fisher, 403/427-5628, Fax: 403/422-1297
Director, Licensing & Certification, Dr. Andy Hendry, 403/427-5609, Fax: 403/427-4185
Director, Post-Secondary Programs, Wayne Shillington, 403/427-5632, Fax: 403/427-4185
Director, System Finance & Information, Phil Gougeon, 403/427-5603, Fax: 403/427-4185

Associated Agencies, Boards & Commissions
- Alberta Council on Admissions & Transfer: #430, 9942 - 108 St., Edmonton AB T5K 2J5
Chair, Terry Moore, 403/422-9021
- Alberta Apprenticeship & Industry Training Board: 10155 - 102 St., 10th Fl., Edmonton AB T5J 4L5 – 403/427-4601
Presiding Officer, Jake Thygesen
- Private Colleges Accreditation Board: #430, 9942 - 108 St., Edmonton AB T5K 2J5
Chair, Dr. Peter J. Krueger, /427-8921
- Private Vocational Schools Advisory Council: Commerce Place, 10155 - 102 St., 10th Fl., Edmonton AB T5J 4L5 – 403/427-5609
Chair, Robert Graesser
- Students Finance Board: Baker Centre, 10025 - 106 St., 10th Fl., Edmonton AB T5J 1G7 – 403/427-2740; Fax: 403/422-4516
Chair, Fred Clarke
CEO, Fred Hemingway

Alberta AGRICULTURE, FOOD & RURAL DEVELOPMENT
7000 - 113 St., Edmonton AB T6H 5T6
403/427-2727; Fax: 403/427-2861; URL: http://www.gov.ab.ca/dept/agric.html

ACTS ADMINISTERED
Agricultural Operation Practices Act
Agricultural Pests Act
Agricultural Service Board Act
Agricultural Societies Act (& Agriculture Grants Amendment Regulation)
Agriculture Financial Services Act
Alberta Agricultural Research Institute Act
Animal Protection Act
Artificial Insemination of Domestic Animals Act
Bee Act
Brand Act
Crop Liens Priorities Act
Crop Payments Act
Dairy Board Act
Dairy Industry Act
Expropriation Act (jointly with Alberta Justice)
Farm Credit Stability Fund Act Amendment, 1989
Farm Implement Act
Federal-Provincial Farm Assistance Act
Feeder Associations Guarantee Act
Fuel Tax Act (jointly with Alberta Treasury)
Fur Farms Act
Government Organization Act, Schedule 2
Horned Cattle Purchases Act
Irrigation Act
Irrigation District Rehabilitation Endowment Fund Act
Line Fence Act
Livery Stable Keepers Act
Livestock Diseases Act
Livestock Identification & Brand Inspection Act
Livestock Industry Diversification Act
Livestock & Livestock Products Act
Marketing of Agricultural Products Act
Meat Inspection Act
Public Lands Act
St. Mary & Milk Rivers Water Agreement (Termination) Act
Soil Conservation Act
Stray Animals Act
Surface Rights Act
Vegetable Sales (Alberta) Act
Weed Control Act
Wheat Board Money Trust Act
Minister, Hon. Walter Paszkowski, 403/427-2137, Fax: 403/422-6035
Deputy Minister, C. Doug Radke, 403/427-2145, Fax: 403/427-6317
Farmers' Advocate, Wallace Daley, 403/427-2433, Fax: 403/422-9690
Director, Administration Division, Mike Mylod, 403/427-2151, Fax: 403/422-6529
Director, Communications Division, Brad Haddrell, 403/427-2127, Fax: 403/427-2861
Director, Internal Audit Division, Ralph Killips, 403/422-9183, Fax: 403/422-5220

FIELD SERVICES SECTOR
Asst. Deputy Minister, Les Lyster, 403/427-2439, Fax: 403/427-6317
Director, Rural Development Division, John Tackaberry, 403/427-2409, Fax: 403/422-7755
Head, Home Economic & 4H Branch, Ted Youck, 403/427-4462, Fax: 403/422-7755
Head, Rural Initiatives, Keith Price, 403/427-4612, Fax: 403/422-3655

Field Service Offices
Central: Provincial Bldg., 3rd Fl., Red Deer AB T4N 6K8 – 403/340-7611; Fax: 403/340-4896, Regional Director, Alan W. Hall
Northeast: PO Box 24, Vermilion AB T9X IJ9 – 403/853-8106; Fax: 403/853-4776, Regional Director, Ralph F. Berkan
Northwest: PO Box 4560, Barrhead AB T7N 1A4 – 403/674-8264; Fax: 403/674-8309, Regional Director, John Knapp
Peace: PO Box 159, Fairview AB T0H 1L0 – 403/835-2291; Fax: 403/835-3600, Regional Director, Yvonne Grabowsky
Southern: Agriculture Centre, Lethbridge AB T1J 4C7 – 403/381-5130; Fax: 403/382-4526, Regional Director, Don Young

PLANNING & DEVELOPMENT SECTOR
Asst. Deputy Minister, Ray Bassett, 403/427-1957, Fax: 403/427-6317
Director, Central Program Support Division, Ken Moholitny, 403/422-9167, Fax: 403/427-5921
Director, Irrigation & Resource Management Division, Brian Colgan, 403/422-4596, Fax: 403/422-0474
Director, Policy Secretariat, Joe Rasario, 403/422-2070, Fax: 403/422-6540
Director, Economic Services Division, Glen Werner, 403/427-7311, Fax: 403/427-5220

PRODUCTION & MARKETING SECTOR
Asst. Deputy Minister, Barry Mehr, 403/427-2442, Fax: 403/422-6317
Director, Animal Industry Division, Dennis Glover, 403/427-2166, Fax: 403/427-1057
Director, Marketing Services Division, Cliff Wulff, 403/427-4241, Fax: 403/422-9746
Director, Plant Industry Division, Don Macyk, 403/427-5341, Fax: 403/422-0783
Director, Processing Industry Division, Dr. T. Church, 403/427-3166, Fax: 403/422-3655

Associated Agencies, Boards & Commissions
- Agricultural Products Marketing Council: 7000 - 113 St., 3rd Fl., Edmonton AB T6H 5T6 – 403/427-2164; Fax: 403/422-9690
General Manager, Brian Rhiness
- Agriculture Financial Service Corporation (AFSC): 4910 - 52 St., PO Box 5000, Camrose AB T4V 4E8 – 403/679-1311 (Lending); Fax: 403/679-1308 – 403/782-8200; Fax: 403/782-5650 (Insurance)
Chair, Bob Splane, 403/679-1300
President & Managing Director, Brian Manning, 403/679-1302
Vice-President, Finance & Administration, Lending Division, David Schurman, 403/679-1327, Fax: 403/782-7510
Vice-President, Insurance Operations, Ray Block, 5718 - 56 Ave., PO Box 16, Lacombe AB T0C 1S0, 403/782-8251; Fax: 403/782-4336

Canadian Almanac & Directory 1997

GOVERNMENT OF ALBERTA

Vice-President, Lending Operations, Andrew Church, 403/679-1301
• Alberta Agricultural Research Institute (AARI): J.G. O'Donoghue Bldg., #300, 7000 - 113 St., Edmonton AB T6H 5T6 – 403/422-5384; Fax: 403/427-1835
Chair, Ed Stelmach, 403/422-5384, Fax: 403/427-1835
Executive Director, Dr. Ralph G. Christian, 403/422-1072, Fax: 403/422-6317, Email: CHRISTI@agric.gov.ab.ca
Research Manager, Dr. Yilma Teklemariam, 403/427-6519, Fax: 403/427-3252
• Alberta Dairy Control Board: 5201 - 50 Ave., Wetaskiwin AB T9A 0S7 – 403/361-1231; Fax: 403/361-1236
Chair, James P. Heron
• Alberta Grain Commission: 7000 - 113 St., Edmonton AB T6H 5T6 – 403/427-3078; Fax: 403/422-9690
Chair, Ken Moholitny
• Irrigation Council: Provincial Bldg., #265, 200 - 5th Ave. S, PO Box 3014, Lethbridge AB T1J 4L1 – 403/381-5176; Fax: 403/382-4406
Chair, John Weing
Council Secretary, Len Ring, 403/381-5176, Fax: 403/382-4406
Administrative Officer, Laurie Hodge
• Land Compensation Board: Phipps-McKinnon Bldg., 10020 - 101A Ave., 18th Fl., Edmonton AB T5J 3G2 – 403/422-2988; Fax: 403/427-5798
Chair, C.J. Purves
• Surface Rights Board: Phipps-McKinnon Bldg., 10020 - 101A Ave., 18th Fl., Edmonton AB T5J 3G2 – 403/427-2444; Fax: 403/427-5798
Chair, C.J. Purves

Agricultural Marketing Boards & Commissions
• Alberta Canola Producers Commission: #170, 14315 - 118 Ave., Edmonton AB T5L 4S6 – 403/454-0844; Fax: 403/451-6933
• Alberta Cattle Commission: #216, 6715 - 8 St. NE, Calgary AB T2E 7H7 – 403/275-4400; Fax: 403/274-0007
Manager, Gary Sargent
• Alberta Chicken Producers' Marketing Board: #101, 11826 - 100 Ave., Edmonton AB T5K 0K3 – 403/488-2125; Fax: 403/488-3570
General Manager, Roger King
• Alberta Egg Producers Board: #15, 1915 - 32 Ave. NE, Calgary AB T2E 7C8 – 403/250-1197; Fax: 403/291-9216
General Manager, W.P. Chorney
• Alberta Fresh Vegetable Marketing Board: 220 - 12A St. North, Lethbridge AB T1H 2J1 – 403/327-0447; Fax: 403/327-0766
• Alberta Hatching Egg Marketing Board: 14815 - 119 Ave., Edmonton AB T5L 2N9 – 403/451-5837; Fax: 403/452-8726
General Manager, Robert Smook
• Alberta Pork Producers' Development Corporation: 10319 Princess Elizabeth Ave., Edmonton AB T5G 0Y5 – 403/474-8288; Fax: 403/471-8065
General Manager, Ed Schultz
• Alberta Pulse Growers Commission: 5030 - 50 St., Lacombe AB T4L 1W8 – 403/986-9398; Fax: 403/986-9398
• Alberta Sheep & Wool Commission: #203, 2916 - 19 St. NE, Calgary AB T2E 6Y9 – 403/735-5111; Fax: 403/735-5113
Manager, Will Verboven
• Alberta Sugar Beet Growers' Marketing Board: 4900 - 50th St., Taber AB T0K 2G0 – 403/223-1110; Fax: 403/223-1022
Manager, Bruce Webster
• Alberta Turkey Growers Marketing Board: #212, 8711A - 50 St., Edmonton AB T6B 1E7 – 403/465-5755; Fax: 403/465-5528
Executive Director, Greg Smith
• Alberta Vegetable Growers Marketing Board: 5217 - 50 St., Taber AB T1G 1V4 – 403/223-4242; Fax: 403/223-4242

General Manager, Terry Cradduck
• Potato Growers of Alberta: Stockman's Centre, #6, 1323 - 44 Ave. NE, Calgary AB T2E 7A6 – 403/291-2430; Fax: 403/291-2641
Manager, Allen Stuart

Alberta Office of the AUDITOR GENERAL
9925 - 109 St., 8th Fl., Edmonton AB T5K 2J8
403/427-4222; Fax: 403/422-9555; URL: http://www.assembly.ab.ca/auditor.gen/auditor.htm
Auditor General, Peter Valentine, F.C.A.
Senior Asst. Auditor General, Andrew J.K. Wingate, C.A.
Asst. Auditor General, Jim Hug, C.A.
Asst. Auditor General, Mike Morgan, C.A.
Asst. Auditor General, Don Neufeld, C.A.
Asst. Auditor General, Nick Shandro, C.A.
Executive Asst. to the Auditor General, L. Shore

Alberta COMMUNITY DEVELOPMENT
Standard Life Centre, 10405 Jasper Ave., 7th Fl., Edmonton AB T5J 4R7
403/427-6530; Fax: 403/427-1496; URL: http://www.gov.ab.ca/dept/mcd.html

ACTS ADMINISTERED
Alberta Alcohol & Drug Abuse Act
Alberta Foundation for the Arts Act
Alberta Order of Excellence Act
Alberta Sport, Recreation, Parks & Wildlife Foundation Act
Amusements Act
Emblems of Alberta Act
Foreign Cultural Property Immunity Act
Glenbow-Alberta Institute Act
Government House Act
Historical Resources Act
Human Rights, Citizenship & Multiculturalism Act
Libraries Act
Protection for Persons in Care Act
Recreation Development Act
Seniors Advisory Council for Alberta Act
Seniors Benefit Act
Wild Rose Foundation Act
Minister, Hon. Shirley McClellan, 403/427-4928, Fax: 403/427-0188
Deputy Minister, Julian Nowicki, 403/427-2921, Fax: 403/427-5362, Email: julian_j_nowicki@mcd_dm_edm@comdev
Senior Director, Systems Branch, Dave Rehill, 403/427-1072, Fax: 403/427-0255
Director, Communications, Gordon Turtle, 403/427-6530, Fax: 403/427-1496, Email: gordon_turtle@mcd_com_edm@comdev
Director, Corporate Planning & Performance Measures, Ken MacLean, 403/427-3114, Fax: 403/422-0553, Email: ken_maclean@fp_edm@comdev_asd

ADMINISTRATIVE SERVICES DIVISION
Executive Director, Rai Batra, 403/427-2925, Fax: 403/427-0255, Email: rai_f_batra@exec_edm@comdev_asd
Director, Financial Services, Douglas Borland, 403/427-5156, Fax: 403/427-0255
Director, FOIP & Records Management Branch, Joe Forsyth, 403/431-2313, Fax: 403/422-1105, Email: joe_forsyth@sis_edm@comdev_asd
Director, Human Resources, Lynn Upshall, 403/427-2546, Fax: 403/422-3142, Email: lynn_upshall@per_edm@comdev_asd

COMMUNITY & CITIZENSHIP SERVICES DIVISION
Asst. Deputy Minister, Murray Finnerty, 403/427-5714, Fax: 403/422-2891, Email: murray_finnerty@adm_edm@comdev_csd

Director, Arts, Recreation & Libraries Branch, Dr. Clive Padfield, Beaver House, 10158 - 103 St., 3rd Fl., Edmonton AB T5J 0X6, 403/427-6315, Fax: 403/422-9132, Email: clive_padfield@arts_edm@comdev_csd
Director, Citizenship & Services Branch, Marie Riddle, 403/422-4927, Fax: 403/422-1105, Email: marie_riddle@wss_wpp_edm@comdev_irc
Director, Development Field Services Branch, Noni Heine, 403/422-2044, Fax: 403/421-0056, Email: Noni_Heine@Exec.Edm@ComDev_CDFS
Director, Human Rights Secretariat, Manuel da Costa, 403/427-3116, Fax: 403/422-3563
Chair, Film Classification Board, Sharon McCann, 403/427-2006

CULTURAL FACILITIES & HISTORICAL RESOURCES DIVISION
Old St. Stephen's College, 8820 - 112 St., Edmonton AB T6G 2P8
403/431-2300; Fax: 403/432-1376
Asst. Deputy Minister, Dr. Bill Byrne, 403/431-2309, Email: bill_byrne@hr_adm_edm@culture
Director, Planning, Marketing & Foundation Services, Mark Rasmussen, Email: mark_rasmussen@hr_adm_edm@culture
Director, Historic Sites Service, Frits Pannekoek, 403/431-2310, Email: frits_pannekoek@hs_dir_edm@culture
Director, Provincial Museum of Alberta, Dr. Philip H.R. Stepney, 12845 - 102 Ave., Edmonton AB T5N 0M6, 403/453-9102, Fax: 403/454-6629
Director, Provincial Archives, Dr. Sandra Thomson, 12845 - 102 Ave., Edmonton AB T5N 0H6, 403/427-1750, Fax: 403/427-4646
Director, Royal Tyrrell Museum of Paleontology, Dr. Bruce Naylor, PO Box 7500, Drumheller AB T0J 0Y0, 403/823-7707, Fax: 403/823-7131
Director, Northern/Southern Alberta Jubilee Auditoria, Ken Graham, 11455 - 87 Ave., Edmonton AB T6G 2T2, 403/427-2760, Fax: 403/422-3750, Email: ken_graham@cd_naja_edm@culture

SENIORS DIVISION
403/427-7876
Executive Director, Ken Wilson, 902/422-0122, Fax: 902/427-1132
Director, Customer Services, Dwight Ganske, 403/422-7264
Director, Operations, Chi Loo, 403/422-7259
Director, Seniors Policy & Special Needs, Dave Arsenault, 403/427-1072

Associated Agencies, Boards & Commissions
• Alberta Alcohol & Drug Abuse Commission (AADAC): Pacific Plaza Bldg., 10909 Jasper Ave., 6th Fl., Edmonton AB T5J 3M9 – 403/427-2837; Fax: 403/423-1419
CEO, Leonard Blumenthal, 403/427-2837
Chair, Bonnie Laing, 403/427-2837
Executive Director, Program Services, Brian Kearns, 403/427-7316, Fax: 403/423-1419
Director, Central Office, Louise Morose, Energy Square Bldg., #803, 10109 - 106 St., Edmonton AB T5J 3L7, 403/427-4263, Fax: 403/427-0456
Director, Northern Office, Corliss Burke, 11333 - 106 St., Grande Prairie AB T8V 6T7, 403/538-5216, Fax: 403/538-5256
Director, Southern Office, Dennis Jones, 1177 - 11th Ave. SW, Calgary AB T2R 0G5, 403/297-3038, Fax: 403/297-3041
• AADAC Recovery Centre: 10302 - 107 St., Edmonton AB T5J 1K2 – 403/427-4291; Fax: 403/422-2881
Manager, Evelyn Kohlman
• Henwood Treatment Centre: 18750 - 18 St., Edmonton AB T5B 4K3 – 403/422-9069; Fax: 403/422-5408

Manager, Betty Roline
Program Manager, Gordon Munro
- Lander Treatment Centre: 43 Ave. & 2nd St. W, Claresholm AB T0L 0T0 – 403/625-1395; Fax: 403/625-1300
Manager, Rob Hale-Matthews
Renfrew Recovery Centre: 1611 Remington Rd. NE, Calgary AB T2E 5K6 – 403/276-8946; Fax: 403/297-4592, Manager, Alan Friesen
- Alberta Historical Resources Foundation
Listed in Section 2, *see* Index.
- Alberta Human Rights, Citizenship & Multiculturalism Commission
Listed alphabetically in detail, this section.
- Alberta Order of Excellence Council: Standard Life Centre, 10405 Jasper Ave., 7th Fl., Edmonton AB T5J 4R7 – 403/427-2925; Fax: 403/427-0255
- Alberta Sport, Recreation, Parks & Wildlife Foundation: Percy Page Centre, 11759 Groat Rd., Edmonton AB T5M 3K9 – 403/427-1976; Fax: 403/488-9755
- Glenbow-Alberta Institute Board of Governors: 130 - 9th Ave. SE, Calgary AB T2G 0P3 – 403/264-8300; Fax: 403/265-9769
- Government House Foundation: 12845 - 102 Ave., Edmonton AB T5N 0M6 – 403/431-2310; Fax: 403/422-1105
- Seniors' Advisory Council for Alberta: 10025 Jasper Ave., Main Fl., Edmonton AB T5J 2N3 – 403/422-2321; Fax: 403/422-3207
Chairman, Jocelyn Burgener

Alberta ECONOMIC DEVELOPMENT & TOURISM

Commerce Place, 10155 - 102 St., Edmonton AB T5J 4L6
403/427-2280; URL: http://www.edt.gov.ab.ca/
Business Line: 1-800-272-9675
Tourism-Visitor Assistance: 1-800-661-8888

ACTS ADMINISTERED
Alberta Opportunity Fund Act
Department of Economic Development & Trade Act
Motion Picture Development Act
Small Business Equity Corporation Act
Vencap Equities Act
Minister, Hon. Dr. Steven West, 403/427-3162, Fax: 403/422-6338
Deputy Minister, Jack Davis
Minister's Executive Asst., Tom Neufeld, 403/427-3162
Director, Corporate & Public Relations, Charlotte Moran, 403/427-0670, Fax: 403/427-1529

BUSINESS FINANCE
403/427-3300; Fax: 403/422-9319
Asst. Deputy Minister, Brian Williams, 403/427-0667
Executive Director, Business Finance, Earl Nent, 403/427-3300
Executive Director, Financial Projects, Don Keech, 403/427-3300

CORPORATE & POLICY DEVELOPMENT
Fax: 403/422-1759
Asst. Deputy Minister, Peter Crerar, 403/427-1946
Executive Director, Finance & Administration, Robert H. Turner, 403/422-0188
Executive Director, Information Management, Neil Taylor, 416/422-1033
Executive Director, Strategic Planning & Policy, Vacant
Administrator, Administrative Services, Linda Gogal, 403/422-9092
Director, Business Policy, Duane Pyear, 403/427-0850
Director, Development Policy, Vacant, 403/427-3627

Director, Human Resources, Gilbert Cleirbaut, 403/422-5498
Director, Electronic Information & Intelligence Services, Greg Yaremko, 403/427-6302
Director, Policy Projects, Carole Shields, 403/427-4443
Director, Research Services, Fred McMullan, 403/422-1063
Director, Economic Scanning & Research Services, Vacant
Manager, Business Planning, Colin Jeffares, 403/422-0531
Manager, Information & Data Retrieval, Greg Yaremko, 403/427-6302
Head Librarian, Library, Donna Gordon, 403/427-0389

INDUSTRY TECHNOLOGY & FORESTRY DEVELOPMENT
Asst. Deputy Minister, Stan Schellenberger, 403/427-6456, Fax: 403/422-3733
Executive Director, Industry Development, Mel Wong, 403/427-2084
Executive Director, Forestry Industry Development, Vacant, 403/422-7011, Fax: 403/427-5299
Executive Director, Technology Development, Rand Harrison, 403/422-0626
Senior Director, Denny Ross-Smith, 403/427-6479
Senior Director & Film Commissioner, Lindsay Cherney, 403/427-6503
Senior Director, Chrys Dmytruk, 403/427-0816
Director, Development Planning, Paul Short, 403/427-6571
Director, Environmental Technologies, Bob Wilkies, 403/427-6620
Director, Financial & Economic Analysis, Nick Gartaganis, 403/427-6582
Director, Investment & Marketing, Shane Pospisil, 403/427-6579
Director, Value-Added Products, Horst Ramanauskas, 403/427-6572

INDEPENDENT BUSINESS & TOURISM DEVELOPMENT
Asst. Deputy Minister, Jim Engel, 403/427-5273, Fax: 403/427-5926
General Manager, Calgary Office, Doug Neil, #300, 639 - 5 Ave. SW, Calgary AB T2P 0M9, 403/297-8910, Fax: 403/297-6168
Executive Director, Business Services, Roger Jackson, 403/427-6987
Executive Director, Development Services, Bruce Wilson, 403/427-6650, Fax: 403/427-0778
Director, Economic Analysis & Planning, Mike Boyd, 403/427-6686
Director, Resource Management & Development, Rick Siddle, 406/427-6656

TOURISM, TRADE & INVESTMENT
Fax: 403/427-1700
Asst. Deputy Minister, Murray Rasmusson, 403/422-2557
Managing Director, The Americas, Jerry Keller, 403/427-6291
Managing Director, Asia/Pacific, Dave Corbett, 403/427-6375
Managing Director, Eastern Region, Doug Lane, 403/427-1905
Managing Director, Europe, Erv Lack, 403/427-6326
Managing Director, Middle East/Africa/India, Bob Hunter, 403/422-2534
Managing Director, Western Region, Don Smithson, 403/427-6059
Acting Managing Director, Division Services, Behrooz Sadre-Hashemi, 403/422-5197
Director, Business Immigration, Peter Carsley, 403/427-6417
Director, Event Promotion, Drew Hutton, 403/427-6433
Director, Investment/IBIS, Joanne Miller, 403/427-6413

Director, Visitor Sales & Services, Barb Spencer, 403/427-4327

Associated Agencies, Boards & Commissions
- Alberta Economic Development Authority (AEDA): Commerce Place, 10155 - 102nd St., 6th Fl., Edmonton AB T5J 4L6 – 403/427-2251; Fax: 403/427-5922
Chair, Hon. Ralph Klein, 403/427-2261, Email: altatalk@censsw.gov.ab.ca
Co-Chair, Doug Mitchell, Q.C., McDougall Centre, 456 - 6th St. SW, Edmonton AB T2P 4E8, 403/297-3022
Co-Chair, Eric Newell, 403/422-5404
Co-Chair, Carlotte Robb, 403/422-5404
Director, Operations (Calgary), Hugh Tadman, 403/422-5404
- Alberta Motion Picture Development Corporation: #690, 10020 - 101A Ave., Edmonton AB T5J 3G2 – 403/424-8855; Fax: 403/424-7669
General Manager, Garry Toth
- Alberta Opportunity Company: 5110 - 49 Ave., PO Box 4040, Ponoka AB T4J 1R5 – 403/783-7011; Fax: 403/783-7032, Toll Free: 1-800-661-3811
Minister Responsible, Hon. Dr. Steven West
President & Managing Director, Jim Anderson
- Alberta Research Council (ARC)
Listed alphabetically in detail, this section.
- Alberta Science & Research Authority (ASRA): 250 Karl Clark Rd., Edmonton AB T6H 5X2 – 403/427-2294; URL: http://www.gov.ab.ca/gov/agency/sara.html
Chair, Dr. Robert B. Church
President, Dr. Robert Fessenden
Director, Communications, Mark Patton, 403/427-2294
- Alberta Tourism Education Council: Sterling Place, 9940 - 106 St., 12th Fl., Edmonton AB T5K 2P6 – 403/422-0781; Fax: 403/422-3430
Executive Director, Vacant
- Alberta Tourism Partnership (ATP): c/o Alberta Economic Development & Tourism, 10155 - 102 St., Edmonton ON T5J 4L6 – 403/531-4671
Agency incorporated on May 30, 1995 to provide an industry-led tourism organization to integrate the industry. Created to simplify distribution & marketing systems, encourage private sector investment & make it easier for Alberta tourism businesses to participate.
Chair, Russ Tynan
Vice-Chair, Ted Kissane
President & CEO, Tom McCabe

Alberta EDUCATION
Devonian Bldg., 11160 Jasper Ave., Edmonton AB T5K 0L2
403/427-7219; Fax: 403/427-0591; URL: http://ednet.edc.gov.ab.ca

ACTS ADMINISTERED
Alberta School Boards Association Act
Barry Creek School Division Act
Government Organization Act, Schedule 4
Northland School Division Act
Remembrance Day Act
School Act
Teachers' Pension Plan Act
Teaching Profession Act
Minister, Hon. Gary G. Mar, 403/427-2025, Fax: 403/427-5582
Deputy Minister, Dr. Leroy Sloan, 403/427-2889, Fax: 403/422-9735
Director, Communications, Carol Chawrun, 403/427-2285, Fax: 403/427-0591
Director, Human Resource Services, Terry Buck, 403/427-2058, Fax: 403/422-2114

GOVERNMENT OF ALBERTA

PLANNING, INFORMATION & FINANCIAL SERVICES DIVISION

Asst. Deputy Minister, Gary Zatko, 403/427-2991, Fax: 403/422-3090

Director, Corporate Services & Information Access, Bruce Aubert, 403/427-2914, Fax: 403/422-3942

Director, Financial Operations, Gary Baron, 403/427-2051, Fax: 403/427-2147

Director, Information Services, Ron Sohnle, 403/427-5739, Fax: 403/427-3201

Director, Policy & Planning, Sharon Campbell, 403/427-8217, Fax: 403/422-5255

Director, School Finance & Facilities, Russ Wiebe, 403/427-7235, Fax: 403/427-5930

Asst. Director, School Business Administration, Steve Bemount, 403/427-7235, Fax: 403/427-5930

Asst. Director, School Facilities, Hoang Le, 403/427-2973, Fax: 403/427-5816

REGIONAL SERVICES DIVISION

Asst. Deputy Minister, Steve Cymbol, 403/427-7484, Fax: 403/422-1400

Director, National & International Education, Amelia Turnbull, 403/427-2035, Fax: 403/422-3014

Director, Native Education, Merv Kowalchuk, 403/427-2043, Fax: 403/422-5256

Regional Manager, Calgary, Gerry Wilson, 403/297-6353, Fax: 403/297-3842

Director, Regional Offices, Ron Smith, 403/427-2952, Fax: 403/422-5256

Director, Special Education Branch, Harvey Finnestad, 403/422-6326, Fax: 403/422-2039

Director, Teacher Certification, Fred Burghardt, 403/427-2045, Fax: 403/422-4199

STUDENT PROGRAMS & EVALUATION DIVISION

Asst. Deputy Minister, Dr. Roger Palmer, 403/422-1608, Fax: 403/422-5129

Director, Alberta Distance Learning Centre, Garry Popowich, 403/674-5333, Fax: 403/674-6561

Acting Director, Curriculum Standards Branch, Keith Wagner, 403/427-2984, Fax: 403/422-3745

Acting Director, Language Services, Ray Lamoureux, 403/427-2940, Fax: 403/422-1947

Director, Learning Resources Distributing Centre, Dr. John Myroon, 403/427-2767, Fax: 403/422-9750

Director, Student Evaluation, Frank Horvath, 403/427-0010, Fax: 403/422-4200

Associated Agencies, Boards & Commissions

- Alberta School Foundation Fund Audit Board: 6908 Fulton Dr., Edmonton AB T6A 3V5
Contact, Janice Rennie
- Alberta Teachers' Retirement Fund Board: #500, 11010 - 142 St., Edmonton AB T2N 2R1
Contact, Dorothy E. Ungstad
- Council on Alberta Teaching Standards: Devonian Bldg., 11160 Jasper Ave., Edmonton AB T5K 0L2
Contact, Fred Burghardt
- School Buildings Board: Devonian Bldg., 11160 Jasper Ave., Edmonton AB T5K 0L2
Contact, Gary Zatko

Alberta Office of the Chief ELECTORAL OFFICER

#100, 11510 Kingsway Ave., Edmonton AB T5G 2Y5
403/427-7191; Fax: 403/422-2900; Email: abelect@compusmart.ab.ca

Chief Electoral Officer, Dermot F. Whelan

Deputy Chief, O. Brian Fjeldheim

Director, Registrations & Financial Operations, W.A. Sage

Alberta ENERGY

Petroleum Plaza, North Tower, 9945 - 108 St., Edmonton AB T5K 2G6
403/427-7425; Fax: 403/427-3198; URL: http://www.gov.ab.ca/dept/enr.html

Ensures that energy & mineral resource development & use occur in an effective, orderly & environmentally responsible manner. The department promotes the accelerated development of the oil sands, & encourages effective & responsible environmental safeguards. Also, reviews current land-use policies to address industry concerns relating to access & ensures economic conservation of resources & prevention of waste to maximize long-term revenue to the province. The agency consists of four divisions & a quasi-judicial regulatory agency called the Alberta Energy & Utilities Board (AEUB).

ACTS ADMINISTERED

Coal Sales Act
Freehold Mineral Rights Tax Act
Gas Utilities Act
Freehold Mineral Rights Tax Act
Gas Utilities Act
Mineral Titles Redemption Act
Mines & Minerals Act
Natural Gas Marketing Act
Natural Gas Price Administration Act
Natural Gas Pricing Agreement Act
Oil Sands Technology & Research Authority Act
Petroleum Incentives Program Act
Petroleum Marketing Act
Public Utilities Act
Willmore Wilderness Park Act

Acts Administered by the Energy Resources Conservation Board

Coal Mines Safety Act
Energy Resources Conservation Act
Gas Resources Preservation Act
Oil & Gas Conservation Act
Oil Sands Conservation Act
Pipeline Act
Turner Valley Unit Operations Act

Minister, Hon. Patricia Black, 403/427-3740, Fax: 403/422-0195

Deputy Minister, Richard Hyndman, 403/427-8032, Fax: 403/427-7737

Senior Solicitor, Legal Services, M. Kaga, 403/427-0940, Fax: 403/422-6068

CORPORATE SERVICES DIVISION

Asst. Deputy Minister, David Luff, 403/427-6342, Fax: 403/427-7737

Chief Financial Officer, Financial Services, Jim Vince, 403/427-3607, Fax: 403/422-4281

Executive Director, Human Resources, Margaret Munsch, 403/427-6768, Fax: 403/422-4299

Executive Director, Information Services, Robin Varley, 403/422-4764, Fax: 403/427-5696

Head, Accomodation Services, Cathryn Landreth, 403/427-4468, Fax: 403/427-4299

Director, Planning Services, Jane Clerk, 403/427-3604, Fax: 403/422-4281

Director, Planning Services, Grant Weismiller, 403/427-0730, Fax: 403/422-4281

MINERAL OPERATIONS DIVISION

Asst. Deputy Minister, David Smith, 403/427-8123, Fax: 403/427-7737

Head, Compliance & Assurance, Steve Slipp, 403/297-8782, Fax: 403/297-5199

Head, Gas Royalty & Mineral Tax, Clif Hetherington, 403/422-9231, Fax: 403/427-3334

Head, Internal Services, Stephen Pugh, 403/422-9135, Fax: 403/422-0382

Head, Mineral Access, Geology & Mapping, Diana Purdy, 403/422-9466

Head, Minerals Tenure, F. David Coombs, 403/422-9430, Fax: 403/422-1123

Head, Petroleum & Other Royalties, Linda White, 403/422-9119, Fax: 403/427-0865

Leader, MRIS Project Office, John McAllister, 403/422-5821, Fax: 403/427-4044

POLICY DIVISION

Asst. Deputy Minister, Larry Morrison, 403/427-0813, Fax: 403/427-7737

Executive Director, Environmental Affairs Branch, John Donner, 403/427-5200, Fax: 403/427-2278

Executive Director, Markets & Regulatory Policy Branch, Paul Precht, 403/427-8038, Fax: 403/422-2548

Acting Executive Director, Royalty & Tenure Branch, Onno DeVries, 403/427-2492, Fax: 403/422-9112

Senior Director, Electricity Branch, Larry Charach, 403/427-8177, Fax: 403/427-8065

RESEARCH & EXTERNAL RELATIONS DIVISION

Asst. Deputy Minister, Ken Bradley, 403/427-0815, Fax: 403/427-7737

Executive Director, External Relations Branch, Elma Spady, 403/427-0226, Fax: 403/422-0800

Executive Director, Research & Technology, Roger Bailey, 403/297-5219, Fax: 403/297-3638

Director, Communications Branch, Alan Roth, 403/422-3667, Fax: 403/422-0698

Director, Engineering & Technical Services, John Scott, 403/297-3627, Fax: 403/297-3638

Director, Funding, Evaluation & Institutional Programs, Dr. Ted J. Cyr, 403/427-7623, Fax: 403/422-0975

Director, Intellectual Property, Doug Komery, 403/297-4375, Fax: 403/297-3638

Coordinator, Freedom of Information & Privacy Office, Mary L. Penny, 403/427-0265, Fax: 403/422-0800

Associated Agencies, Boards & Commissions

- Alberta Energy & Utilities Board (AEUB): 640 - 5 Ave. SW, Calgary AB T2P 3G4 – 403/297-8311; Fax: 403/297-8398; URL: http://www.eub.gov.ab.ca
Chair, Celine Belanger
CEO, Lorne D. Fredlund

Alberta ENVIRONMENTAL PROTECTION (AEP)

9915 - 108 St., Edmonton AB T5K 2G8
403/427-2739, 944-0313 (Information Centre); URL: http://www.gov.ab.ca/ZXenv/
Recycle Information Line: 1-800-463-6326
Pollution Emergency Response Team: 1-800-222-6514
Forest Fire Hotline: 403/427-FIRE (collect)

Provincial ministry responsible for the following: environmental regulatory services; fish & wildlife services & management; program support; enforcement & field services; land & forest services, management & protection; lands & parks administration; water resources services; planning, technical, development & operations services; waste management; natural resource planning & land information services.

ACTS ADMINISTERED

Agricultural & Recreational Land Ownership Act
Alberta Environmental Research Trust Act
Bighorn Agreement Validating Act, 1969
Boundary Surveys Act
Brazeau River Development Act, 1960
Clean Air Act
Clean Water Act
Drainage Districts Act
Environment Council Act
Environmental Protection & Enhancement Act
Fish Marketing Act
Forest Reserves Act
Forests Act
Government Organization Act, Schedule 5

Land Agents Licensing Act
Land Surveyors Act
Natural Resources Conservation Board Act
Provincial Parks Act
Public Lands Act
Special Waste Management Corporation Act
Surveys Act (jointly with Alberta Municipal Affairs)
Water Resources Act (jointly with Alberta Public Works, Supply & Services)
Wilderness Areas, Ecological Reserves & Natural Areas Act
Wildlife Act
Willmore Wilderness Park Act (jointly with Alberta Energy)
Minister, Hon. Ty Lund, 403/427-2391
Deputy Minister, Peter Melnychuk, 403/427-6236, Fax: 403/422-6305
Director, Communications, Lee Funke, 403/427-8636
Executive Director, Financial Services, Bill Simon, 403/427-5971

CORPORATE MANAGEMENT SERVICE
Asst. Deputy Minister, Ron Hicks, 403/427-8155, Fax: 403/422-6305
Director, Education Branch, Bev Yee, 403/427-6310
Director, Financial Planning, Library & Office Support, Ray Duffy, 403/427-6237
Director, Human Resources Division, Morgan Wartenbe, 403/427-6201
Director, Northern Rivers Basin Study Board, Betty Collicott, 403/427-1742
Director, Research & Scientific Support Division, Malcolm Wilson, 403/632-8400
Director, Resource Data Division, Mike Toomey, 403/427-3131
Director, Strategic & Regional Support Division, Annette Trimbee, 403/427-0047
Director, Public Involvement Branch, John Shires, 403/427-5852

Alberta Environmental Centre
PO Box 4000, Vegreville AB T0B 4L0
Fax: 403/632-8385
Director, Malcolm Wilson, 403/632-8400
Acting Head, Physical & Engineering Sciences, Dr. Paul Layte, 403/632-8264
Director, Biological Sciences, Dr. Quereshi Fayyaz, 403/632-8223
Acting Head, Operations Division, Dr. Stan Selinger, 403/632-8412

ENVIRONMENTAL REGULATORY SERVICE
Asst. Deputy Minister, Al Schulz, 403/427-6247, Fax: 403/427-1014
Director, Action on Waste Division, Bruce Taylor, 403/422-8466, Fax: 403/427-1594
Director, Air & Water Approvals Division, David Spink, 403/427-5883
Director, Chemical Assessment Management Division, Jerry Lack, 403/427-5855
Director, Environmental Assessment Division, Bob Stone, 403/427-6270
Director, Land Reclamation Division, Larry Brocke, 403/427-6202
Director, Pollution Control Division, Fred Schulte, 403/427-6209

LAND & FOREST SERVICE
Asst. Deputy Minister, Cliff Henderson, 403/427-3542, Fax: 403/422-6068
Acting Director, Forest Management Division, Dennis Quintilio, 403/427-8474
Director, Forest Protection Division, Con Dermott, 403/427-6807
Manager, Maps Alberta Branch, Eugene Kletke, 403/427-3520 (Order Desk)
Director, Program Support Division, Carson McDonald, 403/427-3549

Director, Land Administration Division, Rick McDonald, 403/427-3570
Director, Clearwater/Bow Forest, Lorne Goff, 403/845-8250
Director, Grande Prairie Forest, Mort Timanson, 403/538-8080
Director, Lac La Biche/Athabaska Forest, Brydon Ward, 403/623-5324
Director, Peace/Footner Forest, Carl Leary, 403/624-6221
Director, Slave Lake Forest, Howard Gray, 403/849-3061
Director, Whitecourt/Edson Forest, Kelly O'Shea, 403/297-8800

NATURAL RESOURCES SERVICE
Asst. Deputy Minister, J.R. Nichols, 403/427-6749, Fax: 403/422-6068
Executive Director, Special Projects, Dave Chabillo, 403/422-2924
Executive Director, Special Projects, Jake Thiessen, 403/427-6252

Fish & Wildlife
Director, Fisheries Management Division, Morley Barrett, 403/427-6730
Director, Enforcement & Field Services Division, Ken Ambrock, 403/427-6735
Director, Program Support Division, Deryl Empson, 403/427-6729
Director, Trust Fund, Tom Smith, 403/427-5192
Director, Wildlife Management Division, Robert Andrews, 403/427-6750

Parks
Director, Management Support, Bruce Duffin, 403/427-7009, Fax: 403/427-5980

Parks Regional Offices
Director, Northern East Slopes Region, Bill Cadre, 403/843-2545
Director, Parkland Region, Bill Cadre, 403/843-2545
Director, Prairie Region, Fred Moffatt, 403/381-5660
Director, Southern East Slopes Region, Dave Nielson, 403/294-0673

Water Resources
Director, Operations Division, Vacant, 403/422-1361
Director, Technical Services Division, Dave Valentine, 403/427-6276
Director, Water Management Division, Doug Tupper, 403/427-6168

Associated Agencies, Boards & Commissions
- Alberta Environmental Appeal Board (EAB): #400, 9925 - 109 St., Edmonton AB T5K 2J8 – 403/427-6207; Fax: 403/427-4693
Chair, William Tilleman
Executive Director, Al Anderson
- Alberta Environmental Research Trust (AERT): #924, 620 - 7 Ave. SW, Calgary AB T2P 0Y8 – 403/297-2360
- Alberta Special Waste Management Corporation Board: Pacific Plaza, #610, 10909 Jasper Ave., Edmonton AB T5J 3L9
- Alberta Special Waste Management Corporation (ASWMC): #600, 10909 Jasper Ave., Edmonton AB T5J 3L9 – 403/422-5029; Fax: 403/428-9627 – Toxic/Chemical Drug Disposal: 1-800-272-8873
Note: This office was closed in the spring of 1996. Most responsibilities were transferred to the Alberta Department of Environmental Protection. The hazardous waste treatment centre near Swan Hills has been privatized & is now operated by Bovar Inc.
- Natural Resources Conservation Board (NRCB): Pacific Plaza, 10909 Jasper Ave., Edmonton AB T5J 2L9 – 403/422-1977; URL: http://www.gov.ab.ca/ZXNRCB/index.html

Chair, Ken R. Smith
Executive Manager, Operations, J. Ingram
Director, Hiske Gerding
- Sustainable Development Coordinating Council (SDCC): South Petroleum Plaza, 9915 - 108 St., 10th Floor, Edmonton AB T5K 2G8 – 403/427-6236; Fax: 403/422-6305
Co-Chair, Peter Melnychuk, 403/427-6236, Fax: 403/422-6305
Co-Chair, Al N. Craig, 403/427-0662
- Tire Recycling Management Board (TRMB): 10060 Jasper Ave., 10th Fl., Edmonton AB T5J 3N4 – 403/990-1111; Fax: 403/990-1122
Executive Director, Doug Wright

Alberta Office of the ETHICS COMMISSIONER
#410, 9925 - 109 St., Edmonton AB T5K 2J8
403/422-2273; Fax: 403/422-2261

ACTS ADMINISTERED
Alberta Conflicts of Interest Act
Alberta Ethics Commissioner, Robert Clark
General Counsel, Frank Work
Senior Administrator, Karen South

Alberta FAMILY & SOCIAL SERVICES
Seventh St. Plaza, 10030 - 107 St., Edmonton AB T5J 3E4
403/427-2734; Fax: 403/422-9044; URL: http://www.gov.ab.ca/dept/fss.html

ACTS ADMINISTERED
Assured Income for the Severely Handicapped Act
Child Welfare Act
Department of Family & Social Services Act
Dependent Adults Act
Income Support Recovery Act
Parentage & Maintenance Act
Social Care Facilities Licensing Act
Social Care Facilities Review Committee Act
Social Development Act
Widows' Pension Act
Acts Administered under the Authority of the Minister
Constitution of Alberta Amendment Act
Métis Settlements Act
Métis Settlements Accord Implementation Act
Métis Settlements Land Protection Act
Minister, Hon. Stockwell Day, 403/427-2606, Fax: 403/427-0954
Deputy Minister, Don Fleming, 403/427-6448, Fax: 403/422-9044
Minister Responsible, Children's Services, Hon. Pearl Calahasen
Special Asst., Native Programs, Tom Ghostkeeper, 403/427-2606
Director, Media & Public Relations, Bob Scott, 403/422-3004
Director, Communications, Kathy Lazowski, 403/427-4801, Fax: 403/422-3071
Children's Advocate, Jean Lafrance, 403/427-8934

ABORIGINAL AFFAIRS
Fax: 403/427-4019
Chief Executive Officer, Cliff Supernault, 403/422-5925
Director, Native Land Claims, Ken Boutillier, 403/427-8407

ADULT SERVICES DIVISION
Asst. Deputy Minister, Pat Boynton, 403/427-1245
Executive Director, Income & Employment Programs, Anne Ward Neville, 403/427-2635
Director, Appeal & Advisory Secretariat, Gordon Thomas, 403/427-2709

Director, Quality Management, Mic Farrell, 403/427-4420
Director, Services to Persons with Disabilities, Norm McLeod, 403/422-0305
Public Guardian, Gordon Cuff, 403/422-1868

CHILDREN'S SERVICES DIVISION
Asst. Deputy Minister, Mat Hanrahan, 403/427-6428
Executive Director, Child Welfare, Sharon Heron, 403/422-5187
Director, Day Care Programs, Neil Irvine, 403/427-4477
Acting Director, Family Violence Prevention, Jane Holliday, 403/422-5916
Director, Legislative Planning, Susan Rankin, 403/427-7267

RESOURCE MANAGEMENT SERVICES
Asst. Deputy Minister, Human Resources & Organizational Planning, Dave Banick, 403/427-7274
Executive Director, Resource Management Services, Frank Wilson, 403/422-3719
Executive Director, Information Resource Services, Al Schut, 403/441-6814
Director, Administration Services, Jack McKendry, 403/427-4506

Associated Agencies, Boards & Commissions
• Metis Settlements Commission: 10525 - 170 St., 3rd Fl., Edmonton AB T5P 4W2 – 403/427-4843; Fax: 403/427-1442
Commissioner, Randy Hardy
• Office of the Commissioner of Services for Children & Families: c/o Alberta Family & Social Services, Seventh St. Plaza, 10030 - 107 St., Edmonton AB T5J 3E4 – 403/422-5011; Fax: 403/422-5036
Commissioner, John Lackey

Alberta FEDERAL & INTERGOVERNMENTAL AFFAIRS
#2200, 10025 Jasper Ave., Edmonton AB T5J 1S6
403/427-2611; Fax: 403/423-6654; URL: http://www.gov.ab.ca/dept/figa.html

ACTS ADMINISTERED
Department of Federal & Intergovernmental Affairs Act
Minister, Hon. Ken Rostad, Q.C., 403/427-2585
Deputy Minister, Oryssia Lennie, 403/427-6644, Fax: 403/423-6654
Director, Communications, Donna Babchishin, 403/422-1510, Fax: 403/423-6654
Information Resource Administrator, Information Resource Centre, Laurel Frank, 403/427-2601

ADMINISTRATIVE SERVICES CENTRE
1201, Legislature Annex, 9718 - 107 St., Edmonton AB T5K 1E4
403/427-1076; Fax: 403/427-0305
Director, Keray Henke, 403/422-4867, Fax: 403/427-5565, Email: khenke@exc.gov.ab.ca
Administrative & Payroll Services, Kathy Miller, 403/422-4091, Email: kmiller@exc.gov.ab.ca
Financial Services, Marilyn Johnston, 403/427-3839, Email: mjohnsto@exc.gov.ab.ca
Information & Technology Services, Carol Coroy, 403/422-2339, Email: coroy@exc.gov.ab.ca

ALBERTA OFFICE (IN OTTAWA)
World Exchange Centre, #1810, 45 O'Connor St., Ottawa ON K1P 1A4
613/237-2615; Fax: 613/563-9934
Research Officer, Marcy Korchinski

CANADIAN FEDERALISM SECTION
AGT Tower II, #2200, 10025 Jasper Ave., Edmonton AB T5J 1S6
Fax: 403/427-0939
Executive Director, Garry Pocock, 403/427-6706, Email: gpo@inter.gov.ab.ca
Director, Aboriginal Affairs, Paul Whittaker, 403/427-6706, Email: pdw@inter.gov.ab.ca
Director, Economic & Resource Policy, Randy Fischer, 403/427-6553, Email: raf@inter.gov.ab.ca
Director, Planning & Coordination, Susan Cribbs, 403/427-6706, Email: sfc@inter.gov.ab.ca
Associate Director, Constitution/Planning, Bruce Tait, 403/427-6706, Email: bta@inter.gov.ab.ca
Senior Intergovernmental Officer, Chinwe Okelu, 403/427-6553, Email: cok@inter.gov.ab.ca

INTERNATIONAL RELATIONS SECTION
Fax: 403/427-0699
Asst. Deputy Minister, Wayne Clifford, 403/427-6543
Managing Director, Russia Canada Collaborative Federalism Project, Rory Campbell
Director, Asia/Pacific, Marvin Schneider
Director, Europe/Latin America/Africa, Daniel Hayward
Director, United States/Mexico, Melanie McCallum

PROTOCOL OFFICE
Fax: 403/422-0786
Chief, Rory Campbell, 403/427-7350
Deputy Chief, Betty Spinks
Director, Operations, Judy Wilson Mahoney, 12845 - 102 Ave., Edmonton AB T5M 0M6, 403/427-2281, Fax: 403/422-6508

SOCIAL & FISCAL POLICY REFORM TEAM
AGT Tower II, #2200, 10025 Jasper Ave., Edmonton AB T5J 1S6
403/427-6553; Fax: 403/427-0939
Executive Officer, Francie Harle
Senior Advisor, Sherry Thompson
Acting Associate Director, Indira Roopnarine, Email: iro@inter.gov.ab.ca

TRADE POLICY TEAM
AGT Tower II, 10025 Jasper Ave., 23rd Fl., Edmonton AB T5J 1S6
Fax: 403/427-0939
Executive Director, International Economic Relations, Helmut Mach, 403/427-6543, Fax: 403/427-0699, Email: hem@inter.gov.ab.ca
Director, International Trade, Jim Ogilvy, 403/427-6553, Email: jao@inter.gov.ab.ca
International Trade Counsel, James Doherty, 403/427-6543, Fax: 403/427-0699, Email: jad@inter.gov.ab.ca
International Trade Counsel, Daryl Hanak, 403/427-6543, Fax: 403/427-0699, Email: dah@inter.gov.ab.ca
Associate Director, Internal Trade, Neil Kirkpatrick, 403/427-6553, Email: nrk@inter.gov.ab.ca

Alberta GAMING & LIQUOR COMMISSION
50 Corriveau Ave., St. Albert AB T8N 3T5
403/447-8600; Fax: 403/447-8916
Minister Responsible, Hon. Dr. Steven West, 403/427-3162, Fax: 403/422-6338
Chair, Bob King, 403/447-8602
Chair's Secretary, Linda Zakowski
Acting CEO, Norman Peterson, 403/447-8657

Alberta GOVERNMENT REORGANIZATION SECRETARIAT
#404, Legislature Bldg., 10800 - 97 Ave., Edmonton AB T5K 2B6
403/427-2585
Minister Responsible, Hon. Ken Rostad, Q.C.

Alberta HEALTH
PO Box 222, Edmonton AB T5J 2P4
403/427-7164; Email: ahinform@mail.health.gov.ab.ca; URL: http://www.gov.ab.ca/dept/health.html
Alberta Health Care Insurance Plan: 403/427-1432 (Edmonton); 403/297-6411 (Calgary)

ACTS ADMINISTERED
Alberta Health Care Insurance Act
Alberta Hospital Association Act
Ambulance Services Act
Blind or Deaf Persons' Rights Act
Cancer Programs Act
Dental Profession Act
Emergency Medical Aid Act
Health Facilities Review Committee Act
Health Insurance Premiums Act
Hospitals Act
Human Tissue Gift Act
Lloydminster Hospital Act
Medical Profession Act
Mental Health Act
M.S.I. Foundation Act
Nursing Homes Act
Nursing Profession Act
Nursing Service Act
Optometry Profession Act
Physical Therapy Profession Act
Premier's Council on the Status of Persons with Disabilities Act
Public Health Act
Regional Health Authorities Act
Registered Dieticians Act
Minister, Hon. Halvar C. Jonson, 403/427-3665, Fax: 403/429-5954
Deputy Minister, Jack Davis, 403/427-7164, Fax: 403/427-1577
Executive Director, Provincial Health Authorities, Mike Higgins, 403/426-8500
Director, Communications, Garth Norris, 403/427-7164, Fax: 403/427-1171

AREA SERVICES DIVISION
Asst. Deputy Minister, Don M. Ford, 403/427-7164
Provincial Health Officer, Dr. John Waters, 403/427-5263
Director, Assurance, Denis Lyons, 403/427-7040
Director, Centre for Disease Control, Mike Reynolds, 403/427-7687
Director, Emergency Health Services, Jon Pascoe, 403/427-4105, Email: ahehsb@mail.health.gov.ab.ca
Director, Environmental Health, Kevin McLeod, 403/427-2643
Director, Health Planning, Ron Dyck, 403/427-2653
Director, Mental Health Services, Henry Borowski, 403/427-2816
Director, Workforce Planning, Harvey Geddes, 403/427-1021
Director, North Area, David Bougher, 403/427-8020
Director, South Area, Vacant, 403/427-6082

CORPORATE SERVICES DIVISION
Asst. Deputy Minister, Aslam Bhatti, 403/427-7164
Director, Finance & Health Planning Administration, Dave Cathro, 403/427-3601
Director, Information Technology, Trevor Hodge, 403/427-7127
Director, Legislation & Contract Services, Bruce Jones, 403/427-6098
Coordinator, Freedom of Information & Privacy, Roger Mariner, 403/427-8028, Email: ahfoip@mail.health.gov.ab.ca

POPULATION HEALTH DIVISION
Asst. Deputy Minister, Nancy Reynolds, 403/427-7164
Provincial Medical Consultant, Dr. David Linklater, 403/427-1562

GOVERNMENT OF ALBERTA 3-101

Director, Health Legislation Review, Evelyn Swanson, 403/427-0407
Director, Health Policy, Jon Brehaut, 403/427-1558
Director, Surveillance, Stephen Gabos, 403/427-4518

Associated Agencies, Boards & Commissions
- Alberta Cancer Board: PO Box 222, Edmonton AB T5J 2P4 – 403/482-9300
President & CEO, Jean-Michel Turc
- Alberta Provincial Mental Health Board: c/o Chair, PO Box 2739, Pincher Creek AB T0K 1W0 – 403/422-2233
Chair, Ron LaJeunesse
- Health Facilities Review Committee: Sterling Place, 9940 - 106 St., 8th Fl., Edmonton AB T5K 2N2 – 403/427-4924
Chair, Denis Herard
- Office of the Mental Health Patient Advocate: Centre West Bldg., 10035 - 108 St., 12th Fl., Edmonton AB T5J 3E1 – 403/422-1812
Director, Dr. Mervyn Hislop
- Premier's Council on the Status of Persons with Disabilities: #250, 11044 - 82 Ave., Edmonton AB T6G 0T2 – 403/422-1095; Fax: 403/422-9691; Email: pcspd@planet.eon.net
Chair, Gary McPherson, 403/422-1095
Executive Director, Fran Vargo, 403/422-1095
Director, Research & Policy Review, Diane Earl

Alberta HUMAN RIGHTS & CITIZENSHIP COMMISSION
Standard Life Centre, #1600, 10405 Jasper Ave., Edmonton AB T5J 4R7
403/427-3116, 427-7661; Fax: 403/422-3563, 427-6013
TTY: 403/427-1597
Southern Alberta Office, #102, 1333 - 8 St. SW, Calgary AB T2R 1M6
403/297-6571, Fax: 403/297-6567
TTY: 403/297-5639

ACTS ADMINISTERED
Alberta Human Rights, Citizenship & Multiculturalism Act
Minister Responsible, Hon. Shirley McClellan, 403/427-4928, Fax: 403/427-0188
Chief Commissioner, Charlach Mackintosh, 403/427-3116, Fax: 403/422-3563
Director, Communications, Carol Chawrun, 403/427-6530, Fax: 403/427-1496

Alberta Office of the INFORMATION & PRIVACY COMMISSIONER
#410, 9925 - 109 St., Edmonton AB T5K 2J8
403/422-6860; Fax: 403/427-5682; Email: ipcab@planet.eon.net
Information & Privacy Commissioner, Robert Clark
Director & General Counsel, Frank Work
Office Administrator, Leanne Levy

Alberta JUSTICE
9833 - 109th St., Edmonton AB T5K 2E8
403/427-2745; Fax: 403/427-6821; URL: http://www.gov.ab.ca/dept/just.html
Legal Research & Analysis: 403/498-3300

ACTS ADMINISTERED
Administration of Estates Act
Administrative Procedures Act
Age of Majority Act
Alberta Evidence Act
Arbitration Act
Civil Enforcement Act
Commissioners for Oaths Act
Conflicts of Interest Act
Contributory Negligence Act
Corrections Act
Court of Appeal Act
Court of Queen's Bench Act
Criminal Injuries Compensation Act
Dangerous Dogs Act
Daylight Saving Time Act
Defamation Act
Devolution of Real Property Act
Domestic Relations Act
Expropriation Act
Extra-provincial Enforcement of Custody Orders Act
Factors Act
Family Relief Act
Fatal Accidents Act
Fatality Inquiries Act
Fraudulent Preferences Act
Frustrated Contracts Act
Government Organization Act, Schedule 9
Guarantees Acknowledgment Act
Innkeepers Act
International Child Abduction Act
International Commercial Arbitration Act
International Conventions Implementation Act
Interpretation Act
Interprovincial Subpoena Act
Intestate Succession Act
Judgement Interest Act
Judicature Act
Jury Act
Justice of the Peace Act
Landlord's Rights on Bankruptcy Act
Languages Act/Loi Linguistique
Legal Profession Act
Legitimacy Act
Limitation of Actions Act
Maintenance Enforcement Act
Maintenance Order Act
Married Women's Act
Masters & Servants Act
Matrimonial Property Act
Mechanical Recording of Evidence Act
Minors' Property Act
Motor Transport Act (jointly with Alberta Transportation & Utilities; Alberta Municipal Affairs)
Motor Transport Act (unproclaimed)
Motor Vehicle Accident Claims Act (jointly with Alberta Municipal Affairs)
Notaries Public Act
Oaths of Office Act
Occupiers' Liability Act
Off-highway Vehicle Act (jointly with Alberta Transportation & Utilities; Alberta Municipal Affairs)
Perpetuities Act
Personal Property Security Act (jointly with Alberta Municipal Affairs)
Petty Trespass Act
Police Act
Powers of Attorney Act
Private Investigators & Security Guards Act
Proceedings Against the Crown Act
Provincial Court Act
Provincial Court Judges Act
Provincial Offences Procedure Act
Public Inquiries Act
Public Trustee Act
Queen's Counsel Act
Reciprocal Enforcement of Judgements Act
Reciprocal Enforcement of Maintenance Orders Act
Regulations Act
Revised Statutes 1980 Act
Road Building Machinery Equipment Act
Sale of Goods Act
Surrogate Court Act
Survival of Actions Act
Survivorship Act
Tort-Feasors Act
Trustee Act
Ultimate Heir Act
Unconscionable Transactions Act
Victims' Programs Assistance Act
Warehouse Receipts Act
Wills Act
Women's Institute Act
Young Offenders Act
Minister & Attorney General, Hon. Brian Evans, 403/427-2339, Fax: 403/422-6621
Deputy Minister & Deputy Attorney General, Neil McCrank, 403/427-5032, Fax: 403/422-9639
Acting Executive Director, Human Resource Services, Sandra Hlus, 403/427-9617, Fax: 403/422-9639
Director, Aboriginal Justice Initiatives, Sylvia Novik, J.E. Brownlee Bldg., 10365 - 97th St., Edmonton AB T5J 3W7, 403/422-2779, Fax: 403/427-4670
Director, Staff College, Peter Nicholson, 16310 - 23rd Ave. NW, Edmonton AB T6R 2H2, 403/422-6598, Fax: 403/422-2854
Chief Medical Examiner, Dr. Graeme Dowling, 7007 - 116th St. NW, Edmonton AB T6H 5R8, 403/427-4987, Fax: 403/422-1265
Asst. Chief Medical Examiner, Dr. Bernard G. Bannach, 7007 - 116th St. NW, Edmonton AB T6H 5R8, 403/427-4987, Fax: 403/422-1265
Asst. Chief Medical Examiner, Dr. Lloyd Denmark, 4070 Bowness Rd. NW, Calgary AB T3B 3R7, 403/297-8123, Fax: 403/297-3429
Chief Legislative Counsel, Peter J. Pagano, 403/427-2217, Fax: 403/422-7366
Public Trustee, Office of the Public Trustee, Jack E. Klinck, Q.C., #400S, 10365 - 97th St., Edmonton AB T5J 3Z8, 403/427-2744, Fax: 403/422-9136
Asst. Public Trustee, William D. Polglase, 403/427-2744
Asst. Public Trustee, Brian M. Smith, #2100, 411 - 1st St. SE, Calgary AB T2G 4Y5, 403/297-6541, Fax: 403/297-2823
For list of Courts & other Legal Offices, including Judicial Officials & Judges *see* Section 10 of this book.

ADMINISTRATION DIVISION
Fax: 403/422-9639
Executive Director, Dennis P. Medwid, 403/427-3301
Director, Administrative Services, Howard A. Brinton, 403/427-5011, Fax: 403/427-6821
Director, Communications, Lesley Gronow, 403/427-8530, Fax: 403/422-7363
Director, Corporate Support Services, Randy Petruk, 10365 - 97th St., Edmonton AB T5J 3W7, 403/422-5969, Fax: 403/427-6002
Director, Finance, D. Ian Hope, 403/427-4997, Fax: 403/422-1648
Director, Internal Audit, Ed Berg, 10365 - 97th St., Edmonton AB T5J 3W7, 403/422-1189, Fax: 403/427-6002
Director, Maintenance Enforcement Program, Gerald C. Leibel, PO Box 2404, Edmonton AB T5J 3Z7, 403/422-5554, Fax: 403/422-1215
Director, Systems & Information Services, Ray Carter, 10365 - 97th St., Edmonton AB T5J 3W7, 403/422-5964, Fax: 403/422-2829

CIVIL LAW DIVISION
Fax: 403/422-9639
Asst. Deputy Minister, Doug Rae, 403/427-0912
Executive Director, Civil Law Branch, R. Neil Dunne, 403/498-3345, Fax: 403/425-0307
Director, Civil & Family Legal Services, Peggy Hartman, 403/498-3390, Fax: 403/425-0307
Director, Constitutional Law, Nolan Steed, 403/498-3323, Fax: 403/425-0307
Director, Legal Research & Analysis, Clark Dalton, 403/498-3305, Fax: 403/425-0307

CORRECTIONAL SERVICES DIVISION
Fax: 403/427-5905
Asst. Deputy Minister, Hank O'Handley, 403/427-3440
Executive Director, Adult Centre Operations Branch, Dave Forbes, J.E. Brownlee Bldg., 10365 - 97 St.,

Canadian Almanac & Directory 1997

Edmonton AB T5J 3W7, 403/427-4703, Fax: 403/427-1904

Executive Director, Community Corrections & Release Programs Branch, Arnold Galet, J.E. Brownlee Bldg., 10365 - 97 St., Edmonton AB T5J 3W7, 403/422-5757, Fax: 403/427-1904

Executive Director, Young Offender Branch, Patricia Meade, 10365 - 97th St., Edmonton AB T5J 3W7, 403/422-5019, Fax: 403/422-0732

COURT SERVICES DIVISION
Fax: 403/422-9639
Asst. Deputy Minister, Rod Wacowich, 403/427-9620
Director, Corporate Services, Dan Mercer, 403/422-6428, Fax: 403/422-6613
Manager, Law Libraries & Provincial Court Librarian, Sandra Perry, Law Courts Bldg., 5th Fl., North, 1A Sir Winston Churchill Square, 2nd Fl. South, Edmonton AB T5J 0R2, 403/427-5579, 5580, Fax: 403/427-0481

CRIMINAL JUSTICE DIVISION
Fax: 403/422-9639
Asst. Deputy Minister, Michael Allen, 403/427-5046
Director, Appeals & Criminal Law Policy, Ken Tjosvold, 403/427-5042, Fax: 403/422-1106
Director, Special Prosecutions Branch, Terry Matchett, 10365 - 97th St., Edmonton AB T5J 3W7, 403/422-0640, Fax: 403/422-1217

PUBLIC SECURITY DIVISION
10365 - 97th St., Edmonton AB T5J 3W7
Fax: 403/427-1194
Asst. Deputy Minister, Robert B. Dunster, 403/427-3457
Acting Director, Policing Services Branch, Judy Mackay, 403/427-3457
Director, Regulatory & Administrative Support Branch, Neil Warner, 403/427-3457, Fax: 403/427-5916
Director, Security Operations Branch, Al Palmer, 403/422-3791, Fax: 403/427-0476
Director, Serious & Violent Crime Initiatives, Gary Hutnan, Bowker Bldg., 9833 - 109 St., Edmonton AB T5K 2E8, 403/427-9030, Fax: 403/422-1330
Manager, Victims' Programs, Barb Pratt, 403/427-3460
Chief Provincial Firearms Officer, George Reid, 403/427-0437, Fax: 403/427-1100

Associated Agencies, Boards & Commissions
• Access to Information & Protection of Privacy Panel: #420, Legislature Bldg., Edmonton AB T5K 2B6 – 403/427-3666
Chair, Hon. Robert Fischer
• Alberta Board of Review: J.E. Brownlee Bldg., 10365 - 97 St., 5th Fl., Edmonton AB T5J 3W7 – 403/422-5994; Fax: 403/427-1762
Chair, Michael Stevens-Guille, Q.C.
Administrator, Lorraine Russell
• Alberta Law Foundation: #300, 407 - 8 Ave. SW, Calgary AB T2P 1E5 – 403/264-4701; Fax: 403/294-9238
Executive Director, O.G. Snider
• Alberta Legal Aid Society: Revlon Bldg., #300, 10320 - 102 Ave., Edmonton AB T5J 4A1 – 403/427-7575; Fax: 403/427-5909
• Crimes Compensation Board: J.E. Brownlee Bldg., 10365 - 97 St., 7th Fl., Edmonton AB T5J 3W7 – 403/427-7217; Fax: 403/422-4213
Chair, Dr. B.A. Nahornick
Secretary to the Board, Linda Unger
• Fatality Review Board: 4070 Bowness Rd. NW, Calgary AB T3B 3R7 – 403/297-8123; Fax: 403/297-3429
Chairperson, Margaret Gowlland
• Law Enforcement Review Board: 10365 - 97 St. 10th Fl., Edmonton AB T5J 3W7 – 403/422-9376; Fax: 403/422-4782
Chair, Patrick Knoll
Secretary to the Board, Barbara Newton

Alberta LABOUR
10808 - 99 Ave., Edmonton AB T5K 0G5
403/427-2723; URL: http://www.gov.ab.ca/dept/lbr.html

ACTS ADMINISTERED
Agrologists Act
Blind Workers' Compensation Act
Burial of the Dead Act
Certified General Accountants Act
Certified Management Accountants Act
Chartered Accountants Act
Chiropractic Profession Act
Dental Disciplines Act
Dental Mechanics Act
Employment Pension Plans Act
Employment Standards Code
Forestry Profession Act
Government Organization Act, Schedule 10
Health Disciplines Act
Labour Relations Code
Managerial Exclusion Act
M.L.A. Compensation Act
Occupational Health & Safety Act
Occupational Therapy Profession Act
Opticians Act
Pharmaceutical Profession Act
Podiatry Act
Police Officers Collective Bargaining Act
Professional & Occupational Associations Registration Act
Psychology Profession Act
Public Service Employees Relations Act
Quarries Regulation Act
Radiation Protection Act
Safety Codes Act
Social Workers Act
Veterinary Profession Act
Workers' Compensation Act
Minsiter, Hon. Murray Smith
Deputy Minister, Robin Ford, 403/427-8305, Fax: 403/422-9205
Director, Communications, Charlotte Moran, 403/427-5585, Fax: 403/427-5988
Director, Personnel, Denis St. Arnaud, 403/427-8391, Fax: 403/422-6615

ISSUES & REGIONAL MANAGEMENT DIVISION
403/427-8301; Fax: 403/427-6327
Asst. Deputy Minister, Shelley Ewart-Johnson, 403/422-3041, Fax: 403/422-9205
Commissioner, Office of the Provincial Fire Commissioner, Tom Makey, 403/427-8392, Fax: 403/422-3562
Superintendent, Pensions, Gail e Armitage, 403/427-8322, Fax: 403/422-4283
Coordinator, Training Services, Linda Fields, 403/427-1173, Fax: 403/422-3091
Director, Information Services, Alec Campbell, 403/427-8531, Fax: 403/422-5070
Director, Work Standards, Mike Kolmatycki, 403/427-8541, Fax: 403/422-3562

Regional Offices
Central: 4920 - 51 St., 2nd Fl., Red Deer AB T4N 6K8 – 403/340-5157; Fax: 403/340-4847, Regional Coordinator, Harry Caufield
North Central: 9940 - 106 Ave., Edmonton AB T5K 2N2 – 403/427-9063; Fax: 403/427-8837, Regional Coordinator, Eric Reitsma
Northwest: 10320 - 99 St., 3rd Fl., Grande Prairie AB T8V 6J4 – 403/538-5243; Fax: 403/538-5462, Regional Coordinator, John MacPherson
South: 727 - 7 Ave., 7th Fl., Calgary AB T2P 0Z2 – 403/427-5765; Fax: 403/297-4174, Regional Coordinator, Peter Hickson

PROFESSIONAL & TECHNICAL SERVICES DIVISION
10011 - 109 St., 5th Fl., Edmonton AB T5J 3S8
403/427-2655; Fax: 403/422-9734
Asst. Deputy Minister, Don Woytowich, 403/427-8387, Fax: 403/422-9205
Senior Technical Adviser, Plumbing & Gas, Ken Fenning, 403/427-8256, Fax: 403/422-0308
Senior Technical Advisor, Building & Fire Safety, Chris Tye, 403/427-8265, Fax: 403/422-3562
Chief Electrical Inspector, Ken McLennan, 403/427-8260, Fax: 403/427-0380
Chief Elevator Inspector, Al Griffin, 403/427-8260, Fax: 403/427-0380

Occupational Health & Safety Services
Fax: 403/427-5698
Director, Occupational Health & Safety, Dr. Roxane Grade, 403/427-6971
Manager, Legislation Standards & Technical Service, Dan Clarke, 403/427-2687

Associated Agencies, Boards & Commissions
• Labour Relations Board/Public Service Employee Relations Board: #503, 10808 - 99 Ave., Edmonton AB T5K 0G5 – 403/427-8547; Fax: 403/422-0970, Toll Free: 1-800-463-2572
Chair, Bob Blair
• Occupational Health & Safety Council: 10808 - 99 Ave., 9th Fl., Edmonton AB T5K 0G5 – 403/427-6971; Fax: 403/427-5698
Chair, Wayne Cameron

Alberta MULTICULTURALISM COMMISSION
Standard Life Centre, 10405 Jasper Ave., 9th Fl., Edmonton AB T5J 4R7
403/427-2927; Fax: 403/422-6348

ACTS ADMINISTERED
Alberta Human Rights, Citizenship & Multiculturalism Act
Minister Responsible, Hon. Shirley McClellan, 403/427-4928, Fax: 403/427-0188
Chair, Yvonne Fritz
Coordinator, Cathy Finlayson

Alberta MUNICIPAL AFFAIRS (AMA)
Commerce Place, 10155 - 102 St., Edmonton AB T5J 4L4
403/427-2732; Fax: 403/422-9105; URL: http://www.gov.ab.ca/dept/ma.html
Communications: 403/427-8862; Fax: 403/422-1419
Provides administrative, financial & planning services to municipalities, sets & enforces marketplace standards, licenses businesses & trades, & offers consumer information & advice.

ACTS ADMINISTERED
Alberta Educational Communications Corporation Act
Alberta Housing Act
Bankruptcy & Insolvency Act (Canada)
Border Areas Act
Builders' Lien Act
Business Corporations Act
Calgary-Canadian Pacific Transit Agreement Act
Calgary (City of) & Calgary Power Agreement Act
Calgary (City of) & Calgary Power Authorization Agreement Act
Calgary Exhibition Stampede Limited - Calgary Lease Authorization Act
Cemeteries Act
Cemetery Companies Act
Change of Name Act
Charitable Fund-raising Act
Collection Practices Act

Companies Act
Condominium Property Act
Consumer Credit Transactions Act
Co-operative Associations Act
Debtors' Assistance Act
Direct Sales Cancellation Act
Dower Act
Edmonton (City of) & Calgary Power Ltd. Agreement Validation Act
Edmonton - Meadowview Agreement Act
Franchises Act
Fuel Oil Licensing Act
Garagemen's Lien Act
Land Titles Act
Law of Property Act
Licensing of Trades & Businesses Act
Lloydminster Municipal Amalgamation Act
Local Authorities Election Act
Marriage Act
Mewata Park Enabling Act
Mobile Homes Sites Tenancies Act
Municipal Government Act
Park Towns Act
Partnership Act
Personal Property Security Act
Possessory Liens Act
Prearranged Funeral Services Act
Public Auctions Act
Real Estate Act
Religious Societies' Land Act
Residential Tenancies Act
Smoky Lake (Town of) Gas Utility Act
Societies Act
Special Areas Act
Spirit River Agreement O.C. Surveys Act
Unfair Trade Practices Act
Vital Statistics Act
Warehousemen's Lien Act
Woodmen's Lien Act
Minister, Hon. Tom Thurber, 403/427-3744
Acting Deputy Minister, John McGowan, 403/427-9660, Fax: 403/427-0453

FINANCE & ADMINISTRATION DIVISION
Asst. Deputy Minister, Ray Reshke, 403/427-1898, Fax: 403/422-9561
Executive Director, Financial Services, Bruce Perry, 403/427-1899, Fax: 403/422-5840
Director, Accounting Services, Bryan Huygen, 403/427-4245, Fax: 403/422-3109
Director, Administrative Services, Ron Todoruk, 403/427-4878, Fax: 403/422-9105
Director, Agencies & Funds, Perry Twaits, 403/427-5942, Fax: 403/427-0453
Director, Budgets & Reporting, Lothar Hellweg, 403/427-4158, Fax: 403/422-5840

HOUSING & CONSUMER AFFAIRS DIVISION
403/427-3917; Fax: 403/427-0418
Asst. Deputy Minister, R.S. Leitch
Executive Director, Field Services, Reegan McCullough, 403/427-3919, Fax: 403/427-0418
Executive Director, Major Projects, Rick Beaupre, 403/422-9528, Fax: 403/427-0418
Executive Director, Program Services, Vacant, 403/427-4517, Fax: 403/427-0418
Director, Divisional Support Services, Penny Stinson
Manager, Grants, Subsidies & Recoveries, Wayne Wendell, 403/427-6897, Fax: 403/427-4315

LOCAL GOVERNMENT SERVICES DIVISION
Asst. Deputy Minister, John McGowan, 403/427-9660, Fax: 403/427-0453
Executive Director, Local Government Advisory, Rae Runge, 403/427-6534, Fax: 403/422-9133
Executive Director, Local Government Development, Brian Quickfall, 403/427-2523, Fax: 403/420-1016

Director, Assessment Standard & Equalizations, Harold Williams, 403/422-1377, Fax: 403/422-3110
Director, Special Services & Management Support, Theresa Ostrum, 403/427-5642, Fax: 403/427-0453

REGISTRIES DIVISION
John E. Brownlee Bldg., 10365 - 97 St., Edmonton AB T5J 3W7
403/422-2362 (Edmonton), 297-8980 (Calgary)
Toll Free: 1-800-465-5009 (in Alberta)
Responsible for motor vehicles, corporate registry, vital statistics & personal property registry. $20.00 each for birth, marriage & death certificates.
Registrar, Inspector, Land Titles & Director, Vital Statistics, Gary Boddez, 403/427-4095, Fax: 403/422-0818
Business Development & Private Agent Support, David Howden, 403/427-0937, Fax: 403/422-0665
Research & Program Development, Laurie Beveridge, 403/427-8250, Fax: 403/422-5018
Registration Services, Calgary, Marvin Schoenleber, 403/297-6525, Fax: 403/297-8641
Registration Services, Edmonton, Bill Campion, 403/427-5166, Fax: 403/422-3105

Associated Agencies, Boards & Commissions
• Alberta Municipal Government Board: 10155 - 102 St., 18th Fl., Edmonton AB T5J 4L4 – 403/427-4864; Fax: 403/427-0986
Director, Administration, Shirley Kwan
• Alberta Social Housing Corporation: 10155 - 102 St., 14th Fl., Edmonton AB T5J 4L4 – 403/422-9222; Fax: 403/427-0961
• Alberta Special Areas Board: PO Box 820, Hanna AB T0J 1P0 – 403/854-5600; Fax: 403/854-5527
Chair, J.J. Stemp

NORTHERN ALBERTA DEVELOPMENT COUNCIL
#206, Provincial Bldg., 9621 - 96 Ave., PO Bag 900-14, Peace River AB T8S 1T4
403/624-6274; Fax: 403/624-6184
Minister Responsible, Hon. Ralph Klein, 403/427-2251, Fax: 403/427-1349, Email: altatalk@censsw.gov.ab.ca
Chair, Wayne Jacques, 403/427-1858, Fax: 403/422-0351

NORTHERN DEVELOPMENT BRANCH
#206, Provincial Bldg., PO Bag 900-14, Peace River AB T8S 1T4
403/624-6277; Fax: 403/624-6184; Email: nadc@ccinet.ab.ca
Executive Director, Rick Sloan
Director, Economic Development, Brian Pountney, 403/624-6276

Alberta Office of the OMBUDSMAN
Phipps-McKinnon Bldg., #1630, 10020 - 101A Ave., Edmonton AB T5J 3G2
403/427-2756; Fax: 403/427-2759
Calgary Office: #850, Ford Tower, 633 - 6 Ave. SW, Calgary AB T2P 2Y5
403/297-6185, Fax: 403/297-5121
Ombudsman, Harley Johnson

Alberta PUBLIC AFFAIRS BUREAU
Park Plaza, 10611 - 98 Ave., 6th Fl., Edmonton AB T5K 2P7
403/427-2754; Fax: 403/422-9704
Minister Responsible, Hon. Ralph Klein, 403/427-2251, Fax: 403/427-1349, Email: altatalk@gov.ab.ca
Managing Director, Gerry Bourdeau, 403/427-4350, Fax: 403/427-1010

COMMUNICATIONS PLANNING & CONSULTING
Director, Communications, Planning & Advertising, Laurie Collins, 403/427-9299
Consultant, Communications, Theresa Lumsdon, 403/427-9352

COMMUNICATIONS SUPPORT SERVICES
Executive Director, Dick Steiner, 403/427-4366, Fax: 403/427-4304
Coordinator, Alberta Communications Network (ACN), Allen MacDonald, 403/427-4374
Director, Print & Graphic Design Services, Marvin Luethe, 403/427-2698
Director, Publication Services & Queen's Printer, Annie Re, 11510 Kingsway Ave., 2nd Fl., Edmonton AB T5G 2Y5, 403/422-2787, Fax: 403/452-0668
Director, Regional Information Telephone Enquiries (RITE), Elainen Dougan, 403/422-4097

Alberta PUBLIC WORKS, SUPPLY & SERVICES (APWSS)
6950 - 113th St., 3rd Fl., Edmonton AB T6H 5V7
403/422-0326; Fax: 403/427-0812; URL: http://www.gov.ab.ca/dept.pwss.html

ACTS ADMINISTERED
Architects Act
Consulting Engineers of Alberta Act
Engineering Geological & Geophysical Professions Act
Freedom of Information & Protection of Privacy Act, 1995
Government Organization Act, Schedule 5 (jointly with Alberta Environmental Protection)
Hospitals Act (jointly with Alberta Health)
Mental Health Act (jointly with Alberta Health)
Nursing Homes Act (jointly with Alberta Health)
Public Works Act (jointly with Alberta Transportation & Utilities)
Water Resources Act (jointly with Alberta Environmental Protection)
Minister, Hon. Stan Woloshyn, 403/427-3666, Fax: 403/427-3649
Deputy Minister, Dan Bader, P.Eng., 403/427-3921, Fax: 403/422-0186
Executive Director, Finance Division, Paul Pellis, 403/427-1990, Fax: 403/422-5141
Executive Director, Human Resources, Gordon Shopland, 403/427-3986, Fax: 403/422-5138
Director, Business Planning, Diane Dalgleish, 403/427-4966, Fax: 403/422-0186
Director, Communications, Jan Berkowski, 403/422-0326, Fax: 403/427-0812

INFORMATION TECHNOLOGY & SUPPLY
Asst. Deputy Minister, Gregg Hook, 403/427-8894, Fax: 403/422-1801, Email: hookg@censsw.gov.ab.ca
Executive Director, Information Technology Division, Stan Petrica, 403/427-4203, Fax: 403/427-1449
Executive Director, Telecommunications Division, Andrew Boys, 403/422-1140, Fax: 403/427-0238
Director, Contracted Services, Ron Caruk, 12360 - 142nd St., Edmonton AB T5L 2H1, 403/427-3222, Fax: 403/427-0834
Director, Purchasing Branch, Mike Long, 403/427-3222
Director, Supplier Development Branch, Wayne Kenny, 403/427-3222

PROPERTY DEVELOPMENT DIVISION
Asst. Deputy Minister, Peter Kruselnicki, P.Eng., 403/427-3835, Fax: 403/427-3873
Executive Director, Capital Projects Division, Malcolm Johnson, 403/427-3927, Fax: 403/422-5832
Executive Director, Civil Projects Division, John Ruttan, 403/427-3928, Fax: 403/422-9594
Executive Director, Health Facility Projects Division, John Bennett, 403/427-7924, Fax: 403/422-9749

Executive Director, Strategic Planning Division, Larry James, 403/427-3928, Fax: 403/422-9043
Executive Director, Technical Resources & Standards Division, Casey Skakun, 403/427-7924, Fax: 403/422-7479
Director, Air Transportation Services, John Tenzer, 11940 - 109th St., Edmonton AB T5G 2T8, 403/427-7341, Fax: 403/422-1232

PROPERTY MANAGEMENT DIVISION
Asst. Deputy Minister, Bob Smith, 403/427-3875, Fax: 403/422-0284
Acting Director, Facility Information & Services Group, Terry Bocirukiw, 403/422-0034, Fax: 403/427-1129
Director, Land Acquisition Branch, Garry Summers, 403/422-1384, Fax: 403/422-5419
Director, Leasing Branch, Bill Hunt, 403/422-0601, Fax: 403/422-2113
Acting Director, Transportation Utility Corridor Management, Dave Bentley, 403/427-3881, Fax: 403/422-2661

Regional Offices
Edmonton & Area: 6950 - 113th St., Edmonton AB T6H 5V7 – 403/427-3881, Director, Dick Polowaniuk, 403/427-3881
Northern: 6950 - 113th St., Edmonton AB T6H 5V7 – 403/427-3881, Director, Lawrence Swabey
Southern: 620 - 7th Ave. SW, Calgary AB T2P 0Y8 – 403/297-3753, Director, John Enns

Alberta RESEARCH COUNCIL (ARC)
250 Karl Clark Rd., PO Box 8330, Edmonton AB T6H 5X2
403/450-5111; Fax: 403/461-2651; URL: http://www.arc.ab.ca
Calgary Office: Digital Bldg., 6815 - 8 St. NE, 3rd Fl., Calgary AB T2E 7H7
403/297-2600, Fax: 403/297-2607
Minister Responsible, Hon. Dianne Mirosh, 403/427-2294
President & CEO, Dr. B.L. Barge, 403/450-5200, Fax: 403/450-1490

ADVANCED TECHNOLOGIES DIVISION
Vice-President, Dr. D.J. Cox, 403/450-5220
Head, Advanced Computing & Engineering, K.I. Gamble, 403/297-7580
Head, Biotechnology, Dr. W.T. Leps, 403/450-5319
Head, Manufacturing Technologies, C.C. Lumb, 403/450-5401
Director, Information Systems, W.J. Neilson, 403/450-5188
General Manager, Electronics Test Centre, B.G. Young, 403/450-5361

DEVELOPMENT & PLANNING DIVISION
Vice-President, Dr. R.J. Fessenden, 403/450-5205
Director, Corporate Marketing, Dr. T.R. Heidrick, 403/450-5218
Manager, Corporate Relations, K.D. Bellveau, 403/450-5203
Manager, Technology Management/Joint Research Venture, R.J. Hipkin, 403/297-2682

RESOURCE TECHNOLOGIES DIVISION
Vice-President, Dr. M.P. du Plessis, 403/297-2604
Head, Alberta Geological Survey, Dr. Jan A. Boon, 403/438-7615
Head, Breakthrough Technologies, Heavy Oil & Oil Sands, Dr. E.E. Isaacs, 403/472-4249
Head, Energy Technologies, Dr. D.M. Nguyen, 403/987-8119
Head, Environmental Technologies, Dr. G.W. Bird, 403/472-4400

Head, Forest Products, R.W.F. Wellwood, 403/450-5419
Head, Pulp & Paper Research, P. Harris, 403/472-4253

Alberta SUCCESSION DUTY OFFICE
J.E. Brownlee Bldg., #400 South, 10365 - 97 St., Edmonton AB T5J 3Z8
403/422-2824; Fax: 403/422-9136
Collector, Succession Duties, Georgette A. Dawes

Alberta TRANSPORTATION & UTILITIES
Twin Atria, 4999 - 98 Ave., Edmonton AB T6B 2X3
403/427-2731; URL: http://www.gov.ab.ca/dept/tu.html
Dangerous Goods Transportation: 1-800-272-9600

ACTS ADMINISTERED
Alberta Resources Railway Corporation Act
City Transportation Act
Department of Transportation & Utilities Act
Highway Traffic Act
Motor Transport Act
Natural Gas Rebates Act
Off-Highway Vehicle Act
Public Highways Development Act
Railway Act
Rural Electrification Long Term Financing Act
Rural Gas Act
Rural Utilities Act
Water, Gas, Electric & Telephone Companies Act
Minister, Hon. Robert Fischer, 403/427-2080, Fax: 403/422-2722
Deputy Minister, Ed McLellan, B.C.E., M.Eng., 403/427-2081, Fax: 403/465-1135
Director, Communications, Jayne Jeneroux, 403/427-7674
Executive Director, Personnel, Ian Pregitzer, 403/427-7756

CONTRACTS & INFRASTRUCTURE MANAGEMENT
Fax: 403/422-6515
Asst. Deputy Minister, Dave Shillabeer, 403/424-0141
Executive Director, Internal Audit Services, Ralph Timleck, 403/427-7678
Director, Contracts & Compliance, Tim Hawnt, 403/427-2091
Acting Head, Equipment Supply & Services, Verne Schneider, 403/427-8310

CORPORATE SERVICES
Fax: 403/422-1070
Asst. Deputy Minister, June A. MacGregor, 413/427-0142
Executive Director, Finance & Facility Services, B. James, 403/427-7396
Executive Director, Policy & Coordination, Tom Brown, 403/427-7944
Executive Director, Rural Utilities, Wayne Brown, 403/427-0125
Solicitor, Legal Services, Jim McFadzen, 403/427-2097
Director, Performance Measures, Les Hempsey, 403/427-7944

REGIONAL COORDINATION
Fax: 403/422-6515
Executive Director, Lyle O'Neill, 403/427-7215
Executive Director, Disaster & Emergency Programs, Ron Wolsey, 403/422-9000
Director, Dangerous Goods Control, Shaun Hammond, 403/427-8901

REGIONAL OPERATIONS
Regional Director, Southern Region - Lethbridge, Alec Waters, 403/381-5426
Regional Director, Central Region - Red Deer, Rob Penny, 403/340-5166

Regional Director, North Central Regiona - Barrhead, John Schroder, 403/674-8221
Regional Director, Peace Region - Peace River, Keith Helberg, 403/624-6280

SAFETY & TECHNICAL SERVICES
Fax: 403/422-6515
Asst. Deputy Minister, Jim Sawchuk, 403/427-7379
Executive Director, Planning & Programming, Brian Marcotte, 403/427-5999
Executive Director, Project Management, J. Ramotar, 403/427-6912
Executive Director, Technical Standards, Allan G. Kwan, 403/427-2087
Executive Director, Transportation Safety & Carrier Services, Roger Clarke, 403/340-5033

TRANSITION MANAGEMENT
Fax: 403/468-5633
Acting Asst. Deputy Minister, Stan Hayter, 403/422-7299
Head, Strategic & Performance Management, Don McTavish, 403/427-7058
Head, Technology Management, Information Management, Bob Ferguson, 403/422-7296

Associated Agencies, Boards & Commissions
• Alberta Gaming & Liquor Commission
Listed alphabetically in detail, this section.
• Alberta Racing Commission: Sloane Square, #507, 5920 - 1A St. SW, Calgary AB T2H 0G3 – 403/297-6551; Fax: 403/255-4078
Chair, Roy Farran
• Alberta Resources Railway: #501, 10130 - 103 St., Edmonton AB T5J 3N9 – 403/427-3165
Managing Director, C. Anderson
• Traffic Safety Board: Twin Atria Bldg., 4999 - 98 Ave., 1st Fl., Edmonton AB T6B 2X3 – 403/427-7178; Fax: 403/427-1740
Chair, George Pedersen
Executive Director, Sherri Thorsen

Alberta TREASURY
Terrace Bldg., 9515 - 107 St., Edmonton AB T5K 2C3
403/427-3035; Fax: 403/422-2463

ACTS ADMINISTERED
Alberta Corporate Tax Act
Alberta Heritage Savings Trust Fund Act
Alberta Income Tax Act
Alberta Municipal Financing Corporation Act
Alberta Securities Commission Reorganization Act
Alberta Stock Savings Plan Act
Alberta Taxpayers Protection Act
Appropriation Acts
Balanced Budget & Debt Retirement Act
Civil Services Garnishee Act
Credit Union Act
Deficit Elimination Act
Farm Credit Stability Fund Act
Financial Administration Act
Financial Consumers Act
Fuel Tax Act
Government Accountability Act
Government Emergency Guarantee Act
Hotel Room Tax Act
Insurance Act
Loan & Trust Corporations Act
Lottery Fund Transfer Act
Members of the Legislative Assembly Pension Plan Act
Municipal Debentures Act
Pari Mutuel Tax Act
Pension Fund Act
Public Sector Pension Plans Act
Securities Act
Small Business Term Assistance Fund Act
Statistics Bureau Act

Tobacco Tax Act
Treasury Branches Act
Trust Companies Act
Utility Companies Income Tax Rebates Act
Provincial Treasurer, Hon. Jim Dinning, 403/427-8809, Fax: 403/428-1341
Executive Asst., Greg Moffatt, 403/427-8809, Fax: 403/428-1341
Deputy Provincial Treasurer, Budget & Management, Al O'Brien, 403/427-4106, Fax: 403/427-0178
Deputy Provincial Treasurer, Finance & Revenue, Allister McPherson, 403/427-3076, Fax: 403/427-0178
Ministerial Projects & Liaison, Paul Taylor, 403/427-3052, Fax: 403/427-0178
Asst. Deputy Provincial Treasurer, Revenue, Len Rokosh, 403/427-3052, Fax: 403/427-0178
Controller, Jim Peters, 403/427-3052, Fax: 403/427-0178

ADMINISTRATION
Corporate Secretary, Michael Faulkner, 403/422-2858, Fax: 403/422-7235
Senior Manager, Financial Services, Terry Eliuk, 403/427-9935 ext.244, Fax: 403/422-2163
Senior Manager, Information Technology Services, David Whitworth, 403/427-4786 ext.236, Fax: 403/422-7235
Senior Manager, Personnel Services, Herb Martin, 403/427-3070 ext.263, Fax: 403/422-0421

BANKING & CASH MANAGEMENT
Director, Mike B. Neuman, 403/427-9766 ext.226, Fax: 403/427-0473
Acting Senior Manager, Securities Administration, Doug de Brujin, 403/427-3041 ext.271
Senior Manager, Securities Systems, J. Allan Benbow, 403/427-9920 ext.247

OFFICE OF BUDGET & MANAGEMENT
Group Leader, Budget Planning, Agriculture & Rural Development, Mike Wevers, 403/427-8741, Fax: 403/426-3951
Group Leader, Budget Planning, Community Services, Larry Bailer, 403/427-8701, Fax: 403/426-4564
Group Leader, Budget Planning, Financial Planning, Bob. Stothart, 403/427-7699, Fax: 403/422-2164
Group Leader, Budget Planning, Natural Resources & Sustainable Development, Mary Gibson, 403/427-8710, Fax: 403/426-4564
Accounting, Richard Lowen, 403/427-8799, Fax: 403/422-0375
Budget Planning & Integration, Alex Fowlie, 403/427-8804, Fax: 403/426-3951
Economics & Public Finance, Grant Robertson, 403/427-7546, Fax: 403/422-2164
Financial & Reporting Standards, Tim Wiles, 403/427-7320, Fax: 403/422-2164
Performance Measurement, Rich Goodkey, 403/427-8417, Fax: 403/422-2164
Special Projects, Doug Porter, 403/427-3052, Fax: 403/427-0178
Tax & Pensions, Virendra Gupta, 403/427-8730, Fax: 403/426-4564

COMMUNICATIONS
Director, Trish Filevich, 403/427-5364, Fax: 403/427-1147

FINANCE PLANNING & ANALYSIS
Director, Robert Bhatia, 403/427-4140 ext.282, Fax: 403/427-2435
Senior Manager, Financial/Economic Analysis, Rod Matheson, 403/427-4140 ext.286
Senior Manager, Financial Sector Policy, Robert Ascah, 403/427-4140 ext.281
Senior Manager, Strategic Financial Planning, Susan Williams, 403/427-4140 ext.277

FINANCIAL INSTITUTIONS
Director, Terry Stroich, 403/427-5064 ext.268, Fax: 403/422-2175

INSURANCE
Superintendent of Insurance, Bernie Rodrigues, 403/422-1592 ext.225, Fax: 403/420-0752
Deputy Superintendent of Insurance, Arthur Hagan, 403/422-1592 ext.226

INVESTMENT MANAGEMENT
Chief Investment Officer, Stan J. Susinski, 403/427-3087, Fax: 403/425-9153
Director, Debt Securities, J. Maurice Husken, 403/427-7981
Director, Equities, John M. Campbell, 403/427-7983
Director, Liability Management, Jai Parihar, 403/427-3088
Director, Structured Investment & Portfolio Research, Rocco Klein, 403/427-3093

LOANS & GUARANTEES
Director, Peter McNeil, 403/427-9722 ext.254, Fax: 403/422-0981
Senior Manager, Financing & Administration, Stan Bebenek, 403/427-9722 ext.264

RISK MANAGEMENT & INSURANCE
Director, Richard Whitehouse, 403/427-4134, Fax: 403/422-5271
Senior Manager, Risk Management Operations, Dick Ewert, 403/427-4134

TAX & REVENUE ADMINISTRATION
Director, Compliance, Terry Burns, 403/427-0540, Fax: 403/422-3770
Director, Internal Support, John Parton, 403/427-9416, Fax: 403/427-5074
Director, Revenue Operations, Rick Callaway, 403/427-3244, Fax: 403/427-0348
Director, Strategic Management & Integration, Peter Tsang, 403/427-9403, Fax: 403/427-9631
Director, Tax Services, Lukas Huisman, 403/427-9425, Fax: 403/427-5074

Alberta Heritage Savings Trust Fund
403/427-3076
The fund manages the province's resource tax revenues & has a mandate to diversify the Alberta economy for the general good of the population. The Deputy Provincial Treasurer, Finance & Revenue has over-all responsibility.

Associated Agencies, Boards & Commissions
• Alberta Pensions Administration: Park Plaza, 3rd Fl., 10611 - 98 Ave., Edmonton AB T5K 2P7 – 403/427-2782; Fax: 403/427-1621; Email: apaco@ibm.net
President & Chief Executive Officer, Robert J. Kallir
Chair, Board of Directors, Jack H. McMahon
Chair, Local Authorities Pension Plan Board, Sandra Weidner
Chair, Management Employees Pension Board, Dianne Keefe
Chair, Public Service Pension Board, Tim Wiles
Chair, Special Forces Pension Board, Michael Dungey
Chair, Universities Academic Pension Board, Dr. Ron Bercov
Secretary, Pension Boards, Leonard R. Morin
• Alberta Municipal Financing Corporation: Terrace Bldg., #403, 9515 - 107 St., Edmonton AB T5K 2C3 – 403/427-9711; Fax: 403/422-2175
President, Robert Splane
• Alberta Securities Commission: 10025 Jasper Ave., 19th Fl., Edmonton AB T5J 3Z5 – 403/422-5201; Fax: 403/427-0777
Chair, W.L. Hess, Q.C., 403/297-4280
Executive Director, R.D. Sczinski, C.A., 403/422-1490
Director, Capital Markets, Darrell Bartlett, C.A., 403/422-1505
Director, Finance & Administration, R.J. Turner, C.A., 403/422-1710
Director, Legal & Policy, Glenda A. Campbell, 403/422-1981
Director, Market Standards, H. Charles Blakey, 403/297-4221
Director, Securities Analysis, Kenneth Parker, C.A., 403/422-0145
Chief Accountant, Matthew Bootie, C.A., 403/297-3251
300 - 5 Ave., S.W., 4th Fl., Calgary AB T2P 3C4 403/297-6454, Fax: 403/297-6156
• Automobile Insurance Board: #407, Terrace Bldg., 9515 - 107 St., Edmonton AB T5K 2C3 – 403/427-5428; Fax: 403/422-2175
Administrator, S. Steeves

Alberta Advisory Council on WOMEN'S ISSUES
This office was closed March 31, 1996.
Minister Responsible, Hon. Shirley McClellan, 403/427-4928, Fax: 403/427-0188
Chair, Marilyn Fleger, 403/422-0668

Alberta WORKERS' COMPENSATION BOARD
9912 - 107 St., PO Box 2415, Edmonton AB T5J 2S5
403/498-4000; Fax: 403/422-0972
Minister Responsible, Hon. Murray Smith, 403/427-3664, Fax: 403/422-9556
President & CEO, Dr. John Cowell, 403/498-4901
Vice-President, Claimant & Health Care Services, John Quince, 403/498-4250
Vice-President, Employer Services, Dieter Brunsch, 403/498-4909
Vice-President, Finance & Administrative Services, David Renwick, 403/498-4188
Secretary & General Counsel, J. Douglas Carr, 403/498-4905
Director, Communications, Anne Marie Downey, 403/498-8680
Director, Organizational Performance & Learning, Michael Plumb, 403/498-8635
Chair, Appeals Commission, George Pheasey, 403/422-9539
Chair, Assessment Review Committee, Kenneth Ogston, 403/498-7830
Chair, Claims Services Review Committee, Dirk Smith, 403/498-4441

GOVERNMENT OF BRITISH COLUMBIA

Seat of Government: Legislative Assembly, Parliament Bldgs., Victoria BC V8V 1X4
URL: http://www.gov.bc.ca/
The Province of British Columbia entered Confederation July 20, 1871. It has an area of 892,677.00 km2, & the StatsCan census population in 1991 was 3,282,061.

Office of the LIEUTENANT GOVERNOR
Government House, 1401 Rockland Ave., Victoria BC V8S 1V9
250/387-2080; Fax: 250/387-2077
Lieutenant Governor, Hon. Garde B. Gardom, Q.C.
Secretary, J. Michael Roberts, L.V.O.

Canadian Almanac & Directory 1997

Office of the PREMIER
#156, West Annex, Legislative Bldgs., Victoria BC V8V 1X4
250/387-1715; Fax: 250/387-0087
Premier & President, Executive Council, Hon. Glen Clark
Deputy Premier, Hon. Dan Miller
Executive Director, Ron Wickstrom
Principal Secretary, Adrian Dix
Director, Communications, Geoff Meggs
Ministerial Asst., Cindy Lowe
Press Secretary, Trish Webb

BRITISH COLUMBIA HOUSE OTTAWA
World Exchange Plaza, #880, 45 O'Connor St., Ottawa ON K1P 1A4
613/237-1966; Fax: 613/237-1636
Senior Representative, Vacant
Intergovernmental Relations Officer, Heather Sheffield, 250/387-0752
Executive Asst. & Office Administrator, Jeanette Gasparini

BRITISH COLUMBIA TRADE DEVELOPMENT CORPORATION (BC Trade)
#730, 999 Canada Place, Vancouver BC V6C 3E1
604/844-1900; Fax: 604/660-2457
Vice-President, Trade Intelligence Division, Margaret Evans, 604/844-1969
Vice-President, Trade Operations Division, Steve Mostardi, 604/844-1936

Out of Province Offices
England: B.C. Trade Development Corporation, British Columbia House, 1 Regent St., London SW1Y 4NS, England – (011-44-171) 930-6857; Fax: (011-44-171) 930-2012; Telex: 51-917369, Director, Paul King
Hong Kong: 901 Hutchison House, 10 Harcourt Rd., Hong Kong – (011-8522) 845-1155; Fax: (011-8522) 845-4114, Agent, H. Dickson Hall
Japan: B.C. Trade Development Corporation, Akasaka KSA Bldg., 2F, 8-10-39 Akasaka, Minato-Ku, Tokyo, Japan 107 – (011-03) 3408-6171; Fax: (011-03) 3408-6340, Director, Trade & Investment, John Tak
Taiwan: B.C. Trade Representative Office, World Trade Centre, PO Box 109-857, 7th Fl., No. 5, Sec. 5, Hsin-Yi Rd., Taipei, Taiwan – (011-886-2) 722-0805; Fax: (011-886-2) 723-9364, Director, Michael K. Craddock
United States: Seattle Trade Office, #930, 720 Olive Way, Seattle WA 98101, USA – 206/628-3023; Fax: 206/447-9004, Director, Michael G. Clark

EXECUTIVE COUNCIL
#156, Parliament Bldgs., Victoria BC V8V 1X4
Premier & Minister Responsible, Youth, Hon. Glen Clark
Minister, Transportation & Highways, Hon. Lois Boone
Minister, Aboriginal Affairs, Hon. John Cashore, 250/387-0886, Fax: 250/356-1124
Attorney General & Minister Responsible, Multiculturalism, Human Rights & Immigration, Hon. Ujjal Dosanjh, 250/356-3027
Minister, Agriculture, Fisheries & Food, Hon. Corky Evans
Minister, Women's Equality, Hon. Sue Hammell
Minister, Health & Minister Responsible, Seniors, Hon. Joy K. MacPhail
Minister, Employment & Investment & Minister, Municipal Affairs & Housing; Deputy Premier, Hon. Dan Miller
Minister, Finance & Corporate Relations & Minister Responsible, Intergovernmental Relations, Hon. Andrew Petter
Minister, Children & Families, Hon. Penny Priddy, 250/356-6348, Fax: 250/356-6595
Minister, Small Business, Tourism & Culture, Hon. Jan Pullinger
Minister, Environment, Lands & Parks, Hon. Paul Ramsey
Minister, Education, Skills & Training & Minister, Labour, Hon. Moe Sihota
Minister, Social Services, Hon. Dennis Streifel, 250/387-3180, Fax: 250/387-5720
Minister, Forests, Hon. David Zirnhelt

Cabinet Operations
#272, West Annex, Legislative Bldgs., Victoria BC V8V 1X4
250/387-0986; Fax: 250/356-7258
Deputy Minister & Secretary to the Executive Council, Douglas McArthur, 250/387-0986, Fax: 250/356-7258
Asst. Deputy Minister, Cabinet Planning Secretariat, Rob Egan
Asst. Deputy Minister & Deputy Secretary, Intergovernmental Relations, Catherine Holt, 250/387-0752, Fax: 250/387-1920
Asst. Deputy Minister, Government Operations, Betty Notar
Director, Cabinet Operations, Elaine Stremlaw-Taylor, 250/387-0784
Deputy Minister's Executive Asst., Christine Peterson

Cabinet Committees
Aboriginal Affairs Working Group of Planning Board
Government Priorities
Land Use Planning Working Group of Planning Board
Planning Board
Planning Board Working Group on Income Security Review
Planning Board Working Group on Legislation
Regulations & Orders in Council
Treasury Board

LEGISLATIVE ASSEMBLY
c/o Clerk's Office, #221 Parliament Bldgs., Victoria BC V8V 1X4
250/387-3785; Fax: 250/387-0942; URL: http://www.legis.gov.bc.ca/
Clerk: E. George MacMinn, Q.C.
Speaker: Dale Lovick, 250/387-3952, Fax: 250/387-2813
Sergeant-at-Arms: Anthony A. Humphreys, 250/356-6966
Chief, Hansard: Peter Robbins, 250/387-3681, Fax: 250/356-5095
Director, Library Administration: Joan Barton, 250/387-6500, Fax: 250/356-1373

Government Caucus Office (NDP)
#166, East Annex, Parliament Bldgs., Victoria BC V8V 1X4
250/387-3655; Fax: 250/356-7156; URL: http://www.bc.ndp.ca
Executive Director, John McInnis

Office of the Official Opposition (Lib.)
#201, Parliament Bldgs., Victoria BC V8V 1X4
250/356-6171; Fax: 250/356-6176
Leader, Gordon Campbell
Executive Director, Judy Kirk
Director, Research, Vacant

Office of the Reform BC Party (Ref.)
Parliament Bldgs., Victoria BC V8V 1X4
250/356-6707; Fax: 250/356-6705
Leader, Jack Weisgerber
Research & Communications, Sarah Bonner

Office of the Progressive Democratic Alliance Party (PDA)
Parliament Bldgs., Victoria BC V8V 1X4
250/356-8176; Fax: 250/387-4088; URL: http://www.xmission.com/ZXseer/pda/pda.html
Leader, Gordon Wilson

Legislative Committees
#224, Parliament Bldgs., Victoria BC V8V 1X4
250/356-2933; Fax: 250/356-8172
Clerk of Committees, C.H. James
Aboriginal Affairs
Justice, Constitutional Affairs & Intergovernmental Relations
Education, Culture & Multiculturalism
Economic Development, Science, Labour, Training & Technology
Environment & Tourism
Finance & Government Services
Health & Social Services
Agriculture & Fisheries
Forests, Energy, Mines & Petroleum Resources
Transportation, Municipal Affairs & Housing
Women's Equality
Public Accounts
Parliamentary Reform, Ethical Conduct, Standing Orders & Private Bills

Special Committee
Selection

THIRTY-SIXTH LEGISLATURE - BRITISH COLUMBIA
250/387-3785
Last General Election, May 28, 1996. Maximum Duration, 5 Years
Party Standings (June 1996):
New Democratic Party (NDP) 39
Liberal (Lib.) 33
BC Reform (Ref.) 2
Progressive Democratic Alliance (PDA) 1
Total 75

Salaries, Indemnities & Allowances: 1993 frozen - Members' annual allowance $32,812 plus a $16,406 expense allowance. In addition to this are the following:
Premier $45,000
Members of Executive Council $39,000 (with portfolio)
Leader of the Official Opposition $39,000
Speaker $39,000
Deputy Speaker; Leader of the Third Party $19,500.

Following is: constituency (number of eligible voters in July, 1993) member, party affiliation. (Address for all is Parliament Bldgs., Victoria, BC V8V 1X4.)

Refer to Cabinet list, Government Caucus Office, Office of the Liberal Party, & Office of the Social Credit Party, above, for **phone** & **Fax** numbers.

MEMBERS BY CONSTITUENCY
Abbotsford (25,630) John Van Dongen, Lib., 250/356-3074, Fax: 250/356-6176
Alberni (18,047) Gerard A. Janssen, NDP, 250/387-0967, Fax: 250/356-0596
Bulkley Valley-Stikine (16,061) Bill Goodacre, NDP, 250/387-3655, Fax: 250/356-7156
Burnaby North (27,516) Pietro Calendino, NDP, 250/387-3655, Fax: 250/356-7156
Burnaby-Edmonds (29,762) Fred G. Randall, NDP, 250/356-3011, Fax: 250/356-7156
Burnaby-Willingdon (32,933) Joan Sawicki, NDP, 250/356-9172, Fax: 250/387-0827
Cariboo North (17,584) John Wilson, Lib., 250/356-6171, Fax: 250/356-6176
Cariboo South (19,679) Hon. David Zirnhelt, NDP, 250/387-6240, Fax: 250/387-1040
Chilliwack (30,867) Barry Penner, Lib., 250/356-6171, Fax: 250/356-6176
Columbia River-Revelstoke (18,822) Jim Doyle, NDP, 250/356-3015, Fax: 250/356-7156
Comox Valley (34,306) Evelyn Gillespie, NDP, 250/387-3655, Fax: 250/356-7156

Coquitlam-Maillardville (32,082) Hon. John Cashore, NDP, 250/387-0886, Fax: 250/356-1124
Cowichan-Ladysmith (29,080) Hon. Jan Pullinger, NDP, 250/387-7165, Fax: 250/356-7156
Delta North (27,051) Reni Masi, Lib., 250/356-6171, Fax: 250/356-6176
Delta South (27,632) Fred Gingell, Lib., 250/356-6587, Fax: 250/356-6176
Esquimalt-Metchosin (31,524) Hon. Moe Sihota, NDP, 250/387-1977, Fax: 250/387-3200
Fort Langley-Aldergrove (25,990) Rich Coleman, Lib., 250/356-6171, Fax: 250/356-6176
Kamloops (28,872) Cathy McGregor, NDP, 250/387-3655, Fax: 250/356-7156
Kamloops-North Thompson (20,328) Kevin Krueger, Lib., 250/356-6171, Fax: 250/356-6176
Kootenay (21,792) Erda Walsh, NDP, 250/387-3655, Fax: 250/356-7156
Langley (24,539) Lynn Stephens, Lib., 250/356-3086, Fax: 250/356-6176
Malahat-Juan de Fuca (25,841) Rick Kasper, NDP, 250/387-0855, Fax: 250/387-0827
Maple Ridge-Pitt Meadows (33,760) Bill Hartley, NDP, 250/356-3033, Fax: 250/356-7156
Matsqui (26,333) Mike de Jong, Lib., 250/356-3082, Fax: 250/356-6176
Mission-Kent (23,556) Hon. Dennis Streifel, NDP, 250/387-3180, Fax: 250/387-5720
Nanaimo (29,778) Dale Lovick, NDP, 250/387-5426, Fax: 250/356-0596
Nelson-Creston (23,234) Hon. Corky Evans, NDP, 250/387-1023, Fax: 250/387-1522
New Westminster (29,323) Graeme Bowbrick, N, NDP, 250/387-3655, Fax: 250/356-7156
North Coast (16,036) Hon. Dan Miller, NDP, 250/356-7020, Fax: 250/356-5587
North Island (23,936) Glenn Robertson, NDP, 250/387-3655, Fax: 250/356-7156
North Vancouver-Lonsdale (26,645) Katherine Whittred, Lib., 250/356-6171, Fax: 250/356-6176
North Vancouver-Seymour (30,346) Daniel Jarvis, Lib., 250/356-3078, Fax: 250/356-6176
Oak Bay-Gordon Head (32,453) Ida Chong, Lib., 250/356-6171, Fax: 250/356-6176
Okanagan East (30,451) John Weisbeck, Lib., 250/356-6171, Fax: 250/356-6176
Okanagan West (38,523) Sindi Hawkins, Lib., 250/356-6171, Fax: 250/356-6176
Okanagan-Boundary (20,379) Bill Barisoff, Lib., 250/356-6171, Fax: 250/356-6176
Okanagan-Penticton (29,602) Rick Thorpe, Lib., 250/356-6171, Fax: 250/356-6176
Okanagan-Vernon (30,431) April Sanders, Lib., 250/356-6171, Fax: 250/356-6176
Parksville-Qualicum (33,142) Paul Reitsma, Lib., 250/356-6171, Fax: 250/356-6176
Peace River North (15,407) Richard Neufeld, Ref., 250/356-6707, Fax: 250/356-6705
Peace River South (18,238) Jack Weisgerber, Ref., 250/356-6707, Fax: 250/356-6705
Port Coquitlam (33,588) Mike Farnworth, NDP, 250/356-1019, Fax: 250/356-7156
Port Moody-Burnaby Mountain (29,917) Christy Clark, Lib., 250/356-6171, Fax: 250/356-6176
Powell River-Sunshine Coast (25,788) Gordon Wilson, PDA, 250/356-3058, Fax: 250/387-4088
Prince George North (20,021) Hon. Paul Ramsey, NDP, 250/387-1187, Fax: 250/387-1356
Prince George-Mount Robson (16,797) Hon. Lois Boone, NDP, 250/387-1978, Fax: 250/356-2290
Prince George-Omineca (19,300) Paul Nettleton, Lib., 250/356-6171, Fax: 250/356-6176
Richmond Centre (25,240) Douglas Symons, Lib., 250/356-3066, Fax: 250/356-6176
Richmond East (22,809) Linda Reid, Lib., 250/356-3056, Fax: 250/356-6176
Richmond Steveston (22,805) Geoff Plant, Lib., 250/356-6171, Fax: 250/356-6176

Rossland-Trail (21,444) Ed Conroy, NDP, 250/356-3052, Fax: 250/356-7156
Saanich North & the Islands (31,903) Murray Robert Coell, Lib., 250/356-6171, Fax: 250/356-6176
Saanich South (29,141) Hon. Andrew Petter, NDP, 250/387-3751, Fax: 250/387-5594
Shuswap (28,800) George Abbott, Lib., 250/356-6171, Fax: 250/356-6176
Skeena (16,828) Helmut Giesbrecht, NDP, 250/356-3029, Fax: 250/387-0827
Surrey-Cloverdale (30,462) Bonnie McKinnon, Lib., 250/356-6171, Fax: 250/356-6176
Surrey-Green Timbers (26,899) Hon. Sue Hammell, NDP, 250/387-1223, Fax: 250/387-4312
Surrey-Newton (32,444) Hon. Penny Priddy, NDP, 250/356-6348, Fax: 250/356-6595
Surrey-Whalley (22,218) Joan Smallwood, NDP, 250/356-9496, Fax: 250/387-0827
Surrey-White Rock (35,942) Wilf Hurd, Lib., 250/356-3076, Fax: 250/356-6176
Vancouver-Burrard (29,952) Tim Stevenson, NDP, 250/387-3655, Fax: 250/356-7156
Vancouver-Fraserview (25,550) Ian Waddell, NDP, 250/387-3655, Fax: 250/356-7156
Vancouver-Hastings (26,368) Hon. Joy K. MacPhail, NDP, 250/387-5394, Fax: 250/387-3696
Vancouver-Kensington (25,521) Hon. Ujjal Dosanjh, NDP, 250/387-1866, Fax: 250/387-6411
Vancouver-Kingsway (24,784) Hon. Glen Clark, NDP, 250/387-1715, Fax: 250/387-0087
Vancouver-Langara (27,493) Val Anderson, Lib., 250/356-3072, Fax: 250/356-6176
Vancouver-Little Mountain (25,990) Gary Farrell-Collins, Lib., 250/356-3060, Fax: 250/356-6176
Vancouver-Mount Pleasant (25,868) Jenny Wai Ching Kwan, NDP, 250/387-3655, Fax: 250/356-7156
Vancouver-Point Grey (28,941) Gordon Campbell, Lib., 250/356-3090, Fax: 250/356-6176
Vancouver-Quilchena (28,941) Colin Hansen, Lib., 250/356-6171, Fax: 250/356-6176
Victoria-Beacon Hill (31,652) Gretchen Brewin, NDP, 250/356-3031, Fax: 250/387-0827
Victoria-Hillside (30,280) Steve Orcherton, NDP, 250/387-3655, Fax: 250/356-7156
West Vancouver-Capilano (29,933) Jeremy Dalton, Lib., 250/356-3070, Fax: 250/356-6176
West Vancouver-Garibaldi (24,706) Ted Nebbeling, Lib., 250/356-6171, Fax: 250/356-6176
Yale-Lillooet (21,468) Harry Lali, NDP, 250/356-3017, Fax: 250/387-0827

MEMBERS (ALPHABETICAL)

George Abbott, Shuswap (28,800)Lib., 250/356-6171, Fax: 250/356-6176
Val Anderson, Vancouver-Langara (27,493)Lib., 250/356-3072, Fax: 250/356-6176
Bill Barisoff, Okanagan-Boundary (20,379)Lib., 250/356-6171, Fax: 250/356-6176
Hon. Lois Boone, Prince George-Mount Robson (16,797)NDP, 250/387-1978, Fax: 250/356-2290
Graeme Bowbrick, N, New Westminster (29,323)NDP, 250/387-3655, Fax: 250/356-7156
Gretchen Brewin, Victoria-Beacon Hill (31,652)NDP, 250/356-3031, Fax: 250/387-0827
Pietro Calendino, Burnaby North (27,516)NDP, 250/387-3655, Fax: 250/356-7156
Gordon Campbell, Vancouver-Point Grey (28,941)Lib., 250/356-3090, Fax: 250/356-6176
Hon. John Cashore, Coquitlam-Maillardville (32,082)NDP, 250/387-0886, Fax: 250/356-1124
Ida Chong, Oak Bay-Gordon Head (32,453)Lib., 250/356-6171, Fax: 250/356-6176
Christy Clark, Port Moody-Burnaby Mountain (29,917)Lib., 250/356-6171, Fax: 250/356-6176
Hon. Glen Clark, Vancouver-Kingsway (24,784)NDP, 250/387-1715, Fax: 250/387-0087
Murray Robert Coell, Saanich North & the Islands (31,903)Lib., 250/356-6171, Fax: 250/356-6176

Rich Coleman, Fort Langley-Aldergrove (25,990)Lib., 250/356-6171, Fax: 250/356-6176
Ed Conroy, Rossland-Trail (21,444)NDP, 250/356-3052, Fax: 250/356-7156
Jeremy Dalton, West Vancouver-Capilano (29,933)Lib., 250/356-3070, Fax: 250/356-6176
Mike de Jong, Matsqui (26,333)Lib., 250/356-3082, Fax: 250/356-6176
Hon. Ujjal Dosanjh, Vancouver-Kensington (25,521)NDP, 250/387-1866, Fax: 250/387-6411
Jim Doyle, Columbia River-Revelstoke (18,822)NDP, 250/356-3015, Fax: 250/356-7156
Hon. Corky Evans, Nelson-Creston (23,234)NDP, 250/387-1023, Fax: 250/387-1522
Mike Farnworth, Port Coquitlam (33,588)NDP, 250/356-1019, Fax: 250/356-7156
Gary Farrell-Collins, Vancouver-Little Mountain (25,990)Lib., 250/356-3060, Fax: 250/356-6176
Helmut Giesbrecht, Skeena (16,828)NDP, 250/356-3029, Fax: 250/387-0827
Evelyn Gillespie, Comox Valley (34,306)NDP, 250/387-3655, Fax: 250/356-7156
Fred Gingell, Delta South (27,632)Lib., 250/356-6587, Fax: 250/356-6176
Bill Goodacre, Bulkley Valley-Stikine (16,061)NDP, 250/387-3655, Fax: 250/356-7156
Hon. Sue Hammell, Surrey-Green Timbers (26,899)NDP, 250/387-1223, Fax: 250/387-4312
Colin Hansen, Vancouver-Quilchena (28,941)Lib., 250/356-6171, Fax: 250/356-6176
Bill Hartley, Maple Ridge-Pitt Meadows (33,760)NDP, 250/356-3033, Fax: 250/356-7156
Sindi Hawkins, Okanagan West (38,523)Lib., 250/356-6171, Fax: 250/356-6176
Wilf Hurd, Surrey-White Rock (35,942)Lib., 250/356-3076, Fax: 250/356-6176
Gerard A. Janssen, Alberni (18,047)NDP, 250/387-0967, Fax: 250/356-0596
Daniel Jarvis, North Vancouver-Seymour (30,346)Lib., 250/356-3078, Fax: 250/356-6176
Rick Kasper, Malahat-Juan de Fuca (25,841)NDP, 250/387-0855, Fax: 250/387-0827
Kevin Krueger, Kamloops-North Thompson (20,328)Lib., 250/356-6171, Fax: 250/356-6176
Jenny Wai Ching Kwan, Vancouver-Mount Pleasant (25,868)NDP, 250/387-3655, Fax: 250/356-7156
Harry Lali, Yale-Lillooet (21,468)NDP, 250/356-3017, Fax: 250/387-0827
Dale Lovick, Nanaimo (29,778)NDP, 250/387-5426, Fax: 250/356-0596
Hon. Joy K. MacPhail, Vancouver-Hastings (26,368)NDP, 250/387-5394, Fax: 250/387-3696
Reni Masi, Delta North (27,051)Lib., 250/356-6171, Fax: 250/356-6176
Cathy McGregor, Kamloops (28,872)NDP, 250/387-3655, Fax: 250/356-7156
Bonnie McKinnon, Surrey-Cloverdale (30,462)Lib., 250/356-6171, Fax: 250/356-6176
Hon. Dan Miller, North Coast (16,036)NDP, 250/356-7020, Fax: 250/356-5587
Ted Nebbeling, West Vancouver-Garibaldi (24,706)Lib., 250/356-6171, Fax: 250/356-6176
Paul Nettleton, Prince George-Omineca (19,300)Lib., 250/356-6171, Fax: 250/356-6176
Richard Neufeld, Peace River North (15,407)Ref., 250/356-6707, Fax: 250/356-6705
Steve Orcherton, Victoria-Hillside (30,280)NDP, 250/387-3655, Fax: 250/356-7156
Barry Penner, Chilliwack (30,867)Lib., 250/356-6171, Fax: 250/356-6176
Hon. Andrew Petter, Saanich South (29,141)NDP, 250/387-3751, Fax: 250/387-5594
Geoff Plant, Richmond Steveston (22,805)Lib., 250/356-6171, Fax: 250/356-6176
Hon. Penny Priddy, Surrey-Newton (32,444)NDP, 250/356-6348, Fax: 250/356-6595
Hon. Jan Pullinger, Cowichan-Ladysmith (29,080)NDP, 250/387-7165, Fax: 250/356-7156

Canadian Almanac & Directory 1997

Hon. Paul Ramsey, Prince George North (20,021)NDP, 250/387-1187, Fax: 250/387-1356
Fred G. Randall, Burnaby-Edmonds (29,762)NDP, 250/356-3011, Fax: 250/356-7156
Linda Reid, Richmond East (22,809)Lib., 250/356-3056, Fax: 250/356-6176
Paul Reitsma, Parksville-Qualicum (33,142)Lib., 250/356-6171, Fax: 250/356-6176
Glenn Robertson, North Island (23,936)NDP, 250/387-3655, Fax: 250/356-7156
April Sanders, Okanagan-Vernon (30,431)Lib., 250/356-6171, Fax: 250/356-6176
Joan Sawicki, Burnaby-Willingdon (32,933)NDP, 250/356-9172, Fax: 250/387-0827
Hon. Moe Sihota, Esquimalt-Metchosin (31,524)NDP, 250/387-1977, Fax: 250/387-3200
Joan Smallwood, Surrey-Whalley (22,218)NDP, 250/356-9496, Fax: 250/387-0827
Lynn Stephens, Langley (24,539)Lib., 250/356-3086, Fax: 250/356-6176
Tim Stevenson, Vancouver-Burrard (29,952)NDP, 250/387-3655, Fax: 250/356-7156
Hon. Dennis Streifel, Mission-Kent (23,556)NDP, 250/387-3180, Fax: 250/387-5720
Douglas Symons, Richmond Centre (25,240)Lib., 250/356-3066, Fax: 250/356-6176
Rick Thorpe, Okanagan-Penticton (29,602)Lib., 250/356-6171, Fax: 250/356-6176
John Van Dongen, Abbotsford (25,630)Lib., 250/356-3074, Fax: 250/356-6176
Ian Waddell, Vancouver-Fraserview (25,550)NDP, 250/387-3655, Fax: 250/356-7156
Erda Walsh, Kootenay (21,792)NDP, 250/387-3655, Fax: 250/356-7156
John Weisbeck, Okanagan East (30,451)Lib., 250/356-6171, Fax: 250/356-6176
Jack Weisgerber, Peace River South (18,238)Ref., 250/356-6707, Fax: 250/356-6705
Katherine Whittred, North Vancouver-Lonsdale (26,645)Lib., 250/356-6171, Fax: 250/356-6176
Gordon Wilson, Powell River-Sunshine Coast (25,788)PDA, 250/356-3058, Fax: 250/387-4088
John Wilson, Cariboo North (17,584)Lib., 250/356-6171, Fax: 250/356-6176
Hon. David Zirnhelt, Cariboo South (19,679)NDP, 250/387-6240, Fax: 250/387-1040

BRITISH COLUMBIA GOVERNMENT DEPARTMENTS & AGENCIES

Ministry of ABORIGINAL AFFAIRS
908 Pandora Ave., Victoria BC V8V 1X4
250/356-8281; Fax: 250/387-1785; URL: http://www.aaf.gov.bc.ca/aaf/

ACTS ADMINISTERED
British Columbia Treaty Commission Act
First Peoples' Heritage, Language & Culture Act
Indian Cut-off Land Disputes Act
Indian Self Government Enabling Act
Sechelt Indian Government Enabling Act
Special Accounts Appropriation & Control Act
Minister, Hon. John Cashore, 250/387-0886, Fax: 250/356-1124
Deputy Minister, Philip Halkett, 250/387-6838
Chief, Treaty Negotiations, Vacant
Executive Coordinator, Ingrid Fee, 250/356-6804

ABORIGINAL RELATIONS DIVISION
Fax: 604/356-6662
Asst. Deputy Minister, Randy Brant, 250/387-5210
Director, Lands & Resources Branch, Linda Martin, 250/356-8282
Director, Social & Economic Incentives Branch, Robert Botterel, 250/356-6599

MANAGEMENT SERVICES
Fax: 604/387-6073
Executive Director, Anne Kirkaldy, 250/356-8699
Director, Finance & Administration Branch, Brian Price, 250/356-1799, Fax: 250/356-0783
Director, Human Resources, Bill Montgomery, 250/356-6247
Director, Information Management Branch, Randy Prokop, 250/356-9518

POLICY, PLANNING & RESEARCH DIVISION
Fax: 604/356-0215
Asst. Deputy Minister, Joy Illington, 250/356-0226
Executive Director, Aboriginal Policy Branch, Deborah McNevin
Executive Director, Treaty Mandates Branch, Nerys Poole, 250/356-2207

PUBLIC AFFAIRS DIVISION
Director, Communications Branch, Tim Myers, 250/356-9090, Fax: 250/387-1785
Director, Public Consultation Branch, Judy Birch, 250/356-8283

Ministry of AGRICULTURE, FISHERIES & FOOD
808 Douglas St., Victoria BC V8W 2Z7
250/387-5121; Fax: 250/387-5130; URL: http://bbs.qp.gov.bc.ca/bcmaff/bcagweb.htm

ACTS ADMINISTERED
Agricultural Credit Act
Agricultural Land Commission Act
Agricultural Produce Grading Act
Agricultural & Rural Development (BC) Act
Agrologists Act
Animal Disease Control Act
Bee Act
BC Wine Act
Cattle Horn Act
Farm Distress Assistance Act
Farm Income Insurance Act
Farm Practices Protection (Right to Farm) Act
Farm Product Industry Act
Farmers' & Womens' Institutes Act
Farming & Fishing Industries Development Act
Fish Inspection Act
Fisheries Act
Food Choice & Disclosure Act
Food Product Standards Act
Fur Farm Act
Game Farm Act
Golf Course Moratorium Act
Grains & Oilseeds Revenue Protectio Plan Trust Fund Act
Grasshopper Control Act
Grazing Enhancement Speical Account Act
Insurance for Crops Act
Livestock Act
Livestock Brand Act
Livestock Industry Act
Livestock Lien Act
Livestock Protection Act
Livestock Public Sale Act
Meat Inspection Act
Milk Industry Act
Ministry of Agriculture & Food Act
Municipal Act (Section 973.1-973.5)
Natural Products Marketing (BC) Act
Okanagan Valley Tree Fruit Authority Act
Pharmacists, Pharmacy Operations & Drug Scheduling Act, ss 49-55
Plant Protection Act
Prevention of Cruelty to Animals Act
Seed Grower Act
Seed Potato Act
Soil Conservation Act
Veterinarians Act
Veterinary Laboratory Act
Weed Control Act
Minister, Hon. Corky Evans, 250/387-1023, Fax: 250/387-1522
Deputy Minister, R. Lorne Seitz, 250/356-1800, Fax: 250/356-7279
Director, Public Affairs Branch, Laura Stringer, 250/356-2862, Fax: 250/387-9105

Policy & Legislation
Executive Director, D.M. Matviw, 250/356-1816

AGRICULTURE DIVISION
Asst. Deputy Minister, Tom Pringle, 250/356-1821
Chief Veterinarian, Abbotsford, Dr. P. Hewitt, 604/854-4400
Director, Crop Protection, W. Wiebe, 250/356-1667
Director, Farm Management (Vernon), T. Peterson, 250/549-5580
Director, Extension Systems, R. Sera, 250/356-1688
Director, Rural Organizations, D. Freed, 250/356-1635
Director, Soils & Engineering, Abbotsford, R. Bertrand, 604/852-5363
Director, North Central Region, Prince George, T. Dever, 250/565-6466
Director, South Coastal Region, Abbotsford, W. Wickens, 604/852-5222
Director, Southern Interior Region, Kelowna, B. Baehr, 250/861-7211

FINANCIAL PROGRAMS & ADMINISTRATION DIVISION
Asst. Deputy Minister, A. Sakalauskas, 406/356-1810
Director, Administration & Finance, D. Davies, 250/356-1849, Fax: 250/387-5130
Director, Farm Income & Crop Insurance, R. Jarvin, 250/356-1615
Acting Director, Financial Development Programs, H. Sasaki, 250/356-1828
Director, Personnel, D. Cherrington, 250/356-1860
Director, Information Technology, D. Evans, 250/356-1668

FISHERIES & FOOD DIVISION
Asst. Deputy Minister, Stuart Culbertson, 250/356-1807
Director, Aquaculture & Commercial Fisheries, Jim Anderson, 250/356-1608, Fax: 250/356-7280
Director, Food Industry, G. Macatee, 250/356-2946
Director, Trade Competition, John Schildroth, 250/387-7183

Associated Agencies, Boards & Commissions
• Provincial Agricultural Land Commission: #133, 4940 Canada Way, Burnaby BC V5G 4K6 – 604/660-7000; Fax: 604/660-7033
Chair, K. Miller
• Okanagan Valley Tree Fruit Authority: PO Box 6000, Summerland BC V0H 1Z0 – 250/494-5021; Fax: 250/494-5024
President & CEO, R. Husdon

Agricultural Marketing Boards & Commissions
• British Columbia Marketing Board: Hartwig Ct., #107, 1208 Wharf St., Victoria BC V8W 3B9 – 250/356-8946; Fax: 250/356-5131
Chair, Doug Kitson
General Manager, James Sandever
• British Columbia Broiler Hatching Egg Commission: 464 Riverside Rd. South, RR#2, Abbotsford BC V2S 4N2 – 604/850-1854; Fax: 604/853-8419
Secretary Manager, John Durham
• British Columbia Chicken Marketing Board: #203, 5752 – 176 St., Surrey BC V3S 4C8 – 604/576-2855; Fax: 604/576-6729
General Manager, R.A. Stafford

Canadian Almanac & Directory 1997

- British Columbia Cranberry Marketing Board: c/o RSW Professional Centre, #200, 8811 Cooney Rd., Richmond BC V6X 3J6 – 250/923-6096; Fax: 250/923-7905
  Chair, Ron May
- British Columbia Egg Marketing Board: 34470 Fraser Way South, PO Box 310, Abbotsford BC V2S 4P2 – 604/853-3348; Fax: 604/853-8714
  Chair, Gerry Zaph
- British Columbia Grape Marketing Board: #5, 1864 Spall Rd., Kelowna BC V1Y 4R1 – 250/762-4652
  Chair, Gerald Moore
- British Columbia Hog Marketing Commission: 2010 Abbotsford Way, Abbotsford BC V2S 6X8 – 604/853-9461; Fax: 604/853-0764
  General Manager, Glen Lucas
- British Columbia Milk Marketing Board: #105, 4664 Lougheed Hwy., Burnaby BC V5C 5T5 – 604/294-6454; Fax: 604/294-4566
  General Manager, Tom Demma
- British Columbia Mushroom Marketing Board: #302, 34252 Marshall Rd., Abbotsford BC V25 5E4 – 604/853-7575; Fax: 604/853-3556
  General Manager, Jack Sharp
- British Columbia Tree Fruit Marketing Board: PO Box 24023, Penticton BC V2A 8L9 – 250/492-0663
  Chair, Brian Karrer
- British Columbia Turkey Marketing Board: #106, 19329 Enterprise Way, Surrey BC V3S 6J8 – 604/534-5644; Fax: 604/534-3651
  Manager, Colyn Welsh
- British Columbia Vegetable Marketing Commission: #201, 7560 Vantage Way, Delta BC V4G 1H1 – 604/940-0188; Fax: 604/940-0661, Toll Free: 1-800-663-1461
  General Manager, Rodger Hughes
- Council of Marketing Boards of British Columbia: 846 Broughton St., Victoria BC V8W 1E4 – 250/383-7171; Fax: 250/383-5031
  Secretary, Andy Dolberg
- Farm Practices Board: Hartwig Ct., #107, 1208 Wharf St., Victoria BC V8W 3B9 – 250/356-8946; Fax: 250/356-5131
  Chair, Doug Kitson
  General Manager, James Sandever

Ministry of the ATTORNEY GENERAL
910 Government St., 5th Fl., Victoria BC V8V 1X4
250/356-9596 (Policy & Education); Fax: 250/356-9037

ACTS ADMINISTERED
Accountants (Management) Act
Adult Guardianship Act
Age of Majority Act
Attorney General Act
Builders Lien Act
Cabinet Appeals Abolition Act
Civil Rights Protection Act
Commercial Appeals Commission Act
Commercial Arbitration Act
Commercial Tenancy Act
Commissioner on Resources & Environment Act
Company Act
Condominium Act
Conflict of Laws Rules for Trusts Act
Constitution Act
Constitutional Question Act
Coroners Act
Correction Act
County Boundary Act
Court Agent Act
Court of Appeal Act
Court Order Enforcement Act
Court Order Interest Act
Court Rules Act
Criminal Injury Compensation Act
Crown Counsel Act
Crown Franchise Act
Crown Proceeding Act
Curfew Act
Disciplinary Authority Protection Act
Election Act
Electoral Boundaries Commission Act
Electoral Districts Act
Emergency Program Act
Enforcement of Canadian Judgments Act
Escheat Act
Estate Administration Act
Estates of Missing Persons Act
Evidence Act
Expropriation Act
Family Compensation Act
Family Maintenance Enforcement Act
Family Relations Act
Federal Courts Jurisdiction Act
Financial Disclosure Act
Firearm Act
Flood Relief Act
Foreign Arbitral Awards Act
Foreign Money Claims Act
Foresters Act
Fraudulent Conveyance Act
Fraudulent Preference Act
Frustrated Contract Act
Good Samaritan Act
Holiday Shopping Regulation Act
Homestead Act
Horse Racing Act
Infants Act
Inquiry Act
International Sale of Goods Act
International Trusts Act
Interpretation Act
Judicial Review Procedure Act
Jury Act
Justice Administration Act
Land (Spouse Protection) Act
Land Title Act
Land Title Inquiry Act
Land Transfer Form Act
Law & Equity Act
Law Reform Commission Act
Legal Profession Act
Legal Services Society Act
Libel & Slander Act
Limitation Act
Liquor Control & Licensing Act
Liquor Distribution Act
Members' Conflict of Interest Act
Ministry of Provincial Secretary & Government Services Act
Motion Picture Act
Motor Carrier Act
Municipal Act
National Cablevision Limited Transfer of Jurisdiction Act
Negligence Act
Notaries Act
Occupiers Liability Act
Offence Act
Ombudsman Act
Pacific Racing Association Act
Parole Act
Partition of Property Act
Patients Property Act
Pawnbrokers Act
Perpetuity Act
Police Act
Power of Appointment Act
Power of Attorney Act
Privacy Act
Private Investigators & Security Agencies Act
Probate Recognition Act
Property Law Act
Provincial Court Act
Public Guardian & Trustee Act
Public Trustee Act
Queen's Counsel Act
Referendum Act
Regulations Act
Rent Distress Act
Representation Agreement Act
Sales on Consignment Act
Senatorial Selection Act
Senior Citizen Automobile Insurance Grant Act
Sheriff Act
Small Claims Act
Statute Revision Act
Statute Uniformity Act
Subpoena (Interprovincial) Act
Supreme Court Act
Survivorship & Presumption of Death Act
Teaching Profession Act
Traffic Victims Indemnity Fund Repeal Act
Transport of Dangerous Goods Act
Trespass Act
Trust & Settlement Variation Act
Trustee Act
Trustee (Church Property) Act
Victims' Rights & Services Act
Wills Act
Wills Variation Act
Young Offenders (British Columbia) Act

Attorney General, Hon. Ujjal Dosanjh, 250/356-3027
Deputy Attorney General, Stephen. Owen, Q.C., 250/387-5211, Fax: 250/387-6224
Deputy Minister, Maureen A. Maloney, 250/356-0149, Fax: 250/387-6224

COMMUNITY JUSTICE BRANCH
Fax: 604/356-1092
Asst. Deputy Minister, Alison MacPhail
Executive Director, Gene Errington, 250/953-3180
Director, Family Justice Reform, Wendy Galloway, 250/387-1111
Program Manager, Victim Services, Kay Charbonneau, 250/387-6848

Consumer Services Division
1019 Wharf St., Victoria BC V8V 1X4
URL: http://www.lcs.gov.bc.ca/
Director, Consumer Operations Branch & Registrar, Motor Dealers, Terry Barnett, 250/387-9112, Fax: 250/953-3533
Director, Debtor Assistance Branch, Harry Atkinson, 250/387-1747, Fax: 250/353-4782
Director, Financial Administration Branch, John Dowler, 250/387-1719, Fax: 250/387-6574
Director, Human Resources Branch, Ernie Kirchgesner, 250/387-3790, Fax: 250/387-6008
Director, Residential Tenancy Branch, Leah Bailey, 250/356-3413, Fax: 250/387-0271
Director, Support Services Branch, Terry Barnett, 250/387-3909, Fax: 250/387-1615
Registrar, Cemeteries, Paul Snickars, 250/387-9114, Fax: 250/953-3533
Registrar, Credit Reporting Agencies, Harry Atkinson, 250/387-1747, Fax: 250/953-4782
Registrar, Travel Services, Chris Saunders, 604/660-3540, Fax: 604/660-3521
Manager, Freedom of Information & Privacy, Mark Grady, 250/387-1736

CORRECTIONS BRANCH
250/387-5059; Fax: 250/387-5698
Asst. Deputy Minister, Don Demers, 250/387-5354
Director, Program Analysis & Evaluation, Alan Markwart, 250/387-1564
Executive Director, Management Services, Brian Mason, 250/356-7930
Director, Resource Analysis, Carol MacKillop, 250/378-6366

GOVERNMENT OF BRITISH COLUMBIA

COURT SERVICES BRANCH
Asst. Deputy Attorney General, Malcolm McAvity, 250/356-1527, Fax: 250/356-8152
Director, Inspections Unit, Doris St. Germain, 250/356-1528
For list of Courts & other Legal Offices, including Judicial Officials & Judges see Section 7 of this book.

CRIMINAL JUSTICE BRANCH
Asst. Deputy Attorney General, Ernie Quantz, Q.C., 250/387-5174, Fax: 250/387-0090

MULTICULTURALISM & IMMIGRATION BRANCH
#309, 703 Broughton St., Victoria BC V8W 1E2
250/387-7970, Fax: 250/356-5316
Executive Director, Ann Bozoian, 250/387-7970
Director, Business Immigration Branch, John Gray, 250/844-1801, Fax: 250/660-4092
Director, Immigration Policy, Gordon Whitehead, 250/387-7951, Fax: 250/356-5316
Director, Multiculturalism BC, Ed Eduljee, 250/660-2395, FAx: 250/660-1150

LAND TITLE BRANCH
910 Government St., 1st Fl., Victoria BC V8V 1X4
250/387-1903; Fax: 250/387-1763
Director, Linda O'Shea, 250/387-6900
Registrar, Kamloops, Ian Smith, #114, 455 Columbia St., Kamloops BC V2C 6K4, 250/828-4455
Acting Registrar, Nelson, Beverly Stevens, 310 Ward St., Nelson BC V1L 5S4, 250/851-1777
Registrar, Prince George, Brian Bigras, #401, 299 Victoria St., Prince George BC V2L 5B8, 250/565-6200
Registrar, Prince Rupert, Kenneth D. Jacques, 730 Second Ave. West, Prince Rupert BC V8J 1H3, 250/627-0530
Registrar, Vancouver/New Westminster, Linda O'Shea, 88 - 6 St., New Westminster BC V3L 5B3, 604/660-2595
Manager, Victoria, Kenneth D. Jacques, Law Courts, 850 Burdett Ave., Victoria BC V8W 1B4, 250/387-6331

LEGAL SERVICES BRANCH
Asst. Deputy Attorney General, Gillian Wallace
Chief Legislative Counsel, Brian Greer, Q.C., 250/356-5751
Senior Counsel, Barristers Division, William Pearce, Q.C., 250/356-8866
Director, Library Services, Jane Taylor, 250/356-8495, Fax: 250/387-5758

LIQUOR CONTROL & LICENSING BRANCH
1019 Wharf St., Victoria BC V8V 1X4
250/387-1254; Fax: 250/387-9184
Responsible for: issuing, renewing & transferring licenses for the sale of liquor; licensing breweries, distilleries, wineries & their agents; inspecting licensed premises; approving & monitoring advertising of beer, wine & liquor; enforcing the Liquor Control & Licensing Act & Regulations.
General Manager, Robert C. Simson

LIQUOR DISTRIBUTION BRANCH
2625 Rupert St., Vancouver BC V5M 3T5
604/252-3021; Fax: 604/252-3026
TLX 04-53470
Solely responsible for the selection, purchasing, pricing & distribution of all alcoholic beverages (wines, spirits & beer) throughout British Columbia in a retail store system of more than 200 government liquor stores & over 70 agency stores.
General Manager, John Nieuwenburg

MANAGEMENT SERVICES BRANCH
Fax: 604/387-0081
Asst. Deputy Minister, Rick McCandless, 250/387-5929

Acting Executive Director, Human Resources Division, Bill White, 530 Fort St., 2nd Fl., Victoria BC V8V 1X4, 250/387-5303, Fax: 250/387-7909
Acting Executive Director, Information Technology Division, Scott Andison, 250/356-8787, Fax: 250/356-7699
Executive Director, Policy & Communications, Mary Beeching, 250/387-8030, Fax: 250/387-3719
Acting Director, Facilities Services, Brian Morin, 1021 Government St., Victoria BC V8V 1X4, 250/387-6821, Fax: 250/356-9528
Director, Finance & Administration Division, Ian Smith, 250/387-4505, Fax: 250/356-8739

Policy & Communications Branch
Executive Director, Mary Beeching, 250/387-8030, Fax: 250/387-3719
Director, Communications Division, Christine McKnight, 250/387-0601, Fax: 250/356-9037
Director, Corporate Planning, Peter Whelan, 250/356-0111, Fax: 250/387-3719
Director, Employment Equity & Women's Programs, Anne Taylor, 250/387-3247, Fax: 250/356-5368
Director, Information & Privacy, Jennifer Kroeker-Hall, 250/387-6898, Fax: 250/953-3559
Director, Issues Management, Vacant, 250/387-9548, Fax: 250/356-9037
Acting Director, Policy & Legislation, Ann Ratel, 250/387-5007, Fax: 250/387-3719

PUBLIC SAFETY & REGULATORY BRANCH
Asst. Deputy Minister, Patti Stockton, 250/387-1292, Fax: 250/356-7747
Executive Director, Coordinated Law Enforcement Unit, Peter Engstad, 250/387-0287
Director, Investigation, Inspection & Standards, Allan Anderson
Director, Police Services, Kevin Begg, 250/356-5483, Fax: 250/356-7747
Director, Provincial Emergency Program, A.J. (Tony) Heemskerk, 250/387-5956, Fax: 250/387-9900
Acting Director, Security Programs, Henry C. Mathias, 250/356-1504, Fax: 250/387-5697

Associated Agencies, Boards & Commissions
- British Columbia Board of Parole: #301, 10090 - 152nd St., Surrey BC V3R 8X8 – 604/660-8846; Fax: 604/660-8877
Chair, Helen M. Joe
Executive Director, D. Bell
- British Columbia Coroner's Service: 4595 Canada Way, 2nd Fl., Burnaby BC V5G 4L9 – 604/660-7739; Fax: 604/660-7776
Chief Coroner, J.V. Cain
- British Columbia Council of Human Rights: 844 Courtney St., 2nd. Fl., Victoria BC V8V 1X4 – 250/387-3710; Fax: 250/387-3643
Chair, Harinder Mahil
Manager, Administrative Services, Shyrl Desjardins
- British Columbia Police Commission: #405, 815 Hornby St., Vancouver BC V6Z 2E6 – 604/660-2385; Fax: 604/660-1223
Chair, J.D.N. Edgar
- British Columbia Review Board: #310, 435 Columbia St., New Westminster BC V3L 5N8 – 604/669-8789; Fax: 604/660-8809
Chair, Norman J. Prelypchan
- Commercial Appeals Commission: #1304, 865 Hornby St., Vancouver BC V6Z 2H4 – 604/660-2987; Fax: 604/660-3372
Chair, Wallace I. Auerbach
- Elections British Columbia
Listed alphabetically in detail, this Section.
- Expropriation Compensation Board: 514 Government St., Victoria BC V8V 2L7 – 250/387-4321; Fax: 250/387-0711
Chair, Jeanne Harvey

- Judicial Council of British Columbia: Pacific Centre, Box 10287, #501, 700 West Georgia St., Vancouver BC V7Y 1E8 – 604/660-2864; Fax: 604/660-1108
Chief Judge, Provincial Court of B.C., Hon. Robert W. Metzger
- Law Courts Education Society of British Columbia: #221, 800 Smithe St., Vancouver BC V6Z 2E1 – 604/660-9870; Fax: 604/660-2420
Executive Director, Rick Craig
- Law Reform Commission: #601, 865 Hornby St., Vancouver BC V6Z 2G3 – 604/660-2366; Fax: 604/660-2378
Chair, Arthur L. Close, Q.C.
Commissioner, Thomas G. Anderson
- Legal Services Society: #300, 1140 West Pender St., PO Box 3, Vancouver BC V6E 4G1 – 604/660-4661; Fax: 604/660-9578
Executive Director, Richard Dalon
- Liquor Appeal Board: #1304, 865 Hornby St., Vancouver BC V6Z 2H4 – 604/660-2987; Fax: 604/660-3372
Chair, Wallace I. Auerbach
- Motion Picture Appeal Board: #310, 435 Columbia St., New Westminster BC V3L 5N8 – 604/660-8789; Fax: 604/660-8809
Chair, Wallace I. Auerbach
- Office of the Public Trustee: #600, 808 West Hastings St., Vancouver BC V6C 3L3 – 604/660-4444; Fax: 604/660-4456
Public Trustee, Dorothy Ewen, 604/660-4489
- Workers' Compensation Board
Listed alphabetically in detail, this Section.

Office of the AUDITOR GENERAL
8 Bastion Sq., Victoria BC V8V 1X4
250/387-6803; Fax: 250/387-1230; URL: http://www.aud.gov.bc.ca/
Auditor General, George Morfitt
Senior Principal, Administration, Terence P. Mackian, 250/356-2625
Asst. Auditor General, Compliance & Special Projects, Gordon Dawson, 250/356-2636
Asst. Auditor General, Financial Statement Attest, Frank Barr, 250/356-2667
Asst. Auditor General, Value-for-Money Audit, J. Peter Gregory, 250/356-2638

Ministry of CHILDREN & FAMILIES (CFAM)
1022 Government St., 2nd Fl., Victoria BC V8V 1X4
604/387-9699
Note: This ministry was announced just prior to publication. Formal organization & structuring had not been decided. The ministry will include certain sectors from the Ministry of Social Services (still listed separately in this book). For more information about the ministry's responsibilities contact the office of the Deputy Minister or contact the Enquiry BC information service, 250/387-6121.
The ministry has been created to "ensure a child centred, integrated approach to promote & protect the healthy development of children & youth, while recognizing their lifelong attachment to family". The development of a Children's Commissioner is expected under the direction of the Ministry. The Commissioner will be responsible for, among other things, reviewing, investigating & responding to complaints, injuries & the death of children.
It has been recommended there be four main branches responsible for the operations of this Ministry, they include: Field Services, Strategic Planning, Corporate Services & Child Protection.
Minister, Hon. Penny Priddy, 250/356-6348, Fax: 250/356-6595
Deputy Minister, Robert Plecas, 604/387-2000

Office of the CONFLICT OF INTEREST COMMISSIONER
#101, 431 Menzies St., Victoria BC V8V 1X4
250/356-9283; Fax: 250/356-6580
Commissioner, Ted Hughes

Ministry of EDUCATION, SKILLS & TRAINING
PO Box 9150, Stn Prov Govt, Victoria BC V8W 9H1
250/356-2500; Fax: 250/356-5945; URL: http://www.educ.gov.bc.ca/

ACTS ADMINISTERED
Accountants (Certified General) Act
Accountants (General) Act
Accountants (Management) Act
Applied Science Technologists & Technicians Act
Architects Act
Architects (Landscape) Act
Barbers Act
College & Institute Act
Engineers & Geoscientists Act
Hairdressers Act
Independent School Act
Institute of Technology Act
Music Teachers (Registered) Act
Open Learning Agency Act
Privated Post-Secondary Education Act
Royal Roads University Act
School Act
Teaching Profession Act
University Act
University Foundations Act
University of Northern British Columbia Act
Workers Compensation Act
Minister, #124, Parliament Bldgs., Victoria BC V8V 1X4, Hon. Moe Sihota, 250/387-1977, Fax: 250/387-3200
Deputy Minister, Don Wright, PO Box 9594, Stn Stn Prov Govt, Victoria BC V8W 9K4, 250/356-2026, Fax: 250/387-8322

EDUCATION PROGRAMS DIVISION
Asst. Deputy Minister, Dr. Sam Lim, 250/356-2499, Fax: 250/356-6063
Acting Director, Career Programs Branch, John Fitzgibbon, 250/387-7044, Fax: 250/387-1418
Acting Director, Curriculum Branch, David Williams, 250/356-2317, Fax: 250/356-2316
Director, Examinations & Assessment Branch, Becky Matthews, 250/356-7269, Fax: 250/387-3682
Director, Field Services Team (K-12), Jerry Mussio, 250/356-2575, Fax: 250/356-8267
Director, Learning Resources Branch, Roy Emperingham, 250/387-5331, Fax: 250/387-1527
Director, Technology & Distance Education Branch, Dr. Barry Carbol, 250/356-2326, Fax: 250/387-5515

MANAGEMENT SERVICES DIVISION
Asst. Deputy Minister, Jim Crone, 250/387-2046, Fax: 250/356-8322
Director, Finance & Administrative Services Branch, Neil Matheson, 250/356-2470, Fax: 250/387-9695
Director, Freedom of Information & Privacy Branch, Rob Langridge, 250/356-7508, Fax: 250/387-6315
Director, Human Resources Branch, Lorie Hunchak, 250/356-2351, Fax: 250/356-1520
Director, Information Management Branch, Dorothy Drislane, 250/387-6155, Fax: 250/356-0033

POLICY, PLANNING & SPECIAL PROGRAMS DIVISION
Asst. Deputy Minister, Paul Pallan, 250/356-2487, Fax: 250/356-2604
Executive Director, Planning & Accountability Section, Derek Sturko, 250/356-7347, Fax: 250/356-9121
Executive Director, Policy, Legislation & Corporate Services Section, Allyson McKay, 250/356-5406, Fax: 250/387-3750
Executive Director, Special Programs Section, Peter Owen, 250/356-0522, Fax: 250/953-4908
Director, Aboriginal Education Branch (K-12), Brian Domney, 250/387-1544, Fax: 250/387-1470
Director, Accountability Branch, Barry Anderson, 250/356-7693, Fax: 250/356-2504
Director, Evaluation & Reporting Branch, Gerald Morton, 250/356-1233, Fax: 250/356-0407
Director, Federal/Provincial Relations & International Education Branch, Gail Thomas, 250/356-7250, Fax: 250/387-0878
Acting Director, French Programs Branch, Raymond Ouimet, 250/356-2524, Fax: 250/387-1470
Inspector, Independent Schools Branch, Gerry Ensing, 250/356-2508, Fax: 250/953-4908
Acting Director, Legislation Branch, Stella Bailey, 250/356-9734, Fax: 250/387-3750
Director, Office for Disability Issues, Frank Jonasen, 250/387-3813, Fax: 250/387-3114, TDD: 387-3555
Director, Planning Branch, Mike Hoebel, 250/356-2332, Fax: 250/356-2504
Acting Director, Policy Branch, Sharon Russell, 250/356-1404, Fax: 250/356-2504
Director, Research & Analysis Branch, Jim Howie, 250/356-7248, Fax: 250/387-0878
Director, School Facilities Branch, Rick Connolly, 250/356-2368, Fax: 250/387-1451
Director, School Finance & Data Management Branch, Joan Axford, 250/356-2586, Fax: 250/387-1451
Director, Social Equity Branch, Robin Syme, 250/356-2565, Fax: 250/356-0580
Director, Special Education Branch, Dr. Shirley McBride, 250/356-2333, Fax: 250/356-7631, TDD: 356-7632

POST SECONDARY EDUCATION DIVISION
Asst. Deputy Minister, Shell Harvey, 250/387-0893, Fax: 250/356-8322
Director, Access & Health Programs Branch, Devron Gaber, 250/387-6198, Fax: 250/356-8851
Director, Business & Technical Programs Branch, Duncan MacRae, 250/387-6191, Fax: 250/356-8131
Director, Facilities Services & Capital Innovations Branch, Jim Parker, 250/387-6450, Fax: 250/387-5259
Director, Innovation & Continuing Education Branch, Jim Soles, 250/356-7740, Fax: 250/387-5259
Director, Post Secondary Finance & Student Assistance, Tom Austin, 250/387-6169, Fax: 250/356-8131
Director, Student Services Branch, Jim Vanstone, 250/387-6100, Fax: 250/356-9455
Director, Universities & Aboriginal Programs Branch, Robin Ciceri, 250/387-6166, Fax: 250/356-8851

SKILLS DEVELOPMENT DIVISION
Asst. Deputy Minister, Betty Notar, 250/356-1379, Fax: 250/387-3296
Executive Director, BC Benefits Transition Team, Heather Dickson, 250/387-4280, Fax: 250/356-8082
Director, Corporate Services Branch, Scott Browning, 634/387-1515, Fax: 634/356-8082
Acting Director, Field Services Branch, Michael Woodcock, 250/387-6012, Fax: 250/356-8082
Director, Program Operations Branch, Kerry Jothen, 250/387-4287, Fax: 250/387-2069
Director, Program Planning & Development Branch, Franki Craig, 250/356-5991, Fax: 250/387-0262

Associated Agencies, Boards & Commissions
• Open Learning Agency: 4355 Mathissi Pl., Burnaby BC V5G 4S8 – 604/431-3000; Fax: 604/431-3333
Chair, Reva Dexter
President, Dr. Glen M. Farrell

ELECTIONS BRITISH COLUMBIA
1075 Pendergast St., Victoria BC V8V 1X4
250/387-5305; Fax: 250/387-3578; URL: http://vvv.com/ZXelectionsbc/
Chief Electoral Officer, Robert A. Patterson

Ministry of EMPLOYMENT & INVESTMENT
712 Yates St., Victoria BC V8V 1X4
250/356-8702; Email: webmaster@eivic.ei.gov.bc.ca; URL: http://www.ei.gov.bc.ca/

Provides an economic framework aimed at strategies for growth & job creation. Ensures safe, efficient & environmentally responsible development of the province's energy & mineral resources. Promotes environmentally sound economic growth & diversification. Encourages increased trade working closely with environmental industry associations & other stakeholders. Establishes new partnerships with the science & technology sectors supplying expertise & scientific services for the development of energy, mineral & petroleum resources.

ACTS ADMINISTERED
British Columbia Buildings Corporation Act
British Columbia Enterprise Corporation Act (other than in relation to the BC Pavilion Corporation)
British Columbia Railway Act
Build BC Act (other than in Part 4, in relation to the BC Transportation Financing Authority)
Coal Act
Community Financial Services Act
Development Corporation Act
Economic Development Electricity Rate Act
Energy Efficiency Act
Expo 86 Corporation Act
Ferry Corporation Act
Fort Nelson Indian Reserve Minerals Revenue Sharing Act
Gas Utility Act
Geothermal Resources Act
Hydro & Power Authority Act
Hydro & Power Authority Privatization Act
Hydro Power Measures Act
Indian Reserve Mineral Resource Act
Industrial Development Incentive Act (other than in relation to the Small Business Incentive Program)
Job Protection Act
Mine Development Assessment Act
Mineral Land Tax Act
Mineral Tax Act
Mineral Tenure Act
Mines Act
Mining Right of Way Act
Ministry of Energy, Mines & Petroleum Resources Act
Ministry of Industry & Small Business Development Act (other than in relation to small business & tourism)
Ministry of International Business & Immigration Act (other than in relation to immigration)
Ministry of International Trade, Science & Investment (other than in relation to small business & tourism)
Ministry of Transportation & Highways Act (Sections 61-67, pertaining to the Victoria Line Ltd.)
Natural Gas Price Act
Natural Resource Community Fund Act
Petroleum & Natural Gas Act
Petroleum & Natural Gas (Vancouver Island Railway Lands) Act
Petroleum Corporation Repeal Act
Pipeline Act
Science Council Act
Science & Technology Fund Act
Special Enterprise Zone & Tax Relief Act
Telephone (Rural) Act
Trade Development Corporation Act
Vancouver Island Natural Gas Pipeline Act

GOVERNMENT OF BRITISH COLUMBIA

Minister, Hon. Dan Miller
Acting Deputy Minister, Blair Redlin, 250/387-0750, Fax: 250/387-5519
Executive Director, Communications Division, Shawn Thomas, 250/356-8712, Fax: 250/356-7042
Director, Corporate Relations Branch, Suzanne Christiansen, 250/356-7013, Fax: 250/387-6145

BRITISH COLUMBIA TRADE & INVESTMENT OFFICE (BCTIO)
250/953-4701; Fax: 250/387-7969; Email: jburnes@eivic.ei.gov.bc.ca
#730, 999 Canada Place, Vancouver BC V6C 3E1
250/844-1900, Fax: 250/660-4048
Asst. Deputy Minister, Chris Nelson, 250/356-2415
Vice-President, Investment & Financial Services Division, Frank Harper
Vice-President, Trade & Industry Division, Richard Poliquin

ENERGY & MINERALS DIVISION (EMD)
1810 Blanshard St., 8th Fl., Victoria BC V8W 9N3
Asst. Deputy Minister, Peter Ostergaard, 250/952-0122, Fax: 250/952-0121
Director, Engineering & Operations Branch, Bou van Oort, 250/952-0302, Fax: 250/952-0291
Director, Mineral Titles Branch, Denis Lieutard, 250/952-0542, Fax: 250/952-0541
Director, Petroleum Geology Branch, John McRae, 250/952-0352, Fax: 250/952-0291
Director, Regional Operations Health & Safety, Fred Hermann, 250/952-0494, Fax: 250/952-0491
Commissioner, Petroleum Titles Branch, Gerald German, 250/952-0334, Fax: 250/952-0331

REVENUE & MANAGEMENT SERVICES DIVISION
1810 Blanshard St., 8th Fl., Victoria BC V8W 9N3
Asst. Deputy Minister, Joan Hesketh, 250/952-0122, Fax: 250/952-0121
Acting Director, Community Development Unit, Jim Green, 604/775-1695, Fax: 604/775-1184
Acting Director, Finance & Administration Branch, Doug Callbeck, 250/952-0162, Fax: 250/952-0161
Assoc. Director, Budgets, Jennifer Smith, 250/952-0161, Fax: 250/952-0161
Director, Human Resources Branch, Barry Turner, 250/952-0142, Fax: 250/952-0141
Director, Information Technology Branch, Barbara Hibbins, 250/387-9466, Fax: 250/387-4410
Director, Resource Revenue Branch, Doug Stangeland, 250/952-0192, Fax: 250/952-0191

POLICY DIVISION
Asst. Deputy Minister, Bruce McRae, 250/952-0115, Fax: 250/952-0111
Division Coordinator, Christine Estes, 250/952-0112
Director, International Branch, Noel Schacter, 250/387-0249, Fax: 250/356-8109
Director, Policy Development Branch, Louise Wilson, 250/356-8160, Fax: 250/356-0380
Director, Resource Planning Branch, Brian Parrott, 250/952-0502, Fax: 250/952-0501

SCIENCE, TECHNOLOGY & CAPITAL DEVELOPMENT DIVISION
250/356-5478; Fax: 250/387-4410
Asst. Deputy Minister, Steve Hollett, 250/356-1282, Fax: 250/356-0105
Asst. Deputy Minister, Deborah George, 250/387-6203, Fax: 250/356-0021
Division Coordinator, Sandra Aitken, 250/387-7969
Acting Director, Capital Project Coordination Branch, Manuel Achadinha, 250/356-7859
Acting Director, Infrastructure & Program Management Branch, Debbie Ainsworth, 250/387-0686
Director, Policy & Planning Branch, Calvin Shantz, 250/356-0678

Acting Director, Program & Agency Coordination Branch, Len Juteau, 250/387-5028

Associated Agencies, Boards & Commissions
- Asia Pacific Foundation: #666, 999 Canada Place, Vancouver BC V6C 3E1 – 604/684-5986; Fax: 604/681-1370
President & CEO, Bill Saywell
- British Columbia Advisory Council on Mining: 1810 Blanshard St., Victoria BC V8W 1X4 – 250/952-0152
- British Columbia Buildings Corporation: 3350 Douglas St., PO Box 1112, Victoria BC V8W 2T4 – 250/387-7211; Fax: 250/387-0024; URL: http://www.bcbc.gov.bc.ca
President & CEO, Dennis Truss, 250/387-7344, Fax: 250/356-2919
Vice-President, Human Resources & Corporate Services, Sharon Halkett
Director, Corporate Communications, Denis Racine
- British Columbia Ferry Corporation: 1112 Fort St., Victoria BC V8V 4V2 – 250/381-1401; Fax: 250/381-5452; URL: http://vvv.com/ferries/index.html
President & CEO, Frank Rhodes
- British Columbia Hydro & Power Authority
Listed alphabetically in detail, this Section.
- British Columbia Mediation & Arbitration Board: 10142 - 101 Ave., Fort St. John BC V1J 2B3 – 250/787-3403; Fax: 250/787-3228
Chair, Ewart Loucks
Vice-Chair, Constance Shortt
- British Columbia Rail Ltd. (BC Rail): PO Box 8770, Vancouver BC V6B 4X6 – 604/984-5001; Fax: 604/984-5201
Chair, Edmond E. Price, 604/986-2012
President & CEO, Paul McElligott
Vice-President, Administration & Corporate Secretary, R. Walter Young, 604/984-5003
Vice-President, Finance & Information Technology, J. Roger Clarke, 604/984-5235
Vice-President, Human Resources & Strategic Planning, Eric Lush, 604/984-5158
Vice-President, Marketing & Sales, Wayne C. Banks, 604/984-5056
Vice-President, Rail Operations, J. Chuck Trainor, 604/984-5238
- Crown Corporations Secretariat: 848 Courtney St., Victoria BC V8W 9N2
Deputy Minister, Lawrie McFarlane
Director, Energy, Insurance Crowns, Bruce Duncan, 250/356-6723
Director, Transportation Crowns, Frank Blasetti, 250/356-6721
- International Commercial Arbitration Centre: #670, 999 Canada Place, Vancouver BC V6C 2E2 – 604/684-2821; Fax: 604/641-1250
Governing Trustee, Graham Clarke
- International Finance Centre - Vancouver Society (IFC): World Trade Centre, #658, 999 Canada Place, Vancouver BC V6C 3E1 – 604/683-6626; Fax: 604/683-6646
Executive Director, Liam Hopkins
- International Maritime Centre: Harbour Centre, #1550, 555 West Hastings St., PO Box 12118, Vancouver BC V6B 4N6 – 604/681-9515; Fax: 604/683-2435
Chair & Director, Graham Clarke
- Job Protection Commission: #369, 1177 West Hastings St., Vancouver BC V6E 2K3 – 604/775-0162; Fax: 604/775-0228, Toll Free: 1-800-665-4605
Commissioner, Doug Kerley
- Mine Accident Reporting System: 1810 Blanshard St., Victoria BC V8V 1X4 – 250/952-0494; Fax: 250/952-0491
- Premiers' Advisory Council on Science & Technology: #501, 168 Chadwick Ct., North Vancouver BC V7M 3L4 – 604/987-8477; Fax: 604/987-5617
Chair, Julia Levy

- Science Council of British Columbia (SCBC): #800, 4710 Kingsway, Burnaby BC V5H 4M2 – 604/438-2752; Fax: 604/438-6564; URL: http://www.scbc.org/, Toll Free: 1-800-665-7222
President, Dr. Jim Reichert
- Victoria Line Limited: #185 Dallas Rd., Victoria BC V8V 1A1 – 250/480-5544; Fax: 250/480-5222
President & CEO, Sandy Peel

Ministry of ENERGY, MINES & PETROLEUM RESOURCES
Note: This ministry was integrated with the Ministry of Employment & Investment in February 1996.

Ministry of ENVIRONMENT, LANDS & PARKS (ELP)
810 Blanshard St., Victoria BC V8V 1X5
250/387-9419; Fax: 250/356-6464; Email: wwwmail@pubaffair.env.gov.bc.ca; URL: http://www.env.gov.bc.ca
General Inquiries: 250/387-1161
Environmental Statutes URL: http://www.env.gov.bc.ca/epd/cpr/admin/cpr.html
Note: Announced changes to personnel structure in November 1996. Provincial department responsible for providing a naturally diverse & healthy environment. BC Environment has management responsibility over air, water, wildlife & wild freshwater fish & sport fish resources. In addition BC Environment regulates waste disposal & pesticide use, assesses major development proposals, enforces environmental legislation & protects resources, property & the public from human & natural hazards.
BC Lands manages & allocates public land to ensure access for industry, commerce, settlement, recreation & conservation uses that are sensitive to both environmental needs & sustainable development.
BC Parks is responsible for the management of parks, recreation areas & ecological reserves with a commitment to the conservation & management of natural features & diverse environments in the province.

ACTS ADMINISTERED
Beaver Lodge Lands Trust Renewal Act
Boundary Act
Commercial River Rafting Safety Act
Creston Valley Wildlife Act
Dogwood, Rhododendron & Trillium Protection Act
Drainage & Dyking Adjustment & Repeal Act, 1965
Drainage, Ditch & Dyke Act
Dyke Maintenance Act
Dyking Authority Act
Ecological Reserve Act
Environment & Land Use Act
Environment Management Act
Environmental Assessment Act
Financial Administration Act (in part)
Greenbelt Act
Industrial Development Act
Industrial Operation Compensation Act
Kootenay Canal Land Acquisition Act
Land Act
Land Survey Act
Land Surveyors Act
Land Title Act
Land (Veterans) Act
Libby Dam Reservoir Act
Litter Act
Ministry of Environment Act
Ministry of Lands, Parks & Housing Act
Park Act
Park (Regional) Act
Pesticide Control Act
Railway Act (in part)
Skagit Environmental Enhancement Act
Sustainable Environment Fund Act

Universities Real Estate Development Corporation Act (in part)
University Endowment Land Act (in part)
University Endowment Land Park Act
Waste Management Act
Water Act
Water Protection Act
Water Utility Act
Weather Modification Act
West Coast National Park Act
Wildlife Act (1982)
Minister, Hon. Paul Ramsey
Deputy Minister, John Allan
Executive Director, Public Affairs & Communications Branch, Mark Stefanson, 250/387-9422, Fax: 250/356-6464
Manager, Communications Services, Jennifer Smyth
Manager, Corporate Services, Monica Collins

ENVIRONMENTAL PROTECTION DEPARTMENT
777 Broughton St., Victoria BC V8V 1X4
250/387-9990; Fax: 250/356-9836
Executive Director, Don A. Fast, 250/387-9993
Acting Director, Air Resources Branch, Prad Khare, 250/387-9987, Fax: 250/356-9836
Director, Industrial Waste & Hazardous Contaminants Branch, Lanny T. Hubbard, 250/387-9992, Fax: 250/387-9935
Director, Municipal Waste Reduction Branch, Ron J. Driedger, 250/387-9974, Fax: 250/356-9974
Director, Pollution Prevention Section, Tom J. Galimberti, 250/356-6027, Fax: 250/356-9836
Acting Director, Water Quality Branch, Shelley Forrester, 250/387-9500, Fax: 250/356-8298
Manager, Laboratory Services & Systems Management Section, Larry Keith, 250/953-3080

ENVIRONMENT REGIONAL OPERATIONS DEPARTMENT
250/356-7223; Fax: 250/387-5669
Asst. Deputy Minister, Dr. Jon O'Riordan, 250/387-9877
Operations Manager, Donna Humphries, 250/953-3735
Director, Forest Practices Code, Dr. Don A. Kasianchuk, 965 Broughton St., 6th Fl., Victoria BC V8V 1X4, 250/387-6989, Fax: 250/953-5170

Regional Offices
Cariboo: 540 Borland St., Williams Lake BC V2G 1R8 – 250/398-4530; Fax: 250/398-4214, Regional Director, Gyl Connaty
Kootenay: #401, 333 Victoria St., Nelson BC V1L 4K3 – 250/354-6333; Fax: 250/354-6332, Regional Director, Dennis McDonald
Lower Mainland: 10334 - 152A St., Surrey BC V3R 7P8 – 604/582-5200; Fax: 604/660-8926, Toll Free: 1-800-665-1118, Regional Director, Jim McCracken
Omineca-Peace: 1011 - 4th Ave., Prince George BC V2L 3H9 – 250/565-6135; Fax: 250/565-6629, Regional Director, Al Sanderson
Skeena: 3726 Alfred Ave., PO Box 5000, Smithers BC V0J 2N0 – 250/847-7260; Fax: 250/847-7591, Acting Regional Director, Jim Yardley
Southern Interior: 1259 Dalhousie Dr., Kamloops BC V2C 5Z5 – 250/371-6200; Fax: 250/828-4000, Regional Director, Dick Anderson
Vancouver Island: 2569 Kenworth Rd., Nanaimo BC V9T 4P7 – 250/758-3100; Fax: 250/755-2473, Regional Director, Earl Warnock

FISHERIES, WILDLIFE & HABITAT PROTECTION DEPARTMENT
810 Blanshard St., 4th Fl., Victoria BC V8V 1X4
250/356-0121; Fax: 250/387-5669
Asst. Deputy Minister, Jim H.C. Walker, 250/356-0139
Director, Fisheries Branch, Dr. Harvey Andrusak, 780 Blanshard St., 2nd Fl., Victoria BC V8V 1X4, 250/387-9711, Fax: 250/387-9750
Director, Forest Renewal Coordination Branch, Al Martin
Director, Habitat Protection Branch, Nancy Wilkin, 780 Blanshard St., 3rd Fl., Victoria BC V8V 1X4, 250/387-9555, Fax: 250/356-5104
Acting Director, Wildlife Branch, D. Ray Halladay, 780 Blanshard St., Victoria BC V8V 1X4, 250/387-9731, Fax: 250/356-9145

LANDS & WATER MANAGEMENT DEPARTMENT
810 Blanshard St., 4th Fl., Victoria BC V8V 1X4
250/387-1288; Fax: 250/387-5669; URL: http://www.env.gov.bc.ca/gdbc/
Asst. Deputy Minister, Frank G. Edgell, 250/387-1282
Director & Surveyor General, Crown Land Registry Services Branch, Greg Roberts, 3400 Davidson Ave., Victoria BC V8V 1X4, 250/387-4461, Fax: 250/387-1830
Director, Geographic Data BC, Gary T. Sawayama, 1802 Douglas St., 4th Fl., 250/387-6316, Fax: 250/356-7831
Director, Hydrology Branch, Jim S. Mattison, 250/387-1112, Fax: 250/356-5496
Acting Director, Information Systems Branch, Ray Allen, 1802 Douglas St., 6th Fl., Victoria BC V8V 1X4, 250/387-6442, Fax: 250/356-1916
Director, Real Estate Services Branch, Brian Clarke, 1802 Douglas St., 3rd Fl., 250/387-1934
Director, Tenure Management Branch, Lynn Kennedy
Director, Water Resources Branch, Jack E. Farrell, 250/387-6945, Fax: 250/356-8298

Lands Regional Operations Department
250/387-1288; Fax: 250/387-5669
Executive Director, Jack Hall, 250/387-1280
Manager, Operations Support, Mike Reimer

Regional Operations Offices
Cariboo: #201, 172 North Second Ave., Williams Lake BC V2G 1Z6 – 250/398-3250; Fax: 250/398-7556, Regional Director, Steve Mazur
Kootenay: 828A Baker St., Cranbrook BC V1C 1A2 – 250/426-1414; Fax: 250/426-1426, Regional Director, Bill Irwin
Lower Mainland: #401, 4603 Kingsway, Burnaby BC V5H 4M4 – 604/660-5500; Fax: 604/660-5538, Regional Director, Dick Roberts
Omineca: #450, 1011 - Fourth Ave., Prince George BC V2L 3H9 – 250/565-6245; Fax: 250/565-6941, Regional Director, Egon Weger
Peace: #400, 10003 - 110th Ave., Fort St. John BC V1J 6M7 – 250/787-3411; Fax: 250/787-3219, Regional Director, John Turner
Skeena: 3726 Alfred Ave., PO Box 5000, Smithers BC V0J 2N0 – 250/847-7334; Fax: 250/847-7556, Acting Regional Director, Ron Creber
Thompson-Okanagan: 478 St. Paul St., Kamloops BC V2C 2J6 – 250/828-4800; Fax: 250/428-4809, Regional Director, John Thompson
Vancouver Island: 851 Yates St., Victoria BC V8V 1X4 – 250/387-5011; Fax: 250/356-1871, Acting Regional Director, Max Nock

MANAGEMENT SERVICES DEPARTMENT
810 Blanshard St., 4th Fl., Victoria BC V8V 1X4
250/387-9878; Fax: 250/387-5669
Asst. Deputy Minister, Greg Koyl, 250/387-9888
Director, Central Services Branch, Wilda F. Dirks, 250/356-9228
Acting Director, Financial Services, Kathy Bryce, 250/356-1377, Fax: 250/356-9239
Director, Human Resources Branch, Ken J. Gower, 250/387-9819, Fax: 250/387-7286
Director, Systems Services Branch, John Roche, 737 Courtney St. 3rd Fl., Victoria BC V8V 1X4, 250/387-9605, Fax: 250/356-7297

PARKS DEPARTMENT/BC Parks
800 Johnson St., 2nd Fl., Victoria BC V8V 1X4
250/387-5002; Fax: 250/387-5757
Asst. Deputy Minister, Denis O'Gorman, 250/387-9997
Director, District Operations Branch, Bob Dalziel, 250/387-3987
Director, Parks Department Services, Wally Eamer, 250/387-3943, Fax: 250/387-5757
Acting Director, Parks & Ecological Reserves Management Branch, Denis Moffatt
Director, Parks & Ecological Reserves Planning, Colin Campbell

Parks Regional Offices
Northern BC: #430, 1011 - 4th Ave., Prince George BC V2L 3H9 – 250/565-6270; Fax: 250/565-6429, Regional Director, S. Robertson
Southern Interior: #101, 1050 West Columbia St., Kamloops BC V2C 1L2 – 250/371-6400; Fax: 250/828-4737, Regional Director, Tom Moore
South Coast: 1610 Mt. Seymour Rd., North Vancouver BC V7G 1L3 – 604/929-2200; Fax: 604/929-2425, Regional Director, George Trachuk

POLICY, PLANNING & LEGISLATION DEPARTMENT
810 Blanshard St., 4th Fl., Victoria BC V8V 1X4
250/356-7223; Fax: 250/387-5669
State of the Environment Report: 250/272-7797
Asst. Deputy Minister, Toby Vigod
Director, Aboriginal Affairs Branch, Margaret Eckenfelder, 250/387-9730, Fax: 250/387-8897
Director, Enforcement & Environmental Emergencies Branch, Nancy Bircher, 250/387-9401, Fax: 250/387-1041
Director, Environmental Assessment Branch, Doug W. Dryden, 250/387-9678, Fax: 250/356-7183
Director, Evaluation & Economics Branch, Ray Payne, 250/356-0204, Fax: 250/356-9836
Director, Land Use Branch, David Johns, 250/387-1850, Fax: 250/356-1916
Director, Strategic Planning, Policy & Legislation Branch, Cindy Brown, 250/356-1907, Fax: 250/387-8894

Associated Agencies, Boards & Commissions
• British Columbia-Alberta Boundary Commission: 3400 Davidson Ave., Victoria BC V8V 1X4 – 250/387-4461; Fax: 250/387-1830
Commissioner, Don Duffy
• British Columbia-Yukon-Northwest Territories Boundary Commission: 3400 Davidson Ave., Victoria BC V8V 1X4 – 250/387-4461; Fax: 250/387-1830
Commissioner, Don Duffy
• Environmental Appeal Board: #125, 911 Yates St., Victoria BC V8V 1X5 – 250/387-3464; Fax: 250/356-9923
Chair, Linda Michaluk

British Columbia ENVIRONMENTAL ASSESSMENT OFFICE
836 Yates St., 2nd Fl., Victoria BC V8V 1X4
250/356-7475; Fax: 250/356-7477; Email: eaoinfo@galaxy.gov.bc.ca; URL: http://www.eao.gov.bc.ca/
Deputy Minister & Executive Director, Sheila Wynn
Director, Aboriginal, Martyn Glassman, 250/387-2206
Director, Corporate Services, Patty Shelton, 250/356-7476
Director, Destination Resorts & Transportation, Ray Crook, 250/356-7492
Director, Energy & Hydro Electric, Derek Griffin, 250/387-1543
Director, Mining, Mike Kent, 604/356-0312
Director, Mining, Norm Ringstad, 250/356-7481
Director, Petroleum & Natural Gas, Marcia Farquhar, 250/356-7484

Canadian Almanac & Directory 1997

Director, Waste Management, Jackie Hamilton, 250/387-1624
Director, Waste Management, Lislie Hildebrant, 250/387-1624
Director, Water, Impoundments & Reservoirs, Daphne Stancil, 250/356-7483

Ministry of FINANCE & CORPORATE RELATIONS (FCR)
617 Government St., Victoria BC V8V 1X4
250/387-9278; URL: http://www.fin.gov.bc.ca/
Enquiry BC: 250/387-6121

ACTS ADMINISTERED
Auditor General Act
Bankruptcy & Insolvency Act (in part)
Bonding Act
British Columbia Endowment Fund Act
British Columbia Enterprise Corporation Loan Privatization Act
British Columbia Payment to Canada of Federal Income Tax on Behalf of Natural Gas Producers Act
British Columbia Railway Finance Act
British Columbia Statistics Act, 1979
Budget Measures Implementation Act
Capital Commission Act
Commodity Contract Act
Company Act, except s. 348
Company Clauses Act
Compensation Fairness Act
Condominium Act, except all matters affecting the powers & duties of the Registrar of Titles
Cooperative Association Act
Corporation Capital Tax Act
Credit Reporting Act
Credit Union Act
Credit Union Incorporation Act
Creditor Assistance Act
Debt Collection Act
Debtor Assistance Act
Document Disposal Act
Educational Institution Capital Finance Act
Esquimalt & Nanaimo Railway Belt Tax Act
Financial Administration Act
Financial Information Act
Financial Institutions Act
Home Acquisition Act
Home Conversion & Leasehold Loan Act
Home Mortgage Assistance Program Act
Home Purchase Assistance Act
Homeowner Interest Assistance Act
Horse Racing Tax Act
Hospital District Finance Act
Hotel Room Tax Act
Housing Construction (Elderly Citizens) Act
Housing & Employment Development Act
Income Tax Act
Insurance Act
Insurance (Captive Company) Act
Insurance (Marine) Act
Insurance Premium Tax Act
International Financial Business Act
International Financial Business (Tax Refund) Act
Land Tax Deferment Act
Legislative Assembly Allowances & Pension Act
Logging Tax Act
Lottery Act
Lottery Corporation Act
Lottery Tax Act
Manufactured Home Act
Mining Tax Act
Miscellaneous Registrations Act, 1992
Ministry of Provincial Secretary & Government Services Act, Ss. 1, 2(3), 4, 8
Mobile Home Act
Mortgage Brokers Act
Motor Dealer Act
Motor Fuel Tax Act
Multilevel Marketing Act
Mutual Fire Insurance Companies Act
Pacific North Coast Native Cooperative Act
Partnership Act
Pension (College) Act
Pension (Municipal) Act
Pension (Public Service) Act
Pension (Teachers) Act
Pension Agreement Act
Pension Society Act
Pension Statutes (Transitional Arrangement) Act
Personal Property Security Act
Privatization Benefits Fund Act
Property Purchase Tax Act
Provincial Municipal Partnership (Taxation Measures) Act
Public Sector Employment Act
Public Service Act. S.B.C., 1985, c. 15
Public Service Act. S.B.C., 1993, c. 66
Public Service Benefit Plan Act
Public Service Bonding Act
Public Service Labour Relations Act
Purchasing Commission Act
Queen's Printer Act
Rate Increase Restraint Act
Real Estate Act
Repairers Lien Act
Residential Tenancy Act
Sale of Goods Act
School District Capital Finance Act
Securities Act, except s. 142
Securities (Forged Transfer) Act
Social Service Tax Act
Society Act
Special Accounts Appropriation & Control Act
Special Appropriation Act
Supply Act (Annual)
Taxation (Rural Area) Act
Taxpayer Protection Act
Tobacco Tax Act
Tourist Accommodation (Assessment Relief) Act
Trade Practice Act
Tugboat Worker's Lien Act
Unclaimed Money Act
Vancouver Stock Exchange Act
Warehouse Lien Act
Warehouse Receipt Act
Woodworker Lien Act

Minister, Hon. Andrew Petter, 250/387-3751
Deputy Minister, Garry Wouters, 250/387-3184
Comptroller General, Alan J. Barnard, 250/387-8543, Fax: 250/356-2001
Executive Director, Communications Branch, Shawn Thomas, 250/356-8712, Fax: 250/356-7042
Director, Communications, Tom Workman, 250/387-9286
Acting Director, Federal-Provincial Relations & Research, Michael Butler, 250/387-9018
Program Manager, Enquiry BC, Susan Park, 525 Superior St., 1st Fl., Victoria BC V8V 1X4, 250/387-9273, Fax: 250/953-4302
Provincial Archivist, BC Archives & Records Services, John A. Bovey, 655 Belleville St., Victoria BC V8V 1X4, 250/387-5885, Fax: 250/387-2072
Deputy Provincial Archivist, BC Archives & Records Services, Gary A. Mitchell, 655 Belleville St., Victoria BC V8V 1X4, 250/387-2992
Director, Protocol & Events Branch, Dianne Lawson, 250/387-4304, Fax: 250/356-2814

BRITISH COLUMBIA PURCHASING AGENCY
Queen's Printer & Executive Director, Product Sales & Services, Vern Burkhardt, 250/655-2400, 250/356-5851

B.C. STATS
EMail: bcstats@fincc04.fin.gov.bc.ca

Acting Director, D. McRae, 250/356-2119, Fax: 250/387-9145
Manager, Business & Economic Statistics, Steve Miller, 250/387-0365, Fax: 250/387-0380
Manager, Data Services, Paul Gosh, 250/387-9221, Fax: 250/387-0329
Manager, Labour & Social Statistics, Anne Kitredge, 250/387-0374, Fax: 250/387-0380
Acting Manager, Population Statistics, Ruth McDougall, 250/387-0337, Fax: 250/387-0380
Cartographer, Heather Glowicki, 250/387-0330
Chief, Demography, David O'Neil, 604/387-0335

INFORMATION TECHNOLOGY SERVICES DIVISION
250/389-3916; Fax: 250/389-3101
This Division was formerly called the British Columbia Systems Corporation.
Head, Chris Boulsbee

PROVINCIAL TREASURY
620 Superior St., Victoria BC V8V 1X4
Asst. Deputy Minister, Chris Trumpy, 250/387-9295, Fax: 250/387-9099
Chief Investment Officer, Doug Pearce, 250/387-7161
Director, Banking & Cash Management, Arn van Iersel, 250/387-9295, Fax: 250/387-3024
Director, Corporate Operations, Janet Fraser, #208, 553 Superior St., Victoria BC V8V 1X4, 250/387-8986, Fax: 250/387-6577
Director, Debt Management, Bruce Sampson, 250/387-6210
Director, Loan Administration, Sheila Ausman, 1312 Blanshard St., Victoria BC V8W 2J1, 250/387-7161, Fax: 250/387-3078
Director, Risk Management Branch, Phil Grewar, 716 Courtney St., 4th Fl., Victoria BC V8V 1X4, 250/387-0521

Treasury Board Staff
Executive Director, Analysis & Evaluation, Har Singh, 250/356-8910
Director, Economic Development Policy, Tony Stark, 250/387-9047
Director, Estimates & Capital Budget, Murray Crowther, 250/387-9052
Director, Fiscal & Economic Analysis, Lois McNabb, 250/387-9023
Acting Director, Program Review, Jim Weir, 250/387-9071
Director, Social Policy, Tom Vincent, 250/387-9038
Director, Tax Policy, Andy Robinson, 250/387-9011

REGISTRIES & MINISTRY SUPPORT SERVICES
Executive Director, Bill Bell, 250/387-3989
Registrar, Corporate & Personal Property, John Powell, 250/356-8658, Corporate Registry Hotline: 604/387-7848; Fax: 604/356-0206
Director, Corporate Development Services, Heather Daynard, 250/387-2719
Director, Financial Services & Administration, Brian Mann, 250/387-8139
Director, Human Resource Services, Grant Price, 250/387-8156
Chief Information Officer, Information Technology Management, Tom Dagg, 250/387-8961, Fax: 250/387-3634

REVENUE DIVISION
Asst. Deputy Minister, E. Lloyd Munro, 250/387-6207
Executive Director, Consumer Taxation, Greg Reimer, 250/387-0666, Fax: 250/387-6218
Director, Income Taxation, Alan Carver, 250/387-3320, Fax: 250/953-3094
Director, Real Property Taxation, Dan Johnstone, 250/387-0352, Fax: 250/356-5347
Director, Revenue Administration, Harold Hilton, 250/387-1667, Fax: 250/356-1090

Associated Agencies, Boards & Commissions

- Auditor Certification Board: 940 Blanshard St., 2nd Fl., Victoria BC V8W 3E6 – 250/356-8658; Fax: 250/387-3055
- British Columbia Educational Institutions Capital Financing Authority: c/o Provincial Treasury, 620 Superior St., Victoria BC V8V 1X4 – 250/387-7132; Fax: 250/387-3024
Contact, Bill Newburg
- British Columbia Housing & Employment Development Financing Authority: c/o Provincial Treasury, 620 Superior St., Victoria BC V8V 1X4 – 250/387-7132; Fax: 250/387-3024
Contact, Bill Newburg
- British Columbia Gaming Commission: 848 Courtney St., Victoria BC V8V 1X4 – 250/356-2797; Fax: 250/356-7949
Chair, Richard Macintosh, 250/387-5311
- British Columbia Lottery Corporation: 74 West Seymour St., Kamloops BC V2C 1E2 – 604/270-0649; Fax: 604/828-5637
President, Guy Simonis
- British Columbia Racing Commission: 4595 Canada Way, 2nd Fl., Burnaby BC V5G 4L9 – 604/660-7400; Fax: 604/660-7414
Chair, Carolyn Askew
Executive Director, Robert E. Collis
- British Columbia Regional Hospital Districts Financing Authority: c/o Provincial Treasury, 620 Superior St., Victoria BC V8V 1X4 – 250/387-7132; Fax: 250/387-3024
Contact, Bill Newburg
- British Columbia School Districts Capital Financing Authority: c/o Provincial Treasury, 620 Superior St., Victoria BC V8V 1X4 – 250/387-7132; Fax: 250/387-3024
Contact, Bill Newburg
- British Columbia Securities Commission: #1100, 865 Hornby St., Vancouver BC V6Z 2H4 – 604/660-4800; Fax: 604/660-2688; Email: inquiries@email.bcsc.gov.bc.ca; URL: http://www.bcsc.bc.ca/, Toll Free: 1-800-373-6393 (outside Vancouver area)
Chair, Doug Hyndman, 604/660-4881
Vice-Chair, Joyce Maykut, 604/660-4886
Superintendent of Brokers, Dean Holley, 604/660-4858
Deputy Superintendent, Compliance & Enforcement, Lang Evans
Deputy Superintendent, Corporate Finance, Wayne Redwick, 604/660-4779
Deputy Superintendent, Exemptions & Orders, Margaret Sheehy, 604/660-4878
Deputy Superintendent, Registration, Ross McLennan, 604/660-4856
Deputy Superintendent, Policy & Legislation, Brenda Benham, 604/660-4853
Senior Counsel, Legal, Mark Skwarok, 604/775-1579
- Financial Institutions Commission (FICOM): #1900, 1050 West Pender St., Vancouver BC V6E 3S7 – 604/660-2947; Fax: 604/660-3170; Email: c/o sastauff@bcsc02.gov.bc.ca; URL: http://www.fic.gov.bc.ca/
Chair, Dale Parker, 604/660-2947
CEO & Superintendent, Bob Hobart, 604/660-2923
Deputy Superintendent, Insurance & IFBs, Larry Neilsen, 604/660-4825
- Insurance Council of BC: #300, 1040 West Georgia St., PO Box 7, Vancouver BC V6E 4H1 – 604/688-0321; Fax: 604/662-7767
General Manager, Jerry Matier
- Provincial Capital Commission (PCC): 613 Pandora Ave., Victoria BC V8W 1N8 – 250/386-1356; Fax: 250/386-1303
Chair, Pamela Charlesworth
Executive Director, Larry Beres, 250/386-1356
- Public Service Commission: 3301 Douglas St., 5th Fl., Victoria BC V8V 1X4 – 250/387-8085; Fax: 250/356-1488
Chair, Graeme Roberts
- Public Service Employee Relations Commission
Commissioner, John Mochrie, 250/387-0512, Fax: 250/356-7074
Director, Labour Relations, Ron McEachern, 250/387-6323, Fax: 250/387-0527
Director, Corporate Personnel Services, Wayne Scale, 250/387-6323
- Real Estate Council of BC: 750 West Pender St., 9th Fl., Vancouver BC V6C 2T8 – 604/683-9664; Fax: 604/683-9017
Chair, Allan Terry, 604/543-7211
- Superannuation Commission: 548 Michigan St., Victoria BC V8V 4R5 – 250/387-1002; Fax: 250/387-4199
Commissioner, John W. Cook, 205/387-8201
Deputy Commissioner, Jerry Woytack, 250/387-0410

Ministry of FORESTS
PO Box 9517, Stn Prov Govt, Victoria BC V8W 9C2
250/387-5255; Fax: 250/387-8485; URL: http://mofwww.for.gov.bc.ca
Physical Address: #300, 1675 Douglas St., Victoria BC V8W 9C2
Forest Practices Code Information: 1-800-565-4838

Also known as the BC Forestry Service, this agency manages provincial forests for an efficient balance of economic, social & environmental benefits. Practices require the effective management of timber, forage, water, fish, wildlife, recreation, tourism, wilderness heritage, energy & minerals. The ministry conducts research in forest renewal, forest productivity & integrated resource management. Provides protection for the province's forests & ranges from fire, insect & dissease. A decentralized organizational structure includes the operation of seven forest regions & 43 forest districts.

The Forest Practices Code was established to regulate & restrict types of logging permitted on private & public lands in the province. Provisions in the Code have been established to ban clear cuts in sensitve areas.

ACTS ADMINISTERED
Boom Chain Brand Act
Carmanah Pacific Park Act
Forest Act
Forest Land Reserve Act
Forest Practices Code of British Columbia Act
Forest Renewal Act
Forest Stand Management Fund Act
Foresters Act
Ministry of Forests Act
Range Act
South Moresby Implementation Account Act
Minister, Hon. David Zirnhelt
Deputy Minister, Gerry Armstrong, 250/387-4809, Fax: 250/387-7065
Director, Public Affairs Branch, Irwin Henderson, 250/387-5255, Fax: 250/387-8485

FORESTRY DIVISION
Chief Forester, Larry Pedersen, 250/387-1296, Fax: 250/356-9499
Director, Forestry Division Services Branch, Tom Lester, 250/387-2517, Fax: 250/387-2513
Director, Inventory Branch, Dave Gilbert, 250/387-1314, Fax: 250/387-5999
Director, Range, Recreation & Forest Practices Branch, Ray Addison, 250/387-6656, Fax: 250/387-6751
Director, Research Branch, Ted Baker, 250/387-6721, Fax: 250/387-0046
Director, Silviculture Practices Branch, Henry Benskin, 250/387-1191, Fax: 250/387-1467
Director, Timber Supply Branch, Gary Townsend, 250/356-5947, Fax: 250/953-3838

REVENUE & CORPORATE SERVICES DIVISION
Asst. Deputy Minister, Harry Powell, 250/387-1300, Fax: 250/387-6267
Director, Audit Services Branch, Ian Birch, 250/387-8671, Fax: 250/356-2085
Director, Financial Management Branch, Bob A. Battles, 250/387-1421, Fax: 250/387-5795
Director, Human Resources Branch, Brian Mader, 250/387-1102, Fax: 250/387-6424
Director, Information Systems Branch, John Ellis, 250/387-8400, Fax: 250/387-5132
Director, Revenue Branch, Bill Howard, 250/387-1701, Fax: 250/387-5670
Acting Director, Technical & Administrative Services Branch, Shirley Robbins, 250/387-6538, Fax: 250/387-5714

OPERATIONS DIVISION
Asst. Deputy Minister, Janna Kumi, 250/387-1236, Fax: 250/953-3687
Director, Business Design Branch, Shelley Sullivan, 250/356-1592, Fax: 250/356-5355
Director, Compliance & Enforcement Branch, Vacant, 250/356-3735, Fax: 250/387-2539
Director, Nursery & Seed Operations Branch, Drew Brazier, 250/387-8955, Fax: 250/387-1467
Director, Protection Branch, Jim Dunlop, 250/387-5965, Fax: 250/387-5685
Director, Resource Tenures & Engineering Branch, Jim Langridge, 250/387-5291, Fax: 250/387-6445

Regional Forestry Offices
Cariboo: 540 Borland St., Williams Lake BC V2G 1R8 – 250/398-4345; Fax: 250/398-4380, Regional Manager, Mike Carlson
Physical Address: #200, 650 Borland St., Williams Lake BC B2G 1R8
Kamloops: 515 Columbia St., Kamloops BC V2C 2T7 – 250/828-4131; Fax: 250/828-4154, Regional Manager, Fred Baxter
Nelson: 518 Lake St., Nelson BC V1L 4C6 – 250/354-6200; Fax: 250/354-6250, Regional Manager, Ross Tozer
Prince George: 1011 - 4th Ave., Prince George BC V2L 3H9 – 250/565-6100; Fax: 250/565-6671, Regional Manager, Al Gorley
Prince Rupert: 3726 Alfred Ave., Bag 5000, Smithers BC V0J 2N0 – 250/847-7500; Fax: 250/847-7217, Regional Manager, Jim Snetsinger
Vancouver: 2100 Labieux Rd., Nanaimo BC V9T 6E9 – 250/751-7001; Fax: 250/751-7190, Regional Manager, Ken Collingwood

POLICY & PLANNING DIVISION
Asst. Deputy Minister, Vacant, 250/387-3656, Fax: 250/387-6267
Director, Aboriginal Affairs Branch, Christie Brown, 250/356-6083, Fax: 250/356-6076
Director, Corporate Policy & Planning Branch, Sue Stephen, 250/356-7880, Fax: 250/356-7903
Director, Economics & Trade Branch, Hartley Lewis, 250/356-9804, Fax: 250/387-5670
Director, Integrated Resources Policy Branch, Ralph Archibald, 250/356-5384, Fax: 250/387-3591

Associated Agencies, Boards & Commissions
- Forest Renewal BC: 727 Fisgard St., Victoria BC V8V 1X4 – 250/387-2500
CEO, Colin Smith
- Timber Export Advisory Committee: 610 Johnson St., 2nd Fl., Victoria BC V8W 3E7 – 250/387-8359
Chair, Don Hammond
Secretary, Don Ruhl

British Columbia GOVERNMENT COMMUNICATIONS OFFICE
612 Government St., Victoria BC V8V 1X4
250/387-1337; Fax: 250/387-3534
This office reports to the Ministry of Finance & Corporate Relations.
Associate Deputy Minister, Evan Lloyd, 250/387-1886, Fax: 250/387-3534
Executive Director, John Usher
Asst. Deputy Minister, Public Issues & Consultation, John Heaney, 614 Government St., Victoria BC V8V 1X4, 250/387-1027, Fax: 250/387-6070
Acting Director, Public & Corporate Relations, Noelle Reeve, 250/387-4315, Fax: 250/387-1399

Ministry of GOVERNMENT SERVICES (MGS)
Note: This agency's operations were integrated with other ministry's operations in a recent government reorganization. Most responsibilities were transferred to the Ministry of Finance & Corporate Relations.

Ministry of HEALTH
1515 Blanshard St., 7th Fl., Victoria BC V8W 3C8
250/952-3456; URL: http://www.hlth.gov.bc.ca
Toll Free: AIDS Hotline 1-800-661-3886
Alcohol & Drug Information: 1-800-663-1441
Cancer Information Line: 1-800-663-4242
Food & Nutrition Information: 1-800-667-DIET
Medical Services Plan Subscriber Information: 1-800-663-7100
Screening Mammography Information Line: 1-800-663-9203, 604/660-3639 (Vancouver)
Travel Assistance Program: 1-800-661-2668
Ensures that health system promotes & provides for the physical, mental, & social well-being of all residents.

ACTS ADMINISTERED
Access to Abortion Services Act
Anatomy Act
British Columbia Health Research Foundation Act
Chiropractors Act
Community Care Facility Act
Continuing Care Act
Dental Technicians & Denturists Act
Dentists Act
Emergency Medical Assistants Act
Forensic Psychiatry Act
Health Act
Health Authorities Act
Health Care (Consent) & Care Facility (Admission) Act (not in force)
Health Emergency Act
Health Professions Act
Hearing Aid Act
Hospital Act
Hospital (Auxiliary) Act
Hospital District Act
Hospital Insurance Act
Human Tissue Gift Act
Marriage Act
Meat Inspection Act
Medical & Health Care Services Act
Medical Practitioners Act
Medicare Protection Act
Mental Health Act
Ministry of Health Act
Name Act
Naturopaths Act
Nurses (Licensed Practical) Act
Nurses (Registered Psychiatric) Act
Optometrists Act
Pharmacists Act
Pharmacists, Pharmacy Operations & Drug Scheduling Act (not in force)
Physiotherapists Act
Podiatrists Act
Psychologists Act
Public Toilet Act
Seniors Advisory Council Act
Tobacco Product Act
Tobacco Sales Act
Venereal Disease Act
Vital Statistics Act
Wills Act (Part II)
Minister & Minister Responsible, Seniors, Hon. Joy K. MacPhail
Deputy Minister, Ken Fyke, 250/952-2609, Fax: 250/952-1909

CORPORATE SERVICES
Asst. Deputy Minister, Robert F. Cronin, 250/952-2601, Fax: 250/952-2205
Chair, Medical Services Commission, John Mochrie, 250/952-3465, Fax: 250/952-3131
Executive Director, BC Ambulance Service, Val Pattee, 1810 Blanshard St., Victoria BC V8V 1X4, 250/952-0885, Fax: 250/952-0905
Executive Director, Communications & Public Affairs, Garth Cramer, 250/952-1889, Fax: 250/952-1883
Executive Director, Design & Construction, Roald Anderson, 1520 Blanshard St., Victoria BC V8W 3C8, 250/952-1204, Fax: 250/952-1202
Executive Director, Finance & Management Services, John D. Herbert, 250/952-2066, Fax: 250/952-1940
Executive Director, Legislation & Professional Regulation, Alan Moyes, 250/952-2281, Fax: 250/952-2205
Executive Director, Pharmacare, Mike Corbeil, 250/952-1706, Fax: 250/952-2235
Executive Director, Policy, Planning & Economics, Vacant
Executive Director, Systems Division, Barry H. Gray, 250/952-2440, Fax: 250/952-2235

Vital Statistics
818 Fort St., Victoria BC V8W 1H8
250/952-2681; Fax: 250/952-2576
Vital Statistics Hotline: 1-800-663-8328
Kelowna: 604/868-7798; Fax: 604/868-7799
Prince George: 604/565-7105; Fax: 604/565-7106
Vancouver: 604/660-2937; Fax: 604/660-2645
For a certificate of a registration or record: $25.00 per copy. For each search for one registration or record for each three-year period or fraction thereof overwhich the search is conducted: $25.00.
Director, Ron J. Danderfer, 250/952-2563, Fax: 250/952-2587

REGIONAL PROGRAMS
Associate Deputy Minister, Thea Vakil, 250/952-1297, Fax: 250/952-1052
Executive Director, Acute Care Programs, Leah Hollins, 250/952-1237, Fax: 250/952-1282
Executive Director, Community Health Programs, Diane Johnston, 250/952-1544, Fax: 250/952-1426
Executive Director, Continuing Care Programs, Rod MacDonald, 250/952-1097, Fax: 250/952-1132
Executive Director, Health Protection & Safety, Andrew G. Hazlewood, 250/952-1731, Fax: 250/952-1486
Executive Director, Mental Health Programs, Brian Copley, 250/952-1608, Fax: 250/952-1589
Executive Director, Program Standards & Information Management, Dr. Doug Bigelow, 1810 Blanshard St., Victoria BC B8B 1X4, 250/952-0937, Fax: 250/952-0942
Executive Director, Provincial Programs, David Babiuk, 250/952-2329, Fax: 250/952-1282
Executive Director, Regional Coordination, Christine Kline, #402 - 1245 West Broadway, Vancouver BC V6H 1G7, 604/775-0661, Fax: 604/775-0596
Executive Director, Regional Funding & Support, Manjit Sidhu, 250/952-1646, Fax: 250/952-1649
Director, Women's Health Bureau, Phyllis Chuly, 250/952-1231, Fax: 250/952-1282

STRATEGIC SERVICES
Asst. Deputy Minister, John Greschener, 250/952-2164, Fax: 250/952-2109
Executive Director, Human Resources, B. White, 250/952-2127, Fax: 250/952-2125
Executive Director, Medical Services Plan Operations, Janet McGregor, 250/952-3187, Fax: 250/952-3131
Executive Director, Medical Services Plan Resource Management, Deborah Shera, 250/952-3122, Fax: 250/952-3131
Executive Director, New Directions Development, Sue Rothwell, 250/952-0980, Fax: 250/952-0985
Director, Information & Privacy Program, Vel Clark, 1810 Blanshard St., Victoria BC V8V 1X4, 250/952-0887, Fax: 250/952-0874
Director, Office for Seniors, Geri Hinton, 250/952-1238, Fax: 250/952-1159
Director, Strategic Labour Services, Rick Fell, 250/952-2245, Fax: 250/952-1795
Director, Strategic Management Services, Deborah Morrow, 250/952-2241, Fax: 250/952-2235
Secretary, Medical Services Commissions, Brenda Stewart, 250/952-3163, Fax: 250/952-3131
Provincial Nurses Advisor, Andrea Henning, 250/952-1111, Fax: 250/952-2235

Associated Agencies, Boards & Commissions
• British Columbia Cancer Foundation
See Canadian Organizations, Section 2.

Ministry of HUMAN RESOURCES
Parliament Bldgs., 614 Humboldt St., 7th Fl., Victoria BC V8V 1X4
250/387-6485; Fax: 250/356-7801
Note: This ministry was announced just prior to publication. Formal organization & structuring had not been decided. The ministry will include certain sectors from the Ministry of Social Services (still listed separately in this book). For more information about the ministry's responsibilities contact the office of the Deputy Minister or contact the Enquiry BC information service, 250/387-6121.
Minister, Hon. Dennis Streifel, 250/387-3180, Fax: 250/387-5720
Deputy Minister, Brenda Eaton, 250/387-3121, Fax: 250/387-5775

British Columbia HYDRO & POWER AUTHORITY
6911 Southpoint Dr., Burnaby BC V3N 4X8
604/528-1600; Fax: 604/623-3901; Email: info.serv@bchydro.bc.ca; URL: http://www.bchydro.bc.ca
Office of the Corporate Secretary, 333 Dunsmuir St., 18th Fl., Vancouver BC V6B 5R3
Provincial Crown corporation established in 1962 to generate, transmit & distribute electricity. B.C. Hydro's Board of Directors is appointed by the Lieutenant-Governor in Council & is responsible for the overall direction of the corporation. The corporation's activities are subject to regulation by the British Columbia Utilities Commission. The third largest electricity utility in Canada, B.C. Hydro serves more than 1.3 million customers in an area containing over 92 percent of British Columbia's population. Most of its customers are served by hydroelectric plants linked together by an interconnected system of transmission lines. Those remote communities not connected to this integrated system are served by small local generating plants.
Chair, Brian Smith, R.O., Q.C., 604/623-4480, Fax: 604/623-4467
Vice-Chair, Dr. Sharon Manson Singer, 604/623-4466
Interim President & CEO, Michael Costello, 604/623-4490

Vice-President, General Counsel & Corporate Secretary, Darlene M. Barnett, 604/623-3600
Senior Vice-President, Corporate & Financial Affairs & CFO, David A. Harrison, 604/623-4129
Senior Vice-President, Customer Services, Gail Sexsmith, 604/528-3373
Acting Senior Vice-President, Human Resources, Aboriginal Relations & Environment, Roy G. Staveley, 604/528-1590
Senior Vice-President, Power Supply, P. Donald Swoboda, 604/528-3218
Senior Vice-President, Transmission & Distribution, Ronald J. Threlkeld, 604/528-2224

Office of the INFORMATION & PRIVACY COMMISSIONER
1675 Douglas St., 4th Fl., Victoria BC V8V 1X4
250/387-5629; Fax: 250/387-1696; URL: http://www.cafe.net/gvc.foi/
Toll Free: 1-800-663-7867 (within BC)
250/660-2421 (outside BC)
Commissioner, David Flaherty
Librarian, Ellinore Barker, Email: ecbarker@galaxy.gov.bc.ca

INSURANCE CORPORATION OF BC (AUTOPLAN)
151 West Esplanade, North Vancouver BC V7M 3H9
604/661-2800; Fax: 604/661-6647
President & CEO, T.M. Thompson
Corporate Secretary & General Counsel, L.K. Robertson
Vice-President, Claims, N.D. Weatherston
Vice-President, Finance & Chief Financial Officer, I. Meharry
Vice-President, Information Services, R.R. Nelson
Vice-President, Insurance, H.G. Reid
Vice-President, Public Affairs & Road Safety, D.K. Hyde
Manager, Strategic Planning & Policy, G.D. Basham

Ministry of LABOUR
825 Fort St., Victoria BC V8W 9K1
250/387-0172; Fax: 250/356-1653; URL: http://www.labour.gov.bc.ca/welcome.htm

ACTS ADMINISTERED
Accountants (Certified General) Act
Accountants (Chartered) Act
Accountants (Management) Act (except s. II-3)
Applied Science Technologists & Technicians Act
Apprenticeship Act
Architects Act (except s. 24-1)
Architects (Landscape) Act
Barbers Act
College & Institute Act
Educational Programs Continuation Act
Employment Standards Act
Engineers & Geoscientists Act (except s. 8-2)
Fire Department Act
Fishers' Collective Bargaining Act
Hairdressers Act
Institute of Technology Act
Labour Education Centre of British Columbia Act
Labour Regulation Act
Labour Relations Code
Ministry of Labour Act (except in relation to gas, electrical, elevating devices, boiler & pressure vessel safety)
Open Learning Agency Act
Pension Benefits Standards Act
Private Post-Secondary Education Act
Skills Development & Fair Wage Act
University Act
University Foundations Act
University of Northern British Columbia Act
Workers' Compensation Act
Workplace Act
Minister, #124, Parliament Bldgs., Victoria BC V8V 1X4, Hon. Moe Sihota, 250/387-1977, Fax: 250/387-3200
Deputy Minister, George Ford, 818 Broughton St., Vicotria BC V8W 9K4, 250/387-3154, Fax: 250/356-5186
Director, Communications Branch, Mike Hughes, 250/387-2699, Fax: 250/356-1653
Office Manager, Communications Branch, Colleen Davis, 250/356-1487

APPRENTICESHIP INITATIVES DIVISION
URL: http://www.labour.gov.bc.ca/apprent/welcome.htm
Executive Director, Stuart Clark, 250/387-6151, Fax: 250/387-1193
Director, Apprenticeship Branch, Greg Biggs, #220, 4946 Canada Way, Burnaby BC V5G 4J6, 604/660-1197
Project Director, Planning & Analysis, Susan McClure, 250/356-6284

LABOUR PROGRAMS
818 Broughton St., 3rd Fl., Victoria BC V8W 9K4
Asst. Deputy Minister, Gary Martin, 250/387-3914, Fax: 250/356-5186
Superintendent of Pensions, Pension Benefits Standards, Sherallyn Miller, #210, 4946 Canada Way, Burnaby BC V5G 4J6, 604/775-1349, Fax: 604/660-6517
Director, Collective Agreement Arbitration Bureau, Geoffrey Crampton, #504, 815 Hornby St., Vancouver BC V6Z 2E6, 604/775-1362, Fax: 604/775-1356
Director, Employers' Advisor, Ray Bozzer, #4003, 8171 Ackroyd Rd., Richmond BC V6X 3K1, 604/660-7253, Fax: 604/660-7486
Director, Employment Standards Headquarters, Jill Walker, 825 Fort St., 2nd Fl., Victoria BC V8W 9K1, 250/387-3300, Fax: 250/356-1886
Director, Labour Policy & Program Development Branch, Jan Rassley, 250/356-0677, Fax: 250/356-5335
Director, Workers' Advisor, Blake Williams, #3000, 8171 Ackroyd Rd., Richmond BC V6X 3K1, 604/660-7888, Fax: 604/660-5284, Toll Free: 1-800-663-4261

LABOUR RELATIONS
818 Broughton St., 3rd Fl., Victoria BC V8W 9K4
Acting Asst. Deputy Minister, Don Cott, 250/387-3161, Fax: 250/356-5186
Director, Labour Services Branch, Anne Burch, 250/356-6346, Fax: 250/356-8322

Associated Agencies, Boards & Commissions
• British Columbia Labour Force Development Board: #221, 560 Johnson St., Victoria BC V8V 1X4 – 250/356-5360; Fax: 250/356-9444; URL: http://www.labour.gov.bc.ca/bclfdb/welcome.htm
CEO, Lee Doney, 250/356-9232
Co-Chair, Business, Stu Noble, 250/356-9232
Co-Chair, Labour, Marion Meagher, 250/356-9232
• Employment Standards Tribunal: #504, 815 Hornby St., Vancouver BC V6Z 2E6 – 604/775-3512; Fax: 604/775-3372
Chair, Geoffrey Crampton
• Labour Relations Board: 1125 Howe St., Vancouver BC V6Z 2K8 – 604/660-1300; Fax: 604/660-1892
Commissioner, Stan Lanyon
Registrar, Margaret Arthur
• Workers' Compensation Board: 6951 Westminster Hwy., Richmond BC V7C 1C6 – 604/273-2266; Fax: 604/276-3151
President & CEO, Dale Parker, 604/276-3190
Vice-President, Prevention Division, Ralph McGinn
Vice-President, Compensation Division, Ron Buchhorn
Vice-President, Finance & Information Services, Sid Fattedad
Vice-President, Human Resources & Corporate Development, David Anderson
Vice-President, Prevention Division, Ralph McGinn
• Workers' Compensation Review Board: #200, 1700 West 75 Ave., Vancouver BC V6P 6G2 – 604/664-7800; Fax: 604/664-7898
Chair, P. Michael O'Brien

Ministry of MUNICIPAL AFFAIRS & HOUSING (MAFF)
Municipal Affairs, PO Box 9490, Victoria BC V8W 9N7
250/387-4089; Fax: 250/356-1070; URL: http://www.marh.gov.bc.ca/
Housing, PO Box 9491, Victoria BC V8W 9N7

ACTS ADMINISTERED
Assessment Act
Assessment Authority Act
Building Safety Standards Act
Cultus Lake Park Act
Electrical Safety Act
Elevating Devices Safety Act
Fire Services Act
Fireworks Act
Gas Safety Act
Greater Nanaimo Water District Act
Greater Vancouver Sewerage & Drainage District Act
Greater Vancouver Water District Act
Home Owner Grant Act
Islands Trust Act
Library Act
Library Foundation of British Columbia Act
Local Government Grants Act
Local Services Act
Manufactured Home Tax Act
Ministry of Labour Act
Ministry of Lands, Parks & Housing Act (sections 5 (c) and 10)
Ministry of Municipal Affairs Act
Mountain Resort Associations Act
Municipal Act (except part 20)
Municipal Aid Act
Municipal Expenditure Restraint Act
Municipal Finance Authority Act
Municipal Improvements Assistance Enabling Act
Municipalities Assistance Act
Municipalities Enabling & Validating Act
Municipalities Enabling & Validaing Act (No.2)
New Westminster Redevelopment Act
Power Engineers & Boiler & Pressure Vessel Safety Act
Provincial-Municipal Partnership Act
Railway Act
Resort Municipality of Whistler Act
Sechelt Indian Government District Enabling Act
Sechelt Indian Government District Home Owner Grant Act
Shelter Aid for Elderly Renters Act
Tourist Accomodation Act
University Endowment Act
Vancouver Charter (not a public act)
Minister, Hon. Dan Miller, 250/387-3602, Fax: 250/387-1334
Deputy Minister, Suzanne Veit, 250/387-4104, Fax: 250/387-7973
Asst. Deputy Minister & Inspector, Office of the Inspector of Municipalities, Ken MacLeod, 205/356-6575, Fax: 205/387-7973
Executive Director, Human & Corporate Development, Lorne Bulmer, 250/387-9193

Canadian Almanac & Directory 1997

LOCAL GOVERNMENT SERVICES
Executive Director, David G. Morris, 250/356-7377, Fax: 250/387-4048
Program Administrator, Downtown Revitalization, Martin Thomas, 250/387-4090
Director, Library Services, Barbara Greeniaus, 250/356-1795, Fax: 250/387-4048
Director, Municipal Administrative Services, Norm McCrimmon, 250/387-4022
Director, Municipal Financial Services, Al Tamblin, 250/387-4067
Director, Municipal Investigations, Fred Thompson, 250/387-4098
Director, Planning Branch, Erik Karlsen, 250/387-4039
Director, Policy & Research, Brian Walisser, 250/387-4050

SAFETY & STANDARDS DEPARTMENT
Asst. Deputy Minister, Gary Harkness, 250/387-4095, Fax: 250/387-7973
Commissioner, Office of the Fire Commissioner, Rick Dumala, 250/356-9000, Fax: 250/356-9019
Director, Boiler & Pressure Vessel Safety, Allan Pringle, 604/660-6251
Director, Building Standards, Jack Robertson, 250/387-4011, Fax: 250/356-9019
Director, Electrical Safety, Roy Broderick, 604/660-6261
Director, Elevating Devices, Allan Pringle, 604/660-6204
Director, Engineering & Inspection, Fleming Christensen, 604/660-5960, Fax: 604/660-5997
Director, Gas Safety, Gordon Cherry, 604/669-6235
Director, Safety Engineering Services, Harry Diemer, 604/660-6294

Associated Agencies, Boards & Commissions
• Assessment Appeal Board: #101, 22356 McIntosh Ave., Maple Ridge BC V2X 3C1 – 604/463-9300; Fax: 604/467-3892
• Board of Examiners: 800 Johnson St., Victoria BC V8V 1X4 – 250/387-4053
Secretary, Mary Harkness
• British Columbia Assessment Authority: 1537 Hillside Ave., Victoria BC V8T 4Y2 – 250/595-6211; Fax: 250/595-6222
Chair, David Driscoll
Assessment Commissioner & CEO, Thomas Johnstone
Director, Communications, Nigel Atkin
• British Columbia Housing Management Commission/BC Housing (BCHMC): #1701, 4330 Kingsway, Burnaby BC V5H 4G7 – 604/433-1711; Fax: 604/439-4722
Acting General Manager, Robert McDiarmid, 604/439-4903
Acting Supervisor, Shelter Aid for Elderly Renters, Debbie Richie, 1175 Douglas St., 4th Fl., Victoria BC V8W 2E1, 250/387-3461, Fax: 250/387-4264
Director, Housing & Community Services Branch, Janet Austin, 604/439-4721
Director, Corporate Services Branch, Peter Stobie, 604/439-4732
Director, Development Services, Jim Woodward, 604/439-4721
• Islands Trust: 1627 Fort St., 2nd. Fl., Victoria BC V8R 1H8 – 250/387-4000; Fax: 250/387-4047
Chair, Graeme Dinsdale
Executive Director, Gordon McIntosh

Office of the OMBUDSMAN
931 Fort St., Victoria BC V8V 3K3
250/387-5855; Fax: 250/387-0198; URL: http://www.ombud.gov.bc.ca/
Toll Free: 1-800-567-3247
Ombudsman, S. Dulcie McCallum, Email: dmccallu@dgvic2.ombd.gov.bc.ca

Deputy Ombudsman, D. Brent Parfitt, Email: bparfitt@dgvic2.ombd.gov.bc.ca
Librarian, Caroline Daniels, 250/356-5725

VANCOUVER OFFICE OF THE OMBUDSMAN
1111 Melville St., Vancouver BC V6E 3V6
250/387-5855; Fax: 250/660-1691
Toll Free: 1-800-567-3247

British Columbia PAVILION CORPORATION
#600, 375 Water St., Vancouver BC V6B 5C6
604/687-3800; Fax: 604/681-9017
President & CEO, Warren Buckley
Vice-President & General Manager, Vancouver Trade & Convention Centre, Barry Smith
Vice-President & General Manager, BC Place Stadium, Neil Campbell
Director, Marketing, Brenda Sandes
Manager, Communications, Ray LeBlond

British Columbia PROVINCIAL EMERGENCY PROGRAM (PEP)
455 Boleskine Rd., Victoria BC V8Z 1E7
250/387-5956; Fax: 250/952-4888; URL: http://hoshi.cic.sfu.ca/ZXpep/
Emergency Coordination Centre (24-hour): 1-800-663-3456

Coordinates emergency planning in provincial government departments throught the Interagency Emergency Preparedness Council.

The Program provides advice, assistance & training to local governments & industry in the preparation of emergency plans. It also promotes public awareness of the need for preparedness & coordinates response to emergencies. PEP operates the Government Emergency Operations Centre for major emergencies. The organization is also responsible for the Disaster Financial Assistance Program (DFA) & supports the Canadian Armed Forces & police in search & rescue through the use of volunteers. PEP operations are administered by the British Columbia Ministry of Attorney General.

ACTS ADMINISTERED
Emergency Program Act & Regulations 1993
Director, A.J. (Tony) Heemskerk, Email: theemske@pep.bc.ca
Manager, Operations, Geoff Amy, Email: gamy@pep.bc.ca
Manager, Policy & Plans, Claude Dalley, Email: cdalley@pep.bc.ca

Ministry of SMALL BUSINESS, TOURISM & CULTURE (SBTC)
1117 Wharf St., Victoria BC V8W 2Z2
250/356-6363 (Tourism); Fax: 250/356-8248; URL: http://www.tbc.gov.bc.ca/homepage.html
250/356-1718 (Culture)

The ministry enhances community & regional development & strengthens the province's small business, tourism & culture sectors. The ministry encourages innovation, leadership & excellence & provides access to government information, programs & services. SBTC also promotes the diversification of local economies & the development of strategic alliances & partnerships with communities, organizations, industry & government.

ACTS ADMINISTERED
British Columbia Enterprise Corporation Act (in relation to the BC Pavilion Corporation)
Cultural Foundation of British Columbia Act
Heritage Conservation Act
Employee Investment Act
Hotel Guest Registration Act
Hotel Keepers Act

Industrial Development Incentive Act (in relation to the Small Business Incentive Program)
Ministry of Industry & Small Business Development Act (in relation to small business)
Ministry of Transportation & Highways Act, sections 61-67
Museum Act
Pacific National Exhibition Incorporation Act
Small Business Venture Capital Act
Travel Regulation Act
Minister, Hon. Jan Pullinger
Deputy Minister, Cassie Doyle, 250/356-2175, Fax: 250/387-1420
Asst. Deputy Minister, Management Services, Rhonda Hunter, 250/387-0111, Fax: 250/387-1420
Director, Central Services, Gary Loat, 250/356-7117, Fax: 250/356-5511
Director, Communications, Patricia Derrick, 250/356-6305, Fax: 250/387-3798

COMMUNITY & REGIONAL DEVELOPMENT DIVISION
1405 Douglas St., 4th Fl., Victoria BC V8W 3C1
250/356-7363; Fax: 250/387-5633
Asst. Deputy Minister, Catherine Read, 250/356-2124
Acting Director, Business Equity Branch, Murray Munro, 250/387-0225, 844-1823 (Vancouver), Fax: 250/387-1080
Director, Client Ministries & Regional Support Services, A. Paxton Mann, 250/356-2038, Fax: 250/387-5633
Director, Economic Analysis & Development Branch, Joan Easton, 250/356-2034, Fax: 250/356-8948
Director, Small Business Development Branch, Murray Munro, 250/387-6025, Fax: 250/387-1080
Businesswomen's Advocate, Kathleen Costello, 250/356-5118, Fax: 250/356-8498

Regional Management Units
Kamloops: #302, 186 Victoria St., Kamloops BC V2C 5R3 – 250/371-3882; Fax: 250/371-3888, Regional Director, John McGuire
Nanaimo: BC Access Centre, 13 Victoria Cres., Nanaimo BC V9R 5B9 – 250/741-3634; Fax: 250/741-3633, Regional Director, John Dyble
Nelson: BC Access Centre, 310 Ward St., Nelson BC V1L 5S4 – 250/354-6113; Fax: 250/354-6680, Regional Director, Peter Levy
Prince George: BC Access Centre, 433 Queensway, Prince George BC V2L 5M2 – 250/565-6998; Fax: 250/565-4222, Regional Director, John Metcalfe
Terrace: BC Access Centre, #102, 3220 Eby St., Terrace BC V8G 5K8 – 250/638-3570; Fax: 250/638-5053, Regional Director, Harold Demetzer

Business Information Centres
Vancouver: 601 Cordova St. West, Vancouver BC V6B 1G1 – 604/660-3900; Fax: 604/660-4166, Marcis Esmits
Victoria: 712 Yates St., 2nd Fl., Victoria BC V8V 1X4 – 250/356-5777; Fax: 250/356-5951, Chuck Dary

CULTURE DIVISION
URL: http://www.tbc.gov.bc.ca/culture/culture-home.html
Asst. Deputy Minister, David Richardson, 250/387-0106, Fax: 250/387-4099
Director, Archaeology Branch, Brian Apland, 250/356-1049, Fax: 250/387-4420
Director, BC Film Commission, Peter Mitchell, 604/660-2732, Fax: 604/660-4790
Director, Cultural Services Branch, Richard Brownsey, 250/356-1721, Fax: 250/387-4420
Director, Heritage Conservation Branch, Wayne Carter, 250/356-1434, Fax: 250/356-7796
Director, Recreation Branch, Russell Irvine, 250/356-1160, Fax: 250/387-4253

Director, Sport Services, Bob Bearpark, 250/356-1178, Fax: 250/387-1407
Executive Director, BC Games Society, Roger Skillings, #200, 990 Fort St., Victoria BC V8V 3K2, 250/387-4684, Fax: 250/387-4489

TOURISM DIVISION
URL: http://www.tbc.gov.bc.ca/tourism/tourism-home.html
Asst. Deputy Minister, Rod Harris, 250/356-2026, Fax: 250/356-6988
Executive Director, Tourism Services, Rick Lemon, 250/387-0130, Fax: 250/356-6988
Director, Industry Development, Denise Hayes, 250/387-6929, Fax: 250/387-2305
Director, Marketing, Don Foxgord, 604/660-3754, Fax: 604/660-3383

Associated Agencies, Boards & Commissions
• British Columbia Arts Council: 800 Johnson St., 5th Fl., Victoria BC V8V 1X4 – 250/356-1718
Chair, Mavor Moore
• British Columbia Festival of the Arts Society: 3577 Douglas St., Victoria BC V8Z 3L6 – 250/383-4214
• British Columbia Heritage Trust: 800 Johnson St., 5th Fl., Victoria BC V8V 1X4 – 250/356-1433; Fax: 250/356-7796
A Crown Corporation providing support for community-based heritage projects through a variety of programs.
Executive Officer, Colin Campbell

Ministry of SOCIAL SERVICES
Parliament Bldgs., 614 Humboldt St., 7th Fl., Victoria BC V8V 1X4
250/387-6485; Fax: 250/356-7801
Note: This ministry was undergoing reorganization at time of publishing. Responsibilities now lie within two newly created ministries, the Ministry of Children & Families & the Ministry of Human Resources. Specific information concerning departmental responsibilities were not known at time of publishing. The names & numbers of individuals listed below should remain relatively intact, however it may be necessary to contact the Deputy Minister's office for more information.

ACTS ADMINISTERED
Adoption Act
Child, Family & Community Service Act
Child, Youth & Family Advocacy Act
Community Resource Board Act
Family & Child Service Act
Guaranteed Available Income for Need Act
Human Resource Facility Act
Ministry of Social Services & Housing Act
Residence & Responsibility Act
Social Workers Act
Minister, Hon. Dennis Streifel, 250/387-3180, Fax: 250/387-5720
Deputy Minister, Brenda Eaton, 250/387-3121, Fax: 250/387-5775
Director, Communications Division, Carol Carman, 250/387-6485, Fax: 250/356-7801
Executive Director, Policy Planning & Research Division, Garry Curtis, 250/387-7036, Fax: 250/387-2418

CHILD, FAMILY & COMMUNITY SERVICE
Asst. Deputy Minister, Chris Haynes, 250/387-6905, Fax: 250/387-2418
Asst. Deputy Director, Rita Maybin, 250/387-7091, Fax: 250/387-7914
Director, Child, Family & Community Services Division, Jeremy Berland, 250/387-7060, Fax: 250/356-7862
Deputy Director, Aboriginal Services, Mavis Henry, 250/387-7091, Fax: 250/387-7914

Director, Audit & Review Division, Judy Hayes, 604/660-1828, Fax: 604/660-2383
Acting Manager, Adoption Programs, Trudy Usher, 250/387-3660, Fax: 250/356-7862

COMMUNITY SUPPORT SERVICES
Asst. Deputy Minister, Theresa Kerin, 250/387-3159, Fax: 250/387-2418
Director, Information & Privacy Division, Al Boyd, 250/387-0820, Fax: 250/387-0817
Director, Community Placement Project (Coquitlam), Gillian Chetty, 604/660-8477, Fax: 604/660-8810
Director, Community Support Services Division, Paula Grant, 250/387-1275, Fax: 250/356-6534
Director, Services for Community Living, Peter Melhuish, 250/952-2722, Fax: 250/952-2723
Manager, Adult Residential Care, Frank Van Zandwijk, 250/387-1275, Fax: 250/356-6534
Manager, Children with Special Needs, Kate Irving, 250/387-1275, Fax: 250/356-6534
Manager, Day Care Subsidies/Community Projects, Pieta Van Dyke, 250/387-1275, Fax: 250/356-6534
Manager, Day Programs (adults with mental handicaps), Randi Mjolsness, 250/387-1275, Fax: 250/356-6534
Coordinator, Senior Citizen Counsellors, Barb Wilson, 250/387-1275, Fax: 250/356-6534

INCOME SUPPORT
Asst. Deputy Minister, Lyn Tait, 7, 250/387-3122, Fax: 250/387-2418
Director, Federal-Provincial Activities Division, Ken Armour, 250/387-4552, Fax: 250/356-8182
Director, Health Services Division, Susan Doyle, 250/387-5664, Fax: 250/356-7290
Director, Income Assistance Division, Isobel Donovan, 250/387-1486, Fax: 250/387-8164
Director, Prevention, Compliance & Enforcement, Mervin Harrower, 250/387-8200, Fax: 250/356-8182
Manager, Emergency Social Services, Ivan Carlson, 250/387-0030, Fax: 250/387-2364

MANAGEMENT SERVICES
Asst. Deputy Minister, Les Foster, 250/387-3124, Fax: 250/387-2418
Director, Administrative Services Division, Morris Wadds, 250/387-3411, Fax: 250/356-7346
Director, Financial Planning Division, Glen Nuttall, 250/387-5035, Fax: 250/356-9799
Director, Financial Services Division, Stew Churlish, 250/387-4415, Fax: 250/356-9637
Director, Human Resources Division, Judith McDonald, 250/387-4511, Fax: 250/387-1610
Director, Systems Services Division (Vancouver), Terry Pollard, 604/660-1600, Fax: 604/660-1821

REGIONAL OPERATIONS
Asst. Deputy Minister, Chris Haynes, 250/387-6905, Fax: 250/387-2418
Regional Director, Fraser North, Jean Macdonald, 604/527-1270, Fax: 604/524-1278
Regional Director, Fraser South, David Young, 604/576-0753, Fax: 604/576-0759
Regional Director, North Vancouver Island, Wayne Ironmonger, 250/741-5600, Fax: 250/741-5606
Regional Director, Okanagan/Kootenays, Larry Ohlmann, 250/470-0888, Fax: 250/470-0890
Regional Director, Prince George & North, Cam Millar, 250/565-6220, Fax: 250/565-6366
Regional Director, Richmond/Burnaby/North Shore/Howe Sound, Elaine Murray, 604/660-0202, Fax: 604/660-5049
Regional Director, South Central Interior, Wrenn Weston, 250/828-4600, Fax: 250/828-4756
Regional Director, South Vancouver Island, Jane Cowell, 250/952-5210, Fax: 250/952-4346
Regional Director, Vancouver, Fred Milowsky, 604/660-2433, Fax: 604/660-4005

Ministry of TRANSPORTATION & HIGHWAYS
940 Blanshard St., Victoria BC V8W 3E6
250/387-7788 (Public Affairs); Fax: 250/356-7706
Provides & maintains safe & efficient movement of people & resources on a multi-modal tranportation network in a socially & environmentally acceptable manner. The ministry also responds to major transportation emergencies & disasters.
The ministry is responsible for the planning, building & maintaining of the provincial road & bridge system. Supports the development of community transportation systems through several programs including: Municipal Restructuring, Urban Renewal, Arterial Highway Beautification, Secondary Highways & Cycling Network Grants.
The Motor Vehicle Branch is the provincial body responsible for issuing & regulating driving standards & drivers licences, & private & commercial enforcement & compliance programs. The branch also levies & collects motor vehicle fees, fines & other applicable taxes.

ACTS ADMINISTERED
British Columbia Railway Act
Coquihalla Highway Construction Acceleration Act
Ferry Act
Highway Act
Highway (Industrial) Act
Highways Scenic Improvements Act
Insurance Corporation Act
Insurance (Motor Vehicle) Act
Motor Carrier Act
Motor Vehicle Act
Railway Act
Riverbank Protection Act
Minister, Hon. Lois Boone
Deputy Minister, Vince Collins, 250/387-3280, Fax: 250/387-6431

ADMINISTRATIVE SERVICES DEPARTMENT
Asst. Deputy Minister, Gordon Hogg, 250/387-5062, Fax: 250/387-7706
Director, Finance & Administration Branch, Bob Buckingham, 250/387-3100
Director, Information Services Branch, Floyd A. Mailhot, 250/387-1457
Director, Personnel Services Branch, Barry T. Wilton, 250/387-5539
Director, Public Affairs Branch, Philip Newton, 250/387-3198

HIGHWAY OPERATIONS DEPARTMENT
Asst. Deputy Minister, Dan Doyle, 250/387-3260, Fax: 250/387-6431
Director, Aboriginal Issues Project, Mary Koyl, 250/387-5925
Chief Highway Engineer, Professional Services Division, Earl A. Lund, 250/387-6772
Director, Bridge Engineering Branch, Peter H. Brett, 250/387-3267
Director, Geotechnical & Materials Engineering Branch, Orlando Tisot, 250/387-1881
Director, Highway Engineering Branch, Merv Clark, 250/356-7747
Director, Highway Safety Branch, Lorne Holowachuk, P.Eng., 250/387-5838
Director, Maintenance Services Branch, W.C. Bedford, 250/387-8626
Director, Properties Branch, Stewart N. Logan, 250/387-1838

MOTOR VEHICLE BRANCH
2631 Douglas St., Victoria BC V8T 5A3
250/387-3140; Fax: 250/387-1169
Asst. Deputy Minister/Superintendent, Steve Rumsey, 250/387-3437

Canadian Almanac & Directory 1997

Executive Director, Operations Division/Deputy Superintendent, Craig Morris, 250/387-6278
Executive Director, Policy & Program Development Division, Mark Medgyesi, 250/387-1752
Director, Information Technology Division, Karen Dellert, 250/356-1274
Director, Inspection & Carrier Safety, Vacant, 250/387-6634, Fax: 250/356-8986
Director, Management Services Division, Brian Sibley, 250/356-6197
Director, Planning & Corporate Development Division, Drew Ritchie, 250/387-1869

PLANNING & MAJOR PROJECTS DEPARTMENT
Asst. Deputy Minister, Bruce McKeown, 250/387-6742, Fax: 250/387-6431
Director, Highway Planning Branch, Tim Stevens, 250/387-7540
Director, Planning Services Branch, Richard H. Dixon, 250/356-5156
Senior Policy Advisor, Policy Branch, Sam Brand, 250/387-5997
Asst. Senior Manager, Major Projects Branch, Dave Ferguson, 250/387-7560

Associated Agencies, Boards & Commissions
•British Columbia Transit: 13401 - 108th Ave., Surrey BC V3T 5T4 – 604/264-5000; Fax: 604/264-5029
President & CEO, Michael O'Connor
General Manager, Victoria Office, Rogert Lingwood, 250/385-2551
•British Columbia Transportation Financing Authority: 2250 Granville Square, Vancouver BC V6C 1S4 – 604/775-1174; Fax: 604/775-2792
President & CEO, Blair Redlin
•Motor Carrier Commission: #200, 703 Broughton St., Victoria BC V8W 1E2 – 250/953-3777; Fax: 250/953-3788
Chair, Donald Johannessen

TREASURY BOARD SECRETARIAT
#248, Legislative Bldgs., Victoria BC V8V 1X4
250/387-6210; Fax: 250/387-9099
Chair, Hon. Andrew Petter, 250/387-3751, Fax: 250/387-5594
Secretary, Garry Wouters, 250/387-6206, Fax: 250/387-9099

British Columbia UTILITIES COMMISSION
900 Howe St., 6th Fl., Vancouver BC V6Z 2N3
604/660-4700; Fax: 604/660-1102; Email: bcuc@pop.gov.bc.ca
Toll Free: 1-800-663-1385 (in B.C. only)
Acts as a regulatory agency for electric, gas & steam utilities & is responsible for major energy project reviews.
Chair & CEO, Dr. Mark K. Jaccard, 604/660-4757
Deputy Chair, Lorna R. Barr
Asst. to Chair & Deputy Chair, Marilyn E. Donn, Email: medonn@pop.gov.bc.ca
Commission Secretary, Robert J. Pellatt

Ministry of WOMEN'S EQUALITY
Parliament Bldgs., 756 Fort St., Victoria BC V8V 1X4
250/387-3600; Fax: 250/356-1396;
URL: http:www.weq.gov.bc.ca/
Agency created with the purpose of providing equality to women by ensuring the consideration of women's concerns in government decisions. The ministry works closely with other government ministries & agencies to develop policy, legislation, services & programs to promote the awareness of women's issues, stop violence against women & promote equality.
Minister, Hon. Sue Hammell, 250/387-1223, Fax: 250/387-4312
Deputy Minister, Eloise Spitzer, 250/387-0413, Fax: 250/356-9377
Asst. Deputy Minister, Policy, Planning & Evaluation, Valerie Mitchell, 250/953-3466, Fax: 250/356-6072, Email: vmitchell@galaxy.gov.bc.ca
Asst. Deputy Minister, Programs, Dyan Dunsmoor-Farley, 250/387-3616, Email: ddunsmoorfar@galaxy.gov.bc.ca
Director, Communications, Sharlene Smith, 250/953-4570, Email: sfsmith@galaxy.gov.bc.ca

GOVERNMENT OF MANITOBA

Seat of Government: Legislative Bldg., Winnipeg MB R3C 0V8
URL: http://www.gov.mb.ca/
Toll Free: URL: http://www.gov.mb.ca
The Province of Manitoba entered Confederation July 15, 1870. It has an area of 547,703.85 km2, and the StatsCan census population in 1991 was 1,091,942.

Office of the LIEUTENANT GOVERNOR
Legislative Bldg., #235, 450 Broadway, Winnipeg MB R3C 0V8
204/945-2753; Fax: 204/945-4329
Lieutenant Governor, Hon. W. Yvon Dumont
Executive Asst., Georgina Buddick

Office of the PREMIER
Legislative Bldg., #204, 450 Broadway, Winnipeg MB R3C 0V8
204/945-3714; Fax: 204/949-1484; Email: premier@leg.gov.mb.ca; URL: http://www.gov.mb.ca/text/quotepg1.html
Premier, Hon. Gary Filmon, Email: premier@leg.gov.mb.ca
Deputy Premier, Hon. James Downey
Clerk of the Executive Council & Deputy Minister, Donald A. Leitch, 204/945-5640, Fax: 204/945-8390
Executive Asst. to the Premier, Lizanne Lachance-Mann, 204/945-2113
Director, Cabinet Communications Secretariat, Bonnie Staples, 204/945-1494
Director, Policy Management Secretariat, Hugh McFadyen, 204/945-0723
Chief of Staff, Taras Sokolyk, 204/945-5642
Secretary, Vacant, 204/945-3593
Secretary to Cabinet for Intergovernmental Relations, Jim Eldridge, 204/945-5343

MANITOBA GOVERNMENT OFFICE - OTTAWA
#512, 90 Sparks St., Ottawa ON K1P 5B4
613/233-4228; Fax: 613/233-3509
Reports to the Clerk of the Executive Council on Federal-Provincial issues & to the Minister of Industry, Trade & Tourism on business & procurement issues.
Senior Representative, John Blackwood

EXECUTIVE COUNCIL
Legislative Bldg., Winnipeg MB R3C 0V8
Premier, President, Executive Council & Minister, Federal-Provincial Relations, Hon. Gary Filmon, 204/945-3714, Fax: 204/949-1484, Email: premier@leg.gov.mb.ca
Deputy Premier & Minister, Industry, Trade & Tourism, Hon. James Downey, 204/945-0067, Fax: 204/945-4882, Email: minitt@leg.gov.mb.ca
Minister, Environment, Hon. J. Glen Cummings, 204/945-3522, Fax: 204/942-1127, Email: minenv@leg.gov.mb.ca
Minister, Rural Development, Hon. Leonard Derkach, 204/945-3788, Fax: 204/945-1383, Email: minrd@leg.gov.mb.ca
Minister, Natural Resources, Hon. Albert Driedger, 204/945-3730, Fax: 204/945-3586, Email: minnr@leg.gov.mb.ca
Minister, Agriculture, Hon. Harry Enns, 204/945-3722, Fax: 204/945-3470, Email: minagr@leg.gov.mb.ca
Minister, Consumer & Corporate Affairs, Minister Responsible, Sport & Government House Leader, Hon. James A. Ernst, 204/945-4256, Fax: 204/945-4009, Email: mincca@leg.gov.mb.ca
Minister, Highways & Transportation, Hon. Glen Findlay, 204/945-3723, Fax: 204/945-7610, Email: minhwy@leg.gov.mb.ca
Minister, Culture, Heritage & Citizenship & Minister Responsible, Multiculturalism, Hon. Harold Gilleshammer, 204/945-3729, Fax: 204/945-5223, Email: minchC@leg.gov.mb.ca
Minister, Health, Hon. James C. McCrae, 204/945-3731, Fax: 204/945-0441, Email: minhlt@leg.gov.mb.ca
Minister, Education & Training, Hon. Linda G. McIntosh, 204/945-3720, Fax: 204/945-1291, Email: minedu@leg.gov.mb.ca
Minister, Family Services, Hon. Bonnie E. Mitchelson, 204/945-4173, Fax: 204/945-5149, Email: minfam@leg.gov.mb.ca
Minister, Government Services, Hon. Brian W. Pallister, 204/945-2979, Fax: 204/945-7331, Email: mings@leg.gov.mb.ca
Minister, Northern Affairs & Minister, Energy & Mines, Hon. Darren T. Praznik, 204/945-3719, Fax: 204/945-8374, Email: minem@leg.gov.mb.ca, Email: minna@leg.gov.mb.ca
Minister, Urban Affairs & Minister, Housing, Hon. Jack F. Reimer, 204/945-0074, Fax: 204/945-1299, Email: minhou@leg.gov.mb.ca, Email: minua@leg.gov.mb.ca
Minister, Finance, Hon. Eric Stefanson, 204/945-3952, Fax: 204/945-6057, Email: minfin@leg.gov.mb.ca
Minister, Labour, Hon. Victor E. Toews, 204/945-4079, Fax: 204/945-8312, Email: minlab@leg.gov.mb.ca
Minister, Justice & Attorney General & Minister Responsible, Status of Women, Hon. Rosemary Vodrey, 204/945-3728, Fax: 204/945-2517, Email: minjus@leg.gov.mb.ca

Cabinet Office
Clerk, Executive Council, Donald A. Leitch, 204/945-5640, Fax: 204/945-8390
Legislative Asst., Agriculture, Frank Pitura, 204/945-4519, Fax: 204/948-2092
Legislative Asst., Culture, Heritage & Citizenship, Michael Radcliffe, 204/945-4609, Fax: 204/945-1284
Legislative Asst., Education & Training, Peter George Dyck, 204/945-4469, Fax: 204/948-2092
Legislative Asst., Industry, Trade & Tourism, Gerry McAlpine, 204/945-1583, Fax: 204/948-2092
Legislative Asst., Justice, David Newman, 204/945-3871, Fax: 204/945-5921
Legislative Asst., Rural Development, Mervin Tweed, 204/945-4198, Fax: 204/948-2092

Cabinet Committees
Assessment Reform
Economic Development Board
Joint Council
Multicultural Affairs
Native Affairs
Provincial Land Use
Regulatory Review
Sustainable Development
Treasure Board Committee
Urban Affairs

LEGISLATIVE ASSEMBLY

c/o Clerk's Office, Legislative Bldg., #237, 450 Broadway Ave., Winnipeg MB R3C 0V8
204/945-3707; Fax: 204/948-2507; URL: http://www.gov.mb.ca/leg-asmb/index1.html
Hansard URL: http://www.gov.mb.ca/leg-asmb/hansard/index.html
Clerk: W.H. Remnant
Speaker: Hon. Louise M. Dacquay
Sergeant-at-Arms: Dennis Gray
Manager, Hansard: Edith McLure
Law Officer, Shirley Strutt
Deputy Clerk, B. Bosiak

Government Caucus Office (PC)
Legislative Bldg., #227, 450 Broadway Ave., Winnipeg MB R3C 0V8
204/945-3709; Fax: 204/945-1284; Email: filmonteam@manpc.nb.ca
Chief of Staff, Heather Campbell-Dewar

Official Opposition Office (NDP)
Legislative Bldg., #234, 450 Broadway Ave., Winnipeg MB R3C 0V8
204/945-3710; Fax: 204/945-0535; Email: ndpmb@mbnet.mb.ca
Leader, Gary Doer, 204/945-4484
Chief of Staff & Director, Research, David Woodbury
Executive Asst., Terry Goertzen, 204/945-4482
Deputy Leader, Jean Friesen
Administrative Secretary, Jeannette Lanthier, 204/945-4484

Office of the Liberal Party (Lib.)
Legislative Bldg., #151, 450 Broadway Ave., Winnipeg MB R3C 0V8
204/945-1793; Fax: 204/945-0874; Email: liberal@freenet.mb.ca
Leader, Paul Edwards, 204/942-3361, Fax: 204/943-4498
Leader's Asst., Julia Panchyshyn, 204/942-3361
Researcher, Andy Drummond, 204/945-1793

Legislative Committees
Legislative Bldg., #249, 450 Broadway Ave., Winnipeg MB R3C 0V8
Fax: 204/245-0038
Committee Contact, Patricia Chaychk, 204/945-0796
Committee Contact, Judy White, 204/945-4729
Agriculture
Economic Development
Industrial Relations
Law Amendments
Municipal Affairs
Private Bills
Privileges & Elections
Public Accounts
Public Utilities & Natural Resources
Rules of the House
Statutory Regulations & Orders

THIRTY-SIXTH LEGISLATURE - MANITOBA
204/945-3707
Last General Election: April 25, 1995. Legal Duration, 5 Years.
Party Standings (June 27, 1995):
Progressive Conservative (PC) 31
New Democratic Party (NDP) 23
Liberal (Lib.) 3
Total 57

Salaries, Indemnities & Allowances: Members' annual indemnity $57,065. In addition to this are the following:
Premier $40,400
Ministers (with portfolio); Leader of the Opposition $25,250
Ministers (without portfolio); Leader of the Second Opposition $25,250
Speaker $21,210
Manitoba has a cost of living indexing system as prescribed by Sec. 53(3) of the Legislative Assembly Act.

Following is: constituency (number of eligible voters at 1995 election) member, party affiliation. (Address for all is Legislative Bldg., Winnipeg, MB R3C 0V8).
Refer to Cabinet List, Caucus Offices, for **phone** & **fax** numbers.

MEMBERS BY CONSTITUENCY
Arthur-Virden (12,045) Hon. James Downey, PC
Assiniboia (11,545) Hon. Linda G. McIntosh, PC
Brandon East (13,037) Leonard S. Evans, NDP
Brandon West (13,407) Hon. James C. McCrae, PC
Broadway (10,883) Conrad Santos, NDP
Burrows (11,103) Doug Martindale, NDP
Charleswood (13,296) Hon. James A. Ernst, PC
Concordia (11,401) Gary Doer, NDP
Crescentwood (14,202) Tim Sale, Lib.
Dauphin (12,460) Stan Struthers, NDP
Elmwood (11,734) Jim Maloway, NDP
Emerson (11,958) Jack Penner, PC
Flin Flon (9,225) Gerard Jennissen, NDP
Fort Garry (17,418) Hon. Rosemary Vodrey, PC
Gimli (14,758) Ed Helwer, PC
Gladstone (12,136) Denis Rocan, PC
Inkster (12,989) Kevin Lamoureaux, Lib.
Interlake (11,602) Clif Evans, NDP
Kildonan (15,106) Dave Chomiak, NDP
Kirkfield Park (13,202) Hon. Eric Stefanson, PC
La Verendrye (12,777) Ben Sveinson, PC
Lac du Bonnet (13,846) Hon. Darren Praznik, PC
Lakeside (11,877) Hon. Harry Enns, PC
Minnedosa (12,593) Hon. Harold Gilleshammer, PC
Morris (13,104) Frank Pitura, PC
Niakwa (15,089) Hon. Jack F. Reimer, PC
Osborne (13,917) Diane McGifford, NDP
Pembina (13,287) Peter George Dyck, PC
Point Douglas (8,569) George Hickes, NDP
Portage la Prairie (11,792) Hon. Brian W. Pallister, PC
Radisson (14,183) Marianne Cerilli, NDP
Riel (12,415) David Newman, PC
River East (13,593) Hon. Bonnie E. Mitchelson, PC
River Heights (13,893) Michael Radcliffe, PC
Roblin-Russell (12,394) Hon. Leonard Derkach, PC
Rossmere (12,234) Hon. Victor E. Toews, PC
Rupertsland (9,924) Eric Robinson, NDP
Seine River (17,525) Hon. Louise M. Dacquay, PC
Selkirk (14,123) Gregory Dewar, NDP
Springfield (15,809) Hon. Glen Findlay, PC
St. Boniface (12,459) Neil Gaudry, Lib.
St. James (11,895) Mary Ann Mihychuk, NDP
St. Johns (11,482) Gord Mackintosh, NDP
St. Norbert (14,971) Marcel Laurendeau, PC
St. Vital (13,037) Shirley Render, PC
Ste. Rose (11,532) Hon. J. Glen Cummings, PC
Steinbach (13,710) Hon. Albert Driedger, PC
Sturgeon Creek (13,710) Gerry McAlpine, PC
Swan River (11,643) Rosann Wowchuk, NDP
The Maples (13,402) Gary Kowalski, Lib.
The Pas (12,056) Oscar Lathlin, NDP
Thompson (10,724) Steve Ashton, NDP
Transcona (13,003) Daryl Reid, NDP
Turtle Mountain (11,800) Mervin Tweed, PC
Tuxedo (18,019) Hon. Gary Filmon, PC
Wellington (10,537) Becky Barrett, NDP
Wolseley (10,670) Jean Friesen, NDP

MEMBERS (ALPHABETICAL)
Steve Ashton, Thompson (10,724)NDP
Becky Barrett, Wellington (10,537)NDP
Marianne Cerilli, Radisson (14,183)NDP
Dave Chomiak, Kildonan (15,106)NDP
Hon. J. Glen Cummings, Ste. Rose (11,532)PC
Hon. Louise M. Dacquay, Seine River (17,525)PC
Hon. Leonard Derkach, Roblin-Russell (12,394)PC
Gregory Dewar, Selkirk (14,123)NDP
Gary Doer, Concordia (11,401)NDP
Hon. James Downey, Arthur-Virden (12,045)PC
Hon. Albert Driedger, Steinbach (13,710)PC
Peter George Dyck, Pembina (13,287)PC
Hon. Harry Enns, Lakeside (11,877)PC
Hon. James A. Ernst, Charleswood (13,296)PC
Clif Evans, Interlake (11,602)NDP
Leonard S. Evans, Brandon East (13,037)NDP
Hon. Gary Filmon, Tuxedo (18,019)PC
Hon. Glen Findlay, Springfield (15,809)PC
Jean Friesen, Wolseley (10,670)NDP
Neil Gaudry, St. Boniface (12,459)Lib.
Hon. Harold Gilleshammer, Minnedosa (12,593)PC
Ed Helwer, Gimli (14,758)PC
George Hickes, Point Douglas (8,569)NDP
Gerard Jennissen, Flin Flon (9,225)NDP
Gary Kowalski, The Maples (13,402)Lib.
Kevin Lamoureaux, Inkster (12,989)Lib.
Oscar Lathlin, The Pas (12,056)NDP
Marcel Laurendeau, St. Norbert (14,971)PC
Gord Mackintosh, St. Johns (11,482)NDP
Jim Maloway, Elmwood (11,734)NDP
Doug Martindale, Burrows (11,103)NDP
Gerry McAlpine, Sturgeon Creek (13,710)PC
Hon. James C. McCrae, Brandon West (13,407)PC
Diane McGifford, Osborne (13,917)NDP
Hon. Linda G. McIntosh, Assiniboia (11,545)PC
Mary Ann Mihychuk, St. James (11,895)NDP
Hon. Bonnie E. Mitchelson, River East (13,593)PC
David Newman, Riel (12,415)PC
Hon. Brian W. Pallister, Portage la Prairie (11,792)PC
Jack Penner, Emerson (11,958)PC
Frank Pitura, Morris (13,104)PC
Hon. Darren Praznik, Lac du Bonnet (13,846)PC
Michael Radcliffe, River Heights (13,893)PC
Daryl Reid, Transcona (13,003)NDP
Hon. Jack F. Reimer, Niakwa (15,089)PC
Shirley Render, St. Vital (13,037)PC
Eric Robinson, Rupertsland (9,924)NDP
Denis Rocan, Gladstone (12,136)PC
Tim Sale, Crescentwood (14,202)Lib.
Conrad Santos, Broadway (10,883)NDP
Hon. Eric Stefanson, Kirkfield Park (13,202)PC
Stan Struthers, Dauphin (12,460)NDP
Ben Sveinson, La Verendrye (12,777)PC
Hon. Victor E. Toews, Rossmere (12,234)PC
Mervin Tweed, Turtle Mountain (11,800)PC
Hon. Rosemary Vodrey, Fort Garry (17,418)PC
Rosann Wowchuk, Swan River (11,643)NDP

MANITOBA GOVERNMENT DEPARTMENTS & AGENCIES

Manitoba AGRICULTURE
Norquay Bldg., #809, 401 York Ave., Winnipeg MB R3C 0P8
204/945-3433 (Administration); Fax: 204/945-5024; Email: minagr@leg.gov.mb.ca

ACTS ADMINISTERED
Agricultural Credit Corporation Act
Agricultural Societies Act
Agricultural Productivity Council Act
Agriculture Producers' Organization Funding Act
Department of Agriculture Act
Agrologists Act
Animal Diseases Act
Animal Husbandry Act
Bee Act
Cattle Producers' Association Act
Coarse Grain Marketing Control Act
Crop Insurance Act
Crown Lands Act, (in part) Sections 6, 7, 10, 12(1), 14, 16, 17, 18, 21, 23, 24 to 28 both inclusive

Canadian Almanac & Directory 1997

Dairy Act
Family Farm Protection Act
Farm Income Assurance Plans Act
Farm Lands Ownership Act
Farm Machinery & Equipment Act
Farm Practices Protection Act
Fruit & Vegetable Sales Act
Horse Racing Regulation Act
Horticultural Society Act
Land Rehabilitation Act
Livestock & Livestock Products Act
Margarine Act
Milk Prices Review Act
Natural Products Marketing Act
Noxious Weeds Act
Pesticides & Fertilizers Control Act
Plant Pests & Diseases Act
Seed & Fodder Relief Act
Veterinary Medical Act
Veterinary Science Scholarship Fund Act
Veterinary Services Act
Wildlife Act, (in part) Section 89(e)
Women's Institute Act
Minister, Hon. Harry Enns, 204/945-3722
Deputy Minister, Don Zasada, 204/945-3734, Fax: 204/948-2095

AGRICULTURAL DEVELOPMENT & MARKETING DIVISION
Asst. Deputy Minister, D.I. Donaghy, 204/945-3736
Director, Animal Industry Branch, Agricultural Services Complex, Univ. of Manitoba, Dr. John Taylor, 204/945-7690, Fax: 204/945-4327
Director, Marketing & Farm Business Management Branch, D. Gingera, 204/945-4521
Director, Soils & Crops Branch, Dr. Barry Todd, 65 - 3rd Ave., PO Box 1149, Carman MB R0G 0J0, 204/745-2040, Fax: 204/745-2299
Director, Veterinary Services Branch, Agricultural Services Complex, Univ. of Manitoba, Vacant, 204/945-7647, Fax: 204/945-8062

MANAGEMENT & OPERATIONS DIVISION
Asst. Deputy Minister, R.L. Baseraba, 204/945-3735
Director, Administrative & Accounting Services, M. Robinson, 204/945-3433, Fax: 204/945-5024
Director, Human Resources, M. Robinson, 204/945-3433
Acting Director, Program & Policy Analysis, G.A. Fearn, 204/945-3979
Manager, Computer Services, R. Takeuchi, 204/945-3435
Manager, Financial Administration, M. Richter, 204/945-3306

POLICY & ECONOMICS DIVISION
Asst. Deputy Minister, C. Lee, 204/945-3910

REGIONAL AGRICULTURAL SERVICES DIVISON
Asst. Deputy Minister, R.L. Baseraba, 204/945-3735
Acting Director, Agricultural Crown Lands Branch, R. Chychota, 36 Centre Ave. West, PO Box 1286, Minnedosa MB R0J 1E0, 204/867-3419, Fax: 204/867-5696
Principal, Agricultural Extension Centre, Keith Levenick, 1129 Queens Ave., Brandon MB R7A 1L9, 204/726-6348, Fax: 204/728-8260

Regional Offices
Central: 25 Tupper St. North, Portage la Prairie MB R1N 3K1 – 204/239-3375; Fax: 204/239-3403, Director, Bryan Yusishen
Eastern/Interlake: 20 - 1 St., PO Box 50, Beausejour MB R0E 0C0 – 204/268-6099; Fax: 204/268-3921, Director, A. Dickson
Northwest: 27 - 2 Ave. SW, Dauphin MB R7N 3E5 – 204/622-2027; Fax: 204/638-7201, Director, R. Chychota

Southwest: Agricultural Extension Centre, 1129 Queen's Ave., Brandon MB R7A 1L9 – 204/726-6359; Fax: 204/726-6260, Director, W. Digby

Associated Agencies, Boards & Commissions
•Agricultural Societies Advisory Board: Norquay Bldg., #810, 401 York Ave., Winnipeg MB R3C 0P8 – 204/945-4522; Fax: 204/945-5024
Superintendent, R. Collins
•Farm Machinery Board: Norquay Bldg., #915, 401 York Ave., Winnipeg MB R3C 0P8 – 204/945-3856; Fax: 204/945-6134
Acting Secretary Manager, R. Ozunko
•Farm Lands Ownership Board: #915 Norquay Bldg., 401 York Ave., Winnipeg MB R3C 0P8 – 204/945-3149; Fax: 204/945-6134
Executive Director, H. Nelson
•Manitoba Agricultural Credit Corporation: #100, 1525 - 1 St., Brandon MB R7A 7A1 – 204/726-6850; Fax: 204/726-6849
General Manager, Gill Shaw
•Manitoba Broiler Hatching Egg Commission: #200, 666 St. James St., Winnipeg MB R3G 3J6 – 204/783-8588; Fax: 204/783-8598
Chair, R.W. Scott
•Manitoba Crop Insurance Corporation: #400, 50 - 24 St. NW, Portage la Prairie MB R1N 3V9 – 204/239-3246; Fax: 204/239-3401
General Manager, B. Manning
•Manitoba Farm Mediation Board: #600, 491 Portage Ave., Winnipeg MB R3B 2E4 – 204/945-0358; Fax: 204/945-1489
Executive Director, H. Nelson
•Manitoba Natural Products Marketing Council: #915 Norquay Bldg., 401 York Ave., Winnipeg MB R3C 0P8 – 204/945-4495; Fax: 204/945-6134
Secretary, G. MacKenzie
•Milk Prices Review Commission: #915 Norquay Bldg., 401 York Ave., Winnipeg MB R3C 0P8 – 204/945-0629; Fax: 204/945-6134
Acting Secretary, A. Khan
•National Tripartite Stabilization Program: #300, 50 - 24 St. NW, Portage la Prairie MB R1N 3V8 – 204/239-3232; Fax: 204/857-6597
Manager, Craig Thomson

Agricultural Marketing Boards & Commissions
•Manitoba Chicken Producer Board: 430-A Dovercourt Dr., Winnipeg MB R3Y 1N4 – 204/489-4603; Fax: 204/489-4907
General Manager, K.L. Dexter
•Manitoba Egg Producers' Marketing Board: #18, Waverley Sq., 5 Scurfield Blvd., Winnipeg MB R3Y 1G3 – 204/488-4888; Fax: 204/488-3544
General Manager, P. Kelly
•Manitoba Honey Producers' Marketing Board: #201, 545 University Cres., Winnipeg MB R3T 5S6 – 204/945-3861; Fax: 204/945-3427
Provincial Apiarist, D. Dixon
•Manitoba Milk Producers' Marketing Board: 36 Scurfield Blvd., Winnipeg MB R3T 3N5 – 204/488-6455; Fax: 204/488-4772
•Manitoba Pork Est.: 750 Marion St., Winnipeg MB R2J 0K4 – 204/233-4991; Fax: 204/233-0049
General Manager, R.L. Sedgwick
•Manitoba Turkey Producers' Marketing Board: 430A Dovercourt Dr., Winnipeg MB R3Y 1N4 – 204/489-4635; Fax: 204/489-4907
General Manager, B.F. Waters
•Manitoba Vegetable Producers' Marketing Board: 1200 King Edward St., Winnipeg MB R3H 0R5 – 204/633-7926; Fax: 204/697-0088
General Manager, T.A. Young

Office of the Provincial AUDITOR
405 Broadway, 12th Fl., Winnipeg MB R3C 3L6
204/945-3790; Fax: 204/945-2169

Provincial Auditor, Vacant, 204/945-3790
Asst. Provincial Auditor, W.A. Johnson, 204/945-3791

Manitoba CONSUMER & CORPORATE AFFAIRS (MCCA)
#317, 450 Broadway, Winnipeg MB R3C 0V8
204/945-1718; Email: mincca@leg.gov.mb.ca

ACTS ADMINISTERED
Administration
Manitoba Evidence Act, Parts II & III
Cooperative, Credit Union Regulation
Cooperatives Act
Credit Unions & Caisses Populaires Act
Consumers' Bureau
Bedding, Upholstered & Stuffed Articles Regulation (of the Public Health Act)
Business Practices Act
Charities Endorsement Act
Consumer Protection Act
Hearing Aid Act & Regulation
Personal Investigations Act
Residential Tenancies
Condominium Act
Landlord & Tenant Act
Residential Tenancies Act
Companies Office
Business Names Registration Act
Corporations Act
Partnership Act
Religious Societies' Lands Act
Deputy Minister
Embalmers' & Funeral Directors' Act
Trade Practices Inquiry Act
Insurance
Insurance Act
Insurance Corporations Tax Act
Marine Insurance Act
Manitoba Securities Commission
Commodity Futures Act
Mortgage Dealers Act
Real Estate Brokers Act
Securities Act
Property Rights
Hudson's Bay Company Land Register Act
Property Security Act
Real Property Act
Registry Act
Revenue Act (part III)
Special Survey Act
Surveys Act
Title to Certain Lands Act
Public Utilities Board
Cemeteries Act
Prearranged Funeral Services Act
Public Utilities Board Act
Residential Tenancies
Condominium Act
Landlord & Tenant Act
Residential Tenancies Act
Trusts & Loans
Part XXIV Corporations Act
Vital Statistics
Change of Name Act
Marriage Act
Vital Statistics Act
Minister, Hon. James A. Ernst, 204/945-4256, Fax: 204/945-4009, Email: mincca@leg.gov.mb.ca
Deputy Minister, A. Morton, 204/945-3742
Acting Superintendent, Insurance, L. Couture, #1142, 405 Broadway, Winnipeg MB R3C 3L6, 204/945-2542
Director General, Property Rights Division, Rick Wilson, 204/945-0446
Commissioner, Residential Tenancies Commission, A. Zivot, 204/945-4242

Director, Administration Office, Fred D. Bryans, 204/945-2653
Director, Consumers' Bureau, Denis Robidoux, #302, 258 Portage Ave., Winnipeg MB R3C 0B6, 204/945-3800, Fax: 204/945-0728
Director, Companies Office, M. Pawlowsky, 204/945-4206
Director, Cooperative & Credit Union Regulations, R. Pozernick, 204/945-2771
Director, Research & Planning, I. Anderson, #1105, 405 Broadway, Winnipeg MB R3C 3L6, 204/945-7892
Director, Residential Tenancies Branch, R. Barsy, 204/945-4069
Director, Trust & Loan, R. Pozernick, 204/945-2771

VITAL STATISTICS
254 Portage Ave., Winnipeg MB R3C 0B8
204/945-2034, 8177; Fax: 204/945-0777
Toll Free: Fax Certificate Requests: 204/948-3128
Provincial agency responsible for the issuance of birth, death, change of name & marriage certificates. Written or faxed requests must be submitted. Fee for each certificate is $25.00.
Director, C. Kaus, 204/945-3701
Manager, Customer Services, D. Whittaker
Supervisor, Application Processing, L. Turzak
Supervisor, Registration Information Systems, F. Beer

Associated Agencies, Boards & Commissions
•Automobile Injury Compensation Appeal Commission: #106, 167 Lombard Ave., Winnipeg MB R3Z 3Z5 – 204/945-4155
Chief Commissioner, R. Taylor, 204/945-4353
•Credit Union Deposit Guarantee Corporation: #100, 233 Portage Ave., Winnipeg MB R3B 2A7 – 204/942-8480; Fax: 204/947-1723
General Manager, George A. Keter
•Hearing Aid Board: 114 Garry St., Winnipeg MB R3C 1G1 – 204/956-2040; Fax: 204/945-0728
Secretary, Denis Robidoux
•Manitoba Liquor Control Commission: 1555 Buffalo Place, PO Box 1023, Winnipeg MB R3C 2X1 – 204/284-2501
Acting President, Al Ahoff
•Manitoba Securities Commission: #1128, 405 Broadway, Winnipeg MB R3C 3L6 – 204/945-2548; Fax: 204/945-0330
Chair, Jocelyn Samson
Counsel, David Cheop
Deputy Director, Corporate Finance, Robert Bouchard
•Public Utilities Board: 280 Smith St., 2nd Fl., Winnipeg MB R3C 1K2 – 204/945-2638; Fax: 204/945-2643
Chair, Gerry D. Forrest, 204/945-2640
Executive Director, G.O. Barron

Manitoba CULTURE, HERITAGE & CITIZENSHIP
213 Notre Dame., Winnipeg MB R3B 1N3
204/945-3729; Email: minchc@leg.gov.mb.ca; URL: http://www.gov.mb.ca/manitoba/chc/immsettl/citz_hom.html

ACTS ADMINISTERED
Amusements Act, Parts I, III to X
Arts Council Act
Centennial Centre Corporation Act
Le Centre Culturel Franco-Manitobain Act
Coat of Arms, Emblems & The Manitoba Tartan Act
Department of Labour Act (in part)
Foreign Cultural Objects Immunity from Seizure Act
Freedom of Information Act
Heritage Manitoba Act
Heritage Resources Act
Legislative Library Act
Manitoba Multiculturalism Act
Museums & Miscellaneous Grants Act
The Museum of Man & Nature Act
Public Libraries Act
Public Printing Act
Minister, Hon. Harold Gilleshammer, 204/945-3729, Fax: 204/945-5223
Deputy Minister, Roxy Freedman, 204/945-4136, Fax: 204/948-3102

ADMINISTRATION & FINANCE DIVISION
Executive Director, Dave Paton, 204/945-2233, Fax: 204/945-5760
Manager, Grants Administration, Pauline Rosmus, 204/945-4580, Fax: 204/945-5760
Manager, Financial Administration, P. Koshyk, 204/945-3946, Fax: 204/945-5760
Manager, Information Systems, Rosemary Unrau, 204/945-4436, Fax: 204/945-5760
Manager, Management Services, K. O'Shaughnessy, 204/945-4215, Fax: 204/945-5760
Director, Community Places Program, Wayne Blackburn, 204/945-1368, Fax: 204/945-2086
Director, Human Resource Services, A. Proulx, 405 Broadway, 9th Fl., Winnipeg MB R3C 3L6, 204/945-2885, Fax: 204/945-6692

CITIZENSHIP DIVISION
Asst. Deputy Minister, Doris Mae Oulton, 204/945-8174, Fax: 204/948-2256
Director, Immigrant Credentials & Labour Market Branch, A. Konopelny, 204/945-3650, Fax: 204/948-2148
Director, Immigration/Settlement Policy & Planning Branch, M. Itzkow, 204/945-2802, Fax: 204/948-2148
Director, Settlement & Adult Language Training Branch, M. Kenny, 204/945-8081, Fax: 204/948-2148
Manager, Citizenship Support Services Branch, N. Kostyshyn-Bailey, 204/945-1649, Fax: 204/948-2148

CULTURE, HERITAGE & RECREATION PROGRAMS DIVISION
Asst. Deputy Minister, Lou-Anne Buhr, 204/945-4078, Fax: 204/945-1684
Director, Arts Branch, Kathleen McMillan, 204/945-4579, Fax: 204/945-1684
Director, Historic Resources, Donna Dul, 204/945-4389, Fax: 204/948-2384
Director, Public Library Services, Sylvia Nicholson, #200, 1595 - 1 St., Brandon MB R7A 7A1, 204/726-6864, Fax: 204/726-6868
Director, Recreation & Wellness Promotion, Jim Hamilton, 204/945-0487, Fax: 204/945-1684
Director, Regional Services, R. de Pencier, 204/945-4396, Fax: 204/945-1684
Acting Manager, Agency Relations, Ann Hultgren-Ryan, 204/945-4509, Fax: 204/945-1684

INFORMATION RESOURCES DIVISION
155 Carlton St., 10th Fl., Winnipeg MB R3C 3H8
Executive Director, Linda Perreault, 204/945-4271, Fax: 204/948-2219
Director, Communication Services, Cindy Stevens, 204/945-4971, Fax: 204/948-2147
Director, Information Services, Dwight MacAulay, 204/945-3746, Fax: 204/945-3988
Associate Director, Advertising Services, Cam McCullough, 204/945-8830, Fax: 204/948-2147
Manager, Business Services, Mike Baudic, 204/945-4392, Fax: 204/948-2219
Manager, Production Services, Heather Coleman, 204/945-7121, Fax: 204/948-2332
Supervisor, Citizens' Inquiry, Liliana Romanowski, 204/945-3744, Fax: 204/945-4261
Supervisor, Statutory Publications, Keith Holness, 204/945-3101, Fax: 204/945-7172

PROVINCIAL SERVICES DIVISION
200 Vaughan St., Winnipeg MB R3C 1T5
Acting Executive Director, S. Bishop, 204/945-3968, Fax: 204/948-2008
Provincial Archivist, Provincial Archives, Peter Bower, 204/945-4233, Fax: 204/948-2008
Legislative Librarian, Legislative Library, S. Bishop, 204/945-3968, Fax: 204/948-2008
Director, Translation Services, M. Freynet, 213 Notre Dame Ave., 2nd Fl., Winnipeg MB R3B 1N3, 204/945-3095, Fax: 204/945-5879

Associated Agencies, Boards & Commissions
•Film Classification Board (& Film Classification Appeal Board): #216, 301 Weston St., Winnipeg MB R3E 3H4 – 204/945-8962; Fax: 204/945-0890
Director, George Rooswinkel
•Heritage Grants Advisory Council: 213 Notre Dame Ave., Winnipeg MB R3B 1N3 – 204/945-4580; Fax: 204/945-5760
Executive Director, P. Rosmus
•Le Centre Culturel Franco-Manitobain/Franco-Manitoban Cultural Centre: 340, boul Provencher, St. Boniface MB R2H 0G7 – 204/233-8972; Fax: 204/233-3324
Executive Director, Alain Boucher
•Manitoba Arts Council: #525, 93 Lombard Ave., Winnipeg MB R3B 3B1 – 204/945-2237
Executive Director, Victor Jerrett-Enns
•Manitoba Centennial Centre Corporation: #117, 555 Main St., Winnipeg MB R3B 1C3 – 204/956-1360; Fax: 204/944-1390
Executive Director, John Walton
•Manitoba Heritage Council: 213 Notre Dame Ave., Main Fl., Winnipeg MB R3B 1N3 – 204/945-4389; Fax: 204/948-2384
Chair, Bill Neville
•Manitoba Museum of Man & Nature
Listed in Section 6; *see* Index.
•Multicultural Grants Advisory Council: 213 Notre Dame Ave., 4th Fl., Winnipeg MB R3B 1N3 – 204/945-4458; Fax: 204/945-1675
Executive Director, R. Taruc
•Multiculturalism Secretariat: 794 Sargent Ave., Winnipeg MB R3E 0B7 – 204/945-1287; Fax: 204/948-2006

Manitoba DEVELOPMENT CORPORATION (MDC)
#555, 155 Carlton St., Winnipeg MB R3C 3H8
204/945-7626; Fax: 204/957-1793
Minister Responsible, Hon. James Downey, 204/945-0067, Fax: 204/945-4882
General Manager, Ian Robertson, 204/945-2472
Corporate Secretary, Jim Kilgour

Manitoba EDUCATION & TRAINING
#168, Legislative Bldg., Winnipeg MB R3C 0P8
204/945-4325; Fax: 204/945-1291; Email: minedu@leg.gov.mb.ca; URL: http://www.gov.mb.ca/educate/main/index.html

ACTS ADMINISTERED
Blind Persons' & Deaf Persons' Maintenance & Education Act
Education Administration Act
Licensed Practical Nurses Act, ss. 14, 15
Private Vocational Schools Act
Public Schools Act
Public Schools Finance Board Act
Teachers' Pension Act
Teachers' Society Act
Universities Establishment Act
Universities Grants Commission Act
University of Manitoba Act

Minister, Hon. Linda G. McIntosh, 204/945-3720, Fax: 204/945-1291

Deputy Minister, Education, J. Carlyle, 204/945-3752, Fax: 204/945-8330

Deputy Minister, Training & Advanced Education, Tom Carson, 204/945-8528, Fax: 204/948-2490

PLANNING & POLICY DEVELOPMENT BRANCH
#409, 1181 Portage Ave., Winnipeg MB R3G 0T3
204/945-6171; Fax: 204/945-0194
Executive Director, John Didyk
Project Coordinator, Distance Education Implementation, Dr. Beth Cruikshank, 204/945-2811, Fax: 204/945-0194

ADMINISTRATION & FINANCE DIVISION
1181 Portage Ave., Winnipeg MB R3G 0T3
Asst. Deputy Minister, Jim Glen, 204/945-6904, Fax: 204/945-8303
Director, Administration & Professional Certification, Brian Hanson, 204/945-7391, Fax: 204/948-2154
Director, Finance, T. Thompson, 204/945-6908, Fax: 204/948-2193
Director, Schools Finance, Gerald Farthing, 204/945-0515, Fax: 204/948-2000
Secretary, Board of Reference, David Yeo, 204/945-8664, Fax: 204/948-2154

BUREAU DE L'EDUCATION FRANÇAISE/French Language Office
#509. 1181 Portage Ave., Winnipeg MB R3C 0T3
Sous-ministre adjoint, Guy Roy, 204/945-6928, Fax: 204/945-1625

SCHOOL PROGRAMS DIVISION
1181 Portage Ave., Winnipeg MB R3G 0T3
Asst. Deputy Minister, Carolyn Loeppky, 204/945-7935, Fax: 204/945-8303
Director, Student Support Services, N.J. Cenerini, 204/945-7911, Fax: 204/945-7914
Coordinator, Assessment & Evaluation Unit, Norman Mayer, 204/945-6157, Fax: 204/945-8303
Program Manager, Independent Study Program, Gerry Gros, Main Plaza, 555 Main St., Winkler MB R6W 1C4, 204/325-2306, Fax: 204/325-4212
Director, Instructional Resources, John Tooth, 204/945-7833, Fax: 204/945-8756
Acting Manager, Manitoba Textbook Bureau, Lanny Kingerski, 130 - 1 Ave. West, Souris MB R0K 2C0
Director, Native Education, Juliette Sabot, 204/945-7883, Fax: 204/948-2010
Director, Program Development Branch, Pat MacDonald, #W120, 1970 Ness Ave., Winnipeg MB R3J 0Y9, 204/945-0926, Fax: 204/945-5060
Acting Director, Program Implementation Branch, Erika Kreis, #W130, 1970 Ness Ave., Winnipeg MB R3J 0Y9, 204/945-1033, Fax: 204/945-5060

TRAINING & ADVANCED EDUCATION
185 Carlton St., 4th Fl., Winnipeg MB R3C 3J1
Asst. Deputy Minister, Tom Carson, 204/945-8528, Fax: 204/948-2490
Director, Apprenticeship, Harvey Miller, 204/945-3339, Fax: 204/948-2346
Acting Director, Employment Development Programs, Pam McConnell, 209 Notre Dame Ave., 4th Fl., Winnipeg MB R3B 1M9, 204/945-6997, Fax: 204/945-0221
Director, Labour Market Support Services, Earl McArthur, 204/945-0608, Fax: 204/945-1792
Acting Director, Manitoba Literacy & Continuing Education, Louise Gordon, 204/945-8571, Fax: 204/945-1792
Acting Director, Workforce 2000 & Youth Programs, B. Knight, 204/945-6195, Fax: 204/945-1792

Acting Manager, Student Financial Assistance Program, Ray Hullen, Box 6, 693 Taylor Ave., Winnipeg MB R3M 3T9, 204/945-8729, Fax: 204/477-5596

ELECTIONS MANITOBA
#302, 379 Broadway, Winnipeg MB R3C 0T9
204/945-3225; Fax: 204/945-6011; Email: election@access.mbnet.mb.ca
Chief Electoral Officer, Richard D. Balasko

Manitoba EMERGENCY MEASURES ORGANIZATION (MEMO)
405 Broadway, 15th Fl., Winnipeg MB R3C 3L6
204/945-4772; Fax: 204/945-4620
Executive Coordinator, Harold Clayton, 204/945-4789
MEMO is a division of Manitoba Government Services, listed separately in this section.

Manitoba ENERGY & MINES
#360, 1395 Ellice Ave., Winnipeg MB R3G 3P2
204/945-4154; Fax: 204/945-0586, 1406; Email: minem@leg.gov.mb.ca; URL: http://www.gov.mb.ca/em/index.html

Develops & administers policies & legislation that foster & promote environmentally sustainable economic development of Manitoba's mineral resources & the development & efficient use of energy resources available to the province.

ACTS ADMINISTERED
Energy Act
Gas Pipe Line Act
Gas Allocation Act
Greater Winnipeg Gas Distribution Act (SM 1988, c. 40)
Homeowners Tax & Insulation Assistance Act (in Part)
Manitoba Natural Resources Development Act (as it applies to Manitoba Resources Ltd.)
Mineral Exploration Incentive Program Act
Mines & Minerals Act
Mining & Metallurgy Compensation Act
Natural Gas Supply Act
Oil & Gas Act
Oil & Gas Production Tax Act
Minister, Hon. Darren Praznik, 204/945-6429
Deputy Minister, Michael Fine, 204/945-4172

PETROLEUM & ENERGY BRANCH
360 - 1395 Ellice Ave, Winnipeg MB R3G 3P2
204/945-6577; Fax: 204/945-0586; Email: htisdale@em.gov.mb.ca; URL: http://www.gov.mb.ca/em/petroleum/index.html
Toll Free: 1-800-282-8069 (Energy)
Petroleum Information: 204/748-1557
Energy Information: 204/945-3760
Director, L.R. Dubreuil, 204/945-6573
Officer, Building Codes, Ken Klassen, 204/945-2792
Officer, Commercial Energy Use & Renewable Alternate Energy, Terry Silcox, 204/945-0757
Officer, Crown Land Sales, Carol Martiniuk, 204/945-6570
Officer, Drilling Licences, Dan Surzyshyn, 204/945-8102
Officer, Geological Information & Residential Energy Use, Harry Klassen, 204/945-6571
Officer, Maps, Reports & Publications, Barb Johnston, 204/748-1557
Officer, Pipelines & Surface Rights, John Fox, 204/945-6574
Officer, Transportation, Marc Arbez, 204/945-0757

GEOLOGICAL SERVICES BRANCH
204/945-6567
Director, W.D. McRitchie, 204/945-6559

MARKETING BRANCH
204/945-8093
Director, K. Thomas, 204/945-1874

MINES BRANCH
204/945-6522
Director, A. Ball, 204/945-6505

Associated Agencies, Boards & Commissions
• Manitoba Mining Board (MMB): #360, 1395 Ellice Ave., Winnipeg MB R3G 3P2 – 204/943-6740
Presiding Member, Doug Abra

Manitoba ENVIRONMENT
Bldg. 2, 139 Tuxedo Ave., Winnipeg MB R3N 0H6
204/945-7100; Email: minenv@leg.gov.mb.ca; URL: http://www.gov.mb.ca/manitoba/environ/index.html

ACTS ADMINISTERED
Dangerous Goods Handling & Transportation Act
Environment Act
High Level Radioactive Waste Act
Manitoba Hazardous Waste Management Corporation Act
Ozone Depleting Substances Act
Public Health Act
Waste Reduction & Prevention (WRAP) Act
Minister, Hon. J. Glen Cummings, 204/945-3522, Fax: 204/942-1127
Deputy Minister, Norman Brandson, 204/945-8807, Fax: 204/945-1256
Director, Administration, Wolf Boehm, 204/945-7006, Fax: 204/948-2338
Director, Legislation & Intergovernmental Affairs, Richard Stephens, 204/945-8152

ENVIRONMENTAL MANAGEMENT DIVISION
204/945-7107; Fax: 204/945-5229
Asst. Deputy Minister, Serge Scrafield
Director, Environmental Approvals Branch, Larry Strachan, 204/945-7071
Director, Environmental Quality Standards Branch, Max Morelli, 204/945-7032
Director, Pollution Prevention Branch, Jerry Spiegel, 204/945-7083

ENVIRONMENTAL OPERATIONS DIVISION
204/945-7008; Fax: 204/945-5229
Environmental Accidents Information: 204/945-7039
Emergency Reporting (24-hour): 204/944-4888
Asst. Deputy Minister, Carl Orcutt
Supervisor, Transportation & Handling of Dangerous Goods, Dave Ediger, 208/945-7039
Senior Operations Consultant, Regional Operations, K. Hawkins, 204/945-7009

Regional Operations
Brandon: Scotia Towers, 1011 Rosser Ave., Brandon MB R7A 0L5 – 204/726-6565, Regional Director, Bernie Chrisp
Steinbach: Town Square, 284 Reimer Ave., Steinbach MB R0A 2A0 – 204/326-3468, Regional Director, Dennis Brown
The Pas: Provincial Bldg., 3rd & Ross Ave., PO Box 2550, The Pas MB R9A 1M4 – 204/627-8362, Regional Director, Steve Davis
Winkler: Southland Mall, 777 Norquay Dr., Winkler MB R6W 2S2 – 204/325-2291, Regional Director, Leslie MacCallum
Winnipeg: Fort Osborne Complex, 139 Tuxedo Ave., 2nd Fl., Winnipeg MB R3N 0H6 – 204/945-7081, Regional Director, Dave Wotton

Manitoba Round Table on the Environment & Economy (MRTEE)
Secretariat: Sustainable Development Coordination Unit, #305, 155 Carlton St., Winnipeg MB R3C 3H8

204/945-1124; Fax: 204/945-0090
Executive Director, Vacant

Associated Agencies, Boards & Commissions
- Clean Environment Commission: Town Square, PO Box 21420, Steinbach MB R0A 2T3 – 204/326-2395; Fax: 204/326-2472
Chair, Dale Stewart
- Manitoba Hazardous Waste Management Corporation (MHWMC)
Note: This agency was privatized in 1995.

Manitoba FAMILY SERVICES
#219, 114 Garry St., Winnipeg MB R3C 4V6
204/945-2324 (Policy & Planning); Fax: 204/945-2156; Email: minfam@leg.gov.mb.ca; URL: http://www.gov.mb.ca/fs/first/ffindex.html

ACTS ADMINISTERED
Child & Family Services Act
Community Child Day Care Standards Act
Department of Labour Act (as it applies to Family Services)
Mental Health Act (in Part)
Parents' Maintenance Act, s. 10
Social Allowances Act
Social Services Administration Act
Minister, Hon. Bonnie E. Mitchelson, 204/945-4173, Fax: 204/945-5149
Deputy Minister, Tannis Mindell, 204/945-6700, Fax: 204/945-1896
Children's Advocate, Office of the Children's Advocate, Wayne Govereau, 204/945-1427, Fax: 204/948-2278
Director, Human Resources Services, Audrey Clifford, 204/945-3165, Fax: 204/945-0601

CHILD & FAMILY SERVICES DIVISION
Asst. Deputy Minister, David Langtry, 204/945-3257, Fax: 204/945-0291
Executive Director, Child Welfare & Family Support, Phil Goodman, 204/945-6948, Fax: 204/945-6717
Director, Child Day Care, Gisella Rempel, 204/945-2668, Fax: 204/948-2143
Director, Children's Special Services, Eleanor Chornoboy, 204/945-3251, Fax: 204/945-2669
Director, Compliance, Bev Ann Murray, 204/945-4272, Fax: 204/945-6717
Director, Family Conciliation, Sandra Dean, 204/945-7235, Fax: 204/948-2142
Director, Family Dispute Services, Marlene Bertrand, 204/945-7259
Director, Seven Oaks Youth Centre, Duncan Michie, 204/339-1934

EMPLOYMENT & INCOME ASSISTANCE DIVISION
Associate Deputy Minister, Doug Sexsmith, 204/945-2692, Fax: 204/948-2153
Executive Director, Administration & Finance, Kim Sharman, 204/945-5600, Fax: 204/948-2153
Executive Director, Client Services, Gerry Schmidt, 204/945-2685, Fax: 204/945-0082
Director, Finance & Administration, Gerry Bosma, 204/945-3080, Fax: 204/945-2760
Director, Income Supplement Programs, Ellen Coates, 204/523-4499
Director, Information Systems, Ken Mason, 204/945-2206, Fax: 204/945-1697
Director, Investigations & Recoveries, Don Feener, 204/945-8627, Fax: 204/945-0082
Director, Municipal Cost-Sharing & Regulation, Sue Bentley, 204/945-2996, Fax: 204/945-0082
Director, Policy & Planning, Drew Perry, 204/945-2324, Fax: 204/945-2156
Director, Welfare Reform, Dan Haughey, 204/945-5795, Fax: 204/945-0082

COMMUNITY LIVING DIVISION
Asst. Deputy Minister, Martin Billinkoff, 204/945-2204, Fax: 204/945-5029
Executive Director, Adult Services, Wes Henderson, 204/945-0172, Fax: 204/945-5668
Executive Director, Regional Operations, Ron Fenwick, 204/945-2120, Fax: 204/945-0082
Director, Residential Care Licensing, Mike McKenzie, 204/945-3576, Fax: 204/944-0254
Chief Executive Officer, Manitoba Developmental Centre, Steve Bergson, 204/856-4237, Fax: 204/856-4258
Commissioner, Vulnerable Persons' Commission Office, Dr. Allen Hansen, 204/945-5039, Fax: 204/948-2603

Manitoba FINANCE
#109, Legislative Bldg., Winnipeg MB R3C 0V8
204/945-3754; Fax: 204/945-8316; Email: minfin@leg.gov.mb.ca; URL: http://www.gov.mb.ca/finance/
Telex: 0636700391

ACTS ADMINISTERED
Corporation Capital Tax Act
Crown Corporations Public Review & Accountability Act
Energy Rate Stabilization Act
Financial Administration Act
Fire Insurance Reserve Fund Act
Fiscal Stabilization Fund Act
Gasoline Tax Act
Health & Post Secondary Education Tax Levy Act
Homeowners Tax & Insulation Assistance Act (Parts I & II)
Hospital Capital Financing Authority Act
Income Tax Act (Manitoba)
Mining Claim Tax Act
Mining Tax Act
Motive Fuel Tax Act
Pari-Mutual Tax Act
Provincial-Municipal Tax Sharing Act
Public Officers Act
Retail Sales Tax Act
Revenue Act, 1964
Succession Duty Act
Suitors' Moneys Act
Tobacco Tax Act
Treasury Branches Act
Minister, Hon. Eric Stefanson, 249/945-3952, Fax: 249/945-6057
Deputy Minister, J.P. Gannon, 204/945-3754, Fax: 204/945-8316
Secretary, Treasury Board, J.D. Benson, #300, 333 Broadway, Winnipeg MB R3C 0S9, 204/945-1100, Fax: 204/945-4878
Associate Secretary, Treasury Board, D. Potter, 204/945-1088, Fax: 204/945-4878

COMPTROLLER DIVISION
#709, 401 York Ave., Winnipeg MB R3C 0P8
Asst. Deputy Minister, E.H. Rosenhek, 204/945-4920, Fax: 204/945-0896
Director, Disbursements & Accounting, Gerry Gaudreau

FEDERAL-PROVINCIAL RELATIONS & RESEARCH DIVISION
#203, 333 Broadway Ave., Winnipeg MB R3C 0S9
Asst. Deputy Minister, E. Boschmann, 204/945-3962, Fax: 204/945-5051

TAXATION DIVISION
401 York Ave., 4th Fl., Winnipeg MB R3C 0P8
Asst. Deputy Minister, S.J. Puchniak, 204/945-3758, Fax: 204/945-0896
Director, Audit Branch, Leon Ballegeer

Director, Tax Administration Branch, Brian Forbes
Director, Taxation Management & Research Branch, Barry Draward

TREASURY DIVISION
Asst. Deputy Minister, Neil S. Benditt, 204/945-3756, Fax: 204/945-1361
Director, Capital Finance, Donald Delisle
Director, Money Management & Banking, William J. Cessford
Director, Treasury Services, Donald Wood

Associated Agencies, Boards & Commissions
- Crown Corporations Council: #320, 530 Kenaston Blvd., Winnipeg MB R3N 1Z4 – 204/949-5270; Fax: 204/949-5283
Chair, John F. Fraser
President & CEO, J. Douglas Sherwood
Vice-President, Finance, Jon Singleton

Manitoba GOVERNMENT SERVICES (MGS)
Woodsworth Bldg., 405 Broadway, 15th Fl., Winnipeg MB R3C 3L6
204/945-3001; Email: mings@leg.gov.mb.ca

ACTS ADMINISTERED
Emergency Measures Act
Expropriation Act
Government House Act
Government Purchases Act
Land Acquisition Act
Public Works Act
Minister, Hon. Brian W. Pallister, 204/945-2979, Fax: 204/945-7331, Email: mings@leg.gov.mb.ca
Deputy Minister, H.G. Eliasson, 204/945-4414, Fax: 204/945-1857
Executive Coordinator, Manitoba Emergency Measures Organization, Harold Clayton, 204/945-4789, Fax: 204/945-4620, Emergencies (24 hour): 204/945-5555

ACCOMMODATION DEVELOPMENT DIVISION
Asst. Deputy Minister, Stephen Kupfer, 204/945-7552, Fax: 204/945-0908
Director, Corporate Accommodation Planning Branch, F. LeClair
Director, Leasing Contracts & Expenditures, C. Shade
Director, Leasing Contracts & Expenditures, M. Shewchuk
Director, Technical Resources Branch, A. Lorimer

ADMINISTRATION & FINANCE DIVISION
Director, Finance, Brian McTaggert
Acting Director, Human Resources, M. Brownscombe
Manager, Systems, D. Primmer

PROPERTY MANAGEMENT DIVISION
Asst. Deputy Minister, Hugh Swan, 204/945-7535, Fax: 204/945-5933
Director, Physical Plant, Vacant

SUPPLY & SERVICES DIVISION
Asst. Deputy Minister, G.W. Berezuk, 204/945-6340, Fax: 204/945-1455
Director, Fleet Vehicles, D. Ducharme, 626 Henry Ave., Winnipeg MB R3A 1P7
Director, Land Acquisition, D. Parnell, 25 Tupper St. North, Portage la Prairie MB R1N 3K1
Director, Materials Supply, T. Danowski, 1680 Church Ave., Winnipeg MB R2X 2W9
Director, Office Equipment Services, J. Emslie, 530 Century St., Winnipeg MB R3H 0Y4
Director, Purchasing, E.F. Baranet, 530 Century St., Winnipeg MB R3H 1A2, 204/945-6380, Fax: 204/245-1455
Director, Telecommunications, F. Cross, 401 York Ave., Winnipeg MB R3C 0P8

Canadian Almanac & Directory 1997

GOVERNMENT OF MANITOBA

Associated Agencies, Boards & Commissions
- Manitoba Disaster Assistance Board: #101, 800 Portage Ave., Winnipeg MB R3G 0N4 – 204/945-3050; Fax: 204/945-4929
Chair, Sydney Reimer
- Manitoba Land Value Appraisal Commission: Norquay Bldg., #408, 900 Portage Ave., Winnipeg MB R3G 0P4 – 204/945-3087; Fax: 204/945-3087
Chair, C. Harvey

Manitoba HEALTH
599 Empress St., PO Box 925, Winnipeg MB R3C 2T6
204/786-7191 (Finance & Administration Branch); Fax: 204/774-1325; Email: minhlt@leg.gov.mb.ca; URL: http://www.gov.mb.ca/health/index.html

ACTS ADMINISTERED
Addictions Foundation Act
Ambulance Services Act
Anatomy Act
Cancer Treatment & Research Foundation Act
Chiropodists Act
Chiropractic Act
Dental Association Act
Dental Health Workers Act
Dental Health Services Act
Denturists Act
Department of Health Act
District Health & Social Services Act
Elderly & Infirm Persons' Housing Act (with respect to personal care homes & infirm persons)
Health Care Directives Act
(Manitoba) Health Research Council Act
Health Sciences Centre Act, 1988-80
Health Services Act
Health Services Insurance Act
Hearing Aid Act
Hospitals Act
Human Tissue Act
Licensed Practical Nurses Act
Medical Act
Mental Health Act (Except Parts II, III, & IV)
Minors Intoxicating Substances Act
Naturopathic Act
Non-Smokers Health Protection Act
Occupational Therapists Act
Ophthalmic Dispensers Act
Optometry Act
Pharmaceutical Act
Physiotherapists Act
Prescription Drugs Cost Assistance Act
Private Hospitals Act
Psychologists Registration Act
Public Health Act
Registered Dieticians Act
Registered Nurses Act
Registered Psychiatric Nurses Act
Registered Respiratory Therapists Act
Sanitorium Board of Manitoba Act
Minister, Hon. James C. McCrae, 204/945-3731, Fax: 204/945-0441
Deputy Minister, John G. Wade, 204/945-3771, Fax: 204/945-4564
Associate Deputy Minister, Health Communities Office, F. DeCock, 204/945-6470, Fax: 204/948-2258

COMMUNITY & MENTAL HEALTH SERVICES DIVISION
599 Empress St., Winnipeg MB R3G 3H2
Asst. Deputy Minister, Sue Hicks, 204/786-7360, Fax: 204/775-3412
Asst. Deputy Minister, Child & Youth Secretariat, Reginald Toews, 447 Portage Ave., 12th Fl., Winnipeg MB R3B 3H5, 204/945-6707
Chief Medical Officer, Dr. John Guilfoyle, #301, 800 Portage Ave., Winnipeg MB R3G 0N4, 204/945-6839

Registrar, Emergency Services, Lorne Charbonneau, 800 Portage Ave., Winnipeg MB R3G 0N4, 204/945-0711
Executive Director, Urban Hospital Services, Sean Drain, 204/786-7138
Director, Administration, Peter Todman, 800 Portage Ave., Winnipeg MB R3G 0N4, 204/945-6690, Fax: 204/947-2040
Director, Cadham Provincial Laboratory, Dr. Trevor Williams, 750 William Ave., PO Box 8450, Winnipeg MB R3C 3Y1, 204/946-2507
Acting Director, Long Term Care, M. Redston, 800 Portage Ave., 2nd Fl., Winnipeg MB R3C 0N4, 204/945-7493, Fax: 204/948-2040
Director, Program Development, L. Thompson, 204/786-7312
Director, Public Health & Epidemiology Branch, Dr. Greg Hammond, #301, 800 Portage Ave., Winnipeg MB R3G 0N4, 204/945-6720, Fax: 204/948-2190
Acting Director, Winnipeg Operations, P. Dubrenski, #5, 189 Evanson St., Winnipeg MB R3G 0N9, 204/945-3302, Fax: 204/945-1735

FINANCE & ADMINISTRATION DIVISION
Asst. Deputy Minister, Tim W. Duprey, 204/786-7263, Fax: 204/783-2171
Director, Finance & Administration Branch, Susan Murphy, 559 Empress St., Winnipeg MB R3C 2T6, 204/788-2508, Fax: 204/774-1325
Director, Human Resources Branch, J. Morris, #602, 330 Graham Ave., Winnipeg MB R3C 4C8, 204/945-5900, Fax: 204/945-1999
Director, Health Information Systems Branch, G.K. Neill, 204/786-7347, Fax: 204/774-1325

HEALTH SERVICES INSURANCE FUND
447 Portage Ave., 12th Fl., Winnipeg MB R3B 3H5
Secretary, Manitoba Health Board, Don B. Nelson, 204/945-8875

MANAGEMENT & PROGRAM SUPPORT SERVICES DIVISION
Fax: 204/783-2171
Executive Director, Insured Benefits, R.H. Harvey, 204/786-7215
Executive Director, Health Information Services, Glenn Alexander, 204/786-7282, Fax: 204/786-8560
Director, Facilities Development Branch, L. Bakken, 800 Portage Ave., Winnipeg MB R3G 0N4, 204/945-3997
Director, Funded Accountability, W. Campbell, 599 Empress St., Winnipeg MB R3G 3H2, 204/786-7149, Fax: 204/775-3412

Associated Agencies, Boards & Commissions
- Addictions Foundation of Manitoba
Listed in Section 2; see Index.
- Drug Standards/Therapeutics Committee: #128, 599 Empress St., PO Box 925, Winnipeg MB R3C 2T6 – 204/786-7233; Fax: 204/783-2171
Secretary, Ken Brown
- Manitoba Council on Aging: #204, 800 Portage Ave., Winnipeg MB R3G 0W5 – 204/945-1997
Director, Gerontology, B. Kyle, 204/945-8731

Manitoba HIGHWAYS & TRANSPORTATION
215 Garry St., Winnipeg MB R3C 3Z1
204/945-3888; Fax: 204/945-7610; Email: minhwy@leg.gov.mb.ca

ACTS ADMINISTERED
Highways & Transportation Department Act
Highway Protection Act
Highway Traffic Act (in part)
Proceeds of Contracts Disbursement Act, 1981
Snowmobile Act
Taxicab Act

Trans-Canada Highway Act
Unsatisfied Judgement Fund Act (in part)
Minister, Hon. Glen Findlay, 204/945-3723, Fax: 204/945-7610
Deputy Minister, Andrew Horosko, 204/945-3768, Fax: 204/945-4766

ADMINISTRATIVE SERVICES DIVISION
215 Garry St., 17th Fl., Winnipeg MB R3C 3Z1
Fax: 204/945-5115
Executive Director, Paul Rochon, 204/945-3887
Director, Personnel Services, D. McIntosh, 204/945-1719, Fax: 204/948-2274
Director, Financial Services, F. Schnerch, 204/945-5869
Budget Coordinator, Financial Services, P. LaRue, 204/945-1996
Director, Computer Services, B. Kirkpatrick, 204/945-4512
Manager, Occupational Health & Safety, G. Mortimer, 204/945-5819
Officer, Claims Investigation, W. McEachaern, 204/945-1429

CONSTRUCTION & MAINTENANCE DIVISION
215 Garry St., 16th Fl., Winnipeg MB R3C 3Z1
Fax: 204/945-3841
Acting Asst. Deputy Minister, B. Tinkler, 204/945-3733
Director, Bridges & Structures, W. Saltzberg, 204/945-5058
Acting Director, Operational Services, R. Mckay, 204/945-3778
Engineer, Maintenance Management, V. Weselak, 204/945-3896
Contract Engineer, Operational Services, G. Tencha, 204/945-3776

DRIVER & VEHICLE LICENSING DIVISION
1075 Portage Ave., Winnipeg MB R3G 0S1
Fax: 204/948-2018
Acting Asst. Deputy Minister/Registrar, M. Zyluk, 204/945-7370
Director/Deputy Registrar, Safety, B. MacMartin, 204/945-8195
Manager, Systems, A. Fulsher, 204/945-7374
Acting Manager, Administration & Finance, D. Puls, 204/945-7362
Director, Transport Safety & Regulation, D. Nelson, 204/945-8925

ENGINEERING & TECHNICAL SERVICES DIVISION
215 Garry St., 14th Fl., Winnipeg MB R3C 3Z1
Fax: 204/945-5539
Asst. Deputy Minister, J. Hosang, 204/945-3772
Director, Materials & Research, R. Van Cauwenberghe, 204/945-8982, Fax: 204/945-2229
Director, Mechanical Equipment Services, C. DeBlonde, 215 Garry St., 17th Fl., Winnipeg MB R3C 3Z1, 204/945-8567, Fax: 204/945-4930
Director, Northern Airports & Marine, D. Selby, 204/945-3421
Director, Traffic Engineering, Ben Rogers, 204/945-3781
Senior Design Engineer, Highway Planning & Design, Vacant, 204/945-4089
Highway Programming Engineer, Programming, T. Curtis, 204/945-3679

TRANSPORTATION POLICY, PLANNING & DEVELOPMENT DIVISION
215 Garry St., 15th Fl., Winnipeg MB R3C 3Z1
Fax: 204/945-5539
Asst. Deputy Minister, Donald Norquay, 204/945-1967
Director, Corporate Services, L. Gibson, 204/945-2886
Director, Policy & Service Development, J. Spacek, 204/945-8617
Director, Systems Planning & Development, A. Chadha, 204/945-2269

REGIONAL OPERATIONS DIVISION
Region 1 (Eastern)
Steinbach Office: #316, 323 Main St., Steinbach MB R0A 2A0 – 204/326-4434; Fax: 204/326-4852, Director, B. Prentice, Technical Services Engineer, L. Vigfusson, Regional Administrator, L. Bilbey
Selkirk: #203, 446 Main St., Selkirk MB R1A 1V7 – 204/785-5248; Fax: 204/785-5249, Maintenance Manager, R. Farrell
Winnipeg: #1, 35 Lakewood Blvd., Winnipeg MB R2J 2M8 – 204/945-8955; Fax: 204/945-6270, Construction Engineer, G. Cooper

Region 2 (South Central)
Portage La Prairie Office: 25 Tupper St. North, Portage La Prairie MB R1N 3K1 – 204/239-3292; Fax: 204/239-3301, Director, B. Petzold, Construction Engineer, R. McKibbin, Technical Services Engineer, R. McKay, Regional Administration, S. Lyons
Carman: 49 Main St., Carman MB R0G 0J0 – 204/745-2086; Fax: 204/745-3439, Maintenance Manager, A. Schollenberg

Region 3 (South Western)
Brandon Office: #1525, 1 St. North, Brandon MB R7C 1B5 – 204/726-6807; Fax: 204/726-6836, Director, R. Scrase, Technical Services Engineer, H. Mahood, Regional Administrator, D. Green
Minnedosa: 36 Center Ave. NW, 2nd Fl., Minnedosa MB R0J 1E0 – 204/867-2744; Fax: 204/867-5096, Construction Engineer, M. Robinson
Boissevain: PO Box 959, Boissevain MB R0K 0E0 – 204/534-2481; Fax: 204/534-6894, Maintenance Manager, K. Dern

Region 4 (West Central)
Dauphin Office: Industrial Rd., Dauphin MB R7N 3B3 – 204/622-2261; Fax: 204/638-6696, Director, A. Safronetz, Technical Services Engineer, R. Dowhey, Maintenance, G. Stary, Regional Administrator, R. Dupas
Swan River: 201 - 4th Ave. South, Swan River MB R0L 1Z0 – 204/734-3413; Fax: 204/734-3886, Construction Engineer, J. Gottfried

Region 5 (Northern)
Thompson Office: 11 Nelson Rd., Thompson MB R8N 0B3 – 204/677-6540; Fax: 204/677-6354, Director, G. Swaine, Technical Services/Construction Engineer, D. McKibbin, Regional Administrator, B. Beavis
The Pas: Otineka Mall, 2nd Fl., The Pas MB R9A 1M4 – 204/623-3803; Fax: 204/623-2893, Construction/Maintenance Engineer, R. Meisters

Associated Agencies, Boards & Commissions
•Highway Traffic Board: #200, 301 Weston St., Winnipeg MB R3E 3H4 – 204/945-6529; Fax: 204/783-6529
Chair, R. Sigurdson, 204/945-3120
Secretary, H.C. Moster, 204/945-1944
•Licence Suspension Appeal Board: #206, 1075 Portage Ave., Winnipeg MB R3G 0S1 – 204/945-7350; Fax: 204/945-0653
Chair, E.R. Guenther
Secretary, D. Hallson
•Manitoba Motor Transport Board: #200, 301 Weston St., Winnipeg MB R3E 3H4 – 204/945-5915; Fax: 204/783-6529
Chair, Donald Norquay, 204/945-1967
Secretary, H.C. Moster, 204/945-0944
•Taxicab Board: #206, 301 Weston St., Winnipeg MB R3E 3H4 – Fax: 204/948-2315
Secretary, G. Cochrane
Chair, G. Orle

Manitoba HOUSING
280 Broadway Ave., Winnipeg MB R3C 0R8
204/945-4109; Email: minhou@leg.gov.mb.ca

ACTS ADMINISTERED
Elderly & Infirm Persons' Housing Act (in part)
Housing & Renewal Corporation Act
Minister, Hon. Jack F. Reimer, 204/945-0074
Deputy Minister, W.J. Kinnear, 204/945-4756
Executive Director, Finance & Administration, G. Julius, 204/945-4694
Director, Client Services, H. Everett, 204/945-4693
Director, Financial Services, H. Bos, 204/945-4703
Director, Personnel, Roger LaFleche, 204/945-4692
Director, Research & Planning, K. Cassin, 204/945-4650

Associated Agencies, Boards & Commissions
•Manitoba Housing Authority: 280 Broadway Ave., 2nd Fl., Winnipeg MB R3C 0R8
General Manager, R. Fallis, 204/945-3935, Fax: 204/945-0546
•Manitoba Housing & Renewal Corporation: 280 Broadway, Winnipeg MB R3C 0R8 – 204/945-4748; Fax: 204/945-3930

Manitoba HYDRO
820 Taylor Ave., PO Box 815, Winnipeg MB R3C 2P4
204/474-3311; Fax: 204/475-9044
Minister Responsible, Hon. Darren Praznik, 204/945-3719
President & CEO, R.B. Brennan, 204/474-3600
Executive Vice-President, Engineering & Environment, Ralph O. Lambert
Vice-President, Corporate Services, Al Snyder
Vice-President, Customer Service, Al Macatavish
Vice-President & Chief Financial Officer, Finance, Vince Warden
General Counsel & Corporate Secretary, Doug Munro
Manager, Public Affairs, Glenn Schneider
Manager, Purchasing, Ray Nixdorf

Manitoba INDUSTRY, TRADE & TOURISM (MITT)
155 Carlton St., 6th Fl., Winnipeg MB R3C 3H8
204/945-2066; Fax: 204/945-1354; Email: minitt@leg.gov.mb.ca

ACTS ADMINISTERED
Convention Centre Corporation Act
Cooperative Association Loans & Loans Guarantee Act
Cooperative Promotion Trust Act
Design Institute Act
Development Corporation Act
Economic Innovation & Technology Council Act
Horse Racing Commission Act
Manitoba Employee Ownership Fund Corporation & Consequential Amendments Act (Crocus Investment Fund)
Manitoba Trading Corporation Act
Statistics Act
Tourism & Recreation Act
Minister, Hon. James Downey, 204/945-0067, Fax: 204/945-4882
Deputy Minister, Fred Sutherland, 204/945-4076, Fax: 204/945-1561
Director, Finance & Administration, J. Dalgliesh, 204/945-2066, Fax: 204/945-1354

AEROSPACE INDUSTRIES DEVELOPMENT INITIATIVE
204/945-0044
Managing Partner, Dennis H. Cleve, 204/945-2455, Fax: 204/945-7592
Development Consultant, R.A. Jack
Development Consultant, B. Manson
Development Consultant, P. Marshall

AGRI-FOOD INDUSTRIES DEVELOPMENT INITIATIVE
204/945-2012
Managing Partner, Brian Walker, 204/945-6668
Development Consultant, S. Davidge
Development Consultant, A. Handford

BUSINESS RESOURCE CENTRE
204/945-7719
Acting Managing Partner, Loretta Clarke, 204/945-7731
Officer, General Information, J. Asselin-Eisner, 204/945-7718

CO-OP DEVELOPMENT
204/945-3748
Managing Partner, Victor Hryshko, 204/945-4455, Fax: 204/945-2804
Director, Research & Economic Services, A. Barber, 204/945-8714, Fax: 204/945-1354
Research Economist, N. Allison, 204/945-2018
Trade Economist, D. Au, 204/945-2398

ENVIRONMENT INDUSTRIES DEVELOPMENT INITIATIVE
204/945-0125
Managing Partner, Valerie Zinger, 204/945-8745
Development Consultant, L. Hendrickson, 204/945-7733
Development Consultant, D. Sprange, 204/945-7938

FINANCIAL SERVICES
204/945-2770
Managing Partner, Stephen Kupfer, 204/945-2472, Fax: 204/945-1193
Acting Asst. Director, J. Kilgour, 204/945-7626

HEALTH INDUSTRIES DEVELOPMENT INITIATIVE
204/945-8206
Acting Managing Partner, Nigel Lilley, 204/945-7241
Consultant, Health Industry Development, M. Settler, 204/945-0498
Consultant, Health Product Development, P. Boulanger, 204/945-0499

INDUSTRY DEVELOPMENT
Managing Partner, Rod Sprange, 204/945-2420
Manager, Manufacturing Sector, B. Brennand, 204/945-7392
Manager, Services Sector, A.E. Jenson, 204/945-8234
Manager, Processing Sector, R.W. Dilay, 204/945-8695
Manager, Resources Sector, G. Hastings, 204/945-1454
Manager, Western Regional Office, G. Ranson, 231 Tenth St., Brandon MB R7A 4E9, 204/726-6253

INFORMATION & TELECOMMUNICATIONS INITIATIVE
204/945-4287
Managing Partner, Stephen Leahey, 204/945-7932, Fax: 204/945-7592
Development Consultant, J. Mickelson, 204/945-3807
Development Consultant, B. Lynch, 204/945-8065
Development Consultant, J. Selymes, 204/945-8501

TOURISM INITIATIVE
204/945-3796; URL: http://www.gov.mb.ca/manitoba/itt/travel/explore/
Toll Free: 1-800-665-0040, ext.TH6
Managing Partner, Hubert Messman, 204/945-4204
Coordinator, Travel Idea Centre, Melanie Bready, 204/945-3916
Manager, Tourism Development, H.D. Goy, 204/945-2307
Manager, Tourism Marketing & Promotions, M. Arbez, 204/945-2392
Manager, Tourism Services, K. Hildebrand, 204/945-8773
Clerk, Master Angler Program, J. Kosie, 204/945-4254

Associated Agencies, Boards & Commissions
•Economic Development Board: #648, 155 Carlton St., Winnipeg MB R3C 3H8 – 204/945-8221; Fax: 204/945-8229; URL: http://www.gov.mb.ca/manitoba/board/board.html

GOVERNMENT OF MANITOBA

Secretary, S. Duncan
- Economic Innovation & Technology Council: #648, 155 Carlton St., Winnipeg MB R3C 3H8 – 204/945-5940; Fax: 204/945-8229; URL: http://www.eitc.mb.ca/eitc.html
Vice-President & CFO, Gail Stephens
- Manitoba Bureau of Statistics: #333, 260 St. Mary Ave., Winnipeg MB R3C 0M6 – 204/945-2982
Director, Wilf Falk, 204/945-2988, Fax: 204/945-0695
Head, Statistical Services, D. Greenwood, 204/945-2989
- Manitoba Development Corporation
Listed alphabetically in detail, this Section.
- Manitoba Trading Corporation (MTC): 155 Carlton St., 4th Fl., Winnipeg MB R3C 3H8 – 204/945-2420
President, Rod Sprange

Manitoba INFORMATION SERVICES
#29, Legislative Bldg., 450 Broadway, Winnipeg MB R3C 0V8
204/945-3746; Fax: 204/945-3988
Provides news releases & television & radio news items.
Minister Responsible, Hon. Harold Gilleshammer, 204/945-3729, Fax: 204/945-5223
Director, Dwight MacAulay
Media Specialist, Carla McLeod
Radio Editor, Joe Czech, Email: jczech@leg.gov.mb.ca
Television Editor, T. Proveda

CITIZENS' INQUIRY SERVICE
#511, 401 York Ave., Winnipeg MB R3C 0P8
204/945-3744; Fax: 204/945-4261
Toll Free: 1-800-282-8060, TDD: 204/945-4796
Answers queries regarding Manitoba's provincial & Federal government departments & agencies.
Manager, Liliana Romanowski

Manitoba Public INSURANCE
234 Donald St., 9th Fl., PO Box 6300, Winnipeg MB R3C 1M8
204/985-7000; Fax: 204/943-9851
Administers Manitoba's Public Automobile Insurance Program & sells extension auto coverage on a competitive basis.
President & General Manager, J.W. Zacharias
Asst. General Manager & Vice-President, Claims, J.P. Broere
Vice-President, Community & Customer Relations, G.D. Newton
Vice-President, Finance & Corporate Information Systems, B.W. Galenzoski
Vice-President, Human Resources, R.B. Best
Vice-President, Insurance Operations, D.R. Kidd
General Counsel & Corporate Secretary, K.M. McCulloch
Manager, Corporate Communications, J.W. Kingdon, 204/985-8247, Fax: 204/942-2216

Manitoba JUSTICE
405 Broadway, 5th Fl., Winnipeg MB R3C 3L6
204/945-2852; Email: minjus@leg.gov.mb.ca

ACTS ADMINISTERED
Canada-United Kingdom Judgements Enforcement Act
Condominium Act (Sections 2 & 3 - with respect to the division of land, Sections 4 & 5 with respect to registration requirements, Section 6 & subsection 7(1))
Constitutional Questions Act
Corrections Act
Court of Appeal Act
Court of Queens' Bench Act
Crime Prevention Foundation Act
Criminal Injuries Compensation Act
Crown Attorneys Act
Child Custody Enforcement Act
Department of Justice Act
Discriminatory Business Practices Act
Escheats Act
Executive Government Organization Act (Subsection 12(2), only, as Keeper of the Great Seal)
Expropriation Act
Fatality Inquiries Act
Hudson's Bay Company Land Register Act
Human Rights Code
International Commercial Arbitration Act
International Sale of Goods Act
Interprovincial Subpoena Act
Intoxicated Persons Detention Act
Jury Act
Justice for Victims of Crime Act
Law Enforcement Review Act
Law Fees Act
Manitoba Women's Advisory Council Act
Mental Health Act (Part IV)
Minors Intoxicating Substances Control Act
Personal Property Security Act
Privacy Act
Private Investigators & Security Guards Act
Proceeding Against in the Crown Act, c P-140
Provincial Court Act, c C-275
Provincial Police Act, c P-150
Public Trustee Act, c P-275
Real Property Act, c R-30
Reciprocal Enforcement of Judgement Act, c J-20
Registry Act, c R-50
Regulations Act, c R-60
Sheriffs Act, c S-100
Special Survey Act, c S-190
Summary Convictions Act, c S-230
Surveys Act, c S-240 (Part I)
Transboundary Pollution Reciprocal Access Act, c T-145
Uniform Law Conference Commissioners Act, c U-30
Vacant Property Act, c V-10
Minister & Attorney General, Hon. Rosemary Vodrey, 204/945-3728, Fax: 204/945-2517, Email: minjus@leg.gov.mb.ca
Deputy Minister & Deputy Attorney General, Bruce MacFarlane, 204/945-3739, Fax: 204/945-4133, Email: dmjus@leg.gov.mb.ca
Executive Director, Administration & Finance Division, P. Sinnott, 204/945-2880

PUBLIC PROSECUTIONS DIVISION
405 Broadway, 5th Fl., Winnipeg MB R3C 3L6
204/945-2852
Asst. Deputy Attorney General, Vacant, Q.C., 204/945-2873
Director, Winnipeg Prosecutions, Vacant, 204/945-2860
Director, Special Prosecutions & Programs, L. Kee, 204/945-3265
Director, Regional Prosecutions, Michael Watson, 204/726-6013
General Counsel, J.G.B. Dangerfield, Q.C., 204/945-2882
General Counsel, Gregg Lawlor, 204/945-2870
General Counsel, J.D. Montgomery, Q.C., 204/945-4425
General Counsel, Rick Saull, 204/945-2863
Coordinator, Victim/Witness Assistance Program, Margaret Bilash, 408 York Ave., 4th Fl., Winnipeg MB R3C 0P9, 204/945-2303
Chief Medical Examiner, Dr. Peter Markesteyn, Office of the Chief Medical Examiner, #607, 330 Graham Ave., Winnipeg MB R3C 4A5, 204/945-0571
For list of Courts & other Legal Offices, including Judicial Officials & Judges *see* Section 10 of this book.

CORRECTIONS DIVISION
405 Broadway, 8th Fl., Winnipeg MB R3C 3L6
Asst. Deputy Minister, Vacant, 204/945-7291, Fax: 204/945-5537
Executive Director, Adult Correctional Services, Jim Wolfe, 204/945-7307
Executive Director, Community & Youth Correctional Services, Ben Thiessen, 204/945-8165, Fax: 204/948-2166
Manager, Fine Option Program, Tom Jennings, 204/945-7894, Fax: 204/488-4173

COURTS DIVISION
405 Broadway, 2nd Fl., Winnipeg MB R3C 3L6
Asst. Deputy Minister, M.W.G. Bruce, 204/945-2049

JUSTICE DIVISION
405 Broadway, 7th Fl., Winnipeg MB R3C 3L6
204/945-2832
Associate Deputy Attorney General, R. Perozzo, 204/945-2847
Director, Civil Legal Services, T. Hague, 204/945-2846
Deputy Director, Civil Legal Services, N.D. Shende, 204/945-2837
Director, Family Law Branch, Joan MacPhail, 204/945-2841
Director, Constitutional Law Branch, Donna Miller, 204/945-0716
Public Trustee, Office of the Public Trustee, Irene Hamilton, 204/945-2703

LEGISLATIVE COUNSEL & LEGAL TRANSLATION DIVISION
405 Broadway, 4th Fl., Winnipeg MB R3C 3L6
204/945-5758
Legislative Counsel & Asst. Deputy Attorney General, Shirley Strutt, 204/945-3708
Director, Legal Translation, Michel Nantel, 204/945-4597

PROPERTY RIGHTS DIVISION
405 Broadway, 14th Fl., Winnipeg MB R3C 3L6
Registrar General, M.A.J. Morton, Q.C., 204/945-2243

Land Titles
General Manager, J.B. Hall, 204/945-2244
Examiner of Surveys, G. Fraser, 204/945-945-2281
Deputy Examiner of Surveys, G. Lund, 204/945-2282

Land Titles Offices
Brandon: 705 Princess Ave., Brandon MB R7A 0P4 – 204/726-6279, District Registrar, J.S. Grewal
Dauphin: 308 Main St. South, Dauphin MB R7N 1K7 – 204/622-2084, District Registrar, Vacant
Morden: 351 Stephen St., Morden MB R0G 1J0 – 204/822-4436, District Registrar, R.E. James
Neepawa: 329 Hamilton St., Neepawa MB R0J 1H0 – 204/476-2106, District Registrar, E. Sims
Portage la Prairie: 25 Tupper St. North, Portage la Prairie MB R1N 3K1 – 204/239-3306, District Registrar, J. Kushniruk
Winnipeg: 405 Broadway, Lower Lobby, Winnipeg MB R3C 3L6 – 204/945-2042, 2043, District Registrar/Deputy Registrar General, R.M. Wilson, 204/945-2242, Senior Deputy District Registrar, H. Armstrong, 204/945-2251, Deputy District Registrar, A. Brown, 204/945-2250, Deputy District Registrar, V. Patel, 204/945-5560

Personal Property
405 Broadway, 15th Fl., Winnipeg MB R3C 3L6
204/945-3123
Registrar, D. Crockatt, 204/945-2656

Associated Agencies, Boards & Commissions
- Board of Review: 408 York St., 2nd Fl., Winnipeg MB R3C 3L6 – 204/945-4438; Fax: 204/945-1260
Secretary, M.A. Ewatski
- Criminal Injuries Compensation Board: 763 Portage Ave., Winnipeg MB R3G 3N2 – 204/775-7821; Fax: 204/784-1452

Executive Director, A. Lovell
- Human Rights Commission: #301, 259 Portage Ave., Winnipeg MB R3B 2A9 – 204/945-3007; Fax: 204/945-1292, TDD: 945-3442

Executive Director, Durlene Germscheid, 204/945-3012
- Law Enforcement Review Agency: 405 Broadway, 12th Fl., Winnipeg MB R3C 3L6 – 204/945-8667; Fax: 204/945-6692

Commissioner, Norm Ralph, 204/945-8696
- Law Reform Commission: 405 Broadway, 12th Fl., Winnipeg MB R3C 3L6 – 204/945-2896; Fax: 204/945-2184

Executive Director, J. Schnoor, 204/945-2900
- Legal Aid Manitoba: #402, 294 Portage Ave., Winnipeg MB R3C 0B9 – 204/985-8505; Fax: 204/944-8582

Executive Director, A. Finebit, 204/945-8508

Manitoba LABOUR

#611, Norquay Bldg., 401 York Ave., Winnipeg MB R3C 0P8
204/945-8190 (Management Services); Fax: 204/948-2085; Email: minlab@leg.gov.mb.ca; URL: http://www.gov.mb.ca/labour/

ACTS ADMINISTERED

Amusements Act (Part II)
Buildings & Mobile Homes Act
Construction Industry Wages Act
Department of Labour Act
Electricians' Licence Act
Elevator Act
Employment Services Act
Employment Standards Act
Fire Departments Arbitration Act
Fires Prevention Act (Part II)
Gas & Oil Burner Act
Labour Relations Act
Municipal Act (sections 301-314)
Pay Equity Act
Payment of Wages Act
Pension Benefits Act
Power Engineers Act
Remembrance Day Act
Retail Business Holiday Closing Act
Steam & Pressure Plants Act
Vacations with Pay Act
Workers Compensation Act (as it relates to Worker Advisors, s 108)
Workplace Safety & Health Act

Minister, Hon. Victor E. Toews, 204/945-4079, Fax: 204/945-8312, Email: vetoews@labour.gov.mb.ca
Deputy Minister, Tom Farrell, 204/945-4039, Fax: 204/945-8312, Email: tfarrell@labour.gov.mb.ca

EMPLOYMENT STANDARDS DIVISION

URL: http://www.gov.mb.ca/labour/standards/index.html
Executive Director, Jim McFarlane, 204/945-3354, Fax: 204/948-2085, Email: jmcfarla@labour.gov.mb.ca
Manager, Worker Advisor Office, Corinne Crawford, 204/945-5035, Fax: 204/948-2020

LABOUR SERVICES DIVISION

Asst. Deputy Minister, Tom Bleasdale, 204/945-3334, Fax: 204/945-1990
Commissioner, Office of the Fire Commissioner, Doug Popowich, 204/945-3328, Fax: 204/948-2089, Email: dpopowic@labour.gov.mb.ca
Director, Conciliation & Mediation Services, Jim Davage, 204/945-3333, Fax: 204/945-3286
Director, Mechanical & Engineering, Wayne Mault, 204/945-3374, Fax: 204/948-2309, Email: wmault@labour.gov.mb.ca
Deputy Superintendent, Pension Commission, Guy Gordon, 204/945-2742, Fax: 204/945-1990

MANAGEMENT SERVICES DIVISION

Executive Director, Jim Nykoluk, 204/945-2295, Fax: 204/948-2085
Director, Financial Services, J. Wood, 204/945-3409
Director, Human Resources & Acting Director, Information Systems, K. Kowalski, 204/945-3316
Director, Legislation & Policy Coordination, P. Bonin, 204/945-2352
Manager, Research Branch, Glenda Segal, 204/945-4889, Fax: 204/948-2085, Email: rbranch@labour.gov.mb.ca

WORKPLACE SAFETY & HEALTH DIVISION

#200, 401 York Ave., Winnipeg MB R3C 0P8
204/945-3446; Fax: 204/945-4556; URL: http://www.gov.mb.ca/labour/safety/index.html
Executive Director, Geoff Bawden, 204/945-3605, Email: gbawden@labour.gov.mb.ca
Director, Mines Inspection Branch, Kesari Reddy, 204/945-0848, Fax: 204/945-4556, Email: kreddy@labour.gov.mb.ca
Director, Workplace Safety & Health Branch, Garry Hildebrand, 204/945-3602, Fax: 204/945-4556, Email: ghildebr@labour.gov.mb.ca
Chief Medical Officer, Occupational Health Branch, Dr. Ted Redekop, 204/945-3608, Email: tredekop@labour.gov.mb.ca

Associated Agencies, Boards & Commissions

- Advisory Council on Workplace Safety & Health: #200, 401 York Ave., Winnipeg MB R3C 0P8 – 204/945-4153; Fax: 204/945-4556

Chair, W.N. Fox-Decent
- Manitoba Civil Service Commission: #935, 155 Carlton St., Winnipeg MB R3C 3H8 – 204/945-4088; Fax: 204/945-1486; Email: rdilts@csc.gov.mb.ca

Commissioner, Paul Hart, 204/945-2098
Chief Financial Officer, Rhett Dilts, 204/945-4088
- Manitoba Labour Board: A.A. Heaps Bldg., #402, 254-258 Portage Ave., Winnipeg MB R3C 0B6 – 204/945-5873; Fax: 204/945-1296

Chair, John Korpesho, Email: korpesho@labour.gov.mb.ca

Manitoba NATURAL RESOURCES

#327, Legislative Bldg., Winnipeg MB R3C 0V8
204/945-3730; Fax: 204/945-3586; Email: minnr@leg.gov.mb.ca; URL: http://www.gov.mb.ca/natres/index.html

ACTS ADMINISTERED

Crown Lands Act
Dutch Elm Disease Act
Dyking Authority Act
Ecological Reserves Act
Endangered Species Act
Fires Prevention Act (Part I)
Fisheries Act (Part III)
Fisherman's Assistance & Polluters' Liability Act
Forest Act
Ground Water & Water Well Act
International Peace Garden Act
Lake of the Woods Control Board Act
Manitoba Habitat Heritage Act
Manitoba Natural Resources Development Act
Manitoba Natural Resources Transfer Act, Amendment Act
Natural Resources Agreement Amendment Act, 1938
Provincial Park Lands Act
Provincial Parks Act
Rivers & Streams Act
Surveys Act (Part II)
Tourism & Recreation Act
Water Commission Act
Water Power Act
Water Resources Administration Act
Water Rights Act
Water Supply Commissions Act
Wildlife Act
Wild Rice Act
Manitoba Fishery Regulations (Section 34 of the Fisheries Act, Canada)

Minister, Hon. Albert Driedger, 204/945-3730, Fax: 204/945-3586
Deputy Minister, David Tomasson, 204/945-3785, Fax: 204/948-2403

LAND INFORMATION CENTRE

1007 Century St., Winnipeg MB R3H 0W4
Executive Director, Jack Schreuder, 204/945-6613, Fax: 204/945-1365
Acting Director, Lands Branch, Bryan Sheridan, 123 Main St. West, PO Box 20000, Neepawa MB R0J 1H0, 204/476-3441, Fax: 204/476-2097
Director, Surveys Branch, Wayne Leeman, 204/945-0011, Fax: 204/945-1365

MANAGEMENT SERVICES DIVISION

1577 Dublin Ave., Winnipeg MB R3E 3J5
Executive Director, W.J. Podolsky, 204/945-4056, Fax: 204/945-2385
Director, Financial Services Branch, Peter Lockett, 204/945-4187, Fax: 204/945-2385
Director, Human Resources Branch, Lorraine Metz, 204/945-2808, Fax: 204/948-2159
Director, Resource Information Systems, Vacant, 200 Saulteaux Crescent, PO Box 90, Winnipeg MB R3J 3W3, 204/945-2929, Fax: 204/945-2385

HEADQUARTERS OPERATIONS

200 Salteaux Cr., Winnipeg MB R3J 3W3
Asst. Deputy Minister, Harvey J. Boyle, 204/945-4842, Fax: 204/945-3125
Director, Wayne Fisher, 204/945-6647, Fax: 204/945-7782

Regional Offices

Central: PO Box 6000, Gimli MB R0C 1B0 – 204/642-6096; Fax: 204/642-6108, Regional Director, Worth Hayden
Eastern: CP 4000, Lac du Bonnet MB R0E 1A0 – 204/345-1433; Fax: 204/345-1440, Regional Director, Bob Enns
Northeastern: 59 Elizabeth Rd., PO Box 28, Thompson MB R8N 1X4 – 204/677-6628; Fax: 204/677-6359, Regional Director, Don Cook
Northwestern: 3rd St. & Ross Ave., PO Box 2550, The Pas MB R9A 1M4 – 204/627-8261; Fax: 204/627-8400, Regional Director, Albert King
Western: #340 - 9th St., PO Box 488, Brandon MB R7A 5Z4 – 204/726-6299; Fax: 204/726-6301, Regional Director, Bob Wooley

RESOURCES DIVISION

URL: http://www.gov.mb.ca/natres/infosys/infosys.html
Parks URL: http://www.gov.mb.ca/natres/parks/homepage.html
Forestry URL: http://www.gov.mb.ca/natres/forestry/forestry.html
Fisheries URL: http://www.gov.mb.ca/natres/fish/fish.html
Asst. Deputy Minister, Dr. Merlin Shoesmith, 200 Saulteaux Crescent, PO Box 80, Winnipeg MB R3J 3W3, 204/945-6829, Fax: 204/945-3125
Director, Fisheries Branch, Joe O'Connor, 200 Saulteaux Cr., PO Box 20, Winnipeg MB R3J 3W3, 204/945-7814, Fax: 204/945-2308
Director, Forestry Branch, A. Hoole, 200 Saulteaux Crescent, PO Box 70, Winnipeg MB R3J 3W3, 204/945-7998, Fax: 204/948-2671
Director, Parks & Natural Areas Branch, Gordon Prouse, 200 Saulteaux Cr., PO Box 50, Winnipeg MB R3J 3W3, 204/945-4362, Fax: 204/945-0012

Director, Policy Coordination Branch, Grant Baker, 200 Saulteaux Cr., PO Box 38, Winnipeg MB R3J 3W3, 204/945-6658, Fax: 204/945-4552
Director, Water Resources Branch, Steven Topping, 1577 Dublin Ave., Winnipeg MB R3E 3J5, 204/945-7488, Fax: 204/945-7419
Director, Wildlife Branch, Brian Gillespie, 200 Saulteaux Cr., PO Box 24, Winnipeg MB R3J 3W3, 204/945-7761, Fax: 204/945-3077

Associated Agencies, Boards & Commissions

• Assiniboine River Management Advisory Board: 200 Saulteaux Cr., PO Box 70, Winnipeg MB R3J 3W3 – 204/945-7950
Chair, Tim Ball
• Ecological Reserves Advisory Committee: PO Box 355, Stn St. Vital, Winnipeg MB R2M 5C8 – 204/942-6617
Chair, David Hatch
• Endangered Species Advisory Committee: 200 Saulteaux Cr., PO Box 80, Winnipeg MB R3J 3W3 – 204/945-6829
Chair, Dr. Merlin Shoesmith
• Lake of the Woods Control Board: c/o Ontario Hydro, 700 University Ave., Toronto ON M5G 1X6
Chair, Joan Eaton
• Lower Red River Valley Water Commission: PO Box 1180, Altona MB R0G 0B0 – 204/324-8365
Chair, R. Martel
• The Manitoba Habitat Heritage Board: #200, 1555 St. James St., Winnipeg MB R3H 1B5 – 204/784-4350
Chair, Ted Poyser
• Prairie Provinces Water Board: #201, 2050 Cornwall St., Regina SK S4P 2K5 – 306/522-6671
Chair, Jim Vollmershausen
• Saskeram Wildlife Management Area Advisory Committee: PO Box 2550, The Pas MB R9A 1M4 – 204/627-8266
Chair, R.C. Uchtmann
• Souris River Water Commission: PO Box 399, Hartney MB R0M 0X0 – 204/858-2590
Chair, Wayne Drummond

Manitoba NORTHERN AFFAIRS
59 Elizabeth Dr., Thompson MB R8N 1X4
204/677-6607; Fax: 204/677-6753; Email: minna@leg.gov.mb.ca

ACTS ADMINISTERED
Communities Economic Development Act
Manitoba Natural Resources Development Act
Northern Affairs Act
Planning Act
Minister, Hon. Darren Praznik, 204/945-6429, Fax: 204/945-8374
Deputy Minister, Michael Fine, 204/945-4172, Fax: 204/945-8374
Director, Administrative Support Division, Rene Gagnon, 204/677-6609, Fax: 204/677-6753

LOCAL GOVERNMENT DEVELOPMENT DIVISION
Asst. Deputy Minister, Oliver Boulette, 204/677-6795, Fax: 204/677-6525
Director, Engineering Services, C. Boyd, 204/677-6683, Fax: 204/677-6525
Director, Inter Regional Services, M. Duval, 204/677-6829, Fax: 204/677-6525

Regional Offices
Dauphin: Provincial Bldg., 27 Second Ave. SW, Dauphin MB RN7 3E5 – 204/622-2152; Fax: 204/622-2305, Regional Director, J. Perchaluk
Selkirk: Rami Bldg., 339A Main St., Selkirk MB R1A 1T3 – 204/785-5089; Fax: 204/785-5218, Regional Director, J. Gordon

The Pas: PO Box 2560, The Pas MB R9A 1M3 – 204/627-8273; Fax: 204/623-4583, Regional Director, K. Barker
Thompson: Provincial Bldg., 59 Elizabeth Dr., PO Box 27, Thompson MB R8N 1X8 – 204/677-6788; Fax: 204/677-6525, Regional Director, K. Vipond

Agreement Management & Coordination
Director, Jeff Polakoff, 204/945-2507, Fax: 204/945-3689
Manager, Northern Flooding, B. Ketcheson, 204/945-2511, Fax: 204/945-3689

Native Affairs Secretariat
Director, Harvey Bostrom, 204/945-0572, Fax: 204/945-3689

Associated Agencies, Boards & Commissions
• Communities Economic Development Fund: 23 Station Rd., Thompson MB R8N 0N6 – 204/778-4138; Fax: 204/778-4313, Toll Free: 1-800-561-4315 (Manitoba)
General Manager, Gerald Offet
Administrative Asst., M. Beckmann

Manitoba Office of the OMBUDSMAN
#750, 500 Portage Ave., Winnipeg MB R3C 3X1
204/786-6483; Fax: 204/942-7803
Toll Free: 1-800-665-0531
Provincial Ombudsman, Barry E. Tuckett
Officer Manager, Laura Foster

Manitoba RURAL DEVELOPMENT
#600, 800 Portage Ave., Winnipeg MB R3G 0N4
Fax: 204/945-1383; Email: mnrd@leg.gov.mb.ca

ACTS ADMINISTERED
Conservation Districts Act
Local Authorities Election Act
Local Government Districts Act
Municipal Act
Municipal Affairs Administration Act
Municipal Assessment Act
Municipal Board Act
Municipal Council Conflict of Interest Act
Municipal Debt Adjustment Act
Municipal Works Assistance Act
Official Time Act
Planning Act
Soldiers' Taxation Relief Act
Surface Rights Act
Unconditional Grants Act
Water Services Board Act
Minister, Hon. Len Derkach, 204/945-3788, Fax: 204/945-1383
Deputy Minister, Winston Hodgins, 204/945-3787, Fax: 204/945-5255
Chief, Financial Services, Brian Johnston, 204/945-2199
Administrator, Personnel, Zinovia Solomon, 204/945-2147

LOCAL GOVERNMENT SERVICES DIVISION
#609, 800 Portage Ave., Winnipeg MB R3G ON4
Asst. Deputy Minister, Marie Elliott, 204/945-2533, Fax: 204/945-3769
Executive Director, Local Government Support Services, Roger Dennis, 204/945-2567
Provincial Municipal Assessor, Assessment Branch, K. Graham, 204/945-2605, Fax: 204/945-1994
Director, Information Systems, Larry Phillips, 204/945-2585
Coordinator, Municipal Services, Fred Butler, 204/945-2570

RURAL ECONOMIC DEVELOPMENT DIVISION
#600, 800 Portage Ave., Winnipeg MB R3G 0N4
204/945-6258
Asst. Deputy Minister, Larry Martin, 204/945-3089, Fax: 204/945-3769
General Manager, Infrastructure Services (Manitoba Water Services Board), Dick Menon, 2022 Currie Blvd., PO Box 22080, Brandon MB R7A 6Y9, 204/726-6073, Fax: 204/726-6290
Director, Community Economic Development Branch, Peter Mah, 204/945-2192, Fax: 204/945-5059
Director, Rural Economic Development Initiative (REDI), Vacant, 204/945-2163, Fax: 204/945-5059
Manager, Grow Bonds Program, Paul Sweatman, PO Box 2000, Altona MB R0G 0B0, 204/324-1957, Fax: 204/324-5151
Director, Corporate Planning & Business Development, Ron Riopka, 204/945-2595, Fax: 204/945-3769

Canada-Manitoba Infrastructure Secretariat
#102A, 800 Portage Ave., Winnipeg MB R3G 0N4
Fax: 204/948-2035
Toll Free: 1-800-268-4883
Program Manager, Jill Vogan, 204/945-4074
Officer, Communications, C. Harvey, 204/945-8778

Manitoba Conservation Districts Commission
Legislative Bldg., #309, 450 Broadway Ave., Winnipeg MB R3C 0V8
204/945-7496; Fax: 204/945-5059
Chair, Winston Hodgins, 204/945-3787
Secretary, Lyle Duguay, 204/945-7496

Conservation Districts
Alonsa: PO Box 33, Alonsa MB R0H 0A0 – 204/767-2101; Fax: 204/767-2301, Manager, Harry Harris
Cooks Creek: 530 Main St., PO Box 100, Oakbank MB R0E 1J0 – 204/444-3652; Fax: 204/444-3652, Manager, B. Lussier
Pembina Valley: 261 Main St., PO Box 659, Manitou MB R0G 1G0 – 204/242-3267; Fax: 204/242-2798, Manager, Thor Thorleifson
Turtle Mountain: 129 Broadway North, PO Box 508, Deloraine MB R0M 0M0 – 204/747-2530; Fax: 204/747-2956, Manager, Gary Davis
Turtle River Watershed: PO Box 449, Ste. Rose du Lac MB R0L 1S0 – 204/447-2139; Fax: 204/447-2278, Manager, M. Boychuk
West Souris River: PO Box 339, Reston MB R0M 1X0 – 204/877-3020; Fax: 204/877-3090, Manager, Glen Campbell
Whitemud Watershed: PO Box 130, Neepawa MB R0J 1H0 – 204/476-5019; Fax: 204/476-2811, Manager, S.W. Hilderbrand

Associated Agencies, Boards & Commissions
• Manitoba Municipal Board: #408, 800 Portage Ave., Winnipeg MB R3G 0N4 – 204/945-1789; Fax: 204/948-2235
Chair, Robert Smellie, Q.C.
• Manitoba Surface Rights Board (MSRB): 2022 Currie Blvd., PO Box 22080, Brandon MB R7A 6Y9 – 204/726-7026; Fax: 204/726-6290
Presiding Member, Thomas A. Cowan
• Manitoba Water Services Board: 2022 Currie Blvd., PO Box 1059, Brandon MB R7A 6A3 – 204/726-6076; Fax: 204/726-6290

Manitoba SENIORS DIRECTORATE
#822, 155 Carlton St., Winnipeg MB R3C 3H8
204/945-2127; Fax: 204/948-2514
Minister Responsible, Hon. Jack F. Reimer, 204/945-0074, Fax: 204/945-1299
Executive Director, Kathy Yurkowski

Manitoba TELEPHONE SYSTEM (MTS)
489 Empress St., Winnipeg MB R3C 3V6
204/941-4111; Fax: 204/956-0836
Minister Responsible, Hon. Glen Findlay
Chair, Tom Stefanson
President & CEO, Bill Fraser
Executive Vice-President, Barry Gordon
Director, Communications, June Kirby

Manitoba TREASURY BOARD
333 Broadway, 3rd Fl., Winnipeg MB R3C 0S9
204/945-1101; Fax: 204/945-4878
Chair, Hon. Eric Stefanson
Secretary, Julian Benson

Manitoba URBAN AFFAIRS
#203, 280 Broadway Ave., Winnipeg MB R3C 0R8
Fax: 204/945-1249; Email: minua@leg.gov.mb.ca

ACTS ADMINISTERED
City of Winnipeg Act
Minister, Hon. Jack F. Reimer, 204/945-0074, Fax: 204/945-1299
Deputy Minister, W.J. Kinnear, 204/945-4278, Fax: 204/948-2555
Asst. Deputy Minister, Heather MacKnight, 204/945-3872
Director, Urban Government & Finance, Marianne Farag, 204/945-4690
Senior Coordinator, Urban Finance, Jon Gunn, 204/945-3864
Senior Coordinator, Urban Policy, Ray Klassen, 204/945-3866

Manitoba WORKERS' COMPENSATION BOARD
333 Maryland St., Winnipeg MB R3G 1M2
204/786-5471; Fax: 204/786-3704
Toll Free: 1-800-362-3340 (Manitoba)
Chair & CEO, Prof. Wally Fox-Decent

ATLANTIC PROVINCES ECONOMIC COUNCIL (APEC)

#500, 5121 Sackville St., Halifax NS B3J 1K1
902/422-6516; Fax: 902/429-6803; Email: apec@fox.nstn.ns.ca
Chief Economist, Elizabeth Beale
Membership Secretary, Kimberly Brown, 902/422-6516

COUNCIL OF MARITIME PREMIERS (CMP)

Council Secretariat, #1006, 5161 George St., PO Box 2044, Halifax NS B3J 2Z1
902/424-7590; Fax: 902/424-8976; Email: premiers@fox.nstn.ns.ca
Council Secretary, Keith Wornell
Information Officer, Kim Thomson
The Premiers of New Brunswick, Nova Scotia & Prince Edward Island constitute the Council. It was established by identical legislation in the three provinces to: promote unity of purpose among their respective Governments; ensure maximum coordination of the activities of the Governments & their agencies &; establish a framework for joint action & undertakings. The Council meets at least four times annually to discuss matters of mutual interest or concern to the three Maritime governments. A Secretariat acts as the focal point for coordinating the efforts of the three Governments in identifying potential benefits that could result from a regional approach to policy formulation & program development.

MARITIME MUNICIPAL TRAINING & DEVELOPMENT BOARD
6100 University Ave., Halifax NS B3H 3J5
902/494-3712, 494-1463; URL: http://ccn.cs.dal.ca/Government/MMTDB/mmtdb-intro.html
Executive Director, A. Donald Smeltzer
In cooperation with municipal associations & local governments, this agency is dedicated to upgrading the administrative capability of municipal employees by encouraging the coordination of efforts & assisting in the establishment of new programs & initiatives.

ATLANTIC PROVINCES EDUCATION FOUNDATION
PO Box 2044, Halifax NS B3J 2Z1
902/424-5352; Fax: 902/424-8976; Email: premiers@fox.nstn.ns.ca
Secretary, Barbara Murray
Coordinates efforts of the four provincial Departments of Education in the development of common curriculum & educational materials for the Atlantic region with a view to increasing the effectiveness & efficiency of the four systems.

MARITIME PROVINCES HIGHER EDUCATION COMMISSION (MPHEC)
PO Box 6000, Fredericton NB E3B 5H1
506/453-2844; Fax: 506/453-2106
Acting Chair, R. Laurence Simpson
An advisory body which assists the provinces & the post-secondary institutions in attaining a more efficient & effective utilization & allocation of resources in the field of higher education.

MARITIME PROVINCES HARNESS RACING COMMISSION
Harbour Quay Bldg., #7, 263 Harbour Dr., Summerside PE C1N 5P1
902/888-3489; Fax: 902/888-2762
Director, Ted Andrews
To govern & regulate harness racing in the Maritime provinces.

GOVERNMENT OF NEW BRUNSWICK

Seat of Government: Legislative Bldg., Legislative Bldg., PO Box 6000, Fredericton NB E3B 5H1
URL: http://www.gov.nb.ca/
The Province of New Brunswick entered Confederation July 1, 1867. It has an area of 713,469.23 km2, and the StatsCan census population in 1991 was 723,900.

Office of the LIEUTENANT GOVERNOR
736 King St., PO Box 6000, Fredericton NB E3B 5H1
506/453-2505; Fax: 506/444-5280
Lieutenant Governor, Hon. Margaret Norrie McCain
Principal Secretary, Corinne Norrad

Office of the PREMIER
Centennial Bldg., 670 King St., PO Box 6000, Fredericton NB E3B 5H1
506/453-2144; Fax: 506/453-7407; Email: premier@gov.nb.ca
Premier, Hon. Frank McKenna, Email: premier@gov.nb.ca
Deputy Minister, Georgio Gaudet
Executive Asst. to the Premier, Ruth McCrea
Director, Communications, Maurice Robichaud

EXECUTIVE COUNCIL
Centennial Bldg., PO Box 6000, Fredericton NB E3B 5H1
Premier, Hon. Frank McKenna, 506/453-2144, Fax: 506/453-7407, Email: premier@gov.nb.ca
Solicitor General, Hon. Jane Barry, 506/453-7414, Fax: 506/453-3870, Email: jbarry@gov.nb.ca
Minister, Finance & Minister of State for Quality, Hon. Edmond Blanchard, Q.C., 506/453-2583, Fax: 506/453-3651, Email: blanchard@gov.nb.ca
Minister, Environment, Hon. Vaughn Blaney, 506/453-2523, Fax: 506/453-3325, Email: vaughnbl@gov.nb.ca
Minister, Municipalities, Culture & Housing, Hon. Ann Breault, 506/457-7866, Fax: 506/453-7478, Email: annb@gov.nb.ca
Minister of State, Literacy & Adult Education & Minister of State, Youth, Hon. Georgie Day, 506/457-6734, Fax: 506/444-5245, Email: gday@gov.nb.ca
Minister of State, Mines & Energy, Hon. Albert Doucet
Minister, Justice & Attorney General, Hon. Paul Duffie, 506/453-3001, Fax: 506/453-3283, Email: pduffie@gov.nb.ca
Deputy Premier, President, Executive Council & Government House Leader, Hon. J. Raymond Frenette
Minister, Natural Resources & Energy, Hon. Alan Graham, 506/453-2510, Fax: 506/453-2930
Minister, Health & Community Services, Hon. Russell H.T. King, M.D., 506/453-2581, Fax: 506/453-5243
Minister, Transportation, Hon. Sheldon Lee, 506/453-2559, Fax: 506/453-2900
Minister, Education, Hon. James Lockyer, Q.C., 506/453-2591, Fax: 506/444-4400, Email: jamesl@gov.nb.ca
Minister, Advanced Education & Labour, Hon. Roland MacIntyre, 506/453-2342
Minister, Human Resources Development & Minister Responsible, Status of Women, Hon. Marcelle Mersereau, 506/453-2558, Fax: 506/453-3377, Email: marcellm@gov.nb.ca
Minister of State, Intergovernmental & Aboriginal Affairs, Hon. Bernard Richard, 506/444-5077, Fax: 506/453-2995, Email: bernardr@gov.nb.ca
Minister of State, Regional Development Corporation & Northern Development, Hon. Jean-Paul Savoie, 506/453-2277, Fax: 506/453-7988, Email: jeanps@gov.nb.ca
Minster, Supply & Services, Hon. Bruce A. Smith
Minister, Fisheries & Aquaculture, Hon. Bernard Thériault, 506/453-2662, Fax: 506/453-5210, Email: bernart@gov.nb.ca
Minister, Economic Development & Tourism & Minister Responsible, Information Highway Secretariat, Hon. Camille Thériault, 506/453-3009, Email: cth@gov.nb.ca
Minister of State, Family & Community Services, Hon. Marilyn Trenholme, M.D.
Minister, Agriculture & Rural Development & Deputy Government House Leader, Hon. Doug Tyler, 506/453-2448, Fax: 506/444-5022

Executive Council Office
Fax: 506/453-2266
Clerk, Executive Council & Secretary, Cabinet, Claire Morris, 506/453-2718
Asst. Clerk, Executive Council & Asst. Secretary, Cabinet, Judith E. Nicholls, 506/453-2985

LEGISLATIVE ASSEMBLY
c/o Clerk's Office, Legislative Bldg., PO Box 6000, Fredericton NB E3B 5H1
506/453-2506; Fax: 506/453-7154; URL: http://www.gov.nb.ca/legis/index.htm
Clerk: Loredana Catalli Sonier
Speaker: Hon. Danny Gay, 506/453-2907
Sergeant-at-Arms: Phyllis A. LeBlanc, 506/453-2527

Director, Hansard & Debates Translation: Valmond LeBlanc
Legislative Librarian: Eric Swanick, 506/453-2338
Clerk's Asst., Donald J. Forestell

Government Caucus Office (Lib.)
506/453-2548; Fax: 506/453-3956
Director, Steven MacKinnon
Officer, Administrative Services, Gabriella Marchetti-Mockler

Office of the Official Opposition (PC)
PO Box 6000, Fredericton NB E3B 5H1
506/453-7494; Fax: 506/453-3461
Leader, Hon. Bernard Valcourt
Executive Asst., Marie-France Pelletier
Director, Administration, Bradley Green

Office of the New Democratic Party (NDP)
PO Box 6000, Fredericton NB E3B 5H1
506/453-3305; Fax: 506/453-3688
Leader, Elizabeth Weir
Executive Asst., Joan Weinman
Provincial Secretary, Roger Couvrette

Standing Committees of the House
Crown Corporations
Law Amendments
Legislative Administration
Ombudsmen
Private Bills
Privileges
Procedure
Public Accounts

Select Committees of the House
Demographics
Electoral Reform
Gasoline Pricing

FIFTY-THIRD LEGISLATURE - NEW BRUNSWICK
506/453-2506
Last General Election, September 11, 1995. Maximum Duration, 5 years.
Party Standings (July, 1996):
Liberal (Lib.) 48
Progressive Conservatives (PC) 6
New Democratic Party (NDP) 1
Total 55

Salaries, Indemnities & Allowances: 1995 - Members' annual indemnity $35,735, plus $14,294 for expenses. In addition to this are the following:
Premier $47,861
Ministers $31,908 (with portfolio); $23,932 (without portfolio)
Leader of the Opposition $31,908
Speaker $23,932

Following is: constituency (number of eligible voters at 1995 election) member, party affiliation. (Address for all is PO Box 6000, Fredericton NB E3B 5H1.)
Refer to Cabinet List, Government Caucus Office, & the Party Listings, for **phone** & **Fax** numbers.

MEMBERS BY CONSTITUENCY
Albert (8,289) Harry Doyle, Lib.
Bathurst (9,634) Hon. Marcelle Mersereau, Lib.
Campbellton (8,755) Hon. Edmond Blanchard, Q.C., Lib.
Caraquet (9,357) Hon. Bernard Thériault, Lib.
Carleton (10,029) Dale Graham, PC
Centre-Péninsule (7,673) Denis Landry, Lib.
Charlotte (7,613) Hon. Sheldon Lee, Lib.
Dalhousie-Restigouche East (9,481) Carolle de Ste-Croix, Lib.
Dieppe-Memramcook (12,467) Greg O'Donnell, Lib.
Edmundston (8,391) Hon. Bernard Valcourt, PC
Fredericton North (11,973) Jim Wilson, Lib.
Fredericton South (10,827) Hon. Russell H.T. King, M.D., Lib.
Fredericton-Fort Nashwaak (8,732) Greg Byrne, Lib.
Fundy Isles (3,418) Eric Allaby, Lib.
Grand Bay-Westfield (7,987) Milton Sherwood, PC
Grand Falls Region/Région de Grand-Sault (8,614) Hon. Paul Duffie, Lib.
Grand Lake (9,277) Hon. Doug Tyler, Lib.
Hampton-Belleisle (10,477) Hon. Georgie Day, Lib.
Kennebecasis (10,580) Peter Leblanc, Lib.
Kent (8,419) Hon. Alan Graham, Lib.
Kent South (10,982) Hon. Camille Thériault, Lib.
Kings East (9,524) Leroy Armstrong, Lib.
Lamèque-Shippagan-Miscou (9,637) Jean-Camille Degrâce, Lib.
Mactaquac (10,049) David Olmstead, Lib.
Madawaska-la-Vallée (8,138) Percy Mockler, PC
Madawaska-les-Lacs (8,618) Jeannot Volpé, CoR
Miramichi Bay (8,739) Hon. Danny Gay, Lib.
Miramichi Centre (10,090) John McKay, Lib.
Miramichi-Bay du Vin (9,604) Hon. Frank McKenna, Lib.
Moncton Crescent (10,315) Ken Macleod, Lib.
Moncton East (11,208) Hon. J. Raymond Frenette, Lib.
Moncton North (11,353) Gene Devereux, Lib.
Moncton South (11,054) Hon. James Lockyer, Q.C., Lib.
Nepisiguit (9,226) Alban Landry, Lib.
New Maryland (10,537) Joan Kingston, Lib.
Nigadoo-Chaleur (9,814) Hon. Albert Doucet, Lib.
Oromocto-Gagetown (10,313) Hon. Vaughn Blaney, Lib.
Petitcodiac (8,131) Hollis Steeves, Lib.
Restigouche West (8,131) Hon. Jean-Paul Savoie, Lib.
Riverview (10,425) Al Kavanaugh, Lib.
Rogersville-Kouchibouguac (7,738) Kenneth Johnson, Lib.
Saint John Champlain (9,830) Hon. Roland MacIntyre, Lib.
Saint John Harbour (9,221) Elizabeth Weir, NDP
Saint John Lancaster (10,075) Hon. Jane Barry, Lib.
Saint John Portland (10,090) Leo A. McAdam, Lib.
Saint John-Fundy (8,495) Stuart Jamieson, Lib.
Saint John-Kings (10,221) Laureen Jarrett, Lib.
Shediac-Cap-Pelé (10,986) Hon. Bernard Richard, Lib.
Southwest Miramichi (8,659) Reg MacDonald, Lib.
Tantramar (7,559) Hon. Marilyn Trenholme, M.D., Lib.
Tracadie-Sheila (9,432) Elvy Robichaud, PC
Victoria-Tobique (8,429) Dr. Larry Kennedy, Lib.
Western Charlotte (8,663) Hon. Ann Breault, Lib.
Woodstock (9,739) Hon. Bruce A. Smith, Lib.
York (9,828) John Flynn, Lib.

MEMBERS (ALPHABETICAL)
Eric Allaby, Fundy Isles (3,418)Lib.
Leroy Armstrong, Kings East (9,524)Lib.
Hon. Jane Barry, Saint John Lancaster (10,075)Lib.
Hon. Edmond Blanchard, Q.C., Campbellton (8,755)Lib.
Hon. Vaughn Blaney, Oromocto-Gagetown (10,313)Lib.
Hon. Ann Breault, Western Charlotte (8,663)Lib.
Greg Byrne, Fredericton-Fort Nashwaak (8,732)Lib.
Hon. Georgie Day, Hampton-Belleisle (10,477)Lib.
Jean-Camille Degrâce, Lamèque-Shippagan-Miscou (9,637)Lib.
Gene Devereux, Moncton North (11,353)Lib.
Hon. Albert Doucet, Nigadoo-Chaleur (9,814)Lib.
Harry Doyle, Albert (8,289)Lib.
Hon. Paul Duffie, Grand Falls Region/Région de Grand-Sault (8,614)Lib.
John Flynn, York (9,828)Lib.
Hon. J. Raymond Frenette, Moncton East (11,208)Lib.
Hon. Danny Gay, Miramichi Bay (8,739)Lib.
Hon. Alan Graham, Kent (8,419)Lib.
Dale Graham, Carleton (10,029)PC
Stuart Jamieson, Saint John-Fundy (8,495)Lib.
Laureen Jarrett, Saint John-Kings (10,221)Lib.
Kenneth Johnson, Rogersville-Kouchibouguac (7,738)Lib.
Al Kavanaugh, Riverview (10,425)Lib.
Dr. Larry Kennedy, Victoria-Tobique (8,429)Lib.
Hon. Russell H.T. King, M.D., Fredericton South (10,827)Lib.
Joan Kingston, New Maryland (10,537)Lib.
Alban Landry, Nepisiguit (9,226)Lib.
Denis Landry, Centre-Péninsule (7,673)Lib.
Peter Leblanc, Kennebecasis (10,580)Lib.
Hon. Sheldon Lee, Charlotte (7,613)Lib.
Hon. James Lockyer, Q.C., Moncton South (11,054)Lib.
Reg MacDonald, Southwest Miramichi (8,659)Lib.
Hon. Roland MacIntyre, Saint John Champlain (9,830)Lib.
Ken Macleod, Moncton Crescent (10,315)Lib.
Leo A. McAdam, Saint John Portland (10,090)Lib.
John McKay, Miramichi Centre (10,090)Lib.
Hon. Frank McKenna, Miramichi-Bay du Vin (9,604)Lib.
Hon. Marcelle Mersereau, Bathurst (9,634)Lib.
Percy Mockler, Madawaska-la-Vallée (8,138)PC
Greg O'Donnell, Dieppe-Memramcook (12,467)Lib.
David Olmstead, Mactaquac (10,049)Lib.
Hon. Bernard Richard, Shediac-Cap-Pelé (10,986)Lib.
Elvy Robichaud, Tracadie-Sheila (9,432)PC
Hon. Jean-Paul Savoie, Restigouche West (8,131)Lib.
Milton Sherwood, Grand Bay-Westfield (7,987)PC
Hon. Bruce A. Smith, Woodstock (9,739)Lib.
Carolle de Ste-Croix, Dalhousie-Restigouche East (9,481)Lib.
Hollis Steeves, Petitcodiac (8,131)Lib.
Hon. Bernard Thériault, Caraquet (9,357)Lib.
Hon. Camille Thériault, Kent South (10,982)Lib.
Hon. Marilyn Trenholme, M.D., Tantramar (7,559)Lib.
Hon. Doug Tyler, Grand Lake (9,277)Lib.
Hon. Bernard Valcourt, Edmundston (8,391)PC
Jeannot Volpé, Madawaska-les-Lacs (8,618)CoR
Elizabeth Weir, Saint John Harbour (9,221)NDP
Jim Wilson, Fredericton North (11,973)Lib.

NEW BRUNSWICK GOVERNMENT DEPARTMENTS & AGENCIES

Department of ADVANCED EDUCATION & LABOUR/Enseignement Supérieur et travail
Chestnut Complex, 470 York St., PO Box 6000, Fredericton NB E3B 5H1
Fax: 506/453-3806; URL: http://www.gov.nb.ca/ael/index.htm

ACTS ADMINISTERED
Adult Education & Training Act
Apprenticeship & Occupational Certification Act
Boiler & Pressure Vessel Act
Electrical Installation & Inspection Act
Elevators & Lifts Act
Employment Development Act
Employment Standards Act
Fisheries Bargaining Act
Higher Education Foundation Act
Hospital Services Act
Human Rights Act
Industrial Relations Act
Labour & Employment Board Act
Labour Market Research Act
Occupational Health & Safety Act
Pension Benefits Act
Plumbing Installation & Inspection Act
Public Service Labour Relations Act
Silicosis Compensation Act

Trade Schools Act
Workers' Compensation Act (administered by Workplace Health, Safety & Compensation Commission)
Workplace Health, Safety & Compensation Commission Act
Youth Assistance Act
Minister, Hon. Roland MacIntyre, 506/453-2342, Fax: 506/453-3038
Minister of State, Literacy & Adult Education & Minister of State, Youth, Hon. Georgie Day, 506/457-6734, Fax: 506/444-5425
Deputy Minister, W. David Ferguson, 506/453-2343, Fax: 506/453-3038
Director, Corporate Communications, Vacant, 506/444-5335, Fax: 506/444-4314
Director, Human Resource Services, Roger Arseneau, 506/453-8209, Fax: 506/453-7913

CORPORATE PROGRAMS DIVISION
Asst. Deputy Minister, Wm. H. Smith, 506/453-8262, Fax: 506/444-4314
Executive Director, Advocacy Services, Maryanne Bourgeois, 506/453-3298, Fax: 506/453-3300
Director, Human Rights Commission, Janet Cullinan, 506/453-2301, Fax: 506/453-2653
Director, Student Services, Don Chevarie, 506/453-3358, Fax: 506/444-4333
Senior Advocate, Office of the Workers' Advocate, Rick Clark, 506/658-2472, Fax: 506/658-3075
Advocate, Office of the Employers' Advocate, Richard Fitzgerald, 506/457-3510, Fax: 506/453-3806
Manager, Employment Services for Persons with Disabilities, Rachel Grant, 506/453-3247, Fax: 506/453-3806
Manager, Learning in the Workplace Initiative & Manager, Literacy Services, Rowena Brooks, 506/444-4331, Fax: 506/453-3300
Manager, Multiculturalism & Immigration, Beverly Woznow, 506/444-4331, Fax: 506/453-3300
Manager, Public Affairs, Shawn Hearn, 506/453-2568, Fax: 506/453-3123

DEPARTMENTAL SERVICES DIVISION
Executive Director, Patrick Doherty, 506/453-2587, Fax: 506/444-4314
Acting Director, Finance, Luc Paulin, 506/453-2519, Fax: 506/453-7913
Director, Information Technology Services, Ken Fitzpatrick, 506/453-2588, Fax: 506/453-3806
Acting Manager, Administration, Bev Bishop, Fax: 506/453-3806
Manager, Facilities Management, Ron LeBlanc, 506/453-8244, Fax: 506/453-7913
Manager, Trade Schools, Gerald Stillwell, 506/453-8214, Fax: 506/453-7913

DIVISION DES SERVICES ÉDUCATIFS (FRANCOPHONE)
Sous-ministre adjoint, Bernard Paulin, 506/444-5732, Fax: 506/444-4314
Directeur éxecutif, TéléÉducation, Rory McGreal, 506/444-4230, Fax: 506/444-4232
Directeur, Services éducatifs, Laurent McLaughlin, 506/453-8237, Fax: 506/444-4960
Directeur, Collège Communautaire du NB, Bathurst, M. Roy, 506/457-2145, Fax: 506/547-7674
Directeur, Collège Communautaire du NB, Campbellton, Edouard Maltais, 506/789-2377, Fax: 506/753-3523
Directeur, Collège Communautaire du NB, Dieppe, Michel Richard, 506/856-2200, Fax: 506/856-2125
Directeur, Collège Communautaire du NB, Edmundston, Michel Laroche, 506/735-2500, Fax: 506/735-1108

EDUCATIONAL SERVICES DIVISION (ANGLOPHONE)
Asst. Deputy Minister, Mike McIntosh, 506/453-8202, Fax: 506/444-4314

Director, Apprenticeship & Occupational Certification, André Ferlatte, 506/453-2260, Fax: 506/453-3806
Principal, NB College of Craft & Design, Janice Gillis, 506/453-2305, Fax: 506/457-7352
Principal, NB Community College, Miramichi, Noreen Lobban, 506/775-6000, Fax: 506/778-6134
Principal, NB Community College, Moncton, John E. Lean, 506/856-2220, Fax: 506/856-3382
Principal, NB Community College, St. Andrews, Gerald Ingersoll, 506/529-5000, Fax: 506/529-5039
Principal, NB Community College, Saint John, Cheryl Robertson, 506/658-6600, Fax: 506/658-6792
Principal, NB Community College, Woodstock, Mac Clendenning, 506/325-4400, Fax: 506/325-2174

LABOUR & EMPLOYMENT DIVISION
Asst. Deputy Minister, John P. Chenier, 506/453-2091, Fax: 506/453-3038
Acting Executive Asst., Employment, Michel Thériault, 506/453-3041, Fax: 506/453-7969
Director, Employment Services, Roger Lévesque, 506/444-4046, Fax: 506/453-7967
Director, Employment Programs, Michel Thériault, 506/453-3818, Fax: 506/453-7967
Director, Employment Administration, Karla Ploude, 506/444-4226, Fax: 506/453-7967
Director, Technical Inspections, Calvin Duncan, 506/453-2336, Fax: 506/457-7394
Chief, Boiler Inspector, Dale Ross, 506/453-4493, Fax: 506/457-7394
Chief, Elevator Inspector, Lee Boudreau, 506/453-2336
Chief, Plumbing Inspector, Fred Holland, 506/453-2336
Executive Director, Planning & Policy Development, Dave Easby, 506/453-2889, Fax: 506/453-3806
Director, Employment Standards Branch, Maurice Boucher, 506/453-3902, Fax: 506/453-3806
Director, Industrial Relations Branch, J. Armand Thomas, 506/453-2261, Fax: 506/453-3806
Director, Labour Market Analysis, Dehorah Burns, 506/457-4859
Director, Planning, Vacant, 506/453-3940
Superintendent, Pensions Branch, Danielle Métivier, 506/453-2055

Associated Agencies, Boards & Commissions
• Apprenticeship & Occupational Certification Board: PO Box 6000, Fredericton NB E3B 5H1 – 506/453-2260; Fax: 506/453-3806
Secretary, Dianne Robinson-Hansen, 506/457-7299
Chair, Darrel LeBlanc, 506/453-2912
• Board of Examiners for Compressed Gas: PO Box 6000, Fredericton NB E3B 5H1 – 506/453-2336; Fax: 506/457-7394
Chair, Michael O'Hearn
• Board of Examiners for Stationary Engineers: PO Box 6000, Fredericton NB E3B 5H1 – 506/453-2336; Fax: 506/457-7394
Chair, Dale Ross
• Ministerial Advisory Committee on Multiculturalism: PO Box 6000, Fredericton NB E3B 5H1 – 506/444-4331; Fax: 506/453-3300
Secretary, Beverly Woznow, 506/444-4331
• New Brunswick Human Rights Commission: 751 Brunswick St., PO Box 6000, Fredericton NB E3B 5H1 – 506/453-2301; Fax: 506/453-2653
Chair, Prof. Constantine Passaris
Director, Janet Cullinan, 506/453-2301, Fax: 506/453-2653
• New Brunswick Labour & Employment Board: 191 Prospect St., PO Box 908, Fredericton NB E3B 1B0 – 506/453-2881; Fax: 506/453-3892
This agency replaces the former Industrial Relations Board, Public Services Labour Relations Board, Employment Standards Tribunal, & Pensions Tribunal.
Chair, Paul Lordon, Q.C.

• New Brunswick Workplace Health, Safety & Compensation Commission (WHSCC): 500 Beaverbrook Ct., 4th Fl., Fredericton NB – 506/453-2467; Fax: 506/453-7982, Toll Free: 1-800-442-9776
President & CEO, John Roushorne, 506/632-2800, Fax: 506/632-4999

Department of AGRICULTURE & RURAL DEVELOPMENT (ARD)/Agriculture et Aménagement rural (AAR)
PO Box 6000, Fredericton NB E3B 5H1
506/453-2666; Fax: 506/453-7978; URL: http//www.gov.nb.ca/agricult/index.htm

ACTS ADMINISTERED
Agricultural Associations Act
Agricultural Commodity Price Stabilization Act
Agricultural Development Act
Agricultural Operation Practices Act
Agricultural Rehabilitation & Development Act
Agricultural Schools Act
Apiary Inspection Act
Artificial Insemination Act
Branding Act
Crop Insurance Act
Dairy Industry Act
Dairy Products Act
Diseases of Animals Act
Drainage of Farm Lands Act
Encouragement of Seed Growing Act
Farm Credit Corporation Assistance Act
Farm Improvement Assistance Loans Act
Farm Income Assurance Act
Farm Machinery Loans Act
Farm Products Boards and Marketing Agencies Act
Farm Products Marketing Act
Fences Act
Harness Racing Commission Act
[M
Imitation Dairy Products Act
Injurious Insect and Pest Act
Keswick Islands Act
Livestock Incentives Act
Livestock Yard Sales Act
Marshland Reclamation Act
Natural Products Grades Act
New Brunswick Grain Act
Oleomargarine Act
Plant Diseases Act
Potato Development and Marketing Council Act
Potato Disease Eradication Act
Poultry Health Protection Act
Pounds Act
Sheep Protection Act
Society for the Prevention of Cruelty Act
Weed Control Act
Women's Institute Act
Minister, Hon. Doug Tyler, 506/453-2448, Fax: 506/444-5022
Deputy Minister, Jack Syroid, 506/453-2450, Fax: 506/444-5022
Asst. Deputy Minister, Planning & Development, Dr. Ibrahim Ghanem, 506/453-2406, Fax: 506/453-7978

MARKETING & FINANCE
Asst. Deputy Minister, Claire LePage, 506/453-3886
Director, Administrative Services Branch, Roger B. Hunter, 506/453-2521
Director, Communications & Education Branch, Serge Michaud, 506/453-2666
Director, Farm Business & Risk Management Branch, D. McQuade, 506/453-2185
Director, Marketing & Business Development Branch, Dr. Brian Dykeman, 506/453-2214
Director, Rural Development Branch, Vacant

GOVERNMENT OF NEW BRUNSWICK

TECHNICAL & FIELD SERVICES
Asst. Deputy Minister, E.T. Pratt, 506/453-2366
Director, Land Resources Branch, Paul Smith, 506/453-2109
Director, Livestock & Livestock Feed Branch, Dr. Mike Maloney, 506/453-2457
Chief, Veterinary Section, Dr. M.F. Maloney, 506/453-2210
Director, Land Resources Branch, Paul Smith, 506/453-2109
Director, Potato & Horticulture Branch, Clair Gartley, 506/453-2172

Regional Offices
Central: Chatham NB – 506/778-6030; Fax: 506/773-4076, Acting Regional Manager, Brian DuPlessis
East: Bathurst NB – 506/547-2088; Fax: 506/547-2064, Regional Manager, V. Taylor
Northeast: Bathurst NB – 506/547-2088; Fax: 506/547-2064, Regional Manager, I. Breau
Northwest: Grand Falls NB – 506/476-5515; Fax: 506/473-6641, Regional Manager, L. Arsenault
South: Sussex NB – 506/432-2000; Fax: 506/432-2044, Regional Manager, J. Herod
Southeast: Moncton NB – 506/856-2277; Fax: 506/856-2669, Regional Manager, P. Jensen
West: Wicklow NB, Regional Manager, C. Gartley

Associated Agencies, Boards & Commissions
• Agricultural Development Board: c/o Department of Agriculture & Rural Development, PO Box 6000, Fredericton NB E3B 5H1 – 506/453-2185; Fax: 506/453-7406
Secretary Manager, Paul Cooper
• Farm Products Marketing Commission: c/o Department of Agriculture & Rural Development, PO Box 6000, Fredericton NB E3B 5H1 – 506/453-3647; Fax: 506/453-7406
Chair, Robert Shannon
Executive Director, Wayne J. Buffett
• Livestock Incentives Act, & Farm Machinery Loans Act: c/o Department of Agriculture & Rural Development, PO Box 6000, Fredericton NB E3B 5H1 – 506/453-2524; Fax: 506/453-7170
Manager, Paul Cooper
• New Brunswick Crop Insurance Commission: c/o Department of Agriculture & Rural Development, PO Box 6000, Fredericton NB E3B 5H1 – 506/453-2185; Fax: 506/453-7406
General Manager, Paul Smith
• New Brunswick Grain Commission: c/o Department of Agriculture & Rural Development, PO Box 6000, Fredericton NB E3B 5H1 – 506/453-2172; Fax: 506/453-7978
Secretary Manager, Dave Walker
• New Brunswick Potato Development & Marketing Council: c/o Incutech Complex, Bag Service 69000, Fredericton NB E3B 6C2 – 506/453-3562
Chair, Don Keenan

Agricultural Marketing Boards & Commissions
• Agence de la pomme de terre du N.B.: CP 2140, Grand-Sault NB E3Z 1E2 – 506/473-3036; Fax: 506/473-4647
Chair, Lionel Poitras
• New Brunswick Apple Marketing Board: #206, 1115 Regent St., Fredericton NB E3B 3Z2 – 506/452-8100; Fax: 506/452-1625
Secretary-Manager, Bruce Thompson
• New Brunswick Cattle Marketing Agency: RR#4, Perth - Andover NB E0J 1V0 – 506/273-6729
Secretary Manager, Neville Delong
• New Brunswick Chicken Marketing Board: #103, 1115 Regent St., Fredericton NB E3B 3Z2 – 506/452-8085; Fax: 506/451-2121
Secretary Manager, Louis Martin
• New Brunswick Cream Marketing Board: RR#5, Sussex NB E0E 1P0 – 506/433-5051

President, Albert Scott
• New Brunswick Egg Marketing Board: 181 Westmorland St., PO Box 126, Stn A, Fredericton NB E3B 4Y2 – 506/458-8885; Fax: 506/453-0645
Secretary Manager, April Sexsmith
• New Brunswick Flue-Cured Tobacco Marketing Board: RR#1, PO Box 516, Bouctouche NB E0A 1G0
President, Normand Poirier
• New Brunswick Greenhouse Products Marketing Board: #206, 1115 Regent St., Fredericton NB E3B 3Z2 – 506/452-8100; Fax: 506/452-1625
Secretary Manager, Bruce Thompson
• New Brunswick Hog Marketing Board: 830 Hanwell Rd., Fredericton NB E3B 6A2 – 506/458-8051; Fax: 506/453-1985
Secretary-Manager, Susan Fox
• New Brunswick Milk Marketing Board: Rochville Rd., PO Box 490, Sussex NB E0E 1P0 – 506/432-9120; Fax: 506/432-9130
Chair, John Robinson
• New Brunswick Potato Agency: PO Box 238, Florenceville NB E0J 1K0 – 506/392-6022; Fax: 506/392-8164
Chair, Lionel Poitras
• New Brunswick Turkey Marketing Board: #103, 1115 Regent St., Fredericton NB E3B 3Z2 – 506/452-8103; Fax: 506/452-1625
President, Bruce Thompson

Office of the AUDITOR GENERAL/Bureau du Vérificateur général
PO Box 758, Fredericton NB E3B 5B4
506/453-2243; Fax: 506/453-3067
Auditor General, Ralph Black, F.C.A., Email: dhu@gov.nb.ca
Deputy Auditor General, Kenneth D. Robinson, C.A., 506/453-2243, Email: kdr@gov.nb.ca

COMMUNICATIONS NEW BRUNSWICK/ Communications Nouveau-Brunswick
225 King St., PO Box 6000, Fredericton NB E3B 5H1
506/453-2240; Fax: 506/453-5329
General Manager, Howie Trainor, 506/453-2240, Email: htrainor@gov.nb.ca
Director, Edit Services, Jim McCarthy, 506/453-2240, Email: mccarthy@gov.nb.ca
Director, Audio-Visual Services Branch, Vacant, 506/453-3042, Fax: 506/457-3556
Director, Design Services Branch, Michel Cote, 506/453-3037

Office of the COMPTROLLER/Bureau du Contrôleur
Centennial Bldg., 670 King St., Fredericton NB E3B 5H1
506/453-2565; Fax: 506/453-2917
Comptroller, Edward L. Mehan
Director, Accounting Services, Michael Ferguson
Manager, Central Accounting Section, Gordon Tuttle
Director, Audit & Consulting Services, Stephen Thompson

Premier's Council on the Status of DISABLED PERSONS/Conseil du Première ministre sur la condition des personnes handicapées
#648, 440 King St., Fredericton NB E3B 5H8
506/452-1112; Fax: 506/450-2747; Email: pcsdp@gov.nb.ca; URL: http://www.gov.nb.ca/pcsdp/english/index.htm
Advises the Minister on matters relating to the status of persons with disabilities & presents to government the public matters of interest & concern to persons with disabilities. The council promotes the prevention of disabling conditions, promotes employment opportunities for persons with disabilities & promotes access by persons with disabilites to all services offered to the citizens of the province.
Executive Director, Randy Dickinson

Department of ECONOMIC DEVELOPMENT & TOURISM/Développement économique et Tourisme
Centennial Bldg., 670 King St., 5th Fl., PO Box 6000, Fredericton NB E3B 5H1
506/453-2850 (Communications & Promotion); Fax: 506/444-4586; URL: http://www.gov.nb.ca/edt/index.htm
Provincial Department responsible for the following: development & marketing of investment opportunities, job creation & the tourism industry; encourages the growth of small & medium-sized businesses in New Brunswick; improves competitiveness in the global marketplace &; assists companies in increasing sales & business in domestic & foreign markets & establishing new markets & export opportunities.

ACTS ADMINISTERED
Economic Development Act
Stock Savings Plan Act
Tourism Development Act
Minister, Hon. Camille Thériault, 506/453-3009, Email: camillet@gov.nb.ca
Deputy Minister, Francis McGuire, 506/453-2795, Email: francism@gov.nb.ca
Director, Corporate Services, Yvon Belliveau, 506/453-2482, Fax: 506/453-5428, Email: yvonb@gov.nb.ca

FINANCE INFRASTRUCTURE & POLICY
Asst. Deputy Minister, Stephen Wheatley, 506/453-2111, Fax: 506/453-5428, Email: gsw@gov.nb.ca
Director, Agreements & Infrastructure, Ray Wilson, 506/453-2489, Fax: 506/453-7904, Email: rayw@gov.nb.ca
Director, Financial Programs, Richard Burgess, 506/453-2474, Fax: 506/453-7904, Email: dickb@gov.nb.ca
Director, Planning & Research, Gary Jochelman, 506/453-2629, Fax: 506/453-7904, Email: garyj@gov.nb.ca

INDUSTRIAL DEVELOPMENT & TOURISM PROGRAMS
Asst. Deputy Minister, George Bouchard, 506/453-2794, Email: georgeb@gov.nb.ca
Director, Industry Services, John Adams, 506/453-2298, Fax: 506/457-4845, Email: johna@gov.nb.ca
Director, Small Business Directorate, Ken Hamilton, 506/453-3890, Fax: 506/457-4845, Email: kenh@gov.nb.ca
Director, Tourism Directorate, Harvey Sawler, 506/453-4283, Fax: 506/453-7127, Email: harveys@gov.nb.ca, URL: http://www.gov.nb.ca/tourism/index.htm
Director, Trade & Investment, Michael MacBride, 506/453-2876, Fax: 506/453-3783, Email: michaelm@gov.nb.ca

INFORMATION HIGHWAY SECRETARIAT
URL: http://www.gov.nb.ca/edt/infohigh/index.htm
Asst. Deputy Minister, Jerrie Fowler, 506/453-3707, Email: jerrief@gov.nb.ca
Director, Paul Aucoin, 506/444-5858, Fax: 506/453-3993

Associated Agencies, Boards & Commissions
• Canada/New Brunswick Business Service Centre: 570 Queen St., Fredericton NB E3B 6Z6 – 506/444-6158, Toll Free: 1-800-668-1010
Information Agent, Paulianne McLellan

- New Brunswick Industrial Development Board: PO Box 6000, Fredericton NB E3B 5H1 – 506/453-2474; Fax: 506/453-7904
- Provincial Holdings Ltd.: PO Box 6000, Fredericton NB E3B 5H1 – 506/453-2474; Fax: 506/453-7904

Secretary-Treasurer, Jim Lovett, Email: jiml@gov.nb.ca

Department of EDUCATION/Éducation
PO Box 6000, Fredericton NB E3B 5H1
506/453-3678; Fax: 506/453-3325; URL: http://www.gov.nb.ca/education/index.htm

ACTS ADMINISTERED
Schools Act

Minister, Hon. James Lockyer, Q.C., 506/453-2591, Fax: 506/444-4400, Email: jamesl@gov.nb.ca
Deputy Minister, Gerald C. Keilty, 506/453-2529, Email: keilty@bov.nb.ca
Deputy Minister, Normand Martin, 506/453-2409, Email: helenef@gov.nb.ca
Director, Communications, Margaret Smith, 506/444-4714, Email: margares@gov.nb.ca
Director, Research & Planning, Mary Jane Richards, 506/453-3090, Email: maryjr@gov.nb.ca

SECTEUR DES SERVICES FRANCOPHONES D'ÉDUCATION
Sous-ministre adjoint, Raymond Daigle, 506/453-2086, Email: dianemc@gov.nb.ca
Directeur, Services aux Élèves, Pierre Dumas, 506/453-2742, Email: pierred@gov.nb.ca
Directeur, Services administratifs, J.-P. Boudreau, 506/453-5365, Email: jpb@gov.nv.ca
Directrice, Services Pédagogiques, Donata Thériault, 506/453-2743, Email: donatat@gov.nb.ca

EDUCATIONAL SERVICES DIVISION (ANGLOPHONE)
Asst. Deputy Minister, Bryon James, 506/453-3326, Email: byronj@gov.nb.ca
Director, Curriculum Development, Barry Lydon, 506/453-2155
Director, District Financial Services, Gordon Wilson, 506/453-2868, Email: gordonw@gov.nb.ca
Director, Evaluation, Cary Grobe, 506/453-2744, Email: caryg@gov.nb.ca
Director, Innovation & Development, Tom Hanley, 506/453-2812
Director, Student Services, Alex Dingwall, 506/453-2816

SUPPORT SERVICES DIVISION
Asst. Deputy Minister, Jolène LeBlanc, 506/453-2085, Email: jolenel@gov.nb.ca
Director, Computer Support Services, Jean Lee, 506/453-7158, Email: jeanl@gov.nb.ca
Director, Educational Facilities, Ronald Breau, 506/453-2242, Email: ronaldb@gov.nb.ca
Director, Finance & Services, James Galvin, 506/453-2752, Email: jamesg@gov.nb.ca
Director, Human Resources, Simon Caron, 506/453-2030, Email: simonc@gov.nb.ca
Director, Instructional Resources, Gérald Breau, 505/453-2319

Office of the Chief ELECTORAL OFFICER/Bureau de la directrice générale des élections
PO Box 6000, Fredericton NB E3B 5H1
506/453-2218; Fax: 506/457-4926
Toll Free: 1-800-308-2922

ACTS ADMINISTERED
Elections Act
Municipal Elections Act

Chief Electoral Officer, Barbara J. Landry
Elections Coordinator, Annise Hollies

Senior Policy Analyst, David Strang
Research & Planning Officer, Mapping, Ron Armitage

Department of the ENVIRONMENT/Environnement
364 Argyle St., PO Box 6000, Fredericton NB E3B 5H1
506/453-3700; Fax: 506/453-3843; URL: http://www.gov.nb.ca/environ/index.htm

ACTS ADMINISTERED
Beverage Containers Act
Clean Environment Act
Clean Water Act
Environmental Trust Fund Act
Pesticides Control Act
Unsightly Premises Act

Minister, Hon. Vaughn Blaney, 506/453-2523, Email: vaughnbl@gov.nb.ca
Deputy Minister, Donald Dennison, 506/453-3095
Director, Administration & Human Resources Branch, Lois Sandwith, 506/453-2020, Fax: 506/453-3843

COMMUNICATIONS & ENVIRONMENTAL EDUCATION
506/453-3700; Fax: 506/453-3843
Director, Gerald N. Hill, 506/453-3700
Information Officer, Kenneth C. Corbett

ENVIRONMENTAL PLANNING & SCIENCES BRANCH
Director, Dr. Nabil D. Elhadi, 506/457-4844, Fax: 506/453-2390
Manager, Land & Water Planning Section, William C. Ayer, 506/457-4846
Manager, Water Resource Monitoring Section, Michael Sprague, 506/457-4844
Manager, Analytical Services Section, David Schellenberg, 506/453-2477
Manager, Environmental Impact Assessment, Kirk Gordon, 506/457-4844

INVESTIGATIONS & ENFORCEMENT BRANCH
Director, Bradford K. Marshall, 506/457-4850, Fax: 506/457-7333
Manager, Investigations Section, Stanley V. Wadden, 506/457-4850

OPERATIONS BRANCH
506/457-4848; Fax: 506/453-2265
Director, James Knight
Manager, Industrial Programs Section, Cheryl Heathwood
Manager, Water & Wastewater Section, Paul Campbell
Manager, Solid Waste & Recycling Section, Perry Haines
Acting Manager, Air Quality Program Section, Michael Murphy
Manager, Hazardous Materials Section, James Shaffner

POLICY & INTERGOVERNMENTAL AFFAIRS BRANCH
506/453-3703; Fax: 506/457-7800
Director, Dr. David I. Besner
Senior Policy Advisor, Parker Gray
Senior Policy Advisor, Dean Mundee

New Brunswick Round Table on Environment & Economy/Table Ronde sur Environnement & Economie
c/o Department of the Environment, PO Box 6000, Fredericton NB E3B 5H1
506/453-3703; Fax: 506/457-7800
Executive Secretary, Dr. David I. Besner

Associated Agencies, Boards & Commissions
- New Brunswick Pesticides Advisory Council: c/o Department of the Environment, PO Box 6000, Fredericton NB E3B 5H1 – 506/457-4848; Fax: 506/453-2893

Coordinator, Pesticides Management Unit, Ken Browne
Manager, Hazardous Materials Section, Dr. Jim Shaffner

Department of FINANCE/Finances
PO Box 6000, Fredericton NB E3B 5H1
506/453-2286; Fax: 506/457-4989; URL: http://www.gov.nb.ca/finance/index.htm

ACTS ADMINISTERED
Admissions & Amusement Tax Act
Appropriation Act
Auditor General Act
Beaverbrook Art Gallery Act (in part)
Beaverbrook Auditorium Act (in part)
Civil Service Act
Crown Construction Contracts Act
Expenditure Management Act, 1991 & 1992
Financial Administration Act
Financial Corporation Capital Tax Act
Fisherman's Disaster Fund Act
Forest Products Loan Act
Gasoline & Motive Fuel Tax Act
Income Tax Act
Liquor Control Act
Loan Act
Lotteries Act
Members' Superannuation Act
Municipalities Act (in part)
New Brunswick Liquor Corporation Act
New Brunswick Municipal Finance Corporation Act
Ombudsman Act (in part)
Pari-Mutual Tax Act
Pay Equity Act
Provincial Court Act
Provincial Loans Act
Public Service Labour Relations Act (in part)
Public Service Superannuation Act
Real Property Tax Act
Real Property Transfer Tax Act
Retirement Plan Benificiaries Act
Revenue Administration Act
Social Services & Education Tax Act
Special Appropriations Act
Special Retirement Program Act
Statistics Act
Teachers' Pension Act
Tobacco Tax Act

Minister, Hon. Edmond Blanchard, Q.C., 506/453-2451, Fax: 506/457-4989, Email: blanchard@gov.nb.ca
Deputy Minister, John Mallory, 506/453-2534

BUDGET PLANNING & FINANCIAL SERVICES
Fax: 506/453-2124
Executive Director, John Campbell, 506/453-3051
Director, Budget Formulation & Planning, John St. Pierre, 506/453-2808
Director, Financial Policy, Terry Christie, 506/453-3075

DEPARTMENT & MANAGEMENT SERVICES
Executive Director, Chris Aiton, 506/453-2962
Director, Information Technology, Jean Lee, 506/454-5411, Fax: 506/444-4724

HUMAN RESOURCES MANAGEMENT
Executive Director, Ellen Barry, 506/453-2799
Director, Compensation Policy, John Cunningham, 506/453-5359
Director, Employee Relations Services, Andrew Kitchen, 506/453-2699
Director, Employee Relations Services, David Pugh, 506/453-2115
Director, Human Resources Development, Madelaine Trenouth, 506/453-2059

Canadian Almanac & Directory 1997

Director, Human Resources Information, Frank Camm, 506/453-2543
Director, Official Languages, Catherine d'Entremont, 506/453-2059
Director, Pensions & Insured Benefits, Cyril Thériault, 506/453-2296

REVENUE DIVISION
Fax: 506/457-7335
Provincial Tax Commissioner, David Morrison, 506/453-2401
Director, Account Management, Larry Bennett, 506/453-2709
Director, Accounting & Central Services, Rick McCullough, 506/453-2138
Director, Customer Services, Donald Thériault, 506/453-2701
Director, Policy & Program Support, Vacant, 506/453-2401

TAXATION & FISCAL POLICY
Executive Director, Norm Campbell, 506/453-2096
Director, Budget Policy & Fiscal Relations, Vacant, 506/453-2097
Director, New Brunswick Statistics Agency, Clifford Marks, 506/453-7970, Fax: 506/453-2381
Director, Tax Policy, James Turgeon, 506/453-2097

TREASURY & DEBT MANAGEMENT
Fax: 506/453-2053
Executive Director, Bryan MacDonald, 506/453-3952
Director, Treasury, Gerry Conroy, 506/453-3859

Associated Agencies, Boards & Commissions
- Atlantic Lottery Corporation (ALC): 770 St. George Blvd., PO Box 5500, Moncton NB E1C 8W6 – 506/867-5800; Fax: 506/388-4246
Chair, Ernest MacKinnon
President, Cluny Macpherson
Vice-President, Sales & Promotion, Bert McWade
Vice-President, Information Technology, Vincent Brunet
- Civil Service Commission of New Brunswick: c/o Office of the Ombudsman, 767 Brunswick St., PO Box 6000, Fredericton NB E3B 5H1 – 506/453-3733; Fax: 506/453-3733
Ombudsman responsible for the CSC, Ellen E. King
- New Brunswick Investment Management Corporation: PO Box 6000, Fredericton NB E3B 5H1 – 506/444-5800
President, Ernest MacKinnon

Department of FISHERIES & AQUACULTURE/Pêches et Aquiculture
York Tower, King's Place, 6th Fl., PO Box 6000, Fredericton NB E3B 5H1
506/453-2251; Fax: 506/453-5210; URL: http://www.gov.nb.ca/dfa/index.htm

ACTS ADMINISTERED
Aquaculture Act
Fish Inspection Act
Fish Processing Act
Fisheries Bargaining Act
Fisheries Development Act
Inshore Fisheries Representation Act
Irish Moss Act
Minister, Hon. Bernard Thériault, 506/453-2662, Fax: 506/453-5210, Email: bernardt@gov.nb.ca
Deputy Minister, Sylvestre McLaughlin, 506/453-2766, Email: sysvestrem@gov.nb.ca

DEVELOPMENT & TRAINING
Executive Director, Maurice Bernier, 506/453-2302, Email: mauriceb@gov.nb.ca
Director, School of Fisheries (Caraquet), Hédard Albert, 506/726-2500, Fax: 506/726-2408

FINANCE & ADMINISTRATION
Asst. Deputy Minister, Alfred Losier, 506/453-2251, Email: losiera@gov.nb.ca
Director, Aquarium & Marine Centre (Shippagan), Clarence LeBreton, 506/336-4771, Fax: 506/336-9646

MARKETING & PROCESSING
Executive Director, Jean-Paul Richard, 506/453-2438, Email: jeanpr@gov.nb.ca

OPERATIONS & SERVICES
Asst. Deputy Minister, David MacMinn, 506/453-2047, Email: macminnd@gov.nb.ca
Director, Aquaculture, John Kershaw, 506/453-2253
Director, Industry Services & Inspection, Kerry Wilson, 506/453-2048, Email: kerryw@gov.nb.ca
Coordinator, Environmental Services, Barry Jones, 506/453-2047, Email: barryj@gov.nb.ca

RESOURCE POLICY & PLANNING
Executive Director, Linda Haché, 506/453-2252, Email: hachel@gov.nb.ca

Associated Agencies, Boards & Commissions
- Fisheries Development Board: PO Box 6000, Fredericton NB E3B 5H1 – 506/453-2302; Fax: 506/453-5210
Executive Director, Maurice Bernier, Email: mauriceb@gov.nb.ca

New Brunswick GEOGRAPHIC INFORMATION CORPORATION/ Corporation d'information géographique du Nouveau-Brunswick
985 College Hill Rd., PO Box 6000, Fredericton NB E3B 5H1
506/457-3581; Fax: 506/453-3898
Chair, Thomas O'Neil
President, Mavis Hurley
Vice-President, Legal, & Chief Registrar of Deeds, Roderick W. MacKenzie, Q.C., 506/453-2963, Email: rwm@gov.nb.ca
Vice-President, Operations, David Jennings, 506/453-2546, Fax: 506/453-3043, Email: dwj@gov.nb.ca
Chief Financial Officer, Carol Macdonald, 506/453-3916, Fax: 506/453-3043, Email: cmm@gov.nb.ca
Communications Officer, Arnold Kearney, 506/453-3804, Email: adk@gov.nb.ca

Department of HEALTH & COMMUNITY SERVICES/Santé et Services communautaires
PO Box 5100, Fredericton NB E3B 5G8
506/453-2536; Fax: 506/444-4697; URL: http://www.gov.nb.ca/hcs/

ACTS ADMINISTERED
Advanced Life Support Services Act
Ambulance Services Act
Anatomy Act
Cemetery Companies Act
Change of Name Act
Family Services Act
Health Act
Hospital Act
Hospital Services Act
Human Tissues Act
Jordan Memorial Home Act
Marriage Act
Medical Consent of Minors Act
Medical Services Payment Act
Mental Health Act
Mental Health Commission of New Brunswick Act
Nursing Homes Act
Prescription Drug Payment Act
Radiological Health Protection Act
Tobacco Sales Act
Treatment of Intoxicated Persons Act
Venereal Disease Act
Vital Statistics Act
Minister, Hon. Russell H.T. King, M.D., 506/453-2581
Deputy Minister, Jean Guy Finn, 506/453-2542
Minister of State, Family & Community Services, Hon. Marilyn Trenholme, M.D., 506/444-5390
Director, Communications, Gerald Weseen, 506/453-2536

ADMINISTRATION & FINANCE DIVISION
Asst. Deputy Minister, Laura Freeman, 506/453-2775
Director, Administrative Support Services, David Gibbs, 506/453-2745
Director, Construction Services, Gérard LeBlanc, 506/444-4804
Director, Financial Services, Dale Wilson, 506/453-2117
Director, Human Resources, Carolyn McKay, 506/453-7961
Director, Information Systems, Jean-Claude Haché, 506/453-2279

Vital Statistics
Fax: 506/453-3245
Registrar General, Alice Garner, 506/453-2714
Administers the Vital Statistics Act, the Change of Name Act & the Marriage Act. For certified Birth, Marriage & Death Certificates, remit $25.00 for each copy required. The fee for wallet size birth certificate or marriage certificate is $20.00. A search costs $10.00.

FAMILY & COMMUNITY SOCIAL SERVICES DIVISION
Asst. Deputy Minister, Gérard Doucet, 506/453-2181
Executive Director, Bob Steele, 506/444-4726
Acting Director, Access/Assessment, Protection & Post Adoption Services, Dick Quigg, 506/453-2040
Director, Executive & Program Support Services, Joy Haines-Bacon, 506/453-2955
Director, Family & Protection Services Office, Edith Doucet, 506/453-2950, Fax: 506/453-2082
Director, Seniors' Office, Norma Pickle, 506/453-2480, Fax: 506/453-2082

INSTITUTIONAL SERVICES DIVISION
Asst. Deputy Minister, James Carter, 506/453-4238
Executive Director, Hospital Services, Jean Castonguay, 506/453-2283
Acting Director, Ambulance Services, Andrew Easton, 506/453-2220
Director, Nursing Homes, Etienne Theriault, 506/453-3821
Director, Program Support Services, Marc Leger, 506/453-3724

MENTAL HEALTH SERVICES DIVISION
Asst. Deputy Minister, Ken Ross, 506/453-3888
Executive Director, Programs, Rachel Bard, 506/444-4442
Director, Quality Management & Executive Support, Claude Allard, 506/444-4442

PLANNING & EVALUATION DIVISION
Fax: 506/444-4697
Executive Director, Bonny Hoyt-Hallett, 506/453-2582
Director, Strategic Planning, Bill Leonard, 506/444-4049
Director, Program Analysis & Evaluation, Aline Saintonge, 506/453-2793
Coordinator, Federal-Provincial Relations, Stephen Chase, 506/453-4050
Coordinator, Legislation Development, Marilyn Born, 506/453-4050

PUBLIC HEALTH & MEDICAL SERVICES DIVISION
Asst. Deputy Minister, John Dicaire, 506/453-2321

Chief Public Health Officer, Dr. Denis Allard, 506/453-2323
Provincial Epidemiologist, Dr. B. Christofer Balram, 506/453-3092
Director, Community & Environmental Health, Mark C. Allen, 506/453-2360
Acting Director, Medicare/Prescription Drug Program, Fay Mackie, 506/453-2415
Acting Director, Prescription Drug Program, Fay Mackie, 506/453-2415

Department of HUMAN RESOURCES DEVELOPMENT/Développement des ressources humaines
PO Box 6000, Fredericton NB E3B 5H1
506/453-2001; Fax: 506/453-7478

ACTS ADMINISTERED
Family Income Security Act
Health Services Act
Vocational Rehabilitation for Disabled Persons Act
Minister, Hon. Marcelle Mersereau, 506/453-2558, Email: marcellm@gov.nb.ca
Deputy Minister, Ernest MacKinnon, 506/453-2590

CORPORATE SERVICES DIVISION
Executive Director, Michael O'Rourke, 506/453-2712
Director, Audit Services, James Church, 506/453-2941
Director, Human Resource Services, Jean Finn, 506/453-2940
Director, Information Systems, Joan Ramsay, 506/453-2866

INCOME SECURITY DIVISION
Asst. Deputy Minister, Karen Mann, 506/453-2379
Director, Income Support, Roger Bourgeois, 506/453-2039

PLANNING & EVALUATION DIVISION
Executive Director, Norma Dubé, 506/453-2460
Director, Programs, Donald Ferguson, 506/453-2379

Associated Agencies, Boards & Commissions
• Social Welfare Appeals Board: PO Box 12999, Fredericton NB E3B 6C2 – 506/444-5182
  Chair, Maurice Harquail

Department of INTERGOVERNMENTAL & ABORIGINAL AFFAIRS/Affaires intergouvernementales et autochtones
PO Box 6000, Fredericton NB E3B 5H1
506/453-2384; Fax: 506/453-2995; URL: http://www.gov.nb.ca/iga/home1_e.htm
Minister of State, Intergovernmental & Aboriginal Affairs, Hon. Bernard Richard
Deputy Minister, Madeleine Delaney-LeBlanc, 506/453-7454
Asst. Deputy Minister, Federal-Provincial Affairs, Kevin Malone, 506/457-7275
Asst. Deputy Minister, Intergovernmental Cooperation, François Rioux, 506/453-2976
Director, Aboriginal Affairs, Dan Horsman, 506/453-2671
Protocol Officer, Office of Protocol, Anne Reynolds, 506/453-2671

Department of JUSTICE/Justice
#412, Centennial Bldg., PO Box 6000, Fredericton NB E3B 5H1
506/453-2719 (Administration); Fax: 506/453-8718; URL: http://www.gov.nb.ca/justice/index.htm

ACTS ADMINISTERED
Absconding Debtors Act
Age of Majority Act
Arbitration Act
Arrest & Examinations Act
Assignment of Book Debts Act
Assignments & Preferences Act
Attorney General Act
Auctioneers Licence Act
Bills of Sale Act
Bulk Sales Act
Business Corporations Act
Charter Compliance Act
Collection Agencies Act
Commissioners for Taking Affidavits Act
Companies Act
Conditional Sales Act
Conflict of Laws Rules for Trusts Act
Consumer Bureau Act
Consumer Product Warranty & Liability Act
Contributory Negligence Act
Controverted Elections Act
Cooperative Associations Act
Corporations Act
Corrupt Practices Inquiries Act
Cost of Credit Disclosures Act
Court Reporters Act
Credit Union Federations Act
Creditors Relief Act
Criminal Prosecution Expenses Act
Crown Debts Act
Crown Prosecutors Act
Defamation Act
Demise of the Crown Act
Devolution of Estates Act
Direct Sellers Act
Divorce Court Act
Easements Act
Entry Warrants Act
Escheats & Forfeitures Act
Evidence Act
Executors & Trustees Act
Expropriation Act
Factors & Agents Act
Family Services Act (Part VII)
Fatal Accidents Act
Federal Courts Jurisdiction Act
Fishermen's Union Act
Foreign Judgments Act
Foreign Resident Corporations Act
Frustrated Contracts Act
Garnishee Act
Great Seal Act
Guardianship of Children Act
Habeas Corpus Act
Infirm Persons Act
Innkeepers Act
Inquiries Act
Insurance Act
International Child Abduction Act
International Commercial Arbitration Act
International Sale of Goods Act
International Trusts Act
Interpretation Act
Interprovincial Subpoena Act
Judges Disqualification Removal Act
Judicature Act
Jury Act
Landlord & Tenant Act
Law Reform Act
Legal Aid Act
Liens on Goods & Chattels Act
Limitation of Actions Act
Limited Partnership Act
Loan & Trust Companies Act
Marine Insurance Act
Marital Property Act
Married Woman's Property Act
Mechanics' Lien Act
Memorials & Executions Act
Merger of Supreme & County Courts of New Brunswick Act
Notaries Public Act
Nova Scotia Grants Act
Partnership Act
Partnership & Business Names Registration Act
Pension Fund Societies Act
Postal Services Interruption Act
Pre-arranged Funeral Services Act
Premium Tax Act
Presumption of Death Act
Probate Court Act
Proceedings Against the Crown Act
Property Act
Protection of Persons Acting Under Statute Act
Provincial Court Act
Provincial Offences Procedure Act
Provincial Offences Procedure for Young Persons Act
Provision for Dependants Act
Public Records Act
Queen's Counsel & Precedence Act
Queen's Printer Act
Quieting of Titles Act
Real Estate Agents Act
Reciprocal Enforcement of Judgments Act
Reciprocal Enforcement of Maintenance Orders Act, 1985
(An Act respecting the Convention Between Canada & the
United Kingdom of Great Britain & Northern Ireland & Providing
for the) Reciprocal Recognition & Enforcement of Judgments in
Civil & Commercial Matters
Recording of Evidence by Sound Recording Machine Act
Regional Savings & Loan Societies Act
Regional Savings & Loan Societies Federation Act
Regulations Act
(An Act Respecting the) Removal of Archaic Terminology from
the Acts of New Brunswick
Residential Tenancies Act
Sale of Goods Act
Sale of Lands Publication Act
Security Frauds Prevention Act
Statute of Frauds Act
Statute Law Amendment Act
Succession Law Amendment Act
Surety Bonds Act
Survival of Actions Act
Survivorship Act
Tortfeasors Act
Trespass Act
Trustees Act
Unconscionable Transactions Relief Act
Wage-Earners Protection Act
Warehouse Receipts Act
  Warehouseman's Lien Act
Wills Act
Winding-up Act
Woodmen's Lien Act
Minister & Attorney General, Hon. Paul Duffie, 506/453-3001, Fax: 506/453-3283
Deputy Minister, Paul M. LeBreton, Q.C., 506/453-2208, Fax: 506/453-3651
Asst. Deputy Minister, Suzanne Bonnell-Burley, 506/453-2458, Fax: 506/453-3651
Director, Research & Planning, Pauline Desrosier-Hickey, 506/453-3693, Fax: 506/453-7483
  For list of Courts & other Legal Offices, including Judicial Officials & Judges *see* Section 10 of this book.

ADMINISTRATIVE SERVICES
Executive Director, Neil Foreman, 506/453-2719, Fax: 506/453-8718
Director, Financial Services, Raymond McLaughlin, 506/453-2719, Fax: 506/453-7483

Director, Human Resource Services, Neil Foreman, 506/453-2719; Fax: 506/453-8718
Provincial Director, Legal Aid New Brunswick, David Potter, 506/451-1424; Fax: 506/451-1429
Director, Legal Services, Richard Burns, Q.C., 506/453-2222; Fax: 506/453-3275
Acting Director, Legislative Services, Elaine Gunter, Q.C., 506/453-2544; Fax: 506/457-7342
Director, Public Legal Education & Information Service, Deborah Doherty, 506/453-5369; Fax: 506/457-7342
Director, Public Prosecutions, Robert Murray, Q.C., 506/453-2784; Fax: 506/453-5364

Office of the Queen's Printer
PO Box 6000, Fredericton NB E3B 5H1
506/453-2520; Fax: 506/453-7408
Queen's Printer, Marie-Ange Lévesque

COURT SERVICES
Executive Director, Carolyn Lovely, 506/453-2935, Fax: 506/453-3651
Registrar, Court of Appeal & Court of Queen's Bench, A. DiGiacinto, 506/453-2452, Fax: 506/453-7921
Director, Operations Court Services, Carolyn Lovely, 506/453-2935, Fax: 506/453-3651
Director, Program Support Court Services, Lynda Richard, 506/453-2452, Fax: 506/453-7921

JUSTICE SERVICES
Director, Consumer Affairs & Chief Rentalsman, Judy Budovitch, 506/453-2682, Fax: 506/444-4494
Director, Corporate Affairs, Charles McAllister, 506/453-3860, Fax: 506/453-2613
Director, Credit Unions, Cooperatives & Trust Companies & Director, Examinations Branch, Pierre LeBlanc, 506/457-4850, Fax: 506/453-7474
Superintendent, Insurance, Reginald Richard, 506/453-2512, Fax: 506/453-2613
Director, Securities Administration, Donne Smith Jr., 506/658-3060, Fax: 506/658-3059

Associated Agencies, Boards & Commissions
• Expropriations Advisory Office: 295 boul St-Pierre ouest, CP 297, Caraquet NB E0B 1K0 – 506/727-3481; Fax: 506/727-4162
Officer, Reginald Leger
• New Brunswick Real Estate Council: PO Box 785, Fredericton NB E3B 5B4 – 506/455-9733; Fax: 506/450-8719
Chair, Carl Sherwood
• Office of the Administrator of Securities: #606, 133 Prince William St., PO Box 5001, Saint John NB E2L 4Y9 – 506/658-3060; Fax: 506/658-3059
Administrator, Donne W. Smith Jr.
Deputy Administrator, Enforcement & Compliance, Edouard LeBlanc

New Brunswick LIQUOR CORPORATION/ Société des alcools du Nouveau-Brunswick
PO Box 20787, Fredericton NB E3B 5B8
506/452-6826; Fax: 506/452-9890
Chair, Wallace Deschenes
President & CEO, Roger J.E. Landry
Vice-President, Operations, Ron Searles
Vice-President, Finance & Administration, D. Jack Dorcas
Secretary, Elizabeth Fairley

LIQUOR LICENSING BRANCH
PO Box 3000, Fredericton NB E3B 5G5
506/453-3732; Fax: 506/457-7335
Policy Advisor, Brian Steeves

Canadian Almanac & Directory 1997

Department of MUNICIPALITIES, CULTURE & HOUSING/Municipalités, culture et habitation
Marysville Place, 20 McGloin St., PO Box 6000, Fredericton NB E3B 5H1
506/453-2690; Fax: 506/457-4991; URL: http://www.gov.nb.ca/mch/index.htm

ACTS ADMINISTERED
Arts Development Trust Fund Act
Assessment Act
Business Improvement Areas Act
Cemetery Companies Act (as it pertains to Non-incorporated Areas)
Closing of Retail Establishments Act
Community Planning Act
Condominium Property Act, s. 7(11)
Control of Municipalities Act
Controverted Elections Act
Days of Rest Act
Elections Act (Provincial)
Emergency Measures Act
Film & Video Act
Fire Prevention Act
Flood & Storm Damage Act
Historic Sites Protection Act
Kings Landing Corporation Act
Le Centre Communautaire Sainte-Anne Act
Legislative Assembly Act, ss. 23/24
Libraries Act
Metric Conversion Act
Municipal Assistance Act
Municipal Capital Borrowing Act
Municipal Debenture Act
Municipal Elections Act
Municipal Heritage Preservation Act
Municipal Thoroughfare Easements Act
Municipalities Act
New Brunswick Arts Board Act
New Brunswick Housing Act
New Brunswick Museum Act
Real Property Tax Act (as it pertains to Assessment)
Registry Act (as it pertains to Affidavits)
Residential Property Tax Relief Act
Sport Development Trust Funds Act
Theatres Cinematographs & Amusements Act
Youth Assistance Act (in part)
Minister, Hon. Ann Breault, 506/453-2313, Email: annb@gov.nb.ca
Deputy Minister, Julian Walker, 506/453-2522
Executive Director, Corporate Services, Michael McKendy, 506/453-3925

CORPORATE SERVICES DIVISION
Asst. Deputy Minister, Lowell Boyle, 506/453-3925
Director, Budget Services, James Murphy, 506/454-4160
Director, Financial Services, George Breau, 506/453-3023
Director, Management Information Services, Dave Brannen, 506/453-3282
Director, Public Affairs, Cathy Garrabb-Read, 506/457-7843

CULTURAL AFFAIRS DIVISION
Fax: 506/453-2416
Asst. Deputy Minister, Louise Gillis, 506/453-7424
Manager, National Exhibition Centre & New Brunswick Sports Hall of Fame, Cynthia Wallace-Casey, 506/453-3747
Director, Archaeology Branch, Dr. Christopher Turnbull, 506/453-2792
Director, Arts Branch, Vacant, 506/453-3610
Director, Heritage Branch, Wayne Burley, 506/453-2324
Director, Kings Landing Historical Settlement, Robert Dallison, 506/363-5090

Director, New Brunswick Museum, Dr. Frank Milligan, 506/635-5356
Director, Village Historique Acadien, Jean-Yves Thériault, 506/727-3467

HOUSING & PUBLIC SAFETY SERVICES DIVISION
506/453-4991
Asst. Deputy Minister, Pauline Rivard, 506/453-3259
Director, Program Support Services, Charles Boulay, 506/453-7450
Chief Engineer, Engineering Services, Vacant, 506/453-2677
Manager, Portfolio Management & Community Services, Vacant, 506/453-7446

New Brunswick Emergency Measures Organization (EMO)
65 Brunswick St., PO Box 6000, Fredericton NB E3B 5H1
506/453-2393; Fax: 506/453-5513; URL: http://www.gov.nb.ca/pss/emo.htm
Director, James O. Stith
Deputy Director, Art Skaling, 506/453-2133
Manager, Plans & Operations, Andrew Morton, 506/453-5515
Manager, Public Information & Communication, Gary Stairs

Office of the Fire Marshall
PO Box 6000, Fredericton NB E3B 5H1
506/453-2004; Fax: 506/457-4899
Executive Director & Provincial Fire Marshal, James O. Stith, 506/453-2393
Deputy Fire Marshal, Philippa Gourley, 506/453-2004
Secretary to the Fire Marshall, Lisa Munn, 506/453-2393

HUMAN RESOURCE SERVICES & ADMINISTRATION DIVISION
Fax: 506/457-4991
Executive Director, Sylvie Levesque-Finn, 506/453-5239

MUNICIPAL SERVICES DIVISION
Fax: 506/457-4991
Asst. Deputy Minister, Paul O'Connell, 506/453-3256
Chief Electoral Officer, Election Branch, Barbara J. Landry
Manager, Downtown Development Branch, Walter Waite, 506/457-4947, Fax: 506/458-9369
Director, Land Use Planning Branch, Gérard Belliveau, 506/453-2171
Director, Local Government Administration Branch, Paul Blackmore, 506/453-2434
Secretary, Municipal Capital Borrowing Board, Dan Rae, 506/453-2154

SPORTS, RECREATION & LIBRARIES DIVISION
Asst. Deputy Minister, James (Jim) Morell, 506/453-2550
Executive Director, Libraries, Jocelyne LeBel, 506/453-2354
Director, Recreation, Normand Léger, 506/453-2312
Director, Sports, Suzanne Mason, 506/453-2928

Associated Agencies, Boards & Commissions
• New Brunswick Film Classification Board: c/o Dept. of Municipalities, Culture & Housing, 20 McGloin St., PO Box 6000, Fredericton NB E3B 5H1 – 506/453-2553
Chair & Director, Vacant
Secretary, Janice Morgan
• Regional Assessment Review Board: PO Box 6000, Fredericton NB E3B 5H1 – 506/453-2126
Chair, Lawrence Garvie

Department of NATURAL RESOURCES & ENERGY (NRE)/Ressources naturelles et énergie (RNE)
PO Box 6000, Fredericton NB E3B 5H1
506/453-2614; Fax: 506/453-3322; URL: http://www.gov.nb.ca/dnre/index.htm

Manages all natural resources within the province including fish & wildlife, timber, minerals, energy, Crown lands & water resources. Responsible for the development, protection, allocation & utilization of resources in a way that is considered economically, environmentally & socially acceptable.

ACTS ADMINISTERED
Bituminous Shale Act
Crown Lands & Forests Act
Ecological Reserves Act
Endangered Species Act
Energy Efficiency Act
Fish & Wildlife Act
Forest Fires Act
Forest Products Act
Gas Distribution Act
Gasoline, Diesel Oil & Home Heating Oil Pricing Act
Maritime Forestry Complex Corporation Act
Metallic Minerals Tax Act
Mining Act
Oil & Natural Gas Act
Ownership of Minerals Act
Oyster Fisheries Act
Parks Act
Pipe Line Act
Quarriable Substances Act
Scalers Act
Surveys Act
Territorial Division Act
Underground Storage Act
Minister, Hon. Alan Graham, 506/453-2510, Fax: 506/453-2930
Minister of State, Mines & Energy, Hon. Albert Doucet
Deputy Minister, Mavis Hurley, 506/453-2501, Fax: 506/453-2930

MINERAL RESOURCES & ENERGY
Asst. Deputy Minister, Don Barnett, 506/453-3862, Fax: 506/453-3671
Director, Geological Surveys Branch, Dr. J. Leslie Davies, 506/453-2206, Fax: 506/453-3671
Director, Mineral Development Branch, Sam McEwan, 506/453-2206, Fax: 506/453-3671
Director, Policy, Planning & Administration Branch, Garry MacEwan, 506/453-2206, Fax: 506/453-3671

REGIONAL RESOURCES
Asst. Deputy Minister, George R. Stevens, 506/453-5417, Fax: 506/453-2930
Executive Director, Corporate Services, Pam Breau, 506/453-2207, Fax: 506/453-2930
Executive Director, Parks, D. John Archibald, 506/453-2730, Fax: 506/453-6630
Executive Director, Policy & Planning, Robert S. Watson, 506/453-2684, Fax: 506/453-2930
Acting Director, Communications, Louella Billings, 506/453-2614, Fax: 506/457-4881
Director, Conservation Services, Richard Monroe, 506/453-2440, Fax: 506/453-6699
Director, Finance & Administration Services, Keith Burgess, 506/453-2468, Fax: 506/453-4279
Director, Forest Fire Management, Tom Reid, 506/453-2530, Fax: 506/453-3322
Director, Information Services & Systems Branch, Peter Andrews, 506/453-5598, Fax: 506/453-6889
Director, Technical Services, Steven Conn, 506/453-2488, Fax: 506/453-3322

RENEWABLE RESOURCES
Asst. Deputy Minister, M. David MacFarlane, 506/453-3063, Fax: 506/453-2930
Executive Director, Fish & Wildlife, Dr. Arnold H. Boer, 506/453-2440, Fax: 506/453-6699
Executive Director, Timber Management, Thomas L. Spinney, 506/453-2432, Fax: 506/453-6689
Director, Crown Lands, J.P. Robichaud, 506/453-2513
Director, Forest Extension Services, Joakim Hermelin, 506/453-3711, Fax: 506/453-3322
Director, Recreation & Environment, Ronald C. Loughrey, 506/453-2383, Fax: 506/453-6689

Associated Agencies, Boards & Commissions
• Board of Examiners under the Scaler's Act: PO Box 6000, Fredericton NB E3B 5H1 – 506/453-2441; Fax: 506/453-6689
• Forest Protection Limited: Comp 5, Site 24, RR#1, Fredericton NB E3B 4X2 – 506/446-6930; Fax: 506/446-6934
• New Brunswick Forest Products Commission: PO Box 6000, Fredericton NB E3B 5H1 – 506/453-2196; Fax: 506/457-4966
Chair, Richard N. Renouf
Executive Director, Linda D. Gould

Office of the OMBUDSMAN/Bureau de l'ombudsman
767 Brunswick St., PO Box 6000, Fredericton NB E3B 5H1
506/453-2789; Fax: 506/453-5599
Ombudsman, Ellen E. King
Asst. Ombudsman & Legal Counsel, Claire Pitre
Secretary, Marielle Goggin

New Brunswick POLICE COMMISSION (NBPC)/Commission de police du Nouveau-Brunswick
#103, 191 Prospect St. West, Fredericton NB E3B 2T7
506/453-2069; Fax: 506/457-3542

The Commission investigates & determines complaints alleging misconduct by municipal & regional police officers; investigates any matter relating to any aspect of policing in any area of the province; determines the adequacy of municipal, regional and RCMP police forces within the province.
Chair, Hon. Stuart G. Stratton, Q.C.
Executive Director, Clem Bolduc

New Brunswick POWER CORPORATION (NBPC)/La société d'énergie du Nouveau-Brunswick
515 King St., PO Box 2000, Fredericton NB E3B 4X1
506/458-3166
President & CEO, James Hannkinson
Senior Vice-President, Chuck Baird
Director, Environmental Affairs, Glen Wilson
Manager, Environmental Assessment & Assurance, Charles Hickman

REGIONAL DEVELOPMENT CORPORATION (RDC)/Société d'aménagement régional (SAR)
836 Churchill Row, PO Box 428, Fredericton NB E3B 5R4
506/453-2277; Fax: 506/453-7988
Minister Responsible, Hon. Jean-Paul Savoie
General Manager, Frank Swift
Asst. General Manager, Finance & Administration, Gordon Gilman
Asst. General Manager, Roland Cormier

New Brunswick RESEARCH & PRODUCTIVITY COUNCIL (RPC)/Conseil de la recherche et de la productivité du Nouveau-Brunswick (CRP)
921 College Hill Rd., Fredericton NB E3B 6Z9
506/452-8994; Fax: 506/452-1395; Email: vjackson@rpc.unb.ca; URL: http://www.rpc.unb.ca
Executive Director, Dr. P. Lewell, 506/452-0585, Email: plewell@rpc.unb.ca
Head, Administration & Finance, Stephen Fox, 506/452-1380, Email: sfox@rpc.unb.ca
Head, Chemical & Biotechnical Services, Dr. Peter Silk, 506/452-1369, Email: psilk@rpc.unb.ca
Head, Engineering Materials & Diagnostics, Jarek Goszczynski, 506/452-1396, Email: jgoszczy@rpc.unb.ca
Head, Food, Fisheries & Aquaculture, Dr. Bev Bacon, 506/452-1368, Email: bbacon@rpc.unb.ca
Head, IRAP, Dr. P. Lewell, 506/452-1385, Email: plewell@rpc.unb.ca
Head, Process & Environmental Technology, Dr. P. Lewell, 526/452-1653, Email: plewell@rpc.unb.ca
Head, Product Innovation, Mike Carr, 506/452-0590, Email: mcarr@rpc.unb.ca
Coordinator, Information Centre, Virginia Jackson, 506/452-1381, Email: vjackson@rpc.unb.ca

Department of the SOLICITOR GENERAL/Solliciteur général
Barker House, 4th Fl., PO Box 6000, Fredericton NB E3B 5H1
506/453-7414; Fax: 506/453-3870; URL: http://www.gov.nb.ca/solgen/index.htm

ACTS ADMINISTERED
Compensation for Victims of Crime Act
Coroners Act
Corrections Act
Criminal Code
Custody & Detention of Young Persons Act
Intoxicated Persons Detention Act
New Brunswick Highway Patrol Act
Parole Act
Police Act
Private Investigators & Security Services Act
Salvage Dealers Licensing Act
Sheriffs Act
Training School Act
Victim Services Act
Young Offenders Act
Minister, Hon. Jane Barry, 506/453-7414
Deputy Solicitor General, Ronald Murray, 506/453-7412
Asst. Deputy Solicitor General, Grant Garneau, 506/453-7142
Chief, Sheriff/Coroner's Office, John Evans, 506/453-3604
Asst. Deputy Minister, Corporate Services, Grant Garneau, 506/453-7142, Fax: 506/453-3870

CORRECTIONAL SERVICES
Asst. Deputy Minister, Nora Kelly, 506/444-4028, Fax: 506/453-3870
Director, Adults Institutional Services, Brian Mackin, 506/453-2846
Acting Director, Institutional & Young Offender Services, Bob Ecktein, 506/453-2846, Fax: 506/453-2307
Director, Victim & Community Services, Doug Naish, 506/453-2846

LAW ENFORCEMENT
Executive Director, Brian Alexander, 506/453-3603, Fax: 506/457-4957
Acting Director, Commercial Vehicle Enforcement, William Adams, 506/453-7157
Coordinator, Transportation of Dangerous Goods, Wayne Hennigar, 506/856-2860

Chief Inspector, Inspections, R. Bliss Noiles, 506/453-2471
Chief, Provincial Firearms Office, R. Bliss Noiles, 506/453-3775

DEPARTMENT OF SUPPLY & SERVICES
Central Purchasing Branch, #205, Marysville Place, PO Box 6000, Fredericton NB E3B 5H1
506/453-2245; URL: http://www.gov.nb.ca/supply/index.htm

ACTS ADMINISTERED
Archives Act
Public Purchasing Act
Public Records Act
Public Works Act
Queen's Printer Act (jointly with Dept. of Justice)
Minister, Hon. Bruce A. Smith
Deputy Minister, G. Stephenson Wheatley, P.Eng.

BUILDINGS DIVISION
Fax: 506/444-4400
Asst. Deputy Minister, Neil Coy, 506/453-2228
Executive Director, Design & Construction, Ashley Cummings, 506/453-2228
Executive Director, Facilities Management, Greg Cook, 506/444-4530
Director, Property Management, Preston Hawkins, 506/453-2221

FINANCE & ADMINISTRATION
Fax: 506/444-4400; URL: http://www.gov.nb.ca/supply/archives/index.htm
Director, Finance & Accounting, Richard Burnett, 506/453-6060
Director, Human Resources, Eric White, 506/453-5952
Director, Information Services Coordination Branch, Tom Harding, 506/457-4938
Manager, Office Administration, Janice York, 506/453-3742
Communications Officer, Donald MacPherson, 506/444-3281

SERVICES DIVISION
URL: http://www.gov.nb.ca/supply/sgs/index.htm (Purchasing)
Asst. Deputy Minister, Vacant
Executive Director, Supply & General Services, Richard Dunphy, 506/453-8737, Fax: 506/444-4200
Chief, Information Technology, Corporate Information Management Services, Lori MacMullen, 506/457-6849, Fax: 506/453-2270
Director, Translation Bureau, Jean-Eudes Levesque, 506/453-2920, Fax: 506/459-7911
Provincial Archivist, Provincial Archives of New Brunswick, Marion Beyea, 506/453-3811, Fax: 506/453-3288
President, Algonquin Properties Ltd., Robert Saintonge, 506/453-2504, Fax: 506/444-4400

Department of TRANSPORTATION/ Transports
King Tower, Kings Pl., 2nd Fl., PO Box 6000, Fredericton NB E3B 5H1
506/453-3626
Motor Vehicles: 506/453-2810

ACTS ADMINISTERED
All-Terrain Vehicle Act
Highway Act
Motor Vehicle Act
New Brunswick Highway Corporation Act
New Brunswick Transportation Authority Act
Public Utilities Act
Minister, Hon. Sheldon Lee, 506/453-2559

Acting Deputy Minister, Donald J. McCrea, 506/453-2549, Email: dot007@gov.nb.ca
Asst. Deputy Minister & Chief Highway Engineer, David J. Johnstone, 506/453-2351, Email: dot004@gov.nb.ca
Executive Director, Administration & Information Systems, Vacant, 506/453-2552, Email: dot007@gov.nb.ca
Executive Director, Engineering Services, D.W. Manuel, 506/453-2849, Email: dot005@gov.nb.ca
Executive Director, Motor Vehicles & Policy, Walter W. Steeves, 506/453-2552, Email: dot008@gov.nb.ca
Executive Director, Operations, George Haines, 506/453-2849, Email: dot006@gov.nb.ca
Executive Director, Vehicle Management, Vacant, 506/453-2552, Email: dot007@gov.nb.ca
Director, Administrative Services, S.C. Andrews-Caron, 506/453-2663, Email: adm046@gov.nb.ca
Director, Construction, K. Lawson, 506/453-2673, Email: con004@gov.nb.ca
Director, Design, C.H. Page, 506/453-2608, Email: des040@gov.nb.ca
Director, Human Resources, Marguerite Levesque, 506/453-2332, Email: hrb004@gov.nb.ca
Director, Information Systems, Kenneth Connell, 506/453-2990, Email: isb002@gov.nb.ca
Director, Maintenance & Traffic, Emilia Rodrigues, 506/453-2600, Email: tec021@gov.nb.ca
Director & Registrar, Motor Vehicles & Officer Responsible, Dangerous/Hazardous Substances Transport, James Morrison, 506/453-2407, Email: dmv022@gov.nb.ca
Director, Planning & Land Management, G.A. Goguen, 506/453-2754, Email: tra007@gov.nb.ca
Director, Quality Initiatives, G.H. Keenan, 506/453-7955, Email: dot012@gov.nb.ca
Director, Structures, Frederick Blaney, 506/453-2674, Email: str031@gov.nb.ca
Acting Director, Transportation Policy, John Palmer, 506/453-2802, Email: pol006@gov.nb.ca
Supervisor, Safety Promotion, Michael Crowther, 506/453-3645

Associated Agencies, Boards & Commissions
• Board of Commissioners of Public Utilities: 110 Charlotte St., PO Box 5001, Saint John NB E2L 4Y9 – 506/658-2504; Fax: 506/633-0163
Chair, D.C. Nicholson
Secretary, Lorraine Legere
• Motor Vehicle Dealer Licensing Board: PO Box 6000, Fredericton NB E3B 5H1 – 506/453-2443
The New Brunswick Motor Carrier Board was abolished on May 15, 1995. Questions concerning public motor bus requirements may be directed to 506/658-2504; transport-related questions may be directed to 506/453-3939.
Officer, T.C. Walton
• New Brunswick Transportation Agency: Kings Place, PO Box 6000, Fredericton NB E3B 5H1 – 506/453-2802; Fax: 506/453-2900
Chair, Vacant, 506/453-2549
Vice-Chair, W.W. Steeves, 506/453-2552

WORKPLACE HEALTH, SAFETY & COMPENSATION COMMISSION OF NEW BRUNSWICK (WHSCC)/Santé, securité et indemnisation des accidents
1 Portland St., PO Box 160, Saint John NB E2L 3X9
506/632-2200; Fax: 506/632-2226; URL: http://www.gov.nb.ca/whscc/index.htm
Toll Free: 1-800-222-9775
Fredericton: 500 Beaverbrook Ct., 4th Fl., Fredericton NB E3B 5X4
506/453-2467, Fax: 506/453-7982
Toll Free: 1-800-442-9776

ACTS ADMINISTERED
Occupational Health & Safety Act
Workers' Compensation Act
President & CEO, John Roushorne
Chair, Médard Collette
Chair, Appeals Tribunal, Léonard Arsenault
Vice-President, Finance & Administration, Frank Chevrier
Vice-President, Operations, Brian Connell
Vice-President, Prevention & Rehabilitation, Dianne Powert
Vice-President, Technology & Planning, David Greason
Manager, Public Affairs, France Haché
Director, Workers' Rehabilitation Centre, Barb Keir

YOUTH COUNCIL OF NEW BRUNSWICK (YCNB)/Conseil de la jeunesse du Nouveau-Brunswick
736 King St., PO Box 6000, Fredericton NB E3B 5H1
506/453-3271; Fax: 506/444-4413
Chair, Corinne Godbout
Executive Director, Beverley J. Barnes

GOVERNMENT OF NEWFOUNDLAND & LABRADOR

Seat of Government: Legislative Assembly, Confederation Bldg., St. John's NF A1B 4J6
URL: http://www.gov.nf.ca/
The Province of Newfoundland entered Confederation March 31, 1949. It has an area of 405,720 km2, and the StatsCan census population in 1991 was 568,474.

Office of the LIEUTENANT GOVERNOR
Government House, Military Rd., PO Box 5517, St. John's NF A1C 5W4
709/729-4494; Fax: 709/729-2234
Lieutenant Governor, Hon. Frederick W. Russell
Private Secretary, Brig. General Gordon C. Barnes

Office of the PREMIER
Confederation Bldg., 8th Fl., PO Box 8700, St. John's NF A1B 4J6
Fax: 709/729-5875; URL: http://www.gov.nf.ca/exec/premier/premier.htm
Premier, Hon. Brian Tobin, 709/729-3570
Acting Chief of Staff, Alphonsus E. Faour, 709/729-3558
Parliamentary Asst., Oliver Langdon, 709/729-2328
Executive Asst., Paul D. Sparkes, 709/729-3961
Executive Asst., Ed Joyce, 709/637-2462
Personal Asst., Margot Brown, 709/729-3972
Director, Communications, Cathy Coady, 709/729-3960
Legislative Asst., Heidi Bonnell, 709/729-0499
Special Asst., Ed Hollett
Special Asst., Gail V. Joy, 709/729-2578
Administrative Officer, Olive White, 709/729-3566

EXECUTIVE COUNCIL
Confederation Bldg., PO Box 8700, St. John's NF A1B 4J6
709/729-5645; URL: http://www.gov.nf.ca/exec/start.htm
Premier & President, Executive Council, Minister Responsible, Intergovernmental Affairs, Hon. Brian Tobin, 709/729-3570, Fax: 709/729-5875
Minister, Social Services, Hon. Joan Marie Aylward, 709/729-3580, Fax: 709/729-6996

Minister, Environment, Hon. Kevin Aylward, M.H.A., 709/729-2574, Fax: 709/729-0112
Minister, Works, Services & Transportation & Minister Responsible, Status of Women, Hon. Julie Bettney, 709/729-3678, Fax: 709/729-4285
Minister, Justice & Attorney General, Hon. Chris D. Decker, 709/729-2869, Fax: 709/729-0469
Minister, Finance & President, Treasury Board, Hon. Paul D. Dicks, Q.C., 709/729-2858, Fax: 709/729-2232
Minister, Fisheries & Aquaculture, Hon. R. John Efford, 709/729-3705, Fax: 709/729-0360
Minister, Development & Rural Renewal, Hon. Judy Foote, 709/729-4729, Fax: 709/729-0654
Minister, Industry, Trade & Technology, Hon. Charles J. Furey, 709/729-2791, Fax: 709/729-2828
Minister, Mines & Energy, Hon. Dr. Rex V. Gibbons, 709/729-2920, Fax: 709/729-0059
Minister, Education, Hon. Roger D. Grimes, 709/729-5040, Fax: 709/729-0414
Minister, Tourism, Culture & Recreation, Hon. Sandra Kelly, 709/729-0659, Fax: 709/729-0662
Minister, Government Services & Lands, Hon. Ernest McLean, 709/729-4713, Fax: 709/729-4754
Minister, Health, Hon. Lloyd Matthews, 709/729-3124, Fax: 709/729-0121
Minister, Municipal & Provincial Affairs, Hon. Arthur D. Reid, 709/729-3048, Fax: 709/729-0943
Minister, Forest Resources & Agrifoods & Government House Leader, Hon. Beaton Tulk, 709/729-4716, Fax: 709/729-2076

Cabinet Secretariat
709/729-5218
Clerk, Executive Council & Secretary to Cabinet, Malcolm Rowe, Q.C., 709/729-2853, Fax: 709/729-5218
Deputy Clerk, Executive Council & Asst. Secretary to Cabinet, Alphonsus E. Faour, 780/729-2844, Fax: 780/729-5218
Asst. Secretary, Economic Policy, Andrew Noseworthy, 709/729-2845, Fax: 709/729-5218
Asst. Secretary, Social Policy, Wayne Green, 709/729-2850, Fax: 709/729-5218
Executive Director, Communications, John Downton, 709/729-4782, Fax: 709/729-0584
Director, Financial Administration, Douglas Heffernan, 709/729-1984, Fax: 709/729-0435

Cabinet Committees
Economic Policy Committee
Planning & Priorities Committee
Social Policy Committee
Treasury Board Committee
Cabinet Committee on Routine Matters & Appointments
Cabinet Committee on Rural Revitalization

Government Programs Office
Fax: 709/729-5038
Director, Social & Fiscal Policy, Bruce Hallett, 709/729-3954
Director, Resource & Economic Policy, Tim Murphy, 709/729-2980

Intergovernmental Affairs Secretariat
709/729-5038
Minister Responsible, Hon. Brian Tobin, 709/729-3570, Fax: 709/729-5875
Secretary, Intergovernmental Affairs, Barbara Knight, 709/729-2134, Fax: 709/729-5038
Asst. Secretary, Intergovernmental Affairs, Brian Bursey, 709/729-3164

Labrador & Aboriginal Affairs Secretariat
Secretary, Harold Marshall, 709/729-4814, Fax: 709/729-4900
Asst. Secretary, Aboriginal Affairs, Raymond Hawco, 709/729-6062, Fax: 709/729-4900

Treasury Board Secretariat
709/729-2156; URL: http://www.gov.nf.ca/exec/Presiden/presiden.htm
President, Hon. Paul D. Dicks, Q.C., 709/729-2858, Fax: 709/729-2232
Secretary, Peter Kennedy, 709/729-3559
Asst. Secretary, Human Resources & Budgeting, Robert Smart, 709/729-2633

HOUSE OF ASSEMBLY
c/o Clerk's Office, Confederation Bldg., PO Box 8700, St.John's NF A1B 4J6
709/729-3405; Fax: 709/729-4820; URL: http://www.gov.nf.ca/house/hoa_ovr.htm
Clerk & Law Clerk: A. John Noel
Speaker: Hon. Lloyd Snow, 709/729-3403
Sergeant-at-Arms: Cyril Kirby
Manager of Hansard: Irene Tapper, 709/729-0960
Librarian, Legislative Library: Norma Jean Richards, 709/729-3604
Deputy Speaker & Chair, Committees, Percy Barrett
Deputy Chair, Committees, Melvin Penney
Clerk Asst., Elizabeth Murphy

Government Caucus Office (Lib.)
PO Box 8700, St. John's NF A1B 4J6
709/729-3400; Fax: 709/729-5774

Office of the Official Opposition (PC)
Confederation Bldg., 5th Fl., PO Box 8700, St. John's NF A1B 4J6
709/729-3391; Fax: 709/729-5202
Leader, Hon. Loyola Sullivan
Opposition House Leader, Harvey Hodder
Chief of Staff, Penny Dobbin

Office of the New Democratic Party (NDP)
PO Box 8700, St. John's NF A1B 4J6
709/729-0270; Fax: 709/576-1443
Leader, Jack Harris

House Committees
Clerk, Committees, Elizabeth Murphy, 709/729-3434
Striking Committee
Standing Committee on Public Accounts
Standing Committee on Privileges & Elections
Government Services Committee
Resource Committee
Social Service Committee
Standing Orders Committee

FORTY-THIRD ASSEMBLY - NEWFOUNDLAND & LABRADOR
709/729-3405
Last General Election, February 22, 1996. Maximum Duration, 5 years.
Party Standings (February 22, 1996):
Liberal (Lib.) 37
Progressive Conservative (PC) 9
New Democratic Party (NDP) 1
Independent 1
Total 48
Salaries, Indemnities & Allowances: 1996 - Members' sessional indemnity $38,028. In addition to this are the following:
Premier $54,843
Ministers; Speaker; Leader of the Opposition $39,834
Government Whip & Opposition Whip $6,000
Chair of Committees (Deputy Speaker) $19,917
Deputy Chair of Committees $9,958
Opposition House Leader $19,917
Following is: constituency (number of eligible voters at 1996 election) member, party affiliation, St. John's telephone number. (Address for all is Confederation Bldg., PO Box 8700, St. John's NF A1B 4J6.)

Refer to Cabinet List, Government Caucus Office, and Opposition Office, for **Fax** numbers.

MEMBERS BY CONSTITUENCY
Baie Verte (7,461) Paul Shelley, PC, 709/729-4841
Bay of Islands (8,041) Hon. Brian Tobin, Lib., 709/729-3570
Bellevue (8,207) Percy Barrett, Lib., 709/729-5204
Bonavista North (8,613) Hon. Beaton Tulk, Lib., 709/729-5106
Bonavista South (9,277) Roger Fitzgerald, PC, 709/729-6131
Burgeo & La Poile (8,864) William Ramsay, Lib., 709/729-5207
Burin-Placentia West (8,609) Mary Hodder, Lib.
Cape St. Francis (7,860) Jack Byrne, PC, 709/729-6979
Carbonear-Harbour Grace (9,069) Hon. Arthur D. Reid, Lib., 709/729-3048
Cartwright-L'Anse au Clair (3,396) Yvonne Jones, Ind., Fax: 709/729-4739
Conception Bay East & Bell Island (8,170) James Walsh, Lib., 709/729-5209
Conception Bay South (8,023) Bob French, PC
Exploits (8,269) Hon. Roger D. Grimes, Lib., 709/729-0659
Ferryland (8,302) Hon. Loyola Sullivan, PC, 709/729-4884
Fortune Bay-Cape la Hune (8,142) Oliver Langdon, Lib., 709/729-6184
Gander (8,237) Hon. Sandra Kelly, Lib.
Grand Bank (8,695) Hon. Judy Foote, Lib.
Grand Falls-Buchans (8,700) Anna Thistle, Lib.
Harbour Main-Whitbourne (8,434) Don Whelan, Lib., 709/729-0140
Humber East (8,514) Robert Mercer, Lib.
Humber Valley (7,728) Rick Woodford, Lib., 709/729-4864
Humber West (7,916) Hon. Paul D. Dicks, Q.C., Lib., 709/729-3403
Kilbride (8,635) Edward Byrne, PC, 709/729-3758
Labrador West (6,803) Perry Canning, Lib.
Lake Melville (6,009) Hon. Ernest McLean, Lib.
Lewisporte (8,397) Melvin Penney, Lib., 709/729-5274
Mount Pearl (8,520) Hon. Julie Bettney, Lib.
Placentia & St. Mary's (8,101) Anthony Sparrow, Lib.
Port au Port (8,334) Gerald Smith, Lib., 709/729-5045
Port de Grave (8,862) Hon. R. John Efford, Lib., 709/729-3678
Signal Hill-Quidi Vidi (6,886) Jack Harris, NDP
St. Barbe (7,720) Hon. Charles J. Furey, Lib., 709/729-2791
St. George's-Stephenville East (8,630) Hon. Kevin Aylward, M.H.A., Lib.
St. John's Centre (8,109) Hon. Joan Marie Aylward, Lib.
St. John's East (7,747) John Ottenheimer, PC
St. John's North (6,703) Hon. Lloyd Matthews, Lib., 709/729-3124
St. John's South (8,452) Tom Osborne, PC
St. John's West (8,642) Hon. Dr. Rex V. Gibbons, Lib., 709/729-2920
Terra Nova (8,777) Tom Lush, Lib., 709/729-4649
The Straits & White Bay South (8,310) Hon. Chris D. Decker, Lib., 709/729-5040
Topsail (8,143) Ralph Wiseman, Lib.
Torngat Mountains (1,233) Wally Anderson, Lib., 709/729-0990
Trinity North (8,982) Doug Oldford, Lib., 709/729-0138
Trinity-Bay de Verde (9,136) Hon. Lloyd Snow, Lib., 709/729-3424
Twillingate & Fogo (9,040) Gerry Reid, Lib.
Virginia Waters (8,592) Walter Noel, Lib., 709/729-5208
Waterford Valley (9,361) Harvey Hodder, PC, 709/729-4234
Windsor-Springdale (8,962) Graham R. Flight, Lib., 709/729-1948

MEMBERS (ALPHABETICAL)

Wally Anderson, Torngat Mountains (1,233)Lib., 709/729-0990
Hon. Joan Marie Aylward, St. John's Centre (8,109)Lib.
Hon. Kevin Aylward, M.H.A., St. George's-Stephenville East (8,630)Lib.
Percy Barrett, Bellevue (8,207)Lib., 709/729-5204
Hon. Julie Bettney, Mount Pearl (8,520)Lib.
Edward Byrne, Kilbride (8,635)PC, 709/729-3758
Jack Byrne, Cape St. Francis (7,860)PC, 709/729-6979
Perry Canning, Labrador West (6,803)Lib.
Hon. Chris D. Decker, The Straits & White Bay South (8,310)Lib., 709/729-5040
Hon. Paul D. Dicks, Q.C., Humber West (7,916)Lib., 709/729-3403
Hon. R. John Efford, Port de Grave (8,862)Lib., 709/729-3678
Roger Fitzgerald, Bonavista South (9,277)PC, 709/729-6131
Graham R. Flight, Windsor-Springdale (8,962)Lib., 709/729-1948
Hon. Judy Foote, Grand Bank (8,695)Lib.
Bob French, Conception Bay South (8,023)PC
Hon. Charles J. Furey, St. Barbe (7,720)Lib., 709/729-2791
Hon. Dr. Rex V. Gibbons, St. John's West (8,642)Lib., 709/729-2920
Hon. Roger D. Grimes, Exploits (8,269)Lib., 709/729-0659
Jack Harris, Signal Hill-Quidi Vidi (6,886)NDP
Harvey Hodder, Waterford Valley (9,361)PC, 709/729-4234
Mary Hodder, Burin-Placentia West (8,609)Lib.
Yvonne Jones, Cartwright-L'Anse au Clair (3,396)Ind., Fax: 709/729-4739
Hon. Sandra Kelly, Gander (8,237)Lib.
Oliver Langdon, Fortune Bay-Cape la Hune (8,142)Lib., 709/729-6184
Tom Lush, Terra Nova (8,777)Lib., 709/729-4649
Hon. Lloyd Matthews, St. John's North (6,703)Lib., 709/729-3124
Hon. Ernest McLean, Lake Melville (6,009)Lib.
Robert Mercer, Humber East (8,514)Lib.
Walter Noel, Virginia Waters (8,592)Lib., 709/729-5208
Doug Oldford, Trinity North (8,982)Lib., 709/729-0138
Tom Osborne, St. John's South (8,452)PC
John Ottenheimer, St. John's East (7,747)PC
Melvin Penney, Lewisporte (8,397)Lib., 709/729-5274
William Ramsay, Burgeo & La Poile (8,864)Lib., 709/729-5207
Hon. Arthur D. Reid, Carbonear-Harbour Grace (9,069)Lib., 709/729-3048
Gerry Reid, Twillingate & Fogo (9,040)Lib.
Paul Shelley, Baie Verte (7,461)PC, 709/729-4841
Gerald Smith, Port au Port (8,334)Lib., 709/729-5045
Hon. Lloyd Snow, Trinity-Bay de Verde (9,136)Lib., 709/729-3424
Anthony Sparrow, Placentia & St. Mary's (8,101)Lib.
Hon. Loyola Sullivan, Ferryland (8,302)PC, 709/729-4884
Anna Thistle, Grand Falls-Buchans (8,700)Lib.
Hon. Brian Tobin, Bay of Islands (8,041)Lib., 709/729-3570
Hon. Beaton Tulk, Bonavista North (8,613)Lib., 709/729-5106
James Walsh, Conception Bay East & Bell Island (8,170)Lib., 709/729-5209
Don Whelan, Harbour Main-Whitbourne (8,434)Lib., 709/729-0140
Ralph Wiseman, Topsail (8,143)Lib.
Rick Woodford, Humber Valley (7,728)Lib., 709/729-4864

Canadian Almanac & Directory 1997

NEWFOUNDLAND & LABRADOR GOVERNMENT DEPARTMENTS & AGENCIES

Office of the AUDITOR GENERAL
Confederation Bldg., PO Box 8700, St. John's NF A1B 4J6
709/729-2700; Fax: 709/729-5970
Auditor General, Elizabeth Marshall, C.A.

CHURCHILL FALLS (LABRADOR) CORPORATION LIMITED
PO Box 12500, St. John's NF A1B 3T5
709/737-1450; Fax: 709/737-1782
CEO, William E. Wells, 709/737-1291
President, T. David Collett, 709/737-1372
Vice-President, Finance & Chief Financial Officer, R. Andrew Grant, 709/737-1452
Vice-President, Human Resources, General Counsel & Secretary, Maureen Greene, 709/737-1465
Vice-President, Operations & Engineering, S.D. Banfield, 709/925-8227
Manager, Corporate Affairs, Donald J. Barrett, 709/737-1370, Fax: 709/737-1816

Department of DEVELOPMENT & RURAL RENEWAL
PO Box 8700, St. John's NF A1B 4J6
URL: http://www.gov.nf.ca/dev.htm
Minister, Hon. Judy Foote, 709/729-4729
Deputy Minister, John Scott, 709/729-4732
Asst. Deputy Miniser, Avalon Region, Burce Saunders, 709/729-7000
Asst. Deputy Minister, Central Region, William MacKenzie, 709/256-5000
Asst. Deputy Miniser, Labrador Region, Harold Marshall, 709/896-2400
Asst. Deputy Miniser, Western Region, Vacant, 709/639-9691
Director, Craft Development, Jim Callahan, 709/729-7182, Fax: 709/729-7160

EMPLOYMENT & REGIONAL ECONOMIC DEVELOPMENT
Asst. Deputy Minister, Sam Kean
Acting Director, Employment Services, Clayton Johnson, 709/729-5675

Associated Agencies, Boards & Commissions
• Economic Recovery Commission (ERC): Beothuck Bldg., 20 Crosbie Pl., 3rd Fl., St. John's NF A1B 3Y8 – 709/729-7255; Email: geoff-meeker@porthole.entnet.nf.ca; URL: http://www.gov.nf.ca/erc/
Chair, Dr. Douglas House
Commissioner, Richard Fuchs
Executive Director, Cathy Duke
• Enterprise Newfoundland & Labrador: 136 Crosbie Rd., St. John's NF A1B 3K3 – 709/729-7000; Fax: 709/729-7135, Toll Free: 1-800-563-9179
President, Philip Wall, 709/729-7051
Vice-President, Patrick Kennedy, 709/729-7060
Vice-President, Regional Economic Development, Sam Kean

Department of EDUCATION
Confederation Bldg., PO Box 8700, St. John's NF A1B 4J6
709/729-5097; Fax: 709/729-5896; URL: http://www.gov.nf.ca/edu/startedu.htm

ACTS ADMINISTERED
Bay St. George Community College Act
College of Fisheries Act
College of Trades & Technology Act
Department of Education Act
Education Apportionment Act
Education (Public Examinations) Act
Education (Teacher Training) Act
Education (Teachers' Pensions) Act
Local School Tax Act
Memorial University Act
Memorial University (Pensions) Act
Memorial University (Property) Act
Newfoundland Teachers' Association Act
Newfoundland Teachers' Collective Bargaining Act
Polytechnical Institute Act
Post Secondary & Vocational Education Act
Regulation of Trade Schools Act
School Attendance Act
Schools Act
Teachers' Loan Act
Technical & Vocational Training Act
University Fees & Allowances Act
Minister, Hon. Roger D. Grimes
Deputy Minister, Deborah E. Fry, 709/729-2723
Associate Deputy Minister, Dr. Robert Crocker, 709/729-0197
Director, Public Relations, Carl Cooper, 709/729-0048

ADVANCED STUDIES BRANCH
Asst. Deputy Minister, Dr. Frank Marsh, 709/729-3026
Director, Institutional & Industrial Education Division, Barry Roberts, 709/729-2350
Director, Student Aid Division, Norman Snelgrove, 709/729-5849
Manager, Human Resource Development Secretariat, Hayward Harris, 709/729-4090

DENOMINATIONAL EDUCATION COUNCILS
133 Crosbie Rd., St. John's NF A1B 1H3
Fax: 709/579-8222
Executive Director, Integrated Education Council, Hubert Norman, 709/753-7260
Executive Director, Pentecostal Education Council, Pastor A.E. Batstone, 709/753-7263
Executive Director, Roman Catholic Education Council, Gerald Fallon, 709/753-4741

FINANCE & ADMINISTRATION BRANCH
Asst. Deputy Minister, Florence Delaney, 709/729-3025
Director, Evaluation, Research & Planning Division, Lenora Perry-Fagan, 709/729-3000
Director, External Financial Relations Division, Jack Thompson, 709/729-3013
Director, Human Resources Division, Glenn Saunders, 709/729-5750
Director, Information Technology Division, Ian Munn, 709/729-5590
Director, Youth Services Division, William J. Wilson, 709/729-3503, Fax: 709/729-3669

PRIMARY, ELEMENTARY & SECONDARY EDUCATION BRANCH
Asst. Deputy Minister, Primary, Elementary & Secondary Education, Dr. Wayne Oakley, 709/729-5720
Director, Program Development Division, Dr. Glen Loveless, 709/729-3004
Director, School Services & Professional Development Division, Gary Hatcher, 709/729-3034
Director, Student Support Services Division, Edward Mackey, 709/729-3023

Associated Agencies, Boards & Commissions
• Literacy Development Council: 238 Blackmarsh Rd., PO Box 8700, St. John's NF A1E 1T2 – 709/738-7323
Executive Director, Wayne Taylor

Office of the Chief ELECTORAL OFFICER
39 Hallett Cr., St. John's NF A1B 4C4
709/729-0712; Fax: 709/729-0679
Chief Electoral Officer, D. Wayne Mitchell

Department of ENVIRONMENT & LABOUR
Confederation Bldg., PO Box 8700, St. John's NF A1B 4J6
709/729-1930; Fax: 709/729-1930; URL: http://www.gov.nf.ca/envlab.htm

ACTS ADMINISTERED
Environment
Act to Amend the Waste Material (Disposal) Act
Act to Amend the Waste Material (Disposal) Act (No. 2)
Department of Environment & Lands Act
Environmental Assessment Act
Packaging Act
Pesticides Control Act
Waste Material Disposal Act
Waters Protection Act
Well Drilling Act
Labour
Department of Employment & Labour Relations Act
Fishing Industry Collective Bargaining Act
Human Rights Code
Industrial Standards Act
Interns & Residents Collective Bargaining Act
Labour Relations Act
Teachers Collective Bargaining Act
Public Service Collective Bargaining Act
Shops' Closing Act
Occupational Health & Safety
Amusement Rides Act & Regulations
(The) Asbestos Abatement Code of Practice
Boiler & Pressure Vessels Act & Regulations
Building Accessibility Act & Regulations
Electrical Regulations
Electrical Inspection Fees Regulations
Elevators Act & Regulations
Occupational Health & Safety Act & Regulations
Radiation Health & Safety Act & Regulations
Mines Act & Mines (Safety of Workmen) Regulations
Workplace Hazardous Materials Inspection System (WHMIS) Regulations
Minister, Hon. Kevin Aylward, M.H.A., 709/729-2577
Deputy Minister, John M. Fleming, 709/729-5722
Public Relations Specialist, Mark Duggan, 709/729-3394
Director, Financial & General Operations, Rick Hayward, 709/729-0939
Director, Human Resources, Kay Mullins, 709/729-0936
Director, Legislation Reform Division, Sean Kelly, 709/729-0047
Director, Occupational Health & Safety Services, Bruce Rogers, 709/729-5548
Director, Policy & Planning Division, Thomas R. Graham, 709/729-0030
Director, Public Relations, Teddy Ryan, 709/729-2575
Director, Youth Strategy & Career Support, Alison Earle, 709/729-2314, Fax: 709/729-6639

ENVIRONMENT BRANCH
Spill Reporting (24-hours): 709/772-2083
Asst. Deputy Minister, David Jeans, 709/729-5732
Director, Civil & Sanitary Environmental Engineering, Kenneth Dominie, 709/729-2556
Director, Environmental Assessment, Phil Graham, 709/729-2562
Director, Environmental Investigations, Carl W. Strong, 709/729-5783
Director, Industrial Environmental Engineering, Derrick Maddocks, 709/729-2555
Director, Water Resource Division, Dr. Wasi Ullah, 709/729-2563

Investigations Regional Offices
St. John's: Elizabeth Towers, PO Box 8700, St. John's NF A1B 4J6

Newfoundland & Labrador Round Table on The Environment & the Economy (NLRTEE)
West Block, Confederation Bldg., PO Box 8700, St. John's NF A1B 4J6
709/729-0027
Chair, Judy Rowell

LABOUR RELATIONS BRANCH
Asst. Deputy Minister, Joseph P. O'Neill, 709/729-2715
Director, Labour Standards, David Kerr, 709/729-2743
CEO, Labour Relations Board, Joseph Noel, 709/729-0911

Associated Agencies, Boards & Commissions
• Human Rights Commission
Listed alphabetically in detail, this Section.
• Labour Relations Board: Metro Place, 261 Kenmount Rd., PO Box 8700, St. John's NF A1B 4J6 – 709/729-2707; Fax: 709/729-5736
Chair, Dennis Browne
CEO, Joe M. Noel
• Labour Standards Board: Confederation Bldg., West Block, PO Box 8700, St. John's NF A1B 4J6 – 709/729-2742; Fax: 709/729-6639
Chair, Frank Tilley
• Workers' Compensation Review Division: Ashley Bldg., 31 Peel St., St. John's NF A1B 3W8 – 709/729-5542; Fax: 709/729-6956
Administrator, Marlene Norman
• Workers' Compensation Commission
Listed alphabetically in detail, this Section.

Department of FINANCE & TREASURY BOARD
Confederation Bldg., PO Box 8700, St. John's NF A1B 4J6
709/729-2858; Fax: 709/729-2856; URL: http://www.gov.nf.ca/fin/startfin.htm
Tax Inquiries: 709/729-3831
The Treasury Board Secretariat is listed with the Executive Council at the beginning of the Newfoundland & Labrador government listings.

ACTS ADMINISTERED
Co-operative Societies Act
Department of Finance Act
Chiropractors Act
Communicable Diseases Act
Control of Foods Distribution Act
Daycare & Homemaker Services Act
Death Duties Act
Dental Act
Denturists Act
Department of Health Act
Dieticians Act
Dispensing Opticians Act
Embalmers & Funeral Directors Act
Emergency Medical Aid Act
Exhumation Act
Food & Drug Act
General Hospital Management Act
Generic Dispensing of Prescription Drugs Act
Grand Falls Hospital (Management) Act
Health & Public Welfare Act
Hearing Aid Dealers Act
Homes for Special Care Act, 1973
Hospital Insurance (Agreement) Act
Hospital & Nursing Home Association Act
Hospitals Act, 1971
Human Tissues Act, 1971
Medical Act, 1974
Medical Care Insurance Act
Mental Health Act, 1971
Mentally Incompetent Persons Act
Midwifery Act
Nurses Training School Building Act
Nursing Assistants Act
Occupational Therapists Act
Old Age Assistance Act
Optometry Act
Pharmaceutical Association Act
Physiotherapy Act
Private Homes for Special Care (Allowances) Act, 1973
Psycologists Act
Registered Nurses Act
Rehabilitation Act
St. Clare's Mercy Hospital Act
Senior Citizens Housing Act
Smoke Free Environment Act
Solemnization of Marriage Act, 1974
Tobacco Control Act
Venereal Disease Prevention Act
Vital Statistics Act
Western Memorial Hospital Corporation Act
Minister, Hon. Paul D. Dicks, Q.C., 709/729-2858, Fax: 709/729-2232
Deputy Minister, Finance, Philip Wall
Comptroller General, Finance, Peter Kennedy, 709/729-3559
Asst. Deputy Minister, Fiscal & Tax Policy, Robert Vardy, 709/729-2944
Asst. Deputy Minister, Debt Management & Pensions, John Bennett, 709/729-2949
Asst. Deputy Minister, Tax Administration, Robert Clarke, 709/729-2966
Asst. Comptroller-General, Financial Controls, Ronald Williams, 709/729-2955
Acting Director, Debt Management, Earl Saunders, 709/729-6848
Director, Fiscal Policy, Bruce Hollett, 709/729-6714
Director, Government Accounts, John Martin, 709/729-2341
Director, Internal Audit, Bernard Howlett, 709/729-2965
Director, Pensions Administration, Maureen McCarthy, 709/729-6093
Director, Pensions Benefit Standards, Vacant, 709/729-6014
Director, Public Relations, Karen Power, 709/729-0110, Fax: 709/729-5645
Director, Support Services (Taxation), William Kean, 709/729-2952, Fax: 709/729-2856
Director, Tax Audit & Compliance, Bernard Cook, 709/729-2352, Fax: 709/729-2856
Director, Tax Policy, Christopher Butt, 709/729-6847

Associated Agencies, Boards & Commissions
• Credit Union Deposit Guarantee Corporation: – 709/753-6498
Executive Director, Doug Laing
Manager, Operations, William Langthorne
• Newfoundland Liquor Corporation: Kenmount Rd., PO Box 8750, Stn A, St. John's NF A1B 3V1 – 709/754-1100; Fax: 709/754-0321
Acting President & Vice-President, Finance, G. . Adams
Vice-President, Operations, M. Clarke
• Newfoundland Municipal Financing Corporation: Confederation Bldg., PO Box 8700, St. John's NF A1B 4J6 – 709/729-6686; Fax: 709/729-2070
Financial Officer, Cynthia LeGrow

Department of FISHERIES & AQUACULTURE
Fisheries Bldg., 30 Strawberry Marsh Rd., PO Box 8700, St. John's NF A1B 4J6
709/729-3707; Fax: 709/729-6082; URL: http://www.gov.nf.ca/fishaq.htm

Note: This Department was undergoing reorganization at time of printing. Major changes & adjustments have been noted below. The new Department of Fisheries & Agriculture consists of all the fisheries related functions of the former Department of Fisheries, Food & Agriculture.

Provides financial assistance & management advice on commercial fisheries & seafood processors; research & development & data dissemination in harvesting & processing methods; market development studies & promotion.

Committed to federal-provincial-industry cooperation to ensure that groundfish & other ocean resource are protected, rebuilt & sustainably harvested; promotes a diverse, multi-species approach to fisheries development (such as the successful harvest of crab, scallops, shrimp & surf clams); establishing a joint industry-government-union task force to develop proposals for solving processing capacity/resource capacity problems.

Provides financial & marketing assistance to new & existing aquaculture enterprises; supports coastal area aquaculture planning; provides aquaculture technology transfer, research & development.

ACTS ADMINISTERED

Aquaculture Act
Fish Inspection Act
Minister, Hon. R. John Efford, 709/729-3705
Deputy Minister, Leslie Dean, 709/729-3707
Director, Administration, Garland Mouland, 709/729-3708
Director, Public Relations, Josephine Cheeseman, 709/729-3733

FISHERIES DEVELOPMENT BRANCH

Fax: 709/729-6082
Asst. Deputy Minister, Reginald Kingsley, 709/729-3713
Director, Harvesting Operations Division, Ron Scaplen, 709/729-3724
Acting Director, Marketing Division, Mike Handrigan, 709/729-3749
Director, Processing Operations Division, Frank Pinhorn, 709/729-3736
Director, Processing Operations Division, F. Pinhorn, 709/729-3736
Acting Director, Technical Services Division, Bert Spracklin, 709/729-2365

AQUACULTURE BRANCH

Fax: 709/729-0360
Asst. Deputy Minister, Alastair O'Rielly, 709/729-3710
Director, Fisheries Adjustment, Bren Condon, 709/729-3732
Director, Planning Services, Mike Warren, 709/729-3712
Director, Resource Analysis, Glenn Blackwood, 709/729-3735

Regional Offices

Avalon: – 709/729-3717
Central: Gander NF – 709/256-1030; Fax: 709/256-1032, Regional Director, Nelson Higdon
Eastern: Grand Bank NF – 709/832-2860, Regional Director, Rex Matthews
Labrador: Goose Bay NF – 709/896-3412; Fax: 709/896-3483, Regional Director, Harvey Best
Western: Port Saunders NF – 709/861-3537; Fax: 709/861-3556, Regional Director, Joseph Kennedy

Department of FOREST RESOURCES & AGRIFOODS

PO Box 8700, St. John's NF A1B 4J6
709/729-4716; URL: http://www.gov.nf.ca/forest.htm

This Department was undergoing reorganization at time of printing. Major changes & adjustments have been noted below. The new Department of Forest Resources & Agrifoods consists of the Forestry & Wildlife sections of the former Department of Natural Resources, & the Agrifoods section of the former Department of Fisheries, Food & Agriculture.

Responsible for the management of the province's mineral, energy, land, forest & wildlife resources in a manner that will ensure optimum benefits for the people of the province.

ACTS ADMINISTERED

Agriculture Societies Act
Agrologists Act
Animal Protection Act
Animal and Poultry Feed Mill Act
Bowater's Newfoundland Act, 1938
Canada-Newfoundland Atlantic Accord Implementation (Newfoundland) Act, 1986
Crop Insurance Act
Department of Forestry and Agriculture Act, 1989
Dog Act
Farm Development Act
Forest Protection Act
Government-Kruger Agreements Act
Hardwood Veneers Act
Industrial Developmnent (Incentives) Act
Labrador Linerboard Limited Agreemnt Act, 1979
Lands Act - Agricultural Development Regulations
Livestock Act
Livestock Community Sales Act
Livestock Health Act
Livestock Insurance Act
Meat Inspection Act
Miscellaneous Financial Provisions Act
Natural Products Marketing Act
Newfoundland Farm Products Corporation Act
Parks Act
Plant Protection Act
Pulp & Paper, An Act to Encourage the manufacture of, 1905, c.10
Poultry and Poultry Products Act
Salt Fish Marketing Act and Regulations
Transportation of Timber over Streams & Lakes Act, 1904-05, as amended
Vegetable Grading Act
Veterinary Medical Act
Minister, Hon. Beaton Tulk, 709/729-4716
Deputy Minister, Hal Stanley, 709/729-4720
Director, Financial Operations Division, Leonard Clarke, 709/729-5054
Director, Human Resources Division, Margaret Power, 709/729-6889
Director, Information Technology Division, Mark Brown, 709/729-2201

AGRIFOODS BRANCH

Provincial Agriculture Bldg., Brookfield Rd., PO Box 8700, St. John's NF A1B 4J6
Asst. Deputy Minister, Martin Howlett, 709/729-3787, Fax: 709/729-0973
Director, Animal Health Division, Dr. Hugh Whitney, 709/729-6879
Director, Farm Business & Evaluation Division, Donna Kelland, 709/729-5090
Director, Production & Marketing Division, David Mackey, 709/729-6758
Director, Soil & Land Management Division, Hazen Scarth, 709/729-6587
Director, Special Projects Division, Philip McCarthy, 709/729-0831

FORESTRY & WILDLIFE BRANCH

Confederation Complex, PO Box 8700, St. John's NF A1B 4J6
Asst. Deputy Minister, Dr. M. Nazir, 709/729-2704, Fax: 709/729-6782

Forestry Branch (Newfoundland Forest Service) (NFS)

Herald Bldg., PO Box 2006, Corner Brook NF A2H 6J8
Director, Forest Management Division, James Taylor, 709/637-2344
Director, Forest Policy & Planning Coordination, Gary Young, 709/729-0023, Fax: 709/729-3374
Director, Forest Products Development Division, Barry Garland, 709/637-2247
Director, Forest Protection & Access Roads Division, G.J. Fleming, 709/637-2349
Director, Forest Regulations & Law Enforcement Division, R.M. Carroll, Forest Protection Centre, PO Box 2222, Gander NF A1V 1N9, 709/256-2892, Fax: 709/256-8869
Director, Silviculture & Research Division, Ivan Downton, 709/637-2284

Forest Regions

Eastern: 30 Airport Blvd., PO Box 2222, Gander NF A1V 2N9 – 709/256-7131; Fax: 709/256-3050, Regional Director, Edward Blackmore
Labrador: Elizabeth Goudie Bldg., Happy Valley, PO Box 3014, Stn B, Goose Bay NF A0P 1E0 – 709/896-3405; Fax: 709/896-3747, Director, K. Colbert
Western: Lundigan Bldg., PO Box 2006, Corner Brook NF A2H 6J8 – 709/637-2409; Fax: 709/637-2264, Director, Allan Masters

Wildlife Branch

709/729-2815
Director, Jim Hancock, 709/729-2817, Fax: 709/729-6629
Acting Chief, Conservation & Habitat, Mike Cahill, 709/729-2548
Chief, Inland Fisheries & Biodiversity, Ken Curnew, 709/729-2540
Chief, Research & Inventories, Shane Mahoney, 709/729-2542
Chief, Wildlife Conservation, Robert Whitten, 709/729-2647

Wildlife Regions

Eastern: 30 Airport Rd., PO Box 2222, Gander NF A1V 2N9 – 709/651-2053, Manager, Randy Trask
Labrador: Happy Valley, PO Box 3014, Stn B, Goose Bay NF A0P 1E0 – 709/896-2732, Manager, Derek LeBoubon
Salmonier Nature Park: Manager, Ralph Jarvis, 709/729-6974
Western: Pasadena NF, Manager, Mike Parsons, 709/686-2071

Agricultural Marketing Boards & Commissions

• Agricultural Products Marketing Board: Provincial Agriculture Bldg., Brookfield Rd., PO Box 8700, St. John's NF A1B 4J6 – 709/729-3799; Fax: 709/729-6040
Chair, Scott Simmons
• Livestock Owners' Compensation Board: Provincial Agriculture Bldg., Brookfield Rd., PO Box 634, St. John's NF A1N 2X1 – 709/729-5090; Fax: 709/729-6046
Chair, Donna Kelland
• Newfoundland Chicken Marketing Board: Donovans Industrial Park, 51 Clyde Ave., St. John's NF A1N 4R8 – 709/747-1493; Fax: 709/747-0544
Manager, A.R. Garland
• Newfoundland Crop Insurance Agency: 35 Hallett Cres., PO Box 634, St. John's NF A1N 2X1 – 709/729-5090; Fax: 709/729-6046
Chair, Donna Kelland
• Newfoundland Egg Marketing Board: PO Box 8453, St. John's NF A1B 3N9 – 709/722-2953; Fax: 709/722-6204
Manager, Ruth Noseworthy

- Newfoundland Farm Products Corporation: Bldg. 902, PO Box 9457, Stn B, St. John's NF A1A 2Y4 – 709/722-3751; Fax: 709/722-7813
President & CEO, Vacant
- Newfoundland Hog Marketing Board: Donovans Industrial Park, 51 Clyde Ave., St. John's NF A1N 4R8 – 709/747-1493; Fax: 709/747-0544
Manager, Rosalind Dyke
- Newfoundland Milk Marketing Board: 655 Topsail Rd., St. John's NF A1E 2E3 – 709/364-6634; Fax: 709/364-8364
Manager, Martin J. Hammond

Department of GOVERNMENT SERVICES & LANDS

PO Box 8700, St. John's NF A1B 4J6
URL: http://www.gov.nf.ca/govtsrv.htm

Note: This Department was undergoing reorganization at time of printing. Major changes & adjustments have been noted below. The new Department of Government Services & Lands combines all Government front-line services to the public. The new department will include: the Commercial & Corporate Affairs Division of the Department of Justice; the Lands Division from the former Department of Natural Resources; & the Motor Vehicle Registration Division from the Department of Works, Services & Transportation; as well as various other services yet to be identified by government review.

Accident & Sickness Insurance Act
Attachment of Wages Act
Automobile Dealers Act
Automobile Insurance Act
Bills of Sale Act
Building Supplies Act
Bulk Sales Act
Collections Act
Corporations (Guarantees) Act
Conditional Sales Act
Consumer Reporting Agencies Act
Direct Sellers Act
Hawkers & Pedlars Act
Income Tax Savings Plan Act
Insurance Adjusters Act
Insurance Adjusters, Agencies & Brokers Act
Insurance Companies Act
Insurance Contracts Act
Investment Contracts Act
Judgement Recovery (Newfoundland) Ltd Act
Landlord & Tenant (Residential Tenancies) Act
Landlords' Taxes Act
Life & Accident Insurance Agents (Licensing) Act
Life Insurance Act
Loan & Finance Corporation (Licensing) Act
Lodgers' Goods Protection Act
Mobile Home Dealers Act
Mortgage Brokers Act
Newfoundland Consumer Protection Act
Pension Plans (Designation of Beneficiaries) Act
Perpetuities & Accumulations Act
Residential Tenancies Act
Real Estate Trading Act
Sale of Goods Act
Salvage Dealers Licensing Act
Tenements (Recovery of Possession) Act
Trade Practices Act
Trust & Loan Companies (Licensing) Act
Trustee Act
Unconscionable Transactions Act
Unsolicited Goods & Credit Cards Act
Warehousemen's Lien Act
Warehouse Receipts Act
Weights & Measures Act
Minister, Hon. Ernest McLean, 709/729-4712
Deputy Minister, Barbara B. Wakeham, 709/729-4752
Director, Finance & Administration, Winston Hiscock, 709/729-3643

Manager, Financial Operations, Felix Croke, 709/720-2041
Manager, General Operations, Doug Sheppard, 709/729-3081
Manager, Human Resources, Doug Redmond, 709/729-4385

COMMERCIAL & CORPORATE AFFAIRS

Asst. Deputy Minister, Winston Morris, 709/729-2571
Registrar, Bills of Sale, Elmer Evans, 709/729-2901
Acting Director, Commercial Relations & Superintendent, Insurance, Doug Connolly, C.A., 709/729-2594
Officer, Consumer Affairs - Corner Brook, Nellie Osmond, 709/637-2444
Officer, Consumer Affairs - Gander, Carl Tessier, 709/256-1020
Director, Criminal Code Licensing, Herbert Vivian, 709/729-2660
Supervisor, Licensing & Enforcement, Gerald O'Neill, 709/729-2595
Director, Real Estate & Landlord-Tenant Relations, Robert LeGrow, 709/729-2608
Chair, Residential Tenancies Board, Martin Howlett, 709/729-5273

GOVERNMENT SERVICE CENTRE

Administers vital statistic information. Fee for each Birth, Marriage, or Death Certificate issued is $10.00.
Asst. Deputy Minister, Michael J. Dwyer, P.Eng., 709/729-3056
Registrar, Vital Statistics, Brenda Andrews, 709/729-3311
Deputy Registrar, Vital Statistics, Rose Evans, 709/729-3313
Director, Clarenville, Guy Perry, Provincial Bldg., PO Box 1148, Clarneville NF A0E 1J0, 709/466-3278, Fax: 709/466-3899
Director, Corner Brook, Shawn Tetford, PO Box 156, Corner Brook NF A2H 6C7, 709/637-2204, Fax: 709/637-2616
Director, Gander, Roger LeDrew, PO Box 2222, Gander NF A1V 2N9, 709/256-1426
Acting Director, Goose Bay, Darryl Johnson, PO Box 903, Stn A, Goose Bay NF A0P 1S0, 709/896-5709, Fax: 709/896-9566
Director, St. John's, Roy Layden, 5 Mews Place, PO Box 8700, St. John's NF A1B 4J6, 709/729-3074, Fax: 709/729-3980

Motor Vehicles Registration

PO Box 8710, St. John's NF A1B 4J5
709/729-2518; Fax: 709/729-6955
Registrar, Motor Vehicles & Provincial Coordinator, Transportation of Dangerous Goods, Max Hussey, 709/729-2958
Deputy Registrar, Corner Brook, Agnes McCarthy, 709/637-2212
Deputy Registrar, Grand Falls-Windsor, Verdon Young
Coordinator, Roadside Enforcement & National Safety Code, Robert Fraize, 709/729-6069

LANDS BRANCH

Asst. Deputy Minister, Wilson Barfoot
Director, Land Use Management Division, John T. Power, 709/729-3227
Director, Surveys & Mapping Division, Neil MacNaughton, 709/729-0602
Manager, Crown Lands Administration, Wayne Boggan, 709/729-3149

Crown Lands Division

Director, Bill Parrott, 709/729-3174
Manager, Crown Lands Administration, Wayne Boggan, 709/729-3149
Regional Lands Manager, Central Region, Joe Blanchard, 709/256-4141

Regional Lands Manager, Eastern Region, Aubrey Rose, 709/729-0345
Regional Lands Manager, Labrador Region, Paul Aylward, 709/896-2488
Regional Lands Manager, Western Region, Don Winsor, 709/637-2393

Associated Agencies, Boards & Commissions
- Newfoundland & Labrador Geographical Names Board: PO Box 8700, St. John's NF A1B 4J6
Secretary, G. Fry, 709/729-3250

Department of HEALTH

West Block, Confederation Bldg., PO Box 8700, St. John's NF A1B 4J6
709/729-5021; Fax: 709/729-5824; URL: http://www.gov.nf.ca/health/starthel.htm

ACTS ADMINISTERED

Cancer Treatment & Research Foundation Act
Chiropractors Act
Communicable Diseases Act
Dental Act
Denturists Act
Department of Health Act
Dieticians Act
Dispensing Opticians Act
Embalmers & Funeral Directors Act
Emergency Medical Aid Act
Food & Drug Act
Generic Dispensing of Prescription Drugs Act
Health & Public Welfare Act (except part XII)
Health & Social Agencies Act
Hearing Aid Dealers Act
Hospital Insurance Agreement Act
Hospital & Nursing Home Association Act
Hospitals Act
Human Tissue Act
Medical Act
Medical Care Insurance Act
Mental Health Act
Mentally Incompetent Persons Act
Midwifery Act
Nursing Assistants Act
Occupational Therapists Act
Optometry Act
Pharmaceutical Association Act
Pharmaceutical Association Act, 1994
Physiotherapy Act
Psychologists Act
Registered Nurses Act
Smoke-free Environment Act
Solemnization of Marriage Act
Tobacco Control Act
Venereal Disease Prevention Act
Vital Statistics Act
Welfare Institutions Act
Minister, Hon. Lloyd Matthews, 709/729-3124
Deputy Minister, Dr. R.J. Williams, 709/729-3125

ADMINISTRATIVE SERVICES & PROGRAMS

Asst. Deputy Minister, Finance & Administration, Christopher Hart, 709/729-0620
Director, Human Resources, Cecil Templeman, 709/729-3141
Director, Institutional Financial Services, David Saunders, 709/729-5277
Director, Public Relations, Jill Sooley, 709/729-1377
Acting Financial Manager, Max Osmond, 709/729-3054
Financial Manager, Cost Shared Programs, Gordon Nash, 709/729-3054

COMMUNITY HEALTH

Asst. Deputy Minister, Joan Dawe, 709/729-3126
Director, Continuing Care, Eleanor Gardner, 709/729-3658

Canadian Almanac & Directory 1997

Director, Disease Control & Epidemiology, Dr. Faith Stratton, 709/729-3430
Director, Drug Dependency Services, Beverley Clarke, 709/729-0623
Director, Environmental Health, Reginald L. Coates, 709/729-3422
Director, Health Promotion, Eleanor Swanson, 709/729-3940
Director, Mental Health Services, Debbie Sue Martin, 709/729-3658
Director, Parent & Child Health, Lynn Vivian-Book, 709/729-3110
Director, Public Health Laboratories, Dr. Sam Ratnam, 709/737-6565
Director, Public Health Nursing, Helen Lawlor, 709/729-3110

INSTITUTIONS
Asst. Deputy Minister, Roy Manuel, 709/729-3127
Acting Director, Hospital Services, Moira Hennessey, 709/729-3105
Director, Personal Care Home Program, Nancy Knight, 709/772-3553
Acting Director, Facilities Planning, Roy Dawe, 709/729-3123
Acting Director, Welfare Institutions Licensing & Inspections, Tom Power, 709/729-3257

POLICY & PROGRAMS
Asst. Deputy Minister, Gerald White, 709/729-3103
Director, Drug Programs & Services, John Downton, 709/729-6507
Director, Health Human Resources, Jeff Young, 709/729-3531
Director, Health Research & Statistics, Catherine Ryan, 709/729-3130
Director, Policy, John Houser, 709/729-3157
Director, Transportation & Special Assistance Programs, Edward Hollett, 709/729-3145

Associated Agencies, Boards & Commissions
•Newfoundland Cancer Treatment & Research Foundation
Listed in Section 2; see Index.
•Newfoundland Medical Care Commission: Elizabeth Towers, 100 Elizabeth Ave., St. John's NF A1C 5J3 – 709/722-6980; Fax: 709/722-0718
Executive Director, Robert Peddigrew
Director, Medical, Dr. Gregory Russell
Director, Dental, Bruce Bowden, B.Sc., D.D.S.

Newfoundland & Labrador HOUSING CORPORATION (NLHC)
2 Canada Dr., PO Box 220, St. John's NF A1C 5J2
709/724-3000; Fax: 709/724-3250; URL: http://www.gov.nf.ca/nlhc/nlhc.htm
Minister Responsible, Hon. Arthur D. Reid
Chair & CEO, Robert Noseworthy
Vice-President, Business Development & Corporate Services, Peter Honeygold
Vice-President, Finance & Executive Services, Edward L. Heath
Vice-President, Human Resources & Information Systems, Mary Marshall
Vice-President, Programs & Regional Operations, Steve McLean

Newfoundland & Labrador HUMAN RIGHTS COMMISSION
PO Box 8700, St. John's NF A1B 4J6
709/729-2709; Fax: 709/729-0790
Executive Director, Gladys Vivian

Newfoundland & Labrador HYDRO
PO Box 12400, St. John's NF A1B 4K7

709/737-1400; Fax: 709/737-1231
President & CEO, William E. Wells
Executive Vice-President, Power Production, T.D. Collett
Vice-President, Corporate Planning, D.W. Osmond
Vice-President, Finance, R. Andrew Grant
Vice-President, Human Resources, General Counsel & Corporate Secretary, Maureen P. Greene
Vice-President, Transmission & Rural Operations, David Reeves
Manager, Corporate Affairs, Donald J. Barrett, 709/737-1370, Fax: 709/737-1816

Department of INDUSTRY, TRADE & TECHNOLOGY
Confederation Annex, 4th Fl., PO Box 8700, St. John's NF A1B 4J6
709/729-5600; Fax: 709/729-5936; Email: info@ditt.gov.nf.ca; URL: http://www.gov.nf.ca/itt/startitt.htm
Toll Free: 1-800-563-2299

Responsible for expanding & diversifying the provincial economy by creating a business environment favorable to private sector expansion & growth. Offers financial support, business analysis, educational opportunities & other assistance to business clients; Monitors & promotes opportunities for investment, assesses & promotes local competitiveness in the wider marketplace, markets the province as an investment location & assists local companies in identifying markets & market requirements, & promotes partnerships between business, goverment & education.

ACTS ADMINISTERED
Economic Diversification & Growth Enterprises (EDGE) Act
Industries Act
Research Council Act
Minister, Hon. Charles J. Furey, 709/729-2791
Deputy Minister, David Oake, 709/729-2787
Asst. Deputy Minister, Advanced Technology & Industry, Sid Blundon, 709/729-0882
Asst. Deputy Minister, Industry, Trade & Investment, David French, 709/729-2788
Asst. Deputy Minister, Policy, Planning & Business Analysis, Lorne Spracklin, 709/729-3613
Director, Public Relations, John Doody, 709/729-0050

ADMINISTRATION
709/729-5600
Director, David Butler, 709/729-2790
Manager, Financial Operations, Randy Snelgrove, 709/729-2786
Manager, Human Resources, Charlie Phillips, 709/729-3943
Manager, Systems & Methods, Vacant
Compliance Officer, Ed Janes, 709/729-1919
Registrar, Maureen Bursey, 709/729-5982

ADVANCED TECHNOLOGY
Director, Linda Cooper, 709/729-5592
Manager, Industrial Technology & Information Industries, Terry Johnstone, 709/729-5592
Manager, Strategic Technologies, Robert Robinson, 709/729-5652

BUSINESS ANALYSIS
Director, Brian Condon, 709/729-5066
Manager, Business Support Programs, Pierre Tobin, 709/729-6223
Senior Industrial Development Officer, Vacant

BUSINESS DEVELOPMENT
Director, Harry Bishop, 709/729-2781

Manager, Business Development, Kirk Tilley, 709/729-4205
Manager, Business Model Development, Jim Cardwell, 709/729-3648

INDUSTRIAL BENEFITS
Director, Fred Murrin, 709/729-5064
Senior Development Officer, Special Projects, David Hallett, 709/729-1044
Industrial Development Officer, Valerie Hillier, 709/729-5641

INDUSTRIAL SUPPORT
Director, Hunter Rowe, 709/729-3296

MARKETING
Director, Geoff Tooton, 709/729-2800
Manager, Marketing Research & Development, Paul Morris, 709/729-2369

POLICY & STRATEGIC PLANNING
Director, Margaret Allan, 709/729-2798
Senior Policy Planning Officer, Vacant, 709/729-5727

PROJECT & PROGRAM ANALYSIS
Director, Brian Hurley, 709/729-3664
Manager, Economic Impact Analysis, Charles Brown, 709/729-4797
Manager, Economic Research, Bryon Hynes, 709/729-6427
Manager, Financial Analysis, Bill Mullaly, 709/729-4363

STRATEGIC PROCUREMENT
Director, Anthony Patey, 709/729-2796
Manager, Trade Policy & Agreements, Dan Fallon, 709/729-2797
Policy & Planning Officer, Tom Fleming, 709/729-5859
Senior Development Officer, Special Projects, Donovan Arnaud

Associated Agencies, Boards & Commissions
•Operation ONLINE: PO Box 8700, St. John's NF A1B 4J6 – 709/729-0050
Established in early 1995 to oversee the implementation of Operation ONLINE (Opportunities for Newfoundland & Labrador in the New Economy), a comprehensive five-year strategy to develop the province's information technology sector.
Co-Chair, David Oake
Co-Chair, Dennis Young
Head, Operational Support, Frank Davis, 709/729-5600

Newfoundland INFORMATION SERVICE
Confederation Bldg., PO Box 8700, St. John's NF A1B 4J6
709/729-4164; Fax: 709/729-0584

Now known as the Communications & Consultation Branch and part of the Cabinet Secretariat of the Newfoundland Executive Council.
Director, Rick Callahan, 709/729-0329
Publications Officer, Bob Powers, 709/729-4023

INTERGOVERNMENTAL AFFAIRS SECRETARIAT
Listed with the Executive Council, this section.

Department of JUSTICE & ATTORNEY GENERAL
Confederation Bldg., PO Box 8700, St. John's NF A1B 4J6
709/729-5942; Fax: 709/729-2129; URL: http://www.gov.nf.ca/just/startjus.htm

GOVERNMENT OF NEWFOUNDLAND & LABRADOR 3-147

ACTS ADMINISTERED
Accident & Sickness Insurance Act
Adult Corrections Act
Agreement for Policing the Province Act
American Bases Act
Apportionment Act
Arbitration Act
Architects Act
Assignment of Books Debts Act
Attachment of Wages Act
Automobile Dealers Act
Automobile Insurance Act
Bankers' Books Act
Bills of Sale Act
Blind Persons' Rights Act
Building Supplies Act
Bulk Sales Act
Canada & United Kingdom Reciprocal Recognition & Enforcement of Judgments Act
Censoring of Moving Pictures Act
Certified General Accountants Act
Certified Public Accountants Act
Chairman of the Board of Commissioners of Public Utilities (Pension) Act
Change of Name Act
Chartered Accountants Act
Chattels Real Act
Children's Law Act
Collections Act
Commissioners for Oaths Act
Conditional Sales Act
Consumer Protection Act
Consumer Reporting Agencies Act
Contributory Negligence Act
Conveyancing Act
Corporations Act
Corporations Guarantees Act
Criminal Injuries Compensation Act
Defamation Act
Department of Justice Act
Detention of Intoxicated Persons Act
Direct Sellers Act
Election Act
Elections Act
Electoral Boundaries Act
Enduring Powers of Attorney Act
Engineers & Geoscientists Act
Evidence Act
Exhumation Act
Family Law Act
Family Relief Act
Fatal Accidents Act
Federal Courts Jurisdiction Act
Fire Insurance Act
Fraudulent Conveyance Act
Freedom of Information Act
Frustrated Contracts Act
Income Tax Savings Plan Act
Industrial and Provident Societies Act
Innkeepers Act
Insurance Adjusters, Agents & Brokers Act
Insurance Companies Act
Insurance Contracts Act
International Commercial Arbitration Act
International Sale of Goods Act
International Trusts Act
Interpretation Act
Interprovincial Subpoena Act
Intestate Succession Act
Investment Contracts Act
Judgment Debts Instalments Act
Judgment Interest Act
Judgment Recovery (Nfld.) Ltd. Act
Judicature Act
Jury Act
Justices Act
Justices & Other Public Authorities Protection Act
Landlords' Taxes Act

Law Reform Commission Act
Law Society Act
Leaseholds in St. John's Act
Legal Aid Act
Life Insurance Act
Limitation of Personal Actions Act
Limitation of Realty Actions Act
Limited Partnership Act
Loan & Finance Corporations Licensing Act
Lodger's Goods Protection Act
Lotteries Act
Management Accountants Act
Mechanics' Lien Act
Mentally Disabled Persons' Estates Act
Minors (Attainment of Majority) Act
Mobile Home Dealers Act
Mortgage Brokers Act
Newfoundland Marine Insurance Company Ltd, An Act to Incorporate the
Notaries Public Act
Oaths Act
Oaths of Office Act
Partnership Act
Pension Plans (Designation of Beneficiaries) Act
Perpetuities & Accumulations Act
Petty Trespass Act
Presumption of Death Act
Prisons Act
Privacy Act
Private Investigation & Security Services Act
Proceedings Against the Crown Act
Proof of Death (Members of Armed Forces) Act
Provincial Court Act
Public Accountancy Act
Public Inquiries Act
Public Investigations Evidence Act
Public Trustee Act
Public Utilities Act
Public Utilities (Acquisition of Lands) Act
Queen's Counsel Act
Quieting of Titles Act
Real Estate Trading Act
Reciprocal Enforcement of Judgments Act
Reciprocal Enforcement of Support Orders Act
Recording of Evidence Act
Registration of Deeds Act
Residential Tenancies Act
Revised Statutes, 1990 Act
Royal Newfoundland Constabulary Act
Sale of Goods Act
Salvage Dealers Licensing Act
Securities Act
Security Interest Registration Act
Sheriff's Act
Small Claims Act
Solicitor General Act
Statutes Act
Statutes Amendments Act
Statutes & Subordinate Legislation Act
Summary Proceedings Act
Support Orders Enforcement Act
Survival of Actions Act
Survivorship Act
Trade Practices Act
Trust & Loan Companies Licensing Act
Trustee Act
Unconscionable Transactions Relief Act
Unified Family Court Act
Unsolicited Goods & Credit Cards Act
Victims of Crime Services Act
Warehouse Receipts Act
Warehouser's Lien Act
Wills Act
Young Persons Offenses Act & Young Offenders Act (Canada) (both with Dept. of Social Services
ACTS ADMINISTERED BY THE DEPARTMENT OF JUSTICE (CONSUMER AFFAIRS DIVISION)
Accident & Sickness Insurance Act

Attachment of Wages Act
Automobile Dealers Act
Automobile Insurance Act
Bills of Sale Act
Building Supplies Act
Bulk Sales Act
Collections Act
Corporations (Guarantees) Act
Conditional Sales Act
Consumer Reporting Agencies Act
Direct Sellers Act
Hawkers & Pedlars Act
Income Tax Savings Plan Act
Insurance Adjusters Act
Insurance Adjusters, Agencies & Brokers Act
Insurance Companies Act
Insurance Contracts Act
Investment Contracts Act
Judgement Recovery (Newfoundland) Ltd Act
Landlord & Tenant (Residential Tenancies) Act
Landlords' Taxes Act
Life & Accident Insurance Agents (Licensing) Act
Life Insurance Act
Loan & Finance Corporation (Licensing) Act
Lodgers' Goods Protection Act
Mobile Home Dealers Act
Mortgage Brokers Act
Newfoundland Consumer Protection Act
Pension Plans (Designation of Beneficiaries) Act
Perpetuities & Accumulations Act
Residential Tenancies Act
Real Estate Trading Act
Sale of Goods Act
Salvage Dealers Licensing Act
Tenements (Recovery of Possession) Act
Trade Practices Act
Trust & Loan Companies (Licensing) Act
Trustee Act
Unconscionable Transactions Act
Unsolicited Goods & Credit Cards Act
Warehousemen's Lien Act
Warehouse Receipts Act
Weights & Measures Act
Minister & Attorney General, Hon. Chris D. Decker, 709/729-2869
Deputy Minister & Deputy Attorney General, Lynn E. Spracklin, Q.C., 709/729-2872
Director, Finance & General Operations Division, Kevin Dicks, 709/729-2890
Director, Accounts Division, Karen Hibbs, 709/729-0271
Director, Information Technology Division, Joan McCarthy-Wiseman, 709/729-3617
Director, Human Resources Division, David Hickey, 709/729-4256
Chief, Forensic Pathology, Dr. Charles Hutton, Health Sciences Complex, 300 Prince Philip Dr., St. John's NF A1B 3V6, 709/737-6402
For list of Courts & other Legal Offices, including Judicial Officials & Judges *see* Section 10 of this book.

CIVIL LAW & RELATED SERVICES
Asst. Deputy Minister, John R. Cummings, 709/729-2880
Director, Civil Law Division, John McCarthy, 709/729-2893
Director, Legal Information Services, Mona Pearce, 709/729-2861
Director, Support Enforcement Division, Cy Simmons, 709/729-2658

PUBLIC PROTECTION & SUPPORT SERVICES
Asst. Deputy Minister, Ralph Alcock, 709/729-4896
Superintendent, Prisons, Donald Saunders, 709/729-0356
Chief Probation Officer, Community Corrections, Wanda Lundrigan, 709/729-0407

Canadian Almanac & Directory 1997

3-148 GOVERNMENT OF NEWFOUNDLAND & LABRADOR

Chief, Royal Newfoundland Constabulary, L.P. Power, 709/729-8151, Inquiries: 709/729-8000
Director, Adult Corrections Division, Marvin McNutt, 709/729-3880, Fax: 709/729-0416
Manager, Victim Services, Jacqueline Lake, 709/729-0885

SENIOR LEGISLATIVE COUNSEL
Asst. Deputy Minister, Calvin Lake, 709/729-2881
Secretary, Gerry Ryan, 709/729-1162

Associated Agencies, Boards & Commissions
- Atlantic Lottery Corporation
See listing under New Brunswick Finance, this Section.
- Newfoundland Legal Aid Commission: Centre Bldg., 21 Church Hill St., St. John's NF A1C 3Z8 – 709/753-7860; Fax: 709/753-6226
Provincial Director, N. Petten
- Newfoundland & Labrador Public Utilities Commission
Listed alphabetically in detail, this section.
- Office of the Chief Electoral Officer
Listed alphabetically in detail, this Section.
- Residential Tenancies Boards: PO Box 8700, St. John's NF A1B 4J6
Chair, St. John's Residential Tenancies Board, Martin Howlett
Chair, Central Residential Tenancies Board, R. Archibald Bonnell
Chair, Eastern Residential Tenancies Board, Philip Sheppard
Chair, Labrador Residential Tenancies Board, Gordie Rendell
Chair, Western Residential Tenancies Board, William J. Gallant
- Royal Newfoundland Constabulary Public Complaints Commission: PO Box 21128, St. John's NF A1A 5B2 – 709/729-0950
Commissioner, Dr. Leslie Harris

LOWER CHURCHILL DEVELOPMENT CORPORATION LIMITED
PO Box 12700, St. John's NF A1B 3T5
709/737-1288; Fax: 709/737-1782
President & CEO, William E. Wells
Manager, Corporate Affairs, Donald J. Barrett, 709/737-1370

Department of MINES & ENERGY
PO Box 8700, St. John's NF A1B 4J6
709/729-2301; URL: http://www.gov.nf.ca/mines.htm

ACTS ADMINISTERED
Mineral Holdings Impost Act
Canada-Newfoundland Atlantic Accord Implementation (Newfoundland) Act, 1986
Crown Lands Act
Department of Mines & Energy Act
Electrical Power Control Act
Emergency Measures Act (Petroleum related emergencies)
Federal-Provincial Power Act, 1962
Industrial Development (Incentives) Act, 1970
Lands Act, 1991
Lower Churchill Development Act, 1979
Mineral Act, 1976
Mineral Lands (Certain) Act
Mineral Vesting in the Crown Act
Miscellaneous Financial Provisions Act, 1975
Natural Products Marketing Act
Natural Products Marketing Act
Newfoundland & Labrador Hydro Act, 1975
Newfoundland & Labrador Power Commission (Water Power) Act, 1970
Newfoundland & Labrador Rural Electricity Act
Parks Act
Petroleum Corporation Act, 1980
Petroleum & Natural Gas Act, 1970
Quarry Materials Act, 1976
Regulations of Mines Act
Rural Electrification Act, 1970
Undeveloped Minerals Areas Act
Buildings Accessibility Act & Regulations
Electrical Regulations
Electrical Inspection Fees Regulations
Elevators Act & Regulations
Occupationsl Health & Safety Act & Regulations
Radiation Health & Safety Act & Regulations
Mines Act & Mines (Safety of Workmen) Regulations
Workplace Hazardous Materials Inspection System (WHMIS) Regulations, 1989
Minister, Hon. Dr. Rex V. Gibbons, 709/729-2920
Deputy Minister, Frederick G. Way, 709/729-2356
Director, Financial Operations Division, Leonard Clarke, 709/729-5054
Director, Human Resources Division, Margaret Power, 709/729-6559
Director, Information Technology Division, Mark Brown, 709/729-2201

ENERGY BRANCH
Asst. Deputy Minister, Martin Sheppard, 709/729-2349
Provincial Coordinator & Chair, Hibernia Project, Gordon Gosse, 709/729-2848
Director, Monitoring & Compliance, Hibernia Project, Brian Maynard, 709/729-0021
Director, Petroleum & Energy Economics Branch, Barry Rodgers, 709/729-3674
Director, Petroleum & Energy Resources Development, David Hawkins, 709/729-2323
Director, Policy, Planning & Coordination, Charles Lester, 709/729-2339

MINES BRANCH
Fax: 709/729-6782
Asst. Deputy Minister, Paul Dean, 709/729-2768
Manager, Engineering Analysis, Fred Morrissey, 709/729-6449
Director, Mineral Lands Division, Ken Andrews, 709/729-6425
Manager, Prospectors Assistance, M.J. Collins, 709/729-2358
Director, Project Management, Wayne Ryder, 709/729-2063

Geological Survey
Fax: 709/729-3493
Director, Vacant, 709/729-2763
Senior Geochemist, Geochemistry/Geophysical & Terrain Sciences, Peter Davenport, 709/729-2171
Senior Geologist, Labrador Mapping, Richard Wardle, 709/729-2107
Senior Geologist, Mineral Deposits, Baxter Kean, 709/729-5946
Senior Geologist, Newfoundland Mapping, Stephen Colman-Sadd, 709/729-3574
Senior Geologist, Publications & Information, Frank Blackwood, 709/729-6541

Associated Agencies, Boards & Commissions
- Canada-Newfoundland Offshore Petroleum Board: TD Place, #500, 140 Water St., St. John's NF A1C 6H6 – 709/778-1400; Fax: 709/778-1473; Email: cnopb@nfld.com; URL: http://canada.gc.ca/depts/agencies/cnpind_e.html
Acting Chair & CEO, John Fitzgerald

Department of MUNICIPAL & PROVINCIAL AFFAIRS
West Block, Confederation Bldg., PO Box 8700, St. John's NF A1B 4J6
709/729-3053; URL: http://www.gov.nf.ca/mpa/startmpa.htm

ACTS ADMINISTERED
Assessment Act
Avian Emblem Act
Building Standards Act
City of Corner Brook Act
City of Mount Pearl Act
City of St. John's Act
Coat of Arms Act
Commemoration Day Act
Crown Corporations Local Taxation Act
Emergency Measures Act
Evacuated Communities Act
Family Homes Expropriation Act
Fire Prevention Act, 1991 (with Government Services & Lands)
Floral Emblem Act
Housing Act
Housing Association Loans Act
Housing Corporation Act
Labrador Act
Mineral Emblem Act
Municipal Affairs Act
Municipalities Act
Provincial Anthem Act
Provincial Flag Act
Rememberence Day Act
Regional Services Boards Act
St. John's Assessment Act
St. John's Centennial Foundation Act
St. John's Municipal Council Parks Act
St. John's Municipal Elections Act
Standard Time Act
Taxation of Utilities & Cable Television Companies Act
Urban & Rural Planning Act (with Government Services & Lands)
Water & Sewerage Corporation of Greater Corner Brook Act, 1951
Minister, Hon. Arthur D. Reid, 709/729-3048
Deputy Minister, John Abbott, 709/729-3049
Director, Emergency Measures Division, Elizabeth Munn, 709/729-3703, Fax: 709/729-3857, 24-hour Emergencies: 709/722-7107
Director, Public Relations, Gary Callahan, 709/729-3142
Coordinator, Canada/Newfoundland Infrastructure Program, Erik Seaward, 709/729-5411

MUNICIPAL SUPPORT SERVICES
Asst. Deputy Minister, A.R. Colbourne, 709/729-3051
Director, Administration, W.O. Hiscock, 709/729-3643
Director, Local Government, John Moore, 709/729-3066
Director, Municipal Engineering Services, Wayne Churchill, 709/729-5328
Director, Municipal Finance, C. Goodland, 709/729-3057
Director, Urban & Rural Planning, Stan Clinton, 709/729-3090
Manager, Finance & General Operations, Felix Croke, 709/729-3096

Associated Agencies, Boards & Commissions
- Newfoundland & Labrador Housing Corporation
Listed alphabetically in detail, this Section.
- Office of the Fire Commissioner: Bldg. 9001, Pleasantville, PO Box 8700, St. John's NF A1B 4J6 – 709/726-1050; Fax: 709/729-2524
Fire Commissioner, Fred Hollett

Newfoundland & Labrador PUBLIC SERVICE COMMISSION
146 - 148 Forest Rd., St. John's NF A1A 1E6
709/729-2751; URL: http://www.gov.nf.ca/psc/psc.htm

Canadian Almanac & Directory 1997

ACTS ADMINISTERED
Conflict of Interest Act and Regulations Public Inquiries Act Public Investigations Evidence Act Public Service Commission Act, 1973
Chair & Deputy Minister, Robert Olivero, 709/729-2650, Email: rolivero@psc.gov.nf.ca
Vice-Chair, Grant Chalker, 709/729-2659, Email: gchalker@psc.gov.nf.ca
Commissioner, Sheila Devine, 709/729-2651, Email: sdevine@psc.gov.nf.ca

Newfoundland & Labrador PUBLIC UTILITIES COMMISSION
PO Box 21040, St. John's NF A1A 5B2
709/726-0955; Fax: 709/726-9604
Chair, David Vardy
Vice-Chair, Leslie E. Galway, C.A., M.B.A.
Clerk, Carol Horwood, 709/726-8600

Department of SOCIAL SERVICES
Confederation Bldg., PO Box 8700, St. John's NF A1B 4J6
709/729-2478; Fax: 709/729-6996; URL: http://www.gov.nf.ca/doss/startdos.htm

ACTS ADMINISTERED
Adoption of Children Act
Child Welfare Act
Day Care Homemaker Services Act
Rehabilitation Act
Social Assistance Act
Social Workers Registration Act
Young Persons Offences Act
Minister, Hon. Joan Marie Aylward
Deputy Minister, Joan Dawe
Director, Public Relations, Glenn Bruce, 709/729-4062

CLIENT & COMMUNITY SERVICES
Asst. Deputy Minister, Noel Browne, 709/729-3585
Director, Community Agencies, Ivy Burt, 709/729-0491

FINANCE & SUPPORT
Asst. Deputy Minister, Dave Roberts, 709/729-3594
Director, Finance & General Operations, J. Strong, 709/729-3584
Director, Human Resources, Elizabeth Horwood, 709/729-2457
Director, Information Systems, Glenn Stokes, 709/729-5101

PROGRAM DEVELOPMENT
Asst. Deputy Minister, George Skinner, 709/729-0217
Director, Child Welfare, Elizabeth Crawford, 709/729-2668
Director, Family & Rehabilitative Services, Don Gallant, 709/729-2436
Director, Income Support, David Lewis, 709/729-3243
Director, Social & Strategic Planning, Vivian Randell, 709/729-0494
Director, Youth Corrections, Sharron Callahan, 709/729-3540

Associated Agencies, Boards & Commissions
• Adoption Appeal Board: Confederation Bldg., PO Box 8700, St. John's NF A1B 4J6
• Child Welfare Board: Confederation Bldg., PO Box 8700, St. John's NF A1B 4J6
• Day Care & Homemaker Services Licensing Board: Confederation Bldg., PO Box 8700, St. John's NF A1B 4J6
• Rehabilitation Appeal Board: Confederation Bldg., PO Box 8700, St. John's NF A1B 4J6
• Social Services Appeal Board: Confederation Bldg., PO Box 8700, St. John's NF A1B 4J6
Executive Secretary, Debbie Loder, 709/729-2479

Provincial Advisory Council on the STATUS OF WOMEN
131 Le Marchant Rd., St. John's NF A1C 2H3
709/753-7270; Fax: 709/753-2606; Email: pacsw@nlnet.nf.ca; URL: http://www.gov.nf.ca/exec/wpo/info.htm
President, Joyce Hancock
Office Administrator, Linda Williams
Policy Analyst, Martha Muzychka
Community Liaison, Provincial Strategy to Address Violence, Jennifer Mercer

Department of TOURISM, CULTURE & RECREATION
Confederation Bldg., PO Box 8700, St. John's NF A1B 4J6
709/729-0928; Fax: 709/729-0662; URL: http://www.gov.nf.ca/tcr/starttcr.htm

ACTS ADMINISTERED
Arts Council Act
Books (Preservation of Copies) Act
Innkeepers Act
Tourist Establishments Act
Minister, Hon. Sandra Kelly
Acting Deputy Minister, Mike Buist
Director, Financial & General Operations, Rick Hayward, 709/729-0851, Fax: 709/729-0870
Director, Human Resources, Kay Mullins, 709/729-0936, Fax: 709/729-0870
Director, Public Relations, Laura Cochrane, 709/729-0928
Director, Systems & Methods, Ray Piercy, 709/729-0315

CULTURAL AFFAIRS, HISTORIC RESOURCES & PROVINCIAL ARCHIVES
Asst. Deputy Minister, Elizabeth Batstone, 709/729-3609, Fax: 709/729-0870
Acting Director, Cultural Affairs, E.A. Channing, 709/729-3650, Fax: 709/729-5952
Director, Historic Resources, David Mills, 709/729-2460, Fax: 709/729-0870
Director, Provincial Archives, David Davis, 709/729-3065, Fax: 709/729-0578
Resource Archaeologist, Martha Drake, 709/729-2462, Fax: 709/729-0870

PARKS & RECREATION
Asst. Deputy Minister, Mike Buist, 709/729-0865, Fax: 709/729-0870
Director, Community Recreation, Sport & Fitness, Vic Janes, 709/729-5261, Fax: 709/729-5293
Director, Parks, Donald Hustins, 709/729-2424, Fax: 709/729-1100

TOURISM & CRAFT DEVELOPMENT
Asst. Deputy Minister, Susan Sherk, 709/729-2821, Fax: 709/729-0870
Director, Tourism Development, Mike Joy, 709/729-2822, Fax: 709/729-0474
Director, Tourism Marketing, Marilyn Butland, 709/729-2831, Fax: 709/729-0057
Director, Tourism Planning & Research, Juanita Keel-Ryan, 709/729-2974, Fax: 709/729-0870

TWIN FALLS POWER CORPORATION
PO Box 12500, St. John's NF A1B 3T5
709/737-1450; Fax: 709/737-1782
President, T. David Collett, P.Eng.
Manager, Corporate Affairs, Donald J. Barrett, 709/737-1370, Fax: 709/737-1816

Newfoundland & Labrador WORKERS' COMPENSATION COMMISSION
#146, 148 Forest Rd., PO Box 9000, St. John's NF A1A 3B8
709/778-1000; Fax: 709/738-1714
CEO, Barbara Taichman

Department of WORKS, SERVICES & TRANSPORTATION
Confederation Bldg., PO Box 8700, St. John's NF A1B 4J6
709/729-3283; Fax: 709/729-0703; URL: http://www.gov.nf.ca/wststart.htm

ACTS ADMINISTERED
Department of Works, Services & Transportation Act
Expropriation Act
Family Homes Expropriation Act
Local Roads Boards Act
Pippy Park Commission Act
Provincial Preference Act
Public Tender Act
Railways Act
Minister, Hon. Julie Bettney, 709/729-3678
Deputy Minister, Clyde Granter, 709/729-3676
Registrar, J. Anthony, 709/729-3284
Chief, Safety & Security, F. Twyne, 709/729-3443
Director, Public Relations, Vacant, 709/729-1968

FINANCE, ADMINISTRATION & SUPPORT SERVICES BRANCH
Asst. Deputy Minister, Vacant, 709/729-3291
Director, Financial & General Operations, Ramona Cole, 709/729-3283
Director, Government Purchasing Agency, Larry Cahill, 709/729-3343
Director, Human Resources, Gordon Murphy, 709/729-3292
Director, Information Systems/Communications, David Penney, 709/729-3367
Acting Director, Printing Services & Queen's Printer, Earl Tucker, 709/729-3210

TRANSPORTATION BRANCH
Asst. Deputy Minister, Terry McCarthy, 709/729-3640
Director, Highway Design & Construction, Keith White, 709/729-3796
Director, Maintenance, Neil Campbell, 709/729-3636
Director, Policy, Planning & Control, Tom Beckett, 709/729-5344
Director, Transportation Services, Tom Prim, P.Eng., 709/729-3278

WORKS BRANCH
Asst. Deputy Minister, George Greenland, 709/729-3999
Director, Accommodations, Martin Balodis, 709/729-3690
Director, Design & Construction, Gunar Leja, 709/729-3355
Director, Engineering Support Services, Keith Noel, 709/729-3019
Director, Realty Services, Kevin Brocklehurst, 709/729-3356

Associated Agencies, Boards & Commissions
• C.A. Pippy Park Commission: PO Box 8861, Stn A, St. John's NF A1B 3T2 – 709/737-3655; Fax: 709/737-3303
Chair & CEO, Dr. Phillip Warren, St. John's North, Lib.
Director, Administration & General Operations, T. Hopkins

GOVERNMENT OF THE NORTHWEST TERRITORIES

Seat of Government: Legislative Assembly, PO Box 1320, Yellowknife NT X1A 2L9
URL: http://www.ssmicro.com/ZXxpsognwt/Net/index.html

The Northwest Territories was reconstituted September 1, 1905. It has an area of 3,426,320 km2, and the StatsCan population in 1991 was 57,649.

The Northwest Territories comprises: 1) all of Canada north of the 60th Parallel of North Latitude, except the portions within the Yukon Territory & the Provinces of Québec & Newfoundland; & 2) the islands of Hudson Bay, James Bay & Ungava Bay, except those islands within the provinces of Manitoba, Ontario & Québec.

The Northwest Territories is governed by a fully elected Legislative Assembly of 24 members elected for a four-year term. Government is by consensus rather than party politics. The Legislature elects the Premier & a seven-member Executive Council, which is charged with the operation of government & the establishment of program & spending priorities.

The Commissioner of the Northwest Territories is appointed by the Federal Government, & serves a role similar to that of a Lieutenant Governor in provincial jurisdictions.

Office of the COMMISSIONER
Courthouse Bldg., 4903 - 49 St., PO Box 1320, Yellowknife NT X1A 2L9
403/873-7210; Fax: 403/873-0223
Commissioner, Hon. Helen Maksagak, 403/873-7400
Deputy Commissioner, Daniel J. Marion
Executive Secretary, Rowena Bower, 403/873-7210

Office of the PREMIER
Lang Bldg., 5003 - 49 St., PO Box 1320, Yellowknife NT X1A 2L9
403/873-7112; Fax: 403/873-0385
Premier, Hon. Don Morin, 403/669-2311, Fax: 403/873-0385
Deputy Premier, Hon. Goo Arlooktoo, 403/669-2399
Executive Asst., Ferne Babiuk, 403/669-2306
Principal Secretary to the Premier, Don Avison, 403/669-2325
Correspondence Secretary, Catherine McLean, 403/669-2322
Press Secretary, Art Sorensen, 403/669-2302
Director, Protocol Office, Terri Boldt, 403/873-7153

EXECUTIVE COUNCIL
PO Box 1320, Yellowknife NT X1A 2L9
Premier & Minister, Executive, Minister Responsible, Intergovernmental Affairs, Hon. Don Morin, 403/689-2311, Fax: 403/873-0385
Minister, Transportation, Minister Responsible, Aboriginal Affairs & Minister, Safety & Public Services, Hon. James Antoine, 403/669-2333, Fax: 403/873-0169
Deputy Premier, Minister Responsible, NWT Housing Coroporation & Minister, Public Works & Services, Hon. Goo Arlooktoo, 403/669-2355, Fax: 403/873-0169
Minister, Education, Culture & Employment, Minister Responsible, Youth & Minister Responsible, NWT Power Corporation, Hon. Charles Dent, 403/669-2355, Fax: 403/873-0169
Minister, Resources, Wildlife & Economic Development & Minister, National Constitutional Affairs, Hon. Stephen Kakfwi, 403/669-2366, Fax: 403/873-0169
Minister, Health & Social Services & Minister, Justice, Hon. Kelvin Ng, 403/669-2388, Fax: 403/873-0169
Minister, Municipal & Community Affairs & Minister Responsible, Women's Directorate, Hon. Manitok Thompson, 403/669-2344, Fax: 403/873-0169
Government House Leader, Minister, Finance & Minister Responsible, Financial Management Board Secretariat, Workers' Compensation Board, Public Utilities Board, Hon. John Todd, 403/669-2377, Fax: 403/873-0169

Cabinet Office
Secretary to Cabinet, Roland Bailey, 403/873-7100, Fax: 403/873-0279
Deputy Secretary to Cabinet, Richard Abernethy, 403/873-7101, Fax: 403/873-0279
Special Advisor to the Premier, Government Operations & Community Initiatives, Al Menard, 403/873-7359, Fax: 403/783-0279
Director, Executive Finance & Administration, Terryl Allen, 403/873-7148, Fax: 403/873-0110
Advisor, Status of Women, Bertha Norwegian, 403/920-3106, Fax: 403/873-0122

Financial Management Board Secretariat
Chair, Hon. John Todd, 403/669-2377
Secretary to the FMB, Lew Voytilla, 403/873-7211, Fax: 403/873-0122
Director, Government Accounting, John Carter, 403/920-3401, Fax: 403/873-0296
Director, Budgeting & Evaluation, Debbie DeLancey, 403/920-6196, Fax: 403/873-0258
Deputy Secretary, Audit & Evaluation, Gordon Robinson, 403/873-7338, Fax: 403/873-0258
Director, Audit Bureau, Doug Hill, 403/873-7106, Fax: 403/873-0209
Director, Information Management, Keith Rogers, 403/920-8962, Fax: 403/873-0128
Deputy Secretary, Human Resource Management, Evelyn Dean, 403/873-7705, Fax: 403/873-0258
Director, Compensation Services & Labour Relations, Herb Hunt, 403/873-7970, Fax: 403/873-0105
Director, Job Evaluation, Gene Kiviaho, 403/920-6983, Fax: 403/873-0175

Legislation & House Planning
Legislative Coordinator, Kevin O'Keefe, 403/669-2239, Fax: 403/873-0139

Office of Official Languages
403/920-6960
Asst. Deputy Minister, Elizabeth Biscaye, 403/920-6960, Fax: 403/873-0122
Official Languages Advisor, Denise Canual, 403/920-6962

Priorities & Planning Secretariat
Secretary, David Colpitts, 403/873-7240, Fax: 403/873-0110
Policy Coordinator, Alan Cash, 403/873-7652

LEGISLATIVE ASSEMBLY
c/o Clerk's Office, PO Box 1320, Yellowknife NT X1A 2L9
403/669-2299, 669-2200; Fax: 403/920-4735; URL: http://www.ssimicro.com/ZXepsognwt/Net/departments/assembly/Gov.html
Toll Free: 1-800-661-0784
Clerk: David M. Hamilton, 403/669-2299
Speaker: Hon. Samuel Gargan, 403/669-2233
Librarian, Legislative Library: Vera Raschke, 403/669-2203
Deputy Speaker, Brian Lewis
Clerk of Committees, Doug Schauerte
Director, Research & Information Services, Lynn Elkin-Hall, 403/669-2213
Coordinator, Public Information, Paul Jones, 403/669-2230

Elections NWT/Plebiscite Office
PO Box 1320, Yellowknife NT X1A 2L9
403/920-6999
Deputy Chief, Rosemary Cairns, 403/920-6140

Office of the Languages Commissioner
PO Box 1320, Yellowknife NT X1A 2L9
403/873-7034
Languages Commissioner, Betty Harnum

Standing Committees of the Legislature
URL: http://www.ssimicro.com/ZXxpsognwt/Net//assembly/committees.html
Government Operations
Infrastructure
Management & Services Board
Resource Management & Development
Rules & Procedures
Social Programs

THIRTEENTH LEGISLATURE - NORTHWEST TERRITORIES
Last election, October 16, 1995. Maximum Duration, four years.
Salaries, Indemnities & Allowances: Members' annual indemnity $39,514; Members' annual guaranteed constituency indemnity (for member's without portfolio) $22,070 plus a non-accountable constituency expense allowance ranging from $16,344 to $30,834 depending on location. In addition t this are the following:
Government Leader $67,715
Ministers $62,275 (with portfolio)
Speaker $62,275
Deputy Speaker $6,000
Following is: constituency (unofficial number of eligible voters in 1995 election) member, constituency phone number (if available). (Address for all is PO Box 1320, Yellowknife NT X1A 2L9.)

MEMBERS
MLA, Mark Evaloarjuk, Amittuq, (1,976)
MLA, Hon. James Antoine, Nahendeh, 403/695-3403
MLA, Kevin J. O'Brien, Kivallivik, (1,291)
MLA, Roy Erasmus, Yellowknife North, (1,621)
MLA, Vince Steen, Nunakput, (635)
MLA, Hon. Charles Dent, Yellowknife Frame Lake, (752), 403/920-3337
MLA, Hon. Samuel Gargan, Deh Cho, (608), 403/874-3230
MLA, Hon. Stephen Kakfwi, Sahtu, (1,571), 403/598-2130
MLA, Floyd K. Roland, Inuvik, (1,175)
MLA, Jake Ootes, Yellowknife Centre, (1,263)
MLA, J. Michael Miltenberger, Thebacha, (1,393)
MLA, Tommy Enuaraq, Baffin Central, (967)
MLA, Hon. Don Morin, Tu Nedhe, (536), 403/394-3172
MLA, David Krutko, Mackenzie Delta, (772)
MLA, Hon. Kelvin Ng, Kitikmeot, (1,114), 403/983-2835
MLA, John Ningark, Natilikmiot, (704), 403/769-6031
MLA, Edward Picco, Iqaluit, (1,428)
MLA, Jane Groenewegen, Hay River, (1,740)
MLA, Hon. Goo Arlooktoo, Baffin South, (768)
MLA, Levi Barnabas, High Arctic, (392)
MLA, Hon. Manitok Thompson, Aivilik, (599), 819/645-2322
MLA, Hon. John Todd, Keewatin Central, (1,148), 819/645-3241
MLA, Seamus Henry, Yellowknife South, (2,339)
MLA, James Rabesca, North Slave, (1,132)

NORTHWEST TERRITORIES GOVERNMENT DEPARTMENTS & AGENCIES

AURORA RESEARCH INSTITUTE (ARI)
c/o Aurora College, PO Box 1430, Inuvik NT X0E 0T0
EMail: maad@inukshuk.gov.nt.ca

Formerly the Science Institute of the Northwest Territories - West. ARI is an arms-length agency of the Territorial Government & a division of Aurora College. Operations were merged with Aurora College in January 1995. The Institute administers the research licensing provisions of the Northwest Territories Scientists Act & provides for seasonal & continuous research projects to be carried out.

Minister Responsible, Hon. Charles Dent, 403/669-2355
Chair, Steven B. Richards
Executive Director, David Malcolm, 403/979-3298, Fax: 403/979-4264
Director, Scientific Services, Gary White, 403/920-6180
Administrator, Yellowknife & Coordinator, NRC IRAP Program, Craig D'Entremont, #500, 5022 - 49th St., Yellowknife NT X1A 3R7, 403/873-7592, Fax: 403/873-0227
Manager, Technology Development, Dr. S.Y. Ahmad, 403/920-3073

Department of EDUCATION, CULTURE & EMPLOYMENT
PO Box 1320, Yellowknife NT X1A 2L9
403/920-6222 (Policy & Planning); Email: info@ece.learnet.nt.ca; URL: http://siksik.learnnet.nt.ca

Minister, Hon. Charles Dent, 403/669-2355, Fax: 403/873-0169
Acting Deputy Minister, Eric Colbourne, 403/873-0456
Director, Policy & Planning, Gail Joyce, 403/920-6221
Director, Financial & Management Services, Paul Devitt, 403/873-7739
Coordinator, Public Affairs, Cathy Jewison, 403/920-6222, Fax: 403/873-0155

CULTURE & CAREERS BRANCH
403/873-7252; Fax: 403/873-0155
Asst. Deputy Minister, Mark Cleveland
Director, Career Development, David Gilday, 403/873-7146
Director, Colleges & Continuing Education, Lesley Allen, 403/920-8827
Director, Culture & Heritage, Charles Arnold, 403/873-7551
Director, Human Resources, Jacqueline McLean, 403/873-7366
Director, Income Support Programs, Dana Heide, 403/920-8922, Fax: 403/873-0443
Director, Language Bureau, Albert Canadien, 403/920-6484
Territorial Archivist, Richard Valpy, 403/873-7657

EDUCATIONAL DEVELOPMENT BRANCH
403/920-8061; Fax: 403/873-0155
Asst. Deputy Minister, Eric Colbourne
Director, Board Operations, Malcolm Farrow, 403/920-8990
Director, Information Networks, Peter Crass, 403/873-7251
Acting Territorial Librarian, NWT Public Library Services, Suliang Feng, PO Box 1100, Hay River NT X0E 0R0, 403/874-6531
Director, Early Childhood & School Services, Anne-Mieke Cameron, 403/920-3491

INCOME SECURITY BRANCH
403/920-6160; Fax: 403/920-0443
Asst. Deputy Minister, Conrad Pilon, 403/920-6160

Associated Agencies, Boards & Commissions
• Northwest Territories Apprenticeship & Trade Certification Board: PO Box 1192, Yellowknife NT X1A 2N8 – 403/873-7357
Acting Chair, Joe Leonardis
Manager, Apprenticeship & Occupational Certification, Felicity Burr, 403/873-7553
• Northwest Territories Arts Council: PO Box 1320, Stn Main, Yellowknife NT X1A 2L9
Contact, Tom Hudson, 403/920-3103

Northwest Territories EMERGENCY MEASURES ORGANIZATION
Northwest Tower, #600, 5201 - 50 Ave., Yellowknife NT X1A 3S9
403/873-7554; Fax: 403/873-8193
Director, Eric Bussey, 403/920-6133
Coordinator, Max Rispin, 403/873-7083
Administration & Operations Officer, Susan Sheck, 403/873-7892

Department of the EXECUTIVE
PO Box 1320, Yellowknife NT X1A 2L9
403/920-3398; Fax: 403/873-0235; URL: http://www.ssimirro.com/ZXxpsognwt/Net/departments/Dept-Executive.HTML

ACTS ADMINISTERED
Financial Administration Act
Legislative Assembly & Executive Council Act
Public Service Act
Minister, Hon. Don Morin, 403/669-2311, Fax: 403/873-0385
Acting Deputy Minister, Darryl Bohnet, 403/920-3398
Director, Staffing Services, Tom Williams, 403/920-8932

Department of FINANCE
PO Box 1320, Yellowknife NT X1A 2L9
URL: http://www.fin.gov.nt.ca

ACTS ADMINISTERED
Borrowing Authorization Act
Income Tax Act
Income Tax Collection Agreement Questions Act
Loan Authorization Act
Payroll Tax Act, 1993
Petroleum Products Tax Act
Property & Assessment Taxation Act
Tobacco Tax Act
Minister, Hon. John Todd, 403/669-2377, Fax: 403/873-0169
Deputy Minister, Eric Nielsen, 403/873-7117, Fax: 403/873-0414
Director, Finance & Administration, William Setchell, 403/873-7158, Fax: 403/873-0325
Director, Fiscal Policy, Margaret Melhorn, 403/873-7303, Fax: 403/873-0381
Director, Treasury, Tony Dawson, 403/873-7308, Fax: 403/873-0325
Senior Policy & Planning Analyst, Joseph La Ferla, 403/920-6364, Fax: 403/873-0414
Territorial Statistician, Ralph Joyce, 403/873-7147, Fax: 403/873-0275
Manager, Tax Administration, Vacant, 403/920-3470, Fax: 403/873-0325

Northwest Territories GOVERNMENT INQUIRIES SERVICE
PO Box 1320, Yellowknife NT X1A 2L9
403/873-7110; Fax: 403/920-4218

Department of HEALTH & SOCIAL SERVICES
Centre Square Tower, 8th Fl., PO Box 1320, Yellowknife NT X1A 2L9
403/920-6173; Fax: 403/873-0266; URL: http://www.hlthss.gov.nt.ca/

ACTS ADMINISTERED
Aboriginal Custom Adoption Recognition Act (assent given, not yet proclaimed)
Adoption Act
Certified Nursing Assistants Act
Child & Family Services Act
Child Welfare Act, Guardianship & Trustee Act (assent given, not yet proclaimed)
Dental Auxiliaries Act
Dental Mechanics Act
Dental Professions Act
Disease Registries Act
Emergency Medical Aid Act
Guardianship & Trusteeship Act
Human Tissue Act
Medical Care Act
Medical Profession Act
Mental Health Act
Nursing Profession Act
Ophthalmic Medical Assistants Act
Optometry Act
Pharmacy Act
Psychologists Act
Public Health Act
Territorial Hospital Insurance Services Act
Minister, Hon. Kelvin Ng, 403/669-2388, Fax: 403/873-0169
Deputy Minister, David Ramsden, 403/920-6173, Fax: 403/873-0266, Email: dave_ramsden@gov.nt.ca
Asst. Deputy Minister, Don Ellis, 403/873-7646, Fax: 403/873-0266, Email: don_ellis@gov.nt.ca
Director, Financial & Management Services, Warren St. Germaine, 403/920-8931, Fax: 403/920-4969, Email: warren_st.germaine@gov.nt.ca
Director, Policy, Planning & Evaluation, Bronwyn Watters, 403/873-7155, Fax: 403/873-0484, Email: bronwyn_watters@inukshuk.gov.nt.ca

HEALTH SERVICES DEVELOPMENT
Chief Medical Health Director, Dr. Ian Gilchrist, 403/920-8946, Fax: 403/873-0266, Email: ian_gilchrist@gov.nt.ca
Director, Health Services Administration, Darrell Bower, 403/873-7714, Fax: 403/873-0280, Email: darrell_bower@gov.nt.ca
Director, Population Health & Board Development, Norman Hatlevik, 403/920-8945, Fax: 403/873-0280, Email: norm_hatlevik@gov.nt.ca

COMMUNITY PROGRAMS & SERVICES
URL: http://siksik.learnnet.nt.ca/HIV-Aids/index.html (HIV/Aids Strategy Info)
Director, Community Health, Cathy Praamsma, 403/873-7738, Fax: 403/873-7706, Email: cathy_praamsma@gov.nt.ca
Director, Family Support & Child Protection, Andrew Langford, 403/920-6255, Fax: 403/873-0444, Email: andrew_langford@gov.nt.ca

Northwest Territories HOUSING CORPORATION
Scotia Centre, 5102 - 50th Ave., 10th Fl., PO Box 2100, Yellowknife NT X1A 2P6
403/873-7850; Fax: 403/870-8024
Minister Responsible, Hon. Kelvin Ng, 403/669-2311, Fax: 403/873-0169
President, Penny Ballantyne, 403/873-7843, Fax: 403/873-9426

Canadian Almanac & Directory 1997

Senior Vice-President, Community & Program Services, Dave Murray, 403/873-7898, Fax: 403/669-7901
Vice-President, Technical Operations, Peter Tremblay, 403/873-7875, Fax: 403/669-7010
Vice-President, Finance, Jim Nelson, 403/873-7873, Fax: 403/873-9426
Comptroller, Finance, Jeff Anderson, 403/873-7864
Director, Community Development Division, David Kravitz, 403/920-6550
Director, Construction Services, Joe Solowy, 403/873-7876
Director, Corporate Services, Chris Lupiano, 403/873-7868
Director, Human Resources, Mike Armstrong, 403/920-6536
Director, Policy & Planning, Penny Ballantyne, 403/920-6504

Ministry of INTERGOVERNMENTAL & ABORIGINAL AFFAIRS
Precambrian Bldg., 7th Fl., PO Box 1320, Yellowknife NT X1A 2L9
403/873-7143; Fax: 403/873-0233
Minister, Hon. James Antoine, 403/669-2333, Fax: 403/669-0399
Deputy Minister, Bob Overvold, 403/873-7143
Executive Secretary, Kathy Green

Department of JUSTICE
PO Box 1320, Yellowknife NT X1A 2L9
403/873-7453; URL: http://pingo.gov.nt.ca/Phone/Dept/dep0013.htm#Il
Minister, Hon. Kelvin Ng, 403/669-2388
Deputy Minister, Donald Cooper, Q.C., 403/920-6197
Asst. Deputy Minister, Attorney General Branch, Miles Pepper, Q.C., 403/920-6300
Asst. Deputy Minister, Solicitor General Branch, Nora Sanders, 403/873-7005
Executive Director, Legal Services Board, Bruce McKay, 403/873-7485
Director, Community Justice, Sue Heron-Herbert, 403/873-7002
Coordinator, Young Offenders, Doug Friesen, 403/920-8823
Director, Constitutional Law Division, Elizabeth Stewart, 403/920-8074
Director, Corrections, Margaret Ravensdale, 403/920-8922
Acting Director, Court Services Administration, Cayley Thomas, 403/920-8852
Director, Financial & Management Services, Louise Dundas Matthews, 403/873-7641
Director, Law Enforcement, Len Davies, 403/873-7002
Director, Legal Division, Reg Tolton, 403/920-8003
Public Trustee, Public Trustee's Office, Larry Pontus, 403/873-7464
Director, Legal Registries/Land Titles, Gary MacDougall, 403/873-7490
Registrar, Legal Securities, Vacant, 403/920-8987
Deputy Registrar, Legal Registries, Nancy Kornichuk, 403/920-8985
Deputy Registrar, Securities, Ann Burry, 403/920-3318
Deputy Registrar, Land Titles, Paul Bachand, 403/873-7491
Deputy Registrar, Land Titles, Kathryn Roy, 403/920-8983
Director, Legislation Division, Mark Aitken, Q.C., 403/873-7462
Director, Policy & Planning, Gerald Sutton, 403/920-6418
Coordinator, Victims Services, Lawrence Norbert, 403/920-6911
Chief Coroner, Coroner's Office, Jo MacQuarrie, 403/873-7460

Chief Territorial Firearms Officer, Firearms Office, Emily Overbo, 403/920-8714
Sheriff, Sheriff's Office, Colin McCluskie, 403/920-6301
For list of Courts & other Legal Offices, including Judicial Officials & Judges see Section 10 of this book.

Associated Agencies, Boards & Commissions
• Judicial Council: PO Box 1439, Yellowknife YT X1A 2P1 – 403/873-7105; Fax: 403/873-0287
Chair, Hon. M. M. de Weerdt
• Legal Services Board of the Northwest Territories: PO Box 1320, Yellowknife NT X1A 2L9 – 403/873-7450; Fax: 403/873-5320
Executive Director, Bruce Mckay, 403/873-7450
Solicitor, Gregory Nearing, 403/873-7450
Solicitor, Jonathan Tarlton, 403/873-7450
• Victims Assistance Committee: c/o Community Justice Division, PO Box 1320, Yellowknife NT X1A 2L9 – 403/920-6911; Fax: 403/873-0299
Chair, Thelma Tees, 403/920-1013
Coordinator, Lawrence Norbert, 403/920-6911

Department of MUNICIPAL & COMMUNITY AFFAIRS
#600, 5201 - 50th Ave., PO Box 1310, Yellowknife NT X1A 2L9
403/873-7118; Fax: 403/873-0309; URL: http://www.maca.gov.nt.ca

ACTS ADMINISTERED
Area Development Act
Charter Communities Act
Cities, Towns & Villages Act
Civil Emergency Measures Act
Commissioner's Land Act
Community Employees Benefits Act
Hamlets Act
Local Authorities Elections Act
Planning Act
Property Assessment & Taxation Act
Senior Citizens' & Disabled Persons' Property Tax Relief Act
Settlements Act
Western Canada Lotteries Act
Minister, Hon. Manitok Thompson, 403/669-2344, Fax: 403/873-0169
Deputy Minister, Penny Ballantyne, 403/873-7118, Fax: 403/873-0169, Email: pballant@maca.gov.nt.ca
Asst. Deputy Minister, Vern Christensen, 403/873-6355, Fax: 403/873-0309, Email: vchriste@maca.gov.nt.ca
Director, Community Development, Moheb Michael, 403/920-3144, Fax: 403/920-6156, Email: mmichael@maca.gov.nt.ca
Director, Community Planning & Lands, Brian Render, 403/920-8916, Fax: 403/920-6343, Email: brender@maca.gov.nt.ca
Director, Emergency Measures Organization, Eric Bussey, 403/920-6133, Fax: 403/873-8193, Email: ebussey@maca.gov.nt.ca
Director, Finance & Administration Services, Jim France, 403/873-7613, Fax: 403/873-0152, Email: jfrance@maca.gov.nt.ca
Director, Policy & Planning, Dennis Adams, 403/873-7977, Fax: 403/873-0152, Email: dadams@maca.gov.nt.ca
Director, Sport & Recreation, Ian Legaree, 403/873-7245, Fax: 403/920-6467, Email: ilegaree@maca.gov.nt.ca

Associated Agencies, Boards & Commissions
• Assessment Appeal Tribunal of the Northwest Territories: PO Box 1320, Yellowknife NT X1A 2L9 – 403/920-6208; Fax: 403/920-6467
Senior Officer, Terry Kozak, Email: tkozak@maca.gov.nt.ca

• Territorial Board of Revision: PO Box 1320, Yellowknife NT X1A 2L9 – 403/873-7997; Fax: 403/920-3159
Senior Officer, Terry Kozak, Email: tkozak@maca.gov.nt.ca
Administrator, Assessment Appeals, Kim Hjelmeland, Email: khjelmel@maca.gov.nt.ca

NUNAVUT RESEARCH INSTITUTE (NRI)
Aeroplex Bldg., PO Box 160, Iqualuit NT X0A 0H0
819/979-4114; Fax: 819/979-4119

Formerly the Science Institute of the Northwest Territories - East. Responsible for science & technology in the Nunavut region. The Institute operates in cooperation with the Nunavut Arctic College & conducts & supports research projects in the Eastern Arctic.
Executive Director, Bruce Rigby
Manager, Science & Technology Services, Richard Isnor, 819/979-4105
Manager, Iqualuit Research Centre, Lynn Peplinski
Manager, Igloolik Research Centre, Leah Otak

Northwest Territories POWER CORPORATION
4 Capital Drive, Hay River NT X0E 1G2
403/874-5200; Fax: 403/874-5251
Minster Responsible, Hon. Charles Dent, 403/669-2355, Fax: 403/873-0169
Chair & CEO, Pierre Alvarez, 403/669-3390, Fax: 403/669-3395
President & COO, Leon Courneya, 403/874-5245, Fax: 403/874-5229
Director, Engineering, Vacant

Department of PUBLIC WORKS & SERVICES
Bldg. YK-7, PO Box 1320, Yellowknife NT X1A 2L9
403/873-7114; Fax: 403/873-0264; URL: http://www.ssimicro.com/ZXxpsognwt/Net/departments/Dept-PublicWorks.HTML
Minister, Hon. Goo Arlooktoo, 403/669-2399, Fax: 403/873-0169
Deputy Minister, Ken Lovely, 403/873-7114
Director, Finance, Dave Waddell, 403/920-8693
Director, Policy & Planning, Gay Kennedy, 403/920-8668
Director, Regional Support Services Division, Sue Bevington, 403/873-7397
Director, Project Management Division, Derek Lovlin, 403/873-7826
Director, Systems & Communications, Peter Bourke, 403/873-7521
Director, Transition Planning, Joe Augc

PETROLEUM PRODUCTS DIVISION
819/645-5165; Fax: 819/945-3554
Director, Merv Homenuik, 819/645-5178

REGIONAL OFFICES
Regional Superintendent, Baffin, Ross Mrazek, 819/979-5150, Fax: 819/979-4748
Regional Superintendent, Fort Smith, Ralph Shelton, 403/872-7260, Fax: 403/872-2830
Regional Superintendent, Inuvik, Brian Lemax, 403/979-7140, Fax: 403/979-4748
Regional Superintendent, Keewatin, Greg Pilgrim, 819/645-5050, Fax: 819/645-2242
Regional Superintendent, Kitikmeot, Brent Boddy, 403/983-7285, Fax: 403/983-2158
Regional Superintendent, Yellowknife, Vince Dixon, 403/873-7650, Fax: 403/873-0257

Department of RESOURCES, WILDLIFE & ECONOMIC DEVELOPMENT
#600, Scotia Centre, Bldg. Box 21, 5102 - 50 Ave., Yellowknife NT X1A 3S8
403/873-7420, 7134; Fax: 403/873-0114; URL: http://www.edt.gov.nt.ca/
Spill Report Line: 403/920-8130

Announced in August 1996 the new Department of Resources, Wildlife & Economic Development, combining the former, Departments of Economic Development & Tourism, Energy, Mines & Petroleum Resources & Renewable Resources. The new department promotes self-sufficiency & growth through the sustainable development of natural resources & enhances the creation of new opportunities in the traditional & wage economy. Aims to protect the condition, quality, diversity & abundance of resources, & the condition & quality of the environment.

ACTS ADMINISTERED
Environmental Protection Act
Environmental Rights Act
Forest Management Act
Forest Protection Act
Herd & Fencing Act
Natural Resources Conservation Trust Act
Pesticide Act
Water Resources Agreement Act
Wildlife Act
Minister, Hon. Stephen Kakfwi, 403/669-2366, Fax: 403/873-0169
Deputy Minister, Andrew Gamble, 403/920-8691, Fax: 403/873-0563
Asst. Deputy Minister, East, Katherine Trumper, W.G. Browne Bldg., PO Box 1000, Iqaluit NT X0A 0H0, 403/979-5071, Fax: 403/979-6026
Executive Director, Resources & Economic Development, Doug Doan, 403/873-7115, Fax: 403/920-2756
Asst. Deputy Minister, West, Robert McLeod, 403/873-7420, Fax: 403/873-0114
Director, Corporate Services, Vacant, 403/873-8920, Fax: 403/873-0563

ENVIRONMENTAL PROTECTION DIVISION
Director, Emery Paquin, 403/873-7654, Fax: 403/873-0221
Manager, Land Protection, Neil Thompson, 403/873-7178
Specialist, Air Quality, Jim Sparling, 403/920-6396
Specialist, Hazardous Substances, Ken Hall, 403/920-6476
Specialist, Industrial Waste, Chris Wolnik, 403/873-7178

FOREST MANAGEMENT DIVISION
Director, Bob Bailey, 403/872-7700, Fax: 403/872-2077
Forest Technician, Marty Sanderson, 403/920-6405
District Forester, Chris Carlisle, PO Box 5, Fort Smith NT X0E 0P0, 403/872-2139
Manager, Air Operations & Administration, Rick Pederson
Supervisor, Fire Operations, Dennis Mahussier
Manager, Fire Science & Planning, Rick Lanoville

MINERALS, OIL & GAS DIVISION
Acting Director, Doug Matthews, 403/920-3214, Fax: 403/873-0254

Energy Policy & Programs
403/920-8944
Director, Joe Ahmad, 403/920-3230
Coordinator, Energy Management Programs, Greg Krysko, 403/873-7203

Mineral Initiatives Office
Manager, Martin Irving, 403/920-3125
Chief Project Geologist, Mike Stubley, 403/920-3344

Mineral Resources
403/920-3222
Director, Michael Cunningham, 403/920-3217
Specialist, Mineral Policy, Kathleen Hearn, 403/920-3204
Advisor, Community Minerals, Rob Johnstone, 403/920-3345
Environmental Analyst, Jane McMullen, 403/873-7086

Resource Policy
Director, Doug Matthews, 403/920-3214, Fax: 403/873-0254
Geologist, Petroleum, Vacant
Specialist, Resource Data, Anna Soininen, 403/920-8679
Economist, Calvin Brackman, 403/873-7735

PARKS & TOURISM DIVISION
Director, Parks & Visitor Services, Robin Reilly, 403/873-7902, Fax: 403/873-0163
Director, Tourism, Marketing & Development, Peter Neugebauer, 403/873-7690, Fax: 403/873-0294
Manager, Capital Programs, Vaugan del Valle, 403/920-8975
Advisor, Licensing & Regulations, David Grindlay, 403/873-7905

POLICY & LEGISLATION DIVISION
Director, Kathryn Emmett, 403/920-8046, Fax: 403/873-0114

STRATEGIC PLANNING DIVISION
Director, Garry Singer, 403/873-7318, Fax: 403/873-0434
Special Advisor, Arts & Crafts, Grant Baker, 403/873-7315
Special Advisor, Business & Technical Services, Chuck Ennis, 403/920-8969
Special Advisor, Government Liaison, Terry Lancaster, 403/873-7360
Special Advisor, Industrial Benefits, Steven Leclair, 403/920-0333
Special Advisor, Natural Resources, John Colford, 403/873-7383

TRADE & INVESTMENT DIVISION
Director, Otto Olah, 403/873-7361, Fax: 403/920-2756

WILDLIFE & FISHERIES DIVISION
Director, Doug Stewart, 403/920-8716, Fax: 403/873-0221
Asst. Director, Wildlife Management Section, Sebastian Oosenbrug, 403/920-8064
Acting Asst. Director, Wildlife Studies Section, Ray Case, 403/873-7765
Supervisor, Conservation Education, Lyn Hartley, 403/873-7134
Supervisor, Fur Management, Ian Ross, 403/873-7771
Supervisor, Resource Development, John Best, 403/920-6401

Regional Offices
Baffin: W.G. Browne Bldg., PO Box 1000, Iqaluit NT X0A 0H0 – 819/979-5072; Fax: 819/979-6026, Regional Superintendent, Clay Buchanan
Deh Cho: Milton Bldg., 2nd Fl., PO Box 240, Fort Simpson NT X0E 0N0 – 403/695-2231; Fax: 403/695-2442, Regional Superintendent, Paul Kraft
Inuvik: Semmler Bldg., 2nd Fl., Bag Service #1, Inuvik NT X0E 0T0 – 403/979-2938; Fax: 403/979-2604, Regional Superintendent, Ed Henderson
Keewatin: Government of the NWT Office, Rankin Inlet NT X0C 0G0 – 819/645-5067; Fax: 819/645-2346, Regional Superintendent, Graeme Dargo
Kitikmeot: PO Bag 200, Cambridge Bay NT X0E 0C0 – 403/982-7241; Fax: 403/982-3701, Regional Superintendent, John Stevenson
North Slave: Tapwe Bldg., 5017 - 49th St., PO Box 1320, Yellowknife NT X1A 2L9 – 403/920-8966; Fax: 403/873-6109, Regional Superintendent, Larry Anderson
Sahtu: Norman Wells NT – 403/587-2310; Fax: 403/587-2204, Regional Superintendent, Gerry LePrieur
South Slave: Sweetgrass Bldg., PO Box 390, Fort Smith NT X0E 0P0 – 403/872-4242; Fax: 403/872-4250, Regional Superintendent, Lloyd Jones

Associated Agencies, Boards & Commissions
• Northwest Territories Business Credit Corporation: Northern United Place, 5004 - 54 St., PO Box 1320, Yellowknife NT X1A 2L9 – 403/920-6454; Fax: 403/873-0101
CEO & Manager, Loan Funds, Afzal Currimbhoy
Manager, Credit & Operations, Ian Collins, 403/920-6452
Lending Officer, East, Gayle Buckel, 403/920-3186
Lending Officer, West, Mike Mageean, 403/920-6453
• Northwest Territories Centre for Remote Sensing: – Fax: 403/873-0221
Director, Helmut Epp, 403/920-3329
Analyst, Remote Sensing, Cindy Squires Taylor, 403/920-3325
GIS Technician, Norm Mair, 403/920-3326
• Northwest Territories Development Corporation (DEVCORP): Tower 7, PO Box 1437, Yellowknife NT X1A 2P1 – 403/920-7700; Fax: 403/920-7701
Chair, Robert Leonard
President, Glenn Soloy
Manager, Capital Projects, George Ehrier
Manager, Investments, David Wallace
• Northwest Territories Workers' Compensation Board Listed alphabetically in detail, this Section.

Department of SAFETY & PUBLIC SERVICES
Panda 2 Mall, 3rd Fl., PO Box 1320, Yellowknife NT X1A 2L9
403/873-7619; Fax: 403/873-0260; URL: http://www.ssimicro.com/ZXepsognwt/Net/departments/dept-Safety.HTML

ACTS ADMINISTERED
Boilers & Pressure Vessels Act
Business Licence Act
Change of Name Act
Consumer Protection Act
Dental Mechanics Act
Dental Profession Act
Electrical Protection Act
Employment Agencies Act
Fire Prevention Act
Gas Protection Act
Insurance Act
Labour Standards Act
Liquor Act
Lotteries Act
Marriage Act
Medical Profession Act
Motion Picture Act
Ophthalmic Medical Assistants Act
Optometry Act
Pawnbrokers & Second Hand Dealers Act
Pharmacy Act
Psychologists Act
Public Utilites Act
Real Estate Agents' Licensing Act
Residential Tenancies Act
Veterinary Profession Act
Vital Statistics Act
Wages Recovery Act
Minister, Hon. James Antoine, 403/669-2333, Fax: 403/873-0169
Deputy Minister, John Quirke, 403/873-7619

Canadian Almanac & Directory 1997

Fire Marshal, Don Gillis, 403/873-7472
Director, Consumer Services, Dorothy Mellor, 403/920-8054, Tenant Hotline: 403/920-8047; Consumer Complaints: 403/873-7125
Director, Finance & Administration Division, Henry Dragon, 403/920-3270

Vital Statistics Office
403/920-3143
Provides territorial birth, marriage & death certificates. Fee for each is $10.00.
Registrar General, Diana Denroche

Associated Agencies, Boards & Commissions
•Northwest Territories Labour Standards Board: PO Box 2804, Yellowknife NT X1A 2R1 – 403/873-7924; Fax: 403/873-0302
Chair, Rosemary Cairns
Executive Secretary, Karyn Dick
•Northwest Territories Liquor Commission: Hay River NT X0E 0R0 – 403/874-2100; Fax: 403/874-2180
General Manager, Ron Courtorielle
Manager, Finance & Administration, Kyle Reid
•Northwest Territories Liquor Licensing Board: Hay River NT X0E 0R0 – 403/874-2906; Fax: 403/873-0302
Executive Secretary, Dorothy Mandeville
Senior Inspector, Paul Craig
Inspector, Jay Ruggles
•Public Utilities Board of the Northwest Territories: PO Bag 5006, Hay River NT X0E 0R0 – 403/874-3944
Chair, John Hill

Department of TRANSPORTATION
Lahm Ridge Bldg., PO Box 1320, Yellowknife NT X1A 2L9
403/920-3460; Fax: 403/873-0363; URL: http://www.ssimicro.com/ZXxpsognwt/Net//departments/Dept-Transport.HTML

ACTS ADMINISTERED
Motor Vehicles Act
Public Highways Act
Public Service Vehicles Act
Transportation of Dangerous Goods Act(s)
Minister, Hon. James Antoine, 403/669-2333, Fax: 403/873-0169
Deputy Minister, Bob Doherty, 403/920-3460, Fax: 403/873-0363
Asst. Deputy Minister, Bruce Rattray, 403/920-3461
Director, Arctic Airports Division, Doug Howard, 403/873-7725
Director, Finance & Administration, Jim Winsor, 403/920-3459
Director, Marine Services Division, Tony MacAlpine, 403/695-3424
Director, Policy & Coordination, John Bunge, 403/920-8754

MOTOR VEHICLES
403/920-8915
Director, Richard MacDonald, 403/920-8915
Asst. Director, Registries, Mike Fahey, 403/920-8633
Asst. Director, Safety & Regulations, Gary Walsh, 403/920-8633
Manager, Registration & Licensing, Dave Buchan, 403/873-7418

TRANSPORTATION HIGHWAYS & ENGINEERING
403/920-8771; Fax: 403/873-0288
Director, Peter Vician, 403/873-7800
Manager, Contracts, Dennis Malloy, 403/920-3434
Project Manager, John Bowen, 403/920-6473

Project Manager, Airports Section, Rob Nelson, 403/873-7809
Head, Structures, Jivko Jivkov, 403/873-7564

TRANSPORTATION PLANNING
403/873-7666; Fax: 403/920-2565
Director, Masood Hassan, 403/873-7934
Manager, Environmental Affairs, Leslie Green, 403/873-7063
Senior Planner, Marine Facilities, Pietro de Bastiani, 403/920-6179
Senior Planner, Transportation, Russell Neudorf, 403/920-3366

Associated Agencies, Boards & Commissions
•Highway Transport Board: Hay River NT X0E 0R0 – 403/874-6763; Fax: 403/874-6088
Director, Mark Schauerte

Northwest Territories WATER BOARD
PO Box 1500, Yellowknife NT X1A 2R3
403/920-8191; Fax: 403/873-9572
Chair, Gordon Wray

STATUS OF WOMEN OF THE NORTHWEST TERRITORIES
PO Box 1320, Yellowknife NT X1A 2L9
403/920-6177
Reports directly to the Executive Council on matters concerning women in the Northwest Territories.
Minister Responsible, Hon. Manitok Thompson, 403/669-2344, Fax: 403/873-0169
President, Rita Arey, PO Box 183, Aklavik NT X0E 0A0
Vice-President (Baker Lake), Rebecca Kudloo
Vice-President (Fort Smith), Sister Agnes Sutherland

Northwest Territories WORKERS' COMPENSATION BOARD
PO Box 8888, Yellowknife NT X1A 2R3
403/920-8686; Fax: 403/873-4596
Minister Responsible, Hon. John Todd, 403/669-2377, Fax: 403/873-0169
Chair, Jeff Gilmour, 403/920-8755
General Manager, Gerry Meier, 403/920-8749
Director, Client Services, Trevor Alexander, 403/920-3817
Director, Corporate Services, Joan Perry, 403/920-3815
Director, Employer Services, John Finley, 403/920-3861
Director, Finance & Administration Services, Dorothy Chattell, 403/920-3850
Project Manager, Claims Management, Mike Swiniarski, 403/920-3827

GOVERNMENT OF NOVA SCOTIA

Seat of Government: Legislative Assembly, Province House, Halifax NS B3J 2T3
URL: http://www.gov.ns.ca/
The Province of Nova Scotia entered Confederation July 1, 1867. It has an area of 52,840.83 km2, and the StatsCan census population in 1991 was 899,942.

Office of the LIEUTENANT GOVERNOR
Government House, 1451 Barrington St., Halifax NS B3J 1Z2
902/425-6300; Fax: 902/424-0537
Lieutenant Governor, Hon. John James Kinley, C.D., S.M., D.Eng., P.Eng., FEIC
Executive Asst., Mary M. McGrath

Office of the PREMIER
One Government Place, 1700 Granville St., PO Box 726, Halifax NS B3J 1X5
902/424-6600; Fax: 902/424-7648;
Email: hlfxgov1.exec.premier@gov.ns.ca;
URL: http://www.gov.ns.ca/govt/prem/
Premier, Hon. John P. Savage, Email: jsavage@fox.nstn.ca
Deputy Premier, Hon. J. William Gillis, Ph.D., 902/424-4044
Deputy Minister, Robert A. Mackay, 902/424-8940
Principal Asst., Suzan Maclean, 902/424-4135
Executive Asst., David Cowan, 902/424-2588
Senior Advisor, Jeanne Wilson Clarke, 902/424-4092
Director, Communications, David Harrigan, 902/424-3750
Coordinator, Administrative Affairs, Arlene D'Eon, 902/424-6604
Coordinator, Scheduling, Stephanie Bennett, 902/424-6601
Media Relations, Ann Graham Walker, 902/424-2590

EXECUTIVE COUNCIL
One Government Place, PO Box 2125, Halifax NS B3J 3B7
902/424-5970; Fax: 902/424-0667
Premier, President, Executive Council & Minister, Intergovernmental Affairs, Hon. John P. Savage, 902/424-6600, Fax: 902/424-7648, Email: jsavage@fox.nstn.ca
Deputy Premier, Deputy President, Executive Council & Minister, Finance, Hon. J. William Gillis, Ph.D., 902/424-5720, Fax: 902/424-0635
Attorney General & Minister, Justice, Hon. Jay F. Abbass, 902/424-4044, Fax: 902/424-0510
Minister, Environment, Hon. F. Wayne Adams, 902/424-2358, Fax: 902/424-0644
Minister, Fisheries, Hon. James A. Barkhouse, 902/424-8953, Fax: 902/424-4671
Minister, Health & Chair, Priorities & Planning Committee, Hon. J. Bernard Boudreau, Q.C., 902/424-3377, Fax: 902/424-0559
Minister, Agriculture & Marketing, Hon. Guy A.C. Brown, 902/424-4388, Fax: 902/424-3948
Minister, Transportation & Public Works, Hon. Donald R. Downe, 902/424-5875, Fax: 902/424-0532
Minister without Portfolio & Minister Responsible, Acadian Affairs, Hon. Wayne J. Gaudet, 902/424-4484, Fax: 902/424-0698
Minister, Education & Culture, Hon. Robert S. Harrison, 902/424-4236, Fax: 902/424-0680
Minister, Business & Consumer Services, Hon. Sandra L. Jolly, 902/424-7579, Fax: 902/424-0754
Minister, Labour, Hon. Manning MacDonald, 902/424-6647, Fax: 902/424-3239
Minister, Community Services, Hon. John MacEachern, 902/424-4304, Fax: 902/424-0549
Minister Responsible, Nova Scotia Economic Renewal Agency, Hon. Richard W. Mann, 902/424-5790, Fax: 902/424-0514
Minister, Natural Resources, Hon. Eleanor E. Norrie, 902/424-4037, Fax: 902/424-0594
Minister Responsible, Technology & Science Secretariat, Hon. Gerald J. O'Malley, 902/424-2900, Fax: 902/424-0500
Minister, Housing & Municipal Affairs, Hon. James A. Smith, M.D., 902/424-5550, Fax: 902/424-0581
Minister, Human Resources, Hon. Allister Surrette, 902/424-5465, Fax: 902/424-0555

Cabinet Office
Secretary to the Executive Council, Robert A. MacKay, Q.C., 902/424-6611, Fax: 902/424-7638
Executive Council Clerk, Brenda Shannon, 902/424-5970, Fax: 902/424-0667

Executive Director, Acadian Affairs, Paul J. Gaudet, 902/424-4484, Fax: 902/424-0698, Yarmouth: 902/742-7234
Director, Intergovernmental Affairs, Dr. Alastair Saunders, 902/424-4899, Fax: 902/424-0728
Chief of Protocol, Colleen MacDonald, 902/424-4463, Fax: 902/424-4309

LEGISLATIVE HOUSE OF ASSEMBLY

c/o Clerk's Office, Province House, 2nd Fl., Halifax NS B3J 2Y3
902/424-5978; Fax: 902/424-0574; URL: http://www.gov.ns.ca/legi/house.htm
Clerk of Assembly: R.K. MacArthur
Speaker: Hon. Paul W. MacEwan, 902/424-5707, Fax: 902/424-0526
Sergeant-at-Arms (Interim): Douglas Giles, 902/424-6603
Legislative Librarian: Margaret Murphy, 902/424-5932
Acting A/Clerk, Arthur Fordham, Q.C.
Director, Legislative T.V., Donald Ledger, 902/424-7992
Director, Administration, Dale Robbins, 902/424-4403
Editor, Hansard, Rodney Caley, 902/424-5706
Acting Chief Legislative Counsel, Gordon D. Hebb

Government Caucus Office (Lib.)
Centennial Bldg., 1660 Hollis St., 10th Fl., PO Box 1617, Halifax NS B3J 2Y3
902/424-8637; Fax: 902/424-0539
Executive Director, George Doucet

Office of the Official Opposition (PC)
Centennial Bldg., 1645 Granville Ave., 8th Fl., PO Box 1617, Halifax NS B3J 2Y3
902/424-2731; Fax: 902/424-7484
Opposition Leader, John F. Hamm
Caucus Chairman, Donald P. McInnes
Chief of Staff, Debi Forsyth-Smith
Administrative Asst., Susan Millard

Office of the New Democratic Party
Roy Bldg., 1657 Barrington St., PO Box 1617, Halifax NS B3J 2Y3
902/424-4134; Fax: 902/424-0504
Leader, Robert Chisholm
Chief of Staff & Director, Richard Starr
Principal Secretary, Bernard Butler

Standing Committees of the House
Committees Office, 1740 Granville St., 3rd Fl., PO Box 2630, Stn M, Halifax NS B3J 3N5
902/424-4432; Fax: 902/424-0513
Chief Clerk, Legislative Committees, Mora Stevens, 902/424-4494
Clerk, Legislative Committees, Darlene Henry, 902/424-5241
  Assembly Matters, Nancy Kinsman, 902/424-5707
  Community Services Committee, Darlene Henry, 902/424-5241
    Economic Development, Darlene Henry, 902/424-5241
      Human Resources, Mora Stevens, 902/424-4494
      Internal Affairs, Mora Stevens, 902/424-4494
      Law Amendments, Gordon Hebb, 902/424-8941
      Private & Local Bills, Arthur Fordham, 902/424-8941
      Public Accounts, Mora Stevens, 902/424-4494
      Resources, Darlene Henry, 902/424-5241
      Veterans Affairs, Mora Stevens, 902/424-4491

FIFTY-SIXTH ASSEMBLY - NOVA SCOTIA
902/424-5978
  Last General Election, May 25, 1993. Maximum Duration, 5 years.
  Party Standings (Sept. 24, 1996):

Liberals (Lib.) 40
Progressive Conservative (PC) 9
New Democratic Party (NDP) 3
Total, 52.

Salaries, Indemnities & Allowances: Members' sessional indemnity $30,130 plus a $15,065 expense allowance. In addition to this are the following:
Premier $52,012
Ministers $37,055
Leader of the Opposition $37,055
Leader of a recognized Party $17,650
Speaker $37,055
Deputy Speaker $18,533

Following is: constituency (number of eligible voters at 1993 election) member, party affiliation. (Address for all is c/o House of Assembly, Province House, Halifax NS B3J 2Y3.)
  Refer to Cabinet List, Government Caucus Office, the Offices of the Official Opposition & of the New Democratic Party, for **phone** & **Fax** numbers.

MEMBERS BY CONSTITUENCY
Annapolis (7,136) Earle Rayfuse, Lib.
Antigonish (7,292) Hon. J. William Gillis, Ph.D., Lib.
Argyle (3,090) Hon. Allister Surrette, Lib.
Bedford-Fall River (4,754) Francene Cosman, Lib.
Cape Breton Centre (5,643) Russell MacNeil, Lib.
Cape Breton East (7,566) Hon. John MacEachern, Lib.
Cape Breton North (5,540) Hon. Ronald D. Stewart, O.C., M.D., Lib.
Cape Breton Nova (6,524) Hon. Paul W. MacEwan, Lib.
Cape Breton South (5,667) Hon. Manning MacDonald, Lib.
Cape Breton The Lakes (6,591) Hon. J. Bernard Boudreau, Q.C., Lib.
Cape Breton West (7,355) Alfie MacLeod, PC
Chester-St. Margarets (5,014) Hon. James A. Barkhouse, Lib.
Clare (3,491) Hon. Wayne J. Gaudet, Lib.
Colchester North (4,984) Ed Lorraine, Lib.
Colchester-Musquodoboit Valley (4,130) Brooke Taylor, PC
Cole Harbour-Eastern Passage (4,734) Dennis Richards, Lib.
Cumberland North (5,676) Hon. Ross Bragg, Lib.
Cumberland South (6,714) Hon. Guy A.C. Brown, Lib.
Dartmouth East (4,912) Hon. James A. Smith, M.D., Lib.
Dartmouth North (3,301) Hon. Sandra L. Jolly, Lib.
Dartmouth South (4,346) Hon. John P. Savage, Lib.
Dartmouth-Cole Harbour (4,097) Alan Mitchell, Lib.
Digby-Annapolis (5,805) Joe Casey, Lib.
Eastern Shore (3,760) Keith Colwell, Lib.
Guysborough-Port Hawkesbury (5,487) Raymond White, Lib.
Halifax Atlantic (4,069) Robert Chisholm, NDP
Halifax Chebucto (3,905) Hon. Jay F. Abbass, Lib.
Halifax Citadel (4,608) Terrence R.B. Donahoe, Q.C., PC
Halifax Fairview (13,702) Eileen O'Connell, NDP
Halifax Needham (4,527) Hon. Gerald J. O'Malley, Lib.
Halifax-Bedford Basin (4,667) Gerry Fogerty, Lib.
Hants East (4,295) Bob Carruthers, Lib.
Hants West (4,152) Ron Russell, PC
Inverness (5,806) Charles MacArthur, Lib.
Kings North (4,137) George Archibald, PC
Kings South (3,069) Hon. Robert S. Harrison, Lib.
Kings West (4,895) George Moody, PC
Lunenburg (3,982) Lila O'Connor, Lib.
Lunenburg West (6,266) Hon. Donald R. Downe, Lib.
Pictou Centre (4,841) John F. Hamm, PC
Pictou East (10,228) Wayne Fraser, Lib.
Pictou West (4,032) Don McInnis, PC
Preston (1,846) Hon. F. Wayne Adams, Lib.
Queens (3,526) John Leefe, PC
Richmond (5,440) Hon. Richard W. Mann, Lib.
Sackville-Beaverbank (3,620) Bill MacDonald, Lib.
Sackville-Cobequid (5,032) John Holm, NDP
Shelburne (5,437) Clifford Huskilson, Lib.
Timberlea-Prospect (3,470) Bruce Holland, Lib.
Truro-Bible Hill (4,357) Hon. Eleanor E. Norrie, Lib.
Victoria (3,119) Kennie MacAskill, Lib.
Yarmouth (5,197) W. Richard Hubbard, Lib.

MEMBERS (ALPHABETICAL)
Hon. Jay F. Abbass, Halifax Chebucto (3,905)Lib.
Hon. F. Wayne Adams, Preston (1,846)Lib.
George Archibald, Kings North (4,137)PC
Hon. James A. Barkhouse, Chester-St. Margarets (5,014)Lib.
Hon. J. Bernard Boudreau, Q.C., Cape Breton The Lakes (6,591)Lib.
Hon. Ross Bragg, Cumberland North (5,676)Lib.
Hon. Guy A.C. Brown, Cumberland South (6,714)Lib.
Bob Carruthers, Hants East (4,295)Lib.
Joe Casey, Digby-Annapolis (5,805)Lib.
Robert Chisholm, Halifax Atlantic (4,069)NDP
Keith Colwell, Eastern Shore (3,760)Lib.
Francene Cosman, Bedford-Fall River (4,754)Lib.
Terrence R.B. Donahoe, Q.C., Halifax Citadel (4,608)PC
Hon. Donald R. Downe, Lunenburg West (6,266)Lib.
Gerry Fogerty, Halifax-Bedford Basin (4,667)Lib.
Wayne Fraser, Pictou East (10,228)Lib.
Hon. Wayne J. Gaudet, Clare (3,491)Lib.
Hon. J. William Gillis, Ph.D., Antigonish (7,292)Lib.
John F. Hamm, Pictou Centre (4,841)PC
Hon. Robert S. Harrison, Kings South (3,069)Lib.
Bruce Holland, Timberlea-Prospect (3,470)Lib.
John Holm, Sackville-Cobequid (5,032)NDP
W. Richard Hubbard, Yarmouth (5,197)Lib.
Clifford Huskilson, Shelburne (5,437)Lib.
Hon. Sandra L. Jolly, Dartmouth North (3,301)Lib.
John Leefe, Queens (3,526)PC
Ed Lorraine, Colchester North (4,984)Lib.
Charles MacArthur, Inverness (5,806)Lib.
Kennie MacAskill, Victoria (3,119)Lib.
Bill MacDonald, Sackville-Beaverbank (3,620)Lib.
Hon. Manning MacDonald, Cape Breton South (5,667)Lib.
Hon. John MacEachern, Cape Breton East (7,566)Lib.
Hon. Paul W. MacEwan, Cape Breton Nova (6,524)Lib.
Alfie MacLeod, Cape Breton West (7,355)PC
Russell MacNeil, Cape Breton Centre (5,643)Lib.
Hon. Richard W. Mann, Richmond (5,440)Lib.
Don McInnis, Pictou West (4,032)PC
Alan Mitchell, Dartmouth-Cole Harbour (4,097)Lib.
George Moody, Kings West (4,895)PC
Hon. Eleanor E. Norrie, Truro-Bible Hill (4,357)Lib.
Eileen O'Connell, Halifax Fairview (13,702)NDP
Lila O'Connor, Lunenburg (3,982)Lib.
Hon. Gerald J. O'Malley, Halifax Needham (4,527)Lib.
Earle Rayfuse, Annapolis (7,136)Lib.
Dennis Richards, Cole Harbour-Eastern Passage (4,734)Lib.
Ron Russell, Hants West (4,152)PC
Hon. John P. Savage, Dartmouth South (4,346)Lib.
Hon. James A. Smith, M.D., Dartmouth East (4,912)Lib.
Hon. Ronald D. Stewart, O.C., M.D., Cape Breton North (5,540)Lib.
Hon. Allister Surrette, Argyle (3,090)Lib.
Brooke Taylor, Colchester-Musquodoboit Valley (4,130)PC
Raymond White, Guysborough-Port Hawkesbury (5,487)Lib.

Canadian Almanac & Directory 1997

NOVA SCOTIA GOVERNMENT DEPARTMENTS & AGENCIES

Department of AGRICULTURE & MARKETING

Joseph Howe Bldg., 1690 Hollis St., 7th Fl., PO Box 190, Halifax NS B3J 2M4
902/424-6734; Fax: 902/424-3948;
  Email: NSDAM_info@nsac.ns.ca; URL: http://www.nsac.ns.ca/nsdam/
Truro Headquarters, PO Box 550, Truro NS B2N 5E3
  Responsible for the administration of programs to enhance competitiveness & excellence in provincial farm production & marketing. The department supports & develops agricultural research & technology transfer. Through three main divisions, the department supplies services to farmers & farm organizations, & technical & continuing education services to farmers.

ACTS ADMINISTERED

Agricultural Operations Protection Act
Agriculture & Marketing Act
Agriculture & Rural Credit Act
Agrologists Act
Animal Health & Protection Act
Baby Chick Protection Act
Bee Industry Act
Beef Commission Act
Brucellosis Control Act
Cold Storage Plants Loan Act
Control of Cattle Pests Act
Crop & Livestock Insurance Act
Dairy Commission Act
Farm Registration Act
Federations of Agriculture Act
Fences & Detention of Stray Livestock Act
Fencing & Impounding of Animals Act
Grain & Forage Commission Act
Imitation Dairy Products Act
Livestock Brands Act
Livestock Health Services Act
Livestock Loans Guarantee Act
Margarine Act
Maritime Provinces Harness Racing Commission Act
Marshland Reclamation Act
Meat Inspection Act
Natural Products Act
Potato Industry Act
Provincial Berry Act
Sheep Protection & Act
Stray Animals Act
Weed Control Act
Wildlife Act, respecting only Deer Farming Regulations
Women's Institute of Nova Scotia, Act Respecting The
Minister, Hon. Guy A.C. Brown, 902/424-4389
Deputy Minister, Dr. L.E. Haley, 902/424-3244, Email: Les.Haley@nsac.ns.ca
Acting Principal, N.S. Agricultural College, Dr. Bernie MacDonald, 902/893-6720, Fax: 902/897-9399, Email: BMacdonald@cadmin.nsac.ns.ca

AGRICULTURAL SERVICES DIVISION

Executive Director, Cynthia Robertson, 902/424-3245, Fax: 902/424-3948, Email: C.Robertson@nsac.ns.ca
Director, Financial Services, R. Mosher, PO Box 550, Truro NS B2N 5E3, 902/893-6599
Director, Land & Credit Services Branch, R.G. Adams, PO Box 550, Truro NS B2N 5E3, 902/893-6500, Fax: 902/895-7693

AGRICULTURAL DEVELOPMENT DIVISION

PO Box 550, Truro NS B2N 5E3
Executive Director, Brian Smith, 902/893-6591, Fax: 902/895-4460, Email: BSmith@fm.nsac.ns.ca

Director, Animal Industry Branch, George Smith, 902/893-6363, Fax: 902/893-6531
Director, Extension Services Branch, Jim Goit, 902/893-6596, Fax: 902/895-7693
Acting Director, Marketing Services Branch, Linda MacDonald, 902/893-6388, Fax: 902/895-9403
Director, Plant Industry Branch, Dave Sangster, 902/893-6555, Fax: 902/893-0244

Associated Agencies, Boards & Commissions

• Nova Scotia Beef Commission: PO Box 550, Truro NS B2N 5E3 – 902/893-6514; Fax: 902/897-9768
Manager, Vacant
• Nova Scotia Crop & Livestock Insurance Commission: PO Box 1092, Truro NS B2N 5G9 – 902/893-6370; Fax: 902/895-4622
Manager, Brian Mahoney
• Nova Scotia Dairy Commission: PO Box 782, Truro NS B2N 5E8 – 902/893-6379; Fax: 902/897-9768
Manager, Gabriel Comeau
• Nova Scotia Farm Loan Board: PO Box 550, Truro NS B2N 5E3 – 902/893-6506; Fax: 902/895-7693
Director, R.G. Adams, 902/893-6500, Email: RAdams@lcs.nsac.ns.ca
Senior Loan Officer, Wayne MacLeod, 902/893-6507
• Nova Scotia Grain & Forage Commission: Kentville Agricultural Centre, 32 Main St., Kentville NS B4N 1J5 – 902/893-6556; Fax: 902/893-0244
Contact, Dwane Mellish

Agricultural Marketing Boards & Commissions

• Natural Products Marketing Council: PO Box 550, Truro NS B2N 5E3 – 902/893-6380; Fax: 902/895-9403
Chair, S.F. Allaby
Acting Secretary, Linda MacDonald
• Nova Scotia Chicken Producers Board: PO Box 338, Canning NS B0P 1H0 – 902/582-7400; Fax: 902/582-7066
Secretary, Robert French
• Nova Scotia Egg & Pullet Producers Marketing Board: PO Box 1096, Truro NS B2N 5G9 – 902/895-6341; Fax: 902/895-6343
Secretary, James Bragg
• Nova Scotia Flue-Cured Tobacco Growers' Marketing Board: Blair House, Kentville Agricultural Centre, PO Box 154, Kentville NS B4N 3W4 – 902/678-0533; Fax: 902/679-1074
Secretary-Manager, Sonya D. MacKillop
• Nova Scotia Grain Marketing Board: PO Box 308, Kentville NS B4N 3X1 – 902/678-5512; Fax: 902/678-1215
Secretary Manager, A. Findlay MacRae
• Nova Scotia Greenhouse Vegetable Marketing Board: PO Box 1422, Truro NS B2N 5V2 – 902/893-3966; Fax: 902/897-9019
Manager, Marie Brody
• Nova Scotia Potato Marketing Board: Blair House, Kentville Agricultural Centre, Kentville NS B4N 1J5 – 902/678-0533; Fax: 902/679-1074
Secretary-Manager, Sonya D. MacKillop
• Nova Scotia Processing Pea & Bean Growers Marketing Board: Blair House, Kentville Agricultural Centre, Kentville NS B4N 1J5 – 902/678-0533; Fax: 902/679-1074
Secretary-Manager, Sonya D. MacKillop
• Nova Scotia Turkey Marketing Board: Blair House, Kentville Agricultural Centre, PO Box 130, Kentville NS B4N 3W4 – 902/678-5836; Fax: 902/679-1074
Operations Manager, Sonya Adams
• Nova Scotia Wool Marketing Board: PO Box 550, Truro NS B2N 5E3 – 902/893-6517; Fax: 902/893-6531
Secretary, Roy MacKenzie

• Pork Nova Scotia: PO Box 1341, Truro NS B2N 5N2 – 902/895-0581; Fax: 902/893-4236
Secretary, John Miller

Office of the AUDITOR GENERAL

#302, 1888 Brunswick St., Halifax NS B3J 3J8
902/424-5907; Fax: 902/424-4350; URL: http://www.gov.ns.ca/legi/audg/
Auditor General, Roy Salmon, F.C.A., 902/424-4046, Email: salmoner@gov.ns.ca
Senior Audit Director, Claude D. Carter, C.A., 902/424-4396
Administrative Asst., Darleen Langille, 902/424-4108

Department of BUSINESS & CONSUMER SERVICES (DBCS)

Joseph Howe Bldg., 1681 Granville St., PO Box 1003, Halifax NS B3J 2X1
902/424-7777; Fax: 902/424-7434; Email: bcs@gov.ns.ca; URL: http://www.gov.ns.ca/bacs/
  Announced in March 1996, the development of the new Department of Business & Consumer Affairs. The new department combines the following services: consumer & corporate relations & financial institutions divisions from the former Department of Housing & Consumer Affairs; vital statistics from the Department of Health; registry of motor vehicles from the former Department of Transortation; provincial tax commission; certain aspects of the Economic Renewal Agency; & the public inquiries service.

ACTS ADMINISTERED

Business & Electronic Filing Act
Cemetary & Funeral Services Act
Change of Name Act
Collection Agenices Act
Companies Act
Condominium Act
Consumer Creditors' Conduct Act
Consumer Protection Act
Consumer Reporting Act
Consumer Services Act
Corporations Registration Act
Corporations Securities Registration Act
Credit Union Act
Dangerous Goods Transportation Act
Direct Sellers' Licensing & Regulation Act
Embalmers & Funeral Directors Act
Future Services Act
Gaming Control Act
Gasoline & Diesel Oil Tax Act
Government Records Act
Health Services Tax Act
Homeowners' Incentive Grants Act
Insurance Act
Insurance Premiums Tax Act
Limited Partnerships Act
Liquor Control Act
Loan Companies Inspection Act
Mortgage Brokers' & Lenders' Registration Act
Motor Carrier Act
Motor Vehicle Act
Mutual Insurance Act
Off-Highway Vehicles Act
Partnerships & Business Names Registration Act
Private Investment Holding Companies Act
Public Accountants Act
Public Highways Act
Real Estate Broker's Licensing Act
Rental Property Conversion Act
Rent Review Act
Residential Tenancies Act
Revenue Act
Societies Act
Solemnization of Marriage Act
Summary Proceedings Act

Theatre & Amusements Act
Trust & Loans Companies Act
Unconscionable Transactions Relief Act
Vital Statistics Act
Minister, Hon. Sandra L. Jolly, 902/424-7579, Fax: 902/424-0754
Deputy Minister, A.A. Rovers, 902/424-7788
Director, Financial Institutions & Revenue, Paul LeBlanc

ACCESS NOVA SCOTIA
Joseph Howe Bldg., 1681 Granville St., Granville Level, PO Box 519, Halifax NS B3J 2X1
902/424-7009; Fax: 902/424-2633; Email: access@gov.ns.ca
Toll Free: 1-800-225-8227
Provincial agency responsible for providing government, community & business information as it pertains to current programs & services.

COMMUNICATIONS SERVICES/PUBLIC INQUIRIES OFFICE
One Government Place, 1700 Granville St., Ground Fl., PO Box 608, Halifax NS B3J 2R7
902/424-5200; Fax: 902/425-3026; Email: burnsca@gov.ns.ca
Toll Free: 1-800-670-4357
Acting Executive Director, Jim Vibert, 902/424-4886
Acting Coordinator, Carla Burns, 902/424-2876

CONSUMER & COMMERCIAL RELATIONS
Alderney Gate, 40 Alderney Dr., PO Box 815, Dartmouth NS B2Y 3Z3
902/424-5602; 5552; Fax: 902/424-8652
Toll Free: 1-800-774-5130
Acting Director, Barbara Jones-Gordon

PROVINCIAL TAX COMMISSION
1723 Hollis St., PO Box 755, Halifax NS B3J 2V4
902/424-4411; Fax: 902/424-0523; Email: keefeg@gov.ns.ca
Toll Free: 1-800-565-2336
Commissioner, Sean O'Connor, Email: OConnorS@gov.ns.ca

REGISTRY OF JOINT STOCK COMPANIES
Centennial Bldg., 1670 Hollis St., PO Box 1529, Halifax NS B3J 2Y4
902/424-7742; Fax: 902/424-4633; Email: jstocks@ra.isisnet.com; URL: http://www.gov.ns.ca/bacs/rjsc/
Acting Registrar, Pearl MacAulay

REGISTRY OF MOTOR VEHICLES
#215, 6061 Young St., PO Box 1652, Halifax NS B3J 2Z3
902/424-5851; Fax: 902/424-0544; Email: rmv@gov.ns.ca; URL: http://www.gov.ns.ca/bacs/rmv/
Toll Free: 1-800-898-7668
Executive Director, Marie Mullally, 902/424-0544

VITAL STATISTICS
Provincial Bldg., 1723 Hollis St., 1st Fl., Halifax NS B3J 2M9
902/424-4381; Fax: 902/424-0678; Email: Vstat@gov.ns.ca; URL: http://www.gov.ns.ca/bacs/vstat/
Responsible for the registration & supply of vital statitics information for the province. Official Birth, Marriage & Death certificates may be obtained through the service. Fee for each ordinary certificate is $20.00.
Deputy Registrar General, Vital Statistics, Betty Etter, 902/424-8907
Administrator, Information Systems & Vital Statistics, Dan Rice

Associated Agencies, Boards & Commissions
•Atlantic Lottery Corporation
See listing under New Brunswick Finance, this Section.

•Nova Scotia Gaming Control Commission: Metropolitan Place, 99 Wyse Rd., PO Box 545, Dartmouth NS B2Y 3Y8 – 902/424-7711; Fax: 902/424-3356
Chair, E. MacNeil
Executive Director, Dennis Kerr

Department of COMMUNITY SERVICES
Johnston Bldg., 5182 Prince St., 5th Fl., PO Box 696, Halifax NS B3J 2T7
902/424-4326; Fax: 902/424-0502

ACTS ADMINISTERED
Adoption Information Act
Adult Protection Act
Children & Family Services Act
Day Care Act
Disabled Persons' Commission Act
Family Benefits Act
Homes for Special Care Act
Infant Custody Act
Senior Citizens' Financial Aid Act
Senior Citizens' Secretariat Act
Social Assistance Act
Social Services Councils Act
Minister, Hon. John MacEachern, 902/424-4304, Fax: 902/424-0549
Deputy Minister, Gordon Gillis, 902/424-4325
Administrative Asst. to Deputy Minister, J.A.A. MacKinnon, 902/424-4326
Administrator, Finance & Administration, George Hudson, 902/424-2750
Director, Audit Services, Colleen Cooper, 902/424-4147
Director, Reform Initiatives & Communications, Donna McCready, 902/424-4326

FAMILY & CHILDREN'S SERVICES
Administrator, Jane Fitzgerald, 902/424-4279
Director, Child Welfare, George Savoury, 902/424-5653
Director, Community Residential & Outreach Services, Trevor Townsend, 902/424-5170
Acting Director, Prevention Services, Joan Parks, 902/424-3204
Director, Transitional Planning & Supply Services & Services to the Mentally Handicapped, William McCarron, 902/424-5863

INCOME & EMPLOYMENT SUPPORT
Administrator, Ron L'Esperance, 902/424-6762
Acting Director, Community Support for Adults, Barbara Carbonnell, 902/424-0930
Director, Employment Support Services, Vacant, 902/424-4329
Director, Income Assistance, Peter Barteaux, 902/424-4262

STRATEGIC PLANNING & POLICY
Administrator, Shulamith Medjock, 902/424-4039
Coordinator, Family Violence Prevention Initiative, Judy Hughes, 902/424-2079
Director, Program Evaluation Review & Research, Elizabeth McNaughton, 902/424-7900
Director, Staff & Management Support Services, Greg Gammon, 902/424-3960

Regional Offices
Eastern: Sydney NS – 902/563-3300, Administrator, Francis Capstick
Halifax: Metro One Bldg., 6061 Young St., Halifax NS B3K 2A3 – 902/424-4755, Administrator, William Campbell
Northern: New Glasgow NS – 902/755-5950, Administrator, Nina Clark
Western: Kentville NS – 902/678-6176, Administrator, F.A. Bowes

Associated Agencies, Boards & Commissions
•Nova Scotia Disabled Persons Commission
Listed alphabetically in detail, this Section.
•Nova Scotia Residential Centre: Truro NS – 902/893-3029
Acting Chief Administrator, Helen Ingraham
•Senior Citizens Secretariat: 1740 Granville St., 4th Fl., PO Box 2065, Halifax NS B3J 2Z1 – 902/424-6322; Fax: 902/424-0561
Director, Brian Vandervaart

Nova Scotia DISABLED PERSONS COMMISSION
#203, 2695 Dutch Village Rd., Halifax NS B3L 4T9
902/424-8280; Fax: 902/424-0592
Toll Free: 1-800-565-8280 (within Nova Scotia)
Chair, Reid Nicholson
Executive Director, Charles Macdonald

Nova Scotia ECONOMIC RENEWAL AGENCY
1800 Argyle St., PO Box 519, Halifax NS B3J 2R7
902/424-8920; Fax: 902/424-0582; Email: econ.era@gov.ns.ca; URL: http://www.gov.ns.ca/ecor/

ACTS ADMINISTERED
Bedford Waterfront Development Act
Business Development Corporation Act
Camping Establishments Regulation Act
Cooperative Associations Act
Economic Renewal Agency Act
Hotel Regulations Act
Industrial Development Act
Industrial Estates Limited Act
Industrial Loan Act
Industry Closing Act
Innovation Corporation Act
Nova Scotia Film Development Corporation Act
Research Foundation Corporation Act
Small Business Development Act
Sydney Waterfront Development Corporation Act
Tartan Act
Trade Development Authority Act
Venture Corporation Act
Voluntary Planning Act
Minister Responsible, Hon. Richard W. Mann, 902/424-5680, Fax: 902/424-0514, Email: econ.minister@gov.ns.ca
Deputy Minister, C.H. (Bert) Loveless, C.A., 902/424-3231, Email: econ.deputy@gov.ns.ca
Special Asst. to Deputy Minister, David Oxner, 902/424-6632
Senior Policy Coordinator, Policy & Coordination, Robert Doherty, 902/424-6624
Senior Advisor, Communications & Public Relations, Steve Warburton, 902/424-0927

COMMUNITY ECONOMIC DEVELOPMENT
EMail: econ.ced@gov.ns.ca
Executive Director, Chris Bryant, 902/424-3545
Director, Regional Operations, Neal Conrad, 902/424-6014
Acting Coordinator, Provincial Employment Program, Brian Watson, 902/424-2106

Canada Nova Scotia Business Service Centre
1575 Brunswick St., Halifax NS B3J 2G1
902/426-8604; Fax: 902/426-6530; Email: halifax@cbsc.ic.gc.ca
Toll Free: 1-800-668-1010
Faxback: 902/426-3201

CORPORATE SERVICES
Executive Director, Brian McDonough, 902/424-7444
Director, Human Resources, Janet Lee, 902/424-7439
Manager, Accounting, David MacKay, 902/424-7446

Canadian Almanac & Directory 1997

GOVERNMENT OF NOVA SCOTIA

INVESTMENT & TRADE
EMail: econ.iat@gov.ns.ca
Trade Development Centre: 902/424-5448; Fax: 902/424-5739
Executive Director, Roy Sherwood, 902/424-3656
Director, Trade, Andy Hare, 902/424-3672
Officer, Investment, Tab Borden, 902/424-3821
Officer, Investment, Marilyn Mullett, 902/424-8282
Officer, Investment, Tom Mulrooney, 902/424-6142
Officer, Investment, Craig Stanfield, 902/424-6140

LENDING & FINANCIAL SERVICES
Executive Director, Donald A. Leet, 902/424-8958
Director, Lending, Doug Giannou, 902/424-6867

NOVA SCOTIA MARKETING AGENCY
Executive Director, Dan Brennan, 902/424-4554
Director, Marketing Policy & Creative Services, Rae Owen, 902/424-0664
Specialist, Attractions & Events, Patricia Lynch, 902/424-4678
Specialist, Market Development, Minto Stewart, 902/424-4646
Specialist, Travel Trade, Rick Young, 902/424-4182

TOURISM NOVA SCOTIA
Executive Director, Michele McKenzie, 902/424-2989
Coordinator, Enquiries, Robert Boyd, 902/424-2906
Supervisor, Tourist Information Centre, Kathryn Malone, 902/424-4576

Foreign Office
United States: 4 Copley Sq., Boston MA 02116, USA – 617/262-7677; Fax: 617/262-7689, Director of Nova Scotia in New England, Gary MacPherson

Associated Agencies, Boards & Commissions
• Innovation Corporation (InNOVAcorp): Woodside Industrial Park, 101 Research Dr., PO Box 790, Dartmouth NS B2Y 3Z7 – 902/424-8670; Fax: 902/424-4679; Email: corpcomm@innovacorp.ns.ca; URL: http:www.innovacorp.ns.ca, Toll Free: 1-800-565-7051
  A technology commercialization corporation formed in 1995 to promote relationships that enable Nova Scotia firms to compete internationally. Offers scientific, engineering & business extension services to assist in developing new technology-based products & services, then helps Nova Scotia companies develop trade ties for these products. Works in cooperation with universities, research institutions & the private sector.
  CEO, Ross McCurdy
  COO, Bob MacNeill, 902/424-8670, ext.114, Email: bmacneill@innovacorp.ns.ca
  CFO, Bob MacNeil
  Executive Director, Corporate Affairs, Kimberly MacDonald-Vibert
  Executive Director, Business Development, Randolf Harrold
• Nova Scotia Business Development Corporation: World Trade & Convention Centre, 1800 Argyle St., 6th Fl., Halifax NS B3J 2R7 – 902/424-6488; Fax: 902/424-6823
  Encourages business development & promote employment opportunities in the province. Offers secured business project financing to companies qualifying for assistance.
• Nova Scotia Film Development Corporation: 1724 Granville St., Halifax NS B3J 1X5 – 902/424-7177, 7185; Email: nsfdc@fox.nstn.ca; URL: http://fox.nstn.ca/ZXnsfdc/
  Chair, Vacant
• Nova Scotia Research Foundation Corporation: Woodside Industrial Park, 101 Research Dr., PO Box 790, Dartmouth NS B2Y 3Z7 – 902/424-8670; Fax: 902/424-4679; Email: coconnell@nsrfc.ns.ca; URL: http://www.nsrfc.ns.ca

President, Dr. Ross McCurdy
• Waterfront Development Corporation Ltd.: 1751 Lower Water St., Halifax NS B3J 1S5 – 902/422-6591; Fax: 902/422-7582
President & CEO, Fred Were
• World Trade & Convention Centre: 1800 Argyle St., PO Box 955, Halifax NS B3J 2V9 – 902/421-8686; Fax: 902/422-2922
President & CEO, Fred MacGillivray

Department of EDUCATION & CULTURE
2021 Brunswick St., PO Box 578, Halifax NS B3J 2S9
902/424-5168; Fax: 902/424-0511; URL: http://www.ednet.ns.ca/

ACTS ADMINISTERED
Apprenticeship & Trades Qualifications Act
Art Gallery Act
Culture, Recreation & Fitness Act, 1973 & amendment in 1981
Degree Granting Act
Education Act & Regulations
Education Assistance Act
Education of the Blind Act
Educational Communications Agency Act
Gaelic College Foundation Act
Handicapped Persons' Education Act & Regulations
Hospital Education Assistance Act
Libraries Act & Regulations
Maritime Provinces Higher Education (Nova Scotia) Act
Multiculturalism Act
Nova Scotia Community College Act
Nova Scotia Museum Act
Nova Scotia School Boards Association Act
Public Archives of Nova Scotia Act
School Boards Act
Sherbrooke Restoration Commission Act
Shubenacadie Canal Commission Act
Special Places Protection Act
Student Aid Act
Tartan Act
Teachers' Collective Bargaining Act
Teaching Profession Act
Trade Schools Regulation Act
Universities Assistance Act
Universities Foundation Act

Minister, Hon. Robert S. Harrison, 902/424-4236, Fax: 902/424-0680
Deputy Minister, Robert P. Moody, 902/424-5643, Email: moodyrp@gov.ns.ca
Communications Officer, Donna MacDonald, 902/424-2615, Fax: 902/424-0680, Email: macdondc@gov.ns.ca
Director, Human Resources, Susan Crandall, 902/424-5766, Fax: 902/424-0657, Email: crandase@gov.ns.ca

ACADIAN & FRENCH LANGUAGE SERVICES BRANCH
Executive Director, Charles Gaudet, 902/424-6097, Fax: 902/424-0613, Email: gaudetcj@gov.ns.ca
Director, Programs Division, Margelaine Holding, 902/424-6327, Email: holdinms@gov.ns.ca

COMMUNITY COLLEGE BRANCH
Executive Director, Gerrie Masters, 902/424-4060, Fax: 902/424-0643, Email: mastermg@gov.ns.ca
Director, Apprenticeship Training Division, Peter Woods, 902/424-8903, Fax: 902/424-0717, Email: woodspr@gov.ns.ca
CEO, Collège de l'Acadie, Réal Samson, PO Box 24, Saulnierville NS B0W 2Z0, 902/769-0851, Fax: 902/769-0165
CEO, Nova Scotia Community College, Jack Buckley, 902/424-4166, Fax: 902/424-0717, Email: bucklejw@gov.ns.ca

FINANCE & OPERATIONS BRANCH
Executive Director, Douglas Nauss, 902/424-3646, Fax: 902/424-0732, Email: naussde@gov.ns.ca
Acting Director, Facilities, Planning & Equipment Division, Charles Clattenburg, 902/424-4386, Email: clattecd@gov.ns.ca
Director, Financial Management Division, Reg Clayton, 902/424-5698, Email: claytowr@gov.ns.ca
Director, Grants & Audit Division, Richard Morris, 902/424-3956, Email: morrisre@gov.ns.ca
Director, Student Assistance Office, Kathleen Thompson, 902/424-8433, Fax: 902/424-0540, Email: thompski@gov.ns.ca

HERITAGE & CULTURE BRANCH (NOVA SCOTIA MUSEUM)
Executive Director, Candace Stevenson, 902/424-6472, Fax: 902/424-0560, Email: stevencj@gov.ns.ca
Director, Cultural Affairs Division, Allison Bishop, 901/425-5929, Fax: 901/424-0710
Director, Maritime Museum of the Atlantic, David Flemming, 902/424-6440, Fax: 902/424-0612, Email: flemmidb@gov.ns.ca
Director, Museum Services Division, Robert Frame, 902/424-6478, Fax: 902/424-0560, Email: framerw@gov.ns.ca
Director, Nova Scotia Museum of Natural History, Debra Burleson, 902/424-7353, Fax: 902/424-0560
Director, Planning & Communications Division, Vacant, 902/424-6471, Fax: 902/424-0560

POLICY BRANCH
Executive Director, Wayne Doggett, 902/424-4377, Fax: 902/424-0626, Email: doggetwf@gov.ns.ca
Director, Planning & Research Division, Maryann Ricketts, 902/424-5631, Fax: 902/424-0626, Email: ricketmh@gov.ns.ca
Acting Director, Publication & Communication Division, Rusty McClelland, 902/424-7747, Fax: 902/424-0519, Email: mcclelrs@gov.ns.ca
Director, Regional Inspection Division, Gail Maclean, 902/424-5829, Fax: 902/424-0519, Email: macleabg@gov.ns.ca
Director, Testing & Evaluation Division, Bette Kelly, 902/424-7746, Fax: 902/424-0614, Email: kellybl@gov.ns.ca
Provincial Librarian, Provincial Library, Marion Pape, 902/424-2457, Fax: 902/424-0633

PROGRAM BRANCH
Executive Director, Tom Rich, 902/424-5799, Fax: 902/424-0749, Email: richt@gov.ns.ca
Acting Director, Education Media Services, Michael Jeffrey, 902/424-2462, Fax: 902/424-0633
Acting Director, English Program Services Division, Robert LeBlanc, 902/424-5745, Fax: 902/424-0613, Email: leblanrm@gov.ns.ca
Director, Extension Services Division, Nancy Hyland, 902/424-8880, Fax: 902/424-0666, Email: hylandnm@gov.ns.ca
Director, Student Services Division, Anne Power, 902/424-7454, Fax: 902/424-0749, Email: powerda@gov.ns.ca

Associated Agencies, Boards & Commissions
• Nova Scotia Council on Higher Education: 2021 Burnswick St., PO Box 2086, Stn M, Halifax NS B3J 3B7 – 902/424-6992; Fax: 902/424-0651; Email: halliwje@gov.ns.ca
Executive Director, Dr. Janet Halliwell
• Nova Scotia Provincial Apprenticeship Board: PO Box 578, Halifax NS B3J 2S9 – 902/424-0872; Fax: 902/424-0717; Email: hlfxtrad.educ.youngsl@gov.ns.ca; URL: http://www.ednet.ns.ca/educ/abc/apprent/apprenhp.htm
Executive Secretary, Bernie Mac Donald

Canadian Almanac & Directory 1997

Nova Scotia ELECTIONS OFFICE
Joseph Howe Bldg., 9th Fl., PO Box 2246, Halifax NS B3J 3C8
902/424-8584; Fax: 902/424-6622
Election Supply Centre, 2543 Barrington St., Halifax NS B3K 2X2
902/424-4375
Acting Chief Electoral Officer, Janet Willwerth

Nova Scotia EMERGENCY MEASURES ORGANIZATION (EMO)
PO Box 2107, Halifax NS B3J 3B7
902/424-5620; Fax: 902/424-5376
Minister Responsible, Hon. F. Wayne Adams, 902/4242358, Fax: 902/424-0644
Director, Michael R. Lester, 902/424-5620, Email: hlfxterm.envi.lestermr@gov.ns.ca
Program Administration Officer, Michael Myette
Coordinator Joint Planning, C.A. Tony Mansell
Training Officer, Tanya Crawford

Zone Offices
Cape Breton: PO Box 714, Sydney NS B1P 6J7 – 902/563-2093; Fax: 902/563-0502, 2319, Zone Controller, Winston Musgrave
Central: PO Box 824, Truro NS B2N 5G6 – 902/893-5896; Fax: 902/893-1648, Zone Controller, William A. Weagle
Western: PO Box 1240, Middleton NS B0S 1P0 – 902/825-2181; Fax: 902/825-4471, Zone Controller, J.A. Andersen

Department of the ENVIRONMENT
PO Box 2107, Halifax NS B3J 3B7
902/424-5300; Fax: 902/424-0644; URL: http://www.gov.ns.ca/envi/

ACTS ADMINISTERED
Clean Nova Scotia Foundation Act
Dangerous Goods & Hazardous Wastes Management Act
Derelict Vehicles Removal Act
Emergency "911" Act
Emergency Measures Act
Environmental Assessment Act
Environmental Protection Act
Environmental Trust Act
Litter Abatement Act
Ozone Layer Protection Act
Pest Control Products (Nova Scotia) Act
Recycling Act
Salvage Yards Licensing Act
Water Act
Well Drilling Act
Youth Conservation Corps Act
Minister, Hon. F. Wayne Adams, 902/424-2358
Deputy Minister, Wayne J. Grady, 902/424-2359, Fax: 902/424-0644
Director, Finance, Scott Nicholson, 902/424-2362, Fax: 902/424-0503
Public Relations, Margaret Murphy, 902/424-2575

ENVIRONMENTAL INDUSTRIES & TECHNOLOGIES DIVISION
902/424-7025; Fax: 902/424-0644; URL: http://www.gov.ns.ca/envi/infoserv/eit/home.htm
Asst. Deputy Minister, Lin Chang, 902/424-3617
Director, Robert Langdon, 902/424-2386
Manager, Trade & Marketing, Mauritz Erhard, 902/424-5205

ENVIRONMENTAL SUPPORT SERVICES DIVISION
902/424-6305; Fax: 902/424-0501
Acting Director, William Smith, 902/424-5071
Acting Manager, Environmental Review Branch, Andrew Kendall, 902/424-6343, Fax: 902/424-0501
Manager, Enforcement Branch, Derek White, 902/424-6341
Manager, Training & Education Services Branch, Lee Lewis, 902/424-6304

POLICY PLANNING & COORDINATION DIVISION
902/424-4944; Fax: 902/424-0501
Director, Frances Martin, 902/424-5695
Asst. Director, Policy & Planning Branch, Frances Martin, 902/424-8695
Director, Research, Statistics & Studies Branch, Vacant

REGIONAL OFFICES DIVISION
902/424-2547; Fax: 902/424-0569
Director, Creighton Brisco, 902/424-2548

Regional Offices
Central: Sunnyside Mall, #307, 1595 Bedford Hwy., Bedford NS B4A 3Y4 – 902/424-3862; Fax: 902/424-0597
Eastern: 295 Charlotte St., Sydney NS B1P 6H7 – 902/563-2100; Fax: 902/563-0502
Northern: IGA Bldg., 44 Inglis St., 2nd Fl., PO Box 824, Truro NS B2N 4G6 – 902/893-5880; Fax: 902/893-0282
Western: Kentville NS – 902/679-6086; Fax: 902/679-6186

RESOURCE MANAGEMENT & POLLUTION CONTROL DIVISION
902/424-2375; Fax: 902/424-0503
Director, Clive Oldreive, 902/424-2385
Manager, Air Quality Branch, Creighton Brisco, 902/424-2550
Manager, Industrial Pollution Control Branch, Dan E. Hiltz, 902/424-2284
Asst. Manager, Pesticide Management Branch, Craig Morrison, 902/424-2541
Manager, Water Resources Branch, Andrew Cameron, 902/424-2554

UTILITIES DIVISION
Fax: 902/424-0503
Director, George Searle, 902/424-2581
Supervisor, Construction, Robert Anderson, 902/424-2580

Nova Scotia Round Table on Environment & Economy
c/o Department of Environment, PO Box 2107, Halifax NS B3J 3B7
902/424-6345; Fax: 902/424-0501
Co-Chair, Hon. F. Wayne Adams
Co-Chair, Hon. John P. Savage, Email: jsavage@fox.nstn.ca
Provincial Coordinator, Patricia Hinch

Associated Agencies, Boards & Commissions
• Nova Scotia Environmental Assessment Board: PO Box 2107, Halifax NS B3J 3B7 – 902/424-2574; Fax: 902/424-0503
CEO, Shirley L. Nicholson
• Nova Scotia Environmental Trust Fund: PO Box 2107, Halifax NS B3J 3B7 – 902/424-6346; Fax: 902/424-0501
Secretariat, Jeanne Bourque
• Nova Scotia Emergency Measures Organization
Listed alphabetically in detail, this section.
• Nova Scotia Resource Recovery Fund Board: PO Box 2107, Halifax NS B3J 3B7 – 902/424-2577; Fax: 902/424-0503
Representatives of groups that contribute to the Fund will consider applications to spend the money for recycling projects & litter abatement.
Administrator, Laurie Lewis

Department of FINANCE
PO Box 187, Halifax NS B3J 2N3
902/424-5554; Fax: 902/424-0635; URL: http://www.gov.ns.ca/fina/

ACTS ADMINISTERED
Appropriations Act
Corporations Capital Tax Act
Equity Tax Act
Expenditure Control Act
Income Tax Act
Members' Retiring Allowances Act
Nova Scotia Stock Savings Plan Act
Pension Benefits Act
Provincial Finance Act
Public Service Superannuation Act
Succession Duty Act
Teachers' Plan Act & Regulations
Minister, Hon. J. William Gillis, Ph.D., 902/424-5720, Fax: 902/424-0635
Deputy Minister, Robert P. Moody, 902/424-5553, Fax: 902/424-0635, Email: moodyrp@gov.ns.ca
Acting Controller, Glenn Hynes, C.A., 902/424-5944, Email: HynesG@gov.ns.ca
Financial Counsel, James Spurr, 902/424-7698
Director, Accounting Services, R. Noble, C.M.A., 902/424-5761
Director, Administration, Ivan Richardson, C.M.A., 902/424-2430
Director, Budget, Lynne Burrell, C.A., 902/424-5029
Director, Internal Audit, Vicki Dimick, 902/424-2407
Director, Management Information Systems, Holly Fancy, 902/424-3993
Director, Payroll Services, S. MacDonald, 902/424-5902

FISCAL & ECONOMIC POLICY BRANCH
Acting Executive Director, Elizabeth Cody, 902/424-4160, Email: codye@gov.ns.ca
Director, Economic Policy Division, Charlie Pye
Acting Director, Fiscal Policy, Bruce Hennebury, 902/424-4168, Fax: 902/424-0590, Email: hennebub@gov.ns.ca
Director, Statistics Division, Paul Dober, 902/424-5691, Fax: 902/424-0714, Email: doberp@gov.ns.ca

INVESTMENTS, PENSIONS & TREASURY SERVICES BRANCH
Executive Director, Richard W. McAloney, CA, CFA, CIA, 902/424-5557, Email: mcaloner@gov.ns.ca
Superintendent, Pension Registration, Nancy MacNeill, 902/424-8915, Email: hlfxprov.fina.macneiln@gov.ns.ca
Director, Investments, Peter Vanloon, 902/424-4140
Director, Liability Management & Treasury Services Division, Douglas Stratton, 902/424-4475, Fax: 902/429-0257, Email: strattod@gov.ns.ca
Director, Pensions, Robert Jack, 902/424-5911

GOVERNMENT PURCHASING AGENCY/PUBLIC TENDERS OFFICE
Central Services Bldg., 6176 Young St., Suite 120, Halifax NS B3K 2A6
902/424-5520; Fax: 902/463-5732; URL: http://www.gov.ns.ca/fina/ptns/index.htm
Director, George Murphy, Email: ssvsgpa.murphyg@gov.ns.ca

Department of FISHERIES
Bank of Montreal Bldg., 5151 George St., 7th Fl., PO Box 2223, Halifax NS B3J 3C4
902/424-4560; Fax: 902/424-4671; URL: http://www.gov.ns.ca/fish/
Pictou Office: 902/485-8031

ACTS ADMINISTERED
Aquaculture Act

GOVERNMENT OF NOVA SCOTIA

Fisheries Act
Fisheries Development Act
Irish Moss Act
Sea Plant Harvesting Act
Minister, Hon. James A. Barkhouse, 902/424-8953
Deputy Minister, Alan Steel, 902/424-0300
Director, Financial Services Division, Frank Dunn, 902/424-4560
Director, Human Resources Division, Frank MacLean, 902/424-4560
Director, Training Division, Barbara Riley, 902/424-0328

AQUACULTURE DIVISION
Acting Director, Alan Chandler, 902/424-3644
Manager, Aquaculture Development, I. Judson, 902/424-3644
Supervisor, Development Unit, C. Reardon, 902/424-0324
Supervisor, Licensing Unit, C. Morrison, 902/424-0354

INLAND FISHERIES DIVISION
Director, Murray Hill, 902/485-7021
Asst. Director, Don A. MacLean, RR#3, St. Andrews NS B0H 1X0, 902/485-7022
Manager, Fraser's Mill Trout Hatchery, D.D. Murrant, RR#3, St. Andrews NS B0H 1X0, 902/783-2926
Manager, Mcgowan Lake Trout Hatchery, Michael MacNeil, PO Box 141, Caledonia NS B0T 1B0, 902/682-2576

MARKETING DIVISION
902/424-0333
Director, Janis Raymond, 902/424-0330
Seafood Consultant, A. Estelle Bryant, 902/424-0331

POLICY, PLANNING DIVISION
902/424-0350
Director, A.A. Longard, 902/424-0347
Advisor, Marine Resources (Groundfish), C. F. MacKinnon, 902/424-0349
Advisor, Marine Resources (Invertebrates), S. Gregory Roach, 902/424-0348
Advisor, Marine Resources (Pelagics), Dr. Robert Crawford, 902/424-0351

TECHNOLOGY & INSPECTION DIVISION
902/424-0343
Director, David Hansen, 902/424-0337
Manager, Technology Development, Marshall Giles, 902/424-0336

Associated Agencies, Boards & Commissions
•Fisheries Loan Board: Bank of Montreal Bldg., 5151 George St., 7th Fl., Halifax NS B3J 3C4 – 902/424-0312; Fax: 902/424-4671
Chair, J.A. Marsters
Director, J.P. Sarty

Department of HEALTH
Joseph Howe Bldg., 1690 Hollis St., 12th Fl., PO Box 488, Halifax NS B3J 2R8
902/424-4310; Fax: 902/424-0559

ACTS ADMINISTERED
Adult Protection Act
AIDS Advisory Commission Act
An Act to Restrict the Privatization of Medical Services
Anatomy Act
Camp Hill Hospital Act
Cancer Treatment & Research Foundation Act
Cape Breton Regional Hospital Act
Change of Name Act
Children & Family Services Act
Chiropractic Act
Cobequid Multi-Service Centre Act
Dental Act
Dental Technicians Act
Denturist Act
Disabled Persons' Commission Act
Dispensing Opticians Act
Drug Dependency Act
Emergency Health Services Act
Fatality Inquiries Act
Halifax Infirmary Act
Health Act
Health Council Act
Health Services & Insurance Act
Homes for Special Care Act
Hospital Services Planning Commission Act
Hospital Trusts Act
Hospitals Act
Human Tissue Gift Act
Incompetent Persons Act
Individual Hospital Acts of Incorporation
Medical Act
Medical Consent Act
Medical Radiation Technologists Act
Medical Services Act
Municipal Hospitals Loan Act
Narcotic Drug Addicts Act
N.S. Hospital Foundation Act
N.S. Sanatorium Act
Nursing Assistants Act
Occupational Therapists Act
Optometry Act
Pharmacy Act
Physiotherapy Act
Professional Dietitians Act
Provincial Health Council Act
Psychologists Act
Regional Health Boards Act
Registered Nurses Association Act
Solemnization of Marriage Act
Tobacco Access Act
Victoria General Hospital Act
Vital Statistics Act
Minister, Hon. J. Bernard Boudreau, Q.C., 902/424-3377, Fax: 902/424-0559
Deputy Minister, Lucy Dobbin, 902/424-7570
Legal Counsel, W.D. Cochrane, 902/424-7729

CORPORATE SERVICES
Executive Director, Don Sweete, 902/424-5948
Director, Revenue & Recovery, Harold McCarthy, 902/424-6202

INSURED PROGRAMS MANAGEMENT
Services include insured programs, pharmaceutical services, ambulance services & administrative services.
Executive Director, Derek Dinham, 902/424-8902, Fax: 902/424-0605

POLICY & PLANNING
Offers program planning, policy development, research statistics & evaluation & AIDS advisory assistance.
Executive Director, Malcolm Maxwell

REGIONAL SUPPORT
Responsible for the delivery of facility, public health, drug dependency & home care services consistent with a regional model.
Executive Director, Dennis P. Holland, 902/424-4270, Fax: 902/424-0550
Administrator, Public Health Services, Janet Braunstein, 902/424-5011

SYSTEMS REFORM
Provides community support services, community planning services, transition planning, & community development services.
Executive Director, Mary Jane Hampton

Associated Agencies, Boards & Commissions
•Cancer Treatment & Research Foundation of Nova Scotia
Listed in Section 2, see Index.
•Nova Scotia Advisory Commission on AIDS: 1740 Granville St., 6th Fl., Halifax NS B3J 1X5 – 902/424-5730; Fax: 902/424-0558
Chair, W.C. Hart, Ph.D.
•Provincial Health Council: #406, Centennial Bldg., 1660 Hollis St., Halifax NS B3J 1V7 – 902/424-7155; Fax: 902/424-0598
Acting Executive Director, Karen Parent
•Emergency Health Services Nova Scotia: c/o Dept. of Health, PO Box 488, Halifax NS B3J 2R8 – 902/424-3928
Jurisdictional responsibilities for all prehospital emergency health services delivery, including ambulance services, first responder & trauma programs, public access & routine critical care inter-hospital transfers.
Commissioner, Dr. Mike Murphy

Department of HOUSING & MUNICIPAL AFFAIRS
PO Box 216, Halifax NS B3J 2M4
902/424-4141; Fax: 902/424-0531; URL: http://www.gov.ns.ca/homa/
Physical Address: Summit Place, 1601 Lower Water St., 4th Fl., Halifax NS B3J 1S2

ACTS ADMINISTERED
Assessment Act
Building Access Act
Building Code Act
Cape Breton Regional Municipality Act
Deed Transfer Tax Act
Ditches & Water Courses Act
Fences & Detention of Stray Livestock Act
Fences & Impounding of Animals Act
Heritage Property Act
Housing Act
Housing Development Corporation Act
Industrial Commissions Act
Louisbourg District Planning & Development Commission Act
Metropolitan Authority Act
Municipal Act
Municipal Affairs Act
Municipal Boundaries & Representation Act
Municipal Conflict of Interest Act
Municipal Elections Act
Municipal Finance Corporation Act
Municipal Grants Act
Municipal Housing Corporations Act
Municipal Loan & Building Fund Act
Planning Act
Regional Transit Authority Act
Registry Act
Rural Fire District Act
Sheep Protection & Dog Regulation Act
Shopping Centre Development Act
Stray Animals Act
Time Definition Act
Towns Act
Village Service Act
Minister, Hon. James A. Smith, M.D., 902/424-5550, Fax: 902/424-0581
Deputy Minister, Edward G. Cramm, 902/424-4100
Executive Director, Assessment Services Division, John MacKay, 902/424-5671
Executive Director, Municipal Services Division, David Darrow, 902/424-7415
Director, Land Information Management Services, Nancy Vanstone, 902/424-7136
Director, Land Use Committee, A. Montgomery, 902/424-4089
Director, Policy Development & Research, Vacant, 902/424-5901

Canadian Almanac & Directory 1997

Asst. Director, Finance & Advisory Services, Vince Smith, 902/424-5744
Departmental Solicitor, Cathleen O'Grady, 902/424-7716
Departmental Solicitor, Christine McCulloch, 902/424-7485
Information Officer, Michelle Whalen, 902/424-6336

NOVA SCOTIA GEOMATICS CENTRE
16 Station St., Amherst NS B4H 3E3
902/667-7231; Fax: 902/667-6008; Email: info@nsgc.gov.ns.ca; URL: http://www.nsgc.gov.ns.ca
Toll Free: 1-800-798-0706
Director, Rob Doiron, Email: rdoiron@fox.nstn.ns.ca
Manager, Client Services, Curt Speight
Manager, Database Development, Bert Seely

REGISTRY OF DEEDS
PO Box 2205, Halifax NS B3J 3C4
902/424-8571
Registrar, R.A. Hickey

Associated Agencies, Boards & Commissions
- Nova Scotia Amusements Regulation Board: PO Box 607, Halifax NS B3J 2R7 – 902/424-4690
Chair, Dennis Kerr
- Nova Scotia Liquor Commission
Listed alphabetically in detail, this Section.
- Nova Scotia Liquor License Board
Listed alphabetically in detail, this Section.
- Nova Scotia Municipal Finance Corporation: Founders Square, #602, 1701 Hollis St., PO Box 850, Stn M, Halifax NS B3J 2V2 – 902/424-4590; Fax: 902/424-0525
Chair, Edward G. Cramm
Secretary, G. Harding
CEO & Treasurer, Shirley Carras
- Nova Scotia Residential Tenancies Board: PO Box 998, Halifax NS B3J 2X3 – 902/424-4690
Acting Director, Barbara Jones-Gordon

Department of HUMAN RESOURCES
One Government Place, 1700 Granville St., PO Box 943, Halifax NS B3J 2V9
902/424-7660; Fax: 902/424-0611;
Email: humr.webmaster@gov.ns.ca; URL: http://www.gov.ns.ca/humr/
TDD: 424-3966

Lead government human resources agency responsible for providing leadership in the development & implementation of human resource policies & practices applicable to civil servants in all agencies of government. The department also provides advisory services to government & the public sector, & is responsible for negotiating & directing the negotiations for specific employee groups paid from public funds.
Minister, Hon. Allister Surrette, 902/424-5465, Fax: 902/424-0555
Deputy Minister, Mildred M. Royer, 902/424-6617, Fax: 902/424-0555
Director, Client Services, Judith Sulliban-Corney, 902/424-5633, Fax: 902/424-0611
Director, Corporate Services, George Fox, 902/424-4086, Fax: 902/424-0956
Director, Research & Organizational Design, B. Bruce MacCharles, 902/424-3924, Fax: 902/424-0589

Associated Agencies, Boards & Commissions
- Advisory Council on the Status of Women
Listed alphabetically in detail, this Section.
- Nova Scotia Sport & Recreation Commission: 1888 Brunswick St., 5th Fl., PO Box 864, Halifax NS B3J 2V2 – 902/424-7512; Fax: 902/424-0520
Executive Director, Dr. William H. White, 902/424-7554
Manager, Recreation Policy, Michael Arthur, 902/424-7629

- Nova Scotia Youth Secretariat: One Government Place, 1700 Granville St., 5th Fl., PO Box 1617, Halifax NS B3J 2Y3 – 902/424-3780; Fax: 902/424-7638
Executive Director, Richard Gilbert

Nova Scotia HUMAN RIGHTS COMMISSION
Lord Nelson Arcade, 5675 Spring Garden Rd., 7th Fl., PO Box 2221, Halifax NS B3J 3C4
902/424-4111; Fax: 902/424-0596; URL: http://www.gov.ns.ca/just/humanrts/
TYY: 902/424-3139

ACTS ADMINISTERED
Human Rights Act
Chair, Mary MacLennan
Executive Director, Wayne Mackay
Public Education Officer, May Lui

Regional Offices
Digby: Basin Place, 68 Water St., PO Box 1029, Digby NS B0V 1A0 – 902/245-4791; Fax: 902/245-5011
New Glasgow: Bridgeview Sq., 115 Maclean St., PO Box 728, New Glasgow NS B2H 4M5 – 902/752-3086; Fax: 902/755-7239
Sydney: Provincial Bldg., Prince St., Sydney NS B1P 5L1 – 902/563-2140; Fax: 902/563-5613

Department of JUSTICE
5151 Terminal Rd., PO Box 7, Halifax NS B3J 2L6
902/424-7125; Fax: 902/424-0510;
Email: hlfxterm.just.wilsonfi@gov.ns.ca;
URL: http://www.gov.ns.ca/just/

ACTS ADMINISTERED
Accountant General of the Supreme Court Act
Age of Majority Act
Alimony Act
Alternative Penalty Act
Anatomy Act
Angling Act
Apportionment Act
Arbitration Act
Architects Act
Assignment of Book Debts Act
Assignments & Preferences Act
Barristers & Solicitors Act
Beneficiaries Designation Act
Bills of Landing Act
Bills of Sale Act
Bulk Sales Act
Canada & the United Kingdom Reciprocal Recognition & Enforcement of Judgments Act
Cape Breton Barristers' Society Act
Child Abduction Act
Collection Act
Companies Act
Companies Winding Up Act
Conditional Sales Act
Constables Act
Constables' Protection Act
Constitutional Questions Act
Contributory Negligence Act
Controverted Elections Act
Conveyancing Act
Corporations Miscellaneous Provisions Act
Corporations Securities Registration Act
Corrections Act
Costs & Fees Act
Court Houses & Lockups Act
Court for Divorce & Matrimonial Causes Act
Court Reporters Act
Court Security Act
Creditors' Relief Act
Defamation Act
Demise of the Crown Act
Ditches & Water Courses Act
Elections Act
Engineering Profession Act
Escheats Act
Estate Actions Act
Estreats Act
Evidence Act
Expropriation Act, 1973
Family Orders Information Release Act
Fatal Injuries Act
Fatal Inquiries Act
Fences & Detention of Stray Livestock Act
Fences & Impounding of Animals Act
Floral Emblem Act
Forcible Entry & Detainer Act
Freedom of Information & Protection of Privacy Act
Gasoline & Fuel Oil Licensing Act
Guardianship Act
Hairdressers Act
Halifax-Dartmouth Bridge Commission Act
House of Assembly Act
Human Tissue Gift Act
Incompetent Persons Act
Indian Lands Act
Indigent Debtors Act
Inebriates' Guardianship Act
Interest on Judgements Act
International Commercial Arbitration Act
Interpretation Act
Intestate Succession Act
Judicature Act
Judicial Disqualifications Removal Act
Juries Act
Justices' & Judges' Protection Act
Justices of the Peace Act
Land Actions Venue Act
Land Holdings Disclosure Act
Land Titles Act
Law Reform Commission Act
Legal Aid Act
Liberty of the Subject Act
Lieutenant Governor & Great Seal Act
Limitation of Actions Act
Limited Partnerships Act
Maintenance Orders Enforcement Act
Margarine Act
Married Women's Deed Act
Married Women's Property Act
Marsh Act
Matrimonial Property Act
Mechanics' Lien Act
Members & Public Employees Disclosure Act
Municipal Conflict of Interest Act
Night Courts Act
Notaries & Commissioners Act
Nova Scotia Tartan Act
Occupiers of Land Liability Act
Official Tree Act
Overholding Tenants Act
Partition Act
Partnership Act
Partnerships & Business Names Registration Act
Payment into Court Act
Pledging of Service Emblems Act
Police Act
Police Services Act
Powers of Attorney Act
Presumption of Death Act
Private Investigators & Private Guards Act
Private Investment Holding Companies Act
Private Ways Act
Probate Act
Proceedings Against the Crown Act
Protection of Property Act
Prothonotaries & Clerks of the Crown Act
Provincial Court Act
Public Accountants Act

GOVERNMENT OF NOVA SCOTIA

Public Archives Act
Public Inquiries Act
Public Offices & Officers Act
Public Prosecutions Act
Public Records Act
Public Records Disposal Act
Public Services Act
Public Subscriptions Act
Public Trustee Act
Quieting Titles Act
Real Property Act
Real Property Transfer Validation Act
Reciprocal Enforcement of Custody Orders Act
Reciprocal Enforcement of Judgments Act
Registered Barbers Act
Registered Nurses' Association Act
Registry Act
Regulations Act
Religious & Charitable Corporations Property Act
Religious Congregations & Societies Act
Remembrance Day Act
Remission of Penalties Act
Residential Tenancies Act
Retail Business Uniform Closing Day Act
Sale of Goods Act
Sale of Land under Execution Act
Salvage Yards Licensing Act
Securities Act
Settlement Act
Sheep Protection & Dog Regulation Act
Sheriffs Act
Slot Machine Act
Small Claims Court Act
Statute of Frauds
Statute Revision Act
Stray Animals Act
Summary Proceedings Act
Supreme Court & Exchequer Court of Canada Act
Sureties Act
Survival of Actions Act
Survivorship Act
Taxing Masters Act
Tenancies & Distress for Rent Act
Testators' Family Maintenance Act
Ticket of Leave Act
Time Definition Act
Tortfeasors Act
Trustee Act
Unclaimed Articles Act
Unconscionable Transactions Relief Act
Uniform Law Act
Unsightly Premises Act
Variation of Trusts Act
Vendors & Purchasers Act
Victims Rights & Services Act
Volunteer Services Act
Warehouse Receipts Act
Warehousemen's Lien Act
Wills Act
Woodmen's Lien Act
Young Persons Summary Proceedings Act
Minister, Hon. Jay F. Abbass, 902/424-4044, Fax: 902/424-0510
Deputy Minister, D. William MacDonald, Q.C., 902/424-4223
Director, Policy Planning & Research, Kit Waters, 902/424-5341, Fax: 902/424-0546, Email: hlfx-term.just.pauls@gov.ns.ca
For list of Courts & other Legal Offices, including Judicial Officials & Judges see Section 10 of this book.

CORRECTIONAL SERVICES DIVISION
PO Box 968, Stn M, Halifax NS
902/424-6290; Fax: 902/424-0692
Acting Director, Fred Hansberger
Administrator, Northern Regional Office, R.G. Parsons, #214, 500 George Place, Sydney NS B1P 1K6, 902/563-2360, Fax: 902/563-3639

Administrator, Southern Regional Office, A.J. Pottier, Lord Nelson Arcade, #800, 5675 Spring Garden Rd., Halifax NS B3J 1H1, 902/424-5776, Fax: 902/424-0693

COURTS & REGISTRIES DIVISION
902/424-7125; Fax: 902/424-0252
Executive Director, Thelma Costello, 902/424-4025
Chief Crown Attorney (Appeals), Kenneth Fiske, 902/424-6794
Director, Public Prosecutions, Vacant, 902/424-8931
Registrar of Probate, Vacant, 902/424-7421, Fax: 902/424-0595

LEGAL SERVICES DIVISION
902/424-8990; Fax: 902/424-0252
Executive Director, Douglas J. Keefe, 902/424-3236
Director, Civil Litigation, Reinhold Endres, 902/424-4024
Registrar, Registry of Regulations, Anna Fried, 902/424-6723
Director, Solicitor Services, Bruce Davidson, Q.C., 902/424-4023

POLICING SERVICES DIVISION
902/424-2504; Fax: 902/424-0700
Executive Director, Robert A. Barss, 902/424-7795
Chief Officer, Licensing & Gun Control, M. Kramers, 902/424-6689, Fax: 902/424-0700

VICTIMS' SERVICES DIVISION
902/424-8785; Fax: 902/424-0252
Acting Director, J. Mariott-Thorne

OFFICE OF THE CHIEF MEDICAL EXAMINER
5788 University Ave., Halifax NS B3H 1V8
902/428-4052; Fax: 902/424-0607
Chief Medical Examiner, Dr. John Butt

Associated Agencies, Boards & Commissions
• Alcohol & Driving Countermeasures Office: 1690 Hollis St., PO Box 217, Stn M, Halifax NS B3J 2M4 – 902/424-4673; Fax: 902/424-0700
Coordinator, Richard James
• Human Rights Commission
Listed alphabetically in detail, this Section.
• Expropriations Compensation Board: 1601 Lower Water St., PO Box 1692, Stn M, Halifax NS B3J 3S3 – 902/424-4448; Fax: 902/424-3919
Chair, S. David Bryson, Q.C.
• Nova Scotia Legal Aid Commission: #401, 5475 Spring Garden Rd., Halifax NS B3J 3T2 – 902/420-6584; Fax: 902/420-3471; URL: http://www.gov.ns.ca/just/lega/
Chair, J. Mark McCrea, 902/420-6584
Executive Director, William Digby, 902/420-6565
• Nova Scotia Police Commission: #300, 1601 Lower Water St., Halifax NS B3J 2Y3 – 902/424-3246; Fax: 902/424-3919; URL: http://www.gov.ns.ca/just/services.htm#POLCOM
Chair, M. Jean Beeler
• Nova Scotia Securities Commission: PO Box 458, Halifax NS B3J 2P8 – 902/424-7768; Fax: 902/424-4625
Chair, Robert B. MacLellan
Vice Chair, H. Leslie O'Brien
Director, Nicholas A. Pittas
Deputy Director, Capital Markets, Elaine Anne MacGregor
Deputy Director, Compliance & Enforcement, Nigel M. Green
Deputy Director, Corporate Finance, J. William Slattery, C.A.

Department of LABOUR
5151 Terminal Rd., PO Box 697, Halifax NS B3J 2T8
902/424-4125; Fax: 902/424-3239; URL: http://www.gov.ns.ca/labr/

ACTS ADMINISTERED
Act to Provide for Pay Equity
Amusement Devices Safety Act
Coal Mines Regulation Act
Electrical Installation Act
Elevators & Lifts Act
Fire Prevention Act
Fireworks Act
Labour Standards Code
Lightning Rod Act
Metalliferous Mines & Quarries Act
Occupational Health & Safety Act
Standard Hose Coupling Act
Stationary Engineers Act
Steam Boiler & Pressure Vessel Act
Trade Union Act
Minister, Hon. Manning MacDonald
Deputy Minister, George Fox, 902/424-4148
Fire Marshall, Robert Cormier, 902/424-4553, Email: cormierr@gov.ns.ca
Director, Administration & Accounting, Peter Horne, 902/424-3967
Solicitor, Pat Clahane, 902/424-5928
Communications Officer, Jennifer McIsaac, 902/424-4680, Email: macisjen@gov.ns.ca

CONCILIATION SERVICES
902/424-4156
Director, Laurie Rantala, 902/424-4156
Conciliator, J.D. Hood, 902/424-8470
Conciliator, Jack O'Brien, 902/424-8469

LABOUR STANDARDS
902/424-4311; Fax: 902/424-0648
Director, Hon. Ross Mitchell, 902/424-5404, Email: mitchelr@gov.ns.ca

OCCUPATIONAL HEALTH & SAFETY
902/424-4328; Fax: 902/424-3239
Toll Free: 1-800-952-2687
Executive Director, Jim LeBlanc, 902/424-8477, Email: leblajim@gov.ns.ca
Director, Mine Safety, Claude White, 902/424-8074
Acting Director, Occupational Health, Stewart Sampson, 902/424-8055
Manager, Occupational Safety, Gerald Muise, 902/424-8478
Acting Director, Safety Training, Stewart Sampson, 902/424-8055

PUBLIC SAFETY
Fax: 902/424-3239
Director, Eugene Chown, 902/424-8479
Acting Chief Inspector, Boiler Safety, Chuck Castle, 902/424-8493
Chief Inspector, Elevators, Lifts & Amusement Devices, Mario Liberatore, 902/424-8487
Inspector, Power Engineers & Crane Operators, Dave Steele, 902/424-8491

RESEARCH
Director, John Patterson, 902/424-4313, Email: pattersj@gov.ns.ca

Associated Agencies, Boards & Commissions
• Construction Industry Panel: PO Box 697, Halifax NS B3J 2T8 – 902/424-6730; Fax: 902/424-3239
Chair, P.E. Darby
CEO, Gary Ross
• Labour Relations Board: PO Box 697, Halifax NS B3J 2T8 – 902/424-6730; Fax: 902/424-3239
Chair, P.E. Darby
CEO, Gary Ross

- Labour Standards Tribunal: PO Box 697, Halifax NS B3J 2T8 – 902/424-6730; Fax: 902/424-3239
Chair, Susan Ashley
Executive Officer, Mary Lou Stewart
- Pay Equity Commission: PO Box 697, Halifax NS B3J 1T8 – 902/424-8595; Fax: 902/424-3239; URL: http://www.gov.ns.ca/labr/pequity.htm
Chair, Patricia Paul
Acting Executive Director, Pat Sherwood
- Stationary Engineers Act, Board of Examiners: PO Box 697, Halifax NS B3J 2T8 – 902/424-7521; Fax: 902/424-3239
Chair, C.W. Purcell
- Workers' Advisers Program: c/o Dept. of Labour, 5151 Terminal Rd., PO Box 697, Halifax NS B3J 2T8
Chief Workers' Adviser, Anne Clarke
- Workers' Compensation Appeal Tribunal: c/o Workers' Compensation Board, PO Box 1150, Halifax NS B3J 2Y2 – 902/424-2257
Chief Appeals Commissioner, Judith Ferguson
- Workers' Compensation Board
Listed alphabetically in detail, this section.
Chief Officer, George Stewart, 902/368-5470

Nova Scotia LIQUOR COMMISSION
93 Chainlake Dr., PO Box 8720, Stn A, Halifax NS B3K 5M4
902/454-5841; Fax: 902/453-1153
Minister Responsible, Hon. Donald R. Downe, 902/424-7579
Chief Commissioner, Douglas A. Caldwell, 902/450-5803, Fax: 902/450-5243
General Manager, G.D. Findlay, 902/450-5802, Fax: 902/450-5225
Executive Director, Corporate Services, L.A. Weagle, 902/450-5901, Fax: 902/450-5225
Executive Director, Retail Services, B.E. Rogers, 902/450-5903, Fax: 902/450-5265

Nova Scotia LIQUOR LICENCE BOARD
PO Box 545, Dartmouth NS B2Y 3Y8
902/424-3660; Fax: 902/424-8987
Minister Responsible, Hon. Eleanor E. Norrie, 902/424-3660
Chair & CEO, Margaret A.M. Shears

Department of NATURAL RESOURCES
Founder's Square, 1701 Hollis St., PO Box 698, Halifax NS B3J 2T9
902/424-5935; Fax: 902/424-7735; URL: http://www.gov.ns.ca/natr/
  Responsible for the administration & management of provincial Crown lands, development of mineral & energy resources, protection & sustainable development of forest resources & operation & maintenance of parks system.

ACTS ADMINISTERED
Act to Confer Certain Powers upon the Lieutenant Governor in Council & to amend the Mines Act
Act to Protect Georges Bank
Beaches Act
Beaches & Foreshores Act
Blueberry Association Act
Bowater Mersey Agreement Act
Canada-Nova Scotia Offshore Petroleum Resources Accord Implementation (Nova Scotia) Act
Coal Mines Regulation Act
Conservation Easements Act
Crown Lands Act
Energy & Mines Resources Conservation Act
Energy-Efficient Appliances Act
Forest Enhancement Act
Forests Act
Gas Storage Exploration Act
Gas Utilities Act
Gypsum Mining Income Tax Act
Halifax Power & Pulp Company Limited Agreement Act, 1962
Indian Lands Act
Kedgemakooge National Park Act
Land Holdings Disclosure Act
Land Surveyors Act
Land Titles Clarification Act
Metalliferous Mines & Quarries Regulation Act
Mineral Resources Act
Natural Resources Advisory Council Act
Offshore Petroleum Royalties Act
Parks Development Act
Petroleum Resources Act
Pipeline Act
Provincial Parks Act
Primary Forest Products Marketing Act
Scalers Act
Scott Maritimes Limited Agreement (1965) Act
Stora Forest Industries Agreement Act
Trails Act
Treasure Trove Act
Wildlife Act
Minister, Hon. Eleanor E. Norrie, 902/424-4037, Fax: 902/424-0594
Deputy Minister, William D. Hogg, C.A., 902/424-4121, Email: wdhogg@gov.ns.ca.
Public Information Officer, Blain Henshaw, 902/424-5252

CORPORATE SERVICES BRANCH
Executive Director, Gary Rix, 902/424-6694, Email: gerix@gov.ns.ca
Director, Financial Services, Jim Morrison, 902/424-5990, Email: j_morris@gov.ns.ca
Acting Director, Fleet Management (Shubenacadie), Colin Gillis, 902/758-3438, Fax: 902/758-3355
Director, Human Resources, Paul Edwards, 902/424-8134, Email: pdedward@gov.ns.ca.
Director, Information Services, Graham Gagne, 902/424-3947, Email: gagagne@gov.ns.ca
Director, Land Administration, Rosalind Penfound, 902/424-4267, Fax: 902/424-3173
Manager, Education & Publication Services (Truro), Emily Gratton, 902/893-5643, Fax: 902/893-6102

MINERALS & ENERGY BRANCH
902/424-5346
Executive Director, Pat Phelan, 902/424-7943, Email: pwphalen@gov.ns.ca.
Director, Mineral & Energy Resources, Scott Swinden, 902/424-2525
Director, Mines & Energy Development, Don Jones, Ph.D., P.Eng., 902/424-5618, Email: dsjones@gov.ns.ca.

PETROLEUM DEVELOPMENT AGENCY
Chief Operating Officer, P. Carey Ryan, 902/424-8203, Email: pcryan@gov.ns.ca.
Director, Planning Secretariat, Vicki Harnish, 902/424-8161, Email: vlharnis@gov.ns.ca.

REGIONAL SERVICES BRANCH
Executive Director, Dan Graham, 902/424-3949, Email: djgraham@gov.ns.ca.
Director, Crown Lands Management, Dan Eidt, 902/424-7594
Director, Extension Services, Gerald Joudrey, 902/424-4445, Email: gtjoudre@gov.ns.ca.
Director, Private Lands Management, Arden Whidden, 902/424-5703
Director, Surveys Division, Keith AuCoin, 902/424-3145
Manager, Enforcement & Hunter Safety, John Mombourquette, 902/424-5254
Manager, Provincial Crown Lands Record Centre, Don Parker, 902/424-8681

Regional Offices
Central: 626 College Rd., Bible Hill NS B2N 2R2 – 902/893-5620; Fax: 902/893-5613, Regional Director, Roger Aggas
Eastern: Beech Hill, RR#7, Antigonish NS B2G 2L4 – 902/863-4513; Fax: 902/863-7342; Email: dnrantig@atcon.com, Regional Director, Fred Delorey
Western: Provincial Bldg., 99 High St., Bridgewater NS B4V 1V8 – 902/543-8167; Fax: 902/543-6157, Regional Director, Brian Gilbert

RENEWABLE RESOURCES BRANCH
Executive Director, John Smith, 902/424-4103, Email: jdsmith@gov.ns.ca.
Director, Forestry, Ed MacAulay, 902/893-5749, Fax: 902/893-6102
Director, Parks & Recreation (Belmont), Barry Diamond, 902/662-3030, Fax: 902/662-2160
Director, Wildlife Division, Barry Sabean, PO Box 516, Kentville NS B4N 3X3, 902/678-6091, Fax: 902/679-6176
Director, Wildlife Management (Kentville), Barry Sabean, 902/679-6091, Fax: 902/679-6176
Manager, Program Development & Evaluation, G. Peter MacQuarrie, 902/424-7708, Email: gpmacqua@gov.ns.ca.

Associated Agencies, Boards & Commissions
- Canada-Nova Scotia Offshore Petroleum Board: TD Centre, 1791 Barrington St., 6th Fl., Halifax NS B3J 3K9 – 902/422-5588; Fax: 902/422-1799; URL: http://Fox.nstn.ca:80/ZXcnsopb/
Chair, Vacant
- Primary Forest Products Marketing Board: Metropolitan Place, #470, 99 Wyse Rd., Dartmouth NS B3A 4S5 – 902/424-7598; Fax: 902/463-0159
Chair, Lee Nauss

Office of the OMBUDSMAN
Lord Nelson Arcade, #300, 5675 Spring Garden Rd., PO Box 2152, Halifax NS B3J 3B7
902/424-6780; Fax: 902/424-6675; URL: http://www.gov.ns.ca/govt/ombu/
Toll Free: 1-800-670-1111
Ombudsman, Douglas G. Ruck
Secretary, Muriel Mappin

Nova Scotia PRIORITIES & PLANNING SECRETARIAT
PO Box 1617, Halifax NS B3J 2Y3
902/424-8910; Fax: 902/424-7638
Chair, Hon. J. Bernard Boudreau, Q.C.
Deputy Minister, Armand Pinard
Director, Aboriginal Affairs, Alan Clark

Nova Scotia RESOURCES LIMITED (NSRL)
#600, 1718 Argyle St., PO Box 2111, Stn M, Halifax NS B3J 3B7
902/420-8800; Fax: 902/425-2195
President & CEO, Donald A. Leet
General Manager, James G. MacDonald
Treasurer & Secretary, Vacant, C.A.
Director, Marketing & Business Development, Vacant

Nova Scotia Advisory Council on the STATUS OF WOMEN
#202, 6169 Quinpool Rd., PO Box 745, Halifax NS B3J 2T3
902/424-8662; Fax: 902/424-0573; URL: http://www.gov.ns.ca/govt/staw/

Operations of the former Women's Directorate & the Advisory Council on the Status of Women have merged. Staff & operations of both agencies are now located at the Advisory Council on the Status of Women's offices. The agency advocates for improved legislation, policies & programs for women. The Women's Directorate portion of operations advises government on ways in which public policies & programs could better serve women.
Minister Responsible, Hon. Eleanor E. Norrie, 902/424-4037
President, Katherine McDonald, 902/424-7548
Coordinator, Regional Services, Marilyn Berry, 902/424-7593
Researcher, Stella Lord, 902/424-8658

SYDNEY STEEL CORPORATION
PO Box 1450, Sydney NS B1P 6K5
902/564-7900; Fax: 902/564-7903
Minister Responsible, Hon. J. Bernard Boudreau, Q.C., 902/424-5720
President & CEO, B.C. Bowman, 902/567-7908
Vice-President & Corporate Secretary, Finance, J.A. Rudderham, 902/564-7920
Vice-President, Marketing, S.H. Didyk, 902/564-7910

Nova Scotia TECHNOLOGY & SCIENCE SECRETARIAT (TSS)
Maritime Centre, 1505 Barrington St., 14th Fl., PO Box 2311, Halifax NS B3J 3C8
902/424-0377; Fax: 902/424-0129; URL: http://www.gov.ns.ca/tss/
Announced the establishment of the Secretariat in March 1996 to help the province define a new framework for developing & instituting technological information transfer within the province. A majority of emphasis is placed on information technology.
Minister, Hon. Gerald J. O'Malley, 902/424-2908
Deputy Minister, Roland MacInnis, 902/424-2902
Executive Director, R.P. MacDonald, 902/424-2888

TIDAL POWER CORPORATION
1701 Hollis St., PO Box 698, Halifax NS B3J 2T9
902/424-7680; Fax: 902/424-7735
Minister Responsible, Hon. Donald R. Downe, 902/424-4037, Fax: 902/424-0594
Corporate Secretary, Allan Parker, 902/424-8175, Email: alparker@gov.ns.ca

Department of TRANSPORTATION & PUBLIC WORKS (TPW)
1969 Upper Water St., PO Box 186, Halifax NS B3J 2N2
902/424-5837
Announced in March 1996, the integration of the former Department of Transportation & Communications with the former Department of Supply & Services to form the Department of Transportation & Public Works. The department is responsible for highway construction & maintenance services, ferry services, & the coordination of provincial programs relating to the transportation of dangerous goods. Provides common services for all government departments & agencies, including real estate services, information & communications, publishing & postal services, & the Provincial Data Centre.

ACTS ADMINISTERED
Dangerous Goods Transportation Act
Highway 104: Western Alignment Act
Off Highway Vehicle Act
Public Highways Act
Surplus Crown Property Disposal Act

Canadian Almanac & Directory 1997

Minister, Hon. Donald R. Downe, 902/424-5875, Fax: 902/424-0171
Deputy Minister, Bruce Atwell, P.Eng., 902/424-4036, Fax: 902/424-2014
Director, Finance, Anna Stuart, 902/424-4126, Fax: 902/424-0722.
Director, Human Resources Division, Patrick Hartling, 902/424-4407, Fax: 902/425-4579
Director, Information Technology, Vacant, 902/424-6999, Fax: 902/424-0570
Director, Internal Audit, Maureen Mansaur, 902/424-3630, Fax: 902/424-0571
Acting Director, Public Affairs & Communications, Angela Poirier, 902/424-8687, Fax: 902/424-0532, Email: dmccready@gov.ns.ca
Director, Transportation Planning & Policy, Don Stonehouse, 902/424-6726, Fax: 902/424-0517

CAPITAL DEVELOPMENT & ENVIRONMENTAL ENGINEERING
Executive Director, Brian Stonehouse, 902/424-2950, Fax: 902/424-0566
Director, Construction Services, Ted Keddy, 902/424-2880
Director, Design Services, Gerald Cullinan, 902/424-2956
Director, Environmental Engineering, Jim Vaughn, 902/424-3018
Director, Project Management, David Seller, 902/424-2961

ENGINEERING SERVICES
Director, Wayne Franklin, 902/424-4589, Fax: 902/424-2014
Acting Director, Engineering, Al MacRae, 902/424-5687, Fax: 902/424-0517, Email: amacrae@gov.ns.ca
Director, Highway Planning, Ralph Spares, 902/424-4193, Fax: 902/424-0572, Email: rwspares@gov.ns.ca
Director, Materials Services, Ray Snair, 902/860-2999, Fax: 902/861-4828
Acting Director, Right-of-Way Claims, Frank Harland, 902/424-5563, Fax: 902/424-0583
Coordinator, Environmental Services, Denis Rushton, 902/424-4082, Fax: 902/424-0570

HIGHWAY PROGRAMS
Acting Executive Director, Ian Foote, 902/424-4059, Fax: 902/424-2014
Director, Equipment, Calvin Archibald, 902/861-1911, Fax: 902/861-1152, Email: carchibald@gov.ns.ca
Director, Operation Services, Don Hoopey, 902/424-4001, Fax: 902/424-0570
District Director, Central, Martin Delaney, 902/424-5328, Fax: 902/424-0568, Email: mdelaney@gov.ns.ca
District Director, Eastern, Tom Hackett, 902/563-2250, Fax: 902/563-0540, Email: thackett@gov.ns.ca
District Director, Northern, Kevin Caines, 902/893-5780, Fax: 902/893-8175
District Director, Western, Vic Coldwell, 902/453-4121, Fax: 902/543-5596, Email: vcoldwell@gov.ns.ca

PROPERTY MANAGEMENT SERVICES
Executive Director, Murray MacGray, 902/424-2904, Fax: 902/424-6257
Director, Accomodation Services, John F. MacLean, 902/424-2808
Director, Facilities Management, Gary Campbell, 902/424-2800

Nova Scotia UTILITY & REVIEW BOARD
#300, 1601 Lower Water St., PO Box 1692, Stn M, Halifax NS B3J 3S3
902/424-4448; Fax: 902/424-3919
Excercises authority over all public utilities in Nova Scotia, including water, electricity & transportation.

ACTS ADMINISTERED
The Assessment Act, RSNS 1989 c. 23 as amended
The Deed Transfer Tax Act, RSNS 1980 c. 121 as amended
Expropriation Act, RSNS 1989 c. 156
Gas Utilities Act, RSNS 1989 c. 182
Gasoline & Diesel Oil Tax Act, RSNS 1989 c. 183
Halifax-Dartmouth Bridge Commission Act, RSNS 1989 c. 192
Health Services Tax Act
Heritage Property Act
Insurance Act (automobile insurance only)
Metropolitan Authority Act
Motor Carrier Act (public passenger only)
Motor Vehicle Transport Act of Canada, 1987 (Federal)
Municipal Boundaries & Representation Act
Nova Scotia Power Corporation Act
Nova Scotia Power Privatization Act
Planning Act
Public Utilities Act
Regional Transit Authority Act
Rural Telephone Act
School Board Act
Shopping Centre Development Act
Tobacco Tax Act
Utility & Review Board Act
Village Services Act
Chair, M. Heather Robertson, Q.C.
Vice-Chair, John A. Morash, C.A., F.C.M.A.
Administrator, Paul G. Allen, C.A.
Senior Advisor, Regulation & Finance, John Murphy, P.Eng.

WORKERS' COMPENSATION BOARD OF NOVA SCOTIA
5668 South St., PO Box 1150, Halifax NS B3J 2Y2
902/424-8440; Fax: 902/424-0509;
Email: donalee.Moulton@wcb.gov.ns.ca;
URL: http://www.pixelmotion.ns.ca/wcb/
Chair, Dr. Robert Elgie
CEO, David Stuewe
Director, Communications, donalee Moulton, 902/424-8339

GOVERNMENT OF ONTARIO

Seat of Government: Legislative Bldgs., Queen's Park, Legislative Bldg., Queen's Park, Toronto ON M7A 1A2
URL: http://www.gov.on.ca/
The Province of Ontario entered Confederation July 1, 1867. It has an area of 1,068,582 km2, and the StatsCan census population in 1991 was 10,084,885.

Office of the LIEUTENANT GOVERNOR
#131, Legislative Bldg., Queen's Park, Toronto ON M7A 1A1
416/325-7780; Fax: 416/325-7787; URL: http://ontla.on.ca/assemsrv/lg.htm
Lieutenant Governor, Hon. Henry N. R. Jackman
Executive Asst., Bryn MacPherson-White
Chief Aide-de-Camp, Col. Roy Beckett, CD
Deputy Chief Aide-de-Camp, LCol. Sandy Cameron, CD
Deputy Chief Aide-de-Camp, Chief Supt. Ken Turriff
Deputy Chief Aide-de-Camp, Cdr. Tony Pitts, CD

Office of the PREMIER
Legislative Bldg., #281, 1 Queen's Park Cres. South, Toronto ON M7A 1A1

416/325-1941; Fax: 416/325-3745; Email: premier@gov.on.ca; URL: http://www.gov.on.ca/premier/office/html
TDD: 416/325-7702

ACTS ADMINISTERED
Executive Council Act
Lieutenant Governor Act
Policy & Priorities Board of Cabinet Act
Representation Act, 1986
Social Contract Act
Premier, Hon. Michael D. Harris, 416/325-1941, Email: premier@gov.on.ca
Deputy Premier & Government House Leader, Hon. Ernie Eves, Frost Bldg. South, 7 Queen's Park Cres., 7th Fl., Toronto ON M7A 1Y7, 416/325-0400
Principal Secretary, David Lindsay, 416/325-7774
Deputy Principal Secretary, Mitch Patten, 416/325-9255
Premier's Secretary, Kitty Knight, 416/325-7796
Executive Asst., Issues Management, Debbie Hutton, 416/325-7804
Policy & Legislative Counsel, Guy Giorno, 416/325-9257
Speech Coordinator, Communications Unit, Glen Stone, 416/325-4173
Support Coordinator, Communications Unit, Liam Scott, 416/325-2675
Senior Media Advisor, Media Unit, Paul Rhodes, 416/325-4332
Press Secretary, Media Unit, Peter Varley, 416/325-7803
Manager, Public Appointments Unit, Toni Arnold, 416/325-9682
Senior Advisor, Scheduling Unit, Scott Munnoch, 416/325-9264
Executive Asst./Caucus Liaison, Special Projects Unit, Bill King, 416/325-7806
Manager, Correspondence, Liz Hickey, 416/325-7798
Senior Officer, Public Enquiries, Vivian Martina, 416/325-1941

THE PREMIER'S COUNCIL
1 Dundas St. West, 25th Fl., Toronto ON M7A 1Y7
416/326-6756; Fax: 416/326-6769
Deputy Minister, Dr. Thomas A. Brzustowski
Administrative Asst., Jane Grier

EXECUTIVE COUNCIL
#4340, Whitney Block, Queen's Park, 99 Wellesley St. West, Toronto ON M7A 1A1
416/325-7641; URL: http://ontla.on.ca/members/exec.htm
Premier & President of the Executive Council, Hon. Michael D. Harris, #281, Legislative Bldg., Queen's Park, Toronto ON M7A 1A1, 416/325-1941, Fax: 416/325-3745, Email: premier@gov.on.ca
Deputy Premier, Government House Leader, Hon. Ernie Eves, Frost Bldg. South, 7 Queen's Park Cres., 7th Fl., Toronto ON M7A 1Y7, 416/325-0400
Minister, Intergovernmental Affairs & Minister Responsible, Women's Issues, Hon. Dianne Cunningham, Mowat Block, 900 Bay St., 6th Fl., Toronto ON M7A 1C2, 416/326-1600, Fax: 416/326-1656
Minister, Community & Social Services, Hon. Janet Ecker
Minister, Attorney General & Minister Responsible, Native Affairs, Hon. Charles Harnick, 720 Bay St., 11th Fl., Toronto ON M5G 2K1, 416/326-4000, Fax: 416/326-4016
Minister, Natural Resources & Northern Development & Mines, Hon. Chris Hodgson, Whitney Block, 99 Wellesley St. West, 6th Fl., Toronto ON M7A 1W3, 416/314-2301, Fax: 416/314-2216
Minister without Portfolio & Minister Responsible, Senior Citizens, Hon. Cameron Jackson, 400 University Ave., 7th Fl., Toronto ON M7A 1T7, 416/326-1460
Minister, Finance, Chair, Management Board of Cabinet & Deputy Minister, Management Board Secretariat, Hon. David Johnson, Ferguson Block, 77 Wellesley St. West, 12th Fl., Toronto ON M7A 1N3, 416/327-2333, Fax: 416/327-3790
Minister, Municipal Affairs & Housing, Hon. Allan Leach, 777 Bay St., 17th Fl., Toronto ON M5G 2E5, 416/585-7000, Fax: 416/585-6470
Minister, Citizenship, Culture & Recreation, Hon. Marilyn Mushinski, 77 Bloor St. West, 6th Fl., Toronto ON M7A 2R9, 416/325-6200, Fax: 416/325-6195
Minister, Transportation, Hon. Al Palladini, Ferguson Block, 77 Wellesley St. West, 3rd Fl., Toronto ON M7A 1N3, 613/927-9200
Minister, Solicitor General & Correctional Services, Hon. Robert W. Runciman, #400, 175 Bloor St. East, Toronto ON M4W 3R8, 416/326-5075, Fax: 416/326-5085
Minister without Portfolio & Minister Responsible, Privatization, Hon. Rob Sampson
Minister, Economic Development, Trade & Tourism, Hon. William Saunderson, Hearst Block, 900 Bay St., 8th Fl., Toronto ON M7A 2E1, 416/325-6900, Fax: 416/325-6918
Minister, Education & Training, Hon. John Snobelen, Mowat Block, 900 Bay St., 22nd Fl., Toronto ON M7A 1L2, 416/325-2600, Fax: 416/325-2608
Minister, Environment & Energy, Hon. Norman W. Sterling, 250 Yonge St., 35th Fl., Toronto TO M5B 2N5, 416/326-8500, Fax: 416/326-8560
Minister, Consumer & Commercial Relations, Hon. David H. Tsubouchi, Hepburn Block, 80 Grosvenor St., 6th Fl., Toronto ON M7A 1E9, 416/325-5225, Fax: 416/325-5221
Minister, Agriculture, Food & Rural Affairs & Minister Responsible, Francophone Affairs, Hon. Noble Villeneuve, 801 Bay St., 11th Fl., Toronto ON M7A 2B2, 416/326-3067, Fax: 416/326-3083
Minister, Health, Hon. James Wilson, Hepburn Block, 80 Grosvenor St., 10th Fl., Toronto ON M7A 2C4, 416/327-4300, Fax: 416/326-1571
Minister, Labour, Hon. Elizabeth Witmer, 400 University Ave., 14th Fl., Toronto ON M7A 1T7, 416/326-7600, Fax: 416/326-1449

Cabinet Office
Whitney Block, Queen's Park, #4340, 99 Wellesley St. West, Toronto ON M7A 1A1
416/325-7641; Fax: 416/314-8980
TDD: 416/314-5721
Secretary of Cabinet & Clerk of Executive Council, Rita Burak, 416/325-7641
Associate Secretary, Susan Waterfield, #1004, 790 Bay St., Toronto ON M7A 1Y7, 416/325-1607
Executive Asst. to Associate Secretary, Scott Bolton, #1004, 790 Bay St., Toronto ON M7A 1Y7, 416/325-1609
Executive Asst., Thom Hagerty, 416/325-4400
Personal Secretary to the Secretary of the Cabinet, Joyce Weylie, 416/325-7618
Executive Secretary (Bilingual), Louise Beaupré, 416/314-4687
Asst. Deputy Minister, Operations, Corporate Issues, David De Launay, 416/325-3767, Fax: 416/325-7631
Asst. Deputy Minister, Operations, Resource Management, Karen Tilford, 416/325-7619, Fax: 416/325-7661
Acting Executive Coordinator, Gord Evans, 416/325-7693, Fax: 416/327-9505
Policy Advisor, Policy & Priorities Board, Kate Andrew, 416/325-7649, Fax: 416/325-7661
Director, Communications Planning, Allan Cohen, 416/325-7623, Fax: 416/325-7627
Director, Information Technology Systems & Services, Ginnie Nelson-Turner, 416/325-7670, Fax: 416/325-3745
Senior Manager, Resources Management, David Whorley, 416/325-4745, Fax: 416/325-7631
Manager, Executive Council Support, Suzanne Wilson, 416/325-7691
Manager, Premier's Correspondence Unit, Aine Scully, 416/325-3736, Fax: 416/325-3745

Cabinet Committees
Economic Development, Executive Coordinator, Judith Wolfe, 416/325-7711, Fax: 416/3258-4836
Environment Policy, Executive Coordinator, Anne Larson, 416/325-4829, Fax: 416/325-4736
Justice, Executive Coordinator, Julie Jai, 416/325-3723, Fax: 416/325-3732
Legislation/Regulation, Committee Secretary, Suzanne Wilson, 416/325-7691, Fax: 416/325-327-9505
Social Policy, Executive Coordinator, John Kenewell, 416/325-9112, Fax: 416/325-3732

LEGISLATIVE ASSEMBLY
c/o Clerk's Office, #104, Legislative Bldg., Queen's Park, Toronto ON M7A 1A2
416/325-7340; Fax: 416/325-7344; Email: assembly@ontla.ola.org.; URL: http://www.ontla.on.ca

ACTS ADMINISTERED
Election Act
Election Finances Act
Freedom of Information & Protection of Privacy Act
Legislative Assembly Act
Legislative Assembly Retirement Allowances Act
Members' Integrity Act
Ombudsman Act
Clerk: Claude DesRosiers, 416/325-7341, URL: http://ontla.on.ca/assemsrv/clerk.htm
Speaker: #180, Legislative Bldg., Queen's Park, Toronto ON M7A 1A8, Chris Stockwell, 416/325-7435, Fax: 416/325-7483
Sergeant-at-Arms: #414, North Wing, Legislative Bldg., Queen's Park, Toronto ON M7A 1A2, Vacant, 416/325-7445, Fax: 416/325-7154, Emergency: 416/325-1111
Director, Hansard Reporting Service: #474, Legislative Bldg., Queen's Park, Toronto ON M71 1A2, Richard Copeland, 416/325-7431, Fax: 416/325-7430, Inquiries: 416/325-7400
Executive Director, Legislative Library: #409, North Wing, Legislative Bldg., Queen's Park, Toronto ON M7A 1A9, Mary E. Dickerson, 416/325-3939, Fax: 416/325-3909, Reference Inquiries: 416/325-3900
Senior Clerk Asst. & Clerk of Journals, Alex D. McFedries, #1407, Whitney Block, Queen's Park, Toronto ON M7A 1A2, 416/325-7350, Fax: 416/325-3534
Clerk Asst. & Clerk of Committees, Deborah Deller, #1405, Whitney Block, Queen's Park, Toronto ON M7A 1A2, 416/325-3502, Fax: 416/325-3505, Inquiries: 416/325-3500
Controller, Finance & Administration, William Ponick, #2503, Whitney Block, Queen's Park, Toronto ON M7A 1A2, 416/325-3568, Fax: 416/314-5995
Executive Director, Assembly Services, Barbara Speakman, #411, North Wing, Legislative Bldg., Queen's Park, Toronto ON M7A 1A2, 416/325-3579, Fax: 416/325-3969

Officers of the Legislative Assembly
Chief Election Officer, W.R. Bailie, 51 Rolark Dr., Scarborough ON M1R 3B1, 416/321-3000, Fax: 416/320-6853
Integrity Commissioner, Hon. G.T. Evans, LL.D., Ph.D., K.C.S.G., 101 Bloor St. West, 4th Fl., Toronto ON M5S 2Z7, 416/314-8983, Fax: 416/314-8987

3-166 GOVERNMENT OF ONTARIO

Election Finances Commissioner, Jack Murray, #1110, 151 Bloor St. West, Toronto ON M5S 1S4, 416/325-9451, Fax: 416/325-9466

Environmental Commissioner, Eva Ligeti, #605, 1075 Bay St., Toronto ON M5S 2W5, 416/325-3377, Fax: 416/325-3370

Information & Privacy Commissioner, Tom Wright, #1700, 80 Bloor St. West, Toronto ON M5S 2V1, 416/326-3333, Fax: 416/325-9195, Toll Free: 1-800-387-0073

Ombudsman, Roberta Jamieson, 125, Queen's Park, Toronto ON M5S 2C7, 416/586-3300, Fax: 416/586-3485

Provincial Auditor, Erik Peters, 1530, 20 Dundas St. West, PO Box 105, Toronto ON M5G 2C2, 416/974-9866, Fax: 416/324-7012

Government Caucus Services

#124, North Wing, Legislative Bldg., Queen's Park, Toronto ON M7A 1A8

416/325-7736; Fax: 416/325-3810; URL: http://ontariopc.on.ca

#249, Legislative Bldg., Queen's Park, Toronto ON M7A 1A8

Chief Government Whip, David Turnbull

Chair, Government Caucus, Margaret Marland

Government House Leader & Deputy Premier, Hon. Ernie Eves, 416/325-0400

Deputy House Leader, Isabel Bassett, 416/325-0367

Executive Coordinator, Research & Communications, Jerry Redmond

Director, Administration, Barbara Cowieson, 416/325-7272

Office of the Official Opposition (Lib.)

#349, Legislative Bldg., Queen's Park, Toronto ON M7A 1A4

416/325-7200; Fax: 416/325-9898; Email: liberal@io.org; URL: http://www.io.org/ZXliberal

Leader, Lyn McLeod, 416/325-7155, Fax: 416/325-9895

Deputy Leader, Sean Conway, #345, Legislative Bldg., Queen's Park, Toronto ON M7A 1A4, 416/325-7197, Fax: 416/325-9001

Chief Opposition Whip, Elinor Caplan, 416/325-3607, Fax: 416/325-3968

Executive Director, Liberal Caucus Service Bureau, Peter Curtis, #1603, Whitney Block, Queen's Park, Toronto ON M7A 1A4, 416/325-7202

Principal Secretary, Bob Richardson, 416/325-7163

Official Opposition House Leader, James Bradley, #331, Legislative Bldg., Queen's Park, Toronto ON M7A 1A4, 416/325-7194, Fax: 416/325-9696

Official Opposition Caucus Chair, David Ramsay, #463, Legislative Bldg., Queen's Park, Toronto ON M7A 1A4, 416/325-7137, Fax: 416/325-9007

Director, Liberal Policy & Communications, Sue Hanna, #1640, Whitney Block, Queen's Park, Toronto ON M7A 1A4, 416/325-7185, Fax: 416/325-9895

Policy Analyst, Financial Institutions, Philip DeMont

Note: The Liberal leadership convention was held on November 30, 1996. Results for the convention were not known at time of publishing.

Office of the New Democratic Party

#381, Legislative Bldg., Queen's Park, Toronto ON M7A 1A5

416/325-7530; Fax: 416/325-8222; Email: ondp@io.org; URL: http://www.ndp.on.ca

Leader, Howard Hampton

Deputy Leader, Floyd Laughren, 416/325-4060, Fax: 416/325-4064

New Democratic Party House Leader, David Cooke, 416/325-3260, Fax: 416/325-3261

New Democratic Party Chief Whip, Frances Lankin, 416/325-6904, Fax: 416/325-3336

New Democratic Party Caucus Chair, Bud Wildman, 416/325-6800, Fax: 416/325-7029

Principal Secretary, Dennis Young, 416/325-8300

Director, Communications, Maria Dyck, 416/325-7310, Fax: 416/325-7111

Standing Committees of the Legislative Assembly

Administration of Justice, Clerk, Donna Bryce, 416/325-3525

Estimates, Clerk, Tannis Manikel, 416/325-3509

Finance & Economic Affairs, Clerk, Franco Carrozza, 416/325-3514

General Government, Clerk, Tonia Grannum, 416/325-3519

Legislative Assembly, Clerk, Lisa Freedman, 416/325-3528

Ombudsman, Clerk, Todd Decker, 416/325-7284

Public Accounts, Clerk, Todd Decker, 416/325-7284

Regulations & Private Bills, Clerk, Lisa Freedman, 416/325-3528

Resources Development, Clerk, Douglas Arnott, 416/325-3506

Social Development, Clerk, Lynn Mellor, 416/325-3522

THIRTY-SIXTH PARLIAMENT - ONTARIO

416/325-7341; URL: http://ontla.on.ca/members/members.htm

Last General Election, June 8, 1995. Maximum Duration, 5 years.

Party Standings (June 24, 1996):

Progressive Conservative (PC) 81

Liberal (Lib.) 31

New Democratic Party (NDP) 16

Independent (Ind.) 2

Total 130

Salaries, Indemnities & Allowances: June 14, 1993 to March 31, 1996 - Members' sessional indemnity $42,218 per annum plus a $14,160 expense allowance. In addition to this are the following:

Premier $42,752 & a leader's allowance of $7,967

Ministers $30,003 (with portfolio); Ministers $15,065 (without portfolio)

Leader of the Opposition $30,902 & a leader's allowance of $5,313

Leaders of Parties with recognized membership of 12 or more in the Assembly $22,000 & a leader's allowance of $2,655

Speaker $22,811

Following is: constituency (number of eligible voters at 1995 election) member, party affiliation, Toronto office address & telephone number.

Refer to Cabinet List, Government Caucus Services Office, Liberal Caucus Services Office, & Office of the Progressive Conservative Party, for **Fax** numbers.

Email addresses for all MPPs are formatted as follows - firstname_lastname-mpp@ontla.ola.org.

MEMBERS BY CONSTITUENCY

Algoma (21,864) Bud Wildman, NDP, 416/325-6800

Algoma-Manitoulin (26,128) Mike Brown, Lib., 416/325-3601

Beaches-Woodbine (38,523) Frances Lankin, NDP, 416/325-6904

Brampton North (69,435) Joe Spina, PC, 416/325-6913

Brampton South (74,364) Tony Clement, PC, 416/314-7782

Brant-Haldimand (48,807) Peter L. Preston, PC, 416/325-8216

Brantford (55,445) Ron Johnson, PC, 416/325-7027

Bruce (46,559) Barb Fisher, PC, 416/325-5617

Burlington South (49,821) Hon. Cameron Jackson, PC, 416/585-6464

Cambridge (62,324) Gerry Martiniuk, PC, 416/325-8451

Carleton (70,780) Hon. Norman W. Sterling, PC, 416/326-8500

Carleton East (61,643) Gilles E. Morin, Lib., 416/325-7216

Chatham-Kent (49,769) Jack Carroll, PC, 416/325-4534

Cochrane North (26,037) Len Wood, NDP, 416/325-7040

Cochrane South (38,584) Gilles Bisson, NDP, 416/325-7122

Cornwall (44,191) John Cleary, Lib., 416/325-3642

Don Mills (42,758) Hon. David Johnson, PC, 416/326-9190

Dovercourt (30,963) Tony Silipo, NDP, 416/325-6311

Downsview (36,926) Annamarie Castrilli, Lib., 416/325-8688

Dufferin-Peel (54,176) David Tilson, PC, 416/326-2485

Durham Centre (66,818) Jim Flaherty, PC, 416/326-8506

Durham East (62,205) John O'Toole, PC, 416/325-6745

Durham West (84,476) Hon. Janet Ecker, PC, 416/325-5246

Durham-York (65,909) Julia Munro, PC, 416/314-5741

Eglinton (48965) Hon. William Saunderson, PC, 416/325-6900

Elgin (54,155) Peter North, Ind., 416/325-7271

Essex South (53,088) Bruce Crozier, Lib., 416/325-7298

Essex-Kent (47,000) Pat Hoy, NDP, 416/325-9099

Etobicoke West (47,256) Chris Stockwell, PC, 416/325-7535

Etobicoke-Humber (48,706) Douglas B. Ford, PC, 416/325-6578

Etobicoke-Lakeshore (50,083) Morley Kells, PC, 416/325-8230

Etobicoke-Rexdale (44,393) John Hastings, PC, 416/325-6001

Fort William (43,643) Lyn McLeod, Lib., 416/325-7155

Fort York (41,147) Rosario Marchese, NDP, 416/325-9092

Frontenac-Addington (51,066) Bill Vankoughnet, Ind., 416/325-8662

Grey-Owen Sound (61,048) Bill Murdoch, PC, 416/327-0616

Guelph (61,691) Brenda Elliott, PC, 416/323-4360

Halton Centre (47,738) Terrence Young, PC, 416/325-2367

Halton North (47,738) Ted Chudleigh, PC, 416/325-8460

Hamilton Centre (40,459) David Christopherson, NDP, 416/325-3188

Hamilton East (44,757) Domenic Agostino, Lib., 416/325-8711

Hamilton Mountain (59,371) Trevor Pettit, PC, 416/325-3715

Hamilton West (49,673) Lillian Ross, PC, 416/325-5562

Hastings-Peterborough (44,719) Harry Danford, PC, 416/326-3057

High Park-Swansea (39,294) Derwyn Shea, PC, 585-4038

Huron (41,549) Helen Johns, PC, 416/327-2419

Kenora (33,061) Frank Miclash, Lib., 416/325-3639

Kingston & The Islands (42,165) John Gerretsen, Lib., 416/325-9210

Kitchener (56,066) Wayne Wettlaufer, PC, 416/325-8220

Kitchener-Wilmot (65,102) Gary Leadston, PC, 416/325-8644

Lake Nipigon (21,708) Gilles Pouliot, NDP, 416/325-4075

Lambton (43,019) Marcel Beaubien, PC, 416/326-3062

Lanark-Renfrew (60,270) Leo Jordan, PC, 416/325-7520

Lawrence (40,099) Joseph Cordiano, Lib., 416/325-3619

Leeds-Grenville (54,953) Hon. Robert W. Runciman, PC, 416/326-5075

Lincoln (54,677) Frank Sheehan, PC, 416/325-8640

London Centre (56,666) Marion Boyd, NDP, 416/325-3170

London North (68,675) Hon. Dianne Cunningham, PC, 416/326-1600

London South (66,875) Bob Wood, PC, 416/325-4928

Markham, Hon. David H. Tsubouchi, PC, 416/325-5225

Middlesex (59,061) Bruce Smith, PC, 416/325-4561
Mississauga East (53,159) Carl DeFaria, PC, 416/325-8502
Mississauga North (81,425) Hon. John Snobelen, PC, 416/325-2600
Mississauga South (51,180) Margaret Marland, PC, 416/325-7731
Mississauga West (96,475) Hon. Rob Sampson, PC, 416/325-0413
Muskoka-Georgian Bay (53,179) Bill Grimmett, PC, 416/325-6955
Nepean (54,832) John Baird, PC, 416/326-1460
Niagara Falls (47,729) Bart Maves, PC, 416/325-5528
Niagara South (38,787) Tim Hudak, PC, 416/325-8454
Nickel Belt (26,850) Floyd Laughren, NDP, 416/325-4060
Nipissing (49,020) Hon. Michael D. Harris, PC, 416/325-1941
Norfolk (56,118) Toby Barrett, PC, 416/325-8404
Northumberland (55,696) Doug Galt, PC, 416/323-4364
Oakville South (48,544) Gary Carr, PC, 416/314-3356
Oakwood (31,493) Mike Colle, Lib., 416/325-8707
Oriole (37,687) Elinor Caplan, Lib., 416/325-3607
Oshawa (54,110) Jerry J. Ouellette, PC, 416/327-9193
Ottawa Centre (44,958) Richard Patten, Lib., 416/325-1628
Ottawa East (48,272) Bernard C. Grandmaître, Lib., 416/325-3610
Ottawa South (43,793) Dalton J.P. McGuinty, Lib., 416/325-7263
Ottawa West (50,027) Robert Chiarelli, Lib., 416/325-3654
Ottawa-Rideau (53,961) Garry J. Guzzo, PC, 416/323-4373
Oxford (55,914) Ernie Hardeman, PC, 416/585-7285
Parkdale (27,999) Tony Ruprecht, Lib., 416/325-7777
Parry Sound (37,484) Hon. Ernie Eves, PC, 416/325-0400
Perth (49,097) Bert Johnson, PC, 416/325-5609
Peterborough (65,678) R. Gary Stewart, PC, 416/325-6639
Port Arthur (47,672) Michael Gravelle, NDP, 416/325-1559
Prescott & Russell (79,574) Jean-Marc Lalonde, Lib., 416/325-7289
Prince Edward-Lennox-South Hastings (47,891) Gary Fox, PC, 416/325-1725
Quinte (50,783) E.J. Douglas Rollins, PC, 416/325-8209
Rainy River (19,406) Howard Hampton, NDP, 416/325-7044
Renfrew North (49,678) Sean Conway, Lib., 416/325-7197
Riverdale (36,682) Marilyn Churley, NDP, 416/325-3250
S.D.G. & East Grenville (46,086) Hon. Noble Villeneuve, PC, 416/326-3067
Sarnia (45,210) Dave Boushy, PC, 416/325-8373
Sault Ste. Marie (57,581) Tony Martin, NDP, 416/325-4014
Scarborough Centre (44,325) Dan Newman, PC, 416/327-9829
Scarborough East (53,750) Steve Gilchrist, PC, 416/325-5055
Scarborough West (42,890) Jim Brown, PC, 416/325-8636
Scarborough-Agincourt (48,203) Gerry Phillips, Lib., 416/325-3628
Scarborough-Ellesmere (43,252) Hon. Marilyn Mushinski, PC, 416/325-6200
Scarborough-North (57,970) Alvin Curling, Lib., 416/325-7277
Simcoe Centre (81,753) Joseph N. Tascona, PC, 416/325-4579
Simcoe East (58,477) Allan K. McLean, PC, 416/325-3855
Simcoe West (56,980) Hon. James Wilson, PC, 416/327-4300

St. Andrew-St. Patrick (48,709) Isabel Bassett, PC, 416/326-9092
St. Catharines (46,146) James Bradley, Lib., 416/325-7194
St. Catharines-Brock (41,047) Tom Froese, PC, 416/325-8227
St. George-St. David (46,174) Hon. Allan Leach, PC, 416/585-7000
Sudbury (49,582) Rick Bartolucci, Lib., 416/325-8716
Sudbury East (49,123) Shelley Martel, NDP, 416/325-9203
Timiskaming (29,037) David Ramsay, Lib., 416/325-7137
Victoria-Haliburton (56,217) Hon. Chris Hodgson, PC, 416/314-2301
Waterloo North (70,170) Hon. Elizabeth Witmer, PC, 416/326-7600
Welland-Thorold (46,713) Peter Kormos, NDP, 416/325-7106
Wellington (50,529) Ted Arnott, PC, 416/325-3880
Wentworth East (56,023) Ed Doyle, PC, 416/325-8411
Wentworth North (54,022) Tony Skarica, PC, 416/325-2505
Willowdale (51,149) Hon. Charles Harnick, PC, 416/326-4000
Wilson Heights (45,228) Monte Kwinter, Lib., 416/325-7208
Windsor-Riverside (50,573) David Cooke, NDP, 416/325-8116
Windsor-Sandwich (51,421) Sandra Pupatello, Lib., 416/325-1496
Windsor-Walkerville (48,141) Dwight Duncan, Lib., 416/325-1398
York Centre (129,108) Hon. Al Palladini, PC, 416/327-9200
York East (44,733) John L. Parker, PC, 416/325-5548, Voice & TTY: 416/425-2329
York Mills (43,180) David Turnbull, PC, 416/325-3877
York South (37,192) Gerard Kennedy, NDP, 416/325-2884
York-Mackenzie (66,558) Frank Klees, PC, 416/314-2193
Yorkview (32,827) Mario Sergio, Lib., 416/325-1404

MEMBERS (ALPHABETICAL)
Domonic Agostino, Hamilton East (44,757)Lib., Ont., 416/325-8711
Ted Arnott, Wellington (50,529)PC, Ont., 416/325-3880
John Baird, Nepean (54,832)PC, Ont., 416/326-1460
Toby Barrett, Norfolk (56,118)PC, Ont., 416/325-8404
Rick Bartolucci, Sudbury (49,582)Lib., Ont., 416/325-8716
Isabel Bassett, St. Andrew-St. Patrick (48,709)PC, Ont., 416/326-9092
Marcel Beaubien, Lambton (43,019)PC, Ont., 416/326-3062
Gilles Bisson, Cochrane South (38,584)NDP, Ont., 416/325-7122
Dave Boushy, Sarnia (45,210)PC, Ont., 416/325-8373
Marion Boyd, London Centre (56,666)NDP, Ont., 416/325-3170
James Bradley, St. Catharines (46,146)Lib., Ont., 416/325-7194
Jim Brown, Scarborough West (42,890)PC, Ont., 416/325-8636
Mike Brown, Algoma-Manitoulin (26,128)Lib., Ont., 416/325-3601
Elinor Caplan, Oriole (37,687)Lib., Ont., 416/325-3607
Gary Carr, Oakville South (48,544)PC, Ont., 416/314-3356
Jack Carroll, Chatham-Kent (49,769)PC, Ont., 416/325-4534
Annamarie Castrilli, Downsview (36,926)Lib., Ont., 416/325-8688
Robert Chiarelli, Ottawa West (50,027)Lib., Ont., 416/325-3654

David Christopherson, Hamilton Centre (40,459)NDP, Ont., 416/325-3188
Ted Chudleigh, Halton North (47,738)PC, Ont., 416/325-8460
Marilyn Churley, Riverdale (36,682)NDP, Ont., 416/325-3250
John Cleary, Cornwall (44,191)Lib., Ont., 416/325-3642
Tony Clement, Brampton South (74,364)PC, Ont., 416/314-7782
Mike Colle, Oakwood (31,493)Lib., Ont., 416/325-8707
Sean Conway, Renfrew North (49,678)Lib., Ont., 416/325-7197
David Cooke, Windsor-Riverside (50,573)NDP, Ont., 416/325-8116
Joseph Cordiano, Lawrence (40,099)Lib., Ont., 416/325-3619
Bruce Crozier, Essex South (53,088)Lib., Ont., 416/325-7298
Hon. Dianne Cunningham, London North (68,675)PC, Ont., 416/326-1600
Alvin Curling, Scarborough-North (57,970)Lib., Ont., 416/325-7277
Harry Danford, Hastings-Peterborough (44,719)PC, Ont., 416/326-3057
Carl DeFaria, Mississauga East (53,159)PC, Ont., 416/325-8502
Ed Doyle, Wentworth East (56,023)PC, Ont., 416/325-8411
Dwight Duncan, Windsor-Walkerville (48,141)Lib., Ont., 416/325-1398
Hon. Janet Ecker, Durham West (84,476)PC, Ont., 416/325-5246
Brenda Elliott, Guelph (61,691)PC, Ont., 416/323-4360
Hon. Ernie Eves, Parry Sound (37,484)PC, Ont., 416/325-0400
Barb Fisher, Bruce (46,559)PC, Ont., 416/325-5617
Jim Flaherty, Durham Centre (66,818)PC, Ont., 416/326-8506
Douglas B. Ford, Etobicoke-Humber (48,706)PC, Ont., 416/325-6578
Gary Fox, Prince Edward-Lennox-South Hastings (47,891)PC, Ont., 416/325-1725
Tom Froese, St. Catharines-Brock (41,047)PC, Ont., 416/325-8227
Doug Galt, Northumberland (55,696)PC, Ont., 416/323-4364
John Gerretsen, Kingston & The Islands (42,165)Lib., Ont., 416/325-9210
Steve Gilchrist, Scarborough East (53,750)PC, Ont., 416/325-5055
Bernard C. Grandmaître, Ottawa East (48,272)Lib., Ont., 416/325-3610
Michael Gravelle, Port Arthur (47,672)NDP, Ont., 416/325-1559
Bill Grimmett, Muskoka-Georgian Bay (53,179)PC, Ont., 416/325-6955
Garry J. Guzzo, Ottawa-Rideau (53,961)PC, Ont., 416/323-4373
Howard Hampton, Rainy River (19,406)NDP, Ont., 416/325-7044
Ernie Hardeman, Oxford (55,914)PC, Ont., 416/585-7285
Hon. Charles Harnick, Willowdale (51,149)PC, Ont., 416/326-4000
Hon. Michael D. Harris, Nipissing (49,020)PC, Ont., 416/325-1941
John Hastings, Etobicoke-Rexdale (44,393)PC, Ont., 416/325-6001
Hon. Chris Hodgson, Victoria-Haliburton (56,217)PC, Ont., 416/314-2301
Pat Hoy, Essex-Kent (47,000)NDP, Ont., 416/325-9099
Tim Hudak, Niagara South (38,787)PC, Ont., 416/325-8454
Hon. Cameron Jackson, Burlington South (49,821)PC, Ont., 416/585-6464
Helen Johns, Huron (41,549)PC, Ont., 416/327-2419
Bert Johnson, Perth (49,097)PC, Ont., 416/325-5609

Canadian Almanac & Directory 1997

GOVERNMENT OF ONTARIO

Hon. David Johnson, Don Mills (42,758)PC, Ont., 416/326-9190

Ron Johnson, Brantford (55,445)PC, Ont., 416/325-7027

Leo Jordan, Lanark-Renfrew (60,270)PC, Ont., 416/325-7520

Morley Kells, Etobicoke-Lakeshore (50,083)PC, Ont., 416/325-8230

Gerard Kennedy, York South (37,192)NDP, Ont., 416/325-2884

Frank Klees, York-Mackenzie (66,558)PC, Ont., 416/314-2193

Peter Kormos, Welland-Thorold (46,713)NDP, Ont., 416/325-7106

Monte Kwinter, Wilson Heights (45,228)Lib., Ont., 416/325-7208

Jean-Marc Lalonde, Prescott & Russell (79,574)Lib., Ont., 416/325-7289

Frances Lankin, Beaches-Woodbine (38,523)NDP, Ont., 416/325-6904

Floyd Laughren, Nickel Belt (26,850)NDP, Ont., 416/325-4060

Hon. Allan Leach, St. George-St. David (46,174)PC, Ont., 416/585-7000

Gary Leadston, Kitchener-Wilmot (65,102)PC, Ont., 416/325-8644

Rosario Marchese, Fort York (41,147)NDP, Ont., 416/325-9092

Margaret Marland, Mississauga South (51,180)PC, Ont., 416/325-7731

Shelley Martel, Sudbury East (49,123)NDP, Ont., 416/325-9203

Tony Martin, Sault Ste. Marie (57,581)NDP, Ont., 416/325-4014

Gerry Martiniuk, Cambridge (62,324)PC, Ont., 416/325-8451

Bart Maves, Niagara Falls (47,729)PC, Ont., 416/325-5528

Dalton J.P. McGuinty, Ottawa South (43,793)Lib., Ont., 416/325-7263

Allan K. McLean, Simcoe East (58,477)PC, Ont., 416/325-3855

Lyn McLeod, Fort William (43,643)Lib., Ont., 416/325-7155

Frank Miclash, Kenora (33,061)Lib., Ont., 416/325-3639

Gilles E. Morin, Carleton East (61,643)Lib., Ont., 416/325-7216

Julia Munro, Durham-York (65,909)PC, Ont., 416/314-5741

Bill Murdoch, Grey-Owen Sound (61,048)PC, Ont., 416/327-0616

Hon. Marilyn Mushinski, Scarborough-Ellesmere (43,252)PC, Ont., 416/325-6200

Dan Newman, Scarborough Centre (44,325)PC, Ont., 416/327-9829

Peter North, Elgin (54,155)Ind., Ont., 416/325-7271

John O'Toole, Durham East (62,205)PC, Ont., 416/325-6745

Jerry J. Ouellette, Oshawa (54,110)PC, Ont., 416/327-9193

Hon. Al Palladini, York Centre (129,108)PC, Ont., 416/327-9200

John L. Parker, York East (44,733)PC, Ont., 416/325-5548, Voice & TTY: 416/425-2329

Richard Patten, Ottawa Centre (44,958)Lib., Ont., 416/325-1628

Trevor Pettit, Hamilton Mountain (59,371)PC, Ont., 416/325-3715

Gerry Phillips, Scarborough-Agincourt (48,203)Lib., Ont., 416/325-3628

Gilles Pouliot, Lake Nipigon (21,708)NDP, Ont., 416/325-4075

Peter L. Preston, Brant-Haldimand (48,807)PC, Ont., 416/325-8216

Sandra Pupatello, Windsor-Sandwich (51,421)Lib., Ont., 416/325-1496

David Ramsay, Timiskaming (29,037)Lib., Ont., 416/325-7137

E.J. Douglas Rollins, Quinte (50,783)PC, Ont., 416/325-8209

Lillian Ross, Hamilton West (49,673)PC, Ont., 416/325-5562

Hon. Robert W. Runciman, Leeds-Grenville (54,953)PC, Ont., 416/326-5075

Tony Ruprecht, Parkdale (27,999)Lib., Ont., 416/325-7777

Hon. Rob Sampson, Mississauga West (96,475)PC, Ont., 416/325-0413

Hon. William Saunderson, Eglinton (48965)PC, Ont., 416/325-6900

Mario Sergio, Yorkview (32,827)Lib., Ont., 416/325-1404

Derwyn Shea, High Park-Swansea (39,294)PC, Ont., 416/585-4038

Frank Sheehan, Lincoln (54,677)PC, Ont., 416/325-8640

Tony Silipo, Dovercourt (30,963)NDP, Ont., 416/325-6311

Tony Skarica, Wentworth North (54,022)PC, Ont., 416/325-2505

Bruce Smith, Middlesex (59,061)PC, Ont., 416/325-4561

Hon. John Snobelen, Mississauga North (81,425)PC, Ont., 416/325-2600

Joe Spina, Brampton North (69,435)PC, Ont., 416/325-6913

Hon. Norman W. Sterling, Carleton (70,780)PC, Ont., 416/326-8500

R. Gary Stewart, Peterborough (65,678)PC, Ont., 416/325-6639

Chris Stockwell, Etobicoke West (47,256)PC, Ont., 416/325-7535

Joseph N. Tascona, Simcoe Centre (81,753)PC, Ont., 416/325-4579

David Tilson, Dufferin-Peel (54,176)PC, Ont., 416/326-2485

Hon. David H. Tsubouchi, MarkhamPC, Ont., 416/325-5225

David Turnbull, York Mills (43,180)PC, Ont., 416/325-3877

Bill Vankoughnet, Frontenac-Addington (51,066)Ind., Ont., 416/325-8662

Hon. Noble Villeneuve, S.D.G. & East Grenville (46,086)PC, Ont., 416/326-3067

Wayne Wettlaufer, Kitchener (56,066)PC, Ont., 416/325-8220

Bud Wildman, Algoma (21,864)NDP, Ont., 416/325-6800

Hon. James Wilson, Simcoe West (56,980)PC, Ont., 416/327-4300

Hon. Elizabeth Witmer, Waterloo North (70,170)PC, Ont., 416/326-7600

Bob Wood, London South (66,875)PC, Ont., 416/325-4928

Len Wood, Cochrane North (26,037)NDP, Ont., 416/325-7040

Terrence Young, Halton Centre (47,738)PC, Ont., 416/325-2367

ONTARIO GOVERNMENT DEPARTMENTS & AGENCIES

Ministry of AGRICULTURE, FOOD & RURAL AFFAIRS (OMAFRA)

Information Centre, 801 Bay St., 1st Fl., Toronto ON M7A 2B2
416/326-3400; Fax: 416/326-3409; URL: http://tdg.uoguelph.ca/omafra/start.html
Toll Free: 1-800-567-8898

ACTS ADMINISTERED

Abandoned Orchards Act
Agricultural & Horticultural Organizations Act
Agricultural Committees Act
Agricultural Rehabilitation & Development Act (Ontario)
Agricultural Representatives Act
Agricultural Research Institute of Ontario Act
Agricultural Tile Drainage Installation Act
Animals for Research Act
Artificial Insemination of Livestock Act
Beef Cattle Marketing Act
Bees Act
Bull Owners Liability Act
Commodity Board Members Act
Commodity Boards & Marketing Agencies Act
Cooperative Loans Act
Crop Insurance Act (Ontario)
Dead Animal Disposal Act
Drainage Act
Edible Oil Products Act
Farm Implements Act
Farm Income Stabilization Act
Farm Practices Protection Act
Farm Products Containers Act
Farm Products Grades & Sales Act
Farm Products Marketing Act
Farm Products Payments Act
Farm Registration & Farm Organizations Funding Act
Fur Farms Act
Grain Corn Marketing Act
Grain Elevator Storage Act
Hunter Damage Compensation Act
Junior Farmer Establishment Act
Livestock & Livestock Products Act
Livestock Branding Act
Livestock Community Sales Act
Livestock Medicines Act
Livestock, Poultry & Honey Bee Protection Act
Meat Inspection Act (Ontario)
Milk Act
Ministry of Agriculture & Food Act
Non-resident Agricultural Interests Registration Act
Oleomargarine Act
Ontario Agricultural Museum Act
Ontario Food Terminal Act
Plant Diseases Act
Pounds Act
Provincial Auctioneers Act
Riding Horse Establishments Act
Seed Potatoes Act
Sheep & Wool Marketing Act
Stock Yards Act
Tile Drainage Act
Topsoil Preservation Act
Veterinarians Act
Weed Control Act
Minister, Hon. Noble Villeneuve, 416/326-3067, Fax: 416/326-3083
Deputy Minister, Kenneth W. Knox, 416/326-3100, Fax: 416/326-3106

Communications Branch

416/326-3103; Fax: 416/326-3106
Director, Joan Krantzberg, 416/326-3027
Manager, Broadcast Services, Graham Howe, #108, Johnston Hall, University of Guelph, Guelph ON N1G 2W1, 519/824-4120, Fax: 519/821-7569
Manager, Finance & Administration, Kathy Goldring, 416/326-3022, Fax: 416/326-3043
Manager, Information Centre, Rita Scagnetti, 416/326-3415, Fax: 416/326-3409
Manager, Media & Editorial Services, Tom Rekstis, 416/326-3031, Fax: 416/326-3043
Manager, Visual Communications & Exhibits, Peter Hume, 52 Royal Rd., Guelph ON N1H 1G3, 519/767-3620, Fax: 519/821-3358

Legal Services Branch
416/326-3384; Fax: 416/326-3385
Director, Louise Stratford, 416/326-3378

AGRICULTURE DIVISION
416/326-3506; Fax: 416/325-1165
Asst. Deputy Minister, Dr. Frank Ingratta, 416/326-3528, Fax: 416/325-1165
Director, Crop Technology & Southern Region, Ralph Shaw, Guelph Agriculture Centre, PO Box 1030, Guelph ON N1H 6N1, 519/767-3172, Fax: 519/837-3049
Acting Director, Farm Business Management & Western Region, Rod Stork, 416/767-3151, Fax: 416/837-3049
Director, Leadership & Organization Development, Central & Northern Region, Gwen Zellen, Guelph Agriculture Centre, PO Box 1030, Guelph ON N1H 6N1, 519/767-3523, Fax: 519/824-6941
Director, Livestock Technology & Eastern Region, Don Taylor, Guelph Agriculture Centre, PO Box 1030, Guelph ON N1H 6N1, 519/767-3112, Fax: 519/837-3049
Director, Resources & Regulations Branch, David Thomson, Guelph Agriculture Centre, PO Box 1030, Guelph ON N1H 1G3, 519/767-3561, Fax: 519/824-6941

Field Offices
Algoma: 341 Trunk Rd., Sault Ste. Marie ON P6A 3S9 – 705/253-1161; Fax: 705/253-8777
Brant: #7, 515 Park Rd. North, Brantford ON N3R 7K8 – 519/759-4190; Fax: 519/759-6857
Bruce: 220 Trillium Ct., RR#3, Walkerton ON N0G 2V0 – 519/881-3301; Fax: 519/881-2739
Carleton: 26 Thorncliffe Pl., Nepean ON K2H 6L2 – 613/828-9167; Fax: 613/828-6083
Cochrane North: Experimental Farm, Kapuskasing ON P5N 2X9 – 705/335-5828; Fax: 705/337-6597
Cochrane South: PO Box 608, Matheson ON P0K 1N0 – 705/273-2509; Fax: 705/273-2967
Dufferin: RR#4, Orangeville ON L9W 2Z1 – 519/941-3830; Fax: 519/941-5689
Dundas: PO Box 488, Winchester ON K0C 2K0 – 613/774-2313; Fax: 613/774-3283
Durham: 60 VanEdward Dr., Port Perry ON L6L 1G3 – 905/985-2003; Fax: 905/985-9599
Elgin: RR#5, PO Box 2027, St. Thomas ON N5P 3X1 – 519/631-4700; Fax: 519/631-8784
Essex: 46 Fox St., Essex ON N8M 2S2 – 519/776-7361; Fax: 519/776-8028
Frontenac: 1055 Princess St., PO Box 651, Kingston ON K7L 4X1 – 613/545-4360; Fax: 613/545-9147
Glengarry: PO Box 579, Alexandria ON K0C 1A0 – 613/525-1046; Fax: 613/525-2457
Grenville: PO Box 2004, Kemptville ON K0G 1J0 – 613/258-8295; Fax: 613/258-8392
Grey: 181 Toronto St., Markdale ON N0C 1H0 – 519/986-2040; Fax: 519/986-3014
Haldimand: PO Box 129, Cayuga ON N0A 1E0 – 905/772-3381; Fax: 905/772-3957
Halton/Peel: 332 Guelph St., Georgetown ON L7G 4B5 – 905/873-9930; Fax: 905/873-9934
Hastings: PO Box 340, Stirling ON K0K 3E0 – 613/395-3393; Fax: 613/395-0739
Huron: 100 Don St., PO Box 159, Clinton ON N0M 1L0 – 519/482-3428; Fax: 519/482-5031
Kenora: Ontario Government Bldg., PO Box 3000, Dryden ON P8N 3B3 – 807/223-2415; Fax: 807/223-2824
Kent: 435 Grand Ave. West, PO Box 726, Chatham ON N7M 5L1 – 519/354-2150; Fax: 519/354-8842
Lambton: PO Box 730, Petrolia ON N0N 1R0 – 519/882-0180; Fax: 519/882-3406
Lanark: 10 Sunset Blvd., Perth ON K7H 2Y2 – 613/267-1063; Fax: 613/267-2264
Leeds: PO Box 635, Brockville ON K6V 5V8 – 613/342-2124; Fax: 613/342-1886
Lennox & Addington: 41 Dundas St. West, Napanee ON K7R 1Z5 – 613/354-3371; Fax: 613/354-3267
Manitoulin: PO Box 328, Gore Bay ON P0P 1H0 – 705/282-2043; Fax: 705/282-2792
Midddlesex: #7, 100 Enterprise Dr., RR#3, Komoka ON N0L 1R0 – 519/473-6480; Fax: 519/473-6431
Muskoka & Parry Sound: PO Box 130, Huntsville ON P0A 1K0 – 705/789-1241; Fax: 705/789-1241
Niagara (Fenwick): 726 Canboro Rd., Fenwick ON L0S 1C0 – 905/892-4741; Fax: 905/892-1472
Niagara (Vineland): Vineland Stn, Vineland ON L0R 2E0 – 905/562-4147; Fax: 905/562-5933
Nipissing: 222 McIntyre St. West, North Bay ON P1B 2Y8 – 705/474-3050; Fax: 705/472-0882
Norfolk: PO Box 587, Simcoe ON N3Y 4N5 – 519/426-7120; Fax: 519/428-1142
Northumberland: 95 Dundas St., PO Box 8200, Brighton ON K0K 1H0 – 613/475-1630; Fax: 613/475-3835
Oxford: PO Box 666, Woodstock ON N4S 7Z5 – 519/537-6621; Fax: 519/539-5351
Perth: 413 Hibernia St., Perth ON N5A 5W2 – 519/271-0820; Fax: 519/273-5278
Peterborough: 55 George St. North, Peterborough ON K9J 3G2 – 705/745-2403; Fax: 705/745-6657
Prescott: PO Box 110, Plantagenat ON K0B 1L0 – 613/673-5115; Fax: 613/673-5578
Prince Edward: PO Box 470, Picton ON K0K 2T0 – 613/476-3224; Fax: 613/476-3370
Rainy River: PO Box 210, Emo ON P0W 1E0 – 807/482-2310; Fax: 807/482-2864
Renfrew: 315 Raglan St. South, Renfrew ON K7V 1R6 – 613/432-4841; Fax: 613/432-7845
Russell: 735 Notre Dame St., PO Box 540, Embrun ON K0A 1W0 – 613/443-3391; Fax: 613/443-5082
Simcoe: Cedar Hill Plaza, 449 Dunlop St. West, Barrie ON L4N 1C3 – 705/725-7288; Fax: 705/725-7296
Stormont: PO Box 97, Avonmore ON K0C 1C0 – 613/346-2143; Fax: 613/346-2689
Sudbury: 1899 LaSalle Blvd., Sudbury ON P3A 1Z6 – 705/566-1630; Fax: 705/566-2689
Thunder Bay: Ontario Government Bldg., 435 James St. South, Thunder Bay ON P7E 6E3 – 807/475-1631; Fax: 807/475-1219
Timiskaming: PO Box G, New Liskeard ON P0J 1P0 – 705/647-6701; Fax: 705/647-6297
Victoria-Haliburton: 322 Kent St. West, Lindsay ON K9V 2Z9 – 705/324-6125; Fax: 705/324-1638
Waterloo: 279 Weber St. North, Waterloo ON N2J 3H8 – 519/884-5390; Fax: 519/884-0241
Wellington: RR#1, Fergus ON N1M 2W3 – 519/846-0941; Fax: 519/846-8178
Wentworth: RR#1, Ancaster ON L9G 3K9 – 416/527-2995; Fax: 416/648-6817
York: #102, 1110 Stellar Dr., Newmarket ON L3Y 7B7 – 416/895-4519; Fax: 416/895-6739

CORPORATE SERVICES DIVISION
416/326-3097; Fax: 416/326-3390
Asst. Deputy Minister, Barb Miller, 416/326-3095
Acting Director, Audit Services, Walter Kent, 416/326-3777, Fax: 416/326-3793
Director, Financial Operations, Pauline Moeller, 416/326-3186, Fax: 416/326-3329
Director, Financial Planning Secretariat, Richard Kirsh, 416/326-3191, Fax: 416/326-3264
Director, Human Resources Branch, Nancy Navkar, 416/326-3717, Fax: 416/326-3128
Director, Management Systems Branch, John Birss, 416/326-3599, Fax: 416/326-3447
Director, Relocation & Administrative Services, Michael Keith, 416/325-1179, Fax: 416/326-6575

RURAL DEVELOPMENT DIVISION
416/326-3085; Fax: 416/326-3747
Supports economic & social sustainability within rural communities; provides resources, expertise & support to community strategic planning, communications planning, capacity building, project evaluation & monitoring; provides protection to Ontario's prime agricultural land areas from competing development & use.
Asst. Deputy Minister, Anne Donohoe, 416/326-3122
Director, Land Use Planning Branch, Neil Smith, 416/326-3126, Fax: 416/326-3065
Acting General Manager, Ontario Agricultural Museum, Tony Price, 144 Town Line, PO Box 38, Milton ON L9T 2Y3, 905/878-8151, Fax: 905/876-4530
Director, Rural Development Secretariat, Keith Pinder, 416/326-3492, Fax: 416/326-3507

EDUCATION, RESEARCH & LABORATORIES DIVISION
95 Stone Rd. West, PO Box 3650, Guelph ON N1H 8J7
519/767-3603; Fax: 519/767-3635
Pesticide/Trace Contaminants Lab: 519/767-6200
Pest Diagnostic Clinic: 519/767-6258
Safety Response Unit: 519/767-6245
Asst. Deputy Minister, Norris Hoag, 519/767-3601, Fax: 519/824-6941
Director, Agriculture & Food Laboratory Services Centre, Dr. Jim Pettit, 519/767-5013, Fax: 519/767-0060
Director, Horticultural Research Institute of Ontario, Dr. Frank Eady, PO Box 7000, Vineland Station ON L0R 2E0, 905/562-4141, Fax: 905/562-3413
Director, Veterinary Laboratory Services, Dr. Deb Stark, 519/837-5081, Fax: 519/767-0015

FOOD INDUSTRY DIVISION
416/326-3759; Fax: 416/326-3747
Asst. Deputy Minister, James Farrar, 416/326-3757
Director, Dairy, Fruit & Vegetable Industry Inspection Branch, Diane Coates Milne, 519/837-5045, Fax: 519/767-0336
Director, Food Industry Competitiveness Branch, James Farrar, 416/326-3047, Fax: 416/326-3094
Acting Director, Market Development Branch, Bill Allen, 416/326-3510, Fax: 416/326-7630
Director, Meat Industry Inspection Branch, Charles Lalonde, 519/837-5060, Fax: 519/767-0305

POLICY & FARM FINANCE DIVISION
416/326-3210; Fax: 416/326-9892
Asst. Deputy Minister, Bob Seguin, 416/326-3204
Director, Farm Assistance Programs, Rolly Stroeter, 416/326-3493, Fax: 416/326-3507
Director, Policy Analysis, Len Roozen, 416/326-3252
Director, Policy & Program Coordination, Bob Kalbfleisch, 416/326-3209

Crop Insurance & Stabilization
Director, Agricorp, Greg Brown, 416/326-3300, Fax: 416/326-3133

Associated Agencies, Boards & Commissions
• Agricultural Research Institute of Ontario (ARIO): 801 Bay St., 6th Fl., Toronto ON M7A 1A3 – 416/326-3396; Fax: 416/326-3394
Director, Norris Hoag
• Cooperative Loans Board of Ontario: #100, 10 Alcorn Ave., Toronto ON M4V 3B3 – 416/326-3493
Chair, Rolly Stroeter
• Council of the College of Veterinarians of Ontario: Guelph Agriculture Centre, 259 Grange Rd., PO Box 1030, Guelph ON N1H 6N1 – 519/767-3116
Contact, Dr. Deb Stark
• Crop Insurance Commission of Ontario: 801 Bay St., 5th Fl., Toronto ON M7A 2B2 – 416/326-3276; Fax: 416/326-3133

Chair, Greg Brown
• Ontario Agricultural Licensing & Registration Review Board: Guelph Agriculture Centre, PO Box 1030, Guelph ON N1H 1G3 – 519/767-3547
Contact, David Thomson
• Ontario Agricultural Museum Advisory Board: PO Box 38, Milton ON L9T 2Y3 – 905/878-8151
Chair, John Wiley
• Ontario Agricultural Rehabilitation & Development Directorate: #100, 10 Alcorn Ave., Toronto ON M4V 3B3 – 416/326-3493
Chair, Rolly Stroeter
• Ontario Beginning Farmer Assistance Program Review Committee: #100, 10 Alcorn Ave., Toronto ON M4V 3B3 – 416/326-3492
Chair, Rolly Stroeter
• Ontario Crop Insurance Arbitration Board: 801 Bay St., 5th Fl., Toronto ON M7A 2B2 – 416/326-3276; Fax: 416/326-3133
Chair, Greg Brown
• Ontario Drainage Tribunal: Guelph Agriculture Centre, 52 Royal Rd., PO Box 1030, Guelph ON N1H 1G3 – 519/767-3552
• Ontario Egg Fund Board: #800, 33 Yonge St., Toronto ON M5E 1X2 – 416/326-7486
Contact, Gloria Marco Borys
• Ontario Farm Family Advisor Program Board: Guelph Agricultural Centre, 52 Royal Rd., PO Box 1030, Guelph ON N1H 6N1 – 519/767-3151
Contact, Rod Stork
• Ontario Farm Implements Board: Guelph Agriculture Centre, 52 Royal Rd., PO Box 1030, Guelph ON N1H 1G3 – 519/767-3547; Fax: 519/824-6941
Chair, David Thomson
• Ontario Farm Income Stabilization Commission: 801 Bay St., 5th Fl., Toronto ON M7A 2B2 – 416/326-3300
Contact, Greg Brown
• Ontario Farm Organizations Accreditation Tribunal: #100, 10 Alcorn Ave., Toronto ON M4V 3B3 – 416/326-3493
Chair, Rolly Stroeter
• Ontario Farm Practices Protection Board: Guelph Agriculture Centre, 52 Royal Rd., PO Box 1030, Guelph ON N1H 1G3 – 519/767-3577
Chair, David Thomson
• Ontario Farm Products Appeal Tribunal: Cooperators Bldg., #303A, 130 Macdonell St., Guelph ON N1H 2Z6 – 519/763-3430; Fax: 519/763-0351
Chair, John Johnston
• Ontario Farm Products Marketing Commission: #800, 33 Yonge St., Toronto ON M5E 1X2 – 416/326-7486; Fax: 416/326-7630
Chair, Jim Wheeler, 519/326-7087
General Manager, David K. Alles, 416/326-7003
• Ontario Farm Tax Rebate Appeal Board: #100, 10 Alcorn Ave., Toronto ON M4V 3B3 – 416/326-3492; Fax: 416/326-3501
Chair, Rolly Stroeter
• Ontario Food Terminal Board: 165 The Queensway, Toronto ON M8Y 1H8 – 416/259-5479; Fax: 416/259-4303
General Manager, C.E. Carsley
• Ontario Grain Financial Protection Board: #800, 33 Yonge St., PO Box 1030, Toronto ON M5E 1X2 – 416/326-7547
Chair, Bill Moore
• Ontario Junior Farmers Establishment Loan Corporation: #100, 10 Alcorn Ave., Toronto ON M4V 3B3 – 416/326-3493; Fax: 416/326-3133
Chair, Rolly Stroeter
• Ontario Livestock Financial Protection Board: #800, 33 Yonge St., Toronto ON M5E 1X2 – 416/326-7547
Chair, Bill Moore
• Ontario Livestock Medicines Advisory Committee: Guelph Agriculture Centre, 52 Royal Rd., PO Box 1030, Guelph ON N1H 1G3 – 519/767-3547
Chair, David Thomson
• Ontario Produce Arbitration Board: Guelph Agriculture Centre, 259 Grange Rd., PO Box 1030, Guelph ON N1H 6N1 – 519/837-5044
Chair, Diane Coates Milne
• Ontario Provincial Decision Committee (Private Mortgage Guarantee Program): #100, 10 Alcorn Ave., Toronto ON M4V 3B3 – 416/326-3492
Contact, Rolly Stroeter
• Ontario Stock Yards Board: 801 Bay St., 4th Fl., Toronto ON M7A 2B2 – 416/326-3015
Chair, Bob Seguin
• Ontario Wolf Damage Assessment Board: #100, 10 Alcorn Ave., Toronto ON M4V 3B3 – 416/326-3492
Contact, Rolly Stroeter

Agricultural Marketing Boards & Commissions

• Ontario Apple Marketing Commission: 7195B Millcreek Dr., Mississauga ON L5A 3R3 – 905/858-1060; Fax: 905/858-3299
• Ontario Asparagus Growers' Marketing Board: 71C Front St. West., Strathroy ON N7G 1X6 – 519/246-1640; Fax: 519/246-1634
Chair, John Jacques
• Ontario Bean Producers' Marketing Board: 140 Raney Cres., London ON N6L 1C3 – 519/652-3566; Fax: 519/652-9607
General Manager, Charles E. Broadwell
• Ontario Broiler Hatching Egg & Chick Commission: 291 Woodlawn Rd. West, Unit 9B, Guelph ON N1H 7L6 – 519/837-0005; Fax: 519/837-0464
General Manager, Roger J. Bennett
• Ontario Chicken Producers' Marketing Board: 3380 South Service Rd., PO Box 5035, Burlington ON L7R 3Y8 – 905/637-0025; Fax: 905/637-3464
General Manager, William V. Doyle
• Ontario Cream Producers' Marketing Board: 6780 Campobello Rd., Mississauga ON L5N 2L8 – 905/821-8970; Fax: 905/821-3160
Secretary Manager, J. Bilyea
• Ontario Egg Producers' Marketing Board: 7195 Millcreek Dr., Mississauga ON L5N 4H1 – 905/858-9790; Fax: 905/821-3160
General Manager, B. Ellsworth
• Ontario Flue-Cured Tobacco Growers' Marketing Board: PO Box 70, Tillsonburg ON N4G 4H4 – 519/842-3661; Fax: 519/842-7813
Secretary, M.E. Lepage
• Ontario Grape Growers' (Fresh & Processing) Marketing Board: PO Box 100, Vineland Stn, Vineland ON L0R 2E0 – 905/688-0990; Fax: 905/688-3211 – (Grapes for Processing)
Secretary, J.R. Rainforth
• Ontario Greenhouse Vegetable Producers' Marketing Board: PO Box 417, Leamington ON N8H 3W5 – 519/326-2604; Fax: 519/326-7842
Secretary, William K. Power
• Ontario Milk Marketing Board: 6780 Campobello Rd., Mississauga ON L5N 2L8 – 905/821-8970; Fax: 905/821-3160
Secretary, H. Parker
• Ontario Pork Producers' Marketing Board: PO Box 740, Etobicoke ON M9C 5H3 – 416/621-1874; Fax: 416/621-6869
Secretary, G. Agnew
• Ontario Potato Growers' (Fresh & Processing) Marketing Board: 570 Brant St., Burlington ON L7R 2G8 – 905/637-5609; Fax: 905/637-7653
Secretary Manager, W.L. Armstrong
• Ontario Processing Tomato Seedling Plant Growers' Marketing Board: PO Box 157, Leamington ON N8H 3W2 – 519/326-4481; Fax: 519/326-3413
Secretary, G. Woodsit
• Ontario Seed Corn Growers' Marketing Board: 785 St. Clair St., RR#7, Chatham ON N7M 5J7 – 519/352-6710; Fax: 519/352-0526
Secretary Manager, Brad Caughy
• Ontario Sheep Marketing Agency: 50 Dovercliffe Rd., Unit 13, Guelph ON N1G 3A6 – 519/836-0043; Fax: 519/824-9101
Secretary Manager, F.E. Winger
• Ontario Soybean Growers' Marketing Board: PO Box 1199, Chatham ON N7M 5L8 – 519/352-7730; Fax: 519/352-8983
Secretary Manager, Fred Brandenburg
• Ontario Tender Fruit Producers' Marketing Board: PO Box 100, Vineland Stn, Vineland ON L0R 2E0 – 905/688-0990; Fax: 905/688-3211
Secretary Manager, J.R. Rainforth
• Ontario Turkey Producers' Marketing Board: 60 New Dundee Rd., RR#2, Kitchener ON N2G 3W5 – 519/748-9636; Fax: 519/748-2742
General Manager, JoAnn White
• Ontario Vegetable Growers' Marketing Board: 435 Consortium Ct., London ON N6E 2S8 – 519/681-1875; Fax: 519/685-5719
Chair, Leonard Harwood
Secretary Manager, John Mumford
• Ontario Wheat Producers' Marketing Board: 880 Richmond St., PO Box 668, Chatham ON N7M 5K8 – 519/354-4430; Fax: 519/354-0675
Secretary Manager, William McClounie

Ministry of the ATTORNEY GENERAL
720 Bay St., 11th Fl., Toronto ON M5G 2K1
416/326-2220; Fax: 416/326-4088

ACTS ADMINISTERED
Absconding Debtors Act
Absentees Act
Accidental Fires Act
Accumulations Act
Administration of Justice Act
Age of Majority & Accountability Act
Aliens' Real Property Act
Anglican Church of Canada
Arbitrations Act
Architects Act
Assessment Review Board Act
Bail Act
Barristers Act
Blind Persons' Rights Act
Bulk Sales Act
Business Records Protection Act
Canada-United Kingdom Convention
Canadian Citizenship & British Status Act
Change of Name Act
Charitable Gifts Act
Charities Accounting Act
Children's Law Reform Act
Commissioners for Taking Affidavits Act
Compensation for Victims of Crime Act
Construction Lien Act
Consultants Act
Conveyance & Law of Property Act
Costs of Distress Act
Court Reform Statute Law Amendment Act
Courts of Justice Act
Creditors' Relief Act
Crown Administration of Estates Act
Crown Agency Act
Crown Attorneys Act
Crown Witnesses Act
Disorderly Houses Act
Dog Owners' Liability Act
English & Wahigoon River Systems Mercury Contamination Settlement Agreement Act
Equality Rights Statute Law Amendment Act
Escheats Act
Estates Act

Estates Administration Act
Evidence Act
Execution Act
Expropriation Act
Family Law Act
Fines & Forfeitures Act
Foreign Arbitral Awards Act
Fraudulent Conveyances Act
Fraudulent Debtors Arrest Act
Frustrated Contracts Act
Gaming Act
Group Defamation Act
Habeas Corpus Act
Hague Convention on Child Abduction
Hague Convention on Service of Documents Abroad
Hospitals & Charitable Institutions Inquiries Act
Hotel Registration of Guests Act
Human Artificial Reproduction Act
Innkeepers Act
International Commercial Arbitration Act
International Sale of Goods Act
Interpretation Act
Interprovincial Subpoenas Act
Intervenor Funding Project Act
Judicial Review Procedure Act
Juries Act
Justices of the Peace Act
Landlord & Tenant Act
Law Society Act
Legal Aid Act
Legal Profession Statute Law Amendment Act
Libel & Slander Act
Limitations Act
Mandatory Retirement Act
Master & Servant Act
Mechanics' Lien Act
Members' Conflict of Interest Act
Mental Incompetency Act
Ministry of the Attorney General Act
Minors' Protection Act
Mortgages Act
Negligence Act
Notaries Act
Occupiers' Liability Act
Ombudsman Act
Ontario Law Reform Commission Act
Ontario Municipal Board Act
Ontario Native Justice of Peace Program Act
Ontario Québec Exchange of Judges Act
Partition Act
Pawnbrokers Act
Perpetuities Act
Police Services Act
Powers of Attorney Act
Proceedings Against the Crown Act
Professional Engineers Act
Profits of Crime Act
Property & Civil Rights Act
Provincial Offences Act
Provincial Residence Mobility Rights Act
Public Accountancy Act
Public Authorities' Protection Act
Public Halls Act
Public Inquiries Act
Public Institutions Inspection Act
Public Officers Act
Public Trustee Act
Race Relations Issues Act
Reciprocal Enforcement of Judgements Act
Reciprocal Enforcement of Judgements (U.K.) Act
Reciprocal Enforcement of Maintenance Orders Act
Regulations Act
Regulations Revision Act
Religious Freedom Act
Religious Organizations' Lands Act
Revised Statutes Confirmation Act
Sale of Goods Act
Search & Seizure Act

Settled Estates Act
Short Forms of Conveyances Act
Short Forms of Leases Act
Short Forms of Mortgages Act
Solicitors Act
South African Trust Investments Act
Statute of Frauds
Statutes Act
Statutes Revision Act
Statutory Powers Procedure Act
Succession Law Reform Act
Support & Custody Orders Enforcement Act
Ticket Speculation Act
Time Act
Transboundary Pollution Reciprocal Access Act
Trespass to Property Act
Trustee Act
Unconscionable Transactions Relief Act
University Expropriation Powers Act
Variation of Trusts Act
Vendors & Purchasers Act
Vienna Sales Convention
Wages Act
Warehouse Receipts Act
Warehousemen's Lien Act
Minister, Hon. Charles Harnick, 416/326-4000, Fax: 416/326-4016
Deputy Minister, Larry Taman, 416/326-2640, Fax: 416/326-4018

Communications Branch
720 Bay St., Main Fl., Toronto ON M5G 2K1
Fax: 416/326-4007
Director, Anji Husain, 416/326-2205
Senior Manager, Client Services, Kimberley Bates, 416/326-2209
Acting Manager, Corporate Communications, Suzanne Kemper, 416/326-3802
Manager, Issues Management, Karen Arnone, 416/326-2604

Drinking/Driving Countermeasures
720 Bay St., 3rd Fl., Toronto ON M5G 2K1
416/326-4408; Fax: 416/326-4007
Manager, John Lefebvre, 416/326-4007

Special Investigations Unit
320 Front St. West, 10th Fl., Toronto ON M5V 3V5
416/314-2915; Fax: 416/314-2925
Director, Graham Reynolds
Communications & Outreach Officer, Sarah Persaud

FINANCE & ADMINISTRATION
Asst. Deputy Attorney General, Richard Monzon, 416/326-2610, Fax: 416/326-2326
Director, Audit Services Branch, Anton M. Odeh, 416/326-4224, Fax: 416/326-4219
Director, Computer & Telecommunications Services Branch, Kalman Brettler, 416/326-2001, Fax: 416/326-4797
Director, Financial & Administrative Services Branch, Helen Hayward, 416/326-4372, Fax: 416/326-4312
Director, Human Resources Branch, Peter W. Clendinneng, 416/326-2700, Fax: 416/326-4009
Coordinator, Freedom of Information & Privacy, Ruth Mallard, 416/326-4300, Fax: 416/326-4307
Acting Manager, Purchasing & Supply Services, Maureen Adamson, 416/326-4067, Fax: 416/326-4085
Manager, Research & Evaluation Services Unit, Tom McCallum, 416/326-2186, Fax: 416/326-2095

Justice Review Project
#205, 101 Bloor St. West, Toronto ON M5S 1P7
416/325-4910; Fax: 416/326-6298
Director, Dick Barnhorst

LEGISLATIVE COUNSEL
Whitney Block, #3600, 99 Wellesley St. West, Toronto ON M7A 1A2
416/326-2841; Fax: 416/326-2806
Chief Legislative Counsel, Donald L. Revell, 416/326-2770
Deputy Chief Legislative Counsel, Administration & Statutes Revision, Sidney Tucker, Q.C., 416/326-2777
Deputy Chief Legislative Counsel, French Language Services, Michael J.B. Wood, 416/326-2766
Deputy Chief Legislative Counsel, Legislative Counsel Services, Corneila Schuh, 416/326-2741
Registrar, Regulations, Lucinda Mifsud, 416/326-2748, Fax: 416/326-2805

COURTS ADMINISTRATION PROGRAM
Asst. Deputy Attorney General, Sandra Lang, 416/326-2609, Fax: 416/326-2652
Director, Facilities & Special Court Services Branch, Matt Veskimets, 416/326-4033, Fax: 416/326-4029
Acting Director, Family Support Plan, Harvey Brownstone, 416/326-4710, Fax: 416/326-4735
Acting Director, Program Development Branch, Axel Frandsen, 416/326-4264, Fax: 416/326-4289

Regional Courts Administration
Executive Director, Metro Toronto, Nestor Yurchuk, 720 Bay St., 2nd Fl., Toronto ON M5G 2K1, 416/326-4250, Fax: 416/326-2073
Acting Regional Director, Central East, Bob Beaudoin, 1091 Gorham St., 2nd Fl., Newmarket ON L3Y 7V1, 905/836-5621, Fax: 905/836-5620
Regional Director, Central South, Donna Silver, 50 Main St. East, Hamilton ON L8N 1E9, 905/577-6866, Fax: 905/577-6877
Regional Director, Central West, Dave Henderson, #302, 201 County Courts Blvd., Brampton ON L6W 4L2, 416/452-7494, Fax: 416/452-9470
Regional Director, East, Bob Beaudoin, #5300, 161 Elgin St., Ottawa ON K2P 2K1, 613/239-1272, Fax: 613/239-1273
Regional Director, Northeast, Andre Clement, #601, 144 Pine St., Sudbury ON PC3 1X3, 705/675-4169, Fax: 705/675-4172
Acting Regional Director, Northwest, Larry Kaplanis, 233 South Court St., 2nd Fl., Thunder Bay ON P7B 2X9, 807/345-2888, Fax: 807/345-6383
Regional Director, Southwest, Walter Chmiel, #2-069, 80 Dundas St. West, London ON N6A 2P3, 519/660-3090, Fax: 519/660-3098

CIVIL LAW DIVISION
416/326-2607; Fax: 416/326-4014
Asst. Deputy Attorney General, Leslie H. Macleod, 416/326-2608
Executive Coordinator, Seconded Legal Services, Brock Grant, 416/326-4020, Fax: 416/326-4019
Acting Public Trustee, Office of the Public Trustee, Susan Himel, 416/314-2690, Fax: 416/314-2716, General Inquiry: 416/314-2800
Official Guardian, Willson McTavish, 393 University Ave., 14th Fl., Toronto ON M5G 1W9, 416/314-8011, Fax: 416/314-8000
Associate Director, Advisory Services, Corey Simpson, 416/326-4098
Associate Director, Litigation, Leah Price, 416/326-4478
Director, Civil Crown Law Office, Heather Cooper, 416/326-4008, Fax: 416/326-4181
General Counsel, T.C. Marshall
General Counsel, Thomas Wickett

CONSTITUTIONAL LAW & POLICY
Director & Chief Counsel, Bonnie J. Wein, 416/326-2584
Acting Director, Constitutional Law, Elizabeth C. Goldberg, 416/326-2624

GOVERNMENT OF ONTARIO

Deputy Director & General Counsel, Carol Creighton, 416/326-4476
Office Administrator, Clita J. Saldanha
Acting Coordinator, Constitutional Information, Michel Y. Hélie, 416/326-4454
Constitutional Information Asst., Heather Janack, 416/326-4474
Criminal Counsel, Susan Chapman, 416/326-4590

CRIMINAL LAW DIVISION
Asst. Deputy Attorney General, Michael Code, 416/326-2616, Fax: 416/326-2063
Provincial Coordinator, Victim-Witness Services, Susan Lee, 416/326-2429
Director, Criminal Crown Law Office, Murray Segal, 416/326-2300, Fax: 416/326-4619
Director, Criminal Prosecutions, Brian Trafford, 416/326-2618, Fax: 416/326-2423
Director, Divisional Planning & Administration, Marnie D. Brown, 416/326-2405
For list of Courts & other Legal Offices, including Judicial Officials & Judges see Section 10 of this book.

POLICY DEVELOPMENT DIVISION
416/326-2500; Fax: 416/326-2699
Director, J. Douglas Ewart, 416/326-2620
Acting Deputy Director, Ann Merritt, 416/326-2509
Deputy Director, Equality Rights Branch, Lori Newton, 416/326-2513

Assessment Review Board
121 Bloor St. East, 3rd Fl., Toronto ON M4W 3H5
416/314-6900; Fax: 416/314-6906
Toll Free: 1-800-263-3237
Registrar, Deborah Guild
Assessment Contact, Theresa E. Camacho
Assessment Contact, Marilyn Gamble
Assessment Contact, Annette Robinson

Associated Agencies, Boards & Commissions
• Board of Negotiation: 720 Bay St., 4th Fl., Toronto ON M5G 2K1 – 416/326-4700
Chair, G.W. Swayze
• Criminal Injuries Compensation Board: 439 University Ave., 4th Fl., Toronto ON M5G 1Y8 – 416/326-2900; Fax: 416/326-2883
Chair, Wendy Calder
Manager, Administration, Dina Alexis
• Office of the Police Complaints Commissioner: 595 Bay St., 9th Fl., PO Box 23, Toronto ON M5G 2C2 – 416/325-4700; Fax: 416/325-4704
Police Complaints Commissioner, Clare E. Lewis
Executive Director, Mark Conacher
• Ontario Criminal Code Review Board: 700 Bay St., 23rd Fl., Toronto ON M5G 1Z6 – 416/327-8868; Fax: 416/327-8867
Chair, John McCamus
Vice Chair, Richard E.B. Simeon
• Ontario Law Reform Commission: 720 Bay St., 11th Fl., Toronto ON M5G 1L9 – 416/326-4200; Fax: 416/326-4693
Chair, John McCamus
Vice Chair, Richard E.B. Simeon
• Royal Commissions & Inquiries: 180 Dundas St. West, 22nd Fl., Toronto ON M5G 1Z8 – 416/598-0411; Fax: 416/325-8739
Coordinator, Inge Sardy

Office of the Provincial AUDITOR
#1530, 20 Dundas St. West, PO Box 105, Toronto ON M5G 2C2
416/327-2381; Fax: 416/327-9862
Provincial Auditor, Erik Peters, 416/327-1325
Asst. Provincial Auditor, Ken Leishman, 416/327-1326
Executive Director, Finance, Public Accounts & General Government Portfolio, Jim McCarter
Director, Community & Social Services Portfolio, Walter Bordne

Director, Crown Agencies, Boards & Commissions Portfolio, John McDowell
Director, Economic Development Portfolio, Gerard Fitzmaurice
Director, Health Portfolio, Nick Mishchenko
Director, Education & Training, Housing & Municipal Affairs Portfolio, Gary Peall
Director, Justice & Regulatory Portfolio, Andrew Cheung
Coordinator, Communications, Margaret Reid

Ministry of CITIZENSHIP, CULTURE & RECREATION (MCCR)
77 Bloor St. West, 6th Fl., Toronto ON M7A 2R9
416/314-6200

ACTS ADMINISTERED
Advocacy Act
Archives Act
Art Gallery of Ontario Act
Arts Council Act
Centennial Centre of Science & Technology Act
Community Recreation Centres Act
Employment Equity
Foreign Cultural Objects Immunity from Seizure Act
George R. Gardiner Museum of Ceramic Art Act
McMichael Canadian Collection Act
Ministry of Citizenship & Culture Act
Ministry of Tourism & Recreation Act
Ontario Heritage Act
Ontario Human Rights Code
Parks Assistance
Public Libraries Act
Royal Ontario Museum Act
Science North Act
Minister, Hon. Marilyn Mushinski, 416/325-6200, Fax: 416/325-6195
Deputy Minister, Naomi Alboim, 416/325-6220, Fax: 416/325-6196
Director, Communications Branch (Citizenship), Bernadette Sulgit, 416/325-7725, Fax: 416/314-4965
Acting Team Leader, Corporate Affairs Branch (Culture & Recreation), André Quenneville, 416/314-7379, Fax: 416/314-4965

CORPORATE SERVICES & ORGANIZATIONAL PLANNING DIVISION
Asst. Deputy Minister, Fran Grant, 416/314-7311
Coordinator, French Language Services, Jeanne Drouillard, 416/325-6214, Fax: 416/314-7277
Includes: Audit & Evaluation Services, Financial & Administrative Services, Human Resources, Information Technology, Legal Services, Organizational Planning, Relocation Project, Budget Planning & Analysis.

CULTURE DIVISION
77 Bloor St. West, 6th Fl., Toronto ON M7A 2R9
416/314-7265
Asst. Deputy Minister, Jane Marlatt, 416/314-7262
Director, Cultural Liaison Branch, Linda Loving, 416/314-7342
Director, Cultural Program Branch, Lyn Hamilton, 416/314-7081
Director, Heritage, Arts & Cultural Industries Policy Branch, Robert Montgomery, 416/314-7115
Acting Director, Libraries & Community Information Branch, Stan Squires

Native Community Branch
Director, Allan Chrisjohn, 416/314-7414, Fax: 416/314-7428

Regional Offices
Fort Frances: 283 Church St., Fort Frances ON P9A 1C9 – 807/274-9732; Fax: 807/274-0671

Geraldton: 303 Main St. East, PO Box 778, Geraldton ON P0T 1M0 – 807/854-0169; Fax: 807/854-2465
Kenora: 227 - 2 St. South, 3rd Fl., Kenora ON P9N 1G1 – 807/468-2864; Fax: 807/468-2788
London: #601, 255 Dufferin Ave., London ON N6A 5K6 – 519/679-7146; Fax: 519/679-7032
Orillia: 15 Matchedash St. North, Orillia ON L3V 4T4 – 705/325-9561; Fax: 705/329-6024
Sault Ste. Marie: 390 Bay St., 3rd Fl., Sault Ste. Marie ON P6A 1X2 – 705/942-0419; Fax: 705/945-6912
Sioux Lookout: 34 Front St. East, Sioux Lookout ON P8T 1A3 – 807/737-1018; Fax: 807/737-3379
Sudbury: 10 Elm St., 4th Fl., Sudbury ON P3C 5N3 – 705/675-4349; Fax: 705/675-4439
Thunder Bay: 1825 East Arthur St., Thunder Bay ON P7E 5N7 – 807/475-1683; Fax: 807/623-6629
Timmins: 22 Wilcox St., 2nd Fl., Timmins ON P4N 3K6 – 705/267-8018; Fax: 705/360-2013
Toronto: 77 Bloor St. West, 20th Fl., Toronto ON M7A 2R9 – 416/314-7429

ONTARIO ANTI-RACISM SECRETARIAT
Asst. Deputy Minister, Ann-Marie Stewart, 416/326-9723, Fax: 416/326-9725
Director, Community Relations Branch, Daniele D'Ignazio, 416/314-6786, Fax: 416/326-9725
Director, Public Sector Support Branch, Selwyn McSween, 416/326-9704, Fax: 416/326-9725

Regional Offices
Hamilton: 119 King St. West, 8th Fl., Hamilton ON L8N 3Z9 – 905/521-7869; Fax: 905/521-7613
Kingston: #202, 1055 Princess St., Kingston ON K7L 1H3 – 613/545-7869; Fax: 613/545-4240
London: #703, 150 Dufferin St., London ON N6A 5K6 – 519/679-7046; Fax: 519/679-7032
Ottawa: One Nicholas St., 6th Fl., Ottawa ON K1N 1H3 – 613/566-3728; Fax: 613/566-2703
Sudbury: 199 Larch St., Sudbury ON P3E 5P9 – 705/675-4127; Fax: 705/675-4439
Thunder Bay: 1825 East Arthur St., Thunder Bay ON P7E 5N7 – 807/623-6234; Fax: 807/623-6629
Toronto: 77 Bloor St. West, 16th Fl., Toronto ON M7A 2R9 – 416/326-9702; Fax: 416/326-9725

POLICY & PLANNING DIVISION
Asst. Deputy Minister, Karen Cohl, 416/314-6046, Fax: 416/314-7599
Director, Corporate Planning Branch, Sharon Cohen, 416/314-4497, Fax: 416/314-7599
Director, Policy & Research Branch, Andrea Maurice, 416/314-7290, Fax: 416/314-7307
Senior Coordinator, Disability Issues Group, Sandra Carpenter, 700 Bay St., 3rd Fl., Toronto ON M5G 1Z6, 416/326-0201, Fax: 416/327-4080, Disability Issues Inquiry/Voice & TDD: 1-800-387-4456; 416/326-0111

PROGRAM MANAGEMENT DIVISION
Asst. Deputy Minister, Clive Joakim, 416/314-7495, Fax: 416/314-7518
Director, Client Services Branch, Edna Rigby, 416/314-7732, Fax: 416/314-7743
Director, Program Development Branch, John DeMarco, 416/326-6214, Fax: 416/326-6265
Senior Manager, Ontario Welcome House Network, Nancy Newton, 132 St. Patrick St., Toronto ON M5T 1V1, 416/314-5747, Fax: 416/314-6707
Senior Coordinator, Seniors' Issues Group, Peter Murchison, 76 College St., 6th Fl., Toronto ON M7A 1N3, 416/327-2441, Fax: 416/327-2425, Toll Free: 1-800-267-7329, TDD: 416/327-2488

Field Offices
Hamilton: 119 King St. West, 8th Fl., Hamilton ON L8N 3Z9 – 905/521-7517; Fax: 905/521-7613

Canadian Almanac & Directory 1997

London: 255 Dufferin St., 6th Fl., London ON N6A 5K6 – 519/679-7146; Fax: 519/679-7032
Ottawa: #612, One Nicholas St., Ottawa ON K1N 7B7 – 613/566-3728; Fax: 613/566-2703
Sault Ste. Marie: 390 Bay St., 3rd Fl., Sault Ste. Marie ON P6A 1X2 – 705/759-8652; Fax: 705/945-6912
Thunder Bay: 1825 East Arthur St., Thunder Bay ON P7E 5N7 – 807/475-1683; Fax: 807/475-1286
Toronto: 35 McCaul St., 4th Fl., Toronto ON M5T 1V7 – 416/314-6793; Fax: 416/314-6646
Windsor: 221 Mill St., Windsor ON N9C 2R1 – 519/256-5486; Fax: 519/256-1637

RECREATION DIVISION
Asst. Deputy Minister, Gillian Platt, 416/314-1547, Fax: 416/314-7461
Includes: Recreation Policy, Recreation Programs, Regional Services

Regional Offices
Central: 35 McCaul St., 4th Fl., Toronto ON M7A 2R9 – 416/314-6685; Fax: 416/314-6686
Eastern: #400, 10 Rideau St., Ottawa ON K1N 9J1 – 613/787-4000; Fax: 613/787-4020
Northeast: #401, 199 Larch St., Sudbury ON P3E 5P9 – 705/688-3035; Fax: 705/688-3043
Northwest: West Arthur Pl., #302, 1265 East Arthur St., Thunder Bay ON P7E 6E7 – 807/623-5592; Fax: 807/475-1297
Western: #406, 30 Duke St. West, Kitchener ON N2H 3W5 – 519/578-3600; Fax: 519/578-1632

Associated Agencies, Boards & Commissions
• Archives of Ontario: 77 Grenville St., Toronto ON M5S 1B3 – 416/327-1600; Fax: 416/327-1999, Toll Free: 1-800-668-9933
Provincial Archivist, Ian E. Wilson
Deputy Archivist, Melanie Goldhar, 416/327-1577
• Art Gallery of Ontario: 317 Dundas St. West, Toronto ON M5T 1G4 – 416/977-0414; Fax: 416/979-6646; URL: http://www.ago.on.ca/
President, Joseph Rotman
Director, Maxwell Anderson
• Conservation Review Board: 77 Bloor St. West, 2nd Fl., Toronto ON M7A 2R9 – 416/314-7125; Fax: 416/314-7175
Chair, Robert Bowes
Secretary, Nancy Smith
• McMichael Canadian Art Collection: 10365 Islington Ave., Kleinburg ON L0J 1C0 – 905/893-1121; Fax: 905/893-2588; URL: http://www.mcmichael.com/
Chair, Joan Goldfarb
Director/CEO, Barbara A. Tyler
Curator, Megan Bice
• Northern Ontario Library Service: 334 Regent St., Sudbury ON P3C 4E2 – 705/675-6467; Fax: 705/675-6108
Chief Executive Officer, Alan Pepper
• Ontario Advisory Council on Disability Issues: 35 McCaul St., 3rd Fl., Toronto ON M5T 1V7 – 416/314-6650 (Voice & TDD); Fax: 416/314-6658
Chair, Dr. Shirley Van Hoof
Executive Officer, Catherine Chandler, 416/314-6654
• Ontario Advisory Council on Multiculturalism & Citizenship: 35 McCaul St., 3rd Fl., Toronto ON M5T 1V7 – 416/314-6650 (Voice & TDD); Fax: 416/314-6658
Chair, Hanny Hassan
Executive Officer, Catherine Chandler, 416/314-6654
• Ontario Advisory Council on Senior Citizens: 35 McCaul St., 3rd Fl., Toronto ON M5T 1V7 – 416/314-6650 (Voice & TDD); Fax: 416/314-6658
Chair, William A. Hughes
Executive Officer, Catherine Chandler, 416/314-6654
• Ontario Arts Council: 151 Bloor St. West, 5th Fl., Toronto ON M5S 1T6 – 416/961-1660; Fax: 416/969-7447; URL: http://www.ffa.ucalgary.ca/oac/index.html
Chair, Paul Hoffert
Executive Director, Gwenlyn Setterfield
• Ontario Film Development Corporation: North Tower, #300, 175 Bloor St. East, Toronto ON M4W 3R8 – 416/314-6858; Fax: 416/314-6876; URL: http://www.to-ontfilm.com/
Chair, Diane Chabot
Chief Executive Director, Alexandra Raffé
• Ontario Heritage Foundation (OHF): 10 Adelaide St. East, Toronto ON M5C 1J3 – 416/325-5000; Fax: 416/325-5071; Email: natural@heritage.gov.on.ca
Chair, Joanna Bedard
Executive Director, Lesley Lewis
Manager, Heritage Community Services, Brian Rogers
Director, Heritage Programs, Richard Moorhouse
Manager, Marketing & Communications, John Ecker
• Ontario Human Rights Commission: 400 University Ave., 12th Fl., Toronto ON M7A 2R9 – 416/314-4500; Fax: 416/314-4533
Chief Commissioner, Rosemary Brown
Executive Director, Remy Beauregard, 416/314-4539
Director, Communication & Education, Pearl Eliadis, 416/314-4522
• Ontario Science Centre: 770 Don Mills Rd., Toronto ON M3C 1T3 – 416/696-2000; Fax: 416/696-3135; URL: http://www.osc.on.ca/
Chair, Phyllis Yaffe
Director General, Emlyn H. Koster
• Ontario Trillium Foundation: 23 Bedford Rd., 3rd Fl., Toronto ON M5R 2J9 – 416/961-0194; Fax: 416/961-9599
Chair, Ron Crawford
Executive Director, Julie White
• Royal Botanical Gardens: PO Box 399, Hamilton ON L8N 3H8 – 905/527-1158; Fax: 905/529-5040
President, Joseph Pigott
Director, Dr. Garry R. Watson
• Royal Ontario Museum (ROM): 100 Queen's Park Cres., Toronto ON M5S 2C6 – 416/586-5549; Fax: 416/586-5863; URL: http://www.rom.on.ca/
Chair, Ken Harrigan
Director, Dr. John McNeill
• Science North: 100 Ramsey Lake Rd., Sudbury ON P3E 5S9 – 705/522-3701; Fax: 705/522-4954
Chair, Lloyd Douglas Reed
CEO, James Marchbank
• Southern Ontario Library Service: #50, 55 West Beaver Creek, Richmond Hill ON L4B 1K5 – 905/771-1522; Fax: 905/771-1526
CEO, Laurie Levine
• Thunder Bay Ski Jumps Ltd.: 11 Little Norway Rd., Site 3, RR#3, Thunder Bay ON P7C 4V2 – 807/475-4402; Fax: 807/475-8315
Chair, John Hatton
General Manager, Lindsay Durno
• TV Ontario: 2180 Yonge St., 5th Fl., Toronto ON M4S 2C1 – 416/484-2600; Fax: 416/484-4234; URL: http://www.tvo.org/
Chair & CEO, Peter Herrndorf

Ministry of COMMUNITY & SOCIAL SERVICES (MCSS)
Hepburn Block, 80 Grosvenor St., 6th Fl., Toronto ON M7A 1E9
416/325-5666; Fax: 416/325-5172, 5171; URL: http://www.gov.on.ca/CSS/
Welfare Fraud Hotline: 1-800-394-7867

ACTS ADMINISTERED
Charitable Institutions Act
Child & Family Services Act
Child Welfare Municipal Payments Continuance Act
Child Welfare Validation of Adoption Orders Act
Day Nurseries Act
Developmental Services Act
District Welfare Administration Boards Act
Family Benefits Act
Financial Administration Act
General Welfare Assistance Act
Homemakers & Nurses Services Act
Homes for Retarded Persons Act
Indian Welfare Services Act
Jewish Family & Child Service of Metro Toronto Act
Soldiers' Aid Commission Act
Vocational Rehabilitation Services Act
Young Offenders Implementation Act
Minister, Hon. Janet Ecker
Deputy Minister, Sandra Lang, 416/325-5233, Fax: 416/325-5240
Director, Communications & Marketing, Michael Kurts, 416/325-5203, Fax: 416/325-5191
Director, Legal Services, Andrea Walker, 416/327-4917

CHILDREN, FAMILY & COMMUNITY SERVICES DIVISION
Asst. Deputy Minister, Lucille Roch, 416/325-5605, Fax: 416/525-5615
Director, Child Care Branch, Ron Bakker, Hepburn Block, 4th Fl., Toronto ON M7A 1E9, 416/327-4865, Fax: 416/327-0563
Director, Children's Services Branch, Nicole Lafrenière-Davis, 416/325-5325, Fax: 416/325-5349
Senior Manager, Community Services Unit, Brad Archer, 416/327-4950, Fax: 416/327-0570
Manager, Aboriginal Healing & Wellness, Carrie Hayward

CORPORATE SERVICES DIVISION
Asst. Deputy Minister, Lynn Macdonald, 416/325-5588, Fax: 416/325-5615
Director, Comprehensive Audit & Investigations Branch, Richard Bradley, 2195 Yonge St., 3rd Fl., Toronto ON M4S 2B1, 416/314-6921, Fax: 416/314-3605
Director, Financial & Administrative Services Branch, Jim Tighe, 880 Bay St., 6th Fl., Toronto ON M7A 2B6, 416/326-8202, Fax: 416/326-8192
Director, Financial & Capital Planning Branch, Alfred Carr, 416/325-5105, Fax: 416/325-5125
Director, Human Resources Branch, Margaret Bodlein, 2 Bloor St. West, 23rd Fl., Toronto ON M7A 1E9, 416/327-4753, Fax: 416/327-0561
Director, Information Systems, Connie McCandless, 5140 Yonge St., 12th Fl., Toronto ON M2N 6L7, 416/730-6647, Fax: 416/730-6628

PROGRAM MANAGEMENT DIVISION
Client Information & Support Services: 416/325-5766; 1-800-665-6129
Responsible for the operation of 12 regional offices.
Asst. Deputy Minister, Suzanne Herbert, 416/325-5579, Fax: 416/325-5432
Director, Development Services Branch, Brian Low, 416/325-5826, Fax: 416/325-5554
Director, Management Support Branch, Barry Whalen, 416/325-5446, Fax: 416/325-5500
Manager, Adoption Operational Services, Collette Kent, 2 Bloor St. West, 24th Fl., Toronto ON M7A 1E9, 416/327-4930
Manager, Office of Child & Family Service Advocacy, Judy Finlay, 416/325-5669, Fax: 416/325-5681

SOCIAL ASSISTANCE & EMPLOYMENT OPPORTUNITIES DIVISION
Asst. Deputy Minister, Kevin Costante, 416/325-5570, Fax: 416/325-3424
Director, Automating Social Assistance Project, Janet Faas
Director, Employment Programs Branch, Cliodhna McMullin
Director, Social Assistance Programs Branch, Mary Kardos-Burton, 416/325-5255, Fax: 416/325-5266

GOVERNMENT OF ONTARIO

Project Director, Social Assistance Delivery Programs, John Rabeau

Associated Agencies, Boards & Commissions
• Child & Family Services Review Board: 2 Bloor St. West, 24th Fl., Toronto ON M7A 1E9 – 416/327-4671
Chair, Dr. Herbert Sohn
• Custody Review Board: 2 Bloor St. West, 24th Fl., Toronto ON M7A 1E9 – 416/327-4673; Fax: 416/327-0558
Chair, Keith Quigg
• Social Assistance Review Board (SARB): 1075 Bay St., 7th Fl., Toronto ON M5S 2B1 – 416/326-5104; Fax: 416/326-5135, Toll Free: 1-800-387-5655
Chair, Laura Bradbury
• Soldiers Aid Commission: 2 Bloor St. West, 24th Fl., Toronto ON M7A 1E9 – 416/327-4674
Chair, Dr. T. Divinec

Ministry of CONSUMER & COMMERCIAL RELATIONS (MCCR)
250 Yonge St., 35th Fl., Toronto ON M5B 2N5
416/326-8555
Toll Free: 1-800-268-1142
416/326-8525 (Communications); Fax: 416/326-8543

ACTS ADMINISTERED
Amusement Devices Act
Apportionment Act
Assignments & Preferences Act
Athletic Control Act
Bailiffs Act
Boilers & Pressure Vessels Act
Boundaries Act
Bread Sales Act
Business Corporations Act
Business Information Statute Law Amendment Act
Business Names Act
Business Practices Act
Cemeteries Act
Certification of Titles Act
Change of Name Act
Collection Agencies Act
Condominium Act
Consumer Protection Act
  Consumer Protection Bureau Act
Consumer Reporting Act
Corporations Act
Corporations Information Act
Debt Collectors Act
Discriminatory Business Practices Act
Elevating Devices Act
Energy Act
Extra-Provincial Corporations Act
Factors Act
Funeral Directors & Establishments Act
Gasoline Handling Act
Land Registration Reform Act
Land Titles Act
Limited Partnerships Act
Liquor Control Act
Liquor Licence Act
Marriage Act
Ministry of Consumer & Commercial Relations Act
Motor Vehicle Dealers Act
Motor Vehicle Repair Act
Ontario New Home Warranties Plan Act
Operating Engineers Act
Paperback & Periodical Distributors Act
Partnerships Act
Partnerships Registration Act
Personal Property Security Act
Prearranged Funeral Services Act
Prepaid Services Act
Racing Commission Act
Real Estate & Business Brokers Act
Registry Act
Repair & Storage Liens Act
Residential Complex Sales Representation Act
Theatres Act
Travel Industry Act
Upholstered & Stuffed Articles Act
Vital Statistics Act
Wine Content Act
and
Criminal Code (Canada), s. 190 (administration dealing with lottery licences issued to charitable & religious organizations to raise money for charitable or religious purposes)
Minister, Hon. David H. Tsubouchi
Deputy Minister, Stien Lal, 416/326-8480, Fax: 416/326-8409
Director, Legal Services, T. Kirk, 416/326-8440

GENERAL INQUIRY UNIT
416/326-8555; Fax: 416/326-8543
Toll Free: 1-800-268-1142
TTY/TTD: 416/326-8566
Manager, B. Darby

Entertainment Standards
1075 Millwood Rd., Toronto ON M4G 1X6
416/314-3626; Fax: 416/314-3632
Senior Manager & Director, Theatres Act, David Scriven
Officer, Policy & Program Development, Molly Acton

Office of the Athletic Commissioner
1075 Millwood Rd., Toronto ON M4G 1X6
416/314-3630; Fax: 416/314-3623
Athletics Commissioner, Ken Hzyzshi

BUSINESS DIVISION
416/326-8575; Fax: 416/325-6192
Asst. Deputy Minister, Art Daniels

Business Affairs Branch
416/326-8835; Fax: 416/326-8859
Director, Angela Longo
Registrar, Bailiffs, Collection Agencies, Reports, Paperbacks & Periodicals, Michael Pepper, 416/326-8805
Registrar, Cemeteries Regulation Branch, Stewart Smith, 416/326-8394
Registrar, Motor Vehicle Dealers, Stewart Smith, 416/326-8670
Registrar, Real Estate & Business Brokers, Gordon Randall, 416/326-8679
Registrar, Travel Industry, R. McKenna, 416/326-8741

Companies Branch
393 University Ave., 2nd Fl., Toronto ON M7A 2H6
416/596-3725; Fax: 416/596-0438
Director, Carol Kirsh, 416/596-3729
Deputy Director, Bev Hawton, 416/314-5150
Manager, Compliance, Ron Hartlen, 416/314-0845
Manager, Corporate Search & BNLP Services, S.K. Lambe, 416/314-0097
Manager, Corporate Services, Robert McLeod, 416/314-0084
Manager, Document Processing, Rita Maio, 416/314-4809

Consumer Affairs Branch
416/326-8600; Fax: 416/326-8665
Director, Brent Gibbs
Supervisor, Compliance Section, Marilyn Gurevsky, 416/326-8639
Acting Manager, Consumer Services Bureau, Vishnu Kangalee, 416/326-8641
Manager, Forensic Accountant, Mike Mouncey, 416/326-8638
Manager, Investigation Section, Brenda Cowley, 416/326-8598

Manager, Resources & Administration, Deborah McCrae, 416/326-8640

TECHNICAL STANDARDS DIVISION
West Tower, 3300 Bloor St. West, 4th Fl., Toronto ON M8X 2X4
Fax: 416/325-2000
Asst. Deputy Minister, John Walter, 416/325-0104
Director, Engineering & Standards Branch, Michael Philip, 416/325-9605
Director, Inspection & Enforcement, E. Stephan, 416/235-0125
Manager, Licensing & Administration Branch, Susan Allain, 416/325-2490

REGISTRATION DIVISION
393 University Ave., 4th Fl., Toronto ON M7A 2H6
416/596-3600; Fax: 416/596-3802
Asst. Deputy Minister, Despina Georges
Director, Personal Property Security Registration, Katharine Smith, 416/596-3771
Director, Real Property Registration, Tony Sharpe, 416/596-3643

Registrar General Branch
189 Red River Rd., PO Box 4600, Thunder Bay ON P7B 6L8
807/343-7414; Fax: 807/343-7411
Toll Free: 1-800-461-2156
Deputy Registrar General, Ted Kelly
  Fees are: Birth Certificate, $11; Marriage Certificate, $11; Death Certificate, $11; Certified Copies, $22; Genealogical Extracts, $22.

Registrations against Personal Property
Security agreements involving personal property - such as chattel mortgages, conditional sales, debentures - are governed by the *Personal Property Security Act, 1989*. Registrations under the *Personal Property Security Act, 1989* may be submitted by mail to the central office or in person at any branch office of the personal property security registration system.
Registration periods are variable. Registrations made under the *Repair & Storage Liens Act, 1989* are also registered in the personal property registration system & may be submitted by mail to the central office or in person to a branch registry office. A central registry has been established for searches.
The *Personal Property Security Act* provides that where collateral is or includes fixtures or goods that may become fixtures, or crops, or oil, gas or other minerals to be extracted, or timber to be cut, a Notice of Security interest may be registered in the proper land registry office.

Land Registrars
Algoma: PO Box 550, Sault Ste. Marie ON P6A 5M8 – 705/253-8887, P.A. Harrison
Brant: Court House, 80 Wellington St., Brantford ON N3T 2L9 – 519/752-8321, P. Gale
Bruce: PO Box 1690, Walkerton ON N0G 2V0 – 519/881-2259, Lee Trevors
Cochrane: PO Box 580, Cochrane ON P0L 1C0 – 705/272-5791; Fax: 705/272-2951, Tim Miedema
Dufferin: 10 Louisa St., Orangeville ON L9W 3P9 – 519/941-1481, Joan Crawford
Dundas: PO Box 645, Morrisburg ON K0C 1X0 – 613/543-2583, Louis Arki
Durham: 590 Rossland Rd. East, Whitby ON L1N 9G5 – 416/430-3452; Fax: 416/666-9806, Terry Brown
Elgin: PO Box 4, St. Thomas ON N5P 3T5 – 519/631-3015, W.W. Burke
Essex: 250 Windsor Ave., Windsor ON N9A 6V9 – 519/971-9980; Fax: 519/971-9979, W.W. Patterson
Frontenac: 1 Court St., Kingston ON K7L 2N4 – 613/548-6767, Desmond Dias
Glengarry: PO Box 668, Alexandria ON K0C 1A0 – 613/525-1315, Jean Claude Brisson

Canadian Almanac & Directory 1997

GOVERNMENT OF ONTARIO 3-175

Grenville: PO Box 1660, Prescott ON K0E 1T0 – 613/925-3177, L.A. Cross
Grey: Court House, 595 - 9 Ave. East, Owen Sound ON N4K 3E3 – 519/376-1637, Paul Nixon
Haldimand: PO Box 310, Cayuga ON N0A 1E0 – 905/772-3531, N.J. Davidson
Haliburton: PO Box 270, Minden ON K0M 2K0 – 705/286-1391, M.L. Flood
Halton: 491 Steeles Ave. East, Milton ON L9T 1Y7 – 905/878-7287; Fax: 905/878-8298, J. Menard
Hastings: 280 Pinnacle St., PO Box 1540, Belleville ON K8N 5J2 – 613/968-4597, Janet Price
Huron: 38 North St., Goderich ON N7A 2T4 – 519/524-9562, P.E. Maclean
Kenora: 220 Main St. South, PO Box 1350, Kenora ON P9N 3X7 – 807/468-2794; Fax: 807/468-2796, Linda McGeachy
Kent: 40 William St. North, Chatham ON N7M 5L8 – 519/352-5520; Fax: 519/352-3222, Elizabeth Wright
Lambton: 700 North Christina St., Sarnia ON N7Y 7N5 – 519/337-2393, Kenneth Doan
Lanark: PO Box 1180, Almonte ON K0A 1A0 – 613/256-1577, Dale Wilson
Leeds: 7 King St. West, Brockville ON K6V 3P7 – 613/345-5751, L.A. Cross
Lennox: 87 Thomas St. East, Napanee ON K7R 1L1 – 613/354-3751, Desmond Dias
Manitoulin: PO Box 265, Gore Bay ON P0P 1H0 – 705/282-2442; Fax: 705/282-3245, R.J. Lane
Middlesex East: New Court House, 80 Dundas St., PO Box 5600, London ON N6A 2P3 – 519/675-7600; Fax: 519/675-7633, Wentworth Newman
Muskoka: PO Box 720, Bracebridge ON P1L 1R6 – 705/645-4415, R.C. Stewart
Niagara North: 59 Church St., St. Catharines ON L2R 3C3 – 905/684-6351, Rolland Gregoire
Niagara South: 200 Division St., PO Box 730, Welland ON L3B 3G1 – 905/735-4011; Fax: 905/735-2430, D. Hill
Nipissing: 360 Plouffe St., North Bay ON P1B 9L5 – 705/474-2270; Fax: 705/474-9155, Rodney C. Wickett
Norfolk: Court House, Simcoe ON N3Y 4K8 – 519/426-2216, N.J. Davidson
Northumberland: #105, 1005 William St., Cobourg ON K9A 5J4 – 905/372-3813, Pauline Green
Ottawa-Carleton: Court House, 161 Elgin St., 4th Fl., Ottawa ON K2P 2K1 – 613/239-1230, Anthony Sharp
Oxford: PO Box 246, Woodstock ON N4S 7W8 – 519/537-6287; Fax: 519/537-3107, R.K. Thomson
Parry Sound: 28 Miller St., Parry Sound ON P2A 1T1 – 705/746-5816, J. Boyer
Peel: 7765 Hurontario St., PO Box 1200, Brampton ON L6V 2L8 – 905/874-4008; Fax: 905/874-4012, Al Cordery
Perth: PO Box 902, Stratford ON N5A 6T1 – 519/271-3343, Corson Wilmot
Peterborough: 160 Charlotte St., 2nd Fl., Peterborough ON K9J 2T8 – 705/876-6690, R.W. Appleton
Prescott: PO Box 302, L'Orignal ON K0B 1K0 – 613/675-4648, Roger Cote
Prince Edward: PO Box 1310, Picton ON K0K 2T0 – 613/476-3219, R.G. Rowe
Rainy River: PO Box 398, Fort Frances ON P9A 3M7 – 807/274-5451; Fax: 807/274-9540, R. Bibby
Renfrew: PO Box 760, Pembroke ON K8A 6X1 – 613/732-8331, R. Price
Russell: PO Box 10, Russell ON K4R 1C8 – 613/445-2138, Anthony Sharp
Simcoe: Court House, 114 Worsley St., Barrie ON L4M 1M1 – 705/734-2722, W.G. Broadhurst
Stormont: 127 Sydney St., Cornwall ON K6H 3H1 – 613/932-4522; Fax: 613/932-4523, Louis Arki
Sudbury: 199 Larch St., 3rd Fl., Sudbury ON P3E 5P9 – 705/675-4300; Fax: 705/675-4148, Walter Zaverucha
Thunder Bay: 189 Red River Rd., 2nd Fl., PO Box 2060, Thunder Bay ON P7B 5E7 – 807/343-7436; Fax: 807/343-7439, Robert Johnson
Timiskaming: PO Box 159, Haileybury ON P0J 1K0 – 705/672-3332; Fax: 705/672-3906, Rodney C. Wickett
Toronto (Metropolitan Registry): #230, 20 Dundas St. West, Toronto ON M5G 2C2 – 416/314-4400; Fax: 416/314-4453, Donna Ball
Toronto (Metropolitan Land Titles): #420, 20 Dundas St. West, PO Box 117, Toronto ON M5G 2C2 – 416/314-4430; Fax: 416/314-4453, Vacant
Victoria: 440 Kent St. West, PO Box 4000, Lindsay ON K9V 4S5 – 705/324-4912, E.A. Legacey
Waterloo: 200 Frederick St., 3rd Fl., Kitchener ON N2H 6N9 – 519/571-6043, Murray Smith
Wellington: PO Box 905, Guelph ON N1H 6M6 – 519/822-0251, Jeff Gilbert
Wentworth: 119 King St. West, PO Box 2112, Hamilton ON L8N 3Z9 – 905/521-7561; Fax: 905/521-7505, Virginia Mattuzzi
York Region: 50 Eagle St. West, Newmarket ON L3Y 6B1 – 905/895-1561, J. Small

Associated Agencies, Boards & Commissions

•Commercial Registration Appeal Tribunal: 1 St. Clair Ave. West, 12th Fl., Toronto ON M4V 1K6 – 416/965-7798; Fax: 416/965-0429
Chair, Judith A. Killoran, Q.C.
Registrar, F. Blais
•Gaming Control Commission: 1099 Bay St., 2nd Fl., Toronto ON M5S 2B3 – 416/326-8880; Fax: 416/326-8711
Chair, Clare Lewis
Executive Director, Duncan Brown
Director, Investigations, Gary Wood, 416/326-8355
Director, Legal, Jerry Cooper, 416/326-8935
Director, Operations, Linda Monzon, 416/326-8703
Counsel, Casino Operations, Jacquie Castel, 416/325-0427
Senior Manager, Native Liaison, Cy Wood, 416/326-8594
•Liquor Control Board of Ontario: 55 Lake Shore Blvd. East, Toronto ON M7A 2H6 – 416/864-2400; Fax: 416/864-2476; URL: http://www.lcbo.com/
Chair, Andrew S. Brandt
Executive Vice-President, Larry Gee
•Liquor Licence Board of Ontario: 55 Lake Shore Blvd. East, Toronto ON M5E 1A4 – Fax: 416/326-0308
Chair & CEO, Andromache Karakatsanis, 416/326-0375
Executive Director, B. Tocher, 416/326-0381
Director, Inspection, Tom Bolton, 416/326-0330
Director, Licensing, Katherine Donnelly, 416/326-0350
•Ontario Film Review Board: 1075 Millwood Rd., Toronto ON M4G 1X6 – 416/314-3626
Chair, Leslie Ann Adams
Office Manager, Linda Sullivan
•Ontario New Home Warranty Program: North East Tower, 6th Fl., 5160 Yonge St., Toronto ON M2N 6L9 – 416/229-9200; Fax: 416/229-3800
•Ontario Racing Commission: #1400, 180 Dundas St. West, Toronto ON M5G 1Z8 – 416/327-0520; Fax: 416/325-3478
Chair, Stan Sandinsky
Director, Jean Major

Ministry of ECONOMIC DEVELOPMENT, TRADE & TOURISM (MEDTT)

Hearst Block, 900 Bay St., Toronto ON M7A 2E1
416/325-6666; Fax: 416/325-6688; URL: gopher://go-vonca.gov.on.ca:70/11/medtt/english

ACTS ADMINISTERED

Acts respecting Development Corporations in Ontario
Historical Parks Act
Metropolitan Toronto Convention Centre Corporation Act
Ministry of Industry & Trade Act
Niagara Parks Act
Ontario International Corporation Act
Ontario Lottery Corporation Act
Ontario Place Corporation Act
Ontario Research Foundation Act
Ottawa Congress Centre Act
St. Clair Parkway Commission Act
St. Lawrence Parks Commission Act
Sheridan Park Corporation Act
Technology Centres Act
Tourism Act

Minister, Hon. William Saunderson, 416/325-6900; Fax: 416/325-6918
Deputy Minister, Vacant, 416/325-6927, Fax: 416/325-6999, Email: wolfsoju@epo.on.ca
Chair, Removing Barriers to Doing Business in Ontario, Peter Barnes, 416/325-6900, Fax: 416/325-6999
Administrative Coordinator, Ontario Investment Fund, Angie Georgakakos, 416/325-3344, Fax: 416/325-6404
Director, Communications Branch, Lee Allison Howe, 416/325-6700, Fax: 416/325-6688
Director, Legal Services Branch, Ingrid Peters, 416/326-1001, Fax: 416/326-1021

BUSINESS DEVELOPMENT & TOURISM DIVISION

Asst. Deputy Minister, Jean Lam
General Manager, Business Development Branch, Peter Friedman, 416/325-6485
Director, Investment, Saad Rafi, 416/325-6926
Director, Tourism, Ruth Cornish
Executive Director, Niagara Gateway Project, Roberta Veley

CORPORATE RESOURCES & AGENCY RELATIONS DIVISION

Asst. Deputy Minister, Brian K. Wood, 416/325-6929, Fax: 416/325-6999
Director, Agency Relations Branch, James Orgill
Director, Audit Services Branch, Gordon H. Aue, 416/326-1702, Fax: 416/326-1712
Director, Finance & Administration Branch, Valerie Wilson, 416/325-6420, Fax: 416/325-6449
Director, Human Resources Branch, Tom Clark, 416/325-6605, Fax: 416/325-6715
Director, Information & Technology Systems Branch, Uma Ganesan, 416/325-6590, Fax: 416/325-6635

MARKETING & TRADE DIVISION

Asst. Deputy Minister, Grahame Richards
Director, International Relations & Protocol Branch, Ernesto Feu, 416/325-8545, Fax: 416/325-8550
Director, Marketing Branch, Geoff Hare, 416/325-6758
Director, Strategic Planning & Coordination Branch, Zahir Janmohamed, 416/325-6673

STRATEGIC ANALYSIS, SECTORS & TECHNOLOGY DIVISION

Asst. Deputy Minister, Peter Sadlier-Brown, 416/325-6962, Fax: 416/325-6985
Director, Capital Goods & Technology Sectors Branch, Joan McCalla, 416/326-9627
Director, Economic Development, Coordination & Analysis Branch, Philip D. Howell, 416/325-6806
Director, Manufacturing Sectors Branch, Penney Dutton
Director, Service Sectors Branch, Ann Whalen
Director, Technology & Training Development Branch, Dr. Chris Riddle
Director, Trade Policy Branch, Katherine McGuire, 416/325-6930, Fax: 416/325-6949

Regional Offices

Central East - Elmvale: General Trust Bldg., 144 Yonge St., PO Box 340, Elmvale ON L0L 1P0 – Fax: 705/322-0740, Toll Free: 1-800-461-9626

Central West - Hamilton: Bank of Montreal Tower, #200, 1 James St. North, Hamilton ON L8R 2K3 – 905/521-7783; Fax: 905/521-7398, Toll Free: 1-800-263-9293

Central East - Metro Toronto: #480, 5 Fairview Mall Dr., North York ON M2J 2Z1 – 416/325-1240; Fax: 416/325-1262

Central West - Peel: 4 Robert Speck Pkwy., 11th Fl., Mississauga ON LHZ 1S1 – 905/277-7771; Fax: 905/279-9160, Toll Free: 1-800-387-5061

Central West - St. Catharines: Corbloc Bldg., #801, 80 King St., St. Catharines ON L2R 7G1 – 416/688-1454; Fax: 416/688-4872, Toll Free: 1-800-263-5670

Eastern - Kingston: #308, 1055 Princess St., Kingston ON K7L 5T3 – 613/545-4444; Fax: 613/545-4439, Toll Free: 1-800-267-7848

Eastern - Ottawa: Tower B, Place de Ville, #870, 112 Kent St., Ottawa ON K1P 5P2 – 613/566-3703; Fax: 613/563-0436, Toll Free: 1-800-267-6592

Eastern - Peterborough: 139 George St. North, Peterborough ON K9J 3G6 – 705/742-3459; Fax: 705/742-3272, Toll Free: 1-800-461-6429

Southwestern - Kitchener: #906, 30 Duke St. West, Kitchener ON N2H 3W5 – 519/744-6391; Fax: 519/571-6104, Toll Free: 1-800-265-2428

Southwestern - London: #607, 195 Dufferin Ave., London ON N6A 1K7 – 519/433-8105; Fax: 519/661-6625, Toll Free: 1-800-265-4743

Southwestern - Owen Sound: 1137 - 2nd Ave. East, Owen Sound ON N4K 2J1 – 519/376-3875; Fax: 519/376-8000, Toll Free: 1-800-265-3796

Southwestern - Sarnia: Polysar Bldg., #503, 201 Front St. North, Sarnia ON N7T 7T9 – 519/332-5030; Fax: 519/332-2836, Toll Free: 1-800-265-1449

Southwestern - Windsor: Ontario Government Bldg., #227, 250 Windsor Ave., Windsor ON N9A 6V9 – 519/252-3475; Fax: 519/973-1378, Toll Free: 1-800-265-1345

Northern - North Bay: 147 McIntyre St., 2nd Fl., North Bay ON P1B 2Y5 – 705/472-9660; Fax: 705/494-4069, Toll Free: 1-800-461-1687

Northern - Sault Ste. Marie: Roberta Bondar Place, #200, 70 Foster Dr., Sault Ste. Marie ON P6A 6V8 – 705/945-5922; Fax: 705/945-5931, Toll Free: 1-800-461-2287

Northern - Sudbury: Ontario Government Bldg., 199 Larch St., 4th Fl., Sudbury ON P3E 5P9 – 705/675-4333; Fax: 705/675-4216, Toll Free: 1-800-461-1196

Northern - Thunder Bay: Ontario Government Bldg., 435 James St. South, 3rd Fl., PO Box 5000, Thunder Bay ON P7C 5G6 – 807/475-1655; Fax: 807/475-1665, Toll Free: 1-800-465-5060

Northern - Timmins: #200, 273 Third Ave., Timmins ON P4N 1E2 – 705/264-1323; Fax: 705/264-5927, Toll Free: 1-800-461-9848

Associated Agencies, Boards & Commissions

- Huronia Historical Advisory Council: PO Box 160, Midland ON L4R 4K8 – 705/526-7838; Fax: 705/526-9193
- Innovation Ontario Corporation: 56 Wellesley St. West, 7th Fl., Toronto ON M7A 2E7 – 416/326-1025; Fax: 416/326-1109

President & Managing Director, James Orgill

- Metro Toronto Convention Centre Corporation: 255 Front St. West, Toronto ON M5V 2W6 – 416/585-8000; Fax: 416/585-8224
- Niagara Parks Commission (NPC): 7400 Portage Rd. South, PO Box 150, Niagara Falls ON L2E 6T2 – 905/356-2241; Fax: 905/354-6041

Chair, Pamela Walker

General Manager, Vacant

- Old Fort William Advisory Committee: Vickers Heights Post Office, Thunder Bay ON P0T 2Z0 – 807/577-8461; Fax: 807/473-2327
- Ontario Development Corporation: 56 Wellesley St. West, 6th Fl., Toronto ON M7A 2E7 – 416/326-1070; Fax: 416/326-1073

President & CEO, Brian K. Wood

President & Managing Director, Innovation Ontario Corporation, James Orgill

- Ontario Lottery Corporation (OLC): #800, 70 Foster Dr., Sault Ste. Marie ON P6A 6V2 – 705/946-6400; Fax: 705/946-6846

President, Garth Manness

- Ontario Place Corporation: 955 Lake Shore Blvd. West, Toronto ON M6K 3B9 – 416/314-9817; Fax: 416/314-9993; URL: http://www.inforamp.net/op/ – General Information: 416/314-9900

General Manager, Maxwell Beck

- Ottawa Congress Centre: 55 Colonel By Dr., Ottawa ON K1N 9J2 – 613/787-5707; Fax: 613/563-7646
- St. Clair Parkway Commission: PO Box 700, Corunna ON N0N 1G0 – 519/862-2291; Fax: 519/862-2294

Chair, Jon Shimizu

General Manager, David Cram

- St. Lawrence Parks Commission: RR#1, Morrisburg ON K0C 1X0 – 613/543-3704; Fax: 613/543-2847

Chair, Gary Clarke

General Manager, Frank G. Shaw

Ministry of EDUCATION & TRAINING

Mowat Block, 900 Bay St., Toronto ON M7A 1L2
416/325-2929; Fax: 416/325-2934;
Email: public.inquiries@edu.gov.on.ca; URL: http://www.edu.gov.on.ca

Toll Free: 1-800-387-5514

Youth Employment Hotline: 1-800-387-0777

Training Hotline: 1-800-387-5656

ACTS ADMINISTERED

Colleges Collective Bargaining Act
Degree Granting Act
Development Charges Act, Part III
Education Act
Essex County French-language Secondary School Act
Lake Superior Board of Education Act
Lambton County Board of Education & Training Dispute Resolution Act
Metropolitan Separate School Board Act
Ministry of Colleges & Universities Act
Municipal & School Board Payments Adjustment Act
Ontario Institute for Studies in Education Act
Ontario School Trustees' Council Act
Ontario Training & Adjustment Board Act
Ottawa-Carleton French Language School Board Transferred Employees Act
Private Vocational Schools Act
Provincial Schools Negotiations Act
School Boards & Teachers Collective Negotiations Act
School Trust Conveyances Act
Teachers Pension Act
Teaching Profession Act
Trades Qualification & Apprenticeship Act
University Foundations Act

Minister, Hon. John Snobelen, 416/325-2600, Fax: 416/325-2608

Deputy Minister, Veronica Lacey, 416/325-2180, Fax: 416/327-9063

Executive Coordinator, Corporate Secretariat, Wilma Provesan

Director, Communications & Marketing Branch, Suzanna Birchwood, 416/325-2947

ELEMENTARY/SECONDARY OPERATIONS & FRENCH-LANAGUAGE EDUCATION

Asst. Deputy Minister, Mariette Carrier-Fraser, 416/325-2132

Director, Capital & Operating Grants Administration, Drew Nameth, 416/325-4030

Director, French-Language Education Policy & Programs, Richard Gauthier, 416/325-2127

Acting Director, Independent Learning Centre, Cynthia Teeter, 416/325-4243

Director, Operations & Field Services, Teresa Gonzalez, 416/325-2470

Director, Provincial Schools Branch, Ruth Taber, 416/325-2507

Manager, Anti-Discrimination & Equal Opportunity Branch, Nora Allingham, 416/325-2152

Acting Manager, Teacher & Student Information Services Unit, Louise Nadeau, 416/325-4328

Regional Offices

Central Ontario: #3201, 2025 Sheppard Ave. East, Toronto ON M2J 1W4 – 416/491-0330; Fax: 416/491-9962, Acting Regional Director, George Demetra

Eastern Ontario: 1580 Merivale Rd., 4th Fl., Ottawa ON K2G 4B5 – 613/225-9210; Fax: 613/225-2881, Regional Director, Maurice Poirier

Midnorthern Ontario: 199 Larch St., 7th Fl., Sudbury ON P3E 5P9 – 705/675-4401; Fax: 705/675-4186, Regional Director, Michel Robineau

Northeastern Ontario: 447 McKeown Ave., PO Box 3020, North Bay ON P1B 8K7 – 705/474-7210; Fax: 705/474-9808, Acting Regional Director, Lise Presseault

Northwestern Ontario: 435 James St. South, PO Box 5000, Thunder Bay ON P7C 5G6 – 807/475-1571; Fax: 807/475-1571, Regional Director, Jacqueline Dojack

Western Ontario: 759 Hyde Park Rd., London ON N6H 3S6 – 519/472-1440; Fax: 519/472-1440, Regional Director, Terry Boucher

ELEMENTARY/SECONDARY POLICY DIVISION

416/325-2135; Fax: 416/325-2381

Asst. Deputy Minister, Jill Hutcheon, 416/325-2135

Acting Director, Curriculum, Learning, & Teaching Branch, Pauline Laing, 416/325-4138

Director, Education Finance Branch, Peter Wright, 416/325-2828

Director, Policy Branch, Marjorie Mercer, 416/325-2660

Director, Secondary School Project, Aryeb Gitterman, 416/325-2538

Acting Director, School Governance Branch, Brian Fleming, 416/327-9057

Manager, Differentiated Staffing Project, Julie Lindhout, 416/325-2390

ORGANIZATION DEVELOPMENT & SERVICES DIVISION

416/325-2772; Fax: 416/325-2778

Asst. Deputy Minister, Garth Jackson, 416/325-2773

Director, Audit, Compliance, & Evaluation, Patrick Madden, 416/325-2140

Director, Finance & Administration Services, Doug Holder, 416/327-9091

Director, Human Resources Planning & Services, Maureen Edgar, 416/327-9003

Director, Information Technology Systems, Bill Vraets, 416/325-2246

Director, Legal Services Unit, Alan Wolfish, 416/325-2399

Acting Director, School Board Technology Transition Project, David Barnes, 416/314-2494

Manager, Corporate Planning Unit, Carol Lawson, 416/325-1818

Project Director, Technology Incentive Partnership Program Project, Bob Kennedy, 416/326-5665

POST SECONDARY EDUCATION DIVISION
Asst. Deputy Minister, David Trick, 416/325-2116
Director, Colleges Branch, Catriona King, 416/325-1815
Director, Post Secondary Education Policy Branch, Vacant
Director, Student Support Branch, Helmut Zisser, 416/325-4181
Director, Universities Branch, B. James Mackay, 416/325-1952

TRAINING DIVISION
Asst. Deputy Minister, Joan Andrew, 416/325-2990
Manager, Adult Education Project, Kay Eastham, 416/325-2577
Director, Apprenticeship Reform Project & Director, Jobs Ontario Training (wind-down), Elisabeth Wagner, 416/314-5166
Director, Labour Market Policy, Planning, & Research, Bruce Baldwin, 416/967-8349
Director, Workplace Preparation, Sante Maurti, 416/326-5883
Director, Workplace Support Services, Judith Robertson, 416/326-5608

Associated Agencies, Boards & Commissions
- College Relations Commission: #400, 111 Avenue Rd., Toronto ON M5R 3J8 – 416/922-7679; Fax: 416/325-4134
CEO, Fred Long
- Conseil de l'Education Franco-Ontarienne/Franco-Ontarian Education Council: #203, 880 Bay St., Toronto ON M7A 1L2 – 416/325-4626; Fax: 416/325-4627
Chair, Rolande Foucher
- Education Relations Commission: #400, 111 Avenue Rd., Toronto ON M5R 3J8 – 416/325-4626; Fax: 416/325-4627
Chair, Paula Knopf
- Languages of Instruction Commission of Ontario: 56 Wellesley St. West, 11th Fl., Toronto ON M7A 2B7 – 416/314-3500; Fax: 416/314-3502
Chair, Keith Reilly
- Ontario Council of Regents for Colleges of Applied Arts & Technology: 790 Bay St., 10th Fl., Toronto ON M5G 1N8 – 416/325-1780; Fax: 416/325-1792
Chair, H. Noble
- Ontario Parent Council: 56 Wellesley St. West, 16th Fl., Toronto ON M7A 2B7 – 416/314-0426; Fax: 416/314-0425, Toll Free: 1-800-361-6483
Chair, Vacant
Executive Secretary, Monique Guibert
Bilingual Secretary, Pascale Demers
- Ontario Teachers' Pension Plan Board: #400, 5650 Yonge St., Toronto ON M2M 4H5 – 416/226-2700; Fax: 416/730-5349
Chair, C.E. Medland

ELECTIONS ONTARIO
51 Rolark Dr., Scarborough ON M1R 3B1
416/321-3000; Fax: 416/321-6853
Toll Free: 1-800-668-2727

ACTS ADMINISTERED
Election Act
Chief Election Officer, W.R. Bailie
Acting Asst. Chief Election Officer, Loren A. Wells
Manager, Operations Section, Alison Carpenter

Ministry of ENVIRONMENT & ENERGY (MOEE)
135 St. Clair Ave. West, Toronto ON M4V 1P5
416/325-4000 (Public Information Centre); Fax: 416/323-4564; URL: http://www.ene.gov.on.ca/
Toll Free: 1-800-565-4923

ACTS ADMINISTERED
Consolidated Hearings Act
Energy Act
Energy Efficiency Act
Environment Statute Law Amendment Act
Environmental Assessment Act
Environmental Protection Act
Ministry of Energy Act
Ministry of the Environment Act
Ontario Energy Board Act
Ontario Energy Corporation Act
Ontario Waste Management Corporation Act
Ontario Water Resources Act
Pesticides Act
Power Corporation Act
Waste Management Act
Minister, Hon. Norman W. Sterling
Deputy Minister, Linda Stevens, 416/323-4271, Fax: 416/323-4513

CONSERVATION & PREVENTION DIVISION
416/323-4320; Fax: 416/323-4481
Asst. Deputy Minister, Judith Wright, 416/323-4319
Director, Environmental Assessment Branch, Chuck Pautler, 250 Davisville Ave., 5th Fl., Toronto ON M4S 1H2, 416/440-3480, Fax: 416/440-3771
Director, Environmental Planning & Analysis Branch, Brian Nixon, 250 Davisville Ave., 3rd Fl., Toronto ON M4S 1H2, 416/440-3772, Fax: 416/440-7039
Director, Industry Conservation Branch, Linda Ploeger, 416/327-1457
Director, Waste Reduction Branch, Bob Breeze, 40 St. Clair Ave. West, 7th Fl., Toronto ON M4V 1M2, 416/325-4440

Green Industry Office
416/323-4578; Fax: 416/323-4436
Manager, Jacquie Maund, 416/323-4688
Senior Business Development Advisor, Brad Defoe, 416/323-4688
Senior Business Development Officer, Nora Gurland, 416/323-4452
Senior Business Development Officer, Rebecca Mckenzie, 416/323-4219
Senior Business Development Advisor, Deborah McKeown, 416/323-4657
Senior International Trade Advisor, Peter Constantino, 416/323-4679
Senior International Trade Advisor, Enrico Di Nino, 416/323-4231

CORPORATE MANAGEMENT DIVISION
Fax: 416/323-4645
Asst. Deputy Minister, André Castel, 416/323-4356
Director, Finance & Administration Branch, Margaret LaPierre, 416/314-4095
Director, Fiscal Planning & Information Management Branch, Carl Griffith, 416/323-4558, Fax: 416/323-4322, General Inquiry: 416/323-4554
Director, Human Resources Branch, MaryEtta Cheney, 416/314-9305, Fax: 416/314-9313
Coordinator, Environmental Youth Corps, Yves Deschénes, 416/314-9387, General Inquiry: 416/314-5906

ENVIRONMENTAL SCIENCES & STANDARDS DIVISION
Fax: 416/323-4396
Acting Asst. Deputy Minister, Ivy Wile, 416/323-4384
Director, Environmental Bill of Rights Office, Helle Tosine, 416/314-3920, Fax: 416/323-5031
Director, Environmental Monitoring & Reporting Branch, Ed Piché, 416/235-6160, Fax: 416/235-6235
Director, Laboratory Services Branch, Dr. Bern Schnyder, 416/235-5747, Fax: 416/235-5744
Director, Program Development & Support Branch, Helle Tosine, 416/314-3920, Fax: 416/314-4128

Director, Science & Technology Branch, Helle Tosine, 416/323-5222, Fax: 416/323-5031
Director, Standards Development Branch, Ivy Wile, 416/323-5096, Fax: 416/323-5166

OPERATIONS DIVISION
Fax: 416/323-4615
Asst. Deputy Minister, Sheila Willis, 416/323-4354
Director, Approvals Branch, Wilfred Ng, 250 Davisville Ave., Toronto ON M4S 1H2, 416/440-3546, Fax: 416/440-6973
Director, Investigations & Enforcement Branch, Patricia Hollett, 250 Davisville Ave., 5th Fl., Toronto ON M4S 1H2, 416/440-3510, Fax: 416/440-3539
Head, Spills Action Centre, Gary Zikovitz, 5775 Yonge St., 10th Fl., Toronto ON M2M 4S1, 416/325-3000, Fax: 416/325-3011, Toll Free: 1-800-268-6060

Regional & District Offices
- Central Region: Toronto Regional & Metro Toronto District Offices, 5775 Yonge St., 8th Fl., North York ON M2M 4J1 – 416/426-6700; Fax: 416/325-6345 – Director, David Crump, 416/326-5596; District Manager, Ken Waldie
Oakville/Halton-Peel District: #401, 1235 Trafalgar Rd., Oakville ON L6H 3P1 – 905/844-5747; Fax: 905/842-1750 - District Manager, J. Budz
- Eastern Region: Kingston Regional & District Office, 133 Dalton Ave., Kingston ON K7K 6C2 – 613/549-4000; Fax: 613/548-6908 – Director, Brian Ward; District Officer, John Bishop
Belleville Sub-Office: Belleville Mall, 470 Dundas St. East, Belleville ON K8N 1G1 - 613/962-9208; Fax: 613/962-6809 - Area Supervisor, John Tooley
Cornwall District: 205 Amelia St., Cornwall ON K6H 3P3 - 613/933-7402; Fax: 613/933-6402 - Acting District Officer, Robert Helliar
Ottawa District: 2435 Holly Lane, Ottawa ON K1V 7P2 - 613/521-3450; Fax: 613/521-5437 - District Officer, Robert A. Dunn
Pembroke Sub-Office: 400A Pembroke St., Pembroke ON K8B 3K8 - 613/732-3643; Fax: 613/732-2668 - Sr. Environmental Officer, A. Polley
Peterborough District: 1477 Lansdowne St. West, Peterborough ON K9J 7M3 - 705/743-2972; Fax: 705/748-4192 - District Officer, Jacques L. Bourque
- Mid-Ontario Region: Sudbury Regional & District Office, #1101, 199 Larch St., Sudbury ON P3E 5P9 – 705/675-4501; Fax: 705/675-4180 - Director, Ron Hore; District Manager, Roger Roy
Barrie District: #1203, 54 Cedar Point Dr., Barrie ON L4N 5R7 - 705/726-1730; Fax: 705/726-5100 - District Manager, I.M. Gray
Muskoka-Haliburton District: 483 Bethune Dr., Gravenhurst ON P1P 1B8 - 705/687-6647; Fax: 705/687-3715 - District Manager, Terrance O'Neill
North Bay District: Northgate Plaza, 1500 Fisher St., North Bay ON P1B 2H3 - 705/476-1001; Fax: 705/476-0207 - District Manager, Gord Miller
Parry Sound Sub-Office: 74 Church St., Parry Sound ON P2A 1Z1 - 705/746-2139; Fax: 705/746-2011 - Senior Environmental Officer, David Packer
- Northern Region: Thunder Bay Regional & District Office, 435 James St. South, 3rd Fl., Thunder Bay ON P7E 6E3 – 807/475-1205; Fax: 807/475-1754 – Director, Wayne Scott; District Manager, Donald Murray
Kenora District: 808 Robertson St., PO Box 5150, Kenora ON P9N 1X9 - 807/468-2718; Fax: 807/468-2735 - District Manager, Peter E. Fox
Sault Ste. Marie District: 747 Queen St., Sault Ste. Marie ON P6A 2A8 - 705/949-4640; Fax: 705/945-6868 - District Manager, Gerry LaHaye
Timmins District: 83 Algonquin Blvd. West, Timmins ON P4N 2R4 - 705/268-3222; Fax: 705/264-7336 - Acting District Manager, Jim Deem

- Southwestern Region: London Regional Office, 985 Adelaide St. South, London ON N6E 1V3 – 519/661-2200; Fax: 519/661-1742 – Director, Jim Janse
- Owen Sound District: 1180 - 20 St. East, Owen Sound ON N4K 6H6 - 519/371-2901; Fax: 519/371-2905 - District Manager, H.W. Page
- Sarnia District: 1094 London Rd., Sarnia ON N7S 1P1 - 519/336-4030; Fax: 519/336-4280 - District Manager, Orrie Wigle
- Windsor District: 250 Windsor Ave., 6th Fl., Windsor ON N9A 6V9 - 519/254-2546; Fax: 519/254-5894 - District Manager, J. Drummond
- West Central Region: Hamilton Regional & District Office, 119 King St. West, 12th Fl., PO Box 2112, Hamilton ON L8N 3Z9 – 905/521-7640; Fax: 905/521-7820 – Director, Hardy Wong, 905/521-7652; District Manager, John Perry
- Cambridge District: 320 Pinebush Rd., PO Box 219, Cambridge ON N1R 5T8 - 519/622-8121; Fax: 519/740-5978 - District Manager, Bill Bardswick
- Welland District: 637 Niagara St. North, Welland ON L3C 1L9 - 905/732-0816; Fax: 905/685-2658 - District Manager, John Mayes

POLICY DIVISION
416/323-4255; Fax: 416/323-4410
Asst. Deputy Minister, Les Horswill, 416/323-4352
Director, Economic Services Branch, Rick Jennings, 416/327-1400, Fax: 416/327-1511
Director, Energy Conservation & Liaison, Tony Rockingham, 416/323-5626, Fax: 416/323-5636
Executive Coordinator, Intergovernmental Relations Office, Ken J. Richards, 416/323-4652; Fax: 416/323-4442
Manager, Aboriginal Affairs Office, Daniel Cayen, 416/323-4260, Fax: 416/323-4442

Associated Agencies, Boards & Commissions
- Environmental Appeal Board: #502, 112 St. Clair Ave. West, Toronto ON M4V 1N3 – 416/314-3300; Fax: 416/314-3299
Chair, John Swaigen
- Environmental Assessment Board: #1201, 2300 Yonge St., PO Box 2382, Toronto ON M4P 1E4 – 416/323-4806; Fax: 416/323-4997
Chair, Grace Patterson, 416/323-4809
- Ontario Clean Water Agency (OCWA): #700, 20 Bay St., Toronto ON M5J 2N8 – 416/314-5600; Fax: 416/314-8300, Toll Free: 1-800-667-6292
CEO & President, Jeff Marshall, 416/314-0757
Director, International Projects, Nick Markettos
- Ontario Energy Board: 2300 Yonge St., 23rd Fl., PO Box 2382, Toronto ON M4P 1E4 – 416/481-1967; Fax: 416/440-7656
Chair, Marie C. Rounding, 416/440-7601
- Ontario Energy Corporation (OEC): South Tower, #905, 175 Bloor St. East, Toronto ON M4W 3R8 – 416/926-4200; Fax: 416/926-9641
Chair, President & CEO, Vacant
- Ontario Hydro
Listed alphabetically in detail, this section.
- Ontario Pesticides Advisory Committee: 40 St. Clair Ave. West, 4th Fl., Toronto ON M4V 1M2 – 416/314-9230; Fax: 416/314-9237
Chair, Dr. C.M. Switzer, 416/314-9233

ENVIRONMENTAL COMMISSIONER OF ONTARIO (ECO)
#605, 1075 Bay St., Toronto ON M5S 2B1
416/325-3377; Fax: 416/325-3370; Email: ecoinfo@pop.web.apc.org
Toll Free: 1-800-701-6454
Commissioner, Eva Ligeti
Coordinator, Communications & Public Affairs, Adrienne Jackson

Ministry of FINANCE
Frost Bldg. South, 7 Queen's Park Cres., Toronto ON M7A 1Y7
416/325-0333 (Communications & Corporate Affairs); Fax: 416/325-0339; URL: http://www.gov.ca/FIN/hmpage.html
Oshawa Office: 33 King St. West, PO Box 627, Oshawa ON L1H 8H5
905/433-6096 (Customer Service Centre), Fax: 905/433-6777
Toll Free: 1-800-263-7965
Ligne sans frais: 1-800-668-5821
TYY: 1-800-263-7776

ACTS ADMINISTERED
Assessment Act
Audit Act
Canadian Insurance Exchange Act
Central Trust Company Act
Commercial Concentration Tax Act
Commodity Futures Act
Compulsory Automobile Insurance Act
Cooperative Corporations Act
Corporations Tax Act
Credit Unions & Caisses Populaires Act
Crown Trust Company Act
Deposits Regulation Act
Employee Share Ownership Plan Act
Employer Health Tax Act
Financial Administration Act
Fuel Tax Act
Gasoline Tax Act
Guarantee Companies Securities Act
Income Tax Act
Insurance Act
Investment Contracts Act
Labour Sponsored Venture Capital Corporations Act
Land Transfer Tax Act
Loan & Trust Corporations Act
Marine Insurance Act
Mining Tax Act
Ministry of Revenue Act
Ministry of Treasury & Economics Act
Mortgage Brokers Act
Motor Vehicle Accident Claims Act
Ontario Credit Union League Limited Act
Ontario Deposit Insurance Corporation Act
Ontario Economic Council Act
Ontario Guaranteed Annual Income Act
Ontario Home Ownership Savings Plan Act
Ontario Loan Act
Ontario Municipal Improvement Corporation Act
Ontario Pensioners Property Tax Assistance Act
Pension Benefits Act
Prepaid Hospital & Medical Services Act
Province of Ontario Savings Office Act
Provincial Land Tax Act
Race Tracks Tax Act
Registered Insurance Brokers Act
Retail Sales Tax Act
Securities Act
Small Business Development Corporations Act
Social Contract Act
Statistics Act
Succession Duty Act
Succession Duty Supplementary Provisions Act
Supply Act
Tobacco Tax Act
Toronto Futures Exchange Act
Toronto Stock Exchange Act
Treasury Board Act
Minister, Hon. David Johnson
Deputy Minister, Michael L. Gourley, 416/325-1590, Fax: 416/325-1595
Deputy Minister, Revenue & Financial Institutions, Dina Palozzi, 416/325-3300, Fax: 416/325-3295

Audit Services Branch
Director, Larry Lindberg, 905/433-6479, Fax: 905/433-5222 (Oshawa), 416/325-8323, Fax: 416/325-5096 (Toronto)

Communications & Corporate Affairs Branch
Director, Don Black, 416/325-0333, Fax: 416/325-0339

Financial Services Policy Branch
Acting Director, Terry Campbell, 250 Yonge St., 30th Fl., Toronto ON M5B 2N7, 416/326-6009, Fax: 416/327-0941

Office of Legal Services
Director, Office of Legal Services, G. Stoodley, 416/325-1450, Fax: 416/325-1460

OFFICE OF THE BUDGET & TAXATION
Asst. Deputy Minister, Vacant, 416/327-0223, Fax: 416/327-0160
Director, Intergovernmental Finance Policy Branch, Harriet De Koven, 416/327-0140, Fax: 416/327-0160
Director, Taxation Policy Branch, Tom Sweeting, 416/327-0228, Fax: 416/327-0260
Director, Tax Design & Legislation Branch, Marion Crane, 416/327-0222, Fax: 416/325-0438

CORPORATE SERVICES DIVISION
Asst. Deputy Minister, Julie Leggatt, 905/433-6994, Fax: 905/433-6688
Director, Administration & Facilities Branch, Jim Ireland, 905/433-5905
Director, Corporate Planning & Finance Branch, Dave Roote, 905/433-5124
Director, Human Resources Branch, Ed Farragher, 905/433-6049
Director, Information Technology Branch, Alan Wilson, 905/433-6823
Director, Taxation Data Centre/Customer Service Centre, Bob Thompson, 905/433-5880

DEPOSIT INSTITUTIONS
Asst. Deputy Minister, Brian Cass, 416/326-9261, Fax: 416/326-9267
Asst. Superintendent & Registrar, Mortgage Brokers Act, Bill Vasiliou, 416/326-9038, Fax: 416/326-9004
Director, Credit Unions & Co-operatives Branch, John Harper, 416/326-9271, Fax: 416/326-9313
Acting Director, Investigations Branch, Robert Barbour, 416/326-9368, Fax: 416/326-9392
Director, Loan & Trust Corporations Branch, Erich Beifuss, 416/326-9002, Fax: 416/326-9004
Manager, Cooperative Development Services, Vacant, 416/326-9242, Fax: 416/326-9313

OFFICE OF ECONOMIC POLICY
Asst. Deputy Minister & Chief Economist, Steve Dorey, 416/325-0850, Fax: 416/325-9224
Director, Labour Economics Branch, Anne Martin, 416/325-0801, Fax: 416/325-0841
Director, Macroeconomics Analysis & Policy Branch, Pat Deutscher, 416/325-0754, Fax: 416/325-0796
Director, Structural Economics Branch, Karen Sadlier-Brown, 416/325-0902, Fax: 416/325-1187

FISCAL & FINANCIAL POLICY DIVISION
Job Security Fund: 416/325-1615, Fax: 416/325-8235
Controller/ADM, Bob Christie, 416/327-2177, Fax: 416/327-2136
Team Leader, Central Accounting Branch, Maurice Cavan, 416/325-8024, Fax: 416/325-8028
Director, Controllership Branch, Robert Siddell, 416/325-8084, Fax: 416/325-8028
Director, Fiscal Planning Branch, Anne Evans, 416/327-0165, Fax: 416/327-0160
Director, Public Sector Labour Market & Productivity Commission, Malcolm Smeaton, 416/325-0888, Fax: 416/325-8235

PROPERTY ASSESSMENT DIVISION
Asst. Deputy Minister, Elizabeth Patterson, 905/433-5772, Fax: 905/436-4513
Director, Appraisal Services Branch, Ian McClung, 905/433-5701, Fax: 905/433-6020
Director, Central & Western Regional Branch, Carl Isenberg, 905/433-5804, Fax: 905/433-6658
Director, Data Services & Development Branch, Chis Lopes, 905/433-5677, Fax: 905/436-4473
Director, Eastern & Northern Regional Operations Branch, Michael O'Dowd, 905/433-6263, Fax: 905/433-5162

OFFICE OF THE TREASURY
Asst. Deputy Minister, Tony Salerno, 416/325-8001, Fax: 416/325-8005

TAX DIVISION
Asst. Deputy Minister, Roy Lawrie, 905/433-5614, Fax: 905/433-6686
Acting Director, Business Services Branch, Tony Ming, 905/433-6617
Director, Collections Branch, John Godden, 905/433-5640
Director, Corporations Tax Branch, Nicole Anidjar, 905/436-4590
Director, Employer Health Tax Branch, Claude Dagenais, 905/433-6495
Director, Motor Fuels & Tobacco Tax Branch, Jay Young, 905/433-6329
Director, Retail Sales Tax Branch, Bob Moxley, 905/433-6156
Acting Director, Special Investigations Branch, Bob Moxley, 905/433-6905
Director, Tax Appeals Branch, Pauline Goral, 905/435-2040
Director, Tax Credits & Grants Branch, Richard Gruchala, 905/433-6941

Associated Agencies, Boards & Commissions
•Ontario Deposit Insurance Corporation: #700, 4711 Yonge St., Toronto ON M2N 6K8
Chair, Lili-Ann Renaud-Foster, 416/325-9444, Fax: 416/325-9568
President & CEO, Andrew Poprawa, 416/325-9580, Fax: 416/325-9568
•Ontario Financing Authority (OFA): #1400, 1 Dundas St. West, Toronto ON M7A 1Y7
Chair/Deputy Minister, Michael L. Gourley, 416/325-1592, Fax: 416/325-1595
Vice-Chair & CEO, Tony Salerno, 416/325-8001, Fax: 416/325-8005
Executive Director, Capital Markets, Gadi Mayman, 416/325-8131, Fax: 416/325-8111
Director, Capital Markets Treasury Division, Christine Moszynski, 416/325-8085, Fax: 416/325-8118
Director, Corporate Finance, Bill Ralph, 416/325-8057
Director, Province of Ontario Savings Office, David Brand, 416/325-9817, Fax: 416/325-8005
Director, Risk Management, Mike Manning, 416/325-8930
Director, Risk Control, David Brand, 416/325-9816, Fax: 416/325-8140
•Ontario Insurance Commission: 5160 Yonge St., PO Box 85, Toronto ON M2N 6L9 – 416/250-7250; Fax: 416/590-7070, Toll Free: 1-800-668-0128
Commissioner, D. Blair Tully, 416/590-7000, Fax: 416/590-8470
Acting Superintendent of Insurance, Grant Swanson, 416/590-7210, Fax: 416/590-7073
Director, Arbitration, Dispute Resolution, Elisabeth Sachs, 416/590-7060
Director, Corporate Licensing & Examinations, Grant Swanson, 416/590-7120
Director, Corporate Operations, Louise Wickson, 416/590-7556
Director, Legal Services, Colleen Parrish, 416/590-7102
Director, Market Conduct, Lea Algar, 416/590-7063
Director, Motor Vehicle Accident Claims Fund, Barbara Dudzinski, 416/590-7080
Director, Rates & Classification, Charles Anderson, 416/590-7061
Commission Actuary, Actuarial Services, Vacant, 416/590-7270
•Ontario Securities Commission: #1800, 20 Queen St. West, Toronto ON M5H 3S8 – 416/597-0681; Fax: 416/593-8240
Chair, Edward Waitzer, 416/593-8200, Fax: 416/593-8241
Executive Director & Deputy Director, Corporate Finance, Brenda Eprile, 416/593-8208, Fax: 416/593-8241
Vice-Chair, Jack Geller, 416/593-8229, Fax: 416/593-8241
Vice-Chair, Joan Smart, 416/593-3666, Fax: 416/593-8241
Chief Accountant, Office of the Chief Accountant, James Saloman, 416/593-8221, Fax: 416/593-8241
Deputy Director, Capital Markets/International Markets, Tanis MacLaren, 416/593-8259, Fax: 416/593-8241
Deputy Director, Corporate Services, Information Technology, Dennis LeFeuvre, 416/593-3676, Fax: 416/593-8188
•Pension Commission of Ontario: 101 Bloor St. West, 9th Fl., Toronto ON M7A 2K2 – 416/314-0660; Fax: 416/314-0620
Acting Chair, Monica Townson, 416/314-0630, Fax: 416/314-1798
Superintendent, Pensions, Ross Peebles, 416/314-0626
Director, Pensions Plans, Nurez Jiwani, 416/314-0588
Director, Policy & Research, Bruce Macnaughton, 416/314-0695
Registrar, Sharon Carr, 416/314-0624
Issue & Correspondence Coordination, Anthony Gullone, 416/314-0605
•Public Sector Labour Market & Productivity Commission: 101 Bloor St. West, 12th Fl., Toronto ON M5S 2Z7
Director, Malcolm A. Smeaton, 416/325-1651

Office of FRANCOPHONE AFFAIRS
Mowat Block, 900 Bay St., 4th Fl., Toronto ON M7A 1C2
416/325-4949; Fax: 416/325-4980
Toll Free: 1-800-268-7507

ACTS ADMINISTERED
French Language Services Act
Minister Responsible, Hon. Noble A. Villeneuve
Executive Director, Denis Fortin
Manager, Community Relations & Communications, Françis Larsen, 416/325-4938
Director, Ministry Services Branch, Jacqueline Frank, 416/325-4943

Ministry of HEALTH
Hepburn Block, 8th Fl., Queen's Park, Toronto ON M7A 1S2
416/327-4327 (Health Information Centre); Fax: 416/327-8781
Toll Free: 1-800-268-1153

ACTS ADMINISTERED
Alcoholism & Drug Addiction [Research Foundation] Act
Ambulance Act
Cancer Act
Cancer Remedies Act
Charitable Institutions Act
Chiropody Act
Chiropractic Act
Community Psychiatric Hospitals Act
Consent to Treatment Act
Dental Hygiene Act
Dental Technology Act
Dentistry Act
Denturism Act
Developmental Services Act (long-term care programs & services only)
Dietetics Act
Drug & Pharmacies Regulation Act
Drugless Practitioners Act
Elderly Persons Centres Act
Fluoridation Act
General Welfare Assistance Act (long-term care programs & services only)
Healing Arts Radiation Protection Act
Health Cards & Numbers Control Act
Health Care Accessibility Act
Health Facilities Special Orders Act
Health Insurance Act
Health Protection & Promotion Act
Homemakers & Nurses Services Act
Homes for the Aged & Rest Homes Act
Homes for Retarded Persons Act (long-term care programs & services only)
Homes for Special Care Act
Hypnosis Act
Immunization of School Pupils Act
Independent Health Facilities Act
Laboratories & Specimen Collection Centre Licensing Act
Long Term Care Act
Massage Therapy Act
Medical Laboratory Technology Act
Medical Radiation Technology Act
Medicine Act
Mental Health Act
Mental Hospitals Act
Midwifery Act
Ministry of Community & Social Services Act (sections 11.1 & 12 re: long-term care programs & services only)
Ministry of Health Act
Municipal Health Services Act
Nursing Act
Nursing Homes Act
Occupational Therapy Act
Ontario Drug Benefit Act
Ontario Medical Association Dues Act
Ontario Mental Health Foundation Act
Opticianary Act
Pharmacy Act
Physiotherapy Act
Prescription Drug Cost Regulation Act
Private Hospitals Act
Psychology Act
Public Hospitals Act
Regulated Health Professions Act
Respiratory Therapy Act
Tobacco Control Act
Toronto Hospital Act
War Veterans Burial Act
Minister, Hon. James Wilson, 416/327-4300, Fax: 416/326-1571
Deputy Minister, Margaret Mottershead, 416/327-4296, Fax: 416/326-1576
Director, Legal Services Branch, G. Sharpe, 416/327-8591, Fax: 416/327-8605
Acting Director, Communications & Information Branch, A. Erland, 416/327-8501, Fax: 416/327-8791
Coordinator, Health Information Centre, Susan Furino, 416/314-8337, Fax: 416/314-8721

Health Economic Development
Head, A. Szénde, 416/327-4531

CORPORATE SERVICES
Asst. Deputy Minister, B. Gibbs, 416/327-0985
Acting Director, Audit Branch, V. Liu, 416/327-7786

GOVERNMENT OF ONTARIO

Director, Fiscal Strategies Branch, L. Steele, 416/327-8674
Acting Director, Human Resources Branch, D. Ferenc, 416/327-8747
Acting Director, Supply & Financial Services Branch, G. Dadd, 416/327-7160
Acting Director, Systems Development Branch, B. McKee, 416/327-8234
Director, Systems Support Branch, Robert Cavanaugh, 613/548-6486
Acting Director, User Support Branch, M. Kerr, 613/548-6566

HEALTH INSURANCE & RELATED PROGRAMS
Asst. Deputy Minister, M.C. Lindberg, 416/327-4266
Acting Director, Drug Programs Branch, L. Tennant, 416/327-8109
Director, Laboratory Services Branch, Dr. Helen Demshar, 416/235-5941
Acting Director, Negotiations Secretariat, N. Ho, 416/327-4490
Director, Provider Services Branch, Marsha Barnes, 613/548-6716 (Kingston)
Director, Registration & Claims Branch, D. Segal, 613/548-6650 (Kingston)

Claims Payment District Offices
Hamilton: 119 King St. West, Hamilton ON L8P 4T9 – 905/521-7547
Kingston: #401, 1055 Princess St., Kingston ON K7L 5T3 – 613/345-0656
London: 217 York St., London ON N6A 1B7 – 519/646-2000
Mississauga: 201 City Centre Dr., Mississauga ON L5B 2T4 – 905/896-6000
Oshawa: 419 King St. West, Oshawa ON L1J 7J2 – 905/576-2870
Ottawa: 75 Albert St., Ottawa ON K1P 5Y9 – 613/237-9100
Sudbury: 199 Larch St., 9th Fl., Sudbury ON P3E 5R1 – 705/675-4010
Thunder Bay: #222, 435 James St. South, Thunder Bay ON P7E 6E3 – 807/475-1351
Toronto: 2195 Yonge St., Toronto ON M4S 2B2 – 416/440-4400

HEALTH STRATEGIES GROUP
Acting Asst. Deputy Minister, Charlie A. Bigenwald, 416/327-0859
Acting Executive Director, Health Human Resources Planning Division, J. Bertram, 416/327-8643
Director, Health Policy Branch, R. Bamhorst, 416/327-8533
Acting Director, Information Planning & Evaluation Branch, M.B. Valentine, 416/327-7482
Director, Northern Health Programs & Planning Branch, E. Mahood, 705/670-7248
Director, Professional Relations Branch, A.R. Burrows, 416/327-8888
Regional Director, Central, B. Sulzenko-Laurie, 416/327-7494
Regional Director, South & Central West, M.B. Valentine, 416/327-7487

INSTITUTIONAL HEALTH
Acting Asst. Deputy Minister, A. Szénde, 416/314-5923
Acting Director, Institutional Services Branch, L. Pisko-Bezruchko, 416/327-7050
Acting Regional Director, Central Hospital Region, A. Garland, 416/327-7115
Regional Director, North/East Hospital Region, G. Monaghan, 416/327-7117
Regional Director, South/West Hospital Region, M. McEwen, 416/327-7156

MENTAL HEALTH PROGRAMS & SERVICES
Asst. Deputy Minister, J. Hill, 416/327-7241
Regional Director, Central, D. Helm, 416/327-7241

Regional Director, North & East, N. Dwyer, 416/327-7235
Regional Director, South & West, M. Gallow, 416/327-7584

POPULATION HEALTH & COMMUNITY SERVICES SYSTEM GROUP
Toll Free: 1-800-668-2437 (AIDS Bureau)
AIDS Information: 416/392-2437
Asst. Deputy Minister, S. Campbell, 416/327-4537, Fax: 416/327-4409
Chief Medical Officer & Director, Health, Dr. R. Schabas, 416/327-7392
Executive Director, Community Health Division, Celia Denov, 416/327-7225, Fax: 416/327-7230
Director, Emergency Health Services Branch, Graham Brand, 416/327-7907
Executive Director, Long-term Care Division, Geoffrey Quirt, 416/327-8370
Director, Assistive Devices Branch, Mark Cox, 416/327-8135
Director, Community Health Branch, Dorothy Loranger, 416/327-7535
Acting Director, Health Promotion Branch, G. Pasut, 416/314-5484
Director, In-Home Services Branch, Tim Young, 416/326-9750
Director, Policy Branch, Patrick T. Laverty, 416/326-9755

Health Boards Secretariat
151 Bloor St. West, 9th Fl., Toronto ON M5S 2T5
416/327-8510; Fax: 416/327-8524
The following Boards can be reached through the Health Boards Secretariat:
Consent & Capality Board
Health Facilities Appeal Board
Health Professions Board
Health Protection Appeal Board
Health Services Appeal Board
Hospital Appeal Board
Laboratory Review Board
Nursing Homes Review Board

Associated Agencies, Boards & Commissions
• Addiction Research Foundation (ARF)
Listed in Section 2, *see* Index.
• Board of Directors of Drugless Therapy-Naturopathy: 4195 Dundas St. West, Etobicoke ON M8X 1V4 – 416/236-4593; Fax: 416/236-4387
Chair, James W. Spring, N.D.
Sec.-Treas., Robert L. Gatis, N.D.
• Chaplaincy Services Ontario: #200, 35 McCaul St., Toronto ON M5T 1V7 – 416/326-6860; Fax: 416/326-6867
Provincial Coordinator, Rev. Michael Steeves
• Healing Arts Radiation Protection Commission (HARP): 5700 Yonge St., 3rd Fl., North York ON M2M 4K5 – 416/327-7952; Fax: 416/327-8805
• Ontario Cancer Institute: Princess Margaret Hospital, 610 University Ave., Toronto ON M5G 2M9 – 416/924-2000
Chair, Ed King
• Ontario Cancer Treatment & Research Foundation: 620 University Ave., 16th Fl., Toronto ON M5G 2L7 – 416/971-9800; Fax: 416/971-6888
• Ontario Mental Health Foundation: #1708, 365 Bloor St. East, Toronto ON M4W 3L4 – 416/920-7721; Fax: 416/920-0026
Executive Director, Dr. Howard Cappell
• Psychiatric Patient Advocate Office: 56 Wellesley St. West, 8th Fl., Toronto ON M5S 2S3 – 416/327-7000; Fax: 416/327-7008
Acting Director, Brock Grant

INFORMATION & PRIVACY COMMISSIONER OF ONTARIO
#1700, 80 Bloor St. West, Toronto ON M5S 2V1
416/326-3333; Fax: 416/325-9195; URL: http://www.ipc.on.ca
Toll Free: 1-800-387-0073
TTY: 416/325-7539
Ensures the public's right of access to information held by provincial & local government organizations; and protects the individual's right of privacy, as it relates to personal information held by provincial & local government organizations. Persons not satisfied with a government decision about access to information may ask the Commissioner to review the government's decision. In addition, the Commissioner investigates complaints from individuals who feel the government has wrongfully collected, used or disclosed their personal information. The Commissioner reports directly to the Legislative Assembly.

ACTS ADMINISTERED
Freedom of Information & Protection of Privacy Act
Municipal Freedom of Information & Protection of Privacy Act
Commissioner, Tom Wright, 416/326-3333
Asst. Commissioner, Access, Tom Mitchinson, 416/326-0012
Asst. Commissioner, Privacy, Dr. Ann Cavoukian, 416/326-3942
Executive Director, Judy Hubert, 416/326-3938
Director, Appeals, Irwin Glasberg, 416/326-0013
Director, Legal Services, Ken Anderson, 416/326-3922
Manager, Communications, Sarah Jones, 416/326-3940

Commission on INTEGRITY
101 Bloor St. West, 4th Fl., Toronto ON M5S 2Z7
416/314-8983; Fax: 416/314-8987
The Commissioner administers the Members' Conflict of Interest Act, 1988, as it applies to members of the Legislative Assembly & Executive Council in Ontario.
Commissioner, Hon. G.T. Evans, LL.D., Ph.D., K.C.S.G.

Ministry of INTERGOVERNMENTAL AFFAIRS
900 Bay St., 6th Fl., Toronto ON M7A 1C2
416/325-4760 (Communications); Fax: 416/325-4759

ACTS ADMINISTERED
Ministry of Intergovernmental Affairs Act
Minister, Hon. Dianne Cunningham, 416/326-1600, Fax: 416/326-1656
Deputy Minister, Judith Wolfson, 416/325-4785, Fax: 416/325-4787
Executive Coordinator, Communications, Laurie Spephens, 416/325-4810, Fax: 416/325-4759
Manager, Finance & Administration Services Branch, Inez Pinder, 416/325-4766
Asst. Deputy Minister, Constitutional Affairs, Michal Ben-Gera, 416/325-4804
Asst. Deputy Minister, Ottawa Office, Vacant, 613/239-1682, Fax: 613/239-1688
Asst. Deputy Minister, Québec Office, Stephen Bornstein, 418/692-1366, Fax: 418/692-1037, Ontario: 416/325-4800

Ministry of LABOUR
400 University Ave., 14th Fl., Toronto ON M7A 1T7
416/326-7565; Fax: 416/326-7406
Toll Free: 1-800-267-9517

ACTS ADMINISTERED
Blind Workmen's Compensation Act
Crown Employees Collective Bargaining Act

Employment Agencies Act
Employment Standards Act
Government Contracts Hours & Wages Act
Hospital Labour Disputes Arbitration Act
Industrial Standards Act
Labour Relations Act
Ministry of Labour Act
Occupational Health & Safety Act
One Day's Rest in Seven Act
Pay Equity Act
Rights of Labour Act
Smoking in the Workplace Act
Workers' Compensation Act
Workmen's Compensation Insurance Act
Minister, Hon. Elizabeth Witmer, 416/326-7600, Fax: 416/326-1449
Deputy Minister, Timothy Millard, 416/326-7606, Fax: 416/326-7599
Director, Communications & Marketing Branch, Tim Nau, 416/326-7400
Director, Legal Services Branch, Nancy Austin, 416/326-7953

BUSINESS & ORGANIZATION SERVICES DIVISION
416/326-7586; Fax: 416/326-7599
Asst. Deputy Minister, Carola Lane, 416/326-7585
Director, Business Management & Accountability Branch, Peter Inokai, 416/326-7271, Fax: 416/326-7274
Acting Director, Client Support Services Branch, Val James, 416/326-7225, Fax: 416/326-7241
Director, Information & Technology Services Branch, Arjun Krishnan, 416/326-7131, Fax: 416/326-7138
Team Leader, Integrated Planning Secretariat, Bruce Stewart, 416/326-1354, Fax: 416/326-7599
Director, Organizational Learning & Effectiveness Branch, Ron Brittain, 416/326-7685, Fax: 416/326-7745
Coordinator, Freedom of Information, Privacy & Records Management Office, Christopher Berzins, 416/326-7786, Fax: 416/314-8749
Coordinator, Occupational Health & Safety, Monica Harding, 416/326-7247, Fax: 416/314-5203

LABOUR MANAGEMENT SERVICES
416/326-7606; Fax: 416/314-8755
Deputy Minister, Vacant, 416/326-7574
Director, Office of Arbitration, Jean M. Read, 416/326-1300, Fax: 416/326-1329
Director, Office of Mediation, Paul G. Gardner, 416/326-7358, Fax: 416/326-7367

LABOUR POLICY DIVISION
416/326-7558; Fax: 416/326-7599
Acting Asst. Deputy Minister, Ron Saunders, 416/326-7555
Director, Employment Conditions & Labour Market Policy Branch, Ron Saunders, 416/314-5853, Fax: 416/314-5855
Director, Labour-Management Policy Branch, Tony Dean, 416/314-5846, Fax: 416/314-5855
Director, Workplace Policies & Practices Branch, Marguerite Rappolt, 416/326-7625, Fax: 416/326-7650

OPERATIONS DIVISION
416/326-7668; Fax: 416/326-7599
Acting Asst. Deputy Minister, Lynn Binette, 416/326-7665
Director, Employment Practices Branch, Pat Coursey, 416/326-7000, Fax: 416/326-7061
Director, Occupational Health & Safety Branch, Ed McCloskey, 416/326-1359, Fax: 416/326-7761
Manager, Information & Administrative Services, Marg Fraser, 416/326-7732, Fax: 416/326-7745
Provincial Coordinator, Construction Health & Safety Program, Ian Carruthers, 416/326-7776
Provincial Coordinator, Industrial Health & Safety Program, John Vander Doelen, 416/326-7904, Fax: 416/326-7761
Provincial Coordinator, Mining Health & Safety Program, Ian Plummer, 705/670-5703, Fax: 705/670-5698
Provincial Coordinator, Professional & Specialized Services, Dr. Om Malik, 416/326-1404
Chief, Materials Testing Laboratory, Marcel D'Jivre, 705/670-5711
Chief, Occupational Health Laboratory Service & Radiation Protection Service, John Tai-Pow, 416/235-5913

Regional Offices
Central: 1290 Central Pkwy. West, 3rd Fl., Mississauga ON L5C 4R3 – 905/615-7030; Fax: 905/615-7098, Area Director, Arthur Gladstone
Eastern: #200, 1111 Prince of Wales Dr., Ottawa ON K2C 3T2 – 613/727-2824; Fax: 613/727-2900, Area Director, Vic Pakalnis
Hamilton/Niagara: 1 Jarvis St., Main Fl., Hamilton ON L8R 3J2 – 905/577-1238; Fax: 905/577-1200, Area Director, Sophie Dennis
Northern: 159 Cedar St., 3rd Fl., Sudbury ON P3E 6A5 – 705/670-7433; Fax: 705/670-7435, Area Director, Paavo Kivisto
Toronto: 2275 Midland Ave., Scarborough ON M1P 3E7 – 416/314-5286; Fax: 416/314-5301, Area Director, Lynn Binette
Western: 130 Dufferin Ave., 4th Fl., London ON N6A 5R2 – 519/439-2210; Fax: 519/672-0268, Area Director, Vic Crew

Associated Agencies, Boards & Commissions
• Industrial Disease Standards Panel: #1004, 69 Yonge St., Toronto ON M5E 1K3 – 416/327-4156; Fax: 416/327-4166
Chair, Nicolette Carlan
• Office of the Employer Advisor: #501, 101 Bloor St. West, Toronto ON M5S 1P5 – 416/327-0020; Fax: 416/327-0726
Director, Jeffrey Stutz
• Office of the Worker Advisor: #1300, 123 Edward St., Toronto ON M5G 1E2 – 416/325-8570; Fax: 416/325-4830
Director, Alec Farquhar
• Ontario Labour Relations Board: 400 University Ave., 4th Fl., Toronto ON M7A 1T7 – 416/326-7500; Fax: 416/326-7531
Chair, Judith McCormack
• Pay Equity Commission: 150 Eglinton Ave. East, 5th Fl., Toronto ON M4P 1E8 – 416/481-4464; Fax: 416/314-8741
Commissioner, Brigid O'Reilly
• Workers' Compensation Board
Listed alphabetically in detail, this section.
• Workplace Health & Safety Agency: #900, 121 Bloor St. East, Toronto ON M4W 3M5 – 416/975-9728; Fax: 416/975-9775
Chair, Bruce Stanton

MANAGEMENT BOARD OF CABINET
Ferguson Block, 77 Wellesley St. West, 12th Fl., Toronto ON M7A 1N3
416/325-1688 (Employment Services); Fax: 416/327-3790
416/326-1234 (Management Board)
Queen's Printer: 416/326-5316

ACTS ADMINISTERED
Management Board of Cabinet Act
Public Service Act
Chair, Hon. David Johnson, 416/327-2333
Executive Director, Ontario Public Service Social Contract Implementation, Richard Lundeen, 416/325-1392
Director, Legal Services Branch, Heather Cooper, 416/325-9391, Fax: 416/325-9404
Chief of Staff, Catherine M. Pead, 416/327-0942
Special Asst., Communications, Valerie Taylor, 416/326-9091
Special Asst., Outreach Constituency, Val Fogarty, 416/327-2944
Special Asst., Policy, Jordan Berger, 416/327-2559
Special Asst., Policy, Andrew Lee, 416/327-4249
Special Asst., Press Secretary, David McCully, 416/327-0948

MANAGEMENT BOARD SECRETARIAT
Secretary, Management Board of Cabinet & Deputy Minister, Management Board Secretariat, Michele M. Noble, 416/327-3805, Fax: 416/327-3809

Communications Services Branch
416/327-2789; Fax: 416/327-2817
Director, Linda Leighton, 416/327-2790
Manager, Customer Accounts Unit, Angela Coke, 416/327-2794
Manager, Issues Management, Corporate Priorities & Media Relations, Vacant, 416/327-2793, Fax: 416/327-2718
Acting Manager, Operational Planning, Production, External Recruitment Advertising, Margaret Cassidy, 416/325-1353, Fax: 416/325-1367
Manager, Publishing Inc., Margaret Cassidy, 416/325-1353, Fax: 416/325-1367
Manager, Strategic Communication Planning & Policy, Elizabeth Lea, 416/325-1363, Fax: 416/327-2817

CORPORATE SERVICES DIVISION
Asst. Deputy Minister, Harold Wu, 416/327-2862, Fax: 416/327-2866
Acting Director, Audit Branch, Marie Davis, 416/314-3448, Fax: 416/314-3467
Director, Finance & Office Services Branch, Ralph Grant, 416/327-2900
Asst. Director, Human Resources, Jane Corbet, 416/327-3814
Director, Information Technology Services Branch, George Radford, 416/327-2828, Fax: 416/327-2530, Helpline: 416/327-2700
Coordinator, Library & Information Services, Marilyn MacKellar, 416/327-2533

EMPLOYMENT EQUITY DIVISION
#393, 595 Bay St., PO Box 51, Toronto ON M5G 2C2
416/325-1300; Fax: 416/325-1313
Asst. Deputy Minister, Vacant, 416/325-1300
Coordinator, Employment Equity Review Committee, Jean-Yves Leduc, 416/314-5576
Director, Employment Equity Branch, Earl Miller, 416/325-1260, Fax: 416/325-1313

INFORMATION & TECHNOLOGY DIVISION
155 University Ave., 8th Fl., Toronto ON M5H 3B7
416/327-3442; Fax: 416/327-3264
Asst. Deputy Minister, David Girvin, 416/327-9696
Director, Customer Service & Support Branch, Bryan Izatt, 416/327-3440, Fax: 416/327-3256
Director, Information & Technology Policy Branch, Trevor Moon, 56 Wellesley St. West, Toronto ON M7A 1Z6, 416/327-3250, Fax: 416/327-3274
Director, Processing Services Branch, Ernie Dark, 1201 Wilson Ave., Toronto ON M3M 1J8, 416/235-4584
Director, Telecommunications Services Branch, Terry Ham, 416/327-3026, Fax: 416/327-3281

OPERATIONS & MINISTRY SUPPORT DIVISION
#1104, 790 Bay St., Toronto ON M7A 1Y7
416/325-1610; Fax: 416/325-1612
Asst. Deputy Minister, Susan Waterfield, 416/325-1607
Director, Freedom of Information & Privacy Branch, Frank White, 101 Bloor St. West, Toronto ON M5S 1P7, 416/327-2084, Fax: 416/327-2190

GOVERNMENT OF ONTARIO

Director, Operational Policy & Program Development Branch, Linda Kahn, 416/325-1617, Fax: 416/325-1753
Director, Ministry Support Branch, Morag Dion, 416/325-1777, Fax: 416/325-1605
Director, Special Programs & Services Branch, Angela Forest, 416/325-0222, Fax: 416/325-0251

PROJECT RENEWAL DIVISION
416/327-9698; Fax: 416/327-3772
Acting Asst. Deputy Minister, Rob Lowry, 416/327-9699
Project Director, Peter Crabtree, 416/327-9729

PROPERTY MANAGEMENT DIVISION
77 Wellesley St. West, 5th Fl., Toronto ON M7A 1N3
416/327-2779; Fax: 416/327-2785
Executive Director, Julie Leggatt, 416/327-2778
Director, Central Operations Branch, Mike Lukacko, 416/327-2660, Fax: 416/327-2695
Director, Client Services & Portfolio Management Branch, Barbara Hewett, 416/327-3722, Fax: 416/327-3772
Director, Contract Management Branch, Vacant, 416/327-2619, Fax: 416/327-2606
Director, Corporate Management & Mortgage Branch, Vern M. Chaves, 77 Grenville St., 9th Fl., Toronto ON M5S 1B3, 416/327-3748, Fax: 416/314-3677
Director, Leasing Services Branch, Del Jackson, 416/327-3943, Fax: 416/327-2694

REAL ESTATE SERVICES DIVISION
777 Bay St., 16th Fl., Toronto ON M5G 2E5
416/585-6777; Fax: 416/585-7577
Executive Director, Kathy Bouey, 416/585-6730
Director, Central Branch, Gordon Laschinger, 416/585-4212, Fax: 416/585-4263
Acting Director, Northern & Eastern Branch, Marie Cardno, 416/585-6742, Fax: 416/585-5263
Director, Western Branch, Peter B. Johansen, 416/585-6770, Fax: 416/585-4005

REALTY GROUP
77 Wellesley St. West, 11th Fl., Toronto ON M7A 1N3
416/327-3937; Fax: 416/327-3942
Asst. Deputy Minister, Tim Casey, 416/327-3933
Acting Director, Design Services Branch, Ann Gabriel, 416/327-1900, Fax: 416/327-1852
Director, Ontario Realty Corporation Transition Team, Ian Veitch, 416/327-2754, Fax: 416/327-4194
Director, Project Management Branch, David McHugh, 720 Bay St., 4th Fl., Toronto ON M5G 2K1, 416/326-4856, Fax: 416/326-4871
Director, Special Projects, Larry Loop, 416/327-2883

STRATEGIC POLICY DIVISION
416/325-1534; Fax: 416/325-1393
Asst. Deputy Minister, Phyllis Clark, 416/325-1531
Executive Director, Agency Reform, Pam Bryant, 416/327-2030, Fax: 416/327-2186
Chief Actuary, Actuarial Services, Clare Pitcher, 416/327-8384, Fax: 416/327-8402
Acting Director, Compensation & Labour Relations Policy Branch, Murray Lapp, 416/325-1488, Fax: 416/327-8402
Director, Data Support Branch, Sheree Davis, 56 Wellesley St. West, 4th Fl., Toronto ON M7A 1Z6, 416/327-2090, Fax: 416/327-1682
Director, Management Structure & Workforce Planning, Wendy Noble, 416/327-2044, Fax: 416/327-2186
Director, Strategic Direction & Planning Branch, Valerie Cook-Jackson, 416/327-3623, Fax: 416/327-2593
Chief Negotiator, Negotiations Secretariat, Angelo Pesce, 416/325-1476, Fax: 416/325-1483

SUPPLY & SERVICE DIVISION
77 Wellesley St. West, 12th Fl., Toronto ON M7A 1N3
416/327-3515; Fax: 416/327-3517
Asst. Deputy Minister, David McGeown, 416/327-3511
Director, (The) Green Workplace, Pat Werner, 416/327-4185, Fax: 416/327-4193, Recycling Hotline: 416/327-3777
Project Director, Strategic Procurement Project, Pat Werner, 416/327-4185
Director, Information Services Branch, Eric Steeves, 416/327-2890, Fax: 416/327-3652
Manager, Access & Inquiry Services, Mary LeFeuvre, 416/325-3444, Fax: 416/325-3407
Manager, Queen's Printer (Publications Ontario), Ruth Hawkins, 416/326-5316
Acting Director, General Services Branch, Gary Vamplew, 416/314-3434, Fax: 416/314-3411
Director, Human Resource Information Services Branch, David Ritcey, 416/327-9210, Fax: 416/327-9254
Director, Purchasing Services Branch, Dan Kusel, 416/327-3518, Fax: 416/327-3573
Manager, Policy & Program Development Section, Gulbaz Khan, 416/327-3580, Environmental Procurement: 416/327-3581
Manager, Supplier Information Service, Brendan Power, 416/327-3552
Manager, Travel Program, Kathy Tortell, 416/327-2568
General Manager, Corporate Contracting Services, Robert Farnley, 416/327-3536
General Manager, Office Products Centre, Bob Hogg, 4375 Chesswood Dr., Toronto ON M3J 2C2, 416/327-3319, General Inquiry: 416/327-3004
Acting Director, Employee Health & Safety Services Branch, Judith Berg, 416/327-1080, Fax: 416/327-1115
Acting Manager, Occupational Health Service, Brenda Brautigam, 416/327-1131
Director, Public Appointments Secretariat, Marilyn Roycroft, 416/327-2640, Fax: 416/327-2640

Citizens' Inquiry Bureau
416/326-1234 (Ontario collect)
TDD: 416/325-3408
Supervisor, Bertha Beniusis

Associated Agencies, Boards & Commissions
• Civil Service Commission: #803, 101 Bloor St. West, Toronto ON M5S 1P7 – 416/325-6314; Fax: 416/325-6317
Chair, Valerie A. Gibbons
Executive Officer & Secretary, Cynthia Bedborough
• Ontario Land Corporation: Ferguson Block, 77 Wellesley St. West, 13th Fl., Toronto ON M7A 1N3 – 416/327-3937
CEO, Tim Casey, 416/327-3933
• Ontario Mortgage Corporation: 62 Wellesley St. West, Toronto ON M5S 2X3 – 416/314-3650
CEO, Tim Casey, 416/327-3933
• Ontario Pension Board: #1200, 1 Adelaide St. East, Toronto ON M5C 2X6 – 416/364-8558; Fax: 416/364-7578, Toll Free: 1-800-668-6203
President, J.J. Wilbee
Chair, W.H. Somerville

Ministry of MUNICIPAL AFFAIRS & HOUSING
777 Bay St., 17th Fl., Toronto ON M5G 2E5
416/585-7041 (Communications Branch); Fax: 416/585-6227; URL: http://nrserv.mmah.gov.on.ca/

ACTS ADMINISTERED
Barrie Innisfil Annexation Act
Barrie-Vespra Annexation Act
Brantford-Brant Annexation Act
Building Code Act
City of Cornwall Annexation Act
City of Gloucester Act
City of Hamilton Act
City of Hazeldean-March Act
City of London Act
City of Nepean Act
City of Ottawa Road Closing & Conveyance Validation Act
City of Port Colborne Act
City of Sudbury Hydro-Electric Service Act
City of Thorold Act
City of Thunder Bay Act
City of Timmins-Porcupine Act
Community Economic Development Act
County of Haliburton Act
County of Oxford Act
County of Simcoe Act
Development Charges Act
District Municipality of Muskoka Act
District of Parry Sound Local Government Act
Geographic Township of Hansen Act
Housing Development Act
International Bridges Municipal Payments Act
Line Fences Act
Local Improvement Act
London-Middlesex Act
Ministry of Municipal Affairs & Housing Act
Moosonee Development Area Board Act
Municipal Act
Municipal Affairs Act
Municipal Arbitrations Act
Municipal Boundary Negotiations Act
Municipal Conflict of Interest Act
Municipal Corporations Quieting Orders Act
Municipal Elderly Residents' Assistance Act
Municipal Elections Act
Municipal Extra Territorial Tax Act
Municipal Franchises Act
Municipal Interest & Discount Rates Act
Municipal Payments in Lieu of Taxes Statute Law Amendment Act
Municipal Private Acts Repeal Act
Municipal & School Tax Credit Assistance Acts
Municipal Subsidies Adjustment Repeal Act
Municipal Tax Assistance Act
Municipal Tax Sales Act
Municipal Unemployment Relief Act
Municipal Works Assistance Act
Municipality of Metropolitan Toronto Act
Municipality of Shuniah Act
Niagara Escarpment Planning & Development Act
Ontario Housing Corporation Act
Ontario Municipal Board Act
Ontario Municipal Employees Retirement System Act
Ontario Planning & Development Act
Ontario Unconditional Grants Act
Ontario Water Resources Act (Clauses 44(2) a, b & c Sec.48)
Ottawa-Carleton Amalgamations & Elections Act
Parkway Belt Planning & Development Act
Planning Act
Police Village of St. George Act
Public Parks Act
Public Utilities Act
Public Utilities Corporations Act
Regional Municipalities Act
Regional Municipality of Durham Act
Regional Municipality of Haldimand-Norfolk Act
Regional Municipality of Halton Act
Regional Municipality of Hamilton-Wentworth Act
Regional Municipality of Niagara Act
Regional Municipality of Ottawa-Carleton Act
Regional Municipality of Ottawa-Carleton Land Acquisition Act
Regional Municipality of Peel Act
Regional Municipality of Sudbury Act
Regional Municipality of Waterloo Act
Regional Municipality of York Act
Rent Control Act

Residential Complexes Financing Costs Restraint Act
Residential Rent Regulation Act
Residential Tenancies Act
Road Access Act
Rural Housing Assistance Act
Sarnia-Lambton Act
Shoreline Property Assistance Act
Snow Roads & Fences Act
Statute Labour Act
Tax Sales Confirmation Act
Territorial Division Act
Tom Longboat Act
Toronto District Heating Corporation Act
Toronto Islands Act
Toronto Islands Residential Community Stewardship Act
Town of Wasaga Beach Act
Township of North Plantagenet Act
Township of South Dumfries Act
Waterfront Regeneration Trust Agency Act
Wharfs & Harbours Act
Minister, Hon. Allan Leach, 416/585-7000, Fax: 416/585-6470
Deputy Minister, Daniel Burns, 416/585-7100, Fax: 416/585-7211
Chair, Board of Negotiation, Gordon Swayze, 416/326-4700
Faciltator, Urban Economic Development, Dale Martin, 416/585-7474
Director, Legal Services Branch, David Spring, 416/585-6724
Executive Coordinator, Communications Branch, Jocelyne Souloudre, 416/585-6900
Manager, Employment Equity Office, Jafar Rasheed, 416/585-7424

CORPORATE MANAGEMENT SERVICES
Asst. Deputy Minister, Larry Close, 416/585-6262
Director, Information Management Branch, Les Fincham, 416/585-7223
Director, Subsidies Management Branch, Vacant, 416/585-6193
Manager, Government Liaison Unit, Bruce McLeod, 416/585-6236
Manager, Office of Francophone Municipal Relations & Ministry Correspondence, Joyce Irvine, 416/585-7556
Manager, Resources Planning Unit, Harvey Regush, 416/585-7193

CORPORATE RESOURCES MANAGEMENT DIVISION
Asst. Deputy Minister, Arnie Temple, 416/585-6670
Director, Administrative Services Branch, Nadia Vakharia, 416/585-7437
Acting Director, Audit Services Branch, Andy Glendenning, 416/585-6550
Director, Financial Controller & Treasurer, Ontario Housing Corporation, Victor Augustine, 416/585-6659
Director, Human Resources Branch, Jim Parker, 416/585-7570
Director, Information & Technology Services Branch, Kurtis Bishop, 416/585-6830
Director, Legal Branch, Andrea Baston, 416/585-6701

HOUSING OPERATIONS DIVISION
Asst. Deputy Minister, Shirley Hoy, 416/585-6373
Chair, Ontario Housing Corporation, William Carson, 416/585-6518, Fax: 416/585-7617
Registrar, Rent Registry, David Braund, 415 Yonge St., 19th Fl., Toronto ON M5B 2E7, 416/326-0923, Fax: 416/326-0930
Acting Executive Director, Housing Field Operations, Peter Schafft, 416/585-6400, Fax: 416/585-7610
Acting Director, Management & Operational Support Branch, Marsha Goldford, 416/585-6847
Director, Program Development & Support Branch, Philip Schwartz, 416/585-7637, Fax: 416/585-4004

HOUSING PLANNING & POLICY DIVISION
Asst. Deputy Minister, Anne Beaumont, 416/585-7482
Director, Housing Development & Buildings Branch, Ann Borooah, 416/585-4238
Director, Housing Policy Branch, Scott Harcourt, 416/585-7019
Director, Strategic Planning & Research Branch, Crom Sparling, 416/585-6360

MUNICIPAL OPERATIONS DIVSION
Asst. Deputy Minister, Brian Riddell, 416/585-6600
Executive Coordinator, Field Management, Peter Boles, 416/585-7251
Director, Community Development Branch, Tania Melnyk, 416/585-6264
Acting Director, Municipal Boundaries Branch, D. Taylor, 416/585-7275
Director, Plans Administration Branch (Central & Southwest), Diana Jardine, 416/585-6025
Director, Plans Administration Branch (North & East), Bryan Hill, 416/585-6093

Field Offices
Central: #207, 47 Sheppard Ave. East, Toronto ON M2N 2Z8 – 416/327-0017; Fax: 416/250-1258
Northeastern: 850 Barrydowne Rd., 3rd Fl., Sudbury ON P3A 3T7 – 705/560-0120; Fax: 705/560-9776
Northwestern: #116, 435 James St. South, Thunder Bay ON P7E 6E3 – 807/475-1651; Fax: 807/475-0898
Southeastern: 1055 Princess St., Kingston ON K7L 5T3 – 613/545-4310; Fax: 613/545-4449
Southwestern: 495 Richmond St., 7th Fl., London ON N6A 5A9 – 519/673-1611; Fax: 519/438-1678

MUNICIPAL POLICY DEVELOPMENT DIVISION
Asst. Deputy Minister, Dana Richardson, 416/585-6321
Director, Canada-Ontario Infrastructure Works, Myra Wiener, 416/585-6296
Director, Local Government Policy Branch, Doug Bonnes, 416/585-7270
Director, Municipal Finance Branch, Nancy Bardecki, 416/585-6951
Acting Director, Municipal Planning Policy Branch, Philip McKinstry, 416/585-6225
Director, Provincial Planning Branch, Meredith Beresford, 416/585-7177

OFFICE FOR THE GREATER TORONTO AREA
Waterpark Pl., #300, 10 Bay St., Toronto ON M5J 2R8
416/314-6400; Fax: 416/314-6440
Asst. Deputy Minister, Elizabeth A. McLaren, 416/314-6417

Associated Agencies, Boards & Commissions
• Office of the Provincial Facilitator: 777 Bay St., 12th Fl., Toronto ON M5G 2E5 – 416/585-6736; Fax: 416/585-7411
Provincial Facilitator, Dale Martin, 416/585-7474
• Ontario Municipal Board (OMB): 655 Bay St., 15th Fl., Toronto ON M5G 1E5 – 416/326-6800
Chair, Helen Cooper
Secretary & COO, Diana Macri
• Ontario Municipal Employees Retirement Board: #100, One University Ave., Toronto ON M5J 2P1 – 416/369-2400; Fax: 416/360-0217
Chair, Gary Mugford
• Rent Review Hearings Board: 77 Bloor St. West, 10th Fl., Toronto ON M5S 1M2 – 416/314-0051; Fax: 416/314-0061
Chair, Brian Goodman
• Waterfront Regeneration Trust: #580, 207 Queen's Quay West, Toronto ON M5J 1A7 – 416/314-9490; Fax: 416/314-9497; Email: info@wrtrust.com.
Commissioner, Hon. David Crombie
Deputy Commissioner, David Carter
Director, Environment Studies, Suzanne Barrett
Information Services Specialist, Janet Hollingsworth

Ontario NATIVE AFFAIRS SECRETARIAT
#1009, 595 Bay St., Toronto ON M5G 2C2
416/326-4740; Fax: 416/326-4017
Minister Responsible, Hon. Charles Harnick
Secretary, Murray Coolican, 416/326-4741
Special Advisor, Corporate Negotiations, Ted Wilson, 416/326-4771
Director, Communications, Sandy Hunter, 416/326-4763
Director, Negotiations Support & Community Relations, Wallis Smith, 416/326-4762
Director, Policy Coordination Branch, Tim Eger, 416/326-4744

Ministry of NATURAL RESOURCES (MNR)
Whitney Block, 99 Wellesley St. West, Toronto ON M7A 1W3
416/314-2000; Fax: 416/314-2051; URL: http://www.mnr.gov.on.ca/mnr/

ACTS ADMINISTERED
Aggregate Resources Act
Algonquin Forestry Authority Act
Algonquin Provincial Park Extension Act
An Act to Confirm the title of the Government of Canada to certain Lands & Indian Lands
An Act for the Settlement of certain Questions between the Governments of Canada and Ontario respecting Indian Reserve Lands
Arboreal Emblem Act
Beds of Navigable Waters Act
Canada Company's Lands Act
Conservation Authorities Act
Conservation Land Act
Crown Forest Sustainability Act
Endangered Species Act
Fish Inspection Act
Fisheries Act (Canada) - Ontario Fishery Regulations
Fisheries Development Act (Canada)
Fisheries Loans Act
Forest Fires Prevention Act
Forest Tree Pest Control Act
Forestry Act
Forestry Workers Employment Act
Forestry Workers Lien for Wages Act
Freshwater Fish Marketing Act (Ontario)
Game & Fish Act
Gananoque Lands Act
Gas & Oil Leases Act
Indian Lands Agreement Confirmation Act
Indian Lands Act
Industrial and Mining Lands Compensation Act
Lac Seul Conservation Act
Lake of the Woods Control Board Act
Lakes & Rivers Improvement Act
Manitoba-Ontario Lake St. Joseph Diversion Agreement Authorization Act
Migratory Birds Convention Act (Canada)
Mineral Emblem Act
Mining Act (Certain Sections)
Ministry of Natural Resources Act
National Radio Observatory Act
North Georgian Bay Recreational Reserve Act
Ontario Geographic Names Board Act
Ontario Harbours Agreement Act
Ottawa River Water Powers Act
Petroleum Resources Act
Provincial Parks Act
Public Lands Act
Seine River Diversion Act
Settlers' Pulpwood Protection Act
Spruce Pulpwood Exportation Act
Steep Rock Iron Ore Development Act
Surveyors Act
Surveys Act
Trees Act
Water Transfer Control Act

Wild Rice Harvesting Act
Wilderness Areas Act
Woodlands Improvement Act
Minister, Hon. Chris Hodgson, 416/314-2301, Fax: 416/314-2216
Deputy Minister, Ron J. Vrancart, 416/314-2150, Fax: 416/314-2159
Director, Communications Services Branch, John McHugh, 416/314-2119
Acting Director, Organizational Development Branch, Michael Williams, 416/314-2306

CORPORATE SERVICES DIVISION (CSD)
416/314-1900; Fax: 416/314-1901
Asst. Deputy Minister, Patricia Malcolmson, 416/314-1897
Director, Corporate Affairs Branch, Larry Douglas, 416/314-1923
Director, Finance & Administration Branch, John Kenrick, 416/314-1893
Director, Human Resources Branch, Gabriella Zillmer, 416/314-1752
Director, Legal Services, Barry G. Jones, 416/314-2025

OPERATIONS DIVISION
Ontario Government Bldg., #224, 435 James St. South, Thunder Bay ON P7E 6E3
807/475-1271; Fax: 807/475-1503
Asst. Deputy Minister, Cam Clark, 807/475-1438
Director, Aviation, Flood & Fire Management, Karan Aquino, #400, 70 Foster Dr., Sault Ste. Marie ON P6A 6V5, 705/945-5937
Manager, Provincial Enforcement Section, Guy Winterton, 705/740-1387
Regional Director, Northeast Region, Dick Hunter, 705/272-7014
Regional Director, Northwest Region, Mike Willick, 807/475-1264
Regional Director, Southcentral Region, Al Stewart, 705/789-9611

POLICY & PLANNING DIVISION
Whitney Block, #6540, 99 Wellesley St. West, Toronto ON M7A 1W3
416/314-6132; Fax: 416/314-1994
Asst. Deputy Minister, Gail Beggs, 416/314-6131
Director, Fish & Wildlife Branch, Andy Houser
Director, Forest Management Branch, Bill Thornton, 705/945-6660
Director, Lands & Natural Heritage Branch, Bob Beecher, 705/755-1212
Director, Land Use Planning Branch, Dave Walton, 705/789-9611
Managing Director, Ontario Parks, Norm Richards, 705/740-1224
Acting Manager, Native Affairs Unit, Monika Turner, 416/314-1188

Water Management & Conservation Authorities
416/314-1977; Fax: 416/314-1995
Manager, John Kinkead, 416/314-1978
Senior Policy Analyst, Ian Crawford, 416/314-1981

Conservation Authorities
Ausable Bayfield: RR#3, Exeter ON N0M 1S5 – 519/235-2610; Fax: 519/235-1963, General Manager, Tom Prout
Cataraqui Region: 1641 Perth Rd., PO Box 160, Glenburnie ON K0H 1S0 – 613/546-4228; Fax: 613/547-6474, General Manager, William Warwick
Catfish Creek: RR#5, Aylmer ON N5H 2R4 – 519/773-9037; Fax: 519/765-1489, General Manager, Kim Smale
Central Lake Ontario: 100 Whiting Ave., Oshawa ON L1H 3T3 – 905/579-0411; Fax: 905/579-0994, Chair, Irv Harrell

Credit Valley: 1255 Derry Rd. West, Meadowvale ON L5N 6R4 – 905/670-1615; Fax: 905/670-2210, General Manager, Vicki Barron
Crowe Valley: PO Box 416, Marmora ON K0K 2M0 – 613/472-3137; Fax: 613/472-5516, General Manager, Kelly Pender
Essex Region: 360 Fairview Ave. West, Essex ON N8M 1Y6 – 519/776-5209; Fax: 519/776-8688, General Manager, Ken Schmidt
Ganaraska Region: PO Box 328, Port Hope ON L1A 3W4 – 905/885-8173; Fax: 905/885-9824, General Manager, Gayle Wood
Grand River: 400 Clyde Rd., PO Box 729, Cambridge ON N1R 5W6 – 519/621-2761; Fax: 519/621-4844, General Manager, Allan Holmes
Grey Sauble: RR#4, Inglis Falls Rd., Owen Sound ON N4K 5N6 – 519/376-3076; Fax: 519/371-0437, General Manager, James Manicom
Halton Region: 2596 Britannia Rd. West, RR#2, Milton ON L9T 2X6 – 905/336-1158; Fax: 905/336-7014, General Manager, Murray Stephen
Hamilton Region: 833 Mineral Springs Rd., PO Box 7099, Ancaster ON L9G 3L3 – 905/525-2181, 648-4427; Fax: 905/525-2214, General Manager, Ben W. Vanderbrug
Kawartha Region: Kenrei Park Rd., RR#1, Lindsay ON K9V 4R1 – 705/328-2271; Fax: 705/328-2286, General Manager, Ian MacNab
Kettle Creek: RR#8, St. Thomas ON N5P 3T3 – 519/631-1270; Fax: 519/631-5026, General Manager, Bryan Hall
Lakehead Region: 1136 Oliver Rd., PO Box 3476, Thunder Bay ON P7B 5J9 – 807/344-5857; Fax: 807/345-9156, General Manager, Mervi Henttonen
Lake Simcoe Region: 120 Bayview Ave., PO Box 282, Newmarket ON L3Y 4X1 – 905/895-1281; Fax: 905/853-5881, Chief, Marilyn Pearce
Long Point Region: RR#3, Simcoe ON N3Y 4K2 – 519/428-4623; Fax: 519/428-1520, General Manager, James Oliver
Lower Thames Valley: 100 Thomas St., Chatham ON N7L 2Y8 – 519/354-7310; Fax: 519/352-3435, General Manager, Jerry Campbell
Lower Trent Region: 441 Front St., Trenton ON K8V 6C1 – 613/394-4829; Fax: 613/394-5226, Acting General Manager, Kelly Pender
Maitland Valley: Marietta St., PO Box 127, Wroxeter ON N0G 2X0 – 519/335-3557; Fax: 519/335-3516, General Manager, Ross Duncan
Mattagami Region: 100 Lakeshore Rd., Timmins ON P4N 8R5 – 705/264-5309; Fax: 705/268-6544, General Manager, Brian Tees
Metro Toronto & Region: 5 Shoreham Dr., North York ON M3N 1S4 – 416/661-6600; Fax: 416/661-6898, General Manager, Craig Mather
Mississippi Valley: Hwy. 511, PO Box 268, Lanark ON K0G 1K0 – 613/259-2491; Fax: 613/259-3468, General Manager, Paul Lehman
Moira River: Wallbridge-Loyalist Rd. & Hwy. 2, PO Box 698, Belleville ON K8N 5B3 – 613/968-3434; Fax: 613/968-8240, General Manager, Terry Murphy
Napanee Region: 25 Ontario St. West, Napanee ON K7R 3S6 – 613/354-3312; Fax: 613/354-5930, General Manager, Terry Murphy
Niagara Peninsula: 2358 Centre St., Allanburg ON L0S 1A0 – 905/227-1013; Fax: 905/227-2998, General Manager, A.L. Burt
Nickel District: 200 Brady St., Sudbury ON P3E 5K3 – 705/674-5249; Fax: 705/674-7939, General Manager, Allen Bonnis
North Bay-Mattawa: RR#5, Site 12, Comp. 5, 233 Birchs Rd., North Bay ON P1B 8Z4 – 705/474-5420; Fax: 705/474-9793, Sec.-Manager, William Beckett
Nottawasaga Valley: RR#1, Hwy. 90, Angus ON L0M 1B0 – 705/424-1479; Fax: 705/424-2115, General Manager, Wayne Wilson

Otanabee Region: Time Sq., #200, 380 Armour Rd., Peterborough ON K9H 7L7 – 705/745-5791; Fax: 705/745-7488, General Manager, Dan White
Prince Edward Region: Union St., PO Box 310, Picton ON K0K 2T0 – 613/476-7408; Fax: 613/476-7146, General Manager, Keith Taylor
Raison Region: County Rd. 18, PO Box 10, Martintown ON K0C 1S0 – 613/528-4823; Fax: 613/528-4825, General Manager, Michel Lalonde
Rideau Valley: Mill St., PO Box 599, Manotick ON K4M 1A5 – 613/692-3571; Fax: 613/692-0831, Toll Free: 1-800-267-3504, General Manager, Dell Hallett
Saugeen Valley: RR#1, Hanover ON N4N 3B8 – 519/364-1255; Fax: 519/364-6990, General Manager, James H. Coffey
Sault Ste. Marie Region: 1100 - 5 Line East, RR#2, Sault Ste. Marie ON P6A 5K7 – 705/946-8530; Fax: 705/946-8533, General Manager, Ralph Yanni
South Nation River: 15 Union St., PO Box 69, Berwick ON K0C 1G0 – 613/984-2948; Fax: 613/984-2872, General Manager, Dennis O'Grady
St. Clair Region: 205 Mill Pond Cres., Strathroy ON N7G 3P9 – 519/245-3710; Fax: 519/245-3348, General Manager, John King
Upper Thames River: RR#6, London ON N6A 4C1 – 519/451-2800; Fax: 519/451-1188, General Manager, Donald Pearson

SCIENCE & INFORMATION RESOURCES DIVISION (SIRD)
90 Sheppard Ave. East, 5th Fl., North York ON M2N 3A1
416/314-1530; Fax: 416/314-1531
Asst. Deputy Minister, Dr. David Balsillie, 416/314-1528
Director, Information Technology Services Branch, Mike Roach, 416/314-1401
Acting Director, Natural Resources Information, Glenn Holder, 416/314-1219
Director, Science Development & Transfer Branch, Jim Maclean, 905/832-7133, Fax: 905/832-7149
Acting Director, Systems Development, Mike Connolly, 416/314-1518

Associated Agencies, Boards & Commissions
• Algonquin Forestry Authority - Huntsville: 222 Main St. West, PO Box 1198, Huntsville ON P0A 1K0 – 705/789-9647; Fax: 705/789-3353
General Manager, W.J. Brown
• Algonquin Forestry Authority - Pembroke: #84, 6 Isabella St., Pembroke ON K8A 5S5 – 613/735-0173; Fax: 613/735-4192
Manager, Operations, B.A. Connelly
• Leslie M. Frost Natural Resources Centre: RR#2, Minden ON K0M 2K0 – 705/766-2451; Fax: 705/766-9677
• Mining & Lands Commissioner: 700 Bay St., 24th Fl., PO Box 330, Toronto ON M5G 1Z6 – 416/314-2320; Fax: 416/314-2327
Commissioner, Linda Kamerman
• Niagara Falls Bridge Commission: PO Box 395, Niagara Falls ON L2E 6T8 – 905/354-5641; Fax: 905/354-3256
General Manager & Sec.-Treas., Allen Gandell
• Office of the Surveyor General: 90 Sheppard Ave. East, 4th Fl., North York ON M2N 3A1 – 416/314-1286; Fax: 416/223-6215
Surveyor General, Pier L. Finos
• Ontario Geographic Names Board: 90 Sheppard Ave. East, Toronto ON M2N 3A1 – 416/314-1278; Fax: 416/314-1338
Executive Secretary, Michael Smart
• Provincial Parks Council: 2450 McDougall St., Windsor ON N8X 3N6 – 519/255-6731; Fax: 519/255-7990
Chair, L.O.W. Burridge

Ministry of NORTHERN DEVELOPMENT & MINES (MNDM)
#1100, 77 Grenville St., Toronto ON M5S 1B3
416/327-0633
Mines & Minerals Information Centre: Macdonald Block, #M2-17, 900 Bay St., Toronto ON M7A 1C3
416/314-3800; Fax: 416/314-3797

ACTS ADMINISTERED
Local Services Boards Act
Mining Act
Ministry of Northern Affairs Act
Northern Ontario Heritage Fund Act
Ontario Mineral Exploration Program Act
Ontario Northland Transportation Commission Act
Minister, Hon. Chris Hodgson, 416/327-0661, Fax: 416/327-0665, Sudbury Fax: 705/670-7013
Deputy Minister, Donald A. Obonsawin, 416/327-0648, Fax: 416/327-0651, Sudbury: 705/670-7007; Fax: 705/670-7057
Manager, Information & Media, Communications, Ronald J. St. Louis, 705/670-7123, Fax: 705/670-7108

CORPORATE SERVICES DIVISION
159 Cedar St., 7th Fl., Sudbury ON P3E 6A5
705/670-7050; Fax: 705/670-7057
Asst. Deputy Minister, Louise Paquette, 705/670-7004, Fax: 705/670-7057

MINES & MINERALS DIVISION
159 Cedar St., 7th Fl., Sudbury ON P3E 6A5
705/670-7188; Fax: 705/670-7046
Asst. Deputy Minister, Dr. John B. Gammon, 705/670-7002
Director, Client Services Branch, Jon Junkin, 933 Ramsey Lake Rd., Sudbury ON P3E 6B5, 705/670-5761, Fax: 705/670-5754
Director, Mineral Sector Analysis Branch, Marc Couse, 705/670-7244, Fax: 705/670-7246
Director, Mining & Land Management Branch, Dr. Dick Cowan, 933 Ramsey Lake Rd., Sudbury ON P3E 6B5, 705/670-5784
Director, Ontario Geological Survey, John Wood, 933 Ramsey Lake Rd., Sudbury ON P3E 6B5, 705/670-7044

NORTHERN DEVELOPMENT DIVISION
#200, 70 Foster Dr., Sault Ste. Marie ON P6A 6V8
705/945-5900; Fax: 705/945-5931
Asst. Deputy Minister, Jim McClure, 705/945-5901
Director, Northern Industry Branch, Russ Sawchuk, 705/945-5903
Director, Northern Regional & Community Development Branch, Royal Poulin, 159 Cedar St., 4th Fl., Sudbury ON P3E 6A5, 705/670-7003, Fax: 705/670-7031
Manager, Economic Analysis & Transportation Branch, George K. Omerod, 705/670-7150, Fax: 705/670-7155
Manager, Program Development Branch, Cal McDonald, 705/670-7139, Fax: 705/670-7155

Regional Offices
Hwy. 17 Area: 159 Cedar St., 4th Fl., Sudbury ON P3E 6A5 – 705/670-7312; Fax: 705/670-7313, Manager, Aime Dimatteo
Thunder Bay Area: 435 James St. South, PO Box 435, Thunder Bay ON P7E 6L3 – 807/475-1509; Fax: 807/475-1589, Manager, Don Moorhouse
Timmins Area: 60 Wilson Ave., Timmins ON P4N 2S7 – 705/267-8455; Fax: 705/360-2000, Manager, Fred Lalonde

Associated Agencies, Boards & Commissions
• Northern Ontario Heritage Fund Corporation: Roberta Bondar Place, #150, 70 Foster Dr., Sault Ste. Marie ON P6A 6V8 – 705/945-6700; Fax: 705/945-6701

General Manager, Dan Kochanowski
• Ontario Northland: 555 Oak St. East, North Bay ON P1B 8L3 – 705/472-4500; Fax: 705/476-5598
President, John Wallace

Office of the OMBUDSMAN
125 Queen's Park, Toronto ON M5S 2C7
416/586-3300; Fax: 416/586-3485
Toll Free: 1-800-263-1830 (English), TDD: 416/586-3510
Ligne sans frais: 1-800-387-2620 (Français)
Ombudsman, Roberta Jamieson
Executive Director, Fiona Crean, 416/586-3438
Director, Investigations & Legal Services, Murray Lapp, 416/586-3358
Coordinator, Communications, Gene Long, 416/586-3402

Regional Offices
Kenora: #12, 308 Second St. South, Kenora ON P9N 1G4 – 807/468-2851; Fax: 807/468-2853, Toll Free: 1-800-417-3255
London: 920 Commissioners Rd. East, London ON N5Z 3J1 – 519/668-0511; Fax: 519/668-7187, Toll Free: 1-800-519-9070
North Bay: #2, 450 Main St. West, North Bay ON P1B 2V2 – 705/476-5800; Fax: 705/497-9931, Toll Free: 1-800-895-3422
Ottawa: 227 Rideau St., Ottawa ON K1N 5X8 – 613/239-1487; Fax: 613/239-1489, Toll Free: 1-800-721-9909
Sault Ste. Marie: #2, 143 Great Northern Rd., Sault Ste. Marie ON P6B 4Y9 – 705/945-6914; Fax: 705/945-6916, Toll Free: 1-800-303-8745
Sudbury: #108, 66 Elm St., Sudbury ON P3C 1R8 – 705/688-3116; Fax: 705/688-3084, Toll Free: 1-800-583-8218
Thunder Bay: 125 North Cumberland St., Thunder Bay ON P7A 4M4 – 807/345-9235; Fax: 807/345-0378, Toll Free: 1-800-430-7663
Timmins: #108, 85 Pine St. South, Timmins ON P4N 2K1 – 705/268-2161; Fax: 705/268-8377, Toll Free: 1-800-459-4660
Windsor: 224 Erie St. West, Main Fl., Windsor ON N9A 6B5 – 519/973-1314; Fax: 519/973-1317, Toll Free: 1-800-592-1887

Ontario HYDRO
700 University Ave., Toronto ON M5G 1X6
416/592-5111; URL: http://www.hydro.on.ca/
Toll Free: 1-800-263-9000
Chair, Bill Farlinger, 416/592-2115, Fax: 416/971-3691
President & CEO, Allan Kupcis, 416/592-2121, Fax: 416/592-4171
Senior Vice-President, General Counsel & Secretary, Larry Leonoff, 416/592-2755, Fax: 416/592-1480
Vice-President, Corporate Communications, Mary McLaughlin, 416/592-2113, Fax: 416/592-2174
Vice-President, Corporate Strategies & Sustainable Development, Rod Taylor, 416/592-3333, Fax: 416/592-3205

CORPORATE BUSINESS GROUP
Executive Vice-President, Chief Financial Officer & Managing Director, Eleanor Clitheroe, 416/592-3453, Fax: 416/592-3190
Acting Vice-President, Business Services, Vipin Suri, 416/592-3505, Fax: 416/592-9407
Vice-President, Human Resources, Susan Wright, 416/592-3009, Fax: 416/592-3556

CUSTOMER SERVICES GROUP
Executive Vice-President & Managing Director, John Fox, 416/592-3321, Fax: 416/592-8490
General Manager, Electricity Exchange, Dave Goulding, 416/592-3277, Fax: 416/592-7265

General Manager, Energy Services, Ron Stewart, 416/592-2936, Fax: 416/592-4044
General Manager, Grid Operations, Tom Rusnov, 416/592-4395, Fax: 416/592-4397
General Manager, Retail System & Vice-President, Aboriginal & Northern Affairs, Larry Doran, 416/592-1999, Fax: 416/592-6552, 3927

GENERATION BUSINESS GROUP
Executive Vice-President & Managing Director, George Hugh
General Manager, Fossil, Jim Burpee, 416/592-5130, Fax: 416/592-5136
General Manager, Hydroelectric, Karen Robinson, 416/592-3514, Fax: 416/592-3526
General Manager, Nuclear, Ron Field, 416/592-2151, Fax: 416/592-3924

ONTARIO HYDRO TECHNOLOGIES
800 Kipling Ave., Toronto ON M82 5S4
416/207-6800; Fax: 416/207-5555
Chair, Peter Barnard, 416/207-6515, Fax: 416/231-4124
President & CEO, Derek Cornthwaite, 416/405-6511
Vice-President, Marketing & New Ventures, Dr. Joe Fox, 416/207-5491
Manager, Natural Sciences, Dr. Michael Sills, 416/207-6815

Ontario Hydro International Inc. (OHI)
20 Dundas St. West, 14th Fl., Toronto ON M5G 2C2
416/506-3761; Fax: 416/506-4684
Chair, Bill Farlinger, 416/506-7611, Fax: 416/506-4688
President, Ian London, 416/506-4920, Fax: 416/506-4688

Ministry of the SOLICITOR GENERAL & CORRECTIONAL SERVICES
200 - 1 Ave. West, North Bay ON P1B 9M3
705/497-9500
Corporate Office: North Tower, #400, 175 Bloor St. East, Toronto ON M4W 3R8
416/326-5000, Fax: 416/326-0498

ACTS ADMINISTERED
Anatomy Act
Coroners Act
Egress from Public Buildings Act
Emergency Plans Act
Fire Accidents Act
Fire Departments Act
Fire Fighters' Exemption Act
Fire Marshals Act
Hotel Fire Safety Act
Lightning Rod Act
Ministry of Correctional Services Act
Ministry of the Solicitor General Act
Ontario Society for the Prevention of Cruelty to Animals Act
Police Services Act
Private Investigators & Security Guards Act
Public Works Protection Act
Retail Business Holidays Act
Solicitor General & Minister, Hon. Robert W. Runciman, 416/326-5075, Fax: 416/326-5085, Email: runciman@epo.gov.on.ca
Deputy Minister, Elaine Todres, 416/326-5060 (Toronto), Fax: 416/327-0469, 705/494-3001 (North Bay)
Director, Communications Branch, Kirk C. Smith, 416/326-5010
Director, Legal Services, Denise Bellamy, 416/326-5044
Director, Race Relations & Policing Unit, Winston Tinglin, 416/326-9333
Acting Manager, Independent Investigations Unit, Brian Scott, 905/826-7335

Canadian Almanac & Directory 1997

Strategic Policy & Planning Division
25 Grosvenor St., 10th Fl., Toronto ON M7A 1Y6
416/314-3355; Fax: 416/325-3465
Executive Director, Dan McIntyre
Director, Corporate Policy, Bev Ward

CORPORATE SERVICES DIVISION
200, First Ave. West, PO Box 4100, North Bay ON P1B 9M3
Asst. Deputy Minister, Michael Jordan, 705/494-3003, Fax: 705/494-3004
Director, Finance & Administrative Services Branch, Gord Jamieson, 705/494-3103
Director, Operational Review, Audit & Investigation Branch, Trinela Cane, 705/494-3429
Director, Human Resources Branch, Nancy Carey, 705/494-3074 (North Bay); 705/329-6604 (Orillia)
Director, Bell Cairn Staff Development Centre, Greg Simmons, 905/548-5000; Fax: 905/548-5001

CORRECTIONAL SERVICES DIVISION
101 Bloor St. West, 7th Fl., Toronto ON M5S 2Z7
Asst. Deputy Minister, Neil McKerrell, 416/327-9911
Director, Operational Support & Coordination Branch, Paul Fleury, 705/494-3339

Regional Operations
Southern: #220, 300 The East Mall, Toronto ON M9B 6B7 – 416/314-0520; Fax: 416/314-0527, Regional Director, David Parker
Eastern: #404, 1055 Princess St., Kingston ON K7L 1H3 – 613/545-4580; Fax: 613/545-1698, Regional Director, John O'Brien
Northern: 957 Cambrian Heights Dr., 2nd Fl., Sudbury ON P3C 5M6 – 705/675-4321; Fax: 705/524-9413, Asst. Regional Director, André Clement
Western: 80 Dundas St., 1st Fl., PO Box 5600, Stn A, London ON N6A 2P3 – 519/675-7757; Fax: 519/679-0699, Regional Director, Pauline Radley

INFORMATION RESOURCES DIVISION
25 Grosvenor St., 11th Fl., Toronto ON M7A 1Y6
416/326-6950; Fax: 416/326-1104
Asst. Deputy Minister, John A. Rollock, 416/326-6952
Director, Computer Operations & Telecommunications Branch, Moy Nahon, 416/326-6967
Director, Information Technology Customer Services Branch, W.D. Gray, 705/494-3230 (North Bay)
Director, Information Technology Development Branch, Ailsa Hamilton, 416/326-6946
Asst. Director, Information Management Services Branch, Kevin Griffin, 416/314-0168, Fax: 416/314-0216
Director, Integrated Justice Project, Kalman Brettler, 416/326-6390, Fax: 416/326-1104
Director, Integrated Safety Project, Frank White, 416/327-6697, Fax: 416/327-6699

ONTARIO PROVINCIAL POLICE (OPP)
50 Andrew St. South, 3rd Fl., Orillia ON L3V 7T5
URL: http://www.gov.on.ca/opp/
Commissioner, T.B. O'Grady, 705/329-6190
Deputy Commissioner, Operations, Gerald Boose, 705/329-6300, Fax: 705/329-6304
Deputy Commissioner, Corporate Support, Diane S. Nagel, 416/314-9376, Fax: 416/314-9433
Chief Superintendent, Administrative Services Division, R.W. Chandler, 705/329-6170
Division Commander & Chief Superintendent, Support Services, E.F. Gibson, 416/314-9174
Chief Superintendent, Investigation Division, G.A. Hawke, 705/329-6310

POLICING SERVICES DIVISION
25 Grosvenor St., 9th Fl., Toronto ON M7A 2H3
Asst. Deputy Minister, Fred Peters, 416/314-3379, Fax: 416/314-3388

Director, Criminal Intelligence Service Ontario, Insp. Roy Teeft, 416/314-3049
Director, Police Support & Programs Branch, Michael Mitchell, 416/314-3015
Director, Standards & New Programs Branch, L.S. Griffiths, 416/314-3072
Coordinator, Public Appointments Unit, Jane Eeles, 416/314-3344

Ontario Police College
County Rd. #32, PO Box 1190, Aylmer ON N5H 2T2
519/773-5361; Fax: 519/773-5762
Director, Noreen Alleyne

PUBLIC SAFETY DIVISION
416/314-3382; Fax: 416/314-3388
Asst. Deputy Minister, James Young, 416/314-3381

Centre of Forensic Sciences
25 Grosvenor St., 2nd Fl., Toronto ON M7A 2G8
416/325-3200; Fax: 416/314-3225
Acting Director, George Cimbura

Emergency Measures Ontario (EMO)
25 Grosvenor St., 19th Fl., Toronto ON M7A 1Y6
416/314-3723; Fax: 416/314-3758
Director, Jim Ellard, 416/314-8621

Office of the Chief Coroner
26 Grenville St., 2nd Fl., Toronto ON M7A 2G9
416/314-4000; Fax: 416/314-4030
Chief Coroner, J.G. Young, M.D.

Office of the Fire Marshal
7 Overlea Blvd., 3rd Fl., Toronto ON M7H 1A8
416/325-3100; Fax: 416/325-3119; Email: http://www.gov.on.ca/OFM/
Fire Marshal, Bernard Moyle, 416/325-3101

Ontario Fire College
PO Box 850, Gravenhurst ON P0C 1G0
705/687-2294; Fax: 705/687-7911
Principal, G.E. Schenk

Associated Agencies, Boards & Commissions
• Ontario Board of Parole: #201, 2195 Yonge St., Toronto ON M4S 2B1 – 416/325-4480; Fax: 416/325-4485
Chair, Ken S. Sandhu
• Ontario Civilian Commission on Police Services (OCCPS): 25 Grosvenor St., 9th Fl., Toronto ON M7A 2H3 – 416/314-3004; Fax: 416/314-0198
Chair, Murray Chitra
Information Contact, Gordon Hampson, 416/314-3013
• Ontario Police Arbitration Commission: 25 Grosvenor St., 1st Fl., Toronto ON M7A 1Y6 – 416/314-3520; Fax: 416/314-3522
Chair, Cindy Dymond

Ministry of TRANSPORTATION (MTO)
1201 Wilson Ave., Downsview ON M3M 1J8
EMail: mtoinf1@epo.gov.on.ca; URL: http://www.gov.on.ca/MTO/
Toll Free: 1-800-268-4686
MTO INFO: 905/704-2000; Fax: 905/704-2002

ACTS ADMINISTERED
Airports Act
Bluewater Bridge Act
Bridges Act
Commuter Services Act
Dangerous Goods Transportation Act
Ferries Act
Highway Traffic Act
Local Roads Boards Act
Ministry of Transportation Act
Motorized Snow Vehicles Act
Off-Road Vehicles Act
Ontario Highway Transport Board Act
Ontario Transportation Development Corporation Act
Public Service Works on Highways Act
Public Transportation and Highway Improvement Act
Public Vehicles Act
Railways Act
Rainbow Bridge Act
Statute Labour Act (part)
Toll Bridges Act
Toronto Area Transit Operating Authority Act
Township of Pelee Act
Truck Transportation Act
Urban Transportation Development Corporation Ltd. Act

Minister, Hon. Al Palladini, 416/327-9200
Deputy Minister, Janet Rush, 416/235-4449, Fax: 416/235-4950
Executive Assistant, Lynn Betzner, 416/235-4451
Director, Communications & Public Education, Marj Welch, 416/235-3904, Fax: 416/235-4841
Director, Customer Service Branch, Wil Vanderelst, 416/235-3908, Fax: 416/235-5072
Director, Internal Audit, Ian Nethercot, 416/235-4316
Director, Legal Services Branch, Anne Marie Gutierrez, 416/235-4404
Manager, MTOInfo Services, Peggy Stewart, 905/704-2041

CORPORATE SERVICES DIVISION
Asst. Deputy Minister, Mary Proc, 416/235-4036, Fax: 416/235-4950
Director, Facilities & Operation Services Branch, John Thorne, 416/235-3754, Fax: 416/235-4000
Director, Financial Planning & Administration Branch, David Aranoff, 416/235-4219, Fax: 416/235-5277
Director, Human Resources Branch, Tatiana Benzaquen, 416/235-3846, Fax: 416/235-4842
Director, Information Systems Branch, Blair Smith, 416/235-3926, Fax: 416/235-4833
Manager, Corporate Operations, John Holland, 416/235-4896
Manager, Greater Toronto Area/Downsview Corporate Services, Joan Crowther, 416/235-5370, Fax: 416/235-4847

OPERATIONS DIVISION
Asst. Deputy Minister, Vacant, 416/235-4457, Fax: 416/235-4950
Director, Operations (Central Region), Denise Evans, 416/235-5185
Director, Planning & Engineering (Central Region), Kevin Pask, 416/235-5400
Director, Resources Management Branch, Ian Oliver, 416/235-4152, Fax: 416/235-4255

Regional Offices
Eastern: 355 Counter St., PO Box 4000, Kingston ON K7L 5A3 – 613/545-4600; Fax: 613/545-4786, Director, Kathryn Moore
Northern: 447 McKeown Ave., PO Box 3030, North Bay ON P1B 8L2 – 705/497-5500; Fax: 705/497-5499, Acting Director, Osmo Ramakko
Northwestern: – 807/473-2050; Fax: 807/473-2165, Director, Larry Lambert
Southwestern: 659 Exeter Rd., PO Box 5338, London ON N6A 5H2 – 519/649-3030; Fax: 519/649-3092, Director, Richard Puccini

POLICY & PLANNING DIVISION
Asst. Deputy Minister, David Guscott, 416/235-3985, Fax: 416/235-3621
Director, Corporate Policy, Linda Clifford, 416/235-4437, Fax: 416/235-5243
Director, Freight Transportation Policy, Rob Bergevin, 416/235-4039

Director, Investment Strategies, Tony Salerno, 416/235-4042
Director, Passenger Transportation Policy, Frank D'Onofrio, 416/235-4050
Director, Transportation Systems Planning, Ravi Girdhar, 416/235-3976
Director, Strategic Transportation Research Branch, Susan Crawford, 416/235-5070

QUALITY & STANDARDS DIVISION
Asst. Deputy Minister, Carl Vervoort, 416/235-4459, Fax: 416/235-4950
Director, Acquisition Standards, Carol Hennum, 416/235-5205
Director, Hwy. 407 Engineering, David Garner, 905/709-2715
Director, Program Development, Bert Vervenne, 416/235-4008
Director, Research & Development, George Gera, 416/235-4707
Director, Transportation Engineering Standards Branch, Steve Radbone, 416/235-4402
Director, Transportation Operations Branch, Colin Rayman, 416/235-3811, Fax: 416/235-4427

RELOCATION DIVISION
Asst. Deputy Minister, Margaret Kelch, 416/235-5312, Fax: 416/235-5368

SAFETY & REGULATION DIVISION
Acting Asst. Deputy Minister, Rudi Wycliffe, 416/235-4453, Fax: 416/235-4153
Director, Business Technology Integration Group, David Mee, 416/235-3589
Director, Compliance Branch & Responsible for Transport of Dangerous Goods, Mike Weir, 416/235-5147
Director, Licensing & Control Branch, Jennifer D'Angelo, 416/235-4793
Director, Road Safety Business Services Group, Blake Forrest, 416/235-3845
Director, Safety Information Technology Branch, Doug Farrar, 416/235-5315
Director, Safety Policy Branch, John Hughes, 416/235-3591

Associated Agencies, Boards & Commissions
• GO Transit: 1120 Finch Ave. West, Toronto ON M3J 3J8 – 416/869-3600; Fax: 416/869-1755
Chair, David Hobbs
Managing Director, Richard Ducharme
• Licence Suspension Appeal Board: 700 Bay St., 24th Fl., PO Box 329, Toronto ON M5G 1Z6 – 416/325-0209
Secretary, Donna Bodok
• Ontario Highway Transport Board: 151 Bloor St. West, 10th Fl., Toronto ON M5S 2T5 – 416/326-6739; Fax: 416/326-6728
Chair, George Samis
Secretary, Marquita McKenzie

Ontario WOMENS DIRECTORATE
2 Carlton St., 12th Fl., Toronto ON M5B 2M9
416/314-0270; Fax: 416/314-0253
Minister Responsible, Hon. Dianne Cunningham, 416/314-0300, Fax: 416/314-0253
Asst. Deputy Minister, Mayann Francis

WORKERS' COMPENSATION BOARD
2 Bloor St. East, 20th Fl., Toronto ON M4W 3C3
416/927-4135; Fax: 416/927-5141; URL: http://www.wcb.on.ca/
Minister Responsible, Hon. Cameron Jackson, 416/326-1460
Chair, Edoardo Di Santo

GOVERNMENT OF PRINCE EDWARD ISLAND

Seat of Government: Legislative Assembly, Province House, PO Box 487, Charlottetown PE C1A 7L1
URL: http://www.gov.pe.ca/
The Province of Prince Edward Island entered Confederation July 1, 1873. It has an area of 5,657 km2, and the StatsCan census population in 1991 was 129,765.

Office of the LIEUTENANT GOVERNOR
Government House, PO Box 846, Charlottetown PE C1A 7L9
902/368-5480; Fax: 902/368-5481; URL: http://www.gov.pe.ca/lg/index.html
Lieutenant Governor, Hon. Gilbert Clements
Private Secretary, Judy Burke, 902/368-5480

Office of the PREMIER
Shaw Bldg., 95 Rochford St., 5th Fl. South, PO Box 2000, Charlottetown PE C1A 7N8
902/368-4400; Fax: 902/368-4416; URL: http://www.gov.pe.ca/premier/index.html
Premier, Hon. Keith W. Milligan
Chief of Staff, D. Spencer Campbell
Private Secretary, Kathy Nicholson
Principal Secretary, Ernest J. Brennan
Officer, Protocol, Rick Brazel

EXECUTIVE COUNCIL
Shaw Bldg., PO Box 2000, Charlottetown PE C1A 7N8
URL: http://www.gov.pe.ca/ec/index.html
Premier & President, Executive Council, Hon. Keith W. Milligan, 902/368-4400, Fax: 902/368-4416
Minister, Agriculture, Fisheries & Forestry, Hon. Walter Bradley, 902/368-4820, Fax: 902/368-4846
Provincial Treasurer, Hon. Wayne D. Cheverie, Q.C., 902/368-4050, Fax: 902/368-6575
Minister without Portfolio & Minister Responsible, Higher Education, Training & Adult Learning, Hon. Paul Connolly, 902/368-5510, Fax: 902/368-5515
Minister, Environmental Resources, Hon. Barry Hicken, 902/368-6410, Fax: 902/368-6488, Email: bwhicken@gov.pe.ca
Minister, Education, Hon. Gordon E. MacInnis, 902/368-4610, Fax: 902/368-4699
Minister, Provincial Affairs & Attorney General, Hon. Lynwood MacPherson, 902/368-5250, Fax: 902/368-4121
Minister, Health & Social Services, Hon. Walter McEwen, Q.C., 902/368-4930, Fax: 902/368-4974
Minister, Economic Development & Tourism, Hon. Robert J. Morrissey, 902/368-4230, Fax: 902/368-4242, Email: rjmorrissey@gov.pe.ca

Executive Council Office
Clerk & Secretary to Cabinet, Barry W. MacMillan, 902/368-4502, Fax: 902/368-6118, Email: bwmacmillan@gov.pe.ca
Clerk Asst., Lynn E. Ellsworth, 902/368-4300, Fax: 902/368-6118, Email: leellsworth@gov.pe.ca
Trade Advisor, Sandy Stewart, 902/368-4504, Fax: 902/368-6118, Email: wastewart@gov.pe.ca

Standing Committees of Cabinet
Community Consultative Committee: PO Box 2000, Charlottetown PE C1A 7N8, Secretary, Susan MacKenzie, 902/368-5510, Fax: 902/368-5737, Email: samackenzie@gov.pe.ca
Management Board: PO Box 2000, Charlottetown PE C1A 7N8, Secretary, Mike Kelly, 902/368-4053, Fax: 902/368-6575, Email: mskelly@gov.pe.ca

LEGISLATIVE ASSEMBLY
c/o Clerk's Office, Province House, PO Box 2000, Charlottetown PE C1A 7N8
902/368-5970; Fax: 902/368-5175; URL: http://www.gov.pe.ca/leg.index.html
Clerk: Allan Rankin, 902/368-5970
Speaker: Hon. Nancy Guptill, 902/368-4310, Fax: 902/368-5175
Sergeant-at-Arms: John Richard
Clerk Asst. & Clerk of Committees, Charles MacKay, Email: cmackay@peinet.pe.ca

Government Members' Office (Lib.)
Coles Bldg., 100 Richmond St., 2nd Fl., PO Box 2890, Charlottetown PE C1A 8C5
902/368-4330; Fax: 902/368-4348; URL: http://www.gov.pe.ca/leg/govmem.html
Caucus Chair, Edward Clark
Caucus Coordinator, Rick Brazel
Caucus Chair Secretary, Lorraine Bartlett
Secretary, Phyllis Arsenault
Secretary, Susan Mooney

Office of the Official Opposition (PC)
Coles Bldg., 100 Richmond St., 3rd Fl., PO Box 338, Charlottetown PE CIA 8C5
902/368-4360; Fax: 902/368-4377
Leader, Hon. Pat Mella
Executive Asst. & Director, Policy & Research, Maurice Rodgerson
Administrative Asst., Colleen Chipman

FIFTY-NINTH GENERAL ASSEMBLY - PRINCE EDWARD ISLAND
URL: http://www.gov.pe.ca/leg/index.html
Last General Election, March 29, 1993. Legal Duration, 5 Years.
Party Standings (June 28, 1996):
Liberal (Lib.) 26
Progressive Conservative (PC) 1
Vacant 5
Total 32
Salaries, Indemnities & Allowances: Effective 1 April, 1996 members' sessional indemnity $30,044 plus a $9,105 tax-free expense & travelling allowance. In addition to this are the following:
Premier $45,253
Ministers $34,738
Speaker $17,205
Deputy Speaker $7,603
Leader of the Opposition, $34,738
Prince Edward Island elects two types of members to the House - Councillors & Assemblymen - a system unaltered since the Legislative Council was merged with the Assembly in 1893. Each of the 16 constituencies elects one councillor & one assemblyman. Each elector is qualified to vote for one councillor & one assemblyman.
Following is: constituency (number of eligible voters at 1993 election) councillor/assemblyman, party affiliation. (Address for all is PO Box 2000, Charlottetown PE C1A 7N8.)
Refer to Cabinet List, Government Members Office, & to Office of the Opposition, for **Fax** numbers.

COUNCILLORS BY CONSTITUENCY
Kings County
First (3,372) Ross Young, Lib., 902/357-2711
Second (2,081) Hon. Walter Bradley, Lib., 902/961-2392
Third (3,030) Roberta Hubley, Lib., 902/838-2780
Fourth (3,467) Vacant,
Fifth (1,995) Hon. Barry Hicken, Lib., 902/962-2809
Prince County
First (7,741) Hector MacLeod, Lib., 902/853-2796
Second (3,258) Vacant,
Third (3,714) Vacant,

Fourth (10,412) Libbe Hubley, Lib., 902/836-3887
Fifth (5,144) Hon. Nancy Guptill, Lib., 902/436-4488
Queens County
First (3,492) Hon. Catherine S. Callbeck, Lib., 902/887-2988
Second (8,656) Ron MacKinley, Lib., 902/566-3963
Third (9,831) Tom Dunphy, Lib., 902/892-0554
Fourth (3,145) Hon. Lynwood MacPherson, Lib., 902/659-2679
Fifth (12,681) Tim Carroll, Lib., 902/566-1784
Sixth (10,132) Hon. Paul Connolly, Lib., 902/892-5615

ASSEMBLYMEN BY CONSTITUENCY
Kings County
First (3,372) Roger Soloman, Lib., 902/687-2845
Second (2,081) Claude Matheson, Lib., 902/961-2401
Third (3,030) Peter Doucette, Lib., 902/838-4505
Fourth (3,467) Stanley Bruce, Lib., 902/838-4666
Fifth (1,995) Rose Marie MacDonald, Lib., 902/853-2729
Prince County
First (7,741) Hon. Robert J. Morrissey, Lib., 902/882-3238
Second (3,258) Hon. Keith W. Milligan, Lib., 902/831-2105
Third (3,714) Robert Maddix, Lib., 902/436-5076
Fourth (10,412) Stavert Huestis, Lib., 902/436-9641
Fifth (5,144) Hon. Walter McEwen, Q.C., Lib., 902/436-7689
Queens County
First (3,492) Marion Murphy, Lib., 902/964-2323
Second (8,656) Hon. Gordon E. MacInnis, Lib., 902/892-6991
Third (9,831) Hon. Pat Mella, PC, 902/569-5076
Fourth (3,145) Vacant,
Fifth (12,681) Hon. Wayne D. Cheverie, Q.C., Lib., 902/892-5719
Sixth (10,132) Vacant,

MEMBERS (ALPHABETICAL)
Hon. Walter Bradley, Kings County - Second (2,081)Lib., 902/961-2392 (Councillor)
Stanley Bruce, Kings County - Fourth (3,467)Lib., 902/838-4666 (Assemblyman)
Hon. Catherine S. Callbeck, Queens County - First (3,492)Lib., 902/887-2988 (Councillor)
Tim Carroll, Queens County - Fifth (12,681)Lib., 902/566-1784 (Councillor)
Hon. Wayne D. Cheverie, Q.C., Queens County - Fifth (12,681)Lib., 902/892-5719 (Assemblyman)
Hon. Paul Connolly, Queens County - Sixth (10,132)Lib., 902/892-5615 (Councillor)
Peter Doucette, Kings County - Third (3,030)Lib., 902/838-4505 (Assemblyman)
Tom Dunphy, Queens County - Third (9,831)Lib., 902/892-0554 (Councillor)
Hon. Nancy Guptill, Prince County - Fifth (5,144)Lib., 902/436-4488 (Councillor)
Hon. Barry Hicken, Kings County - Fifth (1,995)Lib., 902/962-2809 (Councillor)
Libbe Hubley, Prince County - Fourth (10,412)Lib., 902/836-3887 (Councillor)
Roberta Hubley, Kings County - Third (3,030)Lib., 902/838-2780 (Councillor)
Stavert Huestis, Prince County - Fourth (10,412)Lib., 902/436-9641 (Assemblyman)
Rose Marie MacDonald, Kings County - Fifth (1,995)Lib., 902/853-2729 (Assemblyman)
Hon. Gordon E. MacInnis, Queens County - Second (8,656)Lib., 902/892-6991 (Assemblyman)
Ron MacKinley, Queens County - Second (8,656)Lib., 902/566-3963 (Councillor)
Hector MacLeod, Prince County - First (7,741)Lib., 902/853-2796 (Councillor)
Hon. Lynwood MacPherson, Queens County - Fourth (3,145)Lib., 902/659-2679 (Councillor)
Robert Maddix, Prince County - Third (3,714)Lib., 902/436-5076 (Assemblyman)

Claude Matheson, Kings County - Second (2,081)Lib., 902/961-2401 (Assemblyman)
Hon. Walter McEwen, Q.C., Prince County - Fifth (5,144)Lib., 902/436-7689 (Assemblyman)
Hon. Pat Mella, Queens County - Third (9,831)PC, 902/569-5076 (Assemblyman)
Hon. Keith W. Milligan, Prince County - Second (3,258)Lib., 902/831-2105 (Assemblyman)
Hon. Robert J. Morrissey, Prince County - First (7,741)Lib., 902/882-3238 (Assemblyman)
Marion Murphy, Queens County - First (3,492)Lib., 902/964-2323 (Assemblyman)
Roger Soloman, Kings County - First (3,372)Lib., 902/687-2845 (Assemblyman)
Ross Young, Kings County - First (3,372)Lib., 902/357-2711 (Councillor)
Vacant, Kings County - Fourth (3,467) (Councillor)
Vacant, Prince County - Second (3,258) (Councillor)
Vacant, Prince County - Third (3,714) (Councillor)
Vacant, Queens County - Fourth (3,145) (Assemblyman)
Vacant., Queens County - Sixth (10,132) (Assemblyman)

PRINCE EDWARD ISLAND GOVERNMENT DEPARTMENTS & AGENCIES

Department of AGRICULTURE, FISHERIES & FORESTRY
Jones Bldg., 11 Kent St., PO Box 2000, Charlottetown PE C1A 7N8
902/368-4880; Fax: 902/368-4857; URL: http://www.gov.pe.ca/daff/index.html
Pest Information Line: 902/368-5658

ACTS ADMINISTERED
Agricultural Insurance Act
Agricultural Products Standards Act
Agrologists Act
Animal Health & Protection Act
Apiary Inspection Act
Artificial Insemination Act
Dairy Industry Act
Dairy Producers Act
Dog Act
Farm Implement Act
Fences & Detention of Stray Livestock Act
Fish Inspection Act
Forest Management Act
Grain Elevators Corporation Act
Livestock Community Auction Sales Act
Maritime Provinces Harness Racing Commission Act
Natural Products Marketing Act
Pesticides Control Act
Plant Health Act
Potato Crop Mortgage Act
Poultry & Poultry Products Act
Sea Plants Act
Veterinary Profession Act
Weed Control Act
Women's Institute Act
Minister, Hon. Walter Bradley, 902/368-4820, Fax: 902/368-4846, Email: uwbradley@gov.pe.ca
Deputy Minister, Rory Francis, 902/368-4830, Fax: 902/368-4846, Email: rmfrancis@gov.pe.ca
Director, Administration & Income Support Division, Al Hogan, 902/368-5741, Email: jahogan@gov.pe.ca
Director, Communications, Wayne MacKinnon, 902/368-4888, Email: wemackinnon@gov.pe.ca

AGRICULTURE DIVISION
Research Station, PO Box 1600, Stn University, Charlottetown PE C1A 7N3
902/368-5600; Fax: 902/368-5661

Director, Dr. Wendell Grasse, 902/368-5645, Email: wegrasse@gov.pe.ca
Supervisor, Dairy Lab, Boyce MacIsaac, 16 Walker Dr., Charlottetown PE C1A 8S6, 902/368-4480, Fax: 902/368-4486
Manager, Farm Business Management, Jim Newson, 902/368-5613, Email: jfnewson@gov.pe.ca
Manager, Livestock, Feed & Feeding Section, Teresa Mellish, Fax: 902/368-5729
Manager, Research, Resources & Laboratories & Officer Responsible, The Pesticides Act, Richard Veinot, PO Box 306, Kensington PE C0B 1M0, 902/368-5646, Fax: 902/368-5661
Inspector, Pesticides Act, Thane Clarke, 902/836-5450

District Agricultural Offices
Charlottetown: Agricultural Research & Extension Bldg., University Ave., PO Box 1600, Charlottetown PE C1A 7N3 – Fax: 902/368-5729, Farm Management Consultant, Frank Duguay
Montague: Southern Kings Regional Service Centre, PO Box 1500, Montague PE C0A 1R0 – Fax: 902/838-2922, Farm Management Consultant, Colleen Younie
O'Leary: West Prince Regional Services Centre, PO Box 8, O'Leary PE C0B 1V0 – Fax: 902/859-8709, Farm Management Consultant, James Harris
Souris: Johnny Ross Young Regional Services Centre, PO Box 550, Souris PE C0A 2B0 – Fax: 902/687-2026, Farm Management Consultant, Don Sutherland
Summerside: East Prince Regional Services Centre, 109 Water St., Summerside PE C1N 1A9 – Fax: 902/888-8023, Farm Management Consultant, John Coldwill

FISHERIES & AQUACULTURE DIVISION
902/368-5251; Fax: 902/368-5542
Director, Lewie Creed, 902/368-5241, Email: lpcreed@gov.pe.ca
Biologist, Marine Fisheries, Dave Gillis, 902/368-5261, Email: djgillis@gov.pe.ca
Biologist, Shellfish, Richard Gallant, 902/368-5524, Email: rkgallant@gov.pe.ca

FORESTRY DIVISION
J. Frank Gaudet Tree Nursery, Upton Rd., West Royalty, PO Box 2000, Charlottetown PE C1A 7N8
902/368-4700; Fax: 902/368-4713
Forest Fire Emergencies: 1-800-237-5053
Director, Jerry Gavin, 902/368-4705, Email: jpgavin@gov.pe.ca
Manager, Production Development, Bill Butler, 902/368-4711
Manager, Silviculture Development, Bill Glen, 902/368-4703

District Operations
Central: Beach Grove Rd., PO Box 2000, Charlottetown PE C1A 7N8 – 902/368-4800; Fax: 902/368-4806, Manager, Dan McAskill
Eastern: PO Box 29, St. Peter's Bay PE C0A 2A0 – 902/961-2172; Fax: 902/961-3005, Manager, Brian Brown
Western: RR#1, Wellington Station PE C0B 2E0 – 902/854-2155; Fax: 902/888-8402, Manager, Herbert Isherwood

PLANNING & DEVELOPMENT DIVISION
902/368-4840; Fax: 902/368-4857
Director, John MacQuarrie, 902/368-6451, Email: jamacquarrie@gov.pe.ca
Federal/Provincial Relations Officer, Alan Miller, 902/368-6187, Email: acmiller@gov.pe.ca
Officer, Primary Resource Development Agreement Administration, Sandra MacKinnon, 902/368-5593, Email: sjmackinnon@gov.pe.ca

Officer, Trade Relations, Dr. Robert Morrison, 902/
368-5087, Email: wrmorrison@gov.pe.ca

Associated Agencies, Boards & Commissions
• Agricultural Development Corporation: PO Box 2000, Charlottetown PE C1A 7N8 – 902/368-4830; Fax: 902/368-5743
General Manager, Rory Francis
• Grain Elevator Corporation: PO Box 250, Kensington PE COB 1M0 – 902/836-3605; Fax: 902/836-3716
President, Allan Ling

Agricultural Marketing Boards & Commissions
• Prince Edward Island Egg Commodity Marketing Board: Farm Centre, 420 University Ave., Charlottetown PE C1A 7Z5 – 902/892-8401
Manager, Murray Myles
• Prince Edward Island Hog Commodity Marketing Board: Farm Centre, 420 University Ave., Charlottetown PE C1A 7Z5 – 902/892-4201
Manager, Bob Harding
• Prince Edward Island Marketing Council: PO Box 2000, Charlottetown PE C1A 7N8 – 902/368-4816; Fax: 902/368-4846
General Manager, Bob Morrison
• Prince Edward Island Pedigreed Seed Commodity Marketing Board: PO Box 1600, Charlottetown PE C1A 7N3 – 902/368-5633; Fax: 902/368-5661
Secretary, Winston Cousins
• Prince Edward Island Potato Board: Farm Centre, 420 University Ave., Charlottetown PE C1A 7Z5 – 902/892-6551; Fax: 902/566-4914
Manager, Ivan Noonan
• Prince Edward Island Poultry Marketing Board: Baldwin's Rd., RR#6, Cardigan PE C0A 1G0 – 902/838-4108; Fax: 902/838-4108
Manager, Janet Murphy

PEI Public ARCHIVES & RECORDS OFFICE
PO Box 1000, Charlottetown PE C1A 7M4
902/368-4290; Fax: 902/368-5544; Email: htholman@gov.pe.ca
Provincial Archivist, Harry T. Holman

Office of the AUDITOR GENERAL
PO Box 2000, Charlottetown PE C1A 7N8
902/368-4520; Fax: 902/368-4598
Auditor General, J. Wayne Murphy, F.C.A.

Department of ECONOMIC DEVELOPMENT & TOURISM
Shaw Bldg., 95 Rochford St., 5th Fl., PO Box 2000, Charlottetown PE C1A 7N8
902/368-4240; Fax: 902/368-4224; URL: http://www.gov.pe.ca/edt/index.html
Promotes economic development within the province & provides an integrated economic development strategy for the tourism & industrial sectors. The Department cooperates with external development agencies to promote policies & agreements in support of economic development.
Provides leadership in the development, support & implementation of economic development & assists, establishes & maintains profitable wealth-creating enterprises in the province. Assists businesses with planning & offers a full range of financial incentive programs.

ACTS ADMINISTERED
Acadian Purchase Trust Act
Area Industrial Commission Act
Business Development Agency Act
Electric Power & Telephone Act
Energy Corporation Act
Enterprise P.E.I. Act
Georgetown Shipyard Act
Highway Advertisements Act (to be repealed)
Innkeepers Act
Institute of Man & Resources Act
Lending Agency Act
Maritime Economic Cooperation Act
Marketing Agency Act
Mineral Resources Act
National Park Act
Oil & Natural Gas Act
Petroleum Products Act
Recreation Development Act
Roadside Signs Act (to be proclaimed)
Tourism Market Development Act
Minister, Hon. Robert J. Morrissey, 902/368-4230, Email: rjmorrissey@gov.pe.ca
Deputy Minister, Rory Beck, 902/368-4250, Email: rlbeck@gov.pe.ca
Manager, Program Coordination, Susan MacKenzie
Coordinator, Cooperation Agreements, Gary Petitpas, 902/368-4246, Canada/PEI Cooperation Agreement on Industrial Development contact.

ADMINISTRATION & FINANCE
Shaw Bldg., 105 Rochford St., 4th Fl., Charlottetown PE C1A 7N8
902/368-4240; Fax: 902/368-4224
Director, Dianne Bradley, 902/368-5520
Administrative Officer, Karen Fisher

COMMUNITY DEVELOPMENT SECTION
Shaw Bldg., 105 Rochford St., 4th Fl., Charlottetown PE C1A 7N8
902/368-4240; Fax: 902/368-4224
Manager, Birt MacKinnon, 902/368-4244, Email: bwmackinnon@gov.pe.ca
Officer, Community Development, Mel Rossiter
Officer, Economic Development, Joan Auld

DEVELOPMENT DIVISION
Annex 2, West Royalty Park, 2 First Ave., Charlottetown PE C1E 1B0
902/368-6300; Fax: 902/368-6301
Chief Operating Officer, Brian Thompson, 902/360-6306, Email: blthomps@gov.pe.ca
Director, Client Services, Steve Murray, 902/368-6324
Director, Investments, Lennie Kelly, 902/368-5957
Director, Marketing & Communications, Sheri Coles, 902/368-6326
Manager, Finance & Property, Lori Pendleton, 902/368-5963
Acting Manager, Immigration & Procurement, Gerry Ridgeway, 902/368-4265
Manager, Information Technology Development, Lee Brammer
Manager, Research, Dave Bryanton, 902/368-6342
Supervisor, Business Support Programs, Alex Rogers
Representative, Telecommunications Investment, Kevin Lewis
Representative, Trade Development, Patricia Taylor, 902/368-5954
Representative, Trade Development, Shelley Clark, 902/368-6307
Sector Specialist, Agri-food, Patricia Manning
Sector Specialist, Fisheries, Phyllis Duffy
Coordinator, Audio Visual, Nancy George, 902/368-6336
Coordinator, Communications, Ann Stanley, 902/368-6322
Coordinator, Editorial, Carol Horne, 902/368-6332
Coordinator, Media Relations, Glenda Rodd
Coordinator, Publications, Paul Baglole, 902/368-6334
Coordinator, Trade Sales & Promotion, Berni Wood, 902/368-6329

ENERGY, MINERALS & TECHNOLOGY DIVISION
Sullivan Bldg., 16 Fitzroy St., 1st Fl., PO Box 2000, Charlottetown PE C1A 7N8
902/368-5010; Fax: 902/368-6582
Manager, Virginia Bulger, 902/368-5018
Advisor, Energy, Ronald Estabrooks
Officer, Energy, Mike Proud

ENTERPRISE PEI
Holman Bldg., 3rd Fl., 25 University Ave., PO Box 910, Charlottetown PE C1A 7L9
902/368-6300; Fax: 902/368-6301; Email: invest@gov.pe.ca; URL: http://www.gov.pe.ca/edt/epei.html
Toll Free: 1-800-563-3734
Promotes new economic development for the province & solicits & supports investment. Supports small business & encourages entrepreneurship & investment risk sharing. The Department also develops energy & technology strategies, conducts market research, & promotes PEI as a competitive place to do business.
CEO, Rory Beck, 902/368-4250
Chair, Norma MacNeill

LENDING SERVICES DIVISION
Confederation Court Office Bldg., #201, 134 Kent St., PO Box 1420, Charlottetown PE C1A 7N1
902/368-6200; Fax: 902/368-6201
Executive Director, Peter Schurman
Account Manager, Agriculture, Fisheries & Aquaculture, G.F. Gahan
Account Manager, Agriculture, Fisheries & Aquaculture, Hugh Campbell
Account Manager, Small Business, Manufacturing/Processing & Tourism, Peter Wilson
Asst., Resource Lending, Lauraine Simpson
Chair, Credit Review Committee, Tom Cullen

POLICY & PLANNING DIVISION
Shaw Bldg., 105 Rochford St., 4th Fl., PO Box 2000, Charlottetown PE C1A 7N8
902/368-4240; Fax: 902/368-4224
Director, Carol Mayne, 902/368-4264, Email: camayne@gov.pe.ca
Manager, Research, Planning & Evaluation, Charlotte Gorrill, 902/368-4266, Email: clgorrill@gov.pe.ca

TOURISM PEI
Annex 1, West Royalty Industrial Park, 1 First Ave., Charlottetown PE C1E 1B0
902/368-5540; Fax: 902/368-4438
Chief Operating Officer, Frank Butler
Director, Development, Ron MacNeill, 902/368-5505, Email: rnmacnei@gov.pe.ca
Director, Marketing, Rob McCloskey, 902/368-5951
Manager, Acadian Development, Greg Arsenault, 902/368-5513
Manager, Advertising, Greg Arsenault
Manager, Crowbush/Brookvale, Jack Kane, 902/368-4238
Manager, Parks, East, Albert Roche, 902/652-2356
Manager, Parks, West, Greg McKee, 902/859-8790
Officer, Project Development, Doug Murray
Officer, Project Development, Burce Garrity
Coordinator, Festivals & Events, Jill Richardson
Specialist, Tourism Marketing, Les Miller
Officer, Quality Standards, Peter McCrady
Co-Chair, Tourism Marketing Authority, Rory Beck
Co-Chair, Tourism Marketing Authoriy, Dale Larkin

SPECIAL PROJECTS DIVISION
Shaw Bldg., 105 Rochford St., 4th Fl., Charlottetown PE C1A 7N8
902/368-4240; Fax: 902/368-4224
Executive Director, Kim Jay, 902/368-6214
Project Analyst, Fixed Link Bureau, Brian Keefe
Manager, Fixed Link Bureau, Brian Keefe, 902/855-3461

GOVERNMENT OF PRINCE EDWARD ISLAND

Associated Agencies, Boards & Commissions
- East Isle Shipyards Inc.: PO Box 220, Georgetown PE C0A 1L0 – 902/652-2275
Director, Operations, Jim Theriault
- Food Technology Centre: University of PEI Campus, 550 University Ave., Charlottetown PE C1A 4P3 – 902/368-1725; Fax: 902/566-5627; Email: peiftc@peinet.pe.ca; URL: http://www.gov.pe.ca/ftc/index.html
Executive Director, Dr. Richard Ablett
Director, Finance & Development, Colin Marr
Director, Operations, Brenda Tremere
Director, Research & Development Technology, Jim Smith

Department of EDUCATION
Sullivan Bldg., 16 Fitzroy St., PO Box 2000, Charlottetown PE C1A 7N8
902/368-4600; Fax: 902/368-4663; Email: education@gov.pe.ca; URL: http://www.gov.pe.ca/educ/index.html
Management Information: 902/368-4602

ACTS ADMINISTERED
Archeological Sites Protection Act
Archives Act
Fathers of Confederation Buildings Act
Heritage Places Protection Act
Island Regulatory & Appeals Commission Act
Lucy Maud Montgomery Foundation Act
Museum Act
Public Libraries Act
School Act
Sports Commission Act
Teachers' Superannuation Act
Minister, Hon. Gordon E. MacInnis, 902/368-4610, Fax: 902/368-4699, Email: gemacinn@gov.pe.ca
Deputy Minister, Melvin Ostridge, 902/368-4662, Fax: 902/368-4699, Email: mjostridge@gov.pe.ca
Director, Administration & Finance, Gar Andrew, 902/368-4605, Fax: 902/368-4663, Email: agandrew@gov.pe.ca
Director, Culture, Heritage & Recreation, Don LeClair, 902/368-4789, Fax: 902/368-4663, Email: dfleclair@gov.pe.ca
Director, English Programs & Services, Eldon Rogerson, 902/368-4677, Fax: 902/368-4622, Email: eerogers@gov.pe.ca
Director, French Programs & Services, Tilmon Gallant, 902/368-4671, Fax: 902/368-4622, Email: tjgallan@gov.pe.ca
Director, Policy & Evaluation, Dr. Parnell Garland, 902/368-4690, Fax: 902/368-4663, Email: pjgarlan@gov.pe.ca
Director, Provincial Libraries & Archives, Harry T. Holman, 902/368-4227, Fax: 902/961-3203, Email: hthlolman@gov.pe.ca.
Registrar, Teacher Certification & Pensions, Ronald F. Rice, 902/368-4650, Fax: 902/368-4663, Email: rfrice@gov.pe.ca.
Coordinator, Amateur Sport, Ted Lawlor, 902/368-4783, Email: twlawlor@gov.pe.ca
Coordinator, Culture Heritage, Nonie Fraser, 902/888-8000, Email: nefraser@gov.pe.ca
Officer, Francophone Cultural Affairs, Donald DesRoches, 902/368-4788, Email: djdesroches@gov.pe.ca
Coordinator, Professional Development, Lloyd Mallard, 902/368-4283, Email: lfmallar@gov.pe.ca

ELECTIONS PRINCE EDWARD ISLAND
180 Richmond St., 2nd Fl., PO Box 2000, Charlottetown PE C1A 7N8
902/368-5895; Fax: 902/368-6500
Chief Electoral Officer, Merrill H. Wigginton

Prince Edward Island EMERGENCY MEASURES ORGANIZATION
East Prince Regional Service Centre, PO Box 2063, Summerside PE C1N 5L2
902/888-8050, Fax: 902/888-8054
Minister Responsible, Hon. Lynwood MacPherson, 902/368-5250
Acting Director, Albert MacDonald

Prince Edward Island ENERGY CORPORATION
11 Kent St., PO Box 2000, Charlottetown PE C1A 7N8
902/368-4220; Fax: 902/368-5982
Minister Responsible, Hon. Robert J. Morrissey, Email: rjmorrissey@gov.pe.ca
Operations Manager, John te Raa, Ph.D., 902/368-4221

Department of ENVIRONMENTAL RESOURCES
Jones Bldg., 11 Kent St., 4th Fl., PO Box 2000, Charlottetown PE CIA 7N8
902/368-5000; Fax: 902/368-5830; URL: http://www.gov.pe.ca/env/index.html
Environmental Emergencies: 1-800-565-1633

ACTS ADMINISTERED
Automobile Junkyards Act
Environmental Protection Act
Fish & Game Protection Act
Natural Areas Protection Act
Unsightly Property Act
Minister, Hon. Barry Hicken, 902/368-6410, Fax: 902/368-6488, Email: bwhicken@gov.pe.ca
Deputy Minister, Diane Griffin, 902/368-5340, Email: dfgriffin@gov.pe.ca

Cooperation Agreement for Sustainable Economic Development
902/368-6080
Director, H. Arthur Smith, 902/368-4684
Program Planner, Bruce Smith, 902/368-6081

ENVIRONMENTAL PROTECTION DIVISION
902/368-5024
Director, Don Jardine, 902/368-5035, Email: dejardine@gov.pe.ca
Manager, Air Quality & Hazardous Materials Section, Mark Victor, 902/368-5037
Manager, Enforcement Section, Mark Victor, 902/368-5037
Manager, Solid Waste Section, Gerry Stewart, 902/368-5029, Email: gbstewart@gov.pe.ca

FISH & WILDLIFE DIVISION
902/368-4683
Director, H. Arthur Smith, 902/368-6083, Email: hasmith@gov.pe.ca
Chief Conservation Officer, Walter Stewart, 902/368-4808
Manager, Waterfowl & Furbearers Section, Randy Dibblee, 902/368-4666
Manager, Habitat & Natural Areas Section, Rosemary Curley, 902/368-4807

PLANNING & ADMINISTRATION DIVISION
902/368-5320
Director, Andre Lavoie, 902/368-5032, Email: ajlavoie@gov.pe.ca
Coordinator, Environmental Impact Assessment, Alan Godfrey, 902/368-5274, Email: apgodfrey@gov.pe.ca
Coordinator, MIS, Gordon Jenkins, Email: gbjenkins@gov.pe.ca
Coordinator, Policy & Planning, Christine MacKinnon, 902/368-5031, Email: cgmackinnon@gov.pe.ca
Officer, Communications, Lee Bartley, 902/368-5286, Email: elbartley@gov.pe.ca

WATER RESOURCES DIVISION
902/368-5028
Director, Clair Murphy, 902/368-5036, Email: ccmurphy@gov.pe.ca
Manager, Engineering & Utilities Section, Jim Young, 902/368-5034, Email: jjyoung@gov.pe.ca
Manager, Groundwater Section, George Somers, 902/368-5046, Email: ghsomers@gov.pe.ca
Manager, Rivers & Estuaries Section, Bruce Raymond, 902/368-5054, Email: bgraymond@gov.pe.ca
Coordinator, Water Analysis, Cheryl Burke, 902/368-5044, Email: ceburke@gov.pe.ca

Prince Edward Island Round Table on the Environment & Economy
c/o Department of Environmental Resources, PO Box 2000, Charlottetown PE C1A 7N8
902/368-5320; Fax: 902/368-5830
Secretary, Joanne Andrew

Department of HEALTH & SOCIAL SERVICES
Jones Bldg., 11 Kent St., 2nd Fl., PO Box 2000, Charlottetown PE C1A 7N8
902/368-4900; Fax: 902/368-4969; URL: http://www.gov.pe.ca/hss/index.html

ACTS ADMINISTERED
Adoption Act
Adult Protection Act
Change of Name Act
Child Care Facilities Act
Chiropractic Act
Community Care Facilities & Nursing Homes Act
Consent to Treatment & Health Care Directives Act
Correctional Services Act
Dental Profession Act
Dietitians Act
Dispensing Opticians Act
Drug Cost Assistance Act
Family & Child Services Act
Health & Community Services Act
Health Services Payment Act
Hospital & Diagnostic Services Insurance Act
Hospitals Act
Housing Corporation Act
Human Tissue Donation Act
Licensed Nursing Assistants Act
Marriage Act
Medical Act
Mental Health Act
Nurses Act
Occupational Therapists Act
Optometry Act
Pharmacy Act
Physiotherapy Act
Premarital Health Examination Act
Probation Act
Psychologists Act
Public Health Act
Rehabilitation of Disabled Persons Act
Social Work Act
Tobacco Sales to Minors Act
Vital Statistics Act
Welfare Assistance Act
White Cane Act
Minister, Hon. Walter McEwen, Q.C., 902/368-4930, Fax: 902/368-4974, Email: health_min@gov.pe.ca
Deputy Minister, Philip MacDougall, 902/368-4935, Fax: 902/368-4974, Email: wpmacdougall@gov.pe.ca

ADMINISTRATION & FEDERAL-PROVINCIAL RELATIONS
Director, George Mason, 902/368-4926
Officer, Federal Claims, Sandra Howard
Officer, Federal-Provincial Relations & Special Projects, Rick Callaghan
Auditor, Canada Assistance Plan, Belinda Rogers

GOVERNMENT OF PRINCE EDWARD ISLAND

HEALTH POLICY RESEARCH & DEVELOPMENT
Acting Director, Jo-Anne MacDonald, 902/368-4985
Research & Administrative Asst., Judy Morrison
Officer, Public Policy Liaison, Laraine Poole

PUBLIC HEALTH
Chief Health Officer, Lamont Sweet, M.D., 902/368-4996
Epidemiologist, Linda Van Til
Officer, Research & Administrative Support, Connie Cheverie
Research Nurse, Arlenn Walsh

STRATEGIC PLANNING & EVALUATION
Director, Danny Gallant, 902/368-4945
Legislative Specialist, Rob Thomson
Policy Analyst, Dan Pridmore
Research & Evaluation Specialist, Paul Chaulk
Research & Evaluation Specialist, Joanne Ross Keizer

Associated Agencies, Boards & Commissions
• Council on Health & Community Services Policy: Jones Bldg., 2nd Fl., PO Box 2000, Charlottetown PE C1A 7N8 – 902/368-4985; Fax: 902/368-4969
Chair, Debbie Good
Executive Director, Jo-Anne MacDonald
• Health & Community Services Agency: 4 Sydney St., PO Box 2000, Charlottetown PE C1A 7N8 – 902/368-6130; Fax: 902/368-6136
Provincial body responsible for administering all health, social & correctional services for the province. Responsible for the issuance of all provincial birth, death & marriage certificates. Certificate fees are as follows: Birth, $20.00-$30.00; Marriage Licences, $100.00; Death Certificates, $30.00.
Chair, Dr. Don Ling
CEO, Jeanette MacAulay, 902/368-6154
Director, Administrative Services, Ken Ezeard, 902/368-6137
Director, Community Development, Patsy Huggan, 902/368-6152
Director, Economic Development, Peter West, 902/628-5476
Director, Health Informatics, Sandy Sweet, 902/368-6142
Director, Human Resource Development, Bernadette Allan, 902/368-6138
Director, Medical Services, Dr. Pam Forsythe, 902/368-6143
Director, Program Support, Mike Egan, 902/368-6149
Director, Vital Statistics, Thelma Johnston, 902/368-4420

Office of HIGHER EDUCATION, TRAINING & ADULT LEARNING
Shaw Bldg., 105 Rochford St., 3rd Fl., PO Box 2000, Charlottetown PE C1A 7N8
902/368-5988; Fax: 902/368-6144; URL: http://www.gov.pe.ca/ohet/index.html
Minister Responsible, Hon. Paul Connolly, Fax: 902/368-5515
Deputy Minister, Verna Bruce, 902/368-5515
Director, Administration & Finance, Mike Clow, 902/368-4670, Email: gmclow@gov.pe.ca

INTERMINISTERIAL WOMEN'S SECRETARIAT
Senior Policy Advisor, Sandra Bentley, 902/368-4710, Email: scbentley@gov.pe.ca

POLICY & PLANNING
Director, Calvin Caiger, Email: cjcaiger@gov.pe.ca
Coordinator, Transition Initiatives, Judith Holton, 902/368-5556
Manager, Student Aid, Dave MacPherson, 902/368-4640, Email: dwmacphe@gov.pe.ca
Student Aid Officer, Don Currie, 902/368-4604
Student Aid Officer, Joy Livingston-Ford, 902/368-6566
Student Aid Officer, Glenda MacKenzie, 902/368-4640
Planning Officer, Louise Polland, 902/368-5551

TRAINING & ADULT LEARNING
Director, Faye Martin, 902/368-4460, Email: fm-martin@gov.pe.ca
Manager, Apprenticeship & Industrial Training, Louis Dalton, 902/368-4465, Email: lfdalton@gov.pe.ca
Advisor, Adult Education, Barbara Macnutt, 902/368-6286
Officer, Adult Training, Judy Hill, 902/368-6286
Coordinator, Distance Education Initiatives, Anna Sawicki, 902/368-4437
Officer, Employment Training, Pope Connick, 902/888-8020
Apprenticeship Officer, Lou Dalton, 902/368-4465
Apprenticeship Officer, Harvey Hyde, 902/368-4461
Apprenticeship Officer, Joyce Lamont, 902/368-4460
Apprenticeship Officer, Alan Large, 902/368-4464

Prince Edward Island HUMAN RIGHTS COMMISSION
3 Queen St., PO Box 2000, Charlottetown PE C1A 7N8
902/368-4180; Fax: 902/368-4236; Email: jwyatt@peinet.ca
Executive Director, James Wyatt

ISLAND REGULATORY & APPEALS COMMISSION
134 Kent St., PO Box 577, Charlottetown PE C1A 7L1
902/892-3501; Fax: 902/566-4076

ACTS ADMINISTERED
Electric Power & Telephone Act
Lands Protection Act
Planning Act
Real Property Assessment Act
Real Property Tax Act
Rental of Residential Properties Act
Revenue Administration Act
Revenue Tax Act
Roads Act
Unsightly Property Act
Water & Sewerage Act
Chair & CEO, Linda Webber
Vice-Chair, John Blakney
Director, Land & Property Division, Chris Jones
Director, Petroleum Division, H. Doris Pursey
Director, Technical Services Division, Donald G. Sutherland

Prince Edward Island LIQUOR CONTROL COMMISSION
PO Box 967, Charlottetown PE C1A 7M4
902/368-5710; Fax: 902/368-5735
Chair & CEO, Wayne A. MacDougall

Department of PROVINCIAL AFFAIRS & ATTORNEY GENERAL
PO Box 2000, Charlottetown PE C1A 7N8
902/368-5250; Fax: 902/368-5283; 5355; URL: http://www.gov.pe.ca/paag/index.html

ACTS ADMINISTERED
Affidavits Act
Age of Majority Act
Ancient Burial Grounds Act
Appeals Act
Apportionment Act
Arbitration Act
Assignment of Book Debts Act
Auctioneers Act
Bailable Proceedings Act
Bills of Sale Act
Bulk Sales Act
Business Practices Act
Canada-United Kingdom Judgements Recognition Act
Cemeteries Act
Charities Act
Child Status Act
Collection Agencies Act
Commorientes Act
Companies Act
Conditional Sales Act
Condominium Act
Consumer Protection Act
Consumer Reporting Act
Contributory Negligence Act
Controverted Elections (Provincial) Act
Cooperative Associations Act
Coroners Act
Corporation Securities Registration Act
Court Security Act
Court Stenographers Act
Credit Unions Act
Crown Proceedings Act
Custody Jurisdiction & Enforcement Act
Defamation Act
Dependents of a Deceased Person Relief Act
Designation of Beneficiaries under Benefit Plans, An Act Respecting
Direct Sellers Act
Escheats Act, (jointly with Dept. of Transportation & Public Works)
Evidence Act
Factors Act
Family Law Act
Fatal Accidents Act
Films Act
Fire Prevention Act
Foreign Resident Corporations Act
Frauds on Creditors Act
Frustrated Contracts Act
Garage Keeper's Lien Act
Garnishee Act
Habeas Corpus Act
Insurance Act
International Commercial Arbitration Act
International Sale of Goods Act
International Trusts Act
Interpretation Act
Interprovincial Subpoena Act
Investigation of Titles Act
Island Regulatory & Appeals Commission Act
Judgement & Execution Act
Judicial Review Act
Jury Act
Lands Protection Act
Licencing Act
Limited Partnerships Act
Maintenance Enforcement Act
Mechanics' Lien Act
Occupiers' Liability Act
Partnership Act
Pension Benefits Act
Perpetuities Act
Police Act
Powers of Attorney Act
Prearranged Funeral Services Act
Premium Tax Act
Private Investigators & Security Guards Act
Probate Act
Provincial Administrator of Estates Act
Provincial Court Act
Public Trustee Act
Quieting Titles Act
Real Estate Trading Act
Real Property Act
Reciprocal Enforcement of Judgements Act

Canadian Almanac & Directory 1997

Reciprocal Enforcement of Maintenance Orders Act
Sale of Goods Act
Securities Act
Sheriffs Act
Statute of Frauds
Statute of Limitations
Statute Revision Act
Store Hours Act
Summary Proceedings Act
Supreme Court Act
Survival of Actions Act
Time in Public Offices Act
Transboundary Pollution (Reciprocal Access) Act
Trespass to Property Act
Trustee Act
Unclaimed Articles Act
Unconscionable Transactions Relief Act
Uniformity Commissioners Act
Variation of Trusts Act
Warehousemen's Liens Act
Water & Sewerage Act
Winding Up Act
Attorney General & Minister, Hon. Lynwood MacPherson, 902/368-5250, Fax: 902/368-4121
Deputy Minister, Shauna Sullivan Curley, 902/368-5250, Fax: 902/368-4121
Chief Coroner, Office of the Chief Coroner, Dr. H.A. MacMillan, 902/566-4100

CONSUMER, CORPORATE & INSURANCE DIVISION
Director, Edison J. Shea, 902/368-4551, Fax: 902/368-5283
Registrar, Securities & Corporations Officer, Consumer, Corporate & Insurance Services, Ruth Demone, 902/368-4552
Superintendent, Insurance & Real Estate Division, W. Bennett Campbell, 902/368-4564
Public Trustee, Bennett Campbell, 902/368-4564
Manager, Consumer Services, Eric Goodwin, 902/368-4580, Fax: 902/368-5355

CROWN ATTORNEYS DIVISION
Director, Richard Hubley, Q.C., 902/368-4595, Fax: 902/368-5812

LABOUR & INDUSTRIAL RELATIONS DIVISION
Director, Barry Curley, 902/368-5565, Fax: 902/368-5526
Manager, Employment Standards, Wayne S. MacKinnon, 902/368-5550
Officer, Industrial Relations Council, Marlene Clark, 902/368-5553

LEGAL & JUDICIAL SERVICES DIVISION
Director, Charles Thompson, 902/368-4594, Fax: 902/368-4563
Manager, Legal Aid, Kent Brown, 902/368-6042
Legislative Counsel, Raymond Moore, 902/368-4291
Officer, Maintenance Enforcement, Deborah Conway, 902/368-6010
For a list of Courts & other Legal Officers, including Judicial Officials & Judges see Section 10 of this book.

PLANNING & INSPECTION SERVICES DIVISION
902/368-5582; Fax: 902/368-5526
Director, Albert MacDonald, 902/368-4229
Chief Fire Marshal, Office of the Fire Marshal, David Blacquiere, 902/368-4869
Manager, Building & Development Services, Don Walters, 902/368-4874
Manager, Inspection Services, Gerry MacDonald, 902/368-4884, Fax: 902/368-5544
Manager, Provincial Planning, Kingsley Lewis, 902/368-4871, Fax: 902/368-5544
Chief Officer, Boiler & Pressure Vessel, Plumbing & Propane Inspection, Ken Hynes

POLICY & ADMINISTRATION DIVISION
Director, George Likely, 902/368-4233
Manager, Administration, Don Gorveatt, 902/368-4810
Director, Francophone Affairs Secretariat, Claudette Theriault, 902/368-4509
Coordinator, Infrastructure Program, Dennis Friesen, 902/368-4882

Associated Agencies, Boards & Commissions
• Atlantic Lottery Corporation
See listing under New Brunswick Finance, this Section.
• Employment Standards Board: PO Box 2000, Charlottetown PE C1A 7N8 – 902/368-5550; Fax: 902/368-5526
Chair, Michael F. Hennessey
Secretary, Wayne S. MacKinnon
• Labour Relations Board: PO Box 2000, Charlottetown PE C1A 7N8 – 902/368-5550; Fax: 902/368-5526
Chair, George Lyle
CEO, Roy J. Doucette
• Prince Edward Island Emergency Measures Organization
Listed alphabetically in detail, this Section.

Department of the PROVINCIAL TREASURY
PO Box 2000, Charlottetown PE C1A 7N8
902/368-4000; Fax: 902/368-5544; URL: http://www.gov.pe.ca/pt/index.html

ACTS ADMINISTERED
Appropriation Act
Civil Service Act
Civil Service Superannuation Act
Deposit Receipt Act
Environment Tax Act
Financial Administration Act
Financial Corporation Capital Tax Act
Gasoline Tax Act
Health Tax Act
Income Tax Act
Loan Act
Lotteries Commission Act
Northumberland Strait Crossing Act
Public Accounting & Auditing Act
Public Purchasing Act
Public Sector Pay Reduction Act
Queen's Printer Act
Real Property Assessment Act
Real Property Tax Act
Revenue Administration Act
Registry Act
Revenue Tax Act
Supplementary Appropriation Act
Provincial Treasurer, Hon. Wayne D. Cheverie, Q.C., 902/368-4050, Fax: 902/368-6575
Deputy Provincial Treasurer, Mike Kelly, 902/368-4053, Fax: 902/368-6575
Coordinator, Administration, Millie Morrison, 902/368-6215
Director, Policy & Evaluation Division, Bill Harper, 902/368-4202, Fax: 902/368-6622

Office of the Comptroller
Investments: 902/368-4173; Fax: 902/368-4077
Comptroller, K. Scott Stevens, 902/368-4020, Fax: 902/368-4077

FISCAL MANAGEMENT
Fax: 902/368-4034
Director, Roy Spence, 902/368-5802, Fax: 902/368-6622

HUMAN RESOURCES
Director, Marie MacDonald, 902/368-4207, Fax: 902/368-6622
Manager, Employee Assistance - Harbourside, Frank MacAulay, 902/368-5736, Fax: 902/368-5737

Manager, Employee Benefits, Bob Ramsay, 902/368-4002, Fax: 902/368-4383
Manager, Human Resources Development Centre, Craig McDowall, 180 Richmond St., Charlottetown PE C1A 1J2, 902/368-4164, Fax: 902/368-4382
Manager, Personnel Services, Colleen Malone, 902/368-4254, Fax: 902/368-6622
Manager, Occupational Health & Safety, Sheila MacLure, 902/368-4200, Fax: 902/368-6622

SUPPLY & SERVICES
Fax: 902/368-5444
Director, Des Lecky, 902/368-4129, Fax: 902/368-5444
Manager, Communications & Support Services, Daryl Montgomery, 902/368-5080, Fax: 902/368-6243
Manager, Computer Support Services, Lorne Gaudet, 902/368-4124, Fax: 902/368-5444, Help Desk: 902/368-5815
Manager, Information Systems Delivery, Beth Morris, 902/368-4126, Fax: 902/368-5444
Acting Manager, Payment Processing, Daryl Montgomery, 902/368-5080, Fax: 902/368-6243
Manager, Procurement Services, Phil O'Neill, 902/368-4040, Fax: 902/368-5171
Manager, Risk Management & Insurance, Brian Gallant, 902/368-6170, Fax: 902/368-6243
Acting Supervisor, Audio Visual Services, Irwin Campbell, 902/368-5078, Fax: 902/368-6243
Provincial Photographer, Brian Simpson, 902/368-4019, Fax: 902/368-6243
Queen's Printer & Supervisor, Postal Services, Beryl Bujosevich, 902/368-5190, 5084, Fax: 902/368-5544

Island Information Service
11 Kent St., PO Box 2000, Charlottetown PE C1A 7N8
902/368-4000; Fax: 902/368-5544; Email: island@gov.pe.ca
Supervisor, Florine Proud

Regional Service Centres
East Prince: Summerside PE – 902/888-8000; Fax: 902/888-8023, Administrator, Mary Lynn Arsenault, Email: mlarsenault@gov.pe.ca
Evangeline: Wellington PE – 902/854-7250; Fax: 902/854-7255, Administrator, Armand Arsenault, Email: ajasenault@gov.pe.ca
Johnny Ross Young: Souris PE – 902/687-7000; Fax: 902/687-2026, Administrator, Eleanor Avery, Email: emavery@gov.pe.ca
Southern Kings/Queens: Montague OE – 902/838-0600; Fax: 902/838-0610, Administrator, Jim Kinnee, Email: jmkinnee@gov.pe.ca
Tignish & Area: Tingish PE – 902/882-7351; Fax: 902/882-2414, Bilingual Information Secretary, Claudette LeClair
West Prince: O'Leary PE – 902/859-8800; Fax: 902/859-8709, Administrator, Thelma Sweet, Email: thsweete@gov.pe.ca

TAXATION & PROPERTY RECORDS
Provincial Tax Commissioner, James B. Ramsay, 902/368-4070, Fax: 902/368-6164
Registrar, Deeds, Kathy Toole, 902/368-4591, Fax: 902/368-4399
Manager, Client Services, Robert F. Kenny, 902/368-4070, Fax: 902/368-6164
Manager, Commercial & Special Purpose Assessments, William Found, 902/368-4073, Fax: 902/368-6164
Manager, Geomatics Information Centre, Brenda Campbell-Perry, 902/368-5165, Fax: 902/368-4399
Manager, Residential & Farm Assessments, Kevin Dingwell, 902/368-4078, Fax: 902/368-6164
Manager, Tax Administration, Blair White, 902/368-4146, Fax: 902/368-6164
Acting Manager, Tax Audit, Mary Hennessey, 902/368-4174, Fax: 902/368-6164

Associated Agencies, Boards & Commissions
• Prince Edward Island Lotteries Commission: Office of the Deputy Provincial Treasurer, PO Box 2000, Charlottetown PE C1A 7N8 – 902/368-4053; Fax: 902/368-4034
Sec.-Treas., Mike Kelly

Prince Edward Island STAFFING & CLASSIFICATION BOARD
PO Box 2000, Charlottetown PE C1A 7N8
902/368-4080; Fax: 902/368-4383
CEO, Ron Lewis

Advisory Council on the STATUS OF WOMEN
PO Box 2000, Charlottetown PE C1A 7N8
902/368-4510; Fax: 902/368-4516; Email: peiacsw@isn.net
Minister Responsible, Hon. Paul Connolly
Chair, Anne Nicholson
Vice-Chair, Mary Lynn Jenkins
Executive Director, Lisa Murphy

Department of TRANSPORTATION & PUBLIC WORKS
Jones Bldg., PO Box 2000, Charlottetown PE C1A 7N8
902/368-5100; Fax: 902/368-5395; URL: http://www.gov.pe.ca/tpw/index.html

ACTS ADMINISTERED
Access to Public Buildings Act
Architects Act
Crown Building Corporation Act
Dangerous Goods (Transportation) Act
Engineering Profession Act
Expropriation Act
Georgetown Common Land Act
Highway Traffic Act
Judgment Recovery (P.E.I.) Ltd., An Act to Incorporate
Land Survey Act. 1971 (& 1951)
Land Surveyors Act
Motor Carrier Act
Off Highway Vehicle Act
Public Works Act
Roads Act
Vehicle Dealers & Salesmen Act
Minister, Hon. Keith W. Milligan, 902/368-5120
Deputy Minister, Ginger Breedon, 902/368-5130, Fax: 902/368-5385
Director, Administration, P.J. Murphy, 902/368-5125, Fax: 902/368-5395

BUILDINGS DIVISION
Director, Joe Caswell, 902/368-5145
Engineer, Building Construction Section, Foster Millar
Manager, Operations & Maintenance Section, Frank Chiaisson, 902/368-5113
Manager, Properties & Surveys Section, Paul Knox, 902/368-5131
Officer, Surveys, Serge Bernard

HIGHWAY OPERATIONS DIVISION
Chief Engineer, Wayne MacQuarrie, 902/368-6969
Director, Design Section, Allan Bartlett, 902/368-5105
Director, Engineering Services, George Trainor, 902/368-5095
Senior Manager, Materials Laboratory, Terry Kelly, 902/368-4740, Fax: 902/368-5537
Senior Manager, Mechanical, Mark Belfry, 902/368-4750, Fax: 902/368-5537
Manager, Central Region, Gary McLure, 902/368-5182
Manager, East Region, Rick Smith, 902/368-5183
Manager, West Region, Foch McNally, 902/368-5181

HIGHWAY SAFETY DIVISION
17 Haviland St., 1st Fl., Charlottetown PE C1A 3S7
Director, Glen Beaton, 902/368-5200, Fax: 902/368-5236
Registrar, Motor Vehicles, John B. MacDonald, 902/368-5200, Fax: 902/368-5236
Coordinator, Safety, Wilfred MacDonald
Supervisor, Inspection, Charles Easter

Prince Edward Island WORKERS' COMPENSATION BOARD
PO Box 757, Charlottetown PE C1A 7L7
902/368-5680; Fax: 902/368-5696
Chair, Arthur MacDonald
CEO, A.B. Wells
Chief Officer, George Stewart, 902/368-5470
Safety Officer, Wayne Corrigan
Safety Officer, Roger Walsh
Safety Officer, Chris Keefe

GOVERNMENT OF QUÉBEC
Seat of Government: Assemblée Nationale, Hôtel du Parlement, Québec PQ G1A 1A4
URL: http://www.gouv.qc.ca/
The Province of Québec entered Confederation July 1, 1867. It has an area of 1,667,926 km2, and the StatsCan census population in 1991 was 6,895,963.

Cabinet du LIEUTENANT GOUVERNEUR/ Office of the Lieutenant Governor
Édifice André-Laurendeau, 1050, rue St-Augustin, Québec PQ G1A 1A1
418/643-5385; Fax: 418/644-4677
Lieutenant Governor, Vacant
Chef du Cabinet & Aide-de-Camp, Jean-François Provençal

Cabinet du PREMIER MINISTRE/Office of the Premier
Édifice J, 885, Grande-Allée est, 3e étage, Québec PQ G1A 1A2
418/643-5321; Fax: 418/643-3924; URL: http://www.gouv.qc.ca/anglais/premin/premin_intro.html
75, boul René-Lévesque ouest, 17e étage, Montréal PQ H2Z 1A4
514/873-3411, Fax: 514/873-6769
Premier ministre/Premier, Hon. Lucien Bouchard, Email: premier.ministre@gouv.qc.ca
Attachée de presse/Press Attaché, Marthe Lawrence
Adjointe de l'attachée de presse/Deputy Press Attaché, Isabelle Rondeau
Vice-premièr ministre/Deputy Premier, Bernard Landry
Chef de Cabinet/Chief of Staff, Gilbert Charland
Chef de Cabinet adjoint/Deputy Chief of Staff, François Leblanc
Conseiller spécial/Special Advisor, Jean-Rock Boivin
Directrice, Communications, Charles Larochelle

CONSEIL EXÉCUTIF/Executive Council
Hôtel du Parlement, Québec PQ G1A 1A4
URL: http://www.gouv.qc.ca/francais/minorg/mcex/mcex_intro.html
Premier ministre, Hon. Lucien Bouchard, Édifice J, 885, Grande Allée est, 31ème étage, Québec PQ G1A 1A2, 418/643-5321, Fax: 418/643-3924, Email: premier.ministre@gouv.qc.ca, (Premier)
Ministre, Culture et Communications & Ministre responsable, Charte de la langue française, Louise Beaudoin, 225, Grande Allée est, Bloc 1A, Québec PQ G1R 5G5, 418/643-2110, Fax: 418/643-9164, (Minister Culture & Communications & Minister Resp., French Language Charter)
Ministre, Justice & Ministre responsable, Région Côte-Nord, Paul Bégin, 1200, rte de l'Église, 9e étage, Ste-Foy PQ G1V 4M1, 418/643-4210, Fax: 418/646-0027, (Minister, Justice & Minister Resp., Côte-Nord Region)
Leader parlementaire du gouvernement & Ministre délégué, Réforme électorale et parlementaire, Pierre Bélanger, #1.39, Édifice Pamphile-Lemay, Québec PQ G1A 1A5, 418/643-3804, Fax: 418/643-2514, (Leader of Parliament & Minister Resp., Electoral & Parliamentary Reform)
Ministre délégué, Revenu, Roger Bertrand, 3800, rue Marley, 6e étage, Ste-Foy PQ G1X 4A5, 418/652-6835, Fax: 418/643-7379, (Minister Resp., Revenue)
Ministre délégué, Relations avec les citoyens, André Boisclair, #336, 900, boul René-Lévesque est, Québec PQ G1R 2B5, 418/643-6322, Fax: 418/643-8936, (Minister Resp., Public Relations)
Ministre, Transports & Ministre responsable, Affaires intergouvernmentales canadiennes et Région Saguenay Lac-Saint-Jean, Jacques Brassard, Place Haute-Ville, 700, boul René-Lévesque est, 29e étage, Québec PQ G1R 5H1, 418/643-6980, Fax: 418/643-2033, (Minister, Transportation, Minister Resp., Canadian Intergovernmental Affairs & Minister Resp., Saguenay Lac-Saint-Jean Region)
Ministre délégué, Mines, Terres et Forêts & Ministre responsable, Région Chaudière-Appalaches, Denise Carrier-Perreault, Édifice de l'Atrium, 5700, 4e av. ouest, Charlesbourg PQ G1H 6R1, 418/643-7295, Fax: 418/643-4318, (Minister Resp., Mines, Lands & Forests & Minister Resp., Chaudière-Appalaches Region)
Ministre d'État, Ressources naturelles & Ministre responsable, Développement des régions, Affaires autochtones, Réforme électorale et parlementaire et de la Région de Lanaudière, Guy Chevrette, 20, av Chauveau, Secteur B, 3e étage, Québec PQ G1R 4J3, 418/691-2050, Fax: 418/643-1795, (Minister of State, Natural Resources, Minister Resp., Regional Development, Minister Resp., Aboriginal Affairs, Minister Resp., Electoral & Parliamentary Reform & Minister Resp., Lanaudière Region)
Ministre, Environnement et Faune & Ministre responsable, Région de Laval, David Cliche, Édifice Marie-Guyart, 675, boul René-Lévesque est, 30e étage, Québec PQ G1R 5V7, 418/643-8259, Fax: 418/643-4143, (Minister, Environment & Wildlife & Minister Resp., Laval Region)
Ministre déléguée, Industrie et Commerce, Rita Dionne-Marsolais, 710, Place D'Youville, 6e étage, Québec PQ G1R 4Y4, 418/691-5650, Fax: 418/643-8553, (Minister Resp., Industry & Commerce)
Ministre, Relations aveec les citoyens et de l'Immmigation, Ministre d'E@tat, Emploi et Solidarité & Ministre responsable, Condition féminine, Louise Harel, 425, rue Saint-Amable, 4e étage, Québec PQ G1R 4Z1, 418/643-4810, Fax: 418/643-2802, (Minister of State, Employment & Solidarity, Minister Resp., Status of Women)
Ministre, Agriculture, Pêcheries et Alimentation & Ministre responsable, Région Mauricie Bois-Francs, Guy Julien, 200-A, ch Sainte-Foy, 12e étage, Québec PQ G1R 4X6, 418/643-2525, Fax: 418/643-8422, (Minister, Agriculture, Fisheries & Food & Minister Resp., Mauricie Bois-Francs Region)
Vice-premier ministre & Ministre d'État, Économie et Finances et Ministre responsable, Région de l'Estrie, Bernard Landry, 12, rue Saint-Louis, 1er étage, Québec PQ G1R 5L3, 418/643-5270, Fax: 418/643-6626, (Deputy Premier, Minister of State, Finance & Economy & Minister Resp., Estrie Region)
Président, Conseil du trésor & Ministre délégué, Administration à la Fonction publique et Ministre responsable, Région des Laurentides, Jacques Léonard, #4.17, 875, Grande Allée est, Québec PQ

G1R 5R8, 418/643-5926, Fax: 418/643-7824, (President, Treasury Council, Minister Resp., Public Service & Administration & Minister Resp., Laurentides Region)

Ministre, Éducation & Ministre responsable, Région de la Montérégie, Pauline Marois, Édifice Marie-Guyart, 1035, rue de la Chevrotière, 16e étage, Québec PQ G1R 5A5, 418/644-0665, Fax: 418/646-7551, (Minister, Education & Minister Resp., Montérégie Region)

Ministre d'État, Métropole & Ministre responsable, Région de Montréal, Serge Ménard, Édifice H, #2.600, 875, Grande Allée est, Québec PQ G1R 4Y8, 418/646-3018, Fax: 418/643-6377, (Minister of State, Metropolitan Montréal & Minister Resp., Montréal Region)

Ministre, Sécurité publique, Robert Perreault, 2525, boul Laurier, 5e étage, Ste-Foy PQ G1V 2L2, 418/643-2112, Fax: 418/646-6168, (Minister, Public Security)

Ministre, Travail & Ministre responsable, Région du Bas-Saint-Laurent-Gaspésie-Îles-de-la-Madeleine, Matthias Rioux, 200, ch Sainte-Foy, 6e étage, Québec PQ G1R 5S1, 418/643-5297, Fax: 418/644-0003, (Minister, Labour & Minister Resp., Bas-Saint-Laurent-Gaspésie-Îles-de-la-Madeleine Region)

Ministre, Santé et Services sociaux & Ministre responsable, Région de Québec, Jean Rochon, 1075, ch Sainte-Foy, 15e étage, Québec PQ G1S 2M1, 418/643-3160, Fax: 418/644-4534, (Minister, Health & Social Services & Minister Resp., Québec Region)

Ministre, Relations internationales & Ministre responsable, Francophonie et Région de l'Outaouais, Sylvain Simard, 525, boul René-Lévesque est, 4e étage, Québec PQ G1R 5R9, 418/649-2319, Fax: 418/643-4804, (Minister, International Relations, Minister Resp., Francophone Affairs & Minister Resp., Outaouais Region)

Ministre, Affaires municipales & Ministre responsable, Région Abitibi-Témiscamingue et Nord-du-Québec, Rémy Trudel, Édifice Cook-Chauveau, Secteur B, 20, rue Chauveau, 3e étage, Québec PQ G1R 4J3, 418/691-2050, Fax: 418/643-1795

Cabinet Office
885, Grande Allée est, Québec PQ G1A 1A2
Secrétaire général et greffier, Michel Carpentier, 418/643-7355, Fax: 418/646-0866

Cabinet Committees
Secrétariat général, Edifice J, 885, Grande Allée est, 2e étage, Québec PQ G1A 1A2
418/643-7355; Fax: 418/646-0866
Repondant, Colette Gauthier
Comité de législation - Secrétariat à la législation (Legislation Committee)
Comité des priorités (Priorities Committee)
Secrétariat au développement des régions (Regional Development Secretariat)

ASSEMBLÉE NATIONALE/ National Assembly
c/o Secrétariat général, Édifice Honoré-Mercier, #3.57, 1025, rue St-Augustin, Québec PQ G1A 1A3
418/643-2724; Fax: 418/643-5062; URL: http://www.assnat.qc.ca/assnat
Secrétariat Général/Secretary General: Pierre Duchesne
Président/Speaker: Jean-Pierre Charbonneau, 418/646-2820, Fax: 418/643-3423
Adjoint Sergeant-at-Arms: Roger Gagnon, 418/643-2793
Directeur, Bibliothèque et Études documentaires: Gaston Bernier, 418/643-4032, Fax: 418/646-4873
Directeur, Secrétariat des commissions/Clerk of Committees: Vacant, 418/643-2722, Fax: 418/634-0249

Directeur général, Affaires juridiques et législatives/Law Clerk, René Chrétien
Vice-président/Deputy Speaker, Raymond Brouillet
Vice-président/Deputy Speaker, Claude Pinard
Whip en chef du gouvernement/Chief Government Whip, Jean-Pierre Jolivet, 418/643-6018, Fax: 418/643-5462

LES SECRÉTAIRE(E)S RÉGIONAUX/Regional Delegates
Fifteen regional delegates were chosen by the Premier to respond to the specific needs of each region & to assist in the government's task of decentralization. The regions were:
Abitibi/Témiscamingue, André Pelletier
Bas Saint-Laurent, Danielle Doyer
Chaudière-Appalaches, Jean-Guy Paré
Côte-Nord, Denis Perron
Estrie, Claude Boucher
Gaspésie/Îles-de-la-Madeleine, Guy Lelièvre
Lanaudière, Yves Blais
Laurentides, Hélène Robert
Laval, Lyse Leduc
Mauricie/Bois-Francs, Normand Jutras
Montérégie, Roger Paquin
Montréal, André Boulerice
Nord-du-Québec, Michel Létourneau
Québec, Michel Rivard
Saguenay/Lac-Saint-Jean, Gérard-R. Morin

Bureaux de l'opposition/Office of the Official Opposition (Lib.)
#2.83, Hôtel du Parlement, Québec PQ G1A 1A4
418/643-2301; Fax: 418/643-1905
Chef/Leader, Daniel Johnson, 418/643-2743, Fax: 418/643-2957
Chef du Cabinet/Chief of Staff, Martial Fillion
Whip de l'opposition/Opposition Whip, Georges Farrah, 418/643-2301, Fax: 418/643-1905
Coordonnateur, Communications/Director, Communications, Christian Barrette
Coordonnatrice, Service de recherche, Hélène Livernois

THIRTY-FIFTH LEGISLATURE - QUÉBEC
Hôtel du Parlement, Québec PQ G1A 1A4
418/643-2724
Last General Election, September 12, 1994. Maximum Duration, 5 Years.
Party Standings (July 6, 1995):
Parti québécois (PQ) 74
Libéral (Lib.) 47
Action démocratique du Québec (ADQ) 1
Independant (Ind.) 2
Vacant 1
Total 125
Salaries, Indemnities & Allowances (1996): Members' annual indemnity $63,469 plus $11,417 expense allowance. In addition to this are the following:
Premier $66,642
Ministers $47,602
Speaker $47,602
Leader of the Opposition $47,602
Following is: constituency, (number of eligible voters at 1994 election), member, party affiliation. (Address for all is Hôtel du Parlement, Québec, PQ G1A 1A4.)
Refer to Cabinet List, Government Caucus Office, & the Office of the Opposition for **Fax** numbers.

MEMBERS BY CONSTITUENCY
Abitibi-Est (30,462) André Pelletier, PQ, 418/644-4869
Abitibi-Ouest (32,416) François Gendron, PQ, 418/646-8741
Acadie (40,487) Yvan Bordeleau, Lib., 418/644-5990
Anjou (31,878) Pierre Bélanger, PQ, 418/643-3804
Argenteuil (44,509) Régent L. Beaudet, Lib., 418/528-1960
Arthabaska (42,142) Jacques Baril, PQ, 418/644-5905

Beauce-Nord (30,668) Normand Poulin, Lib., 418/528-2847
Beauce-Sud (39,129) Paul-Eugène Quirion, Lib., 418/228-0360
Beauharnois-Huntingdon (39,163) André Chenail, Lib., 418/644-5992
Bellechasse (29,607) Claude Lachance, PQ, 418/528-1215
Berthier (44,574) Gilles Baril, PQ, 418/528-1282
Bertrand (38,854) Robert Thérien, Lib., 418/643-2769
Blainville (36,530) Céline Signori, PQ, 418/528-1349
Bonaventure (29,626) Marcel Landry, PQ, 418/646-0505
Borduas (33,126) Jean-Pierre Charbonneau, PQ, 418/643-2820
Bourassa (31,793) Yvon Charbonneau, Lib., 418/644-8350
Bourget (33,761) Camille Laurin, PQ, 418/528-1657
Brome-Missisquoi (36,354) Pierre Paradis, Lib., 418/643-1275
Châteauguay (39,950) Jean-Marc Fournier, Lib., 418/528-9478
Chambly (47,620) Louise Beaudoin, PQ, 418/643-2110
Champlain (42,908) Yves Beaumier, PQ, 418/528-0555
Chapleau (54,005) Claire Vaive, Lib., 418/528-0759
Charlesbourg (45,931) Jean Rochon, PQ, 418/643-3160
Charlevoix (30,604) Rosaire Bertrand, PQ, 418/528-0986
Chauveau (54,351) Raymond Brouillet, PQ, 418/643-2750
Chicoutimi (44,767) Jeanne L. Blackburn, PQ, 418/646-6362
Chomedey (47,051) Thomas J. Mulcair, Lib., 418/528-2381
Chutes-de-la-Chaudière (49,902) Denise Carrier-Perreault, PQ, 418/643-7295
Crémazie (36,637) Jean Campeau, PQ, 418/646-2619
D'Arcy-McGee (38,868) Lawrence Bergman, Lib., 418/528-2210
Deux-Montagnes (52,644) Hélène Robert, PQ, 418/528-0765
Drummond (45,476) Normand Jutras, PQ, 418/528-1285
Dubuc (34,450) Gérard-R. Morin, PQ, 418/644-5901
Duplessis (36,402) Denis Perron, PQ, 418/643-2446
Fabre (46,899) Joseph Facal, PQ, 418/528-0309
Frontenac (34,353) Roger Lefebvre, Lib., 418/644-6236
Gaspé (29,448) Guy Lelièvre, PQ, 418/528-5818
Gatineau (37,878) Réjean Lafrenière, Lib., 418/644-5980
Gouin (39,276) André Boisclair, PQ, 418/644-2128
Groulx (39,898) Robert Kieffer, PQ, 418/528-2445
Hochelaga-Maisonneuve (31,087) Louise Harel, PQ, 418/643-4810
Hull (43,670) Robert LeSage, Lib., 418/644-9954
Îles-de-la-Madeleine (10,682) Georges Farrah, Lib., 418/643-2301
Iberville (44,299) Richard Le Hir, Ind., 418/643-8474
Jacques-Cartier (44,842) Geoffrey Kelley, Lib., 418/646-6342
Jean-Talon (31,938) Margaret F. Delisle, Lib., 418/646-6349
Jeanne-Mance (36,038) Michel Bissonnet, Lib., 418/528-1488
Johnson (33,877) Claude Boucher, PQ, 418/646-6451
Joliette (41,557) Guy Chevrette, PQ, 418/643-7295
Jonquière (43,614) Hon. Lucien Bouchard, PQ, 418/643-5321
Kamouraska-Témiscouata (33,639) France Dionne, Lib., 418/643-2739
L'Assomption (48,626) Jean-Claude St-André, PQ, 418/528-5474
La Peltrie (49,607) Michel Côté, PQ, 418/646-6506
La Pinière (42,307) Fatima Houda-Pepin, Lib., 418/646-7385
La Prairie (53,079) Monique Simard, PQ, 418/646-4325
Labelle (34,980) Jacques Léonard, PQ, 418/643-5926

Lac-Saint-Jean (37,557) Jacques Brassard, PQ, 418/643-6980
LaFontaine (45,521) Jean-Claude Gobé, Lib., 418/643-4019
Laporte (44,101) André Bourbeau, Lib., 418/644-0093
Laurier-Dorion (41,718) Christos Sirros, Lib., 418/644-0520
Laval-des-Rapides (37,451) Serge Ménard, PQ, 418/646-3018
Laviolette (33,886) Jean-Pierre Jolivet, PQ, 418/643-6018
Lévis (36,866) Jean Garon, PQ, 418/646-3766
Limoilou (43,877) Michel Rivard, PQ, 418/646-0650
Lotbinière (28,906) Jean-Guy Paré, PQ, 418/646-8085
Louis-Hébert (38,649) Paul Bégin, PQ, 418/643-4210
Marguerite-Bourgeoys (40,182) Liza Frulla, Lib., 418/644-7196
Marguerite-D'Youville (41,008) François Beaulne, PQ, 418/644-5965
Marie-Victorin (40,023) Cécile Vermette, PQ, 418/643-5611
Marquette (36,992) François Ouimet, Lib., 418/646-3202
Maskinongé (42,095) Rémy Désilets, PQ, 418/646-5756
Masson (41,397) Yves Blais, PQ, 418/643-5771
Matane (28,055) Matthias Rioux, PQ, 418/643-5297
Matapédia (29,857) Danielle Doyer, PQ, 418/646-6147
Mégantic-Compton (29,896) Madeleine Bélanger, Lib., 418/643-7640
Mercier (39,636) Robert Perreault, PQ, 418/643-2112
Mille-Îles (44,549) Lyse Leduc, PQ, 418/646-1402
Mont-Royal (36,101) John Ciaccia, Lib., 418/643-8695
Montmagny-L'Islet (31,722) Réal Gauvin, Lib., 418/643-9503
Montmorency (51,684) Jean Filion, Ind., 418/528-2272
Nelligan (51,444) Russell Williams, Lib., 418/644-5986
Nicolet-Yamaska (32,530) Michel Morin, PQ, 418/646-3967
Notre-Dame-de-Grâce (36,019) Russell Copeman, Lib., 418/646-5752
Orford (45,802) Robert Benoit, Lib., 418/644-5988
Outremont (42,354) Pierre-Étienne Laporte, Lib., 418/528-5976
Papineau (35,003) Norman MacMillan, Lib., 418/644-6940
Pointe-aux-Trembles (36,932) Vacant,
Pontiac (35,797) Robert Middlemiss, Lib., 418/644-2666
Portneuf (38 312) Roger Bertrand, PQ, 418/652-6835
Prévost (43,417) Daniel Paillé, PQ, 418/646-0245
Richelieu (38,688) Sylvain Simard, PQ, 418/649-2319
Richmond (31,371) Yvon Vallières, Lib., 418/643-8092
Rimouski (37,584) Solange Charest, PQ, 418/646-0999
Rivière-du-Loup (29,252) Mario Dumont, ADQ, 418/644-4560
Robert-Baldwin (42,600) Pierre Marsan, Lib., 418/646-5554
Roberval (41,215) Benoît Laprise, PQ, 418/646-7697
Rosemont (36,518) Rita Dionne-Marsolais, PQ, 418/691-5650
Rousseau (40,316) Lévis Brien, PQ, 418/646-9124
Rouyn-Noranda-Témiscamingue (40,695) Rémy Trudel, PQ, 418/691-2050
Saguenay (35,344) Gabriel-Yvan Gagnon, PQ, 418/646-9851
Saint-François (39,844) Monique Gagnon-Tremblay, Lib., 418/644-2817, Fax: 418/646-6640
Saint-Henri-Sainte-Anne (39,197) Nicole Loiselle, Lib., 418/644-5976
Saint-Hyacinthe (44,389) Léandre Dion, PQ, 418/644-5283
Saint-Jean (47,426) Roger Paquin, PQ, 418/644-5604
Saint-Laurent (41,530) Normand Cherry, Lib., 418/644-7058
Saint-Maurice (33,780) Claude Pinard, PQ, 418/643-2810
Sainte-Marie-Saint-Jacques (41,452) André Boulerice, PQ, 418/643-2327

Salaberry-Soulanges (48,520) Serge Deslières, PQ, 418/644-7844
Sauvé (31,792) Marcel Parent, Lib., 418/643-3067
Shefford (47,958) Bernard Brodeur, Lib., 418/646-4622
Sherbrooke (38,615) Marie Malavoy, PQ, 418/528-2655
Taillon (48,478) Pauline Marois, PQ, 418/644-0664
Taschereau (30,849) André Gaulin, PQ, 418/644-0981
Terrebonne (39,981) Jocelyne Caron, PQ, 418/644-5920
Trois-Rivières (36,391) Guy Julien, PQ, 418/643-2525
Ungava (26,483) Michel Létourneau, PQ, 418/528-1683
Vachon (39,122) David Payne, PQ, 418/644-5195
Vanier (46,924) Diane Barbeau, PQ, 418/644-2640
Vaudreuil (48,829) Daniel Johnson, Lib., 418/643-2743, Fax: 418/643-2957
Verchères (34,854) Bernard Landry, PQ, 418/643-5270
Verdun (41,967) Henri-François Gautrin, Lib., 418/644-5959
Viau (36,378) William Cusano, Lib., 418/643-1874
Viger (35,299) Cosmo Maciocia, Lib., 418/643-7913
Vimont (49,729) David Cliche, PQ, 418/643-8259
Westmount-Saint-Louis (43,275) Jacques Chagnon, Lib., 418/643-4313

MEMBERS (ALPHABETICAL)

Diane Barbeau, Vanier (46,924)PQ, 418/644-2640
Gilles Baril, Berthier (44,574)PQ, 418/528-1282
Jacques Baril, Arthabaska (42,142)PQ, 418/644-5905
Régent L. Beaudet, Argenteuil (44,509)Lib., 418/528-1960
Louise Beaudoin, Chambly (47,620)PQ, 418/643-2110
François Beaulne, Marguerite-D'Youville (41,008)PQ, 418/644-5965
Yves Beaumier, Champlain (42,908)PQ, 418/528-0555
Paul Bégin, Louis-Hébert (38,649)PQ, 418/643-4210
Madeleine Bélanger, Mégantic-Compton (29,896)Lib., 418/643-7640
Pierre Bélanger, Anjou (31,878)PQ, 418/643-3804
Robert Benoit, Orford (45,802)Lib., 418/644-5988
Lawrence Bergman, D'Arcy-McGee (38,868)Lib., 418/528-2210
Roger Bertrand, Portneuf (38 312)PQ, 418/652-6835
Rosaire Bertrand, Charlevoix (30,604)PQ, 418/528-0986
Michel Bissonnet, Jeanne-Mance (36,038)Lib., 418/528-1488
Jeanne L. Blackburn, Chicoutimi (44,767)PQ, 418/646-6362
Yves Blais, Masson (41,397)PQ, 418/643-5771
André Boisclair, Gouin (39,276)PQ, 418/644-2128
Yvan Bordeleau, Acadie (40,487)Lib., 418/644-5990
Hon. Lucien Bouchard, Jonquière (43,614)PQ, 418/643-5321
Claude Boucher, Johnson (33,877)PQ, 418/646-6451
André Boulerice, Sainte-Marie-Saint-Jacques (41,452)PQ, 418/643-2327
André Bourbeau, Laporte (44,101)Lib., 418/644-0093
Jacques Brassard, Lac-Saint-Jean (37,557)PQ, 418/643-6980
Lévis Brien, Rousseau (40,316)PQ, 418/646-9124
Bernard Brodeur, Shefford (47,958)Lib., 418/646-4622
Raymond Brouillet, Chauveau (54,351)PQ, 418/643-2750
Jean Campeau, Crémazie (36,637)PQ, 418/646-2619
Jocelyne Caron, Terrebonne (39,981)PQ, 418/644-5920
Denise Carrier-Perreault, Chutes-de-la-Chaudière (49,902)PQ, 418/643-7295
Jacques Chagnon, Westmount-Saint-Louis (43,275)Lib., 418/643-4313
Jean-Pierre Charbonneau, Borduas (33,126)PQ, 418/643-2820
Yvon Charbonneau, Bourassa (31,793)Lib., 418/644-8350
Solange Charest, Rimouski (37,584)PQ, 418/646-0999
André Chenail, Beauharnois-Huntingdon (39,163)Lib., 418/644-5992
Normand Cherry, Saint-Laurent (41,530)Lib., 418/644-7058

Guy Chevrette, Joliette (41,557)PQ, 418/643-7295
John Ciaccia, Mont-Royal (36,101)Lib., 418/643-8695
David Cliche, Vimont (49,729)PQ, 418/643-8259
Russell Copeman, Notre-Dame-de-Grâce (36,019)Lib., 418/646-5752
Michel Côté, La Peltrie (49,607)PQ, 418/646-6506
William Cusano, Viau (36,378)Lib., 418/643-1874
Margaret F. Delisle, Jean-Talon (31,938)Lib., 418/646-6349
Rémy Désilets, Maskinongé (42,095)PQ, 418/646-5756
Serge Deslières, Salaberry-Soulanges (48,520)PQ, 418/644-7844
Léandre Dion, Saint-Hyacinthe (44,389)PQ, 418/644-5283
France Dionne, Kamouraska-Témiscouata (33,639)Lib., 418/643-2739
Rita Dionne-Marsolais, Rosemont (36,518)PQ, 418/691-5650
Danielle Doyer, Matapédia (29,857)PQ, 418/646-6147
Mario Dumont, Rivière-du-Loup (29,252)ADQ, 418/644-4560
Joseph Facal, Fabre (46,899)PQ, 418/528-0309
Georges Farrah, Îles-de-la-Madeleine (10,682)Lib., 418/643-2301
Jean Filion, Montmorency (51,684)Ind., 418/528-2272
Jean-Marc Fournier, Châteauguay (39,950)Lib., 418/528-9478
Liza Frulla, Marguerite-Bourgeoys (40,182)Lib., 418/644-7196
Gabriel-Yvan Gagnon, Saguenay (35,344)PQ, 418/646-9851
Monique Gagnon-Tremblay, Saint-François (39,844)Lib., 418/644-2817, Fax: 418/646-6640
Jean Garon, Lévis (36,866)PQ, 418/646-3766
André Gaulin, Taschereau (30,849)PQ, 418/644-0981
Henri-François Gautrin, Verdun (41,967)Lib., 418/644-5959
Réal Gauvin, Montmagny-L'Islet (31,722)Lib., 418/643-9503
François Gendron, Abitibi-Ouest (32,416)PQ, 418/646-8741
Jean-Claude Gobé, LaFontaine (45,521)Lib., 418/643-4019
Louise Harel, Hochelaga-Maisonneuve (31,087)PQ, 418/643-4810
Fatima Houda-Pepin, La Pinière (42,307)Lib., 418/646-7385
Daniel Johnson, Vaudreuil (48,829)Lib., 418/643-2743, Fax: 418/643-2957
Jean-Pierre Jolivet, Laviolette (33,886)PQ, 418/643-6018
Guy Julien, Trois-Rivières (36,391)PQ, 418/643-2525
Normand Jutras, Drummond (45,476)PQ, 418/528-1285
Geoffrey Kelley, Jacques-Cartier (44,842)Lib., 418/646-6342
Robert Kieffer, Groulx (39,898)PQ, 418/528-2445
Claude Lachance, Bellechasse (29,607)PQ, 418/528-1215
Réjean Lafrenière, Gatineau (37,878)Lib., 418/644-5980
Bernard Landry, Verchères (34,854)PQ, 418/643-5270
Marcel Landry, Bonaventure (29,626)PQ, 418/646-0505
Pierre-Étienne Laporte, Outremont (42,354)Lib., 418/528-5976
Benoît Laprise, Roberval (41,215)PQ, 418/646-7697
Camille Laurin, Bourget (33,761)PQ, 418/528-1657
Richard Le Hir, Iberville (44,299)Ind., 418/643-8474
Lyse Leduc, Mille-Îles (44,549)PQ, 418/646-1402
Roger Lefebvre, Frontenac (34,353)Lib., 418/644-6236
Guy Lelièvre, Gaspé (29,448)PQ, 418/528-5818
Jacques Léonard, Labelle (34,980)PQ, 418/643-5926
Robert LeSage, Hull (43,670)Lib., 418/644-9954
Michel Létourneau, Ungava (26,483)PQ, 418/528-1683
Nicole Loiselle, Saint-Henri-Sainte-Anne (39,197)Lib., 418/644-5976
Cosmo Maciocia, Viger (35,299)Lib., 418/643-7913

Norman MacMillan, Papineau (35,003)Lib., 418/644-6940
Marie Malavoy, Sherbrooke (38,615)PQ, 418/528-2655
Pauline Marois, Taillon (48,478)PQ, 418/644-0664
Pierre Marsan, Robert-Baldwin (42,600)Lib., 418/646-5554
Serge Ménard, Laval-des-Rapides (37,451)PQ, 418/646-3018
Robert Middlemiss, Pontiac (35,797)Lib., 418/644-2666
Gérard-R. Morin, Dubuc (34,450)PQ, 418/644-5901
Michel Morin, Nicolet-Yamaska (32,530)PQ, 418/646-3967
Thomas J. Mulcair, Chomedey (47,051)Lib., 418/528-2381
François Ouimet, Marquette (36,992)Lib., 418/646-3202
Daniel Paillé, Prévost (43,417)PQ, 418/646-0245
Roger Paquin, Saint-Jean (47,426)PQ, 418/644-5604
Pierre Paradis, Brome-Missisquoi (36,354)Lib., 418/643-1275
Jean-Guy Paré, Lotbinière (28,906)PQ, 418/646-8085
Marcel Parent, Sauvé (31,792)Lib., 418/643-3067
David Payne, Vachon (39,122)PQ, 418/644-5195
André Pelletier, Abitibi-Est (30,462)PQ, 418/644-4869
Robert Perreault, Mercier (39,636)PQ, 418/643-2112
Denis Perron, Duplessis (36,402)PQ, 418/643-2446
Claude Pinard, Saint-Maurice (33,780)PQ, 418/643-2810
Normand Poulin, Beauce-Nord (30,668)Lib., 418/528-2847
Paul-Eugène Quirion, Beauce-Sud (39,129)Lib., 418/228-0360
Matthias Rioux, Matane (28,055)PQ, 418/643-5297
Michel Rivard, Limoilou (43,877)PQ, 418/646-0650
Hélène Robert, Deux-Montagnes (52,644)PQ, 418/528-0765
Jean Rochon, Charlesbourg (45,931)PQ, 418/643-3160
Céline Signori, Blainville (36,530)PQ, 418/528-1349
Monique Simard, La Prairie (53,079)PQ, 418/646-4325
Sylvain Simard, Richelieu (38,688)PQ, 418/649-2319
Christos Sirros, Laurier-Dorion (41,718)Lib., 418/644-0520
Jean-Claude St-André, L'Assomption (48,626)PQ, 418/528-5474
Robert Thérien, Bertrand (38,854)Lib., 418/643-2769
Rémy Trudel, Rouyn-Noranda-Témiscamingue (40,695)PQ, 418/691-2050
Claire Vaive, Chapleau (54,005)Lib., 418/528-0759
Yvon Vallières, Richmond (31,371)Lib., 418/643-8092
Cécile Vermette, Marie-Victorin (40,023)PQ, 418/643-5611
Russell Williams, Nelligan (51,444)Lib., 418/644-5986
Vacant, Pointe-aux-Trembles (36,932)

QUÉBEC GOVERNMENT DEPARTMENTS & AGENCIES

Secrétariat aux AFFAIRES AUTOCHTONES/ Native Affairs
Edifice H, 875, Grande-Allée est, 2e étage, Québec PQ G1R 4Y8
419/644-5848; Fax: 419/644-9659; URL: http://www.gouv.qc.ca/gouv/francais/minorg/saa/index.html
Ministre responsable, Guy Chevrette, 418/643-7295, Fax: 418/643-4318
Sous-ministre associé, André Magny, 418/643-3166, Fax: 418/646-4918
Sous-ministre adjoint, Armand Leblond, 418/643-3166, Fax: 418/646-4918

Secrétariat aux AFFAIRES INTERGOUVERNEMENTALES CANADIENNES/Intergovernmental Affairs
Edifice H, 3e étage, 875, Grande Allée est, Québec PQ G1R 4Y8
418/643-4011; Fax: 418/643-8730; URL: http://www.bouv.qc.ca/francais/minorg/maig/maig_intro.html
Ministre responsable, Jacques Brassard, 418/646-5950
Secrétaire général associé, Hubert Thibault
Secrétaire adjoint, Michel Boivin
Directeur, Affaires économiques, culturelles et sociales, Pierre Dupont
Directeur, Bureaux coopération et francophonie, Line Gagné

Directions régionales/Regional Offices
Moncton: Bureau du Québec, Place l'Assomption, 770, rue Main, Moncton NB E1C 1E7 – 506/857-9851; Fax: 506/857-9883
Ottawa: Bureau du Québec, Place de Ville, Tour B, #700, 112, rue Kent, Ottawa ON K1P 5P2 – 613/238-5322; Fax: 613/563-9137
Toronto: Bureau du Québec, #1504, 20 Queen St. West, PO Box 13, Toronto ON M5H 3S3 – 416/977-6060; Fax: 416/596-1407
Vancouver: Bureau du Québec, World Trade Centre, #640, 999 Canada Place, Vancouver BC V6C 3E1 – 604/844-2833; Fax: 604/844-2834

Ministère des AFFAIRES MUNICIPALES/ Ministry of Municipal Affairs
Édifice Cook-Chauveau, 20, rue Chauveau, Québec PQ G1R 4J3
418/691-2015; Fax: 418/643-7385; URL: http://www.mam.gouv.qc.ca/mam/annuaire.html

ACTS ADMINISTERED
Code municipal du Québec
Loi sur les cités et les villes
Loi sur la Commission municipale
Loi sur le ministère des Affaires municipales
Municipal Organization
Loi sur la Communauté urbaine de l'Outaouais
Loi sur la Communauté urbaine de Montréal
Loi sur la Communauté urbaine de Québec
Loi sur le Conseil régional de zone de la Baie-James
Loi sur les conseils intermunicipaux de transport dans la région de Montréal
Loi sur les corporations municipales & intermunicipales de transport
Loi sur l'entraide municipale contre les incendies
Loi sur les villages cris & le village Naskapi
Loi sur les villages Nordiques & l'Administration régionale Kativik
Loi sur l'organisation territoriale municipale
Fiscal & Financial
Loi sur les dettes & les emprunts municipaux
Loi concernant les droits sur les divertissements
Loi sur la fiscalité municipale
Loi sur les immeubles industriels municipaux
Loi sur l'interdiction de subventions municipales
Loi concernant les droits sur les mutations immobilières
Municipal Administration
Loi sur les cours municipales
Loi sur les régimes de retraite des maires & des conseillers des municipalités
Loi sur le traitement des élus municipaux
Loi sur le régime de retraite des élus municipaux
Loi sur la Société québécoise d'assainissement des eaux
Municipal Democracy
Loi sur les élections & les référendums dans les municipalités
Loi sur le ministère de l'Habitation & de la Protection du consommateur
Loi sur le parc de la Mauricie & ses environs
Loi sur la Régie du logement
Loi sur la Société d'habitation du Québec
Loi sur la Société du parc industriel & commercial aéroportuaire de Mirabel
Planning & Development
Loi sur l'aménagement & l'urbanisme
Loi sur le développement de la région de la Baie-James
Municipal Services
Loi sur l'aide municipale à la protection de public aux traverses de chemin de fer
Loi sur les concessions municipales
Loi sur la contribution municipale à la construction de chemins
Loi sur la Régie de la securité dans le sport
Loi sur les rues publiques
Loi sur les travaux municipaux
Loi sur la vente des services publics municipaux
Miscellaneous Acts
Loi sur les abus préjudiciables à l'agriculture
Loi sur les colporteurs
Ministre, Rémy Trudel, 418/691-2050, Fax: 418/528-0352
Sous-ministre, Paul Champoux-Lesage, 418/691-2040, Fax: 418/644-9863
Sous-ministre adjoint, Affaires juridiques et législatives, Marcel Blanchet, 418/691-2040
Sous-ministre adjointe, Loisir et sports, Diane Lavallée, 418/691-2040
Sous-ministre adjoint, Planification stratégique, Jean-Guy Tessier, 418/691-2040
Directeur général, Gestion et budget, Yvon Verrette, 418/691-2000, Fax: 418/646-0779
Directeur général, Infrastructures et financement municipal, Georges Felli, 418/691-2007, Fax: 418/646-9149
Directeur général, Politiques et fiscalité, Réjean Carrier, 418/691-2043, Fax: 418/643-3204
Directeur, Bureau de coordination des Affaires autochones/Native Affairs, Jean-Guy Blouin, 418/691-2031, Fax: 418/643-8611
Directeur, Bureau de vérification interne, Jean-Guy Morel, 418/691-2029
Directeur, Communications, Philippe Gagnon, 418/691-2019, Fax: 418/643-4385
Secrétaire, Bureaux regionaux, Mario St-Germain, 418/691-2032, Fax: 418/644-6725

Regional Offices
Abitibi-Témiscamingue: #105, 170, av Principale, Rouyn-Noranda PQ J9X 4P7 – 819/764-9581; Fax: 819/797-6803
Bas-Saint-Laurent: 337, rue Moreault, 2e étage, Rimouski PQ G5L 1P4 – 418/727-3629; Fax: 418/727-3537
Chaudière-Appalaches: #510, 580 Grande Allée Est, Québec PQ G1R 2K2 – 418/643-1343; Fax: 418/643-4086
Côte-Nord: #1.801, 625, boul Laflèche, Baie-Comeau PQ G5C 1C5 – 418/589-7241; Fax: 418/589-1955
Estrie: #4.04, 200 rue Belvédère Nord, Sherbrooke PQ J1H 4A9 – 819/820-3244; Fax: 819/820-3979
Gaspésie-Îles-de-la-Madeleine: 220, rue Commerciale Est, CP 310, Chandler PQ G0C 1K0 – 418/689-5024; Fax: 418/689-4108
Mauricie-Bois-Francs: #313, 100, rue Laviolette, Trois-Rivières PQ G9A 5S9 – 819/371-6653; Fax: 819/371-6953
Montréal: 3, Complexe Desjardins, 26e étage, CP 185, Montréal PQ H5B 1B3 – 514/873-5487; Fax: 514/873-3057
Outaouais: #6.380, 170 rue de l'Hôtel-de-Ville, Hull PQ J8X 4C2 – 819/772-3006; Fax: 819/772-3989
Saguenay-Lac-Saint-Jean: #306, 227, rue Racine est, CP 305, Chicoutimi PQ G7H 5C2 – 418/698-3523; Fax: 418/698-3526

Associated Agencies, Boards & Commissions

- Bureau de révision de l'évaluation foncière du Québec/Québec Real Estate Assessment Review Board: #RC10, 575, rue St-Amable, Québec PQ G1R 5R4 – 418/643-3355; Fax: 418/646-0846
Président, Christian Beaudoin, 418/643-6786
- Commission municipale du Québec/Québec Municipal Commission: 20, rue Chauveau, 5e étage, Québec PQ G1R 4J3 – 418/691-2014; Fax: 418/644-4676
Président, Jacques O'Bready
514/873-3031, Fax: 514/873-3764
- Régie du logement/Québec Rental Board: #11.65, 1, rue Notre-Dame est, Montréal PQ H2Y 1B6 – 514/873-6575; Fax: 514/873-6805
Présidente, Louise Thibault
514/643-1697, Fax: 514/646-3570
- Société d'aménagement de l'Outaouais/Outaouais Development: Maison du Citoyen, 25, rue Laurier, CP 1666, Hull PQ J8X 3Y5 – 819/770-1500; Fax: 819/770-3213
- Société d'habitation du Québec/Québec Housing: Bloc 2, 1054, Conroy, 4e étage, Québec PQ G1R 5E7 – 418/643-7676; Fax: 418/643-2166
Président, Jean-Paul Arsenault
514/873-8130, Fax: 514/873-8340
- Société québécoise d'assainissement des eaux (SQAE)/Québec Wastewater Treatment: 1055, boul René-Lévesque est, 10e étage, Montréal PQ H2L 4S5 – 514/873-7411; Fax: 514/873-7879 – Québec: 418/643-2616; Fax: 418/643-0991
Président et Directeur général, Jean-Yves Babin

Ministère de l'AGRICULTURE, DES PÊCHERIES ET DE L'ALIMENTATION (MAPAQ)/Ministry of Agriculture, Fisheries & Food
200, ch Sainte-Foy, Québec PQ G1R 4X6
418/643-2673; Fax: 418/646-0829; Email: info@agr.gouv.qc.ca; URL: http://www.agr.gouv.qc.ca/mapaq/

ACTS ADMINISTERED
Agricultural Abuses Act
Agricultural Merit Act
Agricultural Societies Act
Animal Health Protection Act
An Act respecting commercial fisheries & aquaculture
An Act respecting farmers' & dairymen's associations
An Act respecting municipal taxation (certain sections)
An Act respecting prevention of disease in potatoes
An Act respecting public agricultural lands in the public domain
An Act respecting the bread trade
An Act respecting the École de laiterie & intermediate agricultural schools
An Act respecting the lands in the public domain (certain sections)
An Act respecting the Ministère de l'Agriculture, des Pêcheries & de l'Alimentation
Bees Act
Butter & Cheese Societies Act
Dairy Products & Dairy Products Substitutes Act (certain sections)
Horticultural Societies Act
Maritime Fisheries Credit Act
Mining Act (in part)
Plant Protection Act
Restaurant Merit Act
Stock Breeding Syndicates Act
Thoroughbred Cattle Act
Tourist Establishments Act (certain sections)
Administered by the Société de financement agricole du Québec
An Act respecting farm financing
An Act respecting farm-loan insurance & forestry-loan insurance
An Act respecting the conservation & development of wildlife
An Act respecting the Communauté urbaine de Montréal (certain sections)
An Act respecting the marketing of marine products
An Act to promote forest credit by private institutions
Cities & Towns Act (certain sections)
Farm Credit Act
Farmers' Clubs Act
Forestry Credit Act
Municipal Code of Québec (certain sections)
Fishermen's Merit Act
The Charter of the City of Québec (certain sections)
The Charter of the City of Sherbrooke (certain sections)
The Charter of the City of Trois-Rivières (certain sections)
The Marine Products Processing Act
Administered by the Commission de protection du territoire agricole du Québec
An Act governing the acquisition of farm land by non-residents
An Act to preserve agricultural land
Administered by the Régie des assurances agricoles du Québec
An Act respecting farm income stabilization insurance
Crop Insurance Act
Administered by the Régie des marchés agricoles
An Act respecting the sale price of pulpwood sold by farmers
Dairy Products & Dairy Products Substitutes Act (certain sections)
Farm, Food & Fishery Products Marketing Act
Farm Producers Act
Grain Act
Administered by the Société québécoise d'initiatives agro-alimentaires
An Act respecting la Société québécoise d'initiatives agro-alimentaires
Administered by the Raffinerie de sucre du Québec
An Act respecting the Raffinerie de sucre du Québec
An Act respecting the sale of the Raffinerie de sucre du Québec

Ministre, Guy Julien, 418/643-2525, Fax: 418/643-8422
Sous-ministre, André Vézina, 418/643-2336, Fax: 418/646-7747
Secrétaire du ministère, Luc Boutin, 418/643-2336, Fax: 418/646-7747
Directrice, Affaires juridiques, Huguette Pagé, 418/643-2355, Fax: 418/643-1676
Directrice par intérim, Planification, Jocelyn Cantin, 418/528-1419, Fax: 418/646-7747
Directeur, Vérification interne et des enquêtes, René Laforte, 819/644-4050, Fax: 819/644-4533

AFFAIRES ÉCONOMIQUES/Economic Affairs
Sous-ministre adjoint, Marc Dion, 418/643-2336, Fax: 418/646-7747
Directeur, Analyse de l'information économique, Pascal Van Nieuwenhuyse, 418/643-2460, Fax: 418/646-6564
Directeur, Analyses sectorielles, Louis Vallée, 418/643-2460, Fax: 418/646-6564
Directeur, Appui aux enterprises, Gilles Hains, 418/643-2460, Fax: 418/646-6564
Directeur, Développement des marchés, Zénon Bergeron, 201, boul Crémazie est, 4e étage, Montréal PQ H2L 1M4, 514/873-4410, Fax: 514/873-2364
Directeur, Économie de la production, Daniel Roy, 418/643-2460, Fax: 418/646-6564
Directeur, Politiques commerciales, Gaétan Busque, 418/643-2460, Fax: 418/646-6564

FORMATION, DE LA RECHERCHE ET DU DÉVELOPPEMENT TECHNOLOGIQUE/Research & Development
Sous-ministre adjoint, Louis Bernard, 418/643-2336, Fax: 418/646-7747
Directeur, Environnement et développement durable, Jacques Landry, 418/643-3029, Fax: 418/528-0485
Directrice, Formation et main-d'oeuvre en bioalimentaire, Nadine Girardville, 418/644-1315, Fax: 418/644-3049
Directeur, Institut de technologie agroalimentaire de La Pocatière, André Simard, 401, rue Poiré, La Pocatière PQ G0R 1Z0, 418/856-1110, Fax: 418/856-1719
Directeur, Institut de technologie agroalimentaire de Saint-Hyacinthe, Gilles Vézina, 3230, rue Sicotte, CP 70, Sainy-Hyacinthe PQ J2S 7B3, 514/778-6504, Fax: 514/778-6536
Directeur, Recherche, Daniel Chez, 418/644-1653, Fax: 418/646-0832
Directeur associé, Services technologiques - Productions animales, Yvan Savoie, 418/643-7622, Fax: 418/643-6680
Directeur associé, Services technologiques - Productions animales, Michel Lemay, 418/644-4686, Fax: 418/643-6680

PÊCHES ET AQUICULTURE COMMERCIALES/Commercial Fisheries & Aquaculture
Sous-ministre adjoint, Yvan Rouleau, 418/643-2336, Fax: 418/646-7747
Directeur, Analyses et des politiques, Laval Poulin, 418/528-2877, Fax: 418/643-8820
Directeur, Innovation et des technologies, Lucien Poirier, 96, montée Sandy Beach, CP 1070, Gaspé PQ G0C 1R0, 418/368-7637, Fax: 418/368-1275
Directeur régional, Côte-Nord, Denis Lacerte, 466, rue Arnaud, Sept-Iles PQ G4R 3B1, 418/962-5521, Fax: 418/962-0744
Directeur régional, Estuaire et Eaux intérieures, Michel Lanouette, 460, boul Louis-Fréchette, Nicolet PQ J3T 1Y2, 819/293-5677, Fax: 819/293-8519
Directeur régional, Gaspésie, Jean Carbonneau, 96, montée Sandy Beach, CP 1070, Gaspé PQ G0C 1R0, 418/368-7630, Fax: 418/368-5851
Directeur régional, Iles-de-la-Madeleine, Réjean Richard, 125, rue du Parc, CP 338, Cap-aux-Meules PQ G0B 1B0, 418/986-2098, Fax: 418/986-4421

PRODUCTION ET AFFAIRES RÉGIONALES/Regional Operations
Sous-ministre adjointe, Hélène Alarie, 418/643-2336, Fax: 418/646-7747
Directrice, Analyse et coordination, Hélène Harvey, 418/646-9681, Fax: 418/644-3049

Directions régionales/Regional Offices
Abitibi - Témiscamingue - Nord-du-Québec: #2.01, 180, boul Rideau, Rouyn-Noranda PQ J9X 1N9 – 819/764-3287; Fax: 819/764-5359, Directrice régional, Line Charland
Bas-Saint-Laurent: 337, rue Moreault, Rimouski PQ G5L 1P4 – 418/727-3620; Fax: 418/727-3967, Directeur régional, Gérard Boutin
Chaudière - Appalaches: 1115, av du Palais, Saint-Joseph-de-Beauce PQ G0S 2V0 – 418/397-6825; Fax: 418/397-6345, Directeur régional, Jacques Oliver
Estrie: 4260, boul Bourque, Rock Forest PQ J1N 2A5 – 819/820-3001; Fax: 819/820-3942, Directeur régional, Marcel Normandeau
Gaspésie - Iles-de-la-Madeleine: 94, rue Perron ouest, CP 524, Caplan PQ G0C 1H0 – 418/388-2282; Fax: 418/388-2834, Directeur régional, Yves Buteau
Mauricie - Bois-Francs (Secteur Bois-Francs): 460, boul Louis-Fréchette, 2e étage, Nicolet PQ J3T 1Y2 – 819/293-8501; Fax: 819/293-8446, Directeur régional - Bois Francs, Alain Tremblay
Mauricie - Bois-Francs (Secteur Mauricie): 91, boul Saint-Louis, Saint-Louis-de-France PQ G8T 1E5 – 819/371-6761; Fax: 819/371-6976, Directeur régional - Mauricie, Jean Genest

Montérégie-Est: 3230, rue Sicotte, CP 40, Saint-Hyacinthe PQ J2S 7B2 – 514/778-6530; Fax: 514/778-6540, Directeur régional, Paul Sauvé
Montérégie-Ouest: 177, rue Saint-Joseph, Sainte-Martine PQ J0S 1V0 – 514/427-2000, Fax: 514/427-0407, Directeur régional, Denys Vinet
Montréal - Laval - Lanaudière: 867, boul l'Ange-Gardien, CP 3396, L'Assomption PQ J5W 4M9 – 514/589-5781; Fax: 514/589-7812, Directeur régional, Richard Pelletier
Outaouais - Laurentides: 390, rue Principale, Buckingham PQ J8L 2G7 – 819/986-8541; Fax: 819/986-9299, Directeur régional, Luc Couture
Québec
1140, rue Taillon, 3e étage, Québec PQ G1N 3T9 418/643-0033; Fax: 418/644-8263
Saguenay - Lac-Saint-Jean - Côte-Nord: 801, ch du Pont-Taché, Alma PQ G8B 5W2 – 418/662-6486; Fax: 418/668-8694, Directeur régional, Alain Dessureault

QUALITÉ DES ALIMENTS ET SANTÉ ANIMALE/Food Quality & Animal Health
Sous-ministre adjoint, Jean-Yves Babin, 418/643-2336, Fax: 418/646-7747
Directeur, Laboratoires d'expertises et d'analyses alimentaires, Jacques Boulanger, 2700, rue Einstein, Ste-Foy PQ G1P 3W8, 418/644-5226, Fax: 418/643-0131
Directeur, Normes et programmes, Denis Sanfaçon, 418/646-8083, Fax: 418/644-3049
Directrice, Soutien aux opérations et de la coordination de l'information, Jocelyne Dagenais, 418/646-7693, Fax: 418/644-3049
Directeur régional, Bas-Saint-Laurent - Gaspésie - Iles-de-la-Madeleine, Vacant, 298 boul Thériault, 3e étage, Rivière-du-Loup PQ G5R 4C2, 418/862-6341, Fax: 418/867-4126
Directeur régional, Laurentides - Outaouais - Abitibi-Témiscamingue, Laval Tremblay, 1065, boul de la Carrière, local 110, Hull PQ J8Y 6V5, 819/772-3009, Fax: 819/772-3541
Directeur régional, Mauricie - Bois-Francs - Estrie, Serge Robert, 460, boul Louis-Fréchette, Nicolet PQ J3T 1Y2, 819/-293-8509, Fax: 819/293-2971
Directeur régional, Montérégie, Pierre Chartier, 3220, rue Sicotte, PO Box 3500, Saint-Hyacinthe PQ J2S 7X9, 514/778-6542, Fax: 514/778-6535
Directeur régional, Montréal - Laval - Lanaudière, Yves Proulx, 867, boul l'Ange-Gardien, l'Assomption PQ J5W 4M9, 514/589-5745, Fax: 514/589-0648
Directeur régional, Québec, Robert Clermont, 2700, rue Einstein, Ste-Foy PQ G1P 3W8, 418/644-6140, Fax: 418/644-6327

SERVICES À LA GESTION/Management Services
Directrice, Évaluation de programmes, Mishèle Bérubé, 418/643-7209, Fax: 418/644-4533
Directeur, Ressources financières et matérielles, André Abgral, 418/643-2420, Fax: 418/646-0869
Directeur, Ressources humaines, Jean Hébert, 418/643-7830, Fax: 418/644-4533
Directeur, Ressources informationnelles, André Roy, 418/643-0752, Fax: 418/646-0869
Directrice, Services en communication, Colombe Cliche, 418/643-2517, Fax: 418/643-8307

Associated Agencies, Boards & Commissions
•Commission de protection du territoire agricole/Agricultural Land Preservation: 200, ch Ste-Foy, 2e étage, Québec PQ G1R 4X6 – 418/643-3314; Fax: 418/643-2261
Président, Bernard Ouimet
•Fonds d'Assurance-Prêts Agricoles & Forestiers/Agriculture & Forest Insurance Fund: 1020, rte de l'Eglise, 8e étage, Ste-Foy PQ G1V 4P2 – 418/643-2610; Fax: 418/646-9712
Président, Michel R. St-Pierre
•Régie des assurances agricoles du Québec/Québec Agricultural Insurance Board: 5825, rue St-Georges, Lévis PQ G6V 4L2 – 418/833-5363; Fax: 418/833-6145
Président & directeur général, Luc Roy
•Régie des marchés agricoles & alimentaires du Québec/Québec Agriculture & Food Marketing Board: 201, boul Crémazie est, Montréal PQ H2M 1L3 – 514/873-4024; Fax: 514/873-3984
Président, Jean-Yves Lavoie
•Société de financement agricole du Québec/Québec Agricultural Finance: 1020, rte de l'Église, 8e étage, Ste-Foy PQ G1V 4P2 – 418/643-2610; Fax: 418/646-9712
Président, Michel R. St-Pierre
•Société de promotion de l'industrie des courses de chevaux/Québec Horse Racing: 5400, boul des Galeries, 2e étage, Québec PQ G2K 2B4 – 418/646-1632; Fax: 418/646-2528
Directeur-général, André St-Jean
Montréal Office: #302, 7881, boul Décarie, Montréal PQ H4P 2H2 514/873-5000, Fax: 514/873-0296
•Société québécoise d'initiatives agro-alimentaires (SOQUIA)/Québec Food & Fishing Industries Venture Capital Investment: #284, 1275, ch Ste-Foy, Québec PQ G1S 4S5 – 418/643-2238; Fax: 418/643-2553 – Telex: 051-3023
Président, Lucien Biron
•Tribunal d'Appel en Matière de Protection du Territoire Agricole: 200, ch Ste-Foy, 4e étage, Québec PQ G1R 4X6 – 418/646-3047; Fax: 418/643-0022
Présidente, Rita Bédard

Agricultural Marketing Boards & Commissions
•Centre de développement du porc inc.: 200, ch Ste-Foy, 1er étage, Québec PQ G1R 4X6 – 418/649-5070; Fax: 418/649-5077
Directrice générale, Odile Comeau
•Conseil des productions végétales du Québec inc/Québec Vegetable Products Council: 200 ch Sainte-Foy, 12e étage, Québec PQ GIR 4X6 – 418/646-5766; Fax: 418/646-1830
Directrice générale, Claudine Martel
Conseil des productions animales du Québec inc (CPAQ)/Québec Animal Products Council: 200, ch Sainte-Foy, 12e étage, Québec PQ G1R 4X6 – 418/646-5781; Fax: 418/646-1830, Directeur exécutif, Claude Martin
•Groupe Gestion & économie agricoles inc. (GEAGRI): 200, ch Ste-Foy, 12e étage, Québec PQ G1R 4X6 – 418/646-5772; Fax: 418/646-1830
Directeur exécutif, Claude Tremblay
•L'Union des Producteurs Agricoles: 555, boul Roland-Therrien, Longueuil PQ J4H 3Y9 – 514/679-0530; Fax: 514/679-5436
The following affiliates are at the same address:
Fédération des agricultrices du Québec
Fédération des producteurs acéricoles du Québec (maple syrup)
Fédération des producteurs d'Agneaux & moutons du Québec (sheep & wool)
Fédération des producteurs de Bois du Québec (wood)
Fédération des producteurs de Bovins du Québec (cattle)
Fédération des producteurs de Cultures commerciales du Québec (cash crops)
Fédération des producteurs de Fruits & légumes du Québec (fruit & vegetables)
Fédération des producteurs de Lait du Québec (milk)
Fédération des producteurs Maraîchers du Québec (market gardeners)
Fédération des producteurs de miel du Québec (honey)
Fédération des producteurs d'oeufs de consommation du Québec (eggs)
Fédération des producteurs de Pommes du Québec (apples)
Fédération des producteurs de Pommes de terre du Québec (potatoes)
Fédération des producteurs de Porcs du Québec (pork)
Fédération des producteurs de Volailles du Québec (poultry)
Fédération de la Relève agricole du Québec
Fédération des Syndicats de gestion agricole du Québec
Syndicat des producteurs d'oeufs d'incubation du Québec (eggs)
Président général, Laurent Pellerin
•Office des producteurs de tabac à cigare & à pipe du Québec/Québec Cigar & Pipe Tobacco Producers: 60, rue Vennes, St-Jacques PQ J0K 2R0 – 514/839-3641; Fax: 514/839-2874
Secrétaire, Gaétan Laporte
•Office des producteurs de tabac jaune du Québec: 813, rue Principale, St-Thomas-de-Joliette PQ J0K 3L0 – 514/756-2640
Secrétaire, Jean-Pierre Labyt

Ministère des Relations avec les CITOYENS ET DE L'IMMIGRATION/ Ministry of Citizenship & Immigration
360, rue McGill, 4e étage, Montréal PQ H2Y 2E9
514/873-9940; Fax: 514/864-2899; URL: http://www.immq.gouv.qc.ca/
Québec: #336, 900 boul René-Lévesque est, Québec PQ G1R 2B5
418/644-2428, Fax: 418/528-0829

ACTS ADMINISTERED
Department of Immigration Act
Ministre, Louise Harel, 514/873-9450, Fax: 514/873-1810
Ministre délégué, Relations avec les citoyens, André Boisclair, #336, 900, boul René-Lévesque est, Québec PQ G1R 2B5, 418/643-6322, Fax: 418/643-8936, Email: andre.boisclair/depute/pq@assnat.qa
Sous-ministre, Nicole Fontaine, 514/873-9450, Fax: 514/873-1810
Sous-ministre associée, Nicole Brodeur, 514/873-9447, Fax: 514/864-1930
Sous-ministre adjoint, Robert Trempe
Secrétaire générale, Secteur immigration et communautés culturelles, Francine Émond, 514/499-2199, Fax: 514/873-1810

Secrétariat à la CONDITION FÉMININE/ Québec Women's Secretariat
#2.700, 875, Grande-Allée est, Québec PQ G1R 5W5
418/643-9052; Fax: 418/643-4991
Ministre responsable, Louise Harel, 418/643-4810, Fax: 418/643-2802
Sous-ministre associée, Léa Cousineau
Directrice générale, Michèle Laberge

CONSEIL DU STATUT DE LA FEMME/Status of Women Council
#300, 8, rue Cook, Québec PQ G1R 5J7
418/643-4326; Fax: 418/643-8926
Présidente, Diane Lemieux

Ministère de la CULTURE ET DES COMMUNICATIONS/ Ministry of Culture & Communications
225, Grand-Allée est, Québec PQ G1R 5G5
418/643-2183; Fax: 418/643-4457; URL: http://www.gouv.qc.ca/francais/minorg/mccq/mccq_intro.html

Bureau de Montréal, 480, boul St-Laurent,
  Montréal PQ H2Y 3Y7
514/873-2255, Fax: 514/864-2448

ACTS ADMINISTERED
Loi sur les archives
Loi sur la Bibliothèque nationale du Québec
Loi sur les biens culturels
Charte de la langue française
Loi sur le cinéma
Loi sur les concours artistiques, littéraires et scientifiques
Loi sur le Conseil des arts et des lettres du Québec
Loi sur le Conservatoire
Loi sur le Conservatoire de musique et d'art dramatique du Québec
Loi sur le développement des entreprises québécoises dans le domaine du livre
Loi sur le ministère de la Culture et des Communications
Loi sur le Musée des beaux-arts de Montréal
Loi sur les musées nationaux
Loi sur la programmation éducative
Loi sur la Régie des télécommunications
Loi sur la Société de développement des entreprises culturelles
Loi sur la Société de la Place des Arts de Montréal
Loi sur la Société de radio-télévision du Québec
Loi sur le statut professionnel des artistes des arts visuels, des métiers d'art et de la littérature et sur leurs contrats avec les diffuseurs
Loi sur le statut professionnel et les conditions d'engagement des artistes de la scène, du disque et du cinéma

Ministre, Louise Beaudoin, 418/643-2110, Fax: 418/643-9164
Sous-ministre, Martine Tremblay, 418/643-3310, Fax: 418/643-4023
Secrétariat du ministère, Yves Laliberté, 418/643-4919, Fax: 418/643-4023
Directrice, Affaires juridiques, Julie Gosselin, 418/643-3747, Fax: 418/646-6849
Directeur, Communications, André Dorval, 418/643-6300, Fax: 418/643-4457
Directeur, Secrétariat à la politique linguistique, Guy Dumas
Directeur, Secrétariat de l'autoroute de l'information, Gaétan Poiré

ADMINISTRATION ET SERVICES MINISTÉRIELS/Management Services
Directeur général, Pierre-Denis Cantin, 418/643-7293, Fax: 418/643-4023
Directeur, Personnel et organisation du travail, Jean Cossette, 418/643-6529, Fax: 418/646-6440
Directrice, Recherche, évaluation, statistiques et documentation, Micheline Boivin, 418/643-8824, Fax: 418/643-4080
Directeur, Ressources financières et matérielles, Serge Doyon, 418/643-2101, Fax: 418/646-6440
Directeur, Ressources informationnelles, Gaétan Allard, 418/644-6314, Fax: 418/644-9014

ACTION RÉGIONALE/Regional Operations
Sous-ministre adjoint, Pierre Lafleur, 418/643-3310, Fax: 418/643-4023
Directrice générale, Murielle Doyle, 418/644-4789

Directions
Montréal: 480, boul St-Laurent, Montréal PQ H2Y 3Y7 – 514/873-2255; Fax: 514/864-2448, Directrice, Monique Barriault
Québec: Bloc C, R.C., 225, Grande-Allée est, Québec PQ G1R 5G5 – 418/643-6246; Fax: 418/644-9014, Directeur, André Couture

Directions régionaux
Abitibi-Témiscamingue: #450, 19, rue Perreault ouest, Rouyn-Noranda PQ J9X 6N5 – 819/762-6517; Fax: 819/762-6382, Directrice, Ginette Tremblay
Bas-St-Laurent: 337, rue Moreault, 2e étage, Rimouski PQ G5L 1P4 – 418/727-3650; Fax: 418/727-3824, Directeur, John Michaud
Chaudière-Appalaches: Bloc C, R.C., 225, Grande-Allée est, Québec PQ G1R 5G5 – 418/643-6225; Fax: 418/644-9014, Directrice, Marie-Josée Champagne
Côte-Nord: #1.105, 625, boul Laflèche, Baie-Comeau PQ G5C 1C5 – 418/589-6979; Fax: 418/589-4439, Directeur, Michel Bonneau
Estrie: 740, rue Galt ouest, Sherbrooke PQ J1H 1Z3 – 819/820-3007; Fax: 819/820-3930, Directrice, Carole G. Thibault
Gaspésie-Iles-de-la-Madeleine: 146, av Grand-Pré, PO Box 370, Bonaventure PQ G0C 1E0 – 418/534-4431; Fax: 418/534-4564, Directeur, John Michaud
Laval, Lanaudière et les Laurentides: 480, boul St-Laurent, 5e étage, Montréal PQ H2Y 3Y7 – 514/873-2282; Fax: 514/864-4522, Directeur, Eric Soucy
Mauricie-Bois-Francs: 100, rue Laviolette, 3e étage, Trois-Rivières PQ G9A 5S9 – 819/387-6001; Fax: 819/371-6984, Directrice, Marie-Josée Champagne
Montérégie: #230, 100, rue Richelieu, St-Jean-sur-Richelieu PQ J3B 6X3 – 514/-346-1468; Fax: 514/358-2217, Directrice, Carole G. Thibault
Nord-du-Québec: Bloc B, 225 Grande-Allée est, 2e étage, Québec PQ G1R 5G5 – 418/643-7658; Fax: 418/528-0874, Directrice, Ginette Tremblay
Outaouais: Edifice Jos-Montferrand, 170, rue de l'Hotel-de-Ville, 6e étage, Hull PQ J8X 4C2 – 819/722-3002; Fax: 819/722-3950, Directeur, Eric Soucy
Saguenay-Lac-St-Jean: 930, rue Jacques-Cartier est, 1er étage, Chicoutimi PQ G7H 2A9 – 418/698-3500; Fax: 418/698-3522, Directeur, Michel Bonneau

ACTION STRATÉGIQUE ET PROSPECTIVE
Directeur général, Adélard Guillemette, Québec PQ G1R 5G5, 418/646-4273, Fax: 418/643-6214
Directrice, Arts, médias et technologies de l'information, Hélène Cantin, 418/643-1887, Fax: 418/643-7853
Relations extérieures, Vacant, 418/643-3560, Fax: 418/644-4776

CONCERTATION ET INSTITUTIONS NATIONALES/Policy & Programs
Sous-ministre adjoint, Alain Bruneau, 418/643-3310, Fax: 418/643-4023
Directeur, Formation et concertation, François Paquette, 418/643-7001, Fax: 418/646-5419

Action culturelle et de communications
Sous-ministre adjoint, Pierre Lafleur, 418/643-3310, Fax: 418/643-4023
Coordination des Affaires autochtones, Michel Noël, 418/528-0610, Fax: 418/643-4023
Directeur, Secrétariat administratif, Claude Roy, 418/644-8923, Fax: 418/643-8457
Culture scientifique et technique, Vacant, 418/643-7710, Fax: 418/643-8457
Responsable, Intégration des arts à l'architecture, Nicole Genêt, 418/644-2109, Fax: 418/644-9014

Archives nationales et centre de conservation du Québec
Pavillon Louis-Jacques Casault, 1210 av du Séminaire, Ste-Foy PQ G1N 4V1
418/643-4376, Fax: 418/646-0868
Directeur général, Robert Garon, 418/643-4376, Fax: 418/646-0868
Directeur, Archives nationales de l'ouest du Québec, Normand Gouger, 1945, rue Mullins, Pointe-St-Charles PQ H3K 1N9, 514/873-7606, Fax: 514/873-2980
Directeur, Centre de conservation du Québec, Michel Cauchon, 1825, rue Semple, Québec PQ G1N 4B7, 418/643-7001, Fax: 418/646-5419
Responsable, Centre des documents semi-actifs, Denis Bourassa, 2750 rue Dalton, Sainte-Foy PQ G1P 3S4, 418/646-7696, Fax: 418/646-5421

Conservatoires de musique et d'art dramatique du Québec
580, Grande-Allée, 3e étage, Québec PQ G1R 2K2
Directeur général (par intérim), Alain Bruneau, 418/643-7427, Fax: 418/646-0175
Directeur, Études, Gilles Simard, 418/643-4796, Fax: 418/646-0175

Sociétés d'État et programmation
Directrice générale, Marie-Claire Lévesque, 418/643-4211, Fax: 418/643-4080
Directeur, Arts & Culture, Denis Delangie, 418/644-0485, Fax: 418/643-0380
Directeur, Inforoutes et communications, André Duplessis, 418/643-8096, Fax: 418/528-0874
Directeur, Secrétariat de la propriété intellectuelle, Vacant, 418/644-7194, Fax: 418/643-4080

PROJETS SPÉCIAUX
Directrice, Odette Duplessis, 418/644-7215, Fax: 418/644-4776

Associated Agencies, Boards & Commissions
• Bibliothèque nationale du Québec/Québec National Library
Listed in Section 5 of this book; see Index.
• Commission des biens culturels du Québec/Québec Cultural Property Commission: 12, rue Ste-Anne, 2e étage, Québec PQ G1R 3X2 – 418/643-8378; Fax: 418/643-8591
Président, Cyril Simard, 418/643-8380
• Commission de reconnaissance des associations d'artistes: #910, 425, boul de Maisonneuve ouest, Montréal PQ H3A 1L6 – 514/873-6012; Fax: 514/873-6267
Président, Denis Hardy
• Conseil des arts et des lettres du Québec: 79, boul René-Lévesque est, Québec PQ G1R 5N5 – 418/643-1707; Fax: 418/643-4558, Ligne sans frais: 1-800-897-1707
Président & Directeur-général, Marie Lavigne, 514/864-3351
• Musée d'art contemporain de Montréal/Montréal Museum of Contemporary Art
Listed in Section 6 of this book; see Index.
Président, Roy Lecaud Heenan, 514/847-6202
• Musée de la civilisation/Museum of Civilisation
Listed in Section 6 of this book; see Index.
• Musée du Québec/Museum of Québec
Listed in Section 6 of this book; see Index.
• Régie du Cinéma/Cinema Supervisory Board: 455, rue Ste-Hélène, Montréal PQ H2Y 2L3 – 514/873-2491; Fax: 514/873-8874
Président, Claude Benjamin
• Régie des télécommunications du Québec: #5.00, 900 place d'Youville, Québec PQ G1R 3P7 – 418/643-5560; Fax: 418/643-2960
Président, Vacant
• Secrétariat de l'autoroute de l'information/Information Highway Board: Bloc A, 225, Grande Allée est, 2e étage, Québec PQ G1R 5G5 – 418/528-2640; Fax: 418/528-0339
Sous-ministre associé, Robert Thivierge
• Société de développement des enterprises culturelles (SODEC)/Arts & Cultural Enterprise Development Commission: #200, 1755, boul René-Lévesque est, Montréal PQ H2K 4P6 – 514/873-7768; Fax: 514/873-4388, Ligne sans frais: 1-800-363-0401
Président et Directeur géneral, Pierre Lampron
• Société du Grand Théâtre de Québec/Québec Grand Theatre: 269, boul René-Lévesque est, Québec PQ G1R 2B3 – 418/644-8921; Fax: 418/646-7670

Président, Pierre-Michel Bouchard
- Société de la Place des Arts de Montréal/Montréal Arts: 260, boul de Maisonneuve ouest, Montréal PQ H2X 1Y9 – 514/285-4210; Fax: 514/285-1968

Président, Clément Richard
Directrice générale, France Fortin
- Société de radio-télévision du Québec/Radio-Québec: 1000, rue Fullum, Montréal PQ H2K 3L7 – 514/521-2424; Fax: 514/873-7739, Ligne sans frais: 1-800-361-4301

Président-Directeur général (par intérim), Michel Pagé

Associated Agencies, Boards & Commissions (under the French Language Charter)
- Commission de toponymie/Geographical Names: – 418/644-3688; Fax: 418/644-9466

Président, Henri Dorion, 418/644-6598
- Conseil de la langue française/French Language Council: 800, Place d'Youville, 13e étage, Québec PQ G1R 3P4 – 418/643-2814; Fax: 418/644-7654

Président, Nadia Brédimas-Assimopoulos, 514/873-2285
- Office de la langue français/French Language Board: Tour de la Place-Victoria, 16e étage, CP 316, Montréal PQ H4Z 1G8 – 514/873-0797; Fax: 514/873-3488

Président, Nicole René
- Secrétariat à la politique linguistique: Bloc A - r.-c., 225 Grande Allée est, Québec PQ G1R 5G5 – Fax: 418/646-7832

Directeur, Guy Dumas, 418/643-4248

CURATEUR PUBLIC DU QUÉBEC/ Québec Public Trustee
#500, 600, boul René-Lévesque ouest, Montréal PQ H3B 4W9
514/873-4074; Fax: 514/873-4972
Directeur, Marjolaine Loiselle

Secrétariat au DÉVELOPPEMENT DES RÉGIONS/Regional Affairs Secretariat
Édifice H, #3.600, 875, Grande Allée est, Québec PQ G1R 4Y8
418/528-0930; Fax: 418/644-5610
Ministre d'État, Guy Chevrette, 418/691-2050, Fax: 418/643-1795
Sous-ministre associée, Monique Bégin, 418/528-0930, Fax: 418/644-5610
Ententes gouvernementales, Serge Doyon
Opérations et services, Philippe Vaillancourt
Politiques gouvernementales, Serge Doyon

Délégués régionaux/Regional Delegates
Abitibi-Témiscamingue: #RC03, 180, boul Rideau, Rouyn-Noranda PQ J9X 1N9 – 819/762-3561; Fax: 819/797-1462, Secrétaire adjoint, Vacant
Bas-Saint-Laurent: 337, rue Moreault, Rimouski PQ G5L 1P4 – 418/727-3566; Fax: 418/727-3576, Secrétaire adjoint, Bernard Dussault
Chaudière-Appalaches: 700, av Notre-Dame nord, Suite D, Sainte-Marie-de-Beauce PQ G6E 2K9 – 418/387-6677; Fax: 418/387-4037, Secrétaire adjoint, Simon Chabot
Côte-Nord: #1.802, 625, boul Laflèche, Baie-Comeau PQ G5C 1C5 – 418/589-4345; Fax: 418/589-5199, Secrétaire adjoint, Jacques Tremblay
Estrie: #405, 200, rue Belvedère nord, Sherbrooke PQ J1H 4A9 – 819/820-3155; Fax: 819/820-3929, Secrétaire adjoint, Jean-Paul Gendron
Gaspésie-Îles-de-la-Madeleine: 220, rue Commerciale est, CP 1360, Chandler PQ G0C 1K0 – 418/689-2019; Fax: 418/689-4108, Secrétaire adjoint par intérim, Claude Rioux

Lanaudière: 138, rue Saint-Paul, Joliette PQ J6E 5G3 – 514/752-6866; Fax: 514/752-6877, Secrétaire adjoint, Gérald Durocher
Laurentides: #215, 85, rue De Martigny ouest, Saint-Jérôme PQ J7Y 3R8 – 514/569-3126; Fax: 514/569-3131, Secrétaire adjoint, Jean-Guy Tremblay
Laval: #210, 1555, boul Chomedey, Laval PQ H7V 3Z1 – 514/686-1428; Fax: 514/686-9106, Secrétaire adjointe, Vacant
Mauricie-Bois-Francs: 100, rue Laviolette, 4e étage, Trois-Rivières PQ G9A 5S9 – 819/371-6617; Fax: 819/371-6960, Secrétaire adjoint, Robert De Nobile Verreault
Montérégie: 201, Place Charles-Lemoyne, 2e étage, Longueuil PQ J4K 2T5 – 514/928-7643; Fax: 514/928-7650, Secrétaire adjoint, Yvon Richer
Montréal: Édifice Mercantile, 770, rue Sherbrooke ouest, 4e étage, Montréal PQ H3A 1G1 – 514/873-5845; Fax: 514/873-3224, Secrétaire adjoint, Jean-Pierre Nepveu
Nord-du-Québec: #RC03, 180, boul Rideau, Rouyn-Noranda PQ J9X 1N9 – 819/762-3561; Fax: 819/797-1462, Secrétaire adjoint par interim, Vacant
Outaouais: #7120, 170, rue Hôtel-de Ville, Hull PQ J8X 4C2 – 819/772-3038; Fax: 819/772-3968, Secrétaire adjoint, Paul-André David
Québec: #RC01, 875, Grande Allée est, Québec PQ G1R 4Y8 – 418/643-4957; Fax: 418/528-1410, Secrétaire adjointe, France Boucher
Saguenay-Lac-Saint-Jean: 3950, boul Harvey, 2e étage, Jonquière PQ G7X 8L6 – 418/695-7970; Fax: 418/695-7975, Secrétaire adjoint, Pierre Gauthier

Ministère de l'ÉDUCATION/ Ministry of Education
1035, rue De La Chevrotière, 15e étage, Québec PQ G1R 5A5
418/643-7095; Fax: 418/646-6561; Email: Dir-com@ meq.gouv.qc.ca; URL: http://www.gouv.qc.ca/francais/minorg/medu/medu_intro.html

ACTS ADMINISTERED
Loi sur l'accréditation et le financement des associations d'élèves ou d'étudiants
Loi sur l'aide financière aux étudiants
Charte de la langue française Chap. VIII, La langue de l'enseignement
Loi sur le Collège militaire royal de Saint-Jean
Loi sur les collèges d'enseignement général et professionnel
Loi sur la Commission d'évaluation de l'enseignement collégial et modifiant certaines dispositions législatives
Loi concernant l'Institut Armand-Frappier
Loi sur les concours artistiques, littéraires et scientifiques
Loi sur le Conseil supérieur de l'Éducation
Loi sur les élections scolaires
Loi sur l'enseignement privé
Loi sur les établissements d'enseignement de niveau universitaire
Loi favorisant le développement scientifique et technologique du Québec
Loi sur l'Institut québécois de recherche sur la culture
Loi sur l'instruction publique
Loi sur l'instruction publique pour les autochtones cris, inuit et naskapis
Loi sur les investissements universitaires
Loi sur le ministère de l'Éducation
Loi sur la Société de la maison des sciences et des techniques
Loi sur l'Université du Québec
Ministre, Pauline Marois, 418/644-0664, Fax: 418/646-7551
Sous-ministre, Pierre Lucier, 418/643-3810, Fax: 418/644-4591

Sous-ministre adjoint, Foi catholique, Christine Cadrin-Pelletier, 418/643-3810
Sous-ministre adjoint, Foi protestante, C. Grant Hawley, 418/643-3810

AFFAIRES UNIVERSITAIRES ET SCIENTIFIQUES/ University Affairs
Sous-ministre adjoint, Pierre Nadeau, 418/643-3810
Directeur général, Administration, Lionel Lirette, 418/643-4205
Directeur général, Aide financière aux étudiants, Paul Vachon, 418/646-5315
Directeur général, Ressources informationnelles, Jacques Babin, 418/643-0220

COMMUNAUTÉ ANGLOPHONE/Anglophone Services
600, rue Fullum, Montréal PQ H2K 4L1
514/873-4630; Fax: 514/873-1082
Sous-ministre adjoint & Directrice, Politiques et projets, Élaine Freeland, 514/873-3772
Directeur, Commission de l'éducation en langue anglaise, Walter Duszara, 514/873-5656
Directrice, Production en langue anglaise, Phyllis Koper-Naggiar, 514/873-6073

ENSEIGNEMENT COLLÉGIAL
Sous-ministre adjointe, Pauline C. Lesage, 418/643-3810
Directeur, Affaires éducatives, Jean-Yves Marquis, 418/646-1328
Directeur, Enseignement privé, Régis Malenfant, 418/646-1572
Directrice, Recherche et développement, Claire Prévost-Fournier, 418/643-6671
Directeur, Relations du travail, Gilles Pouliot, 418/646-1572
Directeur, Ressources matétielles et financières, Pierre Malouin, 418/646-4533

FORMATION PROFESSIONNELLE ET TECHNIQUE/Skills Development
Sous-ministre adjoint, Christine Martel, 418/643-3810
Directrice (par intérim), Formation continue, Sylvie Demers, 418/646-1562
Directeur, Organisation pédagogique, Serge Côté, 418/646-5614
Directeur, Programmes de formation professionnelle et technique, Guy Demers, 418/646-1536

RESSOURCES HUMAINES, MATÉRIELLES ET FINANCIÈRES/Finance & Administration
Sous-ministre adjoint, Henri-Paul Chaput, 418/643-3810
Directeur général, Financement et équipements, Réjean Morel, 418/643-3108
Directrice générale, Formation et qualifications, Louise Bussières, 418/643-2535
Directeur général, Relations du travail, Georges-Noël Fortin, 418/643-8610

SERVICES ÉDUCATIFS ET RÉSEAUX/Education & Research
Sous-ministre adjoint, Marcel Théorêt, 418/643-3810
Directeur (par intérim), Coordination des résaux, Jeannot Bordeleau, 418/643-7411
Directeur général, Enseignement privé, Jacques Blouin, 418/646-3939

Associated Agencies, Boards & Commissions
- Centre québécois de valorisation des biomasses et des biotechnologies (CQVB)/Promotion of biomass & biotechnology: #620, 2875, boul Laurier, Ste-Foy PQ G1V 2M2 – 418/657-3853; Fax: 418/657-7934; Email: cqvb@cqvb.gouv.qc.ca; URL: http://www.cqvb.gouv.qc.ca

Président, Marcel Risi, Email: Marcel.Risi@ cqvb.gouv.qc.ca

- Commission consultative de l'enseignement privé/ Advisory Committee on Private Education: 1035, rue De La Chevrotière, 11e étage, Québec PQ G1R 5A5 – 418/646-1249; Fax: 418/643-7752

Président, Jean Poulin

- Commission d'evaluation de l'enseignement collégial: 905, Dufferin-Montmorency, 3e étage, Québec PQ G1R 3M6 – 418/646-5811; Fax: 418/643-9019

Président, Jacques L'Écuyer

- Conseil supérieur de l'Éducation/Education Council: 2050, boul René-Lévesque ouest, 4e étage, Ste-Foy PQ G1V 2K8 – 418/643-3850; Fax: 418/644-2530

Vice-Président, Judith Newman

- Fonds pour la formation de chercheurs et l'aide à la recherche/Researcher Training & Research Assistance Fund: #102, 3700, rue du Campanile, Ste-Foy PQ G1X 4G6 – 418/643-8560; Fax: 418/643-1451

Président (par intérim), Yves Rousseau

ÉLECTIONS DU QUÉBEC/Elections Office
3460, rue de La Pérade, Ste-Foy PQ G1X 3Y5
418/643-5380; Fax: 418/643-7291; Email: DGEQ@DGEQ.QC.CA
#325, 1575, boul Henri-Bourassa ouest, Montréal PQ H3M 3A9
514/956-5475

Directeur général des élections, Pierre-F. Côté, C.R.

Ministère de l'ENVIRONNEMENT ET DE LA FAUNE/Ministry of Environment & Wildlife
Édifice Marie-Guyart, 675, boul René-Lévesque est, Québec PQ G1R 5V7
418/643-3127; Fax: 418/646-5974; Email: info@mef.gouv.qc.ca; URL: http://www.mef.gouv.qc.ca
Ligne sans frais: 1-800-561-1616

ACTS ADMINISTERED
Act approving the Agreement concerning James Bay & Northern Québec
Act respecting acid rain
Act respecting the assistance program for Inuit beneficiaries of the James Bay & Northern Québec Agreement (with respect to hunting, fishing & trapping activities)
Act respecting the Conseil de la conservation et de l'environnement
Act respecting the conservation & development of wildlife
Act respecting Cree Villages & the Naskapi Village
Act respecting hunting, fishing rights in James Bay & Northern Québec Territory
Act respecting the Forillon Park & its surroundings
Act respecting the Mauricie Park & its surroundings
Act respecting the Ministère de l'Environnement
Act respecting the Ministère du Loisir, de la Chasse et de la Pêche
Act respecting the protection of non-smokers in certain public places
Act respecting la Société québecoise de récupération et de recyclage
Act respecting threatened or vulnerable species
Ecological Reserves Act
Environment Quality Act
Fisheries Act (federal)
Migratory Birds Convention Act (federal)
Parks Act
Pesticides Act
Tree Protection Act
Watercourses Act

Ministre, David Cliche, 418/643-8259, Fax: 418/643-4143

Sous-ministre, Jean Pronovost, 418/643-7860, Fax: 418/643-3619

Secrétaire du ministère, Hervé Bolduc, 418/643-7860, Fax: 418/643-3619

Directeur, Affaires intergouvernementales et relations avec les autochtones, Georges Boulet, 418/643-8209, Fax: 418/644-4598

Directeur, Affaires juridiques, Michel Lalande, 418/643-2691, Fax: 418/646-0908

Directeur, Communications et marketing, Luc Poirier, 418/643-2984, Fax: 418/643-3330

Directeur, Enquêtes, René Provencher, 418/643-6185, Fax: 418/643-8923

Directeur, Planification et concertation, Yvon Boudreau, 418/643-1853, Fax: 418/644-4598

DIRECTION GÉNÉRALE DE LA CONNAISSANCE DES ÉCOSYSTÈMES/Knowledge of Ecosystems
Fax: 418/643-7812
Sous-ministre adjoint, Michel Paradis, 418/643-7860
Directrice, Écosystèmes aquatiques, Denyse Gouin, 418/644-3678, Fax: 418/646-8483
Directrice, Information environnementale et de la recherche, Clémence Veillette, 418/643-2073, Fax: 418/646-9262
Directeur, Laboratoires, Aristide Bouchard, 418/643-1301, Fax: 418/528-1091
Directeur, Milieu atmosphérique, Raynald Brulotte, 418/644-3460, Fax: 418/643-9591
Directeur, Milieu hydrique, Normand Trempe, 418/528-2048, Fax: 418/646-2367

DIRECTION GÉNÉRALE DU DÉVELOPPEMENT DURABLE/ Sustainable Development
Fax: 418/643-7812
Sous-ministre adjoint, André Harvey, 418/643-7860
Directeur, Conservation et patrimoine écologique, Léopold Gaudreau, 418/643-5397, Fax: 418/646-6169
Directeur, Promotion du développement durable, Michel Damphousse, 418/643-4115, Fax: 418/643-3754
Directeur, Évaluation environnementale des projets en milieu terrestre, Gilles Plante, 418/643-0519, Fax: 418/644-8222
Directrice, Évaluation environnementale des projets industriels, Suzanne Giguère, 418/643-8424, Fax: 418/646-0266
Directeur, Projets en milieu hydrique et nordique, Pierre Lefebvre, 418/643-7547, Fax: 418/646-0266

DIRECTION GÉNÉRALE DES OPÉRATIONS/Operations
Fax: 418/643-4747
Sous-ministre adjoint aux opérations, Robert Lemieux, 418/643-2207, Fax: 418/646-1800
Directeur, Affaires régionales, Philippe Bussières, 418/644-3987
Directeur, Hydraulique, Yvon Gosselin, 418/644-3556, Fax: 418/643-6900

Directions régionales/Regional Offices
Abitibi-Témiscamingue: 180, boul Rideau, Rouyn-Noranda PQ J9X 1N9 – 819/762-8154; Fax: 819/797-1202, Directeur, Jean-Guy Dugré
Bas-Saint-Laurent: 212, rue Belzile, Rimouski PQ G5L 3C3 – 418/727-3511; Fax: 418/727-3849, Directeur, Pierre Gilbert
Chaudière-Appalaches: 700, rue Notre-Dame nord, Ste-Marie PQ G6E 2K9 – 418/387-4143; Fax: 418/387-7018, Directeur, Jean-Marie Boucher
Côte-Nord: 818 boul Laure, Sept-Îles PQ G4R 3G5 – 418/962-3378; Fax: 418/962-0756, Directeur, Pierre Bertrand
Estrie: 770, rue Goretti, Sherbrooke PQ J1E 3H4 – 819/821-2020; Fax: 819/820-3958, Directeur, Pierre-Huagues Boisvenu
Gaspésie/Îles-de-la-Madeleine: 10, boul Ste-Anne, CP 550, Sainte-Anne-des-Monts PQ G0E 2G0 – 418/763-3301; Fax: 418/763-7810, Directeur, Bernard Dubois

Lanaudière: 6255, 13e av, Montréal PQ H1X 3E6 – 514/374-5840; Fax: 514/873-2100, Directrice, Michelle Page-Melançon
Laurentides: 6255, 13e av, Montréal PQ H1X 3E6 – 514/374-5840; Fax: 514/873-2100, Directeur, Rénald Girard
Laval: #300, 4, Place Laval, Laval PQ H7N 5Y3 – 514/662-2616; Fax: 514/622-3089, Directeur, Roland Mercier
Mauricie-Bois-Francs: 100, rue Laviolette, Trois-Rivières PQ G9A 5S9 – 819/373-4444; Fax: 819/371-6997, Directeur, Alain Verreault
Montérégie: 201, Place Charles-Le Moyne, Longueuil PQ J4K 2T5 – 514/928-7607; Fax: 514/928-7625, Directrice, Kathleen Carrière
Montréal: 5199, rue Sherbrooke est, Montréal PQ H1T 3X9 – 514/873-3636; Fax: 514/873-5662, Directeur, Robert Tétreault
Nord-du-Québec: 150, boul René-Lévesque est, 8e étage, Québec PQ G1R 4Y1 – 418/643-6662; Fax: 418/643-2057, Directeur par intérim, Marc Gauvin
Outaouais: 98, rue Lois, Hull PQ J8Y 3R7 – 819/771-4840; Fax: 819/772-3974, Directeur, Pierre Lévesque
Québec: 9530, rue de la Faune, Charlesbourg PQ G1G 5H9 – 418/622-5151; Fax: 418/622-3014, Directeur, Jacques Rivard
Saguenay/Lac-Saint-Jean: 3950, boul Harvey, 4e étage, Jonquière PQ G7X 8L6 – 418/695-7883; Fax: 418/695-7897, Directrice, Hélène Tremblay

DIRECTION GÉNÉRALE DES POLITIQUES/Policy
Fax: 418/643-7812
Sous-ministre adjoint, Denys Jean, 418/643-7860
Directeur, Coordination, Michel Ouellet, 418/643-4336, Fax: 418/528-1492
Directeur, Politiques des secteurs agricole et naturel, Guy Demers, 418/646-0753, Fax: 418/528-1035
Directeur par intérim, Politiques du secteur municipal, Jean-Maurice Latulippe, 418/644-7434, Fax: 418/644-2003
Directeur, Politiques du secteur industriel, Jean Rivet, 418/528-2363, Fax: 418/644-8562

DIRECTION GÉNÉRALE DE LA RESSOURCE FAUNIQUE ET DES PARCS/Parks & Wildlife
Fax: 418/643-3619
Sous-ministre adjoint, George Arsenault, 418/643-7860
Directeur, Développement et soutien, Eric-Yves Harvey, 418/644-7048, Fax: 418/528-0898
Directeur, Faune et habitats, Richard Chatelain, 418/644-2823, Fax: 418/646-6863
Directeur, Plein air et parcs, Luc Berthiaume, 418/644-9393, Fax: 418/644-8932
Directrice, Réglementation et permis, Claudette Blais, 418/643-7674, Fax: 418/528-0834
Directeur, Territoires fauniques, Luc Samson, 418/643-2846, Fax: 418/528-0834

Associated Agencies, Boards & Commissions
- Bureau d'audiences publiques sur l'environnement (BAPE)/Environmental Public Hearing Board: 625 rue St-Amable, 2e étage, Québec PQ G1R 2G5 – 418/643-7447; Fax: 418/643-9474, Toll Free: 1-800-463-4732 – Montréal: 514/873-7790; Fax: 514/873-5024

Président par intérim, Claudette Journault, 418/643-7447

Directeur, Administration, Michel Brouillard, 418/528-0767

- Comité conjoint de chasse, de pêche et de piégeage/ Hunting, Fishing & Trapping Joint Committee: #369, 393, rue Saint-Jacques, Montréal PQ H2Y 1N9 – 514/224-2151; Fax: 514/224-0039

Président, Kenny Blacksmith

- Comité consultatif de l'environnement Kativik/Katavik Environmental Advisory

Committee: Administration régionale Kativik, CP 75, Kuujjuaq PQ J0M 1C0 – 819/964-2681; Fax: 819/964-2502
Président, Claude Gilbert
Vice-président, Bruno Desbois
Secrétaire de commission, Jacques Lacroix
• Comité consultatif pour l'environnement de la Baie-James (CCEBJ)/James Bay Advisory Committee on the Environment: 3900, rue de Marly, 5e étage, CP 50, Ste-Foy PQ G1X 4E4 – 418/643-8495; Fax: 418/646-0266
Chair, Robert Daigneault
Executive Secretary, Denis Bernatchez
• Fondation de la faune du Québec/Québec Wildlife Foundation: #860, 140, Grande-Allée est, Québec PQ G1R 5M8 – 418/644-7926; Fax: 418/643-7655
Président et Directeur général, Gilles Barras
• Société québécoise de récupération et de recyclage (RECYC-PQ)/Québec Re-Use & Recycling Council: #500, 7171 rue Jean-Talon est, Anjou PQ H1M 3N2 – 514/352-5002; Fax: 514/864-2484
Président, Albert Leblanc

Secrétariat à la FAMILLE/ Family Secretariat
#3.300, 875, Grande-Allée est, Québec PQ G1R 4Y8
418/643-6414; Fax: 418/528-2009; Email: famille@cex.gouv.qc.ca; URL: http://www.gouv.qc.ca/gouv/francais/minorg/sfamille/const.html
Ministre responsable, André Boisclair
Secrétaire général associé, Jean-Louis Bazin

Ministère des FINANCES/ Ministry of Finance
12, rue St-Louis, Québec PQ G1R 5L3
418/691-2233; Fax: 418/646-5643, 1631; URL: http://www.finances.gouv.qc.ca/

ACTS ADMINISTERED
Charter of the Québec Deposit & Investment Fund
Deposit Act
Financial Administration Act
Lotteries & Races Act (Part IV)
Ministre, Bernard Landry, 418/643-5321, Fax: 418/643-3924
Sous-ministre, Gilles Godbout, 418/643-5738, Fax: 418/646-0923
Sous-ministre adjoint et Contrôleur des finances, André Fiset, 418/643-6488, Fax: 418/643-0976
Sous-ministre adjoint, Financement, Jean Laflamme, 418/691-2243
Sous-ministre adjoint, Politiques économiques, Jean-Guy Turcotte, 418/691-2225, Fax: 418/646-6163
Sous-ministre adjoint, Politiques fiscales et budgétaires, Vacant, 418/643-5738, Fax: 418/646-0923
Sous-ministre adjoint, Politiques et institutions financières, Jacques Dumont, 418/691-2274, Fax: 418/643-3572
Sous-ministre associé, Politiques et opérations financières, Marcel Leblanc
Directeur général, Gestion de l'encaisse et de la dette publique, Bob McCollough
Directeur général, Politiques financières & comptables, Jacques Poirer
Directeur général, Politiques intergouvernementales et budgétaires, Bernard Turgeon
Directrice, Politiques-Institutions Financières, Diane Delisle
Directeur, Administration, André Montminy, 418/691-2200
Directeur, Analyse et prévision économique, Abraham Assayag
Directrice, Analyses et synthèses quantitatives, Camille Courchesne

Directeur, Études structurelles, Gilles Demers
Directeur, Marchés de capitaux, Michel Gosselin
Directeur adjoint, Marchés de capitaux, Gaston Simoneau

Associated Agencies, Boards & Commissions
• Bureau de la statistique du Québec/Québec Statistics Office: 200, ch Ste-Foy, 5e étage, Québec PQ G1R 5T4 – 418/691-2401; Fax: 418/643-4129, Toll Free: 1-800-463-4090
Directeur général, Luc Bessette
Directeur général, Statistiques et enquêtes, Guy Savard, 418/691-2407
Directeur général, Statistiques et informatique, Denis Baribeau, 418/691-2407
• Caisse de dépôt et placement du Québec: 1981, av McGill College, Montréal PQ H3A 3C7 – 514/842-3261; Fax: 514/842-4833
Président et chef de la Direction, Jean-Claude Scraire
Premier vice-président, Planification des investissements, Michel Nadeau
• Commission des valeurs mobilières du Québec/Securities Commission: Tour de la Bourse, 800, Place Victoria, 17e étage, Montréal PQ H4Z 1G3 – 514/873-5326; Fax: 514/873-0711
Président, Paul Fortugno, Q.C.
Vice-présidente, Jacynthe Hotte
Vice-président, Martin Labrecque
Vice-président, Guy Lemoine
Membre, G.M. Beaulieu
Membre, Roland Côté
Membre, M. Tremblay
Counseiller spécial, Bureau du président, Gilles Cloutier
Secrétaire général, Jacques Labelle
Directrice, Affaires publiques, Louise Lebel-Chevalier
Directeur, Contentieux, Jean-Pierre Dupont
Directeur, Encadrement du marché, Pierre Lizé
• Société des loteries du Québec/Québec Lotteries: #2000, 500, rue Sherbrooke ouest, Montréal PQ H3A 3G6 – 514/282-8000; Fax: 514/873-8999
Président, Michel Crète

Commission de la FONCTION PUBLIQUE DU QUÉBEC/Public Service Commission
8, rue Cook, 4e étage, Québec PQ G1R 5J8
418/648-3977; Fax: 418/643-7264
Président, Jean-Noël Poulin, 418/643-3977
Secrétaire, Michel Poirier, 418/643-1425
Commissaire, Juliette Barcelo
Commissaire, Jean-Paul Roberge
Commissaire, Gilles R. Tremblay

HYDRO-QUÉBEC
75, boul René-Lévesque ouest, Montréal PQ H2Z 1A4
514/289-2211; Fax: 514/843-3163
Centre d'information & de documentation: 514/289-2316; Fax: 514/985-7304
Minister responsable, François Gendron
Président et chef de l'exploitation, André Caillé
Negotiator, Yves Fortier

Subsidiaries
• Hydro-Québec International: 800, boul de Maisonneuve est, 23e étage, Montréal PQ H2L 4L8 – 514/985-4200; Fax: 514/985-3076
Président-directeur général, Pierre Bolduc
• Société d'Énergie de la Baie-James (SEBJ)/James Bay Energy: 500, boul René-Lévesque ouest, Montréal PQ H2Z 1Z9 – 514/879-8010; Fax: 514/879-8013
Directeur général, Jean-Guy René

Ministère de l'INDUSTRIE, DU COMMERCE, DE LA SCIENCE ET DE LA TECHNOLOGIE/ Ministry of Industry, Commerce, Science & Technology
710, Place d'Youville, 9e étage, Québec PQ G1R 4Y4
418/691-5950 (Renseignements); Fax: 418/644-0118; URL: http://www.gouv.qc.ca/francais/minorg/micst/micst_intro.html
Montréal: 770, rue Sherbrooke ouest, 10e étage, Montréal PQ H3A 1G1
514/982-3000, Fax: 514/873-9913

ACTS ADMINISTERED
Act respecting the Ministère de l'Industrie & du Commerce
Act respecting the Société de développement industriel du Québec
Act respecting the Centre de recherche industrielle du Québec
Act respecting the Société des alcools du Québec
Act respecting the establishment of an integrated steel complex by Sidbec
Act respecting the Société du parc industriel du centre du Québec
Act respecting the Société générale de financement du Québec
Act respecting commercial establishment business hours
Act respecting stuffing & upholstered & stuffed articles
Act respecting the Société de développment des coopératives
Act respecting municipal industrial immovables
Act respecting assistance for tourist development
Act respecting beer & soft drink distributors' permits
Cooperatives Act
Cooperatives Syndicates Act
Act respecting Québec business investment companies
Ministre déléguée, Rita Dionne-Marsolais, 418/691-5650
Sous-ministre, Jacques Brind'Amour, 418/691-5656
Secrétaire du ministère, Celine Olivier, 418/691-5656
Directeur, Gestion des ressources humaines, Michel Gagnon

COMMERCE EXTÉRIEUR
Sous-ministre adjoint, Carl Grenier, 418/691-5656
Directeur général, Amériques/Asie-Pacifique, Harold Mallhot
Directeur général, Développement des marchés, Michel Chevrier
Directeur général, Europe, Afrique, Moyen-orient, François Boullhac
Directeur général, Politique commerciale, Gérald Audet

INDUSTRIE ET DÉVELOPPEMENT TECHNOLOGIQUE
Sous-ministre adjoint, Michel La Salle, 418/691-5656
Directeur général, Chimie, matériaux, santé, mode et textiles, Paul Lussier
Directeur général, Industries des biens d'équipement, André-P. Caron, 418/691-5955
Directeur général, Technologie, promotion de la science et des industries des technologies de l'information, Georges Archambault
Directeur, Fonds de l'Entente de développement industriel, Cyprien Pelletier

INVESTISSEMENTS ÉTRANGERS ET SOCIÉTÉS D'ÉTAT
Sous-ministre adjoint, André Dorr
Directeur général, Investissements étrangers, Marc St-Onge
Directeur, Relations avec les sociétés d'état, Gilbert Delage

OPÉRATIONS RÉGIONALES ET SERVICES AUX ENTREPRISES
Sous-ministre adjoint, Jean-Claude Lafleur, 418/691-5656

Directeur général, Opérations régionales, Pierre Girard, 418/691-5975
Directeur général, Services aux entreprises et aux coopératives, François Paradis, 418/691-5995

POLITIQUES ET ANALYSE ÉCONOMIQUE
Sous-ministre adjoint, Paul Beaulieu, 418/691-5656
Directeur général, Aide à la gestion des entreprises et coopératives, Marc Jean, 418/691-5664
Directeur général, Analyse économique, Yvon Pomerleau, 418/691-5813

Directions régionales/Regional Offices
Abitibi-Témiscamingue: 180, boul Rideau, Rouyn-Noranda PQ J9X 1N9 – 819/762-0865; Fax: 819/762-6496, Directeur, Claude Lecours
Bas-St-Laurent: 92, 2e rue ouest, Rimouski PQ G5L 8B3 – 418/727-3577, Directeur, Réjean Dion
Chaudière/Appalaches: 800, Place D'Youville, 4e étage, Québec PQ G1R 3P4 – 418/643-8993; Fax: 418/643-4099
Directrice, Christine Ellefsen
Côte-Nord et Nord-du-Québec: 625, boul Laflèche, Baie Comeau PQ G5C 1C5 – 418/589-5715; Fax: 418/589-4885, Directeur, Pierre Hébert
Estrie: 200, rue Belvédère nord, Sherbrooke PQ J1H 4A9 – 819/820-3205; Fax: 819/820-3966, Directrice, Diane Lamothe
Gaspèsie/Îles-de-la-Madeleine: 224, rue Principale, New Carlisle PQ G0C 1Z0 – 418/752-2229; Fax: 418/752-2902, Directeur par intérim, Roger Cyr
Lauentides-Lanaudière: 85, rue De Martigny ouest, Saint-Jérôme PQ J7Y 3R8 – 514/569-3031; Fax: 514/569-3039, Directeur, Jacques-A. Gagnon
Mauricie-Bois-Francs: 100, rue Laviolette, Trois-Rivières PQ G9A 5S9 – 519/371-6776; Fax: 519/371-6962, Directeur, Roger Leclerc
Montérégie: #101, 201, Place Charles Lemoyne, Longueuil PQ – 514/928-7456; Fax: 514/928-7465
Directeur, Jacques Quérillon
Montréal: 770, Sherbrooke ouest, 10e étage, Montréal PQ H3A 1G1 – 514/982-3000; Fax: 514/873-9913
Directeur, André Labrie
Outaouais: 170, rue de l'Hôtel-de-Ville, Hull PQ J8X 4C2 – 819/772-3131; Fax: 819/772-3981, Directeur, Richard Picard
Saguenay/Lac-Saint-Jean: 3950, boul Harvey, Jonquière PQ G7X 8L6 – 418/695-7862; Fax: 418/695-7870, Directeur par intérim, Florian Proulx

Associated Agencies, Boards & Commissions
•Centre de recherche industrielle du Québec (CRIQ)/Industrial Research Centre: Parc technologique du Québec métro, 333, rue Franquet, CP 9038, Ste-Foy PQ G1V 4C7 – 418/659-1550; Fax: 418/652-2251, Ligne sans frais: 1-800-667-2386
Président et Directeur général, Pierre Coulombe
•Conseil de la science et de la technologie/Science & Technology Council: 2050, boul René-Lévesque, 5e étage, Ste-Foy PQ G1V 2K8 – 418/644-1165; Fax: 418/646-0920; Email: Camil.Guy@cst.gouv.qc.ca; URL: http://www.cst.gouv.qc.ca/cst/cst_mandatE.html
Président, Louis Berlinguet
•Le Groupe Société générale de financement (SGF)/General Investment Corp.: #1700, 600, rue de la Gauchetière ouest, Montréal PQ H3B 4L8 – 514/876-9290; Fax: 514/395-8055
Président et Chef de la direction, Marc G. Fortier
•Parc technologique du Québec Métropolitain: #390, 2750, rue Einstein, CP 8743, Ste-Foy PQ G1P 4R1
Directeur général, Pierre Prémont
•Service de placement étudiant/Student Placement Service: 2700, boul Laurier, 3e étage, Sainte-Foy PQ G1V 2L8 – 418/643-6965; Fax: 418/643-7901

•La Société des alcools du Québec (SAQ)/Québec Liquor Corp.: 905, rue de Lorimier, Montréal PQ H2K 3V9 – 514/873-2020; Fax: 514/873-6788
Présidente et directrice générale, Jocelyn Tremblay
•Société de développement industriel du Québec (SDI)/Québec Industrial Development: Place Sillery, 1126, ch St-Louis, 5e étage, Québec PQ G1S 1E5 – 418/643-5172
Président et Directeur général, Louis Roquet
•Société du parc industriel & portuaire de Bécancour (SPIPB)/Bécancour Waterfront Industrial Park: 1000, boul Arthur-Sicard, Bécancour PQ G0X 1B0 – 819/294-6656; Fax: 819/294-9020
Président et Directeur général, Pierre Clouâtre
•Société du parc industriel & portuaire Québec-Sud/South Québec Waterfront Industrial Park: 10, rue Giguère, Lévis PQ G1V 1N6 – 418/833-5925
Président, Deny Grenier

L'Inspecteur général des INSTITUTIONS FINANCIÈRES/Inspector General of Financial Institutions
800, place D'Youville, Québec PQ G1R 4Y5
418/694-5016 (Communications); Fax: 418/643-3336; Email: igif@igif.gouv.qc.ca; URL: http://www.igif.gouv.qc.ca/igif
Montréal: 800, Tour de la Place-Victoria, Montréal PQ H4Z 1H9

ACTS ADMINISTERED
Loi sur les assurances (Insurance)
Loi sur les caisses d'entraide économique (Mutual Aid; Economic Assistance)
Loi concernant certaines caisses d'entraide économique (Economic Assistance)
Loi sur les caisses d'épargne et de crédit (Savings & Loan)
Loi sur les compagnies minières (Mining Companies)
Loi sur les corporations de fonds de sécurité (Security Funds)
Loi sur le courtage immobilier (Real Estate Brokerage)
Loi sur les intermédiaires de marché (Market-place Intermediaries)
Loi sur la liquidation des compagnies (Bankruptcy)
Loi sur les pouvoirs spéciaux des corporations (Special Powers of Corporations)
Loi sur la publicité légale des entreprises individuelles, des sociétés et des personnes morales (Legal Publicity of Sole Proprietorships, Partnerships & Legal Persons)
Loi sur les sociétés d'entraide économique (Mutual Aid; Assistance Societies)
Loi sur les sociétés de fiducie et les sociétés d'épargne (Trust & Loan Companies)
Loi sur les sociétés de prêts et de placements (Loans & Investments)
Loi remplaçant la Loi concernant la Confédération des caisses populaires et d'économie Desjardins
Loi concernant certains placements des compagnies d'assurance (Investments of Insurance Companies)

Acts Administered in Part or Jointly with Other Ministries
Code du travail (Labour Code)
Code municipal du Québec (Municipal Code)
Loi sur l'assurance automobile (Auto Insurance)
Loi sur l'assurance-dépôts (Deposit Insurance)
Loi sur les cercles agricoles
Loi sur les cités et villes (Cities & Towns)
Loi sur les clubs de chasse et de pêche (Hunting & Fishing Clubs)
Loi sur les clubs de récréation, (Recreational Clubs)
Loi sur la communauté régionale de l'Outaouais
Loi sur la communauté urbaine de Montréal
Loi sur la communauté urbaine de Québec
Loi sur les compagnies de cimetière (Cemeteries)
Loi sur les compagnies de flottage
Loi sur les compagnies de gaz, d'eau et d'électricité (Gas, Water & Electric Companies)

Loi sur les compagnies de télégraphe et de téléphone
Loi sur la constitution de certaines églises
Loi sur les coopératives
Loi sur les corporations de cimetières catholiques romains (Roman Catholic Cemeteries)
Loi sur les corporations religieuses (Religious Organizations)
Loi sur les évêques catholiques romains (Roman Catholic Bishops)
Loi sur les fabriques (Manufacturing Companies)
Loi constituant le Fonds de solidarité des travailleurs du Québec
Loi sur l'Inspecteur général des institutions financières
Loi sur l'Instruction publique (Public Education)
Loi sur les produits laitiers et leurs succédanés
Loi sur les services de santé et les services sociaux (Health & Social Services)
Loi sur les sociétés agricoles et laitières (Dairy & Agriculture)
Loi sur les sociétés d'agriculture (Agriculture)
Loi sur les sociétés d'horticulture (Horticulture)
Loi sur les sociétés de fabrication de beurre et de fromage (Butter & Cheese)
Loi sur les sociétés nationales de bienfaisance (Charities)
Loi sur les sociétés préventives de cruauté envers les animaux (Associations for prevention of cruelty to animals)
Loi sur les syndicats coopératifs (Cooperatives)
Loi sur les syndicats d'élevage (Breeding)
Loi sur les syndicats professionels (Professional Trade Unions)
Ministre responsable, Bernard Landry, 416/643-5270, Fax: 416/643-6626
L'Inspecteur général par intérim, Institutions financières, Alfred Vaillancourt, 418/694-5015
Surintendant, Assurances, Richard Boivin, 418/694-5011, Fax: 418/528-0835
Surintendant, Intermédiaires de marché et courtage immobilier, Alain Samson, 418/694-5020, Fax: 418/528-0570
Surintendant, Institutions de dépôts, Fernand Gauthier, 418/694-5023, Fax: 418/643-4586
Directrice générale, Administration et entreprises, Louise Milhomme, 418/694-5017
Directeur, Recherche, Alfred Vaillancourt, 418/694-5014

Associated Agencies, Boards & Commissions
•Régie de l'assurance-dépôts du Québec: 800, place D'Youville, Québec PQ G1R 4Y5 – 418/694-5014; Fax: 418/643-3336
Président Directeur général par intérim, Alfred Vaillancourt

Ministère de la JUSTICE/Ministry of Justice
1200, rte de l'Église, Ste-Foy PQ G1V 4M1
418/643-5140 (Communications); Fax: 418/646-4449; URL: http://www.gouv.qc.ca/francais/minorg/mjust/mjust_intro.html

ACTS ADMINISTERED
An Act respecting Access to documents held by public bodies & the protection of personal information
An Act respecting Adoptions of children domiciled in the People's Republic of China
An Act respecting Assistance for victims of crime
An Act respecting Attorney General's prosecutors
An Act respecting Municipal courts
An Act respecting Prearranged funeral services & sepultures
An Act respecting Protection of personal information in the private sector
An Act respecting Public inquiry commissions
An Act respecting Reciprocal enforcement of Maintenance Orders

Canadian Almanac & Directory 1997

An Act respecting Registry offices
An Act respecting the Barreau du Québec (in part)
An Act respecting the Civil aspects of international & interprovincial child abduction
An Act respecting the Class action
An Act respecting the Collection of certain debts
An Act respecting the Consolidation of the statutes & regulations
An Act respecting the Constitution Act
An Act respecting the Examination of complaints from customers of electricity distributors
An Act respecting the Floral emblem
An Act respecting the Implementation of the reform of the Civil Code
An Act respecting the Industrial accidents & occupational diseases (in part)
An Act respecting the Institut québécois de réforme du droit (not in force)
An Act respecting the Judgements rendered in the Supreme Court of Canada on the language of statutes & other instruments of a legislative nature
An Act respecting the Ministère de la Justice
An Act respecting the Official flag
An Act respecting the Payment of certain Crown witnesses
An Act respecting the Payment of certain fines
An Act respecting the Practice of midwifery within the framework of pilot projects
An Act respecting the Public curator
An Act to promote the Reform of the cadastre in Québec (in part)
An Act respecting the Salaries of officers of Justice
An Act respecting the Société québécoise d'information juridique
An Act respecting the United Nations Convention on Contracts for the International Sale of Goods
An Act to promote Good citizenship
An Act to secure the carrying out of the Entente between France & Québec respecting mutual aid in in judicial matters
Bailiffs Act
Charter of Human Rights & Freedoms
Chartered Accountants Act
Chiropractic Act
Civil Code of Québec
Code of Civil Procedure
Code of Penal Procedure
Consumer Protection Act
Court of Appeal Reference Act
Courts of Justice Act
Crime Victims Compensation Act
Crown Payments Prescription Act
Dental Act
Denturologists Act
Disorderly Houses Act
Dispensing Opticians Act
Engineers Act
Expropriation Act (in part)
Forest Engineers Act
Freedom of Worship Act
Hearing-aid Accoustichians Act
Highway Safety Code (in part)
Interpretation Act
Jurors Act
Labour Code (in part)
Land Surveyors Act
Legal Aid Act
Magistrate's Privileges Act
Medical Act
Newspaper Declaration Act
Notarial Act
Nurses Act
Official Time Act
Optometry Act
Pharmacy Act
Podiatry Act
Press Act
Professional Chemists Act

Professional Code
Public Officers Act
Radiology Technicians Act
Regulations Act (in part)
Sheriffs' Act
Special Procedure Act
Stenographers' Act
Territorial Division Act (in part)
Travel Agents Act
Veterinary Surgeons Act
Youth Protection Act (in part)
Ministre, Paul Bégin, 418/643-4210, Fax: 418/646-0027
Sous-ministre, Michel Bouchard, 418/643-4090
Sous-ministre associé, Administration et personnel, Rodrigue Desmeules, 418/643-4314
Directrice, Communications, Nicole Legendre
For list of Courts & other Legal Officers, including Judicial Officials & Judges see Section 10 of this book.

Direction de l'Etat Civil/Civil Status Records Office
418/643-3900; Fax: 418/646-3255
Provincial office responsible for the adminstration of all vital statistics, including birth, death & marriage certificates. Most certificates may be obtained within ten days for a fee of $15.00.

Direction de la réfonte des lois & règlements/Law Reform
1200, rte de l'Église, 4e étage, Ste-Foy PQ G1V 4M1 – 418/643-4808

DIRECTION GÉNÉRALE DES AFFAIRES CRIMINELLES ET PÉNALES/Criminal & Penal Affairs
Sous-ministre associé, Mario Bilodeau, 418/643-4085
Directeur, Direction des affaires criminelles, Paul Monty
Directeur, Direction des affaires pénales, Rosaire Vallières
Directeur, Direction du crime économique, Jean-Paul Roger
Directeur, Direction du droit de la jeunesse, Jean Turmel

DIRECTION GÉNÉRALE DES AFFAIRES JURDIQUES ET LÉGISLATIVES/Judicial & Legislative Affairs
Sous-ministre associé, Jean K. Samson, 418/643-4228
Directeur, Direction des affaires contentieuses, Jean-Yves Bernard
Directeur général adjoint, Direction des affaires juridiques, Jean-Pierre Marcotte
Directrice, Direction des affaires législatives, Marie José Longtin
Directeur, Direction du droit administratif et privé, Serge Lafontaine
Directrice, Direction du droit autochtone et constitutionnel, Dominique Langis

DIRECTION GÉNÉALE DES SERVICES DE JUSTICE/Justice Services
Sous-ministre associé, Gaétan Lemoyne, 418/643-7595
Directrice, Bureau d'aide aux victimes d'actes criminels, Christine Viens
Directeur, Direction des services administratifs, Jean Gauvin
Directeur par interim, Mission de la publicité des droits, Gilles Harvey
Directeur par interim, Mission des services judiciaires, Simon Marcotte
Directrice, Registre des droits personnels et réels mobiliers, Suzanne Potvin-Plamondon

Associated Agencies, Boards & Commissions
•Chambre de la jeunesse: 410, rue Bellechasse est, Montréal PQ H2S 1X3 – 514/495-5817; Fax: 514/873-8938
Juge en chef adjoint, Michel Jasmin
•Commission des affaires sociales/Social Affairs Commission: 1200, rte de l'Église, 2e étage, Ste-Foy PQ – 418/643-3400; Fax: 418/643-5335

Président, Gilles Poirier
•Commission des services juridiques/Legal Services Commission: Tour de l'Est, #1404, 2, Complexe Desjardins, Montréal PQ H5B 1B3 – 514/873-3562; Fax: 514/873-8762
Président, Pierre Lorrain
Secrétaire, Jacques Lemaître-Auger
•Conseil de la Magistrature: #7.45, 1, rue Notre-Dame est, Montréal PQ H2Y 1B6 – 514/393-2045
Président, Louis-Charles Fournier
Secrétaire, Bernard Tellier
•Fonds d'aide aux recours collectifs: #1201, 360, rue St-Jacques ouest, Montréal PQ H2Y 1P5 – 514/864-2750; Fax: 514/864-2998
Président, Jean Bernier
•Société québécoise d'information juridique: 715, Square Victoria, 8e étage, Montréal PQ H2Y 2H7 – 514/842-8741; Fax: 514/844-8984
Président, Jean-Paul Gagné

Ministère de la MÉTROPOLE/Ministry of Mettropolitan Affairs
Édifice H, #2.600, 875, Grande Allée Est, Québec PQ G1R 4Y8
418/646-3018; Fax: 418/643-6377
Ministre, Serge Ménard, 418/646-3018
Sous-ministre, Jacques-Yves Therrien, 418/646-3018
Sous-ministre adjoint, Robert Cournoyer, 418/646-3018, Fax: 418/643-6377
Sous-ministre adjoint, Gaëtan Desrosiers, #3.16, 800 Tour Place Victoria, CP 83, Montréal PQ H4Z 1B7, 514/873-7355, Fax: 514/864-5901
Sous-ministre adjointe, Affaires publiques, Laurette Laurin, #2.50, 800, Tour Place Victoria, CP 83, Montréal PQ H4Z 1B7, 514/873-6710
Sous-ministre adjoint, Paul Saint-Jacques, #3.16, 800, Tour Place Victoria, CP 83, Montréal PQ H4Z 1B7, 514/-873-2622, Fax: 514/864-5901

Office des PROFESSIONS DU QUÉBEC/Occupations Board
Complexe de la Place Jacques-Cartier, 320, rue St-Joseph est, 1er étage, Québec PQ G1K 8G5
418/643-6912; Fax: 418/643-0973
Président, Robert Diamant
Directeur, Communications et secrétariat, Michel Sparer
Directrice, Recherche, Sylvie de Grandmont

PROTECTEUR DU CITOYEN/Ombudsman
2875, boul Laurier, 4e étage, Ste-Foy PQ G1V 2M2
418/643-2688; Fax: 418/643-8759; URL: http://www.ombuds.gouv.qc.ca
Email: protecteur.citoyen@ombuds.gouv.qc.ca
505, rue Sherbrooke est, 3e étage, Montréal PQ H2L 1K2
514/873-2032, Fax: 514/873-4640
Protecteur du citoyen, Daniel Jacoby

Secrétariat à la RÉFORME ÉLECTORALE ET PARLEMENTAIRE/Electoral & Parliamentary Reform
875, Grande Allée est, Québec PQ G1R 4Y8
418/643-2483; Fax: 418/643-5612
Ministre délégué, Pierre Bélanger, 418/643-3804, Fax: 418/643-2514
Secrétaire, Michel Mercier

Ministère des RELATIONS INTERNATIONALES/Ministry of International Relations
Édifice Hector-Fabre, 525, boul Réne-Levesque est, Québec PQ G1R 5R9

418/649-2300; Fax: 418/649-2656; URL: http://www.mri.gouv.qc.ca/introan.htm
Montréal: 380, rue St-Antoine ouest, Montréal PQ H2Y 3X7
514/499-2171, Fax: 514/873-7825
Ministre, Sylvain Simard
Sous-ministre, Michelle Bussières, 418/649-2335, Fax: 418/649-2667
Sous-ministre adjoint, Directions géographiques, Denis Gervais, 418/649-2329, Fax: 418/643-4047
Sous-ministre adjointe, Politiques et aux services à la gestion, Marie Huot, 418/649-2335, Fax: 418/643-4047
Sous-ministre adjoint, Protocole, Jacques Joli-Coeur, 418/649-2346, Fax: 418/649-2657
Sous-ministre adjoint, Gérard P. Latulippe, #5200, 380, rue Saint-Antoine ouest, Montréal PQ H2Y 3X7, 514/987-1807, Fax: 514/987-1257

OPÉRATIONS
380, rue Saint-Antoine ouest, Montréal PQ H2Y 3X7
514/499-2171; Fax: 514/499-2178
Directeur, Aide à l'immigration d'affaires, Gérard Vézina, 514/873-2730, Fax: 514/873-0762
Directeur, Opérations à l'étranger, Gilles-A. Lacroix, 514/873-5760, Fax: 514/864-2926
Directrice, Régionalisation, Ghislain Croft, 514/873-6923, Fax: 514/864-2080
Directeur, Services d'immigration, Louis-E. Prévost, 514/864-9305, Fax: 514/873-9930
Directeur, Services d'intégration socio-économique, Jean-J. Plouffe, 514/873-1879, Fax: 514/873-1275
Directeur, Services pédagogiques, René Jobin, 514/864-9327, Fax: 514/873-3728
Directrice, Support aux opérations, Mimi Pontbriand, 514/873-9840, Fax: 514/864-2080

SECTEUR AFFAIRES INTERNATIONALES/International Affairs
Directeur général, Asie et Océanie, Paul-André Boisclair, 380, rue Saint-Antoine ouest, Montréal PQ H2Y 3X7, 514/499-2150, Fax: 514/873-4200
Directeur général, États-unis, Jean Duquette, 380, rue Saint-Antoine ouest, Montréal PQ H2Y 3X7, 514/499-2189
Directeur général, Europe, François Bouihac, 380, rue Saint-Antoine ouest, Montréal PQ H2Y 3X7, 514/499-2173, Fax: 514/873-4230
Directeur général, France, Vacant, 418/649-2329
Directeur général, Institutions francophones et multi-latérales, Pierre Jolin, 418/649-2341, Fax: 418/649-2664
Directeur général, Relations commerciales, Vacant, 418/649-2328, Fax: 418/649-2658
Directeur général, Services à la gestion, Jean Clavet, 380, rue Saint-Antoine, Montréal PQ H2Y 2E9, 514/873-7448, Fax: 514/873-2354
Directeur, Amérique latine et antilles, Raymonde Saint-Germain, 418/649-2312
Directeur, États-unis, Jean-Marc Blondeau, 418/649-2310
Directeur, Francophonie, René Leduc, 418/649-2344
Directeur, Relations commerciales avec l'Amérique du Nord, Jean-Pierre Furlong, 418/649-2334
Directeur, Relations commerciales intercontinentales, Laurent Cardinal, 418/649-2343

Associated Agencies, Boards & Commissions
• Bureau de révision en immigration: 2055, rue Peel, Montréal PQ H3A 1V4 – 514/864-3010; Fax: 514/864-3181
Directeur, Chahé-Philippe Arslanian
• Conseil des communautés culturelles & de l'immigration/Cultural Communities & Immigration Council: #418, Tour de la Place-Victoria, CP 158, Montréal PQ H4Z 1C3 – 514/873-8501; Fax: 514/873-3469
Présidente, Raymonde Folco, 514/873-5634

Vice-président, Immigration, Jacques Johnson, 514/873-8502
Vice-président, Immigration, Raymond Paquin, 514/873-4802

Ministère des RESSOURCES NATURELLES/ Ministry of Natural Resources
#B-302, 5700 - 4 av ouest, 3e étage, Charlesbourg PQ G1H 6R1
418/646-2727 (Renseignements); Fax: 418/644-7160; URL: http://www.mrn.gouv.qc.ca
Ligne sans frais: 1-800-463-4558

ACTS ADMINISTERED
Loi sur l'Administration régionale Crie
Loi sur les arpentages
Loi sur le cadastre
Loi sur les compagnies de flottage
Loi approuvant la Convention de la Baie James et Nord Québécois
Loi approuvant la Convention du Nord-Est Québécois
Loi favorisant le crédit forestier par les institutions privées
Loi sur le crédit forestier
Loi sur le développement de la région de la Baie James
Loi sur la distribution du gaz
Loi concernant les droits sur les mines
Loi sur l'efficacité énergétique d'appareils fonctionnant à l'éléctricité ou hydrocarbures
Loi sur l'exportation de l'énergie électrique
Loi sur les forêts
Loi sur Hydro-Québec
Loi sur le mérite forestier
Loi sur les mesureurs de bois
Loi sur les mines
Loi sur le Ministère des Ressources Naturelles
Loi sur le mode de paiement des services d'électricité et de gaz dans certains immeubles
Loi favorisant la réforme du cadastre Québécois
Loi sur la régie du gaz naturel
L'article 3 de la section VIII de la loi sur le régime des eaux
Loi concernant le régime des terres dans les territoires de la Baie James et du Nouveau-Québec
Loi sur la Société de Développement Autochtone de la Baie James
Loi sur la Société Eeyou de la Baie James
Loi sur la Société Nationale de l'Amiante
Loi sur la Société Québécoise d'Exploration Minière
Loi sur la Société Québécoise d'Initiatives Pétrolières
Loi sur la Société de Récupération, d'exploitation et de développement Forestiers du Québec
Loi sur les systèmes municipaux et les systèmes privés d'électricité
Loi sur les terres du domaine public
Loi sur les titres de propriété dans certains districts électoraux
Ministre d'État, Guy Chevrette, 418/643-7295, Fax: 418/643-4318
Ministre délégué, Mines, Terres et Forêts, Denise Carrier-Perreault, 418/643-7295, Fax: 418/643-4872
Sous-ministre, Michel Clair, 418/643-4676, Fax: 418/643-1443
Secrétariat du Ministère, Raymond Moisan, 418/643-4676, Fax: 418/643-1443
Directeur générale (par intérim), Gestion, Louis-Gilles Picard, 418/643-4676
Directeur (par intérim), Relations publiques, Raymond Moisan

ÉNERGIE/Energy
Fax: 418/643-8337
Sous-ministre associé, Jacques Lebuis, 418/643-4617
Directeur, Droits hydrauliques et tarifs, René Paquette, 418/646-9273
Directeur, Efficacité énergétique, Gaby Polisois, 418/646-5777

Directeur, Électricité, Florent Côté, 418/643-9755
Directeur, Gaz et pétrole, Alain Lefebvre, 418/644-6711
Directeur, Politiques, Études et Recherche, Claude Desjarlais, 418/643-4561
Directeur, Produits pétroliers, Pierre Lavallée, 418/643-3327

FORÊTS/Forests
880, ch Ste-Foy, Québec PQ G1S 4X4
Sous-ministre associé, Jacques Robitaille, 418/643-3987, Fax: 418/646-4335
Directeur, Conservation des forêts, R. Proulx, 418/643-7735
Directeur, Développement de l'Industrie des Produits Forestiers, Jean-P. Gilbert, 418/644-4364
Directeur, Environnement, Gilles Gaboury, 418/643-8587
Directeur, Gestion des stocks forestiers, Jean Brunet, 418/646-3381
Directeur, Programmes forestiers, Marc Ledoux, 418/646-8945
Directeur, Recherche forestière, Jean-Guy Davidson, 418/643-7994

MINES
Sous-minstre associé, Duc Vu, 418/643-4617, Fax: 418/644-7617
Directeur, Centre de recherche minérale, Jacques Saint-Cyr, 418/643-4540, Fax: 418/643-6706
Directeur, Géologie, Jean-L. Caty, 418/643-5159
Directeur, Industrie minérale, Gilles Mahoney, 418/646-2692
Directeur, Redevances et titres miniers, Raymond Boutin, 418/643-4477

SERVICES RÉGIONAUX/Regional services
880, ch Ste-Foy, Québec PQ G1S 4X4
Directeur général (par intérim), Jacques Caron, 418/643-3987, Fax: 418/528-1278
Directeur, Production des semences et des plants, Guy Bouilianne, 418/644-4484
Directeur, Services administratifs et techniques, André Demers, 418/643-3987

TERRES/Lands
Sous-ministre associé, Remy Girard, 418/643-4685, Fax: 418/644-7617
Directrice, Coordination et diffusion, Francine Beaulieu, 418/643-4685
Directeur, Gestion du territoire public, Jean-Y. Dupéré, 418/643-7685
Directeur, Relevés techniques, Claude de St. Riquier, 418/643-4828
Directrice générale, Direction Générale du cadastre, Jocelyne Lefort, 418/644-6224

Associated Agencies, Boards & Commissions
• Hydro Québec
Listed alphabetically in detail, this Section.
• Régie du gaz naturel/Natural Gas: Tour de la Bourse, #255, 800, Place Victoria, CP 001, Montréal PQ H4Z 1A2 – 514/873-2452; Fax: 514/873-2070
Président, Jean Giroux
• Société de développement de la Baie-James (SDBJ)/ James Bay Development: #110, boul Matagami, CP 970, Matagami PQ J0Y 2A0 – 819/739-4717; Fax: 819/739-4329
Président du conseil, J. Yvon Goyette
Président, Donald Murphy
• Société Nationale de l'Amiante (SNA)/Asbestos: 615, Monfette nord, Thetford Mines PQ G6G 7H4 – 418/338-0131; Fax: 418/338-3856
Président, Benoît Cartier
• Société québécoise d'exploration minière (SO-QUEM)/Québec Mineral Exploration: Place Belle Cour, #2500, 2600, boul Laurier, Ste-Foy PQ G1V 4M6 – 418/658-5400; Fax: 418/658-5459

Président et Directeur général, Yves Harvey
- Société québécoise d'initiatives pétrolières (SOQUIP)/Québec Oil & Gas Exploration: #180, 1175, ave de Lavigerie, Ste-Foy PQ G1V 4P1 – 418/651-9543; Fax: 418/651-2292
- Société de récupération, d'exploitation et de développement forestier (REXFOR)/Québec Forestry Exploitation: 1195, ave de Lavigerie, Ste-Foy PQ G1V 4N3 – 418/659-4530; Fax: 418/643-4037
Président, André L'Ecuyer

Ministère du REVENU/Ministry of Revenue
3800, rue De Marly, Ste-Foy PQ G1X 4A5
3, Complexe Desjardins, CP 3000, Succ Desjardins, Montréal PQ H5B 1A4
Impôt des particuliers: 514/864-6299;1-800-267-6299
Impôt des corps.: 514/864-4155; 1-800-450-4155
TVQ/TPS: 514/873-4692
Retenues à la source: 514/873-6995; 1-800-567-4692
    TVQ/TPS: 514/873-4692; 1-800-567-4692
    Retenues à la source: 514/873-6995; 418/659-7313; 1-800-567-4692
    Impôt des corporations: 514/864-4155; 1-800-450-4155
    Impôt des particuliers: 514/864-6299; 1-800-267-6299

ACTS ADMINISTERED
Act respecting fiscal incentives to industrial development (in part)
Act respecting Income Security (in part)
Act respecting labour standards (in part)
Act respecting municipal taxation (in part)
Act respecting real Estate tax refund
Act respecting the application of the Taxation Act
Act respecting the Ministère du Revenu
Act respecting the Payment of a Allowances to certain self-employed workers
Act respecting the Québec Pension Plan (in part)
Act respecting the Québec sales Tax
Act respecting the Régie de l'assurance-maladie du Québec (in part)
Act to facilitate the payment of support
Act to faster the development of man power training
Act to promote industrial development by means of fiscal advantages
Fuel Tax Act
Land Transfer Duties Act
Licenses Act
Meals & Hotels Tax Act (abrogated)
Taxation Act
Telecommunications Tax Act
Tobacco Tax Act
Ministre d'état, Économie et des Finances, Bernard Landry, 418/643-5270, Fax: 418/643-6266
Ministre délégué, Roger Bertrand, 418/652-6835, Fax: 418/643-7379, 514/287-8283; Fax: 514/873-7502
Sous-ministre, Nicole Malo, F.C.A., 418/652-6833, Fax: 418/643-4962, 514/287-8288; Fax: 514/873-7502

BUREAU DU SOUS-MINISTRE/Deputy Minister
Directeur général, Rénald Dion, 418/652-6868
Directrice, Secrétariat du Ministère, Micheline S. Gravel, 418/652-6834
Directeur, Bureau des plaintes, Gaétan Hallé, 418/652-6159
Directeur, Coordination ministérielle, Bruno Boudreault, 418/652-6864
Directeur, Sécurité et Enquêtes, Claude Gauthier, 418/652-6808
Directeur, Services administratifs, techniques et liaison, Pierre Sarto Blanchard, 418/652-5576

CENTRE DE PERCEPTION FISCALE/Tax Collection
3800 rue De Marly, Secteur 6-4-9, Ste-Foy PQ G1X 4A5
Directeur général, Gabriel Cayer, 418/577-0011, Fax: 418/646-8269
Directeur général adjoint, Montréal, Alain Lambert, 514/287-4431, Fax: 514/873-7346
Directeur général adjoint, Montréal, Pierre Leclerc, 514/287-6875, Fax: 514/864-3265
Directeur général adjoint par intérim, Québec, Claude Rivard, 418/684-2801, Fax: 418/646-0986

DIRECTION GÉNÉRALE DE L'ADMINISTRATION/Administration
Sous-ministre adjoint et directeur général, Onil Roy, 418/652-6884, Fax: 418/643-8482
Directeur, Administration - Montréal, Gilbert Chapleau, 514/287-6841
Directrice, Communications, Michèle Lasanté, 418/652-4935
Directeur, Études et contrôle des revenus, Michel Bordeleau, 418/652-5100
Directeur, Ressources humaines, Yves Cantin, 418/652-6820
Directeur, Ressources matérielles, Pierre Veilleux, 418/652-6801

DIRECTION GÉNÉRALE DES CONTRIBUABLES/Taxpayers
Directeur général par intérim, Michel Vaillancourt, 418/652-6872, Fax: 418/646-8499
Directeur général adjoint, Montréal, Réjean Beaulieu, 514/287-8051
Directeur général adjoint, Québec, Michel Vaillancourt, 418/652-6629
Directeur, Perception automatique des pensions alimentaires, Claude Aubin, 418/643-7040, Fax: 418/646-8270

DIRECTION GÉNÉRALE DE LA LÉGISLATION/Legislation
Sous-ministre adjoint et directeur général, André Brochu, 418/652-6844, Fax: 418/643-9381
Directeur, Affaires juridiques, Jacques Pinsonnault, 418/652-6843
Directeur, Contentieux, Paul Veillette, 514/287-8213, Fax: 514/873-8992
Directeur, Lois sur les impôts, François T. Tremblay, 418/652-6836
Directeur, Lois sur les taxes, Serge Bouchard, 418/652-6837
Directeur, Oppositions - Montréal, Luc R. Gervais, 514/287-8322
Directeur, Oppositions - Québec, Hubert Gaudry, 418/652-6268
Responsable, Service du Contentieux - Montréal, Michel Desrosiers, 514/287-8215
Responsable, Service de Contentieux - Québec, Claude Deamarais, 418/652-6842

DIRECTION GÉNÉRALE DES MANDATAIRES
Sous-ministre adjoint et directeur général, Denis Rheault, 418/652-6876, Fax: 418/646-9965
Directeur général adjoint, Montréal, Roger Pelletier, 514/864-9722
Directeur général adjoint, Québec, Michel Charbonneau, 418/652-4896
Groupe responsable des relations avec Revenu Canada, Pierre Boisvert, 418/652-2795
Groupe responsable des relations avec Revenu Canada, Rodrigue Lachance, 418/652-2794

DIRECTION GÉNÉRALE DES SERVICES EN RÉGIONS/Regional Services
Directrice générale, Francine Martel Vaillancourt, 418/652-6807, Fax: 418/652-5049
Responsable administratif, Abitibi-Témiscamingue, Pierre Bérubé, 75, rue Monseigneur Tessier ouest, Rouyn-Noranda PQ J9X 2S5, 819/764-6753, Fax: 819/797-8537
Responsable administratif, Bas Saint-Laurent, Michel Lepage, 212, rue Belzile, Rimouski PQ G5L 3C3, 514/727-3585, Fax: 514/727-3922
Responsable administratif, Côte-Nord, Serge Ouellet, 456, Arnaud, Sept-Îles PQ G4R 3B1, 418/962-0734, Fax: 418/968-3317
Directeur, Estrie, André Fauteux, 2665, rue King ouest, 7ième étage, Sherbrooke PQ J1L 2H5, 819/566-9750, Fax: 819/820-3115
Directrice, Laval, Jacquie Poissant, 705, ch du Trait-Carré, Laval PQ H7N 1B3, 514/975-3331, Fax: 514/669-4787
Directeur, Mauricie et Bois-Francs, Claude Ricard, #400, 225, rue Des Forges, Trois-Rivières PQ G9A 2G7, 819/371-6050, Fax: 819/371-6410
Directrice, Outaouais, Doris Tessier, 200, Promenade du Portage, Hull PQ J8X 4B7, 819/772-3145, Fax: 819/772-3984
Directeur, Saguenay/Lac St-Jean, Denis Gendron, 2154, rue Deschênes, Jonquière PQ G7S 2A9, 418/548-3566, Fax: 418/695-7999

DIRECTION GÉNÉRALE DES TECHNOLOGIES DE L'INFORMATION/Information Technology
Directeur général, André Gariepy, 418/652-5117, Fax: 418/646-0987
Directeur, Infrastructure systémique, Ghislain Guérin, 418/652-6958
Directeur, Systèmes des entreprises, Jean-Guy Parent, 418/652-5738
Directeur, Systèmes des particuliers, Pierre Bouchard, 418/652-5985

DIRECTION GÉNÉRALE DU TRAITEMENT
Directeur général, Gilles Néron, 418/652-4959, Fax: 418/646-4944
Directrice générale adjointe, Montréal, Renée Méthot, 514/287-3079
Directeur général adjoint, Québec, Guy Morel, 418/652-4726
Directeur, Traitement informatique, Yves Saint-Jacques, 418/652-4901

DIRECTION GÉNÉRALE DE LA VÉRIFICATION ET DES ENQUÊTES
Sous-ministre adjoint et directeur général, Bertrand Croteau, 418/652-6870, Fax: 418/646-0985
Directeur général adjoint, Enquêtes, Alain Dufour, 418/652-5903, Fax: 418/528-2049
Directeur général adjoint, Laval, Assaad Rizk, 705, ch du Trait-Carré, Laval PQ H7N 1B3, 514/975-3301, Fax: 514/669-4707
Directeur général adjoint, Montréal, Michel Lussier, 514/287-8400, Fax: 514/864-1961
Directeur général adjoint, Québec, André Gingras, 418/652-6811

Ministère de la SANTÉ ET DES SERVICES SOCIAUX/
Ministry of Health & Social Services
1075, ch Ste-Foy, Québec PQ G1S 2M1
URL: http://www.gouv.qc.ca/francais/minorg/msss/msss_intro.html
Renseignements généraux, 1088, rue Raymond-Casgrain, Québec PQ G1S 2E4
418/643-3380, Fax: 418/643-3177

ACTS ADMINISTERED
Act respecting the Conseil médical du Québec
Act respecting the Ministère de la Santé et des services sociaux
Act respecting the Ministère des Affaires sociales
Act respecting Health Services & Social Services
Health Insurance Act
Act respecting the Régie de l'assurance maladie du Québec
Hospital Insurance Act
Public Health Act
Act respecting health health services for Cree & Inuit native persons

Act respecting the practice of midwifery within the framework of pilot projects
Youth Protection Act
Mental Patients Protection Act
Public Health Protection Act
Act to secure the handicapped in the exercise of their rights
Act respecting the Commission des affaires sociales
Non-Catholic Cemeteries Act
Act respecting the Conseil de la santé et du bien-être Act
Ministre, Jean Rochon, 418/643-3160, Fax: 418/644-4534
Sous-ministre, Pierre-André Paré, 418/643-6462, Fax: 418/643-9217
Sous-ministre adjointe, Administration et des immobilisations, Cécile Cléroux, 418/643-3224, Fax: 418/643-0596
Sous-ministre adjointe, Planification et à l'évaluation, Sylvie Dillard, 418/644-7304, Fax: 418/646-1956
Sous-ministre adjoint, Relations professionnelles, Hubert Gauthier, 418/643-7463, Fax: 418/643-7472
Sous-ministre adjointe, Santé publique, Christine Colin, 418/646-3487, Fax: 418/528-2651

Associated Agencies, Councils & Commissions
•Bureau des personnes handicapées du Québec/Office for Handicapped Persons: 309, rue Brock, CP 820, Drummondville PQ J2B 6X1 – 819/477-7100; Fax: 819/477-8493
Président et Directeur général, Gaston J. Perreault
•Comité de la santé mentale du Québec: 1075, ch Ste-Foy, Québec PQ G1S 2M1 – 418/643-9210; Fax: 418/646-1956
Président, Robert Paquet
•Commissaire aux plaintes: 5199, rue Sherbrooke est, Québec PQ H1T 3X3 – 418/873-3205; Fax: 418/873-5665
Commissaire, Jean Francoeur
•Commission d'appel pour les Autochtones du Québec/Native Appeals: 2, av du Palais, Rouyn PQ J9X 2N9 – 819/762-2838
Président, Jean-Charles Coutu
•Commission québécoise d'examen (troubles mentaux): 785, av De Salaberry, Québec PQ G1R 2T8 – 418/643-2613; Fax: 418/644-7180
Président, Roch Rioux
•Conseil Consultatif de Pharmacologie/Advisory Council on Pharmacology: 1125, ch St-Louis, 8e étage, Sillery PQ G1S 1E7 – 418/643-3140; Fax: 418/646-8349
Président, Dr. Jacques Le Lorier
•Conseil Consultatif sur les aides technologiques: 845, av Joffre, Québec PQ G1S 4N4 – 418/643-1213; Fax: 418/646-2134
Président, J.-Auguste Mockle
•Conseil de la santé et du bien-être/Health & Welfare Council: 1126, ch St-Louis, Sillery PQ G1S 1E5 – 418/643-3040; Fax: 418/644-0654
Président, Norbert Rodrigue
•Conseil d'évaluation des technologies de la Santé/Health Technology Council: #4205, 800, Place Victoria, CP 215, Montréal PQ H4Z 1E3 – 514/873-2563; Fax: 514/873-1369
Président, Renaldo N. Batiste
•Conseil des aînes/Seniors: 1005, ch Ste-Foy, Québec PQ G1S 4N4 – 418/643-6720; Fax: 418/646-9895
Présidente, Nicole Dumont-Larouche
•Conseil médical du québec: 1005, ch Ste-Foy, Québec PQ G1S 4N4 – 418/646-4379; Fax: 418/646-9895
Président, Juan Roberto Iglesias
•Conseil québécois de la recherche sociale/Québec Social Research Council: 1088, rue Raymond-Casgrain, 1er étage, Québec PQ G1S 2E4 – 418/643-7582; Fax: 418/643-4768
Président, Marc Renaud

•Corporation d'Hébergement du Québec/Québec Social Care Facilities: 2050, boul René-Lévesque Ouest, Ste-Foy PQ G1V 2K8 – 418/643-6112; Fax: 418/644-0563
Président et Directeur général, Conrad Dubuc
•Fonds de la Recherche en Santé du Québec/Québec Health Research Fund: #1950, 550, rue Sherbrooke ouest, Montréal PQ H3A 1B9 – 514/873-2114; Fax: 514/873-8768
Président, Fernand Labrie
•Régie de l'Assurance-maladie du Québec/Québec Health Insurance Board: 1125, ch St-Louis, Québec PQ G1K 7T3 – 418/682-5111
Président et Directeur général par intérim, Denis Morency, 418/682-5162
Adjoint au président et directeur général, Pierre Boucher, 418/682-5162
•Service Ambulancier du Québec/Québec Ambulance Service: 1005, ch Ste-Foy, 5e étage, Québec PQ G1S 4N4 – 418/643-3700
Directeur intérim, Martin Soucy

Ministère de la SÉCURITÉ PUBLIQUE/ Ministry of Public Security
Tour des Laurentides, 2525, boul Laurier, 5e étage, Ste-Foy PQ G1V 2L2
418/643-3500; Fax: 418/643-0275; Email: Infocom@secpub.gouv.qc.ca; URL: http://www.secpub.bouv.qc.ca/secpub/index.html
Montréal Office: 3, Complexe Desjardins, Tour nord, 26e étage, Montréal PQ H5B 1E9
514/873-2112, Fax: 514/873-6597

ACTS ADMINISTERED
Bicycle ownership Act
An Act respecting the Communauté urbaine de Montréal
An Act respecting correctional services
An Act respecting detectives or security agencies
An Act respecting the determination of the causes & circumstances of death
An Act respecting explosives
Fire Investigations Act
Fire Prevention Act
Highway Safety Code (partially administered by the MSP)
An Act respecting liquor permits
An Act respecting lotteries, publicity, contests & amusement machines
An Act respecting the Ministère de la Sécurité publique
An Act respecting Northern Villages & the Kativik regional Government (partially administered by the MSP)
An Act respecting offences relating to Alcoholic Beverages
An Act respecting police organization
Police Act
An Act to promote the parole of inmates
An Act respecting the protection of persons & property in the event of disaster
An Act respecting racing
An Act respecting the Régie des alcools, des courses et des jeux
Safe-Deposit Boxes Act
An Act respecting the Société des alcools du Québec (partially administered by MSP)
An Act respecting the Société des loteries du Québec (partially administered by the MSP)
An Act respecting the Syndical Plan of the Sûreté du Québec
An Act respecting tear bombs
Temperance Act
Ministre, Robert Perreault, 418/643-2112, Fax: 418/646-6168
Sous-ministre, Florent Gagné, 418/643-3500, Fax: 418/643-0275

ADMINISTRATION
Sous-ministre associé, Jean-Louis Lapointe, 418/643-8498, Fax: 418/528-1713
Directrice, Informatique et systèmes, Ann Chamberland, 418/644-0795, Fax: 418/644-4593
Directeur, Organisation et ressources humaines, Jean Demers, 418/528-1431, Fax: 418/643-0645
Directrice, Ressources matérielles et financières, Micheline Biache, 418/528-2897, Fax: 418/528-1713

DIRECTION GÉNÉRALE DE LA SÉCURITÉ ET DE LA PRÉVENTION/Security & Protection
2525, boul Laurier, 2e étage, Ste-Foy PQ G1V 2L2
418/646-8523; Fax: 418/646-5427
Sous-ministre associée, Charles Côté
Directeur (Intérim), Assistance financière, Jacques Gariépy, 418/644-2304
Directeur, Direction des affaires policières et de la sécurité incendie, Daniel St-Onge, 418/644-9774, Fax: 418/646-3564
Directeur, Direction de la sécurité civile et des régions, Jacques Gariépy, 418/646-7950
Responsable, Service général d'inspection, Marc Lizotte, 418/643-8360; 514/864-1900, Fax: 418/644-0132; 514/873-2656

SÉCURITÉ ET PRÉVENTION/Security & Prevention
Directeur, Services de sécurité et de protection, François Côté, 418/643-9353, Fax: 418/646-9265
Chef de service, Service des affaires policières et sécurité privée, Rémy Normand, 418/646-6920, Fax: 418/646-3564
Chef de service, Service de la prévention et de la criminalité, Anne O'Sullivan, 418/646-6628, Fax: 418/646-3564

SERVICES CORRECTIONNELS/Correctional Services
Sous-ministre associé, Normand Carrier, 418/643-3612, Fax: 418/644-7159
Directeur, Centre d'expertise et de coordination en sécurité, Gilles Soucy, 418/643-5141, Fax: 418/643-3426
Directeur, Partenariat et conseil en services correctionnels, Michel Roberge, 418/644-7887, Fax: 418/644-5645
Directeur, Services administratifs, Kevin Walsh, 418/644-3821, Fax: 418/643-3426
Directeur, Direction territoriale Abitibi-Témiscamingue, Nord du Québec, Jean Mercure, 819/797-3790, Fax: 819/797-8882
Directeur, Direction territoriale du Bas-Saint-Laurent, Gaspésie, Côte-Nord, Jocelyn Blais, 418/727-3687, Fax: 418/727-3531
Directeur, Direction territoriale Estrie-Montérégie, Arthur Fauteux, 514/776-7211, Fax: 514/776-7217
Directeur, Direction territoriale Laval, Laurentides, Lanaudière, Outaouais, Roger Giroux, 514/686-9308, Fax: 514/686-6673
Directeur, Direction territoriale de Montréal, Michel Lacoste, 514/864-1800, Fax: 514/873-9362
Directeur, Direction territoriale Québec, Mauricie-Bois-Francs, Chaudière-Appalaches, Marc-André Laliberté, 418/646-0570, Fax: 418/646-9254

Associated Agencies, Boards & Commissions
•Bureau du coroner/Office of the Coroner: Tour Belle Cour, #2350, 2600 boul Laurier, 3e étage, Ste Foy PQ G1V 4M6 – 418/643-1845; Fax: 418/643-6174
Coroner en chef, Pierre Morin
Coroner en chef adjoint, Dr. Serge Turmel, 418/643-1845, Fax: 418/643-6174
•Comité de déontologie policière/Police Ethics Committee: #7.30, 1020, rte de l'Église, Ste-Foy PQ G1V 4W9 – 418/646-1936; Fax: 418/528-0987
Président, Me Claude Brazeau
Commissaire, Denis Racicot, 418/643-7897, Fax: 418/528-9473

Canadian Almanac & Directory 1997

Commissaire adjointe, Marlene Jennings
- **Commissariat aux incendies/Fire Commissioner:** 455, rue Dupont, Québec PQ G1K 6N2 – 418/529-5706; Fax: 418/529-9922

Commissaire, Cyrille Delâge
- **Commission québécoise des libérations conditionnelles/Parole Board:** #200, 2055, rue Peel, Montréal PQ H3A 1V4 – 514/873-2230; Fax: 514/873-7580

Présidente, Renée Collette
Québec: #210, 275, rue de l'Église, Québec PQ G1K 6G7
418/646-8340, Fax: 418/643-7217
- **Institut de police du Québec:** 350, rue Marguerite d'Youville, CP 1120, Nicolet PQ J3T 1X4 – 819/293-8631; Fax: 819/293-4018

Directrice, Louise Gagnon-Gaudreault
- **Laboratoire de sciences judiciaires et de médecine légale/Forensic Science:** 1701, rue Parthenais, 5e étage, CP 1500, Succ C, Montréal PQ H2L 4K6 – 514/873-2704; Fax: 514/873-4847

Directeur, Yves Ste-Marie
- **Régie des alcools, des courses et des jeux/Liquor, Gaming & Racing Board:** 1, rue Notre-Dame est, Montréal PQ H2Y 1B6 – 514/873-3577; Fax: 514/864-9664

Président, Ghislain K. Laflamme
- **Service de médecine légale/Legal Medicine:** 1701, rue Parthenais, 5e étage, CP 1500, Succ C, Montréal PQ H2K 3S7 – 514/873-3300; Fax: 514/873-4847

Chef de service, Dr. André Lauzon
- **Sûreté du Québec/Provincial Police:** 1701, rue Parthenais, Montréal PQ H2L 4K7 – 514/598-4488; Fax: 514/598-4957

Directeur général, Serge Barbeau
Directrice générale associée, Administration, Louise Pagé, 514/598-4545, Fax: 514/596-3681
Directeur général adjoint, Enquêtes criminelles et supports techniques, André Dupré, 514/598-4422, Fax: 514/596-3688
Directeur général adjoint, Planification et téchnologie, Gilles Falardeau, 514/598-4411, Fax: 514/598-4398
Directeur général adjoint, Surveillance du territoire, Georges Boilard, 514/598-4747, Fax: 514/598-4957
Directeur, Communications, Capt. Denis Fiset, 514/598-4848, Fax: 514/598-4917
Directeur, Ethique professionnelle, Insp.-chef Jacques Letendre, 514/598-4900, Fax: 514/598-4886
Directeur, Vérification et contrôle de gestion, Insp.-chef Claude Chagnon, 514/596-3545, Fax: 514/598-4886

Ministère de la SÉCURITÉ DU REVENU/ Ministry of Income Security
425, rue St-Amable, 1er étage, Québec PQ G1R 4Z1
418/643-9818; Fax: 418/646-5426; URL: http://www.gouv.qc.ca/francais/minorg/msp/msp_intro.html
Toll Free: 1-800-361-4743
Montréal: 255, boul Crémazie est, Montréal PQ H2M 1L5

ACTS ADMINISTERED
An Act respecting family assistance allowance
An Act respecting income security
An Act respecting income security for Cree hunters & trappers who are beneficiaries under the Agreement concerning James Bay & Northern Québec
An Act respecting supplementary pension plans
An Act respecting the Commission des affaires sociales
An Act respecting the Ministère de la Sécurité du revenu
An Act respecting the Québec Pension Plan
Supplemental Pension Plans Act
Ministre, Louise Harel, 418/643-4810, Fax: 418/643-2802

Sous-ministre, Michel Noël de Tilly, 418/643-4820, Fax: 418/643-1226
Sous-ministre adjointe, Politiques et des programmes, Suzanne Lévesque, 416/643-9483, Fax: 416/643-0019
Sous ministre adjoint, Réseau Travail-Québec, Claude Simard, 418/643-3390, Fax: 418/644-4599
Directeur général, Administration, Alain Deroy, 418/643-5568, Fax: 418/646-6436
Directeur général et Sous-ministre adjoint, Politiques et programmes, Suzanne Lévesque, 418/643-9483, Fax: 418/643-0019
Directeur général et sous-ministre adjoint, Réseau travail-Québec, Claude B. Simard, 418/643-3390, Fax: 418/644-4599
Directeur général, Technologies de l'Information, André Blondin, 418/646-2876, Fax: 418/644-0120

Associated Agencies, Boards & Commissions
- Office de la sécurité de revenu des chasseurs et piégeurs Cris/Cree Hunters & Trappers Income Security Board: Tour Frontenac, #703, 2700, boul Laurier, Ste-Foy PQ G1V 2L8 – 418/643-7300; Fax: 418/643-6803

Président, Marcel Lesyk
- Régie des rentes/Québec Pension Board: 2600, boul Laurier, Ste-Foy PQ G1V 4T3 – 418/643-8302; Fax: 418/643-9586

Président, Claude Legault

TOURISME QUÉBEC/Tourism Québec
#329, 2, Place Québec, Québec PQ G1R 2B5
418/643-5959; Fax: 418/646-8723; URL: http://www.gouv.qc.ca/francais/minorg/mto/mto_intro.html
Toll Free: 1-800-363-7777 (Tourism Information)
CP 979, Montréal PQ H3C 2W3
514/873-2015, Fax: 514/864-3838

ACTS ADMINISTERED
Loi sur les établissements touristiques (Tourism Establishments)
Ministre déléguée, Industrie et Commerce, Rita Dionne-Marsolais, 418/691-5650, Fax: 418/643-8553
Sous-ministre associée, Tourisme, Lucillee Daoust, 418/643-9141, Fax: 418/643-8499
Directeur, Communications, Marcel Gilbert, 418/643-5959, Fax: 418/646-8723
Note: Tourism representatives are also located in Atlanta, Boston, Chicago, Los Angeles, Brussels, Dusseldorf, London, New York, Paris, Tokyo, & Toronto.
See listings for the Ministry of International Affairs, Immigration & Cultural Communities for addresses.

Associated Agencies, Boards & Commissions
- Société du Centre des congrès de Québec/Québec Convention Centre: #214, 900 boul René-Lévesque est, Québec PQ G1R 2B5 – 418/644-4000; Fax: 418/644-6455

Président et Directeur général (par intérim), François Noël

Ministère des TRANSPORTS (MTQ)/ Ministry of Transportation
700, boul René-Lévesque est, Québec PQ G1R 5H1
418/643-6740; URL: http://www.gouv.qc.ca/francais/minorg/mtrans/mtrans_intro.html

ACTS ADMINISTERED
Loi sur l'assurance automobile
Loi sur les autoroutes
Loi sur les chemins de colonisation
Loi sur les chemins de fer
Code de la sécurité routière
Loi sur les conseils intermunicipaux de transport dans la région de Montréal

Loi sur les corporations municipales & intermunicipales de transport
Loi sur l'expropriation
Loi sur l'indemnisation des victimes d'accidents d'automobiles
Loi sur le ministère des Transports
Loi sur la Société de l'assurance automobile du Québec
Loi sur la Société des traversiers du Québec
Loi sur la Société québécoise des transports
Loi sur le transport par taxi
Loi sur les transports
Loi sur la voirie
Loi sur l'instruction publique (transport des écoliers)
Loi sur la Société de transport de la ville de Laval
Loi sur la Société de transport de la rive Sud de Montréal
Loi sur le camionnage
Loi sur la publicité de long des routes
Ministre, Jacques Brassard, 418/643-6980, Fax: 418/643-2033
Secrétaire du ministère, Pierre Perron
Sous-ministre, Yvan Demers, Fax: 418/643-9836
Sous-ministre adjoint, Planification et technologie, Liguori Hinse, 418/528-0808
Sous-ministre adjoint, Services à la gestion, Jean Mercier, 418/528-0808
Sous-ministre adjoint, Est, Alain Vallières, 418/528-0808, Fax: 418/643-9836
Sous-ministre adjoint, Montréal, Yvon Tourigny, 418/528-0808
Sous-ministre adjoint, Ouest, Luc Crépeault, 418/528-0808
Sous-ministre adjointe, Québec, Micheline Lafrançois, 418/528-0808, Fax: 418/643-9836
Chef de service, Vérification interne, Marcel Plante, 418/643-6591, Fax: 418/643-1269
Directeur, Affaires juridiques, Michel Lalande, 418/643-6937, Fax: 418/643-3980
Directrice adjointe, Affaires juridiques, Huguette Pagé, 418/643-6937, Fax: 418/643-3980

Associated Agencies, Boards & Commissions
- Commission des Transports du Québec/Transport Commission: 200, ch Ste-Foy, 7e étage, Québec PQ G1R 5V5 – 418/644-6041; Fax: 418/643-7404

Président, Louis Gravel
- Conseil de la Recherche et du développement en transport/Transportation Research & Development: #300, 6455, av Christophe-Colomb, Montréal PQ H2S 2G5 – 514/274-3573; Fax: 514/274-9608

Président, Gérard Laganière
Secrétaire général, André Marcil
- Société de l'assurance automobile du Québec/Québec Auto Insurance: 333, boul Jean-Lesage, CP 19600, Québec PQ G1K 8J6 – 418/528-3100; Fax: 418/644-0339

Président et Directeur général, Jean-Yves Gagnon
- Société du port ferroviaire Baie-Comeau-Hauterive/Baie-Comeau-Hauterive Railway Station: 28, Place La Salle, CP 135, Baie-Comeau PQ G4Z 2G9 – 418/296-6785

Président, Jean-Guy Rousseau
- Société québécoise des transports du Québec/Québec Transportation Board: 35, rue de Port-Royal est, Montréal PQ H3L 3T1 – 514/864-1664; Fax: 514/873-7389

Directeur général, Yvan Demers
- Société traversiers du Québec/Ferries Québec: 109, rue Dalhousie, Québec PQ G1K 9A1 – 418/643-2019; Fax: 418/643-7308

Président et Directeur général, Jean-Yves Gagnon

Ministère du TRAVAIL/ Employment Ministry
200, ch Ste-Foy, 6e étage, Québec PQ G1R 5S1
418/643-4817; Fax: 418/644-6969; URL: http://www.travail.gouv.qc.ca/

ACTS ADMINISTERED
Act respecting collective agreement decrees
Act respecting the Ministère du travail
Act respecting the process of negotiating of the collective agreements in the public & parapublic sectors

Acts Administered by Labour Agencies
Act respecting building contractors vocational qualifications
Act respecting complementary social benefits plans in the construction industry
Act respecting electrical installations
Act respecting indemnities for victims of asbestosis or silicosis in mines & quarries
Act respecting industrial accidents & occupational diseases
Act respecting labour relations vocational training & manpower management in the construction industry
Act respecting labour standards
Act respecting manpower vocational training & qualification
Act respecting occupational health & safety
Act respecting piping installations
Act respecting pressure vessels
Act respecting the Conseil consultatif du travail et de la main d'oeuvre
Act respecting the conservation of energy in buildings
Building Act
Master Electricians Act
Master Pipe Mechanics Act
National Holiday Act
Public Buildings Safety Act
Stationary Enginemen Act
Workmen's Compensation Act

Ministre, Matthias Rioux, 418/643-5297, Fax: 418/644-0003
Sous-ministre, Jean-Marc Boily, 418/643-2902, Fax: 418/643-3069
Sous-ministre adjoint, Administration, Pierre Boisvert, 418/643-9004
Sous-ministre adjoint, Planification, recherches et construction, Jacques Henry, 418/643-2902
Sous-ministre adjoint, Relations de travail, Normand Gauthier, 514/873-4678
Secrétaire du Ministère, Christine Barbe, 418/643-2902

Associated Agencies, Boards & Commissions
• Commission de la Construction du Québec/Construction Commission: 3530, Jean-Talon ouest, Montréal PQ H3R 2G3 – 514/341-7740; Fax: 514/341-6354
Président, André Ménard
• Commission des normes du travail/Labour Standards Commission: 400, boul Jean-Lesage, Québec PQ G1K 8W1 – Fax: 514/864-4711, Toll Free: 1-800-265-1414
Président, Jean-Guy Rivard
• Commission de la santé et de la sécurité du travail du Québec (CSST)/Occupational Health & Safety Commission: 1199, rue de Bleury, CP 6056, Succ Centre-Ville, Montréal PQ H3C 4E1 – 514/873-7183; Fax: 514/873-7007; Email: lbeaudoi@riq.qc.ca
Président & chef des opérations, Pierre Gabrièle
Directeur, Bureau du président, Gilles Beauchesne, 418/646-3234
Secrétaire-Général, Pierre Lafrance
Secrétaire général adjoint, Michel Brunet
Directeur général, Planification (Strategic Planning), Pierre Rhéaume
Directeur général, Systèmes, Gérard Bélanger
Vice-président, Finances, Roland Longchamps, 418/646-0496

Vice-président, Opérations, Gérard Bibeau, 418/646-1456
Vice-président, Programmation et expertise-conseil, Alain Albert, 418/646-4057
Vice-président, Relations avec les clientèles et les partenaires, Donald Brisson, 418/644-6083
Vice-présidente, Services, Lynda Durand, 418/646-4057
Directrice, Communications, Richard Thériault
Directeur, Indemnisation des victimes d'actes criminels (Crime Victims Compensati, Rolande Couture
Directrice, Review Office, Micheline Bélanger
Directeur, Services juridiques - Montréal (Legal Services), Yves Panneton
Directeur, Services juridiques - Québec (Legal Services), Pierre Lessard
Directeur, Services médicaux (Medical Services), Colette Fourtier
Responsable, Affaires publiques, Jacques Millette
• Conseil consultatif du travail & de la main d'oeuvre/Advisory Council on Labour & Manpower: #2026, 800, Tour de la Place Victoria, CP 87, Montréal PQ H4Z 1B7 – 514/873-2880; Fax: 514/873-1129
Président, Yves Dulude
• Conseil des services essentiels/Essential Services Council: #2771, 5199, rue Sherbrooke est, Montréal PQ H1T 3X1 – 514/873-7246; Fax: 514/873-3839
Présidente, Madeleine Lemieux
• Institut de recherche & d'information sur la rémunération: #1220, 500, rue Sherbrooke ouest, Montréal PQ H3A 3C6 – 514/288-1394; Fax: 514/288-3536
Présidente, Nicole P. Poupart
• Régie du bâtiment du Québec/Québec Construction Companies Board: 545, boul Crémazie est, Montréal PQ H2M 2V2 – 514/873-0976; Fax: 514/873-7667, Toll Free: 1-800-361-0761
Président, Jean-Claude Riendeau
• Société québécoise de développement de la main-d'oeuvre/Québec Manpower Development: 425, rue St-Amable, Québec PQ G1R 2C5 – 418/643-1892; Fax: 418/643-1714
Présidente, Diane Bellemare

Conseil du TRÉSOR/Treasury Board
Edifice H, 4e étage, 875, Grande Allée est, Québec PQ G1R 5R8
418/643-5926; Fax: 418/643-7824; URL: http://www.riq.qc.ca/scthtml/sct.htm
Secrétariat du conseil du trésor: 418/643-1977; Fax: 418/643-6494

ACTS ADMINISTERED
Loi sur l'emblème aviaire (provincial bird emblem)
Loi sur les services gouvernementaux aux ministères et organismes publics et modifiant diverses dispositions légales (ministries & government organizations)
Loi sur le Services des achats du gouvernement (government purchasing)

Président, Jacques Léonard
Secrétaire, Pierre Roy, 418/643-1977, Fax: 418/643-6494
Secrétaire adjoint, Politiques, Bruno Grégoire, 418/643-1977, Fax: 418/643-4877
Secrétaire associé, Politiques de gestion, Jacques Lafrance, 418/643-9383, Fax: 418/643-4877
Secrétaire associé, Politiques de gestion des technologies de l'information, Jacques S. Roy, 418/643-4482, Fax: 418/644-8528
Secrétaire associé, Ressources humaines, Maurice Charlebois, 418/643-4482, Fax: 418/644-8528
Directeur, Communications, Démosthène Blasi, 418/643-1529, Fax: 418/643-9226

SERVICES GOUVERNEMENTAUX/Government Services
Édifice Lomer-Gouin, 575, rue St-Amable, Québec PQ G1R 5N9
418/643-1529; Fax: 418/643-9226
Secrétaire associé, Jean-Claude Careau, 418/643-2993, Fax: 418/646-4895
Directeur, par intérim, Affaires juridiques, André Samson, 418/691-5964, Fax: 418/528-2338
Directeur, Fichier, Denis Corriveau, 418/644-6249, Fax: 418/643-7544

Administration
Directeur général, Roland Guérin, 418/643-8760, Fax: 418/646-1089
Directeur, Ressources financières, Yvan Bouchard, 418/643-8760, Fax: 418/646-1089
Directeur, Ressources humaines, Jean-Louis Laberge, 418/643-3092, Fax: 418/643-5881
Directeur, Ressources informationnelles, Richard Sirois, 418/643-3918, Fax: 418/646-9880
Directeur, Ressources matérielles, Roland Cloutier, 418/643-6017, Fax: 418/643-6006

Approvisionnements/Purchasing
Édifice Cyrille-Duquette, 1500 H, boul Charest ouest, Ste-Foy PQ G1N 4T5
Secrétaire adjoint, Michel Gagnon, 418/643-3395, Fax: 418/646-5457
Directrice, Acquisitions, Renée M. Beaulieu, 418/643-5457, Fax: 418/643-9192
Directeur, Equipements informatiques, Jacques Darveau, 418/643-3592, Fax: 418/644-2872
Directeur, Fournitures et de l'ameublement, Claude Denis, 418/643-7577, Fax: 418/643-4076
Directeur, Reprographie gouvernementale, Michel C. Tanguay, 418/643-5038, Fax: 418/646-7507

Communication-Québec
1500-C, boul Charest Ouest, 1er étage, Ste-Foy PQ G1N 2E5
418/643-1430; Fax: 418/643-5190
This office is the general information service of the provincial government.
Directrice générale, Marcelle Girard
Directrice, Services centraux, Lise Monette, 418/644-0382

Information gouvernementale/Communication Services
Directrice générale, Marcelle Girard, 418/644-7789, Fax: 418/643-6177
Directeur, Distribution, Roger Hakim, 418/643-1804, Fax: 418/643-6177
Directeur, Edition gouvernementale, Jean-Pierre Lemonde, 418/644-3228, Fax: 418/644-7813
Directeur, Information documentaire, François C. Reny, 418/643-1515, Fax: 418/646-8132
Directeur, Moyens de communication, Maurice Arguin, 418/644-2866, Fax: 418/643-7432

Services aériens et postaux/Postal Services
Directeur général, Gaston Couillard, 418/877-8383, Fax: 418/871-5313
Directeur, Courrier et messagerie, Pierre-André Dupont, 418/644-8902, Fax: 418/646-3660

Services informatiques gouvernementaux/Technical Services
Directeur général, Bernard Beauchemin, 418/644-6108, Fax: 418/646-0988
Directeur, Connexité et gestion des plates-formes mini et réseaux, Paul Lessard, 418/643-5800, Fax: 418/646-0988
Directeur, Opérations, Jean Pellerin, 418/644-4913, Fax: 418/646-0988
Directeur, Planification et gestion, Michel Rochette, Fax: 418/646-0988
Directrice, Services à la clientèle, Danielle Ferland, 418/644-7588, Fax: 418/646-0988

Directeur, Services conseils en informatique, Jacques Proulx, 418/644-1866, Fax: 418/646-0988
Directeur, Soutien technique, Michel Rosciszewski, 418/644-1862, Fax: 418/646-0988

Télécommunications
Directeur général, Raynald Brulotte, 418/643-7774, Fax: 418/646-3566
Directeur, Architecture des réseaux, Roland Grenier, 418/643-2912, Fax: 418/646-3566
Chef de service, Communications radio, René Dagnault, 418/643-4365, Fax: 418/643-0998
Chef de service, Informatiqes, Marcel W. Landry, 418/644-6111, Fax: 418/646-3566
Directeur, Services administratifs, Jacques A. Bilodeau, 418/646-7606, Fax: 418/646-3566
Directeur, Service á la clientéle, Laval Girard, 418/643-2196, Fax: 418/646-3566

Associated Agencies, Boards & Commissions
•Commission de la fonction publique: 8, rue Cook, Québec PQ G1R 5J8 – 418/643-1425; Fax: 418/643-7264
Président, Michel Paquet
•Commission administrative des régimes de retraite & d'assurances: 2875, boul Laurier, 2e étage, Ste-Foy PQ G1V 4J8 – 418/644-8661; Fax: 418/646-8721
Président, Michel Sanschagrin
•Office des ressources humaines
Listed alphabetically in detail, this Section.
•Société immobilière du Québec/Québec Buildings Corp.: 475, rue St-Amable, Québec PQ G1R 4X9 – 418/646-1766 poste 3470; Fax: 418/643-7932
Président et Directeur général, Jean P. Vézina
•Société Parc-autos du Québec métropolitain/Automobile Parking: 17, rue St-Louis, Québec PQ G1R 3Y8 – 418/692-3990; Fax: 418/692-0569
Président et Directeur général, Marc Fortier

VÉRIFICATEUR GÉNÉRAL DU QUÉBEC/ Auditor General
#6.00, 900, Place d'Youville, Québec PQ G1R 3P7
418/691-5900; Fax: 418/646-1307; URL: http://www.sgo.gouv.qc.ca/vgq
Vérificateur général, Guy Breton, 418/691-5901, Email: gbreton@vqg.gouv.qc.ca
Vérificateur général adjoint, Gilles Bédard, 418/691-5903
Vérificateur général adjoint, Jacques Henrichon, 418/691-5904
Directeur, Louis-Phillippe Fiset, 418/691-5930

GOVERNMENT OF SASKATCHEWAN

Seat of Government: Legislative Bldg., Regina SK S4S 0B3
306/781-0222; URL: http://www.gov.sk.ca/
Toll Free: 1-800-667-0666
  The Province of Saskatchewan entered Confederation on September 1, 1905. It has an area of 651,900 km2, and the StatsCan census population in 1991 was 988,928.

Office of the LIEUTENANT GOVERNOR
Government House, 4607 Dewdney Ave., Regina SK S4P 3V7
306/787-4070; Fax: 306/787-7716
Lieutenant Governor, Hon. J.E.N. Wiebe
Private Secretary, Irene White

Office of the PREMIER
2405 Legislative Dr., Regina SK S4S 0B3
306/787-9433; Fax: 306/787-0885; URL: http://www.sasknet.sk.ca
Premier, Hon. Roy Romanow, Q.C., Email: premier@sasknet.sk.ca
Acting Chief of Staff, Judy Samuelson, 306/787-1902
Special Advisor, Carlo Binda
Director, Correspondence, Donna Easto, 306/787-1914
Deputy Premier, Hon. Dwain Lingenfelter

EXECUTIVE COUNCIL
Legislative Bldg., Regina SK S4S 0B3
URL: http://www.gov.sk.ca/execcoun/cabinet.htm#nillson
Premier & President, Executive Council, Hon. Roy Romanow, Q.C., 306/787-0958, Fax: 306/787-0885
Minister, Education, Hon. Patricia Atkinson, 306/787-1684, Fax: 306/787-0237
Minister, Social Services, Hon. Lorne Calvert, 306/787-7363, Fax: 306/787-0656
Minister, Health, Hon. Eric Cline, 306/787-7347, Fax: 306/787-8677
Minister, Indian & Métis Affairs & Minister Responsible, Status of Women & Gaming Authority, Hon. Joanne Crofford, 306/787-0354, Fax: 306/787-2202
Minister, Northern Affairs, Hon. Keith N. Goulet, 306/787-1885, Fax: 306/787-0399
Minister, Energy & Mines, Hon. Eldon Lautermilch, 306/787-0605, Fax: 306/787-8100
Deputy Premier & Minister, Economic Development, Hon. Dwain Lingenfelter, 306/787-9124, Fax: 306/787-9135
Minister, Finance, Hon. Janice MacKinnon, 306/787-6059, Fax: 306/787-6055
Minister, Post-Secondary Education & Skills Training & Minister, Labour, Hon. Robert W. Mitchell, Q.C., 306/787-0659, Fax: 306/787-6946
Minister, Justice & Attorney General, Hon. John Nilson, Q.C., 306/787-0613, Fax: 306/787-1232
Minister, Highways & Transportation, Hon. Andy Renaud, 306/787-6478, Fax: 306/787-6499
Minister, Environment & Resource Management, Hon. Lorne Scott, 306/787-8824, Fax: 306/787-0395
Minister, Responsible for Saskatchewan Property Management (Corporation), Liquor & Gaming, & Saskatchewan Government Insurance, Hon. Clay Serby, 306/787-7387, Fax: 306/787-8747
Provincial Secretary & Minister, Intergovernmental Relations, Hon. Ned Shillington, 306/787-0365, Fax: 306/787-1669
Minister, Municipal Government, Hon. Carol Teichrob, 306/787-0623, Fax: 306/787-0630
Minister, Agriculture & Food, Hon. Eric Upshall, 306/787-0338, Fax: 306/787-1094
Minister, Crown Investments Corporation, Hon. Berny Wiens, 306/787-0394, Fax: 306/787-8487

Department of Executive Council
#135, Legislative Bldg., Regina SK S4S OB3
Fax: 306/787-8338
Cabinet Secretary & Deputy Minister to the Premier, Frank Bogdasavich, 306/787-6338

Cabinet Secretariat
#32, Legislative Bldg., Regina SK S4S 0B3
Fax: 306/787-8299
Acting Clerk, Executive Council & Asst. Cabinet Secretary, Lois Thacyk, 306/787-9621

Chief of Staff's Office
#110, Legislative Bldg., Regina SK S4S 0B3
Fax: 306/787-0883
Acting Chief of Staff, Judy Samuelson, 306/787-1902

Policy & Planning Secretariat
#37, Legislative Bldg., Regina SK S4S 0B3
Fax: 306/787-0012
Associate Deputy Minister to the Premier, Marianne Weston, 306/787-6339

Cabinet Standing Committees
Economic Development Centre, Secretary, Clare Kirkland
Legislative Review, Secretary, Sandra Morgan
Orders in Council Review, Secretary, Sandra Morgan
Planning & Priorities, Secretary, Marianne Weston
Public Sector Bargaining Compensation, Secretary, Michael Shaw
Regulations Review, Secretary, Lois Thacyk
Treasury Board, Secretary, Bill Jones

LEGISLATIVE ASSEMBLY
c/o Clerk's Office, #239, Legislative Bldg., Regina SK S4S 0B3
306/787-2279; Fax: 306/787-0408; URL: http://www.gov.sk.ca/members.htm
Clerk: Gwenn Ronyk, 306/787-2374
Speaker: Hon. Glenn Hagel, 306/787-2282
Sergeant-at-Arms: Patrick Shaw, 306/787-2184
Director, Hansard: Susan Hope, 306/787-2290
Librarian, Legislative Library: Marian Powell, 306/787-2277
Director, Personnel & Administrative Services, Linda Kaminski, 306/787-2338
Director, Broadcast Services, H. Gary Ward, 306/787-2181
Clerk Asst. (Journals), Rose Zerr, 306/787-3992
Legislative Counsel & Law Clerk, Robert Cosman, 306/787-8984

Government Caucus Office (NDP)
#203, Legislative Bldg., Regina SK S4S 0B3
306/787-7388; Fax: 306/787-6247; Email: caucus@sasknet.sk.ca; URL: http://www.sasknet.com/ZX-ndpmla/
Chief of Staff, Jim Fodey
Director, Administration, Gail Fehr

Office of the Official Opposition (Lib.)
#265, Legislative Bldg., Regina SK S4S 0B3
306/787-0860; Fax: 306/787-0250
Leader, Ron Osika
Chief of Caucus Administration, Vacant, 306/787-0860
Deputy Leader, Buckley Belanger

Office of the Third Party (PC)
#140, Legislative Bldg., Regina SK S4S 0B3
306/787-5302; Fax: 306/787-5303; URL: http://www.wbm.ca/actionet/pc/
Leader, Bill Boyd, Email: billboyd@sasknet.sk.ca
Chief of Staff, Reg Downs
Director, Communications, Kathy Peter
Researcher, Lyle Hewitt

Standing Committees of the Legislature
Agriculture
Communication
Constitutional Affairs
Continuing Select
Crown Corporations
Education
Environment
Estimates
Municipal Law
Non-Controversial Bills
Private Members' Bills
Privileges & Elections
Public Accounts

Special Committees of the Legislature
Nominating
Regulations
Rules & Procedures

TWENTY-SECOND LEGISLATURE - SASKATCHEWAN

306/787-2279

Last General Election, June 21, 1995. Maximum Duration 5 Years.
Party Standings (August 1, 1995):
New Democratic Party (NDP) 41
Liberal (Lib.) 10
Progressive Conservative (PC) 5
Independent (Ind.) 1
Vacancy 1
Total 58

Salaries, Indemnities & Allowances: Members' indemnity & expense allowance $59,500. In addition to this are the following:
Premier $49,680
Deputy Premier $39,744
Ministers $34,776
Leader of the Opposition $34,776
Leader of the third Party $17,390
Speaker $29,808
Deputy Speaker $9,936

Following is: constituency, member, party affiliation. (Address for all is 2405 Legislature Dr., Regina SK S4S 0B3.)

MEMBERS BY CONSTITUENCY

Arm River, Harvey McLane, Lib., 306/787-7530, Fax: 306/787-0250
Athabasca, Buckley Belanger, Lib., 306/787-7585, Fax: 306/787-0250
Battleford-Cut Knife, Sharon Murrell, NDP, 306/787-1837, Fax: 306/787-6247
Cannington, Dan D'Autremont, PC, 306/787-5302, Fax: 306/787-5303
Canora-Pelly, Ken Krawetz, Lib., 306/787-7550, Fax: 306/787-0250
Carrot River Valley, Hon. Andy Renaud, NDP, 306/787-6447, Fax: 306/787-6499
Cumberland, Hon. Keith N. Goulet, NDP, 306/787-1885, Fax: 306/787-0399
Cypress Hills, Jack Goohsen, PC, 306/787-5302, Fax: 306/787-5303
Estevan, Larry Ward, NDP, 306/787-1833, Fax: 306/787-6247
Humboldt, Arlene Jule, Lib., 306/787-7583, Fax: 306/787-0250
Indian Head-Milestone, Hon. Lorne Scott, NDP, 306/787-0393, Fax: 306/787-0395
Kelvington-Wadena, June Draude, Lib., 306/787-7501, Fax: 306/787-0250
Kindersley, Bill Boyd, PC, 306/787-9434, Fax: 306/787-5303
Last Mountain-Touchwood, Dale Flavel, NDP, 306/787-0935, Fax: 306/787-6247
Lloydminster, Violet Stanger, NDP, 306/787-0898, Fax: 306/787-6247
Meadow Lake, Maynard Sonntag, NDP, 306/787-0894, Fax: 306/787-6247
Melfort-Tisdale, Rod Gantefoer, Lib., 306/787-7511, Fax: 306/787-0250
Melville, Ron Osika, Lib., 306/787-0860, Fax: 306/787-0250
Moose Jaw North, Hon. Glenn Hagel, NDP, 306/787-2282, Fax: 306/787-2283
Moose Jaw Wakamow, Hon. Lorne Calvert, NDP, 306/787-3661, Fax: 306/787-0656
Moosomin, Donald J. Toth, PC, 306/787-5302, Fax: 306/787-5303
North Battleford, Vacant,
Prince Albert Carlton, Myron Kowalsky, NDP, 306/787-1888, Fax: 306/787-6247
Prince Albert Northcote, Hon. Eldon Lautermilch, NDP, 306/787-0615, Fax: 306/787-8100
Redberry Lake, Walter Jess, NDP, 306/787-0937, Fax: 306/787-6247
Regina Centre, Hon. Joanne Crofford, NDP, 306/787-2207, Fax: 306/787-2202
Regina Coronation Park, Kim Trew, NDP, 306/787-1898, Fax: 306/787-6247
Regina Dewdney, Ed Tchorzewski, NDP, 306/787-7979, Fax: 306/787-6247
Regina Elphinstone, Hon. Dwain Lingenfelter, NDP, 306/787-9124, Fax: 306/787-9135
Regina Lakeview, Hon. John Nilson, Q.C., NDP, 306/787-5353, Fax: 306/787-1232
Regina Northeast, Hon. Ned Shillington, NDP, 306/787-0365, Fax: 306/787-1669
Regina Qu'Appelle Valley, Suzanne Murray, NDP, 306/787-0899, Fax: 306/787-6247
Regina Sherwood, Lindy Kasperski, NDP, 306/787-1802, Fax: 306/787-6247
Regina South, Andrew Thomson, NDP, 306/787-1827, Fax: 306/787-6247
Regina Victoria, Harry Van Mulligen, NDP, 306/787-1900, Fax: 306/787-6247
Regina Wascana Plains, Doreen Hamilton, NDP, 306/787-0891, Fax: 306/787-6247
Rosetown-Biggar, Hon. Berny Wiens, NDP, 306/787-6944, Fax: 306/787-8487
Rosthern, Ben Heppner, PC, 306/787-5302, Fax: 306/787-5303
Saltcoats, Bob Bjornerud, Lib., 306/787-7527, Fax: 306/787-0250
Saskatchewan Rivers, Jack Langford, NDP, 306/787-0985, Fax: 306/787-6247
Saskatoon Eastview, Bob Pringle, NDP, 306/787-8802, Fax: 306/787-6247
Saskatoon Fairview, Hon. Robert W. Mitchell, Q.C., NDP, 306/787-6662, Fax: 306/787-6946
Saskatoon Greystone, Lynda Haverstock, Ind., 306/787-7731, Fax: 306/787-4232
Saskatoon Idylwyld, Hon. Janice MacKinnon, NDP, 306/787-6060, Fax: 306/787-6055
Saskatoon Meewasin, Hon. Carol Teichrob, NDP, 306/787-6100, Fax: 306/787-0630
Saskatoon Mount Royal, Hon. Eric Cline, NDP, 306/787-7345, Fax: 306/787-8677
Saskatoon Northwest, Grant Whitmore, NDP, 306/787-0766, Fax: 306/787-6247
Saskatoon Nutana, Hon. Patricia Atkinson, NDP, 306/787-7360, Fax: 306/787-0237
Saskatoon Riversdale, Hon. Roy Romanow, Q.C., NDP, 306/787-9433, Fax: 306/787-0885
Saskatoon Southeast, Pat Lorje, NDP, 306/787-0895, Fax: 306/787-6247
Saskatoon Sutherland, Mark Koenker, NDP, 306/787-1887, Fax: 306/787-6247
Shellbrook-Spiritwood, Lloyd Johnson, NDP, 306/787-0931, Fax: 306/787-6247
Swift Current, John Wall, NDP, 306/787-0936, Fax: 306/787-6247
Thunder Creek, Gerard Aldridge, Lib., 306/787-7518, Fax: 306/787-0250
Watrous, Hon. Eric Upshall, NDP, 306/787-0338, Fax: 306/787-1094
Weyburn-Big Muddy, Judy Bradley, NDP, 306/787-0897
Wood River, Glen McPherson, Lib., 306/787-0896, Fax: 306/787-0250
Yorkton, Hon. Clay Serby, NDP, 306/787-1889, Fax: 306/787-8747

MEMBERS (ALPHABETICAL)

Gerard Aldridge, Thunder Creek Lib., 306/787-7518, Fax: 306/787-0250
Hon. Patricia Atkinson, Saskatoon Nutana NDP, 306/787-7360, Fax: 306/787-0237
Buckley Belanger, Athabasca Lib., 306/787-7585, Fax: 306/787-0250
Bob Bjornerud, Saltcoats Lib., 306/787-7527, Fax: 306/787-0250
Bill Boyd, Kindersley PC, 306/787-9434, Fax: 306/787-5303
Judy Bradley, Weyburn-Big Muddy NDP, 306/787-0897
Hon. Lorne Calvert, Moose Jaw Wakamow NDP, 306/787-3661, Fax: 306/787-0656
Hon. Eric Cline, Saskatoon Mount Royal NDP, 306/787-7345, Fax: 306/787-8677
Hon. Joanne Crofford, Regina Centre NDP, 306/787-2207, Fax: 306/787-2202
Dan D'Autremont, Cannington PC, 306/787-5302, Fax: 306/787-5303
June Draude, Kelvington-Wadena Lib., 306/787-7501, Fax: 306/787-0250
Dale Flavel, Last Mountain-Touchwood NDP, 306/787-0935, Fax: 306/787-6247
Rod Gantefoer, Melfort-Tisdale Lib., 306/787-7511, Fax: 306/787-0250
Jack Goohsen, Cypress Hills PC, 306/787-5302, Fax: 306/787-5303
Hon. Keith N. Goulet, Cumberland NDP, 306/787-1885, Fax: 306/787-0399
Hon. Glenn Hagel, Moose Jaw North NDP, 306/787-2282, Fax: 306/787-2283
Doreen Hamilton, Regina Wascana Plains NDP, 306/787-0891, Fax: 306/787-6247
Lynda Haverstock, Saskatoon Greystone Ind., 306/787-7731, Fax: 306/787-4232
Ben Heppner, Rosthern PC, 306/787-5302, Fax: 306/787-5303
Walter Jess, Redberry Lake NDP, 306/787-0937, Fax: 306/787-6247
Lloyd Johnson, Shellbrook-Spiritwood NDP, 306/787-0931, Fax: 306/787-6247
Arlene Jule, Humboldt Lib., 306/787-7583, Fax: 306/787-0250
Lindy Kasperski, Regina Sherwood NDP, 306/787-1802, Fax: 306/787-6247
Mark Koenker, Saskatoon Sutherland NDP, 306/787-1887, Fax: 306/787-6247
Myron Kowalsky, Prince Albert Carlton NDP, 306/787-1888, Fax: 306/787-6247
Ken Krawetz, Canora-Pelly Lib., 306/787-7550, Fax: 306/787-0250
Jack Langford, Saskatchewan Rivers NDP, 306/787-0985, Fax: 306/787-6247
Hon. Eldon Lautermilch, Prince Albert Northcote NDP, 306/787-0615, Fax: 306/787-8100
Hon. Dwain Lingenfelter, Regina Elphinstone NDP, 306/787-9124, Fax: 306/787-9135
Pat Lorje, Saskatoon Southeast NDP, 306/787-0895, Fax: 306/787-6247
Hon. Janice MacKinnon, Saskatoon Idylwyld NDP, 306/787-6060, Fax: 306/787-6055
Harvey McLane, Arm River Lib., 306/787-7530, Fax: 306/787-0250
Glen McPherson, Wood River Lib., 306/787-0896, Fax: 306/787-0250
Hon. Robert W. Mitchell, Q.C., Saskatoon Fairview NDP, 306/787-6662, Fax: 306/787-6946
Suzanne Murray, Regina Qu'Appelle Valley NDP, 306/787-0899, Fax: 306/787-6247
Sharon Murrell, Battleford-Cut Knife NDP, 306/787-1837, Fax: 306/787-6247
Hon. John Nilson, Q.C., Regina Lakeview NDP, 306/787-5353, Fax: 306/787-1232
Ron Osika, Melville Lib., 306/787-0860, Fax: 306/787-0250
Bob Pringle, Saskatoon Eastview NDP, 306/787-8802, Fax: 306/787-6247
Hon. Andy Renaud, Carrot River Valley NDP, 306/787-6447, Fax: 306/787-6499
Hon. Roy Romanow, Q.C., Saskatoon Riversdale NDP, 306/787-9433, Fax: 306/787-0885
Hon. Lorne Scott, Indian Head-Milestone NDP, 306/787-0393, Fax: 306/787-0395
Hon. Clay Serby, Yorkton NDP, 306/787-1889, Fax: 306/787-8747
Hon. Ned Shillington, Regina Northeast NDP, 306/787-0365, Fax: 306/787-1669
Maynard Sonntag, Meadow Lake NDP, 306/787-0894, Fax: 306/787-6247

Violet Stanger, Lloydminster NDP, 306/787-0898, Fax: 306/787-6247
Ed Tchorzewski, Regina Dewdney NDP, 306/787-7979, Fax: 306/787-6247
Hon. Carol Teichrob, Saskatoon Meewasin NDP, 306/787-6100, Fax: 306/787-0630
Andrew Thomson, Regina South NDP, 306/787-1827, Fax: 306/787-6247
Donald J. Toth, Moosomin PC, 306/787-5302, Fax: 306/787-5303
Kim Trew, Regina Coronation Park NDP, 306/787-1898, Fax: 306/787-6247
Hon. Eric Upshall, Watrous NDP, 306/787-0338, Fax: 306/787-1094
Harry Van Mulligen, Regina Victoria NDP, 306/787-1900, Fax: 306/787-6247
John Wall, Swift Current NDP, 306/787-0936, Fax: 306/787-6247
Larry Ward, Estevan NDP, 306/787-1833, Fax: 306/787-6247
Grant Whitmore, Saskatoon Northwest NDP, 306/787-0766, Fax: 306/787-6247
Hon. Berny Wiens, Rosetown-Biggar NDP, 306/787-6944, Fax: 306/787-8487
Vacant, North Battleford

SASKATCHEWAN GOVERNMENT DEPARTMENTS & AGENCIES

Saskatchewan AGRICULTURE & FOOD
Walter Scott Bldg., 3085 Albert St., Regina SK S4S 0B1
306/787-5140; Fax: 306/787-0600; URL: http://www.gov.sk.ca/agfood/

ACTS ADMINISTERED
Agri-Food Act
Agri-Food Innovations Fund Act
Agricultural Credit Corporation of Saskatchewan Act
Agricultural Development & Adjustment Act
Agricultural Operations Act
Agricultural Safety Net Act
Agricultural Societies Act
Agriculture Development Fund Act
Agrologists Act, 1994
Animal Identification Act
Animal Products Act
Animal Protection Act
Apiaries Act
Cattle Marketing Deductions Act
Crop Insurance Act
Crop Payment Act
Department of Agriculture Act
Diseases of Animals Act
Drainage Act
Expropriation Act
Expropriation (Rehabilitation Projects) Act
Farm Financial Stability Act
Farmers' Counselling & Assistance Act
Farming Communities Land Act
Grain Charges Limitations Act
Grain & Fodder Conservation Act
Horned Cattle Purchases Act
Horticultural Societies Act
Land Bank Repeal & Temporary Provisions Act
Leafcutting Beekeeping Registration Act
Line Fence Act
Livestock Facilities Tax Credit Act
Livestock Investment Tax Credit Act
Milk Control Act, 1992
Noxious Weeds Act, 1984
Pest Control Act
Pest Control Products (Saskatchewan) Act
Pollution (by Livestock) Control Act, 1984
Prairie Agricultural Machinery Institute Act
Provincial Lands Act
Sale or Lease of Certain Lands Act
Saskatchewan 4-H Foundation Act
Saskatchewan Farm Security Act
Seed Grain Advances Act
Soil Drifting Control Act
Stray Animals Act
Vegetable, Fruit & Honey Sales Act
Veterinarians Act, 1987
Veterinary Services Act
Wildlife Act (subject to O.C. 469/94)
Minister, Hon. Eric Upshall, 306/787-0338, Fax: 306/787-1094
Deputy Minister, Murray McLaughlin, 306/787-5170, Fax: 306/787-2393, Email: mmclaug1@mailer.agr.gov.sk.ca
Asst. Deputy Minister, Financial Support & Program Management, Dale Sigurdson, 306/787-5245, Fax: 306/787-2393, Email: dsigurd1@mailer.agr.gov.sk.ca
Asst. Deputy Minister, Policy & Planning, Terrence Scott, 306/787-5247, Fax: 306/787-2393, Email: tscott1@mailer.agr.gov.sk.ca
Director, Extension Services, Vacant, 306/787-8524, Fax: 306/787-9623

ADMINISTRATIVE SERVICES BRANCH
Fax: 306/787-0600
Director, Jack Zepp, 306/787-5131, Fax: 306/787-0600, Email: jzepp1@mailer.agr.gov.sk.ca
Manager, Financial Services, Ken Petruic, 306/787-5142
Manager, Operations, Ross Johnson, 306/787-5141

AGRICULTURE RESEARCH BRANCH
Director, Martin Wrubleski, 306/787-5960, Fax: 306/787-9623, Email: mwruble1@mailer.agr.gov.sk.ca
Program Coordinator, Engineering, Environment & Economics, Ron Kehrig, 306/933-5094
Program Coordinator, Livestock, Hamid Javed, 306/787-5924
Program Coordinator, Bruce Baumann, 306/787-5107
Program Coordinator, Abdul Jalil, 306/787-8076

COMMUNICATIONS BRANCH
Director, Harvey Johnson, 306/787-6395, Fax: 306/787-0216, Email: hjohnso1@mailer.agr.gov.sk.ca
Asst. Director, Janet Peters, 306/787-5389
Media Relations, Colleen Slater-Smith, 306/787-5155

LANDS BRANCH
Director, Greg Haase, 306/787-5154, Fax: 306/787-5180, Email: ghaase1@mailer.agr.gov.sk.ca

LIVESTOCK & VETERINARY OPERATIONS BRANCH
Director, Ernie Spencer, 306/787-5087, Fax: 306/787-1315, Email: espence1@mailer.agr.gov.sk.ca

MARKETING DEVELOPMENT BRANCH
Director, Ron Dalgliesh, 306/787-8526, Fax: 306/787-0271, Email: rdalgli1@mailer.agr.gov.sk.ca
Marketing Manager, Consumer Products, Ken Evans, 306/787-8537

PASTURES BRANCH
Director, Peter Rempel, 306/787-5191, Fax: 306/787-5180, Email: prempel1@mailer.agr.gov.sk.ca

POLICY & PROGRAM DEVELOPMENT BRANCH
Director, Hal Cushon, 306/787-5961, Fax: 306/787-5134, Email: hcushon1@mailer.agr.gov.sk.ca
Coordinator, Strategic Planning Section, Mitchell Demyen, 306/787-5882
Coordinator, Land Policy Section, Gloria Parisien, 306/787-5207

PORK IMPLEMENTATION TEAM
Provincial Pork Specialist, Dr. Al Theede, 306/933-5096, Fax: 306/933-5323

STATISTICS BRANCH
Director, David Boehm, 306/787-5204, Fax: 306/787-0276, Email: dboehm1@mailer.agr.gov.sk.ca

SUSTAINABLE PRODUCTION BRANCH
Director, J.A. Buchan, 306/787-4661, Fax: 306/787-0428, Email: jbuchan1@mailer.agr.gov.sk.ca
Supervisor, Crop Protection Laboratory, Grant Holzgang, 306/787-8130
Manager, Crop Industry Development Section, Mike McAvoy, 306/787-4668
Manager, Economics & Business Development, Don Barber, 306/787-5962
Manager, Production Technology Section, Doug Billett, 306/787-8061

Associated Agencies, Boards & Commissions
• Agricultural Credit Corporation of Saskatchewan: 350 Cheadle St. West, PO Box 820, Swift Current SK S9H 4Y7 – 306/778-8480; Fax: 306/778-8459
General Manager, Norm Ballagh
• Agri-Food Council: #329, 3085 Albert St., Regina SK S4S 0B1 – 306/787-5952; Fax: 306/787-0271
Secretary, Roy White
• Farm Stress Unit: #329, 3085 Albert St., Regina SK S4S 0B1 – 306/787-5196; Fax: 306/787-9623, Toll Free: 1-800-667-4442
Manager, Ken Imhoff
• Milk Control Board: #1210, 2500 Victoria Ave., Regina SK S4P 3X2 – 306/787-5319; Fax: 306/787-1988
CEO, S.H. Barber
• Prairie Agricultural Machinery Institute: PO Box 1900, Humboldt SK S0K 2A0 – 306/682-2555; Fax: 306/682-5080
Director, Barrie Broad
• Saskatchewan Crop Insurance Corporation: 484 Prince William Dr., PO Box 3000, Melville SK S0A 2P0 – Fax: 306/728-7260
General Manager, Doug Matthies, 306/728-7205
• Saskatchewan Land Allocations Appeal Board: #302, 3085 Albert St., Regina SK S4S 0B1 – 306/787-5955; Fax: 306/787-5134
Administrative Officer, Joe Novak

Agricultural Marketing Boards & Commissions
• Saskatchewan Broiler Hatching Egg Producers Marketing Board: 72 Lindsay Dr., Saskatoon SK S7H 4B4 – 306/955-2740; Fax: 306/374-2041
Sec.-Manager, H. Goodhope
• Saskatchewan Chicken Marketing Board: 1810 - 9th Ave. North, PO Box 1637, Regina SK S4P 3C4 – 306/775-1677; Fax: 306/949-1353
Secretary Manager, Van Stewart
• Saskatchewan Commercial Egg Producers' Marketing Board: 1810 - 9 Ave. North, PO Box 1637, Regina SK S4P 3C4 – 306/924-1505; Fax: 306/924-1515
Secretary Manager, Dave Mackie
• Saskatchewan Pork International Marketing Group (SPI): 502 - 45 St. West, Saskatoon SK S7L 6H2 – 306/653-3014; Fax: 306/244-2918, Toll Free: 1-800-667-2003
General Manager, J. Morris
• Saskatchewan Poultry Council: 502 - 45 St. West, 2nd Fl., Saskatoon SK S7L 6H2 – 306/931-1050; Fax: 306/931-2825
Sec.-Manager, Rose Olsen
• Saskatchewan Pulse Crop Development Board: PO Box 516, Regina SK S4P 3A2 – 306/781-7475; Fax: 306/525-4173
Administrator, Donald R. Jaques
• Saskatchewan Sheep Development Board: 2910 - 11 St. West, PO Box 5025, Saskatoon SK S7K 4E3 – 306/933-5200
Manager, Colleen Sawyer

- Saskatchewan Turkey Producers Marketing Board: 502 - 45 St. West, 2nd Fl., Saskatoon SK S7L 6H2 – 306/931-1050; Fax: 306/931-2825
Secretary Manager, Rose Olsen
- Saskatchewan Vegetable Marketing & Development Board: #101, 2515 Victoria Ave., Regina SK S4P 0T2 – 306/247-2086; Fax: 306/525-4173
Secretary Manager, Tom Hyland

Saskatchewan ARCHIVES BOARD
University of Regina, 3737 Wascana Pkwy., Regina SK S4S 0A2
306/787-4068; Fax: 306/787-1975
University of Saskatchewan, Murray Bldg., 3 Campus Dr., Saskatoon SK S7N 5A4
306/933-5832, Fax: 306/933-7305
Provincial Archivist, Trevor J.D. Powell
Chair, Dr. B. Zagorin, 306/585-4267
Director, Government Records, Don Herperger, 306/787-3864
Acting Director, Historical Records & Director, Saskatoon Office, D'Arcy Hande, 306/933-5833

Saskatchewan ASSESSMENT MANAGEMENT AGENCY (SAMA)
#1600, 1920 Broad St., Regina SK S4P 3V2
306/924-8000; Fax: 306/924-8070
Independent agency responsible for the design & administration of the property assessment system in Saskatchewan.
Minister Responsible, Hon. Carol Teichrob
Chair, Mark Thompson
CEO, Bryan Hebb

Provincial AUDITOR SASKATCHEWAN
#1500, 1920 Broad St., Regina SK S4P 3V7
306/787-6398; Fax: 306/787-6383
Provincial Auditor, Wayne K. Strelioff, 306/787-6360
Asst. Provincial Auditor, Fred Wendel, 306/787-6366
Executive Secretary, Linda Kuntz, 306/787-6361
Executive Director, Brian Atkinson, 306/787-6384
Executive Director, Judy Ferguson, 306/787-6372
Executive Director, Mike Heffernan, 306/787-6364
General Director, Mobashar Ahmad, 306/787-6387
Director, Bob Black, 306/787-6369
Director, Ray Bohn, 306/787-6363
Director, Phil Creaser, 306/787-6388
Director, Ed Montgomery, 306/787-6389
Principal, Jane Knox, 306/787-6368
Manager, Angèle Borys, 306/787-6326
Manager, Lorianne Earis, 306/787-6313
Manager, Rosemarie Evelt, 306/787-6380
Manager, Rod Grabarczyk, 306/787-6373
Manager, Bill Harasymchuk, 306/787-6453
Manager, Rodd Jersak, 306/787-6316
Manager, Shelley Lipon, 306/787-6305
Manager, Dale Markewich, 306/787-6320
Manager, Andrew Martens, 306/787-6374
Manager, Glen Nyhus, 306/787-6385
Manager, Karim Pradhan, 306/787-6386
Manager, Victor Schwab, 306/787-6375
Manager, Leslie Wendel, 306/787-6370

Saskatchewan COMMUNICATIONS NETWORK (SCN)
North Block, 2440 Broad St., Regina SK S4P 3V7
306/787-0490; Fax: 306/787-0496; Email: scn@uregina.ca; URL: http://www.gov.sk.ca/govt/scn/
Minister Responsible, Hon. Robert W. Mitchell, Q.C., 306/787-6662
President/CEO, James Benning, 306/787-2390
Executive Director, Operations, Paul Fudge, 306/787-0447
Executive Director, Programming, Richard Gustin, 306/787-0446
Director, Finance & Human Resources, Garth Ferguson, 306/787-0494
Director, Public Affairs, Iain MacDonald, 306/787-0497

Saskatchewan CROWN INVESTMENTS CORPORATION (CIC)
#400, 2400 College Ave., Regina SK S4P 1C8
306/787-6851; Fax: 306/787-8125; URL: http://www.gov.sk.ca/govt/crowninv/
Acts as a financial holding company & oversees the operations of commercial Crown corporations. Sponsor for the Capital Pension Plan administering pension & benefit services to 37 organizations.
Minister Responsible, Hon. Berny Wiens
President, John Wright
Vice-President, Corporate Services, Don Axtell, 306/787-5841
Vice-President, Finance & Accounting Services, Patti Beatch, 306/787-9309
Vice-President, Human Resources, Bill Hyde, 306/787-1504
Vice-President, Projects, David Hughes, 306/787-5908
Director, Communications, John Miller, 306/787-9039

Saskatchewan ECONOMIC DEVELOPMENT
1919 Saskatchewan Dr., Regina SK S4P 3V7
306/787-2232; URL: http://www.gov.sk.ca/govt/econdev/
The Business Line: 1-800-265-2001
Promotes & administers programs to develop & serve small business in the province. The department provides assistance & guidance to all stages of development & planning of cooperative enterprises & provides support services to new & existing enterprises.
Provides financial assistance to the province's Regional Economic Development Authorities (REDAs), under which municipal governments, cooperatives, development organizations, communities & businesses can coordinate their professional, organizational & financial resources to develop new jobs & create investment.

ACTS ADMINISTERED
Community Bonds Act
Department of Economic Development Act, 1993
Economic Development & Tourism Act
Industry Incentives Program Act
Minister, Hon. Dwain Lingenfelter, 306/787-4864, Fax: 306/787-9135
Deputy Minister, Clare Kirkland, 306/787-9580, Fax: 306/787-2159
Director, Communications Branch, Debbie Wilkie, 306/787-7982

COOPERATIVES DIRECTORATE
Asst. Deputy Minister, Tom Marwick, 306/787-0192, Fax: 306/787-2198

DIVERSIFICATION DIVISION
Asst. Deputy Minister, Tom Douglas, 306/787-8178, Fax: 306/787-3989
Director, Development Services Branch, Lorne Bryden, 306/787-2227, Fax: 306/787-1620
Director, Market Development, Iain Hollier, 306/787-0927
Director, Sector Development, Bryce Baron, 306/787-2246

POLICY & COORDINATION DIVISION
Asst. Deputy Minister, Peter Phillips, 306/787-1672
Director, Business Policy, Laverne Moskal, 306/787-8910
Director, Economic Policy, Dave McQuinn, 306/787-7983

PROGRAMS & CORPORATE SERVICES DIVISION
Asst. Deputy Minister, Janis Rathwell, 306/787-5775
Acting Director, Administrative Services, Donna Johnson, 306/787-1612
Director, Investment Programs, Denise Gustavson, 306/787-3524
Director, Industry Development Programs, Raman Visvanathan, 306/787-9215

REGIONAL ECONOMIC DEVELOPMENT SERVICES DIVISION
306/787-1605; Fax: 306/787-1620
Asst. Deputy Minister, Bob Perrin, 306/787-2171
Asst. Deputy Minister, Special Projects, Brian Hansen, #206, 15 Innovation Pl., Saskatoon SK S7N 2X8, 306/933-7200, Fax: 306/933-8244

Regional Offices
Estevan: 1106 - 6th St., Estevan SK S4A 1A8 – 306/657-4505; Fax: 306/637-4510, Regional Manager, John Slatnik
Moose Jaw: 45 Thatcher Dr., Moose Jaw SK S6H 6V2 – 306/694-3624; Fax: 306/694-3500, Regional Manager, Grant McWilliams
North Battleford: 509 Pioneer Ave., North Battleford SK S9A 1E9 – 306/446-7444; Fax: 306/446-7442, Regional Manager, Jan Swanson
Prince Albert: 800 Central Ave., Prince Albert SK S6V 6G1 – 306/953-2280; Fax: 306/953-2275, Regional Manager, Wayne Phillip
Swift Current: 1 - 1081 Central Ave. North, Swift Current SK S9H 4Z1 – 306/778-8415; Fax: 306/773-4425, Regional Manager, Doug Howorko
Yorkton: 38 - 5th Ave. North, Yorkton SK S3N 0Y8 – 306/786-1415; Fax: 306/786-1417, Regional Manager, Wayne Clarke

Outside Offices
Ottawa: #1306, 155 Queen St., Ottawa ON K1A 1K2 – 613/232-6544; Fax: 613/232-4472
New York: #2107, 630 - 5th Ave., New York NY 10111, U.S.A. – 212/969-9100; Fax: 212/969-9549

Associated Agencies, Boards & Commissions
- Saskatchewan Opportunities Corporation: Grenfell Tower, 1945 Hamilton St., 6th Fl., Regina SK S4P 2C7 – 306/787-8595; Fax: 306/787-8515; URL: http://www.gov.sk.ca/soco/
President, Zach Douglas
Vice-President, Moyez Somani
- Saskatchewan Tourism Authority (STA): #500, 1900 Albert St., Regina SK S4P 4L9 – 306/787-9600; Fax: 306/787-0715, Toll Free: 1-800-667-7191
CEO, Randall Williams, 306/787-9600
Vice President, Marketing & Programs, Stephen Pearce, 306/787-9575
Director, Administration, Neil Brotheridge, 306/787-1535
Director, Education & Training (Saskatchewan Tourism Education Council Division), Carol Lumb, 306/933-5905
Director, Membership Service & Sales, Steve McLellan, 306/933-5902
Director, Operations, Neil Sawatzky, 306/787-2320
- Saskatchewan Trade & Export Partnership (STEP) 1919 Saskatchewan Dr., Regina SK S4P 3V7
306/787-9210; Fax: 306/787-6666
Chairman & CEO, Milton Fair, 306/787-1550

Saskatchewan EDUCATION
2220 College Ave., Regina SK S4P 3V7
306/787-2010; Fax: 306/787-2280;
URL: http://www.sasked.gov.sk.ca

ACTS ADMINISTERED
Education Act
Elementary & Secondary Education Act
Home-based Education Act
Minister, Hon. Patricia Atkinson, 306/787 7360, Fax: 306/787-0237
Deputy Minister, Craig Dotson, 306/787-7071, Fax: 306/787-1300
Executive Director, Communications Branch, Susan Hogarth, 306/787-5271
Executive Director, Finance & Operations Branch, Mae Boa, 306/787-6066
Executive Director, Human Resources Branch, Don Trew, 306/787-5654
Executive Director, Teachers' Superannuation Commission, John McLaughlin, 1870 Albert St., 3rd Fl., Regina SK S4P 3V7, 306/787-9188, Fax: 306/787-1939

EDUCATION DIVISION (K-12)
Asst. Deputy Minister, Ken Horsman, 306/787-6068
Executive Director, Curriculum & Instruction Branch, Margaret Lipp, 306/787-6032
Executive Director, Educational Services Branch, Ernie Cychmistruk, 306/787-5592
Executive Director, Official Minority Language Office Branch, Rene Archambault, 306/787-6089
Executive Director, Planning & Evaluation Branch, Gillian McCreary, 306/787-5863
Director, Third Party Funding Unit, Michael Littlewood, 306/787-1185

Office of the Chief ELECTORAL OFFICER
1702 Park St., Regina SK S4N 6B2
306/787-4000; Fax: 306/787-4052
Chief Electoral Officer, Myron A. Kuziak
Asst. Chief Electoral Officer, Jan Baker

Saskatchewan ENERGY & MINES (SEM)
1914 Hamilton St., Regina SK S4P 4V4
306/787-2526; Fax: 306/787-7338; URL: http://www.gov.sk.ca/govt/enermine/
Saskatchewan Energy Conservation: 1-800-668-4636
Provincial department charged with the responsibility to achieve full & responsible development of Saskatchewan's energy & mineral resources. Delivers services & programs in a manner promoting job creation & developing economic activity in the Province. The department provides valuable revenues to fund government programs and services in all sectors. Produces, promotes, markets, and distributes information on Saskatchewan's resources to the resource industries and the general public.

ACTS ADMINISTERED
Crown Minerals Act, 1985
Department of Energy & Mines Act
Freehold Oil & Gas Production Tax Act
Mineral Resources Act, 1985
Mineral Taxation Act, 1983
Oil & Gas Conservation Act
Pipelines Act
Potash Resources Act
Minister, Hon. Eldon Lautermilch, 306/787-0605
Deputy Minister, Ray Clayton, 306/787-2496, Fax: 306/787-5718

FINANCE & ADMINISTRATION DIVISION
Asst. Deputy Minister, Donald Koop, 306/787-3624, Fax: 306/787-5718
Director, Communications, Marg Moran McQuinn, 306/787-2567, Fax: 306/787-2527
Acting Director, Mineral Revenue Branch, Hal Sanders, 306/787-2832, Fax: 306/787-7338
Director, Personnel & Administration Branch, Lynn Jacobson, 306/787-2525, Fax: 306/787-5718

Director, System Services Branch, Adeline Skwara, 306/787-2548, Fax: 306/787-2333
Supervisor, Accounts, Doug Koepke, 306/787-2505
Supervisor, Purchasing, Ron Robinson, 306/787-2545, Fax: 306/787-7338

EXPLORATION & GEOLOGICAL SERVICES DIVISION
Executive Director, George Patterson, 306/787-2560, Fax: 306/787-2488
Director, Northern Survey Branch, Dr. T.I.I. Sibbald, 306/787-2568, Fax: 306/787-2488
Director, Petroleum Geology Branch, Dr. D.F. Paterson, 201 Dewdney Ave. East, Regina SK S4N 4G3, 306/787-2625, Fax: 306/787-4608
Director, Sedimentary Geodata Branch, Paul Guilov, 306/787-2583, Fax: 306/787-2488
Supervisor & Geological Editor, Support Services, Dr. Charlie T. Harper, 306/787-2578, Fax: 306/787-2488

PETROLEUM & NATURAL GAS DIVISION
Fax: 306/787-2478
Executive Director, Bruce W. Wilson, 306/787-2591
Director, Economic & Fiscal Analysis Branch, Dale Fletcher, 306/787-2605
Director, Engineering Services Branch, Myron Sereda, 306/787-2318
Director, Geology & Petroleum Lands Branch, Gordon Hutch, 306/787-2606
Director, Petroleum Development Branch, Brian Mathieson, 306/787-2593
Director, Petroleum Statistics Branch, Joe Dang, 306/787-2607, Fax: 306/787-8236

RESOURCE POLICY & ECONOMICS DIVISION
Asst. Deputy Minister, Dan McFadyen, 306/787-2523, Fax: 306/787-5718
Director, Energy Development Branch, Malcolm Wilson, 306/787-2618, Fax: 306/787-2333
Director, Energy Economics Branch, Trevor Dark, 306/787-2469, Fax: 306/787-2333
Director, Industrial Minerals Branch, Maurice Hall, 306/787-2521, Fax: 306/787-2333
Director, Metallic Minerals Branch, Jane Forster, 306/787-2501, Fax: 306/787-2333

Saskatchewan ENVIRONMENT & RESOURCE MANAGEMENT
3211 Albert St., Regina SK S4S 5W6
306/787-2700; Fax: 306/787-3941; URL: http://www.gov.sk.ca/govt/environ/
Toll Free: 1-800-667-2757
Environment Resource Network: 1-800-567-4224
Spill Response Centre (24-hour): 1-800-667-7525
Provincial Forest Fires: 1-800-667-9660
Saskatchewan provincial department responsible for the following:
• manages, protects & enhances the province's natural & environmental resources;
• monitors & regulates mining & milling operations & the reclamation & decommissioning of mine sites;
• administers resource conservation services, enforces resource & environmental legislation;
• manages parks & recreation areas;
• maintains & constructs facilities & assists in forest fire management;
• maintains a database of forest resources;
• allocates & manages Crown lands & integrated land resource management &;
• monitors industrial & municipal waste & landfill sites.

ACTS ADMINISTERED
Clean Air Act
Critical Wildlife Habitat Protection Act
Ecological Reserves Act
Environmental Assessment Act
Environmental Management & Protection Act (subject to OC 518/87)
Fisheries Act
Forest Act
Grasslands National Park Act
Litter Control Act
Ozone-depleting Substances Control Act
Parks Act
Prairie & Forest Fires Act
Provincial Lands Act
Regional Parks Act
Renewable Resources, Recreation & Culture Act (subject to OC 177/93)
Sale or Lease of Certain Lands Act
State of the Environment Report Act
Water Appeal Board Act
Water Resources Management Act
Wildlife Act
Minister, Hon. Lorne Scott, Fax: 306/787-0395
Deputy Minister, Stuart Kramer, 306/787-2930, Fax: 306/787-2947, Email: stuart.kramer.erm@govmail.gov.sk.ca

ENVIRONMENTAL ASSESSMENT BRANCH
Executive Director, Ron J. Zukowsky, 306/787-6132, Fax: 306/787-0930, Email: zukowsky.ron@sasknet.sk.ca

MANAGEMENT SERVICES DIVISION
Asst. Deputy Minister, Robert Blackwell, 306/787-2380, Fax: 306/787-2947, EMail robert.blackwell.erm@govmail.gov.sk.ca
Director, Communication Services Branch, Jocelyn Souliere, 306/787-9637, Fax: 306/787-3941, Email: jocelyn.s@sasknet.sk.ca
Director, Financial & Administrative Services Branch, Donna Kellsey, 306/787-8444, Fax: 306/787-8441, Email: donna.kellsey.erm@govmail.gov.sk.ca
Director, Human Resource Services Branch, Nancy Croll, 306/787-9177, Fax: 306/787-9374, Email: nancy.croll.erm@govmail.gov.sk.ca
Director, Information Management Branch, Shelly Vandermey, 306/787-2927, Fax: 306/787-0598, Email: vanderme@mailhost.sasktel.sk.ca

OPERATIONS DIVISION
Asst. Deputy Minister, Ross MacLennan, 306/787-9079, Fax: 306/787-0219, EMail ross.maclennan.erm@govmail.gov.sk.ca
Director, Enforcement & Compliance, Dave Harvey, 306/953-2993, Fax: 306/953-2999, Email: enf@sasknet.sk.ca
Director, Forest Fire Management, Gus MacAuley, 306/953-2206, Fax: 306/953-2530
Executive Director, Regional Operations, Glen Rolles, 306/787-9071, Fax: 306/787-0219, Email: glen.rolles.erm@govmail.gov.sk.ca

POLICY & PROGRAMS DIVISION
Assoc. Deputy Minister, Les Cooke, 306/787-5419, Fax: 306/787-2947, Email: les.cooke@sasknet.sk.ca
Director, Environmental Protection Branch, Bob G. Ruggles, 306/787-6178, Fax: 306/787-5623, Email: bob.ruggles.erm@govmail.gov.sk.ca
Acting Director, Fisheries Branch, Ed Dean, 306/787-2884, Fax: 306/787-0737, Email: ed.dean.erm@govmail.gov.sk.ca
Director, Forestry Branch, Murray Little, 306/953-2486, Fax: 306/953-2360
Director, Parks & Facilities Branch, Don MacAulay, 306/787-2846, Fax: 306/787-7000, Email: don.macaulay.erm@govmail.gov.sk.ca
Director, Policy & Public Involvement, Bruce Smith, 306/787-5760, Fax: 306/787-0024, Email: bruce.smith.erm@govmail.gov.sk.ca
Director, Sustainable Land Management Branch, Doug Mazur, 306/787-7024, Fax: 306/787-1349, Email: doug.mazur.erm@govmail.gov.sk.ca

Director, Wildlife Branch, Dennis Sherratt, 306/787-2309, Fax: 306/787-9544, Email: dennis.sherratt.erm@govmail.gov.sk.ca

Associated Agencies, Boards & Commissions
- Conservation Data Centre: #422, 3211 Albert St., Regina SK S4S 5W6 – 306/787-7197; Fax: 306/787-7196

Coordinator/Zoologist, James Duncan
Ecologist, Joyce Belcher
- Saskatchewan Wetland Conservation Corporation: 3211 Albert St., 2nd Fl., Regina SK S4S 5W6 – 306/787-5419; Fax: 306/787-2847; URL: http://www.wetland.sk.ca/

Chair, Les Cooke
- Wascana Centre Authority: 2900 Wascana Dr., PO Box 7111, Regina SK S4P 3S7 – 306/522-3661; Fax: 306/565-2742

Executive Director, Paul Robinson

Saskatchewan FINANCE
2350 Albert St., Regina SK S4P 4A6
306/787-6768; Fax: 306/787-6544; URL: http://www.gov.sk.ca/govt/finance/

ACTS ADMINISTERED
Accredited Public Accounts Act
Appropriation Act
Certified General Accountants Act
Certified Public Accountants Act
Chartered Accountants Act, 1986
Cooperation Income Tax Collection Agreement Act, 1947
Corporation Capital Tax Act
Crown Corporations Act, 1978
Education & Health Tax Act
Estate Tax Rebate Act, 1969
Estate Tax Rebates Reciprocal Arrangements Act, 1970
Federal-Provincial Agreements Act
Federal-Provincial Administration Act
Financial Administration Act
Fuel Tax Act, 1987
Gift Tax Act, 1972
Heritage Fund (Saskatchewan) Act
Home Energy Loan Act
Horse Racing Regulation Act
Hospital Revenue Act (jointly with Saskatchewan Health)
Hospital Tax Act
Income Tax Act
Industry & Commerce Development Act
Insurance Premiums Tax Act
Labour-sponsored Venture Capital Corporations Act
Liquor Consumption Tax Act
Management Accountants Act
Members of the Legislative Assembly Superannuation Act, 1979
Mortgage Interest Reduction Act
Mortgage Protection Act
Motor Vehicle Insurance Premiums Tax Act
Municipal Employees' Superannuation Act
Municipal Financing Corporation Act
New Grade Energy Inc. Act
Pioneer Trust Company Depositors Assistance Act
Provincial Auditor Act
Public Service Superannuation Act
Revenue & Financial Services Act
Saskatchewan Development Act
Saskatchewan Pension Plan Act
Statistics Act
Stock Savings Plan Tax Credit Act
Succession Duty Act
Superannuation (Supplementary Provisions) Act
Tobacco Tax Act
Minister, Hon. Janice MacKinnon, 306/787-6060, Fax: 306/787-6055

Deputy Minister, Bill Jones, 306/787-6621, Fax: 306/787-7155
Provincial Comptroller, Gerry Kraus, 306/787-6793, Fax: 306/787-9720
Executive Director, Public Employees Benefits Agency, Brian L. Smith, 306/787-6757, Fax: 306/787-0244
General Manager, Saskatchewan Pension Plan, Kathy Strutt, 306/463-5412, Fax: 306/463-3500

ADMINISTRATION DIVISION
Executive Director, Bill Van Sickle, 306/787-6530, Fax: 306/787-6544
Director, Financial Services Branch, Bill Hoover, 306/787-6529
Director, Human Resources Branch, Jim Graham, 306/787-6535
Manager, Administrative Services Branch, Cathy O'Byrne, 306/787-6532, Fax: 306/787-6576
Manager, System Support Branch, Jennifer Hogan, 306/787-7692

BUDGET ANALYSIS DIVISION
Executive Director, Economic & Fiscal Policy Branch, Jim Marshall, 306/787-6724
Executive Director, Taxation & Intergovernmental Affairs Branch, Kirk McGregor, 306/787-6731
Executive Director, Treasury Board Branch, Larry Spannier, 306/787-6780, Fax: 306/787-3482
Director, Bureau of Statistics, Ron McMahon, 306/787-6328
Director, Intergovernmental Affairs, Glen Veikle, 306/787-6735
Director, Planning, Joel Prager, 306/787-6626
Senior Economist, Economics, Fred Young, 306/787-6792
Manager, Fiscal Policy, Joanne Brockman, 306/787-6743

REVENUE DIVISION
Asst. Deputy Minister, Len Rog, 306/787-6685, Fax: 306/787-0241

TREASURY & DEBT MANAGEMENT DIVISION
Asst. Deputy Minister & Registrar, Securities, Sheldon Schwartz, 306/787-6751, Fax: 306/787-8493
Executive Director, Capital Markets Branch, Rae Haverstock, 306/787-6773
Executive Director, Cash & Debt Management Branch, Dennis Polowyk, 306/787-3923
Executive Director, Investment & Liability Management Branch, Vacant, 306/787-9474

Associated Agencies, Boards & Commissions
- Board of Revenue Commissioners: #480, 2151 Scarth St., Regina SK S4P 3V7 – 306/787-6227

Chair, B.G. McNamee
Secretary, Marilyn Turanich
- Saskatchewan Development Fund Corporation: #300, 2400 College Ave., Regina SK S4P 1C8 – 306/787-1645; Fax: 306/787-8125

Chair, Ed Tchorzewski
General Manager, Don Axtel

Saskatchewan HEALTH
3475 Albert St., Regina SK S4S 6X6
306/787-8332; Fax: 306/787-8310; URL: http://www.gov.sk.ca/govt/health/

ACTS ADMINISTERED
Abandoned Refrigerator Act
Ambulance Act
Anatomy Act
Change of Name Act
Dental Care Act
Department of Health Act
Health Districts Act
Health Services Utilization & Research Commission Act
Health Statutes Amendment Act, 1993
Hearing Aid Act
Home Care Act
Hospital Revenue Act
Hospital Standards Act
Housing & Special-care Homes Act
Medical & Hospitalization Tax Repeal Act
Medical Laboratory Licensing Act
Medical Scholarships & Bursaries Act
Mental Health Services Act
Mutual Medical & Hospital Benefit Associations Act
Personal Care Homes Act
Prescription Drugs Act
Public Health Act
Saskatchewan Hospitalization Act
Saskatchewan Medical Care Insurance Act
Union Hospital Act
Venereal Disease Prevention Act
Vital Statistics Act
Acts in which Saskatchewan Health has a Direct Interest
Cancer Foundation Act
Chiropody Profession Act
Chiropractic Act, 1994
Community Health Unit Act
Dental Professions Act
Dental Technicians Act
Dental Therapists Act
Denturists Act
Emergency Medical Aid Act
Human Tissue Gift Act
Licensed Practical Nurses Act
Lloydminster Hospital Act, 1948
Medical Care Insurance Supplementary Provisions Act
Medical Profession Act, 1981
Medical Radiation Technologists Act
Medical Scholarships & Bursaries Act
Naturopathy Act
Opthalmic Dispensers Act
Optometry Act, 1985
Osteopathic Practice Act
Pharmacy Act
Physical Therapists Act, 1984
Professional Dietitians Act
Registered Psychiatric Nurses Act
Registered Nurses Act, 1988
Registered Occupational Therapists Act
Registered Psychologists Act
Residential Services Act
Saskatchewan Embalmers Act
Speech Language Pathologists & Audiologists Act
White Cane Act
Minister, Hon. Eric Cline, 306/787-7345, Fax: 306/787-8677
Deputy Minister, N. Duane Adams, 306/787-3041, Fax: 306/787-4533

INSURED SERVICES DIVISION
Responsible for the issuance of provincial birth, marriage & death certificates. Fee for each certificate is $15.00.
Associate Deputy Minister, Glenda Yeates, 416/787-4695
Executive Director, Medical Care Insurance Branch, Lawrence Krahn, 306/787-3423, Fax: 306/787-3761
Executive Director, Prescription Drug Services Branch, Barb Shea, 306/787-3301, Fax: 306/787-8679
Executive Director, Provincial Laboratory Services, George Peters, 306/787-3629, Fax: 306/787-3112
Director, Vital Statistics & Health Insurance Registration Branch, Ronn Wallace, 1919 Rose St., Regina SK S4P 3V7, 306/787-1167

INTEGRATED HEALTH SERVICES DIVISION
Associate Deputy Minister, Steve Petz, 306/787-4595
Executive Director, District Support Branch, Lois Borden, 306/787-3359

Executive Director, Programs Branch, Danni Boyd, 306/787-6092
Director, Capital & Special Policy Unit, Jim Simmons, 306/787-3235
Service Area Coordinator, Dr. Gary Bell, 306/787-3325

INTERNATIONAL DIVISION
Vice-President, Cy Scheske, 306/787-8339
Executive Director, Communications & Public Information Branch, Mark Seland, 306/787-3825
Executive Director, Finance & Management Services Branch, Kathy Langlois, 306/787-3051
Executive Director, Human Resources & Fee Negotiations Branch, Kelly Kummerfield, 306/787-3070

STRATEGIC SERVICES DIVISION
Senior Associate Deputy Minister, Lorraine Hill, 306/787-3047
Asst. to the Senior Associate Deputy Minister, Dale Bloom, 306/787-3088
Provincial Epidemiologist, Dr. William Osei, 306/787-1580
Executive Director, Corporate Information & Technology Branch, Neil R. Gardner, 306/787-3043, Fax: 306/787-7589
Executive Director, Health Planning & Policy Development Branch, Maureen Yeske, 306/787-3144
Executive Director, Northern Health Services, Kathy Chisholm, 306/425-4517
Executive Director, Provincial Information Network, Bill Morton, 306/787-4635
Executive Director, Strategic Programs Branch, Carol Klassen, 306/787-3200, Fax: 306/787-6113
Director, Wellness & Health Promotion Branch, Pat Bell, 306/787-3083

Associated Agencies, Boards & Commissions
- Provincial Health Council: Faculty of Physical Activity Studies, University of Regina, #100, 3737 Wascana Pkwy., Regina SK S4S 0A2 – 306/585-4876; Fax: 306/585-4854
Chair, Ralph Nilson
- Saskatchewan Health Services Utilization & Research Commission: PO Box 46, Stn 41, Saskatoon SK S7N 0X0 – 306/966-1500; Fax: 306/966-1462

Saskatchewan HIGHWAYS & TRANSPORTATION
1855 Victoria Ave., Regina SK S4P 3V5
306/787-4804; Fax: 306/787-9777; URL: http://www.gov.sk.ca/govt/highways/

ACTS ADMINISTERED
Dangerous Goods Transportation Act
Department of Highways & Transportation Act
Engineering Profession Act
Highways & Transportation Act
Railway Act
Sand & Gravel Act
Minister, Hon. Andy Renaud, 306/787-6447, Fax: 306/787-6499
Deputy Minister, Brian King, 306/787-4950, Fax: 306/787-9777, Email: brian.king.hi0@govmail.gov.sk.ca
Director, Communications & Public Relations, Mike Woods, 306/787-4804, Email: mike.woods.hi0@govmail.gov.sk.ca
Director, Human Resources, Dave Atkinson, 306/787-4757, Email: dave.atkinson.hi0@govmail.gov.sk.ca
Senior Supervisor, Public Relations, John Charlton, 306/787-4805

CORPORATE INFORMATION SERVICES DIVISION
Executive Director, Lynn Tullock, 306/787-4734, Email: lynn.tulloch.hi0@govmail.gov.sk.ca
Director, Geographic Information Services, Roy Chursinoff, 306/787-4857

Director, Information Technology Services, Colin Hodgson, 306/787-4723
Director, Property Services, Jeff Grigg, 306/787-4885

ENGINEERING SERVICES DIVISION
Executive Director, Barry Martin, 306/787-4859, Email: barry.martin.hi0@govmail.gov.sk.ca
Director, Bridges, Herve Bachelu, 306/787-4830
Director, Municipal Services, Larry Johnson, 306/787-2716
Director, Planning & Research, Terry Bloome, 306/787-4838
Director, Testing Services, Bill Pacholka, 306/787-4917

LOGISTICS, PLANNING & COMPLIANCE DIVISION
Executive Director, Bernie Churko, 306/787-4866, Fax: 306/787-9777, Email: bernie.churko.hi0@govmail.gov.sk.ca
Director, Business Support, Greg Gilks, 306/787-4851
Director, Compliance, Peter Hurst, 306/787-4072
Director, Grain & Rail Logistics, Harold Hugg, 306/787-5311
Director, Project Management Team, Mike Hossack, 306/787-4776

Saskatchewan INDIAN & METIS AFFAIRS SECRETARIAT
1870 Albert St., 3rd Fl., Regina SK S4P 3V7
306/787-6250; Fax: 306/787-6336; URL: http://www.gov.sk.ca/govt/indmet/

ACTS ADMINISTERED
Government Organization Act
Indian & Native Affairs Secretariat Act
Minister Responsible, Hon. Joanne Crofford, 306/787-2207, Fax: 306/787-2202
Secretary, Gordon Nystuen, 306/787-6400
Asst. Deputy Minister, Indian Affairs Branch, Ernie Lawton, 306/787-5738
Asst. Deputy Minister, Metis Affairs Branch, Donovan Young, 306/787-6253
Executive Director, Planning, John Reid, 306/787-6678
Executive Director, Policy Development, Bill McLaren, 306/787-5723
Executive Director, Indian Lands & Resources, Glen Benedict, 306/787-6681
Manager, Aboriginal Employment Development, Wayne McKenzie, 306/787-5176
Manager, Policy & Communication, Rob Cunningham, 306/787-6683
Senior Policy Analyst, Mary Tkach, 306/787-5725
Senior Policy Analyst, Indian Lands & Resources, Kay Tootoosis, 306/787-2634
Senior Policy Analyst, Treaty Land Entitlement, Archana Jaiswal, 306/787-0064
Senior Advisor, Inter-Jurisdictional Affairs, John Hill, 306/787-5752
Policy Analyst, Metis Affairs Branch, Doreen Bradshaw, 306/787-6265
Policy Analyst, Metis Affairs Branch, Giselle Marcotte, 306/787-0098
Policy Analyst, Treaty Land Entitlement, Susan Shalapata, 306/787-9706

INFORMATION & PRIVACY COMMISSIONER OF SASKATCHEWAN
#500, 2220 - 12th Ave., Regina SK S4P 0M8
306/787-8350; Fax: 306/757-4858
Commissioner, Derril McLeod, Q.C.
Secretary, Elizabeth Susa

Saskatchewan Government INSURANCE (SGI)
2260 - 11th Ave., Regina SK S4P 0J9
306/751-1200; Fax: 306/787-7477

Minister Responsible, Hon. Clay Serby, 306/787-7387
President, Vacant
Vice-President, Auto Fund, Alan Cookman
Vice-President, Claims, Margaret Anderson
Vice-President, Finance & Administration, Randy Heise
Vice-President, Systems, John Dobie
Vice-President, Underwriting, Larry Fogg
Manager, Driver Licensing, Bill McCallum
Manager, Vehicle Standards & Inspection, Brian Kline

Saskatchewan INTERGOVERNMENTAL AFFAIRS
1919 Saskatchewan Dr., Regina SK S4P 3V7
306/787-1643; Fax: 306/787-1987; URL: http://www.gov.sk.ca/govt/intergov/
Minister & Provincial Secretary, Hon. Ned Shillington
Deputy Minister, Gregory Marchildon, 306/787-1925
Chief, Protocol Office, Michael Jackson, 306/787-3109, Fax: 306/787-1269
General Manager, Information Technology & Telecommunications, Vacant, 306/787-8276, Fax: 306/787-8577
Director, Office of French Language Coordination, Vacant, 306/787-2028, Fax: 306/787-6352
Executive Director, International Relations & Protocol, Paul Osborne, 306/787-6322, Fax: 306/787-7317
Acting Director, Constitutional Relations, Ian Peach, 306/787-8006
Director, Federal/Provincial Affairs, Alan Hilton, 306/787-7962

Saskatchewan JUSTICE
1874 Scarth St., Regina SK S4P 3V7
306/787-7872 (Communications); Fax: 306/787-3874; URL: http://www.gov.sk.ca/govt/justice/

ACTS ADMINISTERED
Justice Related Acts
Aboriginal Courtworkers Commission Act
Absconding Debtors Act
Absentee Act
Age of Majority Act
Agreements of Sale Cancellation Act
Agricultural Leaseholds Act
Arbitration Act, 1992
Assignment of Wages Act
Attachment of Debts Act
Builders' Lien Act
Canada-United Kingdom Judgments Enforcement Act
Canadian Institute of Management (Saskatchewan Division) Act
Children's Law Act
Choices in Action Act
Closing-out Sales Act
Commissioners for Oaths Act
Condominium Property Act, 1993
Constitutional Questions Act
Contributory Negligence Act
Coroners Act
Correctional Services Act
Court Officials Act, 1984
Court of Appeal Act
Creditors' Relief Act
Crown Administration of Estates Act
Crown Employment Contracts Act
Crown Suits (Costs) Act
Department of Justice Act
Dependants' Relief Act
Dependent Adults Act
Devolution of Real Property Act
Distress Act
Enforcement of Foreign Arbitral Awards Act
Enforcement of Maintenance Orders Act
Equality of Status of Married Persons Act

Escheats Act
Executions Act
Exemptions Act
Expropriation Procedures Act
Factors Act
Family Maintenance Act
Fatal Accidents Act
Federal Courts Act
Foreign Judgements Act
Fraudulent Preferences Act
Freedom of Information & Protection of Privacy Act
Frustrated Contracts Act
Garage Keepers Act
Homesteads Act, 1989
Hotel Keepers Act
Improvements under Mistake of Title Act
Indian & Native Affairs Act (subject to O.C.)
International Child Abduction Act
International Commercial Arbitration Act
International Sale of Goods Act
Interpretation Act, 1995
Interprovincial Subpoena Act
Intestate Succession Act
Judgments Extension Act
Judges' Orders Enforcement Act
Jury Act, 1981
Justice of the Peace Act, 1988
Land Contracts (Actions) Act
Land Titles Act
Landlord & Tenant Act
Language Act
Law Reform Commission Act
Laws Declaratory Act
Legal Aid Act
Legal Profession Act, 1990
Libel & Slander Act
Limitation of Actions Act
Limitation of Civil Rights Act
Local Authority Freedom of Information & Protection of Privacy Act
Lord's Day (Saskatchewan) Act
Marriage Act, 1995
Marriage Settlement Act
Matrimonial Property Act
Mechanics' Lien Act
Member Conflict of Interest Act
Mentally Disordered Persons Act
Minors Tobacco Act
Notaries Public Act
Ombudsman Act
Parents' Maintenance Act
Penalties & Forfeitures Act
Pension Benefits Act, 1992
Personal Property Security Act
Police Act, 1990
Police Pension (Saskatoon) Funding Act
Powers of Attorney Act
Pre-judgement Interest Act
Privacy Act
Private Investigators & Security Guards Act
Proceedings Against the Crown Act
Provincial Court Act
Provincial Mediation Board Act
Public Inquiries Act
Public Officers' Protection Act
Public Trustee Act
Public Utilities Easements Act
Queen's Bench Act
Queen's Counsel Act
Queen's Printer's Act
Reciprocal Enforcement of Judgments Act
Reciprocal Enforcement of Maintenance Orders Act, 1983
Recording of Evidence by Sound Recording Machine Act
Recovery of Possession of Land Act
Referendum & Plebiscite Act
Regulations Act, 1995

Residential Tenancies Act
Revised Statutes Act, 1979
Sale of Goods Act
Sales on Consignment Act
Saskatchewan Evidence Act
Saskatchewan Farm Security Act
Saskatchewan Human Rights Code
Saskatchewan Insurance Act
Saskatchewan Natural Resources Transfer Agreement (Treaty Land Entitlement) Act
Securities Act, 1988
Slot Machine Act
Small Claims Act
Summary Offences Procedure Act, 1990
Surface Rights Acquisition & Compensation Act
Survival of Actions Act
Survivorship Act, 1993
Tabling of Documents Act, 1991
Thresher Employees Act
Thresher's Lien Act
Trading Stamp Act
Traffic Safety Council of Saskatchewan Act, 1988
Trustee Act
Trusts Convention Implementation Act
Unconscionable Transactions Relief Act
Variation of Trusts Act
Victims of Crime Act, 1995
Victims of Domestic Violence Act
Warehousemen's Lien Act
Wills Act
Woodmen's Lien Act

Consumer Related Acts

Agricultural Implements Act
Auctioneers Act
Business Corporations Act
Business Names Registration Act
Cemeteries Act
Collection Agents Act
Companies Act
Companies Winding Up Act
Consumer & Commercial Affairs Act (subject to the provisions of O.C. 1134/90 & O.C. 177/93)
Consumer Product Warranties Act
Cooperatives Act, 1989 (except Part XIX)
Cost of Credit Disclosure Act
Credit Reporting Agencies Act
Credit Union Act, 1985 (except Part XVIII)
Direct Sellers Act
Family Farm Credit Act
Film & Video Classification Act
Guarantee Companies Securities Act
Home Owners' Protection Act
Mortgage Brokers Act
Motor Dealers Act
Municipal Hail Insurance Act
Names of Homes Act
Non-profit Corporations Act, 1995
Partnership Act
Prepaid Funeral Services Act
Pyramid Franchises Act
Real Estate Act
Real Estate Brokers Act, 1987
Religious Societies Land Act
Sale of Training Courses Act
Saskatchewan Embalmers Act
Saskatchewan Insurance Act
Trust & Loan Corporations Act
Unsolicited Goods & Credit Cards Act

Minister & Attorney General, Hon. John Nilson, Q.C., 306/787-0613
Deputy Minister & Deputy Attorney General, Brent Cotter, Q.C., 306/787-5351, Fax: 306/787-3874
Associate Deputy Minister, Finance & Administration, Keith Laxdal, 306/787-7869
Acting Director, Administrative Services Branch, Elizabeth Smith, 306/787-5472
Director, Communications, Lisa Ann Wood, 306/787-7872

Registrar of Licensing & Investigations, Consumer Protection Branch, Al Dwyer, 306/787-2952, Fax: 306/787-5550
Acting Deputy Registrar, Consumer Protection Branch, Larry Wilson, 306/787-5712
Superintendent, Insurance & Registrar, Credit Unions, J.M. Hall, 306/787-7881, Fax: 306/787-9779
Deputy Superintendent, Insurance & Deputy Registrar, Credit Unions, Linda Zarzeczny, 306/787-2958, Fax: 306/787-9779
Superintendent of Pensions, Dave Wild, 306/787-2458, Fax: 306/787-9779
Director, Human Resources, Barry Sockett, 306/787-5475, Fax: 306/787-2084
    For list of Courts & other Legal Officers, including Judicial Officials & Judges see Section 10 of this book.

CIVIL LAW DIVISION
Executive Director, Darryl Bogdasavich, Q.C., 306/787-6602, Fax: 306/787-0581

CORRECTIONS DIVISION
Fax: 306/787-8084
Executive Director, Dick Till, 306/787-3573
Director, Regina Correctional Centre, Robert Smerchinski, PO Box 617, Regina SK S4P 3A6, 306/924-9022

PUBLIC LAW & POLICY DIVISION
Executive Director, Doug Moen, Q.C., 306/787-5360
Chief Coroner, Coroner's Branch, John Nyssen, 306/787-5541
Manager, Queen's Printer, Marilyn Lustig-McEwen, 306/787-9345, Fax: 306/787-9111
Executive Director, Law Enforcement Services, John Baker, 306/787-0400
Executive Director, Legislative Services, Doug Moen, Q.C., 306/787-5360
Executive Director, Saskatchewan Police Commission, John Baker, 306/787-0400
Coordinator, Legislative Drafting, Ian Brown, 306/787-9346
Director, Constitutional Branch, Graeme Mitchell, 306/787-8385
Director, Policy, Planning & Evaluation Branch, Betty Ann Pottruff, Q.C., 306/787-8954
Director, Victims Services, Katrine Macaulay, 306/787-0418
Chief, Provincial Firearms Office, Mitch Crumley
Asst. Chief, Provincial Firearms Office, Alan Terry

PUBLIC PROSECUTIONS DIVISION
Executive Director, C. Richard Quinney, Q.C., 306/787-5490

REGISTRY SERVICES DIVISION
Asst. Deputy Minister, Ron Hewitt, Q.C., 306/787-5333, Fax: 306/787-8737
Executive Director, Court Services, Barb Hookenson, 306/787-5680, Fax: 306/787-8737
Executive Director, Property Registration Branch, Beverley Bradshaw, 306/787-5504, Fax: 306/787-8737
Public Trustee, Public Trustees' Office, Ron Kruzeniski, Q.C., 306/787-5427
Director, Corporations Branch, Phil Flory, 306/787-2970, Fax: 306/787-8999
Director, Maintenance Enforcement Office, Lionel McNabb, 306/787-1650, Fax: 306/787-1420
Director, Mediation Services, Ken W. Acton, 306/787-5749, Fax: 306/787-0088

Associated Agencies, Boards & Commissions
• Agricultural Implements Board: 1871 Smith St., Regina SK S4P 3V7 – 306/787-3550; Fax: 306/787-9779
• Law Reform Commission of Saskatchewan: c/o University of Saskatchewan, College of Law, Saskatoon SK S7N 0W0 – 306/966-2699; Fax: 306/966-5574

Canadian Almanac & Directory 1997

Director, Research, K.P.R. Hodges
Legal Research Officer, M.J.W. Finley
- Provincial Mediation Board/Office of the Rentalsman: 2103 - 11 Ave., 5th Fl., Regina SK S4P 3V7 – 306/787-2699; Fax: 306/787 5574
Chair, Terry Chin
- Public & Private Rights Board: 2151 Scarth St., Regina SK S4P 3V7 – 306/787-4071; Fax: 306/787-0088
Chair, Kenneth W. Acton
- Saskatchewan Farm Land Security Board: #207, 3988 Albert St., Regina SK S4S 3R1 – 306/787-5147; Fax: 306/787-8599
Chair, George Lee
General Manager, Dan Patterson
Farm Foreclosure Section, Jim Chernick
Home Quarter Protection, Dick Wellman
- Saskatchewan Farm Security Programs: 122 - 3 Ave. North, Saskatoon SK S7K 2H6 – 306/933-5105; Fax: 306/933-5009
General Manager, Dan Patterson
- Saskatchewan Farm Tenure Arbitration Board: 1871 Smith St., Regina SK SHP 3V7 – 306/787-2101
Manager, Melissa Wallace
- Saskatchewan Film Classification Board: 1871 Smith St., Regina SK S4P 3V7 – 306/787-5884; Fax: 306/787-9779
Chair, Elizabeth Pederson
- Saskatchewan Film Classification Appeal Commission: 1871 Smith St., Regina SK S4P 3V7 – 306/787-5884; Fax: 306/787-9779
Chair, Betsy Bury
- Saskatchewan Human Rights Commission: 122 - 3 Ave. North, 8th Fl., Saskatoon SK S7K 2H6 – 306/933-5952; Fax: 306/933-7863; URL: http://www.gov.sk.ca/govt/hrc/
Chief Commissioner, Donna Greshner
Executive Director, Donalda Ford
- Saskatchewan Police Commission: 1874 Scarth St., 7th Fl., Regina SK S4P 3V7 – 306/787-6534
Director, Tom Savage
- Saskatchewan Police Complaints Investigator: 2151 Scarth St., 3rd Fl., Regina SK S4P 3V7 – 306/787-6519; Fax: 306/787-6528
Investigator, Elton Gritzfeld, Q.C.
Director, Gary Treble
- Saskatchewan Securities Commission: Toronto Dominion Bank Bldg., #850, 1914 Hamilton St., Regina SK S4P 3V7 – 306/787-5645; Fax: 306/787-5899
Chair, Marcel de la Gorgendière, Q.C., 306/787-5630
Vice Chair, Herbert J. Dow, #32, 3415 Calder Cres., Saskatoon SK S7J 5A1
Director, Barbara L. Shourounis, 306/787-5842
Deputy Director, Corporate Finance, Ian McIntosh, 306/787-5867
Deputy Director, Enforcement, Vic Pankratz, 306/787-5850
Deputy Director, Legal, Dean Murrison, 306/787-5879
Deputy Director, Registration, Ann Lorenzen, 306/787-5876
- Saskatoon Child Centre: c/o Saskatchewan Justice, 1874 Scarth St., Regina SK S4P 3V7 – 306/975-8250
A new innovative facility which provides an integrated, coordinated response to child abuse.
Chair, Norm Doell
- Surface Rights Board of Arbitration: 113 - 2nd Ave., PO Box 1597, Kindersley SK S0L 1S0 – 306/463-5447; Fax: 306/463-5449
Chair, Richard Gibbons

Saskatchewan LABOUR
1870 Albert St., Regina SK S4P 3V7
306/787-4496; Fax: 306/787-2208; URL: http://www.gov.sk.ca/govt/labour/
TDD: 306/787-2429

ACTS ADMINISTERED
Building Trades Protection Act
Construction Industry Labour Relations Act, 1992
Employment Agencies Act
Fire Departments Platoon Act
Human Resources, Labour and Employment Act
Labour-Management Disputes (Temporary Provisions) Act
Labour Standards Act
Occupational Health and Safety Act, 1993
Radiation Health and Safety Act, 1985
Trade Union Act
Victims of Workplace Injuries Day of Mourning Act
Wages Recovery Act
Minister, Hon. Robert W. Mitchell, Q.C., 306/787-6662, Fax: 306/787-6946
Deputy Minister, Sandra Morgan, 306/787-2399, Fax: 306/787-2315
Special Advisor, Ted Boyle, 306/787-4156

LABOUR RELATIONS, MEDIATION & CONCILIATION SERVICES DIVISION
Executive Director, Terry Stevens, 306/787-5050, Fax: 306/787-5804

LABOUR SERVICES DIVISION
Executive Director, Graham Mitchell, 306/787-5050, Fax: 306/787-5804

LABOUR SUPPORT DIVISION
Executive Director, N. A. Bamford, 306/787-8414, Fax: 306/787-7229
Acting Director, Human Resources & Administrative Services, Aldene Meis Mason, 306/787-2415, Fax: 306/787-2806
Director, Planning Policy & Communications, John Boyd, 306/787-3370
Acting Manager, Budget & Operations, S. Little, 306/787-4527, Fax: 306/787-1064

OCCUPATIONAL HEALTH & SAFETY DIVISION
306/787-4496; Fax: 306/787-2208
Toll Free: 1-800-567-7233 (Saskatchewan)
Executive Director, Jeff Parr, 306/787-4496, Fax: 306/787-2208, Email: sklab2@sasknet.sk.ca, Toll Free: 1-800-567-7233 (Saskatchewan)
Manager, Hygiene, Risk Assessment & Standards Services, Herb Wooley, 306/787-4506
Acting Manager, Mine & Radiation Safety, Ernie Becker, 306/787-5055
Manager, Workplace Safety, Bob Ross, 306/787-4134
Acting Manager, Workplace Safety, Norm Fengstad

Associated Agencies, Boards & Commissions
- Labour Relations Board: 1914 Hamilton St., Regina SK S4P 4V4 – 306/787-2406; Fax: 306/787-2664
Chair, Beth Bilson
Vice-Chair, Gwen Gray
- Minimum Wage Board: 1870 Albert St., Regina SK S4P 3V7 – 306/787-2474; Fax: 306/787-4780
Chair, Stan Cameron
- Office of the Worker's Advocate: 1870 Albert St., Regina SK S4P 3V7 – 306/787-2456
Acting Director, Wendy Dean

Saskatchewan LIQUOR & GAMING AUTHORITY
2500 Victoria Ave., PO Box 5054, Regina SK S4P 3M3
306/787-4213; Fax: 306/787-8468; URL: http://www.gov.sk.ca/govt/lga/
Minister Responsible, Hon. Joanne Crofford, 306/787-0354
President & CEO, Gordon Nystuen, 306/787-1737
Manager, Public Education & Communications, Lisa Thomson, 306/787-1721

Saskatchewan Government MEDIA SERVICES
#3, Legislative Bldg., Regina SK S4S 0B3
306/787-6281

The central information arm of the government (Executive Council), acting as the coordinating unit for the information sections of the departments.
Director, Vacant

Saskatchewan MUNICIPAL GOVERNMENT
1855 Victoria Ave., Regina SK S4P 3V7
306/787-8282; Fax: 306/787-4181; URL: http://www.gov.sk.ca/govt/munigov/

ACTS ADMINISTERED
Amusement Ride Safety Act
Archives Act
Arts Board Act
Assessment Management Agency Act
Boiler & Pressure Vessel Act
Border Areas Act
Community Planning Profession Act
Controverted Municipal Elections Act
Culture & Recreation Act
Cutknife Reference Act
Department of Rural Development Act
Department of Urban Affairs Act
Doukhobors of Canada C.C.U.B. Trust Fund Act
Electrical Licensing Act
Emergency Planning Act
Fire Prevention Act, 1992
Flin Flon Extension of Boundaries Act, 1952
Gas Licensing Act
Heritage Property Act
House Building Assistance Act
Industrial Towns Act
Interprovincial Lotteries Act, 1984
Jean-Louis Legare Act
Lloydminster Municipal Amalgamation Act, 1930
Local Government Election Act
Local Improvements Act, 1993
Meewasin Valley Authority Act
Municipal Board Act
Municipal Debentures Repayment Act
Municipal Development & Loan Act
Municipal Expropriation Act
Municipal Improvements Assistance (Sask) Act
Municipal Industrial Development Corporation Act
Municipal Reference Act
Municipal Revenue Sharing Program Act
Municipal Tax Sharing (Potash) Act
Northern Affairs Act
Northern Municipalities Act
Passenger & Freight Elevator Act
Planning & Development Act, 1983
Public Libraries Act, 1984
Rural Development Act
Rural Municipal Administrators Act
Rural Municipality Act, 1989
Saskatchewan Centre of the Arts Act
Saskatchewan Heritage Foundation Act
Saskatchewan Housing Corporation Act
Saskatchewan Multicultural Act
Senior Citizens Home Repair Assistance Act, 1984
Subdivisions Act
Tartan Day Act
Tax Enforcement Act
Time Act
Uniform Building & Accessibility Standards Act
Urban Municipal Administrators Act
Urban Municipality Act, 1984
Wakamow Valley Authority Act
Western Development Museum Act
Minister, Hon. Carol Teichrob, 306/787-6100, Fax: 306/787-0630
Deputy Minister, Ken Pontikes, 306/787-2630, Fax: 306/787-1530

Manager, Communications, Maureen Boyle, 306/787-5959, 8282, Fax: 306/787-4181
Director, Finance & Administration, Larry Chaykowski, 306/787-2011, Fax: 306/787-4161
Director, Human Resources, Don Harazny, 306/787-2831, Fax: 306/787-4181

CULTURE & RECREATION DIVISION
URL: http://www.gov.sk.ca/govt/munigov/cult&rec/
Associate Deputy Minister, Ken Alecxe, 306/787-5765, Fax: 306/787-1530
Director, Arts, Cultural Industries & Multiculturalism, Ron Holgerson, 306/787-4753, Fax: 306/787-8560
Director, Heritage Branch, Dean Clark, 306/787-2809, Fax: 306/787-0069
Director, Sport, Recreation & Lotteries, Bill Werry, 306/787-5737, Fax: 306/787-8560
Manager, Government House Heritage Property, Peggy Brunsdon, 4607 Dewdney Ave., Regina SK S4P 3V7, 306/787-5720, Fax: 306/787-5714
Manager, Heritage Foundation, Garth Pugh, 306/787-4188
Manager, Royal Saskatchewan Museum, Ron Borden, College Ave. & Albert St., Regina SK S4P 3V7, 306/787-2813, Fax: 306/787-2820

HOUSING DIVISION
URL: http://www.gov.sk.ca/govt/munigov/housing/
Toll Free: 1-800-667-7567 (Saskatchewan)
Associate Deputy Minister, Ron Styles, 306/787-4200, Fax: 306/787-1530
Director, Financial Operations, Peter Hoffman, 306/787-4174, Fax: 306/787-8571
Director, Intergovernmental Affairs & Northern Housing, Tom Young, 306/787-1791, Fax: 306/787-5166
Executive Director, Program Operations, Ron Sotski, 306/787-7311, Fax: 306/787-5166
Director, Property Management, Craig Marchinko, 306/787-8569

MUNICIPAL SERVICES DIVISION
Asst. Deputy Minister, Ron Davis, 306/787-2674, Fax: 306/787-1530
Director, Municipal Development, Paul Raths, 306/787-2710
Director, Municipal Planning & Advisory Services, Vacant, 306/787-2656
Director, Municipal Policy, Legislative Services & Finance, John Edwards, 306/787-2665
Director, Saskatchewan Infrastructure Program, Russ Krywulak, 306/787-8887, Fax: 306/787-3641
Executive Director, Protection Services Branch, Nick Surtees, 306/787-4509, Fax: 306/787-9273
Director, Emergency Planning, Wayne Marr, 306/787-9567, Fax: 306/787-1694
Chief Building Official, Building Standards Branch, Margaret Miller, 306/787-4517, Fax: 306/787-9273
Commissioner, Office of the Fire Commissioner, Rick McCullough, 306/787-4516, Fax: 306/787-9273
Chair, Board of Examiners, Jean Lazar, 306/787-2643

Associated Agencies, Boards & Commissions
• Saskatchewan Arts Board: T.C. Douglas Bldg., 3475 Albert St., 3rd Fl., Regina SK S4S 6X6 – 306/787-4056; Fax: 306/787-4199, Toll Free: 1-800-667-7526 (Saskatchewan)
Chair, Cheryl Kloppenburg
Vice-Chair, Paul Rezansoff
Executive Director, Valerie Creighton
Director, Operations, Peter Sametz
• Saskatchewan Municipal Board (SMB): 2151 Scarth St., 4th Fl., Regina SK S4P 3V7 – 306/787-6221; Fax: 306/787-1610; URL: http://www.gov.sk.ca/govt/munibrd/
Chair, B.G. McNamee, 306/787-6223
Vice-Chair, J.S. Pass, 306/787-6163

Member, J.D. Robinson, 306/787-6228
Secretary, Assessment Appeals & Condominium Property Act Apportionment Committees, Cindy Schwindt, 306/787-2644
Secretary, Board, Local Government & Property Maintenance Appeals Committee, Marilyn Turanich, 306/787-6227
Secretary, Municipal Boundary & Planning & Fire Prevention Appeals Committees, Barry Fry, 306/787-6244

Saskatchewan NORTHERN AFFAIRS
PO Box 5000, La Ronge SK S0J 1L0
306/425-4200
1919 Saskatchewan Dr., Regina SK S4P 3V7
306/787-2906, Fax: 306/787-2909
Minister, Hon. Keith N. Goulet, 306/787-1885, Fax: 306/787-0399
Deputy Minister, Ray McKay, 306/425-4207
Executive Director, Resource Development Division, Alison Stickland, 1919 Saskatchewan Dr., Regina SK S4P 3V7, 306/787-2908

Saskatchewan OMBUDSMAN
#150, 2401 Saskatchewan Dr., Regina SK S4P 3V7
306/787-6211; Fax: 306/787-9090
Saskatoon: 206 - 4th Ave. South, Saskatoon SK
306/933-5500, Fax: 306/933-8406
Ombudsman, Barbara Tomkins
Asst. Ombudsman, Murray Knoll, 306/787-6210
Asst. Ombudsman, Saskatoon Sub-Office, Glenda Cooney

Saskatchewan POST-SECONDARY EDUCATION & SKILLS TRAINING
2220 College Ave., Regina SK S4P 3V7
306/787-1002; URL: http://www.gov.sk.ca/govt/pseduc/

ACTS ADMINISTERED
Ancillary Dental Personnel Education Act
Apprenticeship & Trade Certification Act
League of Educational Administrators, Directors & Superintendents Act, 1991
Private Vocational Schools Regulation Act
Regional Colleges Act
Registered Music Teachers Act
Saskatchewan Association of School Business Officials Act
SIAST Act
Student Assistance & Student Aid Fund Act, 1985
Teachers' Dental Plan Act
Teachers' Federation Act
Teachers' Life Insurance (Government Contributory) Act
Teachers' Superannuation & Disability Benefits Act
Trade Union Amendment Act
University of Regina Act
University of Saskatchewan Act, 1995
University of Saskatchewan Foundation Act
Minister, Hon. Robert W. Mitchell, Q.C., 306/787-6662, Fax: 306/787-6946
Deputy Minister, Dan Perrins, 306/787-5586, Fax: 306/787-1300
Asst. Deputy Minister, Lily Stonehouse, 306/787-5676
Associate Deputy Minister, Brij Mathur, 250/787-6056, Fax: 250/787-1300
Executive Director, Planning & Policy Coordination, Donna Krawetz, 306/787-7213
Executive Director, Student Support & Employment Services Branch, Linda Smith, 306/787-5896
Executive Director, Training Programs Branch, Wayne McElree, 306/787-2093

Director, Intergovernmental Relations Branch, Barbara MacLean, 306/787-5746
Director, Northern Services Branch, Earl Cook, 306/424-4398
Director, Training Institution Branch, Vacant
Director, University Services Branch, John Biss, 306/787-5900

Saskatchewan POWER CORPORATION (SaskPower)
2025 Victoria Ave., Regina SK S4P 0S1
306/566-2121; Fax: 306/566-2330
Minister Responsible, Hon. Eldon Lautermilch, 306/787-0605, Fax: 306/787-8100
President & CEO, John R. Messer, 306/566-3103
Executive Vice-President, Corporate Affairs, Carole Bryant, 306/566-3515
Vice-President, Customer Services, Roy Yeske, 306/566-3271
Vice-President, Energy Supply & Facilities Planning, Tony Harras, 306/566-2102
Vice-President, Finance, Ken Christensen, 306/566-2620
Vice-President, Human Resources, Kevin Mahoney, 306/566-2161
Vice-President, Major Projects & Facility Enhancements, Lauren Carlson, 306/566-3202
Vice-President, Production & Transmission & Reporting Vice-President, Operations, Rick Patrick, 306/566-2955
Head, Strategy Management & Development, Roy Derrick, 306/566-3104

Saskatchewan PROPERTY MANAGEMENT CORPORATION (SPMC)
1840 Lorne St., Regina SK S4P 3V7
306/787-6911; Fax: 306/787-1061

ACTS ADMINISTERED
Alberta-Saskatchewan Boundary Act, 1939
Architects Act
Geographic Names Board Act
Interior Designers Act
Land Surveys Act
Manitoba-Saskatchewan Boundary Acts, 1937, 1942, 1966, 1978
Purchasing Act
Saskatchewan Land Surveyors Act
Saskatchewan-Northwest Territories Act, 1966
Saskatchewan Property Management Corporation Act
Minister, Hon. Clay Serby, 306/787-7387
Acting President, John Law, 306/787-6520, Fax: 306/787-6547
Vice-President, Accommodation, Garth Rusconi, 306/787-6863
Vice-President, Commercial Services, Al Moffat, 306/787-9909
Vice-President, Finance & Corporate Services, Debbie Koshman, 306/787-1071

Associated Agencies, Boards & Commissions
• Saskatchewan Geographical Names Board: 2045 Broad St., Main Fl., Regina SK S4P 3V7 – 306/787-2800
Secretary, David Arthur

Saskatchewan PUBLIC SERVICE COMMISSION
2103 - 11th Ave., Regina SK S4P 3V7
Fax: 306/787-7533; URL: http://www.gov.sk.ca/govt/psc/
Saskatoon Fax: 306/933-8248
Minister, Hon. Lorne Calvert, 306/787-7363
Chair, Michael Shaw, 306/787-7551, Fax: 306/787-4074

Executive Director, Staffing & Development, Ron Wight, 306/787-8478
Executive Director, Employee Relations, Rick McKillop, 306/787-7606
Director, Administrative & Information Services, Elizabeth Smith, 306/787-7507
Manager, Communications, Don Black, 306/787-7506

Saskatchewan RESEARCH COUNCIL (SRC)
15 Innovation Blvd., Saskatoon SK S7N 2X8
306/933-5400; Fax: 306/933-7896; URL: http://www.src.sk.ca
President & CEO, Ron Woodward, 306/933-5402, Email: woodward@src.sk.ca
Vice-President, Agricultural Biotechnology, Jerome Konecsni, 306/933-6670, Email: konecsni@src.sk.ca
Vice-President, Research, Jim Hutchinson, 306/787-9401, Email: hutchison@src.sk.ca
Vice-President, Technology Transfer, Tony Rawa, 306/933-5499, Email: rawa@src.sk.ca
Director, Analytical Services, Gene Smithson, 306/933-5439, Email: smithson@src.sk.ca
Director, Business Innovation Services, Greg Stevens, 306/933-8152, Email: stevens@src.sk.ca
Director, Building Systems, Mark Bomberg, 306/933-6169, Email: bomberg@src.sk.ca
Director, Corporate Marketing, Rick Tofani, 306/933-5490, Email: tofani@src.sk.ca
Director, Environment, Bryan Schreiner, 306/933-5495, Email: schreiner@src.sk.ca
Director, Fermentation Technologies, Krystyna Sosulski, 306/933-8136, Email: sosulski@src.sk.ca
Director, Genetics Branch, Jeff Kraay, 306/933-8205, Email: kraay@src.sk.ca
DNA Lab, Yves Plante, 306/933-7273, Email: plante@src.sk.ca
Director, Information Technology Applications, Jeff Whiting, 306/933-5423, Email: whiting@src.sk.ca
Director, Instrumentation, Certification & Testing, Steve Tong, 306/933-7160, Email: tong@src.sk.ca
Director, Petroleum & Mineral Exploration, Ernie Pappas, 306/787-9351, Email: pappas@src.sk.ca
Director, Process Development, Ranga Rangnathan, 306/787-9343, Email: rangnathan@src.sk.ca
Director, Product Design & Development, Dave Grier, 306/933-8131, Email: grier@src.sk.ca
Coordinator, Information Services, Colleen MacLeod, 306/933-5489, Email: macleod@src.sk.ca

SASKENERGY INCORPORATED
#1100, 1945 Hamilton St., Regina SK S4P 2C7
306/777-9426; Fax: 306/777-9889
Minister Responsible, Hon. Eldon Lautermilch, 306/787-0605, Fax: 306/787-8100
President & CEO, Ronald S. Clark
Executive Vice-President, TransGas Ltd., Jullian Olenick
Vice-President, Distribution Utility, Russ E. Pratt
Vice-President, Business Development & Marketing, Doug Kelln
Vice-President, Finance & Administration, Elaine Bourassa
General Counsel, Mark Guillet
Director, Gas Supply, Ken From
Vice-President, Human Resources, Robert Haynes
Director, Corporate Affairs, Rosyln Ingram

Many Islands Pipe Lines (Canada) Limited (MIPL)
President, Ronald S. Clark
Acting General Counsel & Corporate Secretary, Mark Guillet

TransGas Limited
President, Ronald S. Clark
Executive Vice-President, Jullian Olenick

Bayhurst Gas Ltd.
President, Ronald S. Clark
Acting General Counsel & Corporate Secretary, Mark Guillet

Saskatchewan SOCIAL SERVICES
1920 Broad St., Regina SK S4P 3V6
306/787-3494; Fax: 306/787-1032; Email: ENVOY 100:cosask.soc.services; URL: http://www.gov.sk.ca/govt/socserv/

ACTS ADMINISTERED
Adoption Act
Child Care Act
Child & Family Services Act
Department of Social Services Act
Family Services Act
Housing & Special-care Homes Act (in part)
Legal Aid Act
Rehabilitation Act
Residential Services Act
Registered Social Workers Act
Saskatchewan Assistance Plan Act
Minister, Hon. Lorne Calvert, 306/787-7363
Deputy Minister, Con Hnatiuk, 306/787-3491, Fax: 306/787-1032
Associate Deputy Minister, Neil Yeates, 306/787-4909
Asst. Deputy Minister, Vic Taylor, 306/787-7357
Director, Communications & Public Education, Virginia Wilkinson, 306/787-0916
Executive Director, Policy & Planning, Brenda Righetti, 306/787-3621
Acting Director, Research & Evaluation, David Rosenbluth, 306/787-7354

COMMUNITY LIVING DIVISION
Central Office, #216, 110 Ominica St. West, Moose Jaw SK S6H 6V2
306/787-694-3800; Fax: 306/694-3842
Executive Director, Larry Moffatt, 306/787-2705
Manager, Income Security, Tony Coughlan, 2151 Scarth St., 1st Fl., Regina SK S4P 3V7, 307/787-3536
Manager, Protection & Children's Services, Dorothea Warren, 2240 Albert St., Regina SK S4P 3V7, 306/787-2928
Manager, Young Offenders, Bob Kary, 306/787-9165

FAMILY & YOUTH SERVICES DIVISION
306/787-7010; Fax: 306/787-0925
Executive Director, Richard Hazel, 306/787-3652
Director, Child & Youth Family Services Programs, Dave Hedlund, 306/787-3647
Director, Community Youth Services, vacant, 306/787-4702
Director, Residential, Custodial & Therapeutic Services, Ron Lisk, 306/787-4701
Director, Dales House, Ken Cameron, 160 McIntosh St., Regina SK S4R 4Z4, 306/787-3617, Fax: 306/787-1750
Director, Kenosee Youth Camp, Tony Yanick, PO Box 699, Carlyle SK S0C 0R0, 306/577-2300
Director, Paul Dojack Youth Centre, Ron Simspson, Ritter & Toothill St., Regina SK S4P 3V7, 306/787-3561, Fax: 306/787-7546

HUMAN RESOURCES DIVISION
306/787-9070; Fax: 306/787-3441
Executive Director, Dave Atkinson, 306/787-3597
Director, Child Day Care Division, Deborah Bryck, 306/787-3855
Director, Federal/Provincial Arrangements, Don Fairbairn, 306/787-3627

INCOME SECURITY PROGRAMS DIVISION
306/787-7469
Executive Director, Phil Walsh, 306/787-9239

Manager, Central Operations, Jan Yaworski, 306/787-3389
Manager, Child Day Care Subsidy Unit, Lorraine Snell, 306/787-3885, Toll Free: 1-800-667-7155
Manager, Family Income Plan (FIP), Lorraine Snell, 306/787-3885, Toll Free: 1-800-667-7552
Manager, Saskatchewan Income Plan (SIP), Jan Yaworski, 306/787-3389, Toll Free: 1-800-667-7161

SUPPORT SERVICES DIVISION
306/787-8667; Fax: 306/787-1600
Executive Director, Wes Mazer, 306/787-8666
Director, Budget Branch, Bob Wihlidal, 306/787-8669
Director, Departmental Services Branch, Joe Makan, 306/787-3106
Director, Financial Services Branch, Bill Duncan, 306/787-3575
Director, Information & Technology Services, Ron Naidu, 306/787-9200

Associated Agencies, Boards & Commissions
• Saskatchewan Legal Aid Commission: #820, 410 - 22 St. East, Saskatoon SK S7K 2H6 – 306/933-5300; Fax: 306/933-6764
Chair, Jane L. Lancaster, Q.C.

Saskatchewan TELECOMMUNICATIONS (SaskTel)
2121 Saskatchewan Dr., Regina SK S4P 3Y2
306/777-3737; Fax: 306/565-8717; URL: http://www.sasktel.com/
Provides telecommunication services throughout Saskatchewan & throughout the world through SaskTel International; provides a full range of national & worldwide long distance communication services.
Minister Responsible, Hon. Carol Teichrob
President & CEO, Don Ching
President, SaskTel International, Kelly Staudt, C.M.A.
Senior Vice-President, Strategic Business Development & Administration, Dan Baldwin
Senior Vice-President, Customs Services, Garry Simons
Vice-President, Corporate Counsel & Regulatory Affairs, John Meldrum
Vice-President, Finance, David Schultz
Vice President, Human Resources/Industrial Relations, Catherine MacKenzie
Vice-President, Mobility, D. Milenkovic
Vice-President, Network Services, Kelvin Shepherd
Vice-President, Sales & Service, Gord Farmer
General Manager, Corporate Affairs, Sean Caragata, 306/777-4105, Fax: 306/359-0305

Saskatchewan WATER CORPORATION (Sask Water)
Victoria Place, 111 Fairford St. East, Moose Jaw SK S6H 7X9
306/694-3900; Fax: 306/694-3944; Email: saskwater.cd@sasknet.sk.ca
Northern Operations Office, 800 Central Ave., PO Box 3003, Prince Albert SK S6V 6G1
306/953-2250, Fax: 306/953-2200
Provincial Crown corporation which manages, protects & develops the province's water & land related resources for the economic & social benefit of the province.
Minister Responsible, Hon. Eldon Lautermilch, 306/787-0605, Fax: 306/787-8100
President, Brian Kaukinen, 306/694-3903
Vice-President, Finance & Corporate Services, Wayne Phillips, 306/694-3909
Vice-President, Irrigation & Agricultural Services, Harvey Fjeld, 306/694-3943

Vice-President, Water Resources Management, Wayne Dybvig, 306/694-3950
Vice-President, Water Supply & Transmission, Al Veroba, 306/694-3905

Regional Water Resource Offices
East Central: 120 Smith St. East, 2nd Fl., Yorkton SK S3N 3V3 – 306/786-1490; Fax: 306/786-1495
Northeast: PO Box 2133, Nipawin SK S0E 1E0 – 306/862-1750; Fax: 306/862-1771
Northwest: Royal Bank Bldg., #402, 1101 - 101st St., North Battleford SK S9A 0Z5 – 306/446-7450; Fax: 306/446-7461
Southeast: Weyburn Square, 110 Souris Ave., Weyburn SK S4H 2Z9 – 306/848-2345; Fax: 306/848-2356
Southwest: E.I. Wood Bldg., 350 Cheadle St. West, Swift Current SK S9H 4G3 – 306/778-8257; Fax: 306/778-8271

Saskatchewan WOMEN'S SECRETARIAT
1914 Hamilton St., 3rd Fl., Regina SK S4P 4V4
306/787-2329; Fax: 306/787-2058; URL: http://www.gov.sk.ca/govt/womsec/
Minister Responsible, Hon. Joanne Crofford, 306/787-2207
Acting Executive Coordinator, Faye Rafter

Saskatchewan WORKERS' COMPENSATION BOARD
#200, 1881 Scarth St., Regina SK S4P 4L1
306/787-4370; Fax: 306/787-0213
Minister Responsible, Hon. Robert W. Mitchell, Q.C., 306/787-6662, Fax: 306/787-6946
Chair, Stan Cameron, 306/787-4378
Director, Planning, Research & Communication, Janice Siekawitch, 303/787-4386

GOVERNMENT OF THE YUKON TERRITORY

Seat of Government: Legislative Assembly, PO Box 2703, Whitehorse YT Y1A 2C6
The Yukon was created as a separate territory June 13, 1898. It has an area of 483,450 km2, and the StatsCan census population in 1991 was 27,797.
A federally appointed commissioner (similar to a provincial lieutenant-governor) oversees federal interests in the territory, but the day-to-day operation of the government rests with the wholly elected executive council (cabinet). The territorial legislature has power to make acts on generally all matters of a local nature in the territory, including the imposition of local taxes, property & civil rights & the administration of justice, education & health & social services.
Legislative powers vested in the provinces but not available to the territory include control of unoccupied Crown land, renewable & non-renewable resources (except wildlife & sport fisheries) & the power to amend the Yukon Act, a federal statute.

Office of the COMMISSIONER
211 Hawkins St., Whitehorse YT Y1A 1X3
403/667-5121; Fax: 403/393-6201
Commissioner, Hon. Judy Gingell
Executive Secretary, Eileen Fry

Office of the GOVERNMENT LEADER
PO Box 2703, Whitehorse YT Y1A 2C6
403/667-5885; Fax: 403/667-3035
Government Leader, John Ostashek, 403/667-5603
Principal Secretary, Gordon Steele

Executive Asst., Elaine Racketti
Administrative Asst., Geri Tuton
Deputy Government Leader, Bill Brewster

EXECUTIVE COUNCIL
PO Box 2703, Whitehorse YT Y1A 2C6
403/667-5812; Fax: 403/393-6202

ACTS ADMINISTERED
Cabinet & Caucus Employees Act
Flag Act
Floral Emblem Act
Intergovernmental Agreements Act
Languages Act
Public Inquiries Act
Yukon Tartan Act
Minister, Executive Council Office, Minister, Land Claims & Minister, Finance, John Ostashek, 403/667-5603
Deputy Government Leader & Minister, Community & Transportation Services, Bill Brewster, 403/667-5651
Government House Leader & Minister, Economic Development, Minister, Health & Social Services & Minister, Renewable Resources, Hon. Mickey Fisher, 403/667-5376
Minister, Government Services & Minister, Education, Hon. Alan Nordling, 403/667-5493
Minister, Justice & Minister, Tourism, Doug Phillips, 403/667-5716

Cabinet Office
Deputy Minister & Cabinet Secretary, John Lawson, 403/667-5866, Fax: 403/393-6214
Deputy Cabinet Secretary, Janet Moodie, 403/667-5866
Asst. Deputy Minister, Federal Relations Office, Glenn Grant, #707, 350 Sparks St., Ottawa ON K1R 7S8, 613/234-3206, Fax: 613/563-9602
Chief Negotiator, Land Claims, Self Government & Devolution, Tim McTiernan, 403/667-5908, Fax: 403/393-6214
Protocol Officer, Pamela Bangart, 403/667-5875
Director, Aboriginal Language Services, Mike Smith, 403/667-3737, Fax: 403/393-6229
Director, Bureau of French Language Services, Harley Trudeau, 403/667-3775, Fax: 403/393-6226
Director, Bureau of Management Improvement, Don Trochim, 403/667-5740
Director, Bureau of Statistics, Gerry Ewert, 403/667-5640, Fax: 403/393-6203
Director, Finance & Management Services, Bonnie Love, 403/667-3539
Director, Policy & Communications, Kimberley Bain, 403/667-5854, 5393, 5939, Fax: 403/393-6202

Associated Agencies, Boards & Commissions
• Yukon Council on the Economy & the Environment: A-8E, PO Box 2703, Whitehorse YT Y1A 2C6 – 403/667-5939; Fax: 403/668-4936
Combines operations with Economic Development, & Renewable Resources.
Chair, Tim Preston
• Yukon Health & Social Services Council: c/o Executive Council Office, PO Box 2703, Whitehorse YT Y1A 2C6 – 403/668-4421
Combines operations with Health, Social Services & Justice.
Chair, Dave Buchan

LEGISLATIVE ASSEMBLY
c/o Clerk's Office, PO Box 2703, Whitehorse YT Y1A 2C6
403/667-5498; Fax: 403/667-4180

ACTS ADMINISTERED
Controverted Elections Act

Elections Act
Electoral District Boundaries Act
Legislative Assembly Act
Legislative Assembly Retirement Allowances Act
Clerk & Chief Electoral Officer: Patrick L. Michael, 403/667-5498
Speaker: John Devries, 403/667-5662
Sergeant-at-Arms: Emery Shilleto
Deputy Clerk, Missy Follwell, 403/667-5499

Office of the Leader of the Opposition
The official opposition party had not been determined by the time of publication. The opposition will be known after the Yukon Legislative Assembly sits in the fall of 1996. Contact the Legislative Assembly for further information.
Leader, Piers McDonald
Executive Asst. to Caucus, Kristina Craig

Standing Committees of the Legislature
Members' Services Board Committee
Public Accounts Committee
Rules, Elections & Privileges Committee
Statutory Instruments Committee

TWENTY-EIGHTH LEGISLATURE - YUKON TERRITORY
403/667-5498
Last General Election, September 30, 1996. Maximum Duration, 4 years.
Party Standings (October 1996):
New Democratic Party (NDP) 11
Yukon Party (YP) 3
Liberal (Lib.) 3
Total 17
Salaries, Indemnities & Allowances: 1994 - Members' indemnity $30,832 plus a $15,416 expense allowance (Whitehorse members receive $13,460). In addition to this are the following:
Premier $28,971
Ministers $21,147
Leader of the Official Opposition $21,147
Leader of the Third Party $4,229
Speaker $7,049
Deputy Speaker $5,287
Following is: constituency, total number of ballots cast in September 1996 election, member, party affiliation. (Address for all is PO Box 2703, Whitehorse YT Y1A 2C6.)

MEMBERS BY CONSTITUENCY
Faro (1,031) Trevor Harding, NDP
Klondike (1,923) Peter Jenkins, YP
Kluane (1,069) Gary McRobb, NDP
Lake Laberge, Doug Livingston, NDP
Mayo-Tatchun (728) Eric Fairclough, NDP
McIntyre-Takhini (1,310) Piers McDonald, NDP
Mount Lorne (1,197) Lois Moorcroft, NDP
Porter Creek North (634) John Ostashek, YP
Porter Creek South (727) Pat Duncan, Lib.
Riverdale North (857) Doug Phillips, YP
Riverdale South (603) Sue Edelman, Lib.
Riverside (380) Jack Cable, Lib.
Ross River-Southern Lakes (1,107) Dave Keenan, NDP
Vuntut Gwitchin (163) Robert Bruce, NDP
Watson Lake (1,373) Dennis Fentie, NDP
Whitehorse Centre (602) Todd Hardy, NDP
Whitehorse West (752) Dave Sloan, NDP

MEMBERS (ALPHABETICAL)
Robert Bruce, Vuntut Gwitchin (163)NDP
Jack Cable, Riverside (380)Lib.
Pat Duncan, Porter Creek South (727)Lib.
Sue Edelman, Riverdale South (603)Lib.
Eric Fairclough, Mayo-Tatchun (728)NDP
Dennis Fentie, Watson Lake (1,373)NDP

Canadian Almanac & Directory 1997

Trevor Harding, Faro (1,031)NDP
Todd Hardy, Whitehorse Centre (602)NDP
Peter Jenkins, Klondike (1,923)YP
Dave Keenan, Ross River-Southern Lakes (1,107)NDP
Doug Livingston, Lake LabergeNDP
Piers McDonald, McIntyre-Takhini (1,310)NDP
Gary McRobb, Kluane (1,069)NDP
Lois Moorcroft, Mount Lorne (1,197)NDP
John Ostashek, Porter Creek North (634)YP
Doug Phillips, Riverdale North (857)YP
Dave Sloan, Whitehorse West (752)NDP

YUKON TERRITORY GOVERNMENT DEPARTMENTS & AGENCIES

Yukon COMMUNITY & TRANSPORTATION SERVICES
PO Box 2703, Whitehorse YT Y1A 2C6
403/667-5431; Fax: 403/667-7056

ACTS ADMINISTERED
Area Development Act
Assessment & Taxation Act
Boiler & Pressure Vessels Act
Building Standards Act
Cemeteries & Burial Sites Act
Civil Emergency Measures Act
Dangerous Goods Transportation Act
Electrical Protection Act
Elevator & Fixed Conveyances Act
Fire Prevention Act
Gas Burning Devices Act
Gasoline Handling Act
Highways Act
Home Owner's Grant Act
Lands Act
Motor Transport Act
Motor Vehicles Act
Municipal Act
Municipal Finance & Community Grants Act
Municipal General Purposes Loan Act
Public Government Act
Public Lotteries Act
Public Service Act
Recreation Act
Subdivision Act
Minister, Bill Brewster, 403/667-5651, Fax: 403/667-3035
Deputy Minister, John Cormie, 403/667-5155, Fax: 403/393-6266
Director, Communications Branch, Dan McArthur, PO Box 2703, Whitehorse YT Y1A 2C6, 403/667-5804, Fax: 403/393-6266
Director, Emergency Measures Organization, Paul Albertson, 403/667-5220, Fax: 403/393-6266

MUNICIPAL & COMMUNITY AFFAIRS DIVISION
Asst. Deputy Minister, Virginia Labelle, 403/667-5636, Fax: 403/667-2658, Email: VLabelle@gov.yk.ca
Director, Community Services Branch, Bill Forsythe, 403/667-5299
Director, Finance, Systems & Administration, Temes Cherinet, 403/667-5311, Fax: 403/393-6264
Director, Engineering & Development, Bryant Yeomans, 403/667-5707, Fax: 403/667-6109
Director, Human Resources, Jean Dell, 403/667-5156, Fax: 403/393-6264
Director, Lands Branch, Lyle Henderson, 403/667-5218, Fax: 403/667-2167
Director, Policy, Planning & Evaluation, Dale Kozmeniuk, 403/667-5941, Fax: 403/393-6266
Director, Public Safety Branch, Bryant Yeomans, 403/667-5707, Fax: 403/393-6249

Director, Sport & Recreation Branch, Peter Milner, 403/667-5608, Fax: 403/393-6416
Fire Marshal, Office of the Fire Marshal, John Holesworth, 403/667-5217

TRANSPORTATION DIVISION
Director, Aviation & Marine Branch, Marc Tremblay, PO Box 2129, Haines Junction YT Y0B 1L0, 403/634-2035, Fax: 403/634-2131
Director, Transportation Engineering, Robin Walsh, 403/633-7928, Fax: 403/677-2647
Director, Transportation Maintenance, Mike Johnson, 403/667-5761, Fax: 403/667-3608
Deputy Registrar, Motor Vehicles, Fred Jennex, 403/667-5315

Associated Agencies, Boards & Commissions
• Yukon Assessment Appeal Board: PO Box 2703, Whitehorse YT Y1A 2C6 – 403/667-5234
Chair, Anne King
• Yukon Driver Control Board: PO Box 2703, Whitehorse YT Y1A 2C6 – 403/667-5313
Chair, Carl Maguire
• Yukon Lottery Corporation: PO Box 2703, Whitehorse YT Y1A 2C6 – 403/667-3749
Chair, Doug Beaumont
• Yukon Motor Transport Board: O Box 2703, Whitehorse YT Y1A 2C6 – 403/667-5782
Chair, Arthur Christensen
• Yukon Municipal Board: PO Box 2703, Whitehorse YT Y1A 2C6 – 403/667-3546
Chair, Craig Tuton

Yukon ECONOMIC DEVELOPMENT
211 Main St., PO Box 2703, Whitehorse YT Y1A 2C6
403/667-5466; Fax: 403/668-8601

ACTS ADMINISTERED
Business Development Assistance Act
Economic Development Act
Economic Development & Regional Development Agreement Act
Economic Development Act
Energy Conservation Act
Energy Conservation Agreement Act
Energy Conservation Assistance Act
Loan Guarantee Act
Minister, Hon. Mickey Fisher, 403/667-5376
Deputy Minister, William Oppen, 403/667-5417
Mining Facilitator, Jesse Duke
Director, Finance & Administration, Val Mather
Senior Planner, Northern Accord Office, Brian Love

ECONOMIC POLICY, PLANNING & RESEARCH BRANCH
Asst. Deputy Minister, Terry Sewell, 403/667-5461
Manager, Economic Research & Analysis, Joe Jeerakathil
Manager, Policy & Planning, Thom Stubbs
Senior Planner, Business & Industry, Richard Lloyd
Senior Planner, Renewable Resources, Bob Kuiper

Energy & Mines Branch
Director, Robert Holmes
Manager, Mineral Resources Development, Rod Hill
Manager, Energy Programs, Doug MacLean
Senior Project Geologist, Geological Surveys, Don Murphy

ECONOMIC PROGRAMS BRANCH
Asst. Deputy Minister, Mike Kenny, 403/667-5470
Director, Industry & Program Development, Rob Snyder
Manager, Financial Programs, Bert Perry
Manager, Rural Business/Community Development Office, Dawson City, John Wierda
Manager, Whitehorse Business/Community Development Office, Guy Cocquyt

Associated Agencies, Boards & Commissions
• Business Development Advisory Board: PO Box 2703, Whitehorse YT Y1A 2C6 – 403/667-5470
Chair, Jose Janssen

Yukon EDUCATION
PO Box 2703, Whitehorse YT Y1A 2C6
403/667-5141; Fax: 403/667-4754

ACTS ADMINISTERED
Access to Information Act
Apprentice Training Act
Archives Act
Canada Student Loans Act (federal)
College Act
Education Act
Employment Expansion & Development Act
Occupational Training Act
Public Libraries Act
Students' Financial Assistance Act
Teaching Profession Act
Trade Schools Regulation Act
Minister, Hon Alan Nordling
Deputy Minister, D.P. Odin, 403/667-5126

ADVANCED EDUCATION DIVISION
Asst. Deputy Minister, Gordon McDevitt, 403/667-5131, Fax: 403/667-6339
Director, Training Services, Ken Smith
Manager, Student Financial Assistance, Carol Theriault
President, Yukon College, Sally Ross, PO Box 2799, Whitehorse YT Y1A 5K4, 403/668-8704, Fax: 403/668-8896

EVALUATION, RESEARCH & PLANNING BRANCH
Director, Gary Ewart
Manager, Legislative Support, Suzzanne Green

FINANCE, MANAGEMENT & INFORMATION SERVICES DIVISION
Asst. Deputy Minister, Florian Lemphers, 403/667-5222, Fax: 403/667-4754
Director, Finance & Systems, George Gartner
Director, Human Resources, Valerie Stehelin
Director, Libraries & Archives, Linda Johnson, 403/667-5309, Fax: 403/667-4253
Territorial Archivist, Dianne Chisholm

PUBLIC SCHOOLS DIVISION
Asst. Deputy Minister, Roland McCaffrey, 403/667-5127, Fax: 403/667-6339
Regional Superintendent, Mavis Fisher
Regional Superintendent, Carol McCauley
Regional Superintendent, Wally Seipp
Regional Superintendent, Fred Smith
Director, French Programs, Mavis Fisher
Director, Policy & Communications, Dr. Sheila Rose
Manager, Computing & Technology, Rose Kelly
Manager, Learning Resources, Terry Burns
Manager, School Services, Gordon deBruyn

Yukon EMERGENCY MEASURES ORGANIZATION (YEMO)
PO Box 2703, Whitehorse YT Y1A 2C6
403/667-5220; Fax: 403/667-4566
Director, Paul Albertson

Yukon ENERGY CORPORATION (YEC)
#304, 204 Lambert St., Whitehorse YT Y1A 1Z4
403/667-5028; Fax: 403/393-6327
Minister Responsible, John Ostashek, 403/667-5603
Chair, B. Ernewein
President, William E. Byers, Q.C., 403/667-8120

Vice-President & CFO, Oliver P. O'Rourke, P.Eng.
Senior Utility Engineer, John F. Maissan, P.Eng., 403/633-7078

Yukon FINANCE
PO Box 2703, Whitehorse YT Y1A 2C6
403/667-5343; Fax: 403/393-6217

ACTS ADMINISTERED
Banking Agency Guarantee Act
Faro Mine Loan Act
Financial Administration Act
Fuel Oil Tax Act
Income Tax Act
Insurance Premium Tax Act
Liquor Tax Act
Loan Agreement Act
Public Sector Compensation Restraint Act
Public Servants Superannuation Act
Tobacco Tax Act
Yukon Development Corporation Loan Guarantee Act
Minister, John Ostashek, 403/667-3767
Deputy Minister, Charles Sanderson, 403/667-3571

FINANCIAL OPERATIONS & REVENUE SERVICES
Acting Asst. Deputy Minister & Director, Accounting Services, Dave Hrycan, 403/667-5279; 5375
Director, Financial Systems, Mederic Tremblay, 403/667-5278
Director, Investments & Debt Services, Jeff Frketich, 403/667-5346
Director, Revenue Services, Norm McIntyre, 403/667-3074

FISCAL RELATIONS & MANAGEMENT BOARD SECRETARIAT
Asst. Deputy Minister, Fiscal Relations & Management Board Secretariat, Leo Chassé, 403/667-5821
Director, Budgets, Joanna Reynolds, 403/667-5344
Director, Fiscal Relations, Tim Shoniker, 403/667-5303
Director, Management Board Secretariat, Helen Bebak, 403/667-5277

Yukon GOVERNMENT SERVICES
PO Box 2703, Whitehorse YT Y1A 2C6
403/667-5436; Fax: 403/393-6218

ACTS ADMINISTERED
Public Printing Act
Minister, Hon. Alan Nordling, 403/667-5493, Fax: 403/667-3035
Deputy Minister, Michael Brandt, 403/667-3732
Acting Asst. Deputy Minister, Corporate Services, Gordon McDevitt, 403/667-3732
Director, Finance & Administration, Christine Mahar, 403/667-5410
Director, Human Resources, Derek Holmes, 403/667-3748
Director, Policy & Planning, Siegfried Fuchsbichler
Officer, Business Incentive Office, Rita MacKenzie-Grieve, 403/667-3505

INFORMATION SERVICES
Fax: 403/667-5304
Director, Vacant, 403/667-3712
Manager, Administration & Communications, Ian Burnett, 403/667-5827
Account Manager, Client Services (Business Services), Peter Dielissen, 403/667-5600
Coordinator, Client Services (Technical Resource Centre), Gaile Trafford, 403/667-5034, Fax: 403/393-6200

Manager, Client Services, Bob Chambers, 403/667-8018
Acting Manager, Production Services, Bob Forward, 403/667-3044, Fax: 403/393-6200

PROPERTY MANAGEMENT
Asst. Deputy Minister, Peter Laight, 403/667-8191, Fax: 403/393-6319
Director, Building Development, Dave Parfitt, 403/667-3064
Director, Facilities Management, Mike Bartsch, 403/667-5966, Fax: 403/393-6319
Director, Realty & Regional Services, Vacant, 403/667-5916, Fax: 403/393-6319
Accounting Supervisor, Elly Lohmann, 403/667-3706, Fax: 403/393-6319
Acting Manager, Project Management, Peter Blum, 403/667-5138
Manager, Realty Services, John Cole, 403/667-5104
Manager, Technical Support, Wayne Rogers, 403/667-3589
Facilities Manager, Heinrich Lohmann, 403/667-3052
Facilities Manager, Jack Robinson, 403/667-3654
Facilities Manager, Jim Tessier, 403/667-8882

SUPPLY SERVICES
Fax: 403/393-6299
Acting Director, Carl Rumscheidt, 403/667-5289
Manager, Purchasing, Al Alcock, 403/667-5459
Manager, Queen's Printer, Carl Rumscheidt, 403/667-3585, Fax: 403/668-3585
Manager, Transportation & Communications, Ray Piloud, 403/667-5793
Asst. Manager, Warehouse, John Debrecini, 403/667-5732

Regional Offices
Eastern: PO Box 2500, Watson Lake YT Y0A 1C0 – 403/536-7494; Fax: 403/536-2784, Regional Manager, Darrell W. Peters
Northern: PO Box 4030, Dawson City YT Y0B 1G0 – 403/993-5499; Fax: 403/993-6814, Regional Manager, Tom Sparrow
Western: PO Box 2068, Haines Junction YT Y0B 1L0 – 403/634-2219; Fax: 403/634-2932, Regional Manager, John Farynowski

Yukon HEALTH & SOCIAL SERVICES
PO Box 2703, Whitehorse YT Y1A 2C6
403/667-3673 (Communications); Fax: 403/667-3096

ACTS ADMINISTERED
Change of Name Act
Child Care Act
Children's Act
Dependants' Relief Act
Disabled Persons' Allowance Act
Health Act
Health Care Insurance Plan Act
Hospital Act
Hospital Insurance Services Act
Marriage Act
Mental Health Act
Pioneer Utility Grant Act
Public Health Act
Rehabilitation Services Act
Seniors' Income Supplement Act
Social Assistance Act
Travel for Medical Treatment Act
Vital Statistics Act
Young Offenders Agreement Act
Young Persons Offences Act
Minister, Hon. Mickey Fisher, 403/667-3769, Fax: 403/667-3035
Deputy Minister, Bruce McLennan, 403/667-5770, Fax: 403/667-3096, Email: mclennan@yknet.yk.ca

Coordinator, Communications, Patricia Living, 403/667-3673, Fax: 403/667-3096, Email: pliving@gov.yk.ca

HEALTH SERVICES BRANCH
Responsible for the administration of vital statistics. Fee for each birth, marriage or death certificate: $10.00.
Asst. Deputy Minister, Malcolm Maxwell, 403/667-5686
Director, Health Care Insurance Services, Joanne Fairlie, 403/667-5202, Fax: 403/668-3786
Deputy Registrar, Vital Statistics, Sylvia Kitching, 403/667-5207

SOCIAL SERVICES BRANCH
Asst. Deputy Minister, Bonnie Clark, 403/667-5684
Director, Family/Children's Services, Anne Sheffield, 403/667-8117, Fax: 403/668-4613

Yukon HOUSING CORPORATION
410A Jarvis St., PO Box 2703, Whitehorse YT Y1A 2C6
403/667-5759; Fax: 403/667-3664
Minister Responsible, Hon. Alan Nordling, 403/667-5493
President, Maurice Albert
Director, Construction & Maintenance, Donald Flinn, 403/667-3549
Director, Corporate Relations, Don Routledge, 403/667-8093
Director, Finance & Administration, Louise Girard, 403/667-5760
Director, Operations, Sandie Romanczak, 403/667-5751

Yukon JUSTICE
PO Box 2703, Whitehorse YT Y1A 2C6
403/667-8292 (Communications); Fax: 403/393-6272

ACTS ADMINISTERED
Age of Majority Act
Business Corporations Act
Business Licence Act
Canada & the United Kingdom Reciprocal Recognition & Enforcement of Judgements Act
Central Trust Company & Crown Trust Company Act
Certified General Accountants Act
Chartered Accountants Act
Chiropractors Act
Choices in Action Act
Collection Act
Compensation of Victims of Crime Act
Condominium Act
Conflict of Laws (Traffic Accidents) Act
Constitutional Questions Act
Consumer Protection Act
Contributory Negligence Act
Cooperative Associations Act
Coroners Act
Corrections Act
Court of Appeal Act
Creditor's Relief Act
Criminal Code of Canada (federal)
Defamation Act
Dental Profession Act
Dental Technicians Act
Devolution of Real Property Act
Distress Act
Divorce Act
Divorce Act (federal)
Employment Agencies Act
Employment Standards Act
Engineering Profession Act
Evidence Act
Executions Act

Exemptions Act
Expropriation Act
Factors Act
Family Property & Support Act
Fatal Accidents Act
Fine Option Act
Foreign Arbitral Awards Act
Fraudulent Preferences & Conveyances Act
Frustrated Contracts Act
Funeral Directors Act
Gaols Act
Garage Keepers' Lien Act
Garnishee Act
Human Rights Act
Human Tissue Gift Act
Insurance Act
International Commercial Arbitration Act
International Sale of Goods Act
Interpretation Act
Interprovincial Subpoena Act
Intestate Succession Act
Judicature Act
Jury Act
Landlord & Tenant Act
Land Titles Act
Legal Profession Act
Legal Services Society Act
Limitation of Actions Act
Lottery Licensing Act
Maintenance & Custody Orders Enforcement Act
Married Women's Property Act
Mechanic's Lien Act
Medical Profession Act
Miner's Lien Act
Noise Prevention Act
Notaries Act
Nursing Assistants Registration Act
Optometrists Act
Partnership Act
Pawnbrokers & Second-hand Dealers Act
Perpetuities Act
Personal Property & Security Act
Pharmacists Act
Presumption of Death Act
Private Investigators & Security Guards Act
Public Utilities Act
Real Estate Agent's Act
Reciprocal Enforcement of Judgements Act
Reciprocal Enforcement of Maintenance Orders Act
Recording of Evidence by Sound Apparatus Act
Registered Nurses Profession Act
Regulations Act
Retirement Plan Beneficiaries Act
Revised Statutes Act
Sale of Goods Act
Securities Act
Small Claims Court Act
Societies Act
Society of Management Accountants Act
Summary Convictions Act
Supreme Court Act
Survivorship Act
Tenants in Common Act
Territorial Court Act
Torture Prohibition Act
Trustee Act
Variation of Trusts Act
Victim Services Act
Warehousemen's Lien Act
Warehouse Receipts Act
Wills Act
Woodmen's Lien Act
Young Offenders Act (federal)
Young Offenders Agreement Act (federal)
Young Offenders Welfare Agreement Act (federal)
Minister, Doug Phillips, 403/667-5716
Deputy Minister, Stuart Whitley, Q.C., 403/393-6272

Director, Finance & Administration, Susan Ryan, 403/667-5446, Fax: 403/667-5790
For list of Courts & other Legal Officers, including Judicial Officials & Judges *see* Section 10 of this book.

CORRECTIONS & COMMUNITY PROGRAMS BRANCH
Director, Joy Waters, 403/667-8293, Fax: 403/393-6326
Director, Community Development & Policing, Robert Cole, 403/667-5962, Fax: 403/667-6826
Manager, Adult Probation Services, Jon. Gaudry, 403/667-5231
Manager, Family Violence Prevention Unit, Michael Hanson, 403/667-3581
Chief Territorial Firearms Officer, Ron Daniels, 403/667-3088, Fax: 403/393-6209

COURT SERVICES BRANCH
Director, Linda Adams, 403/667-5942, Fax: 403/393-6212
Manager, Court Operations, Edna Delisle-Jackson, 406/667-3440
Manager, Judicial Support, Iris Warde, 403/667-3442
Sheriff, Sheriff's Office, Paul Cowan, 403/667-5365

JUSTICE SERVICES BRANCH
Asst. Deputy Minister, Noreen McGowan, 403/667-5256
Chief Coroner, Coroner's Service, R. Kent Stewart, 403/667-5317
Registrar, Land Titles, Dianne Gau, 403/667-5612
Official Guardian & Public Administrator, Official Guardian's Office, Judith Suley, 403/667-5366
Manager, Consumer Services & Superintendent, Insurance, Elsie Bagan, 403/667-5257
Manager, Corporate Affairs & Registrar of Securities, Richard Roberts, 403/667-5225
Manager, Labour Services, Charlene Beauchemin, 403/667-5944

LEGAL SERVICES BRANCH
Director, Howard Kushner, 403/667-3469, Fax: 403/393-6379
Executive Director, Legal Aid, Catherine Buckler, 403/667-5210
Chief, Legislative Counsel, Steven Horn, 403/667-5776

Associated Agencies, Boards & Commissions
- Employment Standards Board: PO Box 2703, Whitehorse YT Y1A 2C6
Chair, Glenis Allen, 403/667-5259
- Yukon Human Rights Commission: 205 Rogers St., Whitehorse YT Y1A 1X1 – 403/667-6226
Chair, Geraldine Hutchings
- Yukon Human Rights Panel of Adjudicators: #202, 208 Main St., Whitehorse YT Y1A 2B2 – 403/667-7667
Chief Adjudicator, Monica Leaske
- Yukon Judicial Council: PO Box 4010, Whitehorse YT Y1A 3S9 – 403/667-3524
Chair, Mr. Justice R.E. Hudson
- Yukon Law Foundation: #201, 302 Steele St., Whitehorse YT Y1A 2C5 – 403/668-4231
Chair, Brian Morris
- Law Society of Yukon - Executive: #201, 302 Steele St., Whitehorse YT Y1A 2C5 – 403/668-4231
President, Kenneth A. Oyler
- Law Society of Yukon - Lawyers' Discipline Committee: #201, 302 Steele St., Whitehorse YT Y1A 2C5 – 403/668-4231
Chair, Terrance W. Boylan
- Yukon Legal Services Society: #167, 2134 - 2 Ave., Whitehorse YT Y1A 5H6 – 403/667-5210
Acting Executive Director, Karen Ruddy
- Yukon Lottery Appeal Board: c/o Consumer Services, PO Box 2703, Whitehorse YT Y1A 2C6 – 403/667-5257
Chair, Raji Millard

- Yukon Medical Council: PO Box 2703, Whitehorse YT Y1A 2C6 – 403/667-5257
Chair, Dr. Lis Densmore
- Nursing Assistants Advisory Committee: Registrar's Office, PO Box 2703, Whitehorse YT Y1A 2C6
Registrar, Elsie Bagan, 403/667-5257
- Yukon Utilities Board: PO Box 6070, Whitehorse YT Y1A 5L7 – 403/667-5058
Chair, Brian Morris

Yukon LIQUOR CORPORATION
PO Box 2703, Whitehorse YT Y1A 2C6
403/667-5245; Fax: 403/668-7806
Minister Responsible, Bill Brewster, 403/667-5651
President & CEO, Jean Besier, 403/667-8923
Chief Liquor Inspector, Jeannine McGregor, 403/667-8926
Director, Corporate Services, David Steele, 403/667-8924
Director, Operations & Purchasing, Bob Morris, 403/667-5244

Yukon PUBLIC SERVICE COMMISSION
PO Box 2703, Whitehorse YT Y1A 2C6
403/667-5252; Fax: 403/667-6705
Minister Responsible, Doug Phillips, 403/667-5716
Commissioner, Patricia N. Cumming
Director, Administration Branch, Richard Wale, 403/667-5861
Director, Benefits Management, Terry Kinney, 403/667-5251
Director, Corporate Human Resource Services, Mal Malloch, 403/667-5250
Director, Planning & Research Branch, Pat Byers, 403/667-3735
Director, Staff Development Branch, Cheryl Van Blaricom, 403/667-8268
Director, Staffing Relations Branch, Megan Slobodin, 403/667-5201

Yukon RENEWABLE RESOURCES (YRR)
PO Box 2703, Whitehorse YT Y1A 2C6
403/667-5237
Toll Free: 1-800-661-0408 (Yukon)

ACTS ADMINISTERED
Agricultural Products Act
Agriculture Development Act
Brands Act
Environment Act
Fisheries Act (Canada) - Administrative agreement for freshwater fisheries
Forest Protection Act
Freshwater Fisheries Agreement Act
Mackenzie River Basin Agreements Act
Parks Act
Pounds Act
Wildlife Act
Yukon River Basin & Alsek River Basin Agreements Act
Yukon River Basin Study Agreement Act
Minister, Hon. Mickey Fisher, 403/667-5376
Deputy Minister, Miriam McTiernan, 403/667-5460, Fax: 403/393-6213
Coordinator, Communications, Dennis Senger

AGRICULTURE BRANCH
Fax: 403/393-6222
Director, Dave Beckman, 403/667-5838

ENVIRONMENT PROTECTION & ASSESSMENT BRANCH
Fax: 403/393-6213
Manager, Joe Ballantyne, 403/667-8177
Manager, Environmental Assessment, Kelvin Leary, 403/667-5409

Manager, Standards & Approvals, Bengt Pettersson, 403/667-5610

FIELD SERVICES BRANCH
Fax: 403/393-6206
Acting Director & Manager, Enforcement & Compliance, Dan Lindsey, 403/667-5786
Regional Resource Manager, North, John Russell, 403/993-6951
Regional Resource Manager, South, Tony Grabowski, 403/667-5115

FINANCE & ADMINISTRATION BRANCH
Director, Stan Marinoske, 403/667-5197, Fax: 403/393-6219
Manager, Financial Services, Darrel March, 403/667-5160
Manager, Information Services & Economic Programs, Steve Smyth, 403/667-5160
Manager, Personnel Services, Nonie Mikeli, 403/667-8659

FISH & WILDLIFE BRANCH
Fax: 403/393-6213
Director, Mark Hoffman, 403/667-5715
Chief, Fisheries, Don Toews, 403/667-5117
Chief, Habitat Management, Manfred Hoefs, 403/667-5671
Chief, Regional Management, Brian Pelchat, 403/667-5720
Chief, Wildlife Management, Doug Larsen, 403/667-5177

PARKS & OUTDOOR RECREATION BRANCH
Fax: 403/668-7823
Director, Jim McIntyre, 403/667-5261
Project Manager, Peter Frankish, 403/667-3057
Regional Superintendent, Klondike, Sandy Sippola, 403/993-6850
Regional Superintendent, Kluane, George Nassiopoulos, 403/634-2026
Regional Superintendent, Liard, Ray Wotton, 403/821-4609

POLICY & PLANNING BRANCH
Fax: 403/667-3641
Director, Jim Connell, 403/667-5634
Manager, Geographic Information Section, Lauren Crooks, 403/667-8137
Manager, Geographic Information Section, Beth Hawkings, 403/667-8137
Manager, Land Claims Coordination Unit, Allan Koprowsky
Manager, Policy Analysis & Development, Michael White

Associated Agencies, Boards & Commissions
- Alsek Renewable Resources Council: PO Box 2077, Haines Junction YT Y0B 1L0

Chair, Mike Crawshay, 403/634-2524
- Mayo Renewable Resources Council: PO Box 249, Mayo YT Y0B 1M0

Chair, Dan McDiarmid, 403/996-2942
- Teslin Renewable Resources Council: PO Box 186, Teslin YT Y0A 1B0

Chair, Denny Denison, 403/390-2323
- Vuntut Gwitchin Renewable Resources Council: PO Box 80, Old Crow YT Y0B 1N0

Chair, Roy Moses, 403/996-3034
- Yukon Fish & Wildlife Management Board: PO Box 5954, Whitehorse YT Y1A 5L7 – 403/667-3754; Fax: 403/667-2099

Chair, Mike Smith, 403/667-3754, Fax: 403/667-2099
Coordinator, Conservation Education, Remy Rodden

Yukon TOURISM
PO Box 2703, Whitehorse YT Y1A 2C6
403/667-5430; Fax: 403/667-3546

ACTS ADMINISTERED
Historic Resources Act
Historic Sites & Monuments Act
Hotels & Tourist Establishments Act
Scientists & Explorers Act
Minister, Doug Phillips, 403/667-5716
Deputy Minister, Vicki Hancock, 403/667-5430

Director, Administration, Cynthia Jenkins, 403/667-3009
Director, Arts Branch, Rick Lemaire, 403/667-8592
Director, Heritage Branch, Jeff Hunston, 403/667-5363
Director, Industry Services Branch, John Spicer, 403/667-5633
Director, Marketing Branch, Klaus W. Roth, 403/667-5390
Coordinator, Historic Sites, Doug Olynyk, 403/667-5295
Yukon Archaeologist, Ruth Gotthardt, 403/667-5983

Yukon WOMEN'S DIRECTORATE
PO Box 2703, Whitehorse YT Y1A 2C6
403/667-3030; Fax: 403/393-6270
Minister Responsible, Doug Phillips, 403/667-5716
Director, Elda Ward, 403/667-5182, Email: eward@gov.yk.ca

Yukon WORKERS' COMPENSATION BOARD
401 Strickland St., Whitehorse YT Y1A 5N8
403/667-5645; Fax: 403/668-2079
Minister Responsible, Hon. Alan Nordling, 403/667-5493
President & CEO, R.M. Farrell, 403/667-5224
Director, Assessments, Dale Schmekel, 403/667-5613
Director, Claims, Isabelle Bordage, 403/667-5319
Director, Client Services, Shannon Borgstrom, 403/667-8185
Director, Finance & Administration, David Tyler, 403/667-5624
Director, Occupational Health & Safety, Mike Tischer, 403/667-8616
Director, Policy, Planning & Evaluation, , Tony Armstrong
Communications Officer, Bonnie King, 403/667-8983
Workers' Advisor, David Brown, 403/667-8695

FOREIGN GOVERNMENT EQUIVALENCY TABLE
CANADIAN GOVERNMENT COMPARISONS WITH MAJOR TRADING PARTNERS

Canada	Belgium	China	France	Germany	Hong Kong	Italy	Japan
Office of the Prime Minister	Office of the Prime Minister	Office of the Premier	Office of the Prime Minister	Office of the Federal Chancellor	Office of the Governor	Office of the Prime Minister	Office of the Prime Minister
House of Commons	Chamber of Representatives	National People's Congress	National Assembly	Federal Assembly	Legislative Council	Chamber of Deputies	House of Representatives
Agriculture & Agri-food	Min. of Agriculture & Small & Medium Size Business	Min. of Agriculture	Min. of Agriculture, Fisheries & Food	Min. of Food, Agriculture & Forestry	Agriculture & Fisheries Dept.	Min. of Agriculture, Food & Forestry Services	Min. of Agriculture, Forestry & Fisheries
Canadian Heritage	Min. of the Interior (in part)	Min. of Culture	Min. of Culture	---	---	Min. of Cultural Heritage/Min. of Natural Patrimony	Min. of Home Affairs
Citizenship & Immigration Canada	Min. of Justice	Min. of Justice	Min. of Justice	Min. of Justice	Immigration Dept.	Min. of National Patrimony	Min. of Justice
Environment Canada	Min. of the Interior	Min. of Forestry/Min. of Water Resources/State Bureau of Environmental Protection	Min. of Environment	Min. for the Environment, Nature Conservation & Nuclear Safety	Environmental Protection Dept./Water Supplies Dept.	Min. of Environment & Public Works/Energy, Environment & New Technology Agency	Min. of Agriculture, Forestry & Fisheries/Japan Environmental Agency
Finance Canada	Min. of the Budget/Min. of Finance	Min. of Finance	Min. of Economy & Finance	Min. of Economic Affairs	Audit Dept./Inland Revenue Dept./Treasury	Min. of Finance	Min. of Finance
Fisheries & Oceans Canada	---	---	Min. of Agriculture, Fisheries & Food	Min. for the Environment, Nature Conservation & Nuclear Safety	Agriculture & Fisheries Dept./Marine Dept.	---	Min. of Agriculture, Forestry & Fisheries/Japanese Fisheries Agency
Foreign Affairs & International Trade Canada	Min. of Foreign Trade/Min. of Foreign Trade	Min. of Foreign Affairs/Min. of Foreign Economic Relations & Trade/Chinese Council for the Promotion of International Trade	Min. of Foreign Affairs	Min. of Foreign Affairs/Federal Office for Foreign Trade Information	Trade Dept./Hong Kong Trade Development Council	Min. of Foreign Affairs/Min. of Foreign Trade/National Inst. for Foreign Trade	Min. of Foreign Affairs/Min. of International Trade & Industry/Japan External Trade Organization
Health Canada	Min. of Pensions & Public Health	Min. of Public Health	Sec. of Health & Social Welfare	Min. of Health	Dept. of Health	Min. of Health	Min. of Health & Welfare
Human Resources Development Canada	Min. of Employment & Labour/Min. of Pensions & Public Health/Min. of Social Affairs	Min. of Labour/Min. of Public Security	Min. of Labour & Social Affairs	Min. of Labour & Social Affairs/Min. of National Education, Secondary School Instruction, Research & Professional Training	Labour Dept./Social Welfare Dept.	Min. of Labour & Social Welfare	Min. of Health & Welfare/Min. of Labour
Indian & Northern Affairs Canada	---	---	Min. of Regional Development, Urban Affairs & Integration	Min. of Regional Planning, Building & Urban Development	Regional Services Dept./Territory Development Dept.	Dept. of Public Administration & Regional Affairs	---
Industry Canada	Min. of Agriculture & Small & Medium Size Business/Min. of Economic Affairs	Min. of the Chemical Industry/Min. of the Electronics Industry/Min. of Machine Building Industry/Min. of Metallurgical Industry/All-China Fedn. of Industry & Commerce	Min. of Economy & Finance/Min. of Industry, Postal Service & Telecommunications/Min. of Small, Medium Business, Trade & Artisans' Activities	Min. of Economic Cooperation & Development/Federal Patent Office	Industry Dept.	Min. of Industry, Commerce & Crafts/Manufacturing Industries Investment & Financing Authority	Min. of International Trade & Industry/Small & Medium Enterprise Agency

Canadian Almanac & Directory 1997

FOREIGN GOVERNMENT EQUIVALENCY TABLE
CANADIAN GOVERNMENT COMPARISONS WITH MAJOR TRADING PARTNERS

México	Netherlands	Norway	South Korea	Switzerland	Taiwan	United Kingdom	United States
Office of the President	Office of the Prime Minister	Office of the Prime Minister	Office of the Prime Minister	Office of the President	Office of the Premier	Office of the Prime Minister	Office of the President
Chamber of Deputies	Second Chamber	Lagting	National Assembly	Federal Assembly	National Assembly	House of Commons	House of Representatives
Sec. of Agriculture, Livestock & Rural Development	Min. of Agriculture, Nature Management & Fisheries	Min. of Agriculture	Min. of Agriculture, Forestry & Fisheries	Dept. of Economic Affairs	Council for Agriculture	Min. of Agriculture, Fisheries & Food	Dept. of Agriculture
Sec. of Social Development/Sec. of Tourism	Min. of Education, Cultural Affairs & Science	Min. of Cultural Affairs	Min. of Culture & Sports	---	---	Dept. of National Heritage/Northern Ireland Office/Scottish Office/Welsh Office	Dept. of State
Sec. of Internal Affairs	Min. of Home Affairs	Min. of Justice	Min. of Justice	---	Min. of Justice	Home Office	Dept. of Justice, Immigration & Naturalization Service
Sec. of Environment, Natural Resources & Fisheries	Min. of Agriculture, Nature Management & Fisheries	Min. of Environment	Min. of the Environment/Korean Environmental Preservation Association	Dept. of the Interior, Office for the Environment, Forests & Countryside	Environment Protection Administration	Dept. of the Environment	Dept. of the Interior/Environmental Protection Agency
Sec. of Finance & Public Credit	Min. of Finance	Min. of Finance	Min. of Government Administration/Economic Planning Board	Dept. of Finance	Min. of Finance	Her Majesty's Treasury	Dept. of Commerce
Sec. of Environment, Natural Resources & Fisheries	Min. of Agriculture, Nature Management & Fisheries	Min. of Fisheries	Min. of Agriculture, Forestry & Fisheries/Korean Maritime Inst./Korean Ocean Research & Development Inst.	---	---	Min. of Agriculture, Fisheries & Food	Dept. of Commerce, Oceans & Atmosphere Office/Dept. of the Interior, U.S. Fish & Wildlife Service
Sec. of Foreign Affairs/National Commercial Exports Council	Min. of Foreign Affairs	Min. of Foreign Affairs/Min. of Trade & Shipping	Min. of Foreign Affairs/Min. of Justice, Korean Customs Service/Korean Inst. for Foreign Economics & Trade	Dept. of Foreign Affairs	Min. of Foreign Affairs	Foreign & Commonwealth Office/Dept. of Trade & Industry/Her Majesty's Treasury, Customs & Excise	Dept. of Commerce/Dept. of State, Foreign Service/International Trade Administration/U.S. International Trade Commn./Advisory Committee for Trade & Policy Negotiations/Office of the U.S. Trade Representative
Sec. of Health	Min. of Health, Welfare & Sports	Min. of Health & Social Affairs	Min. of Health & Welfare/Korean Inst. for Health & Social Affairs	Dept. of the Interior, Office of Public Health	Dept. of Health	Dept. of Health	Dept. of Health & Human Services
Sec. of Labour & Social Welfare	Min. of Social Affairs & Employment	Min. of Health & Social Services/Min. of Local Government & Labour	Min. of Labour Affairs	Dept. of Economic Affairs, Office of Industry, Arts & Labour/Dept. of the Interior, Office of Social Security	Council of Labour Affairs	Dept. of Education & Employment/Dept. of Social Security	Dept. of Health & Human Services, Social Security Administration/Dept. of Labour
---	---	Min. of Development Cooperation	---	---	---	Northern Ireland Office/Scottish Office/Welsh Office	Dept. of the Interior, Bur. of Indian Affairs
Sec. of Commerce & Industrial Development	Min. of Economic Affairs & Foreign Trade	Min. of Development Coordination/Min. of Industry & Energy/Fedn. of Commercial & Service Enterprises	Min. of Trade & Industry	Dept. of Economic Affairs, Office of Industry	Min. of Economic Affairs	Dept. of Trade & Industry	Small Business Administration

Canadian Almanac & Directory 1997

FOREIGN GOVERNMENT EQUIVALENCY TABLE
CANADIAN GOVERNMENT COMPARISONS WITH MAJOR TRADING PARTNERS

Canada	Belgium	China	France	Germany	Hong Kong	Italy	Japan
Justice Canada	Min. of Justice	Min. of Justice	Min. of Justice	Min. of Justice	Judiciary Dept./Legal Dept.	Min. of Justice	Min. of Justice
National Defence Canada	Min. of National Defence	Min. of National Defence	Min. of Defence	Min. of Defence	---	Min. of Defence	Japanese Defence Agency
Natural Resources Canada	Min. of the Interior	Min. of Energy/Min. of Forestry/Min. of Geology & Mineral Resources/Min. of Water Resources	Min. of the Environment/Min. of the Interior	Min. for the Environment, Nature Conservation & Nuclear Safety/Min. of Food, Agriculture & Forestry	Environmental Protection Dept.	Min. of Agriculture, Food & Forestry Resources/Min. of the Interior/Energy Environment & New Technology Agency	Min. of Agriculture, Forestry & Fisheries/Japan Environmental Agency/National Land Agency
Public Works & Govt. Services Canada	Min. of the Interior	Min. of Construction/Min. of Water Resources	Min. of Public Works, Housing, Transportation & Tourism	Min. of Regional Planning, Building & Urban Development	Architectural Services Dept./Building & Lands Dept./Civil Engineering Dept./Fire Services Dept./Govt. Supplies Dept.	Dept. of Public Administration & Regional Affairs	Min. of Construction
Revenue Canada	Min. of Finance/Min. of Pensions & Public Health	State Bureau of Taxation	Min. of Economy & Finance	Min. of Finance	Inland Revenue Dept./Rating & Valuation Dept.	Min. of Budget & Economic Planning	Min. of Finance
Solicitor General Canada	Min. of the Interior	Min. of Public Security/Min. of State Security	Min. of the Interior	Min. of the Interior/Federal Office for Public Security	Correctional Services Dept.	Min. of the Interior	Min. of Home Affairs/Min. of Justice
Statistics Canada	---	---	Sec. for Research	Federal Statistics Office	Census & Statistics Office	---	---
Status of Women Canada	Min. of Social Affairs	---	Min. of Integration & the Fight Against Exclusion	Min. for Women & Youth	---	Dept. of Family & Social Affairs	---
Transport Canada	Min. of Transportation	Min. of Transportation/Civil Aviation Administration/Min. of Public Works, Housing, Transportation & Tourism	Min. of Public Works, Housing, Transportation & Tourism	Min. of Transport/Federal Aviation Office	Civil Aviation Dept./Highways Dept./Marine Dept./Transport Dept./Govt. Land Transport Agency	Min. of Transport & Merchant Marine	Min. of Transport
Treasury Board of Canada	Min. of the Budget/Min. of Finance	Min. of Finance	Min. of Economy & Finance	Min. of Economic Affairs	Audit Dept./Inland Revenue Dept./Treasury	Min. of Finance	Min. of Finance
Veterans Affairs Canada	---	---	---	Min. for Family Affairs & Senior Citizens	Social Welfare Dept.	---	---
Associated Agencies							
Atomic Energy of Canada Ltd.	---	China Nuclear Energy Industry Corp.	France Electricity	Min. for the Environment, Nature Conservation & Nuclear Energy	---	National Nuclear Energy Committee	Japan Atomic Energy Commn.
Bank of Canada	National Bank of Belgium	Bank of China	Bank of France	Bank of the Federal Republic of Germany	Hong Kong/Shanghai Banking Corp.	Bank of Italy	Bank of Japan
Canada Post Corp.	Inst. of Posts & Telecommunications	Min. of Posts & Telecommunications	Min. of Industry, Postal Service & Telecommunications	Min. of Posts & Telecommunications	---	Min. of Posts & Telecommunications	Min. of Posts & Telecommunications

Canadian Almanac & Directory 1997

FOREIGN GOVERNMENT EQUIVALENCY TABLE
CANADIAN GOVERNMENT COMPARISONS WITH MAJOR TRADING PARTNERS

México	Netherlands	Norway	South Korea	Switzerland	Taiwan	United Kingdom	United States
Office of the Attorney General	Min. of Justice	Min. of Justice	Min. of Justice	Min. of Justice & Police	Min. of Justice	Lord Chancellor's Dept./Lord Advocate's Dept.	Dept. of Justice
Sec. of National Defence/Sec. of the Navy	Min. of Defence	Min. of Defence	Min. of National Defence	Dept. of the Military	Min. of National Defence	Min. of Defence	Dept. of Defence/National Security Council
Sec. of Environment, Natural Resources & Fisheries/Mining Sector Development Agency/Council of Mineral Resources Development/National Water Commn.	Min. of Agriculture, Nature Management & Fisheries	Min. of the Environment/Min. of Industry & Energy/National Energy Inst./Norwegian Petroleum Directorate	Min. of Agriculture, Forestry & Fisheries/Min. of the Environment/Korean Inst. for Energy Research/Korean Inst. of Geology, Mining & Materials	Dept. of the Interior, Office for the Environment, Forests & Countryside	Min. of the Interior/Environment Protection Administration	Dept. of the Environment/HM Land Registry/Dept. of National Heritage, Royal Parks	Dept. of Agriculture, Forest Service/Dept. of Energy/Dept. of the Interior, Bureau of Mines, Bureau of Land Management, National Parks Service
Sec. of Internal Affairs	Min. of Transport & Public Works	Min. of Administrative Affairs	Min. of Government Administration/Min. of Transportation & Construction	Dept. of Justice & Police, Federal Intellectual Property Office	Council for Economic Planning & Development	Cabinet Office, The Buying Agency/Office of Public Services & Science/Office of Water Services	General Services Administration
Sec. of Finance & Public Credit	Min. of Finance	Min. of Finance	---	Dept. of Finance, Federal Tax Administration	Min. of Audit	Board of Inland Revenue/National Audit Office	Dept. of the Treasury, Internal Revenue Service
Sec. of Internal Affairs	Min. of Home Affairs/Min. of Justice	Min. of Justice	Min. of Home Affairs/Min. of Justice	Dept. of Justice & Police, Office of Civil Defence, Office of Police Matters	Min. of the Interior	Home Office/Law Officer's Dept.	Dept. of Justice/National Security Council/Central Intelligence Agency
Min. of Internal Affairs, Population & Migration	---	---	Min. of Information & Communications	Dept. of the Interior, Federal Statistics Office	Research, Development & Evaluation Commn.	Office for National Statistics/Home Office, Research & Statistics Directorate	Dept. of Commerce, Economic & Statistics Administration, Bureau of Census
Sec. of Social Development	Min. of Home Affairs	Min. of Children & Family Affairs	---	---	---	Dept. of Education & Employment	Dept. of Labor, Women's Bureau
Sec. of Communications & Transport/National Railways of México	Min. of Transport & Public Works	Min. of Transportation & Communications/Norwegian State Railway	Min. of Transportation & Construction/Korean Maritime Inst./Korean Transport Inst.	Dept. of Transportation, Communications & Energy/Swiss Railway Service	Min. of Communications & Transportation	Dept. of Transport/Associated British Ports/British Railways Board/Civil Aviation Authority	Dept. of Transportation/National Transportation Safety Board
Sec. of Finance & Public Credit	Min. of Finance	Min. of Finance	Min. of Government Administration/Economic Planning Board	Dept. of Finance	Min. of Finance	Her Majesty's Treasury	Dept. of Commerce
---	---	Min. of Health & Social Services	Min. of Patriots & Veterans Affairs	---	Vocational Assistance Commn. for Retired Servicemen	Min. of Defence	Dept. of Veterans Affairs
National Nuclear Development Standards Commn.	---	---	Korean Atomic Energy Research Institute/Korean Nuclear Society	---	Atomic Energy Council	UK Atomic Energy Authority	Nuclear Regulatory Commn.
Bank of México	Bank of the Netherlands	Bank of Korea	Swiss National Bank	Central Bank of China	Bank of England	Federal Reserve System	---
Sec. of Communications & Transport	---	Min. of Transportation & Communications	Min. of Information & Communications	Swiss Post, Telephone & Telegraph Co.	Min. of Communications & Transportation	The Post Office	U.S. Postal Service

Canadian Almanac & Directory 1997

FOREIGN GOVERNMENT EQUIVALENCY TABLE
CANADIAN GOVERNMENT COMPARISONS WITH MAJOR TRADING PARTNERS

Canada	Belgium	China	France	Germany	Hong Kong	Italy	Japan
Canadian Broadcasting Corp.	Inst. of Posts & Telecommunications	Min. of Posts & Telecommunications	France Radio-telephone Company/France Telecom	Min. of Posts & Telecommunications	Radio Television Hong Kong	Min. of Posts & Telecommunications	Min. of Posts & Telecommunications
Canadian National Railway Co.	---	---	---	Govt. Land Transport Agency	---	---	National Railways of México
Canadian Radio-Television & Telecommunications Commn.	Min. of Telecommunications/Inst. of Posts & Telecommunications	Min. of Posts & Telecommunications/Min. of Television, Radio & Cinema	Min. of Industry, Postal Service & Telecommunications	Min. of Posts & Telecommunications	Radio-Television Hong Kong	Min. of Posts & Telecommunications	Min. of Posts & Telecommunications
Canadian Space Agency	---	---	Aerospace Industries	---	---	---	Inst. of Space & Astronautical Science/National Space Development Agency
Correctional Service Canada	Min. of Justice	Min. of Justice	Min. of Justice	Min. of Justice	Correctional Services Dept.	Min. of Institutional Reform	Min. of Justice
Export Development Corp.	Min. of Foreign Trade	Min. of Foreign Economic Relations & Trade/Beijing Foreign Trade Corp.	Min. of Economy & Finance, Foreign Trade	Federal Export Office/Federal Office for Foreign Trade Information	Hong Kong Trade Development Council	Min. of Foreign Trade/National Inst. for Foreign Trade	Japan External Trade Organization
National Energy Board	---	Min. of Energy/China International Water & Electric Corp./China National Petroleum & Natural Gas Corp./China Nuclear Energy Corp.	France Electricity/France Gas Company	---	---	Energy, Environment & New Technology Agency/National Nuclear Energy Committee	---
National Research Council	---	Chinese Academy of Sciences/State Science & Technology Commn.	Sec. for Research	Min. of Education, Science, Research & Technology	----	Min. of Universities, Scientific & Technological Research	Japan Science & Technology Agency
Public Service Commn. of Canada	---	Min. of Personnel	Min. of Civil Service, Administrative Reform & Decentralization	---	---	Dept. of Public Administration & Regional Affairs	---
Royal Canadian Mounted Police	---	Min. of Public Security	---	Min. of the Interior, Academy of State Police	---	---	---

FOREIGN GOVERNMENTS

Following is a listing of government information for those countries which constitute Canada's major trading partners. According to Statistics Canada trade information (see "Principal Trading Partners in 1995", page 1-54) Canada's major trading partners include: Belgium, China, Finland, France, Germany, Hong Kong, Italy, Japan, the Netherlands, Norway, South Korea, Switzerland, Taiwan, the United Kingdom and the United States.

Major trading countries are listed alphabetically and contain information about major government ministries and departments followed by main federal government agencies and corporations. For information about foreign government diplomatic and consular offices in Canada, see "Diplomatic & Consular Representatives in Canada" in the main/general Index.

GOVERNMENT OF BELGIUM/Belgique
Capital: Brussels

Major Political Parties: Flemish Social Christian (CVP); Francophone Socialist (PS); Flemish Socialist (SP); Flemish Liberals & Democrats (VLD)
Currency: Belgian Franc
Total Area: 30,528 km2
Population: 10,131,000 (1994)
Language(s): Dutch, French, German

OFFICE OF THE KING
Palais Royal, Rue de Brèderode, 1000, Brussels, Belgium
(011-32-2) 551-2020
King, H.M. King Albert II
Marshal of the Court, G. Jacques

OFFICE OF THE PRIME MINISTER
16, rue de La Loi, 1000, Brussels, Belgium
(011-32-2) 501-02-11, Fax: (011-32-2) 512-69-53
Prime Minister, Jean-Luc Dehaene
Chief of Cabinet, Paul Maertens
Secretary, Council of Ministers, Steve Dubois

CHAMBER OF REPRESENTATIVES
Palais de la Nation, 1008, Brussels, Belgium
(011-32-2) 419-80-91, Fax: (011-32-2) 519-83-02
President, Charles-Ferdinand Nothomb

SENATE OF BELGIUM
Palais de la Nation, 1009, Brussels, Belgium
(011-32-2) 515-82-11, Fax: (011-32-2) 574-06-85
President, Frank Swaelen

MINISTRY OF AGRICULTURE & SMALL & MEDIUM SIZE BUSINESS
Rue Marie-Thérese 1, Brussels 1040, Belgium
(011-32-2)211-06-11, Fax: (011-32-2) 219-61-30
Minister, Karel Pinxten

MINISTRY OF THE BUDGET
7, Place Quetelet, 1030, Brussels, Belgium
(011-32-2) 219-01-19, Fax: (011-32-2) 219-09-14
Minister, Herman Van Rompuy

MINISTRY OF ECONOMIC AFFAIRS
23, Square de Meeûs, 1040, Brussels, Belgium

FOREIGN GOVERNMENT EQUIVALENCY TABLE
CANADIAN GOVERNMENT COMPARISONS WITH MAJOR TRADING PARTNERS

México	Netherlands	Norway	South Korea	Switzerland	Taiwan	United Kingdom	United States
Telecommunications México	---	Norwegian Telecommunications Authority	Min. of Information & Communications	Swiss Broadcasting & Television Society	Min. of Communications & Transportation	British Broadcasting Corp.	National Telecommunications & Information Admin.
---	Norwegian State Railway	Min. of Transportation & Construction, National Railroad	Swiss Railway Service	---	British Railways Board	Dept. of Transportation, Federal Railway Admin.	---
Sec. of Communications & Transport/Telecommunications México	---	Min. of Transportation & Communications/Norwegian Telecommunications Authority	Min. of Information & Communications/Electronics & Telecommunications Research Inst.	Dept. of Transportation, Communications & Energy/Federal Office of Communications/Swiss Broadcasting & Television Society	Min. of Communications & Transportation	British Telecom International/British Telecommunications PLC/Wireless PLC/Radiotelecommunications Agency	Federal Communications Commn./National Telecommunications & Information Administration
---	---	---	Korean Aerospace Research Inst.	---	---	British Aerospace	National Aeronautics & Space Administration
---	Min. of Justice	Min. of Justice	Min. of Justice	Dept. of Justice & Police	Min. of Justice	Home Office, Her Majesty's Prison Service	Dept. of Justice, Bureau of Prisons
National Commercial Exports Council	Min. of Economic Affairs & Foreign Trade	Min. of Trade & Shipping	Korean Inst. for International Economics & Trade	---	Min. of Economic Affairs, Board of Foreign Trade	Dept. of Trade & Industry/Export Credits Guarantee Dept.	Federal Trade Commn./US Trade & Development Agency
National Council of Mineral Resources Development/National Electricity Commn.	---	National Energy Inst.	Korean Energy Economic Inst./Korean Inst. of Energy Research	Dept. of Transportation, Communications & Energy, Office of Energy	---	Office of Electricity Regulation/Oil & Pipelines Agency	Federal Energy Regulatory Commn.
---	Min. of Education, Cultural Affairs & Science	Min. of Education, Research & Church Affairs	Min. of Science & Technology/Korean Inst. of Advanced Science & Technology	---	National Council of Science	Office of Science & Technology	National Science Fdn./Smithsonian Institution
Sec. of Internal Affairs	---	Min. of Administrative Affairs	Min. of Government Administration	---	Min. of Personnel	Office of Public Services & Science, Civil Service	Office of Personnel Management
Sec. of Internal Affairs	---	---	Min. of Home Affairs, Police Headquarters	Dept. of Justice & Police, Police Matters	Min. of the Interior, National Police Administration	Home Office/UK Police Service/National Criminal Intelligence Service	Federal Bureau of Investigation/Dept. of the Treasury, US Secret Service

(011-32-2) 506-51-11, Fax: (011-32-2) 514-46-83
Minister, Elio Di Rupo

MINISTRY OF EMPLOYMENT & LABOUR
51-53, rue Bélliard, 1040, Brussels, Belgium
(011-32-2) 233-51-11, Fax: (011-32-2) 230-1067
Minister, Miet Smet

MINISTRY OF FINANCE
12, rue de la Loi, 1000, Brussels, Belgium
(011-32-2) 233-81-11, Fax: (011-32-2) 233-80-03
Minister, Philippe Maystadt

MINISTRY OF FOREIGN AFFAIRS
2, rue des Quatre Bras, 1000, Brussels, Belgium
(011-32-2) 516-81-11, Fax: (011-32-2) 511-63-85
Minister, Erik Derycke

MINISTRY OF FOREIGN TRADE
2, rue des Quatre Bras, 1000, Brussels, Belgium
(011-32-2) 516-83-11, Fax: (011-32-2) 512-72-21
Minister, Philippe Maystadt

MINISTRY OF THE INTERIOR
rue des Colonies 56, 7ème étage, 1000, Brussels, Belgium
(011-32-2) 227-0700, Fax: (011-32-2) 219-7930
Minister, Johan Van de Lanotte
State Secretary, Security Secretariat, Jan Peeters, 5, rue Gallilée, 10ème étage, 1030, Brussels, (011-32-2) 210-19-11

MINISTRY OF JUSTICE
115, boul de Waterloo, 1000, Brussels, Belgium
(011-32-2) 542-79-11, Fax: (011-32-2) 538-07-67
Minister, Stefaan De Clerck

MINISTRY OF NATIONAL DEFENCE
Rue Lambermont 8, 1000, Brussels, Belgium
(011-32-2) 516-8211, Fax: (011-32-2) 550-2919
Minister, Jean-Pol Poncelet
Chief of Staff, Air Force, Lt. Gen. Guido Van Hecke, (011-32-2) 243-31-11
Chief of Joint Staff, Armed Forces, V. Adm. Willy Herteleer, (011-32-2) 701-31-11

Chief of Staff, Army, Vacant, (011-32-2) 243-31-11
Chief of Staff, Navy, R. Ad,m. M. Verhulst, (011-32-2) 701-31-19

MINISTRY OF PENSIONS & PUBLIC HEALTH
Bâtiment Amazone, 33, boul Bischoffsheim, 1000, Brussels, Belgium
(011-32-2) 220-20-11, Fax: (011-32-2) 220-20-67
Minister, Marcel Colla
State Secretary, Secretariat for Social Integration & Environment, Jan Peeters, 5, rue Gallilée, 10ème étage, 1030, Brussels, (011-32-2) 210-19-11

MINISTRY OF PUBLIC SERVICE
Résidence Palace, 9ème étage, Rue de la Loi 155, 1040, Brussels, Belgium
(011-32-2) 233-05-11, Fax: (011-32-2) 233-05-90
Minister, Andr@' Flahaut

MINISTRY OF SCIENTIFIC POLICY
66, rue de la Loi, 1040, Brussels, Belgium

(011-32-2) 238-28-11, Fax: (011-32-2) 230-38-62
Minister, Yvan Ylieff

MINISTRY OF SOCIAL AFFAIRS
66, rue de la Loi, 1040, Brussels, Belgium
(011-32-2) 238-28-11, Fax: (011-32-2) 230-38-95
Minister, Magda de Galan

MINISTRY OF TELECOMMUNICATIONS
65, rue de la Loi, 1040, Brussels, Belgium
(011-32-2) 237-67-11, Fax: (011-32-2) 230-18-24
Minister, Elio Di Rupo

MINISTRY OF TRANSPORTATION
65, rue de la Loi, 1040, Brussels, Belgium
(011-32-2) 237-67-11, Fax: (011-32-2) 230-18-24
Minister, Michel Daerden

Associated Agencies
• Belgian Business Federation
4, rue Ravenstein, 1000, Brussels, Belgium
(011-32-2) 515-0811, Fax: (011-32-2) 515-09-99
President, Urbain Devoldere
• Institute of Posts & Telecommunications
5, rue Van Orlay, 1210, Brussels, Belgium
(011-32-2) 213-46-02
• National Bank of Belgium
14, boul de Berlaimont, 1000, Brussels, Belgium
(011-32-2) 221-21-11, Fax: (011-21-2) 221-31-00
Governor, Alfonse Verplaetse

GOVERNMENT OF CHINA/Zhong Guo
Capital: Beijing
Major Political Parties: Chinese Communist Party (CCP)
Currency: Yuan
Total Area: 9,596,960 km2
Population: 1,203,097,268 (1995)
Language(s): Chinese (Mandarin), Yue (Cantonese), Wu (Shanghainese), Minbei (Fuzhou), Minnan (Hokkien-Taiwanese), Xiang, Gan, Hakka

OFFICE OF THE PRESIDENT
c/o State Council Secretariat, Zhong Nan Hai, Beijing, China
(011-86-10) 3098375
President, Jiang Zemin
Vice-President, Rong Yiren

OFFICE OF THE PREMIER
c/o State Council Secretariat, Zhong Nan Hai, Beijing, China
(011-86-10) 666453
Premier, Li Peng
Vice-Premier, Wu Bangguo
Vice-Premier, Jiang Chunyun
Vice-Premier, Zou Jiahua
Vice-Premier, Li Lanqing
Vice-Premier, Qian Qichen
Vice-Premier, Zhu Rongji

THE POLITBURO
Zhong Nan Hai, Beijing, China
(011-86-10) 335987
General Secretary, Jiang Zemin

THE SECRETARIAT
Zhong Nan Hai, Beijing, China
(011-86-10) 335987
General Secretary, Jiang Zemin

NATIONAL PEOPLE'S CONGRESS
Standing Committee, Great Hall of the People, Beijing, China
(011-86-10) 667380
Chair, Qiao Shi

MINISTRY OF AGRICULTURE
11 Nong Zhan Nan Li, East District, Beijing 100017, China
(011-86-10) 5003366, Fax: (011-86-10) 5002448
Minister, Liu Jiang

MINISTRY OF THE CHEMICAL INDUSTRY
No. 16 Bldg., 7th Zone, He Ping Li, East District, Beijing 100013
(011-86-10) 4217784, Fax: (011-86-10) 4215982
Minister, Gu Xiulian

MINISTRY OF CIVIL AFFAIRS
9 Xi Huang Cheng Gen Nen Jie, West District, Beijing 100032, China
(011-86-10) 6016988
Minister, Doje Cering

MINISTRY OF CONSTRUCTION
9 Shan Li He Rd., Hai Dian District, Beijing 100835, China
(011-86-10) 8992833, Fax: (011-86-10) 8313669
Minister, Hou Jie

MINISTRY OF CULTURE
Jia 83 Dong An Men Bei Jie, Beijing 100722, China
(011-86-10) 4013157, Fax: (011-86-10) 4013149
Minister, Liu Zhongde

MINISTRY OF THE ELECTRONICS INDUSTRY
27 Wan Shou Lu, Hai Dian District, Beijing 100846, China
(011-86-10) 8212233, Fax: (011-86-10) 8221838
Minister, Hu Qili

MINISTRY OF ENERGY
187 Fu Yu Jie, Beijing 100091, China
(011-86-10) 654131, Fax: (011-86-10) 8016077
Minister, Shi Dazhen

MINISTRY OF FINANCE
3 San Li He Nan Jie, Fu Xing Men Wai, West District, Beijing 100820, China
(011-86-10) 868731, Fax: (011-86-10) 6013423
Minister, Liu Zhongli

MINISTRY OF FOREIGN AFFAIRS
225 Chao Yang Men Nei Da Jie, Dong Si, East District, Beijing 100701, China
(011-86-10) 5135586
Minister, Qian Qichen

MINISTRY OF FOREIGN ECONOMIC RELATIONS & TRADE
2 Chang An Blvd. East, Beijing 100731, China
(011-86-10) 5126644, Fax: (011-86-10) 5129214
Minister, Wu Yi

MINISTRY OF FORESTRY
18 He Ping Li Dong Jie, East District, Beijing 100714, China
(011-86-10) 4214909, Fax: (011-86-10) 4219149
Minister, Xu Youfang

MINISTRY OF GEOLOGY & MINERAL RESOURCES
64 Fu Chen Men Nei Jie, Beijing 100818, China
(011-86-10) 6024522, Fax: (011-86-10) 6024523
Minister, Song Ruixiang

MINISTRY OF INTERNAL TRADE
45 Fu Xing Men Nei Jie, Beijing 100801, China
(011-86-10) 668581, Fax: (011-86-10) 5017209
Minister, Chen Bangzhu

MINISTRY OF JUSTICE
11 Xia Guang Li, San Yuan Qiao, Chaoyang District, Beijing 100016, China
(011-86-10) 4061351
Minister, Xiao Yang

MINISTRY OF LABOUR
12 He Ping Li Zhong Jie, East District, Beijing 100716, China
(011-86-10) 4211624, Fax: (011-86-10) 4211624
Minister, Li Boyong

MINISTRY OF MACHINE BUILDING INDUSTRY
San Li He, West District, Beijing, China
(011-86-10) 810731
Minister, He Guangyuan

MINISTRY OF METALLURGICAL INDUSTRY
46 Xi Dong Si Jie, Beijing 100711, China
(011-86-10) 5133822, Fax: (011-86-10) 5130074
Minister, Liu Qi

MINISTRY OF NATIONAL DEFENCE
25 Huang Si Da Jie, De Sheng Men Wai, East District, Beijing 100011, China
(011-86-10) 2018356
Minister, Gen. Chi Haotian
Chief of Staff, Department of the People's Liberation Army, Gen. Fu Quanyou
Director, Eastern District, Gen. Yu Yongbo
Director, General Logistics Department, Gen. Wang Ke
Commander, Air Force, Lt. Gen. Yu Zhengwu
Commander, Navy, Adm. Zhang Lianzhong

MINISTRY OF PERSONNEL
12 He Ping Li Zhong Jie, East District, Beijing 100716, China
(011-86-10) 4218719, Fax: (011-86-10) 4218719
Minister, Song Defu

MINISTRY OF POSTS & TELECOMMUNICATIONS
13 West Chang An Ave., Beijing 100804, China
(011-86-10) 6010540, Fax: (011-86-10) 6011250
Minister, Wu Jichuan

MINISTRY OF PUBLIC HEALTH
44 Hou Hai Bei Yan, West District, Beijing 100725, China
(011-86-10) 4012133, Fax: (011-86-10) 4014331
Minister, Chen Minzhang

MINISTRY OF PUBLIC SECURITY
14 Dong Chang An Jie, East District, Beijing 100741, China
(011-86-10) 5121176
Minister, Tao Siju

MINISTRY OF TELEVISION, RADIO & CINEMA
2 Fu Xing Men Wai Jie, PO Box 4501, Beijing 100866, China
(011-86-10) 862753, Fax: (011-86-10) 82122174
Minister, Sun Juazheng

MINISTRY OF STATE SECURITY
14 Dong Chang An Jie, East District, Beijing 100036, China
(011-86-10) 813666
Minister, Jia Chunwang

MINISTRY OF SUPERVISION
4 Chao Jun Miao, Hai Dian District, Beijing 100081, China
(011-86-10) 2566688, Fax: (011-86-10) 2254258
Minister, Cao Qingze

MINISTRY OF TRANSPORTATION
10 Fu Xing Lu, Haidian District, Beijing 100846, China
(011-86-10) 8643369
Minister, Huang Zhendong

MINISTRY OF WATER RESOURCES
1 Bai Guang Lu Er Tiao, Guang An Men, Xuan Wu District, Beijing 100761, China

(011-86-10) 365563, Fax: (011-86-10) 3260365
Minister, Niu Maosheng

Associated Agencies
•All-China Federation of Industry & Commerce
93 Bei He Yan Da Jie, Beijing 100006, China
(011-86-10) 554231
Chair, Wang Zhongfu
•Bank of China
410 Fu Cheng Men Nei Da Jie, Beijing, China
(011-86-10) 6016688
President, Wang Xuebing
•Beijing Foreign Trade Corporation
#12, Yong An Dong Li, Jian Guo Men Wai, Beijing 100022, China
(011-86-10) 5001843
Director, Yu Xiaosong
•China International Water & Electric Corporation
Block 1, Liu Pu Kang, Beijing 100011, China
(011-86-10) 4015511
President, Zhu Jingde
•China National Offshore Oil Corporation
23-F Jing Xin Bldg., Jia 2, North Dong San Huan Rd., Chao Yang District, Beijing 100027, China
(011-86-10) 4663696
President, Wang Yan
•China National Petro-Chemical Corporation
Jia 6, Hui Xin Don Jie, Chao Yang District, Beijing 100013, China
(011-86-10) 4216731
President, Sheng Hauren
•China National Petroleum & Natural Gas Corporation
Liu Pu Kang, Beijing, China
(011-86-10) 2015544
President, Wang Tao
•China Nuclear Energy Industry Corporation
Jia 1, Dong Kou, Yuetan Bei Jie, Beijing, (011-86-10) 867717
(011-86-10) 867717
President, Zhang Xinduo
•Chinese Academy of Sciences
52 Shan Li He Lu, West District, Beijing, China
(011-86-10) 863972
President, Zhou Guangzhao
•Chinese Council for the Promotion of International Trade
1 Fu Xing Men Wai Do Jie, PO Box 4509, Beijing 100860, China
(011-86-10) 8513344
Chair, Zheng Hongye
•Civil Aviation Administration
165 Dong So Zo Da Jie, East District, Beijing 100710, China
(011-86-10) 4012233
Director, Chen Guangyi
•People's Bank of China
32 Cheng Fang St., West District, Beijing 100800, China
(011-86-10) 6016705
Governor, Dai Xianglong
•State Economic & Trade Commission
26 Xuan Wu Men West Ave., Beijing 100053, China
(011-86-10) 8392227
Chair, Wang Zhongyu
•State Education Commission
37 Da Mu Cang Hu Tong, West District, Beijing 100816, China
(011-86-10) 653781
Chair, Zhu Kaixuan
•State Bureau of Environmental Protection
115 Xi Zhi Men Nei, Xiao Jie, East District, Beijing 100035, China
(011-86-10) 6011199
Director, Xie Zhenhua
•State Restructuring of Economic System Commission
22 Xi An Men St., Beijing 100017, China
(011-86-10) 9096363
Chair, Li Tieying

•State Science & Technology Commission
54 San Li He, West District, Beijing 100862, China
(011-86-10) 8515544
Chair, Song Jian
•State Bureau of Taxation
68 Cao Lin Qing Jie, Xuan Wu District, Beijing 100063, China
(011-86-10) 3266836
Director, Liu Zhongli

GOVERNMENT OF FRANCE
Capital: Paris
Major Political Parties: Rally for the Republic (RPR); Union for French Democracy (UDF); Socialist Party (PS); Community Party (PCF)
Currency: French Franc
Total Area: 632,841 km2 with French Overseas Territories
Population: 58,000,000 (1995) Language(s): French

OFFICE OF THE PRESIDENT
Palais de l'Elysée, #55, 57, rue du Faubourg-Saint Honoré, 75008, Paris, France
(011-33-1) 42-92-81-00, Fax: (011-33-1) 47-42-24-65
President, H.E. Jacques Chirac

OFFICE OF THE PRIME MINISTER
Hôtel Matignon, 57, rue de Varenne, 75700, Paris, France
(011-33-1) 42-75-80-00, Fax: (011-33-1) 45-44-15-72
Prime Minister, Alain Juppé
President, Social & Economic Council, Jean Mattéoli, Palais d'Iéna, 1, av d'Iéna, 75775, Paris CEDEX 16, (011-33-1) 44-43-60-00

SENATE
Palais de Luxembourg, 15, rue de Vaugirard, 75291, Paris CEDEX 06, France
(011-33-1) 42-34-20-00, Fax: (011-33-1) 42-14-26-77
President, René Monory

NATIONAL ASSEMBLY
Au Palais-Bourbon, 126, rue de l'Université, 75007, Paris, France
(011-33-1) 40-63-60-00, Fax: (011-331) 42-60-99-03
President, Philippe Séguin

MINISTRY OF AGRICULTURE, FISHERIES & FOOD
78, rue de Varenne, 75007, Paris, France
(011-33-1) 49-55-49-55
Minister, Philippe Vasseur

MINISTRY OF CIVIL SERVICE, ADMINISTRATIVE REFORM & DECENTRALIZATION
32, rue de Babylone, 75700, Paris, France
(011-33-1) 42-75-80-00
Minister, Dominique Perben

MINISTRY OF CULTURE
3, rue de Valois, 75042, Paris, France
(011-33-1) 40-15-80-00, Fax: (011-33-1) 42-61-35-77
Minister, Philippe Douste-Blazy

MINISTRY OF DEFENCE
14, rue Saint-Dominique, 75700, Paris, France
(011-33-1) 42-19-30-11, Fax: (011-33-1) 47-05-40-91
Minister, Charles Millon
Chief of Staff, Armed Forces, Gen. Jean-P. Douin, (011-33-1) 40-65-30-11
Chief of Staff, Air Force, Gen. Jean Rannou, (011-33-1) 45-52-34-56
Chief of Staff, Army, Gen. Mercier, (011-33-1) 42-19-30-11
Chief of Staff, Navy, Adm. Jean Charles Lefebvre, (011-33-1) 42-92-10-00

MINISTRY OF ECONOMY & FINANCE
139, rue de Bercy, 75572, Paris CEDEX 12, France

(011-33-1) 40-04-04-04, Fax: (011-33-1) 43-45-73-89
Minister, Jean Arthuis
Minister Delegate, Budget, Alain Lamassoure
Minister Delegate, Finance & Foreign Trade, Yves Galland

MINISTRY OF ENVIRONMENT
20, av de Ségur, 75700, Paris, France
(011-33-1) 42-19-20-21, Fax: (011-33-1) 42-19-11-23
Minister, Corinne Lepage

MINISTRY OF FOREIGN AFFAIRS
37, qaui d'Orsay, 75700, Paris, France
(011-33-1) 43-17-53-53, Fax: (011-33-1) 45-51-60-12
Minister, Hervé de Charette
Minister Delegate, Cooperation, Jacques Godfrain, 20, rue Monsieur, 75700, Paris, (011-33-1) 47-83-10-10
Minister Delegate, European Affairs, Michel Barnier

MINISTRY OF INDUSTRY, POSTAL SERVICE & TELECOMMUNICATIONS
101, rue de Grenelle, 75537, Paris, France
(011-33-1) 43-19-36-36
Minister, Frank Borotra

MINISTRY DELEGATE OF POST, TELECOMMUNICATIONS & SPACE
20, av de Ségur, 75700, Paris, France
(011-33-1) 43-19-20-20
Minister, François Fillon

MINISTRY DELEGATE OF URBAN AREA & INTEGRATION
8, av de Ségur, 75700, Paris, France
(011-33-1) 40-56-80-00
Minister, Eric Raoult

MINISTRY OF INTERIOR
Place Beauvau, 75800, Paris, France
(011-33-1) 49-27-49-27, Fax: (011-33-1) 43-59-89-50
Minister, Jean-Louis Debré

MINISTRY OF JUSTICE
13, Place Vendôme, 75042, Paris CEDEX 01, France
(011-33-1) 44-77-60-60, Fax: (011-33-1) 42-60-69-38
Minister of State & Keeper of the Seals, Jacques Toubon

MINISTRY OF LABOUR & SOCIAL AFFAIRS
127, rue de Grenelle, 75700, Paris, France
(011-33-1) 40-56-60-00, Fax: (011-33-1) 40-56-67-10
Minister, Jacques Barrot
Minister Delegate, Employment, Anne-Marie Couderc, 40, rue du Bac, 75700, Paris, (011-33-1) 44-39-24-40

MINISTRY OF NATIONAL EDUCATION, SECONDARY SCHOOL INSTRUCTION, RESEARCH & PROFESSIONAL TRAINING
110, rue de Grenelle, 75537, Paris, France
(011-33-1) 49-55-10-10
Minister, François Bayrou

MINISTRY OF PUBLIC WORKS, HOUSING, TRANSPORTATION & TOURISM
3, Place de Fonteroy, Paris 75007, France
(011-33-1) 44-48-80-00, Fax: (011-33-1) 44-49-80-52
Minister, Bernard Pons

MINISTRY OF REGIONAL DEVELOPMENT, URBAN AFFAIRS & INTEGRATION
35, rue Saint-Dominique, 75700, Paris, France
Minister, Jean-Claude Gaudin

MINISTRY OF RELATIONS WITH THE PARLIAMENT
72, rue de Varenne, Paris 75700, France
(011-33-1) 42-75-88-00
Minister, Roger Romani

STATE SECRETARIAT FOR HEALTH & SOCIAL WELFARE
8, av de Ségur, 75700, Paris, France

(011-33-1) 40-56-60-00
Secretary of State, Health & Social Welfare, Hervé Gaymard

STATE SECRETARIAT FOR RESEARCH
21, rue Descartes, 75005, Paris, France
(011-33-1) 46-34-35-35
Secretary of State, Research, François d'Aubert

MINISTRY OF SMALL/MEDIUM BUSINESS & ARTISANS ACTIVITIES
80, rue de Lille, 75700, Paris, France
(011-33-1) 43-19-24-24
Minister, Jean-Pierre Raffarin

Associated Agencies
- Aerospace Industries
37, boul de Montmorency, 75781, Paris CEDEX 16, France
(011-33-1) 42-24-24-24
President, Yves Michot
- Bank of France
1, rue La Vrilière, 75001, Paris, France
(011-33-1) 42-92-42-92, Fax: (011-33-1) 42-96-04-23
Governor, Jean-Claude Trichet
- France Development Fund
35, rue Boissy-d'Anglas, 75379, Paris CEDEX 08, France
(011-33-1) 40-06-31-31, Fax: (011-33-1) 47-42-75-14
Director General, Antoine Pouillieute
- France Electricity
2, rue Louis Murat, 75384, Paris CEDEX 08, France
(011-33-1) 40-42-22-22, Fax: (011-33-1) 40-42-31-83
Chair, Gilles Ménage
- France Gas Company
23, rue Philibert Delorme, 75840, Paris CEDEX 17, France
(011-33-1) 47-54-24-17, Fax: (011-33-1) 47-54-24-85
Director General, Pierre Gadonneix
- France Radio-Telephone Company
116, av du President Kennedy, 75786, Paris CEDEX 16, France
(011-33-1) 42-30-22-22, Fax: (011-33-1) 42-30-14-88
President, Jean Maheu
- France Telecom
6, Place d'Alleray, 75505, Paris CEDEX 15, France
(011-33-1) 44-44-22-22
President, Marcel Roulet

GOVERNMENT OF GERMANY/Deutschland
Capital: Berlin
Major Political Parties: Christian Democratic Union (CDU); Social Democratic Party (SPD); Free Democratic Party (FDP); Christian Social Union (CSU); Party of Democratic Socialism (PDS)
Currency: Deutsche Mark
Land Area: 356,910 km2
Population: 81,337,541 (1995) Language(s): German

OFFICE OF THE PRESIDENT
Sch. Bellevue, Spreeweg 1, 10557, Berlin, Germany
(011-49-30) 39-08-40, (011-49-228) 200-0, Fax: (011-49-228) 200-200, Telex: 886393
President, Prof. Dr. Roman Herzog
State, Secretary, Wilhelm Staudacher

OFFICE OF THE FEDERAL CHANCELLOR
Adenauerallee 141, 53113, Bonn, Germany
(011-49-228) 560, Fax: (011-49-228) 562357, Telex: 886750
Telex: 886750
Chancellor, Dr. Helmut Kohl
Vice-Chancellor, Dr. Klaus Kinkel
Minister of State, Anton Pfeifer
Minister of State, Intelligence Coordination, Bernd Schmidbauer
Minister, Special Tasks & Head of Federal Chancellery, Friedrich Bohl

Press & Information Office of the Federal Government
Welckerstr. 11, 53113, Bonn, Germany
(011-49-228) 2080, Fax: (011-49-228) 2082555, Telex: 886741
Telex: 886741
Director, Peter Hansmann
Deputy Director, Wolfgang G. Gibowski

Federal Intelligence Service
Heilmanstr. 30, 82049, Pullach, Germany
(011-49-89) 7931567
President, Konrad Porzner
Vice-President, Adm. Gerhard Guelich

FEDERAL COUNCIL/Bundesrat
Bendeshaus, Görresstr. 15, 53113, Bonn, Germany
(011-49-228) 9100, Fax: (011-49-228) 9100400
President, Dr. Johannes Rau

FEDERAL ASSEMBLY/Bundestag
Reichstagsgebäude, Scheidemannstr. 2, 10557, Berlin, Germany
(011-49-30) 39770, Fax: (011-49-30) 394751
President, Prof. Dr. Rita Süssmuth

MINISTRY OF DEFENCE
Hardthöhe, Postfach 13 28, 53123, Bonn, Germany
(011-49-228) 1200, Fax: (011-49-228) 125357, Telex: 886575
Telex: 886575
Minister, Volker Rühe
Inspector General, Air Force, Lt. Gen Bernhard Mende, (011-49-228) 4600
Inspector General, Armed Forces, Gen. Hartmut Bagger, (011-49-228) 121
Inspector General, Army, Lt. Gen. Helmut Willmann, (011-49-228) 120
Inspector General, Navy, V. Adm. Hans-Rudolf Böhmer, (011-49-228) 121

MINISTRY OF ECONOMIC AFFAIRS
Villemomblerstr. 76, 53123, Bonn, Germany
(011-49-228) 615-0, Fax: (011-49-228) 6154436, Telex: 886747
Telex: 886747
Minister, Dr. Günter Rexrodt

MINISTRY OF ECONOMIC COOPERATION & DEVELOPMENT
Friedrich-Ebert Allee 40, 53113, Bonn, Germany
(011-49-228) 5350, Fax: (011-49-228) 535-3500, Telex: 8869452
Telex: 8869452
Minister, Carl-Dieter Spranger

MINISTRY OF EDUCATION, SCIENCE, RESEARCH & TECHNOLOGY
Heinemannstr. 2, 53175, Bonn, Germany
(011-49-228) 570, Fax: (011-49-228) 573601, Telex: 2283832
Telex: 2283832
Minister, Dr. Jürgen Rüttgers

MINISTRY FOR THE ENVIRONMENT, NATURE CONSERVATION & NUCLEAR SAFETY
Kennedyallee 5, 53175, Bonn, Germany
(011-49-228) 3050, Fax: (011-49-228) 3053225, Telex: 885790
Telex: 885790
Minister, Dr. Angela Merkel

MINISTRY FOR THE FAMILY & SENIOR CITIZENS
Godesberger Allee 140, 53175, Bonn, Germany
(011-49-228) 3060, Fax: (011-49-228) 3062259, Telex: 885673
Telex: 885673
Minister, Claudia Nolte

MINISTRY OF FINANCE
Graurheindorferstr. 108, 53117, Bonn, Germany
(011-49-228) 6820, Fax: (011-49-228) 6824420, Telex: 886645
Telex: 886645
Minister, Dr. Theodor Waigel

MINISTRY OF FOOD, AGRICULTURE & FORESTRY
Rochusstr. 1, 53123, Bonn, Germany
(011-49-228) 5290, Fax: (011-49-228) 5294262, Telex: 886844
Telex: 886844
Minister, Jochen Borchert

MINISTRY OF FOREIGN AFFAIRS
Adenauerallee 99-103, 53113, Bonn, Germany
(011-49-228) 170, Fax: (011-49-228) 173402, Telex: 886591
Telex: 886591
Minister, Dr. Klaus Kinkel
Minister of State, Europe, Dr. Werner Hoyer
Minister of State, Helmut Schäfer

MINISTRY OF HEALTH
Am Probsthof 78a, 53121, Bonn, Germany
(011-49-228) 9410, Fax: (011-49-228) 9414900, Telex: 8869355
Telex: 8869355
Minister, Horst Seehofer

MINISTRY OF THE INTERIOR
Graurheindorferstr. 198, 53117, Bonn, Germany
(011-49-228) 6810, Fax: (011-49-228) 6814665, Telex: 886896
Telex: 886896
Minister, Manfred Kanther
President, Office of Criminal Investigation, Hans Ludwig Zachert, Thaerstr. 11, P.F. 18 20, 65193, Wiesbaden
President, Office for the Protection of the Constitution, Eckhart Werthebach, Merianstr. 100, P.F. 100553, 50765, Köln
President, Academy of State Police, Dieter Wellershoff, Rosenburgweg, 53115, Bonn

MINISTRY OF JUSTICE
Postfach 200365, Heinemannstr. 6, 53175, Bonn, Germany
(011-49-228) 580, Fax: (011-49-228) 584525, Telex: 886979
Telex: 886979
Minister, Prof. Dr. Edzard Schmidt-Jortzig

MINISTRY OF LABOUR & SOCIAL AFFAIRS
Postfach 140280, Rochusstr. 1, 53123, Bonn, Germany
(011-49-228) 5270, Fax: (011-49-228) 5272965, Telex: 886641
Telex: 886641
Minister, Dr. Norbert Blüm
President, Office of Employment, Bernhard Jagoda, Regensburgerstr. 104, 90478, Nürnberg

MINISTRY OF POSTS & TELECOMMUNICATIONS
Heinrich von Stephan Str. 1, Referat 201, Postfach 8001, 53175, Bonn, Germany
(011-49-228) 140, Fax: (011-49-228) 148872, Telex: 8861101
Telex: 8861101
Minister, Dr. Wolfgang Bötsch

MINISTRY OF REGIONAL PLANNING, BUILDING & URBAN DEVELOPMENT
Deichmanns Aue 31-37, 53179, Bonn, Germany
(011-49-228) 3370, Fax: (011-49-228) 3373060, Telex: 885462
Telex: 885462
Minister, Prof. Dr. Klaus Töpfer

MINISTRY OF TRANSPORT
Robert-Schuman Pl. 1, 53175, Bonn, Germany

(011-49-228) 3000, Fax: (011-49-228) 3003428, Telex: 885700
Telex: 885700
Minister, Mathias Wissman

MINISTRY FOR WOMEN & YOUTH
Rochusstr. 6-10, 53123, Bonn, Germany
(011-49-228) 9300, Fax: (011-49-228) 9303331
Minister, Dr. Angela Merkel

Associated Agencies
• Bank of the Federal Republic of Germany
Wilhelm-Epstein Str. 14, 60431, Frankfurt am Main, Germany
(011-49-69) 95661, Fax: (011-49-69) 5601071
President, Hans Tietmeyer
• Postadamer Str. 1, 56075, Koblenz, Germany
(011-49-261) 5050, Fax: (011-49-261) 505-226
President, Dr. Friedrich Kahlenberg
• Federal Aviation Office
Lilienthalpl. 6, 38108, Braunschweig, Germany
(011-49-531) 23550, Fax: (011-49-531) 2355254
Director, Klaus Koplin
• Federal Export Office
Frankfurter Str. 29-31, 65760, Eschborn, Germany
(011-49-6196) 9080, Fax: (011-49-6196) 908800
President, Dr. Wolfgang Danner
• Federal Office for Foreign Trade Information
Agipastr. 87-93, 53177, Köln, Germany
(011-49-221) 20570, Fax: (011-49-221) 2057212
Director, Hans Diether Dammann
• Federal Office for Public Security
Deutschherrenstr, 93, 53177, Bonn, Germany
(011-49-228) 9400, Fax: (011-49-228) 9401424
President, Hans-Georg Dusch
• Federal Patent Office
Zweibrückenstr. 12, 80331, Munich, Germany
(001-49-89) 21950, Fax: (001-49-89) 21952221
President, Dipl. Ing. Norbert Haugg
• Federal Statistics Office
Gustav-Stresemann-Ring 11, 65189, Wiesbaden, Germany
(011-49-611) 751, Fax: (011-49-611) 724000
President, Johann Hablen

GOVERNMENT OF HONG KONG (HK)
Capital: Victoria
Major Political Parties: Democratic Party; Democratic Alliance for the Betterment of Hong Kong; Hong Kong Democratic Foundation
Currency: Hong Kong Dollar
Total Area: 1,040 km2
Population: 5,542,869 (1995)
Language(s): Cantonese, English

OFFICE OF THE GOVERNOR
Government House, Upper Albert Rd., Hong Kong
(011-852) 523-2031, Fax: (011-852) 810-1592
Governor, H.E. Christopher Patten

OFFICE OF THE EXECUTIVE COUNCIL
Government Secretariat, Lower Albert Rd., Hong Kong
(011-852) 810-2406
President of the Executive Council, Sir David Clive Wilson
Secretary General, K. Fok

LEGISLATIVE COUNCIL
Government House, Hong Kong
(011-852) 844-0700, Fax: (011-852) 845-2444
President, Hon. J.J. Swaine

AGRICULTURE & FISHERIES DEPARTMENT
Government Offices, 393 Canton Rd., Kowloon, Hong Kong
(011-852) 733-2211, Fax: (011-852) 311-3731
Director, Dr. H.Y. Lee

ARCHITECTURAL SERVICES DEPARTMENT
Government Offices, 66 Queensway, Hong Kong
(011-852) 867-3601, Fax: (011-852) 869-0289
Director, P.J. Corser

AUDIT DEPARTMENT
Immigration Tower, 7 Gloucester Rd., 25th/26th Fl., Wan Chai, Hong Kong
(011-852) 829-4210, Fax: (011-852) 824-2087
Director, B.G. Jenney

BUILDING & LANDS DEPARTMENT
Murray Bldg., Mezzanine, Hong Kong
(011-852) 848-2198, Fax: (011-852) 868-4707
Director, D. Chen

CENSUS & STATISTICS DEPARTMENT
Wanchai Tower, 12 Harbour Rd., Wan Chai, Hong Kong
(011-852) 582-4807, Fax: (011-852) 802-4000
Commissioner, R.W.H. Ho

CIVIL AVIATION DEPARTMENT
Government Offices, 66 Queensway, Hong Kong
(011-852) 867-4332, Fax: (011-852) 869-0093
Director, Richard Siegel

CIVIL ENGINEERING DEPARTMENT
Civil Engineering Bldg., 101 Princess Margaret Rd., Ho Man Tin, Kowloon, Hong Kong
(011-852) 848-1111, Fax: (011-852) 714-0064
Director, Dr. E.W. Brand

CORRECTIONAL SERVICES DEPARTMENT
Wanchai Tower, 12 Harbour Rd., 23rd Fl., Wan Chai, Hong Kong
(011-852) 582-5117, Fax: (011-852) 802-0184
Commissioner, F.S. McCosh

CUSTOMS & EXCISE DEPARTMENT
Harbour Bldg., 38 Pier Rd., Central, Hong Kong
(011-852) 852-1411, Fax: (011-852) 542-3334
Commissioner, C.W.B. Oxley

EDUCATION DEPARTMENT
Wu Chung House, 197-221 Queen's Rd. East, Wan Chi, Hong Kong
(011-852) 891-0088, Fax: (011-852) 893-0858
Director, Dominic Wong Shing-wah

ELECTRICAL & MECHANICAL SERVICES DEPARTMENT
98 Caroline Hill Rd., Hong Kong
(011-852) 895-8620, Fax: (011-852) 890-7493
Director, P.K. Kwok

ENVIRONMENTAL PROTECTION DEPARTMENT
Southern Centre, 130 Hennessy Rd., Wan Chai, Hong Kong
(011-852) 835-1018, Fax: (011-852) 838-2155
Director, S.B. Reed

FIRE SERVICES DEPARTMENT
1 Hong Shong Rd., Tsim Sha Tsui, Kowloon, Hong Kong
(011-852) 733-7700, Fax: (011-852) 368-9744
Director, C.Y. Lam

GOVERNMENT SUPPLIES DEPARTMENT
12 Oil St., North Point, Hong Kong
(011-852) 802-6100, Fax: (011-852) 807-2764
Director, N.C.L. Shipman

DEPARTMENT OF HEALTH
Sunning Plaza, Hysan Ave., Causeway Bay, Hong Kong
(011-852) 890-0770, Fax: (011-852) 576-5166
Director, Dr. S.H. Lee

HIGHWAYS DEPARTMENT
Empire Centre, 68 Mody Rd., 10th Fl., Tsim Sha Tsui East, Kowloon, Hong Kong
(011-852) 762-3333, Fax: (011-852) 714-5216
Director, S.K. Kwei

HONG KONG HOUSING AUTHORITY & HOUSING DEPARTMENT
33 Fat Kwong St., Kowloon, Hong Kong
(011-852) 714-5119, Fax: (011-852) 761-0004
Director, T. Fung

IMMIGRATION DEPARTMENT
Immigration Tower, 7 Gloucester Rd., Wai Chai, Hong Kong
(011-852) 824-6111, Fax: (011-852) 824-1133
Director, L.M.Y. Leung

INDUSTRY DEPARTMENT
Ocean Centre, 5 Canton Rd., Kowloon, Hong Kong
(011-852) 737-2208, Fax: (011-852) 730-4633
Director General, T.H. Barma

INFORMATION TECHNOLOGY SERVICES DEPARTMENT
Wanchai Tower, 12 Harbour Rd., Wan Chai, Hong Kong
(011-852) 582-4520, Fax: (011-852) 865-6549
Director, K.H. Lau

INLAND REVENUE DEPARTMENT
Revenue Tower, 5 Gloucester Rd., Wan Chai, Hong Kong
(011-852) 894-5098, Fax: (011-852) 576-6359
Commissioner, Anthony Au-Yeung

JUDICIARY DEPARTMENT
Supreme Court, 38 Queensway, Hong Kong
(011-852) 869-0869, Fax: (011-852) 869-0640
Chief Justice, Sir Ti Liang Yang

LABOUR DEPARTMENT
Harbour Bldg., 38 Pier Rd., Central, Hong Kong
(011-852) 717-1771, Fax: (011-852) 544-3271
Commissioner, K. Fok

LEGAL DEPARTMENT
High Block, Government Offices, 66 Queensway, Hong Kong
(011-852) 567-2198, Fax: (011-852) 877-3978
Attorney General, J.F. Mathews

MARINE DEPARTMENT
Harbour Bldg., 38 Pier Rd., Central, PO Box 4155, Hong Kong
(011-852) 852-3001, Fax: (011-852) 544-9241
Director, A.C. Pyrke

PLANNING DEPARTMENT
Murray Bldg., Garden Rd., Hong Kong
(011-852) 848-2688, Fax: (011-852) 877-0239
Director, K.S. Pun

RATING & VALUATION DEPARTMENT
Hennessy Centre, 500 Hennessy Rd., Causeway Bay, Hong Kong
(011-852) 805-7666, Fax: (011-852) 577-6916
Commissioner, B.J. Woodroffe

REGIONAL SERVICES DEPARTMENT
Regional Council Bldg., 1-3 Pai Tau St., Sha Tin, Hong Kong
(011-852) 414-5555, Fax: (011-852) 311-2667
Director, A.H. Hsu

REGISTRAR GENERAL'S DEPARTMENT
Government Offices, 66 Queensway, Hong Kong
(011-852) 867-2811, Fax: (011-852) 869-0423
Registrar General, N.M. Gellson

SOCIAL WELFARE DEPARTMENT
Wu Chung House, 213 Queen's Rd. East, Wan Chai, Hong Kong
(011-852) 576-1088, Fax: (011-852) 895-4693
Director, I. Strachan

TERRITORY DEVELOPMENT DEPARTMENT
Leighton Centre, 77 Leighton Rd., Causeway Bay, Hong Kong
(011-852) 882-7170, Fax: (011-852) 577-3562
Director, C.K. Chow

TRADE DEPARTMENT
Trade Department Tower, 700 Nathan Rd., Kowloon, Hong Kong
(011-852) 398-5333, Fax: (011-852) 789-2491
Director General, J.A. Miller

TRANSPORT DEPARTMENT
Immigration Tower, 7 Gloucester Rd., 41st Fl., Wan Chai, Hong Kong
(011-852) 829-5258, Fax: (011-852) 824-0433
Commissioner, R.S. Hui

TREASURY
Immigration Tower, 7 Gloucester Rd., Wan Chai, Hong Kong
(011-852) 810-2402, Fax: (011-852) 868-4193
Director, S.H. Chiu

WATER SUPPLIES DEPARTMENT
Immigration Tower, 7 Gloucester Rd., Wan Chai, Hong Kong
(011-852) 829-4400
Director, M.S. Hu

URBAN SERVICES DEPARTMENT
Government Offices, 66 Queensway, Hong Kong
(011-852) 867-5596, Fax: (011-852) 869-0169
Director, H.H. Barma

Associated Agencies
•City & New Territories Administration
Southern Centre, 130 Hennessy Rd., Wan Chai, Hong Kong
(011-852) 835-1444, Fax: (011-852) 834-7649
Secretary, P.K.Y. Tsao
•Government Land Transport Agency
Wanchai Tower I, 12 Harbour Rd., Hong Kong
(011-852) 582-5281, Fax: (011-852) 802-0780
Administrator, P.B. Walker
•Hong Kong/Shanghai Banking Corporation
1 Queen's Rd. Central, PO Box 64, Hong Kong
(011-852) 822-1111, Fax: (011-852) 810-1112
Chair, W. Purves
•Hong Kong Trade Development Council
1 Harbour Rd., Hong Kong
(011-852) 833-4333
Executive Director, J.C.K. So
•Radio Television Hong Kong
Broadcasting House, 30 Broadcast Dr., Kowloon, Hong Kong
(011-852) 339-6441, Fax: (011-852) 338-0279
Director, M.Y. Cheung

GOVERNMENT OF ITALY/Italia
Capital: Rome
Major Political Parties: Northern League; Democratic Party of the Left; Forza Italia; National Alliance; Communist Refounding; Christian Democratic Center; Popular Party
Currency: Italian Lira
Total Area: 301,230 km2
Population: 58,138,394 (1994)
Language(s): Italian, German, French, Slovenian

OFFICE OF THE PRESIDENT
Palazzo del Quirinale, 00187, Rome, Italy
(011-39-6) 46991, Fax: (011-39-6) 46992384
President & Chair, Supreme Defense Council, H.E. Oscar Luigi Scalfaro

OFFICE OF THE PRIME MINISTER
Piazza Colonna, 370, 00187, Rome, Italy
(011-39-6) 6779, Fax: (011-39-6) 6796894
Prime Minister, Lamberto Dini
Deputy Prime Minister, Giuseppe Tatarella
Deputy Prime Minister, Roberto Maroni
Minister without Portfolio, Sergio Berlinguer
Director, Executive Committee for Intelligence & Security, Gen. Giuseppe Tavormina

Senate/Senato della Repubblica
Palazzo Madama, 00186, Rome, Italy
(011-39-6) 67061
President & Speaker, Carlo S. Pasini

Chamber of Deputies/Camera dei Deputati
Piazza Montecitorio, 00186, Rome, Italy
(011-39-6) 67601
Speaker, Irene Pivetti

MINISTRY OF AGRICULTURE, FOOD & FORESTRY RESOURCES
Via XX Settembre, 20, 00187, Rome, Italy
(011-39-6) 4665, Fax: (011-39-6) 4746178
Minister, Michele Pinto

MINISTRY OF BUDGET & ECONOMIC PLANNING
Via XX Settembre, 97, 00187, Rome, Italy
(011-39-6) 47611, Fax: (011-39-6) 4741940
Acting Minister, Carlo Azeglio Ciampi

MINISTRY OF DEFENCE
Palazzo Baracchini, Via XX Settembre, 8, 00187, Rome, Italy
(011-39-6) 4882126, Fax: (011-39-6) 4884759
Minister, Beniamino Andreatta
Chief of Staff, Defence General Staff, Adm. Franco Venturoni, (011-39-6) 46911
Chief of Staff, Air Force, Gen. Adelchi Pillinini, (011-39-6) 49861
Chief of Staff, Army, Lt. Gen. Bonifazio Incisa di Camerana, (011-39-6) 47351
Chief of Staff, Navy, Adm Angelo Mariani, (011-39-6) 36801

MINISTRY OF ENVIRONMENT & PUBLIC WORKS
Piazza Venezia, 11, 00186, Rome, Italy
(011-39-6) 6790151, Fax: (011-39-6) 6786458
Minister, Edo Ronchi
State Secretary, Paolo Gerelli
Director General, Air & Noise Pollution, Dr. Dorrado Clini
Director General, Evaluation of Impact Assessment, Education & information, Costanza Pera
Director General, Nature Preservation, Bruno Agricola
Director General, Water, Waste & Soil, Gianfranco Mascazzini

MINISTRY OF FINANCE
Viale Europa, 00144, Rome, Italy
(011-39-6) 59971, Fax: (011-39-6) 59972067
Minister, Vincenzo Visco

MINISTRY OF EQUAL OPPORTUNITY
Via de Giardino Theodoli, 66, 00186 00186, Rome, Italy
Minister, Anna Finocchiaro

MINISTRY OF FOREIGN AFFAIRS
Palazzo le Farnesina, I, Foro Italico, 00194, Rome, Italy
(011-39-6) 3691, Fax: (011-39-6) 3222850
Minister, Lamberto Dini

MINISTRY OF FOREIGN TRADE
Viale America, 341, 00144, Rome, Italy
(011-39-6) 59931, Fax: (011-39-6) 5921573
Minister, Augusto Fantozzi

MINISTRY OF HEALTH
Viale Dell'Industria, 20, 00144, Rome, Italy
(011-39-6) 59931, Fax: (011-39-6) 5921573
Minister, Rosi Bindi

MINISTRY OF INDUSTRY
Via Molise, 2, 00187, Rome, Italy
(011-39-6) 47051, Fax: (011-39-6) 47053117
Minister, Pierluigi Bersani
Chief of Staff, Commerce, Guiseppe Mazza
Chief of Staff, Industry & Crafts, Guiseppe Barbagallo

MINISTRY OF THE INTERIOR
Palazzo Viminale, Via A. Depretis, 00184, Rome, Italy
(011-39-6) 65101, Fax: (011-39-6) 68802034
Minister, Georgio Napolitano

MINISTRY OF JUSTICE
Via Arenula, 70, Rome 00186, Italy
(011-39-6) 65101, Fax: (011-39-6) 68802034
Minister, Giovanni Maria Flick

MINISTRY OF LABOUR
Via Flavia, 6, 00187, Rome, Italy
(011-39-6) 4683
Minister, Tiziano Treu
Director General, Industrial Relations, Dr. Giuseppe Cacopardi

MINISTRY OF NATIONAL PATRIMONY
Via de Collegio Romano, 27, 00186, Rome, Italy
(011-39-6) 67231
Minister, Walter Veltroni

MINISTRY OF POSTS & TELECOMMUNICATIONS
Viale America, 00144, Rome, Italy
(011-39-6) 59581, Fax: (011-39-6) 5942274
Minister, Antonio Maccanico

MINISTRY OF PUBLIC EDUCATION
Viale Trastevere, 76a, 00153, Rome, Italy
(011-39-6) 58491, Fax: (011-39-6) 5813515
Minister, Luigi Berlinguer

MINISTRY OF PUBLIC WORKS
Piazza dei porti pai, 1, 00198, Rome, Italy
(011-39-6) 44121, Fax: (011-39-6) 442-67275, TELEX 06622314
TELEX 06622314
Minister, Antonio di Pietro

MINISTRY OF TOURISM & ENTERTAINMENT
Via della Ferratella in Laterano, 51, 00184, Rome, Italy
(011-39-6) 8559163, Fax: (011-39-6) 8416609
Minister, Pierluigi Bersani

MINISTRY OF TRANSPORT & MERCHANT MARINE
Piazza della Croce Rossa, 1, 00161, Rome, Italy
(011-39-6) 84901, Fax: (011-39-6) 8417268
Minister, Claudio Burlando

MINISTRY OF THE TREASURY
Via XX Settembre, 97, 00187, Rome, Italy
(011-39-6) 47611, Fax: (011-39-6) 4817716
Minister, Carlo Azeglio Ciampi

MINISTRY OF UNIVERSITIES, SCIENTIFIC & TECHNOLOGICAL RESEARCH
Piazzale Kennedy, 20, 00144, Rome, Italy
(011-39-6) 59991
Minister, Luigi Berlinguer

DEPARTMENT OF EU POLICIES COORDINATION
Via del Giardino Theodoli, 66, 00186, Rome, Italy

(011-39-6) 699831, Fax: (011-39-6) 6991669
Minister, Vacant

DEPARTMENT OF FAMILY & SOCIAL AFFAIRS
Via Barberini, 47, 00187, Rome, Italy
(011-39-6) 4742250, Fax: (011-39-6) 68003238
Minister, Livia Turco

DEPARTMENT OF PUBLIC ADMINISTRATION & REGIONAL AFFAIRS
Corso Vittorio Emanuele, 116, 00186, Rome, Italy
(011-39-6) 680031, Fax: (011-39-6) 68003238
Minister, Franco Bassanini

DEPARTMENT OF RELATIONS WITH PARLIAMENT
Palazzo Ras, Via del Corsa, 184, 00187, Rome, Italy
(011-39-6) 69982830, Fax: (011-39-6) 69982859
Minister, Vacant

Associated Agencies
• Bank of Italy/Banca d'Italia
CP 2484, Via Nazionale, 91, 00184, Rome, Italy
(011-39-6) 47921, Fax: (011-39-6) 47922253
Governor, Antonio Fazio
• Energy, Environment & New Technology Agency
Viale Regina Margherita, 125, 00198, Rome, Italy
(011-39-6) 85281, Fax: (011-39-6) 8528277
President, Nicola Cabibbo
• Manufacturing Industries Investment & Financing Agency
Via XXIV Maggio, 43-45, 00187, Rome, Italy
(011-39-6) 47101, Fax: (011-39-6) 476527
President, Gaetano Mancini
• National Airline Company (Alitalia)
Via della Magliana, 886, 00148, Rome, Italy
(011-39-6) 62621, Fax: (011-39-6) 5920089
CEO & Managing Director, Giovanni Bisignani
• National Institute for Foreign Trade
EUR-Via Liszt, 00100, Rome, Italy
(011-39-6) 599121, Fax: (011-39-6) 5910508
President, Marcello Inghilesi
• National Nuclear Energy Committee
Viale Regina Margherita, 125, 00198, Rome, Italy
(011-39-6) 85281
President, Vacant
• Piassale Enrico Mattei, 1, 00144, Rome, Italy
(011-39-6) 59821, Fax: (011-39-6) 59822141
President, Luigi Meanti
• State Telephone Company
Viale Europa 190, 00100, Rome, Italy
(011-39-6) 54602900, Fax: (011-39-6) 5415492
Director, Giuseppe Parrella

GOVERNMENT OF JAPAN/Nippon
Capital: Tokyo
Major Political Parties: Liberal Democratic Party (LDP); Social Democratic Party of Japan (SDPJ): Clean Government Party (CGP); Japan Communist Party (JCP)
Currency: Yen
Total Area: 377,835 km2
Population: 125,106,937 (1994)
Language(s): Japanese

IMPERIAL HOUSEHOLD AGENCY
1-1 Chiyoda, Chiyada-ku, Tokyo 100, Japan
(011-81-3) 33213-1111
Emperor, H.I.M. Akihito
Grand Master, Ceremonies, Kiyoshi Sumiya

OFFICE OF THE PRIME MINISTER
1-7-1 Nagata-cho, Chiyada-ku, Tokyo 100, Japan
(011-81-3) 33581-2361
Prime Minister, Tomiichi Murayama
Deputy Prime Minister, Yohei Kono

HOUSE OF COUNCILLORS/Sang-in
1-7-1 Nagata-cho, Chiyada-ku, Tokyo 100, Japan
(011-81-3) 33581-3111, Fax: (011-81-3) 33581-2900
President, Bunbei Hara
Speaker, Misao Akagiri

HOUSE OF REPRESENTATIVES/Shugi-in
1-7-1 Nagata-cho, Chiyada-ku, Tokyo 100, Japan
(011-81-3) 33581-5111
Speaker, Takako Doi
Deputy Speaker, Hyosuke Kujiraoka

MINISTRY OF AGRICULTURE, FORESTRY & FISHERIES
1-2-1 Kasumigaseki, Chiyada-ku, Tokyo 100, Japan
(011-81-3) 33502-8111
Minister, Taichiro Okawara

MINISTRY OF CONSTRUCTION
2-1-3 Kasumigaseki, Chiyada-ku, Tokyo 100, Japan
(011-81-3) 33580-4311, Fax: (011-81-3) 33502-3955
Minister, Koken Nosaka

MINISTRY OF EDUCATION
3-2-2 Kasumigaseki, Chiyada-ku, Tokyo 100, Japan
(011-81-3) 33581-4211
Minister, Kaoru Yosano

MINISTRY OF FINANCE
3-1-1 Kasumigaseki, Chiyada-ku, Tokyo 100, Japan
(011-81-3) 33581-4111, Fax: (011-81-3) 35251-2103
Minister, Masayoshi Takemura

MINISTRY OF FOREIGN AFFAIRS
2-2-1 Kasumigaseki, Chiyada-ku, Tokyo 100, Japan
(011-81-3) 33508-7118
Minister, Yohei Kono
Director General, International Economic Relations, Choe Yong-Chin

MINISTRY OF HEALTH & WELFARE
1-2-2 Kasumigaseki, Chiyada-ku, Tokyo 100, Japan
(011-81-3) 33503-1711
Minister, Shoichi Ide

MINISTRY OF HOME AFFAIRS
2-1-2 Kasumigaseki, Chiyada-ku, Tokyo 100, Japan
(011-81-3) 33581-5311
Minister, Hiromu Nonaka

MINISTRY OF INTERNATIONAL TRADE & INDUSTRY
1-3-1 Kasumigaseki, Chiyada-ku, Tokyo 100, Japan
(011-81-3) 33501-1511, Fax: (011-81-3) 33501-1337
Minister, Ryutaro Hashimoto

MINISTRY OF JUSTICE
1-1-1 Kasumigaseki, Chiyada-ku, Tokyo 100, Japan
(011-81-3) 33580-4111
Minister, Isao Maeda

MINISTRY OF LABOUR
1-2-2 Kasumigaseki, Chiyada-ku, Tokyo 1000, Japan
(011-81-3) 33593-1211
Minister, Manso Hamamoto

MINISTRY OF POSTS & TELECOMMUNICATIONS
1-3-2 Kasumigaseki, Chiyada-ku, Tokyo 100, Japan
(011-81-3) 33504-4411, Fax: (011-81-3) 33592-9157
Minister, Hun Oide

MINISTRY OF TRANSPORT
2-1-3 Kasumigaseki, Chiyada-ku, Tokyo 100, Japan
(011-81-3) 33580-3111, Fax: (011-81-3) 33593-0474
Minister, Shizuka Kamei

Associated Agencies
• Bank of Japan/Nippon Ginko
2-1-1 Hongoku-cho, 2 Chome, Nihonbashi, Chuo-ku, Tokyo 103, Japan
(011-81-3) 33279-1111, Fax: (011-81-3) 33245-0358
Governor, Yasuo Matsushita
• Economic Planning Agency
3-1-1 Kasumigaseki, Chiyada-ku, Tokyo 100, Japan
(011-81-3) 33581-0261, Fax: (011-81-3) 33581-3907
Minister of State & Director General, Masahiko Komura
Deputy Director General, Tsutomu Tanaka
• Hokkaido & Okinawa Development Agency
3-1-1 Kasumigaseki, Chiyada-ku, Tokyo 100, Japan
(011-81-3) 3581-9111, Fax: (011-81-3) 3581-1208
Minister of State & Director General, Sadutoshi Ozato
• Institute of Space & Astronautical Science
3-1-1 Yoshinodai, Sagamihara, Kanagawa 229, Japan
(011-81-3) 42751-3911, Fax: (011-81-3) 42759-4255
Director General, Ryojiro Akiba
• Japanese Defence Agency
9-7-45 Akasaka, Minato-ku, Tokyo 107, Japan
(011-81-3) 33408-5211, Fax: (011-81-3) 33408-5211
Minister of State, Tokuichiro Tamazawa
Chair, Joint Staff Council, Self Defence Forces, Gen. Tetsuya Nishimoto, (011-81-3) 33408-5211
Chief of Staff, Air Self Defence Forces, Gen. Isao Ishizuka, (011-81-3) 33408-5211
Chief of Staff, Ground Self Defence Forces, Gen. Hikary Tomizawa, (011-81-3) 33408-5211
Chief of Staff, Maritime Self Defence Forces, Adm. Takeo Fukuchi, (011-81-3) 33408-5211
• Japan Atomic Energy Commission
2-2-1 Kasumigaseki, Chiyada-ku, Tokyo 100, Japan
(011-81-3) 33581-2585, Fax: (011-81-3) 33581-5198
Chair, Makiko Tanaka
• 3-1-1 Kasumigaseki, Chiyada-ku, Tokyo 100, Japan
(011-81-3) 33581-3351, Fax: (011-81-3) 33504-1634
Minister of State & Director General, Sohei Myashita
• Japan External Trade Organization
2-5 Toranomon, Minato-ku, Tokyo 105, Japan
(011-81-3) 33582-5511, Fax: (011-81-3) 33587-0219
President, Noboru Hatekeyama
• Japan Fisheries Agency
1-2-1 Kasumigaseki, Chiyada-ku, Tokyo 100, Japan
(011-81-3) 33502-8111
Director General, Michio Chinzei
• Japan Food Agency
1-2-1 Kasumigaseki, Chiyada-ku, Tokyo 100, Japan
(011-81-3) 33502-8111
Director General, Hirofuji Ueno
• Japan Science & Technology Agency
2-2-1 Kasumigaseki, Chiyada-ku, Tokyo 100, Japan
(011-81-3) 33581-5271
Minister of State & Director General, Makiko Tanaka
• National Land Agency
1-2-2 Kasumigaseki, Chiyada-ku, Tokyo 100, Japan
(011-81-3) 33593-3311
Minister of State & Director General, Kiyoshi Ozawa
• National Space Development Agency of Japan
World Trade Centre Bldg., 2-4-1 Hamamatsu-cho, Minato-ku, Tokyo 105-60, Japan
(011-81-3) 35470-4111, Fax: (011-81-3) 33436-2928
President, Masato Yamano
• Small & Medium Enterprise Agency
1-3-1 Kasumigaseki, Chiyada-ku, Tokyo 100, Japan
(011-81-3) 33581-1511

GOVERNMENT OF MÉXICO (MX)
Capital: Mexico City
Major Political Parties: Institutional Revolutionary Party (PRI); National Action Party (PAN); Democratic Revolutionary Party (PRD); Cardenist Front for the National Reconstruction Party (PFCRN)
Currency: Mexican Peso
Total Area: 1,972,550 km2
Population: 93,985,848 (1995) Language(s): Spanish

OFFICE OF THE PRESIDENT
Palacio nacional, Patio de Honor, 2 Piso, 06067, México, D.F., México
(011-52-5) 522-7489, Fax: (011-52-5) 510-8713
President, H.E. Ernesto Zedillo Ponce de León

CÁMARA DE SENADORES/Senate
Xicoténcatl #9, Ava. Zaragoza y Calle Corregidora, 06018, México, D.F., México
(011-52-5) 521-0020
Chair, Emilio González

CÁMARA DE DIPUTADOS/Chamber of Deputies
Palacio Legislativo, Ava. Congreso de la Unión, Colonia del Parque, 15969, México, D.F., México
(011-52-5) 794-7044
President, Maria de los Angeles Moreno

SECRETARIAT OF AGRARIAN REFORM
Azafran #219, 8 Piso, Col. Granjas México, 08400, México, D.F., México
(011-52-5) 650-6311
Secretary, Arturn Warman Gryj

SECRETARIAT OF AGRICULTURE, LIVESTOCK & RURAL DEVELOPMENT
Ava. Insurgentes Sur #476, 13 Piso, 06760, México, D.F., México
(011-52-5) 584-0096, Fax: (001-52-5) 584-0652
Secretary, Francisco Labastida Ochoa

SECRETARIAT OF COMMERCE & INDUSTRIAL DEVELOPMENT
Alfonso Reyes #30, 10 Piso, Col Hipódromo Condesa, 06140, México, D.F., México
(011-52-5) 286-1823, Fax: (011-52-5) 286-0804
Secretary, Herminio Blanco Morales
Undersecretary, Domestic Trade, Eugenio Carrión Rodríguez
Undersecretary, Foreign Trade & Investigation, Decio de Maria Serrano
Undersecretary, Industries, Raúl Ramos Tercero
Undersecretary, International Trade Negotiations, Jaime Zabludovsky Kuper

SECRETARIAT OF COMMUNICATIONS & TRANSPORT
Ava. Univeridad - Xola, Cuerpo C, 2 Piso, Colonia Navarte, 03028, México, D.F., México
(011-52-5) 519-7456, Fax: (011-52-5) 519-9748
Secretary, Carlos Rojas Sacristán

SECRRETARIAT OF ENERGY, MINES & PARASTATAL INDUSTRY
Colonia Roma Sur, Deleg. Cuauhtémoc, Ava. Insurgentes Sur #552, 3 Piso, Colonia Roma Sur, 06769, México, D.F., México
(011-52-5) 564-9789, Fax: (011-52-5) 564-9769
Secretary, Ignacio Pichardo Pagaza

SECRETARIAT OF ENVIRONMENT, NATURAL RESOURCES & FISHERIES
Lateral del Anillo Periférico Sur, #4209, Fraccionamiento Jardines en la Montana, Delega. Tlalpan, 14210, México, D.F., México
(011-52-5) 628-0602, Fax: (011-52-5) 628-0644
Secretary, Julia Carabias Lillo
Undersecretary, Coordination & Development, Carlos Camacho Gaos
Undersecretary, Fisheries Development, Carlos Camacho Gaos
Undersecretary, Natural Resources, Dr. Oscar González Rodríguez
Undersecretary, Planning, Enrique Provencio Durazo

SECRETARIAT OF FINANCE & PUBLIC CREDIT
Palacio Nacional, Patio Central, 3 Piso, #3025, Col. Centro, Deleg. Cuauhtémoc, 06066, México, D.F., México
(011-52-5) 518-5420, Fax: (011-52-5) 542-221
Secretary, Dr. Guillermo Ortiz Martinez
Comptroller General, Norma Sanamiego, (011-52-5) 575-3983

SECRETARIAT OF FOREIGN AFFAIRS
Ricardo Flores Magón #1, 19 Piso, 06995, México, D.F., México
(011-52-5) 782-3594, Fax: (011-52-5) 254-5549
Secretary, José Angel Gurria Trevino

SECRETARIAT OF HEALTH
Lieja #7, Colonia Juárez, 1 Piso, 06696, México, D.F., México
(011-52-5) 553-6967
Secretary, Juan Ramón de la Fuente Ramírez

SECRETARIAT OF INTERNAL AFFAIRS
Bucareli #99, 1 Piso, 06699, México, D.F., México
(011-52-5) 566-0245
Secretary, Emilio Chuayffet Chemor
Undersecretary, Civil Protection, Humberto Lira Mora
Undersecretary, Government, Arturo Nunez Jimenez
Undersecretary, Political Development, Luis Fernando Aguilar
Undersecretary, Population & Migration, Manuel Rodriguez Arriaga

SECRETARIAT OF LABOUR & SOCIAL WELFARE
Periférico Sur. #4271, Edificio A, Nivel 9, Col. Fuentes del Pedregal, Tlalpan, 14149, México, D.F., México
(011-52-5) 645-5591, Fax: (011-52-5) 645-2345
Minister, Javier Bonilla Garcia

SECRETARIAT OF NATIONAL DEFENCE
Avila Camacho e Industria Militar, Lomas de Sotelo, 11640, México, D.F., México
(011-52-5) 557-4500, Fax: (011-52-5) 395-6766
Secretary, Div. Gen. Enrique Cervantes Aguirre
Undersecretary, Div. Gen. Jaime Contreras Cuerrero
Chief of Staff, Army, Brig. Gen. Enrique Salgado Cordero, (011-52-5) 557-4500
Chief of Staff, Navy, Adm. Alejandro Maldonado Mendoza, (011-52-5) 679-6411
Commander, Air Force, Div. Gen. Humberto Lucero Nevárez, (011-52-5) 557-3310

SECREATARIAT OF THE NAVY
Eje 2 Oriente Trama Heróica, Escuela Naval 861, 04830, México, D.F., México
(011-52-5) 679-6411, Fax: (011-52-5) 685-4266
Secretary, Adm. José Ramón Lorenzo Franco

SECRETARIAT OF PUBLIC EDUCATION
Ava. República de Argentina y González, Obregón #28, 06029, México, D.F., México
(011-52-5) 328-1000
Secretary, Miguel Limón Rojas

SECRETARIAT OF SOCIAL DEVELOPMENT
Ava. Constituyentes #947, Edificio B.P.A., Colonia Belén de las Flores, 01110, México, D.F., México
(011-52-5) 271-8521, Fax: (011-52-5) 271-6614
Secretary, Carlos Rojas Gutiérrez

SECRETARIAT OF TOURISM
Ava. Presidente Masarik #172, 11587, México, D.F., México
(011-52-5) 250-8206
Secreatary, Silvia Hernández Enriquez

Associated Agencies
• Bank of México
Ava. 5 de Mayo #2, Apartado 98, 06059, México, D.F., México
(011-52-5) 237-2000, Fax: (011-52-5) 237-2150
Director General, Miguel Mancera Aguayo
• Energy Policy & Planning Commission
Francisco Márquez 160, Colonia Condesa, México, D.F., México
Chair, Fernando Hiriart Valderrama
• Fruit Industry Commission
Allende 8 Sur., 76007, Querétaro, México
(011-52-463) 570-2499
Director, Francisoco merino Rabago
• Mexican Oil Company (PEMEX)
Ava. Marina Nacional 319, 44 Piso, Colonia Anáhuac, 11311, México, D.F., México
(011-52-5) 531-6239
Director General, Adrián Lajous Vargas
• Mining Sector Development Agency
Puente de Tecamachalco 26, Lomas de Chapultepec, 11000, México, D.F., México
(011-52-5) 540-2906
Director, Luis de Pablo Serno
• National Commercial Exports Council
Edificio de las Instituciones, 7 Piso, O'campo 250, Apartado 2674, Monterrey, México
(011-52-83) 42-2143
President, José Trevito Salinas
• National Council of Mineral Resources Development
Ava. Ninos Heroes, 139, 06720, México, D.F., México
(011-52-5) 568-6112
Director, Renando Castillo Nieto
• National Electricity Commission
Río Ródano 14, 6 Piso, Colonia Cuauhtémoc, 06568, México, D.F., México
(011-52-5) 553-6400
Director, Rogelio Gasca Neri
• National Railways of México
Edificio Administrativo, Ava. Jusús Garcia Corona, #140, Colonia Buenavista, 06358, México, D.F., México
(011-52-5) 327-3600
Director General, Luis de Pable Serna
• National Foreign Investment Commission
Blvd. Avila Camacho, #1, 11 Piso, 11000, México, D.F., México
(011-52-5) 540-1426
Executive Secretary, Dr. Carlos Camacho Gaos
• National Nuclear Development Standards Commission
Dr. Barragán 779, Col. Narvarte, Del. Benito Juárez, 03020, México, D.F., México
(011-52-5) 590-1481
Director General, Miguel Medina Vaillard
• National Water Commission
Insurgentes Sur. 2140, 2 Piso, Co. Ermita, 01070, México, D.F., México
(011-52-5) 661-3806
Director General, Guillermo Guerrero Villalobos
• Office of the Attorney General
Ref.#75 esq., Violeta y Soto, PO Box 06200, Stn Col. Guerrero, México, D.F., México
(011-52-5) 626-4000, Fax: (011-52-5) 626-4419
Attorney General, Fernando Antonio Lozano Gracia
• Telecommunications México
Torre Central de Telecomunicaciones, Eje Central Lázaro Cardenas 567, 11 Piso, Col. Navarte, 03020, México, D.F., México
(011-52-5) 519-4049
Director General, Carlos Minteran Ordiales

GOVERNMENT OF THE NETHERLANDS/ Nederland
Capital: Amsterdam; The Hague
Major Political Parties: Labour Party (PvdA); People's Party for Freedom & Democracy (VVD); Democrats '66 (D'66)
Currency: Netherlands guilder
Total Area: 37,330 km2
Population: 15,367,928 (1994)
Language(s): Dutch

OFFICE OF THE QUEEN
Paleis Noordeinde, PO Box 30412, 2500 GK, The Hague, Netherlands
(011-31-70) 362-4701, Fax: (011-31-70) 361-5214
Armgard, H.M. Queen Beatrix Wilhelmina Armgard

OFFICE OF THE PRIME MINISTER
Binnenhof 20, Postbus 20001, 2500 EA, The Hague, Netherlands
(011-31-70) 356-4100, Fax: (011-31-70) 356-4683

Prime Minister, Wim Kok
First Vice Prime Minister, H.F. Hijkastal
Second Vice President, Hans Van Mierlo

FIRST CHAMBER/Eerste Kamer
Binnenhof 22, PO Box 20017, 2513 AA, s'Gravenhage, Netherlands
(011-31-70) 362-4571, Fax: (011-31-70) 365-3868
Willink, Chair, H.J. Tjeenk

SECOND CHAMBER/Tweede Kamer
Vinnenhof 1A, PO Box 20018, 2500 EA, s'Gravenhage, Netherlands
(011-31-70) 318-2211, Fax: (011-31-70) 365-4122
Chair, Wim Deetman

MINISTRY OF AGRICULTURE, NATURE MANAGEMENT & FISHERIES
Bezuidenhoutseweg 73, 2594 AC, The Hague, Netherlands
(011-31-70) 379-3911, Fax: (011-31-70) 381-5153
Minister, Jozias van Aartsen

MINISTRY OF DEFENCE
Bezuidenhoutseweg 30, Postbus 20701, 2500 ES, The Hague, Netherlands
(011-31-70) 318-8188, Fax: (011-31-70) 318-7888
Minister of Defence, Dr. Jon's Voohoeve
Chief of Staff, Defence Staff, Lt. Gen. Henk G.B. van den Breemen, (011-31-70) 318-7331
Commander-in-Chief, Royal Netherlands Air Force & Chief of Staff, Lt. Gen. Ben Droste, (011-31-70) 349-3591
Commander-in-Chief, Royal Netherlands Army, Lt. Gen. H.A. Couzy
Commander-in-Chief, Royal Netherlands Navy & Chief of Staff, V. Adm. N.W.G. Buis, (011-31-70) 318-8379

MINISTRY OF ECONOMIC AFFAIRS & FOREIGN TRADE
Bezuidenhoutseweg 30, 2594 AV, The Hague, Netherlands
(011-31-70) 379-8911, Fax: (011-31-70) 347-4081
Minister, Economic Affairs, Gerardus I. Wijers
Minister, Foreign Trade, Anneke van Dok-van Weele

MINISTRY OF EDUCATION, CULTURAL AFFAIRS & SCIENCE
Europaweg 4, Postbus 25000, 2700 LZ, Zoetermeer, Netherlands
(011-31-79) 531-911, Fax: (011-31-79) 512-651
Minister, Jozef M.M. Ritzen

MINISTRY OF FINANCE
Korte Voorhout 7, Postbus 20201, 2500 VB, The Hague, Netherlands
(011-31-70) 342-8000, Fax: (011-31-70) 351-7905
Minister, Gerrit Zalm

MINISTRY OF FOREIGN AFFAIRS
Bezuidenhoutseweg 67, Postbus 20061, 2500 EB, The Hague, Netherlands
(011-31-70) 348-6486, Fax: (011-31-70) 348-4848
Minister, Hans Van Mierlo
Minister, Development Cooperation, Jan Proonk

MINISTRY OF HEALTH, WELFARE & SPORTS
Sir Winston Churchillaan 362, Postbus 5406, 2280 HK, Rijswijk, Netherlands
(011-31-70) 340-7911, Fax: (011-31-70) 340-7834
Minister, Else Borst-Eilers

MINISTRY OF HOME AFFAIRS
Schedeldoekshaven 200, Postbus 20011, 2500 EA, The Hague, Netherlands
(011-31-70) 302-6302, Fax: (011-31-70) 363-9153
Minister, Hans F. Dijkstal

MINISTRY HOUSING, PLANNING & ENVIRONMENT
Rijnstraat 8, Postbus 20951, 2500 EZ, The Hague, Netherlands
(011-31-70) 339-3939, Fax: (011-31-70) 339-1352
Minister, Margreeth de Boer

MINISTRY OF JUSTICE
Schedeldoekshaven 100, Postbus 20301, 2500 EH, The Hague, Netherlands
(011-31-70) 370-7911, Fax: (011-31-70) 364-7702
Minister, Winnifred Sorgdrager

MINISTRY FOR NETHERLANDS ANTILLIEAN & ARUBAN AFFAIRS
Herengracht 19A, Postbus 20051, 2500 EB, The Hague, Netherlands
(011-31-70) 362-4301, Fax: (011-31-70) 365-2679
Minister Plenipotentiary, Joris Voorhoeve
Minister Plenipotentiary, Aruba, C.A.S.D. Wever, Paleisstraat 6, 2514 JA, The Hague, (011-31-70) 365-9824, Fax: (011-38-70) 345-1446
Minister Plenipotentiary, Netherlands Antilles, E.A.V. Jesurun, Badhuisweg 175, 2597 JP, The Hague, (011-31-70) 351-2811, Fax: (011-31-70) 351-2722

MINISTRY OF SOCIAL AFFAIRS & EMPLOYMENT
Anna Van Hannoverstraat 4, Postbus 90801, 2500 EV, The Hague, Netherlands
(011-31-70) 333-4444, Fax: (011-31-70) 333-4033
Minister, A.P.W. Melkert

MINISTRY OF TRANSPORT & PUBLIC WORKS
Plesmanweg 1, Postbus 20901, 2500 EX, The Hague, Netherlands
(011-31-70) 351-6171, Fax: (011-31-70) 351-7895
Minister, Annemaria Jorritsma-Lebbink

Associated Agencies
• Bank of the Netherlands/Nederlandsche Bank
Westeinde 1, PO Box 98, 1000 AB, Amsterdam, Netherlands
(011-31-20) 524-9111, Fax: (011-31-20) 620-3426
President, W.F. Duisenberg

GOVERNMENT OF NORWAY/Norge
Capital: Oslo
Major Political Parties: Labour Party; Conservative Party; Center Party
Currency: Norwegian Krone
Total Area: 324,220 km2
Population: 4,314,604 (1994)
Language(s): Norwegian, Lapp, Finnish

OFFICE OF THE KING
Ket. Kgl. Slott, 0010, Oslo 1, Norway
(011-47-22) 44-19-20, Fax: (011-47-22) 55-08-80
H.M. King Harald V
Queen Sonja

OFFICE OF THE PRIME MINISTER
Akersgaten 42, PO Box 8001 Dep., 0030, Oslo 1, Norway
(011-47-22) 34-90-00, Fax: (011-47-22) 34-95-00
Prime Minister, Gro Harlem Brundtland

STORTING/Stortinget
Karl Johansgt. 22, 0026, Oslo 1, Norway
(011-47-22) 31-30-50, Fax: (011-47-22) 31-38-50
President, Kiristi Kolle Grondahl
Vice-President, Edvard Grimstad

LAGTING
Karl Johansgt. 22, 0032, Oslo 1, Norway
(011-47-22) 31-30-50
President, Jan Syse
Vice-President, Dag Jostein Fjaevoll

ODELSTING
Karl Johansgt 22, 0032, Oslo 1, Norway

(011-47-22) 31-30-50, Fax: (011-47-22) 31-38-38
Speaker, Gunnar Skaug

MINISTRY OF ADMINISTRATIVE AFFAIRS
Plesensgate 8, PO Box 8004 Dep., 0030, Oslo 1, Norway
(011-47-22) 34-90-90, Fax: (011-47-22) 27-14-37
Minister, Nils Olav Totland

MINISTRY OF AGRICULTURE
Akersgaten 42, PO Box 8007 Dep., 0030, Oslo 1, Norway
(011-47-22) 34-90-90, Fax: (011-47-22) 34-95-55
Minister, Gunhild Oyangen

MINISTRY OF CHILDREN & FAMILY AFFAIRS
Ploensgate 8, PO Box 8036 Dep., 0030, Oslo 1, Norway
(011-47-22) 34-90-90, Fax: (011-47-22) 34-95-15
Minister, Grete Berget

MINISTRY OF CULTURAL AFFAIRS
PO Box 8030 Dep., 0030, Oslo 1, Norway
(011-47-22) 34-90-90, Fax: (011-47-22) 34-95-50
Minister, Aase Kelveland

MINISTRY OF DEFENCE
Myntgaten 1, PO Box 8126 Dep., 0032, Oslo, Norway
(011-47-22) 40-20-03, Fax: (011-47-22) 40-23-02
Minister, Jorgen Kosmo
Chief of Defence Staff, Armed Forces, Gen. Arne Solli, (011-47-22-49-80-80
Chief of Staff, Air Force, Maj. Gen. Elinar K. Smedsvig
Chief of Staff, Army, Maj. Gen. Sven A. Sved
Chief of Staff, Home Guard, Maj. Gen. Per Mathisen
Chief of Staff, Navy, R. Adm. Hans K. Svensholt

MINISTRY OF DEVELOPMENT COOPERATION
7, Juniplass 1, PO Box 8114 Dep., 0032, Oslo 1, Norway
(011-47-22) 34-36-00, Fax: (011-47-22) 34-95-80
Minister, Karl Nordheim-Larsen

MINISTRY OF EDUCATION, RESEARCH & CHURCH AFFAIRS
Akersgaten 42, PO Box 8119 Dep., 0032, Oslo 1, Norway
(011-47-22) 34-90-90, Fax: (011-47-22) 34-95-40
Minister, Gudmund Hernes

MINISTRY OF THE ENVIRONMENT
Myntgaten 2, PO Box 8013 Dep., 0030, Oslo 1, Norway
(011-47-22) 34-90-90, Fax: (011-47-22) 34-95-60
Minister, Thorbjorn Berntsen

MINISTRY OF FINANCE
Akersgaten 42, PO Box 8008 Dep., 0030, Oslo 1, Norway
(011-47-22) 34-90-90, Fax: (011-47-22) 34-95-05
Minister, Sigbjorn Johnsen

MINISTRY OF FISHERIES
Ovre Slottsgate 2, PO Box 8118 Dep., 0032, Oslo 1, Norway
(011-47-22) 34-90-90, Fax: (011-47-22) 34-95-85
Minister, Jan Henry Olsen

MINISTRY OF FOREIGN AFFAIRS
7, Juniplass 1, PO Box 8114 Dep., 0032, Oslo 1, Norway
(011-47-22) 34-36-00, Fax: (011-47-22) 34-95-80
Minister, Bjorn Tore Godal

MINISTRY OF HEALTH & SOCIAL AFFAIRS
Gruggegaten 10, PO Box 8011 Dep., 0030, Oslo 1, Norway
(011-47-22) 34-90-90, Fax: (011-47-22) 34-95-75
Minister, Hill-Marta Solberg

MINISTRY OF INDUSTRY & ENERGY
Grubbegata 8, PO Box 8148 Dep., 0033, Oslo 1, Norway
(011-47-22) 34-90-90, Fax: (011-47-22) 34-95-25
Minister, Jens Stoltenberg

MINISTRY OF JUSTICE
Akersgaten 42, PO Box 8005 Dep., 0030, Oslo 1, Norway
(011-47-22) 34-90-90, Fax: (011-47-22) 34-95-30
Minister, Grete Faremo

MINISTRY OF LOCAL GOVERNMENT & LABOUR
PO Box 8112 Dep., 0032, Oslo, Norway
(011-47-22) 34-90-90, Fax: (011-47-22) 34-95-45
Minister, Gunnar Berge

MINISTRY OF TRADE & SHIPPING
7, Juniplass 1, PO Box 8114 Dep., 0032, Oslo 1, Norway
(011-47-22) 34-36-00, Fax: (011-47-22) 34-95-80
Minister, Grete Knudsen

MINISTRY OF TRANSPORTATION & COMMUNICATIONS
Mollergaten 1-3, PO Box 8010 Dep., 0030, Oslo 1, Norway
(011-47-22) 34-90-90, Fax: (011-47-22) 34-95-70
Minister, Kjell Opseth

Associated Agencies
• Central Bank of Norway/Norges Bank
Bankplassen 2, PO Box 1179 Sentrum, 0107, Oslo 1, Norway
(011-47-22) 31-60-00, Fax: (011-47-22) 41-31-05
Governor & Chair, Torstein Moland
• Federation of Commercial & Service Enterprises
Drammensveien 30, PO Box 2483, 0202, Oslo 2, Norway
(011-47-22) 55-82-20
President, Vacant
• National Energy Institute
PO Box 40, 2007, Kjeller, Norway
(011-47-6) 80-60-00
Chair, Henrik Ager-Hanssen
• Norwegian Petroleum Directorate
Prof. Olav Hanssensvei 10, PO Box 600, 4001, Stavanger, Norway
(011-47-51) 87-60-00
Director General, Fredrik Hagemann
• Norwegian State Railway
Prinsensgt. 7-9, 0107, Oslo, Norway
(011-47-22) 36-80-00
• Norwegian Telecommunications Authority
PO Box 447 Sentrum, 0104, Oslo, Norway
(011-47-22) 82-46-06
Director General, Roald Ekholdt

GOVERNMENT OF SOUTH KOREA
Capital: Seoul
Major Political Parties: Democratic Liberal Party (DLP); Democratic Party (DP); United People's Party (UPP)
Currency: South Korean Won
Total Area: 98,480 km2
Population: 45,553,882 (1995)
Language(s): Korean, English

OFFICE OF THE PRESIDENT
Chong Wa Dae, 1 Sejong-no, Chongno-ku, Seoul, South Korea
(011-82-2) 770-0011, Fax: (011-82-2) 770-0344
President, H.E. Kim Yong-sam
Chief Secretary, Kim Kwang-Il
Director, National Security Planning Agency, Kwon Yong-hae, 70 Sejong-no, Chongno-ku, Seoul, (011-82-2) 720-2201

OFFICE OF THE PRIME MINSITER
77 Sejong-no, Chongno-gu, Seoul, South Korea
(011-82-2) 720-2006, Fax: (011-82-2) 720-2005
Prime Minister, Lee Soo-Sung
First Minister of State, Political Affairs, Choo Don-Shik
Second Minister of State, Political Affairs, Kim Jang-sook

NATIONAL ASSEMBLY
1-1 Youido-dong, Yongdungpo-gu, Seoul, South Korea
(011-82-2) 784-0911
Speaker, Hwang Nak-joo

MINISTRY OF AGRICULTURE, FORESTRY & FISHERIES
1 Chungang-dong, Kwach'on, Kyonggi, South Korea
(011-82-2) 503-7208, Fax: (011-82-2) 503-7249
Minister, Ghang Wun-Tae
Administrator, Fisheries Administration, Yi Hui-su
Administrator, Forestry Administration, Kwak Mahn-sup
Administrator, Rural Development Administration, Kim Kwang-hui

MINISTRY OF CULTURE & SPORTS
82-1 Sejongno, Chongno-gu, Seoul 110-703, South Korea
(011-82-2) 736-7946, Fax: (011-82-2) 736-8513
Minister, Kim Young-Soo

MINISTRY OF EDUCATION
77 Sejong-no, Chongno-gu, Seoul, South Korea
(011-82-2) 720-3053, Fax: (011-82-2) 736-3402
Minister, Ahn Byung-Young

MINISTRY OF THE ENVIRONMENT
7-16 Shinch'on-dong, Songp'a-Gu, Seoul, South Korea
(011-82-2) 503-7171, Fax: (011-82-2) 503-7522
Minister, Chung Chong-Teck

MINISTRY OF FOREIGN AFFAIRS
77 Sejong-no, Chongno-gu, Seoul, South Korea
(011-82-2) 720-2687, Fax: (011-82-2) 736-7790
Minister, Gong Ro-myung
Director, Institute of Foreign Affairs & National Security, Yi Chong-chae

MINISTRY OF GOVERNMENT ADMINISTRATION
77-6 Sejongno, Chongno-gu, Seoul, South Korea
(011-82-2) 735-7401, Fax: (011-82-2) 720-2948
Minister, Kim Ki-Jae

MINISTRY OF HEALTH & WELFARE
1 Chungang-dong, Kwach'on, Kyonggi, South Korea
(011-82-2) 503-7504, Fax: (011-82-2) 504-6418
Minister, Kim Yang Bae

MINISTRY OF HOME AFFAIRS
77 Sejong-no, Chongno-gu, Seoul, South Korea
(011-82-2) 731-2121, Fax: (011-82-2) 733-2755
Minister, Kim Woo-Suk
Director General, National Police Headquarters, Kim Hwa-nam, 77 Sejong-no, Chongno-ku, Seoul, (011-82-2) 213-2241
Director General, Office of Administrative Control, Kim Si-hyong, (011-82-2) 731-2170

MINISTRY OF INFORMATION
82-1 Sejingno, Chongno-gu, Seoul, South Korea
(011-82-2) 720-1456, Fax: 011-82-2) 392-1883
Minister, Oh In-whan
Director General, Korean Overseas Information Service, Yi Chang-yong, 82-1 Sejong-no, Chongno-ku, 1101-050, Seoul, (011-82-2) 720-4817

MINISTRY OF INFORMATION & COMMUNICATIONS
100 Sejongnom, Chongno-gu, Seoul 110-777, South Korea
(011-82-2) 750-2222, Fax: (011-82-2) 750-2915
Minister, Lee Suk-Chae

MINISTRY OF JUSTICE
1 Chungang-dong, Kwach'on, Kyonggi, South Korea
(011-82-2) 503-7011, Fax: (011-82-2) 504-3337
Minister, Ahn Woo-Mahn

Commissioner, Korean Customs Service, Lee Hwan-kywu, 71 Nonhyun-dong, Kangram-gu, Seoul, (011-82-2) 512-0011

MINISTRY OF LABOUR AFFAIRS
Government Complex II, 1 Chungang-dong, Kwachon-city, Kyonggi-do, South Korea
(011-82-2) 503-9714, Fax: (011-82-2) 503-9771
Minister, Jin Nyum

MINISTRY OF LEGISLATION
77 Sejong-no, Chongno-gu, Seoul 110-760, South Korea
(011-82-2) 720-4484, Fax: (011-82-2) 738-2649
Minister, Kim Ki-suk

MINISTRY OF NATIONAL DEFENCE
77 Sejong-no, Chongno-gu, Seoul, South Korea
(011-82-2) 794-4687, Fax: (011-82-2) 720-2432
Minister, Lee Yang-ho
Chair, Joint Chiefs of Staff, Armed Forces, Gen. Kim Tong-chin, Yongsan-ku, Seoul, (011-82-2) 792-6081
Chief of Staff, Air Force, Gen. Kim Hong-rae, 320-919, PO Box 301, Poonam-ri, Doom-myun, Nonsan-kun, Choongnam
Chief of Staff, Army, Gen. Yun Yong-nam, Bunam-ri, Duma-myun, Nonsan-gun, Choongram
Chief of Naval Operations, Navy, Adm. An Pyong-tae, Bunam-ri, Duma-myun, Nonsan-gun, Choongnam, (011-82-42) 551-3005

MINISTRY OF PATRIOTS & VETERANS AFFAIRS
17-23 Youid-dong, Yongdungp'o-gu, Seoul, South Korea
(011-82-2) 780-9607, Fax: (011-82-2) 784-1087
Minister, Hwang Chang-prong

MINISTRY OF SCIENCE & TECHNOLOGY
Government Complex Bldg. II, Gwacheon, South Korea
(011-82-2) 503-7608, Fax: (011-82-2) 503-7673
Dr. Chung Kunk-mo

MINISTRY OF TRANSPORTATION & CONSTRUCTION
168 2ka, Pongnae-dong, Chung-gu, Seoul, South Korea
(011-82-2) 392-7606, Fax: (011-82-2) 392-9809
Minister, Choo Kynug-suk
Deputy Minister, Construction, Yu Sang-yol
Deputy Minister, Transportation, Ku Pon-yong
Administrator, Maritime & Port, Kim Chol-yong, (011-82-2) 745-7321
Administrator, National Railroad, Dhoe Pyong-uk, (011-82-2) 392-0078

MINISTRY OF STATE FOR POLITICAL AFFAIRS
77 Sejongno, Chongno-gu, Seoul, South Korea
(011-82-2) 720-2271
Minister, Kim Yonn-whan

MINISTRY OF TRADE & INDUSTRY
1 Chungang-dong, Kwach'on, Kyonggi, South Korea
(011-82-2) 503-9404, Fax: (011-82-2) 503-9649
Minister, Park Jae-Yoon
Administrator, Industrial Advancement Administration, Pak Sam-Yyu, (011-82-2) 503-7950
Commissioner, Industrial Property Administration, Park Hong-sik, (011-82-2) 568-5830

Associated Agencies
• Bank of Korea
110, 3ka Namdaemun-no, Chung-ku, PO Box 26, Seoul 100-794, South Korea
(011-82-2) 759-4114, Fax: (011-82-2) 759-4037
Governor, Kim Myong-ho
• Economic Planning Board
1 Chungang-dong, Kwach'on, Kyonggi, South Korea
(011-82-2) 503-9020, Fax: (011-82-2) 503-9033
Minister, Hong Chae-hyung

- PO Box 8, Taedok Science Town, Taejon 305-606, South Korea
- (011-82-2) 587-7001
- President, Yang Seung-taik
- •Environment Management Corporation
- Kangwon Bldg., 1024-4 Daechi-dong, Kangnam-ku, Seoul, South Korea
- (011-82-42) 563-7211
- President, Lee Chang-ki
- •Korean Aerospace Reseach Institute
- PO Box 15, Daeduk Science Town, Taejon 305-606, South Korea
- (011-82-42) 860-2140
- President, Hong Jae-hak
- •Korean Atomic Energy Research Institute
- 150 Duckjin-dong, Yusong-ku, Taejon, South Korea
- (011-82-42) 868-2121
- President, Shin Jae-in
- •Korean Development Institute
- 207-41, Cheongryangri-dong, Dongdaemoon-ku, Seoul 131-101, South Korea
- (011-82-2) 960-0080
- President, Whang In-joung
- •Korean Energy Economic Institute
- 665-1, Naeson-dong, Uiwang City, Kyunggi-do 437-082, South Korea
- (011-82-62) 34321-0681
- President, Lee Hoe-sung
- •Korean Environmental Preservation Association
- Korea Chamber of Commerce Bldg. 45, Nam-daemoonro, 4-ka, Chung-ku, Seoul, South Korea
- (011-82-2) 753-7641
- President, Chung Soo-chang
- •Korean Institute of Advanced Science & Technology
- 373-1, Koosung-dong, Yusung-ku, Taejon 305-701, South Korea
- (011-82-2) 958-3222
- President, Chun Soung-soon
- •Korean Institute of Energy Research
- 71-2, Jang-dong, Yusong-ku, Taejon, South Korea
- (011-82-42) 860-3000
- President, Auh Chung-moo
- •Korean Institute of Geology, Mining & Materials
- 30 Kajeong-dong, Yusong-ku, Taejon 305-350, South Korea
- (011-82-42) 868-3270
- President, Kim Dong-hak
- •Korean Institute for Health & Social Affairs
- San 42-14, Bulkwang-dong, Eunpyung-ku, Seoul 122-040, South Korea
- (011-82-2) 355-8001
- President, Lee Sung-woo
- •Korean Institute of Industry & Technology
- 206-9, Cheongryangri-dong, Dongdaemoon-ku, Seoul, South Korea
- (011-82-2) 962-6211
- President, Park Hong-shik
- •Korean Institute for International Economics & Trade
- 206-9, Cheongryangri-dong, Dongdaemoon-ku, Seoul 131-010, South Korea
- (011-82-2) 962-6211
- President, Cha Dong-se
- •Korean Maritime Institute
- 112-2 Inui-dong, Chongro-gu, Seoul, South Korea
- (011-82-2) 745-7521
- President, Bai Byung-tsi
- •Korean Nuclear Society
- B-109, Keco Nam Seoul Bldg., 21, Yoido-dong, Youngdungpo-ku, Seoul, South Korea
- (011-82-2) 782-0141
- President, Yoon Yong-ku
- •Korean Ocean Research & Development Institute
- PO Box 29, Ansan, Kyunggi-do, Seoul, South Korea
- (011-82-2) 863-4770
- President, Kwak Hee-sang
- •Korean Rural Economic Institute
- 4-102, Hoegi-dong, Dongdaemoon-ku, Seoul 131-050, South Korea
- (011-82-2) 962-7312
- President, Chung Young-il
- •Korean Transport Institute
- Ildong Bldg., 968-5, Daechi-dong, Kangnam-ku, Seoul 135-280
- (011-82-2) 860-1200
- •National Unification Board
- 77 Sejong-no, Chongno-gu, Seoul, South Korea
- (011-82-2) 720-2104, Fax: (011-82-2) 720-2432
- Deputy Prime Minister, Rha Woong-bae

GOVERNMENT OF SWITZERLAND/Schweiz/Suisse

Capital: Bern
Major Political Parties: Radical Democratic Party (FDP); Social Democratic Party (SPS); Christian Democratic Party (SVP); Swiss People's Party
Currency: Swiss Franc
Total Area: 41,290 km2 Population: 7,084,984 (1995)
Language(s): German, French, Italian, Romansch

OFFICE OF THE PRESIDENT
Bundeshaus Ost, 3003, Bern, Switzerland
(011-41-31) 322-22-11, Fax: (011-41-31) 322-32-37
President, Jean-Pascal Delamuraz
Vice President, Arnold Koller
Chancellor, François Couchepin, (011-41-31) 322-37-58, Fax: (011-41-31) 322-37-06

FEDERAL ASSEMBLY
Palais du Parlement, Bundesplatz, 3003, Bern, Switzerland
(011-41-31) 322-97-01, Fax: (011-41-31) 322-99-21
Secretary General, Annmarie Huber

NATIONAL COUNCIL
Parlamentsgebäude, 3003, Bern, Switzerland
(011-41-31) 322-97-11, Fax: (011-41-31) 322-78-04
President, Jean-François Leuba
Vice-President, Judith Slamm

COUNCIL OF STATES
Parlamentsgebäude, 3003, Bern, Switzerland
(011-41-31) 322-97-11, Fax: (011-41-31) 322-99-21
President, Olb Schoch

DEPARTMENT OF FINANCE
Bundesgasse 3, 3003, Bern, Switzerland
(011-41-31) 322-61-11, Fax: (011-41-31) 322-61-87
Chief, Villiger Kaspar
President, Federal Banking Commission, Kurt Haun, (011-41-31) 322-69-11
Senior Director, Federal Customs Administration, Rudolf Dietrich, (011-41-31) 322-65-11
Director, Federal Tax Administration, Dieter Metzger, (011-41-31) 322-71-06

DEPARTMENT OF FOREIGN AFFAIRS
Bundeshaus West, 3003, Bern, Switzerland
(011-41-31) 322-21-11, Fax: (011-41-31) 322-32-37
Chief, Flavio Cotti
Secretary of State, Jakob Kellenberger

DEPARTMENT OF THE INTERIOR
Inselgasse, 3003, Bern, Switzerland
(011-41-31) 322-91-11, Fax: (011-41-31) 322-7901
Chief, Ruth Dreifuss
Director, Office of Culture, Dr. David Streiff
Director, Office for the Environment, Forests & Countryside, Philippe Roch
Director, Office of Public Health, Dr. Thomas Zeltner
Director, Office of Social Security, Dr. Walter Seiler
Director, Federal Statistics Office, Dr. Carlo Malaguerra

DEPARTMENT OF JUSTICE & POLICE
Bundeshaus West, 3003, Bern, Switzerland
(011-41-31) 322-91-11, Fax: (011-41-31) 322-78-32
Chief, Arnold Koller
Attorney General, Carla Del Ponte, (011-41-31) 322-45-11
Director, Federal Intellectual Property Office, Roland Grossenbacher, (011-41-31) 325-25-25, Fax: (011-41-31) 325-25-26
Director, Federal Office of Territorial Planning, Hans Fluckiger, (011-41-31) 322-40-60
Director, Office of Civil Defence, Paul Thüring, (011-41-31) 322-50-11
Director, Office of Justice, Heinrich Koller, (011-41-31) 322-41-43
Director, Office of Police Matters, Anton Widmer, (011-41-31) 322-11-11
Director, Office of Private Insurance, Peter Pfund, (011-41-31) 322-79-11

DEPARTMENT OF THE MILITARY
Bundeshaus Ost, 3003, Bern, Switzerland
(011-41-31) 324-12-11, Fax: (011-41-31) 312-34-63
Chief, Adolf Ogi
Chief of Staff, Lt. Gen. A. Ziener, (011-41-31) 324-52-76

DEPARTMENT OF PUBLIC ECONOMY
Bundeshaus Ost, 3003, Bern, Switzerland
(011-41-31) 322-21-11, Fax: (011-41-31) 322-20-56
Chief, Jean-P. Delamuraz
Secretary of State, Foreign Economic Affairs, Franz Blankart
Director, Office of Industry, Arts & Labour, Jean-Luc Nordmann, (011-41-31) 322-29-44
Director, Office of Agriculture, Hans Burger, (011-41-31) 322-25-11

DEPARTMENT OF TRANSPORTATION, COMMUNICATIONS & ENERGY
Bundeshaus Nord, 3003, Bern, Switzerland
(011-41-31) 322-55-11, Fax: (011-41-31) 322-95-76
Chief, Moritz Leuenberger
Director, Office of Civil Aviation, André Auer, (011-41-31) 325-80-39
Director, Office of Energy, Dr. Eduard Kiener, (011-41-31) 322-56-11

Associated Agencies
- •Federal Office of Communications
- Zurunfststrasse 44, Postfach 1003, 2501, Biel, Switzerland
- (011-41-32) 328-55-11, Fax: (011-41-32) 328-55-55
- Director, Marc Furrer
- •Swiss Broadcasting & Television Society
- Giacomettistr. 3, 3000, Bern, Switzerland
- (011-41-31) 35-09-11, Fax: (011-41-31) 35-09-256
- President, Vacant
- •Swiss Economic Development Company
- Mainaustr. 30, 8034, Zürich, Switzerland
- (011-41-1) 382-22-88, Fax: (011-41-1) 383-82-27
- President, Dr. Hans Jucker
- •Swiss National Bank
- Börsenstr. 15, 8001, Zürich, Switzerland
- (011-41-1) 631-31-11, Fax: (011-41-1) 631-39-11
- President, Markus Lusser
- •Swiss Post, Telephone & Telegraph Company
- Viktoriastr. 21, 3030, Bern, Switzerland
- (011-41-31) 388-11-11, Fax: (011-41-31) 338-25-49
- President, Dieter Syz
- •Swiss Railway Service
- Hochschulstr. 6, 3030, Bern, Switzerland
- (011-41-51) 220-11-11
- President, Benedikt Weibel
- Director General, Infrastructure, Hans Peter Fagagnini

Canadian Almanac & Directory 1997

GOVERNMENT OF TAIWAN/T'ai-wan (ROC)
Capital: Taipei
Major Political Parties: Kuomintang (KMT); Democratic Progressive Party (DPP); Chinese New Party (CNP); Labour Party (LP)
Currency: New Taiwan Dollar
Total Area: 35,980 km2
Population: 21,500,583 (1995)
Language(s): Mandarin, Taiwanese

OFFICE OF THE PRESIDENT
Chiehshou Hall, 122, Chungking S. Rd., Sec. 1, Taipei, Taiwan
(011-886-2) 311-3731, Fax: (011-886-2) 314-0746
President & Chair, National Security Council, H.E. Li Teng-hui
Vice-President, H.E. Li Yuan-zu

OFFICE OF THE PREMIER
1, Chunghsiao E. Rd., Sec. 1, Taipei, Taiwan
(011-886-2) 365-1500, Fax: (011-886-2) 394-8727
Premier, Lien Chan
Vice-Premier, Hsu Li-teh

LEGISLATIVE YÜAN
1, Chungshan S. Rd., Taipei, Taiwan
(011-886-2) 321-1531, Fax: (011-886-2) 322-3557
President, Liu Sung-pan
Vice-President, Wang Chin-p'ing

NATIONAL ASSEMBLY
1, Sui Shan St., Taipei, Taiwan
(011-886-2) 331-1986, Fax: (011-886-2) 361-2515
Secretary General, Chen Chin-jang

OFFICE OF THE PRESIDENT OF THE EXAMINATION YÜAN
1, Shihyuan Rd., Taipei, Taiwan
(011-886-2) 936-3081, Fax: (011-886-2) 938-3240
President, Chiu Chuang-huan

OFFICE OF THE PRESIDENT OF THE CONTROL YÜAN
2, Chunghsiao E. Rd., Sec. 1, Taipei, Taiwan
(011-886-2) 341-3183, Fax: (011-886-2) 394-0910
President, Cheng Shui-chi

COUNCIL FOR AGRICULTURE
37, Nanhai Rd., Taipei, Taiwan
(011-886-2) 381-2997, Fax: (011-886-2) 331-0341
Chair, Paul Sun

MINISTRY OF AUDIT
1, Hangchow N. Rd., Taipei, Taiwan
(011-886-2) 397-1366, Fax: (011-886-2) 397-7884
Auditor General, Su Chen-ping

MINISTRY OF COMMUNICATIONS & TRANSPORTATION
2, Changsha St., Sec. 1, Taipei, Taiwan
(011-886-2) 349-2900, Fax: (011-886-2) 381-2260
Minister, Liu Chao-chiuan
Director General, Civil Aeronautics Administration, Mao Chi-kuo, (011-886-2) 514-2400
Director General, Telecommunications Directorate, Steven Chen, (011-886-2) 344-3691

MINISTRY OF ECONOMIC AFFAIRS
15, Foochow St., Taipei, Taiwan
(011-886-2) 321-2200, Fax: (011-886-2) 391-9398
Minister, Chiang Pin-kung
Director General, Board of Foreign Trade, Lin Yi-fu, (011-886-2) 351-0271
Director, Industrial Development Bureau, Yiin Cheih-min, (011-886-2) 754-1255
Director, Industrial Development & Investment Centre, Chen Yung-hsiang, (011-886-2) 398-2111
Director, International Cooperation Department, Lei Dao-yu, (011-886-2) 391-8198
Chair, Investment Commission, Shen Ke-sheng, (011-886-2) 351-3151

Director General, National Bureau of Standards, Chen Zso-chen, (011-886-2) 738-0007

COUNCIL FOR ECONOMIC PLANNING & DEVELOPMENT
87, Nanking E. Rd., Sec. 2, Taipei, Taiwan
(011-886-2) 552-5300, Fax: (011-886-2) 551-9011
Chair, Hsu Li'teh

MINISTRY OF EDUCATION
5, Chungshan S. Rd., Taipei 10040, Taiwan
(011-886-2) 389-8820, Fax: (011-886-2) 395-2073
Minister, Kuo Wei-fan

ENVIRONMENT PROTECTION ADMINISTRATION
41, Chunghwa Rd., Sec. 1, Taipei, Taiwan
(011-866-2) 311-7722, Fax: (011-866-2) 321-2491
Administrator, Chang Lung-sheng

MINISTRY OF EXAMINATION
1, Shihyuan Rd., Taipei, Taiwan
(011-886-2) 936-3081, Fax: (001-886-2) 938-3240
Minister, Wang Tso-yung

MINISTRY OF FINANCE
2, Aikuo W. Rd., Taipei, Taiwan
(011-886-2) 322-8000, Fax: (011-886-2) 321-1205
Miniser, Lin Chen-kuo

MINISTRY OF FOREIGN AFFAIRS
2, Chiehshou Rd., Taipei, Taiwan
(011-886-2) 311-9292, Fax: (011-886-2) 314-4972
Minister, Frederick Chien-fu

DEPARTMENT OF HEALTH
100, Aikuo E. Rd., Taipei, Taiwan
(011-886-2) 321-0151, Fax: (011-886-2) 312-2907
Director General, Chang Po-ya

GOVERNMENT INFORMATION OFFICE
2, Tientsin St., Taipei, Taiwan
(011-886-2) 322-8888, Fax: (011-886-2) 341-6252
Director General, Jason Hu Chih-chiang

MINISTRY OF THE INTERIOR
5, Hsuchow Rd., Taipei, Taiwan
(011-886-2) 356-5000, Fax: (011-886-2) 397-6850
Minister, Huang Kun-huei
Director, National Police Administration, Lu Yu-chun, (011-886-2) 321-9011

MINISTRY OF JUSTICE
130, Chungking S. Rd., Sec. 1, Taipei, Taiwan
(011-886-2) 314-6871, Fax: (011-886-2) 389-6274
Minister, Ma Ying-jeou

COUNCIL OF LABOUR AFFAIRS
132, Munsheng E. Rd., Sec. 3, Taipei, Taiwan
(011-886-2) 718-2512, Fax: (011-886-2) 514-9240
Chair, Gen. Shieh Shen-san

NATIONAL COUNCIL OF SCIENCE
106, Hoping E. Rd., Sec. 2, Taipei, Taiwan
(011-886-2) 737-7500, Fax: (011-886-2) 737-7668
Chair, Dr. Kuo Nan-hung

MINISTRY OF NATIONAL DEFENCE
Chiehshou Hall, Chungking S. Rd., Taipei 10016, Taiwan
(011-886-2) 311-6117
Minister, Chiang Chung-ling
Commander-in-Chief, General Staff, Gen. Wang Wen-hsiem, (011-886-2) 381-4920
Commander-in-Chief, Air Force, Gen. Huang Hsien-jung, (011-86-2) 771-1744
Commander-in-Chief, Army, Gen. Li Chen-lin, (011-886-2) 479-2111
Commander-in-Chief, Navy, Adm. Ku Chung-lien, (011-886-2) 505-3811

MINISTRY OF PERSONNEL
1, Shihyuan Rd., Taipei, Taiwan
(011-886-2) 936-3081, Fax: (011-886-2) 936-9207
Minister, John Kuan

RESEARCH, DEVELOPMENT & EVALUATION COMMISSION
4, Chunghsiao W. Rd., Sec. 1, Taipei, Taiwan
(011-886-2) 388-0833, Fax: (011-886-2) 392-8133
Chair, Wang Jen-hong

Associated Agencies
- Atomic Energy Council
67 Lane, 144, Keelung Rd., Sec. 4, Taipei, Taiwan
(011-886-2) 363-4180, Fax: (011-886-2) 363-5377
Chair, Hsu Yih-yun
- Central Bank of China
2, Roosevelt Rd. Sec. 1, Taipei, Taiwan
(011-886-2) 393-6161, Fax: (011-886-2) 322-3223
Governor, Y.D. Sheu
- Central Weather Bureau
64, Kungyuan Rd., Taipei, Taiwan
(011-886-2) 371-3181, Fax: (011-886-2) 391-8971
Director, Shieh Shinn-liang
- Taiwan Power Company
242, Roosevelt Rd., Sec. 3, Taipei, Taiwan
(011-886-2) 365-1234, Fax: (011-886-2) 367-8593
President, S.C. Hsi
- Vocational Assistance Commission for Retired Servicemen
222, Chunghsiao E. Rd., Sec. 5, Taipei, Taiwan
(011-886-2) 725-5700, Fax: (011-886-2) 723-0170
Chair, Yang Ting-yung

GOVERNMENT OF THE UNITED KINGDOM
Capital: London
Major Political Parties: Conservative & Unionist Party; Labour Party; Liberal Democratic Party
Currency: British Pound
Total Area: 244,820 km2
Population: 58,295,119 (1995)
Language(s): English, Welsh, Scottish

HER MAJESTY'S HOUSEHOLD
Buckingham Palace, London SW1A 1AA, United Kingdom
(011-44-171) 930-4832, Fax: (011-44-171) 321-0380
Queen, United Kingdom of Great Britain & Northern Ireland, H.M. Queen Elizabeth II
Lord Chamberlain, Earl of Airlie, K.T., G.C.V.O.
Private Secretary, Sir Robert Fellowes, K.C.V.O., K.C.B., (011-44-171) 930-4832
Prince of Wales, Prince Charles, St. Jame's Palace, London SW1 1BS, (011-44-171) 930-4832
Duke of York, Prince Andrew, Buckingham Palace, London SW1A 1AA, (011-44-171) 930-4832

OFFICE OF THE PRIME MINISTER
10 Downing St., London SW1 2AA, United Kingdom
(011-44-171) 270-3000, Fax: (011-44-171) 930-2831
Prime Minister, Rt. Hon. John Major
First Secretary & Deputy Prime Minister, Rt. Hon. Michael Heseltine

HOUSE OF COMMONS
Westminister, London SW1A 0AA, United Kingdom
(011-44-171) 219-3000, Fax: (011-44-171) 219-5839
Lord President of the Council & Leader of the House, Antony Newton
Speaker, Betty Boothroyd

HOUSE OF LORDS
Parliament Office, Westminister SW1A 0PW, United Kingdom
(011-44-171) 219-3000
Leader of the House, Viscount Cranborne
Deputy Leader, Earl Ferrers
Speaker, Lord Mackay of Clashfern

MINISTRY OF AGRICULTURE, FISHERIES & FOOD
Whitehall Place, London SW1A 2HH, United Kingdom
(011-44-171) 270-3000, Fax: (011-44-171) 270-8125
Minister, Rt. Hon. Douglas Hogg, Q.C.
Minister of State, Fisheries & Agriculture, Tony Baldry

MINISTRY OF DEFENCE
Main Bldg., Whitehall, London SW1A 2HB, United Kingdom
(011-44-171) 218-9000
Secretary of State, Rt. Hon. Michael Portillo
Chair & Chief of Staff, Armed Forces, Gen. Sir Peter Inge
Chief of Staff, Air Force, ACM Sir Michael Graydon
Chief of Staff, Army, Gen. Sir Charles H. Guthrie
Chief of Staff, Navy, Adm. Sir Benjamin Bathurst

DEPARTMENT OF EDUCATION & EMPLOYMENT
Sanctuary Bldg., Great Smith St., London SW1P 3BT, United Kingdom
(011-44-171) 925-5000, Fax: (011-44-171) 925-6000
Secretary of State, Rt. Hon. Gillian Shephard
Minister of State, Eric Forth
Minister of State, Lord Henley

DEPARTMENT OF THE ENVIRONMENT
2 Marsham St., London SW1P 3EB, United Kingdom
(011-44-171) 276-3000, Fax: (011-44-171) 276-0818
Secretary of State, Rt. Hon. John Gummer
Minister of State, Local Government, Housing & Urban Regeneration, Rt. Hon. David Curry
Minister of State, Construction & Planning, Robert Jones
Minister, Environment & Countryside, Rt. Hon. The Earl Ferrers

FOREIGN & COMMONWEALTH OFFICE
Downing St., London SW1A 2AL, United Kingdom
(011-44-171) 270-3000, Fax: (011-44-171) 270-3094
Secretary of State, Rt. Hon. Malcolm Rifkind, Q.C.
Minister of State & Minister for Overseas Development, Rt. Hon. The Baroness Lynda Chalker of Wallasey
Minister of State, Sir Nicholas Bonsor
Minister of State, David Davis
Minister of State, Rt. Hon. Jeremy Hanley

DEPARTMENT OF HEALTH
Richmond House, 79 Whitehall, London SW1A 2NS
(011-44-171) 210-3000, Fax: (011-44-171) 210-5523
Secretary of State, Rt. Hon. Stephen Dorrell
Minister of State, Gerald Malone

HOME OFFICE
50 Queen Anne's Gate, London SW1H 9AT, United Kingdom
(011-44-171) 273-3000, Fax: (011-44-171) 273-2190
Secretary of State, Rt. Hon. Michael Howard, Q.C.
Minister of State, Rt. Hon. David Maclean
Minister of State, Rt. Hon. The Baroness Blatch
Minister of State, Ann Widdecombe

LAW OFFICER'S DEPARTMENT
Attorney General's Chambers, 9 Buckingham Gate, London SW1E 6JP, United Kingdom
(011-44-171) 828-7155
Attorney General, Rt. Hon. Sir Nicholas Lyell, Q.C.
Solicitor General, Sir Derek Spencer, Q.C.

LORD ADVOCATE'S DEPARTMENT
2 Carlton Gardens, London SW1Y 5AA, United Kingdom
(011-44-171) 210-1010, Fax: (011-44-171) 210-1025
Lord Advocate, The Lord Rodger of Earlsferry, Q.C.
Solicitor General for Scotland, Paul Cullen, Q.C.

LORD CHANCELLOR'S DEPARTMENT
House of Lords, London SW1A OPW, United Kingdom
(011-44-171) 219-3000
Lord Chancellor, Rt. Hon. The Lord J.P. Mackay of Clashfern

DEPARTMENT OF NATIONAL HERITAGE
Horse Guard's Rd., London SW1P 3AL, United Kingdom
(011-44-171) 270-3000, Fax: (011-44-171) 270-6026
Secretary of State, Rt. Hon. Virginia Bottomley
Minister of State, Iain Sproat

NORTHERN IRELAND OFFICE
Whitehall, London SW1A 2AZ, United Kingdom
(011-44-171) 210-3000
Secretary of State, Rt. Hon. Sir Patrick Mayhew
Minister of State, Rt. Hon. Michael Ancram
Minister of State, Rt. Hon. Sir John Wheeler

OFFICE OF PUBLIC SERVICE
6 Whitehall, London SW1A 2AT, United Kingdom
(011-44-171) 270-5811
Minister, Civil Service & Prime Minister, Rt. Hon. John Major
First Secretary of State & Deputy Prime Minister, Rt. Hon. Michael Heseltine

SCOTTISH OFFICE
Dover House, Whitehall, London SW1A 2AU, United Kingdom
(011-44-171) 270-3000, Fax: (011-44-171) 270-6730
Secretary of State, Rt. Hon. Michael Forsyth
Minister of State, Rt. Hon. The Lord James Douglas Hamilton

DEPARTMENT OF SOCIAL SECURITY
Richmond House, 79 Whitehall, London SW1A 2NS, United Kingdom
(011-44-171) 210-3000, Fax: (011-44-171) 210-5523
Secretary of State, Rt. Hon. Peter Lilley
Minister of State, Social Security & Disabled Persons, Alistair Burt

DEPARTMENT OF TRADE & INDUSTRY
Ashdown House, 123 Victoria St., London SW1E 6RB, United Kingdom
(011-44-171) 215-5000, Fax: (011-44-171) 828-3258
President of the Board of Trade, Rt. Hon. Ian B. Lang
Minister of State, Energy, Rt. Hon. The Lord Fraser of Carmyllic
Minister of State, Industry, Rt. Hon. Greg Knight
Minister of State, Trade, Anthony Nelson

DEPARTMENT OF TRANSPORT
2 Marsham St., London SW1P 3EB, United Kingdom
(011-44-171) 276-3000, Fax: (011-44-171) 276-0818
Secretary of State, Rt. Hon. Sir George Young
Minister of State, Railways & Roads, John Watts

HER MAJESTY'S TREASURY
Parliament St., London SW1P 3AG, United Kingdom
(011-44-171) 270-3000, Fax: (011-44-171) 270-5653
First Lord of the Treasury, Rt. Hon. John Major
Chancellor of the Exchequer, Rt. Hon. Kenneth Clarke, Q.C.

Customs & Excise
New King's Bean House, 22 Upper Ground Rd., London, United Kingdom
(011-44-171) 620-1313
Chair, Sir Brian Unwin

Board of Inland Revenue
Somerset House, Strand, London WC2R 1LB, United Kingdom
(011-44-171) 438-6622
Chancellor of the Exchequer, Kenneth Clarke

WELSH OFFICE
Hwydyr House, Whitehall, London SW1H 9JS, United Kingdom
(011-44-171) 270-3000
Secretary of State, Rt. Hon. William Hague
Minister of State, Roderick Richards

Associated Agencies
•Associated British Ports
150 Holborn St., London EC1N 2LR, United Kingdom
(011-44-171) 486-6621
Chair, J.K. Stuart
•Bank of England
Threadneedle St., London EC2R 8AH, United Kingdom
(011-44-171) 601-4444
Governor, Edward George
•British Aerospace
Warwick House, Farnborough Aerospace Centre, Farnborough, Hants GU14 6YU, United Kingdom
(011-44-1252) 373-232
Chair, R.P. Bauman
•British Airways PLC
Speedbird House, PO Box 10, Heathrow Airport, Hounslow, Middlesex TW6 2JA, United Kingdom
(011-44-181) 759-5511
Chair, Lord King of Wartnaby
•British Broadcasting Corporation
Broadcasting House, London W1A 1AA, United Kingdom
(011-44-171) 580-4468
Chair, Marmaduke Hussey
•British Gas PLC
Rivermill House, 152 Grosvenor Rd., London SW1V 3JL, United Kingdom
(011-44-171) 821-1444
Chair, Sir Dennis Rooke
•Euston House, 24 Eversholt St., PO Box 100, London NW1 1DZ, United Kingdom
(011-44-171) 922-6545
Chair, Sir Bob Reid
•British Telecom International
#820, Holburn Centre, 120 Holburn St., London EC1N 2TE, United Kingdom
(011-44-171) 492-2000
Director, Tom Edwards
•British Telecommunications PLC
British Telecom Centre, 81 Newgate St., London EC1A 7AJ, United Kingdom
(011-44-171) 356-5000
Chair, Sir Ian Vallance
•Cable & Wireless PLC
124 Theobalds Rd., London VC1X 8RX, United Kingdom
(011-44-171) 315-4000
CEO, J. Ross
•Central Office of Information
Hercules Rd., London SE1 7DU, United Kingdom
(011-44-171) 928-2345
CEO, G.M. Devereau
•Civil Aviation Authority
CAA House, 4-12 Queen Anne's Gate, London SW1H 9AZ, United Kingdom
(011-44-171) 379-7311
Chair, Christopher Chataway
•Export Credits Guarantee Department
2 Exchange Tower, Harbour Exchange Square, London E14 9GS
(011-44-171) 512-7887, Fax: (011-44-171) 512-7649
•HM Land Registry
Lincoln's Inn Fields, London WC2A 3PH, United Kingdom
(011-44-171) 405-3488
Chief Land Registrar & CEO, E.J. Pryer
•National Audit Office

197 Buckingham Palace Rd., Victoria, London
 SW1W 9SP, United Kingdom
(011-44-171) 798-7000
Comptroller & Auditor General, John Bourn
•Office of Electricity Regulation
Hagley House, Hagley Rd., Birmingham B16 8QG,
 United Kingdom
(011-44-121) 456-2100
Director General, Prof. S.C. Littlechild
•General Register Office, Trafalgar Rd., Southport
 PR8 2HH, United Kingdom
(011-44-151) 471-4801
Director, Dr. Tim Holt
•Office of Science & Technology (OST)
1 Victoria St., UG.A.35, London SW1 HEOT, United
 Kingdom
(011-44-171) 215-0053, Fax: (011-44-171) 215-0054
•Office of Telecommunications
Export House, Ludgate Hill, London EC4M 7JJ,
 United Kingdom
(011-44-171) 822-1600
Director General, Sir Brian Carsberg
•Centre City Tower, 7 Hill St., Birmingham B5 4UA,
 United Kingdom
Director General, I.C.R. Byatt
•35-38 Portman Square, London W1H 0EU, United
 Kingdom
Director General, Geoffrey Richards
•The Post Office
148 Old St., 4th Fl., London EC1 9HQ, United
 Kingdom
(011-44-171) 490-2888
Chair, Michael Heron
•Radiotelecommunications Agency
Waterloo Bridge House, Waterloo Rd., London
 SE1 8UA, United Kingdom
(011-44-171) 215-5000
CEO, M.J. Mitchell
•Royal Mint
Llantrisant, Pontyclun, Mid-Clamorgan CF7 8YT,
 United Kingdom
(011-44-1433) 222-111
CEO, A.D. Garrett
•UK Atomic Energy Authority
Harwell Laboratory, Oxfordshire 0X11 0RA, United
 Kingdom
(011-44-1325) 821-111
Chair, Sir Anthony Cleaver

GOVERNMENT OF THE UNITED STATES OF AMERICA/United States
Capital: Washington
Major Political Parties: Republican Party; Democratic
 Party
Currency: United States Dollar
Total Area: 9,372,610 km2
Population: 263,814,032 (1995)
Languages: English, Spanish

OFFICE OF THE PRESIDENT
1600 Pennsylvania Ave. NW, Washington DC 20500,
 USA
202/456-2883, Fax: 202/456-2883
President, William J. Clinton
First Lady, Hillary Rodham Clinton
Chief of Staff, Leon Panetta
Whitehouse Spokesperson, Michael McCurry

OFFICE OF THE VICE-PRESIDENT
1600 Pennsylvania Ave. NW, Washington DC 20500,
 USA
202/456-1414, Fax: 202/456-7044
Vice President, Albert Gore Jr.
National Security Advisor, Leon S. Fuerth

SENATE
Capitol Bldg., Washington DC, USA
202/224-3121

President of the Senate, Albert Gore Jr.
Majority Leader, Trent Lott
Minority Leader, Tom Dashle

HOUSE OF REPRESENTATIVES
Capitol Bldg., Washington DC, USA
202/225-3121
Speaker, Hon. Newt Gingrich
Majority Leader, Richard Armey
Minority Leader, Richard Gephardt

Special Agencies
•Advisory Committee for Trade Policy & Negotiations
Windsor Bldg., 600 - 17th St. NW, Washington DC
 20506
202/395-3204, Fax: 202/395-6224
Chair, Susan Hammer
•Central Intelligence Agency
Old Executive Office Bldg., 17th St. & Pennsylvania
 Ave. NW, Washington DC 20500, USA
703/482-1100, Fax: 703/527-5040
Director, John Deutch
•Foreign Intelligence Advisory Board
Old Executive Office Bldg., 17th St. & Pennsylvania
 Ave. NW, Washington DC 20500, USA
202/456-2352, Fax: 202/395-3403
Chair, Les Aspen
•National Security Council
1600 Pennsylvania Ave. NW, Washington DC 20500,
 USA
202/456-2255, Fax: 202/456-1414
Asst. to the President, Anthony Lake
•Office of Science & Technology Policy
17th St. & Pennsylvania Ave. NW, Washington DC
 20500, USA
202/456-7116, Fax: 202/395-3719
Asst. to the President & Director, OSTP, John Gibbons
•Office of the United States Trade Representative
600 - 17th St. NW, Washington DC 20508, USA
202/395-3204, Fax: 202/395-3719
U.S. Trade Representative, Michael Kantor

DEPARTMENT OF AGRICULTURE
Administration Bldg., 14th St. & Independence Ave.
 SW, Washington DC 20250, USA
202/720-3631
Secretary, Daniel Glickman

Forest Service
Auditors Bldg., 201 - 14th St. SW, Washington DC
 20090, USA
202/205-1661, Fax: 202/205-1765
Chief, Jack Ward Thomas

DEPARTMENT OF COMMERCE
Herbert C. Hoover Bldg., 14th St. & Constitution Ave.
 NW, Washington DC 20230, USA
202/482-2000
Secretary, Michael Kantor
Deputy Secretary, David J. Barrum
Undersecretary, Economic & Statistics Administra-
 tion, Evertt M. Ehrilich
Undersecretary, Export Administration, William A.
 Reinsch
Undersecretary, International Trade, Jeffrey E. Garten
Undersecretary, Oceans & Atmosphere, James Baker
Undersecretary, Technology Administration, Mary L.
 Good
Undersecretary, Travel & Tourism, Greg Farmer
•International Trade Administration
Herbert C. Hoover Bldg., 14th St. & Constitution Ave.
 NW, Washington DC 20230, USA
202/482-2867, Fax: 202/482-4821
Undersecretary, Jeffrey Garten

DEPARTMENT OF DEFENCE
The Pentagon, Washington DC 20301, USA
703/545-6700

Secretary, William J. Perry
Office of the Deputy Secretary, John M. Deutch
Chair, Joint Chiefs of Staff, Gen. John M. Shalikashvili,
 703/695-3337
Secretary, Air Force, Sheila E. Widnall, 703/697-7376
Secretary, Army, Togo D. West, 703/695-3211
Secretary, Navy, John H. Dalton, 703/695-3131
Commandant, United States Coast Guard, V. Adm.
 Robert E. Kramek, 202/267-2390
•Defence Intelligence Agency
7400 Defense Pentagon, Washington DC 20301-7400,
 USA
703/695-7353
Director, Lt. Col. James R. Clapper

DEPARTMENT OF EDUCATION
Federal Office Bldg. 6, 400 Maryland Ave. SW,
 Washington DC 20202-0101
202/401-3000
Secretary, Richard W. Riley
Deputy Secretary, Madeleine M. Kunin

DEPARTMENT OF ENERGY
Forrestal Bldg., 1000 Independence Ave. SW,
 Washington DC 20585, USA
202/586-6210, Fax: 202/586-8134
Secretary, Hazel R. O'Leary
Deputy Secretary, William H. White
•Federal Energy Regulatory Commission (FERC)
825 North Capital St. NE, Washington DC 20426, USA
202/208-0000, Fax: 202/208-2106
Chair, Elizabeth Moler

DEPARTMENT OF HEALTH & HUMAN SERVICES
Hubert H. Humphrey Bldg., 200 Independence Ave.
 SW, Washington DC 20201, USA
202/690-7000, Fax: 202/245-3380
Secretary, Donna Shalala
Deputy Secretary, Walter D. Broadnax
•1600 Clifton Rd. NE, Atlanta GA 30333, USA
404/639-3291
Director, David Satcher
•Food & Drug Administration (FDA)
Parklawn Bldg., 5600 Fishers Lane, Rockville MD
 20857, USA
301/827-2410, Fax: 301/443-3100
Commissioner, David Kessler
•Social Security Administration
Altmeyer Bldg., 6401 Security Blvd., Baltimore MD
 21235, USA
410/965-3120, Fax: 410/966-1463
Commissioner, Shirley Chater

DEPARTMENT OF HOUSING & URBAN DEVELOPMENT
HUD Bldg., 451 - 7th St. SW, Washington DC 20410-
 1047, USA
202/708-0417
Secretary, Henry Cisneros
Deputy Secretary, Terrence R. Duvernay Sr.

DEPARTMENT OF THE INTERIOR
Interior Bldg., 1849 C St. NW, Washington DC 20240,
 USA
202/208-7351, Fax: 202/208-5048
Secretary, Bruce Babbitt
Deputy Secretary, John Garamendi
•c/o Dept. of the Interior, Interior Bldg., 1849 C St. SW,
 Washington DC 20240, USA
202/208-3710
Asst. Secretary, Ada Deer
•c/o Dept. of the Interior, Interior Bldg., 1849 C St.
 NW, Washington DC 20240
202/208-3435
Director, Vacant
•National Park Service
1100 Ohio Dr. SW, Washington DC 20242, USA
202/619-7005
Director, Roger Kennedy

- United States Bureau of Mines
810 Seventh St. NW, Washington DC 20241, USA
202/501-9649
Director, Rhea Graham
- United States Fish & Wildlife Service
Arlington Square, 4401 North Fairfax Dr.,
  Arlington VA 22203, USA
202/208-4717
Director, Mollie Beattie

DEPARTMENT OF JUSTICE
Main Justice Bldg., 10th St. & Constitution Ave. NW,
  Washington DC 20530, USA
202/514-2001, Fax: 202/633-4371
Attorney General, Janet Reno
Deputy Attorney General, Philip B. Heymann
- Bureau of Prisons
320 First St. NW, Washington DC 20534, USA
202/307-3198
Director, Kathleen Hawk
- Drug Enforcement Administration (DEA)
600 - 700 Army Navy Dr., Arlington VA 22202, USA
202/307-1000, Fax: 202/367-1000
Administrator, Thomas Consantine
- Federal Bureau of Investigation (FBI)
J. Edgar Hoover FBI Bldg., 9th St. & Pennsylvania
  Ave. NW, Washington DC 20535, USA
202/324-3444, Fax: 202/324-4705
Director, Louis J. Freeh
Deputy Director, David Binney
- Immigration & Naturalization Service
Chester Arthur Bldg., 425 Eye St. NW,
  Washington DC 20536, USA
202/514-1900
Commissioner, Doris Meissner
- United States Marshals Service
Airport Plaza 2, 2611 Jefferson Davis Highway,
  Arlington VA 22202, USA
202/307-9001, Fax: 202/557-9788
Director, Eduardo Gonzalez

DEPARTMENT OF LABOUR
Frances Perkins Bldg., 200 Constitution Ave. NW,
  Washington DC 20210, USA
202/219-8274
Secretary, Robert Reich
Deputy Secretary, Thomas Glynn

DEPARTMENT OF STATE
Main State Dept. Bldg., 2201 C St. NW,
  Washington DC 20520, USA
202/647-4910
Secretary, Warren M. Christopher
Deputy Secretary, Strobe Talbott

DEPARTMENT OF TRANSPORTATION
Nassif Bldg., 400 - 7th St. SW, Washington DC 20590,
  USA
202/366-1111, Fax: 202/366-7256
Secretary, Federico Pena
Deputy Secretary, Mortimer L. Downey
- Federal Aviation Administration (FAA)
800 Independence Ave. SW, Washington DC 20591,
  USA
202/267-3111, Fax: 202/267-3505
Administrator, David Hinson
- Federal Highway Administration
Nassif Bldg., 400 - 7th St. SW, Washington DC 20590,
  USA
202/366-0650, Fax: 202/366-3244
Administrator, Rodney Slater
- Federal Railroad Administration
Nassif Bldg., 400 - 7th St. SW, Washington DC 20590,
  USA
202/366-0710, Fax: 202/366-3055
Administrator, Jolene Molitoris
- Federal Transit Administration

Nassif Bldg., 400 - 7th St. SW, Washington DC 20590,
  USA
202/366-4040, Fax: 202/366-3472
Administation, Gordon Linton

DEPARTMENT OF THE TREASURY
Main Treasury, 1500 Pennsylvania Ave. NW,
  Washington DC 20220, USA
202/622-1100
Secretary, Robert E. Rubin
Deputy Secretary, Lawrence H. Summers
- Internal Revenue Service (IRS)
1111 Constitutional Ave. NW, Washington DC 20224,
  USA
202/622-4115
Commissioner, Margaret Richardson
- Bureau of Alcohol, Tobacco & Firearms
650 Massachusetts Ave. NW, Washington DC 20226,
  USA
202/927-8700, Fax: 202/927-8876
Director, John Magaw
- United States Secret Service
1800 G St. NW, Washington DC 20223, USA
202/435-5700, Fax: 202/435-5246
Director, Eljay Brown
- United States Customs Service
1301 Constitution Ave. NW, Washington DC 20229,
  USA
202/927-1000
Commissioner, George Weise

DEPARTMENT OF VETRANS AFFAIRS
TechWorld Bldg., 801 - 1 St. NW, Washington DC
  20001, USA
202/273-4800
Secretary, Jesse Brown
Deputy Secretary, Hershel Gober

Associated Agencies
- Environmental Protection Agency
Waterside Mall, 401 M St. SW, Washington DC 20460,
  USA
202/260-4700, Fax: 202/260-0279
Administrator, Carol M. Browner
- Federal Communications Commission (FCC)
1919 M St. NW, Washington DC 20554-0001, USA
202/418-1000, Fax: 202/632-0942
Chair, Marsha Martin
- Federal Election Commission
PEPCO Bldg., 999 E St. NW, Washington DC 20463-
  0001, USA
202/219-4100, Fax: 202/219-3880
Chair, Lee Ann Elliott
- Federal Emergency Management Agency
Federal Center Plaza, 500 C St. SW, Washington DC
  20472, USA
202/-646-3923, Fax: 202/646-4086
Director, James Witt
- Federal Reserve System
Federal Reserve Board Bldg., 20th St. & C St. NW,
  Washington DC 20551, USA
202/452-3201, Fax: 202/452-3819
Chair, Alan Greenspan
- Federal Trade Commission
6th St. & Pennsylvania Ave. NW, Washington DC
  20580-0001, USA
202/326-2100, Fax: 202/326-2050
Chair, J.D. Steiger
- General Services Administration
General Services Bldg., Eighteenth & F Sts. NW,
  Washington DC 20405, USA
202/708-5082
Administrator, Roger W. Johnson
- National Aeronautics & Space Administration
  (NASA)
Independence Square, 300 E St. SW, Washington DC
  20546, USA
202/358-0000, Fax: 202/358-2810

Administrator, Daniel Goldin
- National Science Foundation
4201 Wilson Blvd., Arlington VA 22230, USA
703/306-1234
Director, Neal Lane
- National Telecommunications & Information Administration
Herbert C. Hoover Bldg., 14th St. & Constitution Ave.
  NW, Washington DC 20230
202/482-1840
Asst. Secretary, Clarence Irving
- National Transportation Safety Board
490 L'Enfant Plaza East SW, Washington DC 20594,
  USA
202/382-6506, Fax: 202/382-6715
Chair, C.W. Vogt
- Nuclear Regulatory Commission
1717 H St. NW, Washington DC 20555
202/492-7000
Chair & Commissioner, I. Selin
- Office of Personnel Management
1900 E St. NW, Washington DC 20415-0001, USA
202/606-1800
Director, James King
- Peace Corps
Esplande Mall, 1990 K St. NW, Washington DC 20526-
  0001, USA
202/606-3970, Fax: 202/606-4458
Director, Mark Gearan
- Small Business Administration
Washington Office Center, 409 - 3rd St. SW,
  Washington DC 20416, USA
202/205-6605, Fax: 202/205-7064
Administrator, Philip Lader
- Smithsonian Institution
1000 Jefferson Dr. SW, Washington DC 20560, USA
202/357-1300
Secretary, Michael Heyman
Inspector General, Thomas Blair
- United States Arms Control & Disarmament Agency
State Department Bldg., 320 - 21st St. NW,
  Washington DC 20451-0001, USA
202/647-9610, Fax: 202/647-6928
Director, John Holum
- United States Information Agency (USIA)
USIA Bldg., 301 - 4th St. SW, Washington DC 20547,
  USA
202/619-4742, Fax: 202/619-6988
Director, Joseph Duffy
- United States International Trade Commission
  (USITC)
500 E St. SW, Washington DC 20436-0001
202/205-2781, Fax: 202/205-2798
Chair, Peter Watson
- United States Postal Service
475 L'Enfant Plaza SW, Washington DC 20260-0001,
  USA
202/268-4800
Chair, Sam Winters
- United States Trade & Development Agency
#309, State Annex 16, Washington DC 20523-1602,
  USA
703/875-4357
Director, Joseph Grandmaison

THE QUEEN & ROYAL FAMILY

THE HOUSE OF WINDSOR

In 1917 the late King George V, by Proclamation, changed the House name of the Royal Family from Saxe-Coburg-Gotha to the House of Windsor.
THE QUEEN. - Elizabeth the Second, (Elizabeth Alexandra Mary, of Windsor) by the Grace of God, of the United Kingdom, Canada and Her other Realms and Territories Queen; Head of the Commonwealth, Defender of the Faith, Succeeded to the throne Febru-

ary 6th, 1952, and was crowned June 2nd, 1953, at Westminster Abbey. Her Majesty, the elder daughter of the late King George VI and Queen Elizabeth The Queen Mother, was born at 17 Bruton St., London, W.1, on April 21st, 1926, married November 20th, 1947, H.R.H. The Prince Philip, Duke of Edinburgh, K.G., K.T., O.M., G.B.E., A.C., Q.S.O.

THE CHILDREN of Queen Elizabeth and H.R.H. The Prince Philip, Duke of Edinburgh are:

H.R.H. Prince Charles Philip Arthur George, Prince of Wales and Earl of Chester, Duke of Cornwall and Duke of Rothesay, Earl of Carrick and Baron Renfrew, Lord of the Isles, and Great Steward of Scotland, K.G., K.T., G.C.B., A.K., Q.S.O., A.D.C., born November 14th, 1948. Married July 29th, 1981, The Lady Diana Spencer and has issue. Prince William of Wales, born June 21st, 1982 and Prince Henry of Wales, born September 15th, 1984. Marriage dissolved 1996.

H.R.H. The Princess Royal, Anne Elizabeth Alice Louise, K.G., G.C.V.O., Q.S.O., born August 15th, 1950. Married 1st November 14th, 1973 Captain Mark Anthony Peter Phillips, C.V.O., A.D.C. and has issue. Peter Phillips born November 15th, 1977 and Zara Phillips born May 15th, 1981. Marriage dissolved 1992. Married 2nd December 12th, 1993 Commander Timothy James Hamilton Laurence, M.V.O., R.N.

H.R.H. The Prince Andrew Albert Christian Edward, C.V.O., A.D.C., Duke of York, Earl of Inverness and Baron Killyleagh, born February 19th, 1960, married July 23rd, 1986 Miss Sarah Margaret Ferguson and has issue, Princess Beatrice of York, born August 8th, 1988, and Princess Eugenie of York, born March 23rd, 1990. Marriage dissolved 1996.

H.R.H. The Prince Edward Antony Richard Louis, C.V.O., born March 10th, 1964.

THE LATE GEORGE VI. -- George VI succeeded to the Throne December 11th, 1936; and was crowned at Westminster Abbey, May 12th, 1937. Second son of King George V and Queen Mary, he was born at York Cottage, Sandringham, on December 14th, 1895, married, April 26th, 1923, Lady Elizabeth Bowes-Lyon, daughter of the Earl and Countess of Strathmore and Kinghorne. As Heir Presumptive succeeded to the Throne on the abdication of Edward VIII.

QUEEN ELIZABETH, THE QUEEN MOTHER -- born August 4th, 1900, daughter of the 14th Earl of Strathmore and Kinghorne; married, April 26th, 1923.

THE ISSUE of the late King George VI and Queen Elizabeth are:

The reigning Sovereign, Elizabeth the Second (elder daughter).

The Princess Margaret (Rose), Countess of Snowdon, C.I., G.C.V.O., born August 21st, 1930, married Antony Charles Robert Armstrong-Jones, G.C.V.O., (since created Earl of Snowdon) May 6th, 1960, and has issue, Viscount Linley, born November 3rd, 1961 and the Lady Sarah Frances Elizabeth Armstrong-Jones, born May 1st, 1964. Marriage dissolved 1978.

SUCCESSION--The order stands:
The Prince of Wales
Prince William of Wales
Prince Henry of Wales
The Duke of York
Princess Beatrice of York
Princess Eugenie of York
The Prince Edward
The Princess Royal
Mr. Peter Phillips
Miss Zara Phillips
The Princess Margaret, Countess of Snowdon
Viscount Linley
The Lady Sarah Chatto
The Duke of Gloucester
Earl of Ulster
The Lady Davina Windsor
The Lady Rose Windsor
The Duke of Kent
Lord Downpatrick
The Lady Marina Charlotte Windsor
The Lady Amelia Windsor
The Lord Nicholas Windsor
The Lady Helen Taylor
Master Columbus Taylor
The Lord Frederick Windsor
The Lady Gabriella Windsor
Princess Alexandra, The Hon. Lady Ogilvy
Mr. James Ogilvy

HER MAJESTY'S HOUSEHOLD

Lord Chamberlain, The Earl of Airlie, K.T., G.C.V.O.
Lord Steward, The Viscount Ridley, K.G., G.C.V.O., T.D.
Master of the Horse, The Lord Somerleyton, K.C.V.O.
Private Secretary to the Queen, The Rt. Hon. Sir Robert Fellowes, K.C.B., K.C.V.O.
Keeper of the Privy Purse & Treasurer, Mr. Michael Peat, C.V.O.
Master of the Household, Major General Sir Simon Cooper, K.C.V.O.
Crown Equerry, Lt.-Col. Seymour Gilbart-Denham, C.V.O.
Press Secretary, Charles Anson, L.V.O., Esq.

The Lord Chamberlain has the general supervision of the Royal Household.

THE COMMONWEALTH
(COMMONWEALTH OF NATIONS)

The Commonwealth is a voluntary association of 53 independent member countries representing 1.5 billion people around the world -- in Africa, the Americas, Asia, the Caribbean, Europe & the Pacific. It promotes good governance, democracy, sustainable economic & social development, the rule of law & human rights. These & other principles are enshrined in the Harare Commonwealth Declaration of 1991.

There are three principal international organizations of the Commonwealth:

THE COMMONWEALTH SECRETARIAT

Marlborough House, Pall Mall, London SW1Y 5HX, +44 (0)171-839 3411; Fax: +44 (0)171-930 0827
HE Chief Emeka Anyaoku, CON (Nigeria), Commonwealth Secretary-General
Sir Humphrey Maud (Britain), Deputy Commonwealth Secretary-General (Economic & Social Affairs)
Nick Hare (Canada), Deputy Commonwealth Secretary-General (Development Co-operation)
Krishnan Srinivasan (India), Deputy Commonwealth Secretary-General (Political Affairs)
Michael Fathers (New Zealand), Director, Information & Public Affairs

THE COMMONWEALTH FOUNDATION

Marlborough House, Pall Mall, London SW1Y 5HY, +44 (0)171-930 3783; Fax: +44 (0)171-839 8157
Dr. Humayun Khan (Pakistan), Director

The Commonwealth Foundation
#1700-777 Dunsmuir St., PO Box 10428, Pacific Centre, Vancouver BC V7Y 1K4, 604/775-8200; Fax: 604/775-8210, Email: info@col.org, URL: http://www.col.org

For information pertaining to the Commonwealth write to: The Director, Information Division, Commonwealth Secretariat, Marlborough House, Pall Mall, London SW1Y 5HX, U.K.

MEMBER STATES

(showing Capital, Population (1993) & Date of Membership. Dates for Australia, Canada & New Zealand are those on which Dominion Status was acquired):

Antigua & Barbuda - St. John's; 67,000; Nov. 1, 1981
Australia - Canberra; 17,707,000; Jan. 1, 1901
  External territories: Norfolk Island, Coral Sea Islands Territory, Australian Antarctic Territory, Heard Island & McDonald Islands, Cocos (Keeling) Islands, Christmas Island, Territory of Ashmore & Cartier Islands
The Bahamas - Nassau; 266,000; July 10, 1973
Bangladesh - Dhaka; 116,702,000; Apr. 18, 1972
Barbados - Bridgetown; 260,000; Nov. 30, 1966
Belize - Belmopan; 205,000; Sept. 21, 1981
Botswana - Gaborone; 1,402,000; Sept. 30, 1966
Britain - London; 58,040,000
  Dependent territories: Anguilla, Bermuda, British Antarctic Territory, British Indian Ocean Territory, British Virgin Islands, Cayman Islands, Falkland Islands, Gibraltar, Hong Kong, Montserrat, Pitcairn, Henderson, Ducie & Oeno Islands, St. Helena & St. Helena Dependencies (Ascension & Tristan da Cunha), South Georgia & the South Sandwich Islands, & Turks & Caicos Islands
Brunei Darussalam - Bandar Seri Begawan; 281,000; Jan. 1, 1984
Cameroon - Yaoundé; 12,611,000; Nov., 1995
Canada - Ottawa; 27,814,000; July 1, 1867
Cyprus - Nicosia; 726,000; Mar. 13, 1961
Dominica - Roseau; 72,000; Nov. 3, 1978
The Gambia - Banjul; 1,019,000; Feb. 18, 1965
Ghana - Accra; 16,261,000; Mar. 6, 1957
Grenada - Grenada; 91,000; Feb. 7, 1974
Guyana - Georgetown; 812,000; May 26, 1966
India - New Delhi; 900,543,000; Aug. 15, 1947
Jamaica - Kingston; 2,415,000; Aug. 6, 1962
Kenya - Nairobi; 25,376,000; Dec. 12, 1963
Kiribati - Tarawa; 76,000; July 12, 1979
Lesotho - Maseru; 1,899,000; Oct. 4, 1966
Malawi - Lilongwe; 9,303,000; July 6, 1964
Malaysia - Kuala Lumpur; 19,032,000; Aug. 31, 1957
Maldives - Malé; 236,000; July 9, 1982
Malta - Valletta; 362,000; Sept. 21, 1964
Mauritius - Port Louis; 1,111,000; Mar. 12, 1968
Mozambique - Maputo; 16,916,000; Nov., 1995
Namibia - Windhoek; 1,565,000; Mar. 21, 1990
Nauru - Nauru; 8,000; Jan. 31, 1968
New Zealand - Wellington; 3,462,000; Sept. 26, 1907
Includes the territories of Tokelau & the Ross Dependency (Antarctic). Self-governing countries in free association with New Zealand: Cook Islands & Niue.
Nigeria - Abuja; 104,893,000; Oct. 1, 1960 N.B. Under suspension since Nov., 1995.
Pakistan - Islamabad; 122,829,000; Mar. 23, 1989 (previously member 1947-1972)
Papua New Guinea - Port Moresby; 4,148,000; Sept. 16, 1975
St. Kitts & Nevis - Basseterre; 41,000; Sept. 19, 1983
St. Lucia - Castries; 158,000; Feb. 22, 1979
St. Vincent & The Grenadines - Kingstown; 110,000; Oct. 27, 1979
Seychelles - Mahé; 70,000; June 29, 1976
Sierra Leone - Freetown; 4,468,000; Apr. 27, 1961
Singapore - Singapore; 2,867,000; Oct. 16, 1965
Solomon Islands - Honiara; 346,000; July 7, 1978
South Africa - Pretoria; 40,677,000; June 1, 1994
Sri Lanka - Colombo; 17,622,000; Feb. 4, 1948
Swaziland - Mbabane; 888,000; Sept. 6, 1968
Tanzania - Dar es Salaam; 26,743,000; Dec. 9, 1961
Tonga - Nuku'alofa; 93,000; June 4, 1970
Trinidad & Tobago - Port of Spain; 1,282,000; Aug. 31, 1962
Tuvalu - Funafuti; 9,000; Oct. 1, 1978
Uganda - Kampala; 18,026,000; Oct. 9, 1962
Vanuatu - Port Vila; 161,000; July 30, 1980
Western Samoa - Apia; 163,000; Aug. 28, 1970
Zambia - Lusaka; 8,527,000; Oct. 24, 1964
Zimbabwe - Harare; 10,638,000; Apr. 18, 1981

LA FRANCOPHONIE

Member Name, population, national holiday

Belgique (La Royaume de), 10,01 M, 21 juillet
Bénin (République du), 5,215 M, 1er août
Bularie (République de), 8,469 M, 3 mars
Bukina Faso, 9,682, 4 âout
Burundi (République du), 5,958, 1er juillet
Cambodgne, 9,308, 25 juin
Cameroun (République du), 12,547, 20 mai
Canada, 29,248 M, 1er juillet
Canada - Nouveau-Brunswick (Province du), 0,759 M, 15 âout
Canada - Québec (Province du), 7,208 M, 24 juin
Cap-Vert (République du), 0,395 M, 5 juillet
Centrafrique (République), 3,258 M, 1er décembre
Communauté française de Belgique (Wallonie-Bruxelles), 4,5 M, 27 septembre
Comores (République féderale islamique des), 0,607 M, 6 juillet
Congo (République du), 2,441 M, 15 âout
Côte d'Ivoire (République de), 13,397 M, 7 décembre
Djibouti (République de), 0,481 M, 27 juin
Dominique (Commonwealth de), 0,072 M, 27 février
Égypte (République arabe d'), 56,488 M, 23 juillet
France (République française), 57,660 M, 14 juillet
Gabon (République gabonaise), 1,012 M, 17 âout
Guinée (République de), 6,306 M, 2 octobre
Guinée-Bissau (République de Guine'e-Bissao), 1,028 M, 24 septembre
Guinée équatoriale (République de), 0,379 M, 12 octobre
Haiti (République d'), 6,903 M, 1er janvier
Laos (République démocratique populaire lao), 4,605 M, 2 décembre
Liban (République libanaise), 2,901 M,, 22 novembre
Luxembourg (Grande-Duché de), 0,380 M, 23 juin
Madagascar (République de), 13,259 M, 26 juin
Mali (République de), 10,137 M, 22 septembre
Maroc (Royaume de), 26,069 M, 3 mars
Maurice (République de), 1,098 M, 12 mars
Mauritanie (République islamique de), 2,206 M, 28 novembre
Monaco (Principauté de), 0,028 M, 19 novembre
Niger (République du), 8,361 M, 18 décembre
Roumanie, 22,755 M, 1er décembre
Rwanda (République rwandaise), 7,789 M, 1er juillet
Sainte-Lucie, 0,139 M, 22 février
Sénégal (République du), 7,736 M, 4 avril
Seychelles (République des), 0,072 M, 5 juin
Suisse (Confédération), 6,938 M, 1er âout
Tchad (République du), 6,098 M, 11 janvier
Togo (République togolaise), 3,885 M, 27 avril
Tunisie (République tunisienne), 8,579 M, 20 mars
Vanuatu (République du), 0,156 M, 30 juillet
Viêtnam (République socialiste du), 70,902 M, 2 septembre
Zaïre (République du), 41,166 M, 30 juin

INTERNATIONAL ORGANIZATIONS IN CANADA

INTERNATIONAL ATOMIC ENERGY AGENCY
#1702, 365 Bloor St. East, Toronto ON M4W 3L4
416/928-9149; Fax: 416/928-0046
Head, Mr. Godswill Ch. Madueme

INTERNATIONAL CIVIL AVIATION ORGANIZATION
1000 Sherbrooke St. West, Montréal PQ H3A 2R2
514/285-8219; Fax: 514/288-4772
President, Dr Assad Kotaite
Secretary General, Dr. Philippe H.P. Rochat

INTERNATIONAL LABOUR ORGANIZATION
#202, 75 Albert St., Ottawa ON K1P 5E7
613/233-1114; Fax: 613/233-6255
Director, Robert Nadeau

INTERNATIONAL NORTH PACIFIC FISHERIES COMMISSON
6640 North West Marine Dr., Vancouver BC V6T 1X2
604/228-1128; Fax: 604/228-1135
Executive Director, Shigeto Hase

NORTHWEST ATLANTIC FISHERIES ORGANIZATION
PO Box 638, Dartmouth NS B2Y 3Y9
902/469-9105; Fax: 902/469-5729
Executive Secretary, Leonard I. Chepel

PERMANENT JOINT BOARD ON DEFENCE (CANADA-U.S.A.)
International Security & Defence Relations, DFAIT, 125 Sussex Dr., Ottawa ON K1A 0G2
613/992-5457; Fax: 613/992-2482
Secretary, Mervin Meadows

UNITED NATIONS ASSOCIATION IN CANADA
#808, 63 Sparks St., Ottawa ON K1P 5A6
613/232-5751; Fax: 613/563-2455
Executive Director, Angus Archer

UNITED NATIONS CENTRE FOR HUMAN SETTLEMENTS (HABITAT)
Information Office for North America and the Caribbean, #417, 130 Albert St., Ottawa ON K1P 5G4
613/235-6400; Fax: 613/235-6226
Head, Information Office for North America & the Caribbean, Selman Erguden

UNITED NATIONS HIGH COMMISSIONER FOR REFUGEES
#401, 280 Albert St., Ottawa ON K1P 5G8
613/232-0909; Fax: 613/230-1855
Representative, Gary G. Troeller

UNITED NATIONS EDUCATIONAL, SCIENTIFIC & CULTURAL ORGANIZATION (UNESCO)
#400, 56, rue St-Pierre, 4e étage, Québec PQ G1K 4A1
418/692-3333; Fax: 418/692-2562
Representative, Agustin Larrauri

UNITED NATIONS ENVIRONMENT PROGRAMME (UNEP)
Montréal Trust Bldg., 27th Fl., 1800 McGill College Ave., Montréal PQ H3A 3J6
514/282-1122; Fax: 514/282-0068
Chief Officer, Dr. Omar El-Sayed El-Arini

CANADIAN UNICEF COMMITTEE
443 Mount Pleasant Rd., Toronto ON M4S 2L8
416/482-4444; Fax: 416/482-8035
Executive Director, Harry S. Black

CANADIAN PERMANENT MISSIONS AND DELEGATIONS ABROAD

MISSION OF CANADA TO THE EUROPEAN COMMUNITIES
2, av de Tervuren, 1040 Brussels, Belgium
(011-32-2) 735-9125; Fax: (011-32-2) 735-3383
Head of Mission, Ambassador, Gordon S. Smith
Deputy Head of Mission & Minister-Counsellor, W.H. Dowswell
Counsellor, Trade Policy, S. Brereton

NORAD (NORTH AMERICAN AEROSPACE DEFENSE COMMAND)
DNDPA NORAD Headquarters, NORAD PA, Peterson AFB, Colorado Springs, CO USA 80914-5002
719/554-3714; Fax: 719/554-3165

NORTH ATLANTIC COUNCIL
Léopold III Blvd., 1110 Brussels, Belgium
(011-32-2) 216-0346; Fax: (011-32-2) 245-2462
Permanent Representative & Ambassador, James K. Bartleman
Responsible for all NATO (North American Treaty Organization) correspondence.

ORGANIZATION FOR ECONOMIC COOPERATION & DEVELOPMENT
15 bis, rue de Franqueville, 75116 Paris, France
(011-33-1) 40-67-18-45; Fax: (011-33-1) 45-20-30-08
Ambassador & Permanent Representative, Anne Marie Doyle

ORGANIZATION OF AMERICAN STATES
501 Pennsylvania Ave. NW, Washington DC 20001 USA
202/682-1768; Fax: 202/682-7624
Ambassador, Permanent Representative, Brian Dickson, Q.C.

UNITED NATIONS
• Permanent Mission of Canada to the United Nations, One Dag Hammarkjold Plaza, 885 Second Ave., 14th Fl., New York NY 10017-1897 USA. (212) 751-5600; Fax: (212) 486-1295
Ambassador & Permanent Representative, Robert R. Fowler
• Permanent Mission of Canada to the Office of the United Nations at Geneva, 1, rue du Pré-de-la-Bichette, 1202 Geneve, Switzerland – (011-41-22) 733-9000; Fax: (011-41-22) 734-7919
also at this address:
Permanent Mission of Canada to the Secretariat of the General Agreement on Tariffs & Trade (GATT)
Permanent Representative & Ambassador, Gerald E. Shannon
• Permanent Mission of Canada to the International Civil Aviation Organization (ICAO), #876, 1000 Sherbrooke St. West, Montréal PQ H3A 3G4 – (514) 285-8320; Fax: (514) 283-3256
Representative, G.H. Duguay
• Permanent Mission of Canada to the United Nations Centre for Human Settlements (Habitat), Comcraft House, Hailé Sélassie Ave., PO Box 30481, Nairobi – (011-254-2) 33-40-33; Fax: (011-254-2) 33-40-90
also at this address:
Permanent Mission of Canada to the United Nations Environment Program (UNEP)
Representative, Lucie Edwards
• Permanent Mission of Canada to the United Nations Educational, Scientific & Cultural Organization (UNESCO), 1, rue Miollis, 75015 Paris, France – (011-33-1) 45-68-35-17; Fax: (011-33-1) 43-06-87-27
Ambassador & Permanent Delegate, Jacques Demers
• Permanent Mission of Canada to the Food & Agriculture Organization (FAO), Via Zara 30, 00198 Rome, Italy – (011-39-6) 440-3028; Fax: (011-39-6) 440-3063
Permanent Representative, Robert Andrigo
• Permanent Mission of Canada to the International Organizations in Vienna, Dr. Karl Lueger Ring 10, A-1010 Vienna, Austria – (011-43-222) 533-3691; Fax: (011-43-222) 664-4731
Permanent Representative & Ambassador, Peter F. Walker

INTERNATIONAL FISHERIES ORGANIZATIONS
These Commissions are non-governmental organizations whose members are governments or associations of governments.

GREAT LAKES FISHERY COMMISSION
2100 Commonwealth Blvd., #209, Ann Arbor, MI 48105-1563 USA
313/662-3209; Fax: 313/668-2531
Executive Secretary, R.W. Beecher
Canadian Commissioners, F.W.H. Beamish, G. Beggs, P. Sutherland, C. Fraser

Canadian Almanac & Directory 1997

INTERNATIONAL COMMISSION FOR THE CONSERVATION OF ATLANTIC TUNAS
Principe de Vergara 17, 7th Fl., Madrid 28001, Spain
(011-34-1) 431-0329; Fax: (011-34-1) 57-6968
Executive Secretary, Dr. Antonio Fernandez

INTERNATIONAL PACIFIC HALIBUT COMMISSION
PO Box 95009, Seattle WA USA 98145
206/634-1838; Fax: 206/632-2983
Director, Investigation, D.A. McCaughran
Canadian Commissioners, L. Alexander, A. Sheppard, R. Beamish

INTERNATIONAL WHALING COMMISSION
The Red House, 135 Station Rd., Histon, Cambridge, England CB4 4NP
(011-44-223) 233971; Fax: (011-44-223) 232876
Secretary, Dr. R. Gambell

NORTH ATLANTIC SALMON CONSERVATION ORGANIZATION
11 Rutland Sq., Edinburgh, Scotland EH1 2AS
(011-44-31) 228-2551; Fax: (011-44-31) 228-4384
Executive Secretary, Dr. Malcolm Windsor
Canadian Commissioners: J.E. Haché, Dr. W.M. Carter, Jean-Paul Duguay

NORTHWEST ATLANTIC FISHERIES ORGANIZATION
PO Box 638, Dartmouth NS B2Y 3Y9
902/469-9105; Fax: 902/469-5729
Executive Secretary, Dr L.I. Chepel

PACIFIC SALMON COMMISSION
#600, 1155 Robson St., Vancouver BC V6E 1B5
604/684-8081; Fax: 604/666-8707
Executive Secretary, Ian Todd
Canadian Commissioners: B. Buchanan, P.S. Chamut, J. Gosnell, R. Wright

DIPLOMATIC & CONSULAR REPRESENTATIVES IN CANADA

Commonwealth countries are designated by 'High Commissioner'. Foreign countries are designated by 'Ambassador'. It is Almanac editorial style to list Consulates in alphabetical order according to the city of location. Occasionally we have deviated from this style at the special request of the embassy of a particular country and listed their Consulates and Honorary Consulates.

Republic of Albania
Embassy of Albania (to Canada): #1010, 1511 K St. NW., Washington DC 20005
202/222-4942; Fax: 202/628-7342
Ambassador, USA & Canada, His Excellency Lublin Dilja

People's Democratic Republic of Algeria
Embassy of Algeria: 435 Daly Ave., Ottawa ON K1N 6H3
613/789-8505; Fax: 613/789-1406
Ambassador, His Excellency Abdesslam Bedrane
Counsellor, Economic & Commercial Affairs, Ahmed Bouchentouf

Antigua & Barbuda c/o Organization of the Eastern Caribbean States
Dartmouth: Hon. Consul, Castor Williams, 13 Oathill Cr., Dartmouth NS B2Y 4C3, 902/465-8127
Toronto: Consul, Madeline Blackman, #304, 60 St. Clair Ave. East, Toronto ON M4T 1N5, 416/961-3143; Fax: 416/961-7218

Argentine Republic
Embassy of the Argentine Republic: #910, 90 Sparks St., Ottawa ON K1P 5B4
613/236-2351; Fax: 613/235-2659; Commercial Office Fax: 613/563-7925
Ambassador, Her Excellency Lillian O'Connell de Alurralde
Minister, Economic & Commercial Affairs, Guillermo Azrak
Montréal: Consul General, Oscar Galié, #710, 2000, rue Peel, Montréal PQ H3A 2W5, 514/842-6582; Fax: 514/842-5797
Toronto: Consul General, Jorge Vinuela, #5840, 1 First Canadian Place, Toronto ON M5X 1K2, 416/955-0232; Fax: 416/955-0868

Commonwealth of Australia
Australian High Commission: #710, 50 O'Connor St., Ottawa ON K1P 6L2
613/236-0841; Fax: 613/236-4376
High Commissioner, His Excellency Frank C. Murray
Deputy High Commissioner, Pat Hardy
Counsellor, Andrew Engel
Toronto: Consul General, Ian Taylor, #314, 175 Bloor St. East, Toronto ON M4W 3R8, 416/323-1155; Fax: 416/323-3910; Telex: 06-219762
Vancouver: Consul, Graeme South, World Trade Centre Office Complex, #602, 999 Canada Place, Vancouver BC V6C 3E1, 604/684-1177; Fax: 604/684-1856

Republic of Austria
Embassy of Austria: 445 Wilbrod St., Ottawa ON K1N 6M7
613/789-1444; Fax: 613/789-3431
Ambassador, His Excellency Dr. W. Lichem
Calgary: Hon. Consul General, Hans Ockermueller, 1131 Kensington Rd. NW, Calgary AB T2N 3P4, 403/283-6526; Fax: 403/283-1512
Halifax: Hon. Consul, Michael Novac, #710, 1718 Argyle St., Halifax NS B3J 3N6, 902/429-8200; Fax: 902/425-0581
Montréal: Hon. Consul General, Ulrike Billard-Florian, #1030, 1350, rue Sherbrooke ouest, Montréal PQ H3G 1J1, 514/845-8661; Fax: 514/284-3503
Montréal: Trade Commissioner, Peter Paul Schwartz, #1410, 1010, rue Sherbrooke ouest, Montréal PQ H3A 2R7, 514/849-3708; Fax: 514/849-9577
Regina: Hon. Consul, E.F. Anthony Merchant, #100, 2401 Saskatchewan Dr. Plaza, Regina SK S4P 4H9, 306/359-7777; Fax: 306/522-3299
Toronto: Hon. Consul General, Dr. H.G. Abromeit, #1010, 360 Bay St., Toronto ON M5H 2Y6, 416/863-0649; Fax: 416/869-7851
Toronto: Consul (Commercial Affairs), Gerhard Müller, #3330, 2 Bloor St. East, Toronto ON M4W 1A8, 416/967-3348; Fax: 416/967-4101
Vancouver: Hon. Consul General, Graham P. Clarke, #206, 1810 Alberni St., Vancouver BC V6G 1B3, 604/687-3338; Fax: 604/681-3578
Vancouver: Trade Commissioner, Wolfgang Harwalik, #1380, 200 Granville St., Vancouver BC V6C 1S4, 604/683-5808; Fax: 604/662-8528
Winnipeg: Hon. Consul, John Klassen, 330 Saulteaux Cr., Winnipeg MB R3C 3T2, 204/885-2882; Fax: 204/885-7557

Republic of Azerbaijan
Embassy of Azerbaijan (to Canada): #700, 927 - 15th St. NW, Washington DC 20005
202/842-0001; Fax: 202/842-0004; Email: azerbaijan@mcimail.com
Ambassador Designate, His Excellency Hafiz Mir-Jalal Oglu Pashayev

Commonwealth of the Bahamas
High Commission for the Bahamas: #1020, 360 Albert St., Ottawa ON K1R 7X7
613/232-1724; Fax: 613/232-0097
High Commissioner, His Excellency Luther E. Smith
Third Secretary, Melvin V. Claridge

State of Bahrain
Embassy of Bahrain (to Canada): 3502 International Dr. NW, Washington DC 20008
202/342-0741; Fax: 202/362-2192
Ambassador, His Excellency Mohammed Abdel-Ghalfar
Montréal: Consul, Abdulnabi Mussayab Mohamed, 1869, boul René Lévesque ouest, Montréal PQ H3H 1R4, 514/931-7444; Fax: 514/931-5988

People's Republic of Bangladesh
Bangladesh High Commission: #302, 275 Bank St., Ottawa ON K2P 2L6
613/236-0138/9; Fax: 613/567-3213
High Commissioner, Mufleh R. Osmany

Barbados
High Commission for Barbados: #600, 130 Albert St., Ottawa ON K1P 5G4
613/236-9517; Fax: 613/230-4362; Email: barhcott@travel-net.com
High Commissioner, Her Excellency June Clarke
First Secretary, Simone Rudder
North York: Consul General, Errol Humphrey, #1800, 5160 Yonge St., North York ON M2N 6L9, 416/512-6565; Fax: 416/512-6580
Vancouver: Hon. Consul, Annette Goodridge, #401, 2020 Haro St., Vancouver BC V6G 1J3, 604/872-4444; Fax: 604/681-0740
Westmount: Consul, Jennifer V. Barrow, #523, 4800, de Maisonneuve ouest, Westmount PQ H3Z 1M2, 514/932-3206; Fax: 514/932-3775

Kingdom of Belgium
80 Elgin St., 4th Fl., Ottawa ON K1P 1B7
613/236-7267; Fax: 613/236-7882; Telex: 053-3568
Ambassador, His Excellency Christian Fellens
Counsellor, Luc Jacobs
Calgary: Hon. Consul, Bernard Callebut, 908 - 18 Ave. SW, Calgary AB T2P 0H1, 403/265-5777; Fax: 403/244-2094
Edmonton: Hon. Consul, George de Rappard, #107, 4990 - 92 Avenue, Edmonton AB T6B 2W1, 403/425-0184; Fax: 403/466-2832
Halifax: Hon. Consul, Joz de Belie, PO Box 1590, Stn M, Halifax NS B3J 2Y3, 902/423-6324
Montréal: Consul General, Louis Engelen, #850, 999, boul de Maisonneuve ouest, Montréal PQ H3A 3L4, 514/849-7394; Fax: 514/844-3170; Telex: 05-268691
Toronto: Consul General, Claude Rijmenans, #2006, 2 Bloor St. West, PO Box 88, Toronto ON M4W 3E2, 416/944-1422; Fax: 416/944-1421; Telex: 06-23564 CONSUBEL TOR
Vancouver: Hon. Consul, Dirk De Vuyst, 3 Bentall Centre, Vancouver BC V7Y 1J5, 604/691-7566; Fax: 604/688-2827
Winnipeg: Hon. Consul, Paul Deprez, 15 Acadia Bay, Winnipeg MB R3T 3J1, 204/261-1415

Belize
High Commission for Belize: 2535 Massachusetts Ave. NW, Washington DC 20008
202/332-9636; Fax: 202/332-6888
High Commissioner, His Excellency Dean Russell Lindo
Montreal: Hon. Consul General, Harry J.F. Bloomfield, Q.C., 1080 Beaver Hall Hill, Montreal PQ H2Z 1S8, 514/871-4741; Fax: 514/397-0816

Vancouver: Consul General, Pamel Suzanne Picon, 904-1112 West Pender St., Vancouver BC V6E 2S1, (604) 683-4517; Fax: (604) 683-4518

Republic of Benin
Embassy of Benin: 58 Glebe Ave., Ottawa ON K1S 2C3
613/233-4429; Fax: 613/233-8952
Ambassador, Her Excellency Véronique Ahoyo
Calgary: Hon. Consul, Dale M. Simmons, 700, 1207 - 11th Ave. South West, Calgary AB T3C 0M5, 403/245-8405
Montréal: Hon. Consul, Marie B. Archambault, 429, av Viger est, Montréal PQ H2L 2N9, 514/287-1583; Fax: 514/769-6088

Republic of Bolivia
Embassy of Bolivia: #504, 130 Albert St., Ottawa ON K1P 5G4
613/236-5730; Fax: 613/236-8237
Ambassador, Vacant
Minister-Counsellor & Chargé d'Affaires, a.i., Myriam Paz Cerruto
Edmonton: Consul General, Carlos Pechtel, 11231 Jasper Ave., Edmonton AB T5K 0L5, 403/488-1525; Fax: 403/488-0350
Montréal: Hon. Consul, Pilar Ramos de Arto, 18, av Severn, Montréal PQ H3Y 2C7, 514/989-5132; Fax: 514/989-5177
Vancouver: Hon. Consul, Dr. A.S. Andree, 1130, 1040 West Georgia St., Vancouver BC V6E 4H1, 604/685-8121; Fax: 604/685-8120

Republic of Botswana
High Commission for Botswana (to Canada): c/o Republic of Botswana: #7M, Intelsat Bldg., 3400 International Dr. NW, Washngton DC 20008
202/244-4990; Fax: 202/244-4164; Telex: 64221
Ambassador, His Excellency Botsweletse Kingsley Sebele
Toronto: Hon. Consul, Douglas G. Hartle, 14 South Dr., Toronto ON M4W 1R1, 416/978-2495; Fax: 416/324-8239

Federative Republic of Brazil
Embassy of Brazil: 450 Wilbrod St., Ottawa ON K1N 6M8
613/237-1090; Fax: 613/237-6144; Email: BRASEMB@OTTAWA.NET
Ambassador, His Excellency Carlos Augusto R. Santos Neves
Minister-Counsellor, Vacant
Edmonton: Hon. Consul, Peter Elzinga, 8619 Strathearn Dr., Edmonton AB T6C 4C6, 403/466-3130; Fax: 403/465-0247
Halifax: Hon. Consul, Raymond W. Ferguson, 3630 Kempt Rd., PO Box 8870, Stn A, Halifax NS B3K 3Y4, 902/455-9638
Montréal: Consul General, Antonino Porto e Santos, #1700, 2000, rue Mansfield, Montréal PQ H3A 3A5, 514/499-0968; Fax: 514/499-9363
Toronto: Consul General, Luiz Fernando-Gourea de Athayde, #1109, 77 Bloor St. West, Toronto ON M5S 1M2, 416/922-2503; Fax: 416/922-1832
Vancouver: Deputy Consul General, Raul Campos de Castro, #1300, 1300 Pender St. West, Vancouver BC V6E 4G1, 604/687-4589; Fax: 604/681-6534

Brunei Darussalam
High Commission of Brunei Darussalam: #400, 30 Metcalfe St., Ottawa ON K1P 5L4
603/234-5656; Fax: 603/234 4397
High Commissioner, Pengiran Abdul Momin
First Secretary, Magdalene Teo Chee Siong

Republic of Bulgaria
Embassy of the Republic of Bulgaria: 325 Stewart St., Ottawa ON K1N 6K5
613/789-3215; Fax: 613/789-3524
Ambassador, His Excellency Slav Danev
Counsellor & Deputy Head of Mission, Svilen Iliev
Counsellor, Economic & Commercial, Nikolay Babev
Toronto: Consul General, Dimitar Filipov Serafimov, #406, 65 Overlea Blvd., Toronto ON M4H 1P1, 416/696-2420; Fax: 416/696-8019

Burkina-Faso
Embassy of Burkina-Faso: 48 Range Rd., Ottawa ON K1N 8J4
613/238-4796; Fax: 613/238-3812
Ambassador, Mouhoussine Nacro
Counsellor, Eric Tiare
Magog: Hon. Consul, Pierre Bastien, 1718, ch Alfred-Desrochers, RR#2, Magog PQ J1X 3W3, 819/847-1747
Toronto: Hon. Consul, Peter K. Large, #610, 372 Bay St., Toronto ON M5H 2W9, 416/867-8669

Republic of Burundi
Embassy of Burundi: 50 Kaymar St., Rothwell Heights, Gloucester ON K1J 7C7
613/741-8828; Fax: 613/741-2424
Ambassador, Frédéric Ndayegamiye
Ambassador, Hermenegilde Nkurabagaya
Montréal: Hon. Consul, Jean-Guy Laurendeau, 4017 Lacombe St., Montréal PQ H3T 1M7, 514/739-5204
Toronto: Hon. Consul, David Michael Wright, 5 Dewbourne Ave., Toronto ON M5P 1Z1, 416/932-8212; Fax: 416/922-3667
Due to political instability in Burundi, the official Ambassador to Canada was not known at time of publishing.

Republic of Cameroon
Embassy of Cameroon: 170 Clemow Ave., Ottawa ON K1S 2B4
613/236-1522; Fax: 613/236-3885
Ambassador, His Excellency Philémon Y. Yang
Counsellor, Commercial & Economic, Célestin Ngassam

Republic of Cape Verde
Embassy of Cape Verde (to Canada): 3415 Massachusetts Ave. NW, Washington DC 20007
202/965-6820; Fax: 202/965-1207; Telex: 440294 ERCV UI
Ambassador, Vacant
Hon. Consul, Alfredo Luis Evora, Consular Representative of Cape Verde

Central African Republic
Embassy of Central African Republic (to Canada): 1618 - 22nd St. NW, Washington DC 20008
202/483-7800
Ambassador, His Excellency Jean-Pierre Sohahong-Kombet
Counsellor, Ndinga Gaba
Montréal: Hon. Consul General, Jean-François Boisvert, 225, rue St-Jacques St. ouest, Montréal PQ H2Y 1M6, 514/849-8381
Ottawa: Hon. Consul, Stuart E. Hendin, 726, 50 O'Connor St., Ottawa ON K1P 6L2, 613/563-4804; Fax: 613/563-3878
Québec: Hon. Consul, Marc Dorion, #201, 112 Dalhousie St., Québec PQ G1K 4C1, 418/692-1532; Fax: 418/692-5091

Republic of Chad
Embassy of Chad (to Canada): 2002 R St. NW, Washington DC 20009
202/462-4009; Fax: 202/265-1937; Telex: 64225
Ambassador, Vacant
Counsellor, Lémaye Favitsou-Boulandi

Republic of Chile
Embassy of Chile: #605, 151 Slater St., Ottawa ON K1P 5H3
613/235-4402, 9940; Fax: 613/235-1176
Military Attachés Section: #1125, 90 Sparks St., Ottawa ON K1P 5B4, 613/230-7660
Ambassador, His Excellency Fernando Urrutia
Counsellor, Luis Palma
Edmonton: Hon. Consul, Domingo Chavez, 7912 - 104 St., Edmonton AB T6E 4C8, 403/439-9838; Fax: 403/433-2376
Montréal: Consul General, Miguel Poklepovic, #710, 1010, rue Sherbrooke ouest, Montréal PQ H3A 2R7, 514/499-0405; Fax: 514/499-0405
Toronto: Consul General, Rene Faraggi, #800, 170 Bloor St. W., Toronto ON M5R 3L9, 416/924-0106; Fax: 416/924-9563
Vancouver: Consul General, Dennis J. Biggs, #1250, 1185 Georgia Street West, Vancouver BC V6E 4E6, 604/681-9162; Fax: 604/682-2445
Winnipeg: Hon. Consul, Dr. Fernardo Guijon, 59 Emily St., Winnipeg MB R3E 1Y9, 204/787-4259; Fax: 204/889-4410

People's Republic of China
Embassy of China: 515 St. Patrick St., Ottawa ON K1N 5H3
613/789-3434; Fax: 613/789-1911
Ambassador, His Excellency Zhang Yijun
Counsellor, Chen Wenzhou
Counsellor, Commercial Affairs, Yu Zhiting
Counsellor, Science & Technology, Huang Xing
Toronto: Consul General, Tang Fuquan, 240 Saint George St., Toronto ON M5R 2P4, 416/964-7260; Fax: 416/324-6468
Vancouver: Consul General, Yang Zongliang, 3380 Granville St., Vancouver BC V6H 3K3, 604/734-7492; Fax: 604/737-0154

Republic of Colombia
Embassy of Colombia: #1002, 360 Albert St., Ottawa ON K1R 7X7
613/230-3760; Fax: 613/230-4416
Ambassador, His Excellency Alfonso Lopez Caballero
Minister-Counsellor, Hèctor Cacères
Montréal: Consul, Eufracio Morales, #420, 1010, rue Sherbrooke ouest, Montréal PQ H3A 2R7, 514/849-4852; Fax: 514/849-4324
Toronto: Consul General, Clara Maria Leon, #2108, 1 Dundas St. West, Toronto ON M5G 1Z3, 416/977-0098; Fax: 416/977-1025
Toronto: Consul, Commercial Section, James Clemenger, #315, 4100 Yonge St., Toronto ON M2B 2B5, 416/512-9212; Fax: 416/512-9458
Vancouver: Hon. Consul, William Bush, 890, 789 West Pender St., Vancouver BC V6C 1H2, 604/685-6435; Fax: 604/685-6485

Republic of the Congo
Embassy of the Congo (to Canada): 4891 Colorado Ave. NW, Washington DC 20011
202/726-5500; Fax: 202/726-1860; Telex: 197370
Ambassador, His Excellency P.D. Boussoukou-Boumba
Counsellor, Economic Affairs, Ikourou Yoka
Pointe Claire: Hon. Consul, Marcel P. Rigny, 2 Cedar Ave., Pointe Claire PQ H9S 4Y1, 514/697-3781; Fax: 514/697-9860

Republic of Costa Rica
Embassy of Costa Rica: #208, 135 York St., Ottawa ON K1N 5T4
613/562-2855; Fax: 613/562-2582
Ambassador, His Excellency Carlos Miranda
Minister-Counsellor, Francisco Gonzalez
Montréal: Consul General, Monserrat Romero-Royo, 1425, boul René Lévesque ouest, Montréal PQ H3G 1T7, 514/393-1057; Fax: 514/393-1624

Canadian Almanac & Directory 1997

Saskatoon: Hon. Consul General, Ricardo Campbell, 245 Clearwater Ct., Saskatoon SK S7K 3Y9, 306/955-6000; Fax: 306/975-1187
Toronto: Hon. Consul, Peter-Alexander Kircher, 164 Avenue Rd., Toronto ON M5R 2H9, 416/961-6773; Fax: 416/961-6771
Vancouver: Hon. Consul General, William A. Dow, 804, 1550 Alberni St., Vancouver BC V6G 1A5, 604/669-0797; Fax: 604/669-4659

Republic of Croatia
Embassy of Croatia: #1700, 130 Albert St., Ottawa ON K1P 5G4
613/230-7351; Fax: 613/230-7388
Ambassador, His Excellency Zeljko Urban
Minister-Counsellor, Ljerka Alajbeg
Counsellor, Economic, Vesela Mrdjen
First Secretary & Consul, Hrvoje Sagrak
Mississauga: Consul General, Ivan Picukaric, #302, 918 Dundas St. East, Mississauga ON L4Y 2B8, 905/277-9051; Fax: 905/277-5432

Republic of Cuba
Embassy of Cuba: 388 Main St., Ottawa ON K1S 1E3
613/563-0141; Fax: 613/563-0068; Email: cuba@iosphere.net
Ambassador, His Excellency Bienvenido Garcia Negrin
Minister Counsellor, Jorge Lamadrid Mascaro
Third Secretary, Deborah Ojeda Valedon
Montréal: Consul General, Gabriel Tiel, 1415 Pine Ave. West, Montréal PQ H3G 2B2, 514/843-8897; Fax: 514/845-1063
Toronto: Consul General, Jose Menendez, #401, 5353 Dundas St. West, Toronto ON M9B 6H8, 416/234-8181; Fax: 416/234-2754

Republic of Cyprus
High Commission for Cyprus (to Canada): c/o Republic of Cyprus: 2211 R St. NW, Washington DC 20008
202/462-5772; Fax: 202/483-6710
High Commisioner, His Excellency Andreas J. Jacovides
Counsellor, Leonidas Markides
Calgary: Hon. Consul, Alfred A. Balm, 3900 Bankers Hall, 855-2 St. SW, Calgary AB T2P 4J8, 403/264-3400; Fax: 403/237-8675
Montréal: Hon. Consul, Dr. Michael P. Paidoussis, #PH2, 2930, boul Édouard Montpetit, Montréal PQ H3T 1J7, 514/735-7233; Fax: 514/398-7365
Toronto: Consul General, Achillieas Antoniades, Cypress Consulate, #1010, Box 43, 365 Bloor St. East, Toronto ON M4W 3L4, 413/944-0998; Fax: 416/944-9149
Winnipeg: Hon. Consul, Costas P. Ataliotis, 1430 Ellice Ave., Winnipeg MB R3G 0G4, 204/774-6724; Fax: 204/774-2002

Czech Republic
Embassy of the Czech Republic: 541 Sussex Dr., Ottawa ON K1N 6Z6
613/562-3875; Fax: 613/562-3878
Ambassador, His Excellency Stanislav Chylek
Counsellor, Václav Prosec
First Secretary, Economic & Trade Affairs, Jaroslav Zeman
Culture & Press Affairs, Nora Jurkovicová
Consul, Eva Hendrychová
Montréal: Consul-General, Petr Dokladal, 1305, av Pine ouest, Montréal PQ H3G 1B2, 514/849-4495; Fax: 849-4117
Vancouver: Hon. Consul, Miroslav F.M. Hermann, #2100, 1111 West Georgia St., PO Box 48800, Vancouver BC V7X 1K9, 604/661-7530; Fax: 688-0829

Kingdom of Denmark
Embassy of Denmark: #450, 46 Clarence St., Ottawa ON K1N 9K1
613/562-1811; Fax: 613/562-1812
Ambassador, His Excellency Jorgen M. Behnke
Minister-Counsellor, Otto H. Larsen
Calgary: Hon. Consul, Kai Mortensen, 1235 - 11 Ave. SW, Calgary AB T3C 0M5, 403/245-5755; Fax: 403/228-6739
Edmonton: Hon. Consul, Donn Larsen, Oxford Tower, #1112, 10235 - 101 St., Edmonton AB T5J 1G1, 403/426-1457; Fax: 403/420-0005
Halifax: Hon. Consul of Denmark, H.I. Mathers, 1525 Birmingham St., PO Box 3550 South, Halifax NS B3J 3J3, 902/429-5680; Fax: 902/429-5221; Telex: 019-21771
Montréal: Hon. Consul, Michel Blouin, 1, Place Ville Marie, 35th Fl., Montréal PQ H3B 4M4, 514/877-3060; Fax: 514/871-8977
Regina: Consul, Inge Ryan, MacPherson, Leslie & Tyerman, 1919 Saskatchewan Dr., 6th Fl., Regina SK S4P 3V7, 306/787-4750; Fax: 306/787-3989
St. John's: Hon. Consul, Peter Norman Outerbridge, 92 Elizabeth Ave., PO Box 6150, St. John's NF A1C 5X8, 709/726-0020; Fax: 709/726-6013
Toronto: Consul General, Poul Laursen, #310, 151 Bloor St. West, Toronto ON M5S 1S4, 416/962-5661; Fax: 416/962-3668
Vancouver: Hon. Consul, Jorn Bjodstrup Petersen, #755, 777 Hornby St., Vancouver BC V6Z 1S4, 604/684-5171; Fax: 604/684-8054
Winnipeg: Hon. Consul, Anders Bruun, 239 Aubert St., Winnipeg MB R2H 3G8, 204/233-8541; Fax: 204/942-0570

Republic of Djibouti
c/o Embassy of the Republic of Djibouti: #515, 1156 - 15th St. NW, Washington DC 20005
202/331-0270; Fax: 202/331-0302; Telex: 4490085 AMDJ US
Ambassador, His Excellency Roble Olhaye
Counsellor, Dysane Dorani

Commonwealth of Dominica c/o Organization of the Eastern Caribbean States

Dominican Republic
Edmonton: Hon. Consul, Robert W. Hladun, #100, 10187 - 104 St., Edmonton AB, 403/423-1888; Fax: 403/424-0934
Montréal: Consul-General, Esmerelda Villanueva, Central Tower, 1055, St-Mathieu, bur. 241, Montréal PQ H3H 2S3, 514/933-9008; Fax: 514/933-2070
Saint John: Hon. Consul, John Driscoll, 59 Broad St., Saint John NB E2L 1Y3
St. John's: Hon. Consul, M.G. Renouf, 10 Forest Ave., St. John's NF A1C 3J9
Vancouver: Hon. Vice-Consul, Andrew H.S. Leung, #616, 1155 West Georgia St., Vancouver BC V6E 3H4, 604/683-8688; Fax: 683-8033

Organization of the Eastern Caribbean States
High Commission for the Countries of the Eastern Caribbean States: #1610, 112 Kent St., Ottawa ON K1P 5P2
613/236-8952; Fax: 613/236-3042
Acting High Commissioner, Jean-François Michel
First Secretary, Political & Consular, C.O. Dasent
Includes: Antigua & Barbuda, Commonwealth of Dominica, Grenada, Montserrat, Saint Christopher (Saint Kitts) & Nevis, Saint Lucia, Saint Vincent & the Grenadines

Republic of Ecuador
Embassy of Ecuador: #1311, 50 O'Connor St., Ottawa ON K1P 6L2
613/563-8206; Fax: 613/235-5776; Email: MECUACAN@INASEC.CA

Ambassador, His Excellency Alfredo Crespo Cordero
Counsellor, Rafael Paredes
Montréal: Consul General, Gabriel Garcés, #440, 1010, rue Ste-Catherine ouest, Montréal PQ H3B 3R3, 514/874-4071; Fax: 514/874-4071
Okotoks: Hon. Consul, Gordon Lentz, AB Consulate, PO Box 29, Site 6, RR#1, Okotoks AB T0L 1T0, 403/938-8142
Richmond: Hon. Consul, Etienne Walter, #802, 7100 Gilbert Rd., Richmond BC V7C 5C3, 604/273-8577; Fax: 604/273-8576
Toronto: Consul General, Francisco Martinez, #470, 151 Bloor St. West, Toronto ON M5S 1S4, 416/968-2077; Fax: 416/968-3348

Arab Republic of Egypt
Embassy of Egypt: 454 Laurier Ave. East, Ottawa ON K1N 6R3
613/234-4931; Fax: 613/234-9347
Commercial Office: #207, 85 Range Rd., Ottawa ON K1N 8J6, 613/238-6263; Fax: 613/238-2578
Ambassador, His Excellency Mahmoud Mahmoud Farghal
Minister Plenipotentiary, Teymour Moustapha Sirry
Counsellor, Ibrahim Khairat
Montréal: Consul General, Dr. Mohamed Ismail, #2617, 1, Place Ville Marie, Montréal PQ H3B 4S3, 514/866-8455; Fax: 514/866-0835

Republic of El Salvador
Embassy of El Salvador: #504, 209 Kent St., Ottawa ON K2P 1Z8
613/238-2939; Fax: 613/238-6940
Ambassador, Alfredo F. Ungo
Minister-Counsellor, Celina Quinteros
Montréal: Consul-General, Mauricio Suarez-Escalante, 4330, Sherbrooke ouest., Montréal PQ H3Z 1E1, 514/934-3678; Fax: 934-3706
Toronto: Consul, Joaquin Antonio Zaldivar, #320, 151 Bloor St. West, Toronto ON M5S 1T6, 416/975-0812; Fax: 416/975-0283
Vancouver: Hon. Consul, Jeffery Rodd Moore, Sinclair Centre, PO Box 649, Stn A, Vancouver BC V6C 2N5, 604/732-8142

Eritrea
Embassy of Eritrea (to Canada): #400, 910 - 17th St. NW, Washington DC 20006
202/429-1991; Fax: 202/429-9004
Ambassador, Vacant
Ottawa: Second Secretary and Consul, Nura Mohammed Omer, #610, 75 Albert St., Ottawa ON K1P 5E7, 613/234-3989; Fax: 613/234-6213

Republic of Estonia
Embassy of Estonia (to Canada): #1000, 1030 - 16th St. NW, Washington DC 20005
202/789-0320; Fax: 202/789-0471
Ambassador, His Excellency Toomas H. Ilves
Toronto: Hon. Consul General, Ilmar Heinsoo, #202, 958 Broadview Ave., Toronto ON M4K 2R6, 416/461-0764; Fax: 416/461-0448

Democratic Republic of Ethiopia
Embassy of Federal Democratic Republic of Ethiopia: #210, 151 Slater St., Ottawa ON K1P 5H3
613/235-6637; Fax: 613/235-4638; Email: infoethi@magi.com
Ambassador, His Excellency Dr. Fecadu Gadamu
Counsellor, Wahide Belay
Third Secretary, Beleyou Kifelew

European Union
Delegation of the European Commission in Canada: #330, 111 Albert St., Ottawa ON K1P 1A5
613/238-6464; Fax: 613/238-5191
Ambassador & Head of Delegation, His Excellency Jean-Pierre Juneau

Commission of the European Communities
Delegation of the Commission of the European Communities: #1110, 350 Sparks St., Ottawa ON K1R 7S8
613/238-6464; Fax: 613/238-5191
Ambassador & Head of Delegation, His Excellency John R. Beck
Attaché, David Tyson
Counsellor, Economic and Commercial Affairs, Carlos Freitas da Silva

Fiji
Embassy of Fiji (to Canada): One United Nations Plaza, 26th Fl., New York NY 10017
212/355-7316; Fax: 212/319-1896
Ambassador, His Excellency Manasa K. Seniloli
  Ottawa: Hon. Consul, Dr. D. Elaine Pressman, #750, 130 Slater St., Ottawa ON, 613/233-9252
  Vancouver: Hon. Consul, Raj Gopal Pillai, 1840 Clark Dr., Vancouver BC V5N 3G4, 604/254-5544

Republic of Finland
Embassy of Finland: #850, 55 Metcalfe St., Ottawa ON K1P 6L5
613/236-2389; Fax: 613/238-1474
Ambassador, His Excellency Veijo Sampovaara
First Secretary (Deputy Head of Mission), Roy Eriksson
  Calgary: Hon. Consul, Judith M. Romanchuk, Home Oil Tower, #702, 324 - 8 Ave. SW, Calgary AB T2P 2Z2, 403/531-0545; Fax: 403/531-0540
  Edmonton: Hon. Consul, Christian Graefe, Westin Hotel, 10135 - 100 St., Lower Level, Edmonton AB T5J 0N7, 403/426-7865; Fax: 403/428-6964
  Halifax: Hon. Consul, Frank Metcalf, Benjamin Wier House, 1459 Hollis St., Halifax NS B3J 1V1, 902/420-1990; Fax: 902/429-1171
  Montréal: Hon. Consul, James G. Wright, Stock Exchange Tower, #3400, 800 Place Victoria, PO Box 242, Montréal PQ H4Z 1E9, 514/397-7437; Fax: 514/397-7600
  Québec: Hon. Consul, Henri Grondin, Edifice Mérci, #200, 801, ch St-Louis, Québec PQ G1S 1C1, 418/683-3000; Fax: 418/683-8784
  Regina: Hon. Consul, Gordon J. Kuski, Royal Bank Bldg., #700, 2010 - 11th Ave., Regina SK S4P 0J3, 306/757-1641; Fax: 306/359-0785
  Saint John: Hon. Consul, Thomas L. McGloan, PO Box 7174, Stn A, Saint John NB E2L 4S6, 506/634-7450; Fax: 506/634-3612
  Sault Ste. Marie: Hon. Consul, Raimo Viitala, 29 Pageant Dr., Sault Ste. Marie ON P6B 5J7, 705/942-6196
  Sudbury: Hon. Consul, R. Hannu Piironen, 176 McNaughton St., Sudbury ON B3E 1V3, 705/675-0067; Fax: 705/675-0067
  Thunder Bay: Hon. Consul, Seppo K. Paivalainen, Gordon, Vauthier, Paivalainen, 275 Bay St., Thunder Bay ON P7B 1R7, 807/343-9394; Fax: 807/344-1562
  Timmins: Hon. Consul, Margaret Kangas, 5 Birch St. North, Timmins ON P4N 6C8, 705/264-7857; Fax: 705/264-9977
  Toronto: Consul, Helena Lappalainen, #604, 1200 Bay St., Toronto ON M5R 2A5, 416/964-0066; Fax: 416/964-1524; Telex 062-2513
  Vancouver: Hon. Consul General, Lars-Henrik Wrede, #1100, 1188 Georgia St. West, Vancouver BC V6E 4A2, 604/688-4483; Fax: 604/687-8237; Telex 04-55703
  Winnipeg: Hon. Consul, Robert Purves, #127, 167 Lombard Ave., Winnipeg MB R3B 0T6, 204/942-7457; Fax: 204/942-7458

France
Embassy of France: 42 Sussex Dr., Ottawa ON K1M 2C9
613/789-1795; Fax: 613/789-3484
Ambassador, His Excellency Alfred Siefer-Gaillardin
Minister-Counsellor, Jean-François Vallette
Counsellor, Cultural Affairs, Michel Deverge
Counsellor, Economic & Commercial Affairs, Alain Nourissier
  Chicoutimi: Hon. Consul, François Brochet, 1596, Bégin, Chicoutimi PQ G7H 5T6, 418/549-2195
  Edmonton: Consul General, Pierre Marchal, Highfield Place, #300, 10010 - 106 St., Edmonton AB T5J 3L8, 403/428-0232, 0235; Fax: 403/426-1450
  Halifax: Hon. Consul, Roland Bonnel, 6234 Lawrence St., Halifax NS B3L 1J9, 902/494-6804, 429-6562; Fax: 902/494-2319
  Moncton: Consul General, Gérard Perrolet, 250 Lutz St., PO Box 1109, Moncton NB E1C 8P6, 506/857-4191; Fax: 506/858-8169
  Montréal: Consul General, Gérard Leroux, #2601, 1, Place Ville Marie, Montréal PQ H3B 4S3, 514/878-4381; Fax: 514/878-3981; Telex: 0524890
    Commercial Section: #2710, 1000, rue de la Gauchetière ouest, 27e étage, Montréal, PQ, H3B 4W5, 514/878-9851; Fax: 514/878-3677; Telex: 055-61219
  North Sydney: Hon. Vice Consul, Thérèse Goora, North Sydney Consulate, 190 Brook St., PO Box 308, North Sydney NS B2A 3M4, 902/794-3676
  Québec: Consul General, Dominique de Combles de Nayves, Kent House, 25, rue St-Louis, Québec PQ G1R 3Y8, 418/694-2294; Fax: 418/694-2297
    Cultural & Scientific Affairs: 25, rue St-Louis, Québec PQ G1R 3Y8, 418/688-0430
  Saskatoon: Hon. Consul, Bernard M. Michel, Saskatoon Consulate, Cameco Corporation, 2121 - 11th St. West, Saskatoon SK S7M 1J3, 306/956-6305; Fax: 306/956-6302
  St. John's: Hon. Vice Consul, Pierre Morin, St. John's Consulate, 19 Diefenbaker St., St. John's NF A1A 2M2, 709/737-8924
  Sudbury: Hon. Consul, Onésime Tremblay, Sudbury Consulate, 1101 Ramsey Lake Rd., Site 3, PO Box 18, Sudbury ON P3E 5J2, 705/674-8503
  Toronto: Vice Consul, Cultural Affairs & Co-operation, Frédéric Limare, #400, 130 Bloor St. West, Toronto ON M5S 1N5, 416/925-8041; Fax: 416/925-3076; Visa Section: 416/925-8233
    Commercial Section: #2004, 20 Queen St. West, Toronto, ON, M5H 3R3, 416/977-1257; Fax: 416/977-7944
  Vancouver: Consul General and Cultural Affairs, Maryse Berniau, The Vancouver Bldg., #1201, 736 Granville St., Vancouver BC V6Z 1H9, 604/681-4345; Fax: 604/681-4287
    Commercial Section:, 604/681-5875; Fax: 604/681-4287
  Victoria: Hon. Consul, Gordon Denford, 1162 Fort St., Victoria BC V8V 3K8, 250/385-1505; Fax: 250/385-9851
  Whitehorse: Hon. Consul, Rolf Hougen, 305 Main St., Whitehorse YT Y1A 2B4, 403/667-4222; Fax: 403/668-6328; Telex: 036-8274
  Winnipeg: Hon. Consul, Frédéric Granger, Winnipeg Consulate, 64 Athlone Dr., Winnipeg MB R3J 3L2, 204/837-9583

Gabonese Republic
Embassy of Gabon: 4 Range Rd., Ottawa ON K1N 8J3
613/232-5301/02; Fax: 613/232-6916; Telex: 053-4295 AMBGAB OTT
Ambassador, His Excellency Alphonse Oyabi-Gnala
Counsellor, Economic & Financial Affairs, Lucien Moubouvi
  Montréal: Hon. Consul, Luc Benoît, 85, rue Ste-Catherine ouest, Montréal PQ H2X 3P4, 514/287-8500; Fax: 514/287-8643; Telex: 055-60122

Republic of the Gambia
High Commission for Gambia (to Canada): c/o Gambia Embassy: #1000, 1155 - 15th St., NW, Washington DC 20005
202/785-1399; Fax: 202/785-1430; Email: saidy@gambia.com
High Commissioner, Vacant
Chargé d'affaires, His Excellency Tombong Saidy
  Montréal: Hon. Consul, Victor Podd, 255 Beverley Ave., Montréal PQ H3P 1K8, 514/731-5775; Fax: 514/731-4374
  Vancouver: Hon. Consul of Gambia, U. Gary Charlwood, #900, 1199 West Pender St., Vancouver BC V6E 2R1, 604/662-3800; Fax: 604/662-3878

Federal Republic of Germany
Embassy of Germany: 1 Waverley St., Ottawa ON K2P 0T8
613/232-1101; Fax: 613/594-9330; Email: bn555@frenet.carleton.ca; 100440.64@compuserve.com
Postal Address: PO Box 379, Stn A, Ottawa ON K1N 8V4
Ambassador, His Excellency Dr. Hans-Guenter Sulimma
Minister-Counsellor, Dr. Juergen Hellner
Counsellor, Cultural Affairs, Charlotte Schwarzer
Counsellor, Economic & Commercial Affairs, Ulrich Grau
Counsellor, Press & Information Office, Ulrich Koehn
Defence Attaché, Lt. Col. Christian Ibrom
  Calgary: Hon. Consul, Osmar Beltzner, #1970, 700 - 4th Ave. SW, Calgary AB T2P 3J4, 403/269-5900; Fax: 403/269-5901
  Fort St. John: Hon. Consul, Friedrich Eduard Hermann von Ilberg, #9832, 98 A Avenue, Fort St. John BC V1J 1S2, 250/785-4300; Fax: 250/785-5028
  Halifax: Hon. Consul, Prof. Edgar Gold, Bank of Commerce Bldg., #708, 1809 Barrington St., Halifax NS B3J 3K8, 902/420-1599; Fax: 902/422-4713; Telex: 019-21593
  Kitchener: Hon. Consul, Peter D. Kruse, 385 Frederick St., Kitchener ON N2H 2P2, 519/745-6149; Fax: 519/576-0591
  London: Hon. Consul, Barbara Weis, 71 Wharncliff Rd. South, London ON N6J 2J8, 519/432-4133; Fax: 519/667-5187
  Montréal: Consul General, Fritz von Rottenburg, 1250, boul René-Lévesque ouest, Montréal PQ H3B 4W8, 514/931-2277; Fax: 514/931-7239
  Regina: Hon. Consul, Guenter Kocks, 3534 Argyle Rd., Regina SK S4S 2B8, 306/586-8762; Fax: 306/586-8762
  St. John's: Hon. Consul, Gunter K. Sann, 22 Poplar Ave., St. John's NF A1B 1C8, 709/753-7777; Fax: 709/739-6666
  Toronto: Consul General, Roland Fournes, 77 Admiral Rd., Toronto ON M5R 2L4, 416/925-2813; Fax: 416/925-2818; Telex: 06-22866
  Vancouver: Consul General, Franz-Josef Meurer, World Trade Centre, #704, 999 Canada Place, Vancouver BC V6C 3E1, 604/684-8377, 684-4258 (Visas); Fax: 604/684-8334; Telex: 04-507769
  Winnipeg: Hon. Consul, Gerhard Spindler, #208, 310 Donald St., Winnipeg MB R3B 2H4, 204/947-0958; Fax: 204/669-6197

Republic of Ghana
High Commission for Ghana: 1 Clemow Ave., Ottawa ON K1S 2A9
613/236-0871/3; Fax: 613/236-0874
High Commissioner, His Excellency Annan Arkyin Cato
Counsellor, C.K. de Souza
  Montréal: Hon. Consul-General, Joachim Normand, #900, 1420 Sherbrooke St. West, Montréal PQ H3G 1K3, 514/849-1417; Fax: 514/849-2643

North Vancouver: Hon. Consul-General, Dr. William Herbert Lawrence Allsopp, 2919 Eddystone Cr., North Vancouver BC V7H 1B8, 604/929-1496; Fax: 604/929-1860

Hellenic Republic
Embassy of Greece: 76-80 MacLaren St., Ottawa ON K2P 0K6
613/238-6271; Fax: 613/238-5676
Ambassador, His Excellency John Thomoglou
Counsellor, Constantine Giovas
- Montréal: Consul General, Nicholas Vamvounakis, 1170, Place du Frère André, 3e étage, Montréal PQ H3B 3C6, 514/875-2119; Fax: 514/875-8781; Telex: 055-60963 GREEK CONS MTL
- Toronto: Consul General, Christos Kontovounissios, #1800, 365 Bloor St. East, Toronto ON M4W 3L4, 416/515-0133; Fax: 416/515-0209
- Vancouver: Consul, Helen Sourani, #501, 1200 Burrard St., Vancouver BC V6Z 2C7, 604/681-1381; Fax: 604/681-6656

Grenada c/o Organization of the Eastern Caribbean States
Toronto: Consul General, Adrian C.A. Hayes, #820, 439 University Ave., Toronto ON M5G 1Y8, 416/595-1343; Fax: 416/595-8278
Winnipeg: Hon. Consul, Caspar A. Shade, 10 Rice Rd., Winnipeg MB R3T 3N4, 204/269-4788; Fax: 204/452-8491

Republic of Guatemala
Embassy of Guatemala: #1010, 130 Albert St., Ottawa ON K1P 5G4
613/233-7237; Fax: 613/233-0135; Consular Section: 613/233-7188
Ambassador, His Excellency Francisco Villagran de Leon
Minister-Counsellor, Carmen Aida Aguilera
- Norval: Hon. Consul, Roberto Sierra, PO Box 319, Norval ON L0P 1K0, 416/604-0655
- Vancouver: Consul General, Vacant, #760, 777 Hornby St., Vancouver BC V6Z 1S4, 604/688-5209; Fax: 688-5210

Republic of Guinea
Embassy of Guinea: 483 Wilbrod St., Ottawa ON K1N 6N1
613/789-8444; Fax: 613/789-7560
Ambassador, His Excellency Thierno Habib Diallo
First Secretary, Jeanne Bangoura
- Calgary: Hon. Consul, Giovanni De Maria, AB Consulate, 79 Willamette Dr. SE, Calgary AB T2J 2A3, 403/225-2956; Fax: 403/225-2957
- Toronto: Hon. Consul, Charles Arthur Downes, 1 St. John's Rd., Toronto ON M6P 4C7, 416/656-4812; Fax: 416/767-6070
- Vancouver: Hon. Consul, Raymond L. Saunders, 123 Cambie St., Vancouver BC V6B 4R3, 604/327-5550; Fax: 604/684-2100

Republic of Guinea-Bissau
Embassy of Guinea-Bissau (to Canada): 918 - 16th St. NW, Mezzanine Suite, Washington DC 20006
202/872-4222
Ambassador, His Excellency Alfredo Lopes Cabral
- Montréal: Hon. Consul, Nicolas M. Matte, Place Mercantile, 770, rue Sherbrooke ouest, Montréal PQ H3A 1G1, 514/842-9831; Fax: 514/288-7389

Co-operative Republic of Guyana
Burnside Building: #309, 151 Slater St., Ottawa ON K1P 5H3
613/235-7249; Fax: 613/235-1447
High Commissioner, His Excellency Brindley H. Benn
First Secretary, Jennifer Wills

- Willowdale: Hon. Consul, Geoffrey Da Silva, #206, 505 Consumers Rd., Willowdale ON M2J 4V8, 416/494-6040; Fax: 416/494-1530

Republic of Haiti
Embassy of Haiti, Tour B, Place de Ville: #205, 112 Kent St., Ottawa ON K1P 5P2
613/238-1628; Fax: 613/238-2986
Ambassador, His Excellency Emmanuel Ambroise
Minister/Counsellor, Lhande J. Henriquez
- Montréal: Consul, Luciano Pharaon, #1335, 1801 av McGill College, 13e étage, Montréal PQ H3A 2N4, 514/499-1919; Fax: 514/499-1818

Republic of Honduras
Embassy of Honduras: #908, 151 Slater St., Ottawa ON K1P 5H3
613/233-8900; Fax: 613/232-0193; Email: scastell@magmacom.com; breina@magmacom.com
Ambassador, His Excellency Salomé Casstellanos Delgado
Counsellor, Commercial, Bertha M. Reina
First Secretary & Consular Affairs, Marco Tulio Romero
Attaché, Cultural, Nora Bueso
Attaché, Press, Patricia Osorio
- Montréal: Chancellor, Manuel Urbina Bulnes, #306, 1650, boul de Maisonneuve ouest, Montréal PQ H3H 2P3, 514/937-1138
- Québec: Hon. Consul, Thérèse Lacroix, 1334 Maréchal Foch, Québec PQ G1S 2C4, 418/681-5070
- Vancouver: Hon. Consul, Enrique Gonzalez-Calvo, #1026, 510 West Hasting St., Vancouver BC V6B 1L8, 604/685-7711

Republic of Hungary
Embassy of Hungary: 299 Waverley St., Ottawa ON K2P 0V9
613/230-2717; Fax: 613/230-7560; Email: ATTMAIL HUEMBOTT
Ambassador, His Excellency Károly Gedai
Minister Plenipotentiary, István Torzsa
Head, Consular Section, Norbert Konkoly
- Calgary: Hon. Consul, Béla Balázs, 1700 - 96 Ave. SW, Calgary AB T2V 5E5, 403/258-0052; Fax: 403/262-8343
- Montréal: Consul, Judit Nolipa, #2040, 1200, av McGill Collège, Montréal PQ H3B 4G7, 514/393-1048; Fax: 514/393-8226
- Toronto: Consul General, Lajos Illich, #1115, 121 Bloor St. East, Toronto ON M4W 3M5, 416/923-8981; Fax: 416/923-2732
- Vancouver: Hon. Consul, André Molnár, 1650 West 2nd Ave., Vancouver BC V6J 4R2, 604/734-6698
- Vancouver: Hon. Vice-Consul, Brigitte A. Farkas, #203, 1076 Richards St., Vancouver BC V6B 3E1, 604/681-5936; Fax: 604/681-3466

Republic of Iceland
Embassy of Iceland (to Canada): #1200, 1156 - 15 St. NW, Washington DC 20005
202/265-6653; Fax: 202/265-6656; Email: idemb.wash@utn.stjr.is
Ambassador, His Excellency Einar Benediktsson
Minister-Counsellor, Petur G. Thorsteinsson
- Edmonton: Hon. Consul, Gudmundur A. Arnason, 14434 McQueen Rd., Edmonton AB T5N 3L6, 403/455-7946
- Montréal: Hon. Consul General, William I.M. Turner Jr., #575, 1981, av McGill College, Montréal PQ H3A 2X1, 514/982-0188; Fax: 514/982-0190
- Ottawa: Hon. Consul General, E.T. Lahey, #300, 246 Queen St., Ottawa ON K1P 5E4, 613/238-7412; Fax: 613/238-1799

- Regina: Hon. Consul, Jon Orn Jonsson, 4705 Castle Rd., Regina SK S4S 4W9, 306/586-7737; Fax: 306/359-1885
- St. John's: Hon. Consul, Avalon M. Goodridge, 20 Glasgow Place, St. John's NF A1B 2B4, 709/753-2787; Fax: 709/754-0699
- Timberlea: Hon. Consul, Lawrence J. Cooke, 14 Bay Ct., Timberlea NS B3T 1C4, 902/876-0657; Fax: 902/876-0657
- Toronto: Hon. Consul, J. Ragnar Johnson, #2400, 250 Yonge St., Toronto ON M5B 2M6, 416/979-6740; Fax: 416/979-1234
- West Vancouver: Hon. Consul, Heather Alda Ireland, 940 Younette Dr., West Vancouver BC V7T 1S9, 604/922-0854; Fax: 604/925-2524
- Winnipeg: Hon. Consul General, Neil Bardal, 984 Portage Ave., Winnipeg MB R3G 0R6, 204/949-2200; Fax: 204/783-5916

Republic of India
High Commission of India: 10 Springfield Rd., Ottawa ON K1M 1C9
613/744-3751; Fax: 613/744-0913; Email: hicomind@Ottawa.net
High Commissioner, His Excellency Prem Kumar Budhwar
High Commissioner (Designate), His Excellency G.S. Bedi
Deputy High Commissioner & Minister, A.K. Banerjee
- Toronto: Consul General, Rajiv Kumar Bhatia, #500, 2 Bloor St. West, Toronto ON M4W 3E2, 416/960-0751, 2377; Fax: 416/960-9812; Email: cgindia@pathcom.com
- Vancouver: Consul General, Jawahar Lal, 325 Howe St., 2nd Fl., Vancouver BC V6C 1Z7, 604/662-8811; Fax: 604/682-2471; Email: indiaadm@axionet.com

Republic of Indonesia
55 Parkdale Ave., Ottawa ON K1Y 1E5
613/724-1100; Fax: 613/724-1105; Email: kbri@prica.org
Ambassador, His Excellency Benjamin Parwoto
Counsellor, Economic, Chaidir Siregar
- Toronto: Consul, Titiek S.A. Suyono, 129 Jarvis St., Toronto ON M5C 2H6, 416/360-4020; Fax: 416/360-4295
- Vancouver: Consul, Jacky D. Wahyu, 1455 West Georgia St., 2nd Fl., Vancouver BC V6G 2T3, 604/682-8855; Fax: 604/662-8396

Islamic Republic of Iran
Embassy of the Islamic Republic of Iran: 245 Metcalfe St., Ottawa ON K2P 2K2
613/235-4726, 233-4726; Fax: 613/232-5712; Email: iranemb@sonetis.com
Deputy Chief of Mission, Parvis Afshari
Ambassador, His Excellency M.H. Lavassani

Republic of Iraq
Embassy of Iraq: 215 McLeod St., Ottawa ON K2P 0Z8
613/236-9177; Fax: 613/567-1101
Ambassador, Vacant
Chargé d'Affaires, Haitham Taufiq Al-Najjar
Attaché, Mohammed Fakhri

Ireland
Embassy of Ireland: #1105, 130 Albert St., Ottawa ON K1P 5G4
613/233-6281; Fax: 613/233-5835
Ambassador, His Excellency Paul Dempsey
First Secretary, Ronan Corvin
Third Secretary, Stephen Dawson

State of Israel
Embassy of Israel: #1005, 50 O'Connor St., Ottawa ON K1P 6L2
613/567-6450; Fax: 613/237-8865

Chargé d'affaires, Eli Yerushalmi
　Montréal: Consul General, Daniel Gal, #2620, 1155, boul René-Lévesque ouest, Montréal PQ H3B 4S5, 514/393-9372; Fax: 514/393-8795
　Toronto: Consul General, Yehudi Kinar, #700, 180 Bloor St. West, Toronto ON M5S 2V6, 416/961-1126; Fax: 416/961-7737

Italian Republic
Embassy of Italy: 275 Slater St., 21st Fl., Ottawa ON K1P 5H9
613/232-2401; Fax: 613/233-1484
Ambassador, His Excellency Andrea Negrotto
Minister-Counsellor, Sandro de Bernadin
　Brantford: Hon. Vice Consul, Arcangelo Martino, 288 Murray St., Brantford ON N3S 5T1, 519/753-0404
　Calgary: Hon. Consular Agent, Augusto Ambrosino, 326 - 27 Ave. NE, Calgary AB T2E 2A2, 403/248-3457
　Edmonton: Vice Consul, Pierfrancesco De Cerchio, #1900, Midland Walwyn Tower, Edmonton Centre, Edmonton AB T5J 2Z2, 403/423-5153; Fax: 403/423-5214
　Guelph: Hon. Vice-Consul, Imelda Porcellato, 127 Ferguson St., Guelph ON N1E 2Y9, 519/763-2228
　Halifax: Hon. Vice Consul, Rodolfo Meloni, #7, 1574 Argyle St., PO Box 12, Halifax NS B3J 2B3, 902/422-0066
　Hamilton: Vice Consul, Salvatore Di Venezia, #509, 105 Main St. East, Hamilton ON L8N 1G6, 905/529-5030; Fax: 905/529-7028
　Kingston: Hon. Vice Consul, Nicla A. d'Anna Sivilotti, 221 King St. East, Kingston ON K7L 3A6, 613/548-4380
　London: Hon. Vice Consul, Luigi Rossetti, 344 Richmond St. 2nd Fl., London ON N6A 3C3, 519/438-6740
　Montréal: Consul General, Carlo Selvaggi, 3489, av Drummond ouest, 2e étage, Montréal PQ H3G 1X6, 514/849-8351; Fax: 514/499-9471
　Niagara Falls: Hon. Vice Consul, Domenico Morabito, 4904 Victoria Ave., Niagara Falls ON L2E 4C6, 905/356-2231
　Prince Rupert: Hon. Consular Agent, Mario Giovanni Marogna, PO Box 640, Prince Rupert BC V8T 3S1, 250/624-6282; Fax: 250/624-6613
　Québec: Hon. Consul, Riccardo Rossini, 355 - 23e rue, Québec PQ G1L 1W8, 418/529-9801; Fax: 418/529-2996
　Regina: Hon. Vice Consul, Lucia Papini, 82 Lowry Place, Regina SK S4S 4P5, 306/586-6832; Fax: 306/585-4894
　Sarnia: Hon. Vice Consul, Antonio Domenichini, #210, 785 Exmouth St., Sarnia ON N7T 5P7, 519/336-0101
　Sault Ste. Marie: Hon. Vice Consul, Rudolph C. Peres, Professional Place, #201, 212 Queen St. East, Sault Ste. Marie ON P6A 5X8, 705/949-0704
　St. John's: Hon. Consular Agent, Gordon S. Lono, 8 Hunt Place, St. John's NF A1B 2J9, 709/739-8809
　Sudbury: Hon. Vice Consul, Dr. Roberto Grosso, 96 Larch St., Sudbury ON P3E 1C1, 705/674-4922
　Sydney: Hon. Consular Agent, Leonardo D'Addario, Sydney NS
　Thunder Bay: Hon. Vice Consul, Giovanna Pirotta Zovatto, #205, 105 May St. North, Thunder Bay ON P7C 3N9, 807/622-9052
　Timmins: Hon. Vice Consul, Rino Charles Bragagnolo, #131, 101 Mall, 38 Pine St. South, Timmins ON P4N 6K6, 705/264-1285
　Toronto: Consul General, Leonardo Sampoli, 136 Beverley St., Toronto ON M5T 1Y5, 416/977-1566; Fax: 416/977-1119
　Trail: Hon. Consular Agent, Gemma Merlo, 128 Colley St., Trail BC V1R 2M2, 250/364-1826
　Vancouver: Consul General, Arnaldo Abeti, #705, 1200 Burrard St., Vancouver BC V6Z 2C7, 604/684-7288; Fax: 604/685-4263
　Victoria: Hon. Vice Consul, Yolanda Pagnotta McKimmie, #207, 1050 Park Blvd., Victoria BC V8V 2T4, 250/386-3277; Fax: 250/595-5812
　Windsor: Hon. Vice Consul, Liliana Scotti Busi, 1145 Erie St. East, Windsor ON N9A 3Z6, 519/256-0092
　Winnipeg: Hon. Vice Consul, Bruno Esposito, #309, 283 Portage Ave., Winnipeg MB R3B 2B5, 204/943-7637

Republic of Ivory Coast
Embassy of Ivory Coast: 9 Marlborough Ave., Ottawa ON K1N 8E6
613/236-9919; Fax: 613/563-8287
Ambassador, His Excellency Julien Kacou
　Montréal: Hon. Consul, André Vannerum, #602, 417, rue St-Pierre, Montréal PQ H2Y 2N4, 514/845-8121; Fax: 514/688-7473
　Toronto: Hon. Consul, Peter J. Dawes, 260 Adelaide St. East, PO Box 110, Toronto ON M5A 1N1, 416/366-8490; Fax: 416/947-1534
　Vancouver: Hon. Consul, Jim O'Hara, 1531 Haywood Ave. West, Vancouver BC V7W 1W4, 604/291-5182; Fax: 604/291-5225

Jamaica
Jamaican High Commission: #800, 275 Slater St., Ottawa ON K1P 5H9
613/233-9311; Fax: 613/233-0611
High Commissioner, Her Excellency Maxine Eleanor Roberts
Counsellor, Ann Scott
First-Secretary, Caroline Blake
　St. Albert: Hon. Consul, Dolli Booth, 36 Windermere Cres., St. Albert AB T8N 3S5, 403/459-8440
　Toronto: Consul General, Margarietta St. Juste, #482, 214 King St. West, Toronto ON M5H 3S6, 416/598-3008
　Winnipeg: Hon. Consul, Prof. D.K. Gordon, 11 Wadham Bay, Winnipeg MB R3T 3K2, 204/269-5319

Japan
Embassy of Japan: 255 Sussex Dr., Ottawa ON K1N 9E6
613/241-8541; Fax: 613/241-2232; Email: http://emb@japan.magi.com
Ambassador, His Excellency Takashi Tajima
Minister, Naoto Amaki
Minister, Kiyoshi Araki
Counsellor, Hiroshi Matsumura
　Edmonton: Consul General, Shigeru Ise, ManuLife Place, #2480, 10180 - 101 St., Edmonton AB T5J 3S4, 403/422-3752; Fax: 403/424-1635
　Halifax: Hon. Consul General, Bruce S.C. Oland, Lindwood Holdings Ltd., Keith Hall, 1475 Hollis St., PO Box 2066, Halifax NS B3J 2Z1, 902/429-6530
　Montréal: Consul General, Yuji Kurokawa, #2120, 600, rue de La Gauchetière ouest, Montréal PQ H3B 4L8, 514/866-3429; Fax: 514/395-6000
　Regina: Hon. Consul General, Arthur Tsuneo Wakabayashi, 3234 Mountbatten Cres., Regina SK S4V 0Z4, 306/789-3221; Fax: 306/761-0766
　St. John's: Hon. Consul General, Aidan Maloney, 2 Laughlin Cres., St. John's NF A1A 2G2, 709/722-3016
　Toronto: Consul General, Hajime Tsujimoto, #2702, Toronto Dominion Bank Tower, Toronto Dominion Centre, PO Box 10, Toronto ON M5K 1A1, 416/363-7038; Fax: 416/367-9392
　Vancouver: Consul General, Yasuo Nozaka, #900, 1177 Hastings St. West, Vancouver BC V6E 2K9, 604/684-5868; Fax: 604/684-6939
　Winnipeg: Hon. Consul General, Otto Lang, 680 Wellington Cres., Winnipeg MB R3M 0C2, 204/284-0478

Hashemite Kingdom of Jordan
Embassy of Jordan: #701, 100 Bronson Ave., Ottawa ON K1R 6G8
613/238-8090; Fax: 613/232-3341
Ambassador, Michael Molloy
Second Secretary, Karim Wael Masri

Republic of Kazakhstan
Consulate General of Kazakhstan: 7777 Keele St., Concord ON L4K 1Y7
Hon. Consul General, Robert P. Kaplan, P.C., Q.C., LL.B.

Republic of Kenya
High Commission for Kenya: 415 Laurier Ave. East, Ottawa ON K1N 6R4
613/563-1773; Fax: 613/233-6599
High Commissioner, His Excellency Mwanyengela Ngali
Counsellor, Danielo Mayaka

Republic of Korea
Embassy of Korea: 151 Slater St., 5th Fl., Ottawa ON K1P 5H3
613/232-1715; Fax: 613/232-0928
Ambassador, His Excellency Kee Bock Shin
Minister, Young-Jo Jung
　Montréal: Consul General, Tae Kyu Yang, #2500, 1002, rue Sherbrooke ouest, Montréal PQ H3A 3G4, 514/845-3243; Fax: 514/845-8517
　Toronto: Consul General, Kyoung-Bo Shim, 555 Avenue Rd., Toronto ON M4V 2J7, 416/920-3809; Fax: 416/924-7305
　Vancouver: Consul General, Johng Won Kang, #830, 1066 Hastings St. West, Vancouver BC V6E 3X1, 604/681-9581; Fax: 604/681-4864

State of Kuwait
Embassy of Kuwait: 80 Elgin St., Ottawa ON K1P 1C6
613/780-9999; Fax: 613/780-9905
Ambassador, His Excellency Abdulmoshin Yousef Al-Duaij
Counsellor, Abdullatif A. Al-Mawwash

Kyrgyz Republic
Embassy of Kyrgyzstan (to Canada): #705, 1511 K St. NW, Washington DC 20005
202/347-3732; Fax: 202/347-3718; Email: kyrgyz@aol.com
Chargé d'Affaires, a.i., Almas Chukin

Lao People's Democratic Republic
Embassy of Laos (to Canada): 2222 - 5 St. NW, Washington DC 20008
202/332-6416; Fax: 202/332-4923
Ambassador, Hiem Phommachanh
First Secretary, Seng Soukhathivong

Republic of Latvia
Embassy of Latvia, Tower B: #208, 112 Kent St., Ottawa ON K1P 5P2
613/238-6014; Fax: 613/238-7044; Email: latvia-embassy@magmacom.com; Consular Division: 613/238-6868
Ambassador, Dr. Georges Andrevevs
Chargé d'Affaires, Martins Lacis

Lebanese Republic
Embassy of Lebanon: 640 Lyon St., Ottawa ON K1S 3Z5
613/236-5825; Fax: 613/232-1609
Ambassador, His Excellency Dr. Assem Salman Jaber
Counsellor, Michel Haddad

Outremont: Consul General, Charbel Wehbi, 40, ch Côte Ste Catherine, Outremont PQ H2V 2A2, 514/276-2638; Fax: 514/276-0090

Kingdom of Lesotho
High Commission for Lesotho: 202 Clemow Ave., Ottawa ON K1S 2B4
613/236-9449; Fax: 613/238-3341
High Commissioner, Dr. Gwendoline M Malahleha, Ph.D.
Counsellor, Boomo Frank Sofonia
  Montréal: Hon. Consul General, Louis D. Burke, 4750, The Boulevard, Montréal PQ H3Y 1V3, 514/482-6568; Fax: 514/483-6595
  Vancouver: Hon. Consul, Kenneth L. Burke, 2046 - 14 Ave. West, Vancouver BC V6J 2K4, 604/734-2729; Fax: 604/734-0627

Republic of Liberia
Embassy of Liberia, Ottawa ON
  Burlington: Hon. Consul, Edward A. Collis, 1441 Ontario St., Burlington ON L7S 1G5, 905/333-4000; Fax: 905/632-4000
  Montréal: Hon. Consul General, H.J.F. Bloomfield, #1720, 1080 Beaver Hall Hill, Montréal PQ H2Z 1S8, 514/871-4741; Fax: 514/397-0816
  Ste-Foy: Hon. Consul, Philip Berlach, 400, rue Morse, Ste-Foy PQ G1N 4L4
  Toronto: Hon. Consul General, Erwin Singer, Toronto ON
  Vancouver: Hon. Consul General, Philip Garratt, #502, 815 Hornby St., Vancouver BC V6Z 2E6, 604/684-5988; Fax: 604/684-0367
Embassy temporarily closed.

Socialist People's Libyan Arab Jamahiriya
c/o Permanent Mission of Libya to the U.N.: #309, 315 East 48th St., New York NY 10017
212/752-5775; Fax: 212/593-4787
Ambassador, His Excellency Mohamed Azwai
Chargé d'Affaires, Ibrahim A. Omar

Liechtenstein c/o Swiss Confederation

Republic of Lithuania
Embassy of Lithuania (to Canada): 2622 - 16th St. NW, Washington DC 20009
202/234-5860; Fax: 202/328-0460
Ambassador designate, A. Eidintas
  Toronto: Hon. Consul General of Lithuania, Haris Lapas, Toronto, 416/538-2992

Grand Duchy of Luxembourg
Embassy of Luxembourg (to Canada): 2200 Massachusetts Ave. NW, Washington DC 20008
202/265-4171; Fax: 202/328-8270
Ambassador, His Excellency Alphonse Berns
Minister-Counsellor, Jean-Paul Munchen
  Calgary: Hon. Consul, Z.G. (Dan) Havlena, c/o Cec Papke Sales & Rentals Ltd., #216, 816 - 7 Ave. SW, Calgary AB T2P 1A1, 403/262-5576; Fax: 403/262-3556
  Montréal: Hon. Consul General, Marie-Claire Lefort, 3877 Draper Ave., Montréal PQ H4A 2N9, 514/489-6052
  Vancouver: Hon. Consul, Klaus Priebe, #300, 1111 Melville St., Vancouver BC V6E 4H7, 604/682-3664; Fax: 604/688-3830

Republic of Madagascar
Embassy of Madagascar: 282 Somerset St. West, Ottawa ON K2P 0J6
613/563-2506; Fax: 613/231-3261
Ambassador, His Excellency René Fidèle Rajaonah
  Brossard: Hon. Vice Consul, Julien Randrianarivony, 8530, rue Saguenay, Brossard PQ J4X 1M6, 514/672-0353; Fax: 514/466-1552

Calgary: Hon. Consul, Zdenek Geoffrey Havlena, c/o Cec Papke Sales & Rentals Ltd., #216, 816 - 7 Ave. SW, Calgary AB T2P 1A1, 403/262-5576; Fax: 403/262-3556

Republic of Malawi
High Commission for Malawi: 7 Clemow Ave., Ottawa ON K1S 2A9
613/236-8931; Fax: 613/236-1054
High Commissioner, His Excellency Emmanuel C.R. Gondwe
First Secretary, David Ntonya
  St-Lambert: Hon. Consul, Yvon Maloney, 5437, boul Plamondon, St-Lambert PQ J4S 1W4, 514/466-9543
  Toronto: Hon. Consul, Robert A. Elek, #544, 21 Dale Ave., Toronto ON M4W 1K3, 416/234-9333

Malaysia
High Commission of Malaysia: 60 Boteler St., Ottawa ON K1N 8Y7
613/241-5182; Fax: 613/241-5214; Telex: 053-3520
High Commissioner, His Excellency Dato Abdullah Zawawi Bin Haji Mohamed
Counsellor, Saipul Anuar Bin Abd Muin
  Toronto: Consul, Sahban Bin Haji Muksan, #1110, 150 York St., Toronto ON M5H 3S5, 416/947-0004; Fax: 416/947-0006
  Vancouver: Consul General, Ali Bin Abdullah, #1900, 925 Georgia St. West, Vancouver BC V6C 3L2, 604/685-9550; Fax: 604/685-9520

Republic of Mali
Embassy of Mali: 50 Goulburn Ave., Ottawa ON K1N 8C8
613/232-1501; Fax: 613/232-7429
Ambassador, His Excellency Diakité Manassa Danioko
Counsellor, Mohamed Maiga
  Montréal: Hon. Consul, Paul Fortin, #1810, 1 Westmount Sq., Montréal PQ H3Z 2P9, 514/939-1267; Fax: 514/489-0379
  Toronto: Hon. General Consul, Paul John Tuz, 519 Spadina Rd., Toronto ON M5P 2W6, 416/489-4849; Fax: 416/766-1970

Malta
High Commission for Malta (to Canada); c/o Embassy of Malta: 2017 Connecticut Ave. NW, Washington DC 20008
202/462-3611; Fax: 202/387-5470; Email: 102475.2476@compuserve.com; Telex: 64231 MALTAREP
High Commissioner, His Excellency Dr. Albert Borg Olivier de Puget
  Etobicoke: Hon. Consul General, Milo Vassallo, West Tower, Mutual Group Centre, #730, 3300 Bloor St. West, Etobicoke ON M8X 2X2, 416/207-0922; Fax: 416/207-0986
  Montréal: Hon. Consul, Edward G. Abela, 3461 Northcliffe, Montréal PQ H4A 3K8, 514/284-3627; Fax: 514/284-1860
  St. John's: Hon. Consul General, Charles E. Puglisevich, Crosbie Bldg., PO Box 186, Stn C, St. John's NF A1C 5J2, 709/722-2744; Fax: 709/722-3208
  Vancouver: Hon. Consul General, Joachim Grubner, #310, 1001 Broadway West, Vancouver BC V6H 4B1, 604/732-4453; Fax: 604/738-4796

Islamic Republic of Mauritania
Embassy of Mauritania: 249 McLeod St., Ottawa ON K2P 1A1
613/237-3283; Fax: 613/237-3287
Ambassador, His Excellency Abdel Majid Kamil
Counsellor, Sidi Ould Mohamed Lagdhaf

Republic of Mauritius
High Commission for Mauritius (to Canada): c/o Embassy of Mauritius: #441, 4301 Connecticut Ave. NW, Washington DC 20008
202/244-1491; Fax: 202/966-0983
High Commissioner, His Excellency Anund Priyay Neewoor
Second Secretary, M. Nagub Soomauroo
  Montréal: Hon. Consul, Richard Gervais, #200, 606, rue Cathcart, Montréal PQ H3B 1K9, 514/393-9500; Fax: 514/393-9324

United Mexican States
Embassy of Mexico: #1500, 45 O'Connor St., Ottawa ON K1P 1A4
613/233-8988, 9272; Fax: 613/235-9123
  Commercial Section, 613/235-7782; Fax: 613-235-1129
Ambassador, Her Excellency Sandra Fuentes-Berain
Minister & Deputy Head of Mission, Francisco Olguin Uribe
Minister, Commercial Affairs, Jose Poblano
  Calgary: Hon. Consul, Patrick H.M.D. Coquet, #830, 540 - 5 Ave. SW, Calgary AB T2P 0M2, 403/263-7077; Fax: 403/263-7075
  Montréal: Consul General, Celso H. Delgado Ramirez, #1015, 2000, rue Mansfield, Montréal PQ H3A 2Z7, 514/288-2502; Fax: 514/288-8287; Tourist section: 514/871-1052
  Commercial Section: #1540, 1501 McGill College, Montréal, PQ, H3H 2T5, 514/287-1669; Fax: 514/287-1844
  Sillery: Hon. Consul, Madelaine Therrien, #1407, 380, rue Saint-Louis, Sillery PQ G1S 4M1, 418/681-3192
  Toronto: Consul General, Sergio Aguilera Beteta, #4440, 99 Bay St., PO Box 266, Toronto ON M5L 1E9, 416/368-2875; Fax: 416/368-1672
  Vancouver: Consul General, Roberto Gamboa, #810, 1130 Pender St. West, Vancouver BC V6E 4A4, 604/684-3547; Fax: 604/684-2485; Telex: 04-55634
  Winnipeg: Hon. Consul, Gary Thomas Brazzell, Winnipeg MB

Principality of Monaco
  Montréal: Hon. Consul General, Michel Pasquin, #1500, 1155 Sherbrooke St. West, Montréal PQ H3A 2W1, 514/849-0589; Fax: 514/631-2771
  Vancouver: Hon. Consul General, Fritz A.W. Ziegler, #500, 1111 Melville St., Vancouver BC V6E 4H7, 604/682-4633; Fax: 604/684-0015

Mongolian People's Republic
Embassy of Mongolia (to Canada): c/o U.S. Embassy of Mongolia: 2833 M St. NW, Washington DC 20007
202/333-7117; Fax: 202/298-9227
Ambassador, His Excellency Luvsandorj Dawagiv

Montserrat c/o Organization of the Eastern Caribbean States

Kingdom of Morocco
Embassy of Morocco: 38 Range Rd., Ottawa ON K1N 8J4
613/236-7391; Fax: 613/236-6164
Ambassador, His Excellency Tajeddine Baddou
Minister/Plenipotentiary, Abbas El Mokri
  Montréal: Consul General, Elyazid El Kadiri, #1510, 1010, rue Sherbrooke ouest, Montréal PQ H3A 2R7, 514/288-8750; Fax: 514/288-4859
  Vancouver: Hon. Consul, Percy Von Lipinsky, 3357 Pt. Grey Rd., Vancouver BC V6K 1A4, 604/671-6501; Fax: 604/689-8913

Republic of Mozambique
Embassy of Mozambique (to Canada): #570, 1990 M St. NW, Washington DC 20036
202/293-7146; Fax: 202/835-0245

Ambassador, His Excellency Hipolito Pereira Zozimo Patricio

Union of Myanmar
Embassy of Myanmar: #902, 85 Range Rd., Ottawa ON K1N 8J6
613/232-6434; Fax: 613/232-6435
Ambassador, His Excellency Dr. Kyaw Winung

Republic of Namibia
High Commission for Namibia (to Canada): 1605 New Hampshire Ave. NW, Washington DC 20009
202/986-0540; Fax: 202/986-0443
High Commissioner, His Excellency Tuliameni Kalomoh
    Waterloo: Hon. Consul, Walter McLean, 122 Avondale Ave. South, Waterloo ON N2L 2G3, 519/578-5932; Fax: 519/578-7799

Kingdom of Nepal
Royal Nepalese Embassy (to Canada): c/o Embassy of Nepal: 2131 Leroy Place NW, Washington DC 20008
202/667-4550; Fax: 202/667-5534; Telex 440085 EVER UI
Ambassador, Vacant
Chargé d'Affaires, Pradep Khapitwada
    Toronto: Hon. Consul General, Kunjar Sharma, BDO Dunwoody Ward Mallette, Royal Bank Plaza, PO Box 33, Toronto ON M5J 2J9, 416/865-0210; Fax: 416/865-0904

Kingdom of the Netherlands
Royal Netherlands Embassy: #2020, 350 Albert St., Ottawa ON K1R 1A4
613/237-5030; Fax: 613/237-6471
Ambassador, His Excellency Johannes H.W. Fietelaars
Counsellor & Deputy Head of Mission, Arend H. Huitzing
Counsellor, Economic & Commercial Affairs, Aart Jan M. Verdegaal
    Calgary: Hon. Consul, G.A. Van Wielingen, Canada Trust Tower, #2103, 421 - 7 Ave. SW, Calgary AB T2P 4K9, 403/266-2710; Fax: 403/265-8180
    Edmonton: Hon. Consul, R. Dootjes, 10214 - 112 St., Edmonton AB T5K 1M5, 403/428-7513; Fax: 403/424-2053
    Halifax: Hon. Consul, Gavin Joseph Rainnie, Purdy's Wharf, #1306, 1959 Upper Water St., Halifax NS B3J 3N2, 902/422-1485; Fax: 902/420-1787
    Kingston: Hon. Vice Consul, Dr. H. Westenberg, 115 Lower Union St., Kingston ON K7L 2N3, 613/542-7095
    London: Hon. Vice Consul, Dr. R.D. ter-Vrugt, 650 Colborne St., London ON N5A 5A1, 519/551-0453; Fax: 519/432-7431
    Montréal: Consul General, Hans van Dam, #1500, 1245, rue Sherbrooke ouest, Montréal PQ H3G 1G2, 514/849-4247; Fax: 514/849-8260
    Québec: Hon. Consul, E.A. Price, 10, rue Ste-Anne, PO Box 833, Québec PQ G1R 3X1, 418/692-2175; Fax: 418/692-4161
    Regina: Hon. Consul, W.B.C. de Lint, #100, 2400 College Ave., Regina SK S4P 1C8, 306/522-8577
    Saint John: Hon. Consul, C.D. Whelly, #1600, 1 Brunswick Sq., PO Box 1324, Stn A, Saint John NB E2L 4H8, 506/632-8900; Fax: 506/632-8809; Telex: 014-47252
    St. John's: Hon. Consul, A.A. Bruneau, 55 Kenmount Rd., PO Box 8910, St. John's NF A1B 3P6, 709/737-5616; Fax: 709/737-5832
    Thunder Bay: Hon. Vice Consul, R.P. Welter, 179 South Algoma St., Thunder Bay ON P7B 3C1, 807/344-5721
    Toronto: Consul General, P.W.A. Schellekeus, #2106, 1 Dundas St. West, Toronto ON M5G 1Z3, 416/598-2520; Fax: 416/598-8064
    Vancouver: Consul General, Baron M. Van Aerssen Beijeren Van Voshol, Crown Trust Bldg., #821, 475 Howe St., Vancouver BC V6C 2B3, 604/684-6448; Fax: 604/684-3549
    Winnipeg: Hon. Consul, Hans Hasenack, 69 Shorecrest Dr., Winnipeg MB R3P 1N9, 204/489-0467; Fax: 204/489-4219

New Zealand
New Zealand High Commission: #727, 99 Bank St., Ottawa ON K1P 6G3
613/238-5991; Fax: 613/238-5707
High Commissioner, The Hon. Stephen Jacobs
Deputy High Commissioner, Craig A. Rickit
First Secretary, Barbara Bridge
    Vancouver: Consul General & Trade Commissioner, Stephen Bryant, #1200, 888 Dunsmuir St., Vancouver BC V6C 3K4, 604/684-7388; Fax: 604/684-7333

Republic of Nicaragua
Embassy of Nicaragua: #407, 130 Albert St., Ottawa ON K1P 5G4
613/234-9361; Fax: 613/238-7666; Consular Section: 613/238-7677
Ambassador, His Excellency Dr. René Sandino Arguello
Minister-Counsellor Chargé d'affaires, A.I., Susan Grigsby de Fonseca
First Secretary, Consular Affairs, Juan Manuel Siero Cantarero
    Laval: Hon. Consul, Noel Lacayo Barreto, 495 Josiane, Laval PQ H7P 5RL, 514/484-9694; Fax: 514/625-5132
    Toronto: Hon. Consul, Ilse Mendieta de McGrath, 2351 Poplar Cr., Toronto ON L5J 4H2, 905/855-3960; Fax: 905/855-1513

Republic of Niger
Embassy of Niger: 38 Blackburn Ave., Ottawa ON K1N 8A2
613/232-4291; Fax: 613/230-9808
Ambassador, His Excellency Aboubacar Abdou
Counsellor, Boubacar Adarnor
Second Secretary, M. Saley Brah
    Montréal: Hon. Consul, Pierre Thomas, #850, 231, rue St-Jacques ouest, Montréal PQ H2Y 1M6, 514/844-4428
    Toronto: Hon. Consul, Jean Michel Beck, Toronto ON
    Vancouver: Hon. Consul, John Akerley, Vancouver BC

Federal Republic of Nigeria
High Commission for Nigeria: 295 Metcalfe St., Ottawa ON K2P 1R9
613/236-0521; Fax: 613/236-0529
High Commissioner, Vacant
Minister-Counsellor & Acting High Commissioner, M.A.B. Adeyanju

Kingdom of Norway
Royal Norwegian Embassy: #532, 90 Sparks St., Ottawa ON K1P 5B4
613/238-6571; Fax: 613/238-2765
Ambassador, His Excellency Bjorn Inge Kristvik
Attaché, Elna Verheyleweghen
    Calgary: Hon. Consul, L.E. Bjornsen, North Tower, Western Canadian Place, #1753, 707 - 8th Ave. SW, PO Box 6525, Stn D, Calgary AB T2P 3G7, 403/263-2270; Fax: 403/298-6081
    Dartmouth: Hon. Consul, Steinar J. Engeset, #206, 11 Morris Dr., Dartmouth NS B3B 1M2, 902/468-1330; Fax: 902/468-7200
    Edmonton: Hon. Consul, Roar Tungland, 2310 - 80 Ave., PO Box 5584, Edmonton AB T6C 4E9, 403/440-2292; Fax: 403/440-1241
    Mississauga: Hon. Consul General, Trygve Husebye, 2600 South Sheridan Way, Mississauga ON L5J 2M4, 905/822-2339; Fax: 905/855-1450
    Montréal: Hon. Consul General, Richard Pound, #3900, 1155, boul René Lévesque ouest, Montréal PQ H3B 3V2, 514/874-9087; Fax: 514/397-3063
    Québec: Hon. Consul, Gaétan Thivierge, 2 Nouvelle France, Wolves Crove, PO Box 40, Stn B, Québec PQ G1K 7A2, 418/525-8171; Fax: 418/525-9940
    Regina: Hon. Consul, John T. Nilson, McCallum Hill Center, #1500, 1874 Scarth St., Regina SK S4P 4E9, 306/347-8000; Fax: 306/352-5250
    Saint John: Hon. Consul, Donald F. MacGowan, Q.C., 40 Wellington Row, PO Box 6850, Stn A, Saint John NB E2L 4S3, 506/633-3800; Fax: 506/633-3811
    St. John's: Hon. Consul, Robert I. Collingwood, Baine Johnston Centre, #800, 10 Fort William Place, PO Box 5367, St. John's NF A1C 5W2, 709/576-1780; Fax: 709/576-1273
    Vancouver: Hon. Consul General, Bjorn Hareid, Waterfront Centre, #1200, 200 Burrard St., Vancouver BC V6C 3L6, 604/682-7977; Fax: 604/682-8376
    Victoria: Consul, Cecil P. Ridout, Hartwig Court, #401, 1208 Wharf St., PO Box 577, Victoria BC V8W 2P5, 250/384-1174; Fax: 250/382-3231
    Ville de la Baie: Hon. Consul, C.J. Tremblay, 1522 - 6e av, Ville de la Baie PQ G7B 1R6, 418/544-1488
    Winnipeg: Hon. Consul, Astrid Walker, 336 Lindenwood Dr. East, Winnipeg MB R3P 2H1, 204/489-1626

Sultanate of Oman
Embassy of Oman (to Canada): 2342 Massachusetts Ave. NW, Washington DC 20008
202/387-1980; Fax: 202/745-4933
Ambassador, His Excellency Awadh Bader Al-Shanfari

Islamic Republic of Pakistan
High Commission for Pakistan: #608, 151 Slater St., Ottawa ON K1P 5H3
613/238-7881; Fax: 613/238-7296; Email: hcpak@magi.com
High Commissioner, Farouk A. Rana
First Secretary/Head of Chancery, Muhammad Sarfraz A. Khanzada
    Montréal: Consul General, Muhammad Ashraf, 3421, rue Peel, Montréal PQ H3A 1W7, 514/845-2297; Fax: 514/845-1354; Telex: 055-62154
    Willowdale: Consul General, Yusuf Shah, #810, 4881 Yonge St., Willowdale ON M2N 5X3, 416/250-1255; Fax: 416/250-1321

Republic of Panama
Embassy of Panama (to Canada): 2862 McGill Terrace NW, Washington DC 20008
202/483-1407; Fax: 202/483-8413
Ambassador, His Excellency Ricardo Alberto Arias
    Montréal: Consul General, Luis E. Uribe, #904, 1425, boul René-Lévesque ouest, Nun's Island, Montréal PQ H3G 1T7, 514/874-1929
    Vancouver: Hon. Consul, Dr. John Stuart Gladwell, #700, 555 West Hastings St., Vancouver BC V6B 4N5, 604/893-7033; Fax: 604/687-2043

Papua New Guinea
Embassy of Papua New Guinea: #300, 1615 New Hampshire Ave., Washington DC 20009
202/745-3680; Fax: 202/745-3679
Ambassador, His Excellency Nagora Bogan
    Toronto: Hon. Consul, David Beatty, Old Canada Investment Corp. Ltd., #2700, 145 King St. West, Toronto ON M5H 1J8, 416/865-0470

Republic of Paraguay
Embassy of Paraguay: #401, 151 Slater St., Ottawa ON K1P 5H3
613/567-1283; Fax: 613/567-1679
Ambassador, Washington Ashwell
First Secretary, Marta Elvira Marsiaj
 Montréal: Hon. Consul, Claude J.Y. Le Gris, #2820, 1, Place Ville Marie, Montréal PQ H3B 4R4, 514/398-0465; Fax: 514/487-0188

Republic of Peru
Embassy of Peru: #1901, 130 Albert St., Ottawa ON K1P 5G4
613/238-1777; Fax: 613/232-3062; Email: emperuca@magi.com; Telex: 053-3754 LEPRU OTT
Ambassador, His Excellency Hernan Couturier Mariategui
 Montréal: Consul General, Raul A. Rivera Maravi, La Tour Ouest, #376, 550, rue Sherbrooke ouest, Montréal PQ H3A 1B9, 514/844-5123; Fax: 514/843-8425
 Toronto: Consul General, Dora Salazar-Watkins, #301, 10 Saint Mary St., Toronto ON M4Y 1P9, 416/963-9696; Fax: 416/963-9074
 Vancouver: Consul, Amador Velasquez, #1850, 505 Burrard St., Vancouver BC V7X 1M6, 604/662-8880; Fax: 604/662-3564

Republic of the Philippines
Embassy of the Philippines: #606-608, 130 Albert St., Ottawa ON K1P 5G4
613/233-1121; Fax: 613/233-4165
Ambassador, His Excellency Pacifico A. Castro
Minister-Counsellor & Consul General, Antonio P. Villamayor
 Edmonton: Hon. Consul, Victoriano K. Cui, 8458 - 182 St., Edmonton AB T5T 2Y7, 403/444-5743
 Saint-Laurent: Hon. Consul General, Jose M. Reyes, #202, 3300, Cote Vertu, Saint-Laurent PQ H4R 2B7, 514/335-0478; Fax: 514/335-2786
 Toronto: Consul General, Clemencio F. Montesa, #365, 151 Bloor St. West, Toronto ON M5S 1S4, 416/922-7181; Fax: 416/922-2638
  Trade Section: #409, 60 Bloor St. West, Toronto, ON, M4W 3B8, 416/967-1788; Fax: 416/967-6236
 Vancouver: Consul General, Lourdes G. Morales, #301-308, 470 Granville St., Vancouver BC V6C 1V5, 604/685-7645; Fax: 604/685-9945; Telex: 04-51390
 Winnipeg: Hon. Consul, Dr. Rolando D. Guzman, 714 Medical Arts Bldg., #708, 233 Kennedy St., Winnipeg MB R3C 3J5, 204/942-7870

Republic of Poland
Embassy of Poland: 443 Daly Ave., Ottawa ON K1N 6H3
613/789-0468; Fax: 613/789-1218; Email: aj201@freenet.carleton.ca
Ambassador, His Excellency Tadeusz Diem
Counsellor, Maksymilian Podstawski
 Montréal: Consul General, Malgorzata Dzieduszycka-Ziemilska, 1500, av Pine ouest, Montréal PQ H3G 1B4, 514/937-9481; Fax: 514/937-7272
  Commercial Section: 3501, av Musée, Montréal, PQ, H3G 2C8, 514/937-9481; Fax: 514/937-7272
 Toronto: Consul General, Wojciech Tycinski, 2603 Lake Shore Blvd. West, Toronto ON M8V 1G5, 416/252-5471; Fax: 416/252-0509
  Commercial Section: #2860, 3300 Bloor St. West, Centre Tower, Toronto, ON, M8X 2W8, 416/233-6571; Fax: 416/233-9578
 Vancouver: Consul General, Krzysztof Kasprzyk, #1600, 1177 Hastings St. West, Vancouver BC V6E 2K3, 604/688-3530; Fax: 604/688-3537

Portugal
Embassy of Portugal: 645 Island Park Dr., Ottawa ON K1Y 0B8
613/729-0883; Fax: 613/729-4236; Consular Section: Tel: 613/729-2270
Ambassador, His Excellency Fernando Manuel da Silva Marques
Counsellor, Vera Maria Fernandes
 Edmonton: Hon. Consul, Luis Filipe da Rocha Rodrigues Freire, 398 Clearview Rd., Edmonton AB T5A 4G6, 403/473-1005; Fax: 403/473-2985
 Halifax: Hon. Consul, Arthur R. Moreira, 1646 Barrington St., PO Box 355, Halifax NS B3J 2N7, 902/423-7211
 Montréal: Consul General, Antonio Jorge Jacob de Carvalho, #1725, 2020, rue University, Montréal PQ H3A 2A5, 514/499-0359; Fax: 514/499-0366
  Commercial Section: #940, 500, rue Sherbrooke ouest, Montréal PQ H3A 3C6, 514/282-1264; Fax: 514/499-1450
 Québec: Hon. Consul, Fernao Mendonça Perestrelo, #710, 775, av Murray, Québec PQ G1S 4T2, 418/681-8650
 St. John's: Hon. Consul, Hernani Eurico da Silva Martins, 40 Mansfield Cres., PO Box 5249, St. John's NF A1E 5A8, 709/726-2440, 745-2271
 Toronto: Consul General, José Manuel da Encarnaçao Pessanha Vieigas, 121 Richmond St. West, 7th Fl., Toronto ON M5H 2K1, 416/360-8260; Fax: 416/360-0350
  Commercial & Tourism Sections: #1005, 60 Bloor St. West, Toronto, ON, M4W 3B8, 416/921-4925; Fax: 416/921-1353
 Vancouver: Consul, Walid Maciel Chaves Saad, #904, 700 West Pender St., Vancouver BC V6C 1G8, 604/688-6514; Fax: 604/685-7042
 Winnipeg: Consul, Gustavo Uriel da Roza, Jr., #908, 167 Lombard Ave., Winnipeg MB R3B 1N7, 204/943-8941

State of Qatar
Embassy of Qatar (to Canada), c/o Mission to the United Nations: #1180, 600 New Hampshire Ave. NW, Washington DC 20037
202/338-0111; Fax: 202/337-2989
Ambassador, His Excellency Sheikh Abdulrahman bin Saud al-Thani

Republic of Romania
Embassy of Romania: 655 Rideau St., Ottawa ON K1N 6A3
613/789-3709; Fax: 613/789-4365
Ambassador, His Excellency Valeriu Eugen Pop
Chargé d'Affairs, Adrian Petrescu
Minister-Counsellor, Economic Affairs, Viorel Onel
 Montréal: Consul General, Romulus-Patrus Bena, #M01.04, 1111, rue St. Urbain, Montréal PQ H2Z 1X6, 514/876-1792; Fax: 514/876-1797
 Toronto: Consul General, Ilie Puscas, #530, 111 Peter St., Toronto ON M5V 2H1, 416/585-5802; Fax: 416/585-4798

Russian Federation
Embassy of the Russian Federation: 285 Charlotte St., Ottawa ON K1N 8L5
613/235-4341; Fax: 613/236-6342
 Consular Section: 52 Range Rd., Ottawa K1N 8J5, 613/236-7220; Fax: 613/238-6158
Ambassador, His Excellency Alexander M. Belonogov
Minister-Counsellor, Vassili D. Sredin
Counsellor, Commercial, Valeri Makharadze
Counsellor, Consular, Vladimir Shillin
 Montréal: Consul General, Nikoli Smirnov, 3685, av du Musée, Montréal PQ H3G 2E1, 514/843-5901; Fax: 514/842-2012
  Trade Section: 95 Wurtemburg St., Ottawa ON K1N 8Z7, 613/236-1222; Fax: 613/238-2951

Rwandese Republic
121 Sherwood Dr., Ottawa ON K1Y 3V1
613/722-5835; Fax: 613/729-3291
Ambassador, His Excellency Maximin Mazimpaka Segasayo
Counsellor, Faustin Kanyamibwa
 Montréal: Hon. Consul General, Pierre Valcour, 1600 Delorimier St., Montréal PQ H2K 3W5, 514/526-1392; Fax: 514/521-7081
 North York: Hon. Consul, Ronald Heynneman, #102, 211 Consumers St., North York ON M2J 4G8, 416/493-5474; Fax: 416/493-8171

Saint Kitts & Nevis c/o Organization of the Eastern Caribbean States
Halifax: Hon. Consul, E. Anthony Ross, CLL Group Building, #602, 2695 Dutch Village Rd., Halifax NS B3L 4T9, 902/455-9090

Saint Lucia c/o Organization of the Eastern Caribbean States
Markham: Consul, Dunstan Fontenelle, 3 Dewberry Dr., Markham ON L3S 2R7, 416/472-1423; Fax: 416/472-6379

Saint Vincent & the Grenadines c/o Organization of the Eastern Caribbean States
North York: Consul for Saint Vincent & the Grenadines, Burns Bonadie, 210 Sheppard Ave. East, Ground Fl., North York ON M2N 3A9, 416/222-0745; Fax: 416/222-3830

San Marino
Montréal: Hon. Consul General, Raymond Lette, 27, av McNider, Montréal PQ H2V 3X4, 514/871-3838; Fax: 514/876-4217
Toronto: Hon. Consul, Germano Valle, #1104, 15 McMurrich St., Toronto ON M5R 3M6, 416/925-7777, 971-4848; Fax: 416/964-8937

Democratic Republic of Sao Tomé & Principe
c/o Permanent Mission of Sao Tomé & Principe to the U.N.: #1604, 122 East 42nd St., New York NY 10168
First Secretary, Domingos Ferreira
 Montréal: Hon. Consul, Alain Berranger, 4068, av Beaconsfield, Montréal PQ H4A 2H3

Kingdom of Saudi Arabia
Royal Embassy of Saudi Arabia: #901, 99 Bank St., Ottawa ON K1P 6B9
613/237-4100; Fax: 613/237-0567; Telex: 053-4285; Consular Section: 613/237-4104
Ambassador, His Excellency Asaad Al-Zuhair
First Secretary, Ghazi Hassad Eid

Republic of Senegal
Embassy of Senegal: 57 Marlborough Ave., Ottawa ON K1N 8E8
613/238-6392; Fax: 613/238-2695
Counsellor, Alioune Diagne
Ambassador, His Excellency Pierre Diouf
 Montréal: Hon. Consul, Louis-Philippe Lavoie, 3700, rue St-Christophe, Montréal PQ H2L 3X5, 514/526-8183
 North York: Hon. Consul, Dr. Gérard Bastien, 2472 Bayview Ave., North York ON M2L 1A7, 416/444-7492
 Vancouver: Hon. Consul, Kenneth John Bodnarchuk, 320 Industrial Ave., Vancouver BC V6A 2P5, 604/682-2121

Serbia c/o Federal Republic of Yugoslavia

Republic of Seychelles
High Commission for Seychelles (to Canada): #900F, 820 Second Ave., New York NY 10017
212/687-9766; Fax: 212/808-4975
High Commissioner, His Excellency Marc Marengo

Republic of Singapore
c/o Permanent Mission of the Republic of Singapore to the U.N.: 231 East 51st St., New York NY 10022
212/826-0840; Fax: 212/826-2964; Telex: 421283 SGWA UI
High Commissioner, Chew Tai Soo
  Vancouver: Hon. Consul General, Hon. N.T. Nemetz, C.C., Q.C., #1305, 999 Hastings St. West, Vancouver BC V6C 2W2, 604/669-5115; Fax: 604/669-5153

Slovak Republic
Embassy of the Slovak Republic: 50 Rideau Terrace, Ottawa ON K1M 2A1
613/749-4442; Fax: 613/749-4989; Email: slovakem@fox.nstn.ca
Ambassador, His Excellency Anton Hykisch
Counsellor, Economic and Commercial Affairs, Jozef Horsky
Counsellor, Political & Press Affairs, Stanislav Opiela
  Calgary: Hon. Consul, Ludovit Zanzotto, 208 Scenic Glen Place NW, Calgary AB T3L 1K3, 403/239-3543
  Montréal: Hon. Consul, Mark Kmec, 3700, rue de la Montagne, Montréal PQ H3G 2A8, 514/843-3700; Fax: 514/987-5460
  Toronto: Hon. Consul, John Stephens, #407, 1280 Finch Ave. West, Toronto ON M3J 3K6, 416/665-1499; Fax: 416/665-7488
  Vancouver: Hon. Consul, Stanislav Lisiak, 905 - 8 Ave. West, Vancouver BC V5Z 1E4, 604/732-4431; Fax: 604/732-4439
  Winnipeg: Hon. Consul, Jozef Kiska, 99 Grace St., Winnipeg MB R3B 0E4, 204/947-1728

Republic of Slovenia
Embassy of Slovenia: #2101, 150 Metcalfe St., Ottawa ON K2P 1P1
613/565-5781; Fax: 613/565-5783
Ambassador, His Excellency Marijan Majcen
Minister-Plenipotentiary, Mitja Strukelj

Solomon Islands
High Commission c/o Permanent Mission to the U.N.: #800B, 820 - 2 Ave., New York NY 10017
212/599-6194
High Commissioner, His Excellency Francis Bugotu

Republic of South Africa
High Commission for South Africa: 15 Sussex Dr., Ottawa ON K1M 1M8
613/744-0330; Fax: 613/741-1639; Email: safrica@ottawa.net
High Commissioner, His Excellency B.l.L. Modise
  Montréal: Consul, Heyn van Rooyen, #2615, 1, Place Ville Marie, Montréal PQ H3B 4S3, 514/878-9217; Fax: 514/878-4751
  Toronto: Consul General, Patrick Evans, #2300, 2 First Canadian Place, PO Box 424, Toronto ON M5X 1E3, 416/364-0314; Fax: 416/364-1737

Kingdom of Spain
Embassy of Spain: 74 Stanley Ave., Ottawa ON K1M 1P4
613/747-2252, 7293; Fax: 613/744-1224; Email: spain@ott.hookup.net
Ambassador, His Excellency Fernando M. Valenzuela
Minister-Counsellor, Ramón Sáenz de Heredia
Defence Attaché, Col. Antonio Diaz rojas
Counsellor, Cultural, Enrique Viguera
Counsellor, Commercial, Alfonso Carbajo
Couseellor, Labour, Carlos Solinis
Attaché, Education, José Félix Barrio
  Burnaby: Hon. Consul, Joaquin Ayala, 3736 Parker St., Burnaby BC V5C 3B1, 604/299-7760; Fax: 604/255-2532
  Calgary: Hon. Consul, Steve Jaksi, #2402, 835 6th Ave. SW, Calgary AB T2P 0V4, 403/237-5975
  Halifax: Hon. Vice Consul, Louis Holmes, 82 Bedford Hills Rd., Halifax NS B4A IJ9, 902/835-4900; Fax: 902/835-9439
  Montréal: Consul General, José Maria Castroviejo, #1456, 1 Westmount Sq., Montréal PQ H3Z 2P9, 514/935-5235; Fax: 514/935-4655
  Montréal: Consul, Commercial, Fernando Baijet, Place Bonaventure, Mart E, CP 1137, Montréal PQ H5A 1G4, 514/866-4914
  Sillery: Hon. Vice Consul, François Robitaille St-Cyr, 1085, av Bougainville, Sillery PQ G1S 3B1, 418/688-9872
  St. John's: Hon. Vice Consul, Nathanaiel J. Cooper, 87 Water St., PO Box 5128, St. John's NF A1C 5V6, 709/726-8000; Fax: 709/726-9891
  Toronto: Consul General, Jose Antonio Zorrilla, #400, 1200 Bay St., Toronto ON M5R 2A5, 416/967-4949; Fax: 416/925-4949
  Toronto: Consul, Commercial, Arturo Pina, #1204, 55 Bloor St. West, Toronto ON M4W 1A5, 416/967-0488; Fax: 416/968-9547
  Toronto: Consul, Tourism, Ignacio Ducasse, 2 Bloor St. West, 34th Fl., Toronto ON M4W 3E2, 416/961-3131; Fax: 416/961-1992
  Winnipeg: Hon. Vice Consul, Donald Allan Green, 1025 Buchanan Blvd., Winnipeg MB R2Y 1N7, 204/831-6033

Democratic Socialist Republic of Sri Lanka
High Commission of the Democratic Socialist Republic of Sri Lanka: #1204, 333 Laurier Ave. West, Ottawa ON K1P 1C1
613/233-8449; Fax: 613/238-8448; Email: lankacom@magi.com
High Commissioner, His Excellency A.C. Goonasekera
First Secretary, Commercial, Sonali Wjeratne
Minister-Counsellor, S.B. Weragama
Third Secretary, A.L. Ratnapala
Attaché, L.G. Silva
  Vancouver: Hon. Consul, Mir Ihor Huculak, #807, 938 Howe St., Vancouver BC V6Z 1N9, 604/331-2505; Fax: 604/331-2515

Republic of The Sudan
Embassy of The Sudan: #507, 85 Range Rd., Ottawa ON K1N 8J6
613/235-4000, 4999; Fax: 613/235-6880
Chargé d'Affaires, Elfadil O.M. Ahmed

Republic of Suriname
Embassy of Suriname (to Canada): #108, 4301 Connecticut Ave. NW, Washington DC 20008
202/244-7488; Fax: 202/244-5878
Ambassador, Willem A. Udenhout

Kingdom of Swaziland
High Commission for Swaziland: #1204, 130 Albert St., Ottawa ON K1P 5G4
613/567-1480; Fax: 613/567-1058; Telex: 053-3185
High Commissioner, His Excellency Bremer M. Nxumalo
First Secretary, S. Ntshangase
Third Secretary, Ambrose H. Maziya
Administrative Attaché, Khetsiwe V. Maseko

Kingdom of Sweden
Embassy of Sweden: 377 Dalhousie St., Ottawa ON K1N 9N8
613/241-8553; Fax: 613/241-2277; Telex: 053-3331 SVENSK OTT
Ambassador, His Excellency Jan Stahl
Counsellor, Lisette Lindahl Owens
  Calgary: Hon. Consul, Gunilla Mungan, 1039 Durham Ave. SW, Calgary AB T2T 0P8, 403/541-0354; Fax: 403/244-7728
  Edmonton: Hon. Consul, Donald G. Bishop, c/o Bishop & McKenzie, #2500, 10104 - 103 Ave., Edmonton AB T5J 1V3, 403/426-5550; Fax: 403/426-1305
  Fredericton: Hon. Consul, Rhona Ruben, c/o Ruben & Kingston, 259 Brunswick St., PO Box 1142, Fredericton NB E3B 5C2, 506/458-0000; Fax: 506/451-8766
  Halifax: Hon. Consul, Kaj Nielsen, c/o Volvo, PO Box 2027, Halifax NS B3J 2Z1, 902/450-5252; Fax: 902/450-5272
  Montréal: Hon. Consul, Marie Giguère, c/o Martineau Walker, #3400, 800, Place Victoria, Montréal PQ H4Z 1E9, 514/866-4019; Fax: 514/397-7600
  Québec: Hon. Consul General, Paule Gauthier, c/o Desjardins Ducharme Stein Monast Le St-Amable, #300, 1150 Claire Fontaine, Québec PQ G1R 5G4, 418/640-4437; Fax: 418/523-5391
  Regina: Hon. Consul, Ronald E. Shirkey, #325, 2550 - 15 Ave., Regina SK S4P 1A5, 306/359-1000; Fax: 306/359-3300
  St. John's: Hon. Consul, Albert Hickman, 85 Kenmount Rd., PO Box 8340, Stn A, St. John's NF A1B 3N7, 709/726-6990; Fax: 709/726-4003
  Toronto: Hon. Consul, Robert Stocks, #1504, 2 Bloor St. West, Toronto ON M4W 3E2, 416/963-8768; Fax: 416/923-8809
  Vancouver: Hon. Consul General, Magnus Ericson, #1100, 1188 West Georgia St., Vancouver BC V6E 4A2, 604/683-5838; Fax: 604/687-8237; Telex: 04-51451
  Winnipeg: Hon. Consul, Neil E. Carlson, 1035 Mission St., Winnipeg MB R2J 0A4, 204/233-3373; Fax: 204/233-6938

Swiss Confederation
Embassy of Switzerland: 5 Marlborough Ave., Ottawa ON K1N 8E6
613/235-1837; Fax: 613/563-1394; Telex: 053-3648
Ambassador, His Excellency Daniel Dayer
Counsellor, Georges Martin
  Calgary: Hon. Consul, Klaus D. Zahnd, #700, 140 - 4 Ave. SW, Calgary AB T2P 3N3, 403/233-8919; Fax: 403/269-3048
  Edmonton: Hon. Consul, Bruno Dobler, 4926 - 89 St., Edmonton AB T6E 5K1, 403/462-9221; Fax: 403/463-6319
  Montréal: Consul General, Max Heller, 1572, av Dr. Penfield, Montréal PQ H3G 1C4, 514/932-7181; Fax: 514/932-9028; Telex: 055-60026
  Québec: Hon. Consul, Jean-Pierre Beltrami, 3293, 1er av, Québec PQ G1L 3R2, 418/623-9864; Fax: 418/623-6644
  Toronto: Consul General, Claude Duboulet, #601, 154 University Ave., Toronto ON M5H 3Y9, 416/593-5371; Fax: 416/593-5083; Telex: 065-24624
  Vancouver: Consul General, Robert Wenger, World Trade Centre, #790, 999 Canada Place, Vancouver BC V6C 3E1, 604/684-2231; Fax: 604/684-2806; Telex: 04-51184

Syrian Arab Republic
Embassy of Syria (to Canada): 2215 Wyoming Ave. NW, Washington DC 20008
202/232-6313; Fax: 202/234-9548
Ambassador, His Excellency Walid Al-Moualem

United Republic of Tanzania
High Commission for Tanzania: 50 Range Rd., Ottawa ON K1N 8J4
613/232-1500; Fax: 613/232-5184; Telex: 053-3569
High Commissioner, His Excellency Fadhil D. Mbaga

Kingdom of Thailand
Royal Thai Embassy: 180 Island Park Dr., Ottawa ON K1Y 0A2
613/722-4444; Fax: 613/722-6624; Telex: 053-3975 THAIDUTO OTT

Commercial Section: 1801, 275 Slater St., Ottawa ON
K1P 5H9, 613/238-4002; Fax: 613/238-6226
Ambassador, His Excellency Virasakdi Futrakul
Minister, Cholchineepan Chiranond
Minister-Counsellor, Commercial, Vira Boonsri
    Edmonton: Hon. Consul, Kurt Beier, 8625 - 112 St., Edmonton AB T6G 1K8, 403/469-3576; Fax: 403/432-1387
    Montréal: Hon. Consul General, Marc J. Besso, #1500, 666, rue Sherbrooke ouest, Montréal PQ H3A 1E7, 514/982-0777; Fax: 514/282-7435
    Toronto: Hon. Consul General, Richard C. Meech, Q.C., 44th Fl., Scotia Plaza, 40 King St. West, Toronto ON M5H 3Y4, 416/367-6750; Fax: 416/367-6749; Telex: 06-22687
    Vancouver: Hon. Consul General, Horst G.P. Koehler, C.M., #106, 736 Granville St., Vancouver BC V6Z 1G3, 604/687-1143; Fax: 604/687-4434

Republic of Togo
Embassy of Togo: 12 Range Rd., Ottawa ON K1N 8J3
613/238-5916,5917; Fax: 613/235-6425; Telex: 053-4564 AMBATOGO OTT
Ambassador, His Excellency Kossivi Osseyi
First Secretary, Economic and Commercial, Hodgo Biam
    Calgary: Hon. Consul, Garry Tarrant, #700, 1207 - 11 Ave., Calgary AB T3C 0M5, 403/229-0103; Fax: 403/245-5156
    Toronto: Hon. Consul, Paul John Tuz, #403, 1 St. Johns Rd., Toronto ON M6P 4C7, 416/766-5744; Fax: 416/766-1970
    Verdun: Hon. Consul, Gérard Shanks, Verdun Consulate, 484 - 5 Ave., Verdun PQ H4G 2K1, 514/769-4888

Republic of Trinidad & Tobago
High Commission for Trinidad & Tobago: #508, 75 Albert St., Ottawa ON K1P 5E7
613/232-2418; Fax: 613/232-4349; Email: tthcotta@travel-net.com
High Commissioner, Her Excellency Shastri Ali
Deputy High Commissioner, Stephen Kangal
First Secretary, Dennison Webster
    North York: Consul General, Cyril Blanchfield, #303, 2005 Sheppard Ave. East, North York ON M2J 5B4, 416/495-9442; Fax: 416/495-6934

Republic of Tunisia
Embassy of Tunisia: 515 O'Connor St., Ottawa ON K1S 3P8
613/237-0330; Fax: 613/237-7939
Ambassador, His Excellency Khalifa El Hafdhi
    Montréal: Consul, Hachem Ben Achour, #600, 511, Place d'Armes, Montréal PQ H2Y 2W7, 514/289-8633; Fax: 514/288-6469

Republic of Turkey
Embassy of Turkey: 197 Wurtemburg St., Ottawa ON K1N 8L9
613/789-4044; Fax: 613/789-3442
Ambassador, His Excellency Omer Ersun
Counsellor, Hasan Servet Oktem
Counsellor, Economic & Commercial, Erdogan Hurbas
    Montréal: Hon. Consul General, Ali T. Argun, #2500, 1100, boul René-Lévesque ouest, Montréal PQ H3B 5C9, 514/397-6903; Fax: 514/397-5815

Republic of Uganda
High Commission for Uganda: 231 Cobourg St., Ottawa ON K1N 8J2
613/789-7797; Fax: 613/789-8909; Telex: 053-4469
High Commissioner, His Excellency Dr. Tibamanya mwene Mushanga
Counsellor, James H.O. Okullo

Republic of Ukraine
Embassy of Ukraine: 310 Somerset St. West, Ottawa ON K2P 0J9
613/230-2961; Fax: 613/230-2400; Consular Section: 613/230-8015
Ambassador, His Excellency Volodymyz Furkalo
Commissioner, Trade, Igor Sanin

United Arab Emirates
c/o Permanent Mission of the United Arab Emirates to the U.N.: 747 Third Ave., New York NY 10017
212/371-0480; Fax: 212/371-4923
Ambassador, His Excellency Mohammed J. Samhan
First Secretary, Khalid K. Al-Mualla
First Secretary, Yacub Y. Al-Hosani
Third Secretary, Omar S. Ghobash

United Kingdom of Great Britain & Northern Ireland
British High Commission: 80 Elgin St., Ottawa ON K1P 5K7
613/237-1530; Fax: 613/237-7980
High Commissioner, His Excellency Anthony M. Goodenough, K.C.M.G.
Deputy High Commissioner, Linda Duffield
Counsellor, Economic & Commercial, Boyd McCleary
Counsellor, Robert M.F. Kelly
    Dartmouth: Hon. Consul, L. Straughan, 1 Canal St., PO Box 605, Stn M, Dartmouth NS B2Y 3YB, 902/422-0313; Fax: 902/463-7678
    Montréal: Consul General, I. Rawlinson, #4200, 1000, rue De La Gauchetière ouest, Montréal PQ H3B 4W5, 514/866-5863; Fax: 514/866-0202
    St. John's: Hon. Consul, Frank D. Smith, 113 Topsail Rd., St. John's NF A1E 2A9, 709/579-2002; Fax: 709/579-0475
    Toronto: Consul General, Peter D.R. Davies, College Park, #2800, 777 Bay St., Toronto ON M5G 2G2, 416/593-1290; Fax: 416/593-1229
    Vancouver: Consul General, B.P. Austin, #800, 1111 Melville St., Vancouver BC V6E 3V6, 604/683-4421; Fax: 604/681-0693
    Winnipeg: Hon. Consul, R.E.M. Hill, 229 Athlone Dr., Winnipeg MB R3J 3L6, 204/896-1380; Fax: 204/896-3025

United States of America
Embassy of U.S.A.: 100 Wellington St., PO Box 866, Stn B, Ottawa ON K1P 5T1
613/238-5335; Fax: 613/238-8750
Consular Section: 85 Albert St., Ottawa ON K1P 6A4, 613/238-5335
Ambassador, The Hon. James J. Blanchard
Minister, The Hon. James Walsh
Minister-Counsellor, Economic Affairs, Marshall Casse
Minister-Counsellor, Environment, Science & Technological Affairs, Thomas J. Wajda
    Calgary: Consul General, William N. Witting, #1050, 615 Macleod Trail SE, Calgary AB T2G 4T8, 403/266-8962; Fax: 403/264-6630
    Halifax: Consul General, Roger A. Meece, Scotia Square, 910 Cogswell Tower, Halifax NS B3J 3K1, 902/429-2480; Fax: 902/423-6861
    Montréal: Consul General, R. Susan Wood, 455, boul René-Lévesque, CP 65, Stn Desjardins, Montréal PQ H2Z 1Z2, 514/398-9695; Fax: 514/398-0973
    Québec: Consul General, Marie T. Huhtala, 2, Place Terrasse Dufferin, CP 939, Québec PQ G1R 4T9, 418/692-2095; Fax: 418/692-4640; Telex: 051-2275
    Toronto: Consul General, G. Alfred Kennedy, 360 University Ave., Toronto ON M5G 1S4, 416/595-1700; Fax: 416/595-0051
    Vancouver: Consul General, David T. Johnson, 1095 Pender St. West, Vancouver BC V6E 2M6, 604/685-4311; Fax: 604/685-5285

Eastern Republic of Uruguay
Embassy of Uruguay: #1905, 130 Albert St., Ottawa ON K1P 5G4
613/234-2727; Fax: 613/233-4670; Email: urott@iosphere.net; Consular Section: 234-2937
Ambassador, Elbio Rosselli
First Secretary, Eduardo Anon
Second Secretary, Carlos Gitto
    North York: Hon. Consul, Carlos Garcia, #1610, 2 Sheppard Ave. East, North York ON M2N 5Y7, 416/221-7799; Fax: 416/221-7199
    Vancouver: Hon. Consul, Conrado Beckerman, 2331 Granville St., Vancouver BC V6H 3G4, 604/739-0389; Fax: 604/731-6702

Holy See
Apostolic Nunciature: 724 Manor Ave., Rockcliffe Park, Ottawa ON K1M 0E3
613/746-4914; Fax: 613/746-4786
Apolistic Nuncio, His Excellency The Most Rev. Carlo Curis
First Secretary, The Right Rev. Vito Rallo

Republic of Venezuela
Embassy of Venezuela: 32 Range Rd., Ottawa ON K1N 8J4
613/235-5151; Fax: 613/746-2571
Counsellor, Marisol Black
Minister-Counsellor, Beatrice Gerbasi
Ambassador, His Excellency Felix Rossi Guerrero
    Montréal: Consul General, Nelly Pulido de Tagliaferro, #400, 2055, rue Peel, Montréal PQ H3A 1V4, 514/842-3417; Fax: 514/287-7101; Telex: 05-267523
    Toronto: Consul General, Hilda Hernandez, #1904, 365 Bloor St. East, Toronto ON M4W 3L4, 416/960-6070; Fax: 416/960-6077

Socialist Republic of Viet Nam
Embassy of Vietnam: 25B Davidson Dr., Gloucester ON K1J 6L7
613/744-4963 Consular Section 745-9735; Fax: 613/744-1709 Consular Section 744-5072
Ambassador, His Excellency Dang Nghiem Bai
Counsellor, Commercial, Tran Ve

Western Samoa
High Commission for Western Samoa (to Canada): #800D, 820 Second Ave., New York NY 10017
212/599-6196; Fax: 212/599-0797
High Commissioner, His Excellency Tuiloma Neroni Slade

Republic of Yemen
Embassy of Yemen: #1100, 350 Sparks St., Ottawa ON K1R 7S8
613/232-8525; Fax: 613/232-8276
Ambassador, His Excellency Dr. Mohamed Saed Ali
First Secretary, Abdullah Fadhel

Federal Republic of Yugoslavia
Embassy of Yugoslavia: 17 Blackburn Ave., Ottawa ON K1N 8A2
613/233-6289; Fax: 613/233-7850
First Secretary & Chargé d'Affaires, A. Mitic
Ambassador, Vacant
    Montréal: Hon. Consul, Kalman Samuels, 1200, rue du Fort, Montréal PQ H3H 2B3, 514/939-1200

Republic of Zaire
Embassy of Zaire: 18 Range Rd., Ottawa ON K1N 8J3
613/236-7103; Fax: 613/567-1404; Telex: 053-4314
Minister-Counsellor, Kalombo Kabundi Lukusa
Ambassador, His Excellency Kaweta Milombe Sampassa
    Montréal: Hon. Consul General, Luc-Jacques Pirard, Montréal Consulate, #504, 410, rue St-Nicolas, Montréal PQ H2Y 2P5, 514/845-0271

Republic of Zambia
High Commission for Zambia: #1610, 130 Albert St., Ottawa ON K1P 5G4
High Commissioner, His Excellency Joshua S. Siyolwe
First Secretary, I.B.L. Tompwe

Republic of Zimbabwe
High Commission for the Republic of Zimbabwe: 332 Somerset St. West, Ottawa ON K2P 0J9
613/237-4388; Fax: 613/563-8269
High Commissioner, Her Excellency Lillie Chitauro
Counsellor, Commercial, Wilbert C.T.T. Dumba
Counsellor, Erasmus Moyo

CANADIAN DIPLOMATIC REPRESENTATIVES ABROAD

Republic of Albania c/o **Republic of Hungary**

People's Democratic Republic of Algeria
Canadian Embassy: 27 bis, rue des Frères Benhafid, Hydra
(011-213-2) 69-16-11; Fax: (011-213-2) 69-39-20; Email: MITNET: 380-0000; Telex: 266043; (66043 CANAD DZ)
Postal Address: PO Box 225, Alger-Gare, 1600 Alger, Algeria
Ambassador, Jacques Noiseux
Counsellor, Commercial, W.A. McKenzie
Commercial Officer, Zahra Bensalah, Email: zahra.bensalah@paris03.x400.gc.ca

Principality of Andorra c/o **Kingdom of Spain**

People's Republic of Angola c/o **Republic of Zimbabwe**
Luanda: Hon. Consul, Allan Cain, Honourary Consulate of Canada, Rua Rei Katyavala #113, Luanda, Angola, (011-244-2) 330-243; Fax: (011-244-2) 343-754 (2100-0800hrs Angola time); Telex: 0991-4072/-4073/-4081 (CIAM AN)

Anguilla c/o **Barbados**

Antigua & Barbuda c/o **Barbados**

Argentine Republic
Canadian Embassy: Tagle 2828, 1425, Buenos Aires
(011-54-1) 805-3032; Fax: (011-54-1) 806-209; Email: MITNET: 381-0000
Postal Address: Casilla de Correo 1598, Buenos Aires, Argentina
Ambassador, Robert G. Clark
First Secretary, Commercial & Economic, S. Harper
Ambassador, Uruguay, Roland Goulet
Commercial Officer, Elena Masciarelli, Email: elena.masciarelli@bairs01.x400.gc.ca

Republic of Armenia c/o **Russian Federation**

Aruba c/o **Republic of Venezuela**

Commonwealth of Australia
Canadian High Commission: Commonwealth Ave., Canberra ACT 2600
(011-61-6) 273-3844; Fax: (011-61-2) 273-3285; Email: MITNET: 342-0000
High Commissioner, Brian Schumacher
Deputy High Commissioner, G.J. Wilson
Counsellor, Commercial, J.F. Donaghy
Commercial Officer, Robert G. Gow, Email: Bob.Gow@sydny01.x400.gc.ca
Perth: Hon. Consul, R.B. Blake, Honorary Consulate of Canada, 267 St. George's Terrace, 3rd Fl., Perth WA 6000, Australia, (011-61-09) 322-7930
South Melbourne: Hon. Consul, T. Moore, Honorary Consulate of Canada, DMR Bldg., Level 8, 1 Southbank Blvd., South Melbourne VIC 3205, Australia, (011-61-03) 645-8643; Fax: (011-61-03) 645-8647
Sydney: Consul General, Alan Virtue, Canadian Consulate General, Quay West Bldg, Level 5, 111 Harrington St., Sydney NSW 2000, Australia, (011-61-2) 364-3000; Fax: (011-61-2) 364-3098; Cable: CANADIAN SYDNEY; MITNET: 351-0000

Republic of Austria
Canadian Embassy: Laurenzerber 2, A-1010, Vienna
(011-43-1) 531-38-3000; Fax: (011-43-1) 531-38-3321; Email: MITNET: 459-3321; Cable: DOMCAN VIENNA
Ambassador, Peter F. Walker
Counsellor, Commercial, T. Marr
Minister-Counsellor, P. McKellar
Commercial Officer, Roland J. Rossi, Email: roland.rossi@vienn02.x400.gc.ca

Republic of Azerbaijan c/o **Republic of Turkey**

Azores c/o **Portuguese Republic**

Commonwealth of the Bahamas c/o **Jamaica**
Nassau: Hon. Consul, H.A. Jacobsen, Honorary Consulate of Canada, Shirley Street Plaza, PO Box SS-6371, Nassau, Bahamas, 809/393-2123; Fax: 809/393-1305; Telex: 20246 (BEAVER BAH)

State of Bahrain c/o **State of Kuwait**

People's Republic of Bangladesh
Canadian High Commission: House CWN 16/A, Rd. 48, Gulshan Ave., Dhaka
(011-880-2) 88-36-39; Fax: (011-88-2) 88-30-43; Email: MITNET: 319-0000; Cable: DOMCAN DHAKA
Postal Address: GPO Box 569, Dhaka, Bangladesh
High Commissioner, Nicholas Etheridge
Counsellor, Development, J. Deyell
Senior Commercial Officer, Syed Shamimur Rahman, Email: syed.rahman@dhaka01.x400.gc.ca

Barbados
Canadian High Commission: Bishop's Court Hill, St. Michael
809/429-3550; Fax: 809/437-8474; Email: MITNET: 318-0000; Telex: 2247 (2247 CANADA WB); Cable: DOMCAN BRIDGETOWN
Postal Address: PO Box 404, Bridgetown, Barbados
High Commissioner, Colleen Swords
Counsellor, K. Harley
Counsellor, Commercial, P. Hermant
Counsellor, Development, N. Norcott
Trade Commissioner, Peter Hermant

Republic of Belarus c/o **Russian Federation**

Kingdom of Belgium
Canadian Embassy: 2, av de Tervuren, 1040, Brussels
(011-32-2) 741-0606; Fax: (011-32-2) 741-0613; Email: MITNET: 448-3211; Cable: DOMCAN BRUSSELS
Ambassador, Jean-Paul Hubert
Minister/Counsellor, G. Béchard
Counsellor, Commercial/Economic, S. Doyon
Commercial Officer, Bart Roefmans

Belize c/o **Jamaica**
Belize City: Lester Young, Hon. Consul, Honorary Consulate of Canada, 85 North Front St., PO Box 610, Belize City, Belize, (011-501-02) 33-722; Fax: (011-501-02) 30-060

Republic of Benin c/o **Federal Republic of Nigeria**

Bermuda c/o **United States of America**

Republic of Bolivia c/o **Republic of Peru**
La Paz: Hon. Consul, Hector Arduz, Honorary Consulate of Canada, Av 20 de octubre 2475, Plaza Avaroa, Sopocachi, PO Box 13045, La Paz, Bolivia, (011-591-2) 37-52-24; Fax: (011-591-2) 43-23-30

Republic of Botswana c/o **Republic of Zimbabwe**
Gaborone: Hon. Consul, D. Leonard, Honorary Consulate of Canada, PO Box 1009, Gaborone, Botswana, (011-267) 371-659

Federative Republic of Brazil
Canadian Embassy: Setor de Embaixadas Sul, #803, Ava das Naçcoes, lote 16, 70410-900, Brasilia, D.F.
(011-55-61) 321-2171; Fax: (011-55-61) 321-4529; Email: MITNET: 384-0000
Postal Address: Caixa Postal 00961, 70359-900 Brasilia D.F., Brazil
Ambassador, Nancy M. Stiles
Counsellor & Consul, B. Wilkin
Counsellor, Commercial/Economic, P. Williams
Commercial Officer (Sao Paulo), Mariangela Olivieri de Lima, Email: td.spalo@spalo01.x400.gc.ca
Rio de Janeiro: Hon. Consul, Jack Delmar, Honourary Consulate of Canada, Rua Lauro Muller 166, #2707, Torre Rio Sul, Botafogo, 22290-160, Rio de Janeiro, Brazil, (011-55-21) 542-7593; Fax: (011-55-21) 275-2195
Sao Paulo: Consul General, Michael C. Spencer, Canadian Consulate General, Edificio Top Centre, Ava Paulista 854, 5th Fl., 01310-913, Sao Paulo, Brazil, (011-55-11) 287-2122; Fax: (011-55-11) 251-5057; MITNET: 376-0000

British Virgin Islands c/o **Barbados**

Brunei
Canadian High Commission: #219, Sheraton Utama Hotel, Jalan Tasek, Bandar Seri Begawn
(011-673-2) 22-00-43; Fax: (011-673-2) 22-00-40
Postal Address: PO Box 2808, Bandar Seri Begawan 1928, Brunei
High Commissioner, Richard Belliveau
Counsellor, Development, M. Archambault
Counsellor, Development, T. Broughton

Republic of Bulgaria c/o **Republic of Romania**

Burkina-Faso
Canadian Embassy: Agostino Neto St., PO Box 548, Ouagaougou
(011-226) 31-18-94; Fax: (011-226) 31-19-00; Telex: 5264 (DOMCAN BF)
Postal Address: PO Box 548, Ouagadougou 01, Kadiogo, Burkina-Faso
Ambassador, Louise Ouimet
First Secretary, Development, S. Ostiguy

Republic of Burundi c/o **Republic of Kenya**
Bujumbura: Hon Consul, J.M.A. Persoons, Honorary Consulate of Canada, boul du 28 novembre, CP 5, Bujumbura, Burundi, (011-257) 22-16-32; Fax: (011-257) 22-28-16

Canadian Almanac & Directory 1997

Kingdom of Cambodia
Canadian Embassy: Villa II, St. 254, Chartaumuk Ward, District Daun Penh, Phnom Penh
(011-855-23) 426-000; Fax: (011-855-23) 362-429
Ambassador, Gordon Longmuir

Republic of Cameroon
Canadian Embassy: Immeuble Stamatiades, Place de l'Hôtel de Ville, Yaoundé
(011-237) 22-19-36; Fax: (011-237) 22-10-90;
Email: MITNET: 317-0000; Cable: DOMCAN YAOUNDÉ
Postal Address: PO Box 572, Yaoundé, Cameroon
Ambassador, Pierre Giguère
Counsellor, Development, P. Marion

Republic of Cape Verde c/o Republic of Senegal

Cayman Islands c/o Jamaica

Central African Republic c/o Republic of Cameroon
Quartier Sissongo Bangui: Hon. Consul, Lyne Godmaire, Honorary Consulate of Canada, PO Box 973, Quartier Sissongo Bangui, Central African Republic

Republic of Chad c/o Republic of Cameroon

Republic of Chile
Canadian Embassy: Ahumada 11, 10th Fl., Santiago
(011-56-2) 696-2256; Fax: (011-56-2) 696-2424;
Email: stago.td@stago01.x400.gc.ca; MITNET: 386-0000; Telex: 240341 (DOMCAN CL); Cable: DOMCAN SANTIAGO DE CHILE
Postal Address: Casilla 427, Santiago, Chile
Ambassador, Marc Lortie
Counsellor, Commercial, P. Furesz
Commercial Officer, Margot Edwards
Conception: Honorary Consulate of Canada, a/s ABN AMRO Bank, PO Box 425, Conception, Chile, Fax: (011-56-2) 696-0738

People's Republic of China
Canadian Embassy: 19 Dong Zhi Men Wai St., Chao Yang District, Beijing 100600
(011-86-10) 532-3536; Fax: (011-86-10) 532-4072;
Email: td.bejing@bejing03.x400.gc.ca; MITNET: 341-0000; Cable: DOMCAN PEKING
Ambassador, Howard Balloch
Minister, Commercial, K. Sunquist
Minister-Counsellor & Consul, G. Saint-Jacques
Third Secretary (Commercial), David Murphy, Email: david.murphy@bejing03.x400.gc.ca
Commercial Officer/Interpreter, Q. Chen, Email: qi.chen@bejing03.x400.gc.ca
Guangzhou: Consul, M.C. Boyd, Consulate of Canada, China Hotel Office Tower, #1563-4, Liu Hua Lu, Guangzhou 510015, P.R. China, (011-86-20) 666-0569; Fax: (011-86-20) 667-2401
Shanghai: Consul General, Ted Lipman, Canadian Consulate General, American International Centre, Shanghai Centre, West Tower, #604, 1376 Nanjing Xi Lu, Shanghai 200040, P.R. China, (011-86-21) 6279-8400; Fax: (011-1-86-21) 6279-8401; Telex: 33608 (33608 CANAD CN)

Republic of Colombia
Canadian Embassy: Calle 76, No. 11-52, Bogota
(011-57-1) 313-1355; Fax: (011-57-1) 316-3046; Cable: CANADIAN BOGOTA
Postal Address: Apartado Aéreo 53531, Bogotá 2, Colombia
Ambassador, C. William Ross
Counsellor, Commercial, Z.W. Burianyk
Counsellor & Consul, D. Gillett

Commercial Officer, Carlos E. Rivera, Email: carlos.rivera@bgota01.x400.gc.ca

Islamic Federal Republic of the Comoros c/o United Republic of Tanzania

People's Republic of the Congo c/o Republic of Zaire

Republic of Costa Rica
Canadian Embassy: Apartado Postal 351-1007, San José
(011-506) 296-4149; Fax: (011-506) 296-4270;
Email: MITNET: 388-0000
Ambassador, Dan Goodleaf
Counsellor & Consul, G. Lapointe
Firest Secretary & Consul, Commercial, M. Lebleu
Commercial Officer, Adolfo Quesada V., Email: adolfo.quesada@sjose01.x400.gc.ca

Republic of Croatia
Canadian Embassy, Hotel Esplanade: Mihanoviceva 1, 10000, Zagreb
(011-385-1) 457-7885; Fax: (011-385-1) 457-7913
Ambassador, Graham N. Green
Counsellor & Consul, Commercial, R. Lecoq

Republic of Cuba
Canadian Embassy: Calle 30, No. 518, Esquina a 7a, Miramar, Havana
(011-53-7) 33-25-16; Fax: (011-53-7) 33-20-44;
Email: MITNET: 389-0000; Telex: 51-1586 (51-1586 CANCU); Cable: DOMCAN HAVANA
Ambassador, Mark Entwistle
Counsellor & Consul, Commercial, R. Mailhot
Varadero: Hon. Consul, Y. des Hayes, Honorary Consulate of Canada, Granma Hotel, Bloque 18, apt. 210, Varadero, Cuba, (011-56) 64-177; Fax: (011-56) 33-7149

Republic of Cyprus c/o State of Israel
Nicosia: Hon. Consul, M. G. Ioannides, Honorary Consulate of Canada, Margarita House, #403, 15 Thermistocles Dervis St., Nicosia, Cyprus, (011-357-2) 45-16-30; Fax: (011-357-2) 45-90-96; Telex: 2110 (MARCO CY)
Postal Address: PO Box 2125, Nicosia, Cyprus

Czech Republic
Canadian Embassy: Mickiewiczova 6, 125 33, Prague 6
(011-42-2) 2431-1108; Fax: (011-42-2) 2431-0294;
Email: MITNET: 395-0000; Telex: 121061 (911308 DMCN CH); Cable: DOMCAN PRAGUE
Ambassador, Alain Dudoit
Counsellor & Consul, Y. Jobin
Counsellor, Commercial, R. Bélanger
Commercial Officer, Pavel Szappanos, Email: pavel.szappanos@prgue01.x400.gc.ca

Kingdom of Denmark
Canadian Embassy: Kr. Bernikowsgade 1, 1105, Copenhagen K
(011-45-33) 12-22-99; Fax: (011-45-33) 12-42-10;
Email: copen.td@copen.01x400.gc.ca; MITNET: 460-0000
Ambassador, Brian Baker
R.C.D., Looye, Counsellor & Consul
Counsellor, Commercial, G. Cadieux
Commercial Officer, David Horup

Republic of Djibouti c/o Democratic Republic of Ethiopia
Djibouti: Hon. Consul, R. Arsenault, Honorary Consulate of Canada, c/o SNC-Lavalin, House No. 233, Kampala St., PO Box 914, Djibouti, Djibouti, (011-253) 35-11-59; Fax: (011- 253) 35-44-23

Commonwealth of Dominica c/o Barbados

Dominican Republic
Canadian Embassy: Maximo Gomez 30, Santo Domingo
809/689-0002; Fax: 809/682-2691; Telex: 3460270
Postal Address: PO Box 2054, Santo Domingo 1, Dominican Republic
Ambassador (resident in Caracas, Venezuela), Yves Gagnon
Counsellor & Consul, Commercial (Caracas, Venezuela), P. Giroux
First Secretary & Consul, Commercial (Caracas, Venezuela), G. Lemieux
Puerto Plata: Hon. Consul, T. Hall, Honorary Consulate of Canada, #3, Beller 51, Puerto Plata, Dominican Republic, 809/586-5761; Fax: 809/586-5762; Telex: 3462022

Republic of Ecuador
Edificio Josueth Gonzalez, 4th Fl.: Ava. 6 de Diciembre, 2816, Quito
(011-593-2) 564-795; Fax: (011-593-2) 503-108
Postal Address: PO Box 17-11-6512, Quito, Ecuador
Ambassador, David Adam
Third Secretary & Consul, Administration, M. Felisiak
Guayaquil: Hon. Consul, F. Costa, Honorary Consulate of Canada, Edificio Torres de la Merced, Piso 21, General Cordova 800 y Victor Manuel Rendon, Guayaquil, Ecuador, (011-593-4) 566-747; Fax: (011-593-4) 314-562; Telex: 42513

Arab Republic of Egypt
Canadian Embassy: 5 Midan El Saraya el Kobra St., Garden City, Cairo
(011-20-2) 354-3110; Fax: (011-20-2) 354-7659;
Email: MITNET: 392-0000
Postal Address: PO Box 1667, Cairo, Egypt
Ambassador, Michael D. Bell
Counsellor & Consul, Commercial/Economic, D. Paterson
Counsellor, Development, J. Sinclair
Commercial Officer, Hany W. Ibrahim, Email: hany.h.w.i.ibrahim@cairo01.x400.gc.ca
Alexandria: Hon. Consul, A.M.M. Khairy, Honorary Consulate of Canada, Arab Express Shipping Co., 59 El Horria St., Alexandria, Egypt, (011-50-2) 203-493-9142; Fax: (011-50-2) 203-490-9695

Republic of El Salvador
Canadian Embassy: Ava Las Palmas no. 111, Colonia San Benito, San Salvador
(011-503-2) 794-655; Fax: (011-503-2) 790-765
Postal Address: Apartado Postal 3078, Centro de Gobierno, San Salvador, El Salvador
Ambassador (located in Guatamala City), James Fox
Hon. Consul, J.D. Hunter
Counsellor, Development (located in Guatamala City), E.W.E. Doe
Counsellor, Development (located in Tegulcigalpa, Honduras), J. Touzel
San Salvador: Hon. Consul, James D. Hunter, Canadian Consulate, 111 Av. Las Palmas, Colonia San Benito, San Salvador, El Salvador, (011-503) 241-648; Fax: (011-503) 790-765
Postal Address: Apartado Postal 3078, Centro de Gobierno, San Salvador

England c/o United Kingdom of Great Britain & Northern Ireland

Republic of Equatorial Guinea c/o Gabonese Republic

Eritrea c/o Democratic Republic of Ethiopia

Republic of Estonia
Canadian Embassy: Toom Kooli 13, 2nd Fl., 0100, Tallinn

(011-372) 631-3570; Fax: (011-372) 631-3573
Ambassador (located in Stockholm, Sweden), William L. Clarke
Minister-Counsellor (located in Riga, Latvia), G.R. Skinner
First Secretary, Commercial (located in Latvia), H.J. Kunzer

Democratic Republic of Ethiopia
Canadian Embassy: Old Airport Area, Higher 23, Kebele 12, #122, Addis Ababa
(011-251-1) 71-30-22; Fax: (011-251-1) 71-30-33; Telex: 21053 (DOMCAN ET); Cable: DOMCAN ADDIS
 Postal Address: PO Box 1130, Addis Ababa, Ethiopia
Ambassador, Gabriel M. Lessard
Counsellor & Consul, Development, P. Hitschfeld
First Secretary & Consul, T. Martin

European Union
The Mission of Canada to the European Union: av de Tervuren 2, 1040, Brussels
(011-32-2) 741-0660; Fax: (011-32-2) 741-0629;
 Email: MITNET: 448-3274
Head of Mission, Ambassador, Jacques Roy
Deputy Head of Mission & Minister-Counsellor, R. Hage
Counsellor, Economic Affairs, R. Stewart
Counsellor, Science & Technology, W. Coderre
Counsellor, Trade Policy, S. Brereton

Falkland Islands c/o Argentine Republic

Faroe Islands c/o Kingdom of Denmark

Fiji c/o New Zealand
Suva: Hon. Consul, Michael T. Brook, Honorary Consulate of Canada, L.I.C.I. Bldg., 7th Fl., Butt St., Suva, Fiji, (011-679) 30-05-89; Fax: (011-679) 30-02-96
 Postal Address: PO Box 2193, Govt. Bldg., Suva, Fiji

Republic of Finland
Canadian Embassy: P. Esplanadi 25B, 00100, Helsinki
(011-358-0) 17-11-41; Fax: (011-358-0) 60-10-60;
 Email: MITNET: 443-0000
 Postal Address: PO Box 779, 00101 Helsinki, Finland
Ambassador, Isabelle Massip
Counsellor & Consul, Commercial, Leopold Battel
Commercial Officer, Risto Pakarinen

French Republic
Canadian Embassy: 35, av Montaigne, 75008, Paris
(011-33-1) 44-43-29-00; Fax: (011-33-1) 44-43-29-99;
 Email: MITNET: 447-2900; Telex: 651806 (CANADA 280806F/CANADB 280806F); Cable: STADACONA PARIS
Ambassador, Jacques Roy
Minister, Noble, J.J. Noble
Minister-Counsellor, Commercial & Economic, B. Côté
Commercial Officer, Linda Bernard
 La Wantzenau: Hon. Consul, Jean-Jacques Hetzel, Honorary Consulate of Canada, Polysar France, rue de Ried, La Wantzenau, France, (011-33) 88-96-65-02; Fax: (011-33) 88-96-64-54
  Postal Address: CP 7, 67610 La Wantzenau, France
 Lyon: Consul, Anne-Marie Viarouge-Sagala, Consulate of Canada, Bonnel Bldg., Part-Dieu, 74, rue de Bonnel, 3e étage, 69003, Lyon, France, (011-33-4) 72-61-15-25; Fax: (011-33-4) 78-62-09-36
 Nice: Hon. Consul, M. Felizzola, Honorary Consulate of Canada, c/o Agence de Voyages French Med'Tours, 64, av Jean Médecin, 06000, Nice, France, (011-33-4) 88-96-65-02; Fax: (011-33-4) 88-96-64-54
 St. Pierre: Hon. Consul, F. Park, Honorary Consulate of Canada, Institut Frecher, CP 903, St. Pierre, St. Pierre et Miquelon, F-97500, (508) 41-55-10; Fax: (508) 41-55-01
 Toulouse: Hon. Consul, Jacques Guibert, Honorary Consulate of Canada, 30, boul de Strasbourg, 31014, Toulouse, France, (011-33-5) 61-99-30-16; Fax: (011-33-5) 61-63-43-37
  Postal Address: CP 138, Toulouse, France

French Polynesia c/o French Republic

Gabonese Republic
Canadian Embassy, PO Box 4037, Libreville
(011-241) 74-34-64; Fax: (011-241) 74-34-66;
 Email: MITNET: 326-0000; Telex: 5527 GO (DOMCAN 5527 GO)
Ambassador, Louise Charron Fortin
Attaché & Consul, Administration, Y. Levesque

Republic of the Gambia c/o Republic of Senegal

Republic of Georgia c/o Republic of Turkey

Federal Republic of Germany
Canadian Embassy: Friedrich-Wilhelm-Strasse 18, 53113, Bonn
(011-49-228) 968-0; Fax: (011-49-228) 968-3904;
 Email: MITNET: 449-0000; Telex: 886421 (886421 DOMCA D); Cable: DOMCAN BONN
Ambassador, Gaétan Lavertu
Minister, L. Friedlaender
Minister-Counsellor, Commercial, Ed Mallory
Technology Development Officer, Jutta Zillgen-Schaefer
 Berlin: Minister, Adriaan de Hoog, Canadian Embassy Office, Friedrich-Strasse 95, 10117, Berlin, Germany, (011-49-30) 261-1161; Fax: (011-49-30) 262-9206; Telex: 305099 (305099 CANAD D)
 Düsseldorf: Consul, R.M. Bollman, Canadian Consulate, Prinz-Georg-Strasse 126, 40479, Düsseldorf, Germany, (011-49-211) 17-21-70; Fax: (011-49-211) 35-91-65
 Hamburg: Consul & Senior Trade Commissioner, D. Baker, Canadian Consulate, Canadian Consulate, ABC Strasse, 45, 20534, Hamburg, Germany, (011-49-40) 355-56290; Fax: (011-49-40) 355-66294
 Munich: Consul & Senior Trade Commissioner, J. Lang, Canadian Consulate, Tal 29, 80331, Munich, Germany, (011-49-89) 29-06-50; Fax: (011-49-89) 228-065-199

Republic of Ghana
Canadian High Commission: 42 Independence Ave., Accra
(011-233-21) 77-37-91; Fax: (011-233-21) 77-37-92;
 Email: MITNET: 313-0000
 Postal Address: PO Box 1639, Accra, Ghana
High Commissioner, John Schram
First Secretary, W. Gusen
First Secretary, Development, A. Lavender
First Secretary, Development, C. Thiruchittampalamj

Gibraltar c/o United Kingdom of Great Britain & Northern Ireland

Hellenic Republic
Canadian Embassy: 4 Ioannou Gennadiou St., Athens
(011-30-1) 725-4011; Fax: (011-30-1) 725-3994;
 Email: MITNET: 451-0000; Cable: DOMCAN ATHENS
Ambassador, Derek Fraser
Counsellor, Commercial, D. Cohen
Commercial Officer, Marianna Saropoulous

Greenland c/o Kingdom of Denmark
Nuuk: Hon. Consul, Lars Peter Danielsen, Canadian Honorary Consulate, Groenlandsfly A/S, 3900, Nuuk, Greenland, (011-299) 28888; Fax: (011-299) 27288; Telex: 90602
 Postal Address: PO Box 1012, 3900 Nuuk, Greenland

Grenada c/o Barbados

Saint Vincent & the Grenadines c/o Barbados

Guadeloupe c/o Barbados

Guam c/o Japan

Republic of Guatemala
Canadian Embassy: 13 calle 8-44, Zone 10, Edyma Plaza, Guatemala City
(011-52-2) 33-61-04; Fax: (011-52-2) 33-61-61;
 Email: MITNET: 312-0000; Telex: 5206 (5206 CANADA GU); Cable: CANADIAN GUATEMALA CITY
 Postal Address: PO Box 400 Guatemala City, Guatemala
Ambassador, Daniel Livermore
Counsellor & Consul, Commercial, R. Shaw-Wood
Counsellor & Consul, Development, E.W.E. Doe
Commercial Assistant, Margo Dannemiller, Email: margo.dannemiller@gtmla01.x400.gc.ca

Republic of Guinea
Canadian Embassy, PO Box 99, Conakry
(011-224) 41-23-95; Fax: (011-224) 41-42-36;
 Email: MITNET: 311-3000; Telex: 2170 (2170 DOMCAN GE)
Ambassador, Denis Briand
Counsellor & Consul, Development, J.-C. Mailhot

Republic of Guinea-Bissau c/o Republic of Senegal

Co-operative Republic of Guyana
Canadian High Commission: High & Young Sts., Georgetown
(011-592-2) 72081; Fax: (011-592-2) 58380;
 Email: MITNET: 398-0000; Cable: DOMCAN GEORGETOWN
 Postal Address: PO Box 10880, Georgetown, Guyana
High Commissioner, Alan Bowker
First Secretary, Development, S. Greaves
First Secretary, Development, D.J. Ross

Republic of Haiti
Canadian Embassy, Édifice Banque de Nova Scotia: rte de Delmas, Port-au-Prince
(011-509) 23-2358; Fax: (011-509) 23-8720;
 Email: MITNET: 310-0000; Telex: (203) 20069 (20069 DOMCAN HN); Cable: DOMCAN PORT-AU-PRINCE
 Postal Address: CP 826, Port-au-Prince, Haiti
Ambassador, J. Christopher Poole
Counsellor & Consul, L.-R. Daigle
Counsellor, Development, M. Apollon
Counsellor, Development, S. Fortin

Republic of Honduras
Canadian Embassy, Edificio Comercial Los Castatnos: 60 piso, Blvd. Morazán, Tegucigalpa
(011-504) 31-45-35; Fax: (011-504) 31-57-93; Telex: 1683 (DOMCA H0)
 Postal Address: Apartado Postal 3552, Tegucigalpa, Honduras
Ambassador (located in San José, Costa Rica), Dan Goodleaf
Counsellor & Consul (located in Costa Rica), G. Lapointe

Counsellor, Development (located in Costa Rica), J. Touzel

Hong Kong
Commission for Canada, Tower 1, Exchange Square: 8 Connaught Place, 11th Fl., Hong Kong
(011-852) 2810-4321; Fax: (011-852) 2810-6736; Email: td.hkong@hkong02.x400.gc.ca; Cable: DOMCAN HONG KONG
 Postal Address: GPO Box 11142, Hong Kong, Hong Kong
Commissioner, Garrett C.M. Lambert
Counsellor, Commercial, S. Mullin
First Secretary (Commercial), Martin Charron, Email: martin.charron@hkong.02.400.gc.ca
Commercial Officer, Zita Yau

Republic of Hungary
Canadian Embassy: Budakeszi ut. 32, 1121, Budapest
(011-36-1) 275-1200; Fax: (011-36-1) 275-1210; Email: MITNET: 393-0000
Ambassador, Susan M.W. Cartwright
Counsellor, S. Marcoux
Counsellor & Consul, Commercial, R. Lecoq
Commercial Officer, Ilona Csete-Horvath, Email: ilona.csete-horvath@bpestanx01.400.gc.ca

Republic of Iceland c/o Kingdom of Norway
Reykjavik: Hon. Consul General, J.H. Bergs, Honorary Consulate General of Canada, Suourlandsbraut 10, 108, Reykjavik, Iceland, (011-354-5) 680-820; Fax: (011-354-5) 680-899; Telex: 94014879 (CAND G)
 Postal Address: PO Box 8094, 128 Reykjavik, Iceland

Republic of India
Canadian High Commission: 7/8 Shantipath, Chanakyapuri, New Delhi 110021
(011-91-11) 687-6500; Fax: (011-91-11) 687-6579; Email: MITNET: 355-0000; Cable: DOM-CANADA NEW DELHI
 Postal Address: PO Box 5207, New Delhi, India
High Commissioner, Stanley Gooch
Deputy High Commissioner, D. Waterfall
Counsellor, Commercial, D. Summers
Counsellor, Development, S. Gibbons
Commercial Officer, Viney Gupta, Email: viney.gupta@delhi01.x400.gc.ca
 Bangalore: Canadian Trade Office, 103 Prestige Meridien 1, 29 M.G. Rd., Bangalore, India, (011-91-80) 559-9418; Fax: (011-91-80) 559-9424
 Bombay: Consul & Trade Commissioner, D.C Dix, Canadian Consulate, 41/42 Maker Chambers VI, 6 Jamnalal Bajaj Marg, Nariman Point, Bombay, 400 021, India, (011-91-22) 287-6027; Fax: (011-91-22) 287-5514; Telex: 011-85122 (COC IN)
 Madras: Hon. Consul, V. Srinivasan, Honorary Consulate of Canada, c/o W.S. Industries Limited, Karumuttu Centre, 498 Anna Salai, 2nd Fl., Nandanam, Madras 600 035, India, 434-9295; Fax: 434-0847

Republic of Indonesia
Canadian Embassy: Wisma Metropolitan, Jalan Jendral Sudirman, 5th Fl., Jakarta 12084
(011-62-21) 525-0709; Fax: (011-62-21) 571-2251; Email: MITNET: 344-0000
 Postal Address: PO Box 8324/JKS.MP, Jakarta 12084, Indonesia
Ambassador, Gary Smith
Counsellor & Consul, A. McNiven
Counsellor, Development, R. Woodhouse
Counsellor & Consul, Commercial, G. Rishchynski
Commercial Officer, Husni Djaelani, Email: djaelani.husni@jkrta02.x400.gc.ca

Canadian Almanac & Directory 1997

 Surabaya: A. Markus, Hon. Consul, Honorary Consulate of Canada, c/o P.T. Maspion, Head Office, JL. Kembang Jepun, No. 38-40, Surabaya, Indonesia, 031-330333; Fax: 031-333055

Islamic Republic of Iran
Canadian Embassy: 57 Shahid Sarafraz, Ostad-Motahari Ave., 15868, Tehran
(011-98-21) 873-2623; Fax: (011-98-21) 873-3202; Email: MITNET: 330-3920
 Postal Address: PO Box 11365-4647, Tehran, Iran
Ambassador, Michel de Salaberry
Counsellor & Consul, G. Jacoby
Counsellor, Commercial, G. Rassman
Third Secretary (Commercial), Emmanuel Kamarianakis, Email: emmanuel.kamarianakis@teran01.x400.gc.ca

Republic of Iraq c/o Hashemite Kingdom of Jordan

Republic of Ireland
Canadian Embassy: 65 St. Stephen's Green, Dublin 2
(011-353-1) 478-1988; Fax: (011-353-1) 478-1285; Email: MITNET: 441-0000; Cable: DOMCAN DUBLIN
Ambassador, Michael B. Phillips
Counsellor, Commercial, K. Dewolf
Commercial Officer, John Sullivan

State of Israel
Canadian Embassy: 220 Rehov Hayarkon, Tel Aviv 63405
(011-972-3) 527-2929; Fax: (011-972-3) 527-2333; Email: MITNET: 399-0000
 Postal Address: PO Box 6410, Tel Aviv 63405, Israel
Ambassador, David Berger
Counsellor & Consul, D. Viveash
High Commissioner, Cyprus, David Berger
Counsellor, Commercial, R. Zeisler
Canadian Forces Attaché, Col. T.S.M. Humphries
Commercial Officer, Atalia Kahan, Email: atalia.kahan@taviv.01.x400.gc.ca

Italian Republic
Canadian Embassy: Via G.B. de Rossi 27, 00161, Rome
(011-39-6) 44598-1; Fax: (011-39-6) 44598-750; Email: rome@rome01.x400.gc.ca; MITNET: 455-0000; Cable: DOMCAN ROME
Ambassador, Jeremy Kinsman
Minister-Counsellor, R.F. Andrigo
Minister-Counsellor, Economic/Commercial, N. Kalisch
Counsellor, Development, G. Saint Cyr
Commercial Officer, Alex L. Jones, Email: alex.jones@rome01.x400.gc.ca
 Milan: Consul General, Ian McLean, Canadian Consulate General, Via Vittor Pisani 19, 20124, Milan, Italy, (011-39-2) 6758-1; Fax: (011-39-2) 6758-3900; URL: http://www.Agora.stm.it/canaca/homepage.htm; Email: milan@milan01x400.gc.ca

Republic of the Ivory Coast
Canadian Embassy, Immeuble Trade Centre: 23, av Noguès, Le Plateau, Abidjan
(011-225) 21-20-09; Fax: (011-225) 22-05-30; Email: MITNET: 325-0000; Telex: 23593 (DOMCAN CI); Cable: DOMCAN CI
 Postal Address: PO Box 4104, Abidjan 01, Côte d'Ivoire.
Ambassador, Suzanne Laporte
Counsellor & Consul, G. Paquet
First Secretary, Commercial, P. Veilleux
Commercial Officer, Ousmane Somali

Jamaica
Canadian High Commission, Mutual Security Bank Bldg.: 30-36 Knutsford Blvd., Kingston 5
809/926-1500; Fax: 809/926-1702; Email: MITNET: 333-0000; Telex: 2130 (2130 BEAVER JA); Cable: BEAVER KINGSTONJA
 Postal Address: PO Box 1500, Kingston 10, Jamaica
High Commissioner, Gavin Stewert
Counsellor, Commercial, P. Molson
 Montego Bay: Hon. Consul, L. Crichton, Consulate of Canada, 29 Gloucester Ave., Montego Bay, Jamaica, 809/952-6198; Fax: 809/952-3953

Japan
Canadian Embassy: 3-38 Akasaka 7-chome, Minato-ku, Tokyo 107
(011-81-3) 3408-2101; Fax: (011-81-3) 3479-5320; Telex: (72) 22218 (DOMCAN J22218); Cable: CANADIAN TOKYO
Trade & Investment Section, (011-81-3) 3470-7280
Ambassador, Donald W. Campbell
Minister, Economic/Commercial, J. Tennant
Counsellor, Commercial, R. Brocklebank
Commercial Officer, Yoshio Tamai, Email: yoshio.tamai@tokyo04.x400.gc.ca
 Fukuoka: Consul & Trade Commissioner, B. Préfontaine, Consulate of Canada, FT Bldg., 9F, 4-8-28 Watanabe-Dori, Chuo-Ku, Fukuoka, Japan 810, (011-81-92) 752-6055; Fax: (011-81-92) 752-6077
 Nagoya: Consul & Trade Commissioner, Robert Mason, Consulate of Canada, Nakato Marunouchi Bldg., 6F, 3-7-16 Marunouchi, Naka-Ku, Nagoya, Japan, (011-81-52) 972-0450; Fax: (011-81-52) 972-0453
 Osaka 542: Consul General, Peter Campbell, Consulate General of Canada, Daisan Shoho Bldg., 12th Fl., 2-2-3, Nishi-Shinsaibashi, Chuo-ku, Osaka 542, Japan, (011-81-6) 212-4910; Fax: (011-81-6) 212-4914
 Postal Address: PO Box 150, Osaka Minami 542-91, Japan

Hashemite Kingdom of Jordan
Canadian Embassy, Pearl of Shmeisani Bldg., Amman
(011-962-6) 66-61-24; Fax: (011-962-6) 68-92-27; Email: MITNET: 391-0000
 Postal Address: PO Box 815403, Amman 11180, Jordan
Ambassador, Michel de Salaberry
Counsellor & Consul, Political, P.A. Bakewell
First Secretary, Development, D. Joly
Commercial Officer, Hala Helou

Republic of Kazakhstan
Canadian Embassy: 34 Vinagradova St., Almaty
(011-7-327) 250-11-51; Fax: (011-7-327) 581-14-93
Ambassador, Richard Mann
Minister-Counsellor, Commercial (located in Russia), M.L. Morin
Counsellor, Commercial (located in Russia), G. Jones

Republic of Kenya
Canadian High Commission, Comcraft House: Hailé Sélassie Ave., Nairobi
(011-254-2) 21-48-04; Fax: (011-254-2) 22-69-87; Email: MITNET: 331-3400; Telex: 22198 (22198 DOMCAN); Cable: DOMCAN NAIROBI
 Postal Address: PO Box 30481, Nairobi, Kenya
High Commissioner, Bernard Dussault
Counsellor, J. Wall
Counsellor, Development, J. Lobsinger
Senior Commercial Assistant, Thelma R. Staussi

Kiribati c/o New Zealand

Republic of Korea
Canadian Embassy, 10th Fl., Kolon Bldg.: 45 Mugyo-Dong, 10th/11th Fls., Jung-Ku, Seoul 100-170
(011-82-2) 753-2605; Fax: (011-82-2) 755-0686;
Email: MITNET: 348-0000; Cable: DOMCAN SEOUL
Postal Address: PO Box 6299, Seoul 100-662, Korea
Ambassador, Michel Perrault
Minister, Counsellor & Consul, Commercial, M. Hladik
Counsellor, Commercial, M. Woods
Third Secretary, Commercial, Jean-Dominique Ieraci, Email: jean-dominique.j.d.i.ieraci@seoul02.x400.gc.ca
Commercial Officer, Y.H. Choi
Pusan: Hon. Consul, H.-W. Koo, Honorary Consulate of Canada, c/o Bumin Mutual Savings & Finance Corporation, #32-1, 2-GA, Daecheung-Dong, Chung-Ku, Pusan, Korea, (011-8251) 246-7024; Fax: (011-8251) 247-8443

State of Kuwait
Canadian Embassy, Block 4, House No. 24: Al-Mutawakel, Da Aiyah, Kuwait City
(001 965) 256-3025; Fax: (001-965) 256-4167;
Email: MITNET: 332-0000
Postal Address: PO Box 25281, Safat 13113, Kuwait City, Kuwait
Ambassador, Terry Colfer
Counsellor & Consul, Commercial, J.N. Guérin
Counsellor & Consul, Commercial, R. Banerjee
Commercial Officer, Ibtissam Hajj

Republic of Kyrgyzstan c/o Republic of Kazakhstan

Lao People's Democratic Republic c/o Kingdom of Thailand

Republic of Latvia
Canadian Embassy: Doma laukums 4, 4th Fl., Riga
(011-371) 783-0141; Fax: (011-371) 783-0140
Ambassador (located in Sweden), William L. Clarke
First Secretary, Commercial, H.J. Kunzer

Lebanese Republic
Office of the Canadian Embassy, Coolrite Bldg., 1st Fl.: 434 Autostrade Jall-El-Dib, Beirut
(011-961-1) 521-163; Fax: (011-961-1) 521-167
Postal Address: PO Box 60163, Jal-El-Dib, Beirut, Lebanon
Ambassador, Daniel Marchand
Second Secretary & Vice Counsel, Commercial, M. Poirier
Counsellor, Commercial, M. Abou Guendia
Second Secretary, Commerical, Mario Poirier

Kingdom of Lesotho c/o Republic of South Africa
Maseru: Hon. Consul, Z.M. Bam, Honorary Consulate of Canada, Canadian Consulate, Maseru Book Centre Kingsway, 1st Fl., PO Box 1165, Maseru, Lesotho, (011-266) 311-256; Fax: (011-266) 310-462

Republic of Liberia c/o Republic of Ghana

Social People's Libyan Arab Jamahiriya c/o Republic of Tunisia

Principality Liechtenstein c/o Swiss Confederation

Republic of Lithuania
Canadian Embassy: Didzioji 8-5, 2001, Vilnius
(011-370-2) 220-898; Fax: (011-370-2) 220-884
Ambassador (located in Sweden), William L. Clarke
Minister-Counsellor (located in Latvia), G.R. Skinner

First Secretary, Commercial (located in Latvia), J.H. Kunzer

Grand Duchy of Luxembourg c/o Kingdom of Belgium
Luxembourg: Hon. Consul, P. Krier, Honorary Consulate of Canada, c/o Price-Waterhouse & Co., 24-26, av de la Liberté, Luxembourg L-1930, Luxembourg, (011-352) 40-24-20; Fax: (011-352) 40-24-55 ext.600

Macao c/o Hong Kong

Democratic Republic of Madagascar c/o United Republic of Tanzania
Antananarivo 101: Hon. Consul, Serge P. Lachapelle, Honorary Consulate of Canada, c/o QIT-Madagascar Minerals, Villa Paula Androhibe, Lot II-J-169, Antananarivo 101, Madagascar, (011-261-2) 425-59; Fax: (011-261-2) 425-06; Telex: 22474 BAWDEN MG
Postal Address: Canadian Consulate, CP 4003, Antananarivo 101, Madagascar

Madeira c/o Portuguese Republic

Republic of Malawi c/o Republic of Zambia
Blantyre-Limbe: Hon. Consul, K. Okhai, Honorary Consulate of Canada, Comet Ltd., PO Box 51146, Blantyre-Limbe, Malawi, (011-265) 643-277; Fax: (011-265) 643-446

Malaysia
Canadian High Commission, Plaza MBF: 172 Jalan Ampang, 7th Fl., 50450, Kuala Lumpur
(011-60-3) 261-2000; Fax: (011-60-3) 261-3248;
Email: tradcan@po.jaring.my; MITNET: 345-0000
Postal Address: PO Box 10990, 50732, Kuala Lumpur, Malaysia
High Commissioner, André Simard
Counsellor, Commercial, P.S. Lau
Counsellor, Commercial, B. Reid
First Secretary, Commercial, Paul Bailey

Republic of Maldives c/o Democratic Socialist Republic of Sri Lanka

Republic of Mali
Canadian Embassy, PO Box 198, Bamako
(011-223) 22-22-36; Fax: (011-223) 22-43-62; Telex: 2530 (DOMCAN BAMAKO)
Ambassador, Susan McCoy
Counsellor & Consul, Development, Denis G. Beaudoin

Republic of Malta c/o Italian Republic
Valletta: Hon. Consul, J.M. Demajo, Honorary Consulate of Canada, Demajo House, 103 Archbishop St., Valletta, Malta, (011-356) 233-121; Fax: (011-356) 235-145

Marshall Islands c/o Republic of the Philippines

Martinique c/o Barbados

Islamic Republic of Mauritania c/o Republic of Senegal
Nouakchott: Hon. Consul, J. Chauvin, Honorary Consulate of Canada, PO Box 428, Nouakchott, Mauritania, (011-222-2) 534-48; Fax: (011-222-2) 540-09

Republic of Mauritius c/o Republic of South Africa
Port Louis: Hon. Consul, M.P. Birger, Canadian Consulate, 18 Jules Koenij St., Port Louis, Mauritius, (011-230) 208-0821; Fax: (011-230) 208-3391

United Mexican States
Canadian Embassy: Calle Schiller no. 529, Colonia Polanco, 11560, Mexico City
(011-52-5) 724-7900; Fax: (011-52-5) 724-7981;
Email: MITNET: 379-3000
Postal Address: Apartado Postal 105-05, 11580 Mexico City, D.F. Mexico
Ambassador, Marc Perron
Minister-Counsellor, Economic/Commercial, D. Thibault
Counsellor, Commercial, J. Prévost
Counsellor, Commercial, M. Wondergem
Counsellor, Commerce, B. Hood
Second Secretary, Commercial, Sophie Legendre
Acapulco: Hon. Consul, Diane McLean, Honorary Consulate of Canada, Hotel Club del Sol, Costera Miguel Aleman, esq. Reyes Católicos, Acapulco, Mexico, (011-52-74) 85-66-21; Fax: (011-52-74) 85-74-17
Postal Address: Apartado Postal 94-C, 39300, Acapulco, Guerrero, Mexico
Ajijic: Hon. Consul, A.C. Rose, Honorary Consulate of Canada, Hotel de Chapala, Paseo del Prado 20, Ajijic, Mexico, (011-52-376) 62-288; Fax: (011-52-376) 62-420
Cancun: Hon. Consul, Daniel Lavoie, Honorary Consulate of Canada, Centro Comercial Plaza Mexico, Local 312, Ava. Tulum 200, esq. Agua, 77500, Cancun, Mexico, (011-52-98) 84-37-16; Fax: (011-52-98) 84-67-16
Guadalajara: Consul & Trade Commissioner, J. Daubeny, Canadian Consulate, Hotel Fiesta Americana, Local 31, Aurelio Aceves 225, Col. Vallarta Poniente, 44100, Guadalajara, Mexico, (011-52-36) 16-56-42; Fax: (011-52-36) 15-86-65
Mazatlan: Hon. Consul, F. Balcarcel, Honorary Consulate of Canada, Hotel Playa Mazatlan, Zona Dorada, Rodolfo Loaiza 202, Mazatlan, Mexico, (011-52-69) 13-73-20; Fax: (011-52-69) 14-66-55
Postal Address: Apartado Postal 614, 82210, Mazatlan, Sinaloa, Mexico
Monterrey: Vice-Consul & Trade Commissioner, T.G. Cullen, Canadian Consulate, Edificio Kalos, Piso C-1, Local 108-A, Zaragoza 1300 Sur y Constitucion, 6400, Monterrey, Mexico, (011-52-83) 44-27-53; Fax: (011-52-83) 44-30-48
Oaxaca: Hon. Consul, Frances May, Honorary Consulate of Canada, 119 Dr. Liceaga #8, 68000, Oaxaca, Mexico, (011-52-95) 13-37-77; Fax: (011-52-95) 15-21-47
Postal Address: Apartado Postal 29 Sucursal C, Col. Reforma, 68050 Oaxaca, Mexico
Puerto Vallarta: Hon. Consul, L. Benoit, Honorary Consulate of Canada, Calle Hidalgo 226, 160 Zaragoza, Interior 10, Col. Centro, 48300, Puerto Vallarta, Mexico, (011-52-32) 22-53-98; Fax: (011-52-32) 22-35-17
San Miguel de Allende: Hon. Consul, G. Bisaillon, Honorary Consulate of Canada, Mesones 38, Interior 15, 37700, San Miguel de Allende, Mexico, (011-52-41) 52-30-25; Fax: (011-52-41) 52-68-56
Tijuana: Hon. Consul, R.E. Ripa, Honorary Consulate of Canada, German Gedovius 10411-101, Condominio del Parque, Zona Rio, 22320, Tijuana, Mexico, (011-52-66) 84-04-61; Fax: (011-52-66) 84-03-01

Republic of Moldova c/o Republic of Romania

Principality of Monaco c/o French Republic

Mongolian People's Republic c/o People's Republic of China

Montenegro c/o Federal Republic of Yugoslavia

Montserrat c/o **Barbados**

Kingdom of Morocco
Canadian Embassy: 13 bis, rue Jaafar As-Sadik, Rabat-Agdal
(011-212-7) 67-28-80; Fax: (011-212-7) 67-21-87
 Postal Address: CP 709, Rabat-Agdal, Morocco
Ambassador, Jean-Guy St-Martin
Counsellor, Commercial, Roger Marceau
Counsellor, Development, M. Faucher
Commercial Officer, Najat Benyahia, Email: majat.benyahia@rabat01.x400.gc.ca

Republic of Mozambique
Canadian Embassy: 1345, rue Thomas Nduda, Maputo
(011-258-1) 492-623; Fax: (011-258-1) 492-667; Telex: 6684 ACDI MO
 Postal Address: CP 1578, Maputo, Mozambique
Ambassador (located in Zimbabwe), Art Wright
Counsellor & Consul, Development (located in Zimbabwe), J. Copland
Counsellor, Development (located in Kenya), R. Benoit

Union of Myanmar c/o **Kingdom of Thailand**

Republic of Namibia c/o Republic of South Africa
Windhoek: Hon. Consul, I. Swanepoel, Honorary Consulate of Canada, PO Box 9704, Windhoek, Namibia, (0926-461) 235-841; Fax: (0926-461) 235-841

Nauru c/o **Commonwealth of Australia**

Kingdom of Nepal c/o **Republic of India**

Kingdom of the Netherlands
Canadian Embassy: Sophialaan 7, 2514 JP, The Hague
(011-31-70) 361-4111; Fax: (011-31-70) 365-1111; Email: MITNET: 442-0000; Cable: DOMCAN THE HAGUE
Ambassador, Marie Bernard-Meunier
Minister-Counsellor, Commercial/Economic, C. Fontaine
Commercial Officer, Chris J. Rowley
 Curaçao: Hon. Consul, L.K. Lynch, Honorary Consulate of Canada, PO Box 305, Curaçao, Netherlands Antilles, (011-599-9) 66-11-15; Fax: (011-599-9) 66-11-22; Telex: 1127 MCBNK/NA; Cable: MADUROBANK

Netherlands Antilles c/o Republic of Venezuela
Curaçao: Hon. Consul, L.K. Lynch, Canadian Consulate, Maduro and Curiels Bank N.V., Plaza JoJo Correa 2-4, Willemstad, Curaçao, (011-599-9) 66-11-15; Fax: (011-599-9) 66-11-22; Telex: 1127 MCBNK/NA

New Caledonia c/o **Commonwealth of Australia**

New Zealand
Canadian High Commission: 61 Molesworth St., 3rd Fl., Thorndon, Wellington
(011-64-4) 473-9577; Fax: (011-64-4) 471-2082; Email: MITNET: 352-0000; Cable: DOMCAN WELLINGTON
 Postal Address: PO Box 12-049, Thorndon, Wellington, New Zealand
High Commissioner, Rob Wright
Counsellor, B.E. Armstrong
Commercial Officer (Auckland), Brian Emsley
 Auckland: Consul & Trade Commissioner, K. McFarlane, Canadian Consulate, Jetset Centre, Level 9, 44-48 Emily Place, Auckland, New Zealand, (011-64-9) 309-3690; Fax: (011-64-9) 307-3111
 Postal Address: PO Box 6186, Wellesley Street, Auckland, New Zealand

Republic of Nicaragua c/o Republic of Costa Rica
Managua: Hon. Consul, Alberto E. Belli, Honorary Consulate of Canada, Frente Plazoleta Telcor Central, 208 Calle de Triunfo, Managua, Nicaragua, (011-505-2) 28-75-74; Fax: (011-505-2) 28-48-21
 Postal Address: Apartado 514, Managua, Nicaragua

Republic of Niger
Canadian Embassy, Édifice Sonara II.: av du Premier Pont, Niamey
(011-227) 73-36-86; Fax: (011-227) 75-31-01; Telex: 5264 (DOMCAN 5264 NI)
 Postal Address: CP 362, Niamey, Niger
Ambassador (located in Côte d'Ivoire), Suzanne Laporte
Counsellor & Consul, Development, J.G. Lépine

Federal Republic of Nigeria
Canadian High Commission, Committee of Vice-Chancellors Bldg.: Plot 8A, 4 Idowa-Taylor St., Victoria Island, Lagos
(011-234-1) 262-2512; Fax: (011-234-1) 262-2517; Telex: 21275 (DOMCAN NG); Cable: DOMCAN LAGOS
 Postal Address: PO Box 54506, Ikoyi Station, Lagos, Nigeria
High Commissioner, Vacant
Counsellor, G.L. Ohlsen
 Abuja: Liaison Officer, J. Frik, Canadian High Commission, Liaison Office, Plot 622, Gana St., Zone A5, Maitama, Abuja, Nigeria, (011-234-090) 803-249; Fax: (011-234-090) 803-249
 Postal Address: PO Box 6924 WUSE, Abuja, FCT, Nigeria

Niue c/o **New Zealand**

Northern Ireland c/o **United Kingdom of Great Britain & Northern Ireland**

Northern Marianas c/o **Republic of the Philippines**

Kingdom of Norway
Canadian Embassy: Oscars Gate 20, Oslo 0244
(011-47) 22-46-69-55; Fax: (011-47) 22-69-34-67; Email: td.oslo@oslo01.x400.gc.ca
Ambassador, François Mathys
Counsellor & Consul, M.A. Godfrey
First Secretary, Commercial, C. Dickson
Second Secretary, Commercial, Lisa Pezzack

Sultanate of Oman c/o State of Kuwait
Muscat: Hon. Consul, M.A. Moosa, Honourary Consulate of Canada, Flat #310, Bldg. 477, Moosa Abdul Rahman Hassan Bldg., Way 2907, A'Noor St., Ruwi, Muscat, Oman, (011-968) 791-738; Fax: (011-968) 791-740
 Postal Address: PO Box 8275, Muttrah, Sultanate of Oman

Islamic Republic of Pakistan
Canadian High Commission: Diplomatic Enclave, Sector G-5, Islamabad
(011-92-51) 21-11-01; Fax: (011-92-51) 21-15-40; Cable: DOMCAN ISLAMABAD
 Postal Address: GPO Box 1042, Islamabad, Pakistan
High Commissioner, Marie-Andrée Beauchemin
Counsellor, D.K. Hallman
Counsellor, Development, M. Paterson
Commercial Officer, Ali Khan
 Karachi 0227: Hon. Consul, B. Avari, Honourary Consulate of Canada, c/o #120, Beach Luxury Hotel, Moulvi Tamiz Uddin Khan Rd., Karachi 0227, Pakistan, (011-92-21) 55-11-00; Fax: (011-92-21) 55-12-22

Republic of Panama
Edificio Banco Central Hispano: Ava. Samuel Lewis, 4th Fl., Panama City
(011-507) 264-9731; Fax: (011-507) 264-0451
 Postal Address: Apartado 3658, Balboa Ancon, Panama City, Panama
Ambassador, Louise Léger
Conseller & Consul (located in Costa Rica), G. Lapointe
Counsellor, Development (located in Costa Rica), J. Touzel
First Secretary & Consul, Commercial, M. Lebleu
 Panama City: Hon. Consul, Ruth Lister de Denton, Canadian Consulate, Edificio Proconsa, Aero Peru, Piso 5B, Calle Manuel y Caza, Campo Alegre, Panama City, Panama, (011-507) 64-70-14; Fax: (011-507) 23-54-70
 Postal Address: Apartado Postal 3658, Balboa, Panama

Papua New Guinea c/o Commonwealth of Australia
Port Moresby: Hon. Consul, R. Hiatt, Honourary Consulate of Canada, The Lodge, Brampton St., 2nd Fl., Port Moresby, Papua New Guinea, (011-675) 21-35-99; Fax: (011-675) 21-36-12
 Postal Address: PO Box 851, Port Moresby, Papua New Guinea

Republic of Paraguay c/o Republic of Chile
Asunción: Hon. Consul, B. Wiebe, Honourary Consulate of Canada, El Paraguayo Independiente 995, Entrepiso, Oficinas 1 y 2, Asunción, Paraguay, (011-595-21) 49-95-05; Fax: (011-595-21) 44-95-06; Telex: 652-PY (652-PY COTMO)
 Postal Address: Casilla 2577, Asunción, Paraguay

Republic of Peru
Canadian Embassy: Calle Federico Gerdes 130 (antes Libertad), Miraflores, Lima
(011-51-1) 444-4015; Fax: (011-51-1) 444-4347; Telex: 25323 (25323 PE DOMCAN); Cable: CANADIAN LIMA
 Postal Address: Casilla 18-1126, Correo Miraflores, Lima 18, Peru
Ambassador, Anthony G. Vincent
Counsellor & Consul, D. Bickford
Counsellor & Consul, Development, P. Chambers
Counsellor, Development, G. Rivard
First Secretary & Consul, Commercial, D. Ayotte
Commercial Officer, Oscar G. Vásquez, Email: oscar.vasquez@lima01.x400.gc.ca

Republic of the Philippines
Canadian Embassy, Allied Bank Centre, 9th & 11th Fls.: 6754 Ayala Ave., Makati City, Manila Metro
(011-63-2) 810-8861; Fax: (011-63-2) 810-8839; Email: byron.lee@manil01.x400.gc.ca; Telex: 63676 (63676 DOMCAN PN); Cable: DOMCAN MANILA
 Postal Address: PO Box 2168, Makati Central Post Office, 1299 Makati, Manila Metro, Philippines
Ambassador, Stephen Heeney
Counsellor, Commercial, C.D. Caldwell
Counsellor, Commercial, A. Fraser
Counsellor, Development, R. Beadle
Commercial Officer, Byron C. Lee, Email: byron.lee@manil01.x400.gc.ca

Republic of Poland
Canadian Embassy: Ulica Jana Matejki 1/5, Warsaw 00-481
(011-48-22) 629-80-51; Fax: (011-48-22) 629-64-57; Email: wsaw.td@wsa01.x400.gc.ca
Ambassador, Serge April

Counsellor & Consul, Commercial, L. McDonald
Commercial Officer, Ewa Gawron-Dobroczynska, Email: ewa.gawron-dobroczynska@wsaw01.x400.gc.ca

Portuguese Republic
Canadian Embassy: Ava. da Liberdade 144/56, 4th Fl., Lisbon 1250
(011-351-1) 347-4892; Fax: (011-351-1) 347-6466; Cable: DOMCAN LISBON
Ambassador, Patricia Marsden-Dole
Counsellor & Consul, Commercial, L.M. Gaetan
Commercial Officer, Luis S. Dâmaso, Email: luis.damaso@lsbon01.x400.gc.ca
- Faro: Hon. Consul, L. Filipe Afonso, Honourary Consulate of Canada, Rua Frei Lourenço de Sta Maria No. 1, 1st Fl., Apt. 79, Faro 8001, Portugal, (011-351-89) 80-37-57; Fax: (011-351-89) 80-47-77; Telex: 56566 (MEFALP)

Principe c/o Gabonese Republic

Puerto Rico c/o United States of America

State of Qatar c/o State of Kuwait

Republic of Romania
Canadian Embassy: 36 Nicolae Iorga, Bucharest 71118
(011-40-1) 222-9845; Fax: (011-40-1) 312-0366; Telex: 10690 (10690 CANAD R)
Postal Address: PO Box 117, Post Office No. 22, Bucharest, Romania
Ambassador, Gilles Duguay
Counsellor & Consul, Commercial, M.R. Vlad
Commercial Officer, Octavian Bonea

Russian Federation
Canadian Embassy: 23 Starokonyushenny Pereulok, Moscow 121002
(011-7-095) 956-6666; Fax: (011-7-095) 241-4400; Cable: CANADA MOSCOW
Ambassador, Anne Leahy
Minister-Counsellor, Commercial, M.L. Morin
Minister-Counsellor & Consul, F. de Kerckhove
Counsellor, L. Heuckroth
Counsellor, Commercial, G. Jones
Commercial Officer, Lilya Panova, Email: lilya.panova@mosco01.x400.gc.ca
- St. Petersburg: Consul General, Ann Collins, Canadian Consulate, 32 Malodetskoselsky Pkt., St. Petersburg 198147, Russia, (011-7-812) 119-8448; Fax: (011-7-812) 119-8393

Rwandese Republic
Canadian Embassy: rue Akagera, PO Box 1177, Kigali
(011-250) 73210; Fax: (011-250) 72719; Telex: 22592 (22592 DOMCAN RW)
Ambassador (located in Kenya), Bernard Dussault
Counsellor, Development (located in Kenya), J. Lobsinger
Counsellor, Development, C. Latulippe

Saint Kitts and Nevis c/o Barbados

Saint Lucia c/o Barbados

Republic of San Marino c/o Italian Republic

Democratic Republic of Sao Tomé & Principe c/o Gabonese Republic

Kingdom of Saudi Arabia
Canadian Embassy: Diplomatic Quarter, Riyadh
(011-966-1) 488-2288; Fax: (011-966-1) 488-1997; Telex: 404893 (DOMCAN SJ); Cable: DOMCAN RIYADH
Postal Address: PO Box 94321, Riyadh 11693, Saudi Arabia
Ambassador, Daniel Edward Hobson
Minister-Counsellor, Commercial, M. Esselmont
Counsellor, Commercial, R.J. Shalka
Third Secretary (Commercial), David McGregor, Email: david.d.m.mcgregor@ryadh01.X400.gc.ca
- Jeddah: Hon. Consul, T.Y. Zahid, Honourary Consulate of Canada, Headquarters Bldg., Zahid Corporate Group, Jeddah, Saudi Arabia, (011-966-2) 667-1156; Fax: (011-966-2) 669-0727
Postal Address: PO Box 8928, Jeddah 21492, Saudi Arabia

Scotland c/o United Kingdom of Great Britain & Northern Ireland

Republic of Senegal
Canadian Embassy: 45, av de la République, Dakar
(011-221) 23-92-90; Fax: (011-221) 23-87-49
Postal Address: CP 3373, Dakar, Senegal
Ambassador, Wilfrid-Guy Licari
Counsellor, Development, P. Lachance
Counsellor & Consul, Development, J. Laberge

Serbia c/o Federal Republic of Yugoslavia

Republic of Seychelles c/o United Republic of Tanzania

Republic of Sierra Leone c/o Republic of Ghana

Republic of Singapore
Canadian High Commission, IBM Towers: 80 Anson Rd., 14th/15th Fls., Singapore 0207
(011-65) 225-6363; Fax: (011-65) 225-2450; Email: cdatanjs@signet.com.sg; Cable: CANADIAN SINGAPORE
Postal Address: Robinson Rd., PO Box 845, Singapore 9016, Singapore
High Commissioner, Barry Carin
Counsellor, Commercial, W. Roberts
Counsellor, Development, M. Archambault
Counsellor, Development, T. Broughton
Third Secretary, Commercial, Alain Gendron

Slovak Republic c/o Czech Republic
Bratislava: Hon. Consul, P. Erben, Honourary Consulate of Canada, Kolarska 4, 81106, Bratislava, Slovakia, (011-42-07) 361-277

Republic of Slovenia c/o Republic of Hungary

Solomon Islands c/o Commonwealth of Australia

Somali Democratic Republic c/o Republic of Kenya

Republic of South Africa
Canadian High Commission: 1103 Arcadia St., Hatfield 0083, Pretoria
(011-27-12) 342-6923; Fax: (011-27-12) 342-3837; Telex: 5322112 (5322112 CANAD SA); Cable: CANDOM PRETORIA
Postal Address: Private Bag X13, Hatfield 0028, Pretoria, South Africa
High Commissioner, Arthur Perron
Minister-Counsellor, C. McMaster
Counsellor, Economic, R. Sandor
Counsellor, Development, R. Benoit
Counsellor, Development, G. Hawes
First Secretary, Commercial (located in Johannesburg), R. Harwood
Commercial Officer (Johannesburg), Ronelle de Wet, Email: ronelle.r.d.dewet@pret01.x400.gc.ca
- Capetown: Canadian High Commission, Reserve Bank Bldg., 30 St. George's Mall St., Capetown 8001, South Africa, (011-27-21) 23-5240; Fax: (011-27-21) 23-4893
Postal Address: PO Box 683, Capetown 8000, South Africa
- Durban: Hon. Consul, R.B. McElligott, Honourary Consulate of Canada, PO Box 5448, Durban 4000, South Africa, (011-322) 301197; Fax: (011-322) 031024
- Johannesburg: Canadian High Commission Trade Office, Cradock Place, 10 Arnold St., 1st Fl., Rosebank, Johannesburg, South Africa
Postal Address: Canadian High Commission Trade Office, PO Box 1394, Parklands 2121, Johannesburg, South Africa

Kingdom of Spain
Canadian Embassy, Edificio Goya: Calle Nunez de Balboa 35, Madrid 28001
(011-34-1) 431-4300; Fax: (011-34-1) 431-3893; Cable: CANADIAN MADRID
Postal Address: Apartado 587, 28080 Madrid, Spain
Ambassador, David Wright
Counsellor, Commercial, G. Bruneau
Counsellor & Consul, P. Wilcox
Commerical Officer, Isidro Garcia, Email: isidro.garcia@mdrid01.X400.gc.ca
- Barcelona: Consul, R.F. Désmoré, Canadian Consulate, Travessera de les Corts, 265, Barcelona 08014, Spain, (011-34-3) 410-6699; Fax: (011-34-3) 410-7755
- Bilbao: Hon. Consul, S. Gardiner, Honourary Consulate of Canada, Ava. Juan Antonio Zunzunegui, 2, 1, Bilbao 48013, Spain, (011-34-4) 427-69-22; Fax: (011-34-4) 427-15-78
- Malaga: Hon. Consul, John Schwarzmann, Honourary Consulate of Canada, Plaza de la Malagueta 3, 1st Fl., Malaga 29016, Spain, (011-34-52) 22-33-46; Fax: (011-34-52) 22-40-23
- Seville: Hon. Consul, Julian Garcia-Hidalgo, Honourary Consulate of Canada, Ava. de la Constitución 30, 2nd Fl., local 4-41001, Seville, Spain, (011-34-54) 22-94-13

Democratic Socialist Republic of Sri Lanka
Canadian High Commission: 6 Gregory's Rd., Cinnamon Gardens, Colombo 7
(011-94-1) 69-58-41; Fax: (011-94-1) 68-70-49; Cable: DOMCANADA COLOMBO
Postal Address: PO Box 1006, Colombo, Sri Lanka
High Commissioner, Konrad Sigurdson
Counsellor, Development, J. Murray

St. Martin/St-Marten c/o Barbados

Republic of The Sudan c/o Democratic Republic of Ethiopia

Republic of Suriname c/o Co-operative Republic of Guyana
Paramaribo: Hon. Consul, A.F. Smit, Honourary Consulate of Canada, Waterkant 90-94, PO Box 1849-1850, Paramaribo, Suriname, (011-597) 471-222; Fax: (011-597) 475-718

Kingdom of Swaziland c/o Republic of South Africa

Kingdom of Sweden
Canadian Embassy: Tegelbacken 4, 7th Fl., Stockholm
(011-46-8) 453-3000; Fax: (011-46-8) 24-24-91; Email: stlkm@stklm01.X400.gc.ca
Postal Address: PO Box 16129, 10323 Stockholm, Sweden
Ambassador, William L. Clark
Counsellor, Commercial, J. Sotvedt
Commercial Officer, Inga-Lill Olsson, Email: inga.olsson@stkhm01.x400.gc.ca

Goteborg: Hon. Consul, K.S.U. Granander, Honorary Consulate of Canada, c/o ACL Sweden AB, S-403 36, Goteborg, Sweden

Swiss Confederation
Canadian Embassy: Kirchenfeldstr. 88, Berne 3005
(011-41-31) 352-63-81; Fax: (011-41-31) 352-73-15; Email: bern.cda@ping.ch
  Postal Address: PO Box 3000, Berne 6, Switzerland
Ambassador, Réjean Frenette
Counsellor & Consul, P. Ducharme
First Secretary & Consul, Commercial, J. Schwartzburg
Senior Commercial Officer, Werner Naef

Syrian Arab Republic
Canadian Embassy: Lot 12, Mezzeh Autostr., Damascus
(011-963-11) 611-6892; Fax: (011-963-11) 611-8034
  Postal Address: PO Box 3394, Damascus, Syria
Ambassador, John A. McNee
Counsellor & Consul, C. Sheck
Counsellor, Commercial, T. Greenwood

Republic of Tajikistan c/o Republic of Kazakhstan

United Republic of Tanzania
Canadian High Commission: 38 Mirambo St., Dar-es-Salaam
(011-255-51) 46000; Fax: (011-255-51) 46005; Telex: 41015 (41015 DOMCAN TZ)
  Postal Address: PO Box 1022, Dar-es-Salaam, Tanzania
High Commissioner, Verona Edelstein
Counsellor, J. Gauthier
Counsellor, Development, A. Poplawski
First Secretary, Development, D. Foxall

Kingdom of Thailand
Boonmitr Bldg.: 138 Silom Rd., 11th Fl., Bangkok 10500
(011-66-2) 237-4125; Fax: (011-66-2) 236-6463
  Postal Address: PO Box 2090, Bangkok 10500, Thailand
Ambassador, Manfred G. von Nostitz
Counsellor & Consul, Commercial, K. Lewis
Counsellor & Consul, Commercial, D. Cameron
Counsellor, Development, I. Knutson
Commercial Officer, Viyada Vanichrojanarat
  Chiang Mai: Hon. Consul, N. Wangviwat, Honorary Canadian Consulate, c/o Raming Tea Co. Ltd., 151 Super Hwy., Tasala, Chiang Mai 5000, Thailand, (011-66-53) 24-22-92; Fax: (011-66-53) 24-26-16

Republic of Togo c/o Republic of Ghana

Kingdom of Tonga c/o New Zealand

Republic of Trinidad & Tobago
Canadian High Commission, Huggins Bldg.: 72 South Quay, Port-of-Spain
809/623-7254; Fax: 809/624-4016; Cable: DOMCAN PORT OF SPAIN
  Postal Address: PO Box 1246, Port-of-Spain, Trinidad
High Commissioner, Marc Lemieux

Republic of Tunisia
Canadian Embassy: 3, rue du Sénégal, Place d'Afrique, Tunis
(011-216-1) 796-577; Fax: (011-216-1) 792-371; Telex: 15324 (15324 DOMCAN TN); Cable: DOMCAN TUNIS
  Postal Address: PO Box 31, Belvédère, 1002 Tunis, Tunisia
Ambassador, Arsène Després
First Secretary & Consul, Commercial, J.-P. Hamel
Counsellor, Development, G. Barchechat

Republic of Turkey
Canadian Embassy: Nenehatun Caddesi No. 75, Gaziosmanpasa 06700, Ankara
(011-90-312) 436-1275; Fax: (011-90-312) 446-4437; Telex: 42369 (DCAN TR)
Ambassador, Michael Mace
Counsellor, Commercial, B. Desjardins
Second Secretary (Commercial), David Usher, Email: david.usher@ankra.01.x400.gc.ca
Commercial Officer, Akin Kosetorunu, Email: akin.kosetorunu@ankra.01.x400.gc.ca
  Istanbul: Hon. Consul, Z.B. Tesal, Honourary Consulate of Canada, Büyükdere Cad. 107/3, Begün Han, 80300 Gayrettepe, Istanbul, Turkey, (011-90-1) 271-5174; Fax: (011-90-1) 272-3427; Telex: 26133 TR

Turkmenistan c/o Republic of Kazakhstan

Turks & Caicos Islands c/o Jamaica

Tuvalu c/o New Zealand

U.S. Virgin Islands c/o United States of America

Republic of Uganda c/o Republic of Kenya
Kampala: Hon. Consul, D. Campbell, Honourary Consulate of Canada, 92/94 - 5 St., Industrial Area, Kampala, Uganda, (011-256-41) 25-81-41; Fax: (011-256-41) 24-13-80
  Postal Address: c/o Uganda Bata, PO Box 422, Kampala, Uganda

Republic of Ukraine
Canadian Embassy: 31 Yaroslaviv Val St., Kiev 252034
(011-7-044) 212-0412; Fax: (011-7-044) 212-2339; Telex: 131479 (131479 UYUT SU)
Ambassador, Christopher W. Westdal
Counsellor, Commercial, D. Goresky
Commercial Officer, Nicole Abiaad Zaroubi

United Arab Emirates c/o State of Kuwait
Bur Dubai: Consul & Trade Commissioner, R. Farrell, Canadian Consulate, Juma Al Majid Bldg.,, #708, Khalid Ibn Al Waleed St., Bur Dubai, United Arab Emirates, (011-971-4) 52-17-17; Fax: (011-971-4) 51-77-22
  Postal Address: PO Box 52472, Dubai, United Arab Emirates

United Kingdom of Great Britain & Northern Ireland
Canadian High Commission, Macdonald House: One Grosvenor Sq., London W1X OAB
(011-44-171) 258-6600; Fax: (011-44-171) 258-6333; Email: MITNET: 445-0000
High Commissioner, The Hon. Royce Frith, Q.C.
Minister, Commercial/Economic, R. Burchill
Minister, Political/Public Affairs, J. Wright
Counsellor, Commercial/Economic, J.-M. Roy
Commercial Officer, Giles C.H. Scott, Email: giles.scott@ldn02.x400.gc.ca
  Birmingham: Hon. Consul, E. Birch, Honorary Consulate of Canada, 55 Colmore Row, Birmingham B3 2AS, United Kingdom, (011-44) 121-236-6474
  Edinburgh: Hon. Consul, A.S. Bell, Honorary Consulate of Canada, 3 George St., Edinburgh, (011-32) 220-4333

United States of America
Canadian Embassy: 501 Pennsylvannia Ave. NW, Washington DC 20001
202/682-1740; Fax: 202/682-7726; Email: MITNET: 456-0000; URL: http://www.nstn.ca/wshdc; Telex: 89664 (DOMCAN A WSH)
Ambassador, Raymond A.J. Chrétien
Minister, Deputy Head of Mission, Douglas G. Waddell
Counsellor, Commercial, D. Brown
Counsellor, Commercial, D. Horton
Counsellor, Commercial Agriculture & Fisheries, D. Plunkett
Counsellor, Science & Technology, D. Strange
First Secretary, Commercial, Kathy Aleong, Email: kathryn.aleong@wshdc01.x400.gc.ca
First Secretary, Commercial, R. Cairns
First Secretary, Commercial, R. Rutherford
  Atlanta: Consul General, Allan Stewart, Canadian Consulate General, #400, South Tower, One CNN Center, Atlanta GA 30303-2705, USA, 404/577-6810; Fax: 404/524-5046; Telex: MITNET: 467-0000
  Boston: Consul General, Donald W. Cameron, Canadian Consulate General, #400, 3 Copley Place, Boston MA 02116, USA, 617/262-3760; Fax: 617/262-3415; MITNET: 468-0000
  Buffalo: Consul General, Mark Romoff, Canadian Consulate General, #3000, 1 Marine Midland Center, Buffalo NY 14203-2884, USA, 716/858-9500; Fax: 716/852-4340; MITNET: 469-0000
  Chicago: Consul General, Allan N. Lever, Canadian Consulate General, 2 Prudential Plaza, #2400, 180 North Stetson Ave., Chicago IL 60601, USA, 312/616-1860; Fax: 312/616-1877; MITNET: 470-0000
  Dallas: Consul General, Jon Swanson, Canadian Consulate General, St. Paul Place, #1700, 750 North St. Paul St., Dallas TX 75201-3247, USA, 214/922-9806; Fax: 214/922-9815; Cable: CANADIAN DALLAS; MITNET: 472-0000
  Detroit: Consul General, Donald Wismer, Canadian Consulate General, #1100, 600 Renaissance Center, Detroit MI 48243-1798, USA, 313/567-2340; Fax: 313/567-2164; URL: http://www.bizserve.com/canadian-detroit; MITNET: 473-0000
  Los Angeles: Consul General, Kim Campbell, Canadian Consulate General, 550 South Hope St., 9th Fl., Los Angeles CA 90071-2627, USA, 213/346-2700; Fax: 213/620-8827; Telex: 674119 (DOMCAN LSA); MITNET: 476-0000
  Miami: Consul & Trade Commissioner, D. Campbell, Canadian Consulate General, #1600, 200 South Biscayne Blvd., Miami FL 33131, USA, 305/579-1600; Fax: 305/368-3900; MITNET: 368-0000
  Minneapolis: Consul General, Robert Déry, Canadian Consulate General, 701 - 4th Ave. South, Minneapolis MN 55415, USA, 612/333-4641; Fax: 612/332-4061; MITNET: 474-0000
  New York: Consul General, George. Haynal, Canadian Consulate General, 1251 Ave. of the Americas, 16th Fl., New York NY 10020-1175, USA, 212/596-1600; Fax: 212/596-1790; URL: http://www.canada-ny.org; MITNET: 457-0000
  San Juan: Hon. Consul, R.D.K. Seymour, Honourary Consulate of Canada, 107 Cereipo St., Alt. de Santa Maria, Guaynabo, San Juan, Puerto Rico, 809/790-2210; Fax: 809/790-2205
  Seattle: Consul General, J. Thomas Boehm, Canadian Consulate General, 412 Plaza 600, Sixth & Stewart, Seattle WA 98101-1286, USA, 206/443-1777; Fax: 206/443-1782; MITNET: 477-0000

Eastern Republic of Uruguay
Edifio Torre Libertad: Plaza Cagangha 1335, off. 1105, 11100, Montevideo
(011-598-2) 92-20-30; Fax: (011-598-2) 92-20-29
Ambassador, Roland Goulet
First Secretary, Commercial & Economic (located in Argentina), S. Harper
  Montevideo: Hon. Consul, R.M.R. Sanguinetti, Honourary Consulate of Canada, Edificio Torre Libertad, Plaza Cagancha 1335, Piso 10, 11100,

Montevideo, Uruguay, (011-598-2) 92-20-29; Fax: (011-598-2) 92-02-23

Republic of Uzbekistan c/o Republic of Kazakhstan

Republic of Vanuatu c/o Commonwealth of Australia

Holy See
Canadian Embassy: Via della Conciliazione 4/D, 00193, Rome
(011-39-6) 6830-7316; Fax: (011-39-6) 6880-6283; Email: MITNET: 464-0000
Ambassador, Léonard Legault
Counsellor, Y. Saint-Hilaire

Republic of Venezuela
Canadian Embassy, Edificio Torre Europa: Ava. Francisco de Miranda, Piso 7, Campo Alegre, Caracas
(011-58-2) 951-6166; Fax: (011-58-2) 951-4950; Email: MITNET: 394-0000; Telex: 23377 (DOMCA VE); Cable: DOMCA CARACAS
 Postal Address: Apt. 62302, Caracas 1060A, Venezuela
Ambassador, Yves Gagnon
First Secretary & Consul, Commercial, G. Lemieux
Third Secretary & Vice Consul, Peter Lundy, Email: peter.lundy@crcas01.x400.gc.ca
 Porlamar: Hon. Consul, R.B. Todd, Canadian Consulate, Conj. Residencial Mediterraneo, Torre Tirreno PH-A, Urb. Bella Vista, Porlamar, Venezuela, (011-58-95) 636-568

Socialist Republic of Viet Nam
Canadian Embassy: 31 Hung Vuong St., Hanoi
(011-84-4) 235-500; Fax: (011-84-4) 235-351
Ambassador, Christine Desloges
Counsellor, Commercial, W. Hughes
Counsellor, Development, W.A. Young
Third Secretary (Commercial), Nathalie Dubé, Email: natalie.n.d.dube@paris03.x400.gc.ca
 Ho Chi Minh City: Consul & Trade Commissioner, I. Burney, Canadian Consulate, #102, 203 Dong Khoi St., Dist. 1, Ho Chi Minh City, Viet Nam, (011-84-8) 242-000; Fax: (011-84-8) 294-528

Wales c/o United Kingdom of Great Britain & Northern Ireland

Independent State of Western Samoa c/o New Zealand

Republic of Yemen c/o Kingdom of Saudi Arabia
Sanaa: Hon. Consul, A.A. Zabarah, Honourary Consulate of Canada, c/o Yemen Computer Co., Ltd., Bldg 4, Street 11 (near Haddah St.), Sanaa, Yemen, (011-967-1) 20-88-14; Fax: (011-967-1) 20-95-23; Telex: 2406 YCC YE
Postal Address: PO Box 340, Sanaa, Yemen

Federal Republic of Yugoslavia
Canadian Embassy: Kneza Milosa 75, 11000, Belgrade
(011-381-11) 64-46-66; Fax: (011-381-11) 64-14-80; Telex: 11137 (11137 DOMCA YU); Cable: DOMCAN BELGRADE
Ambassador, Dennis Snider

Republic of Zaire
Canadian Office c/o Embassy of the USA: 310, av des Aviateurs, Kinshasa
(011-243-12) 21-532; Fax: (011-243-88) 43-805; Cable: AMEMBASSY KINSHASA
Head, Canadian Office, Counsellor & Consul, Denis Grégoire-de-Blois

Republic of Zambia
Canadian High Commission: 5199 United Nation Ave., Lusaka
(011-260-1) 25-08-33; Fax: (011-260-1) 25-41-76; Telex: ZA 42480 (DOMCAN ZA 42480); Cable: DOMCAN LUSAKA
 Postal Address: PO Box 31313, Lusaka, Zambia
High Commissioner, Mary Mosser

Republic of Zimbabwe
Canadian High Commission: 45 Baines Ave., Harare
(011-263-4) 25-08-33; Fax: (011-263-4) 25-41-76; Telex: 24465 (24465 CANADA ZW); Cable: CANAD HARARE
 Postal Address: PO Box 1430, Harare, Zimbabwe
High Commissioner, Anne M. Charles
Counsellor, Development, J. Copland
Commercial Officer, Josée Lanctôt

SECTION 4

MUNICIPALITIES DIRECTORY

MUNICIPALITIES BY PROVINCE	1	**NEWFOUNDLAND**	29	**QUÉBEC**	77
ALBERTA	1	NORTHWEST TERRITORIES	37	SASKATCHEWAN	134
BRITISH COLUMBIA	12	NOVA SCOTIA	39	YUKON TERRITORY	152
MANITOBA	18	ONTARIO	42	**MAJOR MUNICIPALITIES**	153
NEW BRUNSWICK	24	PRINCE EDWARD ISLAND	74	**REGIONAL MUNICIPALITIES**	171

See ADDENDA at the back of this book for late changes & additional information.

MUNICIPAL GOVERNMENT

The Municipal Section of the Almanac is in three parts. *Part 1* is a list of local municipalities in Canada, arranged by provinces, and including population and electoral districts. Each provincial list is preceded by notes about local municipal organization and elections. *Part 2* includes in-depth listings for major municipalities in Canada, listed alphabetically. *Part 3* includes regional governments in large population areas, in British Columbia, Ontario, and Québec.

Part 1 (Cities, Towns Villages, etc., with Officials, listed by Province)

ALBERTA

The major legislation concerning municipal government in Alberta is the Municipal Government Act.

Municipal government in Alberta is either rural or urban. Rural municipal governments are organized into Municipal Districts, with Specialized Municipalities created to meet the unique needs of a specific municipality. Elected councils are responsible for all municipal functions and levying taxes. Two other rural categories are Improvement Districts and Special Areas, which are geographically large, sparsely populated areas for which the provincial government levies and collects all taxes and provides services.

Urban municipalities include Summer Villages, Villages, Towns and Cities. These are fully autonomous municipal units, each with an elected council. They are responsible for providing all municipal services within their corporate limits and for levying taxes and rates.

In addition to the above forms of municipal government there are eight Metis Settlements established under the Metis Settlements Act.

Types of Municipalities that may be formed:

Municipal District: A majority of the buildings used as dwellings are on parcels of land with an area of at least 1,850 square metres and there is a population of 1,000 or more.

Summer Village: There are at least sixty parcels of land that have buildings used as dwellings located on them; a majority of the persons who would be electors of the proposed summer village do not reside in the area; there is a population of less than 300.

Village: A majority of the buildings are on parcels of land smaller than 1,850 square metres and there is a population of 1,000 or more.

Town: A majority of the buildings are on parcels of land smaller than 1,850 square metres and there is a population of 1,000 or more.

City: A majority of the buildings are on parcels of land smaller than 1,850 square metres and there is a population of 10,000 or more.

Specialized Municipality: An area in which the Minister is satisfied that a type of municipality (as listed above) does not meet the needs of the proposed municipality. Incorporation and changes in status are determined by the Lieutenant Governor in Council (Provincial Cabinet) on the recommendation of the Minister of Municipal Affairs. It is not necessary to change status by reason of population change.

Cities in CAPITALS; Towns marked †; Villages marked (V); Summer Villages marked (SV). Alberta Counties & Municipal Districts, Specialized Municipalities and Improvement Districts follow this list. An in-depth listing for municipalities marked with * appears in Part 2 (check Index for page numbers).

MUNICIPALITY	1994 POP.	FEDERAL ELECTORAL DISTRICT	PROVINCIAL ELECTORAL DISTRICT	CONTACT PERSON WITH ADDRESS, PHONE & FAX
Acme (V)	527	Wild Rose	Three Hills-Airdrie	Joanne Weller, Adm., PO Box 299, Acme T0M 0A0 – 403/546-3783, Fax: 403/546-3014
AIRDRIE	14,506	Wild Rose	Three Hills-Airdrie	Deryl Kloster, Mgr., PO Box 5, Airdrie T4B 2C9 – 403/948-8800, Fax: 403/948-6567, URL: http://www.airdrie.com/
Alberta Beach (SV)	562	Yellowhead	Whitecourt-Ste. Anne	Lori Donner, CAO, PO Box 278, Alberta Beach T0E 0A0 – 403/924-3181, Fax: 403/924-3313
Alix (V)	782	Crowfoot	Lacombe-Stettler	Richard Kutt, Adm., PO Box 87, Alix T0C 0B0 – 403/747-2495, Fax: 403/747-3663

Canadian Almanac & Directory 1997

4-2 ALBERTA MUNICIPALITIES

Cities in CAPITALS; Towns marked †; Villages marked (V); Summer Villages marked (SV). Alberta Counties & Municipal Districts, Specialized Municipalities and Improvement Districts follow this list. An in-depth listing for municipalities marked with * appears in Part 2 (check Index for page numbers).

MUNICIPALITY	1994 POP.	FEDERAL ELECTORAL DISTRICT	PROVINCIAL ELECTORAL DISTRICT	CONTACT PERSON WITH ADDRESS, PHONE & FAX
Alliance (V)	230	Vegreville	Wainright	Tamina Miller, Adm., PO Box 149, Alliance T0B 0A0 – 403/879-3911, Fax: 403/879-2235
Amisk (V)	198	Vegreville	Wainwright	Joyce DeBord, Adm., PO Box 72, Amisk T0B 0B0 – 403/856-3980, Fax: 403/856-3980
Andrew (V)	520	Vegreville	Vegreville-Viking	John K. Woychuk, Adm., PO Box 180, Andrew T0B 0C0 – 403/365-3687, Fax: 403/365-2061
Argentia Beach (SV)	2	Wetaskiwin	Drayton Valley-Calmar	Ken D. Armstrong, Adm., 9322 - 73 Ave., Edmonton T6E 1A7 – 403/433-4969, Fax: 403/433-4969
Arrowwood (V)	156	Macleod	Little Bow	Denise Kuntz, Sec.-Treas., PO Box 36, Arrowwood T0L 0B0 – 403/534-3821, Fax: 403/534-3821
Athabasca †	2,278	Athabasca	Athabasca-Wabasca	Cliff Sawatzky, Mgr., 4705 - 49 Ave., Athabasca T9S 1B7 – 403/675-2063, Fax: 403/675-4242
Banff †	7,615	Wild Rose	Banff-Cochrane	James Bennett, Mgr., PO Box 1260, Banff T0L 0C0 – 403/762-1200, Fax: 403/762-1260
Barnwell (V)	531	Medicine Hat	Taber-Warner	Wendy Bateman, Adm., PO Box 159, Barnwell T0K 0B0 – 403/223-4018, Fax: 403/223-2373
Barons (V)	262	Lethbridge	Little Bow	Darrell Garceau, Adm., PO Box 129, Barons T0L 0G0 – 403/757-3633, Fax: 403/757-3633
Barrhead †	4,160	Yellowhead	Barrhead-Westlock	John M. MacLean, Municipal Sec., PO Box 4189, Barrhead T7N 1A2 – 403/674-3301, Fax: 403/674-5648
Bashaw †	807	Crowfoot	Ponoka-Rimbey	Orlene Wigglesworth, Mgr., PO Box 510, Bashaw T0B 0H0 – 403/372-3911, Fax: 403/372-2335
Bassano †	1,190	Medicine Hat	Bow Valley	Gerry Neighbour, Adm., PO Box 299, Bassano T0J 0B0 – 403/641-3788, Fax: 403/641-2585
Bawlf (V)	360	Crowfoot	Ponoka-Rimbey	Myrna Schapansky, Adm., PO Box 40, Bawlf T0B 0J0 – 403/373-3797
Beaumont †	5,685	Elk Island	Leduc	Connie McKinney, Sec., 5600 - 49 St., Beaumont T4X 1A1 – 403/929-8782, Fax: 403/929-8729
Beaverlodge †	1,779	Peace River	Grande Prairie-Wapiti	Ivan Hegland, Mgr., PO Box 30, Beaverlodge T0H 0C0 – 403/354-2202, Fax: 403/354-2207
Beiseker (V)	640	Wild Rose	Three Hills-Airdrie	Wendy Ramberg, Adm., PO Box 349, Beiseker T0M 0G0 – 403/947-3774, Fax: 403/947-2146
Bentley (V)	930	Wetaskiwin	Rocky Mountain House	Elizabeth Smart, CAO, PO Box 179, Bentley T0C 0J0 – 403/748-4044, Fax: 403/748-3213
Berwyn (V)	606	Peace River	Dunvegan	Harry Aspin, Adm., PO Box 250, Berwyn T0H 0E0 – 403/338-3922, Fax: 403/338-2224
Betula Beach (SV)	4	Yellowhead	Stony Plain	Jeanette Killips, Sec.-Treas., 10544 - 55 Ave., Edmonton T6H 0W7 – 403/434-9975
Big Valley (V)	303	Crowfoot	Lacombe-Stettler	Yvette Cassidy, Adm., PO Box 236, Big Valley T0J 0G0 – 403/876-2269, Fax: 403/876-2223
Birch Cove (SV)	16	Yellowhead	Whitecourt-Ste Anne	Wes Romanchuk, Adm., 5312 - 56 St., Barrhead T7N 1C3 – 403/674-6638, Fax: 403/674-5648
Birchcliff (SV)	63	Red Deer	Rocky Mountain House	Marianne Whitehead, Adm., #104, 4505 - 50 Av.., Sylvan Lake T4S 1V9 – 403/887-2822, Fax: 403/887-2897
Bittern Lake (V)	169	Wetaskiwin	Wetaskiwin-Camrose	Anne Hoyme, Sec.-Treas., General Delivery, Bittern Lake T0C 0L0 – 403/672-7373, Fax: 403/672-7373
Black Diamond †	1,727	Macleod	Highwood	Dianne Kreh, Mgr., PO Box 10, Black Diamond T0L 0H0 – 403/933-4348, Fax: 403/933-5865
Blackfalds †	1,769	Red Deer	Lacombe-Stettler	Jerry Bagozzi, CAO, PO Box 220, Blackfalds T0M 0J0 – 403/885-4677, Fax: 403/885-4610
Blackie (V)	303	Macleod	Highwood?	Sharlene Shaw, Adm., PO Box 220, Blackie T0L 0J0 – 403/684-3688, Fax: 403/684-3308
Bon Accord †	1,460	Beaver River	Redwater	Judy Meredith, CAO, PO Box 100, Bon Accord T0A 0K0 – 403/921-3550, Fax: 403/921-3585
Bondiss (SV)	67	Athabasca	Athabasca-Wabasca	John H. Crowston, Adm., 16411 – 79A Ave., Edmonton T5R 3J2 – 403/483-8817
Bonnyville †	5,132	Beaver River	Bonnyville	Olga Cross, Sec., PO Box 1006, Bonnyville T9N 2J7 – 403/826-3496, Fax: 403/826-4806
Bonnyville Beach (SV)	60	Beaver River	Bonnyville	Dollard L. Demers, Adm., PO Box 6439, Bonnyville T9N 2G3 – 403/826-2925, Fax: 403/826-3734
Botha (V)	174	Crowfoot	Lacombe-Stettler	Josie Hunter, Adm., PO Box 160, Botha T0C 0N0 – 403/742-5079, Fax: 403/742-6586
Bow Island †	1,509	Medicine Hat	Cypress-Medicine Hat	Kenneth Hollinger, Adm., PO Box 100, Bow Island T0K 0G0 – 403/545-2522, Fax: 403/545-6642
Bowden †	936	Wild Rose	Innisfail-Sylvan Lake	Frances Berggren, Clerk, PO Box 338, Bowden T0M 0K0 – 403/224-3395, 2133, Fax: 403/224-2244
Boyle (V)	784	Athabasca	Athabasca-Wabasca	Charlie Sheen, Adm., PO Box 9, Boyle T0A 0M0 – 403/689-3642, 3643, Fax: 403/689-3998
Breton (V)	532	Wetaskiwin	Drayton Valley-Calmar	Charlene Freeson, Adm., PO Box 480, Breton T0C 0P0 – 403/696-3636, Fax: 403/696-3590
Brooks †	9,433	Medicine Hat	Bow Valley	Kevin Bridges, Mgr., PO Box 880, Brooks T1R 1B7 – 403/362-3333, Fax: 403/362-4787

Canadian Almanac & Directory 1997

ALBERTA MUNICIPALITIES 4-3

Cities in CAPITALS; Towns marked †; Villages marked (V); Summer Villages marked (SV). Alberta Counties & Municipal Districts, Specialized Municipalities and Improvement Districts follow this list. An in-depth listing for municipalities marked with * appears in Part 2 (check Index for page numbers).

MUNICIPALITY	1994 POP.	FEDERAL ELECTORAL DISTRICT	PROVINCIAL ELECTORAL DISTRICT	CONTACT PERSON WITH ADDRESS, PHONE & FAX
Bruderheim †	1,208	Elk Island	Vegreville-Viking	Keith Miller, CAO, PO Box 280, Bruderheim T0B 0S0 – 403/796-3731, Fax: 403/796-3037
Burdett (V)	267	Medicine Hat	Cypress-Medicine Hat	Roselyn Pahl, Adm., PO Box 37, Burdett T0K 0J0 – 403/833-3794, Fax: 403/833-3794
Burnstick Lake (SV)	2	Red Deer	Rocky Mountain House	Sharon Plett, Adm., PO Box 5754, High River T1V 1P3 – 403/652-4636, Fax: 403/652-3125
*CALGARY	767,059 ('96)	Calgary Centre; Calgary North; Calgary Northeast; Calgary Southeast; Calgary Southwest; Calgary West	Cal.-Bow; Cal.-Buffalo; Cal.-Currie; Cal.-Egmont; Cal.-Elbow; Cal.-Fish Creek; Cal.-Cross; Cal.-East.; Cal.-Foothills; Cal.-Forest Lawn; Cal.-Glenmore; Cal.-Lougheed; Cal.-McCall; Cal -McKnight; Cal.-Millican; Cal.-Montrose; Cal.-Mountain View; Cal.-North Hill; Cal.-Nose Creek; Cal.-NW.; Cal.-Shaw; Cal.-Varsity; Cal. W.	D. L. Garner, Clerk, PO Box 2100, Calgary T2P 2M5 – 403/268-2111, Fax: 403/268-2633, URL: http://www.gov.calgary.ab.ca/
Calmar †	1,779	Wetaskiwin	Drayton Valley-Calmar	Shirley Melnikel, Mgr., PO Box 750, Calmar T0C 0V0 – 403/985-3604, Fax: 403/985-3039
CAMROSE	13,701	Crowfoot	Wetaskiwin-Camrose	J. Neil Brodie, Clerk, City Hall, 5204 - 50 Ave., Camrose T4V 0S8 – 403/672-4426, Fax: 403/672-2469
Canmore †	7,161	Wild Rose	Banff-Cochrane	Martin Buckley, Sec., PO Box 460, Canmore T0L 0M0 – 403/678-1502, Fax: 403/678-1534
Carbon (V)	437	Crowfoot	Drumheller	Wendy J. Sowerby, Adm., PO Box 249, Carbon T0M 0L0 – 403/572-3244, Fax: 403/572-3778
Cardston †	3,480	Lethbridge	Cardston-Chief Mountain	Gregory D. Burt, Adm., PO Box 280, Cardston T0K 0K0 – 403/653-3366, Fax: 403/653-2499
Carmangay (V)	257	Macleod	Little Bow	Audrey Wilcox, Adm., PO Box 130, Carmangay T0L 0N0 – 403/643-3595, Fax: 403/643-2007
Caroline (V)	452	Red Deer	Rocky Mountain House	Velma Keeler, Adm., PO Box 148, Caroline T0M 0M0 – 403/722-3781, Fax: 403/722-4050
Carstairs †	1,796	Wild Rose	Olds-Didsbury	Daphne Turner, CAO, PO Box 370, Carstairs T0M 0N0 – 403/337-3341, Fax: 403/337-3343
Castle Island (SV)	6	Yellowhead	Whitecourt-Ste Anne	Leo D. Ludwig, Adm., 9615 - 152 St., Edmonton T5P 1W7 – 403/484-4213, Fax: 403/481-2887
Castor †	933	Crowfoot	Chinook	Michael Yakielashek, CAO, PO Box 479, Castor T0C 0X0 – 403/882-3215, Fax: 403/882-3454
Cayley (V)	243	Macleod	Highwood	Leslie Fitzgerald, Adm., PO Box 70, Cayley T0L 0P0 – 403/395-3731, Fax: 403/395-2352
Cereal (V)	216	Crowfoot	Chinook	Carol Hok, Adm., PO Box 160, Cereal T0J 0N0 – 403/326-3823, Fax: 403/326-3823
Champion (V)	401	Macleod	Little Bow	Marjorie Robinson, Adm., PO Box 367, Champion T0L 0R0 – 403/897-3833, Fax: 403/897-2250
Chauvin (V)	372	Vegreville	Wainwright	Betty Swanson, Adm., PO Box 160, Chauvin T0B 0V0 – 403/858-3881, Fax: 403/858-2125
Chestermere †	1,603	Wild Rose	Drumheller	Frank Kosa, CAO, 156 East Chestermere Dr., Chestermere T1X 1C1 – 403/272-9744, Fax: 403/272-9745
Chipman (V)	208	Elk Island	Vegreville-Viking	Pat Tomkow, Adm., PO Box 176, Chipman T0B 0W0 – 403/363-3982, Fax: 403/363-3766
Claresholm †	3,297	Macleod	Pincher Creek-MacLeod	Larry Flexhaug, Town Coordinator, PO Box 1000, Claresholm T0L 0T0 – 403/625-3381, Fax: 403/625-3869
Clive (V)	497	Wetaskiwin	Lacombe-Stettler	Karen Kane, Adm., PO Box 90, Clive T0C 0Y0 – 403/784-3366, Fax: 403/784-2012
Cluny (V)	103	Macleod	Drumheller	Sharon Papp, Adm., PO Box 189, Cluny T0J 0S0 – 403/734-3753, Fax: 403/734-2660
Clyde (V)	441	Athabasca	Barrhead-Westlock	Trudy Ferguson, Clerk, PO Box 190, Clyde T0G 0P0 – 403/348-5356, Fax: 403/348-5356
Coaldale †	5,507	Lethbridge	Taber-Warner	Ray Coad, Mgr., 1920 - 17 St., Coaldale T1M 1M1 – 403/345-4417, Fax: 403/345-4083
Coalhurst (V)	1,389	Lethbridge	Little Bow	Marge Williams, Adm., PO Box 456, Coalhurst T0L 0V0 – 403/381-3033, Fax: 403/381-2924
Cochrane †	6,612	Wild Rose	Banff-Cochrane	Julian deCocq, CAO, PO Box 10, Cochrane T0L 0W0 – 403/932-2075, Fax: 403/932-6032
Cold Lake † [a]	4,250	Beaver River	Bonnyville	Denis H. Lafond, CAO, PO Box 8098, Cold Lake T0A 0V0 – 403/639-3351, Fax: 403/639-2510
Consort (V)	714	Crowfoot	Chinook	Jack P. Trieber, Adm., PO Box 490, Consort T0C 1B0 – 403/577-3623, Fax: 403/577-2024
Coronation †	1,184	Crowfoot	Chinook	Terrence Schneider, Adm., PO Box 219, Coronation T0C 1C0 – 403/578-3679, Fax: 403/578-3020
Coutts (V)	355	Lethbridge	Taber-Warner	Shirley A. Heather-Kalau, CAO, PO Box 202, Coutts T0K 0N0 – 403/344-3848, Fax: 403/344-4360

Canadian Almanac & Directory 1997

4-4 ALBERTA MUNICIPALITIES

Cities in CAPITALS; Towns marked †; Villages marked (V); Summer Villages marked (SV). Alberta Counties & Municipal Districts, Specialized Municipalities and Improvement Districts follow this list. An in-depth listing for municipalities marked with * appears in Part 2 (check Index for page numbers).

MUNICIPALITY	1994 POP.	FEDERAL ELECTORAL DISTRICT	PROVINCIAL ELECTORAL DISTRICT	CONTACT PERSON WITH ADDRESS, PHONE & FAX
Cowley (V)	277	Macleod	Pincher Creek-MacLeod	Laurie Wilgosh, Adm., PO Box 40, Cowley T0K 0P0 – 403/628-3808, Fax: 403/628-3808
Cremona (V)	393	Wild Rose	Olds-Didsbury	Cleta Haggerty, Mgr., PO Box 10, Cremona T0M 0R0 – 403/637-3762, Fax: 403/637-2101
Crossfield †	1,800	Wild Rose	Olds-Didsbury	Brian L. Irvine, CAO, PO Box 500, Crossfield T0M 0S0 – 403/946-5565, Fax: 403/946-4523
Crowsnest Pass †	6,679	Macleod	Pincher Creek-MacLeod	John Kapalka, Adm., PO Box 600, Blairmore T0K 0E0 – 403/562-8833, Fax: 403/563-5474
Crystal Springs (SV)	40	Wetaskiwin	Drayton Valley-Calmar	Bernie Bawol, Adm., 46 Mission St., Sherwood Park T8A 0V7 – 403/464-2346, Fax: 403/464-2346
Czar (V)	176	Vegreville	Wainwright	Tricia Strang, Adm., PO Box 30, Czar T0B 0Z0 – 403/857-3740, Fax: 403/857-2353
Daysland †	674	Vegreville	Wainwright	Avril Crossley, Adm., PO Box 610, Daysland T0B 1A0 – 403/374-3767, Fax: 403/374-2455
Delburne (V)	564	Crowfoot	Innisfail-Sylvan Lake	David Sarsfield, Adm., PO Box 341, Delburne T0M 0V0 – 403/749-3606, Fax: 403/749-2800
Delia (V)	198	Crowfoot	Drumheller	Velma V. Kalhs, Sec.-Treas., PO Box 206, Delia T0J 0W0 – 403/364-3787, Fax: 403/364-2089
Derwent (V)	109	Vegreville	Vermillion-Lloydminster	Shirley Crabbe, Sec.-Treas., PO Box 102, Derwent T0B 1C0 – 403/741-3792, Fax: 403/741-3792
Devon †	4,380	Wetaskiwin	Leduc	Gerald Rhodes, Mgr., PO Box 400, Devon T0C 1E0 – 403/987-3366, Fax: 403/987-4778
Dewberry (V)	203	Vegreville	Vermillion-Lloydminster	Anne Elliott, Sec.-Treas., PO Box 30, Dewberry T0B 1G0 – 403/847-3053
Didsbury †	3,399	Wild Rose	Olds-Didsbury	Evan Parliament, CAO, PO Box 790, Didsbury T0M 0W0 – 403/335-3391, Fax: 403/335-9794
Donalda (V)	232	Crowfoot	Lacombe-Stettler	Deborah Hiller, Adm., PO Box 160, Donalda T0B 1H0 – 403/883-2345, Fax: 403/883-2022
Donnelly (V)	421	Peace River	Dunvegan	Denis Maisonneuve, Adm., PO Box 200, Donnelly T0H 1G0 – 403/925-3835, Fax: 403/925-2100
Drayton Valley †	5,983	Yellowhead	Drayton Valley-Calmar	Manny Deol, Mgr., PO Box 6837, Drayton Valley T7A 1A1 – 403/542-5327, Fax: 403/542-5753
DRUMHELLER	6,277	Crowfoot	Drumheller	Raymond Romanetz, Mgr., 703 - 2 Ave. West, Drumheller T0J 0Y3 – 403/823-6300, Fax: 403/823-7739
Duchess (V)	588	Medicine Hat	Bow Valley	Karen Grove, Sec.-Treas., PO Box 158, Duchess T0J 0Z0 – 403/378-4452, Fax: 403/378-3860
Eaglesham (V)	184	Peace River	Dunvegan	Hope Mazurek, Sec.-Treas., PO Box 209, Eaglesham T0H 1H0 – 403/359-3895, Fax: 403/359-2550
Eckville †	899	Red Deer	Rocky Mountain House	Therese Kleeberger, Adm., PO Box 578, Eckville T0M 0X0 – 403/746-2171, Fax: 403/746-2900
Edberg (V)	145	Crowfoot	Ponoka-Rimbey	Bernice McAmmond, Adm., PO Box 160, Edberg T0B 1J0 – 403/877-3999, 3959, Fax: 403/877-2562
Edgerton (V)	389	Vegreville	Wainwright	Mary Trefiak, CAO, PO Box 57, Edgerton T0B 1K0 – 403/755-3933, Fax: 403/755-3750
*EDMONTON	637,442 ('95)	Edmonton East; Edmonton North; Edmonton Northwest; Edmonton Southeast; Edmonton Southwest; Edmonton-Strathcona	Edmonton-Avonmore; Ed.-Beverly-Belmont; Ed.-Centre; Ed.-Ellerslie; Ed.-Glengarry; Ed.-Glenora; Ed.-Gold Bar; Ed.-Highlands-Beverly; Ed.-Manning; Ed.-Mayfield; Ed.-McClung; Ed.-Meadowlark; Ed.-Mill Woods; Ed.-Norwood; Ed.-Roper; Ed.-Rutherford; Ed.-Strathcona; Ed.-Whitemud	Ulli S. Watkiss, Clerk, City Hall, 1 Sir Winston Churchill Sq., Edmonton T5J 2R7 – 403/496-8222, Fax: 403/496-8220, URL: http://www.gov.edmonton.ab.ca
Edmonton Beach (SV)	352	St. Albert	Stony Plain	Lori Donner, CAO, Box 77, Site 3, RR#4, Stony Plain T7Z 1X4 – 403/963-4211, Fax: 403/963-4260
Edson †	7,323	Yellowhead	West Yellowhead	Clarence Joly, Mgr., PO Box 6300, Edson T7E 1T7 – 403/723-4401, Fax: 403/723-3508
Elk Point †	1,341	Beaver River	Lac La Biche-St Paul	J. Curt Svendsen, Mgr., PO Box 448, Elk Point T0A 1A0 – 403/724-3810, Fax: 403/724-2762
Elnora (V)	262	Crowfoot	Innisfail-Sylvan Lake	Gwen Renouf, Adm., PO Box 629, Elnora T0M 0Y0 – 403/773-3922, Fax: 403/773-3922
Empress (V)	189	Medicine Hat	Bow Valley	Wendi Miller, Sec., PO Box 159, Empress T0J 1E0 – 403/565-3938, Fax: 403/565-2010
Entwistle (V)	460	Yellowhead	Stony Plain	Elsie Patterson, Adm., PO Box 270, Entwistle T0E 0S0 – 403/727-3652, Fax: 403/727-2168
Evansburg (V)	723	Yellowhead	Whitecourt-Ste Anne	Lauren Donald Craven, Adm., PO Box 39, Evansburg T0E 0T0 – 403/727-3583, Fax: 403/727-2384
Fairview †	3,262	Peace River	Dunvegan	Larry Chorney, Mgr., PO Box 730, Fairview T0H 1L0 – 403/835-5461, Fax: 403/835-3576

Cities in CAPITALS; Towns marked †; Villages marked (V); Summer Villages marked (SV). Alberta Counties & Municipal Districts, Specialized Municipalities and Improvement Districts follow this list. An in-depth listing for municipalities marked with * appears in Part 2 (check Index for page numbers).

MUNICIPALITY	1994 POP.	FEDERAL ELECTORAL DISTRICT	PROVINCIAL ELECTORAL DISTRICT	CONTACT PERSON WITH ADDRESS, PHONE & FAX
Falher †	1,183	Peace River	Dunvegan	Gerard A. Nicolet, Adm., PO Box 155, Falher T0H 1M0 – 403/837-2247, Fax: 403/837-2647
Ferintosh (V)	129	Crowfoot	Ponoka-Rimbey	Myrna Fankhanel, Adm., PO Box 160, Ferintosh T0B 1M0 – 403/877-3767, Fax: 403/877-3767
Foremost (V)	582	Medicine Hat	Cypress-Medicine Hat	Kelly Calhoun, Adm., PO Box 159, Foremost T0K 0X0 – 403/867-3733, Fax: 403/867-2031
Forestburg (V)	967	Vegreville	Wainwright	Marion Oberg Riise, Adm., PO Box 210, Forestburg T0B 1N0 – 403/582-3668, Fax: 403/582-2233
Fort Macleod †	3,112	Macleod	Pincher Creek-MacLeod	Lane McLaren, Mgr., PO Box 1420, Fort Macleod T0L 0Z0 – 403/553-4425, Fax: 403/553-2426
FORT SASKATCHEWAN	12,313	Elk Island	Clover Bar-Fort Saskatchewan	Laurine Gunness, Clerk, 10005 - 102 St., Fort Saskatchewan T8L 2C5 – 403/992-6200, Fax: 403/998-4774
Fox Creek †	2,260	Yellowhead	Grande Prairie-Smoky	Blaine Alexander, Mgr., PO Box 149, Fox Creek T0H 1P0 – 403/622-3896, Fax: 403/622-4247
Gadsby (V)	26	Crowfoot	Lacombe-Stettler	Lavone Smith, Sec.-Treas., PO Box 80, Gadsby T0C 1K0 – 403/574-3793
Galahad (V)	158	Vegreville	Wainwright	Donna Schroeder, Adm., PO Box 66, Galahad T0B 1R0 – 403/583-3741, Fax: 403/583-2230
Ghost Lake (SV)	53	Wild Rose	Banff-Cochrane	Ernest Janzen, Adm., PO Box 207, Carseland T0J 0M0 – 403/934-5008, Fax: 403/934-5008
Gibbons †	2,762	Beaver River	Redwater	Maisie Metrunec, Mgr., PO Box 68, Gibbons T0A 1N0 – 403/923-3331, Fax: 403/923-3691
Girouxville (V)	349	Peace River	Dunvegan	Estelle Girard, Adm., PO Box 276, Girouxville T0H 1S0 – 403/323-4270, Fax: 403/323-4110
Gleichen †	331	Wild Rose	Little Bow	Phyllis Allen, Adm., PO Box 159, Gleichen T0J 1N0 – 403/734-3732, Fax: 403/734-2660
Glendon (V)	404	Beaver River	Bonnyville	Tammy Hellum, Sec., PO Box 177, Glendon T0A 1P0 – 403/635-3807, Fax: 403/653-2100
Glenwood (V)	310	Macleod	Cardston-Chief Mountain	Gordon Burt, Adm., PO Box 1084, Glenwood T0K 2R0 – 403/626-3233, Fax: 403/626-3233
Golden Days (SV)	65	Wetaskiwin	Drayton Valley-Calmar	John F. Tyler, CAO, 16815 - 117 Av., Edmonton T5M 3V6 – 403/483-4129, Fax: 403/451-0221
Grande Cache †	3,842	Yellowhead	West Yellowhead	Duane J. Dukart, Adm., PO Box 300, Grande Cache T0E 0Y0 – 403/827-3362, Fax: 403/827-2406
GRANDE PRAIRIE	29,242	Peace River	Grande Prairie-Smoky; Grande Prairie-Wapiti	Janette Ferguson, City Clerk, City Hall, PO Bag 4000, Grande Prairie T8V 6V3 – 403/538-0300, Fax: 403/539-1056; URL: http://www.ccinet.ab.ca/city-of-gp/homepage.html
Grandview (SV)	50	Wetaskiwin	Drayton Valley-Calmar	Kathy Graber, Adm., PO Box 99, Ma Me O Beach T0C 1X0 – 403/586-2251, Fax: 403/586-3615
Granum †	371	Macleod	Pincher Creek-MacLeod	Ruth Lindsay, Adm., PO Box 88, Granum T0L 1A0 – 403/687-3822, Fax: 403/687-2285
Grassy Lake (V)	284	Medicine Hat	Taber-Warner	Diane Skiba, Adm., PO Box 629, Grassy Lake T0K 0Z0 – 403/655-2377, Fax: 403/655-2444
Grimshaw †	2,812	Peace River	Dunvegan	Jenny Cole, Sec., PO Box 377, Grimshaw T0H 1W0 – 403/332-4626, Fax: 403/332-1250
Gull Lake (SV)	108	Wetaskiwin	Rocky Mountain House	Larry E. Waud, Adm., #2, 22 Bruns Rd., Lacombe T4L 1N9 – 403/782-2510, Fax: 403/782-2510
Hairy Hill (V)	54	Vegreville	Vegreville-Viking	Don Laing, Adm., PO Box 83, Hairy Hill T0B 1S0 – 403/768-3840, Fax: 403/768-3840
Half Moon Bay (SV)	51	Beaver River	Rocky Mountain House	Marianne Whitehead, Adm., #104, 4505 - 50 Av., Sylvan Lake T4S 1V9 – 403/887-2822, Fax: 403/887-2897
Halkirk (V)	150	Crowfoot	Chinook	H. Jean Anderson, Sec.-Treas., PO Box 126, Halkirk T0C 1M0 – 403/884-2464, Fax: 403/884-2113
Hanna †	2,996	Crowfoot	Chinook	J. Duff Carroll, Mgr., PO Box 430, Hanna T0J 1P0 – 403/854-4433, Fax: 403/854-2772
Hardisty †	656	Vegreville	Wainwright	Debbie Johannesson, Adm., PO Box 10, Hardisty T0B 1V0 – 403/888-3623, Fax: 403/888-2200
Hay Lakes (V)	327	Elk Island	Leduc	Jennifer Grahn, Adm., PO Box 40, Hay Lakes T0B 1W0 – 403/878-3200, Fax: 403/878-3200
Heisler (V)	186	Vegreville	Wainwright	Bonnie Bendfeld, Adm., PO Box 60, Heisler T0B 2A0 – 403/889-3774, Fax: 403/889-2280
High Level †	2,921	Peace River	Peace River	Anna Neustaeter, Sec., PO Box 485, High Level T0H 1Z0 – 403/926-2201, Fax: 403/926-2899
High Prairie †	2,932	Athabasca	Lesser Slave Lake	Kevin Greig, Mgr., PO Box 179, High Prairie T0G 1E0 – 403/523-3388, Fax: 403/523-5930
High River †	6,893	Macleod	Highwood	Gary Hudson, Mgr., 129 - 3 Ave. West, High River T1V 1M9 – 403/652-2110, Fax: 403/652-2396
Hill Spring (V)	238	Macleod	Cardston-Chief Mountain	Karen Folsom, Adm., PO Box 40, Hill Spring T0K 1E0 – 403/626-3876, Fax: 403/626-3876
Hines Creek (V)	423	Peace River	Dunvegan	Hazel Reintjes, Mgr., PO Box 421, Hines Creek T0H 2A0 – 403/494-3690, Fax: 403/494-3605

Cities in CAPITALS; Towns marked †; Villages marked (V); Summer Villages marked (SV). Alberta Counties & Municipal Districts, Specialized Municipalities and Improvement Districts follow this list. An in-depth listing for municipalities marked with * appears in Part 2 (check Index for page numbers).

MUNICIPALITY	1994 POP.	FEDERAL ELECTORAL DISTRICT	PROVINCIAL ELECTORAL DISTRICT	CONTACT PERSON WITH ADDRESS, PHONE & FAX
Hinton †	9,341	Yellowhead	West Yellowhead	Bernie Kreiner, Mgr., 813 Switzer Dr., Hinton T7V 1V1 – 403/865-6016, Fax: 403/865-5706, URL: http://www.ycs.ab.ca/market/hinton/index.htm
Holden (V)	411	Vegreville	Vegreville-Viking	Christine B. Mackay, CAO, PO Box 357, Holden T0B 2C0 – 403/688-3928, Fax: 403/688-2091
Horseshoe Bay (SV)	29	St. Paul	Lac La Biche-St Paul	Ken Parsons, Adm., 15035 - 80 St., Edmonton T5C 1M4 – 403/475-2407, Fax: 403/475-2407
Hughenden (V)	285	Vegreville	Wainwright	Trudy Pelsey, Adm., PO Box 26, Hughenden T0B 2E0 – 403/856-3830, Fax: 403/856-2034
Hussar (V)	150	Wild Rose	Drumheller	Valerie Allan, Adm., PO Box 100, Hussar T0J 1S0 – 403/787-3766
Hythe (V)	623	Peace River	Grande Prairie-Wapiti	Christene Livingstone, Adm., PO Box 219, Hythe T0H 2C0 – 403/356-3888, Fax: 403/356-2009
Innisfail †	5,858	Red Deer	Innisfail-Sylvan Lake	Dale P. Mather, CAO, 4945 - 53 St., Innisfail T4G 1A1 – 403/227-3376, Fax: 403/227-4045
Innisfree (V)	254	Vegreville	Vermilion-Lloydminster	Andrea Stepanik, Adm., PO Box 69, Innisfree T0B 2G0 – 403/592-3886, Fax: 403/592-3729
Irma (V)	442	Vegreville	Wainwright	Myron J. Goyan, CAO, PO Box 419, Irma T0B 2H0 – 403/754-3665, Fax: 403/754-3668
Irricana (V)	801	Wild Rose	Three Hills-Airdrie	Rosemary Wittevrongel, CAO, PO Box 100, Irricana T0M 1B0 – 403/935-4672, Fax: 403/935-4270
Irvine †	326	Medicine Hat	Cypress-Medicine Hat	Jo-Anne Lambert, Adm., PO Box 90, Irvine T0J 1V0 – 403/834-3923, Fax: 403/834-3894
Island Lake (SV)	122	Athabasca	Athabasca-Wabasca	Shelley Bowles, Adm., PO Box 119, Legal T0J 1L0 – 403/961-2487, Fax: 403/961-2024
Island Lake South (SV)	76	Athabasca-Lac la Biche	Athabasca-Wabasca	Ken Parsons, Adm., 15035 - 80 St., Edmonton T5C 1M4 – 403/475-2407, Fax: 403/475-2407
Itaska Beach (SV)	3	Wetaskiwin	Drayton Valley-Calmar	John F. Tyler, CAO, #73, 51559 RR 225, Sherwood Park T8C 1H5 – 403/464-0365, Fax: 403/464-4193
Jarvis Bay (SV)	33	Red Deer	Rocky Mountain House	Marianne Whitehead, Adm., #104, 4505 - 50 Av., Sylvan Lake T4S 1V9 – 403/464-0365, Fax: 403/464-4193
Kapasiwin (SV)	10	Yellowhead	Stony Plain	Jolly Drever, Adm., PO Box 3, Kapasiwin T0E 2Y0 – 403/892-2879
Killam †	1,053	Vegreville	Wainwright	Vera Engel, Adm., PO Box 189, Killam T0B 2L0 – 403/385-3977, Fax: 403/385-2120
Kinuso (V)	254	Athabasca	Lesser Slave Lake	June Roe, Adm., PO Box 57, Kinuso T0G 1K0 – 403/775-3570, Fax: 403/775-3910
Kitscoty (V)	622	Vegreville	Vermilion-Lloydminster	Jean E. Buha, Adm., PO Box 128, Kitscoty T0B 2P0 – 403/846-2221, Fax: 403/846-2221
Lac La Biche †	2,737	Beaver River	Lac la Biche-St Paul	Richard Persson, Sec., PO Box 387, Lac La Biche T0A 2C0 – 403/623-4323, Fax: 403/623-3510
Lacombe †	7,580	Wetaskiwin	Lacombe-Stettler	Robert Jenkins, CAO, 5034 - 52 St., Lacombe T4L 1A1 – 403/782-6666, Fax: 403/782-5655
Lakeview (SV)	27	Yellowhead	Stony Plain	Jeanette Killips, Sec.-Treas., 10544 - 55 Ave., Edmonton T6H 0W7 – 403/434-9975
Lamont †	1,574	Elk Island	Vegreville-Viking	Dean Pickering, CAO, PO Box 330, Lamont T0B 2R0 – 403/895-2010, Fax: 403/895-2595
Larkspur (SV)	9	Athabasca-Lac la Biche	Barrhead-Westlock	Don Baillie, Adm., PO Box 339, Boyle T0A 0M0 – 403/689-2080, Fax: 403/689-3998
Lavoy (V)	109	Vegreville	Vegreville-Viking	Shirley Rattray, Sec.-Treas., PO Box 179, Lavoy T0B 2S0 – 403/658-3788
LEDUC	14,117	Wetaskiwin	Leduc	Laura Reichert, Acting City Clerk, 1 Alexandra Park, Leduc T9E 4C4 – 403/980-7177, Fax: 403/980-7127
Legal (V)	945	St. Albert	Redwater	Wilma Weiss, Adm., PO Box 390, Legal T0G 1L0 – 403/961-3773, Fax: 403/961-4133
*LETHBRIDGE	64,938	Lethbridge	Lethbridge-East; Lethbridge-West	Dianne Nemeth, City Clerk, City Hall, 910 - 4 Ave. South, Lethbridge T1J 0P6 – 403/320-3900, Fax: 403/320-9369; URL: http://www.city.lethbridge.ab.ca
Linden (V)	504	Wild Rose	Three Hills-Airdrie	Ross Dean, Adm., PO Box 213, Linden T0M 1J0 – 403/546-3888, Fax: 403/546-2112
LLOYDMINSTER	10,042 ('94)	Vegreville	Vermillion-Lloydminster	Tom Lysyk, Clerk, City Hall, 5011 - 49 Ave., Lloydminster S9V 0T8 – 306/825-6184, Fax: 306/825-7170
Lomond (V)	167	Macleod	Little Bow	Tracy Doram, CAO, PO Box 268, Lomond T0L 1G0 – 403/792-3611, Fax: 403/792-3782
Longview (V)	304	Macleod	Highwood	Leslie Fitzgerald, Adm., PO Box 147, Longview T0L 1H0 – 403/558-3922, Fax: 403/558-3743
Lougheed (V)	266	Vegreville	Wainwright	Stan Towers, Sec.-Treas., PO Box 5, Lougheed T0B 2V0 – 403/386-3970, Fax: 403/386-2136
Ma Me O Beach (SV)	76	Wetaskiwin	Drayton Valley-Calmar	Kathy Graber, Adm., PO Box 99, Ma Me O Beach T0C 1X0 – 403/586-2251, Fax: 403/586-3615
Magrath †	1,743	Lethbridge	Cardston-Chief Mountain	Rodney Bly, Adm., PO Box 520, Magrath T0K 1J0 – 403/758-3212, Fax: 403/758-6333

ALBERTA MUNICIPALITIES 4-7

Cities in CAPITALS; Towns marked †; Villages marked (V); Summer Villages marked (SV). Alberta Counties & Municipal Districts, Specialized Municipalities and Improvement Districts follow this list. An in-depth listing for municipalities marked with * appears in Part 2 (check Index for page numbers).

MUNICIPALITY	1994 POP.	FEDERAL ELECTORAL DISTRICT	PROVINCIAL ELECTORAL DISTRICT	CONTACT PERSON WITH ADDRESS, PHONE & FAX
Manning †	1,139	Peace River	Peace River	Penny Kary, Sec.-Treas., PO Box 125, Manning T0H 2M0 – 403/836-3606, 3728, Fax: 403/836-3570
Mannville (V)	774	Vegreville	Vermilion-Lloydminster	Kent Staden, Adm., PO Box 180, Mannville T0B 2W0 – 403/763-3500, Fax: 403/763-3643
Marwayne (V)	484	Vegreville	Vermilion-Lloydminster	G.T. Horton, CAO, PO Box 113, Marwayne T0B 2X0 – 403/847-3962, Fax: 403/847-3896
Mayerthorpe †	1,692	Yellowhead	Whitecourt-Ste Anne	Ed Mitchell, Mgr., PO Box 420, Mayerthorpe T0E 1N0 – 403/786-2416, Fax: 403/786-4590
McLennan †	1,026	Peace River	Dunvegan	Richard Duncan, Mgr., PO Box 356, McLennan T0H 2L0 – 403/324-3065, Fax: 403/324-2288
MEDICINE HAT	45,892	Medicine Hat	Cypress-Medicine Hat; Medicine Hat	Larry P. Godin, Clerk, City Hall, 580 - 1 St. SE, Medicine Hat T1A 8E6 – 403/529-8222, 8220, Fax: 403/526-9030
Mewatha Beach (SV)	53	Athabasca	Athabasca-Wabasca	Don Baillie, Adm., PO Box 339, Boyle T0A 0M0 – 403/689-2080, Fax: 403/689-3998
Milk River †	926	Lethbridge	Taber-Warner	Lavinia Henderson, CAO, PO Box 270, Milk River T0K 1M0 – 403/647-3773, Fax: 403/647-3772
Millet †	2,005	Wetaskiwin	Wetaskiwin-Camrose	Michael E. (Mike) Storey, CAO, PO Box 270, Millet T0C 1Z0 – 403/387-4554, Fax: 403/387-4459
Milo (V)	120	Macleod	Little Bow	Colleen Deitz, Adm., PO Box 65, Milo T0L 1L0 – 403/599-3883, Fax: 403/599-2201
Minburn (V)	105	Vegreville	Vermilion-Lloydminster	Sherri-Anne Doolaege, Sec.-Treas., PO Box 65, Minburn T0B 3B0 – 403/593-3939, Fax: 403/593-2195
Mirror (V)	478	Crowfoot	Lacombe-Stettler	Lavern Clark, Adm., PO Box 130, Mirror T0B 3C0 – 403/788-3011, Fax: 403/788-2345
Morinville †	6,255	St. Albert	Spruce Grove-Sturgeon-St Albert	Angie Gibeault, Mgr., 10125 - 100 Ave., Morinville T8R 1L6 – 403/939-4361, Fax: 403/939-5633
Morrin (V)	251	Crowfoot	Drumheller	Annette Plachner, Sec.-Treas., PO Box 149, Morrin T0J 2B0 – 403/772-3870, Fax: 403/772-2123
Mundare †	596	Vegreville	Vegreville-Viking	Peter Polischuk, Adm., PO Box 348, Mundare T0B 3H0 – 403/764-3929, Fax: 403/764-2003
Munson (V)	159	Crowfoot	Drumheller	Ken Raduenz, Adm., PO Box 10, Munson T0J 2C0 – 403/823-6987, Fax: 403/823-6987
Myrnam (V)	342	Vegreville	Vermillion-Lloydminster	Gloria Yaremchuk, Sec.-Treas., PO Box 278, Myrnam T0B 3K0 – 403/366-3910, Fax: 403/366-3910
Nakamun Park (SV)	9	Yellowhead	Whitecourt-Ste Anne	Shelley Bowles, Sec.-Treas., Site 1, RR#1, Onoway T0E 1V0 – 403/961-2024, Fax: 403/961-2024
Nampa (V)	496	Peace River	Peace River	Sharon Unrau, Adm., PO Box 69, Nampa T0H 2R0 – 403/322-3852, Fax: 403/322-2100
Nanton †	1,612	Macleod	Little Bow	Karen G. Harty, Adm., PO Box 609, Nanton T0L 1R0 – 403/646-2029, Fax: 403/646-2653
New Norway (V)	273	Crowfoot	Ponoka-Rimbey	Anne Flynn, Adm., PO Box 60, New Norway T0B 3L0 – 403/855-3915, Fax: 403/855-3915
New Sarepta (V)	404	Elk Island	Leduc	Orville Borys, Adm., PO Box 278, New Sarepta T0B 3M0 – 403/941-3929, Fax: 403/941-3929
Nobleford (V)	573	Lethbridge	Little Bow	Darrell Garceau, Adm., PO Box 67, Nobleford T0L 1S0 – 403/824-3555, Fax: 403/824-3555
Norglenwold (SV)	186	Red Deer	Rocky Mountain House	Marianne Whitehead, Adm., #104, 4505 - 50 Av., Sylvan Lake T4S 1V9 – 403/887-2822, Fax: 403/887-2897
Norris Beach (SV)	20	Wetaskiwin	Drayton Valley-Calmar	John B. Ludwig, Adm., 9615 - 152 St., Edmonton T5P 1W7 – 403/484-4213, Fax: 403/481-2887
Okotoks †	7,789	Macleod	Highwood	Richard Quail, Acting Mun. Commr., PO Box 220, Okotoks T0L 1T0 – 403/938-4404, Fax: 403/938-7387
Olds †	5,542	Wild Rose	Olds-Didsbury	Garry Gelech, CAO, 4911 - 51 Ave., Olds T4H 1R5 – 403/556-6981, Fax: 403/556-6537
Onoway (V)	681	Yellowhead	Whitecourt-Ste Anne	Catherine Dunn, Director of Municipal Operations, PO Box 540, Onoway T0E 1V0 – 403/967-5338, Fax: 403/967-3226
Oyen †	1,070	Crowfoot	Chinook	Debbie Kovitch, Adm., PO Box 360, Oyen T0J 2J0 – 403/664-3511, 3585, Fax: 403/664-3712
Paradise Valley (V)	136	Vegreville	Vermillion-Lloydminster	Barbara Viel, Adm., PO Box 24, Paradise Valley T0B 3R0 – 403/745-2287, Fax: 403/745-2287
Parkland Beach (SV)	66	Ponoka-Rimbey	Wetaskiwin	Susan Koots, Adm., PO Box 130, Rimbey T0C 2J0 – 403/843-2055, Fax: 403/843-6499
Peace River †	6,696	Peace River	Peace River	Gordon Lundy, Mgr., PO Box 6600, Peace River T8S 1S4 – 403/624-2574, Fax: 403/624-4664
Pelican Narrows (SV)	95	Athabasca	Bonnyville	Padey Lapointe, Adm., PO Box 7878, Bonnyville T9N 2J2 – 403/826-5907
Penhold †	1,590	Red Deer	Innisfail-Sylvan Lake	Linda See, Adm., PO Box 10, Penhold T0M 1R0 – 403/886-4567, Fax: 403/886-4039
Picture Butte †	1,559	Lethbridge	Little Bow	Nona C. Housenga, Adm., PO Box 670, Picture Butte T0K 1V0 – 403/732-4555, 4482, Fax: 403/732-4335
Pincher Creek †	3,660	Macleod	Pincher Creek-MacLeod	Sandy Chrapko, Mgr., PO Box 159, Pincher Creek T0K 1W0 – 403/627-3156, Fax: 403/627-4784

Canadian Almanac & Directory 1997

ALBERTA MUNICIPALITIES

Cities in CAPITALS; Towns marked †; Villages marked (V); Summer Villages marked (SV). Alberta Counties & Municipal Districts, Specialized Municipalities and Improvement Districts follow this list. An in-depth listing for municipalities marked with * appears in Part 2 (check Index for page numbers).

MUNICIPALITY	1994 POP.	FEDERAL ELECTORAL DISTRICT	PROVINCIAL ELECTORAL DISTRICT	CONTACT PERSON WITH ADDRESS, PHONE & FAX
Plamondon (V)	253	Beaver River	Lac la Biche-St Paul	Collette Borgen, Adm., PO Box 98, Plamondon T0A 2T0 – 403/798-3883, Fax: 403/789-2400
Point Alison (SV)	1	Yellowhead	Stony Plain	Birch Nero, Adm., 112 Langholm Dr., St. Albert T8N 3N9 – 403/458-0285
Ponoka †	5,861	Wetaskiwin	Ponoka-Rimbey	Dave Dmytryshyn, Mgr., 5102 - 48 Ave., Ponoka T4J 1P7 – 403/783-4431, Fax: 403/783-6745
Poplar Bay (SV)	47	Wetaskiwin	Drayton Valley-Calmar	John B. Ludwig, Adm., 9615 - 152 St., Edmonton T5P 1W7 – 403/484-4213, Fax: 403/481-2887
Provost †	1,893	Vegreville	Wainwright	Lynda P. Berry, Adm., PO Box 449, Provost T0B 3S0 – 403/753-2261, Fax: 403/753-6889
Radway (V)	173	Beaver River	Redwater	Jeanette Kruhlak, Adm., PO Box 280, Radway T0A 2V0 – 403/736-3574, Fax: 403/736-3858
Rainbow Lake †	880	Peace River	Peace River	J. Melville Burge, Mgr., PO Box 149, Rainbow Lake T0H 2Y0 – 403/956-3934, Fax: 403/956-3570
Raymond †	3,130	Lethbridge	Cardston-Chief Mountain	Scott Barton, CAO, PO Box 629, Raymond T0K 2S0 – 403/752-3322, Fax: 403/752-4379
*RED DEER	59,834 ('96)	Red Deer	Red Deer-North; Red Deer-South	Kelly Kloss, Clerk, City Hall, PO Box 5008, Red Deer T4N 3T4 – 403/342-8111, 8132, Fax: 403/346-6195
Redcliff †	3,806	Medicine Hat	Bow Valley	Randy Giesbrecht, Mgr., PO Box 40, Redcliff T0J 2P0 – 403/548-3618, Fax: 403/548-6623
Redwater †	2,090	Beaver River	Redwater	Don McLeod, Mgr., PO Box 397, Redwater T0A 2W0 – 403/942-3519, Fax: 403/942-4321
Rimbey †	2,133	Wetaskiwin	Ponoka-Rimbey	Greg Gayton, Mgr., PO Box 350, Rimbey T0C 2J0 – 403/843-2113, Fax: 403/843-6599
Rochon Sands (SV)	36	Crowfoot	Lacombe-Stettler	Harvey Kassian, Adm., PO Box 1746, Stettler T0C 2L0 – 403/742-4717, 4668
Rocky Mountain House †	5,684	Red Deer	Rocky Mountain House	Larry Holstead, Mgr., PO Box 1509, Rocky Mountain House T0M 1T0 – 403/845-2866, Fax: 403/845-3230
Rockyford (V)	331	Wild Rose	Drumheller	Lois Mountjoy, Adm., PO Box 294, Rockyford T0J 2R0 – 403/533-3950, Fax: 403/533-3950
Rosalind (V)	192	Crowfoot	Ponoka-Rimbey	Maxine King, Adm., General Delivery, Rosalind T0B 3Y0 – 403/375-3996, Fax: 403/375-3996
Rosemary (V)	337	Medicine Hat	Bow Valley	Wanda Lepp, Sec.-Treas., PO Box 128, Rosemary T0J 2W0 – 403/378-4246, Fax: 403/378-3144
Ross Haven (SV)	83	Yellowhead	Whitecourt-Ste Anne	Dennis Evans, Adm., 16, 26213 Township Rd. 512, Spruce Grove T7Y 1C6 – 403/987-3204, 495-4747, Fax: 403/987-3204
Rumsey (V)	60	Crowfoot	Drumheller	Debra Anderson, Sec., PO Box 110, Rumsey T0J 2Y0 – 403/368-3952
Rycroft (V)	634	Peace River	Dunvegan	Sandra Isaac, Adm., PO Box 360, Rycroft T0H 3A0 – 403/765-3652, Fax: 403/765-2002
Ryley (V)	432	Vegreville	Vegreville-Viking	Bob Luross, Adm., PO Box 230, Ryley T0B 4A0 – 403/663-3653, Fax: 403/663-3541
ST. ALBERT	45,985	St. Albert	Spruce Grove-Sturgeon-St Albert; St Albert	Fiona Daniel, Clerk, 5 St. Anne St., St. Albert T8N 3Z9 – 403/459-1500, Fax: 403/458-1974; URL: http://www.city.st-albert.ab.ca
St. Paul †	5,021	Beaver River	Lac La Biche-St Paul	Wayne C. Horner, Adm., PO Box 1480, St. Paul T0A 3A0 – 403/645-4481, Fax: 403/645-5076
Sandy Beach (SV)	116	Yellowhead	Whitecourt-Ste Anne	Shelley Bowles, Adm., Site 1, RR#1, PO Box 63, Onoway T0E 1V0 – 403/967-2873, Fax: 403/967-2873
Sangudo (V)	405	Yellowhead	Whitecourt-Ste Anne	Pamela Nelson, Adm., PO Box 190, Sangudo T0E 2A0 – 403/785-2258, Fax: 403/785-3393
Seba Beach (SV)	118	Yellowhead	Stony Plain	Susan Dzus, Adm., PO Box 190, Seba Beach T0E 2B0 – 403/797-3863, Fax: 403/797-3800
Sedgewick †	874	Vegreville	Wainwright	Colin J. Dean Craven, Adm., PO Box 129, Sedgewick T0B 4C0 – 403/384-3504, Fax: 403/384-3545
Sexsmith †	1,354	Peace River	Grande Prairie-Smoky	Irene Basisty, Mgr., PO Box 420, Sexsmith T0H 3C0 – 403/568-3681, Fax: 403/568-2200
Silver Beach (SV)	36	Wetaskiwin	Drayton Valley-Calmar	Ken D. Armstrong, Adm., 9322 - 73 Ave., Edmonton T6E 1A7 – 403/433-4969, Fax: 403/433-4969
Silver Sands (SV)	84	Yellowhead	Whitecourt-Ste Anne	Mark T. Anker, Adm., 14403 - 110A Ave., Edmonton T5N 1J7 – 403/454-9414
Slave Lake †	5,607	Athabasca	Lesser Slave Lake	Pat Vincent, Mgr., PO Box 1030, Slave Lake T0G 2A0 – 403/849-8000, Fax: 403/849-2633
Smoky Lake †	1,057	Beaver River	Redwater	Harvey Prockiw, Mgr., PO Box 460, Smoky Lake T0A 3C0 – 403/656-3674, Fax: 403/656-3675
South Baptiste (SV)	84	Athabaska	Athabasca-Wabasca	Don Baillie, Adm., PO Box 339, Boyle T0A 0M0 – 403/689-2080, Fax: 403/689-3998
South View (SV)	43	Yellowhead	Whitecourt-Ste Anne	Mark T. Anker, Adm., 14403 - 110A Ave., Edmonton T5N 1J7 – 403/454-9414
Spirit River †	1,102	Peace River	Dunvegan	Ron Thompson, Mgr., PO Box 130, Spirit River T0H 3G0 – 403/864-3998, Fax: 403/864-3433

ALBERTA MUNICIPALITIES 4-9

Cities in CAPITALS; Towns marked †; Villages marked (V); Summer Villages marked (SV). Alberta Counties & Municipal Districts, Specialized Municipalities and Improvement Districts follow this list. An in-depth listing for municipalities marked with * appears in Part 2 (check Index for page numbers).

MUNICIPALITY	1994 POP.	FEDERAL ELECTORAL DISTRICT	PROVINCIAL ELECTORAL DISTRICT	CONTACT PERSON WITH ADDRESS, PHONE & FAX
SPRUCE GROVE	13,076	St. Albert	Spruce Grove-Sturgeon-St Albert	Diane Roy, Clerk, 315 Jespersen Ave., Spruce Grove T7X 3E8 – 403/962-2611, Fax: 403/962-2526
Standard (V)	359	Wild Rose	Drumheller	Evelyn Larsen, CAO, PO Box 249, Standard T0J 3G0 – 403/644-3968, Fax: 403/644-2284
Stavely †	528	Macleod	Little Bow	Sheryl Fath, Adm., PO Box 249, Stavely T0L 1Z0 – 403/549-3761, Fax: 403/549-3743
Stettler †	4,947	Vegreville	Lacombe-Stettler	Robert Stoutenberg, Mgr., PO Box 280, Stettler T0C 2L0 – 403/742-8305, Fax: 403/742-1404
Stirling (V)	810	Lethbridge	Taber-Warner	J. Scott Barton, Adm., PO Box 360, Stirling T0K 2E0 – 403/756-3379, Fax: 403/756-2262
Stony Plain †	7,405	St. Albert	Stony Plain	Phil Hamel, Mgr., 4905 - 51 Ave., Stony Plain T7Z 1Y1 – 403/963-2151, Fax: 403/963-0935
Strathmore †	4,880	Wild Rose	Drumheller	Dwight Stanford, Mgr., 680 Westchester Rd., Strathmore T1P 1J1 – 403/934-3133, Fax: 403/934-4713
Strome (V)	274	Vegreville	Wainwright	Betty Mohler, Adm., PO Box 51, Strome T0B 4H0 – 403/376-3558, Fax: 403/376-3558
Sunbreaker Cove (SV)	76	Red Deer	Rocky Mountain House	Marianne Whitehead, Adm., #104, 4505 - 50 Av., Sylvan Lake T4S 1V9 – 403/887-2822, Fax: 403/887-2897
Sundance Beach (SV)	22	Wetaskiwin	Drayton Valley-Calmar	Ken Armstrong, Adm., 9322 - 73 Ave., Edmonton T6E 1A7 – 403/433-4969, Fax: 403/433-4969
Sundre †	2,027	Wild Rose	Olds-Didsbury	Harvey Doering, Adm., PO Box 420, Sundre T0M 1X0 – 403/638-3551, Fax: 403/638-2100
Sunrise Beach (SV)	80	Yellowhead	Whitecourt-Ste Anne	Shelley Bowles, Adm., Site 1, RR#1, PO Box 18, Onoway T0E 1V0 – 403/967-5473, Fax: 403/967-2873
Sunset Beach (SV)	46	Athabasca	Athabasca-Wabasca	Jim Pollock, Adm., Site 1, RR#1, PO Box 39, Onoway T0E 1V0 – 403/967-5473, Fax: 403/967-5473
Sunset Point (SV)	89	Yellowhead	Whitecourt-Ste Anne	Robert L. Tessier, CAO, 120 Country Club Place, Edmonton T6M 2H7 – 403/481-5017
Swan Hills †	2,348	Yellowhead	Barrhead-Westlock	Brad Watson, Mgr., PO Box 149, Swan Hills T0G 2C0 – 403/333-4477, Fax: 403/333-4547
Sylvan Lake †	4,815	Red Deer	Innisfail-Sylvan Lake	Lyle Wack, Mgr., 4926 - 50 Ave., Sylvan Lake T4S 1A1 – 403/887-2141, Fax: 403/887-3660
Taber †	6,660	Medicine Hat	Taber-Warner	Bill Landiuk, Acting Mgr., 4900A - 50 St., Taber T1G 1T1 – 403/223-5500, Fax: 403/223-5530
Thorhild (V)	502	Beaver River	Redwater	Debbie Hamilton, Adm., PO Box 310, Thorhild T0A 3J0 – 403/398-3688, Fax: 403/398-2100
Thorsby (V)	708	Wetaskiwin	Drayton Valley-Calmar	Elizabeth Megyesi, CAO, PO Box 297, Thorsby T0C 2P0 – 403/789-3935, Fax: 403/789-3779
Three Hills †	3,298	Crowfoot	Three Hills-Airdrie	Jack Ramsden, Mgr., PO Box 610, Three Hills T0M 2A0 – 403/443-5822, Fax: 403/443-2616
Tilley (V)	331	Medicine Hat	Bow Valley	Debbie Guilbault, Sec., PO Box 155, Tilley T0J 3K0 – 403/377-2203, Fax: 403/377-2203
Tofield †	1,660	Vegreville	Vegreville-Viking	Cindy Neufeld, Adm., PO Box 30, Tofield T0B 4J0 – 403/662-3269, Fax: 403/662-3929
Torrington (V)	177	Wild Rose	Three Hills-Airdrie	Irene Wilson, Adm., PO Box 10, Torrington T0M 2B0 – 403/631-3866, Fax: 403/631-2140
Trochu †	907	Crowfoot	Three Hills-Airdrie	Maureen Malaka, Adm., PO Box 340, Trochu T0M 2C0 – 403/442-3085, Fax: 403/442-2528
Turner Valley †	1,458	Macleod	Highwood	Sharon Plett, Mgr., PO Box 330, Turner Valley T0L 2A0 – 403/933-4944, Fax: 403/933-5377
Two Hills †	1,108	Vegreville	Vegreville-Viking	Jerry Taschuk, Adm., PO Box 630, Two Hills T0B 4K0 – 403/657-3395, Fax: 403/657-2158
Val Quentin (SV)	115	Yellowhead	Whitecourt Ste-Anne	Lori Donner, CAO, PO Box 128, Alberta Beach T0E 0A0 – 403/924-3085, Fax: 403/963-4260
Valleyview †	2,039	Peace River	Grande Prairie-Smoky	Doug Topinka, Mgr., PO Box 270, Valleyview T0H 3N0 – 403/524-5150, Fax: 403/524-2727
Vauxhall †	996	Medicine Hat	Little Bow	Earla Wagar, Adm., PO Box 509, Vauxhall T0K 2K0 – 403/654-2174, Fax: 403/654-4110
Vegreville †	5,138	Vegreville	Vegreville-Viking	Richard Binnendyk, Mgr., PO Box 640, Vegreville T9C 1R7 – 403/632-2606, Fax: 403/632-3088
Vermilion †	4,258	Vegreville	Vermilion-Lloydminster	Robert Watt, Mgr., PO Box 328, Vermilion T0B 4M0 – 403/853-5358, Fax: 403/853-4910
Veteran (V)	297	Crowfoot	Chinook	Betty A. Christianson, Adm., PO Box 439, Veteran T0C 2S0 – 403/575-3954, Fax: 403/575-3954
Viking †	1,109	Vegreville	Vegreville-Viking	Lydia Hanson, CAO, PO Box 369, Viking T0B 4N0 – 403/336-3466, Fax: 403/336-2660
Vilna (V)	314	Beaver River	Lac La Biche-St Paul	Linda Kolewaski, Adm., PO Box 10, Vilna T0A 3L0 – 403/636-3620
Vulcan †	1,466	Macleod	Little Bow	George Balash, Adm., PO Box 360, Vulcan T0L 2B0 – 403/485-2417, Fax: 403/485-2914
Wabamun (V)	600	Yellowhead	Stony Plain	Leagh Randle, Adm., PO Box 240, Wabamun T0E 2K0 – 403/892-2699, Fax: 403/892-2669

Canadian Almanac & Directory 1997

Cities in CAPITALS; Towns marked †; Villages marked (V); Summer Villages marked (SV). Alberta Counties & Municipal Districts, Specialized Municipalities and Improvement Districts follow this list. An in-depth listing for municipalities marked with * appears in Part 2 (check Index for page numbers).

MUNICIPALITY	1994 POP.	FEDERAL ELECTORAL DISTRICT	PROVINCIAL ELECTORAL DISTRICT	CONTACT PERSON WITH ADDRESS, PHONE & FAX
Wainwright †	4,891	Vegreville	Wainwright	Ray Poulin, Adm., 1018 - 2 Ave, Wainwright T9W 1R1 – 403/842-3381, Fax: 403/842-2898
Waiparous (SV)	53	Wild Rose	Banff-Cochrane	Sharon Plett, Adm., PO Box 5754, High River T1V 1P3 – 403/652-4636, Fax: 403/652-3125
Wanham (V)	216	Peace River	Dunvegan	Tara L. Foote, Adm., PO Box 189, Wanham T0H 3P0 – 403/694-3946, Fax: 403/694-2647
Warburg (V)	519	Wetaskiwin	Drayton Valley-Calmar	Chris Pankewitz, Adm., PO Box 29, Warburg T0C 2T0 – 403/848-2841, Fax: 403/848-2296
Warner (V)	450	Lethbridge	Taber-Warner	Arlene B. Gerard, Adm., PO Box 88, Warner T0K 2L0 – 403/642-3877, Fax: 403/642-2011
Warspite (V)	73	Beaver River	Redwater	Joan Prusak, Sec.-Treas., PO Box 96, Warspite T0A 3N0 – 403/383-3838, Fax: 403/383-3757
Waskatenau (V)	257	Beaver River	Redwater	Bernice Macyk, Adm., PO Box 99, Waskatenau T0A 3P0 – 403/358-2208, Fax: 403/358-2208
Wembley †	1,424	Peace River	Grande Prairie-Wapiti	Karen Steinke, Adm., PO Box 89, Wembley T0H 3S0 – 403/766-2269, Fax: 403/766-2868
West Baptiste (SV)	36	Athabasca-Lac la Biche	Athabasca-Wabasca	Ken Parsons, Adm., 15035 - 80 St., Edmonton T5C 1M4 – 403/475-2407, Fax: 403/475-2407
West Cove (SV)	81	Yellowhead	Whitecourt-Ste Anne	Mark T. Anker, Adm., 14403 - 110A Ave., Edmonton T5N 1J7 – 403/454-9414
Westlock †	4,719	Athabasca	Barrhead-Westlock	Garth Bancroft, Adm., PO Box 2220, Westlock T0G 2L0 – 403/349-4444, Fax: 403/349-4436
WETASKIWIN	10,771	Wetaskiwin	Wetaskiwin-Camrose	Shelley Klinger, Clerk, 4904 - 51 St., Wetaskiwin T9A 1L2 – 403/352-3344, Fax: 403/352-0930
Whispering Hills (SV)	69	Athabasca	Athabasca-Wabasca	Norm Milke, Adm., #1502, 12319 Jasper Ave., Edmonton T5N 4A7 – 403/488-5603
White Gull (SV)	20	Athabasca	Athabasca-Wabasca	Don Baillie, Adm., PO Box 339, Boyle T0A 0M0 – 403/689-2080, Fax: 403/689-3998
White Sands (SV)	21	Crowfoot	Lacombe-Stettler	Robert J. Krejci, Sec.-Tres., PO Box 460, Stettler T0C 2L0 – 403/742-4431, Fax: 403/742-1266
Whitecourt †	7,056	Yellowhead	Whitecourt-Ste Anne	W.L. (Bud) Winger, Mgr., PO Box 509, Whitecourt T7S 1N6 – 403/778-2273, Fax: 403/778-4166
Willingdon (V)	355	Vegreville	Vegreville-Viking	Olivia Walcheske, Adm., PO Box 210, Willingdon T0B 4R0 – 403/367-2337, Fax: 403/367-2167
Yellowstone (SV)	97	Yellowhead	Whitecourt-Ste Anne	Mark T. Anker, Adm., 14403 - 110A Ave., Edmonton T5N 1J7 – 403/454-9414
Youngstown (V)	245	Crowfoot	Chinook	Evelyn Blagen, Adm., PO Box 99, Youngstown T0J 3P0 – 403/779-3873, Fax: 403/779-2279

a. The towns of Cold Lake and Grand Centre were amalgamated to form a new municipality on October 1, 1996.

ALBERTA MUNICIPAL DISTRICTS

MUNICIPAL DISTRICTS	1994 POP.	CONTACT PERSON WITH ADDRESS, PHONE & FAX
Acadia No. 34	522	Murray Peers, Sec.-Treas., PO Box 30, Acadia Valley T0J 0A0 – 403/972-3808, Fax: 403/972-3833
Athabasca County No. 12	6,049	Jim Woodward, Mgr., 3602 - 48 Ave., Athabasca T9S 1M8 – 403/675-2273, 423-0592, Fax: 403/675-5512
Badlands No. 7	1,228	Kay Brink, Adm., PO Box 1588, Drumheller T0J 0Y0 – 403/823-1200, Fax: 403/823-2550
Barrhead County No. 11	5,591	Doug Tymchyshyn, Mgr., 5306 - 49 St., Barrhead T7N 1N5 – 403/674-3331, Fax: 403/674-2777
Beaver County No. 9	5,430	Ron Pepper, CAO, PO Box 140, Ryley T0B 4A0 – 403/663-3730, 421-4058, Fax: 403/663-3602
Big Lakes No. 125	3,848	John Eriksson, CAO, Provincial Bldg., PO Box 239, High Prairie T0G 1E0 – 403/523-5955, Fax: 403/523-6566
Bighorn No. 8	1,292	D. Sam Hall, Mgr., PO Box 310, Exshaw T0L 2C0 – 403/673-3611, 233-7678, Fax: 403/673-3895
Birch Hills No. 19	1,378	Don Spink, Acting Mgr., Birch Hills Service Centre, PO Box 157, Wanham T0H 3P0 – 403/694-3793, Fax: 403/694-3788
Bonnyville No. 87	10,269	R.A. (Roy) Doonanco, Mgr., PO Box 1010, Bonnyville T9N 2J7 – 403/826-3171, Fax: 403/826-4524
Brazeau No. 77	6,301	Layne Johnson, Mgr., PO Box 77, Drayton Valley T7A 1R1 – 403/542-7777, 428-7826, Fax: 403/542-7770
Camrose County No. 22	7,475	Brian D. Austrom, Adm., 3755 - 43 Ave., Camrose T4V 3S8 – 403/672-4446, 424-1239, Fax: 403/672-1008
Cardston No. 6	4,490	M. Vern Quinton, Adm., PO Box 580, Cardston T0K 0K0 – 403/653-4977, 328-4062, Fax: 403/653-1126
Clear Hills No. 21	2,903	Faye Kary, Sec.-Treas., PO Box 240, Worsley T0H 3W0 – 403/685-3925, Fax: 403/685-3960
Clearwater No. 99	10,131	Brian Irmen, Mgr., PO Box 550, Rocky Mountain House T0M 1T0 – 403/845-4444, Fax: 403/845-7330
Cypress No. 1	5,022	Lutz Perschon, Mgr., PO Box 108, Dunmore T0J 1A0 – 403/526-2888, Fax: 403/526-8958
East Peace No. 131	2,445	Kelly Bunn, CAO, PO Box 1300, Peace River T8S 1Y9 – 403/624-6580, Fax: 403/624-6595
Fairview No. 136	1,812	Lloyd Brattly, Sec.-Treas., PO Box 189, Fairview T0H 1L0 – 403/835-4903, Fax: 403/835-3131
Flagstaff County No. 29	4,099	Shelly Armstrong, Mgr., PO Box 358, Sedgewick T0B 4C0 – 403/384-3537, Fax: 403/384-3635
Foothills No. 31	12,476	Harry Riva Cambrin, Mgr., PO Box 5605, High River T1V 1M7 – 403/652-2341, Fax: 403/652-7880
Forty Mile County No. 8	3,193	Shirley R. Leverton, Adm., PO Box 160, Foremost T0K 0X0 – 403/867-3530, Fax: 403/867-2242
Grande Prairie County No. 1	12,314	Ron Pfau, Adm., 8611 - 108 St., Grande Prairie T8V 4C5 – 403/532-9722, Fax: 403/532-4234
Greenview No. 16	5,269	Gordon Frank, Mgr., PO Box 1079, Valleyview T0H 3N0 – 403/524-3193, Fax: 403/524-4307
Kneehill No. 48	4,713	John C. Jeffery, Adm., PO Box 400, Three Hills T0M 2A0 – 403/443-5541, Fax: 403/443-5115
Lac Ste. Anne County No. 28	8,059	Len Szybunka, Adm., PO Box 219, Sangudo T0E 2A0 – 403/785-3411, 459-1900, Fax: 403/785-2359
Lacombe County No. 14	9,283	Edwin E. Koberstein, Commr., 5432 - 56 Ave., Lacombe T4L 1E9 – 403/782-6601, Fax: 403/782-3820
Lamont County No. 30	4,266	Helen Patterson, Mgr., General Delivery, Lamont T0B 2R0 – 403/895-2233, Fax: 403/895-7404
Leduc County No. 25	11,503	Larry R. Majeski, Mgr., #101, 1101 - 5 St., Nisku T9E 2X3 – 403/955-3555, 986-2251, Fax: 403/955-3444
Lesser Slave River No. 124	2,564	Jack Ramme, Mgr., PO Box 722, Slave Lake T0G 2A0 – 403/849-7130, Fax: 403/849-4939
Lethbridge County No. 26	8,442	Sheldon Steinke, Mgr., 904 - 4 Ave. South, Lethbridge T1J 4E4 – 403/328-5525, Fax: 403/328-5602

Canadian Almanac & Directory 1997

MUNICIPAL DISTRICTS	1994 POP.	CONTACT PERSON WITH ADDRESS, PHONE & FAX
Mackenzie No. 23	7,260	Dennis Litke, CAO, PO Box 640, Fort Vermillion T0H 1N0 – 403/927-3717, Fax: 403/927-4266
Minburn County No. 27	3,490	David Marynowich, Mgr., PO Box 550, Vegreville T9C 1R6 – 403/632-2082, Fax: 403/632-6296
Mountain View County No.17	9,951	Herman Epp, Commr., PO Box 100, Didsbury T0M 0W0 – 403/335-3311, Fax: 403/335-9207
Newell County No. 4	6,014	Marlene Bowen, Adm., PO Box 130, Brooks T1R 1B2 – 403/362-3266, Fax: 403/362-8681
Northern Lights No. 22	3,789	Ian Becker, CAO, PO Box 200, Peace River T8S 1Z1 – 403/624-6121, Fax: 403/624-6494
Opportunity No. 17		Jim Kincaid, Mgr, PO Box 60, Wabasca T0G 2K0 – 403/891-3778, Fax: 403/891-3772
Paintearth County No. 18	2,324	W. Tim Peterson, Adm., PO Box 509, Castor T0C 0X0 – 403/882-3211, 3156, Fax: 403/882-3560
Parkland County	22,550	Delmar Kulak, Mgr. Admin. Services, 4601 - 48 St., Stony Plain T7Z 1R1 – 403/963-2231, Fax: 403/963-2980
Peace No. 135	1,559	Joyce Sydnes, Adm., PO Box 34, Berwyn T0H 0E0 – 403/338-3845, Fax: 403/338-2222
Pincher Creek No. 9	3,108	Ron Leaf, CAO, PO Box 279, Pincher Creek T0K 1W0 – 403/627-3130, Fax: 403/627-5070
Ponoka County No. 3	7,896	Charlie Cutforth, Adm., PO Box 5500, Ponoka T4J 1P6 – 403/783-3333, Fax: 403/783-6965
Provost No. 52	2,536	Rod Hawken, Adm., PO Box 300, Provost T0B 3S0 – 403/753-2434, Fax: 403/753-6432
Ranchland No. 66		Twyla Cyr, Adm., PO Box 906, Nanton T0L 1R0 – 403/646-3131, Fax: 403/646-3141
Red Deer County No.23	15,049	Lorne McLeod, Commr., 4758 - 32 St., Red Deer T4N 0M8 – 403/350-2150, Fax: 403/346-9840
Rocky View No. 44	19,888	Peter Kivisto, Mgr., PO Box 3009, Calgary T2M 4L6 – 403/230-1401, Fax: 403/277-5977
Saddle Hills No. 20	2,722	Don Spink, Acting Mgr., PO Box 69, Spirit River T0H 3G0 – 403/864-3760, Fax: 403/864-3904
St. Paul County No. 19	6,489	Robert Krawchuk, Adm., 5015 - 49 Ave., St. Paul T0A 3A4 – 403/645-3301, Fax: 403/645-3104
Smoky Lake County No. 13	2,689	Cary Smigerowsky, Mgr., PO Box 310, Smoky Lake T0A 3C0 – 403/656-3730, 424-7103, Fax: 403/656-3768
Smoky River No. 130	2,613	Lucien G. Turcotte, Adm., PO Box 210, Falher T0H 1M0 – 403/837-2221, Fax: 403/837-2453
Spirit River No. 133	812	Veronica Andruchiw, Adm., PO Box 389, Spirit River T0H 3G0 – 403/864-3500, Fax: 403/864-4303
Starland No. 47	2,055	Ross D. Rawlusyk, Adm., PO Box 249, Morrin T0J 2B0 – 403/772-3793, Fax: 403/772-3807
Stettler County No. 6	5,251	Tim Timmons, Commr., PO Box 1270, Stettler T0C 2L0 – 403/742-4441, Fax: 403/742-1277
Strathcona County	61,559	Eric McGhan, Commr., 2001 Sherwood Dr., Sherwood Park T8A 3W7 – 403/464-8111, Fax: 403/464-8050
Sturgeon No. 90	15,465	Gilbert J. Boddez, Adm., 9601 - 100 St., Morinville T8R 1L9 – 403/939-4321, 460-8903, Fax: 403/939-3003
Taber No. 14	5,317	Clarence F. Schile, Adm., 4900B - 50 St., Taber T1G 1T2 – 403/223-3541, Fax: 403/223-1799
Thorhild County No. 7	2,912	Bill Kostiw, Adm., PO Box 10, Thorhild T0A 3J0 – 403/398-3741, 429-3928, Fax: 403/398-3748
Two Hills County No. 21	2,776	Gary Popowich, Adm., PO Box 490, Two Hills T0B 4K0 – 403/657-3358, Fax: 403/657-3504
Vermilion River County No. 24	7,714	Karen Gartner, Adm., PO Box 69, Kitscoty T0B 2P0 – 403/846-2244, 2269, Fax: 403/846-2716
Vulcan County No. 2	3,648	Elaine Schneider, Acting Adm., PO Box 180, Vulcan T0L 2B0 – 403/485-2241, Fax: 403/485-2920
Wainwright No. 61	3,919	Tim Timmons, Adm., 717 - 14 Ave., Wainwright T9W 1B3 – 403/842-4454, Fax: 403/842-2463
Warner County No. 5	3,677	Allan K. Romeril, Adm., PO Box 90, Warner T0K 2L0 – 403/642-3635, Fax: 403/642-3631
Westlock No. 92	6,994	Wyatt Glebe, Adm., PO Box 219, Westlock T0G 2L0 – 403/349-3346, 429-1135, Fax: 403/349-2012
Wetaskiwin County No. 10	9,816	Frank Coutney, Adm., PO Box 6960, Wetaskiwin T9A 2G5 – 403/352-3321, Fax: 403/352-3486
Wheatland County	5,779	Ernie Maser, Mgr., 435B Hwy#1, Strathmore T1P 1J4 – 403/934-3321, Fax: 403/934-4889
Willow Creek No. 26	4,764	Cindy Zabolotney, Adm., PO Box 550, Claresholm T0L 0T0 – 403/625-3351, Fax: 403/625-3886
Wood Buffalo	34,706	Glen Laubenstein, Mgr., 9909 Franklin Ave., 3rd Fl., Fort McMurray T9H 2K4 – 403/743-7000, 743-7023, Fax: 403/743-7028
Woodlands No. 15	2,980	Norm Kjemhus, Adm., Provincial Bldg., #210, 5020 - 52 Ave., Whitecourt T7S 1N2 – 403/778-7102, Fax: 403/778-7209
Yellowhead No. 94	8,692	Terry Broome, Mgr., 2716 - 1st Ave., Edson T7E 1N9 – 403/723-4800, 665-6030, Fax: 403/723-5066

ALBERTA IMPROVEMENT DISTRICTS AND NATIVE SERVICES DIVISON

Rural & Improvement Districts Association of Alberta, Shirley Mercier, Sec-T., Box 36, Site 206, RR#2, St. Alberta AB T8N 1M9; 403/973-6762

DISTRICTS	CONTACT PERSON WITH ADDRESS, PHONE & FAX
Districts 4 (Waterton), 6, 9 (Banff), 12 (Jasper), 13 (Elk Island), 24	Rick Grimson, ID Mgr., Local Government Advisory Branch, 10155-102 St., 15th Fl., Edmonton T5J 4L4 – 403/427-2225, Fax: 403/422-9133
Jasper Improvement District	George Krefting, Mgr., PO Box 520, Jasper T0E 1E0 – 403/852-3356, Fax: 403/852-4019
Kananaskis Country	Dave Nielsen, Mgr., PO Box 70, Kananaskis T0L 2H0 – 403/591-8800, Fax: 403/591-7495

ALBERTA METIS SETTLEMENTS

Metis Settlements General Council, Thomas Droege, Executive Director, 649, Princeton Place, 10339 - 124 St., Edmonton AB T5N 1R1; 403/488-6500, Fax: 403/488-5700

SETTLEMENT	1994 POP.	CONTACT PERSON WITH ADDRESS, PHONE & FAX
Buffalo Lake	534	Ernie Hawk, Adm., PO Box 20, Caslan T0A 0R0 – 403/689-2170, Fax: 403/689-2024
East Prairie	260	Robert L'Hirondelle, Adm., PO Box 1289, High Prairie T0G 1E0 – 403/523-2594, Fax: 403/523-2777
Elizabeth	539	Richard Power, Adm., PO Box 420, Grand Centre T0A 1T0 – 403/594-5026, Fax: 403/594-5452
Fishing Lake	283	Barbara Fayant, Adm., General Delivery, Sputinow T0A 3G0 – 403/943-2202, Fax: 403/943-2575
Gift Lake	697	Gerry Peardon, Adm., PO Box 60, Gift Lake T0G 1B0 – 403/767-3894, Fax: 403/767-3888
Kikino	821	Roger Littlechilds, Adm., General Delivery, Kikino T0A 2B0 – 403/623-7868, Fax: 403/623-7080
Paddle Prairie	470	Barbara Auger, Adm., General Delivery, Paddle Prairie T0H 2W0 – 403/981-2227, Fax: 403/981-3737
Peavine	363	Sherry Cunningham, Adm., PO Box 238, High Prairie T0G 1E0 – 403/523-2557, Fax: 403/523-5616

BRITISH COLUMBIA

Incorporated municipalities in British Columbia include Villages, Towns, Cities, and District Municipalities as well as one Indian Government District. Twenty-seven regional districts provide local government services to the unincorporated areas and, in many cases, co-ordinate service delivery between such areas and the incorporated municipalities included within the regional district boundaries.

Municipal elections in all municipalities are held on the third Saturday of November. Terms of office are three years (1996, 1999, etc.).

Legislation: The Municipal Act, excluding the City of Vancouver, which is regulated under the provisions of the Vancouver Charter.

Cities in CAPITALS; District municipalities marked (DM); Districts marked (D); Towns marked †; Villages marked (V). British Columbia Regional Districts follow this list. An in-depth listing for municipalities marked with * appears in Part 2 (check Index for page numbers).

MUNICIPALITY	1991 POP.	COUNTY OR DISTRICT	FEDERAL ELECTORAL DISTRICT	PROVINCIAL ELECTORAL DISTRICT	CONTACT PERSON WITH ADDRESS, PHONE & FAX
*ABBOTSFORD	110,000 ('96)	Fraser Valley	Fraser Valley East	Abbotsford; Matsqui	Toiressa O. Strong, City Clerk, 32315 South Fraser Way, Abbotsford V2T 1W7 – 604/853-2281, 857-1251, Fax: 604/853-1934
Alert Bay (V)	628	Mount Waddington	North Island-Powell River	North Island	John Rowell, Clerk, PO Box 28, Alert Bay V0N 1A0 – 250/974-5213, Fax: 250/974-5470
Anmore (V)	741	Greater Vancouver	Port Moody-Coquitlam	Port Moody-Burnaby Mountain	Howard Carley, Clerk, 2697 Sunnyside Rd., Port Moody V3H 3C8 – 604/469-9877, Fax: 604/469-0537
ARMSTRONG	3,200	North Okanagan	Okanagan-Shuswap	Shuswap	Barry Gagnon, Clerk-Treas., PO Box 40, Armstrong V0E 1B0 – 250/546-3023, Fax: 250/546-3710
Ashcroft (V)	1,714	Thompson-Nicola	Cariboo-Chilcotin	Yale-Lillooet	Al Benson, Sec.-Treas., PO Box 129, Ashcroft V0K 1A0 – 250/453-9161, Fax: 250/453-9664
Belcarra (V)	586	Greater Vancouver	Port Moody-Coquitlam	Port Moody-Burnaby Mountain	Moira McGregor, Sec.-Treas., 4084 Bedwell Bay Rd., Belcarra V3H 4P8 – 604/939-4411, Fax: 604/939-5034
*BURNABY	168,000 ('95)	Greater Vancouver	Burnaby-Kingsway; New Westminster-Burnaby	Burnaby-Edmonds; Burnaby North; Burnaby-Willingdon	Debbie Comis, City Clerk, 4949 Canada Way, Burnaby V5G 1M2 – 604/294-7944, Fax: 604/294-7537
Burns Lake (V)	1,682	Bulkley-Nechako	Prince George-Bulkley Valley	Bulkley Valley-Stikine	Lonny Miller, Sec.-Treas., PO Box 570, Burns Lake V0J 1E0 – 250/692-7587, Fax: 250/692-3059
Cache Creek (V)	1,007	Thompson-Nicola	Cariboo-Chilcotin	Yale-Lillooet	Gordon Daily, Clerk, PO Box 7, Cache Creek V0K 1H0 – 250/457-6237, Fax: 250/457-9192
Campbell River (DM)	28,000 ('95)	Comox-Strathcona	North Island-Powell River	North Island	William Halstead, Clerk, 301 St. Ann's Rd., Campbell River V9W 4C7 – 250/286-5700, Fax: 250/286-5760
CASTLEGAR	6,579	Central Kootenay	Kootenay West-Revelstoke	Rossland-Trail	Dianne Hunter, Clerk, 460 Columbia Ave., Castlegar V1N 1G7 – 250/365-7227, Fax: 250/365-8566
Central Saanich (DM)	13,684	Capital	Saanich-Gulf Islands	Saanich North & the Islands	Gary C. Nason, Clerk-Adm., 1903 Mt. Newton Cross Rd., Saanichton V8M 2A9 – 250/652-4444, Fax: 250/652-0135
Chase (V)	2,083	Thompson-Nicola	Kamloops	Shuswap	Christopher Coates, Sec.-Treas., PO Box 440, Chase V0E 1M0 – 250/679-3238, Fax: 250/679-3070
Chetwynd (DM)	2,843	Peace River	Prince George-Peace River	Peace River South	Jannene Disher, Clerk, PO Box 357, Chetwynd V0C 1J0 – 250/788-2281, Fax: 250/788-2299
Chilliwack (DM)	49,531	Fraser Valley	Fraser Valley East	Chilliwack	David W. Hampson, Clerk, 8550 Young Rd. South, Chilliwack V2P 4P1 – 604/792-9311, Fax: 604/795-8443, URL: http://www.gov.chilliwack.bc.ca/
Clinton (V)	662	Thompson-Nicola	Cariboo-Chilcotin	Cariboo South	Isabell Hadford, Sec.-Treas., PO Box 309, Clinton V0K 1K0 – 250/459-2261, Fax: 250/459-2227
Coldstream (DM)	7,999	North Okanagan	Okanagan-Shuswap	Okanagan-Vernon	Greg Betts, Clerk, 9901 Kalamalka Rd., Vernon V1B 1L6 – 250/545-5304, Fax: 250/545-4733
COLWOOD	13,468	Capital	Esquimalt-Juan de Fuca	Esquimalt-Metchosin	Barry Bennett, Clerk, 3300 Wishart Rd., Victoria V9C 1R1 – 250/478-5541, Fax: 250/478-7516
Comox †	8,253	Comox-Strathcona	Comox-Alberni	Comox Valley	Helen M. Dale, Clerk, 1809 Beaufort Ave., Comox V9M 1R9 – 250/339-2202, Fax: 250/339-7110
*COQUITLAM	100,946 ('96)	Greater Vancouver	Port Moody-Coquitlam	Mission-Coquitlam; Port Coquitlam	Warren Jones, Clerk, 1111 Brunette Ave., Coquitlam V3K 1E9 – 604/664-1400, Fax: 604/664-1650, URL: http://www.gov.coquitlam.bc.ca/
COURTENAY	11,652	Comox-Strathcona	Comox-Alberni	Comox Valley	John E. Wilson, Clerk, 750 Cliffe Ave., Courtenay V9N 2J7 – 250/334-4441, Fax: 250/334-4241
CRANBROOK	16,447	East Kootenay	Kootenay East	Kootenay	Carmen Biafore, Adm., 40 - 10 Ave. South, Cranbrook V1C 2M8 – 250/426-4211, Fax: 250/426-4026; URL: http://cyberlink.bc.ca/~pthiessen/cranb1.htm
Creston †	4,205	400 Central Kootenay	Kootenay East	Nelson-Creston	Bill Hutchinson, Sec.-Treas., PO Box 1339, Creston V0B 1G0 – 250/428-2214, Fax: 250/428-9164

Cities in CAPITALS; District municipalities marked (DM); Districts marked (D); Towns marked †; Villages marked (V). British Columbia Regional Districts follow this list. An in-depth listing for municipalities marked with * appears in Part 2 (check Index for page numbers).

MUNICIPALITY	1991 POP.	COUNTY OR DISTRICT	FEDERAL ELECTORAL DISTRICT	PROVINCIAL ELECTORAL DISTRICT	CONTACT PERSON WITH ADDRESS, PHONE & FAX
Cumberland (V)	2,220	Comox-Strathcona	Comox-Alberni	Comox Valley	Richard Kanigan, Clerk, PO Box 340, Cumberland V0R 1S0 – 250/336-2291, Fax: 250/336-2321
DAWSON CREEK	10,981	Peace River	Prince George-Peace River	Peace River South	Jim Noble, Clerk, PO Box 150, Dawson Creek V1G 4G4 – 250/782-3351, Fax: 250/782-3352
*Delta (Corp.)	90,000 ('93)	Greater Vancouver	Delta	Delta North; Delta South	J.C. Lambie, Acting Clerk, 4500 Clarence Taylor Cres., Delta V4K 3E2 – 604/946-4141, Fax: 604/946-3390
DUNCAN	4,301	Cowichan Valley	Nanaimo-Cowichan	Cowichan-Ladysmith	Paul Douville, Clerk, PO Box 820, Duncan V9L 3Y2 – 250/746-6126, Fax: 250/746-6129
Elkford (DM)	2,846	East Kootenay	Kootenay East	Kootenay	Betty-Lou Wyatt, Clerk-Treas., PO Box 340, Elkford V0B 1H0 – 250/865-2241, Fax: 250/865-2429
ENDERBY	2,128	North Okanagan	Okanagan-Shuswap	Shuswap	Robert W. Watson, Clerk-Treas., PO Box 400, Enderby V0E 1V0 – 250/838-7230, Fax: 250/838-6007
Esquimalt †	16,192	Capital	Esquimalt-Juan de Fuca	Esquimalt-Metchosin	Robert Seright, Clerk, 1229 Esquimalt Rd., Victoria V9A 3P1 – 250/385-2461, Fax: 250/385-6668
FERNIE	5,012	East Kootenay	Kootenay East	Kootenay	Jennifer Bridarolli, Clerk, PO Box 190, Fernie V0B 1M0 – 250/423-6817, Fax: 250/423-3034
Fort Nelson †	3,804	Fort Nelson-Liard	Prince George-Peace River	Peace River North	Patricia A. Bailey, Clerk, PO Box 399, Fort Nelson V0C 1R0 – 250/774-2541, Fax: 250/774-6794
Fort St. James (D)	2,058	Bulkley-Nechako	Prince George-Bulkley Valley	Prince George-Omineca	Dan Zabinsky, Clerk, PO Box 640, Fort St. James V0J 1P0 – 250/996-8233, Fax: 250/996-2248
FORT ST. JOHN	14,156	Peace River	Prince George-Peace River	Peace River North	Colin Griffith, Acting Clerk, 10631 - 100 St., Fort St. John V1J 3Z5 – 250/787-8150, Fax: 250/787-8181
Fraser Lake (V)	1,302	Bulkley-Nechako	Prince George-Bulkley Valley	Prince George-Omineca	Angus Davis, Clerk, PO Box 430, Fraser Lake V0J 1S0 – 250/702-5000, Fax: 250/699-6469
Fruitvale (V)	2,062	Kootenay Boundary	Kootenay West-Revelstoke	Rossland-Trail	Vince Morelli, Clerk, PO Box 370, Fruitvale V0G 1L0 – 250/367-7551, Fax: 250/367-9267
Gibsons †	3,138	Sunshine Coast	North Island-Powell River	Powell River-Sunshine Coast	Terry Lester, Acting Clerk, PO Box 340, Gibsons V0N 1V0 – 604/886-2274, Fax: 604/886-9735
Gold River (V)	2,166	Comox-Strathcona	North Island-Powell River	North Island	Larry Plourde, Acting Clerk, PO Box 610, Gold River V0P 1G0 – 250/283-2202, Fax: 250/283-7500
Golden †	3,721	Columbia-Shuswap	Kootenay East	Columbia River-Revelstoke	Ian Fremantle, Clerk, PO Box 350, Golden V0A 1H0 – 250/344-2271, Fax: 250/344-6577
GRAND FORKS	3,610	Kootenay Boundary	Okanagan-Similkameen-Merritt	Okanagan-Boundary	Lynne Burch, Clerk, PO Box 220, Grand Forks V0H 1H0 – 250/442-8266, Fax: 250/442-8000
Granisle (V)	803	Bulkley-Nechako	Prince George-Bulkley Valley	Bulkley Valley-Stikine	Robert Jackman, Sec.-Treas., PO Box 128, Granisle V0J 1W0 – 250/697-2248, Fax: 250/697-2306
GREENWOOD	725	Kootenay Boundary	Okanagan-Similkameen-Merritt	Okanagan-Boundary	Monique Beaudry, Clerk-Treas., PO Box 129, Greenwood V0H 1J0 – 250/445-6644, Fax: 250/445-6441
Harrison Hot Springs (V)	655	Fraser Valley	Fraser Valley East	Mission-Kent	Mark Brennan, Sec.-Treas., PO Box 160, Harrison Hot Springs V0M 1K0 – 604/796-2171, Fax: 604/796-2192
Hazelton (V)	339	Kitimat-Stikine	Skeena	Bulkley Valley-Stikine	Amy Brown, Deputy Clerk, PO Box 40, Hazelton V0J 1Y0 – 250/842-5991, Fax: 250/842-5152
Highlands (DM)	1,201	Capital	Esquimalt-Juan de Fuca, Saanich-Gulf Islands	Malahat-Juan de Fuca, Saanich South	Bruce Woodbury, Clerk-Treas., 1564 Millstream Rd., Victoria V9B 5T9 – 250/474-1773, Fax: 250/474-3677
Hope (DM)	3,147	Fraser Valley	Fraser Valley East	Yale-Lillooet	Eric McMurran, Clerk, PO Box 609, Hope V0X 1L0 – 604/869-5671, Fax: 604/869-2275
Houston (DM)	3,628	Bulkley-Nechako	Prince George-Bulkley Valley	Bulkley Valley-Stikine	Bill Beamish, Clerk, PO Box 370, Houston V0J 1Z0 – 250/845-2238, Fax: 250/845-3429
Hudson's Hope (DM)	985	Peace River	Prince George-Peace River	Peace River North	Fay Lavallee, Clerk-Treas., PO Box 330, Hudson's Hope V0C 1V0 – 250/783-9901, Fax: 250/783-5741
Invermere (DM)	2,207	East Kootenay	Kootenay East	Columbia River-Revelstoke	Bill Lindsay, Clerk, PO Box 339, Invermere V0A 1K0 – 250/342-9281, Fax: 250/342-2934
*KAMLOOPS	79,000 ('96)	Thompson-Nicola	Kamloops	Kamloops; Kamloops-North Thompson	Wayne Vollrath, City Clerk-Asst. Adm., 7 Victoria St. West, Kamloops V2C 1A2 – 250/828-3311, Fax: 250/828-3578
Kaslo (V)	863	Central Kootenay	Kootenay West-Revelstoke	Nelson-Creston	Rae Sawyer, Sec.-Treas., PO Box 576, Kaslo V0G 1M0 – 250/353-2311, Fax: 250/353-7767

Canadian Almanac & Directory 1997

Cities in CAPITALS; District municipalities marked (DM); Districts marked (D); Towns marked †; Villages marked (V). British Columbia Regional Districts follow this list. An in-depth listing for municipalities marked with * appears in Part 2 (check Index for page numbers).

MUNICIPALITY	1991 POP.	COUNTY OR DISTRICT	FEDERAL ELECTORAL DISTRICT	PROVINCIAL ELECTORAL DISTRICT	CONTACT PERSON WITH ADDRESS, PHONE & FAX
*KELOWNA	88,559 ('94)	Central Okanagan	Okanagan Centre	Okanagan East; Okanagan West	David L. Shipclark, Clerk, City Hall, 1435 Water St., Kelowna V1Y 1J4 – 250/763-6011, Fax: 250/862-3399
Kent (DM)	4,322	Fraser Valley	Fraser Valley East	Mission-Kent	Anthony C. Lewis, Clerk-Treas., PO Box 70, Agassiz V0M 1A0 – 604/796-2235, Fax: 604/796-9854
Keremeos (V)	933	Okanagan-Similkameen	Okanagan-Similkameen-Merritt	Okanagan-Boundary	Andrew Verigin, Sec.-Treas., PO Box 160, Keremeos V0X 1N0 – 250/499-2711, Fax: 250/499-5477
KIMBERLEY	6,531	East Kootenay	Kootenay East	Columbia River-Revelstoke	Mike Cave, Clerk, 340 Spokane St., Kimberley V1A 2E8 – 250/427-5311, Fax: 250/427-5252
Kitimat (DM)	11,305	Kitimat-Stikine	Skeena	Skeena	Walter McLellan, Clerk, 270 City Centre, Kitimat V8C 2H7 – 250/632-2161, Fax: 250/632-4995
Ladysmith †	4,875	Cowichan Valley	Nanaimo-Cowichan	Cowichan-Ladysmith	Patrick Durban, Clerk, Town Hall, PO Box 220, Ladysmith V0R 2E0 – 250/245-6400, Fax: 250/245-6411
Lake Country (D)			Okanagan Centre	Okanagan East	Randy Rose, Clerk, 3051 Woodsdale Rd., Winfield V4V 1X9 – 250/766-5650, Fax: 250/766-0116
Lake Cowichan (V)	2,241	Cowichan Valley	Nanaimo-Cowichan	Cowichan-Ladysmith	Ed Gilman, Sec.-Treas., PO Box 860, Lake Cowichan V0R 2G0 – 250/749-6681, Fax: 250/749-3900
Langford (D)			Esquimalt-Juan de Fuca	Equimalt-Metchasin Malahat-Juan de Fuca	Geoff Pearce, Clerk, 2805 Carlow Rd., Victoria V9B 5V9 – 250/478-7882, Fax: 250/478-7864
LANGLEY	22,500 ('94)	Fraser Valley	Fraser Valley West	Langley	Robert Wilson, Clerk, 5549 - 204 St., Langley V3A 1Z4 – 604/530-3131, Fax: 604/530-4371
*Langley (DM)	80,000 ('96)	Fraser Valley, Langley, Surrey-White Horse	Fraser Valley West; Langley; Surrey-White Rock-South Langley	Fort Langley-Aldergrove	Rodney T. Edwards, Municipal Clerk, 4914 - 221 St., Langley V3A 3Z8 – 604/534-3211, Fax: 604/533-6098
Lillooet (D)	1,782	Squamish-Lillooet	Cariboo-Chilcotin	Yale-Lillooet	Terry Johnston, Clerk, PO Box 610, Lillooet V0K 1V0 – 250/256-4289, Fax: 250/256-4288
Lions Bay (V)	1,328	Greater Vancouver	Capilano-Howe Sound	West Vancouver-Garibaldi	Bernice Pullen, Sec.-Treas., PO Box 141, Lions Bay V0N 2E0 – 604/921-9333, Fax: 604/921-6643
Logan Lake (DM)	2,379	Thompson-Nicola	Kamloops	Yale-Lillooet	Doug Fleming, Clerk-Treas., PO Box 190, Logan Lake V0K 1W0 – 250/523-6225, Fax: 250/523-6678
Lumby (V)	1,265	North Okanagan	Okanagan-Shuswap	Okanagan-Vernon	Lynda Shykora, Sec.-Treas., PO Box 430, Lumby V0E 2G0 – 250/547-2171, Fax: 250/547-6894
Lytton (V)	335	Thompson-Nicola	Cariboo-Chilcotin	Yale-Lillooet	Hedley Crowther, Clerk, PO Box 100, Lytton V0K 1Z0 – 250/455-2355, Fax: 250/455-2142
Mackenzie (DM)	5,796	Fraser-Fort George	Prince George-Peace River	Peace River South	Brian Ritchie, Clerk, PO Box 340, Mackenzie V0J 2C0 – 250/997-3221, Fax: 250/997-5186
Maple Ridge (DM)	48,023	Fraser Valley	Mission-Coquitlam	Maple Ridge-Pitt Meadows	Jim McBride, Clerk, 11995 Haney Place, Maple Ridge V2X 6A9 – 604/463-5221, Fax: 604/467-7329
Masset (V)	1,476	Skeena-Queen Charlotte	Skeena	North Coast	Alfred Brockley, Sec.-Treas., PO Box 68, Masset V0T 1M0 – 250/626-3995, Fax: 250/626-3968
McBride (V)	580	Fraser-Fort George	Prince George-Bulkley Valley	Prince George-Mount Robson	Ronald V. Brown, Sec.-Treas., PO Box 519, McBride V0J 2E0 – 250/569-2229, Fax: 250/569-3276
MERRITT	6,253	Thompson-Nicola	Okanagan-Similkameen-Merritt	Yale-Lillooet	Yvonne Porada, Clerk, PO Box 189, Merritt V0K 2B0 – 250/378-4224, Fax: 250/378-2600
Metchosin (DM)	4,232	Capital	Esquimalt-Juan de Fuca	Esquimalt-Metchosin	Gerald Mellott, Clerk-Treas., 4450 Happy Valley Rd., RR#4, Victoria V9B 5T6 – 250/474-3167, Fax: 250/474-6298
Midway (V)	611	Kootenay Boundary	Okanagan-Similkameen-Merritt	Okanagan-Boundary	Robert J. Hatton, Sec.-Treas., PO Box 160, Midway V0H 1M0 – 250/449-2222, Fax: 250/449-2258
Mission (DM)	26,202	Fraser Valley	Mission-Coquitlam	Mission-Kent	Jacqueline Fennellow, Clerk, PO Box 20, Mission V2V 4L9 – 604/820-3700, Fax: 604/826-1363
Montrose (V)	1,197	Kootenay Boundary	Kootenay West-Revelstoke	Rossland-Trail	Gerry A. Henke, Sec.-Treas., PO Box 510, Montrose V0G 1P0 – 250/367-7234, Fax: 250/367-7288
Nakusp (V)	1,374	Central Kootenay	Kootenay West-Revelstoke	Nelson-Creston	Malcolm Buckley, Clerk, PO Box 280, Nakusp V0G 1R0 – 250/265-3689, Fax: 250/265-3788
*NANAIMO	72,000 ('95)	Nanaimo	Nanaimo-Cowichan	Nanaimo; Parksville-Qualicum	Jim Bowden, Clerk, 455 Wallace St., Nanaimo V9R 5J6 – 250/754-4251, Fax: 250/755-4436, URL: http://www.sd68.nanaimo.bc.ca/nol/
NELSON	8,760	Central Kootenay	Kootenay West-Revelstoke	Nelson-Creston	Victor Kumar, Clerk, 502 Vernon St., Nelson V1L 4E8 – 250/352-5511, Fax: 250/352-2131

Cities in CAPITALS; District municipalities marked (DM); Districts marked (D); Towns marked †; Villages marked (V). British Columbia Regional Districts follow this list. An in-depth listing for municipalities marked with * appears in Part 2 (check Index for page numbers).

MUNICIPALITY	1991 POP.	COUNTY OR DISTRICT	FEDERAL ELECTORAL DISTRICT	PROVINCIAL ELECTORAL DISTRICT	CONTACT PERSON WITH ADDRESS, PHONE & FAX
New Denver (V)	571	Central Kootenay	Kootenay West-Revelstoke	Nelson-Creston	Carol Gordon, Sec.-Treas., PO Box 40, New Denver V0G 1S0 – 250/358-2316, Fax: 250/358-7251
New Hazelton (DM)	786	Kitimat-Stikine	Skeena	Bulkley Valley-Stikine	Brian Fassnidge, Clerk-Treas., PO Box 340, New Hazelton V0J 2J0 – 250/842-6571, Fax: 250/842-6077
NEW WESTMINSTER	44,443 ('92)	Greater Vancouver	New Westminster-Burnaby	New Westminster	Cathie Bruce, Clerk, 511 Royal Ave., New Westminster V3L 1H9 – 604/521-3711, Fax: 604/521-3895
North Cowichan (DM)	21,373	Cowichan Valley	Nanaimo-Cowichan	Cowichan-Ladysmith	Mark Ruttan, Clerk, PO Box 278, Duncan V9L 3X4 – 250/746-3100, Fax: 250/746-3133
North Saanich (DM)	9,645	Capital	Saanich-Gulf Islands	Saanich North & the Islands	Pam Hilchie, Clerk, PO Box 2639, Sidney V8L 4C1 – 250/656-0781, Fax: 250/656-3155
*North Vancouver (DM)	78,161 ('95)	Greater Vancouver	Capilano-Howe Sound; North Vancouver	N. Vancouver-Lonsdale; N. Vancouver-Seymour; W. Vancouver-Capilano	Agnes S. Hilsen, Acting Clerk, 355 West Queens Rd., North Vancouver V7L 4K1 – 604/987-7131, Fax: 604/984-9637, URL: http://www.district.north-van.bc.ca/
NORTH VANCOUVER	38,436	Greater Vancouver	North Vancouver	N. Vancouver-Lonsdale; N. Vancouver-Seymour; W. Vancouver-Capilano	Bruce Hawkshaw, Clerk, 141 - 14 St. West, North Vancouver V7M 1H9 – 604/985-7761, Fax: 604/985-9417
Oak Bay (DM)	17,815	Capital	Victoria	Oak Bay-Gordon Head	Tom MacDonald, Clerk, 2167 Oak Bay Ave., Victoria V8R 1G2 – 250/598-3311, Fax: 250/598-9108
Oliver †	3,743	Okanagan-Similkameen	Okanagan-Similkameen-Merritt	Okanagan-Boundary	Debbie McGinn, Clerk, PO Box 638, Oliver V0H 1T0 – 250/498-3404, Fax: 250/498-4466
100 Mile House (DM)	1,866	Cariboo	Cariboo-Chilcotin	Cariboo South	Ronald Haggstrom, Clerk-Treas., PO Box 340, 100 Mile House V0K 2E0 – 250/395-2434, Fax: 250/395-3625
Osoyoos †	3,403	Okanagan-Similkameen	Okanagan-Similkameen-Merritt	Okanagan-Boundary	Karl Newholm, Clerk, PO Box 3010, Osoyoos V0H 1V0 – 250/495-6515, Fax: 250/495-2400
PARKSVILLE	7,306	Nanaimo	Comox-Alberni	Parksville-Qualicum	Shirley E. Hine, Clerk, PO Box 1390, Parksville V9P 2H3 – 250/248-6144, Fax: 250/248-6650
Peachland (DM)	3,459	Central Okanagan	Okanagan Centre	Okanagan-Penticton	Bill Brown, Clerk, PO Box 390, Peachland V0H 1X0 – 250/767-2647, Fax: 250/767-3433
Pemberton (V)	502	Squamish-Lillooet	Capilano-Howe Sound	West Vancouver-Garibaldi	Bryan Kirk, Sec.-Treas., PO Box 100, Pemberton V0N 2L0 – 604/894-6135, Fax: 604/894-5708
PENTICTON	27,258	Okanagan-Similkameen	Okanagan-Similkameen-Merritt	Okanagan-Penticton	Leo den Boer, Clerk, 171 Main St., Penticton V2A 5A9 – 250/490-2400, Fax: 250/490-2402
Pitt Meadows (DM)	11,147	Fraser Valley	Mission-Coquitlam	Maple Ridge-Pitt Meadows	Brian E. Strong, Clerk, 12007 Harris Rd., Pitt Meadows V3Y 2B5 – 604/465-5454, Fax: 604/465-2404
PORT ALBERNI	18,403	Alberni-Clayoquot	Comox-Alberni	Alberni	George Wiley, Clerk, 4850 Argyle St., Port Alberni V9Y 1V8 – 250/723-2146, Fax: 250/723-1003
Port Alice (V)	1,371	Mount Waddington	North Island-Powell River	North Island	Jane Kennedy, Clerk, PO Box 130, Port Alice V0N 2N0 – 250/284-3391, Fax: 250/284-3416
Port Clements (V)	483	Skeena-Queen Charlotte	Skeena	North Coast	Jukka Efraimsson, Sec.-Treas., PO Box 198, Port Clements V0T 1R0 – 250/557-4295, Fax: 250/557-4568
PORT COQUITLAM	36,773	Greater Vancouver	Mission-Coquitlam; Port Moody-Coquitlam	Port Coquitlam	Susan Rauh, Clerk, 2580 Shaughnessy St., Port Coquitlam V3C 2A8 – 604/944-5411, Fax: 604/944-5402
Port Edward (DM)	739	Skeena-Queen Charlotte	Skeena	North Coast	Robert Earl, Clerk-Treas., 770 Pacific Av., Port Edward V0V 1G0 – 250/628-3667, Fax: 250/628-9225
Port Hardy (DM)	5,082	Mount Waddington	North Island-Powell River	North Island	Joseph A. Fernandez, Clerk, PO Box 68, Port Hardy V0N 2P0 – 250/949-6665, Fax: 250/949-7433
Port McNeill †	2,641	Mount Waddington	North Island-Powell River	North Island	Margaret Page, Clerk, PO Box 728, Port McNeill V0N 2R0 – 250/956-3111, Fax: 250/956-4300
PORT MOODY	20,000 ('94)	Greater Vancouver	Port Moody-Coquitlam	Port Moody-Burnaby Mountain	Lynne Watson, Acting Clerk, PO Box 36, Port Moody V3H 3E1 – 604/469-4500, Fax: 604/469-4550
Pouce Coupé (V)	832	Peace River	Prince George-Peace River	Peace River South	Diana Chorney, Sec.-Treas., PO Box 190, Pouce Coupé V0C 2C0 – 250/786-5794, Fax: 250/786-5257
Powell River (DM)	12,991	Powell River	North Island-Powell River	Powell River-Sunshine Coast	Victor Petersen, Clerk, 6910 Duncan St., Powell River V8A 1V4 – 604/485-6291, Fax: 604/485-2913

Cities in CAPITALS; District municipalities marked (DM); Districts marked (D); Towns marked †; Villages marked (V). British Columbia Regional Districts follow this list. An in-depth listing for municipalities marked with * appears in Part 2 (check Index for page numbers).

MUNICIPALITY	1991 POP.	COUNTY OR DISTRICT	FEDERAL ELECTORAL DISTRICT	PROVINCIAL ELECTORAL DISTRICT	CONTACT PERSON WITH ADDRESS, PHONE & FAX
*PRINCE GEORGE	75,000 ('96)	Fraser-Fort George	Prince George-Bulkley Valley; Prince George-Peace River	Pr. George-Mt. Robson; Pr. George N.; Pr. George-Omineca	Allan Chabot, City Clerk, City Hall, 1100 Patricia Blvd., Prince George V2L 3V9 – 250/561-7600, Fax: 250/561-0183
PRINCE RUPERT	16,620	Skeena-Queen Charlotte	Skeena	North Coast	Patti Sawka, Clerk, 424 West Third Av., Prince Rupert V8J 1L7 – 250/627-0934, Fax: 250/627-0999
Princeton †	2,796	Okanagan-Similkameen	Okanagan-Similkameen-Merritt	Yale-Lillooet	Cornelius Froese, Clerk, PO Box 670, Princeton V0X 1W0 – 250/295-3135, Fax: 250/295-3477
Qualicum Beach †	4,418	Nanaimo	Comox-Alberni	Parksville-Qualicum	Mark D. Brown, Clerk, PO Box 130, Qualicum Beach V9K 1S7 – 250/752-6921, Fax: 250/752-1243
QUESNEL	8,179	Cariboo	Cariboo-Chilcotin	Cariboo North	Doug Ruttan, Clerk, 405 Barlow Ave., Quesnel V2J 2C3 – 250/992-2111, Fax: 250/992-2206
Radium Hot Springs (V)	395	East Kootenay	Kootenay East	Columbia River-Revelstoke	Laura Green, Sec.-Treas., PO Box 340, Radium Hot Springs V0A 1M0 – 250/347-6455, Fax: 250/347-9068
REVELSTOKE	7,729	Columbia-Shuswap	Kootenay West-Revelstoke	Columbia River-Revelstoke	Rick Butler, Clerk, PO Box 170, Revelstoke V0E 2S0 – 250/837-2161, Fax: 250/837-4930
*RICHMOND	140,024 ('94)	Greater Vancouver	Richmond	Richmond-Centre; Richmond E.; Richmond-Steveston	Richard McKenna, City Clerk, 6911 - No. 3 Rd., Richmond V6Y 2C1 – 604/276-4000, Fax: 604/278-5139
ROSSLAND	3,557	Kootenay Boundary	Kootenay West-Revelstoke	Rossland-Trail	Andre Carrel, Clerk, PO Box 1179, Rossland V0G 1Y0 – 250/362-7396, Fax: 250/362-5451
*Saanich	105,100 ('95)	Capital	Saanich-Gulf Islands	Oak Bay-Gordon Head; Saanich N. & the Islands; Saanich S.	Terry R. Kirk, Municipal Clerk, 770 Vernon Ave., Victoria V8X 2W7 – 250/475-1775, Fax: 250/475-5400
Salmo (V)	1,069	Central Kootenay	Kootenay West-Revelstoke	Rossland-Trail	Brian Ryder, Sec.-Treas., PO Box 1000, Salmo V0G 1Z0 – 250/357-9433, Fax: 250/357-9633
Salmon Arm (DM)	12,115	Columbia-Shuswap	Okanagan-Shuswap	Shuswap	Wayne Buchanan, Clerk, PO Box 40, Salmon Arm V1E 4N2 – 250/832-6021, Fax: 250/832-5584
Sayward (V)	406	Comox-Strathcona	North Island-Powell River	North Island	Jean Phye, Sec.-Treas., PO Box 29, Sayward V0P 1R0 – 250/282-5512, Fax: 250/282-5511
Sechelt (DM)	6,123	Sunshine Coast	North Island-Powell River	Powell River-Sunshine Coast	Michael P. Vaughn, Clerk, PO Box 129, Sechelt V0N 3A0 – 604/885-1986, Fax: 604/885-7591
Sicamous (DM)	2,501	Columbia-Shuswap	Okanagan-Shuswap	Shuswap	Karen Smith, Clerk, PO Box 219, Sicamous V0E 2V0 – 250/836-2477, Fax: 250/836-4314
Sidney †	10,082	Capital	Saanich-Gulf Islands	Saanich N. & the Islands	David W. Bartley, Clerk, 2440 Sidney Ave., Sidney V8L 1Y7 – 250/656-1184, Fax: 250/655-4508
Silverton (V)	231	Central Kootenay	Kootenay West-Revelstoke	Nelson-Creston	Dorothy Mellen, Sec.-Treas., PO Box 14, Silverton V0G 2B0 – 250/358-2472, Fax: 250/358-2321
Slocan (V)	263	Central Kootenay	Kootenay West-Revelstoke	Nelson-Creston	Bonnie St. Thomas, Sec.-Treas., PO Box 50, Slocan V0G 2C0 – 250/355-2277, Fax: 250/355-2666
Smithers †	5,029	Bulkley-Nechako	Skeena	Bulkley Valley-Stikine	Terri-Anne Barge, Clerk, PO Box 879, Smithers V0J 2N0 – 250/847-3251, Fax: 250/847-9643
Spallumcheen (DM)	4,719	North Okanagan	Okanagan-Shuswap	Shuswap	George Sawada, Clerk-Treas., PO Box 100, Armstrong V0E 1B0 – 250/546-3013, Fax: 250/546-8878
Sparwood (DM)	4,211	East Kootenay	Kootenay East	Kootenay	Loretta Montemurro, Clerk, PO Box 520, Sparwood V0B 2G0 – 250/425-6271, Fax: 250/425-7277
Squamish (DM)	11,709	Squamish-Lillooet	Capilano-Howe Sound	West Vancouver-Garibaldi	Joe Barry, Clerk, PO Box 310, Squamish V0N 3G0 – 604/892-5217, Fax: 604/892-1083
Stewart (DM)	1,151	Kitimat-Stikine	Skeena	North Coast	Brian Woodward, Clerk-Treas., PO Box 460, Stewart V0T 1W0 – 250/636-2251, Fax: 250/636-2417
Summerland (DM)	9,253	Okanagan-Similkameen	Okanagan-Similkameen-Merritt	Okanagan-Penticton	George Redlich, Clerk, PO Box 159, Summerland V0H 1Z0 – 250/494-6451, Fax: 250/494-1415
*SURREY	274,000 ('94)	Greater Vancouver	Delta; Surrey North; Surrey-White Rock-South Langley	Surrey-Cloverdale; Surrey-Green Timbers; Surrey-Newton; Surrey-Whalley; Surrey-White Rock	Donna Kenny, City Clerk & General Mgr., Legislative Services, 14245 - 56 Ave., Surrey V3X 3A2 – 604/591-4011, Fax: 604/591-4357, URL: http://www.city.surrey.bc.ca/
Tahsis (V)	1,053	Comox-Strathcona	North Island-Powell River	North Island	Paul R. Edgington, Sec.-Treas., PO Box 519, Tahsis V0P 1X0 – 250/934-6344, Fax: 250/934-6622
Taylor (DM)	821	Peace River	Skeena	Peace River North	Robert Kelly, Clerk-Treas., PO Box 300, Taylor V0C 2K0 – 250/789-3392, Fax: 250/789-3543

Cities in CAPITALS; District municipalities marked (DM); Districts marked (D); Towns marked †; Villages marked (V). British Columbia Regional Districts follow this list. An in-depth listing for municipalities marked with * appears in Part 2 (check Index for page numbers).

MUNICIPALITY	1991 POP.	COUNTY OR DISTRICT	FEDERAL ELECTORAL DISTRICT	PROVINCIAL ELECTORAL DISTRICT	CONTACT PERSON WITH ADDRESS, PHONE & FAX
Telkwa (V)	959	Bulkley-Nechako	Skeena	Bulkley Valley-Stikine	Arlene de Gelder, Sec.-Treas., PO Box 220, Telkwa V0J 2X0 – 250/846-5212, Fax: 250/846-9572
TERRACE	11,433	Kitimat-Stikine	Skeena	Skeena	Robert Hallsor, Clerk, 3215 Eby St., Terrace V8G 2X8 – 250/635-6311, Fax: 250/638-4777
Tofino (DM)	1,103	Alberni-Clayoquot	Comox-Alberni	Alberni	Charles Hamilton, Clerk, PO Box 9, Tofino V0R 2Z0 – 250/725-3229, Fax: 250/725-3775
TRAIL	7,919	Kootenay Boundary	Kootenay West-Revelstoke	Rossland-Trail	James D. Forbes, Clerk, 1394 Pine Ave., Trail V1R 4E6 – 250/364-1262, Fax: 250/364-0830
Tumbler Ridge (DM)	4,650	Peace River	Prince George-Peace River	Peace River South	Norma Everett, Clerk, PO Box 100, Tumbler Ridge V0C 2W0 – 250/242-4242, Fax: 250/242-3993
Ucluelet (V)	1,595	Alberni-Clayoquot	Comox-Alberni	Alberni	Wallace Mah, Clerk, PO Box 999, Ucluelet V0R 3A0 – 250/726-7744, Fax: 250/726-7335
Valemount (V)	1,128	Fraser-Fort George	Prince George-Bulkley Valley	Prince George-Mount Robson	Dennis Goddard, Clerk, PO Box 168, Valemount V0E 2Z0 – 250/566-4435, Fax: 250/566-4249
*VANCOUVER	508,814 ('94)	Greater Vancouver	Burnaby-Kingsway; Vancouver Centre; Vanc. E.; Vanc. Quadra; Vanc. S.	Vancouver Burrard; Vanc.-Fraserview; Vanc.-Hastings; Vanc.-Kensington; Vanc.-Kingsway; Vanc.-Langara; Vanc.-Little Mtn.; Vanc.-Mt. Pleasant; Vanc.-Point Grey; Vanc.-Quilchena	Maria Kinsella, Clerk, 453 West 12 Ave., Vancouver V5Y 1V4 – 604/873-7011, Fax: 604/873-7419, URL: http://www.city.vancouver.bc.ca/
Vanderhoof (DM)	4,023	Bulkley-Nechako	Prince George-Bulkley Valley	Prince George-Omineca	Mike Redfearn, Clerk, PO Box 900, Vanderhoof V0J 3A0 – 250/567-4711, Fax: 250/567-9169
VERNON	31,000 ('95)	North Okanagan	Okanagan-Shuswap	Okanagan-Vernon	Marg Bailey, Clerk, 3400 - 30 St., Vernon V1T 5E6 – 250/545-1361, Fax: 250/545-7876
*VICTORIA	71,228	Capital	Victoria	Esquimalt-Metchosin; Oak Bay-Gordon Head; Victoria-Beacon Hill; Victoria-Hillside	Mark Johnston, Clerk & Director, Administration, One Centennial Sq., Victoria V8W 1P6 – 250/385-5711, Fax: 250/361-0348, URL: http://www.city.victoria.bc.ca/
View Royal †	5,925	Capital	Esquimalt-Juan de Fuca	Esquimalt-Metchosin	Heinz Burki, Clerk, 45 View Royal Ave., Victoria V9B 1A6 – 250/479-6800, Fax: 250/727-9551
Warfield (V)	1,814	Kootenay Boundary	Kootenay West-Revelstoke	Rossland-Trail	Shirley A. Tognotti, Sec.-Treas., 555 Schofield Hwy., Trail V1R 2G7 – 250/368-8202, Fax: 250/368-9354
West Vancouver (DM)	38,783	Greater Vancouver	Capilano-Howe Sound	N. Vancouver-Lonsdale; W. Vancouver-Capilano; W. Vancouver-Garibaldi	Margaret K. Warwick, Clerk, 750 - 17 St., West Vancouver V7V 3T3 – 604/922-1211, Fax: 604/925-7006
Whistler (DM)	4,459	Squamish-Lillooet	Cariboo-Chilcotin	West Vancouver-Garibaldi	Brenda M. Sims, Clerk, 4325 Blackcomb Way, Whistler V0N 1B4 – 604/932-5535, Fax: 604/932-6636
WHITE ROCK	16,314	Greater Vancouver	Surrey-White Rock-South Langley	Surrey-White Rock	Diane A. Middler, Clerk, 15322 Buena Vista Ave., White Rock V4B 1Y6 – 604/531-9111, Fax: 604/541-2118
WILLIAMS LAKE	10,385	Cariboo	Cariboo-Chilcotin	Cariboo North; Cariboo South	Wayne Thiessen, Clerk, 450 Mart St., Williams Lake V2G 1N3 – 250/392-2311, Fax: 250/392-4408
Zeballos (V)	220	Comox-Strathcona	North Island-Powell River	North Island	Tara Gilbert, Sec.-Treas., PO Box 127, Zeballos V0P 2A0 – 250/761-4229, Fax: 250/761-4331

BRITISH COLUMBIA REGIONAL DISTRICTS

REG. DISTRICTS	1991 POP.	CONTACT PERSON WITH ADDRESS, PHONE & FAX
Alberni-Clayoquot	31,224	Bob Harper, Sec., 3008 - 5 Ave., Port Alberni V9Y 2E3 – 250/720-2700, Fax: 250/723-1327
Bulkley-Nechako	38,343	Jay J. Simons, Sec., PO Box 820, Burns Lake V0J 1E0 – 250/692-3195, Fax: 250/692-3305
Capital	308,720 ('93)	William Jordan, Executive Director, 524 Yates St., PO Box 1000, Victoria V8W 2S6 – 250/360-3000, Fax: 250/360-3130; URL: http://vvv.com/crd/
Cariboo	61,059	Bob Long, Sec., 525 Borland St., Williams Lake V2G 1R9 – 250/392-3351, Fax: 250/392-2812
Central Coast	3,482	Donna Mikkelson, Sec., PO Box 186, Bella Coola V0T 1C0 – 250/799-5291, Fax: 250/799-5750
Central Kootenay	51,073	Barry Baldigara, Sec.-Asst. Adm., 601 Vernon St., Nelson V1L 4E9 – 250/352-6665, Fax: 250/352-9300
Central Okanagan	134,000 ('95)	Al Harrison, Sec., 1450 KLO Rd., Kelowna V1W 3Z4 – 250/763-4918, Fax: 250/763-0606
Columbia-Shuswap	41,665	Al Kuroyama, Sec., PO Box 978, Salmon Arm V1E 4P1 – 250/832-8194, Fax: 250/832-3375
Comox-Strathcona	82,729	Wayne d'Easum, Sec., PO Box 3370, Courtenay V9N 5N5 – 250/334-6000, Fax: 250/334-4358
Cowichan Valley	60,560	Jennifer Forrest, Sec., 137 Evans St., Duncan V9L 1P5 – 250/746-2500, Fax: 250/746-5612
East Kootenay	52,368	Wayne McNamar, Sec., 19 - 24 Ave. South, Cranbrook V1C 3H8 – 250/489-2791, Fax: 250/489-3498

Canadian Almanac & Directory 1997

REG. DISTRICTS	1991 POP.	CONTACT PERSON WITH ADDRESS, PHONE & FAX
Fort Nelson-Liard	5,038	Patricia A. Bailey, Sec., PO Box 399, Fort Nelson V0C 1R0 – 250/774-2541, Fax: 250/774-6794
Fraser-Fort George	90,739	Dave N. Wilson, Sec., 987 - 4 Ave., Prince George V2L 3H7 – 250/960-4400, Fax: 250/563-7520
Fraser Valley [a.]	186,251	Robert Moore, Clerk-Sec., 8430 Cessna Drive, Chilliwack V2P 7K4 – 250/702-5000, Fax: 250/792-9684
Greater Vancouver	1,713,393 ('93)	Paulette Vetleson, Sec., 4330 Kingsway, Burnaby V5H 4G8 – 604/432-6200, Fax: 604/432-6248 URL: http://www.gvrd.bc.ca/index.html
Kitimat-Stikine	42,053	Bob Marcellin, Sec., #300, 4545 Lazelle Ave., Terrace V8G 4E1 – 250/635-7251, Fax: 250/635-9222
Kootenay Boundary	31,194	Larry Robinson, Sec., #202, 843 Rossland Ave., Trail V1R 4S8 – 250/368-9148, Fax: 250/368-3990
Mount Waddington	13,896	Rosemary Fromson, Sec., PO Box 729, Port McNeill V0N 2R0 – 250/956-3161, Fax: 250/956-3232
Nanaimo	119,596 ('94)	Carol Mason, Sec., PO Box 40, Lantzville V0R 2H0 – 250/390-4111, Fax: 250/390-4163
North Okanagan	61,744	Peter Mackiewich, Sec.-Treas., 9848 Aberdeen Rd., Vernon V1B 2K9 – 250/545-5368, Fax: 250/545-1445
Okanagan-Similkameen	66,701	Vanessa Sutton, Adm.-Sec., 101 Martin St., Penticton V2A 5J9 – 250/492-0237, Fax: 250/492-0063
Peace River	53,317	Moray Stewart, Sec., PO Box 810, Dawson Creek V1G 4H8 – 250/784-3200, Fax: 250/784-3201
Powell River	18,477	Frances Ladret, Sec., 5776 Marine Ave., Powell River V8A 2M4 – 604/483-3231, Fax: 604/483-2229
Skeena-Queen Charlotte	23,769	Bryce Barnewall, Sec., #115 West 1st Av., Prince Rupert V8J 4K8 – 250/624-2002, Fax: 250/627-8493
Squamish-Lillooet	23,421	Rick Beauchamp, Sec., PO Box 219, Pemberton V0N 2L0 – 604/894-6371, Fax: 604/894-6526
Sunshine Coast	20,785	Larry Jardine, Sec., PO Box 800, Sechelt V0N 3A0 – 604/885-2261, Fax: 604/885-7909
Thompson-Nicola	117,000 ('94)	Eric Shishido, Sec., 2079 Falcon Rd., Kamloops V2C 4J2 – 250/372-9336, Fax: 250/372-5048

a. Effective December 12, 1995 the new Fraser Valley Regional District was created through an amalgamation of the regional districts of Central Fraser Valley, Dewdney-Alouette & Fraser-Cheam.

MANITOBA

All municipalities in Manitoba (except Winnipeg) are governed by the Manitoba Municipal Act. Winnipeg is governed by the City of Winnipeg Act.

In Manitoba there are no counties or regional governments; there are incorporated cities, towns, villages, and rural municipalities. Incorporation is determined by population and assessment. In order to incorporate into a village, a community requires 750 people and a tax base of $3,000,000. For a town the requirement is 1,500 people and $6,000,000 assessment. For a city it is 10,000 population.

All municipal elections are held every three years; thus, October 1995, October 1998, October 2001.

Cities in CAPITALS; Towns marked †; Villages marked (V); Rural Municipalities marked (RM). An in-depth listing for municipalities marked with * appears in Part 2 (check Index for page numbers).

MUNICIPALITY	1991 POP.	FEDERAL ELECTORAL DISTRICT	PROVINCIAL ELECTORAL DISTRICT	CONTACT PERSON WITH ADDRESS, PHONE & FAX
Albert (RM)	526	Brandon-Souris	Arthur-Virden	Rick Branston, Sec.-Treas., PO Box 70, Tilston R0M 2B0 – 204/686-2271, Fax: 204/686-2335
Altona †	3,060	Provencher	Emerson	Jim Spencer, Municipal Adm., 111 Centre Av. East, PO Box 1630, Altona R0G 0B0 – 204/324-6468, Fax: 204/324-1550
Arborg (V)	1,039	Portage-Interlake	Interlake	Roger Huel, Mun. Adm., 337 River Rd., PO Box 159, Arborg R0C 0A0 – 204/376-2647, Fax: 204/376-5379
Archie (RM)	490	Dauphin-Swan River	Roblin-Russell	Allen W. Cole, Sec.-Treas., Qu'Appelle St., PO Box 67, McAuley R0M 1H0 – 204/722-2053, Fax: 204/722-2027
Argyle (RM)	1,307	Portage-Interlake	Turtle Mountain	Gord Dearsley, Adm., 132 - 2 St. North, PO Box 40, Baldur R0K 0B0 – 204/535-2176, Fax: 204/535-2176
Arthur (RM)	581	Brandon-Souris	Arthur-Virden	Joan Cooper, Sec.-Treas., 138 Main St., PO Box 429, Melita R0M 1L0 – 204/522-3263, Fax: 204/522-8706
Beauséjour †	2,651	Selkirk-Red River	Lac du Bonnet	Jack Douglas, Sec.-Treas., 639 Park Av., PO Box 1028, Beauséjour R0E 0C0 – 204/268-2008, Fax: 204/268-3107
Benito (V)	427	Dauphin-Swan River	Swan River	Karon Harness, Sec.-Treas., 126 Main St., PO Box 369, Benito R0L 0C0 – 204/539-2634, Fax: 204/539-2221
Bifrost (RM)	2,750	Portage-Interlake	Interlake	L. Grant Thorsteinson, Sec.-Treas., 329 River Rd., PO Box 70, Arborg R0C 0A0 – 204/376-2391, Fax: 204/376-2742
Binscarth (V)	469	Dauphin-Swan River	Roblin-Russell	Bonnie Cozens, Sec.-Treas., 116 Russell St., PO Box 54, Binscarth R0J 0G0 – 204/532-2223, Fax: 204/532-2153
Birtle †	802	Dauphin-Swan River	Roblin-Russell	Joan E. Taylor, Sec.-Treas., PO Box 57, Birtle R0M 0C0 – 204/842-3234, Fax: 204/842-3496
Birtle (RM)	866	Dauphin-Swan River	Roblin-Russell	Debbie Jensen, Sec.-Treas., 678 Main St., PO Box 70, Birtle R0M 0C0 – 204/842-3403, Fax: 204/842-3622
Blanshard (RM)	643	Dauphin-Swan River	Minnedosa	Diane Kuculym, Sec.-Treas., 10 Cochrane St., PO Box 179, Oak River R0K 1T0 – 204/566-2146, Fax: 204/566-2126
Boissevain †	1,484	Brandon-Souris	Turtle Mountain	Lloyd Leganchuk, Sec.-Treas., 420 South Railway, PO Box 490, Boissevain R0K 0E0 – 204/534-2433, Fax: 204/534-3710
Boulton (RM)	378	Dauphin-Swan River	Roblin-Russell	Raymond G. Bomback, Sec.-Treas., PO Box 110, Inglis R0J 0X0 – 204/564-2589, Fax: 204/564-2643
Bowsman (V)	382	Dauphin-Swan River	Swan River	Laurie Maidy, Sec.-Treas., 105 - 2 St., PO Box 244, Bowsman R0L 0H0 – 204/238-4351, Fax: 204/238-4351
*BRANDON	38,573	Brandon-Souris	Brandon East; Brandon West	W. Ian Ford, Clerk, 410 - 9 St., Brandon R7A 6A2 – 204/729-2186, Fax: 204/729-8244
Brenda (RM)	801	Brandon-Souris	Arthur-Virden	Ron Bertholet, Sec.-Treas., PO Box 40, Waskada R0M 2E0 – 204/673-2401, Fax: 204/673-2663
Brokenhead (RM)	3,310	Selkirk-Red River	Lac du Bonnet	Wayne Omichinski, Sec.-Treas., PO Box 490, Beauséjour R0E 0C0 – 204/268-1624, Fax: 204/268-1504
Cameron (RM)	538	Brandon-Souris	Arthur-Virden	Brad Coe, Sec.-Treas., 315 East Railway St., PO Box 399, Hartney R0M 0X0 – 204/858-2590, Fax: 204/858-2681

Canadian Almanac & Directory 1997

Cities in CAPITALS; Towns marked †; Villages marked (V); Rural Municipalities marked (RM). An in-depth listing for municipalities marked with * appears in Part 2 (check Index for page numbers).

MUNICIPALITY	1991 POP.	FEDERAL ELECTORAL DISTRICT	PROVINCIAL ELECTORAL DISTRICT	CONTACT PERSON WITH ADDRESS, PHONE & FAX
Carberry †	1,481	Lisgar-Marquette	Gladstone	Ernest J.W. McCallum, Sec.-Treas., 122 Main St., PO Box 130, Carberry R0K 0H0 – 204/834-2195, Fax: 204/834-2795
Carman †	2,567	Lisgar-Marquette	Morris	Cheryl Young, Sec.-Treas., 12 - 2 Ave. SW, PO Box 160, Carman R0G 0J0 – 204/745-2443, 1-800-207-2721, Fax: 204/745-2903
Cartier (RM)	3,115	Portage-Interlake	Lakeside	Andre C. Carriere, Sec.-Treas., PO Box 117, Elie R0H 0H0 – 204/353-2214, Fax: 204/353-2335
Cartwright (V)	329	Lisgar-Marquette	Turtle Mountain	Colleen Mullin, Sec.-Treas., 485 Curwen, PO Box 9, Cartwright R0K 0L0 – 204/529-2363, Fax: 204/529-2288
Clanwilliam (RM)	481	Lisgar-Marquette	Minnedosa	Colleen Synchyshyn, Mun. Adm., 44 Main St. NW, PO Box 40, Erickson R0J 0P0 – 204/636-2431, Fax: 204/636-2516
Coldwell (RM)	1,394	Portage-Interlake	Lakeside	Diane Jacobs, Sec.-Treas., 35 Main St., PO Box 90, Lundar R0C 1Y0 – 204/762-5421, Fax: 204/762-5177
Cornwallis (RM)	4,216	Brandon-Souris	Minnedosa	Daryl J. Check, Clerk, Site 500, RR#5, PO Box 10, Brandon R7A 5Y5 – 204/727-2436, Fax: 204/725-3659
Crystal City (V)	437	Lisgar-Marquette	Turtle Mountain	Douglas E. Cavers, Adm., 26 South Railway Av. East, PO Box 310, Crystal City R0K 0N0 – 204/873-2591, Fax: 204/873-2459
Daly (RM)	880	Lisgar-Marquette	Minnedosa	John B. MacLellan, Sec.-Treas., 615 - 2 Av., PO Box 538, Rivers R0K 1X0 – 204/328-7410, Fax: 204/328-7410
Dauphin †	8,453	Dauphin-Swan River	Dauphin	Jim Puffalt, Adm., 21 - 2 Ave. NW, Dauphin R7N 1H1 – 204/638-3938, Fax: 204/638-5790
Dauphin (RM)	2,669	Dauphin-Swan River	Dauphin	Gail Anderson, Mun. Adm., PO Box 574, Dauphin R7N 2V4 – 204/638-4531, Fax: 204/638-7598
De Salaberry (RM)	2,985	Provencher	Emerson; Morris	Ron Musick, Sec.-Treas., 466 Sabourin St., PO Box 40, St. Pierre Jolys R0A 1V0 – 204/433-7406, Fax: 204/433-7063
Deloraine †	1,045	Brandon-Souris	Arthur-Virden	Ronald H. Amey, Sec.-Treas., 102 Broadway St. South, PO Box 510, Deloraine R0M 0M0 – 204/747-2655, Fax: 204/747-2927
Dufferin (RM)	2,431	Lisgar-Marquette	Morris	Linda Colpitts, Sec.-Treas., 12 - 2 Av. SW, PO Box 100, Carman R0G 0J0 – 204/745-2301, Fax: 204/745-6348
Dunnottar (V)	307	Selkirk-Red River	Gimli	Nora L. Rentz, Sec.-Treas., #210, 1839 Main St., Winnipeg R2V 2A4 – 204/339-1639, Fax: 204/339-1630
East St. Paul (RM)	5,820	Selkirk-Red River	Springfield	Janet Nylen, Sec.-Treas., 3021 Birds Hill Rd., East St. Paul R2E 1A7 – 204/668-8112, Fax: 204/668-1987
Edward (RM)	789	Lisgar-Marquette	Arthur-Virden	Rob Trott, Sec.-Treas., PO Box 100, Pierson R0M 1S0 – 204/634-2231, Fax: 204/634-2479
Elkhorn (V)	505	Lisgar-Marquette	Arthur-Virden	Garth Mitchell, Sec.-Treas., 10 Grange St., PO Box 280, Elkhorn R0M 0N0 – 204/845-2161, Fax: 204/845-2312
Ellice (RM)	494	Dauphin-Swan River	Roblin-Russell	J. C. Chartier, Sec.-Treas., Main St. North, PO Box 100, St. Lazare R0M 1Y0 – 204/683-2241, Fax: 204/683-2317
Elton (RM)	1,322	Lisgar-Marquette	Minnedosa	Kathleen E.I. Steele, Sec.-Treas., Forrest R0K 0W0 – 204/728-7834, Fax: 204/725-1865
Emerson †	721	Provencher	Emerson	Pat Ihme, Sec.-Treas., 104 Church, PO Box 340, Emerson R0A 0L0 – 204/373-2002, Fax: 204/373-2486
Erickson (V)	544	Lisgar-Marquette	Minnedosa	Colleen Synchyshyn, Mun. Adm., 44 Main St. NW, PO Box 40, Erickson R0J 0P0 – 204/636-2431, Fax: 204/636-2516
Eriksdale (RM)	977	Portage-Interlake	Lakeside	Debra Surgenor, Sec., 16 Main St., PO Box 10, Eriksdale R0C 0W0 – 204/739-2666, Fax: 204/739-2073
Ethelbert (V)	364	Dauphin-Swan River	Swan River	Eleanor Kuzyk, Sec.-Treas., PO Box 185, Ethelbert R0L 0T0 – 204/742-3301, Fax: 204/742-3228
Ethelbert (RM)	548	Dauphin-Swan River	Swan River	Dennis Puchailo, Sec.-Treas., PO Box 115, Ethelbert R0L 0T0 – 204/742-3212, Fax: 204/742-3642
FLIN FLON	7,119	Churchill	Flin Flon	Ken Shoemaker, Sec.-Treas., 20 - 1 Av., PO Box 100, Flin Flon R8A 1M6 – 204/687-7511, Fax: 204/687-5133
Franklin (RM)	1,651	Lisgar-Marquette	Emerson	Helen I. Robbins, Sec.-Treas., 115 Waddell Av., PO Box 66, Dominion City R0A 0H0 – 204/427-2557, Fax: 204/427-2224
Garson (V)	320	Selkirk-Red River	Lac du Bonnet	Eileen Boonstra, Sec.-Treas., 13 Thompson Av., PO Box 97, Garson R0E 0R0 – 204/268-2382
Gilbert Plains (V)	741	Dauphin-Swan River	Dauphin	Ernie Mouck, Mun. Admin., 114 Main St. North, PO Box 39, Gilbert Plains R0L 0X0 – 204/548-2761
Gilbert Plains (RM)	1,071	Dauphin-Swan River	Dauphin	Joan E. Priest, Sec.-Treas., 115 Main St. North, PO Box 220, Gilbert Plains R0L 0X0 – 204/548-2326, Fax: 204/548-2564
Gimli †	1,579	Portage-Interlake	Gimli	Danny Jo Sigmundson, Sec.-Treas., 64 - 2 Av., PO Box 88, Gimli R0C 1B0 – 204/642-5210, Fax: 204/642-7151
Gimli (RM)	2,737	Portage-Interlake	Gimli	Christopher Fulsher, Mun. Adm., PO Box 1246, Gimli R0C 1B0 – 204/642-8593, Fax: 204/642-8149
Gladstone †	928	Lisgar-Marquette	Gladstone	Louise Blaire, Sec.-Treas., 48 Dennis St., PO Box 25, Gladstone R0J 0T0 – 204/385-2332, Fax: 204/385-2391
Glenboro (V)	674	Lisgar-Marquette	Gladstone	Donald E. Foster, Sec.-Treas., 109 Broadway St., PO Box 190, Glenboro R0K 0X0 – 204/827-2083, Fax: 204/827-2553
Glenella (RM)	660	Lisgar-Marquette	Ste. Rose	Aaren Robertson, Sec.-Treas., PO Box 10, Glenella R0J 0V0 – 204/352-4281, Fax: 204/352-4281
Glenwood (RM)	722	Brandon-Souris	Turtle Mountain	Dennis Bauldic, Mun. Adm., 100 - 2 St. South, PO Box 487, Souris R0K 2C0 – 204/483-2822, Fax: 204/483-2062

4-20 MANITOBA MUNICIPALITIES

Cities in CAPITALS; Towns marked †; Villages marked (V); Rural Municipalities marked (RM). An in-depth listing for municipalities marked with * appears in Part 2 (check Index for page numbers).

MUNICIPALITY	1991 POP.	FEDERAL ELECTORAL DISTRICT	PROVINCIAL ELECTORAL DISTRICT	CONTACT PERSON WITH ADDRESS, PHONE & FAX
Grandview †	870	Dauphin-Swan River	Dauphin	James W. Wilson, Sec.-Treas., 436 Main St., PO Box 219, Grandview R0L 0Y0 – 204/546-2792, Fax: 204/546-2589
Grandview (RM)	1,003	Dauphin-Swan River	Dauphin	Joan Scott, Sec.-Treas., 414 Main St., PO Box 340, Grandview R0L 0Y0 – 204/546-2564, Fax: 204/546-3019
Gretna (V)	620	Provencher	Emerson	Mary Harder, Sec.-Treas., 568 Hespeler Av., PO Box 280, Gretna R0G 0V0 – 204/327-5578, Fax: 204/327-5458
Grey (RM)	2,104	Lisgar-Marquette	Lakeside	Ronald D. Hayward, Sec.-Treas., 34 Main St. North, PO Box 99, Elm Creek R0G 0N0 – 204/436-2014, Fax: 204/436-2543
Hamiota (V)	823	Dauphin-Swan River	Roblin-Russell	Ernest G. Buhler, Sec.-Treas., 44 - 4 St., PO Box 100, Hamiota R0M 0T0 – 204/764-2779, Fax: 204/764-2671
Hamiota (RM)	590	Dauphin-Swan River	Roblin-Russell	Ernest G. Buhler, Sec.-Treas., 44 - 4 St., PO Box 100, Hamiota R0M 0T0 – 204/764-2779, Fax: 204/764-2671
Hanover (RM)	8,889	Provencher	Steinbach	Charles Teetaert, Sec.-Treas., PO Box 1720, Steinbach R0A 2A0 – 204/326-4488, Fax: 204/326-4830
Harrison (RM)	900	Dauphin-Swan River	Minnedosa	Shelley Glenn, Sec.-Treas., 106 Main St., PO Box 220, Newdale R0J 1J0 – 204/849-2107, Fax: 204/849-2107
Hartney †	477	Brandon-Souris	Arthur-Virden	Garry McBrien, Sec.-Treas., 237 East Railway, PO Box 339, Hartney R0M 0X0 – 204/858-2429, Fax: 204/858-2429
Headingley (RM)	1,603	Winnipeg St. James	Charleswood	Lorne F. Erb, Sec.-Treas., 1-126 Bridge Rd., PO Box 310, Headingley R4H 1G9 – 204/837-5766, Fax: 204/831-7207
Hillsburg (RM)	613	Dauphin-Swan River	Roblin-Russell	Eleanor Nykolaishyn, Sec.-Treas., 130 - 2 Av. NW, PO Box 1180, Roblin R0L 1P0 – 204/937-2155
Killarney †	2,163	Brandon-Souris	Turtle Mountain	Harold A. Lamb, Sec.-Treas., 415 Broadway Av., PO Box 10, Killarney R0K 1G0 – 204/523-7120, Fax: 204/523-4637
La Broquerie (RM)	2,038	Provencher	Steinbach	Laurent Tétrault, Sec.-Treas., 94 Principale St., PO Box 130, La Broquerie R0A 0W0 – 204/424-5251, Fax: 204/424-5193
Lac du Bonnet (V)	1,089	Provencher	Lac du Bonnet	Colleen L. Johnson, Sec.-Treas., 84 - 2 St., PO Box 339, Lac du Bonnet R0E 1A0 – 204/345-8693, Fax: 204/345-8694
Lac du Bonnet (RM)	2,218	Provencher	Lac du Bonnet	Rose-Marie Blanchette, Sec.-Treas., PO Box 100, Lac du Bonnet R0E 1A0 – 204/345-2619, Fax: 204/345-6716
Lakeview (RM)	460	Lisgar-Marquette	Ste. Rose	Viola K. Wild, Sec.-Treas., 103 Main St., PO Box 100, Langruth R0H 0N0 – 204/445-2243, Fax: 204/445-2162
Langford (RM)	733	Lisgar-Marquette	Ste. Rose	Vinetta Hannaburg, Sec.-Treas., 282 Hamilton St., PO Box 280, Neepawa R0J 1H0 – 204/476-5775, Fax: 204/476-5431
Lansdowne (RM)	999	Lisgar-Marquette	Ste. Rose	Carol Henderson, Sec.-Treas., PO Box 141, Arden R0J 0B0 – 204/368-2202, Fax: 204/368-2202
Lawrence (RM)	648	Dauphin-Swan River	Dauphin	Elizabeth Tymchuk, Sec.-Treas., PO Box 220, Rorketon R0L 1R0 – 204/732-2333, Fax: 204/732-2557
Leaf Rapids †	1,613	Churchill	Flin Flon	Ernie Epp, Adm., PO Box 340, Leaf Rapids R0B 1W0 – 204/473-2436, Fax: 204/473-2566
Lorne (RM)	2,128	Lisgar-Marquette	Gladstone	Val Turner, Sec.-Treas., PO Box 10, Somerset R0G 2L0 – 204/744-2133, Fax: 204/744-2349
Louise (RM)	1,147	Lisgar-Marquette	Turtle Mountain	Douglas E. Cavers, Sec.-Treas., 26 South Railway Av. East, PO Box 310, Crystal City R0K 0N0 – 204/873-2591, Fax: 204/873-2459
Macdonald (RM)	3,999	Portage-Interlake	Morris	W. Tom Raine, Sec.-Treas., 161 Mandan Dr., PO Box 100, Sanford R0G 2J0 – 204/736-2255, Fax: 204/736-4335
MacGregor (V)	852	Lisgar-Marquette	Gladstone	Lawrence Hart, Sec.-Treas., 27 Hampton St. East, PO Box 190, MacGregor R0H 0R0 – 204/685-2211, Fax: 204/685-2616
Manitou (V)	811	Lisgar-Marquette	Pembina	Jacalyn Clayton, Sec.-Treas., 418 Main St., PO Box 280, Manitou R0G 1G0 – 204/242-2515, Fax: 204/242-2599
McCreary (V)	554	Dauphin-Swan River	Ste. Rose	Wendy L. Turko, Sec.-Treas., 436 - 2 Av., PO Box 267, McCreary R0J 1B0 – 204/835-2341, Fax: 204/835-2658
McCreary (RM)	646	Dauphin-Swan River	Ste. Rose	Linda Cripps, Sec.-Treas., PO Box 338, McCreary R0J 1B0 – 204/835-2309, Fax: 204/835-2649
Melita †	1,134	Brandon-Souris	Arthur-Virden	Clifford E. Hicks, Sec.-Treas., 79 Main St., PO Box 364, Melita R0M 1L0 – 204/522-3413, Fax: 204/522-3587
Miniota (RM)	1,048	Dauphin-Swan River	Roblin-Russell	Doug McAulay, Sec.-Treas., PO Box 70, Miniota R0M 1M0 – 204/567-3683, Fax: 204/567-3807
Minitonas (V)	544	Dauphin-Swan River	Swan River	Brent J. Fowler, Adm., 305 Main St., PO Box 9, Minitonas R0L 1G0 – 204/525-4461, Fax: 204/525-4857
Minitonas (RM)	1,227	Dauphin-Swan River	Swan River	Brent J. Fowler, Adm., 305 Main St., PO Box 9, Minitonas R0L 1G0 – 204/525-4461, Fax: 204/525-4857
Minnedosa †	2,526	Lisgar-Marquette	Minnedosa	Gail V. Graves, Mun. Adm., 103 Main St. East, PO Box 426, Minnedosa R0J 1E0 – 204/867-2727, Fax: 204/867-2686
Minto (RM)	665	Brandon-Souris	Minnedosa	Susan Hoglund, Mun. Adm., 49 Main St. South, PO Box 247, Minnedosa R0J 1E0 – 204/867-3865, Fax: 204/867-1937
Montcalm (RM)	1,606	Provencher	Emerson	Michel Duval, Sec.-Treas., 46 First St. East, PO Box 300, Letellier R0G 1C0 – 204/737-2271, Fax: 204/737-2032
Morden †	5,273	Lisgar-Marquette	Pembina	Abe Bergmann, Town Mgr., #100, 195 Stephen St., Morden R6M 1V3 – 204/822-4434, Fax: 204/822-6494

Canadian Almanac & Directory 1997

Cities in CAPITALS; Towns marked †; Villages marked (V); Rural Municipalities marked (RM). An in-depth listing for municipalities marked with * appears in Part 2 (check Index for page numbers).

MUNICIPALITY	1991 POP.	FEDERAL ELECTORAL DISTRICT	PROVINCIAL ELECTORAL DISTRICT	CONTACT PERSON WITH ADDRESS, PHONE & FAX
Morris †	1,616	Provencher	Morris	Conrad Nicholson, Sec.-Treas., 233 Main St. North, PO Box 28, Morris R0G 1K0 – 204/746-2531, Fax: 204/746-6009
Morris (RM)	2,865	Provencher	Morris; Emerson	Grant MacAulay, Sec.-Treas., 207 Main St. N., PO Box 518, Morris R0G 1K0 – 204/746-2642, Fax: 204/746-8801
Morton (RM)	848	Brandon-Souris	Turtle Mountain	Lloyd Leganchuk, Sec.-Treas., 420 South Railway, PO Box 490, Boissevain R0K 0E0 – 204/534-2433, Fax: 204/534-3710
Mossey River (RM)	819	Dauphin-Swan River	Swan River	John E. Pascal, Sec.-Treas., PO Box 80, Fork River R0L 0V0 – 204/657-2331, Fax: 204/657-2202
Neepawa †	3,258	Lisgar-Marquette	Ste. Rose	Ken Jenkins, Sec.-Treas., 282 Hamilton St., PO Box 339, Neepawa R0J 1H0 – 204/476-2317, Fax: 204/476-5431
Niverville †	1,530	Provencher	Steinbach	G. Jim Buys, Adm., PO Box 267, Niverville R0A 1E0 – 204/388-4600, Fax: 204/388-6110
North Cypress (RM)	2,028	Lisgar-Marquette	Gladstone	Ernest J.W. McCallum, Sec.-Treas., 122 Main St., PO Box 130, Carberry R0K 0H0 – 204/834-2195, Fax: 204/834-2795
North Norfolk (RM)	2,967	Lisgar-Marquette	Gladstone	Lawrence Hart, Sec.-Treas., 27 Hampton St. E., PO Box 190, MacGregor R0H 0R0 – 204/685-2211, Fax: 204/685-2616
Notre Dame de Lourdes (V)	614	Lisgar-Marquette	Gladstone	Roger Fouasse, Sec.-Treas., 55 Rodgers St., PO Box 89, Notre Dame de Lourdes R0G 1M0 – 204/248-2348, Fax: 204/248-2348
Oak Lake †	350	Brandon-Souris	Arthur-Virden	Mary Smith, Sec.-Treas., 293 - 2 Av. West, PO Box 100, Oak Lake R0M 1P0 – 204/855-2423, Fax: 204/855-2836
Oakland (RM)	990	Brandon-Souris	Turtle Mountain	Doug Boake, Sec.-Treas., PO Box 28, Nesbitt R0K 1P0 – 204/824-2374, Fax: 204/824-2374
Ochre River (RM)	991	Dauphin-Swan River	Dauphin	Ilene Mayne, Mun. Adm., 206 MacKenzie Av., PO Box 40, Ochre River R0L 1K0 – 204/733-2423, Fax: 204/733-2259
Odanah (RM)	519	Lisgar-Marquette	Minnedosa	Susan Hoglund, Mun. Adm., 49 Main St., PO Box 1197, Minnedosa R0J 1E0 – 204/867-3282, Fax: 204/867-1937
Pembina (RM)	1,928	Lisgar-Marquette	Pembina	Judy D. Young, Sec.-Treas., 315 Main St., PO Box 189, Manitou R0G 1G0 – 204/242-2838, Fax: 204/242-2798
Pilot Mound (V)	747	Lisgar-Marquette	Turtle Mountain	Tannis Stevenson, Sec.-Treas., 219 Broadway Av., PO Box 39, Pilot Mound R0G 1P0 – 204/825-2587, Fax: 204/825-2362
Pipestone (RM)	1,795	Brandon-Souris	Arthur-Virden	William W. Busby, Sec.-Treas., 401 - 3 Av., PO Box 99, Reston R0M 1X0 – 204/877-3327, Fax: 204/877-3999
Plum Coulee (V)	676	Provencher	Emerson	Ron Wm. Wiebe, Sec.-Treas., 253 Main Av., PO Box 36, Plum Coulee R0G 1R0 – 204/829-3419, Fax: 204/829-3436
*PORTAGE LA PRAIRIE	13,186	Portage-Interlake	Portage la Prairie	Dale Lyle, City Mgr., 97 Saskatchewan Ave. East, Portage la Prairie R1N 0L8 – 204/239-8337, Fax: 204/239-1532
Portage la Prairie (RM)	7,156	Portage-Interlake	Portage la Prairie; Lakeside	Richard C. Locke, Sec.-Treas., 35 Tupper St. South, Portage la Prairie R1N 1W7 – 204/857-3821, Fax: 204/239-0069
Powerview (V)	724	Provencher	Lac du Bonnet	Janice Thevenot, Sec.-Treas., PO Box 220, Powerview R0E 1P0 – 204/367-8483, Fax: 204/367-4747
Rapid City †	406	Dauphin-Swan River	Minnedosa	Valerie P. Irving, Sec.-Treas., 410 - 3 Av., PO Box 146, Rapid City R0K 1W0 – 204/826-2679, Fax: 204/826-2679
Rhineland (RM)	4,150	Provencher	Emerson	Jake Bergen, Sec.-Treas., 72 - 2 St. NE, PO Box 270, Altona R0G 0B0 – 204/324-5357, Fax: 204/324-1516
Ritchot (RM)	5,146	St. Boniface	La Verendrye; Morris	Yves Sabourin, Sec.-Treas., 352 Main St., St. Adolphe R5A 1B9 – 204/883-2293, Fax: 204/883-2674
Rivers †	1,076	Lisgar-Marquette	Minnedosa	Shirley Warkentin, Sec.-Treas., 670 - 2 Av., PO Box 520, Rivers R0K 1X0 – 204/328-5250, Fax: 204/328-5374
Riverside (RM)	883	Lisgar-Marquette	Turtle Mountain	Susan Lamont, Sec.-Treas., PO Box 126, Dunrea R0K 0S0 – 204/776-2113, Fax: 204/776-2228
Riverton (V)	584	Portage-Interlake	Interlake	Nadine Eyjolfson, Sec.-Treas., 56 Laura St., PO Box 250, Riverton R0C 2R0 – 204/378-2281, Fax: 204/378-5616
Roblin †	1,838	Dauphin-Swan River	Roblin-Russell	Marna J. Ellwood, Mun. Adm., 125 - 1 Av. NW, PO Box 730, Roblin R0L 1P0 – 204/937-8333, Fax: 204/937-4382
Roblin (RM)	954	Lisgar-Marquette	Turtle Mountain	Colleen Mullin, Sec.-Treas., 485 Curwen, PO Box 9, Cartwright R0K 0L0 – 204/529-2363, Fax: 204/529-2288
Rockwood (RM)	6,990	Portage-Interlake	Gimli	Janis L. Gluchi, Sec.-Treas., 33 Main St., PO Box 902, Stonewall R0C 2Z0 – 204/467-2272, Fax: 204/467-5329
Roland (RM)	968	Lisgar-Marquette	Morris	Dianne R. Toews, Sec.-Treas., 45 - 3 St., PO Box 119, Roland R0G 1T0 – 204/343-2061, Fax: 204/343-2001
Rosedale (RM)	1,614	Lisgar-Marquette	Ste. Rose	Harold McConnell, Sec.-Treas., 282 Hamilton St., PO Box 100, Neepawa R0J 1H0 – 204/476-5414, Fax: 204/476-5431
Rossburn (V)	609	Dauphin-Swan River	Roblin-Russell	Leonard A. Mackedenski, Sec.-Treas., 43 Main St. North, PO Box 70, Rossburn R0J 1V0 – 204/859-2762, Fax: 204/859-2959
Rossburn (RM)	658	Dauphin-Swan River	Roblin-Russell	Ernie Antonow, Sec.-Treas., 39 Main St., PO Box 100, Rossburn R0J 1V0 – 204/859-2779, Fax: 204/859-2959
Rosser (RM)	1,364	Portage-Interlake	Lakeside	Linda Van De Walle, Sec.-Treas., Rosser R0H 1E0 – 204/467-5711, Fax: 204/467-5958
Russell †	1,616	Dauphin-Swan River	Roblin-Russell	Wally R. Melnyk, Sec.-Treas., 135 Pelly Av. North, PO Box 10, Russell R0J 1W0 – 204/773-2253, Fax: 204/773-3370

Cities in CAPITALS; Towns marked †; Villages marked (V); Rural Municipalities marked (RM). An in-depth listing for municipalities marked with * appears in Part 2 (check Index for page numbers).

MUNICIPALITY	1991 POP.	FEDERAL ELECTORAL DISTRICT	PROVINCIAL ELECTORAL DISTRICT	CONTACT PERSON WITH ADDRESS, PHONE & FAX
Russell (RM)	528	Dauphin-Swan River	Roblin-Russell	Louise Ewankiw, Sec.-Treas., 362 Main St. North, PO Box 220, Russell R0J 1W0 – 204/773-2294, Fax: 204/773-2294
St. Andrews (RM)	9,461	Selkirk-Red River	Selkirk; Gimli	Marilyn S. Regiec, Sec.-Treas., General Delivery, Clandeboye R0C 0P0 – 204/738-2264, Fax: 204/738-2500
Ste. Anne (V)	1,477	Provencher	La Verendrye	J. Guy Levesque, Sec.-Treas., 181 Central Av., Ste. Anne R5H 1G3 – 204/422-5293, Fax: 204/422-5459
Ste. Anne (RM)	3,810	Provencher	La Verendrye	Alice De Baets, Sec.-Treas., 141 Central Av., Ste. Anne R5H 1C3 – 204/422-5929, Fax: 204/422-9723
St. Claude (V)	613	Portage-Interlake	Lakeside	Simone Dupasquier, Sec.-Treas., 12 - 1 St., PO Box 249, St. Claude R0G 1Z0 – 204/379-2382, Fax: 204/379-2072
St. Clements (RM)	7,870	Selkirk-Red River	Lac du Bonnet; Springfield	Tom Mollard, Mgr., Grp. 35, RR#1, PO Box 2, East Selkirk R0E 0M0 – 204/482-3300, Fax: 204/482-3098
St. François Xavier (RM)	898	Portage-Interlake	Lakeside	Colleen Sinkewicz, Sec.-Treas., 1060, Hwy 26, St. François Xavier R4L 1A5 – 204/864-2092, Fax: 204/864-2390
St. Laurent (RM)	1,115	Portage-Interlake	Lakeside	Lisa Wurm, Sec.-Treas., General Delivery, St. Laurent R0C 2S0 – 204/646-2259, Fax: 204/646-2705
St. Lazare (V)	315	Dauphin-Swan River	Roblin-Russell	Claude Chartier, Sec.-Treas., Main St. N., PO Box 100, St. Lazare R0M 1Y0 – 204/683-2241, Fax: 204/683-2317
St. Pierre-Jolys (V)	907	Provencher	Morris	Rita I. Bazin, Sec.-Treas., 466 Sabourin St., PO Box 218, St. Pierre-Jolys R0A 1V0 – 204/433-7832, Fax: 204/433-7053
Ste. Rose (RM)	1,008	Dauphin-Swan River	Ste. Rose	Michelle Denys, Sec.-Treas., 630 Central Av., PO Box 30, Ste. Rose du Lac R0L 1S0 – 204/447-2633, Fax: 204/447-2278
Ste. Rose du Lac (V)	1,008	Dauphin-Swan River	Ste. Rose	Marlene M. Bouchard, Adm., 580 Central Av., PO Box 445, Ste. Rose du Lac R0L 1S0 – 204/447-2229, Fax: 204/447-2875
Saskatchewan (RM)	677	Dauphin-Swan River	Minnedosa	Beverley Wells, Sec.-Treas., 435 - 3 Av., PO Box 9, Rapid City R0K 1W0 – 204/826-2515
Selkirk †	9,815	Selkirk-Red River	Selkirk	James Fenske, Mgr., 200 Eaton Ave., Selkirk R1A 0W6 – 204/785-4900, Fax: 204/482-5448
Shell River (RM)	1,165	Dauphin-Swan River	Roblin-Russell	Twyla Ludwig, Sec.-Treas., 213 - 2 Av. NW, PO Box 998, Roblin R0L 1P0 – 204/937-4430, Fax: 204/937-8496
Shellmouth (RM)	760	Dauphin-Swan River	Roblin-Russell	Raymond G. Bomback, Sec.-Treas., PO Box 62, Inglis R0J 0X0 – 204/564-2589, Fax: 204/564-2643
Shoal Lake (V)	784	Dauphin-Swan River	Roblin-Russell	Ernie Pushkarenko, Sec.-Treas., PO Box 342, Shoal Lake R0J 1Z0 – 204/759-2270, Fax: 204/759-2690
Shoal Lake (RM)	703	Dauphin-Swan River	Roblin-Russell	Thelma Chegwin, Sec.-Treas., 306 Elm St., PO Box 278, Shoal Lake R0J 1Z0 – 204/759-2565, Fax: 204/759-2740
Sifton (RM)	769	Dauphin-Swan River	Arthur-Virden	Mary Smith, Sec.-Treas., 293 - 2 Av. West, PO Box 100, Oak Lake R0M 1P0 – 204/855-2423, Fax: 204/855-2836
Siglunes (RM)	1,560	Portage-Interlake	Interlake	Mel Bullerwell, Sec.-Treas., 38 Main St., PO Box 370, Ashern R0C 0E0 – 204/768-2641, Fax: 204/768-2301
Silver Creek (RM)	594	Dauphin-Swan River	Roblin-Russell	Sophia Smith, Sec.-Treas., PO Box 130, Angusville R0J 0A0 – 204/773-2449, Fax: 204/773-2449
Snow Lake †	1,598	Churchill	Flin Flon	Chuck Dunning, Sec.-Treas., 113 Elm St., PO Box 40, Snow Lake R0B 1M0 – 204/358-2551, Fax: 204/358-2112
Somerset (V)	496	Lisgar-Marquette	Gladstone	Linda L. Talbot, Sec.-Treas., 291 Carlton Av., PO Box 187, Somerset R0G 2L0 – 204/744-2171
Souris †	1,662	Brandon-Souris	Turtle Mountain	Elwin W. Swan, Sec.-Treas., 100 - 2 St. South, PO Box 518, Souris R0K 2C0 – 204/483-2169, Fax: 204/483-2129
South Cypress (RM)	862	Lisgar-Marquette	Gladstone	Eric Plaetinck, Sec.-Treas., 618 Railway Av., PO Box 219, Glenboro R0K 0X0 – 204/827-2252, Fax: 204/827-2553
South Norfolk (RM)	1,234	Lisgar-Marquette	Gladstone	Sheila Mowatt, Sec.-Treas., 180 Broadway, PO Box 30, Treherne R0G 2V0 – 204/723-2044, Fax: 204/723-2719
Springfield (RM)	11,102	Selkirk-Red River	Springfield	Eric Towler, Sec.-Treas., 628 Main St., PO Box 219, Oakbank R0E 1J0 – 204/444-3321, Fax: 204/444-2137
Stanley (RM)	4,558	Lisgar-Marquette	Pembina	Rick Klippenstein, Sec.-Treas., #100, 379 Stephen St., Morden R6M 1V1 – 204/822-6251, Fax: 204/822-3596
Steinbach †	8,213	Provencher	Steinbach	Jack Kehler, Sec.-Treas., 225 Reimer Av., PO Box 1090, Steinbach R0A 2A0 – 204/326-9877, Fax: 204/326-4171
Stonewall †	2,997	Portage-Interlake	Gimli	Robert J. Potter, Sec.-Treas., 377 Main St., PO Box 250, Stonewall R0C 2Z0 – 204/467-5561, Fax: 204/467-9129
Strathclair (RM)	1,055	Dauphin-Swan River	Minnedosa	E. Jo-Ann McKerchar, Sec.-Treas., 127 Minnedosa Av., PO Box 160, Strathclair R0J 2C0 – 204/365-2196, Fax: 204/365-2056
Strathcona (RM)	878	Lisgar-Marquette	Turtle Mountain	Barrie McGill, Sec.-Treas., PO Box 100, Belmont R0K 0C0 – 204/537-2241
Swan River †	3,917	Dauphin-Swan River	Swan River	Harry Showdra, Mun. Adm., 135 - 5 Av. North, PO Box 879, Swan River R0L 1Z0 – 204/734-4586, Fax: 204/734-5166
Swan River (RM)	2,947	Dauphin-Swan River	Swan River	Betty Nemetchek, Sec.-Treas., PO Box 610, Swan River R0L 1Z0 – 204/734-3344, Fax: 204/734-3701
Taché (RM)	7,576	Provencher	La Verendrye	Ernest A. Lajoie, Sec.-Treas., 450 Dawson Rd., PO Box 100, Lorette R0A 0Y0 – 204/878-3321, Fax: 204/878-9977
Teulon (V)	1,016	Portage-Interlake	Gimli	Laura L. Humbert, Adm., 44 - 4 Av. SE, PO Box 69, Teulon R0C 3B0 – 204/886-2314, Fax: 204/886-3918

Cities in CAPITALS; Towns marked †; Villages marked (V); Rural Municipalities marked (RM). An in-depth listing for municipalities marked with * appears in Part 2 (check Index for page numbers).

MUNICIPALITY	1991 POP.	FEDERAL ELECTORAL DISTRICT	PROVINCIAL ELECTORAL DISTRICT	CONTACT PERSON WITH ADDRESS, PHONE & FAX
THOMPSON	14,977	Churchill	Thompson	Lynn Taylor, City Mgr., City Hall, 226 Mystery Lake Rd, Thompson R8N 1S6 – 204/677-7910, Fax: 204/677-7981
Thompson (RM)	1,262	Lisgar-Marquette	Morris	Mary Riddell, Adm., 531 Norton Av., PO Box 190, Miami R0G 1H0 – 204/435-2114, Fax: 204/435-2067
Treherne (V)	661	Lisgar-Marquette	Gladstone	Sheila Mowatt, Sec.-Treas., 180 Broadway Av., PO Box 30, Treherne R0G 2V0 – 204/723-2044, Fax: 204/723-2719
Turtle Mountain (RM)	1,142	Brandon-Souris	Turtle Mountain	Harold A. Lamb, Sec.-Treas., 415 Broadway Av., PO Box 160, Killarney R0K 1G0 – 204/523-7058, Fax: 204/523-4637
Victoria (RM)	1,405	Lisgar-Marquette	Gladstone	Yvon P. L. Bruneau, Sec.-Treas., 130 Broadway St., PO Box 40, Holland R0G 0X0 – 204/526-2423, Fax: 204/526-2028
Victoria Beach (RM)	196	Selkirk-Red River	Lac du Bonnet	Raymond Moreau, Sec.-Treas., #303, 960 Portage Ave., Winnipeg R3G 0R4 – 204/774-4263, Fax: 204/774-9834
Virden †	2,894	Brandon-Souris	Arthur-Virden	Robert Eslinger, Sec.-Treas., 236 Wellington St. West, PO Box 310, Virden R0M 2C0 – 204/748-2440, Fax: 204/748-2501
Wallace (RM)	1,889	Brandon-Souris	Arthur-Virden	Don Stephenson, Sec.-Treas., 304 Nelson St. West, PO Box 2200, Virden R0M 2C0 – 204/748-1239, Fax: 204/748-3450
Waskada (V)	289	Brandon-Souris	Arthur-Virden	Ron Bertholet, Sec.-Treas., PO Box 40, Waskada R0M 2E0 – 204/673-2401, Fax: 204/673-2663
Wawanesa (V)	482	Brandon-Souris	Turtle Mountain	Barbara Roney, Sec.-Treas., 106 - 4 St., PO Box 278, Wawanesa R0K 2G0 – 204/824-2244, Fax: 204/824-2244
West St. Paul (RM)	3,658	Selkirk-Red River	Selkirk	Mel Didyk, Sec.-Treas., 3550 Main St., West St. Paul R4A 5A3 – 204/338-0306, Fax: 204/338-3539
Westbourne (RM)	1,957	Lisgar-Marquette	Gladstone; Ste. Rose	Patricia Pugh, Sec.-Treas., PO Box 150, Gladstone R0J 0T0 – 204/385-2388, Fax: 204/385-2388
Whitehead (RM)	1,421	Brandon-Souris	Minnedosa	James F. Madder, Sec.-Treas., PO Box 107, Alexander R0K 0A0 – 204/752-2261, Fax: 204/752-2129
Whitemouth (RM)	1,714	Provencher	La Verendrye	Rita E. Bell, Sec.-Treas., PO Box 248, Whitemouth R0E 2G0 – 204/348-2221, Fax: 204/348-2576
Whitewater (RM)	787	Brandon-Souris	Turtle Mountain	Murray R. Jackson, Sec.-Treas., PO Box 53, Minto R0K 1M0 – 204/776-2172, Fax: 204/776-2252
Winchester (RM)	661	Brandon-Souris	Arthur-Virden	Leona Williams, Sec.-Treas., 129 Broadway St. North, PO Box 387, Deloraine R0M 0M0 – 204/747-2572, Fax: 204/747-2883
Winkler †	6,397	Lisgar-Marquette	Pembina	Vince Anderson, Mun. Adm., 185 Main St., Winkler R6W 1B4 – 204/325-9524, Fax: 204/325-9515
*WINNIPEG	641,700 ('94)	Winnipeg North; Winnipeg North Centre; Winnipeg St. James; Winnipeg South; Winnipeg South Centre; Winnipeg Transcona	Assiniboia; Broadway; Burrows; Charleswood; Concordia; Crescentwood; Elmwood; Fort Garry; Inkster; Kildonan; Kirkfield Park; Niakwa; Osborne; Point Douglas; Radisson; Riel; River East; River Heights; Rossmere; St. Boniface; St. James; St. Johns; St. Norbert; St. Vital; Seine River; Sturgeon Creek; The Maples; Transcona; Tuxedo; Wellington; Wolseley	Dorothy E. Browton, City Clerk, Council Building, Civic Centre, 510 Main St., Winnipeg R3B 1B9 – 204/986-2196, Fax: 204/949-0566
Winnipeg Beach †	641	Portage-Interlake	Gimli	Valerie D. Moore, Mun. Adm., 29 Robinson, PO Box 160, Winnipeg Beach R0C 3G0 – 204/389-2698, Fax: 204/389-2019
Winnipegosis †	771	Dauphin-Swan River	Swan River	Terry Tomlinson, Sec.-Treas., 130 - 2 St., PO Box 370, Winnipegosis R0L 2G0 – 204/656-4791, Fax: 204/656-4751
Woodlands (RM)	3,334	Portage-Interlake	Lakeside	A. Eilene Myskiw, Sec.-Treas., Woodlands R0C 3H0 – 204/383-5679, Fax: 204/383-5169
Woodworth (RM)	1,051	Brandon-Souris	Arthur-Virden	Howard J. Norek, Sec.-Treas., PO Box 148, Kenton R0M 0Z0 – 204/838-2317, Fax: 204/838-2000
The Pas †	6,166	Churchill	The Pas	John F. Marnock, Mun. Adm., 81 Edwards Av., PO Box 870, The Pas R9A 1K8 – 204/623-6481, Fax: 204/623-5506

MANITOBA LOCAL GOVERNMENT DISTRICTS

Incorporated under "The Local Government Districts Act," January 1st, 1945. Local Government Districts have basically the same powers, functions and purposes as regular municipalities except that although they have an elected council, they are ultimately responsible to the Minister of Rural Development. Effective January 1, 1997 a proposed change to legislation will transfer most of the Local Government Districts to full municipal status. Roger Dennis, Executive Director, Local Government Support Services Branch, #508, 800 Portage Ave., Winnipeg; 204/945-2572

DISTRICTS	1991 POP.	CONTACT PERSON WITH ADDRESS, PHONE & FAX
Alexander	2,399	Rose Beaudry, Adm., PO Box 100, St. Georges R0E 1V0 – 204/367-2235, Fax: 204/367-2257
Alonsa	1,952	Carol Szewczyk, Adm., PO Box 127, Alonsa R0H 0A0 – 204/767-2054, Fax: 204/767-2044
Armstrong	1,888	Don Rybachuk, Adm., PO Box 69, Inwood R0C 1P0 – 204/278-3377, Fax: 204/278-3437
Churchill	1,143	Rod McKenzie, Adm., 180 La Verendrye Av., PO Box 459, Churchill R0B 0E0 – 204/675-8871, Fax: 204/675-2934
Consol	3,037	Leona Axcell, Adm., 264 Fischer Av., PO Box 578, The Pas R9A 1K6 – 204/623-7474, Fax: 204/623-4546

DISTRICTS	1991 POP.	CONTACT PERSON WITH ADDRESS, PHONE & FAX
Fisher	2,145	Linda Podaima, Adm., PO Box 280, Fisher Branch R0C 0Z0 – 204/372-6393, Fax: 204/372-8470
Gillam	1,893	Hilda M. Price, Adm., 323 Railway Av., PO Box 100, Gillam R0B 0L0 – 204/652-2121, Fax: 204/652-2338
Grahamdale	1,812	Beverley Yaworsky, Resident Adm., PO Box 160, Moosehorn R0C 2E0 – 204/768-2858, Fax: 204/768-3374
Grand Rapids	506	Lillian Turner, Adm., PO Box 301, Grand Rapids R0C 1E0 – 204/639-2260, Fax: 204/639-2475
Lynn Lake	834	Fred Salter, Adm., 503 Sherrit Av., PO Box 100, Lynn Lake R0B 0W0 – 204/356-2418, Fax: 204/356-8297
Mountain	2,043	Christine Playfoot, Adm., PO Box 155, Birch River R0L 0E0 – 204/236-4222, Fax: 204/236-4773
Mystery Lake	2	Don C. Taylor, Adm., PO Box 189, Thompson R8N 1N1 – 204/677-4075, Fax: 204/778-7642
Park	1,330	Sylvester Yakielashek, Adm., PO Box 190, Onanole R0J 1N0 – 204/848-7614, Fax: 204/848-2082
Pinawa	1,806	Gary Hanna, Resident Adm., 36 Burrows Rd., PO Box 100, Pinawa R0E 1L0 – 204/753-2331, Fax: 204/753-2770
Piney	1,559	Reynald Preteau, Adm., PO Box 48, Vassar R0A 2J0 – 204/437-2060, Fax: 204/437-2556
Reynolds	1,297	Jeanne Kozak, Adm., General Delivery, Hadashville R0E 0X0 – 204/426-5305, Fax: 204/426-5552
Stuartburn	1,517	Judy Reimer, Adm., PO Box 59, Vita R0A 2K0 – 204/425-3218, Fax: 204/425-3513

NEW BRUNSWICK

The provincial government of New Brunswick provides all services of a municipal nature for the rural area of the province while municipalities provide these services to their residents. For the rural area, an advisory committee may be elected at public meetings biennially to assist and advise the Minister. Municipal councils are elected to look after the affairs of the municipalities.

Acts of the legislature governing municipalities are the Municipalities Act, the Municipal Assistance Act, the Community Planning Act, the Assessment Act, the Municipal Capital Borrowing Act, the Municipal Elections Act, and the Control of Municipalities Act.

Population requirements for incorporation of municipalities are 10,000 for cities and 1,500 for towns. There are no specified requirements for villages.

Municipal elections are held every three years on the second Monday in May; thus, May 1995, May 1998, May 2001.

Cities in CAPITALS; Towns marked †; Villages marked (V). An in-depth listing for municipalities marked with * appears in Part 2 (check Index for page numbers).

MUNICIPALITY	1991 POP.	COUNTY	FEDERAL ELECTORAL DISTRICT	PROVINCIAL ELECTORAL DISTRICT	CONTACT PERSON WITH ADDRESS, PHONE & FAX
Alma (V)	308	Albert	Fundy-Royal	Albert	Louise Butland, Clerk-Treas., Main St., PO Box 38, Alma E0A 1B0 – 506/887-2203, Fax: 506/887-2239
Aroostook (V)	409	Victoria	Madawaska-Victoria	Victoria-Tobique	Darlene Francoeur, Clerk, PO Box 90, Aroostook E0J 1B0 – 506/273-6443, Fax: 506/273-3025
Atholville (V)	1,474	Restigouche	Restigouche-Chaleur	Campbellton	Jeannette Gould, Gref, 247, rue Notre-Dame, CP 10, Atholville E0K 1A0 – 506/789-1213, Fax: 506/789-0290
Baker Brook (V)	649	Madawaska	Madawaska-Victoria	Madawaska-les-Lacs	Gertrude Albert, Gref., 3677, rue Principale, pièce A, Baker Brook E7A 1V3 – 506/258-3250, Fax: 506/258-1023
Balmoral (V)	1,949	Restigouche	Restigouche-Chaleur	Dalhousie-Restigouche-East	Laurent Bujold, Gref., 625, av des Pionniers, CP 60, Balmoral E0B 1C0 – 506/826-2826, Fax: 506/826-1180
Bas-Caraquet (V)	1,849	Gloucester	Acadie-Bathurst	Caraquet	Richard Frigault, Adm., 8185, rue St-Paul, CP 60, Bas-Caraquet E0B 1E0 – 506/727-4411, Fax: 506/727-4006
Bath (V)	653	Carleton	Carleton-Charlotte	Carleton	Sharon Olmstead, Clerk, 161 School St., PO Box 38, Bath E0J 1E0 – 506/278-5293, Fax: 506/278-5932
BATHURST	14,409	Gloucester	Acadie-Bathurst	Bathurst	Louise C. Wafer, Clerk, 256 St. Andrew St., PO Box 116, Bathurst E2A 2Z1 – 506/548-0400, Fax: 506/548-0435
Belledune (V)	488	Gloucester	Restigouche-Chaleur	Nigadoo-Chaleur	Donald C. McAlister, Clerk-Treas., 931 Main St., Belledune E0B 1G0 – 506/522-5613, Fax: 506/522-9804
Beresford †	4,367	Gloucester	Restigouche-Chaleur	Nigadoo-Chaleur	Norval Godin, Adm.-Gref., 855, rue Principale, CP 600, Beresford E0B 1H0 – 506/542-2000, Fax: 506/542-1880
Bertrand (V)	1,310	Gloucester	Acadie-Bathurst	Caraquet	M.J. Léonel Thériault, Adm., 651, boul des Acadiens, CP 119, Bertrand E0B 1J0 – 506/727-2239, Fax: 506/727-7312
Blacks Harbour (V)	1,139	Charlotte	Carleton-Charlotte	Charlotte	Deanna Hunter, Clerk-Mgr., 881 Main St., CP 90, Blacks Harbour E0G 1H0 – 506/456-3324, Fax: 506/456-1052
Blackville (V)	938	Northumberland	Miramichi	Southwest Miramichi	Kurt Marks, Adm., PO Box 17, Blackville E0C 1C0 – 506/843-6337, Fax: 506/843-6043
Bouctouche †	2,364	Kent	Beauséjour	Kent South	Jean-Clovis Collette, Gref., 211, boul Irving, CP 370, Bouctouche E0A 1G0 – 506/743-1480, Fax: 506/743-1481
Bristol (V)	724	Carleton	Carleton-Charlotte	Carleton	Nancy Shaw, Clerk, 104 Juniper Rd., PO Box 57, Bristol E0J 1G0 – 506/392-6013, Fax: 506/392-5211
Cambridge-Narrows (V)	534	Queens	Fundy-Royal	Oromocto-Gagetown	Marilyn Powell, Clerk, Municipal Bldg., Cambridge-Narrows E0E 1B0 – 506/488-3155, Fax: 506/488-1018
CAMPBELLTON	8,699	Restigouche	Restigouche-Chaleur	Campbellton	Ronald F. Mahoney, Clerk-Adm., Campbellton City Centre, PO Box 100, Campbellton E3N 3G1 – 506/789-2700, Fax: 506/759-7403

Canadian Almanac & Directory 1997

Cities in CAPITALS; Towns marked †; Villages marked (V). An in-depth listing for municipalities marked with * appears in Part 2 (check Index for page numbers).

MUNICIPALITY	1991 POP.	COUNTY	FEDERAL ELECTORAL DISTRICT	PROVINCIAL ELECTORAL DISTRICT	CONTACT PERSON WITH ADDRESS, PHONE & FAX
Canterbury (V)	422	York	Carleton-Charlotte	Woodstock	Eva Mott, Clerk, 95 Main St., PO Box 90, Canterbury E0H 1C0 – 506/279-2048, Fax: 506/279-2920
Cap Pelé (V)	2,181	Westmorland	Beauséjour	Shediac-Cap-Pelé	Michel Mélanson, Gref.-Adm., 31, ch St-André, CP 540, Cap-Pelé E0A 1J0 – 506/577-4157, Fax: 506/577-2602
Caraquet †	4,556	Gloucester	Acadie-Bathurst	Caraquet	Pierre Doiron, Gref., 50, rue Du Colisée, CP 420, Caraquet E0B 1K0 – 506/727-1717, Fax: 506/727-7719
Centreville (V)	529	Carleton	Carleton-Charlotte	Carleton	Cynthia R. Gray, Clerk, Main St., PO Box 117, Centreville E0J 1H0 – 506/276-3671, Fax: 506/276-9891
Charlo (V)	1,597	Restigouche	Restigouche-Chaleur	Dalhousie-Restigouche-East	Adolphe Goulette, Gref.-Adm., 616, rue Chaleur, CP 62, Charlo E0B 1M0 – 506/684-3597, Fax: 506/684-4481
Chipman (V)	1,615	Queens	Fundy-Royal	Grand Lake	Brenda Barton, Clerk, PO Box 149, Chipman E0E 1C0 – 506/339-6601, Fax: 506/339-6197
Clair (V)	903	Madawaska	Madawaska-Victoria	Madawaska-les-Lacs	Nicole Michaud, Gref., 809E, rue Principale, Clair E7A 2H7 – 506/992-2181, Fax: 506/992-0021
Dalhousie †	4,775	Restigouche	Restigouche-Chaleur	Dalhousie-Restigouche East	Michael Allain, Clerk-Adm., 111 Hall St., PO Box 250, Dalhousie E0K 1B0 – 506/684-5554, Fax: 506/684-5213
Dieppe †	10,463	Westmorland	Moncton	Dieppe-Memramcook	Rolande Gallant, Gref., 333 Acadia Ave., Dieppe E1A 1G9 – 506/857-0440, Fax: 506/853-4965
Doaktown (V)	1,090	Northumberland	Miramichi	Southwest Miramichi	Marilyn Price, Clerk, PO Box 97, Doaktown E0C 1G0 – 506/365-7970, Fax: 506/365-7111
Dorchester (V)	848	Westmorland	Beauséjour	Tantramar	Simonne Malenfant-Edgett, Clerk-Treas., 3 Main St., PO Box 80, Dorchester E0A 1M0 – 506/379-2582, Fax: 506/379-1116
Drummond (V)	1,007	Victoria	Madawaska-Victoria	Grand Falls Region; Region de Grand-Sault	Chantal McCarthy, Gref., Site 59, Bôite 6, 1412 ch Tobique, Drummond E0J 1M0 – 506/473-2660, Fax: 506/473-4543
East Riverside-Kingshurst (V)	1,049	Kings	Fundy-Royal	Saint John-Kings	T. Thomas Newcombe, Clerk, 70 Hampton Rd., Rothesay E2E 5L5 – 506/847-7140, Fax: 506/847-9367
EDMUNDSTON	10,835	Madawaska	Madawaska-Victoria	Edmundston	Paul Lavoie, Secrétaire municipal, 7, ch Canada, Edmundston E3V 1T7 – 506/739-2115, Fax: 506/737-6820
Eel River Crossing (V)	1,467	Restigouche	Restigouche-Chaleur	Dalhousie-Restigouche East	Kim Bujold, Clerk, 20, rue Savoie, CP 159, Eel River Crossing E0B 1P0 – 506/826-2490, Fax: 506/826-3912
Fairvale (V)	5,041	Kings	Fundy-Royal	Saint John-Kings	Sandra Shields, Clerk, PO Box 538, Rothesay E2E 5A6 – 506/847-4758, Fax: 506/847-1288
Florenceville (V)	694	Carleton	Carleton-Charlotte	Carleton	Bernice Beaulieu, Clerk, PO Box 152, Florenceville E0J 1K0 – 506/392-5249, Fax: 506/392-6143
*FREDERICTON	47,016	York	Fredericton-York-Sunbury	Fredericton North; Fredericton South; Fredericton-Fort Nashwaak	Donna Lavigne, City Clerk, PO Box 130, Fredericton E3B 4Y7 – 506/452-9500, Fax: 506/452-9509
Fredericton Junction (V)	714	Sunbury	Carleton-Charlotte	New Maryland	Jocelyn Nason, Clerk, 195A Sunbury Dr., Fredericton Junction E0G 1T0 – 506/368-2628, Fax: 506/368-1900
Gagetown (V)	607	Queens	Fundy-Royal; Fredericton-York-Sunbury; Carleton-Charlotte	Oromocto-Gagetown	Allison Blair, Clerk, Front St., PO Box 189, Gagetown E0G 1V0 – 506/488-3167
Gondola Point (V)	4,218	Kings	Fundy-Royal	Kennebecasis	Sandra Ryall, Clerk-Treas., Meenans Cove Rd., PO Box 579, Rothesay E2E 5A6 – 506/849-2588, Fax: 506/849-0702
Grand Bay †	3,613	Kings	Fundy-Royal	Grand Bay-Westfield	Sandra M. Gautreau, Clerk-Mgr., 77 River Valley Dr., PO Box 180, Grand Bay E0G 1W0 – 506/738-8457, Fax: 506/738-1824
Grand Falls-Grand-Sault †	6,083	Victoria	Madawaska-Victoria	Grand Falls Region; Région de Grand-Sault	Joseph L. Côté, Adm.-Gref., 142 Court St., PO Box 800, Grand Falls E3Z 1C3 – 506/475-7777, Fax: 506/475-7779
Grand Manan (V)	598	Charlotte	Carleton-Charlotte	Fundy Isles	Geraldine Ingalls, Clerk, Ingalls Head, Grand Manan E0G 2C0 – 506/662-8109, Fax: 506/662-8737
Grande-Anse (V)	981	Gloucester	Acadie-Bathurst	Nepisiguit	Thérèse Haché, Adm., 19, rue Acadie, CP 147, Grande Anse E0B 1R0 – 506/732-5411, Fax: 506/732-5267
Hampton †	3,590	Kings	Fundy-Royal	Hampton-Belleisle	Margaret Clarke, Clerk, 10 DeMille Ct., PO Box 370, Hampton E0G 1Z0 – 506/832-7661, Fax: 506/832-7621

Canadian Almanac & Directory 1997

Cities in CAPITALS; Towns marked †; Villages marked (V). An in-depth listing for municipalities marked with * appears in Part 2 (check Index for page numbers).

MUNICIPALITY	1991 POP.	COUNTY	FEDERAL ELECTORAL DISTRICT	PROVINCIAL ELECTORAL DISTRICT	CONTACT PERSON WITH ADDRESS, PHONE & FAX
Hartland †	890	Carleton	Carleton-Charlotte	Carleton	Judy Dee, Clerk, Orser St., PO Box 358, Hartland E0J 1N0 – 506/375-4357, Fax: 506/375-8265
Harvey (V)	372	York	Fundy-Royal	York	Ellen Bransfield, Clerk, PO Box 125, Harvey Station E0H 1H0 – 506/366-6240, Fax: 506/366-6242
Hillsborough (V)	1,239	Albert	Fundy-Royal	Albert	Danny Jonah, Adm.-Clerk, 197 Main St., PO Box 100, Hillsborough E0A 1X0 – 506/734-3100, Fax: 506/734-1990
Kedgwick (V)	1,118	Restigouche	Restigouche-Chaleur	Restigouche West	Diane Thompson, Gref., 12, rue Notre-Dame, CP 267, Kedgwick E0K 1C0 – 506/284-2160, Fax: 506/284-2859
Lac Baker (V)	229	Madawaska	Madawaska-Victoria	Madawaska-les-Lacs	Paul Ouellette, Gref., 69, rue de la Pointe, Lac Baker E7A 1J1 – 506/992-2531, Fax: 506/992-3045
Lamèque †	1,687	Gloucester	Acadie-Bathurst	Lamèque-Shippagan-Miscou	Henri-Paul Guignard, Adm.-Gref., 28, rue De L'Hôpital, CP 58, Lamèque E0B 1V0 – 506/344-2246, Fax: 506/344-2296
Le Goulet (V)	1,087	Gloucester	Acadie-Bathurst	Lamèque-Shippagan-Miscou	Alvine Bulger, Gref.-Trés., 917, rue Principale, CP 300, Le Goulet E0B 1W0 – 506/336-9711, Fax: 506/336-2499
Maisonnette (V)	675	Gloucester	Acadie-Bathurst	Caraquet	Nicole Boudreau, Gref.-Trés., CP 248, Maisonnette E0B 1X0 – 506/727-6888, Fax: 506/727-4290
McAdam (V)	1,600	York	Carleton-Charlotte	York	Ann Donahue, Clerk, 146 Saunders Rd., PO Box 299, McAdam E0H 1K0 – 506/784-2293, Fax: 506/784-1402
Meductic (V)	248	York	Carleton-Charlotte	Woodstock	Reta Cummings, Clerk, PO Box 27, Meductic E0H 1L0 – 506/272-2106
Memramcook (V)	4,678	Westmorland	Beasèjour	Dieppe-Memramcook	Louis Arthur Gaudet, Adm.-Gref., 612, rue Centrale, CP 300, Saint Joseph E0A 2Y0 – 506/758-2078, Fax: 506/758-9544
Millville (V)	334	York	Carleton-Charlotte	York	Christine Myshrall, Clerk, PO Box 39, Millville E0H 1M0 – 506/463-8251, Fax: 506/463-8262
Minto (V)	3,096	Sunbury-Queens	Fundy-Royal	Grand Lake	Rose Collette, Clerk, 19 Maple St., PO Box 7, Minto E0E 1J0 – 506/327-3383, Fax: 506/327-3041
MIRAMICHI	22,000	Northcumberland	Miramichi	Miramichi Bay; Miramichi-Bay Duvin; Miramichi-Centre	James F. Lamkey, Clerk, 406 Water St., Miramichi E1N 1B7 – 506/778-1200, Fax: 506/773-6040
*MONCTON	57,010	Westmorland	Moncton	Moncton E.; Monc. N.; Monc. S.; Monc. Crescent	Elizabeth Reade, Clerk, 655 Main St., Moncton E1C 1E8 – 506/853-3333, Fax: 506/859-4225
Nackawic †	1,224	York	Carleton-Charlotte	York	William MacLean, Clerk, 115 Otis Dr., PO Box 638, Nackawic E0H 1P0 – 506/575-2241, Fax: 506/575-2035
Néguac (V)	1,745	Northumberland	Miramichi	Miramichi Bay	Georges R. Savoie, Adm., 1175, rue Principale, CP 106, Néguac E0C 1S0 – 506/776-8328, Fax: 506/776-3500
New Maryland (V)	5,751	York	Fredericton-York-Sunburry	New Maryland	Connie Saulnier, Clerk, 429 New Maryland Hwy., New Maryland E3C 1G2 – 506/451-8508, Fax: 506/450-1605
Nigadoo (V)	950	Gloucester	Restigouche-Chaleur	Nigadoo-Chaleur	Bill Lévesque, Gref., 385, rue Principale, CP 190, Nigadoo E0B 2A0 – 506/783-2488, Fax: 506/783-2989
Norton (V)	1,476	Kings	Fundy-Royal	Hampton-Belleisle	Bev Wilcox, Clerk, Route 124, PO Box 240, Norton E0G 2N0 – 506/839-2373, Fax: 506/839-5560
Oromocto †	9,325	Sunbury	Fredericton-York-Sunbury	Oromocto-Gagetown	A. Wayne Carnell, Adm., 137 MacDonald Ave., Oromocto E2V 1A6 – 506/357-4400, Fax: 506/357-6723
Paquetville (V)	688	Gloucester	Acadie-Bathurst	Centre-Péninsule	Muriel Gallien, Adm., 1094, rue du Parc, CP 159, Paquetville E0B 2B0 – 506/764-5493, Fax: 506/764-5240
Perth-Andover (V)	1,877	Victoria	Madawaska-Victoria	Victoria-Tobique	Murray Watters, Clerk-Adm., 344 East Riverside Dr., PO Box 219, Perth-Andover E0J 1V0 – 506/273-2235, Fax: 506/273-6351
Petit-Rocher (V)	1,988	Gloucester	Restigouche-Chaleur	Nigadoo-Chaleur	Guy Clavette, Gref., 582, rue Principale, CP 270, Petit-Rocher E0B 2E0 – 506/783-8711, Fax: 506/783-3946
Petitcodiac (V)	1,342	Westmorland	Moncton	Petitcodiac	Pam Cochrane, Clerk, 63 Main St., PO Box 479, Petitcodiac E0A 2H0 – 506/756-3376, Fax: 506/756-8294

Cities in CAPITALS; Towns marked †; Villages marked (V). An in-depth listing for municipalities marked with * appears in Part 2 (check Index for page numbers).

MUNICIPALITY	1991 POP.	COUNTY	FEDERAL ELECTORAL DISTRICT	PROVINCIAL ELECTORAL DISTRICT	CONTACT PERSON WITH ADDRESS, PHONE & FAX
Plaster Rock (V)	1,246	Victoria	Madawaska-Victoria	Victoria-Tobique	Barbara Wishart-Fawcett, Adm., 81 Ridgewell, PO Box 129, Plaster Rock E0J 1W0 – 506/356-6070, Fax: 506/356-6081
Pointe-Verte (V)	1,193	Gloucester	Restigouche-Chaleur	Nigadoo-Chaleur	Donald Hammond, Gref.-Adm., 375, rue Principale, CP 89, Pointe-Verte E0B 2H0 – 506/783-7973, Fax: 506/783-8950
Port Elgin (V)	490	Westmorland	Beauséjour	Tantramar	Sonia M. Wells, Clerk-Treas., PO Box 180, Port Elgin E0A 2K0 – 506/538-2221, Fax: 506/538-2263
Quispamsis †	8,446	Kings	Fundy-Royal	Kennebecasis	Catherine Snow, Clerk, Municipal Dr., PO Box 21085, Quispamsis E2E 4Z4 – 506/847-8878, Fax: 506/849-5025
Renforth (V)	1,474	Kings	Fundy-Royal	Saint John-Kings	Joan Fitzgerald, Clerk-Admin., 95 Shore Rd., Renforth E2H 1K7 – 506/847-2288, Fax: 506/847-2286
Rexton (V)	940	Kent	Beauséjour	Kent	Barry Glencross, Clerk-Admin., 96 Main St., PO Box 100, Rexton E0A 2L0 – 506/523-6921, Fax: 506/523-7383
Richibucto †	1,469	Kent	Beauséjour	Rogersville-Kouchibouguac	Jean-Paul Mazerolle, Gérant, 31, rue Principale, CP 337, Richibucto E0A 2M0 – 506/523-4467, Fax: 506/523-1826
Riverside-Albert (V)	485	Albert	Fundy-Royal	Albert	Deborah Murray, Clerk-Treas., PO Box 59, Riverside-Albert E0A 1A0 – 506/882-2086, Fax: 506/882-2038
Riverview †	16,270	Albert	Moncton	Riverview	Charles S. Shannon, Clerk-Mgr., 30 Honour House Ct., Riverview E1B 3Y9 – 506/387-2020, Fax: 506/387-2033
Rivière-Verte (V)	988	Madawaska	Madawaska-Victoria	Madawaska-la-Vallée	Evelyn Therrien, Gref., 78, rue Principale, CP 100, Rivière-Verte E0L 1E0 – 506/263-8028, Fax: 506/263-5610
Rogersville (V)	1,385	Kent	Miramichi	Rogersville-Kouchibouguac	Hélène LeBlanc, Adm.-Gref., 4, rue de l'École, CP 70, Rogersville E0A 2T0 – 506/775-1200, Fax: 506/775-6544
Rothesay †	1,647	Kings	Fundy-Royal	Saint-John-Kings	Tom Newcombe, Clerk-Mgr., PO Box 4699, Rothesay E2E 5X4 – 506/847-7132, Fax: 506/847-9367
Sackville †	5,494	Westmorland	Beauséjour	Tantramar	Bob Cooling, CAO, 2 Main St. East, PO Box 660, Sackville E0A 3C0 – 506/364-0400, Fax: 506/364-0414
Saint-André (V)	424	Madawaska	Madawaska-Victoria	Grand Falls Region; Région de Grand-Sault	Giselle Ouellette, Secrétaire-Gref., Boîte 1, Site 155, RR#4, Grand-Sault E0J 1M0 – 506/473-4868, Fax: 506/473-7159
St. Andrews †	1,652	Charlotte	Carleton-Charlotte	Western Charlotte	212 Water St., PO Box 160, St. Andrews E0G 2X0 – 506/529-1820, Fax: 506/529-3383
Sainte-Anne-de-Madawaska (V)	1,341	Madawaska	Madawaska-Victoria	Madawaska-la-Vallée	Jocelyn Roy, Gref., 75, rue Principale, CP 99, Sainte-Anne-de-Madawaska E0L 1G0 – 506/445-2449, Fax: 506/445-2405
Saint-Antoine (V)	1,380	Kent	Beauséjour	Kent South	Bernadine Maillet, Gref., 51, rue Principale, CP 180, Saint-Antoine E0A 2X0 – 506/525-2212, Fax: 506/525-9531
Saint-Basile †	3,332	Madawaska	Madawaska-Victoria	Madawaska-la-Vallée	Doreen Banville, Gref., 540, rue Principale, CP 261, Saint-Basile E0L 1H0 – 506/263-5583, Fax: 506/263-4200
Saint-François-de-Madawaska (V)	661	Madawaska	Madawaska-Victoria	Madawaska-les-Lacs	Colette Lévesque, Gref., 2033, rue Commerciale, Saint-François-de-Madawaska E7A 1B3 – 506/992-3121, Fax: 506/992-3894
St. George †	1,345	Charlotte	Carleton-Charlotte	Charlotte	Ross Norman, Mgr., 1 School St., PO Box 148, St. George E0G 2Y0 – 506/755-1020, Fax: 506/755-1029
Saint-Hilaire (V)	273	Madawaska	Madawaska-Victoria	Madawaska-les-Lacs	Jacqueline Ouellet, Gref., RR#1, Edmundston E3V 3K3 – 506/258-3307
Saint-Isidore (V)	2,701		Acadie-Bathurst	Centre-Péninsule	Louis LeBouthillier, Gref, CP 145, Saint-Isidore E0B 2L0 – 506/358-6356, Fax: 506/358-2020
Saint-Jacques (V)	2,505	Madawaska	Madawaska-Victoria	Madawaska-Les-Lacs	Pauline Grondin, Gref., 12, rue Rivière à la Truite, CP 150, Saint-Jacques E0L 1K0 – 506/735-3341, Fax: 506/735-6924

Cities in CAPITALS; Towns marked †; Villages marked (V). An in-depth listing for municipalities marked with * appears in Part 2 (check Index for page numbers).

MUNICIPALITY	1991 POP.	COUNTY	FEDERAL ELECTORAL DISTRICT	PROVINCIAL ELECTORAL DISTRICT	CONTACT PERSON WITH ADDRESS, PHONE & FAX
*SAINT JOHN	74,969	Saint John	Carleton-Charlotte; Fundy-Royal; Saint John	S. John-Fundy; S. John-Kings; S. John-Champlain; S. John-Harbour; S. John-Portland; S. John-Lancaster; Grand Bay-Westfield	Mary L. Munford, Common Clerk, City Hall, Market Sq., PO Box 1971, Saint John E2L 4L1 – 506/658-2800, Fax: 506/658-2802; URL: http://www.city.saint-john.nb.ca
Saint-Léolin (V)	856	Gloucester	Acadie-Bathurst	Caraquet	Gérard Battah, Gref., CP 8, Saint-Léolin E0B 2M0 – 506/732-5367, Fax: 506/732-3177
Saint Léonard †	1,545	Madawaska	Madawaska-Victoria	Madawaska-la-Vallée	Julie Pelletier, Gref.-Trés., 108, rue du Pont, CP 390, Saint Léonard E0L 1M0 – 506/423-6381, Fax: 506/423-7615
Saint-Louis-de-Kent (V)	1,009	Kent	Beauséjour	Rogersville-Kouchibouguac	Léo-Paul Frigault, Gref., 33, rue Beauséjour, CP 220, Saint-Louis-de-Kent E0A 2Z0 – 506/876-2441, Fax: 506/876-4530
Sainte-Marie-Saint-Raphaël (V)	1,201	Gloucester	Acadie-Bathurst	Lamèque-Shippagan-Miscou	Denis Ducharme, Adm., 274, boul De La Mer, CP 91, Sainte-Marie-Saint-Raphaël E0B 2N0 – 506/344-2258, Fax: 506/344-2542
St. Martins (V)	411	Saint John	Fundy-Royal	Saint John-Fundy	Sandra Roy, Clerk, St. Martins E0G 2Z0 – 506/833-4430, Fax: 506/833-4430
Saint-Quentin (V)	2,269	Restigouche	Restigouche-Chaleur	Restigouche West	Roger Cyr, Gref., 10, rue Deschênes, CP 489, Saint-Quentin E0K 1J0 – 506/235-2425, Fax: 506/235-1952
St. Stephen †	4,931	Charlotte	Carleton-Charlotte	Western Charlotte	Wayne Tallon, Mgr., 34 Milltown Blvd., St. Stephen E3L 1G3 – 506/466-1566, Fax: 506/466-5558
Salisbury (V)	1,805	Westmorland	Moncton	Petitcodiac	Carol Wortman, Clerk-Admin., 56, rue Douglas, PO Box 270, Salisbury E0A 3E0 – 506/372-5011, Fax: 506/372-1013
Shediac †	4,343	Westmorland	Beauséjour	Shediac-Cap-Pelé	Jeannette Bourque, Gref., 170, rue Main, CP 969, Shediac E0A 3G0 – 506/532-7000, Fax: 506/532-6156
Shippagan †	2,760	Gloucester	Acadie-Bathurst	Lamèque-Shippagan-Miscou	Éloi Haché, Gref., 200, av Hôtel de Ville, CP 280, Shippagan E0B 2P0 – 506/336-2310, Fax: 506/336-4848
Stanley (V)	429	York	Fredericton-York-Sunbury	Mataquac	Lorna Pinnock, Clerk, 17 Glen Rd., PO Box 149, Stanley E0H 1T0 – 506/367-3245, Fax: 506/367-3245
Sussex †	4,132	Kings	Fundy-Royal	Kings East	Paul Maguire, Clerk, 22 Maple Ave., PO Box 1057, Sussex E0E 1P0 – 506/433-7200, Fax: 506/432-6116
Sussex Corner (V)	1,346	Kings	Fundy-Royal	Kings East	Sandra Daigle, Clerk, 179 Post Rd., Sussex Corner E0E 1R0 – 506/433-5184, Fax: 506/433-3785
Tide Head (V)	1,156	Restigouche	Restigouche-Chaleur	Campbellton	Christine Babcock, Clerk, 4 Mountain St., PO Box 60, Tide Head E0K 1K0 – 506/753-5738, Fax: 506/753-7347
Tracadie-Sheila †	4,319	Gloucester	Acadie-Bathurst	Tracadie-Sheila	Cécile Rousselle, Gref., 4293, rue Beauregard, CP 3600, Tracadie-Sheila E1X 1G5 – 506/393-4020, Fax: 506/393-4025
Tracy (V)	576	Sunbury	Carleton-Charlotte	New Maryland	Geraldine Harris, Clerk, Tracy E0G 3C0 – 506/368-2878, Fax: 506/368-1014
Verret (V)	737	Madawaska	Madawaska-Victoria	Madawaska-les-Lacs	Nicole Lévesque, Gref., 122 Rte 120, Verret E3V 3K3 – 506/739-7175, Fax: 506/735-2654
Westfield (V)	1,203	Kings	Fundy-Royal	Grand Bay-Westfield	Linda Thompson, Clerk-Treas., RR#2, PO Box 2158, Westfield E0G 3J0 – 506/757-2500, Fax: 506/757-8463
Woodstock †	4,631	Carleton	Carleton-Charlotte	Woodstock	Ken Harding, CAO, 824 Main St., PO Box 1059, Woodstock E0J 2B0 – 506/328-3307, Fax: 506/328-8344

NEWFOUNDLAND

The provincial government of Newfoundland and Labrador exercises control over the activities of all municipalities in accordance with the Executive Council Act and the Municipal Affairs Act. Under the provisions of the Municipalities Act, the Department exercises a certain degree of financial and administrative control over all municipalities with the exception of the Cities of St. John's, Corner Brook and Mount Pearl. The towns and communities incorporated under the Municipalities Act do not require ministerial approval of their annual budgets, but the Department employs inspectors to oversee municipal activities. The province assumes responsibility for public health, welfare and law enforcement which are elsewhere generally considered to be municipal functions.

The cities, towns and communities incorporated in Newfoundland are authorized to levy taxes and to provide a wide range of municipal services and to make appropriate bylaws or regulations for the implementation and administration of these services. Towns and community councils have virtually the same powers with one significant exception being that community councils can avail of a more simplified election process and the fact that community councils are elected for two-year terms as opposed to four-year terms for both town and city councils.

City and town councils in Newfoundland are elected on the second Tuesday in November every four years (1997, 2001, etc.). Community councils are elected on the second Tuesday in November every second year or at every second annual general meeting of the community which must be held between January 1 and March 31 each year.

Cities in CAPITALS; Towns marked †; Communities marked ‡; Regional Municipalities marked (RG). An in-depth listing for municipalities marked with * appears in Part 2 (check Index for page numbers).

MUNICIPALITY	1991 POP.	FEDERAL ELECTORAL DISTRICT	PROVINCIAL ELECTORAL DISTRICT	CONTACT PERSON WITH ADDRESS, PHONE & FAX
Admiral's Beach ‡	275	St. John's West	Placentia & St. Mary's	Vacant, Clerk, PO Box 196, Admiral's Beach A0B 3A0 – 709/521-2671
Anchor Point ‡	380	Humber-St. Barbe-Baie Verte	St. Barbe	Elizabeth Genge, Clerk, PO Box 117, Anchor Point A0K 1A0 – 709/456-2149
Appleton †	526	Gander-Grand Falls	Gander	Mavis Simms, Clerk, Site 4, RR#1, PO Box 31, Appleton A0G 2K0 – 709/679-2289, Fax: 709/679-5552
Aquaforte ‡	188	St. John's West	Ferryland	Darlene George, Clerk, Aquaforte A0A 1A0 – 709/363-2253
Arnold's Cove †	1,106	St. John's West	Bellevue	Wayne Slade, Clerk, PO Box 70, Arnold's Cove A0B 1A0 – 709/463-2323, Fax: 709/463-2323
Avondale †	802	St. John's East	Harbour Main-Whitbourne	Carol Ann Cantwell, Clerk, PO Box 59, Avondale A0A 1B0 – 709/229-4201, Fax: 709/229-4446
Badger †	1,073	Gander-Grand Falls	Grand Falls-Buchans	Pansy Hurley, Clerk, PO Box 130, Badger A0H 1A0 – 709/539-2406, Fax: 709/539-5262
Badger's Quay et al †	3,230	Bonavista-Trinity-Conception	Bonavista North	Harry Winter, Clerk, PO Box 64, Badger's Quay A0G 1B0 – 709/536-2010, Fax: 709/536-3481
Baie Verte †	1,913	Humber-St. Barbe-Baie Verte	Baie Verte	Ruth Burton, Clerk, PO Box 218, Baie Verte A0K 1B0 – 709/532-8222, Fax: 709/532-4134
Baine Harbour ‡	189	Burin-St. George's	Burin-Placentia West	John Bryant, Clerk, General Delivery, Baine Harbour A0E 1A0 – 709/443-2646
Bauline †	386	St. John's East	Cape St. Francis	Gail Tobin, Clerk, 2 Brook Path, Bauline A1K 1E9 – 709/335-2483
Bay Bulls †	1,065	St. John's West	Ferryland	Andrea Norman, Clerk, PO Box 70, Bay Bulls A0A 1C0 – 709/334-3454, Fax: 709/334-3454
Bay de Verde †	679	Bonavista-Trinity-Conception	Trinity-Bay de Verde	Molly Walsh, Clerk, PO Box 10, Bay de Verde A0A 1E0 – 709/587-2260, Fax: 709/587-2049
Bay L'Argent †	403	Burin-St. George's	Bellevue	Wanda Stewart, Clerk, PO Box 29, Bay L'Argent A0E 1B0 – 709/461-2606, Fax: 709/461-2608
Bay Roberts †	5,474	Bonavista-Trinity-Conception	Port de Grave	Daphne Earle, Clerk, PO Box 114, Bay Roberts A0A 1G0 – 709/786-2126, Fax: 709/786-2128
Baytona ‡	366	Gander-Grand Falls	Lewisporte	Linda Budden, Clerk, PO Box 29, Baytona A0G 2J0 – 709/659-6101
Beachside ‡	280	Gander-Grand Falls	Baie Verte	Mary Bennett, Clerk, 112 Bayview Rd., Beachside A0J 1T0 – 709/267-5251
Bellburns ‡	123	Humber-St. Barbe-Baie Verte	St. Barbe	Miriam House, Clerk, Bellburns A0K 1H0 – 709/898-2468
Belleoram †	739	Burin-St. George's	Fortune Bay-Cape La Hune	Hilda Gould, Clerk, PO Box 29, Belleoram A0H 1B0 – 709/881-6161, Fax: 709/881-6161
Bide Arm ‡	325	Humber-St. Barbe-Baie Verte	The Straits & White Bay North	Phyllis Randell, Clerk, Bide Arm A0K 1J0 – 709/457-2811, Fax: 709/457-2253
Birchy Bay †	768	Gander-Grand Falls	Lewisporte	Ruby Pollard, Clerk, PO Box 40, Birchy Bay A0G 1E0 – 709/659-3221, Fax: 709/659-2121
Bird Cove ‡	349	Humber-St. Barbe-Baie Verte	St. Barbe	Sharon Pittman, Clerk, 67 Michaels Dr., Bird Cove A0K 1L0 – 709/247-2256, Fax: 709/247-2128
Biscay Bay ‡	97	St. John's West	Ferryland	Fred White, Clerk, PO Box 14, Biscay Bay A0A 4B0 – 709/438-2425
Bishop's Cove ‡	292	Bonavista-Trinity-Conception	Port de Grave	Joan Smith, Clerk, PO Box 141, Bishop's Cove A0A 3X0 – 709/589-2194
Bishop's Falls †	4,232	Gander-Grand Falls	Exploits	Josephine Budgell, Clerk, PO Box 310, Bishop's Falls A0H 1C0 – 709/258-6581, Fax: 709/258-6346
Bonavista †	4,597	Bonavista-Trinity-Conception	Bonavista South	David Hiscock, Clerk, PO Box 279, Bonavista A0C 1B0 – 709/468-7816, Fax: 709/468-2495
Botwood †	3,663	Gander-Grand Falls	Exploits	Audrey Rowsell, Clerk, PO Box 490, Botwood A0H 1E0 – 709/257-2839, Fax: 709/257-3330
Branch ‡	382	St. John's West	Placentia & St. Mary's	Augustine Power, Clerk, PO Box 129, Branch A0B 1E0 – 709/338-2920, Fax: 709/338-2921
Brent's Cove ‡	310	Humber-St. Barbe-Baie Verte	Baie Verte	Ellen Butler, Clerk, Brent's Cove A0K 1R0 – 709/661-5301
Brighton ‡	297	Gander-Grand Falls	Windsor-Springdale	Donna Ince, Clerk, Brighton A0J 1B0 – 709/263-7391

Canadian Almanac & Directory 1997

NEWFOUNDLAND MUNICIPALITIES

Cities in CAPITALS; Towns marked †; Communities marked ‡; Regional Municipalities marked (RG). An in-depth listing for municipalities marked with * appears in Part 2 (check Index for page numbers).

MUNICIPALITY	1991 POP.	FEDERAL ELECTORAL DISTRICT	PROVINCIAL ELECTORAL DISTRICT	CONTACT PERSON WITH ADDRESS, PHONE & FAX
Brigus †	929	St. John's East	Harbour Main-Whitbourne	Wayne Rose, Clerk, PO Box 220, Brigus A0A 1K0 – 709/528-4588, Fax: 709/528-4588
Bryant's Cove ‡	441	Bonavista-Trinity-Conception	Port de Grave	Louise Noseworthy, Clerk, Site 5, PO Box 2, Bryant's Cove A0A 3P0 – 709/596-2291
Buchans †	1,164	Gander-Grand Falls	Grand Falls-Buchans	Margaret Hamilton, Clerk, PO Box 190, Buchans A0H 1G0 – 709/672-3972, Fax: 709/672-3702
Burgeo †	2,400	Burin-St. George's	Burgeo & La Poile	Stanley Cossar, Clerk, PO Box 220, Burgeo A0M 1A0 – 709/886-2250, Fax: 709/886-2166
Burin †	2,940	Burin-St. George's	Burin-Placentia West	Beth Hanrahan, Clerk, PO Box 370, Burin A0E 1E0 – 709/891-1760, Fax: 709/891-2069
Burlington ‡	456	Humber-St. Barbe-Baie Verte	Baie Verte	Velma Young, Clerk, Burlington A0K 1S0 – 709/252-2607, Fax: 709/252-3062
Burnt Islands †	1,024	Burin-St. George's	Burgeo & La Poile	Rosetta Glover, Clerk, PO Box 39, Burnt Islands A0M 1B0 – 709/698-3512
Campbellton †	687	Gander-Grand Falls	Lewisporte	Elaine Hart, Clerk, PO Box 70, Campbellton A0G 1L0 – 709/261-2300
Cape Broyle ‡	693	St. John's West	Ferryland	Andrew O'Brien, Clerk, Cape Broyle A0A 1P0 – 709/432-2288, Fax: 709/432-2288
Cape St. George ‡	1,140	Burin-St. George's	Port au Port	Sandra Jesso, Clerk, PO Box 130, Cape St. George A0N 1E0 – 709/644-2290, Fax: 709/644-2291
Carbonear †	5,259	Bonavista-Trinity-Conception	Carbonear-Harbour Grace	Niall C. Butt, Clerk, PO Box 999, Carbonear A1Y 1C5 – 709/596-3831, Fax: 709/596-5021
Carmanville †	942	Gander-Grand Falls	Bonavista North	Mary Sheppard, Clerk, PO Box 239, Carmanville A0G 1N0 – 709/534-2814
Cartwright ‡	611	Labrador	Cartwright-L'Anse au Clair	Charlotte Dyson, Clerk, PO Box 129, Cartwright A0K 1V0 – 709/938-7259, Fax: 709/938-7454
Catalina †	1,205	Bonavista-Trinity-Conception	Bonavista South	Valerie Rogers, Clerk, PO Box 2, Catalina A0C 1J0 – 709/469-2615, Fax: 709/469-2772
Centreville et al †	1,472	Bonavista-Trinity-Conception	Bonavista North	Selena Brown, Clerk, PO Box 130, Centreville A0G 4P0 – 709/678-2840, Fax: 709/678-2536
Chance Cove †	435	Bonavista-Trinity-Conception	Bellevue	Debbie Collett, Clerk, Chance Cove A0B 1K0 – 709/460-4151
Change Islands †	524	Gander-Grand Falls	Twillingate & Fogo	Doris Hoffe, Clerk, PO Box 67, Change Islands A0G 1R0 – 709/621-4181, Fax: 709/621-4181
Channel-Port aux Basques †	5,644	Burin-St. George's	Burgeo & La Poile	Donna Bragg, Clerk, PO Box 70, Port aux Basques A0M 1C0 – 709/695-2214, Fax: 709/695-9852
Chapel Arm †	638	Bonavista-Trinity-Conception	Bellevue	Phyllis Pretty, Clerk, Chapel Arm A0B 1L0 – 709/592-2720
Charlottetown ‡	292	Labrador	Cartwright-L'Anse au Clair	Jessie Nippard, Clerk, Charlottetown A0K 5Y0 – 709/949-0229, Fax: 709/949-0355
Clarenville †	4,473	Bonavista-Trinity-Conception	Trinity North	Vacant, Clerk, PO Box 66, Clarenville A0E 1J0 – 709/466-7937, Fax: 709/466-2276
Clarke's Beach †	1,192	Bonavista-Trinity-Conception	Harbour Main-Whitbourne	Joan Wilcox, Clerk, PO Box 159, Clarke's Beach A0A 1W0 – 709/786-3993, Fax: 709/786-3993
Coachman's Cove ‡	208	Humber-St. Barbe-Baie Verte	Baie Verte	Marina Bryan, Clerk, Coachman's Cove A0K 1X0 – 709/253-2142
Colinet ‡	232	St. John's West	Placentia & St. Mary's	Maureen Didham, Clerk, Colinet A0B 1M0 – 709/521-2300
Colliers †	808	St. John's East	Harbour Main-Whitbourne	Geraldine Whelan-Hawco, Clerk, PO Box 84, Colliers A0A 1Y0 – 709/229-4333, Fax: 709/229-4333
Come By Chance †	296	St. John's West	Bellevue	Patsy Smith, Clerk, PO Box 89, Come By Chance A0B 1N0 – 709/542-3240, Fax: 709/542-3121
Comfort Cove-Newstead ‡	625	Gander-Grand Falls	Lewisporte	Mary Lou Ginn, Clerk, PO Box 10, Comfort Cove-Newstead A0G 3K0 – 709/244-4121
Conception Bay South †	17,590	St. John's East	Conception Bay South; Topsail	Maureen Harvey, Clerk, PO Box 280, Manuels A0A 2Y0 – 709/834-2093, Fax: 709/834-8337
Conception Harbour †	907	St. John's East	Harbour Main-Whitbourne	Colleen Wade, Clerk, Conception Harbour A0A 1Z0 – 709/229-4781
Conche ‡	417	Humber-St. Barbe-Baie Verte	The Straits & White Bay North	Laboura Whelan, Clerk, PO Box 59, Conche A0K 1Y0 – 709/622-4531, Fax: 709/622-4491
Cook's Harbour †	359	Humber-St. Barbe-Baie Verte	The Straits & White Bay North	Margaret Elliott, Clerk, Cook's Harbour A0K 1Z0 – 709/249-3111
Cormack ‡	788	Burin-St. George's	Humber Valley	Cynthia Fry, Clerk, Site 26, RR#2, PO Box 4, Deer Lake A0K 2E0 – 709/635-7025, Fax: 709/635-7363
CORNER BROOK	22,410	Humber-St. Barbe-Baie Verte	Humber East; Humber West; Bay of Islands	James Kennedy, City Clerk, City Hall, PO Box 1080, Corner Brook A2H 6E3 – 709/637-1630, Fax: 709/637-1625
Cottlesville †	375	Gander-Grand Falls	Twillingate & Fogo	Shelly Philpott, Clerk, PO Box 10, Cottlesville A0G 1S0 – 709/629-3505, Fax: 709/629-7411
Cow Head †	696	Humber-St. Barbe-Baie Verte	St. Barbe	Eura Curtis, Clerk, PO Box 40, Cow Head A0K 2A0 – 709/243-2446

Cities in CAPITALS; Towns marked †; Communities marked ‡; Regional Municipalities marked (RG). An in-depth listing for municipalities marked with * appears in Part 2 (check Index for page numbers).

MUNICIPALITY	1991 POP.	FEDERAL ELECTORAL DISTRICT	PROVINCIAL ELECTORAL DISTRICT	CONTACT PERSON WITH ADDRESS, PHONE & FAX
Cox's Cove ‡	941	Humber-St. Barbe-Baie Verte	Bay of Islands	Sandra Warren, Clerk, PO Box 100, Cox's Cove A0L 1C0 – 709/688-2900
Crow Head ‡	280	Gander-Grand Falls	Twillingate & Fogo	Meta J. Hamlyn, Clerk, PO Box 250, Crow Head A0G 4M0 – 709/884-5651, Fax: 709/884-2344
Cupids †	868	St. John's East	Harbour Main-Whitbourne	Linda Noseworthy, Clerk, PO Box 99, Cupids A0A 2B0 – 709/528-4428
Daniel's Harbour ‡	428	Humber-St. Barbe-Baie Verte	St. Barbe	Melda House, Clerk, PO Box 68, Daniel's Harbour A0K 2C0 – 709/898-2300, Fax: 709/898-2593
Deer Lake †	5,134	Humber-St. Barbe-Baie Verte	Humber Valley	Maxine Hayden, Clerk, PO Box 940, Deer Lake A0K 2E0 – 709/635-2451, Fax: 709/635-5857
Dover †	881	Bonvavista-Trinity-Conception	Terra Nova	Daphne Collins, Clerk, PO Box 10, Dover A0G 1X0 – 709/537-2139, Fax: 709/537-2018
Duntara ‡	102	Bonavista-Trinity-Conception	Bonavista South	Dorothy Power, Clerk, Duntara A0C 1M0 – 709/447-3190
Eastport †	601	Bonavista-Trinity-Conception	Terra Nova	Cynthia Lane, Clerk, PO Box 119, Eastport A0G 1Z0 – 709/677-2161, Fax: 709/677-2144
Elliston †	533	Bonavista-Trinity-Conception	Bonavista South	Bonnie Critch, Clerk, PO Box 115, Elliston A0C 1N0 – 709/468-2649
Embree †	846	Gander-Grand Falls	Lewisporte	Maxine Lane, Clerk, Embree A0G 2A0 – 709/535-8712
Englee †	984	Humber-St. Barbe-Baie Verte	The Straits & White Bay North	Doris Randell, Clerk, PO Box 160, Englee A0K 2J0 – 709/866-2711, Fax: 709/866-2357
English Harbour East ‡	288	Burin-St. George's	Bellevue	Daphne Hynes, Clerk, PO Box 21, English Harbour East A0E 1M0 – 709/245-4271
Fermeuse ‡	505	St. John's West	Ferryland	Patrick Walsh, Clerk, Fermeuse A0A 2G0 – 709/363-2400, Fax: 709/363-2308
Ferryland ‡	717	St. John's West	Ferryland	Doris Kavanagh, Clerk, PO Box 75, Ferryland A0A 2H0 – 709/432-2127, Fax: 709/432-2209
Flatrock †	1,044	St. John's East	Cape St. Francis	Rita Farrell, Clerk, 663 Wind Gap Rd., Flatrock A1K 1C7 – 709/437-6312
Fleur de Lys †	463	Humber-St. Barbe-Baie Verte	Baie Verte	Judy Traverse, Clerk, Fleur de Lys A0K 2M0 – 709/253-3131
Flower's Cove †	372	Humber-St. Barbe-Baie Verte	The Straits & White Bay North	Bruce Way, Clerk, PO Box 149, Flower's Cove A0K 2N0 – 709/456-2124
Fogo †	1,030	Gander-Grand Falls	Twillingate & Fogo	Bruce Pomeroy, Clerk, PO Box 57, Fogo A0G 2B0 – 709/266-2237, Fax: 709/266-2972
Fogo Island Region				Sandra Cull, Clerk, PO Box 159, Joe Batt's Arm A0G 2X0 – 709/266-1212
Forteau ‡	518	Labrador	Cartwright-L'Anse au Clair	Gail Flynn, Clerk, PO Box 99, Forteau A0K 2P0 – 709/931-2481, Fax: 709/931-2037
Fortune †	2,177	Burin-St. George's	Grand Bank	Basil Collier, Clerk, PO Box 159, Fortune A0E 1P0 – 709/832-2810, Fax: 709/832-2210
Fox Cove †	464	Burin-St. George's	Burin-Placentia West	Gladys Kavanagh, Clerk, Site 25, PO Box 17, Burin A0E 1E0 – 709/891-1500, Fax: 709/891-1500
Fox Harbour ‡	434	St. John's West	Placentia & St. Mary's	Patricia Quilty, Clerk, PO Box 64, Fox Harbour A0B 1V0 – 709/227-2271
Frenchman's Cove ‡	229	Burin-St. George's	Grand Bank	Miriam Power, Clerk, Frenchman's Cove A0E 1R0 – 709/826-2190
Gallants ‡	73	Burin-St. George's	Humber West	Beverley Hickey, Clerk, Gallants A0L 1G0 – 709/646-2912
Gambo †	2,496	Bonavista-Trinity-Conception	Terra Nova	Scott Pritchett, Clerk, PO Box 250, Gambo A0G 1T0 – 709/674-4476, Fax: 709/674-5399
Gander †	10,339	Gander-Grand Falls	Gander	James Butler, Clerk, PO Box 280, Gander A1V 1W6 – 709/651-2949, Fax: 709/256-2124
Garnish †	716	Burin-St. George's	Grand Bank	Steven Grandy, Clerk, PO Box 70, Garnish A0E 1T0 – 709/826-2330, Fax: 709/826-2330
Gaskiers ‡	508	St. John's West	Placentia & St. Mary's	Gertrude Kielley, Clerk, RR#1, PO Box 122, St. Mary's A0B 3B0 – 709/525-2430
Gaultois †	516	Burin-St. George's	Fortune Bay-Cape La Hune	Sylvin Rose, Clerk, PO Box 101, Gaultois A0H 1N0 – 709/841-6546
Gillams ‡	496	Humber-St. Barbe-Baie Verte	Bay of Islands	Lois Blanchard, Clerk, RR#2, PO Box 3968, Corner Brook A2H 6B9 – 709/783-2800
Glenburnie ‡	365	Humber-St. Barbe-Baie Verte	Humber Valley	Eulah Raike, Clerk, Birchy Head A0K 1K0 – 709/453-7220, Fax: 709/453-2594
Glenwood †	984	Gander-Grand Falls	Gander	Cynthia Davis, Clerk, PO Box 130, Glenwood A0G 2K0 – 709/679-2159
Glovertown †	2,276	Bonavista-Trinity-Conception	Terra Nova	Joanne Perry, Clerk, PO Box 224, Glovertown A0G 2L0 – 709/533-2351, Fax: 709/533-2225
Goose Cove East ‡	373	Humber-St. Barbe-Baie Verte	The Straits & White Bay North	Gertrude Troy, Clerk, PO Box 208, St. Anthony A0K 4S0 – 709/454-8393
Grand Bank †	3,528	Burin-St. George's	Grand Bank	Cathy Trimm, Clerk, PO Box 640, Grand Bank A0E 1W0 – 709/832-1600, Fax: 709/832-1636

NEWFOUNDLAND MUNICIPALITIES

Cities in CAPITALS; Towns marked †; Communities marked ‡; Regional Municipalities marked (RG). An in-depth listing for municipalities marked with * appears in Part 2 (check Index for page numbers).

MUNICIPALITY	1991 POP.	FEDERAL ELECTORAL DISTRICT	PROVINCIAL ELECTORAL DISTRICT	CONTACT PERSON WITH ADDRESS, PHONE & FAX
Grand Falls-Windsor †	14,693	Gander-Grand Falls	Grand Falls-Buchans; Windsor-Springdale	Rod Flench, Clerk, PO Box 439, Grand Falls-Windsor A2A 2J8 – 709/489-0412, Fax: 709/489-6301
Grand Le Pierre ‡	356	Burin-St. George's	Bellevue	Martha Bolt, Clerk, PO Box 35, Grand La Pierre A0E 1Y0 – 709/662-2702
Great Harbour Deep ‡	203	Humber-St. Barbe-Baie Verte	Humber Valley	Gaye Newman, Clerk, Great Harbour Deep A0K 2Z0 – 709/843-3481
Greenspond †	435	Bonavista-Trinity-Conception	Bonavista North	Derrick Bragg, Clerk, PO Box 100, Greenspond A0G 2N0 – 709/269-3111
Hampden ‡	716	Humber-St. Barbe-Baie Verte	Humber Valley	Ruth Jenkins, Clerk, PO Box 9, Hampden A0K 2Y0 – 709/455-4212
Hant's Harbour †	531	Bonavista-Trinity-Conception	Trinity-Bay de Verde	Doris J. Short, Clerk, PO Box 40, Hant's Harbour A0B 1Y0 – 709/586-2741
Happy Adventure ‡	323	Bonavista-Trinity-Conception	Terra Nova	Kim Holloway, Clerk, PO Box 106, Eastport A0G 1Z0 – 709/677-2593, Fax: 709/677-2058
Happy Valley-Goose Bay †	8,610	Labrador	Lake Melville	Valerie Sheppard, Clerk, PO Box 40, Happy Valley-Goose Bay A0P 1E0 – 709/896-3321, Fax: 709/896-9454, URL: http://www.happyvalley-goosebay.com/
Harbour Breton †	2,418	Burin-St. George's	Fortune Bay-Cape La Hune	Bernice Herritt, Clerk, PO Box 130, Harbour Breton A0H 1P0 – 709/885-2354, Fax: 709/885-2095
Harbour Grace †	3,917	Bonavista-Trinity-Conception	Carbonear-Harbour Grace	Sean O'Brien, Clerk, PO Box 310, Harbour Grace A0A 2M0 – 709/596-3631
Harbour Main †	1,278	St. John's East	Harbour Main-Whitbourne	Gloria Brazil, Clerk, PO Box 40, Harbour Main A0A 2P0 – 709/229-6822, Fax: 709/229-6234
Hare Bay †	1,387	Bonavista-Trinity-Conception	Terra Nova	George R. Collins, Clerk, PO Box 130, Hare Bay A0G 2P0 – 709/537-2187
Hawke's Bay †	564	Humber-St. Barbe-Baie Verte	St. Barbe	Yvonne House, Clerk, Hawkes Bay A0K 3B0 – 709/248-5216, Fax: 709/248-5201
Heart's Content †	567	Bonavista-Trinity-Conception	Trinity-Bay de Verde	Alice Cumby, Clerk, PO Box 31, Heart's Content A0B 1Z0 – 709/583-2491, Fax: 709/583-2226
Heart's Delight †	878	Bonavista-Trinity-Conception	Trinity-Bay de Verde	Sherry Chislett, Clerk, PO Box 129, Heart's Delight A0B 2A0 – 709/588-2708, Fax: 709/588-2280
Heart's Desire †	363	Bonavista-Trinity-Conception	Trinity-Bay de Verde	Eleanor Andrews, Clerk, Heart's Desire A0B 2B0 – 709/588-2280
Hermitage ‡	756	Burin-St. George's	Fortune Bay-Cape La Hune	Myrtle Kendall, Clerk, PO Box 126, Hermitage A0H 1S0 – 709/883-2343, Fax: 709/883-2150
Holyrood †	2,075	St. John's East	Concession Bay South; Harbour Main-Whitbourne	Germaine Crawley, Clerk, PO Box 100, Holyrood A0A 2R0 – 709/834-7600, Fax: 709/834-7600
Hopedale ‡	515	Labrador	Torngat Mountains	Judy Dicker, Clerk, Hopedale A0P 1G0 – 709/933-3864, Fax: 709/933-3800
Howley †	363	Humber-St. Barbe-Baie Verte	Humber Valley	Blanche Gilley, Clerk, PO Box 40, Howley A0K 3E0 – 709/635-5555
Hughes Brook ‡	166	Humber-St. Barbe-Baie Verte	Bay of Islands	Debbie White, Clerk, RR#2, PO Box 2527, Corner Brook A2H 6B9 – 709/783-2921
Humber Arm South †	2,182	Humber-St. Barbe-Baie Verte	Bay of Islands	Marion Evoy, Clerk, Benoit's Cove A0L 1A0 – 709/789-2981, Fax: 709/789-3308
Indian Bay ‡	215	Bonavista-Trinity-Conception	Bonavista North	Jackie Cook, Clerk, Indian Bay A0G 2V0 – 709/678-2727
Irishtown-Summerside †	1,560	Humber-St. Barbe-Baie Verte	Bay of Islands	Geraldine Wheeler, Clerk, RR#2, PO Box 2795, Corner Brook A2H 6B9 – 709/783-2146
Isle aux Morts †	1,146	Burin-St. George's	Burgeo & La Poile	Richard Lillington, Clerk, PO Box 110, Isle aux Morts A0M 1J0 – 709/698-3441, Fax: 709/698-3449
Jackson's Arm ‡	533	Humber-St. Barbe-Baie Verte	Humber Valley	Alfreda Osmond, Clerk, PO Box 10, Jackson's Arm A0K 3H0 – 709/459-3122, Fax: 709/459-3173
Joe Batt's Arm †	1,164	Gander-Grand Falls	Twillingate & Fogo	Vacant, Clerk, PO Box 28, Joe Batt's Arm A0G 2X0 – 709/658-3490, Fax: 709/658-3408
Keels ‡	128	Bonavista-Trinity-Conception	Bonavista South	Glenys Byrne, Clerk, PO Box 20, Keels A0C 1R0 – 709/447-3126
King's Cove ‡	214	Bonavista-Trinity-Conception	Bonavista South	Gerald Barron, Clerk, King's Cove A0C 1S0 – 709/477-4361
King's Point †	869	Gander-Grand Falls	Baie Verte	Nellie Richards, Clerk, King's Point A0J 1H0 – 709/268-3838
Kippens †	1,767	Burin-St. George's	Port au Port	Norma Childs, Clerk, Kippens A2N 3H8 – 709/643-5281, Fax: 709/643-9773
La Scie †	1,412	Humber-St. Barbe-Baie Verte	Baie Verte	Vida Short, Clerk, PO Box 130, La Scie A0K 3M0 – 709/675-2266
Labrador City †	9,061	Labrador	Labrador West	Joyce Narduzzi, Clerk, PO Box 280, Labrador City A2V 2K5 – 709/944-2621, Fax: 709/944-6353
Lamaline †	482	Burin-St. George's	Grand Bank	Shelley Lovell, Clerk, PO Box 40, Lamaline A0E 2C0 – 709/857-2341
L'Anse au Clair ‡	263	Labrador	Cartwright-L'Anse au Clair	Loretta Griffin, Clerk, L'Anse au Clair A0K 3K0 – 709/931-2481, Fax: 709/931-2481

Canadian Almanac & Directory 1997

Cities in CAPITALS; Towns marked †; Communities marked ‡; Regional Municipalities marked (RG). An in-depth listing for municipalities marked with * appears in Part 2 (check Index for page numbers).

MUNICIPALITY	1991 POP.	FEDERAL ELECTORAL DISTRICT	PROVINCIAL ELECTORAL DISTRICT	CONTACT PERSON WITH ADDRESS, PHONE & FAX
L'Anse au Loup ‡	630	Labrador	Cartwright-L'Anse au Clair	Doreen Belbin, Clerk, PO Box 101, L'Anse au Loup A0K 3L0 – 709/927-5573, Fax: 709/927-5263
Lark Harbour ‡	755	Humber-St. Barbe-Baie Verte	Bay of Islands	Debra Park, Clerk, PO Box 40, Lark Harbour A0L 1H0 – 709/681-2270
Lawn †	1,005	Burin-St. George's	Grand Bank	Ruth M. Bennett, Clerk, PO Box 29, Lawn A0E 2E0 – 709/873-2439, Fax: 709/873-3006
Leading Tickles West ‡	564	Gander-Grand Falls	Exploits	Kimberly Newman, Clerk, PO Box 39, Leading Tickles West A0H 1T0 – 709/483-2180
Lewin's Cove ‡	609	Burin-St. George's	Grand Bank	Linda Inkpen, Clerk, PO Box 40, Lewin's Cove A0E 2G0 – 709/894-4777
Lewisporte †	3,848	Gander-Grand Falls	Lewisporte	Helen Combden, Clerk, PO Box 219, Lewisporte A0G 3A0 – 709/535-2737, Fax: 709/535-2695
Little Bay ‡	154	Gander-Grand Falls	Baie Verte	Stella Simms, Clerk, PO Box 39, Little Bay A0J 1J0 – 709/267-5257
Little Bay East ‡	201	Burin-St. George's	Bellevue	Gail Clarke, Clerk, Little Bay East A0E 2J0 – 709/461-2724
Little Bay Islands ‡	261	Gander-Grand Falls	Baie Verte	Betty Tucker, Clerk, PO Box 64, Little Bay Islands A0J 1K0 – 709/626-3511
Little Burnt Bay †	436	Gander-Grand Falls	Lewisporte	Maisie Wells, Clerk, PO Box 40, Little Burnt Bay A0G 3B0 – 709/535-6415
Little Catalina †	710	Bonavista-Trinity-Conception	Bonavista South	Marilyn Reid, Clerk, PO Box 59, Little Catalina A0C 1W0 – 709/469-2795
Logy Bay et al. †	1,882	St. John's East	Cape St. Francis	Barbara Power, Clerk, SS#3, PO Box 51428, St. John's A1B 4M2 – 709/726-7930, Fax: 709/726-2178
Long Harbour †	522	St. John's West	Bellevue	Loretta Keating, Clerk, PO Box 40, Long Harbour A0B 2J0 – 709/228-2920, Fax: 709/228-2900
Lord's Cove ‡	329	Burin-St. George's	Grand Bank	Christina Lundrigan, Clerk, Lord's Cove A0E 2C0 – 709/857-2316
Lourdes ‡	858	Burin-St. George's	Port au Port	Loretta Snook, Clerk, PO Box 29, Lourdes A0N 1R0 – 709/642-5812, Fax: 709/642-5812
Lumsden †	675	Bonavista-Trinity-Conception	Bonavista North	Edison Goodyear, Clerk, PO Box 100, Lumsden A0G 3E0 – 709/530-2309, Fax: 709/530-2144
Lushes Bight et al. ‡	397	Gander-Grand Falls	Windsor-Springdale	Madeline Burton, Clerk, Beaumont A0J 1A0 – 709/264-3271, Fax: 709/264-3191
Main Brook †	458	Humber-St. Barbe-Baie Verte	The Straits & White Bay North	Ella R. Pilgrim, Clerk, PO Box 28, Main Brook A0K 3N0 – 709/865-6561, Fax: 709/865-3279
Makkovik ‡	370	Labrador	Torngat Mountains	S. David Dyson, Clerk, PO Box 68, Makkovik A0P 1J0 – 709/923-2221
Mary's Harbour ‡	470	Labrador	Cartwright-L'Anse au Clair	Glenys Rumbolt, Clerk, Mary's Harbour A0K 3P0 – 709/921-6281, Fax: 709/921-6255
Marystown †	6,739	Burin-St. George's	Burin-Placentia West	Dennis P. Kelly, Clerk, PO Box 918, Marystown A0E 2M0 – 709/279-1661, Fax: 709/279-2862
Massey Drive †	619	Humber-St. Barbe-Baie Verte	Humber East	Phyllis Stratton, Clerk, Massey Dr., Massey Drive A2H 7A2 – 709/634-2742, Fax: 709/634-2899
McIvers ‡	725	Humber-St. Barbe-Baie Verte	Bay of Islands	Bernice E. Parsons, Clerk, RR#2, PO Box 4375, Corner Brook A2H 6B9 – 709/688-2603
Meadows ‡	719	Humber-St. Barbe-Baie Verte	Bay of Islands	Phyllis Brake, Clerk, RR#2, PO Box 3529, Corner Brook A2H 6B9 – 709/783-2339
Melrose ‡	423	Bonavista-Trinity-Conception	Bonavista South	Rosemary Donovan, Clerk, Melrose A0C 1Y0 – 709/469-2882
Middle Arm ‡	622	Humber-St. Barbe-Baie Verte	Baie Verte	Neta Mitchell, Clerk, PO Box 51, Middle Arm A0K 3R0 – 709/252-2521
Miles Cove ‡	223	Gander-Grand Falls	Windsor-Springdale	Nellie Reid, Clerk, Miles Cove A0J 1L0 – 709/652-3505
Millertown ‡	158	Gander-Grand Falls	Grand Falls-Buchans	Judy Menchenton, Clerk, PO Box 56, Millertown A0H 1V0 – 709/852-6216, Fax: 709/852-5431
Milltown †	1,161	Burin-St. George's	Fortune Bay-Cape La Hune	Gerry Glover, Clerk, PO Box 70, Milltown A0H 1W0 – 709/882-2232, Fax: 709/882-2636
Ming's Bight ‡	456	Humber-St. Barbe-Baie Verte	Baie Verte	Glenda Regular, Clerk, PO Box 59, Ming's Bight A0K 3S0 – 709/254-6516, Fax: 709/254-6516
Morrisville ‡	201	Burin-St. George's	Fortune Bay-Cape La Hune	Derrick McDonald, Clerk, PO Box 19, Morrisville A0H 1W0 – 709/882-2322
Mount Carmel et al. †	619	St. John's West	Placentia & St. Mary's	Bernadette Didham, Clerk, Mount Carmel A0B 2M0 – 709/521-2040, Fax: 709/521-2258
Mount Moriah †	726	Humber-St. Barbe-Baie Verte	Bay of Islands	Carol Hussey, Clerk, PO Box 31, Mount Moriah A0L 1J0 – 709/785-5232
MOUNT PEARL	23,689	St. John's West	Mount Pearl; Waterford Valley	Gerard Lewis, City Clerk, 3 Centennial St., Mount Pearl A1N 1G4 – 709/748-1043, Fax: 709/364-8935
Musgrave Harbour †	1,528	Gander-Grand Falls	Bonavista North	Sophie Mercer, Clerk, PO Box 159, Musgrave Harbour A0G 3J0 – 709/655-2119, Fax: 709/655-2064
Musgravetown †	726	Bonavista-Trinity-Conception	Terra Nova	Charlotte Wiseman, Clerk, PO Box 129, Musgravetown A0C 1Z0 – 709/467-2726

Canadian Almanac & Directory 1997

Cities in CAPITALS; Towns marked †; Communities marked ‡; Regional Municipalities marked (RG). An in-depth listing for municipalities marked with * appears in Part 2 (check Index for page numbers).

MUNICIPALITY	1991 POP.	FEDERAL ELECTORAL DISTRICT	PROVINCIAL ELECTORAL DISTRICT	CONTACT PERSON WITH ADDRESS, PHONE & FAX
Nain †	1,069	Labrador	Torngat Mountains	Dasi Ikkusek, Clerk, PO Box 59, Nain A0P 1L0 – 709/922-2842, Fax: 709/922-2295
New Perlican †	281	Bonavista-Trinity-Conception	Trinity-Bay de Verde	Donna Piercey, Clerk, PO Box 39, New Perlican A0B 2S0 – 709/583-2500
Nipper's Harbour ‡	243	Humber-St. Barbe-Baie Verte	Baie Verte	Beth Prole, Clerk, PO Box 10, Nipper's Harbour A0K 3T0 – 709/255-3151
Norman's Cove †	1,054	Bonavista-Trinity-Conception	Bellevue	Diane Hudson, Clerk, PO Box 70, Norman's Cove A0B 2T0 – 709/592-2490, Fax: 709/592-2106
Norris Arm †	1,089	Gander-Grand Falls	Lewisporte	Regina Organ, Clerk, PO Box 70, Norris Arm A0G 3M0 – 709/653-2519, Fax: 709/653-2163
Norris Point ‡	927	Humber-St. Barbe-Baie Verte	St. Barbe	Regina Organ, Clerk, PO Box 119, Norris Point A0K 3V0 – 709/458-2207
North River ‡	542	Bonavista-Trinity-Conception	Harbour Main-Whitbourne	Beverly Sparkes, Clerk, PO Box 104, North River A0A 3C0 – 709/786-6216
North West River †	528	Labrador	Lake Melville	Melinda Baikie, Clerk, PO Box 100, North West River A0P 1M0 – 709/497-8533, Fax: 709/497-8228
Northern Arm †	391	Gander-Grand Falls	Exploits	Ella Humphries, Clerk, PO Box 2006, Northern Arm A0H 1E0 – 709/257-3482, Fax: 709/257-3482
Old Perlican †	745	Bonavista-Trinity-Conception	Trinity-Bay de Verde	Judi Barter, Clerk, PO Box 39, Old Perlican A0A 3G0 – 709/587-2266, Fax: 709/587-2261
Pacquet ‡	326	Humber-St. Barbe-Baie Verte	Baie Verte	Janet Sacrey, Clerk, Pacquet A0K 3X0 – 709/251-5496, Fax: 709/251-5497
Paradise †	4,747	St. John's East	Conception Bay East & Bell Island; Topsail	Joyce Moss, Clerk, PO Box 100, Paradise A1L 1C4 – 709/782-1400, Fax: 709/782-3601
Parkers Cove ‡	441	Burin-St. George's	Burin-Placentia West	Bernadette Synard, Clerk, Parker's Cove A0E 1H0 – 709/443-2216
Parson's Pond ‡	582	Humber-St. Barbe-Baie Verte	St. Barbe	Joan Parsons, Clerk, PO Box 39, Parson's Pond A0K 3Z0 – 709/243-2564
Pasadena †	3,428	Humber-St. Barbe-Baie Verte	Humber East	Melvina Tracey, Clerk, 18 Tenth Ave., Pasadena A0L 1K0 – 709/686-2075, Fax: 709/686-2507
Peterview †	1,011	Gander-Grand Falls	Exploits	Venus Samson, Clerk, PO Box 10, Peterview A0H 1Y0 – 709/257-2926, Fax: 709/257-2926
Petty Harbour †	974	St. John's West	Ferryland	Noreen Hearn, Clerk, PO Box 70, Petty Harbour A0A 3H0 – 709/368-3959
Pilley's Island ‡	465	Gander-Grand Falls	Windsor-Springdale	Betty Traverse, Clerk, PO Box 70, Pilley's Island A0J 1M0 – 709/652-3555
Pinware ‡	175	Labrador	Cartwright-L'Anse au Clair	Vacant, Clerk, Pinware A0K 5S0 – 709/927-5588
Placentia †	5,394	St. John's West	Placentia & St. Mary's	Margie Hatfield, Clerk, PO Box 99, Placentia A0B 2Y0 – 709/227-2151, Fax: 709/227-2048
Plate Cove East ‡	145	Bonavista-Trinity-Conception	Bonavista South	Barry Mavin, Adm., Plate Cove East A0C 2C0
Plate Cove West ‡	322	Bonavista-Trinity-Conception	Bonavista South	Barry Mavin, Adm., Plate Cove West A0C 2E0
Point au Gaul ‡	130	Burin-St. George's	Grand Bank	Peter M. Lockyer, Clerk, PO Box 20, Point au Gaul A0E 2C0 – 709/857-2514
Point Lance ‡	161	St. John's West	Placentia & St. Mary's	Bernadette Careen, Clerk, PO Box 23, Point Lance A0B 1E0 – 709/337-2355
Point Leamington †	852	Gander-Grand Falls	Exploits	Patricia Earle, Clerk, PO Box 39, Point Leamington A0H 1Z0 – 709/484-3421, Fax: 709/484-3556
Point May ‡	435	Burin-St. George's	Grand Bank	Darlene Hewitt, Clerk, Site 5, PO Box 19, Point May A0E 2C0 – 709/857-2640
Point of Bay ‡	209	Gander-Grand Falls	Exploits	Sybil Boone, Clerk, Point of Bay A0H 2A0 – 709/257-3171
Pool's Cove ‡	258	Burin-St. George's	Fortune Bay-Cape La Hune	Lloyd Spurrell, Clerk, PO Box 10, Pool's Cove A0H 2B0 – 709/665-3371
Port Anson ‡	209	Gander-Grand Falls	Windsor-Springdale	Daphne Hewlett, Clerk, Port Anson A0J 1N0 – 709/652-3656
Port au Bras ‡	319	Burin-St. George's	Burin-Placentia West	Beatrice Abbott, Clerk, RR#1, PO Box 359, Burin A0E 1E0 – 709/891-1195, Fax: 709/891-1195
Port au Choix †	1,260	Humber-St. Barbe-Baie Verte	St. Barbe	Maurice Kelly, Clerk, PO Box 89, Port au Choix A0K 4C0 – 709/861-3406, 3409, Fax: 709/861-3061
Port au Port East ‡	785	Burin-St. George's	Port au Port	Theresa Hann, Clerk, PO Box 39, Port au Port East A0N 1T0 – 709/648-2731, Fax: 709/648-9481
Port-au-Port-West †	718	Burin-St. George's	Port au Port	Daniel McCann, Clerk, PO Box 89, Aguathuna A0N 1A0 – 709/648-2891
Port Blandford †	676	Bonavista-Trinity-Conception	Terra Nova	Vida Greening, Clerk, PO Box 70, Port Blandford A0C 2G0 – 709/543-2170, Fax: 709/543-2153
Port Hope Simpson ‡	614	Labrador	Cartwright-L'Anse au Clair	Glynes Penney, Clerk, Port Hope Simpson A0K 4E0 – 709/960-0236, Fax: 709/960-0387
Port Kirwan ‡	120	St. John's West	Ferryland	Lucy Bosch, Clerk, Site 2, PO Box 40, Port Kirwan A0A 2G0 – 709/363-2417

Cities in CAPITALS; Towns marked †; Communities marked ‡; Regional Municipalities marked (RG). An in-depth listing for municipalities marked with * appears in Part 2 (check Index for page numbers).

MUNICIPALITY	1991 POP.	FEDERAL ELECTORAL DISTRICT	PROVINCIAL ELECTORAL DISTRICT	CONTACT PERSON WITH ADDRESS, PHONE & FAX
Port Rexton ‡	482	Bonavista-Trinity-Conception	Trinity North	Lois Long, Clerk, PO Box 55, Port Rexton A0C 2H0 – 709/464-2006, Fax: 709/464-2006
Port Saunders †	822	Humber-St. Barbe-Baie Verte	St. Barbe	Judy Quinlan, Clerk, PO Box 39, Port Saunders A0K 4H0 – 709/861-3105, Fax: 709/861-2137
Port Union †	638	Bonavista-Trinity-Conception	Bonavista South	Thomas Sutton, Clerk, PO Box 91, Port Union A0C 2J0 – 709/469-2571, Fax: 709/469-3444
Portugal Cove-St Philip's †	4,701 ('92)	St. John's East; St. John's West	Conception Bay East & Bell Island	Loretta Tucker, Clerk, PO Box 144, Portugal Cove A0A 3K0 – 709/895-6594, Fax: 709/895-3780
Portugal Cove South ‡	341 ('92)	St. John's West	Ferryland	Mary O'Leary, Clerk, Site 11, PO Box 8, Trepassey A0A 4B0 – 709/438-2092
Postville ‡	231	Labrador	Torngat Mountains	Shirley Goudie, Clerk, Postville A0P 1N0 – 709/479-9830, Fax: 709/479-9888
Pouch Cove †	1,976	St. John's East	Cape St. Francis	Nora Hughes, Clerk, PO Box 59, Pouch Cove A0A 3L0 – 709/335-2848, Fax: 709/335-2840
Raleigh ‡	389	Humber-St. Barbe-Baie Verte	The Straits & White Bay North	Ricky Elliott, Clerk, PO Box 119, Raleigh A0K 4J0 – 709/452-4461
Ramea †	1,224	Burin-St. George's	Fortune Bay-Cape La Hune	Wilfred Cutler, Clerk, PO Box 69, Ramea A0M 1N0 – 709/625-2280, Fax: 709/625-2010
Red Bay ‡	288	Labrador	Cartwright-L'Anse au Clair	Josie Moores, Clerk, Red Bay A0K 4K0 – 709/920-2197, Fax: 709/920-2197
Red Harbour ‡	252	Burin-St. George's	Burin-Placentia West	Walter Kenway, Clerk, Red Harbour A0E 2R0 – 709/443-2599
Reidville ‡	585	Humber-St. Barbe-Baie Verte	Humber Valley	Gail King, Clerk, Site 14, RR#2, PO Box 5, Deer Lake A0K 2E0 – 709/635-5232
Rencontre East ‡	212	Burin-St. George's	Fortune Bay-Cape La Hune	Barbara Caines, Clerk, Rencontre East A0H 2C0 – 709/848-3186, Fax: 709/848-3231
Renews ‡	551	St. John's West	Ferryland	Doris Moriarty, Clerk, PO Box 40, Renews A0A 3N0 – 709/363-2500, Fax: 709/363-2143
Rigolet ‡	334	Labrador	Torngat Mountains	Paula Flowers, Clerk, Rigolet A0P 1L0 – 709/947-3382, Fax: 709/947-3360
River of Ponds ‡	341	Humber-St. Barbe-Baie Verte	St. Barbe	Margaret House-Hoddinott, Clerk, River of Ponds A0K 4M0 – 709/225-3161
Riverhead ‡	398	St. John's West	Placentia & St. Mary's	Ann Lee, Clerk, Riverhead A0B 3B0 – 709/525-2106
Robert's Arm †	994	Gander-Grand Falls	Windsor-Springdale	Ada Rowsell, Clerk, PO Box 10, Robert's Arm A0J 1R0 – 709/652-3331, Fax: 709/652-3079
Rocky Harbour ‡	1,138	Humber-St. Barbe-Baie Verte	St. Barbe	Beatrice Pittman, Clerk, PO Box 24, Rocky Harbour A0K 4N0 – 709/458-2376
Roddickton †	1,153	Humber-St. Barbe-Baie Verte	The Straits & White Bay North	Arthur Locke, Clerk, PO Box 10, Roddickton A0K 4P0 – 709/457-2413, Fax: 709/457-2663
Rose Blanche †	918	Burin-St. George's	Burgeo & La Poile	Ivy Cokes, Clerk, PO Box 159, Rose Blanche A0M 1P0 – 709/956-2540
Rushoon ‡	482	Burin-St. George's	Burin-Placentia West	Jacqueline Gaulton, Clerk, Rushoon A0E 2S0 – 709/443-2572
St. Alban's †	1,586	Burin-St. George's	Fortune Bay-Cape La Hune	Genevieve Tremblett, Clerk, PO Box 10, St. Alban's A0H 2E0 – 709/538-3132, Fax: 709/538-3683
St. Anthony †	3,164	Humber-St. Barbe-Baie Verte	The Straits & White Bay North	Brenda Ricketts, Clerk, PO Box 430, St. Anthony A0K 4S0 – 709/454-3454, Fax: 709/454-4154
St. Bernard's †	852	Burin-St. George's	Bellevue	Marie McCarthy, Clerk, PO Box 70, St. Bernard's A0E 2T0 – 709/461-2257, Fax: 709/461-2179
St. Brendan's ‡	378	Bonavista-Trinity-Conception	Terra Nova	Rita White, Clerk, PO Box 43, St. Brendan's A0G 3V0 – 709/669-4271
St. Bride's ‡	586	St. John's West	Placentia & St. Mary's	Joan McGrath, Clerk, St. Bride's A0B 2Z0 – 709/337-2160
St. George's †	1,678	Burin-St. George's	St. George's-Stephenville East	Francis Alexander, Clerk, PO Box 250, St. George's A0N 1Z0 – 709/647-3283, Fax: 709/647-3180
St. Jacques †	701	Burin-St. George's	Fortune Bay-Cape La Hune	Francis Courtney, Clerk, PO Box 102, English Harbour W. A0M 1M0 – 709/888-6141, Fax: 709/888-5101
*ST. JOHN'S	103,502 ('92)	St. John's East; St. John's West	Kilbride; Signal Hill-Quidi Vidi; St. J. Centre; St. J. East; St. J. North; St. J. South; St. J. West; Virginia Waters; Waterford Valley	Damian Ryan, City Clerk & Director, Administrative Services, City Hall, PO Box 908, St. John's A1C 5M2 – 709/576-8600, Fax: 709/576-8474
St. Joseph's ‡	205	St. John's West	Placentia & St. Mary's	Joseph Dobbin, Clerk, PO Box 9, St. Joseph's A0B 3A0 – 709/521-2486
St. Lawrence †	1,743	Burin-St. George's	Grand Bank	Gregory Quirke, Clerk, PO Box 128, St. Lawrence A0E 2V0 – 709/873-2222, Fax: 709/873-3352
St. Lewis ‡	339	Labrador	Cartwright-L'Anse au Clair	Ruby Poole, Clerk, St. Lewis A0K 4W0 – 709/939-2282, Fax: 709/939-2810
St. Lunaire-Griquet †	1,020	Humber-St. Barbe-Baie Verte	The Straits & White Bay North	Glenda Burden, Clerk, PO Box 9, St. Lunaire-Griquet A0K 2X0 – 709/623-2323, Fax: 709/623-2170

NEWFOUNDLAND MUNICIPALITIES

Cities in CAPITALS; Towns marked †; Communities marked ‡; Regional Municipalities marked (RG). An in-depth listing for municipalities marked with * appears in Part 2 (check Index for page numbers).

MUNICIPALITY	1991 POP.	FEDERAL ELECTORAL DISTRICT	PROVINCIAL ELECTORAL DISTRICT	CONTACT PERSON WITH ADDRESS, PHONE & FAX
St. Mary's ‡	637	St. John's West	Placentia & St. Mary's	Theresa Power, Clerk, PO Box 15, St. Mary's A0B 3B0 – 709/525-2586, Fax: 709/525-2641
St. Pauls ‡	448	Humber-St. Barbe-Baie Verte	St. Barbe	Ruth Bennett, Clerk, PO Box 9, St. Pauls A0K 4Y0 – 709/243-2279
St. Shotts ‡	232	St. John's West	Placentia & St. Mary's	Raymond Molloy, Clerk, St. Shotts A0A 3R0 – 709/438-2454
St. Vincent's et al. †	674	St. John's West	Placentia & St. Mary's	Madonna Stamp, Clerk, PO Box 39, St. Vincent's A0B 3C0 – 709/525-2540
Sally's Cove ‡	49	Humber-St. Barbe-Baie Verte	St. Barbe	Inez Roberts, Clerk, PO Box 14, Sally's Cove A0K 4Z0 – 709/458-2529
Salmon Cove †	791	Bonavista-Trinity-Conception	Carbonear-Harbour Grace	Jacqueline Deering, Clerk, General Delivery, Salmon Cove A0A 3S0 – 709/596-2101
Salvage †	246	Bonavista-Trinity-Conception	Terra Nova	Cynthia Burden, Clerk, Salvage A0G 3X0 – 709/677-3535
Sandringham ‡	308	Bonavista-Trinity-Conception	Terra Nova	Audrey Penney, Clerk, Sandringham A0G 3Y0 – 709/677-2317
Sandy Cove ‡	174	Bonavista-Trinity-Conception	Terra Nova	Anne Benger, Clerk, Site 8, PO Box 37, Eastport A0G 1Z0 – 709/677-2731
Seal Cove (Fortune Bay) ‡	467	Burin-St. George's	Fortune Bay-Cape La Hune	Emily Loveless, Clerk, PO Box 69, Seal Cove A0H 2G0 – 709/851-4431
Seal Cove (White Bay) †	656	Humber-St. Barbe-Baie Verte	Baie Verte	Lily Miller, Clerk, PO Box 119, Seal Cove A0K 5E0 – 709/531-2550
Seldom-Little Seldom †	590	Gander-Grand Falls	Twillingate & Fogo	Shirley Penney, Clerk, PO Box 100, Seldom A0G 3Z0 – 709/627-3246, Fax: 709/627-3489
Small Point †	505	Bonavista-Trinity-Conception	Carbonear-Harbour Grace	Loretta Diamond, Clerk, Site 6, PO Box 24, Adam's Cove A0A 1T0 – 709/598-2610
South Brook †	720	Gander-Grand Falls	Windsor-Springdale	Hope Rowsell, Clerk, PO Box 63, South Brook A0J 1S0 – 709/657-2206, Fax: 709/657-2206
South River †	786	Bonavista-Trinity-Conception	Harbour Main-Whitbourne	Sheila Bowering, Clerk, PO Box 40, South River A0A 3W0 – 709/786-6761
Southern Harbour †	716	St. John's West	Bellevue	Linda Ryan, Clerk, PO Box 10, Southern Harbour A0B 3H0 – 709/463-2329, Fax: 709/463-2208
Spaniard's Bay †	2,779 ('92)	Bonavista-Trinity-Conception	Port de Grave	Wayne Smith, Clerk, PO Box 190, Spaniard's Bay A0A 3X0 – 709/786-3568, Fax: 709/786-7273
Springdale †	3,545	Gander-Grand Falls	Windsor-Springdale	Kathleen Parewick, Clerk, PO Box 57, Springdale A0J 1T0 – 709/673-3439, Fax: 709/673-4969
Steady Brook †	421	Humber-St. Barbe-Baie Verte	Humber East	Wanda Baggs, Clerk, PO Box 117, Steady Brook A2H 2N2 – 709/634-7601, Fax: 709/634-7547
Stephenville †	7,621	Burin-St. George's	St. George's-Stephenville East; Port au Port	Barry Coates, Clerk, PO Box 420, Stephenville A2N 2Z5 – 709/643-8360, Fax: 709/643-2770
Stephenville Crossing †	2,172	Burin-St. George's	St. George's-Stephenville East	Yvonne Young, Clerk, PO Box 68, Stephenville Crossing A0N 2C0 – 709/646-2600, Fax: 709/646-2605
Summerford †	1,157	Gander-Grand Falls	Twillingate & Fogo	Vicky Anstey, Clerk, PO Box 59, Summerford A0G 4E0 – 709/629-3419, Fax: 709/629-7532
Sunnyside †	622	Bonavista-Trinity-Conception	Bellevue	Joan Sheppard, Clerk, PO Box 89, Sunnyside A0B 3J0 – 709/472-4506, Fax: 709/472-4182
Terra Nova ‡	38	Bonavista-Trinity-Conception	Terra Nova	Walter Calloway, Sec., Site 1, PO Box 8, Terra Nova A0C 1L0 – 709/265-6311
Terrenceville †	818	Burin-St. George's	Bellevue	Lucy Hickey, Clerk, PO Box 54, Terrenceville A0E 2X0 – 709/662-2204
Tilt Cove ‡	17	Humber-St. Barbe-Baie Verte	Baie Verte	Margaret Collins, Clerk, PO Box 22, Tilt Cove A0K 3M0 – 709/675-2641
Tilting ‡	379	Gander-Grand Falls	Twillingate & Fogo	Mary O'Keefe, Clerk, PO Box 40, Tilting A0G 4H0 – 709/658-7236, Fax: 709/658-7239
Torbay †	4,707	St. John's East	Cape St. Francis	Mary Thorne, Clerk, PO Box 190, Torbay A1K 1E3 – 709/437-6532, Fax: 709/437-1309
Traytown ‡	374	Bonavista-Trinity-Conception	Terra Nova	Elizabeth Carter, Clerk, Traytown A0G 4K0 – 709/533-2156
Trepassey †	1,198	St. John's West	Ferryland	Yvonne Power, Clerk, PO Box 129, Trepassey A0A 4B0 – 709/438-2641, Fax: 709/438-2749
Trinity ‡	326	Bonavista-Trinity-Conception	Trinity North	Joanne Mackey, Clerk, PO Box 42, Trinity A0C 2S0 – 709/464-3836
Triton et al. †	1,273	Gander-Grand Falls	Windsor-Springdale	Astrid Fudge, Clerk, PO Box 10, Triton A0J 1V0 – 709/263-2264, Fax: 709/263-2381
Trout River ‡	763	Humber-St. Barbe-Baie Verte	Humber Valley	Glenda Aubert, Clerk, PO Box 89, Trout River A0K 5P0 – 709/451-5376, Fax: 709/451-2127
Twillingate †	2,969	Gander-Grand Falls	Twillingate & Fogo	David Burton, Clerk, PO Box 220, Twillingate A0G 4M0 – 709/884-2438, Fax: 709/884-5278
Upper Island Cove †	2,038	Bonavista-Trinity-Conception	Port de Grave	Baxter Drover, Clerk, PO Box 149, Upper Island Cove A0A 4E0 – 709/589-2503, Fax: 709/589-2522
Victoria †	1,831	Bonavista-Trinity-Conception	Carbonear-Harbour Grace	Sharon Snooks, Clerk, PO Box 130, Victoria A0A 4G0 – 709/596-3783, Fax: 709/596-5020

Canadian Almanac & Directory 1997

NORTHWEST TERRITORIES MUNICIPALITIES 4-37

Cities in CAPITALS; Towns marked †; Communities marked ‡; Regional Municipalities marked (RG). An in-depth listing for municipalities marked with * appears in Part 2 (check Index for page numbers).

MUNICIPALITY	1991 POP.	FEDERAL ELECTORAL DISTRICT	PROVINCIAL ELECTORAL DISTRICT	CONTACT PERSON WITH ADDRESS, PHONE & FAX
Wabana †	3,608	St. John's East	Conception Bay East & Bell Island	Diane Butler, Clerk, PO Box 1229, Bell Island A0A 4H0 – 709/488-2990, Fax: 709/488-3181
Wabush †	2,331	Labrador	Labrador West	Florence Harnett, Clerk, PO Box 190, Wabush A0R 1B0 – 709/282-5696, Fax: 709/282-5142
West St. Modeste ‡	202	Labrador	Cartwright-L'Anse au Clair	Robin O'Dell, Clerk, West St. Modeste A0K 5S0 – 709/927-5583, Fax: 709/927-5898
Westport ‡	469	Humber-St. Barbe-Baie Verte	Baie Verte	Peggy Randell, Clerk, PO Box 29, Westport A0K 5R0 – 709/224-5501
Whitbourne †	1,036	St. John's West	Harbour Main-Whitbourne	Wanda Lynch, Clerk, General Delivery, Whitbourne A0B 3K0 – 709/759-2780, Fax: 709/759-2016
Whiteway ‡	333	Bonavista-Trinity-Conception	Trinity-Bay de Verde	Melinda Legge, Clerk, Whiteway A0B 3L0 – 709/588-2948, Fax: 709/588-2837
Winterland ‡	272	Burin-St. George's	Grand Bank	Marlyese Simms, Clerk, Winterland A0E 2Y0 – 709/279-3701, Fax: 709/583-2010
Winterton †	667	Bonavista-Trinity-Conception	Trinity-Bay de Verde	Joan Hiscock, Clerk, PO Box 59, Winterton A0B 3M0 – 709/583-2010, Fax: 709/583-2099
Witless Bay †	1,064	St. John's West	Ferryland	Joan Yard, Clerk, PO Box 147, Witless Bay A0A 4K0 – 709/334-3407, Fax: 709/334-2377
Woodstock ‡	311	Humber-St. Barbe-Baie Verte	Baie Verte	Cora-Lee Decker, Clerk, Woodstock A0K 5X0 – 709/251-3176
Woody Point ‡	405	Humber-St. Barbe-Baie Verte	Humber Valley	Judy Goosney, Clerk, PO Box 76, Bonne Bay A0K 1P0 – 709/453-2273
York Harbour ‡	415	Humber-St. Barbe-Baie Verte	Bay of Islands	Vida Robinson, Clerk, York Harbour A0L 1L0 – 709/681-2280

NORTHWEST TERRITORIES

LEGISLATION: The Cities, Towns and Villages Act; Hamlets Act; Charter Communities Act; Property Assessment and Taxation Act; Local Authorities Elections Act.

Incorporation as a City, Town or Village is determined by assessed value of all assessable land. In order to incorporate as a village, a community requires total assessed value of more than $10 million; as a town an assessed value of more than $50 million; and as a city an assessed value of more than $200 million.

Municipal elections in cities, towns and villages are held on the third Monday of October; in hamlets, elections are held on the second Monday of December; in charter communities, election dates vary, depending on what has been established in the community's charter; and in a settlement, the election date is fixed in the settlement corporation's establishment order. The term of office for a mayor and councillor in a city, town or village is three years, unless a by-law has been enacted to reduce the term to two years; in a hamlet, the term of office for a mayor is two years, unless a by-law has been enacted to establish the term at three years, and for councillors the term of office is two years and terms are staggered. In charter communities the term of office for members of council are established in the community's charter. The term of office for council members of a settlement is two years and may be staggered. The chairperson of a settlement council is chosen by the members of the council.

In cities, towns and villages members of council commence their term of office at 12 noon on the first Monday in November following their election; in hamlets the term of office commences at 12 noon on the first Monday in January; and in charter communities the commencement of terms is established in the community's charter.

Cities in CAPITALS; Towns marked †; Villages marked (V); Hamlets marked (H). An in-depth listing for municipalities marked with * appears in Part 2 (check Index for page numbers).

MUNICIPALITY	1991 POP.	FEDERAL ELECTORAL DISTRICT	TERRITORIAL ELECTORAL DISTRICT	CONTACT PERSON WITH ADDRESS, PHONE & FAX
Aklavik (H)			Mackenzie Delta	Nellie Gruben, Sr. Admin. Officer, PO Box 88, Aklavik X0E 0A0 – 403/978-2361, 978-2351 (Band Office), Fax: 403/978-2434
Arctic Bay (H)			High Arctic	Mike Richards, Sr. Admin. Officer, PO Box 150, Arctic Bay X0A 0A0 – 403/439-9917, 9918, Fax: 403/439-8767
Arviat (H)			Kivallivik	Darren Flynn, Sr. Admin. Officer, General Delivery, Arviat X0C 0E0 – 819/857-2841, Fax: 819/857-2519
Baker Lake (H)			Kivallivik	Dennis Zettler, Sr. Admin. Officer, PO Box 149, Baker Lake X0C 0A0 – 819/793-2874, Fax: 819/793-2509
Broughton Island (H)			Baffin Central	Don Pickle, Sr. Admin. Officer, General Delivery, Broughton Island X0A 0B0 – 819/927-8832, 8117, Fax: 819/927-8120
Cambridge Bay (H)			Kitikmeot	Henry Brown, Sr. Admin. Officer, PO Box 16, Cambridge Bay X0E 0C0 – 403/983-2337, Fax: 403/983-2193
Cape Dorset (H)			Baffin South	Timoon Toonoo, Sr. Admin. Officer, PO Box 30, Cape Dorset X0A 0C0 – 819/897-8943, 8981, Fax: 819/897-8030
Chesterfield Inlet (H)			Aivilik	Roy Mullins, Sr. Admin. Officer, General Delivery, Chesterfield Inlet X0E 0B0 – 819/898-9951, Fax: 819/898-9108
Clyde River (H)			Baffin Central	Jonathon Palluq, Sr. Admin. Officer, General Delivery, Clyde River X0A 0E0 – 819/924-6220, 6301, Fax: 819/924-6293
Coral Harbour (H)			Aivilik	Louis Primeau, Sr. Admin. Officer, General Delivery, Coral Harbour X0C 0C0 – 819/925-8867, Fax: 819/925-8233
Fort Liard (H)			Nahendeh	John McKee, Sr. Admin. Officer, General Delivery, Fort Liard X0G 0A0 – 403/770-4104, Fax: 403/770-4004
Fort McPherson (H)			Mackenzie Delta	Paul Fraser, Sr. Admin. Officer, PO Box 57, Fort McPherson X0E 0J0 – 403/952-2428, Fax: 403/952-2725
Fort Providence (H)			Deh Cho	Albert Lafferty, Sr. Admin. Officer, General Delivery, Fort Providence X0E 0L0 – 403/699-3441, Fax: 403/699-3210
Fort Simpson (V)	1,142	Western Arctic	Nahendeh	John Crisp, Sr. Admin. Officer, PO Box 438, Fort Simpson X0E 0N0 – 403/695-2253, 2254, Fax: 403/695-2005

Canadian Almanac & Directory 1997

NORTHWEST TERRITORIES MUNICIPALITIES

Cities in CAPITALS; Towns marked †; Villages marked (V); Hamlets marked (H). An in-depth listing for municipalities marked with * appears in Part 2 (check Index for page numbers).

MUNICIPALITY	1991 POP.	FEDERAL ELECTORAL DISTRICT	TERRITORIAL ELECTORAL DISTRICT	CONTACT PERSON WITH ADDRESS, PHONE & FAX
Fort Smith †	2,480	Western Arctic	Thebacha	Roy Scot, Sr. Admin. Officer, PO Box 147, Fort Smith X0E 0P0 – 403/872-2014, 2045, Fax: 403/872-4345
Gjoa Haven (H)			Natilikmiot	Greg Morash, Sr. Admin. Officer, General Delivery, Gjoa Haven X0E 1J0 – 403/360-7141, Fax: 403/360-6309
Grise Fiord (H)			High Arctic	Lizzie Pallituq, Sr. Admin. Officer, General Delivery, Grise Fiord X0A 0J0 – 819/980-9959, 9060, Fax: 819/980-9052
Hall Beach (H)			Amittuq	Marie Kringuk, Sr. Admin. Officer, General Delivery, Hall Beach X0A 0K0 – 819/928-8829, 8945, Fax: 819/928-8871
Hay River †	3,206	Western Arctic	Hay River	Charles Scarborough, Sr. Admin. Officer, 73 Woodland Dr., Hay River X0E 1G1 – 403/874-6522, Fax: 403/874-3237
Holman (H)			Nunakput	Eleanor Young, Sr. Admin. Officer, General Delivery, Holman X0E 0S0 – 403/396-3511, Fax: 403/396-3256
Igloolik (H)			Amittuq	Nicole Tessier, Sr. Admin. Officer, General Delivery, Igloolik X0A 0L0 – 819/934-8940
Inuvik †	3,206	Western Arctic	Inuvik	Don Howden, Sr. Admin. Officer, PO Box 1160, Inuvik X0E 0T0 – 403/979-2607, Fax: 403/979-2071
Iqaluit †	3,552	Nunatsiaq	Iqaluit	John Raycroft, Sr. Admin. Officer, PO Box 460, Iqaluit X0A 0H0 – 819/979-5600, Fax: 819/979-5922
Kimmirut (formerly Lake Harbour) (H)				Raymond Kaslak, Sr. Admin. Officer, General Delivery, Kimmirut X0A 0N0 – 819/939-2247, 2002, Fax: 819/939-2045
Kugluktuk (formerly Coppermine) (H)				Vacant, Sr. Admin. Officer, PO Box 271, Kugluktuk X0E 0E0 – 403/982-4461, 4471, Fax: 403/982-3060
Norman Wells †	627	Western Arctic	Sahtu	Alec Simpson, Sr. Admin. Officer, PO Box 5, Norman Wells X0E 0V0 – 403/587-2238, 2205, Fax: 403/587-2678
Pangnirtung (H)			Baffin Central	Rita Mike, Sr. Admin. Officer, PO Box 253, Pangnirtung X0A 0R0 – 819/473-8953, 8831, Fax: 819/473-8832
Paulatuk (H)			Nunakput	Ken Thompson, Sr. Admin. Officer, General Delivery, Paulatuk X0E 1N0 – 403/580-3531, Fax: 403/580-3703
Pelly Bay (H)			Natilikmiot	Nick Carter, Sr. Admin. Officer, General Delivery, Pelly Bay X0E 1K0 – 403/769-6281, Fax: 403/769-6069
Pond Inlet (H)			Amittuq	Jake Anaviapik, Sr. Admin. Officer, General Delivery, Pond Inlet X0A 0S0 – 819/899-8934, 8935, Fax: 819/899-8940
Rae-Edzo (H)				Ralph Butterworth, Sr. Admin. Officer, PO Box 68, Rae X0E 0Y0 – 403/392-6500, 6561, Fax: 403/392-6139
Rankin Inlet (H)			Keewatin Central	Antonio Masone, Sr. Admin. Officer, PO Box 310, Rankin Inlet X0C 0G0 – 819/645-2953, Fax: 819/645-2146
Repulse Bay (H)			Aivilik	Sheldon Dorey, Sr. Admin. Officer, General Delivery, Repulse Bay X0C 0H0 – 819/462-9952
Resolute (H)			High Arctic	Susan Salluviniq, Sr. Admin. Officer, General Delivery, Resolute Bay X0A 0V0 – 819/252-3616, 3689, Fax: 819/252-3749
Sachs Harbour (H)			Nunakput	Jackie Kuptana, Sr. Admin. Officer, General Delivery, Sachs Harbour X0E 0Z0 – 403/690-4351, Fax: 403/690-4802
Sanikiluaq (H)			Baffin South	Brian Fleming, Sr. Admin. Officer, General Delivery, Sanikiluaq X0A 0W0 – 819/266-8874, 8996, Fax: 819/266-8903
Taloyoak (formerly Spence Bay) (H)			Natilikmiot	Elwood Johnson, Sr. Admin. Officer, General Delivery, Taloyoak X0E 1B0 – 403/561-6341, Fax: 403/561-5057
Tuktoyaktuk (H)				Lucy Kuptana, Sr. Admin. Officer, PO Box 120, Tuktoyaktuk X0E 1C0 – 403/977-2286, Fax: 403/977-2110
Tulita (formerly Fort Norman) (H)				Sheila Bassi, Sr. Admin. Officer, General Delivery, Tulita X0E 0K0 – 403/588-4471
Wha Ti (formerly Lac La Martre) (H)				Thomas Matus, Sr. Admin. Officer, General Delivery, Wha Ti X0E 1P0 – 403/573-3401, Fax: 403/573-3018
Whale Cove (H)			Keewatin Central	Terry Rogers, Sr. Admin. Officer, General Delivery, Whale Cove X0C 0J0 – 819/896-9961, Fax: 819/896-9109
*YELLOWKNIFE	15,179	Western Arctic	Yellowknife South; Yellowknife North; Yellowknife Centre; Yellowknife Frame Lake	Brian Chambers, City Clerk-Asst. City Adm., PO Box 580, Yellowknife X1A 2N4 – 403/920-5600, Fax: 403/920-5649; URL: http://www.city.yellowknife.nt.ca

Canadian Almanac & Directory 1997

NOVA SCOTIA

Nova Scotia is geographically divided into 18 counties. Twelve of these constitute separate municipalities. The remaining six are each divided into two districts and each of these constitutes a separate municipality. Thus there are 24 rural municipalities. Within these areas are autonomous incorporated towns and the regional municipalities (Cape Breton, Halifax and Queens), and other local organizations with limited jurisdiction, including school boards, boards of school trustees, village commissions, local service commissions, rural fire districts and other special purpose forms.

Incorporation of a town is governed by the Municipal Boundaries & Representation Act.

The organization of towns is specified in the Towns Act and that of rural municipalities in the Municipal Act. Villages are governed by the Village Service Act. Additional regulation is provided by the Municipal Affairs Act, the Municipal Boundaries & Representation Act, the Municipal Finance Corporation Act, and the Planning Act.

All general and special municipal elections, including elections for school board members, are governed by the Municipal Elections Act, 1979. The term of office for mayors, councillors, aldermen, and elective school board members is three years. Elections take place on the third Saturday in October, every third year, thus: October 1997, October 2000, October 2003.

Cities in CAPITALS; Regional Municipalities marked (RG); Towns marked †; Villages marked (V); Rural Municipalities marked (RM). An in-depth listing for municipalities marked with * appears in Part 2 (check Index for page numbers).

MUNICIPALITY	1991 POP.	COUNTY	FEDERAL ELECTORAL DISTRICT	PROVINCIAL ELECTORAL DISTRICT	CONTACT PERSON WITH ADDRESS, PHONE & FAX
Amherst †	9,742	Cumberland	Cumberland-Colchester	Cumberland North	Eric Mourant, Town Mgr., Ratchford St., PO Box 516, Amherst B4H 4A1 – 902/667-3352, Fax: 902/667-3356
Annapolis County (RM)	20,168	Annapolis; South West Nova	Annapolis East	Annapolis; Digby-Annapolis Royal	Jacquie Lawrence, Municipal Clerk, 752 George St., PO Box 100, Annapolis Royal B0S 1A0 – 902/532-2331, Fax: 902/532-2096, URL: http://www.munofann@clan.tartannet.ns.ca/
Annapolis Royal †	633	Annapolis	South West Nova	Digby-Annapolis Royal	Sherman Hudson, Clerk-Treas., 285 St. George St., PO Box 310, Annapolis Royal B0S 1A0 – 902/532-2043, Fax: 902/532-7443
Antigonish †	4,924	Antigonish	Cape Breton Highlands-Canso	Antigonish	Brian MacNeil, Clerk-Treas., 274 Main St., Antigonish B2G 2C4 – 902/863-1312, Fax: 902/863-9201
Antigonish County (RM)	14,302	Antigonish	Cape Breton Highlands-Canso	Antigonish	Alan Bond, Clerk-Treas., 42 West St., Antigonish B2G 2H5 – 902/863-1117, Fax: 902/863-5751
Argyle District (RM)	9,215	Yarmouth	South West Nova	Argyle	Robert Thibault, Clerk-Treas., 27 Courthouse St., PO Box 10, Tusket B0W 3M0 – 902/648-2311, Fax: 902/648-0367
Aylesford (V)	1,121	Kings	Annapolis Valley-Hants	Kings West	Dianne Steele, Clerk-Treas., PO Box 91, Aylesford B0P 1C0 – 902/847-9876
Baddeck (V)	1,067	Victoria	Cape Breton Highlands-Canso	Victoria	Mabel MacEachern, Clerk-Treas., PO Box 370, Baddeck B0E 1B0 – 902/295-3231, Fax: 902/295-3331
Barrington District (RM)	7,774	Shelburne	South Shore	Shelburne	J.R. Fry, Clerk-Treas., PO Box 100, Barrington B0W 1E0 – 902/637-2015, Fax: 902/637-2075
Berwick †	2,150	Kings	Annapolis Valley-Hants	Kings West	Judith Mitchell, Clerk-Treas., 236 Commercial St., PO Box 130, Berwick B0P 1E0 – 902/538-8068, Fax: 902/538-3724
Bible Hill (V)		Colchester	Cumberland-Colchester	Truro-Bible Hill	Robert Christianson, Clerk-Treas., 39 Pictou Rd., Bible Hill B2N 2R9 – 902/893-8083, Fax: 902/897-0430
Bridgetown †	1,021	Annapolis	South West Nova	Annapolis	William F. Hamilton, Clerk-Treas., 271 Granville St., PO Box 609, Bridgetown B0S 1C0 – 902/665-4637, Fax: 902/665-4039
Bridgewater †	7,248	Lunenburg	South Shore	Lunenburg West	Lisa Rhuland, Clerk, 60 Pleasant St., PO Box 9, Bridgewater B4V 2W7 – 902/543-4651, Fax: 902/543-6876
Canning (V)	908	Kings	Annapolis Valley-Hants	Kings North	Gloria Porter, Clerk-Treas., PO Box 9, Canning B0P 1H0 – 902/582-3768
Canso †	1,228	Guysborough	Cape Breton Highlands-Canso	Guysborough-Port Hawkesbury	Scott Conrod, Clerk-Treas., 2 Telegraph St., PO Box 189, Canso B0H 1H0 – 902/366-2525, Fax: 902/366-3093
*Cape Breton (RG)			Cape Breton East Richmond; Cape Breton Highlands-Canso; Cape Breton-The Sydneys	Cape Breton Centre; Cape Breton East; Cape Breton North; Cape Breton Nova; Cape Breton South; Cape Breton-The Lakes	Bernie White, Clerk, 320 Esplanade, Sydney B1P 1A7 – 902/564-6302, 6306, Fax: 902/567-6839
Chester (V)	1,249	Lunenburg	South Shore	Lunenburg East	Annette Collicutt, Clerk-Treas., RR#1, Chester B0J 1J0 – 902/275-2118
Chester District (RM)	10,789	Lunenburg	South Shore	Chester-St. Margaret's	Barry Lenihan, Clerk-Treas., 151 King St., PO Box 369, Chester B0J 1J0 – 902/275-3554, Fax: 902/275-4771
Clare District (RM)	9,654	Digby	South West Nova	Clare	Delphis J. Comeau, Clerk-Treas., PO Box 458, Little Brook B0W 1Z0 – 902/769-2031, Fax: 902/769-3773
Clark's Harbour †	1,076	Shelburne	South Shore	Shelburne	Linda Symonds, Clerk-Treas., 2648 Main St., PO Box 160, Clark's Harbour B0W 1P0 – 902/745-2390, Fax: 902/745-1772

Canadian Almanac & Directory 1997

4-40 NOVA SCOTIA MUNICIPALITIES

Cities in CAPITALS; Regional Municipalities marked (RG); Towns marked †; Villages marked (V); Rural Municipalities marked (RM). An in-depth listing for municipalities marked with * appears in Part 2 (check Index for page numbers).

MUNICIPALITY	1991 POP.	COUNTY	FEDERAL ELECTORAL DISTRICT	PROVINCIAL ELECTORAL DISTRICT	CONTACT PERSON WITH ADDRESS, PHONE & FAX
Colchester County (RM)	34,694	Colchester	Cumberland-Colchester	Colchester-Musquodoboit Valley; Colchester North; Truro-Bible Hill	Andrew Beckett, Executive Director, PO Box 697, Truro B2N 5E7 – 902/897-3160, Fax: 902/895-9983
Cornwallis Square (V)		Kings	Annapolis Valley-Hants	Kings West	Robyn Peterson, Clerk-Treas., PO Box 129, Waterville B0P 1V0 – 902/679-0632, Fax: 902/678-9543
Cumberland County (RM)	17,151	Cumberland	Cumberland-Colchester	Cumberland North; Cumberland South	Rennie Bugley, CAO, PO Box 428, Amherst B4H 3Z5 – 902/667-2313, Fax: 902/667-1352
Digby †	2,311	Digby	South West Nova	Digby-Annapolis Royal	Mike Ireland, Clerk-Treas., 147 First Ave., PO Box 579, Digby B0V 1A0 – 902/245-4769, Fax: 902/245-2121
Digby District (RM)	9,285	Digby	South West Nova	Digby-Annapolis Royal	W.L. McMillan, Clerk-Treas., PO Box 429, Digby B0V 1A0 – 902/245-4777, Fax: 902/245-5748
Dover (V)	607	Halifax	Cape Breton Highlands-Canso	Guysborough-Port Hawkesbury	Leslie Boudreau Jr., Chairman, Little Dover B0H 1V0
Freeport (V)	397	Digby	South West Nova	Digby-Annapolis	Dale Tibert, Clerk-Treas., PO Box 31, Freeport B0V 1B0 – 902/839-2144
Greenwood (V)		Kings	Annapolis Valley-Hants	Kings West	Sharon Robertson, Clerk-Treas., 904 Central Ave., PO Box 1068, Greenwood B0P 1N0 – 902/765-8788
Guysborough District (RM)	6,518	Guysborough	Cape Breton Highlands-Canso	Guysborough-Port Hawkesbury	Shirley Nixon, Clerk-Treas., Municipal Bldg., 33 Pleasant St., PO Box 79, Guysborough B0H 1N0 – 902/533-3705, Fax: 902/533-2749
*Halifax (RG) [a]	330,000		Dartmouth; Halifax; Halifax West	Bedford-Fall River; Chester-St. Margaret's; Colchester-Musquidoboit Valley; Cole Harbour-Eastern Passage; Dartmouth Cole Harbour; Dartmouth East; Dartmouth North; Dartmouth South; Eastern Shore; Halifax Atlantic; Halifax Bedford Basin; Halifax Chebucto; Halifax Citadel; Halifax Fairview; Halifax Needham; Preston; Sackville Beaverbank; Sackville Cobequid; Timberlea-Prospect	Barry Coopersmith, City Mgr., 1841 Argyle St., PO Box 1749, Halifax B3J 3A5 – 902/496-2000, Fax: 902/425-1466; URL: http://www.ccn.cs.dal.ca/Government/HRM/HRM-Home.html/
Hants East District (RM)	18,560	Hants	Annapolis Valley-Hants	Hants East	Ian Glasgow, Clerk, PO Box 190, Shubenacadie B0N 2H0 – 902/758-2299, Fax: 902/758-3497
Hants West District (RM)	13,611	Hants	Annapolis Valley-Hants	Hants West	Dwight Bennett, Clerk-Treas., Industrial Mall, 76 Morrison Dr., PO Box 3000, Windsor B0N 2T0 – 902/798-8391, Fax: 902/798-8553
Hantsport †	1,274	Hants	Annapolis Valley-Hants	Hants West	Joseph D. McGinn, Clerk-Treas., 3 Oak St., PO Box 399, Hantsport B0P 1P0 – 902/684-3211, Fax: 902/684-3417
Havre Boucher (V)	481	Antigonish	Cape Breton Highlands-Canso	Antigonish	Raymond Carpenter, Clerk-Treas., Havre Boucher B0P 1P0 – 902/232-3088
Hebbville (V)	815	Lunenburg	South Shore	Lunenburg West	Dave Steele, Clerk-Treas., RR#4, Bridgewater B4V 2W3 – 902/543-8181, Fax: 902/543-7123
Inverness County (RM)	17,629	Inverness	Cape Breton Highlands-Canso	Guysborough-Port Hawkesbury; Inverness; Victoria	A.A. Murray, Clerk-Treas., PO Box 179, Port Hood B0E 2W0 – 902/787-2274, Fax: 902/787-3110
Kentville †	5,506	Kings	Annapolis Valley-Hants	Kings North	William Boyd, Clerk-Treas., 354 Main St., PO Box 218, Kentville B4N 3W4 – 902/679-2500, Fax: 902/679-2375
Kings County (RM)	45,186	Kings	Annapolis Valley-Hants	Kings North; Kings South; Kings West	R.G. Ramsay, CAO, 87 Cornwallis St., PO Box 100, Kentville B4N 3W3 – 902/678-6141, Fax: 902/679-2820
Kingston (V)	62	Kings	Annapolis Valley-Hants	Kings West	Pat Fleury, Clerk-Treas., 522 Victoria Dr., PO Box 254, Kingston B0P 1R0 – 902/765-2800, Fax: 902/765-2800
Lawrencetown (V)	427 ('81)	Annapolis	South West Nova	Annapolis	Dene Marshall, Clerk-Treas., 83 Lawrencetown Lane, PO Box 38, Lawrencetown B0S 1M0 – 902/584-3559, Fax: 902/584-3559

Canadian Almanac & Directory 1997

Cities in CAPITALS; Regional Municipalities marked (RG); Towns marked †; Villages marked (V); Rural Municipalities marked (RM). An in-depth listing for municipalities marked with * appears in Part 2 (check Index for page numbers).

MUNICIPALITY	1991 POP.	COUNTY	FEDERAL ELECTORAL DISTRICT	PROVINCIAL ELECTORAL DISTRICT	CONTACT PERSON WITH ADDRESS, PHONE & FAX
Lockeport †	798	Shelburne	South Shore	Shelburne	Maureen Lewis, Clerk-Treas., 26 North St., PO Box 189, Lockeport B0T 1L0 – 902/656-2216, Fax: 902/656-2935
Lunenburg †	2,781	Lunenburg	South Shore	Lunenburg	Beatrice Renton, Town Mgr., 119 Cumberland St., PO Box 129, Lunenburg B0J 2C0 – 902/634-4410, Fax: 902/634-4416, URL: http://www.isisnet.com/life/lunenberg/
Lunenburg District (RM)	25,720	Lunenburg	South Shore	Cheester-St. Margaret's Lunenburg; Lunenburg West	D.E. Steele, CAO, 210 Aberdeen Rd., PO Box 200, Bridgewater B4V 2W8 – 902/543-8181, Fax: 902/543-7123
Mahone Bay †	1,096	Lunenburg	South Shore	Lunenburg	Kyle Hiltz, Clerk-Treas., 493 Main St., PO Box 530, Mahone Bay B0J 2E0 – 902/624-8327, Fax: 902/624-8069
Middleton †	1,819	Annapolis	South West Nova	Annapolis	E.L. Bennett, Clerk-Treas., 131 Commercial St., PO Box 340, Middleton B0S 1P0 – 902/825-4841, Fax: 902/825-6460
Mulgrave †	935	Guysborough	Cape Breton Highlands-Canso	Guysborough-Port Hawkesbury	Nathan Gorall, Clerk-Treas., 457 MacLeod St., PO Box 129, Mulgrave B0E 2G0 – 902/747-2243, Fax: 902/747-2585
New Glasgow †	9,905	Pictou	Central Nova	Pictou Centre	Jim Langille, Clerk-Treas., 111 Provost St., PO Box 7, New Glasgow B2H 5E1 – 902/755-7788, Fax: 902/755-6242
New Minas (V)	896	Kings	Annapolis Valley-Hants	Kings South	Linda Lockhart, Clerk-Treas., 9209 Commercial St., New Minas B4N 3G1 – 902/681-6972, Fax: 902/681-0779
Oxford †	1,384	Cumberland	Cumberland-Colchester	Cumberland South	H.M. McCormack, Clerk-Treas., PO Box 338, Oxford B0M 1P0 – 902/447-2170, Fax: 902/447-2485
Parrsboro †	1,634	Cumberland	Cumberland-Colchester	Cumberland South	Ashley Brown, Clerk-Treas., 1 Eastern Ave., PO Box 400, Parrsboro B0M 1S0 – 902/254-2036, Fax: 902/254-2313
Pictou †	4,134	Pictou	Central Nova	Pictou West	David L. Steele, Clerk-Treas., PO Box 640, Pictou B0K 1H0 – 902/485-4372, Fax: 902/485-8110
Pictou County (RM)	23,190	Pictou	Central Nova	Pictou Centre; Pictou East; Pictou West	Clyde A. Purvis, Clerk, 28 Willow St., PO Box 910, Pictou B0K 1H0 – 902/485-4311, Fax: 902/485-6475
Port Hawkesbury †	3,991	Inverness	Cape Breton Highlands-Canso	Guysborough-Port Hawkesbury	Colin J. MacDonald, Clerk-Treas., Provincial Bldg., MacSween St., PO Box 10, Port Hawkesbury B0E 2V0 – 902/625-2746, Fax: 902/625-0040
Port Williams (V)	1,009	Kings	Annapolis Valley-Hants	Kings North	Glenda Clark, Clerk-Treas., 1045 Main St., PO Box 153, Port Williams B0P 1T0 – 902/542-4411
Pugwash (V)	775	Cumberland	Cumberland-Colchester	Cumberland North	Katheryne Langille, Clerk-Treas., 124 Water St., PO Box 220, Pugwash B0K 1L0 – 902/243-2946, Fax: 902/243-2126
*Queens (RG)		Queens	South Shore	Queens	Clerk, PO Box 1264, Liverpool B0T 1K0 – 902/354-3453, Fax: 902/354-7473
Richmond County (RM)	11,260	Richmond	Cape Br.-E. Richmond; Cape Br. Highlands-Canso	Richmond	Louis Digout, CAO, PO Box 120, Arichat B0E 1A0 – 902/226-2400, Fax: 902/226-1510
River Hebert (V)	773 ('86)	Cumberland	Cumberland-Colchester	Cumberland South	Judy Rector, Clerk-Treas., River Hebert B0L 1G0 – 902/251-2368
St. Mary's District (RM)	3,043	Guysborough	Cape Breton Highlands-Canso	Guysborough-Port Hawkesbury	Helen MacDonald, Clerk-Treas., PO Box 296, Sherbrooke B0J 3C0 – 902/522-2049, Fax: 902/522-2309
St. Peter's (V)	748	Richmond	Cape Breton Highlands-Canso	Richmond	Maura Calder, Clerk-Treas., PO Box 452, St. Peter's B0E 3B0
Shelburne †	2,245	Shelburne	South Shore	Shelburne	Wilmont Hardy, Clerk-Treas., 168 Water St., PO Box 670, Shelburne B0T 1W0 – 902/875-2991, Fax: 902/875-3932
Shelburne District (RM)	5,450	Shelburne	South Shore	Shelburne	Alan Merritt, Clerk-Treas., 136 Hammond Rd., PO Box 280, Shelburne B0T 1W0 – 902/875-3083, Fax: 902/875-1278
Springhill †	4,373	Cumberland	Cumberland-Colchester	Cumberland South	Donald Tabor, Clerk-Treas., 29 Main St., PO Box 1000, Springhill B0M 1X0 – 902/597-3751, Fax: 902/597-3637
Stellarton †	5,237	Pictou	Central Nova	Pictou Centre	A.A. Pearson, Clerk-Treas., 250 Ford St., PO Box 2200, Stellarton B0K 1S0 – 902/752-2114, Fax: 902/755-4105
Stewiacke †	1,306	Colchester	Cumberland-Colchester	Colchester-Musqodoboit Valley	Lillian Smith, Clerk-Treas., PO Box 8, Stewiacke B0N 2J0 – 902/639-2231, Fax: 902/639-2221

Cities in CAPITALS; Regional Municipalities marked (RG); Towns marked †; Villages marked (V); Rural Municipalities marked (RM). An in-depth listing for municipalities marked with * appears in Part 2 (check Index for page numbers).

MUNICIPALITY	1991 POP.	COUNTY	FEDERAL ELECTORAL DISTRICT	PROVINCIAL ELECTORAL DISTRICT	CONTACT PERSON WITH ADDRESS, PHONE & FAX
Tatamagouche (V)	726 ('86)	Colchester	Cumberland-Colchester	Colchester North	Michelle Cameron, Clerk-Treas., Tatamagouche B0K 1V0 – 902/657-3696
Tiverton (V)	261 ('86)	Digby	South West Nova	Digby-Annapolis	Mary Cossaboom, Clerk-Treas., PO Box 16, Tiverton B0V 1G0 – 902/839-2369
Trenton †	2,957	Pictou	Central Nova	Pictou Centre	Robin Campbell, Clerk-Treas., 120 Main St., PO Box 328, Trenton B0K 1X0 – 902/752-5311, Fax: 902/752-0090
Truro †	11,683	Colchester	Cumberland-Colchester	Truro-Bible Hill	D.G. Gilroy, Clerk-Treas., 730 Prince St., PO Box 427, Truro B2N 5C5 – 902/895-4484, Fax: 902/893-0501
Victoria County (RM)	8,708	Victoria	Cape Breton Highlands-Canso; Cape Breton-The Sydneys	Victoria	Mabel S. MacEachern, Clerk-Treas., Chebucto St., PO Box 370, Baddeck B0E 1B0 – 902/295-3231, Fax: 902/295-3331
Westport (V)	321	Digby	South West Nova	Digby-Annapolis	Caroline Norwood, Clerk-Treas., PO Box 1192, Westport B0V 1H0 – 902/839-2219
Westville †	4,228	Pictou	Central Nova	Pictou East	Jim Langille, Clerk-Treas., 111 Provost St., PO Box 7, New Glasgow B2H 5E1 – 902/752-4245, Fax: 902/755-6242
Weymouth (V)	380	Digby	South West Nova	Digby-Annapolis	Clyde Cossman, Clerk-Treas., PO Box 121, Weymouth B0W 3T0 – 902/837-5257
Windsor †	3,625	Hants	Annapolis Valley-Hants	Hants West	Lawrence Armstrong, Clerk-Treas., 100 King St., PO Box 158, Windsor B0N 2T0 – 902/798-2275, Fax: 902/798-5679
Wolfville †	3,475	Kings	Annapolis Valley-Hants	Kings South	Roy Brideau, Town Mgr., 195 Main St., PO Box 1030, Wolfville B0P 1X0 – 902/542-5767, Fax: 902/542-4789
Yarmouth †	7,781	Elgin	South West Nova	Yarmouth	Raymond Gallant, CAO, 400 Main St., Yarmouth B5A 1G2 – 902/742-8565, Fax: 902/742-6244
Yarmouth District (RM)	10,895	Yarmouth	South West Nova	Yarmouth	Ken Moses, Clerk-Treas., 403 Main St., PO Box 152, Yarmouth B5A 4B2 – 902/742-7159, Fax: 902/742-3164

a. Effective April 1, 1996, Halifax Regional Municipality was created through the amalgamation of the cities of Halifax & Dartmouth, the town of Bedford, & Halifax County municipality.

ONTARIO

Southern Ontario is divided into upper-tier municipal units including the counties, the regional municipalities, the Municipality of Metropolitan Toronto, the District Municipality of Muskoka and the Restructured County of Oxford.

The cities, except for the City of Sarnia in the County of Lambton, and separated towns located within the counties do not come within the jurisdiction of the county councils. The municipalities within the other areas have been restructured and are all included in the upper-tier system.

County councils consist of the reeves of all the local municipalities and, in the cases of larger communities, the deputy reeves. Restructured upper-tier councils have representation established by individual statute based generally on representation by population.

Restructured units, which contain about two-thirds of the Provincial population, generally have fewer and larger local municipalities within them than do the counties. The functions of the upper-tier councils of restructured areas are more extensive than those of the counties (i.e. water supply, sewage treatment, waste management, regional planning, social services, long term financing and, in most areas, policing).

Northern Ontario consists of one regional municipality (Sudbury) and a number of local municipalities (cities, towns, villages, townships and improvement districts). The north is divided into 10 territorial districts which do not serve any municipal purpose. A large part of Northern Ontario is unorganized for municipal purposes.

Under the Municipal Elections Act, local government elections in Ontario are normally held on the second Monday in November. A standard three-year term of office is provided for all municipal councils, school boards and other local boards. Regional Chairs in Ottawa-Carleton and Hamilton-Wentworth are directly elected as well.

The preliminary list of electors is based on information obtained through triennial enumeration by mail-out questionnaire by provincial assessment commissioners during the month of May.

A mandatory advance poll is held by all municipalities on the Saturday, nine days before polling day and the Wednesday immediately before polling day. Additional advance polls may be held as provided by a by-law passed by the council of a municipality before Nomination Day. Contact the Local Government Policy Branch for any further information (Local Government Policy Branch, Ministry of Municipal Affairs, 777 Bay St., Toronto ON M5G 2E5, 416/585-7266).

Cities in CAPITALS; Towns marked †; Separated Towns marked (SE); Villages marked (V); Townships marked Twp; Restructured Counties marked (RS); United Counties marked (U); Development Areas (DA); • means separated for municipal purposes from county. An in-depth listing for municipalities marked with * appears in Part 2 (check Index for page numbers).

MUNICIPALITY	1994 POP.	COUNTY OR DISTRICT	FEDERAL ELECTORAL DISTRICT	PROVINCIAL ELECTORAL DISTRICT	CONTACT PERSON WITH ADDRESS, PHONE & FAX
Adelaide Twp	2,000	Middlesex	Lambton-Middlesex	Middlesex	J. Michael Bett, Adm.-Clerk-Treas., RR#5, Strathroy N7G 3H6 – 519/247-3687, Fax: 519/247-3411
Adjala-Tosorontio Twp	8,896	Simcoe	York-Simcoe	Simcoe West	Michael A. Clark, Clerk, PO Box 94, Loretto L0G 1L0 – 905/936-3471, Fax: 905/936-3041
Admaston Twp	1,528	Renfrew	Renfrew-Nipissing-Pembroke	Lanark-Renfrew	Beverly Briscoe, Clerk-Treas., RR#2, Renfrew K7V 3Z5 – 613/432-2885, Fax: 613/432-4052
Adolphustown Twp	848	Lennox & Addington	Hastings-Frontenac-Lennox & Addington	Prince Edward-Lennox-South Hastings	Kathy Purcell, Clerk-Treas., RR#1, Bath K0H 1G0 – 613/373-2859, Fax: 613/373-2110

Canadian Almanac & Directory 1997

Cities in CAPITALS; Towns marked †; Separated Towns marked (SE); Villages marked (V); Townships marked Twp; Restructured Counties marked (RS); United Counties marked (U); Development Areas (DA); • means separated for municipal purposes from county. An in-depth listing for municipalities marked with * appears in Part 2 (check Index for page numbers).

MUNICIPALITY	1994 POP.	COUNTY OR DISTRICT	FEDERAL ELECTORAL DISTRICT	PROVINCIAL ELECTORAL DISTRICT	CONTACT PERSON WITH ADDRESS, PHONE & FAX
Ailsa Craig (V)	947	Middlesex	Lambton-Middlesex	Middlesex	Joyce D. Coursey, Clerk-Treas., PO Box 29, Ailsa Craig N0M 1A0 – 519/293-3401, Fax: 519/293-3475
Airy Twp	796	Nipissing District	Renfrew-Nipissing-Pembroke	Renfrew North	Harold Luckasavitch, Adm.-Clerk-Treas., Post St., Whitney K0J 2M0 – 613/637-2650, Fax: 613/637-5368
*Ajax †	59,500 ('96)	Durham Reg. Mun.	Ontario	Durham West	Martin J. de Rond, Clerk, 65 Harwood Ave. South, Ajax L1S 2H9 – 905/683-4550, Fax: 905/683-1061
Albemarle Twp	1,127	Bruce	Bruce-Grey	Bruce	Rhonda J. Cook, Clerk-Treas., RR#6, Wiarton N0H 2T0 – 519/534-2668, Fax: 519/534-4941
Alberton Twp	904	Rainy River District	Kenora-Rainy River	Rainy River	Barbara Stevens, Clerk-Treas., RR#1 - B2, PO Box 759, Fort Frances P9A 3M2 – 807/274-6053, Fax: 807/274-8449
Aldborough Twp	3,772	Elgin	Elgin-Norfolk	Elgin	Joanne Groch, Clerk-Treas., RR#1, PO Box 490, Rodney N0L 2C0 – 519/785-0560, Fax: 519/785-0644
Alexandria †	3,272	Stormont, Dundas & Glengarry	Stormont	Dundas & Glengarry	Leo Poirier, Clerk-Adm., 90 Main St. South, PO Box 700, Alexandria K0C 1A0 – 613/525-1110, Fax: 613/525-1649
Alfred (V)	1,212	Prescott & Russell	Glengarry-Prescott-Russell	Prescott & Russell	Pierre Lemay, Clerk-Treas., 265 St. Philippe St., PO Box 70, Alfred K0B 1A0 – 613/679-2292, Fax: 613/679-4939
Alfred Twp	2,216	Prescott & Russell	Glengarry-Prescott-Russell	Prescott & Russell	Diane Thauvette, Clerk-Treas., PO Box 220, Lefaivre K0B 1J0 – 613/679-2750, Fax: 613/679-1156
Alice & Fraser Twp	3,955	Renfrew	Renfrew-Nipissing-Pembroke	Renfrew North	Bruce Lloyd, Clerk-Treas., RR#4, Pembroke K8A 6W5 – 613/735-6291, Fax: 613/735-5820
Almonte †	4,352	Lanark	Lanark-Carleton	Lanark-Renfrew	J. Des Houston, Adm.-Clerk-Treas., 14 Bridge St., PO Box 400, Almonte K0A 1A0 – 613/256-1685, Fax: 613/256-5759
Alnwick Twp	973	Northumberland	Northumberland	Northumberland	Michael Rutter, Clerk-Treas., PO Box 34, Roseneath K0K 2X0 – 905/352-2841, Fax: 905/352-2032
Alvinston (V)	977	Lambton	Lambton-Middlesex	Lambton	Robert G. Alderman, Clerk-Treas., 3236 River St., PO Box 28, Alvinston N0N 1A0 – 519/898-2173, Fax: 519/898-5656
Amabel Twp	3,577	Bruce	Bruce-Grey	Bruce	William E. Johnston, Clerk-Adm., RR#1, Sauble Beach N0H 2G0 – 519/422-1551, Fax: 519/422-2844
Amaranth Twp	3,187	Dufferin	Wellington-Grey-Dufferin-Simcoe	Dufferin-Peel	William Bospoort, Clerk-Treas., RR#7, Orangeville L9W 2Z3 – 519/941-1007, Fax: 519/941-1802
Ameliasburgh Twp	5,119	Prince Edward	Prince Edward-Hastings	Prince Edward-Lennox-South Hastings	Richard L. Woodley, Clerk-Treas., PO Box 66, Ameliasburgh K0K 1A0 – 613/962-2551, Fax: 613/962-1514
Amherst Island Twp	386	Lennox & Addington	Kingston & the Islands	Kingston & the Islands	Diane Pearce, Clerk-Treas., Stella K0H 2S0 – 613/389-3393, Fax: 613/389-0040
Amherstburg †	9,707	Essex	Essex-Windsor	Essex South	Thomas C. Kilgallin, Clerk-Adm., 271 Sandwich St. South, PO Box 159, Amherstburg N9V 2Z3 – 519/736-0012, Fax: 519/736-5403
Ancaster †	22,496	Hamilton-Wentworth Reg. Mun.	Hamilton-Wentworth	Wentworth North	Trish Sweeney, Clerk-Treas., 300 Wilson St. East, Ancaster L9G 2B9 – 905/648-4611, Fax: 905/648-3557
Anderdon Twp	5,596	Essex	Essex-Windsor	Essex South	David Mailloux, CAO & Clerk., 3400 Middle Side Rd., RR#4, Amherstburg N9V 2Y9 – 519/736-5495, Fax: 519/736-8445
Anson, Hindon & Minden Twp	3,160 ('95)	Haliburton	Victoria-Haliburton	Victoria-Haliburton	Tammy McKelvey, Clerk-Treas., 7 Milne St., PO Box 359, Minden K0M 2K0 – 705/286-1260, Fax: 705/286-4917
The Archipelago Twp	634	Parry Sound District	Parry Sound-Muskoka	Parry Sound	Bruce B. Leclaire, Clerk & CAO, 9 James St., Parry Sound P2A 1T4 – 705/746-4243, Fax: 705/746-7301
Arkona (V)	511	Lambton	Lambton-Middlesex	Lambton	Robert Jefferson, Clerk-Treas., 16 Smith St., PO Box 95, Arkona N0M 1B0 – 519/828-3947, Fax: 519/828-3268
Armour Twp	1,289	Parry Sound District	Parry Sound-Muskoka	Parry Sound	Laura Rowley, Clerk-Treas., PO Box 533, Burk's Falls P0A 1C0 – 705/382-3332, Fax: 705/382-2068
Armstrong Twp	1,303	Timiskaming District	Timiskaming-French River	Timiskaming	Gilles Richard, Adm.-Clerk-Treas., 35 - 10th St., PO Box 546, Earlton P0J 1E0 – 705/563-2375, Fax: 705/563-2093

Cities in CAPITALS; Towns marked †; Separated Towns marked (SE); Villages marked (V); Townships marked Twp; Restructured Counties marked (RS); United Counties marked (U); Development Areas (DA); • means separated for municipal purposes from county. An in-depth listing for municipalities marked with * appears in Part 2 (check Index for page numbers).

MUNICIPALITY	1994 POP.	COUNTY OR DISTRICT	FEDERAL ELECTORAL DISTRICT	PROVINCIAL ELECTORAL DISTRICT	CONTACT PERSON WITH ADDRESS, PHONE & FAX
Arnprior †	6,376	Renfrew	Renfrew-Nipissing-Pembroke	Lanark-Renfrew	Gary M. Buffam, Clerk-Adm., 105 Elgin St. West, PO Box 130, Arnprior K7S 3H4 – 613/623-4231, Fax: 613/623-8091
Arran Twp	1,621	Bruce	Bruce-Grey	Bruce	Stan Dolphin, Clerk-Treas., RR#2, Tara N0H 2N0 – 519/934-2051, Fax: 519/934-3595
Artemesia Twp	2,506	Grey	Bruce-Grey	Grey	Margaret Russell, Clerk-Treas., RR#2, Flesherton N0C 1E0 – 519/924-2208, 924-3019, Fax: 519/924-3806
Arthur (V)	1,960	Wellington	Wellington-Grey-Dufferin-Simcoe	Wellington	Marlene M. Ternan, Clerk-Treas., 146 George St., PO Box 490, Arthur N0G 1A0 – 519/848-2120, Fax: 519/848-3551
Arthur Twp	2,472	Wellington	Wellington-Grey-Dufferin Simcoe	Wellington	Cathy More, Clerk-Treas., General Delivery, Kenilworth N0G 2E0 – 519/848-3620, Fax: 519/848-3228
Ashfield Twp	1,836	Huron	Huron-Bruce	Huron	Linda Andrew, Clerk-Treas., RR#7, Lucknow N0G 2H0 – 519/529-7383, Fax: 519/529-1024
Asphodel Twp	2,418	Peterborough	Peterborough	Hastings-Peterborough	John M. Duchene, Clerk-Treas., RR#3, Hastings K0L 1Y0 – 705/696-2161, Fax: 705/696-3783
Assiginack Twp	751	Manitoulin District	Algoma	Algoma-Manitoulin	Sheila M. Keys, Clerk-Treas., Spragge St., PO Box 238, Manitowaning P0P 1N0 – 705/859-3196, Fax: 705/859-3010
Athens (V)	947	Leeds & Grenville	Leeds-Grenville	Leeds-Grenville	Betty-Ann Hayes, Clerk-Treas., 1 Main St. West, PO Box 159, Athens K0E 1B0 – 613/924-2044, Fax: 613/924-2091
Athol Twp	1,290	Prince Edward	Prince Edward-Hastings	Prince Edward-Lennox-South Hastings	Beverly Williams, Clerk-Treas., PO Box 124, Cherry Valley K0K 1P0 – 613/476-6709, Fax: 613/476-6709
Atikokan Twp	3,632	Rainy River District	Thunder Bay-Atikokan	Rainy River	Susan Bryk, Clerk-Treas., 120 Mark St., PO Box 1330, Atikokan P0T 1C0 – 807/597-2738, Fax: 807/597-6186
Atwood Twp	241	Rainy River District	Kenora-Rainy River	Rainy River	Patrick Giles, Clerk-Treas., 211 - 4 St., PO Box 427, Rainy River P0W 1L0 – 807/852-3529, Fax: 807/852-3529
Augusta Twp	7,285	Leeds & Grenville	Leeds-Grenville	Leeds-Grenville	Ray Gilmour, Adm.-Clerk-Treas., RR#2, Prescott K0E 1T0 – 613/925-4231, Fax: 613/925-3499
Aurora †	34,320	York Reg. Mun.	York North	York North	Lawrence Allison, Clerk, 100 John West Way, PO Box 1000, Aurora L4G 6J1 – 905/727-1375, Fax: 905/841-3483
Aylmer †	6,275	Elgin	Elgin-Norfolk	Elgin	Phyllis Ketchabaw, Clerk, 46 Talbot St. West, Aylmer N5H 1J7 – 519/773-3164, Fax: 519/765-1446
Bagot & Blythfield Twp	1,256	Renfrew	Renfrew-Nipissing-Pembroke	Lanark-Renfrew	Cathy Reddy, Clerk-Treas., PO Box 180, Calabogie K0J 1H0 – 613/752-2222, Fax: 613/752-2617
Baldwin Twp	646	Sudbury District	Algoma	Nickel Belt	Joan Seidel, Clerk-Treas., PO Box 7095, McKerrow P0P 1M0 – 705/869-0225, Fax: 705/869-5049
Bancroft †	2,280	Hastings	Hastings-Frontenac-Lennox & Addington	Hastings-Peterborough	Dean F. Paterson, CAO, 24 Flint St., PO Box 790, Bancroft K0L 1C0 – 613/332-3331, Fax: 613/332-0384
Bangor, Wicklow & McClure Twp	1,007	Hastings	Hastings-Frontenac-Lennox & Addington	Hastings-Peterborough	Donald C. Bloom, Clerk-Treas., PO Box 130, Maynooth K0L 2S0 – 613/338-2811, Fax: 613/338-3292
Barclay Twp	1,416	Kenora	Kenora-Rainy River	Rainy River	Mabel A. Korkola, Clerk-Treas., Site 108, RR#1, PO Box 75, Dryden P8N 2Y4 – 807/937-6200, Fax: 807/937-2045
*BARRIE	71,413	Simcoe	Simcoe Centre	Simcoe Centre	John E. Craig, City Clerk, 70 Collier St., PO Box 400, Barrie L4M 4T5 – 705/726-4242, Fax: 705/739-4243; URL: http://www.city.barrie.on.ca/
Barrie Twp	706	Frontenac	Hastings-Frontenac-Lennox & Addington	Frontenac-Addington	Lynne Dodds, Clerk-Treas., PO Box 250, Cloyne K0H 1K0 – 613/336-8633, Fax: 613/336-9840
Barrie Island Twp	59	Manitoulin District	Algoma	Algoma-Manitoulin	Pam Bond, Clerk-Treas., PO Box 30, Gore Bay P0P 1H0 – 705/282-2991
Barry's Bay (V)	1,055	Renfrew	Renfrew-Nipissing-Pembroke	Renfrew North	Robert J. Norlock, Clerk-Treas., 10 Bay St. South, PO Box 940, Barry's Bay K0J 1B0 – 613/756-2747, Fax: 613/756-0553
Bastard & S. Burgess Twp	2,508	Leeds & Grenville	Leeds-Grenville	Leeds-Grenville	Troy J. McHarg, Clerk, PO Box 500, Delta K0E 1G0 – 613/928-2251, Fax: 613/928-3097
Bath (V)	1,274	Lennox & Addington	Hastings-Frontenac-Lennox & Addington	Prince Edward-Lennox-South Hastings	Sandra E. McNamee, Adm.-Clerk-Treas., 352 Academy St., PO Box 100, Bath K0H 1G0 – 613/352-3361, Fax: 613/352-5726
Bathurst Twp	2,971	Lanark	Lanark-Carleton	Lanark-Renfrew	Cathic Ritchie, Clerk-Treas., RR#4, Perth K7H 3C6 – 613/267-5353, Fax: 613/264-8516

ONTARIO MUNICIPALITIES 4-45

Cities in CAPITALS; Towns marked †; Separated Towns marked (SE); Villages marked (V); Townships marked Twp; Restructured Counties marked (RS); United Counties marked (U); Development Areas (DA); • means separated for municipal purposes from county. An in-depth listing for municipalities marked with * appears in Part 2 (check Index for page numbers).

MUNICIPALITY	1994 POP.	COUNTY OR DISTRICT	FEDERAL ELECTORAL DISTRICT	PROVINCIAL ELECTORAL DISTRICT	CONTACT PERSON WITH ADDRESS, PHONE & FAX
Bayfield (V)	847	Huron	Huron-Bruce	Huron	Patrick M. Graham, Clerk-Treas., PO Box 99, Bayfield N0M 1G0 – 519/565-2455, Fax: 519/565-2333
Bayham Twp	4,152	Elgin	Elgin-Norfolk	Elgin	Donald W. MacLeod, Clerk-Treas., PO Box 160, Straffordville N0J 1Y0 – 519/866-5521, Fax: 519/866-3884
Beachburg (V)	803	Renfrew	Renfrew-Nipissing-Pembroke	Renfrew North	Phyllis McLeese, Clerk-Treas., 181 Main St., PO Box 100, Beachburg K0J 1C0 – 613/582-3625, Fax: 613/582-7046
Beardmore Twp	391	Thunder Bay District	Thunder Bay-Nipigon	Lake Nipigon	Margaret E. Dupuis, Clerk-Treas., 226 Main St., PO Box 270, Beardmore P0T 1G0 – 807/875-2639, Fax: 807/875-2726
Beckwith Twp	4,689	Lanark	Lanark-Carlton	Lanark Renfrew	Yvonne L. Robert, Clerk-Treas., RR#2, Carleton Place K7C 3P2 – 613/257-1539, Fax: 613/257-8996
Bedford Twp	945	Frontenac	Hastings-Frontenac-Lennox & Addington	Frontenac-Addington	M.Micheline Grondin, Clerk, RR#2, Godfrey K0H 1T0 – 613/374-2066, Fax: 613/374-1584
Belle River †	4,353	Essex	Essex-Windsor	Essex-Kent	Austin L. Mousseau, Clerk-Treas., 419 Notre Dame St., PO Box 580, Belle River N0R 1A0 – 519/728-2700, Fax: 519/728-4577
BELLEVILLE	34,954	Hastings	Prince Edward-Hastings	Quinte	William C. Moreton, City Clerk, City Hall, 169 Front St., Belleville K8N 2Y8 – 613/968-6481, Fax: 613/968-9534
Belmont (V)	1,474	Elgin	Elgin-Norfolk	Elgin	Allan Hovi, Clerk-Treas., 189 Main St., Belmont N0L 1B0 – 519/644-1071, Fax: 519/644-0766
Belmont & Methuen Twp	2,877	Peterborough	Peterborough	Hastings-Peterborough	Stephen Kaegi, Clerk-Treas., RR#3, PO Box 10, Havelock K0L 1Z0 – 705/778-2308, Fax: 705/778-5248
Bentinck Twp	3,396	Grey	Bruce-Grey	Grey	Mark Turner, Clerk-Deputy Treas., RR#1, Elmwood N0G 1S0 – 519/364-1909, Fax: 519/364-3785
Bexley Twp	1,209	Victoria	Victoria-Haliburton	Victoria-Haliburton	Helen A. Russell, Clerk-Treas., Grandy Rd., PO Box 90, Coboconk K0M 1K0 – 705/454-3322, Fax: 705/454-2392
Bicroft Twp	543	Haliburton	Victoria-Haliburton	Victoria-Haliburton	Sandra A. McColl, Clerk-Treas., Monck Rd., PO Box 160, Cardiff K0L 1M0 – 613/339-2442, Fax: 613/339-2442
Biddulph Twp	2,194	Middlesex	London-Middlesex	Middlesex	Lawrence G. Hotson, Clerk-Treas., PO Box 190, Lucan N0M 2J0 – 519/227-4491, Fax: 519/227-4998
Billings Twp	481	Manitoulin District	Algoma	Algoma-Manitoulin	Jessie M. Graham, Clerk-Treas., PO Box 34, Kagawong P0P 1J0 – 705/282-2611, Fax: 705/282-3199
Black River-Matheson Twp	3,178	Cochrane District	Timiskaming-French River	Cochrane South	Thomas E. Monahan, Clerk, 429 Park Lane, PO Box 601, Matheson P0K 1N0 – 705/273-2313, Fax: 705/273-2140
Blandford-Blenheim Twp	7,157	Oxford	Oxford	Oxford	Keith I. Reibling, Clerk-Treas., 47 Wilmot St. South, PO Box 100, Drumbo N0J 1G0 – 519/463-5347, Fax: 519/463-5881
Blanshard Twp	1,953	Perth	Perth-Wellington-Waterloo	Perth	Anthony Serpa, Clerk-Treas., RR#6, St Marys N4X 1C8 – 519/229-8707, Fax: 519/229-8928
Blenheim †	4,567	Kent	Essex-Kent	Essex-Kent	Elinor Mifflin, Clerk-Treas., 35 Talbot St. West, PO Box 2128, Blenheim N0P 1A0 – 519/676-5405, Fax: 519/676-0244
Blind River †	3,911	Algoma District	Algoma	Algoma	Ken Corbiere, Clerk-Adm., 11 Hudson St., PO Box 640, Blind River P0R 1B0 – 705/356-2251, Fax: 705/356-7343
Bloomfield (V)	667	Prince Edward	Prince Edward-Hastings	Prince Edward-Lennox-South Hastings	Kim White, Clerk-Treas., 45 Main St., PO Box 190, Bloomfield K0K 1G0 – 613/393-2424, Fax: 613/393-1323
Blue Twp	87	Rainy River District	Kenora-Rainy River	Rainy River	Patrick W. Giles, Clerk-Treas., PO Box 427, Rainy River P0W 1L0 – 807/852-3529, Fax: 807/852-3529
Blyth (V)	964	Huron	Huron-Bruce	Huron	John Stewart, Clerk-Treas., 103 Queen St. South, PO Box 393, Blyth N0M 1H0 – 519/523-4545
Bobcaygeon (V)	2,472	Victoria	Victoria-Haliburton	Victoria-Haliburton	M. Mardelle Braine, Clerk-Treas., 123 East St. South, PO Box 250, Bobcaygeon K0M 1A0 – 705/738-2363, Fax: 705/738-5623
Bonfield Twp	2,027	Nipissing District	Nipissing	Parry Sound	Lise I. McMillan, Adm.-Clerk-Treas., 365 Hwy 531, Bonfield P0H 1E0 – 705/776-2641, Fax: 705/776-1154

Canadian Almanac & Directory 1997

Cities in CAPITALS; Towns marked †; Separated Towns marked (SE); Villages marked (V); Townships marked Twp; Restructured Counties marked (RS); United Counties marked (U); Development Areas (DA); • means separated for municipal purposes from county. An in-depth listing for municipalities marked with * appears in Part 2 (check Index for page numbers).

MUNICIPALITY	1994 POP.	COUNTY OR DISTRICT	FEDERAL ELECTORAL DISTRICT	PROVINCIAL ELECTORAL DISTRICT	CONTACT PERSON WITH ADDRESS, PHONE & FAX
Bosanquet †	4,899	Lambton	Lambton-Middlesex	Lambton	Carol P. McKenzie, Clerk, Louisa St., PO Box 269, Thedford N0M 2N0 – 519/296-4953, Fax: 519/296-5666
Bothwell †	912	Kent	Kent	Chatham-Kent	Attie Dewit, Clerk-Treas., 320 Main St., PO Box 400, Bothwell N0P 1C0 – 519/695-2722, Fax: 519/695-5079
Bracebridge †	11,675	Muskoka Dist. Mun.	Parry Sound-Muskoka	Muskoka-Georgian Bay	R.M. Clarke, CAO, 23 Dominion St. North, PO Box 360, Bracebridge P1L 1R6 – 705/645-5264, Fax: 705/645-7525
Bradford West Gwillimbury †	18,222	Simcoe	York-Simcoe	Simcoe Centre	Juanita Dempster-Evans, Clerk-Adm., 61 Holland St. East, PO Box 160, Bradford L3Z 2A8 – 905/775-5303, Fax: 905/775-0153
Braeside (V)	546	Renfrew	Renfrew-Nipissing-Pembroke	Lanark-Renfrew	Noreen C. Mellema, Clerk-Treas., Centre St., PO Box 40, Braeside K0A 1G0 – 613/623-5433, Fax: 613/623-9423
*BRAMPTON	236,319	Peel Reg. Mun.	Brampton; Bramalea-Gore-Malton	Brampton North; Brampton South	Leonard Mikulich, City Clerk & Director, Administration, 2 Wellington St. West, Brampton L6Y 4R2 – 905/874-2500, Fax: 905/874-2119
Brant Twp	3,267	Bruce	Bruce-Grey	Bruce	Gary Napper, Clerk-Treas., RR#1, Elmwood N0G 1S0 – 519/881-0188
*BRANTFORD	84,500	Brant	Brant	Brantford	Wilf Coulson, City Clerk, City Hall, 100 Wellington Sq., Brantford N3T 2M3 – 519/759-4150, Fax: 519/754-0742
Brantford Twp	6,241	Brant	Brant	Brant-Haldimand	Margaret E. Kiernan, Clerk, 80 Chatham St., PO Box 1295, Brantford N3T 5T6 – 519/756-7470, Fax: 519/756-0662
Brethour Twp	170	Timiskaming District	Timiskaming-French River	Timiskaming	Roland Lachapelle, Clerk-Treas., Belle Vallée P0J 1A0 – 705/647-7632, Fax: 705/647-7632
Brighton †	4,199	Northumberland	Northumberland	Northumberland	Christine Boutilier, Clerk-Treas., 36 Alice St., PO Box 189, Brighton K0K 1H0 – 613/475-0670, Fax: 613/475-3453
Brighton Twp	3,418	Northumberland	Northumberland	Northumberland	Donald J. O'Neil, Clerk-Treas., RR#7, Brighton K0K 1H0 – 613/475-2894, Fax: 613/475-2599
Brock Twp	10,991	Durham Reg. Mun.	Victoria-Haliburton	Durham York	George S. Graham, Clerk, 1 Cameron St. East, PO Box 10, Cannington L0E 1E0 – 705/432-2681, Fax: 705/432-3487
BROCKVILLE	21,582	Leeds & Grenville	Leeds-Grenville	Leeds-Grenville	Brian C. Switzer, CAO-Clerk, Victoria Bldg., 1 King St. West, PO Box 5000, Brockville K6V 7A5 – 613/342-8772, Fax: 613/498-2793; URL: http://www.brockville.com
Bromley Twp	1,170	Renfrew	Renfrew-Nipissing-Pembroke	Renfrew North	Lauretta Rice, Clerk-Treas., RR#1, Douglas K0J 1S0 – 613/649-2342, Fax: 613/649-2770
Brooke Twp	1,877	Lambton	Lambton-Middlesex	Lambton	Gloria Ruth Bedford, Clerk-Treas., RR#7, Alvinston N0N 1A0 – 519/847-5566, Fax: 519/847-5468
Broughan Twp	227	Renfrew	Renfrew-Nipissing-Pembroke	Renfrew North	Murray Hanes, Clerk-Treas., Dacre K0J 1N0 – 613/649-2379, Fax: 613/649-2744
Bruce Twp	1,515	Bruce	Huron Bruce	Bruce	Bob Waram, Clerk-Treas., RR#3, Tiverton N0G 2T0 – 519/368-7066, Fax: 519/368-5196
Bruce Mines †	589	Algoma District	Algoma	Algoma	Kerry Vasey, Clerk-Treas., 56 Taylor St., PO Box 220, Bruce Mines P0R 1C0 – 705/785-3493, Fax: 705/785-3170
Brudenell & Lyndoch Twp	734	Renfrew	Renfrew-Nipissing-Pembroke	Renfrew North	Corinna Frew, Clerk-Treas., PO Box 91, Quadeville K0J 2G0 – 613/758-2651, Fax: 613/758-2192
Brussels (V)	1,127	Huron	Huron-Bruce	Huron	Donna M. White, Clerk-Treas., 399 Turnberry St., PO Box 119, Brussels N0G 1H0 – 519/887-6572, Fax: 519/887-6572
Burford Twp	5,712	Brant	Oxford	Brant Haldimand	John R. Innes, Clerk-Treas., 116 King St. East, PO Box 249, Burford N0E 1A0 – 519/449-2434, Fax: 519/449-1380
Burk's Falls (V)	669	Parry Sound District	Parry Sound-Muskoka	Parry Sound	Jarvis W. Osborne, Clerk-Treas., 172 Ontario St., PO Box 160, Burk's Falls P0A 1C0 – 705/382-3138, Fax: 705/382-2273
Burleigh & Anstruther Twp	1,391	Peterborough	Victoria-Haliburton	Hastings-Peterborough	Gayle P. Bates, CAO, PO Box 128, Apsley K0L 1A0 – 705/656-4445, Fax: 705/656-4446
*BURLINGTON	128,453	Halton Reg. Mun.	Burlington; Halton-Peel	Burlington South-Halton Centre	Ronald C. Lathan, City Clerk, City Hall, 426 Brant St., PO Box 5013, Burlington L7R 3Z6 – 905/335-7777, Fax: 905/335-7881; URL: http://worldchat.com/cob
Burpee Twp	219	Manitoulin District	Algoma	Algoma-Manitoulin	M. Jeanette Clark, Clerk-Treas., General Delivery, Evansville P0P 1E0 – 705/282-3099

Canadian Almanac & Directory 1997

ONTARIO MUNICIPALITIES 4-47

Cities in CAPITALS; Towns marked †; Separated Towns marked (SE); Villages marked (V); Townships marked Twp; Restructured Counties marked (RS); United Counties marked (U); Development Areas (DA); • means separated for municipal purposes from county. An in-depth listing for municipalities marked with * appears in Part 2 (check Index for page numbers).

MUNICIPALITY	1994 POP.	COUNTY OR DISTRICT	FEDERAL ELECTORAL DISTRICT	PROVINCIAL ELECTORAL DISTRICT	CONTACT PERSON WITH ADDRESS, PHONE & FAX
Cache Bay †	673	Nipissing District	Nipissing	Nipissing	Pauline Pinkas, Clerk-Adm., 55 Cache St., PO Box 40, Cache Bay P0H 1G0 – 705/753-1220, Fax: 705/753-5100
Caldwell Twp	1,569	Nipissing District	Timiskaming-French River	Nipissing	Marcelin L. Tellier, Clerk-Treas., 20 Hwy 64, PO Box 12, Verner P0H 2M0 – 705/594-2318, Fax: 705/594-9153
Caledon †	38,894	Peel Reg. Mun.	Halton-Peel	Dufferin-Peel	Marjory Morden, Clerk, 6311 Old Church Rd., PO Box 1000, Caledon East L0N 1E0 – 905/584-2272, Fax: 905/857-7217
Caledonia Twp	1,441	Prescott & Russell	Glengarry-Prescott-Russell	Prescott & Russell	Joanne Bougie-Normand, Clerk-Treas., 6950 County Rd. #22, RR#1, St. Bernardin K0B 1N0 – 613/678-2100, Fax: 613/678-2990
Calvin Twp	562	Nipissing District	Nipissing	Parry Sound	Kathleen Moore, Clerk-Treas., RR#2, Mattawa P0H 1V0 – 705/744-2700, Fax: 705/744-0309
*CAMBRIDGE	100,000 ('96)	Waterloo Reg. Mun.	Cambridge	Cambridge	James Anderson, City Clerk, 73 Water St. North, PO Box 669, Cambridge N1R 5W8 – 519/623-1340, Fax: 519/740-3011
Cambridge Twp	6,002	Prescott & Russell	Glengarry-Prescott-Russell	Prescott & Russell	Roger Brunette, Clerk-Adm., 985 Hwy. 500 West, RR#3, Casselman K0A 1M0 – 613/764-5444, Fax: 613/764-3310
Camden Twp	2,067	Kent	Kent	Chatham-Kent	Shelley Wilkins, Clerk-Adm.-Treas., 25367 Kent Bridge Rd., RR#6, Dresden N0P 1M0 – 519/683-4921, Fax: 519/683-2438
Camden East Twp	4,518	Lennox & Addington	Hastings-Frontenac-Lennox & Addington	Frontenac-Addington	Dorothy Wilson, Clerk-Adm., Centreville K0K 1N0 – 613/378-2475, Fax: 613/378-0033
Campbellford †	3,305	Northumberland	Northumberland	Northumberland	James Timlin, Adm.-Clerk-Treas., 36 Front St. South, PO Box 1056, Campbellford K0L 1L0 – 705/653-1900, Fax: 705/653-5203
Capreol †	3,621	Sudbury Reg. Mun.	Nickel Belt	Sudbury East	Edgar Bérubé, Clerk-Treas., 9 Morin St., PO Box 700, Capreol P0M 1H0 – 705/858-1212, Fax: 705/858-1085
Caradoc Twp	6,117	Middlesex	Lambton-Middlesex	Middlesex	Marion Loker, Clerk-Treas., PO Box 190, Mt. Brydges N0L 1W0 – 519/264-1001, Fax: 519/264-9634
Carden Twp	803	Victoria	Victoria-Haliburton	Victoria-Haliburton	Jean M. Jones, Clerk-Treas., RR#1, Sebright L0K 1W0 – 705/833-2811, Fax: 705/833-2815
Cardiff Twp	674	Haliburton	Hastings-Frontenac-Lennox & Addington	Victoria-Haliburton	Roger J. Hogan, Clerk, RR#3, Bancroft K0L 1C0 – 613/339-2323, Fax: 613/339-3098
Cardinal (V)	1,580	Leeds & Grenville	Leeds-Grenville	SDG & East Grenville	John Walsh, Acting Clerk-Treas., 331 Walter St., PO Box 400, Cardinal K0E 1E0 – 613/657-3266, Fax: 613/657-3001
Carleton Place †	7,483	Lanark	Lanark-Carleton	Lanark-Renfrew	Duncan H. Rogers, Clerk, 175 Bridge St., Carleton Place K7C 2V8 – 613/257-3101, Fax: 613/257-8170
Carling Twp	989	Parry Sound District	Parry Sound-Muskoka	Parry Sound	Susan Murphy, Clerk-Adm., RR#1, Nobel P0G 1G0 – 705/342-5856, Fax: 705/342-9527
Carlow Twp	422	Hastings	Hastings-Frontenac-Lennox & Addington	Hastings-Peterborough	Arlene Douglas, Clerk-Treas., Boulter K0L 1G0 – 613/332-1760, Fax: 613/332-2175
Carnarvon Twp	1,043	Manitoulin District	Algoma	Algoma-Manitoulin	Mary-Ann McCutcheon, Clerk-Treas., PO Box 187, Mindemoya P0P 1S0 – 705/377-5726, Fax: 705/377-5585
Carrick Twp	2,365	Bruce	Bruce-Grey	Bruce	Alex T. Mitchell, Clerk-Treas., PO Box 400, Mildmay N0G 2J0 – 519/367-5330, Fax: 519/367-5252
Casey Twp	411	Timiskaming District	Timiskaming-French River	Timiskaming	Michel Lachapelle, Clerk-Treas., PO Box 460, Belle Vallée P0J 1A0 – 705/647-7257, Fax: 705/647-7257
Casimir, Jennings & Appleby Twp	1,142	Sudbury District	Timiskaming-French River	Sudbury East	Gaétane D. Lemieux, CAO & Clerk-Treas., PO Box 70, St. Charles P0M 2W0 – 705/867-2032, Fax: 705/867-5789
Casselman (V)	2,586	Prescott & Russell	Glengarry-Prescott-Russell	Prescott & Russell	Gilles R. Lortie, Clerk, 751 St. Jean St., PO Box 710, Casselman K0A 1M0 – 613/764-3139, Fax: 613/764-5709
Cavan Twp	5,344	Peterborough	Peterborough	Peterborough	Nancy Davis, Clerk, 1 King St. East, PO Box 189, Millbrook L0A 1G0 – 705/932-2929, Fax: 705/932-3458
Chalk River (V)	923	Renfrew	Renfrew-Nipissing-Pembroke	Renfrew North	Pauline G. Rantz, Clerk-Treas., 15 Main St., PO Box 59, Chalk River K0J 1J0 – 613/589-2985, Fax: 613/589-2015
Chamberlain Twp	366	Timiskaming District	Timiskaming-French River	Timiskaming	Susan Renaud, Clerk-Treas., RR#3, Englehart P0J 1H0 – 705/544-8088, Fax: 705/544-8088

Canadian Almanac & Directory 1997

Cities in CAPITALS; Towns marked †; Separated Towns marked (SE); Villages marked (V); Townships marked Twp; Restructured Counties marked (RS); United Counties marked (U); Development Areas (DA); • means separated for municipal purposes from county. An in-depth listing for municipalities marked with * appears in Part 2 (check Index for page numbers).

MUNICIPALITY	1994 POP.	COUNTY OR DISTRICT	FEDERAL ELECTORAL DISTRICT	PROVINCIAL ELECTORAL DISTRICT	CONTACT PERSON WITH ADDRESS, PHONE & FAX
Chandos Twp	633	Peterborough	Victoria-Haliburton	Hastings-Peterborough	Dorothy Walke, CAO, RR#1, Apsley K0L 1A0 – 705/656-4936, Fax: 705/656-1557
Chapleau Twp	2,872	Sudbury District	Timmins-Chapleau	Nickel Belt	Allan D. Pellow, Clerk & CAO, 20 Pine St., PO Box 129, Chapleau P0M 1K0 – 705/864-1330, Fax: 705/864-1824
Chapman Twp	594	Parry Sound District	Parry Sound-Muskoka	Parry Sound	Linda Saunders, Clerk-Treas., PO Box 70, Magnetawan P0A 1P0 – 705/387-4680, Fax: 705/387-4875
Chapple Twp	893	Rainy River District	Kenora-Rainy River	Rainy River	Doris I. Dyson, Clerk-Treas., PO Box 4, Barwick P0W 1A0 – 807/487-2354, Fax: 807/487-2406
Charlottenburgh Twp	7,670	Stormont, Dundas & Glengarry	Glengarry-Prescott-Russell	Cornwall	Marcel J. Lapierre, Adm.-Clerk, 19687 William St., PO Box 40, Williamstown K0C 2J0 – 613/347-2444, Fax: 613/347-3411
Charlton †	275	Timiskaming District	Timiskaming-French River	Timiskaming	Carolyn M. Ryan, Clerk-Treas., PO Box 50, Charlton P0J 1B0 – 705/544-2363, Fax: 705/544-8188
CHATHAM	39,815	Kent	Kent	Chatham-Kent	Brian W. Knott, City Clerk, Civic Centre, 315 King St. West, PO Box 640, Chatham N7M 5K8 – 519/352-4500, Fax: 519/436-3237
Chatham Twp	5,987	Kent	Kent	Chatham-Kent	Nelson J. Praill, Adm.-Clerk-Treas., 785 St. Clair St. Ext., Chatham N7M 5J7 – 519/352-8260, Fax: 519/352-4188
Chatsworth (V)	482	Grey	Bruce-Grey	Grey	Elizabeth Thompson, Clerk-Treas., 184 Garafraxa St., PO Box 150, Chatsworth N0H 1G0 – 519/794-3232, Fax: 519/794-4654
Chesley †	1,815	Bruce	Bruce-Grey	Bruce	Joan Albright, Clerk-Treas., 112 First Ave. South, PO Box 70, Chesley N0G 1L0 – 519/363-2524
Chesterville (V)	1,458	Stormont	Dundas & Glengarry	Stormont-Dundas	Howard F. Smith, Clerk-Treas., 1 Mill St., Chesterville K0C 1H0 – 613/448-2342, Fax: 613/448-1232
Chisholm Twp	1,191	Nipissing District	Nipissing	Parry Sound	Linda M. Ringler, Clerk-Treas., RR#4, Powassan P0H 1Z0 – 705/724-3526, Fax: 705/724-5099
Christie Twp	541	Parry Sound District	Parry Sound-Muskoka	Parry Sound	Craig Jeffery, Clerk, RR#3, Parry Sound P2A 2W9 – 705/732-2355, Fax: 705/732-1274
Clarence Twp	10,069	Prescott & Russell	Glengarry-Prescott-Russell	Prescott & Russell	415 Lemay St., Clarence Creek K0A 1N0 – 613/488-2570, Fax: 613/488-2324
Clarendon & Miller Twp	483	Frontenac	Hastings-Frontenac-Lennox & Addington	Frontenac-Addington	Donna Gemmill, Clerk-Treas., PO Box 97, Plevna K0H 2M0 – 613/479-2231, Fax: 613/479-2352
*Clarington (Mun.)	57,000 ('96)	Durham Reg. Mun.	Durham	Durham East	Patti Barrie, Clerk, 40 Temperance St., Bowmanville L1C 3A6 – 905/623-3379, Fax: 905/623-4169
Clearview Twp	11,684	Simcoe	Wellington-Grey-Dufferin-Simcoe	Simcoe West	Robert Campbell, Clerk, 217 Gideon St., PO Box 200, Stayner L0M 1S0 – 705/428-6230, Fax: 705/428-0288
Clifford (V)	722	Wellington	Wellington-Grey-Dufferin-Simcoe	Wellington	Dianne Epworth, Clerk-Treas., PO Box 29, Clifford N0G 1M0 – 519/327-8141, Fax: 519/327-8148
Clinton †	3,182	Huron	Huron-Bruce	Huron	C. Marie Jefferson, Clerk-Treas., 23 Albert St., PO Box 400, Clinton N0M 1L0 – 519/482-3997, Fax: 519/482-9183
Cobalt †	1,371	Timiskaming District	Timiskaming-French River	Timiskaming	Bill Rayburn, CAO-Clerk-Treas., 18 Silver St., PO Box 70, Cobalt P0J 1C0 – 705/679-8877, Fax: 705/679-5050
Cobden (V)	902	Renfrew	Renfrew-Nipissing-Pembroke	Renfrew North	Dean Sauriol, Clerk-Treas., 44 Main St., PO Box 40, Cobden K0J 1K0 – 613/646-2282, Fax: 613/646-2283
Cobourg †	15,037	Northumberland	Northumberland	Northumberland	Richard G. Stinson, Clerk, 55 King St. West, Cobourg K9A 2M2 – 905/372-4301, Fax: 905/372-1533
Cochrane †	4,339	Cochrane District	Cochrane-Superior	Cochrane North	Pierre Demers, Clerk & CAO, 171 - 4 Ave., PO Box 490, Cochrane P0L 1C0 – 705/272-4361, Fax: 705/272-6068
Cockburn Island Twp	2	Manitoulin District	Algoma	Algoma-Manitoulin	Austin Clipperton, Clerk-Treas., Walford P0P 2E0 – 705/844-2289, Fax: 705/865-2736
Colborne (V)	1,968	Northumberland	Northumberland	Northumberland	Jean Kernaghan, Clerk-Treas., 1 Toronto St., PO Box 357, Colborne K0K 1S0 – 905/355-2821, Fax: 905/355-3430
Colborne Twp	2,030	Huron	Huron-Bruce	Huron	John Stewart, Clerk, RR#5, Goderich N7A 3Y2 – 519/524-4669, Fax: 519/524-1951
Colchester North Twp	3,891	Essex	Essex-Kent	Essex-South	Norma F. Meloche, Clerk-Treas., 2610 City Road #12, RR#2, Essex N8M 2X6 – 519/776-6476, Fax: 519/776-7171

Cities in CAPITALS; Towns marked †; Separated Towns marked (SE); Villages marked (V); Townships marked Twp; Restructured Counties marked (RS); United Counties marked (U); Development Areas (DA); • means separated for municipal purposes from county. An in-depth listing for municipalities marked with * appears in Part 2 (check Index for page numbers).

MUNICIPALITY	1994 POP.	COUNTY OR DISTRICT	FEDERAL ELECTORAL DISTRICT	PROVINCIAL ELECTORAL DISTRICT	CONTACT PERSON WITH ADDRESS, PHONE & FAX
Colchester South Twp	5,625	Essex	Essex-Kent	Essex-South	Michael W. Girard, Clerk-Adm., 44 King St. East, PO Box 449, Harrow N0R 1G0 – 519/738-2282, Fax: 519/738-3404
Coleman Twp	489	Timiskaming District	Timiskaming-French River	Timiskaming	Claire Bigelow, Clerk-Treas., 10 Prospect Ave., PO Box 40, Cobalt P0J 1C0 – 705/679-8833, Fax: 705/679-8300
Collingwood †	14,673	Simcoe	Wellington-Grey-Dufferin-Simcoe	Simcoe West	Carman K. Morrison, Clerk-Adm., 97 Hurontario St., PO Box 157, Collingwood L9Y 3Z5 – 705/445-1030, Fax: 705/445-2448
Collingwood Twp	3,251	Grey	Wellington-Grey-Dufferin-Simcoe	Grey	Chris Fawcett, Clerk-Mgr., Hillcrest Dr., PO Box 40, Clarksburg N0H 1J0 – 519/599-3070, Fax: 519/599-2474
Conmee Twp	682	Thunder Bay District	Thunder Bay-Nipigon	Port Arthur	Karen Bazilewich, Clerk-Treas., RR#1, Kakabeka Falls P0T 1W0 – 807/475-5229, Fax: 807/475-5229
CORNWALL	46,802	Stormont, Dundas & Glengarry	Stormont-Dundas	Cornwall	Richard Allaire, Clerk & CAO, 360 Pitt St., PO Box 877, Cornwall K6H 5T9 – 613/932-6252, Fax: 613/932-8145; URL: http://www.city.cornwall.on.ca
Cornwall Twp	6,608	Stormont, Dundas & Glengarry	Stormont-Dundas	Cornwall	Bernard J. Chisholm, Clerk-Treas., RR#1, Long Sault K0C 1P0 – 613/933-1162, Fax: 613/933-7876
Cosby, Mason & Martland Twp	1,493	Sudbury District	Timiskaming-French River	Sudbury East	Jody E. Lundy, CAO-Clerk, 17 Dollard St., PO Box 156, Noelville P0M 2N0 – 705/898-2294, Fax: 705/898-2181
Cramahe Twp	3,060	Northumberland	Northumberland	Northumberland	Trudy Merrill, Clerk, PO Box 39, Castleton K0K 1M0 – 905/344-7352, Fax: 905/344-5040
Culross Twp	1,647	Bruce	Huron-Bruce	Bruce	G. Elizabeth Stobo, Clerk-Treas., Gordon St., PO Box 10, Teeswater N0G 2S0 – 519/392-6623, Fax: 519/392-6266
CUMBERLAND	46,368 ('96)	Ottawa-Carleton Reg. Mun.	Carleton-Gloucester	Prescott & Russell	Carmelle Bédard, Clerk, #100, 255 Centrum Blvd., Orleans K1E 3V8 – 613/830-6200, Fax: 613/830-8741; URL: http://www.municipality.cumberland.on.ca
Dack Twp	462	Timiskaming District	Timiskaming-French River	Timiskaming	Louise Williams, Clerk-Treas., RR#2, Englehart P0J 1H0 – 705/544-7525
Dalton Twp	426	Victoria	Victoria-Haliburton	Victoria-Haliburton	Jean M. Jones, Clerk-Treas., RR#1, Sebright L0K 1W0 – 705/833-2011
Darling Twp	499	Lanark	Lanark-Carleton	Lanark-Renfrew	Della Ranger, Clerk-Treas., RR#4, Lanark K0G 1K0 – 613/259-5263, Fax: 613/259-2694
Dawn Twp	1,503	Lambton	Lambton-Middlesex	Lambton	Donna MacDougall, Clerk-Treas., 4591 Lambton Line, RR#4, Dresden N0P 1M0 – 519/692-5148, Fax: 519/692-5511
Day & Bright Add'l. Twp	255	Algoma District	Algoma	Algoma	Deborah Tonelli, Clerk-Treas., RR#2, Thessalon P0R 1L0 – 705/842-5102, Fax: 705/842-5102
Deep River †	4,278	Renfrew	Renfrew-Nipissing-Pembroke	Renfrew North	Larry Simmons, Clerk-Treas., 100 Deep River Rd., PO Box 400, Deep River K0J 1P0 – 613/584-2000, Fax: 613/584-3237
Delaware Twp	2,465	Middlesex	Lambton-Middlesex	Middlesex	Marilyn Loeb, Clerk, 30 Main St., PO Box 70, Delaware N0L 1E0 – 519/652-5441, Fax: 519/652-0412
Delhi Twp	15,134	Haldimand-Norfolk Reg. Mun.	Haldimand-Norfolk	Norfolk	Betteanne M. Cadman, Clerk, 183 Main St., PO Box 182, Delhi N4B 2W9 – 519/582-2100, Fax: 519/582-4571
Deloro (V)	156	Hastings	Hastings-Frontenac-Lennox & Addington	Hastings-Peterborough	Frank Mills, Clerk-Treas., Township of Marmora & Lake, PO Box 459, Marmora K0K 2M0 – 613/472-2629, Fax: 613/472-5330
Denbigh Abinger & Ashby Twp	628	Lennox & Addington	Hastings-Frontenac-Lennox & Addington	Frontenac-Addington	Jack Pauhl, Clerk-Treas., Denbigh K0H 1L0 – 613/333-2736, Fax: 613/333-2736
Derby Twp	2,856	Grey	Bruce-Grey	Grey	Bruce Hoffman, Clerk-Treas., RR#3, Owen Sound N4K 5N5 – 519/376-2672, Fax: 519/376-5284
Deseronto †	1,728	Hastings	Prince Edward-Hastings	Prince Edward-Lennox-South Hastings	Richard J. Beare, Clerk-Adm., 331 Main St., PO Box 310, Deseronto K0K 1X0 – 613/396-2440, Fax: 613/396-3141
Dilke Twp	144	Rainy River District	Kenora-Rainy River	Rainy River	Lise Langlais, Clerk-Treas., PO Box 106, Pinewood P0W 1K0 – 807/483-5891, Fax: 807/483-5891
Dorion Twp	465	Thunder Bay District	Thunder Bay-Nipigon	Lake Nipigon	Helena Tamminen, Clerk-Treas., Dorion Loop Rd., RR#1, Dorion P0T 1K0 – 807/857-2289, Fax: 807/857-2203
Douro Twp	3,511	Peterborough	Peterborough	Hastings-Peterborough	Robert C. Allen, Clerk-Treas. & CAO, Douro K0L 1S0 – 705/652-3374, Fax: 705/652-5061

Cities in CAPITALS; Towns marked †; Separated Towns marked (SE); Villages marked (V); Townships marked Twp; Restructured Counties marked (RS); United Counties marked (U); Development Areas (DA); • means separated for municipal purposes from county. An in-depth listing for municipalities marked with * appears in Part 2 (check Index for page numbers).

MUNICIPALITY	1994 POP.	COUNTY OR DISTRICT	FEDERAL ELECTORAL DISTRICT	PROVINCIAL ELECTORAL DISTRICT	CONTACT PERSON WITH ADDRESS, PHONE & FAX
Dover Twp	3,973	Kent	Kent	Chatham-Kent	M. Dianne Caryn, CAO & Clerk, 515 Grand Ave. West, Chatham N7L 1C5 – 519/354-3350, Fax: 519/354-1664
Downie Twp	2,338	Perth	Perth-Wellington-Waterloo	Perth	Muriel King, Clerk-Treas., PO Box 181, St. Pauls Station N0K 1V0 – 519/271-0619, Fax: 519/271-0647
Drayton (V)	1,333	Wellington	Perth-Wellington-Waterloo	Wellington	Deborah LucasSwitzer, Clerk-Treas., 22 John St., PO Box 160, Drayton N0G 1P0 – 519/638-3097, Fax: 519/638-5102
Dresden †	2,492	Kent	Kent	Chatham-Kent	James L. Babcock, Adm.-Clerk-Treas., 485 St. George St., PO Box 730, Dresden N0P 1M0 – 519/683-4306, Fax: 519/683-6623
Drummond Twp	2,866	Lanark	Lanark-Carleton	Lanark-Renfrew	Linda Vanalstine, Clerk-Treas., RR#6, Perth K7H 3C8 – 613/267-5444, Fax: 613/267-3911
Dryden †	6,300	Kenora District	Kenora-Rainy River	Kenora	Linda R. Lemieux, Clerk, 30 Van Horne Ave., Dryden P8N 2A7 – 807/223-2225, Fax: 807/223-3999
Dubreuilville Twp	864	Algoma District	Timmins-Chapleau	Algoma	Patrice Viel, Clerk-Treas., 23 Pine St., PO Box 149, Dubreuilville P0S 1B0 – 705/884-2340, Fax: 705/884-2626
Dummer Twp	2,847	Peterborough	Peterborough	Hastings-Peterborough	David Clifford, Adm.-Clerk-Treas., 894 South St., PO Box 92, Warsaw K0L 3A0 – 705/652-8392, Fax: 705/652-5044
Dundalk (V)	1,566	Grey	Wellington-Grey-Dufferin-Simcoe	Grey	Bonnie Riddell, Clerk-Adm., 80 Main St. East, PO Box 249, Dundalk N0C 1B0 – 519/923-2144, Fax: 519/923-2685
Dundas †	22,154	Hamilton-Wentworth Reg. Mun.	Hamilton-Wentworth	Wentworth North	Susan Steele, Clerk, 60 Main St., PO Box 8584, Dundas L9H 5E7 – 905/628-6327, Fax: 905/628-5077
Dungannon Twp	1,285	Hastings	Hastings-Frontenac-Lennox & Addington	Hastings-Peterborough	Peter Degeer, Clerk-Treas., L'Amable K0L 2L0 – 613/332-3711, Fax: 613/332-3154
Dunnville †	11,908	Haldimand-Norfolk Reg. Mun.	Haldimand-Norfolk	Brant-Haldimand	Ronald T. Sparks, Clerk-Adm., 111 Broad St. East, PO Box 187, Dunnville N1A 2X5 – 905/774-7595, Fax: 905/774-4294
Dunwich Twp	2,279	Elgin	Elgin-Norfolk	Elgin	Ken Loveland, Clerk-Treas., 156 Main St., PO Box 329, Dutton N0L 1J0 – 519/762-2204, Fax: 519/762-2278
Durham †	2,546	Grey	Bruce-Grey	Grey	Dan Sullivan, Clerk-Treas., 137 Garafraxa St. North, PO Box 639, Durham N0G 1R0 – 519/369-2200, Fax: 519/369-5962
Dutton (V)	1,198	Elgin	Elgin-Norfolk	Elgin	Kim V.H. Watson, Clerk-Treas., 199 Main St., PO Box 59, Dutton N0L 1J0 – 519/762-2736, Fax: 519/762-3739
Dymond Twp	1,242	Timiskaming District	Timiskaming-French River	Timiskaming	John A. Telfer, Clerk-Treas., PO Box 5030, New Liskeard P0J 1P0 – 705/647-6044, Fax: 705/647-6686
Dysart et al Twp	4,702	Haliburton	Victoria-Haliburton	Victoria-Haliburton	Donna L. McCallum, Adm.-Clerk-Treas., Maple Ave., PO Box 389, Haliburton K0M 1S0 – 705/457-1740, Fax: 705/457-1964
Ear Falls Twp	1,097	Kenora District	Kenora-Rainy River	Kenora	Dennis Kristjanson, Clerk-Treas., 15 Spruce St., PO Box 309, Ear Falls P0V 1T0 – 807/222-3624, Fax: 807/222-2384
East Ferris Twp	4,153	Nipissing District	Nipissing	Parry Sound	F. Brad Claridge, Adm.-Clerk-Treas., RR#1, Corbeil P0H 1K0 – 705/752-2740, Fax: 705/752-2452
East Garafraxa Twp	2,012	Dufferin	Wellington-Grey-Dufferin-Simcoe	Dufferin-Peel	Susan M. Stone, Clerk-Treas., RR#3, Orton L0N 1N0 – 519/928-5298; 855-9833, Fax: 519/928-2345
East Gwillimbury †	18,820	York Reg. Mun.	York-Simcoe	Durham-York	Beth A. McKay, Clerk-Adm., 19000 Leslie St., Sharon L0G 1V0 – 905/478-4282, Fax: 905/478-2808
East Hawkesbury Twp	3,153	Prescott & Russell	Glengarry-Prescott-Russell	Prescott & Russell	Réjeanne Clermont, Clerk-Treas., PO Box 340, St. Eugene K0B 1P0 – 613/674-2170, Fax: 613/674-2989
East Luther Grand Valley Twp [a]	2,537	Dufferin	Wellington-Grey-Dufferin-Simcoe	Dufferin-Peel	Jane M. Wilson, Clerk-Treas., 5 Main St. North, PO Box 249, Grand Valley L0N 1G0 – 519/928-5652, Fax: 519/928-2275
East Wawanosh Twp	1,137	Huron	Huron-Bruce	Huron	Winona E. Thompson, Clerk-Treas., PO Box 160, Belgrave N0G 1E0 – 519/357-2880, Fax: 519/357-4214

ONTARIO MUNICIPALITIES 4-51

Cities in CAPITALS; Towns marked †; Separated Towns marked (SE); Villages marked (V); Townships marked Twp; Restructured Counties marked (RS); United Counties marked (U); Development Areas (DA); • means separated for municipal purposes from county. An in-depth listing for municipalities marked with * appears in Part 2 (check Index for page numbers).

MUNICIPALITY	1994 POP.	COUNTY OR DISTRICT	FEDERAL ELECTORAL DISTRICT	PROVINCIAL ELECTORAL DISTRICT	CONTACT PERSON WITH ADDRESS, PHONE & FAX
East Williams Twp	1,311	Middlesex	Lambton-Middlesex	Middlesex	Linda Turmel, Clerk-Treas., 4427 Queen St., RR#1, Ailsa Craig N0M 1A0 – 519/232-4506, Fax: 519/232-9095
*East York (Borough)	98,594	Metro Mun.	Beaches-Woodbine; Broadview-Greenwood; Don Valley East; Don Valley West; Rosedale	Don Mills; York East	William Alexander, Borough Clerk, 850 Coxwell Ave., East York M4C 5R1 – 416/778-2000, Fax: 416/778-9134
East Zorra-Tavistock Twp	7,370	Oxford	Oxford	Oxford	Jeff Carswell, Clerk & Dep. Treas., 90 Loveys St. East, PO Box 100, Hickson N0J 1L0 – 519/462-2697, Fax: 519/462-2961
Eastnor Twp	1,743	Bruce	Bruce-Grey	Bruce	Kelly Thompson, Clerk-Treas., RR#2, PO Box 40, Lion's Head N0H 1W0 – 519/793-3227, Fax: 519/793-3725
Edwardsburgh Twp	4,566	Leeds & Grenville	Leeds-Grenville	SDG & East Grenville	Richard Bennett, Clerk-Treas., 18 Centre St., PO Box 129, Spencerville K0E 1X0 – 613/658-3055, Fax: 613/658-3445
Eganville (V)	1,255	Renfrew	Renfrew-Nipissing-Pembroke	Renfrew North	Richard K. Schilling, Clerk-Adm., 85 Bonnechere St., PO Box 249, Eganville K0J 1T0 – 613/628-3101, Fax: 613/628-1336
Egremont Twp	2,391	Grey	Wellington-Grey-Dufferin-Simcoe	Grey	Brenda Anderson, Clerk-Treas., PO Box 183, Mount Forest N0G 2L0 – 519/334-3480, Fax: 519/334-3388
Ekfrid Twp	2,202	Middlesex	Lambton-Middlesex	Middlesex	Janneke Newitt, Clerk-Treas., 48 Wellington St., PO Box 276, Appin N0L 1A0 – 519/289-2016, Fax: 519/289-2331
Elderslie Twp	1,158	Bruce	Bruce-Grey	Bruce	Connie McKinnon, Clerk-Treas., PO Box 57, Chesley N0G 1L0 – 519/363-3039, Fax: 519/363-2604
Eldon Twp	2,804	Victoria	Victoria-Haliburton	Victoria-Haliburton	Donald A. Grant, Adm.-Clerk-Treas., PO Box 247, Kirkfield K0M 2B0 – 705/438-3141, Fax: 705/438-5212
Elizabethtown Twp	7,240	Leeds & Grenville	Leeds-Grenville	Leeds-Grenville	Stephen McDonald, Adm. & Clerk-Treas., 6544 New Dublin Rd., RR#2, Addison K0E 1A0 – 613/345-7480, Fax: 613/345-7235
Ellice Twp	3,104	Perth	Perth-Wellington-Waterloo	Perth	Arnold Siroen, Clerk-Treas., Rostock N0K 1T0 – 519/393-6237, Fax: 519/593-5445
ELLIOT LAKE	12,387	Algoma District	Algoma	Algoma-Manitoulin	Larry E. Burling, Clerk, 45 Hillside Dr. North, Elliot Lake P5A 1X5 – 705/848-2287, Fax: 705/461-7244
Elma Twp	3,978	Perth	Lanark-Carleton	Perth	George S. Tucker, Clerk-Treas., 194 King St., Atwood N0G 1B0 – 519/356-2231, Fax: 519/356-2161
Elora (V)	3,116	Wellington	Wellington-Grey-Dufferin-Simcoe	Wellington	Donald D. Wilson, Adm.-Clerk-Treas., 1 MacDonald Sq., PO Box 508, Elora N0B 1S0 – 519/846-9691, Fax: 519/846-2074
Elzevir & Grimsthorpe Twp	731	Hastings	Hastings-Frontenac-Lennox & Addington	Hastings-Peterborough	Jane Sopha, Clerk-Treas., RR#3, PO Box 63, Tweed K0K 3J0 – 613/478-5818, Fax: 613/478-5818
Emily Twp	6,254	Victoria	Victoria-Haliburton	Victoria-Haliburton	Nancy Paish, Clerk-Treas., RR#4, Omemee K0L 2W0 – 705/799-5254, Fax: 705/799-5957
Emo Twp	1,197	Rainy River District	Kenora-Rainy River	Rainy River	Brenda J. Cooke, Clerk-Adm., 39 Queen St., PO Box 358, Emo P0W 1E0 – 807/482-2378, Fax: 807/482-2741
Englehart †	1,655	Timiskaming District	Timiskaming-French River	Timiskaming	Brian Koski, Adm.-Clerk-Treas., 61 Fifth Ave., PO Box 399, Englehart P0J 1H0 – 705/544-2244, Fax: 705/544-8737
Enniskillen Twp	3,159	Lambton	Lambton-Middlesex	Lambton	Duncan McTavish, Clerk-Adm., 4465 Rokeby Line, RR#1, Petrolia N0N 1R0 – 519/882-2490, Fax: 519/882-3335
Ennismore Twp	4,239	Peterborough	Peterborough	Peterborough	Norman K. Kyle, Adm.-Clerk-Treas., 549 Ennis Rd., Ennismore K0L 1T0 – 705/292-8903, Fax: 705/292-8964
Eramosa Twp	5,764	Wellington	Guelph-Wellington	Wellington	Virginia Sinnott, Clerk & CAO, RR#1, Rockwood N0B 2K0 – 519/856-9951, Fax: 519/856-2240
Erie Beach (V)	236	Kent	Essex-Kent	Essex-Kent	Lisa Enid Docherty, Clerk, PO Box 100, Erieau N0P 1N0 – 519/676-3681, Fax: 519/676-1050
Erieau (V)	482	Kent	Essex-Kent	Essex-Kent	Verne M. Burke, Clerk-Treas., Ross Lane, PO Box 121, Erieau N0P 1N0 – 519/676-3681, Fax: 519/676-1050

Canadian Almanac & Directory 1997

Cities in CAPITALS; Towns marked †; Separated Towns marked (SE); Villages marked (V); Townships marked Twp; Restructured Counties marked (RS); United Counties marked (U); Development Areas (DA); • means separated for municipal purposes from county. An in-depth listing for municipalities marked with * appears in Part 2 (check Index for page numbers).

MUNICIPALITY	1994 POP.	COUNTY OR DISTRICT	FEDERAL ELECTORAL DISTRICT	PROVINCIAL ELECTORAL DISTRICT	CONTACT PERSON WITH ADDRESS, PHONE & FAX
Erin (V)	2,414	Wellington	Guelph-Wellington	Wellington	Kathryn Ironmonger, Clerk-Adm., 109 Main St., PO Box 149, Erin N0B 1T0 – 519/833-2604, Fax: 519/833-7458
Erin Twp	7,468	Wellington	Guelph-Wellington	Wellington	R. Murray Clarke, Clerk-Adm., 5684 Hwy.25, PO Box 250, Hillsburgh N0B 1Z0 – 519/855-4407, Fax: 519/855-4821
Ernestown Twp	11,343	Lennox & Addington	Hastings-Frontenac-Lennox & Addington	Prince Edward-Lennox-South Hastings	Michael G. Wade, CAO, 263 Main St., PO Box 70, Odessa K0H 2H0 – 613/386-7351, Fax: 613/386-3833
Escott, Front of Twp	1,194	Leeds & Grenville	Leeds-Grenville	Leeds-Grenville	Marilyn Noseworthy, Clerk-Treas., 1367 County Rd. 2, Mallorytown K0E 1R0 – 613/659-3455
Espanola †	5,144	Sudbury District	Algoma	Algoma-Manitoulin	Merwyn P. Sheppard, Clerk-Treas.-Adm., #2, 100 Tudhope St., PO Box 638, Espanola P5E 1S6 – 705/869-1540, Fax: 705/869-0083
Essa Twp	15,400	Simcoe	Simcoe Centre	Simcoe West	Brenda Sigouin, Clerk-Adm., PO Box 10, Angus L0M 1B0 – 705/424-9770, Fax: 705/424-2367
Essex †	6,745	Essex	Essex-Windsor	Essex-South	Wayne Miller, Clerk-Adm., 33 Talbot St. South, Essex N8M 1A8 – 519/776-7336, Fax: 519/776-8811
*ETOBICOKE	316,800	Metro Mun.	Etobicoke Centre; Etobicoke-Lakeshore; Etobicoke North; York West	Etobicoke-Rexdale; Etobicoke West; Etobicoke-Lakeshore; Etobicoke-Humber	Brenda Glover, Clerk-Treas. & Commissioner, Administrative Services, City Hall, 399 The West Mall, Etobicoke M9C 2Y2 – 416/394-8000, Fax: 416/394-8895
Euphemia Twp	1,076	Lambton	Lambton-Middlesex	Lambton	Joan Webster, Clerk-Treas., RR#2, Bothwell N0P 1C0 – 519/695-2312, Fax: 519/695-3705
Euphrasia Twp	1,374	Grey	Bruce-Grey	Grey	Debbie Robertson, Clerk-Treas., RR#2, Meaford N4L 1W6 – 519/538-2030, Fax: 519/538-5651
Evanturel Twp	513	Timiskaming District	Timiskaming-French River	Timiskaming	Lorne A. LaCarte, Clerk-Treas., PO Box 209, Englehart P0J 1H0 – 705/544-8200, Fax: 705/544-8200
Exeter †	4,384	Huron	Huron-Bruce	Huron	Elizabeth Bell, Clerk-Treas., PO Box 759, Exeter N0M 1S6 – 519/235-0310, Fax: 519/235-3304
Faraday Twp	1,416	Hastings	Hastings-Frontenac-Lennox & Addington	Hastings-Peterborough	Elizabeth Mackey, Clerk-Treas., PO Box 929, Bancroft K0L 1C0 – 613/332-3638, Fax: 613/332-3006
Fauquier-Strickland Twp	671	Cochrane District	Cochrane-Superior	Cochrane North	Louisette Morin, Deputy Clerk-Treas., 25 Grzela Rd., PO Box 40, Fauquier P0L 1G0 – 705/339-2521, Fax: 705/339-2421
Fenelon Twp	5,567	Victoria	Victoria-Haliburton	Victoria-Haliburton	Nancy Wright-Laking, Clerk, Cameron K0M 1G0 – 705/887-3880, Fax: 705/887-3946
Fenelon Falls (V)	1,806	Victoria	Victoria-Haliburton	Victoria-Haliburton	Joanne Young, Clerk, 21 Market St., PO Box 179, Fenelon Falls K0M 1N0 – 705/887-3133, Fax: 705/887-4337
Fergus †	8,008	Wellington	Wellington-Grey-Dufferin-Simcoe	Wellington	William J. Tigert, Clerk-Treas. & CAO, 198 St. Andrew St. West, PO Box 10, Fergus N1M 2W7 – 519/843-3250, Fax: 519/843-7601
Field Twp	639	Nipissing District	Timiskaming-French River	Nipissing	Robert Courchesne, Clerk-Treas., 110 Morin St., PO Box 70, Field P0H 1M0 – 705/758-6659, Fax: 705/758-9529
Finch (V)	441	Stormont, Dundas & Glengarry	Stormont-Dundas	SDG & East Grenville	Madeleine Brown, Clerk-Treas., PO Box 200, Finch K0C 1K0 – 613/984-2525, Fax: 613/984-0168
Finch Twp	2,582	Stormont, Dundas & Glengarry	Stormont-Dundas	SDG & East Grenville	Arnott V. Empey, Clerk-Treas., 2 Victoria St., PO Box 99, Berwick K0C 1G0 – 613/984-2821, Fax: 613/984-2908
Flamborough †	30,972	Hamilton-Wentworth Reg. Mun.	Hamilton-Wentworth	Wentworth North	M. Jane Lee, Clerk, 163 Dundas St. East, PO Box 50, Waterdown L0R 2H0 – 905/689-7351; Ham. line 524-0322; Tor. line 825-217, Fax: 905/689-3310
Flesherton (V)	575	Grey	Bruce-Grey	Grey	Christine C. Kinsman, Clerk-Treas., 4 Elizabeth St., PO Box 99, Flesherton N0C 1E0 – 519/924-2609, Fax: 519/924-2938
Foley Twp	1,427	Parry Sound District	Parry Sound-Muskoka	Parry Sound	William B. Fox, Clerk-Adm., RR#2, Parry Sound P2A 2W8 – 705/378-2485, Fax: 705/378-5121
Forest †	2,795	Lambton	Lambton-Middlesex	Lambton	John Byrne, Clerk-Adm., 40 King St. West, PO Box 610, Forest N0N 1J0 – 519/786-2335, Fax: 519/786-2135
Fort Erie †	26,221	Niagara Reg. Mun.	Erie	Niagara South	Carolyn Booth, Clerk, 1 Civic Centre, Fort Erie L2A 2S6 – 905/871-1600, Fax: 905/871-4022

ONTARIO MUNICIPALITIES 4-53

Cities in CAPITALS; Towns marked †; Separated Towns marked (SE); Villages marked (V); Townships marked Twp; Restructured Counties marked (RS); United Counties marked (U); Development Areas (DA); • means separated for municipal purposes from county. An in-depth listing for municipalities marked with * appears in Part 2 (check Index for page numbers).

MUNICIPALITY	1994 POP.	COUNTY OR DISTRICT	FEDERAL ELECTORAL DISTRICT	PROVINCIAL ELECTORAL DISTRICT	CONTACT PERSON WITH ADDRESS, PHONE & FAX
Fort Frances †	8,514	Rainy River District	Kenora-Rainy River	Rainy River	Glenn W. Treftlin, Clerk, 320 Portage Ave., PO Box 38, Fort Frances P9A 3M5 – 807/274-5323, Fax: 807/274-8479
Frankford (V)	1,971	Hastings	Prince Edward-Hastings	Quinte	David Pearson, Clerk-Treas., 12 Trent St. North, PO Box 388, Frankford K0K 2C0 – 613/398-6200, Fax: 613/398-8826
Fullarton Twp	1,627	Perth	Perth-Wellington-Waterloo	Perth	Donald Feeney, Clerk-Treas., Fullarton N0K 1H0 – 519/229-8828, Fax: 519/229-8914
Galway & Cavendish Twp	685	Peterborough	Victoria-Haliburton	Hastings-Peterborough	Joan McCausland, Clerk-Treas., Kinmount K0M 2A0 – 705/488-2981, Fax: 705/488-2993
Gananoque (SE)	4,973	Leeds & Grenville	Leeds-Grenville	Leeds-Grenville	Corinne Wendt, Clerk-Treas., 30 King St. East, PO Box 100, Gananoque K7G 2T6 – 613/382-2149, Fax: 613/382-8587
Gauthier Twp	134	Timiskaming District	Timiskaming-French River	Timiskaming	Dianne Quinn, Sec.-Treas., 82 McPherson St., PO Box 65, Dobie P0K 1B0 – 705/568-8951, Fax: 705/568-8951
Georgian Bay Twp	2,074	Muskoka Dist. Mun.	Parry Sound-Muskoka	Muskoka-Georgian Bay	Winanne Grant, Clerk-Adm., RR#1, Port Severn L0K 1S0 – 705/538-2337, Fax: 705/538-1850
Georgina †	30,802	York Reg. Mun.	York-Simcoe	Durham-York	Larry R. Simpson, Clerk, Civic Centre, RR#2, Keswick L4P 3G1 – 905/476-4301, Fax: 905/476-8100
Geraldton †	2,578	Thunder Bay District	Cochrane-Superior	Lake Nipigon	Roy T. Sinclair, Clerk & CAO, 301 East St., PO Box 70, Geraldton P0T 1M0 – 807/854-1100, Fax: 807/854-1947
Gillies Twp	487	Thunder Bay District	Thunder Bay-Atikokan	Fort William	Orma Kempe, Clerk-Treas., South Gillies P0T 2V0 – 807/475-3185, Fax: 807/473-0767
Glackmeyer Twp	1,059	Cochrane District	Cochrane-Superior	Cochrane North	Jean-Pierre Ouellette, Clerk-Treas.-CAO, PO Box 1867, Cochrane P0L 1C0 – 705/272-4313, Fax: 705/272-2885
Glamorgan Twp	619	Haliburton	Victoria-Haliburton	Victoria-Haliburton	Glen Madill, Clerk-Treas., PO Box 70, Gooderham K0M 1R0 – 705/447-2410, Fax: 705/447-3180
Glanbrook Twp	10,149	Hamilton-Wentworth Reg. Mun.	Hamilton-Wentworth	Wentworth East	Harry Kooyman, Clerk, 4280 Binbrook Rd., RR#1, Binbrook L0R 1C0 – 905/692-9191, Fax: 905/692-9199
Glencoe (V)	2,054	Middlesex	Lambton-Middlesex	Middlesex	William Black, Clerk-Treas., 153 McKellar St., PO Box 218, Glencoe N0L 1M0 – 519/287-2015, Fax: 519/287-2359
Glenelg Twp	1,030	Grey	Bruce-Grey	Grey	John S. Black, Clerk-Treas., RR#1, Markdale N0C 1H0 – 519/369-5131
*GLOUCESTER	110,000 ('95)	Ottawa-Carleton Reg. Mun.	Carleton-Gloucester; Ottawa South; Ottawa Vanier	Carleton East; Ottawa East; Ottawa-Rideau	Michèle Giroux, Clerk, 1400 Blair Pl., PO Box 8333, Gloucester K1G 3V5 – 613/748-4100, Fax: 613/748-0235; URL: http://www.city.gloucester.on.ca/
Goderich †	7,500	Huron	Huron-Bruce	Huron	Larry J. McCabe, Clerk-Adm., 57 West St., Goderich N7A 2K5 – 519/524-8344, Fax: 519/524-7209
Goderich Twp	2,503	Huron	Huron-Bruce	Huron	Suzanne Vodden, Clerk-Treas., RR#3, Clinton N0M 1L0 – 519/482-9804, Fax: 519/482-9516
Golden Twp	2,183	Kenora District	Kenora-Rainy River	Kenora	Sten Lif, CAO & Clerk, PO Box 190, Balmertown P0V 1C0 – 807/735-2096, Fax: 807/735-2286
Gordon Twp	448	Manitoulin District	Algoma	Algoma-Manitoulin	Dorothy Field, Clerk-Treas., PO Box 120, Gore Bay P0P 1H0 – 705/282-2702, Fax: 705/282-2702
Gore Bay †	895	Manitoulin District	Algoma	Algoma-Manitoulin	Joyce Foster, Clerk-Treas. & CAO, 15 Water St., PO Box 298, Gore Bay P0P 1H0 – 705/282-2420, Fax: 705/282-3076
Gosfield North Twp	4,500	Essex	Essex-Kent	Essex-South	Brian Weaver, Clerk-Adm., 122 Fox St., PO Box 130, Cottam N0R 1B0 – 519/839-4844, Fax: 519/839-5566
Gosfield South Twp	7,604	Essex	Essex-Kent	Essex-South	Dan M. DiGiovanni, Clerk-Adm., 2021 Division Rd. North, Kingsville N9Y 2Y9 – 519/733-2305, Fax: 519/733-8108
Goulbourn Twp	19,350 ('95)	Ottawa-Carleton Reg. Mun.	Nepean	Carleton	Moira A. Winch, Clerk, PO Box 189, Stittsville K2S 1A3 – 613/836-4864, Fax: 613/831-2279
Grand Bend (V)	954	Lambton	Lambton-Middlesex	Lambton	Paul Turnbull, Clerk-Treas., 4 Ontario St. North, PO Box 340, Grand Bend N0M 1T0 – 519/238-8461, Fax: 519/238-8577
Grattan Twp	1,248	Renfrew	Renfrew-Nipissing-Pembroke	Renfrew North	Thomas J. Gallagher, Clerk-Treas., RR#2, Eganville K0J 1T0 – 613/628-2728, Fax: 613/628-2855
Gravenhurst †	8,941	Muskoka Dist. Mun.	Parry Sound-Muskoka	Muskoka-Georgian Bay	William E. Winegard, CAO-Clerk, 190 Harvie St., Gravenhurst P1P 1S9 – 705/687-3412, Fax: 705/687-7016

Canadian Almanac & Directory 1997

Cities in CAPITALS; Towns marked †; Separated Towns marked (SE); Villages marked (V); Townships marked Twp; Restructured Counties marked (RS); United Counties marked (U); Development Areas (DA); • means separated for municipal purposes from county. An in-depth listing for municipalities marked with * appears in Part 2 (check Index for page numbers).

MUNICIPALITY	1994 POP.	COUNTY OR DISTRICT	FEDERAL ELECTORAL DISTRICT	PROVINCIAL ELECTORAL DISTRICT	CONTACT PERSON WITH ADDRESS, PHONE & FAX
Greenock Twp	1,684	Bruce	Bruce-Grey	Bruce	Audrey E. Wells, Clerk-Treas., RR#1, Cargill N0G 1J0 – 519/366-2226, Fax: 519/366-2484
Grey Twp	2,036	Huron	Huron-Bruce	Huron	Brad Knight, Clerk-Treas., RR#3, Brussels N0G 1H0 – 519/887-6268, Fax: 519/887-6231
Griffith & Matawatchan Twp	339	Renfrew	Renfrew-Nipissing-Pembroke	Renfrew North	Audrey Youmans, Clerk-Treas., Hwy. 41, Griffith K0J 2R0 – 613/333-2789, Fax: 613/333-5213
Grimsby †	18,925	Niagara Reg. Mun.	Lincoln	Lincoln	Kathryn Vout, Clerk, 160 Livingston Ave., PO Box 159, Grimsby L3M 4G3 – 905/945-9634, Fax: 905/945-5010
*GUELPH	93,000	Wellington	Guelph-Wellington	Guelph	Lois A. Giles, Clerk & Director, Information Services, 59 Carden St., Guelph N1H 3A1 – 519/822-1260, Fax: 519/763-1269
Guelph Twp	3,045	Wellington	Guelph-Wellington	Wellington	Janice Sheppard, Clerk-Adm., PO Box 20030, Guelph N1H 6H6 – 519/822-4661, Fax: 519/822-4044
Hagar Twp	881	Sudbury District	Timiskaming-French River	Sudbury East	Lorraine Demore, Clerk-Treas., 21 Main St. South, PO Box 79, Markstay P0M 2G0 – 705/853-4536, Fax: 705/853-4964
Hagarty & Richards Twp	1,604	Renfrew	Renfrew-Nipissing-Pembroke	Renfrew North	Lorna Hudder, Clerk-Treas., RR#2, Killaloe K0J 2A0 – 613/757-2344, Fax: 613/757-2927
Hagerman Twp	452	Parry Sound District	Parry Sound-Muskoka	Parry Sound	Muriel Junck, Clerk-Treas., General Delivery, Dunchurch P0A 1C0 – 705/389-2466, Fax: 705/389-1855
Haileybury †	4,666	Timiskaming District	Timiskaming-French River	Timiskaming	Diane R. Beatty, Clerk-Treas., 451 Meridian Ave., Bag D, Haileybury P0J 1K0 – 705/672-3363, Fax: 705/672-3200
Haldimand †	21,151	Haldimand-Norfolk Reg. Mun.	Haldimand-Norfolk	Brant-Haldimand	Janis Lankester, Clerk, 45 Munsee St. North, PO Box 400, Cayuga N0A 1E0 – 905/772-3324, Fax: 905/772-3542
Haldimand Twp	4,131	Northumberland	Northumberland	Northumberland	Terrence J. Korotki, Clerk-Treas. & CAO, PO Box 70, Grafton K0K 2G0 – 905/349-2822, Fax: 905/349-3259
Hallowell Twp	4,101	Prince Edward	Prince Edward-Hastings	Prince Edward-Lennox-South Hastings	Malcolm G. (Mac) MacDonald, Clerk-Treas., RR#1, Picton K0K 2T0 – 613/393-2011, Fax: 613/393-5792
Halton Hills †	38,763	Halton Reg. Mun.	Halton-Peel	Halton North	Janet Lunn Stewart, Clerk, 1 Halton Hills Dr., PO Box 128, Georgetown L7G 5G2 – 905/873-2600, Fax: 905/873-2347
*HAMILTON	318,947	Hamilton-Wentworth Reg. Mun.	Hamilton East; Ham. Mountain; Ham.-Wentworth; Ham. West; Lincoln	Ham. Centre; Ham. East; Ham. West; Ham. Mountain; Wentworth East	Joseph J. Schatz, City Clerk, City Hall, 71 Main St. West, Hamilton L8N 3T4 – 905/546-2700, Fax: 905/546-2095
Hamilton Twp	9,470	Northumberland	Northumberland	Northumberland	Peggy Cramp, Clerk & CAO, PO Box 1060, Cobourg K9A 4W5 – 905/342-2810, Fax: 905/342-2818
Hanover †	6,538	Grey	Bruce-Grey	Grey	Robert Casselman, Clerk-Adm., 341 - 10 St., Hanover N4N 2P1 – 519/364-2780, Fax: 519/364-6456
Harley Twp	617	Timiskaming District	Timiskaming-French River	Timiskaming	Michel Lachapelle, Clerk-Treas., RR#2, New Liskeard P0J 1P0 – 705/647-5439, Fax: 705/647-5439
Harris Twp	535	Timiskaming District	Timiskaming-French River	Timiskaming	Wilda A. Gibson, Clerk-Treas., RR#3, Site 4-96, New Liskeard P0J 1P0 – 705/647-5094
Harriston †	1,900	Wellington	Wellington-Grey-Dufferin-Simcoe	Wellington	Eleanore Gordon, Clerk-Treas., 68 Elora St., PO Box 10, Harriston N0G 1Z0 – 519/338-3444, Fax: 519/338-2359
Harrow †	2,656	Essex	Essex-Kent	Essex-South	Jerome E. Marion, Adm. & Clerk-Treas., 44 King St. East, PO Box 129, Harrow N0R 1G0 – 519/738-2523, Fax: 519/738-9040
Harvey Twp	3,059	Peterborough	Victoria-Haliburton	Hastings-Peterborough	John W. Millage, Adm.-Clerk-Treas., PO Box 130, Buckhorn K0L 1J0 – 705/657-8883, Fax: 705/657-9077
Harwich Twp	6,116	Kent	Kent-Essex	Essex-Kent	W. Michael Phipps, Adm.-Clerk, 21633 Communication Rd., PO Box 2022, Chatham N7M 5L9 – 519/436-1122, Fax: 519/436-1127
Hastings (V)	1,106	Northumberland	Northumberland	Northumberland	Margaret Montgomery, Clerk-Treas., 6 Albert St. East, PO Box 250, Hastings K0L 1Y0 – 705/696-2351, Fax: 705/696-2323
Havelock (V)	1,307	Peterborough	Peterborough	Hastings-Peterborough	Donald L. Kelloway, Adm.-Clerk-Treas., 1 Oak St., PO Box 190, Havelock K0L 1Z0 – 705/778-2282, Fax: 705/778-5129

ONTARIO MUNICIPALITIES 4-55

Cities in CAPITALS; Towns marked †; Separated Towns marked (SE); Villages marked (V); Townships marked Twp; Restructured Counties marked (RS); United Counties marked (U); Development Areas (DA); • means separated for municipal purposes from county. An in-depth listing for municipalities marked with * appears in Part 2 (check Index for page numbers).

MUNICIPALITY	1994 POP.	COUNTY OR DISTRICT	FEDERAL ELECTORAL DISTRICT	PROVINCIAL ELECTORAL DISTRICT	CONTACT PERSON WITH ADDRESS, PHONE & FAX
Hawkesbury †	9,871	Prescott & Russell	Glengarry-Prescott-Russell	Prescott & Russell	J. Jacques Poulin, Clerk, 600 Higginson St., Hawkesbury K6A 1H1 – 613/632-4888, Fax: 613/632-2463
Hay Twp	2,184	Huron	Huron-Bruce	Huron	Janisse Zimmerman, Clerk-Treas., Mill St., PO Box 250, Zurich N0M 2T0 – 519/236-4351, Fax: 519/236-4329
Head, Clara & Maria Twp	264	Renfrew	Renfrew-Nipissing-Pembroke	Renfrew North	Diane Beauchamp, Clerk-Treas., Stonecliffe K0J 2K0 – 613/586-2526, Fax: 613/586-2596
Hearst †	5,529	Cochrane District	Cochrane-Superior	Cochrane North	Louis Corbeil, Clerk, 925 Alexandra St., PO Bag 5000, Hearst P0L 1N0 – 705/362-4341, Fax: 705/362-5902
Hensall (V)	1,210	Huron	Huron-Bruce	Huron	Luanne F. Phair, Clerk-Treas., 108 King St., PO Box 279, Hensall N0M 1X0 – 519/262-2812, Fax: 519/262-2821
Hepworth (V)	462	Bruce	Bruce-Grey	Bruce	William Johnston, Clerk, PO Box 69, Hepworth N0H 1P0 – 519/935-2911, Fax: 519/935-2911
Herschel Twp	1,226	Hastings	Hastings-Frontenac-Lennox & Addington	Hastings-Peterborough	Erma Dafoe, Clerk-Treas., RR#2, Bancroft K0L 1C0 – 613/332-3757, Fax: 613/332-5609
Hibbert Twp	1,340	Perth	Perth-Wellington-Waterloo	Perth	Patricia Taylor, Clerk-Treas., PO Box 129, Dublin N0K 1E0 – 519/345-2931, Fax: 519/345-2901
Highgate (V)	418	Kent	Kent	Essex-Kent	Rita Jackson, Clerk-Treas., 291 King St., PO Box 198, Highgate N0P 1T0 – 519/678-3936, Fax: 519/678-3936
Hilliard Twp	245	Timiskaming District	Timiskaming-French River	Timiskaming	Janet Gore, Clerk-Treas., RR#3, PO Box 12, Thornloe P0J 1S0 – 705/563-2593, Fax: 705/563-2593
Hillier Twp	1,700	Prince Edward	Prince Edward-Hastings	Prince Edward-Lennox-South Hastings	Brian M Quibell, Clerk-Treas., PO Box 20, Hillier K0K 2J0 – 613/399-3377
Hilton Twp	223	Algoma District	Algoma	Algoma	E. Ann Langer, Clerk-Treas., PO Box 205, Hilton Beach P0R 1G0 – 705/246-2472, Fax: 705/246-0132
Hilton Beach (V)	223	Algoma District	Algoma	Algoma	Gloria Fischer, Clerk-Treas., PO Box 25, Hilton Beach P0R 1G0 – 705/246-2242, Fax: 705/246-2913
Himsworth North Twp	2,993	Parry Sound District	Parry Sound-Muskoka	Parry Sound	Virginia Onley, Clerk, 280 Main St. North, PO Box 100, Callander P0H 1H0 – 705/752-1410, Fax: 705/752-3116
Himsworth South Twp	1,518	Parry Sound District	Parry Sound-Muskoka	Parry Sound	Judith Gauthier, Clerk-Treas., 196 Main St. West, PO Box 159, Powassan P0H 1Z0 – 705/724-2740, Fax: 705/724-3872
Hinchinbrooke Twp	1,118	Frontenac	Hastings-Frontenac-Lennox & Addington	Frontenac-Addington	Heather J. Fox, Clerk-Treas., RR#2, Godfrey K0H 1T0 – 613/374-2619, Fax: 613/374-1399
Holland Twp	2,748	Grey	Bruce-Grey	Grey	Arnold Rosenburg, Clerk-Treas., RR#3, Holland Centre N0H 1R0 – 519/794-2307
Hope Twp	3,612	Northumberland	Northumberland	Northumberland	Frances (Fran) Aird, Adm.-Clerk-Treas., 5325 County Road 10, PO Box 85, Port Hope L1A 3V9 – 905/753-2230, Fax: 905/753-2434
Hornepayne Twp	1,424	Algoma District	Cochrane-Superior	Algoma	Susan Smith, Clerk, 68 Front St., PO Box 370, Hornepayne P0M 1Z0 – 807/868-2020, Fax: 807/868-2787
Horton Twp	2,325	Renfrew	Renfrew-Nipissing-Pembroke	Lanark-Renfrew	Mackie J. McLaren, Clerk-Treas., RR#5, Renfrew K7V 3Z8 – 613/432-6271, Fax: 613/432-7298
Howard Twp	2,249	Kent	Kent	Essex-Kent	James A. Campbell, Clerk-Treas., 57 Main St. East, PO Box 369, Ridgetown N0P 2C0 – 519/674-3315, Fax: 519/674-5108
Howe Island Twp	421	Frontenac	Hastings-Frontenac-Lennox & Addington	Kingston & the Islands	Carol Dwyre, Clerk-Treas., RR#4, Gananoque K7G 2V6 – 613/544-6348, Fax: 613/548-7545
Howick Twp	3,546	Huron	Huron-Bruce	Huron	Mary Ellen Greb, Clerk-Treas., RR#1, PO Box 89, Gorrie N0G 1X0 – 519/335-3208, Fax: 519/335-6208
Howland Twp	928	Manitoulin District	Algoma	Algoma-Manitoulin	E.O. (Ned) Martin, Clerk-Treas., Sheguiandah P0P 1W0 – 705/368-2009, Fax: 705/368-3017
Hudson Twp	455	Timiskaming District	Timiskaming-French River	Timiskaming	Stephan Palmateer, Clerk-Treas., RR#1, New Liskeard P0J 1P0 – 705/647-5568, Fax: 705/647-6373
Hullett Twp	1,843	Huron	Huron-Bruce	Huron	Beverly M. Shaddick, Clerk-Treas., PO Box 226, Londesboro N0M 2H0 – 519/523-4340, Fax: 519/523-9787
Humphrey Twp	1,049	Parry Sound District	Parry Sound-Muskoka	Parry Sound	Donna L. Besman, CAO, RR#2, Parry Sound P2A 2W8 – 705/732-4300, Fax: 705/732-6347

Canadian Almanac & Directory 1997

Cities in CAPITALS; Towns marked †; Separated Towns marked (SE); Villages marked (V); Townships marked Twp; Restructured Counties marked (RS); United Counties marked (U); Development Areas (DA); • means separated for municipal purposes from county. An in-depth listing for municipalities marked with * appears in Part 2 (check Index for page numbers).

MUNICIPALITY	1994 POP.	COUNTY OR DISTRICT	FEDERAL ELECTORAL DISTRICT	PROVINCIAL ELECTORAL DISTRICT	CONTACT PERSON WITH ADDRESS, PHONE & FAX
Hungerford Twp	3,024	Hastings	Prince Edward-Hastings	Hastings-Peterborough	Gary P. Thompson, Clerk-Treas., 63 Victoria St. North, PO Box 568, Tweed K0K 3J0 – 613/478-3035, Fax: 613/478-1145
Huntingdon Twp	2,216	Hastings	Hastings-Frontenac-Lennox & Addington	Hastings-Peterborough	Bonnie E. Jones, Clerk-Treas., RR#5, Madoc K0K 2K0 – 613/473-4030, Fax: 613/473-5444
Huntsville †	14,342	Muskoka Dist. Mun.	Parry Sound-Muskoka	Muskoka-Georgian Bay	Robert W. Small, Clerk-Adm., 37 Main St. East, PO Box 2700, Huntsville P0A 1K0 – 705/789-1751, Fax: 705/789-6689
Huron Twp [b]	3,061	Bruce	Huron-Bruce	Bruce	S. Susan Stevenson, Clerk, PO Box 130, Ripley N0G 2R0 – 519/395-3735, Fax: 519/395-4107
Ignace Twp	1,605	Kenora District	Kenora-Rainy River	Rainy River	David W. Hatch, Clerk-Treas., 200 Beaver St., PO Box 248, Ignace P0T 1T0 – 807/934-2202, Fax: 807/934-2864
Ingersoll †	9,545	Oxford	Oxford	Oxford	Edward Hunt, Clerk-Adm., PO Box 340, Ingersoll N5C 3V3 – 519/485-0120, Fax: 519/485-3543
Innisfil †	22,523	Simcoe	Simcoe Centre	Simcoe Centre	Paul G. Landry, Clerk, PO Box 5000, Stroud L0L 2M0 – 705/436-3710, Fax: 705/436-7120
Iron Bridge (V)	716	Algoma District	Algoma	Algoma	Noella Brown, Clerk-Treas., 10 John St., PO Box 460, Iron Bridge P0R 1H0 – 705/843-2033, Fax: 705/843-2035
Iroquois (V)	1,206	Stormont, Dundas & Glengarry	Stormont-Dundas	SDG & East Grenville	Elizabeth A. Marlin, Adm.-Clerk-Treas., PO Box 249, Iroquois K0E 1K0 – 613/652-4422, Fax: 613/652-4636
Iroquois Falls †	5,581	Cochrane District	Timmins-Chapleau	Cochrane South	John J. Buchan, Clerk-Adm., 235 Main St., PO Box 230, Iroquois Falls P0K 1G0 – 705/232-5700, Fax: 705/232-4241
Jaffray Melick †	4,012	Kenora District	Kenora-Rainy River	Kenora	Gordon R. Meads, Clerk & CAO, 243 Rabbit Lake Rd., RR#2, Kenora P9N 3W8 – 807/548-4234, Fax: 807/548-1728
James Twp	491	Timiskaming District	Timiskaming-French River	Timiskaming	Myrna J. Hayes, Clerk-Treas., Pine St., PO Box 10, Elk Lake P0J 1G0 – 705/678-2237, Fax: 705/678-2495
Jocelyn Twp	248	Algoma District	Algoma	Algoma	Janet Boucher, Clerk-Treas., RR#1, Richards Landing P0R 1J0 – 705/246-2025, Fax: 705/246-3282
Johnson Twp	667 ('95)	Algoma District	Algoma	Algoma	Jo-Ann McDiarmid, Clerk-Treas., Canadian Pacific Ave., PO Box 160, Desbarats P0R 1E0 – 705/782-6601, Fax: 705/782-6780
Joly Twp	258	Parry Sound District	Parry Sound-Muskoka	Parry Sound	Susan Webster, Clerk-Treas., PO Box 519, Sundridge P0A 1Z0 – 705/384-5428, Fax: 705/384-5428
Kaladar, Anglesea & Effingham Twp	1,429	Lennox & Addington	Hastings-Frontenac-Lennox & Addington	Frontenac-Addington	Margaret Wood, Clerk-Treas., PO Box 89, Flinton K0H 1P0 – 613/336-2286, Fax: 613/336-2847
KANATA	43,362	Ottawa-Carleton Reg. Mun.	Lanark-Carleton	Carleton	Gord Kemp, Acting Clerk, 580 Terry Fox Dr., Kanata K2L 4C2 – 613/592-4281, Fax: 613/592-8183
Kapuskasing †	9,658	Cochrane District	Cochrane-Superior	Cochrane North	Nancy Montpellier, Clerk-Treas., 88 Riverside Dr., Kapuskasing P5N 1B3 – 705/335-2341, Fax: 705/337-1741
Kearney †	706	Parry Sound District	Parry Sound-Muskoka	Parry Sound	Elwood Varty, Clerk-Treas. & CAO, Monteith Rd., PO Box 38, Kearney P0A 1M0 – 705/636-7752, Fax: 705/636-0527
Keewatin †	1,994	Kenora District	Kenora-Rainy River	Kenora	Warren D. Spencer, Clerk & CAO, 221 Main St., PO Box 139, Keewatin P0X 1C0 – 807/547-2881, Fax: 807/547-2284
Kemptville †	2,721	Leeds & Grenville	Leeds-Grenville	SDG & East Grenville	Cahl Pominville, Clerk, 15 Water St., PO Box 130, Kemptville K0G 1J0 – 613/258-3483, Fax: 613/258-4322
Kennebec Twp	733	Frontenac	Hastings-Frontenac-Lennox & Addington	Frontenac-Addington	Shirley Conner, Clerk-Treas., PO Box 70, Arden K0H 1B0 – 613/335-2000, Fax: 613/335-2922
Kenora †	9,715	Kenora District	Kenora-Rainy River	Kenora	William E. Preisentanz, Clerk & CAO, 1 Main St. South, Kenora P9N 3X2 – 807/467-2000, Fax: 807/467-2045
Kenyon Twp	3,336	Stormont, Dundas & Glengarry	Glengarry-Prescott-Russell	SDG & East Grenville	Johanna (Annie) Levac, Acting Clerk-Treas., RR#5, PO Box 11, Alexandria K0C 1A0 – 613/527-2090, Fax: 613/527-2019
Keppel Twp	3,751	Grey	Bruce-Grey	Grey	Clerk, RR#1, Wiarton N0H 2T0 – 519/534-2247, Fax: 519/534-4970
Kerns Twp	408	Timiskaming District	Timiskaming-French River	Timiskaming	Stephan Palmateer, Clerk-Treas., RR#1, New Liskeard P0J 1P0 – 705/647-5568, Fax: 705/647-6373

Canadian Almanac & Directory 1997

Cities in CAPITALS; Towns marked †; Separated Towns marked (SE); Villages marked (V); Townships marked Twp; Restructured Counties marked (RS); United Counties marked (U); Development Areas (DA); • means separated for municipal purposes from county. An in-depth listing for municipalities marked with * appears in Part 2 (check Index for page numbers).

MUNICIPALITY	1994 POP.	COUNTY OR DISTRICT	FEDERAL ELECTORAL DISTRICT	PROVINCIAL ELECTORAL DISTRICT	CONTACT PERSON WITH ADDRESS, PHONE & FAX
Killaloe (V)	656	Renfrew	Renfrew-Nipissing-Pembroke	Renfrew North	Susan Sheridan, Clerk-Treas., 1 John St., PO Box 39, Killaloe K0J 2A0 – 613/757-2300, Fax: 613/757-3634
Kincardine †	6,318	Bruce	Huron-Bruce	Bruce	Maureen A. Couture, Clerk-Adm., 707 Queen St., Kincardine N2Z 1Z9 – 519/396-3468, Fax: 519/396-8288
Kincardine Twp	2,894	Bruce	Huron-Bruce	Bruce	Muriel P. Eskrick, Clerk-Treas., RR#5, PO Box 14, Kincardine N2Z 2X6 – 519/396-8100, Fax: 519/396-8432
King Twp	17,504	York Reg. Mun.	York-Simcoe; York North	York North	Cameron H. Duncan, Clerk, 3565 King Rd., King City L7B 1A1 – 905/833-5321, Fax: 905/833-2300
*KINGSTON	59,624	Frontenac	Kingston & the Islands	Kingston & the Islands	Sheila Birrell, City Clerk, City Hall, 216 Ontario St., Kingston K7L 2Z3 – 613/546-4291, Fax: 613/546-5232
Kingston Twp	39,679	Frontenac	Kingston & the Islands	Frontenac-Addington	Susan A. McLean, Clerk, 1425 Midland Ave., PO Box 3400, Kingston K7L 5L8 – 613/384-1770, Fax: 613/384-7106
Kingsville †	5,841	Essex	Essex-Kent	Essex-South	Victoria Sim, Clerk-Adm., 41 Division St. South, Kingsville N9Y 1P4 – 519/733-2315, Fax: 519/733-5588
Kinloss Twp	1,172	Bruce	Huron-Bruce	Bruce	Mark Becker, Clerk-Treas., Holyrood N0G 2B0 – 519/395-3575, Fax: 519/395-4920
Kirkland Lake †	10,330	Timiskaming District	Timiskaming-French River	Timiskaming	J. Bev Bennetts, Clerk, 3 Kirkland St. West, PO Box 1757, Kirkland Lake P2N 3K3 – 705/567-9361, Fax: 705/567-3535
*KITCHENER	184,600 ('96)	Waterloo Reg. Mun.	Cambridge; Kitchener; Waterloo	Kitchener; Kitchener-Wilmot	Robert W. Pritchard, City Clerk & Commissioner, General Services, City Hall, 200 King St. West, PO Box 1118, Kitchener N2G 4G7 – 519/741-2286, Fax: 519/741-2705; URL: http://www.oceta.on.ca/city.kitchener
Kitley Twp	2,236	Leeds & Grenville	Leeds-Grenville	Leeds-Grenville	Atty Jones, Clerk-Treas., 424 Hwy. 29, Toledo K0E 1Y0 – 613/275-2277, Fax: 613/275-2093
La Vallée Twp	1,036	Rainy River District	Kenora-Rainy River	Rainy River	Laurie A. Witherspoon, Clerk-Treas., Main St., PO Box 99, Devlin P0W 1C0 – 807/486-3452, Fax: 807/486-3863
Laird Twp	986	Algoma District	Algoma	Algoma	Phyllis L. MacKay, Clerk-Treas., RR#4, Echo Bay P0S 1C0 – 705/248-2395, Fax: 705/248-1138
Lake of Bays Twp	2,588	Muskoka Dist. Mun.	Parry Sound-Muskoka	Muskoka-Georgian Bay	S. Faye Tibbel, Clerk-Adm., 3 Dwight Bay Rd., Dwight P0A 1H0 – 705/635-2272, Fax: 705/635-2132
Lakefield (V)	2,387	Peterborough	Peterborough	Hastings-Peterborough	William L. Mitchell, Clerk-Treas. & Adm., 1 Bridge St., PO Box 400, Lakefield K0L 2H0 – 705/652-3381, Fax: 705/652-3995
Lanark (V)	815	Lanark	Lanark-Carleton	Lanark-Renfrew	Laurie Cordick, Clerk-Treas., 75 George St., PO Box 20, Lanark K0G 1K0 – 613/259-2398, Fax: 613/259-2291
Lanark Twp	1,461	Lanark	Lanark-Carleton	Lanark-Renfrew	Paul Snider, Clerk, RR#2, Lanark K0G 1K0 – 613/259-5686, Fax: 613/259-2583
Lancaster (V)	727	Stormont, Dundas & Glengarry	Glengarry-Prescott-Russell	SDG & East Grenville	Marilyn LeBrun, Clerk-Treas., Pine St., PO Box 220, Lancaster K0C 1N0 – 613/347-2023, Fax: 613/347-1146
Lancaster Twp	3,684	Stormont, Dundas & Glengarry	Glengarry-Prscsott-Russell	SDG & East Grenville	Michel J. Samson, Clerk-Treas., North Lancaster K0C 1Z0 – 613/347-2476, Fax: 613/347-2477
Larder Lake Twp	925	Timiskaming District	Timiskaming-French River	Timiskaming	Robert E. Emmell, Clerk-Treas., 13 Godfrey St., PO Box 40, Larder Lake P0K 1L0 – 705/643-2158, Fax: 705/643-2311
LaSalle †	18,797	Essex	Essex-Windsor	Windsor-Sandwich	Kenneth M. Antaya, Clerk-Adm., 5950 Malden Rd., LaSalle N9H 1S4 – 519/969-7770, Fax: 519/969-4469
Latchford †	328	Timiskaming District	Timiskaming French River	Timiskaming	Lynn M. Godden, Adm.-Clerk-Treas., 10 Main St., PO Box 10, Latchford P0J 1N0 – 705/676-2416, Fax: 705/676-2121
Lavant, Dalhousie & N. Sherbrooke Twp	1,360	Lanark	Lanark-Carleton	Lanark-Renfrew	Mary L. Kirkham, Clerk-Treas., Bag Service, McDonald's Corners K0G 1M0 – 613/278-2694, Fax: 613/278-2694
Laxton, Digby & Longford Twp	994	Victoria	Victoria-Haliburton	Victoria-Haliburton	Brenda A. Greer, Clerk-Treas., PO Box 70, Norland K0M 2L0 – 705/454-3418, Fax: 705/454-3279
Leamington †	14,629	Essex	Essex-Kent	Essex South	Brian R. Sweet, Clerk, 38 Erie St. North, Leamington N8H 2Z3 – 519/326-5761, Fax: 519/326-2481

4-58 ONTARIO MUNICIPALITIES

Cities in CAPITALS; Towns marked †; Separated Towns marked (SE); Villages marked (V); Townships marked Twp; Restructured Counties marked (RS); United Counties marked (U); Development Areas (DA); • means separated for municipal purposes from county. An in-depth listing for municipalities marked with * appears in Part 2 (check Index for page numbers).

MUNICIPALITY	1994 POP.	COUNTY OR DISTRICT	FEDERAL ELECTORAL DISTRICT	PROVINCIAL ELECTORAL DISTRICT	CONTACT PERSON WITH ADDRESS, PHONE & FAX
Leeds & Lansdowne, Front of Twp	4,798	Leeds & Grenville	Leeds-Grenville	Leeds-Grenville	Diane Hall, Clerk-Adm., 129 Jessie St., PO Box 129, Lansdowne K0E 1L0 – 613/659-2415, Fax: 613/659-3619
Leeds & Lansdowne, Rear of Twp	2,689	Leeds & Grenville	Leeds-Grenville	Leeds-Grenville	Eileen Watson, Clerk-Treas., PO Box 160, Lyndhurst K0E 1N0 – 613/928-2423, Fax: 613/928-3116
Limerick Twp	322	Hastings	Hastings-Frontenac-Lennox & Addington	Hastings-Peterborough	Carlene Baker, Clerk-Treas., RR#2, Gilmour K0L 1W0 – 613/474-2863, Fax: 613/474-0478
Lincoln †	17,318	Niagara Reg. Mun.	Lincoln	Lincoln	Kyle S. Kruger, Clerk, 4800 South Service Rd., Beamsville L0R 1B1 – 905/563-8205, Fax: 905/563-6566
Lindsay †	16,590	Victoria	Victoria-Haliburton	Victoria-Haliburton	Percy Luther, Acting Clerk, 180 Kent St. West, Lindsay K9V 2Y6 – 705/324-6171, Fax: 705/324-2051
Lindsay Twp	484	Bruce	Bruce-Grey	Bruce	Norma Brinkman, Clerk-Treas., RR#2, Lion's Head N0H 1W0 – 519/793-3522, Fax: 519/793-3823
Lion's Head (V)	520	Bruce	Bruce-Grey	Bruce	Janet Morrow, Clerk-Treas., 90 Main St., PO Box 310, Lion's Head N0H 1W0 – 519/793-3731, Fax: 519/793-4222
Listowel †	5,262	Perth	Perth-Wellington-Waterloo	Perth	R. Les Tervit, Adm.-Clerk-Treas., 330 Wallace Ave. North, Listowel N4W 1L3 – 519/291-2950, Fax: 519/291-5611
Little Current †	1,450	Manitoulin District	Algoma	Algoma-Manitoulin	Edwin Bond, Clerk-Treas., 50 Meredith St. West, Little Current P0P 1K0 – 705/368-2277, Fax: 705/368-2245
Lobo Twp	5,464	Middlesex	London-Middlesex	Middlesex	Sharon A. McMillan, Clerk-Adm., 10227 Ilderton Rd., RR#2, Ilderton N0M 2A0 – 519/666-0190, Fax: 519/666-0271
Lochiel Twp	2,921	Stormont, Dundas & Glengarry	Glengarry-Prescott-Russell	SDG & East Grenville	Rhéal M. (Ray) Charbonneau, Clerk-Treas., RR#1, Alexandria K0C 1A0 – 613/525-3283, Fax: 613/525-5052
Logan Twp	2,184	Perth	Perth-Wellington-Waterloo	Perth	Karen McLagan, Clerk-Treas., RR#1, Bornholm N0K 1A0 – 519/347-2404, Fax: 519/347-2939
*LONDON	331,600 ('95)	Middlesex	London East; London-Middlesex; London West	London Centre; London North; London South; Middlesex	Kenneth W. Sadler, City Clerk, City Hall, 300 Dufferin Ave., PO Box 5035, London N6A 4L9 – 519/661-4500, Fax: 519/661-4892, URL: http://www.city.london.on.ca/
London Twp	4,741	Middlesex	London-Middlesex	Middlesex	Albert F. Bannister, Clerk-Adm., 14361 Medway Rd., Arva N0M 1C0 – 519/660-0092, Fax: 519/660-3653
Longlac †	1,833	Thunder Bay District	Cochrane-Superior	Lake Nipigon	Jane Jantunen, Clerk-Treas., 105 Hamel Ave., PO Box 640, Longlac P0T 2A0 – 807/876-2316, Fax: 807/876-2396
Longueuil Twp	1,336	Prescott & Russell	Glengarry-Prescott-Russell	Prescott & Russell	Jeanne Charlebois, Clerk-Treas., 925 Hwy 17, PO Box 343, L'Orignal K0B 1K0 – 613/675-4727, Fax: 613/675-1050
L'Orignal (V)	1,971	Prescott & Russell	Glengarry-Prescott-Russell	Prescott & Russell	Diane Lalonde, Clerk-Treas., 36 Court St., PO Box 271, L'Orignal K0B 1K0 – 613/675-2294, Fax: 613/675-2830
Loughborough Twp	4,436	Frontenac	Hastings-Frontenac-Lennox & Addington	Frontenac-Addington	Carolyn Holland, Clerk., PO Box 100, Sydenham K0H 2T0 – 613/376-3027, Fax: 613/376-6657
Lucan (V)	1,845	Middlesex	London-Middlesex	Middlesex	Ronald J. Reymer, Clerk, 161 Main St., PO Box 449, Lucan N0M 2J0 – 519/227-4253, Fax: 519/227-1755
Lucknow (V)	1,162	Bruce	Huron-Bruce	Bruce	Bertha M. Whitcroft, Clerk-Treas., 526 Campbell St., PO Box 40, Lucknow N0G 2H0 – 519/528-3539, Fax: 519/528-3630
Lutterworth Twp	900	Haliburton	Victoria-Haliburton	Victoria-Haliburton	Mary Jane Irwin, Clerk-Treas., PO Box 850, Minden K0M 2K0 – 705/286-1541, Fax: 705/286-6005
MacDonald, Meredith & Aberdeen; Add'l Twp	1,504	Algoma District	Algoma	Algoma	Jean V. Robbins, Clerk-Treas., 208 Church St., PO Box 10, Echo Bay P0S 1C0 – 705/248-2441, Fax: 705/248-3091
Machar Twp	868	Parry Sound District	Parry Sound-Muskoka	Parry Sound	Brenda Sinclair Paul, Clerk-Treas., Municipal Rd. North, PO Box 70, South River P0A 1X0 – 705/386-7741, Fax: 705/386-0765
Machin Twp	1,037	Kenora District	Kenora-Rainy River	Kenora	D. Marie Wiebe, Adm.-Clerk-Treas., PO Box 249, Vermilion Bay P0V 2V0 – 807/227-2633, Fax: 807/227-5443

Canadian Almanac & Directory 1997

ONTARIO MUNICIPALITIES 4-59

Cities in CAPITALS; Towns marked †; Separated Towns marked (SE); Villages marked (V); Townships marked Twp; Restructured Counties marked (RS); United Counties marked (U); Development Areas (DA); • means separated for municipal purposes from county. An in-depth listing for municipalities marked with * appears in Part 2 (check Index for page numbers).

MUNICIPALITY	1994 POP.	COUNTY OR DISTRICT	FEDERAL ELECTORAL DISTRICT	PROVINCIAL ELECTORAL DISTRICT	CONTACT PERSON WITH ADDRESS, PHONE & FAX
Madoc (V)	1,296	Hastings	Hastings-Frontenac-Lennox & Addington	Hastings-Peterborough	Doug Parks, Clerk-Treas., 107 St. Lawrence St. West, PO Box 310, Madoc K0K 2K0 – 613/473-5211, Fax: 613/473-5446
Madoc Twp	1,831	Hastings	Hastings-Frontenac-Lennox & Addington	Hastings-Peterborough	Bill G. Lebow, Clerk-Treas., PO Box 503, Madoc K0K 2K0 – 613/473-2677, Fax: 613/473-5580
Magnetawan (V)	230	Parry Sound District	Parry Sound-Muskoka	Parry Sound	Sharon Sohm, Clerk-Treas., PO Box 70, Magnetawan P0A 1P0 – 705/387-3947, Fax: 705/387-3947
Maidstone Twp	10,714	Essex	Essex-Windsor	Essex-Kent	Csop Toth, Clerk, 1089 Puce Rd., RR#3, Essex N8M 2X7 – 519/727-6668, Fax: 519/727-3757
Malahide Twp	5,671	Elgin	Elgin-Norfolk	Elgin	Randall R. Millard, Clerk-Adm., 87 John St. South, Aylmer N5H 2C3 – 519/773-5344, Fax: 519/773-5334
Malden Twp	3,220	Essex	Essex-Windsor	Essex-South	Garth Poulain, Clerk-Treas., 6744 Concession #6, RR#2, Amherstburg N9V 2Y8 – 519/736-3141, Fax: 519/736-7787
Manitouwadge Twp	3,554	Thunder Bay District	Cochrane-Superior	Lake Nipigon	Ken Taniwa, CAO-Treas., 1 Mississauga Dr., Manitouwadge P0T 2C0 – 807/826-3227, Fax: 807/826-4592
Manvers Twp	5,157	Victoria	Victoria-Haliburton	Durham East	D.M. Peggy Whitteker, Clerk-Treas., PO Box 210, Bethany L0A 1A0 – 705/277-2321, Fax: 705/277-1580
Marathon †	4,702	Thunder Bay District	Cochrane-Superior	Lake Nipigon	Kathy Dallaire, Clerk, 4 Hemlo Dr., PO Box TM, Marathon P0T 2E0 – 807/229-1340, Fax: 807/229-1999
Mariposa Twp	6,839	Victoria	Victoria-Haliburton	Victoria-Haliburton	Sandra Lloyd, Clerk, PO Box 70, Oakwood K0M 2M0 – 705/953-9900, Fax: 705/953-9184
Markdale (V)	1,193	Grey	Bruce-Grey	Grey	Geoffrey A. Barlow, Clerk-Treas., 50 Lorne St., PO Box 439, Markdale N0C 1H0 – 519/986-2811, Fax: 519/986-3643
*Markham †	160,000 ('95)	York Reg. Mun.	Markham-Whitchurch-Stouffville	Markham	Bob Panizza, Clerk, 101 Town Centre Blvd., Markham L3R 9W3 – 905/477-7000, Fax: 905/479-7771
Marmora (V)	1,442	Hastings	Hastings-Frontenac-Lennox & Addington	Hastings-Peterborough	Carol D. Church, Adm.-Clerk-Treas., 12 Bursthall St., PO Box 417, Marmora K0K 2M0 – 613/472-2533, Fax: 613/472-3015
Marmora & Lake Twp	2,054	Hastings	Hastings-Frontenac-Lennox & Addington	Hastings-Peterborough	Frank Mills, Clerk & CAO, PO Box 459, Marmora K0K 2M0 – 613/472-2629, Fax: 613/472-5330
Maryborough Twp	2,573	Wellington	Wellington-Grey-Dufferin-Simcoe	Wellington	Robert Skeoch, Clerk-Treas., 1 Hilwood Dr., PO Box 39, Moorefield N0G 2K0 – 519/638-3043, Fax: 519/638-2200
Massey †	1,063	Sudbury District	Algoma	Algoma-Manitoulin	Alton Hobbs, Clerk-Treas., 205 Sable St., PO Box 490, Massey P0P 1P0 – 705/865-2181, Fax: 705/865-2514
Matachewan Twp	427	Timiskaming District	Timiskaming-French River	Timiskaming	Jacqueline Walkingshaw, Clerk-Treas., PO Box 177, Matachewan P0K 1M0 – 705/565-2274, Fax: 705/565-2564
Matilda Twp	3,321	Stormont, Dundas & Glengarry	Stormont-Dundas	SDG & East Grenville	Wilmont E. (Bill) Horner, Clerk-Treas., Brinston K0E 1C0 – 613/652-4403, Fax: 613/652-2279
Mattawa †	2,428	Nipissing District	Nipissing	Parry Sound	Wayne P. Belter, Clerk & CAO, 160 Water St., PO Box 390, Mattawa P0H 1V0 – 705/744-5611, Fax: 705/744-0104
Mattawan Twp	102	Nipissing District	Nipissing	Parry Sound	Irvine J. Burke, Clerk-Treas., PO Box 610, Mattawa P0H 1V0 – 705/744-5737, Fax: 705/744-5365
Mattice-Val Côté Twp	888	Cochrane District	Cochrane-Superior	Cochrane North	Gilbert Brisson, Clerk-Adm., 500 Hwy.11, PO Box 129, Mattice P0L 1T0 – 705/364-6511, Fax: 705/364-6431
Maxville (V)	826	Stormont, Dundas & Glengarry	Glengarry-Prescott-Russell	SDG & East Grenville	Connie A. Charbonneau, Clerk-Treas., 2 Spring St., PO Box 277, Maxville K0C 1T0 – 613/527-2705, Fax: 613/527-2066
Mayo Twp	384	Hastings	Hastings-Frontenac-Lennox & Addington	Hastings-Peterborough	Vivian McMunn, Clerk-Treas., RR#4, Bancroft K0L 1C0 – 613/332-2637, Fax: 613/332-2637
McCrosson & Tovell Twp	208	Rainy River District	Kenora-Rainy River	Rainy River	Patrick W. Giles, Clerk-Treas., 211 - 4 St., PO Box 427, Rainy River P0W 1L0 – 807/852-3529, Fax: 807/852-3529
McDougall Twp	2,162	Parry Sound District	Parry Sound-Muskoka	Parry Sound	Norma Bryant, Clerk-Adm., RR#3, Parry Sound P2A 2W9 – 705/342-5252, Fax: 705/342-5573
McGarry Twp	1,050	Timiskaming District	Timiskaming-French River	Timiskaming	Ardene Lefebvre, Clerk-Treas., 27 Webster St., PO Box 99, Virginiatown P0K 1X0 – 705/634-2145, Fax: 705/634-2700

Canadian Almanac & Directory 1997

Cities in CAPITALS; Towns marked †; Separated Towns marked (SE); Villages marked (V); Townships marked Twp; Restructured Counties marked (RS); United Counties marked (U); Development Areas (DA); • means separated for municipal purposes from county. An in-depth listing for municipalities marked with * appears in Part 2 (check Index for page numbers).

MUNICIPALITY	1994 POP.	COUNTY OR DISTRICT	FEDERAL ELECTORAL DISTRICT	PROVINCIAL ELECTORAL DISTRICT	CONTACT PERSON WITH ADDRESS, PHONE & FAX
McGillivray Twp	1,843	Middlesex	Lambton-Middlesex	Middlesex	Shirley Scott, Clerk-Treas., RR#3, Ailsa Craig N0M 1A0 – 519/293-3686, Fax: 519/293-3878
McKellar Twp	854	Parry Sound District	Parry Sound-Muskoka	Parry Sound	Shawn Boggs, Clerk-Treas., PO Box 69, McKellar P0G 1C0 – 705/389-2842, Fax: 705/389-1244
McKillop Twp	1,427	Huron	Huron-Bruce	Huron	Marion McClure, Clerk-Treas., RR#1, Seaforth N0K 1W0 – 519/527-1916, Fax: 519/527-1916
McMurrich Twp	552	Parry Sound District	Parry Sound-Muskoka	Parry Sound	Richard Gibb, Clerk-Treas., PO Box 70, Sprucedale P0A 1Y0 – 705/685-7901, Fax: 705/685-7393
McNab Twp	5,523	Renfrew	Renfrew-Nipissing-Pembroke	Lanark-Renfrew	Murray Yantha, Clerk-Treas., RR#2, Arnprior K7S 3G8 – 613/623-5756, Fax: 613/623-9138
Meaford †	4,330	Grey	Bruce-Grey	Grey	Graham D. Shaw, Clerk-Treas., 12 Nelson St. East, Meaford N4L 1A1 – 519/538-1060, Fax: 519/538-5240
Melancthon Twp	2,286	Dufferin	Wellington-Grey-Dufferin-Simcoe	Dufferin-Peel	Marion A. Hunter, Clerk-Treas., RR#6, Shelburne L0N 1S9 – 519/925-5525, Fax: 519/925-1110
Merrickville (V)	995	Leeds & Grenville	Leeds-Grenville	Leeds-Grenville	Wayne T. Kirby, Clerk-Treas., 317 Brock St. West, PO Box 340, Merrickville K0G 1N0 – 613/269-4791, Fax: 613/269-4793
Mersea Twp	8,494	Essex	Essex-Kent	Essex-South	Lynn Foster, Clerk-Adm., 38 Erie St. North, Leamington N8H 2Z3 – 519/326-5725, Fax: 519/322-1441
Metcalfe Twp	1,033	Middlesex	Lambton-Middlesex	Middlesex	Raymond G. Wilson, Clerk-Treas., RR#3, Strathroy N7G 3H5 – 519/247-3868, Fax: 519/247-3868
Michipicoten Twp	3,744	Algoma District	Timmins-Chapleau	Algoma	Grant E. Southwell, CAO-Clerk, 40 Broadway Ave., PO Box 500, Wawa P0S 1K0 – 705/856-2244, Fax: 705/856-2120
Midland †	14,284	Simcoe	Simcoe North	Muskoka-Georgian Bay	Fred G. Flood, CAO, 575 Dominion Ave., Midland L4R 1R2 – 705/526-4275, Fax: 705/526-9971
Mildmay (V)	1,069	Bruce	Bruce-Grey	Bruce	David H. Johnston, Clerk-Treas., 16 Peter St., PO Box 128, Mildmay N0G 2J0 – 519/367-2617, Fax: 519/367-2155
Millbrook (V)	1,210	Peterborough	Victoria-Haliburton	Peterborough	Gail A. Empey, Adm.-Clerk-Treas., 7 King St. East, PO Box 58, Millbrook L0A 1G0 – 705/932-2780, Fax: 705/932-2595
Milton †	30,278	Halton Reg. Mun.	Oakville-Milton; Halton-Peel	Halton North; Halton Centre	William Roberts, Clerk, Victoria Park Square, PO Box 1005, Milton L9T 4B6 – 905/878-7211, Fax: 905/878-6995
Milverton (V)	1,539	Perth	Perth-Wellington-Waterloo	Perth	Arthur J. Brubacher, Clerk-Treas., 25 Mill St. East, Milverton N0K 1M0 – 519/595-8321, Fax: 519/595-8765
Minto Twp	2,357	Wellington	Wellington-Grey-Dufferin-Simcoe	Wellington	Frances Hale, Clerk-Treas., 5941 Hwy.89, PO Box 160, Harriston N0G 1Z0 – 519/338-2511, Fax: 519/338-2005
*MISSISSAUGA	500,000	Peel Reg. Mun.	Bramalea-Gore-Malton; Mississauga East; Mississauga South; Mississauga West	Mississauga East; Mississauga North; Mississauga South; Mississauga West	Arthur Grannum, Deputy City Clerk, 300 City Centre Dr., Mississauga L5B 3C1 – 905/896-5000, Fax: 905/896-5220; URL: http://www.city.mississauga.on.ca
Mitchell †	3,518	Perth	Perth-Wellington-Waterloo	Perth	Donald J. Eplett, Clerk-Treas., 169 St. David St., Mitchell N0K 1N0 – 519/348-8429, Fax: 519/348-4155
Monmouth Twp	767	Haliburton	Victoria-Haliburton	Victoria-Haliburton	Sharon Stoughton-Craig, Clerk-Treas., PO Box 10, Wilberforce K0L 3C0 – 705/448-2981, Fax: 705/448-2532
Mono Twp	5,980	Dufferin	Wellington-Grey-Dufferin-Simcoe	Dufferin-Peel	Keith H. McNenly, Clerk-Adm., RR#1, Orangeville L9W 2Y8 – 519/941-3599, Fax: 519/941-9490
Montague Twp	2,830	Lanark	Lanark-Carleton	Lanark-Renfrew	Judy Nesbitt, Clerk-Adm., Roger Stevens Rd., PO Box 755, Smiths Falls K7A 4W6 – 613/283-7478, Fax: 613/283-3112
Monteagle Twp	1,186	Hastings	Hastings-Frontenac-Lennox & Addington	Hastings-Peterborough	Eleanor N. Tully, Clerk-Treas., Township Garage, RR#5, Bancroft K0L 1C0 – 613/338-3193, Fax: 613/338-2752
Moonbeam Twp	1,185	Cochrane District	Cochrane-Superior	Cochrane North	Carole Gendron, Clerk-Treas., 53 St. Aubin Ave., PO Box 330, Moonbeam P0L 1V0 – 705/367-2244, Fax: 705/367-2610
Moore Twp	10,684	Lambton	Sarnia-Lambton	Lambton	Ron H. Whitman, Clerk, 1155 Emily St., Mooretown N0N 1M0 – 519/867-2021, Fax: 519/867-5509
Moosonee (DA)	1,800 ('91)				Laurie McGoldrick, Clerk, PO Box 127, Moosonee P0L 1Y0 – 705/336-2993, Fax: 705/336-2426

Canadian Almanac & Directory 1997

Cities in CAPITALS; Towns marked †; Separated Towns marked (SE); Villages marked (V); Townships marked Twp; Restructured Counties marked (RS); United Counties marked (U); Development Areas (DA); • means separated for municipal purposes from county. An in-depth listing for municipalities marked with * appears in Part 2 (check Index for page numbers).

MUNICIPALITY	1994 POP.	COUNTY OR DISTRICT	FEDERAL ELECTORAL DISTRICT	PROVINCIAL ELECTORAL DISTRICT	CONTACT PERSON WITH ADDRESS, PHONE & FAX
Morley Twp	500	Rainy River District	Kenora-Rainy River	Rainy River	Anna H.M. Boily, Clerk-Treas., PO Box 40, Stratton P0W 1N0 – 807/483-5455, Fax: 807/483-5882
Mornington Twp	3,381	Perth	Perth-Waterloo-Wellington	Perth	Constance Flanagan, Clerk-Treas., PO Box 70, Newton N0K 1R0 – 519/595-8917, Fax: 519/595-8778
Morris Twp	1,771	Huron	Huron-Bruce	Huron	Nancy Michie, Clerk-Treas., RR#4, Brussels N0G 1H0 – 519/887-6137, Fax: 519/887-6424
Morrisburg (V)	2,362	Stormont, Dundas & Glengarry	Stormont-Dundas	SDG & East Grenville	Cheryl V. Tynski, Clerk-Treas., 6 - 5 St. West, PO Box 737, Morrisburg K0C 1X0 – 613/543-2504, Fax: 613/543-4430
Morson Twp	188	Rainy River District	Kenora-Rainy River	Rainy River	Patrick M. Giles, Clerk-Treas., 211 - 4 St., PO Box 427, Rainy River P0W 1L0 – 807/852-3529, Fax: 807/852-3529
Mosa Twp	1,304	Middlesex	Lambton-Middlesex	Middlesex	Betty Ann MacKinnon, Clerk-Treas., RR#1, Glencoe N0L 1M0 – 519/693-4403, Fax: 519/693-4404
Mount Forest †	4,164	Wellington	Wellington-Grey-Dufferin-Simcoe	Wellington	E.C. (Al) Brubacher, Adm.-Clerk-Treas., 102 Main St. South, PO Box 188, Mount Forest N0G 2L0 – 519/323-2150, Fax: 519/323-2930
Mountain Twp	3,319	Stormont, Dundas & Glengarry	Stormont-Dundas	SDG & East Grenville	Glenna A. MacIntosh, Clerk-Treas., PO Box 9, Mountain K0E 1S0 – 613/989-2915, Fax: 613/989-3294
Mulmur Twp	2,509	Dufferin	Wellington-Grey-Dufferin-Simcoe	Dufferin-Peel	Terry M. Horner, Clerk-Treas., RR#2, Lisle L0M 1M0 – 705/466-3341, Fax: 705/466-2922
Murray Twp	6,841	Northumberland	Northumberland	Northumberland	C. Ken Rose, Clerk & CAO, RR#1, Trenton K8V 5P4 – 613/392-4435, Fax: 613/392-7151
Muskoka Lakes Twp	5,397	Muskoka Dist. Mun.	Parry Sound-Muskoka	Muskoka-Georgian Bay	Paul H. Davidson, Clerk-Adm., PO Box 129, Port Carling P0B 1J0 – 705/765-3156, Fax: 705/765-6755
Nairn Twp	400	Sudbury District	Algoma	Nickel Belt	Robert Deschene, Clerk-Treas., 64 McIntyre St., Nairn Centre P0M 2L0 – 705/869-4232, Fax: 705/869-5248
Nakina Twp	536	Thunder Bay District	Cochrane-Superior	Lake Nipigon	W. Terrance Dowhaniuk, Adm.-Clerk-Treas., 168 Centre Ave., PO Box 210, Nakina P0T 2H0 – 807/329-5361, Fax: 807/329-5982
NANTICOKE	22,401	Haldimand-Norfolk Reg. Mun.	Haldimand-Norfolk	Norfolk	David M. Kilpatrick, City Clerk, 230 Main St., Port Dover N0A 1N0 – 519/583-0890, Fax: 519/583-1431
Napanee †	4,955	Lennox & Addington	Hastings-Frontenac-Lennox & Addington	Prince Edward-Lennox-South Hastings	John C. (Jack) McNamee, Adm.-Clerk-Treas., 124 John St., PO Box 97, Napanee K7R 3L4 – 613/354-3351, Fax: 613/354-6545
Neebing Twp	902	Thunder Bay District	Thunder Bay-Atikokan	Fort William	Claudette Levac, Clerk-Treas., RR#7, Thunder Bay P7C 5V5 – 807/964-2092, Fax: 807/964-2076
*NEPEAN	116,000	Ottawa-Carleton Reg. Mun.	Nepean	Nepean; Ottawa-Rideau	John LeMaistre, City Clerk, Nepean Civic Square, 101 Centrepointe Dr., Nepean K2G 5K7 – 613/727-6600, Fax: 613/727-6613
Neustadt (V)	542	Grey	Bruce-Grey	Grey	Janice M. McLeod, Clerk-Treas., 449 Mill St., PO Box 66, Neustadt N0G 2M0 – 519/799-5758, Fax: 519/799-5353
New Liskeard †	4,986	Timiskaming District	Timiskaming-French River	Timiskaming	Kenneth D.N. Boal, CAO & Clerk, 90 Whitewood Ave., PO Box 730, New Liskeard P0J 1P0 – 705/647-4367, Fax: 705/647-4442
New Tecumseth †	20,767	Simcoe	Simcoe-Centre	Simcoe West	Sterling W. Zeran, Clerk, 10 Wellington St. East, PO Box 910, Alliston L9R 1A1 – 705/435-6219, Fax: 705/435-2873
Newboro (V)	283	Leeds & Grenville	Leeds-Grenville	Leeds-Grenville	Dianne G. Bresee, Clerk-Treas., PO Box 10, Newboro K0G 1P0 – 613/272-2265, Fax: 613/272-3299
Newburgh (V)	712	Lennox & Addington	Hastings-Frontenac-Lennox & Addington	Frontenac-Addington	Darlene Plumley, Clerk-Treas., PO Box 189, Newburgh K0K 2S0 – 613/378-6617, Fax: 613/378-6617
Newbury (V)	404	Middlesex	Lambton-Middlesex	Middlesex	Betty D. Gordon, Clerk-Treas., 54 Hagerty Rd., PO Box 130, Newbury N0L 1Z0 – 519/693-4941, Fax: 519/693-4902
Newmarket †	49,645	York Reg. Mun.	York-Simcoe	York North	Robert M. Prentice, Clerk, 465 Davis Dr., PO Box 328, Newmarket L3Y 4X7 – 905/895-5193, Fax: 905/895-6004

Cities in CAPITALS; Towns marked †; Separated Towns marked (SE); Villages marked (V); Townships marked Twp; Restructured Counties marked (RS); United Counties marked (U); Development Areas (DA); • means separated for municipal purposes from county. An in-depth listing for municipalities marked with * appears in Part 2 (check Index for page numbers).

MUNICIPALITY	1994 POP.	COUNTY OR DISTRICT	FEDERAL ELECTORAL DISTRICT	PROVINCIAL ELECTORAL DISTRICT	CONTACT PERSON WITH ADDRESS, PHONE & FAX
*NIAGARA FALLS	74,915	Niagara Reg. Mun.	Niagara Falls	Niagara Falls; Niagara South	Elwood Wagg, City Clerk, City Hall, 4310 Queen St., PO Box 1023, Niagara Falls L2E 6X5 – 905/356-7521, Fax: 905/356-9083; URL: http://www.niagara.com:80/city.niagara_falls/
Niagara on the Lake †	12,695	Niagara Reg. Mun.	Niagara Falls	St. Catharines-Brock	Robert Howse, Clerk, PO Box 100, Virgil L0S 1T0 – 905/468-3266, Fax: 905/468-2959
Nichol Twp	3,999	Wellington	Wellington-Grey-Dufferin-Simcoe	Wellington	Barbara Hodsman, Clerk-Treas., 485 Washington St., Site 1, PO Box 23, Elora N0B 1S0 – 519/846-5317, Fax: 519/846-9553
Nickel Centre †	12,129	Sudbury Reg. Mun.	Nickel Belt	Sudbury East	Sandra Olson, Clerk, 190 Church St., Garson P3L 1T8 – 705/693-2771, Fax: 705/693-2710
Nipigon Twp	2,095	Thunder Bay District	Thunder Bay-Nipigon	Lake Nipigon	Ronald J. Lanigan, Adm.-Clerk-Treas., 25 - 2nd St., PO Box 160, Nipigon P0T 2J0 – 807/887-3135, Fax: 807/887-3564
Nipissing Twp	1,501	Parry Sound District	Parry Sound-Muskoka	Parry Sound	Charles H. Barton, Clerk-Treas., Nipissing P0H 1W0 – 705/724-2144, Fax: 705/724-5385
Norfolk Twp	11,096	Haldimand-Norfolk Reg. Mun.	Elgin-Norfolk	Norfolk	Merlin House, Clerk-Adm., PO Box 128, Langton N0E 1P0 – 519/875-4485, Fax: 519/875-4789
Normanby Twp	2,550	Grey	Bruce-Grey	Grey	Susan Shannon, Clerk-Treas., PO Box 60, Ayton N0G 1C0 – 519/665-7550, Fax: 519/665-2284
North Algona Twp	596	Renfrew	Renfrew-Nipissing-Pembroke	Renfrew North	Edith Frew, Clerk-Treas., PO Box 99, Golden Lake K0J 1X0 – 613/625-2561, Fax: 613/625-2561
*NORTH BAY	55,960	Nipissing District	Nipissing	Nipissing	Bonny Harrison, City Clerk, City Hall, 200 McIntyre St. East, PO Box 360, North Bay P1B 8H8 – 705/474-0400, Fax: 705/495-4353
North Burgess Twp	1,134	Lanark	Lanark-Carleton	Lanark-Renfrew	Verna Poole, Clerk-Treas., RR#3, Perth K7H 3C5 – 613/267-7922, Fax: 613/267-7922
North Crosby Twp	983	Leeds & Grenville	Leeds-Greenville	Leeds-Grenville	Alison Fath, Clerk-Treas., RR#2, Westport K0G 1X0 – 613/273-2097, Fax: 613/273-2794
North Dorchester Twp	8,144	Middlesex	London-Middlesex	Middlesex	Robert G. Lacroix, Clerk-Adm., 4305 Hamilton Rd., PO Box 209, Dorchester N0L 1G0 – 519/268-7334, Fax: 519/268-3928
North Dumfries Twp	7,090	Waterloo Reg. Mun.	Cambridge	Brant-Haldimand	Marvin Bosetti, Clerk, RR#4, Cambridge N1R 5S5 – 519/621-0340, Fax: 519/623-7641
North Easthope Twp	2,102	Perth	Perth-Wellington-Waterloo	Perth	William R. Hoffard, Clerk-Treas., RR#1, Stratford N5A 6S2 – 519/625-8726, Fax: 519/625-8732
North Elmsley Twp	2,824	Lanark	Lanark-Carleton	Lanark-Renfrew	Judy M. Carroll, Clerk, RR#5, Perth K7H 3C7 – 613/267-6500, Fax: 613/267-2083
North Fredericksburgh Twp	3,095	Lennox & Addington	Hastings-Frontenac-Lennox & Addington	Prince Edward-Lennox-South Hastings	Dianne B. Parks, Clerk-Treas., RR#2, Napanee K7R 3K7 – 613/354-2186, Fax: 613/354-2750
North Marysburgh Twp	1,165	Prince Edward	Prince Edward-Hastings	Prince Edward-Lennox-South Hastings	Wanda C. Thissen, Clerk-Treas., RR#4, Picton K0K 2T0 – 613/476-4436, Fax: 613/476-2635
North Monaghan Twp	1,158	Peterborough	Peterborough	Peterborough	Linda Levitt, Clerk-Treas., 2199 Davis Rd., RR#3, Peterborough K9J 6X4 – 705/749-1688, Fax: 705/749-1787
North Plantagenet Twp	3,294	Prescott & Russell	Glengarry-Prescott-Russell	Prescott & Russell	Elise Campbell, Clerk-Treas., PO Box 271, Plantagenet K0B 1L0 – 613/673-4797, Fax: 613/673-4812
The North Shore Twp	665	Algoma District	Algoma	Algoma-Manitoulin	Dugal G. McQuarrie, Clerk-Treas., PO Box 108, Algoma Mills P0R 1A0 – 705/849-2213, Fax: 705/849-2428
*NORTH YORK	549,115	Metro Mun.	Don Valley East; Don Valley North; Don Valley West; Eglinton-Lawrence; Willowdale; York Centre; York South-Weston; York West	Don Mills; Downsview; Lawrence; Oriole; Willowdale; Wilson Heights; York Mills; Yorkview	Denis G. Kelly, City Clerk, 5100 Yonge St., North York M2N 5V7 – 416/395-6910, Fax: 416/395-6920
Norwich Twp	10,302	Oxford	Oxford	Oxford	Robert C. Watkins, Clerk-Adm., 10 Main St. East, PO Box 100, Otterville N0J 1R0 – 519/879-6568, Fax: 519/879-6385
Norwood (V)	1,441	Peterborough	Peterborough	Hastings-Peterborough	Glenn Girven, Adm.-Clerk-Treas., 78 Colborne St., PO Box 29, Norwood K0L 2V0 – 705/639-5343, Fax: 705/639-1880
Oakland Twp	1,336	Brant	Haldimand-Norfolk	Brant-Haldimand	David Brenneman, Clerk-Treas., General Delivery, Oakland N0E 1L0 – 519/446-2924, Fax: 519/446-2924

Canadian Almanac & Directory 1997

ONTARIO MUNICIPALITIES 4-63

Cities in CAPITALS; Towns marked †; Separated Towns marked (SE); Villages marked (V); Townships marked Twp; Restructured Counties marked (RS); United Counties marked (U); Development Areas (DA); • means separated for municipal purposes from county. An in-depth listing for municipalities marked with * appears in Part 2 (check Index for page numbers).

MUNICIPALITY	1994 POP.	COUNTY OR DISTRICT	FEDERAL ELECTORAL DISTRICT	PROVINCIAL ELECTORAL DISTRICT	CONTACT PERSON WITH ADDRESS, PHONE & FAX
*Oakville †	118,063	Halton Reg. Mun.	Oakville-Milton	Halton Centre; Oakville South	Judith Muncaster, Town Clerk, 1225 Trafalgar Rd., PO Box 310, Oakville L6J 5A6 – 905/845-6601, Fax: 905/815-2025
O'Connor Twp	708	Thunder Bay District	Thunder Bay-Atikokan	Fort William	Ruby Delyea, Clerk-Treas., RR#1, Kakabeka Falls P0T 1W0 – 807/475-4761, Fax: 807/473-0891
Oil Springs (V)	728	Lambton	Lambton-Middlesex	Lambton	Marilyn G. Sanderson, Clerk-Treas., PO Box 22, Oil Springs N0N 1P0 – 519/834-2939, Fax: 519/834-2333
Olden Twp	830	Frontenac	Hastings-Frontenac-Lennox & Addington	Frontenac-Addington	Judy C. Gray, Clerk-Treas., RR#1, PO Box 74, Mountain Grove K0H 2E0 – 613/335-5539, Fax: 613/335-2480
Oliver Twp	2,488	Thunder Bay District	Thunder Bay-Nipigon	Port Arthur	Sharron Martyn, Clerk-Treas., Municipal Office, PO Box 10, Murillo P0T 2G0 – 807/935-2613, Fax: 807/935-2161
Omemee (V)	1,097	Victoria	Victoria-Haliburton	Victoria-Haliburton	Judy Currins, Clerk-Treas., 1 King St. West, PO Box 1000, Omemee K0L 2W0 – 705/799-5032, Fax: 705/799-2020
Onaping Falls †	5,068	Sudbury Reg. Mun.	Nickel Belt	Nickel Belt	Richard Demers, Clerk-Treas., 53 Hwy#144, PO Box 400, Dowling P0M 1R0 – 705/855-4583, Fax: 705/855-2591
Onondaga Twp	1,625	Brant	Brant	Brant-Haldimand	Arlene Jackson, Clerk-Treas., 734 Hwy#54, RR#7, Brantford N3T 5L9 – 519/758-1143, Fax: 519/758-1619
Opasatika Twp	358	Cochrane District	Cochrane-Superior	Cochrane North	Benoit Sigouin, Clerk-Treas. & CAO, 50 Government Rd., PO Box 100, Opasatika P0L 1Z0 – 705/369-4531, Fax: 705/369-2002
Ops Twp	4,107	Victoria	Victoria-Haliburton	Victoria-Haliburton	Sandra Richardson, Clerk-Treas., RR#5, PO Box 337, Lindsay K9V 4S3 – 705/324-5132, Fax: 705/328-2086
Orangeville †	21,373 ('96)	Dufferin	Wellington-Grey-Dufferin-Simcoe	Dufferin-Peel	Ann E. Armstrong, Clerk, 87 Broadway St., Orangeville L9W 1K1 – 519/941-0439, Fax: 519/941-9033
Orford Twp	1,283	Kent	Kent	Essex-Kent	Jane Smith, Clerk-Treas., Main St., PO Box 196, Highgate N0P 1T0 – 519/678-3961, Fax: 519/678-3694
ORILLIA	26,072	Simcoe	Simcoe North	Simcoe East	Ronald Ellett, City Clerk, 35 West St. North, PO Box 340, Orillia L3V 6J1 – 705/325-1311, Fax: 705/325-5178
Oro-Medonte Twp	15,516	Simcoe	Simcoe North	Simcoe East	Darlene Shoebridge, Clerk, PO Box 100, Oro L0L 2X0 – 705/487-2171, Fax: 705/487-0133
Osgoode Twp	15,207	Ottawa-Carleton Reg. Mun.	Carleton-Gloucester	Carleton	Wayne Robinson, Clerk, 8243 Victoria St., PO Box 130, Metcalfe K0A 2P0 – 613/821-1107, Fax: 613/821-4359
*OSHAWA	132,500 ('95)	Durham Reg. Mun.	Durham; Oshawa	Durham East; Oshawa; Durham Centre	B. Suter, City Clerk, City Hall, 50 Centre St. South, Oshawa L1H 3Z7 – 905/725-7351
Osnabruck Twp	4,568	Stormont, Dundas & Glengarry	Stormont-Dundas	SDG & East Grenville	Betty de Haan, Clerk-Treas., PO Box 340, Ingleside K0C 1M0 – 613/537-2362, Fax: 613/537-8113
Oso Twp	1,189	Frontenac	Hasting-Frontenac-Lennox & Addington	Frontenac-Addington	Cathy MacMunn, Clerk-Treas., PO Box 89, Sharbot Lake K0H 2P0 – 613/279-2935, Fax: 613/279-2422
Osprey Twp	1,996	Grey	Wellington-Grey-Dufferin-Simcoe	Grey	Linda Fry, Clerk-Treas., Maxwell N0C 1J0 – 519/922-2551, Fax: 519/922-2502
Otonabee Twp	5,060	Peterborough	Peterborough	Hastings-Peterborough	Christine A. Wright, Adm.-Clerk-Treas., PO Box 70, Keene K0L 2G0 – 705/295-6852, Fax: 705/295-6405
*OTTAWA	313,971	Ottawa-Carleton Reg. Mun.	Carleton-Gloucester; Ottawa Centre; Ottawa South; Ottawa Vanier; Ottawa West	Carleton East; Ottawa-Rideau; Ottawa Centre; Ottawa East; Ottawa South; Ottawa West	Pierre Pagé, City Clerk, City Hall, 111 Sussex Dr., Ottawa K1N 5A1 – 613/244-5300, Fax: 613/244-5396, URL: http://www.ottawa.com/
OWEN SOUND	20,399	Grey	Bruce-Grey	Grey	Glen E. Henry, City Clerk, City Hall, 808 - 2 Ave. East, Owen Sound N4K 2H4 – 519/376-1440, Fax: 519/371-0511
Oxford-on-Rideau Twp	6,160	Leeds & Grenville	Leeds-Grenville	SDG & East Grenville	Martha Sladek, Clerk-Treas., PO Box 2010, Oxford Mills K0G 1S0 – 613/258-3995, Fax: 613/258-9366
Paipoonge Twp	3,064	Thunder Bay District	Thunder Bay-Atikokan	Fort William	Jocelyn MacKinnon, Clerk-Treas., RR#6, Thunder Bay P7C 5N5 – 807/939-1543, Fax: 807/939-1550
Paisley (V)	1,024	Bruce	Huron-Bruce	Bruce	Joanne Marklewitz, Clerk-Treas., 338 Goldie St., PO Box 460, Paisley N0G 2N0 – 519/353-5609, Fax: 519/353-7145

Canadian Almanac & Directory 1997

Cities in CAPITALS; Towns marked †; Separated Towns marked (SE); Villages marked (V); Townships marked Twp; Restructured Counties marked (RS); United Counties marked (U); Development Areas (DA); • means separated for municipal purposes from county. An in-depth listing for municipalities marked with * appears in Part 2 (check Index for page numbers).

MUNICIPALITY	1994 POP.	COUNTY OR DISTRICT	FEDERAL ELECTORAL DISTRICT	PROVINCIAL ELECTORAL DISTRICT	CONTACT PERSON WITH ADDRESS, PHONE & FAX
Pakenham Twp	1,872	Lanark	Lanark-Carleton	Lanark-Renfrew	Diane Smithson, Clerk-Treas., Municipal Office, PO Box 40, Pakenham K0A 2X0 – 613/624-5430, Fax: 613/624-5646
Palmerston †	2,350	Wellington	Wellington-Grey-Dufferin-Simcoe	Wellington	Larry C. Adams, Clerk-Treas., 250 Daly St., PO Box 190, Palmerston N0G 2P0 – 519/343-2340, Fax: 519/343-2278
Palmerston & N. & S. Canonto Twp	348	Frontenac	Wellington-Grey-Dufferin-Simcoe	Frontenac-Addington	Heather Gemmill, Clerk-Treas., RR#1, Ompah K0H 2J0 – 613/479-2811, Fax: 613/479-2364
Papineau-Cameron Twp	925	Nipissing District	Nipissing	Parry Sound	Sandra J. Morin, Clerk-Treas., PO Box 630, Mattawa P0H 1V0 – 705/744-5610, Fax: 705/744-0434
Paris †	8,552	Brant	Brant	Brant-Haldimand	Gloria Taylor, Clerk-Adm., 66 Grand River St. North, Paris N3L 2M2 – 519/442-6324, Fax: 519/442-3461
Parkhill †	1,677	Middlesex	Lambton-Middlesex	Middlesex	Vivian L. Gunness, Adm.-Clerk-Treas., 229 Main St., PO Box 9, Parkhill N0M 2K0 – 519/294-6244, Fax: 519/294-0573
Parry Sound †	5,991	Parry Sound District	Parry Sound-Muskoka	Parry Sound	Ian Mollett, CAO, 52 Seguin St., Parry Sound P2A 1B4 – 705/746-2101, Fax: 705/746-7461
Peel Twp	4,294	Wellington	Perth-Wellington-Waterloo	Wellington	Christine Oosterveld, Clerk-Treas., PO Box 119, Drayton N0G 1P0 – 519/638-3314, Fax: 519/638-5113
Pelee Twp	261	Essex	Essex-Kent	Essex-South	Brett Kelly, Clerk-Treas., Pelee Island N0R 1M0 – 519/724-2931, Fax: 519/724-2470
Pelham †	13,956 ('95)	Niagara Reg. Mun.	Erie	Lincoln	Murray Hackett, Clerk-Adm., 20 Pelham Town Square, PO Box 400, Fonthill L0S 1E0 – 905/892-2607, Fax: 905/892-5055
PEMBROKE	13,445	Renfrew	Renfrew-Nipissing-Pembroke	Renfrew North	Raymond J. Brazeau, CAO, 1 Pembroke St. East, PO Box 277, Pembroke K8A 6X3 – 613/735-6821, Fax: 613/735-3660
Pembroke Twp	1,891	Renfrew	Renfrew-Nipissing-Pembroke	Renfrew North	Darrel J. Ryan, Adm.-Clerk-Treas., RR#4, Pembroke K8A 6W5 – 613/735-2319, Fax: 613/735-6614
Penetanguishene †	6,794	Simcoe	Simcoe North	Simcoe East	George N. Vadeboncoeur, CAO-Clerk, 10 Robert St. West, PO Box 580, Penetanguishene L9M 2E4 – 705/549-7453, Fax: 705/549-3743
Percy Twp	3,062	Northumberland	Northumberland	Northumberland	Ria Colquhoun, Clerk & CAO, 40 Main St., PO Box 129, Warkworth K0K 3K0 – 705/924-2931, Fax: 705/924-3139
Perry Twp	2,023	Parry Sound District	Parry Sound-Muskoka	Parry Sound	Peter Lafantaisie, CAO-Clerk, Old Government Rd., PO Box 70, Emsdale P0A 1J0 – 705/636-5941, Fax: 705/636-5759
Perth †	5,524	Lanark	Lanark-Carleton	Lanark-Renfrew	Thomas G. Kent, Clerk-Adm., 80 Gore St. East, Perth K7H 1H9 – 613/267-3311, Fax: 613/267-7351
Petawawa (V)	6,016	Renfrew	Renfrew-Nipissing-Pembroke	Renfrew North	Robert W. Rantz, Clerk-Treas., 30 Victoria St., PO Box 69, Petawawa K8H 2X1 – 613/687-5536, Fax: 613/687-5973
Petawawa Twp	8,430	Renfrew	Renfrew-Nipissing-Pembroke	Renfrew North	Mitchell W. (Mitch) Stillman, Adm.-Clerk-Treas., 680 Hwy. 17 West, Pembroke K8A 7H5 – 613/735-2591, Fax: 613/735-7335
*PETERBOROUGH	66,494	Peterborough	Peterborough	Peterborough	Steven F. Brickell, City Clerk, 500 George St. North, Peterborough K9H 3R9 – 705/742-7771, Fax: 705/743-7825
Petrolia †	4,809	Lambton	Lambton-Middlesex	Lambton	Brad Loosley, Adm.-Clerk-Treas., 4201 Petrolia St., PO Box 1270, Petrolia N0N 1R0 – 519/882-2350, Fax: 519/882-3373
*Pickering †	70,733	Durham Reg. Mun.	Ontario	Durham West	Bruce J. Taylor, Town Clerk, Pickering Civic Complex, One The Esplanade, Pickering L1V 6K7 – 905/683-2760, Fax: 905/420-0515
Pickle Lake Twp	489	Kenora District	Kenora-Rainy River	Lake Nipigon	Heather B. Brown, Clerk-Treas., PO Box 340, Pickle Lake P0V 3A0 – 807/928-2034, Fax: 807/928-2708
Picton †	4,077	Prince Edward	Prince Edward-Hastings	Prince Edward-Lennox-South Hastings	Sterling P. Johnston, Clerk-Treas., 74 King St., PO Box 1670, Picton K0K 2T0 – 613/476-5966, Fax: 613/476-8144
Pilkington Twp	2,369	Wellington	Wellington-Grey-Dufferin-Simcoe	Wellington	Caroline Hacking, Clerk-Treas., RR#2, Elora N0B 1S0 – 519/846-9801, Fax: 519/846-9858
Pittsburgh Twp	10,675	Frontenac	Hastings-Frontenac-Lennox & Addington; Kingston & the Islands	Frontenac-Addington; Kingston & the Islands	Beulah N. Webb, Clerk, 900 McLean Crt., PO Box 966, Kingston K7L 4X8 – 613/546-3283, Fax: 613/546-0908

Cities in CAPITALS; Towns marked †; Separated Towns marked (SE); Villages marked (V); Townships marked Twp; Restructured Counties marked (RS); United Counties marked (U); Development Areas (DA); • means separated for municipal purposes from county. An in-depth listing for municipalities marked with * appears in Part 2 (check Index for page numbers).

MUNICIPALITY	1994 POP.	COUNTY OR DISTRICT	FEDERAL ELECTORAL DISTRICT	PROVINCIAL ELECTORAL DISTRICT	CONTACT PERSON WITH ADDRESS, PHONE & FAX
Plantagenet (V)	964	Prescott & Russell	Glengarry-Prescott-Russell	Prescott & Russell	Sylvio Simard, Clerk-Treas., 220 Main St., PO Box 350, Plantagenet K0B 1L0 – 613/673-4859, Fax: 613/673-1021
Plummer, Add'l Twp	664	Algoma District	Algoma	Algoma	Betty Mills, Clerk-Treas., RR#1, Bruce Mines P0R 1C0 – 705/785-3479, Fax: 705/785-3135
Plympton Twp	5,119	Lambton	Lambton-Middlesex	Lambton	Archie W. McKinlay, Clerk, PO Box 400, Wyoming N0N 1T0 – 519/845-3939, Fax: 519/845-0597
Point Edward (V)	2,277	Lambton	Sarnia-Lambton	Sarnia	Joe Simon, Clerk-Treas., 36 St. Clair St., Point Edward N7V 4G8 – 519/337-3021, Fax: 519/337-5963
Port Burwell (V)	882	Elgin	Elgin-Norfolk	Elgin	David Free, Clerk-Adm., 21 Pitt St., PO Box 10, Port Burwell N0J 1T0 – 519/874-4343, Fax: 519/874-4948
PORT COLBORNE	18,389	Niagara Reg. Mun.	Erie	Niagara South	Len C. Hunt, Clerk-Treas., 239 King St., Port Colborne L3K 4G8 – 905/835-2900, Fax: 905/834-5746
Port Elgin †	6,772	Bruce	Huron-Bruce	Bruce	Martin Parker, Clerk, 515 Goderich St., Port Elgin N0H 2C4 – 519/832-2008, Fax: 519/832-2140
Port Hope †	11,040	Northumberland	Northumberland	Northumberland	Mike Rostetter, Clerk & CAO, 56 Queen St., PO Box 117, Port Hope L1A 3V9 – 905/885-4544, Fax: 905/885-7698
Port Stanley (V)	2,183	Elgin	Elgin-Norfolk	Elgin	Donald N. Leitch, Clerk-Adm., 302 Bridge St., Port Stanley N5L 1J7 – 519/782-3383, Fax: 519/782-5142
Portland Twp	4,529	Frontenac	Hastings-Frontenac-Lennox & Addington	Frontenac-Addington	Deborah Bracken, Clerk-Treas., PO Box 1000, Hartington K0H 1W0 – 613/372-2743, Fax: 613/372-1108
Powassan †	1,122	Parry Sound District	Parry Sound-Muskoka	Parry Sound	Traven D. Reed, Adm., 270 King St., PO Box 250, Powassan P0H 1Z0 – 705/724-2813, Fax: 705/724-5533
Prescott (SE)	3,999	Leeds & Grenville	Leeds-Grenville	Leeds-Grenville	Andrew Brown, Clerk & CAO, 360 Dibble St. West, PO Box 160, Prescott K0E 1T0 – 613/925-2812, Fax: 613/925-4381
Prince Twp	965	Algoma District	Algoma	Algoma	Rachel Tyczinski, Adm.-Clerk-Treas., 3042 2nd Line West, RR#6, Sault Ste. Marie P6A 6K4 – 705/779-2992, Fax: 705/779-2725
Proton Twp	1,783	Grey	Wellington-Grey-Dufferin-Simcoe	Grey	Helgi Scott, Clerk, RR#1, Dundalk N0C 1B0 – 519/923-2110, Fax: 519/923-9262
Puslinch Twp	4,585	Wellington	Guelph-Wellington	Wellington	Brenda Law, Clerk-Treas., RR#3, Guelph N1H 6H9 – 519/763-1226, Fax: 519/763-5846
Radcliffe Twp	1,058	Renfrew	Renfrew-Nipissing-Pembroke	Renfrew North	Pat E. Pilgrim, Clerk-Treas., Farmer Rd., PO Box 70, Combermere K0J 1L0 – 613/756-3704, Fax: 613/756-3704
Raglan Twp	834	Renfrew	Renfrew-Nipissing-Pembroke	Renfrew North	Evaliene Krieger, Clerk-Treas., Palmer Rapids K0J 2E0 – 613/758-2061, Fax: 613/758-2235
Rainy River †	921	Rainy River District	Kenora-Rainy River	Rainy River	Irwin E. Johnston, Clerk-Treas., 200 Atwood Ave., PO Box 488, Rainy River P0W 1L0 – 807/852-3978, Fax: 807/852-3553
Raleigh Twp	5,209	Kent	Essex-Kent	Essex-Kent	Stu Cuthbert, Adm.-Clerk-Treas., RR#5, Merlin N0P 1W0 – 519/689-4206, Fax: 519/689-4870
Ramara Twp	9,757	Simcoe	Simcoe North	Simcoe East	Francis B. Mangan, Clerk, PO Box 130, Brechin L0K 1B0 – 705/484-5374, Fax: 705/484-0441
Ramsay Twp	3,624	Lanark	Lanark-Carleton	Lanark-Renfrew	Ross E. Trimble, Adm.-Clerk-Treas., RR#2, Almonte K0A 1A0 – 613/256-2064, Fax: 613/256-4887
Ratter & Dunnet Twp	1,248	Sudbury District	Timiskaming-French River	Sudbury East	Katherine McCauley, Clerk-Treas., 38 Rutland Ave., PO Box 250, Warren P0H 2N0 – 705/967-2174, Fax: 705/967-2177
Rawdon Twp	2,618	Hastings	Hastings-Frontenac-Lennox & Addington	Hastings-Peterborough	Cheryl Robson, Clerk-Treas. & Adm., General Delivery, Springbrook K0K 3C0 – 613/395-3962, Fax: 613/395-0672
Rayside-Balfour †	14,816	Sudbury Reg. Mun.	Nickel Belt	Nickel Belt	Gary J. Michalak, Clerk, 108 Hwy#144, PO Box 639, Chelmsford P0M 1L0 – 705/855-9061, Fax: 705/855-5737
Red Lake Twp	2,061	Kenora District	Kenora-Rainy River	Kenora	Arthur Osborne, CAO-Clerk, 117 Howey St., PO Box 308, Red Lake P0V 2M0 – 807/727-2311, Fax: 807/727-3980
Red Rock Twp	1,237	Thunder Bay District	Thunder Bay-Nipigon	Lake Nipigon	Michael W. Groulx, Adm. & Clerk-Treas., 42 Salls St., PO Box 447, Red Rock P0T 2P0 – 807/886-2245, Fax: 807/886-2793

Canadian Almanac & Directory 1997

Cities in CAPITALS; Towns marked †; Separated Towns marked (SE); Villages marked (V); Townships marked Twp; Restructured Counties marked (RS); United Counties marked (U); Development Areas (DA); • means separated for municipal purposes from county. An in-depth listing for municipalities marked with * appears in Part 2 (check Index for page numbers).

MUNICIPALITY	1994 POP.	COUNTY OR DISTRICT	FEDERAL ELECTORAL DISTRICT	PROVINCIAL ELECTORAL DISTRICT	CONTACT PERSON WITH ADDRESS, PHONE & FAX
Renfrew †	7,665	Renfrew	Renfrew-Nipissing-Pembroke	Lanark-Renfrew	Dorian Laurier, Clerk, 127 Raglan St. South, PO Box 2000, Renfrew K7V 4G7 – 613/432-4848, Fax: 613/432-8265
Richmond Twp	3,829	Lennox & Addington	Hastings-Frontenac-Lennox & Addington	Prince Edward-Lennox-South Hastings	Doreen Doupe, Clerk-Treas., PO Box 100, Selby K0K 2Z0 – 613/388-2603, Fax: 613/388-2790
*Richmond Hill †	87,000	York Reg. Mun.	York North	York Centre	Robert Douglas, Town Clerk, 225 East Beaver Creek Rd., PO Box 300, Richmond Hill L4C 4Y5 – 905/771-8800, Fax: 905/771-2400
Rideau Twp	12,106	Ottawa-Carleton Reg. Mun.	Carleton-Gloucester	Carleton	J. David Ball, Clerk, 2155 Roger Stevens Dr., North Gower K0A 2T0 – 613/489-3314, Fax: 613/489-2880
Ridgetown †	3,234	Kent	Kent	Essex-Kent	Gerald P. Secord, Adm.-Clerk-Treas., 45 Main St. East, PO Box 550, Ridgetown N0P 2C0 – 519/674-5583, Fax: 519/674-0660
Rochester Twp	4,384	Essex	Essex-Windsor	Essex-Kent	Annette Drouillard, Clerk-Adm., 958 Hwy#2, St. Joachim N0R 1S0 – 519/728-2213, Fax: 519/728-4614
Rockcliffe Park (V)	2,183	Ottawa-Carleton Reg. Mun.	Ottawa Vanier	Carleton East	Murray MacLean, Clerk-Adm., 350 Springfield Rd., Rockcliffe Park K1M 0K7 – 613/749-9791, Fax: 613/749-0127
Rockland †	7,547	Prescott & Russell	Glengarry-Prescott-Russell	Prescott & Russell	Diane Labelle, Clerk-Adm., 1560 Laurier St., PO Box 909, Rockland K4K 1P7 – 613/446-6022, Fax: 613/446-7320
Rolph, Buchanan, Wylie & McKay Twp	1,822	Renfrew	Renfrew-Nipissing-Pembroke	Renfrew North	Mary Mysyk, Clerk-Treas. & CAO, RR#1, Deep River K0J 1P0 – 613/584-3114, Fax: 613/584-3285
Romney Twp	1,946	Kent	Essex-Kent	Essex-Kent	Earl R. Waites, Clerk-Treas., 994 Talbot Trail, RR#1, Wheatley N0P 2P0 – 519/825-4618, Fax: 519/825-4619
Ross Twp	1,873	Renfrew	Renfrew-Nipissing-Pembroke	Renfrew North	Eleanor Tabbert, Clerk-Treas., PO Box 1, Forester's Falls K0J 1V0 – 613/646-7428, Fax: 613/646-7332
Rosseau (V)	284	Parry Sound District	Parry Sound-Muskoka	Parry Sound	Yvonne Mullen, Clerk-Treas., Victoria St., PO Box 8, Rosseau P0C 1J0 – 705/732-4231, Fax: 705/732-1817
Roxborough Twp	3,383	Stormont, Dundas & Glengarry	Stormont-Dundas	SDG & East Grenville	Paulette Valley, Deputy Clerk-Treas., 2594 Tolmies Corners Rd., PO Box 189, Moose Creek K0C 1W0 – 613/538-2531, Fax: 613/538-2650
Russell Twp	11,417	Prescott & Russell	Glengarry-Prescott-Russell	Prescott & Russell	Jean-Guy Bourdeau, Adm.-Clerk, 717 Notre Dame St., Embrun K0A 1W1 – 613/443-3066, Fax: 613/443-1042
Rutherford & George Island Twp	379	Manitoulin District	Algoma	Algoma-Manitoulin	Jeannette Roque, Clerk-Treas., 32 Commissioner St., Killarney P0M 2A0 – 705/287-2424, Fax: 705/287-2660
Ryerson Twp	582	Parry Sound District	Parry Sound-Muskoka	Moosomin	Judy McCarty, Clerk-Treas., RR#1, Burk's Falls P0A 1C0 – 705/382-3232, Fax: 705/382-3286
*ST CATHARINES	125,887	Niagara Reg. Mun.	St. Catharines; Welland-St. Catharines-Thorold	St. Catharines-Brock; St. Catharines; Lincoln	Kenneth R. Todd, City Clerk & Director, Corporate Support Services, City Hall, 50 Church St., PO Box 3012, St. Catharines L2R 7C2 – 905/688-5600, Fax: 905/682-3631
St. Clair Beach (V)	3,495	Essex	Windsor-St. Clair	Windsor-Riverside	Andre M. Barrette, Clerk-Treas., 13677 St. Gregory's Rd., Windsor N8N 3E4 – 519/735-6261, Fax: 519/735-8388
St. Edmunds Twp	929	Bruce	Bruce-Grey	Bruce	Cathy Robins, Clerk-Adm., PO Box 70, Tobermory N0H 2R0 – 519/596-2430, Fax: 519/596-2536
St. Isidore (V)	740	Prescott & Russell	Glengarry-Prescott-Russell	Prescott & Russell	Norman Bonneville, Clerk-Treas., 25 rue de l'Église, PO Box 10, St. Isidore K0C 2B0 – 613/524-2155, Fax: 613/524-3406
St. Joseph Twp	1,108	Algoma District	Algoma	Algoma	A. Michael Jagger, Clerk-Treas., 1511 - 10 Side Rd., PO Box 187, Richards Landing P0R 1J0 – 705/246-2625, Fax: 705/246-3142
St. Marys †	5,493	Perth	Perth-Wellington-Waterloo	Perth	Kenneth G. Storey, Adm.-Clerk-Treas., 175 Queen St. East, PO Box 998, St. Marys N4X 1B6 – 519/284-2340, Fax: 519/284-2881
ST. THOMAS	29,758	Elgin	Elgin-Norfolk	Elgin	Peter Leack, Clerk, City Hall, 545 Talbot St., PO Box 520, St. Thomas N5P 3V7 – 519/631-1680, Fax: 519/633-9019
St. Vincent Twp	2,296	Grey	Bruce-Grey	Grey	Jim Foster, Clerk-Treas., RR#1, Meaford N4L 1W5 – 519/538-2421, Fax: 519/538-5599

Cities in CAPITALS; Towns marked †; Separated Towns marked (SE); Villages marked (V); Townships marked Twp; Restructured Counties marked (RS); United Counties marked (U); Development Areas (DA); • means separated for municipal purposes from county. An in-depth listing for municipalities marked with * appears in Part 2 (check Index for page numbers).

MUNICIPALITY	1994 POP.	COUNTY OR DISTRICT	FEDERAL ELECTORAL DISTRICT	PROVINCIAL ELECTORAL DISTRICT	CONTACT PERSON WITH ADDRESS, PHONE & FAX
Sandfield Twp	245	Manitoulin District	Algoma	Algoma-Manitoulin	Ruth F. Legge, Clerk-Treas., RR#1, Mindemoya P0P 1C0 – 705/377-5621, Fax: 705/377-5621
Sandwich South Twp	6,260	Essex	Essex-Windsor	Essex-Kent	Gerald Sykes, Clerk-Adm., 3455 North Talbot Rd., Oldcastle N0R 1L0 – 519/737-6971, Fax: 519/737-1975
Sarawak Twp	2,727	Grey	Bruce-Grey	Grey	Kenneth J. Clarke, Adm. & Clerk-Treas., RR#2, Owen Sound N4K 5N4 – 519/376-2729, Fax: 519/372-1620
*SARNIA	69,657	Lambton	Sarnia-Lambton	Sarnia	Ann Tuplin, City Clerk & Commissioner, Administrative Services, City Hall, 255 North Christina St., PO Box 3018, Sarnia N7T 7N2 – 519/332-0330, Fax: 519/332-3995
Saugeen Twp	1,759	Bruce	Huron-Bruce	Bruce	Linda White, Clerk-Dep. Treas., PO Box 249, Port Elgin N0H 2C0 – 519/389-5550, Fax: 519/389-4305
*SAULT STE. MARIE	78,399	Algoma District	Sault Ste. Marie; Algoma	Sault Ste. Marie	Donna P. Irving, City Clerk, Civic Centre, 99 Foster Dr., PO Box 580, Sault Ste Marie P6A 5N1 – 705/759-2500, Fax: 705/759-2310
*SCARBOROUGH	510,000 ('96)	Metro Mun.	Scarborough-Agincourt; Scarborough Centre; Scarborough East; Scarborough-Rouge River; Scarborough West	Scarborough-Agincourt; Scarborough Centre; Scarborough East; Scarborough-Ellesmere; Scarborough North; Scarborough West	W. Drew Westwater, City Clerk, Civic Centre, 150 Borough Dr., Scarborough M1P 4N7 – 416/396-7111, Fax: 416/396-6920
Schreiber Twp	1,762	Thunder Bay District	Cochrane-Superior	Lake Nipigon	Dawn Halcrow, Clerk-Treas.-Adm., 608 Winnipeg St., Schreiber P0T 2S0 – 807/824-2711, Fax: 807/824-3231
Scugog Twp	17,880	Durham Reg. Mun.	Durham	Durham East	Earl S. Cuddie, Adm.-Clerk, 181 Perry St., PO Box 780, Port Perry L9L 1A7 – 905/985-7346, Fax: 905/985-1931
Seaforth †	2,223	Huron	Huron-Bruce	Huron	James D. Crocker, CAO & Clerk-Treas., 72 Main St. South, Seaforth N0K 1W0 – 519/527-0160, Fax: 519/527-2561
Sebastopol Twp	559	Renfrew	Renfrew-Nipissing-Pembroke	Renfrew North	Sandra Yonin, Clerk-Treas., Foymount K0J 1W0 – 613/754-2825, Fax: 613/754-2825
Severn Twp	9,757	Simcoe	Simcoe North	Simcoe East	James B. Mather, Clerk & CAO, PO Box 159, Orillia L3V 6J3 – 705/325-2315, Fax: 705/327-5818
Seymour Twp	4,226	Northumberland	Northumberland	Northumberland	Shirley M. Preston, Clerk-Treas., 66 Front St. South, PO Box 1027, Campbellford K0L 1L0 – 705/653-2330, Fax: 705/653-5413
Shallow Lake (V)	457	Grey	Bruce-Grey	Grey	Rosemary Buchanan, Clerk-Treas., 12 Cruickshank St., Shallow Lake N0H 2K0 – 519/935-3164, Fax: 519/935-3164
Shedden Twp	809	Algoma District	Elgin-Norfolk	Algoma-Manitoulin	Mary Bray, Clerk-Treas.-Adm., 8 Trunk Rd., PO Box 70, Spanish P0P 2A0 – 705/844-2300, Fax: 705/844-2622
Sheffield Twp	1,367	Lennox & Addington	Hastings-Frontenac-Lennox & Addington	Frontenac-Addington	Susan Beckel, Clerk, Ottawa St., PO Box 3, Tamworth K0K 3G0 – 613/379-2923, Fax: 613/379-2789
Shelburne †	3,450	Dufferin	Wellington-Grey-Dufferin-Simcoe	Dufferin-Peel	Susan McKenzie, Clerk-Treas., 203 Main St. East, PO Box 69, Shelburne L0N 1S0 – 519/925-2600, Fax: 519/925-6134
Sherborne et al Twp	553	Haliburton	Victoria-Haliburton	Victoria-Haliburton	Diane J. Griffin, Adm.-Clerk-Treas., PO Box 99, Dorset P0A 1E0 – 705/766-2211, Fax: 705/766-9688
Sherwood, Jones & Burns Twp	2,047	Renfrew	Renfrew-Nipissing-Pembroke	Renfrew North	Valerie R. Jahn, Clerk-Treas., RR#2, Barry's Bay K0J 1B0 – 613/756-2741, Fax: 613/756-0251
Shuniah Twp	2,144	Thunder Bay District	Thunder Bay-Nipigon	Port Arthur	Janice C. Ross, Clerk-Treas., 420 Leslie Ave., Thunder Bay P7A 1X8 – 807/683-3611, Fax: 807/683-6982
Sidney Twp	12,890	Hastings	Prince Edward-Hastings	Quinte	James R. (Jim) Pine, CAO, RR#5, Belleville K8N 4Z5 – 613/966-8330, Fax: 613/966-4973
Simcoe †	14,896	Haldimand-Norfolk Reg. Mun.	Haldimand-Norfolk	Norfolk	Lori Heinbuch, Clerk, 50 Colborne St. South, PO Box 545, Simcoe N3Y 4N5 – 519/426-5870, Fax: 519/426-8573
Sioux Lookout †	3,073	Kenora District	Kenora-Rainy River	Kenora	Mary L. MacKenzie, Clerk, 25 - 5 Ave., PO Box 158, Sioux Lookout P8T 1A4 – 807/737-2700, Fax: 807/737-3436

Canadian Almanac & Directory 1997

Cities in CAPITALS; Towns marked †; Separated Towns marked (SE); Villages marked (V); Townships marked Twp; Restructured Counties marked (RS); United Counties marked (U); Development Areas (DA); • means separated for municipal purposes from county. An in-depth listing for municipalities marked with * appears in Part 2 (check Index for page numbers).

MUNICIPALITY	1994 POP.	COUNTY OR DISTRICT	FEDERAL ELECTORAL DISTRICT	PROVINCIAL ELECTORAL DISTRICT	CONTACT PERSON WITH ADDRESS, PHONE & FAX
Sioux Narrows Twp	360	Kenora District	Kenora-Rainy River	Kenora	Debbie Sinclair, Clerk-Treas., PO Box 417, Sioux Narrows P0X 1N0 – 807/226-5241, Fax: 807/226-5712
Smith Twp	8,692	Peterborough	Peterborough	Peterborough	Derick A. Holyoake, Adm.-Clerk-Treas., PO Box 270, Bridgenorth K0L 1H0 – 705/292-9507, Fax: 705/292-6491
Smiths Falls (SE)	9,001	Lanark	Lanark-Carleton	Lanark-Renfrew	Kathy L. Coulthart-Dewey, Clerk, 77 Beckwith St. North, PO Box 695, Smiths Falls K7A 4T6 – 613/283-4124, Fax: 613/283-4764
Smooth Rock Falls †	1,877	Cochrane District	Cochrane-Superior	Cochrane North	Roger Labelle, Clerk & CAO, 142 - 1 St., PO Box 249, Smooth Rock Falls P0L 2B0 – 705/338-2717, Fax: 705/338-2584
Snowdon Twp	803	Halburton	Victoria-Haliburton	Victoria-Haliburton	Ernest A. Hills, Clerk-Treas., RR#1, Minden K0M 2K0 – 705/286-2657, Fax: 705/286-1685
Sombra Twp	4,081	Lambton	Lambton-Middlesex	Lambton	John De Mars, Clerk-Adm., PO Box 40, Sombra N0P 2H0 – 519/892-3637, Fax: 519/892-3543
Somerville Twp	2,092	Victoria	Victoria-Haliburton	Victoria-Haliburton	Elinor Burke, Clerk-Treas., PO Box 59, Kinmount K0M 2A0 – 705/488-2571, Fax: 705/488-2576
Sophiasburgh Twp	2,067	Prince Edward	Prince Edward-Hastings	Prince Edward-Lennox-South Hastings	Gordon A. Way, Clerk-Treas., Demorestville K0K 1W0 – 613/476-2209, Fax: 613/476-2220
South Algona Twp	328	Renfrew	Renfrew-Nipissing-Pembroke	Renfrew North	Brenda Jolicoeur, Clerk-Treas., RR#4, Killaloe K0J 2A0 – 613/625-2323, Fax: 613/625-2538
South Crosby Twp	1,771	Leeds & Grenville	Leeds-Grenville	Leeds-Grenville	Myrna Stearry, Clerk-Treas., RR#1, Elgin K0G 1E0 – 613/359-5830, Fax: 613/359-5849
South Dorchester Twp	1,806	Elgin	Elgin-Norfolk	Elgin	Jane Knapp, Clerk-Treas., RR#2, Springfield N0L 2J0 – 519/765-4175, Fax: 519/765-4153
South Dumfries Twp	5,103	Brant	Brant	Brant-Haldimand	James G. Wilson, Clerk-Treas., 13 Main St. South, PO Box 40, St. George N0E 1N0 – 519/448-1432, Fax: 519/448-3105
South Easthope Twp	1,837	Perth	Perth-Wellington-Waterloo	Perth	Margaret Hislop, Clerk-Treas., 37 William St. West, PO Box 269, Shakespeare N0B 2P0 – 519/625-8372, Fax: 519/625-8498
South Elmsley Twp	3,312	Leeds & Grenville	Leeds-Grenville	Leeds-Grenville	Sharon Seward, Clerk-Treas., RR#1, Smiths Falls K7A 5B8 – 613/283-5427, Fax: 613/283-5918
South Fredericks-burgh Twp	1,147	Lennox & Addington	Hastings-Frontenac-Lennox & Addington	Prince Edward-Lennox-South Hastings	Lorraine Patterson, Clerk-Treas., RR#2, Napanee K7R 3K7 – 613/354-2420, Fax: 613/354-7682
South Gower Twp	2,280	Leeds-Grenville	Leeds & Grenville	SDG & East Grenville	Dorothy McCargar, Clerk-Treas., RR#3, Kemptville K0G 1J0 – 613/258-2781, Fax: 613/258-5574
South Marysburgh Twp	848	Prince Edward	Prince Edward-Hastings	Prince Edward-Lennox-South Hastings	Clifford Walker, Clerk-Treas., PO Box 12, Milford K0K 2P0 – 613/476-6771, Fax: 613/476-6771
South Monaghan Twp	1,250	Peterborough	Peterborough	Peterborough	June M. Buettner, Clerk-Treas., 199 Highway 28, Bailieboro K0L 1B0 – 705/939-6079, Fax: 705/939-1096
South Plantagenet Twp	1,788	Prescott & Russell	Glengarry-Prescott-Russell	Prescott & Russell	Calista Nicholas, Clerk-Treas., 3248 County Rd. #9, RR#1, Fournier K0B 1G0 – 613/524-2932, Fax: 613/524-3351
South River (V)	1,080	Parry Sound District	Parry Sound-Muskoka	Parry Sound	Richard V. Clouthier, Clerk-Adm., 209 Ottawa Ave., PO Box 310, South River P0A 1X0 – 705/386-2573, Fax: 705/386-0702
South Sherbrooke Twp	670	Lanark	Lanark-Carleton	Lanark-Renfrew	Allan Burn, Clerk-Treas., RR#1, Maberly K0H 2B0 – 613/268-2194, Fax: 613/268-2478
South-West Oxford Twp	8,422	Oxford	Oxford	Oxford	Allen Forrester, Clerk-Treas.-Adm., RR#1, Mount Elgin N0J 1N0 – 519/485-0477, Fax: 519/485-2932
Southampton †	3,065	Bruce	Huron-Bruce	Bruce	Ronald G. Brown, Clerk-Adm., 201 High St., PO Box 340, Southampton N0H 2L0 – 519/797-2015, Fax: 519/797-3088
Southwold Twp	4,431	Elgin	Elgin-Norfolk	Elgin	R. Alex Pow, Clerk, General Delivery, Fingal N0L 1K0 – 519/769-2010, Fax: 519/769-2837
The Spanish River Twp	1,476	Sudbury District	Algoma	Algoma-Manitoulin	Austin H. Clipperton, Clerk-Treas., Site 1, RR#3, PO Box 5, Massey P0P 1P0 – 705/865-2646, Fax: 705/865-2736
Springer Twp	2,434	Nipissing District	Nipissing; Timiskaming-French River	Nipissing	Normand Roberge, Clerk-Treas. & CAO, 245 Hwy 17 East, PO Box 1390, Sturgeon Falls P0H 2G0 – 705/753-0570, Fax: 705/753-1034

ONTARIO MUNICIPALITIES 4-69

Cities in CAPITALS; Towns marked †; Separated Towns marked (SE); Villages marked (V); Townships marked Twp; Restructured Counties marked (RS); United Counties marked (U); Development Areas (DA); • means separated for municipal purposes from county. An in-depth listing for municipalities marked with * appears in Part 2 (check Index for page numbers).

MUNICIPALITY	1994 POP.	COUNTY OR DISTRICT	FEDERAL ELECTORAL DISTRICT	PROVINCIAL ELECTORAL DISTRICT	CONTACT PERSON WITH ADDRESS, PHONE & FAX
Springfield (V)	669	Elgin	Elgin-Norfolk	Elgin	Catherine Bearss, Clerk-Treas., 106 Main St., PO Box 29, Springfield N0L 2J0 – 519/765-4222, Fax: 519/765-4222
Springwater Twp	14,073	Simcoe	Simcoe Centre	Simcoe Centre	Eleanor Rath, Clerk, County of Simcoe Administrative Centre, Midhurst L0L 1X0 – 705/728-4784, Fax: 705/728-6957
Stafford Twp	2,712	Renfrew	Renfrew-Nipissing-Pembroke	Renfrew North	Darrel J. Ryan, Adm.-Clerk-Treas., RR#4, Pembroke K8A 6W5 – 613/735-3955, Fax: 613/735-6614
Stanhope Twp	1,174	Haliburton	Victoria-Haliburton	Victoria-Haliburton	Gerald C. Bain, Adm.-Clerk-Treas., RR#2, Minden K0M 2K0 – 705/489-2379, Fax: 705/489-3491
Stanley Twp	1,613	Huron	Huron-Bruce	Huron	E. Ansberth Willert, Clerk-Treas., RR#1, Varna N0M 2R0 – 519/233-7907, Fax: 519/233-3111
Stephen Twp	4,215	Huron	Huron-Bruce	Huron	Laurence R. Brown, CAO & Clerk-Treas., 38 Victoria St. East, Crediton N0M 1M0 – 519/234-6331, Fax: 519/234-6301
Stirling (V)	2,998	Hastings	Hastings-Frontenac-Lennox & Addington	Hastings-Peterborough	Kathy Reid, Adm.-Clerk-Treas., 98 Front St. East, PO Box 40, Stirling K0K 3E0 – 613/395-3380, Fax: 613/395-0864
*STONEY CREEK	51,865	Hamilton-Wentworth Reg. Mun.	Lincoln	Wentworth East	Rose Caterini, City Clerk, 777 Hwy. 8, PO Box 9940, Stoney Creek L8G 4N9 – 905/643-1261, Fax: 905/643-6161
Storrington Twp	3,940	Frontenac	Hastings-Frontenac-Lennox & Addington	Frontenac-Addington	David Bass, Adm. & Clerk-Treas., RR#1, Battersea K0H 1H0 – 613/353-2222, Fax: 613/353-1225
STRATFORD	27,563	Perth	Perth-Wellington-Waterloo	Perth	Ron Shaw, Clerk-Adm., City Hall, One Wellington St., PO Box 818, Stratford N5A 6W1 – 519/271-0250, Fax: 519/273-5041
Strathroy †	10,981	Middlesex	Lambton-Middlesex	Middlesex	Arden Royce, Clerk-Adm., 52 Frank St., Strathroy N7G 2R4 – 519/245-1070, Fax: 519/245-6353
Strong Twp	1,349	Parry Sound District	Parry Sound-Muskoka	Parry Sound	Diana Georgie, Clerk-Treas., Hwy 11 South, PO Box 420, Sundridge P0A 1Z0 – 705/384-5819, Fax: 705/384-5892
Sturgeon Falls †	6,161	Nipissing District	Nipissing	Nipissing	Guy Savage, Adm.-Clerk-Treas., 225 Holditch St., PO Box 270, Sturgeon Falls P0H 2G0 – 705/753-2250, Fax: 705/753-3950
Sturgeon Point (V)	89	Victoria	Victoria-Haliburton	Victoria-Haliburton	Marlyn Beggs, Clerk-Treas., RR#3, Fenelon Falls K0M 1N0 – 705/887-2343, Fax: 705/887-9340
*SUDBURY	87,087	Sudbury Reg. Mun.	Nickel Belt; Sudbury	Sudbury; Sudbury East	Thom M. Mowry, Clerk, City Hall, Civic Square, 200 Brady St., PO Box 5000, Sudbury P3A 5P3 – 705/674-3141
Sullivan Twp	2,655	Grey	Bruce-Grey	Grey	Will Moore, Clerk-Treas., PO Box 92, Desboro N0H 1K0 – 519/794-3024, Fax: 519/794-4499
Sundridge (V)	979	Parry Sound District	Parry Sound-Muskoka	Parry Sound	Lillian S. Fowler, Clerk-Treas., 110 Main St., PO Box 129, Sundridge P0A 1Z0 – 705/384-5316, Fax: 705/384-7874
Sydenham Twp	2,997	Grey	Bruce-Grey	Grey	Richard Holland, Clerk-Treas., RR#8, Owen Sound N4K 5W4 – 519/376-8487, Fax: 519/376-8090
Tara (V)	863	Bruce	Bruce-Grey	Bruce	Holly M. MacArthur, Clerk-Treas., 39 Yonge St., PO Box 238, Tara N0H 2N0 – 519/934-2544, Fax: 519/934-2651
Tarbutt & Tarbutt Add'l Twp	432	Algoma District	Algoma	Algoma	Ruth Kelso, Clerk-Treas., RR#1, Desbarats P0R 1E0 – 705/782-6776, Fax: 705/782-4274
Tay Twp	10,058	Simcoe	Simcoe North	Muskoka-Georgian Bay	Ted Walker, Clerk & CAO, Park St., PO Box 100, Victoria Harbour L0K 2A0 – 705/534-7248, Fax: 705/534-4493
Tecumseh †	11,913	Essex	Windsor-St. Clair	Windsor-Riverside	Leo A. Lessard, Clerk-Treas., 917 Lesperance Rd., Tecumseh N8N 1W9 – 519/735-2184, Fax: 519/735-6712
Teeswater (V)	1,027	Bruce	Huron-Bruce	Bruce	Kendra J. Reinhart, Clerk-Treas., 2 Clinton St. South, PO Box 369, Teeswater N0G 2S0 – 519/392-6818, Fax: 519/392-6819
Tehkummah Twp	339	Manitoulin District	Algoma	Algoma-Manitoulin	Shirley Pyette, Clerk-Treas., Municipal Bldg., Tehkummah P0P 2C0 – 705/859-3293, Fax: 705/859-2605
Temagami Twp	864	Nipissing District	Timiskaming-French River	Timiskaming	John Hodgson, Clerk-Treas. & CAO, PO Box 220, Temagami P0H 2H0 – 705/569-3421, Fax: 705/569-2834
Terrace Bay Twp	2,309	Thunder Bay District	Cochrane-Superior	Lake Nipigon	M. Heather Adams, Clerk & CAO, 12 Simcoe Plaza, PO Box 40, Terrace Bay P0T 2W0 – 807/825-3315, Fax: 807/825-9576

Canadian Almanac & Directory 1997

ONTARIO MUNICIPALITIES

Cities in CAPITALS; Towns marked †; Separated Towns marked (SE); Villages marked (V); Townships marked Twp; Restructured Counties marked (RS); United Counties marked (U); Development Areas (DA); • means separated for municipal purposes from county. An in-depth listing for municipalities marked with * appears in Part 2 (check Index for page numbers).

MUNICIPALITY	1994 POP.	COUNTY OR DISTRICT	FEDERAL ELECTORAL DISTRICT	PROVINCIAL ELECTORAL DISTRICT	CONTACT PERSON WITH ADDRESS, PHONE & FAX
Thamesville (V)	925	Kent	Kent	Essex-Kent	Violet Harry, Clerk-Treas., London Rd., PO Box 280, Thamesville N0P 2K0 – 519/692-3991, Fax: 519/692-5915
Thedford (V)	814	Lambton	Lambton-Middlesex	Lambton	Jackie Mason, Clerk-Treas., 89 Main St., PO Box 70, Thedford N0M 2N0 – 519/296-4980, Fax: 519/296-4648
Thessalon †	1,371	Algoma District	Algoma	Algoma	Robert MacLean, Clerk-Treas., 169 Main St., PO Box 220, Thessalon P0R 1L0 – 705/842-2217, Fax: 705/842-2572
Thessalon Twp	709	Algoma District	Algoma	Algoma	Lorna M. Hagan, Adm.-Clerk-Treas., RR#1, Thessalon P0R 1L0 – 705/842-3800, Fax: 705/842-3800
Thompson Twp	105	Algoma District	Algoma	Algoma	Sandra Leach, Clerk-Treas., RR#1, Blind River P0R 1B0 – 705/356-7393, Fax: 705/356-7393
Thornbury †	1,612	Grey	Wellington-Grey-Dufferin-Simcoe	Grey	Janette Scott, Clerk, 26 Bridge St., Thornbury N0H 2P0 – 519/599-3250, Fax: 519/599-7723
Thornloe (V)	130	Timiskaming District	Timiskaming-French River	Timiskaming	Gordon Edwards, Clerk-Treas., Main St., PO Box 30, Thornloe P0J 1S0 – 705/563-8303, Fax: 705/563-8192
THOROLD	17,586	Niagara Reg. Mun.	Welland-St. Catharines-Thorold	Welland-Thorold	Kenneth Todd, City Clerk, 8 Carleton St. South, PO Box 1044, Thorold L2V 4A7 – 905/227-6613, Fax: 905/227-3666
*THUNDER BAY	113,562	Thunder Bay District	Thunder Bay-Atikokan; Thunder Bay-Nipigon	Fort William; Port Arthur	M. Elaine Bahlieda, City Clerk, City Hall, 500 Donald St. East, Thunder Bay P7E 5V3 – 807/625-2230, Fax: 807/623-5468
Thurlow Twp	7,327	Hastings	Prince Edward-Hastings	Prince Edward-Lennox-South Hastings	Gary King, Clerk-Adm., General Delivery, River Road South, Corbyville K0K 1K0 – 613/968-5553, Fax: 613/968-2930
Tilbury †	4,254	Kent	Essex-Kent	Essex-Kent	Robert J. Bourassa, Clerk-Adm., 17 Superior St., PO Box 1299, Tilbury N0P 2L0 – 519/682-2583, Fax: 519/682-3123
Tilbury East Twp	2,273	Kent	Essex-Kent	Essex-Kent	George Darnley, Clerk-Treas., RR#1, Merlin N0P 1W0 – 519/682-0803, Fax: 519/682-1611
Tilbury North Twp	3,469	Essex	Essex-Windsor	Essex-Kent	M. Daniel Perdu, Clerk-Treas., 6690 Tecumseh Rd., PO Box 70, Stoney Point N0R 1N0 – 519/798-3115, Fax: 519/798-5976
Tilbury West Twp	1,655	Essex	Essex-Windsor	Essex-Kent	Donald H. McMillan, Clerk-Treas., 6400 Main St., PO Box 158, Comber N0P 1J0 – 519/687-2240, Fax: 519/687-2911
Tillsonburg †	12,729	Oxford	Oxford	Norfolk	David C. Morris, Clerk-Adm., 200 Broadway St., 2nd Fl., Tillsonburg N4G 5A7 – 519/842-6428, Fax: 519/842-9431
TIMMINS	45,692	Cochrane District	Timmins-Chapleau	Cochrane South	R. Jack Watson, City Clerk, 220 Algonquin Blvd. East, Timmins P4N 1B3 – 705/264-1331, Fax: 705/360-1392
Tiny Twp	8,204	Simcoe	Simcoe North	Simcoe East	Vicki Robertson, Clerk-Adm., 130 Balm Beach, RR#1, Perkinsfield L0L 2J0 – 705/526-4204, Fax: 705/526-2372
Tiverton (V)	796	Bruce	Huron-Bruce	Bruce	Sharon Mooser, Clerk-Treas., PO Box 130, Tiverton N0G 2T0 – 519/368-7860, Fax: 519/368-5535
*TORONTO	590,838	Metro Mun.	Beaches-Woodbine; Broadview-Greenwood; Davenport; Don Valley West; Parkdale-High Park; Rosedale; St. Paul's; Trinity-Spadina; York South-Weston	Beaches-Woodbine; Dovercourt; Eglinton; Fort York; High Park-Swansea; Oakwood; Parkdale; Riverdale; St. Andrew-St. Patrick; St. George-St. David	Barbara G. Caplan, City Clerk, City Hall, 100 Queen St. West, Toronto M5H 2N2 – 416/392-9111, URL: http://www.city.toronto.on.ca/
TRENTON	16,404	Hastings	Northumberland	Quinte	Beverley A. Mansfield, Clerk-Adm., 65 Dundas St. West, PO Box 490, Trenton K8V 5R6 – 613/392-2841, Fax: 613/392-0714
Trout Creek †	669	Parry Sound District	Parry Sound-Muskoka	Parry Sound	Betty Young, Clerk-Treas., Main St. West, PO Box 99, Trout Creek P0H 2L0 – 705/723-5253, Fax: 705/723-1034
Tuckersmith Twp	3,036	Huron	Huron-Bruce	Huron	John R. McLachlan, Clerk-Treas., 42 - 1 Ave., Vanastra N0M 1L0 – 519/482-9523, Fax: 519/482-7621
Tudor & Cashel Twp	598	Hastings	Hastings-Frontenac-Lennox & Addington	Hastings-Peterborough	Andrew J. McMurray, Clerk-Treas., RR#1, Gilmour K0L 1W0 – 613/474-2583

Canadian Almanac & Directory 1997

ONTARIO MUNICIPALITIES 4-71

Cities in CAPITALS; Towns marked †; Separated Towns marked (SE); Villages marked (V); Townships marked Twp; Restructured Counties marked (RS); United Counties marked (U); Development Areas (DA); • means separated for municipal purposes from county. An in-depth listing for municipalities marked with * appears in Part 2 (check Index for page numbers).

MUNICIPALITY	1994 POP.	COUNTY OR DISTRICT	FEDERAL ELECTORAL DISTRICT	PROVINCIAL ELECTORAL DISTRICT	CONTACT PERSON WITH ADDRESS, PHONE & FAX
Turnberry Twp	1,739	Huron	Huron-Bruce	Huron	Dorothy R. Kelly, Clerk-Treas., 100 Queen St., Bluevale N0G 1G0 – 519/357-2991, Fax: 519/357-4106
Tweed (V)	1,477	Hastings	Hastings-Frontenac-Lennox-Addington	Hastings-Peterborough	Martha Murphy, Clerk-Treas., 320 Colborne St., PO Box 729, Tweed K0K 3J0 – 613/478-2535, Fax: 613/478-6457
Tyendinaga Twp	3,201	Hastings	Prince Edward-Hastings	Prince Edward-Lennox-South Hastings	Carman J. Milligan, Clerk-Treas., RR#1, Shannonville K0K 3A0 – 613/968-5445
Usborne Twp	1,529	Huron	Huron-Bruce	Huron	Sandra J. Strang, Clerk-Treas., RR#3, Exeter N0M 1S5 – 519/235-2900
Uxbridge Twp	14,672	Durham Reg. Mun.	Durham	Durham	W.E. Taylor, Clerk, 51 Toronto St. South, PO Box 190, Uxbridge L9P 1T1 – 905/852-9181, Fax: 905/852-9674
Val Rita-Harty Twp	1,085	Cochrane District	Cochrane-Superior	Cochrane North	Christiane Potvin, Clerk-Treas., 2, avenue de l'Église, PO Box 100, Val Rita P0L 2G0 – 705/335-6146, Fax: 705/337-6292
Valley East †	22,102	Sudbury Reg. Mun.	Nickel Belt	Sudbury East	Roland O. Chenier, Clerk, 1679 Main St., PO Box 430, Val Caron P3N 1P6 – 705/897-4938, Fax: 705/897-2667
VANIER	17,562	Ottawa-Carleton Reg. Mun.	Ottawa Vanier	Ottawa East	Daniel J.P. Ouimet, CAO-Clerk, 300 des Pèresblancs Ave., Vanier K1L 7L5 – 613/746-8105, Fax: 613/745-2985
Vankleek Hill †	1,941	Prescott & Russell	Glengarry-Prescott-Russell	Prescott & Russell	Gerard Sauvé, Clerk-Treas., 11 Queen St., PO Box 40, Vankleek Hill K0B 1R0 – 613/678-2206, Fax: 613/678-2988
*VAUGHAN	116,360	York Reg. Mun.	York North	York Centre	J.D. Leach, City Clerk, 2141 Major Mackenzie Dr., Vaughan L6A 1T1 – 905/832-2281, Fax: 905/832-8535, URL: http://www.city.vaughan.on.ca/
Verulam Twp	3,950	Victoria	Victoria-Haliburton	Victoria-Haliburton	Barbara Meacham, Clerk-Treas., 21 Canal St. East, PO Box 820, Bobcaygeon K0M 1A0 – 705/738-2431, Fax: 705/738-6026
Vienna (V)	443	Elgin	Elgin-Norfolk	Elgin	Lynda Millard, Clerk-Treas., PO Box 133, Vienna N0J 1Z0 – 519/874-4225, Fax: 519/874-4225
Wainfleet Twp	6,139	Niagara Reg. Mun.	Erie	Niagara South	Albert Guiler, Clerk-Treas., PO Box 40, Wainfleet L0S 1V0 – 905/899-3463, Fax: 905/899-2340
Walden †	9,753	Sudbury Reg. Mun.	Nickel Belt	Nickel Belt	Richard Bois, Clerk-Adm., 25 Black Lake Rd., PO Box 910, Walden P3Y 1J3 – 705/692-3613, Fax: 705/692-3225
Walkerton †	4,735	Bruce	Bruce-Grey	Bruce	Richard Radford, Clerk, 111 Jackson St., PO Box 68, Walkerton N0G 2V0 – 519/881-2223, Fax: 519/881-2991
Wallace Twp	2,382	Perth	Perth-Wellington-Waterloo	Perth	Gordon M. Burns, Clerk-Treas., Gowanstown N0G 1Y0 – 519/291-2760, Fax: 519/291-1902
Wallaceburg †	10,992	Kent	Kent	Chatham-Kent	Sheldon W. Parsons, Clerk, 786 Dufferin Ave., Wallaceburg N8A 2V3 – 519/627-1603, Fax: 519/627-1212
Wardsville (V)	423	Middlesex	Lambton-Middlesex	Middlesex	Janet Salliss, Clerk-Treas., 156 Hagerty Rd., PO Box 64, Wardsville N0L 2N0 – 519/693-4962, Fax: 519/693-4962
Warwick Twp	2,446	Lambton	Lambton-Middlesex	Lambton	Donald I. Craig, Clerk-Treas., 6332 Nauvoo Rd., RR#8, Watford N0M 2S0 – 519/849-3926, Fax: 519/849-6136
Wasaga Beach †	7,463	Simcoe	Simcoe Centre	Simcoe West	Eric E. Collingwood, Clerk-Treas.-Adm., 30 Lewis St., PO Box 110, Wasaga Beach L0L 2P0 – 705/429-3844, Fax: 705/429-6732
*WATERLOO	75,274	Waterloo Reg. Mun.	Waterloo	Waterloo North	Lew Ayers, City Clerk, City Hall, 100 Regina St. South, PO Box 337, Waterloo N2J 4A8 – 519/886-1550, Fax: 519/747-8760
Watford (V)	1,633	Lambton	Lambton-Middlesex	Lambton	Frances Woods, Clerk-Treas., 5288 Nauvoo Rd., PO Box 10, Watford N0M 2S0 – 519/876-2740, Fax: 519/876-3531
Webbwood †	554	Sudbury District	Algoma	Algoma-Manitoulin	Judy Van Norman, Clerk-Treas., 16 Main St., PO Box 10, Webbwood P0P 2G0 – 705/869-3861, Fax: 705/869-1394
WELLAND	47,423	Niagara Reg. Mun.	Erie; Welland-St. Catharines-Thorold	Welland-Thorold	Craig A. Stirtzinger, City Clerk, 411 East Main St., Welland L3B 3K4 – 905/735-1700, Fax: 905/732-1919
Wellesley Twp	8,309	Waterloo Reg. Mun.	Waterloo	Waterloo North	Gordon Ludington, Clerk, RR#1, Clements N0B 2M0 – 519/699-4611, Fax: 519/699-4540

Canadian Almanac & Directory 1997

4-72 ONTARIO MUNICIPALITIES

Cities in CAPITALS; Towns marked †; Separated Towns marked (SE); Villages marked (V); Townships marked Twp; Restructured Counties marked (RS); United Counties marked (U); Development Areas (DA); • means separated for municipal purposes from county. An in-depth listing for municipalities marked with * appears in Part 2 (check Index for page numbers).

MUNICIPALITY	1994 POP.	COUNTY OR DISTRICT	FEDERAL ELECTORAL DISTRICT	PROVINCIAL ELECTORAL DISTRICT	CONTACT PERSON WITH ADDRESS, PHONE & FAX
Wellington (V)	1,470	Prince Edward	Prince Edward-Hastings	Prince Edward-Lennox-South Hastings	Doreen Kendall, Clerk-Treas., 28 East St., PO Box 160, Wellington K0K 3L0 – 613/399-3424, Fax: 613/399-1802
West Carleton Twp	15,625	Ottawa-Carleton Reg. Mun.	Lanark-Carleton	Carleton	Monica Ceschia, Clerk, 5670 Carp Rd., Kinburn K0A 2H0 – 613/832-5644, Fax: 613/832-3341
West Garafraxa Twp	3,341	Wellington	Wellington-Grey-Dufferin-Simcoe	Wellington	Dianne Smith, Clerk-Treas., Belwood N0B 1J0 – 519/843-2259, Fax: 519/843-6614
West Hawkesbury Twp	2,957	Prescott & Russell	Glengarry-Prescott-Russell	Prescott & Russell	Robert Lefebvre, Clerk-Treas., 948 Pleasant Corners Rd. East, Vankleek Hill K0B 1R0 – 613/678-3003, Fax: 613/678-3363
West Lincoln Twp	11,060	Niagara Reg. Mun.	Erie	Lincoln	Salter Hayden, Clerk, 318 Canborough St., PO Box 400, Smithville L0R 2A0 – 905/957-3346, Fax: 905/957-3219
West Lorne (V)	1,367	Elgin	Elgin-Norfolk	Elgin	Brenda Fleming, Clerk-Treas., 223 Graham St., PO Box 309, West Lorne N0L 2P0 – 519/768-1234, Fax: 519/768-2783
West Luther Twp	1,114	Wellington	Wellington-Grey-Dufferin-Simcoe	Wellington	Dea Baker-Pearce, Clerk-Treas., RR#4, Kenilworth N0G 2E0 – 519/848-3451, Fax: 519/848-9350
West Nissouri Twp	3,347	Middlesex	London-Middlesex	Middlesex	Stewart M. Findlater, Clerk-Adm., 160 King St., Thorndale N0M 2P0 – 519/461-0750, Fax: 519/461-1427
West Wawanosh Twp	1,453	Huron	Huron-Bruce	Huron	Liliane Nolan, Clerk-Treas., RR#2, Lucknow N0G 2H0 – 519/528-2903, Fax: 519/528-3327
West Williams Twp	911	Middlesex	Lambton-Middlesex	Middlesex	Beverley LeCouteur, Clerk-Treas., RR#2, Parkhill N0M 2K0 – 519/294-0001, Fax: 519/294-0021
Westmeath Twp	2,442	Renfrew	Renfrew-Nipissing-Pembroke	Renfrew North	Randi Keith, Clerk-Treas., Westmeath K0J 2L0 – 613/587-4464, Fax: 613/587-4229
Westport (V)	645	Leeds & Grenville	Leeds-Grenville	Leeds-Grenville	Scott Bryce, Clerk-Treas., PO Box 68, Westport K0G 1X0 – 613/273-2191, Fax: 613/273-3460
Wheatley (V)	1,557	Kent	Essex-Kent	Essex-Kent	W. Tim Jackson, Clerk-Treas., 25 Erie St. South, PO Box 530, Wheatley N0P 2P0 – 519/825-4819, Fax: 519/825-4045
*Whitby †	67,324	Durham Reg. Mun.	Durham; Ontario	Durham East; Durham Centre	D.G. McKay, Town Clerk, 575 Rossland Rd. East, Whitby L1N 2M8 – 905/668-5803, Fax: 905/686-7005
Whitchurch-Stouffville †	17,796	York Reg. Mun.	Markham-Whitchurch-Stouffville	Durham-York	Michele Kennedy, Clerk, 19 Civic Ave., PO Box 419, Stouffville L4A 7Z6 – 905/640-1900, Fax: 905/640-7957
White River Twp	933	Algoma District	Timmins-Chapleau	Algoma	Marilyn Parent Lethbridge, Clerk-Adm., 102 Durnham St., PO Box 307, White River P0M 3G0 – 807/822-2450, Fax: 807/822-2719
Wiarton †	2,291	Bruce	Bruce-Grey	Bruce	R. Ruthann Carson, Clerk, 315 George St., PO Box 310, Wiarton N0H 2T0 – 519/534-1400, Fax: 519/534-4862
Wilberforce Twp	1,796	Renfrew	Renfrew-Nipissing-Pembroke	Renfrew North	Marilyn Schruder, Clerk-Treas., RR#1, Eganville K0J 1T0 – 613/628-2080, Fax: 613/628-3341
Williamsburgh Twp	3,335	Stormont, Dundas & Glengarry	Stormont-Dundas	SDG & East Grenville	Michael S. Waddell, Adm.-Clerk-Treas., PO Box 160, Williamsburgh K0C 2H0 – 613/535-2673, Fax: 613/535-2099
Wilmot Twp	13,135	Waterloo Reg. Mun.	Perth-Wellington-Waterloo	Kitchener-Wilmot	Jane M. Steller, Clerk, 60 Snyder's Rd. West, Baden N0B 1G0 – 519/634-8444, Fax: 519/634-5522
Winchester (V)	2,275	Stormont, Dundas & Glengarry	Stormont-Dundas	SDG & East Grenville	Bonnie Dingwall, Adm. & Clerk-Treas., 547 St. Lawrence St., PO Box 489, Winchester K0C 2K0 – 613/774-2105, Fax: 613/774-5699
Winchester Twp	3,445	Stormont, Dundas & Glengarry	Stormont-Dundas	SDG & East Grenville	Nancy Krisjanis, Clerk-Treas., RR#4, Winchester K0C 2K0 – 613/448-2772, Fax: 613/448-1470
*WINDSOR	199,000 ('95)	Essex	Essex-Windsor; Windsor-St. Clair; Windsor West	Windsor-Riverside; Windsor-Sandwich; Windsor-Walkerville	Thomas W. Lynd, City Clerk, City Hall, 350 City Hall Sq., PO Box 1607, Windsor N9A 6S1 – 519/255-6500, Fax: 519/255-6868
Wingham †	2,921	Huron	Huron-Bruce	Huron	J. Byron Adams, Clerk-Treas., 274 Josephine St., PO Box 90, Wingham N0G 2W0 – 519/357-3550, Fax: 519/357-1110
Wolfe Island Twp	1,093	Frontenac	Kingston & the Islands	Kingston & the Islands	Terry J. O'Shea, Clerk-Treas., PO Box 130, Wolfe Island K0H 2Y0 – 613/385-2216, Fax: 613/385-1032
Wolford Twp	1,455	Leeds & Grenville	Leeds-Grenville	Leeds-Grenville	Margaret R. Bates, Adm.-Clerk-Treas., RR#3, PO Box 1, Jasper K0G 1G0 – 613/283-8683, Fax: 613/283-6087

Canadian Almanac & Directory 1997

Cities in CAPITALS; Towns marked †; Separated Towns marked (SE); Villages marked (V); Townships marked Twp; Restructured Counties marked (RS); United Counties marked (U); Development Areas (DA); • means separated for municipal purposes from county. An in-depth listing for municipalities marked with * appears in Part 2 (check Index for page numbers).

MUNICIPALITY	1994 POP.	COUNTY OR DISTRICT	FEDERAL ELECTORAL DISTRICT	PROVINCIAL ELECTORAL DISTRICT	CONTACT PERSON WITH ADDRESS, PHONE & FAX
Wollaston Twp	622	Hastings	Hastings-Frontenac-Lennox & Addington	Hastings-Peterborough	Jacqueline Dalby, Clerk-Treas., PO Box 99, Coe Hill K0L 1P0 – 613/337-5731, Fax: 613/337-5789
WOODSTOCK	31,252	Oxford	Oxford	Oxford	John McGinnis, City Clerk, 500 Dundas St., PO Box 40, Woodstock N4S 7W5 – 519/539-1291, Fax: 519/539-7705
Woodville (V)	688	Victoria	Victoria-Haliburton	Victoria-Haliburton	Heather Muir, Clerk, 78 King St., PO Box 9, Woodville K0M 2T0 – 705/439-2505, Fax: 705/439-2319
Woolwich Twp	16,711	Waterloo Reg. Mun.	Waterloo	Waterloo North	Kris Fletcher, Clerk, 69 Arthur St. South, PO Box 158, Elmira N3B 2Z6 – 519/669-1647, Fax: 519/669-1820
Worthington Twp	110	Rainy River District	Kenora-Rainy River	Rainy River	Patrick Giles, Clerk-Treas., PO Box 427, Rainy River P0W 1L0 – 807/852-3529, Fax: 807/852-3529
Wyoming (V)	2,077	Lambton	Lambton-Middlesex	Lambton	Caroline DeSchutter, Clerk-Treas., 546 Niagara St., PO Box 250, Wyoming N0N 1T0 – 519/845-3351, Fax: 519/845-0730
Yarmouth Twp	7,733	Elgin	Elgin-Norfolk	Elgin	Ken G. Sloan, Clerk-Adm., 1229 Talbot St., St. Thomas N5P 1G8 – 519/631-4860, Fax: 519/631-4036
Yonge & Escott, Rear of Twp	1,868	Leeds & Grenville	Leeds-Grenville	Leeds-Grenville	Darlene Noonan, Clerk-Treas., 5 Central St., PO Box 189, Athens K0E 1B0 – 613/924-9049, Fax: 613/924-1958
Yonge, Front of Twp	2,337	Leeds & Grenville	Leeds-Grenville	Leeds-Grenville	Nancy A. Petri, Clerk-Treas., 1514 County Road #2, PO Box 130, Mallorytown K0E 1R0 – 613/923-2251, Fax: 613/923-2421
*YORK	134,977	Metro Mun.	Davenport; Eglinton-Lawrence; Parkdale-High Park; St. Paul's; York South-Weston	Oakwood; St. Andrew-St. Patrick; York South	Ron W. Maurice, City Clerk, 2700 Eglinton Ave. West, Toronto M6M 1V1 – 416/394-2700, Fax: 416/394-2803
Zone Twp	987	Kent	Kent	Chatham-Kent	Wynnona Revell, Clerk-Treas., RR#3, Bothwell N0P 1C0 – 519/695-2307, Fax: 519/695-2307
Zorra Twp	8,182	Oxford	Oxford	Oxford	Wayne A. Johnson, Clerk-Adm., PO Box 306, Ingersoll N5C 3K5 – 519/485-2490, Fax: 519/485-2520
Zurich (V)	845	Huron	Huron-Bruce	Huron	Maureen Simmons, Clerk-Treas., 22 Main St. West, PO Box 280, Zurich N0M 2T0 – 519/236-4974, Fax: 519/236-7687

a. Formerly the township of East Luther & the village of Grand Valley.
b. Formerly the township of Huron & the village of Ripley.

ONTARIO COUNTIES

COUNTY	1994 POP.	CONTACT PERSON WITH ADDRESS, PHONE & FAX
Brant	109,643	Dan Ciona, Clerk-Treas., 1249 Colborne St. West, PO Box 160, Burford N0E 1A0 – 519/449-2451, Fax: 519/449-2454
Bruce	61,459	Bettyanne Bray, Clerk, 30 Park St., PO Box 70, Walkerton N0G 2V0 – 519/881-1291, Fax: 519/881-1619
Dufferin	40,997	Scott A. Wilson, Clerk-Adm., 51 Zina St., Orangeville L9W 1E5 – 519/941-2816, Fax: 519/941-4565
Elgin	74,093	Mark G. McDonald, Clerk, 450 Sunset Dr., St. Thomas N5R 5V1 – 519/631-1460, Fax: 519/633-7661
Essex	337,466	John H. Curran, CAO & Clerk, 360 Fairview Ave. West, Essex N8M 1Y6 – 519/776-6441, Fax: 519/776-4455
Frontenac	127,038	Sylvia G. Coburn, Clerk, Court House, Court St., Kingston K7L 2N4 – 613/548-4202, Fax: 613/548-8193
Grey	81,523	Sharon Vokes, Clerk-Treas., County Bldg., 595 Ninth Ave. East, Owen Sound N4K 3E3 – 519/376-2205, Fax: 519/376-7970
Haliburton	13,895	Ross Rigney, Acting Clerk-Treas., 11 Newcastle St., PO Box 399, Minden K0M 2K0 – 705/286-1333, Fax: 705/286-4829
Hastings	108,066	Bill Bouma, CAO & Clerk, 235 Pinnacle St., PO Box 4400, Belleville K8N 3A9 – 613/966-1311, Fax: 613/966-2574
Huron	59,068	Lynn Murray, Clerk-Adm., Court House Sq., Goderich N7A 1M2 – 519/524-8394, Fax: 519/524-2044
Kent	101,974	Chuck L. Knapp, Clerk-Adm., 435 Grand Ave. West, PO Box 1230, Chatham N7M 5L8 – 519/351-1010, Fax: 519/351-9669
Lambton	122,106	H. Wayne Kloske, CAO, 789 Broadway St., PO Box 3000, Wyoming N0N 1T0 – 519/845-0801, Fax: 519/845-3160
Lanark	54,451	Cynthia Moyle, Acting Treas. & Dep. Clerk, County Admin. Bldg., Sunset Blvd., PO Box 37, Perth K7H 3E2 – 613/267-4200, Fax: 613/267-2964; URL: http://www.county.lanark.on.ca
Leeds & Grenville	89,943	Fred W. Dollman, Adm.-Clerk-Treas., Court House, PO Box 729, Brockville K6V 5V8 – 613/342-3840, Fax: 613/342-2101
Lennox & Addington	35,531	Larry Keech, Clerk & CAO, 97 Thomas St. East, PO Box 1000, Napanee K7R 3S9 – 613/354-4883, Fax: 613/354-3112
Middlesex	61,687	Donald Hudson, Clerk-Treas., 399 Ridout St. North, London N6A 2P1 – 519/434-7321, Fax: 519/434-0638
Northumberland	75,448	Lynda Mitchell, CAO-Clerk-Treas., 860 William St., Cobourg K9A 3A9 – 905/372-0141, Fax: 905/372-3046
Oxford	94,959	Kenneth J. Whiteford, CAO-Clerk, Court House, 415 Hunter St., PO Box 397, Woodstock N4S 7Y3 – 519/539-5688, Fax: 519/537-3024
Perth	69,604	James A. Bell, Clerk-Treas., Court House, 1 Huron St., Stratford N5A 5S4 – 519/271-0531, Fax: 519/271-6265
Peterborough	115,911	W. Douglas (Doug) Armstrong, Adm.-Clerk-Treas., County Court House, 470 Water St., Peterborough K9H 3M3 – 705/743-0380, Fax: 705/876-1730
Prescott & Russell	70,505	Jean-Pierre Pitre, Clerk-Treas. & CAO, 59 Court St., PO Box 304, L'Orignal K0B 1K0 – 613/675-4661, Fax: 613/675-2519
Prince Edward	22,504	Donald Ward, Clerk-Treas., 332 Main St., PO Box 1550, Picton K0K 2T0 – 613/476-2148, Fax: 613/476-8356
Renfrew	90,481	Michael J. Johnson, Adm.-Clerk-Treas., 9 International Dr., Pembroke K8A 6W5 – 613/735-7288, Fax: 613/735-2081
Simcoe	303,475	Al F. Pelletier, Clerk, Admin Centre, Midhurst L0L 1X0 – 705/726-9300, Fax: 705/726-3991

COUNTY	1994 POP.	CONTACT PERSON WITH ADDRESS, PHONE & FAX
Stormont, Dundas & Glengarry	107,541	Raymond J. Lapointe, Co-ordinator-Clerk-Treas., 20 Pitt St., Cornwall K6J 3P2 – 613/932-4302, Fax: 613/936-2913
Victoria	62,994	George Brown, Clerk, 26 Francis St., PO Box 9000, Lindsay K9V 5R8 – 705/324-1750, Fax: 705/324-1750
Wellington	69,348	James C. Andrews, Clerk & CAO, 74 Woolwich St., Guelph N1H 3T9 – 519/837-2600, Fax: 519/837-1909

ONTARIO DISTRICTS

DISTRICTS	1994 POP.	LOCATION
Algoma	127,269	Sault Ste. Marie
Cochrane	93,917	Cochrane
Kenora	58,748	Kenora
Manitoulin	11,192	Gore Bay
Nipissing	84,723	North Bay
Parry Sound	38,423	Parry Sound
Rainy River	22,997	Fort Frances
Sudbury	26,178	Espanola
Thunder Bay	158,810	Thunder Bay
Timiskaming	38,983	Haileybury

ONTARIO REGIONAL MUNICIPALITIES

An in-depth listing for regional districts marked with * appears in Part 3 (check Index for page numbers).

MUNICIPALITY	1994 POP.	CONTACT PERSON WITH ADDRESS, PHONE & FAX
Durham	421,824	Cecil W. Lundy, Clerk, 605 Rossland Rd. East, PO Box 623, Whitby L1N 6A3 – 905/668-7711, Fax: 905/668-9963
Haldimand-Norfolk	96,586	Gerald van der Wolf, Regional Clerk, 70 Town Centre Dr., Townsend N0A 1S0 – 519/587-4911, Fax: 519/587-5554
Halton	315,557	Joan A. Eaglesham, Regional Clerk, 1151 Bronte Rd., Oakville L6M 3L1 – 905/825-6000, Fax: 905/825-8838, URL: http//www.region.halton.on.ca
Hamilton-Wentworth	459,656 ('96)	Robert C. Prowse, Regional Clerk, 119 King St. West, PO Box 910, Hamilton L8N 3V9 – 905/546-4154, Fax: 905/546-2546
Metropolitan Toronto	2,317,400	Novina Wong, Metropolitan Clerk, Metro Hall, Station 1071, 55 John St., 7th Fl., Toronto M5V 3C6 – 416/392-8000, Fax: 416/392-2980; URL: http://www.metrotor.on.ca
Muskoka	45,017	William C. (Bill) Calvert, Clerk & Chief Administrative Officer, 70 Pine St., Bracebridge P1L 1N3 – 705/645-2231, Fax: 705/645-5319
Niagara	415,200	Thomas R. Hollick, Regional Clerk, 2201 St. David's Rd., PO Box 1042, Thorold L2V 4T7 – 905/685-1571, Fax: 905/687-4977; URL: http://www.regional.niagara.on.ca/niagara/
Ottawa-Carleton	696,045 ('93)	Mary Jo Woollam, Regional Clerk, Cartier Sq., 111 Lisgar St., Ottawa K2P 2L7 – 613/560-1335, Fax: 613/560-6055
Peel	879,100 ('95)	Bonnie J. Zeran, Regional Clerk, 10 Peel Centre Dr., Brampton L6T 4B9 – 905/791-9400, Fax: 905/791-4792URL: http://www.region.peel.on.ca
Sudbury	162,000	Angie Haché, Regional Clerk, 200 Brady St., PO Box 3700, Sudbury P3A 5W5 – 705/673-2171, Fax: 705/673-2960
Waterloo	387,000	Evelyn L. Stettner, Regional Clerk, Regional Administration Bldg., 150 Frederick St., Kitchener N2G 4J3 – 519/575-4400, Fax: 519/575-4481; URL: http://www.oceta.on.ca/region.waterloo/gov/
York	577,960 ('96)	Dennis Hearse, Regional Clerk, 17250 Yonge St., PO Box 147, Newmarket L3Y 6Z1 – 905/731-0201, Fax: 905/895-3031

PRINCE EDWARD ISLAND

Enabling legislation in P.E.I. includes the City of Charlottetown Incorporation Act, the Town of Summerside Incorporation, and the Municipalities Act (replaces the former Village Service Act, the Town Act, and the Community Improvement Act). There are no population considerations for incorporation of a municipality, but a petition must be made by at least 25 residents of an area indicating their desire to incorporate; stating the boundaries of the area, whether it is to be a town or a community, and the services which are to be provided.

Municipal Elections are held every three years in November.

Cities in CAPITALS; Towns marked †; Communities marked ‡. An in-depth listing for municipalities marked with * appears in Part 2 (check Index for page numbers).

MUNICIPALITY	1994 POP.	FEDERAL ELECTORAL DISTRICT	PROVINCIAL ELECTORAL DISTRICT	CONTACT PERSON WITH ADDRESS, PHONE & FAX
Abram's Village ‡	311	Egmont	Evangeline-Miscouche	Desmond Arsenault, Adm., PO Box 104, Abram's Village C0B 2E0 – 902/854-2501
Afton ‡	826	Malpeque	Tracadie-Fort Augustus	Jean LePage, Adm., RR#2, Cornwall C0A 1H0 – 902/675-4355
Alberton †	1,068	Egmont	Alberton-Miminegash	Susan Wallace, Adm., PO Box 153, Alberton C0B 1B0 – 902/853-2720, Fax: 902/853-2720
Alexandra ‡	259	Cardigan	Belfast-Pownal Bay	Sheila White, Adm., PO Box 2683, Charlottetown C1A 8C3 – 902/569-4760
Annandale--Little Pond--Howe Bay ‡	352	Cardigan	Georgetown-Baldwin's Road	Jim Mills, Adm., Annandale-Little Pond, RR#4, Souris C0A 2B0 – 902/583-2220
Bedeque ‡	151	Malpeque	Borden-Kinkora	Clara Lockhart, Adm., PO Box 4007, Bedeque C0B 1C0 – 902/887-2244
Belfast ‡	1,839	Cardigan	Belfast-Pownal Bay	Janice MacDonald, Adm., RR#3, Belle River C0A 1B0 – 902/659-2813, Fax: 902/659-2813
Bonshaw ‡	186	Malpeque	Crapaud-Hazel Grove	Leo MacLeod, Adm., RR#3, Bonshaw C1E 1Z3 – 902/675-3670, Fax: 902/368-1239
Borden-Carleton ‡		Malpeque	Borden-Kinkora	C. Fred Leard, Adm., PO Box 89, Borden C0B 1X0 – 902/855-2225, Fax: 902/855-2225

Canadian Almanac & Directory 1997

PRINCE EDWARD ISLAND MUNICIPALITIES 4-75

Cities in CAPITALS; Towns marked †; Communities marked ‡. An in-depth listing for municipalities marked with * appears in Part 2 (check Index for page numbers).

MUNICIPALITY	1994 POP.	FEDERAL ELECTORAL DISTRICT	PROVINCIAL ELECTORAL DISTRICT	CONTACT PERSON WITH ADDRESS, PHONE & FAX
Brackley ‡	327	Malpeque	Stanhope-East Royalty	Joanne Jay, Adm., 1 Cudmore Lane, Brackley C0A 2H0 – 902/368-8283
Breadalbane ‡		Malpeque	Crapaud-Hazel Grove	Sandy MacKay, Adm., Breadalbane C0A 1E0 – 902/964-2500
Brudenell ‡	358	Cardigan	Montague-Kilmuir	Gordon Nixon, Adm., PO Box 836, Montague C0A 1R0 – 902/838-4044
Cardigan ‡	359	Cardigan	Georgetown-Baldwin's Road	Margaret Forgarty, Adm., Cardigan C0A 1G0 – 902/583-2459
Central Bedeque ‡	181	Malpeque	Borden-Kinkora	Doug MacMurdo, Adm., Central Bedeque, RR#3, Summerside C1N 4J9 – 902/887-3185
Central Kings ‡	563	Cardigan		Marion Trowbridge, Adm., RR#5, Cardigan C0A 1G0 – 902/583-2834
*CHARLOTTETOWN	32,400 ('95)	Hillsborough	Sherwood-Hillsborough; Parkdale-Belvedere; Charlottetown-Kings Square; Charlottetown-Rochefort Square; Charlottetown-Spring Park	Harry Gaudet, Chief Administrative Officer, PO Box 98, Charlottetown C1A 7K2 – 902/566-5548, Fax: 902/566-4701
Clyde River ‡	554	Malpeque	Crapaud-Hazel Grove	Janice McAlduff, Adm., PO Box 644, Cornwall C0A 1H0 – 902/628-1550
Cornwall †	2,038	Malpeque	North River-Rice Point	Eldon Sentner, Adm., PO Box 430, Cornwall C0A 1H0 – 902/566-2354, Fax: 902/566-5228
Crapaud ‡	323	Malpeque	Crapaud-Hazel Grove; Borden-Kinkora	Susan Williams, Adm., Crapaud C0A 1J0 – 902/658-2297
Darlington ‡	78	Malpeque	Crapaud-Hazel Grove	Cindy Nicholson, Adm., Darlington, North Wiltshire C0A 1Y0 – 902/964-3489
Eastern Kings ‡	1,272	Cardigan		Kay Sweeny, Adm., RR#1, Elmira C0A 1K0 – 902/357-2534
Ellerslie-Bideford ‡	463	Egmont	Cascumpec-Grand River	Linda MacKinnon, Adm., PO Box 43, Tyne Valley C0B 2C0 – 902/831-3476
Georgetown †	716	Cardigan	Georgetown-Baldwin's Road	Patsy Gotell, Adm., PO Box 89, Georgetown C0A 1L0 – 902/652-2924, Fax: 902/652-2701
Grand Tracadie ‡	543	Cardigan	Tracadie-Fort Augustus	Patsy McKinnon, Adm., Grand Tracadie, Little York C0A 1P0 – 902/672-2698
Greenmount-Montrose ‡	323	Egmont	Tignish-DeBlois	June Pridham, Adm., RR#2, Alberton C0B 1B0 – 902/853-2870
Hampshire ‡	327	Malpeque	North River-Rice Point; Crapaud-Hazel Grove	Gail Stewart, Adm., RR#2, North Wiltshire C0A 1Y0 – 902/368-1144, Fax: 902/368-1144
Hazelbrooke ‡	216	Cardigan	Belfast-Pownal Bay; Tracadie-Fort Augustus	Frank Curran, Adm., Hazelbrooke, RR#1, Charlottetown C1A 7J6 – 902/569-3792
Hunter River ‡	356	Malpeque	Crapaud-Hazel Grove; Park Corner-Oyster Bed	Desi Nantes, Adm., PO Box 74, Hunter River C0A 1N0 – 902/964-2417
Kensington †	1,332	Malpeque	Kensington-Malpeque	Frances Salsman, Adm., PO Box 418, Kensington C0B 1M0 – 902/836-3781, Fax: 902/836-3781
Kingston ‡	685	Malpeque	Noth River-Rice Point; Crapaud-Hazel Grove	Teresa Hughes, Adm., RR#4, North Wiltshire C0A 1Y0 – 902/675-2889
Kinkora ‡	253	Malpeque	Borden-Kinkora	Leonard Keefe, Adm., PO Box 38, Kinkora C0B 1N0 – 902/887-2868, Fax: 902/887-3514
Lady Slipper ‡	809	Egmont		Julie Whitehead, Adm., RR#2, Ellerslie C0B 1J0 – 902/831-2921
Linkletter ‡	289	Egmont	St. Eleanors-Summerside	Gary Linkletter, Adm., Glen Dr., Linkletter C1N 5N2 – 902/436-6922
Lorne Valley ‡	91	Cardigan	Georgetown-Baldwin's Road	Louise Sheppard, Adm., PO Box 81, Cardigan C0A 1G0 – 902/583-2352
Lot 11 and Area ‡	780	Egmont	Cascumpec-Grand River	Mary Williams, Adm., RR#2, Ellerslie C0B 1J0 – 902/831-2787
Lower Montague ‡	450	Cardigan	Montague-Kilmuir	Elizabeth Nicholson, Adm., PO Box 821, Montague C0A 1R0 – 902/838-3359
Malpeque Bay ‡	1,238	Malpeque	Kensington-Malpeque	Joanne. McGarvill, Adm., RR#5, Kensington C0B 1M0 – 902/836-4255
Meadowbank ‡	306	Malpeque	North River-Rice Point	Lawson Drake, Adm., Meadowbank, RR#2, Cornwall C0A 1H0 – 902/566-2736
Miltonvale Park ‡	1,106	Malpeque		Judy K. MacDonald, Adm., RR#10, PO Box 38, Winsloe C1E 1Z4 – 902/368-3090
Miminegash ‡	249	Egmont	Alberton-Miminegash	Shirley Perry, Adm., Miminegash C0B 1S0 – 902/882-3237
Miscouche ‡	672	Egmont	Evangeline-Miscouche	Judy Gallant, Adm., PO Box 70, Miscouche C0B 1T0 – 902/436-4962, Fax: 902/436-4692

Canadian Almanac & Directory 1997

4-76 PRINCE EDWARD ISLAND MUNICIPALITIES

Cities in CAPITALS; Towns marked †; Communities marked ‡. An in-depth listing for municipalities marked with * appears in Part 2 (check Index for page numbers).

MUNICIPALITY	1994 POP.	FEDERAL ELECTORAL DISTRICT	PROVINCIAL ELECTORAL DISTRICT	CONTACT PERSON WITH ADDRESS, PHONE & FAX
Montague †	1,901	Cardigan	Montague-kilmuir	Laurel Halstrum, Adm., PO Box 546, Montague C0A 1R0 – 902/838-2528, Fax: 902/838-3392
Morell ‡	349	Cardigan	Morell-Fortune Bay	George Morrison, Adm., PO Box 173, Morell C0A 1S0 – 902/961-2420
Mount Stewart ‡	315	Cardigan	Tracadie-Fort Augustus	Muriel Jay Matheson, Adm., PO Box 143, Mount Stewart C0A 1T0 – 902/676-2881
Murray Harbour ‡	390	Cardigan	Murray River-Gaspereaux	Jill Harris, Adm., PO Box 119, Murray Harbour C0A 1V0 – 902/962-3835
Murray River ‡	485	Cardigan	Murray River-Gaspereaux	Doris White, Adm., Murray River C0A 1W0 – 902/962-2633
New Haven-Riverdale ‡	473	Malpeque	Crapaud-Hazel Grove	Diane Dowling, Adm., RR#3, Bonshaw C0A 1C0 – 902/675-3670, Fax: 902/368-1239
North Rustico ‡	614	Malpeque	Park Corner-Oyster Bed	Freda Pineau, Adm., PO Box 38, North Rustico C0A 1X0 – 902/963-3211
North Shore ‡		Malpeque		Wanda Myers, Adm., RR#1, York C0A 1P0 – 902/672-2363
North Wiltshire ‡	208	Egmont	Crapaud-Hazel Grove	Wendell Clark, Adm., North Wiltshire C0A 1Y0 – 902/621-0397
Northport ‡		Egmont	Alberton-Miminegash	Paula Foley, Adm., RR#2, Alberton C0A 1B0 – 902/853-2551
O'Leary ‡	856	Egmont	West Point-Bloomfield	Beverley Coughlin, Adm., PO Box 130, O'Leary C0B 1V0 – 902/859-3311, Fax: 902/859-3311
Pleasant Grove ‡	194	Malpeque	Stanhope-East Royalty	Art Chaisson, Adm., Pleasant Grove, RR#1, Little York C0A 1P0 – 902/672-2417
Richmond ‡	248	Egmont	Cascumpec-Grand River; Evangeline-Miscouche	May McNeill, Adm., Richmond C0B 1Y0 – 902/854-2011
St. Felix ‡	359	Egmont	Tignish-DeBlois	Barb Pitre, Adm., PO Box 22, Tignish C0B 2B0 – 902/882-3443
St. Louis ‡	124	Egmont	Alberton-Miminegash; Tignish-DeBlois	Dorothy Doucette, Adm., PO Box 33, St. Louis C0B 1Z0 – 902/882-3305
St. Nicholas ‡		Egmont	Evangeline-Miscouche	Yvonne Poirier, Adm., RR#2, Miscouche C0B 1T0 – 902/854-2731
St. Peters Bay ‡	284	Cardigan	Morell-Fortune Bay	Mary Burge, Adm., PO Box 51, St. Peters Bay C0A 2A0 – 902/961-2268, Fax: 902/961-3148
Sherbrooke ‡	613	Egmont	Kensington-Malpeque	Robin Wiley-Hoyt, Adm., PO Box 1344, Summerside C1N 4K2 – 902/436-7005, Fax: 902/436-7723
Souris †	1,333	Cardigan	Souris-Elmira	Mildred Ehler, Adm., 75 Main St., Souris C0A 2B0 – 902/687-2157, Fax: 902/687-4426
Souris West ‡	327	Cardigan	Souris-Elmira	Margaret MacDonald, Adm., PO Box 680, Souris C0A 2B0 – 902/687-2251
Southport ‡	1,665	Hillsborough		Carol Lowther, Adm., 13 Glenn Stewart Dr., Charlottetown C1A 8X9 – 902/569-3914, Fax: 902/569-3331
Stanley Bridge et al	256	Egmont	Park Corner-Oyster Bed	Brenda Larter, Adm., PO Box 157, Hunter River C0A 1N0 – 902/963-2698, Fax: 902/963-2698
Stratford †		Cardigan; Hillsborough	Glen Stewart-Bellevue Cove	Carol Lowther, Adm., 110 Mason Rd., Stratford C1A 7J7
SUMMERSIDE	13,600 ('95)	Egmont	Wilmot-Summerside; St. Eleanors-Summerside	Terry Murphy, Chief Administrative Officer, PO Box 1510, Summerside C1N 4K4 – 902/436-4222, Fax: 902/436-9296
Tignish ‡	893	Egmont	Tignish-DeBlois	Karen Buote, Adm., PO Box 57, Tignish C0B 2B0 – 902/882-2600, Fax: 902/882-2414
Tignish Shore ‡	72	Egmont		Donna Pitre, Adm., Kildare Cape, Tignish C0B 2B0 – 902/882-3811
Tyne Valley ‡	215	Egmont	Cascumpec-Grand River	Marie Barlow, Adm., PO Box 39, Tyne Valley C0B 2C0 – 902/831-2719
Union Road ‡	187	Malpeque	Georgetown-Baldwin's Road	Ian MacArthur, Adm., Union Road, RR#3, Charlottetown C1A 7J7 – 902/368-8213
Valleyfield ‡	648	Cardigan	Georgetown-Baldwin's Road; Montague-Kilmuir; Belfast-Pownal Bay	Donald Nicholson, Adm., RR#3, Montague C0A 1R0 – 902/838-4238
Victoria ‡	172	Malpeque	Crapaud-Hazel Grove	Kaye MacVittie, Adm., Victoria C0A 2G0 – 902/658-2085
Warren Grove ‡	296	Malpeque	North River-Rice Point	Mike Beamish, Adm., Warren Grove, RR#4, Cornwall C0A 1H0 – 902/566-4300
Wellington ‡	408	Egmont	Cascumpec-Grand River; Evangeline-Miscouche	Sharon MacNeill, Adm., PO Box 26, Wellington C0B 2E0 – 902/854-3028, Fax: 902/436-2838
West River ‡	538	Malpeque		Billy Grant, Adm., PO Box 1008, Charlottetown C1A 8C3 – 902/675-3675
Winsloe ‡	1,105	Malpeque	Winsloe-West Royalty	Betty Pryor, Adm., PO Box 121, Winsloe C0A 2H0 – 902/628-1598

Canadian Almanac & Directory 1997

MUNICIPALITY	1994 POP.	FEDERAL ELECTORAL DISTRICT	PROVINCIAL ELECTORAL DISTRICT	CONTACT PERSON WITH ADDRESS, PHONE & FAX
Winsloe South ‡	197	Malpeque	Winsloe-West Royalty	Joanne Turner, Adm., RR#1, Winsloe C0A 2H0 – 902/368-1444
York ‡		Malpeque	Stanhope-East Royalty	Sharon MacKinnon, Adm., PO Box 8819, York C0A 1P0 – 902/629-1313

QUÉBEC

(Source: Ministère des Affaires municipales)

Québec municipalities are governed either by the Municipal Code, by the Cities and Towns Act, by special legislation or specific charter.

Local municipalities divide into three broad categories, each comprising different types of municipalities. Rural municipalities come under the Municipal Code. Urban municipalities are ruled by the Cities and Towns Act. In spite of the double designation in the Act, cities and towns have the same powers. Municipalities governed by special legislation include the Cree and Northern villages created following the 1975 James Bay Agreement, as well as the cities of Montréal and Québec, which are governed almost exclusively by their own Pre-Confederation charters. There are also over 100 unorganized areas which are included in the territory of regional county municipalities and are directly administered by them.

Each municipality is administered by a Council including a Mayor and at least six councillors. The term of each individual Council member is four years. In a rural municipality, all members of council are generally elected at large but may adopt a by-law providing for the rotation of half of its councillors every two or three years. Urban municipalities are usually divided into wards.

In addition to local municipalities, there are three types of second-tier or regional municipalities, and every local municipality is a member of a second-tier municipality.

Urban communities have existed since 1970. There are three of them, one including all 29 municipalities on the island of Montréal, one for the Québec City metropolitan area, and one for the Hull-Gatineau metropolitan area. Each urban community has been established by a separate Act.

Regional county municipalities (RCM) constitute another type of second-tier municipality. They have been established by letters patent since 1980, by virtue of the 1979 Act respecting land use planning and development. The whole settled part of the province is covered by 96 such regional county municipalities, except for the municipalities included in the urban communities. The council of an RCM or an urban community is composed of members of all the municipalities included in the territory.

The third type of regional municipality is represented by the Kativik Regional Administration established in 1980. It provides local services to 12 Inuit villages located along the extreme northern shore of Québec.

Cities (Villes) in CAPITALS; Villages marked (V); Townships/Cantons marked (Canton);United townships/Cantons unis marked (Cantons); Parishes (Paroisses) marked (P); Municipalities marked (Mun.).; Northern villages/Villages nordiques marked (NV); Cree Villages/Villages Cris marked (VC); Naskapi Villages/Villages Naskapi marked (VN); In the third column, Urban Community/Communauté Urbaine marked Urb. Com. An in-depth listing for municipalities marked with * appears in Part 2 (check Index for page numbers).

MUNICIPALITY	1993 POP.	REGIONAL COUNTY MUN.	FEDERAL ELECTORAL DISTRICT	PROVINCIAL ELECTORAL DISTRICT	CONTACT PERSON WITH ADDRESS, PHONE & FAX
Abercorn (V)	335	Brome-Missisquoi	Brome-Missisquoi	Brome-Missisquoi	Lyne Vaillancourt, Sec.-Trés., 10, ch des Églises ouest, Abercorn J0E 1B0 – 514/538-2664, Fax: 514/538-6295
ACTON-VALE	4,798	Acton	St-Hyacinthe-Bagot	Johnson	Rita Parent, Gref., 1025, rue Boulay, CP 640, Acton-Vale J0H 1A0 – 514/546-2703, Fax: 514/546-4865
Aguanish (Mun.)	417	Minganie	Manicouagan	Duplessis	Marie-Paule Chevarie, Sec.-Trés., 106, rte Jacques-Cartier, CP 47, Aguanish G0G 1A0 – 418/533-2323, Fax: 418/533-2205
Akulivik (NV)	380	Kativik	Abitibi	Ungava	Adamie Qumak, Sec.-Trés., Akulivik J0M 1V0 – 819/496-2073, Fax: 819/496-2200
Albanel (Mun.)	2,567	Maria-Chapdelaine	Roberval	Roberval	Gilles Lambert, Sec.-Trés., 160, rue Principale, Albanel G8M 3J5 – 418/279-5250, Fax: 418/279-3147
Alleyn-et-Cawood (Cantons)	203	Pontiac	Pontiac-Gatineau-Labelle	Gatineau	Line Gagnon, Sec.-Trés., CP 75, Danford Lake J0X 1P0 – 819/467-2941, Fax: 819/467-2941
ALMA	26,467	Lac-St-Jean-Est	Lac-St-Jean	Lac-St-Jean	Jean Paradis, Gref., Hôtel de Ville, 140, rue St-Joseph sud, Alma G8B 3R1 – 418/669-5000, Fax: 418/669-5019
Amherst (Canton)	966	Les Laurentides	Argenteuil-Papineau	Labelle	Bernard Davidson, Sec.-Trés., 124, rue St-Louis, CP 30, St-Rémi-d'Amherst J0T 2L0 – 819/687-3355, Fax: 819/687-8430
AMOS	13,996	Abitibi	Abitibi	Abitibi-Ouest	France Beaulieu, Gref., Hôtel de Ville, 182, 1e rue est, Amos J9T 2G1 – 819/732-3254, Fax: 819/727-9792
AMQUI	6,467	La Matapédia	Matapédia-Matane	Matapédia	Mario Lavoie, Gref., 20, promenade de l'Hôtel-de-Ville, CP 1030, Amqui G0J 1B0 – 418/629-4242, Fax: 418/629-4090
Angliers (V)	314	Témiscamingue	Témiscamingue	Rouyn-Noranda-Témiscamingue	Aline Arsenault, Sec.-Trés., 14, de la Baie Miller, CP 9, Angliers J0Z 1A0 – 819/949-4351, Fax: 819/949-2112
ANJOU	37,700	Montréal (Urb. Com.)	Anjou-Rivière-des-Prairies	Anjou	Robert Ménard, Gref., 7701, boul Louis-H. Lafontaine, Anjou H1K 4B9 – 514/493-8000, Fax: 514/493-8009
Armagh (Mun.)	1,667	Bellechasse	Bellechasse	Bellechasse	Christian Noël, Sec.-Trés., 5, rue de la Salle, CP 87, Armagh G0R 1A0 – 418/466-2916, Fax: 418/466-2409
Arntfield (Mun.)	447	Rouyn-Noranda	Témiscamingue	Rouyn-Noranda-Témiscamingue	Sylvain Munger, Sec.-Trés., 15, av Fugère, CP 46, Arntfield J0Z 1B0 – 819/279-2241, Fax: 819/279-2481
Arundel (Canton)	602	Les Laurentides	Argenteuil-Papineau	Argenteuil	Bernice Goulet, Sec.-Trés., 2, rue du Village, CP 40, Arundel J0T 1A0 – 819/687-3991, Fax: 819/687-8760
ASBESTOS	6,674	Asbestos	Richmond-Wolfe	Richmond	Yvan Provencher, Gref., 185, rue du Roi, Asbestos J1T 1S4 – 819/879-7171, Fax: 819/879-2343

Canadian Almanac & Directory 1997

4-78 QUÉBEC MUNICIPALITIES

Cities (Villes) in CAPITALS; Villages marked (V); Townships/Cantons marked (Canton);United townships/Cantons unis marked (Cantons); Parishes (Paroisses) marked (P); Municipalities marked (Mun.).; Northern villages/Villages nordiques marked (NV); Cree Villages/Villages Cris marked (VC); Naskapi Villages/Villages Naskapi marked (VN); In the third column, Urban Community/Communauté Urbaine marked Urb. Com. An in-depth listing for municipalities marked with * appears in Part 2 (check Index for page numbers).

MUNICIPALITY	1993 POP.	REGIONAL COUNTY MUN.	FEDERAL ELECTORAL DISTRICT	PROVINCIAL ELECTORAL DISTRICT	CONTACT PERSON WITH ADDRESS, PHONE & FAX
Ascot (Mun.)	8,662	Sherbrooke	Mégantic-Compton-Stanstead	St-François	Mario Boily, Sec.-Trés., 600, rue Thibault, Ascot J1H 6G7 – 819/563-3993, Fax: 819/563-3203
Ascot-Corner (Mun.)	2,375	Le Haut-St-François	Mégantic-Compton-Stanstead	Mégantic-Compton	Suzanne B.-Jacques, Sec.-Trés., 5655, route 112, CP 209, Ascot-Corner J0B 1A0 – 819/566-5436, Fax: 819/566-8526
Aston-Jonction (V)	208	Nicolet-Yamaska	Drummond	Nicolet-Yamaska	Line Camiré, Sec.-Trés., 235, rue Vigneault, CP 27, Aston-Jonction G0Z 1A0 – 819/226-3459, Fax: 819/226-3013
Aubert-Gallion (Mun.)	2,047	Beauce-Sartigan	Beauce	Beauce-Sud	Claude Dutil, Sec.-Trés., #335, 15e rue, St-Georges-Ouest G5Y 4X2 – 418/227-0383, Fax: 418/227-0383
Auclair (Mun.)	542	Témiscouata	Rimouski-Témiscouata	Kamouraska-Témiscouata	Ginette Levasseur, Sec.-Trés., 49, rue des Pionniers, Auclair G0L 1A0 – 418/899-2834, Fax: 418/899-6958
Audet (Mun.)	748	Le Granit	Mégantic-Compton-Stanstead	Mégantic-Compton	Jean-Louis Boucher, Sec.-Trés., 251, rue Principale, CP 27, Audet G0Y 1A0 – 819/583-1596
Aumond (Canton)	627	La Vallée-de-la-Gatineau	Pontiac-Gatineau-Labelle	Gatineau	Johanne Grondin, Sec.-Trés., 679, rte Principale, Aumond J0W 1W0 – 819/449-4006, Fax: 819/449-7448
Aupaluk (NV)	132	Kativik	Manicouagan	Ungava	Sec.-Trés., Aupaluk J0M 1X0 – 819/491-7070, Fax: 819/491-7035
Austin (Mun.)	904	Memphrémagog	Brome-Missisquoi	Brome-Missisquoi	Anne-Marie Ménard, Sec.-Trés., 21, ch Millington, CP 10, Austin J0B 1B0 – 819/843-2388, Fax: 819/843-8211
Authier (Mun.)	371	Abitibi-Ouest	Témiscamingue	Abitibi Ouest	Louise Lambert, Sec.-Trés., 605, av Principale, CP 90, Authier J0Z 1C0 – 819/782-3093
Authier-Nord (Mun.)	381	Abitibi-Ouest	Témiscamingue	Abitibi-Ouest	Carole Lefebvre, Sec.-Trés., 452A, 9e Rang, Authier-Nord J0Z 1E0 – 819/782-3914, Fax: 819/782-3009
Ayer's Cliff (V)	878	Memphrémagog	Mégantic-Compton-Stanstead	Orford	Ginette Savard-Gauvin, Sec.-Trés., 958, rue Main, CP 36, Ayer's Cliff J0B 1C0 – 819/838-5006, Fax: 819/838-4411
AYLMER	34,927	Outaouais (Urb. Com.)	Hull-Aylmer	Pontiac	Suzanne Ouellet, Gref., Hôtel de Ville, 115, rue Principale, Aylmer J9H 3M2 – 819/685-5005, Fax: 819/685-5019
BAIE-COMEAU	26,905	Manicouagan	Charlevoix	Saguenay	Sylvain Ouellet, Gref., 19, av Marquette, Baie-Comeau G4Z 1K5 – 418/296-4931, Fax: 418/296-3759
Baie-de-Shawinigan (V)	307	Le Centre-de-la-Mauricie	St-Maurice	St-Maurice	Réjeanne Jacob, Sec.-Trés., 2, rue de l'Édifice-Municipal, Baie-de-Shawinigan G9N 1Z3 – 819/536-2217, Fax: 819/536-3449
Baie-des-Sables (Mun.)	698	Matane	Matapédia-Matane	Matane	Myriam Mercier, Sec.-Trés., 20, rue du Couvent, CP 39, Baie-des-Sables G0J 1C0 – 418/772-6218
Baie-du-Febvre (Mun.)	1,296	Nicolet-Yamaska	Richelieu	Nicolet-Yamaska	Maryse Baril, Sec.-Trés., 420A, rte Marie-Victorin, Baie-du-Febvre J0G 1A0 – 514/783-6422, Fax: 514/783-6423
BAIE-D'URFÉ	3,901	Montréal (Urb. Com.)	Vaudreuil	Nelligan	Françoise Lange, Gref., 20410, ch Lakeshore, Baie d'Urfé H9X 1P7 – 514/457-5324, Fax: 514/457-5671
Baie-James (Mun.)	3,216	Terr. du Nouveau-Québec	Abitibi	Ungava	Robert L'Africain, Gref., 110, boul Matagami, CP 500, Matagami J0Y 2A0 – 819/739-2030, Fax: 819/739-2713
Baie-Johan-Beetz (Mun.)	113	Minganie	Manicouagan	Duplessis	Jean Devost, Sec.-Trés., Baie-Johan-Beetz G0G 1B0 – 418/539-0125
Baie-Ste-Catherine (Mun.)	316	Charlevoix-Est	Charlevoix	Charlevoix	Ève Savard, Sec.-Trés., 488, rte 138, Baie-Ste-Catherine G0T 1A0 – 418/237-4354, Fax: 418/237-4223
Baie-St-Paul (P)	2,318	Charlevoix	Charlevoix	Charlevoix	Emilien Bouchard, Sec.-Trés., 6, ch de l'Équerre, RR#4, Boite 7, Baie-St-Paul G0A 1B0 – 418/435-3125, Fax: 418/435-2608
BAIE-ST-PAUL	3,765	Charlevoix	Charlevoix	Charlevoix	Maurice Lavoie, Sec.-Trés., 6, rue St-Jean-Baptiste, CP 969, Baie-St-Paul G0A 1B0 – 418/435-2205, Fax: 418/435-2688
Baie-Trinité (V)	672	Manicouagan	Manicouagan	Saguenay	Monique C.-Chouinard, Sec.-Trés., 51, route 138 ouest, CP 100, Baie-Trinité G0H 1A0 – 418/939-2231, Fax: 418/939-2616
Barford (Canton)	648	Coaticook	Mégantic-Compton-Stanstead	Mégantic-Compton	Solange Dupont, Sec.-Trés., CP 200, Coaticook J1A 2T7 – 819/849-4853, Fax: 819/849-4854
BARKMERE	65	Les Laurentides	Argenteuil-Papineau	Argenteuil	Robert Mearns, Sec.-Trés., 182, ch de Barkmere, CP 11, Arundel J0T 1A0 – 819/687-3373
Barnston (Canton)	1,500	Coaticook	Mégantic-Compton-Stanstead	Orford	Marie Dagenais, Sec.-Trés., 1525, ch Riendeau, Barnston J1A 2S5 – 819/849-9186, Fax: 819/849-3952
Barnston-Ouest (Mun.)	606	Coaticook	Mégantic-Compton-Stanstead	Orford	Wanda Rozynska, Sec.-Trés., 2133, ch de Ways Mills, RR#1, Ayer's Cliff J0B 1C0 – 819/838-4321
Barraute (Mun.)	2,229	Abitibi	Abitibi	Abitibi-Est	Richard Nantel, Sec.-Trés., 481, 8e av, CP 299, Barraute J0Y 1A0 – 819/734-6574, Fax: 819/734-5186

Canadian Almanac & Directory 1997

QUÉBEC MUNICIPALITIES 4-79

Cities (Villes) in CAPITALS; Villages marked (V); Townships/Cantons marked (Canton);United townships/Cantons unis marked (Cantons); Parishes (Paroisses) marked (P); Municipalities marked (Mun.).; Northern villages/Villages nordiques marked (NV); Cree Villages/Villages Cris marked (VC); Naskapi Villages/Villages Naskapi marked (VN); In the third column, Urban Community/Communauté Urbaine marked Urb. Com. An in-depth listing for municipalities marked with * appears in Part 2 (check Index for page numbers).

MUNICIPALITY	1993 POP.	REGIONAL COUNTY MUN.	FEDERAL ELECTORAL DISTRICT	PROVINCIAL ELECTORAL DISTRICT	CONTACT PERSON WITH ADDRESS, PHONE & FAX
Batiscan (Mun.)	905	Francheville	Champlain	Champlain	Sylvie Brousseau, Sec.-Trés., 395, rue Principale, Batiscan G0X 1A0 – 418/362-2421, Fax: 418/362-3174
BEACONSFIELD	19,873	Montréal (Urb. Com.)	Lachine-Lac-St-Louis	Jacques-Cartier	Johanne Legault, Gref., 303, boul Beaconsfield, Beaconsfield H9W 4A7 – 514/428-4400, Fax: 514/428-4424
Béarn (Mun.)	1,045	Témiscamingue	Abitibi	Rouyn-Noranda-Témiscamingue	Lynda Gaudet, Sec.-Trés., 28, 2e rue nord, CP 69, Béarn J0Z 1G0 – 819/726-4121, Fax: 819/726-4121
BEAUCEVILLE	3,959	Robert-Cliche	Beauce	Beauce-Nord	Roger Longchamps, Sec.-Trés., 540, 1re av Renault, CP 579, Beauceville G0S 1A0 – 418/774-9137, Fax: 418/774-9141
Beaudry (Mun.)	1,126	Rouyn-Noranda	Témiscamingue	Rouyn-Noranda-Témiscamingue	Fleurette Lefebvre, Sec.-Trés., 667, rue Principale, CP 10, Beaudry J0Z 1J0 – 819/797-5333, Fax: 819/797-2108
BEAUHARNOIS	6,665	Beauharnois-Salaberry	Beauharnois-Salaberry	Beauharnois-Huntingdon	Jean Beaulieu, Gref., #400, 600, rue Ellice, Beauharnois J6N 3P7 – 514/429-3546, Fax: 514/429-6663
Beaulac (V)	389	L'Amiante	Richmond-Wolfe	Richmond	Claude Jacques, Sec.-Trés., 22B, rue St-Jacques, CP 40, Beaulac G0Y 1B0 – 418/458-2375, Fax: 418/458-2375
*BEAUPORT	72,259	Québec (Urb. Com.)	Beauport-Montmorency-Orléans	Montmorency; Limoilou	Josette Tessier, Gref., 10, rue de l'Hôtel-de-Ville, CP 5187, Beauport G1E 6P4 – 418/666-2121, Fax: 418/667-8936
BEAUPRÉ	2,811	La Côte-de-Beaupré	Beauport-Montmorency-Orléans	Charlevoix	Jean-Paul Paré, Sec.-Trés., 216, rue Prévost, Beaupré G0A 1E0 – 418/827-4541, Fax: 418/827-3818
Beaux-Rivages (Mun.)	1,052	Antoine-Labelle	Lévis	Labelle	Nicole Sarrasin, Sec.-Trés., 330, rte 117 est, CP 30, Lac-des-Écorces J0W 1H0 – 819/585-4600, Fax: 819/585-4610
BÉCANCOUR	11,411	Bécancour	Richelieu	Nicolet-Yamaska	France Leclerc, Gref., 1295, av Nicolas-Perrot, Bécancour G0X 1B0 – 819/294-6500, Fax: 819/294-6535
Bedford (Canton)	832	Brome-Missisquoi	Brome-Missisquoi	Brome-Missisquoi	Thérèse Lanctôt, Sec.-Trés., 820, ch de-la-Rivière, Bedford J0J 1A0 – 514/248-3627, Fax: 514/248-4678
BEDFORD	2,788	Brome-Missisquoi	Brome-Missisquoi	Brome-Missisquoi	Bertrand Déry, Sec.-Trés., 14, rue Philippe-Côté, CP 420, Bedford J0J 1A0 – 514/248-2440, Fax: 514/248-3220
Bégin (Mun.)	985	Le Fjord-du-Saguenay	Lac-St-Jean	Dubuc	Alain Coudé, Sec.-Trés., 126, rue Brassard, Bégin G0V 1B0 – 418/672-4270, Fax: 418/672-6161
Belcourt (Mun.)	300	Vallée-de-l'Or	Abitibi	Abitibi-Est	Nathalie Lizotte, Sec.-Trés., 219, rue Communautaire, CP 22, Belcourt J0Y 2M0 – 819/737-8894, Fax: 819/737-8894
Bellecombe (Mun.)	776	Rouyn-Noranda	Témiscamingue	Rouyn-Noranda-Témiscamingue	Lise Plourde, Sec.-Trés., 1161, rte des Pionniers, CP 55, Bellecombe J0Z 1K0 – 819/797-8302, Fax: 819/797-6585
Bellefeuille (P)	12,038	La Rivière-du-Nord	Labelle	Prévost	Claudette Pion, Sec.-Trés., 999, rue de l'Église, Bellefeuille J0R 1A0 – 514/436-7447, Fax: 514/436-8422
BELLETERRE	427	Témiscamingue	Témiscamingue	Rouyn-Noranda-Témiscamingue	Liliane Rochon, Sec.-Trés., 265, 1re av, CP 130, Belleterre J0Z 1L0 – 819/722-2122, Fax: 819/722-2527
BELOEIL	19,609	La Vallée-du-Richelieu	Chambly	Borduas	Sylvie Piérard, Gref., 777, rue Laurier, Beloeil J3G 4S9 – 514/467-2835, Fax: 514/464-5445
Bergeronnes (Canton)	212	La Haute Côte-Nord	Charlevoix	Saguenay	Hervé Simard, Sec.-Trés., 424, rue de la Mer, CP 189, Grandes-Bergeronnes G0T 1G0 – 418/232-6735, Fax: 418/232-6671
BERNIÈRES-ST-NICOLAS	15,615	Les Chutes-de-la-Chaudière	Lévis	Chutes-de-la-Chaudière	Marcel Frigon, Greffe, 1240, ch Filteau, Bernières-St-Nicolas G7A 1A5 – 418/831-2877, Fax: 418/831-8907
Bernierville (V)	1,960	L'Érable	Frontenac	Frontenac	Sylvie Tardif, Sec.-Trés., 821, rue Principale, CP 340, St-Ferdinand G0N 1N0 – 418/428-9404, Fax: 418/428-9724
Berry (Mun.)	523	Abitibi	Abitibi	Abitibi-Ouest	Vacant, Sec.-Trés., 271, rang 1 et 10, Berry J0Y 2G0 – 819/732-1815, Fax: 819/732-1815
Berthier-sur-Mer (P)	1,132	Montmagny	Bellechasse	Montmagny-L'Islet	Suzanne Blais, Sec.-Trés., 8, boul Blais est, Berthier-sur-Mer G0R 1E0 – 418/259-7343, Fax: 418/259-2038
BERTHIERVILLE	4,183	D'Autray	Berthier-Montcalm	Berthier	Céline Lahaie, Gref., 588, rue De Montcalm, CP 269, Berthierville J0K 1A0 – 514/836-7035, Fax: 514/836-1446
Béthanie (Mun.)	403	Acton	Shefford	Johnson	Claire Petit, Sec.-Trés., 745, ch du Dixième-Rang, Valcourt J0E 2L0 – 514/548-2826, Fax: 514/548-5693
Biencourt (Mun.)	761	Témiscouata	Rimouski-Témiscouata	Rimouski	Lucette Viel, Sec.-Trés., 2, rue St-Marc, CP 70, Biencourt G0K 1T0 – 418/499-2423, Fax: 418/499-2708

Canadian Almanac & Directory 1997

4-80 QUÉBEC MUNICIPALITIES

Cities (Villes) in CAPITALS; Villages marked (V); Townships/Cantons marked (Canton);United townships/Cantons unis marked (Cantons); Parishes (Paroisses) marked (P); Municipalities marked (Mun.).; Northern villages/Villages nordiques marked (NV); Cree Villages/Villages Cris marked (VC); Naskapi Villages/Villages Naskapi marked (VN); In the third column, Urban Community/Communauté Urbaine marked Urb. Com. An in-depth listing for municipalities marked with * appears in Part 2 (check Index for page numbers).

MUNICIPALITY	1993 POP.	REGIONAL COUNTY MUN.	FEDERAL ELECTORAL DISTRICT	PROVINCIAL ELECTORAL DISTRICT	CONTACT PERSON WITH ADDRESS, PHONE & FAX
BLACK LAKE	4,552	L'Amiante	Frontenac	Frontenac	Réjean Martin, Sec.-Trés., 350, rue St-Hubert, Black Lake G6H 1R5 – 418/423-2773, Fax: 418/423-4707
BLAINVILLE	24,758	Thérèse-de-Blainville	Blainville-Deux Montagnes	Blainville	Gisèle Gauvreau, Gref., 1001, ch du Camp-Bouchard, Blainville J7C 4N4 – 514/434-5200, Fax: 514/434-5229
Blanc-Sablon (Mun.)	1,252		Manicouagan	Duplessis	Rollande Russell, Sec.-Trés., 1149, boul Dr. Camille Marcoux, CP 400, Lourdes-de-Blanc-Sablon G0G 1W0 – 418/461-2707, Fax: 418/461-2529
Blue-Sea (Mun.)	548	La Vallée-de-la-Gatineau	Pontiac-Gatineau-Labelle	Gatineau	France Carpentier, Sec.-Trés., 7, rue Principale, CP 99, Blue Sea Lake J0X 1C0 – 819/463-2261, Fax: 819/463-4345
Boileau (Mun.)	239	Papineau	Argenteuil-Papineau	Papineau	Nicole Bourret, Sec.-Trés., RR#1, Namur J0V 1N0 – 819/687-3436, Fax: 819/687-3745
BOIS-DES-FILION	6,921	Thérèse-de-Blainville	Terrebonne	Blainville	Nadon Martin, Greffe, 60, 36e av sud, Bois-des-Filion J6Z 2G6 – 514/621-1460, Fax: 514/621-8483
Bois-Franc (Mun.)	458	La Vallée-de-la-Gatineau	Pontiac-Gatineau-Labelle	Gatineau	Isabelle Caron, Sec.-Trés., 466, rte 105, Bois-Franc J9E 3A9 – 819/449-2252, Fax: 819/449-4407
BOISBRIAND	23,060	Thérèse-de-Blainville	Blainville-Deux Montagnes	Groulx	Lucie Mongeau, Gref., 940, boul de la Grande-Allée, Boisbriand J7G 2J7 – 514/435-1954, Fax: 514/435-6398
Boischatel (Mun.)	4,069	La Cote de Beaupré	Beauport-Montmorency-Orléans	Montmorency	Michel Lefebvre, Sec.-Trés., 9, côte de l'Église, Boischatel G0A 1H0 – 418/822-0721, Fax: 418/822-2373
Bolton-Est (Mun.)	622	Memphrémagog	Brome-Missisquoi	Brome-Missisquoi	Michael Merovitz, Sec.-Trés., 858, rue Missisquoi, Bolton-Centre J0E 1G0 – 514/292-3444, Fax: 514/292-4224
Bolton-Ouest (Mun.)	654	Brome-Missisquoi	Brome-Missisquoi	Brome-Missisquoi	Carrol Kralik, Sec.-Trés., CP 711, Knowlton J0E 1V0 – 514/242-2704
Bonaventure (Mun.)	2,963	Bonaventure	Bonaventure-Îles-de-la-Madeleine	Bonaventure	Roy Rollande, Sec.-Trés., 127, av Louisbourg, CP 428, Bonaventure G0C 1E0 – 418/534-2313, Fax: 418/534-4336
Bonne-Espérance (Mun.)	923		Manicouagan	Duplessis	René Fequet, Sec.-Trés., CP 40, Rivière St-Paul G0G 1V0 – 418/379-2911, Fax: 418/379-2959
Bonsecours (Mun.)	505	Le Val-St-François	Richmond-Wolfe	Brome-Missisquoi	Suzanne Tessier, Sec.-Trés., 605, rue du Couventise, CP 119, Bonsecours J0E 1H0 – 514/532-3139, Fax: 514/532-3953
Boucher (Mun.)	545	Mékinac	Champlain	Laviolette	Nicole Léveillé, Sec.-Trés., 610, rte Principale, St-Joseph-de-Mékinac G0X 2E0 – 819/646-5686, Fax: 819/646-5686
BOUCHERVILLE	36,198	Lajemmerais	Verchères	Marguerite-D'Youville	Claude Caron, Gref., 500, rue de la Rivière-aux-Pins, Boucherville J4B 2Z7 – 514/449-3131, Fax: 514/655-0086
Bouchette (Mun.)	722	La Vallée-de-la-Gatineau	Pontiac-Gatineau-Labelle	Gatineau	Christine Lacroix, Sec.-Trés., 36, rue Principale, CP 59, Bouchette J0X 1E0 – 819/465-2555, Fax: 819/465-2318
Bowman (Mun.)	521	Papineau	Gatineau-La Lièvre	Papineau	Denise Wilson, Sec.-Trés., CP 29, Val-des-Bois J0X 3C0 – 819/454-2421, Fax: 819/454-2133
Brébeuf (P)	661	Les Laurentides	Laurentides	Labelle	Lynda Foisy, Sec.-Trés., 217, rte 323, Brébeuf J0T 1B0 – 819/425-9833, Fax: 819/425-6611
Brigham (Mun.)	2,390	Brome-Missisquoi	Brome-Missisquoi	Brome-Missisquoi	Jacqueline Giroux, Sec.-Trés., 118, av des Cèdres, CP 70, Brigham J0E 1J0 – 514/263-5942, Fax: 514/263-8380
Bristol (Canton)	1,161	Pontiac	Pontiac-Gatineau-Labelle	Pontiac	Keith R. Emmerson, Sec.-Trés., RR#1, Bristol J0X 1G0 – 819/647-5555, Fax: 819/647-2424
Brome (V)	303	Brome-Missisquoi	Brome-Missisquoi	Brome-Missisquoi	Linda Flanagan, Sec.-Trés., 330, ch Stage Coach, CP 2, Brome J0E 1K0 – 514/243-0489, Fax: 514/243-0489
BROMONT	3,601	La Haute-Yamaska	Brome-Missisquoi	Brome-Missisquoi	Pierre Simoneau, Gref., 88, boul de Bromont, Bromont J0E 1L0 – 514/534-2021, Fax: 514/534-1025
Brompton (Canton)	2,107	Le Val-St-François	Richmond-Wolfe	Johnson	Réjeanne Gagnon, Sec.-Trés., 30, rue du Couvent, CP 900, Bromptonville J0B 1H0 – 819/846-6811, Fax: 819/846-6812
BROMPTONVILLE	3,286	Le Val-St-François	Richmond-Wolfe	Johnson	Michel Dupont, Sec.-Trés., 133, rue Laval, CP 610, Bromptonville J0B 1H0 – 819/846-2757, Fax: 819/846-6621
*BROSSARD	68,414	Champlain	La Prairie	Lapinière	Daniel Carrier, Gref., 2001, boul Rome, Brossard J4W 3K5 – 514/923-7000, Fax: 514/923-7016
Brownsburg (V)	2,592	Argenteuil	Argenteuil-Papineau	Argenteuil	Line Ross, Sec.-Trés., 300, rue de l'Hôtel de Ville, CP 40, Brownsburg J0V 1A0 – 514/533-6687, Fax: 514/533-5795
Bryson (V)	797	Pontiac	Pontiac-Gatineau-Labelle	Pontiac	Jean-Guy Lallemand, Sec.-Trés., 770, rue Centrale, CP 119, Bryson J0X 1H0 – 819/648-5940

Canadian Almanac & Directory 1997

QUÉBEC MUNICIPALITIES 4-81

Cities (Villes) in CAPITALS; Villages marked (V); Townships/Cantons marked (Canton); United townships/Cantons unis marked (Cantons); Parishes (Paroisses) marked (P); Municipalities marked (Mun.).; Northern villages/Villages nordiques marked (NV); Cree Villages/Villages Cris marked (VC); Naskapi Villages/Villages Naskapi marked (VN); In the third column, Urban Community/Communauté Urbaine marked Urb. Com. An in-depth listing for municipalities marked with * appears in Part 2 (check Index for page numbers).

MUNICIPALITY	1993 POP.	REGIONAL COUNTY MUN.	FEDERAL ELECTORAL DISTRICT	PROVINCIAL ELECTORAL DISTRICT	CONTACT PERSON WITH ADDRESS, PHONE & FAX
BUCKINGHAM	11,429	Outaouais (Urb. Com.)	Gatineau	Papineau	Serge Gauthier, Gref., 515, rue Charles, Buckingham J8L 2K4 – 819/986-3351, Fax: 819/986-8336
Bury (Mun.)	1,177	Le Haut-St-François	Mégantic-Compton-Stanstead	Mégantic-Compton	Marilyn Matheson, Sec.-Trés., 563, rue Main, CP 179, Bury J0B 1J0 – 819/872-3692
CABANO	3,215	Témiscouata	Rimouski-Témiscouata	Kamouraska-Témiscouata	Gilles Ruest, Sec.-Trés., 79, rue Commerciale, CP 188, Cabano G0L 1E0 – 418/854-2116, Fax: 418/854-0118
CADILLAC	1,003	Rouyn-Noranda	Abitibi	Abitibi-Est	Réal Maranda, Sec.-Trés., 2, rue Dumont est, CP 185, Cadillac J0Y 1C0 – 819/759-3606, Fax: 819/759-3607
Calixa-Lavallée (P)	482	Lajemmerais	Verchères	Verchères	Monique Pigeon, Sec.-Trés., 771, ch de la Beauce, Calixa-Lavallée J0L 1A0 – 514/583-6470, Fax: 514/583-6470
Calumet (V)	679	Argenteuil	Argenteuil-Papineau	Argenteuil	Carole Constantineau, Sec.-Trés., 105, rue des Érables, CP 10, Calumet J0V 1B0 – 819/242-4966, Fax: 819/242-1232
Campbell's Bay (V)	953	Pontiac	Pontiac-Gatineau-Labelle	Pontiac	Colleen Saint-Jean, Sec.-Trés., 207, rue Leslie, CP 157, Campbell's Bay J0X 1K0 – 819/648-5811, Fax: 819/648-2045
CANDIAC	11,735	Roussillon	La Prairie	La Prairie	Carole Lemaire, Gref., 100, boul Montcalm nord, Candiac J5R 3L8 – 514/444-6000, Fax: 514/444-6009
Cantley (Mun.)	4,733	Les Collines-de-l'Outaouais	Gatineau-La Lièvre	Chapleau	Lucie Gendron, Sec.-Trés., 8, ch River, Cantley J8V 2Z9 – 819/827-3434, Fax: 819/827-4328
Cap-à-l'Aigle (V)	775	Charlevoix-Est	Charlevoix	Charlevoix	Robert Lapointe, Sec.-Trés., 760, rue St-Raphaël, CP 10, Cap-à-l'Aigle G0T 1B0 – 418/665-7596, Fax: 418/665-7597
Cap-aux-Meules (V)	1,648	Les Îles-de-la-Madeleine	Bonaventure-Îles-de-la-Madeleine	Îles-de-la-Madeleine	Hubert Poirier, Sec.-Trés., 460, ch Principal, CP 309, Cap-aux-Meules G0B 1B0 – 418/986-2460, Fax: 418/986-6962
CAP-CHAT	2,907	Denis-Riverin	Gaspé	Matane	Claudette Lemieux-Soucy, Gref., 53, rue Notre-Dame, CP 279, Cap-Chat G0J 1E0 – 418/786-5537, Fax: 418/786-5540
CAP-DE-LA-MADELEINE	35,070	Francheville	Champlain	Champlain	Yolaine Tremblay, Gref., 10, rue de l'Hôtel-de-Ville, CP 220, Cap-de-la-Madeleine G8T 7W4 – 819/375-1661, Fax: 819/375-3101
CAP-ROUGE	14,738	Québec (Urb. Com.)	Louis-Hébert	La Peltrie	Marcel Laroche, Gref., 4473, rue St-Félix, Cap-Rouge G1Y 3A6 – 418/650-7777, Fax: 418/651-9528
Cap-St-Ignace (Mun.)	2,983	Montmagny	Bellechasse	Montmagny-L'Islet	Donald Bernier, Sec.-Trés., 850, rte du Souvenir, Cap-St-Ignace G0R 1H0 – 418/246-5631, Fax: 418/246-5663
Cap-Santé (Mun.)	2,857	Portneuf	Portneuf	Portneuf	Jacques Blais, Sec.-Trés., 194, rte 138, Cap-Santé G0A 1L0 – 418/285-1207, Fax: 418/285-0009
Caplan (Mun.)	2,182	Bonaventure	Bonaventure-Îles-de-la-Madeleine	Bonaventure	Argée Garant, Sec.-Trés., 17, boul Perron est, CP 360, Caplan G0C 1H0 – 418/388-2075, Fax: 418/388-2429
Capucins (Mun.)	288	Denis-Riverin	Gaspé	Matane	Maryse Lavoie, Sec.-Trés., 294, rue du Village, Capucins G0J 1H0 – 418/786-5021, Fax: 418/786-5517
CARIGNAN	5,703	La Vallée-du-Richelieu	Champlain	Chambly	Vacant, Sec.-Trés., 2555, ch Bellevue, Carignan J3L 6G8 – 514/658-1066, Fax: 514/658-6079
Carillon (V)	204	Argenteuil	Argenteuil-Papineau	Argenteuil	Danielle Jacques-Roy, Sec.-Trés., 21, rue Kelly, Carillon J0V 1C0 – 514/537-8400, Fax: 514/537-8400
CARLETON	2,883	Avignon	Bonaventure-Îles-de-la-Madeleine	Bonaventure	André Allard, Sec.-Trés., CP 237, Carleton G0C 1J0 – 418/364-7073, Fax: 418/364-7314
CAUSAPSCAL	2,144	La Matapédia	Matapédia-Matane	Matapédia	Jean-Noël Barriault, Gref., 1, rue Saint-Jacques nord, Causapscal G0J 1J0 – 418/756-5588, Fax: 418/756-3344
Cayamant (Mun.)	580	La Vallée-de-la-Gatineau	Pontiac-Gatineau-Labelle	Gatineau	Suzanne Vallières, Sec.-Trés., ch Lachapelle, Lac-Cayamant J0X 1Y0 – 819/463-3587, Fax: 819/463-4020
CHAMBLY	16,834	La Vallée-du-Richelieu	Chambly	Chambly	Louise Bouvier, Gref., 56, rue Martel, Chambly J3L 1V3 – 514/658-8788, Fax: 514/658-4214
Chambord (Mun.)	1,786	Le Domaine-du-Roy	Roberval	Roberval	Mario Gagnon, Sec.-Trés., 104, rue Principale, CP 70, Chambord G0W 1G0 – 418/342-6274, Fax: 418/342-8438
Champlain (Mun.)	1,675	Francheville	Champlain	Champlain	Jean Houde, Sec.-Trés., 819, rue Notre-Dame, CP 250, Champlain G0X 1C0 – 819/295-3979, Fax: 819/295-3032
Champneuf (Mun.)	188	Abitibi	Abitibi	Abitibi-Ouest	Diane Fleurent, Sec.-Trés., 12, 6e av nord, Champneuf J0Y 1E0 – 819/754-2053
CHANDLER	3,455	Pabok	Gaspé	Gaspé	Léandre Savoie, Gref., 35, rue Commerciale ouest, CP 459, Chandler G0C 1K0 – 418/689-2221, Fax: 418/689-4963

Canadian Almanac & Directory 1997

4-82 QUÉBEC MUNICIPALITIES

Cities (Villes) in CAPITALS; Villages marked (V); Townships/Cantons marked (Canton);United townships/Cantons unis marked (Cantons); Parishes (Paroisses) marked (P); Municipalities marked (Mun.).; Northern villages/Villages nordiques marked (NV); Cree Villages/Villages Cris marked (VC); Naskapi Villages/Villages Naskapi marked (VN); In the third column, Urban Community/Communauté Urbaine marked Urb. Com. An in-depth listing for municipalities marked with * appears in Part 2 (check Index for page numbers).

MUNICIPALITY	1993 POP.	REGIONAL COUNTY MUN.	FEDERAL ELECTORAL DISTRICT	PROVINCIAL ELECTORAL DISTRICT	CONTACT PERSON WITH ADDRESS, PHONE & FAX
CHAPAIS	2,423	Terr. du Nouveau-Québec	Roberval	Ungava	Daniel Dufour, Sec.-Trés., 145, boul Springer, CP 380, Chapais G0W 1H0 – 418/745-2511, Fax: 418/745-3871
Chapeau (V)	463	Pontiac	Pontiac-Gatineau-Labelle	Pontiac	Richard Vaillancourt, Sec.-Trés., 37, rue St-Joseph, CP 100, Chapeau J0X 1M0 – 819/689-2266, Fax: 819/689-5619
Charette (Mun.)	1,003	Le Centre-de-la-Mauricie	St-Maurice	Maskinongé	Claire Gélinas, Sec.-Trés., 390, rue St-Édouard, Charette G0X 1E0 – 819/221-2095, Fax: 819/221-3493
CHARLEMAGNE	6,376	L'Assomption	Terrebonne	Masson	Léo M. Lepage, Gref., 84, rue du Sacré-Coeur, Charlemagne J5Z 1W8 – 514/581-2541, Fax: 514/581-0597
*CHARLES-BOURG	73,962	Québec (Urb. Com.)	Charlesbourg	Charlesbourg; Chauveau	Jacques Dorais, Gref., 160, 76e rue est, Charlesbourg G1H 7H5 – 418/624-7500, Fax: 418/624-7525
CHARNY	11,081	Les Chutes-de-la-Chaudière	Lévis	Les Chutes-de-la-Chaudière	Michel Hallé, Gref., 5333, rue de la Symphonie, Charny G6X 3B6 – 418/832-4695, Fax: 418/832-4978
Chartierville (Mun.)	322	Le Haut-St-François	Mégantic-Compton-Stanstead	Mégantic-Compton	Monique Bissonnette, Sec.-Trés., 27, rue St-Jean-Baptiste, Chartierville J0B 1K0 – 819/656-2323
CHÂTEAU-RICHER	3,870	La Côte-de-Beaupré	Beauport-Montmorency-Orléans	Montmorency	François Gravel, Sec.-Trés., 8006, av Royale, Château-Richer G0A 1N0 – 418/824-4294, Fax: 418/824-3277
CHÂTEAUGUAY	42,246	Roussillon	Châteauguay	Châteauguay	Vacant, Gref., 5, boul d'Youville, Châteauguay J6J 2P8 – 514/698-3000, Fax: 514/698-3019
Chatham (Canton)	3,746	Argenteuil	Argenteuil-Papineau	Argenteuil	Jackline Williams, Sec.-Trés., 270, rte du Canton, St-Philippe-d'Argenteuil J8G 1R4 – 514/562-9121, Fax: 514/562-1482
Chazel (Mun.)	381	Abitibi-Ouest	Argenteuil-Papineau	Abitibi-Ouest	Florianne Trépanier, Sec.-Trés., 335, rue Principale, Chazel J0Z 1N0 – 819/333-4758, Fax: 819/333-4758
Chelsea (Mun.)	5,451	Les Collines-de-l'Outaouais	Pontiac-Gatineau-Labelle	Gatineau	Alcide Cloutier, Sec.-Trés., 100, ch Old Chelsea, CP 330, Chelsea J0X 1N0 – 819/827-1124, Fax: 819/827-2672
Chénéville (V)	689	Papineau	Argenteuil-Papineau	Papineau	Claire Blais, Sec.-Trés., 63, rue de l'Hôtel-de-Ville, CP 70, Chénéville J0V 1E0 – 819/428-3583, Fax: 819/428-3583
Chertsey (Mun.)	3,133	Matawinie	Laurentides	Bertrand	Pierre Mercier, Sec.-Trés., 333, av de l'Amitié, CP 120, Chertsey J0K 3K0 – 514/882-2920, Fax: 514/882-3333
Chester-Est (Canton)	315	Arthabaska	Richmond-Wolfe	Arthabaska	Jeanne-d'Arc Guillemette, Sec.-Trés., 130, rue Guillemette, RR#1, Ste-Hélène-de-Chester G0P 1H0 – 819/382-2650, Fax: 819/382-9933
Chesterville (Mun.)	798	Arthabaska	Richmond-Wolfe	Arthabaska	Lyse Côté, Sec.-Trés., 261, rue de l'Accueil, Chesterville G0P 1J0 – 819/382-2059, Fax: 819/382-2059
CHIBOUGAMAU	8,978	Terr. du Nouveau-Québec	Roberval	Ungava	Jean Fraser, Gref., 650, 3e rue, Chibougamau G8P 1P1 – 418/748-2688, Fax: 418/748-6562
Chichester (Canton)	479	Pontiac	Pontiac-Gatineau-Labelle	Pontiac	Richard Vaillancourt, Sec.-Trés., 37, rue St-Joseph, CP 158, Chapeau J0X 1M0 – 819/689-2266, Fax: 819/689-5619
*CHICOUTIMI	64,616 ('95)	Le Fjord-du-Saguenay	Chicoutimi	Chicoutimi	Hélène Savard, Gref., Services juridiques, 201, rue Racine est, CP 129, Chicoutimi G7H 5B8 – 418/698-3000, Fax: 418/698-3129
Chisasibi (VC)			Abitibi	Ungava	CP 150, Chisasibi J0M 1E0 – 819/855-2878, Fax: 819/855-2875
Chute-aux-Outardes (V)	2,234	Manicouagan	Charlevoix	Saguenay	Michel Deschênes, Sec.-Trés., 44, rue Jean, CP 490, Chute-aux-Outardes G0H 1C0 – 418/567-2144, Fax: 418/567-4478
Chute-St-Philippe (Mun.)	728	Antoine-Labelle	Pontiac-Gatineau-Labelle	Labelle	Marie-Andrée Bouchard, Sec.-Trés., 592, ch du Progrès, Chute-St-Philippe J0W 1A0 – 819/585-3397, Fax: 819/585-3397
Clarendon (Canton)	1,552	Pontiac	Pontiac-Gatineau-Labelle	Pontiac	Lorna Younge, Sec.-Trés., CP 777, Shawville J0X 2Y0 – 819/647-3862, Fax: 819/647-3862
Clermont (Canton)	539	Abitibi-Ouest	Témiscamingue	Abitibi-Ouest	Yvette Portelance, Sec.-Trés., 722, 4e rang, St-Vital-de-Clermont J0Z 3M0 – 819/333-6129
CLERMONT	3,450	Charlevoix-Est	Charlevoix	Charlevoix	Guy-Raymond Savard, Sec.-Trés., 2, rue de Maisonneuve, Clermont G4A 1G6 – 418/439-3931, Fax: 418/439-4889
Clerval (Mun.)	351	Abitibi-Ouest	Témiscamingue	Abitibi-Ouest	Lise Roy, Sec.-Trés., 579, 2e rang, Clerval J0Z 1R0 – 819/783-2640, Fax: 819/783-2640
Cleveland (Canton)	1,659	Le Val-St-François	Richmond-Wolfe	Richmond	Jacques St-Jean, Sec.-Trés., 292, ch de la Rivière, Richmond J0B 2H0 – 819/826-3546, Fax: 819/826-2827

QUÉBEC MUNICIPALITIES **4-83**

Cities (Villes) in CAPITALS; Villages marked (V); Townships/Cantons marked (Canton);United townships/Cantons unis marked (Cantons); Parishes (Paroisses) marked (P); Municipalities marked (Mun.).; Northern villages/Villages nordiques marked (NV); Cree Villages/Villages Cris marked (VC); Naskapi Villages/Villages Naskapi marked (VN); In the third column, Urban Community/Communauté Urbaine marked Urb. Com. An in-depth listing for municipalities marked with * appears in Part 2 (check Index for page numbers).

MUNICIPALITY	1993 POP.	REGIONAL COUNTY MUN.	FEDERAL ELECTORAL DISTRICT	PROVINCIAL ELECTORAL DISTRICT	CONTACT PERSON WITH ADDRESS, PHONE & FAX
Clifton-Est (Canton)	364	Le Haut-St-François	Mégantic-Compton-Stanstead	Mégantic-Compton	Adèle Madore, Sec.-Trés., 207, rte 253, St-Isidore-d'Auckland J0B 2X0 – 819/889-2706, Fax: 819/889-2706
Cloridorme (Canton)	1,184	La Côte-de-Gaspé	Gaspé	Gaspé	Marie Dufresne, Sec.-Trés., CP 100, Cloridorme G0E 1G0 – 418/395-2808, Fax: 418/395-2228
Cloutier (Mun.)	375	Rouyn-Noranda	Témiscamingue	Rouyn-Noranda-Témiscamingue	Denis Grenier, Sec.-Trés., CP 100, Cloutier J0Z 1S0 – 819/797-5598, Fax: 819/797-5598
COATICOOK	6,942	Coaticook	Mégantic-Compton-Stanstead	Orford	Roma Fluet, Gref.è, 150, rue Child, Coaticook J1A 2B3 – 819/849-2721, Fax: 819/849-9669
Colombier (Mun.)	1,006	La Haute-Côte-Nord	Charlevoix	Saguenay	Max Brisson, Sec.-Trés., 568, rue Principale, CP 69, Colombier G0H 1P0 – 418/565-3343, Fax: 418/565-3289
Colombourg (Mun.)	808	Abitibi-Ouest	Témiscamingue	Abitibi-Ouest	Nicole Bouffard, Sec.-Trés., 705, rang 3, CP 27, Colombourg J0Z 1T0 – 819/333-5783, Fax: 819/333-1075
Compton (Mun.)	2,159	Coaticook	Mégantic-Compton-Stanstead	St-François	Nicole Couture, Sec.-Trés., #201, 3, ch de Hatley, Compton J0B 1L0 – 819/835-5584, Fax: 819/835-5750
Compton Station (Mun.)	899	Coaticook	Mégantic-Compton-Stanstead	St-François	Réginald Rémillard, Sec.-Trés., #202, 3, ch de Hatley, CP 190, Compton J0B 1L0 – 819/835-5345, Fax: 819/835-0015
Contrecoeur (Mun.)	5,891	Lajemmerais	Verchères	Verchères	Yves Beaulieu, Sec.-Trés., 5000, rte Marie-Victorin, Contrecoeur J0L 1C0 – 514/587-5901, Fax: 514/587-5855
COOKSHIRE	1,636	Le Haut-St-François	Mégantic-Compton-Stanstead	Mégantic-Compton	André Croisetière, Sec.-Trés., 220, rue Principale est, CP 430, Cookshire J0B 1M0 – 819/875-3165, Fax: 819/875-5311
Côte-Nord-du-Golfe-St-Laurent (Mun.)	1,392		Argenteuil-Papineau	Duplessis	Richmond Monger, Adm., Chevery G0G 1G0 – 419/787-2244, Fax: 419/787-2241
CÔTE-ST-LUC	30,890 ('94)	Montréal (Urb. Com.)	Mont Royal	D'Arcy McGee	Jocelyne Habra, Gref., 5801, boul Cavendish, Côte-St-Luc H4W 3C3 – 514/485-6800, Fax: 514/485-6963
Coteau-du-Lac (Mun.)	4,559	Vaudreuil-Soulanges	Vaudreuil	Salaberry-Soulanges	Guy Lauzon, Sec.-Trés., 191, rte 338, Coteau-du-Lac J0P 1B0 – 514/763-5822, Fax: 514/763-0938
Courcelles (P)	982	Le Granit	Mégantic-Compton-Stanstead	Beauce-Sud	Renée Mathieu, Sec.-Trés., 116, av du Domaine, CP 160, Courcelles G0M 1C0 – 418/483-5540, Fax: 418/483-5540
COWANSVILLE	12,533	Brome-Missisquoi	Brome-Missisquoi	Brome-Missisquoi	Claude Deschênes, Gref., 220, place Municipale, Cowansville J2K 1T4 – 514/263-0141, Fax: 514/263-9357
Crabtree (Mun.)	2,273	Joliette	Joliette	Joliette	Sylvie Malo, Sec.-Trés., 412 - 1re av, CP 660, Crabtree J0K 1B0 – 514/754-3434, Fax: 514/754-2172
D'Alembert (Mun.)	792	Rouyn-Noranda	Témiscamingue	Rouyn-Noranda-Témiscamingue	Diane Pépin, Sec.-Trés., 1007, ch des Pins, D'Alembert J9X 5A3 – 819/797-0007, Fax: 819/797-2136
DANVILLE	1,908	Asbestos	Richmond-Wolfe	Richmond	René Allard, Sec.-Trés., 52, rue Daniel-Johnson, CP 310, Danville J0A 1A0 – 819/839-2966, Fax: 819/839-3734
Daveluyville (Mun.)	1,170	Arthabaska	Lotbinière	Nicolet-Yamaska	Gaston Bélanger, Sec.-Trés., 337, rue Principale, CP 187, Daveluyville G0Z 1C0 – 819/367-3395, Fax: 819/367-3395
Deauville (V)	2,283	Sherbrooke	Richmond-Wolfe	Orford	Vacant, Sec.-Trés., 7894, boul Bourque, Deauville J1N 3L1 – 819/864-4213, Fax: 819/864-6266
DÉGELIS	3,424	Témiscouata	Rimouski-Témiscouata	Kamouraska-Témiscouata	Claire Bérubé, Gref., 369, av Principale, Dégelis G5T 2G3 – 418/853-2332, Fax: 418/853-3464
Déléage (Mun.)	2,023	La Vallée-de-la-Gatineau	Pontiac-Gatineau-Labelle	Gatineau	Jacinthe St-Amour-Labelle, Sec.-Trés., 175, route 107, RR#1, Maniwaki J9E 3A8 – 819/449-1979, Fax: 819/449-7441
Delisle (Mun.)	4,372	Lac-St-Jean-Est	Lac-St-Jean	Lac-St-Jean	Florent Côté, Sec.-Trés., 4800, av Grande-Décharge, CP 158, Delisle G0W 1L0 – 418/347-3307, Fax: 418/347-3967
DELSON	6,432	Roussillon	Châteauguay	La Prairie	Nicole Lafontaine, Gref., 50, rue Ste-Thérèse, Delson J0L 1G0 – 514/632-1050, Fax: 514/632-1571
Denholm (Canton)	427	La Vallée-de-la-Gatineau	Pontiac-Gatineau-Labelle	Gatineau	Lorraine Paquette, Sec.-Trés., 419, ch du Poisson-Blanc, Denholm J0X 2S0 – 819/457-2992, Fax: 819/457-9862
Des Ruisseaux (Mun.)	4,630	Antoine-Labelle	Charlevoix	Labelle	Normand Bélanger, Sec.-Trés., 1269, boul des Ruisseaux, Des Ruisseaux J9L 3G6 – 819/623-5451, Fax: 819/623-6810
DESBIENS	1,292	Lac-St-Jean-Est	Lac-St-Jean	Lac-St-Jean	Fernand Lapointe, Sec.-Trés., 925, rue Hébert, CP 9, Desbiens G0W 1N0 – 418/346-5571, Fax: 418/346-5422

Canadian Almanac & Directory 1997

4-84 QUÉBEC MUNICIPALITIES

Cities (Villes) in CAPITALS; Villages marked (V); Townships/Cantons marked (Canton);United townships/Cantons unis marked (Cantons); Parishes (Paroisses) marked (P); Municipalities marked (Mun.).; Northern villages/Villages nordiques marked (NV); Cree Villages/Villages Cris marked (VC); Naskapi Villages/Villages Naskapi marked (VN); In the third column, Urban Community/Communauté Urbaine marked Urb. Com. An in-depth listing for municipalities marked with * appears in Part 2 (check Index for page numbers).

MUNICIPALITY	1993 POP.	REGIONAL COUNTY MUN.	FEDERAL ELECTORAL DISTRICT	PROVINCIAL ELECTORAL DISTRICT	CONTACT PERSON WITH ADDRESS, PHONE & FAX
Deschaillons-sur-St-Laurent (Mun.)	1,119	Bécancour	Lotbinière	Lotbinière	Sylvie Dubois, Sec.-Trés., 1056, rte Marie-Victorin, CP 176, Deschaillons-sur-Saint-Laurent G0S 1G0 – 819/292-2085, Fax: 819/292-3194
Deschambault (Mun.)	1,353	Portneuf	Portneuf	Portneuf	Claire St-Arnaud, Sec.-Trés., 120, rue St-Joseph, CP 220, Deschambault G0A 1S0 – 418/286-4511, Fax: 418/286-6511
Destor (Mun.)	432	Rouyn-Noranda	Témiscamingue	Rouyn-Noranda-Témiscamingue	Brigitte Drapeau, Sec.-Trés., 921, ch du Parc, CP 13, Destor J9X 5A3 – 819/637-2073, Fax: 819/637-5512
DEUX-MON-TAGNES	14,481	Deux-Montagnes	Blainville-Deux-Montagnes	Deux-Montagnes	Luc Amireault, Gref., 803, ch d'Oka, CP 55, Deux-Montagnes J7R 4K1 – 514/473-2796, Fax: 514/473-3412
Disraëli (P)	1,038	L'Amiante	Richmond-Wolfe	Frontenac	Magda Matteau, Sec.-Trés., 8306, route 112, CP 760, Disraëli G0N 1E0 – 418/449-5329, Fax: 418/449-5329
DISRAËLI	2,813	L'Amiante	Richmond-Wolfe	Frontenac	Jocelyn Turcotte, Sec.-Trés., 550, av Jacques-Cartier, CP 2050, Disraëli G0N 1E0 – 418/449-2771, Fax: 418/449-4299
Ditton (Canton)	523	Le Haut-St-François	Mégantic-Compton-Stanstead	Mégantic-Compton	Lucie Lortitch, Sec.-Trés., 18, rue Chartier, CP 90, La Patrie J0B 1Y0 – 819/888-2691, Fax: 819/888-2691
Dixville (Mun.) [a]	836 ('95)	Coaticook	Mégantic-Compton-Stanstead	Mégantic-Compton	Mary Brus, Sec.-Trés., 251, ch Parker, Dixville J0B 1P0 – 819/849-3037, Fax: 819/849-3037
DOLBEAU	8,417	Maria-Chapdelaine	Roberval	Roberval	André Côté, Gref., 1100, boul Wallberg, Dolbeau G8L 1G7 – 418/276-0160, Fax: 418/276-8312
DOLLARD-DES-ORMEAUX	47,538	Montréal (Urb. Com.)	Pierrefonds-Dollard	Robert-Baldwin	Louise Pinault, Gref., 12001, boul de Salaberry, Dollard-des-Ormeaux H9B 2A7 – 514/684-1010, Fax: 514/684-1273
DONNACONA	6,304	Portneuf	Portneuf	Portneuf	Denis Roy, Gref., 138, av Pleau, CP 609, Donnacona G0A 1T0 – 418/285-0110, Fax: 418/285-0020
DORVAL	17,477	Montréal (Urb. Com.)	Lachine-Lac-St-Louis	Jacques Cartier	Marcel Guérin, Gref., 60, av Martin, Dorval H9S 3R4 – 514/633-4040, Fax: 514/633-4138
DRUMMOND-VILLE	45,554 ('94)	Drummond	Drummond	Drummond	Thérèse Cajolet, Gref.è, 413, rue Lindsay, CP 398, Drummondville J2B 1G8 – 819/478-6554, Fax: 819/478-3363
Dubuisson (Mun.)	1,504	Vallée-de-l'Or	Abitibi	Abitibi-Est	Robert Cadieux, Sec.-Trés., 128, rue Margeurite-Bourgeois, Dubuisson J9P 4N7 – 819/738-4892, Fax: 819/738-4017
Dudswell (Mun.) [b]	1,614 ('95)	Le Haut-St-François	Mégantic-Compton-Stanstead	Mégantic-Compton	Hélène Leroux, Sec.-Trés., 76, rue Principale, CP 149, Bishopton J0B 1G0 – 819/884-5926, Fax: 819/884-5916
Duhamel (Mun.)	429	Papineau	Argenteuil-Papineau	Papineau	Claire Dinel, Sec.-Trés., 1899, rue Principale, CP 117, Duhamel J0V 1G0 – 819/428-7100, Fax: 819/428-1941
Duhamel-Ouest (Mun.)	612	Témiscamingue	Témiscamingue	Rouyn-Noranda-Témiscamingue	Lise Gosselin, Sec.-Trés., 9, rue Notre-Dame-de-Lourdes, CP 1499, Ville-Marie J0Z 3W0 – 819/629-2522, Fax: 819/629-3215
Dundee (Canton)	395	Le Haut-St-Laurent	Beauharnois-Salaberry	Beauharnois-Huntingdon	Diane L'Écuyer, Sec.-Trés., 3296, montée Smallman, Dundee J0S 1L0 – 514/264-4674, Fax: 514/264-4674
DUNHAM	3,374	Brome-Missisquoi	Brome-Missisquoi	Brome-Missisquoi	Pierre Loiselle, Gref., 3777, rue Principale, CP 70, Dunham J0E 1M0 – 514/295-2418, Fax: 514/295-2182
DUPARQUET	692	Abitibi-Ouest	Témiscamingue	Abitibi-Ouest	Andrée Cloutier, Sec.-Trés., CP 190, Duparquet J0Z 1W0 – 819/948-2266, Fax: 819/948-2466
Dupuy (Mun.)	1,180	Abitibi-Ouest	Témiscamingue	Abitibi-Ouest	Hélène Ayotte, Sec.-Trés., 2 av. du chemin de fer, CP 59, St-Jacques-de-Dupuy J0Z 1X0 – 819/783-2595, Fax: 819/783-2595
Durham-Sud (Mun.)	1,113	Drummond	Drummond	Johnson	France Gagon-Noël, Sec.-Trés., 70, rue de l'Hôtel-de-Ville, CP 70, Durham-Sud J0H 2C0 – 819/858-2044, Fax: 819/858-2044
EAST-ANGUS	3,837	Le Haut-St-François	Mégantic-Compton-Stanstead	Mégantic-Compton	Michel Roy, Sec.-Trés., 146, rue Angus nord, CP 400, East Angus J0B 1R0 – 819/832-2868, Fax: 819/832-2938
East Broughton (Mun.)	2,526	L'Amiante	Frontenac	Frontenac	Marc-André Grondin, Sec.-Trés., 600 - 10e av sud, East Broughton G0N 1H0 – 418/427-2608, Fax: 418/427-3414
East Farnham (V)	554	Brome-Missisquoi	Brome-Missisquoi	Brome-Missisquoi	Ginette B.-Lafrance, Sec.-Trés., 228, rue Principale, East Farnham J0E 1N0 – 514/263-4252, Fax: 514/263-9405
East Hereford (Mun.)	361	Coaticook	Mégantic-Compton-Stanstead	Mégantic-Compton	Diane Lauzon-Rioux, Sec.-Trés., 15, rue de l'Église, East Hereford J0B 1S0 – 819/844-2463, Fax: 819/844-2463

Cities (Villes) in CAPITALS; Villages marked (V); Townships/Cantons marked (Canton);United townships/Cantons unis marked (Cantons); Parishes (Paroisses) marked (P); Municipalities marked (Mun.).; Northern villages/Villages nordiques marked (NV); Cree Villages/Villages Cris marked (VC); Naskapi Villages/Villages Naskapi marked (VN); In the third column, Urban Community/Communauté Urbaine marked Urb. Com. An in-depth listing for municipalities marked with * appears in Part 2 (check Index for page numbers).

MUNICIPALITY	1993 POP.	REGIONAL COUNTY MUN.	FEDERAL ELECTORAL DISTRICT	PROVINCIAL ELECTORAL DISTRICT	CONTACT PERSON WITH ADDRESS, PHONE & FAX
Eastmain (VC)			Abitibi	Ungava	Mark Stewart, Sec.-Trés., 147, Shabow Meskino, Baie-James J0M 1W0 – 819/977-0211, Fax: 819/977-0281
Eastman (V)	742	Memphrémagog	Brome-Missisquoi	Brome-Missisquoi	Bénédict Fortin, Sec.-Trés., 395, rue Principale, CP 150, Eastman J0E 1P0 – 514/297-2114, Fax: 514/297-2398
Eaton (Canton)	2,744	Le Haut-St-François	Mégantic-Compton-Stanstead	Mégantic-Compton	Jean Hivert, Sec.-Trés., 375, rte 253, RR#3, Cookshire J0B 1M0 – 819/875-3554, Fax: 819/875-5646
Egan-Sud (Mun.)	548	La Vallée-de-la-Gatineau	Pontiac-Gatineau-Labelle	Gatineau	Louise Saint-Amour, Sec.-Trés., 95, rte 105, Egan-Sud J9E 3A9 – 819/449-1702, Fax: 819/449-7423
Elgin (Canton)	488	Le Haut-St-Laurent	Beauharnois-Salaberry	Beauharnois-Huntingdon	Diane L'Écuyer, Sec.-Trés., 933, 2e Concession, Athelstan J0S 1A0 – 514/264-2320, Fax: 514/264-2320
Entrelacs (Mun.)	680 ('94)	Matawinie	Laurentides	Bertrand	Jean-François René, Sec.-Trés., 2351, ch d'Entrelacs, Entrelacs J0T 2E0 – 514/228-2529, Fax: 514/228-4866
Escuminac (Mun.)	660	Avignon	Bonaventure-Îles-de-la-Madeleine	Bonaventure	Barbara Borris, Sec.-Trés., CP 5, Pointe-à-la-Garde G0C 2M0 – 418/788-2613
Esprit-Saint (Mun.)	525	Rimouski-Neigette	Rimouski-Témiscouata	Rimouski	Diane Ouellet, Sec.-Trés., 121, rue Principale, Esprit-Saint G0K 1A0 – 418/779-2716, Fax: 418/779-2716
ESTÉREL	130	Les Pays-d'en-Haut	Laurentides	Bertrand	Richard Gagné, Sec.-Trés., 115, ch Dupuis, CP 8, Estérel J0T 1E0 – 514/228-2501, Fax: 514/228-3268
Évain (Mun.)	3,769	Rouyn-Noranda	Témiscamingue	Rouyn-Noranda-Témiscamingue	Michèle Morel, Sec.-Trés., 200, rue Côté ouest, CP 330, Évain J0Z 1Y0 – 819/768-5818, Fax: 819/768-5040
FARNHAM	6,428	Brome-Missisquoi	Brome-Missisquoi	Iberville	Jean-Bernard Luneau, Gref., 477, rue de l'Hôtel-de-Ville, Farnham J2N 2H3 – 514/293-3178, Fax: 514/293-2989
Fassett (Mun.)	548	Papineau	Argenteuil-Papineau	Papineau	Hélène Larente, Sec.-Trés., 19, rue Gendron, CP 70, Fassett J0V 1H0 – 819/423-5388
Fatima (Mun.)	3,160	Îles-de-la-Madeleine	Bonaventure-Îles-de-la-Madeleine	Îles-de-la-Madeleine	Jacques Arseneault, Sec.-Trés., 395, ch de l'Hôpital, CP 610, Îles-de-la-Madeleine G0B 1G0 – 418/986-3341, Fax: 418/986-3803
Ferland-et-Boilleau (Mun.)	691	Le Fjord-du-Saguenay	Chicoutimi	Dubuc	Sylvie Gagnon, Sec.-Trés., 462, rte 381, Ferland-et-Boilleau G0V 1H0 – 418/676-2282, Fax: 418/676-2282
Ferme-Neuve (P)	947	Antoine-Labelle	Pontiac-Gatineau-Labelle	Labelle	Thérèse Boivin, Sec.-Trés., 53, rang No 2 pope, CP 179, Ferme-Neuve J0W 1C0 – 819/587-4115, Fax: 819/587-3049
Ferme-Neuve (V)	2,356	Antoine-Labelle	Pontiac-Gatineau-Labelle	Labelle	Claude Campeau, Sec.-Trés., 280, 6e av, CP 370, Ferme-Neuve J0W 1C0 – 819/587-3400, Fax: 819/587-4733
FERMONT	3,860	Caniapiscau	Manicouagan	Duplessis	Gervais Boucher, Sec.-Trés., 100, Place Daviault, CP 520, Fermont G0G 1J0 – 418/287-5411, Fax: 418/287-5413
FLEURIMONT	15,309	Sherbrooke	Sherbrooke	St-François	Thérèse Beaubien, Gref., 1735, ch Galvin, Fleurimont J1G 3E7 – 819/565-9954, Fax: 819/565-5476
Fontainebleau (Mun.)	174	Le Haut-St-François	Mégantic-Compton-Stanstead	Mégantic-Compton	Sonia Poulin, Sec.-Trés., 34, ch de la Mine, Fontainebleau J0B 3J0 – 819/877-2723
FORESTVILLE	4,071	La Haute Côte-Nord	Charlevoix	Saguenay	Yvan Fortin, Sec.-Trés., 1, 2e av, CP 70, Forestville G0T 1E0 – 418/587-2285, Fax: 418/587-6212
Fort-Coulonge (V)	1,713	Pontiac	Pontiac-Gatineau-Labelle	Pontiac	Ken Rose, Sec.-Trés., 134, rue Principale, CP 640, Fort Coulonge J0X 1V0 – 819/683-2259, Fax: 819/683-3627
Fort Rupert (VC)			Abitibi	Ungava	CP 60, Fort Rupert J0M 1R0 – 819/895-8650, Fax: 819/895-8901
Fortierville (V)	408	Bécancour	Lotbinière	Lotbinière	Nicole Laveaux, Sec.-Trés., 198, rue de la Fabrique, Fortierville G0S 1J0 – 819/287-5922, Fax: 819/287-5922
FOSSAMBAULT-SUR-LE-LAC	877	La Jacques-Cartier	Portneuf	Portneuf	Johanne Bédard, Sec.-Trés., 145, rue Gingras, Fossambault-sur-le-Lac G0A 3M0 – 418/875-3133, Fax: 418/875-3544
Franklin (Mun.)	1,807	Le Haut-St-Laurent	Manicouagan	Beauharnois-Huntingdon	Nancy Westerman, Sec.-Trés., 1670, rte 202, CP 84, Franklin Centre J0S 1E0 – 514/827-2538, Fax: 514/827-2640
Franquelin (Mun.)	383	Manicouagan	Manicouagan	Saguenay	Ginette Plante, Sec.-Trés., 27, rue des Érables, CP 10, Franquelin G0H 1E0 – 418/296-1406, Fax: 418/296-1406
Frelighsburg (Mun.)	1,114	Brome-Missisquoi	Brome-Missisquoi	Brome-Missisquoi	Anne Pouleur, Sec.-Trés., 2, pl. de l'Hôtel-de-Ville, Frelighsburg J0J 1C0 – 514/298-5133, Fax: 514/298-5557
Frontenac (Mun.)	1,399	Le Granit	Mégantic-Compton-Stanstead	Mégantic-Compton	Bruno Turmel, Sec.-Trés., 2430, rue St-Jean, Frontenac G6B 2S1 – 819/583-3295, Fax: 819/583-0855

QUÉBEC MUNICIPALITIES

Cities (Villes) in CAPITALS; Villages marked (V); Townships/Cantons marked (Canton);United townships/Cantons unis marked (Cantons); Parishes (Paroisses) marked (P); Municipalities marked (Mun.).; Northern villages/Villages nordiques marked (NV); Cree Villages/Villages Cris marked (VC); Naskapi Villages/Villages Naskapi marked (VN); In the third column, Urban Community/Communauté Urbaine marked Urb. Com. An in-depth listing for municipalities marked with * appears in Part 2 (check Index for page numbers).

MUNICIPALITY	1993 POP.	REGIONAL COUNTY MUN.	FEDERAL ELECTORAL DISTRICT	PROVINCIAL ELECTORAL DISTRICT	CONTACT PERSON WITH ADDRESS, PHONE & FAX
Fugèreville (Mun.)	412	Témiscamingue	Témiscamingue	Rouyn-Noranda-Témiscamingue	Marlène L'Heureux, Sec.-Trés., 43, rue Principale, CP 831, Fugèreville J0Z 2A0 – 819/748-3241, Fax: 819/748-2114
Gallichan (Mun.)	488	Abitibi-Ouest	Témiscamigue	Abitibi-Ouest	Yvette Fournier-Boutin, Sec.-Trés., 219, ch de la Rivière ouest, CP 38, Gallichan J0Z 2B0 – 819/787-6092
Gallix (Mun.)	522	Sept-Rivières	Manicouagan	Duplessis	Lise Chiasson, Sec.-Trés., 524, rue Lapierre, Gallix G0G 1L0 – 418/766-3161, Fax: 418/766-3264
Garthby (Canton)	399	L'Amiante	Richmond-Wolfe	Richmond	Marcel Bilodeau, Sec.-Trés., 6599, rte 112, Garthby G0Y 1B0 – 418/458-2363, Fax: 418/458-2363
GASPÉ	16,670	La Côte-de-Gaspé	Gaspé	Gaspé	Judith Desmeules, Gref., 25, rue de l'Hôtel-de-Ville, CP 618, Gaspé G0C 1R0 – 418/368-2104, Fax: 418/368-4871
*GATINEAU	105,000 ('95)	Outaouais (Urb. Com.)	Gatineau-La Lièvre	Gatineau; Chapleau	J.C. Laurin, Gref., 144, boul. de l'Hôpital, Gatineau J8T 7S7 – 819/243-2345, Fax: 819/243-2338, URL: http://gamma.omnimage.ca/clients/gatineau
Gayhurst-Partie-Sud-Est (Canton)	198	Le Granit	Beauce	Beauce-Sud	Yvette Roy, Sec.-Trés., 234, rang 2 sud, St-Ludger G0M 1W0 – 819/548-5145, Fax: 819/548-5145
Girardville (Mun.)	1,430	Maria-Chapdelaine	Roberval	Roberval	Denis Desmeules, Sec.-Trés., 180, rue Principale, CP 340, Girardville G0W 1R0 – 418/258-3293, Fax: 418/258-3473
Godbout (V)	409	Manicouagan	Manicouagan	Saguenay	Carolle Vallée, Sec.-Trés., 144, rue Pascal-Comeau, CP 248, Godbout G0H 1G0 – 418/568-7581, Fax: 418/568-7718
Godmanchester (Canton)	1,615	Le Haut-St-Laurent	Beauharnois-Salaberry	Beauharnois-Huntingdon	Élaine Duhème, Sec.-Trés., 2282, ch Ridge, CP 1508, Huntingdon J0S 1H0 – 514/264-4116, Fax: 514/264-9749
Gore (Canton)	1,024	Argenteuil	Richmond-Wolfe	Argenteuil	Louise Rochon-McGarr, Sec.-Trés., 9, ch Cambria, Lakefield J0V 1K0 – 514/562-2025, Fax: 514/562-5424
Gracefield (V)	743	La Vallée-de-la-Gatineau	Pontiac-Gatineau-Labelle	Gatineau	Sylvain Bertrand, Sec.-Trés., 3, rue de la Polyvalente, CP 329, Gracefield J0X 1W0 – 819/463-3458, Fax: 819/463-4236
Granby (Canton)	11,219	La Haute-Yamaska	Shefford	Shefford	Réal Paré, Sec.-Trés., 735, rue Dufferin, CP 579, Granby J2G 8E9 – 514/372-3442, Fax: 514/372-7345
GRANBY	45,194	La Haute-Yamaska	Shefford	Shefford	Alain Noël, Gref., 87, rue Principale, Granby J2G 2T8 – 514/776-8282, Fax: 514/776-8211
Grand-Calumet (Canton)	818	Pontiac	Pontiac-Gatineau-Labelle	Pontiac	Jacques Mantha, Sec.-Trés., 8, rue Brizard, CP 130, L'Île-du-Grand-Calumet J0X 1J0 – 819/648-5965, Fax: 819/648-2659
GRAND-MÈRE	14,841	Le Centre-de-la-Mauricie	St-Maurice	Laviolette	Christiane Houle, Gref., 333 - 5e av, CP 350, Grand-Mère G9T 5L1 – 819/538-9543, Fax: 819/538-7244
Grand-Métis (Mun.)	300	La Mitis	Matapédia-Matane	Matane	Claudette Michaud, Sec.-Trés., 155 - 2e rang ouest, Grand-Métis G0J 1Z0 – 418/775-2860
Grand-Remous (Canton)	1,249	La Vallée-de-la-Gatineau	Pontiac-Gatineau-Labelle	Gatineau	Betty McCarthy, Sec.-Trés., 1567, Transcanadienne, Grand-Remous J0W 1E0 – 819/438-2877, Fax: 819/438-2364
Grand-St-Esprit (Mun.)	578	Nicolet-Yamaska	Richelieu	Nicolet-Yamaska	Nicole Larochelle, Sec.-Trés., 5410, route Principale, Grand-St-Esprit J0G 1B0 – 819/289-2410, Fax: 819/289-2410
Grande-Cascapédia (Mun.)	281	Bonaventure	Bonaventure-Îles-de-la-Madeleine	Bonaventure	Holly McColm, Sec.-Trés., 161A, rte 299, CP 70, Grande-Cascapédia G0C 1T0 – 418/392-4338
Grande-Entrée (Mun.)	733	Îles-de-la-Madeleine	Bonaventure-Îles-de-la-Madeleine	Îles-de-la-Madeleine	Roméo Bénard, Sec.-Trés., CP 58, Grande-Entrée G0B 1H0 – 418/985-2277, Fax: 418/985-2149
Grande-Île (Mun.)	4,309	Beauharnois-Salaberry	Beauharnois-Salaberry	Salaberry-Soulanges	Alain Gagnon, Sec.-Trés., 1155, boul. Mgr-Langlois, Grande-Ile J6S 1B9 – 514/373-8860, Fax: 514/373-1630
GRANDE-RIVIÈRE	4,069	Pabok	Gaspé	Gaspé	Éliane Hotton-Beaulieu, Gref., 108, rue de l'Hôtel de Ville, CP 188, Grande-Rivière G0C 1V0 – 418/385-2282, Fax: 418/385-2290
Grande-Vallée (P)	1,443	La Côte-de-Gaspé	Gaspé	Gaspé	Diane Côté, Sec.-Trés., 3, rue St-François-Xavier est, CP 98, Grande-Vallée G0E 1K0 – 418/393-2161, Fax: 418/393-2274
Grandes-Bergeronnes (V)	640	La Haute Côte-Nord	Charlevoix	Saguenay	Hélène Hervieux, Sec.-Trés., 424, rue de la Mer, CP 158, Grandes-Bergeronnes G0T 1G0 – 418/232-6244, Fax: 418/232-6602
Grandes-Piles (V)	386	Mékinac	Champlain	Laviolette	Pierrette Fontaine, Sec.-Trés., 620 - 5e av, Grandes-Piles G0X 1H0 – 819/538-9708, Fax: 819/538-6947
GREENFIELD-PARK	18,637	Champlain	St-Hubert	Laporte	Carole Leroux, Gref., 156, boul Churchill, Greenfield-Park J4V 2M3 – 514/671-5955, Fax: 514/671-0517

Cities (Villes) in CAPITALS; Villages marked (V); Townships/Cantons marked (Canton);United townships/Cantons unis marked (Cantons); Parishes (Paroisses) marked (P); Municipalities marked (Mun.).; Northern villages/Villages nordiques marked (NV); Cree Villages/Villages Cris marked (VC); Naskapi Villages/Villages Naskapi marked (VN); In the third column, Urban Community/Communauté Urbaine marked Urb. Com. An in-depth listing for municipalities marked with * appears in Part 2 (check Index for page numbers).

MUNICIPALITY	1993 POP.	REGIONAL COUNTY MUN.	FEDERAL ELECTORAL DISTRICT	PROVINCIAL ELECTORAL DISTRICT	CONTACT PERSON WITH ADDRESS, PHONE & FAX
Grenville (Canton)	1,902	Argenteuil	Argenteuil-Papineau	Argenteuil	Murial Nixon, Sec.-Trés., 40, ch Maple, Grenville J0V 1J0 – 819/242-8762, Fax: 819/242-9341
Grenville (V)	1,421	Argenteuil	Argenteuil-Papineau	Argenteuil	Chantale Rheault, Sec.-Trés., 21, rue Tri-Jean, CP 220, Grenville J0V 1J0 – 819/242-2146, Fax: 819/242-5891
Grondines (Mun.)	724	Portneuf	Portneuf	Portneuf	Jean Gravel, Sec.-Trés., 220, rue Principale, Grondines G0A 1W0 – 418/268-8583, Fax: 418/268-5553
Gros-Mécatina (Mun.)	684		Manicouagan	Duplessis	Rita Collier, Sec.-Trés., La Tabatière G0G 1T0 – 418/773-2263
Grosse-Île (Mun.)	575	Les Îles-de-la-Madeleine	Bonaventure-Îles-de-la-Madeleine	Îles-de-la-Madeleine	John Dewey, Sec.-Trés., CP 30, Leslie G0B 1M0 – 418/985-2510, Fax: 418/985-2297
Grosses-Roches (Mun.)	514	Matane	Matapédia-Matane	Matane	Linda Imbeault, Sec.-Trés., 122, rue de la Mer, CP 69, Grosses-Roches G0J 1K0 – 418/733-4273, Fax: 418/733-4273
Guérin (Canton)	283	Témiscamingue	Témiscamingue	Rouyn-Noranda-Témiscamingue	Jacqueline Arbour, Sec.-Trés., 516A, rue St-Gabriel, CP 1040, Guérin J0Z 2E0 – 819/784-7011, Fax: 819/784-5231
Halifax-Nord (Canton)	360	L'Érable	Frontenac	Frontenac	Doris Turgeon, Sec.-Trés., 10, rue de l'Église, Ste-Sophie-de-Mégantic G0P 1L0 – 819/362-2225
Ham-Nord (Canton)	1,039	Arthabaska	Richmond-Wolfe	Richmond	Sombeleine Martel, Sec.-Trés., 474, rue Principale, CP 29, Ham-Nord G0P 1A0 – 819/344-2424, Fax: 819/344-2805
Hampden (Canton)	143	Le Haut-St-François	Compton	Mégantic-Compton	Germaine Lapointe, Sec.-Trés., 863, ch Ditton, route 257, CP 212, Scotstown J0B 3B0 – 819/657-4942, Fax: 819/657-4942
HAMPSTEAD	7,333	Montréal (Urb. Com.)	Mont Royal	D'Arcy McGee	Maurice Guay, Gref., 5569, ch Reine-Marie, Hampstead H3X 1W5 – 514/369-8200, Fax: 514/369-8229
Harrington (Canton)	763	Argenteuil	Argenteuil-Papineau	Argenteuil	Luc Lafontaine, Sec.-Trés., CP 176, Arundel J0T 1A0 – 819/687-2122, Fax: 819/687-8610
Hatley (Canton)	753	Memphrémagog	Mégantic-Compton-Stanstead	Orford	France Boisvert, Sec.-Trés., CP 570, North Hatley J0B 2C0 – 819/842-2977, Fax: 819/842-2639
Hatley (Mun.) c	705 ('95)	Memphrémagog	Mégantic-Compton-Stanstead	Orford	Shirley R. Knapp, Sec.-Trés., CP 360, Ayer's Cliff J0B 1C0 – 819/838-4646
Havelock (Canton)	768	Le Haut-St-Laurent	Beauharnois-Salaberry	Beauharnois-Huntingdon	Linda Hébert, Sec.-Trés., 481, rte 203, Havelock J0S 2C0 – 514/826-4741, Fax: 514/826-4800
Havre-aux-Maisons (Mun.)	2,259	Les Îles-de-la-Madeleine	Bonaventure-Îles-de-la-Madeleine	Îles-de-la-Madeleine	Jean Richard, Sec.-Trés., 37, ch Central, CP 128, Havre-aux-Maisons G0B 1K0 – 418/969-2222, Fax: 418/969-2872
Havre-St-Pierre (Mun.)	3,608	Minganie	Manicouagan	Duplessis	André Cyr, Sec.-Trés., 1081, rue de la Digue, CP 910, Havre-St-Pierre G0G 1P0 – 418/538-2717, Fax: 418/538-3439
Hébertville (Mun.)	2,452	Lac-St-Jean-Est	Lac-St-Jean	Lac-St-Jean	Sabin Larouche, Sec.-Trés., 351, rue Turgeon, Hébertville G8N 1S8 – 418/344-1302, Fax: 418/344-4618
Hébertville-Station (V)	1,405	Lac-St-Jean-Est	Lac-St-Jean	Lac-St-Jean	Yvon Baril, Sec.-Trés., 6, rue Tremblay, CP 69, Hébertville Station G0W 1T0 – 418/343-3961, Fax: 418/343-2349
Hemmingford (Canton)	1,785	Les Jardins-de-Napierville	Beauharnois-Salaberry	Beauharnois-Huntingdon	Margaret Hess, Sec.-Trés., #3, 505, rue Frontière, CP 576, Hemmingford J0L 1H0 – 514/247-2050, Fax: 514/247-3283
Hemmingford (V)	763	Les Jardins-de-Napierville	Beauharnois-Salaberry	Beauharnois-Huntingdon	Diane Lawrence, Sec.-Trés., #5, 505, rue Frontière, Hemmingford J0L 1H0 – 514/247-3310, Fax: 514/247-2389
Henryville (Mun.)	835	Le Haut-Richelieu	Brome-Missisquoi	Iberville	Christiane Veilleux, Sec.-Trés., 133, rue St-Georges, CP 180, Henryville J0J 1E0 – 514/299-2655, Fax: 514/299-2655
Henryville (V)	718	Le Haut-Richelieu	Brome-Missisquoi	Iberville	Sonia Côté, Sec.-Trés., 165, rue de l'Église, CP 120, Henryville J0J 1E0 – 514/299-2833, Fax: 514/299-2833
Hérouxville (P)	1,327	Mékinac	Champlain	Laviolette	Denise Cossette, Sec.-Trés., 1060, rue St-Pierre, CP 10, Hérouxville G0X 1J0 – 418/365-7135, Fax: 418/365-7041
Hinchinbrooke (Canton)	2,482	Le Haut-St-Laurent	Beauharnois-Salaberry	Beauharnois-Huntingdon	Kevin Neal, Sec.-Trés., 1056, ch Brook, Athelstan J0S 1A0 – 514/264-5353, Fax: 514/264-3787
Honfleur (Mun.)	851	Bellechasse	Bellechasse	Bellechasse	Jérôme Fortier, Sec.-Trés., 320, rue St-Jean, Honfleur G0R 1N0 – 418/885-9195, Fax: 418/885-9195
Hope (Canton)	896	Bonaventure	Bonaventure-Îles-de-la-Madeleine	Bonaventure	Roland Chapados, Sec.-Trés., 330, rte 132, CP 729, Paspébiac G0C 2K0 – 418/752-3526, Fax: 418/752-6986

Canadian Almanac & Directory 1997

Cities (Villes) in CAPITALS; Villages marked (V); Townships/Cantons marked (Canton);United townships/Cantons unis marked (Cantons); Parishes (Paroisses) marked (P); Municipalities marked (Mun.).; Northern villages/Villages nordiques marked (NV); Cree Villages/Villages Cris marked (VC); Naskapi Villages/Villages Naskapi marked (VN); In the third column, Urban Community/Communauté Urbaine marked Urb. Com. An in-depth listing for municipalities marked with * appears in Part 2 (check Index for page numbers).

MUNICIPALITY	1993 POP.	REGIONAL COUNTY MUN.	FEDERAL ELECTORAL DISTRICT	PROVINCIAL ELECTORAL DISTRICT	CONTACT PERSON WITH ADDRESS, PHONE & FAX
Hope Town (Mun.)	391	Bonaventure	Bonaventure-Îles-de-la-Madeleine	Bonaventure	Gladys Grenier, Sec.-Trés., CP 146, St-Godefroi G0C 3C0 – 418/752-2137, Fax: 418/752-2137
Howick (V)	659	Le Haut-St-Laurent	Beauharnois-Salaberry	Beauharnois-Huntingdon	Claudette Provost, Sec.-Trés., 51, rue Colville, CP 40, Howick J0S 1G0 – 514/825-2032, Fax: 514/825-0026
Huberdeau (Mun.)	976	Les Laurentides	Argenteuil-Papineau	Argenteuil	Mona St-Georges, Sec.-Trés., 101, rue Dupont, CP 72, Huberdeau J0T 1G0 – 819/687-8321, Fax: 819/687-8808
HUDSON	5,249	Vaudreuil-Soulanges	Vaudreuil	Vaudreuil	Louise L.-Villandré, Sec.-Trés., 481, rue Principale, CP 550, Hudson J0P 1H0 – 514/458-5348, Fax: 514/458-4922
*HULL	65,764 ('95)	Outaouais (Urb. Com.)	Hull-Aylmer	Hull	Jean-Pierre Chabot, Directeur général adjoint, 25, rue Laurier, CP 1970, Hull J8X 3Y9 – 819/595-7180, Fax: 819/595-7192
HUNTINGDON	2,970	Le Haut-St-Laurent	Beauharnois-Salaberry	Beauharnois-Huntingdon	Diane Taillon, Sec.-Trés., 16, rue Prince, Huntingdon J0S 1H0 – 514/264-5389, Fax: 514/264-6826
IBERVILLE	9,882	Le Haut-Richelieu	St-Jean	Iberville	François Lapointe, Gref., 855, 1re rue, Iberville J2X 3C7 – 514/347-2318, Fax: 514/347-7550
Inukjuak (NV)	1,060	Kativik	Abitibi	Ungava	Caroline Naktialuk, Sec.-Trés., Inukjuak J0M 1M0 – 819/254-8845, Fax: 819/254-8779
Inverness (Canton)	592	L'Érable	Frontenac	Lotbinière	Marie Turcotte, Sec.-Trés., 1799, route Dublin, CP 129, Inverness G0S 1K0 – 418/453-2512, Fax: 418/453-2554
Inverness (V)	283	L'Érable	Frontenac	Lotbinière	Johanne Tardif, Sec.-Trés., 1831, rue Dublin, CP 128, Inverness G0S 1K0 – 418/453-2108
Irlande (Mun.)	1,059	L'Amiante	Frontenac	Frontenac	Céline Roy, Sec.-Trés., 157, ch Gosford, St-Ferdinand G0N 1N0 – 418/428-9216, Fax: 418/428-9216
Ivry-sur-le-Lac (Mun.)	336	Les Laurentides	Laurentides	Bertrand	Chantale Marion, Sec.-Trés., 601, ch de la Gare, Ivry-sur-le-Lac J8C 2Z8 – 819/326-0554, Fax: 819/326-8618
Ivujivik (NV)	264	Kativik	Abitibi	Ungava	Mark Airnaituk, Sec.-Trés., Ivujivik J0M 1H0 – 819/922-9940, Fax: 819/922-3045
JOLIETTE	18,308	Joliette	Joliette	Joliette	Louis-André Garceau, Gref., 614, boul Manseau, Joliette J6E 6J3 – 514/753-8000, Fax: 514/753-8199
*JONQUIÈRE	59,734 ('95)	Le Fjord-du-Saguenay	Jonquière	Jonquière	Pierre Brassard, Gref., Hôtel de Ville, 2890, Place Davis, CP 2000, Jonquière G7X 7W7 – 418/546-2222, Fax: 418/699-6018
Kamouraska (Mun.)	778	Kamouraska	Kamouraska-Rivière-du-Loup	Kamouraska-Témiscouata	Marie Drapeau, Sec.-Trés., 67, av Morel, CP 130, Kamouraska G0L 1M0 – 418/492-6523, Fax: 418/492-6523
Kangiqsualujjuaq (NV)	537	Kativik	Manicouagan	Ungava	Tommy Annanack, Sec.-Trés., Kangiqsualujjuaq J0M 1N0 – 819/337-5271, Fax: 819/337-5200
Kangiqsujuaq (NV)	411	Kativik	Manicouagan	Ungava	Anthony Nemeth, Sec.-Trés., Kangiqsujuaq J0M 1K0 – 819/338-3342, Fax: 819/338-3237
Kangirsuk (NV)	355	Kativik	Manicouagan	Ungava	Marc Carrier, Sec.-Trés., Kangirsuk J0M 1A0 – 819/935-4388, Fax: 819/935-4287
Kazabazua (Mun.)	669	La Vallée-de-la-Gatineau	Pontiac-Gatineau-Labelle	Gatineau	Eleonore Wilson, Sec.-Trés., 30, ch Begley, CP 10, Kazabazua J0X 1X0 – 819/467-2852, Fax: 819/467-3872
Kiamika (Mun.)	691	Antoine-Labelle	Pontiac-Gatineau-Labelle	Labelle	Josée Lacasse, Sec.-Trés., 3, ch Valiquette, Kiamika J0W 1G0 – 819/585-3225, Fax: 819/585-3992
Kingsbury (V)	155	Le Val-St-François	Richmond-Wolfe	Johnson	Horace Nadeau, Sec.-Trés., 370, rue du Moulin, Kingsbury J0B 1X0 – 819/826-2527
Kingsey (Canton)	1,435	Drummond	Richmond-Wolfe	Richmond	Marie-Sylvie Janelle, Sec.-Trés., 1205, rue de l'Église, CP 29, St-Félix-de-Kingsey J0B 2T0 – 819/848-2321, Fax: 819/848-2202
Kingsey Falls (Mun.)	530	Arthabaska	Richmond-Wolfe	Richmond	Nicole Henrichon, Sec.-Trés., 57, boul Kingsey, CP 59, Kingsey Falls J0A 1B0 – 819/363-2480, Fax: 819/363-2480
Kingsey Falls (V)	1,239	Arthabaska	Lotbinière	Richmond	Hélène Laroche, Sec.-Trés., 15, rue Caron, CP 270, Kingsey Falls J0A 1B0 – 819/363-3810, Fax: 819/363-3819
Kinnear's Mills (Mun.)	368	L'Amiante	Frontenac	Frontenac	Lucien Trépanier, Sec.-Trés., 120, rue des Églises, Kinnear's Mills G0N 1K0 – 418/424-3377, Fax: 418/424-3015
Kipawa (Mun.)	520	Témiscamingue	Témiscamingue	Rouyn-Noranda-Témiscamingue	Marie-Rose Tremblay, Sec.-Trés., 15, rue Principale, Tee Lake J0Z 3P0 – 819/627-3500, Fax: 819/627-1067
KIRKLAND	17,725	Montréal (Urb. Com.)	Vaudreuil	Nelligan	Lise Labrosse, Gref., 17200, boul Hymus, Kirkland H9J 3Y8 – 514/694-4100, Fax: 514/630-2711
Kuujjuaq (NV)	1,425	Kativik	Manicouagan	Ungava	Ian Robertson, Sec.-Trés., CP 58, Kuujjuaq J0M 1C0 – 819/964-2943, Fax: 819/964-2980

QUÉBEC MUNICIPALITIES 4-89

Cities (Villes) in CAPITALS; Villages marked (V); Townships/Cantons marked (Canton);United townships/Cantons unis marked (Cantons); Parishes (Paroisses) marked (P); Municipalities marked (Mun.).; Northern villages/Villages nordiques marked (NV); Cree Villages/Villages Cris marked (VC); Naskapi Villages/Villages Naskapi marked (VN); In the third column, Urban Community/Communauté Urbaine marked Urb. Com. An in-depth listing for municipalities marked with * appears in Part 2 (check Index for page numbers).

MUNICIPALITY	1993 POP.	REGIONAL COUNTY MUN.	FEDERAL ELECTORAL DISTRICT	PROVINCIAL ELECTORAL DISTRICT	CONTACT PERSON WITH ADDRESS, PHONE & FAX
Kuujjuarapik (NV)	613	Kativik	Abitibi	Ungava	Pierre Roussel, Sec.-Trés., Kuujjuarapik J0M 1G0 – 819/929-3360, Fax: 819/929-3453
LA BAIE	21,647	Le Fjord-du-Saguenay	Chicoutimi	Dubuc	Dominique Tremblay, Gref., 422, rue Victoria, La Baie G7B 3M4 – 418/697-5000, Fax: 418/697-5059
La Baleine (Mun.)	287	Charlevoix	Charlevoix	Charlevoix	Kathia Parent, Sec.-Trés., 145, ch Principale, La Baleine G0A 2A0 – 418/438-2878, Fax: 418/438-2878
La Bostonnais (Mun.)	494	Le Haut-St-Maurice	Champlain	Laviolette	Estelle Giguère, Sec.-Trés., BG 2, La Tuque G9X 3N6 – 819/523-6091
La Conception (Mun.)	782	Les Laurentides	Laurentides	Labelle	Jean-Denis Larocque, Sec.-Trés., 1371, boul. du Centenaire, La Conception J0T 1M0 – 819/686-3016, Fax: 819/686-5808
La Corne (Mun.)	629	Abitibi	Abitibi	Abitibi-Ouest	Suzanne McLaughlin-Dionne, Sec.-Trés., 324, route 111, La Corne J0Y 1R0 – 819/799-3571, Fax: 819/799-3571
La Doré (P)	1,714	Le Domaine-du-Roy	Roberval	Roberval	Laurent-Paul Dallaire, Sec.-Trés., 5000, rue des Peupliers, La Doré G8J 1E8 – 418/256-3545, Fax: 418/256-3496
La Durantaye (P)	700	Bellechasse	Bellechasse	Bellechasse	Rachel Lamontagne, Sec.-Trés., 539, rue Piedmont, La Durantaye G0R 1W0 – 418/884-3465, Fax: 418/884-3048
La Guadeloupe (V)	1,760	Beauce-Sartigan	Beauce	Beauce-Sud	Marc-André Doyle, Sec.-Trés., 483 - 9e rue est, CP 279, La Guadeloupe G0M 1G0 – 418/459-3342, Fax: 418/459-3507
La Macaza (Mun.)	936	Antoine-Labelle	Pontiac-Gatineau-Labelle	Labelle	Guy Goudreau, Sec.-Trés., 53, rue des Pionniers, CP 28, La Macaza J0T 1R0 – 819/275-2077, Fax: 819/275-3429
La Malbaie-Pointe-au-Pic (V)[d]	5,009 ('95)	Charlevoix-Est	Charlevoix	Charlevoix	Roger Arpin, Sec.-Trés., 280, rue Nairn, La Malbaie G5A 1L9 – 418/665-3747, Fax: 418/665-4935
La Martre (Mun.)	333	Denis-Riverin	Gaspé	Matane	Marielle Cloutier-Gagnon, Sec.-Trés., 10, av du Phare, La Martre G0E 2H0 – 418/288-5605, Fax: 418/288-5144
La Minerve (Canton)	954	Les Laurentides	Laurentides	Labelle	Robert Charette, Sec.-Trés., 6, rue Mailloux, La Minerve J0T 1S0 – 819/274-2364, Fax: 819/274-2031
La Morandière (Mun.)	335	Abitibi	Abitibi	Abitibi-Ouest	Sandra Hardy, Sec.-Trés., 204, rte 397, La Morandière J0Y 1S0 – 819/734-6143, Fax: 819/734-6143
La Motte (Mun.)	421	Abitibi	Abitibi	Abitibi-Ouest	Lyne Daigle, Sec.-Trés., 349, ch St-Luc, CP 644, La Motte J0Y 1T0 – 819/732-2878, Fax: 819/732-2878
La Patrie (V)	354	Le Haut-St-François	Mégantic-Compton-Stanstead	Mégantic-Compton	Ghislaine Giard, Sec.-Trés., 44, rue Garneau, CP 180, La Patrie J0B 1Y0 – 819/888-2514, Fax: 819/888-2514
La Pêche (Mun.)	6,265	Les Collines-de-l'Outaouais	Pontiac-Gatineau-Labelle	Gatineau	Charles Ricard, Sec.-Trés., CP 70, Ste-Cécile-de-Masham J0X 2W0 – 819/456-2161, Fax: 819/456-4534
LA PLAINE	11,840	Les Moulins	Terrebonne	Masson	Louise Langlois, Sec.-Trés., 675, rue de l'Église, CP 90, La Plaine J0N 1B0 – 514/478-2555, Fax: 514/478-4496
LA POCATIÈRE	4,925	Kamouraska	Kamouraska-Rivière-du-Loup	Kamouraska-Témiscouata	Claude Crête, Sec.-Trés., 412 - 9e rue, CP 668, La Pocatière G0R 1Z0 – 418/856-3394, Fax: 418/856-5465
LA PRAIRIE	15,839	Roussillon	La Prairie	La Prairie	Bernard Blain, Gref., #400, 170, boul Taschereau, La Prairie J5R 5H6 – 514/444-0540, Fax: 514/444-0548
La Présentation (P)	1,855	Les Maskoutains	St-Hyacinthe-Bagot	Verchères	André Charron, Sec.-Trés., 772, rue Principale, La Présentation J0H 1B0 – 514/796-2317, Fax: 514/796-1707
La Rédemption (P)	606	La Mitis	Matapédia-Matane	Matapédia	Gaétane Viens, Sec.-Trés., 68, rue Soucy, CP 39, La Rédemption G0J 1P0 – 418/776-5311, Fax: 418/776-5711
La Reine (Mun.)	483	Abitibi-Ouest	Témiscamingue	Abitibi-Ouest	Diane Sévigny-East, Sec.-Trés., 1, 3e av ouest, CP 40, La Reine J0Z 2L0 – 819/947-5271, Fax: 819/947-5271
LA SARRE	8,660	Abitibi-Ouest	Témiscamingue	Abitibi-Ouest	François Casaubon, Sec.-Trés., 6, 4e av est, La Sarre J9Z 1J9 – 819/333-2282, Fax: 819/333-3090
La Trinité-des-Monts (P)	362	Rimouski-Neigette	Rimouski-Témiscouata	Rimouski	Thérèse Dumont, Sec.-Trés., 12, rue Principale ouest, CP 9, La Trinité-des-Monts G0K 1B0 – 418/779-2421, Fax: 418/779-2421
LA TUQUE	13,211	Le Haut-St-Maurice	Champlain	Laviolette	Yves Tousignant, Gref., 558, rue Commerciale, La Tuque G9X 3A9 – 819/523-5110, Fax: 819/523-5419
La Visitation-de-l'Île-Dupas (Mun.)	564	D'Autray	Berthier-Montcalm	Berthier	Claire Hérard, Sec.-Trés., 113, rue de l'Église, La Visitation-de-l'Île-Dupas J0K 2P0 – 514/836-6019, Fax: 514/836-6019

Canadian Almanac & Directory 1997

4-90 QUÉBEC MUNICIPALITIES

Cities (Villes) in CAPITALS; Villages marked (V); Townships/Cantons marked (Canton);United townships/Cantons unis marked (Cantons); Parishes (Paroisses) marked (P); Municipalities marked (Mun.).; Northern villages/Villages nordiques marked (NV); Cree Villages/Villages Cris marked (VC); Naskapi Villages/Villages Naskapi marked (VN); In the third column, Urban Community/Communauté Urbaine marked Urb. Com. An in-depth listing for municipalities marked with * appears in Part 2 (check Index for page numbers).

MUNICIPALITY	1993 POP.	REGIONAL COUNTY MUN.	FEDERAL ELECTORAL DISTRICT	PROVINCIAL ELECTORAL DISTRICT	CONTACT PERSON WITH ADDRESS, PHONE & FAX
La Visitation-de-Yamaska (Mun.)	416	Nicolet-Yamaska	Richelieu	Nicolet-Yamaska	Lucie Lambert, Sec.-Trés., 21, rue Principale, La Visitation J0G 1C0 – 514/564-2818, Fax: 514/564-2818
Labelle (Mun.)	2,200	Les Laurentides	Laurentides	Labelle	Pierre Delage, Sec.-Trés., CP 390, Labelle J0T 1H0 – 819/686-2144, Fax: 819/686-3820
Labrecque (Mun.)	1,205	Lac-St-Jean-Est	Lac-St-Jean	Lac-St-Jean	Suzanne Couture, Sec.-Trés., 3425, rue Ambroise, CP 9, St-Léon G0W 2S0 – 418/481-2022, Fax: 418/481-1210
Lac-à-la-Croix (Mun.)	991	Lac-St-Jean-Est	Lac-St-Jean	Lac-St-Jean	Marie-Hélène Boily, Sec.-Trés., 353, rue St-Jean, Lac-à-la-Croix G0W 1W0 – 418/349-2892, Fax: 418/349-8724
Lac-à-la-Tortue (Mun.)	2,969	Le Centre-de-la-Mauricie	St-Maurice	St-Maurice	Madeleine Lahaie, Sec.-Trés., 1082, 37e av, CP 129, Lac-à-la-Tortue G0X 1L0 – 819/538-5882, Fax: 819/538-5340
Lac-au-Saumon (V)	1,300	La Matapédia	Matapédia-Matane	Matapédia	Nadia Saint-Pierre, Sec.-Trés., 24, Place de la Municipalité, CP 98, Lac-au-Saumon G0J 1M0 – 418/778-3378, Fax: 418/778-3706
Lac-aux-Sables (P)	1,512	Mékinac	Portneuf	Portneuf	Benoit Beaupré, Sec.-Trés., 820, rue St-Alphonse, Lac-aux-Sables G0X 1M0 – 418/336-2331, Fax: 418/336-2500
Lac-Beauport (Mun.)	4,800	La Jacques-Cartier	Charlesbourg	Chauveau	Jean-François Parent, Sec.-Trés., 65, ch du Tour-du-Lac, CP 159, Lac-Beauport G0A 2C0 – 418/849-7141, Fax: 418/849-0361
Lac-Bouchette (Mun.)	1,524	Le Domaine-du-Roy	Roberval	Roberval	Serge Martel, Sec.-Trés., 186, rue Principale, CP 40, Lac-Bouchette G0W 1V0 – 418/348-6306, Fax: 418/348-9477
LAC-BROME	5,048	Brome-Missisquoi	Brome-Missisquoi	Brome-Missisquoi	Catherine Bouchard, Gref., 122, ch Lakeside, CP 60, Knowlton J0E 1V0 – 514/243-6111, Fax: 514/243-5300
Lac-Carré (V)	867	Les Laurentides	Laurentides	Labelle	Danielle Gauthier, Sec.-Trés., 64, rue de l'Hôtel-de-Ville, CP 270, Lac-Carré J0T 1J0 – 819/688-3104, Fax: 819/688-2405
LAC-DELAGE	361	La Jacques-Cartier	Charlesbourg	Chauveau	Guylaine Thibault, Sec.-Trés., 24, rue Pied-des-Pentes, Lac-Delage G0A 4P0 – 418/848-2417, Fax: 418/848-2417
Lac-des-Aigles (Mun.)	695	Témiscouata	Rimouski-Témiscouata	Rimouski	Sylvie Samson, Sec.-Trés., 75, rue Principale, CP 70, Lac-des-Aigles G0K 1V0 – 418/779-2300, Fax: 418/779-3024
Lac-des-Écorces (V)	988	Antoine-Labelle	Pontiac-Gatineau-Labelle	Labelle	Guy Legault, Sec.-Trés., 111, boul St-François sud, CP 60, Lac-des-Écorces J0W 1H0 – 819/585-9155, Fax: 819/585-2555
Lac-des-Plages (Mun.)	407	Papineau	Argenteuil-Papineau	Papineau	Denis Dagenais, Sec.-Trés., 2053, ch Tour du Lac, Lac-des-Plages J0T 1K0 – 819/426-2391
Lac-des-Seize-Îles (Mun.)	221	Les Pays-d'en-Haut	Argenteuil-Papineau	Argenteuil	Luce Bergeron, Sec.-Trés., 47, rue de l'Église, CP 360, Lac-des-Seize-Iles J0T 2M0 – 514/226-3117, Fax: 514/226-3117
Lac-Drolet (Mun.)	1,170	Le Granit	Mégantic-Compton-Stanstead	Mégantic-Compton	Ronald Leclerc, Sec.-Trés., 685, rue Principale, CP 148, Lac-Drôlet G0Y 1C0 – 819/549-2332
Lac-du-Cerf (Mun.)	427	Antoine-Labelle	Pontiac-Gatineau-Labelle	Labelle	Jacinthe Valiquette, Sec.-Trés., 15, rue Émard, Lac-du-Cerf J0W 1S0 – 819/597-2424, Fax: 819/597-2424
Lac-Dufault (Mun.)	771	Rouyn-Noranda	Témiscamingue	Rouyn-Noranda-Témiscamingue	Lise Bélair, Sec.-Trés., 34, rue Principale, Lac-Dufault J9X 5A3 – 819/797-3068, Fax: 819/797-5236
Lac-Édouard (Mun.)	168	Le Haut-St-Maurice	Champlain	Laviolette	Lise Côté, Sec.-Trés., 195, rue Principale, CP 4049, Lac-Édouard G0X 3N0 – 819/653-2238, Fax: 819/653-2017
LAC-ETCHEMIN	2,698	Les Etchemins	Bellechasse	Bellechasse	Marcel Lachance, Sec.-Trés., 208, 2e av, CP 370, Lac-Etchemin G0R 1S0 – 418/625-4521, Fax: 418/625-3175
Lac-Frontière (Mun.)	185	Montmagny	Bellechasse	Montmagny-L'Islet	Dany Robert, Sec.-Trés., 22, rue de l'Église, Lac-Frontière G0R 1T0 – 418/245-3553
Lac-Kénogami (Mun.)	1,418	Le Fjord-du-Saguenay	Jonquière	Jonquière	Germain Girard, Sec.-Trés., 3000, ch de l'Église, Lac-Kénogami G7X 7V6 – 418/547-8869, Fax: 418/547-6158
LAC-MÉGANTIC	5,941	Le Granit	Mégantic-Compton-Stanstead	Mégantic-Compton	Jean Perreault, Gref., #200, 5527, rue Frontenac, Lac-Mégantic G6B 1H6 – 819/583-2441, Fax: 819/583-5920
Lac-Nominingue (Mun.)	1,836	Antoine-Labelle	Pontiac-Gatineau-Labelle	Labelle	Yves Légaré, Sec.-Trés., 2110, ch Tour-du-Lac, CP 390, Lac-Nominingue J0W 1R0 – 819/278-3384, Fax: 819/278-4967
Lac-Poulin (V)	56	Beauce-Sartigan	Beauce	Beauce-Sud	Paul Poulin, Sec.-Trés., 1855, 127e rue, CP 186, St-Georges G5Y 5C7 – 418/228-6115

Canadian Almanac & Directory 1997

QUÉBEC MUNICIPALITIES 4-91

Cities (Villes) in CAPITALS; Villages marked (V); Townships/Cantons marked (Canton);United townships/Cantons unis marked (Cantons); Parishes (Paroisses) marked (P); Municipalities marked (Mun.).; Northern villages/Villages nordiques marked (NV); Cree Villages/Villages Cris marked (VC); Naskapi Villages/Villages Naskapi marked (VN); In the third column, Urban Community/Communauté Urbaine marked Urb. Com. An in-depth listing for municipalities marked with * appears in Part 2 (check Index for page numbers).

MUNICIPALITY	1993 POP.	REGIONAL COUNTY MUN.	FEDERAL ELECTORAL DISTRICT	PROVINCIAL ELECTORAL DISTRICT	CONTACT PERSON WITH ADDRESS, PHONE & FAX
Lac-Saguay (V)	317	Antoine-Labelle	Pontiac-Gatineau-Labelle	Labelle	Richard Gagnon, Sec.-Trés., 257A, rte 117, Lac-Saguay J0W 1L0 – 819/278-3972, Fax: 819/278-0260
Lac-St-Charles (Mun.)	7,858	Québec (Urb. Com.)	Charlesbourg	Chauveau	Jacques Lacombe, Sec.-Trés., 510, rue Delage, CP 8, Lac-St-Charles G0A 2H0 – 418/849-2811, Fax: 418/849-2849
LAC-ST-JOSEPH	151	La Jacques-Cartier	Portneuf	Portneuf	Armand Létourneau, Sec.-Trés., 4417, rue des Lierres, Charlesbourg G1G 1S2 – 418/626-3598, Fax: 418/624-0997
Lac-Ste-Marie (Mun.)	485	La Vallée-de-la-Gatineau	Pontiac-Gatineau-Labelle	Gatineau	Johanne D'Amour, Sec.-Trés., CP 97, Lac-Ste-Marie J0X 1Z0 – 819/467-5437, Fax: 819/467-3691
Lac-St-Paul (Mun.)	401	Antoine-Labelle	Pontiac-Gatineau-Labelle	Labelle	Francine Bélec, Sec.-Trés., 388, rue Principale, Lac-St-Paul J0W 1K0 – 819/587-4283, Fax: 819/587-4892
LAC-SERGENT	245	Portneuf	Portneuf	Portneuf	Nicole Lacasse, Sec.-Trés., 1149, ch Tour du Lac Nord, Lac-Sergent G0A 2J0 – 418/875-4854, Fax: 418/875-4854
Lac-Simon (Mun.)	635	Papineau	Argenteuil-Papineau	Papineau	Gisèle Prévost, Sec.-Trés., CP 220, Chénéville J0V 1E0 – 819/428-3906, Fax: 819/428-3455
Lac-Supérieur (Mun.)	1,030	Les Laurentides	Laurentides	Labelle	Clarisse Daoust, Sec.-Trés., 1281, ch du lac-Supérieur, Lac-Supérieur J0T 1J0 – 819/688-2208, Fax: 819/688-3010
Lac-Tremblant-Nord (Mun.)		Labelle	Laurentides	Labelle	Michèle Dutrisac-Kilburn, Sec.-Trés., CP 150, Mont-Tremblant H3Z 2H6 – 514/937-3528, Fax: 514/938-9274
L'Acadie (Mun.)	5,356	Le Haut-Richelieu	St-Jean	St-Jean	Denis L'Heureux, Sec.-Trés., 1161, ch du Clocher, L'Acadie J2Y 1A1 – 514/347-8221, Fax: 514/347-6642
LACHENAIE	16,878	Les Moulins	Terrebonne	Terrebonne	Judith Viens, Gref., 3060, boul St-Charles, Lachenaie J6V 1A1 – 514/471-2424, Fax: 514/471-9872
LACHINE	35,729	Montréal (Urb. Com.)	Lachine-Lac-St-Louis	Marquette	Sylvie Aubin, Gref., 1800, boul St-Joseph, Lachine H8S 2N4 – 514/634-3471, Fax: 514/634-8164, URL: http://www.cum.qc.ca/LACHINE
LACHUTE	12,016 ('94)	Argenteuil	Argenteuil-Papineau	Argenteuil	Vacant, Gref., 380, rue Principale, Lachute J8H 1Y2 – 514/562-3781, Fax: 514/562-1431
Lacolle (V)	1,474	Le Haut-Richelieu	St-Jean	St-Jean	Georgette Chevrefils, Sec.-Trés., 1, rue de l'Église sud, CP 400, Lacolle J0J 1J0 – 514/246-3201, Fax: 514/246-4412
Lafontaine (V)	8,056	La Rivière-du-Nord	Laurentides	Prévost	Fernand Campbell, Sec.-Trés., 70 - 106e av, Lafontaine J7Y 1G5 – 514/438-2264, Fax: 514/438-4355
Laforce (Mun.)	484	Témiscamingue	Témiscamingue	Rouyn-Noranda-Témiscamingue	Yves Nolet, Sec.-Trés., CP 25, Laforce J0Z 2J0 – 819/722-2461
Lamarche (Mun.)	572	Lac-St-Jean-Est	Lac-St-Jean	Lac-St-Jean	Aline Perron, Sec.-Trés., 100, rue Principale, Lamarche G0W 1X0 – 418/481-2861, Fax: 418/481-1412
Lambton (Mun.)	1,511	Le Granit	Mégantic-Compton-Stanstead	Mégantic-Compton	Claire Bédard, Sec.-Trés., 230, rue du Collège, CP 206, Lambton G0M 1H0 – 418/486-7438, Fax: 418/486-7440
L'ANCIENNE-LORETTE	15,929	Québec (Urb. Com.)	Québec-Est	La Peltrie	Serge Morin, Gref., 1575, rue Turmel, L'Ancienne-Lorette G2E 3J5 – 418/872-9811, Fax: 418/872-1962
Landrienne (Canton)	1,056	Abitibi	Abitibi	Abitibi-Ouest	Jacques Perron, Sec.-Trés., 158, av Principale est, Landrienne J0Y 1V0 – 819/732-4357, Fax: 819/732-4357
L'Ange-Gardien (Mun.)	3,014	Les Collines-de-l'Outaouais	Gatineau-La Lièvre	Papineau	Paul St-Louis, Sec.-Trés., 870, ch Donaldson, L'Ange-Gardien J8L 2W7 – 819/986-7470, Fax: 819/986-8349
L'Ange-Gardien (P)	2,952	La Côte-de-Beaupré	Beauport-Montmorency-Orléans	Montmorency	Jacques Villeneuve, Sec.-Trés., 6405, av Royale, L'Ange-Gardien G0A 2K0 – 418/822-1555, Fax: 418/822-2526
L'Ange-Gardien (V)	594	Rouville	Shefford	Iberville	André Parent, Sec.-Trés., 249, rue St-Joseph, CP 120, L'Ange-Gardien J0E 1E0 – 514/293-7575, Fax: 514/293-6635
Langelier (Canton)	525	Le Haut-St-Maurice	Champlain	Laviolette	Manon Shallow, Sec.-Trés., 47, rue Principale, CP 2010, La Croche G0X 1R0 – 819/523-2061, Fax: 819/523-2061
L'Annonciation (V)	2,247	Antoine-Labelle	Pontiac-Gatineau-Labelle	Labelle	Lise Cadieux, Sec.-Trés., 84, rue Principale sud, CP 398, L'Annonciation J0T 1T0 – 819/275-2929, Fax: 819/275-3676
Lanoraie-d'Autray (Mun.)	1,942	D'Autray	Berthier-Montcalm	Berthier	Robert Coolidge, Sec.-Trés., 57, rue Laroche, CP 308, Lanoraie J0K 1E0 – 514/887-2364, Fax: 514/887-2077
L'Anse-St-Jean (Mun.)	1,309	Le Fjord-du-Saguenay	Chicoutimi	Dubuc	Lolita Boudreault, Sec.-Trés., 3, rue du Couvent, L'Anse-St-Jean G0V 1J0 – 418/272-2633, Fax: 418/272-3148

Canadian Almanac & Directory 1997

4-92 QUÉBEC MUNICIPALITIES

Cities (Villes) in CAPITALS; Villages marked (V); Townships/Cantons marked (Canton);United townships/Cantons unis marked (Cantons); Parishes (Paroisses) marked (P); Municipalities marked (Mun.).; Northern villages/Villages nordiques marked (NV); Cree Villages/Villages Cris marked (VC); Naskapi Villages/Villages Naskapi marked (VN); In the third column, Urban Community/Communauté Urbaine marked Urb. Com. An in-depth listing for municipalities marked with * appears in Part 2 (check Index for page numbers).

MUNICIPALITY	1993 POP.	REGIONAL COUNTY MUN.	FEDERAL ELECTORAL DISTRICT	PROVINCIAL ELECTORAL DISTRICT	CONTACT PERSON WITH ADDRESS, PHONE & FAX
Lantier (Mun.)	732	Les Laurentides	Laurentides	Bertrand	Lise Loiseau, Sec.-Trés., 118, 29e av, CP 39, Lantier J0T 1V0 – 819/326-2674, Fax: 819/326-5204
Larouche (P)	1,036	Le Fjord-du-Saguenay	Jonquière	Lac-St-Jean	Paul-Henri Munger, Sec.-Trés., 709, rue Gauthier, Larouche G0W 1Z0 – 418/695-2201, Fax: 418/695-4989
*LASALLE	74,777	Montréal (Urb. Com.)	LaSalle-Émard	Marguerite-Bourgeoys; Marquette	Nicole Herby, Gref., 55, av Dupras, LaSalle H8R 4A8 – 514/367-1000, Fax: 514/367-3520
L'Ascension (P)	692	Antoine-Labelle	Pontiac-Gatineau-Labelle	Labelle	Sylvain Michaudville, Sec.-Trés., 59, rue de l'Hôtel-de-Ville, CP 30, L'Ascension J0T 1W0 – 819/275-3027, Fax: 819/275-3489
L'Ascension-de-Notre-Seigneur (P)	1,859	Lac-St-Jean-Est	Lac-St-Jean	Lac-St-Jean	Roger Boily, Sec.-Trés., 51, 4e av est, L'Ascension-de-Notre-Seigneur G0W 1Y0 – 418/347-3482, Fax: 418/347-4253
L'Ascension-de-Patapédia (Mun.)	320	Avignon	Bonaventure-Îles-de-la-Madeleine	Bonaventure	Lorraine Gallant, Sec.-Trés., 82, rue Principale, CP 9, L'Ascension-de-Patapédia G0J 1R0 – 418/299-2024, Fax: 418/299-2024
L'ASSOMPTION	12,341	L'Assomption	Joliette	L'Assomption	Suzanne Dubé, Gref., 399, rue Dorval, L'Assomption J5W 1A1 – 514/589-5671, Fax: 514/589-4512
LATERRIÈRE	4,836	Le Fjord-du-Saguenay	Jonquière	Dubuc	Normand Girard, Gref., 6166, rue Notre-Dame, CP 69, Laterrière G0V 1K0 – 418/678-2216, Fax: 418/678-2647
Latulipe-et-Gaboury (Cantons)	376	Témiscamingue	Témiscamingue	Rouyn-Noranda-Témiscamingue	Gisèle Gauthier, Sec.-Trés., 1, rue Principale est, CP 9, Latulipe J0Z 2N0 – 819/747-4281, Fax: 819/747-2194
Launay (Canton)	279	Abitibi	Abitibi	Abitibi-Ouest	Claudette Laroche, Sec.-Trés., 843, rue des Pionniers, Launay J0Y 1W0 – 819/796-2545
LAURENTIDES	2,627	Montcalm	Joliette	Rousseau	Jean-Guy Champoux, Sec.-Trés., 250 - 12e av, CP 128, Laurentides J0R 1C0 – 514/439-2539, Fax: 514/439-6384
Laurier-Station (V)	2,266	Lotbinière	Lotbinière	Lotbinière	Réjean Tousignant, Sec.-Trés., 137, rue de la Station, Laurier Station G0S 1N0 – 418/728-3852, Fax: 418/728-4801
Laurierville (V)	911	L'Érable	Frontenac	Lotbinière	Réjean Gingras, Sec.-Trés., 140, rue Grenier, CP 159, Laurierville G0S 1P0 – 819/365-4646, Fax: 819/365-4200
*LAVAL	344,700 ('95)	Laval	Laval-Centre; Laval-Est; Laval-Ouest	Chomedey; Fabre; Laval-des-Rapides; Mille-Îles; Vimont	Guy Collard, Gref., Hôtel de Ville, 1, Place du Souvenir, CP 422, Laval H7V 1W7 – 514/978-8000, Fax: 514/978-5943
Lavaltrie (V)	4,735	D'Autray	Berthier-Montcalm	Berthier	Réjean Nantais, Sec.-Trés., 1370, rue Notre-Dame, Lavaltrie J0K 1H0 – 514/586-2921, Fax: 514/586-3939
L'Avenir (Mun.)	1,229	Drummond	Drummond	Johnson	Andrée Béland, Sec.-Trés., 575, rue Principle, CP 112, L'Avenir J0C 1B0 – 819/394-2422, Fax: 819/394-2222
Laverlochère (P)	880	Témiscamingue	Témiscamingue	Rouyn-Noranda-Témiscamingue	Monique Rivest, Sec.-Trés., 11, rue St-Isidore ouest, CP 159, Laverlochère J0Z 2P0 – 819/765-5111, Fax: 819/765-5111
Lawrenceville (V)	628	Le Val-St-François	Richmond-Wolfe	Brome-Missisquoi	René Majella, Sec.-Trés., 1525, rue Principale, CP 60, Lawrenceville J0E 1W0 – 514/535-6398, Fax: 514/535-6398
Le Bic (Mun.)	3,190	Rimouski-Neigette	Rimouski-Témiscamingue	Rimouski	Camille Roussel, Sec.-Trés., 149, rue Ste-Cécile, CP 99, Le Bic G0L 1B0 – 418/736-5833, Fax: 418/736-4834
LE GARDEUR	15,743	L'Assomption	Joliette	Masson	Céline Girard, Gref., 1, Montée des Arsenaux, Le Gardeur J5Z 2C1 – 514/585-1140, Fax: 514/585-7679
LEBEL-SUR-QUÉVILLON	3,463	Terr. du Nouveau-Québec	Abitibi	Ungava	Serge Woods, Gref., 500, Place Quévillon, CP 430, Lebel-sur-Quévillon J0Y 1X0 – 819/755-4826, Fax: 819/755-8124
Leclercville (V)	328	Lotbinière	Lotbinière	Lotbinière	Rachel Héroux, Sec.-Trés., 182, rue St-Jean-Baptiste, Leclercville G0S 2K0 – 819/292-2769, Fax: 819/292-2736
Lefebvre (Mun.)	712	Drummond	Drummond	Johnson	Carole Côté, Sec.-Trés., 186, 10e rang, Lefebvre J0H 2C0 – 819/394-2782, Fax: 819/394-2782
Lejeune (Mun.)	409	Témiscouata	Rimouski-Témiscouata	Kamouraska-Témiscouata	Lynda Caron-Damboise, Sec.-Trés., 69, rue de la Grande-Coulée, CP 40, Lejeune G0L 1S0 – 418/855-2428, Fax: 418/855-2428
Lemieux (Mun.)	350	Bécancour	Lotbinière	Lotbinière	France Hénault, Sec.-Trés., 530, rue de l'Église, Lemieux G0X 1S0 – 819/283-2506, Fax: 819/283-2506
LEMOYNE	5,718	Champlain	St-Hubert	Laporte	André Bellefeuille, Sec.-Trés., 2205, rue St-Georges, Lemoyne J4R 1V7 – 514/671-5940, Fax: 514/671-1578

Canadian Almanac & Directory 1997

Cities (Villes) in CAPITALS; Villages marked (V); Townships/Cantons marked (Canton);United townships/Cantons unis marked (Cantons); Parishes (Paroisses) marked (P); Municipalities marked (Mun.).; Northern villages/Villages nordiques marked (NV); Cree Villages/Villages Cris marked (VC); Naskapi Villages/Villages Naskapi marked (VN); In the third column, Urban Community/Communauté Urbaine marked Urb. Com. An in-depth listing for municipalities marked with * appears in Part 2 (check Index for page numbers).

MUNICIPALITY	1993 POP.	REGIONAL COUNTY MUN.	FEDERAL ELECTORAL DISTRICT	PROVINCIAL ELECTORAL DISTRICT	CONTACT PERSON WITH ADDRESS, PHONE & FAX
LENNOXVILLE	4,209	Sherbrooke	Sherbrooke	St-François	Johanne Henson, Gref., 150, rue Queen, Lennoxville J1M 1J6 – 819/569-9388, Fax: 819/563-3705
L'Épiphanie (P)	2,758	L'Assomption	Joliette	Rousseau	Nicole Renaud, Sec.-Trés., 331, rang du Bas-de-l'Achigan, L'Épiphanie J5X 1E1 – 514/588-5547, Fax: 514/588-6050
L'ÉPIPHANIE	3,954	L'Assomption	Joliette	Rousseau	Johane Ducharme, Gref., 66, rue Notre-Dame, L'Épiphanie J0K 1J0 – 514/588-5515, Fax: 514/588-6171
LÉRY	2,572	Roussillon	Beauharnois-Salaberry	Châteauguay	Rose-Hélène Langlais, Sec.-Trés., 1, rue de l'Hôtel-de-Ville, Léry J6N 1E8 – 514/692-6861, Fax: 514/692-6881
Les Boules (Mun.)	414	La Mitis	Matapédia-Matane	Matane	Yolande Marcheterre, Sec.-Trés., 28, rte 132, Les Boules G0J 1S0 – 418/936-3479
Les Cèdres (Mun.)	4,168	Vaudreuil-Soulanges	Vaudreuil	Salaberry-Soulanges	Normand Meilleur, Sec.-Trés., 1060, ch du Fleuve, Les Cèdres J0P 1L0 – 514/452-4340, Fax: 514/452-4605
Les Coteaux (Mun.)	2,837	Vaudreuil-Soulanges	Vaudreuil	Salaberry-Soulanges	Claude Madore, Sec.-Trés., 65, route 338, Coteau-Landing J0P 1C0 – 514/267-3531, Fax: 514/267-3532
Les Éboulements (Mun.)	1,023	Charlevoix	Charlevoix	Charlevoix	André Girard, Sec.-Trés., 248, rue du Village, CP 130, Les Éboulements G0A 2M0 – 418/635-2755, Fax: 418/635-2755
Les Escoumins (Mun.)	2,280	La Haute-Côte-Nord	Charlevoix	Saguenay	Micheline Savard, Sec.-Trés., 2, rue Sirois, CP 160, Les Escoumins G0T 1K0 – 418/233-2766, Fax: 418/233-3273
Les Hauteurs (Mun.)	725	La Mitis	Matapédia-Matane	Matapédia	Diane Bernier, Sec.-Trés., 50, rue de l'Église, CP 69, Les Hauteurs G0K 1C0 – 418/798-8266, Fax: 418/798-8266
Les Méchins (Mun.)	1,337	Matane	Matapédia-Matane	Matane	Lyne Fortin, Sec.-Trés., 108, rte des Fonds, Les Méchins G0J 1T0 – 418/729-3952, Fax: 418/729-3952
Leslie Clapham-et-Huddersfield (Cantons)	958	Pontiac	Pontiac-Gatineau-Labelle	Pontiac	Anita Lafleur, Sec.-Trés., CP 70, Otter Lake J0X 2P0 – 819/453-7049, Fax: 819/453-7311
L'Étang-du-Nord (Mun.)	3,099	Les Îles-de-la-Madeleine	Bonaventure-Îles-de-la-Madeleine	Îles-de-la-Madeleine	Dominique Delaney, Sec.-Trés., 1589, ch Étang-du-Nord, CP 689, L'Étang-du-Nord G0B 1E0 – 418/986-3321, Fax: 418/986-6231
LÉVIS	42,635	Desjardins	Lévis	Lévis	Sylvie Dionne, Gref., 225, côte du Passage, Lévis G6V 5T4 – 418/838-4000, Fax: 418/838-4051
L'Île-aux-Coudres (Mun.)	1,114	Charlevoix	Charlevoix	Charlevoix	Marcelle Pedneault, Sec.-Trés., 23, rue Royale ouest, CP 14, L'Île-aux-Coudres G0A 3J0 – 418/438-2583, Fax: 418/438-2750
L'Île-Bizard (V)	11,499	Montréal (Urb. Com.)	Notre-Dame-de-Grâce	Nelligan	Martin Claveau, Sec.-Trés., 350, rue de l'Église, St-Raphaël-de-Île-Bizard H9C 1G9 – 514/620-6331, Fax: 514/620-2189
L'ÎLE-CADIEUX	152	Vaudreuil-Soulanges	Vaudreuil	Vaudreuil	Annie Herrbach, Sec.-Trés., 50, ch de l'Île, L'Ile-Cadieux J7V 8P3 – 514/424-4273, Fax: 514/424-6327
L'Île-d'Anticosti (Mun.)	273	Minganie	Manicouagan	Duplessis	Alain Descarreaux, Sec.-Trés., CP 119, Port-Menier G0G 2Y0 – 418/535-0311, Fax: 418/535-0381
L'Île-d'Entrée (V)	178	Les Îles-de-la-Madeleine	Bonaventure-Îles-de-la-Madeleine	Îles-de-la-Madeleine	Clara Chenell, Sec.-Trés., L'Ile-d'Entrée G0B 1C0 – 418/986-4179, Fax: 418/986-3764
L'ÎLE-DORVAL	3	Montréal (Urb. Com.)	Lachine-Lac-St-Louis	Jacques-Cartier	Claire Robinson, Sec.-Trés., CP 53061, Dorval H9S 5W4 – 514/633-0182, Fax: 514/344-2615
L'Île-du-Havre-Aubert (Mun.)	2,580	Les Îles-de-la-Madeleine	Bonaventure-Îles-de-la-Madeleine	Îles-de-la-Madeleine	Jean-Yves Lebreux, Sec.-Trés., CP 37, Havre-Aubert G0B 1J0 – 418/937-5205, Fax: 418/937-5558
L'ÎLE-PERROT	8,759	Vaudreuil-Soulanges	Vaudreuil	Vaudreuil	Albert Portelance, Gref., 110, boul Perrot, L'Île-Perrot J7V 3G1 – 514/453-1751, Fax: 514/453-2432
Lingwick (Canton)	459	Le Haut-St-François	Mégantic-Compton-Stanstead	Mégantic-Compton	Suzanne Blais, Sec.-Trés., 72, rte 108, Lingwick J0B 2Z0 – 819/877-3311, Fax: 819/877-3311
L'Isle-aux-Allumettes (Canton)	568	Pontiac	Pointe-Gatineau-Labelle	Pontiac	Richard Vaillancourt, Sec.-Trés., 37, rue St-Joseph, CP 100, Chapeau J0X 1M0 – 819/689-2266, Fax: 819/689-5619
L'Isle-aux-Allumettes Est (Canton)	458	Pontiac	Pontiac-Gatineau-Labelle	Pontiac	Dennis Czmielewski, Sec.-Trés., RR#4, Chapeau J0X 1M0 – 819/689-2586, Fax: 819/689-2586
L'Isle-Verte (V)	1,040	Rivière-du-Loup	Kamouraska-Rivière-du-Loup	Rivière-du-Loup	Guy Bérubé, Sec.-Trés., 141, rue St-Jean-Baptiste, CP 159, Isle-Verte G0L 1K0 – 418/898-2812, Fax: 418/898-2788
L'ISLET	954	L'Islet	Bellechasse	Montmagny-L'Islet	Marie-Josée Bernier, Sec.-Trés., 92, 7e rue, CP 68, L'Islet G0R 2C0 – 418/247-5345, Fax: 418/247-5345

4-94 QUÉBEC MUNICIPALITIES

Cities (Villes) in CAPITALS; Villages marked (V); Townships/Cantons marked (Canton); United townships/Cantons unis marked (Cantons); Parishes (Paroisses) marked (P); Municipalities marked (Mun.).; Northern villages/Villages nordiques marked (NV); Cree Villages/Villages Cris marked (VC); Naskapi Villages/Villages Naskapi marked (VN); In the third column, Urban Community/Communauté Urbaine marked Urb. Com. An in-depth listing for municipalities marked with * appears in Part 2 (check Index for page numbers).

MUNICIPALITY	1993 POP.	REGIONAL COUNTY MUN.	FEDERAL ELECTORAL DISTRICT	PROVINCIAL ELECTORAL DISTRICT	CONTACT PERSON WITH ADDRESS, PHONE & FAX
L'Islet-sur-Mer (Mun.)	1,806	L'Islet	Bellechasse	Montmagny-L'Islet	Colette Lord, Sec.-Trés., 130, rue Notre-Dame, CP 99, L'Islet-sur-Mer G0R 2B0 – 418/247-3060, Fax: 418/247-5009
Litchfield (Canton)	516	Pontiac	Pontiac-Gatineau-Labelle	Pontiac	Claire Romain, Sec.-Trés., 201, route 148, CP 340, Campbell's Bay J0X 1K0 – 819/648-5511, Fax: 819/648-5575
Lochaber (Canton)	564	Papineau	Gatineau-La Lièvre	Papineau	Marthe Thibaudeau, Sec.-Trés., 164, rte 148 est, Thurso J0X 3B0 – 819/985-3291
Lochaber-Ouest (Canton)	510	Papineau	Gatineau-La Lièvre	Papineau	Mario Bélisle, Sec.-Trés., 1021, rue de Liesse, Angers J8M 1H7 – 819/986-3321, Fax: 819/986-1516
Longue-Pointe (Mun.)	567	Minganie	Manicouagan	Duplessis	Célyne B.-Loiselle, Sec.-Trés., 20, ch du Roi ouest, Longue-Pointe G0G 1V0 – 418/949-2053, Fax: 418/949-2166
*LONGUEUIL	137,134	Champlain	Longueuil; St-Hubert	Marie-Victorin; Taillon	Claude Comtois, Gref., 777, rue d'Auverge, CP 5000, Longueuil J4K 4Y7 – 514/646-8218, Fax: 514/646-8080
LORETTEVILLE	14,858	Québec (Urb. Com.)	Charlesbourg	Chauveau	Gilles Martel, Gref., 305, rue Racine, Loretteville G2B 1E7 – 418/842-1921, Fax: 418/842-2585
LORRAINE	9,180	Thérèse-de-Blainville	Blainville-Deux-Montagnes	Blainville	Brenda Bernard, Gref., 33, boul De Gaulle, Lorraine J6Z 3W9 – 514/621-8550, Fax: 514/621-4763
Lorrainville (Mun.)	1,492	Témiscamingue	Témiscamingue	Rouyn-Noranda-Témiscamingue	Monique Bastien, Sec.-Trés., 2, rue St-Jean-Baptiste est, CP 218, Lorrainville J0Z 2R0 – 819/625-2167, Fax: 819/625-2380
Lotbinière (Mun.)	1,016	Lotbinière	Lotbinière	Lotbinière	Bernard Lepage, Sec.-Trés., 7523, route Marie-Victorin, CP 70, Lotbinière G0S 1S0 – 418/796-2103, Fax: 418/796-2103
LOUISEVILLE	8,276	Maskinongé	Berthier-Montcalm	Maskinongé	Aline Corriveau-Lambert, Greffe, 105, rue Saint-Laurent, Louiseville J5V 1J6 – 819/228-9437, Fax: 819/228-2263
Low (Canton)	938	La Vallée-de-la-Gatineau	Pontiac-Gatineau-Labelle	Gatineau	Liette Hickey, Sec.-Trés., CP 100, Low J0X 2C0 – 819/422-3528, Fax: 819/422-3796
Luceville (V)	1,450	La Mitis	Rimouski-Témiscouata	Matapedia	Marie-Andrée Jeffrey, Sec.-Trés., 67, boul St-Pierre, CP 310, Luceville G0K 1E0 – 418/739-3566, Fax: 418/739-3566
Lyster (Mun.)	1,790	L'Érable	Frontenac	Lotbinière	Pierre Dubois, Sec.-Trés., 2375, rue Bécancour, CP 220, Lyster G0S 1V0 – 819/389-5787, Fax: 819/389-5981
Lytton (Canton)	253	La Vallée-de-la-Gatineau	Pontiac-Gatineau-Labelle	Gatineau	Marie-Paule Gosselin, Sec.-Trés., 189, ch Montcerf, Lytton J0W 1N0 – 819/449-5205, Fax: 819/449-5205
Macamic (P)	589	Abitibi-Ouest	Témiscamingue	Abitibi-Ouest	Joëlle Rancourt, Sec.-Trés., 6, 7e av est, CP 277, Macamic J0Z 2S0 – 819/782-4867, Fax: 819/782-4886
MACAMIC	1,867	Abitibi-Ouest	Témiscamingue	Abitibi-Ouest	Denis Bédard, Sec.-Trés., 1, 7e av ouest, CP 128, Macamic J0Z 2S0 – 819/782-4604, Fax: 819/782-4283
Maddington (Canton)	457	Arthabaska	Lotbinière	Nicolet-Yamaska	Robert Desaulniers, Sec.-Trés., 572, rue Principale, CP 339, Daveluyville G0Z 1C0 – 819/367-2818, Fax: 819/367-2143
Magog (Canton)	4,745	Memphrémagog	Brome-Missisquoi	Orford	Gilbert Cyr, Sec.-Trés., 61, ch Southière, Magog J1X 5R9 – 819/843-3339, Fax: 819/843-9840
MAGOG	14,669	Memphrémagog	Brome-Missisquoi	Orford	Michel Pinault, Gref., 7, rue Principale est, Magog J1X 1Y4 – 819/843-6501, Fax: 819/843-1091
MALARTIC	4,394	Vallée-de-l'Or	Abitibi	Abitibi-Est	Réjean Hamel, Gref., 901, rue Royale, CP 3090, Malartic J0Y 1Z0 – 819/757-3611, Fax: 819/757-3084
MANIWAKI	4,853	La Vallée-de-la-Gatineau	Pontiac-Gatineau-Labelle	Gatineau	Roger Riel, Gref., 186, rue Principale sud, Maniwaki J9E 1Z9 – 819/449-2800, Fax: 819/449-7078
Manseau (V)	622	Bécancour	Lotbinière	Lotbinière	Mario Geoffroy, Sec.-Trés., 200, rue Roux, CP 200, Manseau G0X 1V0 – 819/356-2450, Fax: 819/356-2721
Mansfield-et-Pontefract (Cantons)	1,984	Pontiac	Pontiac-Gatineau-Labelle	Pontiac	Donald Marion, Sec.-Trés., CP 880, Mansfield J0X 1V0 – 819/683-2944, Fax: 819/683-3590
MAPLE GROVE	2,511	Beauharnois-Salaberry	Beauharnois-Salaberry	Châteauguay	Guylaine Côté, Gref., 149, rue St-Laurent, Maple Grove J6N 1K2 – 514/225-5061, Fax: 514/429-6540
Marchand (Mun.)	1,280	Antoine-Labelle	Pontiac-Gatineau-Labelle	Labelle	Claire Coulombe, Sec.-Trés., 106, rue Principale sud, CP 695, L'Annonciation J0T 1T0 – 819/275-3202, Fax: 819/275-1318
Maria (Mun.)	2,610	Avignon	Bonaventure-Îles-de-la-Madeleine	Bonaventure	Gilbert Leblanc, Sec.-Trés., 26, route des Geais, Maria G0C 1Y0 – 418/759-3883, Fax: 418/759-3059
Maricourt (Mun.)	448	Le Val-St-François	Abitibi	Johnson	Lucille Boissonneault, Sec.-Trés., RR#1, Racine J0E 1Y0 – 514/532-2243, Fax: 514/532-2243

Canadian Almanac & Directory 1997

Cities (Villes) in CAPITALS; Villages marked (V); Townships/Cantons marked (Canton);United townships/Cantons unis marked (Cantons); Parishes (Paroisses) marked (P); Municipalities marked (Mun.).; Northern villages/Villages nordiques marked (NV); Cree Villages/Villages Cris marked (VC); Naskapi Villages/Villages Naskapi marked (VN); In the third column, Urban Community/Communauté Urbaine marked Urb. Com. An in-depth listing for municipalities marked with * appears in Part 2 (check Index for page numbers).

MUNICIPALITY	1993 POP.	REGIONAL COUNTY MUN.	FEDERAL ELECTORAL DISTRICT	PROVINCIAL ELECTORAL DISTRICT	CONTACT PERSON WITH ADDRESS, PHONE & FAX
MARIEVILLE	5,426	Rouville	Shefford	Iberville	Sylvie Dolbec, Gref., 682, rue St-Charles, Marieville J3M 1P9 – 514/460-4444, Fax: 514/460-2770
Marsoui (V)	472	Denis-Riverin	Gaspé	Matane	Nancy Leclerc, Sec.-Trés., 1, rue du Quai, CP 130, Marsoui G0E 1S0 – 418/288-5552, Fax: 418/288-5104
Marston (Canton)	499	Le Granit	Mégantic-Compton-Stanstead	Mégantic-Compton	Jeanne-Mance Roy, Sec.-Trés., 344, rte 263 sud, RR#1, Nantes G0Y 1G0 – 819/583-0435
Martinville (Mun.)	507	Coaticook	Mégantic-Compton-Stanstead	Mégantic-Compton	Roland Gascon, Sec.-Trés., 233, rue Principale est, Martinville J0B 2A0 – 819/835-5390, Fax: 819/835-5390
MASCOUCHE	28,913	Les Moulins	Terrebonne	Masson	Danielle Lord, Gref., 3034, ch Ste-Marie, Mascouche J7K 1P1 – 514/474-4133, Fax: 514/474-6401
Maskinongé (V)	1,055	Maskinongé	Berthier-Montcalm	Maskinongé	Marie-Josée Cournoyer, Sec.-Trés., 36B, rue St-Denis, Maskinongé J0K 1N0 – 819/227-2515, Fax: 819/227-2061
MASSON-ANGERS	6,229	Outaouais (Urb. Com.)	Gatineau-La Lièvre	Papineau	Pierre Hayes, Sec.-Trés., 57, ch de Montréal est, CP 670, Masson-Angers J8M 1K7 – 819/986-1250, Fax: 819/986-9539
Massueville (V)	649	Le Bas-Richelieu	Richelieu	Richelieu	Bernard Choquette, Sec.-Trés., 973, rue Royale, CP 90, Massueville J0G 1K0 – 514/788-2957, Fax: 514/788-2966
MATAGAMI	2,499	Terr. du Nouveau-Québec	Abitibi	Ungava	Jean-Robert Gagnon, Gref., 195, boul Matagami, CP 160, Matagami J0Y 2A0 – 819/739-2541, Fax: 819/739-4278
MATANE	12,725	Matane	Matapédia-Matane	Matane	André Lavoie, Gref., 230, av St-Jérôme, Matane G4W 3A2 – 418/562-2333, Fax: 418/562-4869
Matapédia (P)	828	Avignon	Bonaventure-Îles-de-la-Madeleine	Bonaventure	Aimée Firth, Sec.-Trés., 1, rue de l'Hôtel-de-Ville, CP 207, Matapédia G0J 1V0 – 418/865-2917, Fax: 418/865-2828
Mayo (Mun.)	402	Papineau	Gatineau-La Lièvre	Papineau	Michel Vézina, Sec.-Trés., CP 300, Buckingham J8L 2X5 – 819/986-2586, Fax: 819/986-2586
McMasterville (Mun.)	3,908	La Vallée-du-Richelieu	Chambly	Borduas	Pierre Landry, Sec.-Trés., 255, boul Constable, McMasterville J3G 1S5 – 514/467-3580, Fax: 514/467-2493
McWatters (Mun.)	1,860	Rouyn-Noranda	Témiscamingue	Rouyn-Noranda-Témiscamingue	Lise Paquet, Sec.-Trés., 3361, ch du Vieux-Pont ouest, McWatters J9X 5B7 – 819/762-2725, Fax: 819/762-1842
Melbourne (Canton)	1,087	Le Val-St-François	Johnson	Johnson	John Barley, Sec.-Trés., 1257, route 243, CP 4, Melbourne J0B 2B0 – 819/826-3555, Fax: 819/826-3981
Melbourne (V)	525	Le Val-St-François	Richmond-Wolfe	Johnson	Nicole B.-Circé, Sec.-Trés., 22, rue Principale, CP 70, Melbourne J0B 2B0 – 819/826-6200, Fax: 819/826-6200
Melocheville (V)	2,366	Beauharnois-Salaberry	Beauharnois-Salaberry	Salaberry-Soulanges	Normand Charette, Sec.-Trés., 380, boul Edgar-Hébert, Melocheville J0S 1J0 – 514/429-6426, Fax: 514/429-2346
MERCIER	8,723	Roussillon	Châteauguay	Châteauguay	Chantal Bergeron, Gref., 794, boul St-Jean-Baptiste, Mercier J6R 2L3 – 514/691-6090, Fax: 514/691-6529
Messines (Mun.)	1,317	La Vallée-de-la-Gatineau	Pontiac-Gatineau-Labelle	Gatineau	Paul Beaudoin, Sec.-Trés., 3, ch de la Ferme, CP 69, Messines J0X 2J0 – 819/465-2323, Fax: 819/465-2943
MÉTABETCHOUAN	3,453	Lac-St-Jean-Est	Lac-St-Jean	Lac-St-Jean	Laurent Rheault, Gref., 81, rue St-André, CP 99, Métabetchouan G0W 2A0 – 418/349-2060, Fax: 418/349-2395
Métis-sur-Mer (V)	243	La Mitis	Matapédia-Matane	Matane	Karen Turriff, Sec.-Trés., 31, rue de la Station, CP 44, Métis-sur-Mer G0J 1W0 – 418/936-3420, Fax: 418/936-3838
Milan (Mun.)	249	Le Granit	Mégantic-Compton-Stanstead	Mégantic-Compton	Suzanne Durivage, Sec.-Trés., 403, rang Ste-Marie, CP 54, Milan G0Y 1E0 – 819/657-4527, Fax: 819/657-4527
Mille-Isles (Mun.)	988	Argenteuil	Argenteuil-Papineau	Argenteuil	Chantal St-Pierre, Sec.-Trés., 1262, ch de Mille-Isles, Mille-Isles J0R 1A0 – 514/438-2958, Fax: 514/438-6157
MIRABEL	19,980	Mirabel	Argenteuil-Papineau	Argenteuil	Suzanne Mireault, Gref., 14111, rue St-Jean, Mirabel J0N 1R0 – 514/476-0360, Fax: 514/475-7195
MISTASSINI	7,038	Roberval	Roberval	Roberval	Christian Painchaud, Gref., 173, boul St-Michel, Mistassini G8M 1E9 – 418/276-3685, Fax: 418/276-8164
Mistassini (VC)			Abitibi	Ungava	Annie Cheechoo, Sec.-Trés., 187, rue Main, Mistassini G0W 1C0 – 418/923-3461, Fax: 418/923-3115
Moffet (Mun.)	252	Témiscamingue	Témiscamingue	Rouyn-Noranda-Témiscamingue	Linda Roy, Sec.-Trés., CP 89, Moffet J0Z 2W0 – 819/747-3116

Canadian Almanac & Directory 1997

Cities (Villes) in CAPITALS; Villages marked (V); Townships/Cantons marked (Canton);United townships/Cantons unis marked (Cantons); Parishes (Paroisses) marked (P); Municipalities marked (Mun.).; Northern villages/Villages nordiques marked (NV); Cree Villages/Villages Cris marked (VC); Naskapi Villages/Villages Naskapi marked (VN); In the third column, Urban Community/Communauté Urbaine marked Urb. Com. An in-depth listing for municipalities marked with * appears in Part 2 (check Index for page numbers).

MUNICIPALITY	1993 POP.	REGIONAL COUNTY MUN.	FEDERAL ELECTORAL DISTRICT	PROVINCIAL ELECTORAL DISTRICT	CONTACT PERSON WITH ADDRESS, PHONE & FAX
MOISIE	806	Sept-Rivières	Manicouagan	Duplessis	Ronald Bernatchez, Sec.-Trés., 1085, rue Lamothe, CP 340, Moisie G0G 2B0 – 418/927-2122, Fax: 418/927-2653
Mont-Carmel (Mun.)	1,382	Kamouraska	Kamouraska-Rivière-du-Loup	Kamouraska-Témiscouata	Léa Lévesque, Sec.-Trés., 22, rue de la Fabrique, Mont-Carmel G0L 1W0 – 418/498-2050, Fax: 418/489-2522
MONT-JOLI	6,489	La Mitis	Matapédia-Matane	Matapédia	Gilles Thibault, Gref., 40, av de l'Hôtel-de-Ville, Mont-Joli G5H 1W8 – 418/775-7285, Fax: 418/775-6320
MONT-LAURIER	8,177	Antoine-Labelle	Pontiac-Gatineau-Labelle	Labelle	Blandine Boulianne, Gref., 485, rue Mercier, Mont-Laurier J9L 3N8 – 819/623-1221, Fax: 819/623-4840
Mont-Lebel (Mun.)	336	Rimouski-Neigette	Rimouski-Témiscouata	Rimouski	Denise Pelletier, Sec.-Trés., 63, 3e rang ouest, CP 130, Sainte-Blondine G0K 1J0 – 418/735-5772, Fax: 418/735-5772
Mont-Rolland (V)	2,647	Les Pays-d'en-Haut	Laurentides	Bertrand	Yves Desmarais, Sec.-Trés., 1425, rue Morin, CP 280, Mont-Rolland J0R 1G0 – 514/229-2200, Fax: 514/229-6842
MONT-ROYAL	18,450	Montréal (Urb. Com.)	Mont-Royal	Mont-Royal	Josée C.-Katz, Gref., 90, av Roosevelt, Mont-Royal H3R 1Z5 – 514/734-2900, Fax: 514/737-3080
Mont-St-Grégoire (Mun.)	3,190	Le Haut-Richelieu	St-Jean	Iberville	Christianne Pouliot, Sec.-Trés., 225, rue St-Joseph sud, CP 120, Mont-St-Grégoire J0J 1K0 – 514/347-5376, Fax: 514/347-9200
MONT-ST-HILAIRE	12,995	La Vallée-du-Richelieu	Chambly	Borduas	Estelle Simard, Gref., 100, rue du Centre-Civique, Mont-St-Hilaire J3H 3M8 – 514/467-2854, Fax: 514/467-6460
Mont-St-Michel (Mun.)	676	Antoine-Labelle	Pontiac-Gatineau-Labelle	Labelle	Lucie Gagnon, Sec.-Trés., 94, rue de l'Église, Mont-St-Michel J0W 1P0 – 819/587-3093, Fax: 819/587-3781
Mont-St-Pierre (V)	273	Denis-Riverin	Gaspé	Gaspé	Marianne Ouellet, Sec.-Trés., 102, rue Cloutier, CP 9, Mont-St-Pierre G0E 1V0 – 418/797-2898, Fax: 418/797-2307
Mont-Tremblant (Mun.)	764	Les Laurentides	Laurentides	Labelle	Daniel-G. Décarie, Sec.-Trés., 1875, ch Principal, CP 179, Mont-Tremblant J0T 1Z0 – 819/425-8671, Fax: 819/425-5091
Montbeillard (Mun.)	586	Rouyn-Noranda	Témiscamingue	Rouyn-Noranda-Témiscamingue	Marie Grimard-Dugon, Sec.-Trés., 551, rue du Village, CP 10, Montbeillard J0Z 2X0 – 819/797-2985, Fax: 819/797-2390
Montcalm (Mun.)	401	Les Laurentides	Argenteuil-Papineau	Argenteuil	Lucie Tremblay-Côté, Sec.-Trés., 10, rue de l'Hôtel-de-Ville, Weir J0T 2V0 – 819/687-2836, Fax: 819/687-2836
Montcerf (Mun.)	511	La Vallée-de-la-Gatineau	Pontiac-Gatineau-Labelle	Gatineau	Liliane Crytes, Sec.-Trés., 18, rue Principale nord, Montcerf J0W 1N0 – 819/449-4578, Fax: 819/449-7310
Montebello (V)	1,113	Papineau	Argenteuil-Papineau	Papineau	Charles-Guy Beauchamp, Sec.-Trés., 550, rue Notre-Dame, CP 190, Montebello J0V 1L0 – 819/423-5123, Fax: 819/423-5703
MONTMAGNY	11,830	Montmagny	Bellechasse	Montmagny-L'Islet	Louise Bhérer, Gref., 134, rue St-Jean-Baptiste est, Montmagny G5V 1K6 – 418/248-3361, Fax: 418/248-0923
Montpellier (Mun.)	795	Papineau	Argenteuil-Papineau	Papineau	Henriette Dupuis, Sec.-Trés., 4, rue du Bosquet, Montpellier J0V 1M0 – 819/428-3663, Fax: 819/428-1221
*MONTRÉAL	1,017,666	Montréal (Urb. Com.)	Ahuntsic; Anjou-Rivière-des-Prairies; Hochelaga-Maisonneuve; LaSalle-Émard; Laurier-Ste-Marie; Mercier; Mont-Royal; Notre-Dame-de-Grâce; Outremont; Papineau-St-Michel; Rosemont; St-Denis; St-Henri-Westmount; St-Laurent-Cartierville; St-Léonard; Verdun St-Paul	Acadie; Anjou; Bourassa; Bourget; Crémazie; D'Arcy McGee; Gouin; Hochelaga-Maisonneuve; Jeanne-Mance; LaFontaine; Laurier-Dorion; Mercier; Mont-Royal; Notre-Dame de Grâce; Outremont; Pointe-aux-Trembles; Rosemont; St-Henri-Ste-Anne; St-Laurent; Ste-Marie-St-Jacques; Viau; Viger; Westmount-St-Louis	Léon Laberge, Gref., Hôtel de Ville, 275, rue Notre-Dame est, Montréal H2Y 1C6 – 514/872-1111, Fax: 514/872-5655, URL: http://www.ville.montreal.qc.ca/

Canadian Almanac & Directory 1997

Cities (Villes) in CAPITALS; Villages marked (V); Townships/Cantons marked (Canton);United townships/Cantons unis marked (Cantons); Parishes (Paroisses) marked (P); Municipalities marked (Mun.).; Northern villages/Villages nordiques marked (NV); Cree Villages/Villages Cris marked (VC); Naskapi Villages/Villages Naskapi marked (VN); In the third column, Urban Community/Communauté Urbaine marked Urb. Com. An in-depth listing for municipalities marked with * appears in Part 2 (check Index for page numbers).

MUNICIPALITY	1993 POP.	REGIONAL COUNTY MUN.	FEDERAL ELECTORAL DISTRICT	PROVINCIAL ELECTORAL DISTRICT	CONTACT PERSON WITH ADDRESS, PHONE & FAX
MONTRÉAL-EST	3,815	Montréal (Urb. Com.)	Mercier	Pointe-aux-Trembles	André Lesage, Gref., 11370, rue Notre-Dame est, Montréal-Est H1B 2W6 – 514/645-7431, Fax: 514/645-0107
*MONTRÉAL-NORD	86,641 ('94)	Montréal (Urb. Com.)	Bourassa	Bourassa; Sauvé	Hélène Simoneau, Greffe, 4242, Place de l'Hôtel-de-Ville, Montréal-Nord H1H 1S5 – 514/328-4000, Fax: 514/328-4299
MONTRÉAL-OUEST	5,248	Montréal (Urb. Com.)	Notre-Dame-de-Grâce	Notre-Dame-de-Grâce	Georgina Mastromonaco, Gref., 50, av Westminster sud, Montréal-Ouest H4X 1Y7 – 514/481-8125, Fax: 514/481-4554
Morin-Heights (Mun.)	2,117	Les Pays-d'en-Haut	Argenteuil-Papineau	Argenteuil	Dominique Valiquette, Sec.-Trés., 823, rue du Village, Morin-Heights J0R 1H0 – 514/226-3232, Fax: 514/226-8786
Mulgrave-et-Derry (Cantons)	255	Papineau	Gatineau-La Lièvre	Papineau	Michel-A. Vézina, Sec.-Trés., 140, rue Joseph, CP 300, Buckingham J8L 2X5 – 819/986-2586, Fax: 819/986-2586
MURDOCHVILLE	1,713	La Côte-de-Gaspé	Gaspé	Gaspé	Daniel Bujold, Sec.-Trés., 635, 5e rue, CP 1120, Murdochville G0E 1W0 – 418/784-2536, Fax: 418/784-2607
Namur (Mun.)	559	Papineau	Argenteuil-Papineau	Papineau	Sharon Besson, Sec.-Trés., 331, rue de l'Hôtel-de-Ville, Namur J0V 1N0 – 819/426-2457, Fax: 819/426-3074
Nantes (Mun.)	1,272	Le Granit	Mégantic-Compton-Stanstead	Mégantic-Compton	Robert Busque, Sec.-Trés., 1244, rue Principale, CP 60, Nantes G0Y 1G0 – 819/547-3655
Napierville (V)	3,044	Les Jardins-de-Napierville	St-Jean	Beauharnois-Huntingdon	Ginette Leblanc-Pruneau, Sec.-Trés., 260, rue de l'Église, CP 1120, Napierville J0J 1L0 – 514/245-7210, Fax: 514/245-7691
Natashquan (Canton)	392	Minganie	Manicouagan	Duplessis	Lorraine Hounsell, Sec.-Trés., 29, ch d'en-Haut, CP 99, Natashquan G0G 2E0 – 418/726-3362, Fax: 418/726-3698
Nédélec (Canton)	473	Témiscamingue	Témiscamingue	Rouyn-Noranda-Témiscamingue	Anny Cloutier, Sec.-Trés., 33, rue Principale, CP 70, Nédélec J0Z 2Z0 – 819/784-3311, Fax: 819/784-3311
Nemiscau (VC)			Abitibi	Ungava	1, rue Lakeshore, Nemiscau J0M 3B0 – 819/673-2512, Fax: 819/673-2542
Neuville (V)	1,125	Portneuf	Portneuf	Portneuf	Ysa Brochu, Sec.-Trés., 230, rue du Père-Rhéaume, Neuville G0A 2R0 – 418/876-2280, Fax: 418/876-3349
New Carlisle (Mun.)	1,635	Bonaventure	Bonaventure-Îles-de-la-Madeleine	Bonaventure	Donald Kerr, Sec.-Trés., 138, rue Main, CP 40, New Carlisle G0C 1Z0 – 418/752-3141, Fax: 418/752-3140
New Glasgow (V)	180	La Rivière-du-Nord	Joliette	Rousseau	France Massé, Sec.-Trés., 819, rue Raby, CP 35, New Glasgow J0R 1J0 – 514/436-2894, Fax: 514/436-2894
NEW RICHMOND	4,182	Bonaventure	Bonaventure-Îles-de-la-Madeleine	Bonaventure	Line Cormier, Gref., 99, Place Suzanne-Guité, CP 338, New Richmond G0C 2B0 – 418/392-7001, Fax: 418/392-5331
Newport (Canton)	786	Le Haut-St-François	Mégantic-Compton-Stanstead	Mégantic-Compton	Myrna MacDonald, Sec.-Trés., CP 730, Cookshire J0B 1M0 – 819/875-5475, Fax: 819/875-5884
Newport (Mun.)	2,208	Pabok	Gaspé	Bonaventure	Georges-Walter Smith, Sec.-Trés., 300, rte 132, CP 7, Newport G0C 2A0 – 418/777-2281, Fax: 418/777-2865
NICOLET	5,041	Nicolet-Yamaska	Richelieu	Nicolet-Yamaska	Monique Corriveau, Gref., 180, rue de Mgr-Panet, Nicolet J3T 1S6 – 819/293-6901, Fax: 819/293-6767
Nicolet-Sud (Mun.)	411	Nicolet-Yamaska	Richelieu	Nicolet-Yamaska	Claude Bouchard, Sec.-Trés., CP 26, St-Célestin J0C 1G0 – 819/229-3642, Fax: 819/229-1149
Norbertville (V)	283	Arthabaska	Lotbinière	Arthabaska	Gilles Gauvreau, Sec.-Trés., 17, rue Landry, Norbertville G0P 1B0 – 819/369-9294
NORMANDIN	4,075	Maria-Chapdelaine	Roberval	Roberval	Florian Girard, Gref., 1048, rue St-Cyrille, Normandin G8M 4R9 – 418/274-2004, Fax: 418/274-7171
Normétal (Mun.)	1,215	Abitibi-Ouest	Témiscamingue	Abitibi-Ouest	Gaétan Petit, Sec.-Trés., 59, 1re rue, CP 308, Normétal J0Z 3A0 – 819/788-2550, Fax: 819/788-2730
North-Hatley (V)	737	Memphrémagog	Mégantic-Compton-Stanstead	Orford	Solange Morisette, Sec.-Trés., 210, rue Main, CP 30, North Hatley J0B 2C0 – 819/842-2754, Fax: 819/842-4501
Northfield (Mun.)	543	La Vallée-de-la-Gatineau	Pontiac-Gatineau-Labelle	Gatineau	Yvon Blanchard, Sec.-Trés., RR#1, Gracefield J0X 1W0 – 819/463-2182, Fax: 819/463-2757
Notre-Dame-Auxiliatrice-Buckland (P)	821	Bellechasse	Bellechasse	Bellechasse	Danielle Wagner, Sec.-Trés., 4340, rue Principale, CP 40, Buckland G0R 1G0 – 418/789-3119, Fax: 418/789-3535
Notre-Dame-de-Bon-Secours (Mun.)	1,455	Rouville	Chambly	Chambly	Lucie Sabourin, Sec.-Trés., 387, ch Marieville, Notre-Dame-De-Bon-Secours J3L 4A7 – 514/658-2662, Fax: 514/658-5954

QUÉBEC MUNICIPALITIES

Cities (Villes) in CAPITALS; Villages marked (V); Townships/Cantons marked (Canton);United townships/Cantons unis marked (Cantons); Parishes (Paroisses) marked (P); Municipalities marked (Mun.).; Northern villages/Villages nordiques marked (NV); Cree Villages/Villages Cris marked (VC); Naskapi Villages/Villages Naskapi marked (VN); In the third column, Urban Community/Communauté Urbaine marked Urb. Com. An in-depth listing for municipalities marked with * appears in Part 2 (check Index for page numbers).

MUNICIPALITY	1993 POP.	REGIONAL COUNTY MUN.	FEDERAL ELECTORAL DISTRICT	PROVINCIAL ELECTORAL DISTRICT	CONTACT PERSON WITH ADDRESS, PHONE & FAX
Notre-Dame-de-Bon-Secours Nord (P)	266	Papineau	Argenteuil-Papineau	Papineau	Gilles Gignac, Sec.-Trés., CP 310, Montebello J0V 1L0 – 819/423-5575, Fax: 819/423-5575
Notre-Dame-de-la-Merci (Mun.)	577	Matawinie	Laurentides	Bertrand	Jean-Maurice Gadoury, Sec.-Trés., 1900, montée de la Réserve, Notre-Dame-de-la-Merci J0T 2A0 – 819/424-2113, Fax: 819/424-7347
Notre-Dame-de-la-Paix (P)	716	Papineau	Argenteuil-Papineau	Papineau	Hugues Servant, Sec.-Trés., 283, rue Notre-Dame, CP 10, Notre-Dame-de-la-Paix J0V 1P0 – 819/522-6610, Fax: 819/522-6610
Notre-Dame-de-la-Salette (Mun.)	707	Les Collines-de-l'Outaouais	Gatineau-La Lièvre	Papineau	Jean-Pierre Valiquette, Sec.-Trés., 2, rue Rollin, CP 59, Notre-Dame-de-la-Salette J0X 2L0 – 819/766-2533, Fax: 819/766-2533
Notre-Dame-de-l'Île-Perrot (P)	5,841	Vaudreuil-Soulanges	Vaudreuil	Vaudreuil	Serge Jolin, Sec.-Trés., 21, rue de l'Église, Notre-Dame-de-l'Île-Perrot J7V 8P4 – 514/453-4128, Fax: 514/453-8961
Notre-Dame-de-Lorette (Mun.)	268	Maria-Chapdelaine	Québec-Est	Roberval	Michèle Tremblay, Sec.-Trés., 54, rue Principale, Notre-Dame-de-Lorette G0W 1B0 – 418/276-1934, Fax: 418/276-1934
Notre-Dame-de-Lourdes (P)	736	L'Érable	Frontenac	Lotbinière	Gervaise Côté, Sec.-Trés., 830, rue Principale, Lourdes G0S 1T0 – 819/385-4315, Fax: 819/385-4315
Notre-Dame-de-Lourdes (P)	2,168	Joliette	Joliette	Joliette	François Hétu, Sec.-Trés., 4050, rue Principale, Notre-Dame-de-Lourdes J0K 1K0 – 514/759-2277, Fax: 514/759-2055
Notre-Dame-de-Lourdes-de-Ham (Mun.)	357	Arthabaska	Richmond-Wolfe	Richmond	Christiane Leblanc, Sec.-Trés., 25, rue de l'Église, Notre-Dame-de-Lourdes-de-Ham G0P 1C0 – 819/344-5806
Notre-Dame-de-Montauban (Mun.)	946	Mékinac	Portneuf	Portneuf	Manon Frenette, Sec.-Trés., 555, av des Loisirs, CP 69, Montauban G0X 1W0 – 418/336-2640, Fax: 418/336-2353
Notre-Dame-de-Pierreville (P)	838	Nicolet-Yamaska	Richelieu	Nicolet-Yamaska	Micheline Bénard, Sec.-Trés., 48, rue Principale, Notre-Dame-de-Pierreville J0G 1G0 – 514/568-2087, Fax: 514/568-6059
Notre-Dame-de-Pontmain (Mun.)	572	Antoine-Labelle	Pontiac-Gatineau-Labelle	Labelle	Micheline Grenier, Sec.-Trés., 1027, rue Principale, Notre-Dame-de-Pontmain J0W 1S0 – 819/597-2382, Fax: 819/597-2382
Notre-Dame-de-Portneuf (P)	1,866	Portneuf	Portneuf	Portneuf	Jacques Chevalier, Sec.-Trés., 500, rue Notre-Dame, CP 218, Notre-Dame-de-Portneuf G0A 2Z0 – 418/286-6641, Fax: 418/286-4493
Notre-Dame-de-St-Hyacinthe (P)	899	Les Maskoutains	St-Hyacinthe-Bagot	St-Hyacinthe	Jean-Luc Giard, Sec.-Trés., 4740, rue Gouin, St-Hyacinthe J2S 1E1 – 514/773-3720, Fax: 514/773-5611
Notre-Dame-de-Stanbridge (P)	847	Brome-Missisquoi	Brome-Missisquoi	Brome-Missisquoi	Gaétan Lanoue, Sec.-Trés., 900, rue Principale, CP 40, Notre-Dame-de-Stanbridge J0J 1M0 – 514/296-4710, Fax: 514/296-4710
Notre-Dame-des-Anges (P)	475	Portneuf	Taschereau	Taschereau	Colette Huot, Sec.-Trés., 260, boul Langelier, Québec G1K 5N1 – 418/529-0931, Fax: 418/529-0813
Notre-Dame-des-Bois (Mun.)	626	Le Granit	Mégantic-Compton-Stanstead	Mégantic-Compton	Guylaine Blais, Sec.-Trés., 35, côte de l'Église, Notre-Dame-des-Bois J0B 2E0 – 819/888-2724, Fax: 819/888-2904
Notre-Dame-des-Monts (Mun.)	938	Charlevoix-Est	Charlevoix	Charlevoix	Nicole Williams, Sec.-Trés., 15, rue Principale, Notre-Dame-des-Monts G0T 1L0 – 418/439-3452, Fax: 418/439-3452
Notre-Dame-des-Neiges des Trois-Pistoles (P)	1,208	Les Basques	Kamouraska-Rivière-du-Loup	Rivière-du-Loup	Danielle Ouellet, Sec.-Trés., 4, 2e rang Centre, CP 729, Trois-Pistoles G0L 4K0 – 418/851-3009, Fax: 418/851-3169
Notre-Dame-des-Pins (P)	1,003	Beauce-Sartigan	Beauce	Beauce-Sud	Claude Poulin, Sec.-Trés., 2790, 1re av, Notre-Dame-des-Pins G0M 1K0 – 418/774-9718, Fax: 418/774-9718
Notre-Dame-des-Prairies (Mun.)	6,803	Joliette	Joliette	Joliette	Yves Poirier, Sec.-Trés., 225, boul Antonio-Barrette, Notre-Dame-des-Prairies J6E 1E7 – 514/759-7741, Fax: 514/759-6255
Notre-Dame-des-Sept-Douleurs (P)	41	Rivière-du-Loup	Kamouraska-Rivière-du-Loup	Rivière-du-Loup	Gérald Dionne Jr., Sec.-Trés., École Fraser, ch Principal, Île-Verte G0L 1K0 – 418/898-3451, Fax: 418/898-3492
Notre-Dame-du-Bon-Conseil (P)	1,055	Drummond	Drummond	Richmond	Pierrette Bourgeois-Richard, Sec.-Trés., 1428, route 122, CP 239, Notre-Dame-du-Bon-Conseil J0C 1A0 – 819/336-5374, Fax: 819/336-2389
Notre-Dame-du-Bon-Conseil (V)	1,314	Drummond	Drummond	Richmond	Lucette Descôteaux, Sec.-Trés., 541, rue Notre-Dame, CP 128, Notre-Dame-du-Bon-Conseil J0C 1A0 – 819/336-2744, Fax: 819/336-2030

Cities (Villes) in CAPITALS; Villages marked (V); Townships/Cantons marked (Canton);United townships/Cantons unis marked (Cantons); Parishes (Paroisses) marked (P); Municipalities marked (Mun.).; Northern villages/Villages nordiques marked (NV); Cree Villages/Villages Cris marked (VC); Naskapi Villages/Villages Naskapi marked (VN); In the third column, Urban Community/Communauté Urbaine marked Urb. Com. An in-depth listing for municipalities marked with * appears in Part 2 (check Index for page numbers).

MUNICIPALITY	1993 POP.	REGIONAL COUNTY MUN.	FEDERAL ELECTORAL DISTRICT	PROVINCIAL ELECTORAL DISTRICT	CONTACT PERSON WITH ADDRESS, PHONE & FAX
NOTRE-DAME-DU-LAC	2,182	Témiscouata	Rimouski-Témiscouata	Kamouraska-Témiscouata	Hermel Roussel, Gref., 5, rue de l'Hôtel-de-Ville, CP 158, Notre-Dame-du-Lac G0L 1X0 – 418/899-6743, Fax: 418/899-2041
Notre-Dame-du-Laus (Mun.)	1,295	Antoine-Labelle	Gatineau-La Lièvre	Labelle	Yves Larocque, Sec.-Trés., 66, rue Principale, CP 10, Notre-Dame-du-Laus J0X 2M0 – 819/767-2247, Fax: 819/767-3102
Notre-Dame-du-Mont-Carmel (P)	4,801	Le Centre-de-la-Mauricie	St-Maurice	St-Maurice	Jean Lachance, Sec.-Trés., 3860, rue de l' Hôtel de Ville, Notre-Dame-du-Mont-Carmel G0X 3J0 – 819/375-9856, Fax: 819/373-4045
Notre-Dame-du-Mont-Carmel (P)	882	Le Haut-Richelieu	St-Jean	St-Jean	Sylvie Larose-Asselin, Sec.-Trés., 82, rte 202, Notre-Dame-du-Mont-Carmel J0J 1J0 – 514/246-2692, Fax: 514/246-2692
Notre-Dame-du-Nord (Mun.)	1,281	Témiscamingue	Témiscamingue	Rouyn-Noranda-Témiscamingue	Lucien Beauregard, Sec.-Trés., 71, rue Principale, CP 160, Notre-Dame-du-Nord J0Z 3B0 – 819/723-2294, Fax: 819/723-2483
Notre-Dame-du-Portage (P)	1,193	Rivière-du-Loup	Kamouraska-Rivière-du-Loup	Rivière-du-Loup	Eric Bérubé, Sec.-Trés., 560, route de la Montagne, CP 69, Notre-Dame-du-Portage G0L 1Y0 – 418/862-9163, Fax: 418/862-9163
Notre-Dame-du-Rosaire (Mun.)	374	Montmagny	Lac-St-Jean	Montmagny-L'Islet	Maryse Bernard, Sec.-Trés., 22, rue Jolicoeur, Notre-Dame-du-Rosaire G0R 2H0 – 418/469-2802, Fax: 418/469-2802
Notre-Dame-du-Sacré-Coeur-d'Issoudun (P)	771	Lotbinière	Lotbinière	Lotbinière	Suzanne Therrien-Croteau, Sec.-Trés., 455, route de l'Église, Issoudun G0S 1L0 – 418/728-2006, Fax: 418/728-2303
Nouvelle (Mun.)	2,217	Avignon	Bonaventure-Îles-de-la-Madeleine	Bonaventure	Lise Castilloux, Sec.-Trés., 470, rue Francoeur, CP 68, Nouvelle G0C 2E0 – 418/794-2253, Fax: 418/794-2076
Noyan (Mun.)	961	Le Haut-Richelieu	Brome-Missisquoi	Iberville	Brenda McDonald, Sec.-Trés., 1312, ch de la Petite-France, CP 8, Noyan J0J 1B0 – 514/294-2689, Fax: 514/294-2175
Ogden (Mun.)	784	Memphrémagog	Mégantic-Compton-Stanstead	Orford	Faye Dustin, Sec.-Trés., 70, ch Ogden, Beebe J0B 1E0 – 819/876-7117, Fax: 819/876-2121
Oka (Mun.)	1,839	Deux-Montagnes	Argenteuil-Papineau	Deux-Montagnes	Marie Daoust, Sec.-Trés., 183, rue des Anges, CP 369, Oka J0N 1E0 – 514/479-8388, Fax: 514/479-1886
Oka (P)	1,844	Deux-Montagnes	Argenteuil-Papineau	Deux-Montagnes	Jacques Fournier, Sec.-Trés., 2017, ch Oka, CP 38, Oka J0N 1E0 – 514/479-8333, Fax: 514/479-6869
Omerville (V)	1,934	Memphrémagog	Brome-Missisquoi	Orford	Jean-Paul Bergeron, Sec.-Trés., 51, rue St-Jacques ouest, Omerville J1X 4H4 – 819/843-5744, Fax: 819/843-5303
Orford (Canton)	1,029	Memphrémagog	Sherbrooke	Orford	Jean-Marie Beaupré, Sec.-Trés., 2530, ch du Parc, Orford J1X 3W3 – 819/843-3111, Fax: 819/843-2707
Ormstown (V)	1,635	Le Haut-St-Laurent	Beauharnois-Salaberry	Beauharnois-Huntingdon	Jean-Claude Marcil, Sec.-Trés., 81, rue Lambton, Ormstown J0S 1K0 – 514/829-2625, Fax: 514/829-4162
OTTERBURN-PARK	6,402	La Vallée-du-Richelieu	Chambly	Borduas	Jean Tremblay, Sec.-Trés., 472, av Prince-Edward, Otterburn Park J3H 1W4 – 514/536-0303, Fax: 514/467-8260
OUTREMONT	23,237 ('94)	Montréal (Urb. Com.)	Outremont	Outremont	Mario Gerbeau, Gref., 543, ch Côte Ste-Catherine, Outremont H2V 2R2 – 514/495-6200, Fax: 514/495-6290
Pabos (Mun.)	1,508	Pabok	Gaspé	Gaspé	David A. Duguay, Sec.-Trés., 440, boul Pabos, CP 39, Pabos G0C 2H0 – 418/689-4920, Fax: 418/689-5644
Pabos Mills (Mun.)	1,595	Pabok	Gaspé	Gaspé	Raymond Cyr, Sec.-Trés., 151, rte 132, Pabos Mills G0C 2J0 – 418/689-3523, Fax: 418/689-4664
Packington (P)	634	Témiscouata	Rimouski-Témiscouata	Kamouraska-Témiscouata	Denis Moreau, Sec.-Trés., 35A, rue Principale, Packington G0L 1Z0 – 418/853-2269, Fax: 418/853-2269
Padoue (Mun.)	342	La Mitis	Matapédia-Matane	Matane	Marc-André Lavoie, Sec.-Trés., 494, 8e rang, Padoue G0J 1X0 – 418/775-5486
Palmarolle (Mun.)	1,597	Abitibi-Ouest	Témiscamingue	Abitibi-Ouest	Hélène Larivière, Sec.-Trés., 499, route 393, CP 309, Palmarolle J0Z 3C0 – 819/787-2303, Fax: 819/787-2303
Papineauville (V)	1,775	Papineau	Argenteuil-Papineau	Papineau	Paula Pagé, Sec.-Trés., 266, rue Viger, CP 248, Papineauville J0V 1R0 – 819/427-5511, Fax: 819/427-5590
Parent (V)	436	Le Haut-St-Maurice	Champlain	Laviolette	Sylvie Ruel, Sec.-Trés., 2, rue de l'Hôtel-de-Ville, CP 8, Parent G0X 3P0 – 819/667-2323, Fax: 819/667-2542
Parisville (P)	617	Bécancour	Lotbinière	Lotbinière	Ginette C.-Bisaillon, Sec.-Trés., 1260, rue St-Jacques, Parisville G0S 1X0 – 819/292-2222, Fax: 819/292-2222

QUÉBEC MUNICIPALITIES

Cities (Villes) in CAPITALS; Villages marked (V); Townships/Cantons marked (Canton);United townships/Cantons unis marked (Cantons); Parishes (Paroisses) marked (P); Municipalities marked (Mun.).; Northern villages/Villages nordiques marked (NV); Cree Villages/Villages Cris marked (VC); Naskapi Villages/Villages Naskapi marked (VN); In the third column, Urban Community/Communauté Urbaine marked Urb. Com. An in-depth listing for municipalities marked with * appears in Part 2 (check Index for page numbers).

MUNICIPALITY	1993 POP.	REGIONAL COUNTY MUN.	FEDERAL ELECTORAL DISTRICT	PROVINCIAL ELECTORAL DISTRICT	CONTACT PERSON WITH ADDRESS, PHONE & FAX
Paspébiac (Mun.)	3,141	Bonaventure	Bonaventure-Îles-de-la-Madeleine	Bonaventure	Jean-Guy Duguay, Sec.-Trés., 178, 9e rue, CP 130, Paspébiac G0C 2K0 – 418/752-2277, Fax: 418/752-6566
Paspébiac-Ouest (Mun.)	766	Bonaventure	Bonaventure-Îles-de-la-Madeleine	Bonaventure	Céline Poirier-Berthelot, Sec.-Trés., 11, route Scott, CP 99, Paspébiac-Ouest G0C 2K0 – 418/752-6777, Fax: 418/752-6777
PERCÉ	4,120	Pabok	Gaspé	Gaspé	Bruno Cloutier, Sec.-Trés., 137, rte 132 ouest, CP 99, Percé G0C 2L0 – 418/782-2933, Fax: 418/782-5487
Péribonka (Mun.)	635	Maria-Chapdelaine	Roberval	Roberval	Normand Fortin, Sec.-Trés., 312, rue Édouard-Niquet, Péribonka G0W 2G0 – 418/374-2967, Fax: 418/374-2355
Petit-Matane (Mun.)	1,287	Matane	Matapédia-Matane	Matane	Lise Gauthier, Sec.-Trés., 676, ch de la Grève, Petit-Matane G0J 1Y0 – 418/566-2135
Petit-Saguenay (Mun.)	1,026	Le Fjord-du-Saguenay	Chicoutimi	Dubuc	Alexis Lavoie, Sec.-Trés., 35, ch du Quai, CP 40, Petit-Saguenay G0V 1N0 – 418/272-2323, Fax: 418/272-2346
Petite-Rivière-St-François (Mun.)	811	Charlevoix	Charlevoix	Charlevoix	Francine Dufour, Sec.-Trés., 1067, rue Principale, CP 10, Petite-Rivière-St-François G0A 2L0 – 418/632-5831, Fax: 418/632-5886
Petite-Vallée (Mun.)	229	La Côte-de-Gaspé	Gaspé	Gaspé	Simon Côté, Sec.-Trés., 45, rue Principale, CP 1067, Petite-Vallée G0E 1Y0 – 418/393-2949, Fax: 418/393-2592
Philipsburg (V)	298	Brome-Missisquoi	Brome-Missisquoi	Brome-Missisquoi	Ginette Laroche, Sec.-Trés., 203, rue Philips, CP 360, Philipsburg J0J 1N0 – 514/248-2124, Fax: 514/248-2124
Piedmont (Mun.)	1,624	Les Pays-d'en-Haut	Laurentides	Bertrand	Gilbert Aubin, Sec.-Trés., 670, rue Principale, Piedmont J0R 1K0 – 514/227-1888, Fax: 514/227-6716
PIERREFONDS	49,483	Montréal (Urb. Com.)	Pierrefonds-Dollard	Nelligan; Robert Baldwin	Chantal Gauvreau, Gref., 13665, boul Pierrefonds, CP 2500, Pierrefonds H9H 4N2 – 514/624-1124, Fax: 514/624-1300
Pierreville (V)	1,119	Nicolet-Yamaska	Richelieu	Nicolet-Yamaska	Michel Gagnon, Sec.-Trés., 26, rue Ally, CP 300, Pierreville J0G 1J0 – 514/568-2139, Fax: 514/568-0689
PINCOURT	10,477	Vaudreuil-Soulanges	Vaudreuil	Vaudreuil	Gilles Chamberland, Sec.-Trés., 919, ch Duhamel, Pincourt J7V 4G8 – 514/453-8981, Fax: 514/453-0934
Pintendre (Mun.)	5,445	Desjardins	Lévis	Lévis	Hervé Tremblay, Sec.-Trés., 344, 10e av, Pintendre G6C 1G7 – 418/838-6070, Fax: 418/838-6085
Piopolis (Mun.)	331	Le Granit	Mégantic-Compton-Stanstead	Mégantic-Compton	Gaby Grenier-Richard, Sec.-Trés., 433, rue Principale, Piopolis G0Y 1H0 – 819/583-3953, Fax: 819/583-3953
Plaisance (Mun.)	1,080	Papineau	Argenteuil-Papineau	Papineau	Ghislain Ménard, Sec.-Trés., 281, rue Desjardins, Plaisance J0V 1S0 – 819/427-5363, Fax: 819/427-5015
Plessisville (P)	2,768	L'Érable	Frontenac	Arthabaska	Roger Chandonnet, Sec.-Trés., 290, route 165 sud, CP 245, Plessisville G6L 2Y7 – 819/362-2712, Fax: 819/362-9185
PLESSISVILLE	7,151	L'Érable	Frontenac	Arthabaska	René Turcotte, Sec.-Trés., 1700, rue St-Calixte, Plessisville G6L 1R3 – 819/362-3284, Fax: 819/362-6421
POHÉNÉGAMOOK	3,322	Témiscouata	Kamouraska-Rivière-du-Loup	Kamouraska-Témiscouata	Georges Comeau, Sec.-Trés., 1309, rue Principale, Pohénégamook G0L 1J0 – 418/859-2533, Fax: 418/859-3465
Pointe-à-la-Croix (Mun.)	1,840	Avignon	Bonaventure-Îles-de-la-Madeleine	Bonaventure	Gaby Guidry, Sec.-Trés., 30, rue Chouinard, CP 159, Pointe-à-la-Croix G0C 1L0 – 418/788-2011, Fax: 418/788-2916
POINTE-AU-PÈRE	4,197	Rimouski-Neigette	Rimouski-Témiscouata	Matapédia	Mario Caron, Sec.-Trés., 315, av Dionne, Pointe-au-Père G5M 1M8 – 418/724-7723, Fax: 418/724-6112
Pointe-aux-Outardes (V)	1,148	Manicouagan	Charlevoix	Saguenay	Dania Hovington, Sec.-Trés., 471, ch Principal, Les Buissons G0H 1H0 – 418/567-2203, Fax: 418/567-4409
Pointe-aux-Trembles (P)	2,194	Portneuf	Portneuf	Portneuf	Yves Raymond, Sec.-Trés., 230, rue Père-Rhéaume, CP 158, Neuville G0A 2R0 – 418/876-2233, Fax: 418/876-3349
Pointe-Calumet (V)	4,977	Deux-Montagnes	Argenteuil-Papineau	Deux-Montagnes	Chantal Pilon, Sec.-Trés., 300, av Basile-Routhier, Pointe-Calumet J0N 1G2 – 514/473-5930, Fax: 514/473-6571
POINTE-CLAIRE	28,014	Montréal (Urb. Com.)	Lachine-Lac-St-Louis	Jacques-Cartier	Jean-Denis Jacob, Greffe, 451, boul St-Jean, Pointe-Claire H9R 3J3 – 514/630-1200, Fax: 514/630-1227
Pointe-des-Cascades (V)	750	Vaudreuil-Soulanges	Vaudreuil	Salaberry-Soulanges	Christiane Cyr, Sec.-Trés., 52, ch du Fleuve, Pointe-des-Cascades J0P 1M0 – 514/455-9671, Fax: 514/455-3414

QUÉBEC MUNICIPALITIES 4-101

Cities (Villes) in CAPITALS; Villages marked (V); Townships/Cantons marked (Canton);United townships/Cantons unis marked (Cantons); Parishes (Paroisses) marked (P); Municipalities marked (Mun.).; Northern villages/Villages nordiques marked (NV); Cree Villages/Villages Cris marked (VC); Naskapi Villages/Villages Naskapi marked (VN); In the third column, Urban Community/Communauté Urbaine marked Urb. Com. An in-depth listing for municipalities marked with * appears in Part 2 (check Index for page numbers).

MUNICIPALITY	1993 POP.	REGIONAL COUNTY MUN.	FEDERAL ELECTORAL DISTRICT	PROVINCIAL ELECTORAL DISTRICT	CONTACT PERSON WITH ADDRESS, PHONE & FAX
Pointe-du-Lac (Mun.)	5,950	Francheville	Trois-Rivières	Maskinongé	Martial Beaudry, Trés., 1597, ch Ste-Marguerite, Pointe-du-Lac G0X 1Z0 – 819/377-1121, Fax: 819/377-2415
Pointe-Fortune (V)	446	Vaudreuil-Soulanges	Vaudreuil	Vaudreuil	Hélène Therrien, Sec.-Trés., 694, rue du Tisseur, CP 60, Pointe-Fortune J0P 1N0 – 514/451-5178, Fax: 514/451-5178
Pointe-Lebel (V)	1,877	Manicouagan	Charlevoix	Saguenay	Patricia Huet, Sec.-Trés., 365, rue Granier, Pointe-Lebel G0H 1N0 – 418/589-8073, Fax: 418/589-6154
Pont-Rouge (V)	4,605	Portneuf	Portneuf	Portneuf	Marc-André Trudel, Sec.-Trés., 212, rue Dupont est, CP 1240, Pont-Rouge G0A 2X0 – 418/873-4481, Fax: 418/873-3494
Pontbriand (Mun.)	910	L'Amiante	Frontenac	Frontenac	Aline Turmel, Sec.-Trés., 1279, rue de l'Église, Pontbriand G0N 1K0 – 418/338-0432, Fax: 418/338-6008
Pontiac (Mun.)	4,819	Les Collines-de-l'Outaouais	Pontiac-Gatineau-Labelle	Pontiac	Germain Clairoux, Sec.-Trés., 2024, rte 148, Pontiac J0X 2G0 – 819/455-2401, Fax: 819/455-9756
PORT-CARTIER	7,633	Sept-Rivières	Manicouagan	Duplessis	Guylaine Morissette, Gref., 40, av Parent, Port-Cartier G5B 2G5 – 418/766-2343, Fax: 418/766-6236
Port-Daniel (Mun.)	1,845	Pabok	Bonaventure-Îles-de-la-Madeleine	Bonaventure	Conrad Jones, Sec.-Trés., 490, route 132, CP 130, Port-Daniel G0C 2N0 – 418/396-5225, Fax: 418/396-5588
Portage-du-Fort (V)	307	Pontiac	Pontiac-Gatineau-Labelle	Pontiac	Fernand Roy, Sec.-Trés., CP 59, Portage-du-Fort J0X 2T0 – 819/683-3027, Fax: 819/683-2694
PORTNEUF	1,554	Portneuf	Portneuf	Portneuf	Dominique Lavallée, Sec.-Trés., 100, rue Paquin, CP 100, Portneuf G0A 2Y0 – 418/286-3844, Fax: 418/286-4304
Poste-de-la-Baleine (VC)			Abitibi	Ungava	CP 390, Poste-de-la-Baleine J0M 1G0 – 819/929-3384, Fax: 819/929-3677
Potton (Canton)	1,672	Memphrémagog	Brome-Missisquoi	Brome-Missisquoi	Jacques Hébert, Sec.-Trés., CP 330, Mansonville J0E 1X0 – 514/292-3313, Fax: 514/292-5555
Poularies (Mun.)	849	Abitibi-Ouest	Témiscamingue	Abitibi-Ouest	Hélène Richer, Sec.-Trés., 990, rue Principale, CP 58, Poularies J0Z 3E0 – 819/782-5159, Fax: 819/782-5063
Preissac (Mun.)	538	Abitibi	Abitibi	Abitibi-Ouest	François Roch, Sec.-Trés., 6, rue des Rapides, Preissac J0Y 2E0 – 819/732-4938, Fax: 819/732-4938
Prévost (Mun.)	6,585	La Rivière-du-Nord	Laurentides	Prévost	2870, boul Curé-Labelle, Prévost J0R 1T0 – 514/224-2981, Fax: 514/224-8323
Price (V)	2,030	La Mitis	Matapédia-Matane	Matapédia	Louise Furlong, Sec.-Trés., 18, rue Fournier, CP 340, Price G0J 1Z0 – 418/775-2144, Fax: 418/775-2459
Princeville (P)	1,765	L'Érable	Lotbinière	Arthabaska	Jean-Marc Bédard, Sec.-Trés., 101, rue Demers est, Princeville G6L 4E8 – 819/364-3092, Fax: 819/364-3970
PRINCEVILLE	4,028	L'Érable	Lotbinière	Arthabaska	Mario Juaire, Sec.-Trés., 50, av St-Jacques ouest, Princeville G6L 4Y5 – 819/364-5179, Fax: 819/364-5198
Puvirnituq (NV)	1,105	Kativik	Abitibi	Ungava	Mary Angiyou, Sec.-Trés., Povungnituk J0M 1P0 – 819/964-2825, Fax: 819/988-2751
Quaqtaq (NV)	243	Terr. du Nouveau Québec	Manicouagan	Ungava	Sammy Tukkiapik, Sec.-Trés., Quaqtaq J0M 1J0 – 819/492-9912, Fax: 819/492-9935
*QUÉBEC	175,039	Québec (Urb. Com.)	Charlesbourg; Portneuf; Québec; Québec-Est	Chauveau; Jean-Talon; La Peltrie; Limoilou; Taschereau; Vanier	Antoine Carrier, Gref., Hôtel de ville, 2, rue des Jardins, CP 700, Québec G1R 4S9 – 418/691-7041, Fax: 418/691-2346
Racine (Mun.)[e]	1,010 ('95)	Le Val-St-François	Richmond-Wolfe	Johnson	André Courtemanche, Sec.-Trés., 136, rte 222, CP 120, Racine J0E 1Y0 – 514/532-2876, Fax: 514/532-2865
Ragueneau (P)	1,779	Manicouagan	Charlevoix	Saguenay	Alain Landry, Sec.-Trés., 523, rte 138, CP 190, Ragueneau G0H 1S0 – 418/567-2345, Fax: 418/567-2344
Rainville (Mun.)	1,805	Brome-Missisquoi	Brome-Missisquoi	Iberville	Marie-Josée Lepage, Sec.-Trés., 1810, rue Principale est, Rainville J2N 1N4 – 514/293-3326, Fax: 514/293-4341
Rapide-Danseur (Mun.)	208	Abitibi-Ouest	Témiscamingue	Abitibi-Ouest	Yvette Fournier-Boutin, Sec.-Trés., 535, route du Village, CP 459, Rapide-Danseur J0Z 3G0 – 819/948-2152, Fax: 819/948-2152
Rapides-des-Joachims (Mun.)	187	Pontiac	Pontiac-Gatineau-Labelle	Pontiac	Fernand Roy, Sec.-Trés., RR#1, CP 92, Rapides-des-Joachims J0X 3M0 – 819/683-3027, Fax: 819/683-2694
Rawdon (Canton)	3,820	Matawinie	Berthier-Montcalm	Rousseau	Ginette Filion, Sec.-Trés., 3647, rue Queen, CP 730, Rawdon J0K 1S0 – 514/834-2587, Fax: 514/834-3031
Rawdon (V)	3,561	Matawinie	Berthier-Montcalm	Rousseau	Jean-Guy Charest, Sec.-Trés., 3647, rue Queen, CP 550, Rawdon J0K 1S0 – 514/834-2596, Fax: 514/834-2329

Canadian Almanac & Directory 1997

QUÉBEC MUNICIPALITIES

Cities (Villes) in CAPITALS; Villages marked (V); Townships/Cantons marked (Canton);United townships/Cantons unis marked (Cantons); Parishes (Paroisses) marked (P); Municipalities marked (Mun.).; Northern villages/Villages nordiques marked (NV); Cree Villages/Villages Cris marked (VC); Naskapi Villages/Villages Naskapi marked (VN); In the third column, Urban Community/Communauté Urbaine marked Urb. Com. An in-depth listing for municipalities marked with * appears in Part 2 (check Index for page numbers).

MUNICIPALITY	1993 POP.	REGIONAL COUNTY MUN.	FEDERAL ELECTORAL DISTRICT	PROVINCIAL ELECTORAL DISTRICT	CONTACT PERSON WITH ADDRESS, PHONE & FAX
Rémigny (Mun.)	391	Témiscamingue	Témiscamingue	Rouyn-Noranda-Témiscamingue	Paquerette Roy, Sec.-Trés., 1304, ch de l'Église, Rémigny J0Z 3H0 – 819/761-2421, Fax: 819/761-2421
*RÉPENTIGNY	56,555	L'Assomption	Terrebonne	L'Assomption	Jean Fafard, Gref., 435, boul Iberville, Répentigny J6A 2B6 – 514/654-2323, Fax: 514/654-2421
RICHELIEU	2,989	Rouville	Chambly	Chambly	Richard Blouin, Gref., 200, boul Richelieu, Richelieu J3L 3R4 – 514/658-1157, Fax: 514/658-5096
RICHMOND	3,219	Le Val-St-François	Richmond-Wolfe	Richmond	Gilles Ducharme, Sec.-Trés., 745, rue Gouin, CP 1250, Richmond J0B 2H0 – 819/826-3789, Fax: 819/826-6281
Rigaud (Mun.) f	6,276 ('95)	Vaudreuil-Soulanges	Vaudreuil	Vaudreuil	Diane Desjardins, Sec.-Trés., 391, ch de la Mairie, CP 580, Rigaud J0P 1P0 – 514/451-0869, Fax: 514/451-4227
RIMOUSKI	32,397	Rimouski-Neigette	Rimouski-Témiscouata	Rimouski	Marc Doucet, Gref., 205, av de la Cathédrale, CP 710, Rimouski G5L 7C7 – 418/723-3313, Fax: 418/724-3180
Rimouski-Est (V)	2,246	Rimouski-Neigette	Rimouski-Témiscouata	Rimouski	Denis Ouellet, Sec.-Trés., 540, rue St-Germain est, Rimouski-Est G5L 1E9 – 418/723-8388, Fax: 418/722-0226
Ripon (Canton)	671	Papineau	Argentenuil-Papineau	Papineau	Danièle Migneault, Sec.-Trés., 31, rue Coursol, CP 40, Ripon J0V 1V0 – 819/983-2000, Fax: 819/983-1327
Ripon (V)	657	Papineau	Argenteuil-Papineau	Papineau	Danièle Mignault, Sec.-Trés., 31, rue Coursol, CP 100, Ripon J0V 1V0 – 819/983-6685, Fax: 819/983-1327
Risborough (Mun.)	961	Le Granit	Beauce	Beauce-Sud	Pierrette Morin, Sec.-Trés., CP 129, St-Ludger G0M 1W0 – 819/548-5408, Fax: 819/548-5408
Ristigouche Sud-Est (Canton)	162	Avignon	Bonaventure-Îles-de-la-Madeleine	Bonaventure	Suzanne Bourdages, Sec.-Trés., 35, ch Kempt, RR#2, Matapédia G0J 1V0 – 418/788-5769
Rivière-à-Claude (Mun.)	204	Denis-Riverin	Gaspé	Matane	Claudine Auclair, Sec.-Trés., 520, rue Principale est, Rivière-à-Claude G0E 1Z0 – 418/797-2422, Fax: 418/797-2455
Rivière-à-Pierre (Mun.)	752	Portneuf	Portneuf	Portneuf	Yolande Gauvreau, Sec.-Trés., 830, rue Principale, Rivière-à-Pierre G0A 3A0 – 418/323-2112, Fax: 418/323-2111
Rivière-au-Tonnerre (Mun.)	546	Minganie	Manicouagan	Duplessis	Carmelle Anglehart, Sec.-Trés., 473, rue Jacques Cartier, CP 129, Rivière-au-Tonnerre G0G 2L0 – 418/465-2255, Fax: 418/465-2956
Rivière-Beaudette (Mun.)	1,402	Vaudreuil-Soulanges	Vaudreuil	Salaberry-Soulanges	Céline Chayer, Sec.-Trés., 663, ch de la Frontière, Rivière-Beaudette J0P 1R0 – 514/269-2931, Fax: 514/269-2815
Rivière-Bleue (Mun.)	1,676	Témiscouata	Rimouski-Témiscouata	Kamouraska-Témiscouata	Claude A. Dubé, Sec.-Trés., 32, rue des Pins est, CP 98, Rivière-Bleue G0L 2B0 – 418/893-5559, Fax: 418/893-5530
Rivière-du-Gouffre (Mun.)	1,315	Charlevoix	Charlevoix	Charlevoix	Jean Bergeron, Sec.-Trés., CP 1431, Baie-St-Paul G0A 1B0 – 418/435-5113, Fax: 418/435-5493
RIVIÈRE-DU-LOUP	14,354 ('95)	Rivière-du-Loup	Kamouraska-Rivière-du-Loup	Rivière-du-Loup	Georges Deschênes, Gref., 65, rue de l'Hôtel-de-Ville, CP 37, Rivière-du-Loup G5R 3Y7 – 418/862-9810, Fax: 418/862-2817
Rivière-Éternité (Mun.)	634	Le Fjord-du-Saguenay	Chicoutimi	Dubuc	Denis Houde, Sec.-Trés., 418, rte Principale, Rivière-Éternité G0V 1P0 – 418/272-2860, Fax: 418/272-3454
Rivière-Héva (Mun.)	1,057	Vallée-de-l'Or	Abitibi	Abitibi-Est	Chantal Côté, Sec.-Trés., 740, route St-Paul nord, CP 60, Rivière-Héva J0Y 2H0 – 819/735-3521, Fax: 819/735-4251
Rivière-Malbaie (Mun.)	2,100	Charlevoix-Est	Charlevoix	Charlevoix	Daniel Lavoie, Sec.-Trés., 250, ch de la Vallée, Rivière-Malbaie G5A 1V4 – 418/665-3218, Fax: 418/665-7353
Rivière-Ouelle (Mun.)	1,313	Kamouraska	Kamouraska-Rivière-du-Loup	Kamouraska-Témiscouata	André Lacombe, Sec.-Trés., 106, rue de l'Église, CP 99, Rivière-Ouelle G0L 2C0 – 418/856-1790
Rivière-Pentecôte (Mun.)	760	Sept-Rivières	Manicouagan	Duplessis	Lise Gauthier, Sec.-Trés., 4344, route Jacques-Cartier, CP 3, Rivière-Pentecôte G0H 1R0 – 418/799-2262, Fax: 418/799-2263
Rivière-St-Jean (Mun.)	325	Minganie	Manicouagan	Duplessis	Sylvie Edwards, Sec.-Trés., 116, rue du Quai, Rivière-St-Jean G0G 2N0 – 418/949-2464, Fax: 418/949-2489
Robertsonville (V)	1,877	L'Amiante	Frontenac	Frontenac	Robert Perreault, Sec.-Trés., 184, rue Notre Dame sud, Robertsonville G0N 1L0 – 418/338-6177, Fax: 418/338-5553
ROBERVAL	11,929	Le Domaine-du-Roy	Roberval	Roberval	Jean-Guy Tardif, Gref., 851, boul St-Joseph, Roberval G8H 2L6 – 418/275-0202, Fax: 418/275-5031

Cities (Villes) in CAPITALS; Villages marked (V); Townships/Cantons marked (Canton);United townships/Cantons unis marked (Cantons); Parishes (Paroisses) marked (P); Municipalities marked (Mun.).; Northern villages/Villages nordiques marked (NV); Cree Villages/Villages Cris marked (VC); Naskapi Villages/Villages Naskapi marked (VN); In the third column, Urban Community/Communauté Urbaine marked Urb. Com. An in-depth listing for municipalities marked with * appears in Part 2 (check Index for page numbers).

MUNICIPALITY	1993 POP.	REGIONAL COUNTY MUN.	FEDERAL ELECTORAL DISTRICT	PROVINCIAL ELECTORAL DISTRICT	CONTACT PERSON WITH ADDRESS, PHONE & FAX
Rochebaucourt (Mun.)	244	Abitibi	Abitibi	Abitibi-Ouest	Louise Noël, Sec.-Trés., 20, rue Chanoine-Girard, Rochebaucourt J0Y 2J0 – 819/754-2083, Fax: 819/754-2083
ROCK FOREST	15,119	Sherbrooke	Richmond-Wolfe	Orford	Pierre Ménard, Gref., 1000, rue Haut-Bois, Rock Forest J1N 3V4 – 819/564-7444, Fax: 819/564-8144
Rollet (Mun.)	370	Rouyn-Noranda	Témiscamingue	Rouyn-Noranda-Témiscamingue	Paulette Lemay, Sec.-Trés., 761, rue Principale, CP 10, Rollet J0Z 3J0 – 819/493-4141, Fax: 819/493-4141
Roquemaure (Mun.)	463	Abitibi-Ouest	Témiscamingue	Abitibi-Ouest	Lise Roy, Sec.-Trés., 15, rue Raymond est, CP 40, Roquemaure J0Z 3K0 – 819/787-6311, Fax: 819/787-6311
ROSEMÈRE	12,226	Thérèse-de-Blainville	Blainville-Deux-Montagnes	Groulx	Sylvie Trahan, Gref., 100, rue Charbonneau, Rosemère J7A 3W1 – 514/621-3500, Fax: 514/621-7601
Rougemont (V)	1,219	Rouville	Shefford	Iberville	Louise Berthiaume, Sec.-Trés., 839, rue Principale, Rougemont J0L 1M0 – 514/469-3484, Fax: 514/469-5232
Rouyn-Noranda (V) [g]	29,774 ('95)	Rouyn-Noranda	Témiscamingue	Rouyn-Noranda-Témiscamingue	Daniel Samson, Gref., 100, rue Taschereau est, CP 220, Rouyn-Noranda J9X 5C3 – 819/797-7111, Fax: 819/797-7120
ROXBORO	5,957	Montréal (Urb. Com.)	Pierrefonds-Dollard	Robert-Baldwin	Sophie Valois, Gref., 13, rue Centre-Commercial, Roxboro H8Y 2N9 – 514/684-0555, Fax: 514/684-0705
Roxton (Canton)	1,198	Acton	Shefford	Johnson	Denise Audet, Sec.-Trés., 216, rang Ste-Geneviève, CP 278, Roxton Falls J0H 1E0 – 514/548-2500, Fax: 514/548-2412
Roxton Falls (V)	1,434	Acton	Shefford	Johnson	Hélène Lussier, Sec.-Trés., 189, rue Notre-Dame, CP 180, Roxton Falls J0H 1E0 – 514/548-5790, Fax: 514/548-5881
Roxton Pond (P)	2,239	La Haute-Yamaska	Shefford	Shefford	Raymond Loignon, Sec.-Trés., 901, rue St-Jean, CP 60, Roxton Pond J0E 1Z0 – 514/372-6875, Fax: 514/372-1205
Roxton Pond (V)	1,024	La Haute-Yamaska	Shefford	Shefford	Raymond Loignon, Sec.-Trés., CP 60, Roxton Pond J0E 1Z0 – 514/372-6875, Fax: 514/372-1205
Sacré-Coeur (Mun.)	2,059	La Haute-Côte-Nord	Rimouski-Témiscouata	Saguenay	Sarto Simard, Sec.-Trés., 88, rue Principale nord, CP 159, Sacré-Coeur G0T 1Y0 – 418/236-4621, Fax: 418/236-9144
Sacré-Coeur-de-Crabtree (Mun.)	1,205	Joliette	Joliette	Joliette	Chantale Mercier, Sec.-Trés., 97, ch St-Michel, Crabtree J0K 1B0 – 514/754-2686, Fax: 514/754-2686
Sacré-Coeur-de-Jésus (P)	583	L'Amiante	Frontenac	Frontenac	Marie-France Létourneau, Sec.-Trés., 4118, rte 112, Sacré-Coeur-de-Jésus G0N 1G0 – 418/427-3447, Fax: 418/427-3447
Sacré-Coeur-de-Marie-Sud (P)	685	L'Amiante	Frontenac	Frontenac	Jean-Rock Turgeon, Sec.-Trés., 11, 8e rang sud, Sacré-Coeur-de-Marie-Sud G0N 1W0 – 418/335-3968, Fax: 418/335-2667
St-Adalbert (Mun.)	751	L'Islet	Bellechasse	Montmagny-L'Islet	Normande Chouinard, Sec.-Trés., 55, rue Principale, St-Adalbert G0R 2M0 – 418/356-5271, Fax: 418/356-5271
STE-ADÈLE	5,314	Les Pays-d'en-Haut	Laurentides	Bertrand	Michel Rousseau, Gref., 1381, boul de Ste-Adèle, CP 1108, Ste-Adèle J0R 1L0 – 514/229-2921, Fax: 514/229-4179
St-Adelme (P)	569	Matane	Matapédia-Matane	Matane	Rita Bernier, Sec.-Trés., 231, rue Principale, CP 39, St-Adelme G0J 2B0 – 418/733-4044, Fax: 418/733-4111
St-Adelphe (P)	1,105	Mékinac	Champlain	Laviolette	Daniel Bacon, Sec.-Trés., 150, rue Baillargeon, St-Adelphe G0X 2G0 – 418/322-5721, Fax: 418/322-5434
St-Adolphe-d'Howard (Mun.)	2,263	Les Pays-d'en-Haut	Argenteuil-Papineau	Argenteuil	Lise B.-Villeneuve, Sec.-Trés., 1881, ch du Village, CP 180, St-Adolphe-d'Howard J0T 2B0 – 819/327-2044, Fax: 819/327-2282
St-Adrien (Mun.)	556	Asbestos	Richmond-Wolfe	Richmond	Henriette Giguère, Sec.-Trés., 1589, rue Principale, St-Adrien J0A 1C0 – 819/828-2872, Fax: 819/828-0442
St-Adrien-d'Irlande (Mun.)	399	L'Amiante	Frontenac	Frontenac	Doris Lessard, Sec.-Trés., 152, rue Municipale, St-Adrien-d'Irlande G0N 1M0 – 418/335-2585, Fax: 418/335-2585
St-Agapit (Mun.)	3,104	Lotbinière	Lotbinière	Lotbinière	Denis Pelletier, Sec.-Trés., 1186, rue Principale, St-Agapit G0S 1Z0 – 418/888-4620, Fax: 418/888-4791
Ste-Agathe (P)	578	Lotbinière	Frontenac	Lotbinière	Ghislaine Gravel, Sec.-Trés., 254, rue St-Pierre, CP 159, St-Agathe G0S 2A0 – 418/599-2605, Fax: 418/599-2605
Ste-Agathe (V)	724	Lotbinière	Frontenac	Lotbinière	Rolande Viger, Sec.-Trés., 46, rue St-Jacques, CP 125, Ste-Agathe G0S 2A0 – 418/599-2548, Fax: 418/599-2548

Cities (Villes) in CAPITALS; Villages marked (V); Townships/Cantons marked (Canton);United townships/Cantons unis marked (Cantons); Parishes (Paroisses) marked (P); Municipalities marked (Mun.).; Northern villages/Villages nordiques marked (NV); Cree Villages/Villages Cris marked (VC); Naskapi Villages/Villages Naskapi marked (VN); In the third column, Urban Community/Communauté Urbaine marked Urb. Com. An in-depth listing for municipalities marked with * appears in Part 2 (check Index for page numbers).

MUNICIPALITY	1993 POP.	REGIONAL COUNTY MUN.	FEDERAL ELECTORAL DISTRICT	PROVINCIAL ELECTORAL DISTRICT	CONTACT PERSON WITH ADDRESS, PHONE & FAX
STE-AGATHE-DES-MONTS	5,908	Les Laurentides	Laurentides	Bertrand	Maurice Hews, Sec.-Trés., 50, rue St-Joseph, Ste-Agathe-des-Monts J8C 1M9 – 819/326-4595, Fax: 819/326-5784
Ste-Agathe-Nord (Mun.)	1,322	Les Laurentides	Labelle	Bertrand	Charlotte Champagne, Sec.-Trés., 1155, route 329 nord, CP 126, Ste-Agathe-Nord J8C 3A1 – 819/326-3187, Fax: 819/326-1578
Ste-Agathe-Sud (V)	2,076	Les Laurentides	Laurentides	Bertrand	Benoît Fugère, Sec.-Trés., 1700, rue Principale est, Ste-Agathe-Sud J8C 1M2 – 819/326-3920, Fax: 819/326-9157
Ste-Agnès (P)	652	Charlevoix-Est	Charlevoix	Charlevoix	Micheline Murray, Sec.-Trés., 11, rue Principale, Ste-Agnès G0T 1R0 – 418/439-4155, Fax: 418/439-4155
St-Aimé (P)	613	Le Bas-Richelieu	Richelieu	Richelieu	Claire Lassonde, Sec.-Trés., 285, rue Bonsecours, CP 240, Massueville J0G 1K0 – 514/788-2737, Fax: 514/788-2737
St-Aimé-des-Lacs (Mun.)	928	Charlevoix-Est	Charlevoix	Charlevoix	Suzanne Gaudreault, Sec.-Trés., 119, rue Principale, St-Aimé des Lacs G0T 1S0 – 418/439-2229, Fax: 418/439-2229
St-Aimé-du-Lac-des-Îles (Mun.)	754	Antoine-Labelle	Pontiac-Gatineau-Labelle	Labelle	Claude Comtois, Sec.-Trés., 123, ch du Village, CP 1, St-Aimé-du-Lac-des-Iles J0W 1J0 – 819/597-2047, Fax: 819/597-2554
St-Alban (Mun.)	1,309	Portneuf	Portneuf	Portneuf	Myriam Falardeau, Sec.-Trés., 204, rue Principale, St-Alban G0A 3B0 – 418/268-8026, Fax: 418/268-5073
St-Albert-de-Warwick (P)	1,370	Arthabaska	Lotbinière	Richmond	Suzanne Crête-Corriveau, Sec.-Trés., CP 100, St-Albert J0A 1E0 – 819/353-3300, Fax: 819/353-3313
St-Alexandre (P)	1,933	Kamouraska	Kamouraska-Rivière-du-Loup	Kamouraska-Témiscouata	Lyne Dumont, Sec.-Trés., 723, route 289, CP 10, St-Alexandre G0L 2G0 – 418/495-2440, Fax: 418/495-2659
St-Alexandre (Mun.)	2,065	Le Haut-Richelieu	St-Jean	Iberville	Maryse Boucher, Sec.-Trés., 453, rue St-Denis, CP 60, St-Alexandre J0J 1S0 – 514/346-6641, Fax: 514/346-0538
St-Alexandre-des-Lacs (P)	382	La Matapédia	Matapédia-Matane	Matapédia	Rita Angers-Rioux, Sec.-Trés., 17, rue de l'Église, St-Alexandre-des-Lacs G0J 2C0 – 418/778-3532, Fax: 418/778-3532
St-Alexis (P)	832	Montcalm	Berthier-Montcalm	Rousseau	Rémy Lanoue, Sec.-Trés., 232, rue Principale, St-Alexis J0K 1T0 – 514/839-7277, Fax: 514/839-6241
St-Alexis (V)	540	Montcalm	Berthier-Montcalm	Rousseau	Rémy Lanoue, Sec.-Trés., 232, rue Principale, St-Alexis J0K 1T0 – 514/839-7277, Fax: 514/839-6241
St-Alexis-de-Matapédia (P)	823	Avignon	Bonaventure-Îles-de-la-Madeleine	Bonaventure	Lise Pitre, Sec.-Trés., 121, rue Rustico nord, CP 99, St-Alexis-de-Matapédia G0J 2E0 – 418/299-2030, Fax: 418/299-3011
St-Alexis-des-Monts (P)	2,855	Maskinongé	St-Maurice	Maskinongé	Gilles Frappier, Sec.-Trés., 101, rue de l'Hôtel-de-Ville, CP 300, St-Alexis-des-Monts J0K 1V0 – 819/265-2046, Fax: 819/265-2481
St-Alfred (Mun.)	450	Robert-Cliche	Beauce	Beauce-Nord	Jacques Diane, Sec.-Trés., 194, rang Ste-Marie, St-Alfred G0M 1L0 – 418/774-2068, Fax: 418/774-2068
St-Alphonse (Mun.)	901	Bonaventure	Bonaventure-Îles-de-la-Madeleine	Bonaventure	Reina Goulet, Sec.-Trés., 127, rue Principale est, CP 40, St-Alphonse G0C 2V0 – 418/388-5214, Fax: 418/388-2435
St-Alphonse (P)	2,719	La Haute-Yamaska	Shefford	Brome-Missisquoi	Danielle Bonneau, Sec.-Trés., 360, rue Principale, St-Alphonse J0E 2A0 – 514/375-4570, Fax: 514/375-4717
St-Alphonse-Rodriguez (Mun.)	2,320	Matawinie	Berthier-Montcalm	Berthier	Jacques-Y. Lachapelle, Sec.-Trés., 101, rue de la Plage, St-Alphonse-Rodriguez J0K 1W0 – 514/883-2264, Fax: 514/883-0833
St-Amable (Mun.)	6,218	Lajemmerais	Verchères	Verchères	Michel Martel, Sec.-Trés., 616, rue de l'Église, St-Amable J0L 1N0 – 514/649-3555, Fax: 514/922-0728
St-Ambroise (Mun.)	3,696	Le Fjord-du-Saguenay	Lac-St-Jean	Dubuc	Jean-Rock Claveau, Sec.-Trés., 330, rue Gagnon, CP 190, St-Ambroise G0V 1R0 – 418/672-4765, Fax: 418/672-6126
St-Ambroise-de-Kildare (P)	3,304	Joliette	Berthier-Montcalm	Joliette	Yvon Ducharme, Sec.-Trés., 740, rue Principale, CP 57, Kildare J0K 1C0 – 514/755-4782, Fax: 514/755-4784
St-Anaclet-de-Lessard (P)	2,587	Rimouski-Neigette	Rimouski-Témiscouata	Rimouski	Alain Lapierre, Sec.-Trés., 318, rue Principale ouest, CP 99, St-Anaclet G0K 1H0 – 418/723-2816, Fax: 418/723-0436
St-André (Mun.)	731	Kamouraska	Kamouraska-Rivière-du-Loup	Kamouraska-Témiscouata	Claudine Lévesque, Sec.-Trés., 143, rue Principale, St-André-de-Kamouraska G0L 2H0 – 418/493-2085
St-André-Avellin (P)	1,520	Papineau	Argenteuil-Papineau	Papineau	Claire Tremblay, Sec.-Trés., 119, rue Principale, CP 490, St-André-Avellin J0V 1W0 – 819/983-2318, Fax: 819/983-2344

Cities (Villes) in CAPITALS; Villages marked (V); Townships/Cantons marked (Canton);United townships/Cantons unis marked (Cantons); Parishes (Paroisses) marked (P); Municipalities marked (Mun.).; Northern villages/Villages nordiques marked (NV); Cree Villages/Villages Cris marked (VC); Naskapi Villages/Villages Naskapi marked (VN); In the third column, Urban Community/Communauté Urbaine marked Urb. Com. An in-depth listing for municipalities marked with * appears in Part 2 (check Index for page numbers).

MUNICIPALITY	1993 POP.	REGIONAL COUNTY MUN.	FEDERAL ELECTORAL DISTRICT	PROVINCIAL ELECTORAL DISTRICT	CONTACT PERSON WITH ADDRESS, PHONE & FAX
St-André-Avellin (V)	1,683	Papineau	Argenteuil-Papineau	Papineau	Claire Tremblay, Sec.-Trés., CP 490, St-André-Avellin J0V 1W0 – 819/983-2318, Fax: 819/983-2344
St-André-d'Acton (P)	2,487	Acton	St-Hyacinthe-Bagot	Johnson	Marthe Gauthier, Sec.-Trés., 1053, boul St-André, Acton-Vale J0H 1A0 – 514/546-2406, Fax: 514/546-3275
St-André-d'Argenteuil (P)	1,108	Argenteuil	Argenteuil-Papineau	Argenteuil	Nancy Le Moignan, Sec.-Trés., 10, rue de la Mairie, CP 179, St-André-Est J0V 1X0 – 514/537-3676, Fax: 514/537-3070
St-André-de-Restigouche (Mun.)	236	Avignon	Bonaventure-Îles-de-la-Madeleine	Bonaventure	Blandine Beaulieu, Sec.-Trés., 163, rue Principale, CP 4, St-André-de-Restigouche G0J 2G0 – 418/865-2234
St-André-du-Lac-St-Jean (V)	621	Le Domaine-du-Roy	Roberval	Lac-St-Jean	Marcel Lapointe, Sec.-Trés., 11, rue du Collège, St-André-du-Lac-St-Jean G0W 2K0 – 418/349-8167, Fax: 418/349-2040
St-André-Est (V)	1,437	Argenteuil	Argenteuil-Papineau	Argenteuil	Linne Roquebrune, Sec.-Trés., 10, rue de la Mairie, CP 149, St-André-Est J0V 1X0 – 514/537-3527, Fax: 514/537-3070
St-Ange-Gardien (P)	1,360	Rouville	Shefford	Iberville	André Parent, Sec.-Trés., 249, rue St-Joseph, CP 120, L'Ange-Gardien-de-Rouville J0E 1E0 – 514/293-7575, Fax: 514/293-6635
Ste-Angèle-de-Mérici (Mun.)	1,212	La Mitis	Matapédia-Matane	Matapédia	Laureine Ouellet, Sec.-Trés., 23, rue de la Fabrique, CP 129, Ste-Angèle-de-Mérici G0J 2H0 – 418/775-7733, Fax: 418/775-5722
Ste-Angèle-de-Monnoir (P)	1,465	Rouville	Shefford	Iberville	Jacqueline Houle, Sec.-Trés., 7, ch du Vide, CP 30, Ste-Angèle-de-Monnoir J0L 1P0 – 514/460-7838, Fax: 514/460-3853
Ste-Angèle-de-Prémont (Mun.)	626	Maskinongé	Berthier-Montcalm	Maskinongé	Gilles Gerbeau, Sec.-Trés., 2451, rue Camirand, Ste-Angèle-de-Prémont J0K 1R0 – 819/268-5526, Fax: 819/268-5526
Ste-Angélique (P)	646	Papineau	Portneuf	Papineau	Jacqueline Paul, Sec.-Trés., 266, rue Viger, CP 279, Papineauville J0V 1R0 – 819/427-5221, Fax: 819/427-8318
St-Anicet (P)	2,300	Le Haut-St-Laurent	Beauharnois-Salaberry	Beauharnois-Huntingdon	Claudette Génier-Leblanc, Sec.-Trés., 335, av Jules-Léger, St-Anicet J0S 1M0 – 514/264-2555, Fax: 514/264-2395
STE-ANNE-DE-BEAUPRÉ	3,298	La Côte-de-Beaupré	Beauport-Montmorency-Orléans	Charlevoix	Claude Boissonnault, Sec.-Trés., 9336, av Royale, Ste-Anne-de-Beaupré G0A 3C0 – 418/827-3191, Fax: 418/827-8275
STE-ANNE-DE-BELLEVUE	4,083	Montréal (Urb. Com.)	Vaudreuil	Nelligan	Jacques Turgeon, Gref., 109, rue Ste-Anne, CP 40, Ste-Anne-de-Bellevue H9X 1M2 – 514/457-5500, Fax: 514/457-6087
Ste-Anne-de-la-Pérade (Mun.)	2,299	Francheville	Champlain	Champlain	René Roy, Sec.-Trés., 200, rue Principale, CP 308, Ste-Anne-de-la-Pérade G0X 2J0 – 418/325-2841, Fax: 418/325-3070
Ste-Anne-de-la-Pocatière (P)	1,935	Kamouraska	Kamouraska-Rivière-du-Loup	Kamouraska-Témiscouata	René Pelletier, Sec.-Trés., 175, ch des Sables est, Ste-Anne-de-la-Pocatière G0R 1Z0 – 418/856-3192
Ste-Anne-de-la-Rochelle (Mun.)	587	Le Val-St-François	Richmond-Wolfe	Brome-Missisquoi	France Lagrandeur, Sec.-Trés., 142, rue Lagrandeur, Ste-Anne-de-la-Rochelle J0E 2B0 – 514/539-1654, Fax: 514/539-1654
Ste-Anne-de-Portneuf (Mun.)	1,063	La Haute-Côte-Nord	Charlevoix	Saguenay	Gontran Tremblay, Sec.-Trés., 170, rue Principale, CP 98, Ste-Anne-de-Portneuf G0T 1P0 – 418/238-2642, Fax: 418/238-5319
Ste-Anne-de-Sabrevois (P)	1,833	Le Haut-Richelieu	St-Jean	Iberville	Michèle Dupuis, Sec.-Trés., 1218, rte 133, Sabrevois J0J 2G0 – 514/347-0066, Fax: 514/347-4040
Ste-Anne-de-Sorel (P)	2,954	Le Bas-Richelieu	Richelieu	Richelieu	Luc Papillon, Sec.-Trés., 1685, ch du Chenal-du-Moine, Ste-Anne-de-Sorel J3P 5N3 – 514/742-1616, Fax: 514/742-1118
Ste-Anne-des-Lacs (P)	1,792	Les Pays-d'en-Haut	Laurentides	Bertrand	Claude Panneton, Sec.-Trés., 773, ch de Ste-Anne-des-Lacs, Ste-Anne-des-Lacs J0R 1B0 – 514/224-2675, Fax: 514/224-8672
STE-ANNE-DES-MONTS	5,616	Denis-Riverin	Gaspé	Matane	Sylvie Lepage, Sec.-Trés., 6, 1re av ouest, CP 458, Ste-Anne-des-Monts G0E 2G0 – 418/763-5511, Fax: 418/763-3473
STE-ANNE-DES-PLAINES	11,773	Thérèse-de-Blainville	Joliette	Blainville	Serge Lepage, Gref., 139, boul Ste-Anne, Ste-Anne-des-Plaines J0N 1H0 – 514/478-0211, Fax: 514/478-5660
Ste-Anne-du-Lac (Mun.)	666	Antoine-Labelle	Pontiac-Gatineau-Labelle	Labelle	Denise Beaudry, Sec.-Trés., 1, rue St-François-Xavier, Ste-Anne-du-Lac J0W 1V0 – 819/586-2110, Fax: 819/586-2110

Canadian Almanac & Directory 1997

Cities (Villes) in CAPITALS; Villages marked (V); Townships/Cantons marked (Canton);United townships/Cantons unis marked (Cantons); Parishes (Paroisses) marked (P); Municipalities marked (Mun.).; Northern villages/Villages nordiques marked (NV); Cree Villages/Villages Cris marked (VC); Naskapi Villages/Villages Naskapi marked (VN); In the third column, Urban Community/Communauté Urbaine marked Urb. Com. An in-depth listing for municipalities marked with * appears in Part 2 (check Index for page numbers).

MUNICIPALITY	1993 POP.	REGIONAL COUNTY MUN.	FEDERAL ELECTORAL DISTRICT	PROVINCIAL ELECTORAL DISTRICT	CONTACT PERSON WITH ADDRESS, PHONE & FAX
Ste-Anne-du-Lac (V)	51	L'Amiante	Frontenac	Frontenac	Richard Samson, Sec.-Trés., 421, rue des Tulipes, CP 112, Thetford Mines G6G 5R9 – 418/338-0467, Fax: 418/338-6784
Ste-Anne-du-Sault (P)	1,359	Arthabaska	Lotbinière	Nicolet-Yamaska	Vital Gosselin, Sec.-Trés., CP 38, Daveluyville G0Z 1C0 – 819/367-2210, Fax: 819/367-2210
St-Anselme (P)	1,395	Bellechasse	Bellechasse	Bellechasse	Louis Felteau, Sec.-Trés., 134, rue Principale, St-Anselme G0R 2N0 – 418/885-4442, Fax: 418/885-4442
St-Anselme (V)	1,874	Bellechasse	Bellechasse	Bellechasse	Louis Felteau, Sec.-Trés., 678, rue Ste-Anne, CP 400, St-Anselme G0R 2N0 – 418/885-4977, Fax: 418/885-6779
ST-ANTOINE	11,190	La Rivière-du-Nord	Gaspé	Prévost	Serge Forget, Gref., 854, boul St-Antoine, St-Antoine J7Z 3C5 – 514/436-1762, Fax: 514/436-3057
St-Antoine-de-Lavaltrie (P)	3,320	D'Autray	Berthier-Montcalm	Berthier	Yvon Mousseau, Sec.-Trés., 49, ch de Lavaltrie, St-Antoine-de-Lavaltrie J0K 1H0 – 514/586-1331, Fax: 514/586-4060
St-Antoine-de-l'Isle-aux-Grues (P)	200	Montmagny	Bellechasse	Montmagny-L'Islet	Adèle Roy-Lavoie, Sec.-Trés., l'Isle-aux-Grues G0R 1P0 – 418/248-8060, Fax: 418/248-8060
St-Antoine-de-Tilly (Mun.)	1,422	Lotbinière	Lotbinière	Lotbinière	Mario Léonard, Sec.-Trés., 3837, ch de Tilly, St-Antoine-de-Tilly G0S 2C0 – 418/886-2441, Fax: 418/886-2075
St-Antoine-sur-Richelieu (Mun.)	1,668	La Vallée-du-Richelieu	Verchères	Verchères	Gisèle Collette, Sec.-Trés., 1060, rue des Ormes, CP 208, St-Antoine-sur-Richelieu J0L 1R0 – 514/787-3497, Fax: 514/787-2852
St-Antonin (P)	3,349	Rivière-du-Loup	Kamouraska-Rivière-du-Loup	Rivière-du-Loup	Gina Dionne, Sec.-Trés., 261, rue Principale, CP 340, St-Antonin G0L 2J0 – 418/862-1056, Fax: 418/862-3268
St-Apollinaire (Mun.)	3,755	Lotbinière	Lotbinière	Lotbinière	Jean Blais, Sec.-Trés., 94, rue Principale, St-Apollinaire G0S 2E0 – 418/881-3996, Fax: 418/881-4152
Ste-Apolline-de-Patton (P)	718	Montmagny	Bellechasse	Montmagny-L'Islet	Raynald Bernard, Sec.-Trés., 497, route Principale, Ste-Apolline de-Patton G0R 2P0 – 418/469-3031, Fax: 418/469-3031
St-Armand (Mun.)	1,072	Brome-Missisquoi	Brome-Missisquoi	Brome-Missisquoi	Jacqueline C.-Chisholm, Sec.-Trés., 414, ch Luke, St-Armand J0J 1T0 – 514/248-2344, Fax: 514/248-2344
St-Arsène (P)	1,214	Rivière-du-Loup	Kamouraska-Rivière-du-Loup	Rivière-du-Loup	François Michaud, Sec.-Trés., #201, 49, rue de l'Église, St-Arsène G0L 2K0 – 418/867-2205, Fax: 418/867-2205
St-Athanase (Mun.)	394	Témiscouata	Kamouraska-Rivière-du-Loup	Kamouraska-Témiscouata	Francine Morin-Bélanger, Sec.-Trés., 6081, ch de l'Église, CP 40, St-Athanase G0L 2L0 – 418/859-2575, Fax: 418/859-3415
St-Athanase (P)	6,771	Le Haut-Richelieu	St-Jean	Iberville	Carole Bergeron-Laurin, Sec.-Trés., 90, rte 104, Ste-Athanase J2X 1H1 – 514/347-9716, Fax: 514/347-0703
St-Aubert (Mun.)	1,293	L'Islet	Bellechasse	Montmagny-L'Islet	Serge Roussel, Sec.-Trés., 14, rue des Loisirs, St-Aubert G0R 2R0 – 418/598-3368, Fax: 418/598-3369
St-Augustin (Mun.)	980	Manicouagan	Duplessis	Duplessis	Nicole Driscoll, Sec.-Trés., CP 279, St-Augustin G0G 2R0 – 418/947-2404, Fax: 418/947-2533
St-Augustin (P)	550	Maria-Chapdelaine	Roberval	Roberval	Maud Larouche, Sec.-Trés., 686, rue Principale, St-Augustin G0W 1K0 – 418/374-2147, Fax: 418/374-2984
St-Augustin-de-Desmaures (Mun.)	13,249	Québec (Urb. Com.)	Portneuf	La Peltrie	Michel Beauchemin, Sec.-Trés., 200, rte Fossambault, St-Augustin-de-Desmaures G3A 2E3 – 418/878-2955, Fax: 418/878-4986
St-Augustin-de-Woburn (P)	748	Le Granit	Mégantic-Compton-Stanstead	Mégantic-Compton	Gaétane Allard-Lavoie, Sec.-Trés., 590, rue St-Augustin, CP 120, Woburn G0Y 1R0 – 819/544-4211, Fax: 819/544-9236
Ste-Aurélie (Mun.)	943	Les Etchemins	Beauce	Beauce-Sud	Tancrède Allen, Sec.-Trés., 6, rue des Saules, Ste-Aurélie G0M 1M0 – 418/593-3021, Fax: 418/593-3961
Ste-Barbe (P)	1,360	Le Haut-St-Laurent	Beauharnois-Salaberry	Beauharnois-Huntingdon	Marc Rémillard, Sec.-Trés., 470, ch de l'Église, Ste-Barbe J0S 1P0 – 514/371-2504, Fax: 514/371-2575
St-Barnabé (P)	1,303	Maskinongé	Trois-Rivières	Maskinongé	Denis Gélinas, Sec.-Trés., 70, rue Duguay, St-Barnabé G0X 2K0 – 819/264-2085, Fax: 819/264-2079
St-Barnabé-Sud (P)	920	Les Maskoutains	St-Hyacinthe-Bagot	St-Hyacinthe	Nicole Bélanger, Sec.-Trés., 251, rang de Michaudville, St-Barnabé-Sud J0H 1G0 – 514/792-3030, Fax: 514/792-3759
St-Barthélemy (P)	2,110	D'Autray	Berthier-Montcalm	Berthier	Jean Charland, Sec.-Trés., 1980, rue Bonin, St-Barthélemy J0K 1X0 – 514/885-3511, Fax: 514/885-2165
St-Basile (P)	919	Portneuf	Portneuf	Portneuf	Roger Proulx, Sec.-Trés., 39, av Garnier, CP 70, St-Basile G0A 3G0 – 418/329-2969, Fax: 418/329-3743
ST-BASILE-LE-GRAND	10,723	La Vallée-du-Richelieu	Chambly	Chambly	Luce Doucet, Gref., 204, rue Principale, St-Basile le-Grand J3N 1M1 – 514/653-4261, Fax: 514/653-8028

Cities (Villes) in CAPITALS; Villages marked (V); Townships/Cantons marked (Canton);United townships/Cantons unis marked (Cantons); Parishes (Paroisses) marked (P); Municipalities marked (Mun.).; Northern villages/Villages nordiques marked (NV); Cree Villages/Villages Cris marked (VC); Naskapi Villages/Villages Naskapi marked (VN); In the third column, Urban Community/Communauté Urbaine marked Urb. Com. An in-depth listing for municipalities marked with * appears in Part 2 (check Index for page numbers).

MUNICIPALITY	1993 POP.	REGIONAL COUNTY MUN.	FEDERAL ELECTORAL DISTRICT	PROVINCIAL ELECTORAL DISTRICT	CONTACT PERSON WITH ADDRESS, PHONE & FAX
St-Basile-Sud (V)	1,932	Portneuf	Portneuf	Portneuf	Paulin Leclerc, Sec.-Trés., 40, av Garnier, CP 370, St-Basile G0A 3G0 – 418/329-2204, Fax: 418/329-2788
Ste-Béatrix (Mun.)	1,532	Matawinie	Berthier-Montcalm	Berthier	Danielle Lambert, Sec.-Trés., 861, rue de l'Église, Ste-Béatrix J0K 1Y0 – 514/883-2245, Fax: 514/883-1772
St-Benjamin (Mun.)	938	Les Etchemins	Beauce	Beauce-Sud	France Veilleux, Sec.-Trés., 440, av du Collège, CP 100, St-Benjamin G0M 1N0 – 418/594-8156, Fax: 418/594-6068
St-Benoît-du-Lac (Mun.)	57		Brome-Missisquoi	Brome-Missisquoi	Jacques Bolduc, Directeur général, Abbaye-St-Benoît, St-Benoît-du-Lac J0B 2M0 – 819/843-4080, Fax: 819/843-3199
St-Benoît-Labre (Mun.)	1,484	Beauce-Sartigan	Beauce	Beauce-Sud	Gaétane Vallée, Sec.-Trés., 216, boul des Érables, St-Benoît-Labre G0M 1P0 – 418/228-9250, Fax: 418/228-0518
St-Bernard (Mun.)	2,054	La Nouvelle-Beauce	Beauce	Beauce-Nord	Madeleine Nadeau, Sec.-Trés., 551, rue Vaillancourt, CP 70, St-Bernard G0S 2G0 – 418/475-6060, Fax: 418/475-6069
St-Bernard-de-Lacolle (P)	1,590	Les Jardins-de-Napierville	St-Jean	Beauharnois-Huntingdon	Daniel Striletsky, Sec.-Trés., 113, rang Saint-Claude, St-Bernard-de-Lacolle J0J 1V0 – 514/246-3348, Fax: 514/246-4380
St-Bernard-Sud (P)	617	Les Maskoutains	St-Hyacinthe-Bagot	Richelieu	Sylvie Chaput, Sec.-Trés., 410, rue Principale, St-Bernard-de-Michaudville J0H 1C0 – 514/792-3190, Fax: 514/792-3591
St-Blaise-sur-Richelieu (Mun.)	2,002	Le Haut-Richelieu	St-Jean	St-Jean	Francine Leblanc, Sec.-Trés., 795, rue des Loisirs, St-Blaise-sur-Richelieu J0J 1W0 – 514/291-5944, Fax: 514/291-3832
Ste-Blandine (P)	2,036	Rimouski-Neigette	Rimouski-Témiscouata	Rimouski	Monique Sénéchal, Sec.-Trés., 3, rue du Collège, Ste-Blandine G0K 1J0 – 418/735-2752, Fax: 418/735-2708
St-Bonaventure (Mun.)	1,140	Drummond	Drummond	Nicolet-Yamaska	Claire Côté, Sec.-Trés., 720, rue Plante, St-Bonaventure J0C 1C0 – 819/396-2335, Fax: 819/396-2335
St-Boniface-de-Shawinigan (V)	3,962	Le Centre-de-la-Mauricie	St-Maurice	St-Maurice	Jacques Caron, Sec.-Trés., 140, rue Guimont, St-Boniface-de-Shawinigan G0X 2L0 – 819/535-3811, Fax: 819/535-1242
Ste-Brigide-d'Iberville (Mun.)	1,373	Le Haut-Richelieu	St-Jean	Iberville	Réjeanne Giroux, Sec.-Trés., 480, rue de l'Hôtel-de-Ville, CP 9, Ste-Brigide J0J 1X0 – 514/293-7511, Fax: 514/293-7511
Ste-Brigitte-de-Laval (Mun.)	3,051	La Jacques-Cartier	Beauport-Montmorency-Orléans	Montmorency	Jacques Vallée, Sec.-Trés., 1, rue Auclair, Ste-Brigitte-de-Laval G0A 3K0 – 418/825-2515, Fax: 418/825-3114
Ste-Brigitte-des-Saults (P)	807	Drummond	Drummond	Nicolet-Yamaska	Nicole Comtois, Sec.-Trés., 400, rue Principale, CP 1038, Ste-Brigitte-des-Saults J0C 1E0 – 819/336-4460, Fax: 819/336-4410
St-Bruno (Mun.)	2,628	Lac-St-Jean-Est	Lac-St-Jean	Lac-St-Jean	Claude Moisan, Sec.-Trés., 541, av St-Alphonse, CP 39, St-Bruno G0W 2L0 – 418/343-2303, Fax: 418/343-2662
St-Bruno-de-Guigues (Mun.)	1,101	Témiscamingue	Témiscamingue	Rouyn-Noranda-Témiscamingue	Serge Côte, Sec.-Trés., 21, rue Principale nord, CP 130, St-Bruno-de-Guigues J0Z 2G0 – 819/728-2186, Fax: 819/728-2404
St-Bruno-de-Kamouraska (Mun.)	609	Kamouraska	Kamouraska-Rivière-du-Loup	Kamouraska-Témiscouata	Suzanne Dionne, Sec.-Trés., rue du Couvent, CP 28, St-Bruno-de-Kamouraska G0L 2M0 – 418/492-2612, Fax: 418/492-2612
ST-BRUNO-DE-MONTARVILLE	25,259	La Vallée-du-Richelieu	Chambly	Chambly	Chantal Sainte-Marie, Gref., 1585, rue Montarville, St-Bruno-de-Montarville J3V 3T8 – 514/653-2443, Fax: 514/461-3649
St-Calixte (Mun.)	4,365	Montcalm	Berthier-Montcalm	Rousseau	Denis Malouin, Sec.-Trés., 6230, rue de l'Hôtel-de-Ville, St-Calixte J0K 1Z0 – 514/222-2782, Fax: 514/222-2789
St-Camille (Canton)	473	Asbestos	Richmond-Wolfe	Richmond	Marie Pigeon, Sec.-Trés., 85, rue Desrivières, St-Camille J0A 1G0 – 819/828-3222, Fax: 819/828-3723
St-Camille-de-Lellis (P)	1,014	Les Etchemins	Bellechasse	Bellechasse	Nicole Mathieu, Sec.-Trés., 7, rue Carrier, CP 70, St-Camille-de-Lellis G0R 2S0 – 418/595-2233, Fax: 418/595-2233
St-Casimir (P)	479	Portneuf	Portneuf	Portneuf	Ginette Paquin, Sec.-Trés., 220, boul de la Montagne, 3e étage, CP 250, St-Casimir G0A 3L0 – 418/339-2676, Fax: 418/339-3105
St-Casimir (Mun.)	1,481	Portneuf	Portneuf	Portneuf	Carole Germain, Sec.-Trés., 220, boul de la Montagne, CP 220, St-Casimir G0A 3L0 – 418/339-2543, Fax: 418/339-3105

Canadian Almanac & Directory 1997

QUÉBEC MUNICIPALITIES

Cities (Villes) in CAPITALS; Villages marked (V); Townships/Cantons marked (Canton);United townships/Cantons unis marked (Cantons); Parishes (Paroisses) marked (P); Municipalities marked (Mun.).; Northern villages/Villages nordiques marked (NV); Cree Villages/Villages Cris marked (VC); Naskapi Villages/Villages Naskapi marked (VN); In the third column, Urban Community/Communauté Urbaine marked Urb. Com. An in-depth listing for municipalities marked with * appears in Part 2 (check Index for page numbers).

MUNICIPALITY	1993 POP.	REGIONAL COUNTY MUN.	FEDERAL ELECTORAL DISTRICT	PROVINCIAL ELECTORAL DISTRICT	CONTACT PERSON WITH ADDRESS, PHONE & FAX
STE-CATHERINE	10,399	Roussillon	Châteauguay	La Prairie	Carole Cousineau, Gref., 5465, boul Marie-Victorin, Ste-Catherine J0L 1E0 – 514/632-0590, Fax: 514/632-3298
Ste-Catherine-de-Hatley (Mun.)	1,808	Memphrémagog	Mégantic-Compton-Stanstead	Orford	François Bachand, Sec.-Trés., CP 30, Katevale J0B 1W0 – 819/843-1935, Fax: 819/843-8527
Ste-Catherine-de-la-Jacques-Cartier (Mun.)	4,321	La Jacques-Cartier	Portneuf	Portneuf	Marcel Grenier, Sec.-Trés., 1, rue Rouleau, CP 250, Ste-Catherine-de-la-Jacques-Cartier G0A 3M0 – 418/875-2758, Fax: 418/875-2170
Ste-Cécile-de-Lévrard (P)	445	Bécancour	Lotbinière	Lotbinière	Réjean Poisson, Sec.-Trés., 235, rue Principale, Ste-Cécile-de-Lévrard G0X 2M0 – 819/263-2104
Ste-Cécile-de-Milton (Canton)	1,843	La Haute-Yamaska	Shefford	Shefford	Ronald Sauriol, Sec.-Trés., 136, rue Principale, CP 33, Ste-Cécile-de-Milton J0E 2C0 – 514/378-1942, Fax: 514/378-4621
Ste-Cécile-de-Whitton (Mun.)	870	Le Granit	Mégantic-Compton-Stanstead	Mégantic-Compton	Linda Deschiever, Sec.-Trés., 4557, rue Principale, Ste-Cécile-de-Whitton G0Y 1J0 – 819/583-0770, Fax: 819/583-0770
St-Célestin (Mun.)	765	Nicolet-Yamaska	Richelieu	Nicolet-Yamaska	Gisèle P.-Morin, Sec.-Trés., 990, rang du Pays-Brûlé, St-Célestin J0C 1G0 – 819/229-3745, Fax: 819/229-1386
St-Célestin (V)	765	Nicolet-Yamaska	Richelieu	Nicolet-Yamaska	Claude Bouchard, Sec.-Trés., 420, rue Houde, CP 47, St-Célestin J0C 1G0 – 819/229-3642, Fax: 819/229-1149
St-Césaire (P)	2,069	Rouville	Shefford	Iberville	Louise Benoit, Sec.-Trés., 2046, rte 112, St-Césaire J0L 1T0 – 514/469-3700, Fax: 514/469-2398
ST-CÉSAIRE	3,057	Rouville	Shefford	Iberville	Pierre Despars, Sec.-Trés., 1111, av St-Paul, St-Césaire J0L 1T0 – 514/469-3108, Fax: 514/469-5275
St-Charles-Borromée (Mun.)	10,164	Joliette	Joliette	Joliette	François Thériault, Sec.-Trés., 525, rue Visitation, St-Charles-Borromée J6E 4P2 – 514/759-4415, Fax: 514/759-3393
St-Charles-de-Bellechasse (Mun.)	2,181 ('94)	Bellechasse	Bellechasse	Bellechasse	Denis Labbé, Sec.-Trés., 25, av Commerciale, St-Charles G0R 2T0 – 418/887-6600, Fax: 418/887-6779
St-Charles-de-Bourget (Mun.)	732	Le Fjord-du-Saguenay	Lac-St-Jean	Dubuc	Colombe Bergeron, Sec.-Trés., 357, 2e rang, St-Charles-de-Bourget G0V 1G0 – 418/672-2624, Fax: 418/672-4403
St-Charles-de-Drummond (Mun.)	4,511	Drummond	Drummond	Drummond	Gilles Proulx, Sec.-Trés., 1250, rue Proulx, St-Charles-de-Drummond J2C 5A2 – 819/477-4530, Fax: 819/477-0697
St-Charles-de-Mandeville (Mun.)	1,872	D'Autray	Berthier-Montcalm	Berthier	Francine Bergeron, Sec.-Trés., 162, boul Desjardins, St-Charles-de-Mandeville J0K 1L0 – 514/835-2055, Fax: 514/835-7795
St-Charles-Garnier (P)	383	La Mitis	Matapédia-Matane	Matapédia	Francine Roy, Sec.-Trés., CP 39, St-Charles-Garnier G0K 1K0 – 418/798-4305, Fax: 418/798-4305
St-Charles-sur-Richelieu (Mun.)	1,727 ('95)	La Vallée-du-Richelieu	Verchères	Verchères	Anne Tremblay, Sec.-Trés., 12, rue Union, St-Charles-sur-Richelieu J0H 2G0 – 514/584-3484, Fax: 514/584-2965
Ste-Christine (P)	790	Acton	St-Hyacinthe-Bagot	Johnson	Bernadette Rodier-Chagnon, Sec.-Trés., 629, rue des Loisirs, Ste-Christine J0H 1H0 – 819/858-2828
Ste-Christine-d'Auvergne (Mun.)	351	Portneuf	Portneuf	Portneuf	Réjeanne Plamondon, Sec.-Trés., 80, Principale, CP 639, Ste-Christine-d'Auvergne G0A 1A0 – 418/329-3304, Fax: 418/329-3356
St-Christophe-d'Arthabaska (P)	2,236	Arthabaska	Lotbinière	Arthabaska	Francine Moreau, Sec.-Trés., 418, route Pie X, Arthabaska G6P 6S1 – 819/357-9031, Fax: 819/357-9087
St-Chrysostome (V)	934	Le Haut-St-Laurent	Beauharnois-Salaberry	Beauharnois-Huntingdon	Pauline Primeau, Sec.-Trés., #10, 124, rue Notre-Dame, CP 190, St-Chrysostome J0S 1R0 – 514/826-3035, Fax: 514/826-3607
Ste-Claire (Mun.)	3,128	Bellechasse	Bellechasse	Bellechasse	Serge Gagnon, Sec.-Trés., 55, rue de la Fabrique, CP 189, Ste-Claire G0R 2V0 – 418/883-3314, Fax: 418/883-3845
St-Claude (Mun.)	984	Le Val-St-François	Richmond-Wolfe	Richmond	France Lavertu, Sec.-Trés., 295, rte de l'Église, St-Claude J0B 2N0 – 819/845-7795, Fax: 819/845-2479
St-Clément (P)	596	Les Basques	Kamouraska-Rivière-du-Loup	Rivière-du-Loup	Line Caron, Sec.-Trés., 25A, rue St-Pierre, CP 40, St-Clément G0L 2N0 – 418/963-2258, Fax: 418/963-2619
St-Cléophas (P)	437	La Matapédia	Matapédia-Matane	Matapédia	Lise Turbide, Sec.-Trés., 350, rue Principale, St-Cléophas G0J 3N0 – 418/536-3023
St-Cléophas (P)	282	D'Autray	Berthier-Montcalm	Berthier	Chantal Piette, Sec.-Trés., 750, rue Principale, St-Cléophas-de-Brandon J0K 2A0 – 514/889-5683, Fax: 514/889-8007

Cities (Villes) in CAPITALS; Villages marked (V); Townships/Cantons marked (Canton);United townships/Cantons unis marked (Cantons); Parishes (Paroisses) marked (P); Municipalities marked (Mun.).; Northern villages/Villages nordiques marked (NV); Cree Villages/Villages Cris marked (VC); Naskapi Villages/Villages Naskapi marked (VN); In the third column, Urban Community/Communauté Urbaine marked Urb. Com. An in-depth listing for municipalities marked with * appears in Part 2 (check Index for page numbers).

MUNICIPALITY	1993 POP.	REGIONAL COUNTY MUN.	FEDERAL ELECTORAL DISTRICT	PROVINCIAL ELECTORAL DISTRICT	CONTACT PERSON WITH ADDRESS, PHONE & FAX
St-Clet (Mun.)	1,511	Vaudreuil-Soulanges	Vaudreuil	Salaberry-Soulanges	Nathalie Pharand, Sec.-Trés., 4, rue du Moulin, St-Clet J0P 1S0 – 514/456-3363, Fax: 514/456-3879
Ste-Clothilde-de-Horton (P)	866	Arthabaska	Lotbinière	Richmond	Marlène Langlois, Sec.-Trés., rue du Parc, CP 29, Ste-Clothilde-de-Horton J0A 1H0 – 819/336-5344, Fax: 819/336-5440
Ste-Clotilde-de-Beauce (Mun.)	593	L'Amiante	Beauharnois-Salaberry	Beauce-Sud	Marcel Pomerleau, Sec.-Trés., 1045, rue Principale, Ste-Clotilde-de-Beauce G0N 1C0 – 418/427-2637, Fax: 418/427-2637
Ste-Clotilde-de-Châteauguay (P)	1,606	Les Jardins-de-Napierville	Beauharnois-Salaberry	Beauharnois-Huntingdon	Nicole Marcil-Lefebvre, Sec.-Trés., 2452, ch de l'Église, Ste-Clotilde-de-Châteauguay J0L 1W0 – 514/826-3129, Fax: 514/826-3217
Ste-Clotilde-de-Horton (V)	388	Arthabaska	Lotbinière	Richmond	Roger Boissonneault, Sec.-Trés., 11, rte 122, CP 189, Ste-Clotilde-de-Horton J0A 1H0 – 819/336-2033
St-Colomban (P)	3,987	La Rivière-du-Nord	Argenteuil-Papineau	Argenteuil	Suzanne Rainville, Sec.-Trés., 330, montée de l'Église, St-Colomban J0R 1N0 – 514/436-1453, Fax: 514/436-5955
St-Côme (P)	1,845	Matawinie	Berthier-Montcalm	Berthier	Alice Riopel, Sec.-Trés., 1673, 55e rue, St-Côme J0K 2B0 – 514/883-2726, Fax: 514/883-6431
St-Côme-Linière (P)	3,178	Beauce-Sartigan	Beauce	Beauce-Sud	Yvan Bélanger, Sec.-Trés., 1375, 18e rue, CP 219, St-Côme-de-Linière G0M 1J0 – 418/685-3825, Fax: 418/685-2566
ST-CONSTANT	19,535	Roussillon	Châteauguay	La Prairie	Martine Savard, Gref., 147, rue St-Pierre, CP 130, St-Constant J5A 2G2 – 514/638-2010, Fax: 514/638-5919
Ste-Croix (P)	870	Lotbinière	Lotbinière	Lotbinière	Hélène Boucher, Sec.-Trés., 6310, rue Principale, CP 100, Ste-Croix G0S 2H0 – 418/926-2212, Fax: 418/926-2212
Ste-Croix (V)	1,719	Lotbinière	Lotbinière	Lotbinière	Bertrand Fréchette, Sec.-Trés., 6310, rue Principale, CP 609, Ste-Croix G0S 2H0 – 418/926-3494, Fax: 418/926-2570
St-Cuthbert (P)	1,785	D'Autray	Berthier-Montcalm	Berthier	Richard Lauzon, Sec.-Trés., 1891, rue Principale, CP 100, St-Cuthbert J0K 2C0 – 514/836-4852, Fax: 514/836-4833
St-Cyprien (Mun.)	1,270	Témiscouata	Kamouraska-Rivière-du-Loup	Rivière-du-Loup	André Roy, Sec.-Trés., 101B, rue Collin, CP 9, St-Cyprien G0L 2P0 – 418/963-2730, Fax: 418/963-3490
St-Cyprien (P)	675	Les Etchemins	St-Cyprien	Bellechasse	Pauline Fortier, Sec.-Trés., 399, rue Principale, CP 100, St-Cyprien G0R 1B0 – 418/383-5274, Fax: 418/383-5269
St-Cyprien-de-Napierville (P)	1,320	Les Jardins-de-Napierville	St-Jean	Beauharnois-Huntingdon	Pauline Roy, Sec.-Trés., 121, rang Cyr, St-Cyprien-de-Napierville J0J 1L0 – 514/245-3658, Fax: 514/245-3658
St-Cyrille-de-Lessard (P)	842	L'Islet	Bellechasse	Montmagny-L'Islet	Raymonde Dubé, Sec.-Trés., CP 87, St-Cyrille-de-L'Islet G0R 2W0 – 418/247-5186, Fax: 418/247-5186
St-Cyrille-de-Wendover (Mun.)	3,888	Drummond	Drummond	Richmond	Mario Picotin, Sec.-Trés., 4055, rue Principale, St-Cyrille-de-Wendover J1Z 1C8 – 819/397-4226, Fax: 819/397-5505
St-Damase (P)	432	La Matapédia	Matapédia-Matane	Matane	Colette Dastous, Sec.-Trés., 18, av du Centenaire, St-Damase G0J 2J0 – 418/776-2103, Fax: 418/776-5705
St-Damase (V)	1,406	Les Maskoutains	St-Hyacinthe-Bagot	St-Hyacinthe	Yvon Tétreault, Sec.-Trés., 223, rue Principale, St-Damase J0H 1J0 – 514/797-3341, Fax: 514/797-3543
St-Damase (V)	1,134	Les Maskoutains	St-Hyacinthe-Bagot	St-Hyacinthe	Yvon Tétreault, Sec.-Trés., 223, rue Principale, St-Damase J0H 1J0 – 514/797-3341, Fax: 514/797-3543
St-Damase-de-L'Islet (Mun.)	654	L'Islet	Bellechasse	Montmagny-L'Islet	Paulette Lord-Lapointe, Sec.-Trés., 26, rue du Villlage est, CP 10, St-Damase-de-L'Islet G0R 2X0 – 418/598-9370
St-Damien (P)	1,624	Matawinie	Berthier-Montcalm	Berthier	Michel St-Laurent, Sec.-Trés., 6850, rte 347, CP 240, St-Damien J0K 2E0 – 514/835-3419, Fax: 514/835-5538
St-Damien-de-Buckland (P)	2,231	Bellechasse	Bellechasse	Bellechasse	Jacques Thibault, Sec.-Trés., 55, rte St-Gérard, St-Damien-de-Buckland G0R 2Y0 – 418/789-2526, Fax: 418/789-2125
St-David (P)	993	Le Bas-Richelieu	Lévis	Nicolet-Yamaska	Sylvie Letendre, Sec.-Trés., 11, rue Rivière David, St-David J0G 1L0 – 514/789-2288, Fax: 514/789-3023
St-David-de-Falardeau (Mun.)	2,031	Le Fjord-du-Saguenay	Lac-St-Jean	Dubuc	Daniel Hudon, Sec.-Trés., 140, boul St-David, CP 130, St-David-de-Falardeau G0V 1C0 – 418/673-4647, Fax: 418/673-3266
St-Denis (P)	486	Kamouraska	Kamouraska-Rivière-du-Loup	Kamouraska-Témiscouata	Thérèse Dumais-Charest, Sec.-Trés., 23, rte 132 ouest, CP 69, St-Denis G0L 2R0 – 418/498-2280
St-Denis (P)	1,218	La Vallée-du-Richelieu	Verchères	Verchères	Lise Leduc, Sec.-Trés., #200, 636, ch des Patriotes, St-Denis J0H 1K0 – 514/787-2092, Fax: 514/787-2635

Canadian Almanac & Directory 1997

Cities (Villes) in CAPITALS; Villages marked (V); Townships/Cantons marked (Canton);United townships/Cantons unis marked (Cantons); Parishes (Paroisses) marked (P); Municipalities marked (Mun.).; Northern villages/Villages nordiques marked (NV); Cree Villages/Villages Cris marked (VC); Naskapi Villages/Villages Naskapi marked (VN); In the third column, Urban Community/Communauté Urbaine marked Urb. Com. An in-depth listing for municipalities marked with * appears in Part 2 (check Index for page numbers).

MUNICIPALITY	1993 POP.	REGIONAL COUNTY MUN.	FEDERAL ELECTORAL DISTRICT	PROVINCIAL ELECTORAL DISTRICT	CONTACT PERSON WITH ADDRESS, PHONE & FAX
St-Denis (V)	1,096	La Vallée-du-Richelieu	Verchères	Verchères	Pierre Pétrin, Sec.-Trés., 601, ch des Patriotes, St-Denis-sur-Richelieu J0H 1K0 – 514/787-2244, Fax: 514/787-3721
St-Denis-de-Brompton (P)	2,174	Le Val-St-François	Richmond-Wolfe	Johnson	Marc Laflamme, Sec.-Trés., 2050, Ernest-Camiré, CP 120, St-Denis-de-Brompton J0B 2P0 – 819/846-2744, Fax: 819/846-0915
St-Didace (P)	629	D'Autray	Berthier-Montcalm	Berthier	André Allard, Sec.-Trés., 380, rue Principale, St-Didace J0K 2G0 – 514/835-4184, Fax: 514/835-4184
St-Dominique (V)	2,200	Les Maskoutains	Vaudreuil	St-Hyacinthe	Agnès Archambault, Sec.-Trés., 467, rue Deslandes, St-Dominique J0H 1L0 – 514/774-9939, Fax: 514/774-1595
St-Dominique-du-Rosaire (Mun.)	487	Abitibi	Abitibi	Abitibi-Ouest	Lucille Ferron, Sec.-Trés., 235A, rue Principale, St-Dominique-du-Rosaire J0Y 2K0 – 819/727-9544, Fax: 819/727-9544
St-Donat (P)	787	La Mitis	Rimouski-Témiscouata	Matapedia	Gil Bérubé, Sec.-Trés., 194, av Mont-Comi, CP 70, St-Donat G0K 1L0 – 418/739-4634, Fax: 418/739-5003
St-Donat (Mun.)	3,178	Matawinie	Rimouski-Témiscouata	Bertrand	Jean Robidoux, Sec.-Trés., 475, rue Desrochers, CP 460, St-Donat J0T 2C0 – 819/424-2383, Fax: 819/424-5020
St-Edmond (Mun.)	238	La Matapédia	Matapédia-Matane	Matapédia	Philippe Lavigne, Sec.-Trés., 880, 4e rang, Lac-au-Saumon G0J 1M0 – 418/778-3478
St-Edmond (Mun.)	612	Maria-Chapdelaine	Roberval	Roberval	Danielle Bernard, Sec.-Trés., 561, ch Principale, St-Edmond-les-Plaines G0W 2M0 – 418/274-3069, Fax: 418/274-5629
St-Edmond-de-Grantham (P)	575	Drummond	Drummond	Drummond	Hervé Lafleur, Sec.-Trés., 393, Notre-Dame-de-Lourdes, St-Edmond-de-Grantham J0C 1K0 – 819/395-2562, Fax: 819/395-2562
St-Édouard (P)	1,316	Les Jardins-de-Napierville	Champlain	Beauharnois-Huntingdon	Daniel Théroux, Sec.-Trés., 405C, montée Lussier, CP 120, St-Édouard J0L 1Y0 – 514/454-6333, Fax: 514/454-6333
St-Édouard-de-Fabre (P)	746	Témiscamingue	Témiscamingue	Rouyn-Noranda-Témiscamingue	Anita Pelchat, Sec.-Trés., 1323, rue Principale, CP 70, Fabre J0Z 1Z0 – 819/634-4441, Fax: 819/634-4441
St-Édouard-de-Frampton (P)	1,323	La Nouvelle-Beauce	Beauce	Beauce-Nord	Josée Audet, Sec.-Trés., 107, rue Ste-Anne, CP 40, St-Édouard-de-Frampton G0R 1M0 – 418/479-5363, Fax: 418/479-5363
St-Édouard-de-Lotbinière (P)	1,359	Lotbinière	Lotbinière	Lotbinière	Anna Blondin, Sec.-Trés., 105, route Soucy, CP 188, St-Édouard G0S 1Y0 – 418/796-2971, Fax: 418/796-2228
St-Édouard-de-Maskinongé (Mun.)	760	Maskinongé	Berthier-Montcalm	Maskinongé	Gilles Gerbeau, Sec.-Trés., 3800, rue St-André, St-Édouard-de-Maskinongé J0K 2H0 – 819/268-2833, Fax: 819/268-2833
Ste-Edwidge-de-Clifton (Canton)	591	Coaticook	Mégantic-Compton-Stanstead	Mégantic-Compton	Réjean Fauteux, Sec.-Trés., 203, rue Principale Nord, Ste-Edwidge-de-Clifton J0B 2R0 – 819/849-7740, Fax: 819/849-7740
St-Élie (P)	1,435	Le Centre-de-la-Mauricie	St-Maurice	Maskinongé	Micheline Allard, Sec.-Trés., 22, ch des Loisirs, CP 39, St-Élie G0X 2N0 – 819/221-2839, Fax: 819/221-4039
St-Élie-d'Orford (P)	5,046	Sherbrooke	Richmond-Wolfe	Orford	Pierre Auger, Sec.-Trés., 161, ch St-Roch, St-Élie-d'Orford J0B 2S0 – 819/566-5466, Fax: 819/566-1163
Ste-Élisabeth (P)	1,638	D'Autray	Berthier-Montcalm	Berthier	Pauline Ladouceur, Sec.-Trés., 2270, rue Principale, Ste-Élizabeth J0K 2J0 – 514/759-2875, Fax: 514/756-4312
Ste-Élisabeth-de-Warwick (P)	446	Arthabaska	Lotbinière	Richmond	Lucille Gosselin, Sec.-Trés., 230, 4e rang, CP 75, Ste-Élisabeth-de-Warwick J0A 1M0 – 819/358-5162, Fax: 819/358-5162
St-Éloi (P)	360	Les Basques	Kamouraska-Rivière-du-Loup	Rivière-du-Loup	Annie Roussel, Sec.-Trés., 183, rue Principale, CP 9, St-Éoi G0L 2V0 – 418/898-2734, Fax: 418/898-2734
St-Elphège (P)	333	Nicolet-Yamaska	Richelieu	Nicolet-Yamaska	France Dionne, Sec.-Trés., 245, rang St-Antoine, St-Elphège J0G 1J0 – 514/568-0288, Fax: 514/568-0288
St-Elzéar (Mun.)	578	Bonaventure	Bonaventure-Îles-de-la-Madeleine	Bonaventure	Lucille Ferlatte, Sec.-Trés., 148, ch Principal, CP 40, St-Elzéar G0C 2W0 – 418/534-2611, Fax: 418/534-2611
St-Elzéar (Mun.)	414	Témiscouata	Rimouski-Témiscouata	Kamouraska-Témiscouata	Nanny Lévesque, Sec.-Trés., 209, rue de l'Église, St-Elzéar G0L 2W0 – 418/854-7690, Fax: 418/854-7690
St-Elzéar (Mun.)	1,584	La Nouvelle-Beauce	Beauce	Beauce-Nord	Solange Marcoux, Sec.-Trés., 672, av Principale, St-Elzéar G0S 2J0 – 418/387-2534, Fax: 418/387-4378
Ste-Émélie-de-l'Énergie (Mun.)	1,392	Matawinie	Berthier-Montcalm	Berthier	Guylaine Comtois, Sec.-Trés., 241, rue Coutu, Ste-Émélie-de-L'Énergie J0K 2K0 – 514/886-3823, Fax: 514/886-3824
ST-ÉMILE	7,231	Québec (Urb. Com.)	Charlesbourg	Chauveau	Jean Savard, Gref., 6180, rue des Érables, St-Émile G3E 1K6 – 418/842-3000, Fax: 418/842-7081

Cities (Villes) in CAPITALS; Villages marked (V); Townships/Cantons marked (Canton);United townships/Cantons unis marked (Cantons); Parishes (Paroisses) marked (P); Municipalities marked (Mun.).; Northern villages/Villages nordiques marked (NV); Cree Villages/Villages Cris marked (VC); Naskapi Villages/Villages Naskapi marked (VN); In the third column, Urban Community/Communauté Urbaine marked Urb. Com. An in-depth listing for municipalities marked with * appears in Part 2 (check Index for page numbers).

MUNICIPALITY	1993 POP.	REGIONAL COUNTY MUN.	FEDERAL ELECTORAL DISTRICT	PROVINCIAL ELECTORAL DISTRICT	CONTACT PERSON WITH ADDRESS, PHONE & FAX
St-Émile-de-Suffolk (Mun.)	508	Papineau	Argenteuil-Papineau	Papineau	Gisèle Éthier, Sec.-Trés., 299, rte des Cantons, Saint-Émile-de-Suffolk J0V 1Y0 – 819/426-2987, Fax: 819/426-2947
Ste-Emmélie (P)	344	Lotbinière	Lotbinière	Lotbinière	Francine Demers, Sec.-Trés., 189, rang du Portage, Leclercville G0S 2K0 – 819/292-2331, Fax: 819/292-2639
St-Éphrem-de-Beauce (P)	1,295	Beauce-Sartigan	Beauce	Beauce-Sud	Charlotte Longchamps, Sec.-Trés., #1, 34, rue de la Station, CP 369, St-Éphrem-de-Beauce G0M 1R0 – 418/484-5716, Fax: 418/484-5715
St-Éphrem-de-Tring (V)	1,146	Beauce-Sartigan	Beauce	Beauce-Sud	Thérèse Bolduc, Sec.-Trés., 34, rue de la Station, CP 87, St-Éphrem-de-Tring G0M 1R0 – 418/484-2114, Fax: 418/484-2305
St-Éphrem-d'Upton (P)	868	Acton	St-Hyacinthe-Bagot	Johnson	Robert Leclerc, Sec.-Trés., 863, rue Lanoie, St-Éphrem-d'Upton J0H 2E0 – 514/549-4361, Fax: 514/549-5045
St-Épiphane (Mun.)	963	Rivière-du-Loup	Kamouraska-Rivière-du-Loup	Rivière-du-Loup	Denis Lagacé, Sec.-Trés., 280, rue Bernier, CP 69, St-Épiphane G0L 2X0 – 418/862-0052, Fax: 418/862-7753
St-Esprit (P)	2,075	Montcalm	Berthier-Montcalm	Rousseau	Nathalie Rochon, Sec.-Trés., 21, rue Principale, St-Esprit J0K 2L0 – 514/839-3629, Fax: 514/839-6070
St-Étienne-de-Beauharnois (Mun.)	837	Beauharnois-Salaberry	Beauharnois-Salaberry	Beauharnois-Huntingdon	Ginette Prud'homme, Sec.-Trés., 489, ch St-Louis, St-Étienne-de-Beauharnois J0S 1S0 – 514/225-1000, Fax: 514/225-1011
St-Étienne-de-Beaumont (P)	2,025	Bellechasse	Bellechasse	Bellechasse	Richard Serge, Sec.-Trés., 6, boul Mercier, Beaumont G0R 1C0 – 418/833-3369, Fax: 418/833-4788
St-Étienne-de-Bolton (Mun.)	392	Memphrémagog	Brome-Missisquoi	Brome-Missisquoi	Sylvain Demers, Sec.-Trés., 9, rang de la Montagne, St-Étienne-de-Bolton J0E 2E0 – 514/297-3353, Fax: 514/297-0412
St-Étienne-de-Lauzon (Mun.)	7,851	Les Chutes-de-la-Chaudière	Lévis	Chutes-de-la-Chaudière	Sébastien Hamel, Sec.-Trés., 1, place Chamberland, CP 339, St-Étienne-de-Lauzon G6J 1M5 – 418/831-4023, Fax: 418/831-7198
St-Étienne-des-Grès (P)	3,719	Francheville	St-Maurice	Maskinongé	Hélène Boisvert, Sec.-Trés., 1230, rue Principale, CP 130, St-Étienne-des-Grès G0X 2P0 – 819/535-3113, Fax: 819/535-1246
St-Eugène (P)	1,238	L'Islet	Bellechasse	Montmagny-L'Islet	Ginette Gagné, Sec.-Trés., 79, rue Mgr-Bernier, St-Eugène G0R 1X0 – 418/247-5340, Fax: 418/247-5052
St-Eugène (Mun.)	1,039	Drummond	Drummond	Drummond	Chantal Herman, Sec.-Trés., 1065, rang de l'Église, CP 30, St-Eugène J0C 1J0 – 819/396-3000, Fax: 819/396-3576
St-Eugène (Mun.)	715	Maria-Chapdelaine	Roberval	Roberval	Frédéric Lemieux, Sec.-Trés., 439, rue Principale, CP 70, St-Eugène G0W 1B0 – 418/276-1787, Fax: 418/276-1787
St-Eugène-de-Guigues (Mun.)	427	Témiscamingue	Témiscamingue	Rouyn-Noranda-Témiscamingue	Raynald Julien, Sec.-Trés., 4, rue Notre-Dame ouest, CP 1070, St-Eugène-de-Guigues J0Z 3L0 – 819/785-2301, Fax: 819/785-3512
St-Eugène-de-Ladrière (P)	540	Rimouski-Neigette	Rimouski-Témiscouata	Rimouski	Huguette Proulx, Sec.-Trés., 159, rue Principale, St-Eugène-de-Ladrière G0L 1P0 – 418/869-2582, Fax: 418/869-2582
Ste-Eulalie (Mun.)	848	Nicolet-Yamaska	Lotbinière	Nicolet-Yamaska	Laurent Champagne, Sec.-Trés., 488, rang des Érables, CP 70, Ste-Eulalie G0Z 1E0 – 819/225-4345, Fax: 819/225-4078
Ste-Euphémie-sur-Rivière-du-Sud (Mun.)	364	Montmagny	Bellechasse	Montmagny-L'Islet	Benoit Roth, Sec.-Trés., 220, rue Principal est, Ste-Euphémie-sur-Rivière-du-Sud G0R 2Z0 – 418/469-3427, Fax: 418/469-3427
St-Eusèbe (P)	675	Témiscouata	Rimouski-Témiscouata	Kamouraska-Témiscouata	Andréa Deschamps, Sec.-Trés., 222, rue Principale, St-Eusèbe G0L 2Y0 – 418/899-2762, Fax: 418/899-0194
ST-EUSTACHE	41,409	Deux-Montagnes	Blainville-Deux-Montagnes	Deux-Montagnes	Gilles Gougeon, Gref., 145, rue St-Louis, St-Eustache J7R 5C2 – 514/974-5000, Fax: 514/974-5229
St-Évariste-de-Forsyth (Mun.)	604	Beauce-Sartigan	Frontenac	Beauce-Sud	Claude Poulin, Sec.-Trés., 495, rue Principale, CP 38, St-Évariste-de-Forsyth G0M 1S0 – 418/459-6488, Fax: 418/459-6268
St-Fabien (P)	1,910	Rimouski-Neigette	Rimouski-Témiscouata	Rimouski	Murielle Cloutier, Sec.-Trés., 10, 7e av, CP 9, St-Fabien G0L 2Z0 – 418/869-2950, Fax: 418/869-2950
St-Fabien-de-Panet (P)	983	Montmagny	Bellechasse	Montmagny-L'Islet	Claude Saint-Pierre, Sec.-Trés., 195, rue Bilodeau, CP 9, St-Fabein-de-Panet G0R 2J0 – 418/249-4471, Fax: 418/249-4471
Ste-Famille (P)	978	L'Île-d'Orléans	Beauport-Montmorency-Orléans	Montmorency	Lise Lapointe, Sec.-Trés., 3894, ch Royal, Ste-Famille G0A 3P0 – 418/829-3572, Fax: 418/829-2513

QUÉBEC MUNICIPALITIES

Cities (Villes) in CAPITALS; Villages marked (V); Townships/Cantons marked (Canton);United townships/Cantons unis marked (Cantons); Parishes (Paroisses) marked (P); Municipalities marked (Mun.).; Northern villages/Villages nordiques marked (NV); Cree Villages/Villages Cris marked (VC); Naskapi Villages/Villages Naskapi marked (VN); In the third column, Urban Community/Communauté Urbaine marked Urb. Com. An in-depth listing for municipalities marked with * appears in Part 2 (check Index for page numbers).

MUNICIPALITY	1993 POP.	REGIONAL COUNTY MUN.	FEDERAL ELECTORAL DISTRICT	PROVINCIAL ELECTORAL DISTRICT	CONTACT PERSON WITH ADDRESS, PHONE & FAX
St-Faustin (Mun.)	1,528	Les Laurentides	Laurentides	Labelle	Gaetan Charette, Sec.-Trés., 100, Place de la Mairie, CP 120, St-Faustin J0T 2G0 – 819/688-2161, Fax: 819/688-6791
ST-FÉLICIEN	9,584	Le Domaine-du-Roy	Roberval	Roberval	Luc Bergeron, Gref., 1058, boul Sacre-Coeur, CP 7000, St-Félicien G8K 2R5 – 418/679-0251, Fax: 418/679-1449
Ste-Félicité (Mun.)	533	L'Islet	Bellechasse	Montmagny-L'Islet	Denise M.-Morneau, Sec.-Trés., 5, route de l'Église nord, Ste-Félicité G0R 4P0 – 418/359-2321, Fax: 418/359-2321
Ste-Félicité (P)	663	Matane	Matapédia-Matane	Matane	Denise Banville-Otis, Sec.-Trés., 114, rue St-Jean, CP 130, Ste-Félicité G0J 2K0 – 418/733-4230
Ste-Félicité (V)	758	Matane	Matapédia-Matane	Matane	Yves Chassé, Sec.-Trés., 192, rue St-Joseph, CP 9, Ste-Félicité G0J 2K0 – 418/733-4628, Fax: 418/733-8377
St-Félix-de-Dalquier (Mun.)	975	Abitibi	Abitibi	Abitibi-Ouest	Richard Michaud, Sec.-Trés., 20, rue Principale sud, St-Félix-de-Dalquier J0Y 1G0 – 819/727-1732, Fax: 819/727-1732
St-Félix-de-Valois (P)	3,782	Matawinie	Berthier-Montcalm	Berthier	Gaston Charette, Sec.-Trés., 600, ch Joliette, CP 220, St-Félix-de-Valois J0K 2M0 – 514/889-5589, Fax: 514/889-5259
St-Félix-de-Valois (V)	1,753	Matawinie	Berthier-Montcalm	Berthier	Suzanne Ricard, Sec.-Trés., 4881, rue Principale, CP 69, St-Félix-de-Valois J0K 2M0 – 514/889-5581, Fax: 514/889-5293
St-Félix-d'Otis (Mun.)	711	Le Fjord-du-Saguenay	Chicoutimi	Dubuc	Bertrand Boudreault, Sec.-Trés., 455, rue Principale, CP 38, St-Félix-d'Otis G0V 1M0 – 418/544-5543, Fax: 418/544-9122
St-Ferdinand (Mun.)	756	L'Érable	Frontenac	Frontenac	Michèle Lacroix, Sec.-Trés., 821, rue Principale, CP 160, St-Ferdinand G0N 1N0 – 418/428-3480, Fax: 418/428-9724
St-Ferréol-les-Neiges (Mun.)	2,092	La Côte-de-Beaupré	Beauport-Montmorency-Orléans	Charlevoix	François Drouin, Sec.-Trés., 33, rue de l'Église, St-Ferréol-les-Neiges G0A 3R0 – 418/826-2253, Fax: 418/826-0489
St-Fidèle-de-Mont-Murray (P)	1,014	Charlevoix-Est	Charlevoix	Charlevoix	Raynald Tremblay, Sec.-Trés., 79, rue Principale, CP 40, St-Fidèle G0T 1T0 – 418/434-2447, Fax: 418/434-2315
Ste-Flavie (P)	901	La Mitis	Matapédia-Matane	Matapédia	Suzanne Landreville, Sec.-Trés., 775, rte Jacques-Cartier, Ste-Flavie G0J 2L0 – 418/775-7050, Fax: 418/775-5672
St-Flavien (P)	698	Lotbinière	Lotbinière	Lotbinière	Mario Roy, Sec.-Trés., 6, rue Caux, St-Flavien G0S 2M0 – 418/728-4190, Fax: 418/728-4190
St-Flavien (V)	760	Lotbinière	Lotbinière	Lotbinière	Mario Roy, Sec.-Trés., 6, rue Caux, St-Flavien G0S 2M0 – 418/728-4190, Fax: 418/728-4190
Ste-Florence (Mun.)	551	La Matapédia	Matapédia-Matane	Matapédia	Huguette Gagné, Sec.-Trés., CP 9, Ste-Florence G0J 2M0 – 418/756-3491, Fax: 418/756-3491
St-Fortunat (Mun.)	276	L'Amiante	Richmond-Wolfe	Richmond	Alcide Bédard, Sec.-Trés., 107, rue Principale, St-Fortunat G0P 1G0 – 819/344-5431, Fax: 819/344-5431
*STE-FOY	74,328	Québec (Urb. Com.)	Louis-Hébert	Jean-Talon; La Peltrie; Louis-Hébert	René Damphousse, Gref. et Directeur général adjoint, 1130, rte de l'Église, CP 218, Ste-Foy G1V 4E1 – 418/650-7925, Fax: 418/650-7972
St-François (P)	515	L'Île-d'Orléans	Beauport-Montmorency-Orléans	Montmorency	Roland Gosselin, Sec.-Trés., 337, rue Lemelin, St-François G0A 3S0 – 418/829-3100, Fax: 418/829-1004
St-François-d'Assise (P)	928	Avignon	Bonaventure-Îles-de-la-Madeleine	Bonaventure	Suzanne Roy, Sec.-Trés., 457, ch Central, CP 39, St-François-d'Assise G0J 2N0 – 418/299-2066, Fax: 418/299-3037
St-François-de-Beauce (Mun.)	1,268	Robert-Cliche	Beauce	Beauce-Nord	Dorothy Fortin-Thibodeau, Sec.-Trés., CP 5, Beauceville-Est G0S 1A0 – 418/774-5259, Fax: 418/774-5259
St-François-de-la-Rivière-du-Sud (Mun.)	1,616	Montmagny	Bellechasse	Montmagny-L'Islet	Yves Laflamme, Sec.-Trés., 534, ch St-François ouest, CP 68, St-François G0R 3A0 – 418/259-7228, Fax: 418/259-2056
St-François-de-Pabos (Mun.)	782	Pabok	Gaspé	Gaspé	Nancy Huard, Sec.-Trés., 168, route St-François, CP 219, St-François-de-Pabos G0C 2H0 – 418/689-6620, Fax: 418/689-7082
St-François-de-Sales (Mun.)	857	Le Domaine-du-Roy	Roberval	Roberval	Renaud Blanchette, Sec.-Trés., 541, rue Principale, St-François de Sales G0W 1M0 – 418/348-6736, Fax: 418/348-9439
St-François-du-Lac (P)	1,056	Nicolet-Yamaska	Richelieu	Nicolet-Yamaska	Claire Roy, Sec.-Trés., 56, route Marie-Victorin, CP 240, St-François-du-Lac J0G 1M0 – 514/568-2124, Fax: 514/568-2124

Cities (Villes) in CAPITALS; Villages marked (V); Townships/Cantons marked (Canton);United townships/Cantons unis marked (Cantons); Parishes (Paroisses) marked (P); Municipalities marked (Mun.).; Northern villages/Villages nordiques marked (NV); Cree Villages/Villages Cris marked (VC); Naskapi Villages/Villages Naskapi marked (VN); In the third column, Urban Community/Communauté Urbaine marked Urb. Com. An in-depth listing for municipalities marked with * appears in Part 2 (check Index for page numbers).

MUNICIPALITY	1993 POP.	REGIONAL COUNTY MUN.	FEDERAL ELECTORAL DISTRICT	PROVINCIAL ELECTORAL DISTRICT	CONTACT PERSON WITH ADDRESS, PHONE & FAX
St-François-du-Lac (V)	952	Nicolet-Yamaska	Richelieu	Nicolet-Yamaska	Carmen Forcier, Sec.-Trés., 480, rue Notre Dame, CP 60, St-François-du-Lac J0G 1M0 – 514/568-3728, Fax: 514/568-1130
St-François-Ouest (Mun.)	1,274	Robert-Cliche	Beauce	Beauce-Nord	Huguette Rodrigue, Sec.-Trés., 345, rang du Bord-de-l'Eau, Beauceville-Ouest G0M 1A0 – 418/774-5177, Fax: 418/774-5177
St-François-Xavier-Brompton (P)	1,890	Le Val-St-François	Richmond-Wolfe	Johnson	Mario Chabot, Sec.-Trés., 94, rue Principale, CP 10, St-François-Xavier-de-Brompton J0B 2V0 – 819/845-3954, Fax: 819/845-7711
St-François-Xavier-de-Viger (Mun.)	328	Rivière-du-Loup	Kamouraska-Rivière-du-Loup	Rivière-du-Loup	Yvette Beaulieu, Sec.-Trés., 123, rue Principale, St-François-Xavier-de-Viger G0L 3C0 – 418/497-2302, Fax: 418/497-2302
Ste-Françoise (Mun.)	544	Bécancour	Lotbinière	Lotbinière	Isabelle Dubois, Sec.-Trés., 563, 11e rang est, Ste-Françoise G0S 2N0 – 819/287-5755, Fax: 819/287-5838
Ste-Françoise (P)	524	Les Basques	Kamouraska-Rivière-du-Loup	Rivière-du-Loup	Andrée Rioux, Sec.-Trés., 156, rue Jérémie-Beaulieu, Ste-Françoise G0L 3B0 – 418/851-1502
St-Frédéric (P)	1,033	Robert-Cliche	Beauce	Beauce-Nord	Jacqueline Lehoux, Sec.-Trés., 389, rue du Parc, CP 87, St-Frédéric G0N 1P0 – 418/426-3357, Fax: 418/426-3357
St-Fulgence (Mun.)	2,237	Le Fjord-du-Saguenay	Lac-St-Jean	Dubuc	Gilles Tremblay, Sec.-Trés., 253, rue Saguenay, CP 70, St-Fulgence G0V 1S0 – 418/674-2588, Fax: 418/674-9213
St-Gabriel (Mun.)	1,259	La Mitis	Matapédia-Matane	Matapédia	Marie-Paule Rioux, Sec.-Trés., 248, rue Principale, CP 10, St-Gabriel G0K 1M0 – 418/798-4938, Fax: 418/798-4108
ST-GABRIEL	2,946	D'Autray	Berthier-Montcalm	Berthier	Raymond Gagnon, Sec.-Trés., 45, rue Beausoleil, CP 750, St-Gabriel-de-Brandon J0K 2N0 – 514/835-2212, Fax: 514/835-9852
St-Gabriel-de-Brandon (P)	2,338	D'Autray	Berthier-Montcalm	Berthier	André Comtois, Sec.-Trés., 5111, ch du Lac, CP 929, St-Gabriel-de-Brandon J0K 2N0 – 514/835-3494, Fax: 514/835-3495
St-Gabriel-de-Valcartier (Mun.)	2,965	La Jacques-Cartier	Charlesbourg	Chauveau	Joan Sheehan, Sec.-Trés., 1743, boul Valcartier, St-Gabriel-de-Valcartier G0A 4S0 – 418/844-1218, Fax: 418/844-3030
St-Gabriel-Lalemant (Mun.)	953	Kamouraska	Kamouraska-Rivière-du-Loup	Kamouraska-Témiscouata	Gina Lévesque, Sec.-Trés., CP 9, Kamouraska G0L 3E0 – 418/852-2801, Fax: 418/852-3390
St-Gédéon (Mun.)	1,839	Lac-St-Jean-Est	Lac-St-Jean	Lac-St-Jean	Dany Dallaire, Sec.-Trés., 208, ch Dequen, St-Gédéon G0W 2P0 – 418/345-8001, Fax: 418/345-2306
St-Gédéon (P)	604	Beauce-Sartigan	Beauce	Beauce-Sud	Jean-Paul Jolin, Sec.-Trés., 102, 1re av, CP 429, St-Gédéon G0M 1T0 – 418/582-6435, Fax: 418/582-6016
St-Gédéon (V)	1,750	Beauce-Sartigan	Beauce	Beauce-Sud	Pierre-Alain Pelchat, Sec.-Trés., 102 - 1re av sud, St-Gédéon G0M 1T0 – 418/582-3341, Fax: 418/582-6016
STE-GENEVIÈVE	3,242	Montréal (Urb. Com.)	Pierrefonds-Dollard	Nelligan	Rita Allaire, Gref., 13, rue Chauret, Ste-Geneviève H9H 2X2 – 514/626-2535, Fax: 514/626-0312
Ste-Geneviève-de-Batiscan (P)	1,134	Francheville	Champlain	Champlain	Robert Néron, Sec.-Trés., 30, rue St-Charles, CP 70, Ste-Geneviève-de-Batiscan G0X 2R0 – 418/362-2078, Fax: 418/362-2111
Ste-Geneviève-de-Berthier (P)	2,458	D'Autray	Berthier-Montcalm	Berthier	Lincoln LeBreton, Sec.-Trés., 400, rang de la Rivière Bayonne sud, Ste-Geneviève-de-Berthier J0K 1A0 – 514/836-4333, Fax: 514/836-7260
St-Georges (V)	4,091	Le Centre-de-la-Mauricie	St-Maurice	Laviolette	Royal Duchemin, Sec.-Trés., 505 - 105e av, St-Georges G9T 3H3 – 819/538-8631, Fax: 819/538-8634
ST-GEORGES	20,043 ('96)	Beauce-Sartigan	Beauce	Beauce-Sud	Laurent Nadeau, Gref., 11700, boul Lacroix, St-Georges G5Y 1L3 – 418/228-5555, Fax: 418/228-3855
St-Georges-de-Cacouna (P)	696	Rivière-du-Loup	Kamouraska-Rivière-du-Loup	Rivière-du-Loup	Thérèse Dubé, Sec.-Trés., 263, rte 132, CP 40, St-Georges-de-Cacouna G0L 1G0 – 418/862-1937, Fax: 418/862-0136
St-Georges-de-Cacouna (V)	1,168	Rivière-du-Loup	Kamouraska-Rivière-du-Loup	Rivière-du-Loup	Jacques St-Pierre, Sec.-Trés., 415, rue St-Georges, CP 249, Cacouna G0L 1G0 – 418/867-1781, Fax: 418/867-5677
St-Georges-de-Clarenceville (Mun.)	967	Le Haut-Richelieu	Brome-Missisquoi	Iberville	Thérèse Lacombe, Sec.-Trés., 1350, ch Middle, St-Georges-de-Clarenceville J0J 1B0 – 514/294-2464, Fax: 514/294-2016
St-Georges-de-Windsor (Mun.)	875	Asbestos	Richmond-Wolfe	Richmond	Lise Roy, Sec.-Trés., 485, rue Principale, St-Georges-de-Windsor J0A 1J0 – 819/828-2716, Fax: 819/828-0213

Canadian Almanac & Directory 1997

4-114 QUÉBEC MUNICIPALITIES

Cities (Villes) in CAPITALS; Villages marked (V); Townships/Cantons marked (Canton);United townships/Cantons unis marked (Cantons); Parishes (Paroisses) marked (P); Municipalities marked (Mun.).; Northern villages/Villages nordiques marked (NV); Cree Villages/Villages Cris marked (VC); Naskapi Villages/Villages Naskapi marked (VN); In the third column, Urban Community/Communauté Urbaine marked Urb. Com. An in-depth listing for municipalities marked with * appears in Part 2 (check Index for page numbers).

MUNICIPALITY	1993 POP.	REGIONAL COUNTY MUN.	FEDERAL ELECTORAL DISTRICT	PROVINCIAL ELECTORAL DISTRICT	CONTACT PERSON WITH ADDRESS, PHONE & FAX
St-Georges-Est (P)	3,060	Beauce-Sartigan	Beauce	Beauce-Sud	Yvon Gilbert, Sec.-Trés., #154, 80, boul Lacroix, St-Georges G5Y 1R7 – 418/228-2925, Fax: 418/228-2925
St-Gérard (V)	560	Le Haut-St-François	Mégantic-Compton-Stanstead	Mégantic-Compton	Francine Blanchette, Sec.-Trés., 183, rue Principale, CP 3B C3, St-Gérard G0Y 1K0 – 819/877-2839, Fax: 819/877-2839
St-Gérard-des-Laurentides (P)	2,154	Le Centre-de-la-Mauricie	St-Maurice	St-Maurice	Denis Brodeur, Sec.-Trés., 431, rue des Frênes, St-Gérard-des-Laurentides G9N 6T6 – 819/539-9121, Fax: 819/539-8622
St-Gérard-Majella (P)	3,675	L'Assomption	Joliette	Rousseau	Marius Savoie, Sec.-Trés., 2700, ch du Roy, St-Gérard-Majella J5X 1B1 – 514/588-5536, Fax: 514/588-7161
St-Gérard-Majella (P)	278	Le Bas-Richelieu	Richelieu	Nicolet-Yamaska	Roger Proulx, Sec.-Trés., 370, rang Ste-Catherine, St-Gérard-d'Yamaska J0G 1X0 – 514/789-2630, Fax: 514/789-0336
St-Germain (P)	344	Kamouraska	Kamouraska-Rivière-du-Loup	Kamouraska-Témiscouata	Hélène B.-Bernier, Sec.-Trés., 146, rang des Côtes, St-Germain G0L 3G0 – 418/492-5203
St-Germain-de-Grantham (Mun.) [h]	3,466 ('95)	Drummond	Drummond	Drummond	Danielle S.-Gauthier, Sec.-Trés., 233, ch Yamaska, CP 190, St-Germain-de-Grantham J0C 1K0 – 819/395-5496, Fax: 819/395-5200
Ste-Germaine-Boulé (Mun.)	1,134	Abitibi-Ouest	Témiscamingue	Abitibi-Ouest	Gisèle Bisson-Lapointe, Sec.-Trés., 199, rue Roy, CP 5, Ste-Germaine-Boulé J0Z 1M0 – 819/787-6221, Fax: 819/787-6221
Ste-Germaine-de-l'Anse-aux-Gascons (P)	1,314	Pabok	Bonaventure-Îles-de-la-Madeleine	Bonaventure	Thérèse Chapados, Sec.-Trés., 63, route 132 ouest, CP 39, Gascons G0C 1P0 – 418/396-5400, Fax: 418/396-2333
Ste-Germaine-du-Lac-Etchemin (P)	1,577	Les Etchemins	Bellechasse	Bellechasse	Eudore Poulin, Sec.-Trés., 208, 2e av, Sainte-Germaine-du-Lac-Etchemin G0R 1S0 – 418/625-2291, Fax: 418/625-2292
Ste-Gertrude-Manneville (Mun.)	792	Abitibi	Abitibi	Abitibi-Ouest	Gertrude Bilodeau, Sec.-Trés., 391, rte 395, Ste-Gertrude J0Y 2L0 – 819/727-2244, Fax: 819/727-2244
St-Gervais (Mun.)	1,884	Bellechasse	Bellechasse	Bellechasse	Gilles Breton, Sec.-Trés., 36, rue de la Fabrique, CP 69, St-Gervais G0R 3C0 – 418/887-6116, Fax: 418/887-6312
St-Gilbert (P)	351	Portneuf	Portneuf	Portneuf	Michelle Robitaille, Sec.-Trés., 3, rue Principale, St-Gilbert G0A 3T0 – 418/268-8194, Fax: 418/268-8194
St-Gilles (P)	1,875	Lotbinière	Lotbinière	Lotbinière	Aline Martin, Sec.-Trés., 161, rue O'Hurley, St-Gilles G0S 2P0 – 418/888-3198, Fax: 418/888-5145
St-Godefroi (Canton)	589	Bonaventure	Bonaventure-Îles-de-la-Madeleine	Bonaventure	Jocelyne Joseph, Sec.-Trés., 109, route 132, CP 157, St-Godefroi G0C 3C0 – 418/752-6316, Fax: 418/752-6316
St-Grégoire-de-Greenlay (V)	634	Le Val-St-François	Richmond-Wolfe	Johnson	Bernice McAdams, Sec.-Trés., #201, 3, rue Greenlay sud, Greenlay J1S 2S1 – 819/845-7667, Fax: 819/845-2644
St-Guillaume (Mun.) [i]	1,731 ('95)	Drummond	Drummond	Nicolet-Yamaska	Hélène Philips, Sec.-Trés., 106, rue St-Jean-Baptiste, CP 295, St-Guillaume J0C 1L0 – 819/396-2403, Fax: 819/396-0184
St-Guy (Mun.)	159	Les Basques	Kamouraska-Rivière-du-Loup	Rimouski	Lisa Caron, Sec.-Trés., 54, rue Principal, St-Guy G0K 1W0 – 418/963-2601, Fax: 418/963-2601
Ste-Hedwidge (Mun.)	903	Le Domaine-du-Roy	Roberval	Roberval	Gilles Toulouse, Sec.-Trés., 1090, rue Principale, Ste-Hedwidge G0W 2R0 – 418/275-3020, Fax: 418/275-4163
Ste-Hélène (P)	996	Kamouraska	Kamouraska-Rivière-du-Loup	Kamouraska-Témiscouata	Nathalie Blais, Sec.-Trés., 531, rue de l'Église sud, CP 216, Ste-Hélène G0L 3J0 – 418/492-6830, Fax: 418/492-1854
Ste-Hélène-de-Bagot (Mun.)	1,565	Les Maskoutains	St-Hyacinthe-Bagot	Johnson	Denise P.-Arsenault, Sec.-Trés., 379, 7e av, Ste-Hélène-de-Bagot J0H 1M0 – 514/791-2455, Fax: 514/791-2550
Ste-Hélène-de-Breakeyville (P)	3,246	Les Chutes-de-la-Chaudière	Lévis	Chutes-de-la-Chaudière	Jean-Guy Brassard, Sec.-Trés., 22, rue Ste-Hélène, Ste-Hélène-de-Breakeyville G0S 1E2 – 418/832-0356, Fax: 418/832-0358
Ste-Hélène-de-Mancebourg (P)	407	Abitibi-Ouest	Témiscamingue	Abitibi-Ouest	Sylvie Boutin-Bergeron, Sec.-Trés., 686, rang 1, Mancebourg J0Z 2T0 – 819/333-5766, Fax: 819/333-5766
Ste-Hénédine (P)	1,252	La Nouvelle-Beauce	Beauce	Beauce-Nord	Yvon Marcoux, Sec.-Trés., 111, rue Principale, CP 6, Ste-Hénédine G0S 2R0 – 418/935-7125, Fax: 418/935-7125
St-Henri (Mun.)	4,206	Desjardins	Lévis	Lévis	Jacques Risler, Sec.-Trés., 219, rue Commerciale, St-Henri-de-Lévis G0R 3E0 – 418/882-2401, Fax: 418/882-0302

Canadian Almanac & Directory 1997

Cities (Villes) in CAPITALS; Villages marked (V); Townships/Cantons marked (Canton);United townships/Cantons unis marked (Cantons); Parishes (Paroisses) marked (P); Municipalities marked (Mun.).; Northern villages/Villages nordiques marked (NV); Cree Villages/Villages Cris marked (VC); Naskapi Villages/Villages Naskapi marked (VN); In the third column, Urban Community/Communauté Urbaine marked Urb. Com. An in-depth listing for municipalities marked with * appears in Part 2 (check Index for page numbers).

MUNICIPALITY	1993 POP.	REGIONAL COUNTY MUN.	FEDERAL ELECTORAL DISTRICT	PROVINCIAL ELECTORAL DISTRICT	CONTACT PERSON WITH ADDRESS, PHONE & FAX
St-Henri-de-Taillon (Mun.)	730	Lac-St-Jean-Est	Lac-St-Jean	Lac-St-Jean	Léonard Dufour, Sec.-Trés., 401, rue de l'Hôtel-de-Ville, St-Henri-de-Taillon G0W 2X0 – 418/347-3243, Fax: 418/347-3243
St-Herménégilde (Mun.)	601	Coaticook	Mégantic-Compton-Stanstead	Mégantic-Compton	Céline Bessette-Dubois, Sec.-Trés., 776, rue Principale, St-Herménégilde J0B 2W0 – 819/849-4443, Fax: 819/849-4443
St-Hilaire-de-Dorset (P)	128	Beauce-Sartigan	Beauce	Beauce-Sud	Raymond Lamontagne, Sec.-Trés., 648, rue Principale, St-Hilaire-de-Dorset G0M 1G0 – 418/459-6872, Fax: 418/459-6872
St-Hilarion (P)	1,194	Charlevoix	Charlevoix	Charlevoix	Joseph Rochefort, Sec.-Trés., 215, ch Principale, St-Hilarion G0A 3V0 – 418/457-3463, Fax: 418/457-3463
St-Hippolyte (P)	5,136	La Rivière-du-Nord	Joliette	Bertrand	Yvon Veillette, Sec.-Trés., 2253, ch des Hauteurs, St-Hippolyte J0R 1P0 – 514/563-2505, Fax: 514/563-2362
St-Honoré (Mun.)	3,908	Le Fjord-du-Saguenay	Lac-St-Jean	Dubuc	Hugues Blackburn, Sec.-Trés., 3611, boul Martel, CP 250, St-Honoré G0V 1L0 – 418/673-3405, Fax: 418/673-3871
St-Honoré (Mun.)	864	Témiscouata	Rimouski-Témiscouata	Kamouraska-Témiscouata	Lucie April, Sec.-Trés., 99, rue Principale, CP 70, St-Honoré G0L 3K0 – 418/497-2588, Fax: 418/497-1656
St-Honoré (P)	768	Beauce-Sartigan	Beauce	Beauce-Sud	Francine Talbot, Sec.-Trés., 289, route de Shenley ouest, CP 249, St-Honoré G0M 1V0 – 418/485-6781, Fax: 418/485-6781
St-Hubert (P)	1,413	Rivière-du-Loup	Kamouraska-Rivière-du-Loup	Rivière-du-Loup	Lisette Claveau, Sec.-Trés., 4, ch Taché est, CP 218, St-Hubert G0L 3L0 – 418/497-3394, Fax: 418/497-1187
*ST-HUBERT	78,171 ('95)	Champlain	St-Hubert	Laporte; Vachon	Bernard Houle, Directeur, Sécretariat administratif et juridique, 5900, boul Cousineau, St-Hubert J3Y 7K8 – 514/445-7600, Fax: 514/445-7847
St-Hugues (Mun.)	1,343	Les Maskoutains	St-Hyacinthe-Bagot	St-Hyacinthe	Raymonde Gauvin, Sec.-Trés., 508, rue Notre-Dame, St-Hugues J0H 1N0 – 514/794-2030, Fax: 514/794-2474
ST-HYACINTHE	41,063 ('96)	Les Maskoutains	St-Hyacinthe-Bagot	St-Hyacinthe	Hélène Beauchesne, Gref., 700, av de l'Hôtel-de-Ville, CP 10, St-Hyacinthe J2S 5B2 – 514/778-8300, Fax: 514/778-8628
St-Hyacinthe-le-Confesseur (P)	1,202	Les Maskoutains	St-Hyacinthe-Bagot	St-Hyacinthe	Lise Lemonde, Sec.-Trés., 345, rue Mondor, St-Hyacinthe J2S 5A6 – 514/774-9666, Fax: 514/774-9666
St-Ignace-de-Loyola (P)	1,986	D'Autray	Berthier-Montcalm	Berthier	Fabrice Saint-Martin, Sec.-Trés., 25, rue Laforest, St-Ignace-de-Loyola J0K 2P0 – 514/836-3376, Fax: 514/836-1400
St-Ignace-de-Stanbridge (P)	748	Brome-Missisquoi	Brome-Missisquoi	Brome-Missisquoi	Monique Aubry-Santerre, Sec.-Trés., 678, rang de l'Église nord, St-Ignace-de-Stanbridge J0J 1Y0 – 514/296-4467, Fax: 514/296-4467
Ste-Irène (P)	362	La Matapédia	Matapédia-Matane	Matapédia	Lucie Desjardins, Sec.-Trés., 362, rue de la Fabrique, Ste-Irène G0J 2P0 – 418/629-5705, Fax: 418/629-5705
St-Irénée (P)	759	Charlevoix-Est	Charlevoix	Charlevoix	Marie-Claude Lavoie, Sec.-Trés., 128, rue Principale, CP 68, St-Irénée G0T 1V0 – 418/452-3231, Fax: 418/452-8221
St-Isidore (P)	2,621	Roussillon	Châteauguay	Châteauguay	Daniel Vinet, Sec.-Trés., 671, rue St-Régis, CP 240, St-Isidore J0L 2A0 – 514/454-3919, Fax: 514/454-7485
St-Isidore (Mun.)	2,621	La Nouvelle-Beauce	Beauce	Beauce-Nord	Nancy Labrecque, Sec.-Trés., 128, rte Coulombe, St-Isidore G0S 2S0 – 418/882-5670, Fax: 418/882-5902
St-Isidore-d'Auckland (Mun.)	633	Le Haut-St-François	Mégantic-Compton-Stanstead	Mégantic-Compton	Gaétan Perron, Sec.-Trés., 66, ch Auckland, St-Isidore-d'Auckland J0B 2X0 – 819/658-3637, Fax: 819/658-9070
St-Jacques (P)	1,738	Montcalm	Berthier-Montcalm	Joliette	See/Voir St-Jacques (V)
St-Jacques (V)	2,531	Montcalm	Berthier-Montcalm	Joliette	Gilles Sincerny, Sec.-Trés., 16, rue Maréchal, St-Jacques J0K 2R0 – 514/839-3671, Fax: 514/839-2387
St-Jacques-de-Horton (Mun.)	236	Arthabaska	Lotbinière	Richmond	Jean-Paul Fleurant, Sec.-Trés., 711, rue St-Antoine, Notre-Dame-du-Bon-Conseil J0C 1A0 – 819/336-5402
St-Jacques-de-Leeds (Mun.)	757	L'Amiante	Frontenac	Frontenac	Nathalie Laflamme, Sec.-Trés., 430, rue Principale, CP 9, Leeds G0N 1J0 – 418/424-3321, Fax: 418/424-3321
St-Jacques-le-Majeur-de-Causapscal (P)	700	La Matapédia	Matapédia-Matane	Matapédia	Jacques Tremblay, Sec.-Trés., 677, route 132 ouest, CP 400, Causapscal G0J 1J0 – 418/756-3996, Fax: 418/756-3996
St-Jacques-le-Majeur-de-Wolfeston (P)	205	L'Amiante	Richmond-Wolfe	Frontenac	Linda Bolduc, Sec.-Trés., 877, route 263, Saint-Jacques-le-Majeur G0N 1E0 – 418/449-1531

Canadian Almanac & Directory 1997

4-116 QUÉBEC MUNICIPALITIES

Cities (Villes) in CAPITALS; Villages marked (V); Townships/Cantons marked (Canton);United townships/Cantons unis marked (Cantons); Parishes (Paroisses) marked (P); Municipalities marked (Mun.).; Northern villages/Villages nordiques marked (NV); Cree Villages/Villages Cris marked (VC); Naskapi Villages/Villages Naskapi marked (VN); In the third column, Urban Community/Communauté Urbaine marked Urb. Com. An in-depth listing for municipalities marked with * appears in Part 2 (check Index for page numbers).

MUNICIPALITY	1993 POP.	REGIONAL COUNTY MUN.	FEDERAL ELECTORAL DISTRICT	PROVINCIAL ELECTORAL DISTRICT	CONTACT PERSON WITH ADDRESS, PHONE & FAX
St-Jacques-le-Mineur (P)	1,363	Les Jardins-de-Napierville	Châteauguay	St-Jean	Chantal Guinois, Sec.-Trés., 91, rue Principale, St-Jacques-le-Mineur J0J 1Z0 – 514/347-5446, Fax: 514/347-5754
St-Janvier-de-Joly (Mun.)	990	Lotbinière	Lotbinière	Lotbinière	Céline Biron, Sec.-Trés., 729, rue des Loisirs, CP 70, Joly G0S 1M0 – 418/728-2984, Fax: 418/728-2984
St-Jean (P)	869	L'Île-d'Orléans	St-Jean	Montmorency	Roch Lemieux, Sec.-Trés., 2336, ch Royal, St-Jean G0A 3W0 – 418/829-2206, Fax: 418/829-2206
St-Jean-Baptiste (Mun.)	777	La Mitis	Matapédia-Matane	Matapédia	Madeleine Roy, Sec.-Trés., 251, ch du Sanatorium, Mont-Joli G5H 1V6 – 418/775-8678, Fax: 418/775-8566
St-Jean-Baptiste (P)	3,099	Rouville	St-Hyacinthe-Bagot	Borduas	Denis Meunier, Sec.-Trés., 3100, rue Principale, St-Jean-Baptiste J0L 2B0 – 514/467-3456, Fax: 514/467-8813
St-Jean-Baptiste-de-l'Isle-Verte (Mun.)	615	Rivière-du-Loup	Charlevoix	Rivière-du-Loup	Léonard Dion, Sec.-Trés., 141, rue St-Jean-Baptiste, CP 248, L'Isle-Verte G0L 1K0 – 418/898-3284, Fax: 418/898-2788
St-Jean-Baptiste-de-Nicolet (P)	2,806	Nicolet-Yamaska	Richelieu	Nicolet-Yamaska	Sylvie Provencher, Sec.-Trés., 525, rte du Port, St-Jean-Baptiste-de-Nicolet J3T 1W3 – 819/293-6161, Fax: 819/293-6616
St-Jean-Chrysostome (P)	1,765	Le Haut-St-Laurent	Beauharnois-Salaberry	Beauharnois-Huntingdon	Céline Ouimet, Sec.-Trés., 124, rang Notre-Dame, CP 70, St-Chrysostome J0S 1R0 – 514/826-3911, Fax: 514/826-0568
ST-JEAN-CHRYSOSTOME	13,764	Les Chutes-de-la-Chaudière	Lévis	Chutes-de-la-Chaudière	Jacques Leblond, Gref., 959, rue de l'Hôtel-de-Ville, St-Jean-Chrysostome G6Z 2N8 – 418/839-9417, Fax: 418/839-4244
St-Jean-de-Brébeuf (Mun.)	419	L'Amiante	Frontenac	Frontenac	Solange Bolduc-Dostie, Sec.-Trés., 344, ch Craig, St-Jean-de-Brébeuf G6G 5R5 – 418/453-7774, Fax: 418/453-2339
St-Jean-de-Cherbourg (P)	229	Matane	Matapédia-Matane	Matane	Jacinthe Imbeault, Sec.-Trés., 121, 8e rang ouest, St-Jean-de-Cherbourg G0J 2R0 – 418/733-4716, Fax: 418/733-4716
St-Jean-de-Dieu (Mun.)	1,943	Les Basques	Kamouraska-Rivière-du-Loup	Rivière-du-Loup	Normand Morency, Sec.-Trés., 32, rue Principale sud, St-Jean-de-Dieu G0L 3M0 – 418/963-3529, Fax: 418/963-2903
St-Jean-de-la-Lande (Mun.)	363	Témiscouata	Rimouski-Témiscouata	Kamouraska-Témiscouata	Francine Dubé, Sec.-Trés., 810A, rue Principale, St-Jean-de-la-Lande G0L 3N0 – 418/853-3475, Fax: 418/853-3703
St-Jean-de-la-Lande (P)	675	Beauce-Sartigan	Beauce	Beauce-Sud	Claudette Deschénes, Sec.-Trés., 600, rue Principale, St-Jean-de-la-Lande G0M 1E0 – 418/227-4363, Fax: 418/227-9266
St-Jean-de-Matha (Mun.)	3,517	Matawinie	Berthier-Montcalm	Berthier	D. Nicole Archambault, Sec.-Trés., 170, rue Ste-Louise, CP 60, St-Jean-de-Matha J0K 2S0 – 514/886-3867, Fax: 514/886-3398
St-Jean-des-Piles (P)	608	Le Centre-de-la-Mauricie	St-Maurice	Laviolette	Maryse Flageole, Sec.-Trés., 1594, rue Principale, St-Jean des Piles G0X 2V0 – 819/538-3829, Fax: 819/538-3155
St-Jean-Port-Joli (Mun.)	3,414	L'Islet	Bellechasse	Montmagny-L'Islet	Denis Gaudreault, Sec.-Trés., 7, Place de l'Église, CP 488, St-Jean-Port-Joli G0R 3G0 – 418/598-3084, Fax: 418/598-3085
ST-JEAN-SUR-RICHELIEU	39,724	Le Haut-Richelieu	St-Jean	St-Jean	Jacques Jutras, Gref., 188, rue Jacques-Cartier nord, CP 1025, St-Jean-sur-Richelieu J3B 7B2 – 514/357-2100, Fax: 514/357-2285
Ste-Jeanne-d'Arc (P)	378	La Mitis	Matapédia-Matane	Matapédia	Madeleine Lévesque, Sec.-Trés., 205, rue Principale, CP 40, Ste-Jeanne-d'Arc G0J 2T0 – 418/776-5660, Fax: 418/776-5660
Ste-Jeanne-d'Arc (V)	1,142	Maria-Chapdelaine	Roberval	Roberval	Régis Martin, Sec.-Trés., 378, rue François-Bilodeau, CP 39, Ste-Jeanne-d'Arc G0W 1E0 – 418/276-3166, Fax: 418/276-7648
Ste-Jeanne-de-Pont-Rouge (Mun.)	2,188	Portneuf	Portneuf	Portneuf	Line Morasse, Sec.-Trés., 17, rue du College, CP 638, Pont-Rouge G0A 2X0 – 418/873-4243, Fax: 418/873-3870
ST-JÉRÔME	25,574	La Rivière-du-Nord	Laurentides	Prévost	Louise Pepin, Gref., 280, rue Labelle, St-Jérôme J7Z 5L1 – 514/436-1511, Fax: 514/436-6626
St-Jérôme-de-Matane (P)	1,183	Matane	Matapédia-Matane	Matane	Cécile Dion, Sec.-Trés., 378, av St-Jérôme, Matane G4W 3B2 – 418/562-2548, Fax: 418/562-2548
St-Joachim (P)	1,552	La Côte-de-Beaupré	Beauport-Montmorency-Orléans	Charlevoix	Danielle Paré-Lessard, Sec.-Trés., 172, rue de l'Église, St-Joachim G0A 3X0 – 418/827-3755, Fax: 418/827-8574

Canadian Almanac & Directory 1997

Cities (Villes) in CAPITALS; Villages marked (V); Townships/Cantons marked (Canton);United townships/Cantons unis marked (Cantons); Parishes (Paroisses) marked (P); Municipalities marked (Mun.).; Northern villages/Villages nordiques marked (NV); Cree Villages/Villages Cris marked (VC); Naskapi Villages/Villages Naskapi marked (VN); In the third column, Urban Community/Communauté Urbaine marked Urb. Com. An in-depth listing for municipalities marked with * appears in Part 2 (check Index for page numbers).

MUNICIPALITY	1993 POP.	REGIONAL COUNTY MUN.	FEDERAL ELECTORAL DISTRICT	PROVINCIAL ELECTORAL DISTRICT	CONTACT PERSON WITH ADDRESS, PHONE & FAX
St-Joachim-de-Courval (P)	670	Drummond	Drummond	Nicolet-Yamaska	Monique-M. Richard, Sec.-Trés., 550, rue Principale, St-Joachim-de-Courval J0C 1H0 – 819/397-2334, Fax: 819/397-4648
St-Joachim-de-Shefford (P)	1,172	La Haute-Yamaska	Shefford	Shefford	Réal Pitt, Sec.-Trés., 567, 1er rang ouest, St-Joachim-de-Shefford J0E 2G0 – 514/539-3201, Fax: 514/539-3145
St-Joseph-de-Beauce (P)	1,184	Robert-Cliche	Beauce	Beauce-Nord	Jean-Louis Lessard, Sec.-Trés., 289, rte 276, St-Joseph-de-Beauce G0S 2V0 – 418/397-5858, Fax: 418/397-4390
ST-JOSEPH-DE-BEAUCE	3,245	Robert-Cliche	Beauce	Beauce-Nord	Hélène Renaud, Sec.-Trés., 843, av du Palais, CP 850, St-Joseph-de-Beauce G0S 2V0 – 418/397-4358, Fax: 418/397-5715
St-Joseph-de-Blandford (P)	486	Bécancour	Lotbinière	Lotbinière	Mario Geoffroy, Sec.-Trés., 200, rue Roux, CP 200, Manseau G0X 1V0 – 819/356-2450, Fax: 819/356-2721
St-Joseph-de-Cléricy (Mun.)	535	Rouyn-Noranda	Témiscamingue	Rouyn-Noranda-Témiscamingue	Charlène Ferron, Sec.-Trés., 931, rue du Souvenir, Clericy J0Z 1P0 – 819/637-2131, Fax: 819/637-2133
St-Joseph-de-Coleraine (Mun.)	1,811	L'Amiante	Frontenac	Frontenac	Eloy Gravel, Sec.-Trés., 88, rue St-Patrick, CP 40, Coleraine G0N 1B0 – 418/423-4000, Fax: 418/423-4150
St-Joseph-de-Ham-Sud (P)	237	Asbestos	Richmond-Wolfe	Richmond	Monique Polard, Sec.-Trés., 9, ch Gosford sud, St-Joseph-de-Ham-Sud J0B 3J0 – 819/877-3258, Fax: 819/877-5121
St-Joseph-de-Kamouraska (P)	440	Kamouraska	Kamouraska-Rivière-du-Loup	Kamouraska-Témiscouata	Ginette Castonguay, Sec.-Trés., 161, 5e rang est, St-Joseph-de-Kamouraska G0L 3P0 – 418/493-2214, Fax: 418/493-2214
St-Joseph-de-la-Pointe-de-Lévy (P)	859	Desjardins	Lévis	Lévis	Michel Blais, Sec.-Trés., 910, rte Mgr Bourget, St-Joseph-de-la-Pointe-de-Lévy G6V 6N4 – 418/833-3882, Fax: 418/833-7895
St-Joseph-de-la-Rive (V)	227	Charlevoix	Charlevoix	Charlevoix	Nicole Girard, Sec.-Trés., 183, rue des Saules, CP 39, St-Joseph-de-la-Rive G0A 3Y0 – 418/635-2742, Fax: 418/635-2742
St-Joseph-de-Lanoraie (P)	1,698	D'Autray	Berthier-Montcalm	Berthier	Michel Dufort, Sec.-Trés., 361, rue Notre-Dame, CP 400, Lanoraie J0K 1E0 – 514/887-2381, Fax: 514/887-7593
St-Joseph-de-Lepage (P)	611	La Mitis	Matapédia-Matane	Matapédia	Renée Roy, Sec.-Trés., 70, rue de la Rivière, Mont-Joli G5H 3N8 – 418/775-4171, Fax: 418/775-3004
St-Joseph-de-Maskinongé (P)	1,272	Maskinongé	Berthier-Montcalm	Maskinongé	Gisèle Lemyre, Sec.-Trés., 154, rte 138, St-Joseph-de-Maskinongé J0K 1N0 – 819/227-2243, Fax: 819/227-2097
ST-JOSEPH-DE-SOREL	2,126	Le Bas-Richelieu	Richelieu	Richelieu	Martin Valois, Sec.-Trés., 700, rue Montcalm, St-Joseph-de-Sorel J3R 1C9 – 514/742-3744, Fax: 514/742-1315
St-Joseph-des-Érables (Mun.)	455	Robert-Cliche	Beauce	Beauce-Nord	Raymonde Tardif, Sec.-Trés., 224, route des Fermes, St-Joseph-de-Beauce G0S 2V0 – 418/397-6617
St-Joseph-du-Lac (P)	4,788	Deux-Montagne	Argenteuil-Papineau	Deux-Montagnes	Fernand Larocque, Sec.-Trés., 1110, ch Principal, St-Joseph-du-Lac J0N 1M0 – 514/623-1072, Fax: 514/623-2889
St-Jovite (P)	1,382	Les Laurentides	Laurentides	Labelle	François Perreault, Sec.-Trés., 75, ch Napoléon, St-Jovite J0T 2H0 – 819/425-8641, Fax: 819/425-9414
ST-JOVITE	4,461	Les Laurentides	Laurentides	Labelle	Lise Julien, Sec.-Trés., 1145, rue Ouimet, CP 159, St-Jovite J0T 2H0 – 819/425-8614, Fax: 819/425-9247
St-Jude (P)	1,186	Les Maskoutains	St-Hyacinthe-Bagot	Richelieu	Francine Gilbert, Sec.-Trés., 940, rue du Centre, St-Jude J0H 1P0 – 514/792-3855, Fax: 514/792-3828
St-Jules (Mun.)	391	Bonaventure	Bonaventure-Îles-de-la-Madeleine	Bonaventure	Susan Legouffe, Sec.-Trés., 55, route Gallagher, Saint-Jules G0C 1T0 – 418/392-4042, Fax: 418/392-4042
St-Jules (P)	568	Robert-Cliche	Beauce	Beauce-Nord	Maurice Cloutier, Sec.-Trés., 390, route Principale, St-Jules G0N 1R0 – 418/397-5444, Fax: 418/397-5444
Ste-Julie (Mun.)	720	L'Érable	Frontenac	Lotbinière	Danielle B.-Bilodeau, Sec.-Trés., 140, rue Grenier, Laurierville G0S 1P0 – 819/365-4200, Fax: 819/365-4200
STE-JULIE	22,097 ('94)	Lajemmerais	Verchères	Marguerite-D'Youville	Brigitte Boisvert, Sec.-Trés., 1580, ch du Fer-à-Cheval, Ste-Julie J3E 1Y2 – 514/922-7111, Fax: 514/922-7108
St-Julien (P)	430	L'Amiante	Richmond-Wolfe	Frontenac	Raymonde Gouin, Sec.-Trés., 2409, 2e rang est, St-Julien G0N 1B0 – 418/423-4525, Fax: 418/423-4525
Ste-Julienne (P)	6,856	Montcalm	Berthier-Montcalm	Rousseau	Jimmy L. Laveaux, Sec.-Trés., 1400, route 125, CP 250, Ste-Julienne J0K 2T0 – 514/831-2688, Fax: 514/831-4433

Canadian Almanac & Directory 1997

4-118 QUÉBEC MUNICIPALITIES

Cities (Villes) in CAPITALS; Villages marked (V); Townships/Cantons marked (Canton);United townships/Cantons unis marked (Cantons); Parishes (Paroisses) marked (P); Municipalities marked (Mun.).; Northern villages/Villages nordiques marked (NV); Cree Villages/Villages Cris marked (VC); Naskapi Villages/Villages Naskapi marked (VN); In the third column, Urban Community/Communauté Urbaine marked Urb. Com. An in-depth listing for municipalities marked with * appears in Part 2 (check Index for page numbers).

MUNICIPALITY	1993 POP.	REGIONAL COUNTY MUN.	FEDERAL ELECTORAL DISTRICT	PROVINCIAL ELECTORAL DISTRICT	CONTACT PERSON WITH ADDRESS, PHONE & FAX
St-Just-de-Bretenières (Mun.)	943	Montmagny	Bellechasse	Montmagny-L'Islet	Isabelle Simard, Sec.-Trés., 250, rue Principale, CP 40, St-Just-de-Bretenières G0R 3H0 – 418/244-3637, Fax: 418/244-3637
St-Juste-du-Lac (Mun.)	654	Témiscouata	Rimouski-Témiscouata	Kamouraska-Témiscouata	Nicole Dubé-Chouinard, Sec.-Trés., 28, ch Principale, CP 38, St-Juste-du-Lac G0L 3R0 – 418/899-2855, Fax: 418/899-2938
St-Justin (P)	1,195	Maskinongé	Berthier-Montcalm	Maskinongé	Raymonde Baril, Sec.-Trés., 1281, rue Gérin, St-Justin J0K 2V0 – 819/227-2838, Fax: 819/227-4876
Ste-Justine (Mun.)	1,932	Les Etchemins	Bellechasse	Bellechasse	Gilles Vézina, Sec.-Trés., 167, rte 204, CP 10, Ste-Justine G0R 1Y0 – 418/383-5397, Fax: 418/383-5398
Ste-Justine-de-Newton (P)	1,005	Vaudreuil-Soulanges	Vaudreuil	Vaudreuil	Denis Perrier, Sec.-Trés., 2627, rue Principale, CP 28, Ste-Justine-de-Newton J0P 1T0 – 514/764-3573, Fax: 514/764-3180
St-Lambert (P)	310	Abitibi-Ouest	Témiscamingue	Abitibi-Ouest	Nicole Garant, Sec.-Trés., RR#1, Des Méloizes J0Z 1V0 – 819/788-2491
ST-LAMBERT	22,148	Champlain	La Prairie	Laporte	Louise Grégoire-Marsh, Gref., 55, rue Argyle, St-Lambert J4P 2H3 – 514/672-4444, Fax: 514/672-3732
St-Lambert-de-Lauzon (P)	4,485	Les Chutes-de-la-Chaudière	Lévis	Chutes-de-la-Chaudière	Magdalen Blanchet, Sec.-Trés., 1200, rue du Pont, CP 160, St-Lambert-de-Lévis G0S 2W0 – 418/889-9715, Fax: 418/889-0660
St-Laurent (P)	1,612	L'Île-d'Orléans	Beauport-Montmorency-Orléans	Montmorency	Claudette Pouliot, Sec.-Trés., 1430, ch Royale, St-Laurent G0A 3Z0 – 418/828-2322, Fax: 418/828-2170
*SAINT-LAURENT	73,358 ('94)	Montréal (Urb. Com.)	St-Laurent-Cartierville	Acadie; St-Laurent	Édith Baron-Lafrenière, Gref., 777, boul Marcel-Laurin, Saint-Laurent H4M 2M7 – 514/855-6000, Fax: 514/855-5999
St-Lazare (P)	9,846	Vaudreuil-Soulanges	Vaudreuil	Vaudreuil	Gaétan Prévost, Sec.-Trés., 1960, ch Ste-Angelique, CP 360, St-Lazare J0P 1V0 – 514/424-8000, Fax: 514/455-4712
St-Lazare-de-Bellechasse (Mun.)	1,310	Bellechasse	Bellechasse	Bellechasse	Richard Côté, Sec.-Trés., 114, rue Leroux, CP 159, St-Lazare-de-Bellechasse G0R 3J0 – 418/883-3841, Fax: 418/883-2551
St-Léandre (P)	394	Matane	Matapédia-Matane	Matane	Carmen Laderoute, Sec.-Trés., 3025, rue Principale, St-Léandre G0J 2V0 – 418/737-4973, Fax: 418/737-4973
St-Léon-de-Standon (P)	1,279	Bellechasse	Bellechasse	Bellechasse	Gérald Patry, Sec.-Trés., 100A, rue St-Pierre, CP 130, St-Léon-de-Standon G0R 4L0 – 418/642-5034, Fax: 418/642-2570
St-Léon-le-Grand (P)	1,141	La Matapédia	Matapédia-Matane	Matapédia	Suzanne Poirier, Sec.-Trés., 277, rue Plourde, CP 188, St-Léon-le-Grand G0J 2W0 – 418/743-2914, Fax: 418/743-2914
St-Léon-le-Grand (P)	957	Maskinongé	Berthier-Montcalm	Maskinongé	Gabrielle Lampron, Sec.-Trés., 49, rue de la Fabrique, St-Léon-le-Grand J0K 2W0 – 819/228-3236, Fax: 819/228-8088
*ST-LÉONARD	74,083 ('94)	Montréal (Urb. Com.)	St-Léonard	Jeanne-Mance; Viger	Georges Larivée, Gref., 8400, boul Lacordaire, St-Léonard H1R 3B1 – 514/328-8400, Fax: 514/328-8479
St-Léonard-d'Aston (Mun.)	2,316	Nicolet-Yamaska	Drummond	Nicolet-Yamaska	Ginette L.-Richard, Sec.-Trés., 370, rue Principale, CP 520, St-Léonard-d'Aston J0C 1M0 – 819/399-2596, Fax: 819/399-2333
St-Léonard-de-Portneuf (Mun.)	1,108	Portneuf	Portneuf	Portneuf	Eddy Alain, Sec.-Trés., 260, rue Pettigrew, St-Léonard-de-Portneuf G0A 4A0 – 418/337-6741, Fax: 418/337-6742
St-Liboire (Mun.)	2,393	Les Maskoutains	St-Hyacinthe-Bagot	St-Hyacinthe	Denise Breton, Sec.-Trés., 121, rue Paquette, CP 120, St-Liboire J0H 1R0 – 514/793-2811, Fax: 514/793-4428
St-Liguori (P)	1,693	Montcalm	Berthier-Montcalm	Joliette	Gilles Fredette, Sec.-Trés., 750, rue Principale, St-Liguori J0K 2X0 – 514/753-3570, Fax: 514/753-4638
St-Lin (Mun.)	7,571	Montcalm	Joliette	Rousseau	Linda Duquette, Sec.-Trés., 250, 12e av, CP 220, Laurentides J0R 1C0 – 514/439-3130, Fax: 514/439-1525
St-Louis (P)	742	Les Maskoutains	Richelieu	Richelieu	Jocelyne Brouillard, Sec.-Trés., 765B, rue St-Joseph, St-Louis J0G 1K0 – 514/788-2631, Fax: 514/788-2231
St-Louis-de-Blandford (P)	850	Arthabaska	Lotbinière	Lotbinière	Danielle B.-Bédard, Sec.-Trés., 80, rue Principale, CP 140, St-Louis de Blandford G0Z 1B0 – 819/364-7007, Fax: 819/364-2781
ST-LOUIS-DE-FRANCE	7,016	Francheville	Champlain	Champlain	Gilles Toupin, Gref., 100, rue de la Mairie, St-Louis-de-France G8W 1S1 – 819/374-6550, Fax: 819/374-0659
St-Louis-de-Gonzague (Mun.)	497	Les Etchemins	Beauce	Bellechasse	Colombe Bilodeau, Sec.-Trés., 103, rue de l'Église, Ravignan G0R 2L0 – 418/267-5931, Fax: 418/267-5930

Canadian Almanac & Directory 1997

Cities (Villes) in CAPITALS; Villages marked (V); Townships/Cantons marked (Canton);United townships/Cantons unis marked (Cantons); Parishes (Paroisses) marked (P); Municipalities marked (Mun.).; Northern villages/Villages nordiques marked (NV); Cree Villages/Villages Cris marked (VC); Naskapi Villages/Villages Naskapi marked (VN); In the third column, Urban Community/Communauté Urbaine marked Urb. Com. An in-depth listing for municipalities marked with * appears in Part 2 (check Index for page numbers).

MUNICIPALITY	1993 POP.	REGIONAL COUNTY MUN.	FEDERAL ELECTORAL DISTRICT	PROVINCIAL ELECTORAL DISTRICT	CONTACT PERSON WITH ADDRESS, PHONE & FAX
St-Louis-de-Gonzague (P)	1,462	Beauharnois-Salaberry	Beauharnois-Salaberry	Salaberry-Soulanges	Micheline J.-Carrière, Sec.-Trés., 140, rue Principale, CP 99, St-Louis-de-Gonzague J0S 1T0 – 514/371-0523, Fax: 514/371-6229
St-Louis-de-Gonzague-du-Cap-Tourmente (P)	5	La Côte-de-Beaupré	Beauport-Montmorency-Orléans	Charlevoix	Roberge Jacques, Administrateur, 1, rue des Remparts, Québec G1R 5L7 – 418/692-3981, Fax: 418/692-4345
St-Louis-du-Ha!-Ha! (P)	1,513	Témiscouata	Rimouski-Témiscouata	Kamouraska-Témiscouata	Gratien Ouellet, Sec.-Trés., 95, rue St-Charles, St-Louis-du-Ha!-Ha! G0L 3S0 – 418/854-2260, Fax: 418/854-0717
Ste-Louise (P)	847	L'Islet	Kamouraska-Rivière-du-Loup	Kamouraska-Témiscouata	Ghislain Lizotte, Sec.-Trés., 80, rte de la Station, Ste-Louise G0R 3K0 – 418/354-2509, Fax: 418/354-7730
St-Luc (P)	912	Matane	Matapédia-Matane	Matane	Guylaine Labrie, Sec.-Trés., #100, 3, rue de l'Église, St-Luc-de-Matane G0J 2X0 – 418/562-2916, Fax: 418/562-8754
St-Luc (P)	568	Les Etchemins	Bellechasse	Bellechasse	Lorette S.-Jolin, Sec.-Trés., 230A, rue Principale, St-Luc G0R 1L0 – 418/636-2176, Fax: 418/636-2176
ST-LUC	15,856	Le Haut-Richelieu	St-Jean	St-Jean	Lise Bigonesse, Gref.è., 347, boul St-Luc, St-Luc J2W 2A2 – 514/348-7348, Fax: 514/348-5889
St-Luc-de-Vincennes (Mun.)	640	Francheville	Champlain	Champlain	Rita Massicotte, Sec.-Trés., 600, rue Principale, CP 450, St-Luc-de-Vincennes G0X 3K0 – 819/295-3782, Fax: 819/295-3782
Ste-Luce (P)	1,367	La Mitis	Rimouski-Témiscouata	Matapédia	Gaétan Ross, Sec.-Trés., 1, rue Langlois, CP 40, Ste-Luce G0K 1P0 – 418/739-4317, Fax: 418/739-4823
Ste-Lucie-de-Beauregard (Mun.)	404	Montmagny	Bellechasse	Montagny-L'Islet	Yvon Leclerc, Sec.-Trés., 146, rue Principale, Ste-Lucie-de-Beauregard G0R 3L0 – 418/223-3122, Fax: 418/223-3122
Ste-Lucie-des-Laurentides (Mun.)	965	Les Laurentides	Laurentides	Bertrand	Monique Paiement, Sec.-Trés., 2057, 10e rue, Ste-Lucie-des-Laurentides J0T 2J0 – 819/326-3198, Fax: 819/326-0592
St-Lucien (P)	1,208	Drummond	Drummond	Richmond	Louise Tessier, Sec.-Trés., 5350, route 255, St-Lucien J0C 1N0 – 819/397-4679, Fax: 819/397-4679
St-Ludger (V)	183	Le Granit	Beauce	Beauce-Sud	Ghislaine Poulin-Duquette, Sec.-Trés., 158, rue des Fleurs, CP 24, St-Ludger G0M 1W0 – 819/548-5843
St-Ludger-de-Milot (Mun.)	741	Lac-St-Jean-Est	Roberval	Lac-St-Jean	Rita Ouellet, Sec.-Trés., 739, rue Gaudreault, CP 9, St-Ludger-de-Milot G0W 2B0 – 418/373-2266, Fax: 418/373-2554
Ste-Madeleine (V)	1,944	Les Maskoutains	St-Hyacinthe-Bagot	Verchères	Sylvie Fréchette, Sec.-Trés., 850, rue St-Simon, CP 30, Ste-Madeleine J0H 1S0 – 514/795-3822, Fax: 514/795-3736
Ste-Madeleine-de-la-Rivière-Madeleine (Mun.)	537	Denis-Riverin	Gaspé	Gaspé	Martine Fournier, Sec.-Trés., 142, rte Principale, Madeleine-Centre G0E 1P0 – 418/393-2428, Fax: 418/393-2869
St-Magloire-de-Bellechasse (Mun.)	882	Les Etchemins	Bellechasse	Bellechasse	Irène Mercier, Sec.-Trés., 130, rue Principale, CP 40, St-Magloire G0R 3M0 – 418/257-4421, Fax: 418/257-4421
St-Majorique-de-Grantham (P)	918	Drummond	Drummond	Drummond	Colette Tessier, Sec.-Trés., 1966, boul St-Joseph ouest, RR#5, Saint-Majorique-de-Grantham J2B 8A8 – 819/478-7058, Fax: 819/478-8479
St-Malachie (P)	1,219	Bellechasse	Bellechasse	Bellechasse	Hélène Bissonnette, Sec.-Trés., 610, 7e rue, CP 99, St-Malachie G0R 3N0 – 418/642-2102, Fax: 418/642-2231
St-Malachie-d'Ormstown (P)	2,186	Le Haut-St-Laurent	Beauharnois-Salaberry	Beauharnois-Huntingdon	Jean-Claude Marcil, Sec.-Trés., 81, rue Lambton, Ormstown J0S 1K0 – 514/829-2625, Fax: 514/829-4162
St-Malo (Mun.)	428	Le Haut-St-François	Mégantic-Compton-Stanstead	Mégantic-Compton	Jean-Paul Roy, Sec.-Trés., 116A, rue Principale, St-Malo J0B 2Y0 – 819/658-3556, Fax: 819/658-9010
St-Marc-de-Figuery (P)	594	Abitibi	Abitibi	Abitibi-Ouest	Aline Guénette, Sec.-Trés., 10, av Michaud, CP 12, St-Marc-de-Figuery J0Y 1J0 – 819/732-8501, Fax: 819/732-8501
St-Marc-des-Carrières (V)	3,169	Portneuf	Portneuf	Portneuf	Maryon Leclerc, Sec.-Trés., 965, av Bona Dussault, CP 157, St-Marc-des-Carrières G0A 4B0 – 418/268-3862, Fax: 418/268-8776
St-Marc-du-Lac-Long (P)	521	Témiscouata	Rimouski-Témiscouata	Kamouraska-Témiscouata	Claudette Beaulieu, Sec.-Trés., 12, rue de l'Église, St-Marc-du-Lac-Long G0L 1T0 – 418/893-2643, Fax: 418/893-7228
St-Marc-sur-Richelieu (Mun.)	1,959	Le Vallée-du-Richelieu	Verchères	Verchères	Sylvie Burelle, Sec.-Trés., 102, rue de la Fabrique, St-Marc-sur-Richelieu J0L 2E0 – 514/584-2258, Fax: 514/584-2795
St-Marcel (Mun.)	517	L'Islet	Bellechasse	Montmagny-L'Islet	Angèle Bélanger, Sec.-Trés., 48, rue Taché est, CP 10, St-Marcel-de-L'Islet G0R 3R0 – 418/356-2691, Fax: 418/356-2820

4-120 QUÉBEC MUNICIPALITIES

Cities (Villes) in CAPITALS; Villages marked (V); Townships/Cantons marked (Canton);United townships/Cantons unis marked (Cantons); Parishes (Paroisses) marked (P); Municipalities marked (Mun.).; Northern villages/Villages nordiques marked (NV); Cree Villages/Villages Cris marked (VC); Naskapi Villages/Villages Naskapi marked (VN); In the third column, Urban Community/Communauté Urbaine marked Urb. Com. An in-depth listing for municipalities marked with * appears in Part 2 (check Index for page numbers).

MUNICIPALITY	1993 POP.	REGIONAL COUNTY MUN.	FEDERAL ELECTORAL DISTRICT	PROVINCIAL ELECTORAL DISTRICT	CONTACT PERSON WITH ADDRESS, PHONE & FAX
St-Marcel-de-Richelieu (Mun.)	643	Les Maskoutains	St-Hyacinthe-Bagot; Richelieu	Nicolet-Yamaska	Sylvie Viens, Sec.-Trés., 500, rue de l'École, St-Marcel-de-Richelieu J0H 1T0 – 514/794-2832, Fax: 514/794-1140
St-Marcellin (P)	304	Rimouski-Neigette	Rimouski-Témiscouata	Rimouski	Brigitte Couturier, Sec.-Trés., 337, rte 234, St-Marcellin G0K 1R0 – 418/798-4382, Fax: 418/798-4382
Ste-Marcelline-de-Kildare (Mun.)	1,187	Matawinie	Berthier-Montcalm	Joliette	Micheline Miron, Sec.-Trés., 435 - 1re av, Pied-de-la-Montagne, Ste-Marcelline J0K 2Y0 – 514/883-2241, Fax: 514/883-2242
Ste-Marguerite (Mun.)	258	La Matapédia	Matapédia-Matane	Matapédia	Odette Corbin, Sec.-Trés., 15, rte de La Vérendrye, Ste-Marguerite-Marie G0J 2Y0 – 418/756-3364, Fax: 418/756-3364
Ste-Marguerite (P)	1,002	La Nouvelle-Beauce	Beauce	Beauce-Nord	Jacqueline Giroux, Sec.-Trés., 235, rue St-Jacques, Ste-Marguerite G0S 2X0 – 418/935-7103, Fax: 418/935-3709
Ste-Marguerite-du-Lac-Masson (P)	1,701	Les Pays-d'en-Haut	Laurentides	Bertrand	Pierre Landreville, Sec.-Trés., 414, boul Baron-Empain, CP 180, Lac Masson J0T 1L0 – 514/228-2543, Fax: 514/228-4008
STE-MARIE	10,862 ('94)	La Nouvelle-Beauce	Beauce	Beauce-Nord	Benoît Fecteau, Gref., 270, av Marguerite-Bourgeois, CP 1750, Ste-Marie G6E 3C7 – 418/387-2301, Fax: 418/387-2454
Ste-Marie-de-Blandford (Mun.)	507	Bécancour	Lotbinière	Lotbinière	Josée Charest, Sec.-Trés., 473, rue des Bosquets, Ste-Marie-de-Blandford G0X 2W0 – 819/283-2127, Fax: 819/283-2127
Ste-Marie-de-Monnoir (P)	2,311	Rouville	Shefford	Iberville	Francine Guertin, Sec.-Trés., 146, ch Ruisseau-Barré, Ste-Marie-de-Monnoir J3M 1P2 – 514/460-2251, Fax: 514/460-4532
Ste-Marie-Madeleine (P)	2,188	Les Maskoutains	St-Hyacinthe-Bagot	Verchères	Sylvie McDuff, Sec.-Trés., 3541, boul Laurier, Ste-Marie-Madeleine J0H 1S0 – 514/795-6272, Fax: 514/795-3180
Ste-Marie-Salomé (P)	1,254	Montcalm	Joliette	Joliette	Gérard Martin, Sec.-Trés., 690, ch St-Jean, Ste-Marie-Salomé J0K 2Z0 – 514/839-6212, Fax: 514/839-6106
Ste-Marthe (Mun.)	1,147	Vaudreuil-Soulanges	Vaudreuil	Vaudreuil	Josée Lalonde, Sec.-Trés., 776, rue des Loisirs, Ste-Marthe J0P 1W0 – 514/459-4284, Fax: 514/459-4627
Ste-Marthe-du-Cap (Mun.)	6,028	Francheville	Champlain	Champlain	Marcel Milot, Sec.-Trés., 1001, rang St-Malo, CP 158, Ste-Marthe-du-Cap G8T 7W2 – 819/378-5949, Fax: 819/378-0561
STE-MARTHE-SUR-LE-LAC	8,232	Deux-Montagnes	Blainville-Deux-Montagnes	Deux-Montagnes	Vacant, Gref.è, 3000, ch Oka, Ste-Marthe-sur-le-Lac J0N 1P0 – 514/472-7310, Fax: 514/472-4283
St-Martin (P)	2,502	Beauce-Sartigan	Laval-Centre	Beauce-Sud	Carmelle Veilleux, Sec.-Trés., 1, 1e av est, CP 99, St-Martin G0M 1B0 – 418/382-5035, Fax: 418/382-5035
Ste-Martine (Mun.)	2,304	Beauharnois-Salaberry	Beauharnois-Salaberry	Beauharnois-Huntingdon	Claudette Lefebvre-Dubuc, Sec.-Trés., 3, rue des Copains, Ste-Martine J0S 1V0 – 514/427-3050, Fax: 514/427-7331
St-Mathias-sur-Richelieu (Mun.)	3,729	Rouville	Chambly	Chambly	Normande Vigeant, Sec.-Trés., 37, ch des Épinettes, St-Mathias-sur-Richelieu J3L 5Z7 – 514/658-2841, Fax: 514/447-1416
St-Mathieu (Mun.)	1,861	Roussillon	Châteauguay	La Prairie	Francine Fleurent, Sec.-Trés., 299, ch Saint-Édouard, St-Mathieu J0L 2H0 – 514/632-9528, Fax: 514/632-9544
St-Mathieu (P)	1,118	Le Centre-de-la-Mauricie	Kamouraska-Rivière-du-Loup	St-Maurice	Hélène Richard-Chateauvert, Sec.-Trés., 561, ch Déziel, St-Mathieu-du-Parc G0X 1N0 – 819/532-2205, Fax: 819/532-2415
St-Mathieu-de-Beloeil (P)	2,060	La Vallée-du-Richelieu	Verchères	Borduas	Monique Beaudry, Sec.-Trés., 5000, rue des Loisirs, St-Mathieu-de-Beloeil J3G 2C9 – 514/467-7490, Fax: 514/467-2999
St-Mathieu-de-Rioux (P)	576	Les Basques	Kamouraska-Rivière-du-Loup	Rimouski	Michelle Lafontaine, Sec.-Trés., 224A, rue de l'Église, CP 40, St-Mathieu-de-Rioux G0L 3T0 – 418/738-2953, Fax: 418/738-2454
St-Mathieu-d'Harricana (Mun.)	665	Abitibi	Abitibi	Abitibi-Ouest	Nathalie Savard, Sec.-Trés., 203, ch des 3e et 4e rang, CP 63, Harricana-Ouest J0Y 1M0 – 819/727-9557, Fax: 819/727-9557
St-Maurice (P)	2,283	Francheville	Champlain	Champlain	Gisèle Lefèbvre, Sec.-Trés., 2510, rang St-Jean, CP 9, St-Maurice G0X 2X0 – 819/374-4525, Fax: 819/374-9132
St-Maxime-du-Mont-Louis (Mun.)	1,571	Denis-Riverin	Gaspé	Gaspé	Hilaire Lemieux, Sec.-Trés., 1, 1re av ouest, CP 130, Mont-Louis G0E 1T0 – 418/797-2310, Fax: 418/797-2928
St-Médard (Mun.)	329	Les Basques	Kamouraska-Rivière-du-Loup	Rimouski	Nancy Rioux, Sec.-Trés., 64, rue Principale est, CP 9, St-Médard G0L 3V0 – 418/963-6276, Fax: 418/963-6276

Canadian Almanac & Directory 1997

Cities (Villes) in CAPITALS; Villages marked (V); Townships/Cantons marked (Canton);United townships/Cantons unis marked (Cantons); Parishes (Paroisses) marked (P); Municipalities marked (Mun.).; Northern villages/Villages nordiques marked (NV); Cree Villages/Villages Cris marked (VC); Naskapi Villages/Villages Naskapi marked (VN); In the third column, Urban Community/Communauté Urbaine marked Urb. Com. An in-depth listing for municipalities marked with * appears in Part 2 (check Index for page numbers).

MUNICIPALITY	1993 POP.	REGIONAL COUNTY MUN.	FEDERAL ELECTORAL DISTRICT	PROVINCIAL ELECTORAL DISTRICT	CONTACT PERSON WITH ADDRESS, PHONE & FAX
Ste-Mélanie (P)	2,399	Joliette	Berthier-Montcalm	Berthier	Réjean Marsolais, Sec.-Trés., 10, rue Louis-Charles-Panet, Ste-Mélanie J0K 3A0 – 514/889-5871, Fax: 514/889-4527
St-Méthode (Mun.)	1,072	Le Domaine-du-Roy	Roberval	Roberval	Michel Légaré, Sec.-Trés., 880, rue Principale, St-Méthode G0W 2Y0 – 418/679-1387, Fax: 418/679-9227
St-Méthode-de-Frontenac (Mun.)	1,642	L'Amiante	Frontenac	Frontenac	Bernardin Hamann, Sec.-Trés., 24, rue Principale ouest, CP 10, St-Méthode-de-Frontenac G0N 1S0 – 418/422-2135, Fax: 418/422-2135
St-Michel (P)	2,227	Les Jardins-de-Napierville	Châteauguay	Beauharnois-Huntingdon	Micheline Lemay, Sec.-Trés., 410, Place St-Michel, CP 60, St-Michel J0L 2J0 – 514/454-4502, Fax: 514/454-4502
St-Michel-de-Bellechasse (P)	1,662	Bellechasse	Bellechasse	Bellechasse	Ronald Gonthier, Sec.-Trés., 129, rte 132 est, St-Michel-de-Bellechasse G0R 3S0 – 418/884-2865, Fax: 418/884-2866
St-Michel-de-Rougemont (P)	1,423	Rouville	St-Hyacinthe-Bagot	Iberville	Marielle Guertin, Sec.-Trés., 61, ch Marieville, Saint-Michel-de-Rougemont J0L 1M0 – 514/469-3790, Fax: 514/469-0309
St-Michel-des-Saints (Mun.)	2,455	Matawinie	Berthier-Montcalm	Berthier	Alain Bellerose, Sec.-Trés., 390, rue Matawin, CP 160, St-Michel-des-Saints J0K 3B0 – 514/833-6941, Fax: 514/833-6081
St-Michel-du-Squatec (P)	1,426	Témiscouata	Rimouski-Témiscouata	Kamouraska-Témiscouata	Gilles Morin, Sec.-Trés., 150, rue St-Joseph, CP 280, Squatec G0L 4H0 – 418/855-2185, Fax: 418/855-2935
St-Michel-d'Yamaska (P)	1,091	Le Bas-Richelieu	Richelieu	Richelieu	Brigitte Vachon, Sec.-Trés., 137, rue Principale, CP 120, Yamaska J0G 1W0 – 514/789-2489, Fax: 514/789-2970
St-Modeste (P)	891	Rivière-du-Loup	Kamouraska-Rivière-du-Loup	Rivière-du-Loup	Diane Castonguay, Sec.-Trés., 312, rue Principale, St-Modeste G0L 3W0 – 418/867-2352, Fax: 418/867-5359
St-Moïse (P)	665	La Matapédia	Matapédia-Matane	Matapédia	Simone Beaulieu, Sec.-Trés., 62, rue Principale, CP 8, St-Moïse G0J 2Z0 – 418/776-2833, Fax: 418/776-2833
Ste-Monique (Mun.)	930	Lac-St-Jean-Est	Lac-St-Jean	Lac-St-Jean	Jean-Claude Duchesne, Sec.-Trés., 101, rue Honfleur, CP 9, Ste-Monique G0W 2T0 – 418/347-3592, Fax: 418/347-4368
Ste-Monique (P)	494	Nicolet-Yamaska	Richelieu	Nicolet-Yamaska	Marthe L.-Ouellet, Sec.-Trés., 931, Le Petit-St-Esprit, Ste-Monique J0G 1N0 – 819/289-2467
Ste-Monique (V)	234	Nicolet-Yamaska	Richelieu	Nicolet-Yamaska	Lucie Lambert, Sec.-Trés., 310, rue St-Antoine, Ste-Monique J0G 1N0 – 819/289-2051
St-Narcisse (P)	2,075	Francheville	Champlain	Champlain	René Pinard, Sec.-Trés., 353, rue Notre-Dame, CP 139, St-Narcisse G0X 2Y0 – 418/328-8645, Fax: 418/328-4348
St-Narcisse-de-Beaurivage (P)	1,109	Lotbinière	Lévis	Lotbinière	Solange Boulanger, Sec.-Trés., #1, 508, rue de l'École, St-Narcisse-de-Beaurivage G0S 1W0 – 418/475-6842, Fax: 418/475-6842
St-Narcisse-de-Rimouski (P)	1,049	Rimouski-Neigette	Rimouski-Témiscouata	Rimouski	Gilles Lepage, Sec.-Trés., 7, rue du Pavillon, CP 1040, St-Narcisse-de-Rimouski G0K 1S0 – 418/735-6021, Fax: 418/735-2638
St-Nazaire (Mun.)	2,063	Lac-St-Jean-Est	Lac-St-Jean	Lac-St-Jean	Roger Bouchard, Sec.-Trés., 199, rue Principale, CP 130, St-Nazaire-du Lac-Saint-Jean G0W 2V0 – 418/662-4154, Fax: 418/662-5467
St-Nazaire-d'Acton (P)	962	Acton	St-Hyacinthe-Bagot	Johnson	Guylaine Bourgoin, Sec.-Trés., 371, rue Principale, St-Nazaire-d'Acton J0H 1V0 – 819/392-2347, Fax: 819/392-2039
St-Nazaire-de-Dorchester (P)	398	Bellechasse	Bellechasse	Bellechasse	Jacques Bruneau, Sec.-Trés., 98, rte Émile-Lachance, St-Nazaire G0R 3T0 – 418/642-2249
St-Nérée (P)	881	Bellechasse	Bellechasse	Bellechasse	Jean-Louis Chabot, Sec.-Trés., 1990, rte Principale, St-Nérée G0R 3V0 – 418/243-2735, Fax: 418/243-2136
St-Nicéphore (Mun.)	8,537	Drummond	Drummond	Drummond	Bernard Parenteau, Sec.-Trés., 4677, av Traversy, CP 1123, St-Nicéphore J2A 2G2 – 819/477-5144, Fax: 819/474-6766
St-Noël (V)	506	La Matapédia	Matapédia-Matane	Matane	Manon Caron, Sec.-Trés., 51, rue de l'Église, CP 88, St-Noël G0J 3A0 – 418/776-2936, Fax: 418/776-5521
St-Norbert (P)	1,053	D'Autray	Berthier-Montcalm	Berthier	Martine Laberge, Sec.-Trés., 2150, rue Principale, St-Norbert J0K 3C0 – 514/836-4700, Fax: 514/836-4700
St-Norbert-d'Arthabaska (Mun.)	882	Arthabaska	Lotbinière	Arthabaska	René Savoie, Sec.-Trés., 250, route de la Rivière, Norbertville G0P 1B0 – 819/369-9318, Fax: 819/369-9318

QUÉBEC MUNICIPALITIES

Cities (Villes) in CAPITALS; Villages marked (V); Townships/Cantons marked (Canton);United townships/Cantons unis marked (Cantons); Parishes (Paroisses) marked (P); Municipalities marked (Mun.).; Northern villages/Villages nordiques marked (NV); Cree Villages/Villages Cris marked (VC); Naskapi Villages/Villages Naskapi marked (VN); In the third column, Urban Community/Communauté Urbaine marked Urb. Com. An in-depth listing for municipalities marked with * appears in Part 2 (check Index for page numbers).

MUNICIPALITY	1993 POP.	REGIONAL COUNTY MUN.	FEDERAL ELECTORAL DISTRICT	PROVINCIAL ELECTORAL DISTRICT	CONTACT PERSON WITH ADDRESS, PHONE & FAX
St-Norbert-de-Mont-Brun (Mun.)	596	Rouyn-Noranda	Témiscamingue	Rouyn-Noranda-Témiscamingue	Marielle Fortier-Migneault, Sec.-Trés., Maison du Partage, 956, rue Principale, Mont-Brun J0Z 2Y0 – 819/637-7045, Fax: 819/637-7045
St-Octave-de-Dosquet (P)	948	Lotbinière	Lotbinière	Lotbinière	Louisette Chartrand, Sec.-Trés., 179, rue St-Joseph sud, Dosquet G0S 1H0 – 418/728-3653, Fax: 418/728-3338
St-Octave-de-Métis (P)	606	La Mitis	Matapédia-Matane	Matane	Line-Hélène Bérubé, Sec.-Trés., 220, 3e rang ouest, CP 107, St-Octave-de-Métis G0J 3B0 – 418/775-2996, Fax: 418/775-2996
Ste-Odile-sur-Rimouski (P)	1,296	Rimouski-Neigette	Rimouski-Témiscouata	Rimouski	Dolorès Beaulieu, Sec.-Trés., 160, ch des Pointes, Ste-Odile-sur-Rimouski G5L 7B5 – 418/724-4925, Fax: 418/724-7388
St-Odilon-de-Cranbourne (P)	1,488	Robert-Cliche	Beauce	Beauce-Nord	André Fecteau, Sec.-Trés., 106, rue de l'Hôtel-de-Ville, CP 100, St-Odilon G0S 3A0 – 418/464-4801, Fax: 418/464-4800
St-Omer (P)	1,431	Avignon	Bonaventure-Îles-de-la-Madeleine	Bonaventure	Michelyne Leblanc, Sec.-Trés., 303, rte 132 ouest, CP 157, St-Omer G0C 2Z0 – 418/364-3682, Fax: 418/364-6049
St-Omer (Mun.)	375	L'Islet	Bellechasse	Montmagny-L'Islet	Lise B. Guillot, Sec.-Trés., 243, ch des Pelletier, CP 1765, Saint-Omer G0R 4R0 – 418/356-5634, Fax: 418/356-5081
St-Onésime-d'Ixworth (P)	641	Kamouraska	Kamouraska-Rivière-du-Loup	Kamouraska-Témiscouata	Isabelle St-Laurent, Sec.-Trés., 12, rte de l'Église, St-Onésime-d'Ixworth G0R 3W0 – 418/856-3018
ST-OURS	1,672	Le Bas-Richelieu	Richelieu	Richelieu	France Blain, Sec.-Trés., 2540, rue de l'Immaculée-Conception, CP 129, St-Ours J0G 1P0 – 514/785-2203, Fax: 514/785-2254
St-Pacôme (Mun.)	1,991	Kamouraska	Kamouraska-Rivière-du-Loup	Kamouraska-Témiscouata	Madeleine Saint-Amant, Sec.-Trés., 27, rue St-Louis, CP 370, St-Pacôme G0L 3X0 – 418/852-2356, Fax: 418/852-2977
ST-PAMPHILE	2,993	L'Islet	Bellechasse	Montmagny-L'Islet	Richard Pelletier, Sec.-Trés., 3, rte Elgin sud, CP 638, St-Pamphile G0R 3X0 – 418/356-5501, Fax: 418/356-5502
St-Pascal (Mun.)	1,467	Kamouraska	Kamouraska-Rivière-du-Loup	Kamouraska-Témiscouata	Réjean Pelletier, Sec.-Trés., 506, rue Taché, 2e étage, CP 756, St-Pascal G0L 3Y0 – 418/492-3817
ST-PASCAL	2,733	Kamouraska	Kamouraska-Rivière-du-Loup	Kamouraska-Témiscouata	Louise Saint-Pierre, Gref., 405, rue Taché, CP 250, St-Pascal G0L 3Y0 – 418/492-2312, Fax: 418/492-9862
St-Patrice-de-Beaurivage (Mun.)	1,182	Lotbinière	Lotbinière	Lotbinière	Lise Demers, Sec.-Trés., 530, rue Principale, St-Patrice-de-Beaurivage G0S 1B0 – 418/596-2362, Fax: 418/596-2362
St-Patrice-de-la-Rivière-du-Loup (P)	3,272	Rivière-du-Loup	Kamouraska-Rivière-du-Loup	Rivière-du-Loup	Adryen Sénéchal, Sec.-Trés., 252, rue Fraser, St-Patrice-de-la-Rivière-du-Loup G5R 3Y4 – 418/862-8722, Fax: 418/862-2287
St-Patrice-de-Sherrington (P)	2,053	Les Jardins-de-Napierville	Châteauguay	Beauharnois-Huntingdon	Lucie Riendeau, Sec.-Trés., 300, rue St-Patrice, CP 210, Sherrington J0L 2N0 – 514/454-4959, Fax: 514/454-5677
St-Paul (Mun.)	3,835	Joliette	Joliette	Joliette	Richard B. Morasse, Sec.-Trés., 18, boul Brassard, St-Paul J0K 3E0 – 514/759-4040, Fax: 514/759-6396
St-Paul-d'Abbotsford (P)	2,847	Rouville	Shefford	Iberville	Daniel Rainville, Sec.-Trés., 926, rue Principale est, CP 69, St-Paul-d'Abbotsford J0E 1A0 – 514/379-5408, Fax: 514/379-9905
St-Paul-de-Châteauguay (Mun.)	1,411	Beauharnois-Salaberry	Beauharnois-Salaberry	Beauharnois-Huntingdon	Léopold Vanier, Sec.-Trés., #1C, 55, rue Saint-Joseph, Ste-Martine J0S 1V0 – 514/427-3703, Fax: 514/427-2548
St-Paul-de-la-Croix (P)	456	Rivière-du-Loup	Kamouraska-Rivière-du-Loup	Rivière-du-Loup	Hélène Malenfant, Sec.-Trés., 3, route de l'Église nord, CP 70, St-Paul-de-la-Croix G0L 3Z0 – 418/898-2031, Fax: 418/898-2322
St-Paul-de-l'Île-aux-Noix (P)	1,864	Le Haut-Richelieu	St-Jean	St-Jean	Marie-Lili Lenoir, Sec.-Trés., 959, rue Principale, St-Paul-de-l'Île-aux-Noix J0J 1G0 – 514/291-3166, Fax: 514/291-5930
St-Paul-de-Montminy (Mun.)	973	Montmagny	Bellechasse	Montmagny-L'Islet	René Gagné, Sec.-Trés., 309 - 4e av, CP 160, St-Paul-de-Montminy G0R 3Y0 – 418/469-3120, Fax: 418/469-3120
St-Paul-du-Nord (Mun.)	815	La Haute-Côte-Nord	Charlevoix	Saguenay	Marguerite Plourde, Sec.-Trés., 201, rte 138, CP 39, St-Paul-du-Nord G0T 1W0 – 418/231-2344, Fax: 418/231-2577
Ste-Paule (Mun.)	190	Matane	Matapédia-Matane	Matane	Gilles Desjardins, Sec.-Trés., 191, rue de l'Église, Ste-Paule G0J 3C0 – 418/737-4296, Fax: 418/737-9460
St-Paulin (Mun.)	1,609	Maskinongé	St-Maurice	Maskinongé	Ghislain Lemay, Sec.-Trés., 3051, rue Bergeron, CP 120, St-Paulin J0K 3G0 – 819/268-2026, Fax: 819/268-2890

Canadian Almanac & Directory 1997

QUÉBEC MUNICIPALITIES 4-123

Cities (Villes) in CAPITALS; Villages marked (V); Townships/Cantons marked (Canton);United townships/Cantons unis marked (Cantons); Parishes (Paroisses) marked (P); Municipalities marked (Mun.).; Northern villages/Villages nordiques marked (NV); Cree Villages/Villages Cris marked (VC); Naskapi Villages/Villages Naskapi marked (VN); In the third column, Urban Community/Communauté Urbaine marked Urb. Com. An in-depth listing for municipalities marked with * appears in Part 2 (check Index for page numbers).

MUNICIPALITY	1993 POP.	REGIONAL COUNTY MUN.	FEDERAL ELECTORAL DISTRICT	PROVINCIAL ELECTORAL DISTRICT	CONTACT PERSON WITH ADDRESS, PHONE & FAX
Ste-Perpétue (Mun.)	2,085	L'Islet	Bellechasse	Montmagny-L'Islet	Marie-Claude Chouinard, Sec.-Trés., 368, av Principale, 2ième Étage, Ste-Perpétue G0R 3Z0 – 418/359-2966, Fax: 418/359-2707
Ste-Perpétue (P)	1,056	Nicolet-Yamaska	Drummond	Nicolet-Yamaska	Silvie Leclerc, Sec.-Trés., 2480, rang Ste-Anne, CP 98, Ste-Perpétue J0C 1R0 – 819/336-6740, Fax: 819/336-6770
Ste-Pétronille (V)	1,170	L'Île-d'Orléans	Beauport-Montmorency-Orléans	Montmorency	Gaston Lebel, Sec.-Trés., 3, ch de l'Église, Ste-Pétronille G0A 4C0 – 418/828-2270, Fax: 418/828-1364
St-Philémon (P)	891	Bellechasse	Bellechasse	Bellechasse	Diane Labrecque, Sec.-Trés., 1531, rue Principale, CP 10, St-Philémon G0R 4A0 – 418/469-2890, Fax: 418/469-2890
St-Philibert (Mun.)	363	Beauce-Sartigan	Beauce	Beauce-Sud	Marie-Jeanne O.-Rodrigue, Sec.-Trés., 329, rue Principale, CP 9, St-Philibert G0M 1X0 – 418/228-8759, Fax: 418/228-3906
St-Philippe (P)	3,791	Roussillon	Châteauguay	La Prairie	Alfred Trudeau, Sec.-Trés., 141, boul Edouard VII, CP 30, St-Philippe J0L 2K0 – 514/659-7701, Fax: 514/659-7702
St-Philippe-de-Néri (P)	1,017	Kamouraska	Kamouraska-Rivière-du-Loup	Kamouraska-Témiscouata	Pierre Leclerc, Sec.-Trés., 12, côte de l'Église, CP 130, St-Philippe-de-Néri G0L 4A0 – 418/498-2744, Fax: 418/498-2193
Ste-Philomène-de-Fortierville (P)	282	Bécancour	Lotbinière	Lotbinière	Claude Martel, Sec.-Trés., 405, route 265, Ste-Philomène-de-Fortierville G0S 1J0 – 819/287-4577, Fax: 819/287-4577
St-Pie (P)	2,466	Les Maskoutains	St-Hyacinthe-Bagot	Iberville	Cécile Charron, Sec.-Trés., 70, rue St-François, CP 519, St-Pie J0H 1W0 – 514/772-2481, Fax: 514/772-2482
St-Pie (V)	2,179	Les Maskoutains	Saint-Hyacinthe-Bagot	Iberville	Christiane Côté, Sec.-Trés., 77, rue Saint-Pierre, St-Pie J0H 1W0 – 514/772-2488, Fax: 514/772-2233
St-Pie-de-Guire (P)	528	Drummond	Richelieu	Nicolet-Yamaska	René Dumont, Sec.-Trés., 100 - 9e rang, St-Pie-de-Guire J0G 1R0 – 514/784-2278, Fax: 514/784-0133
St-Pierre (P)	2,075	L'Île-d'Orléans	Beauport-Montmorency-Orléans	Montmorency	Marie-Paule Corriveau, Sec.-Trés., 515, route des Prêtres, CP 100, St-Pierre G0A 4E0 – 418/828-2855, Fax: 418/828-2855
St-Pierre (V)	374	Joliette	Joliette	Joliette	Chantale Mercier, Sec.-Trés., 485, ch Village de St-Pierre nord, Joliette J6E 3Z1 – 514/756-2592, Fax: 514/756-2592
ST-PIERRE	5,035	Montréal (Urb. Com.)	Notre-Dame-de-Grâce	Marquette	Pierre Bernardin, Gref., 69, 5e av, St-Pierre H8R 1P1 – 514/368-5700, Fax: 514/368-5717
St-Pierre-Baptiste (P)	489	L'Érable	Frontenac	Lotbinière	Suzanne Savage, Sec.-Trés., 1051, rue Principale, St-Pierre-Baptiste G0P 1K0 – 418/453-2286, Fax: 418/453-2286
St-Pierre-de-Broughton (Mun.)	941	L'Amiante	Frontenac	Frontenac	Berthe Boulanger, Sec.-Trés., 29, rue de la Fabrique, CP 68, St-Pierre-de-Broughton G0N 1T0 – 418/424-3572, Fax: 418/424-3572
St-Pierre-de-la-Rivière-du-Sud (P)	903	Montmagny	Bellechasse	Montmagny-L'Islet	Georges Baillargeon, Sec.-Trés., 645 - 2e av, St-Pierre-de-la-Rivière-du-Sud G0R 4B0 – 418/248-8277, Fax: 418/248-7068
St-Pierre-de-Lamy (Mun.)	184	Témiscouata	Rimouski-Témiscouata	Kamouraska-Témiscouata	Odette Caron, Sec.-Trés., 115, route de l'Église, St-Pierre de Lamy G0L 4B0 – 418/497-2447, Fax: 418/497-1840
St-Pierre-de-Véronne-à-Pike-River (Mun.)	670	Brome-Missisquoi	Brome-Missisquoi	Brome-Missisquoi	Lucie Fortin, Sec.-Trés., 548, rte 202, CP 93, St-Pierre-de-Véronne-à-Pike-River J0J 1P0 – 514/248-2120, Fax: 514/248-4772
St-Pierre-les-Becquets (Mun.)	1,396	Bécancour	Lotbinière	Lotbinière	Marcelle Lafleur, Sec.-Trés., 110, rue des Loisirs, St-Pierre-les-Becquets G0X 2Z0 – 819/263-2622, Fax: 819/263-2622
St-Placide (Mun.)	1,539	Deux-Montagnes	Argenteuil-Papineau	Deux-Montagnes	Françoise Duplessis, Sec.-Trés., 281, rang St-Vincent, CP 60, St-Placide J0V 2B0 – 514/476-9021, Fax: 514/258-3059
St-Polycarpe (Mun.)	1,782	Vaudreuil-Soulanges	Vaudreuil	Salaberry-Soulanges	Fleurette Pilon-Sauvé, Sec.-Trés., 1263, ch Élie-Auclair, CP 380, St-Polycarpe J0P 1X0 – 514/265-3777, Fax: 514/265-3010
Ste-Praxède (P)	353	L'Amiante	Richmond-Wolfe	Frontenac	Josée Vachon, Sec.-Trés., 5695, rte 263, Lambton G0M 1H0 – 418/449-2250, Fax: 418/449-2250
St-Prime (Mun.)	2,586	Le Domaine-du-Roy	Roberval	Roberval	Régis Girard, Sec.-Trés., 599, rue Principale, St-Prime G8J 1T2 – 418/251-2116, Fax: 418/251-2823
St-Prosper (Mun.)	3,682	Les Etchemins	Beauce	Beauce-Sud	Johanne Nadeau, Sec.-Trés., 2025 - 29e rue, St-Prosper G0M 1Y0 – 418/594-8135, Fax: 418/594-8865
St-Prosper (P)	609	Francheville	Champlain	Champlain	Jeannine Mongrain, Sec.-Trés., 375, rue St-Joseph, CP 68, St-Prosper G0X 3A0 – 418/328-8449, Fax: 418/328-4267

Canadian Almanac & Directory 1997

4-124 QUÉBEC MUNICIPALITIES

Cities (Villes) in CAPITALS; Villages marked (V); Townships/Cantons marked (Canton);United townships/Cantons unis marked (Cantons); Parishes (Paroisses) marked (P); Municipalities marked (Mun.).; Northern villages/Villages nordiques marked (NV); Cree Villages/Villages Cris marked (VC); Naskapi Villages/Villages Naskapi marked (VN); In the third column, Urban Community/Communauté Urbaine marked Urb. Com. An in-depth listing for municipalities marked with * appears in Part 2 (check Index for page numbers).

MUNICIPALITY	1993 POP.	REGIONAL COUNTY MUN.	FEDERAL ELECTORAL DISTRICT	PROVINCIAL ELECTORAL DISTRICT	CONTACT PERSON WITH ADDRESS, PHONE & FAX
St-Raphaël (Mun.)	2,201	Bellechasse	Bellechasse	Bellechasse	Armand Picard, Sec.-Trés., 19, av Chanoine-Audet, CP 159, St-Raphaël G0R 4C0 – 418/243-2853, Fax: 418/243-2605
St-Raphaël-d'Albertville (P)	397	La Matapédia	Matapédia-Matane	Matapédia	Diane Petrie, Sec.-Trés., 1058, rue Principale, CP 8, Albertville G0J 1A0 – 418/756-3554, Fax: 418/756-3554
St-Raphaël-Sud (P)	234	Nicolet-Yamaska	Lotbinière	Nicolet-Yamaska	Jacqueline Laplante, Sec.-Trés., 1360 - 3e rang, Aston-Jonction G0Z 1A0 – 819/226-3232, Fax: 819/226-3013
ST-RAYMOND j	9,049 ('95)	Portneuf	Portneuf	Portneuf	Réjeanne Julien, Sec.-Trés., 375, rue St-Joseph, CP 880, St-Raymond G0A 4G0 – 418/337-2202, Fax: 418/337-2203
ST-RÉDEMPTEUR	6,341	Les Chutes-de-la-Chaudière	Lévis	Chutes-de-la-Chaudière	Jean Marion, Gref., 95, 19e rue, St-Rédempteur G6K 1E5 – 418/831-4488, Fax: 418/831-7550
ST-RÉMI	6,070	Les Jardins-de-Napierville	Châteauguay	Beauharnois-Huntingdon	Serge Brazeau, Gref., 105, rue Perras, CP 578, St-Rémi J0L 2L0 – 514/454-3993, Fax: 514/454-7978
St-Rémi-de-Tingwick (P)	462	Arthabaska	Richmond-Wolfe	Richmond	Élise Gendron, Sec.-Trés., 141A, rue Principale, St-Rémi-de-Tingwick J0A 1K0 – 819/359-2731, Fax: 819/359-2731
St-René (P)	532	Beauce-Sartigan	Beauce	Beauce-Sud	Michel Drouin, Sec.-Trés., 533, rte Principale, St-René G0M 1Z0 – 418/382-5461, Fax: 418/382-3655
St-René-de-Matane (Mun.)	1,077	Matane	Matapédia-Matane	Matane	Diane Gagnon, Sec.-Trés., #2, 136, av St-René, CP 58, St-René-de-Matane G0J 3E0 – 418/224-3306, Fax: 418/224-3259
Ste-Rita (Mun.)	411	Les Basques	Kamouraska-Rivière-du-Loup	Rivière-du-Loup	Brigitte Pelletier, Sec.-Trés., #25, 1, rue de l'Église est, CP 39, Ste-Rita G0L 4G0 – 418/963-2967, Fax: 418/963-6539
St-Robert (P)	1,904	Le Bas-Richelieu	Richelieu	Richelieu	Éloi Lemoine, Sec.-Trés., 650, ch de Saint-Robert, CP 150, St-Robert J0G 1S0 – 514/782-2844, Fax: 514/782-2844
St-Robert-Bellarmin (Mun.)	687	Le Granit	Beauce	Beauce-Sud	Suzanne Lescomb, Sec.-Trés., 10, rue Nadeau, CP 27, St-Robert-Bellarmin G0M 2E0 – 418/582-3420, Fax: 418/582-3420
St-Roch-de-l'Achigan (P)	4,269	Montcalm	Joliette	Rousseau	Philippe Riopelle, Sec.-Trés., 30, rue du Dr Wilfrid Locat nord, CP 480, St-Roch-de-l'Achigan J0K 3H0 – 514/588-2211, Fax: 514/588-4478
St-Roch-de-Mékinac (P)	312	Mékinac	Champlain	Laviolette	Robert Jourdain, Sec.-Trés., 1210, rte Ducharme, St-Roch-de-Mékinac G0X 2E0 – 819/646-5635, Fax: 819/646-5635
St-Roch-de-Richelieu (P)	1,740	Le Bas-Richelieu	Verchères	Verchères	Clément Boutin, Sec.-Trés., 1111, rue du Parc, St-Roch de Richelieu J0L 2M0 – 514/785-2755, Fax: 514/785-3098
St-Roch-des-Aulnaies (P)	1,073	L'Islet	Kamouraska-Rivière-du-Loup	Kamouraska-Témiscouata	Cécile Morin, Sec.-Trés., 379, rte de l'Église, St-Roch-des-Aulnaies G0R 4E0 – 418/354-2892, Fax: 418/354-2059
St-Roch-Ouest (Mun.)	399	Montcalm	Terrebonne	Rousseau	Christiane Archambault, Sec.-Trés., 840, ch du Ruisseau-St-Jean, St-Roch-Ouest J0K 3H0 – 514/588-2146, Fax: 514/588-6060
St-Romain (Mun.)	702	Le Granit	Mégantic-Compton-Stanstead	Mégantic-Compton	Benoit Bernier, Sec.-Trés., 355, rue Principale, CP 90, St-Romain G0Y 1L0 – 418/486-7374, Fax: 418/486-7875
ST-ROMUALD	10,637	Les Chutes-de-la-Chaudière	Lévis	Chutes-de-la-Chaudière	Danielle Bilodeau, Gref.è., 2175, ch du Fleuve, CP 43100, St-Romuald G6W 7W9 – 418/839-4141, Fax: 418/839-5548
St-Rosaire (P)	808	Arthabaska	Lotbinière	Arthabaska	Jacques Boucher, Sec.-Trés., 9, rue St-Pierre, CP 125, St-Rosaire G0Z 1K0 – 819/752-6178, Fax: 819/752-3959
Ste-Rosalie (P)	1,646	Les Maskoutains	St-Hyacinthe-Bagot	St-Hyacinthe	Johanne Beaudoin, Sec.-Trés., 1115, rue du Centre, Ste-Rosalie J0H 1X0 – 514/799-3707, Fax: 514/799-1707
Ste-Rosalie (V)	3,908	Les Maskoutains	St-Hyacinthe-Bagot	St-Hyacinthe	Jacques DesOrmeaux, Sec.-Trés., 3205, rue Morissette, Ste-Rosalie J0H 1X0 – 514/799-4141, Fax: 514/799-3835
Ste-Rose-de-Watford (Mun.)	827	Les Etchemins	Beauce	Bellechasse	Sylvie Alexandre, Sec.-Trés., 495, rue Principale, CP 39, Ste-Rose-de-Watford G0R 4G0 – 418/267-5811, Fax: 418/267-5330
Ste-Rose-du-Nord (P)	423	Le Fjord-du-Saguenay	Lac-St-Jean	Dubuc	Maryse Girard, Sec.-Trés., 126, rue de la Descente-des-Femmes, Ste-Rose-du-Nord G0V 1T0 – 418/675-2250, Fax: 418/675-2250

Canadian Almanac & Directory 1997

Cities (Villes) in CAPITALS; Villages marked (V); Townships/Cantons marked (Canton);United townships/Cantons unis marked (Cantons); Parishes (Paroisses) marked (P); Municipalities marked (Mun.).; Northern villages/Villages nordiques marked (NV); Cree Villages/Villages Cris marked (VC); Naskapi Villages/Villages Naskapi marked (VN); In the third column, Urban Community/Communauté Urbaine marked Urb. Com. An in-depth listing for municipalities marked with * appears in Part 2 (check Index for page numbers).

MUNICIPALITY	1993 POP.	REGIONAL COUNTY MUN.	FEDERAL ELECTORAL DISTRICT	PROVINCIAL ELECTORAL DISTRICT	CONTACT PERSON WITH ADDRESS, PHONE & FAX
Ste-Sabine (P)	462	Les Etchemins	Bellechasse	Bellechasse	Gaétan Lemieux, Sec.-Trés., 4, rue Saint-Charles, Ste-Sabine G0R 4H0 – 418/383-5488
Ste-Sabine (P)	1,046	Brome-Missisquoi	Brome-Missisquoi	Brome-Missisquoi	Francine Surprenant, Sec.-Trés., 185, rue Principale, Ste-Sabine J0J 2B0 – 514/293-7686, Fax: 514/293-7686
St-Samuel (P)	740	Arthabaska	Lotbinière	Richmond	Lucie Arel-Constant, Sec.-Trés., 141, rue de l'Église, St-Samuel-de-Horton G0Z 1G0 – 819/353-1242, Fax: 819/353-1242
St-Sauveur (P)	2,932	Les Pays-d'en-Haut	Laurentides	Bertrand	René Lachance, Sec.-Trés., 125, ch Jean-Adam, Saint-Sauveur J0R 1R2 – 514/227-4633, Fax: 514/227-8564
St-Sauveur-des-Monts (V)	2,749	Les Pays-d'en-Haut	Laurentides	Bertrand	Normand Patrice, Sec.-Trés., 30, av Filion, St-Sauveur-des-Monts J0R 1R0 – 514/227-2668, Fax: 514/227-8818
St-Sébastien (Mun.)	829	Le Granit	Mégantic-Compton-Stanstead	Mégantic-Compton	Martine Rouleau, Sec.-Trés., 582, rue Principale, St-Sébastien G0Y 1M0 – 819/652-2727, Fax: 819/652-2584
St-Sébastien (P)	845	Le Haut-Richelieu	Brome-Missisquoi	Iberville	Micheline Benoit, Sec.-Trés., 176, rue Dussault, CP 126, St-Sébastien J0J 2C0 – 514/244-5237, Fax: 514/244-6264
Ste-Séraphine (P)	436	Arthabaska	Lotbinière	Richmond	Denise Gaudreau, Sec.-Trés., 2660, rue du Centre Communautaire, Ste-Séraphine J0A 1E0 – 819/336-3200, Fax: 819/336-3200
St-Sévère (P)	383	Maskinongé	Trois-Rivières	Maskinongé	Anne-Marie Sauvageau, Sec.-Trés., 47, rue Principale, St-Sévère G0X 3B0 – 819/264-5656, Fax: 819/264-5656
St-Séverin (P)	297	Robert-Cliche	Beauce	Beauce-Nord	Georgette L.-Grégoire, Sec.-Trés., 900, rue des Lacs, St-Séverin G0N 1V0 – 418/426-2423, Fax: 418/426-2423
St-Séverin (P)	1,026	Mékinac	Champlain	Laviolette	Ginette Hamelin, Sec.-Trés., 1986, pl du Centre, CP 120, St-Séverin G0X 2B0 – 418/365-5844, Fax: 418/365-7544
St-Siméon (P)	1,344	Bonaventure	Bonaventure-Îles-de-la-Madeleine	Bonaventure	Jean-Pierre Gauthier, Sec.-Trés., 107D, av de l'Église, CP 39, St-Siméon G0C 3A0 – 418/534-2155, Fax: 418/534-3830
St-Siméon (P)	525	Charlevoix-Est	Charlevoix	Charlevoix	Gérald Bouchard, Sec.-Trés., 500, rue St-Laurent, CP 116, St-Siméon G0T 1X0 – 418/638-2451, Fax: 418/638-5177
St-Siméon (V)	1,040	Charlevoix-Est	Charlevoix	Charlevoix	Sylvie Foster, Sec.-Trés., 502, rue St-Laurent, CP 98, St-Siméon G0T 1X0 – 418/638-2691, Fax: 418/638-5145
St-Simon (P)	504	Les Basques	Rimouski-Témiscouata	Rimouski	Johanne Bélisle, Sec.-Trés., 54, rue Principale est, CP 40, St-Simon G0L 4C0 – 418/738-2896, Fax: 418/738-2934
St-Simon (P)	1,254	Les Maskoutains	St-Hyacinthe-Bagot	St-Hyacinthe	Sylvain Drolet, Sec.-Trés., 45, rue du Couvent, Saint-Simon J0H 1Y0 – 514/798-2276, Fax: 514/798-2498
St-Simon-les-Mines (Mun.)	414	Beauce-Sartigan	Beauce	Beauce-Sud	Francine P.-Thibodeau, Sec.-Trés., 3384, rue Principale, St-Simon-les-Mines G0M 1K0 – 418/774-3317
St-Sixte (Mun.)	499	Papineau	Gatineau-La Lièvre	Papineau	Alain Hotte, Sec.-Trés., 5, rue Emery, Saint-Sixte J0X 3B0 – 819/983-3155, Fax: 819/983-3409
Ste-Sophie (Mun.)	298	L'Érable	Frontenac	Frontenac	Réjean Gosselin, Sec.-Trés., 505, rue Principale, Ste-Sophie G0P 1L0 – 819/362-3465, Fax: 819/362-3465
Ste-Sophie (Mun.)	8,067	La Rivière-du-Nord	Joliette	Rousseau	Martial Fillion, Sec.-Trés., 2212, rue de l'Hôtel-de-Ville, CP 69, Ste-Sophie J0R 1S0 – 514/438-7784, Fax: 514/438-1080
Ste-Sophie-de-Lévrard (P)	805	Bécancour	Lotbinière	Lotbinière	Micheline St-Onge, Sec.-Trés., 184A, Saint-Antoine, Ste-Sophie-de-Lévrard G0X 3C0 – 819/288-5804, Fax: 819/288-5804
St-Stanislas (Mun.)	1,279	Francheville	Champlain	Champlain	Raymonde Bordeleau, Sec.-Trés., 33, rue du Port, CP 96, St-Stanislas G0X 3E0 – 418/328-3245, Fax: 418/328-4121
St-Stanislas (Mun.)	334	Maria-Chapdelaine	Roberval	Roberval	Majella Gagnon, Sec.-Trés., 955, rue Principale, St-Stanislas G0W 2C0 – 418/276-4476, Fax: 418/276-4476
St-Stanislas-de-Kostka (P)	1,643	Beauharnois-Salaberry	Beauharnois-Salaberry	Salaberry-Soulanges	Lucille Benoit, Sec.-Trés., 221, rue Centrale, CP 120, St-Stanislas-de-Kostka J0S 1W0 – 514/373-8944, Fax: 514/373-8949
St-Sulpice (P)	2,900	L'Assomption	Joliette	L'Assomption	Huguette Archambault, Sec.-Trés., 1089, rue Notre-Dame, St-Sulpice J5W 1G1 – 514/589-4450, Fax: 514/589-9647

Cities (Villes) in CAPITALS; Villages marked (V); Townships/Cantons marked (Canton);United townships/Cantons unis marked (Cantons); Parishes (Paroisses) marked (P); Municipalities marked (Mun.).; Northern villages/Villages nordiques marked (NV); Cree Villages/Villages Cris marked (VC); Naskapi Villages/Villages Naskapi marked (VN); In the third column, Urban Community/Communauté Urbaine marked Urb. Com. An in-depth listing for municipalities marked with * appears in Part 2 (check Index for page numbers).

MUNICIPALITY	1993 POP.	REGIONAL COUNTY MUN.	FEDERAL ELECTORAL DISTRICT	PROVINCIAL ELECTORAL DISTRICT	CONTACT PERSON WITH ADDRESS, PHONE & FAX
St-Sylvère (Mun.)	947	Bécancour	Lotbinière	Nicolet-Yamaska	Ginette Richard, Sec.-Trés., 837, 8e rang, St-Sylvère G0Z 1H0 – 819/285-2075, Fax: 819/285-2075
St-Sylvestre (P)	635	Lotbinière	Frontenac	Lotbinière	Céline Bilodeau, Sec.-Trés., 21, rte Beaurivage, St-Sylvestre G0S 3C0 – 418/596-2596, Fax: 418/596-2596
St-Sylvestre (V)	370	Lotbinière	Frontenac	Lotbinière	Chantal Therrien, Sec.-Trés., 824, rue Principale, CP 70, St-Sylvestre G0S 3C0 – 418/596-2384, Fax: 418/596-2384
St-Télésphore (P)	837	Vaudreuil-Soulanges	Vaudreuil	Salaberry-Soulanges	Danielle Bourgon, Sec.-Trés., 1425, rte 340, St-Télésphore J0P 1Y0 – 514/269-2999, Fax: 514/269-2257
St-Tharcisius (P)	566	La Matapédia	Matapédia-Matane	Matapédia	Sophie Fournier, Sec.-Trés., 55, rue Principale, CP 10, St-Tharcisius G0J 3G0 – 418/629-4727, Fax: 418/629-4727
Ste-Thècle (Mun.)	2,923	Mékinac	Champlain	Laviolette	Louise T.-Rompré, Sec.-Trés., 301, rue St-Jacques, CP 244, Ste-Thècle G0X 3G0 – 418/289-2070, Fax: 418/289-3014
St-Théodore-d'Acton (P)	1,703	Acton	St-Hyacinthe-Bagot	Johnson	Florence Gauthier, Sec.-Trés., 1661, rue Principale, CP 150, St-Théodore-d'Acton J0H 1Z0 – 514/546-2634, Fax: 514/546-2526
St-Théophile (Mun.)	855	Beauce-Sartigan	Beauce	Beauce-Sud	Paula Lacoursière, Sec.-Trés., 644, rue du Collège, CP 10, St-Théophile G0M 2A0 – 418/597-3998, Fax: 418/597-3015
STE-THÉRÈSE	26,373	Thérèse-de-Blainville	Blainville-Deux-Montagnes	Groulx	Jean-Luc Berthiaume, Gref., 6, rue de l'Église, CP 100, Ste-Thérèse J7E 4H7 – 514/434-1440, Fax: 514/434-1499
Ste-Thérèse-de-Gaspé (Mun.)	1,309	Pabok	Gaspé	Gaspé	Luc Lambert, Sec.-Trés., 374, route 132, CP 160, Ste-Thérèse-de-Gaspé G0C 3B0 – 418/385-3313, Fax: 418/385-3799
Ste-Thérèse-de-la-Gatineau (Mun.)	400	La Vallée-de-la-Gatineau	Pontiac-Gatineau-Labelle	Gatineau	Mariette Rochon, Sec.-Trés., CP 155, Ste-Thérèse-de-la-Gatineau J0X 2X0 – 819/449-4134, Fax: 819/449-2194
St-Thomas (Mun.)	2,978	Joliette	Berthier-Montcalm	Joliette	Roger Drainville, Sec.-Trés., 770, rue Principale, CP 390, St-Thomas J0K 3L0 – 514/759-3405, Fax: 514/759-0059
St-Thomas-d'Aquin (P)	3,736	Les Maskoutains	St-Hyacinthe-Bagot	St-Hyacinthe	Murielle Archambault, Sec.-Trés., 105, rue Prévert, St-Thomas-d'Aquin J0H 2A0 – 514/796-5885, Fax: 514/796-1851
St-Thomas-de-Pierreville (P)	687	Nicolet-Yamaska	Richelieu	Nicolet-Yamaska	Carmelle L. Dupuis, Sec.-Trés., 82, rue Shooner, CP 428, Pierreville J0G 1J0 – 514/568-3366, Fax: 514/568-0021
St-Thomas-Didyme (Mun.)	972	Maria-Chapdelaine	Roberval	Roberval	Jean-Marc Paradis, Sec.-Trés., 9, av du Moulin, CP 40, St-Thomas-Didyme G0W 1P0 – 418/274-3638, Fax: 418/274-4176
St-Thuribe (P)	457	Portneuf	Portneuf	Portneuf	Lise Labonté, Sec.-Trés., 378, rue Principale, CP 69, St-Thuribe G0A 4H0 – 418/339-2171
ST-TIMOTHÉE	8,572	Beauharnois-Salaberry	Beauharnois-Salaberry	Salaberry-Soulanges	Annie Bouchard, Gref., 88, rue St-Laurent, CP 69, St-Timothée J6S 6J9 – 514/371-4013, Fax: 514/371-4771
St-Tite (P)	1,528	Mékinac	Champlain	Laviolette	Benoit Cadotte, Sec.-Trés., 540, rue Notre Dame, 2e étage, St-Tite G0X 3H0 – 418/365-5093, Fax: 418/365-4296
ST-TITE	2,802	Mékinac	Champlain	Laviolette	Pierre Massicotte, Sec.-Trés., 540, rue Notre-Dame, St-Tite G0X 3H0 – 418/365-5143, Fax: 418/365-4020
St-Tite-des-Caps (Mun.)	1,594	La Côte-de-Beaupré	Beauport-Montmorency-Orléans	Charlevoix	Gilles Ménard, Sec.-Trés., 1, rue Leclerc, St-Tite-des-Caps G0A 4J0 – 418/823-2239, Fax: 418/823-2527
St-Ubalde (Mun.)	1,732	Portneuf	Portneuf	Portneuf	Serge Deraspe, Sec.-Trés., 427B, boul Chabot, St-Ubalde G0A 4L0 – 418/277-2124, Fax: 418/277-2055
St-Ulric (V)	768	Matane	Matapédia-Matane	Matane	Michèle Paquet, Sec.-Trés., 128, av Ulric-Tessier, CP 130, St-Ulric G0J 3H0 – 418/737-4341, Fax: 418/737-4341
St-Ulric-de-Matane (P)	983	Matane	Matapédia-Matane	Matane	France Gagné, Sec.-Trés., 302, route Centrale, St-Ulric-de-Matane G0J 3H0 – 418/737-4051, Fax: 418/737-4051
St-Urbain (P)	1,613	Charlevoix	Charlevoix	Charlevoix	Guy Bouchard, Sec.-Trés., 989, rue St-Edouard, CP 100, St-Urbain G0A 4K0 – 418/639-2467, Fax: 418/639-2467
St-Urbain-Premier (P)	1,183	Beauharnois-Salaberry	Beauharnois-Salaberry	Beauharnois-Huntingdon	Nicole Sainte-Marie, Sec.-Trés., 204, rue Principale, St-Urbain-Premier J0S 1Y0 – 514/427-3987, Fax: 514/427-3987

Cities (Villes) in CAPITALS; Villages marked (V); Townships/Cantons marked (Canton);United townships/Cantons unis marked (Cantons); Parishes (Paroisses) marked (P); Municipalities marked (Mun.).; Northern villages/Villages nordiques marked (NV); Cree Villages/Villages Cris marked (VC); Naskapi Villages/Villages Naskapi marked (VN); In the third column, Urban Community/Communauté Urbaine marked Urb. Com. An in-depth listing for municipalities marked with * appears in Part 2 (check Index for page numbers).

MUNICIPALITY	1993 POP.	REGIONAL COUNTY MUN.	FEDERAL ELECTORAL DISTRICT	PROVINCIAL ELECTORAL DISTRICT	CONTACT PERSON WITH ADDRESS, PHONE & FAX
Ste-Ursule (P)	1,459	Maskinongé	Berthier-Montcalm	Maskinongé	Diane Faucher, Sec.-Trés., 215, rue Lessard, CP 60, Ste-Ursule J0K 3M0 – 819/228-4345, Fax: 819/228-8326
St-Valentin (P)	539	Le Haut-Richelieu	St-Jean	St-Jean	Caroline Rousselet, Sec.-Trés., 790, ch de la Quatrième Ligne, St-Valentin J0J 2E0 – 514/291-5422, Fax: 514/291-5327
St-Valère (Mun.)	1,349	Arthabaska	Lotbinière	Arthabaska	Jocelyn Jutras, Sec.-Trés., 1641A, rte 161, St-Valère G0P 1M0 – 819/353-2219, Fax: 819/353-2219
St-Valérien (P)	839	Rimouski-Neigette	Rimouski-Témiscouata	Rimouski	Marie-Paule Cimon, Sec.-Trés., 181, route Centrale, CP 9, St-Valerien G0L 4E0 – 418/736-5047, Fax: 418/736-5922
St-Valérien-de-Milton (Canton)	1,850	Les Maskoutains	Shefford	Johnson	Fernande Bessette, Sec.-Trés., 1384, rue Principale, CP 150, St-Valérien J0H 2B0 – 514/549-2463, Fax: 514/549-2993
St-Vallier (Mun.)	1,078	Bellechasse	Bellechasse	Bellechasse	Jean Lemieux, Sec.-Trés., 375, montée de la Station, St-Vallier G0R 4J0 – 418/884-2559, Fax: 418/884-2454
St-Venant-de-Paquette (Mun.)	115	Coaticook	Mégantic-Compton-Stanstead	Mégantic-Compton	Robert Plante, Sec.-Trés., 5, ch du Village, St-Venant-de-Paquette J0B 1S0 – 819/658-3660
Ste-Véronique (V)	1,072	Antoine-Labelle	Pontiac-Gatineau-Labelle	Labelle	Suzanne Ranger-Dubé, Sec.-Trés., 341, boul F. Lafontaine, CP 150, Ste-Véronique J0W 1X0 – 819/275-3256, Fax: 819/275-2095
St-Vianney (Mun.)	601	La Matapédia	Matapédia-Matane	Matapédia	Adrien Beaupré, Sec.-Trés., 140, av Centrale, CP 39, St-Vianney G0J 3J0 – 418/629-4082, Fax: 418/629-1342
St-Viateur (P)	250	D'Autray	Berthier-Montcalm	Berthier	Jean Charland, Sec.-Trés., 1980, rue Bonin, St-Barthelemy J0K 1X0 – 514/885-3511, Fax: 514/885-2165
Ste-Victoire-de-Sorel (P)	2,213	Le Bas-Richelieu	Richelieu	Richelieu	Michel Saint-Martin, Sec.-Trés., 517, ch Ste-Victoire, Ste-Victoire-de-Sorel J0G 1T0 – 514/782-3111, Fax: 514/782-2687
St-Victor (V)	1,182	Robert-Cliche	Beauce	Beauce-Nord	Marc Bélanger, Sec.-Trés., 257, rue Marchand, St-Victor G0M 2B0 – 418/588-6854, Fax: 418/588-6855
St-Victor-de-Tring (Mun.)	1,212	Robert-Cliche	Beauce	Beauce-Nord	Marc Bélanger, Sec.-Trés., 287, rue Marchand, St-Victor G0M 2B0 – 418/588-6854, Fax: 418/588-6855
St-Wenceslas (Mun.) k	1,239 ('95)	Nicolet-Yamaska	Drummond	Nicolet-Yamaska	Lucie Allard, Sec.-Trés., 1240, rue Principale, CP 68, St-Wenceslas G0Z 1J0 – 819/224-7784, Fax: 819/224-7784
St-Zacharie (Mun.)	2,242	Les Etchemins	Beauce	Beauce-Sud	Martin Roy, Sec.-Trés., 735 - 15e rue, CP 249, St-Zacharie G0M 2C0 – 418/593-3185, Fax: 418/593-3085
St-Zénon (P)	1,149	Matawinie	Berthier-Montcalm	Berthier	Michel Sirois, Sec.-Trés., 6101, rue Principale, St-Zénon J0K 3N0 – 514/884-5987, Fax: 514/884-5285
St-Zénon-du-Lac-Humqui (P)	491	La Matapédia	Matapédia-Matane	Matapédia	Claudine Dechamplain, Sec.-Trés., 156, rte 195, Lac-Humqui G0J 1N0 – 418/743-2177
St-Zéphirin-de-Courval (P)	822	Nicolet-Yamaska	Richelieu	Nicolet-Yamaska	Christiane Réné, Sec.-Trés., 1471, rue St-Pierre, CP 40, St-Zéphirin-de-Courval J0G 1V0 – 514/564-2188, Fax: 514/564-2339
St-Zotique (V)	2,733	Vaudreuil-Soulanges	Vaudreuil	Salaberry-Soulanges	Louise Viau-Perron, Sec.-Trés., 1250, rue Principale, St-Zotique J0P 1Z0 – 514/267-9335, Fax: 514/267-0907
Saints-Anges (P)	848	La Nouvelle-Beauce	Beauce	Beauce-Nord	Marie-Paule Marquis, Sec.-Trés., 317, rte des Érables, CP 157, Saints-Anges G0S 3E0 – 418/253-5230, Fax: 418/253-5230
Saints-Martyrs-Canadiens (P)	194	Arthabaska	Richmond-Wolfe	Richmond	Thérèse Lemay, Sec.-Trés., 13, ch du Village, CP 27, Saint-Martyrs G0Y 1B0 – 819/344-5171, Fax: 819/344-5171
SALABERRY-DE-VALLEYFIELD	28,516	Beauharnois-Salaberry	Beauharnois-Salaberry	Salaberry-Soulanges	Claude Barrette, Sec.-Trés., 61, rue Ste-Cécile, Salaberry-de-Valleyfield J6T 1L8 – 514/370-4300, Fax: 514/370-4343
Salluit (NV)	836	Kativik	Abitibi	Ungava	Donald C. Caméron, Sec.-Trés., Salluit J0M 1S0 – 819/255-8953, Fax: 819/255-8802
Sault-au-Mouton (V)	727	La Haute-Côte-Nord	Charlevoix	Saguenay	France Brassard, Sec.-Trés., 70, route 138, CP 99, Sault-au-Mouton G0T 1Z0 – 418/231-2710, Fax: 418/231-2163
Sawyerville (V)	950	Le Haut-St-François	Mégantic-Compton-Stanstead	Mégantic-Compton	Lise Houle, Sec.-Trés., 11, ch Clifton, CP 186, Sawyerville J0B 3A0 – 819/889-2252, Fax: 819/889-2252
Sayabec (Mun.)	2,075	La Matapédia	Matapédia-Matane	Matapédia	Joël Harrisson, Sec.-Trés., 3, rue Keable, CP 39, Sayabec G0J 3K0 – 418/536-5440, Fax: 418/536-5572
Schefferville (VN)	315	Caniapiscau	Manicouagan	Duplessis	Nicole Saint-Amand, Sec.-Trés., 505, rue Fleming, CP 1600, Schefferville G0G 2T0 – 418/585-2471, Fax: 418/585-2256

Cities (Villes) in CAPITALS; Villages marked (V); Townships/Cantons marked (Canton);United townships/Cantons unis marked (Cantons); Parishes (Paroisses) marked (P); Municipalities marked (Mun.).; Northern villages/Villages nordiques marked (NV); Cree Villages/Villages Cris marked (VC); Naskapi Villages/Villages Naskapi marked (VN); In the third column, Urban Community/Communauté Urbaine marked Urb. Com. An in-depth listing for municipalities marked with * appears in Part 2 (check Index for page numbers).

MUNICIPALITY	1993 POP.	REGIONAL COUNTY MUN.	FEDERAL ELECTORAL DISTRICT	PROVINCIAL ELECTORAL DISTRICT	CONTACT PERSON WITH ADDRESS, PHONE & FAX
SCOTSTOWN	660	Le Haut-St-François	Mégantic-Compton-Stanstead	Mégantic-Compton	Armand Charest, Sec.-Trés., 101, ch Victoria ouest, CP 130, Scotstown J0B 3B0 – 819/657-4965, Fax: 819/657-4965
Scott (Mun.) [l]	1,477 ('95)	La Nouvelle-Beauce	Beauce	Beauce-Nord	Lucie Pomerleau, Sec.-Trés., 132, rte du Président Kennedy, Scott-Jonction G0S 3G0 – 418/387-2037, Fax: 418/387-1837
Senneterre (P)	1,102	Vallée-de-l'Or	Abitibi	Abitibi-Est	Georgette Dumont, Sec.-Trés., 171, rte 113 sud, CP 700, Senneterre J0Y 2M0 – 819/737-2842, Fax: 819/737-2842
SENNETERRE	3,622	Vallée-de-l'Or	Abitibi	Abitibi-Est	Hélène Veillette, Gref., 551 - 10e av, CP 789, Senneterre J0Y 2M0 – 819/737-2296, Fax: 819/737-4215
Senneville (V)	973	Montréal (Urb. Com.)	Vaudreuil	Nelligan	35, ch Senneville, Senneville H9X 1B8 – 514/457-6020, Fax: 514/457-0447
SEPT-ÎLES	25,683	Sept-Rivières	Manicouagan	Duplessis	Claude Bureau, Gref., 546, av De Quen, Sept-Iles G4R 2R4 – 418/962-2525, Fax: 418/964-3213
Shannon (Mun.)	3,804	La Jacques-Cartier	Portneuf	Chauveau	Dale Feeney, Sec.-Trés., 50, ch St-Patrick, Shannon G0A 4N0 – 418/844-3778, Fax: 418/844-2111
SHAWINIGAN	20,723	Le Centre-de-la-Mauricie	St-Maurice	St-Maurice	Louise Panneton, Gref., 550, av de l'Hôtel-de-Ville, CP 400, Shawinigan G9N 6V3 – 819/536-7211, Fax: 819/536-7255
SHAWINIGAN-SUD	12,038	Le Centre-de-la-Mauricie	St-Maurice	St-Maurice	Yves Vincent, Gref., 1550 - 118e rue, Shawinigan-Sud G9P 3G8 – 819/536-5671, Fax: 819/536-5225
Shawville (V)	1,656	Pontiac	Pontiac-Gatineau-Labelle	Pontiac	Charles Dale, Sec.-Trés., 350, rue Main, CP 339, Shawville J0X 2Y0 – 819/647-2979, Fax: 819/647-3732
Sheen-Esher-et-Malakoff (Cantons)	104	Pontiac	Pontiac-Gatineau-Labelle	Pontiac	Donald Marion, Sec.-Trés., Sheenboro J0X 2Z0 – 819/683-2944, Fax: 819/683-3590
Shefford (Canton)	3,896	La Haute-Yamaska	Shefford	Shefford	Sylvie Gougeon, Sec.-Trés., CP 1300, Waterloo J0E 2N0 – 514/539-2258, Fax: 514/539-4951
Shenley (Canton)	1,013	Beauce-Sartigan	Beauce	Beauce-Sud	Roger LeBlond, Sec.-Trés., 499, rue Principale, CP 128, St-Honoré G0M 1V0 – 418/485-6738, Fax: 418/485-6738
*SHERBROOKE	79,432 ('94)	Sherbrooke	Sherbrooke	St-François; Sherbrooke	Pierre Huard, Gref. et Directrice, Services juridiques, 191, rue Palais, CP 610, Sherbrooke J1H 5H9 – 819/821-5700, Fax: 819/822-6064, URL: http://ville.sherbrooke.qc.ca
Shigawake (Mun.)	448	Bonaventure	Bonaventure-Îles-de-la-Madeleine	Bonaventure	Elton Hayes, Sec.-Trés., CP 334, Shigawake G0C 3E0 – 418/752-2474, Fax: 418/752-2676
Shipshaw (Mun.)	2,851	Le Fjord-du-Saguenay	Jonquière	Dubuc	Gary James, Sec.-Trés., 3760, route St-Léonard, Shipshaw G7P 1G9 – 418/542-4533, Fax: 418/542-6173
Shipton (Mun.)	3,001	Asbestos	Richmond-Wolfe	Richmond	Michel Lecours, Sec.-Trés., 150, rue Water, CP 209, Danville J0A 1A0 – 819/839-2771, Fax: 819/839-2918
SILLERY	13,082	Québec (Urb. Com.)	Louis-Hébert	Jean Talon; Louis-Hébert	Constance Corriveau, Gref., 1445, av Maguire, Sillery G1T 2W9 – 418/684-2100, Fax: 418/684-2199
SOREL	24,964	Le Bas-Richelieu	Richelieu	Richelieu	Jean Charbonneau, Gref., 71, rue Charlotte, CP 368, Sorel J3P 7K1 – 514/780-5600, Fax: 514/780-5625
Stanbridge (Canton)	900	Brome-Missisquoi	Brome-Missisquoi	Brome-Missisquoi	Vera Gendreau, Sec.-Trés., CP 240, Stanbridge-Est J0J 2H0 – 514/248-3188, Fax: 514/248-3188
Stanbridge-Station (Mun.)	382	Brome-Missisquoi	Brome-Missisquoi	Brome-Missisquoi	Serge Therrien, Sec.-Trés., 229, ch Principale, Stanbridge-Station J0J 2J0 – 514/248-2125, Fax: 514/248-1132
Stanstead (V) [m]	3,240 ('95)	Memphrémagog	Mégantic-Compton-Stanstead	Orford	Monique Pépin, Sec.-Trés., 96, rue Main, Stanstead J0B 2K0 – 819/876-7181, Fax: 819/876-5560
Stanstead (Canton)	883	Memphrémagog	Mégantic-Compton-Stanstead	Orford	Thérèse McCutcheon, Sec.-Trés., 778, ch Sheldon, Magog J1X 3W4 – 819/876-2948, Fax: 819/876-7007
Stanstead-Est (Mun.)	716	Coaticook	Mégantic-Compton-Stanstead	Orford	Scott Lothrop, Sec.-Trés., 2310, ch Curtis, Stanstead-Est J0B 3E0 – 819/876-7292, Fax: 819/876-7292
Stoke (Mun.)	2,354	Le Val-St-François	Richmond-Wolfe	Johnson	Diane Roy-Dubois, Sec.-Trés., 403, rue Principale, CP 30, Stoke J0B 3G0 – 819/878-3790, Fax: 819/878-3804
Stoneham-et-Tewkesbury (Cantons)	4,714	La Jacques-Cartier	Charlesbourg	Chauveau	Denis Robitaille, Sec.-Trés., 325, ch du Hibou, Stoneham-et-Tewkesbury G0A 4P0 – 418/848-2381, Fax: 418/848-1748
Stornoway (Mun.)	554	Le Granit	Mégantic-Compton-Stanstead	Mégantic-Compton	Diane Mercier, Sec.-Trés., 507, route 108 ouest, CP 98, Stornoway G0Y 1N0 – 819/652-2800, Fax: 819/652-2105

Cities (Villes) in CAPITALS; Villages marked (V); Townships/Cantons marked (Canton);United townships/Cantons unis marked (Cantons); Parishes (Paroisses) marked (P); Municipalities marked (Mun.).; Northern villages/Villages nordiques marked (NV); Cree Villages/Villages Cris marked (VC); Naskapi Villages/Villages Naskapi marked (VN); In the third column, Urban Community/Communauté Urbaine marked Urb. Com. An in-depth listing for municipalities marked with * appears in Part 2 (check Index for page numbers).

MUNICIPALITY	1993 POP.	REGIONAL COUNTY MUN.	FEDERAL ELECTORAL DISTRICT	PROVINCIAL ELECTORAL DISTRICT	CONTACT PERSON WITH ADDRESS, PHONE & FAX
Stratford (Canton)	799	Le Granit	Mégantic-Compton-Stanstead	Mégantic-Compton	Hélène Lessard, Sec.-Trés., 165, av Centrale nord, Stratford G0Y 1P0 – 418/443-2307, Fax: 418/443-2603
Stukely (Mun.)	256	Memphrémagog	Brome-Missisquoi	Brome-Missisquoi	Élise Guertin, Sec.-Trés., CP 209, Eastman J0E 1P0 – 514/297-3440, Fax: 514/297-3448
Stukely-Sud (Mun.)	789	Memphrémagog	Brome-Missisquoi	Brome-Missisquoi	Lise Côté, Sec.-Trés., 101, pl de la Mairie, CP 30, Stukely-Sud J0E 2J0 – 514/297-3407, Fax: 514/297-3759
Sullivan (Mun.)	3,094	Vallée-de-l'Or	Abitibi	Abitibi-Est	Houle Réal, Sec.-Trés., 456, rue de l'Hôtel-de-Ville, CP 40, Sullivan J0Y 2N0 – 819/874-4576, Fax: 819/874-3175
Sutton (Canton)	1,569	Brome-Missisquoi	Brome-Missisquoi	Brome-Missisquoi	Suzanne Lessard-Gilbert, Sec.-Trés., 11, rue Principale sud, CP 160, Sutton J0E 2K0 – 514/538-2290, Fax: 514/538-0930
SUTTON	1,663	Brome-Missisquoi	Brome-Missisquoi	Brome-Missisquoi	Nicole Bonnal, Gref., 11A, rue Principale sud, CP 959, Sutton J0E 2K0 – 514/538-2230, Fax: 514/538-0955
Tadoussac (V)	856	La Haute-Côte-Nord	Charlevoix	Saguenay	Gaétan Turcotte, Sec.-Trés., 162, rue des Jésuites, Tadoussac G0T 2A0 – 418/235-4446, Fax: 418/235-4433
Taschereau (Mun.)	692	Abitibi-Ouest	Témiscamingue	Abitibi-Ouest	Linda Chabot, Sec.-Trés., 780A, ch des Pionniers, CP 30, Taschereau J0Z 3N0 – 819/796-2744, Fax: 819/796-2744
Taschereau (V)	692	Abitibi-Ouest	Témiscamingue	Abitibi-Ouest	Yves Aubut, Sec.-Trés., 52, rue Morin, CP 150, Taschereau J0Z 3N0 – 819/796-2219, Fax: 819/796-2219
Tasiujaq (V)	152	Kativik	Manicouagan	Ungava	Jeannie Cain, Sec.-Trés., Tasiujaq J0M 1T0 – 819/633-9924, Fax: 819/633-5026
TÉMISCAMING	3,026	Témiscamingue	Témiscamingue	Rouyn-Noranda-Témiscamingue	Sylvie Bourque, Gref., 451, ch Kipawa, CP 730, Témiscaming J0Z 3R0 – 819/627-3273, Fax: 819/627-3019
Terrasse-Vaudreuil (Mun.)	1,896	Vaudreuil-Soulanges	Vaudreuil	Vaudreuil	Gaétan Lemieux, Sec.-Trés., 74 - 7e av, Terrasse-Vaudreuil J7V 3M9 – 514/453-8120, Fax: 514/453-1180
TERREBONNE	44,425	Les Moulins	Terrebonne	Terrebonne	Denis Bouffard, Gref., 775, rue St-Jean-Baptiste, Terrebonne J6W 1B5 – 514/471-4192, Fax: 514/471-4482
THETFORD MINES	18,669	L'Amiante	Frontenac	Frontenac	Denise Veilleux, Gref., 144, rue Notre-Dame sud, CP 489, Thetford Mines G6G 5T3 – 418/335-2981, Fax: 418/335-7089
Thetford-Partie-Sud (Canton)	3,156	L'Amiante	Frontenac	Frontenac	Lucie Picard, Sec.-Trés., 2093, rue Notre-Dame nord, Thetford-Partie-Sud G6G 2V9 – 418/338-3533, Fax: 418/338-9443
Thorne (Canton)	375	Pontiac	Pontiac-Gatineau-Labelle	Pontiac	Robert Charette, Sec.-Trés., rte 366, Ladysmith J0X 2A0 – 819/647-3206, Fax: 819/647-3206
THURSO	2,687	Papineau	Gatineau-La Lièvre	Papineau	Mario Boyer, Trés., 161, rue Galipeau, CP 1140, Thurso J0X 3B0 – 819/985-2701, Fax: 819/985-0134
Tingwick (P)	1,265	Arthabaska	Richmond-Wolfe	Richmond	Chantal Cantin, Sec.-Trés., 48, rue de l'Hôtel-de-Ville, CP 150, Tingwick J0A 1L0 – 819/359-2454, Fax: 819/359-2233
Tourelle (Mun.)	1,501	Denis-Riverin	Gaspé	Matane	Murielle Tanguay, Sec.-Trés., 9, boul Perron est, CP 39, Tourelle G0E 2J0 – 418/763-2629, Fax: 418/763-9004
Tourville (Mun.)	842	L'Islet	Bellechasse	Montmagny-L'Islet	Normand Blier, Sec.-Trés., 946, rue Principale, CP 206, Tourville G0R 4M0 – 418/359-2106, Fax: 418/359-2106
TRACY	13,568	Le Bas-Richelieu	Richelieu	Richelieu	Laval Tardif, Gref., 3025, boul de la Mairie, Tracy J3R 1C2 – 514/742-5671, Fax: 514/742-5770
Trécesson (Canton)	1,081	Abitibi	Abitibi	Abitibi-Ouest	Marlène Fortin, Sec.-Trés., 314, rue Sauvé, Villemontel J0Y 2S0 – 819/732-8524, Fax: 819/732-8524
Tremblay (Canton)	3,645	Le Fjord-du-Saguenay	Bellechasse	Dubuc	Chantal Girard, Sec.-Trés., 1215, rte Martel, Tremblay G7H 5B2 – 418/543-6875, Fax: 418/543-6803
Très-St-Rédempteur (P)	619	Vaudreuil-Soulanges	Vaudreuil	Vaudreuil	Lise Couët, Sec.-Trés., 769, rte Principale, Très-St-Rédempteur J0P 1P0 – 514/451-5203, Fax: 514/451-5203
Très-St-Sacrement (P)	1,339	Le Haut-St-Laurent	Beauharnois-Salaberry	Beauharnois-Huntingdon	Suzanne Côté, Sec.-Trés., 63, rue Lambton, CP 192, Howick J0S 1G0 – 514/825-0192, Fax: 514/825-0193
Tring-Jonction (V)	1,401	Robert-Cliche	Beauce	Beauce-Nord	Marcel Poulin, Sec.-Trés., 100, av Commerciale, CP 10, Tring-Jonction G0N 1X0 – 418/426-2497, Fax: 418/426-2497
Trois-Lacs (Mun.)	515	Asbestos	Richmond-Wolfe	Richmond	Ghyslaine Leroux, Sec.-Trés., 134, rue Larochelle, Trois-Lacs J1T 3M7 – 819/879-5783, Fax: 819/879-7175

Cities (Villes) in CAPITALS; Villages marked (V); Townships/Cantons marked (Canton);United townships/Cantons unis marked (Cantons); Parishes (Paroisses) marked (P); Municipalities marked (Mun.).; Northern villages/Villages nordiques marked (NV); Cree Villages/Villages Cris marked (VC); Naskapi Villages/Villages Naskapi marked (VN); In the third column, Urban Community/Communauté Urbaine marked Urb. Com. An in-depth listing for municipalities marked with * appears in Part 2 (check Index for page numbers).

MUNICIPALITY	1993 POP.	REGIONAL COUNTY MUN.	FEDERAL ELECTORAL DISTRICT	PROVINCIAL ELECTORAL DISTRICT	CONTACT PERSON WITH ADDRESS, PHONE & FAX
TROIS-PISTOLES	3,995	Les Basques	Kamouraska-Rivière-du-Loup	Rivière-du-Loup	Gabriel Desjardins, Sec.-Trés., 5, rue Notre-Dame est, CP 550, Trois-Pistoles G0L 4K0 – 418/851-1995, Fax: 418/851-3567
TROIS-RIVIÈRES	51,412 ('94)	Francheville	Trois-Rivières	Trois-Rivières	Gilles Poulin, Gref., 1325, Place de l'Hôtel-de-Ville, CP 368, Trois-Rivières G9A 5H3 – 819/374-3521, Fax: 819/372-4631
TROIS-RIVIÈRES-OUEST	20,887	Francheville	Trois-Rivières	Maskinongé	Claude Touzin, Gref., 500, côte Richelieu, Trois-Rivières-Ouest G9A 2Z1 – 819/375-7731, Fax: 819/375-2815
Ulverton (Mun.)	317	Drummond	Drummond	Johnson	France Turcotte, Sec.-Trés., 151, rte 143, Ulverton J0B 2B0 – 819/826-5049, Fax: 819/826-5181
Umiujaq (NV)	289	Kativik	Abitibi	Ungava	Annie Kasudluak, Sec.-Trés., Umiujaq J0M 1Y0 – 819/331-7000, Fax: 819/331-7057
Upton (V)	1,005	Acton	St-Hyacinthe-Bagot	Johnson	Louise Quintal, Sec.-Trés., 863, rue Lanoie, Upton J0H 2E0 – 514/549-5611, Fax: 514/549-5045
Val-Alain (Mun.)	927	Lotbinière	Lotbinière	Lotbinière	France Bisson, Sec.-Trés., 1245 - 2e rang, CP 10, Val-Alain G0S 3H0 – 819/744-3222, Fax: 819/744-3222
Val-Barrette (V)	572	Antoine-Labelle	Pontiac-Gatineau-Labelle	Labelle	Claude Meilleur, Sec.-Trés., 135, rue St-Joseph, CP 60, Val-Barrette J0W 1Y0 – 819/585-3131, Fax: 819/585-4915
VAL-BÉLAIR	17,951	Québec (Urb. Com.)	Portneuf	Chauveau	Suzanne Paquet, Sec.-Trés., 1105, av de l'Église nord, Val-Bélair G3K 1X5 – 418/842-7184, Fax: 418/842-1945
Val-Brillant (Mun.)	1,017	La Matapédia	Matapédia-Matane	Matapédia	Louise Bérubé, Sec.-Trés., 11, rue St-Pierre ouest, CP 220, Val-Brillant G0J 3L0 – 418/742-3212, Fax: 418/742-3624
Val-David (V)	3,225	Les Laurentides	Laurentides	Bertrand	André Desjardins, Sec.-Trés., 2579, de l'Église, Val-David J0T 2N0 – 819/322-2900, Fax: 819/322-6327
Val-des-Bois (Mun.)	678	Papineau	Gatineau-La Lièvre	Papineau	Lynda Melanson, Sec.-Trés., 595, route 309, CP 69, Val-des-Bois J0X 3C0 – 819/454-2280, Fax: 819/454-2211
Val-des-Lacs (Mun.)	537	Les Laurentides	Laurentides	Bertrand	Réjane Gagnon, Sec.-Trés., 349, ch de Val-des-Lacs, Val-des-Lacs J0T 2P0 – 819/326-5624, Fax: 819/326-7065
Val-des-Monts (Mun.)	5,943	Les Collines-de-l'Outaouais	Gatineau-La Lièvre	Papineau	Patricia Fillet, Sec.-Trés., 1, route du Carrefour, Val-des-Monts J8N 4E9 – 819/457-9400, Fax: 819/457-4141
VAL-D'OR	24,227 ('95)	Vallée-de-l'Or	Abitibi	Abitibi-Est	Normand Gélinas, Gref., 855, 2e av, CP 400, Val-d'Or J9P 4P4 – 819/824-9613, Fax: 819/825-6650
Val-Joli (Mun.)	1,556	Le Val-St-François	Richmond-Wolfe	Johnson	Lucie Camiré, Sec.-Trés., 500, rte 249, Val-Joli J1S 2L5 – 819/845-7663, Fax: 819/845-7663
Val-Morin (Mun.)	1,480	Les Laurentides	Laurentides	Bertrand	Manon Bernard, Sec.-Trés., 6120, rue Morin, CP 210, Val-Morin J0T 2R0 – 819/322-3635, Fax: 819/322-3923
Val-Racine (P)	112	Le Granit	Mégantic-Compton-Stanstead	Mégantic-Compton	Denise Hallé, Sec.-Trés., 2991, ch St-Léon, CP 1, Val-Racine G0Y 1E0 – 819/657-4790, Fax: 819/657-4790
Val-St-Gilles (Mun.)	208	Abitibi-Ouest	Témiscamingue	Abitibi-Ouest	Hélène Richer, Sec.-Trés., 801, rue Principale, Val-St-Gilles J0Z 3T0 – 819/333-5676, Fax: 819/333-3116
Val-Senneville (Mun.)	2,179	Vallée-de-l'Or	Abitibi	Abitibi-Est	Nicole Guilbert, Sec.-Trés., 656, route des Campagnards, CP 30, Val-Senneville J0Y 2P0 – 819/824-2910, Fax: 819/824-5549
Valcourt (Canton)	1,154	Le Val-St-François	Richmond-Wolfe	Johnson	Lucie Beauchemin, Sec.-Trés., 9040B, rue de la Montagne, CP 219, Valcourt J0E 2L0 – 514/532-2688, Fax: 514/532-5570
VALCOURT	2,349	Le Val-St-François	Richmond-Wolfe	Johnson	Manon Beauchemin, Gref., 1155, rue St-Joseph, CP 340, Valcourt J0E 2L0 – 514/532-3313, Fax: 514/532-3424
Vallée-Jonction (Mun.)	1,952	La Nouvelle-Beauce	Beauce	Beauce-Nord	Gervais Boily, Sec.-Trés., 218, rue Labbé, CP 218, Vallée-Jonction G0S 3J0 – 418/253-5515, Fax: 418/253-6731
VANIER	11,321	Québec (Urb. Com.)	Québec-Est	Vanier	Marie-Josée Dumais, Gref., 233, boul Pierre-Bertrand, Vanier G1M 2C7 – 418/687-3530, Fax: 418/681-9433
VARENNES	15,809	Lajemmerais	Verchères	Verchères	Yves G. Vincent, Gref., 175, rue Ste-Anne, CP 5000, Varennes J3X 1T5 – 514/652-9888, Fax: 514/652-2655
Vassan (Mun.)	1,031	Vallée-de-l'Or	Abitibi	Abitibi-Est	Brigitte Grandmont, Sec.-Trés., 479, rte 111, CP 610, Vassan J0Y 2R0 – 819/824-8550, Fax: 819/824-5623
VAUDREUIL-DORION	18,595	Vaudreuil-Soulanges	Vaudreuil	Vaudreuil	Lise Roy, Gref., 2555, rue Dutrisac, Vaudreuil-Dorion J7V 7E6 – 514/455-3371, Fax: 514/455-0087

Cities (Villes) in CAPITALS; Villages marked (V); Townships/Cantons marked (Canton);United townships/Cantons unis marked (Cantons); Parishes (Paroisses) marked (P); Municipalities marked (Mun.).; Northern villages/Villages nordiques marked (NV); Cree Villages/Villages Cris marked (VC); Naskapi Villages/Villages Naskapi marked (VN); In the third column, Urban Community/Communauté Urbaine marked Urb. Com. An in-depth listing for municipalities marked with * appears in Part 2 (check Index for page numbers).

MUNICIPALITY	1993 POP.	REGIONAL COUNTY MUN.	FEDERAL ELECTORAL DISTRICT	PROVINCIAL ELECTORAL DISTRICT	CONTACT PERSON WITH ADDRESS, PHONE & FAX
Vaudreuil-sur-le-Lac (V)	951	Vaudreuil-Soulanges	Vaudreuil	Vaudreuil	Claudia Chebin, Sec.-Trés., 44, rue de l'Église, Vaudreuil-sur-le-Lac J7V 8P3 – 514/455-1133, Fax: 514/455-8614
Venise-en-Québec (Mun.)	988	Le Haut-Richelieu	Brome-Missisquoi	Iberville	Diane Bégin, Sec.-Trés., 237, 16e av ouest, CP 270, Venise-en-Québec J0J 2K0 – 514/244-5838, Fax: 514/244-5550
Verchères (Mun.)	5,125	Lajemmerais	Verchères	Verchères	Luc Forcier, Sec.-Trés., 581, boul Marie-Victorin, Verchères J0L 2R0 – 514/583-3307, Fax: 514/583-3637
*VERDUN	62,112	Montréal (Urb. Com.)	Verdun-St-Paul	Verdun	Gérard Cyr, Gref., 4555, rue de Verdun, Verdun H4G 1M4 – 514/765-7000, Fax: 514/765-7006
Vianney (Mun.)	211	L'Érable	Frontenac	Frontenac	Constant Marcoux, Sec.-Trés., 522, rue Principale, CP 12, Vianney G0N 1N0 – 418/428-3461, Fax: 418/428-3016
VICTORIAVILLE	38,191	Arthabaska	Lotbinière	Arthabaska	Jean Poirier, Gref., 1, rue Notre-Dame ouest, CP 370, Victoriaville G6P 6T2 – 819/758-1571, Fax: 819/758-9292
VILLE-MARIE	2,655	Témiscamingue	Témiscamingue	Rouyn-Noranda-Témiscamingue	Pierre Genest, Sec.-Trés., 9, rue Notre-Dame-de-Lourdes, CP 730, Ville-Marie J0Z 3W0 – 819/629-2881, Fax: 819/629-3215
VILLEROY	556	L'Érable	Lotbinière	Lotbinière	Angèle Germain, Sec.-Trés., 380, rue Principale, Villeroy G0S 3K0 – 819/385-4605, Fax: 819/385-4605
Vinoy (Mun.)	136	Papineau	Argenteuil-Papineau	Papineau	Denise Imbeault, Sec.-Trés., 63, rue de l'Hôtel-de-Ville, CP 309, Chénéville J0V 1E0 – 819/428-3372, Fax: 819/428-3583
Waltham-et-Bryson (Cantons)	484	Pontiac	Pontiac-Gatineau-Labelle	Pontiac	Fernand Roy, Sec.-Trés., CP 29, Waltham Station J0X 3H0 – 819/683-3027, Fax: 819/683-2694
Warden (V)	359	La Haute-Yamaska	Shefford	Shefford	Danielle Corriveau-Verhoef, Sec.-Trés., 172, rue Principale, CP 90, Warden J0E 2M0 – 514/539-1349
Warwick (Canton)	1,994	Arthabaska	Lotbinière	Richmond	Lise Lemieux, Sec.-Trés., 281A, rue St-Louis ouest, CP 160, Warwick J0A 1M0 – 819/358-6197, Fax: 819/358-2164
WARWICK	2,976	Arthabaska	Lotbinière	Richmond	Jacques Hamel, Sec.-Trés., 8, rue de l'Hôtel-de-Ville, CP 70, Warwick J0A 1M0 – 819/358-4300, Fax: 819/358-4309
Waswanipi (VC)			Abitibi	Ungava	Robert Ottereyes, Sec.-Trés., Édifice Diom Blacksmith, Waswanipi J0Y 3C0 – 819/753-2587, Fax: 819/753-2555
WATERLOO	4,187	La Haute-Yamaska	Shefford	Shefford	Denyse Bélanger, Gref., 417, rue de la Cour, CP 50, Waterloo J0E 2N0 – 514/539-2282, Fax: 514/539-3257
WATERVILLE	1,387	Sherbrooke	Mégantic-Compton-Stanstead	St-François	Gilles Boisvert, Sec.-Trés., 170, rue Principale sud, CP 40, Waterville J0B 3H0 – 819/837-2456, Fax: 819/837-2456
Weedon (Canton)	691	Le Haut-St-François	Mégantic-Compton-Stanstead	Mégantic-Compton	Robert Tardif, Sec.-Trés., 450 - 2e av, Weedon J0B 3J0 – 819/877-2727, Fax: 819/877-2255
Weedon-Centre (V)	1,262	Le Haut-St-François	Mégantic-Compton-Stanstead	Mégantic-Compton	Robert Tardif, Sec.-Trés., 450 - 2e av, Weedon-Centre J0B 3J0 – 819/877-2727, Fax: 819/877-2255
Wemindji (VC)			Abitibi	Mégantic-Compton	16, rue Beaver, CP 60, Wemindji J0M 1L0 – 819/978-0264, Fax: 819/978-0258
Wentworth (Canton)	340	Argenteuil	Argenteuil-Papineau	Argenteuil	Louise Bruneau, Sec.-Trés., 114, ch Lac-Louisa, Lachute J8H 3W8 – 514/562-0701, Fax: 514/562-0703
Wentworth-Nord (Mun.)	853	Les Pays-d'en-Haut	Argenteuil-Papineau	Argenteuil	Daniel Jetté, Sec.-Trés., 3488, rue Principale, Laurel J0T 1Y0 – 514/226-2416, Fax: 514/226-2109
Westbury (Canton)	1,008	Le Haut-St-François	Mégantic-Compton-Stanstead	Mégantic-Compton	Chantal Bellavance, Sec.-Trés., CP 40, East Angus J0B 1R0 – 819/832-3966, Fax: 819/832-3966
WESTMOUNT	20,506	Montréal (Urb. Com.)	St-Henri-Westmount	Westmount-St-Louis	Marie-France Paquet, Gref., 4333, rue Sherbrooke, Westmount H3Z 1E2 – 514/989-5200, Fax: 514/989-5480
Wickham (Mun.)	2,311	Drummond	Drummond	Johnson	Réal Dulmaine, Sec.-Trés., 893, rue Moreau, CP 9, Wickham J0C 1S0 – 819/398-6878, Fax: 819/398-7166
WINDSOR	4,960	Le Val-St-François	Richmond-Wolfe	Johnson	Joseph Plante, Gref., 22, rue St-Georges, Windsor J1S 1J3 – 819/845-7888, Fax: 819/845-7606
Wotton (Mun.)	1,595	Asbestos	Richmond-Wolfe	Richmond	Carole Vaillancourt, Sec.-Trés., 400, rue Mgr-L'Heureux, CP 60, Wotton J0A 1N0 – 819/828-2112, Fax: 819/828-3594
Wright (Canton)	1,222	La Vallée-de-la-Gatineau	Pontiac-Gatineau-Labelle	Gatineau	Louise Carpentier, Sec.-Trés., 185, route 105, RR#3, Gracefield J0X 1W0 – 819/463-2143, Fax: 819/463-1050

4-132 QUÉBEC MUNICIPALITIES

Cities (Villes) in CAPITALS; Villages marked (V); Townships/Cantons marked (Canton);United townships/Cantons unis marked (Cantons); Parishes (Paroisses) marked (P); Municipalities marked (Mun.).; Northern villages/Villages nordiques marked (NV); Cree Villages/Villages Cris marked (VC); Naskapi Villages/Villages Naskapi marked (VN); In the third column, Urban Community/Communauté Urbaine marked Urb. Com. An in-depth listing for municipalities marked with * appears in Part 2 (check Index for page numbers).

MUNICIPALITY	1993 POP.	REGIONAL COUNTY MUN.	FEDERAL ELECTORAL DISTRICT	PROVINCIAL ELECTORAL DISTRICT	CONTACT PERSON WITH ADDRESS, PHONE & FAX
Yamachiche (Mun.)	2,876	Maskinongé	Trois-Rivières	Maskinongé	Paul Desaulniers, Sec.-Trés., 366, rue Ste-Anne, CP 430, Yamachiche G0X 3L0 – 819/296-3795, Fax: 819/296-3542
Yamaska (V)	463	Le Bas-Richelieu	Richelieu	Richelieu	France Nadeau, Sec.-Trés., 110, rue de Mgr-Parenteau, Yamaska J0G 1W0 – 514/789-2333, Fax: 514/789-2998
Yamaska-Est (V)	268	Le Bas-Richelieu	Richelieu	Richelieu	Diane Bibeau-Desmarais, Sec.-Trés., 43, rue Guilbault, Yamaska-Est J0G 1X0 – 514/789-2175, Fax: 514/789-2175

a. Effective March 27, 1995 the new municipality of Dixville was created through the amalgamation of the municipality of St-Mathieu-de-Dixville & the village of Dixville.
b. Effective October 11, 1995 the new municipality of Dudswell was created through the amalgamation of the canton of Dudswell & the villages of Bishopton & Marbleton.
c. Effective September 27, 1995 the new municipality of Hatley was created through the amalgamation of the village of Hatley & the canton of Hatley-Ouest.
d. Effective February 15, 1995, the new village of La Malbaie-Pointe-au-Pic was created through the amalgamation of the village of La Malbaie & the village of Pointe-au-Pic.
e. Effective February 15, 1995 the new municipality of Racine was created through the amalgamation of the municipality of Racine & the municipality of Brompton Gore.
f. Effective November 29, 1995 the new municipality of Rigaud was created through the amalgamation of the village of Rigaud & the paroisse of Ste-Madeleine-de-Rigaud.
g. Effective December 13, 1995 the new village of Rouyn-Noranda was created through the amalgamation of the village of Rouyn-Noranda & the municipality of St-Guillaume-de-Granada.
h. Effective February 22, 1995 the new municipality of St-Germain-de-Grantham was created through the amalgamation of the village of St-Germain-de-Grantham & the Paroisse of St-Germain-de-Grantham.
i. Effective November 8, 1995 the new municipality of St-Guillaume was created through the amalgamation of the paroisse of St-Guillaume & the village of St-Guillaume.
j. Effective March 29, 1995 the new city of St-Raymond was created through the amalgamation of the village of St-Raymond & the Paroisse of St-Raymond.
k. Effective October 11, 1995 the new municipality of St-Wenceslas was created through the amalgamation of the municipality of St-Wenceslas & the village of St-Wenceslas.
l. Effective March 29, 1995 the new municipality of Scott was created through the amalgamation of the municipality of Taschereau-Fortier & the village of Scott.
m. Effective February 15, 1995 the new village of Stanstead was created through the amalgamation of the villages of Rock Island, Beebe Plain, & Stanstead Plain.

REGIONAL COUNTY MUNICIPALITIES/MUNICIPALITÉS DE COMTÉ, QUEBEC

MUNICIPALITY	1993 POP.	CONTACT PERSON WITH ADDRESS & PHONE
Abitibi	25,327	Michel Roy, Gref., 571 - 1re rue est, CP 214, Amos J9T 2H3 – 819/732-5356
Abitibi-Ouest	24,508	Nicole Breton, Gref., #105, 6 - 8e av est, La Sarre J9Z 1N6 – 819/339-5671
Acton	15,648	Yvan Talbot, Gref., 1037, rue Beaugrand, CP 1590, Acton Vale J0H 1A0 – 514/546-3256
Antoine-Labelle	33,322	Pierre Borduas, Gref., 400, boul Albiny-Paquette, Mont-Laurier J9L 1J9 – 819/623-3485
Argenteuil	28,462	Marc Carrière, Gref., 430, rue Grâce, Lachute J8H 1M6 – 514/562-2474
Arthabaska	63,236	Gilles Gagnon, Gref., 40, Grande-Ligne, Victoriaville G6P 6R9 – 819/752-2444
Asbestos	15,834	Madeleine Lamoureux, Gref., #303, 185, rue du Roi, Asbestos J1T 1S4 – 819/879-6661
Avignon	14,941	Gaétan Bernatchez, Gref., 470, rue Francoeur, CP 128, Nouvelle G0C 2E0 – 418/794-2221
Beauce-Sartigan	45,280	Gilles Piché, Gref., 12220 - 2e av, St-Georges G5Y 1X4 – 418/228-8418
Beauharnois-Salaberry	61,779	Jean Tétrault, Gref., #300, 600, rue Ellice, Beauharnois J6N 3P7 – 514/225-0870
Bécancour	19,939	Laval Dubois, Gref., 3691, Pl le Jardin, Gentilly G0X 1G0 – 819/298-2070
Bellechasse	29,676	Clément Fillion, Gref., 100, rue Mgr-Bilodeau, CP 130, St-Lazare G0R 3J0 – 418/883-3347
Bonaventure	20,688	Anne-Marie Flowers, Gref., 138, rue Principale, CP 40, New Carlisle G0C 1Z0 – 418/752-6601
Brome-Missisquoi	47,353	Robert Desmarais, Gref., 3, rue Principale, CP 150, Bedford J0J 1A0 – 514/248-3326
Caniapiscau	4,175	Nancy Malouin, Gref., 100, place Daviault, CP 1420, Fermont G0G 1J0 – 418/287-5339
Champlain	330,222	Sylvie Cossette, Gref., #100, 1000, rue de Sérigny, Longueuil J4K 5B1 – 514/646-6199
Charlevoix	13,672	Sylvain Boulianne, Gref., 4, Place de l'Église, CP 549, Baie-St-Paul G0A 1B0 – 418/435-2639
Charlevoix-Est	17,734	Pierre Girard, Gref., 172, boul Notre-Dame, CP 610, Clermont G0T 1C0 – 418/439-3947
Coaticook	16,481	Guy Charland, Gref., #106, 57, rue Main est, Coaticook J1A 1N1 – 819/849-9166
D'Autray	35,790	Claude Joyal, Gref., 180, rue Champlain, CP 1500, Berthierville J0K 1A0 – 514/836-7007
Denis-Riverin	13,926	Michel Thibeault, Gref., 122 - 1re av ouest, CP 969, Ste-Anne-des-Monts G0E 2G0 – 418/763-7791
Desjardins	53,186	André Roy, Gref., 229A, rue St-Omer, Lévis G6V 6N4 – 418/833-1519
Deux-Montagnes	79,109	Yvon Bélair, Gref., #201, 400, boul de Deux-Montagnes, Deux-Montagnes J7R 7C2 – 514/491-1818
Drummond	84,058	Raymond Malouin, Gref., 436, rue Lindsay, Drummondville J2B 1G6 – 819/477-2230
Francheville	142,981	Pierre St-Onge, Gref., 3275, rue Foucher, CP 367, Trois-Rivières G9A 5G4 – 819/378-8088
Joliette	53,811	Alain Beaulieu, Gref., 632, rue de Lanaudière, Joliette J6E 3M7 – 514/759-2237
Kamouraska	24,654	Guy Lavoie, Gref., 425, av Patry, CP 1120, St-Pascal G0L 3Y0 – 418/492-1660
La Côte-de-Beaupré	22,248	Jacques Pichette, Gref., 7007, av Royale, Château-Richer G0A 1N0 – 418/824-3444
La Côte-de-Gaspé	21,239	Henri Preston, Gref., 37, rue du Banc, CP 57, Rivière-au-Renard G0E 2A0 – 418/269-7718
La Haute-Côte-Nord	13,729	Alain Tremblay, Gref., #1, 9, rue Roussel, CP 790, Les Escoumins G0T 1K0 – 418/233-2102
La Haute-Yamaska	77,453	Johanne Gaouette, Gref., 739, rue Dufferin, Granby J2H 2H5 – 514/378-9975
La Jacques-Cartier	25,055	Claude Hallé, Gref., 1020, boul du Lac, Lac-Beauport G0A 2C0 – 418/849-2885
La Matapédia	20,773	Jean-Pierre Morneau, Gref., 123, rue Desbiens, CP 2020, Amqui G0J 1B0 – 418/629-2053
La Mitis	20,880	Gilles Goulet, Gref., 300, av du Sanatorium, Mont-Joli G5H 1V7 – 418/775-8445
La Nouvelle-Beauce	24,885	Ghislain Poulin, Gref., 700, rue Notre-Dame nord, Ste-Marie G6E 2K9 – 418/387-3444
La Rivière-du-Nord	80,813	Carole Leduc, Gref., #204, 236, av du Palais, St-Jérôme J7Z 1X8 – 514/436-9321
La Vallée-de-la-Gatineau	19,116	André Beauchemin, Gref., 42, rue Principale, CP 307, Gracefield J0X 1W0 – 819/463-3241
La Vallée-du-Richelieu	111,161	Pierre Bélanger, Gref., 630, rue Richelieu, Beloeil J3G 5E8 – 514/464-0339
Lac-St-Jean-Est	53,066	Guy Gagnon, Gref., 675, rue Collard ouest, Alma G8B 1N1 – 418/668-3023
Lajemmerais	91,820	Maryse Vermette, Gref., 609, rte Marie-Victorin, Verchères J0L 2R0 – 514/583-3301
L'Amiante	46,901	Serge Nadeau, Gref., 320, boul Frontenac, Black-Lake G0N 1A0 – 418/423-2757
L'Assomption	104,302	Roger Carrier, Gref., 300A, rue Dorval, CP 5057, L'Assomption J0K 1G0 – 514/589-2288

MUNICIPALITY	1993 POP.	CONTACT PERSON WITH ADDRESS & PHONE
Laval	335,009	Ronald Bourcier, Gref., 1, Place du Souvenir, CP 422, Laval H7V 3Z4 – 514/662-4101
Le Bas-Richelieu	55,496	Denis Boisvert, Gref., 1275, ch des Patriotes, Sorel J3P 2N4 – 514/743-2703
Le Centre-de-la-Mauricie	70,050	Lyne Ricard, Gref., 550, av de l'Hôtel-de-Ville, CP 127, Shawinigan G9N 6T8 – 819/536-4477
Le Domaine-du-Roy	32,581	Denis Taillon, Gref., #101, 901, boul St-Joseph, Roberval G8H 2L8 – 418/275-5044
Le Fjord-du-Saguenay	178,176	Rénald Gaudreault, Gref., 475, boul Talbot, Chicoutimi G7H 4A3 – 418/696-2521
Le Granit	21,371	Serge Bilodeau, Gref., 5090, rue Frontenac, Lac-Mégantic G6B 1H3 – 819/583-0181
Le Haut-Richelieu	98,125	Joane Saulnier, Gref., 380, 4e av, CP 90, Iberville J2X 1W9 – 514/346-3636
Le Haut-St-François	22,700	Claude Brochu, Gref., 85, rue Principale ouest, CP 250, Cookshire J0B 1M0 – 819/875-3966
Le Haut-St-Laurent	22,703	François Landreville, Gref., 23, rue King, CP 1600, Huntingdon J0S 1H0 – 514/264-5411
Le Haut-St-Maurice	15,160	Daniel Prince, Gref., 800, rue Réal, La Tuque G9X 2S9 – 819/523-6111
Le Val-St-François	33,271	Martin Lafleur, Gref., 810, montée du Parc, CP 1869, Richmond J0B 2H0 – 819/826-6505
L'Érable	25,374	Victoire Renaud, Gref., 1636, av St-Louis, Plessisville G6L 2M9 – 819/362-6395
Les Basques	10,605	François Gosselin, Gref., 122, rue Notre-Dame ouest, CP 399, Trois-Pistoles G0L 4K0 – 418/851-3206
Les Chutes-de-la-Chaudière	73,020	Benoît Chevalier, Gref., 8100, rue du Blizzard, Charny G6X 1C9 – 418/832-2496
Les Collines-de-l'Outaouais	30,932	Norman Vachon, Gref., 216, ch Old Chelsea, Old Chelsea J0X 1N0 – 819/827-0516
Les Etchemins	18,937	Maryse Breton, Gref., 495, rue de l'Édifice-Municipal, CP 100, Ste-Rose-de-Watford G0R 4G0 – 418/267-5152
Les Îles-de-la-Madeleine	14,232	Lise Chevrier, Gref., CP 339, Cap-aux-Meules G0B 1B0 – 418/986-4251
Les Jardins-de-Napierville	23,137	Nicole Inkel, Gref., 361, rue St-Jacques, CP 1030, Napierville J0J 1L0 – 514/245-7527
Les Laurentides	34,220	Denis Savard, Gref., 1111, ch du Lac-Colibri, CP 30, St-Faustin J0T 2G0 – 819/688-3661
Les Maskoutains	80,339	Alain Beauregard, Gref., #200, 2200, rue Pratte, St-Hyacinthe J2S 4B6 – 514/774-3141
Les Moulins	102,056	Daniel Pilon, Gref., 148, rue St-André, Terrebonne J6W 3C3 – 514/471-9576
Les Pays-d'en-Haut	24,268	Yvan Genest, Gref., #200, 1332, boul Ste-Adèle, CP 1380, Ste-Adèle J0R 1L0 – 514/229-6637
L'Île-d'Orléans	7,219	Jules Prémont, Gref., 3893, ch Royal, Ste-Famille G0A 3P0 – 418/829-3104
L'Islet	20,217	Benoît Lévesque, Gref., 364, rue Verreault, CP 790, St-Jean-Port-Joli G0R 3G0 – 418/598-3076
Lotbinière	27,750	Daniel Patry, Gref., CP 430, Ste-Croix G0S 2H0 – 418/926-3407
Manicouagan	35,438	André Blais, Gref., 1384, rue Anticosti, Baie-Comeau G5C 3R2 – 418/589-9594
Maria-Chapdelaine	28,980	Christian Bouchard, Gref., 209, boul des Pères, Mistassini G0W 2C0 – 418/276-2131
Maskinongé	24,626	Janyse Pichette, Gref., 121, rue Petite-Rivière, Louiseville J5V 2H3 – 819/228-2193
Matane	24,287	Michel Barriault, Gref., 572, rue du Phare est, Matane G4W 1B1 – 418/562-6734
Matawinie	37,609	Yves Gaillardetz, Gref., 3184 - 1re av, CP 1239, Rawdon J0K 1S0 – 514/834-5441
Mékinac	14,412	Claude Beaulieu, Gref., 560, rue Notre-Dame, CP 490, St-Tite G0X 3H0 – 418/365-5151
Memphrémagog	37,599	Guy Jauron, Gref., 455, rue Macdonald, Magog J1X 1M2 – 819/843-9292
Minganie	6,241	Martin Larue, Gref., 8788, boul de l'Escale, CP 1146, Havre-St-Pierre G0G 1P0 – 418/538-2732
Mirabel	19,980	Suzanne Mireault, Gref., 14111, rue St-Jean, CP 60, Ste-Monique J0N 1R0 – 514/476-0360
Montcalm	36,750	Gaétan Hudon, Gref., 1530, rue Albert, CP 308, Ste-Julienne J0K 2T0 – 514/831-2182
Montmagny	23,608	Bernard Létourneau, Gref., 159, rue St-Louis, CP 38, Montmagny G5V 1N5 – 418/248-5985
Nicolet-Yamaska	24,514	Donald Martel, Gref., 400, rue Notre-Dame, CP 420, St-François-du-Lac J0G 1M0 – 514/568-3144
Pabok	22,205	Gaétan Lelièvre, Gref., 46, boul René-Lévesque ouest, CP 128, Chandler G0C 1K0 – 418/689-4313
Papineau	21,188	Louise Perrier, Gref., 266, rue Viger, CP 278, Papineauville J0V 1R0 – 819/427-6243
Pontiac	15,737	Luc Séguin, Gref., CP 460, Campbell's Bay J0X 1K0 – 819/648-5689
Portneuf	48,110	Yves Laroche, Gref., 185, rte 138, Cap-Santé G0A 1L0 – 418/285-3744
Rimouski-Neigette	53,819	Louise Audet, Gref., 220, av de la Cathédrale, CP 1297, Rimouski G5L 5J2 – 418/724-5154
Rivière-du-Loup	32,263	André Guay, Gref., 310, rue St-Pierre, CP 938, Rivière-du-Loup G5R 3V3 – 418/867-2485
Robert-Cliche	19,016	Gilbert Caron, Gref., 111A, 107e rue de la Station, Beauceville G0S 1A0 – 418/774-9828
Roussillon	125,519	Pierre Largy, Gref., 50, rue Ste-Thérèse, Delson J0L 1G0 – 514/638-1221
Rouville	33,043	Rosaire Marcil, Gref., #100, 500, rue Desjardins, Marieville J3M 1E1 – 514/460-2127
Rouyn-Noranda	43,222	Pierre Monfette, Gref., 332, rue Perreault est, Rouyn-Noranda J9X 3C6 – 819/762-6541
Sept-Rivières	35,492	Suzanne Cyr, Gref., #200, 106, rue Napoléon, Sept-Îles G4R 3L7 – 418/962-1900
Sherbrooke	131,447	Gilles Moreau, Gref., 390, rue King ouest, Sherbrooke J1H 1R4 – 819/821-2446
Témiscamingue	17,366	Denis Clermont, Gref., 21, rue Notre-Dame-de-Lourdes, CP 548, Ville-Marie J0Z 3W0 – 819/629-2829
Témiscouata	23,868	Jean-Pierre Laplante, Gref., 3, rue Hôtel de Ville, CP 460, Notre-Dame-du-Lac G0L 1X0 – 418/899-6725
Thérèse-de-Blainville	114,291	Lucille Vincelli, Gref., 100, rue Charbonneau, Rosemère J7A 3W1 – 514/621-4752
Vallée-de-l'Or	43,059	Louis Bourget, Gref., 42, Place Hammond, Val-d'Or J9P 3A9 – 819/825-7733
Vaudreuil-Soulanges	91,838	André Boisvert, Gref., #200, 420, av Roche, Vaudreuil-Dorion J7V 2N1 – 514/455-5753

QUÉBEC URBAN COMMUNITIES (REGIONAL GOVERNMENTS)

An in-depth listing for regional districts marked with * appears in Part 3 (check Index for page numbers).

MUNICIPALITY	POP.	CONTACT PERSON WITH ADDRESS & PHONE
Montréal	1,779,254 ('94)	Gérard Divay, Gref., 1550, rue Metcalfe, Montréal H3A 1X6 – 514/280-3522, Fax: 514/280-4243, URL: http://www.cum.qc.ca/
l'Outaouais	217,658 ('95)	Jacques Tremblay, Gref., #500, 25, rue Laurier, CP 2210, Hull J8X 3Z4 – 819/770-1380, Fax: 819/770-8479
Québec	493,694 ('94)	Serge Allen, Gref., 399, rue St-Joseph est, Québec G1K 8E2 – 418/529-8771, Fax: 418/529-2219
Administration Régionale Kativik		CP 9, Kuujjuaq J0M 1C0 – 819/964-2964, Fax: 819/964-2956

SASKATCHEWAN

Acts governing the municipal system in Saskatchewan are The Urban Municipality Act, 1984; The Rural Municipality Act, 1989; and The Northern Municipalities Act. In the province there are the following types of incorporated municipalities: Rural Municipalities, Villages, Resort Villages, Towns, and Cities, as well as Northern Towns, Northern Villages, Northern Hamlets and Northern Settlements. The incorporation of these municipalities is voluntary. Thus a Village that qualifies to be named a Town, can remain a Village if the population so wishes.

Rural Municipalities: are divided into divisions. A Reeve is elected at large every two years. Councillors are also elected every two years but in "staggered" sequence.

Villages: are defined as communities with not less than 100 permanent residents and not less than 50 dwellings and/or business premises. The Village is represented by a Mayor and two to four Councillors. They Mayor and Councillors are elected by the eligible electorate every three years.

Towns: are defined as communities with not less that 500 permanent residents. They are represented by a Mayor and six Councillors elected at large by the eligible electorate every three years.

Cities: are defined as communities with not less than 5,000 residents. They are represented by a Mayor and Councillors (the number varies).

Northern Municipalities: have similar criteria as above.

Elections for all are every three years.

Rural municipal nominations are received until the third Monday in October and elections are held on the third Wednesday after the nomination period. Nominations are held in Urban Municipalities on the second Wednesday in October and elections on the fourth Wednesday in October.

Cities in CAPITALS; Towns marked †; Villages marked (V); Northern Villages marked (NV); Resort Villages not listed. An in-depth listing for municipalities marked with * appears in Part 2 (check Index for page numbers).

MUNICIPALITY	1991 POP.	FEDERAL ELECTORAL DISTRICT	PROVINCIAL ELECTORAL DISTRICT	CONTACT PERSON WITH ADDRESS, PHONE & FAX
Abbey (V)	190	Swift Current-Maple Creek-Assiniboia	Cypress Hills	Richard B. Sylvestre, Adm., PO Box 210, Abbey S0N 0A0 – 306/689-2412, Fax: 306/689-2901
Aberdeen †	474	Saskatoon-Humboldt	Humboldt	Donna May, Adm., PO Box 130, Aberdeen S0K 0A0 – 306/253-4311, Fax: 306/253-4744
Abernethy (V)	243	Regina-Qu'Appelle	Melville	Leona Ward, Clerk, PO Box 95, Abernethy S0A 0A0 – 306/333-2271, Fax: 306/333-2271
Adanac (V)	17	Kindersley-Lloydminster	Battleford-Cut Knife	Victoria Ralston, Clerk, PO Box 1736, Unity S0K 4L0 – 306/228-2037
Admiral (V)	23	Swift Current-Maple Creek-Assiniboia	Wood River	Madeleine Spetz, Clerk, PO Box 44, Admiral S0N 0B0 – 306/297-6356
Air Ronge (NV)	782	Prince Albert-Churchill River	Cumberland	Joyce L. Forrest, Adm., PO Box 100, Air Ronge S0J 3G0 – 306/425-2107, Fax: 306/425-3108
Alameda †	317	Souris-Moose Mountain	Cannington	Ron Burness, Adm., PO Box 36, Alameda S0C 0A0 – 306/489-2077, Fax: 306/489-4602
Albertville (V)	149	Prince Albert-Churchill River	Saskatchewan Rivers	Colleen Lavoie, Clerk, General Delivery, Albertville S0J 0A0 – 306/929-2110, Fax: 306/929-4791
Alida (V)	179	Souris-Moose Mountain	Cannington	Tammy McCannell, Clerk, PO Box 6, Alida S0C 0B0 – 306/443-2228
Allan †	765	Saskatoon-Dundurn	Watrous	Christine Dyck, Adm., PO Box 159, Allan S0K 0C0 – 306/257-3272, Fax: 306/257-3337
Alsask (V)	319	Kindersley-Lloydminster	Kindersley	Ronald A. Henry, Clerk, PO Box 219, Alsask S0L 0A0 – 306/968-2394, Fax: 306/968-2300
Alvena (V)	79	Saskatoon-Humboldt	Humboldt	Sheri Schitka, Adm., PO Box 8, Alvena S0K 0E0 – 306/943-2101
Aneroid (V)	98	Swift Current-Maple Creek-Assiniboia	Wood River	M.B. Thibault, Clerk, PO Box 226, Aneroid S0N 0C0 – 306/588-2300
Annaheim (V)	185	Saskatoon-Humboldt	Kelvington-Wadena	Brenda Nagy, Adm., PO Box 70, Annaheim S0K 0G0 – 306/598-2122, Fax: 306/598-4526
Antler (V)	71	Souris-Moose Mountain	Cannington	Yvonne Bauche, Adm., PO Box 83, Antler S0C 0E0 – 306/452-6155
Arborfield †	433	Mackenzie	Carrot River Valley	Allan Frisky, Adm., PO Box 280, Arborfield S0E 0A0 – 306/769-8533, Fax: 306/769-8301
Archerwill (V)	272	Mackenzie	Kelvington-Wadena	Paulette Althouse, Clerk, PO Box 130, Archerwill S0E 0B0 – 306/323-2161, Fax: 306/323-2101
Arcola †	496	Souris-Moose Mountain	Cannington	Sheila Sim, Adm., PO Box 359, Arcola S0C 0G0 – 306/455-2212, Fax: 306/455-2445
Arelee (V)	25	Kindersley-Lloydminster	Redberry Lake	Lloyd R. Cross, Adm., PO Box 100, Arelee S0K 0H0 – 306/237-4424, Fax: 306/237-4294
Arran (V)	59	Yorkton-Melville	Canora-Pelly	Mike Burtnack, Clerk, PO Box 40, Arran S0A 0B0 – 306/595-4521
Asquith †	525	Kindersley-Lloydminster	Redberry Lake	Holly Cross, Acting Adm., PO Box 160, Asquith S0K 0J0 – 306/329-4341, Fax: 306/329-4969
Assiniboia †	2,774	Swift Current-Maple Creek-Assiniboia	Wood River	Bruce L. Masur, Adm., PO Box 670, Assiniboia S0H 0B0 – 306/642-3382, Fax: 306/642-5622
Atwater (V)	31	Yorkton-Melville	Saltcoats	Doreen D. Rausch, Clerk, PO Box 58, Atwater S0A 0C0 – 306/745-3809
Avonlea (V)	405	Moose Jaw-Lake Centre	Thunder Creek	Tim Forer, Adm., PO Box 209, Avonlea S0H 0C0 – 306/868-2221, Fax: 306/868-2221
Aylesbury (V)	63	Moose Jaw-Lake Centre	Arm River	Dorothy M. Wright, Clerk, PO Box 151, Aylesbury S0G 0B0 – 306/734-5125
Aylsham (V)	104	Mackenzie	Carrot River Valley	Dorothy E. Blue, Clerk, PO Box 71, Aylsham S0E 0C0 – 306/862-9415
Balcarres †	661	Regina-Qu'Appelle	Melville	Don A. Warner, Clerk, PO Box 130, Balcarres S0G 0C0 – 306/334-2566, Fax: 306/334-2907
Balgonie †	1,096	Regina-Qu'Appelle	Regina Wascana Plains	Barbara Marcia, Adm., PO Box 310, Balgonie S0G 0E0 – 306/771-2284, Fax: 306/771-2899

Cities in CAPITALS; Towns marked †; Villages marked (V); Northern Villages marked (NV); Resort Villages not listed. An in-depth listing for municipalities marked with * appears in Part 2 (check Index for page numbers).

MUNICIPALITY	1991 POP.	FEDERAL ELECTORAL DISTRICT	PROVINCIAL ELECTORAL DISTRICT	CONTACT PERSON WITH ADDRESS, PHONE & FAX
Bangor (V)	54	Yorkton-Melville	Saltcoats	Joan C. Bomerak, Clerk, PO Box 35, Bangor S0A 0E0 – 306/728-4084
Battleford †	4,107	The Battlefords-Meadow Lake	Battleford-Cut Knife	Sheryl Ballendine, Adm., PO Box 40, Battleford S0M 0E0 – 306/937-6200, Fax: 306/937-2450
Beatty (V)	112	Saskatoon-Humboldt	Melfort-Tisdale	James D. Mason, Clerk, PO Box 51, Beatty S0J 0C0 – 306/752-3980
Beauval (NV)	717	The Battlefords-Meadow Lake	Athabasca	Dorothy M. Alcrow, Clerk, PO Box 19, Beauval S0M 0G0 – 306/288-2110, Fax: 306/288-2348
Beechy (V)	298	Kindersley-Lloydminster	Rosetown-Biggar	Heather Meaden, Clerk, PO Box 153, Beechy S0L 0C0 – 306/859-2205, Fax: 306/859-2238
Belle Plaine (V)	80	Moose Jaw-Lake Centre	Thunder Creek	Reg E. McKee, Clerk, PO Box 63, Belle Plaine S0G 0G0 – 306/692-3390
Bengough †	527	Swift Current-Maple Creek-Assiniboia	Weyburn-Big Muddy	Wanda McGonigal, Adm., PO Box 188, Bengough S0C 0K0 – 306/268-2927, Fax: 306/268-2927
Benson (V)	85	Souris-Moose Mountain	Estevan	Nadine Leclair, Clerk, PO Box 27, Benson S0C 0L0 – 306/634-4904
Bethune (V)	369	Moose Jaw-Lake Centre	Arm River	Patti Garrett, Clerk, PO Box 209, Bethune S0G 0H0 – 306/638-3188, Fax: 306/638-3188
Bienfait †	799	Souris-Moose Mountain	Estevan	Helen Gurski, Adm., PO Box 220, Bienfait S0C 0M0 – 306/388-2969, Fax: 306/388-2960
Big River †	809	The Battlefords-Meadow Lake	Shellbrook-Spiritwood	Bernice Swanson, Adm., PO Box 220, Big River S0J 0E0 – 306/469-2112, Fax: 306/469-5755
Biggar †	2,351	Kindersley-Lloydminster	Rosetown-Biggar	R.G. Tyler, Adm., PO Box 489, Biggar S0K 0M0 – 306/948-3317, Fax: 306/948-5134
Birch Hills †	939	Saskatoon-Humboldt	Saskatchewan Rivers	Darlene Cochrane, Adm., PO Box 206, Birch Hills S0J 0G0 – 306/749-2232, Fax: 306/749-2220
Birsay (V)	65	Kindersley-Lloydminster	Rosetown-Biggar	Murray Cook, Clerk, PO Box 106, Birsay S0L 0G0 – 306/573-2047, Fax: 306/573-2111
Bjorkdale (V)	251	Mackenzie	Carrot River Valley	Joanne Kehrig, Clerk, PO Box 27, Bjorkdale S0E 0E0 – 306/886-2167, Fax: 306/886-4446
Bladworth (V)	111	Moose Jaw-Lake Centre	Arm River	Marion Bessey, Clerk, PO Box 90, Bladworth S0G 0J0 – 306/567-4364
Blaine Lake †	575	The Battlefords-Meadow Lake	Redberry Lake	Eleanora Boyko, Adm., PO Box 10, Blaine Lake S0J 0J0 – 306/497-2531, Fax: 306/497-2511
Borden (V)	215	The Battlefords-Meadow Lake	Redberry Lake	Sandra Long, Adm., PO Box 210, Borden S0K 0N0 – 306/997-2134
Bounty (V)	28	Kindersley-Lloydminster	Rosetown-Biggar	Kay Logan, Clerk, RR#1, PO Box 16, Bounty S0L 0L0 – 306/856-4825
Bracken (V)	48	Swift Current-Maple Creek-Assiniboia	Wood River	Donna Peakman, Clerk, PO Box 41, Bracken S0N 0G0 – 306/293-2945
Bradwell (V)	148	Saskatoon-Dundurn	Watrous	Robert Thurmeier, Adm., PO Box 100, Bradwell S0K 0P0 – 306/257-4141, Fax: 306/257-3303
Bredenbury †	394	Yorkton-Melville	Saltcoats	Olga Mosiman, Clerk, PO Box 87, Bredenbury S0A 0H0 – 306/898-2055, Fax: 306/898-2103
Briercrest (V)	140	Moose Jaw-Lake Centre	Thunder Creek	Eileen Jeffery, Clerk, PO Box 25, Briercrest S0H 0K0 – 306/799-2053
Broadview †	797	Souris-Moose Mountain	Moosomin	Phil Boivin, Adm., PO Box 430, Broadview S0G 0K0 – 306/696-2533, Fax: 306/696-3573
Brock (V)	157	Kindersley-Lloydminster	Kindersley	Barry Knight, Clerk, PO Box 70, Brock S0L 0H0 – 306/379-2116, Fax: 306/379-2024
Broderick (V)	93	Moose Jaw-Lake Centre	Arm River	Elaine Nadeau, Clerk, PO Box 29, Broderick S0H 0L0 – 306/867-8009, Fax: 306/867-9271
Brownlee (V)	100	Moose Jaw-Lake Centre	Arm River	Linda Smith, Clerk, PO Box 89, Brownlee S0H 0M0 – 306/759-2302
Bruno †	656	Saskatoon-Humboldt	Humboldt	Vicky Serblowski, Adm., PO Box 370, Bruno S0K 0S0 – 306/369-2514, Fax: 306/369-2514
Buchanan (V)	338	Yorkton-Melville	Canora-Pelly	Eleanor Hadubiak, Adm., PO Box 479, Buchanan S0A 0J0 – 306/592-2144
Buena Vista (V)	276	Regina-Lumsden	Arm River	Anne Fink, Clerk, PO Box 154, Regina Beach S0G 4C0 – 306/729-4385, Fax: 306/729-4518
Buffalo Narrows (NV)	1,060	Prince Albert-Churchill River	Athabasca	Laura Durocher, Clerk, PO Box 98, Buffalo Narrows S0M 0J0 – 306/235-4225, Fax: 306/235-4699
Bulyea (V)	122	Regina-Qu'Appelle	Last Mountain-Touchwood	Kelly Hansen, Clerk, PO Box 37, Bulyea S0G 0L0 – 306/725-4936
Burstall †	451	Swift Current-Maple Creek-Assiniboia	Cypress Hills	Elaine K. Brodie, Adm., PO Box 250, Burstall S0N 0H0 – 306/679-2000, Fax: 306/679-2275
Cabri †	561	Swift Current-Maple Creek-Assiniboia	Cypress Hills	Anne P. Francis, Adm., PO Box 200, Cabri S0N 0J0 – 306/587-2500
Cadillac (V)	134	Swift Current-Maple Creek-Assiniboia	Wood River	Twila St. Jacques, Clerk, PO Box 189, Cadillac S0N 0K0 – 306/785-2100
Calder (V)	155	Yorkton-Melville	Saltcoats	Helen Tkachuk, Clerk, PO Box 47, Calder S0A 0K0 – 306/742-2158

Cities in CAPITALS; Towns marked †; Villages marked (V); Northern Villages marked (NV); Resort Villages not listed. An in-depth listing for municipalities marked with * appears in Part 2 (check Index for page numbers).

MUNICIPALITY	1991 POP.	FEDERAL ELECTORAL DISTRICT	PROVINCIAL ELECTORAL DISTRICT	CONTACT PERSON WITH ADDRESS, PHONE & FAX
Cando (V)	96	Kindersley-Lloydminster	Battleford-Cut Knife	Dora Beckman, Clerk, PO Box 6, Cando S0K 0V0 – 306/937-3052
Canora †	2,381	Yorkton-Melville	Canora-Pelly	Patrick N. Dergousoff, Adm., PO Box 717, Canora S0A 0L0 – 306/563-5773, Fax: 306/563-4336
Canwood (V)	367	The Battlefords-Meadow Lake	Shellbrook-Spiritwood	Terry Lofstrom, Clerk, PO Box 172, Canwood S0J 0K0 – 306/468-2016, Fax: 306/468-2666
Carievale (V)	234	Souris-Moose Mountain	Cannington	Donalene McMillen, Clerk, PO Box 154, Carievale S0C 0P0 – 306/928-2033, Fax: 306/928-2021
Carlyle †	1,181	Souris-Moose Mountain	Cannington	Norm Riddell, Adm., PO Box 10, Carlyle S0C 0R0 – 306/453-2363, Fax: 306/453-6380
Carmichael (V)	33	Swift Current-Maple Creek-Assiniboia	Cypress Hills	Collette Jones, Clerk, PO Box 503, Gull Lake S0N 1A0 – 306/672-3501, Fax: 306/672-3879
Carnduff †	1,062	Souris-Moose Mountain	Cannington	Kevin Stephenson, Adm., PO Box 100, Carnduff S0C 0S0 – 306/482-3300, Fax: 306/482-3422
Caronport (V)	889	Moose Jaw-Lake Centre	Thunder Creek	Mildred From, Adm., PO Box 550, Caronport S0H 0S0 – 306/756-2225, Fax: 306/756-2225
Carragana (V)	47	Mackenzie	Kelvington-Wadena	Olga Smith, Clerk, PO Box 42, Carragana S0E 0K0 – 306/278-3487
Carrot River †	1,027	Mackenzie	Carrot River Valley	Duril Touet, Adm., PO Box 147, Carrot River S0E 0L0 – 306/768-2515, Fax: 306/768-2930
Central Butte †	562	Moose Jaw-Lake Centre	Arm River	Don Wildeman, Adm., PO Box 10, Central Butte S0H 0T0 – 306/796-2288, Fax: 306/796-2223
Ceylon (V)	163	Souris-Moose Mountain	Weyburn-Big Muddy	Vaughan B. McClarty, Adm., PO Box 188, Ceylon S0C 0T0 – 306/454-2202, Fax: 306/454-2627
Chamberlain (V)	129	Moose Jaw-Lake Centre	Arm River	Rhonda Lang, Clerk, PO Box 8, Chamberlain S0G 0R0 – 306/638-4680
Chaplin (V)	332	Moose Jaw-Lake Centre	Thunder Creek	Carol Andrews, Clerk, PO Box 210, Chaplin S0H 0V0 – 306/395-2221, Fax: 306/395-2221
Choiceland †	434	Mackenzie	Saskatchewan Rivers	Colleen Digness, Adm., PO Box 279, Choiceland S0J 0M0 – 306/428-2070, Fax: 306/428-2424
Christopher Lake (V)	199	Prince Albert-Churchill River	Saskatchewan Rivers	Cheryl Heleta, Adm., PO Box 163, Christopher Lake S0J 0N0 – 306/982-4242, Fax: 306/982-4242
Churchbridge †	919	Yorkton-Melville	Saltcoats	Dawn Dressler, Adm., PO Box 256, Churchbridge S0A 0M0 – 306/896-2240, Fax: 306/896-2240
Clavet (V)	359	Saskatoon-Dundurn	Watrous	Susan Bonokoski, Clerk, PO Box 68, Clavet S0K 0Y0 – 306/933-2425, Fax: 306/933-2425
Climax (V)	226	Swift Current-Maple Creek-Assiniboia	Wood River	Ronald James Johnson, Adm., PO Box 30, Climax S0N 0N0 – 306/293-2124, Fax: 306/293-2702
Coderre (V)	68	Moose Jaw-Lake Centre	Thunder Creek	Faye Johnstone, Clerk, PO Box 9, Coderre S0H 0X0 – 306/394-2070
Codette (V)	293	Mackenzie	Carrot River Valley	Eunice Rudy, Clerk, PO Box 100, Codette S0E 0P0 – 306/862-9551, Fax: 306/862-9551
Cole Bay (NV)	163	The Battlefords-Meadow Lake	Athabasca	Delphine Bouvier, Adm., General Delivery, Cole Bay S0M 0M0 – 306/829-4232, Fax: 306/829-4312
Coleville (V)	372	Kindersley-Lloydminster	Kindersley	Gloria Johnson, Adm., PO Box 249, Coleville S0L 0K0 – 306/965-2281, Fax: 306/965-2466
Colgate (V)	45	Souris-Moose Mountain	Estevan	Laurie Bell, Clerk, PO Box 5, Colgate S0C 0V0 – 306/456-2472, Fax: 306/456-2512
Colonsay †	453	Moose Jaw-Lake Centre	Watrous	Joanne Binsfeld, Adm., PO Box 190, Colonsay S0K 0Z0 – 306/255-2313, Fax: 306/255-2000
Conquest (V)	224	Kindersley-Lloydminster	Rosetown-Biggar	Margaret Latimer, Clerk, PO Box 250, Conquest S0L 0L0 – 306/856-2114
Consul (V)	114	Swift Current-Maple Creek-Assinboia	Cypress Hills	Carrie Funk, Adm., PO Box 185, Consul S0N 0P0 – 306/299-2030
Coronach †	944	Swift Current-Maple Creek-Assiniboia	Wood River	Murray H. Setrum, Adm., PO Box 90, Coronach S0H 0Z0 – 306/267-2150, Fax: 306/267-2296
Craik †	481	Moose Jaw-Lake Centre	Arm River	Nora Bakken, Clerk, PO Box 60, Craik S0G 0V0 – 306/734-2250
Craven (V)	267	Regina-Qu'Appelle	Last Mountain-Touchwood	Linda Stevens, Clerk, PO Box 30, Craven S0G 0W0 – 306/731-3452
Creelman (V)	134	Souris-Moose Mountain	Indian Head-Milestone	May Allan, Clerk, PO Box 177, Creelman S0G 0X0 – 306/433-2011
Creighton †	1,668	Prince Albert-Churchill River	Cumberland	Therese Wheeler, Adm., PO Box 100, Creighton S0P 0A0 – 306/688-8253, Fax: 306/688-4764
Cudworth †	727	Saskatoon-Humboldt	Humboldt	Judy P.M. Trischuk, Clerk, PO Box 69, Cudworth S0K 1B0 – 306/256-3492, Fax: 306/256-3515
Cumberland House (NV)	738	Mackenzie	Cumberland	Pat McKenzie, Adm., PO Box 190, Cumberland House S0E 0S0 – 306/888-2066, Fax: 306/888-2103
Cupar †	636	Regina-Qu'Appelle	Last Mountain-Touchwood	Cecile Daradich, Adm., PO Box 397, Cupar S0G 0Y0 – 306/723-4324, Fax: 306/723-4324
Cut Knife †	588	The Battlefords-Meadow Lake	Battleford-Cut Knife	Richard Emanuel, Adm., PO Box 338, Cut Knife S0M 0N0 – 306/398-2363, Fax: 306/398-2568

Cities in CAPITALS; Towns marked †; Villages marked (V); Northern Villages marked (NV); Resort Villages not listed. An in-depth listing for municipalities marked with * appears in Part 2 (check Index for page numbers).

MUNICIPALITY	1991 POP.	FEDERAL ELECTORAL DISTRICT	PROVINCIAL ELECTORAL DISTRICT	CONTACT PERSON WITH ADDRESS, PHONE & FAX
Dafoe (V)	20	Mackenzie	Watrous	Lana M. Bolt, Clerk, PO Box 142, Dafoe S0K 1C0 – 306/554-3250
Dalmeny †	1,436	Saskatoon-Clark's Crossing	Rosthern	Shelley Funk, Adm., PO Box 400, Dalmeny S0K 1E0 – 306/254-2133, Fax: 306/254-2142
Davidson †	1,115	Moose Jaw-Lake Centre	Arm River	Gary Edom, Adm., PO Box 340, Davidson S0G 1A0 – 306/567-2040, Fax: 306/567-4730
Debden (V)	416	The Battlefords-Meadow Lake	Shellbrook-Spiritwood	Carmen Jean, Adm., PO Box 400, Debden S0J 0S0 – 306/724-2040, Fax: 306/724-2220
Delisle †	874	Kindersley-Lloydminster	Redberry Lake	Mark Dubkowski, Adm., PO Box 40, Delisle S0L 0P0 – 306/493-2242
Denare Beach (NV)	822	Prince Albert-Churchill River	Cumberland	Beverley J. Wheeler, Clerk, PO Box 70, Denare Beach S0P 0B0 – 306/362-2054, Fax: 306/362-2257
Denholm (V)	85	The Battlefords-Meadow Lake	Redberry Lake	Beverley Shumlich, Clerk, PO Box 71, Denholm S0M 0R0 – 306/445-7330
Denzil (V)	207	Kindersley-Lloydminster	Kindersley	Janet Vetter, Adm., PO Box 100, Denzil S0L 0S0 – 306/358-2118, Fax: 306/358-4828
Deschambault Lake (NH)	607	Prince Albert-Churchill River	Cumberland	Laura Clarke, Clerk, General Delivery, Deschambault Lake S0P 0C0 – 306/632-4522, Fax: 306/632-4507
Dilke (V)	98	Moose Jaw-Lake Centre	Arm River	Colleen R. Duesing, Clerk, PO Box 100, Dilke S0G 1C0 – 306/488-4866
Dinsmore (V)	374	Kindersley-Lloydminster	Rosetown-Biggar	Jim Main, Clerk, PO Box 278, Dinsmore S0L 0T0 – 306/846-2220, Fax: 306/846-2999
Disley (V)	60	Regina-Lumsden	Arm River	Patti Garrett, Clerk, PO Box 203, Bethune S0G 0H0 – 306/638-3188, Fax: 306/638-3188
Dodsland (V)	269	Kindersley-Lloydminster	Kindersley	Wendy L. Davis, Clerk, PO Box 400, Dodsland S0L 0V0 – 306/356-2055, Fax: 306/356-2055
Dollard (V)	33	Swift Current-Maple Creek-Assiniboia	Cypress Hills	Richard E. Goulet, Adm., PO Box 1115, Shaunavon S0N 2M0 – 306/297-2108, Fax: 306/297-2108
Domremy (V)	150	Saskatoon-Humboldt	Humboldt	Lil Georget, Clerk, PO Box 208, Domremy S0K 1G0 – 306/423-5244
Dore Lake (NH)	41	The Battlefords-Meadow Lake	Athabasca	Eugenie Aubichon, Clerk, PO Box 608, Big River S0J 0E0 – 306/832-4528, Fax: 306/832-4525
Dorintosh (V)	100	The Battlefords-Meadow Lake	Meadow Lake	Barbara Galger, Clerk, PO Box 40, Dorintosh S0M 0T0 – 306/236-5166
Drake (V)	243	Moose Jaw-Lake Centre	Watrous	Elsie Schroeder, Clerk, PO Box 18, Drake S0K 1H0 – 306/363-2109
Drinkwater (V)	78	Moose Jaw-Lake Centre	Thunder Creek	Shelly Large, Clerk, PO Box 66, Drinkwater S0H 1G0 – 306/693-5093
Dubuc (V)	99	Yorkton-Melville	Melville	Leona Kaczur, Clerk, PO Box 126, Dubuc S0A 0R0 – 306/877-2172
Duck Lake †	661	Saskatoon-Humboldt	Shellbrook-Spiritwood	Betty Fiolleau, Adm., PO Box 430, Duck Lake S0K 1J0 – 306/467-2277
Duff (V)	52	Yorkton-Melville	Melville	Reta M. Schick, Clerk, PO Box 57, Duff S0A 0S0 – 306/728-3592
Dundurn †	496	Saskatoon-Dundurn	Arm River	Marion D. Beaucage, Adm., PO Box 185, Dundurn S0K 1K0 – 306/492-2202, Fax: 306/492-2202
Duval (V)	108	Regina-Qu'Appelle	Last Mountain-Touchwood	Leonard Wm. Jones, Clerk, PO Box 70, Duval S0G 1G0 – 306/725-3767
Dysart (V)	243	Regina-Qu'Appelle	Last Mountain-Touchwood	Bernadette Rothecker, Clerk, PO Box 70, Dysart S0G 1H0 – 306/432-2100
Earl Grey (V)	289	Regina-Qu'Appelle	Last Mountain-Touchwood	Shelley Mohr, Adm., PO Box 100, Earl Grey S0G 1J0 – 306/939-2062
Eastend †	622	Swift Current-Maple Creek-Assiniboia	Cypress Hills	Karen Mack, Adm., PO Box 520, Eastend S0N 0T0 – 306/295-3322, Fax: 306/295-3571
Eatonia †	505	Kindersley-Lloydminster	Kindersley	Darlene L. Olson, Adm., PO Box 237, Eatonia S0L 0Y0 – 306/967-2582, Fax: 306/967-2267
Ebenezer (V)	182	Yorkton-Melville	Yorkton	Norman Zayshley, Clerk, PO Box 97, Ebenezer S0A 0T0 – 306/782-5758
Edam (V)	425	The Battlefords-Meadow Lake	Lloydminster	Trudy McMurphy, Adm., PO Box 203, Edam S0M 0V0 – 306/397-2223, Fax: 306/397-2626
Edenwold (V)	175	Regina-Qu'Appelle	Indian Head-Milestone	Liz Kletzel, Clerk, PO Box 130, Edenwold S0G 1K0 – 306/771-4121
Elbow (V)	328	Moose Jaw-Lake Centre	Arm River	Valerie C. Hundeby, Adm., PO Box 8, Elbow S0H 1J0 – 306/854-2277, Fax: 306/854-2229
Elfros (V)	181	Mackenzie	Last Mountain-Touchwood	Mary Corby, Clerk, PO Box 40, Elfros S0A 0V0 – 306/328-2123
Elrose †	577	Kindersley-Lloydminster	Rosetown-Biggar	Barb Trayhorne, Adm., PO Box 458, Elrose S0L 0Z0 – 306/378-2202, Fax: 306/378-2966
Elstow (V)	104	Saskatoon-Dundurn	Watrous	Elva Greschuk, Clerk, PO Box 29, Elstow S0K 1M0 – 306/257-3889
Endeavour (V)	173	Yorkton-Melville	Kelvington-Wadena	Cindy Greba, Adm., PO Box 307, Endeavour S0A 0W0 – 306/547-3484

Cities in CAPITALS; Towns marked †; Villages marked (V); Northern Villages marked (NV); Resort Villages not listed. An in-depth listing for municipalities marked with * appears in Part 2 (check Index for page numbers).

MUNICIPALITY	1991 POP.	FEDERAL ELECTORAL DISTRICT	PROVINCIAL ELECTORAL DISTRICT	CONTACT PERSON WITH ADDRESS, PHONE & FAX
Englefeld (V)	219	Saskatoon-Humboldt	Kelvington-Wadena	Roman Zimmerman, Clerk, PO Box 44, Englefeld S0K 1N0 – 306/287-3151, Fax: 306/287-3139
Ernfold (V)	64	Swift Current-Maple Creek-Assiniboia	Thunder Creek	Diane Marie McLaren, Clerk, PO Box 100, Ernfold S0H 1K0 – 306/629-3866, 3881
Esterhazy †	2,896	Yorkton-Melville	Saltcoats	Brian Sych, Adm., PO Box 490, Esterhazy S0A 0X0 – 306/745-3942, Fax: 306/745-6797
ESTEVAN	10,240	Souris-Moose Mountain	Estevan	Marcel Hoste, Clerk, 1102 - 4 St., Estevan S4A 0W7 – 306/634-1802, Fax: 306/634-9790
Eston †	1,210	Kindersley-Lloydminster	Kindersley	Helen M. Cowan, Adm., PO Box 757, Eston S0L 1A0 – 306/962-4444, Fax: 306/962-4224
Evesham (V)	38	Kindersley-Lloydminster	Battleford-Cut Knife	Marge Wells, Clerk, PO Box 29, Evesham S0L 1B0 – 306/753-2614
Eyebrow (V)	169	Moose Jaw-Lake Centre	Arm River	Joy Harms, Clerk, PO Box 159, Eyebrow S0H 1L0 – 306/759-2167
Fairlight (V)	68	Souris-Moose Mountain	Moosomin	Diana Sauter, Clerk, PO Box 55, Fairlight S0G 1M0 – 306/646-5709
Fenwood (V)	65	Yorkton-Melville	Melville	Doreen Dohms, Clerk, PO Box 66, Fenwood S0A 0Y0 – 306/728-4069
Fife Lake (V)	68	Swift Current-Maple Creek-Assiniboia	Wood River	Cecil L. Keast, Clerk, PO Box 688, Coronach S0H 0Z0 – 306/267-3234, Fax: 306/267-3234
Fillmore (V)	328	Souris-Moose Mountain	Indian Head-Milestone	Brian Beare, Adm., PO Box 185, Fillmore S0G 1N0 – 306/722-3330, Fax: 306/722-3370
Findlater (V)	55	Moose Jaw-Lake Centre	Arm River	Heather Paul, Clerk, PO Box 10, Findlater S0G 1P0 – 306/638-4630
Flaxcombe (V)	123	Kindersley-Lloydminster	Kindersley	Charlotte Helfrich, Clerk, PO Box 136, Flaxcombe S0L 1E0 – 306/463-6397
Fleming †	118	Souris-Moose Mountain	Moosomin	Joan Mills, Clerk, PO Box 62, Fleming S0G 1R0 – 306/435-4244
Flin Flon (V)	330	Prince Albert-Churchill River	Cumberland	
Foam Lake †	1,359	Mackenzie	Canora-Pelly	G. Emily Kreuger, Adm., PO Box 57, Foam Lake S0A 1A0 – 306/272-3359, Fax: 306/272-3738
Forget (V)	68	Souris-Moose Mountain	Cannington	Sharon Wilkes, Clerk, PO Box 100, Forget S0C 0X0 – 306/457-2808
Fort Qu'Appelle †	1,953	Regina-Qu'Appelle	Indian Head-Milestone	Sandra Schlamp, Adm., PO Box 309, Fort Qu'Appelle S0G 1S0 – 306/332-5266, Fax: 306/332-5087
Fosston (V)	87	Mackenzie	Kelvington-Wadena	John Reschny, Clerk, PO Box 160, Fosston S0E 0V0 – 306/322-4521
Fox Valley (V)	360	Swift Current-Maple Creek-Assiniboia	Cypress Hills	Michelle Sehn, Clerk, PO Box 207, Fox Valley S0N 0V0 – 306/666-3020
Francis †	205	Regina-Wascana	Indian Head-Milestone	Joyce A. Carroll, Clerk, PO Box 128, Francis S0G 1V0 – 306/245-3624
Frobisher (V)	158	Souris-Moose Mountain	Estevan	Diane Truscott, Clerk, PO Box 235, Frobisher S0C 0Y0 – 306/486-2140, Fax: 306/486-2140
Frontier (V)	385	Swift Current-Maple Creek-Assiniboia	Cypress Hills	Raymond J. Dubé, Adm., PO Box 30, Frontier S0N 0W0 – 306/296-2030, Fax: 306/296-2175
Gainsborough (V)	301	Souris-Moose Mountain	Cannington	Valerie A. Olney, Adm., PO Box 120, Gainsborough S0C 0Z0 – 306/685-2010, Fax: 306/685-2161
Gerald (V)	186	Yorkton-Melville	Saltcoats	Karen Assailly, Clerk, PO Box 155, Gerald S0A 1B0 – 306/745-6786
Girvin (V)	43	Moose Jaw-Lake Centre	Arm River	Marcia Palmer, Clerk, PO Box 70, Girvin S0G 1X0 – 306/567-4337, Fax: 306/567-4236
Gladmar (V)	53	Souris-Moose Mountain	Weyburn-Big Muddy	Darlene Petterson, Clerk, PO Box 92, Gladmar S0C 1A0 – 306/969-4837
Glaslyn (V)	435	The Battlefords-Meadow Lake	Shellbrook-Spiritwood	Linda Sandwick, Adm., PO Box 279, Glaslyn S0M 0Y0 – 306/342-2144, Fax: 306/342-2144
Glen Ewen (V)	152	Souris-Moose Mountain	Cannington	Darlene Carefoot, Clerk, PO Box 99, Glen Ewen S0C 1C0 – 306/925-2211
Glenavon (V)	237	Souris-Moose Mountain	Moosomin	James Hoff, Adm., PO Box 327, Glenavon S0G 1Y0 – 306/429-2011, Fax: 306/429-2260
Glenside (V)	80	Moose Jaw-Lake Centre	Arm River	Ethel Rooke, Clerk, General Delivery, PO Box 99, Glenside S0H 1T0 – 306/867-8932
Glentworth (V)	81	Swift Current-Maple Creek-Assiniboia	Wood River	E.P. Gasper, Clerk, PO Box 70, Glentworth S0H 1V0 – 306/266-4920, Fax: 306/266-2077
Glidden (V)	49	Kindersley-Lloydminster	Kindersley	Lois Haug, Clerk, PO Box 26, Glidden S0L 1H0 – 306/463-3338, Fax: 306/463-4748
Golden Prairie (V)	67	Swift Current-Maple Creek-Assiniboia	Cypress Hills	Quinton Jacksteiit, Adm., PO Box 9, Golden Prairie S0N 0Y0 – 306/662-2883, Fax: 306/662-2883
Goodeve (V)	77	Yorkton-Melville	Melville	Louise Rathgeber, Clerk, PO Box 160, Goodeve S0A 1C0 – 306/876-4633
Goodsoil (V)	288	The Battlefords-Meadow Lake	Meadow Lake	Donna Weinkauf, Clerk, PO Box 176, Goodsoil S0M 1A0 – 306/238-2094, Fax: 306/238-2094

Canadian Almanac & Directory 1997

Cities in CAPITALS; Towns marked †; Villages marked (V); Northern Villages marked (NV); Resort Villages not listed. An in-depth listing for municipalities marked with * appears in Part 2 (check Index for page numbers).

MUNICIPALITY	1991 POP.	FEDERAL ELECTORAL DISTRICT	PROVINCIAL ELECTORAL DISTRICT	CONTACT PERSON WITH ADDRESS, PHONE & FAX
Goodwater (V)	34	Souris-Moose Mountain	Estevan	Kevin Melle, Adm., PO Box 280, Weyburn S4H 2K1 – 306/456-2566, Fax: 306/456-2566
Govan †	318	Regina-Qu'Appelle	Last Mountain-Touchwood	Cal C. Shaw, Adm., PO Box 160, Govan S0G 1Z0 – 306/484-2011, Fax: 306/484-2113
Grand Coulee (V)	276	Regina-Lumsden	Regina Qu'Appelle Valley	Patrick Seeley, Clerk, RR#2, Site 1, Box 72, Regina S4P 2Z2 – 306/352-8694
Gravelbourg †	1,226	Swift Current-Maple Creek-Assiniboia	Thunder Creek	Aline Kirk, Adm., PO Box 359, Gravelbourg S0H 1X0 – 306/648-3301, Fax: 306/648-3400
Grayson (V)	256	Yorkton-Melville	Melville	Eileen Parker, Clerk, PO Box 69, Grayson S0A 1E0 – 306/794-2044, Fax: 306/794-4655
Green Lake (NV)	513	The Battlefords-Meadow Lake	Athabasca	Moise Lafond, Adm., PO Box 128, Green Lake S0M 1B0 – 306/832-2131, Fax: 306/832-2124
Grenfell †	1,164	Souris-Moose Mountain	Moosomin	Leslie McGhie, Adm., PO Box 1120, Grenfell S0G 2B0 – 306/697-2815, Fax: 306/697-2484
Guernsey (V)	161	Moose Jaw-Lake Centre	Watrous	Eleanor Uchacz, Clerk, PO Box 93, Guernsey S0K 1W0 – 306/365-4356
Gull Lake †	1,050	Swift Current-Maple Creek-Assiniboia	Cypress Hills	Abe Funk, Adm., PO Box 150, Gull Lake S0N 1A0 – 306/672-3361, Fax: 306/672-3777
Hafford †	478	The Battlefords-Meadow Lake	Redberry Lake	Charles W. Linnell, Adm., PO Box 220, Hafford S0J 1A0 – 306/549-2331, Fax: 306/549-2331
Hague †	655	Saskatoon-Clark's Crossing	Rosthern	Ivan M. Gabrysh, Adm., PO Box 180, Hague S0K 1X0 – 306/225-2155, Fax: 306/225-4410
Halbrite (V)	111	Souris-Moose Mountain	Estevan	Gail Silver, Clerk, PO Box 10, Halbrite S0C 1H0 – 306/458-2252
Handel (V)	38	Kindersley-Lloydminster	Rosetown-Biggar	Dean Evanisky, Clerk, PO Box 19, Handel S0K 1Y0 – 306/658-4244
Hanley †	499	Moose Jaw-Lake Centre	Arm River	Tony Obrigewitch, Adm., PO Box 270, Hanley S0G 2E0 – 306/544-2223, Fax: 306/544-2223
Hardy (V)	18	Souris-Moose Mountain	Weyburn-Big Muddy	Marie Fettes, Clerk, General Delivery, Hardy S0C 1J0 – 306/869-2800
Harris (V)	214	Kindersley-Lloydminster	Rosetown-Biggar	Peggy Garner, Clerk, PO Box 124, Harris S0L 1K0 – 306/656-2122, Fax: 306/656-2151
Hawarden (V)	102	Moose Jaw-Lake Centre	Arm River	Darice Carlson, Clerk, PO Box 37, Hawarden S0H 1Y0 – 306/855-2020
Hazenmore (V)	89	Swift Current-Maple Creek-Assiniboia	Wood River	D. Koenig, Clerk, PO Box 36, Hazenmore S0N 1C0 – 306/264-3218
Hazlet (V)	129	Swift Current-Maple Creek-Assiniboia	Cypress Hills	Scott Spicer, Adm., PO Box 150, Hazlet S0N 1E0 – 306/678-2131, Fax: 306/678-2131
Hepburn (V)	463	Saskatoon-Clark's Crossing	Rosthern	Karen Kosowan, Adm., PO Box 217, Hepburn S0K 1Z0 – 306/947-2170
Herbert †	941	Swift Current-Maple Creek-Assiniboia	Thunder Creek	Sandra MacArthur, Adm., PO Box 370, Herbert S0H 2A0 – 306/784-2400, Fax: 306/784-2402
Herschel (V)	53	Kindersley-Lloydminster	Rosetown-Biggar	Deborah C. Rea, Clerk, PO Box 88, Herschel S0L 1L0 – 306/377-2014
Heward (V)	25	Souris-Moose Mountain	Cannington	Dolores Mitchall, Clerk, PO Box 10, Heward S0G 2G0 – 306/457-2852
Hodgeville (V)	258	Swift Current-Maple Creek-Assiniboia	Thunder Creek	Sheila Cooper, Clerk, PO Box 307, Hodgeville S0H 2B0 – 306/677-2223, Fax: 306/677-2466
Holdfast (V)	239	Moose Jaw-Lake Centre	Arm River	Harvey Hemingway, Clerk, PO Box 160, Holdfast S0G 2H0 – 306/488-2000
Hubbard (V)	56	Regina-Qu'Appelle	Melville	Bruce Lamming, Clerk, PO Box 148, Hubbard S0A 1J0 – 306/795-2880
Hudson Bay †	1,868	Mackenzie	Carrot River Valley	Richard Dolezsar, Adm., PO Box 730, Hudson Bay S0E 0Y0 – 306/865-2261, Fax: 306/865-2800
Humboldt †	4,989	Saskatoon-Humboldt	Humboldt	Robert G. Smith, Adm., PO Box 640, Humboldt S0K 2A0 – 306/682-2525, Fax: 306/682-3144
Hyas (V)	135	Yorkton-Melville	Canora-Pelly	Robert Newman, Clerk, PO Box 40, Hyas S0A 1K0 – 306/594-2817, Fax: 306/594-2817
Île à la Crosse (NV)	1,284	Prince Albert-Churchill River	Athabasca	Rose Daigneault, Adm., PO Box 280, Ile à la Crosse S0M 1C0 – 306/833-2122, Fax: 306/833-2132
Imperial †	364	Moose Jaw-Lake Centre	Arm River	Sheila Newlove, Adm., PO Box 90, Imperial S0G 2J0 – 306/963-2220, Fax: 306/963-2445
Indian Head †	1,827	Regina-Qu'Appelle	Indian Head-Milestone	Lawrence Natyshak, Adm., PO Box 460, Indian Head S0G 2K0 – 306/695-3344, Fax: 306/695-2398
Insinger (V)	28	Yorkton-Melville	Canora-Pelly	Bettie Thompson, Adm., PO Box 179, Insinger S0A 1L0 – 306/647-2422, Fax: 306/647-2422
Invermay (V)	328	Yorkton-Melville	Kelvington-Wadena	Veronica L. Wolski, Clerk, PO Box 234, Invermay S0A 1M0 – 306/593-2242, Fax: 306/593-2242
Ituna †	803	Regina-Qu'Appelle	Melville	Lawrence Skoretz, Adm., PO Box 580, Ituna S0A 1N0 – 306/795-2272, Fax: 306/795-2272
Jans Bay (V)	195	Prince Albert-Churchill River	Athabasca	Rose Morin, Clerk, General Delivery, Canoe Narrows S0M 0K0 – 306/829-4320, Fax: 306/829-4424

Canadian Almanac & Directory 1997

4-140 SASKATCHEWAN MUNICIPALITIES

Cities in CAPITALS; Towns marked †; Villages marked (V); Northern Villages marked (NV); Resort Villages not listed. An in-depth listing for municipalities marked with * appears in Part 2 (check Index for page numbers).

MUNICIPALITY	1991 POP.	FEDERAL ELECTORAL DISTRICT	PROVINCIAL ELECTORAL DISTRICT	CONTACT PERSON WITH ADDRESS, PHONE & FAX
Jansen (V)	210	Mackenzie	Watrous	Elaine Kral, Clerk, PO Box 116, Jansen S0K 2B0 – 306/364-2148
Jedburgh (V)	18	Yorkton-Melville	Melville	Jerry T. Kuziak, Adm., PO Box 10, Jedburgh S0A 1R0 – 306/647-2450, Fax: 306/647-2450
Kamsack †	2,323	Yorkton-Melville	Saltcoats	Bruno Kossman, Adm., PO Box 729, Kamsack S0A 1S0 – 306/542-2155, Fax: 306/542-2975
Keeler (V)	27	Moose Jaw-Lake Centre	Arm River	Reg E. McKee, Clerk, PO Box 33, Keeler S0H 2E0 – 306/692-3390
Kelfield (V)	7	Kindersley-Lloydminster	Rosetown-Biggar	Patti Turk, Adm., PO Box 8, Kelfield S0K 2C0 – 306/932-4931
Kelliher (V)	368	Regina-Qu'Appelle	Last Mountain-Touchwood	Elizabeth A. Clark, Clerk, PO Box 190, Kelliher S0A 1V0 – 306/675-2226, Fax: 306/675-2226
Kelvington †	1,109	Mackenzie	Kelvington-Wadena	Beverly Anne Link, Adm., PO Box 10, Kelvington S0A 1W0 – 306/327-4482, Fax: 306/327-4946
Kenaston (V)	309	Moose Jaw-Lake Centre	Arm River	Mark J. Zdunich, Adm., PO Box 129, Kenaston S0G 2N0 – 306/252-2211, Fax: 306/252-2240
Kendal (V)	90	Regina-Qu'Appelle	Indian Head-Milestone	Nadine Jensen, Clerk, PO Box 97, Kendal S0G 2P0 – 306/424-2722
Kennedy (V)	296	Souris-Moose Mountain	Cannington	Amaret Smyth, Clerk, PO Box 93, Kennedy S0G 2R0 – 306/538-2194
Kenosee Lake (V)	163	Souris-Moose Mountain	Cannington	Jane Laich, Adm., PO Box 30, Kenosee Lake S0C 2S0 – 306/577-2139
Kerrobert †	1,143	Kindersley-Lloydminster	Kindersley	Sharon Pope, Adm., PO Box 558, Kerrobert S0L 1R0 – 306/834-2361, Fax: 306/834-2633
Khedive (V)	21	Souris-Moose Mountain	Weyburn-Big Muddy	Wayne Lozinsky, Adm., PO Box 189, Pangman S0C 2C0 – 306/442-2131, Fax: 306/442-2131
Killaly (V)	103	Yorkton-Melville	Melville	Vern Huber, Clerk, PO Box 69, Killaly S0A 1X0 – 306/748-2311
Kincaid (V)	197	Swift Current-Maple Creek-Assiniboia	Wood River	Diana Lott, Clerk, PO Box 177, Kincaid S0H 2J0 – 306/264-3910
Kindersley †	4,572	Kindersley-Lloydminster	Kindersley	James V. Toye, Adm., PO Box 1269, Kindersley S0L 1S0 – 306/463-2675, Fax: 306/463-4577
Kinistino †	701	Saskatoon-Humboldt	Melfort-Tisdale	Shirley Jackson, Adm., PO Box 10, Kinistino S0J 1H0 – 306/864-2461, Fax: 306/864-3465
Kinley (V)	32	Kindersley-Lloydminster	Redberry Lake	Melanie Burwell, Adm., PO Box 51, Kinley S0K 2E0 – 306/237-4359
Kipling †	1,005	Souris-Moose Mountain	Moosomin	Dave Petz, Adm., PO Box 299, Kipling S0G 2S0 – 306/736-2515, Fax: 306/736-8448
Kisbey (V)	219	Souris-Moose Mountain	Cannington	Verna Reed, Clerk, PO Box 249, Kisbey S0C 1L0 – 306/462-2212
Krydor (V)	34	The Battlefords-Meadow Lake	Redberry Lake	W. Grewa, Clerk, PO Box 195, Krydor S0J 1K0 – 306/931-2393
Kyle †	533	Kindersley-Lloydminster	Rosetown-Biggar	Marlene Pederson, Adm., PO Box 520, Kyle S0L 1T0 – 306/375-2525, Fax: 306/375-2525
La Loche (NV)	1,691	Prince Albert-Churchill River	Athabasca	Doug Gailey, Clerk, PO Box 310, La Loche S0M 1G0 – 306/822-2032, Fax: 306/822-2078
La Ronge †	2,578	Prince Albert-Churchill River	Cumberland	John Wade, Adm., PO Box 5680, La Ronge S0J 1L0 – 306/425-2066, Fax: 306/425-3883
Lafleche †	466	Swift-Current-Maple Creek-Assiniboia	Wood River	Lorraine McIvor, Adm., PO Box 250, Lafleche S0H 2K0 – 306/472-5292
Laird (V)	221	Saskatoon-Humboldt	Rosthern	Grant Peters, Clerk, PO Box 189, Laird S0K 2H0 – 306/223-4343, Fax: 306/223-4220
Lake Alma (V)	66	Souris-Moose Mountain	Estevan	Myrna Lohse, Clerk, PO Box 163, Lake Alma S0C 1M0 – 306/447-2002
Lake Lenore (V)	336	Saskatoon-Humboldt	Humboldt	Barb Politeski, Clerk, PO Box 148, Lake Lenore S0K 2J0 – 306/368-2344, Fax: 306/368-2226
Lampman †	647	Souris-Moose Mountain	Cannington	Rodney Audette, Adm., PO Box 70, Lampman S0C 1N0 – 306/487-2462, Fax: 306/487-2285
Lancer (V)	94	Swift Current-Maple Creek-Assiniboia	Cypress Hills	Bertha E. Hopfauf, Clerk, PO Box 3, Lancer S0N 1G0 – 306/689-2925, Fax: 306/689-2890
Landis (V)	228	Kindersley-Lloydminster	Battleford-Cut Knife	Beryl Hart, Clerk, PO Box 153, Landis S0K 2K0 – 306/658-2155
Lang (V)	206	Souris-Moose Mountain	Indian Head-Milestone	Colleen Christopherson, Clerk, PO Box 97, Lang S0G 2W0 – 306/464-2024, Fax: 306/464-2210
Langenburg †	1,156	Yorkton-Melville	Saltcoats	Howard McCullough, Adm., PO Box 400, Langenburg S0A 2A0 – 306/743-2432, Fax: 306/743-2723
Langham †	1,185	Kindersley-Lloydminster	Redberry Lake	Randy J. Sherstobitoff, Adm., PO Box 289, Langham S0K 2L0 – 306/283-4842, Fax: 306/283-4842
Lanigan †	1,397	Moose Jaw-Lake Centre	Watrous	Jack R. Dvernichuk, Adm., PO Box 280, Lanigan S0K 2M0 – 306/365-2809, Fax: 306/365-2960
Lashburn †	748	Kindersley-Lloydminster	Lloydminster	Vicki Seabrook, Adm., PO Box 328, Lashburn S0M 1H0 – 306/285-3533, Fax: 306/285-3358

Canadian Almanac & Directory 1997

Cities in CAPITALS; Towns marked †; Villages marked (V); Northern Villages marked (NV); Resort Villages not listed. An in-depth listing for municipalities marked with * appears in Part 2 (check Index for page numbers).

MUNICIPALITY	1991 POP.	FEDERAL ELECTORAL DISTRICT	PROVINCIAL ELECTORAL DISTRICT	CONTACT PERSON WITH ADDRESS, PHONE & FAX
Leader †	999	Swift Current-Maple Creek-Assiniboia	Cypress Hills	R. Kim Hauta, Adm., PO Box 39, Leader S0N 1H0 – 306/628-3868, Fax: 306/628-4337
Leask (V)	442	The Battlefords-Meadow Lake	Redberry Lake	Rick Poole, Adm., PO Box 190, Leask S0J 1M0 – 306/466-2229, Fax: 306/466-2000
Lebret (V)	201	Regina-Qu'Appelle	Melville	Bernadette Huber, Clerk, PO Box 40, Lebret S0G 2Y0 – 306/332-6545, Fax: 306/332-5338
Lemberg †	395	Yorkton-Melville	Melville	Joyce Hauck, Clerk, PO Box 399, Lemberg S0A 2B0 – 306/335-2244, Fax: 306/335-2911
Leoville (V)	370	The Battlefords-Meadow Lake	Shellbrook-Spiritwood	Mona Chalifour, Clerk, PO Box 280, Leoville S0J 1N0 – 306/984-2140, Fax: 306/984-2337
Leross (V)	91	Regina-Qu'Appelle	Last Mountain-Touchwood	Elaine Klyne, Clerk, PO Box 68, Leross S0A 2C0 – 306/675-4429
Leroy †	456	Mackenzie	Watrous	Mark Fedak, Adm., PO Box 40, Leroy S0K 2P0 – 306/286-3288, Fax: 306/286-3400
Leslie (V)	43	Mackenzie	Last Mountain-Touchwood	Norman Casement, Clerk, PO Box 97, Leslie S0A 2E0 – 306/272-3959
Lestock (V)	313	Regina-Qu'Appelle	Last Mountain-Touchwood	Luelle Frisko, Clerk, PO Box 209, Lestock S0A 2G0 – 306/274-2277
Liberty (V)	128	Moose Jaw-Lake Centre	Arm River	Michele Cruise, Clerk, PO Box 59, Liberty S0G 3A0 – 306/847-2033
Limerick (V)	155	Swift Current-Maple Creek-Assiniboia	Wood River	Mary Jean Alligham, Adm., PO Box 129, Limerick S0H 2P0 – 306/263-2020, Fax: 306/263-2013
Lintlaw (V)	223	Yorkton-Melville	Kelvington-Wadena	Dorothy Procyk, Clerk, PO Box 10, Lintlaw S0A 2H0 – 306/325-2006
Lipton (V)	352	Regina-Qu'Appelle	Last Mountain-Touchwood	Marlene L. Bausmer, Clerk, PO Box 219, Lipton S0G 3B0 – 306/336-2505
LLOYDMINSTER	7,241	Kindersley-Lloydminster	Lloydminster	Tom Lysyk, Clerk, 5011 - 49 Ave., Lloydminster S9V 0T8 – 306/825-6184, Fax: 306/825-7170
Lockwood (V)	26	Moose Jaw-Lake Centre	Watrous	Irene Hurley, Clerk, PO Box 55, Lockwood S0K 2R0
Loon Lake (V)	366	The Battlefords-Meadow Lake	Meadow Lake	Norman G. Friesen, Clerk, PO Box 220, Loon Lake S0M 1L0 – 306/837-2090, Fax: 306/837-4735
Loreburn (V)	170	Moose Jaw-Lake Centre	Arm River	Muriel Stronski, Clerk, PO Box 177, Loreburn S0H 2S0 – 306/644-2097, Fax: 306/644-2099
Love (V)	94	Mackenzie	Saskatchewan Rivers	Valerie Rodgers, Clerk, PO Box 94, Love S0J 1P0 – 306/276-2525
Loverna (V)	21	Kindersley-Lloydminster	Kindersley	Beverly A. Dahl, Adm., PO Box 70, Marengo S0L 2K0 – 306/968-2922, Fax: 306/968-2278
Lucky Lake (V)	341	Kindersley-Lloydminster	Rosetown-Biggar	Edna A. Laturnus, Adm., PO Box 99, Lucky Lake S0L 1Z0 – 306/858-2234, Fax: 306/858-2234
Lumsden †	1,477	Regina-Lumsden	Regina Qu'Appelle Valley	Wayne Zerff, Adm., PO Box 160, Lumsden S0G 3C0 – 306/731-2404, Fax: 306/731-3572
Luseland †	658	Kindersley-Lloydminster	Kindersley	Donna Gerrard, Adm., PO Box 130, Luseland S0L 2A0 – 306/372-4218, Fax: 306/372-4218
Macklin †	1,117	Kindersley-Lloydminster	Battleford-Cut Knife	Kim G. Gartner, Adm., PO Box 69, Macklin S0L 2C0 – 306/753-2256, Fax: 306/753-3234
MacNutt (V)	103	Yorkton-Melville	Saltcoats	Cheryl Peppler, Clerk, PO Box 10, MacNutt S0A 2K0 – 306/742-4391
Macoun (V)	157	Souris-Moose Mountain	Estevan	Bernice Mohns, Clerk, PO Box 58, Macoun S0C 1P0 – 306/634-9352
Macrorie (V)	126	Kindersley-Lloydminster	Rosetown-Biggar	Noreen Andrew, Clerk, PO Box 37, Macrorie S0L 2E0 – 306/243-2010
Madison (V)	20	Kindersley-Lloydminster	Kindersley	Judy E. Douglas, Clerk, PO Box 70, Madison S0L 2G0 – 306/962-3888
Maidstone †	985	Kindersley-Lloydminster	Lloydminster	Donna Bendig, Adm., PO Box 208, Maidstone S0M 1M0 – 306/893-2373, Fax: 306/893-2373
Major (V)	64	Kindersley-Lloydminster	Kindersley	Louise Kollman, Clerk, PO Box 94, Major S0L 2H0 – 306/834-5390
Makwa (V)	113	The Battlefords-Meadow Lake	Meadow Lake	Penny L. Barker, Clerk, PO Box 67, Makwa S0M 1N0 – 306/236-3919
Mankota (V)	381	Swift Current-Maple Creek-Assiniboia	Wood River	Jody Penna, Adm., PO Box 336, Mankota S0H 2W0 – 306/478-2331, Fax: 306/478-2525
Manor (V)	326	Souris-Moose Mountain	Cannington	Joan Mills, Adm., PO Box 295, Manor S0C 1R0 – 306/448-2273
Mantario (V)	20	Kindersley-Lloydminster	Kindersley	Beverly A. Dahl, Adm., PO Box 47, Mantario S0L 2J0 – 306/968-2922, Fax: 306/968-2278
Maple Creek †	2,334	Swift Current-Maple Creek-Assiniboia	Cypress Hills	Tim Leson, Adm., PO Box 428, Maple Creek S0N 1N0 – 306/662-2244, Fax: 306/662-4131
Marcelin (V)	193	The Battlefords-Meadow Lake	Redberry Lake	Brenda Desjardins, Clerk, PO Box 39, Marcelin S0J 1R0 – 306/226-2168, Fax: 306/226-2168
Marengo (V)	69	Kindersley-Lloydminster	Kindersley	Beverly A. Dahl, Adm., PO Box 70, Marengo S0L 2K0 – 306/968-2922, Fax: 306/968-2278

4-142 SASKATCHEWAN MUNICIPALITIES

Cities in CAPITALS; Towns marked †; Villages marked (V); Northern Villages marked (NV); Resort Villages not listed. An in-depth listing for municipalities marked with * appears in Part 2 (check Index for page numbers).

MUNICIPALITY	1991 POP.	FEDERAL ELECTORAL DISTRICT	PROVINCIAL ELECTORAL DISTRICT	CONTACT PERSON WITH ADDRESS, PHONE & FAX
Margo (V)	151	Mackenzie	Kelvington-Wadena	Vivian G. Rothlander, Clerk, PO Box 28, Margo S0A 2M0 – 306/324-2134
Markinch (V)	81	Regina-Qu'Appelle	Last Mountain-Touchwood	Rita T. Orb, Adm., PO Box 29, Markinch S0G 4P0 – 306/726-4355
Marquis (V)	105	Moose Jaw-Lake Centre	Arm River	Ronald J. Gasper, Adm., PO Box 40, Marquis S0H 2X0 – 306/788-2022
Marsden (V)	242	Kindersley-Lloydminster	Battleford-Cut Knife	Jason Boyle, Adm., PO Box 69, Marsden S0M 1P0 – 306/826-5215, Fax: 306/826-5512
Marshall (V)	573	Kindersley-Lloydminster	Lloydminster	Lorne Kachur, Adm., PO Box 125, Marshall S0M 1R0 – 306/387-6340, Fax: 306/387-6161
Martensville †	3,310	Saskatoon-Clark's Crossing	Rosthern	Phillip W. Ratzlaff, Adm., PO Box 970, Martensville S0K 2T0 – 306/931-2166, Fax: 306/933-2468
Maryfield (V)	408	Souris-Moose Mountain	Moosomin	Ward Fraser, Adm., PO Box 58, Maryfield S0G 3K0 – 306/646-2143
Maymont (V)	188	The Battlefords-Meadow Lake	Redberry Lake	E. Lynne Tolley, Adm., PO Box 160, Maymont S0M 1T0 – 306/389-2051, Fax: 306/389-2051
Mazenod (V)	48	Swift Current-Maple Creek-Assiniboia	Thunder Creek	Mary-Ellen McKechnie, Clerk, PO Box 427, Mossbank S0H 3G0 – 306/354-2878
McLean (V)	262	Regina-Qu'Appelle	Indian Head-Milestone	Lyla Grad, Clerk, PO Box 56, McLean S0G 3E0 – 306/699-7279, Fax: 306/699-2347
McTaggart (V)	122	Souris-Moose Mountain	Weyburn-Big Muddy	Nichol Lynch, Adm., PO Box 134, McTaggart S0G 3G0 – 306/842-5911
Meacham (V)	116	Saskatoon-Humboldt	Watrous	Elizabeth Saretzky, Clerk, PO Box 9, Meacham S0K 2V0 – 306/376-2003
Meadow Lake †	4,318	The Battlefords-Meadow Lake	Meadow Lake	Richard Levesque, Adm., PO Box 610, Meadow Lake S0M 1V0 – 306/236-3622, Fax: 306/236-4299
Meath Park (V)	228	Prince Albert-Churchill River	Saskatchewan Rivers	Elaine Esopenko, Adm., PO Box 255, Meath Park S0J 1T0 – 306/929-2112, Fax: 306/929-2281
Medstead (V)	172	The Battlefords-Meadow Lake	Shellbrook-Spiritwood	Darrin Beaudoin, Clerk, PO Box 148, Medstead S0M 1W0 – 306/342-4609
MELFORT	5,628	Mackenzie	Melfort-Tisdale	Joanne Forer, Clerk, PO Box 2230, Melfort S0E 1A0 – 306/752-5911, Fax: 306/752-5556
MELVILLE	4,905	Yorkton-Melville	Melville	Ron J. Walton, City Clerk, PO Box 1240, Melville S0A 2P0 – 306/728-6840, Fax: 306/728-5911
Mendham (V)	43	Swift Current-Maple Creek-Assiniboia	Cypress Hills	Sandra Ehnisz, Clerk, PO Box 55, Mendham S0N 1P0 – 306/628-3505
Meota (V)	268	The Battlefords-Meadow Lake	North Battleford	Allie R. Raycraft, Adm., PO Box 80, Meota S0M 1X0 – 306/892-2061, Fax: 306/892-2061
Mervin (V)	156	The Battlefords-Meadow Lake	Lloydminster	Donald Cormack, Clerk, PO Box 35, Mervin S0M 1Y0 – 306/845-2784
Meyronne (V)	56	Swift Current-Maple Creek-Assiniboia	Wood River	Hazel Diebel, Clerk, PO Box 119, Meyronne S0H 3A0 – 306/264-3773
Michel Village (NH)	87	Prince Albert-Churchill River	Athabasca	Rita Maurice, Clerk, General Delivery, Michel Village via Dillon S0M 0S0 – 306/282-4401, 4402, Fax: 306/282-2155
Midale †	497	Souris-Moose Mountain	Estevan	Bonnie Ludwig, Adm., PO Box 128, Midale S0C 1S0 – 306/458-2400, Fax: 306/458-2588
Middle Lake (V)	245	Saskatoon-Humboldt	Humboldt	Carol Winkel, Clerk, PO Box 119, Middle Lake S0K 2X0 – 306/367-2149
Milden (V)	228	Kindersley-Lloydminster	Rosetown-Biggar	Barb Barteski, Clerk, PO Box 70, Milden S0L 2L0 – 306/935-2131, Fax: 306/935-2020
Milestone †	593	Regina-Wascana	Indian Head-Milestone	Ernest P. Audette, Adm., PO Box 74, Milestone S0G 3L0 – 306/436-2130, Fax: 306/436-2051
Minton (V)	124	Souris-Moose Mountain	Weyburn-Big Muddy	Joyce Axten, Clerk, PO Box 52, Minton S0C 1T0 – 306/969-2144, Fax: 306/969-2244
Missinipe (NH)	40	Prince Albert-Churchill River	Cumberland	Shirley Glass, Clerk, PO Box 1617, La Ronge S0J 1L0 – 306/635-4540, Fax: 306/635-4434
Mistatim (V)	114	Mackenzie	Carrot River Valley	Elsie Leblanc, Clerk, PO Box 145, Mistatim S0E 1B0 – 306/889-2114
Montmartre (V)	471	Regina-Wascana	Indian Head-Milestone	Dale Brenner, Adm., PO Box 146, Montmartre S0G 3M0 – 306/424-2040, Fax: 306/424-2040
*MOOSE JAW	33,803 ('95)	Moose Jaw--Lake Centre	Moose Jaw North; Moose Jaw Wakamow	Brian Hamblin, City Clerk, 228 Main St. North, Moose Jaw S6H 3J8 – 306/694-4400, Fax: 306/692-4518, 691-0292
Moosomin †	2,436	Souris-Moose Mountain	Moosomin	Paul Listrom, Adm., PO Box 730, Moosomin S0G 3N0 – 306/435-2988, Fax: 306/435-3343
Morse †	313	Swift Current-Maple Creek-Assiniboia	Thunder Creek	Darlene Klassen, Adm., PO Box 270, Morse S0H 3C0 – 306/629-3300
Mortlach (V)	296	Moose Jaw-Lake Centre	Thunder Creek	Maureen Grajczyk, Clerk, PO Box 10, Mortlach S0H 3E0 – 306/355-2229
Mossbank †	400	Moose Jaw-Lake Centre	Thunder Creek	Judy L. Bolton, Adm., PO Box 370, Mossbank S0H 3G0 – 306/354-2294, Fax: 306/354-7725
Muenster (V)	385	Saskatoon-Humboldt	Kelvington-Wadena	Cheryl Chapman, Clerk, PO Box 98, Muenster S0K 2Y0 – 306/682-2794

Canadian Almanac & Directory 1997

Cities in CAPITALS; Towns marked †; Villages marked (V); Northern Villages marked (NV); Resort Villages not listed. An in-depth listing for municipalities marked with * appears in Part 2 (check Index for page numbers).

MUNICIPALITY	1991 POP.	FEDERAL ELECTORAL DISTRICT	PROVINCIAL ELECTORAL DISTRICT	CONTACT PERSON WITH ADDRESS, PHONE & FAX
Naicam †	826	Mackenzie	Kelvington-Wadena	Ruby J. Lindsay, Adm., PO Box 238, Naicam S0K 2Z0 – 306/874-2280, Fax: 306/874-5444
Neilburg (V)	355	Kindersley-Lloydminster	Battleford-Cut Knife	Dale Bryden, Adm., PO Box 280, Neilburg S0M 2C0 – 306/823-4321, Fax: 306/823-4477
Netherhill (V)	48	Kindersley-Lloydminster	Kindersley	Judy Shaver, Clerk, PO Box 70, Netherhill S0L 2M0 – 306/463-3562
Neudorf (V)	373	Yorkton-Melville	Melville	Donna Litzenberger, Clerk, PO Box 187, Neudorf S0A 2T0 – 306/748-2551
Neville (V)	89	Swift Current-Maple Creek-Assiniboia	Thunder Creek	Susan Fehr, Clerk, PO Box 88, Neville S0N 1T0 – 306/627-3255
Nipawin †	4,419	Mackenzie	Carrot River Valley	Peter M. Cannon, Adm., PO Box 2134, Nipawin S0E 1E0 – 306/862-9866, Fax: 306/862-3076
Nokomis †	459	Moose Jaw-Lake Centre	Watrous	Iv-Lee Kane, Clerk, PO Box 189, Nokomis S0G 3R0 – 306/528-2010, Fax: 306/528-2010
Norquay †	524	Yorkton-Melville	Cabora-Pelly	Rodney C. Johnson, Adm., PO Box 327, Norquay S0A 2V0 – 306/594-2101, Fax: 306/594-2347
NORTH BATTLEFORD	14,350	The Battlefords-Meadow Lake	North Battleford	Doug McEwen, City Clerk, PO Box 460, North Battleford S9A 2Y6 – 306/445-1732, Fax: 306/445-0411
North Portal (V)	164	Souris-Moose Mountain	Estevan	George Fuchs, Clerk, PO Box 81, North Portal S0C 1W0 – 306/927-2315
Odessa (V)	239	Regina-Qu'Appelle	Indian Head-Milestone	Sheila Leurer, Clerk, PO Box 91, Odessa S0G 3S0 – 306/957-2020, Fax: 306/957-2075
Ogema †	383	Swift Current-Maple Creek-Assiniboia	Weyburn-Big Muddy	Peggy Tumback, Adm., PO Box 159, Ogema S0C 1Y0 – 306/459-2230, Fax: 306/459-2762
Osage (V)	33	Regina-Wascana	Indian Head-Milestone	Linda Kreutzer, Clerk, PO Box 96, Osage S0G 3T0 – 306/722-3747
Osler †	634	Saskatoon-Clark's Crossing	Rosthern	Sarah Peters, Adm., PO Box 190, Osler S0K 3A0 – 306/239-2155, Fax: 306/239-2155
Outlook †	2,091	Moose Jaw-Lake Centre	Arm River	Lawrence W. Zarubiak, Adm., PO Box 518, Outlook S0L 2N0 – 306/867-8663, Fax: 306/867-9898
Oxbow †	1,132	Souris-Moose Mountain	Cannington	Geraldine Gervais, Adm., PO Box 149, Oxbow S0C 2B0 – 306/483-2300, Fax: 306/483-5277
Paddockwood (V)	177	Prince Albert-Churchill River	Saskatchewan Rivers	Lillian Sauer, Clerk, PO Box 188, Paddockwood S0J 1Z0 – 306/989-2033
Palmer (V)	40	Swift Current-Maple Creek-Assiniboia	Thunder Creek	Mary-Ellen McKechnie, Clerk, PO Box 368, Palmer S0H 1X0 – 306/354-2878
Pangman (V)	248	Souris-Moose Mountain	Weyburn-Bug Muddy	Wayne Lozinsky, Clerk, PO Box 189, Pangman S0C 2C0 – 306/442-2131, Fax: 306/442-2131
Paradise Hill (V)	455	The Battlefords-Meadow Lake	Meadow Lake	Marion Hougham, Clerk, PO Box 270, Paradise Hill S0M 2G0 – 306/344-2206, Fax: 306/344-4941
Parkside (V)	127	The Battlefords-Meadow Lake	Shellbrook-Spiritwood	Gwen Olson, Clerk, PO Box 48, Parkside S0J 2A0 – 306/747-2235
Patuanak (NH)	99	Prince Albert-Churchill River	Athabasca	Beverly Maurice, Clerk, General Delivery, Patuanak S0M 2H0 – 306/396-2020, Fax: 306/396-2092
Paynton (V)	182	The Battlefords-Meadow Lake	Lloydminster	Gina Bernier, Clerk-Adm., PO Box 10, Paynton S0M 2J0 – 306/895-2023
Pelican Narrows (NV)	252	Prince Albert-Churchill River	Cumberland	John M. Merasty, Clerk, PO Box 10, Pelican Narrows S0P 0E0 – 306/632-2225, Fax: 306/632-2006
Pelly (V)	376	Yorkton-Melville	Canora-Pelly	Ella Klimm, Clerk, PO Box 160, Pelly S0A 2Z0 – 306/595-2124
Pennant (V)	156	Swift Current-Maple Creek-Assiniboia	Cypress Hills	Kim Valentine, Clerk, PO Box 57, Pennant S0N 1X0 – 306/626-3316
Pense (V)	556	Regina-Lumsden	Thunder Creek	Carol Bellefeuille, Adm., PO Box 125, Pense S0G 3W0 – 306/345-2332, Fax: 306/345-2343
Penzance (V)	52	Moose Jaw-Lake Centre	Arm River	Brenda Olson, Clerk, PO Box 86, Penzance S0G 3X0 – 306/488-4683
Perdue (V)	395	Kindersley-Lloydminster	Redberry Lake	Pam McMahon, Clerk, PO Box 190, Perdue S0K 3C0 – 306/237-4337, Fax: 306/237-4202
Piapot (V)	61	Swift Current-Maple Creek-Assiniboia	Cypress Hills	Nicole Drinkwater, Clerk, PO Box 129, Piapot S0N 1Y0 – 306/558-2007
Pierceland (V)	475	The Battlefords-Meadow Lake	Meadow Lake	Jane Eistetter, Clerk, PO Box 39, Pierceland S0M 2K0 – 306/839-2015, Fax: 306/839-2057
Pilger (V)	102	Saskatoon-Humboldt	Humboldt	Luella Bregenser, Clerk, PO Box 70, Pilger S0K 3G0 – 306/367-4927
Pilot Butte †	1,450	Regina-Qu'Appelle	Regina Wascana Plains	Ed Sigmeth, Adm., PO Box 253, Pilot Butte S0G 3Z0 – 306/781-4547, Fax: 306/781-4477
Pinehouse (NV)	820	Prince Albert-Churchill River	Athabasca	Marie Lavallee, Clerk, General Delivery, Pinehouse Lake S0J 2B0 – 306/884-2030, Fax: 306/884-2021
Plato (V)	21	Kindersley-Lloydminster	Rosetown-Biggar	Judy Mathers, Acting Clerk, PO Box 57, Plato S0L 2P0 – 306/574-2110
Pleasantdale (V)	105	Mackenzie	Kelvington-Wadena	Dianne M. Dodd, Adm., PO Box 147, Pleasantdale S0K 3H0 – 306/874-5743

Cities in CAPITALS; Towns marked †; Villages marked (V); Northern Villages marked (NV); Resort Villages not listed. An in-depth listing for municipalities marked with * appears in Part 2 (check Index for page numbers).

MUNICIPALITY	1991 POP.	FEDERAL ELECTORAL DISTRICT	PROVINCIAL ELECTORAL DISTRICT	CONTACT PERSON WITH ADDRESS, PHONE & FAX
Plenty (V)	170	Kindersley-Lloydminster	Kindersley	Maxine Woods, Clerk, PO Box 177, Plenty S0L 2R0 – 306/932-2045
Plunkett (V)	118	Moose Jaw-Lake Centre	Watrous	Helen Miller, Clerk, PO Box 149, Plunkett S0K 3J0 – 306/944-4514
Ponteix †	631	Swift Current-Maple Creek-Assiniboia	Wood River	Daniel Gervais, Adm., PO Box 330, Ponteix S0N 1Z0 – 306/625-3222, Fax: 306/625-3204
Porcupine Plain †	803	Mackenzie	Kelvington-Wadena	Barry Warsylewicz, Clerk, PO Box 310, Porcupine Plain S0E 1H0 – 306/278-2262, Fax: 306/278-3378
Preeceville †	1,205	Yorkton-Melville	Canora-Pelly	Connie Hryciuk, Adm., PO Box 560, Preeceville S0A 3B0 – 306/547-2810, Fax: 306/547-3116
Prelate (V)	191	Swift Current-Maple Creek-Assiniboia	Cypress Hills	Darlene Wagner, Clerk, PO Box 40, Prelate S0N 2B0 – 306/673-2340, Fax: 306/673-2340
Primate (V)	70	Kindersley-Lloydminster	Kindersley	Dianne Latendresse, Clerk, PO Box 6, Primate S0L 2S0 – 306/753-2897
*PRINCE ALBERT	34,181	Prince Albert--Churchill River	Prince Albert Carlton; Prince Albert Northcote	Charmaine Code, Director & City Clerk, Legislative Services, City Hall, 1084 Central Ave., Prince Albert S6V 7P3 – 306/953-4305, Fax: 306/953-4313
Prud'homme (V)	184	Saskatoon-Humboldt	Humboldt	Kim Sopotyk, Clerk, PO Box 38, Prud'homme S0K 3K0 – 306/654-2001, Fax: 306/654-2001
Punnichy (V)	365	Mackenzie	Last Mountain-Touchwood	Nancy L. Benko, Clerk, PO Box 250, Punnichy S0A 3C0 – 306/835-2135, Fax: 306/835-2100
Qu'Appelle †	671	Regina-Qu'Appelle	Indian Head-Milestone	Carol Wickenheiser, Adm., PO Box 60, Qu'Appelle S0G 4A0 – 306/699-2279, Fax: 306/699-2306
Quill Lake (V)	464	Mackenzie	Watrous	Judy L. Kanak, Adm., PO Box 9, Quill Lake S0A 3E0 – 306/383-2592
Quinton (V)	168	Mackenzie	Last Mountain-Touchwood	Ralph Brockman, Clerk, PO Box 128, Quinton S0A 3G0 – 306/835-2515
Rabbit Lake (V)	157	The Battlefords-Meadow Lake	Redberry Lake	Ian McLennan, Adm., PO Box 9, Rabbit Lake S0M 2L0 – 306/824-2044, Fax: 306/824-2044
Radisson †	390	The Battlefords-Meadow Lake	Redberry Lake	Kimberly Waterhouse, Clerk, PO Box 69, Radisson S0K 3L0 – 306/827-2218, Fax: 306/827-2218
Radville †	846	Souris-Moose Mountain	Weyburn-Big Muddy	Lyle R. Fisher, Clerk, PO Box 339, Radville S0C 2G0 – 306/869-2477, Fax: 306/869-3100
Rama (V)	121	Yorkton-Melville	Canora-Pelly	Lorraine Kaminski, Clerk, PO Box 205, Rama S0A 3H0 – 306/593-6065
Raymore †	668	Mackenzie	Last Mountain-Touchwood	Elaine Perry, Adm., PO Box 10, Raymore S0A 3J0 – 306/746-2100, Fax: 306/746-4314
Redvers †	936	Souris-Moose Mountain	Cannington	Janice Burnett, Adm., PO Box 249, Redvers S0C 2H0 – 306/452-3533, Fax: 306/452-3701
*REGINA	184,000 ('95)	Regina-Lumsden; Regina-Qu'Appelle; Regina-Wascana	Regina Centre; Regina Coronation Park; Regina Dewdney; Regina Elphinstone; Regina Lakeview; Regina Northeast; Regina Qu'Appelle Valley; Regina Sherwood; Regina South; Regina Victoria; Regina Wascana Plains	Randy Markewich, City Clerk, PO Box 1790, Regina S4P 3C8 – 306/777-7000, Fax: 306/777-6802
Regina Beach †	921	Regina-Lumsden	Arm River	Pearl Peters, Adm., PO Box 10, Regina Beach S0G 4C0 – 306/729-2202, Fax: 306/729-3411
Rhein (V)	218	Yorkton-Melville	Saltcoats	Val Kyba, Clerk, PO Box 233, Rhein S0A 3K0 – 306/273-2155
Richard (V)	29	The Battlefords-Meadow Lake	Redberry Lake	Ed A. Sargent, Clerk, 1541 - 94 St., North Battleford S9A 0E6 – 306/446-4475, Fax: 306/446-4475
Richmound (V)	236	Swift Current-Maple Creek-Assiniboia	Cypress Hills	Shelly Dirk, Clerk, PO Box 29, Richmound S0N 2E0 – 306/669-2166
Ridgedale (V)	122	Mackenzie	Melfort-Tisdale	Bev Sochaski, Clerk, PO Box 27, Ridgedale S0E 1L0 – 306/277-2002
Riverhurst (V)	174	Moose Jaw-Lake Centre	Arm River	Jo-ann Shooter, Clerk, PO Box 116, Riverhurst S0H 3P0 – 306/353-2220
Robsart (V)	26	Swift Current-Maple Creek-Assiniboia	Cypress Hills	W.D. Olmsted, Clerk, PO Box 119, Robsart S0N 2G0
Rocanville †	842	Souris-Moose Mountain	Moosomin	Mel Strong, Adm., PO Box 265, Rocanville S0A 3L0 – 306/645-2022, Fax: 306/645-2022
Roche Percée (V)	154	Souris-Moose Mountain	Estevan	Charlotte Wrigley, Clerk, PO Box 237, Bienfait S0C 0M0 – 306/634-4661
Rockglen †	507	Swift Current-Maple Creek-Assiniboia	Wood River	Diane Griffin, Adm., PO Box 267, Rockglen S0H 3R0 – 306/476-2144, Fax: 306/476-2339
Rockhaven (V)	36	The Battlefords-Meadow Lake	Battleford-Cut Knife	Louise Denton, Clerk, PO Box 9, Rockhaven S0M 2R0 – 306/398-2734, Fax: 306/398-2868
Rose Valley †	409	Mackenzie	Kelvington-Wadena	Marvin H. Holm, Adm., PO Box 460, Rose Valley S0E 1M0 – 306/322-2232, Fax: 306/322-4461

SASKATCHEWAN MUNICIPALITIES 4-145

Cities in CAPITALS; Towns marked †; Villages marked (V); Northern Villages marked (NV); Resort Villages not listed. An in-depth listing for municipalities marked with * appears in Part 2 (check Index for page numbers).

MUNICIPALITY	1991 POP.	FEDERAL ELECTORAL DISTRICT	PROVINCIAL ELECTORAL DISTRICT	CONTACT PERSON WITH ADDRESS, PHONE & FAX
Rosetown †	2,519	Kindersley-Lloydminster	Rosetown-Biggar	Gary W. Crowder, Adm., PO Box 398, Rosetown S0L 2V0 – 306/882-2214, Fax: 306/882-3166
Rosthern †	1,560	Saskatoon-Humboldt	Rosthern	Brenda Kereluke, Adm., PO Box 416, Rosthern S0K 3R0 – 306/232-4826, Fax: 306/232-5638
Rouleau †	480	Moose Jaw-Lake Centre	Thunder Creek	Elizabeth Busby, Adm., PO Box 250, Rouleau S0G 4H0 – 306/776-2270, Fax: 306/776-2270
Ruddell (V)	31	The Battlefords-Meadow Lake	Redberry Lake	B. Lynne Tolley, Clerk, PO Box 7, Ruddell S0M 2S0 – 306/389-2051
Rush Lake (V)	77	Swift Current-Maple Creek-Assiniboia	Thunder Creek	Adeline Steinley, Clerk, PO Box 120, Rush Lake S0H 3S0 – 306/784-3504
Ruthilda (V)	19	Kindersley-Lloydminster	Rosetown-Biggar	Pat Richards, Clerk, PO Box 37, Ruthilda S0K 3S0 – 306/932-4426
St. Benedict (V)	144	Saskatoon-Humboldt	Humboldt	Joan Martin, Clerk, PO Box 99, St. Benedict S0K 3T0 – 306/289-2072, Fax: 306/289-2125
St. Brieux (V)	400	Saskatoon-Humboldt	Humboldt	Gailene Gallais, Adm., PO Box 280, St. Brieux S0K 3V0 – 306/275-2257, Fax: 306/275-4949
St. George's Hill (NH)	124	Prince Albert-Churchill River	Athabasca	Nicole Sylvestre, Clerk, General Delivery, Dillon S0M 0S0 – 306/282-4408, Fax: 306/282-2002
St. Gregor (V)	136	Saskatoon-Humboldt	Kelvington-Wadena	Ann-Marie Block, Clerk, PO Box 19, St. Gregor S0K 3X0 – 306/366-2134
St. Louis (V)	433	Saskatoon-Humboldt	Humboldt	Rita Ferland, Adm., PO Box 99, St. Louis S0J 2C0 – 306/422-8171
St. Victor (V)	56	Swift Current-Maple Creek-Assiniboia	Wood River	Evelyn Ducharme, Clerk, PO Box 25, St. Victor S0H 3T0 – 306/642-3257
St. Walburg †	746	The Battlefords-Meadow Lake	Meadow Lake	Muriel G. Rosser-Swift, Adm., PO Box 368, St. Walburg S0M 2T0 – 306/248-3430, Fax: 306/248-3484
Saltcoats †	545	Yorkton-Melville	Saltcoats	Joyce Morgan, Clerk, PO Box 120, Saltcoats S0A 3R0 – 306/744-2212, Fax: 306/744-2212
Salvador (V)	50	Kindersley-Lloydminster	kindersley	Leona Sieben, Clerk, PO Box 10, Salvador S0L 2W0 – 306/372-4757
Sandy Bay (NV)	770	Prince Albert-Churchill River	Cumberland	Elwood H. Hennings, Adm., PO Box 130, Sandy Bay S0P 0G0 – 306/754-2165, 2181, Fax: 306/754-2157
*SASKATOON	195,597 ('94)	Saskatoon-Humboldt; Saskatoon-Clark's Crossing	Saskatoon Eastview; Saskatoon Fairview; Saskatoon Greystone; Saskatoon Idylwyld; Saskatoon Meewasin; Saskatoon Mount Royal; Saskatoon Northwest; Saskatoon Nutana; Saskatoon Riversdale; Saskatoon Southest; Saskatoon Sutherland	Janice Mann, City Clerk, City Hall, 222 - 3 Ave. North, Saskatoon S7K 0J5 – 306/975-3200
Sceptre (V)	168	Swift Current-Maple Creek-Assiniboia	Cypress Hills	Sherry Egeland, Clerk, PO Box 128, Sceptre S0N 2H0 – 306/623-4244, Fax: 306/623-4229
Scott †	118	Kindersley-Lloydminster	Kindersley	Linda F. Nielsen, Clerk, PO Box 96, Scott S0K 4A0 – 306/247-2100
Sedley (V)	342	Regina-Wascana	Indian Head-Milestone	Helen Weinberger, Clerk, PO Box 130, Sedley S0G 4K0 – 306/885-2133, Fax: 306/885-2133
Semans (V)	333	Mackenzie	Watrous	Sharon Church, Adm., PO Box 113, Semans S0A 3S0 – 306/524-2144, Fax: 306/524-2145
Senlac (V)	94	Kindersley-Lloydminster	Wilkie	Thomas J. Forbes, Adm., PO Box 93, Senlac S0L 2Y0 – 306/228-4330
Shackleton (V)	12	Swift Current-Maple Creek-Assiniboia	Cypress Hills	Marjorie A. Cator, Clerk, PO Box 7, Shackleton S0N 2L0 – 306/587-2910
Shamrock (V)	34	Moose Jaw-Lake Centre	Thunder Creek	Cathy Marchessault, Clerk, PO Box 119, Shamrock S0H 3W0 – 306/648-2736
Shaunavon †	1,913	Swift Current-Maple Creek-Assiniboia	Wood River	Charmaine Bernath, Adm., PO Box 820, Shaunavon S0N 2M0 – 306/297-2605, Fax: 306/297-2608
Sheho (V)	212	Yorkton-Melville	Canora-Pelly	Pamela Hawreluik, Clerk, PO Box 130, Sheho S0A 3T0 – 306/849-2044
Shell Lake (V)	172	The Battlefords-Meadow Lake	Shellbrook-Spiritwood	Brian C. Fisher, Clerk, PO Box 280, Shell Lake S0J 2G0 – 306/427-2272, Fax: 306/427-2060
Shellbrook †	1,173	Prince Albert-Churchill River	Shellbrook-Spiritwood	Kenneth G. Danger, Adm., PO Box 40, Shellbrook S0J 2E0 – 306/747-2177, Fax: 306/747-3111
Silton (V)	77	Regina-Qu'Appelle	Last Mountain-Touchwood	Brenda Small, Clerk, PO Box 1, Silton S0G 4L0 – 306/731-3222
Simpson (V)	212	Moose Jaw-Lake Centre	Watrous	Donn Bergsveinson, Adm., PO Box 10, Simpson S0G 4M0 – 306/836-2020
Sintaluta †	185	Regina-Qu'Appelle	Indian Head-Milestone	Ann B. Dolter, Clerk, PO Box 150, Sintaluta S0G 4N0 – 306/727-2100
Smeaton (V)	225	Prince Albert-Churchill River	Saskatchewan Rivers	Levina Pearse, Clerk, PO Box 70, Smeaton S0J 2J0 – 306/426-2044, Fax: 306/426-2291

Canadian Almanac & Directory 1997

Cities in CAPITALS; Towns marked †; Villages marked (V); Northern Villages marked (NV); Resort Villages not listed. An in-depth listing for municipalities marked with * appears in Part 2 (check Index for page numbers).

MUNICIPALITY	1991 POP.	FEDERAL ELECTORAL DISTRICT	PROVINCIAL ELECTORAL DISTRICT	CONTACT PERSON WITH ADDRESS, PHONE & FAX
Smiley (V)	71	Kindersley-Lloydminster	Kindersley	Don M. Fizell, Clerk, PO Box 90, Smiley S0L 2Z0 – 306/838-2020, Fax: 306/838-4343
Southend Reindeer (NH)	142	Prince Albert-Churchill River	Cumberland	Bella Cook, Clerk, General Delivery, Southend S0J 2L0 – 306/758-2044, Fax: 306/758-2044
Southey †	693	Regina-Qu'Appelle	Last Mountain-Touchwood	Connie C. Hall, Adm., PO Box 248, Southey S0G 4P0 – 306/726-2202, Fax: 306/726-2202
Sovereign (V)	66	Kindersley-Lloydminster	Rosetown-Biggar	Lenora Anton, Clerk, PO Box 2, Sovereign S0L 3A0 – 306/882-3704
Spalding (V)	287	Mackenzie	Kelvington-Wadena	Olinda Elsasser, Adm., PO Box 280, Spalding S0K 4C0 – 306/872-2276, Fax: 306/872-2100
Speers (V)	91	The Battlefords-Meadow Lake	Redberry Lake	Ronald Tanchak, Adm., PO Box 974, Speers S0M 2V0 – 306/246-2114, Fax: 306/246-2171
Spiritwood †	973	The Battlefords-Meadow Lake	Shellbrook-Spiritwood	Jack Klamot, Adm., PO Box 460, Spiritwood S0J 2M0 – 306/883-2161, Fax: 306/883-3212
Springside †	591	Yorkton-Melville	Melville	Joan M. Popoff, Adm., PO Box 414, Springside S0A 3V0 – 306/792-2022
Springwater (V)	25	Kindersley-Lloydminster	Rosetwon-Biggar	Judy Hammond, Clerk, PO Box 39, Springwater S0K 0M0 – 306/948-2340, Fax: 306/948-2335
Spruce Lake (V)	76	The Battlefords-Meadow Lake	Meadow Lake	Sharon Mork, Clerk, PO Box 13, Spruce Lake S0M 2W0 – 306/845-2291
Spy Hill (V)	297	Yorkton-Melville	Saltcoats	Audrey Clark, Clerk, PO Box 69, Spy Hill S0A 3W0 – 306/534-2255
Stanley Mission (NH)	199	Prince Albert-Churchill River	Cumberland	Marilyn Butler, Clerk, General Delivery, Stanley Mission S0J 2P0 – 306/635-2222, Fax: 306/635-2145
Star City †	507	Mackenzie	Melfort-Tisdale	Laurie Guderyan, Clerk, PO Box 250, Star City S0E 1P0 – 306/863-2282, Fax: 306/863-2277
Stenen (V)	120	Yorkton-Melville	Canora-Pelly	Donna Lee Olson, Clerk, PO Box 160, Stenen S0A 3X0 – 306/548-4334, Fax: 306/548-4334
Stewart Valley (V)	115	Swift Current-Maple Creek-Assiniboia	Swift Current	Valerie L. Ferguson, Clerk, PO Box 10, Stewart Valley S0N 2P0 – 306/778-3611
Stockholm (V)	391	Yorkton-Melville	Saltcoats	Mona M. Jacob, Adm., PO Box 265, Stockholm S0A 3Y0 – 306/793-2151
Stony Rapids (NH)		Prince Albert-Churchill River	Athabasca	Linda Ball, Clerk, General Delivery, Stony Rapids S0J 2R0 – 306/439-2173, Fax: 306/439-2098
Stornoway (V)	14	Yorkton-Melville	Saltcoats	Peter Mandzuik, Clerk, PO Box 100, Stornoway S0A 3Z0 – 306/273-4718
Storthoaks (V)	129	Souris-Moose Mountain	Cannington	Elaine R. Morgan, Adm., PO Box 40, Storthoaks S0C 2K0 – 306/449-2262, Fax: 306/449-2210
Stoughton †	721	Souris-Moose Mountain	Cannington	Gerald W. Figler, Adm., PO Box 397, Stoughton S0G 4T0 – 306/457-2413, Fax: 306/457-3162
Strasbourg †	802	Regina-Qu'Appelle	Last Mountain-Touchwood	W. Doug Hunter, Adm., PO Box 369, Strasbourg S0G 4V0 – 306/725-3707, Fax: 306/725-3613
Strongfield (V)	58	Moose Jaw-Lake Centre	Arm River	Doreen Kennedy, Clerk, PO Box 87, Strongfield S0H 3Z0 – 306/857-2150
Sturgis †	701	Yorkton-Melville	Canora-Pelly	Louise Baht, Adm., PO Box 520, Sturgis S0A 4A0 – 306/548-2108, Fax: 306/548-2948
Success (V)	46	Swift Current-Maple Creek-Assiniboia	Cypress Hills	Rhonda Theise, Clerk, PO Box 40, Success S0N 2R0 – 306/773-7909
SWIFT CURRENT	15,200 ('93)	Swift Current-Maple Creek-Assiniboia	Swift Current	Delores Cox, Clerk, PO Box 340, Swift Current S9H 3W1 – 306/778-2777, Fax: 306/778-2194
Tantallon (V)	161	Yorkton-Melville	Saltcoats	Heather Godwin, Clerk, PO Box 70, Tantallon S0A 4B0 – 306/643-2112
Tessier (V)	39	Kindersley-Lloydminster	Rosetown-Biggar	Paula Richmond, Clerk, PO Box 34, Tessier S0L 3G0 – 306/656-4580
Theodore (V)	473	Yorkton-Melville	Canora-Pelly	Ron Sebulsky, Clerk, PO Box 417, Theodore S0A 4C0 – 306/647-2315, Fax: 306/647-2476
Timber Bay (NH)	119	Prince Albert-Churchill River	Cumberland	Vacant, Clerk, General Delivery, Timber Bay S0J 2T0 – 306/663-5885, Fax: 306/663-5052
Tisdale †	3,045	Mackenzie	Melfort-Tisdale	Merv T. Vey, Adm., PO Box 1090, Tisdale S0E 1T0 – 306/873-2681, Fax: 306/873-5700
Togo (V)	165	Yorkton-Melville	Saltcoats	Rosemarie G. Hamell, Clerk, PO Box 100, Togo S0A 4E0 – 306/597-2114
Tompkins (V)	227	Swift Current-Maple Creek-Assiniboia	Cypress Hills	Denise Willows, Clerk, PO Box 247, Tompkins S0N 2S0 – 306/622-2020, Fax: 306/622-2139
Torquay (V)	285	Souris-Moose Mountain	Estevan	Linda M. Dugan, Clerk, PO Box 6, Torquay S0C 2L0 – 306/923-2172, Fax: 306/923-2172
Tramping Lake (V)	143	Kindersley-Lloydminster	Kindersley	Rose Simon, Clerk, PO Box 157, Tramping Lake S0K 4H0 – 306/755-2002
Tribune (V)	64	Souris-Moose Mountain	Estevan	Dallas Locken, Clerk, PO Box 61, Tribune S0C 2M0 – 306/456-2213, Fax: 306/456-2213
Tugaske (V)	157	Moose Jaw-Lake Centre	Arm River	Darrel Dean, Adm., PO Box 159, Tugaske S0H 4B0 – 306/759-2211, Fax: 306/759-2249

Cities in CAPITALS; Towns marked †; Villages marked (V); Northern Villages marked (NV); Resort Villages not listed. An in-depth listing for municipalities marked with * appears in Part 2 (check Index for page numbers).

MUNICIPALITY	1991 POP.	FEDERAL ELECTORAL DISTRICT	PROVINCIAL ELECTORAL DISTRICT	CONTACT PERSON WITH ADDRESS, PHONE & FAX
Turnor Lake (NH)	185	Prince Albert-Churchill River	Athabasca	Victorina Montgrand, Clerk, General Delivery, Turnor Lake S0M 3E0 – 306/894-2080, 2023, Fax: 306/894-2138
Turtleford †	459	The Battlefords-Meadow Lake	Lloydminster	Deanna Kahl-Lundberg, Adm., PO Box 38, Turtleford S0M 2Y0 – 306/845-2156, Fax: 306/845-3320
Tuxford (V)	92	Moose Jaw-Lake Centre	Arm River	Reg E. McKee, Clerk, PO Box 28, Tuxford S0H 4C0 – 306/692-3390
Unity †	2,227	Kindersley-Lloydminster	Battleford-Cut Knife	Jim Weninger, Adm., PO Box 1030, Unity S0K 4L0 – 306/228-2621, Fax: 306/228-4221
Val Marie (V)	219	Swift Current-Maple Creek-Assiniboia	Wood River	John Billington, Clerk, PO Box 178, Val Marie S0N 2T0 – 306/298-2022, Fax: 306/298-2062
Valparaiso (V)	30	Mackenzie	Melfort-Tisdale	Ann Campbell, Clerk, PO Box 473, Star City S0E 1P0 – 306/863-2522, Fax: 306/863-2255
Vanguard (V)	249	Swift Current-Maple Creek-Assiniboia	Thunder Creek	Ronald W. Kehoe, Adm., PO Box 187, Vanguard S0N 2V0 – 306/582-2010, Fax: 306/582-4811
Vanscoy (V)	331	Kindersley-Lloydminster	Redberry Lake	Beatrice V. Thomas, Adm., PO Box 223, Vanscoy S0L 3J0 – 306/668-2008
Vawn (V)	51	The Battlefords-Meadow Lake	Lloydminster	Sylvia Duhaime, Clerk, PO Box 22, Vawn S0M 2Z0 – 306/397-2885, Fax: 306/397-2213
Veregin (V)	126	Yorkton-Melville	Canora-Pelly	Eva D. Moskal, Clerk, PO Box 160, Veregin S0A 4H0 – 306/542-4338
Vibank (V)	375	Regina-Qu'Appelle	Indian Head-Milestone	Jeanette Schaeffer, Adm., PO Box 204, Vibank S0G 4Y0 – 306/762-2130
Viceroy (V)	64	Swift Current-Maple Creek-Assiniboia	Weyburn-Big Muddy	Mervin A. Guillemin, Adm., PO Box 95, Viceroy S0H 4H0 – 306/268-4555, Fax: 306/268-4547
Viscount (V)	299	Moose Jaw-Lake Centre	Watrous	Lloyd Wilkie, Clerk, PO Box 99, Viscount S0K 4M0 – 306/944-2199, Fax: 306/944-2199
Vonda †	267	Saskatoon-Humboldt	Humboldt	Lionel Diederichs, Clerk, PO Box 190, Vonda S0K 4N0 – 306/258-2035, Fax: 306/258-2035
Wadena †	1,599	Mackenzie	Kelvington-Wadena	Michael Hotsko, Adm., PO Box 730, Wadena S0A 4J0 – 306/338-2145, Fax: 306/338-3804
Wakaw †	965	Saskatoon-Humboldt	Humboldt	Sheri Schitka, Adm., PO Box 669, Wakaw S0K 4P0 – 306/233-4223, Fax: 306/233-5234
Waldeck (V)	333	Swift Current-Maple Creek-Assiniboia	Thunder Creek	Kathy Lang, Clerk, PO Box 97, Waldeck S0H 4J0 – 306/773-9778
Waldheim †	812	Saskatoon-Humboldt	Rosthern	D. Chris Adams, Adm., PO Box 460, Waldheim S0K 4R0 – 306/945-2161, Fax: 306/945-2360
Waldron (V)	35	Yorkton-Melville	Melville	Karen Handke, Clerk, PO Box 87, Waldron S0A 4K0 – 306/728-5366
Wapella †	429	Souris-Moose Mountain	Moosomin	Nancy Campbell, Clerk, PO Box 189, Wapella S0G 4Z0 – 306/532-4343
Warman †	2,644	Saskatoon-Clark's Crossing	Rosthern	John Janeson, Adm., PO Box 340, Warman S0K 4S0 – 306/933-2133, Fax: 306/933-1987
Waseca (V)	152	Kindersley-Lloydminster	Lloydminster	Rachael Gustafson, Clerk, PO Box 128, Waseca S0M 3A0 – 306/893-2211
Watrous †	1,872	Moose Jaw-Lake Centre	Watrous	Willard Struck, Clerk, PO Box 730, Watrous S0K 4T0 – 306/946-3369, Fax: 306/946-2974
Watson †	884	Mackenzie	Watrous	Jacqueline Lamarre, Adm., PO Box 276, Watson S0K 4V0 – 306/287-3224, Fax: 306/287-3442
Wawota †	654	Souris-Moose Mountain	Cannington	Lynne Swanson, Adm., PO Box 58, Wawota S0G 5A0 – 306/739-2216, Fax: 306/739-2222
Webb (V)	64	Swift Current-Maple Creek-Assiniboia	Cypress Hills	Don Haley, Adm., PO Box 100, Webb S0N 2X0 – 306/674-2230, Fax: 306/674-2324
Weekes (V)	104	Mackenzie	Kelvington-Wadena	Brenda Kipling, Clerk, PO Box 159, Weekes S0E 1V0 – 306/278-2800
Weirdale (V)	72	Prince Albert-Churchill River	Saskatchewan Rivers	Elizabeth Gatley, Clerk, General Delivery, Weirdale S0J 2Z0 – 306/929-2329, Fax: 306/929-2239
Weldon (V)	243	Saskatoon-Humboldt	Saskatchewan Rivers	Fanuel Lima, Adm., PO Box 190, Weldon S0J 3A0 – 306/887-2070
Welwyn (V)	161	Souris-Moose Mountain	Moosomin	Elaine Olsen, Adm., PO Box 118, Welwyn S0A 4L0 – 306/733-2077, Fax: 306/733-2022
West Bend (V)	13	Mackenzie	Canora-Pelly	Valerie Dlugan, Clerk, PO Box 11, West Bend S0A 4M0 – 306/675-4554
Weyakwin (NH)	167	Prince Albert-Churchill River	Cumberland	Jemima Nelson, Clerk, PO Box 295, Weyakwin S0J 1W0 – 306/663-5820, Fax: 306/663-5112
WEYBURN	9,673	Souris-Moose Mountain	Weyburn-Big Muddy	Fred C. Martyn, City Clerk, PO Box 370, Weyburn S4H 2K6 – 306/848-3209, Fax: 306/842-2001
White City (V)	862	Regina-Qu'Appelle	Regina Wascana Plains	Darlene Woloshyn, Clerk, PO Box 220, White City S0G 5B0 – 306/781-2355, Fax: 306/781-2194
White Fox (V)	442	Mackenzie	Carrot River Valley	Wendy Nycholat, Adm., PO Box 38, White Fox S0J 3B0 – 306/276-2106, Fax: 306/276-2131
Whitewood †	1,064	Souris-Moose Mountain	Moosomin	Patricia Henry, Adm., PO Box 129, Whitewood S0G 5C0 – 306/735-2210, Fax: 306/735-2262

4-148 SASKATCHEWAN MUNICIPALITIES

Cities in CAPITALS; Towns marked †; Villages marked (V); Northern Villages marked (NV); Resort Villages not listed. An in-depth listing for municipalities marked with * appears in Part 2 (check Index for page numbers).

MUNICIPALITY	1991 POP.	FEDERAL ELECTORAL DISTRICT	PROVINCIAL ELECTORAL DISTRICT	CONTACT PERSON WITH ADDRESS, PHONE & FAX
Wilcox (V)	230	Regina-Wascana	Indian Head-Milestone	K.S. Ritchie, Adm., PO Box 130, Wilcox S0G 5E0 – 306/732-2030, Fax: 306/732-4495
Wilkie †	1,401	The Battlefords-Meadow Lake	Battleford-Cut Knife	Julie Brooks, Adm., PO Box 580, Wilkie S0K 4W0 – 306/843-2692, Fax: 306/843-3151
Willow Bunch †	476	Swift Current-Maple Creek-Assiniboia	Wood River	Collette Walter, Clerk, PO Box 189, Willow Bunch S0H 4K0 – 306/473-2450, Fax: 306/473-2450
Willowbrook (V)	36	Yorkton-Melville	Melville	M.J. Kowal, Clerk, PO Box 60, Willowbrook S0A 4P0 – 306/783-6751
Windthorst (V)	246	Souris-Moose Mountain	Moosomin	Martha J. Hassler, Clerk, PO Box 98, Windthorst S0G 5G0 – 306/224-2033
Wiseton (V)	120	Kindersley-Lloydminster	Rosetown-Biggar	Sandra E. Elliott, Clerk, PO Box 160, Wiseton S0L 3M0 – 306/357-2022
Wishart (V)	194	Mackenzie	Last Mountain-Touchwood	Jim Turanich, Adm., PO Box 160, Wishart S0A 4R0 – 306/576-2252, Fax: 306/576-2132
Wollaston Lake (NH)	250	Prince Albert-Churchill River	Cumberland	Vacant, Clerk, General Delivery, Wollaston Lake S0J 3C0 – 306/633-2193, Fax: 306/633-2020
Wolseley †	853	Regina-Qu'Appelle	Moosomin	Norman R. Hicks, Clerk, PO Box 310, Wolseley S0G 5H0 – 306/698-2477, Fax: 306/698-2953
Wood Mountain (V)	46	Swift Current-Maple Creek-Assiniboia	Wood River	Jocelyn Beauregard, Clerk, PO Box 89, Wood Mountain S0H 0B0 – 306/266-2002, Fax: 306/266-2020
Woodrow (V)	39	Swift Current-Maple Creek-Assiniboia	Wood River	Pauline Crone, Clerk, PO Box 68, Woodrow S0H 4M0
Wroxton (V)	65	Yorkton-Melville	Saltcoats	Linda Napady, Clerk, PO Box 160, Wroxton S0A 4S0 – 306/742-4557
Wynyard †	2,022	Mackenzie	Last Mountain-Touchwood	Sheila Hitchings, Adm., PO Box 220, Wynyard S0A 4T0 – 306/554-2123, Fax: 306/554-3224
Yarbo (V)	135	Yorkton-Melville	Saltcoats	Joan Kerr, Clerk, PO Box 96, Yarbo S0A 4V0 – 306/745-3532
Yellow Creek (V)	90	Saskatoon-Humboldt	Melfort-Tisdale	Sally Wojcichowsky, Adm., PO Box 219, Yellow Creek S0K 4X0 – 306/279-2191
Yellow Grass †	535	Souris-Moose Mountain	Indian Head-Milestone	Gail Blaney, Adm., PO Box 270, Yellow Grass S0G 5J0 – 306/465-2400, Fax: 306/465-2802
YORKTON	15,315	Yorkton-Melville	Yorkton	Laurie-Anne Rusnak, Clerk, PO Box 400, Yorkton S3N 2W3 – 306/786-1700, Fax: 306/786-6880
Young (V)	352	Moose Jaw-Lake Centre	Watrous	Jean Jack, Clerk, PO Box 359, Young S0K 4Y0 – 306/259-2242
Zealandia †	137	Kindersley-Lloydminster	Rosetown-Biggar	Nora Hoffman, Clerk, PO Box 52, Zealandia S0L 3N0 – 306/882-3825
Zelma (V)	69	Moose Jaw-Lake Centre	Watrous	Maxine Fischer, Clerk, Zelma GMB #14, Allan S0K 0C0 – 306/257-3927
Zenon Park (V)	254	Mackenzie	Melfort-Tisdale	Lisa Archer, Clerk, PO Box 278, Zenon Park S0E 1W0 – 306/767-2233, Fax: 306/767-2226

Rural Municipalities in Saskatchewan

MUNICIPALITY	1991 POP.	CONTACT PERSON WITH ADDRESS & PHONE
Aberdeen No. 373	730	Mary Glenister, Adm., PO Box 40, Aberdeen S0K 0A0 – 306/253-4312, Fax: 306/253-4445
Abernethy No. 186	515	Evan G. Behrns, Adm., PO Box 183, Abernethy S0A 0A0 – 306/333-2044, Fax: 306/333-2285
Antelope Park No. 322	193	Beverly A. Dahl, Adm., PO Box 70, Marengo S0L 2K0 – 306/968-2922, Fax: 306/968-2278
Antler No. 61	655	John H.J. Eberl, Adm., PO Box 70, Redvers S0C 2H0 – 306/452-3263, Fax: 306/452-3518
Arborfield No. 456	548	Allan Frisky, Adm., PO Box 280, Arborfield S0E 0A0 – 306/769-8633, Fax: 306/769-8301
Argyle No. 1	360	Valerie A. Olney, Adm., PO Box 120, Gainsborough S0C 0Z0 – 306/685-2010, Fax: 306/685-2161
Arlington No. 79	351	Richard E. Goulet, Adm., PO Box 1115, Shaunavon S0N 2M0 – 306/297-2108, Fax: 306/297-2108
Arm River No. 252	335	Norman Sagen, Adm., PO Box 250, Davidson S0G 1A0 – 306/567-3103, Fax: 306/567-3266
Auvergne No. 76	447	Linda J. Linnen, Adm., PO Box 60, Ponteix S0N 1Z0 – 306/625-3210, Fax: 306/625-3681
Baildon No. 131	679	Debra A. Kerfoot, Adm., PO Box 1902, Moose Jaw S6H 7N6 – 306/693-2166, Fax: 306/693-2166
Barrier Valley No. 397	702	Fern Lucas, Adm., PO Box 246, Archerwill S0E 0B0 – 306/323-2101, Fax: 306/323-2101
Battle River No. 438	866	Betty Johnson, Adm., PO Box 148, Battleford S0M 0E0 – 306/937-2235, Fax: 306/937-2235
Bayne No. 371	698	Lonnie Sowa, Adm., PO Box 130, Bruno S0K 0S0 – 306/369-2511, Fax: 306/369-2511
Beaver River No. 622	1,103	Debra Johnson, Adm., PO Box 129, Pierceland S0M 2K0 – 306/839-2060, Fax: 306/839-2178
Bengough No. 40	467	Dale L. Leflar, Adm., PO Box 429, Bengough S0C 0K0 – 306/268-2055, Fax: 306/268-2055
Benson No. 35	496	Laureen Keating, Adm., PO Box 69, Benson S0C 0L0 – 306/634-9410, Fax: 306/634-9410
Big Arm No. 251	330	Walter Krawchuk, Adm., PO Box 10, Stalwart S0G 4R0 – 306/963-2402
Big Quill No. 308	840	Glenn Thompson, Adm., PO Box 898, Wynyard S0A 4T0 – 306/554-2533, Fax: 306/554-2533
Big River No. 555	848	Wendy Gowda Drummond, Adm., PO Box 219, Big River S0J 0E0 – 306/469-2323
Big Stick No. 141	259	Quinton Jacksteit, Adm., PO Box 9, Golden Prairie S0N 0Y0 – 306/662-2883, Fax: 306/662-2883
Biggar No. 347	1,057	Adele McLeod, Adm., PO Box 280, Biggar S0K 0M0 – 306/948-2422, Fax: 306/948-2250
Birch Hills No. 460	836	Sandra Barber, Adm., PO Box 369, Birch Hills S0J 0G0 – 306/749-2233, Fax: 306/749-2220
Bjorkdale No. 426	1,253	Spencer H. Abbs, Adm., PO Box 10, Crooked River S0E 0R0 – 306/873-2470, Fax: 306/873-2470
Blaine Lake No. 434	423	James V. Burak, Adm., PO Box 38, Blaine Lake S0J 0J0 – 306/497-2282, Fax: 306/497-2511
Blucher No. 343	1,225	Robert Thurmeier, Adm., PO Box 100, Bradwell S0K 0P0 – 306/257-3344, Fax: 306/257-3303
Bone Creek No. 108	435	Rhonda Bellefeuille, Adm., PO Box 459, Shaunavon S0N 2M0 – 306/297-2570, Fax: 306/297-2570

Canadian Almanac & Directory 1997

MUNICIPALITY	1991 POP.	CONTACT PERSON WITH ADDRESS & PHONE
Bratt's Lake No. 129	391	Kevin S. Ritchie, Adm., PO Box 130, Wilcox S0G 5E0 – 306/732-2030, Fax: 306/732-4495
Britannia No. 502	1,332	B. Bonnie Mills-Midgley, Adm., PO Box 661, Lloydminster S9V 0Y7 – 306/825-2610, Fax: 306/825-2610
Brock No. 64	329	Bruce F. Waddell, Adm., PO Box 247, Kisbey S0C 1L0 – 306/462-2010, Fax: 306/462-2010
Brokenshell No. 68	348	Lorelei Zdunich, Adm., PO Box 10, Trossachs S0C 2N0 – 306/842-5820, Fax: 306/842-7530
Browning No. 34	550	Greg Wallin, Adm., PO Box 40, Lampman S0C 1N0 – 306/487-2444, Fax: 306/487-2496
Buchanan No. 304	669	Karren Statchuk, Adm., PO Box 10, Buchanan S0A 0J0 – 306/592-2055
Buckland No. 491	3,556	C. Lorne Marshall, Adm., 99 River St. E., Prince Albert S6V 0A1 – 306/763-2585, Fax: 306/763-6369
Buffalo No. 409	518	Jeanette Nicholson, Adm., PO Box 100, Wilkie S0K 4W0 – 306/843-2301, Fax: 306/843-2342
Calder No. 241	638	Rona Seidle, Adm., PO Box 10, Wroxton S0A 4S0 – 306/742-4233, Fax: 306/742-4559
Caledonia No. 99	462	Ernest P. Audette, Adm., PO Box 328, Milestone S0G 3L0 – 306/436-2050, Fax: 306/436-2051
Cambria No. 6	391	Dale Shauf, Adm., PO Box 210, Torquay S0C 2L0 – 306/923-2000
Cana No. 214	1,129	John B. Chesney, Adm., PO Box 550, Melville S0A 2P0 – 306/728-5645, Fax: 306/728-3807
Canaan No. 225	204	Edna A. Laturnus, Adm., PO Box 99, Lucky Lake S0L 1Z0 – 306/858-2234, Fax: 306/858-2234
Canwood No. 494	1,811	Hugh Otterson, Adm., PO Box 10, Canwood S0J 0K0 – 306/468-2014, Fax: 306/468-2666
Carmichael No. 109	558	Collette Jones, Adm., PO Box 420, Gull Lake S0N 1A0 – 306/672-3501, Fax: 306/672-3879
Caron No. 162	541	Sandra Sparkes, Adm., PO Box 85, Caron S0H 0R0 – 306/756-2353, Fax: 306/756-2250
Chaplin No. 164	231	Doris Bauck, Adm., PO Box 60, Chaplin S0H 0V0 – 306/395-2244
Chester No. 125	588	James R. Hoff, Adm., PO Box 180, Glenavon S0G 1Y0 – 306/429-2110, Fax: 306/429-2260
Chesterfield No. 261	646	Garry Ritsco, Adm., PO Box 70, Eatonia S0L 0Y0 – 306/967-2222, Fax: 306/967-2424
Churchbridge No. 211	1,015	Casmer P. Chyz, Adm., PO Box 211, Churchbridge S0A 0M0 – 306/896-2522, Fax: 306/896-2743
Clayton No. 333	1,050	Douglas W. Ferder, Adm., PO Box 220, Hyas S0A 1K0 – 306/594-2832
Clinworth No. 230	347	Naida Dillman, Adm., PO Box 120, Sceptre S0N 2H0 – 306/623-4229, Fax: 306/623-4229
Coalfields No. 4	440	Terry Erdelyan, Adm., PO Box 190, Bienfait S0C 0M0 – 306/388-2323, Fax: 306/388-2330
Colonsay No. 342	357	Katherine Templeman, Adm., PO Box 130, Colonsay S0K 0Z0 – 306/255-2233, Fax: 306/255-2291
Connaught No. 457	865	Keith Hummel, Adm., PO Box 25, Tisdale S0E 1T0 – 306/873-2657, Fax: 306/873-4442
Corman Park No. 344	6,800	Fred J. Sutter, Adm., 111 Pinehouse Dr., Saskatoon S7K 5W1 – 306/242-9303, Fax: 306/242-6965
Cote No. 271	760	Kim McIvor, Adm., PO Box 669, Kamsack S0A 1S0 – 306/542-2121, Fax: 306/542-2121
Coteau No. 255	529	Murray Cook, Adm., PO Box 30, Birsay S0L 0G0 – 306/573-2047, Fax: 306/573-2111
Coulee No. 136	663	Mollie Weinbender, Adm., 1680 Chaplin St. East, Swift Current S9H 1K8 – 306/773-5420
Craik No. 222	393	Tim Fox, Adm., PO Box 420, Craik S0G 0V0 – 306/734-2242, Fax: 306/734-2688
Cupar No. 218	660	Loretta Young, Adm., PO Box 40, Markinch S0G 3J0 – 306/726-2063, Fax: 306/726-2063
Cut Knife No. 439	509	Donald McCallum, Adm., PO Box 70, Cut Knife S0M 0N0 – 306/398-2353, Fax: 306/398-2839
Cymri No. 36	531	Curtis. Herzberg, Adm., PO Box 238, Midale S0C 1S0 – 306/458-2244, Fax: 306/458-2699
Deer Forks No. 232	258	Rodney J. Quinton, Adm., PO Box 250, Burstall S0N 0H0 – 306/679-2000, Fax: 306/679-2275
Douglas No. 436	521	Ronald A. Tanchak, Adm., PO Box 964, Speers S0M 2V0 – 306/246-2171, Fax: 306/246-2171
Duck Lake No. 463	982	Lois McCormick, Adm., PO Box 250, Duck Lake S6V 5R1 – 306/467-2011, Fax: 306/476-4423
Dufferin No. 190	574	Rick Hicks, Adm., PO Box 67, Bethune S0G 0H0 – 306/638-3112, Fax: 306/638-3112
Dundurn No. 314	569	Violet P. Barna, Adm., PO Box 159, Dundurn S0K 1K0 – 306/492-2132, Fax: 306/492-2132
Eagle Creek No. 376	554	Lloyd Cross, Adm., PO Box 100, Arelee S0K 0H0 – 306/237-4424, Fax: 306/237-4294
Edenwold No. 158	2,349	Donna L. Strudwick, Adm., PO Box 10, Balgonie S0G 0E0 – 306/771-2522, Fax: 306/771-2631
Elcapo No. 154	732	Mervin J. Schmidt, Adm., PO Box 668, Broadview S0G 0K0 – 306/696-2474, Fax: 306/696-2474
Eldon No. 471	882	Gordon R. Fullerton, Adm., PO Box 130, Maidstone S0M 1M0 – 306/893-2391, Fax: 306/893-2391
Elfros No. 307	684	Mary Corby, Adm., PO Box 40, Elfros S0A 0V0 – 306/328-2011
Elmsthorpe No. 100	405	Lawrence Harty, Adm., PO Box 240, Avonlea S0H 0C0 – 306/868-2011, Fax: 306/868-2011
Emerald No. 277	774	Jim Turanich, Adm., PO Box 160, Wishart S0A 4R0 – 306/576-2002, Fax: 306/576-2132
Enfield No. 194	438	Joe Van Leuken, Adm., PO Box 70, Central Butte S0H 0T0 – 306/796-2025, Fax: 306/796-2025
Enniskillen No. 3	545	Bill J. Ringguth, Adm., PO Box 179, Oxbow S0C 2B0 – 306/483-2277, Fax: 306/483-2277
Enterprise No. 142	299	Darryl Altman, Adm., PO Box 150, Richmound S0N 2E0 – 306/669-2000, Fax: 306/669-2052
Estevan No. 5	1,139	Dale Malmgren, Adm., 1329 - 4 St., Estevan S4A 0X1 – 306/634-2222, Fax: 306/634-2223
Excel No. 71	630	Mervin Guillemin, Adm., PO Box 100, Viceroy S0H 4H0 – 306/268-4555, Fax: 306/268-4547
Excelsior No. 166	945	Christina Patoine, Adm., PO Box 180, Rush Lake S0H 3S0 – 306/784-3121, Fax: 306/784-3121
Eye Hill No. 382	713	Calvin Giggs, Adm., PO Box 69, Macklin S0L 2C0 – 306/753-2075, Fax: 306/753-3234
Eyebrow No. 193	379	Herbert A. White, Adm., PO Box 99, Eyebrow S0H 1L0 – 306/759-2101
Fertile Belt No. 183	1,091	B. Darlene Maier, Adm., PO Box 190, Stockholm S0A 3Y0 – 306/793-2061, Fax: 306/793-2063
Fertile Valley No. 285	657	Donna G. Haug, Adm., PO Box 70, Conquest S0L 0L0 – 306/856-2037, Fax: 306/856-2211
Fillmore No. 96	422	Allan Dionne, Adm., PO Box 130, Fillmore S0G 1N0 – 306/722-3251, Fax: 306/722-3775
Fish Creek No. 402	434	Richard W. Kindrachuk, Adm., PO Box 160, Wakaw S0K 4P0 – 306/233-4412, Fax: 306/233-4412
Flett's Springs No. 429	899	Clinton W. Tetarenko, Adm., PO Box 160, Melfort S0E 1A0 – 306/752-3606, Fax: 306/752-3882
Foam Lake No. 276	953	Ron Kostiuk, Adm., PO Box 490, Foam Lake S0A 1A0 – 306/272-3334, Fax: 306/272-4722
Fox Valley No. 171	400	Daniel S. Buye, Adm., PO Box 190, Fox Valley S0N 0V0 – 306/666-2055, Fax: 306/666-2174
Francis No. 127	803	Claude A. Caron, Adm., PO Box 36, Francis S0G 1V0 – 306/245-3256, Fax: 306/245-3203
Frenchman Butte No. 501	1,397	Isabelle Jasper, Adm., PO Box 180, Paradise Hill S0M 2G0 – 306/344-2034, Fax: 306/344-4434
Frontier No. 19	338	Raymond Dubé, Adm., PO Box 30, Frontier S0N 0W0 – 306/296-2030, Fax: 306/296-2175
Garden River No. 490	711	Francine Kenzle, Adm., PO Box 70, Meath Park S0J 1T0 – 306/929-2020, Fax: 306/929-2281
Garry No. 245	682	Jerry T. Kuziak, Adm., PO Box 10, Jedburgh S0A 1R0 – 306/647-2450, Fax: 306/647-2450
Glen Bain No. 105	419	Dianne Debert, Adm., PO Box 61, Glen Bain S0N 0X0 – 306/264-3607, Fax: 306/264-3607
Glen McPherson No. 46	202	Michael E. Sherven, Adm., PO Box 277, Mankota S0H 2W0 – 306/478-2323, Fax: 306/478-2606
Glenside No. 377	425	Pamela Urton, Adm., PO Box 1084, Biggar S0K 0M0 – 306/948-3681, Fax: 306/948-3684
Golden West No. 95	526	Edward A. Mish, Adm., PO Box 70, Corning S0G 0T0 – 306/224-4456, Fax: 306/224-4456
Good Lake No. 274	733	David W. Popowich, Adm., PO Box 896, Canora S0A 0L0 – 306/563-5244, Fax: 306/563-5244
Grandview No. 349	503	Patti Turk, Adm., PO Box 39, Kelfield S0K 2C0 – 306/932-4911, Fax: 306/932-4911
Grant No. 372	560	Lionel J. Diederichs, Adm., PO Box 190, Vonda S0K 4N0 – 306/258-2022, Fax: 306/258-2035
Grass Lake No. 381	560	Brenda M. Kasas, Adm., PO Box 40, Reward S0K 3N0 – 306/228-2988, Fax: 306/228-4188
Grassy Creek No. 78	437	L. Marcel Meloche, Adm., PO Box 400, Shaunavon S0N 2M0 – 306/297-2520
Gravelbourg No. 104	549	Shirley M. Parker, Adm., PO Box 510, Gravelbourg S0H 1X0 – 306/648-2412, Fax: 306/648-2603
Grayson No. 184	763	Eileen M. Parker, Adm., PO Box 69, Grayson S0A 1E0 – 306/794-2044, Fax: 306/794-4655

MUNICIPALITY	1991 POP.	CONTACT PERSON WITH ADDRESS & PHONE
Great Bend No. 405	546	Ken Tanchak, Adm., PO Box 150, Borden S0K 0N0 – 306/997-2101, Fax: 306/997-2101
Griffin No. 66	465	Audrey L. Trombley, Adm., PO Box 70, Griffin S0C 1G0 – 306/842-6298, Fax: 306/842-6400
Gull Lake No. 139	307	Ida-Mae Leek, Adm., PO Box 58, Gull Lake S0N 1A0 – 306/672-4430, Fax: 306/672-3879
Happy Valley No. 10	222	Louise A. Brown, Adm., PO Box 39, Big Beaver S0H 0G0 – 306/267-4540
Happyland No. 231	457	Joseph C. Ries, Adm., PO Box 339, Leader S0N 1H0 – 306/628-3800, Fax: 306/628-4228
Harris No. 316	295	Jim Angus, Adm., PO Box 146, Harris S0L 1K0 – 306/656-2072, Fax: 306/656-2151
Hart Butte No. 11	385	Vernon Palmer, Adm., PO Box 210, Coronach S0H 0Z0 – 306/267-2005, Fax: 306/267-2391
Hazel Dell No. 335	903	G. Urban McLaughlin, Adm., PO Box 87, Okla S0A 2X0 – 306/325-4315
Hazelwood No. 94	415	Gary Vargo, Adm., PO Box 270, Kipling S0G 2S0 – 306/736-8121, Fax: 306/736-8121
Heart's Hill No. 352	410	Vern Gintaut, Adm., PO Box 458, Luseland S0L 2A0 – 306/372-4224, Fax: 306/372-4224
Hillsborough No. 132	166	James W. Nichols, Adm., #3, 54 Stadacona St. West, Moose Jaw S6H 1Z1 – 306/693-1329
Hillsdale No. 440	610	Dale M. Bryden, Adm., PO Box 280, Neilburg S0M 2C0 – 306/823-4321, Fax: 306/823-4477
Hoodoo No. 401	699	Lloyd Wedewer, Adm., PO Box 250, Cudworth S0K 1B0 – 306/256-3281, Fax: 306/256-7147
Hudson Bay No. 394	1,889	Linda Purves, Adm., PO Box 520, Hudson Bay S0E 0Y0 – 306/865-2691, Fax: 306/865-2857
Humboldt No. 370	1,065	Fred W. Saliken, Adm., PO Box 420, Humboldt S0K 2A0 – 306/682-2242, Fax: 306/682-3239
Huron No. 223	277	Darrel Dean, Adm., PO Box 159, Tugaske S0H 4B0 – 306/759-2421, Fax: 306/759-2249
Indian Head No. 156	486	Jody Crossman, Adm., PO Box 39, Indian Head S0G 2K0 – 306/695-3464, Fax: 306/695-3462
Insinger No. 275	634	Bettie Thompson, Adm., PO Box 179, Insinger S0A 1L0 – 306/647-2422, Fax: 306/647-2422
Invergordon No. 430	811	Barry Kuzyk, Adm., PO Box 40, Crystal Springs S0K 1A0 – 306/749-2852, Fax: 306/749-2499
Invermay No. 305	611	Greg Wolkowski, Adm., PO Box 130, Invermay S0A 1M0 – 306/593-2152, Fax: 306/593-2152
Ituna Bon Accord No. 246	631	Diane M. Olech, Adm., PO Box 190, Ituna S0A 1N0 – 306/795-2202, Fax: 306/795-2202
Kellross No. 247	734	Robert Jorgensen, Adm., PO Box 10, Leross S0A 2C0 – 306/675-4423, Fax: 306/675-4423
Kelvington No. 366	759	Tim G. Leurer, Adm., PO Box 519, Kelvington S0A 1W0 – 306/327-4222, Fax: 306/327-4222
Key West No. 70	514	Peggy Tumback, Adm., PO Box 159, Ogema S0C 1Y0 – 306/459-2262, Fax: 306/459-2762
Keys No. 303	543	Sharon Ciesielski, Adm., PO Box 899, Canora S0A 0L0 – 306/563-5331, Fax: 306/563-6759
Kindersley No. 290	1,083	Douglas C. Empey, Adm., PO Box 1210, Kindersley S0L 1S0 – 306/463-2524, Fax: 306/463-4197
King George No. 256	309	Jamie McIntosh, Adm., PO Box 100, Dinsmore S0L 0T0 – 306/846-2022, Fax: 306/846-2022
Kingsley No. 124	584	Tim C. Lozinsky, Adm., PO Box 239, Kipling S0G 2S0 – 306/736-2272, Fax: 306/736-2272
Kinistino No. 459	954	Larry W. Edeen, Adm., PO Box 310, Kinistino S0J 1H0 – 306/864-2474, Fax: 306/864-2880
Kutawa No. 278	402	Marlene I. Benko, Adm., PO Box 40, Punnichy S0A 3C0 – 306/835-2110, Fax: 306/835-2100
Lac Pelletier No. 107	515	Rose Lawrence, Adm., PO Box 70, Neville S0N 1T0 – 306/627-3226
Lacadena No. 228	888	Johann F.H. Penner, Adm., PO Box 39, Lacadena S0L 1V0 – 306/574-4753, Fax: 306/574-4753
Laird No. 404	1,102	Brenda Strembicki, Adm., PO Box 160, Waldheim S0K 4R0 – 306/945-2133
Lajord No. 128	1,032	Rod J. Heise, Adm., PO Box 36, Lajord S0G 2V0 – 306/781-2744, Fax: 306/781-2744
Lake Alma No. 8	345	Darlene Lund, Adm., PO Box 100, Lake Alma S0C 1M0 – 306/447-2022, Fax: 306/447-2022
Lake Johnston No. 102	242	H. Sam Edgerton, Adm., PO Box 160, Mossbank S0H 3G0 – 306/354-2414, Fax: 306/354-7725
Lake Lenore No. 399	579	Gailene Gallais, Adm., PO Box 280, St. Brieux S0K 3V0 – 306/275-2066, Fax: 306/275-4949
Lake of the Rivers No. 72	413	F.A. Kornfeld, Adm., PO Box 610, Assiniboia S0H 0B0 – 306/642-3533, Fax: 306/642-4382
Lakeland No. 521	594	Howard Paterson, Adm., PO Box 27, Christopher Lake S0J 0N0 – 306/982-2010, Fax: 306/982-2589
Lakeside No. 338	606	Judy Kanak, Adm., PO Box 9, Quill Lake S0A 3E0 – 306/383-2261, Fax: 306/383-2255
Lakeview No. 337	689	J. Ann Sanderson, Adm., PO Box 220, Wadena S0A 4J0 – 306/338-2341, Fax: 306/338-2341
Langenburg No. 181	855	Adam Faul, Adm., PO Box 489, Langenburg S0A 2A0 – 306/743-2341, Fax: 306/743-2341
Last Mountain Valley No. 250	430	Cal Shaw, Adm., PO Box 160, Govan S0G 1Z0 – 306/484-2011, Fax: 306/484-2113
Laurier No. 38	471	Darlene J. Paquin, Adm., PO Box 219, Radville S0C 2G0 – 306/869-2255, Fax: 306/869-2524
Lawtonia No. 135	550	Art Thompson, Adm., PO Box 10, Hodgeville S0H 2B0 – 306/677-2266, Fax: 306/677-2446
Leask No. 464	913	Rick Poole, Adm., PO Box 190, Leask S0J 1M0 – 306/466-2000, Fax: 306/466-2000
Leroy No. 339	750	Joan Fedak, Adm., PO Box 100, Leroy S0K 2P0 – 306/286-3261, Fax: 306/286-3400
Lipton No. 217	607	Melony K. Materi, Adm., PO Box 40, Lipton S0G 3B0 – 306/336-2244, Fax: 306/336-2244
Livingston No. 331	556	Mike Burtnack, Adm., PO Box 40, Arran S0A 0B0 – 306/595-4521
Lomond No. 37	436	Kevin Melle, Adm., PO Box 280, Weyburn S4H 2K1 – 306/456-2566, Fax: 306/456-2566
Lone Tree No. 18	238	Ronald J. Johnson, Adm., PO Box 30, Climax S0N 0N0 – 306/293-2124, Fax: 306/293-2702
Longlaketon No. 219	1,035	Shelly Mohr, Adm., PO Box 100, Earl Grey S0G 1J0 – 306/939-2144
Loon Lake No. 561	930	Darren D. Elder, Adm., PO Box 40, Loon Lake S0M 1L0 – 306/837-2076, Fax: 306/837-2282
Loreburn No. 254	473	Nona Stronski, Adm., PO Box 40, Loreburn S0H 2S0 – 306/644-2022, Fax: 306/644-2064
Lost River No. 313	260	Christine Dyck, Adm., PO Box 159, Allan S0K 0C0 – 306/257-3272, Fax: 306/257-3337
Lumsden No. 189	1,279	John E. Spicer, Adm., PO Box 160, Lumsden S0G 3C0 – 306/731-2231, Fax: 306/731-3572
Manitou Lake No. 442	631	Jason Boyle, Adm., PO Box 69, Marsden S0M 1P0 – 306/826-5215, Fax: 306/826-5512
Mankota No. 45	559	Michael E. Sherven, Adm., PO Box 148, Mankota S0H 2W0 – 306/478-2323, Fax: 306/478-2606
Maple Bush No. 224	223	Garry L. Gross, Adm., PO Box 160, Riverhurst S0H 3P0 – 306/353-2292, Fax: 306/353-2292
Maple Creek No. 111	1,213	Debbie Kusler, Adm., PO Box 188, Maple Creek S0N 1N0 – 306/662-2300, Fax: 306/662-3566
Mariposa No. 350	337	Joe Fruhstuk, Adm., PO Box 39, Tramping Lake S0K 4H0 – 306/834-5037, Fax: 306/834-5037
Marquis No. 191	478	Ronald J. Gasper, Adm., PO Box 40, Marquis S0H 2X0 – 306/788-2022, Fax: 306/788-2168
Marriott No. 317	598	Jim P. Reiter, Adm., PO Box 366, Rosetown S0L 2V0 – 306/882-4030, Fax: 306/882-4401
Martin No. 122	387	Holly J. McFarlane, Adm., PO Box 99, Wapella S0G 4Z0 – 306/532-4332, Fax: 306/435-4313
Maryfield No. 91	489	Doreen Jurkovic, Adm., PO Box 70, Maryfield S0G 3K0 – 306/646-2033, Fax: 306/646-2033
Mayfield No. 406	528	Laurie DuBois, Adm., PO Box 100, Maymont S0M 1T0 – 306/389-2112, Fax: 306/389-2112
McCraney No. 282	513	Gregory M. Brkich, Adm., PO Box 129, Kenaston S0G 2N0 – 306/252-2240, Fax: 306/252-2240
McKillop No. 220	573	W. Doug Hunter, Adm., PO Box 369, Strasbourg S0G 4V0 – 306/725-3230, Fax: 306/725-3613
McLeod No. 185	743	Murray J. Hanowski, Adm., PO Box 130, Neudorf S0A 2T0 – 306/748-2233, Fax: 306/748-2647
Meadow Lake No. 588	2,445	Darryl J. Wilkinson, Adm., #1, 225 Centre St., Meadow Lake S9X 1L5 – 306/236-5651, Fax: 306/236-3115
Medstead No. 497	689	Darrin Beaudoin, Adm., PO Box 148, Medstead S0M 1W0 – 306/342-4609
Meeting Lake No. 466	696	Debbie L. Wohlberg, Adm., PO Box 26, Mayfair S0M 1S0 – 306/246-4228, Fax: 306/246-4228
Meota No. 468	799	Allie R. Raycraft, Adm., PO Box 80, Meota S0M 1X0 – 306/892-2061, Fax: 306/892-2061
Mervin No. 499	1,219	L. Ryan. Domotor, Adm., PO Box 130, Turtleford S0M 2Y0 – 306/845-2045, Fax: 306/845-2950
Milden No. 286	328	Melody Nieman, Adm., PO Box 206, Milden S0L 2L0 – 306/935-2181
Milton No. 292	247	Beverly A. Dahl, Adm., PO Box 70, Marengo S0L 2K0 – 306/968-2922, Fax: 306/968-2278

Canadian Almanac & Directory 1997

MUNICIPALITY	1991 POP.	CONTACT PERSON WITH ADDRESS & PHONE
Miry Creek No. 229	586	Richard B. Sylvestre, Adm., PO Box 210, Abbey S0N 0A0 – 306/689-2281, Fax: 306/689-2901
Monet No. 257	667	Lori A. McDonald, Adm., PO Box 370, Elrose S0L 0Z0 – 306/378-2212, Fax: 306/378-2212
Montmartre No. 126	649	Dale Brenner, Adm., PO Box 120, Montmartre S0G 3M0 – 306/424-2040, Fax: 306/424-2040
Montrose No. 315	714	Raymond N. French, Adm., PO Box 755, Delisle S0L 0P0 – 306/493-2694, Fax: 306/493-2694
Moose Creek No. 33	460	Betty Ann Rattray, Adm., PO Box 10, Alameda S0C 0A0 – 306/489-2044, Fax: 306/489-2112
Moose Jaw No. 161	1,959	James W. Nichols, Adm., 170 Fairford St. West, Moose Jaw S6H 1V3 – 306/692-3446, Fax: 306/691-0015
Moose Mountain No. 63	581	Ron Matsalla, Adm., PO Box 445, Carlyle S0C 0R0 – 306/453-6175, Fax: 306/453-2430
Moose Range No. 486	1,408	Richard C. Colborn, Adm., PO Box 699, Carrot River S0E 0L0 – 306/768-2212, Fax: 306/768-2211
Moosomin No. 121	522	Holly J. McFarlane, Adm., PO Box 1109, Moosomin S0G 3N0 – 306/435-3113, Fax: 306/435-4313
Morris No. 312	494	Rolande Davis, Adm., PO Box 130, Young S0K 4Y0 – 306/259-2211, Fax: 306/259-2225
Morse No. 165	556	Mark Wilson, Adm., PO Box 340, Morse S0H 3C0 – 306/629-3282, Fax: 306/629-3212
Mount Hope No. 279	700	Jim Down, Adm., PO Box 190, Semans S0A 3S0 – 306/524-2055, Fax: 306/524-2055
Mount Pleasant No. 2	486	Brian R. Miller, Adm., PO Box 278, Carnduff S0C 0S0 – 306/482-3313, Fax: 306/482-5278
Mountain View No. 318	413	Glenda Giles, Adm., PO Box 130, Herschel S0L 1L0 – 306/377-2144, Fax: 306/377-2144
Newcombe No. 260	368	Lois L. Haug, Adm., PO Box 40, Glidden S0L 1H0 – 306/463-3338, Fax: 306/463-4748
Nipawin No. 487	1,389	Eunice Rudy, Adm., PO Box 250, Codette S0E 0P0 – 306/862-9551, Fax: 306/862-9551
North Battleford No. 437	1,036	Bruce W. Kosolofski, Adm., 1101 - 101 St., North Battleford S9A 0Z5 – 306/445-3604, Fax: 306/445-3604
North Qu'Appelle No. 187	717	Beverly van der Breggen, Adm., PO Box 99, Fort Qu'Appelle S0G 1S0 – 306/332-5202, Fax: 306/332-6028
Norton No. 69	346	Wayne Lozinsky, Adm., PO Box 189, Pangman S0C 2C0 – 306/442-2131, Fax: 306/442-2131
Oakdale No. 320	388	Gloria Johnson, Adm., PO Box 249, Coleville S0L 0K0 – 306/965-2281, Fax: 306/965-2466
Old Post No. 43	628	Doreen Koester, Adm., PO Box 70, Wood Mountain S0H 4L0 – 306/266-2002, Fax: 306/266-2020
Orkney No. 244	1,899	Grant Doupe, Adm., 26 - 5 Ave. North, Yorkton S3N 0Y8 – 306/782-2333, Fax: 306/782-5177
Paddockwood No. 520	1,053	Carole Moritz, Adm., PO Box 187, Paddockwood S0J 1Z0 – 306/989-2124, Fax: 306/989-2124
Parkdale No. 498	746	Marvin L. Bates, Adm., PO Box 310, Glaslyn S0M 0Y0 – 306/342-2015, Fax: 306/342-2015
Paynton No. 470	354	Gina Bernier, Adm., PO Box 10, Paynton S0M 2J0 – 306/895-2020
Pense No. 160	559	Julia M. Foster, Adm., PO Box 190, Pense S0G 3W0 – 306/345-2303, Fax: 306/345-2583
Perdue No. 346	482	John de Gooijer, Adm., PO Box 208, Perdue S0K 3C0 – 306/237-4202, Fax: 306/237-4202
Piapot No. 110	392	Sidney C. McGillivray, Adm., PO Box 100, Piapot S0N 1Y0 – 306/558-2011, Fax: 306/558-2125
Pinto Creek No. 75	301	Henrietta J. Lott, Adm., PO Box 239, Kincaid S0H 2J0 – 306/264-3277, Fax: 306/264-3277
Pittville No. 169	309	Scott G. Spicer, Adm., PO Box 150, Hazlet S0N 1E0 – 306/678-2131, Fax: 306/678-2131
Pleasant Valley No. 288	462	Jim P. Reiter, Adm., PO Box 2080, Rosetown S0L 2V0 – 306/882-2722, Fax: 306/882-5303
Pleasantdale No. 398	781	Lowell Prefontaine, Adm., PO Box 70, Pleasantdale S0K 3H0 – 306/874-5732, Fax: 306/874-5732
Ponass Lake No. 367	854	Bonnie W. Lengyel, Adm., PO Box 98, Rose Valley S0E 1M0 – 306/322-2162
Poplar Valley No. 12	309	Evan Strelioff, Adm., PO Box 190, Rockglen S0H 3R0 – 306/476-2062, Fax: 306/476-2062
Porcupine No. 395	1,321	Ed F. Poniatowski, Adm., PO Box 190, Porcupine Plain S0E 1H0 – 306/278-2368, Fax: 306/278-2368
Prairie No. 408	578	Raymond W. Toews, Adm., PO Box 159, Battleford S0M 0E0 – 306/937-2321
Prairie Rose No. 309	411	Dennis C. McBurney, Adm., PO Box 89, Jansen S0K 2B0 – 306/364-2013, Fax: 306/364-2088
Prairiedale No. 321	362	Donald M. Fizell, Adm., PO Box 90, Smiley S0L 2Z0 – 306/838-2020, Fax: 306/838-4343
Preeceville No. 334	1,300	Lynn Kardynal, Adm., PO Box 439, Preeceville S0A 3B0 – 306/547-2029, Fax: 306/547-2081
Prince Albert No. 461	3,340	Terry-Lynn Zahara, Adm., 99 River St. East, Prince Albert S6V 0A1 – 306/763-2469, Fax: 306/763-6369
Progress No. 351	423	Donna Gerrard, Adm., PO Box 130, Luseland S0L 2A0 – 306/372-4322, Fax: 306/372-4218
Reciprocity No. 32	497	Lyle McDonald, Adm., PO Box 70, Alida S0C 0B0 – 306/443-2212, Fax: 306/443-2287
Redberry No. 435	584	Alan Tanchak, Adm., PO Box 160, Hafford S0J 1A0 – 306/549-2333, Fax: 306/549-2333
Redburn No. 130	336	Elizabeth Busby, Adm., PO Box 250, Rouleau S0G 4H0 – 306/776-2270, Fax: 306/776-2270
Reford No. 379	417	Helen Dietz, Adm., PO Box 689, Wilkie S0K 4W0 – 306/843-2342, Fax: 306/843-2342
Reno No. 51	574	Grace Potter, Adm., PO Box 90, Consul S0N 0P0 – 306/299-2133, Fax: 306/299-4433
Riverside No. 168	619	Sharlene Higginson, Adm., PO Box 129, Pennant S0N 1X0 – 306/626-3255, Fax: 306/626-3661
Rocanville No. 151	679	G. Dennis Giegle, Adm., PO Box 298, Rocanville S0A 3L0 – 306/645-2055, Fax: 306/645-2697
Rodgers No. 133	226	Linda K. Coates, Adm., PO Box 70, Courval S0H 1A0 – 306/394-4305, Fax: 306/394-4305
Rosedale No. 283	524	Darlene Walker, Adm., PO Box 150, Hanley S0G 2E0 – 306/544-2202, Fax: 306/544-2202
Rosemount No. 378	223	Gary A. Dziadyk, Adm., PO Box 184, Landis S0K 2K0 – 306/658-2034, Fax: 306/658-2034
Rosthern No. 403	1,817	James F. Spriggs, Adm., PO Box 126, Rosthern S0K 3R0 – 306/232-4393, Fax: 306/232-5321
Round Hill No. 467	461	Ian McLennan, Adm., PO Box 9, Rabbit Lake S0M 2L0 – 306/824-2044, Fax: 306/824-2044
Round Valley No. 410	517	Mervin Bosch, Adm., PO Box 538, Unity S0K 4L0 – 306/228-2248, Fax: 306/228-3483
Rudy No. 284	415	Larry W. Hubbard, Adm., PO Box 1010, Outlook S0L 2N0 – 306/867-9349, Fax: 306/867-8038
St. Andrews No. 287	585	Darcy Olson, Adm., PO Box 488, Rosetown S0L 2V0 – 306/882-2314, Fax: 306/882-3287
St. Louis No. 431	1,307	Leo G. Gareau, Adm., PO Box 28, Hoey S0J 1E0 – 306/422-6170, Fax: 306/422-8520
St. Peter No. 369	1,086	Brenda Nagy, Adm., PO Box 70, Annaheim S0K 0G0 – 306/598-2122, Fax: 306/598-4526
St. Philips No. 301	402	Victoria McKohoniuk, Adm., PO Box 220, Pelly S0A 2Z0 – 306/595-2050, Fax: 306/595-2050
Saltcoats No. 213	967	Ronald R.. Risling, Adm., PO Box 150, Saltcoats S0A 3R0 – 306/744-2202, Fax: 306/744-2455
Sarnia No. 221	365	Harvey Hemingway, Adm., PO Box 160, Holdfast S0G 2H0 – 306/488-2033
Saskatchewan Landing No. 167	509	Caroll Wallace, Adm., PO Box 40, Stewart Valley S0N 2P0 – 306/778-2105, Fax: 306/778-2105
Sasman No. 336	1,205	Jim Little, Adm., PO Box 130, Kuroki S0A 1Y0 – 306/338-2263, Fax: 306/338-3328
Scott No. 98	343	Paul P. Thiele, Adm., PO Box 210, Yellow Grass S0G 5J0 – 306/465-2512
Senlac No. 411	360	Janet Leibel, Adm., PO Box 130, Senlac S0L 2Y0 – 306/228-3339, Fax: 306/228-2264
Shamrock No. 134	386	Edwin A. Henry, Adm., PO Box 40, Shamrock S0H 3W0 – 306/648-3594, Fax: 306/648-3687
Shellbrook No. 493	1,834	Kenneth G. Danger, Adm., PO Box 40, Shellbrook S0J 2E0 – 306/747-2177, Fax: 306/747-3111
Sherwood No. 159	1,093	Donna Rollie, Adm., 1840 Cornwall St., Regina S4P 2K2 – 306/525-5237, Fax: 306/352-1760
Silverwood No. 123	639	Eileen Grassl, Adm., PO Box 700, Whitewood S0G 5C0 – 306/735-2500, Fax: 306/735-2524
Sliding Hills No. 273	784	Todd Steele, Adm., PO Box 70, Mikado S0A 2R0 – 306/563-5285, Fax: 306/563-5285
Snipe Lake No. 259	686	Barbara L. Allen, Adm., PO Box 786, Eston S0L 1A0 – 306/962-3214, Fax: 306/962-4330
Souris Valley No. 7	444	Jo Ann Larsen, Adm., PO Box 40, Oungre S0C 1Z0 – 306/456-2676, Fax: 306/456-2480
South Qu'Appelle No. 157	1,128	Sandra Drinnan, Adm., PO Box 66, Qu'Appelle S0G 4A0 – 306/699-2257, Fax: 306/699-2257
Spalding No. 368	768	Robert J. McPherson, Adm., PO Box 10, Spalding S0K 4C0 – 306/872-2166, Fax: 306/872-2166
Spiritwood No. 496	1,694	Gloria Teer, Adm., PO Box 340, Spiritwood S0J 2M0 – 306/883-2034, Fax: 306/883-2034
Spy Hill No. 152	553	Tracy L. Johnson, Adm., PO Box 129, Spy Hill S0A 3W0 – 306/534-2022, Fax: 306/534-2022

4-152 YUKON TERRITORY MUNICIPALITIES

MUNICIPALITY	1991 POP.	CONTACT PERSON WITH ADDRESS & PHONE
Stanley No. 215	782	Marie Steiner, Adm., PO Box 70, Melville S0A 2P0 – 306/728-2818, Fax: 306/728-2818
Star City No. 428	1,081	Ann T. Campbell, Adm., PO Box 370, Star City S0E 1P0 – 306/863-2522, Fax: 306/863-2255
Stonehenge No. 73	659	Mary Jean Allingham, Adm., PO Box 129, Limerick S0H 2P0 – 306/263-2020, Fax: 306/263-2013
Storthoaks No. 31	478	Elaine R. Morgan, Adm., PO Box 40, Storthoaks S0C 2K0 – 306/449-2262, Fax: 306/449-2210
Surprise Valley No. 9	274	Joyce Axten, Adm., PO Box 52, Minton S0C 1T0 – 306/969-2144, Fax: 306/969-2244
Sutton No. 103	384	H. Sam Edgerton, Adm., PO Box 100, Mossbank S0H 3G0 – 306/354-2414, Fax: 306/354-7725
Swift Current No. 137	1,605	Dave Dmytruk, Adm., PO Box 1210, Swift Current S9H 3X4 – 306/773-7314, Fax: 306/773-9538
Tecumseh No. 65	383	Zandra Slater, Adm., PO Box 300, Stoughton S0G 4T0 – 306/457-2277
Terrell No. 101	396	Ernest P. Karlson, Adm., PO Box 60, Spring Valley S0H 3X0 – 306/475-2803, Fax: 306/475-2803
Three Lakes No. 400	736	Tim Schmidt, Adm., PO Box 100, Middle Lake S0K 2X0 – 306/367-2172, Fax: 306/367-2011
Tisdale No. 427	1,163	Terry Hvidston, Adm., PO Box 128, Tisdale S0E 1T0 – 306/873-2334, Fax: 306/873-4442
Torch River No. 488	2,022	Jacques A. Bertrand, Adm., PO Box 40, White Fox S0J 3B0 – 306/276-2066, Fax: 306/276-2099
Touchwood No. 248	482	Marlene I. Benko, Adm., PO Box 160, Punnichy S0A 3C0 – 306/835-2110, Fax: 306/835-2100
Tramping Lake No. 380	390	Karen Wiley, Adm., PO Box 129, Scott S0K 4A0 – 306/247-2033, Fax: 306/247-2055
Tullymet No. 216	378	Darwin Chatterson, Adm., PO Box 190, Balcarres S0G 0C0 – 306/334-2366, Fax: 306/334-2930
Turtle River No. 469	409	Joseph McMurphy, Adm., PO Box 128, Edam S0M 0V0 – 306/397-2311, Fax: 306/397-2311
Usborne No. 310	618	Keith Schulze, Adm., PO Box 310, Lanigan S0K 2M0 – 306/365-2924, Fax: 306/365-2808
Val Marie No. 17	531	Barry W. Dixon, Adm., PO Box 59, Val Marie S0N 2T0 – 306/298-2009, Fax: 306/298-2224
Vanscoy No. 345	2,308	Shawn Antosh, Adm., PO Box 187, Vanscoy S0L 3J0 – 306/668-2060, Fax: 306/668-1338
Victory No. 226	573	Rita Fraser, Adm., PO Box 100, Beechy S0L 0C0 – 306/859-2270, Fax: 306/859-2270
Viscount No. 341	549	Patrick T. Clavelle, Adm., PO Box 100, Viscount S0K 4M0 – 306/944-2044, Fax: 306/944-2044
Wallace No. 243	1,051	Grant Doupe, Adm., 26 - 5 Ave. North, Yorkton S3N 0Y8 – 306/782-2333, Fax: 306/782-5177
Walpole No. 92	527	Rhonda M. Hall, Adm., PO Box 117, Wawota S0G 5A0 – 306/739-2545, Fax: 306/739-2777
Waverley No. 44	416	Ed P. Gasper, Adm., PO Box 70, Glentworth S0H 1V0 – 306/266-4920, Fax: 306/266-2077
Wawken No. 93	737	Jane Laich, Acting Adm., PO Box 90, Wawota S0G 5A0 – 306/739-2332, Fax: 306/739-2222
Webb No. 138	441	Don Haley, Adm., PO Box 100, Webb S0N 2X0 – 306/674-2230, Fax: 306/674-2324
Wellington No. 97	424	Janice E. Mus, Adm., PO Box 1390, Weyburn S4H 3J9 – 306/842-5606
Weyburn No. 67	885	Lloyd E. Muma, Adm., 23 - 6 St. NE, Weyburn S4H 1A7 – 306/842-2314, Fax: 306/842-1002
Wheatlands No. 163	276	Gary Wapple, Adm., PO Box 129, Mortlach S0H 3E0 – 306/355-2233
Whiska Creek No. 106	479	Kathy Countryman, Adm., PO Box 10, Vanguard S0N 2V0 – 306/582-2133, Fax: 306/582-4950
White Valley No. 49	641	Yvonne Wilton, Adm., PO Box 520, Eastend S0N 0T0 – 306/295-3553, Fax: 306/295-3571
Willner No. 253	397	Norman Sagen, Adm., PO Box 250, Davidson S0G 1A0 – 306/567-3103, Fax: 306/567-3266
Willow Bunch No. 42	535	Margaret L. Brown, Adm., PO Box 220, Willow Bunch S0H 4K0 – 306/473-2302, Fax: 306/473-2302
Willow Creek No. 458	1,002	Bert Ross, Adm., PO Box 5, Brooksby S0E 0H0 – 306/863-4143, Fax: 306/863-2366
Willowdale No. 153	499	C. Marlene Tebbutt, Adm., PO Box 58, Whitewood S0G 5C0 – 306/735-2344, Fax: 306/735-4495
Wilton No. 472	1,651	Trent Michelman, Adm., PO Box 40, Marshall S0M 1R0 – 306/387-6244, Fax: 306/387-6598
Winslow No. 319	447	Wendy Davis, Adm., PO Box 310, Dodsland S0L 0V0 – 306/356-2106, Fax: 306/356-2085
Wise Creek No. 77	315	L. Marcel Meloche, Adm., PO Box 400, Shaunavon S0N 2M0 – 306/297-2520
Wolseley No. 155	577	Dale A. Harvey, Adm., PO Box 370, Wolseley S0G 5H0 – 306/698-2522, Fax: 306/698-2664
Wolverine No. 340	641	Coleen Bowman, Adm., PO Box 28, Burr S0K 0T0 – 306/682-3640, Fax: 306/682-3640
Wood Creek No. 281	394	Donn Bergsveinson, Adm., PO Box 10, Simpson S0G 4M0 – 306/836-2020
Wood River No. 74	487	Derek Thiele, Adm., PO Box 250, Lafleche S0H 2K0 – 306/472-5235
Wreford No. 280	269	Lois M. Friend, Adm., PO Box 99, Nokomis S0G 3R0 – 306/528-2202
The Gap No. 39	320	Vaughan B. McClarty, Adm., PO Box 188, Ceylon S0C 0T0 – 306/454-2202, Fax: 306/454-2627

YUKON TERRITORY

LEGISLATION: Municipal Act, Municipal Finance & Community Grants Act, Assessment and Taxation Act.

Requirements for incorporation in the Yukon are based on population: village 300-1,000, town 500-3,000, city over 2,500. Any community may become a hamlet, an advisory body to the minister, as a first step towards becoming a municipality.

Municipal elections are held every three years and polling day is the third Thursday of October in each election year. Mayors and councillors are elected for a three-year period.

Cities in CAPITALS; Towns marked †; Villages marked (V); Hamlets marked (H). An in-depth listing for municipalities marked with * appears in Part 2 (check Index for page numbers).

MUNICIPALITY	1994 POP.	FEDERAL ELECTORAL DISTRICT	TERRITORIAL ELECTORAL DISTRICT	CONTACT PERSON WITH ADDRESS, PHONE & FAX
Beaver Creek (H)	143	Yukon	Kluane	Gary Knickle, President, Community Club, Beaver Creek Y0B 1A0 – 403/862-7211
Burwash Landing (H)	76	Yukon	Kluane	Liz Johnson, Mgr., Kluane First Nation, Mile 1093, General Delivery, Burwash Landing Y1A 3V4 – 403/841-4274, Fax: 403/841-5900
Carcross (H)	421	Yukon	Ross River-Southern Lakes	Rhonda Passmore, President, Community & Curling Club, PO Box 48, Carcross Y0B 1B0 – 403/821-3101
Carmacks (V)	470	Yukon	Mayo-Tatchun	Village of Carmacks Y0B 1C0 – 403/863-6271, Fax: 403/863-6606
Dawson City †	2,019	Yukon	Klondike	Jim Kincaid, CAO, PO Box 308, Dawson City Y0B 1G0 – 403/993-7400, Fax: 403/993-7434
Destruction Bay (H)	45	Yukon	Kluane	Jim Flumerfelt, President, Kluane Lake Athletic Assn., Destruction Bay Y0B 1C0 – 403/841-4211
Faro †	515	Yukon	Faro	Olga Payne, Clerk, PO Box 580, Faro Y0B 1K0 – 403/994-2728, Fax: 403/994-3154
Haines Junction (V)	796	Yukon	Kluane	Sheila O'Hanion, Clerk-Treas., PO Box 53329, Haines Junction Y0B 1L0 – 403/634-2291, Fax: 403/634-2008
Ibex Valley (H)	230	Yukon	Kluane	RR#2, Site 3, Comp 24, Whitehorse Y1A 5W2 – 403/633-6131, Fax: 403/633-5213

Canadian Almanac & Directory 1997

YUKON TERRITORY MUNICIPALITIES 4-153

Cities in CAPITALS; Towns marked †; Villages marked (V); Hamlets marked (H). An in-depth listing for municipalities marked with * appears in Part 2 (check Index for page numbers).

MUNICIPALITY	1994 POP.	FEDERAL ELECTORAL DISTRICT	TERRITORIAL ELECTORAL DISTRICT	CONTACT PERSON WITH ADDRESS, PHONE & FAX
Mayo (V)	472	Yukon	Mayo-Tatchun	Margarit Wozniak, CAO, PO Box 160, Mayo Y0B 1M0 – 403/996-2317, Fax: 403/996-2907
Mount Lorne (H)		Yukon	Mount Lorne	RR#1, Site 20, Comp 9, Whitehorse Y1A 4Z6 – 403/668-6310, Fax: 403/633-5884
Old Crow (H)	263	Yukon	Vuntut Gwichin	Robert Bruce Jr., Chief, Vuntut Gwichin First Nation, Old Crow Y0B 1N0 – 403/966-3261, Fax: 403/966-3800
Pelly Crossing (H)	291	Yukon	Mayo-Tatchun	Pat Van Bibber, Chief, Selkirk First Nation, Pelly Crossing Y0B 1P0 – 403/537-3331, Fax: 403/537-3902
Ross River (H)	392	Yukon	Ross River-Southern Lakes	Pat Moore, Sec., Ross River Community Club, Ross River Y0B 1S0 – 403/969-2536, Fax: 403/969-2903
Stewart Crossing (H)	42	Yukon	Mayo-Tatchun	Dan McDiarmid, President, Stewart Crossing Community Club, Stewart Crossing Y1A 4N1 – 403/996-2514
Tagish (H)	134	Yukon	Ross River-Southern Lakes	Edith Sanders, President, Tagish Community Association, Tagish Y0B 1T0 – 403/399-3407
Teslin (V)	465	Yukon	Ross River-Southern Lakes	Jerry Bruce, CAO, Village of Teslin Y0A 1B0 – 403/390-2530, Fax: 403/390-2104
Upper Liard (H)	162	Yukon	Watson Lake	Fran Byers, Mgr., Liard First Nation, PO Box 328, Watson Lake Y0A 1C0 – 403/536-2131, Fax: 403/536-2332
Watson Lake †	1,749	Yukon	Watson Lake	Andy Nichols, CAO, PO Box 590, Watson Lake Y0A 1C0 – 403/536-2246, Fax: 403/536-2498
*WHITEHORSE	23,474 ('95)	Yukon	Lake Laberge Whitehorse C; McIntyre-Takhini; Porter Creek N; Porter Creek S; Riverdale N; Riverdale S; Riverside; Whitehorse W	Dee Balsam, City Clerk, 2121 - 2 Ave., Whitehorse Y1A 1C2 – 403/667-6401, Fax: 403/668-8384

MAJOR MUNICIPALITIES

Part 2 (Alphabetical list of major cities, including Council & senior administrative officials)

Editor's Note: The population figures given here for (1991) are StatsCan census figures. Any others (with a different year) are estimates provided by the municipality or province.

Each local municipality listing here includes a main address & general phone & fax number. Some listings include email and websites (URLs). Use these addresses & numbers if no other phone or fax follows the name of listed persons.

Election results from autumn 1996 municipal elections held in British Columbia & Québec were not available for these pages at time of going to press; please refer to the Addenda at the back of this book for updates.

City of ABBOTSFORD
32315 South Fraser Way, Abbotsford BC V2T 1W7
604/853-2281, 857-1251, Fax: 604/853-1934
Incorporated: January 1, 1995
Area: 35,851 ha
Population: 110,000 (1996)

COUNCIL
Editor's Note: Results of the November 1996 election were not available at press time; up to date results may appear in the Addenda at the back of this book.
Next Election: November 1999 (3 year terms)

ADMINISTRATION
City Clerk, Toiressa O. Strong
Treasurer, Dan Bottrill, Fax: 604/853-7968
City Manager, Hedda Cochran
Chief Constable, Barry Daniel, 604/859-5225; Fax: 604/859-4812
Director, Development Services, Richard Danziger, Fax: 604/853-4981
Director, Engineering, Ed Regts, P.Eng., Fax: 604/853-2219
Director, Finance, Dan Bottrill, Fax: 604/853-7968
Director, Parks & Recreation, Ken Yates, 604/859-3134; Fax: 604/854-5077
Economic Development Officer, Malcolm Harvey
Fire Chief, Lex Haagen, 604/853-3566; Fax: 604/853-7941

Town of AJAX
65 Harwood Ave. South, Ajax ON L1S 2H9
905/683-4550, Fax: 905/683-1061
Incorporated: 1950
Area: 65.3 sq. km
Population: 59,500 (1996)

COUNCIL
Mayor, Steve Parish
Councillors & Wards: 1) F.T. Schaper; 2) S.A. Crawford; 3) J. Atkinson; 4) P.A. Brown
Regional Councillors & Wards: 1 & 2) Roger Anderson; 3 & 4) J.G. McMaster
Next Election: November 1997 (3 year terms)

ADMINISTRATION
Clerk, Martin J. de Rond
Treasurer, G.D. Kirkbride
Chief Administrative Officer, Barry E. Malmsten, Fax: 905/686-8352
Director, Business Development, G. Whittington, Fax: 905/686-0360
Director, Engineering & Works, F.J. Hull, Fax: 905/686-0360
Director, Human Resources, Richard Parisotto, Fax: 905/686-8352
Director, Parks & Recreation, T.W. Flood, 905/427-8811; Fax: 905/427-3821
Director, Planning, Peter Tollefsen, M.C.I.P., Fax: 905/686-0360
Director, Transit, T. Barnett, 905/427-5710; Fax: 905/427-3473
Fire Chief (Emergency Response), Randall J. Wilson, 905/683-3050

City of BARRIE
70 Collier St., PO Box 400, Barrie ON L4M 4T5
705/726-4242, Fax: 705/739-4243, URL: http://www.city.barrie.on.ca/citymin.htm
Incorporated: 1853
Area: 27 sq. mi (7,265 ha)
Population: 71,413 (1994)

COUNCIL
Mayor, Janice Laking
Aldermen & Wards: 1) Jim Perri; 2) Aileen Carroll; 3) Rob Warman, 4) Al Burns; 5) Dave Morrison; 6) Steve Trotter; 7) Mary Florence Bartley; 8) Don Kirkpatrick; 9) Anne Black; 10) Mike Ramsay
Next Election: November 1997 (3 year terms)

ADMINISTRATION
City Clerk, John E. Craig
Treasurer, Lorne Knowles, Fax: 705/739-4237
City Administrator, Peter Lee, Fax: 705/739-4244
Administrator, Social Services, Gary Calvert, Fax: 705/739-4245
Director, Municipal Works, Kerry Columbus, Fax: 705/739-4247
Director, Parks & Recreation, Sid Armatage, Fax: 705/739-4238
Director, Planning & Development, Jim Taylor, Fax: 705/739-4240
Fire Chief, Jim Lemieux, 705/728-1277; Fax: 705/728-4439
Manager, Public Utilities, Don Dowds, 705/722-6168; Fax: 722-6159
Manager, Traffic, Transit & Parking, George Kaveckas, Fax: 705/726-8503
Police Chief, Jack Delcourt, Fax: 705/728-2971
Purchasing Agent, Noel Banavage, Fax: 705/726-8392
Economic Development Officer, Nancy Tuckett, Fax: 705/726-8433

Ville de BEAUPORT
10, rue de l'Hôtel-de-Ville, CP 5187, Beauport PQ G1E 6P4
418/666-2121, Fax: 418/667-8936

Canadian Almanac & Directory 1997

Incorporée: 1855
Superficie: 90.4 sq. km
Population: 72,259 (1993)

CONSEIL

Editor's Note: Results of the November 1996 election were not available at press time; for up to date results refer to the Addenda at the back of this book.
Prochaine election: novembre 2000 (mandat de 4 ans)

ADMINISTRATION

Greffière, Josette Tessier
Trésorier, Paul Lepage, c.a.
Directeur général, André Letendre
Directeur, Approvisionnements, Pierre Tessier
Directeur, Communications, Yves Marchand
Directeur, Développement économique, Bernard Auger
Directeur, Loisirs et parcs, Paul-André Lavigne
Directeur, Personnel, Louis-Philippe Hébert
Directeur, Police, Normand Bergeron
Directeur, Services Environnementaux, Jean Vézina
Directeur, Services techniques/Génie, Roger Robert, ing.
Asst. Directeur, Incendies, Gaétan Boily
Asst. Directeur, Travaux publics, Clement Villeneuve, ing.
Procureur, Jean-Charles Lord
Urbaniste, Jacques Dompierre

City of BRAMPTON
2 Wellington St. West, Brampton ON L6Y 4R2
905/874-2500, Fax: 905/874-2119
Incorporated: January 1, 1974
Area: 103.5 sq. mi
Population: 236,319 (1994)

COUNCIL

Mayor, Peter Robertson
City Councillors & Wards: 1) Bob Hunter; 2) Linda Jeffrey; 3) Bob Linton; 4) Malcolm Moore; 5) Grant Gibson; 6) John Hutton; 7) Bill Cowie; 8) Peter Richards; 9) Dick Metzak; 10) John Sprovieri; 11) Sandra Hames
Regional Councillors & Wards: 1 & 5) Lorna Bissell; 3 & 4) Susan Fennell; 7 & 11) Gael Miles; 8 & 9) Rhoda Begley; 2, 6 & 10) Paul Palleschi
Next Election: November 1997 (3 year terms)

ADMINISTRATION

City Clerk & Director, Administration, Leonard Mikulich
Treasurer, Paul Caine
City Manager, Al Solski
Commissioner, Community Services, M.J. Neeb
Commissioner, Legal Services, J.G. Metras, Q.C.
Commissioner, Planning & Building, J. Marshall, 905/874-2055
Commissioner, Public Works & Transportation, Larry T. Koehle
Chief Building Official, Building, Percy Hornblow
Chief Economic Development Officer, Dennis Cutjar, 905/874-2662
Director, Human Resources, Mariann Love
Director, Information Technology, J. Wright
Director, Parks Development, K. Walsh
Director, Planning & Development Services, J. Corbett
Director, Recreation Facilities & Programs, H. Newlove
Director, Transit, G. Marshall
Director, Urban Design & Zoning, W. Lee
Fire Chief & EMO, V. Clark
Manager, Supply & Services, Martin Lingard, 905/874-2271

City of BRANDON
410 - 9 St., Brandon MB R7A 6A2
204/729-2186, Fax: 204/729-8244
Incorporated: May 30, 1882
Area: 25.88 sq. miles
Population: 38,573 (1991)

COUNCIL

Mayor, Richard N. Borotsik
Councillors & Wards: 1. Assiniboine) Joe Kay; 2. Rosser) Drew Caldwell; 3. Victoria) Don Kille; 4. University) Rick Chrest; 5. Meadows) Laurie MacKenzie; 6. South Centre) Jim Reid; 7. Linden Lanes) Scott Smith; 8. Richmond) Margo Campbell; 9. Riverview) Ross Martin; 10. Green Acres) Don Jessiman
Next Election: October 1998 (3 year terms)

ADMINISTRATION

Clerk, W. Ian Ford, 204/729-2210
Treasurer, Rod Burkard, 204/729-2209
City Manager, Earl E. Backman, 204/729-2204; Fax: 204/729-0975
City Engineer, Environmental Services, Ted Snure, 204/729-2214
City Solicitor, Robyn Singleton, 204/729-2246
Coordinator, Safety & EMO, Brian Kayes, 204/729-2239
Director, Human Resources, Rick J. Boyd, 204/729-2242; Fax: 204/729-1904
Director, Parks & Recreation, Brian LePoudre, 204/729-2268
Director, Social Services, Edna Thomassen, 204/729-2293
Fire Chief, Garry Winters, 204/729-2401
Manager, Economic Development, Don Allan, 204/728-3287
Manager, Public Works, Glen Newton, 204/729-2277; Fax: 204/726-8546
Manager, Transportation Services, Robert C. MacDonald, 204/729-2195; Fax: 204/726-8546
Officer, Planning & Development, Dave Wallace, 204/729-2295
Police Chief, Richard B. Scott, 204/729-2305; Fax: 204/726-1323
Supervisor, Purchasing, Scotty McIntosh, 204/729-2251; Fax: 204/726-8546

City of BRANTFORD
City Hall, 100 Wellington Sq., Brantford ON N3T 2M3
519/759-4150, Fax: 519/754-0742
Incorporated: May 31, 1877
Area: 17,227.5 acres
Population: 84,500 (1994)

COUNCIL

Mayor, Chris Friel
Councillors & Wards: 1) Jo Brennan, Paul Urbanowicz; 2) Vince Bucci, John Sless; 3) Mike Hancock, Max Sherman; 4) Richard Carpenter, Andy Woodburn; 5) Marguerite Ceschi-Smith, Wally Lucente
Next Election: November 1997 (3 year terms)

ADMINISTRATION

City Clerk, Wilf Coulson, Fax: 519/759-7840
Treasurer, Calvin Hawke
Chief Administrative Officer, Geoff Wilson
Administrator, Parks & Recreation, Hans Loewig
Chief Building Official, D. Ferguson, Fax: 519/752-1874
City Engineer, A. Gretzinger, P.Eng., 519/759-1350
Director, Economic Development, D. Amos, Fax: 519/752-6775
Director, Environmental Services, Terry Spiers, P.Eng., 519/759-1350
Director, Human Resources, David Clarke
Director, Parks & Properties, V. Hergott, 519/756-1500
Director, Planning, P. Atcheson, Fax: 519/752-6977

Director, Recreation, Eric Finkelstein
Director, Tourism & Entertainment, P. Sales, 519/752-9910, 6541
Purchasing Officer, G. Sturgeon
Superintendent, Works, W. Garabedian, 519/752-4832

Ville de BROSSARD
2001, boul Rome, Brossard PQ J4W 3K5
514/923-7000, Fax: 514/923-7016
Incorporée: 14 fevrier, 1958
Superficie: 44.77 sq. km
Population: 68,414 (1993)

CONSEIL

Maire, Paul Leduc
Conseillers et Districts: 1) Nicole Carrier; 2) Claude Moses; 3) Claude Dufresne; 4) Pierre Gauthier; 5) Louis-Philippe Blain; 6) Louis-Carol Duchesne; 7) Breda Nadon; 8) Joseph Vassallo; 9) Yves Lampron; 10) Noë Leclerc
Prochaine election: novembre 1998 (mandat de 4 ans)

ADMINISTRATION

Greffier, Daniel Carrier
Trésorier, André Paquette
Directeur général, Richard Labrecque
Directeur, Incendie, Robert Imbeault
Directeur, Loisirs, André Montpetit
Directeur, Mesures d'urgence, Richard Labrecque
Directeur, Police, Gilles Frigon
Directeur, Travaux publics et génie, Mark-B. Laroche
Directeur, Urbanisme, Michel Boyer

City of BURLINGTON
City Hall, 426 Brant St., PO Box 5013, Burlington ON L7R 3Z6
905/335-7777, Fax: 905/335-7881, cob@worldchat.com, URL: http://worldchat.com/cob
Incorporated: January 1, 1974
Area: 72.65 sq. miles
Population: 128,453 (1994)

COUNCIL

Mayor, Walter Mulkewich
City Councillors & Wards: 1) Leslie Bullock, Robert MacIsaac; 2) Jack Dennison, John Edwards; 3) Mark Carr, Ralph Scholtens; 4) Barry Quinn, John Taylor; 5) Carol D'Amelio, Dennis Lee; 6) Don Carter, Joan Lougheed; 7) Bob Brechin, David Trueman; 8) Mike Wallace, Bob Wood
Regional Councillors & Wards: 1) Robert S. MacIssac; 2) Jack Dennison; 3) Ralph Scholtens; 4) Barry Quinn; 5) Dennis Lee; 6) Don Carter; 7) Bob Brechin; 8) Bob Wood
Next Election: November 1997 (3 year terms)

ADMINISTRATION

City Clerk, Ronald C. Lathan, 905/335-7705
Director, Finance, Robert Carrington, 905/335-7654; Fax: 905/335-7877
City Manager, Tim Dobbie, 905/335-7609
General Manager, Business Affairs, Douglas Brown, 905/335-7614; Fax: 905/335-7842
General Manager, Community Services, Gary Goodman, 905/335-7642; Fax: 905/335-7880
General Manager, Development & Infrastructure, Edward Sajecki, 905/335-7883; Fax: 905/335-7842
Director, Building, Dan Mousseau, 905/335-7731; Fax: 905/335-7876
Director, Engineering, Vacant, 905/335-7687
Director, Environmental & Maintenance Services, Bob Young, 905/335-7873
Director, Management Information Services, Rick Kawai, 905/335-7743
Director, Parks & Recreation, James E. Olmstead, 905/335-7736; Fax: 905/335-7782

Director, Planning, Michael Hall
Director, Transit & Traffic, Vince Mauceri, 905/335-7797; Fax: 905/335-7878
Economic Development Officer, Office of Business Development, Gary Ridgway, 905/335-7712
Fire Chief, Glen Peace, 905/335-1867; Fax: 905/333-1570
Supervisor, Buying, Ken Charles, 905/335-7710

City of BURNABY
4949 Canada Way, Burnaby BC V5G 1M2
604/294-7944, Fax: 604/294-7537
Incorporated: September 22, 1892
Population: 168,000 (1995)

COUNCIL
Editor's Note: Results of the November 1996 election were not available at press time; up to date results may appear in the Addenda at the back of this book.
Next Election: November 1999 (3 year terms)

ADMINISTRATION
City Clerk, Debbie Comis, 604/294-7283; Fax: 604/294-7537
Treasurer, Rick Earle
City Manager, R.H. Moncur, 604/294-7103; Fax: 604/294-7733
Deputy City Manager, Corporate Labour Relations, George Harvie, 604/294-7684; Fax: 604/294-7733
Deputy City Manager, Corporate Services, Chad Turpin, 604/294-7285; Fax: 604/294-7733
Chief Building Inspector, G.R. Humphrey, 604/294-7158; Fax: 604/294-7220
Coordinator, Emergency Program, John Plesha, 604/294-7105; Fax: 604/294-7733
Director, Engineering, W.Craig Sinclair, 604/294-7468; Fax: 604/294-7425
Director, Planning & Building Inspection, D.G. Stenson, 604/294-7413; Fax: 604/294-7220
Director, Recreation & Cultural Services, Dennis Gaunt, 604/294-7102; Fax: 604/294-7710
Fire Chief, W. Brassington, 604/294-7195; Fax: 604/294-0490
Medical Health Officer, Dr. Nadine Loewen, 604/294-7280; Fax: 604/660-7050
Municipal Solicitor, P.W. Flieger, 604/294-7380; Fax: 604/294-7985
Purchasing Agent, John Vissers, 604/294-7377; Fax: 604/294-7529

City of CALGARY
PO Box 2100, Stn M, Calgary AB T2P 2M5
403/268-2111, Fax: 403/268-2633; URL: http// www.gov.calgary.ab.ca/
Incorporated: January 1, 1894
Area: 721.36 sq. km
Population: 767,059 (1996)

COUNCIL
Mayor, Al Duerr, 403/268-5622; Fax: 403/268-8130
Aldermen & Wards: 1) Dale Hodges; 2) Joanne Kerr; 3) John Schmal; 4) Bob Hawkesworth; 5) Ray Jones; 6) David Bronconnier; 7) Bev Longstaff; 8) Jon Lord; 9) Joe Ceci; 10) Ray Clark; 11) Barry Erskine; 12) Sue Higgins; 13) Patti Grier; 14) Linda Fox-Mellway
Next Election: October 1998 (3 year terms)

ADMINISTRATION
Clerk, D. L. Garner, 403/268-5861; Fax: 403/268-2362; EMail: dgarner@gov.calgary.ab.ca
Commissioner, Finance & Administration, A.J. Habstritt, 403/268-5631; Fax: 403/268-1581; EMail: ahabstritt@gov.calgary.ab.ca
Chief Commissioner, Paul Dawson, 403/268-5631; Fax: 403/268-1581; EMail: pdawson@gov.calgary.ab.ca
Commissioner, Operations & Utilities, R.L. Ward, 403/268-5631; Fax: 403/268-1581; EMail: lward@gov.calgary.ab.ca
Commissioner, Planning, Transportation & Community Services, R.J. Holmes, 403/268-5631; Fax: 403/268-1581; EMail: rjholmes@gov.calgary.ab.ca
Chief of Police, C. Silverberg, 403/265-5900; Fax: 403/268-4552; EMail: csilverberg@gov.calgary.ab.ca
City Assessor & Director, Assessment, I.W. McClung, 403/268-4609; Fax: 403/268-8278; EMail: imcclung@gov.calgary.ab.ca
City Solicitor, Law Dept., A. Abougoush, Q.C., 403/268-2441; Fax: 403/268-4634; EMail: aaabougoush@gov.calgary.ab.ca
Acting Director, Data Processing Services, J. Umbach, 403/268-4811; Fax: 403/268-2456; EMail: jumbach@gov.calgary.ab.ca
Director, Emergency Medical Services, S.W. Cartwright, 403/268-2785; Fax: 403/268-4696; EMail: scartwright@gov.calgary.ab.ca
Acting Engineer, Engineering & Environmental Services, G. Lamb, P.Eng., 403/268-5700; Fax: 403/403/268-8291, Email: glamb@gov.calgary.ab.ca
Director, Finance, B. Loach, 403/268-2601; Fax: 403/268-2578; EMail: bloach@gov.calgary.ab.ca
Director, Fleet Services, M. Bamford, 403/268-1122; Fax: 403/266-2496; EMail: mbamford@gov.calgary.ab.ca
Director, Human Resources, S. Mallon, 403/268-8110; Fax: 403/268-4680; EMail: smallon@gov.calgary.ab.ca
Director, Management Audit, R.D. MacLean, 403/268-5670; Fax: 403/268-5411; EMail: rmaclean@gov.calgary.ab.ca
Acting Director, Parks & Recreation, K. Knights, 403/268-5200; Fax: 403/268-5265; EMail: kknights@gov.calgary.ab.ca
Director, Planning & Building, R. Parker, 403/268-5311; Fax: 403/268-1528; EMail: rparker@gov.calgary.ab.ca
Director, Public Information, M. Kaiser, 403/268-8844; Fax: 403/268-8105; EMail: mkaiser@gov.calgary.ab.ca
Director, Social Services, J. Bader, 403/268-5111; Fax: 403/268-8275; EMail: jbader@gov.calgary.ab.ca
Director, Supply Management Services, J.B. Trahan, 403/268-5540; Fax: 403/268-5523; EMail: btrahan@gov.calgary.ab.ca
Director, Transportation, Oliver Bowen, 403/268-1574; Fax: 403/268-1633; EMail: obowen@gov.calgary.ab.ca
Fire Chief, J.C. Ross, 403/287-4299; Fax: 403/243-9947; EMail: jross@gov.calgary.ab.ca
Acting General Manager, Electric System, K. Bosma, 403/268-2820; Fax: 403/265-8419; EMail: kbosma@gov.calgary.ab.ca
Leader, Corporate Properties Group, R.J. Shaw, 403/268-2700; Fax: 403/268-1948; EMail: bshaw@gov.calgary.ab.ca
President, Calgary Economic Development Authority, J. Jong, 403/221-7831; Fax: 403/221-7837

City of CAMBRIDGE
73 Water St. North, PO Box 669, Cambridge ON N1R 5W8
519/623-1340, Fax: 519/740-3011
Incorporated: January, 1973
Area: 44.5 sq. mi
Population: 100,000 (1996)

COUNCIL
Mayor, Jane Brewer
Councillors & Wards: 1) Bill Brown; 2) Greg Durocher; 3) Karl Kiefer; 4) Robert Adshade; 5) Victoria Clark; 6) Gary Price
Regional Councillors: Doug Craig; Ted Fairless; Fred Kent; Bill Struck

Next Election: November 1997 (3 year terms)

ADMINISTRATION
City Clerk, James Anderson, 519/740-4584
Treasurer, John McIntyre, 519/740-4500
Chief Administrative Officer, Don Smith, 519/740-4518
Commissioner, Community Services, Wayne Taylor, 519/740-4596
Commissioner, Engineering & Public Works, Garth James, 519/740-4546; Fax: 519/622-6184
Commissioner, Planning, Wendy Wright, 519/740-4576; Fax: 519/622-6184
Director, Public Works, Brian Jones, 519/740-4547; Fax: 519/622-8032
Director, Purchasing & Inventory, David Farrar, 519/740-4293; Fax: 519/740-0834
Fire Chief, Emergency Response, Terry Allen, 519/621-6001; Fax: 519/621-4521
General Manager, Business Development, Don Eastwood, 519/740-4535; Fax: 519/740-4512

Regional Municipality of CAPE BRETON
320 Esplanade, Sydney NS B1P 1A7
902/564-6302, 6306, Fax: 902/567-6839
Incorporated: August 1, 1995

COUNCIL
Mayor, John Coady
Councillors & Districts: 1) Dannie Hansen; 2) Kevin Saccary; 3) Gerard Burke; 4) Ron Burrows; 5) Art MacDonald; 6) Ray Kavanaugh; 7) Frankie Morrison; 8) Bill Kyte; 9) Jim MacLeod; 10) Douglas MacDonald; 11) Ray Paruch; 12) Jim MacEachern; 13) Arnie Mombourquette; 14) Ivan Doncaster; 15) Claire Dethridge; 16) Rod MacArthur; 17) Mike White; 18) Murray Johnston; 19) Clarence Prince; 20) J. Wesley Stubbert; 21) Doug Young

ADMINISTRATION
Clerk, Bernie White
Director, Finances, Rick Farmer
Chief Administrative Officer, Jerry Ryan, 902/563-5006
Internal Audit, Bob MacNeil
Administrator, Corporate Services, Jim MacCormack
Administrator, Public Services, Gordon MacInnis
Chief of Police, Edgar MacLeod
Director, Engineering, Frank Potter
Director, Fire, Rescue & Building Services, Bernie MacKinnon
Director, Human Resources, Rhona Green
Director, Planning, Doug Foster
Director, Public Works, Kevin MacDonald
Director, Recreation, Culture & Facilities, John Fraser
Director, Technology & Communications, Debbie Rudderham

Ville de CHARLESBOURG
160, 76e rue est, Charlesbourg PQ G1H 7H5
418/624-7500, Fax: 418/624-7525
Incorporée: 1 janvier, 1855
Superficie: 67.31 sq. km
Population: 73,962 (1993)

CONSEIL
Editor's Note: Results of the November 1996 election were not available at press time; for up to date results refer to the Addenda at the back of this book.
Prochaine election: novembre 2000 (mandat de 4 ans)

ADMINISTRATION
Greffier, Jacques Dorais
Directeur, Finances, Clément Guay, 418/624-7550; Fax: 418/624-7655
Directeur général, Michel Lavoie, 418/624-7804
Directeur, Communications, Richard Sévigny, 418/624-7520

Directeur, Loisirs, Serge Paquin, 418/624-7760
Directeur, Travaux publics, Serge Côté, 418/624-7700; Fax: 418/624-7707
Directeur, Urbanisme, Jean-Laval Gagné, 418/624-7512

City of CHARLOTTETOWN
PO Box 98, Charlottetown PE C1A 7K2
902/566-5548, Fax: 902/566-4701
Incorporated: 1855
Area: 42.18 sq. km
Population: 32,400 (1995)

COUNCIL
Mayor, Ian MacDonald
Councillors: Roger Birt; Richard Brown; Mike Duffy; Regis Duffy; Clifford Lee; George MacDonald; Brendon McCloskey; Jim McQuaid; Allan Poulton; Mitchell Tweel
Next Election: November 1997 (3 year terms)

ADMINISTRATION
Chief Administrative Officer, Harry Gaudet
Treasurer, Doug Morton
Chief of Police, Paul Smith
Director, Corporate Services, Donna Waddell
Director, Public Services, Joe Coady
Manager, Fire Services, Bill Hogan
Manager, Human Resources, Phil Handrahan
Manager, Parks & Recreation, Sue Hendricken
Manager, Public Works, Paul Johnston
Utility Manager, Reagh Clark

Ville de CHICOUTIMI
201, rue Racine est, CP 129, Chicoutimi PQ G7H 5B8
418/698-3000, Fax: 418/698-3129
Incorporée: 1 janvier, 1976
Population: 64,616 (1995)

CONSEIL
Maire, Ulric Blackburn
Conseillers et Districts: 1) Jean-Guy Villeneuve; 2) Carl Savard; 3) Marina Larouche; 4) Florian Pilote; 5) Jean-Guy Girard; 6) Jacques Fortin; 7) André Belley; 8) Jacques Bouchard; 9) René Girard; 10) Jacques Cleary; 11) Marcel Jean
Prochaine election: novembre 1997 (mandat de 4 ans)

ADMINISTRATION
Greffière, Services juridiques, Hélène Savard
Trésorière et Directrice, Services financiers, Rina Zampieri
Directeur général, Coordonnateur Mesures d'urgence, Marcel Demers, Fax: 418/698-3019
Directeur général adjoint, Robert Bouchard
Directeur général adjoint, Louison Lepage
Directeur, Ressources humaines, Roger Gonthier
Directeur, Sûreté municipale, Christian Harvey
Directeur, Service technique, Daniel Richard, 150, boul du Saguenay Est, CP 129, Chicoutimi PQ G7H 5B8, 418/698-3131
Directeur, Service des incendies, Denis Simard, 2587, rue Roussel, CP 129, Chicoutimi PQ G7H 5B8, 418/698-3382; Fax: 418/698-3389
Directeur, Service d'urbanisme, François Hains, 150, boul du Saguenay est, CP 129, Chicoutimi PQ G7H 5B8, 418/698-3116
Directeur, Service des travaux publics, Guy St-Gelais, 504, boul Saguenay ouest, CP 129, Chicoutimi PQ G7H 5B8, 418/698-3183; Fax: 418/698-3189

Municipality of CLARINGTON
40 Temperance St., Bowmanville ON L1C 3A6
905/623-3379, Fax: 905/623-4169
Population: 57,000 (1996)

COUNCIL
Mayor, Diane Hamre
Local & Regional Councillors: 1) Larry Hannah, Mary Novak; 2) Carson Elliott, Pat Pingle; 3) Ann Dreslinski, David Scott
Next Election: November 1997 (3 year terms)

ADMINISTRATION
Clerk, Patti Barrie
Treasurer, Marie Marano
Chief Administrative Officer, W. H. (Bill) Stockwell
Chief Building Officer, Howard Wight, Fax: 905/623-0830
Director, Community Services, Joe Caruana
Director, Planning & Development, Frank Wu
Director, Public Works, Stephen Vokes
Fire Chief, Mike Creighton
Officer, Tourism & Marketing, Jennifer Cooke
Purchasing Agent, Lou-Ann Birkett
Senior Planner, Community Planning Branch, Janice Auger Szwarz, ext.319; Fax: 905/623-0830

City of COQUITLAM
1111 Brunette Ave., Coquitlam BC V3K 1E9
604/664-1400, Fax: 604/664-1650, URL: http://www.gov.coquitlam.bc.ca/
Incorporated: December 1, 1992
Area: 69 sq. mi
Population: 100,946 (1996)

COUNCIL
Editor's Note: Results of the November 1996 election were not available at press time; up to date results may appear in the Addenda at the back of this book.
Next Election: November 1999 (3 year terms)

ADMINISTRATION
Clerk, Warren Jones
Treasurer, Robin D. Hicks
City Manager, Dr. N. Cook
City Engineer, Neil Nyberg, 604/664-1531; Fax: 604/664-1654
City Planner, Deb Day, 604/664-1481; Fax: 604/664-1652
City Solicitor, Deborah Brown
Director, Corporate Services, Don Buchanan
Director, Leisure & Parks Services, Barry Elliott, 604/937-6014; Fax: 604/936-3975
Director, Permits & Licences, K. Wright
Director, Personnel, S. Haines
Fire Chief, K.D. Johnson
Purchasing Agent, Richard Baller

Corporation of DELTA
4500 Clarence Taylor Cres., Delta BC V4K 3E2
604/946-4141, Fax: 604/946-3390
Incorporated: November 10, 1879
Population: 90,000 (1993)

COUNCIL
Mayor, Beth Johnson
Editor's Note: Results of the November 1996 election were not available at press time; up to date results may appear in the Addenda at the back of this book.
Next Election: November 1999 (3 year terms)

ADMINISTRATION
Acting Clerk, J.C. Lambie
Chief Administrative Officer, Tom Fletcher
Director, Corporate Services, Rick Elligott
Director, Engineering, Peter Steblin
Director, Human Resources, J.C. Lambie
Director, Parks & Recreation, David Kalinovich
Acting Director, Permits & Licences, Ron Everett
Director, Planning, Wayne Dickinson
Fire Chief, Randy Wolsey
Police Chief, Jim Cessford

Borough of EAST YORK
850 Coxwell Ave., East York ON M4C 5R1
416/778-2000, Fax: 416/778-9134
Incorporated: January 1, 1967
Area: 8.3 sq. miles
Population: 98,594 (1994)

COUNCIL
Mayor, Michael D. Prue, 416/778-2022
Councillors & Wards: 1) Norm Crone, Michael Tziretas; 2) Paul Robinson, George Vasilopoulos; 3) John Antonopoulos, Bob Dale; 4) Tim Cholvat, Lorna Krawchuk
Metro Councillor: Case Ootes
Next Election: November 1997 (3 year terms)

ADMINISTRATION
Borough Clerk, William Alexander, Jr., 416/778-2001
Treasurer & Director, Finance, Glenn Kippen, 416/778-2063
Chief Administrative Officer, Virginia West, 416/778-2160
Commissioner, Development Services, Richard Tomaszewicz, 416/778-2041
Commissioner, Parks, Recreation & Operations, Clair Tucker-Reid, 416/778-2180
Director, Human Resources, Earl Hough
Director, Parks & Operations, Don Boyle
Director, Transportation & Engineering Services, John W. Thomas
Environmental Engineer, Victor A. Chao-Ying, 416/778-2218; Fax: 416/466-9877
Fire Chief, John Miller, 416/396-3750
Manager, Planning, David Oikawa
Solicitor, Charles Loopstra, 416/778-2065

City of EDMONTON
City Hall, 1 Sir Winston Churchill Sq., Edmonton AB T5J 2R7
403/496-8222, Fax: 403/496-8220, URL: http://www.gov.edmonton.ab.ca/city/
Incorporated: 1904
Area: 700.64 sq. km
Population: 637,442 (1995)

COUNCIL
Mayor, Bill Smith
Aldermen & Wards: 1) Leroy Chahley, Wendy Kinsella; 2) Allan Bolstad, Rose Rosenberger; 3) Brian Mason, Robert Noce; 4) Michael Phair, Jim Taylor; 5) Larry Langley, Brent Maitson; 6) Terry Cavanagh, Dick Mather
Next Election: October 1998 (3 year terms)

ADMINISTRATION
Clerk, Ulli S. Watkiss, 403/496-8151
Chief Financial Officer, Finance, Bob Ardiel, 403/496-5353; Fax: 403/496-5109
City Manager, Richard Picherack, 403/496-8222
General Manager, Community & Family Services, Joyce Tustian, Centennial Library, 7 Sir Winston Churchill Sq., 5th Fl., Edmonton AB T5J 2V4, 403/496-5804; Fax: 403/496-5996
General Manager, Computing Resources, J. Mills, Century Place, 9803 - 102A Ave., 18th Fl., Edmonton AB T5J 3A3, 403/496-4200; Fax: 403/496-4014
Acting General Manager, Parks & Recreation Dept., Maria David-Evans, Revillon Bldg., 5th Fl., PO Box 2359, Edmonton AB T5J 2R7, 403/496-4858; Fax: 403/496-4944
General Manager, Personnel, W. Wetterberg, Centennial Bldg., 10015 - 103 Ave., 17th Fl., Edmonton AB T5J 0H1, 403/496-7800; Fax: 403/496-8063
General Manager, Planning Dept., B. Duncan, Exchange Building, 10250 - 101 St., 2nd Fl., Edmonton AB T5J 3P4, 403/496-6050; Fax: 403/496-6104

General Manager & City Engineer, Public Works Dept., A.B. Maurer, Century Place, 9803 - 102A Ave., 3rd Fl., Edmonton AB T5J 3A3, 403/496-5656; Fax: 403/496-5636
General Manager, Transportation Dept., R. Millican, Century Place, 9803 - 102A Ave., 15th Fl., Edmonton AB T5J 3A3, 403/496-2808; Fax: 403/496-2803
Auditor General, Office of the Auditor General, A. Bolduc, Centennial Bldg., 10015 - 103 Ave., 6th Fl., Edmonton AB T5J 0H1, 403/496-8303; Fax: 403/496-8062
City Solicitor, Law Dept., Ron Liteplo, Chancery Hall, 3 Sir Winston Churchill Sq., 9th Fl., Edmonton AB T5J 2C3, 403/496-7201; Fax: 403/496-7267
Chief of Police, Police Services, John Lindsay, 9620 - 103A Ave., Edmonton AB T5H 0H7, 403/421-3460; Fax: 403/425-9963
Fire Chief, Emergency Response, F. Sherburne, 10351 - 96 St., Edmonton AB T5H 2H5, 403/496-3801; Fax: 403/496-1518

City of ETOBICOKE
City Hall, 399 The West Mall, Etobicoke ON M9C 2Y2
416/394-8000, Fax: 416/394-8895
Incorporated: June 29, 1983
Area: 48.3 sq. miles (125 sq. km)
Population: 316,800 (1994)

COUNCIL
Mayor, Douglas C. Holyday
Councillors & Wards: 1) Irene Jones; 2) Peter Milczyn; 3) Connie Micallef; 4) Michael O'Rourke; 5) Brian Flynn; 6) Agnes Potts; 7) Gloria Luby; 8) Mario Giansante; 9) Alex Marchetti; 10) Brian Ineson; 11) Elizabeth Brown; 12) Vincent Crisanti
Metro Councillors: Dennis Flynn; Lois Griffin; Blake Kinahan; Dick O'Brien
Next Election: November 1997 (3 year terms)

ADMINISTRATION
Clerk-Treas. & Commissioner, Administrative Services, Brenda Glover, 416/394-8070
City Manager, David G. Deaves, 416/394-8921; Fax: 416/394-6067
Commissioner, Parks & Recreation Services, J.T. Riley, 416/394-8501
Commissioner, Planning, Karen Bricker, 416/394-8213; Fax: 416/394-6063
Commissioner, Works, Tom G. Denes, 416/394-8341; Fax: 416/394-8942
Director, Business Development & Corporate Affairs, Rick A. Field, 416/394-8949
Director, Purchasing Services, Tim Collet, 416/394-8155; Fax: 416/394-6065
Medical Officer of Health, A. Egbert, 416/394-8263; Fax: 416/394-8893
Sec.-Treas., Committee of Adjustment, D. Mungovan, 416/394-8063; Fax: 416/394-6042

City of FREDERICTON
PO Box 130, Fredericton NB E3B 4Y7
506/452-9500, Fax: 506/452-9509
Incorporated: 1848
Area: 53 sq. miles
Population: 47,016 (1991)

COUNCIL
Mayor, Brad Woodside
Councillors & Wards: 1) G. Skead; 2) R.W. Turnbull; 3) M.J. Smith; 4) P.R. Bird; 5) W. Brown; 6) T. Cameron; 7) D.I. Bentley; 8) R.W. Jackson; 9) T.J. Jellinek; 10) B. Sansom; 11) J. Burns; 12) D.E. Kelly
Next Election: May 1998 (3 year terms)

ADMINISTRATION
City Clerk, Donna Lavigne

City Treasurer, M. Marven Grant
City Administrator, Paul R. Stapleton
Chief Building Inspector, M.A. Rickard
City Engineer, E. John Bliss
City Solicitor, Bruce A. Noble
Director, Economic Development, Jacques Dubé
Director, Human Resources, J. David King
Director, Planning & Development, Jake Rudolph
Director, Recreation, Robert A. Mabie, 506/458-8530
Director, Transit & Parking, Ronald Steeves
Fire Chief, Bert Fusk, 506/450-7210
Manager, Purchasing, Bob Cormier
Manager, Tourism, Nancy Lockerbie
Police Chief, Gordon M. Carlisle, 905/452-9701

Ville de GATINEAU
144, boul. de l'Hôpital, Gatineau PQ J8T 7S7
819/243-2345, Fax: 819/243-2338, URL: http://gamma.omnimage.ca/clients/gatineau/
Incorporée: 1975
Superficie: 141 sq. km (54.4 sq. miles)
Population: 105,000 (1995)

CONSEIL
Maire, Guy Lacroix
Conseillers et Districts: 5) Jean Deschênes; 6) Jacques Forget; 8) Richard Migneault; 9) Jean René Mouette; 12) Yvon Boucher; Bellevue) Richard Côté; De Touraine) Thérèse Cyr; Des Belles-Rives) Jean-Pierre Charette; Du Ruisseau) Marcel Schryer; La Baie) Berthe Miron; Le Baron) Richard Canuel; Limbour) Simon Racine
Prochaine election: novembre 1999 (mandat de 4 ans)

ADMINISTRATION
Greffier, J.C. Laurin, 819/243-2350
Directeur, Services financiers et DGA, Robert Bélair, 819/243-2313
Directeur général, Claude Doucet, 819/243-2310
Directrice, Approvisionnements, Lynda Gariépy, 819/243-2380
Directeur, Communications, Jean Boileau, 819/243-2330
Directeur, Cour municipale, Jacques Dionne, 819/669-2541
Directeur, Incendies, Pierre Bertrand, 819/246-6065
Directrice, Loisirs et Culture, Hélène Grand'Maître, 819/243-4343
Directeur, Ressources humaines, Jean Gervais, 819/243-2490
Directeur, Sécurité publique et mesures d'urgence, Joël Chéruet, 819/568-5550; Fax: 819/568-9561
Directeur, Services techniques, Georges Raymond, 819/669-2500; Fax: 819/669-2399
Directeur, Urbanisme, Jacques Perrier, 819/243-2450

City of GLOUCESTER
1400 Blair Pl., PO Box 8333, Gloucester ON K1G 3V5
613/748-4100, Fax: 613/748-0235, URL: http://www.city.gloucester.on.ca/
Incorporated: January 1, 1981
Area: 29,526 ha
Population: 110,000 (1995)

COUNCIL
Mayor, Claudette Cain
Councillors in Wards: 1) Michael Denny; 2) Patricia Clark; 3) Rainer Bloess; 4) René Danis; 5) Frank J. Cauley; 6) George Barrett
Next Election: November 1997 (3 year terms)

ADMINISTRATION
Clerk, Michèle Giroux, 613/748-4104
Treasurer, Karen Tippett, 613/748-4158
City Manager, Pierre Tessier, 613/748-4125

Deputy City Manager, Community Development, D.J. Darch, P.Eng., 613/748-4191
Deputy City Manager, Corporate Services, Jo-Anne Poirier, 613/748-4293
Deputy City Manager, Operations & Fire, Brian Futterer, 613/748-4235
Director, Economic Development, Len Romanica, 613/748-4194
Director, Information Systems, Brenda Esson, 613/748-4196
Director, Recreation & Culture, Clem Pelot, 613/748-4138
Director, Human Resources, Gail Horsman, 613/748-4108
Fire Chief, Hubert Labelle, 613/748-4204
General Manager, Economic Adjustment, Don Loguisto, 613/748-4300
Manager, Corporate Communications, Liz Fauteux, 613/748-4259
Manager, Purchasing & Risk, Ted Allan, 613/748-4201

City of GUELPH
59 Carden St., Guelph ON N1H 3A1
519/822-1260, Fax: 519/763-1269
Incorporated: 1879
Area: 26.53 sq. miles
Population: 93,000 (1994)

COUNCIL
Mayor, Joe Young
Councillors & Wards: 1) John Carere, Karen Farbridge; 2) Sean Farrelly, Gary Walton; 3) Norm Jary, Dan Schnurr; 4 & 5) Cathy Downer, Bill McAdams; 6) Walter Bilanski, John Pate
Next Election: November 1997 (3 year terms)

ADMINISTRATION
Clerk & Director, Information Services, Lois A. Giles, 519/837-5603
Director, Finance, David Kennedy, 519/837-5610; Fax: 519/837-5631
City Administrator, D.R. Creech, 519/837-5602; Fax: 519/822-8277
City Solicitor, Lois Payne, 519/837-5637; Fax: 519/822-8217
Director, Business Development, Vacant, 519/837-5600; Fax: 519/837-5636
Director, Community Services, Gus Stahlmann, 519/837-5618; Fax: 519/763-9240
Director, Electric-Guelph Hydro, J.A. MacKenzie, 519/822-3017
Director, Personnel, J.D. Kentner, 519/837-5601; Fax: 519/763-2685
Director, Planning & Development, Vacant, 519/837-5616; Fax: 519/837-5640
Director, Works, R.D. Funnell, P.Eng., 519/837-5604; Fax: 519/837-5635
Fire Chief, Art Cutten
Medical Officer of Health, Dr. D. Kittle, 519/837-5611
Police Chief, Lenna Bradburn
Purchasing Agent, Mark Bolzon, 519/837-5611; Fax: 519/837-5631
Transportation, Robert Coghill, 50 Municipal St., Guelph ON N1G 1G9

Regional Municipality of HALIFAX
1841 Argyle St., PO Box 1749, Halifax NS B3J 3A5
902/496-2000, Fax: 902/425-1466, URL: http://www.ccn.cs.dal.ca/Government/HRM/HRM-Home.html/
Population: 330,000

COUNCIL
Mayor, Walter R. Fitzgerald, 902/490-4010; Fax: 902/490-4012

Councillors: Stephen Adams; Barry Barnet; Jerry Blumenthal; Ron Cooper; John Cunningham; Bill Dooks; Graham L. Downey; Howard Epstein; Jack Greenough; Ron Hanson; Bob Harvey; David Hendsbee; Bruce Hetherington; Peter J. Kelly; Harry McInroy; Jack Mitchell; Reg Rankin; Condo Sarto; Clint Schofield; Gordon Snow; Bill Stone; Larry Uteck; Russell Walker
Editor's Note: Effective April 1, 1996, Halifax Regional Municipality was created through the amalgamation of the cities of Halifax & Dartmouth, the town of Bedford, & Halifax County municipality.

ADMINISTRATION
City Manager, Barry Coopersmith, 902/421-6500
Chief, Police, Vincent J. MacDonald
Chief Administrative Officer, Kenneth R. Meech, 902/490-4026; Fax: 902/490-4044
Commissioner, Community Services, Dan English
Commissioner, Corporate Services, Lawrence Corrigan
Commissioner, Fire Services, Garry Greene
Commissioner, Policy & Planning, Valerie Spencer
Commissioner, Regional Operations, George McLellan
Director, Administrative & Legal Services, Wayne Anstey
Director, Engineering Services, Kulvinder Dhillon, P.Eng.
Director, Finance, Ron Singer
Director, Human Resources, Christine Birchall
Director, Information Services, Chuck Keith
Director, Operations, Doug Quinn
Director, Transportation, Brian Smith
General Manager, Business Parks, Tom Rath
Manager, Tourism, Lewis M. Rogers

City of HAMILTON
City Hall, 71 Main St. West, Hamilton ON L8N 3T4
905/546-2700, Fax: 905/546-2095
Incorporated: 1846
Area: 54.38 sq. miles
Population: 318,947 (1994)

COUNCIL
Mayor, Bob Morrow, 905/546-2095
Aldermen & Wards: 1) Marvin Caplan, Mary Kiss; 2) V.J. Agiro, W.M. McCulloch; 3) Don Drury, Bernie Morelli; 4) Geraldine Copps, Dave Wilson; 5) Fred Eisenberger; 6) Bob Charters, Tom Jackson; 7) Terry Anderson, Henry Merling; 8) Frank D'Amico, Don Ross
Next Election: November 1997 (3 year terms)

ADMINISTRATION
City Clerk, Joseph J. Schatz, 905/546-4605
Treasurer, Allan Ross, 905/546-4524
Chief Administrative Officer, Joseph Pavelka, 905/546-4535
Commissioner, Building, Len King, 905/546-2775
Commissioner, Human Resources, John Johnston, 905/546-4462
City Solicitor, P. Noë-Johnson, 905/546-4635
Commissioner, Public Works & Traffic, Doug Lobo, 905/546-4623; Fax: 905/546-3972
Director, Culture & Recreation, Ross Fair, 905/546-4616
Director, Information Systems, Jim Hindson, 905/546-4563
Director, Planning, Victor Abraham, 905/546-4134
Director, Property, D. Vyce, 905/546-4501
Fire Chief, Gary Smith, 905/546-3346

Ville de HULL
25, rue Laurier, CP 1970, Succ B, Hull PQ J8X 3Y9
819/595-7180, Fax: 819/595-7192

Incorporée: 1875
Superficie: 37.32 sq. km
Population: 65,764 (1995)

CONSEIL
Maire, Yves Ducharme
Conseillers et Districts: Georges-Vanier) Denise Gagné; Hautes-Plaines) Roch Cholette; Lafontaine) Pierre Chénier; Laurier) Pierre Leduc; Montcalm) Roland Michaud; Parc-de-la-Montagne) Lynus Godin; Saint-Raymond) Pierre Philion; Verchères) Claude Bonhomme; Wright) Ghislaine Boucher; de l'Université) Claude Millette
Prochaine election: novembre 1999 (mandat de 4 ans)

ADMINISTRATION
Directeur, Finances, Michel Tremblay, 819/595-7210; Fax: 819/595-7215
Directeur général, Paul Préseault, o.m.a, 819/595-7131; Fax: 819/595-7138
Directeur général adjoint, Jean-Pierre Chabot, 819/595-7147; Fax: 819/595-7138
Directeur général adjoint, François Trottier, 819/595-7145; Fax: 819/595-7138
Directeur, Approvisionnements, François Bellemare, 819/595-7501; Fax: 819/595-7519
Directrice, Arts et culture, Jacqueline Tardif, 819/595-7429; Fax: 819/595-7425
Directeur, Bibliothèque, Denis Boyer, 819/595-7461; Fax: 819/595-7487
Directeur, Communications, Louis-Paul Guindon, 819/595-7172; Fax: 819/595-7178
Directeur, Développement économique et touristique, Rock Lapointe, 819/595-8001; Fax: 819/595-7784
Directeur, Développement immobilier, André Croteau, 819/595-7291; Fax: 819/595-7888
Directeur, Développement organisationnel, Serge Brousseau, 819/595-7151; Fax: 819/595-7849
Directeur, Incendie, Jean-Maurice Roy, 819/595-7521; Fax: 819/595-7546
Directeur, Loisirs, Gilbert Séguin, 819/595-7401; Fax: 819/595-7425
Directeur, Police, Claude Papineau, 819/595-7601; Fax: 819/595-7824
Directeur, Travaux publics et Ingénierie, Yves Patry, 819/595-7321; Fax: 819/595-7321
Directeur, Urbanisme, Pierre Tanguay, 819/595-7331; Fax: 819/595-7326
Greffière, Cour municipale, Lucie Poulin, 819/595-7270; Fax: 819/595-7280
Responsable, Services congrès & tourisme, Pierre Normandin, 819/595-8013; Fax: 819/595-9755

Ville de JONQUIÈRE
Hôtel de Ville, 2890, Place Davis, CP 2000, Jonquière PQ G7X 7W7
418/546-2222, Fax: 418/699-6018
Incorporée: January 1, 1975
Superficie: 208.28 sq. km
Population: 59,734 (1995)

CONSEIL
Maire, Marcel Martel
Conseillers et districts: Lucie Gagnon; Sylvie Gaudreault; Réginald Gervais; Daniel Giguère; Jean-Eudes Girard; Gaston Laforest; Réjean Laforest; Robert Lavoie; Huguette Poirier; Claude Tremblay
Prochaine election: novembre 1999 (mandat de 4 ans)

ADMINISTRATION
Greffier, Pierre Brassard, 418/699-6005; Fax: 418/699-6119
Trésorier, Serges Chamberland, 418/546-2040; Fax: 418/546-2043
Chef du cabinet du Maire, Marcel Fortin, 418/699-6053; Fax: 418/699-6057
Directeur général, Jean-Marc Gagnon, 418/699-6012

Directeur général adjoint, Gérard Leroux, 418/699-6013
Commissaire Industriel, Developpement économique, Daniel Larouche
Directrice du Contentieux, Jocelyne Trépanier, 418/699-6052; Fax: 418/699-6057
Directeur, Personnel, Benoît Boulianne, 418/699-6016
Directeur, Service des incendies, Normand Laplante, 418/546-2102; Fax: 418/546-2043
Directeur, Services des loisirs, Laval Boucher, 418/699-6078; Fax: 418/699-6095
Directeur, Service de la protection publique, Gaston Tardif, 418/546-2007; Fax: 418/546-2038
Directeur, Services techniques, Daniel Gaudreault, 418/699-6033; Fax: 418/699-6097
Directeur, Travaux publics, Roger Lavoie, 418/546-2122; Fax: 418/546-2118
Chef de division, Approvisionnements, Gaytan Charest, 418/546-2110; Fax: 418/546-2114
Chef de division, Atelier mécanique, Lionel Débigaré, 418/546-2230; Fax: 418/546-2229
Chef de division, Budget et rémunération, Gaytan Charest, 418/546-2062; Fax: 418/546-2043
Chef de division, Comptabilité, Trésorerie, André Cyr, 418/546-2044; Fax: 418/546-2043
Chef de division, Inspection et permis, Alain Jean, 418/546-2149; Fax: 418/546-2161
Coordonnateur, Communications, Jeannot Allard, 418/699-6017; Fax: 418/699-6018

City of KAMLOOPS
7 Victoria St. West, Kamloops BC V2C 1A2
250/828-3311, Fax: 250/828-3578
Incorporated: 1893
Area: 31,142.2 ha
Population: 79,000 (1996)

COUNCIL
Editor's Note: Results of the November 1996 election were not available at press time; up to date results may appear in the Addenda at the back of this book.
Next Election: November 1999 (three year terms)

ADMINISTRATION
City Clerk/Asst. Administrator, Wayne Vollrath, 250/828-3446
Treasurer & Director, Finance, Wayne Ridgway, 250/828-3413; Fax: 250/828-0845; EMail: wridgway@city.kamloops.bc.ca
City Administrator, J.E. Martignago, 250/828-3498
Asst. Administrator, City Engineer, E.G. Kurtz, 250/828-3452; Fax: 250/828-0952
Director, Development Services, R.H. Diehl, 250/828-3566; Fax: 250/828-7848
Director, Human Resources, K.D. Stinson, 250/828-3439; Fax: 250/372-1351
Director, Parks & Recreation Services, D.E. Kujat, 250/828-3489
Fire Chief & EMO, Doug Norman, 250/828-3490; Fax: 250/372-1447
Collector, R.O. Gowing, 250/828-3432
Manager, Engineering & Environmental Services, M. Gravelle, 250/828-3464; Fax: 250/828-0952
Manager, Tourism, Karen McLaughlin, 250/828-3488; Fax: 250/828-7848
Purchasing Agent, E. Wild, 250/828-3503; Fax: 250/828-1766

City of KELOWNA
City Hall, 1435 Water St., Kelowna BC V1Y 1J4
250/763-6011, Fax: 250/862-3399
Incorporated: May 4, 1905
Area: 87.7 sq. miles
Population: 88,559 (1994)

MAJOR MUNICIPALITIES

COUNCIL

Editor's Note: Results of the November 1996 election were not available at press time; up to date results may appear in the Addenda at the back of this book.
Next Election: November 1999 (three year terms)

ADMINISTRATION

Clerk, David L. Shipclark, 250/862-3308
Treasurer, Cliff P. Kraft, Fax: 250/470-0690
City Administrator, R.A. Born
Director, Corporate Services, Vacant
Director, Human Resources, R.W. Baker, 250/862-3376; Fax: 250/862-3318
Director, Leisure Services, David Graham, 250/862-3383; Fax: 250/470-0699
Director, Planning & Development Services, Ron Mattiussi, Fax: 250/862-3320
Director, Works & Utilities, Rod McCrae, 250/862-3341; Fax: 250/862-3349
Fire Chief, Gerry Zimmermann, 250/860-6419; Fax: 250/862-3571
Police Chief, RCMP City Detachment, Supt. Rod MacKay, 350 Doyle Ave., Kelowna BC V1Y 6V7, 250/762-3300; Fax: 250/762-3751
Assessor, J. Farkas, #201, 1665 Ellis St., Kelowna BC, 250/763-8300; Fax: 250/861-6136
Manager, Information Services, D. Rasmussen
Medical Health Officer, Dr. B. Muirhead, 250/868-7700; Fax: 250/868-7760
Supervisor, Purchasing & Stores, R. Reiter, 250/862-3346

City of KINGSTON

City Hall, 216 Ontario St., Kingston ON K7L 2Z3
613/546-4291, Fax: 613/546-5232
Incorporated: 1846
Area: 11.69 sq. miles
Population: 59,624 (1994)

COUNCIL

Mayor, Gary Bennett
Councillors & Wards: 1. Sydenham) Don Rogers; 2. Ontario) Dick Myers; 3. St. Lawrence) Dave Clarke; 4. Cataraqui) Don Bristol; 5. Frontenac) Mary Fleming; 6. Rideau) Carol Allison-Burra; 7. Victoria) Patricia Hodge; 8. Portsmouth) Jim Neill; 9. Kingscourt) Joe Hawkins; 10. Riverview) Dave Meers
Next Election: November 1997 (3 year terms)

ADMINISTRATION

City Clerk, Sheila Birrell
City Treasurer, Vacant
Chief Administrative Officer, Richard Fiebig
Commissioner, Kingston Municipal Operations, B. Sheridan, ext.225
Administrator, Social Services, B. Mason
Chief Building Official, T. Beltrami
City Solicitor, Norm Jackson, ext.208
Director, Human Resources, B. Bishop
Director, Planning & Urban Renewal, Rupert Dobbin, ext.278
Director, Purchasing, R. Plumley, ext.236
Fire Chief, R. Thurlby
Manager, Public Utilities Commission, G. Jarvis
Officer, Home Improvement Program, D. Werden
Police Chief, W. Closs, Fax: 613/549-3111

City of KITCHENER

City Hall, 200 King St. West, PO Box 1118, Kitchener ON N2G 4G7
519/741-2286, Fax: 519/741-2705, Email kcouncil@hookup.net, URL: http://www.oceta.on.ca/city.kitchener
Incorporated: June 10, 1912
Area: 13,382 ha
Population: 184,600 (1996)

COUNCIL

Mayor, Richard D. Christy
Councillors & Wards: 1. Centre) Karen Redman; 2. Rockway-St. Mary's) Mike Wagner; 3. Victoria Park) Mark Yantzi; 4. Bridgeport-North) John Smola; 5. Stanley Park) Jake Smola; 6. Chicopee) Berry Vrbanovic; 7. Fairview) James Ziegler; 8. South) Tom Galloway; 9. Forest) Geoff L.J. Lorentz; 10. West) Christina Weylie
Next Election: November 1997 (3 year terms)

ADMINISTRATION

City Clerk & Commissioner, General Services, Robert W. Pritchard, 519/741-2280; EMail: robertpr@hookup.net
Commissioner, Finance, John A. Gazzola, 519/741-2350; Fax: 519/741-2750; EMail: jgazzola@hookup.net
Chief Administrative Officer, Tom McKay, 519/741-2290
General Manager, Parks & Recreation, Tom Clancy, 519/741-2394; Fax: 519/741-2723
General Manager, Planning & Development, Tim McCabe, 519/741-2320; Fax: 519/741-2624
General Manager, Public Works, Ed Kovacs, 519/741-2420; Fax: 519/741-2633
City Solicitor, James Shivas, 519/741-2263; Fax: 519/741-2702
Director, Economic Development, V. Gibaut, 519/741-2291; Fax: 519/741-2722
Director, Human Resources, Doug Paterson, 519/741-2252; Fax: 519/741-2400
Director, Transit, Walter Beck, 519/741-2560; Fax: 519/741-2640
Environmental Engineer, Chris Ford, 519/741-2215; Fax: 519/741-2222; EMail: cford@hookup.net
Fire Chief, James Hancock, 519/741-2500; Fax: 519/741-2697; EMail: jhancock@mgl.ca

District of LANGLEY

4914 - 221 St., Langley BC V3A 3Z8
604/534-3211, Fax: 604/533-6098
Incorporated: 1873
Area: 303.05 sq. km
Population: 80,000 (1996)

COUNCIL

Editor's Note: Results of the November 1996 election were not available at press time; up to date results may appear in the Addenda at the back of this book.
Next Election: November 1999 (three year terms)

ADMINISTRATION

Municipal Clerk, Rodney T. Edwards, 604/533-6003
Acting Director, Finance, Frank Clark Jones, 604/533-6030
Administrator, J.F. Godfrey, 604/533-6002
Director, Community Development, Kurt Alberts, 604/533-6059
Director, Engineering, P. Anderson, 604/533-6072
Director, Human Resources, Mike Zora, 604/533-6121
Director, Parks & Recreation, Doug Brimacombe, 604/533-6087
Fire Chief, W. Markel, 604/888-7755; Fax: 604/888-7088

Ville de LASALLE

55, av Dupras, LaSalle PQ H8R 4A8
514/367-1000, Fax: 514/367-3520
Incorporée: 1912
Superficie: 4,789 arpents
Population: 74,777 (1993)

CONSEIL

Maire, Michel Leduc, m.d.
Conseillers et Districts: 1) Gilbert Vachon; 2) Pierre Lussier; 3) François Dupuis; 4) Ross Blackhurst; 5) Manon Barbe; 6) Antonio Massana; 7) Monique Vallée; 8) Me Daniel Zizian; 9) Vincenzo Cesari; 10) Alvaro Farinacci; 11) Frank Talarico; 12) Alain Chénier
Prochaine élection: novembre 1999 (mandat de 4 ans)

ADMINISTRATION

Greffière, Nicole Herby, 514/367-6392; Fax: 514/367-6607
Trésorier, Service des finances, Gervais Lemay, 514/367-6230; Fax: 514/367-3520
Directeur général, Georges Kremery, 514/367-6200
Chef de Cabinet du Maire, Pierre Guérin, 514/367-6209
Chef, Génie, Yvon Rousseau, 514/367-6770; Fax: 514/367-6602
Chef, Service des achats, Robert Martineau, 514/367-6470; Fax: 514/367-6602
Commissaire, Corporation de développement économique de LaSalle, Gilles Léonard, 514/367-6380
Directrice, Service de la culture, Rachel Laperrière, 514/367-6370; Fax: 514/367-5840
Directeur, Service de protection contre l'incendie, Pierre Damico, 514/367-6320; Fax: 514/368-1436
Directeur, Service des communications, Gérald Lawrence, 514/367-6490; Fax: 514/367-6607
Directeur, Service des loisirs, Mario Vachon, 514/367-6350; Fax: 514/367-6606
Directeur, Service des ressources humaines, Michel Beaudoin, 514/367-6400; Fax: 514/367-5840
Directeur, Services techniques, André Traversy, 514/367-6700; Fax: 514/367-6602

Ville de LAVAL

Hôtel de Ville, 1, Place du Souvenir, CP 422, Succ St-Martin, Laval PQ H7V 1W7
514/978-8000, Fax: 514/978-5943
Incorporée: 6 aout, 1965
Superficie: 242.41 sq. km (93.6 sq. miles)
Population: 344,700 (1995)

CONSEIL

Maire, Gilles Vaillancourt
Conseillers: 1) Jacques St-Jean; 2) André Gervais; 3) Maurice Clermont; 4) Monique Gauthier; 5) Georges Gauthier; 6) Jacques Lapierre; 7) Georges Gagné; 8) Micheline Hamel; 9) Yves Gratton; 10) Jocelyne Guertin; 11) Michelle Major; 12) Pierrette Patenaude; 13) Richard Lagrois; 14) Savas Fortis; 15) Richard Goyer; 16) Pierre Cléroux; 17) Jean-Jacques Beldié; 18) Robert Plante; 19) André Boileau; 20) Robert Masseau; 21) Guy Cyr; 22) Denis Goulet; 23) Yvon Martineau; 24) Norman Girard
Prochaine élection: novembre 1997 (mandat de 4 ans)

ADMINISTRATION

Greffier, Guy Collard, 514/978-3950; Fax: 514/978-3966
Budget, Richard Beaudry, 514/978-3901; Fax: 514/978-3915
Directeur général, Claude Asselin, 514/978-3676; Fax: 514/978-3692
Achats et magasins, Marcel Boucher, 514/662-4555; Fax: 514/662-4580
Communications, Mesures d'urgences, Pierre René de Cotret
Contentieux, Jean Allaire, 514/978-5866; Fax: 514/978-5871
Évaluation, Claude Globensky, 514/978-8777; Fax: 514/978-8710
Finances, André Bourgeois, 514/978-5704; Fax: 514/978-5789
Génie et Environnement, Pierre Lafrance, 514/662-4550; Fax: 514/662-5091
Incendies, Alain Vaillancourt, 514/662-4450; Fax: 514/967-8306

Informatique, André Lafferrière, 514/662-4040; Fax: 514/662-7473
Loisirs, Paul Lemay, 514/662-4343; Fax: 514/669-4729
Police, Jean Marc-Aurèle, 514/662-4242; Fax: 514/662-7282
Ressources humaines, Pierre Comeau, 514/978-6560; Fax: 514/978-6561
Travaux publics, André Perrault, 514/662-4666; Fax: 514/662-7279
Urbanisme, Normand Garièpy, 514/662-4333; Fax: 514/662-7250

City of LETHBRIDGE
City Hall, 910 - 4 Ave. South, Lethbridge AB T1J 0P6
403/320-3900, Fax: 403/320-9369, URL: http://www.city.lethbridge.ab.ca
Incorporated: 1906
Area: 48 sq. miles (12,413 ha)
Population: 64,938 (1994)

COUNCIL
Mayor, David B. Carpenter, Fax: 403/320-7575; EMail: mayor@city.lethbridge.ab.ca
Aldermen: Jeffrey Coffman; Barbara Lacey; Don M. Lebaron; Ed J. Martin; Joe Mauro; Frank Peta; Shaun Ward; Greg Weadick
Next Election: October 1998 (3 year terms)

ADMINISTRATION
City Clerk, Dianne Nemeth, 403/320-3821; Fax: 403/320-7575; EMail: cclerk@city.lethbridge.ab.ca
Director, Finance & Utilities, Garth Sherwin, 403/320-3985; Fax: 403/320-6571
City Manager, Bryan Horrocks
Director, Community Services, Tom Hudson, 403/320-3002; Fax: 403/380-2512
Chief of Police, John LaFlamme, 403/327-2210; Fax: 403/328-6999
City Solicitor, Douglas Hudson, 403/320-3903
Comptroller, Barry Sawada, 403/320-3981; Fax: 403/327-6571; EMail: bsawada@city.lethbridge.ab.ca
Fire Chief, Tom Wickersham, 403/320-3803; Fax: 403/327-3503; EMail: fire@city.lethbridge.ab.ca
Deputy Fire Chief, Disaster Services, Ted Bochan, 403/320-3802; Fax: 403/327-3503
General Manager, Development Services, Felix Michna, 403/320-3921; Fax: 403/320-6571; EMail: fmichna@city.lethbridge.ab.ca
General Manager, Environmental Utilities, Henry Bosman, 403/320-3096; Fax: 403/320-9703; EMail: hbosman@city.lethbridge.ab.ca
Infrastructure Steward, Bud Hogeweide, 403/320-3094; Fax: 403/329-4657; EMail: hogeweid@city.lethbridge.ab.ca
Land Administrator, Gary Weikum, 403/320-3922; Fax: 403/327-6571; EMail: gweikum@city.lethbridge.ab.ca
Manager, Assessment & Taxation, Barrie Hosack, 403/320-3951; Fax: 403/320-6571
Manager, Computer Services, Joe Feller, 403/320-3971; Fax: 403/327-6571; EMail: jfeller@city.lethbridge.ab.ca
Manager, Economic Development, Darrel McKenzie, 1-800-332-1801; Fax: 403/320-9369; EMail: ecodev@city.lethbridge.ab.ca
Manager, Fleet Services, Doug Brandvold, 403/329-7368; Fax: 403/328-4467
Manager, Human Resources, Paul Petry, 403/320-3912
Manager, Leisure & Human Services, Brian Bourassa, 403/320-3010; Fax: 403/380-2512
Manager, Leisure Facilities, Tom Hopkins, 403/320-3012; Fax: 403/380-2512; EMail: thopkins@city.lethbridge.ab.ca
Manager, Lethbridge Power, Juergen Renter, 403/320-3933; Fax: 403/380-2541; EMail: powerline@city.lethbridge.ab.ca

Manager, Parks, Ron Peterson, 403/320-3017; Fax: 403/320-2823
Manager, Purchasing, Al Burghardt, 403/320-3961; Fax: 403/328-0501
Manager, Risk & Insurance, Leo VandenHeuval, 403/320-3902; Fax: 403/320-6571; EMail: vandenhe@city.lethbridge.ab.ca
Manager, Solid Waste & Recycling, Walter Brodowski, 403/320-3090; Fax: 403/329-4657
Manager, Sportsplex, Ashley Matthews, 403/320-4040; Fax: 403/327-3620
Manager, Traffic Operations, Brian Johnson, 403/320-3092; Fax: 403/329-4657; EMail: bjohnson@city.lethbridge.ab.ca
Manager, Transit, Ed Granger, 403/320-3884; Fax: 403/380-3876
Medical Health Officer, Community & Wellness, Dr. Paul Hasselback, 403/382-6014; Fax: 403/382-6011; EMail: phassel@crha.sas.ab.ca

City of LONDON
City Hall, 300 Dufferin Ave., PO Box 5035, London ON N6A 4L9
519/661-4500, Fax: 519/661-4892, http://www.city.london.on.ca
Incorporated: 1855
Area: 43,667 ha
Population: 331,600 (1995)

COUNCIL
Mayor, Dianne Haskett
Councillors & Wards: 1) Joseph V. Avola, Sheila Davenport; 2) Robert Beccarea, Joseph B. Swan; 3) E. Howard, Bernard R. MacDonald; 4) William Armstrong, W.J. Polhill; 5) Anne Marie DeCicco, Gary E. Williams; 6) Ben Veel, Megan Walker; 7) Martha E. Joyce, E.L. Wernham
Next Election: November 1997 (3 year terms)

ADMINISTRATION
City Clerk, Kenneth W. Sadler
City Treasurer & Commissioner, Linda H. Reed
City Administrator, John E. Fleming
Commissioner, Planning & Development, Victor A. Coté
Chief of Police, J. Fanino
Commissioner & City Engineer, John W. Jardine
Director, Economic Development, Matthew H. Fischer
Director, Human Resources, H. Ross Rowe
Director & Medical Officer of Health, Dr. G.L. Pollett
Fire Chief, Gary W. Weese
Manager, Parks & Recreation, J.G. Lohuis

Ville de LONGUEUIL
777, rue d'Auverge, CP 5000, Longueuil PQ J4K 4Y7
514/646-8218, Fax: 514/646-8080
Incorporée: 1874
Superficie: 45 sq. km
Population: 137,134 (1993)

CONSEIL
Maire, Claude Gladu, 514/646-8215; Fax: 514/646-8203
Conseillers et Districts: 1. Charles-Lemoyne) Joël Gamache; 2. Pierre d'Iberville) Cécile Langevin; 3. Fernand-Bouffard) Henri Dubois; 4. St.Pierre-Apôtre) Sylvie Robidas; 5. Coteau-Rouge) Nicole Béliveau-Zeitter; 6. Octavien-Vincent) Normand Caisse; 7. Hubert-Perron) Alain St-Pierre; 8. St-Vincent-de-Paul) Johane Fontaine Deshais; 9. Adrien-Laflamme) Nicole Lafontaine; 10. Christ-Roi) Manon Hénault; 11. Emérillon) Serge Sévigny; 12. Sieur-de-Roberval) Lise Sauvé; 13. Lionel-Groulx) Bertrand Girard; 14. Adrien-Gamache) Michel Timpiero; 15. Saint-Pie-X) Florent Charest; 16. Saint-Antoine) Pierre Beaudry; 17. Fatima) Pierre Racicot; 18. Bellerive) Jacques Milette; 19. Gentilly)

Claudette Tessier; 20. Du Tremblay) Simon Crochetière
Prochaine election: novembre 1998 (mandat de 4 ans)

ADMINISTRATION
Greffier, Claude Comtois, 514/646-8225
Directeur général, Massimo Iezzoni, Fax: 514/646-8255
Directeur général adjoint et directeur des services financiers, Pierre Pouliot, 514/646-8710
Chef de division, Hygiène du milieu, Pierre Lemoyne, 514/646-8404
Directeur, Communications, Jean Racicot, 514/646-8669
Directeur, Contentieux, Me Claude Séguin, 514/646-8235
Directeur, Loisirs et culture, Martin Lelievre, 514/646-8647
Directeur, Police, Marc Quimper, 514/646-8510; Fax: 514/646-8497
Directeur, Prévention des incendies, Gilles Lamadeleine, 514/646-8270
Directeur, Ressources humaines, Raymond Patry, 514/646-8790
Directeur, Urbanisme et permis, Claude Doyon, 514/646-8420

Town of MARKHAM
101 Town Centre Blvd., Markham ON L3R 9W3
905/477-7000, Fax: 905/479-7771
Incorporated: January 1, 1971
Area: 52,890 acres
Population: 160,000 (1995)

COUNCIL
Mayor, Don Cousens, 905/470-6622; Fax: 905/479-7775
Regional Councillors: Carole Bell; Fred Cox; Bill Fisch; Gordon Landon
Ward Councillors: 1) Bill O'Donnell; 2) Stan Daurio; 3) Jim Jones; 4) George McKelvey; 5) Ralph Aselin; 6) Ron Maheu; 7) Randy Barber; 8) Alex Chiu
Next Election: November 1997 (3 year terms)

ADMINISTRATION
Clerk, Bob Panizza
Treasurer & Commissioner, Finance & Administration, John W. McCormack, Fax: 905/479-7764
Chief Administrative Officer, Lorne V. McCool, ext.263; Fax: 905/479-7764
Commissioner, Community Services, Dalo Keliar, ext.265; Fax: 905/479-7766
Commissioner, Development Services, Mary-Francis Turner
Commissioner & Town Solicitor, Legal Services, Robert Swayze, Fax: 905/479-7764
Director, Economic Development, Stephen Chait
Director, Human Resources, Jim Hamill
Director, Recreation, Barbara Roth
Director, Roads, Ted Mortson
Fire Chief, Ken Beckett
Manager, Administrative Services, Andrew Vickery

City of MISSISSAUGA
300 City Centre Dr., Mississauga ON L5B 3C1
905/896-5000, Fax: 905/896-5220, URL: http://www.city.mississauga.on.ca
Incorporated: January 1, 1974
Area: 111 sq. miles
Population: 500,000 (1994)

COUNCIL
Mayor, Hazel McCallion
Councillors & Wards: 1) Carmen Corbasson; 2) Patricia Mullin; 3) Maja Prentice; 4) Frank Dale; 5) Frank McKechnie; 6) David Culham; 7) Nando Iannicca; 8) Katie Mahoney; 9) Pat Saito
Next Election: November 1997 (3 year terms)

ADMINISTRATION
Deputy City Clerk, Arthur Grannum, 905/896-5419
Treasurer & Commissioner, Finance, William H. Munden, 905/896-5262
City Manager, David S. O'Brien, 905/896-5550; Fax: 905/615-3376
Commissioner, Community Services, Paul Mitcham, 905/615-3100
Commissioner, Corporate Services, Margaret Rodrigues, 905/896-5392
Commissioner, Human Resources, David Bray, 905/896-5023
Commissioner, Planning & Building, Thomas Mokrzycki, 905/896-5561; Fax: 905/896-5553
Commissioner, Transportation & Works, Angus McDonald, 905/896-5112; Fax: 905/896-5504
City Solicitor, Shelley Pohjola, 905/896-5393; Fax: 905/896-5106
Director, Economic Development, Karen Campbell, 905/896-5012; Fax: 905/615-3376
Acting Director, Public Affairs, Susan Amring, 905/896-5047; Fax: 905/615-3078
Director, Recreation & Parks, John Lohwis, 905/615-3700; Fax: 905/615-3469
Director, Works, Martin Powell, 905/896-5086; Fax: 905/896-5583
Fire Chief, Cyril Hare, 905/615-3750; Fax: 905/615-3773
General Manager, Mississauga Transit, Ed Dowling, 905/615-3840; Fax: 905/615-3833
Acting Manager, Materiel Management, Norm Baxter, 905/615-3268

City of MONCTON
655 Main St., Moncton NB E1C 1E8
506/853-3333, Fax: 506/859-4225
Incorporated: 1890
Area: 58.06 sq. miles
Population: 57,010 (1991)

COUNCIL
Mayor, Léopold F. Belliveau
Councillors & Wards: 1) Norman H. Crossman, Brian Murphy; 2) S. Boyd Anderson, Joan MacAlpine; 3) John W. Betts, George H. LeBlanc; 4) Charles J. Gillespie, Q.C., Yvon Goguen
Councillors at Large: Judith E. Jacobson; Stan McGrath
Next Election: May 1998 (3 year terms)

ADMINISTRATION
Clerk, Elizabeth Reade, 506/853-3550; EMail: elizabeth.reade@moncton.org
Commissioner, Finance & Administration, H.T. Eno, Fax: 506/859-2676; EMail: tom.eno@moncton.org
City Manager, L.E. Strang, 506/853-3550; EMail: al.strang@moncton.org
Commissioner, Engineering & Public Works, J.G. Greenough, Fax: 506/853-3543; EMail: geoff.greenough@moncton.org
Commissioner, Policy & Corporate Resources, M.B. Sullivan; EMail: mike.sullivan@moncton.org
Chief of Police, G.D.J. Cohoon, 506/857-2400; Fax: 506/857-2414; EMail: greg.cohoon@moncton.org
City Solicitor, William E. Cooper, Fax: 506/859-2610; EMail: bill.cooper@moncton.org
Director, Community Services/Community Development & Partnership, Ian. Fowler, Fax: 506/859-2629; EMail: ian.fowler@moncton.org
Director, Community Services/Operations, Rod Higgins, Fax: 506/859-2629; EMail: rod.higgins@moncton.org
Director, Greater Moncton District Planning Commission, Kenneth D. Stevens
Director, Purchasing, Connie O'Brien, Fax: 506/859-2675
Director, Special Projects, Ron LeBlanc, Fax: 506/853-3543; EMail: ron.leblanc@moncton.org
Fire Chief, Bruce Morrison, 506/857-8800; Fax: 506/856-4353; EMail: bruce.morrison@moncton.org
Chair, EMO, & Manager, Codiac Transit Commission, John Allain, 280 Pacific Ave., Moncton NB E1E 2G8, 506/857-2008; Fax: 506/859-2680
General Manager, Moncton Industrial Development, Peter Belliveau, #102, 910 Main St., Moncton NB E1C 1G6, 506/857-0700; Fax: 506/859-7206
President, Greater Moncton Economic Commission, Ron Gaudet

Ville de MONTRÉAL
Hôtel de Ville, 275, rue Notre-Dame est, Montréal PQ H2Y 1C6
514/872-1111, Fax: 514/872-5655, URL: http://www.ville.montreal.qc.ca/
Incorporée: 1832
Superficie: 192.47 sq. km (74.2 sq. mi)
Population: 1,017,666 (1993)

CONSEIL
Maire, Pierre Bourque
Conseillers et Districts: 1. Cartierville) Pierre Gagnier; 2. L'Acadie) Noushig Eloyan; 3. Ahuntsic) Hasmig Belleli; 4. Saint-Sulpice) Maurice Beauchamp; 5. Fleury) Colette St-Martin; 6. Sault-au-Récollet) Serge-Éric Bélanger; 7. Saint-Michel) Paolo Tamburello; 8. Jean-Rivard) Daniel Boucher; 9. François-Perreault) Vittorio Capparelli; 10. Villeray) Sylvain Lachance; 11. Octave-Crémazie) Anie Samson; 12. Jarry) Achille Polcaro; 13. Parc-Extension) Konstantinos Georgoulis; 14. Saint-Édouard) Pierre Goyer; 15. Père-Marquette) Robert Laramée; 16. Louis-Hébert) Hubert Deraspe; 17. Étienne-Desmarteau) Michelle Daines; 18. Marie-Victorin) Kettly Beauregard; 19. Bourbonnière) Andrée Lavallée; 20. Rosemont) Robert Côté; 21. de Lorimier) Richard Théorêt; 22. Plateau Mont-Royal) Jean Doré; 23. Laurier) Louise Roy; 24. Mile-End) Helen Fotopulos; 25. Jeanne-Mance) Michel Prescott; 26. Peter McGill) Georgine Coutu; 27. Cote-des-Neiges) Pierre-Yves Melançon; 28. Darlington) Jack Chadirdjian; 29. Victoria) Saulie Zajdel; 30. Snowdon) Marvin Rotrand; 31. Notre-Dame-de-Grâce) Michael Applebaum; 32. Loyola) Jeremy Searle; 33. Décarie) Sam Boskey; 34. Émard) Robert Gagnon; 35. Saint-Paul) Philippe Bissonnette; 36. Saint-Henri) Germain Prégent; 37. Pointe-Saint-Charles) Marcel Sévigny; 38. Saint-Jacques) Sammi Forcillo; 39. Sainte-Marie) Martin Lemay; 40. Hochelaga) Luc Larivée; 41. Maisonneuve) Nathalie Malépart; 42. Pierre-de-Coubertin) Benoît Parent; 43. Louis-Riel) Jacques Charbonneau; 44. Longue-Pointe) Claire St-Arnaud; 45. Honoré-Beaugrand) Ivon Le Duc; 46. Tétreaultville) Jean-Guy Deschamps; 47. Marc-Aurèle-Fortin) Giovanni De Michele; 48. Rivière-des-Prairies) Aimé Charron; 49. Pointe-aux-Trembles) Marie Lebeau; 50. La Rousselière) Colette Paul; 51. du Bout-de-l'Île) Johanne Lorrain
Prochaine election: novembre 1998 (mandat de 4 ans)

ADMINISTRATION
Greffier, Léon Laberge, 514/872-3142
Secrétariat administratif, Danielle Rondeau, 872-8155; Fax: 872-8433
Avocate en Chef & Directrice, Service du contentieux, Suzanne Jalbert, 514/872-2919; Fax: 514/872-2828
Directeur, Service des finances et du contrôle, Roger Galipeau, #207, 155, rue Notre-Dame est, Montréal PQ H2Y 1B5, 514/872-6630; Fax: 514/872-3145
Directrice, Service de la gestion financière des caisses de retraite, Thieu Quan Hoang, 413, rue St-Jacques, 7e étage, Montréal PQ H2Y 1N9
Directeur, Service de l'approvisionnement et du soutien technique, André Drolet, 9515, rue St-Hubert, Montréal PQ H2M 1Z4, 514/872-7014; Fax: 514/872-7510
Directeur, Service de la circulation & du transport, Yann Davies, #1.220, 700, rue St-Antoine est, Montréal PQ H2Y 1A6, 514/872-3130; Fax: 514/872-1727
Directrice, Service de la culture, Janine Beaulieu, 5650, rue d'Iberville, 5e étage, Montréal PQ H2G 3E4, 514/872-1149; Fax: 514/872-0425
Directeur, Service du développement économique, Jean-Marc Lajoie, 500, Place d'Armes, 13e étage, Montréal PQ H2Y 1N9, 514/872-6404; Fax: 514/872-9812
Directeur, Service du génie, Bruno Gauthier, #1.230, 700, rue St-Antoine est, Montréal PQ H2Y 1A6, 514/872-3945; Fax: 514/872-1721
Directeur, Service de l'habitation, Fabien Cournoyer, #4.100, 303, rue Notre-Dame est, Montréal PQ H2Y 3Y8, 514/872-3882; Fax: 514/872-3883
Directeur, Service des immeubles, André Blain, 385, rue Sherbrooke est, Montréal PQ H2X 1E3, 514/872-5380; Fax: 514/872-4049
Directrice, Service des parcs, jardins & espaces verts, Lise Cormier, #200, 4590, rue d'Orléans, Montréal PQ H1X 2K4, 514/872-1457; Fax: 514/872-1458
Directrice, Service des permits & inspections, Céline Topp, #2.100, 303, rue Notre-Dame est, Montréal PQ H2Y 2Y8, 514/872-3111; Fax: 514/872-3587
Directeur, Service du personnel, Jean Des Trois Maisons, 413, rue St-Jacques, 4e étage, Montréal PQ H2Y 1N9, 514/872-5809; Fax: 514/872-8430
Directeur, Service de la prévention des incendies, Roméo Noël, 4040, av du Parc, Montréal PQ H1M 2S6, 514/872-3761; Fax: 514/868-3180
Directeur, Service de la propreté, Michel Jodoin, #1.100, 700, rue St-Antoine est, Montréal PQ H2Y 1A6, 514/872-1266; Fax: 514/872-3505
Directeur, Service de la sécurité du revenu, Robert Guay, 1125, rue Ontario est, 2e étage, Montréal PQ H2L 1R2, 514/872-4940; Fax: 514/872-6020
Directrice, Service des sports, des loisirs & du développement social, Stella Guy, #201, 7400, boul St-Michel, Montréal PQ H2A 2Z8, 514/872-2465; Fax: 514/872-4561
Directrice, Service des travaux publics, Johanne Falcon, #R-230, 700, rue St-Antoine est, Montréal PQ H2Y 1A6, 514/872-9278; Fax: 514/872-8990
Directeur, Service de l'urbanisme, Pierre Ouellet, 303, rue Notre-Dame est, 5e étage, Montréal PQ H2Y 3Y8, 514/872-4523; Fax: 514/872-0024
Vérificateur, Bureau du Vérificateur, Guy Lefebvre, c.a., #605, 276, rue St-Jacques, Montréal PQ H2Y 1N3, 514/872-2208; Fax: 514/872-6950

Ville de MONTRÉAL-NORD
4242, Place de l'Hôtel-de-Ville, Montréal-Nord PQ H1H 1S5
514/328-4000, Fax: 514/328-4299
Incorporée: 15 mars, 1915
Superficie: 427.6 ha
Population: 86,641 (1994)

CONSEIL
Maire, Yves Ryan
Conseillers et Districts: 1) Antonin Dupont; 2) Michelle Allaire; 3) Pierre Blain; 4) Georgette Morin; 5) Maurice Bélanger; 6) Jean-Marc Gibeau; 7) Jean-Paul Lessard; 8) Normand Fortin; 9) James V. Infantino; 10) André Coulombe; 11) Raymond Paquin; 12) Robert Guerriero
Prochaine election: novembre 1998 (mandat de 4 ans)

ADMINISTRATION
Greffe, Hélène Simoneau
Directeur, Finances, Michel Labrecque
Directeur général, Michel Archambault
Chef, Approvisionnement, Yvon Ménard, 514/328-4051; Fax: 514/328-4055

Chef, Informatique, Jean-Claude Bérubé
Chef, Personnel, Jean-Pierre Masse
Directeur, Génie, Yvon Paquette, ing., 514/328-4007; Fax: 514/328-4055
Directeur, Protection incendie, André Morin
Directeur, Services des Loisirs et de la Vie Communautaire, François Boucher, 514/328-4166; Fax: 514/328-4064
Directeur, Travaux publics, Environnement et Mesures d'urgence, Roland de Grandpré, ing., 514/328-4104; Fax: 514/328-4065
Directice, Centres biblio-culturels, Céline Dénommée

City of MOOSE JAW
228 Main St. North, Moose Jaw SK S6H 3J8
306/694-4400, Fax: 306/692-4518, 691-0292
Incorporated: November 20, 1903
Area: 17.25 sq. miles
Population: 33,803 (1995)

COUNCIL
Mayor, Ray Boughen
Aldermen: Frank Abdou; Graham Chute; Mike Hataley; John Livingston; Peter Norys; Al Schwinghamer
Next Election: October 1997 (3 year terms)

ADMINISTRATION
City Clerk, Brian Hamblin, 306/694-4424
Director, Finance, Paul Meginbir
City Commissioner, Jim Penrod, 306/694-4427
Chief of Police, Richard Baum, 306/694-1588
Director, Parks & Recreation, Garry McKay, 306/694-4447
EMO Coordinator, Capt. Dale Hall, 306/692-2792
Engineer, Planning & Utilities, Mike Caswell, 306/694-4473
Engineer, Public Works, Ed Fredeen, 306/694-4437
Fire Chief, Barry Dewald, 306/692-2792
Manager, Assessment, Land & Licensing, Dave Pierce, 306/694-4477
Supervisor, Personnel, Karen Ireland, 306/694-4464
Supervisor, Transit, Kim Burnside, 306/694-4454

City of NANAIMO
455 Wallace St., Nanaimo BC V9R 5J6
250/754-4251, Fax: 250/755-4436, URL: http://www.sd68.nanaimo.bc.ca/nol/welcome.html
Incorporated: December 24, 1874
Area: 88.19 sq. km
Population: 72,000 (1995)

COUNCIL
Editor's Note: Results of the November 1996 election were not available at press time; up to date results may appear in the Addenda at the back of this book.
Next Election: November 1999 (3 year terms)

ADMINISTRATION
Clerk, Jim Bowden, 250/755-4404; Fax: 250/755-4435
Director, Finance, C.L. Davis, 250/755-4413; Fax: 250/755-4440
Administrator, Gerald D. Berry, 250/755-4401
General Manager, Corporate Services, A.C. Kenning, 250/755-4410; Fax: 250/755-4440
General Manager, Operations, K.B. Davis, 250/758-5222; Fax: 250/756-5326
Director, Development Services, B.N. Mehaffey, 250/755-4409; Fax: 250/755-4439
Director, Human Resources, J.M. Constable, 250/755-4427; Fax: 250/755-4449
Director, Parks, Recreation & Culture, A.W. Laidlaw, 250/755-7516; Fax: 250/753-7277
Director, Strategic Planning, Engineering & Economic Development, D.L. (Les) King, 250/755-4428
Fire Chief, Ray Digby, 250/753-7311; Fax: 250/753-5480

Managing Director, Public Works, M. Mackenzie, 250/758-5222; Fax: 250/756-5326
Economic Development, M. Entwistle, 250/755-4465; Fax: 250/755-4403

City of NEPEAN
Nepean Civic Square, 101 Centrepointe Dr., Nepean ON K2G 5K7
613/727-6600, Fax: 613/727-6613
Incorporated: 1850
Area: 78.84 sq. miles (50,400 acres)
Population: 116,000 (1994)

COUNCIL
Mayor, Ben Franklin
Councillors & Wards: 1) Mervin Sullivan; 2) Rick Chiarelli; 3) Molly McGoldrick-Larsen; 4) Margaret Rywak; 5) Lee-Ann Farnworth; 6) Doug Collins
Next Election: November 1997 (3 year terms)

ADMINISTRATION
City Clerk, John LeMaistre, 613/727-6612
Commissioner, Finance, Lloyd Russell, 613/727-6615
Chief Administrative Officer, Robert R. Letourneau, 613/727-6607
Commissioner, Human Resources, Grant Armstrong, 613/727-6624
Commissioner, Planning, Jack D. Stirling, 613/727-6626
Commissioner, Public Works, A. Clarke Bellinger, 613/727-6630
Director, Parks & Recreation, R.J. (Bob) Sulpher, 613/727-6635
Director, Information Services, Andrea McCormick, 613/727-6634
Director, Purchasing & Risk Management, John Harris, ext.420
Fire Chief & Commissioner, Emergency Services, Chris Powers, 613/825-2020

City of NIAGARA FALLS
City Hall, 4310 Queen St., PO Box 1023, Niagara Falls ON L2E 6X5
905/356-7521, Fax: 905/356-9083, URL: http://www.niagara.com:80/city.niagara_falls/
Incorporated: January 1, 1904
Area: 80.92 sq. miles
Population: 74,915 (1994)

COUNCIL
Mayor, Wayne Thomson
Aldermen & Wards: 1) Wayne Campbell, Kim Craitor, Patrick Cummings, Gary Hendershot, Paisley Janvary, Judy Orr, Norman Puttick, Selina Volpatti; 2) Shirley Fisher, Bruce Ward; 3) Femino Susin; 4) Victor Pietroangelo
Next Election: November 1997 (3 year terms)

ADMINISTRATION
City Clerk, Elwood Wagg
Director, Finance, Paul Jacques
Chief Administrative Officer, Edward P. Lustig
City Solicitor, R. Kallio
Director, Municipal Works, Larry A. Oates
Director, Parks & Recreation, Adele Kon
Director, Planning & Development, Doug Darbyson
Manager, Business Development, Serge Felicetti
Manager, Human Resources, A. (Tony) Ravenda
Fire Chief, Fire Dept., Pete Corfield, 5815 Morrison St., Niagara Falls ON L2E 2E8, 905/356-1324

City of NORTH BAY
City Hall, 200 McIntyre St. East, PO Box 360, North Bay ON P1B 8H8
705/474-0400, Fax: 705/495-4353, http://www.canadore.on.ca/northbay.htm

Incorporated: 1925
Area: 128.9 sq. miles
Population: 55,960 (1994)

COUNCIL
Mayor, Jack Burrows
Councillors: Jay Aspin; Lynne Bennett; Peter Handley; Laurie Kidd; George Maroosis; Wayne Poeta; Anthony Rota; Arne Schmidt; Jack Smylie; Terry Talentino
Next Election: November 1997 (3 year terms)

ADMINISTRATION
City Clerk, Bonny Harrison
Treasurer, Brian Rogers
Administrator, Vacant
Chief Building Inspector, Brian Horsman
Chief of Police, Ron Nagel
City Solicitor, M.B. Burke
Director, Engineering & Environmental Services, Vacant
Director, Human Resources, R.A. Young
Director, Parks & Recreation, Vacant
Director, Planning & Economic Development, Steve M. Sajatovic
Director, Transportation & Works, Brian A. Baker
Fire Chief, E. (Ted) McCullough
Manager, Economic Development, Rick Evans
Manager, Environmental Services, Peter Bullock
Manager, Transit, Terry Brent
Medical Officer of Health, Dr. Catherine Whiting

District of NORTH VANCOUVER
355 West Queens Rd., North Vancouver BC V7L 4K1
604/987-7131, Fax: 604/984-9637, URL: http://www.district.north-van.bc.ca/
Incorporated: 1891
Area: 40,121 acres
Population: 78,161 (1995)

COUNCIL
Editor's Note: Results of the November 1996 election were not available at press time; up to date results may appear in the Addenda at the back of this book.
Next Election: November 1999 (3 year terms)

ADMINISTRATION
Acting Clerk, Agnes S. Hilsen
Director, Financial Services, M.S. Hoskin
Municipal Manager, G.M. Howie
Chief, Fire Services, R.A. Grant
Director, Corporate Services, D.C. Stuart
Director, Parks & Engineering Services, E.J. Bremner
Director, Planning & Development Services, R.E. Plunkett
Director, Recreation, Gary Young, 604/984-4181; Fax: 604/984-4294
Manager, Parks, Cameron Cairncross, 604/986-9141; Fax: 604/986-7968
Manager, Permits & Licenses, D.E. Pawson
Manager, Purchasing, Mike Chapman, 604/990-2261; Fax: 604/987-7185
Coordinator, North & West Vancouver Emergency Program, G.R. Peterson, 165 East 13th St., North Vancouver BC V7L 2L3, 604/985-3713; Fax: 604/985-3733
Medical Health Officer, Dr. Brian O'Connor, 132 West Esplanade, North Vancouver BC V7M 1A2, 604/983-6701; Fax: 604/983-6839
Project Manager, North Shore Economic Development Commission, Judy Perkins, 604/984-3580; Fax: 604/984-3563

City of NORTH YORK
5100 Yonge St., North York ON M2N 5V7
416/395-6910, Fax: 416/395-6920

Incorporated: February 14, 1979
Area: 69.5 sq. miles
Population: 549,115 (1994)

COUNCIL
Mayor, Mel Lastman
Councillors & Wards: 1) George Mammoliti; 2) Gina Severino; 3) Peter Li Preti; 4) Frank Di Giorgio; 5) Maria Rizzo; 6) Milton Berger; 7) Michael Feldman; 8) Joanne Flint; 9) Ronald Summers; 10) Don Yuill; 11) John Filion; 12) Denzil Minnan-Wong; 13) David Shiner; 14) Paul Sutherland
Metro Councillors & Wards: Black Creek) Maria Augimeri; Centre) Norman Gardner; Centre South) Bev Salmon; Don Parkway) Gordon Chong; Humber) Judy Sgro; Seneca Heights) Joan King; Spadina) Howard Moscoe
Next Election: November 1997 (3 year terms)

ADMINISTRATION
City Clerk, Denis G. Kelly, 416/395-7372; Fax: 416/395-7337
Treasurer & Commissioner, Finance, Wanda A. Liczyk, 416/395-6700; Fax: 416/395-6703
Commissioner, Building, E. Yarman Uzumeri, P.Eng, 416/395-7513; Fax: 416/395-7589
Commissioner, City Hall Building Services, Bob West, 416/395-6903
Commissioner, Human Resources, Ron Yarwood, 416/395-6970; Fax: 416/395-6985
Commissioner, Parks & Recreation, Joe Halstead, 416/395-6188
Commissioner, Planning, Paula Dill, 416/395-7150; Fax: 416/395-7155
Commissioner, Public Works, Alan Wolfe, P.Eng., 416/395-6242; Fax: 416/395-6200
Commissioner, Transportation, Jim Kinrade, 416/395-7474; Fax: 416/395-7482
City Solicitor, George M. Dixon, 416/395-7055; Fax: 416/395-7056
Fire Chief, Alan Speed, 416/395-7241; Fax: 416/395-7200
Medical Officer of Health, Public Health, Dr. Barbara Yaffe, 416/395-7611; Fax: 416/395-7691
Senior Officer, Economic Development, John Tracogna, 416/395-7407; Fax: 416/395-7431

Town of OAKVILLE
1225 Trafalgar Rd., PO Box 310, Oakville ON L6J 5A6
905/845-6601, Fax: 905/815-2025
Incorporated: May 27, 1857
Area: 55 sq. miles
Population: 118,063 (1994)

COUNCIL
Mayor, Ann Mulvale
Councillors & Wards: 1) Ralph Robinson; 2) Linda Hardacre; 3) Tedd Smith; 4) Mark Brown; 5) Sean Weir; 6) Mark Farrow
Local & Regional Councillors & Wards: 1) Kevin Flynn; 2) Kathy Graham; 3) Keith Bird; 4) Stephen Sparling; 5) Liz Behrens; 6) Anne Fairfield
Next Election: November 1997 (3 year terms)

ADMINISTRATION
Town Clerk, Judith Muncaster, 905/338-4178
Treasurer & Director, Finance, Michelle A. Séguin, ext.3062
Town Manager, Harry E. Henderson, 905/338-4176
Deputy Town Manager, Administrative Services, M.K. Wood, ext.3166
Deputy Town Manager, Community Services, P.F. Wagland, ext.3165
Deputy Town Manager, Development & Community Planning, R.H.B. Foy, ext.3164
Commissioner, By-law Enforcement & Licensing, P.J. Bouillon, ext.3252; Fax: 905/338-4230
Director, Human Resources, G.M. Zubyk, 905/338-4400
Director, Parks & Recreation, R.G. Perkins, ext.3112
Director, Planning Services, E.C. (Ted) Salisbury, 905/338-4185
Director, Public Works, Ray Green, ext.3300
Director, Purchasing & Office Services, R.J. Cournoyer, ext.3087
Fire Chief, D. Wayne Gould, 905/338-4426
General Manager, Economic Development Office, John Meyerstein, ext.3030
Town Solicitor, D.L. Gates, Fax: 905/338-4184

City of OSHAWA
City Hall, 50 Centre St. South, Oshawa ON L1H 3Z7
905/725-7351
Incorporated: March 8, 1924
Area: 14,245 ha (143 sq. km)
Population: 132,500 (1995)

COUNCIL
Mayor, Nancy Diamond, Fax: 905/436-5691
City Councillors & Wards: Central) D. Dykstra; North) J. Wiley; South) J. Kolodzie; Southeast) A. Mason; West) J. Spring
Regional & City Councillors & Wards: 1) B. Nicholson; 2) P. Beal; 3) R. Lutczyk; 4) N. Pidwerbecki; 5) J. Gray; 6) B. Boychyn; 7) C. Clarke; 8) J. Aker; 9) J. Potticary; 10) I. Harrell
Next Election: November 1997 (3 year terms)

ADMINISTRATION
City Clerk, B. Suter, Fax: 905/436-5697
City Treasurer, N. Tellis, Fax: 905/436-5618
City Manager, J. Brown, 905/436-5622; Fax: 905/436-5623
Commissioner, Community Services, S. Bedford, Fax: 905/436-5692
Commissioner, Development & Planning Services, T. Goodchild, Fax: 905/436-5699
Commissioner, Corporate Services, J. Baker, Fax: 905/436-5689
Commissioner, Public Works Services, A. Myklebost, Fax: 905/436-5694
Director, Budget Services, R. Stockman
Director, Economic Development, Don O'Leary
Director, Engineering, J. Simmonds
Director, Information Management Services, D. Powell
Director, Legal Services, R. Holland, Fax: 905/436-5689
Acting Director, Operations, M. Sims
Director, Parks & Facilities, N. Hutchinson
Director, Personnel, B.D. Gough, Fax: 905/436-5698
Director, Treasury & Fiscal Services, A.P. Geboers
Fire Chief (Emergency Response), M. Wilson, Fax: 905/433-0276
Maintenance Engineer, Byron Simmons, Fax: 905/436-5694
Manager, Buildings, G.N. Bilous
Manager, Planning, B. Hunt
Tax Collector, T. Dwyer
Manager, Oshawa Transit, N. Tweedle, 710 Raleigh Ave., Oshawa ON L1H 3T2, 905/579-2471; Fax: 905/579-1050

City of OTTAWA
City Hall, 111 Sussex Dr., Ottawa ON K1N 5A1
613/244-5300, Fax: 613/244-5396, http://www.ottawa.com/
Incorporated: December 18, 1854
Area: 110.15 sq. km
Population: 313,971 (1994)

COUNCIL
Mayor, Jacquelin Holzman
Councillors & Wards: 1) Ron Kolbus; 2) Brian Mackey; 3) Diane Deans; 4) Richard Cannings; 5) Stéphane Émard-Chabot; 6) Elisabeth Arnold; 7) Joan Wong; 8) Karin Howard; 9) Jim Watson; 10) Allan Higdon
Next Election: November 1997 (3 year terms)

ADMINISTRATION
City Clerk, Pierre Pagé, Fax: 613/244-5417
Treasurer & Director, Corporate Finances, George Montgomery
Chief Administrative Officer, David O'Brien
Commissioner, Corporate Services, Suzanne McGlashan
Commissioner, Engineering & Works Dept., Ted Robinson, 111 Sussex Dr., Ottawa ON K1N 5A1, 613/ext. 3035
Commissioner, Housing, 11 Holland Ave., Ottawa ON K1Y 4S1, 613/564-8432; Fax: 613/564-8558
Commissioner, Planning, Economic Development & Housing, James L. Sevigny, ext.3046; Fax: 613/244-5619
Commissioner, Recreation & Culture, Don Gamble, 11 Holland Ave., 613/564-1893; Fax: 613/564-8427
Chief of Police, B. Ford
City Auditor, Peter O'Callaghan
City Solicitor & Director, Corporate Law, Douglas R. Wallace
Director, Human Resources, Pierre Charette
Civic Complaints Bureau, 1600 Scott St., 2nd Fl., Ottawa ON K1Y 4N7, 613/564-1111; Fax: 613/564-2688
Fire Chief, Ronald Horrocks, 1445 Carling Ave., Ottawa ON K1Z 7L9, 613/564-1675; Fax: 613/564-8043
General Manager, Non-Profit Housing, 11 Holland Ave., Ottawa ON K1Y 4S1, 613/564-8432; Fax: 613/564-8558

City of PETERBOROUGH
500 George St. North, Peterborough ON K9H 3R9
705/742-7771, Fax: 705/743-7825
Incorporated: 1850
Area: 51.82 sq. km
Population: 66,494 (1994)

COUNCIL
Mayor, Jack Doris
Aldermen & Wards: Ashburnham) D. Paul Ayotte, Patti S. Peeters; Monaghan) Michael McIntyre, George G. Mitchell; Northcrest) Dean Wasson, Roy Wood; Otonabee) Jeffrey Leal, Glenn Pagett; Town) Sean Eyre, Paul Wilson
Next Election: November 1997 (3 year terms)

ADMINISTRATION
City Clerk, Steven F. Brickell, 705/748-8816
City Treasurer, B. Horton, 705/748-8863
City Administrator, R. Chittick, 705/748-8810
Chief of Police, K. McAlpine, 705/876-1122
City Engineer, Barry Poulton, 705/748-8885; Fax: 705/876-4610
City Solicitor, J. Hart, 705/748-8896; Fax: 705/742-3947
Director, Community Services, R. Browne, 705/748-8822
Director, Planning & Development, Malcolm Hunt, 705/748-8881; Fax: 705/742-5218
Emergency Planning Officer, R. Manley, 705/748-8820
Fire Chief, L. Grant, 705/745-2460
Manager, Public Works, P. Heffernan, 705/745-1386; Fax: 705/743-3223
Manager, Purchasing, Stephen MacPhee, 705/748-8855
Manager, Transportation, J. Kimble, 705/748-8895

Town of PICKERING
Pickering Civic Complex, One The Esplanade, Pickering ON L1V 6K7
905/683-2760, Fax: 905/420-0515
Incorporated: early 1800s

Canadian Almanac & Directory 1997

Area: 55,974 acres (22,652 ha)
Population: 70,733 (1994)

COUNCIL
Mayor, Wayne Arthurs
Local Councillors & Wards: 1) Dave Ryan; 2) Sherry Senis; 3) Enrico Pistritto
Regional Councillors & Wards: 1) Maurice Brenner; 2) David Farr; 3) Rick Johnson
Next Election: November 1997 (3 year terms)

ADMINISTRATION
Town Clerk, Bruce J. Taylor, 905/420-4611
Treasurer-Collector, Jim Walls, 905/420-4614
Executive Director, Operations, Thomas J. Quinn, 905/420-4648; Fax: 905/420-7648
Town Manager, C.M. Timothy Sheffield, 905/420-4620; Fax: 905/420-6064
Director, Culture & Recreation, Stephen Reynolds, 905/420-4620
Director, Human Resources, Dayle Cameron
Director, Legal Services, Penny Wyger, 905/420-4626; Fax: 905/420-7648
Director, Parks & Facilities, Everett Buntsma, 905/420-4624; Fax: 905/420-7648
Director, Personnel, H. Duane Reid
Director, Planning, Neil Carroll, 905/420-4617; Fax: 905/420-7648
Director, Public Works, Richard Holborn, 905/420-4360; Fax: 905/420-4650
Fire Chief, Rick Pearsall, 905/839-8095; Fax: 905/839-6327
Transit Supervisor, Transportation Services, Neil Killens, 905/683-1179; Fax: 905/683-5314

City of PORTAGE LA PRAIRIE
97 Saskatchewan Ave. East, Portage la Prairie MB R1N 0L8
204/239-8337, Fax: 204/239-1532
Incorporated: 1907
Population: 13,186 (1991)

COUNCIL
Mayor, Glenn Carlson
Aldermen: Harold Clayton; Bill Hamilton; Hugh Kennedy; Ian MacKenzie; Dave Quinn; Ross Smith
Next Election: October 1998 (3 year terms)

ADMINISTRATION
City Manager, Dale Lyle
Director, Finance & Administration, Vacant
Director, Economic & Community Development, Dean Yaremchuk
Director, Operations, Kelly Braden
Director, Public Safety, Wayne Christie

City of PRINCE ALBERT
City Hall, 1084 Central Ave., Prince Albert SK S6V 7P3
306/953-4305, Fax: 306/953-4313
Incorporated: October 8, 1904
Area: 64.97 sq. km
Population: 34,181 (1991)

COUNCIL
Mayor, Don Cody
Councillors: 1) Lawrence Joseph; 2) Phil West; 3) Grethyll Adams; 4) Jim Stiglitz; 5) Frank Harris; 6) Arne Lindberg; 7) Jack Matheson; 8) James Bristowe
Next Election: October 1997 (3 year terms)

ADMINISTRATION
Director & City Clerk, Charmaine Code, 306/953-4305
City Commissioner, Terry Topping, 306/953-4300
Chief of Police, Greg McCullagh, 306/953-4240
City Engineer, Arnie McKay, 306/953-4900
Asst City Engineer, Operations, Jack Jensen

City Solicitor, Jean Maksymiuk, 306/953-4315
Director, Assessment & Taxation, D. Bell, 306/953-4320
Director, Financial Services, Ken Enion, 306/953-4330
Director, Human Resources & Corporate Communication Services, Laurent Mougeot, 306/953-4310
Director, Parks & Recreation, Blair Hoffman, 306/953-4800
Director, Planning & Economic Development, Denton Yeo, 306/953-4370
Fire Chief/EMO Coordinator, Brian Shand, 306/953-4202
Manager, Collection-Distribution, Kevin Callaghan, 306/953-4900
Manager, Sanitation, Robert Burns, 306/953-4900
Manager, Surface Works, Verden Jeancart, 306/953-4900
Manager, Transportation, Ron Liebreich, 306/953-4900
Purchasing Agent, Terry Tolley, 306/953-4350
Environmental Committee, 1084 Central Ave., Prince Albert SK S6V 7P3, 306/953-4900; Fax: 306/953-4353

City of PRINCE GEORGE
City Hall, 1100 Patricia Blvd., Prince George BC V2L 3V9
250/561-7600, Fax: 250/561-0183, http://vortex.net-bistro.com/pg/index.html
Incorporated: 1915
Area: 123 sq. miles
Population: 75,000 (1996)

COUNCIL
Editor's Note: Results of the November 1996 election were not available at press time; up to date results may appear in the Addenda at the back of this book.
Next Election: November 1999 (3 year terms)

ADMINISTRATION
City Clerk, Allan Chabot, 250/561-7250
Treasurer & Director, Bill Kennedy, 250/561-7603
City Engineer, Dwayne Halldorson, P.Eng., 250/561-7660; Fax: 250/561-7720
City Manager, George Paul, 250/561-7607
Director, Development Services, Peter Bloodoff, 250/561-7616; Fax: 250/561-7721
Director, Fire Services, Mike Dornbierier, 250/561-7670; Fax: 250/561-7703
Director, Human Resources, Kathleen Soltis, 250/561-7626; Fax: 250/561-7719
Director, Leisure Services, Tom Madden, 250/561-7644; Fax: 250/561-7718
Director, Public Works, Gary Champagne, 250/561-7500; Fax: 250/561-7502
Manager, Bylaw Services, Norm Hudon, 250/561-7623; Fax: 250/561-7724
Manager, Police Services, Carol Wells, 250/561-3306
Purchasing Agent, Scott Bone, 250/561-7511; Fax: 250/563-8420

Ville de QUÉBEC
Hôtel de ville, 2, rue des Jardins, CP 700, Succ Haute-Ville, Québec PQ G1R 4S9
418/691-7041, Fax: 418/691-2346
Incorporée: 25 avril, 1883
Superficie: 88.9 sq. km
Population: 175,039 (1993)

CONSEIL
Maire, Jean-Paul L'Allier
Conseillers et Districts: 1) Donald Baillargeon; 2) Claude Larose; 3) André Forgues; 4) Françoise Viger; 5) Francine Roberge; 6) Alain Delwaide; 7) Réjean Lemoine; 8) Jacques Fiset; 9) Pierre-André Gaudreault; 10) André Marier; 11) Lynda Cloutier; 12) Lyse Poirier; 13) Richard Dugas; 14) Yvon Bussières; 15) Gilles Trudel; 16) Gérald Poirier; 17) Charlotte M. Munger; 18) Bruno Maltais; 19) Claude Cantin; 20) Jacques Jobin
Prochaine election: novembre 1997 (mandat de 4 ans)

ADMINISTRATION
Greffier, Me. Antoine Carrier, LL.B., 418/691-6076
Trésorier et Directeur, Finances et Administration, Guy Martineau, c.a., 418/691-6024; Fax: 418/691-6088
Directeur général, Serge Viau, ing., Fax: 418/691-6313
Directeur général adjoint, Hervé Brosseau, LL.B., Fax: 418/691-6313
Avocat, Contentieux, Me Denis Boutin, Fax: 418/691-7622
Directeur, Approvisionnement, Jean Chabot, Fax: 418/691-7025
Directeur, Commission de l'exposition provinciale, René Proulx, Fax: 418/691-7249
Directeur, Communications et Relations extérieures, Gilbert Athot, 418/691-7672; Fax: 418/691-7219
Directeur, Développement économique et urbain, Réal Charest, Fax: 418/691-4683
Directeur, Entretien des équipements, Michel Hallé, ing., Fax: 418/691-7421
Directrice, Environnement, Madeleine Paulin, 418/691-6899; Fax: 418/691-7642
Directeur, Gestion de l'information, André Boucher, Fax: 418/691-7681
Directeur, Ingénierie, Claude Goulet, ing., 418/691-6702; Fax: 418/691-4684
Directeur, Loisir, culture et vie communautaire, Michel Choquette, Fax: 418/691-4683
Directeur (par intérim), Office municipal d'habitation de Québec, Jacques Mathieu, Fax: 418/691-7358
Directeur, Planification, Pierre-Paul Gingras, 418/691-6425; Fax: 418/691-6161
Directeur, Police, Normand Bergeron, Fax: 418/691-4747
Directeur, Protection contre l'incendie, Henri Labadie, 418/691-6720; Fax: 418/691-6989
Directeur, Ressources humaines, François Jutras, Fax: 418/691-7635
Directeur (par intérim), SOM-HADEC, Brigitte Mercier, ing., Fax: 418/691-7508
Directeur, Travaux Publics, Jean Lavoie, ing, 418/691-6392; Fax: 418/691-6707
Vérificateur, Lambert Legaré, c.a.

City of RED DEER
City Hall, PO Box 5008, Red Deer AB T4N 3T4
403/342-8111, 8132, Fax: 403/346-6195
Incorporated: March 25, 1913
Area: 59.5 sq. km
Population: 59,834 (1996)

COUNCIL
Mayor, Gail Surkan
Councillors: Jeffrey Dawson; Morris Flewwelling; Bev Hughes; Bill Hull; Dennis Moffat; Robert E. Schnell; Jason Volk; Lorna Watkinson-Zimmer
Next Election: October 1998 (3 year terms)

ADMINISTRATION
Clerk, Kelly Kloss, 403/342-8134
Manager, Treasury Services, Doug Norris, 403/342-8203
City Manager, H.M.C. (Mike) Day, 413/342-8156
City Assessor, Al Knight, 403/342-8120
Director, Community Services, Lowell Hodgson, 403/342-8323
Director, Corporate Services, Alan Wilcock, 403/342-8203
Director, Development Services, Bryon Jeffers, 403/342-8158
Fire Chief, Robert Oscroft, 403/346-5511; Fax: 403/343-1866

Inspector, RCMP City Detachment, Scott Sutton, 403/341-2000
Manager, Engineering Development, Ken Haslop, 403/342-8158
Manager, Information Technology Services, Dale Smith, 403/342-8392
Manager, Inspections & Licensing, Ryan Strader, 403/342-8195; Fax: 403/347-1138
Manager, Land & Economic Development, Alan Scott, 403/342-8106
Manager, Personnel, Grant Howell, 403/342-8148
Manager, Public Works, Gordon Stewart, 403/342-8238; Fax: 403/343-7074
Manager, Recreation, Parks & Culture, Don Batchelor, 403/342-8159
Manager, Transit, Kevin Joll, 403/342-8225
Acting Purchasing Agent, Shirley McKenzie, 403/342-8293

City of REGINA
PO Box 1790, Regina SK S4P 3C8
306/777-7000, Fax: 306/777-6802
Incorporated: June 19, 1903
Area: 110 sq. km
Population: 184,000 (1995)

COUNCIL
Mayor, Doug Archer
Councillors: Mike Badham; Fred Clipsham; Rob Deglau; Bill Gray; Ray Hamilton; Darlene Hincks; Bill Hutchison; Vic McDougall; Linda McKay; Bill Wells
Next Election: October 1997 (3 year terms)

ADMINISTRATION
City Clerk, Randy Markewich, 306/777-7264
Director, Finance, Doug Fisher, 306/777-7317
City Manager, Bob Linner, 306/777-7314
Director, Support Services, Randy Garvey, 306/777-7038
City Auditor General, Wolfgang Langenbacher, 306/777-7619
City Solicitor, Leslie Shaw, 306/777-7472
Director, Community Services, Bland Brown, 306/777-7318
Director, Fire Services, Hugh Gordon, 306/777-7833
Director, Human Resources, Cal Barks, 403/777-7703
Acting Director, Information Services, D. Scott, 306/777-7258
Director, Municipal Engineering, David Calam, 306/777-7438; Fax: 306/777-6806
Director, Planning & Building, M. Afsar, 306/777-7551; Fax: 306/777-6823
Director, Property Development, L. Boyko, 306/777-7491
Director, Public Affairs, M. Gregory, 306/777-7499
Director, Public Works, Bill Aldcorn, 306/777-7650; Fax: 306/777-6801
Director, Transit, Don Hnetka, 306/777-7775

City of RICHMOND
6911 - No. 3 Rd., Richmond BC V6Y 2C1
604/276-4000, Fax: 604/278-5139
Incorporated: 1879
Area: 16,818 ha (41,529 acres)
Population: 140,024 (1994)

COUNCIL
Editor's Note: Results of the November 1996 election were not available at press time; up to date results may appear in the Addenda at the back of this book.
Next Election: November 1999 (3 year terms)

ADMINISTRATION
City Clerk, Richard McKenna, 604/276-4007
Finance Administrator, Jim Bruce, 604/276-4095
Administrator, Johnny Carline, 604/276-4153
Deputy Administrator, Gord Howie, 604/276-4153
Administrator, Community Services, Mike Brow, 604/276-4107
Administrator, Public Works, George Duncan, 604/244-1204
Administrator, Urban Development, Ron Mann, 604/276-4082
City Solicitor, Paul Kendrick, 604/276-4104
Director, Information Services, Brian Sameshima, 604/276-4080
Director, Permits & Licenses, Bob Switzer, 604/278-5575
Director, Personnel, Anne Smith, 604/276-4105
Fire Chief, John Lysholm, 604/278-5131
Manager, Environment & Land Use, Eleanor G. Atienza, 604/276-4139; Fax: 276-4177
Medical Health Officer, Dr. John Garry, 604/276-4050
RCMP Officer-in-Charge, Supt. Ernie MacAulay, 604/278-1212

Town of RICHMOND HILL
225 East Beaver Creek Rd., PO Box 300, Richmond Hill ON L4C 4Y5
905/771-8800, Fax: 905/771-2400
Incorporated: 1957
Area: 25,167 acres
Population: 87,000 (1994)

COUNCIL
Mayor, William Bell, 905/884-1179
Councillors & Wards: 1) Vito Spadafora; 2) Brenda Hogg; 3) David L. Cohen; 4) Jane Robertson; 5) Nick Papa; 6) Bryon Wilfert
Regional & Local Councillors: Gail Blackburn; Janet Mabley
Next Election: November 1997 (3 year terms)

ADMINISTRATION
Town Clerk, Robert Douglas, Fax: 905/771-2502
Treasurer & Commissioner, Finance, S. Zorbas, Fax: 905/771-2501
Chief Administrative Officer, C.D. Weldon, Fax: 905/771-2406
Commissioner, Parks & Recreation, Lynton Friedberg, 905/771-8870; Fax: 905/771-2481
Commissioner, Planning & Development, J.E. Babcock, 905/771-8910; Fax: 905/771-2404
Commissioner, Transportation & Works, M.A. McCauley, 905/771-8830; Fax: 905/771-2405
Fire Chief, R.G. Kennedy, 905/883-5444; Fax: 905/883-0866
Manager, Corporate Communications, C. Moore
Manager, Transit, W.J. Newton, Fax: 905/771-2408
Town Solicitor, A.T. Kowalishin, Fax: 905/771-2408

Corporation of SAANICH
770 Vernon Ave., Victoria BC V8X 2W7
250/475-1775, Fax: 250/475-5400
Incorporated: March 1, 1906
Area: 41.42 sq. miles
Population: 105,100 (1995)

COUNCIL
Editor's Note: Results of the November 1996 election were not available at press time; up to date results may appear in the Addenda at the back of this book.
Next Election: November 1999 (3 year terms)

ADMINISTRATION
Municipal Clerk, Terry R. Kirk, ext.3500; Fax: 250/475-5440
Controller-Treasurer, Ronald Porter
Administrator, R.M. Sharp
Chief of Police, W. Nixon
City Solicitor, C.G. Nation
Director, Parks & Recreation, D.W. Hunter, ext.5422; Fax: 250/475-5450
Director, Personnel, L. Teal
Fire Chief, David W. Hill, 250/475-5500, ext.3612; Fax: 250/475-5505
Manager, Engineering Services, H. McKay, ext.3450; Fax: 250/475-5450
Manager, Purchasing, N. Duckworth, ext.3480
Municipal Planner, A. Hopper, ext.3400; Fax: 250/475-5450

City of ST CATHARINES
City Hall, 50 Church St., PO Box 3012, St. Catharines ON L2R 7C2
905/688-5600, Fax: 905/682-3631
Incorporated: 1876
Area: 38.38 sq. miles
Population: 125,887 (1994)

COUNCIL
Mayor, Alan L. Unwin
Councillors & Wards: 1) Wendy Patriquin, William Wiley; 2) Judy Casselman, Joseph Kushner; 3) Alex Christie, Michael Collins; 4) Rick Dykstra, Jackie Phelan; 5) Brian Heit, Brian McMullan; 6) Erick R. Roberts, Bruce Williamson
Next Election: November 1997 (3 year terms)

ADMINISTRATION
City Clerk & Director, Corporate Support Services, Kenneth R. Todd, C.M.O.
City Treasurer & Director, Financial Management Services, Colin E. Briggs
Chief Administrative Officer, B. Robert Puhach
City Engineer & Director, Transportation & Environmental Services, Paul Mustard
Director, Recreation & Community Services, William Fenwick
Superintendent, Operations, Gord Harry
Building Inspector, John Fisher
Environmental Coordinator, Jim Horton
Fire Chief, Thomas Johnson
Solicitor, A. Poulin
General Manager, St. Catharines Transit Commission, Eric Gillespie, 2012 First St. South, RR#3, St. Catharines ON L2S 3V9, 905/685-4228; Fax: 905/685-4050

Ville de STE-FOY
1130, rte de l'Église, CP 218, Ste-Foy PQ G1V 4E1
418/650-7925, Fax: 418/650-7972
Incorporée: 1949
Superficie: 83.32 sq. km
Population: 74,328 (1993)

CONSEIL
Mairesse, Andrée P.-Boucher
Conseillers et Districts: 1) Gilles Lavoie; 2) Élie Duchesneau; 3) Georges Trépanier; 4.) Jean Normand; 5) Gilles Bolduc; 6) Odette Fleming; 7) Claude Allard; 8) Denis Racine; 9) Armand Thibodeau; 10) Gilles Latulippe; 11) Guy Filion; 12) Thomas Hughes
Prochaine election: 3 novembre 1997 (mandat de 4 ans)

ADMINISTRATION
Greffier et Directeur général adjoint, René Damphousse, 418/650-7925
Directeur, Trésorerie, Rémi Beaudoin, 418/650-7949
Directeur général, Alain Marcoux, 418/650-7958
Chef, Incendies, Pierre Leclair
Coordonnateur, Communications, Gilles Noël, 418/650-7906
Coordonnateur, Contentieux, Me Serge Giasson, 418/650-7927
Directeur, Approvisionnement et Équipement, René Lachance, 418/650-7910

Directeur, Contrôle du développement et de la cartographie, Roch Laliberté, 418/650-7902
Directrice, Loisirs, Pascale Guimont, 418/650-7935
Directeur, Personnel, Pierre-André Thomas, 418/650-7936
Directeur, Protection publique, Pierre Leclair, 418/654-4261
Directeur, Service du génie, Clément Bérubé, 418/650-7922
Directeur, Systèmes, Claude Hudon, 418/650-7907
Directeur, Travaux publics, Jacques Tessier, 418/650-7955

Ville de ST-HUBERT
5900, boul Cousineau, St-Hubert PQ J3Y 7K8
514/445-7600, Fax: 514/445-7847
Incorporée: 1860
Superficie: 68 sq. km
Population: 78,171 (1995)

CONSEIL
Editor's Note: Results of the November 1996 election were not available at press time; for up to date results refer to the Addenda at the back of this book.
Prochaine election: novembre 2000 (mandat de 4 ans)

ADMINISTRATION
Directeur général, Guy Benedetti
Directrice, Communications, Lise Gagnon Hosson
Directeur, Loisir et de la vie communautaire, Donald Courcy
Directeur, Permis et évaluation, Gilles Rodrigue
Directrice, Planification et développement, Huguette Béland
Directeur, Police, incendies et mesures d'urgence, Pierre Trudeau
Directeur, Secrétariat administratif et juridique, Bernard Houle
Directeur, Services administratifs, Pierre Archambault
Directeur, Services techniques, Denis Gélinas, ing.
Directeur, Travaux publics, Michel Sarrazin, ing.F.
Directeur adjoint, Informatique, Daniel Doiron
Chef de division, Permis et évaluation, Jean Larose
Commissaire, Développement économique, Francis Thibeault
Conseiller, Développement et projets spéciaux, Roger Inkel

City of SAINT JOHN
City Hall, Market Sq., PO Box 1971, Saint John NB E2L 4L1
506/658-2800, Fax: 506/658-2802, URL: http://www.city.saint-john.nb.ca
Incorporated: May 18, 1785
Area: 121.69 sq. miles
Population: 74,969 (1991)

COUNCIL
Mayor, Shirley McAlary
Councillors: Shirley Arthurs; Walter Ball; Sterling Brown; Derek Chase; Stephen Fitzpatrick; Arthur L. Gould; Dennis R. Knibb; Peter Trites; M.A. Vincent; Christopher Waldschutz
Next Election: May 1998 (3 year terms)

ADMINISTRATION
Common Clerk, Mary L. Munford, 506/658-2862
Commissioner, Finance, Daryl Wilson, 506/658-2951
City Manager, Terrence Totten, 506/658-2913
Commissioner, Municipal Operations, Charles Robichaud, P.Eng., 506/658-2818; Fax: 506/658-2852
Commissioner, Community Services, William Butler, P.Eng., Fax: 506/658-2879
Commissioner, Environment & Development Services, Claude MacKinnon, P.Eng., 506/658-2876; Fax: 506/658-2837

Commissioner, Human Resources, Paul Groody, 506/658-2866
Building Inspector, Bill Edwards, P.Eng., 506/658-2911; Fax: 506/658-2879
City Solicitor, John Nugent, 506/658-2860
Director, Engineering, Stuart Armstrong, P.Eng., 506/658-2818; Fax: 506/658-2852
Director, Municipal Works, Shayne Galbraith, P.Eng., 506/658-2826; Fax: 506/658-4740
Director, Parks, Bernard Morrison, 506/658-2841; Fax: 506/658-2902
Director, Recreation, J. Brownell, 506/658-2908
Director, Tourism & Communications, Yvonne Huntington, 506/658-2990; Fax: 506/632-6118
Fire Chief, Glen Tait, 506/658-2910; Fax: 506/658-2916
General Manager, Economic Development, Steve Carson
General Manager, Transit, Frank McCarey, PO Box 3860, Saint John NB E2M 5C2, 506/658-4700; Fax: 506/658-4704
Manager, Planning, Jim Baird
Police Chief, D. Sherwood, Fax: 506/648-3304
Purchasing Agent, David Logan, Fax: 506/658-4742

City of ST. JOHN'S
City Hall, PO Box 908, St. John's NF A1C 5M2
709/576-8600, Fax: 709/576-8474
Incorporated: 1888
Area: 493 sq. km
Population: 103,502 (1992)

COUNCIL
Mayor, John J. Murphy
Councillors: Jeffrey Brace; Raymond O'Neill; Marie White; Dorothy Wyatt; 1) Sean Hanrahan; 2) Shawn Skinner; 3) Keith Coombs; 4) Gerard Colbert; 5) John Dinn
Deputy Mayor: Andrew Wells
Next Election: November 1997 (4 year terms)

ADMINISTRATION
City Clerk & Director, Administrative Services, Damian Ryan
Treasurer & Director, Finance, Robert Bishop, C.A., 709/576-8347; Fax: 709/576-8564
City Manager, Vacant, 709/576-8671
Chief Commisssioner & City Solicitor, Ron Penney, 709/576-8641; Fax: 709/576-8561
Assoc. Commissioner & Director, Building & Property Management, Wayne Purchase, 709/576-8701; Fax: 709/576-8160
Assoc. Commissioner & Director, Engineering & Planning, Art Cheeseman, 709/576-8658
Director, Human Resources, Guy Annable, 709/576-8213; Fax: 709/576-8575
Director, Public Works & Parks, Paul Mackey, 709/576-8303; Fax: 709/576-8026
Manager, Economic Development, Ed Breen, 709/576-8572; Fax: 709/576-8246
Manager, Environmental Initiatives, Geraldine King, 709/576-8613
Manager, Parks Service, Jim Clark, 709/576-8541; Fax: 709/576-8073
Manager, Tourism Division, Kevin Gushue, 709/567-8545; Fax: 709/576-8246
Purchasing Agent, Melvin Rowe, 709/576-8152; Fax: 709/576-8470
Real Estate Officer, Garth Griffiths, C.E.T., 709/576-8440; Fax: 709/576-8561
Staff Engineer, Transportation, Robin King, 709/576-8625; Fax: 709/576-8604
St. John's Transportation Commission, 245 Freshwater Rd., St. John's NF A1B 1B3, 709/722-3929; Fax: 709/722-0018

Ville de SAINT-LAURENT
777, boul Marcel-Laurin, Saint-Laurent PQ H4M 2M7
514/855-6000, Fax: 514/855-5999
Incorporée: 27 février, 1893
Superficie: 43 sq. km (16.6 sq. mi)
Population: 73,358 (1994)

CONSEIL
Maire, Dr. Bernard Paquet
Conseillers et Districts: 1) Ivette Biondi; 2) Michèle D. Biron; 3) Pierre Lambert; 4) René Dussault; 5) Micheline Roy; 6) Roland Bouchard; 7) Charles. Benchimol; 8) Jean-René Taschereau; 9) Alan DeSousa; 10) Ronald Moreau; 11) Irving Grundman; 12) Maurice Cohen; 13) Alfred Giannetti; 14) François Ghali
Prochaine election: novembre 1998 (mandat de 4 ans)

ADMINISTRATION
Greffière, Édith Baron-Lafrenière
Trésorier, Jean Kahalé, c.g.a.
Directeur général, Pierre Lebeau, c.g.a.
Directeur, Communications, Jacques Viens, 514/855-5701; Fax: 514/855-5709
Directeur, Ingénierie et Environnement, Douglas B. Floreani, ing., 514/855-5960; Fax: 514/855-5959
Directeur, Loisirs, Guy Bourgon
Directeur, Prévention de l'incendie, Charles St-Onge, 514/956-2504; Fax: 514/855-5838
Directeur, Travaux publics, Jacques Brassard
Directeur, Urbanisme, Claude Charette, ing., urb.
Directeur adjoint, Inspection et permis, Mario Duchesne, arch., 514/855-5975

Ville de ST-LÉONARD
8400, boul Lacordaire, St-Léonard PQ H1R 3B1
514/328-8400, Fax: 514/328-8479
Incorporée: 1886
Superficie: 13.63 sq. km
Population: 74,083 (1994)

CONSEIL
Maire, Frank Zampino
Conseillers et Districts: 1) John Valentini; 2) Tommaso Nanci; 3) Mario Battista; 4) Italo Barone; 5) Alexandre Pacetti; 6) Dominic Perri; 7) Yvette Bissonnet; 8) Vincenzo Arciresi; 9) André Chrétien; 10) Domenico Moschella; 11) Jean-Jacques Goyette; 12) Robert L. Zambito
Prochaine election: novembre 1998 (mandat de 4 ans)

ADMINISTRATION
Greffier, Georges Larivée, o.m.a.
Finances, Sylvie A. Brunet
Directeur général, Pierre Santamaria, ing.
Directeur général adjoint, Gérard Soulard
Génie, Pierre Egesbourg, ing.
Loisirs communautaires, Claude Martineau
Personnel, Jean-Claude Durand
Prévention des incendies, André Medzalabanleth
Services techniques, Vilis Preiss, ing., 514/328-8345
Urbaniste, M.F. Frigon

City of SARNIA
City Hall, 255 North Christina St., PO Box 3018, Sarnia ON N7T 7N2
519/332-0330, Fax: 519/332-3995
Incorporated: May 7, 1914
Area: 43,762 acres
Population: 69,657 (1994)

COUNCIL
Mayor, Mike Bradley
City & County Aldermen & Wards: 1) Jim Foubister; 3) Terry Burrell; 4) John Kowalyshyn

City Aldermen & Wards: 1) John Vollmar; 2) Dave Brown; 3) Pat O'Brien; 4) Andy Bruziewicz
Next Election: November 1997 (3 year terms)

ADMINISTRATION
City Clerk & Commissioner, Administrative Services, Ann Tuplin
City Treasurer, Dean A. Anderson
City Manager, Ronald E. Brooks
Administrator, Legal Services, Valerie M'Garry
Director, Building Services, Jacques Skutt
Director, Community Services, Terry McCallum, ext.200
Director, Development Planning, Michael Shnare
Director, Engineering, Reg McMichael, ext.284
Director, Human Resources, Jim Colquhoun
Director, Information Services, Ronald Marshall
Director, Operations, A.J. Morrison
Director, Parks & Facilities, Colleen Johnston
Director, Policy Planning, Peter Hungerford
Director, Transit, Lorraine George
EMO Officer, Bruce Middleton
Fire Chief, Owen Forsythe
Police Chief, Murray McMaster
Purchasing Officer, M. José

City of SASKATOON
City Hall, 222 - 3 Ave. North, Saskatoon SK S7K 0J5
306/975-3200
Incorporated: May 26, 1906
Area: 14,574.04 ha
Population: 195,597 (1994)

COUNCIL
Mayor, Henry Dayday
Councillors: Jill Postlethwaite; 1) Herve Langlois; 2) Anita Langford; 3) Rik Steernberg; 4) Myles Heidt; 5) Peter McCann; 6) Kate Waygood; 7) Patricia Roe; 9) Donna Birkmaier; 10) Done Atchinson
Next Election: October 1997 (3 year terms)

ADMINISTRATION
City Clerk, Janice Mann, 306/975-3240; Fax: 306/975-2784
General Manager, Asset Management, Larry Ollenberger, 306/975-2990; Fax: 306/975-3034
Auditor General, Bob Prosser, 306/975-3274; Fax: 306/975-2784
City Solicitor, Theresa Dust, 306/975-3270; Fax: 306/975-7828
Director, Planning & Development, K. Pontikes, 306/975-3208; Fax: 306/975-3048
General Manager, Environmental Services, Randy Munch, P.Eng., 306/975-2562; Fax: 306/975-2553
General Manager, Finance, Phil Richards, 306/975-3206; Fax: 306/975-7975
General Manager, Fire & Protective Services, William Hewitt, 306/975-2575; Fax: 306/975-2589
General Manager, Human Resources, Shelley Chirpilo, 306/975-3265; Fax: 306/975-3073
General Manager, Leisure Services, Paul Gauthier, 306/975-3337; Fax: 306/975-3185
General Manager, Planning & Building, Lee Ann Coveyduck, 306/975-2654; Fax: 306/975-7712
General Manager, Public Works, Stewart Uzelman, P. Eng., 306/975-2450; Fax: 306/975-2971
General Manager, Transportation, Tom Mercer, P. Eng., 306/975-2630; Fax: 306/975-7672
Police Chief, Dave Scott, 306/975-8286; Fax: 306/975-8319

City of SAULT STE. MARIE
Civic Centre, 99 Foster Dr., PO Box 580, Sault Ste Marie ON P6A 5N1
705/759-2500, Fax: 705/759-2310
Incorporated: 1912
Area: 92 sq. miles
Population: 78,399 (1994)

COUNCIL
Mayor, Stephen E. Butland
Councillors & Wards: 1) Jack Moore, Charles Swift; 2) Jack Cameletti, Udo Rauk; 3) Mary Borowicz, John Solski; 4) Rick Niro, Michael Sanzosti; 5) Walter Chisholm, Wayne DeLuca; 6) Ed Szczepanik, Gary Trembinski
Next Election: November 1997 (3 year terms)

ADMINISTRATION
City Clerk, Donna P. Irving, 705/759-5388
Treasurer & Commissioner, Finance, William Freiburger, 705/759-5350
Chief Administrative Officer, Joseph M. Fratesi, 705/759-5347
Commissioner, Administrative Services, Walter Lamming, 705/759-5283
Commissioner, Community Services, Reginald B. Avery, 705/759-5310
Acting Commissioner, Engineering & Planning, Patrick M. McAuley, 705/759-5378
Commissioner, Personnel, John Luszka, 705/759-5361
Commissioner, Public Works & Traffic, Melvin W. Brechin, 705/541-7000; Fax: 705/541-7010
Commissioner, Social Services, John Maccarone, 705/759-5266
Executive Director, Economic Development Corporation, Bruce Strapp, 705/759-5432; Fax: 705/759-2185
Chief Building Official, Joseph D. LaRue, 705/759-5410
Chief of Police, Robert McEwen, 705/949-6300; Fax: 705-759-7820
City Solicitor, Lorie A. Bottos, 705/759-5400
City Tax Collector, Garry B. Mason, 705/759-5290
Director, Environmental Engineering, Jim Elliott, 705/759-5381
Director, Planning, John M. Bain, 705/759-5368
Fire Chief, David J. Fluke, 705/949-3335; Fax: 705/949-2341
Manager, Purchasing, Iain Little, 705/759-5299
Manager, Transit, Art Gagnon, 705/759-5438; Fax: 705/759-4534

City of SCARBOROUGH
Civic Centre, 150 Borough Dr., Scarborough ON M1P 4N7
416/396-7111, Fax: 416/396-6920, Hazardous Waste: 416/392-4330; Recycling: 416/396-7372
Incorporated: June 29, 1983
Area: 72.5 sq. miles
Population: 510,000 (1996)

COUNCIL
Mayor, Frank Faubert, 416/396-7222; Fax: 416/396-4286
Councillors & Wards: 1) Harvey Barron; 2) Gerry Altobello; 3) Mike Tzekas; 4) Lorenzo Berardinetti; 5) Brad Duguid; 6) Paul Mushiniski; 7) Fred Johnson; 8) David Soknacki; 9) Ron Moeser; 10) Ron Watson; 11) Sherene Shaw; 12) Doug Mahood; 13) Bas Balkissoon; 14) Edith Montgomery
Metro Councillors: Agincourt) Scott Cavalier; City Centre) Brian Harrison; Highland Creek) Ken Morrish; Malvern) Raymond Cho; Scarborough Bluffs) Brian Ashton; Wexford) Norm Kelly
Next Election: November 1997 (3 year terms)

ADMINISTRATION
City Clerk, W. Drew Westwater, 416/396-7279; Fax: 416/395-4301
Treasurer & Commissioner, Finance & Corporate Services, Estelle Lo, 416/396-7248; Fax: 416/396-5677
City Manager, Vacant, 416/396-7278; Fax: 416/396-4301
Commissioner, Planning & Building, Lorne Ross, 416/396-7343; Fax: 416/396-4265
Commissioner, Recreation, Parks & Culture, Bruce F. Fleury, 416/396-7404; Fax: 416/396-5399
Commissioner, Works & Environment, Michael A. Price, 416/396-7344; Fax: 416/396-5681
City Solicitor, John R. Ratchford, 416/396-7124; Fax: 416/396-4262
Director, Central Services (Purchasing), Bill Adams, 416/396-7228; Fax: 416/396-5677
Acting Executive Director, Economic Development, Brenda Librecz, 416/396-7744; Fax: 416/396-4241
Fire Chief, Thomas Powell, 416/396-7786; Fax: 416/396-7665
Medical Officer of Health, Dr. Colin D'Cunha, 416/396-7445; Fax: 416/396-5150
Senior Director, Human Resource Services, Alan Deans, 416/396-7759; Fax: 416/396-7217

Ville de SHERBROOKE
191, rue Palais, CP 610, Sherbrooke PQ J1H 5H9
819/821-5700, Fax: 819/822-6064, URL: http://ville.sherbrooke.qc.ca
Superficie: 22 sq. miles
Population: 79,432 (1994)

CONSEIL
Maire, Jean Perrault
Conseillers et Districts: 1. Le Triolet) Jean François Rouleau; 2. Mont-Bellevue) Laurier Custeau; 3. Immaculée-Conception) Lise Drouin-Paquette; 4. Centre-Ville) Serge Paquin; 5. Vieux-Nord) Alain Leclerc; 6. St-Jean-Baptiste) Michel Carrier; 7) Sylvie Lapointe; 8. Jardins-Fleuris) Bernard F. Tanguay; 9. Parc-Victoria) Serge Cardin; 10. St-Alphonse) Camille Fortier; 11) Jean-Luc Lavoie; 12. Carrefour) Jacques Jubinville
Prochaine election: novembre 1998 (mandat de 4 ans)

ADMINISTRATION
Greffière et Directrice, Services juridiques, Me Pierre Huard, 819/821-5425; Fax: 819/822-6064
Trésorier, François Poulette, 819/821-5490; Fax: 819/822-6091
Directeur général, Jean-Claude Boucher, 819/821-1950
Directeur général adjoint-population, Gilles Veilleux, 819/821-5910; Fax: 819/823-5121
Directeur général adjoint-administration, Jacques Lacroix, 819/821-5618; Fax: 819/823-5121
Chef de Cabinet - Mairie, Jean-Yves LaFlamme, 819/821-5969; Fax: 819/822-6131
Chef de division, Communications, Charlotte Gosselin, 819/821-5572; Fax: 819/823-5153
Chef de division, Évaluation, Richard Gagné, 819/821-5708; Fax: 819/821-5777
Chef de division, Informatique, Denis Dore, 819/821-5623; Fax: 819/821-5470
Chef de division, Ingénierie, Claude Cinq-Mars, 819/821-5925
Directeur, Hydro-Sherbrooke, Roger Vachon, 819/821-5718; Fax: 819/822-6085
Directeur, Planification et Travaux publics, Guy Labbé, 819/821-5798; Fax: 819/822-6070
Directeur, Protection contre les incendies, Jacques Denault, 819/821-5514; Fax: 819/821-5516
Directeur, Ressources financières, Denys Maurice, 819/821-5490; Fax: 819/821-6091
Directeur, Ressources humaines, Claude Lessard, 819/821-5689; Fax: 819/821-6086
Directeur, Ressources matérielles, Marc Latendresse, 819/821-5666; Fax: 819/821-5426
Directeur, Sécurité publique, Michel Carpentier, 819/821-1985
Directeur, Services récréatifs & communautaires, Alvin Doucet, 819/821-5772; Fax: 819/823-5168
Président, SDRS - Industrie, Jean Perrault, 819/821-5969; Fax: 819/822-6131

City of STONEY CREEK
777 Hwy. 8, PO Box 9940, Stoney Creek ON L8G 4N9
905/643-1261, Fax: 905/643-6161
Population: 51,865 (1994)

COUNCIL
Mayor, Anne Bain
Councillors & Wards: 1) Doug Conley; 2) Georgina Beattie; 3) Maria Pearson; 4) John Santarelli; 5) Larry Di Ianni; 6) John Copland; 7) Paul Miller
Next Election: November 1997 (3 year terms)

ADMINISTRATION
City Clerk, Rose Caterini
Treasurer, Frank Carrocci
Chief Administrative Officer, William F. Allcock
Chief Building Official, Henry Dekker
Chief Municipal Law Enforcement Officer, Susan McGrath
Director, Engineering, Ian Neville
Director, Human Resources, Mary A. Adamson
Director, Planning, Ronald Marini
Director, Recreation & Parks, Philip J. Bruckler
Fire Chief, Richard Playfair
Manager, Operations, Murray Dinning

City of SUDBURY
City Hall, Civic Square, 200 Brady St., PO Box 5000, Stn A, Sudbury ON P3A 5P3
705/674-3141
Incorporated: 1972
Area: 26,723 ha
Population: 87,087 (1994)

COUNCIL
Mayor, Jim Gordon, Fax: 705/671-9327
Councillors & Wards: 1) Ted Nicholson; 2) Ted Callaghan; 3) Ron G. MacDonald; 4) Jim Ilnitski; 5) Gerry McIntaggart; 6) J. Austin Davey; 7) Dr. Ricardo de la Riva; 8) Peter Dow; 9) Doug Craig
Regional Councillors: Ron Bradley; Tom Davies; John Fera; Eldon Gainer; Jim Gordon; Jim Griffin; Stan Hayduk; Terry Kett; Lionel Lalonde; Frank Mazzuca; Bob Parker; John Robert
Next Election: November 1997 (3 year terms)

ADMINISTRATION
Clerk, Thom M. Mowry, Fax: 705/671-8118
Director & City Treasurer, Finance, Larry Laplante
City Manager & Asst. City Manager, Corporate Services, Gary Polano, Fax: 705/671-9327
Asst. City Manager, Community Services, Brian Cottam
Asst. City Manager, Physical Services, Richard Hinton
City Solicitor, W. Fred Dean
Director, Administrative Services, Lise Poratto-Mason
Director, Engineering & Construction, Angelo D'Agostino
Director, Human Resources, Wayne Baker
Director, Information Services, Bruno Mangiardi
Director, Leisure Services, Don Waddell
Director, Maintenance, Greg Clausen
Fire Chief, Don McLean
Chief Executive Officer, Sudbury Public Library, Marian Ridge
Executive Director, Sudbury Metro Centre, Maureen M. Luoma

City of SURREY
14245 - 56 Ave., Surrey BC V3X 3A2
604/591-4011, Fax: 604/591-4357, URL: http://www.city.surrey.bc.ca/
Incorporated: November 10, 1879
Area: 132 sq. miles
Population: 274,000 (1994)

COUNCIL
Editor's Note: Results of the November 1996 election were not available at press time; up to date results may appear in the Addenda at the back of this book.
Next Election: November 1999 (3 year terms)

ADMINISTRATION
City Clerk & General Manager, Legislative Services, Donna Kenny, 604/591-4113; Fax: 604/591-8731
General Manager, Finance, Dennis Atkinson, 604/591-4156; Fax: 604/591-3654
City Manager, D. Lychak, 604/591-4122; Fax: 604/591-4357
General Manager, Corporate Services, G. Samson, 604/591-4331; Fax: 604/591-4451
General Manager, Engineering, U. Mital, 604/591-4219; Fax: 604/591-8693
General Manager, Human Resources, Len Posyniak, 604/591-4114; Fax: 604/591-4517
General Manager, Parks & Recreation, Brian MacRae, 604/591-4418; Fax: 604/591-9566
General Manager, Planning & Development, L. Walker, 604/591-4474; Fax: 604/591-2507
Director & Medical Health Officer, Dr. Roland Guasparini, 604/572-2600; Fax: 604/594-0949
Fire Chief, James Bale, 604/543-6701; Fax: 604/543-6715
Manager, Economic Development, Bruce Riddick, 604/591-4333
Manager, Engineering Planning, Paul Ham, 604/591-4243
Manager, Operations, Jamie Umploby, 604/590-7211

City of THUNDER BAY
City Hall, 500 Donald St. East, Thunder Bay ON P7E 5V3
807/625-2230, Fax: 807/623-5468
Incorporated: January 1, 1970
Area: 156 sq. miles
Population: 113,562 (1994)

COUNCIL
Mayor, David Hamilton
Aldermen & Wards: Current River) Dick Waddington; McIntyre) Frank Pullia; McKellar) Betty Kennedy; Neebing) J.D. Polhill; Northwood) Sargon Khubyar; Red River) Lorne Allard; Westfort) Ed Metzler
Aldermen at Large: Ken Boshcoff; Evelyn Dodds; John Ranta; Lawrence Timko; Joe Vander Wees
Next Election: November 1997 (3 year terms)

ADMINISTRATION
City Clerk, M. Elaine Bahlieda, 807/625-2480
General Manager, Finance, P. Milligan, 807/625-2242; Fax: 807/622-7963
City Manager, Vacant, 807/622-2224; Fax: 807/622-6669
Chief of Police, Protective Services, B. Chambers, 807/625-1304; Fax: 807/623-9242
General Manager, Community Services, G. Davies, 807/625-3320; Fax: 807/625-3292
General Manager, Corporate Services, G. Alexander, 807/625-3525; Fax: 807/625-0181
General Manager, Planning & Building Services, J. Favron, 807/625-2544; Fax: 807/623-2206
General Manager, Telephone & Information Services, S. Hacio, 807/625-2121; Fax: 807/623-0518
General Manager, Transportation & Works, R.H. Wright, 807/625-2137; Fax: 807/625-3588
Manager, Transit, A. Grant, 570 Fort William Rd., Thunder Bay ON P7B 2Z8, 807/625-2187; Fax: 807/345-5744

City of TORONTO
City Hall, 100 Queen St. West, Toronto ON M5H 2N2
416/392-9111, TDD: 416/392-7354; Telex: 06-219570, URL: http://www.city.toronto.on.ca/
Incorporated: March 6, 1834
Area: Land 101 sq. km
Population: 590,838 (1994)

COUNCIL
Mayor, Barbara Hall
Councillors & Wards: 1) David Hutcheon; 2) Chris Korwin-Kuczynski; 3) Mario Silva; 4) Martin Silva; 5) Dan Leckie; 6) Kyle Rae; 7) Pamela McConnell; 8) Peter Tabuns; 9) Steve Ellis; 10) Tom Jakobek; 11) Rob Maxwell; 12) Betty Disero; 13) John Adams; 14) Howard Joy; 15) Kay Gardner; 16) Michael Walker
Metro Councillors: Davenport) Dennis Fotinos; Don River) Jack Layton; Downtown) Olivia Chow; East Toronto) Paul Christie; High Park) David Miller; Midtown) Ila Bossons; North Toronto) Anne Johnston; Trinity-Niagara) Joe Pantalone
Next Election: November 1997 (3 year terms)

BOARD OF MANAGEMENT
Commissioner, City Works Services, Barry Gutteridge
Commissioner, Community Services, Tom Greer
Commissioner, Corporate Services, Margaret Rogrigues
Commissioner, Urban Development Services, John Morand

ADMINISTRATION
City Clerk, Barbara G. Caplan, 416/392-7020
Treasurer & Commissioner, Finance, Nick Kristoffy, 416/392-7051; Fax: 416/392-0920
City Auditor, John S. Woods, 416/392-7171; Fax: 416/392-7959
Commissioner, Buildings & Inspections, Michael Nixon, 416/392-0495; Fax: 416/392-0677
Acting Commissioner, City Property, Herb Pick, 416/392-7132; Fax: 416/392-0029
Commissioner, Housing, William P. Clarkin, 416/392-7885; Fax: 416/392-0560
Commissioner, Parks & Recreation, Herb Pirk, 416/392-7284; Fax: 416/392-0023
Commissioner, Planning & Development, Robert E. Millward, 416/392-7182; Fax: 416/392-0797
Acting Commissioner, Public Works & the Environment, David Bailey, 416/392-7708; Fax: 416/392-0816
Acting City Engineer, Werner Wichmann, 416/392-7701; Fax: 416-392-0816
City Solicitor, Dennis Y. Perlin, Q.C., 416/392-7221; Fax: 416/392-1199
City Surveyor, Wally Kowalenko, 416/392-7755; Fax: 416-392-0081
Coordinator, Information Services, City Clerk's, Mary Lynn Sackrule, 416/392-7341; Fax: 416/392-1553
Director, Economic Development, Peter G. Tomlinson, 416/392-7987; Fax: 416/392-0675
Director, Labour Relations, Vacant, 416/392-7497; Fax: 416/392-0652
Director, Operations, Mayor's Office, George Smitherman, 416/392-7001; Fax: 416/392-0026
Acting Fire Chief, Peter Ferguson, 416/392-0150; Fax: 416/392-0161
Acting Medical Officer of Health, Public Health, Dr. David McKeown, 416/392-2716; Fax: 416/392-0713

City of VANCOUVER
453 West 12 Ave., Vancouver BC V5Y 1V4
604/873-7011, Fax: 604/873-7419, http://www.city.vancouver.bc.ca/
Incorporated: 1886
Area: 44 sq. miles
Population: 508,814 (1994)

COUNCIL

Editor's Note: Results of the November 1996 election were not available at press time; up to date results may appear in the Addenda at the back of this book.
Next Election: November 1999 (3 year terms)

ADMINISTRATION

Clerk, Maria Kinsella, 604/873-7266
General Manager, Corporate Services, Penny J. Bruin, 604/873-7220; Fax: 604/873-7107
City Manager, Ken Dobell, 604/873-7627; Fax: 604/873-7641
General Manager, Engineering Services, Dave Rudberg, 604/873-7300; Fax: 604/871-6119
General Manager, Fire & Rescue Services, Glen Maddess, 604/665-6051; Fax: 604/665-6016
General Manager, Parks, Vic Kondrosky, 604/257-8448; Fax: 604/257-8427
Chief Constable, Raymond Canuel, 604/665-3444; Fax: 604/665-3417
City Planner, Ann McAfee, 604/873-7451
Communications Advisor, Scott MacRae, 604/874-7270
Corporation Counsel, Terrance R. Bland, 604/873-7505; Fax: 604/873-7445
Director, Civic Theatres, Rae Ackerman, 604/665-3020; Fax: 604/665-3001
Director, Emergency Management, John Oakley, 604/873-7756; Fax: 604/871-6116
Director, Equal Opportunity Employment Program, Lorna McCreath, 604/873-7799; Fax: 604/871-6251
Director, Legal Services, Francie Connell, 604/873-7508; Fax: 604/873-7445
Director, Permits & Licences, Jack Perri, 604/873-7520; Fax: 604/873-7100
Director, Social Planning, Burke Taylor, 604/871-6004; Fax: 604/871-6048
General Manager, Community Services, Ted Droettboom, 604/873-6254; Fax: 604/873-7898
General Manager, Human Resource Services, Marilyn Clark, 604/873-7655; Fax: 604/873-7696

City of VAUGHAN

2141 Major Mackenzie Dr., Vaughan ON L6A 1T1
905/832-2281, Fax: 905/832-8535, URL: http://www.city.vaughan.on.ca/
Incorporated: January 1, 1971
Area: 101 sq. miles
Population: 116,360 (1994)

COUNCIL

Mayor, Lorna Jackson, 905/851-1478
Local Councillors & Wards: 1) Peter Meffe; 2) Tony Carella; 3) Bernard Di Vona; 4) Mario G. Racco; 5) Bernie Green
Regional Councillors: Michael Di Biase; Joyce Frustaglio
Next Election: November 1997 (3 year terms)

ADMINISTRATION

City Clerk, J.D. Leach
Treasurer & Commissioner, Finance, Clayton D. Harris
Chief Administrative Officer, S.C. Somerville
Commissioner, Community Services, G.D. Haist
Commissioner, Economic Development, Frank Miele, 905/832-8521, ext.8244; Fax: 905/832-6248
Commissioner, Legal & Corporate Services, T.A. Caron
Commissioner, Planning, John Stevens, 905/832-8565, ext.8208; Fax: 905/832-6080
Commissioner, Works, George Todd, ext.8639
Director, Building Services, M.M. Navabi
Director, Engineering, Bill Robinson, 905/832-8525, ext.8247; Fax: 905/832-6145
Director, Human Resources, R.G. Nagel

Director, Management Info Services, Operational Audit & Review, S.R. Thompson
Director, Operations, David Moy, 905/832-8562, ext.6116; Fax: 905/303-2005
Director, Parks, Domenic Lunardo, 905/832-8639, ext.8795; Fax: 905/660-7907
Director, Property & Facilities, J. Piccolo
Director, Recreation, J.S. Epstein
Fire Chief, J.B. Sutton, ext.8205; Fax: 905/832-8572
Manager, Purchasing, G.A. Wilson, 905/832-8555, ext.8269; Fax: 905/832-8522

Ville de VERDUN

4555, rue de Verdun, Verdun PQ H4G 1M4
514/765-7000, Fax: 514/765-7006
Incorporée: 1907
Superficie: 9.96 sq. km
Population: 62,112 (1993)

CONSEIL

Maire, Georges Bossé
Conseillers et Quartiers: 1) Arthur Benarroch; 2) Marvin Reisler; 3) Jacques Lauzon; 4) Ginette Patry; 5) Alain Tassé; 6) Danielle Mimeault; 7) Laurent Dugas; 8) Claude Ravary; 9) Nicole Santerre; 10) France Lecocq; 11) Louis Leblanc; 12) Suzanne Dunne; 13) John Gallagher
Prochaine election: novembre 1997 (mandat de 4 ans)

ADMINISTRATION

Greffier, Gérard Cyr
Finances, Gilles Champagne
Directeur général, Gaétan Laberge
Méthodes & Procédures, Jean Roy
Prévention des incendies et Sécurité publique, Raymond Therrien, 514/765-7118
Ressources humaines, Johanne Jolicoeur
Service développement de la communauté, Daniel L'Écuyer
Services techniques, Raymond Fréchette, 514/765-7075
Travaux publics, Pierre Boutin, 514/765-7181
Urbanisme et environnement, Dany Tremblay, 514/765-7080

City of VICTORIA

One Centennial Sq., Victoria BC V8W 1P6
250/385-5711, Fax: 250/361-0348, URL: http://www.city.victoria.bc.ca/
Incorporated: August 2, 1862
Area: 4,641 acres
Population: 71,228 (1991)

COUNCIL

Editor's Note: Results of the November 1996 election were not available at press time; up to date results may appear in the Addenda at the back of this book.
Next Election: November 1999 (3 year terms)

ADMINISTRATION

Clerk & Director, Administration, Mark Johnston
Director, Finance, David Gawley
City Manager, Don Roughley
Chief Constable, Doug Richardson
City Engineer, Steve Yoshino
City Solicitor, John Basey, 250/361-0212; Fax: 250/385-3592
Director, Human Resources, Ron Longbottom
Director, Parks & Recreation, John Plantinga, 250/361-0361; Fax: 250/361-0385
Director, Planning, Len Vopnfjord, 250/361-0382; Fax: 250/361-0386
Fire Chief, Victoria Emergency Program, Michael Heppell, 250/920-3350; Fax: 920-3370

City of WATERLOO

City Hall, 100 Regina St. South, PO Box 337, Waterloo ON N2J 4A8
519/886-1550, Fax: 519/747-8760
Incorporated: January 1, 1948
Area: 6.646 ha (25.7 sq. miles)
Population: 75,274 (1994)

COUNCIL

Mayor, Brian Turnbull
Councillors & Wards: 1. West) Craig Hoddle; 2. Lakeshore) Dave Roeder; 3. Lexington) Bruce Anderson; 4. Columbia) Morty Taylor; 5. Westmount) Scott Jones; 6. Uptown) Tricia Siemens; 7. Glenridge) Bruce Alexander
Councillors at Large: Mike Connelly; Bruce McKenty; Joan McKinnon
Next Election: November 1997 (3 year terms)

ADMINISTRATION

City Clerk, Lew Ayers, 519/747-8704; Fax: 519/747-8510
City Treasurer, Bob Mavin
Chief Administrative Officer, Tom Stockie, 519/747-8702; Fax: 519/747-8500
General Manager, Operations, Kathy Durst, 519/747-8735; Fax: 519/747-8754
City Engineer, Gordon Lemon, 519/747-8741; Fax: 519/747-8775
Director, Human Resources, Don Ceré
Director, Planning, Greg Romanick
Director, Purchasing, Jim Walsh, 519/747-8725; Fax: 519/886-5788
Fire Chief, Max Hussey, 519/884-2121; Fax: 519/884-0242
Manager, Landscape Architect Group, Barb Magee-Turner, 519/747-8757; Fax: 519/747-8792

Town of WHITBY

575 Rossland Rd. East, Whitby ON L1N 2M8
905/668-5803, Fax: 905/686-7005
Incorporated: 1968
Area: 56.87 sq. miles (36,400 acres)
Population: 67,324 (1994)

COUNCIL

Mayor, Tom Edwards
Councillors: Dennis Fox; Judi Longfield; Don Mitchell; Shirley Scott
Regional Councillors: Marcel Brunelle; Joe Drumm; Gerry Emm
Next Election: November 1997 (3 year terms)

ADMINISTRATION

Town Clerk, D.G. McKay
Treasurer, R.A. Claringbold
Administrator, Wm. H. Wallace
Director, Marketing & Economic Development, P.G. Lebel
Director, Parks & Recreation, L.J. Morrow
Director, Personnel, H.D. Reid
Director, Planning, R.B. Short
Director, Public Works, W.J. Hancock
Fire Chief, A.J. VanDoleweerd

City of WHITEHORSE

2121 - 2 Ave., Whitehorse YT Y1A 1C2
403/667-6401, Fax: 403/668-8384
Incorporated: 1950
Area: 162 sq. miles
Population: 23,474 (1995)

COUNCIL

Councillors: Dan Boyd; Barb Harris; Katie Hayhurst; Bernie Philips; Dave Stockdale; Jared Storey
Next Election: October 1997 (3 year terms)

ADMINISTRATION

City Clerk, Dee Balsam, 403/668-8660
Director, Finance, Patricia Burke, 403/668-8611
City Manager, Bill Newell, 403/668-8638; Fax: 403/668-8639
City Engineer, Mitchell Moroziuk, 403/668-8307; Fax: 403/668-8386
Director, Community Services, Rob Roycroft, 403/668-8624
Director, Human Resources, Glenis Allen, 403/668-8619
Director, Municipal Services, Doug Raines, 403/668-8300; Fax: 403/668-8386
Fire Chief, Brian Monahan, 403/668-8383; Fax: 403/668-8389
Chief Building Inspector, Ken Hyatt, 403/668-8340; Fax: 403/668-8395
Manager, Building Maintenance, George White, 403/668-8302
Manager, By-laws, Ernie Stagg, 403/668-8318; Fax: 403/668-8386
Manager, Information Services, Larry Baran, 403/668-8670
Manager, Parks & Recreation, Cathy Carlile, 403/668-8326; Fax: 403/668-8324
Manager, Planning Services, Dennis Shewfelt, 403/668-8338; Fax: 403/668-8395
Manager, Purchasing, Robert Chisholm, 403/668-8642; Fax: 403/668-8387
Manager, Transportation, George Snider, 403/668-8351; Fax: 403/668-8386
Manager, Utilities, George Mair, 403/668-8352; Fax: 403/668-8386

City of WINDSOR

City Hall, 350 City Hall Sq., PO Box 1607, Windsor ON N9A 6S1
519/255-6500, Fax: 519/255-6868
Incorporated: 1854
Area: 49.6 sq. miles
Population: 199,000 (1995)

COUNCIL

Mayor, Mike Hurst
Councillors & Wards: 1) Dan Allen, Margaret Williams; 2) Peter Carlesimo, Sheila Wisdom; 3) Donna Gamble, Fulvio Valentinis; 4) Dave Cassivi, Bill Marra; 5) Rick Limoges, Tom Wilson
Next Election: November 1997 (3 year terms)

ADMINISTRATION

City Clerk, Thomas W. Lynd, 519/255-6211
Acting Commissioner, Finance, Gerry Pinsonneault, 519/255-6253; Fax: 519/255-7310
Chief Administrative Officer, Chuck Wills, 519/255-6311; Fax: 519/255-1861
Commissioner, Building, E. Link, 519/255-6267; Fax: 519/255-7170
Commissioner, Human Resources, Archie Glajch, 519/255-6206; Fax: 519/255-6874
Commissioner, Parks & Recreation Dept., Lloyd Burridge, 2450 McDougall St., Windsor ON N8X 3N6, 519/253-2300; Fax: 519/255-7990
Commissioner, Planning, John Atkins, 519/255-6281; Fax: 519/255-6680
Acting Commissioner, Property Dept., Bill Salzer, 68 Chatham St. East, Windsor ON N9A 2W1, 519/255-6400; Fax: 519/255-7910
Commissioner, Public Works & Emergency Planning, Gord Harding, 519/255-6257; Fax: 519/255-9847
Commissioner, Social Services, D. Howe, 755 Louis Ave., Windsor ON N9A 1X3, 519/255-5200; Fax: 519/255-7619
Commissioner, Traffic Engineering, J. Tofflemire, 1269 Mercer St., Windsor ON N8X 3P4, 519/255-6248; Fax: 519/255-7371

Commissioner, Windsor-Essex County Development Commission, Paul Bondy, #215, 333 Riverside Dr. West, Windsor ON N9A 7C5, 519/255-9200; Fax: 519/255-9987
City Solicitor, A.S. Kellerman, 519/255-6468; Fax: 519/255-6933
Manager, Environmental Services, Ron McConnell, 519/974-1010 ext.223
Chief of Police, Police Dept., John Kousik, 445 City Hall Sq., Windsor ON N9A 1K5, 519/255-6630; Fax: 519/255-6191
Fire Chief, Fire Dept., David Fields, 815 Goyeau St., Windsor ON N9A 1H7, 519/253-6573; Fax: 519/255-6832
General Manager, Windsor Utilities Commission, K.L. Edwards, 787 Ouellette Ave., Windsor ON N9A 4J4, 519/255-2727; Fax: 519/255-2767
Manager, Purchasing Dept., Don Mills, 185 City Hall Sq., Windsor ON N9A 6W5, 519/255-6272; Fax: 519/255-9891
Medical Officer of Health, Metro Windsor-Essex County Health Unit, Dr. Allen Heimann, 1005 Ouellette Ave., Windsor ON N9A 4J8, 519/258-2146; Fax: 519/258-6003

City of WINNIPEG

Council Building, Civic Centre, 510 Main St., Winnipeg MB R3B 1B9
204/986-2196, Fax: 204/949-0566, http://www.Remcan.CA/tourismw/
Incorporated: November 8, 1873
Area: 570 sq. km (57.053 ha)
Population: 641,700 (1994)

COUNCIL

Mayor, Susan A. Thompson
Councillors & Wards: Daniel McIntyre) Amaro Silva; Elmwood) Lillian Thomas; Fort Rouge) Glen Murray; North Kildonan) Mark Lubosch; Old Kildonan) Mike O'Shaughnessy; Point Douglas) John Prystanski; River Heights) Garth Steek; St. Boniface) Daniel Vandal; St. Charles) Pat Phillips; St. James) Jae Eadie; St. Norbert) John Angus; St. Vital) Allan Golden; Transcona) Shirley Timm-Rudolph
Next Election: October 1998 (3 year terms)

ADMINISTRATION

City Clerk, Dorothy E. Browton, 204/986-2436; Fax: 204/947-3452
Director, Corporate Finance, K. Dowdall, 204/986-2510; Fax: 204/949-9301
Commissioner, Planning & Community Services, T. Yauk, 204/986-2376; Fax: 204/949-1174
Commissioner, Protection, Parks & Culture, L.H. Reynolds, 204/986-2379; Fax: 204/949-1174
Commissioner, Works & Operations, W.D. Carroll, 204/986-2377; Fax: 204/949-1174
Coordinator, Emergency Program, M. Bennett, 204/986-4691; Fax: 204/942-5082
Chief of Police, David Cassels, Public Safety Bldg., 151 Princess St., Winnipeg MB R3B 1L1, 204/986-6037; Fax: 204/986-6077
City Assessor, Assessment, Vacant, 65 Garry St., Winnipeg MB R3C 4K4, 204/986-2951; Fax: 204/986-6105
City Solicitor & Manager, Legal Services, U. Goeres, 185 King St., 3rd Fl., Winnipeg MB R3B 1J1, 204/986-2408; Fax: 204/947-9155
Director, Business Liaison & Intergovernmental Affairs, D. Kalcsics, 204/986-5160; Fax: 204/986-7196
Director, Land & Development Services, P.A. Hamilton, 65 Garry St., 2nd Fl., Winnipeg MB R3C 4K4, 204/986-5235; Fax: 204/944-8476
Director, Materials Management Division, Corporate Finance, E. Van Mierlo, 185 King St., 1st Fl., Winnipeg MB R3B 1J1, 204/986-2451; Fax: 204/949-1178

Director, Parks & Recreation Dept., J. Hreno, 2799 Roblin Blvd., Winnipeg MB R3B 0B8, 204/986-3800; Fax: 204/832-7134
Director, Streets & Transportation Dept., J. Thomson, 100 Main St., Winnipeg MB R3C 1A4, 204/986-5285; Fax: 204/942-4811
Director, Social Services Dept., L. King, 705 Broadway, Winnipeg MB R3G 0X2, 204/986-5600; Fax: 204/944-8451
Director, Transit Dept., R.L. Borland, 421 Osborne St., Winnipeg MB R3L 2A2, 204/986-5724; Fax: 204/986-6863
Fire Chief, Fire Dept., B.J. Lough, Public Safety Bldg., 151 Princess St., Winnipeg MB R3B 1L1, 204/986-6330; Fax: 204/947-0164
General Manager, Winnipeg Hydro, R.J. Linton, 1315 Notre Dame Ave., Winnipeg MB R3G 3E2, 204/986-2320; Fax: 204/772-3872
Manager, Financial Planning & Budgets, J. Ferrier, 204/986-2186; Fax: 204/986-2237
Medical Health Officer, Community Services, Dr. M. Frost, 280 William Ave., Winnipeg MB R3B 0R1, 204/986-3440; Fax: 204/947-3957

City of YELLOWKNIFE

PO Box 580, Yellowknife NT X1A 2N4
403/920-5600, Fax: 403/920-5649, Email: eda@city.yellowknife.nt.ca, URL: http://www.city.yellowknife.nt.ca
Incorporated: January 1, 1970
Area: 13,857 ha
Population: 15,179 (1991)

COUNCIL

Mayor, Dave Lovell
Aldermen: Vi Beck; John Dalton; Trevor Kasteel; Blake Lyons; Jo MacQuarrie; Dick Peplow; Ruth Spence; Merlyn Williams
Next Election: October 1997 (3 year terms)

ADMINISTRATION

City Clerk/Asst. City Administrator, Brian Chambers, 403/920-5685
Director, Finance, Joe Kronstal, 403/920-5645
City Administrator, Douglas B. Lagore, 403/920-5624
Director, Community Services, Max Hall, 403/920-5634
Director, Human Resources, Sheila Dunn, 403/920-5677
Director, Planning & Lands, Bob McKinnon, 403/920-5672
Director, Public Safety, Dave Nicklen, 403/920-5669
Director, Public Works & Engineering, Neil Jamieson, 403/920-5653
Executive Director, Economic Development, Archie Gillies, 403/873-5772

City of YORK

2700 Eglinton Ave. West, Toronto ON M6M 1V1
416/394-2700, Fax: 416/394-2803
Incorporated: July 1, 1973
Area: 2,335 ha
Population: 134,977 (1994)

COUNCIL

Mayor, Frances Nunziata
Councillors & Wards: 1) Roz Mendelson; 2) Joe Mihevc; 3) Rob Davis; 4) Joan Roberts; 5) Barry Rowland; 6) Michael McDonald; 7) Randy Leach; 8) William Saundercook
Metro Councillors & Wards: Eglinton) Caroline Di Giovanni; York Humber) Alan Tonks
Next Election: November 1997 (3 year terms)

ADMINISTRATION

City Clerk, Ron W. Maurice
Treasurer & Director, Finance, Wendy Tysall

Commissioner, Buildings, P. Hansen
Commissioner, Human Resources, Elma Lobo
Commissioner, Planning, E. Sajecki
Senior Director, Parks & Recreation, Ken Dickin
Senior Director, Public Works, Bill Dunford
Director, Economic Development, Bill Steiss
Director, Purchasing, J. Price
Fire Chief, S. Stewart
Medical Officer of Health, Dr. J.W. Mitchell
Solicitor, G. Bartlett

REGIONAL GOVERNMENT

Part 3 (Alphabetical list of regional municipalities in major population areas of British Columbia, Ontario & Québec)

BRITISH COLUMBIA REGIONAL GOVERNMENTS

For a complete list of Regional Governments in BC see part 1 of this Section

CAPITAL Regional District
524 Yates St., PO Box 1000, Victoria BC V8W 2S6
250/360-3000, Fax: 250/360-3130, Email for general enquiries only snorrington@wpo.gov.bc.ca, URL: http://vvv.com/crd/
Incorporated: February 1, 1966
Area: 934 sq. miles
Population: 308,720 (1993)
Member Areas include: Dist. of Central Saanich; City of Colwood; Town of Esquimalt; Dist. of Highlands; Langford; Dist. of Metchosin; Dist. of North Saanich; Dist. of Oak Bay; Corp. of Saanich; Town of Sidney; City of Victoria; Town of View Royal
Chairperson, Bob Clark
Executive Director, William Jordan, 250/360-3124
Director, Finance (Purchasing), Diana Lokken, 250/360-3010; Fax: 250/360-3023
General Municipal Services, Yoon Chee, 250/642-1620; Fax: 250/642-5274
Health Planning, Jeremy Tate, 250/360-3145; Fax: 250/360-3120
Health Services, Dr. Richard Stanwick, 250/360-3116; Fax: 250/360-3023
Administrator, Regional Parks, Lloyd Rushton, 250/478-3344; Fax: 250/478-5416
Chief Engineer, Michael Williams, 250/360-3092; Fax: 250/360-3079
Community Relations Officer, Ron Kirstein, 250/360-3133; Fax: 250/360-3226
Director, Human Resources, Bill Eccleston, 250/360-3073; Fax: 250/360-3076
Acting Head, Environmental Services, Trevor Smyth, 250/360-3082; Fax: 250/360-3254
Manager, Regional Planning & Services, Jane Seright, 250/360-3162; Fax: 250/360-3159

GREATER VANCOUVER Regional District
4330 Kingsway, Burnaby BC V5H 4G8
604/432-6200, Fax: 604/432-6248, URL: http://www.gvrd.bc.ca/index.html
Incorporated: June 29, 1967
Area: 2,931.4 sq. km
Population: 1,713,393 (1993)
Member Areas include: Village of Anmore; Village of Belcarra; City of Burnaby; City of Coquitlam; Delta; City of Langley; Dist. of Langley; Village of Lions Bay; Dist. of Maple Ridge; City of New Westminster; Dist. of North Vancouver; City of North Vancouver; Dist. of Pitt Meadows; City of Port Coquitlam; City of Port Moody; City of Richmond; City of Surrey; City of Vancouver; Dist. of West Vancouver; City of White Rock
Chair, Greg Halsey-Brandt
Secretary, Paulette Vetleson
Manager, Finance, Administration & Properties, Ian Jarvis
Manager, Air Quality, Barrie Mills, P.Eng.
Manager, Communications & Education, Deborah Trouten
Manager, Personnel & Labour Relations, Mark Leffler
Manager, Regional Parks, R.A. Hankin
Manager, Sewerage & Drainage, Hew McConnell, P.Eng.
Manager, Solid Waste, Len Hayton, P.Eng.
Manager, Strategic Planning, Kenneth D. Cameron
Manager, Water Engineering & Construction, John Morse, P.Eng.
Regional Manager & Commissioner, Water District, Sewerage & Drainage District, Ben Marr, P.Eng.
Administrator, Hospitals, Greg Stump
Administrator, Housing, Perry Staniscia

ONTARIO REGIONAL GOVERNMENTS

Regional Municipality of DURHAM
605 Rossland Rd. East, PO Box 623, Whitby ON L1N 6A3
905/668-7711, Fax: 905/668-9963
Incorporated: January 1, 1974
Area: 954 mi^2 (2,471 sq. km)
Population: 421,824 (1994)
Member Areas include: Town of Ajax; Twp. of Brock; Clarington; City of Oshawa; Town of Pickering; Twp. of Scugog; Twp. of Uxbridge; Town of Whitby
Regional Chair, Gary Herrema
Clerk, Cecil W. Lundy
Commissioner, Economic Development Department, P.W. Olive, 1615 Dundas St. East, Whitby ON, 905/723-0023; Fax: 905/436-5359
Commissioner, Finance Department, J.L. Gartley, 60 Bond St. West, Oshawa ON, 905/571-3311; Fax: 905/571-7460
Commissioner, Planning Department, A.L. Georgieff, 1615 Dundas St. East, Whitby ON, 905/728-7731; Fax: 905/436-6612
Commissioner, Works Department, V.A. Silgailis, 105 Consumers Dr., Whitby ON, 905/668-7721; Fax: 905/668-2051
Medical Officer of Health, Health Department, Dr. R.J. Kyle, 1615 Dundas St. East, Whitby ON, 905/723-8521; Fax: 905/723-6026
Director, Information Systems, J. Hermes, 60 Bond St. West, Oshawa ON, 905/571-3311; Fax: 905/571-7307

Regional Municipality of HALDIMAND-NORFOLK
70 Town Centre Dr., Townsend ON N0A 1S0
519/587-4911, Fax: 519/587-5554
Incorporated: April 1, 1974
Area: 1,103 mi^2
Population: 96,586 (1994)
Member Areas include: Twp. of Delhi; Town of Dunnville; Town of Haldimand; City of Nanticoke; Twp. of Norfolk; Town of Simcoe
Regional Clerk, Gerald van der Wolf
Treasurer & Commissioner, Finance, Robert Johnstone
Chief Administrative Officer, Gerry Taylor
Regional Chair, John Harrison
Commissioner, Engineering, Eric D'Hondt
Commissioner, Human Resources, Rick Beaumont
Commissioner, Planning & Economic Development, Lee Kennaley
Medical Officer of Health, Dr. Sandor Demeter
Regional Solicitor, Thomas A. Cline

Regional Municipality of HALTON
1151 Bronte Rd., Oakville ON L6M 3L1
905/825-6000, Fax: 905/825-8838, http://www.region.halton.on.ca
Incorporated: January 1, 1974
Area: 987 sq. km
Population: 315,557 (1994)
Member Areas include: City of Burlington; Town of Halton Hills; Town of Milton; Town of Oakville
Chief Administrative Officer, John S. Burke, ext. 7236; Fax: 905/825-8839
Regional Clerk, Joan A. Eaglesham, ext.7237
Commissioner, Corporate Services, Joseph Rinaldo, Fax: 905/825-8820
Commissioner, Planning & Public Works, Art Leitch, 905/825-6030; Fax: 905/825-2067
Commissioner, Social & Community Services, Bonnie Ewart, Fax: 905/825-8836
Commissioner & Medical Officer of Health, Dr. Bob Nosal, 905/825-6060; Fax: 905/825-8588
Chief of Police, Peter Campbell, 905/825-4777
Director, Human Resources, Greg Hughes, Fax: 905/825-4032
Manager, Purchasing, Andrea Mindenhall, Fax: 905/825-8820
Regional Solicitor, Mark Meneray, ext.6010
Fire Chief, Fire Dept., Terry Edwards, 905/335-1867; Fax: 905/333-1570

Regional Municipality of HAMILTON-WENTWORTH
119 King St. West, PO Box 910, Hamilton ON L8N 3V9
905/546-4154, Fax: 905/546-2546
Incorporated: January 1, 1974
Area: 280,764 acres
Population: 459,656 (1996)
Member Areas include: Town of Ancaster; Town of Dundas; Town of Flamborough; Twp. of Glanbrook; City of Hamilton; City of Stoney Creek
Regional Chair, Terry Cooke
Regional Clerk, Robert C. Prowse
Acting Treasurer & Commissioner, Finance, Jim Bruzzese, 905/546-4270; Fax: 905/546-2584
Chief Administrative Officer, Michael Fenn, 905/546-4152; Fax: 905/546-2340
Chief, Hamilton-Wentworth Regional Police Dept., R. Middaugh, 905/546-4925
Commissioner, Human Resource Services, John Johnston, 905/546-4462; Fax: 905/546-2650
Commissioner, Regional Environment Dept., J.D. Thoms, 905/546-4339; Fax: 905/546-4473
Commissioner, Regional Transportation Dept., Dale Turvey, 905/528-4200; Fax: 905/546-6050
Commissioner, Social Services, Mike Schuster, 905/546-4800; Fax: 905/577-0115
Commissioner & Corporate Counsel, Regional Legal Services, Rand Roszell, 905/546-4248; Fax: 905/546-4370
Director, Economic Development, Nick Catalano, 905/546-4222; Fax: 905/546-4107
Director, Information Systems, Jim Hindson, 905/546-4276; Fax: 905/546-2573
Medical Officer of Health, Regional Public Health Dept., Dr. Marilyn James, 905/546-3500; Fax: 905/528-2205

MUSKOKA District Municipality
70 Pine St., Bracebridge ON P1L 1N3
705/645-2231, Fax: 705/645-5319
Incorporated: January 1, 1971
Area: 4,035.29 sq. km
Population: 45,017 (1994)
Member Areas include: Town of Bracebridge; Twp. of Georgian Bay; Town of Gravenhurst; Town of Huntsville; Twp. of Lake of Bays; Twp. of Muskoka Lakes

Canadian Almanac & Directory 1997

Clerk & Chief Administrative Officer, William C. (Bill) Calvert
Treasurer & Commissioner, Finance & Administration, John McRae
Commissioner, Engineering & Public Works, Tony White, Fax: 705/645-7599
Commissioner, Human Services, I. Turnbull
Commissioner, Planning & Economic Development, James Green, Fax: 705/646-2207
Secretary, Land Division Committee, M. Wylie
Solicitor, D. Royston

Regional Municipality of NIAGARA
2201 St. David's Rd., PO Box 1042, Thorold ON L2V 4T7
905/685-1571, Fax: 905/687-4977, Toll Free: 1-800-263-7215, URL: http://www.regional.niagara.on.ca/niagara/
Incorporated: January 1, 1970
Area: 1,850 sq. km
Population: 415,200 (1994)
Member Areas include: Town of Fort Erie; Town of Grimsby; Town of Lincoln; City of Niagara Falls; Town of Niagara on the Lake; Town of Pelham; City of Port Colborne; City of St Catharines; City of Thorold; Twp. of Wainfleet; City of Welland; Twp. of West Lincoln
Chief Administrative Officer, Michael H. Boggs; EMail: mboggs@regional.niagara.on.ca
Regional Clerk, Thomas R. Hollick; EMail: rhollick@regional.niagara.on.ca
Director, Finance, Michael T. Trojan
Director, Human Resources, John Nicol
Director, Planning, Alan Veale
Director, Public Works, John Kernahan
Director, Social Services & Senior Citizens, Susan R. Reid, 905/984-6900; Fax: 905/984-8760
Medical Officer of Health, Dr. Robin C. Williams, 905/688-3762; Fax: 905/682-3901; EMail: williams@regional.niagara.on.ca
Purchasing, Pat Crow
Solicitor, Bruce Banting
Niagara Economic Tourism Corporation (NET Corp.), Mike Duffy
Police Chief, Niagara Regional Police Dept., Grant Waddell, 68 Church St., St. Catherines ON L2R 3C6

Regional Municipality of OTTAWA-CARLETON
Cartier Sq., 111 Lisgar St., Ottawa ON K2P 2L7
613/560-1335, Fax: 613/560-6055, http://resudox.net/rmoc/region.html
Incorporated: January 1, 1969
Area: 2,766 sq. km
Population: 696,045 (1993)
Member Areas include: City of Cumberland; City of Gloucester; Twp. of Goulbourn; City of Kanata; City of Nepean; Twp. of Osgoode; City of Ottawa; Twp. of Rideau; Village of Rockcliffe Park; City of Vanier; Twp. of West Carleton
Chair, Peter D. Clark, 613/560-2068; Fax: 613/560-6010
Regional Clerk, Mary Jo Woollam, 613/560-2058; Fax: 613/560-1380
Commissioner, Finance, Jack C. LeBelle, 613/560-2069; Fax: 613/560-6004
Chief Administrative Officer, C. Mervyn Beckstead, 613/560-1214; Fax: 613/560-6047
Commissioner, Environmental Services, Michael Sheflin, 613/560-2050, ext.1285; Fax: 613/560-6009
Commissioner, Homes for the Aged, Garry Armstrong, 613/560-2081; Fax: 613/560-6008
Commissioner, Human Resources, Joyce Potter, 613/560-2060; Fax: 560-1392
Commissioner, Planning & Property Services, Nick Tunnacliffe, 613/560-2053; Fax: 613/560-6006

Commissioner, Social Services Department, Dick Stewart, 495 Richmond Rd., Ottawa ON K2A 0G3, 613/728-3913; Fax: 613/724-4223
Acting Medical Officer of Health, Health Department, Dr. Ed Ellis, 495 Richmond Rd., Ottawa ON K2A 0G3, 613/722-2328; Fax: 613/724-4191
Director, Information & Public Affairs, Rob Dolan, 613/560-1337; Fax: 613/560-6017
Regional Internal Auditor, Internal Audit, Richard Palmer, 613/560-1388; Fax: 613/560-6047
Regional Solicitor, Douglas Cameron, 613/560-2056; Fax: 613-560-1383

Regional Municipality of PEEL
10 Peel Centre Dr., Brampton ON L6T 4B9
905/791-9400 (for assistance), Fax: 905/791-4792, 905/791-7800 (for automated attendant), URL: http://www.region.peel.on.ca
Incorporated: October 15, 1973
Area: 1,257.2 sq. km
Population: 879,100 (1995)
Member Areas include: City of Brampton; Town of Caledon; City of Mississauga
Chief Administrative Officer, M. Garrett, ext. 4312; Fax: 905/791-2567
Regional Clerk, Bonnie J. Zeran, ext.4325
Treasurer, Joseph Pennachetti, ext.4528; Fax: 905/791-4195
Commissioner, Corporate Services & Regional Solicitor, R.K. Gillespie, ext.4315; Fax: 905/791-2567
Commissioner, Planning, Peter E. Allen, ext.4349; Fax: 905/791-7920
Commissioner, Public Works, Donald J. Markle, ext.4395; Fax: 905/791-0728
Commissioner, Social Services, P. Vezina
Commissioner & Medical Officer of Health, Dr. P. Cole, ext.2215; Fax: 905/796-0970
Commissioner, Housing & General Manager, Peel Living, R. Maloney, ext.2246; Fax: 905/796-0972
Director, Engineering & Construction, Mitchell Zamojc, ext.4382
Director, Human Resources, Paul Vivian, ext.4201; Fax: 905/791-6118
Director, Operations, John Savage, ext.4578
Manager, Emergency Program, J. Moore, ext.4730
Sec.-Treas., Land Division Committee, D.B. Cowtan, ext. 4328
Chief of Police, R. Lunney, 7755 Huronontario St., Brampton ON, 905/453-3311

Regional Municipality of SUDBURY
200 Brady St., PO Box 3700, Stn A, Sudbury ON P3A 5W5
705/673-2171, Fax: 705/673-2960
Incorporated: January 1, 1973
Area: 1,088 mi^2
Population: 162,000 (1994)
Member Areas include: Town of Capreol; Town of Nickel Centre; Town of Onaping Falls; Town of Rayside-Balfour; City of Sudbury; Town of Valley East; Town of Walden
Chief Administrative Officer, Jim R. Rule
Regional Clerk, Angie Haché
Regional Treasurer & Director, Financial Services, Sandra Jonasson
Commissioner, Corporate Services, Doug Wuksinic
Commissioner, Health & Social Services, M. Mieto
Commissioner, Planning & Development, Bill Lautenbach
Commissioner, Public Works, Patrick J. Morrow
Chief Building Official, Guido Mazza
Chief of Police, Regional Police Services, Alex McCauley
Communications & Public Relations Officer, Paul Philion, ext.507

Coordinator, Environmental Services, David Caverson, 705/674-4455 ext.4327
Director, Human Resources, Patrick Thomson
Director, Legal Services, R. Swiddle
Director, Operations, Brian Bilodeau, 705/560-2022; Fax: 705/560-9641
Director, Recreational Services, James Cappadocia
General Manager, Sudbury Regional Development Corp., Frank Hess, ext.308; Fax: 705/671-6767

Municipality of METROPOLITAN TORONTO
Metro Hall, Station 1071, 55 John St., 7th Fl., Toronto ON M5V 3C6
416/392-8000, Fax: 416/392-2980, URL: http://www.metrotor.on.ca/
Incorporated: April 15, 1953
Area: 240 mi^2
Population: 2,317,400 (1994)
Member Areas include: Borough of East York; City of Etobicoke; City of North York; City of Scarborough; City of Toronto; City of York
Metropolitan Chairman, Alan Tonks, 416/392-8001; Fax: 416/392-3799
Metropolitan Clerk, Novina Wong, 416/392-8016; Fax: 416/392-2980; EMail: metroclerk@metrodesk.metrotor.on.ca
Treasurer & Commissioner, Finance, Louise Eason, 416/392-8077; Fax: 416/392-3649
Chief Administrative Officer, Robert Richards, 416/392-8673; Fax: 416/392-3751
Commissioner, Ambulance Services, John Dean, 416/392-2000; Fax: 416/392-2115
Commissioner, Community Services, Shirley Hoy, 416/397-7325; Fax: 416/392-8492
Commissioner, Corporate & Human Resource Services, Earl Rowe, 416/397-0820; Fax: 416/392-3966
Commissioner, Parks & Culture, Ray Biggart, 416/392-9186; Fax: 416/392-3355
Commissioner, Planning, David Gurin, 416/392-8101; Fax: 416/392-3821
Commissioner, Transportation, Douglas P. Floyd, 416/392-8300; Fax: 416/392-4426
Commissioner, Works, Michael Thorne, 416/392-8211; Fax: 416/392-4540
Chair, Metropolitan Toronto Police Services Board, Maureen Prinsloo, 416/808-2222; Fax: 416/808-8082
Chair, Board of Management, The Guild Inn, Bernard Rasch, 416/266-4449; Fax: 416/266-4375
Chief Admin. Officer/Sec.-Treas., Metropolitan Toronto & Region Conservation Authority, Craig Mather, 416/661-6600; Fax: 416/661-6898
Chief General Manager, Exhibition Place, Peter Moore, 416/393-6000; Fax: 416/393-6372
Chief General Manager, Toronto Transit Commission, David Gunn, 416/393-4000; Fax: 416/488-6198
Chief of Police, Metropolitan Toronto Police, David Boothby, 416/324-2222; Fax: 416/324-6345
Director, Catholic Children's Aid Society of Metropolitan Toronto, Dr. C.J. Maloney, 416/925-2115; Fax: 416/395-1581
Director, Metropolitan Library Board, Frances Schwenger, 416/393-7000; Fax: 416/392-3102
Executive Director, Children's Aid Society of Metropolitan Toronto, Bruce Rivers, 416/924-4646; Fax: 416/324-2485
Executive Director, Community Information Centre of Metro Toronto, Allison Hewitt, 416/392-0505; Fax: 416/392-4404
Executive Director, Economic Development, Don M. Baxter, 416/392-3377; Fax: 416/397-0906
General Manager, Metropolitan Licensing Commission, Carol Ruddell-Foster, 416/392-3000; Fax: 416/392-3102
General Manager, Metropolitan Toronto Housing Co. Ltd., Joanne Campbell, 416/392-6000; Fax: 416/392-3974

General Manager, Metropolitan Toronto Zoo, Calvin White, 416/392-5900; Fax: 416/392-5934
General Manager, O'Keefe Centre, Elizabeth Bradley, 416/393-7469; Fax: 416/393-7454
Metropolitan Auditor, Allan G. Andrews, 416/392-8030; Fax: 416/392-3754
Metropolitan Solicitor, H.W. Osmond Doyle, 416/392-8047; Fax: 416/392-5624
President, Metropolitan Toronto Convention & Visitors Association, Kirk Shearer, 416/203-2600; Fax: 416/203-7943

Regional Municipality of WATERLOO
Regional Administration Bldg., 150 Frederick St., Kitchener ON N2G 4J3
519/575-4400, Fax: 519/575-4481, URL: http://www.oceta.on.ca/region.waterloo/gov/
Incorporated: January 1, 1973
Area: 1,345 sq. km
Population: 387,000 (1994)
Member Areas include: City of Cambridge; City of Kitchener; Twp. of North Dumfries; City of Waterloo; Twp. of Wellesley; Twp. of Wilmot; Twp. of Woolwich
Regional Clerk, Evelyn L. Stettner, 519/575-4410
Commissioner, Finance, Malcolm Gregg, 519/575-4545; Fax: 519/575-4448
Chief Administrative Officer, Gerald A. Thompson, 519/575-4425; Fax: 519/575-4440
Asst. Chief Administrative Officer, Human Resources, Cheryl Lowe, 519/575-4485; Fax: 519/575-4454
Commissioner, Corporate Resources & Regional Solicitor, C.P. Giller, 519/575-4460; Fax: 519/575-4466
Commissioner, Engineering, William R. Pyatt, 519/575-4540; Fax: 519/575-4453
Commissioner, Planning & Culture, Sally A. Thorsen, 519/575-4535; Fax: 519/575-4449
Commissioner, Social Services, P. Johnston, 99 Regina St. South, PO Box 1612, Waterloo ON N2J 4G6, 519/883-2170; Fax: 519/519/883-2234
Director, Child Care, M. Parker, 519/883-2177; Fax: 519/883-2234
Director, Client Services, L. Snyder, 519/883-2175; Fax: 519/883-2234
Director, Communicable Disease, J. Daley, 519/883-2250; Fax: 519/883-2248
Director, Community Health Administration, A. Schlorff, 519/883-2242; Fax: 519/883-2241
Director, Design & Construction, W. Brodribb, 519/575-4457; Fax: 519/575-4430
Director, Employee Development, C. VanAndel, 519/575-4701; Fax: 519/575-4454
Director, Employee Relations, P. Mellor, 519/575-4461; Fax: 519/575-4454
Director, Facilities Management & Fleet Services, K. Noonan, 519/575-4711; Fax: 519/575-4430
Director, Financial Services, L. Ryan, 519/575-4542; Fax: 519/575-4547
Director, Healthy Environments, B. Hatton, 519/883-2270; Fax: 519/883-2241
Director, Healthy Lifestyles, T. Schumilas, 519/883-2554; Fax: 519/883-2241
Director, Income Maintenance, F. Pizzuto, 519/883-2179; Fax: 519/883-2234
Director, Information Systems, W. Gasparini, 519/575-4570, ext.3077
Director, Legal Services, D. Fisher, 519/575-4518; Fax: 519/575-4466
Director, Library Services, K. Manley, 519/575-4589; Fax: 519/634-5371
Director, Planning & Development, Paul Mason, 519/575-4512; Fax: 519/575-4449
Director, Transportation, J. Hammer, 519/575-4401; Fax: 519/575-4453
Coordinator, Community Safety & Crime Prevention, C. Sadeler, 519/575-4794; Fax: 519/575-4440
Coordinator, Emergency Planning, M. Verbeek, 519/575-4740; Fax: 519/575-4440
Coordinator, Social Planning & Administration, B. Blowes, 519/883-2190; Fax: 519/883-2234
Medical Officer of Health & Commissioner, Community Health, Dr. R. Sax, 99 Regina St. South, Waterloo ON N2J 4V3, 519/883-2000; Fax: 519/883-2241

Regional Municipality of YORK
17250 Yonge St., PO Box 147, Newmarket ON L3Y 6Z1
905/731-0201, Fax: 905/895-3031
Incorporated: January 1, 1971
Area: 663 mi^2
Population: 577,960 (1996)
Member Areas include: Town of Aurora; Town of East Gwillimbury; Town of Georgina; Twp. of King; Town of Markham; Town of Newmarket; Town of Richmond Hill; City of Vaughan; Town of Whitchurch-Stouffville
Regional Chair, Eldred King, 905/640-2876
Regional Clerk, Dennis Hearse
Commissioner & Regional Treasurer, Finance, S. Cartwright
Chief Administrative Officer, Alan Wells
Commissioner, Planning & Development Services, J. Livey
Commissioner, Transportation & Works, K. Schipper
Commissioner & Medical Officer of Health, Health Services, Dr. H. Jaczek
Commissioner & Regional Solicitor, Corporate & Legal Services, P. Carlyle
Administrator, Social Services, J. Simmons
Chief of Police, Bryan Cousineau
Director, Human Resources, Sheila Tyndall
Fire Coordinator, Ken Beckett

QUÉBEC REGIONAL GOVERNMENTS

COMMUNAUTÉ URBAINE DE MONTRÉAL
1550, rue Metcalfe, Montréal PQ H3A 1X6
514/280-3522, Fax: 514/280-4243, URL: http://www.cum.qc.ca/
Incorporée: December 23, 1969
Superficie: 1,190.88 mi^2
Population: 1,779,254 (1994)
Member Areas include: Ville d'Anjou; Ville de Baie-d'Urfé; Ville de Beaconsfield; Ville de Côte-St-Luc; Ville de Dollard-des-Ormeaux; Ville de Dorval; Ville de Hampstead; Ville de Kirkland; Ville de Lachine; Ville de LaSalle; Village de L'Île-Bizard; Ville de Mont-Royal; Ville de Montréal; Ville de Montréal-Est; Ville de Montréal-Nord; Ville de Montréal-Ouest; Ville d'Outremont; Ville de Pierrefonds; Ville de Pointe-Claire; Ville de Roxboro; Ville de Ste-Anne-de-Bellevue; Ville de Ste-Geneviève; Ville de Saint-Laurent; Ville de St-Léonard; Ville de St-Pierre; Village de Senneville; Ville de Verdun; Ville de Westmount
Director General, Gérard Divay, 514/280-3535; Fax: 514/280-4232
Treasurer, Michel Bélanger, 514/280-3600; Fax: 514/280-3693
Secretary, Nicole Lafond, 514/280-3445; Fax: 514/280-3594
Director, 911 Emergency Centre, Louise Cherry, 514/280-6750; Fax: 514/280-2649
Director, Air & Water Purification, Fernand Cadieux, 514/280-4321; Fax: 514/280-4318
Director, Communications, Robert Laurier, 514/280-3522; Fax: 514/280-4243
Director, Economic Development Office, Tour Scotia, 1002, rue Sherbrooke ouest, Montréal PQ, 514/280-4251; Fax: 514/280-4266
Director, Emergency Services Bureau, Jean-Bernard Guindon, 514/280-4040; Fax: 514/280-4044
Director, Planning, Vacant, 514/280-6700; Fax: 514/280-6744
Director, Police, Jacques Duchesneau, 514/280-2000; Fax: 514/280-2008
Director, Regional Parks, Daniel Malo, 514/280-6704; Fax: 514/280-6787
Director, Technical Services, Serge Allie, 514/280-3530; Fax: 514/280-3597
Director, Valuation, Jean Bélanger, 514/280-3800; Fax: 514/280-3899
Director, Wastewater Treatment Plant, Réjean Levesque, 514/280-4355; Fax: 514/280-4346
Director General & Secretary, Arts Council, Jacques Cleary, 514/280-3580; Fax: 514/280-3789
Deputy Director, Food Inspection, Jean Troalen, 514/280-4283; Fax: 514/280-4318
Auditor's Office, Gaétan Foisy, 514/280-3540; Fax: 514/280-4090

COMMUNAUTÉ URBAINE DE L'OUTAOUAIS
#500, 25, rue Laurier, CP 2210, Succ B, Hull PQ J8X 3Z4
819/770-1380, Fax: 819/770-8479
Population: 217,658 (1995)
Member Areas include: Ville de Aylmer; Ville de Buckingham; Ville de Gatineau; Ville de Hull; Ville de Masson-Angers
Directeur général, Jacques Tremblay
Trésorière, Gladys Guérin
Président du conseil, Marc Croteau
Vice-président du conseil, Luc Montreuil
Conseiller juridique, Me Michel Pharand
Directeur, Évaluation & Ressources humaines, Michel Hervieux
Directeur, Environnement (Génie), Claude Robert
Directeur, Environnement (Opérations), Lawrence Gangur
Directeur, Planification, Nelson Tochon

COMMUNAUTÉ URBAINE DE QUÉBEC
399, rue St-Joseph est, Québec PQ G1K 8E2
418/529-8771, Fax: 418/529-2219
Incorporée: December 23, 1969
Superficie: 575 sq. km
Population: 493,694 (1993)
Member Areas include: Ville de Beauport; Municipalité de Boischatel; Ville de Cap-Rouge; Ville de Charlesbourg; Lac-St-Charles; Ville de L'Ancienne-Lorette; Ville de Loretteville; Ville de Québec; Paroisse de St-Augustin; Ville de St-Émile; Ville de Ste-Foy; Ville de Sillery; Ville de Val-Bélair; Ville de Vanier
Chair, Executive Committee, Jean-Paul L'Allier, Fax: 418/529-4655
General Manager, Serge Allen, Fax: 418/529-4655
Treasurer, Raynald Bédard
Sec.-Treas., Pierre Rousseau
Chair, Transport Commission, Claude Larose
Directeur, Aménagement du territoire, Jean Guyard
Director, Assessment, Jean-Guy Kirouac
Director, Communications, France Lagacé, Fax: 418/529-8327
Director, Environmental Services, René Gélinas, Fax: 418/529-4299
Director, Human Resources, Pierre Lemay
Director, Information Management, Gilles Bélanger
Director, Legal, Estelle Alain
Director, Tourism & Convention Office, Pierre Labrie

Canadian Almanac & Directory 1997

4-174 REGIONAL GOVERNMENT

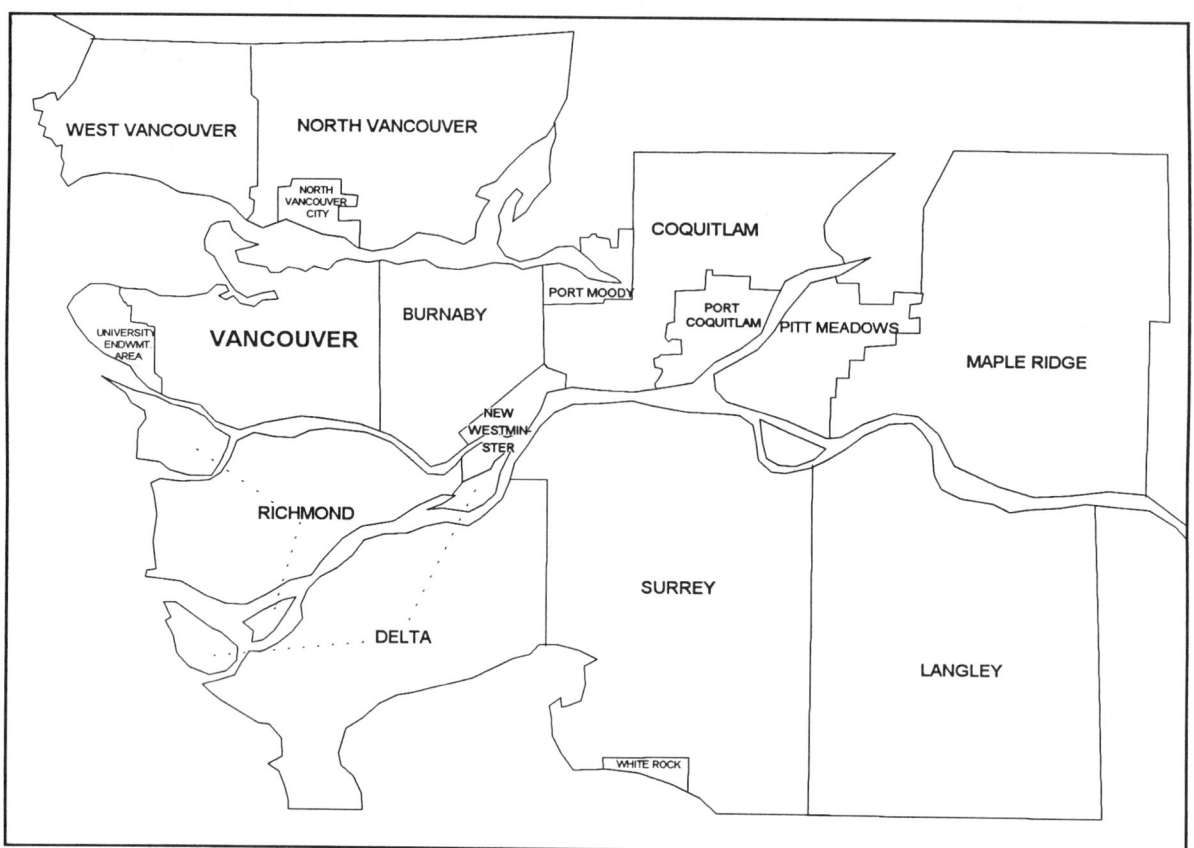

REGIONAL GOVERNMENT 4-175

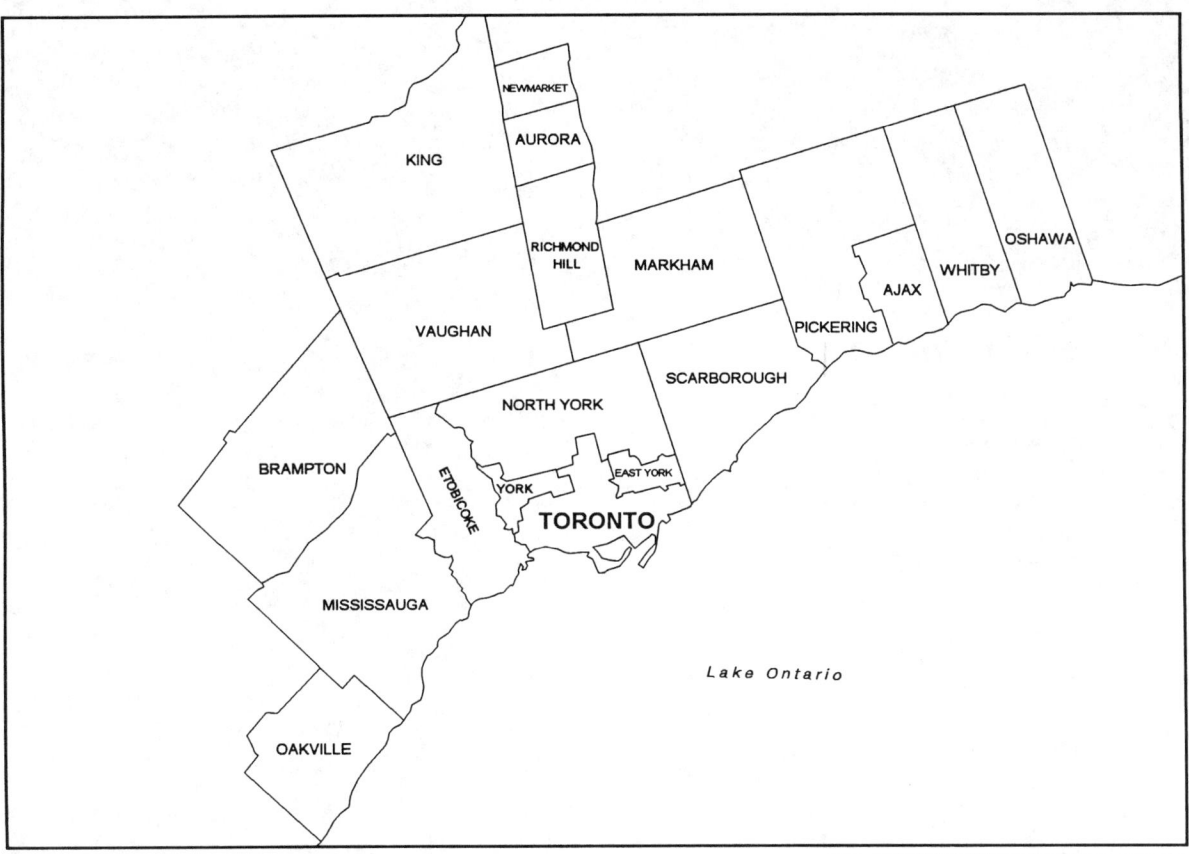

© Copyright DATAMAP Electronic Mapping, Toronto

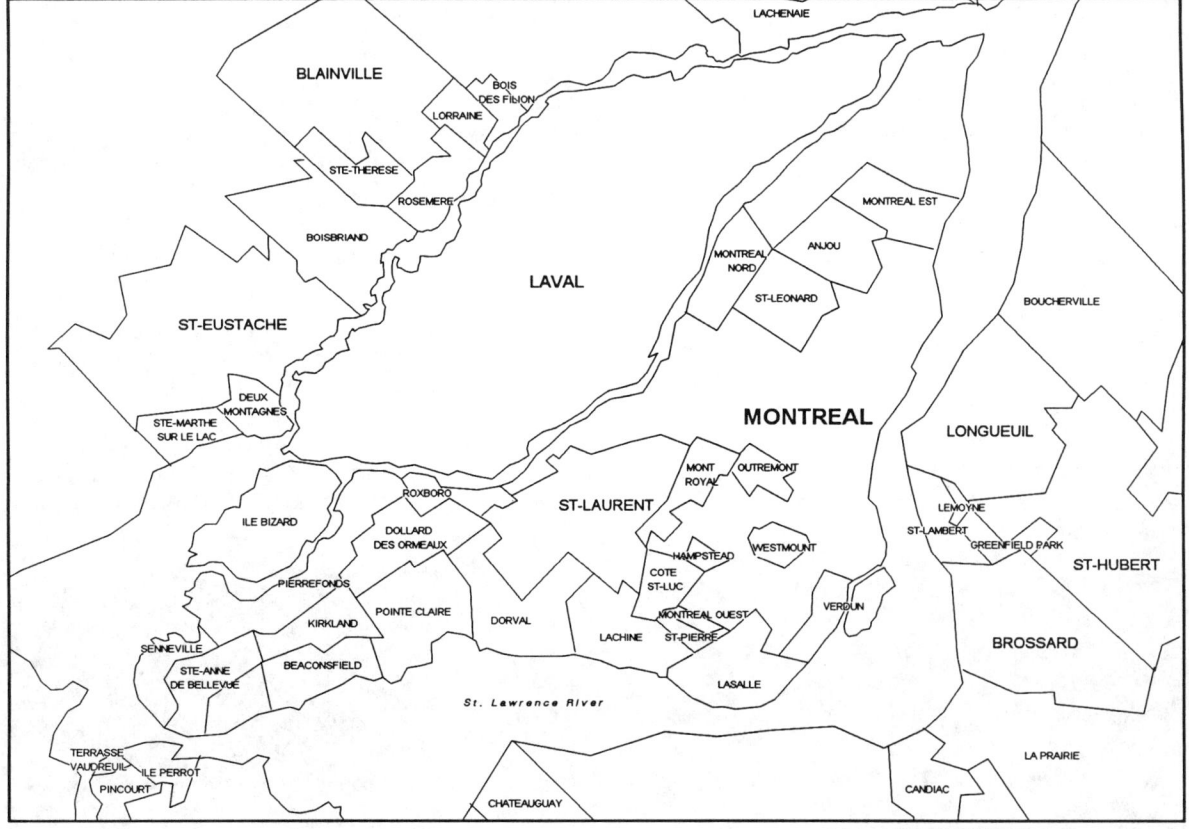

© Copyright DATAMAP Electronic Mapping, Toronto

Canadian Almanac & Directory 1997

SECTION 5

COMMUNICATIONS & INFORMATION MANAGEMENT DIRECTORY

LIBRARIES	1	MAGAZINES	159	SPECIALTY & PAY SERVICES	223
ARCHIVES	112	BROADCASTING STATIONS	198	CABLE STATIONS	223
BOOK PUBLISHERS	115	AM BROADCASTING STATIONS	199	ONLINE SERVICE PROVIDERS	230
NEWSPAPERS	130	FM BROADCASTING STATIONS	206	FREENETS	232
MAGAZINE INDEX	148	TELEVISION STATIONS	213	WEBSITE DIRECTORY	233

See ADDENDA at the back of this book for late changes & additional information.

LIBRARIES

The National Library of Canada/Bibliothèque nationale du Canada
395 Wellington St., Ottawa ON K1A 0N4
613/995-9481; TTY 613/992-6969; Fax: 613/943-1112; Email: ENVOY 100: OONL.REFERENCE; reference@nlc-bnc.ca; URL: http://www.nlc-bnc.ca/ Symbol: OONL
National Librarian, Marianne Scott, Email: mfs@nlo.nlc-bnc.ca
Acquisitions & Bibliographic Services, Director General, Ingrid Parent, 819/994-6887, Email: ingrid.parent@nlc-bnc.ca
Corporate Policy & Communications, Director General, Tom Delsey, 613/943-1939, Email: tom.delsey@nlc-bnc.ca
Information Technology Services, Director General, Louis Forget, 819/997-7223, Email: louis.forget@nlc-bnc.ca
Information Resource Management, Director General, Rolande Blair, 613/996-2892, Email: rolande.blair@nlc-bnc.ca
National & International Program, Director General, Gwynneth Evans, 613/995-3904, Email: gwynneth.evans@nlc.bnc.ca
Research & Information Services, Director General, Mary Jane Starr, 613/996-0680, Email: mary-jane.starr@nlc-bnc.ca

The National Library is governed by the National Library Act, 1969; primary functions are: to promote knowledge & use of the published heritage of Canada; to ensure its acquisition & preservation & to support Canadian studies; to foster library development throughout Canada; to facilitate Canadian library & information resource-sharing. Offers interlibrary loan, reference, info. & advisory services; administers the legal deposit regulations which require that two copies of current Canadian publications be deposited with the Library; publishes national bibliography, Canadiana, (lists new publications relating to Canada); maintains online union catalogues of Canadian libraries; enters into agreements with libraries & coordinates the development of Canadian bibliographic & communications networking to facilitate the sharing of library resources. Collections of Canadian materials include monographs, microforms, newspapers, periodicals, government publications, educational kits, sound recordings, videos & CD-ROMs.

Access AMICUS, 819/997-7227, Fax: 819/994-6835, Email: ENVOY 100: its.cic; cic@nlc-bnc.ca
Canadian Book Exchange Centre, 613/952-8902, Fax: 613/954-9891, Email: cbecccel@nlc-bnc.ca
Canadian Literature Research Service, 613/947-0827, Fax: 613/995-1969, Email: clrssrlc@nlc-bnc.ca
Canadian Thesis Service, 819/953-6221, Fax: 819/997-7517, Email: theses@nlc-bnc.ca
Canadiana (The National Bibliography), 819/994-6918, Fax: 819/953-0291, Email: canadiana@nlc-bnc.ca
Cataloguing Standards - CAN/MARC Office, 819/994-6936, Fax: 819/994-6835, Email: canmarc@nlc-bnc.ca
Cataloguing Standards - Standards & Support, 819/994-6934, Fax: 819/953-0291, Email: cataloguing.standards@nlc-bnc.ca
Cataloguing in Publication (CIP), 819/994-6881, Fax: 819/997-7517, Email: cip@nlc-bnc.ca
Children's Literature Service, 613/996-7774, Fax: 613/995-1969, Email: ENVOY 100: OONL.CLS; clsslj@nlc-bnc.ca
Gifts & Exchanges, 819/994-6955, Fax: 819/997-2395, Email: exchanges@nlc-bnc.ca; gifts@nlc-bnc.ca
Interlibrary Loan (ILL), 613/996-3566, Fax: 613/996-4424, Email: ENVOY 100: OONL.ILL.PEB
International Standard Numbers - Canadian ISBN & ISMN, 819/953-8508, Fax: 819/997-7519, Email: isbn@nlc-bnc.ca
International Standard Numbers - ISSN Canada, 819/994-6895, Fax: 819/953-0291, Email: issn@nlc-bnc.ca
Jacob M. Lowy Collection, 613/995-7960, Fax: 613/995-1969, Email: lowy@ncl-bnc.ca
Legal Deposit, 819/997-9565, Fax: 819/953-8508, Email: legal.deposit@nlc-bnc.ca
Library Information Service, 613/995-8717, Fax: 613/943-2946, Email: ENVOY 100: OONL.LDC; lissib@nlc-bnc.ca
Literary Manuscript Collection, 613/947-0827, Fax: 613/995-1969, Email: litmss@nlc-bnc.ca
MARC Records Distribution Service (MRDS), 819/994-6913, Fax: 819/953-0291, Email: mrds@nlc-bnc.ca
Marketing & Publishing, 613/995-7969, Fax: 613/991-9871, Email: publications@nlc-bnc.ca
Music Division, 613/996-2300, Fax: 613/952-2895, Email: ENVOY 100: OONL.MUS; music@nlc-bnc.ca
Preservation, 613/996-3945, Fax: 613/996-7941
Public Programs, 613/992-9988, Fax: 613/943-2343, Email: public.programs@nlc-bnc.ca
Rare Book Collection, 613/947-0828, Fax: 613/995-1969, Email: rare.books.livres.rares@nlc-bnc.ca
Reading Room (2nd Fl.), 613/996-7428, Fax: 613/943-1112, Email: reference@nlc-bnc.ca
Reference & Information Services, 613/995-9481; TTY: 613/992-6969, Fax: 613/943-1112, Email: reference@nlc-bnc.ca
Union Catalogue, 819/997-7990; 819/953-0291, Fax: 819/947-2706, Email: union.catalogue@nlc-bnc.ca

GOVERNMENT DEPARTMENTS IN CHARGE OF LIBRARIES
ALBERTA: Alberta Community Development-Libraries Section, Arts, Recreation & Libraries Branch, Beaver House, 10158 - 103 St., 3rd Fl., Edmonton AB T5J 0X6 – 403/427-2556; Fax: 403/422-9132; Email: ENVOY:ILL.AECLS – Manager, Punch Jackson
BRITISH COLUMBIA: British Columbia Ministry of Municipal Affairs-Library Services Branch, Administration, PO Box 9490, Victoria BC V8W 9N7 – 250/356-1791; Fax: 250/387-4048; Toll Free: 1-800-663-7051 – Director, Barbara Greeniaus, Email: bgreeniaus@hq.marh.gov.bc.ca; Policy & Legislation, Manager, Chris Peppler, 250/387-4133, Email: cpeppler@hq.marh.gov.bc.ca; Technology & Information Services, Manager, Jim Looney, 250/660-7346, Email: jlooney@hq.marh.gov.bc.ca; Technical Services/ILL, Manager, Laurel Prysiazny, 250/387-5277, Email: lprysiazny@hq.marh.gov.bc.ca; Library Consultant, Barbara Chouinard, 250/356-0413,

Canadian Almanac & Directory 1997

Email: bchouinard@hq.marh.gov.bc.ca; Library Consultant, Dawn Stoppard, 250/356-1790, Email: dstoppard@hq.marh.gov.bc.ca

MANITOBA: Manitoba Culture, Heritage & Citizenship-Public Library Services, #200, 1525 - 1 St., Brandon MB R7A 7A1 – 204/726-6590; Fax: 204/726-6868; Email: ENVOY:ILL.MWPL – Director, Sylvia Nicholson

NEW BRUNSWICK: New Brunswick Library Services, PO Box 6000, Fredericton NB E3B 5H1 – 506/453-2354; Fax: 506/453-2416; Email: ENVOY:ILL.NBFC – Director, Jocelyne LeBel

NEWFOUNDLAND: Newfoundland Provincial Public Libraries Board, Arts & Culture Centre, 125 Allendale Rd., St. John's NF A1B 3A3 – 709/737-3964; Fax: 709/737-3009; Email: dagale@calvin.stemnet.nf.ca – Director, David Gale

NORTHWEST TERRITORIES: Northwest Territories Library Services, 62 Woodland Dr., PO Box 1100, Hay River NT X0E 1G1 – 403/874-6531; Fax: 403/874-3321; Email: ENVOY: NWT.Library.Services – A/Territorial Librarian, Suliang Feng; Administrative Secretary, Heather Beck; Technical Services, Head, Brian Dawson; Order Clerk, Theresa Lafferty; Technical Service Clerk, Shannon Coady; Shipping Clerk, Alison Kilgour

NOVA SCOTIA: Nova Scotia Provincial Library, 3770 Kempt Rd., Halifax NS B3K 4X8 – 902/424-2400; Fax: 902/424-0633; Email: admin@nshpl.library.ns.ca; Symbol: NSHPL – Provincial Librarian, Marion L. Pape; User Services, Andrea John; Administration & Systems, Elizabeth Armstrong; Technical Services, Bridget Turner

ONTARIO: Ministry of Citizenship, Culture & Recreation-Cultural Partnerships Branch, 77 Bloor St. West, 3rd Fl., Toronto ON M7A 2R9 – 416/314-7611; Fax: 416/314-7635 – Director, Michael Langford

PRINCE EDWARD ISLAND: Prince Edward Island Provincial Library, Red Head Rd., PO Box 7500, Morell PE C0A 1S0 – 902/961-7320; Fax: 902/961-7322; TLX: 014-44154; Email: ENVOY:ILL.PC – Director of Archives & Libraries, Harry Holman

QUÉBEC: Ministère de la culture et des communications-Direction des arts, bibliothèques et industries culturelles, Bloc A, 225, Grande Allée est, 3e étage, Québec PQ G1R 5G5 – 418/644-7206; Fax: 418/644-0380 – Directeur, François Paquette

SASKATCHEWAN: Saskatchewan Provincial Library, 1352 Winnipeg St., Regina SK S4P 3V7 – 306/787-2976; Fax: 306/787-2029; Email: srp.admin@provlib.lib.sk.ca; URL: http://www.lib.sk.ca/provlib/; http://www.lib.sk.ca/pleis/; Symbol: SRP – Provincial Librarian, Maureen Woods; Public Library & Client Services, Director, Joylene Campbell; Client Projects & Assessment, Head, Marie Sakon; Client Services, Reference & Interlibrary Loans, Head, Ved Arora; Multitype Coordinator Services, Coordinator, Marilyn Jenkins; Technical & Internal Services, Director, Gloria Materi

YUKON TERRITORY: Government of Yukon, Dept. of Education, Libraries & Archives Division, PO Box 2703, Whitehorse YT Y1A 2C6 – 403/667-5309; Fax: 403/393-6253; Email: ILL.Yukon – Director, Linda R. Johnson, Email: Ljohnson@gov.yk.ca; Manager, Public Library Services, Julianne Ourom, 403/667-5447, Fax: 403/667-2666

Library Associations, refer to page 2-116.

ALBERTA

Regional Library Systems with Member Libraries

CHINOOK ARCH REGIONAL LIBRARY SYSTEM
2902 - 7th Ave. North, Lethbridge AB T1H 5C6 – 403/380-1500; Fax: 403/380-3550; Symbol: ALCA
CEO, Maggie Macdonald

Arrowwood Municipal Library, PO Box 88, Arrowwood AB T0L 0B0 – 403/534-3932; Fax: 403/534-3932 – Librarian, Mary Block

Cardston & District Public Library, PO Box 1560, Cardston AB T0K 0K0 – 403/653-4775 – Head Librarian, Lei Shimbashi-Ellet

Cardston Municipal District No. 6 Library Board, PO Box 580, Cardston AB T0K 0K0 – 403/653-4977 – Sec.-Treas., Vern Quinton

Carmangay & District Municipal Library, PO Box 67, Carmangay AB T0L 0N0 – 403/643-3777 – Head Librarian, Marion Schibbelhute

Vulcan County Municipal Library Board, PO Box 84, Carmangay AB T0L 0N0 – Secretary, Margaret Shaw

Champion Municipal Library, PO Box 177, Champion AB T0L 0R0 – 403/897-3099 – Head Librarian, Grete Christiansen

Claresholm Municipal Library, PO Box 548, Claresholm AB T0L 0T0 – 403/625-4168 – Head Librarian, Kathy Bantle

Coaldale Public Library, PO Box 1207, Coaldale AB T1M 1N1 – 403/345-1340; Fax: 403/345-1342 – Head Librarian, Frieda Boschman

Fort MacLeod RCMP Centennial Library, PO Box 1479, Fort Macleod AB T0L 0Z0 – 403/553-3880; Fax: 403/553-2643 – Librarian, Sharon Edwards

Glenwood Municipal Library, PO Box 1156, Glenwood AB T0K 2R0 – 403/626-3660 – Librarian, Twylla Oviatt

Granum Municipal Library, PO Box 300, Granum AB T0L 1A0 – 403/687-3912 – Head Librarian, Linda DeMaere

Lethbridge Municipal Library, 810 - 5 Ave. South, Lethbridge AB T1J 4C4 – 403/380-7341; Fax: 403/329-1478; Email: ENVOY: ILL.AL – Head Librarian, Duncan Rand

Lomond Public Library, PO Box 290, Lomond AB T0L 1G0 – 403/792-3934 – Head Librarian, Donna Dietrich

Magrath Public Library, PO Box 295, Magrath AB T0K 1J0 – 403/758-6498; Fax: 403/758-6333 – Head Librarian, Marilyn Grusendorf

Milo Municipal Library, PO Box 30, Milo AB T0L 1L0 – 403/599-3850 – Head Librarian, Barbara Godkin

Picture Butte Municipal Library, PO Box 1130, Picture Butte AB T0K 1V0 – 403/732-4141 – Head Librarian, Bonnie Lewis; Circulation Librarian, Anne Withage

Raymond Public Library, PO Box 258, Raymond AB T0K 2S0 – 403/752-4785 – Head Librarian, Linda Sheen

Stavely Municipal Library, PO Box 100, Stavely AB T0L 1Z0 – 403/549-2190 – Head Librarian, Jean Cochlan

Theodore Bradley Library, PO Box 100, Stirling AB T0K 2E0 – 403/756-3665 – Head Librarian, Donna Clawson

Taber Public Library, PO Box 2019, Taber AB T0K 2G0 – 403/223-4343 – Head Librarian, Renée Husdal

Vauxhall Public Library, PO Box 265, Vauxhall AB T0K 2K0 – 403/654-2370 – Head Librarian, Vera Lowen

Vulcan Municipal Library, PO Box 1120, Vulcan AB T0L 2B0 – 403/485-2571 – Head Librarian, Patricia Crosby

MARIGOLD LIBRARY SYSTEM
710 - 2 St., Strathmore AB T1P 1K4 – 403/934-5334; Fax: 403/934-5331; Toll Free: 1-800-332-1077; Email: rlunn@freenet.calgary.ab.ca;
Symbol: ASMLS
Director, Rowena Lunn
Public Services Librarian, Laurie Harrison
Technical Services Librarian, Arlene Hammer

Acme Municipal Library, PO Box 326, Acme AB T0M 0A0 – 403/546-3845; Fax: 403/546-2248 – Librarian, Connie Rieger

Banff Public Library, PO Box 996, Banff AB T0L 0C0 – 403/762-2661; Fax: 403/762-3805; Email: jfish@awine.com – Librarian, Jeannette Fish

Beiseker Municipal Library, PO Box 8, Beiseker AB T0M 0G0 – 403/947-3230; Fax: 403/947-2146 – Librarian, Cherry Greer

Sheep River Municipal Library, PO Box 90, Black Diamond AB T0L 0H0 – 403/933-3278; Fax: 403/933-7373 – Librarian, Tracey Nicoll

Berry Creek Community Library, RR#2, Cessford, Brooks AB T1R 1E2 – 403/566-3743; Fax: 403/566-3736 – Librarian, Gina Lundquist

Canmore Public Library, PO Box 757, Canmore AB T0L 0M0 – 403/678-2468; Fax: 403/678-2165 – Librarian, Jean Luthy

Carbon Municipal Library, PO Box 70, Carbon AB T0M 0L0 – 403/572-3440 – Librarian, Elaine Murphy

Cereal & District Municipal Library, PO Box 218, Cereal AB T0J 0N0 – 403/326-3853 – Librarian, Rose-Marie Rude

Consort Municipal Library, General Delivery, Consort AB T0C 1B0 – 403/577-3003; Fax: 403/566-3736 – Librarian, Shelley Beier

Delia Municipal Library, PO Box 302, Delia AB T0J 0W0 – 403/364-3777; Fax: 403/364-3805; URL: delia@schnet.edc.gov.ab.ca – Librarian, Leah Hunter

Drumheller Public Library, PO Box 1599, Drumheller AB T0J 0Y0 – 403/823-5382; Fax: 403/823-4469; Email: drumli@dns.magtech.ab.ca – Librarian, Linde Turner

East Coulee Community Library, PO Box 600, East Coulee AB T0J 1B0 – 403/822-2158 – Librarian, Beatrice Foose

Empress Municipal Library, PO Box 188, Empress AB T0J 1E0 – 403/565-3023 – Librarian, Wilma Schafer

Exshaw Community Library, PO Box 157, Exshaw AB T0L 2C0 – 403/673-3571 – Librarian, Rosie Reid

Gleichen Municipal Library, PO Box 160, Gleichen AB T0J 1N0 – 403/734-2390 – Librarian, Dorien Jackson

Hanna Municipal Library, PO Box 878, Hanna AB T0J 1P0 – 403/854-3865; Fax: 403/854-2772 – Librarian, Mary McKay

High River Centennial Library, 909 - 1st St. West, High River AB T1V 1A5 – 403/652-2917; Fax: 403/652-7203 – Librarian, Deborah Gardiner

Hussar Municipal Library, General Delivery, Hussar AB T0J 1S0 – 403/787-3766; Fax: 403/787-3922 – Librarian, Myrtle Pentelchuk

Irricana & District Municipal Library, PO Box 299, Irricana AB T0M 1B0 – 403/935-4818 – Librarian, Kathleen Beagle

Linden Community Library, PO Box 120, Linden AB T0M 1J0 – 403/546-3863; Fax: 403/546-4220 – Librarian, Debbie Martin

Longview Municipal Library, PO Box 189, Longview AB T0L 1H0 – 403/558-3631 – Librarian, Lise Robert

Millarville Community Library, PO Box 59, Millarville AB T0L 1K0 – 403/931-3919 – Librarian, Norma Dawson

Morrin Municipal Library, PO Box 284, Morrin AB T0J 2B0 – 403/772-3922 – Librarian, Faye Edwards

Okotoks Public Library, PO Box 310, Okotoks AB T0L 1T0 – 403/938-2220; Fax: 403/938-4317 – Librarian, Marg Proctor

Oyen Municipal Library, PO Box 328, Oyen AB T0J 2J0 – 403/664-3580; Fax: 403/664-2520 – Librarian, Charlotte Lester

Rockyford Municipal & District Library, PO Box 277, Rockyford AB T0J 2R0 – 403/533-3801 – Librarian, Kelly-Anne Nickle

Rumsey Community Library, PO Box 113, Rumsey AB T0J 2Y0 – 403/368-3939 – Librarian, Isabella Taylor

Standard Municipal Library, PO Box 305, Standard AB T0J 3G0 – 403/644-3995 – Librarian, Betty Christensen

Strathmore Municipal Library, 85 Lakeside Blvd., Strathmore AB T1P 1A0 – 403/934-5440 – Librarian, Margie Lavoie

Three Hills Municipal Library, PO Box 207, Three Hills AB T0M 2A0 – 403/443-2360 – Librarian, Sharon Wood

Trochu Municipal Library, PO Box 396, Trochu AB T0M 2C0 – 403/442-2458 – Librarian, Brenda Cunningham

Youngstown Municipal Library, PO Box 39, Youngstown AB T0J 3P0 – 403/779-3864; Fax: 403/779-2279 – Librarian, Wendy Mainhood

NORTHERN LIGHTS LIBRARY SYSTEM
PO Box 8, Elk Point AB T0A 1A0 – 403/724-2596; Fax: 403/724-2597; Email: nlls@ccinet.ab.ca; Symbol: AEPNL
Director, Kolette Taber
Public Services Librarian, Linda MacCallum
Finance & Administrative Officer, Don Isert

Bonnyville Municipal District Municipal Library Board, PO Box 1010, Bonnyville AB T9N 2J7 – 403/826-3710; Fax: 403/826-4524; Symbol: ABM – Chair, Polly Kopala

Cold Lake Public Library, #1301 - 8th Ave., Cold Lake AB T0A 0V2 – 403/639-3967; Fax: 403/639-3963 – Librarian, Hansa Thaleshvar

Elk Point Public Library, PO Box 750, Elk Point AB T0A 1A0 – 403/724-3737; Fax: 403/724-3737 – Librarian, Michele Duczek

Grand Centre & District Public Library, PO Box 1049, Grand Centre AB T0A 1T0 – 403/594-5101; Fax: 403/594-0007 – Librarian, Mary Anne Penner

Kitscoty Municipal Library, PO Box 300, Kitscoty AB T0B 2P0 – 403/846-2121; Fax: 403/846-2930 – Librarian, Wanda Berg

Lloydminster Public Library, 5010 - 49 Ave., Lloydminster AB T9V 0K2 – 403/875-0850; 306/825-2618 (Sask.); Fax: 403/875-6523; Email: Lloydlib@supernet.ab.ca – Chief Librarian, Ron Gillies

Marwayne Public Library, PO Box 174, Marwayne AB T0B 2X0 – 403/847-3930; Fax: 403/847-3796 – Clerk Librarian, Carol Killam

Medley Public Library, PO Box 1400, Medley AB T0A 2M0 – 403/594-4254 – Librarian, Dale Gratton

County of Two Hills #21 Municipal Library Board, PO Box 204, Myrnam AB T0B 3K9 – 403/366-3302 – Secretary, Beverly Myroniuk

Myrnam Community Library, General Delivery, Myrnam AB T0B 3K0 – 403/366-3801; Fax: 403/366-2332 – Librarian, Anne Godziuk

Three Cities Public Library, PO Box 60, Paradise Valley AB T0B 3R0 – 403/745-2277 (school); Fax: 403/745-2641 – Librarian, Sandra Babcock

St. Paul Municipal Library, PO Box 1328, St. Paul AB T0A 3A0 – 403/645-5198; Fax: 403/645-5790 – Librarian, Rachel Holman

Smoky Lake Municipal Library, PO Box 460, Smoky Lake AB T0A 3C0 – 403/656-4212; Fax: 403/656-4212 – Chair, Carole Carpenter

Alice Melnyk Public Library, PO Box 460, Two Hills AB T0B 4K0 – 403/657-3553; Fax: 403/657-3553 – Chair, Esther Zayak

Vermilion Public Library, PO Box 476, Vermilion AB T0B 4M0 – 403/853-4288; Fax: 403/853-1783 – Librarian, Karla Palichuk

Anne Chorney Public Library, PO Box 130, Waskatenau AB T0A 3P0 – 403/358-2777; Fax: 403/358-2332 – Librarian, Cathy Zon

PARKLAND REGIONAL LIBRARY SYSTEM
5404 - 56 Ave., Lacombe AB T4L 1G1 – 403/782-3850; Fax: 403/782-4650; URL: http://www.rtt.ab.ca/rtt/prl; Symbol: ALAP
Director, Margaret Law
Assistant Director, Clive Maishment
Reference Librarian, Patricia Silver

Alix Public Library, PO Box 69, Alix AB T0C 0B0 – 403/747-3233 – Librarian, Debra Cowan

Alliance Municipal Library, PO Box 185, Alliance AB T0B 0A0 – 403/879-3733 – Librarian, Mandy Fuller

Bashaw Municipal Library, PO Box 669, Bashaw AB T0B 0H0 – 403/372-4055 – Librarian, Beth Richardson

Bawlf Public Library, PO Box 33, Bawlf AB T0B 0J0 – 403/373-3882 – Librarian, Linda Nikiforuk

Bentley Municipal Library, PO Box 361, Bentley AB T0C 0J0 – 403/748-4626 – Librarian, Valerie Anderson

Blackfalds Public Library, PO Box 70, Blackfalds AB T0M 0J0 – 403/885-2343 – Librarian, Darlene Stone

Bowden Public Library, PO Box 218, Bowden AB T0M 0K0 – 403/224-3688 – Librarian, Doreen Lee

Camrose Public Library, 4710 - 50 Ave., Camrose AB T4V 0R8 – 403/672-4214; Fax: 403/672-9165 – Librarian, Robin Brown

Caroline Municipal Library, PO Box 339, Caroline AB T0M 0M0 – 403/722-4060; Fax: 403/722-4050 – Librarian, Viola Larsen

Bob Clarke Municipal Library, PO Box 941, Carstairs AB T0M 0N0 – 403/337-3943 – Librarian, Anne Strilchuk

Clive Public Library, PO Box 82, Clive AB T0C 0Y0 – 403/784-3131 – Librarian, Donna Hunter

Cremona Municipal Library, General Delivery, Cremona AB T0M 0R0 – 403/637-3763; Fax: 403/637-2101 – Librarian, Sandra Herbert

Daysland Public Library, PO Box 700, Daysland AB T0B 1A0 – 403/374-3730 – Librarian, Carol Pennycook

Delburne Municipal Library, PO Box 405, Delburne AB T0M 0V0 – 403/749-3848; Fax: 403/749-2800 – Librarian, Sheila Reczseidler

Didsbury Municipal Library, PO Box 305, Didsbury AB T0M 0W0 – 403/335-3142; Fax: 403/335-3142 – Librarian, Mark Fischer

Lone Pine Public Library, RR#2, Didsbury AB T0M 0W0 – 403/337-2888 – Librarian, Ruth Good

Eckville Municipal Library, PO Box 492, Eckville AB T0M 0X0 – 403/746-3240 – Librarian, Cathy Rolfsen

Edberg Public Library, General Delivery, Edberg AB T0B 1J0 – 403/877-2538; Fax: 403/877-2562 – Librarian, Amanda McCrea

Elnora Public Library, General Delivery, Elnora AB T0M 0Y0 – 403/773-3922 – Librarian, Christine Hunter

Forestburg Public Library, PO Box 579, Forestburg AB T0B 1N0 – 403/582-4110 – Librarian, Judy Oberg

Galahad Public Library, PO Box 58, Galahad AB T0B 1R0 – 403/583-3917 – Librarian, Lori Wegenast

Hardisty & District Public Library, General Delivery, Hardisty AB T0B 1V0 – 403/888-3947 – Librarian, Trudy Vickerman

Hay Lakes Municipal Library, PO Box 69, Hay Lakes AB T0B 1W0 – 403/878-3366 – Librarian, Nora Klappstein

Heisler Municipal Library, PO Box 111, Heisler AB T0B 2A0 – Fax: 403/889-2280 – Librarian, Linda Calon

Innisfail Public Library, 4949 - 49 St., PO Box 220, Innisfail AB T4G 1A5 – 403/227-4407; Fax: 403/227-3122 – Librarian, Virginia Robblee

Killam & District Municipal Library, PO Box 329, Killam AB T0B 2L0 – 403/385-3032 – Librarian, Karen Auburn

Lacombe Public Library, #6, 5033 - 52 St., Lacombe AB T4L 2A6 – 403/782-7572 – Librarian, Christina Landry

Lougheed & District Public Library, PO Box 179, Lougheed AB T0B 2V0 – 403/386-3730 – Librarian, Debra Smith

Mirror Municipal Library, PO Box 254, Mirror AB T0B 3C0 – 403/788-3044 – Librarian, Jeanne Kingston

Nordegg Public Library, General Delivery, Nordegg AB T0M 2H0 – 403/721-3949; Fax: 403/721-2057 – Librarian, Heather Clement

Olds Municipal Library, 5217 - 52 St., Olds AB T4H 1S8 – 403/556-6460; Fax: 403/556-6692 – Librarian, Donna Phillips

Penhold & District Public Library, PO Box 10, Penhold AB T0M 1R0 – 403/886-2636 – Librarian, Gertrude Hingley

Ponoka Jubilee Library, PO Box 4160, Ponoka AB T4J 1R6 – 403/783-3843; Fax: 403/783-6745 – Librarian, Norma-Jean Colquhoun

Rimbey Municipal Library, PO Box 1130, Rimbey AB T0C 2J0 – 403/843-2841 – Librarian, Susan Grieshaber-Otto

Rocky Mountain House Memorial Library, PO Box 1497, Rocky Mountain House AB T0M 1T0 – 403/845-2042; Fax: 403/845-5633 – Librarian, Myrna G. Speers

Sedgewick & District Municipal Library, PO Box 569, Sedgewick AB T0B 4C0 – 403/384-3003 – Librarian, Judy Ferrier

Sundre Municipal Library, PO Box 539, Sundre AB T0M 1X0 – 403/638-4000; Fax: 403/638-4000 – Librarian, Charlene Siegfried

Sylvan Lake Municipal Library, PO Box 46, Sylvan Lake AB T0M 1Z0 – 403/887-2130; Fax: 403/887-3660; Email: sylvan-lake-library@ccinet.ab.ca – Librarian, Alice Swabey

Water Valley Public Library, General Delivery, Water Valley AB T0M 2E0 – 403/637-3899 – Librarian, Harriet Green

PEACE LIBRARY SYSTEM
8301 - 110 St., Grande Prairie AB T8W 6T2 – 403/538-4656; Fax: 403/539-5285; Email: pls@terranet.ab.ca
Acting Director, Sharon Siga
Public Services Librarian, Linda Duplessis
Public Services Librarian, Beth Walker
Technical Services Librarian, Sharon Siga
Acquisitions Librarian, Lyn Bjerke

Bear Point Community Library, General Delivery, Bear Canyon AB T0H 0B0 – 403/595-3771; Fax: 403/595-3777; Email: bearcan@schnet.edc.gov.ab.ca – Librarian, Shirley Fredrickson

Alberta RCMP Century Public Library, PO Box 119, Beaverlodge AB T0H 0C0 – 403/354-2569 – Librarian, Linda Senenko

Berwyn Women's Institute Municipal Library, PO Box 89, Berwyn AB T0H 0E0 – 403/338-3616 – Librarian, Kirsten Bettenson

Menno-Simons Community School Library, General Delivery, Cleardale AB T0H 3Y0 – 403/585-3623; Fax: 403/685-3665; Email: menno@schnet.edc.gov.ab.ca – Librarian, Ida May McLarty

Fairview Public Library, PO Box 248, Fairview AB T0H 1L0 – 403/835-2613; Fax: 403/835-3281 – Librarian, Chris Burkholder

Canadian Almanac & Directory 1997

Bibliothèque Dentinger, CP 60, Falher AB T0H 1M0 – 403/837-2776 – Bibliothécaire, Cecile Johnson

Grande Prairie County Library Board, 8611 - 108 St., Grande Prairie AB T8V 4C5 – 403/532-9722 – Secretary, Jean Rycroft

Grande Prairie Municipal Library, 9910 - 99 Ave., Grande Prairie AB T8V 0R5 – 403/532-3580; Fax: 403/538-4983; Email: gppl@terranet.ab.ca – Librarian, Rick Leech

Grimshaw Municipal Library, PO Box 588, Grimshaw AB T0H 1W0 – 403/332-4553 – Librarian, Linda Chmilar

High Level Municipal Library, PO Box 1380, High Level AB T0H 1Z0 – 403/926-2097; Email: hlplsys@ccinet.ab.ca – Librarian, Sheryl Pelletier

High Prairie Municipal Library, PO Box 890, High Prairie AB T0G 1E0 – 403/523-3838 – Librarian, Janet G. Lemay

Hines Creek Municipal Library, PO Box 750, Hines Creek AB T0H 2A0 – 403/494-3879; Fax: 403/494-3605 – Librarian, Betty Ann Tachit

Hythe Municipal Library, PO Box 601, Hythe AB T0H 2C0 – 403/356-3014 – Librarian, Karen Bass

Kinuso Municipal Library, PO Box 60, Kinuso AB T0G 1K0 – 403/775-3694 – Librarian, Susan Moody

La Glace Community Library, PO Box 209, La Glace AB T0H 2J0 – 403/568-4696 – Librarian, Doris Fast

Manning Municipal Library, PO Bag 1400, Manning AB T0H 2M0 – 403/836-3054 – Librarian, Barbara Mulcahy

McLennan Municipal Library, PO Box 298, McLennan AB T0H 2L0 – 403/324-3767; Fax: 403/324-2288 – Librarian, Mariette Limoges

Nampa Municipal Library, PO Box 509, Nampa AB T0H 2R0 – 403/322-3805; Fax: 403/322-2100 – Librarian, Netah Schmalz

Peace River Municipal Library, 9807 - 97 Ave., Peace River AB T8S 1H6 – 403/624-4076 – Librarian, Sharon Keene

Rainbow Lake Municipal Library, PO Box 266, Rainbow Lake AB T0H 2Y0 – 403/956-3656 – Librarian, Mary Grace

Sexsmith Shannon Municipal Library, PO Box 266, Sexsmith AB T0H 3C0 – 403/568-4333; Fax: 403/568-2200 – Librarian, Sherrill Robinson

Spirit River Municipal Library, PO Box 490, Spirit River AB T0H 3G0 – 403/864-4038 – Librarian, Carol Bergstrom

Valhalla Centre Community Library, PO Box 68, Valhalla Centre AB T0H 3M0 – 403/356-3834 – Librarian, Gail Perry

Valleyview Municipal Library, PO Box 897, Valleyview AB T0H 3N0 – 403/524-3033; Fax: 403/524-2727 – Librarian, Sophie Major

Worsley & District Library, PO Box 210, Worsley AB T0H 3W0 – 403/685-3842; Fax: 403/685-3766 – Librarian, Sandra Wasylciw

SHORTGRASS LIBRARY SYSTEM

2375 - 10 Ave. SW, Medicine Hat AB T1A 8E2 – 403/529-0550; Fax: 403/528-2473; Email: ENVOY: SHORTGRASS

Director, Raymond Lusty

Bow Island Municipal Library, PO Box 608, Bow Island AB T0K 0G0 – 403/545-2828; Fax: 403/545-6642 – Librarian, Susan Andersen

Brooks Municipal Library, PO Box 1149, Brooks AB T0J 0J0 – 403/362-2947; Fax: 403/362-8111 – Librarian, Karen Armbruster

Foremost Municipal Library, PO Box 397, Foremost AB T0K 0X0 – 403/867-3855 – Librarian, Betty Van Staalduine

Manyberries Library, c/o Manyberries School, General Delivery, Manyberries AB T0K 1L0 – 403/868-3762 (School) – School Secretary, Karen Jakubowsky

Medicine Hat Public Library, 414 First St. SE, Medicine Hat AB T1A 0A8 – 403/527-5528; Fax: 403/527-4595 – Librarian, Bruce Evans

Redcliff Municipal Library, PO Box 280, Redcliff AB T0J 2P0 – 403/548-3335 – Librarian, Reita Wilson

YELLOWHEAD REGIONAL LIBRARY SYSTEM

433 King St., PO Box 400, Spruce Grove AB T7X 2Y1 – 403/962-2003; Fax: 403/962-2770; Email: yellowhd@freenet.edmonton.ab.ca; Symbol: ASGY

Director, Linda Cook

Assistant Director, Louise Fiolek

Alberta Beach Public Library, PO Box 186, Alberta Beach AB T0E 0A0 – 403/924-3545 – Librarian, Anne Allen

Alder Flats Public Library, PO Box 148, Alder Flats AB T0C 0A0 – 403/388-3898; Fax: 403/388-3887 – Librarian, Ivy Seeley

Barrhead Public Library, 5103 - 53 Ave., Barrhead AB T7N 1N9 – 403/674-8519; Fax: 403/674-8520; Email: yslemko@ls.barrhead.ab.ca – Coordinator of Libraries, Yvonne Slemko; Library Technician, Darlene Bush

Bibliothèque de Beaumont Library, 5202 - 50 St., Beaumont AB T4X 1K7 – 403/929-2665 – Librarian, Valerie McGillivray

Breton Public Library, PO Box 447, Breton AB T0C 0P0 – 403/696-3740; Fax: 403/696-3590 – Librarian, Diane Shave

Calmar Public Library, PO Box 328, Calmar AB T0C 0V0 – 403/985-3472; Fax: 403/985-3039 – Librarian, Carol Nystrom

Clyde Public Library, PO Box 190, Clyde AB T0G 0P0 – 403/348-5356 – Librarian, Wanda Tollenaar

Darwell Public Library, PO Box 206, Darwell AB T0E 0L0 – 403/892-3199 – Librarian, E. Vienna Johnson

Drayton Valley Municipal Library, 5120 - 52 St., PO Box 6240, Drayton Valley AB T0E 0M0 – 403/542-2228; Fax: 403/542-5753; Email: nnaidoo@ccinet.ab.ca – Librarian, Nesen Naidoo

Duffield Community Library, PO Box 479, Duffield AB T0E 0N0 – 403/892-2644; Fax: 403/892-3344 – Librarian, Jutta Kube

Keephills Community Library, RR#1, Duffield AB T0E 0N0 – 403/731-3965; Fax: 403/731-2433 – Librarian, Catherine Wagner

Sunwapta Shores Public Library, Box 4, Site 4, RR#1, Duffield AB T0E 0N0 – 403/797-2424 – Librarian, Vicki Richardson

Entwistle Public Library, PO Box 323, Entwistle AB T0E 0S0 – 403/727-4332 – Librarian, Judy Spring

M. Alice Frose Library, PO Box 150, Fawcett AB T0G 0Y0 – 403/954-3827; Fax: 403/954-2570 – Library Clerk, Marie Meyn

Flatbush Public Library, PO Box 82, Flatbush AB T0G 0Z0 – 403/681-3773 – Librarian, Rose Pichota

Fort Assiniboine Library, General Delivery, Fort Assiniboine AB T0G 1A0 – 403/584-3876; Fax: 403/584-2227 – Librarian, Louise Davison

Grande Cache Municipal Library, PO Box 809, Grande Cache AB T0E 0Y0 – 403/827-2081 – Library Coordinator, Gabriella Fleissner

Rich Valley Public Library, RR#1, Site 6, PO Box 6, Gunn AB T0E 1A0 – 403/967-3525 – Librarian, Sylvia Fitzgerald

Jarvie Community Library, PO Box 119, Jarvie AB T0G 1H0 – 403/954-2513 – Librarian, Kim Klein

Leduc Public Library, #2, Alexandra Park, Leduc AB T9E 4C4 – 403/986-2637; Fax: 403/986-3462; Email: bat@freenet.edmonton.ab.ca – Librarian, Beth Anne Thomas

Mayerthorpe Public Library, PO Box 810, Mayerthorpe AB T0E 1N0 – 403/786-2440; Fax: 403/786-4590 – Librarian, Karen Watson

Millet Public Library, PO Box 30, Millet AB T0C 1Z0 – 403/387-5222 – Librarian, Claudia Wagner

Neerlandia Public & School Library, PO Box 10, Neerlandia AB T0G 1R0 – 403/674-5581; Fax: 403/674-2927 – Librarian, Sandra Olthuis

New Sarepta Municipal Library, PO Box 10, New Sarepta AB T0B 3M0 – 403/941-3924; Fax: 403/941-2224 – Librarian, Judy Appleby

Onoway Public Library, PO Box 484, Onoway AB T0E 1V0 – 403/967-2445; Email: onowaypl@freenet.edmonton.ab.ca – Librarian, Barb McIntyre

Sangudo Public & High School Library, PO Box 524, Sangudo AB T0E 2A0 – 403/785-3431 – Librarian, Helga Jossy

Seba Beach Public Library, PO Box 159, Seba Beach AB T0E 2B0 – 403/797-3940; Fax: 403/797-3800 – Librarian, Chris Newson

Spruce Grove Public Library, #15, 420 King St., Spruce Grove AB T7X 2C6 – 403/962-4423; Fax: 403/962-4826; Email: sgpl@freenet.edmonton.ab.ca – Librarian, Nancy Jones

Stony Plain Public Library, PO Box 1680, Stony Plain AB T7X 2C6 – 403/963-5440; Fax: 403/963-5439 – Librarian, Rosemary Coyle

Thorsby Municipal Library, PO Box 319, Thorsby AB T0C 2P0 – 403/789-3808 – Librarian, Carolyn Hoffman

Tomahawk Community School Library, PO Box 69, Tomahawk AB T0E 2H0 – 403/339-2433 – Librarian, Chris Worden Goerz

Vimy Public Library, PO Box 29, Vimy AB T0G 2J0 – 403/961-3014 – Librarian, Pauline Despins

Wabamun Municipal Library, PO Box 89, Wabamun AB T0E 2K0 – 403/892-2713 – Librarian, Donna Holliday

Warburg Public Library, PO Box 299, Warburg AB T0C 2T0 – 403/848-2391 – Librarian, Meta Siemens

Lakedell Area Community Library, RR#1, Westerose AB T0C 2V0 – 403/586-2246 – Librarian, Yvonne M. Adair

Linaria Public Library, RR#1, Westlock AB T0G 2L0 – 403/349-2558 – Librarian, Olga Hadley

Westlock Municipal Library, PO Box 1198, Westlock AB T0G 2L0 – 403/349-3060; Fax: 403/349-3306 – Librarian, Carolyne Musterer

Wetaskiwin Municipal Library, 5002 - 51 Ave., Wetaskiwin AB T9A 0V1 – 403/352-4055; Fax: 403/352-3266 – Librarian, Ivy Breitkreuz

Whitecourt & District Public Library, PO Box 150, Whitecourt AB T7S 1N3 – 403/778-2900; Fax: 403/778-4166 – Librarian, Thyra Ferguson

Winfield Community Library, PO Box 360, Winfield AB T0C 2X0 – 403/682-2213 – Librarian, Ileane Cox

Municipal, Public & Community Libraries

Airdrie Municipal Library, PO Box 3310, Airdrie AB T4B 2B6 – 403/948-0600; Fax: 403/948-6567 – Head Librarian, Mary Westcott; Public Services Librarian, Vivyan Oneil; Technical Services Librarian, Debbie Hobberfield

Amisk Public Library, PO Box 71, Amisk AB T0B 0B0 – 403/856-3980 – Librarian, Donna Holte

Andrew Municipal Library, PO Box 449, Andrew AB T0B 0C0 – 403/365-3501; Fax: 403/365-3734 – Librarian, Denise Dorland

Ashmont Public Library, PO Box 330, Ashmont AB T0A 0C0 – 403/726-3877; Fax: 403/726-3777 – Librarian, Donna Karpyshyn – Branch of St. Paul County Municipal Library Board

Athabasca County Municipal Library Board, PO Box 540, Athabasca AB T0G 0B0 – 403/675-2285; Fax: 403/675-3544 – Secretary, Robert Tannas – See also following branches: Grassland Community Library, Rochester Community Library

Athabasca: Alice B. Donahue Library & Archives, PO Box 2099, Athabasca AB T0G 0B0 – 403/675-2735; Fax: 403/675-5933 – Librarian, Judy Flax

LIBRARIES — ALBERTA

Barnwell Public Library, 490 Cottonwood St., PO Box 261, Barnwell AB T0K 0B0 – 403/223-3626 – Librarian, Karenne Stuckart

Bassano Municipal Memorial Library, PO Box 658, Bassano AB T0J 0B0 – 403/641-4065 – Librarian, Anne MacPhail

Bellevue Public Library, PO Box 489, Bellevue AB T0K 0C0 – 403/564-5201 – Librarian, Doreen Glavin – Branch of Crowsnest Pass Municipal Library Board (see Blairmore)

Big Valley Municipal Library, PO Box 205, Big Valley AB T0J 0G0 – 403/876-2642 – Librarian, Cheryl Wildman

Blairmore: Crowsnest Pass Municipal Library Board, PO Box 1177, Blairmore AB T0K 0E0 – 403/562-8393 – Secretary, Sandra Brokofsky – See also following branches: Bellevue Public Library, Blairmore Public Library

Blairmore Public Library, PO Box 1177, Blairmore AB T0K 0E0 – 403/562-8408 – Librarian, Jessie Arbuckle; Librarian, Judy Bradley – Branch of Crowsnest Pass Municipal Library Board

Bodo Community Library, PO Box 93, Bodo AB T0B 0M0 – 403/753-6647 – Librarian, Kelly Paulgaard – Branch of Provost Municipal District Library Board

Bon Accord Public Library, PO Box 749, Bon Accord AB T0A 0K0 – 403/921-2540; Fax: 403/921-3585 – Librarian, Julie Saunders

Bonnyville Municipal Library, PO Box 8058, Bonnyville AB T9N 2J3 – 403/826-3071; Fax: 403/826-2058 – Librarian, Gil Heney

Boyle Public Library, PO Box 450, Boyle AB T0A 0M0 – 403/689-4161 – Head Librarian, Katherine Bulmer

Brocket: Oldman River Cultural Centre Library, PO Box 70, Brocket AB T0J 0H0 – 403/965-3939 – Librarian, Jo-Ann YellowHorn

Brownfield Community Library, PO Box 54, Brownfield AB T0C 0R0 – 403/578-2487 – Librarian, Annette Barnes

Brownvale: Municipal District of Peace #135 Municipal Library Board, PO Box 57, Brownvale AB T0H 0L0 – 403/597-2250 – Sec.-Treas., Maureen Osowetski – See also following branches: Brownvale Public Library

Brownvale Public Library, General Delivery, Brownvale AB T0H 0L0 – 403/597-3781 – Librarian, Faye McEachnie – Branch of Municipal District of Peace #135 Municipal Library Board

Bruderheim Municipal Library, PO Box 250, Bruderheim AB T0B 0S0 – 403/796-3032 – Librarian, Annette Bjorkquist

Cadogan Public Library, General Delivery, Cadogan AB T0B 0T0 – 403/753-2434 – Librarian, Avis Jickling – Branch of Provost Municipal District Library Board

Calgary Public Library, 616 Macleod Trail SE, Calgary AB T2G 2M2 – 403/260-2600; Fax: 403/237-5393; Email: ENVOY: ILL.AC; Symbol: AC – Director, Gerry Meek; Collection & Electronic Resources, Manager, Beth Barlow, 403/260-2607; Support Services, Manager, Anne Sawa, 403/260-2668; Planning, Manager, Barbara Killick, 403/260-2634; Human Resources, Manager, Ellen Humphrey, 403/260-2627; Youth Services, Manager, J. Hardman, 403/260-2679 – See also following branches: Alexander Calhoun Branch Library, Bowness Branch Library, Chinook Branch Library, Fish Creek Area Library, Forest Lawn Branch Library, Georgina Thomson Branch Library, Louise Riley Branch Library, Memorial Park Branch Library, Millican-Ogden Branch Library, Nose Hill Area Library, Shaganappi Branch Library, Southwood Branch Library, Thorn-Hill Branch Library, Village Square Area Library, W.R. Castell Central Library

Calgary: Alexander Calhoun Branch Library, 3223 - 14 St. SW, Calgary AB T2T 3V8 – 403/221-2010 – Manager, Barbara Lake – Branch of Calgary Public Library

Calgary: Bowness Branch Library, 7930 Bowness Rd. NW, Calgary AB T3B 0H3 – 403/221-2022 – Jean Ludlam – Branch of Calgary Public Library

Calgary: Chinook Branch Library, Chinook Centre, Bowladrome Level, 6455 MacLeod Trail South, Calgary AB T2H 0K8 – 403/221-2072 – Manager, Janet MacKinnon – Branch of Calgary Public Library

Calgary: Fish Creek Area Library, 11161 Bonaventure Dr. SE, Calgary AB T2J 6S1 – 403/221-2090; Fax: 403/225-2526 – Manager, Susan Beatty – Branch of Calgary Public Library

Calgary: Forest Lawn Branch Library, 4807 - 8 Ave. SE, Calgary AB T2A 4M1 – 403/221-2070 – Manager, Janet MacKinnon – Branch of Calgary Public Library

Calgary: Georgina Thomson Branch Library, 51 Cornell Rd. NW, Calgary AB T2L 0L4 – 403/221-2040 – Jean Ludlam – Branch of Calgary Public Library

Calgary: Louise Riley Branch Library, 1904 - 14 Ave. NW, Calgary AB T2N 1M5 – 403/221-2046 – Manager, Marilyn Wallace – Branch of Calgary Public Library

Calgary: Memorial Park Branch Library, 1221 - 2 St. SW, Calgary AB T2R 0W5 – 403/221-2006 – Manager, Aruna Marthe – Branch of Calgary Public Library

Calgary: Millican-Ogden Branch Library, 7005 - 18 St. SE, Calgary AB T2C 1Y1 – 403/221-2080 – Manager, Aruna Marathe – Branch of Calgary Public Library

Calgary: Nose Hill Area Library, 1530 Northmount Dr. NW, Calgary AB T2G 0G6 – 403/221-2030 – Manager, Jane Haney – Branch of Calgary Public Library

Calgary: Shaganappi Branch Library, Shaganappi Multi-Service Centre, 3415 - 8 Ave. SW, Calgary AB T3C 0E8 – 403/221-2020 – Manager, Carolyn Murray – Branch of Calgary Public Library

Calgary: Southwood Branch Library, 924 Southland Dr. SW, Calgary AB T2W 0J9 – 403/221-2082 – Manager, Mary Enright – Branch of Calgary Public Library

Calgary: Thorn-Hill Branch Library, Thorn-Hill Community Centre, 6617 Centre St. North, Calgary AB T2K 4Y5 – 403/221-2050 – Manager, Ann Austin – Branch of Calgary Public Library

Calgary: Village Square Area Library, Village Square Leisure Centre, 2623 - 56 St. NE, Calgary AB T1Y 6E7 – 403/221-2060; Fax: 403/280-8965 – Manager, Carole McCloy – Branch of Calgary Public Library

Calgary: W.R. Castell Central Library, 616 McLeod Trail SE, Calgary AB T2G 2M2 – 403/260-2600; Fax: 403/237-5393 – Manager, Central & Area Libraries, Peg Hofmann – Branch of Calgary Public Library

Castor Municipal Library, PO Box 699, Castor AB T0C 0X0 – 403/882-3999 – Librarian, Wendy Bozek

Chauvin Municipal Library, PO Box 129, Chauvin AB T0B 0V0 – 403/858-3744; Fax: 403/858-2392; Email: folkin@schnt.gov.ab.ca – Librarian, Linda Granigan

Chestermere Municipal Library, 156 East Chestermere Dr., Chestermere AB T1X 1C1 – 403/272-9744; Fax: 403/569-0512 – Municipal Administrator, Kathy Nikkel

Clyde Municipal Library, PO Box 190, Clyde AB T0G 0P0 – 403/348-5356 (Village Office) – Librarian, Wanda Tollenaar

Cochrane: Nan Boothby Memorial Library, PO Box 996, Cochrane AB T0L 0W0 – 403/932-4353; Fax: 403/932-4353 – Librarian, Brenda J. Hughes

Coronation Memorial Library, PO Box 453, Coronation AB T0C 1C0 – 403/578-3445 – Librarian, Eileen Merchant

Coutts Municipal Library, PO Box 216, Coutts AB T0K 0N0 – 403/344-3804; Fax: 403/344-3815 – Librarian, Sharon Wollersheim

Crossfield Municipal Library, PO Box 355, Crossfield AB T0M 0S0 – 403/946-4232 – Librarian, Sylvia Ramage

Czar Municipal Library, PO Box 127, Czar AB T0B 0Z0 – 403/857-3870 – Librarian, Robyn Long

Debolt Public Library, PO Box 480, Debolt AB T0H 1B0 – 403/957-3770 – Librarian, Karen Downey

Derwent Public Library, General Delivery, Derwent AB T0B 1C0 – 403/741-3792 – Librarian, Leona Bielech

Devon Public Library, PO Box 398, Devon AB T0C 1E0 – 403/987-3720 (School) – Librarian, Audrey Benjamin

Donalda Municipal Library, PO Box 40, Donalda AB T0B 1H0 – 403/883-2345; Fax: 403/883-2022 – Librarian, Leigh-Ann Ensign

Duchess Public Library, PO Box 88, Duchess AB T0J 0Z0 – 403/378-4369 – Librarian, Cathy Neufeld

Eaglesham Public Library, PO Box 206, Eaglesham AB T0H 1H0 – 403/359-3792; Fax: 403/359-3745 – Library Clerk, Norma Bolster

Edgerton Public Library, General Delivery, Edgerton AB T0B 1K0 – 403/755-3820 (res.) – Sec.-Treas., Brenda Redhead

Edmonton Public Library, 7 Sir Winston Churchill Sq., Edmonton AB T5J 2V4 – 403/496-7000; Fax: 403/496-1885; Email: penny@freenet.edmonton.ab.ca – Director, Penelope McKee; Reference Librarian, Louise Reimer; Circulation Librarian, Michael Dell; Children's Librarian, Joanne Griener; Deputy Director, Public Services, Keith Turnbull; Deputy Director, Support Services, Al Davis; Acquisitions Librarian, Mary Flannagan – See also following branches: Calder Branch Library, Capilano Branch Library, Castledowns Branch Library, Highlands Branch Library, Idylwylde Branch Library, Jasper Place Branch Library, Londonderry Branch Library, Millwoods Branch Library, Southgate Branch Library, Sprucewood Branch Library, Strathcona Branch Library, Woodcroft Branch Library

Edmonton: Calder Branch Library, 12522 - 132 Ave., Edmonton AB T5L 3P9 – 403/496-7090; Fax: 403/496-1453 – Branch Manager, Jack de Graaf – Branch of Edmonton Public Library

Edmonton: Capilano Branch Library, 201 Capilano Mall, Edmonton AB T6A 0A1 – 403/496-1803; Fax: 403/496-7009 – Branch Manager, Barbara Bulat – Branch of Edmonton Public Library

Edmonton: Castledowns Branch Library, 15333 Castledowns Rd. #9, Edmonton AB T5X 3Y7 – 403/496-1805; Fax: 403/496-7005 – Branch Manager, Jack de Graaf – Branch of Edmonton Public Library

Edmonton: Highlands Branch Library, 6710 - 118 Ave., Edmonton AB T5B 0P3 – 403/496-1806; Fax: 403/496-7012 – Branch Manager, Howard Saunders – Branch of Edmonton Public Library

Edmonton: Idylwylde Branch Library, 8310 - 88 Ave., Edmonton AB T6C 1L1 – 403/496-1809; Fax: 403/496-7092 – Branch Manager, Barbara Bulat – Branch of Edmonton Public Library

Edmonton: Jasper Place Branch Library, 9010 - 156 St., Edmonton AB T5R 5X7 – 403/496-1810; Fax: 403/496-7004 – Branch Manager, Skip Wilson – Branch of Edmonton Public Library

Edmonton: Londonderry Branch Library, L10A Londonderry Mall, Edmonton AB T5C 3C8 – 403/496-1816; Fax: 403/496-1452; Symbol: LON – Branch Manager, Andrea Smith – Branch of Edmonton Public Library

Edmonton: Millwoods Branch Library, 601 Millwoods Town Centre, 2331 - 66 St., Edmonton AB T6K 4B5 – 403/496-1820; Fax: 403/496-1450 – Branch Manager, Hazel Spratt – Branch of Edmonton Public Library

Edmonton: Southgate Branch Library, 48 Southgate Mall, Edmonton AB T6H 4M6 – 403/496-1825; Fax: 403/496-7007 – Branch Manager, Joanne Griener – Branch of Edmonton Public Library

Edmonton: Sprucewood Branch Library, 11555 - 95 St., Edmonton AB T5G 1L5 – 403/496-7098; Fax: 403/496-7010 – Branch Manager, Howard Saunders – Branch of Edmonton Public Library

Edmonton: Strathcona Branch Library, 8331 - 104 St., Edmonton AB T6E 4E9 – 403/496-1828; Fax: 403/496-1451 – Branch Manager, Pat Arnold – Branch of Edmonton Public Library

Edmonton: Woodcroft Branch Library, 13420 - 114 Ave., Edmonton AB T5M 2Y5 – 403/496-1831; Fax: 403/496-7089 – Branch Manager, Pat Arnold – Branch of Edmonton Public Library

Edson & District Public Library, 4726 - 8 Ave., Edson AB T7E 1S8 – 403/723-6691; Fax: 403/723-3508 – Head Librarian, Lisbeth J. Booth

Enchant Public Library, PO Box 3000, Enchant AB T0K 0V0 – 403/739-3835 – Librarian, Sandy Severtson – Branch of Taber Municipal District Library Board

Evansburg & District Municipal Library, PO Box 339, Evansburg AB T0E 0T0 – 403/727-3872; Fax: 403/727-2437 – Librarian, E. Lauer

Falher: Municipal District of Smoky River No. 130 Municipal Library Board, PO Box 210, Falher AB T0H 1M0 – 403/837-2221 – Secretary, Roger Laflamme

Fort McMurray Public Library, Jubilee Centre, 9907 Franklin Ave., Fort McMurray AB T9H 2K4 – 403/743-7800; Fax: 403/743-7037; Email: ENVOY: ILL.FOR – Director, Carol Cooley; Public Services Librarian, Paula Lacroix

Fort Saskatchewan Public Library, 10011 - 102 St., Fort Saskatchewan AB T8L 2C5 – 403/998-4275; Fax: 403/998-4774 – Library Director, Marcia E. Redford

Fort Vermilion Community Library, PO Box 4, Fort Vermilion AB T0H 1N0 – 403/927-4279; Symbol: AFVC – Librarian, Anne Martens

Fox Creek Municipal Library, PO Box 1078, Fox Creek AB T0H 1P0 – 403/622-2343; Fax: 403/622-3482 – Librarian, Carol Downing

Gem: County of Newell Library Board, PO Box 35, Gem AB T0J 1M0 – 403/641-2155 – Sec.-Treas., Betty Neufeld – See also following branches: Alcoma Public Library, Gem Jubilee Library, Rolling Hills Public Library

Gem: Gem Jubilee Library, PO Box 37, Gem AB T0J 1M0 – 403/641-2261 – Librarian, Shelly Heryford – Branch of County of Newell Library Board

Gibbons Public Library, PO Box 510, Gibbons AB T0A 1N0 – 403/923-2004; Fax: 403/923-3691 – Librarian, Julie Saunders

Grassland Community Library, PO Box 57, Grassland AB T0A 1V0 – 403/525-3733; Fax: 403/525-3750 – Librarian, Lori Zachkewich – Branch of Athabasca County Municipal Library Board

Grassy Lake Community Library, PO Box 690, Grassy Lake AB T0K 0Z0 – 403/655-2232; Fax: 403/655-2259 – Librarian, Cindy Orr

Hairy Hill Municipal Library, PO Box 126, Hairy Hill AB T0B 1S0 – 403/768-3840; Email: dlaing@agt.net – Librarian, Don Laing

Hays: Taber Municipal District Library Board, PO Box 63, Hays AB T0K 1B0 – 403/725-3750 – Sec.-Treas., Diane Wickenheiser – See also following branches: Enchant Public Library, Hays Public Library

Hays Public Library, PO Box 36, Hays AB T0K 1B0 – 403/725-3744 – Librarian, Diane Wickenheiser – Branch of Taber Municipal District Library Board

Heinsburg: St. Paul County Municipal Library Board, General Delivery, Heinsburg AB T0A 1X0 – Chair, Bob Smith – See also following branches: Ashmont Public Library, Bibliothèque Mallaig Community Library, Heinsburg Public Library, Lafond Public Library

Heinsburg Public Library, General Delivery, Heinsburg AB T0A 1X0 – 403/943-3913; Fax: 403/943-3773 – Librarian, Cathy Botting – Branch of St. Paul County Municipal Library Board

High Level: Zama Community Library, PO Box 1453, High Level AB T0H 1Z0 – 403/683-2448 – Librarian, Janet Forrest

Hinton Municipal Library, 803 Switzer Dr., Hinton AB T7V 1V1 – 403/865-2363; Fax: 403/865-4292; Email: Library@yes.ab.ca – Librarian, Hetty Wilderdijk

Holden Municipal Library, PO Box 26, Holden AB T0B 2C0 – 403/688-3838; Fax: 403/688-2091 – Librarian, Sandy Kluczny

Hughenden Public Library, PO Box 36, Hughenden AB T0B 2E0 – 403/856-3830 – Librarian, Leslie McDevitt

Irma Municipal Library, PO Box 340, Irma AB T0B 2H0 – 403/754-3752; Fax: 403/754-3802 – Librarian, Marj Guiltner

Irvine Municipal Library, PO Box 67, Irvine AB T0J 1V0 – Chairperson, Joan Côté

Jasper Municipal Library, PO Box 1170, Jasper AB T0E 1E0 – 403/852-3652; Fax: 403/852-5841 – Librarian, Judy Krefting

Keg River Community Library, PO Box 3, Keg River AB T0H 2G0 – 403/981-2128 – Librarian, Janice Freeman

La Crete Community Library, PO Box 609, La Crete AB T0H 2H0 – 403/928-3166; Fax: 403/928-3000 – Librarian, Helen Wiebe

Lac La Biche & District Public Library, PO Box 2039, Lac La Biche AB T0A 2C0 – 403/623-7467; Fax: 403/623-3510 – Librarian, Ron Weir

Lafond Public Library, PO Box 20, Lafond AB T0A 2G0 – 403/645-2432 – Librarian, Joanne Ternovoy – Branch of St. Paul County Municipal Library Board (*see* Heinsburg)

Lamont Public Library, PO Box 180, Lamont AB T0B 2R0 – 403/895-2228; Fax: 403/895-2600 – Librarian, Rosemarie Konsorada

Lethbridge: County of Lethbridge Municipal Library, 905 - 4 Ave. South, Lethbridge AB T1J 4E4 – 403/328-5525 – Sec.-Treas., S. Steinke

Mallaig: Bibliothèque Mallaig Community Library, CP 90, Mallaig AB T0A 2K0 – 403/635-3858; Téléc: 403/635-3938 – Librarian, Anne-Marie Amyotte – Branch of St. Paul County Municipal Library Board (*see* Heinsburg)

Mannville Municipal Library, PO Box 186, Mannville AB T0B 2W0 – 403/763-3611 – Librarian, Theresa Myroniuk

Milk River: Warner County Municipal Library Board, PO Box 8, Milk River AB T0K 1M0 – 403/344-2128 – Treasurer, Joy Nett – See also following branches: Wrentham Public Library

Milk River Municipal Library, PO Box 579, Milk River AB T0K 1M0 – 403/647-3793 – Librarian, Velora Kundert

Morinville Public Library, 10119 - 100 Ave., Morinville AB T8R 1S1 – 403/939-3292; Email: mvillep@freenet.edmonton.ab.ca – Librarian, Mark Oberg

Nanton: Municipal District of Willow Creek Library Board, PO Box 751, Nanton AB T0L 1R0 – 403/646-5467 – Secretary, Colleen Kindt

Nanton: Thelma Fanning Memorial Library, PO Box 310, Nanton AB T0L 1R0 – 403/646-5535; Fax: 403/646-2653 – Librarian, Llizabet K. Dwwyor

Newbrook Community Public Library, PO Box 208, Newbrook AB T0A 2P0 – 403/576-3771; Fax: 403/576-2115 – Librarian, Jan Rosenthal – Branch of Thorhild County Municipal Library Board

Niton Junction: Green Grove Community Library, PO Box 219, Niton Junction AB T0E 1S0 – 403/795-3782; Fax: 403/795-3933 – Librarian, Wendy Langard

Pincher Creek Municipal Library, PO Box 2020, Pincher Creek AB T0K 1W0 – 403/627-3813 – Librarian, Gwendy Donegani

Plamondon Municipal Library, PO Box 90, Plamondon AB T0A 2T0 – 403/798-3852; Fax: 403/798-3850; Email: plamonee@schnet.edc.gov.ab.ca – Librarian, Emilie Chevigny

Provost Municipal District Library Board, PO Box 300, Provost AB T0B 3S0 – 403/753-2774 – Secretary, Kelly Paulgaard – See also following branches: Bodo Community Library, Cadogan Public Library

Provost Municipal Library, PO Box 449, Provost AB T0B 3S0 – 403/753-2801 – Librarian, Colleen Vaughan

Radway & District Municipal Library, PO Box 220, Radway AB T0A 2V0 – 403/736-3548 (Rec. Centre) – Librarian, Fern Mulyk

Rainier: Alcoma Public Library, General Delivery, Rainier AB T0J 2M0 – 403/362-3741; Fax: 403/362-3741 – Librarian, Joyce Aasen – Branch of County of Newell Library Board (*see* Gem)

Ralston: Graham Community Library, PO Box 40, Ralston AB T0J 2N0 – 403/544-3670 – Librarian, Barbara Janecke

Red Deer Public Library, 4818 - 49 St., Red Deer AB T4N 1T9 – 403/346-4576; Fax: 403/341-3110; Email: info@rdpl.red-deer.ab.ca; URL: http://www.rdpl.red-deer.ab.ca – Director, Dean Frey; Children's Librarian, Donna Alberts, 403/346-7470; Adult Services Librarian, Cynthia Belanger, 403/346-2100; Information Technology, Scott Stanley – See also following branches: Dawe Public Library

Red Deer: Dawe Public Library, 56 Holt St., Red Deer AB T4N 6A6 – 403/341-3822; Fax: 403/343-2120 – Jill Griffith – Branch of Red Deer Public Library

Redwater Public Library, PO Box 384, Redwater AB T0A 2W0 – 403/942-3464 – Librarian, Anne Schmidt

Rochester Community Library, PO Box 309, Rochester AB T0G 1Z0 – 403/698-3970; Fax: 403/698-2290 – Librarian, Doris Briggs – Branch of Athabasca County Municipal Library Board

Rolling Hills Public Library, PO Box 40, Rolling Hills AB T0J 2S0 – 403/964-3640; Fax: 403/964-3659 – Librarian, Johnene Amulung – Branch of County of Newell Library Board (*see* Gem)

Rosemary Municipal Library, PO Box 210, Rosemary AB T0J 2W0 – 403/378-4493 – Librarian, Donna Janzen

Rycroft Municipal Library, PO Box 248, Rycroft AB T0H 3A0 – 403/765-3973; Fax: 403/765-2002 – Librarian, Valerie Twelvetree

Ryley: Beaver County No. 9 Municipal Library Board, PO Box 140, Ryley AB T0B 4A0 – 403/663-3730 – Sec.-Treas., Margaret Jones

Ryley: McPherson Municipal Library, PO Box 139, Ryley AB T0B 4A0 – 403/663-3999 – Librarian, Lori Yachimec

St. Albert Public Library, 5 St. Anne St., St. Albert AB T8N 3Z9 – 403/459-1530; Fax: 403/458-5772; Email: sapl@freenet.edmonton.ab.ca – Library Director, Pamela Forsyth, 403/459-1681; Adult Services/Reference Librarian, Jill Armitage, 403/459-1682; Circulation Librarian, Rosanne Delaney, 403/459-1537; Children's Librarian, Arlene Kissau, 403/459-1536; Systems/Technical Services Librarian, David Rushton, 403/459-1684

St. Isidore Community Library, PO Box 1168, St Isidore AB T0H 3B0 – 403/624-8182 – Librarian, Marie Lavoie

Sherwood Park: Strathcona County Municipal Library, 104 Sherwood Park Mall, 2020 Sherwood Dr., Sherwood Park AB T8A 5P7 – 403/449-5800; Fax: 403/467-6861; Email: scml@freenet.edmonton.ab.ca; Symbol: SPS – Library Director, Marilyn Corbett; Children's Librarian, Mary Card, 403/449-5809; Public Relations & Programming Librarian, Joan Urshel, 403/449-5807

Silver Valley: Savanna Community Library, PO Box 49, Silver Valley AB T0H 3E0 – 403/351-3808 – Librarian, Sandra Lario

Slave Lake Municipal Library, PO Box 540, Slave Lake AB T0G 2A0 – 403/849-5250; Fax: 403/849-2633 – Librarian, Anne McMeekin

Spirit River: Municipal District of Spirit River No. 133 Municipal Library, PO Box 389, Spirit River AB T0H 3G0 – 403/864-2463 – Secretary, Giselle Lewchuk

Stettler Public Library, 6202 - 44 Ave., 2nd Fl., Stettler AB T0C 2L1 – 403/742-2292; Fax: 403/742-3480 – Head Librarian, Eileen Scheerschmidt

Swan Hills Public Library, PO Box 386, Swan Hills AB T0G 2C0 – 403/333-4505 – Head Librarian, Su Balog; Children's Librarian, Vickie Erickson

Tangent Community Library, PO Box 70, Tangent AB T0H 3J0 – 403/359-2126 – Librarian, Annie Laurin

Thorhild County Municipal Library Board, PO Box 615, Thorhild AB T0A 3J0 – 403/576-2180 – Chairperson, Barb Koistinen – See also following branches: Newbrook Community Public Library

Thorhild & District Municipal Library, PO Box 658, Thorhild AB T0A 3J0 – 403/398-3502; Fax: 403/398-2100 – Librarian, Rose Alexander

Tilley & District Public Library, PO Box 225, Tilley AB T0J 3K0 – 403/377-2233; Fax: 403/377-2703 – Librarian, Brenda Arnold

Tofield Municipal Library, PO Box 479, Tofield AB T0B 4J0 – 403/662-3838; Fax: 403/662-3929; Email: ehubbard@freenet.edmonton.ab.ca – Librarian, Elizabeth Hubbard

Vegreville Public Library, PO Box 129, Vegreville AB T9C 1R1 – 403/632-3491; Fax: 403/632-3423 – Librarian, Janet Kolisniak

Veteran Municipal Library, PO Box 527, Veteran AB T0C 2S0 – 403/575-3915 – Librarian, Shirley Kary

Viking Municipal Library, PO Box 300, Viking AB T0B 4N0 – 403/336-4992; Fax: 403/334-2660 – Library Clerk, Kaye Roddick

Vilna & District Municipal Library, PO Box 119, Vilna AB T0A 3L0 – 403/636-3667 – Librarian, Frank D. Barry

Wainwright: Municipal District of Wainwright Municipal Library Board, 717 - 14 Ave., Wainwright AB T9W 1B3 – 403/842-4454; Fax: 403/842-2463 – Secretary, Janice Frost

Wainwright Public Library, PO Box 1358, Wainwright AB T0B 4P0 – 403/842-2673; Fax: 403/842-2340; Email: wainlib@agt.net – Librarian, Ava Nickel

Wandering River Women's Institute Community Library, General Delivery, Wandering River AB T0A 3M0 – 403/771-3928 – Chairperson, Gerda Rebkowich

Wanham Community Library, General Delivery, Wanham AB T0H 3P0 – 403/694-3828 – Librarian, Alice Hillaby

Warner Memorial Municipal Library, PO Box 270, Warner AB T0K 2L0 – 403/642-3988 – Librarian, Julie A. Hutchinson

Waskatenau: Anne Chorney Public Library, PO Box 130, Waskatenau AB T0A 3P0 – 403/358-2777 – Librarian, Cathy Zon

Wildwood Community Public Library, PO Box 243, Wildwood AB T0E 2M0 – 403/325-2108; Fax: 403/325-3783 – Librarian, Ann Myrholm

Willingdon & District Public Library, PO Box 270, Willingdon AB T0B 4R0 – 403/367-2222 – Librarian, Frances Hols

Wrentham Public Library, PO Box 111, Wrentham AB T0K 2P0 – 403/222-2485 – Librarian, Brenda Jurgens – Branch of Warner County Municipal Library Board (see Milk River)

Special & College Libraries & Resource Centres

AIRDRIE
Kids First Parent Association of Canada – Library, PO Box 5256, Airdrie AB T4B 2B3 – 403/289-1440 – National Secretary, Cathy Buchanan

ATHABASCA
Athabasca University - Library, 1 University Dr., PO Box 10000, Athabasca AB T9S 1A1 – 403/675-6254; Fax: 403/675-6477; Toll Free: 1-800-788-9041; Email: library@admin.athabascau.ca; ENVOY: ATHA.U.LIB.
  Library Services, Director, Steve Schafer, 403/675-6259
  Technical Services & Systems, Head, Doug Kariel, 403/675-6261
  Cataloguing & Reference Librarian, Kevin Furniss, 403/675-6232
  Circulation Supervisor, Eileen Hendy, 404/675-6271
  Interlibrary Loans Supervisor, Judy Stady, 403/675-6251

BANFF
The Banff Centre for the Arts - Library, PO Box 1020, Banff AB T0L 0C0 – 403/762-6265; Fax: 403/762-6236; Email: Envoy: LIBRARY.BNFFCNTR; URL: http://www.banffcentre.ab.ca;
  Symbol: ABSFA
  Head Librarian, Bob Foley
  Music Librarian, P. Lawless

Banff Mineral Springs Hospital – Library, PO Box 1050, Banff AB T0L 0C0 – 403/762-2222 – Director, Health Records, Eldene Heikkila

Planned Parenthood of Banff – CRC Resource Centre, Community Resource Centre, YWCA, PO Box 520, Banff AB T0L 0C0 – 403/762-4511 – Administrative Assistant, Janet Harris

Whyte Museum of the Canadian Rockies - Archives Library, 111 Bear St., PO Box 160, Banff AB T0L 0C0 – 403/762-2291; Fax: 403/762-8919; Symbol: ABA – Librarian, Mary Andrews

BARRHEAD
Alberta Distance Learning Centre - Library, PO Box 4000, Barrhead AB T7N 1P4 – 403/674-5333; Fax: 403/674-6561; Email: Dhagan@edc.gov.ab.ca – Librarian, Dawn I. Hagan

Barrhead & District Historical Society – Library, PO Box 4122, Barrhead AB T7N 1A1 – 403/674-5203 – Curator of Museum, Mable Gravel

BEAVERLODGE
Beaverlodge Research Centre - Library, PO Box 29, Beaverlodge AB T0H 0C0 – 403/354-2212; Fax: 403/354-8171; Symbol: ABEAG – Librarian, Shelley M. Pirnak, Email: pirnaks@em.agr.ca

BIG VALLEY
Canadian Northern Society – Library, PO Box 142, Big Valley AB T0J 0G0 – 403/672-3099 – Lori Pratt

BLAIRMORE
Crowsnest Pass Symphony – Library, PO Box 567, Blairmore AB T0K 0E0 – 403/562-2127 – Librarian, C. Kovach

CALGARY
Acres International Limited - Library, 10201 Southport Rd. SW, 5th Fl., Calgary AB T2W 4X9 – 403/253-9161, ext.300; Fax: 403/255-2444 – Librarian, Evelyn Ross

AIDS Calgary Awareness Association – Library, #300, 1021 - 10 Ave. SW, Calgary AB T2R 0B7 – 403/228-0198 – Education Coordinator, Pia Anderson

Alberta Association of Rehabilitation Centres – Library, Box 105, 2725 - 12 St. NE, Calgary AB T2E 7J2 – 403/250-9495

Alberta College of Art & Design - Luke Lindoe Library, 1407- 14 Ave. NW, Calgary AB T2N 4R3 – 403/284-7631; Fax: 403/289-6682; Toll Free: 1-800-251-8290; Symbol: ACAA – Director, Christine E. Sammon, Email: christine.sammon@sait.ab.ca

Alberta Energy & Utilities Board - Library, 640 - 5 Ave. SW, Calgary AB T2P 3G4 – 403/297-8242; Fax: 403/297-3517; Email: ENVOY: ERCB.LIB; Symbol: ACER – Librarian, Liz Johnson

Alberta Energy Co. Ltd. - Library, 3900, 421 - 7 Ave SW, Calgary AB T5K 2P6 – 403/422-1306; Fax: 403/266-8185
  Library Acquisitions, Catherine Vrielink, Email: cvrielink@aec.ca
  Supervisor, Information Centre, June Crichton

Alberta Justice - Law Society of Alberta Library, Courthouse, 611 - 4 St. SW, Calgary AB T2P 1T5 – 403/297-6148; Fax: 403/297-5171; Email: lawseare@cia.com – Regional Librarian, Robert Leigh
  Office of the Chief Medical Examiner, Southern Region - Library, 4070 Bowness Rd. NW, Calgary AB T3B 3R7 – 403/297-8123; Fax: 403/297-3429; Symbol: ACCME – Librarian, Karen McManus
  Southern Alberta Region, Provincial Court Library, 323 - 6 Ave. SE, 5th Fl., Calgary AB T2G 4V1 – 403/297-3126; Fax: 403/297-2981 – Librarian, Susan Powelson, Email: sepowelson@freenet.calgary.ab.ca

Alberta Natural Gas Co. Ltd. - Information Centre, Amoco Centre, #2900, 240 - 4 Ave. SW, 27th Fl., Calgary AB T2P 4L7 – 403/691-7760; Fax: 403/691-7888; Email: ENVOY: ACAS.ILL – Administrator, Paul Mankelow

Alberta Playwrights' Network – Script Library/Reading Room, 1134 - 8 Ave. SW, 2nd Fl., Calgary AB T2P 1J5 – 403/269-8564; Toll Free: 1-800-268-8564

Alberta Sulphur Research Ltd. – Library, Chemistry Department, University of Calgary, 2500 University Dr. NW, Calgary AB T2N 1N4 – 403/220-5372; Email: asrinfo@chem.ucalgary.ca

Alberta Wheat Pool – Library, 505 - 2 St. SW, PO Box 2700, Calgary AB T2P 2P5 – 403/290-5581 – Librarian, Jane Fournier

Alberta Wilderness Association – Library, 455 - 12 St. NW, PO Box 6398, Calgary AB T2P 2E1 – 403/492-2311

Arusha Centre Society – Resource Centre, 233 - 10 St. NW, Calgary AB T2N 1V5 – 403/270-3200 – Linda Grandinetti

Baptist Leadership Training School - Library, 4330 - 16 St. SW, Calgary AB T2T 4H9 – 403/243-3770; Fax: 403/287-1930; Toll Free: 1-800-549-4675 – Principal, Myrna Sears

Bennett Jones Verchere - Law Library, Bankers Hall East, #4500, 855 - 2 St. SW, Calgary AB T2P 4K7 – 403/298-3165; Fax: 403/265-7219
  Chief Librarian, Shelagh Mikulak, Email: mikulaks@bjv.ca
  Reference Librarian, Bernadette Gunn, 403/298-3691
  Reference Services Librarian, Kathy Kurceba, 403/298-3691
  Librarian, Kathleen Hogan, 403/298-3692
  Senior Library Technician, Bonnie Buchanan, 403/298-3143
  Library Technician, Yolanda Jung, 403/298-3006
  Library Clerk, Lorie Larry, 403/298-3226

Blake, Cassels & Graydon Law Office - Library, Bankers Hall East, #3500, 855 - 2 St. SW, Calgary AB T2P 4J8 – 403/260-9600; Fax: 403/263-9895 – Librarian, Jane Hillard

Building Owners & Managers Association of Calgary – Library, #401, 131 - 9 Ave. SW, Calgary AB T2P 1K1 – 403/237-0559 – Executive Assistant, Jean Douglas

Canadian Almanac & Directory 1997

Burnet, Duckworth & Palmer, Barristers & Solicitors - Research & Library Services, First Canadian Centre, #1400, 350 - 7 Ave. SW, Calgary AB T2P 3N9 – 403/260-0187; Fax: 403/260-0332
   Research Lawyer/Director of Research & Information Services, Penelope F. Hamilton
   Assistant Librarian, Diane Shackleton
   Library Assistant, Susan Russell
Calgary Board of Education - Educational Resources & Services, 3610 - 9 St. SE, Calgary AB T2G 3C5 – 403/294-8542; Fax: 403/287-9739
   Acquisitions, Head, Frankie Steele, 403/294-8539
   Biblio Systems & Services, Head, Yasmin Peerani, 403/294-8589
   Circulation (Film & Video), Head, Doreen Johnson, 403/294-8733
   Processing, Head, Maureen Akins, 403/294-8590
   Media Production, Head, Penny Dowswill, 403/294-8576
   School Library Technology, Frank Karas, 403/294-8559
The Calgary Herald - Library, 215 - 16 St. SE, PO Box 2400, Calgary AB T2P 0W8 – 403/235-7361; Fax: 403/235-7379 – Library Team Manager, Karen Crosby
Calgary Horticultural Society – Library, 208 - 50 Ave. SW, Calgary AB T2S 2S1 – 403/287-3469 – Director, Library/Books, Barbara Nobert
Calgary Learning Centre - Library, 3930 - 20 St. SW, Calgary AB T2T 4Z9 – 403/686-9300; Fax: 403/686-0627
   Librarian, Carolyn Patterson, 403/686-9300, Email: cpatters@acs.ucalgary.ca
   Library Technician, Janice Caskey
Calgary Philharmonic Society – Library, 205 - 8 Ave. SE, Calgary AB T2G 0K9 – 403/571-0270 – Librarian, Rob Grewcock
Calgary Regional Health Authority - Bow Valley Centre Hospital Library, 841 Centre Ave. East, Calgary AB T2E 0A1 – 403/268-9237; Fax: 403/268-9283
   Reference Librarian, Steven Paschold, 403/268-9236
   Circulation Librarian, Melanie Heaton, 403/268-9237
   Public Services Librarian/ILL, Debbie Clark
   Technical Services Librarian, Spencer Stevens, 403/268-9737
   Library Clerk, Ana Petrunic, 403/268-9237
   Peter Lougheed Centre - Hospital Library, 3500 - 26 Ave. NE, Calgary AB T1Y 6J4 – 403/291-8736; Fax: 403/291-8888; Email: ENVOY: ILL.ACPLC; Symbol: ACPLC – Medical Library Technician, Kathie Gaudes
Calgary Society for Students with Learning Difficulties – Learning Centre Library, 3930 - 20 St. SW, Calgary AB T2T 4Z9 – 403/686-9322 – Librarian, Carolyn Patterson
Calgary Sun - Library, 2615 - 12 St. NE, Calgary AB T2E 7W9 – 403/250-4200; Fax: 403/291-4116; URL: http://www.canoe.ca/CalgarySun/home.html – Chief Librarian, Kathryn Dilts, 403/250-4135
Canadian Association for Suicide Prevention – Library, #201, 1615 - 10th Ave. SW, Calgary AB T3C 0J7 – 403/245-3900 – Karen Kiddey
Canadian Association of Oilwell Drilling Contractors – Library, #800, 540 - 5 Ave. SW, Calgary AB T2P 0M2 – 403/264-4311 – Coordinator, Economic Analysis, Alan Laws
Canadian Energy Research Institute – I.N. McKinnon Memorial Library, #150, 3512 - 33 St. NW, Calgary AB T2L 2A6 – 403/282-8876; Email: ENVOY: ILL.ACINM – Library Technician, Lynne Buist
Canadian Heritage - Parks Canada, Western Region - Library, #551, 220 - 4 Ave. SE, Calgary AB T2P 3H8 – 403/292-4455; Fax: 403/292-6679; Email: bitzl@pk-swro.dots.doe.ca; Symbol: ACIA – Librarian, Leonard Bitz, Email: Len_Bitz@pch.gc.ca

Canadian Holistic Nurses Association – Archives, 7535 Hunterview Dr. NW, Calgary AB T2K 4P7 – 403/451-0043; Fax: 403/452-3276
Canadian Hunter Exploration Ltd. - Library, #2000, 605 - 5 Ave. SW, Calgary AB T2P 3H5 – 403/260-1772; Fax: 403/260-1899; Symbol: ACHE – Library Coordinator, Wendy Mayer
Canadian Institute of Resources Law – Library, PF-B 3330, University of Calgary, 2500 University Dr. NW, Calgary AB T2N 1N4 – 403/220-3200 – Secretary, Susan Parsons
Canadian Nazarene College - Thomson Library, #610, 833 - 4th Ave. SW, Calgary AB T2P 3T5 – 403/571-2550; Fax: 403/571-2556; Toll Free: 1-800-363-6896
   Head Librarian, Carolyn J. Alho
   Administrative Assistant, Heather J. Liebenberg
Canadian Occidental Petroleum Ltd. - Library, #1500, 635 - 8 Ave. SW, Calgary AB T2P 3Z1 – 403/234-6437; Fax: 403/263-8673; Symbol: ACCO – Librarian, Marlene Robertson
City of Calgary - Engineering & Environmental Library, #8026, 800 Macleod Trail SE, PO Box 2100, Calgary AB T2P 2M5 – 403/268-2793; Fax: 403/268-8260; Symbol: ACE – Library Specialist, Allisen Stubbs
City of Calgary Electric System - Resource Centre, PO Box 2100, Calgary AB T2P 2M5 – 403/268-1100; Fax: 403/269-1833 – Supervisor, Shannon-Dean Christoffersen, 403/268-1268
City of Calgary Planning & Building Department - Information Centre, PO Box 2100, Calgary AB T2P 2M5 – 403/268-5438; Fax: 403/268-5623 – Linda D. Read
City of Calgary Social Services Dept. - Library, PO Box 8116, Calgary AB T2P 2M5 – 403/268-5115; Fax: 403/268-5765 – Research Social Planner, Judith Rempel
Clean Calgary Association – Clean Calgary Environmental Resource Library, #100, 3811 Edmonton Trail NE, Calgary AB T2E 3P5 – 403/230-1443
Code Hunter Wittmann - Library, #1200, 700 - 2nd Ave. SW, Calgary AB T2P 4V5 – 403/298-1000; Fax: 403/263-9193; Symbol: CODH – Librarian, Susan Hammer, 403/298-1088
Commonwealth Microfilm - Library, 901 - 10 Ave. SW, Calgary AB T2R 0B5 – 403/245-2555; Fax: 403/244-6426 – Regional General Manager, Irene Price
Cook Snowdon Law Office - Library, #2000, 421 - 7 Ave. SW, Calgary AB T2P 4K9 – 403/298-2000; Fax: 403/298-2085 – Librarian, Ann Wright
Cottonwood Consultants Ltd. – Library, 615 Deercroft Way SE, Calgary AB T2J 5V4 – 403/271-1408 – Environmental Researcher, Cliff Wallis
Deloitte & Touche - Library, Scotia Centre, #2400, 700 - 2 St. SW, Calgary AB T2P 0S7 – 403/267-1783; Fax: 403/264-2871; Email: gellnerh@cia.com; Symbol: ACTR
   Library Technician, Heather Gellner
   Library Technician, Andrea Taylor
Developmental Disabilities Resource Centre of Calgary, 4631 Richardson Way SW, Calgary AB T3E 7B7 – 403/240-3111; Fax: 403/240-3230
DeVry Institute of Technology - Library, 803 Manning Rd. NE, Calgary AB T2E 7M8 – 403/235-3450; Fax: 403/273-3554; Toll Free: 1-800-363-5558 – LRC Coordinator, Darlene Hittel, 403/235-3450, ext. 145, Email: dhittel@acs.ucalgary.ca
Ernst & Young - Business Information Services, #1300, 707 - 7 Ave. SW, Calgary AB T2P 3H6 – 403/290-4183, 4216; Fax: 403/290-4265; Symbol: ACCG
   Manager, Joan Faulk
   Library Technician, Liz Henry
Family Life Education Council of Calgary – Library, 233 - 12 Ave. SW, Calgary AB T2R 0G9 – 403/262-1117 – Resource Coordinator, Deborah Bray
Fluor Daniel Canada Inc. - Technical Information Centre, 10101 Southport Rd. SW, Calgary AB T2W 3N2 – 403/259-1110; Fax: 403/259-1222;

Email: ENVOY: FLUOR.LIB – Supervisor, Nancy Topper
Foothills Pipe Lines Ltd. - Library, #3100, 707 - 8 Ave. SW, Calgary AB T2P 3W8 – 403/294-4471; Fax: 403/294-4171; Symbol: ACF – Library Technician, Leslie Confrancisco
Glenbow Museum - Library, 130 - 9 Ave. SE, Calgary AB T2G 0P3 – 403/268-4197; Fax: 403/232-6569; Email: GLENBOW.LIB; Symbol: ACG
   Senior Librarian, Lindsay Moir
   Reference Librarian, Catherine Myhr
Grace Women's Health Centre – Dr. Alfred Rothwell Library, 1441 - 29 St. NW, Calgary AB T2N 4JB – 403/670-2200; Fax: 403/284-0228 – Shirley A. Thistlewood
Gulf Canada Resources - Library, PO Box 130, Calgary AB T2P 2H7 – 403/233-3905; Fax: 403/233-3070; Symbol: ACGO
   Team Leader - Library/Record Management, Susan Lowe
   Reference Librarian, Guy Trott
   Library Technician, Sherri Querengesser
Heart & Stroke Foundation of Alberta – Library, 1825 Park Rd. SE, Calgary AB T2G 3Y6 – 403/264-5549 – Tracey Ginn
Howard, Mackie Law Office - Library, Canterra Tower, #1000, 400 - 3 Ave. SW, Calgary AB T2P 4H2 – 403/232-9500; Fax: 403/266-1395, 1397 – Joan Scilley
Husky Oil Limited - Library, PO Box 6525, Calgary AB T2P 3G7 – 403/298-7057; Fax: 403/298-7464 – Librarian, Wanda Oleszkiwicz
Immigration & Refugee Board - Documentation Centre, 205 - 9th Ave. SE, Calgary AB T2G 0R3 – 403/292-6130; Fax: 403/292-6116 – Chief, Michael Embaie
Imperial Oil Limited - Information Resources, 237 - 4 Ave. SW, 12th Fl., Calgary AB T2P 0H6 – 403/237-4520; Fax: 403/237-3728; Email: ENVOY: ILL.ESSO.MAIN; Symbol: ACI – Information Resources Manager, Jane St. Germain
   Research Library, 3535 Research Rd. NW, Calgary AB T2L 2K8 – 403/284-7417; Fax: 403/284-7589; Email: ENVOY: ILL.ESSO.RESEARCH; Symbol: ACIPRD – Information Specialist, Abe Cohen
Institute of Sedimentary & Petroleum Geology - Library, 3303 - 33 St. NW, Calgary AB T2L 2A7 – 403/292-7165; Fax: 403/292-5377; Symbol: ACSP – Head Librarian, John McIsaac, 403/292-7169
Insurance Institute of Southern Alberta – Library, #801, 1015 - 4 St. SW, Calgary AB T2R 1J4 – 403/266-3427 – Frances Lang
International Association of Hydrogeologists - Canadian Chapter – Library, c/o Dept. of Geology & Geophysics, University of Calgary, 2500 University Dr. NW, Calgary AB T2N 1N4 – 403/220-4512 – Librarian, Beverley Foss
MacKimmie Matthews Law Office - Library, Gulf Canada Sq., #700, 401 - 9 Ave. SW, PO Box 2010, Calgary AB T2P 2M2 – 403/232-0765; Fax: 403/232-0888 – Manager of Library Services, Judy Harvie
Macleod, Dixon - Law Library, Canterra Tower, #3700, 400 - 3 Ave. SW, Calgary AB T2P 4H2 – 403/267-8141; Fax: 403/264-5973; Symbol: ACMD – Librarian, Lana Barrett, 403/267-8141
Manalta Coal Ltd. - Resource Centre, 700 - 9 Ave. SW, Calgary AB T2P 3V4 – 403/231-7100; Fax: 403/269-8075
   Teresa Harper
   Josie Christopher
McCarthy Tétrault - Library, #3200, 421 - 7 Ave. SW, Calgary AB T2P 4K9 – 403/260-3500; Fax: 403/260-3501 – Librarian, Colleen A. Maier
McManus Anderson Miles Law Office - Library, Bow Valley Square, #2200, 250 - 6 Ave. SW, Calgary AB T2P 3H7 – 403/263-2190; Fax: 403/263-6840 – Librarian, Leila Lukowski

Milner Fenerty Law Office - Library, Fifth Avenue Pl., 30th Fl., 237 - 4th Ave. SW, Calgary AB T2P 4X7 – 403/268-7055; Fax: 403/268-3100 – Head Librarian, Anil Tiwari

Mobil Oil Canada - Library, PO Box 800, Calgary AB T2P 2J7 – 403/260-7857; Fax: 403/260-7600; Email: ENVOY: ILL.ACM; Symbol: ACM – Senior Legal Secretary & Law Librarian, June A. Lux

Monenco AGRA Inc. - Information Resource Centre, #900, Monenco Place, 801 - 6 Ave. SW, Calgary AB T2P 3W3 – 403/298-4673; Fax: 403/298-4125; Email: ENVOY: MONENCO.LIBRARY – Manager, Lyn McCluskey

Mount Royal College - Learning Resources Centre, 4825 Richard Rd. SW, Calgary AB T3E 6K6 – 403/240-6124; Fax: 403/240-6698; Email: ENVOY: ADMIN/ILL.ACMR – Director of Library Services, Madeleine Bailey

National Energy Board-Environment Branch – Library, 311 - 6th Ave. SW, Calgary AB T2P 3H2 – 403/299-3561 – Manager, Helen Booth

National Energy Board - Library, 311 - 6 Ave. SW, Calgary AB T2P 3H2 – 403/299-3561; Fax: 403/292-5576; Symbol: ACNEB – Manager, Library Services, Helen Booth

Natural Resources Canada - GSC Regional Library - Calgary, Institute of Sedimentary & Petroleum Geology, 3303 - 33rd St. NW, Calgary AB T2L 2A7 – 403/292-7165; Fax: 403/292-5377; Symbol: ACSP – Head Librarian, John McIssac, 403/292-7169

Norcen Energy Resources Ltd. - Library, 715 - 5 Ave. SW, Calgary AB T2P 2X7 – 403/231-0886; Fax: 403/231-0383; Symbol: ACNER – Librarian, Robert McLauchlin

Nova - An Alberta Corporation - Business Information Centre, 801 - 7 Ave. SW, PO Box 2535, Calgary AB T2P 2N6 – 403/290-6718; Fax: 403/290-8940; Symbol: ACNA – Team Leader, Jody Barrett, 403/290-7505

Nova Gas Transmission - Business Information Centre, 801 - 7 Ave. SW, PO Box 2535, Calgary AB T2P 2N6 – 403/290-7505; Fax: 403/290-8940 – Acquisitions Librarian, Jody Barrett

Novacor Chemicals Ltd. - Technical Information Services, 2928 - 16 St. NE, Calgary AB T2E 7K7 – 403/250-4794; Fax: 403/291-3208; Email: library@mail.novacor.com; Symbol: ACNH – Team Leader, Shirley Veness

PanCanadian Petroleum Ltd. - Corporate Library, 150 - 9th Ave. SW, PO Box 2850, Calgary AB T2P 2S5 – 403/268-7645; Fax: 403/268-7649; Email: Pat_Bolander@pcp.ca; Symbol: ACPP – Library Technician, Pat Bolander

Parlee McLaws, Barristers & Solicitors - Library, Western Canadian Place, #3400, 707 - 8 Ave. SW, Calgary AB T2P 1H5 – 403/294-7000; Fax: 403/265-8263; Symbol: ACPML – Reference Technician, Phyllis L. Thornton, 403/294-7059

Petro-Canada - Library, PO Box 2844, Calgary AB T2P 3E3 – 403/730-2659; Fax: 403/296-3030 – Librarian, Joyce Johnson

Petroleum Communication Foundation – Library, #214, 311 - 6th Ave. SW, Calgary AB T2P 3H2 – 403/264-6064 – Communication Advisor, Jennifer O'Brien

Petroleum Industry Training Service – Library, #13, 2115 - 27 Ave. NE, Calgary AB T2E 7E4 – 403/250-0883; Toll Free: 1-800-667-5557 – Library Technician, Brad Tickell

Planned Parenthood Alberta – Reproductive Health Resource Centre, #301, 1220 Kensington Rd. NW, Calgary AB T2N 3P5 – 403/283-8591

Price Waterhouse - Calgary Library, #1200, 425 - 1 St. SW, Calgary AB T2P 3V7 – 403/267-1200; Fax: 403/233-0883 – Library Technician, Laureen Matthews

Ranson, Smith, Neef & Barnes - Library, #1700, 633 - 6 Ave. SW, Calgary AB T2P 2Y5 – 403/269-5400; Fax: 403/265-8118 – Partner, Ronald R. Neef

Reid Crowther & Partners Ltd. – Library, #210, 340 Midpark Way SE, Calgary AB T2X 1P1 – 403/254-3301, ext.653 – Technical Librarian, Doreen Munsie

Revenue Canada - Research & Library Services, #382, 220 - 4 Ave. SE, Calgary AB T2G 0L1 – 403/691-8711; Fax: 403/691-8712; Symbol: ACRCT – Librarian, Pat Sandercock

Rigel Oil & Gas Ltd. - Library, Bow Valley Square 3, #1900, 255 - 5 Ave. SW, Calgary AB T2P 3G6 – 403/267-3057; Fax: 403/267-3087; Symbol: ACTP – Librarian, Cheryl Morrisey

Rocky Mountain College - Library, 4039 Brentwood Rd. NW, Calgary AB T2L 1L1 – 403/284-5100; Fax: 403/220-9567 – Head Librarian, Ronald A. Fox

Rockyview General Hospital – Library Services, 7007 - 14th St. SW, Calgary AB T2V 1P9 – 403/541-3143; Fax: 403/541-3486; Email: Tuyet.Lam@crha-health.ab.ca; Symbol: ACRVH – Librarian, Kim Polvi

Sceptre Resources Limited - Engineering Library, #2000, 400 - 3 Ave. SW, Calgary AB T2P 4H2 – 403/298-9800; Fax: 403/290-1106 – Supervisor, Library Services, Terry-Lyn Martin

Singleton Urquhart Scott Law Office - Library, #203, 200 Barclay Parade SW, Calgary AB T2P 4R5 – 403/261-9043; Fax: 403/265-4632 – Office Services, Cris Salazar

Society for Technology & Rehabilitation – Technical Resource Centre, #200, 1201 - 5 St. SW, Calgary AB T2R 0Y6 – 403/262-9445

Southern Alberta Institute of Technology - Educational Resources Centre, 1301 - 16 Ave. NW, Calgary AB T2L 0M4 – 403/284-8616, 8860; Fax: 403/284-8619; Email: rthornboroug@admn.sait.ab.ca; Symbol: ACSA
  Educational Resources, Manager, R. Thornborough
  Instructional Services, D. Weber, 403/284-8408
  Media Production, M. Sinotte, 403/284-8381
  Reference Librarian, J. Hill, 403/284-8432
  Resource Access, H. Green, 403/284-8372
  Resource Development, M. Chan, 403/284-8617
  Resource Provision, Gwen Chrapko, 403/284-8648
  Technology & Systems Services/Resource Assistance, T. Skinner, 403/284-8701

Sproule Associates Ltd. Library, North Tower, Sun Life Plaza, 140 - 4 Ave. SW, 9th Fl., Calgary AB T2P 3N3 – 403/269-7951; Fax: 403/237-0201 – Supervisor, Marilyn Marsden

Statistics Canada - Prairie Regional Reference Centre, #401, First Street Plaza, 138 - 4 Ave. SE, Calgary AB T2G 4Z6 – 403/292-6717; Fax: 403/292-4958; Toll Free: 1-800-563-7828

Stikeman, Elliott Law Office - Library, Bankers Hall, #1500, 855 - 2nd St. SW, Calgary AB T2P 4J7 – 403/266-9000; Fax: 403/266-9034 – Librarian, Lynne Gibson

Suicide Information & Education Centre – Resource Centre, #201, 1615 - 10 Ave. SW, Calgary AB T3C 0J7 – 403/245-3900; Symbol: ACSIEC – Library Coordinator, Karen Kiddey

Suncor Inc. - Library, 112 - 4th Ave. SW, Calgary AB T2P 2V5 – 403/269-8128; Fax: 403/269-6200 – Information Specialist, Dave Yadav, Email: yadavd@tcel.com

Talisman Energy Inc. - Information Resources Centre, #2400, 855 - 2 St. SW, Calgary AB T2P 4J9 – 403/237-1040; Fax: 403/237-1902 – Coordinator, Cathy Ross

Toronto-Dominion Bank - Corporate & Investment Banking Group Library, #800, Home Oil Tower, Toronto-Dominion Sq., 324 - 8 Ave. SW, Calgary AB T2P 2Z2 – 403/292-1296; Fax: 403/292-2772 – Librarian, V. Swanson

Towers Perrin - Information Centre, #3700, 150 - 8 Ave. SW, Calgary AB T2P 3Y7 – 403/261-1400; Fax: 403/237-6733 – Librarian, Mary Davey

TransAlta Utilities Corporation - Library, PO Box 1900, Calgary AB T2P 2M1 – 403/267-7388; Fax: 403/267-3727; Symbol: ACTU Librarian, Shamin Kassam, 403/267-3636 Reference Librarian, Jean Khusardeo

TransCanada Pipelines - Library, PO Box 1000, Calgary AB T2P 4K5 – 403/267-6498; Fax: 403/267-6266; Symbol: ACTRPL – Librarian, Tracy Angel

University of Calgary - Library, 2500 University Dr. NW, Calgary AB T2N 1N4 – 403/220-5953; Fax: 403/282-6837, 1218
  Director, Library, Tom Eadie, 403/220-5953
  Medical Library, Medical Librarian, John Cole, 403/220-6858
  Law Library, Law Librarian, Olga-Margaret Kizlyk Scarpari, 403/220-5090
  Gallagher Library of Geology & Geophysics, Geosciences Librarian, Darlene Warren, 403/220-6043
  Management Resource Centre, Librarian, Laurie Moffat, 403/220-7577
  Administrative Services, Coordinator, Yvonna Hinks, 403/220-3767
  Client Services, Coordinator, Elaine Bouey, 403/220-7373
  Collection & Technical Services, Coordinator, Ada-Marie Atkins Nechka, 403/220-3755
  Information Technology Services, Coordinator, Mary Westell, 403/220-3764
  Access, Manager, Arden Matheson, 403/220-5084
  Collections, Manager, Joanne Henning, 403/220-3796
  Acquisitions, Manager, Sandra Telfer, 403/220-7215
  Bibliographic Services, Manager, Vacant, 403/220-3479

Vocational & Rehabilitation Research Institute – Resource Centre/Library, 3304 - 33 St. NW, Calgary AB T2L 2A6 – 403/284-1121,ext.431 – Librarian, Bob McGowan

Walsh Wilkins, Barristers & Solicitors - Library, #2800, 801 - 6 Ave. SW, Calgary AB T2P 4A3 – 403/267-8400; Fax: 403/264-9400 – Librarian, Frankie Wilson

Western Gas Marketing Ltd. - Library, 530 - 8 Ave. SW, PO Box 500, Calgary AB T2P 3V6 – 403/269-5792; Fax: 403/264-7257; Email: ENVOY: ILL.ACTCP/WESTERN.GAS.MKTG – Supervisor, Library Services, Liz Varsek

Zenith Hookenson Boyle Law Office - Library, #520, 10333 Southport Rd. SW, Calgary AB T2W 3X6 – 403/259-5041; Fax: 403/258-0719 – Receptionist, Carole Sabados

CAMROSE

Augustana University College - Library, 4901 - 46 Ave., Camrose AB T4V 2R3 – 403/679-1189; Fax: 403/679-1594; Symbol: ACAL
  Head Librarian, Nancy Goebel
  Reference Librarian, Paul Neff

Camrose International Institute – Library, 5061 - 50 St., Camrose AB T4V 1R3 – 403/672-2660 – Librarian, Susan Wolfe

CANMORE

Alpine Club of Canada – Library, PO Box 2040, Canmore AB T0L 0M0 – 403/678-5940 – Librarian, Bev Bendell

CLARESHOLM

Appaloosa Horse Club of Canada – APHCC Museum & Archives, PO Box 940, Claresholm AB T0L 0T0 – 403/625-3326

COLLEGE HEIGHTS

Canadian Union College - Library, 50 Ramona Dr., College Heights AB T4L 2B7 – 403/782-3381; Fax: 403/782-3977; Email: cuclibrary@ccinet.ab.ca
  Librarian, Joyce Van Scheik
  Assistant Librarian, Carol Nicks

DIDSBURY

Didsbury & District Historical Society – Library, PO Box 1175, Didsbury AB T0M 0W0 – 403/335-9295 – Office Coordinator, Susan Sloan

DRAYTON VALLEY

The Pembina Institute for Appropriate Development – Library, PO Box 7558, Drayton Valley AB T7A 1S7 – 403/542-6272

DRUMHELLER

Royal Tyrrell Museum of Palaeontology - Library, PO Box 7500, Drumheller AB T0J 0Y0 – 403/823-7707; Fax: 403/823-7131; Email: rtmp@dns.magtech.ab.ca; Symbol: ADTMP
   Library Technician, Deborah Frey, 403/823-7707, ext.328
   Public Services, Lorna Johnston Hodge

Solicitor General Canada - Drumheller Institution - Library, PO Box 3000, Drumheller AB T0J 0Y0 – 403/823-5101, ext.166; Symbol: AADI – Librarian, Sharen Nadasdi

EDMONTON

Alberta Research Council – Library, 250 Karl Clark Rd., PO Box 8330, Edmonton AB T6H 5X2 – 403/450-5260; Fax: 403/450-8996; Email: STORMS@arc.ab.ca – Library Contact, Barb Storms

ACCESS - Media Resource Centre, 3720 - 76 Ave, Edmonton AB T6B 2N9 – 403/440-7777; Fax: 403/440-8899; Toll Free: 1-800-352-8293; URL: http://www.ccinet.ab.ca/access – Librarian, Darnell Waldner

AGT Limited - Corporate Library, 10020 - 100 St., 23-H Fl., Edmonton AB T5J 0N5 – 403/493-6134; Symbol: AEGT

Alberta Advanced Education & Career Development - Labour Market Information Centre, 10030 - 107 St., South Tower, Edmonton AB T5J 4X7 – 403/427-3722; Fax: 403/427-4778
   Coordinator, Dorothy Humphrey
   Administrative Support, Lorelei Pritchard

Alberta Agriculture, Food & Rural Development & Alberta Public Works, Supply & Services - Neil Crawford Provincial Centre Library, 7000 - 113 St., Edmonton AB T6H 5T6 – 403/422-2104; Fax: 403/422-2484; Symbol: AEAG
   Head Librarian, Robert Bateman, Email: bateman@agric.gov.ab.ca
   Reference Librarian, Connie Hruday
   Reference Librarian, Jennifer Fullen
   Technical Services Librarian, Jane Starr
   Interlibrary Loan Technician, Fran Harris

Alberta Arbitration & Mediation Society – Library, #408, McLeod Building, 10136 - 100 St., Edmonton AB T5J 0P1 – 403/426-0650; Toll Free: 1-800-232-7214 – Librarian, Kay Forsyth

Alberta Association for Community Living – Reg Peters Resource Centre, 11724 Kingsway Ave., Edmonton AB T5G 0X5 – 403/451-3055; Toll Free: 1-800-252-7556 – Information Resource Coordinator, Marta Carmona

Alberta Association of Architects – Library, Duggan House, 10515 Saskatchewan Dr., Edmonton AB T6E 4S1 – 403/432-0224 – Assistant Registrar, Nurjehan Jamal

Alberta Associations for Bright Children – Bright Site, The Bright Site, #1280, 6240 - 113 St., Edmonton AB T6H 3L2 – 403/413-1630

Alberta Band Association – R. Bruce Marsh Memorial Library, #808, 10136 - 100 St., Edmonton AB T5J 0P1 – 403/429-0482

Alberta Choral Federation – Choral Lending Library, #209, 14218 Stony Plain Rd., Edmonton AB T5N 3R3 – 403/488-7645 – Patricia Cook

Alberta Citizenship & Women's Secretariat - Library, Standard Life Centre, #901, 10405 Jasper Ave., Edmonton AB T5J 4R7 – 403/422-4927; Fax: 403/422-6348; Symbol: AEAC – Library Technician, Mary Louise Mitchell, Email: mlmitchell@mcd.gov.ab.ca

Alberta Economic Development & Tourism - Library, 10155 - 102 St., 5th Fl., Edmonton AB T5J 4L6 – 403/427-4957; Fax: 403/427-0610 – Librarian, Donna M. Gordon, Email: gordonon@censsw.gov.ab.ca

Alberta Education - Library, Devonian Building, West Tower, 11160 Jasper Ave., 4th Fl., Edmonton AB T5K 0L2 – 403/427-2985; Fax: 403/427-5927; Email: librarian@edc.gov.ab.ca; Symbol: AEE – Manager, Library Services, Christina Andrews
   Materials Resource Centre for the Visually Impaired, 12360 - 142 St., Edmonton AB T5L 4X9 – 403/427-4681; Fax: 403/427-6683; Email: KRibeiro@edc.gov.ab.ca; Symbol: AEEM – Manager, Kathryn Ribeiro, 403/427-5212

Alberta Energy - Oil Sands Information Services, North Petroleum Plaza, 9945 - 108 St., Edmonton AB T5K 2G6 – 403/427-8382; Fax: 403/427-3198; Symbol: AOSIS
   Manager, Helga Petri
   Technical Information Officer, Dagmar Losert
   Technical Information Officer, James Li
   Administrative Assistant, Valerie Pinkoski
   Information Clerk, May Fallis
   Calgary Branch, Technical Information Officer, Gary Whitehead, 403/297-3380
   Calgary Branch, Library Assistant, Brenda Belland, 403/297-3380

Alberta Environmental Protection - Library, 9920 - 108 St., 6th Fl., Edmonton AB T5K 2M4 – 403/427-5870; Fax: 403/422-0170; Email: library@env.gov.ab.ca; Symbol: AEEN

Alberta Health - Library Services Branch, 10025 Jasper Ave., 9th Fl., Edmonton AB T5J 2P4 – 403/427-8720; Fax: 403/427-1643; Email: ahlib2@mail.health.gov.ab.ca; Symbol: AEHE
   Health Librarian, Peggy Yeh
   Librarian, Linda Bumstead
   ILL, Anna Duerr

Alberta Health Record Association – Library, PO Box 1752, Edmonton AB T5J 2P1 – Toll Free: 1-800-863-8613

Alberta Junior Forest Warden Association – Library, Bramalea Building, 9920 - 108 St., 10th Fl., Edmonton AB T5K 2M4 – 403/427-3551 – Rena Lee

Alberta Justice - Library, Bowker Bldg., #403, 9833 - 109 St., Edmonton AB T5K 2E8 – 403/498-3413; Fax: 403/427-6821; Symbol: AEATCA – Justice Law Librarian, Andrew Balázs
   Office of the Chief Medical Examiner, Northern Region - Library, 7007 - 116 St., Edmonton AB T6H 5R8 – 403/427-4987; Fax: 403/422-1265; Symbol: AEOCME – Librarian, Cathy Woodside

Alberta Labour - Library, #302, 10808 - 99 Ave., Edmonton AB T5K 0G5 – 403/427-8533; Fax: 403/420-0084; Symbol: AEML – Librarian, Debbie Hunter

Alberta Legislative Assembly - Library, #216, Legislative Bldg., Edmonton AB T5K 2B6 – 403/427-2473; Fax: 403/427-6016 – Librarian, Lorne Buhr

Alberta Municipal Affairs - Library, Commerce Place, 10155 - 102 St., 17th Fl., Edmonton AB T5J 4L4 – 403/427-4829; Fax: 403/420-1016 – Library Technician, Lynda Meyer

Alberta Museums Association – Library, Rosedale House, 9829 - 103 St., Edmonton AB T5J 0X9 – 403/424-2626 – Education Coordinator, Gail Rydman

Alberta Pensions Administration Board - Library, Park Plaza Bldg., 10611 - 98 Ave., 4th Fl., Edmonton AB T5K 2P7 – 403/427-3354; Fax: 403/421-1652 – Librarian, Theresa Frauenfeld

Alberta Public Works, Supply & Services - Standards & Specifications Library, 12360 - 142 St., 2nd Fl, Edmonton AB T5L 2H1 – 403/427-3222, ext.274; Fax: 403/427-0834 – Administrator, Wendy Proch

Alberta Registered Dietitians Association – Library, 18104 - 102 Ave., Edmonton AB T5S 1S7 – 403/448-0059

Alberta Rehabilitation Council for the Disabled – Resource Centre, #400, 10909 Jasper Ave., Edmonton AB T5J 3L9 – 403/429-0137 – Library Technician, Gwen Sanderson

Alberta Safety Council – Library, #201, 10526 Jasper Ave., Edmonton AB T5J 1Z7 – 403/428-7555 – Office Manager, Carol Reimer

Alberta School for the Deaf Library, 6240 - 113 St., Edmonton AB T6H 3L2 – 403/422-0244; Fax: 403/422-2036

Alberta Securities Commission - Library, 10025 Jasper Ave., 19th Fl., Edmonton AB T5J 3Z5 – 403/427-5201; Fax: 403/422-0777 – Librarian, Richard Farrelly

Alberta Teachers' Association – Library, Barnett House, 11010 - 142 St., Edmonton AB T5N 2R1 – 403/453-2411 – Librarian, Elaine Atwood

Alberta Treasury - Tax Resource Library, Sir Frederick Haltain Bldg., 9811 - 109 St., 2nd Fl. NE, Edmonton AB T5K 2L5 – 403/427-9425; Fax: 403/427-0348 – Librarian, M. Davies

Association canadienne-française de l'Alberta – Bibliothèque, #200, 8923 - 82 Ave., Edmonton AB T6C 1Z2 – 403/466-1680 – Louise Lavallée

Baptist General Conference of Canada – BGC Canada Archives, 4306 - 97 St., Edmonton AB T6E 5R9 – 604/855-6147 – Volunteer Archivist, Rev. Bill Funk

Bishop & McKenzie Law Office - Library, #2500, 10104 - 103 Ave., Edmonton AB T5J 1V3 – 403/426-5550; Fax: 403/426-1305 – Librarian, Catherine Mackenzie

Brownlee Fryett Law Office - Library, Commerce Place, #2200, 10155 - 102 St., Edmonton AB T5J 4G8 – 403/497-4800; Fax: 403/424-3254 – Librarian, Tara Veylan

Bryan & Company Law Office - Library, Manulife Place, #2600, 10180 - 101 St., Edmonton AB T5J 3Y2 – 403/423-5730; Fax: 403/428-6324 – Janet Anderson

Canadian Broadcasting Corporation - Record Library, PO Box 555, Edmonton AB T5J 2P4 – 403/468-7465; Fax: 403/468-7471 – Music Librarian, Shirley Thorvaldson

Canadian Institute of Ukrainian Studies – Library, 352 Athabasca Hall, University of Alberta, Edmonton AB T6G 2E8 – 403/492-2972; TLX: 037-2979

Canadian Libraries in Occupational Safety & Health – Library, c/o Alberta Labour Library, 10808 - 99 Ave, 3rd Fl., Edmonton AB T5K 0G5 – 403/427-8533; Email: AECOH.ILL; Symbol: AEOH

Canadian Organization of Small Business Inc. – Library, PO Box 11246, Edmonton AB T5H 3J5 – 403/423-2672 – Administrative Coordinator, Linda Stevens

Canadian Utilities Ltd. - Library Services, 10035 - 105 St., Edmonton AB T5J 2V6 – 403/420-7039; Fax: 403/420-7772; Symbol: AECU – Corporate Librarian, Reneé Hartel-Mohrmann, 403/420-7746

CANSPEC Group - Library, 7450 - 18 St., Edmonton AB T6P 1N8 – 403/440-2131; Fax: 403/440-1167; Toll Free: 1-800-663-9729; Symbol: AEHM – Head of Library Services, Connie Vogler

Communitas Group Ltd. - Resource Centre, #200, 12120 - 106 Ave., Edmonton AB T5N 0Z2 – 403/482-5467; Fax: 403/488-5102 – Librarian, Lesley Connley

Cross Cancer Institute - Abdul Khaliq Library, 11560 University Ave., 3rd Fl., Edmonton AB T6G 1Z2 – 403/432-8593; Fax: 403/432-8411; Email: ILL.ZJU; Symbol: AECCI – Medical Librarian, Linda Harris

Cruickshank Karvellas Law Office - Library, Manulife Pl., #3400, 10180 - 101 St., Edmonton AB T5J 4W9 – 403/970-5279; Fax: 403/424-1311 – Librarian, Lyla Reid

Deloitte & Touche - Information Centre, #2000, 10180 - 101 St., Edmonton AB T5J 4E4 – 403/421-3790;

Fax: 403/421-3782; Email: cengbers@planet.eon.net – Librarian, Cea Engbers

Earthkeeping: Food & Agriculture in Christian Perspective – Earthkeeping Resource Centre, #205, 10711 - 107 Ave., Edmonton AB T5H 0W6 – 403/428-6981

Edmonton Archives - Library, 10440 - 108 Ave., Edmonton AB T5H 3Z9 – 403/496-8710 – City Archivist, Bruce Ibsen

Edmonton Catholic Schools - District Library, 10425 - 84 Ave., Edmonton AB T6E 2H3 – 403/439-7356; Fax: 403/433-0181 – District Librarian, Vivianne Fagnon

Edmonton Social Planning Council – Roger Soderstrom Resource Library, #41, 9912 - 106 St., Edmonton AB T5K 1C5 – 403/423-2031

Edmonton Stamp Club – Library, PO Box 399, Edmonton AB T5J 2J6 – 403/479-6067 – Librarian, Maurice Hampson

Edmonton Symphony Society – Library, 10160 - 103 St., Edmonton AB T5J 0X6 – 403/428-1108 – Librarian, Sheila Jones

Emery Jamieson Law Office - Library, #1700, Oxford Tower, Edmonton Centre, 10235 - 101 St., Edmonton AB T5J 3G1 – 403/426-5220; Fax: 403/420-6277 – Librarian, Ana San Miguel

Enviro-Test Laboratories - Division of ETL Chemspec Analytical Ltd. - Library, 9936 - 67 Ave., Edmonton AB T6E 0P5 – 403/413-5227; Toll Free: 1-800-668-9878 – Inside Sales, Sylvia Ouellette

Environment Canada - Atmospheric Environment Service, Prairie & Northern Region - Library, #200, 4999 - 98 Ave., Edmonton AB T6B 2X3 – 403/951-8817, 8818; Fax: 403/951-8819; Symbol: AEEPS; AEEAE – Chief Librarian, Terri Fraser

The Environmental Law Centre (Alberta) Society – Library, #204, 10709 Jasper Ave., Edmonton AB T5J 3N3 – 403/482-4891; Toll Free: 1-800-661-4238; Symbol: AEELC – Librarian, Dolores Noga

Environmental Services Association of Alberta – Library, #250, 10508 - 82 Ave., Edmonton AB T6E 2A4 – 403/439-6363; Toll Free: 1-800-661-9278 – Program Coordinator, Renée LaBoucane

Fédération des parents francophones de l'Alberta – Centre de ressources préscolaires Guy-Lacombe, #205, 8925 - 82 Ave., Edmonton AB T6C 0Z2 – 403/468-6934 – Coordonnateur, Richard Vaillancourt

FEESA - An Environmental Education Society – Library, #900, 10150 - 100 St., Edmonton AB T5J 0P6 – 403/421-1497

Field & Field Perraton Law Office - Library, Oxford Tower, Edmonton Centre, #2000, 10235 - 101 St., Edmonton AB T5J 3G1 – 403/423-3003; Fax: 403/428-9329; 424-7116 – Librarian, Linda Statt, 403/423-3003, ext.249

German-Canadian Association of Alberta – Library, Deutsch-Kanadische Assoziation von Alberta, #203, 8708 - 48 Ave., Edmonton AB T6E 5L1 – 403/465-7466

Glenrose Rehabilitation Hospital – Library Services, 10230 - 111 Ave., Edmonton AB T5G 0B7 – 403/471-2262; Email: pschoenberg@grhosp.ab.ca; Symbol: AEG – Librarian, Peter Schoenberg

Grant MacEwan Community College - Resource Centre for Voluntary Organizations, #5-132, 10700 - 104 Ave., Edmonton AB T5J 4S2 – 403/497-5616; Fax: 403/497-5209; Email: robertsonl@admin.gmcc.ab.ca; Symbol: RCVO Coordinator, Lynda Robertson, 403/497-5617 Coordinator, Karen Spiess

Grey Nuns Community Health Centre – Library, 1100 Youville Dr. West, Edmonton AB T6L 5X8 – 403/450-7301; Fax: 403/450-7202 – Librarian, Sheila Fynn

H.W. Kuckertz Law Office - Library, 9959 - 82 Ave., Edmonton AB T6E 1Z1 – 403/432-9308; Fax: 403/439-9950 – Harold Kuckertz

Institute for Peace & Global Education – Library, Department of Secondary Education, University of Alberta, 57 University Campus, Edmonton AB T6G 2G5 – 403/492-5504 – Vimbi Nhundu

Judo Alberta – Video Library, Percy Page Centre, 11759 Groat Rd., Edmonton AB T5M 3K6 – 403/453-8679 – Joyce Syrenne

Justice Canada - Prairies & Northwest Territories Region, Edmonton Regional Office - Law Library, #211, 10199 - 101 St., Edmonton AB T5J 3Y4 – 403/495-2973; Fax: 403/495-2964; Symbol: AEJ
Law Librarian, Suzan A. Hebditch, Email: suzan.hebditch@justice.x400.gc.ca
Library Technician, Eve Poirier

Natural Resources Canada-Canadian Forest Service: Northwest Region – Library, 5320 - 122 St., Edmonton AB T6H 3S5 – 403/435-7323, 7324; Fax: 403/435-7356; Email: ill@nofc.forestry.ca; Symbol: AEF – Head, Library Services, Edith M. Hopp

North American Baptist Conference - Canadian Headquarters – Schalm Memorial Library, 11525 - 23 Ave., Edmonton AB T6J 4T3 – 403/437-1960; Email: library@nabcebs.ab.ca – Librarian, Aileen Wright

Northern Alberta Institute of Technology - McNally Library, 11762 - 106 St., Edmonton AB T5G 2R1 – 403/471-8844; Fax: 403/471-8813; Symbol: AENA – Helga Kinnaird

Planned Parenthood Association of Edmonton – Phyllis Harris Library, #50, 9912 - 106 St., Edmonton AB T5K 1C5 – 403/423-3737 – Counselling Coordinator, Jeni Adler

Society for the Retired & Semi-Retired – Heritage Library, 15 Sir Winston Churchill Sq., Edmonton AB T5J 2E5 – 403/423-5510 – Resource Librarian, A. Webster

Solicitor General Canada - Edmonton Institution - Library, PO Box 2290, Edmonton AB T5J 3H7 – 403/472-6052, ext.265; Fax: 403/495-6036;
Symbol: AEEIS – Librarian, Sikhumbuzo Maqubela

Stanley Technology Group Inc. – Library, 10160 - 112 St., Edmonton AB T5K 2L6 – 403/423-4777; Fax: 403/421-4300; Symbol: AESAE – Librarian, Donna Meen

Statistics Canada - Prairie Regional Reference Centre, Park Sq., 10001 Bellamy Hill, 9th Fl., Edmonton AB T5J 3B6 – 403/495-3027; Fax: 403/495-5318; Toll Free: 1-800-563-7828
Assistant Director, Advisory Services, Connie Leclair
Data Dissemination, Officer, Carmel Forbes
Data Dissemination, Officer, Nadia Danyliuk

Tarrabain & Company - Law Library, #2150, Tower One, Scotia Place, Edmonton AB T5J 3R8 – 403/429-1010; Fax: 403/429-0101 – Barrister, M. Deborah Stewart

Toxics Watch Society of Alberta – Resource Centre, 10511 Saskatchewan Dr., Edmonton AB T6E 4S1 – 403/433-4808

Transport Canada - Airworthiness Technical Reference Centre, Canada Place, #1100, 9700 Jasper Ave., Edmonton AB T5J 4E6 – 403/495-5223; Fax: 403/495-6659 – Librarian, David J.S. Robinson
Regional Library Edmonton, #1100, 9700 Jasper Ave., 11th Fl., Edmonton AB T5J 4E6 – 403/495-3801; Fax: 403/495-6460; Symbol: AETR – Regional Librarian, Patricia Nelson, Email: nelsopj@tc.gc.ca

United Nurses of Alberta – Library, Park Plaza, 10611 - 98 Ave., 9th Fl., Edmonton AB T5K 2P7 – 403/425-1025 – Melanie Chapman

University of Alberta - Libraries, Edmonton AB T6G 2J8 – 403/492-3790; Fax: 403/492-8302; Email: ENVOY: UILLS; URL: http://www.library.ualberta.ca/library.html; Symbol: AEU
Learning Systems, Executive Director, Ernie Ingles, 403/492-5569

Academic Planning & Liaison, Associate Director, B.J. Busch, 403/492-0073
Operational Support Services, Associate Director, S. Rooney, 403/492-3793
Library Development & Public Relations, Assistant Director, M. Distad, 403/492-1429
Herbert T. Coutts (Education) Library, Education Librarian, Kathleen DeLong, 403/492-5759, Fax: 403/492-8367, Email: educref@library.ualberta.ca
Humanities & Social Sciences Library, Librarian, Deborah Dancik, 403/492-1405, Fax: 403/492-5083
Government Publications, Coordinator, Sally Manwaring, 403/492-2632
John Alexander Weir Memorial Law Library, Acting Law Librarian, D. Dancik, 403/492-1569, Fax: 403/492-7546
John W. Scott Health Sciences Library, Acting Health Sciences Librarian, M. Young, 403/492-7918, Fax: 403/492-6960
Science & Technology Library, Librarian, Margo Young, 403/492-7912, Fax: 403/492-2721
Canadian Circumpolar Library, Head Librarian, Robin Minion, 403/492-4409
Mathematics Library, Supervisor, Masood Ahmad, 403/492-3529
William C. Wonders Map Collection, University Map Curator, R. Whistance-Smith, 403/492-4760
Winspear Business Reference Room, Head, Kathy West, 403/492-7931
Dept. of Biochemistry, C.J. Smith Reading Room, Librarian, Susan Smith, 403/492-3358
Data Library, Data Library Coordinator, Chuck Humphrey, 403/492-5212
Music Resources Centre, Librarian, James Whittle, 403/492-5708
Rural Economy Library, Librarian, Barbara Johnson, 403/492-4225
Information Technology Services, Head, D. Poff, 403/492-4770, Fax: 403/492-9243
Interlibrary Loans & Document Delivery, Head, A. Gibb, 403/492-7882, Fax: 403/492-4327
Bibliothèque Saint-Jean, Bibliothécaire, Juliette Henley, 403/465-8710, Fax: 403/468-2550
Bruce Peel Special Collections Library, Head, John Charles, 403/492-7928
Dept. of Extension, Legal Resource Centre Library, Administrative Librarian, Elaine Hutchinson, 403/492-5732
Development Disabilities Centre Library, Librarian, H. de Groot, 403/492-4439
Faculty of Extension, Educational Media Services, Head, James Shaw, 403/492-5047 (Adult Studies); 5039 (Film & Video)
MacLeod Memorial Library, Librarian, Theresa Burwell, 403/492-8337
St. Joseph's College Library, Librarian, Paula Sheedy, 403/492-7681

Willson & Associates Law Office - Library, 10316 - 121 St., Edmonton AB T5N 1K8 – 403/482-6670; Fax: 403/482-2518

World Trade Center Edmonton – Resource Center, PO Box 1480, Edmonton AB T5J 2N5 – 403/471-7283 – Secretary, Kathy Jansen

Writers Guild of Alberta – Library, Percy Page Centre, 11759 Groat Rd., 3rd Fl., Edmonton AB T5M 3K6 – 403/422-8174; Toll Free: 1-800-665-5354

HINTON

Johnson & McClelland Law Office - Library, 221 Pembina Ave., PO Box 6060, Hinton AB T7V 1X4 – 403/865-2222; Fax: 403/865-8857

INNISFAIL

Solicitor General Canada - Bowden Institution - Library, PO Box 6000, Innisfail AB T0M 1A0 – 403/

227-3391, ext.361; Fax: 403/227-6022; Symbol: AIBI – Librarian, Frank Turner

JASPER
Alberta Speleological Society – Library, PO Box 2474, Jasper AB T0E 1E0 – 403/234-8829(evenings) – Librarian, John Chaychuk

Jasper-Yellowhead Historical Society – Library, PO Box 42, Jasper AB T0E 1E0 – 403/852-3013 – Museum Manager, Roben Nuraitz

LACOMBE
Interpretation Canada - An Association for Heritage Interpretation – Library, PO Box 398, Lacombe AB T0C 1S0 – 403/853-8400 – Sandra A. Pyper

LETHBRIDGE
Agriculture & Agri-Food Canada-Lethbridge Research Centre – Library, Hwy. 3 East, PO Box 3000, Lethbridge AB T1J 4B1 – 403/327-4561; Email: library@ABRSLE.gov.ca; Symbol: ALAG – Librarian, Cheryl M. Ronning-Mains

Native Counselling Services of Alberta – Library, #208, 324 - 7 St. South, Lethbridge AB T1J 2G2 – 403/423-2141 – Librarian, Alexandra Nowacka

University of Lethbridge - Library, 4401 University Dr., Lethbridge AB T1K 3M4 – 403/327-2263 – Library Contact, Business, Andrea Glover

MEDICINE HAT
Defence Research Establishment - Suffield - Scientific Information Section, PO Box 4000, Medicine Hat AB T1A 8K6 – 403/544-4662; Fax: 403/544-3388; Email: ENVOY: DRES.LIBRARY; Symbol: ARS – A/Head, J. Fitzgerald

Unisphere Global Resource Centre – Library, 101 - 6 St. SE, Medicine Hat AB T1A 1G7 – 403/529-2656

MEDLEY
National Defence - Aerospace Engineering Test Establishment - Technical Reference Library, CFB Cold Lake, Medley AB T0A 2M0 – 403/840-8000, ext.8062; Fax: 403/840-7381; Email: reflib@aete.coldlake.dnd.ca; Symbol: AMECFA – Librarian, John MacIntyre

RALSTON
National Defence (Canada)-Research Centre: Suffield – Library, General Delivery, Ralston AB T0J 2N0 – 403/544-4000

RED DEER
Red Deer College - Library, PO Box 5005, Red Deer AB T4N 5H5 – 403/342-3300; Fax: 403/346-8500; Symbol: ARDC

STETTLER
Buffalo Lake Naturalists Club – Library, Box 1802, Stettler AB T0C 2L0 – 403/742-1837 – Librarian, Lloyd Lohr

VEGREVILLE
Alberta Environmental Protection - Alberta Environmental Centre – Library, PO Bag 4000, Vegreville AB T9C 1T4 – 403/632-8415; Fax: 403/632-8379; Email: library@aec.env.gov.ab.ca; Symbol: AVEE – Librarian, Fabian Harrison

BRITISH COLUMBIA

Municipal Public Libraries
Burnaby Public Library, 6100 Willingdon Ave., Burnaby BC V5H 4N5 – 604/436-5427; Fax: 604/436-2961; Email: ENVOY: F.BPL - Paul Whitney – Chief Librarian, Paul Whitney; Assistant Chief Librarian, Jon O'Grady, 604/436-5432; Circulation Supervisor, Betty Lamarche; Children's Services, Coordinator, Joyce Pinsker; Technical Services Librarian, Carolyn Hoffman, 604/436-5424; Acquisitions Librarian, John Davenport, 604/436-5435 – See also following branches: Bob Prittie Metrotown Branch Library, Cameron Branch Library, Kingsway Branch Library, McGill Branch Library

Burnaby: Bob Prittie Metrotown Branch Library, 6100 Willingdon Ave., Burnaby BC V5H 4N5 – 604/436-5410; Fax: 604/436-2961; Email: ENVOY: F.BPL; Symbol: BB – Branch Librarian, Jon O'Grady – Branch of Burnaby Public Library

Burnaby: Cameron Branch Library, 9523 Cameron St., Burnaby BC V3J 1L6 – 604/421-5454; Fax: 604/436-2961 – Branch Librarian, Linda Shineton – Branch of Burnaby Public Library

Burnaby: Kingsway Branch Library, 7252 Kingsway, Burnaby BC V5E 1G3 – 604/522-3971; Fax: 604/436-2961 – Branch Librarian, Caroline Christie – Branch of Burnaby Public Library

Burnaby: McGill Branch Library, 4595 Albert St., Burnaby BC V5C 2G6 – 604/299-8955; Fax: 604/299-5167 – Branch Librarian, Linnea Gibbs – Branch of Burnaby Public Library

Coquitlam Public Library, 575 Poirier St., Coquitlam BC V3J 6A9 – 604/931-2416; Fax: 604/931-6739; Email: ENVOY: ILL.BCOQ – Director, Stan Pukesh – See also following branches: Lincoln Branch Library, Poirier St. Main Library

Coquitlam: Lincoln Branch Library, 3020 Lincoln Ave., Coquitlam BC V3J 6B4 – 604/464-1112; Fax: 604/464-3380 – Branch Supervisor, Marlene Winters – Branch of Coquitlam Public Library

Coquitlam: Poirier St. Main Library, 575 Poirier St., Coquitlam BC V3J 6A9 – 604/931-1293; Fax: 604/931-1460 – Branch Head, Elspeth Richmond, 604/931-1293; Reference Librarian, Gillian Campbell, 604/931-1444; Children's Librarian, Deborah Duncan, 604/931-1292; Public Services Librarian, Leslie Utsunomiya, 604/937-0455 – Branch of Coquitlam Public Library

Dawson Creek Public Library, 1001 McKellar Ave., Dawson Creek BC V1G 4W7 – 250/782-4661; Fax: 250/782-4667; Email: ENVOY: ILL.BDC – Librarian, Mary Short; Assistant Librarian, Jenny Snyder

Mackenzie Public Library, 400 Skeena Dr., Mackenzie BC V0J 2C0 – 250/997-6343; Email: ENVOY: ILL.BMK – Librarian, Patricia Dauphinee

Nelson Municipal Library, 602 Stanley St., Nelson BC V1L 1N4 – 250/352-6333; Fax: 250/354-1799; Email: dthomas@netidea.com; Symbol: BNE – Chief Librarian, Deborah Thomas; Reference Librarian, Martha Scott; Circulation & Acquisitions Librarian, Deb Thomas; Children's Librarian, Nancy Radonich

New Westminster Public Library, 716 - 6 Ave., New Westminster BC V3M 2B3 – 604/521-8874; Fax: 604/521-6647; URL: http://www.nwpl.new-westminster.bc.ca; Symbol: BNW – City Librarian, Ron Clancy, Email: rclancy@nwpl.new-westminster.bc.ca; Reference Librarian, Joan G. Halverson; Circulation Librarian, Maureen Allen; Children's Librarian, Ellen Heaney; Public Services Librarian, Debra Nelson; Technical Services Librarian, Jean Simpson

North Vancouver District Public Library, 1280 East 27 St., North Vancouver BC V7J 1S1 – 604/984-0286; Fax: 604/984-7600; Email: ENVOY: F.NVD – Chief Librarian, Noreen A. Ballantyne; Reference Coordinator, Vicki Ringe; Adult Coordinator, Blair G. Thompson; Children's & Young Adult Coordinator, Allison Haupt; Manager, Collections & Services, Barbara Jo May; Manager, Technical Services, Alison J. Hill; Manager, Systems & Technology, Jacqueline Van Dyk; Audiovisual Coordinator, Jean McCarran – See also following branches: Capilano Branch Library, Lynn Valley Branch Library, Parkgate Branch Library

North Vancouver: Capilano Branch Library, 3045 Highland Blvd., North Vancouver BC V7R 2X4 – 604/987-4471; Fax: 604/987-0956 – Branch Manager, Teresa James, Email: tjames@nvdpl.north-van.bc.ca – Branch of North Vancouver District Public Library

North Vancouver: Lynn Valley Branch Library, 1280 East 27 St., North Vancouver BC V7J 1S1 – 604/984-0286; Fax: 604/984-7600; Email: pforsyth-manchester@nvdpl.north-van.bc.ca – Branch Manager, Penny Forsyth-Manchester – Branch of North Vancouver District Public Library

North Vancouver City Library, 121 - 14th St. West, North Vancouver BC V7M 1P2 – 604/980-0581; Fax: 604/983-3624; Email: ENVOY: F.NVC – Chief Librarian, Joe Lavery

North Vancouver: Parkgate Branch Library, 3675 Banff Ct., North Vancouver BC V7H 2Y7 – 604/929-3727; Fax: 604/929-0758 – Branch Manager, Helen Kaiser, Email: hgk@nvdpl.north-van.bc.ca – Branch of North Vancouver District Public Library

Penticton Public Library, 785 Main St., Penticton BC V2A 5E3 – 250/492-0024; Fax: 250/492-0440; Email: ENVOY: ILL.BP – Director, R.M. McIvor; Children's Librarian, K. Kellerman; Systems Librarian, S. Murphy; Assistant Director, L. Little

Port Moody Public Library, 240 Ioco Rd., PO Box 37, Port Moody BC V3H 2E1 – 604/469-4575; Fax: 604/469-4576; Email: bpulham@wimsey.com – Director, Brian Pulham; Children's Librarian, Vicki Donaghue; Public Services Librarian, Eva Lederer

Pouce Coupe Municipal Public Library, PO Box 75, Pouce Coupe BC V0C 2C0 – 250/786-5765; Fax: 250/786-5257; Email: ENVOY: ILL.BPOC – Librarian, Faye Randall

Prince George Public Library, 887 Dominion St., Prince George BC V2L 5L1 – 250/563-9251; Fax: 250/563-0892; Email: PG.LIBRARY; Symbol: BPG – Director, Edel Toner-Rogala, 250/563-9251, ext.129; Adult Services Manager, Nancy E. Black, 250/563-9251, ext.125; Children's Services Manager, Barb Dean, 250/563-9251, ext.105; Support Services Manager, Joseph Stibrany, 250/563-9251, ext.130; Finance & Administrative Services Manager, Noreen Redman, 250/563-9251, ext.134; Community Relations Manager, Joan Jarman, 250/563-9251, ext.128

Prince Rupert Library, 101 - 6 Ave. West., Prince Rupert BC V8J 1Y9 – 250/627-1345; Fax: 250/627-7743; Email: library@citytel.net; Symbol: BPR – Librarian, Michele Cook; Deputy Librarian, Michael Purcell

Richmond Public Library, #100, 7700 Minoru Gate, Richmond BC V6Y 1R9 – 604/231-6422; Fax: 604/273-0459; Email: ENVOY: F.RPL; URL: http://www.rpl.richmond.bc.ca – Chief Librarian, Greg Buss – See also following branches: Shellmont Branch Library, Steveston Branch Library

Richmond: Shellmont Branch Library, #166, 11080 Williams Rd., Richmond BC V7A 1X8 – 604/277-2815 – Branch Head, Andrée Duval – Branch of Richmond Public Library

Richmond: Steveston Branch Library, 4111 Moncton St., Richmond BC V7E 3A8 – 604/274-2012 – Branch Head, Andrée Duval – Branch of Richmond Public Library

Surrey Public Library, 13742 - 72 Ave., Surrey BC V3W 2P4 – 604/572-8269; Fax: 604/596-8523; Email: ENVOY: STAN.SMITH or ILL.BSUR – Librarian, Stan Smith – See also following branches: Cloverdale Branch, Guildford Branch, Newton Branch Library, Ocean Park Branch Library, Port Kells Branch Library, Whalley Branch Library

Surrey: Cloverdale Branch, 5642 - 176A St., Surrey BC V3S 4G9 – 604/576-1384; Fax: 604/576-0120 –

Branch Manager, Jennifer Herfst – Branch of Surrey Public Library

Surrey: Guildford Branch, 15105 - 105 Ave., Surrey BC V3R 7G8 – 604/588-5015; Fax: 604/588-5627 – Branch Manager, Jane Knight – Branch of Surrey Public Library

Surrey: Newton Branch Library, 13795 - 70 Ave., Surrey BC V3W 0E1 – 604/596-7401; Fax: 604/597-3792 – Branch Manager, Melanie Houlden – Branch of Surrey Public Library

Surrey: Ocean Park Branch Library, 12854 - 17th Ave., Surrey BC V4A 1T5 – 604/531-5044; Fax: 604/531-3951 – Community Librarian, Jane Gifford – Branch of Surrey Public Library

Surrey: Port Kells Branch Library, 18885 - 88th Ave., Surrey BC V4N 3G5 – 604/882-0733; Fax: 604/882-0733 – Community Librarian, Sharon Ward – Branch of Surrey Public Library

Surrey: Whalley Branch Library, 10347 - 135th St., Surrey BC V3T 4C3 – 604/588-5951; Fax: 604/588-0457 – Branch Manager, Patricia Miller – Branch of Surrey Public Library

Trail & District Public Library, 1051 Victoria St., Trail BC V1R 3T3 – 250/364-1731; Fax: 250/364-2176; Email: ENVOY: ILL.BT – Director, Julie Spurrell

Vancouver Public Library, 350 West Georgia St., Vancouver BC V6B 6B1 – 604/331-4001; Fax: 604/331-4080; Email: ENVOY: VPL.ILL; Symbol: VPL – Director, Madeleine Aalto; Circulation Librarian, Susan Everall; Technical Services Librarian, Pat Haffenden – See also following branches: Britannia Community Branch Library, Carnegie Branch Library, Champlain Heights Branch Library, Collingwood Branch Library, Dunbar Branch Library, Firehall Branch Library, Fraserview Branch Library, Hastings Branch Library, Joe Fortes Branch Library, Kensington Community Library, Kerrisdale Branch Library, Kitsilano Branch Library, Marpole Branch Library, Mount Pleasant Branch Library, Oakridge Branch Library, Renfrew Branch, Riley Park Branch Library, South Hill Branch Library, Strathcona Branch Library, West Point Grey Branch Library

Vancouver: Britannia Community Branch Library, 1661 Napier St., Vancouver BC V5L 4X4 – 604/665-2222 – Branch Head, Catherine Connell – Branch of Vancouver Public Library

Vancouver: Carnegie Branch Library, 401 Main St., Vancouver BC V6A 2T7 – 604/665-3010 – Branch Head, Eleanor Kelly – Branch of Vancouver Public Library

Vancouver: Champlain Heights Branch Library, #101, 3200 East 54th Ave., Vancouver BC V5S 3T8 – 604/665-3955 – Branch Head, Susan Watson – Branch of Vancouver Public Library

Vancouver: Collingwood Branch Library, 2985 Kingsway, Vancouver BC V5R 5J4 – 604/665-3953 – Branch Head, Janet Wynne-Edwards – Branch of Vancouver Public Library

Vancouver: Dunbar Branch Library, 4515 Dunbar St., Vancouver BC V6S 2G7 – 604/665-3968 – Branch Head, Andrew Kevlahan – Branch of Vancouver Public Library

Vancouver: Firehall Branch Library, 1455 West 10th Ave., Vancouver BC V6H 1J8 – 604/665-3970 – Branch Head, Judi Walker – Branch of Vancouver Public Library

Vancouver: Fraserview Branch Library, 1950 Argyle Dr., Vancouver BC V5P 2A8 – 604/665-3957 – Branch Head, Marsha Robinson – Branch of Vancouver Public Library

Vancouver: Hastings Branch Library, 2674 Hastings St. East, Vancouver BC V5K 1Z6 – 604/665-3959 – Branch Head, Donna Meadwell – Branch of Vancouver Public Library

Vancouver: Joe Fortes Branch Library, 870 Denman St., Vancouver BC V6G 2L8 – 604/665-3972 – Branch Head, Thomas Quigley – Branch of Vancouver Public Library

Vancouver: Kensington Community Library, 3927 Knight St., Vancouver BC V5N 3L8 – 604/665-3961 – Branch Head, Anne Kyler – Branch of Vancouver Public Library

Vancouver: Kerrisdale Branch Library, 2112 West 42nd Ave., Vancouver BC V6M 2B6 – 604/665-3974 – Branch Head, Jane White – Branch of Vancouver Public Library

Vancouver: Kitsilano Branch Library, 2425 MacDonald St., Vancouver BC V6K 3Y9 – 604/665-3976; Fax: 604/731-6931 – Branch Head, Linda Kalman – Branch of Vancouver Public Library

Vancouver: Marpole Branch Library, 8386 Granville St., Vancouver BC V6P 4Z7 – 604/665-3978 – Branch Head, Chris Middlemass – Branch of Vancouver Public Library

Vancouver: Mount Pleasant Branch Library, 370 East Broadway, Vancouver BC V5T 4G5 – 604/665-3962 – Branch Head, Del Tait – Branch of Vancouver Public Library

Vancouver: Oakridge Branch Library, Oakridge Shopping Centre, #191, 650 West 41 Ave., Vancouver BC V5Z 2M9 – 604/665-3980 – Branch Head, Peter Archibald – Branch of Vancouver Public Library

Vancouver: Renfrew Branch, 2969 East 22nd Ave., Vancouver BC V5M 2Y3 – 604/257-8705 – Branch Head, Stephanie Bohlin – Branch of Vancouver Public Library

Vancouver: Riley Park Branch Library, Little Mountain Neighbourhood House, 3981 Main St., Vancouver BC V5V 3P3 – 604/665-3964 – Branch Head, Anne Kyler – Branch of Vancouver Public Library

Vancouver: South Hill Branch Library, 6076 Fraser St., Vancouver BC V5W 2Z7 – 604/665-3965 – Branch Head, Tish McMurtry – Branch of Vancouver Public Library

Vancouver: Strathcona Branch Library, 592 East Pender St., Vancouver BC V6A 1V5 – 604/665-3967 – Branch Head, Heather Scoular – Branch of Vancouver Public Library

Vancouver: West Point Grey Branch Library, 4480 West 10th Ave., Vancouver BC V6R 2H9 – 604/665-3982 – Head Librarian, Susan Bridgman – Branch of Vancouver Public Library

Victoria: Greater Victoria Public Library, 735 Broughton St., Victoria BC V8W 3H2 – 250/382-7241; Fax: 250/382-7125; Email: ENVOY: VICT.P.L. – Chief Librarian, Sandra Anderson; Children's Librarian, Colleen Stewart; Technical Services Librarian, Barbara Irwin; Acquistions Librarian, Glenda Payzant – See also following branches: Bruce Hutchison Branch Library, Esquimalt Branch Library, Juan de Fuca Branch at Royal Roads University, Nellie McClung Branch Library, Oak Bay Branch Library, Saanich-Victoria Branch Library

Victoria: Bruce Hutchison Branch Library, 4636 Elk Lake Dr., Victoria BC V8Z 7K2 – 250/727-0104 – Branch Head, Ruth Scott, Email: rscott@gvpl.victoria.bc.ca – Branch of Greater Victoria Public Library

Victoria: Esquimalt Branch Library, 1149 Esquimalt Rd., Victoria BC V9A 3N6 – 250/385-1021 – Branch Head, Cheryl Osborn, Email: cosborn@gvpl.victoria.bc.ca – Branch of Greater Victoria Public Library

Victoria: Juan de Fuca Branch at Royal Roads University, 2005 Sooke Rd., Victoria BC V9B 5Y2 – 250/391-0653; Fax: 250/391-0879 – Branch Head, Gillian Pearson, Email: gpearson@gvpl.victoria.bc.ca – Branch of Greater Victoria Public Library

Victoria: Nellie McClung Branch Library, 3950 Cedar Hill Rd., Victoria BC V8P 3Z9 – 250/477-7111 – Branch Head, Barbara Hutcheson, Email: bhutches@gvpl.victoria.bc.ca – Branch of Greater Victoria Public Library

Victoria: Oak Bay Branch Library, 1442 Monterey Ave., Victoria BC V8S 4W1 – 250/592-2489 – Branch Head, H. Wetselaar, Email: hwetsela@gvpl.victoria.bc.ca – Branch of Greater Victoria Public Library

Victoria: Saanich-Victoria Branch Library, 3500 Blanshard St., Victoria BC V8X 1W3 – 250/475-6100 – Branch Head, Diane Brittain, Email: dbrittai@gvpl.victoria.bc.ca – Branch of Greater Victoria Public Library

West Vancouver Memorial Library, 1950 Marine Dr., West Vancouver BC V7V 1J8 – 604/925-7400; Fax: 604/925-5933; Email: ENVOY: F.WVML; Symbol: BWV – Chief Librarian, Jack Mounce; Reference Services, Head, Ted Benson; Adult Services, Head, Cheryl McGregor; Youth Services, Head, Julia Hedley; Support Services, Head, Lauren Henderson; Technical Services/Systems, Head, Roy Hunter; Acquisitions, Head, Devona Hanlin

Regional Library Districts with Member Libraries

FRASER VALLEY REGIONAL LIBRARY

34589 Delair Rd., Abbotsford BC V2S 5Y1 – 604/859-7141; Fax: 604/852-5701; Email: ENVOY: FVRL.ILL

Executive Director, Judith Hare
Manager of Public Services, Maria Jarvie
Manager, Systems & Technical Services, Diana Guinn
Collection Development Coordinator, Sybil Harrison

Abbotsford MSA Centennial Branch Library, 33660 South Fraser Way, Abbotsford BC V2S 2B9 – 604/853-1753 – Community Librarian, Judy Casey

Clearbrook Branch Library, 32383 South Fraser Way, Abbotsford BC V2T 1W6 – 604/859-7814 – Area Coordinator, Barbara Emerson

Agassiz Branch Library, 7110 Cheam Ave., PO Box 7, Agassiz BC V0M 1A0 – 604/796-9510 – Community Librarian, Earla Legault

Aldergrove Branch Library, 26770 - 29 Ave., Aldergrove BC V0X 1A0 – 604/856-6415; Fax: 604/856-6816 – Community Librarian, Yvonne Holden

Boston Bar Branch Library, 47643 Old Boston Bar Rd., PO Box 67, Boston Bar BC V0K 1C0 – 604/867-8855 – Community Librarian, Cora Dunlop

Chilliwack Branch Library, 45860 - 1 Ave., Chilliwack BC V2P 7K1 – 604/792-1941 – Area Coordinator, Kathy Brown

George Mackie Branch Library, 8440 - 112 St., Delta BC V4C 4W8 – 604/594-8155 – Area Coordinator, Barbara Hynek

Ladner (Delta Pioneer) Branch Library, 4683 - 51 St., Delta BC V4K 2V8 – 604/946-6215 – Community Librarian, Cecilia Duncan

South Delta Branch Library, 1321A - 56 St., Delta BC V4L 2A6 – 604/943-2271 – Community Librarian, Shirley Featherstone

Fort Langley Branch Library, 9167 Glover Rd., PO Box 312, Fort Langley BC V1M 2R6 – 604/888-0722 – Community Librarian, Mary Marquette

Hope Branch Library, 325 Wallace St., PO Box 609, Hope BC V0X 1L0 – 604/869-2313 – Community Librarian, Sydney Mason

Brookswood Branch Library, 20045 - 40 Ave., Langley BC V3A 2W2 – 604/534-7055 – Community Librarian, Marina Kristjanson

Langley Centennial Branch Library, 20355 Douglas Cres., Langley BC V3A 4B3 – 604/534-3284 – Area Coordinator, Mary Kierans

Walnut Grove Branch Library, 8889 Walnut Grove Dr., Langley BC V1M 2N7 – 604/882-0410 – Community Librarian, Bea Rawlings

Maple Ridge Branch Library, 22420 Dewdney Trunk Rd., Maple Ridge BC V2X 3J5 – 604/467-4922 – Branch Librarian, Kathryn Feeney

Canadian Almanac & Directory 1997

Mission Branch Library, 33247 - 2 Ave., Mission BC V2V 1J9 – 604/826-6610 – Branch Librarian, Rhian Piprell

Mount Lehman Branch Library, 5875 Mt. Lehman Rd., Mount Lehman BC V0X 1V0 – 604/856-4988 – Community Librarian, Mary Iverson

Pitt Meadows Branch Library, 12047 Harris Rd., Pitt Meadows BC V3Y 1Z2 – 604/465-4113 – Community Librarian, Sandra Richardson

Terry Fox Branch Library, 2470 Mary Hill Rd., Port Coquitlam BC V3C 3B1 – 604/927-7999 – Area Co-ordinator, Ada Con

White Rock Branch Library, 15342 Buena Vista Ave., White Rock BC V4B 1Y6 – 604/541-2201 – Community Librarian, Mary Anne Johnson

Yale Branch Library, c/o Yale Elementary School, 65050 Albert St., Yale BC V0K 2S0 – 604/863-2262 – Community Librarian, Karen Rushlow

Yarrow Public Library, 4670 Community St., PO Box 370, Yarrow BC V0X 2A0 – 604/823-4664 – Community Librarian, Gail Berger

OKANAGAN REGIONAL LIBRARY
1430 KLO Rd., Kelowna BC V1W 3P6 – 250/860-4033; Fax: 250/861-8696; Email: ENVOY: OK.LIBRARY; Symbol: BKO
Executive Director, Lesley Dieno
Public Services Manager, Lorraine Hladik
Technical Services Librarian, Paula Neumann
Children's Services Coordinator, Judy Arter
Media Librarian, Georgia McKay

Armstrong Branch Library, PO Box 189, Armstrong BC V0E 1B0 – 250/546-8311 – Community Librarian, Charlene Woodbury

Celista Branch, PO Box 233, Celista BC V0E 1L0 – 250/955-8198 – Community Librarian, Angela Stevenson

Cherryville Branch, RR#1-6E, Lumby BC V0E 2G0 – 250/547-9776 – Librarian, Colleen Primley

Enderby Branch, City Hall Complex, Hwy. 97, PO Box 226, Enderby BC V0E 1V0 – 250/838-6488 – Community Librarian, Kathleen Moerman

Falkland Branch, PO Box 33, Falkland BC V0E 1W0 – 250/379-2705 – Community Librarian, Julie Schoenberger

Golden Branch, PO Box 750, Golden BC V0A 1H0 – 250/344-6516 – Community Librarian, Lynda Whitwell

Hedley Branch, PO Box 155, Hedley BC V0X 1K0 – 250/292-8209 – Community Librarian, Martha Chambers

Kaleden Branch, PO Box 370, Kaleden BC V0H 1K0 – 250/497-8066 – Community Librarian, Louise Gardiner

Kelowna Resource Centre, 1626 Richter St., Kelowna BC V1Y 2M3 – 250/762-2800 – Kelowna Area Librarian, Beth McKee

Mission Branch, #5, 3818 Gordon Dr., Kelowna BC V1W 3G8 – 250/868-3391 – Community Librarian, Sharron Cooper

Keremeos Branch, PO Box 330, Keremeos BC V0X 1N0 – 250/499-2313 – Community Librarian, Isabel Chatfield

Lumby Branch, Lumby Community Centre, 2250 Shields Ave., PO Box 116, Lumby BC V0E 2G0 – 250/547-9528 – Community Librarian, Darlene Gudeit

Naramata Branch, PO Box 190, Naramata BC V0H 1N0 – 250/496-5679 – Community Librarian, Carol A. McGibney

Okanagan Falls Branch, PO Box 299, Okanagan Falls BC V0H 1R0 – 250/497-5886 – Community Librarian, Ruell Smith

Oliver Branch, PO Box 758, Oliver BC V0H 1T0 – 250/498-2242 – Community Librarian, Kaye-Marie Yuckin

Osoyoos Branch, PO Box 1038, Osoyoos BC V0H 1V0 – 250/495-7637 – Community Librarian, Kathy Burton

Oyama Branch, PO Box 55, Oyama BC V0H 1W0 – 250/548-3377 – Community Librarian, Helen Edgar

Peachland Branch, PO Box 21, Peachland BC V0H 1X0 – 250/767-9111 – Community Librarian, Pat Fowler

Princeton Branch, PO Box 958, Princeton BC V0X 1W0 – 250/295-6495 – Community Librarian, Joan Muir

Revelstoke Branch, PO Box 1289, Revelstoke BC V0E 2S0 – 250/837-5095 – Community Librarian, Joan Holzer

Rutland Branch, PO Box 2104, Rutland BC V1X 3B2 – 250/765-8165 – Community Librarian, Sheila Mitchell

Salmon Arm Branch, PO Box 1630, Salmon Arm BC V1E 4P7 – 250/832-6161 – Librarian, Leslie Stafford

Silver Creek Branch, RR#1, Site 9, Comp. 60, Salmon Arm BC V1E 4M1 – 250/832-4719 – Community Librarian, Marlene Campbell

Seymour Arm Branch, RR#2, Sicamous BC V0E 2V0 – 250/832-8775 – Community Librarian, Holly MacKenzie

Sicamous Branch, PO Box 15, Sicamous BC V0E 2V0 – 250/836-4845 – Community Librarian, Sharon Dyck

Sorrento Branch, PO Box 54, Sorrento BC V0E 2W0 – 250/675-4818 – Community Librarian, Glenna Hines

Summerland Branch, PO Box 1198, Summerland BC V0H 1Z0 – 250/494-5591 – Community Librarian, Jan Carlson

Trout Lake Branch, PO Box 46, Trout Lake BC V0G 1R0 – Community Librarian, Nancy Savage

Vernon Branch, 3001 - 32 Ave., Vernon BC V1T 2L8 – 250/542-7610 – Vernon Area Librarian, Wendy Stevens

Westbank Branch, PO Box 46, Westbank BC V4T 1Z1 – 250/768-4369 – Community Librarian, Marnie Keath

Winfield Branch, PO Box 477, Winfield BC V0H 2C0 – 250/766-3141 – Community Librarian, Angela MacPherson

VANCOUVER ISLAND REGIONAL LIBRARY
6250 Hammond Bay Rd., PO Box 3333, Nanaimo BC V9R 5N3 – 250/758-4697; Fax: 250/758-2482; Email: ENVOY: ILL.VIRL; DF.MEADOWS; Symbol: ORCA
Director, Donald F. Meadows
Coordinator, Reference Service, Marion Wildin
Coordinator, Catalogue & Compilation Service, Gloria Novak
Coordinator, Collections, Sher O'Hara
Personnel Officer, Ann Lowrie

Bella Coola Branch Library, PO Box 68, Bella Coola BC V0T 1C0 – 250/799-5330; Fax: 250/799-5330 – Branch Head, Linda Baker

Brentwood/Central Saanich Branch Library, 1209 Clarke Rd., Brentwood Bay BC V8M 1P8 – 250/652-2013; Fax: 250/652-6224 – Branch Head, Katherine Day

Campbell River Branch Library, 1240 Shopper's Row, Campbell River BC V9W 2C8 – 250/287-3655; Fax: 250/287-2119 – Branch Head, Julia Clausen

Chemainus Branch Library, 2592 Legion St., PO Box 72, Chemainus BC V0R 1K0 – 250/246-9471; Fax: 250/246-9411 – Branch Head, Heather Aikenhead

Comox Branch Library, 1729 Comox Ave., Comox BC V9M 3M2 – 250/339-2971; Fax: 250/339-2940 – Branch Head, Judy Van Sickle

Courtenay Branch Library, 410 Cliffe Ave., Courtenay BC V9N 2J2 – 250/334-3369; Fax: 250/334-0910 – Branch Head, Diane Taggart

Cumberland Branch Library, PO Box 378, Cumberland BC V0R 1S0 – 250/336-8121; Fax: 250/336-8121 – Branch Head, Ellen Wise

Cowichan Branch Library, 2687 James St., Duncan BC V9L 2X5 – 250/746-7661; Fax: 250/746-5595 – Branch Head, Fyvie Weeks

Gold River Branch Library, 396 Nimpkish Dr., PO Box 309, Gold River BC V0P 1G0 – 250/283-2502; Fax: 250/283-2502 – Branch Head, Ann Henkelman

Hornby Island Branch Library, 1765 Sollans Rd., PO Box 37, Hornby Island BC V0R 1Z0 – 250/335-0044; Fax: 250/335-0044 – Branch Head, Denyse Wallace

Ladysmith Branch Library, #3, 740 - 1st Ave., PO Box 389, Ladysmith BC V0R 2E0 – 250/245-2322; Fax: 250/245-2393 – Branch Head, Florence Edgar

Lake Cowichan Branch Library, #1, 38 King George, PO Box 918, Lake Cowichan BC V0R 2G0 – 250/749-3431; Fax: 250/749-3401 – Branch Head, Deborah Maher

Masset Branch Library, 2123 Collison, PO Box 710, Masset BC V0T 1M0 – 250/626-3663; Fax: 250/626-3663 – Branch Head, Andrea Gee

South Cowichan Branch Library, #33, 2720 Mill Bay Rd., PO Box 2000, Mill Bay BC V0R 2P0 – 250/743-5436; Fax: 250/743-5506 – Branch Head, Pat Fiddis

Nanaimo Branch Library, 580 Fitswilliam St., Nanaimo BC V9R 3B2 – 250/753-1154; Fax: 250/754-1483 – Branch Head, Dorrit Olesen

Wellington Branch Library, 3032 Barons Rd., Nanaimo BC V9T 4B5 – 250/758-5544; Fax: 250/758-7513 – Branch Head, Elise Hoy

Parksville Branch Library, 162 Morrison Ave., PO Box 508, Parksville BC V9P 2G6 – 250/248-3841; Fax: 250/248-0170 – Branch Head, Vivienne Wilson

Port Alberni Branch Library, 4245 Wallace St., Port Alberni BC V9Y 3Y6 – 250/723-9511; Fax: 250/723-5366 – Branch Head, Mary Howarth

Port Alice Branch Library, Marine Dr., PO Box 190, Port Alice BC V0N 2N0 – 250/284-3554; Fax: 250/284-3554 – Branch Head, Cheryl Reaume

Port Clements Branch Library, 35 Cedar Ave. West, PO Box 283, Port Clements BC V0T 1R0 – 250/557-4402; Fax: 250/557-4402 – Branch Head, Sheila Heit

Port Hardy Branch Library, 7110 Market St., PO Box 251, Port Hardy BC V0N 2P0 – 250/949-6661; Fax: 250/949-6600 – Branch Head, Barbara Bruner

Port McNeill Branch Library, #4, Broughton Plaza, PO Box 786, Port McNeill BC V0N 2R0 – 250/956-3669; Fax: 250/956-3669 – Branch Head, Bonita Vandervalk

Port Renfrew Branch Library, General Delivery, Port Renfrew BC V0S 1K0 – 250/647-5423; Fax: 250/647-5534 – Branch Head, Joan Levy

Quadra Island Branch Library, Heriot Bay, 712 Cramer Rd., PO Box 310, Quadra Island BC V0P 1H0 – 250/285-2216; Fax: 250/285-2216 – Branch Head, Barbara Van Orden

Qualicum Beach Branch Library, 133 West Fern Rd., PO Box 397, Qualicum Beach BC V9K 1S9 – 250/752-6121; Fax: 250/752-6630 – Branch Head, Diana Wilson

Queen Charlotte Branch Library, 138 Bay St., PO Box 339, Queen Charlotte City BC V0T 1S0 – 250/559-4518; Fax: 250/559-4518 – Branch Head, Marnie Andrews

Sandspit Branch Library, Seabreeze Plaza, PO Box 228, Sandspit BC V0T 1T0 – 250/637-2247; Fax: 250/637-2247 – Branch Head, Adriana Spighi

Sayward Branch Library, Sayward Centre Mall, 641C Kelsey Way, PO Box 310, Sayward BC V0P 1R0 – 250/282-5551; Fax: 250/282-5551 – Branch Head, Heather Sprout

Sidney/North Saanich Branch Library, 10091 Resthaven Dr., Sidney BC V8L 3G3 – 250/656-0944; Fax: 250/656-6400 – Branch Head, Wendy Gibbs

Sointula Branch Library, PO Box 187, Sointula BC V0N 3E0 – 250/973-6493; Fax: 250/973-6493 – Branch Head, Linda Burrows

Sooke Branch Library, 6686 Sooke Rd., PO Box 468, Sooke BC V0S 1N0 – 250/642-3022; Fax: 250/642-3994 – Branch Head, Sonia Desrosiers

Tahsis Branch Library, 977 South Maquinna Rd., PO Box 458, Tahsis BC V0P 1X0 – 250/934-6621; Fax: 250/943-6621 – Branch Head, Penelope Leach

Tofino Branch Library, 385 Main St., PO Box 97, Tofino BC V0R 2Z0 – 250/725-3713; Fax: 250/725-3713 – Branch Head, Linda White

Ucluelet Branch Library, 1768 Peninsula, PO Box 247, Ucluelet BC V0R 3A0 – 250/726-4642; Fax: 250/726-4642 – Branch Head, Ann Novak

Union Bay Branch Library, 5527 Island Hwy., PO Box 81, Union Bay BC V0R 3B0 – 250/335-2433; Fax: 250/335-2433 – Branch Head, Bryanna Grogan

Colwood Branch Library, Colwood Plaza, 1913 Sooke Rd., Victoria BC V9B 1V9 – 250/478-6711; Fax: 250/478-7900 – Branch Head, Gerald Brookall

Langford Branch Library, #11, 721 Station Rd., Victoria BC V9B 2S1 – 250/474-1722; Fax: 250/474-1730 – Branch Head, Rosanne Rowan

Woss Public Branch Library, PO Box 5280, Woss BC V0N 3P0 – 250/281-2263; Fax: 250/281-2263 – Branch Head, Lori Kaube

Integrated Public Library System with Member Libraries

CARIBOO LIBRARY NETWORK

Network Office, #2, 487 Borland St., Williams Lake BC V2G 1R9 – 250/392-7399; Fax: 250/392-3637
Librarian, Lil Mack

100 Mile House Library, PO Box 278, 100 Mile House BC V0K 2E0 – Wendy Hamblin

Alexis Creek Branch, General Delivery, Alexis BC V0L 1A0 – 250/394-4346

Alkali Lake Branch, General Delivery, Alkali Lake BC V0L 1B0 – 250/440-5618

Anahim Lake Branch, General Delivery, Anahim Lake BC V0L 1C0 – 250/742-3235 – Librarian, Sue Glenn

Big Lake Branch, General Delivery, Big Lake BC V0L 1G0

Bridge Lake Branch, General Delivery, Bridge Lake BC V0K 1E0 – 250/593-4545

Forest Grove Branch, PO Box 8, Forest Grove BC V0K 1M0 – 250/397-2927 – Librarian, Mary Bourne

Horsefly Branch, PO Box 48, Horsefly BC V0L 1L0 – 250/620-3345

Lac La Hache Branch, PO Box 246, Lac La Hache BC V0K 1T0 – 250/396-7642 – Librarian, Elva Ogden

Likely Branch, PO Box 86, Likely BC V0L 1N0 – 250/790-2234 – Librarian, Janis Ulrich

McLeese Lake Branch, PO Box 100, McLeese Lake BC V0L 1P0 – 250/297-6533 – Librarian, Evelyn Suski

Nazko Branch, RR#5, Quesnel BC V2J 3H9 – Librarian, Marlene Cline, 604/992-8626

Quesnel Library, 593 Barlow Ave., Quesnel BC V2J 2C5 – 250/992-7912; Fax: 250/992-9882 – Librarian, Barbara McKenzie

Tatla Lake Branch, General Delivery, Tatla Lake BC V0L 1V0 – 250/476-1242 – Librarian, Jean Fell

Wells Branch, PO Box 35, Wells BC V0K 2R0 – 250/994-3424

Williams Lake Branch, 110 Oliver St., Williams Lake BC V2G 1L8 – 250/392-3630; Fax: 250/392-3518 – Librarian, Lillian Mack

THOMPSON-NICOLA REGIONAL DISTRICT LIBRARY SYSTEM

Administration Centre, 906 Laval Cres., Kamloops BC V2C 5P5 – 250/374-8866; Fax: 250/374-8355; Email: postmaster@tnrdlib.bc.ca
Director of Libraries, Alice Dalton
Reference Librarian, Alex MacDonald
Manager of Library & Support Services, Kevin Kierans

Ashcroft Library, 201 Brink St., PO Box 789, Ashcroft BC V0K 1A0 – 250/453-9042; Fax: 250/453-9042 – Branch Head, Margaret Vallance

Barrière Library, 643 Barrière Town Rd., PO Box 100, Barrière BC V0E 1E0 – 250/672-5811; Fax: 250/672-5811 – Branch Head, Betty Uppenborn

Blue River Library, PO Box 2, Blue River BC V0E 1J0 – 250/673-8235 – Branch Head, Judith Mitchell

Cache Creek Library, 1390 Quartz Rd., PO Box 429, Cache Creek BC V0K 1H0 – 250/457-9953 – Branch Head, Lillian Liesch

Chase Library, 614 Shuswap Ave., PO Box 590, Chase BC V0E 1M0 – 250/679-3331; Fax: 250/679-3331 – Branch Head, Jill Bewza

Clearwater Library, RR#1, PO Box 1913, Clearwater BC V0E 1N0 – 250/674-2543; Fax: 250/674-2543 – Branch Head, Darlene Cowie

Clinton Library, 1506 Tingley St., PO Box 550, Clinton BC V0K 1K0 – 250/459-7752 – Branch Head, Catheryn Munro

Kamloops Library, #101, 63 Victoria St. West, Kamloops BC V2C 6L4 – 250/372-5145; Fax: 250/372-5614 – Branch Head, Alex MacDonald

Logan Lake Library, #70, 150 Opal Dr., PO Box 310, Logan Lake BC V0K 1W0 – 250/523-6745; Fax: 250/523-6745 – Branch Head, Sophie Douglas

Lytton Library, PO Box 220, Lytton BC V0K 1Z0 – 250/455-2521 – Branch Head, Shirley Mountford

Merritt Library, 2058 Granite Ave., PO Box 1510, Merritt BC V0K 2B0 – 250/378-4737; Fax: 250/378-3706 – Branch Head, Deborha Merrick

North Kamloops Library, 795 Tranquille Rd., North Kamloops BC V2B 3J3 – 250/554-1124; Fax: 250/376-3825 – Branch Head, Michael Killick

Savona Library, 640 Tingley St., PO Box 169, Savona BC V0K 2J0 – 250/373-2666; Fax: 250/373-2666 – Branch Head, Sandra Rawson

Federated Public Library System

Burnaby: Interlink Federated Public Library System, #110, 6545 Bonsor Ave., Burnaby BC V5H 1H3 – 604/437-8441; Fax: 604/430-8595; Email: ENVOY: ADMIN/INTERLINK – Director, Gordon Ray

Public Library Associations

Alert Bay Public Library, PO Box 208, Alert Bay BC V0N 1A0 – 250/974-5721; Email: ENVOY: ILL.BABM – Librarian, Joyce Wilby

Bowen Island Public Library, 6 Cates Hill, 495 Mt. Gardner Rd., PO Box 10, Bowen Island BC V0N 1G0 – 604/947-9788; Fax: 604/947-2008; Email: ENVOY: ILL.BBI – Librarian, Tina Nielsen

Burns Lake Public Library, 613 Government St., PO Box 449, Burns Lake BC V0J 1E0 – 250/692-3192; Fax: 250/692-7488; Email: ENVOY: ILL.BBUL; Symbol: BBUL – Chief Librarian, Gwynne Nelson; Children's Librarian, Linda Palmer

Castlegar & District Public Library, 1005 - 3 St., Castlegar BC V1N 2A2 – 250/365-7765;
Email: ENVOY: ILL.BCD – Librarian, Judy Wearmouth; Assistant Librarian, Kay Ross; Assistant Librarian, Julie Kalesnikoff

Chetwynd Public Library, 5012 - 46 St., PO Box 1420, Chetwynd BC V0C 1J0 – 250/788-2559; Fax: 250/788-2186; Email: ENVOY: ILL.BCHE – Librarian, Fay Asleson

Cranbrook Public Library, 20 - 17 Ave. North, Cranbrook BC V1C 3W8 – 250/426-4063; Fax: 250/426-2098; Symbol: BCR – Director, Patricia Adams

Creston Public Library, 205 - 7 Ave. North, PO Box 1639, Creston BC V0B 1G0 – 250/428-4141; Fax: 250/428-4703 – Chief Librarian, Michelle Demopoulos

Elkford Public Library, 816 Michel Rd., PO Box 280, Elkford BC V0B 1H0 – 250/865-2912; Fax: 250/865-2460; Email: ENVOY: ILL.BELK – Librarian, Sharon Gumowsky

Fernie Public Library, 592 - 3 Ave., PO Box 448, Fernie BC V0B 1M0 – 250/423-4458; Fax: 250/423-3050; Email: ENVOY: ILL.BF; Symbol: BF – Librarian, Diane Sharp

Fort Nelson Public Library, PO Box 330, Fort Nelson BC V0C 1R0 – 250/774-6777; Fax: 250/774-6777; Symbol: BFN – Librarian, Nola Newman

Fort St. James Public Library, 389 Stuart Dr., PO Box 729, Fort St. James BC V0J 1P0 – 250/996-7431; Email: ENVOY: ILL.BFSJA – Librarian, Kay Biron

Fort St. John Public Library, 10015 - 100 Ave., Fort St. John BC V1J 1Y7 – 250/785-3731; Fax: 250/785-1510; Symbol: BFSJ – Director, Angela Mehmel

Fraser Lake Public Library, PO Box 520, Fraser Lake BC V0J 1S0 – 250/699-8888; Fax: 250/699-8899; Email: ENVOY: ILL.BFRL – Head Librarian, Judith Loza

Fruitvale: Beaver Valley Public Library, PO Box 429, Fruitvale BC V0G 1L0 – 250/367-7114; Fax: 250/367-7130; Email: ENVOY: ILL.BFBV; Symbol: BFBV – Librarian, Bette Michaux

Gibsons & District Public Library, 470 South Fletcher Rd., PO Box 109, Gibsons BC V0N 1V0 – 604/886-2130; Email: ENVOY: ILL.BGI – Chief Librarian, Myrna Baba

Goldbridge Public Library, General Delivery, Goldbridge BC V0K 1P0 – 250/238-2437 – Contact, Sheena Aitken – Branch of Lillooet Area Library Association

Grand Forks & District Public Library, PO Box 1539, Grand Forks BC V0H 1H0 – 250/442-3944; Fax: 250/442-2645; Email: ENVOY: ILL.BGF – Librarian, Lorraine Kelley

Granisle Public Library, PO Box 550, Granisle BC V0J 1W0 – 250/697-2713; Symbol: BGR – Community Librarian, Sherry Smith

Greenwood Public Library, 346 South Copper St., PO Box 279, Greenwood BC V0H 1J0 – 250/445-6111; Email: ENVOY: ILL.BGRE; Symbol: BGRE – Librarian, Judy Foucher

Hazelton District Public Library, PO Box 323, Hazelton BC V0J 1Y0 – 250/842-5961; Fax: 250/842-5069; Email: ENVOY: ILL.BHA; Symbol: BHA – Librarian, Janet Willson

Houston Public Library, PO Box 840, Houston BC V0J 1Z0 – 250/845-2256; Fax: 250/845-2088; Email: library2@netshop.net; Symbol: BH – Librarian, Janet Marren

Hudson's Hope Library, PO Box 269, Hudson's Hope BC V0C 1V0 – 250/783-9414; Email: ENVOY: ILL.BHH – Librarian, Wendy McIver

Invermere Public Library, PO Box 989, Invermere BC V0A 1K0 – 250/342-6416; Fax: 250/342-6416; Email: ENVOY: ILL.BIN – Librarian, Elizabeth Burke

Kaslo & District Public Library, PO Box 760, Kaslo BC V0G 1M0 – 250/353-2942; Email: ENVOY: ILL.BKASL – Community Librarian, Denise Fournier

Kemano Public Library, PO Box 90, Kemano BC V0T 1K0 – 250/634-5495; Fax: 250/634-5255; Email: ENVOY: ILL.BKE; Symbol: BKE – Librarian, Judith Halland

Kimberley Public Library, 115 Spokane St., Kimberley BC V1A 2E5 – 250/427-3112; Fax: 250/427-7157; Email: ENVOY: ILL.BKI; Symbol: BKI – Librarian, Beverley J. Varty

Kitimat Public Library, 940 Wakashan Ave., Kitimat BC V8C 2G3 – 250/632-2665; Fax: 250/632-2630; Email: ENVOY: ILL.BKIT – Chief Librarian, Mike Burris

Lillooet Area Library Association, PO Box 939, Lillooet BC V0K 1V0 – 250/256-7944 – Librarian, Sheila Pfeiffer – See also following branches: Bridge River Public Library, Goldbridge Public Library

McBride Public Library, 241 Dominion St., PO Box 489, McBride BC V0J 2E0 – 250/569-2411;

5-16 LIBRARIES — BRITISH COLUMBIA

Email: ENVOY: ILL.BMB – Librarian, Margaret Griffiths

Midway Public Library, PO Box 268, Midway BC V0H 1M0 – 250/449-2620; Email: ENVOY: ILL.BM – Librarian, Rosemary Santopinto

Nakusp Public Library, 92 - 6 Ave. NW, PO Box 297, Nakusp BC V0G 1R0 – 250/265-3363; Email: ENVOY: ILL.BNA – Librarian, Evelyn Goodell

Pemberton & District Public Library, PO Box 430, Pemberton BC V0N 2L0 – 604/894-6916; Email: ENVOY: ILL.BPE – Librarian, Janet Naylor

Pender Island Public Library, RR#1, PO Box 12, Pender Island BC V0N 2M0 – 250/629-3722; Email: ENVOY: ILL.BPI – Chair, Johanna Timmermans

Powell River District Public Library, 4411 Michigan Ave., Powell River BC V8A 2S3 – 604/485-4796; Fax: 604/485-2913; Email: ENVOY: ILL.BPRDP – Chief Librarian, Elaine Julian

Rossland Public Library, PO Box 190, Rossland BC V0G 1Y0 – 250/362-7611; Email: ENVOY: ILL.BR; Symbol: BR – Librarian, Lois Haynes

Salmo Public Library, 120 - 4th St., PO Box 458, Salmo BC V0G 1Z0 – 250/357-2312; Fax: 250/357-2596; Email: ENVOY: ILL.BSA – Librarian, June Stockdale

Salt Spring Island Public Library Association, 129 McPhillips Ave., Salt Spring Island BC V8K 2T6 – 250/537-4666; Email: ENVOY: ILL.BGSI – Chairman, Anthony M. Burridge; Chief Librarian, Michael Wheaton; Reference Librarian, June Perry, 250/537-9838; Children's Librarian, Merle Sheffield, 250/537-9520

Sechelt Public Library Association, 5520 Trail Ave., PO Box 2104, Sechelt BC V0N 3A0 – 604/885-3260; Email: ENVOY: ILL.BSE – Librarian, Rose Toenders

Shalalth: Bridge River Public Library, PO Box 19, Shalalth BC V0N 3C0 – 250/259-8242 – Contact, Edith Lovey – Branch of Lillooet Area Library Association

Smithers Public Library, PO Box 55, Smithers BC V0J 2N0 – 250/847-3043; Email: ENVOY: ILL.BS – Librarian, David Anson

Sparwood Public Library, 110 Pine Ave., PO Box 1060, Sparwood BC V0B 2G0 – 250/425-2299; Fax: 250/425-0229; Email: ENVOY: ILL.BSPA – Librarian, James Bertoia

Squamish Public Library, PO Box 1039, Squamish BC V0N 3G0 – 604/892-3110; Email: ENVOY: ILL.BSQ – Librarian, Maureen Painter

Stewart Public Library, PO Box 546, Stewart BC V0T 1W0 – 250/636-2380; Email: ENVOY: ILL.BSP – Librarian, Dorean Neisner

Terrace Public Library, 4610 Park Ave., Terrace BC V8G 1V6 – 250/638-8177; Fax: 250/635-6207; Email: ENVOY: ILL.BTE – Librarian, Ed Curell

Tumbler Ridge Library, 340 Front St., PO Box 70, Tumbler Ridge BC V0C 2W0 – 250/242-4778; Fax: 250/242-5669; Email: tr_lib@Pris.bc.ca; ENVOY: ILL.BTR – Librarian, Peggy Holden

Valemount Public Library, 1070 Main St., PO Box 368, Valemount BC V0E 2Z0 – 250/566-4367; Fax: 250/566-4278; Email: ENVOY: ILL.BVALE – Librarian, Linda Hedberg

Vanderhoof Public Library, PO Bag 6000, Vanderhoof BC V0J 3A0 – 250/567-4060; Fax: 250/567-4060; Email: ENVOY: ILL.BVDH – Librarian, Jane Gray

Victoria: View Royal Public Library, 279 Island Hwy., Victoria BC V9B 1G4 – 250/479-2723; Email: ENVOY: ILL.BVIVR – Librarian, Sara Cook

Whistler Public Library, 4329 Main St., PO Box 95, Whistler BC V0N 1B0 – 604/932-5564; Fax: 604/932-0664; Email: ENVOY: ILL.BW – Head Librarian, Joan Richoz

Reading Centres

Atlin Public Library, PO Box 208, Atlin BC V0W 1A0 – 250/651-7572 – Librarian, Carol Boyko

Brisco Reading Centre, PO Box 50, Brisco BC V0A 1B0 – 250/346-3229 – Librarian, Betty Dreyer

Burton Community Reading Centre, PO Box 142, Burton BC V0G 1E0 – 250/265-4161 – Librarian, Elaine Marshall

Crawford Bay: Eastshore Community Library, PO Box 85, Crawford Bay BC V0B 1E0 – 250/227-9496 – Librarian, Cathy Poch

Dease Lake Reading Centre, PO Box 237, Dease Lake BC V0C 1L0 – 250/771-3636 – Librarian, Carolyn Moore

Edgewater Public Library, PO Box 129, Edgewater BC V0A 1E0 – 250/347-9558 – Chair, Susan Fahrni

Edgewood: Inonoaklin Valley Reading Centre, PO Box 129, Edgewood BC V0G 1J0 – 250/269-7212; Fax: 250/269-7633 – Librarian, Susan Bampton

Fauquier Community Reading Centre, PO Box 99, Fauquier BC V0G 1K0 – 250/269-7348 – Librarian, Anna Siebold

Fort Steele: Steeples' View Reading Centre, PO Box 56, Fort Steele BC V0B 1N0 – 250/429-3981 – Librarian, Judi-Lynn Haskett-Getty

Grasmere Reading Centre, PO Box 36, Grasmere BC V0B 1R0 – 250/887-3433 – Librarian, Betty Sinclair

Lions Bay Library, 400 Centre Rd., PO Box 326, Lions Bay BC V0N 2E0 – 604/921-6944 – Librarian, Mansje More

Madeira Park: Pender Harbour Reading Centre, PO Box 271, Madeira Park BC V0N 2H0 – 604/883-2983 – Librarian, Maud Hayes

Moyie Reading Centre, General Delivery, PO Box 124, Moyie BC V0B 2A0 – 250/829-0522 – Librarian, Arlene Pervin

New Denver Reading Centre, PO Box 432, New Denver BC V0G 1S0 – 250/358-2221 – Chairperson, Agnes Emary

Riondel Community Library, PO Box 29, Riondel BC V0B 2B0 – 250/225-3494 – Librarian, Edith Nelson

Roberts Creek Public Library, General Delivery, Roberts Creek BC V0N 2W0 – 604/886-2577

Telkwa Reading Centre, PO Box 313, Telkwa BC V0J 2X0 – 250/846-9286 – Librarian, Christine Tessier

Special & College Libraries & Resource Centres

ABBOTSFORD

Solicitor General Canada - Matsqui Institution - Library, PO Box 2500, Abbotsford BC V2S 4P3 – 604/859-4841, ext.313; Fax: 604/850-8375; Symbol: BAMIS – Librarian, Jill Hummerstone

Regional Headquarters (Pacific) - Library, PO Box 4500, Abbotsford BC V2T 4M8 – 604/854-2570; Fax: 604/854-2612; Symbol: BASG – Librarian, Monika McEwen

Regional Psychiatric Centre (Pacific) - Library, PO Box 3000, Abbotsford BC V2S 4P4 – 604/853-7464, ext.259; Fax: 604/853-6992; Symbol: BARP – Contract Librarian, Jennifer Joslin

University College of the Fraser Valley - Library, 33844 King Rd., RR#2, Abbotsford BC V2S 7M9 – 604/854-4510; Fax: 604/853-8055; Email: harris@ucfv.bc.ca; Symbol: BCLF

Director of Libraries, W.E. Harris
Technical Services, Judy Inouye
Public Services, Anne Knowlan

Western Pentecostal Bible College - Lorne Philip Hudson Memorial Library, PO Box 1700, Abbotsford BC V2S 7E7 – 604/853-7491, local 30; Fax: 604/853-8951

Librarian, Laurence M. Van Kleek
Library Work Supervisor, Lorraine Craddock
Library Work Supervisor, Darlene H. Van Kleek
Library Technologist, Leona Krause

AGASSIZ

Agassiz Research Centre - Library, 6947 Hwy. 7, PO Box 1000, Agassiz BC V0M 1A0 – 604/796-2221, ext.250; Fax: 604/796-0359; Email: boydl@em.agr.ca; Symbol: BAGAG – Librarian, Lyne Stack Boyd

Solicitor General Canada - Kent Institution - Library, PO Box 1500, Agassiz BC V0M 1A0 – 604/796-2121, ext.467; Fax: 604/796-9563; Symbol: BAKI – Librarian, Catherine Ings

Mountain Institution - Library, PO Box 1600, Agassiz BC V0M 1A0 – 604/796-2231, ext.484; Fax: 604/796-1450; Symbol: BAMI – Librarian, Joanne Bean

ALERT BAY

U'mista Cultural Society – Library, PO Box 253, Alert Bay BC V0N 1A0 – 250/974-5403 – Collections Manager, Juanita Pascos

BURNABY

Association of British Columbia Teachers of English as an Additional Language – Mel Henderson Collection, #177, 4664 Lougheed Hwy., Burnaby BC V5C 5T5 – 604/294-8325 – Librarian, Diane Jones

BC Hydro - Info Centre, #B02, 6911 Southpoint Dr., Burnaby BC V3N 4X8 – 604/528-3065; Fax: 604/528-3137; Symbol: BCH – Librarian, H. Elizabeth McLaren

BC Tel Information - Resource Centre, #5, 3777 Kingsway, Burnaby BC V5H 3Z7 – 604/432-2671; Fax: 604/435-0510; Symbol: BVABT – Manager, IRC, Shelley Tegart

British Columbia Institute of Technology - Library Services, 3700 Willingdon Ave., Burnaby BC V5G 3H2 – 604/432-8371; Fax: 604/430-5443; Email: ENVOY: BCIT; Symbol: BBIT

Chief Librarian, Paula Pick, 604/432-8360
Public/Technical Services, Coordinator, Robert Roy, 604/432-8364
Cataloguer, Yu Mei Choi, 604/432-8922
Systems Librarian, Merilee MacKinnon, 604/432-8647
BusinessGerry Weeks, 604/432-8856
Electronics & Computing, Frank Knor, 604/432-8508
Engineering, Margot Allingham, 604/432-8793
Health, Ana Ferrinho, 604/432-8546
Trades, Tony Kelly, 604/432-8764
Film, 604/432-8367
Pacific Marine Training Institute, Librarian, Linda Matsuba, 604/985-0622, ext.330

Burnaby Hospital – H.H.W. Brooke Memorial Library, 3935 Kincaid St., Burnaby BC V5G 2X6 – 604/431-4734; Fax: 604/431-4734; Email: hlim@a.teleserve.ca – Librarian, Houng Lim

Columbia College - Library, 6037 Marlborough Ave., Burnaby BC V5H 3L6 – 604/430-6422; Fax: 604/430-6761 – Head Librarian, Yvonne de Souza

Golder Associates Ltd. - Library, #500, 4260 Still Creek Dr., Burnaby BC V5C 6C6 – 604/298-6623; Fax: 604/298-5253; Email: lwills@golder.com; Symbol: GA – Librarian, Lisa Wills

Greater Vancouver Regional District - Library, 4330 Kingsway, Burnaby BC V5H 4G8 – 604/432-6335; Fax: 604/432-6445; Symbol: BBGV – Chief Librarian, Frances Christopherson, Email: fchristo@gvrd.bc.ca

Health Canada - Health Protection Branch - Regional Library, 3155 Willingdon Green, Burnaby BC V5G 4P2 – 604/666-3147; Fax: 604/666-3149 – Librarian, Elizabeth Hardacre

Kerfoot, Cameron & Company Law Office - Library, #314, 9600 Cameron St., Burnaby BC V3J 7N3 – 604/421-7144; Fax: 604/421-2912 – Berry Kerfoot

MacMillan Bloedel Research (MB Research) - Technical Library, 4225 Kincaid St., Burnaby BC V5G 4P5 – 604/439-8601; Fax: 604/439-1259; Symbol: MACB
  Supervisor, Judy M. O'Mara, Email: jmomara@macblo.ca
  Research Librarian, Marjory Jardine, Email: mejardine@macblo.ca
  Library Technician, Lana Sloan
Mechanical Contractors Association of British Columbia – Library, 3210 Lake City Way, Burnaby BC V5A 3A4 – 604/420-9714
MPR Teltech Ltd. - Information Resources Centre, 8999 Nelson Way, Burnaby BC V5A 4B5 – 604/293-5381; Fax: 604/293-5787; Email: ENVOY: MPR.LIB Patrice Hall; Symbol: BBMT – Reference Librarian, Patrice Hall
Simon Fraser University - W.A.C. Bennett Library, Burnaby BC V5A 1S6 – 604/291-3265; Fax: 604/291-4908; Email: libloan@sfu.ca; URL: http://www.lib.sfu.ca/; Symbol: BVAS
  University Librarian, Ted C. Dobb
  Collections Management, Division Head, Sharon Thomas, 604/291-3263
  Loans/Circulation, Head, Giselle Pomerleau, 604/291-3274
  Processing Division, Head, Mary Harris, 604/291-3184
  Reference, Head, Perce Groves, 604/291-3252
  Research Data Library, Librarian, Walter Piovesan, 604/291-1313
  Systems & Monographs, Head, Vacant, 604/291-3184
  Belzberg Branch, Head Librarian, Karen Marotz, 604/291-5054
  Business, Librarian, Elaine Fairey, 604/291-3044
  Business, Librarian, Sylvia Bell, 604/291-3044
  Inter-Library Loans, Head, Todd Mundle, 604/291-5596

BURNS LAKE
BC Courthouse Library Society, 508 Yellowhead Hwy., PO Box 244, Burns Lake BC V0J 1E0

CAMPBELL RIVER
BC Courthouse Library Society – Library, Courthouse, 500 - 13 Ave., Campbell River BC V9W 6P1
North Island College - Campbell River Campus Library, 1480 Elm St., Campbell River BC V9W 3A6 – 250/286-8957; Fax: 250/287-4537;
  Symbol: BCOMN – Library Clerk, Marion Summerer, Email: summerer@nic.bc.ca
Strathcona Park Lodge & Outdoor Education Centre – Library, PO Box 2160, Campbell River BC V9W 5C9 – 250/286-3122 – Owner, Myrna Boulding

CASTLEGAR
Selkirk College - Library, 301 Frank Beinder Way, PO Box 1200, Castlegar BC V1N 3J1 – 250/365-1229; Fax: 250/365-7259; Symbol: BCS
  Library Director, John Mansbridge, 250/365-7292, ext.263
  Reference Librarian, Ron Welwood
  Technical Services Librarian, Judy Deon
West Kootenay/Boundry AIDS Network, Outreach & Support Society – Library, 903 - 4th St., Castlegar BC V1N 3P3 – Toll Free: 1-800-421-2737

CHETWYND
Northern Lights College - Chetwynd Campus Library, PO Box 1180, Chetwynd BC V0C 1J0 – 250/788-2248 – Patty Krawczyk

CHILLIWACK
BC Courthouse Library Society, Courthouse, 9391 College St., Chilliwack BC V2P 4L7

University College of the Fraser Valley - Library, 45635 Yale Rd., Chilliwack BC V2P 6T4 – 604/792-0025; Fax: 604/792-2388; Symbol: BCLF
  Director, W.E. Harris, Email: Harris@ucfu.bc.ca
  Public Services Librarian, Anne Knowlan

CLEARBROOK
Columbia Bible College - Library, 2940 Clearbrook Rd., Clearbrook BC V2T 2Z8 – 604/853-3358; Fax: 604/853-3063 – Librarian, David Giesbrecht, 604/853-3567
CSC Regional Headquarters (Pacific) - Library & Information Resource Centre, PO Box 4500, Clearbrook BC V2S 4P4 – 604/854-2570

COQUITLAM
Pacific Institute for Advanced Study – Library, 936 Thermal Dr., Coquitlam BC V3J 6R8 – 604/469-7964
Registered Psychiatric Nurses Association of British Columbia – Library, #251, 3041 Anson Ave., Coquitlam BC V3B 2H6 – 604/294-6539
Warnock Hersey Professional Services Ltd. - Library, 211 Schoolhouse St., Coquitlam BC V3K 4X9 – 604/520-3321; Fax: 604/524-9186 – Librarian, Regina Frackowiak

COURTENAY
BC Courthouse Library Society, Courthouse, 420 Cumberland, Courtenay BC V9N 5M6
North Island College - Comox Valley Campus Library, 2300 Ryan Rd., Courtenay BC V9N 8N6 – 250/334-5001; Fax: 250/334-5291; Email: thomas@nic.bc.ca; Symbol: BCOMN
  Librarian, Shiloa Thomas
  Library Assistant, Helen Wickins
  Library Clerk, Debby Scott

CRANBROOK
BC Courthouse Library Society, Courthouse, 102 - 11 Ave. South, Cranbrook BC V1C 2P2
College of the Rockies - Library, PO Box 8500, Cranbrook BC V1C 5L7 – 250/489-2751; Fax: 250/489-8256; Email: reference@cotr.bc.ca; Symbol: BCRK
  Director, Learning Resources Centre, Heather Schneider
  Public Services Librarian, Barbara Janzen
  Coordinator LRC-Teleconferencing, Jim Duncan

DAWSON CREEK
BC Courthouse Library Society, Courthouse, 1201 - 103 Ave., Dawson Creek BC V1G 4J2
Northern Lights College - Dawson Creek Campus Library, 11401 - 8 St., Dawson Creek BC V1G 4G2 – 250/784-7533; Fax: 250/782-6069; Symbol: BDCNL – Regional Librarian, Mary Anne Guenther

DELTA
BC Courthouse Library Society, 4450 Clarence Taylor Cres., Delta BC V4K 3W3
British Columbia Waterfowl Society – Library, 5191 Robertson Rd., RR#1, Delta BC V4K 3N2 – 604/946-6980
Souch Severide Law Office - Library, #220, 4977 Trennant St., Delta BC V4K 2K5 – 604/946-1249

DEWDNEY
The Canadian Orthodox Church – Library, 37323 Hawkins Pickle Rd., Dewdney BC V0M 1H0 – 604/826-9336 – Librarian, Father Moses Armstrong

DUNCAN
BC Courthouse Library Society, Courthouse, 238 Government St., Duncan BC V9L 1A5
BC School District 65 - District Resource Centre, 2557 Beverly St., Duncan BC V9L 2X3 – 250/748-0321, ext.243; Fax: 250/748-3497 – Coordinator, John Caldwell

FORT LANGLEY
Eagle's Nest - Resource Centre, 23195 - 96 Ave., PO Box 1120, Fort Langley BC V1M 2S5 – 604/888-9887; Fax: 604/888-9899

FORT NELSON
Northern Lights College - Fort Nelson Campus Library, PO Box 860, Fort Nelson BC V0C 1R0 – 250/774-2741

FORT ST. JOHN
BC Courthouse Library Society, Courthouse, 10600 - 100 St., Fort St. John BC V1J 4L6
Fort St. John Community Arts Council – Library, 10003 - 100 St., Fort St. John BC V1J 3Y5 – 250/785-1991 – Artspace Administrator, Sue Popesky
Northern Lights College - Fort St. John Campus - Library Resource Centre, PO Box 1000, Fort St. John BC V1J 6K1 – 250/785-6981;
  Email: ENVOY:NLS.ILL

FORT STEELE
Fort Steele Heritage Town - Research Library & Archives, General Delivery, Fort Steele BC V0B 1N0 – 250/489-3351; Fax: 250/489-2624;
  Symbol: OTHSC – Archivist/Librarian, Derryll White

KAMLOOPS
BC Courthouse Library Society, Courthouse, 455 Columbia St., Kamloops BC V2C 6K4 – 250/828-4385; Fax: 250/828-4734 – Denise Caldwell
BC School District 24 - Henry Grube Education Centre, 245 Kitcherner Cres., Kamloops BC V2B 1B9 – 250/376-2260; Fax: 250/376-7966 – Teacher/Librarian, Corinne Paravantes
Morelli, Chertkow Law Office - Library, #300, 180 Seymour St., Kamloops BC V2C 2E3 – 250/374-3344; Fax: 250/374-1144 – Library Assistant, Mary Buchanan
Royal Inland Hospital – Library, 311 Columbia St., Kamloops BC V2C 2T1 – 250/314-2234 – Manager, Library Services, Teresa Prior
University College of the Cariboo - Library, PO Box 3010, Kamloops BC V2C 5N3 – 250/828-5300; Fax: 250/828-5313; Symbol: CR
  Director, Nancy Levesque, 250/828-5305
  Reference Librarian, Peter Peller, 250/828-5304
  Technical Services Librarian, John Weller, 250/828-5303

KASLO
Kaslo Arts Council – Langham Arts Instruction Library, PO Box 1000, Kaslo BC V0G 1M0 – 250/353-2661

KELOWNA
BC Courthouse Library Society, Courthouse, 1355 Water St., Kelowna BC V1Y 9R3 – 250/470-6980; Fax: 250/470-6858
Okanagan Symphony Society – Library, PO Box 1120, Kelowna BC V1Y 7P8 – 250/763-7018 – Librarian, David Benda
Okanagan University College - Library, 1000 KLO Rd., Kelowna BC V1Y 4X8 – 250/762-5445; Fax: 250/762-9743; Email: ENVOY: G/ZILM;
  Symbol: AKOC – Director of Library Services, G. Zilm
  North Kelowna Campus Library, 3333 College Way, Kelowna BC V1V 1V7 – 250/762-5445; Fax: 250/470-6003; Symbol: AKOC
Salloum Doak Law Office - Library, #200, 537 Leon Ave., Kelowna BC V1Y 2A9 – 250/763-4323; Fax: 250/763-4780
Weddell, Horn & Company Law Office - Library, #1, 1737 Pandosy St., Kelowna BC V1Y 1R2 – 250/762-2011; Fax: 250/861-3980 – Librarian, Jennifer Finlay

Canadian Almanac & Directory 1997

KITIMAT

Alcan Smelters & Chemicals Ltd. - Kitimat Works, Technical Library, PO Box 1800, Kitimat BC V8C 2H2 – 250/639-8560; Fax: 250/639-8644 – Nora Brown

Wozney & Donaldson Law Office - Library, #366, City Centre, Kitimat BC V8C 1T6 – 250/632-7151; Fax: 250/632-7100 – Manager, R.W. Wozney

LAKE COWICHAN

School District 66 (Lake Cowichan) - District Resource Center, PO Box 980, Lake Cowichan BC V0R 2G0 – 250/749-3822; Fax: 250/749-3543 – Coordinator, Linda Nelson

LANGLEY

Fleming, Olson & Taneda - Library, 4038 - 200B St., Langley BC V3A 1N9 – 604/533-3411; Fax: 604/533-8749

Northwest Baptist Theological College - ACTS Library, PO Box 790, Langley BC V3A 8B8 – 604/888-7511,ext.2906; Fax: 604/888-3354 – Librarian, W.B. Badke, Email: badke@charity.twu.ca

Recreation Vehicle Dealers Association of British Columbia – Library, #201, 19623 - 56 Ave., Langley BC V3A 3X7 – 604/533-4200

Roofing Contractors Association of British Columbia – Library, 9734 - 201st St., Langley BC V1M 3E8 – 604/882-9734

Society of Christian Schools in BC – Library, 7600 Glover Rd., Langley BC V3A 6H4 – 604/888-6366 – Education Coordinator, J. Vanderhoek

Trinity Western University - Norma Marion Alloway Library, 7600 Glover Rd., Langley BC V2Y 1Y1 – 604/888-7511; Fax: 604/888-3786
Chief Librarian, David Twiest
Reference Librarian, Ron Braid
Media Librarian, Ted Goshdak
Systems Librarian, Stan Olson

MAPLE RIDGE

Dewdney-Alouette Railway Society – Library, 22520 - 116 Ave., Maple Ridge BC V2X 8Y4 – 604/463-5311 – Archivist, John R. Maughan

MASSET

BC Courthouse Library Society, 1666 Orr St., PO Box 230, Masset BC V0T 1M0

MISSION

Solicitor General Canada - Mission Institution - Library, PO Box 60, Mission BC V2V 4L8 – 604/826-1231, ext.325; Symbol: BMMI – Librarian, J. Joslin

University College of the Fraser Valley - Mission Campus Library, 33046 Fourth Ave., Mission BC V2V 1S5 – 604/826-6286; Fax: 604/826-4517

Westminster Abbey - Seminary of Christ the King Library, PO Box 30, Mission BC V2V 4L8 – 604/826-8975 – Librarian, Boniface Aicher

NANAIMO

BC Courthouse Library Society, Courthouse, 35 Front St., Nanaimo BC V9R 5J1

Fisheries & Oceans Canada-Pacific Biological Station – Library, Hammond Bay Rd., PO Box 3190, Nanaimo BC V9R 5K6 – 250/756-7071; Email: library@pbs.dfo.ca; Envoy: DFO.LIB.NANAIMO; Symbol: BNP – Head, Library Services, Gordon Miller

NELSON

BC Courthouse Library Society, Courthouse, 320 Ward St., Nelson BC V1L 1S6

Chamber of Mines of Eastern British Columbia – Library of Government Geological Reports, 215 Hall St., Nelson BC V1L 5X4 – 250/352-5242

The Daily News Library, 266 Baker St., Nelson BC V1L 4H3 – 250/352-3552

Selkirk College - Nelson Campus, 2001 Silver King Rd., Nelson BC V1L 1C8 – 250/352-6601, ext.254 – Campus Librarian, Barb Cavalier

NEW WESTMINSTER

BC Courthouse Library Society, The Law Courts, Begbie Sq., New Westminster BC V3M 1C9 – 604/660-8577; Fax: 604/660-1715 – Josephine Lord

Douglas College - Library, PO Box 2503, New Westminster BC V3L 5B2 – 604/527-5568; Fax: 604/527-5095; Symbol: CABNWD
Director, Virginia Chisholm, 604/527-5182
Reference Librarian, Jean Cockburn, 604/527-5184
Audio Visual Librarian, Susan Ashcroft, 604/527-5189
Technical Services Librarian, Penny Swanson, 604/527-5259
Collections Librarian, Joan Wenman, 604/527-5181
Circulation Librarian, Patti Romanko, 604/527-5183
Serials Librarian, Len McIver, 604/527-5190
Extension Librarian, Mary Matthews, 604/527-5190
Orientation Librarian, Sandra Hochstein, 604/527-5181
Public Service Librarian, Diane Hewitt, 604/527-5184

Econotech Services Ltd. – Library, 852 Derwent Way, New Westminster BC V3M 5R1 – 604/526-4221; Toll Free: 1-800-463-5700; Symbol: ECON – Librarian, Norma Becker

HOPE International Development Agency – Hope Global Resource Centre, 214 - 6 St., New Westminster BC V3L 3A2 – 604/525-5481 – Coordinator/Resource Centre, Leah Libsekal

Justice Institute of British Columbia – Library, 715 McBride Blvd., New Westminster BC V3L 5T4 – 604/528-5594; Fax: 604/660-9637; Email: april_haddad@sfu.ca; Symbol: BVAJI – Librarian, April Haddad

Royal Columbian Hospital – Library, 330 Columbia St. East, New Westminster BC V3L 3W7 – 604/520-4281; Fax: 604/520-4804 – Manager, S. Abzinger

NORTH VANCOUVER

Capilano College - Library, 2055 Purcell Way, North Vancouver BC V7J 3H5 – 604/984-4944; Fax: 604/984-1728; Email: ENVOY: CP/ILL.BVAC; URL: http://www.capcollege.bc.ca; Symbol: BVAC
College Librarian, Frieda Wiebe, 604/984-4943
Reference Coordinator, George Modenesi, 604/986-1911, ext.2111
Circulation Coordinator, David Lambert, 604/986-1911, ext.2108
Collections Coordinator, Karin Hall, 604/986-1911, ext.2141
Technical Services Librarian, Sidney Myers, 604/986-1911, ext.2127
Systems Librarian, Annette Lorek, 604/986-1911, ext.2143
Media Production Supervisor, Edna Sakata, 604-986-1911, ext.2117

Environment Canada - Pacific & Yukon Region, 224 West Esplanade, North Vancouver BC V7M 3H7 – 604/666-5914; Fax: 604/666-1788; Email: ENVOY: EPSPACIFIC; Symbol: BVAEP – Librarian, Andrew Fabro

EVS Consultants Ltd. - Library, 195 Pemberton Ave., North Vancouver BC V7P 2R4 – 604/986-4331; Fax: 604/662-8548 – Librarian, Rhona Karbusicky

Insurance Corporation of BC - Information Resource Center, #249, 151 West Esplanade, North Vancouver BC V7M 3H9 – 604/661-6322; Fax: 604/443-7304; Email: ENVOY: ICBC.LIB; Symbol: ICBC Librarian/Manager, Grace Makarewicz
Information Technician, Ida Bradd

Lions Gate Hospital – Carson Memorial Library, 231 East 15 St., North Vancouver BC V7L 2L7 – 604/988-3131 – Director, Sharon Lyons

PENTICTON

BC Courthouse Library Society, Courthouse, 100 Main St., Penticton BC V2A 5A5

PORT ALBERNI

BC Courthouse Library Society, Courthouse, 2999 - 4 Ave., Port Alberni BC V9Y 8A5

North Island College - Port Alberni Campus Library, 3699 Roger St., Port Alberni BC V9Y 8E3 – 250/724-8733; Fax: 250/724-8780
Library Assistant, Sherry Van Bavel
Library Technician, Monica Mooney

PORT COQUITLAM

BC Courthouse Library Society, 2620 Mary Hill Rd., Port Coquitlam BC V3C 3B2

Riverview Hospital - Library Services, 500 Lougheed Hwy., Port Coquitlam BC V3C 4J2 – 604/524-7576; Fax: 604/524-7021; Email: library@bcmhs.bc.ca – Manager, Library Services, Patricia Fortin, 604/524-7018

PORT HARDY

North Island College - Port Hardy Campus Library, PO Box 901, Port Hardy BC V0N 2P0 – 250/949-7912; Fax: 250/949-2617 – Diane Newman

POWELL RIVER

BC Courthouse Library Society, Courthouse, 6953 Alberni St., Powell River BC V8A 2B8

PRINCE GEORGE

BC Courthouse Library Society, Courthouse, 1600 - 3 Ave., Prince George BC V2L 3G6 – 250/565-6357; Fax: 250/565-6946 – Julie Loerke

BC Ministry of Environment, Lands & Parks - Northern BC Region Library, #430, 1011 - 4th Ave., Prince George BC V2L 3H9 – 250/565-6342 – Evelyn Malgunas

The Citizen Newspaper - Library, PO Box 5700, Prince George BC V2L 5K9 – 250/562-2441; Fax: 250/562-7453 – Librarian, Leslie Barclay

College of New Caledonia - Library, 3330 - 22 Ave., Prince George BC V2N 1P8 – 250/562-2131; Fax: 250/561-5845; Email: cnclibrary@cnc.bc.ca; Symbol: BPGC
Associate Director, Resource Centres, Katherine Plett
Reference Librarian, Kathryn Ruffle
Technical Services Librarian, Brenda Yee
Orientation/Instruction Librarian, Sandra Chulka

Hope Heinrich Law Office - Library, 1598 - 6 Ave., Prince George BC V2L 5G7 – 250/563-0681; Fax: 250/562-3761 – Administrator, Ruth Langner

Prince George Regional Hospital – Medical Library, 2000 - 15 Ave., Prince George BC V2M 1S2 – 250/565-2219; Fax: 604/563-6850 – Librarian, Anne M. Allgaier

PRINCE RUPERT

BC Courthouse Library Society, Courthouse, 100 Market Pl., Prince Rupert BC V8J 1B8

QUESNEL

BC Courthouse Library Society, Courthouse, 350 Barlow Ave., Quesnel BC V2J 2C1

REVELSTOKE

Canadian Avalanche Association – Library, PO Box 2759, Revelstoke BC V0E 2S0 – 250/837-2435; Toll Free: 1-800-667-1105

RICHMOND

British Columbia Genealogical Society – BCGS Resource Centre, PO Box 88054, Lansdowne Mall, Richmond BC V6X 3T6 – 604/988-6075

Klohn-Crippen Consultants Ltd. – Library, 10200 Shellbridge Way, Richmond BC V6X 2W7 – 604/

279-4315; Email: dawsone@rmd.klohn.com; Symbol: KLL – Library/Records Coordinator, Elaine Dawson

MacDonald Dettwiler and Associates Ltd. – Library, 13800 Commerce Pkwy., Richmond BC V6V 2Y3 – 604/278-3411; Symbol: MD – Librarian, Darlene Cripps

Triton Environmental Consultants Ltd. – Library, #120, 13511 Commerce Pkwy., Richmond BC V6V 2L1 – 604/279-2093; Email: louisea@Triton-Env.com; Symbol: BVAEN – Librarian, Louise Archibald

Union of BC Municipalities – Library, #15, 10551 Shellbridge Way, Richmond BC V6X 2W9 – 604/270-8226 – Technical Services Librarian, Frank Storey

Workers' Compensation Board - Library, 6951 Westminster Hwy., Richmond BC V7C 1C6 – 604/231-8450; Fax: 604/279-7608; Email: library@wcb.bc.ca; Symbol: BVAWC – Librarian, Lance Nordstrom

ROSSLAND
BC Courthouse Library Society, PO Box 1448, Rossland BC V0G 1Y0

SAANICHTON
BC School District 63 - District Resource Centre, 2125 Keating Cross Rd., Saanichton BC V8M 2A5 – 250/652-7320; Fax: 250/544-1254; Email: lcoupal@cln.etc.bc.ca; URL: http://www.sd63.bc.ca – Teacher-Librarian, Linda Coupal

SALMON ARM
BC Courthouse Library Society, c/o Court Registry, PO Box 100, Salmon Arm BC V1E 4S4

SECHELT
Capilano College - Sechelt Campus Library, 5627 Inlet Ave., Sechelt BC V0N 3A0 – 604/885-9310 – Becky Wayte

SIDNEY
Esperanto Association of Canada – Libraro Ludovika, PO Box 2159, Sidney BC V8L 3S6 – 902/477-5251 – Librarian, Stevens T. Norvell Jr.

Fisheries & Oceans Canada-Institute of Ocean Sciences – Library, 9860 West Saanich Rd., PO Box 6000, Sidney BC V8L 4B2 – 250/363-6392; Fax: 604/363-6390; Symbol: BVIEM – Librarian, Sharon Thomson

Natural Resources Canada - GSC Regional Library, Pacific Geoscience Centre, 9860 Saanich Rd. West, PO Box 6000, Sidney BC V8L 4B2 – 250/363-6392

World Esperanto Association – Library, 765 Braemar Ave., Sidney BC V8L 5G5 – 514/495-8442 – Normand Fleury

SMITHERS
BC Courthouse Library Society, PO Box 5000, Smithers BC V0J 2N0

SQUAMISH
Capilano College - Squamish Campus Library, 1150 Carson Pl., Squamish BC V0N 3G0 – 604/892-5322 – Regional Assistant, Susan Herity

SUMMERLAND
Agriculture & Agri-Food Canada-Summerland Research Centre – Canadian Agriculture Library, Hwy. 97, Summerland BC V0H 1Z0 – 250/494-7711; Email: lbbsuag@ncccot.agr.ca; Symbol: BSUAG – Librarian, Margaret A. Watson

SURREY
BC Hydro - Powertech Laboratories Inc. – Library, 12388 - 88 Ave., Surrey BC V3M 7R7 – 604/590-7456 – Librarian, Janet Kibblewhite

BC Courthouse Library Society, Courthouse, 14340 - 57 Ave., Surrey BC V3X 1B2

British Columbia Forestry Association – Library, 9800A - 140 St., Surrey BC V3T 4M5 – 604/582-0100 – Cheryl Zida

Forest Education BC – Green Timbers Forest Education Centre, 9800A - 140th St., Surrey BC V3T 4M5 – 604/582-7170 – Environmental Education Assistant, Liz Fontaine

Learning Disabilities Association of British Columbia – Resource Centre, #203, 15463 - 104 St., Surrey BC V3R 1N9 – 604/588-6322

Surrey Memorial Hospital – Library, 13750 - 96th Ave., Surrey BC V3V 1Z2 – 604/585-5666, ext.2467; Fax: 604/585-5540; Email: lhoward@smhpo1.hosp.gov.bc.ca; Symbol: SMH – Librarian, Linda Howard

Western Canada Fertilizer Association – Business Information Centre, #101, 9250 - 120 St., Surrey BC V3V 4B7 – 604/584-2270

TERRACE
BC Courthouse Library Society, Courthouse, 3408 Kalum St., Terrace BC V8G 2N6

Northwest Community College - Learning Resource Centre, 5331 McConnell Ave., Terrace BC V8G 4C2 – 250/638-5407; Fax: 250/635-3511; Email: barnes@noradm.nwcc.bc.ca; Symbol: BTENW Coordinator, Patricia Barnes Technical Services Librarian, Liz Ball

TRAIL
Cominco Ltd. - Central Technical Library, Cominco Research, PO Box 2000, Trail BC V1R 4S4 – 250/364-4408; Fax: 250/364-4456; Symbol: BTC Licensing & Information Specialist, Stan Greenwood
Library Assistant, Randi Holford

VANCOUVER
Affiliation of Multicultural Societies & Service Agencies of B.C. – Resource Centre, 385 Boundary Rd., Vancouver BC V5K 4S1 – 604/298-5949 – Research Coordinator, Bernard Bouska

AIDS Vancouver – PARC Library, c/o Pacific AIDS Resource Centre, 1107 Seymour St., Vancouver BC V6B 5S8 – 604/681-2122; Symbol: AV – Librarian, Janice Linton

Alexander, Holburn, Beaudin & Lang Law Office - Library, #2700, 700 West Georgia St., PO Box 10057, Vancouver BC V7Y 1B8 – 604/688-1351; Fax: 604/669-7642; Email: ahblinfo@ahbl.bc.ca – Librarian, Susan Daly

Armstrong & Company Law Office - Library, #480, Scotia Tower, 650 West Georgia St., PO Box 11622, Vancouver BC V6B 4N9 – 604/683-7361; Fax: 604/662-3231 – Carol Brownie

Asia Pacific Foundation of Canada – Library, #666, 999 Canada Pl., Vancouver BC V6C 3E1 – 604/684-5986 – Rachel Charron

Association for Educators of Gifted, Talented & Creative Children – Library, c/o British Columbia Teachers' Federation, #100, 550 - 6th Ave. West, Vancouver BC V5Z 4P2 – 604/871-1848

Association of Book Publishers of British Columbia – Library, #107, 100 West Pender St., Vancouver BC V6B 1R8 – 604/684-0228 – Margaret Reynolds

Autism Society of British Columbia – Library, 1584 Rand Ave., Vancouver BC V6P 3G2 – 604/261-8888 – Librarian, Leslie Jones

BC Courthouse Library Society – Vancouver Courthouse Library, 800 Smithe St., Vancouver BC V6Z 2E1 – 604/660-2841; Fax: 604/660-2821; Toll Free: 1-800-665-2570

BC Lung Association – Film Library, 2675 Oak St., Vancouver BC V6H 2K2 – 604/731-5864

BC Music Educators' Association – Library, c/o British Columbia Teachers' Federation, #100, 550 - 6th Ave. West, Vancouver BC V6J 3H9 – 604/871-1848

BC Rail - Library, PO Box 8770, Vancouver BC V6B 4X6 – 604/984-5090; Fax: 604/984-5090; Symbol: BCRL – Librarian, Kathryn Boegel

BC Research Inc. – Library, 3650 Westbrook Mall, Vancouver BC V6S 2L2 – 604/224-4331; Email: glass@bcl.bc.ca; Symbol: BVAR – Research Librarian, Nancy Glass

BC Securities Commission - Library, 865 Hornby St., 10th Fl., Vancouver BC V6Z 2H4 – 604/660-9692; Fax: 604/660-5473; Email: carol_s_williams@email.bcse.gov.bc.ca; Symbol: BVASEC – Business Librarian, Carol Williams

The Bible Holiness Movement – Library, PO Box 223, Vancouver BC V6C 2M3 – 250/498-3895

Blake, Cassels & Graydon Law Office - Library, #1700, 1030 West Georgia St., Vancouver BC V6E 2Y3 – 604/631-3300; Fax: 604/631-3309, 3305 – Librarian, Maureen Hall

British Columbia Health Association – Library, #600, 1333 Broadway West, Vancouver BC V6H 4C7 – 604/734-2423; TLX: 04-54300 – Librarian, Carolyn Hall

British Columbia Real Estate Association – Library, #309, 1155 Pender St. West, Vancouver BC V6E 2P4 – 604/683-7702; Symbol: BCREA – Director of Research, Theresa Murphy

British Columbia Teachers' Federation – Information Centre, #100, 550 - 6th Ave. West, Vancouver BC V5Z 4P2 – 604/871-2283; Email: dbroome@bctf.bc.ca; Symbol: BVATF – Librarian, Diana Broom

British Columbia Trade Development Corporation - Trade Resource Centre, #730, 999 Canada Place, Vancouver BC V6C 3E1 – 604/844-1983; Fax: 604/660-2457 – Manager, Karen Calderbank

Bull, Housser & Tupper Law Office - Library, Royal Centre, 1055 Georgia St. West, PO Box 11130, Vancouver BC V6E 3R3 – 604/687-6575; Fax: 604/641-4949; Symbol: BHT – Chief Librarian, Catherine Ryan

Campney & Murphy, Barristers & Solicitors - Library, #2100, 1111 Georgia St. West, PO Box 48800, Vancouver BC V7X 1K9 – 604/688-8022; Fax: 604/688-0829; Email: cmlaw@campneymurphy.com; Symbol: CM – Law Librarian, Anna Holeton

Canadian Broadcasting Corporation - TV News Library, 700 Hamilton St., PO Box 4600, Vancouver BC V6B 4A2 – 604/662-6855; Fax: 604/662-6878; Symbol: BVACBV – Librarian, Colin Preston

Le Centre culturel francophone de Vancouver – Bibliothèque, 1551 - 7 Ave. West, Vancouver BC V6J 1S1 – 604/736-9806 – Dominique Dupont

Centre for Human Settlements - Disaster Preparedness Resource Centre, 2206, The East Mall, Vancouver BC V6T 1Z3 – 604/822-5518; Fax: 604/822-6164; Symbol: DPRC

Chemetics International Company – Library, 1818 Cornwall Ave., Vancouver BC V6J 1C7 – 604/734-1200 – Librarian, Claudia Chandler

Clark, Wilson Law Office - Library, #800, 885 West Georgia St., Vancouver BC V6C 3H1 – 604/687-5700; Fax: 604/687-6314; Email: central@cwilson.com – Library Assistant, Diane Snyder

College Institute Educators' Association of BC – Library, #301, 555 - 8 Ave. West, Vancouver BC V5Z 1C6 – 604/873-8988 – Administrative Assistant, Nancy Yip

College of Physicians & Surgeons of British Columbia – Medical Library Service, 1383 - 8th Ave. West, Vancouver BC V6H 4C4 – 604/733-6671; Email: ENVOY: BCMLS; Symbol: BCMLS – Director, Jim Henderson

Cominco Ltd. - Corporate/Legal Library, 200 Burrard St., Vancouver BC V6C 3L7 – 604/685-3055; Fax: 604/844-2509; Email: ENVOY: COMLIB; Cominco_Library@mindlink.bc.ca; Symbol: BVACOM – Librarian, Keith Low

Canadian Almanac & Directory 1997

The Commonwealth of Learning – Information Resource Centre, Pacific Centre, Box 10428, #1700, 777 Dunsmuir St., PO Box 10428, Vancouver BC V7Y 1K4 – 604/775-8234; Symbol: VACL – Library Technician, Sue Parker

Connell Lightbody - Library, Box 11161, Royal Centre, #1900, 1055 Georgia St. West, Vancouver BC V6E 4J2 – 604/684-1181; Fax: 604/641-3916 – Librarian, Carole F. Burley

Continuing Legal Education Society of BC – Library, #300, 845 Cambie St., Vancouver BC V6B 5T2 – 250/699-3544; Toll Free: 1-800-663-0437 – Karen Imeson

Coopers & Lybrand - Library, 1111 Hastings St. West, Vancouver BC V6E 3R2 – 604/661-5700; Fax: 604/661-5709; Symbol: CLY – Librarian, Jane Moxon

Deloitte & Touche - Library, 4 Bentall Centre, Bental IV, #2000, 1055 Dunsmuir St., PO Box 49279, Vancouver BC V7X 1P4 – 604/669-4466; Fax: 604/685-0458; Symbol: DT – Librarian, Iona Douglas

D.F. Dickins Associates Ltd. – Library, #210, 1290 Hornby St., Vancouver BC V6Z 1W2 – 604/684-0516 – Sandra Peters

Douglas, Symes & Brissenden Law Office - Library, One Bentall Centre, Box 2100, #2100, 505 Burrard St., Vancouver BC V7X 1R4 – 604/683-6911; Fax: 604/669-1337 – Librarian, Rochelle Matheson

Early Childhood Multicultural Services – Westcoast Child Care Resource Centre, #201, 1675 - 4th Ave. West, Vancouver BC V6J 1L8 – 604/739-9456 – Coordinator, Bayla Greenspoon

EcoDesign Resource Society – Resource Centre, #201, 1102 Homer St., PO Box 3981, Vancouver BC V6B 3Z4 – 604/689-7622

Edwards, Kenny & Bray Law Office - Library, 1040 Georgia St. West, 19th Fl., Vancouver BC V6E 4H3 – 604/689-1811; Fax: 604/689-5177 – Librarian, Stephanie Taggart

Emily Carr Institute of Art & Design - Library, Granville Island, 1399 Johnston St., Vancouver BC V6H 3R9 – 604/844-3840; Fax: 604/844-3801; URL: http://www.eciad.bc.ca/ – Library Director, Sheila Wallace

Ernst & Young, Pacific Centre, 700 Georgia St. West, PO Box 10101, Vancouver BC V7Y 1C7 – 604/683-7133; Fax: 604/643-5422; Symbol: EY – Librarian, Ellen Roth

The Family History Association of Canada – Library, #301, 2245 West Broadway, Vancouver BC V6K 2E4 – 250/223-2112

Farris, Vaughan, Wills & Murphy Law Office - Library, Pacific Centre South, 700 West Georgia St., PO Box 10026, Vancouver BC V7Y 1B3 – 604/684-9151; Fax: 604/661-9349
Librarian, Johanna Sigurdson
Technical Services Librarian, Wilma Macfarlane

Federation of British Columbia Writers – Reference Library, #600, 890 West Pender St., PO Box 2206, Vancouver BC V6B 3W2 – 604/683-2057

Feller Drysdale Law Office - Library, #1550, 400 Burrard St., PO Box 58, Vancouver BC V6C 3A6 – 604/689-2626; Fax: 604/681-5354 – Receptionist, Carol White

Fisheries & Oceans Canada - Fisheries Management Regional Library, 555 West Hastings St., Vancouver BC V6E 5G3 – 604/666-3851; Fax: 604/666-3450; Email: ENVOY: DFO.LIB.VANCOUVER; Symbol: BVAFI – Coordinator, Library & Information Services, Marcia Croy Vanwely, Email: vanwelym@mailhost.pac.dfo.ca

Fluor Daniel – Technical Information Centre, #500, 1075 West Georgia St., Vancouver BC V6E 4M7 – 604/488-2270 – Librarian, Leonie Page

Forest Alliance of British Columbia – Library, 1055 Dunsmuir St., PO Box 49312, Vancouver BC V7X 1L3 – 604/685-7507; Toll Free: 1-800-567-8733 – Information Services Manager, Kit Tam

Forintek Canada Corp. – Western Laboratory Library, 2665 East Mall, Vancouver BC V6T 1W5 – 604/222-5668; Email: holder@van.forintek.ca; Symbol: BVAFP – Librarian, Barbara Holder

Fraser & Beatty Law Office - Library, Grosvenor Bldg., 1040 Georgia St. West, 15th Fl., Vancouver BC V6E 4H8 – 604/687-4460; Fax: 604/683-5214 – Library Assistant, Lynda Mitchell

The Fraser Institute – Library, 626 Bute St., 2nd Fl., Vancouver BC V6E 3M1 – 604/688-0221; Toll Free: 1-800-665-3558 – Marie Morris

Freeman & Company Law Office - Library, 885 Georgia St. West, 19th Fl., Vancouver BC V6C 3H4 – 604/683-4201; Fax: 604/631-2288 – Librarian, Annabel Hooten

Geological Survey of Canada - Cordilleran Geoscience Library, Natural Resources Canada, 100 Pender St. West, 5th Fl., Vancouver BC V6B 1R8 – 604/666-3812; Fax: 604/666-7186; Symbol: BVAG
Library Services, Manager, Mary Akehurst, 604/666-1147, Email: makehurst@gsc.emr.ca
Library Technician, Fontaine Hwang, 604/666-3812

Goethe-Institut/German Cultural Centre (Vancouver) – Library, 944 - 8th Ave. West, Vancouver BC V5Z 1E5 – 604/732-3966 – Librarian, Ingrid Cuk

Gordon Spratt & Associates Ltd. – Library, 2348 Yukon St., Vancouver BC V5Y 3T6 – 604/872-1211 – Senior Technician, M. McCaull

H.A. Simons Ltd. – Library, #400, 111 Dunsmuir St., Vancouver BC V6B 5W3 – 604/664-4311; Fax: 604/664-3368; Email: jwallace@hasimons.com; Symbol: HAS – Corporate Librarian, Jan Wallace

Harper Grey Easton Law Office - Library, #3100, Vancouver Centre, 650 West Georgia St., PO Box 11504, Vancouver BC V6B 4P7 – 604/687-0411; Fax: 604/669-9385; Email: hge@hgelaw.com – Librarian, Liisa Tella

Hospital Employees Union (CLC) – Library, 2006 - 10 Ave. West, Vancouver BC V6J 4P5 – 604/734-3431 – Librarian, Elaine Samwald

Human Resources Development Canada - Regional Economic Services Branch - Library, 1055 West Georgia St., 11th Fl., PO Box 11145, Stn Royal Centre, Vancouver BC V6E 2P8 – 604/666-2611; Symbol: BVAMI – Statistical Officer, Tom Caspersen

Immigration & Refugee Board - Documentation Centre, #1510, 1600 - 800 Burrard St., Vancouver BC V6Z 2J9 – 604/666-5945; Fax: 604/666-7370 – Chief, Alta Haggarty

Institute of Asian Research – Asian Library, Asian Centre - University of British Columbia, 1871 West Mall, Vancouver BC V6T 1Z2 – 604/822-5905; Email: ljoe@unixg.ubc.ca – Head, Asian Library, Linda Joe

Institute of Certified Management Consultants of British Columbia – Library, #1501, 650 Georgia St. West, PO Box 11606, Vancouver BC V6B 4N9 – 604/681-1419

International Development Education Resource Association – Library, #200, 2678 Broadway Ave. West, Vancouver BC V6K 2G3 – 604/732-1496; Film Line: 604/739-8815

Jewish Historical Society of BC – Nemetz Jewish Community Archive, #206, 950 - 41 Ave. West, Vancouver BC V5Z 2N7 – 604/257-5199 – Archivist, Diane Rogers

Jones McCloy Peterson Law Office - Library, #1700, Three Bentall Centre, 595 Burrard St., PO Box 49117, Vancouver BC V7X 1G4 – 604/682-1851; Fax: 604/682-7329

Justice Canada - Vancouver Regional Office - Library, #900, 840 Howe St., Vancouver BC V6Z 2S9 – 604/666-0549; Fax: 604/666-2760; Symbol: BVAJ – Librarian, Judy Deavy, Email: judy.deavy@justice.x400.gc.ca

Killam, Whitelaw & Twining - Law Library, #100, 200 Granville St., PO Box 25, Vancouver BC V6C 1S4 – 604/682-5466; Fax: 604/682-5217 – Phyllis Gordon

KPMG Peat Marwick Thorne - Library, Pacific Centre, 777 Dunsmuir St., PO Box 10426, Vancouver BC V7Y 1K3 – 604/691-3000, ext.4067; Fax: 604/691-3031 – Librarian, Diane Lee, 604/691-3292

Labour Relations Board of BC - Library, 1125 Howe St., Vancouver BC V7X 1K9 – 604/660-1300; Fax: 604/660-1892; Symbol: IRC
Librarian, Astrid Kenning
Technician, Krystyna Kwiatkowska
Assistant, Carole Choquette

Ladner Downs Law Office - Library, Waterfront Centre, #900, 200 Burrard St., PO Box 48600, Vancouver BC V7X 1T2 – 604/640-4012; Fax: 604/687-1415 – Librarian, Anne Beresford

Lang Michener Lawrence & Shaw - Library, 2500 Three Bentall Centre, 595 Burrard St., PO Box 49200, Vancouver BC V7X 1L1 – 604/689-9111; Fax: 604/685-7084; Email: library@lmls.com – Library Technician, Anne Ikeda

Langara College - Library, 100 - 49 Ave. West, Vancouver BC V5Y 2Z6 – 604/323-5384; Fax: 604/323-5512
College Librarian, Judith Neamtan, 604/323-5386, Fax: 604/323-5512
Public Services Librarian, Niina Mitter, 604/323-5290, Fax: 604/323-5512
Technical Services Librarian, Jo Toon, 604/323-5457, Fax: 604/323-5649
Acquisitions, Charlotte Wynne, 604/323-5385, Fax: 604/323-5649
Media Services, Linda Prince, 604/323-5459, Fax: 604/323-5577
Systems, Halina Mitton, 604/323-5243, Fax: 604/323-5649

The Laurier Institution – Library, #608, 1030 West Georgia St., Vancouver BC V6E 2Y3 – 604/669-3638 – A. Roberts

Lawson, Lundell, Lawson & McIntosh Law Office - Library, #1600, 925 Georgia St. West, Vancouver BC V6C 3L2 – 604/685-3456; Fax: 604/669-1620; Email: library@lawsonlundell.com
Librarian, Gwendoline Hoar, 604/631-9167
Library Technician, Cecilia Hui

Lindsay Kenney Law Office - Library, 700 West Pender St., 17th Fl., Vancouver BC V6C 1G8 – 604/687-1323; Fax: 604/687-2347; Email: info@lindsaykenney.bc.ca; URL: http://www.lindsaykenney.bc.ca – Library Manager, Lynn Smith

MacMillan Bloedel Ltd. Research Library, 925 Georgia St. West, 5th Fl., Vancouver BC V6C 3L2 – 604/439-8601; Symbol: BVAMB – Librarian, Judy O'Mara

McCarthy Tétrault - Library, Pacific Centre, #1300, 777 Dunsmuir St., PO Box 10424, Vancouver BC V7Y 1K2 – 604/643-7100; Fax: 604/643-7900; URL: http://www.mccarthy.ca
Head Librarian, Susan Crysler, 604/643-7931, Email: smc@mccarthy.ca
Reference Librarian, Debbie Benson, 604/643-7178
Technician, Natasha Lyndon, 604/643-7199

Muslim Education & Welfare Foundation of Canada – Jannat Bibi Library, 2580 McGill St., Vancouver BC V5K 1H1 – 604/255-9941 – Dr. Nazih Kamal Hammad

Myasthenia Gravis Foundation of British Columbia – Library, 2805 Kingsway Ave., Vancouver BC V5R 5H9 – 604/451-5511

Norecol, Dames & Moore Inc. - Vancouver – Library, #1900, 650 West Georgia St., PO Box 11507, Vancouver BC V6B 4NT – 604/681-1672;
Symbol: NORE – Manager, Business Admin., Starlet Lum

Northwest Wildlife Preservation Society – NWPS Wildlife Library, PO Box 34129, Vancouver BC V6J 4M1 – 604/736-8750

Owen, Bird Law Office - Library, Three Bentall Centre, #2900, 595 Burrard St., PO Box 49130, Vancouver BC V7X 1J5 – 604/688-0401; Fax: 604/688-2827 – Library Technician, Nancy Connor

Pacific Salmon Commission - Library, #600, 1155 Robson St., Vancouver BC V6E 1B5 – 604/684-8081; Fax: 604/666-8707; Email: PACSALM.LIB; tarita@psc.org; Symbol: PSAL – Librarian, Teri Tarita

Persons with AIDS Society of British Columbia – Pacific AIDS Resource Centre, c/o Pacific AIDS Resource Centre, 1107 Seymour St., Vancouver BC V6B 5S8 – 604/681-2122 – PWA Librarian, Ted Erikson

Planned Parenthood Association of British Columbia – Library, #201, 1001 West Broadway, Vancouver BC V6K 2G8 – 604/731-4252; Toll Free: 1-800-739-7367 – Education Director, Faye Bebb

Price Waterhouse - Vancouver Library, #1400, 601 Hastings St. West, Vancouver BC V6B 5A5 – 604/443-2631; Fax: 604/443-2635; Symbol: PW – Librarian, Janet Parkinson

Pulp & Paper Research Institute of Canada - UBC Pulp & Paper Centre, 2385 East Mall, Vancouver BC V6T 1Z4 – 604/822-8568; Fax: 604/822-8563; Symbol: BVAPPC – Librarian, Rita M. Penco

Vancouver Laboratory Library, 3800 Westbrook Mall, Vancouver BC V6S 2L9 – 604/222-3200; Fax: 604/222-3207; Symbol: BVAPPR – Librarian, Linda Everett

Recycling Council of British Columbia – Waste Reduction Library, #201, 225 Smithe St., Vancouver BC V6B 4X7 – 604/683-6009; Toll Free: 1-800-667-4321 – Library Coordinator, Jo Bergstrand

Registered Nurses Association of British Columbia – Library, 2855 Arbutus St., Vancouver BC V6J 3Y8 – 604/736-7331 – Library Manager, Joan Andrews

Revenue Canada - Research & Library Services, 1166 West Pender St., Vancouver BC V6E 3H8 – 604/691-4782; Fax: 604/689-7536; Email: ENVOY: TAYLOR.EV; Symbol: BVATC – Team Coordinator, Library Services, Evelyn Taylor

Russell & DuMoulin Law Office - Library, #2100, 1075 Georgia St. West, Vancouver BC V6E 3G2 – 604/631-3131; Fax: 604/631-3232; Email: rdlibrary@rd-counsel.com; Symbol: BVARD – Manager, Library Services, Joan D. Bilsland

Sandwell Inc. – Library, 1190 Hornby St., Vancouver BC V6Z 2H6 – 604/684-9311 – Librarian, Joyce White

Seva Service Society – Library, #104, 1926 Broadway Ave. West, Vancouver BC V6J 1Z2 – 604/733-4284 – Administrative Assistant, B.J. Telford

Sierra Legal Defence Fund – Library, #214, 131 Water St., Vancouver BC V6B 1H6 – 604/685-5618 – Office Administrator, Carol McDonald

Singleton Urquhart Scott Law Office - Library, #1200, 1125 Howe St., Vancouver BC V6Z 2K8 – 604/682-7474; Fax: 604/682-1283; URL: http://www.singleton.com – Librarian, Claudia Goldman

SNC-Lavalin Inc. - Vancouver Library, 1075 Georgia St. West, 12th Fl., Vancouver BC V6E 3C9 – 604/662-3555; Fax: 604/683-1672 – Librarian, Brenda Oscar

Sobolewski Anfield Law Office - Library, Stock Exchange Twr., Pacific Centre, #1600, 609 Granville St., PO Box 10068, Vancouver BC V7Y 1C3 – 604/669-1322 – Rosemary Keelan

Society of Kabalarians of Canada – Resource Centre, 908 - 7 Ave. West, Vancouver BC V5Z 1C3 – 604/736-2875

Society Promoting Environmental Conservation – Library, 2150 Maple St., Vancouver BC V6J 3T3 – 604/737-7732

Statistics Canada - Pacific Regional Reference Centre, Sinclair Centre, #600, 300 West Georgia St., Vancouver BC V6B 6C7 – 604/666-3691; Fax: 604/666-4863; Toll Free: 1-800-263-1136 – Manager, Data Dissemination, D.G. Meakins

Swinton & Company Law Office - Library, Robson Ct., #1000, 840 Howe St., Vancouver BC V6Z 2M1 – 604/687-2242; Fax: 604/643-1200 – Librarian, Elizabeth Kinersly

Teck Corporation Library, #600, 200 Burrard St., Vancouver BC V6C 3L9 – 604/687-1117; Fax: 604/687-6100 – Librarian, Mary-Anne Pomphrey

Teck Mining Group Ltd., #600, 200 Burrard St., Vancouver BC V6C 3L9 – 604/687-1117; Fax: 604/687-6100 – Librarian, Mary-Anne Pamphrey

Thorsteinssons Law Office - Library, Three Bentall Centre, 595 Burrard St., 27th Fl., PO Box 49123, Vancouver BC V7X 1J2 – 604/689-1261; Fax: 604/688-4711; Email: 73742.3144@compuserve.com – Librarian, Yoko Beriault

Towers Perrin - Information Centre, #1600, 1100 Melville St., Vancouver BC V6E 4A6 – 604/691-1034; Fax: 604/691-1062; Email: lepagec@towers.com; Symbol: TPF&C
Information Specialist, Carey LePage
Information Services Analyst, Judy MacKenzie

Trade Union Research Bureau - Library, #170, 111 Victoria Dr., Vancouver BC V5L 4C4 – 604/255-7346; Fax: 604/255-0971; Symbol: TURB – Office Manager, Susan Lockhart

Trans Mountain Pipe Line Company Ltd. Library, #900, 1333 Broadway West, Vancouver BC V6H 4C2 – 604/739-5286; Fax: 604/739-5008; Email: janetg@vcr.tmpl.ca; Symbol: TMPL – Library/Records Coordinator, Janet Graham

Transport Canada - Library, Pacific Region, #620, 800 Burrard St., Vancouver BC V6Z 2J8 – 604/666-5868; Fax: 604/666-2320; Email: rowland@unixg.ubc.ca; Symbol: BVATCA – Regional Librarian, J. Jill Rowland

Turtle Island Earth Stewards – Library, #101, 5810 Battison St., Vancouver BC V5R 5X8 – 604/432-9473

Union of British Columbia Indian Chiefs – Library, 342 Water St., 5th Fl., Vancouver BC V6B 1B6 – 604/684-0231 – Librarian, Sarah Torsky

University of British Columbia - Libraries, 1956 Main Mall, Vancouver BC V6T 1Z1 – 604/822-3871; Fax: 604/822-3893; Email: ENVOY: R.PATRICK@UNIXG.UBC.CA
University Librarian, Dr. Ruth Patrick, 604/822-2298
Administrative Services, Assistant Librarian, Erik de Bruijn, 604/822-4555
Catalogue Division, Head, N.E. Omelusik, 604/822-9103
Government Publications/Humanities & Social Sciences, Head, Jocelyn Godolphin, 604/822-2160
Interlibrary Loans, Head, Patrick Dunn, 604/822-4430
Order Division, Head, Nadine Baldwin, 604/822-5038
Public Services, Assistant Librarian, Heather Keate, 604/822-2396
Technical Services, Assistant Librarian, Nadine Baldwin, 604/822-2740
Asian Library, Head, Linda Joe, 604/822-2427
Biomedical Branch, Librarian, Nancy Forbes, 604/875-4505
Crane Library for the Blind, Head Librarian, Paul Thiele, 604/822-6111
Data Library, Head, Hilde Colenbrander, 604/822-6742
Education Library, Head, Howard Hurt, 604/822-8680
Eric Hamber Memorial Branch, Librarian, Pat Lysyk, 604/875-2153
Fine Arts/Music/Special Collections, Head, Hans Burndorfer, 604/228-2720
Law Library, Head, Thomas Shorthouse, 604/822-2275
MacMillan Forestry/Agriculture Library, Head, Lore Brongers, 604/822-6333
Map Library, Map Librarian, Tim Ross, 604/822-2231
School of Library, Archival & Information Studies, Director, Dr. Ken Haycock, 604/822-2404
Science & Engineering Division Library, Head, Bonita Stableford, 604/228-3295
Sedgewick Undergraduate Library, Coordinator, Julie Stevens, 604/822-3098
St. Paul's Hospital Branch, Librarian, Barbara Saint, 604/631-5425
Woodward Biomedical Library, Head, Johann van Reenen, 604/822-2762
David Lam Library Management Research Library, Librarian, Elizabeth Caskey, 604/822-9399

Urban Development Institute of Canada – Library, 717 Pender St. West, 3rd Fl., Vancouver BC V6C 1G9 – 604/669-9585; Symbol: UDI – Librarian, David Helem

Vancouver Aquarium - Robin Best Library, PO Box 3232, Vancouver BC V6B 3X8 – 604/685-3364; Fax: 604/631-2529; Symbol: VAQ – Librarian, Treva Ricou

Vancouver Board of Trade – Library, #400, 999 Canada Place, Vancouver BC V6C 3C1 – 604/681-2111 – Librarian, Lucia Park

Vancouver Community College - Libraries, 1155 East Broadway, PO Box 24620, Vancouver BC V5N 5T9 – 604/871-7318; Fax: 604/871-7100; Email: bappleton@vcc.bc.ca; Symbol: BVAVCC
College Librarian, Brenda Appleton
Acquisitions, Head, Charlotte Wynne, 604/324-5385, Fax: 604/324-5512
Technical Services, Department Chair, J. Toon, 604/324-5457, Fax: 604/324-5512
City Centre Library, Campus Librarian, Eva Sharel, 604/443-8349, Fax: 604/443-8329
King Edward Campus, Campus Librarian, Aphrodite Harris, 604/871-7319, Fax: 604/871-7446

Vancouver Holocaust Centre Society - A Museum for Education & Remembrance – Resource Centre, 950 - 41 Ave. West, Vancouver BC V5Z 2N7 – 604/734-5325

The Vancouver Maritime Museum Society, 1905 Ogden Ave., Vancouver BC V6J 1A3 – 604/257-8300 – Curator of Collections, J. Thornley

Vancouver Symphony Society – VSO Library, 601 Smithe St., Vancouver BC V6B 5G1 – 604/684-9100 – Librarian, Mirella Leeson

Vancouver Youth Symphony Orchestra – Library, #204, 3737 Oak St., Vancouver BC V6H 2M4 – 604/737-0714 – C. Epp

VanDusen Botanical Gardens Association – VanDusen Library, 5251 Oak St., Vancouver BC V6M 4H1 – 604/257-8668 – Librarian, Barbara J. Fox

Victory Square Law Office - Library, #200, 198 West Hastings St., Vancouver BC V6B 1H2 – 604/684-8421; Fax: 604/684-8427 – Betty Wong

Watson Goepel Maledy Law Office - Library, #3023, 595 Burrard St., PO Box 49096, Vancouver BC V7X 1G4 – 604/688-1301; Fax: 604/688-8193 – Administrator, Deborah A. Welch

West Coast Environmental Law Research Foundation – Library, #1001, 207 Hastings St. West, Vancouver BC V6B 1H7 – 604/684-7378 – Research Coordinator, Catherine Ludgate

West Coast Women & Words Society – Library, #219, 1675 - 8th Ave. West, Vancouver BC V6J 1V2 – 604/730-1034

Westcoast Energy Inc. - Library, 1333 Georgia St. West, 14th Fl., Vancouver BC V6E 3K9 – 604/691-5517; Fax: 604/691-5994; Symbol: WEI – Librarian, Beatrice Yakimchuk

Western Canada Wilderness Committee – Library, 20 Water St., Vancouver BC V6B 1A4 – 604/683-8220; Toll Free: 1-800-661-9453 – Sue Fox

Canadian Almanac & Directory 1997

Women's Legal Education & Action Fund - West Coast LEAF – Library, #905, 207 Hastings St. West, Vancouver BC V6B 1H7 – 604/684-8772

VANDERHOOF
Yinka Dene Language Institute – Library, RR#2, Hospital Rd., Vanderhoof BC V0J 3A0 – 250/567-9236 – Ruby Ephrom

VERNON
BC Courthouse Library Society – Library, Courthouse, 3001 - 27th St., Vernon BC V1T 4W5

Edward F. Kenny Barrister & Solicitor - Library, 3009 - 28 St., Vernon BC V1T 4Z7 – 250/545-0587; Fax: 250/545-8660 – Office Manager, Joyce Hodgson

VICTORIA
BC Ministry of Environment, Lands & Parks - Environmental Protection Department – Library, 777 Broughton St., Victoria BC V8V 1X4
Fisheries Branch, 810 Blanshard St., Victoria BC V8V 1X5 – 604/660-1812

BC Ministry of Forests - Research Branch – Library, 1450 Government St., Victoria BC V8W 3E7 – 250/387-3628; Fax: 604/953-3079; Symbol: BVIFO – Manager, Susanne Barker

AIDS Vancouver Island – Library, #304, 733 Johnston St., Victoria BC V8W 3C7 – 250/384-2366; Toll Free: 1-800-665-2437 – Aaron Severs

BC Courthouse Library Society, Courthouse, 850 Burdett Ave., Victoria BC V8W 1B4 – 250/387-3239; Fax: 250/387-0698 – Sheila Folka

BC Employment & Investment - Library Services, 712 Yates St., 2nd Fl., Victoria BC V8V 1X4 – 250/387-0341; Fax: 250/356-8212
Librarian, Margaret Palmer, Email: mpalmer@eivic.ei.gov.bc.ca
Kathy Gower, Email: kgower@eivic.ei.gov.bc.ca
Jennifer Siemens

BC Legislative Library, #214, Parliament Bldgs., Victoria BC V8V 1X4 – 250/387-6510; Fax: 250/356-1373
Director, Joan A. Barton, 250/387-6500
Manager, Reference Services, Maureen Lawson

BC Ministry Labour - Library, 818 Broughton St., Victoria BC V8V 1X4 – 250/953-3378; Fax: 250/356-8322; Symbol: BVIML – Librarian, Vivienne Bruce

BC Ministry of Energy, Mines & Petroleum Resources - Library, 1810 Blanshard St., 8th Fl., Victoria BC V8V 1X4 – 250/952-0581
Head Librarian, Margaret Palmer
Librarian, Sharon Ferris

BC Ministry of Environment, Lands & Parks - BC Parks Library, 800 Johnson St., 2nd Fl., Victoria BC V8V 1X4 – 250/389-3974; Fax: 250/387-5757; Email: ENVOY: PARKSLIB; Symbol: VIPB
Librarian, Shirley Desrosiers
ILL Library Assistant, John Pinn
Circulation, A/V Library Assistant, Louise Noble
Library, 810 Blanshard St., 1st Fl., Victoria BC V8V 1X4 – 250/387-9747; Fax: 250/387-9741;
Email: ENVOY: ENVLIB.BC;
Symbol: BVILFW
Reference Librarian, Kathy Neer, Email: kneer@pubaffair.env.gov.bc.ca
ILL Technician, Bonnie Brugger
Acquisitions Clerk, Carol Smith

BC Ministry of Health & Ministry Responsible for Seniors - Library/Audio Visual Resource Centre, 1515 Blanshard St., Main Fl., Victoria BC V8W 3C8 – 250/387-6468; Fax: 250/356-9937 – Head Librarian, Elizabeth Woodworth

BC School District 61 - Greater Victoria School Board Learning Resource Centre, 923 Topaz Ave., Victoria BC V8T 2M2 – 250/360-4300; Fax: 250/360-4370 – Learning Resource Officer, Shannon Glover, 250/360-4302

BC School District 62 - District Resource Centre, 3143 Jacklin Rd., Victoria BC V9B 5R1 – 250/474-9800; Fax: 250/474-9825

British Columbia Museums Association – Library, 514 Government St., Victoria BC V8V 4X4 – 250/387-3315

Camosun College - Library, 3100 Foul Bay Rd., Victoria BC V8P 5J2 – 250/370-3604; Fax: 250/370-3624; URL: http://www.camosun.bc.ca/~library – Coordinator, Catherine Winter, Email: winter@camosun.bc.ca

Centre for Curriculum & Professional Development – Library, 1483 Douglas St., 5th Fl., Victoria BC V8W 3K4 – 250/387-6065 – Coordinator, Publications, JoAnne Pasquale

Defence Research Establishment - Pacific - Information Services Library, Forces Mail Office, Victoria BC V0S 1B0 – 250/380-2854; Fax: 250/363-2856; Symbol: BEPN – Head, Antony Cheung

Ecoforestry Institute Society – Library, PO Box 5783, Victoria BC V8R 6S8 – 250/388-5459; Fax: 604/388-5123 – Lara Lamport

Gordon & Velletta Law Office - Library, #203, 919 Fort St., Victoria BC V8V 3K3 – 250/383-9104; Fax: 250/383-1922 – Legal Assistant, Lori Adams

Greater Victoria Chamber of Commerce – Library, 525 Fort St., Victoria BC V8W 1E8 – 250/383-7191 – Business Information Officer, Lynda Boyd

Inter-Cultural Association of Greater Victoria – Multicultural Division Library, #200, 2540 Government St., Victoria BC V8T 4P7 – 250/388-4728 – Multicultural Coordinator, Alvaro Moreno

Island Deaf & Hard of Hearing Centre – Library, #300, 1627 Fort St., Victoria BC V8R 1H8 – 250/592-8144 – Wendy Dobbie

McConnan, Bion, O'Connor & Peterson Law Office - Library, #420, 880 Douglas St., Victoria BC V8W 2B7 – 250/385-1383; Fax: 250/385-2841

Natural Resources Canada-Canadian Forest Service: Pacific Forestry Centre – Library, 506 West Burnside Rd., Victoria BC V8Z 1M5 – 250/363-0600; Fax: 604/363-6035; Email: asolyma@a1.pfc.forestry.ca; Symbol: BVIF – Head, Library Services, Alice Solyma

The Right to Die Society of Canada – Library, PO Box 39018, Victoria BC V8V 4X8 – 250/380-1112 – Head Librarian, Evelyn Martens

Royal Roads University - Library & Learning Resources Centre, 2005 Sooke Rd., Victoria BC V9B 5Y2 – 250/391-2575; Fax: 250/391-2594; URL: http://www.royalroads.ca/docs/library/home.html
Manager, Barry Jensen, MLS, 250/391-2596, Email: bjensen@post.royalroads.ca
Assistant, Aquisitions, Rachanee Tannas, 250/391-2595, Email: rtannas@post.royalroads.ca
Assistant, Circulation & Interlibrary Loan, Melanie Martens, 250/391-2575, Email: mmartens@post.royalroads.ca

Royal United Services Institute of Vancouver Island – CFB Esquimalt Library, Bay Street Armoury, 715 Bay St., Victoria BC V8T 1R1 – 250/384-1331

Smith, Hutchison Law Office - Library, 747 Fort St., 11th Fl., Victoria BC V8W 3E9 – 250/388-6666; Fax: 250/389-0400 – J. Michael Hutchison

Solicitor General Canada – William Head Institution - Library, PO Box 4000, Victoria BC V8X 3Y8 – 250/363-4642, ext.245; Fax: 250/363-5983; Symbol: BVIW – Librarian, Kim Rempel

South Pacific Peoples Foundation of Canada – Resource Centre, #415, 620 View St., Victoria BC V8W 1J6 – 250/381-4131 – Resource Centre Coordinator, Margaret Argue

Thurber Environmental Consultants Ltd. – Library, #210, 4475 Viewmont Ave., Victoria BC V8Z 6L8 – 250/727-2201; Symbol: BVIT – Librarian, Rose Mary Ormerod

United World Colleges – Library, Lester B. Pearson College of the Pacific, RR#1, Victoria BC V9B 5T7 – 250/478-5591 – Bette Kirchner

University of Victoria - McPherson Library, PO Box 1800, Victoria BC V8W 3H5 – 250/721-8211; Fax: 250/721-8215; Symbol: CABVIV
University Librarian, Marnie Swanson
Access Services, Head, Jessie Kurtz
Bibliographic & Authorities Records Unit, Coordinator, Hugh Irving
Business Librarian, Hazel Cameron
Cataloguing Database Management Unit, Coordinator, John Dell
Cataloguing Librarian, Sam Acquila
Collection Management Services, Head, Donna Signori
Communications Librarian/Reference Librarian, Betty Gibb
Continuing Studies Library Services, Program Director, Sandy Slade
External Services Librarian, Kathryn Paul
Humanities Librarian, Ken Cooley
Library Staff Relations, Manager, Wendie McHenry
Library Systems & Budget, Manager, L. Declerck
Public Services, Director, Joan Sandllands
Reference, Head, Don White
Science Librarian, Katy Nelson
Serials Management Unit, Coordinator, Elena Romaniuk
Systems Librarian, Kathleen Matthews
Technical Services, Director, Hana Komorous
University Archivist & Head, Special Collections, Chris Petter
Reference/ILL Librarian, Cheryl Lumley

Victoria International Development Education Association – Resource Centre, #407, 620 View St., Victoria BC V8W 1J6 – 250/385-2333

Victoria Persons with AIDS Society – AIDS Treatment Information Library, 613 Superior St., Victoria BC V8V 1V1 – 250/383-7494; Toll Free: 1-800-434-2959 – David Hillman

WEST VANCOUVER
Fisheries & Oceans Canada - West Vancouver Laboratory Library, 4160 Marine Dr., West Vancouver BC V7V 1N6 – 604/666-4813; Fax: 604/666-3497; Email: DFO.LIB.WESTVAN; Symbol: BVAPE – Librarian, Mei-Shuen Fok

WILLIAMS LAKE
BC Courthouse Library Society – Library, Courthouse, 540 Borland St., Williams Lake BC V2G 1R8

Council of Forest Industries – Library, #203, 197 Second Ave. North, Williams Lake BC V2G 1Z5 – 250/392-7770; Symbol: COFI – Librarian, Sheila Foley

University College of the Cariboo - Williams Lake Campus, 351 Hodgson Rd., Williams Lake BC V2G 3P7 – 250/392-8030; Fax: 250/392-8032; Email: mcoyne@cariboo.bc.ca; Symbol: BWLCC – Librarian, Michael Coyne

MANITOBA

Regional Library Systems with Member Libraries

BORDER REGIONAL LIBRARY
312 Seventh Ave. South, PO Box 970, Virden MB R0M 2C0 – 204/748-3862; Symbol: MVE
Regional Library Coordinator, Della Scott
Librarian, Linda Grant-Braybrook

Elkhorn Branch Library, 110 Richhill Ave. East, PO Box 370, Elkhorn MB R0M 0N0 – 204/845-2292 – Librarian, Ellen Rae Overand

Mc Auley Branch Library, PO Box 234, Mc Auley MB R0M 1H0 – 204/722-2221 – Librarian, Carolyn Grant

EVERGREEN REGIONAL LIBRARY
63 - 1 Ave., PO Box 1140, Gimli MB R0C 1B0 – 204/642-7912; Fax: 204/642-8056; Symbol: MGE
Head Librarian, Valerie Eyolfson

Arborg Branch Library, PO Box 4053, Arborg MB R0C 0A0 – 204/376-5388; Fax: 204/642-8056 – Branch Head, Linda Hegg
Riverton Branch Library, Riverton MB R0C 2R0 – 204/378-2988; Fax: 204/642-8056 – Branch Head, Sigrid Palsson

JOLYS REGIONAL LIBRARY
PO Box 118, St-Pierre-Jolys MB R0A 1V0 – 204/433-7729; Email: stplibrary@pli.mb.ca; Symbol: MSTP
Head Librarian, Claudette Desharnais

St. Malo Library, Chalet Malouin, St. Malo MB R0A 1T0 – 204/347-5606; Email: stmlibrary@pli.mb.ca – Librarian, Carole Arpin

LAKELAND REGIONAL LIBRARY
318 Williams Ave., PO Box 970, Killarney MB R0K 1G0 – 204/523-4949; Symbol: MKL
Librarian, Lil Hysop

Cartwright Branch Library, Railway Ave., Cartwright MB R0K 0L0 – 204/529-2261; Symbol: MCCB – Branch Head, Gloria Kinley
Pilot Mound Branch Library, PO Box 126, Pilot Mound MB R0G 1P0 – 204/825-2035; Symbol: MPM – Branch Head, Allison MacAulay

NORTH-WEST REGIONAL LIBRARY
PO Box 999, Swan River MB R0L 1Z0 – 204/734-3880; Symbol: MSRNW
Head Librarian, Bonnie Ray

Benito Branch Library, General Delivery, Benito MB R0L 0C0 – 204/539-2446; Symbol: MBB – Branch Head, Mabel Cooke

PARKLAND REGIONAL LIBRARY
504 Main St. North, Dauphin MB R7N 1C9 – 204/638-6410; Fax: 204/638-9483; Symbol: MDP
Director, Glenn Butchart

Siglunes District Library, PO Box 368, Ashren MB R0C 0E0 – 204/768-2048 – Librarian, Kathi Budge
Birch River & District Branch Library, 3rd St., PO Box 245, Birch River MB R0L 0E0 – 204/236-4419 – Attendant, Gwenda Wotton
Birtle Branch Library, PO Box 207, Birtle MB R0M 0C0 – 204/842-3418 – Librarian, Susan Barteaux
Bowsman Branch Library, PO Box 209, Bowsman MB R0L 0H0 – 204/238-4615 – Librarian, Fern De Groot
Dauphin Branch Library, 504 Main St. North, Dauphin MB R7N 1C9 – 204/638-3055 – Librarian, Lynn Innerst
Erickson District Library, PO Box 385, Erickson MB R0J 0P0 – 204/636-2325 – Librarian, Imeke Kerr
Foxwarren Branch Library, PO Box 204, Foxwarren MB R0J 0R0 – 204/847-2030 – Librarian, Pearl Clunie
Gilbert Plains Branch Library, Gilbert Plains MB R0L 0X0 – 204/548-2733 – Librarian, Sudesh Malik
Gladstone District Library, PO Box 720, Gladstone MB R0J 0T0 – 204/385-2641 – Librarian, Margaret Broadfoot
Grandview Branch Library, General Delivery, Grandview MB R0L 0Y0 – 204/546-2398 – Librarian, Marion Storozinski
Hamiota Centennial Library, PO Box 610, Hamiota MB R0M 0T0 – 204/764-2680 – Librarian, Gladys Mathison

Langruth Library, PO Box 154, Langruth MB R0H 0N0 – 204/445-2030 – Librarian, Karen Dick
McCreary District Library, PO Box 297, McCreary MB R0J 1B0 – 204/835-2629 – Attendant, Germaine Longtin
Minitonas Branch Library, Minitonas MB R0L 1G0 – 204/525-4840 – Librarian, Betty MacCumber
Ochre River Branch Library, General Delivery, Ochre River MB R0L 1K0 – 204/733-2293 – Librarian, Orla Berkvens
Roblin & District Library, PO Box 1342, Roblin MB R0L 1P0 – 204/937-2443 – Librarian, Marlene Beattie
Shoal Lake Community Library, PO Box 428, Shoal Lake MB R0J 1Z0 – 204/759-2242 – Librarian, Donna Charney
Winnipegosis Branch Library, Winnipegosis MB R0L 2G0 – 204/656-4876 – Librarian, Kim Fehr

PORTAGE PLAINS REGIONAL LIBRARY
170 Saskatchewan Ave. West, Portage la Prairie MB R1N 0M1 – 204/857-4271; Fax: 204/239-4387; Symbol: MPLP
Head Librarian, Pat Mutala
Assistant Librarian, Percy Gregoire-Voskamp

Regional Municipality of Victoria Branch Library, Holland MB R0G 0X0 – 204/526-2011; Symbol: MHP – Librarian, Linda Clark

RUSSELL & DISTRICT REGIONAL LIBRARY
PO Box 340, Russell MB R0J 1W0 – 204/773-3127; Fax: 204/773-3759; Symbol: MRD
Librarian, Florence Pushka
Librarian, Louise Sidoryk

Binscarth Branch Library, General Delivery, Binscarth MB R0J 0G0 – 204/532-2342 – Librarian, Doris Barrett

SOUTH CENTRAL REGIONAL LIBRARY
Civic Centre, 185 Main St., Winkler MB R6W 1B4 – 204/325-5864; Fax: 204/325-5915; Email: irisloew@mbnet.mb.ca; Symbol: MMOW
Head Librarian, Iris Loewen

Altona Branch Library, PO Box 650, Altona MB R0G 0B0 – 204/324-1503; URL: scrla@altona.man.net; Symbol: MWOW – Librarian, Liz Forrester
Morden Branch Library, 514 Stephen St., Morden MB R6M 1T7 – 204/822-4092; Email: scrlbm@mbnet.mb.ca – Branch Librarian, Kathy Ginter
Winkler Branch Library, Civic Centre, 185 Main St., Winkler MB R6W 1B4 – 204/325-7174; Fax: 204/325-5915; Email: scrlibw@mbnet.mb.ca; Symbol: MAOW – Branch Librarian, Lori Friesen

SOUTH INTERLAKE REGIONAL LIBRARY
385 Main St., Stonewall MB R0C 2Z0 – 204/467-8415; Symbol: MSTOS
Chief Librarian/Administrator, Heather Kowalchuk
Bookmobile Contact, Peggy Armstrong

Teulon Branch Library, 70 Main St., Teulon MB R0C 3B0 – 204/886-3648; Symbol: MTSIR – Branch Librarian, Barb Bowman

SOUTHWESTERN MANITOBA REGIONAL LIBRARY
73 Main St., PO Box 670, Melita MB R0M 1L0 – 204/522-3923; Email: swmblib@mail.techplus.com; Symbol: MMES
Head Librarian, Valorie Wray

Napinka Branch Library, Napinka MB R0M 1N0 – 204/665-2282 – Librarian, Deb Green
Pierson Branch Library, PO Box 39, Pierson MB R0M 1S0 – 204/634-2215 – Librarian, Viki Miner

WESTERN MANITOBA REGIONAL LIBRARY
638 Princess Ave., Brandon MB R7A 0P3 – 204/727-6648; Fax: 204/727-4447; Symbol: MBW
Chief Librarian, Kathy Thornborough
Children's Librarian, Shelley Mortensen

Brandon Public Library, 638 Princess Ave., Brandon MB R7A 0P3 – 204/727-6648 – Chief Librarian, Kathy Thornborough
Carberry/North Cypress Branch Library, PO Box 382, Carberry MB R0K 0H0 – 204/834-3043 – Branch Supervisor, Isabel Cathcart
Glenboro/South Cypress Branch Library, PO Box 429, Glenboro MB R0K 0X0 – 204/827-2874; Fax: 204/827-2127 – Branch Supervisor, Jackie Steele
Neepawa Branch Library, PO Box 759, Neepawa MB R0J 1H0 – 204/476-5648; Fax: 204/476-5939 – Branch Supervisor, Jean Forsman

Public Libraries

Baldur: Regional Municipality of Argyle Public Library, PO Box 358, Baldur MB R0K 0B0 – 204/535-2314; Fax: 204/535-2242; Symbol: MBA – Librarian, Cheri McLaren
Beausejour: Brokenhead River Regional Library, PO Box 1087, Beausejour MB R0E 0C0 – 204/268-3588; Symbol: MBBR – Head Librarian, Diane Sienema
Boissevain & Morton Regional Library, PO Box 340, Boissevain MB R0K 0E0 – 204/534-6478; Symbol: MBOM – Director, Phyllis Hallett
Carman: Boyne Regional Library, 15 - 1st Ave. SW, PO Box 788, Carman MB R0G 0J0 – 204/745-3504; Symbol: MCB – Head Librarian, Helen Stewart
Churchill Public Library, PO Box 730, Churchill MB R0B 0E0 – 204/675-2731; Symbol: MCH – Librarian, Juliette Lee; Archivist, Anne Gould; Part-time Librarian, Beverley Mulhern
Deloraine: Bren Del Win Centennial Library, PO Box 584, Deloraine MB R0M 0M0 – 204/747-2415; Symbol: MDB – Librarian, Lorraine Stovin
Flin Flon Public Library, 58 Main St., Flin Flon MB R8A 1J8 – 204/687-3397; Fax: 204/687-4233; Symbol: MFF – Library Administrator, Gretta Redahl
Gillam Public Library, PO Box 400, Gillam MB R0B 0L0 – 204/652-2617; Symbol: MGI – Head Librarian, Gerry Belbas
Headingley Municipal Library, 121 Alboro St., Headingley MB R4J 1A3 – 204/888-5410; Symbol: MHH – Librarian, Audrey Teichroeb
La Broquerie: Bibliothèque St. Joachim, PO Box 10, La Broquerie MB R0A 0W0 – 204/424-5287; Fax: 204/424-5610 – Library Technician, Gisele Balcaen
Lac du Bonnet Regional Library, 84 - Third St., PO Box 216, Lac du Bonnet MB R0E 1A0 – 204/345-2653; Symbol: MLDB – Head Librarian, Rosalind M. Burt
Leaf Rapids Public Library, PO Box 190, Leaf Rapids MB R0B 1W0 – 204/473-2742; Symbol: MLR – Head Librarian, Traci Dunn
Lynn Lake Centennial Library, PO Box 1127, Lynn Lake MB R0B 0W0 – Librarian, Margaret Thomson
MacGregor: North Norfolk MacGregor Regional Library, PO Box 6722, MacGregor MB R0H 0R0 – 204/685-2796; Symbol: MMNN – Librarian, Lorraine Burt
Manitou Public Library, PO Box 432, Manitou MB R0G 1G0 – 204/242-3134; Symbol: MMA – Librarian, Beverly Boote
Minnedosa Regional Library, PO Box 1226, Minnedosa MB R0J 1E0 – 204/867-2585; Symbol: MMR – Librarian, Georgina Johnson
Morris: Valley Regional Library, PO Box 397, Morris MB R0G 1K0 – 204/746-2136; Symbol: MMVR – Librarian, Diane DeKezel
Norway House: Ayamiscikawikamik Public Library, Culture Centre, Norway House MB R0B 1B0 – 204/

359-6047; Fax: 204/359-6262; Symbol: MNHA – Librarian, Geraldine Simpson
Notre Dame de Lourdes: Bibliothèque Père Champagne, Centre Dom Benoit, 55, rue Rodgers, CP 399, Notre Dame de Lourdes MB R0G 1M0 – 204/248-2386; Symbol: MNDP – Président, Denis Bibault; Bibliothécaire, Colette Compté
Pinawa Public Library, Pinawa MB R0E 1L0 – 204/753-2496; Email: plibrary@eastman.freenet.mb.ca; Symbol: MP – Librarian, Brenda Johnson
Rapid City Regional Library, PO Box 8, Rapid City MB R0K 1W0 – 204/826-2732; Symbol: MRA – Librarian, Jocelyn Aimoe
Reston District Library, PO Box 340, Reston MB R0M 1X0 – 204/877-3673; Symbol: MRP – Librarian, Onagh Williamson
Rivers: Prairie Crocus Regional Library, PO Box 609, Rivers MB R0K 1X0 – 204/328-7613; Symbol: MRIP – Librarian, Beth Schafer
Rossburn Regional Library, PO Box 87, Rossburn MB R0J 1V0 – 204/859-2687; Symbol: MRO – Librarian, Ann Hrycak
St Adolphe: Bibliothèque Ritchot, CP 123, St Adolphe MB R5A 1AY – 204/388-4016; Symbol: MIBR – Librarian, Lee Anne David
Ste-Anne: Bibliothèque Ste-Anne Library, PO Box 220, Ste-Anne MB R0A 1R0 – 204/422-9958; Symbol: MSA – Librarian, Denise Van Den Bussche
St-Claude: Bibliothèque Saint-Claude Library, 50 - 1 St., PO Box 203, St-Claude MB R0G 1Z0 – 204/379-2524; Symbol: MSCL – Librarian, Lynn Gobin
St-Georges: Bibliothèque Allard Library, St-Georges Community Club, PO Box 157, St-Georges MB R0E 1V0 – 204/367-8443; Email: sgplibr@eastman.freenet.mb.ca; Symbol: MSTG – Head Librarian, Janet Roberts
St-Jean-Baptiste: Bibliothèque Montcalm Library, CP 345, St-Jean-Baptiste MB R0G 2B0 – 204/758-3137; Symbol: MSJB – Head Librarian, Diane Bérard
Ste-Rose-du-Lac: Ste. Rose Regional Library, Ste-Rose-du-Lac MB R0L 1S0 – 204/447-2527; Symbol: MSTR – Librarian, Sonja Saquet
Selkirk Community Library, 303 Main St., Selkirk MB R1A 1S7 – 204/482-3522; Email: ENVOY: ILL.MSEL; Symbol: MSEL – Librarian, Linda Pleskach
Snow Lake Community Library, PO Box 760, Snow Lake MB R0B 1M0 – 204/358-2322; Symbol: MSL – Librarian, Dorothy Salahub
Somerset: Bibliothèque Somerset/Somerset Library, 289 Carlton St., PO Box 279, Somerset MB R0G 2L0 – 204/744-2170; Symbol: MS – Librarian, Lucille Labossière
Souris: Glenwood & Souris Regional Library, PO Box 760, Souris MB R0K 2C0 – 204/483-2757; Symbol: MSOG – Librarian, Margaret Greaves
Steinbach Public Library, 304 - 2 St., PO Box 2050, Steinbach MB R0A 2A0 – 204/326-6841; Fax: 204/326-6859; Symbol: MSTE – Librarian, Valerie Kasper
The Pas Public Library, 53 Edwards St., PO Box 4100, The Pas MB R9A 1R2 – 204/623-2023; Fax: 204/623-4594; Email: ILL.MTP; Symbol: MTP – Library Administrator, Roberta Day
Thompson Public Library, 81 Thompson Dr. North, Thompson MB R8N 0C3 – 204/677-3717; Email: ThompsonPublib@NorCom.mb.ca; Symbol: MTH – Administrator, Edward Reece; Children's Librarian, Carole Parenteau
Winnipeg Public Library, 251 Donald St., Winnipeg MB R3C 3P5 – 204/986-6462; Fax: 204/942-5671; Email: ENVOY: ILL.MW; Symbol: MW – City Librarian, David Weismiller; Circulation Supervisor, Lesley Herrington, 204/986-6461; Children's Librarian, Laura Fowler, 204/986-2803; Reference Librarian, Eric Hunt, 204/986-2801; Manager, Branch Offices, Carol Mahe, 204/986-6473; Acquisitions Librarian, Betty Parry, 204/986-5002 – See also following branches: Bibliothèque de St-Boniface, Brooklands Branch Library, Charleswood Branch Library, Cornish Branch Library, Fort Garry Branch Library, Henderson Branch Library, Louis Riel Branch Library, McPhillips Branch Library, Munroe Branch Library, Osborne Branch Library, Pembina Trail Branch Library, River Heights Branch Library, St. James-Assiniboia Branch Library, St. John's Branch Library, St. Vital Branch Library, Transcona Branch Library, West End Branch Library, West Kildonan Branch Library, Westwood Branch Library, Windsor Park Branch Library, Winnipeg Centennial Library
Winnipeg: Bibliothèque de St-Boniface, #100, 131, boul Provencher, Winnipeg MB R2H 0G2 – 204/986-4330; Téléc: 204/942-5671 – Coordinator of French Language Services, Danielle Chagnon; Reference Librarian, Liv Thorseth, 204/986-4331; Email: lthorset@city.winnipeg.mb.ca; Children's Librarian, Édith Boulet, 204/986-4332; Email: eboulet@city.winnipeg.mb.ca – Branch of Winnipeg Public Library
Winnipeg: Brooklands Branch Library, 9 Dee St., Winnipeg MB R2R 0K8 – 204/986-4681 – Branch Head, Ken Horobin – Branch of Winnipeg Public Library
Winnipeg: Charleswood Branch Library, 5014 Roblin Blvd., Winnipeg MB R3R 0G7 – 204/986-3069; Fax: 204/986-3545; Email: tfurmani@city.winnipeg.mb.ca – Branch Head, Terry Furmaniuk – Branch of Winnipeg Public Library
Winnipeg: Cornish Branch Library, 20 West Gate, Winnipeg MB R3C 2E1 – 204/986-4679; Fax: 204/986-7126; Email: rwatkins@city.winnipeg.mb.ca – Branch Head, Rick Watkins – Branch of Winnipeg Public Library
Winnipeg: Fort Garry Branch Library, 1360 Pembina Hwy., Winnipeg MB R3T 2B4 – 204/986-4910; Fax: 204/986-3399; Email: kborland@city.winnipeg.mb.ca – Acting Branch Head, Karin Borland – Branch of Winnipeg Public Library
Winnipeg: Henderson Branch Library, #1, 1050 Henderson Hwy., Winnipeg MB R2K 2M5 – 204/986-4314; Fax: 204/986-3065; Email: rwalker@city.winnipeg.mb.ca – Area Head, Rick Walker – Branch of Winnipeg Public Library
Winnipeg: Louis Riel Branch Library, 1168 Dakota St., Winnipeg MB R2N 3T9 – 204/986-4568; Fax: 204/986-3274; Email: epiush@city.winnipeg.mb.ca – Branch Head, Evelyn Piush – Branch of Winnipeg Public Library
Winnipeg: McPhillips Branch Library, 1120 McPhillips St., Winnipeg MB R2X 2L3 – 204/986-3729; Fax: 204/986-3764; Email: jfernie@city.winnipeg.mb.ca – Branch Head, Janice Fernie – Branch of Winnipeg Public Library
Winnipeg: Munroe Branch Library, 489 London St., Winnipeg MB R2K 2Z4 – 204/986-3736; Fax: 204/986-7125; Email: ggrainge@city.winnipeg.mb.ca – Branch Head, Gale Grainger – Branch of Winnipeg Public Library
Winnipeg: Osborne Branch Library, 625 Osborne St. South, Winnipeg MB R3L 2B3 – 204/986-4775; Fax: 204/986-1124; Email: jjohnsto@city.winnipeg.mb.ca – Branch Head, C. Jill Johnston – Branch of Winnipeg Public Library
Winnipeg: Pembina Trail Branch Library, 2724 Pembina Hwy., Winnipeg MB R3T 2H7 – 204/986-4370; Fax: 204/986-3290; Email: kmadansi@city.winnipeg.mb.ca – Branch Head, Kamini Madansingh – Branch of Winnipeg Public Library
Winnipeg: River Heights Branch Library, 1520 Corydon Ave., Winnipeg MB R3N 0J6 – 204/986-4394; Fax: 204/986-3544; Email: rgeorge@city.winnipeg.mb.ca – Branch Head, Rosemary George – Branch of Winnipeg Public Library
Winnipeg: St. James-Assiniboia Branch Library, 1910 Portage Ave., Winnipeg MB R3J 0J2 – 204/986-5583; Fax: 204/986-3798; Email: bnorquay@city.winnipeg.mb.ca – Acting Branch Head, Brenda Norquay – Branch of Winnipeg Public Library
Winnipeg: St. John's Branch Library, 500 Salter St., Winnipeg MB R2W 4M5 – 204/986-4689; Fax: 204/986-7123; Email: lcarmich@city.winnipeg.mb.ca – Branch Head, Lynn Carmichael – Branch of Winnipeg Public Library
Winnipeg: St. Vital Branch Library, 6 Fermor Ave., Winnipeg MB R2M 0Y2 – 204/986-5625; Fax: 204/986-3173; Email: sgarbett@city.winnipeg.mb.ca – Acting Branch Head, Susan Garbett-Snidal – Branch of Winnipeg Public Library
Winnipeg: Transcona Branch Library, 111 Victoria Ave. West, Winnipeg MB R2C 1S6 – 204/986-3950; Fax: 204/986-3172; Email: dfillion@city.winnipeg.mb.ca – Branch Head, Doris Fillion – Branch of Winnipeg Public Library
Winnipeg: West End Branch Library, 823 Ellice Ave., Winnipeg MB R3G 0C3 – 204/987-4677; Fax: 204/986-7129; Email: jturnbul@city.winnipeg.mb.ca – Branch Head, Joan Turnbull – Branch of Winnipeg Public Library
Winnipeg: West Kildonan Branch Library, 365 Jefferson Ave., Winnipeg MB R2V 0N3 – 204/986-4384; Fax: 204/986-3729; Email: tgretzin@city.winnipeg.mb.ca – Acting Branch Head, Tannis Gretzinger – Branch of Winnipeg Public Library
Winnipeg: Westwood Branch Library, 66 Allard Ave., Winnipeg MB R3K 0T3 – 204/986-4742; Fax: 204/986-3799; Email: dbates@city.winnipeg.mb.ca – Branch Head, Diane Bates – Branch of Winnipeg Public Library
Winnipeg: Windsor Park Branch Library, 955 Cottonwood Rd., Winnipeg MB R2J 1G3 – 204/986-4945; Fax: 204/986-7122; Email: dsouchan@city.winnipeg.mb.ca – Branch Head, Diane Souchan – Branch of Winnipeg Public Library
Winnipeg Centennial Library, 251 Donald St., Winnipeg MB R3C 3P5 – 204/986-6450; Fax: 204/942-5671; Email: dweismil@city.winnipeg.mb.ca; Symbol: MW – Manager, Vera Andrysiak – Branch of Winnipeg Public Library

Special & College Libraries & Resource Centres

BRANDON

Agriculture & Agri-Food Canada-Brandon Research Centre – Library, RR#3, 18th St. & Valley Rd., Brandon MB R7A 5Y3 – 204/726-7650; Email: lbmbag@ncccot.agr.ca – Aquisition Librarian, Carol Enns
Assiniboine Community College - Library, 1430 Victoria Ave. East, Brandon MB R7A 2A9 – 204/726-6635; Fax: 204/726-7014; Email: armstrong@accnet.assiniboinec.mb.ca
  Librarian, Sandra Armstrong
  Library Technician, Anni de Cangas
  Library Clerk, Dory Yorobe
Brandon General Hospital – Library Services, 150 McTavish Ave. East, Brandon MB R7A 2B3 – 204/727-2257; Fax: 204/727-0317; Email: Envoy: ILL.MBGH; Symbol: MBGH – Director of Library Services, Dianna Derouin
Brandon Mental Health Centre – Reference & Lending Library, PO Box 420, Brandon MB R7A 5Z5 – 204/726-2713; Fax: 204/726-6089 – Library Assistant, Betsy Playter
Brandon University - John E. Robbins Library, 270 - 18th St., Brandon MB R7A 6A9 – 204/727-9645; Fax: 204/726-1072; Email: ENVOY 100: ILL.MBC; Symbol: MBC
  Acting University Librarian, Terry Mitchell
  Music Librarian, June Jones
  Public Services, Head, Linda Burridge
  Extension Librarian, Carmen Kazakoff

Child & Family Services of Western Manitoba – Library, #100, 340 - 9 St., Brandon MB R7A 6C2 – 204/726-6030; Toll Free: 1-800-483-8980 – Executive Assistant, Joan Kennedy

Hunt, Miller & Combs Law Office - Library, 148 - 8 St., PO Box 22108, Brandon MB R7A 6Y9 – 204/727-8491; Fax: 204/727-4350 – Partner, J.D. Cram

The Marquis Project, Inc. – Laura Delamater Resource Centre, #200, 107 - 7 St., Brandon MB R7A 3S5 – 204/727-5675 – Resource Coord./Educator, Debra Jennings

CHURCHILL

Churchill Health Centre – Library, Churchill Town Centre, General Delivery, Churchill MB R0B 0E0 – 204/675-8881 – Wanda O'Brien

Churchill Northern Studies Centre - Library, PO Box 610, Churchill MB R0B 0E0 – 204/675-2307; Fax: 204/675-2139 – Executive Director, Michael Carter

DAUPHIN

Manitoba Heritage Federation Inc. – MHF Heritage Library, 21 - 2nd Ave. NW, 2nd Fl., Dauphin MB R7N 1H1 – 204/638-9154 – Administrative Assistant, Sheila Goraluk

Western Christian College - Library, PO Box 5000, Dauphin MB R7N 2V5 – 204/638-8801; Fax: 204/638-7054; Email: w.ulrich@mts.net
Teacher Librarian, Loreen Husband
Library Clerk, Donna Gannon

HAMIOTA

Hamiota District Health Centre – Library, 177 Birch Ave., Hamiota MB R0M 0T0 – 204/764-2412 – Health Educator, Jody Allan

MANITOU

Selby & Jones Law Office - Library, PO Box 279, Manitou MB R0G 1G0 – 204/242-2801; Fax: 204/242-2923

MORDEN

Agriculture & Agri-Food Canada - Canadian Agriculture Library, #100-101, Route 100, Morden MB R6M 1Y5 – 204/822-4471; Fax: 204/822-6841 – Secretary/Librarian, Cheryl Sharf

OAK HAMMOCK MARSH

Ducks Unlimited Canada – Library, Oak Hammock Marsh Conservation Centre, 1 Mallard Bay at Hwy. 220, PO Box 1160, Oak Hammock Marsh MB R0C 2Z0 – 204/467-3295; Toll Free: 1-800-665-3825 – Patti Preston

OTTERBURNE

Providence College & Seminary - Library, Otterburne MB R0A 1G0 – 204/433-7488; Fax: 204/433-7158; Email: lwild@providence.mb.ca; URL: http://www.providence.mb.ca
Head Librarian, Larry Wild
Circulation Librarian, Murray Harrison
Technical Services Librarian, Martha Loeppky

PINAWA

Atomic Energy of Canada Limited-Whiteshell Laboratories – WL Information Centre, General Delivery, Pinawa MB R0E 1L0 – 204/753-2311; Fax: 204/753-8490; Email: ENVOY: WNRE.LIBRARY; refdesk@wl.aecl.ca; Symbol: MPW – Library Supervisor, Sharon Taylor

PORTAGE LA PRAIRIE

The Daily Graphic & Herald Leader Press - Library, 1941 Saskatchewan Ave. West, PO Box 130, Portage La Prairie MB R1N 3B4 – 204/857-3427; Fax: 204/239-1270
Office Manager, M. Barter

Chief Librarian, Tom Tenszen
Reference Librarian, Simon Blake
Public Services Librarian, Ian White

David Winton Bell Memorial Library - Delta Waterfowl & Wetlands Research Station, RR#1, Box 1, Portage La Prairie MB R1N 3A1 – 204/239-1900; Fax: 204/239-5950; Email: dw4ducks@portage.net; Symbol: MDW – Library Technician, Heidi den Haan

Economic Innovation & Technology Council - National Agri-Food Technology Centre, 810 Phillips St., PO Box 1240, Portage La Prairie MB R1N 3J9 – 204/239-3162; Fax: 204/239-3180; Toll Free: 1-800-870-1040; Email: INET: ILL.CFPDC; lpetriuk@eitc.mb.ca; URL: http://www.eitc.mb.ca/naf/; Symbol: MPCFP – Library Technician, Joan Ransom

Manitoba Developmental Centre - Memorial Library, PO Box 1190, Portage La Prairie MB R1N 3C6 – 204/856-4205, ext.213; Fax: 204/856-4258; Symbol: MPLPM – Library Technician, Jo-Anne Doan

Portage La Prairie & District Arts Council – Library, 160 Saskatchewan Ave. West, Portage La Prairie MB R1N 0M1 – 204/239-6029 – Librarian, Mary Anne Beaton

SELKIRK

Selkirk Mental Health Centre – Library, 825 Manitoba Ave. West, PO Box 9600, Selkirk MB R1A 2B5 – 204/482-3810, ext.411 – Library Technician, Lorna Weiss

STEINBACH

Red River Apiarists' Association – Library, PO Box 1448, Steinbach MB R0A 2A0 – 204/326-3763 – Librarian, Ron Rudiak

Steinbach Bible College - Library, PO Box 1420, Steinbach MB R0A 2A0 – 204/326-6451; Fax: 204/326-6908
Librarian, Myrna Friesen, Email: mfriesen@sbcollege.mb.ca
Technical Services Librarian, Lois Loeppky

STONEWALL

Goodman & Grantham Law Office - Library, Westside Plaza, 15 - 353 Main St., PO Box 1400, Stonewall MB R0C 2Z0 – 204/467-5527; Fax: 204/467-5550

THE PAS

Keewatin Community College - Library, PO Box 3000, The Pas MB R9A 1M7 – 204/623-3416, ext.261; Fax: 204/623-7316
Librarian, Elena Ruivivar
Library Technician, Sharyl Latta
Library Technician, John Schoen

The Sam Waller Museum - Library, 306 Fischer Ave., PO Box 185, The Pas MB R9A 1K4 – 204/623-3802; Fax: 204/623-5506 – Curator, Paul Thistle

THOMPSON

Keewatin Community College - Thompson Campus Library, 504 Princeton Dr., Thompson MB R8N 0A5 – 204/677-6408; Fax: 204/677-6439 – Librarian, Shelly Doman, Email: sdoman@kccnet.keewatincc.mb.ca

Thompson Citizenship Council – Multi Culture Centre, 97 McGill Pl., Thompson MB R8N 0H9 – 204/677-3981

WINNIPEG

Economic Innovation & Technology Council - Environmental Sciences Centre – Library, Environmental Research, 745 Logan Ave., Winnipeg MB R3E 3L5 – 204/945-3804 – Librarian, Helen Woo

Aboriginal Women's Network Inc. – Aboriginal Women's Resource Centre, 181 Higgins Ave., 3rd Fl., Winnipeg MB R3A 3G1 – 204/942-2711

Addictions Foundation of Manitoba – William Potoroka Memorial Library, 1031 Portage Ave., Winnipeg MB R3G 0R8 – 204/944-6233;
Symbol: MAFM – Library Services Manager, Rita Shreiber

Agriculture & Agri-Food Canada-Winnipeg Research Centre – Canadian Agriculture Library, 195 Dafoe Rd., Winnipeg MB R3T 2M9 – 204/983-0721; Email: lbmwag@ncccot.agr.ca – Librarian, Mike Malyk

Aikins, MacAulay & Thorvaldson Law Office - Library, Commodity Exchange Tower, 360 Main St., 30th Fl., Winnipeg MB R3C 4G1 – 204/957-4785; Fax: 204/957-0840 – Librarian, Shu Huang

Ancient, Free & Accepted Masons of Canada - Grand Lodge of Manitoba – Grand Lodge of Manitoba Library, Masonic Memorial Temple, 420 Corydon Ave., Winnipeg MB R3L 0N8 – 204/453-7410 – Grand Librarian, Charles A. Merrick

Arcor Resource Library, 265 Notre Dame Ave., Winnipeg MB R3B 1N9 – 204/943-9400; Fax: 204/943-4088 – Librarian, Arthur Short

Benedictine Sisters of Manitoba – St. Benedict's Monastery Library, 225 Masters Ave., Winnipeg MB R4A 2A1 – 204/338-4601

Bethania Mennonite Personal Care Home Inc. – Library, 1045 Concordia Ave., Winnipeg MB R2K 3S7 – 204/667-0795 – Staff Education Coordinator, Esther Fransen

Boeing Canada Technology Ltd. - Technical Library, 99 Murray Park Rd., Winnipeg MB R3J 3M6 – 204/888-2300, ext.3374; Fax: 204/888-2951 – Library Technician, Stephen Porrior

Buchwald Asper Gallagher Henteleff Barristers & Attorneys-at-Law - Library, Commodity Exchange Tower, 360 Main St., 25th Fl., Winnipeg MB R3C 4H6 – 204/956-0560, ext.373; Fax: 204/957-0227 – Librarian, Edie Biberdorf

Canadian Artists' Representation Manitoba – Library, #221, 100 Arthur St., Winnipeg MB R3B 1H3 – 204/943-7211; Symbol: VARC – Program Coordinator, Helma Rogge

Canadian Brain Injury Coalition – Library, 29 Pearce Ave., Winnipeg MB R2V 2K3 – 204/334-0471

Canadian Broadcasting Corporation - Music & Record Library, 541 Portage Ave., PO Box 160, Winnipeg MB R3C 2H1 – 204/788-3222; Fax: 204/788-3685; Symbol: MWC – Senior Librarian, Mary Worobec

Canadian Coalition for Ecology, Ethics & Religion – Library, 22 Carriage Bay, Winnipeg MB R2Y 0M5 – 204/832-1882

Canadian Disability Rights Council – Resources Centre, #208, 428 Portage Ave., Winnipeg MB R3C 0E2 – 204/943-4787

Canadian Federation of Genealogical & Family History Societies Inc. – Library, 227 Parkville Bay, Winnipeg MB R2M 2J6 – 204/256-6176 – Secretary, Cécile Skene

Canadian Grain Commission - Library, #300, 303 Main St., Winnipeg MB R3C 3G8 – 204/983-0878; Fax: 204/983-6098; Email: ENVOY: CGC.LIBRARY; simundss@mbnet.mb.ca;
Symbol: MWGR
Chief Librarian, Elva Simundsson
Technical Services & Acquisitions Technician, C. MacDonald Deda
Circulation Technician, C. Wallmann

Canadian Heritage - Parks Canada, Prairie & Northern Region Library, 457 Main St., Winnipeg MB R3B 3E8 – 204/983-5941; Fax: 204/983-2014; Email: PARKS.ILLMWIAP; Symbol: MWIAP – Regional Librarian, Blair Kuntz, Email: blair_kuntz@pch.gc.ca

Canadian Home Economics Association Foundation – Gwenyth Bailey Simpson Video Resource Library, 303 Ashland Ave., Winnipeg MB R3L 1L6 – 204/475-1508

Canadian Mennonite Bible College - Library, 600 Shaftesbury Blvd., Winnipeg MB R3P 0M4 – 204/888-6781; Fax: 204/831-5675 – Librarian, Paul Friesen

Canadian Wheat Board - Library, 423 Main St., PO Box 816, Winnipeg MB R3C 2P5 – 204/983-3437; Fax: 204/983-4031; Email: library@cwb.ca; Symbol: MWCWB – Librarian, Ruth Reedman, Email: ruth_reedman@cwb.ca

Catherine Booth Bible College - Library, 447 Webb Place, Winnipeg MB R3B 2P2 – 204/947-6701; Fax: 204/942-3856; Symbol: CBBA – Director of Library Services, Adrian Dalwood

Centre for Mennonite Brethren Studies – Library, 169 Riverton Ave., Winnipeg MB R2L 2E5 – 204/669-6575; Fax: 204/654-1865; Email: adueck@cdnmb-conf.ca
Director, Abe Dueck
Archivist, Alf Redekop

City of Winnipeg - Waterworks, Waste & Disposal Dept. - Resource Centre, 1500 Plessis Rd., Winnipeg MB R2C 2Z9 – 204/986-3250, 4481; Fax: 204/224-0032; Email: JdaSilva@City.Winnipeg.MB.CA.; Symbol: MWWW – Library Technician, Joann de Silva

Collège universitaire de Saint-Boniface - Bibliothèque Alfred-Monnin, 200, av de la Cathedrale, Winnipeg MB R2H 0H7 – 204/235-4403; Téléc: 204/233-9472; Symbol: MSC
Bibliothécaire en chef, Marcel Boulet, 204/235-4402
Bibliothécaire, Madeleine Samuda
Bibliothécaire, Marcel Lemieux

Community Therapy Services Inc. - Library, 35 King St., 5th Fl., Winnipeg MB R3B 1H4 – 204/949-0533; Fax: 204/942-1428 – Education Coordinator, Monica Brechka

Concord College - Library, 169 Riverton Ave., Winnipeg MB R2L 2E5 – 204/669-6583; Fax: 204/663-2468; Email: thiessen@uwpg02.uwinnipeg.ca; Symbol: MWMBC – Librarian, Richard Thiessen

Concordia Hospital – Library, 1095 Concordia Ave., Winnipeg MB R2K 3S8 – 204/661-7163; Fax: 204/663-7301 – Library Technician, Peggy Prins

Council on Homosexuality & Religion – Library, PO Box 1912, Winnipeg MB R3C 3R2 – 204/474-0212 – Resource Officer, Jeremy Buchner

Crafts Guild of Manitoba Inc. – Library, 183 Kennedy St., Winnipeg MB R3C 1S6 – 204/943-1190 – Librarian, M. Wilson

Deer Lodge Centre – J.W. Crane Memorial Library, 2109 Portage Ave., Winnipeg MB R3J 0L3 – 204/831-2152; Fax: 204/888-1805; Email: inglis@mbnet.mb.ca; URL: http://www.mbnet.mb.ca/cvm/health/deerlod2.html; Symbol: MWDL
Director, Judy Inglis
Technical Services/Systems Librarian, Laurie Blanchard
Library Technician, Janice Saunders
Library Technician, Christine Shaw-Daigle

Economic Innovation & Technology Council - Industrial Technology Centre Library, 1329 Niakwa Rd. East, Winnipeg MB R2J 3T4 – 204/945-1413; Fax: 204/945-1784; Email: ENVOY: ILL.MWMRC; URL: http://itc.mb.ca; Symbol: MWMRC – Librarian, Betty J. Dearth, Email: bdearth@itc.mb.ca

Environment Canada - Atmospheric Environment Service, Central Region - Library, #1000, 266 Graham Ave., Winnipeg MB R3C 3V4 – 204/983-2024; Fax: 204/983-4884 – Secretary, Scientific Services, Patti Graham

Epilepsy Manitoba – Resource Centre, 825 Sherbrook St., Winnipeg MB R3A 1M5 – 204/783-0466 – Resource Coordinator, Cateland Penner

Fédération provinciale des comités de parents du Manitoba – Centre de ressources éducatives à l'enfance (CRÉE), 531 Marion St., Winnipeg MB R2J 0J9 – 204/237-9666 – Directrice, Suzanne Lagassé

Fillmore & Riley - Law Library, #1700, 360 Main St., Winnipeg MB R3C 3Z3 – 204/956-2970; Fax: 204/957-0516 – Librarian, Christine Stewart

Fire Fighters Historical Society of Winnipeg, Inc. – Library, Winnipeg Fire Department, 151 Princess St., 5th Fl., Winnipeg MB R3B 1L1 – 204/888-8021 – Barb Kuryluk

Fisheries & Oceans Canada-Freshwater Institute – Eric Marshall Aquatic Research Library, 501 University Cr., Winnipeg MB R3T 2N6 – 204/983-5170; Fax: 204/983-6285; Email: library@fwi.dfo.ca; Symbol: MWFW – Acting Manager, Mary Layton

Folk Arts Council of Winnipeg – Library, 375 York Ave., Winnipeg MB R3C 3J3 – 204/944-9793 – Resources Officer, Eslyn Glasgow

Freshwater Institute - Eric Marshall Aquatic Research Library, Fisheries & Oceans Canada, 501 University Cres., Winnipeg MB R3T 2N6 – 204/983-5169; Fax: 204/983-6285 – Librarian, Mary Layton

Gays for Equality – Gay/Lesbian Resource Centre, #1, 222 Osborne St., PO Box 1661, Winnipeg MB R3C 2Z6 – 204/474-0212

German Society of Winnipeg – Library, 121 Charles St., Winnipeg MB R2W 4A6 – 204/589-7724 – Secretary, K. Turner

Gould Goszer Law Office - Library, 175 Carlton St., 2 Fl., Winnipeg MB R3C 3H9 – 204/943-0571; Fax: 204/943-4498

The Great-West Life Assurance Company – Library, 100 Osborne St. North, PO Box 6000, Winnipeg MB R3C 3A5 – 204/946-8906; Email: ENVOY: D.NELSON; Symbol: MWGW – Corporate Librarian, Dale Nelson

Heritage Winnipeg – Library, #509, 63 Albert St., Winnipeg MB R3B 1G4 – 204/942-2663

Human Resources Development Canada - Manitoba Region Resource Centre, #500, 259 Portage Ave., Winnipeg MB R3B 3L4 – 204/983-7229; Fax: 204/983-2117 – Technical Services Assistant, Donna Martin, 204/983-7229

Industry Canada - Canada Business Service Centre, #800, 330 Portage Ave., Winnipeg MB R3C 2V2 – 204/984-2272; Fax: 204/983-3852; Toll Free: 1-800-665-2019
Chief Librarian, Oliver Bernuetz, 204/983-6182
Manager, Shannon Coughlin
Business & Trade Services Officer, Lee Gregg, 204/983-8036
Library Technician, Lisanne Wood

Institute of Urban Studies – Library, University of Winnipeg, 346 Portage Ave., Winnipeg MB R3C 0C3 – 204/982-1145 – Librarian, Nancy Klos

Intercultural Development Education Association – Resource Centre, 60 Maryland St., Winnipeg MB R3G 1K7 – 204/786-2030

International Institute for Sustainable Development – Library, 161 Portage Ave. East, 6th Fl., Winnipeg MB R3B 0Y4 – 204/958-7724; Email: mroy@iisd-post.iisd.ca – Project Officer, Marlene Roy

Islamic Ahamdiyya – Library, 525 Kylemore Ave., Winnipeg MB R3L 1B5 – 204/475-2642

Jewish Historical Society of Western Canada – Archives, #404, 365 Hargrave St., Winnipeg MB R3B 2K3 – 204/942-4822 – Archivist, Bonnie Tregobon

Jewish Public Library, 1725 Main St., Winnipeg MB R2V 1Z4 – 204/338-8408 – Librarian, Nina Thompson

The John Howard Society of Manitoba – Justice Resource Centre, 583 Ellice Ave., Winnipeg MB R3B 1Z7 – 204/775-1514 – Volunteer Coordinator, Stephen Murphy

Justice Canada - Winnipeg Regional Office - Library, #301, 310 Broadway, Winnipeg MB R3C 0S6 – 204/983-2391; Fax: 204/983-3636 – Barbara Shields

Law Society of Manitoba – Library, 219 Kennedy St., Winnipeg MB R3C 1S8 – 204/942-5571

League for Life in Manitoba – Library, 579 Des Meurons St., Winnipeg MB R2H 2P6 – 204/233-8047, 7283; Toll Free: 1-800-665-0570 – Barbara Gommerman

Learning Disabilities Association of Manitoba – Resource Centre, 60 Maryland St., 2nd Fl., Winnipeg MB R3G 1K7 – 204/774-1821

Legal Aid Manitoba - Library, #402, 294 Portage Ave., Winnipeg MB R3C 0B9 – 204/985-8500; Fax: 204/944-8582

Manitoba Archaeological Society Inc. – Library, PO Box 1171, Winnipeg MB R3C 2Y4 – 204/942-7243

Manitoba Association for the Promotion of Ancestral Languages – Resource Centre, 1574 Main St., Winnipeg MB R2W 5J8 – 204/338-7951 – Secretary, Leanna Burgess

Manitoba Association of Playwrights – Library, #503, 100 Arthur St., Winnipeg MB R3B 1H3 – 204/942-8941

Manitoba Blind Sports Association – Library, 200 Main St., Winnipeg MB R3C 4M2 – 204/925-5694

Manitoba Cancer Treatment & Research Foundation – Library, 100 Olivia St., Winnipeg MB R3E 0V9 – 204/787-2136; Symbol: MWCT

Manitoba Child Care Association – Resource Library, 364 McGregor St., Winnipeg MB R2W 4X3 – 204/586-8587 – Resource/Research Dev. Officer, Katalin Nagy

Manitoba Crafts Council – Library, #003, 100 Arthur St., Winnipeg MB R3B 1H3 – 204/942-1816

Manitoba Culture, Heritage & Citizenship - Legislative Library, 200 Vaughan St., Winnipeg MB R3C 1T5 – 204/945-4330; Fax: 204/948-2008; Email: refserv@mbnet.mb.ca; URL: http://www.gov.mb.ca/manitoba/leg-lib/contents.html; Symbol: MWP
Legislative Librarian, Susan Bishop, 204/945-3968
Reference Services, Head, Rick MacLowick
Collection Development, Head, Doreen Schafer
Technical Services, Head, Paul Nielson

Manitoba Eco-Network Inc. – Library, 116 Sherbrook St., PO Box 26007, Winnipeg MB R3G 4K9 – 204/772-7542

Manitoba Education & Training - Direction des Resources éducatives françaises, #S208, 200 Cathedral Ave., Winnipeg MB R2H 0H7 – 204/945-8594; Téléc: 204/945-0092; Symbol: MWDRE
Acting Director, Doris Lemoine, 204/945-8554
Librarian, Gemma Boily, 204/945-2010
Reference Librarian, Norma Rocan, 204/945-4782
Acquisitions Librarian, Nicole Baudry, 204/945-2743
Instructional Resources, 1181 Portage Ave., Winnipeg MB R3G 0T3 – 204/945-7833; Fax: 204/945-8756; Email: irb@minet.gov.mb.ca; Symbol: MWE
Coordinator, John Tooth
Resource Sharing, Phyllis Barich, 204/945-5764
Collection Management, Lorrie Andersen, 204/945-7823
Circulation, Debbie Somerville, 204/945-5371
Technical Services, Atarrha Wallace, 204/945-7834
Information Services, Diane Dwarka, 204/945-4015
Assistant Coordinator/Marketing, Elaine Seepish, 204/945-7830
Special Materials Services, #215, 1181 Portage Ave., Winnipeg MB R3G 0T3 – 204/945-7842; Fax: 204/945-7914; Toll Free: 1-800-282-8069 – Circulation Supervisor, Denise Speliers

Manitoba Energy & Mines - Library, #360, 1395 Ellice Ave., Winnipeg MB R3G 3P2 – 204/945-6569; Fax: 204/945-0586; Email: emlib@energymines.gov.mb.ca; Symbol: MWEMM
Library Technician, Monique Lavergne
Library Technician, Debbie Rind

Manitoba Environment - Resource Centre, Bldg. 2, 139 Tuxedo Ave., Winnipeg MB R3N 0H6 – 204/945-7125; Fax: 204/945-5229; Email: ENVOY 100:

ILL.MWEM; URL: http://www.gov.mb.ca/manitoba/environ/; Symbol: MEW
   Head Librarian, Helen Woo, Email: woo@mbnet.mb.ca
   Library Technician, Wendy Barber
Manitoba Federation of Labour – Occupational Health Centre, #101, 275 Broadway, Winnipeg MB R3C 4M6 – 204/949-0811 – Library Technician, Pat Hebert
Manitoba Finance - Federal-Provincial Relations & Research Library, #203, 333 Broadway, Winnipeg MB R3C 0S9 – 204/945-3757; Fax: 204/945-5051 – Librarian, Beatrice Miller
Manitoba Genealogical Society Inc. – Resource Centre, PO Box 2066, Winnipeg MB R3C 3R4 – 204/944-1153
Manitoba Health - Library, 599 Empress St., Winnipeg MB R3G 3H2 – 204/786-7124; Fax: 204/945-5063; Email: ENVOY: ILL.MWHP; Symbol: MWHP
   Manager, Marilyn Brooke, 204/786-7192
   Customer Services Support, Gail Kohut, 204/945-7198
   Customer Services Technician, Vera Ott, 204/786-7109
Manitoba Health Record Association – Library, PO Box 1544, Winnipeg MB R3C 2Z4 – 204/235-3188 – Georgina Lendvoy
Manitoba Highways & Transportation - Library, 215 Garry St., 16th Fl., Winnipeg MB R3C 3Z1 – 204/945-3772 – Gladys Bronevitch
Manitoba Hydro - Library, 820 Taylor Ave., PO Box 815, Winnipeg MB R3C 2P4 – 204/474-3614; Fax: 204/453-1838; Email: ENVOY: MAN.HYDRO.1; Symbol: MWH
   Corporate Librarian, Rhona Lapierre
   Reference Librarian, Ruth Epp, 204/474-3212
Manitoba Indian Cultural Education Centre – People's Library, 119 Sutherland Ave., Winnipeg MB R2W 3C9 – 204/942-0228 – Vi Chalmers
Manitoba Industry, Trade & Tourism - Audio Visual Library, #510, 155 Carlton St., Winnipeg MB R3C 3H8 – 204/945-3998; Fax: 204/945-2302 – Manager, John W.G. Giesbrecht, 204/945-2036
   Business Library, 155 Carlton St., 5th Fl., Winnipeg MB R3C 3H8 – 204/945-2036; Fax: 204/945-2804 Manager, Business Library, John W.G. Giesbrecht
   Public Services Technician, P. Jane Bullied
Manitoba Justice - Attorney General's Library, 405 Broadway, 6th Fl., Winnipeg MB R3C 3L6 – 204/945-2895 – Librarian, Brian Chesworth
   Great Library, Law Courts Bldg., #331, 408 York Ave., Winnipeg MB R3C 0P9 – 204/945-1958; Fax: 204/948-2138 – Chief Librarian, Garth Niven
   Legal Library Resources, 405 Broadway, 2nd Fl., Winnipeg MB R3C 3L6 – 204/945-0968 – Director, Legal Library Resources, Marilyn Hernandez
Manitoba Labour - Research & Planning Library, #409, 401 York Ave., Winnipeg MB R3C 0P8 – 204/945-3412; Fax: 204/948-2085 – Research Analyst, Glenda Segal
   Workplace Safety & Health Library, #200, 401 York Ave., Winnipeg MB R3C 0P8 – 204/945-0580; Fax: 204/945-4556; Toll Free: 1-800-282-8069; URL: http://www.gov.mb.ca/manitoba/safety; Symbol: MWLW – Librarian, Jean Van Walleghem, Email: jvan@labour.gov.mb.ca
Manitoba Labour Board - Library, #402, 258 Portage Ave., Winnipeg MB R3C 0B6 – 204/945-3783; Fax: 204/945-1296 – Research Analyst, Jodi Gilmore, 204/945-5046
Manitoba Legislative Assembly - Library, 200 Vaughan St., Winnipeg MB R3C 1T5 – 204/945-4330; Fax: 204/948-2008; Email: refserv@mbnet.mb.ca; URL: http://www.gov.mb.ca/leg-lib/contents.html; Symbol: MWP
   Librarian, Susan Bishop

Reference Services, Head, F.B. MacLowick
Manitoba Library Association – Library, #208, 100 Arthur St., Winnipeg MB R3B 1H3 – 204/943-4567
Manitoba Museum of Man & Nature - Library, 190 Rupert Ave., Winnipeg MB R3B 0N2 – 204/988-0692, 0662; Fax: 204/942-3679; Email: steffan@museummannature.mb.ca; Symbol: MWMM
   Head Librarian, Cindi Steffan
   Library Technician, Judy Carnegie
Manitoba Natural Resources - Land Information Centre - Air Photo Library, 1007 Century St., Winnipeg MB R3H 0W4 – 204/945-6670; Fax: 204/945-1365 – Manager, Product Distribution, Valerie Borkowsky
   Library, 1495 St. James St., PO Box 44, Winnipeg MB R3H 0W9 – 204/945-6610 – Library Assistant, Debbie Oliver
Manitoba Ombudsman - Library, #750, 500 Portage Ave., Winnipeg MB R3C 3X1 – 204/786-6483; 1-800-665-0531 (Manitoba); Fax: 204/942-7803 – Office Manager, L. Foster
Manitoba Society of Artists – Archives, 504 Daer Blvd., Winnipeg MB R3K 1C5 – 204/837-1754 – Secretary, Barbara K. Endres
Manitoba Society of Pharmacists Inc. – Pharmacy House Library, 187 St. Mary's Rd., Winnipeg MB R2H 1J2 – 204/233-1411 – Director, Continuing Education, Janet McGillivray
Manitoba Telephone System - Corporate Library, 489 Empress St., PO Box 6666, Winnipeg MB R3C 3V6 – 204/941-6344; Fax: 204/772-2155; Email: ENVOY: MTS.LIBRARY; Symbol: MWTS – Tanya L. Evancio
Manitoba Trucking Association – Library, 25 Bunting St., Winnipeg MB R2X 2P5 – 204/632-6600 – Research Coordinator, D. Milton
Manitoba Writers' Guild – MWG Resource Centre, #206, 100 Arthur St., Winnipeg MB R3B 1H3 – 204/942-6134 – Administrative Assistant, Kathie Axtill
Meadowood Manor – Nursing Resource Centre, 577 St. Anne's Rd., Winnipeg MB R2M 5B2 – 204/257-2394; Fax: 204/254-5402 – Education Coordinator, Elaine Wardrop
Meltzer Essers Duboff Schachter Law Office - Library, 175 Carlton St., 2nd Fl., Winnipeg MB R3C 3H9 – 204/942-3361; Fax: 204/943-4498 – Neil Duboff
Mennonite Central Committee Canada – Library, 134 Plaza Dr., Winnipeg MB R3T 5K9 – 204/261-6381 – Resource Librarian, Kathleen Hull
Mentoring Artists for Women's Art – Library, 175 McDermot Ave., Winnipeg MB R3B 0S1 – 204/949-9490
Mines Accident Prevention Association of Manitoba – Film & Reference Library, #700, 305 Broadway, Winnipeg MB R3C 3J7 – 204/942-2789
Misericordia General Hospital – Library, 99 Cornish Ave., Winnipeg MB R3C 1A2 – 204/788-8109; Fax: 204/744-7834 – Sharon Allentuck
National Defence - CFB Winnipeg - Base Recreational Library, 3 Jameswood Dr., Winnipeg MB R3J 0T0 – 204/831-7252 – Head Librarian, L. Schaffer
National Energy Conservation Association – Library, PO Box 3214, Winnipeg MB R3C 4E7 – 204/783-1273; Toll Free: 1-800-263-5974
The National Testing Laboratories Ltd. – Library, 199 Henlow Bay, Winnipeg MB R3Y 1G4 – 204/488-6999
Pitblado & Hoskin Law Office - Library, #1900, 360 Main St., Winnipeg MB R3C 3Z3 – 204/944-2580; Fax: 204/957-1790 – Librarian, Carla Moore
Polish Combatants Association - Winnipeg – SPK Library, 1364 Main St., Winnipeg MB R2X 0P2 – 204/586-6223
Recycling Council of Manitoba – Resource Centre, Powers Bldg., #501, 428 Portage Ave., Winnipeg MB R3C 1N7 – 204/925-3777 – Information Officer, Darrell Keating

Red River Community College - Library, 2055 Notre Dame Ave., Winnipeg MB R3H 0J9 – 204/632-2322; Fax: 204/697-4791; Email: ENVOY: ILL.MWRR; Symbol: MWRR
   Director, Library Services, Patricia Bozyk
   Head, Technical Services, Martin Beckwith
   Coordinator, Reference Services, Norman Beattie
   Coordinator, Access Services, Karen Hunt
Revenue Canada - Research & Library Services, 325 Broadway, 5th Fl., Winnipeg MB R3C 4T4 – 204/983-1013; Fax: 204/983-1015; Symbol: MWRE – Librarian, Don Albright
Royal Canadian Mounted Police Forensic Laboratory - Scientific Information Centre, 621 Academy Rd., Winnipeg MB R3N 0E7 – 204/983-6586; Fax: 204/983-6399 – Librarian, June Poitras
St. Amant Centre - Medical Library, 440 River Rd., Winnipeg MB R2M 3Z9 – 204/256-4301 – Pauline Dufresne
St. Boniface General Hospital – Carolyn Sifton - Helene Fuld Library, 409 Tache Ave., Winnipeg MB R2H 2A6 – 204/237-2807; Fax: 204/235-3339; Email: rabnett@sbrc.umanitoba.ca; Symbol: MWSBM – Head Librarian, Mark Rabnett
The Salvation Army Grace General Hospital – Winnipeg Library, 300 Booth Dr., Winnipeg MB R3J 3M7 – 204/837-0127; Fax: 204/885-7905; Email: jkochan@mbnet.mb.ca; Symbol: MWGH – Library Technician, Janet Kochan
Seven Oaks General Hospital – Library, 2300 McPhillips St., Winnipeg MB R2V 3M3 – 204/632-3107; Fax: 204/694-9469 – Library Technician, Arthur Short
Société historique de Saint-Boniface – Centre de documentation, 200, av de la Cathédrale, Winnipeg MB R2H 0H7 – 204/233-4888
Society for Manitobans with Disabilities Inc. – Stephen Sparling Resource Library, 825 Sherbrook St., Winnipeg MB R3A 1M5 – 204/786-5601 ext.319; Toll Free: 1-800-282-8041 – Librarian, Edith Konoplenko
Solicitor General Canada - Stony Mountain Institution - Library, PO Box 4500, Winnipeg MB R3C 3W8 – 204/453-5541, ext.5673; Fax: 204/453-5541; Symbol: MWSM – Librarian, Peter Kulyk
Spina Bifida Association of Canada – Library, #220, 388 Donald St., Winnipeg MB R3B 2J4 – 204/957-1784; Toll Free: 1-800-565-9488 – Mary Meldrum
Sport Manitoba – Library, 200 Main St., Winnipeg MB R3C 4M2 – 204/925-5605 – Ken Faulder
Statistics Canada - Prairie Regional Reference Centre, MacDonald Bldg., 344 Edmonton St., 3rd Fl., Winnipeg MB R3B 3l9 – 204/983-4020; Fax: 204/983-7543; Toll Free: 1-800-563-7828
   Assistant Regional Director, B. Gloyn
   Data Dissemination Officer, Ron Wonneck
Taylor McCaffrey Law Office - Library, 400 St. Mary Ave., 9th Fl., Winnipeg MB R3C 4K5 – 204/988-0463; Fax: 204/957-0945; Email: taylorm@mbnet.mb.ca – Librarian, Jane Bridle
Thompson Dorfman Sweatman Law Office - Library, Toronto-Dominion Centre, 2200 - 201 Portage Ave., Winnipeg MB R3B 3L3 – 204/957-1930; Fax: 204/943-6445 – Librarian, P. Betcher
Transport Canada - Central Region Library, Aviation Audio Visual Library, 333 Main St., 16th Fl., PO Box 8550, Winnipeg MB R3C 0P6 – 204/983-6853; Fax: 204/984-2255; Symbol: MWTCR – A/Regional Librarian, Lisa Wong
Ukrainian Cultural & Educational Centre - Library, 184 Alexander Ave. East, Winnipeg MB R3B 0L6 – 204/942-0218; Fax: 204/943-2857 – Librarian, Larissa Tolchinsky
Ukrainian National Home Association – Library, 582 Burrows Ave., Winnipeg MB R2W 2A6 – 204/582-4528 – Librarian, Helen Mayba
Ukrainian Orthodox Church of Canada – Library, 9 St. John's Ave., Winnipeg MB R2W 1G8 – 204/586-3093 – Archivist/Librarian, Wolodymyr G. Senchuk

UMA Engineering Ltd. - Library, 1479 Buffalo Pl., Winnipeg MB R3T 1L7 – 204/284-0580; Fax: 204/475-3646 – Bernice Kandrac

United Grain Growers Ltd. – Corporate Library, #2800, 201 Portage Ave., PO Box 6600, Winnipeg MB R3C 3A7 – 204/944-5754; Fax: 204/944-5415 – Librarian, Jackie Garrity

University of Manitoba - Libraries, Winnipeg MB R3T 2N2 – 204/474-9881; Fax: 204/261-1515; URL: http://www.cc.umanitoba.ca/academic_support/libraries/
 Director of Libraries, Carolynne Presser
 Automated Systems & Services, Associate Director, Pat Nicholls
 Bibliographic Database Management, Coordinator, Ganga Dakshinamurti
 Collections Management, Coordinator, Donna Breyfogle
 Collections, Associate Director, Michael Angel
 Finance & Planning, Executive Assistant, Janice Chaturvedi
 Personnel, Executive Assistant, Linda Lassman
 Public Services, Associate Director, Susan Suart
 Albert D. Cohen Management Library, Head, Dennis Felbel, 204/474-8440
 Architecture & Fine Arts Library, Head, Mary Lochhead, 204/474-9216
 D.S. Woods Education Library, Head, David Thirlwall, 204/474-9976
 Donald W. Craik Engineering Library, Head, Norma Godavari, 204/474-9445
 E.K. Williams Law Library, Head, Neil A. Campbell, 204/474-9995
 Eckhardt-Gramatté Music Library, Head, Vladimir Simosko, 204/474-9567
 Elizabeth Dafoe Library, Head, Nicole Michaud-Oystryk, 204/474-9211
 Medical Library, Acting Head, Michael Tennenhouse, 204/789-3342
 Science Library, Head, Ada Ducas, 204/474-8171
 St. Andrew's College Library, Head, Raisa Moroz, 204/474-8901
 St. John's College Library, Head, Patrick Wright, 204/474-8542
 St. Paul's College Library, Head, Earle Ferguson, 204/474-8585
 Neil John Maclean Health Sciences Library, 770 Bannatyne Ave., Winnipeg MB R3E 0W3 – 204/789-3342; Fax: 204/772-0094; Email: infodesk@bldghsc.1an1.umanitoba.ca; URL: http://www.cc.umanitoba.ca/libraries/medical/main.html

University of Winnipeg - Library, 515 Portage Ave., Winnipeg MB R3B 2E9 – 204/786-9801; Fax: 204/783-8910, 786-1824; Email: libadmin@uwpg02.uwinnipeg.ca; Symbol: MWUC
 University Librarian, W.R. Converse, 204/786-9801
 Associate University Librarian, Coreen Koz, 204/786-9802
 Acquisitions, Head, Kathy Buschhausen, 204/786-9806
 Circulation, Head, Pat Russell, 204/786-9807
 Computerized Information Systems & Networks, Head, William Pond, 204/786-9812
 Interlending & Document Supply Services (IDSS), Allison Sproul Dixon, 204/786-9031
 Reference/Public Services & Systems, Head, William Pond, 204/786-9812
 Technical Services, Head, Joan Scanlon, 204/786-9803
 Cataloguing Librarian, Kam Wing Lee
 Collection Librarian, Linwood DeLong, 204/786-9124
 Government Documents/Reference Librarian, Linda Dixon
 Special Projects Librarian, Sandra Zuk, 204/786-9813

Victoria General Hospital – Library, 2340 Pembina Hwy., Winnipeg MB R3T 2E8 – 204/477-3307 – Lynne Hardy

Visual Arts Manitoba – Library, #221, 100 Arthur St., Winnipeg MB R3B 1H3 – 204/943-1056

Walsh, Micay and Company Law Office - Library, Richardson Bldg., One Lombard Pl., 10th Fl., Winnipeg MB R3B 3H1 – 204/942-0081; Fax: 204/957-1261 – Partner, A. Dalmyn

William Molloy Memorial Library, 19 Linacre Rd., Winnipeg MB R3T 3G5 – 204/261-9366 – Sandra Konrad

Winnipeg Art Gallery - The Clara Lander Library, 300 Memorial Blvd., Winnipeg MB R3C 1V1 – 204/786-6641; Fax: 204/788-4998 – Librarian, Catherine Shields

Winnipeg Clinic - Library, 425 St. Mary Ave., Winnipeg MB R3C 0N2 – 204/957-1900, ext.512; Fax: 204/943-2164 – Librarian, S. Loeppky

Winnipeg Free Press - Library, 1355 Mountain Ave., Winnipeg MB R2X 3B6 – 204/697-7289; Fax: 204/697-7412; Email: library@freepress.mb.ca – Librarian, J. Williamson, 204/697-7290

Winnipeg Gay/Lesbian Resource Centre, #1, 222 Osborne St. South, Winnipeg MB R3C 2Z6 – 204/284-5208; 474-0212; Fax: 204/478-1160 – Services Coordinator, Jeremy Buckner

The Winnipeg Sun - Library, 1700 Church Ave., Winnipeg MB R2X 3A2 – 204/694-2022 – Marcia P. Stephenson

Winnipeg Symphony Orchestra Inc. – Music Library, #101, 555 Main St., Winnipeg MB R3B 1C3 – 204/949-3950; Box Office: 949-3999 – Margo Hodgson

YM-YWCA - Women's Resource Centre, 301 Vaughan St., Winnipeg MB R3B 2N7 – 204/989-4140; Fax: 204/943-6159 – Volunteer Librarian, Babs Friesen

NEW BRUNSWICK

Regional Library Systems with Member Libraries

ALBERT-WESTMORLAND-KENT REGIONAL LIBRARY
#201, 644 Main St., Moncton NB E1C 1E2 – 506/857-1932; Fax: 506/857-1922; Email: potvin@gov.nb.ca
Regional Librarian, Claude Potvin
Reference Librarian, Thérèse Arsenault
Children's Librarian, Nancy Cohen

Bibliothèque publique de Bouctouche, 84, boul Irving, Bouctouche NB E0A 1G0 – 506/743-1483 – Bibliothécaire, Carmen Leger

Bibliothèque publique de Dieppe, 333, av Acadie, Dieppe NB E1A 1G9 – 506/859-8526 – Bibliothécaire, Claudia Losier

Dorchester Public Library, Dorchester NB E0A 1M0 – 506/379-6611 – Librarian, Daphne Holmes

Hillsborough Public Library, Hillsborough NB E0A 1X0 – 506/734-1896 – Barbara Alcorn

Hopewell Cape Public Library, Hopewell Cape NB E0A 1Y0 – Librarian, Shirley Teahan

Moncton Public Library, #101, 644 Main St., Moncton NB E1C 1E2 – 506/857-8731; Fax: 506/857-1922 – Librarian, Jeanne Maddix

Petitcodiac Public Library, 31 Main St., PO Box 369, Petitcodiac NB E0A 2H0 – 506/756-8079 – Librarian, Janet Coates-Mason

Port Elgin Public Library, Port Elgin NB E0A 2K0 – 506/538-2221 – Librarian, Betty Davis

Bibliothèque publique de Richibuctou, 81, rue Main, CP 397, Richibuctou NB E0A 2M0 – 506/523-1825 – Bibliothécaire, Michele-Ann Goguen

Riverview Public Library, 34 Honour House Ct., Riverview NB E1B 3Y9 – 506/387-2108 – Librarian, Lynn Cormier

Sackville Public Library, 33 West Main St., PO Box 1769, Sackville NB E0A 3C0 – 506/536-3184 – Librarian, Allan Alward

Bibliothèque publique de St-Antoine, 11, av Jeanne d'Arc, CP 328, St-Antoine NB E0A 2X0 – 506/525-2331 – Bibliothécaire, Paulette Leger

Bibliothèque publique de Memramcook, CP 98, St-Joseph NB E0A 2Y0 – 506/758-9829 – Bibliothécaire, Jocelyne Leblanc

Salisbury Public Library, 205 Main St., PO Box 419, Salisbury NB E0A 3E0 – 506/372-9106 – Librarian, Margaret Crosthwaite

Bibliothèque publique de Shediac, 161, rue Main, CP 1448, Shediac NB E0A 3G0 – 506/532-7014 – Bibliothécaire, Gabrielle LeBlanc

CHALEUR REGIONAL LIBRARY
88, Val D'Amour Rd., PO Box 607, Campbellton NB E3N 3H1 – 506/759-8551; Fax: 506/789-1620; Email: libcr@gov.nb.ca
Regional Director, James Violette

Bibliothèque publique d'Atholville, 272, rue Notre-Dame, PO Box 142, Atholville NB E0K 1A0 – 506/789-0300; Fax: 506/789-0300 – Responsable, A.M. Bernard

Bibliothèque publique de Bas-Caraquet, 8185, rue St-Paul, CP 149, Bas-Caraquet NB E0B 1E0 – 506/727-9305; Téléc: 506/727-9300 – Responsable, M. David

Bibliothèque du Centenaire Népisiguit, 360, av Douglas, CP 86, Bathurst NB E2A 3Z1 – 506/548-0706; Téléc: 506/548-0708 – Bibliothécaire, Jacques Filiatrault

Bibliothèque publique Mgr. Robichaud, 855, rue Principale, CP 600, Beresford NB E0B 1H0 – 506/542-1830; Téléc: 506/542-1880 – Responsable, M. Imbeault

Campbellton Centennial Library, 2, rue Aberdeen, PO Box 130, Campbellton NB E3N 3G1 – 506/753-5253; Fax: 506/759-3803 – Librarian, James Katan

Bibliothèque publique Mgr. Paquet, 10A, rue Colisée, Caraquet NB E1W 1A5 – 506/727-1701; Téléc: 506/727-6021 – Responsable, C. Hébert-LeBouthillier

Bibliothèque du centenaire de Dalhousie, 405, rue Adelaide, CP 1980, Dalhousie NB E0K 1B0 – 506/684-1344; Téléc: 506/684-1210 – Bibliothécaire, Myrian Doiron

Bibliothèque publique de Lamèque, 46, rue du Pêcheur nord, CP 922, Lamèque NB E0B 1V0 – 506/344-0362; Téléc: 506/344-0363 – Responsable, J.M. Noël

Bibliothèque publique de Petit-Rocher, 702, rue Principale, CP 490, Petit-Rocher NB E0B 2E0 – 506/783-7331; Téléc: 506/783-8845 – Responsable par intérim, J. Cormier

Bibliothèque publique de Shippagan, 244, boul J.D. Gauthier, CP 739, Shippagan NB E0B 2P0 – 506/336-3920; Téléc: 506/336-3921 – Responsable, P. Godin

Bibliothèque municipale de Tracadie, 776, ch Pointe des Ferguson, CP 3654, Tracadie-Sheila NB E1X 1G5 – 506/393-4005; Téléc: 506/395-4009 – Responsable, I. Aubie

BIBLIOTHÈQUE RÉGIONALE DU HAUT-SAINT-JEAN
135A, rue St-François, Edmundston NB E3V 1E8 – 506/739-7331; Téléc: 506/735-2745; Courrier électronique: libhr@gov.nb.ca; ENVOY: BIBLIO.HSJ; Symbol: NBEBR
Bibliothécaire régional, Guy Lefrançois

Bibliothèque publique Mgr. W.J. Conway, 74, rue Canada, Edmundston NB E3V 1V5 – 506/735-4713; 6422; Téléc: 506/737-6848 – Bibliothécaire, J. Robert Daigle

Bibliothèque publique de Grand-Sault, 136, rue Church, CP 850, Grand-Sault NB E3Z 1C3 – 506/473-1248; Téléc: 506/473-7160 – Bibliothécaire, Patricia Toner

Bibliothèque publique de Kedgwick, 17, rue Jeanne-Mance, CP 250, Kedgwick NB E0K 1C0 – 506/284-2757; Téléc: 506/284-4557 – Responsable, Mariette St-Pierre

Bibliothèque publique Mgr. Plourde, 15, rue Bellevue, St-François de Madawaska NB E7A 1A4 – 506/992-0132; Téléc: 506/992-0133 – Responsable, Bertin Nadeau

Bibliothèque publique Dr. Lorne J. Violette, 180, rue St-Jean, CP 789, St-Léonard NB E0L 1M0 – 506/423-7787; Téléc: 506/423-1190 – Responsable, Nicole Malenfant

Bibliothèque publique La Moisson de St-Quentin, 206, rue Canada, St-Quentin NB E0K 1J0 – 506/235-1955; Téléc: 506/235-1952 – Responsable, Y. Quimper

SAINT JOHN REGIONAL LIBRARY

1 Market Sq., Saint John NB E2L 4Z6 – 506/648-1191; Fax: 506/658-2903; Symbol: NBS

Regional Librarian, Eileen Travis

Information Technology/Branch Development, Manager, Barbara A. Malcolm

Public Relations/Development Librarian, Jean Cunningham

Youth Services Librarian, Joann Hamilton-Barry

Information Services Librarian, Diane Buhay

Campobello Public Library, PO Box 51, Welshpool, Campobello NB E0G 3H0 – 506/752-2268; Fax: 506/752-1015 – Branch Manager, Glenna Cline

Kennebecasis Public Library, One Landing Ct., Quispamsis NB E2E 4R2 – 506/849-2043; Fax: 506/849-0122 – Branch Manager, Leslye McVicar

Ross Memorial Library, 110 King St., PO Box 367, St. Andrews NB E0G 2X0 – 506/529-1825; Fax: 506/529-1829 – Branch Supervisor, Lesa Pomeroy

Bibliothèque Le Cormoran, Centre Samuel de Champlain, ch Boar's Head, RR#1, Saint John NB E2L 3W2 – 506/658-4610; Fax: 506/658-3984 – Branch Supervisor, Mireille Mercure

East Branch Public Library, Westmorland Place, 545 Westmorland Rd., Saint John NB E2J 2G5 – 506/658-2968 – Branch Manager, Valerie Bauer

Saint John Free Public Library, 1 Market Sq., Saint John NB E2L 4Z6 – 506/648-1191; Fax: 506/658-2903 – City Librarian, Ian A. Wilson

West Branch Public Library, Lancaster Mall, 621 Fairville Blvd., Saint John NB E2M 4X5 – 506/658-2974 – Branch Manager, Barbara Mackay

St. Croix Public Library, 1 Budd Ave., St. Stephen NB E3L 1E8 – 506/466-4781; Fax: 506/466-1510 – Branch Manager, Elva Hatt

Sussex Public Library, Main St., PO Box 1496, Sussex NB E0E 1P0 – 506/433-7215; Fax: 506/433-2538; Symbol: NBS – Branch Manager, Pauline Giberson

YORK REGIONAL LIBRARY

4 Carleton St., Fredericton NB E3B 5P4 – 506/453-5380; Fax: 506/457-4878; Email: libyr@gov.nb.ca; Symbol: NBFYR

Regional Librarian, Laurette Mackey

Reference Librarian, Greg Blake

Children's Librarian, Marilyn Dennis

Technical Services Librarian, Geraldine Stanaway

Boiestown Community-School Library, PO Box 99, Boiestown NB E0H 1A0 – 506/369-2022; Fax: 506/369-2023 – Branch Manager, Gail Ross

Chatham Public Library, PO Box 446, Chatham NB E1N 3A8 – 506/773-6274; Fax: 506/773-6963 – Branch Manager, Patricia Clancy

Chipman Public Library, Chipman NB E0E 1C0 – 506/338-5842; Fax: 506/339-6197 – Branch Manager, Krista Blyth

Doaktown Community-School Library, 438 Main St., PO Box 58, Doaktown NB E0C 1G0 – 506/365-2018; Fax: 506/365-2019 – Branch Manager, Belva Brown

Andrew & Laura McCain Public Library, PO Box 270, Florenceville NB E0J 1K0 – 506/392-5294; Fax: 506/392-6143 – Branch Manager, Lorena Green

Bibliothèque Dr Marguerite Michaud, Centre communautaire Ste-Anne, 715, rue Priestman, Fredericton NB E3B 5W1 – 506/455-1740; Téléc: 506/453-3958 – Bibliothécaire, Françoise Caron

Fredericton Public Library, 12 Carleton St., Fredericton NB E3B 5P4 – 506/458-8154; Fax: 506/450-6167 – City Librarian, William Molesworth

Minto Public Library, 19 Maple St., Minto NB E0E 1J0 – 506/327-3220; Fax: 506/327-3041 – Branch Manager, Mary Lambropoulos

Nashwaaksis Public School Library, 324 Fulton Ave., Fredericton NB E3A 2C3 – 506/453-3241; Fax: 506/444-4129 – Branch Manager, Ruth Russell

Dr. Walter Chestnut Public Library, PO Box 120, Hartland NB E0J 1N0 – 506/375-4876; Fax: 506/375-4938 – Branch Manager, Ann Ellis

Harvey Community Library, Harvey Station NB E0H 1H0 – 506/366-2206; Fax: 506/366-2210 – Branch Manager, Joanne Cole

McAdam Public Library, 146 Saunders Rd., McAdam NB E0H 1K0 – 506/784-1403; Fax: 506/784-3218 – Branch Manager, Catherine Dougherty

Nackawic Public & School Library, Nackawic NB E0H 1P0 – 506/575-2336; Fax: 506/575-2336 – Branch Manager, Carolyn Munroe

Bibliothèque Père-Louis-Lamontagne, Carrefour-Beausoleil, 300, ch Beaverbrook, Newcastle NB E1V 1A1 – 506/627-4084; Téléc: 506/622-6361 – Bibliothécaire, Sylvan Lavoie

Newcastle Public Library, 100 Fountain Head Lane, Newcastle NB E1V 4A1 – 506/627-2545; Fax: 506/622-6503 – Librarian, Catherine Reid

Oromocto Public Library, 54 Miramichi Rd., Oromocto NB E2L 1S2 – 506/357-3320; Fax: 506/357-2266 – Librarian, Muriel Morton

Perth-Andover Public Library, PO Box 128, Perth-Andover NB E0J 1V0 – 506/273-2843; Fax: 506/273-1913 – Branch Manager, Tammie De Merchant

Plaster Rock Public-School Library, Tobique Valley High School, Plaster Rock NB E0J 1W0 – 506/356-6018; Fax: 506/356-6019 – Branch Manager, Carolyn Knowlton

Stanley Public Library, PO Box 108, Stanley NB E0H 1T0 – 506/367-2492; Fax: 506/367-3166 – Contact, Rhonda Smith

L.P. Fisher Public Library, 679 Main St., PO Box 1540, Woodstock NB E0J 2B0 – 506/328-8660; Fax: 506/325-4486 – Branch Manager, Jonathan Tait

Sub Headquarters, 113 Cedar St., PO Box 2050, Woodstock NB E0J 2B0 – 506/325-4485; Fax: 506/325-4486 – Supervising Librarian, Meredith MacKeen

Special & College Libraries & Resource Centres

BATHURST

Chaleur Regional Hospital – Library, 1750 Sunset Dr., Bathurst NB E2A 4L7 – 506/344-2261 – Suzanne Doucet

New Brunswick Community College - Bathurst Campus Library, rue Collège, CP 266, Bathurst NB E2A 3Z2 – 506/547-7495; Fax: 506/547-2174; Symbol: NBBCC – Bibliothécaire, Lucien Chassé

CAMPBELLTON

New Brunswick Community College - Campbellton Campus Library, rue Village, PO Box 309, Campbellton NB E3N 3G7 – 506/789-2377; Fax: 506/753-3523 – Librarian, Pierre Paul Chausse

CARAQUET

Fédération des caisses populaires acadiennes ltée – Bibliothèque, Place de l'Acadie, 295, boul St-Pierre ouest, CP 920, Caraquet NB E0B 1K0 – 506/727-6565, 1300 – Conseiller en gestion doc., Steve Godin

CHATHAM

New Brunswick Community College - Miramichi Campus Library, 80 University Ave., PO Box 1053, Chatham NB E1N 3W4 – 506/778-9451 – Librarian, Samuel Inch

DIEPPE

New Brunswick Community College - Dieppe Campus Library, 505, rue du Collège, PO Box 4519, Dieppe NB E1A 6G1 – 506/856-2200; Fax: 506/856-2125

DORCHESTER

Solicitor General Canada - Dorchester Penitentiary - Library, PO Box A, Dorchester NB E0A 1M0 – 506/857-6363, ext.2508; Symbol: NBDD – Librarian, Bill Geier

Westmorland Institution - Library, PO Box 130, Dorchester NB E0A 1M0 – 506/379-2471, ext.3503; Symbol: NBDW – Librarian, Tim Atkinson

EDMUNDSTON

Centre Universitaire Saint-Louis Mallet, 165, boul Hebert, Edmundston NB E3V 2S8 – 506/737-5050; Téléc: 506/737-5373 – Bibliotechnicienne, Claire Charest

Fraser Inc. – Central Technical Research Library, 27 Rice St., Edmundston NB E3V 1S9 – 506/735-5551 – Manager, Jean-Claude Martin

New Brunswick Community College - Edmundston Campus Library, PO Box 70, Edmundston NB E3V 3K7 – 506/735-2500; Fax: 506/735-1108; Symbol: NBECC – Librarian, Kenda Clark-Gorey

FREDERICTON

New Brunswick Department of Agriculture - Land Resources Branch – Library, PO Box 6000, Fredericton NB E3B 5H1 – 506/453-2109

New Brunswick Research & Productivity Council – RPC Info Centre, 921 College Hill Rd., Fredericton NB E3B 6Z9 – 506/452-1381; Fax: 506/452-1395; Email: vjackson@rpc.unb.ca; Symbol: NPFRP – Co-ordinator, Virginia Jackson

ADI Group Inc. – Library, PO Box 44, Fredericton NB E3B 4Y2 – 506/452-9000; Email: dee@adi.ca – Librarian, Debra Edmondson

Agriculture & Agri-Food Canada-Fredericton Research Centre – Library, 850 Lincoln Rd., PO Box 20280, Fredericton NB E3B 4Z7 – 506/452-3260; Email: lbnbfag@ncccot.agr.ca; Symbol: NBFAG – Librarian, Richard Anderson

AIDS New Brunswick – Bibliothèque, 65 Brunswick St., Fredericton NB E3B 1G5 – 506/459-7518, 506/450-2620 – Caroline Ploem

Association des enseignantes et des enseignants francophones du Nouveau-Brunswick – Bibliothèque, CP 712, Fredericton NB E3B 5B4 – 506/452-8921 – Germaine Burns

Association Museums New Brunswick – Resource Centre, 503 Queen St., PO Box 116, Fredericton NB E3B 4Y2 – 506/452-2908

Canada/New Brunswick Service Centre - Resource Centre, 570 Queen St., Fredericton NB E3B 6Z6 – 506/444-6158; Toll Free: 1-800-668-1010 – Information Agent, Paulianne McLellan

Conservation Council of New Brunswick – Library, 180 St. John St., Fredericton NB E3B 4A9 – 506/458-8747

Dr. Everett Chalmers Hospital – Health Sciences Library, PO Box 9000, Fredericton NB E3B 5N5 – 506/452-5432; Fax: 506/452-5571; Email: ENVOY: ILL.NBFDEC – Librarian, Paul Clark

Fraser, Smith & Townsend Law Office - Library, Toronto-Dominion Tower, #430, 77 Westmorland St., PO Box 38, Fredericton NB E3B 4Y2 – 506/452-9900; Fax: 506/452-6726 – Bernice MacGregor

Law Society of New Brunswick – Library, #206, 1133 Regent St., Fredericton NB E3B 3Z2 – 506/453-

2500; Fax: 506/453-9438 – Law Librarian, Diane Hanson

Natural Resources Canada-Canadian Forest Service: Atlantic Centre – Library, Hugh John Flemming Forestry Centre, College Hill, PO Box 4000, Fredericton NB E3B 5P7 – 506/452-3541; Fax: 506/452-3525; Email: mrenner@fcmr.forestry.ca; Symbol: NBFE – Regional Librarian, Melinda Renner

New Brunswick Advanced Education & Labour - Library, 470 York St., PO Box 6000, Fredericton NB E3B 5H1 – 506/453-8247; Fax: 506/453-3806; Email: mcomeau@gov.nb.ca – Administrative Services Officer, Mary Comeau

New Brunswick Agriculture - Publication Centre, PO Box 6000, Fredericton NB E3B 5H1 – 506/453-2333; Fax: 506/453-7978 – Information Officer, Amrik Jaswal

New Brunswick College of Craft & Design - Library, PO Box 6000, Fredericton NB E3B 5H1 – 506/453-2305; Fax: 506/457-7352 – Honorary Librarian, Barbara M. Smith

New Brunswick Department of the Environment - Library, 364 Argyle St., 2nd Fl., Fredericton NB E3B 1T9 – 506/453-2566; Fax: 506/453-3843; Symbol: NBFME – Librarian, Gail Darby

New Brunswick Economic Development & Tourism - Records Management/Library, PO Box 6000, Fredericton NB E3B 5H1 – 506/453-2187; Fax: 506/444-5299
   Records Manager, Sandra Thomas
   Departmental Library, Frances Scott

New Brunswick Education - Library, PO Box 6000, Fredericton NB E3B 5H1 – 506/453-3229; Fax: 506/453-3325; Symbol: NBFED – Librarian, Judith Colter, M.L.S.

New Brunswick Electric Power Commission - Reference Centre, 527 King St., Fredericton NB E3B 4X1 – 506/458-4027; Fax: 506/458-4390 – Julie A. Robinson

New Brunswick Federation of Agriculture – Library, #201, 1115 Regent St., Fredericton NB E3B 3X2 – 506/452-8101 – Policy Officer, Bruce Oliver

New Brunswick Finance - Library, #373, Centennial Bldg., PO Box 6000, Fredericton NB E3B 5H1 – 506/453-2511 – Chief Librarian, Katherine Brennan

New Brunswick Health & Community Services - Library, Carleton Place, 3rd Fl., PO Box 5100, Fredericton NB E3B 5G8 – 506/453-3715; Fax: 506/453-2958; Email: librarydoh@gov.nb.ca; Symbol: NBFH – Chief Librarian, Carole Ford, 506/453-3715

New Brunswick Healthcare Association – Library, 861 Woodstock Rd., RR#3, Fredericton NB E3B 4X4 – 506/451-0750

New Brunswick Legislative Library, Legislative Bldg., PO Box 6000, Fredericton NB E3B 5H1 – 506/453-2338; Fax: 506/444-5889; Email: bibleglib@gov.nb.ca; Symbol: NBFL
   Chief Librarian, Eric L. Swanick
   Reference Librarian, Margaret Pacey
   Government Publications Librarian, Janet McNeil
   Technical Services Librarian, Jean-Claude Arcand

New Brunswick Lung Association – Library, Victoria Health Centre, #257, 65 Brunswick St., Fredericton NB E3B 1G5 – 506/455-8961; Toll Free: 1-800-565-5864 – Program Coordinator, Susan Kelso

New Brunswick Natural Resources & Energy - Library, PO Box 6000, Fredericton NB E3B 5H1 – 506/453-5478; Fax: 506/444-4367; Email: ENVOY: ILL.NBFNR – Library Technician, Sheila Robinson

New Brunswick Occupational Health & Safety Commission - Library, PO Box 6000, Fredericton NB E3B 5H1 – 506/453-2467; Fax: 506/453-7982 – Director, Administration & Human Resources, Joanne Walker

New Brunswick Ombudsman - Library, PO Box 6000, Fredericton NB E3B 5H1 – 506/453-2789; Fax: 506/444-4087; Toll Free: 1-800-561-4021 – Secretary, Giséle Girouard

New Brunswick Statistics Agency - Library, Centennial Bldg., #248, 670 King St., Fredericton NB E3B 5H1 – 506/453-2381; Fax: 506/453-7970 – Secretary, Mary Lou Farris

New Brunswick Supply & Services - Information Services Group Library, #200, Westmorland Pl., PO Box 6000, Fredericton NB E3B 5H1 – 506/453-3807; Fax: 506/453-2270; Email: ENVOY: NBFDSS; Symbol: NBFDSS – Librarian, David Campbell

New Brunswick Teachers' Association – Library, PO Box 752, Fredericton NB E3B 5R6 – 506/452-1726 – Germaine Burns

New Brunswick Translation Bureau - Library, Marysville Place, PO Box 6000, Fredericton NB E3B 5H1 – 506/453-2920; Fax: 506/459-7911; Symbol: NBFT
   Chief Librarian, Lucie Laperrière
   Assistant Librarian, Suzanne Pelletier

New Brunswick Transportation - Library, PO Box 6000, Fredericton NB E3B 5H1 – 506/453-2535; Fax: 506/444-5790; Email: adm041@gov.nb.ca; Symbol: NBFTR
   Library Manager, Bonnie Ellis
   Library Assistant, Lisette Dionne

Nurses Association of New Brunswick – Library, 165 Regent St., Fredericton NB E3B 3W5 – 506/458-8731 – Librarian, Barbara Thompson

Tourism Industry Association of New Brunswick Inc. – Library, Prospect Place, #206, 191 Prospect St., Fredericton NB E3B 2T7 – 506/458-5646 – Program Director, Karen Richard

University of New Brunswick - Harriet Irving Library, PO Box 7500, Fredericton NB E3B 5H5 – 506/453-4572; Fax: 506/453-4595; Symbol: NBFU
   Director of Libraries, John D. Teskey
   Associate Director of Libraries, Dr. Alan Burk
   Technical Services, Head, Judith Aldus
   Collection Development, Head, Judith Colson
   Engineering Library, Head, Doris Rauch, 506/453-4747
   Science & Forestry Library, Head, Eszter Schwenke, 506/453-4601
   Education Resource Centre, Head, Patricia Johnston, 506/453-3516
   Research & Information Services, Coordinator, John Neilson, 506/453-4749

Writers' Federation of New Brunswick – Library, PO Box 37, Fredericton NB E3B 4Y2 – 506/459-7228 – Project Coordinator, Anna Mae Snider

GRAND-SAULT

New Brunswick Community College - Grand-Sault Campus Library, 160, rue Réservoir, PO Box 1270, Grand-Sault NB E3Z 1C6 – 506/473-7733; Fax: 506/473-7769 – Librarian, Kenda Clark-Gorey

MONCTON

Association des conseillers et conseillères scolaires francophones du Nouveau-Brunswick – Bibliothèque, 27, rue John, Moncton NB E1C 2G7 – 506/857-2263 – Secrétaire administrative, Léon Richard

Atlantic Baptist University - George A. Rawlyk Memorial Library, PO Box 6004, Moncton NB E1C 9L7 – 506/858-8970; Fax: 506/858-9694; Email: douthwri@nbnet.nb.ca; ENVOY: ATL.BAP.COL; Symbol: NBMAB – Librarian, Ivan W. Douthwright

Atlantic Lottery Corporation - Library, PO Box 5500, Moncton NB E1C 8W6 – 506/867-5846; Fax: 506/867-5616; Email: atloto6@nbnet.nb.ca – Librarian, Wendy Donnahee

Canadian Air Transport Administration - Atlantic Regional Library, Place Heritage Court, 95 Foundry St., 5th Fl., PO Box 42, Moncton NB E1C 8K6 – 506/857-7360; Fax: 506/851-3018; Symbol: NBMOTA

Embroiderers' Association of Canada, Inc. – Leonida Leatherdale Library, 1311 Salisbury Rd., RR#1, Moncton NB E1C 8J5 – 506/852-8816 – Helen McCrindle

Environment Canada-Environmental Conservation Service - Environmental Quality Laboratories - Moncton – Library, Environmental Science Centre, PO Box 23005, Moncton NB E1A 6S8 – 506/851-6606 – Administrative Assistant, L. Boulter

Fisheries & Oceans Canada - Atlantic Fisheries, Gulf Region Library, 343 Archibald St., PO Box 5030, Moncton NB E1C 9B6 – 506/851-6264; Fax: 506/857-7732; Email: ENVOY: DFO.LIB.MONCTON; Symbol: NBMF – Librarian, Paulette Lévesque, 506/857-6226

Fowler & Fowler Law Office - Library, #11, 885 Main St., PO Box 721, Moncton NB E1C 8M9 – 506/857-8811; Fax: 506/857-9297 – James E. Fowler

Hôpital Dr. Georges L. Dumont – Bibliothèque des sciences de la santé, 330, rue Archibald, Moncton NB E1C 2Z3 – 506/862-4247; Courrier électronique: ENVOY: ILL.NBMHD; Symbol: NBMHD – Bibliothécaire, Marthe Brideau

Moncton Hospital – Health Sciences Library – South-East Health Care Corp., 135 MacBeath Ave., Moncton NB E1C 6Z8 – 506/857-5447; Email: ENVOY: NBMMH; mctnhosp@nbnet.nb.ca; Symbol: NBMMH – Librarian, S.P. Libby

New Brunswick Community College - Moncton Campus Library, 1234 Mountain Rd., Moncton NB E1C 8H9 – 506/856-2226; Fax: 506/856-3288; Symbol: NBMOCC – Librarian, Bill Hegan

Public Works & Government Services Canada - Superannuation Branch - Reference Library, PO Box 5010, Moncton NB E1C 8Z5 – 506/533-5681; Fax: 506/533-5558; Symbol: NBMOS – Documentation Coordinator, Marie-Marthe Sarrazin

Université de Moncton - Bibliothèque Champlain, Centre universitaire de Moncton, 165, av Massey, Moncton NB E1A 3E9 – 506/858-4012; Téléc: 506/858-4086; Symbol: NBMOU
   Bibliothécaire en chef, Albert Lévesque
   Bibliothèque de droit, Directrice, S. Clermont, 506/858-4547
   Centre d'études acadiennes, Bibliothécaire, Gilles Chiasson, 506/858-4085
   Centre de ressources pédagogiques, Directrice, Berthe Boudreau, 506/858-4356
   Centre universitaire de Shippagan, Directrice, Rose-Marie Gauthier
   Centre universitaire St-Louis-Maillet, Directeur, Joanine Michaud, 506/737-5050

NEWCASTLE

Newcastle Hospital – Library, 673 King George Hwy., PO Box 420, Newcastle NB E1V 3M5 – 506/627-7041; Fax: 506/627-7029; Email: mirhslib@nbnet.nb.ca; Symbol: NBNM – Health Sciences Librarian, Nancy McAllister

PRINCE WILLIAM

Kings Landing Library, Route 2, Exit 259, Prince William NB E0H 1S0 – 506/363-5090; Fax: 506/363-5757; Email: cnbkl@chin.cycor.ca
   Director, Bob Dallison
   Curator of Collections, Don Lemon

RENOUS

Solicitor General Canada - Atlantic Institution - Library, PO Box 74, Renous NB E0C 1X0 – 506/623-4060; Fax: 506/623-4017; Symbol: NBRA – Librarian, Murray Baillie

ROTHESAY

Colin Mackay Memorial Library - RCS-Netherwood, Rothesay NB E0G 2W0 – 506/847-8224; Fax: 506/849-9101; Email: rcsnthwd@nbnet.nb.ca – Librarian, Jennifer Leger, M.L.I.S.

SACKVILLE

Environment Canada - Canadian Wildlife Service, Atlantic Region - Library, PO Box 1590, Sackville NB E0A 3C0 – 506/364-5019; Fax: 506/364-5062; Email: sealyj@ns.doe.ca; Symbol: NBSACW – Librarian, Jean Sealy

Mount Allison University - Ralph Pickard Bell Library, Sackville NB E0A 3C0 – 506/364-2562; Fax: 506/364-2617; Email: ENVOY: ILL.NBSAM
University Librarian, Sara Lochhead
Technical Services, Head, Ruthmary MacPherson

ST. ANDREWS

Atlantic Salmon Federation – Library, PO Box 429, St. Andrews NB E0G 2X0 – 506/529-4581 – Librarian, Carol James

Fisheries & Oceans Canada-St. Andrews Biological Station – Library, Dept. of Fisheries & Oceans, Brandy Cove Rd., St. Andrews NB E0G 2X0 – 506/529-8854; Email: library@sta.dfo.ca; Symbol: NBAB – Librarian, Marilynn Rudi

New Brunswick Community College - St. Andrews Campus Library, PO Box 427, St. Andrews NB E0G 2X0 – 506/529-5070; Fax: 506/529-5009; Symbol: NBSTAC – Librarian, Mary Doon, 506/529-5070

SAINT JOHN

Centre communautaire Samuel-de-Champlain, Boar's Head, RR#1, Saint John NB E2L 3W2 – 506/658-4600

New Brunswick Community College - Saint John Campus - L.R. Fulton Library & Audio Visual Centre, PO Box 2270, Saint John NB E2L 3V1 – 506/658-6727; Fax: 506/658-6792 – Librarian, Dewan Sachdeva

New Brunswick Museum - Library, 277 Douglas Ave., Saint John NB E2K 1E5 – 506/643-2322; Fax: 506/643-2360; Symbol: NBSM – Coordinator, Gary Hughes, 506/643-2322

New Brunswick Youth Orchestra – Library, 38 Cliff St., Saint John NB E2L 3A7 – 506/657-1498 – Librarian, Charles Estabrooks

Region 2 Hospital Corporation – Library Services, c/o Saint John Regional Hospital, PO Box 2100, Saint John NB E2L 4L2 – 506/648-6763; Fax: 506/648-6764; Symbol: NBSRH – Director, Anne Kilfoil

Saint John Jewish Historical Museum – Jewish Museum Library, 29 Wellington Row, Saint John NB E2L 3H4 – 506/633-1833 – Assistant to the Curator, Katherine Biggs

Saint John Law Society – Library, 110 Charlotte St., Saint John NB E2L 2J3 – 506/658-2542 – Librarian, Marilyn Brown

The Telegraph-Journal/The Evening Times-Globe - Library, 210 Crown St., PO Box 2350, Saint John NB E2L 3V8 – 506/632-8888

University of New Brunswick - Ward Chipman Library, PO Box 5050, Saint John NB E2L 4L5 – 506/648-5700; Fax: 506/648-5701; Symbol: NBSU
Reference Librarian, William Kerr, Email: kerr@unbst.ca
Director, Susan Collins

ST. MARTINS

Carson Memorial Library, St. Martins NB E0G 2Z0 – 506/833-4740 – Librarian, Elizabeth Thibodeau, 506/833-4324

SUSSEX

Bethany Bible College - Rogers Memorial Library, Sussex NB E0E 1P0 – 506/432-4400, ext.470; Fax: 506/432-4425
Director, Library Services, Howard Cogswell
Library Assistant, Eileen Gavel

WOODSTOCK

New Brunswick Community College - Woodstock Library, PO Box 1175, Woodstock NB E0J 2B0 – 506/325-4400; Fax: 506/328-8426; Email: NBCCWood@nbnet.nb.ca; Symbol: NBCC – Librarian, Margaret McAllister

NEWFOUNDLAND

Regional Library Systems with Member Libraries

CENTRAL NEWFOUNDLAND LIBRARY DIVISION

PO Box 3333, Gander NF A1V 1X2 – 709/651-2781; Fax: 709/256-2194; Email: ENVOY 100: ADMIN.CR
Librarian, Patricia Parsons
Librarian, Ralph Dale

Baie Vertep Public Library, PO Box 178, Baie Verte NF A0K 1B0 – 709/532-8361 – Library Technician, Debbie Yetman

Bishop's Falls Public Library, PO Box 329, Bishop's Falls NF A0H 1C0 – 709/258-6244 – Library Technician, Cora Stanley

Botwood Public Library, PO Box 749, Botwood NF A0H 1E0 – 709/257-2091 – Library Technician, Mariem Gill

Buchans Public Library, PO Box 99, Buchans NF A0H 1G0 – 709/672-3859 – Library Technician, Diane Burton

Carmanville Public Library, Carmanville NF A0G 1N0 – 709/534-2370 – Library Technician, Kay Butt

Centreville Public Library, PO Box 100, Wareham-Centreville NF A0G 4P0 – 709/678-2700 – Library Technician, Gertrude Collins

Change Islands Public Library, PO Box 40, Change Islands NF A0G 1R0 – 709/621-5566 – Library Technician, Christine Hoffe

Dover Public Library, PO Box 250, Dover NF A0G 1X0 – 709/537-5763 – Library Technician, Linda Rogers

Fogo Island Public Library, Fogo Island NF A0G 2B0 – 709/266-2210 – Library Technician, Marion Foley

Gambo Public Library, PO Box 10, Gambo NF A0G 1T0 – 709/674-5052 – Librarian, Sylvia Collins

Gander Public Library, PO Box 4444, Gander NF A1V 1X2 – 709/256-3282 – Library Technician, Glenda Peddle

Gaultois Public Library, PO Box 100, Gaultois NF A0H 1N0 – Library Technican, Phyllis Harris

Glenwood Public Library, PO Box 40, Glenwood NF A0G 2K0 – 709/679-5700 – Library Technician, Michelle Stuckless

Alexander Bay Public Library, PO Box 70, Glovertown NF A0G 2L0 – 709/533-6688 – Library Technician, Audrey Lane

Harmsworth Public Library, Arts & Culture Centre, Cromer Ave., Grand Falls-Windsor NF A2A 1W9 – 709/489-2303 – Library Technician, Elizabeth Waye

Greenspond Public Library, PO Box 70, Greenspond NF A0G 2N0 – Library Technician, Mae Dyke

Harbour Breton Public Library, PO Box 569, Harbour Breton NF A0H 1P0 – 709/885-2165 – Library Technician, Vivian Bennett

Hare Bay Public Library, Hare Bay NF A0G 2P0 – 709/537-2391 – Library Technician, Sylvia Collins

Harry's Harbour Public Library, Harry's Harbour NF A0J 1E0 – Library Technician, Ellen King

Hermitage Public Library, PO Box 159, Hermitage NF A0H 1S0 – 709/883-2421 – Library Technician, Bernice Willmott

Tilley Memorial Public Library, PO Box 23, Kings Point NF A0J 1H0 – 709/268-2282 – Library Technician, Greta Noble

La Scie Public Library, La Scie NF A0K 3M0 – 709/675-2004 – Library Technician, Mrs. Jackie Sheppard

Lewisporte Public Library, Lewisporte NF A0G 3A0 – 709/535-2519 – Library Technician, Judy Snow

Lumsden Public Library, Lumsden NF A0G 3E0 – 709/530-2617 – Library Technician, Beatrice Stagg

John B. Wheeler Public Library, PO Box 130, Musgrave Harbour NF A0G 3J0 – 709/655-2730 – Library Technician, Donna Noseworthy

Norris Arm Public Library, PO Box 100, Norris Arm NF A0G 3M0 – 709/653-2531 – Library Technician, Judy Rowsell

Point Leamington Public Library, PO Box 76, Point Leamington NF A0H 1Z0 – 709/484-3541 – Library Technician, Emma Rolfe

Roberts Arm Public Library, PO Box 119, Roberts Arm NF A0J 1R0 – 709/652-3100 – Library Technician, Brenda Taylor

St Albans Public Library, PO Box 70, St Albans NF A0H 2E0 – 709/538-3034 – Library Technician, Melinda Walsh

Seal Cove Public Library, PO Box 70, Seal Cove NF A0K 5E0 – 709/531-2505 – Library Technician, Madeline Parsons

Naskapi School Public Library, Sops Arm NF A0K 5K0 – 709/482-2422 – Library Technician, Beatrice Pinksen

Springdale Public Library, PO Box 100, Springdale NF A0J 1T0 – 709/673-4169 – Library Technician, Golda Burton

Summerford Public Library, Summerford NF A0G 4E0 – 709/629-3244; Fax: 709/629-3419 – Library Technician, Mavis Boyd

Twillingate Public Library, PO Box 338, Twillingate NF A0G 4M0 – 709/884-2353 – Library Technician, Barbara Hamlyn

Wesleyville Public Library, Wesleyville NF A0G 4R0 – 709/536-5777 – Library Technician, Beverley Hounsell; Library Technician, Marion Hennebury

EASTERN NEWFOUNDLAND LIBRARY DIVISION

Arts & Culture Centre, Allendale Rd., St. John's NF A1B 3A3 – 709/737-3505; 3508; Fax: 709/737-2660; Symbol: NFED
Regional Librarian, John White, Email: jfwhite@calvin.stemnet.nf.ca

Arnold's Cove Public Library, Arnold's Cove NF A0B 1A0 – 709/463-8707 – Library Technician, Lisa Giles

Bay Roberts Public Library, Water St., PO Box 610, Bay Roberts NF A0A 1G0 – 709/786-9629 – Library Technician, Linda Miller

Bell Island Public Library, Wabana, Bell Island NF A0A 4H0 – 709/488-2413 – Library Technician, Lois Clarke

Bonavista Memorial Library, PO Box 400, Bonavista NF A0C 1B0 – 709/468-2185 – Library Technician, Brenda Wilton

Brigus Public Library, Brigus NF A0A 1K0 – 709/528-3156 – Library Technician, Elsie Percy

Burin Memorial Library, PO Box 306, Burin NF A0E 1E0 – 709/891-1924 – Library Technician, Marilyn Beazley

Carbonear Public Library, PO Box 928, Carbonear NF A1Y 1C4 – 709/596-3382 – Library Technician, Brenda Peach

Joseph Clouter Memorial Library, Catalina NF A0C 1J0 – 709/469-3045 – Library Technician, Kimberley Johnson

Clarenville Public Library, PO Box 2550, Clarenville NF A0E 1J0 – 709/466-7634 – Library Technician, Marvin Pitts

Fortune Memorial Library, Fortune NF A0E 1P0 – 709/832-0232 – Library Technician, Fay Dominie

Fox Harbour Public Library, Fox Harbour NF A0B 1V0 – 709/227-2271 – Library Technician, Catherine Murray

G. Hollett Memorial Library, Garnish NF A0E 1T0 – 709/826-2371 – Library Technician, Anne Riley

Canadian Almanac & Directory 1997

Grand Bank Memorial Library, PO Box 1000, Grand Bank NF A0E 1W0 – 709/832-0310 – Library Technician, Mildred Watts
Harbour Grace Public Library, Harbour Grace NF A0A 2M0 – 709/596-3894 – Library Technician, Doreen Quinn
Holyrood Public Library, PO Box 263, Holyrood NF A0A 2R0 – 709/229-7852 – Library Technician, Diane Mann
Conception Bay South Public Library, PO Box 580, Manuels NF A1W 1N1 – 709/834-4241 – Library Technician, Bertha Rideout
Marystown Memorial Library, PO Box 1270, Marystown NF A0E 2M0 – 709/279-1507 – Library Technician, Patricia Mayo
Mount Pearl Public & Resource Library, PO Box 880, Mount Pearl NF A1N 3C8 – 709/368-3603 – Library Technician, Linda Quinn
Old Perlican Public Library, Old Perlican NF A0A 3G0 – 709/587-2639 – Library Technician, Christina McNeil
Placentia Public Library, Placentia NF A0B 2Y0 – 709/227-3621 – Library Technician, Doris Bowering
Pouch Cove Public Library, PO Box 40, Pouch Cove NF A0A 3L0 – 709/335-2652 – Library Technician, Diane Mulley
Cape Shore Public Library, St. Bride's NF A0B 2Z0 – 709/337-2360 – Library Technician, Mary Coffey
St. Lawrence Public Library, Memorial Dr., St. Lawrence NF A0E 2V0 – 709/873-2650 – Library Technician, Meta Turpin
Southern Harbour Public Library, Southern Habour NF A0B 3H0 – 709/463-8814 – Library Technician, Bride Whiffen
Spaniard's Bay Public Library, Spaniard's Bay NF A0A 3X0 – 709/786-3568 – Library Technician, Marilyn Clarke
E. Morey Memorial Public Library, 1288A Torbay Rd., Torbay NF A1K 1B2 – 709/437-6571 – Library Technician, Marie Evans
Trepassey Public Library, Trepassey NF A0A 4B0 – 709/438-2224 – Library Technician, Ted Winter
Upper Island Cove Public Library, Upper Island Cove NF A0A 4E0 – 709/589-2090 – Library Technician, Clara Peckford
Victoria Public Library, Victoria NF A0A 4G0 – 709/596-3682 – Library Technician, Mary Sutton
Whitbourne Public Library, Whitbourne NF A0B 3K0 – 709/759-2461 – Library Technician, Gloria Somerton
Winterton Public Library, Winterton NF A0B 3M0 – 709/583-2810 – Library Technician, Betty Pitcher

NEWFOUNDLAND PROVINCIAL RESOURCE LIBRARY

Arts & Culture Centre, Allendale Rd., St. John's NF A1B 3A3 – 709/737-3946; Fax: 709/737-2660; Email: cameron@morgan.ucs.mun.ca
Manager, Charles Cameron
Reference Librarian, Anne Lawson
Circulation & Branch Librarian, Victoria Murphy
Children's Librarian, Heather Myers
Newfoundland Collection Librarian, Brenda Parmenter

A.C. Hunter Library, Arts & Culture Centre, Allendale Rd., St. John's NF A1B 3A3 – 709/737-3950 (Adults); 737-3953 (Children); Fax: 709/737-3953
Marjorie Mews Library, Highland Plaza, 18 Highland Dr., St. John's NF A1A 3C5 – 709/737-2621 – Library Technician, Glenda Quinn
Michael Donovan Library, 655 Topsail Rd., St. John's NF A1E 2E3 – 709/737-2621 – Library Technician, Rita Roberts

WEST NEWFOUNDLAND-LABRADOR LIBRARY DIVISION

5 Union St., Corner Brook NF A2H 5M7 – 709/634-7333; Fax: 709/634-7313; Email: ENVOY 100: ADMIN.WR

Librarian, Elinor Benjamin, Email: elinorb@morgan.ucs.mun.ca
Librarian, Sandy Chilcote

Burgeo Public Library, PO Box 370, Burgeo NF A0M 1A0 – 709/886-2730 – Library Technician, Freda MacDonald
Cape St. George Public Library, PO Box 191, Cape St. George NF A0N 1E0 – 709/644-2852; Email: cmstuckl@calvin.stemnet.nf.ca – Library Technician, Cynthia Stuckless
Cartwright Public Library, PO Box 166, Cartwright NF A0K 1V0 – 709/938-7219 – Library Technician, Robyn Holwell
Churchill Falls Public Library, PO Box 160, Churchill Falls NF A0R 1A0 – 709/925-3281 – Library Technician, Anne Murphy
Corner Brook City Library, Sir Richard Squires Bldg., Mt. Bernard Ave., Corner Brook NF A2H 6J8 – 709/634-0013; Fax: 709/634-0330; Email: lwest@calvin.stemnet.nf.ca – Librarian, Lynne West
Cow Head Public Library, Cow Head NF A0K 2A0 – 709/243-2467 – Library Technician, Nora Shears
Daniel's Harbour Public Library, PO Box 39, Daniel's Harbour NF A0K 2C0 – 709/898-2283 – Library Technician, Edith Guinchard
Cormack Public Library, RR#2, PO Box 524, Deer Lake NF A0K 2E0 – 709/635-7022 – Library Technician, Marie Morris
Deer Lake Public Library, PO Bag 2002, Deer Lake NF A0K 2E0 – 709/635-3671; Email: wcramm@calvin.stemnet.nf.ca – Library Technician, Worneta Cramm
Codroy Valley Public/School Library, General Delivery, Doyles NF A0N 1J0 – 709/955-2940; Fax: 709/955-2620 – Library Technician, Wilfreida Bungay
Melville Public Library, Elizabeth Goudie Bldg., Happy Valley NF A0P 1E0 – 709/896-8045 – Library Technician, Hyra Skoglund
Labrador City Public Library, 306 Hudson Dr., Labrador City NF A2V 1L5 – 709/944-2190; Fax: 709/944-3674; Email: efoley@calvin.stemnet.nf.ca – Library Technician, Ethel Foley
Labrador South Public Library, L'Anse au Loup NF A0K 3L0 – 709/927-5542 – Library Technician, Phyllis O'Brien
Blow-Me-Down Public/School Library, Lark Harbour NF A0L 1H0 – 709/681-2620; Email: npickett@calvin.stemnet.nf.ca – Library Technician, Norma Pickett
Lourdes Public/School Library, PO Box 129, Lourdes NF A0N 1R0 – 709/642-5248; Email: esnook@calvin.stemnet.nf.ca – Library Technician, Elizabeth Snook
Norris Point Public Library, Norris Point NF A0K 3V0 – Email: jsamms@calvin.stemnet.nf.ca – Library Technician, Judy Samms
Pasadena Public Library, 16 Tenth Ave., Pasadena NF A0L 1K0 – 709/686-2792 – Library Technician, Gloria Campbell
Curran Memorial Library, Port au Port East NF A0N 1T0 – 709/648-9401 – Shirley Crane
Port Au Port West Public/School Library, General Delivery, Port au Port NF A0N 1T0 – Library Technician, Maureen Abbott
Channel-Port-aux-Basques Public Library, PO Box 790, Port-aux-Basques NF A0M 1C0 – 709/695-3471; Email: bingram@calvin.stemnet.nf.ca – Library Technician, Brenda Ingram
Ingornachoix Public Library, PO Box 59, Port Saunders NF A0K 4H0 – 709/861-3690 – Library Technician, Evelyn Biggin
Marie S. Penney Memorial Library, PO Box 59, Ramea NF A0M 1N0 – 709/625-2344 – Library Technician, Marlene Augustus
Rocky Harbour Public Library, Rocky Harbour, St. Barbe South NF A0K 4N0 – 709/458-2900; Email: besmith@calvin.stemnet.nf.ca – Library Technician, Margaret Parsons
St. Anthony Public Library, PO Box 129, St. Anthony NF A0K 4S0 – 709/454-3025 – Library Technician, Bernice Smith
Bay St. George South Public/School Library, PO Box 70, St. Fintan's NF A0N 1Y0 – 709/645-2780, ext.35; 645-2052 – Library Technician, Anita MacInnis
St Georges Public Library, PO Box 249, St Georges NF A0N 1Z0 – 709/647-3808 – Library Technician, Joan Downey
St. Lunaire-Griquet Public Library, St. Lunaire NF A0K 2X0 – 709/623-2904 – Library Technician, Mae Bussey
Kindale Public Library, 45 Carolina Ave., Stephenville NF A2N 3P8 – 709/643-4262; Fax: 709/643-5781; Email: ymcisaac@calvin.stemnet.nf.ca – Library Technician, Yvonne McIsaac
Stephenville Crossing Public Library, PO Box 610, Stephenville Crossing NF A0N 2C0 – 709/646-2086 – Library Technician, Joan Downey
Wabush Public Library, PO Box 179, Wabush NF A0R 1B0 – 709/282-3479 – Library Technician, Alfreda Harkins
Edgar L. Roberts Memorial Library, PO Box 179, Woody Point NF A0K 1P0 – 709/453-2556 – Library Technician, Dianna Brown

Special & College Libraries & Resource Centres

BONAVISTA

Eastern College of Applied Arts, Technology & Continuing Education - Bonavista Campus Library, PO Box 670, Bonavista NF A0C 1B0 – 709/468-2610

BURIN

Eastern College of Applied Arts, Technology & Continuing Education - Burin Campus Library, PO Box 369, Burin NF A0E 1E0 – 709/891-1253; Fax: 709/891-2256 – Librarian, Gary Peschell

CARBONEAR

Eastern College of Applied Arts, Technology & Continuing Education - Carbonear Campus, PO Box 60, Carbonear NF A1Y 1B5 – 709/596-6139; Fax: 709/596-2688; Email: agoff@calvin.stemnet.nf.ca
Learning Resources Specialist, Alexandra Goff
Library Technician, Sophie Colbourne

CLARENVILLE

Eastern College of Applied Arts, Technology & Continuing Education - Clarenville Campus Library, PO Box 308, Clarenville NF A0E 1J0 – 709/466-0328; Fax: 709/466-2771 – Learning Resources Coordinator, Lynn Cuff

CORNER BROOK

Newfoundland & Labrador Department of Natural Resources - Newfoundland Forest Service - Library, Herald Bldg., PO Box 2006, Corner Brook NF A2H 6J8 – 709/637-2307; Fax: 709/637-2403; Email: bboland@atcon.com; Symbol: NFCBF
Newfoundland & Labrador Environmental Network – Library, PO Box 944, Corner Brook NF A2H 6J2 – 709/634-2520 – Martin von Mirbach
Sir Wilfred Grenfell College - Ferriss Hodgett Library, Memorial University of Newfoundland, University Dr., Corner Brook NF A2H 3A3 – 709/637-6236; Fax: 709/639-8125; Email: ENVOY: GRENFELL.COLLEGE; Symbol: NFCBM – Associate University Librarian, Elizabeth Behrens, Email: ebehrens@beothuk.swgc.mun.ca
Western Memorial Regional Hospital – Health Sciences Library, PO Box 2005, Corner Brook NF A2H 6J7 – 709/637-5395; Fax: 709/634-2649; Email: ENVOY: ILL.WMRH – Librarian, Kimberly Hancock

Westviking College - Corner Brook Campus Library, PO Box 822, Corner Brook NF A2H 6H6 – 709/637-8528; Fax: 709/634-2126 – Librarian, Marian Burnett

GANDER
James Paton Memorial Hospital – Medical Library, 125 TransCanada Hwy., Gander NF A1V 1P7 – 709/256-5760 – Library Technician, Marion Brake

GRAND FALLS-WINDSOR
Central Newfoundland Regional Health Centre – Medical Library, 50 Union St., Grand Falls-Windsor NF A2A 2E1 – 709/292-2228 – Head Librarian, Ellen C Fewer

HAPPY VALLEY-GOOSE BAY
Melville Hospital – Medical Library, Happy Valley-Goose Bay NF A0P 1E0 – 709/896-2417 – Secretary, Glenda Simon

Them Days Inc. – Library, 3 Courtemanche, PO Box 939, Happy Valley-Goose Bay NF A0P 1E0 – 709/896-8531 – Office Manager/Archivist, Gillian H. Saunders

LABRADOR CITY
Captain William Jackman Memorial Hospital – Medical Library, 410 Booth Ave., Labrador City NF A2V 2K1 – 709/944-2632 – Librarian, Margaret Sullivan

MOUNT PEARL
Heywood, Kennedy, Belbin Law Office - Library, 184 Park Avenue, PO Box 250, Mount Pearl NF A1N 2C3 – 709/747-9613; Fax: 709/747-9723 – Jackie Brazil, LL.B.

PLACENTIA
Eastern College of Applied Arts, Technology & Continuing Education - Placentia Campus Library, PO Box 190, Placentia NF A0B 1J0 – 709/227-2037

ST ANTHONY
Charles S. Curtis Memorial Hospital – Library, St Anthony NF A0K 4S0 – 709/454-3333 – Joan Hillier

ST. JOHN'S
Newfoundland & Labrador Department of Environment & Labour - Industrial Environmental Engineering – Library, Confederation Bldg., PO Box 8700, St. John's NF A1B 4J6 – 709/729-2110

Newfoundland & Labrador Department of Fisheries, Food & Agriculture - Soil, Plant & Feed Laboratory – Library, Brookfield Rd., PO Box 8700, St. John's NF A1B 4J6 – 709/729-6587

Action: Environment – Resource Centre, PO Box 2549, St. John's NF A1C 6K1 – 709/579-3729

Agriculture & Agri-Food Canada-St. John's Research Centre – Canadian Agriculture Library, 308 Brookfield Rd., PO Box 7098, St. John's NF A1N 2C1 – 709/772-4169; Fax: 709/772-6064; Email: library@nfrssj.agr.ca; Symbol: LBNFSA – Librarian, Hélène Sabourin

Association of Newfoundland & Labrador Archives – Library, Colonial Building, Military Rd., St. John's NF A1C 2C9 – 709/726-2867

Cabot College of Applied Arts, Technology & Continuing Education - Prince Philip Drive Campus Library, PO Box 1693, St. John's NF A1C 5P7 – 709/778-2547; Fax: 709/778-2648; Email: bneable@admin.cabot.nf.ca
  Librarian, Beverley Neable
  Bell Island Campus Library, Librarian, Marg Hawco, 709/488-2991
  Engineering Technology Centre Library, Librarian, Chitra Paranjape, 709/758-7099
  Parade Street Campus Library, Librarian, Joan Roberts, 709/758-7573
  Seal Cove Campus Library, Librarian, Jerome McGrath, 709/744-2047
  Topsail Road Campus Library, Librarian, Joan Roberts, 709/758-7622

Canada-Newfoundland Offshore Petroleum Board - Library, #500, TD Place, 140 Water St., St. John's NF A1C 6H6 – 709/778-1450; Fax: 709/778-1473
  Librarian, Eileen Blanchard
  Library Technician/Clerk, Lisa Clarke

Canadian Broadcasting Corporation - Broadcast Materials Library, PO Box 12010, St. John's NF A1B 3T8 – 709/576-5049; Fax: 709/576-5011 – Supervisor, Larry O'Brien

City of St. John's - Planning Library, City Hall, New Gower St., PO Box 908, St. John's NF A1C 5M2 – 709/576-8401; Fax: 709/576-8604 – Planner/Research & Information, Robert Butt

Community Services Council, Newfoundland & Labrador – Library, #101, Virginia Park Plaza, Newfoundland Dr., St. John's NF A1A 3E9 – 709/753-9860

Enterprise Newfoundland & Labrador - Business Resource Centre, Viking Building, 136 Crosbie Rd., St. John's NF A1B 3K3 – 709/729-7150; Fax: 709/729-7183; Symbol: NFSNLD
  Manager, Business Resource Centre, Corinne Hynes
  Reference Librarian, Darlene Abbott
  Online Librarian, Heather Roberts

Environment Canada-Environmental Conservation Service - Environmental Quality Laboratories - St. John's – Library, Northwest Atlantic Fisheries Centre, PO Box 5037, St. John's NF A1C 5V3 – 709/772-5488

Environmental Design Consultants - Division of BFL Consultants Ltd. – Library, BFL Place, 133 Crosbie Rd., PO Box 12070, St. John's NF A1B 1H3 – 709/753-6252 – Documents Clerk, Debbie Dooley

Fisheries & Oceans Canada-Northwest Atlantic Fisheries Centre – Library, PO Box 5667, St. John's NF A1C 5X1 – 709/772-2022; Email: conroy@nflorc.nwafc.nf.ca; Symbol: NFSF – Library Contact, Audrey Conroy

The General Hospital/Health Sciences Centre – Health Sciences Library, 300 Prince Philip Dr., St. John's NF A1B 3V6 – 709/758-1308 – Librarian, Cathy Sheehan

Heritage Foundation of Newfoundland & Labrador – Library, PO Box 5171, St. John's NF A1C 5V5 – 709/739-1892

The Hub - Specialized Information Centre, PO Box 13788, St. John's NF A1B 4G3 – 709/754-0352; Fax: 709/722-2110 – Coordinator, Donna Underhay

Law Society of Newfoundland – Library, Atlantic Place, 5th Fl., PO Box 1028, St. John's NF A1C 5M3 – 709/753-7770; Fax: 709/753-0054 – Law Librarian, Gail A. Hogan

Learning Disabilities Association of Newfoundland, PO Box 26036, St. John's NF A1E 5T9 – 709/754-3665 – Nancy Galway

Leonard A. Miller Centre – Library, St. John's NF A1A 1E5 – 709/778-4344; Fax: 709/778-4333 – Librarian, Sheila Mensinkai

Marine Institute - Library, 155 Ridge Rd., PO Box 4920, St. John's NF A1C 5R3 – 709/778-0662; Fax: 709/778-0346; Symbol: NFSCF – Librarian, D.E. Taylor-Harding, Email: dharding@inseine.ifmt.nf.ca

Memorial University - Libraries, 234 Elizabeth St., St. John's NF A1B 3Y1 – 709/737-7428; Fax: 709/737-3118; Email: ENVOY: QEII.LIB
  University Librarian, Richard H. Ellis
  Acquisitions/Periodicals, Head, Victoria Ripley, 709/737-7438
  Cataloguing, Head, Charles Pennell, 709/737-7433
  Collections, Head, Dorothy Milne, 709/737-7421
  Information Services, Head, Joy Tillotson, 709/737-7427
  Lending Services, Head, Louise White, 709/737-4352
  Maps, Head, Alberta Auringer Wood, 709/737-8892
  Systems, Head, Slavko Manojlovich, 709/737-7470
  Centre for Cold Ocean Resources Engineering, Researcher, Judith Whittick, 709/737-8351, Email: ENVOY: C.CORE
  Centre for Newfoundland Studies, Head, Anne Hart, 709/737-7475
  Health Sciences, Librarian, George Beckett, 709/737-6670
  Collections, Coordinator, Michael Lenardo, 709/737-7421
  Ocean Engineering Information Centre, Bartlett Bldg., K-1000, St. John's NF A1B 3X5 – 709/737-8377; Fax: 709/737-4706; Email: ccore@kean.ucs.mun.ca; Symbol: NFSMO
  Information Researcher, Barbara Bodden
  Information Researcher, Sherry Well

Morris & Pittman Law Office - Library, 139 Water St., PO Box 2355, St. John's NF A1C 6E7 – 709/754-8474; Fax: 709/754-8036 – Barbara Hearn

National Research Council-Institute for Marine Dynamics – Library, PO Box 12093, St. John's NF A1B 3T5 – 709/772-2468; Fax: 709/772-3670; Email: library@minnie.imd.nrc.ca; Symbol: NFSNM – Librarian, Susan Salo

Natural Resources Canada-Canadian Forest Service: Atlantic Region – Library, Pleasantville Complex, Bldg. 304, PO Box 6028, St. John's NF A1C 5X8 – 709/772-4672; Fax: 709/772-2576; Email: ENVOY: ILL.NFRC; Symbol: NFSEC – Librarian, Patricia Tilley

Newfoundland & Labrador Alliance of Technical Industries – NATI Library, Atlantic Place, #602, 215 Water St., PO Box 41, St. John's NF A1C 6C9 – 709/722-3069

Newfoundland & Labrador Department of Education & Training - Learning Resources Distribution Centre, Bldg. 951, St. John's NF A1A 1R2 – 709/729-2619; Fax: 709/729-2177 – Jewel S. Cousens

Newfoundland & Labrador Department of Environment & Labour - Environment Library, Confederation Bldg., West Block, 4th Fl., PO Box 4750, St. John's NF A1C 5T7 – 709/729-3394; Fax: 709/729-1930

Newfoundland & Labrador Department of Finance - Departmental Library, PO Box 8700, St. John's NF A1B 4J6 – 709/729-2341 – Director, Government Accounting, Ron Williams

Newfoundland & Labrador Department of Fisheries, Food & Agriculture - Library, Provincial Fisheries Bldg., 30 Strawberry Marsh Rd., PO Box 8700, St. John's NF A1B 4J6 – 709/729-3723; Fax: 709/729-6082 – Library Technician, Sandra Hallett

Newfoundland & Labrador Department of Justice - Law Library, Confederation Bldg., PO Box 8700, St. John's NF A1B 4J6 – 709/729-2912; Fax: 709/729-1370; Symbol: NFSJL
  Library Director, Mona B. Pearce
  Library Technician, Brenda Blundon

Newfoundland & Labrador Department of Mines & Energy - Geological Survey Library, 95 Bonaventure Ave., St. John's NF A1B 4J6 – 709/729-3159; Fax: 709/729-3493; URL: http://www.geosurv.gov.nf.ca; Symbol: NFSMEM – Geologist, Catherine Patey

Newfoundland & Labrador Department of Municipal & Provincial Affairs - Urban & Rural Planning Division Library, Confederation Bldg., West Block, PO Box 8700, St. John's NF A1B 4J6 – 709/729-3090; Fax: 709/729-2609

Newfoundland & Labrador Department of Tourism, Culture & Recreation - Parks & Wildlife Division Library, PO Box 8700, St. John's NF A1B 4J6 – 709/729-6205

Newfoundland & Labrador Genealogical Society Inc. – Newfoundland & Labrador Genealogical Resource Centre, Colonial Building, Military Rd., St. John's NF A1C 2C9 – 709/754-9525 – Administrator, Resource Cenre, Elsa Hochwald

Newfoundland & Labrador Teachers' Association – Information Centre, 3 Kenmount Rd., St. John's NF A1B 1W1 – 709/726-3223; Toll Free: 1-800-563-3599 – Judy Handrigan

Newfoundland Association of Public Employees – Library, PO Box 8100, St. John's NF A1B 3M9 – 709/754-0700; Toll Free: 1-800-563-4442 – Research Officer, Trudi Brake

Newfoundland House of Assembly - Legislative Library, Confederation Bldg., PO Box 8700, St. John's NF A1B 4J6 – 709/729-3604; Fax: 709/729-0234 – Legislative Librarian, N.J. Richards

Pentecostal Assemblies of Newfoundland – Library, PO Box 8248, St. John's NF A1B 3N4 – 709/753-6314 – General Manager, Dept. of Lit., C. Buckle

Provincial Archives of Newfoundland & Labrador – Library, Military Rd., St. John's NF A1C 2C9 – 709/729-3065; Fax: 709/729-0578; Symbol: PANL

Director, Provincial Archives, David J. Davis, 709/729-0724, Email: ddavis@tourism.gov.nf.ca

Reference Archivist, R. Calvin Best, 709/729-0475

Pre-1949, Government Records Archivist, Anthony Murphy, 709/729-0496

Post-1949, Government Records Archivist, John Mowbray

Still & Moving Images Archivist, Ann Devlin-Fischer

Records Manager, Paul Kenny

Queen's College - Library, Prince Philip Dr., St. John's NF A1B 3R6 – 709/753-0116; Fax: 709/753-1214; Symbol: NFSQ – Rev. Dr. D. Davis

St. Clare's Mercy Hospital – Library, 154 Lemarchant Rd., St. John's NF A1C 5B8 – 709/778-3414 – Librarian, Catherine Lawton

School of Nursing, 250 Waterford Bridge Rd., St. John's NF A1E 1E3 – 709/778-3577; Fax: 709/754-4160; Email: cathy@nurse.nf.ca – Instructional Materials Specialist, Cathy Ryan

St. John's Board of Trade – Community Data Centre, 159 Water St., PO Box 5127, St. John's NF A1C 5V5 – 709/726-2961 – Manager, Member Services, Kyran Pittman Snair

Salvation Army Grace General Hospital - C.A. Pippy Jr. Medical Library, 241 Le Marchant Rd., St. John's NF A1E 1P9 – 709/778-6796 – Librarian, Elizabeth Duggan

Statistics Canada - Atlantic Regional Reference Centre, Viking Bldg., Crosbie Rd., 3rd Fl., St. John's NF A1B 3P2 – 709/772-6433; Toll Free: 1-800-565-7192

Waterford Hospital – Library Services - Health Care Corporation of St. John's, 306 Waterford Bridge Rd., St. John's NF A1E 4J8 – 709/758-3368; Fax: 709/758-3988; Email: dkearsey@nlnet.nf.ca; Symbol: WTFD – Library Technician, Debra Kearsey

Women's Enterprise Bureau – Library, 30 Harvey Rd., St. John's NF A1C 2G1 – 709/754-5555; Email: ACOA/ENTERPRISE.NETWORK – Faye Worthman

STEPHENVILLE

Sir Thomas Roddick Hospital – Library, 89 Ohio Dr., Stephenville NF A2N 2V6 – 709/643-7400; Fax: 709/643-2700 – Regional Director, Education Services, Karen Alexander

Westviking College of Applied Arts, Technology & Continuing Education - Library, PO Box 5400, Stephenville NF A2N 2Z6 – 709/643-7752; Fax: 709/643-5407; Email: vfurge@calvin.stemnet.nf.ca; Symbol: NFSBS

Main Campus, Librarian, Valerie Furge

Library Technician, Tina Foote

L.A. Bown Campus, Library Technician, Cathy Ash

Stephenville Crossing Campus, Library Technician, Barb King

TWILLINGATE

Notre Dame Bay Memorial Health Centre – Library, Twillingate NF A0G 4M0 – 709/884-2131 – Library Technician, Barbara Hamlyn

NORTHWEST TERRITORIES

Public Libraries

Arviat: Donald Suluk Library, PO Bag 4000, Arviat NT X0C 0E0 – 819/857-2579; Fax: 819/857-2743 – Local Librarian, Sally Kritaliak

Baker Lake: Thomas Tapatai Library, PO Box 189, Baker Lake NT X0C 0A0 – 819/793-2909; Fax: 819/793-2509 – Local Librarian, Sarah Segova

Cambridge Bay: May Hakongak Community Library, General Delivery, Cambridge Bay NT X0E 0C0 – 403/983-2028; Fax: 403/983-2553; TLX: 034-45652 – Local Librarian, Kim Crockatt

Clyde River Community Library, PO Box 150, Clyde River NT X0A 0E0 – 819/924-6266; Fax: 819/924-6247 – Local Librarian, Yvonne Earle – Branch of Baffin Regional Library

Coppermine Community Library, PO Box 190, Coppermine NT X0E 0E0 – 403/982-3098; Fax: 403/982-3060 – Local Librarian, Lucy Nivingalok

Fort Norman Community Library, General Delivery, Fort Norman NT X0E 0K0 – 403/588-4361; Fax: 403/588-3912 – Local Librarian, Nancy Norn-Lennie

Fort Simpson: John Tetso Memorial Library, PO Box 258, Fort Simpson NT X0E 0N0 – 403/695-3276; Fax: 403/695-2035; TLX: 034-4324 – Local Librarian, Natasha McCagg

Fort Smith: Mary Kaeser Library, PO Box 630, Fort Smith NT X0E 0P0 – 403/872-2296; Fax: 403/872-4345 – Local Librarian, Jeri Miltenberger

Hay River Dene Village Library, c/o Adult Education Centre, PO Box 1638, Hay River NT X0E 0R0 – 403/874-2128; Fax: 403/874-3229 – Local Librarian, Barbara Low

Hay River: Northwest Territories Centennial Library, PO Box 5003, Hay River NT X0E 0R0 – 403/874-6486; Fax: 403/874-3321 – Local Librarian, Marilyn Barnes

Igloolik: Amitturmiut Library, PO Box 260, Igloolik NT X0A 0L0 – 819/934-8812; Fax: 819/934-8779 – Local Librarian, Sylvia Ivalu – Branch of Baffin Regional Library

Inuvik Centennial Library, PO Box 1640, Inuvik NT X0C 0T0 – 403/979-2749; Fax: 403/979-3221 – Librarian, Deb Sullivan

Iqaluit: Baffin Regional Library, PO Bag 189A, Iqaluit NT X0A 0H0 – 819/979-5401; Fax: 819/979-1373; Email: mye@inukshuk.gov.nt.ca – Regional Manager, Yvonne Earle; Library Technician, Carol Rigby – See also following branches: Amitturmiut Library, Clyde River Community Library, Iqaluit Centennial Library, Nanisivik Community Library, Qimiruvik Library

Iqaluit Centennial Library, PO Box 189A, Iqaluit NT X0A 0H0 – 819/979-5400; Fax: 819/979-1373 – Local Librarian, David Kurtz – Branch of Baffin Regional Library

Nanisivik Community Library, PO Box 115, Nanisivik NT X0A 0X0 – 819/436-7445; Fax: 819/436-7588 – Local Librarian, Ruth Borst-Boyd – Branch of Baffin Regional Library

Norman Wells Community Library, PO Box 377, Norman Wells NT X0E 0V0 – 403/587-2956; Fax: 403/587-2956 – Co-Local Librarian, Linda Craig; Co-Local Librarian, Michelle Smith

Pangnirtung: Qimiruvik Library, PO Box 403, Pangnirtung NT X0A 0R0 – 819/473-8678; Fax: 819/473-8685 – Local Librarian, Rita Kisa – Branch of Baffin Regional Library

Pond Inlet: Rebecca P. Idlout Library, PO Bag 212, Pond Inlet NT X0A 0S0 – 819/899-8972; Fax: 819/899-8175 – Local Librarian, Philippa Ootoowak

Rankin Inlet: John Ayaruaq Library, PO Bag 002, Rankin Inlet NT X0C 0G0 – 819/645-5034; Fax: 819/645-2889; Email: INET: KEE.Sc.RI – Local Librarian, Linda Huisman

Rankin Inlet: Keewatin Regional Library, PO Bag 002, Rankin Inlet NT X0C 0G0 – 819/645-5035; Fax: 819/645-2889 – Regional Manager, Denise Anderson

Yellowknife Public Library, PO Box 694, Yellowknife NT X1A 2N5 – 403/920-5642; Fax: 403/920-5671; Email: leen@inukshuk.gov.nt.ca; libser@inuksuk.gov.nt.ca; Symbol: NWY – Library Manager, Eileen Murdoch; Public Services Librarian, Mike Burris; Library Technician, Fred Coppin

Special & College Libraries & Resource Centres

FORT SMITH

Science Institute of the NWT - South Slave Research Centre – Library, PO Box 45, Fort Smith NT X0E 0P0 – 403/872-4909

Aurora College - Thebacha Campus Library, Bag Service #2, Fort Smith NT X0E 0P0 – 403/872-7544; Fax: 403/872-4511; Email: ENVOY: ACTC.LIBRARY; Symbol: NWFST

Librarian, Alexandra Hook

Library Technician, Janet Lanoville

Canadian Heritage - Wood Buffalo National Park Library, PO Box 750, Fort Smith NT X0E 0P0 – 403/872-2349; Fax: 403/872-3910; Symbol: NWFSW – Librarian, Jenny Belyea

HAY RIVER

Northwest Territories Court Library - Hay River Branch, PO Box 1276, Hay River NT X0E 0R0

IGLOOLIK

Nunavut Research Institute - Igloolik Research Centre – Library, PO Box 210, Igloolik NT X0A 0L0 – 819/934-8836

INUVIK

Aurora Research Institute - Inuvik Research Centre – Library, PO Box 1430, Inuvik NT X0E 0T0 – 403/979-3838; Symbol: NWII – Library Manager, Vanessa Bebee

Ingamo Hall Friendship Centre – Resource Centre, PO Box 1293, Inuvik NT X0E 0T0 – 403/979-2166 – Coordinator, Bryan Edwards

Inuvik Research Centre - Library, College West, PO Box 1430, Inuvik NT X0E 0T0 – 403/979-3838; Fax: 403/979-3570

Northwest Territories Court Library - Inuvik Branch, PO Box 1965, Inuvik NT X0E 0T0

IQALUIT

Nunavut Research Institute - Iqaluit Research Centre – Library, Aeroplex Bldg., PO Box 160, Iqaluit NT X0A 0H0 – 819/979-4114

Northwest Territories Association of Provincial Court Judges – Law Library, Court House, PO Box 297, Iqaluit NT X0A 0H0 – 403/979-5450 – Chief Librarian, Sue Baer

Northwest Territories Court Library - Iqaluit Branch, Iqaluit Courthouse, PO Box 297, Iqaluit NT X0A 0H0

Nunavut Arctic College - Nunatta Campus Library, PO Box 600, Iqaluit NT X0A 0H0 – 819/979-7220; Fax: 819/979-4579; Email: ENVOY: AC.IQ.LIB; Symbol: NWIAC

Librarian, Gayle Jessop

Library Technician, Brenda Mowbray

YELLOWKNIFE

Ecology North – Recycling Resource Centre, PO Box 2888, Yellowknife NT X1A 2N1 – 403/873-6019 – Resource Centre Manager, Paula Webber

Environment Canada - Prairie & Northern Region, Library, PO Box 637, Yellowknife NT X1A 2N5 – 403/920-8531; Fax: 403/873-8185; Symbol: NWYECW – In Charge, Kevin McCormick

Fédération franco-ténoise – Bibliothèque, CP 1325, Yellowknife NT X1A 2N9 – 403/920-2919 – Caroline Millette

Indian & Northern Affairs Canada-Northern Affairs Sector - Northwest Territories – Library, PO Box 1500, Yellowknife NT X1A 2R3 – 403/920-1111

National Defence - Northern Region Headquarters - Library, PO Box 6666, Yellowknife NT X1A 2R3 – 403/873-4011, ext.817; Fax: 403/873-0856; Email: CSN: 620-1961, ext.540; Symbol: NWYND – Library Clerk, Evans Block

Northwest Territories Court Library, Courthouse, 4903 - 49 St., 1st Fl., PO Box 1320, Yellowknife NT X1A 2L9 – 403/873-7618; Fax: 403/873-0368; Email: NWT.COURT.LIB; Symbol: NWYC – Librarian, Susan Baer, 403/920-8617
Library Technician, Kelly Chiu

Northwest Territories Federation of Labour – Library, PO Box 2787, Yellowknife NT X1A 2R1 – 403/873-3695; Symbol: NWTFL – Researcher, Peter Atamanenko

Northwest Territories Health - Dr. Otto Schaefer Health Resource Centre, The Centre Square Tower, 2nd Fl., PO Box 1320, Yellowknife NT X1A 2L9 – 403/873-7713; Fax: 403/873-7706; Email: NWT.Health.Lib; Symbol: NWYOS – Florrie Cook

Northwest Territories Intergovernmental & Aboriginal Affairs - Library, Precambrian Bldg., 7th Fl., PO Box 1320, Yellowknife NT X1A 2L9 – 403/873-7143; Fax: 403/873-0233 – Executive Secretary, Kathy Green

Northwest Territories Legislative Branch Library, Centre Square Tower, 2nd Fl., PO Box 1320, Yellowknife NT X1A 2L9 – 403/873-7628; Fax: 403/873-0395
Branch Librarian, Bev Speight
Library Technician, Marni McDonald

Northwest Territories Legislative Library, Legislative Assembly Building, PO Box 1320, Yellowknife NT X1A 2L9 – 403/669-2202, 2203; Fax: 403/873-0207; Email: NWT.GOVTLIB; Symbol: NWYGI
Legislative Librarian, Vera Raschke
Legislative Branch Library, Branch Librarian, Bev Speight

Northwest Territories Renewable Resources - Library, Scotia Centre-5, PO Box 1320, Yellowknife NT X1A 2L9 – 403/920-8606; Fax: 403/873-0293; Email: ALISON.WELCH; Symbol: NWYRR – Librarian, Alison Welch

Northwest Territories Safety & Public Services - Resource Centre Library, Government of NWT, Box 1320, PA-3, Yellowknife NT X1A 2L9 – 403/873-7470; Fax: 403/873-0262
Library Technician, Rita Denneron
Manager, Occupational Safety & Health Section, Al Schreiner

Prince of Wales Northern Heritage Centre - Culture & Heritage Division, Yellowknife NT X1A 2L9 – 403/873-7177; Fax: 403/873-0205; Email: pwnhcl@gov.nt.ca; Symbol: NWYWNH – Librarian, Carolynn Kobelka

NOVA SCOTIA

Regional Library Systems with Member Libraries

ANNAPOLIS VALLEY REGIONAL LIBRARY
PO Box 640, Bridgetown NS B0S 1C0 – 902/665-2995; Fax: 902/662-4899; Email: avradmin@nsar.library.ns.ca; Symbol: NSAR
Reference Librarian, Corinne Frantel

Annapolis Royal Branch Library, St. George St., PO Box 579, Annapolis Royal NS B0S 1A0 – 902/532-2226 – Branch Librarian, Dorothy Abbott
Berwick Branch Library, 236 Commercial St., Berwick NS B0P 1E0 – 902/538-9517 – Branch Librarian, Marian Prout
Bridgetown Branch Library, Town Hall, 271 Granville St., PO Box 39, Bridgetown NS B0S 1C0 – 902/665-2758 – Branch Librarian, Betty Chazalon
Mobile Branch #1, PO Box 640, Bridgetown NS B0S 1C0 – 902/665-2995; Fax: 902/665-4899
Hantsport Branch Library, Hantsport School, 11 School St., Box 542, Hantsport NS B0P 1P0 – 902/584-3488 – Branch Librarian, Diana Thompson
Kentville Branch Library, 95 Cornwallis St., PO Box 625, Kentville NS B4N 3X7 – 902/679-2544 – Branch Contact, Winnie Stephen-Wills
Mobile Branch #2, PO Box 625, Kentville NS B4N 3X7 – 902/679-6653; Fax: 902/679-6653
Kingston Branch Library, 671 Main St., PO Box 430, Kingston NS B0P 1R0 – 902/765-3631 – Branch Librarian, Andrea Leeson
Lawrencetown Branch Library, 479 Main St., PO Box 88, Lawrencetown NS B0S 1M0 – 902/584-3044 – Branch Librarian, Dene Marshall
Middleton Branch Library, 45 Gates Ave., PO Box 667, Middleton NS B0S 1P0 – 902/825-4835 – Branch Librarian, Susan Aldred
Port Williams Branch Library, Community Centre, 131 Main St., Port Williams NS B0P 1T0 – 902/542-3005; Fax: 902/542-3005 – Branch Librarian, Connie Millett
Windsor Branch Library, 78 Thomas St., Windsor NS B0N 2T0 – 902/798-5424 – Branch Librarian, Peggy Hamilton
Wolfville Branch Library, 21 Elm Ave., PO Box 880, Wolfville NS B0P 1X0 – 902/542-5760; Fax: 902/542-5780 – Branch Librarian, Sharon Wendt

CAPE BRETON REGIONAL LIBRARY
50 Falmouth St., Sydney NS B1P 6X9 – 902/562-3279; Fax: 902/564-0765; Email: inssc@nssc.library.ns.ca; Symbol: NSSC
Regional Librarian, Ian R. MacIntosh

Baddeck Branch Library, Chebucto St., PO Box 88, Baddeck NS B0E 1B0 – 902/295-2055
Victoria County Bookmobile, Chebucto St., Baddeck NS B0E 1B0 – 902/295-2055
Dominion Branch Library, 78 Commercial St., Dominion NS B0A 1E0 – 902/849-3590
Donkin Branch Library, Donkin Elementary School, 81 Centre Ave., Donkin NS B0A 1G0 – 902/737-1154
Florence Branch Library, 380 Main St., Florence NS B0C 1J0 – 902/736-1988
Glace Bay Library, 121 Union St., Glace Bay NS B1A 2P8 – 902/849-8657
Louisbourg Branch Library, 10 Upper Warren St., Louisbourg NS B0A 1M0 – 902/733-3608
Main-A-Dieu Branch Library, Credit Union Bldg., Main-A-Dieu NS B0A 1N0 – 902/733-2555
New Waterford Branch Library, 3390 Plummer Ave., PO Box 12, New Waterford NS B1H 4K4 – 902/862-2892
Ingonish Branch Library, Cabot Trail, North Ingonish NS B0C 1K0 – 902/285-2544
Wilfred Oram Centennial Library, 299 Commercial St., North Sydney NS B2A 1B9 – 902/794-3272
Tompkins Memorial Library, 2249 Sydney Rd., Reserve Mines NS B0A 1V0 – 902/849-6685
Martha Hollett Memorial Library, 113 Main St., PO Box 102, Sydney Mines NS B1V 2L4 – 902/736-3219
Cape Breton County Bookmobile, 50 Falmouth St., Sydney NS B1P 6X9 – 902/562-3279
James McConnell Memorial Library, 50 Falmouth St., Sydney NS B1P 6X9 – 902/562-3161

COLCHESTER-EAST HANTS REGIONAL LIBRARY
754 Prince St., Truro NS B2N 1G9 – 902/895-4183; Fax: 902/895-7149; Email: anstc@nstc.library.ns.ca; Symbol: NSTC
Regional Library Director, Janet D. Pelley
Adult Services, Administrator, Daphne Cragg
Children's Services, Administrator, M. Lynda Marsh
Technical & Automated Services, Administrator, Michelle G. Walters

Elmsdale Branch Library, Elmsdale NS B0N 1M0 – 902/883-9838 – Branch Assistant, Rosalind Morrison
Stewiacke Branch Library, Stewiacke NS B0N 2J0 – 902/639-2481 – Branch Assistant, Evelyn Caldwell
Tatamagouche Branch Library, Tatamagouche NS B0K 1V0 – 902/657-3064 – Branch Assistant, Glenn Hamilton
Truro Branch Library, 754 Prince St., Truro NS B2N 1G9 – 902/895-4183; Fax: 902/895-7149

CUMBERLAND REGIONAL LIBRARY
Confederation Memorial Bldg., Ratchford St., PO Box 220, Amherst NS B4H 3Z2 – 902/667-2135; Fax: 902/667-1360; Email: insamc@rs6000.nshpl.library.ns.ca
Chief Librarian, Beverly True
Assistant Librarian, Frances Newman

Advocate Branch Library, Fundy Tides Recreation Centre, Advocate Harbour NS B0M 1A0 – 902/392-2214
Four Fathers Memorial Library, Acadia St., PO Box 220, Amherst NS B3H 3Z2 – 902/667-2549; Fax: 902/667-1360; Email: ILL.NSAMC
Oxford Branch Library, Water St., PO Box 309, Oxford NS B0M 1P0 – 902/447-2440
Parrsboro Branch Library, Queen St., PO Box 397, Parrsboro NS B0M 1S0 – 902/254-2046
Pugwash Branch Library, Durham St., Pugwash NS B0K 1L0 – 902/243-3331
River Hebert Miners Memorial Branch Library, Tidal View Health Centre, 2730 Barrons Field Rd., River Hebert NS B0L 1G0 – 902/251-2324
Springhill Branch Library, Main St., Springhill NS B0M 1X0 – 902/597-2211

DARTMOUTH NORTH COMMUNITY CENTRE LIBRARY
Highfield Park Drive, 134 Pinecrest Dr., Dartmouth NS B3A 2J9 – 902/490-5840; Fax: 902/490-5842
Branch Head, Troy Myers

Woodlawn Branch Library, Woodlawn Centre, 114 Woodlawn Rd., Dartmouth NS B2W 2S7 – 902/435-8352; Fax: 902/435-8380 – Branch Head, Darlene Beck

EASTERN COUNTIES REGIONAL LIBRARY
390 Murray St., PO Bag 2500, Mulgrave NS B0E 2G0 – 902/747-2597; Fax: 902/747-2500; Email: info@nsme.library.ns.ca; Symbol: NSME
Acting Chief Librarian, David Cumby
User Services Librarian, Heather Halliday
Coordinatrice des services en langue française, Lorraine Fennell

Canso Branch Library, 18 School St., PO Box 44, Canso NS B0H 1H0 – 902/366-2955; Fax: 902/366-2955

Canadian Almanac & Directory 1997

Cyril Ward Memorial Library, 27 Pleasant St., PO Box 191, Guysborough NS B0H 1N0 – 902/533-3586; Fax: 902/533-3586

Drs. Coady & Tompkins Memorial Library, 7972 Cabot Trail, General Delivery, Margaree Forks NS B0E 2A0 – 902/248-2821; Fax: 902/248-2821

Mulgrave Branch Library, 390 Murray St., PO Box 2500, Mulgrave NS B0E 2G0 – 902/747-2597; Fax: 902/747-2500

Petit de Grat Branch Library, PO Box 151, Petit de Grat NS B0E 2L0 – 902/226-3534; Fax: 902/226-3534

Port Hawkesbury Branch Library, 304 Pitt St., PO Box 996, Port Hawkesbury NS B0E 2V0 – 902/625-2729; Fax: 902/625-2729

Sherbrooke Branch, Main St., PO Box 177, Sherbrooke NS B0J 3C0 – 902/522-2180; Fax: 902/522-2180

HALIFAX REGIONAL LIBRARY

60 Alderney Dr., Dartmouth NS B2Y 4P8 – 902/490-5744; Fax: 902/490-5762; Email: ansh@nsh.library.ns.ca; Symbol: NSH

Acting Director, Susan McLean

Administrative Services, Acting Assistant Director, Aileen Lewis

Youth Services Coordinator, Linda Hodgins, 902/490-5748

Adult Services Coordinator, Laura Jantek, 902/490-5700

Information Services Coordinator, Michael Colborne

Branch Services Coordinator, Paula Saulnier

Community Services Coordinator, Joan Brown Hicks, 902/490-5718

Technical Services/Systems Coordinator, Deborah Nicholson, 902/490-5726

Branches East, Head, Andrew Poplawski

Branches West, Head, Ranjani Masih

Rural Services, Head, Janet Channing

Bedford Branch Library, Wardour Centre, 15 Dartmouth Rd., Bedford NS B4A 3X6 – 902/490-5740; Fax: 902/490-5752 – Branch Head, Sarah Wenning

Cole Harbour Library, Cole Harbour Place, Forest Hills Parkway, Cole Habour NS – 902/434-7228; Reference: 902/434-6177; Fax: 902/434-7448 – Branch Head, Penny Logan

Alderney Gate Library, 60 Alderney Dr., Dartmouth NS B2Y 4P8 – 902/490-5745

Captain William Spry Public Library, Captain William Spry Community Centre, 10 Kidston Rd., Halifax NS B3R 2J7 – 902/490-5734; Fax: 902/490-5741 – Branch Head, Jennifer Evans

Halifax North Branch Library, 2285 Gottingen St., Halifax NS B3K 3B7 – 902/490-5723; Fax: 902/490-5737 – Branch Head, Tracey Jones

Spring Garden Road Library, 5381 Spring Garden Rd., Halifax NS B3J 1E9 – 902/490-5700; Reference Services: 902/490-5710; Fax: 902/490-5746; Email: ansh@nsh.library.ns.ca; Symbol: NSH – Contact, Michael Colborne

Thomas Raddall Public Library, 255 Lacewood Dr., Halifax NS B3M 4G2 – 902/490-5738; Fax: 902/490-5739 – Branch Head, Jean Morgan

J.D. Shatford Memorial Library, Hubbards NS B0J 1T0 – 902/857-9176; Fax: 902/857-1397 – Branch Head, Paige Rockwell

Sackville Branch Library, Sackville Commercial Centre, 636 Sackville Dr., Lower Sackville NS B4C 2E1 – 902/865-8653; Reference: 902/865-3744; Fax: 902/865-2370 – Acting Branch Head, Helen Thexton

Musquodoboit Harbour & District Branch Library, The Strip Mall, Musquodoboit Harbour NS B0J 1T0 – 902/889-2227; Fax: 902/889-3799 – Branch Head, Sue Brown

Sheet Harbour Branch Library, Blue Water Business Centre, Sheet Harbour NS B0J 3B0 – 902/885-2391; Fax: 902/885-2749 – Branch Head, Vickie Josey

PICTOU-ANTIGONISH REGIONAL LIBRARY

PO Box 276, New Glasgow NS B2H 5E3 – 902/755-6031; Fax: 902/755-6775; Email: insngp@nsngp.library.ns.ca; Symbol: NSNGP

Director, Ann Ripley

Children's Librarian, Linda Arsenault

Technical Services Librarian, Fred Popowich

Systems Librarian, Eric Stackhouse

Antigonish Library, PO Box 1741, Antigonish NS B2G 2M5 – 902/863-4276; Email: antigoni@nsngp.library.ns.ca – Contact, Rhynda Tudor

New Glasgow Library, PO Box 276, New Glasgow NS B2H 5E3 – 902/752-8233; Email: newglaso@nsngp.library.ns.ca – Branch Supervisor, Carol A. MacMillan

Pictou Library, PO Box 622, Pictou B0K 1H0 – 902/485-5021; Email: pictou@nsngp.library.ns.ca – Contact, Bonnie Allan

River John Library, PO Box 104, River John NS B0K 1N0 – 902/351-2599 – Contact, Margaret MacLean

Stellarton Library, PO Box 1372, Stellarton NS B0K 1S0 – 902/755-1638 – Contact, Gail Meikle; Peggy Vienneau

Trenton Library, Main St., PO Box 612, Trenton NS B0K 1X0 – 902/752-5181 – Contact, Shelley MacLean

Westville Library, Queen St., PO Box 627, Westville NS B0K 2A0 – 902/396-5022 – Contact, Gina Snell

SOUTH SHORE REGIONAL LIBRARY

PO Box 34, Bridgewater NS B4V 2W6 – 902/543-2548; Fax: 902/543-8191; Email: ansbs@nsbs.library.ns.ca; Symbol: NSBS

Chief Librarian, Janet Clark

Branch/Extension Librarian, Frances Anderson

Mobile Branch/Technical Services Librarian, Cathy MacDonald

Bridgewater Branch Library, 547 King St., Bridgewater NS B4V 1B3 – 902/543-9222

DeWolfe Memorial Library, Gorham St., PO Box 9, Liverpool NS B0T 1K0 – 902/354-5270

Lunenburg Branch Library, 19 Pelham St., Lunenburg NS B0J 2C0 – 902/634-8008

WESTERN COUNTIES REGIONAL LIBRARY

405 Main St., Yarmouth NS B5A 1G3 – 902/742-2486; Fax: 902/742-6920; Email: ansy@nsy.library.ns.ca; Symbol: NSY

Regional Library Director, Trudy Amirault

Reference Librarian, Virginia Stoddard

Children's Librarian, Joanne Head

French Services Librarian, Janice Boudreau

Barrington Branch Library, PO Box 310, Barrington Passage NS B0W 1G0 – 902/637-3348; Email: barringt@nsy.library.ns.ca – Contact, Margo Chetwynd

Clarks Harbour Branch Library, PO Box 189, Clarks Harbour NS B0W 1P0 – 902/745-2885; Email: clarksha@nsy.library.ns.ca – Contact, Shelly Smith

Digby Branch Library, Town Hall, Sydney St., PO Box 730, Digby NS B0V 1A0 – 902/245-2163; Email: digby@nsy.library.ns.ca – Contact, Thelma Pulsifer

Lockeport Branch Library, PO Box 265, Lockeport NS B0T 1L0 – 902/656-2817; Email: lockepor@nsy.library.ns.ca – Contact, Mary Anne Turner

Clare Branch Library, PO Box 265, Meteghan NS B0W 2J0 – 902/645-3350; Email: clare@nsy.library.ns.ca – Contact, Aline Deveau

Pubnico Branch Library, PO Box 22, Pubnico NS B0W 2W0 – 902/762-2204; Fax: 902/762-3208; Email: pubnico@nsy.library.ns.ca – Contact, Beatrice Adams

Shelburne Branch Library, PO Box 158, Shelburne NS B0T 1W0 – 902/875-3615; Fax: 902/875-1015; Email: mckaymem@nsy.library.ns.ca – Branch Head, Edith Bower

Westport Branch Library, PO Box 1194, Westport NS B0V 1H0 – 902/839-2955; Email: westport@nsy.library.ns.ca – Branch Head, Charlotte Dixon

Weymouth Branch Library, PO Box 340, Weymouth NS B0W 3T0 – 902/837-4596; Email: weymouth@nsy.library.ns.ca – Contact, Marguerite Thibault

Yarmouth Branch Library, 405 Main St., Yarmouth NS B5A 1G3 – 902/742-5040; Fax: 902/742-6920; Email: yarmouth@nsy.library.ns.ca – Librarian, Joanne Head

Special & College Libraries & Resource Centres

AMHERST

Amherst Township Historical Society – Genealogical Archives, c/o Cumberland County Museum, 150 Church St., Amherst NS B4H 3C3 – 902/667-2561 – Education Officer, Alexander Graham

Cumberland County Family Planning Association – Library, 16 Church St., Lower Level, PO Box 661, Amherst NS B4H 4B8 – 902/667-7500 – Community Director, Ruthie Patriquin

Indian & Northern Affairs Canada - Library, 40 Havelock St., PO Box 160, Amherst NS B4H 3Z3 – 902/661-6233; Fax: 902/667-9947; Symbol: NSAIN – Public Inquiries Officer, Debbi Adams

ANTIGONISH

Coady International Institute – Marie Michael Library, St. Francis Xavier University, PO Box 5000, Antigonish NS B2G 2W5 – 902/867-3964; Fax: 902/867-3907; Email: sadams@juliet.stfx.ca; Symbol: NSASF – Librarian, Sue Adams

St. Francis Xavier University - Angus L. Macdonald Library, PO Box 5000, Antigonish NS B2G 2W5 – 902/867-2267; Fax: 902/867-5153; Email: interlibloan@essex.stfx.ca; Symbol: NSAS

Chief Librarian, Rita Campbell

Reference Librarian, Barbara Phillips, 902/867-2242

Circulation Supervisor, Jane Synishin, 902/867-2228

Systems Librarian, Mark Leggott, 902/867-2114

Acquisitions Supervisor, Kevin MacNeil, 902/867-2168

ARMDALE

Nova Scotia Teachers Union – Library, 3106 Dutch Village Rd., Armdale NS B3L 4L7 – 902/477-5621; Toll Free: 1-800-565-6788 – Librarian, Maureen Phinney

BEDFORD

Environment Canada - Atmospheric Environment Service, Atlantic Region - Library, 1496 Bedford Hwy., Bedford NS B4A 1E5 – 902/426-9278; Fax: 902/426-9158; Symbol: NSHW – Librarian, Joan Backer, 902/426-9187

BERWICK

Western Kings Memorial Health Centre – Library, PO Box 490, Berwick NS B0P 1E0 – 902/538-3111; Symbol: NSBWK – Chief Librarian, Jacinta Harvey

CHURCH POINT

Université Sainte-Anne - Bibliothèque Louis R. Comeau, Church Point NS B0W 1M0 – 902/769-2114, ext.161; Fax: 902/769-0137; Email: ENVOY: ILL.NSCS; Symbol: NSCS

University Librarian, Mildred Comeau

Reference Librarian, Cecile Pothier

Circulation, Rejeanne LeBlanc-Comeau

ILL, Corinne Arsenault

LIBRARIES — NOVA SCOTIA 5-37

DARTMOUTH

Nova Scotia Research Foundation Corporation – Library, 101 Research Dr., PO Box 790, Dartmouth NS B2Y 3Z7 – 902/424-8670, ext.181; Toll Free: 1-800-565-7051; Email: library@nsrfc.ns.ca; ill@nsrfc.ns.ca; Symbol: NSHR – Information Services Coordinator, Mary Veling

Black Cultural Centre for Nova Scotia – Library, 1149 Main St., Dartmouth NS B2Z 1A8 – 902/434-6223; Fax: 902/434-2306 – Curator, Henry Bishop

Boyne Clarke Law Office - Library, Belmont House, #700, 33 Alderney Dr., PO Box 876, Dartmouth NS B2Y 3Z5 – 902/469-9500; Fax: 902/463-7500 – Chair, Library Committee, Larry Gratan

Cole Harbour Rural Heritage Society – Library, 471 Poplar Dr., Dartmouth NS B2W 4L2 – 902/434-0222 – Curator, Terry Eyland

Defence Research Establishment - Atlantic - Reference Library, 9 Grove St., PO Box 1012, Dartmouth NS B2Y 3Z7 – 902/426-3100, ext.135; Fax: 902/426-9654; Email: ENVOY: DREA.INFO.SVCS; Symbol: NSHN – Information Services, Iris Ouellette, Email: Ouellette@drea.dnd.ca

Environment Canada-Environmental Conservation Service - Environmental Quality Laboratories - Dartmouth – Library, Bedford Institute of Oceanography, 1 Challenger Dr., PO Box 1006, Dartmouth NS B2Y 4A2 – 902/426-3288 – Librarian, Dawn Taylor-Prime

Environment Canada - Atlantic Region Library, Queen Sq., 45 Alderney Dr., 5th Fl., Dartmouth NS B2Y 2N6 – 902/426-7219; Fax: 902/426-6143; Email: library@ns.doe.ca; Symbol: NSDE
Librarian, Dawn Taylor-Prime, 902/426-7219, Email: primed@ns.doe.ca
Interlibrary Loans, ILL Librarian, Rebecca Arsenault

Fisheries & Oceans Canada-Bedford Institute of Oceanography – Maritimes Regional Library, 1 Challenger Dr., PO Box 1006, Dartmouth NS B2Y 4A2 – 902/426-3675; Fax: 902/496-1544; Email: biolib@maritimes.dfo.ca; Symbol: NSDB – Chief, Library Services, Anna Fiander

Health Canada - Health Protection Branch - Library, PO Box 1060, Dartmouth NS B2Y 3Z7 – 902/426-6694; Fax: 902/426-6676 – Librarian, Adeline MacDonald

Lupus Society of Nova Scotia – Library, 71 Penhorn Dr., Dartmouth NS B2W 1K8 – 902/434-4511 – Librarian, Carol Benard

Nova Scotia Community College - Akerley Campus Library, 21 Woodlawn Rd., Dartmouth NS B2W 2R7 – 902/434-2020, ext.336; Fax: 902/462-4320; Symbol: NSDRV – Librarian, P.T.H. Huang

Nova Scotia Hospital – Health Sciences Library, 300 Pleasant St., PO Box 1004, Dartmouth NS B2Y 3Z9 – 902/464-3254; Fax: 902/464-4804; Symbol: NSDNSH – Library Technician, Myrna Lawson

Nova Scotia Housing & Consumer Affairs - Library, PO Box 815, Dartmouth NS B2Y 3Z3 – 902/424-8090; Fax: 902/424-5327 – Janet M. Baker

Schizophrenia Society of Nova Scotia – Library, Administration Office, Nova Scotia Hospital, #1120, Mount Hope Ctr., PO Box 1004, Dartmouth NS B2Y 3Z9 – 902/465-2601, 464-3456; Toll Free: 1-800-465-2601 – Librarian, Geri Cooper

Transport Canada - Maritimes Regional Library, Queen's Square Bldg., #1215, 45 Alderney Dr., PO Box 1013, Dartmouth NS B2Y 4K2 – 902/426-5182; Fax: 902/426-8337; Symbol: NSHMT – Library Technician, Gary Keirstead

DIGBY

Digby General Hospital – Health Records Library, PO Box 820, Digby NS B0V 1A0 – 902/245-2501; Symbol: NSDG – Shirley Dugas

HALIFAX

AIDS Coalition of Nova Scotia – Library, #300, 5675 Spring Garden Rd., Halifax NS B3J 1H1 – 902/425-4882 – Rosanne LeBlanc

Alzheimer Society of Nova Scotia – Alzheimer Resource Centre, 5954 Spring Garden Rd., Halifax NS B3H 1Y7 – 902/422-7961 – Program Coordinator, Johnann Macgillivray

Armbrae Academy - Library, 1400 Oxford St., Halifax NS B3H 3Y8 – 902/423-7920; Fax: 902/423-9731 – Headmaster, Eric T. MacKnight

Atlantic School of Theology – Library, 640 Francklyn St., Halifax NS B3H 3B5 – 902/423-7986; Fax: 902/423-7941; Email: ENVOY: nshph.ill; URL: http://novanet.ns.ca/ast/homepage.html; Symbol: NSHPH
Head Librarian, Dr. D. Davis
Cataloguing, Technical Services Librarian, Lloyd J. Melanson
Reference, Librarian, Elaine Murray
Assistant Technical Services Librarian, Michael Bramah

Bio-Response Systems Ltd. – Library, PO Box 2564, Halifax NS B3J 3N5 – 902/422-5949 – Chief Librarian, Nick Wright

Burchell, MacAdam & Hayman Law Office - Library, 1646 Barrington St., PO Box 36, Halifax NS B3J 2L4 – 902/423-6361; Fax: 902/420-9326 – Michael Wood

Cambridge Military Library, RA Park, 1565 Queen St., Halifax NS B3J 2H9 – 902/427-7193 – M.Cpl. Ralph Sweetman

Canadian Broadcasting Corporation - Broadcasting Materials Library, 5600 Sackville St., PO Box 3000, Halifax NS B3J 2E9 – 902/420-4186; Fax: 902/420-4281; Email: kirby@halifax.cbc.ca – Senior Broadcast Material Librarian, Doug Kirby, 902/420-4160
Music & Record Library, 5600 Sackville St., PO Box 3000, Halifax NS B3J 3E9 – 902/420-4404; Fax: 902/420-4414; Symbol: NSHCB – Senior Record Librarian, Caroline Grant

Canadian Heritage - Parks Canada, Atlantic Region Library, Historic Properties, Upper Water St., Halifax NS B3J 1S9 – 902/426-8951; Fax: 902/426-7012; Email: ENVOY: PARKSATLANTIC.LB; Symbol: NSHIAP
Chief, Information Holdings Management, David Palmer, 902/426-8951, Email: palmerd@pksaro.dots.doe.ca
Librarian, Lynn O'Brien, 902/426-4621
Library Clerk, Shirley McNeil, 902/426-7266
Records Management, Coordinator, Gail Collins, 902/426-7327
Records, Clerk, Linda Soulis, 902/426-3426
Records, Clerk, Wayne O'Melia, 902/426-3426
Parks Canada, Halifax Citadel National Historic Site - Library, PO Box 9080, Halifax NS B3K 5M7 – 902/426-1992; Fax: 902/426-4228; Symbol: NSHCN – Head, Ron McDonald

The Chronicle-Herald & The Mail Star - Herald Information Services, 1650 Argyle St., PO Box 610, Halifax NS B3J 2T2 – 902/426-3080; Fax: 902/426-2810; Email: online@herald.ns.ca; URL: http://www.herald.ns.ca
Librarian, Alberta Dubé
Library Assistant, Debbie Reid

The Clean Nova Scotia Foundation – Library, 1675 Bedford Row, PO Box 2528, Halifax NS B3J 3N5 – 902/420-3474; Toll Free: 1-800-665-5377 – Information Officer, Rochelle Owen

Cooperative Housing Federation of Nova Scotia – Library, #609, 5251 Duke St., Halifax NS B3J 1P3 – 902/492-3881 – Tom Waters

Council of Nova Scotia Archives – Library, c/o Public Archives of Nova Scotia, 6016 University Ave., Halifax NS B3H 1W4 – 902/424-7093 – Archivist, Johanna Smith

Cox Downie Law Office - Library, PO Box 2380, Halifax NS B3J 3E5 – 902/421-6262; Fax: 902/421-3130; Email: coxdowni@fox.nstn.ca
Librarian, Linda Matte
Librarian, Rachelane DeWolf-Swetnam

Daley, Black & Moreira Law Office - Library, #400, TD Centre, 1791 Barrington St., PO Box 355, Halifax NS B3J 2N7 – 902/423-7211; Fax: 902/420-1744 – Librarian, Mary Gibson

Dalhousie University - Killam Library, 6225 University Ave., Halifax NS B3H 4H8 – 902/494-3601; Fax: 902/494-2062; Symbol: NSHD
University Librarian, Dr. William F. Birdsall, Email: bill.birdsall@dal.ca
Collections Development, Head, Holly Melanson
Technical Services, Head, Elaine Boychuk
Science Services, Head, Patricia Lutley
Law Library, Law Librarian, Christian L. Wiktor, 902/424-2124, Fax: 902/494-6669, Email: ENVOY: ILL.WELDON
Pharmacy Library, Information Officer, Elizabeth Foy, 902/494-1671
W.K. Kellogg Health Sciences Library, Librarian, Elizabeth Sutherland, 902/494-3787, Fax: 902/494-3750, Email: ENVOY: ILL.KELLOGG
School for Resource & Environmental Studies Library, Information Specialist/Publications, Judith G. Reade, 902/494-3632, Fax: 902/494-3728

Development Education Resource & Information Centre – Library, 3115 Veith St., Halifax NS B3K 3G9 – 902/454-4874

Ecology Action Centre – Library, #31, 1568 Argyle St., Halifax NS B3J 2B3 – 902/429-2202

Fisheries & Oceans Canada - Scotia-Fundy Regional Library, Halifax Fisheries Library, 1707 Lower Water St., PO Box 550, Halifax NS B3J 2S7 – 902/426-7160; Fax: 902/426-1862; Email: hfxlib@bionet.bio.dfo.ca; Symbol: NSHF
Head Librarian, Lori Collins
ILL, Diane Stewart

Health Canada - Library, 1557 Hollis St., Halifax NS B3J 3V4 – 902/426-8440 – Library, Anne MacAlpine

Heart & Stroke Foundation of Nova Scotia – Library, City Centre Atlantic, #204, 5523 Spring Garden Rd., Halifax NS B3J 3T1 – 902/423-7530; Toll Free: 1-902-422-8111 – Education Coordinator, Helen Greenough

International Education Centre - Saint Mary's University – Resource Centre, Saint Mary's University, 923 Robie St., Halifax NS B3H 3C3 – 902/420-5525 – Ron Houlihan

IWK-Grace Health Centre for Children, Women & Families – Izaak Walton Killam Children's Hospital Health Sciences Library, 5980 University Ave., Halifax NS B3H 4N1 – 902/420-3058; Email: Library@gracehosp.ns.ca; ILL.I; Symbol: NSHGH – Manager, Library Services, Darlene Chapman

Justice Canada - Halifax Regional Office - Library, #1400, 5251 Duke St., Halifax NS B3J 1P3 – 902/426-3260; Fax: 902/426-2329 – Administrative Assistant, Samantha Boorman

Lane Environment Limited – Library, 1663 Oxford St., Halifax NS B3H 3Z5 – 902/423-8197 – Administrative Assistant, Suzanne Sleigh

Lester Pearson Institute for International Development – Library, 1321 Edward St., Halifax NS B3H 3H5 – 902/494-2038; TLX: 019 21 863 – David Redwood

Maritime Conservatory of Music - Library, 5820 Spring Garden Rd., Halifax NS B3H 1X8 – 902/423-6995; Fax: 902/423-6029 – Office Manager, Janet Hillier

Maritime Museum of the Atlantic - Library, 1675 Lower Water St., Halifax NS B3J 1S3 – 902/424-7890; Fax: 902/424-0612; Symbol: NSHMM

McInnes Cooper & Robertson - Law Library, 1601 Lower Water St., PO Box 730, Halifax NS B3J 2V1

Canadian Almanac & Directory 1997

– 902/424-1340, 1320; Fax: 902/425-6386, 6350; Email: mcrhfx@mcrlaw.com; Symbol: NSHMCR
Librarian, Lindy L. Stephens
Library Technician, Elizabeth McPhee

Mount Saint Vincent University - Library, 166 Bedford Hwy., Halifax NS B3M 2J6 – 902/457-6120; Fax: 902/457-3175; Email: ENVOY: ADMIN/MT.ST.VINCENTUNIV; URL: http://www.msvu.ca/; Symbol: NSHV
Reference Services/Collections Development, Head, Terrence Paris, 902/457-6526
User Services Librarian, Meg Raven, 902/457-6403
Bibliographic Services Librarian, Peter Glenister, 902/457-6402
Chief Librarian, Lillian Beltaos, 902/457-6121

National Defence - CFB Halifax - Reference & Recreation Library, Forces Mail Office, Halifax NS B3K 2X0 – 902/427-8398; Symbol: NSHN – Base Librarian, Jackie Lombard

Nova Scotia Association of Health Organizations – Library, Bedford Professional Centre, 2 Dartmouth Rd., Halifax NS B4A 2K7 – 902/832-8500

Nova Scotia Barristers' Society – Library, #1101, 1645 Granville St., Halifax NS B3J 1X3 – 902/425-2665; Fax: 902/422-1697 – Director, Library Services, Barbara Campbell

Nova Scotia College of Art & Design - Library, 5163 Duke St., Halifax NS B3J 3J6 – 902/494-8196; Fax: 902/425-2420; Email: ilga@nscad.ns.ca; Symbol: NSHCA – Director of Library Services, Ilga Leja, 902/494-8181

Nova Scotia Community College - Halifax Campus Library, 1825 Bell Rd., Halifax NS B3H 2Z4 – 902/424-7972; Fax: 902/424-0553 – Deborah Costelo
Institute of Technology Library, 5685 Leeds St., PO Box 2210, Halifax NS B3J 3C4 – 902/424-4224; Fax: 902/424-0534; Symbol: NSHTI
Librarian, Nola Brennan
Library Clerk, Veronica Paris

Nova Scotia Community Services - Library, PO Box 696, Halifax NS B3J 2T7 – 902/424-7906; Fax: 902/424-0502; Email: coms.phillija@gov.ns.ca; Symbol: NSHSS – Librarian, Jane Phillips

Nova Scotia Confederation of University Faculty Associations – Library, #404, 1646 Barrington St., Halifax NS B3J 2A3 – 902/422-1204 – Rose Norman

Nova Scotia Department of Health - Library, Joseph Howe Bldg., 1681 Granville St., 10th Fl., Halifax NS B3J 2R8 – 902/424-8694; Fax: 902/424-0663; Email: library@gov.ns.ca; Symbol: NSHH – Librarian, Ruth Vaughan

Nova Scotia Economic Renewal Agency - Library, 1800 Argyle St., PO Box 519, Halifax NS B3J 2R7 – 902/424-5807, 6178; Fax: 902/424-0748; Email: econ.library@gov.ns.ca; Symbol: NSHDD
Librarian, Donald Purcell
Library Assistant, Eileen Dunphy

Nova Scotia Education & Culture - Library, #402, 2021 Brunswick St., PO Box 587, Halifax NS B3J 2S9 – 902/424-5264; Fax: 902/424-0519; Email: hlfxtrad.educ.arbuckkl@gov.ns.ca; Symbol: NSHVTT
Librarian, K. Arbuckle, Email: arbuckkl@gov.ns.ca
Information Services Librarian, A. Roman, Email: romancd@gov.ns.ca
Library Assistant, Jennifer Millman, Email: millmajl@gov.ns.ca

Nova Scotia Environment - Library, 5151 Terminal Rd., 5th Fl., PO Box 2107, Halifax NS B3J 3B7 – 902/424-5300; Fax: 902/424-2372; Symbol: NSHDE – Research & Statistics Officer, Janice E. Laufer, 902/424-2372

Nova Scotia Finance - Federal-Provincial Taxation & Fiscal Relations Library, PO Box 187, Halifax NS B3J 2N3 – 902/424-2595; Fax: 902/424-0590 – Sheila Crummell

Nova Scotia Fisheries - Library, Purdy's Wharf, 1959 Upper Water St., 3rd Fl., PO Box 2223, Halifax NS B3J 3C4 – 902/424-4560, 4561; Fax: 902/424-4671

Nova Scotia Housing & Consumer Affairs - Library, PO Box 998, Halifax NS B3J 2X3 – 902/424-4690; Fax: 902/424-0533 – Charlene Titus

Nova Scotia Human Rights Commission - Library, PO Box 2221, Halifax NS B3J 3C4 – 902/424-4111; Fax: 902/424-0596; Symbol: NSHRC
Public Education Officer, May Lui
Central Registry Clerk, Jennifer Downey

Nova Scotia Justice - Library, 5151 Terminal Rd., 3rd Fl., PO Box 7, Halifax NS B3J 2L6 – 902/424-7699; Fax: 902/424-4556; Symbol: NSHOL – Library Contact, Marie DeYoung

Nova Scotia Labour - Library, PO Box 697, Halifax NS B3J 2T8 – 902/424-8474; Fax: 902/424-3239; Email: ENVOY 100: ILL.NSHDOL; Symbol: NSHDOL – Librarian, JoAnn Richling

Nova Scotia Legislative Library, Province House, PO Box 396, Halifax NS B3J 2P8 – 902/424-5932; Fax: 902/424-0574; Email: ENVOY: ILL.NSHL; nsleglib@fox.nstn.ca
Legislative Librarian, Margaret F. Murphy
Reference Librarian, Sandra Scott, 902/424-5625
Technical Services Librarian, Jean Sawyer

Nova Scotia Municipal Affairs - Library, PO Box 216, Halifax NS B3J 2M4 – 902/424-5965; Fax: 902/424-0531; Symbol: NSHMA – Librarian, Audrey Manzer, Email: amanzer@gov.ns.ca

Nova Scotia Museum - Library, 1747 Summer St., Halifax NS B3H 3A6 – 902/424-7198; Fax: 902/424-0560; Symbol: NSHM – Librarian, Susan Whiteside

Nova Scotia Natural Resources - Library, 1701 Hollis St., 3rd Fl., PO Box 698, Halifax NS B3J 2T9 – 902/424-8633; Fax: 902/424-4735; Symbol: NSHDOM
Head, Library Services, Valerie Brisco
Reference Librarian, Barbara DeLory

Nova Scotia Ombudsman - Library, PO Box 2152, Halifax NS B3J 3B7 – 902/424-6780; Fax: 902/424-6675; Toll Free: 1-800-670-1111 – Secretary, Muriel Mappin

Nova Scotia Safety Council – Library, Bloomfield Centre, #207, 2786 Agricola St., Halifax NS B3K 4E1 – 902/454-9621

Nova Scotia Youth Orchestra – Library, #200, 1541 Barrington St., Halifax NS B3J 1Z5 – 902/423-5984

Nova Scotian Institute of Science – Library, Dalhousie University, Science Services University Library, Halifax NS B4H 4H8 – 902/494-2384 – Librarian, Sharon Longard

Oxfam-Canada - Halifax Office – Deveric Library, 3115 Veith St., Halifax NS B3K 3G9 – 902/454-5182 – Carolyn Van Gurp

Patterson Palmer Hunt Murphy - Library, #1600, 5151 George St., PO Box 247, Halifax NS B3J 2N9 – 902/492-2000; Fax: 902/429-5215 – Librarian, Lynda Feetham

Public Archives of Nova Scotia - Library, 6016 University Ave., Halifax NS B3H 1W4 – 902/424-6060; Fax: 902/424-0628 – Provincial Archivist, Carman V. Carroll

Public Legal Education Society of Nova Scotia – Reference Library, #911, 6080 Young St., Halifax NS B3K 5L2 – 902/454-2198; Toll Free: 1-800-665-9779

Queen Elizabeth II Health Sciences Centre - Health Sciences Library, 1335 Queen St., Halifax NS B3J 2H6 – 902/496-3458; Fax: 902/496-2168; Symbol: NSHHI – Director, Anitra Laycock, Email: alaycock@fox.nstn.ca

Queen Elizabeth II Health Sciences Centre (Camp Hill Hospital) – Health Sciences Library, 1763 Robie St., Halifax NS B3H 3G2 – 902/496-4287; Fax: 902/496-2168; Email: ENVOY: CHH.LIB; chh.lib@resonet.com; Symbol: NSHCH – Director, Anitra Laycock

Queen Elizabeth II Health Sciences Centre (Victoria General Hospital) – Health Sciences Library - Bethune Bldg., 1278 Tower Rd., Halifax NS B3H 2Y9 – 902/428-2429; Fax: 902/428-7456; Email: vghl@fox.nstn.ca; Symbol: NSHVGH – Director, Anitra Laycock

Ringette Nova Scotia – Resource Library, 5516 Spring Garden Rd., PO Box 3010, Stn South, Halifax NS B3J 3G6 – 902/425-5450, ext.350

St. Mary's University - Patrick Power Library, Halifax NS B3H 3C3 – 902/420-5544; Fax: 902/420-5561; Email: ENVOY: ILL.NSHS; Symbol: NSHS
Acting University Librarian, Margot E. Schenk, 902/420-5532
Reference/Research Librarian, Douglas Vaisey, 902/420-5540
Systems & Training Librarian, Rashid Tayyeb, 902/420-5545

SNC-Lavalin Inc. - Nova Scotia Branch Library, #200, Park Lane Terraces, 5657 Spring Garden Rd., Halifax NS B3J 3R4 – 902/492-4544; Fax: 902/492-4540 – Librarian, Aubrey Reynolds

Statistics Canada - Atlantic Regional Reference Centre, North American Life Centre, 1770 Market St., Halifax NS B3J 3M3 – 902/426-5331; Fax: 902/426-9538; Toll Free: 1-800-565-7192

Stewart McKelvey Stirling Scales - Library, 1959 Upper Water St., 9th Fl., PO Box 997, Halifax NS B3J 2X2 – 902/420-3200; Fax: 902/420-4143; Symbol: NSHSMC
Coordinator, Information Services, Cynthia Murphy, 902/420-3373
Library Assistant, Christine Johannesen, 902/420-3200, ext.104

Technical University of Nova Scotia - Library, PO Box 1000, Stn Central RPO, Halifax NS B3J 2X4 – 902/420-7700; Fax: 902/420-7831; Email: library@tuns.ca; Symbol: NSHT
University Librarian, Donna Richardson
Public Services Librarian, Helen Powell, 902/420-7595
Reference Librarian, Michelle Clairmont, 902/420-2614
Head of Circulation, Bill Slauenwhite, 902/420-2630
Technical Services Librarian, Mark Bartlett, 902/420-7562

Tourism Industry Association of Nova Scotia – Library, The World Trade & Convention Centre, #402, 1800 Argyle St., Halifax NS B3J 3N8 – 902/423-4480

Union of Nova Scotia Municipalities – Library, #1106, 1809 Barrington St., Halifax NS B3J 3K8 – 902/423-8331

The United Church of Canada - Maritime Conference Archives, 640 Francklyn St., Halifax NS B3H 3B5 – 902/429-4819 – Conference Archivist, Carolyn Earle

University of King's College - Library, 6350 Coburg Rd., Halifax NS B3H 2A1 – 902/422-1271, ext.171; Fax: 902/423-3357; Symbol: NSHK
Chief Librarian, H. Drake Petersen, 902/422-1271, ext.173
Circulation, Head, M. Elaine Galey, 902/422-1271, ext.171
Collections, Head, Patricia L. Chalmers, 902/422-1271, ext.174
Reference, Head, Gillian Frances-Barlow, 902/422-1271, ext.175
Serials/Acquisitions, Head, Paulette C. Drisdelle, 902/422-1271, ext.172

Visual Arts Nova Scotia – Resource Centre, #901, 1809 Barrington St., Halifax NS B3J 3K8 – 902/423-4694 – Executive Secretary, Dinah Simmons

Writers' Federation of Nova Scotia – Library, #901, 1809 Barrington St., Halifax NS B3J 3K8 – 902/423-8116

KENTVILLE

Agriculture & Agri-Food Canada-Kentville Research Centre – Library, 32 Main St., Kentville NS B4N 1J5 – 902/679-5508; Fax: 902/679-2311;

Email: melansonpa@em.agr.ca; minerj@em.agr.ca; Symbol: NSKR – Librarian, Jerry R. Miner

Efamol Research Inc. - Library, Annapolis Valley Industrial Park, Chipman Dr., Unit 2, PO Box 818, Kentville NS B4N 4H8 – 902/678-5534, ext.165; Fax: 902/678-9440; Email: bjstaili@fox.nstn.ns.ca; Symbol: NSKER – Research Library Manager, Barbara J. Stailing

Kemic Bioresearch Laboratories Ltd. – Library, 70 Exhibition St., PO Box 878, Kentville NS B4N 4H8 – 902/678-8195 – Librarian, Susan Goodall, B.Sc.

Nova Scotia Community College - Kingstec Campus Library, PO Box 487, Kentville NS B4N 3X3 – 902/678-7341; Fax: 902/679-1141; Email: ENVOY: NSKKR.ILL – Library Technician, Paula Coldwell

Valley Regional Hospital – Library, 150 Exhibition St., Kentville NS B4N 5E3 – 902/679-2657, ext.3299; Email: kublin@fox.nstn.ca; Symbol: NSKVH – Librarian, Joyce Kublin

LAWRENCETOWN

College of Geographic Sciences - J.B. Hall Memorial Library, 50 Elliott Rd., RR#1, Lawrencetown NS B0S 1M0 – 902/584-2226; Fax: 902/584-7211; Symbol: NSLAL – Librarian, Donna M. Eisner

LOUISBOURG

Canadian Heritage - Fortress of Louisbourg - Library, PO Box 160, Louisbourg NS B01 1M0 – 902/733-2280; Fax: 902/733-2362; URL: http://fortress.uccb.ns.ca; Symbol: NSLF – Historical Records Supervisor, Eric Krause, Email: krausee@pkslhs.dots.doe.ca

LUNENBURG

D.W.T. Brattston Law Office - Library, PO Box 1599, Lunenburg NS B0J 2C0 – 902/634-8474; Fax: 902/634-9400

Lunenburg Marine Museum Society – Library, 68 Bluenose Dr., PO Box 1363, Lunenburg NS B0J 2C0 – 902/634-4794 – Heather Getson

MIDDLETON

Annapolis Valley Historical Society – Library, PO Box 925, Middleton NS B0S 1P0 – 902/825-6116 – Library Assistant, Krista Toole

Soldiers' Memorial Hospital – Library, PO Box 730, Middleton NS B0S 1P0 – 902/825-3411, ext.357; Email: medical@soldiersmem.ns.ca; Symbol: NSMS – Librarian, Joyce Kublin

NEW GLASGOW

Aberdeen Hospital – Dr. G.R. Douglas Memorial Library, 835 East River Rd., New Glasgow NS B2H 3S6 – 902/752-7600,ex.213; Fax: 902/755-2356

PORT HASTINGS

Port Hastings Historical Society – Genealogy Records, PO Box 115, Port Hastings NS B0E 2T0 – 902/625-1295

PORT HAWKESBURY

Nautical Institute - Library, PO Box 1225, Port Hawkesbury NS B0E 2V0 – 902/625-2380; Fax: 902/625-0193 – Librarian, Lana MacLean

Nova Scotia Community College - Nautical Institute Library, 226 Reeves St., PO Box 1225, Port Hawkesbury NS B0E 2V0 – 902/625-2380; Fax: 902/625-0193 Librarian, Lana B. MacLean
Library Clerk, Glenda Charlton
Acting Library Clerk, Margaret Eager

SPRINGHILL

Correctional Service Canada - Springhill Institution - Library, PO Box 2140, Springhill NS B0M 1X0 – 902/597-8651, ext.301; Fax: 902/597-3888; Symbol: NSSS

Library Supervisor, Donna Morrison
Library Assistant, Carolyn Mooring

STELLARTON

Nova Scotia Community College - Pictou Campus Library, PO Box 820, Stellarton NS B0K 1S0 – 902/752-2002; Fax: 902/752-5446; Email: hratch@north.nsis.com – Librarian, Harvey Ratchford

SYDNEY

Canadian Coast Guard College - Library, 1990 Westmount Rd., PO Box 4500, Sydney NS B1L 6L1 – 902/564-3660; Fax: 902/564-3672; URL: http://www.cgc.ns.ca; Symbol: NSSCG – Librarian, D.N. MacSween, Email: macsween@cgc.ns.ca

Canadian Music Educators' Association – Library, 43 Victoria Hill, Sydney NS B1R 1N9 – 902/567-2398

Cape Breton Health Care Complex – Health Sciences Library, 1482 George St., Sydney NS B1P 1P3 – 902/567-8000, ext.2738; Symbol: NSSSRH – Library Assistant, Patricia Foley

Cape Breton Regional Hospital - Health Sciences Library, 1492 George St., Sydney NS B1P 1P2 – 902/562-2322, ext.137; Fax: 902/562-8593; Symbol: NSSSRH – Librarian, Patricia Colford Keough

Centre for International Studies (Nova Scotia) – Library, #256, Campus Centre, University College of Cape Breton, PO Box 5300, Sydney NS B1P 6L2 – 902/562-6090 – Program Assistant, Celia Lorway

Community Economic Development Institute – Library, University College of Cape Breton, PO Box 5300, Sydney NS B1P 6L2 – 902/564-1366 – Manager, Cecil Cameron

University College of Cape Breton - Library, PO Box 5300, Sydney NS B1P 6L2 – 902/564-1353; Fax: 902/562-6949; Email: 31128: LIB.UCCB; Symbol: NSSX
University College Librarian, Penelope Marshall, 902/539-5300, ext.388
Public Services Librarian, Laura Pervill
Technical Services Librarian, Mary Dobson

TATAMAGOUCHE

Tatamagouche Historical & Cultural Society – Library, Main St., Tatamagouche NS B0K 1V0 – Librarian, Glen Hamilton

TRURO

Nova Scotia Department of Agriculture & Marketing - Plant Industry Branch – Library, PO Box 550, Truro NS B2N 5E3 – 902/895-1571

Burchell MacDougall - Law Library, 710 Prince St., PO Box 1128, Truro NS B2N 5H1 – 902/895-1561; Fax: 902/895-7709 – Krista McNutt

Colchester Historical Society – Library, PO Box 412, Truro NS B2N 5C5 – 902/895-6284 – Archivist, Nan Harvey

Native Council of Nova Scotia – Library, Abenaki Rd., PO Box 1320, Truro NS B2N 5N2 – 902/895-1524, 1525; Toll Free: 1-800-565-4372 – Communication Support Sec., Shirley Mitchell

Nova Scotia Agricultural College - MacRae Library, PO Box 550, Truro NS B2N 5E3 – 902/893-6669; Fax: 902/895-0934; Email: Telnet: lib.nsac.ns.ca, Login: public, Password: pub.lib; Symbol: NSTA
Chief Librarian, Bonnie Waddell, 902/893-6670, Email: hwaddell@ca.nsac.ns.ca
Systems Librarian, F. Lai, 902/893-6669

Nova Scotia Teachers' College - Learning Resources Centre, PO Box 810, Truro NS B2N 5G5 – 902/893-5326; Fax: 902/893-5610; Email: ptiwana@fox.nstn.nsw.ca; Symbol: NSTT
Acquisitions & SerialsPaul Tiwana
Circulation & ReferenceSheila Pearl
CataloguingTom Acker, 902/895-5306, ext.259

WINDSOR JUNCTION

Nova Scotia Transportation & Communications - Materials Laboratory Library, Site #37, RR#1, Windsor Junction NS B0N 2V0 – 902/861-1911, ext.56; Fax: 902/861-4828 – Librarian, M. Reid

WOLFVILLE

Acadia University - Vaughan Memorial Library, Wolfville NS B0P 1X0 – 902/542-2200, ext.1510; Fax: 902/542-2128; Symbol: NSWA
University Librarian, Lorraine McQueen, Email: lorraine.mcqueen@acadian.ca
Acquisitions, Roni Fenwick, 902/542-2200, ext.1248
Information Services, Betty Jeffrey, 902/542-2200, ext.1403
Electronic Resources, Mary MacLeod, 902/542-2200, ext.1734

Wolfville Historical Society – WHS Library, PO Box 38, Wolfville NS B0P 1X0 – 902/542-9775 – Librarian, Shirley Meliott

YARMOUTH

Yarmouth County Historical Society – Library, 22 Collins St., Yarmouth NS B5A 3C8 – 902/742-5539 – Librarian/Archivist, Laura Bradley

ONTARIO

Public Libraries

Acton Public Library, 17 River St., Acton ON L7J 1C2 – 519/853-0301; Fax: 519/853-3110 – Branch Head, Catherine Yestadt – Branch of Halton Hills Public Library (*see* Georgetown)

Addison: Elizabethtown Twp. Public Library Board, RR#2, Addison ON K0E 1A0 – 613/924-9525 – Librarian, Ruth Blanchard – See also following branches: Lyn Branch Library

Ailsa Craig Branch Library, 160 Main St., Ailsa Craig ON N0M 1A0 – 519/293-3441; Fax: 519/293-3441 – Supervisor, Joan McDonald – Branch of Middlesex County Library (*see* Arva)

Ailsa Craig: Beechwood Library, RR#1, Ailsa Craig ON N0M 1A0 – Supervisor, Elizabeth McLachlan – Branch of Middlesex County Library (*see* Arva)

Ajax Public Library, 65 Harwood Ave. South, Ajax ON L1S 2H8 – 905/683-4000; Fax: 905/683-6960; URL: http://www.io.org/~bruin/; Symbol: OAJ – CEO/Librarian, Geoffrey P. Nie; Support Services Manager, Dan Gioiosa – See also following branches: Administration & Technical Services, McLean Community Branch Library, Pickering Village Branch Library

Ajax: Administration & Technical Services, 539 Westney Rd. South, Ajax ON L1S 4N7 – 905/683-6632; Fax: 905/683-6944; Email: nieg@gov.on.ca – Branch of Ajax Public Library

Ajax: McLean Community Branch Library, 95 Magill Dr., Ajax ON L1T 3K7 – 905/428-8489; Fax: 905/428-3743 – Branch Head, Cindy Kimber – Branch of Ajax Public Library

Ajax: Pickering Village Branch Library, 58 Church St. North, Ajax ON L1T 2W6 – 905/683-1140; Fax: 905/683-1140 – Branch Head, Cindy Kimber – Branch of Ajax Public Library

Alexandria Branch Library, PO Box 1030, Alexandria ON K0C 1A0 – 613/525-3241 – Supervisor/Branch Head, Colombe Raymond – Branch of Stormont, Dundas & Glengarry County Library (*see* Finch)

Alliston: New Tecumseth Public Library, PO Box 1199, Alliston ON L9R 1T3 – 705/435-0250; Fax: 705/435-2873 – CEO, Sandra Kendall – See also following branches: Alliston Memorial Branch Library, Beeton Branch Library, Tottenham Branch Library

Alliston Memorial Branch Library, 17 Victoria St. East, Alliston ON L9R 1T3 – 705/435-5651 – Branch of New Tecumseth Public Library

Canadian Almanac & Directory 1997

Almonte Public Library, PO Box 820, Almonte ON K0A 1A0 – 613/256-1037; Fax: 613/256-4423; Email: pnelson@almonte.library.on.ca; Symbol: OA – Head Librarian, Peter Nelson; Children's Librarian, Monica Blackburn

Alton Branch, 15 Station St., Alton ON L0N 1A0 – 519/941-5480; Fax: 519/941-5480 – Branch Head, Donna St. Jacques – Branch of Caledon Public Library (*see* Bolton)

Alvinston Library, 3251 River St., PO Box 44, Alvinston ON N0N 1A0 – 519/898-2921 – Librarian, Ruth Leitch – Branch of Lambton County Library (*see* Wyoming)

Ameliasburgh Twp. Library, Site 1-0, RR#1, Ameliasburg ON K0K 1A0 – 613/968-9327, 962-2551; Fax: 613/962-1514; Email: pleavey@ameliasburgh.library.on.ca; Symbol: OAAP – CEO/Chief Librarian, Peggy Leavey – See also following branches: Consecon Branch Library

Amherstburg Library, 232 Sandwich St. South, Amherstburg ON N9V 2A4 – 519/736-4632 – Supervisor, Jean Hunt – Branch of Essex County Library

Ancaster Public Library, 300 Wilson St. East, Ancaster ON L9G 2B9 – 905/648-6911; Fax: 905/648-2961 – Branch Head, Kay McDonald – Branch of Wentworth Libraries (*see* Hamilton)

Angus: Essa Centennial Library, 36 King St., PO Box 280, Angus ON L0M 1B0 – 705/424-6531; Fax: 705/424-6531 – CEO/Administrator, Loretta Metcalfe; Administrative Assistant/ILLO, Angie Wishart

Apsley: Burleigh, Anstruther & Chandos Union Public Library, Main St., PO Box 335, Apsley ON K0K 1A0 – 705/656-4333 – Chief Librarian, Susan Mycroft

Arden Branch Library, General Delivery, Arden ON K0H 1B0 – 613/335-2570 – Sue DesRosiers – Branch of Frontenac County Library (*see* Kingston)

Arkona Library, 16 Smith St., PO Box 12, Arkona ON N0M 1B0 – 519/828-3406 – Librarian, Helen Batten – Branch of Lambton County Library (*see* Wyoming)

Arnprior Public Library, 21 Madawaska St., Arnprior ON K7S 1R6 – 613/623-2279; Fax: 613/623-9882; Email: j.barker@sauron.globalx.net; Symbol: OAR – Chief Librarian, Judy Barker; Children's Librarian, Patricia Bouchard; ILL Librarian, Gail Whalen

Arthur Branch Library, 183 George St., Arthur ON N0G 1A0 – 519/848-3999; Fax: 519/846-2066 – Branch Supervisor, Trudy Gohn – Branch of Wellington County Library (*see* Fergus)

Arva: Middlesex County Library, Centennial Bldg., 11 St. John's Dr., Arva ON N0M 1C0 – 519/660-8368; Fax: 519/660-6511 – County Librarian, Margaret Rule; Reference Librarian, Carol Roberts; Systems Librarian, Beverly Sweezie – See also following branches: Ailsa Craig Branch Library, Avon Library, Beechwood Library, Coldstream Library, Delaware Library, Dorchester Library, Glencoe Library, Harrietsville Library, Komoka Library, London Twp. Library, Lucan Library, Melbourne Library, Mount Brydges Library, Newbury Library, Parkhill Library, Putnam Library, Wardsville Library, West Nissouri Library

Astorville: East Ferris Twp. Public Library Board, Astorville Public Library, Astorville ON P0H 1B0 – 705/752-2042 – CEO, Claudette Quinn

Athens Public Library, PO Box 309, Athens ON K0E 1B0 – 613/924-2048 – CEO, Freda Schaafsma

Atikokan Public Library, Civic Centre, Atikokan ON P0T 1C0 – 807/597-4406; Fax: 807/597-1514 – Librarian, Doris B. Brown

Auburn Branch Library, Auburn ON N0M 1E0 – Branch Supervisor, Laura May Chamney – Branch of Huron County Library (*see* Goderich)

Aurora Public Library, 56 Victoria St., Aurora ON L4G 1R2 – 905/727-9493; Fax: 905/727-9374 – Librarian, Colleen Abbott

Avonmore Branch Library, PO Box 70, Avonmore ON K0C 1C0 – 613/346-2137 – Supervisor/Branch Head, Beverley J. Campbell – Branch of Stormont, Dundas & Glengarry County Library (*see* Finch)

Avon Library, Avon ON N0L 2J0 – 519/269-3652 – Supervisor, Anita Crandall – Branch of Middlesex County Library (*see* Arva)

Aylmer Old Town Hall Library, 38 John St. South, Aylmer ON N5H 2C2 – 519/773-2439 – Supervisor, Christina Mayhew – Branch of Elgin County Library (*see* St. Thomas)

Ayr: Ayr Branch Library, Stanley St., PO Box 339, Ayr ON N0B 1E0 – 519/632-7298 – Branch Supervisor, Diane Schmidt – Branch of Waterloo Regional Library (*see* Kitchener)

Ayton: Normanby Twp. Public Library, Ayton ON N0G 1C0 – 519/665-7784 – Librarian, Janet Byers

Azilda Branch Library, PO Box 818, Azilda ON P0M 1B0 – 705/983-2650 – Librarian, Solange Jolicoeur – Branch of Rayside-Balfour Library (*see* Chelmsford)

Baden Branch Library, 115 Snyder's Rd. East, PO Box 214, Baden ON N0B 1G0 – 519/634-8933 – Asst. Branch Supervisor, Connie Miller – Branch of Waterloo Regional Library (*see* Kitchener)

Baillieboro Branch Library, 199 Hwy. 28, Baillieboro ON K0L 1B0 – 705/939-6510; Fax: 705/939-1096 – Branch Head, Vilda Nurse – Branch of Cavan, Millbrook, South Monaghan Union Library (*see* Millbrook)

Bala Public Library, Bala Community Centre, PO Box 50, Bala ON P0C 1A0 – 705/762-0576 – Librarian, Mari Carson – Branch of Port Carling Public Library

Bala: Wahta Mohawks Library, PO Box 327, Bala ON P0C 1A0 – 416/762-3343; Fax: 416/762-5744 – CEO, Lila Commandant

Balmertown: Twp. of Golden - Balmertown Public Library, PO Box 280, Balmertown ON P0V 1C0 – 807/735-2110; Fax: 807/735-2110 – CEO/Librarian, Arlene Johnson

Bancroft Public Library, 14 Flint St., PO Box 127, Bancroft ON K0L 1C0 – 613/332-3380 – CEO, Betty Lambeck

Bancroft: United Public Library, c/o Herman Public School, RR#4, Bancroft ON K0L 1C0 – 613/332-2897 – CEO, Ursula O'Connor

Barrie Public Library, 60 Worsley St., Barrie ON L4M 1L6 – 705/728-1010; Fax: 705/728-4322 – Director of Library Services, Adele Kostiak; Circulation Services, Joanne Comper; Children's & Adult Services, Katherine Wallis; Technical Services Librarian, Dunja Conroy

Barrie: Southern Ontario Library Service - Barrie, 30 Morrow Rd., Barrie ON L4N 3V8 – 705/733-0051; Fax: 705/733-1143

Barry's Bay Public Library, Opeongo Line, PO Box 970, Barry's Bay ON K0J 1B0 – 613/756-2000 – Librarian, A. Lorbetskie – See also following branches: Sherwood Jones & Burns Branch

Barwick Community Library, PO Box 4, Barwick ON P0W 1A0 – 807/487-2354 – Librarian, Doris Dyson

Batawa: Sidney Twp. Public Library, 1 Haig St., PO Box 1057, Batawa ON K0K 1E0 – 613/398-7344 – CEO, Robert Amesse – See also following branches: Bayside Branch Library

Bath Branch Library, PO Box 400, Bath ON K0H 1G0 – 613/352-3361 – Supervisor, Phyllis Strain – Branch of Lennox & Addington County Library (*see* Napanee)

Bath: Sandhurst Branch Library, RR#1, Bath ON K0H 1G0 – 613/352-5007 – Supervisor, Phyllis Strain – Branch of Lennox & Addington County Library (*see* Napanee)

Battersea: Storrington Twp., Sunbury Branch Library, RR#2, Battersea ON K0H 1H0 – 613/353-6333 – Carol Lee Riley – Branch of Frontenac County Library (*see* Kingston)

Bayfield Branch Library, PO Box 2090, Bayfield ON N0M 1G0 – 519/565-2886 – Branch Supervisor, Anny Johnston – Branch of Huron County Library (*see* Goderich)

Baysville: Lake of Bays Public Library, University Ave., Baysville ON P0B 1A0 – 705/767-2361; Fax: 705/767-3933; Email: linla@muskoka.com – CEO, Linda Lacroix – See also following branches: Dwight Public Library

Beachburg Public Library, 202 Main St., PO Box 159, Beachburg ON K0J 1C0 – 613/582-7090 – CEO, Marilyn Labow

Beachville Library, Beachville ON N0J 1A0 – 519/423-6533 – Supervisor, Teresa Van Rees – Branch of Oxford County Library (*see* Woodstock)

Beamsville: Lincoln Public Library, 4996 Beam St., PO Box 460, Beamsville ON L0R 1B0 – 905/563-7014; Fax: 905/563-1810 – CEO, A. Lorene Sims; Children's Librarian, Elizabeth Peters – See also following branches: Moses F. Rittenhouse Branch Library

Beardmore Public Library, 185 Main St., PO Box 240, Beardmore ON P0T 1G0 – 807/875-2212; Fax: 807/875-2212 – Head Librarian, Lucie Lavigne

Bearskin Lake Public Library, Bearskin Lake ON P0V 1E0 – 807/363-2518; Fax: 807/363-1066

Beaverton Branch, 401 Simcoe St., PO Box 310, Beaverton ON L0K 1A0 – 705/426-9283 – Librarian, Brigitta Johnston – Branch of Brock Twp. Public Library (*see* Sunderland)

Beeton Branch Library, 38 Main St. West, PO Box 305, Beeton ON L0G 1A0 – 905/729-3726 – Branch of New Tecumseth Public Library (*see* Alliston)

Belfountain Branch, 17239 - 5th Line West, Belfountain ON L0N 1B0 – 519/927-5701; Fax: 519/927-5662 – Branch Assistant, Glenda Dolan – Branch of Caledon Public Library (*see* Bolton)

Belle River Public Library, 467 Notre Dame St., PO Box 459, Belle River ON N0R 1A0 – 519/728-2324 – CEO, Christina Ouellette

Belleville Public Library, 223 Pinnacle St., Belleville ON K8N 3A7 – 613/968-6731; Fax: 613/968-6841; Symbol: OBE – CEO, Leona Hendry; Reference Librarian, Elizabeth Mitchell; Circulation Supervisor, Fanny Tom; Children's Librarian, Barbara Coulman; Technical Services Librarian, Brian Naulls; Systems Manager, Carlene Martin – See also following branches: East Branch Library

Belleville: Bayside Branch Library, RR#2, Belleville ON K8N 4Z2 – 613/962-5695 – Branch Head, Iris Claveau – Branch of Sidney Twp. Public Library (*see* Batawa)

Belleville: East Branch Library, 495 Victoria Ave., Belleville ON K8N 2G4 – 613/962-1681 – Branch Head, Winnifred Voogt – Branch of Belleville Public Library

Belmont Public Library, PO Box 149, Belmont ON N0L 1B0 – 519/644-1560 – Supervisor, Maria Smit – Branch of Elgin County Library (*see* St. Thomas)

Binbrook Public Library, Hwy. 56, PO Box 89, Binbrook ON L0R 1C0 – 905/692-3323; Fax: 905/692-3323 – Branch Head, Carolyne Timms – Branch of Wentworth Libraries (*see* Hamilton)

Birch Island: Whitefish River First Nation Public Library, General Delivery, Birch Island ON P0P 1A0 – 705/285-0028; Fax: 705/285-4532 – Librarian, Rose Jacko

Blenheim Branch Library, George St., Blenheim ON N0P 1A0 – 519/676-3174 – Branch Librarian, Diane Sanford – Branch of Kent County Library (*see* Chatham)

Blind River Public Library, 17 Michigan Ave., PO Box 880, Blind River ON P0R 1B0 – 705/356-7616; Fax: 705/356-7343 – Librarian, Rhea Marcellus

Canadian Almanac & Directory 1997

Blind River: Mississauga First Nation Library, PO Box 1299, Blind River ON P0R 1B0 – 705/356-1621; Fax: 705/356-1740 – CEO, Clifford Niganobe

Bloomfield-Hallowell Union Library, 36 Main St., PO Box 9, Bloomfield ON K0K 1G0 – 613/393-3400; Fax: 613/393-1323 – Librarian, Barbara Sweet

Bloomingdale Branch Library, Bloomingdale ON N0B 1K0 – 519/745-3151 – Asst. Branch Supervisor, Janice Martin – Branch of Waterloo Regional Library (see Kitchener)

Bluevale Branch Library, Bluevale ON N0G 1G0 – Branch Supervisor, Bonnie Grieg – Branch of Huron County Library (see Goderich)

Blyth Branch Library, PO Box 388, Blyth ON N0M 1H0 – 519/523-4400 – Branch Supervisor, Pat Brigham – Branch of Huron County Library (see Goderich)

Bobcaygeon Branch Library, Bobcaygeon ON K0M 1A0 – 705/738-2088; Fax: 705/738-2088 – Librarian, Valerie Garland – Branch of Victoria County Public Library (see Lindsay)

Bolton: Caledon Public Library, Albion-Bolton Community Centre, 150 Queen St. South, Bolton ON L7E 1E3 – 905/857-1400; Fax: 905/857-8280; Email: CNCP: lb EHQ 010 – Chief Librarian, Rod Hall; Reference/Acquisitions Librarian, Louisa Cooper, 519/927-5662; Children's Librarian, Rose Paulovich; Public Services Librarian, Gladys Rennie; Technical Services Librarian, Margaret Fleetwood – See also following branches: Albion-Bolton Branch, Alton Branch, Belfountain Branch, Caledon East Branch, Caledon Village Branch, Inglewood Library

Bolton: Albion-Bolton Branch, Albion-Bolton Community Centre, 150 Queen St. South, Bolton ON L7E 1E3 – 905/857-1400; Fax: 905/857-8280 – Branch Head, Les Szollosy – Branch of Caledon Public Library

Bond Head Branch, Bond Head Community Centre, PO Box 58, Bond Head ON L0G 1B0 – 905/775-6875 – Lynn Flack – Branch of Bradford West Gwillimbury Public Libraries

Bonfield Public Library, Hwy. 531, Bonfield ON P0H 1E0 – 705/776-2641 – Librarian, Jeanette Shields

Borden: Base Borden Public & Military Library, PO Box 430, Borden ON L0M 1C0 – 705/424-1200 – Head Librarian, Terri Bristow

Bothwell Branch Library, Main St., Bothwell ON N0P 1C0 – 519/695-2844 – Branch Librarian, Marianne Buchanan – Branch of Kent County Library (see Chatham)

Bothwell: Caldwell First Nation Library, 215 Main St., PO Box 250, Bothwell ON N0P 1C0 – 519/695-3920; Fax: 519/695-2358 – Librarian, Larry Johnson

Bourget: Bibliothèque publique de Canton de Clarence, CP 143, Bourget ON K0A 1E0 – Librarian, Marthe Boileau – See also following branches: Succursale de Bourget, Succursale de Clarence Creek, Succursale de Hammond, Succursale de St-Pascal-Baylon

Bourget: Succursale de Bourget, 11 Laval St. East, CP 98, Bourget ON K0A 1E0 – Bibliothécaire, Thérèse D. Lalonde – Branch of Bibliothèque publique de Canton de Clarence

Bowmanville: Clarington Public Library, 62 Temperance St., Bowmanville ON L1C 3A8 – 905/623-7322; Fax: 905/623-9905 – Library Director, Cynthia Mearns – See also following branches: Clarke Branch Library, Newcastle Village Branch Library

Bracebridge Public Library, 94 Manitoba St., PO Box 1537, Bracebridge ON P1L 1S1 – 705/645-4171; Fax: 705/645-1262 – Chief Librarian, Ann-Marie Mathieu

Bradford West Gwillimbury Public Libraries, 100 Holland Crt., PO Box 130, Bradford ON L3Z 2A7 – 905/775-3328; Fax: 905/775-1236 – CEO, Alannah Hegedus; Reference/Children's, Anita Sikma; Circulation, Adrienne Price; Technical Services, Liz Fenwick; ILL, Flora Nydam – See also following branches: Bond Head Branch, Newton Robinson Branch

Bradford: Newton Robinson Branch, Site #5, RR#2, PO Box 27, Bradford ON L3Z 2A7 – 705/458-4515 – Gwen Taylor – Branch of Bradford West Gwillimbury Public Libraries

Brampton Public Library, 65 Queen St. East, Brampton ON L6W 3L6 – 905/453-2444; Fax: 905/453-4602; Symbol: BRAM – CEO, Tom Drynan, Email: dryant@gov.on.ca – See also following branches: Chinguacousy Resource Branch, Cyril Clark Branch Library, Fletcher's Creek Branch Library, Four Corners Branch Library

Brampton: Chinguacousy Resource Branch, 150 Central Park Dr., Bramalea ON L6T 1B4 – 905/793-4636; Fax: 905/793-0506; Symbol: OBRA – Branch Manager, Cynthia Toniolo – Branch of Brampton Public Library

Brampton: Cyril Clark Branch Library, 20 Loafer's Lake Lane, Brampton ON L6Z 1X9 – 905/846-7310; Fax: 905/846-4278 – Branch Supervisor, Catherine Carreiro – Branch of Brampton Public Library

Brampton: Fletcher's Creek Branch Library, City South Plaza, #308A, 7700 Hurontario St., Brampton ON L6V 3N2 – 905/453-1038; Fax: 905/453-8425 – Branch Supervisor, Arleta Wang – Branch of Brampton Public Library

Brampton: Four Corners Branch Library, 65 Queen St. East, Brampton ON L6W 3L6 – 905/453-2444; Fax: 905/453-4602 – Manager, Branch Libraries, Gary Baumbach – Branch of Brampton Public Library

Brantford Public Library, 173 Colborne St., Brantford ON N3T 2G8 – 519/756-2220; Fax: 519/756-4979 – CEO, Wendy Newman; Circulation, Mary Varga; Reference & Branch Services, Christopher Stanley; Technical Services, June Hibbert; Business Administrator, Shirley Allan; Public Services, Lorie Macdonald-Milton – See also following branches: St. Paul Avenue Branch Library

Brantford: St. Paul Avenue Branch Library, 441 St. Paul Ave., Brantford ON N3R 4N8 – 519/753-2179 – Reference & Branch Services, Christopher Stanley – Branch of Brantford Public Library

Brechin: Mara Twp. Public Library, Brechin ON L0K 1B0 – 705/484-0476 – Librarian, A. Lambert – See also following branches: Atherley Branch Library

Bridgenorth: Smith Twp. Public Library, Ward St., PO Box 500, Bridgenorth ON K0L 1H0 – 705/292-5065; Fax: 705/292-6695; Symbol: OBRIS – Library Technician, Joan MacDonald

Brigden Library, 1540 Duncan St., PO Box 339, Brigden ON N0N 1B0 – 519/864-1142 – Head Librarian, Janet Eves – Branch of Lambton County Library (see Wyoming)

Brighton Public Library, PO Box 129, Brighton ON K0K 1H0 – 613/475-2511 – CEO, Maureen Venton

Brights Grove Library, 2600 Hamilton Rd., PO Box 339, Brights Grove ON N0N 1C0 – 519/869-2351 – Librarian, Mavis Schmid – Branch of Lambton County Library (see Wyoming)

Brinston Branch Library, PO Box 40, Brinston ON K0E 1C0 – 613/652-2045 – Supervisor/Branch Head, Elaine Horner – Branch of Stormont, Dundas & Glengarry County Library (see Finch)

Britt Area Public Library, PO Box 2, Britt ON P0G 1A0 – 705/383-2292 – Librarian, Barbara Wohleber

Britt: Magnetawan First Nation Public Library, RR#1, PO Box 15, Britt ON P0G 1A0 – 705/383-2477; Fax: 705/383-2566 – CEO, Faye Lachapelle

Brockville: Augusta Twp. Public Library, RR#2, Brockville ON K6V 5T2 – 613/926-2449; Fax: 613/926-0440 – Head Librarian, Denise Maloney; Reference Librarian, Linda Parrott

Brockville Public Library, 21 George St., PO Box 100, Brockville ON K6V 5T7 – 613/342-3936; Fax: 613/342-9598 – CEO, Margaret Williams; Reference Librarian, Monica Fazekas; Children's Librarian, Maureen Wharton

Brooklin Branch Library, PO Box 430, Brooklin ON L0B 1C0 – 905/655-3191 – Branch Head, Margaret Edwards – Branch of Whitby Public Library

Brownsville Library, Brownsville ON N0L 1C0 – 519/877-2938 – Supervisor, Dora Sykes – Branch of Oxford County Library (see Woodstock)

Bruce Mines & Plumber Additional Union Library, Desbarats St., PO Box 249, Bruce Mines ON P0R 1C0 – 705/785-3370; Fax: 705/785-3370 – Librarian, Gail Bennett

Brussels Branch Library, PO Box 80, Brussels ON N0G 1H0 – 519/887-6448 – Branch Supervisor, Susan Nichol – Branch of Huron County Library (see Goderich)

Brussels: Cranbrook Branch Library, RR#3, Brussels ON N0G 1H0 – Branch Supervisor, Carmie Newman – Branch of Huron County Library (see Goderich)

Buckhorn: Harvey Twp. Public Library, General Delivery, Buckhorn ON K0L 1J0 – 705/657-3695; Fax: 705/657-9077; Symbol: OBH – CEO, Maria Bradburn

Burford Twp. Public Library, 120 King St., PO Box 255, Burford ON N0E 1A0 – 519/449-5371 – Librarian, E. Strond

Burgessville Library, PO Box 70, Burgessville ON N0J 1C0 – 519/424-2404 – Supervisor, Linda Visser – Branch of Oxford County Library (see Woodstock)

Burk's Falls Armour & Ryerson Union Public Library, Yonge & Copeland Sts., PO Box 620, Burk's Falls ON P0A 1C0 – 705/382-3327; Fax: 705/382-2497 – CEO, Margaret Ross, 705/382-2852

Burlington Public Library, 2331 New St., Burlington ON L7R 1J4 – 905/639-3611; Fax: 905/681-7277; Email: schickw@haltonbe.on.ca; Symbol: OBU – CEO, Wendy M. Schick; Adult Services Librarian, Judy Walker; Children's Librarian, Andrea Gordon; Technical Services Librarian, Gwen Forsyth – See also following branches: Aldershot Branch Library, Kilbride Branch Library, New Appleby Branch Library, Tyandaga Branch Library

Burlington: Aldershot Branch Library, 335 Plains Rd. East, Burlington ON L7T 2C7 – 905/333-9995; Fax: 905/681-7277 – Branch Head, Diane Warrick – Branch of Burlington Public Library

Burlington: New Appleby Branch Library, 676 Appleby Line, Burlington ON L7L 5Y1 – 905/639-6373; Fax: 905/681-7277 – Branch Head, Laura Williams – Branch of Burlington Public Library

Burlington: Tyandaga Branch Library, 1500 Upper Middle Rd., Burlington ON L7P 3P5 – 905/335-2209; Fax: 905/681-7277 – Branch Head, Marilyn Powell – Branch of Burlington Public Library

Burnt River Branch Library, Burnt River ON K0M 1C0 – 705/454-8045 – Branch Head, June Hunter – Branch of Victoria County Public Library (see Lindsay)

Burritt's Rapids: Oxford-on-Rideau Twp. Public Library, PO Box 119, Burritt's Rapids ON K0G 1B0 – 613/269-3636 – Librarian, Olivia Mills – See also following branches: Burritt's Rapids Library, Oxford Mills Library

Burritt's Rapids Library, PO Box 119, Burritt's Rapids ON K0G 1B0 – 613/269-3636 – Librarian, Olivia Mills – Branch of Oxford-on-Rideau Twp. Public Library

Cache Bay Public Library, 77 Cache St., Cache Bay ON P0H 1G0 – CEO, Clare Lisk

Calabogie: Bagot & Blythfield Twp. Public Library, Calabogie ON K0J 1H0 – 613/752-2317 – Librarian, Lois Mulvihill

Caledon East Branch, 24 Church St., Caledon East ON L0N 1E0 – 905/584-2094; Fax: 905/584-2094 – Branch Head, Gerry Lawlor – Branch of Caledon Public Library (see Bolton)

Caledon Village Branch, 18313 Hwy. 10, Caledon Village ON L0N 1C0 – 519/927-5800 – Branch Head, Jean Douglas – Branch of Caledon Public Library (see Bolton)

Caledonia: Haldimand Public Libraries, 25 Caithness St. West, Caledonia ON N3W 1B7 – 905/772-5467; Fax: 905/772-3542 – Librarian, Janet Martin – See also following branches: Caledonia Public Library, Cayuga Public Library, Hagersville Public Library

Caledonia Public Library, 25 Caithness St. West, Caledonia ON N3W 1B7 – 905/765-2634 – Library Head, Mary Edwards – Branch of Haldimand Public Libraries (see Caledonia)

Callander: North Himsworth Twp. Public Library, Catherine St., PO Box 149, Callander ON P0H 1H0 – 705/752-2544 – CEO, Helen McDonnell

Cambray Branch Library, Cambray ON K0M 1E0 – 705/374-4900 – Branch Head, Isabel Barton – Branch of Victoria County Public Library (see Lindsay)

Cambridge Public Library, 20 Grand Ave. North, Cambridge ON N1S 2K6 – 519/621-0460; Fax: 519/621-2080 – Head, Information Services, Barbara Carlton; Circulation & Children's Librarian, Dixie Alkier; Automation Systems Librarian, Christine Wilson – See also following branches: Hespeler Branch, Preston Branch

Cambridge: Hespeler Branch, 5 Tannery St., Cambridge ON N3C 2C1 – 519/658-4412; Fax: 519/621-2080 – Librarian, Liz Krist – Branch of Cambridge Public Library

Cambridge: Preston Branch, 435 King St. East, Cambridge ON N3H 3N1 – 519/653-3632; Fax: 519/621-2080 – Librarian, Angela Caretta – Branch of Cambridge Public Library

Camden East Branch, PO Box 10, Camden East ON K0K 1J0 – 613/378-2101 – Supervisor, Mary Lou Fraser – Branch of Lennox & Addington County Library (see Napanee)

Camlachie Library, 6707 Camlachie Sideroad, PO Box 130, Camlachie ON N0N 1E0 – 519/899-2202 – Librarian, Anne Ross – Branch of Lambton County Library (see Wyoming)

Campbellcroft: Garden Hill Branch Library, RR#1, Campbellcroft ON L0A 1B0 – 905/797-2473 – Branch Head, Merrylin Caldwell – Branch of Northumberland County Public Library (see Hastings)

Campbellford/Seymour Branch Library, Bridge St., Campbellford ON K0L 1L0 – 705/653-3611 – Branch Head, Mae Bailey – Branch of Northumberland County Public Library (see Hastings)

Canfield: Caistorville Branch Library, RR#2, Canfield ON N0A 1C0 – 905/692-4290 – Branch Head, Barb Stolys – Branch of West Lincoln Public Library (see Smithville)

Cannington Branch, Ann St. North, Cannington ON L0E 1E0 – 705/432-2867 – Branch Head, Susan Ross – Branch of Brock Twp. Public Library (see Sunderland)

Capreol Public Library, Morin St., PO Box 520, Capreol ON P0M 1H0 – 705/858-1622 – Librarian, Barbara Finnson

Cardiff: Bicroft Branch Library, Cardiff ON K0L 1M0 – 613/339-2804 – Supervisor, Cathy Passaretti – Branch of Haliburton County Public Library

Cardinal Public Library, Lewis St., PO Box 490, Cardinal ON K0E 1E0 – 613/657-3822 – Librarian, Betty Donaldson

Cargill Branch Library, King St., Cargill ON N0G 1J0 – 519/366-2259 – Branch Supervisor, Cheryl Parker – Branch of Bruce County Public Library (see Port Elgin)

Carleton Place Public Library, 101 Beckwith St., Carleton Place ON K7C 2T3 – 613/257-2702 – Librarian, Janet French-Baril

Carlisle Library, PO Box 320, Carlisle ON L0R 1H0 – 905/689-8769 – Branch Head, Elizabeth Vervaeke – Branch of Wentworth Libraries (see Hamilton)

Carp: West Carleton Twp. Public Library, 3911 Carp Rd., Carp ON K0A 1L0 – 613/839-5412; Fax: 613/839-0179; Email: wmckay@westcarleton.twp.library.on.ca – CEO, Wendy McKay; Main Branch Supervisor, Barbara Enright – See also following branches: Constance & Buckham's Bay Branch, Fitzroy Harbour Branch

Carp: Constance & Buckham's Bay Branch, c/o Constance & Buckham's Bay Community Centre, 262 Len Purcell Dr., Constance Bay ON K0A 1L0 – 613/839-5412; Fax: 613/839-0179 – Supervisor, Mary Porritt – Branch of West Carleton Twp. Public Library

Carp: Fitzroy Harbour Branch, Fitzroy Harbour Community Centre, 100 Victoria St., PO Box 220, Carp ON K0A 1L0 – 613/839-5412; Fax: 613/839-0179 – Supervisor, Mary Porritt – Branch of West Carleton Twp. Public Library

Cartier Public Library, Cartier ON P0M 1J0 – 705/965-2001; Fax: 705/965-2500 – Librarian, Simonne McGowan

Casselman Public Library, PO Box 340, Casselman ON K0A 1M0 – 613/764-5505 – Librarian, Thérèse Chenier

Castleton: Cramahe Twp. Public Library, Town Hall, PO Box 82, Castleton ON K0K 1M0 – 905/344-7320 – Chief Librarian, Suzanne LaBerge

Cavan: Mount Pleasant Branch Library, RR#2, Cavan ON L0A 1C0 – 705/799-7841 – Librarian, Bonnie Bullock – Branch of Cavan, Millbrook, South Monaghan Union Library (see Millbrook)

Cayuga Public Library, 28 Cayuga St., PO Box 550, Cayuga ON N0A 1E0 – 905/772-5726; Symbol: EBHA – Library Head, Donna Armstrong – Branch of Haldimand Public Libraries (see Caledonia)

Chalk River Public Library, PO Box 160, Chalk River ON K0J 1J0 – 613/589-2966 – Librarian, Judy Field

Chapleau Public Library, PO Box 910, Chapleau ON P0M 1K0 – 705/864-0852 – Chief Librarian, Diane Collings

Chatham: Kent County Library, 455 Grand Ave. West, Chatham ON N7L 1C5 – 519/351-1010, ext.301; Fax: 519/351-9669 – Director, Margaret Scott – See also following branches: Blenheim Branch Library, Bothwell Branch Library, Dresden Branch Library, Highgate Branch Library, Merlin Branch Library, North Maple Mall Branch Library, Ridgetown Branch Library, Thamesville Branch Library, Tilbury Branch Library, Wallaceburg Branch Library, Wheatley Branch Library

Chatham Public Library, 120 Queen St., Chatham ON N7M 2G6 – 519/354-2940; Fax: 519/436-3237; Email: OPLIN CN/CP DIALCOM OLS002; Symbol: OCHA – Director, Library Services, Sally Scherer; Children's Librarian, Dianne Thompson; Public Services Coordinator, Sheila Gibbs; Technical Services Coordinator, Pam Sojczynski; Acquisitions Coordinator, Lynne Brown

Chatham: North Maple Mall Branch Library, 801 St. Clair St., Chatham ON N7M 5J7 – 519/354-7922 – Branch Librarian, Karen Charbonneau – Branch of Kent County Library (see Chatham)

Chelmsford: Rayside-Balfour Library, PO Box 1720, Chelmsford ON P0M 1L0 – 705/855-9333; Fax: 705/855-4629 – Librarian, Jacqueline Vaillancourt – See also following branches: Azilda Branch Library

Chesley Branch Library, 102 - 1 Ave. Southibrary, PO Box 220, Chesley ON N0G 1L0 – 519/363-2239 – Branch Supervisor, Mary Witzke – Branch of Bruce County Public Library (see Port Elgin)

Chesterville Branch Library, PO Box 120, Chesterville ON K0C 1H0 – 613/448-2616 – Supervisor/Branch Head, Verla Levere – Branch of Stormont, Dundas & Glengarry County Library (see Finch)

Christian Island: Beausoleil First Nation Library, Cedar Point PO, Christian Island ON L0K 1C0 – 705/247-2011; Fax: 705/247-2239 – Librarian, Carlene Montague

Churchill Branch Library, RR#1, Churchill ON L0L 1K0 – 705/456-2671; Fax: 705/456-4467 – Branch Head, Paula Wright – Branch of Innisfil Public Library (see Stroud)

Clarence Creek: Succursale de Clarence Creek, Clarence Creek ON K0A 1N0 – Bibliothécaire, Raymond Lafleur – Branch of Bibliothèque publique de Canton de Clarence (see Bourget)

Clarence Creek: Succursale de Hammond, CP 102, Hammond ON K0A 2A0 – Bibliothécaire, Pierrette Hillier – Branch of Bibliothèque publique de Canton de Clarence (see Bourget)

Clarksburg: L.E. Shore Memorial Library, 175 Bruce St. South, PO Box 357, Thornbury ON N0H 2P0 – 519/599-3681; Fax: 519/599-7951; Email: leonard@georgian.net – CEO, Ken Haigh

Clifford Branch Library, Clifford ON N0G 1M0 – 519/327-8328; Fax: 519/846-2066 – Branch Supervisor, Henny Derbecker – Branch of Wellington County Library (see Fergus)

Clinton Branch Library, 27 Albert St., PO Box 370, Clinton ON N0M 1L0 – 519/482-3673 – Branch Supervisor, Ingrid Bos – Branch of Huron County Library (see Goderich)

Cloyne: Barrie Twp., Cloyne Branch Library, PO Box 190, Cloyne ON K0H 1K0 – 613/336-8744 – Janet Black – Branch of Frontenac County Library (see Kingston)

Cobalt Public Library, PO Box 170, Cobalt ON P0J 1C0 – 705/679-8120 – CEO, B. Eno

Cobden Public Library, 44 Main St., PO Box 40, Cobden ON K0J 1K0 – 613/646-7592 – Librarian, Shirley A. Sutherland

Coboconk Branch Library, PO Box 73, Coboconk ON K0M 1K0 – 705/454-1777; Fax: 705/454-1777 – Branch Head, Laurie Campbell – Branch of Victoria County Public Library (see Lindsay)

Cobourg Public Library, 200 Ontario St. South, Cobourg ON K9A 5P4 – 905/372-9271; Fax: 905/372-4538 – Chief Librarian, Valerie Scott

Cochrane Public Library, 143 - 3rd St., PO Box 700, Cochrane ON P0L 1C0 – 705/272-4178; Fax: 705/272-4165 – CEO, Audrey Andrews; Children's Librarian, Beatrice Fortin; Head, Interlibrary Loans, Carole Bernard

Codrington: Brighton Twp. Branch Library, RR#2, Codrington ON K0K 1R0 – Branch Head, Grace McLean – Branch of Northumberland County Public Library (see Hastings)

Coe Hill: Wollaston & Limerick Union Public Library, Coe Hill Public School, PO Box 100, Coe Hill ON K0L 1P0 – 613/337-5711 – Librarian, Catherine Giroux

Colborne Public Library, 1 Toronto St., PO Box 190, Colborne ON K0K 1S0 – 905/355-3722; Fax: 905/355-3430; Email: ocolb@eagle.ca; Symbol: OCOLB – Librarian, Pat Johnson

Coldwater Memorial Public Library, 31 Coldwater Rd., PO Box 278, Coldwater ON L0K 1E0 – 705/686-3601 – CEO, Shirley Jennett

Collingwood Public Library, 100 Second St., Collingwood ON L9Y 1E5 – 705/445-1571; Fax: 705/445-3704; Email: clib@georgian.net – Chief Librarian/CEO, Kerri Robinson; Reference Librarian, Debra Kuehl; Children's Librarian, Lynda Reid; Technical Services Librarian, Judith Koenig; Audio Visual, Ruth Branget; Public Relations Coordinator, Kathy Frizell; Systems Administrator, Karen Berry

Comber Branch Library, 6400 Main St., PO Box 250, Comber ON N0P 1J0 – 519/687-2832 – Supervisor, Gisèle Lévesque – Branch of Essex County Library

Coniston Branch Library, 30 Second Ave., Coniston ON P0M 1M0 – 705/694-5511; Fax: 705/694-0992 – Head Librarian, Jane Shannon – Branch of Nickel Centre Public Library (*see* Garson)

Consecon Branch Library, PO Box 130, Consecon ON K0K 1T0 – 613/392-1106; Fax: 613/962-1514 – Branch of Ameliasburgh Twp. Library

Cookstown Branch Library, 19 Queen St., PO Box 261, Cookstown ON L0L 1L0 – 705/458-1273; Fax: 705/458-1294; Email: sbaues@innisfil.library.on.ca – Branch Head, Susan Baues – Branch of Innisfil Public Library (*see* Stroud)

Copper Cliff Centennial Library, 11 Balsam St., PO Box 790, Copper Cliff ON P0M 1N0 – 705/673-1155, ext.280; Fax: 705/682-4520 – Branch Supervisor, Heini Heinonen-Kari; Branch Assistant, Joanne Charbonneau – Branch of Sudbury Public Library

Cornwall: Akwesasne Library, PO Box 579, Cornwall ON K6H 5T3 – 518/358-2240; Fax: 518/358-2649 – Director/Circulation Librarian, Carol C. White, 518/358-2240; Acquisitions Librarian, Corinne White, 518/358-2240

Cornwall Public Library, 208 Second St. East, PO Box 939, Cornwall ON K6H 5V1 – 613/932-4796; Fax: 613/932-2715; Symbol: OC – CEO/Chief Librarian, Robert Hubsher; Deputy Chief Librarian, Magdalene Albert; Reference Librarian, Brenda Smith; Head of Administration, Janet Harwood; Children's Librarian, Kae Elgie

Corunna Library, 417 Lyndock St., PO Box 460, Corunna ON N0N 1G0 – 519/862-1132 – Librarian, Elizabeth Cusden – Branch of Lambton County Library (*see* Wyoming)

Cottam Branch Library, 122 Fox St., PO Box 159, Cottam ON N0R 1B0 – 519/839-5040 – Supervisor, Emily Somerville – Branch of Essex County Library

Courtright Library, 1534 - 4th St., PO Box 182, Courtright ON N0N 1H0 – 519/867-2712 – Librarian, Diane Leizert – Branch of Lambton County Library (*see* Wyoming)

Creemore Branch, 165 Jane St., PO Box 279, Creemore ON L0M 5G0 – 705/466-3011; Fax: 705/466-3011 – Branch Head, Joyce Smith – Branch of Clearview Public Library (*see* Stayner)

Crysler Branch Library, PO Box 190, Crysler ON K0A 1R0 – 613/987-2090 – Supervisor/Branch Head, Lucille Quenneville – Branch of Stormont, Dundas & Glengarry County Library (*see* Finch)

Curve Lake Band Library, Curve Lake PO, Curve Lake ON K0L 1R0 – 705/657-3217; Fax: 705/657-8707 – CEO, Kathleen Taylor

Cutler: Serpent River First Nation Public Library, Village Rd., Cutler ON P0P 1B0 – 705/844-2131; Fax: 705/844-2757 – Librarian, Virginia McLeod

Dalkeith Branch Library, PO Box 70, Dalkeith ON K0B 1E0 – 613/874-2337 – Supervisor/Branch Head, Lillian Crooks – Branch of Stormont, Dundas & Glengarry County Library (*see* Finch)

Deep River: Rolph, Buchanan, Wylie & McKay Twp. Public Library, Municipal Hall, RR#1, Deep River ON K0J 1P0 – 613/584-2714; Fax: 613/584-3285; Symbol: OROLP – Librarian, Maureen L. Bakewell

Deep River: W.B. Lewis Public Library, 55 Ridge Rd., PO Box 278, Deep River ON K0J 1P0 – 613/584-4244; Fax: 613/584-1405; Symbol: RYDR – CEO, Jill Foster; Children's Librarian, Jane Linauskas

Delaware Library, Lion's Park, Young St., Delaware ON N0L 1E0 – 519/652-9978 – Supervisor, Linda Verberne – Branch of Middlesex County Library (*see* Arva)

Delhi Twp. Public Library, 192 Main St., Delhi ON N4B 2M2 – 519/582-1791; Fax: 519/582-4571; Email: ERDE; Symbol: DE – CEO, Gwen Wood; Circulation Librarian, Kim Handsaeme; Technical Services Librarian, Jennifer Grohs

Delta Branch Library, Delta ON K0E 1G0 – 613/928-2991 – Librarian, Lois Braidwood – Branch of Rideau Lakes Union Library (*see* Elgin)

Deseronto Public Library, Main St. West, PO Box 302, Deseronto ON K0K 1X0 – 613/396-2744 – Librarian, R. Glendon Brant

Deseronto: Ka:nhiote Tyendinaga Territory Public Library, Tyendinaga Mohawk Territory, RR#1, Deseronto ON K0K 1X0 – 613/967-6264; Fax: 613/396-3627 – CEO, Karen Lewis

Devlin: Naicatchewenin Band Library, Rainy Lake Indian Reserve 17A, RR#1, PO Box 15, Devlin ON P0W 1C0 – 807/486-3407; Fax: 807/486-3704 – Librarian, Darlene Smith

Dobie: Gauthier Public Library, PO Box 11, Dobie ON P0K 1B0 – 705/567-1189 – Librarian, Jim Malherbe

Dorchester Library, 54 Dorchester Rd., Dorchester ON N0L 1G0 – 519/268-3451; Fax: 519/268-3451 – Supervisor, Margaret Trevitt – Branch of Middlesex County Library (*see* Arva)

Dorion Public Library, RR#1, Dorion ON P0T 1K0 – 807/857-2318 – Librarian, Betty Chambers, 807/857-2290; Librarian's Assistant, Janet Harris; Librarian's Assistant, Gale Ellis

Dorset: Sherborne Branch Library, PO Box 195, Dorset ON P0A 1E0 – 705/766-9969 – Branch Head, Carol Anger – Branch of Haliburton County Public Library

Douglas: Bromley-St. Michael Community Library, Hwy. 60, PO Box 130, Douglas ON K0J 1S0 – 613/649-2576 – Librarian, Anne English

Douro Twp. Public Library, General Delivery, Douro ON K0L 1S0 – 705/745-6803 – Librarian, Pauline Beyer

Dowling: Lionel Rheaume Public Library, 31 Sturgeon St., PO Box 520, Dowling ON P0M 1R0 – 705/855-9028; Fax: 705/855-7702 – Librarian, Bonnie Rhude – See also following branches: Earle Jarvis Public Library, Levack Branch Library

Drayton Branch Library, PO Box 130, Drayton ON N0G 0P0 – 519/638-3788; Fax: 519/846-2066 – Branch Supervisor, B. Van Soest – Branch of Wellington County Library (*see* Fergus)

Dresden Branch Library, 187 Brown St., Dresden ON N0P 1M0 – 519/683-4922 – Branch Librarian, Carol Richmond – Branch of Kent County Library (*see* Chatham)

Drumbo Library, PO Box 69, Drumbo ON N0J 1G0 – 519/463-5321 – Supervisor, Barbara Blake – Branch of Oxford County Library (*see* Woodstock)

Dryden Public Library, 36 Van Horne Ave., Dryden ON P8N 2A7 – 807/223-1475; Fax: 807/223-4312 – CEO, Bryan C. Buffett

Dubreuilville (Bibliothèque publique), 23, rue des Pins, Dubreuilville ON P0S 1B0 – 705/884-2284 – Bibliothécaire, Denise B. Gagné

Dunchurch: Hagerman Twp. Public Library, General Delivery, Dunchurch ON P0A 1G0 – 705/389-3311 – Librarian, Marlane Andersen

Dundalk Public Library, Main St., PO Box 190, Dundalk ON N0C 1B0 – 519/923-3248; Fax: 519/923-2685; Symbol: DD – CEO/Librarian, Dianne Walker

Dundas Public Library, 18 Ogilvie St., Dundas ON L9H 2S2 – 905/627-3507; Fax: 905/627-4391 – Interim CEO, D. Varley

Dunnville Public Library, 317 Chestnut St., Dunnville ON N1A 2H4 – 905/774-4240; Fax: 905/774-4294 – Librarian, Debra Jackson; Circulation Librarian, Ann Hemming; Children's Librarian, Donna Hoedt

Dunsford Branch Library, Dunsford Community Centre, PO Box 82, Dunsford ON K0M 1L0 – 705/793-3037 – Branch Librarian, Shelley Ferguson – Branch of Victoria County Public Library (*see* Lindsay)

Durham Public Library, PO Box 706, Durham ON N0G 1R0 – 519/369-2107; Fax: 519/369-5962; Symbol: DU – Chief Librarian, Marlaine Elvidge

Dutton Public Library, PO Box 69, Dutton ON N0L 1J0 – 519/762-2780 – Supervisor, Mary Lou McMillan – Branch of Elgin County Library (*see* St. Thomas)

Dwight Public Library, PO Box 172, Dwight ON P0A 1H0 – 705/635-3319; Fax: 705/635-3319; Email: lakebay@muskoka.com – Librarian, Peggy Hurley – Branch of Lake of Bays Public Library (*see* Baysville)

Ear Falls Twp. Public Library, 1 Balsalm St., PO Box 369, Ear Falls ON P0V 1T0 – 807/222-3209 – Librarian, Krishna Singh

Earlton: Bibliothèque publique du canton d'Armstrong, 35 - 10th St., CP 39, Earlton ON P0J 1E0 – 705/563-2717; Téléc: 705/563-2093 – Directrice générale, Aline Lefebvre

East York Public Library, #34, 2 Thorncliffe Park Dr., East York ON M4H 1H2 – 416/396-3800; Fax: 416/396-3812 – CEO, Alice R. Lorriman; Technology & Support Services, Manager, Carol Ufford; User Services, Nancy Chavner – See also following branches: Dawes Rd. Library, Leaside Library, S. Walter Stewart Library, Thorncliffe Library, Todmorden Library

East York: Dawes Rd. Library, 416 Dawes Rd., East York ON M4B 2E8 – 416/396-3820; Fax: 416/396-3825 – Branch Librarian, Caroline Ingvaldsen – Branch of East York Public Library

East York: Leaside Library, 165 McRae Dr., East York ON M4G 1S8 – 416/396-3835; Fax: 416/396-3840 – Branch Manager, Mary Ann San Juan – Branch of East York Public Library

East York: S. Walter Stewart Library, 170 Memorial Park Ave., East York ON M4J 2K5 – 416/396-3975; Fax: 416/396-3842 – Branch Manager, Nancy Chavner – Branch of East York Public Library

East York: Thorncliffe Library, 48 Thorncliffe Park Dr., East York ON M4H 1J7 – 416/396-3865; Fax: 416/396-3866 – Branch Librarian, Margaret Adair – Branch of East York Public Library

East York: Todmorden Library, Pape Community Centre, 1081-1/2 Pape Ave., East York ON M4K 3W6 – 416/396-3875 – Branch Manager, Nancy Chavner – Branch of East York Public Library

Eganville: Bonnechere Union Public Library, 75 Wallace St., PO Box 39, Eganville ON K0J 1T0 – 613/628-2400 – Librarian, T. Smith

Elgin: Rideau Lakes Union Library, Halladay St., PO Box 189, Elgin ON K0G 1E0 – 613/359-5315 – Coordinator, Susan Warren – See also following branches: Delta Branch Library, Elgin Branch Library, Lyndhurst Branch Library, Portland Branch Library, Seeley's Bay Branch

Elgin Branch Library, Elgin ON K0G 1E0 – 613/359-5315 – Librarian, Marjorie Keates – Branch of Rideau Lakes Union Library

Elk Lake Public Library, PO Box 218, Elk Lake ON P0J 1G0 – 705/678-2340 – Librarian, Dorothy Tessier

Elliot Lake Public Library, Algo Centre Mall, 151 Ontario Ave., Elliot Lake ON P5A 2T2 – 705/461-7204; Fax: 705/461-7244 – Librarian, Barbara Fazekas

Elmira Branch Library, 65 Arthur St. South, Elmira ON N3B 2M6 – 519/669-5477 – Branch Supervisor, Mary Anne Kirkness – Branch of Waterloo Regional Library (*see* Kitchener)

Elmvale: Flos-Elmvale Public Library, 64 Queen St. West, PO Box 430, Elmvale ON L0L 1P0 – 705/322-1482 – Branch Head, Lynn Patkau – Branch of Springwater Public Library (*see* Midhurst)

Elora Branch Library, Elora ON N0B 1S0 – 519/846-0190; Fax: 519/846-2066 – Branch Supervisor, Bonnie Moebus – Branch of Wellington County Library (*see* Fergus)

Embro Library, James St., Embro ON N0J 1G0 – 519/475-4172 – Supervisor, Josephine St. Clair – Branch of Oxford County Library (*see* Woodstock)

Embrun: Russell Twp. Public Library, 993 Notre Dame St., PO Box 297, Embrun ON K0A 1W0 – 613/443-3636; Fax: 613/443-0668; Symbol: OERT – Directrice générale, Lucille Legault – See also following branches: Marionville Branch Library, Russell Branch Library

Emeryville Library, 104 Emery Dr., PO Box 160, Emeryville ON N0R 1C0 – 519/727-6464 – Supervisor, Angela Rice – Branch of Essex County Library

Emo: Emo Public Library, Mill St., PO Box 490, Emo ON P0W 1E0 – 807/482-2575; Fax: 807/482-2575 – CEO/Librarian, Shirley D. Sheppard

Emo: Manitou Library, PO Box 450, Emo ON P0W 1E0 – 807/482-2479

Emsdale: Perry Twp. Public Library, PO Box 39, Emsdale ON P0A 1J0 – 705/636-5454 – Librarian, Bessie Marshall

Englehart Public Library, 71 Fourth Ave., Englehart ON P0J 1H0 – 705/544-2100; Email: englib@nt.net; Symbol: OENG – Librarian/CEO, Betty Lafferty

Ennismore Twp. Public Library, Ennismore PO, Ennismore ON K0L 1T0 – 705/292-8022; Fax: 705/292-8022 – Librarian, Carol Crough

Enterprise Branch Library, PO Box 163, Enterprise ON K0K 1Z0 – 613/358-2058 – Supervisor, Joan Larkin – Branch of Lennox & Addington County Library (see Napanee)

Erin Village Branch Library, 140 Main St., Unit 4, Erin ON N0B 1T0 – 519/833-2216; Fax: 519/846-2066 – Branch Supervisor, Virginia Hogan – Branch of Wellington County Library (see Fergus)

Espanola Public Library, 245 Avery Dr., Espanola ON P5E 1S4 – 705/869-2940; Fax: 705/869-6463; Email: library@etown.net – Chief Librarian, Mark Gagnon, Email: markg@engrg.uwo.ca

Essex County Library, 360 Fairview Ave. West, Essex ON N8M 1Y3 – 519/776-5241; Fax: 519/776-4455 – Chief Librarian, Edward R. George; Manager of Technical Services, Patricia Knight – See also following branches: Amherstburg Library, Comber Branch Library, Cottam Branch Library, Emeryville Library, Essex Library, Harrow Branch Library, Kingsville Library, LaSalle Library, Malden Road Library, McGregor Library, Ruthven Library, St. Clair Beach Library, Stoney Point Library, Tecumseh Branch Library, Woodslee Library

Essex Library, 18 Gordon Ave., Essex ON N8M 2M4 – 519/776-8962 – Supervisor, Judy Ward – Branch of Essex County Library

Etobicoke Public Libraries, 65 Hartsdale Dr., PO Box 501, Etobicoke ON M9R 2S8 – 416/394-5000; Fax: 416/394-5050 – CEO, Jennifer Milne; Public Services, Director, Anne Bailey; Collection Development, Director, Judy Paisley – See also following branches: Albion Library, Alderwood Library, Brentwood Public Library, Eatonville Library, Elmbrook Park Library, Humber Bay Library, Humberwood Library, Long Branch Library, Mimico Centennial Library, New Toronto Library, Northern Elms Library, Rexdale Library, Richview Central Library

Etobicoke: Albion Library, 1515 Albion Rd., Etobicoke ON M9V 1B2 – 416/394-5170; Fax: 416/394-5185 – Branch Manager, Lesley North – Branch of Etobicoke Public Libraries

Etobicoke: Alderwood Library, 525 Horner Ave., Etobicoke ON M8W 2B9 – 416/394-5310 – Branch Manager, Cathy Richardson – Branch of Etobicoke Public Libraries

Etobicoke: Brentwood Public Library, 36 Brentwood Rd. North, Etobicoke ON M8X 2B5 – 416/394-5240; Fax: 416/394-5257 – Branch Manager, Virginia Van Vliet – Branch of Etobicoke Public Libraries

Etobicoke: Eatonville Library, 430 Burnhamthorpe Rd., Etobicoke ON M9B 2B1 – 416/394-5270 – Branch Manager, Peter Moffet – Branch of Etobicoke Public Libraries

Etobicoke: Elmbrook Park Library, 2 Elmbrook Cres., Etobicoke ON M9C 5B4 – 416/394-5290 – Branch Manager, Sue Patrick – Branch of Etobicoke Public Libraries

Etobicoke: Humber Bay Library, 200 Parklawn Rd., Etobicoke ON M8Y 3J1 – 416/394-5300 – Branch Manager, Mark Gaudet – Branch of Etobicoke Public Libraries

Etobicoke: Humberwood Library, 850 Humberwood Blvd., Etobicoke ON M9W 7A6 – 416/394-5210; Fax: 416/394-5215 – Branch Manager, Anne Campbell – Branch of Etobicoke Public Libraries

Etobicoke: Long Branch Library, 3500 Lake Shore Blvd. West, Etobicoke ON M8W 1N6 – 416/394-5320 – Branch Manager, Bert Crandall – Branch of Etobicoke Public Libraries

Etobicoke: Mimico Centennial Library, 47 Station Rd., Etobicoke ON M8V 2R1 – 416/394-5330; Fax: 416/394-5338 – Branch Manager, Margaret Rice – Branch of Etobicoke Public Libraries

Etobicoke: New Toronto Library, 110 - 11 St., Etobicoke ON M8V 3G5 – 416/394-5350; Fax: 416/394-5358 – Branch Manager, Susan Humphries – Branch of Etobicoke Public Libraries

Etobicoke: Northern Elms Library, Rexdale Plaza, 2267 Islington Ave., Etobicoke ON M9W 3W7 – 416/394-5230 – Branch Manager, Marliese Patrick – Branch of Etobicoke Public Libraries

Etobicoke: Rexdale Library, 2243 Kipling Ave., Etobicoke ON M9W 4L5 – 416/394-5200 – Branch Manager, Pat Llabbe – Branch of Etobicoke Public Libraries

Etobicoke: Richview Central Library, 1806 Islington Ave., Etobicoke ON M9C 5H8 – 416/394-5120; Fax: 416/394-5158 – Branch Manager, Ilka Abbott – Branch of Etobicoke Public Libraries

Exeter Branch Library, PO Box 610, Exeter ON N0M 1S6 – 519/235-1890 – Branch Supervisor, Helen Hodgins – Branch of Huron County Library (see Goderich)

Falconbridge Branch Library, Edison St. Community Centre, PO Box 460, Falconbridge ON P0M 1S0 – 705/693-2423 – Branch Head, Marlene Bilsborough – Branch of Nickel Centre Public Library (see Garson)

Fauquier-Strickland Public Library, PO Box 100, Fauquier ON P0L 1G0 – 705/339-2521; Fax: 705/339-2421 – Librarian, Odile Tremblay

Fenelon Falls Branch Library, 21 Market St., PO Box 867, Fenelon Falls ON K0M 1N0 – 705/887-6300; Fax: 705/887-6300 – Branch Head, Valerie Garland – Branch of Victoria County Public Library (see Lindsay)

Fenwick: Maple Acre Branch Library, 782 Canboro Rd., General Delivery, Fenwick ON L0S 1C0 – 905/892-5226 – Librarian, Peggy Grady – Branch of Pelham Public Library (see Fonthill)

Fergus: Wellington County Library, Wellington Pl., RR#1, Fergus ON N1M 2W3 – 519/846-0918; Fax: 519/846-2066; Email: path@county.wellington.on.ca; Symbol: OFERW – CEO, Patrick Harvie – See also following branches: Arthur Branch Library, Centre Wellington Branch Library, Clifford Branch Library, Drayton Branch Library, Elora Branch Library, Erin Village Branch Library, Harriston Branch Library, Mount Forest Branch Library, Palmerston Branch Library, Puslinch Branch Library

Fergus: Centre Wellington Branch Library, RR#1, Fergus ON N1M 2W3 – 519/846-0918; Fax: 519/846-2066 – Branch of Wellington County Library

Fergus Public Library, 190 St. Andrew St. West, Fergus ON N1M 1N5 – 519/843-1180; Fax: 519/843-7601 – Librarian, G. Kozak Selby

Field Public Library, 59 Ecole St., Field ON P0H 1M0 – 705/758-6610; Fax: 705/758-9529 – CEO, Lucienne Desjardins

Finch: Stormont, Dundas & Glengarry County Library, PO Box 217, Finch ON K0C 1K0 – 613/346-2501; Fax: 613/246-2461 – CEO, Leanne Glendenning – See also following branches: Alexandria Branch Library, Avonmore Branch Library, Brinston Branch Library, Chesterville Branch Library, Crysler Branch Library, Dalkeith Branch Library, Finch Branch Library, Glen Robertson Branch, Ingleside Branch Library, Lancaster Branch Library, Lancaster Twp. Branch Library, Long Sault Branch Library, Maxville Branch Library, Moose Creek Branch Library, Morewood Branch Library, Morrisburg Branch Library, South Mountain Branch Library, St. Andrews West Branch, Williamsburg Branch Library, Williamstown Branch Library, Winchester Branch Library

Finch Branch Library, PO Box 250, Finch ON K0C 1K0 – 613/984-2807 – Supervisor/Branch Head, Janet Stephens – Branch of Stormont, Dundas & Glengarry County Library

Flesherton Public Library, 10 Elizabeth St., Flesherton ON N0C 1E0 – 519/924-2241 – Librarian, Wilda Allen

Flinton: Kaladar, Anglesea & Effingham Twps. Public Library, Main St., Flinton ON K0H 1P0 – Librarian, Yvonne Brushey

Florence Library, 531 Florence Rd., PO Box 102, Florence ON N0P 1R0 – 519/692-3213 – Librarian, Mary Emerick – Branch of Lambton County Library (see Wyoming)

Florence: Shetland Library, 1279 Shetland Rd., Florence ON N0P 1R0 – 519/695-3330 – Librarian, Barbara Beckett – Branch of Lambton County Library (see Wyoming)

Foleyet Public Library, PO Box 147, Foleyet ON P0M 1T0 – 705/899-2280 – Librarian, William J. Kilgour

Fonthill: Pelham Public Library, PO Box 830, Fonthill ON L0S 1E0 – 905/892-6443; Fax: 905/892-3392; Symbol: OFP – CEO, Hugh D. Molson – See also following branches: Maple Acre Branch Library

Fordwich Branch Library, RR#1, Fordwich ON N0G 1V0 – Branch Supervisor, Marion Feldskov – Branch of Huron County Library (see Goderich)

Forester's Falls: Ross Twp. Public Library, Forester's Falls ON K0J 1V0 – 613/646-2543 – Librarian, Debbie Byce, 613/646-2496

Forest: Chippewas of Kettle & Stony Point Library, RR#2, 53 Indian Lane, Forest ON N0N 1J0 – 519/786-6903; Fax: 519/786-6904; Email: lhenry@xcelco.on.ca – CEO, Linda Henry

Forest Library, 61 King St. West, PO Box 370, Forest ON N0N 1J0 – 519/786-5152 – Librarian, M. Wallace – Branch of Lambton County Library (see Wyoming)

Fort Erie Public Library, 136 Gilmore Rd., Fort Erie ON L2A 2M1 – 905/871-2546; Fax: 905/871-9884 – CEO, Elizabeth Rossnagel; Reference Librarian, Lorne Featherston; Children's Librarian, Hazel Reinhart; Adult Services Librarian, Lynda Goodridge; Technical Services Librarian, Dee Thompson – See also following branches: Crystal Ridge Branch Library, Stevensville Branch Library

Fort Erie: Crystal Ridge Branch Library, c/o 136 Gilmore Ave., Fort Erie ON L2A 2M1 – 905/894-1281 – Branch of Fort Erie Public Library

Fort Erie: Stevensville Branch Library, c/o 136 Gilmore Ave., Fort Erie ON L2A 2M1 – 905/382-2051 – Branch of Fort Erie Public Library

Fort Frances Public Library, 363 Church St., Fort Frances ON P9A 1C9 – 807/274-9879; Fax: 807/274-4496 – Librarian, Margaret Sedgwick

Frankford Public Library, 12 Trent St. North, PO Box 550, Frankford ON K0K 2C0 – 613/398-7572 – Librarian, C. Fox

Frankville: Kitley Twp. Public Library, Frankville ON K0E 1H0 – 613/275-2093 – CEO, Judi Osler

Freelton Library, PO Box 15, Freelton ON L0R 1K0 – 905/659-7639 – Branch Head, Valerie Lawson – Branch of Wentworth Libraries (see Hamilton)

Gananoque Public Library, 100 Park St., Gananoque ON K7G 2Y5 – 613/382-2436 – Librarian, J. Love

Gananoque: Howe Island Branch Library, Gananoque ON K7G 2V6 – 613/549-7972 – Yvonne Kane – Branch of Frontenac County Library (see Kingston)

Garson: Nickel Centre Public Library, 214 Orell St., Garson ON P3L 1V2 – 705/693-2729; Fax: 705/693-5540 – CEO, Lillian Bergeron – See also following branches: Coniston Branch Library, Falconbridge Branch Library, Garson Branch Library, Skead Branch Library

Garson Branch Library, 214 Orell St., Garson ON P3L 1V2 – 705/693-2729; Fax: 705/693-5540 – Head Librarian, Verna Thompson – Branch of Nickel Centre Public Library

Georgetown: Halton Hills Public Library, 9 Church St., Georgetown ON L7G 2A3 – 905/798-4730, ext.288; Fax: 905/873-6118; Email: ENHH-(INFO); Symbol: CAOGTN – Reference Librarian, Geoffrey Cannon; Children's/Public Services Librarian, Cindy Cooper; Support Services Librarian, Walter Lewis – See also following branches: Acton Public Library, Georgetown Branch Library

Georgetown Branch Library, 9 Church St., Georgetown ON L7G 2A3 – 905/873-2681; Fax: 905/873-6118 – Branch Head, Pamela Payne – Branch of Halton Hills Public Library (see Georgetown)

Geraldton Centennial Public Library, PO Box 40, Geraldton ON P0T 1M0 – 807/854-1490; Fax: 807/854-2351 – Librarian, Donna Mae Mikkonen

Gilmour: Tudor & Cashel Public Library, RR#2, PO Box 435, Gilmour ON K0L 1W0 – 613/474-2583 – Librarian/CEO, Norma J. Sedgwick

Glanworth Library, 2950 Glanworth Dr., Glanworth ON N0L 1L0 – 519/681-6797; Fax: 519/663-5396 – Branch Head, Judy Shaw – Branch of London Public Library

Glen Morris Branch Library, Glen Morris ON N0B 1W0 – 519/740-2122 – Branch Head, Kelly Dinsmore – Branch of South Dumfries Twp. Public Library

Glen Morris Public Library, Glen Morris ON N0B 1W0 – 519/740-2122 – Librarian, Marlene Thompson

Glen Robertson Branch, PO Box 92, Glen Robertson ON K0B 1H0 – 613/874-2250 – Supervisor/Branch Head, James Findlayson – Branch of Stormont, Dundas & Glengarry County Library (see Finch)

Glencoe Library, 178 McKellar St., PO Box 490, Glencoe ON N0L 1M0 – 519/287-2735; Fax: 519/287-2735 – Supervisor, Karen J. Kendrick-Diamond – Branch of Middlesex County Library (see Arva)

Gloucester: Bibliothèque publique de Gloucester, 1400 Blair Place, 5th Fl., CP 8333, Gloucester ON K1J 3V5 – 613/748-4226; Téléc: 613/748-4114; Courrier électronique: ao682@freenet.carleton.ca; Symbol: BPG – Director, Arch Campbell; Deputy Director, Elaine Condos – See also following branches: Services Techniques, Succursale Blackburn Hamlet, Succursale Blossom Park, Succursale Hôtel de Ville, Succursale Orléans

Gloucester: Services Techniques, #7, 2950 Bank St., Gloucester ON K1T 1N8 – 613/523-2957; Téléc: 613/523-9378 – Chef des services techniques, Marie Desaulniers; Chef de cataloguage, Céline Lefebvre-Turcotte – Branch of Bibliothèque publique de Gloucester

Gloucester: Succursale Blackburn Hamlet, 199 Glen Park Dr., Gloucester ON K1B 5B8 – 613/824-6926; Téléc: 613/824-8848; Symbol: OGBH – Branch Head, Marcia Aronson – Branch of Bibliothèque publique de Gloucester

Gloucester: Succursale Blossom Park, #7, 2950 Bank St., Gloucester ON K1T 1N8 – 613/731-9907; Fax: 613/731-0744 – Branch Head, Sonia Chippendale – Branch of Bibliothèque publique de Gloucester

Gloucester: Succursale Hôtel de Ville, 1400 Blair Pl., CP 8333, Gloucester ON K1G 3V5 – 613/748-4208; Téléc: 613/748-4314; Symbol: OGO – Branch Head, Dave Thomas – Branch of Bibliothèque publique de Gloucester

Gloucester: Succursale Orléans, 1705 Orléans Blvd., Gloucester ON K1C 4W2 – 613/824-1962; Téléc: 613/748-4114; Symbol: OGB – Branch Head, Abe Schwartz – Branch of Bibliothèque publique de Gloucester

Goderich: Huron County Library, RR#5, Clinton ON N0M 1L0 – 519/482-5457; Fax: 519/482-7820; Email: ht001@hometown.on.ca; Symbol: OGOH – County Librarian, Beth Ross; Deputy County Librarian, Sharon Cox – See also following branches: Auburn Branch Library, Bayfield Branch Library, Bluevale Branch Library, Blyth Branch Library, Brussels Branch Library, Centralia Branch Library, Clinton Branch Library, Cranbrook Branch Library, Exeter Branch Library, Fordwich Branch Library, Goderich Branch Library, Gorrie Branch Library, Hensall Branch Library, Kirkton Branch Library, Seaforth Branch Library, Wingham Branch Library, Zurich Branch Library

Goderich Branch Library, 52 Montreal St., Goderich ON N7A 2G4 – 519/524-9261 – Branch Supervisor, Marg Bushell – Branch of Huron County Library (see Goderich)

Gogama Public Library, PO Box 238, Gogama ON P0M 1W0 – 705/894-2448 – Volunteer Head Librarian/CEO, Sue Primeau

Gogama: Mattagami Indian Band Library, PO Box 250, Gogama ON P0M 1W0 – 705/894-2003

Golden Lake First Nation Library, PO Box 100, Golden Lake ON K0J 1X0 – 613/625-2402; Fax: 613/625-2332 – Librarian, Linda Sarazin

Gooderham: Glamorgan Branch Library, Gooderham ON K0M 1R0 – 705/447-3163 – Branch Head, Marilyn Billings – Branch of Haliburton County Public Library

Gore Bay Union Public Library, 15 Water St., PO Box 225, Gore Bay ON P0P 1H0 – 705/282-2221; Fax: 705/282-3076 – CEO/Librarian, Johanna Allison

Gorrie Branch Library, Gorrie ON N0G 1X0 – Branch Supervisor, Jackie Gowdy – Branch of Huron County Library (see Goderich)

Grafton: Centreton Branch Library, RR#1, Grafton ON K0K 2G0 – 905/349-2976 – Branch Head, Heather Viscount – Branch of Northumberland County Public Library (see Hastings)

Grafton Branch Library, PO Box 12, Grafton ON K0K 2G0 – 905/349-2424 – Branch Head, Bette LeBarr – Branch of Northumberland County Public Library (see Hastings)

Grand Bend Library, 22-81 Gill Rd., PO Box 117, Grand Bend ON N0M 1T0 – 519/238-2067 – Librarian, Cathy Smith – Branch of Lambton County Library (see Wyoming)

Grand Valley Public Library, 4 Amaranth St., PO Box 129, Grand Valley ON L0N 1G0 – 519/928-5622; Email: gvpl@flexnet.com – Librarian, S. Leighton

Gravenhurst Public Library, 275 Muskoka Rd. South, Gravenhurst ON P1P 1J1 – 705/687-3382; Email: gplib@muskoka.com – CEO/Librarian, Robena Kirton – See also following branches: Morrison Library Outpost, Ryde Library Outpost

Gravenhurst: Ryde Library Outpost, RR#3, Gravenhurst ON P1P 1R3 – 705/687-2633 – Branch Head, Barb Holden – Branch of Gravenhurst Public Library

Gravenhurst: Walker's Point Public Library, Walker's Point Community Centre, RR#2, Gravenhurst ON P0C 1G0 – 705/687-9965 – Librarian, Linda Schell – Branch of Port Carling Public Library

Greely Branch Library, 7008 Parkway Rd., PO Box 159, Greely ON K0A 1Z0 – 613/821-3609 – Librarian, Alison Surinskis – Branch of Osgoode Twp. Public Library Board

Greensville Library, #5, 59 Kirby St., Greensville ON L9H 4H6 – 905/627-4951 – Branch Head, Gaye Robinson – Branch of Wentworth Libraries (see Hamilton)

Grimsby Public Library, 25 Adelaide St., Grimsby ON L3M 1X2 – 905/945-5142 – Librarian, Barry Church

Guelph Public Library, 100 Norfolk St., Guelph ON N1H 4J6 – 519/824-6220; Fax: 519/824-8342 – Chief Librarian, Norman McLeod; Reference Librarian, Steven Kraft; Circulation Librarian, Barbara Baxter; Children's Librarian, Kerry Hannah; Technical Services Librarian, Cathy McInnis; Systems Librarian, Linda J. Kearns – See also following branches: Bullfrog Mall Library, Scottsdale Centre Branch Library

Guelph: Bullfrog Mall Library, #36, 380 Eramosa Rd., Guelph ON N1E 6R2 – 519/824-6220; Fax: 519/824-8342 – Librarian, Kate Gilchrist – Branch of Guelph Public Library

Guelph: Puslinch Branch Library, RR#3, Guelph ON N1H 6H9 – 519/763-8026; Fax: 519/846-2066 – Branch Supervisor, F.E. Shaw – Branch of Wellington County Library (see Fergus)

Guelph: Scottsdale Centre Branch Library, #1, 650 Scottsdale Dr., Guelph ON N1G 2M3 – 519/824-6220; Fax: 519/824-8342 – Librarian, Robin Tunney – Branch of Guelph Public Library

Hagersville Public Library, 13 Alma St. North, PO Box 219, Hagersville ON N0A 1H0 – 905/768-5941 – Library Head, L. Diane McKeen – Branch of Haldimand Public Libraries (see Caledonia)

Hagersville: Mississaugas of New Credit Band Library, RR#6, Hagersville ON N0A 1H0 – 905/768-5686; Fax: 905/768-1225 – CEO, Carolyn King

Haileybury Public Library, 545 Lakeshore, PO Bag O, Haileybury ON P0J 1K0 – 705/672-3707; Fax: 705/672-5966; Symbol: JHAB – CEO, Elizabeth A. Bishop

Haliburton County Public Library, 2001 Mountain St., PO Box 119, Haliburton ON K0M 1S0 – 705/457-2241; Email: joel-levis@canrem.com; Symbol: OHAL – Director, Joel Levis; Technical Services Librarian, Carol Madill; ILL, Arlene Robinson – See also following branches: Bicroft Branch Library, Cardiff Branch Library, Dysart Branch Library, Glamorgan Branch Library, Minden Branch Library, Monmouth Branch Library, Sherborne Branch Library, Snowdon Twp., Lochlin Library, Stanhope Branch Library

Haliburton: Dysart Branch Library, PO Box 119, Haliburton ON K0M 1S0 – 705/457-1791 – Branch Head, Victoria Ross – Branch of Haliburton County Public Library

Haliburton: Stanhope Branch Library, RR#1, Haliburton ON K0M 2K0 – 705/489-2402 – Branch Head, Marjorie Cowen – Branch of Haliburton County Public Library

Hamilton Public Library, 55 York Blvd., PO Box 2700, Stn LCDI, Hamilton ON L8N 4E4 – 905/546-3200; Fax: 905/546-3202; Email: ENVOY: HAM.PUB.LIB. – CEO, Ken Roberts; Deputy CEO, Don Kilpatrick; Youth Services Librarian, Helen Benoit; Acquisitions Librarian, Pamela Haley – See also following branches: Barton Library, Concession Library, Kenilworth Library, Locke Library, Picton Branch Library, Red Hill Library, Sherwood Library, Terryberry Library, Westdale Library

Hamilton: Wentworth Libraries, 69 Sanders Blvd., Hamilton ON L8S 3J8 – 905/546-4126; Fax: 905/522-9083; Symbol: CAOHWL – Chief Librarian, Barbara Baker; Reference Librarian, Jane Skeates; Acquisitions/Technical Services Librarian, Frances Rukavina; Public Services/Circulation Librarian, Leslie Muirhead – See also following branches: Ancaster Public Library, Binbrook Public Library, Carlisle Library, Freelton Library, Greensville Library, Lynden Public Library, Millgrove Public Library,

LIBRARIES — ONTARIO

Mount Hope Public Library, Rockton Public Library, Saltfleet Public Library, Sheffield Public Library, Stoney Creek Public Library, Valley Park Library, Waterdown Public Library, Winona Public Library

Hamilton: Barton Library, 571 Barton St. East, Hamilton ON L8L 2Z4 – 905/546-3450; Fax: 905/546-3453 – Librarian, Debbie Rudderham – Branch of Hamilton Public Library

Hamilton: Concession Library, 565 Concession St., Hamilton ON L8V 1A8 – 905/546-3415; Fax: 905/546-3491 – Librarian, Jean Lyall – Branch of Hamilton Public Library

Hamilton: Kenilworth Library, 103 Kenilworth Ave. North, Hamilton ON L8H 4R6 – 905/546-3960; Fax: 905/546-4010 – Librarian, Rita Bozz – Branch of Hamilton Public Library

Hamilton: Locke Library, 285 Locke St. South, Hamilton ON L8P 4C2 – 905/546-3492; Fax: 905/546-3447 – Librarian, Karen Peter – Branch of Hamilton Public Library

Hamilton: Picton Branch Library, 502 James St. North, Hamilton ON L8L 1J4 – 905/546-3494; Fax: 905/546-3496 – Librarian, Debbie Rudderham – Branch of Hamilton Public Library

Hamilton: Red Hill Library, 695 Queenston Rd., Hamilton ON L8G 1A1 – 905/546-2069; Fax: 905/546-3973 – Librarian, Yvonne Patch – Branch of Hamilton Public Library

Hamilton: Sherwood Library, 467 Upper Ottawa, Hamilton ON L8T 3T4 – 905/546-3267; Fax: 905/546-3268 – Librarian, Sheila Gamble – Branch of Hamilton Public Library

Hamilton: Terryberry Library, 100 Mohawk Rd. West, Hamilton ON L9C 1W1 – 905/546-3921; Fax: 905/546-3953 – Librarian, Karen Cooper – Branch of Hamilton Public Library

Hamilton: Valley Park Library, 970 Paramount Dr., Hamilton ON L8J 1Y2 – 905/573-3141 – Branch Head, Jane Henderson – Branch of Wentworth Libraries

Hamilton: Westdale Library, 955 King St. West, Hamilton ON L8S 1K9 – 905/546-3456; Fax: 905/546-3458 – Librarian, Karen Peter – Branch of Hamilton Public Library

Hanmer: Valley East Public Library, 4100 Elmview Dr., Hanmer ON P3P 1J7 – 705/969-5565; Fax: 705/969-7787; Email: vallylib@cyberbeach.net; Symbol: OVC – CEO, Charles Grayson; Public Services Librarian, Lynn Imbeau; Technical Services Librarian, L. Roberts

Hanover Public Library, 341 - 10 St., Hanover ON N4N 1P5 – 519/364-1420 – Librarian, Linda Manchester

Harrietsville Library, 201 Main St., Harrietsville ON N0L 1N0 – 519/269-3089 – Supervisor, Sharon Churchill – Branch of Middlesex County Library (see Arva)

Harriston Branch Library, Elora St., PO Box 130, Harriston ON N0G 1Z0 – 519/338-2396; Fax: 519/846-2066 – Branch Supervisor, Dorothy Pike – Branch of Wellington County Library (see Fergus)

Harrow Branch Library, 140 King St. West, PO Box 550, Harrow ON N0R 1G0 – 519/738-6362 – Supervisor, Hilda Enns – Branch of Essex County Library

Hartington: Portland Twp., Hartington Branch Library, Hartington ON K0H 1W0 – 613/372-2524 – Joan Leonard – Branch of Frontenac County Library (see Kingston)

Hastings: Northumberland County Public Library, General Delivery, Hastings ON K0L 1Y0 – 705/696-3630; Fax: 705/696-1806 – CEO, Judy Howard; Reference Librarian, Catherine McLeod; Technical Services Librarian, Lily Griffiths – See also following branches: Brighton Twp. Branch Library, Campbellford/Seymour Branch Library, Centreton Branch Library, Garden Hill Branch Library, Grafton Branch Library, Hastings Branch Library, Murray Twp. (Wooler) Branch Library, Roseneath Branch Library, Warkworth (Percy Twp.) Branch Library

Hastings Branch Library, 6 Albert St., PO Box 130, Hastings ON K0L 1Y0 – 705/696-2111 – Branch Head, Ann Sullivan – Branch of Northumberland County Public Library

Havelock Public Library, 13 Quebec St., PO Box 464, Havelock ON K0L 1Z0 – 705/778-2621 – Librarian, Beth LaBarre

Hawkesbury: Bibliothèque publique de Hawkesbury, 550, rue Higginson, Hawkesbury ON K6A 1H1 – 613/632-6656; Téléc: 613/632-8314 – Directeur par intérim, Yvon Léonard; Référence, Frances Pâlin; Prêt entre bibliothèques, Lynn Belle-Isle Guindon; Services techniques, Sophie Pageau

Hearst Public Library, PO Bag 5000, Hearst ON P0L 1N0 – 705/362-4700; Fax: 705/362-5902 – Chief Library Technician, Jeannette Lecours Levesque

Hensall Branch Library, 198 King St., PO Box 249, Hensall ON N0M 1X0 – 519/262-2445 – Branch Supervisor, Susan Hartman – Branch of Huron County Library (see Goderich)

Hepworth Branch Library, 465 Bruce St., PO Box 83, Hepworth ON N0H 1P0 – 519/935-2030 – Branch Supervisor, Barbara Wong – Branch of Bruce County Public Library (see Port Elgin)

Hepworth: Sauble Beach Branch Library, RR#1, Sauble Beach ON N0H 2G0 – 519/422-1283; Fax: 519/422-1283 – Branch Supervisor, Bonnie Phair – Branch of Bruce County Public Library (see Port Elgin)

Heron Bay: Pic River First Nation Public Library, Pic Day School, Heron Bay ON P0T 1R0 – 807/229-0630 – CEO, Alanna R. Starr

Hickson Library, Hickson ON N0J 1L0 – 519/462-2927 – Supervisor, Louise Ross – Branch of Oxford County Library (see Woodstock)

Highgate Branch Library, King St., Highgate ON N0P 1T0 – 519/678-3313 – Branch Librarian, Vera Leverton – Branch of Kent County Library (see Chatham)

Highland Grove: Cardiff Branch Library, Highland Grove ON K0L 2A0 – 705/448-2652 – Branch Head, Joanne Burroughs – Branch of Haliburton County Public Library

Hillsburgh: Erin Twp. Public Library, 115 Main St., PO Box 490, Hillsburgh ON N0B 1Z0 – 519/855-4010; Fax: 519/855-4873 (call first) – Librarian, Barb Thompson

Hilton Union Library, PO Box 117, Hilton Beach ON P0R 1G0 – 705/246-2557 – CEO, Diane Gerhart

Hogansburg: Akwesasne Library & Cultural Centre, St. Regis Mohawk Reservation, Rte. 37, RR#1, PO Box 14C, Hogansburg NY 13655-9705 USA – 518/358-2240; Fax: 518/358-2649 – CEO, Carol White

Holland Landing: East Gwillimbury Public Library, 19513 Yonge St., PO Box 1609, Holland Landing ON L9N 1P2 – 905/836-6492; Fax: 905/836-6499 – CEO, Karen McLean; Reference Librarian, Alexandra Gutelius; Children's Librarian, Linne Thompson – See also following branches: Mount Albert Branch Library

Honey Harbour Branch Library, Honey Harbour ON P0E 1E0 – 705/756-8851; Fax: 705/756-8851 – Librarian, Billie Hewitt – Branch of Georgian Bay Twp. Public Library

Hornepayne Public Library, 200 Front St., PO Box 539, Hornepayne ON P0M 1Z0 – 807/868-2332 – Librarian, L. Kahara

Huntsville Public Library, 7 Minerva St. East, PO Box 1029, Huntsville ON P0A 1K0 – 705/789-5232; Fax: 705/789-0732 – Chief Librarian/CEO, Marguerite Urban

Huron Park: Centralia Branch Library, 117 Wellington Cres., Huron Park ON N0M 1Y0 – Branch Supervisor, Maxine Hyde – Branch of Huron County Library (see Goderich)

Ignace Public Library, 36 Main St., PO Box 480, Ignace ON P0T 1T0 – 807/934-2280; Fax: 807/934-6452; Symbol: NZIG – Librarian, Catherine Penney

Ilderton: Coldstream Library, RR#2, Ilderton ON N0M 2A0 – 519/666-1201 – Supervisor, Mary Higgs – Branch of Middlesex County Library (see Arva)

Ilderton: London Twp. Library, 40 Heritage Dr., Ilderton ON N0M 2A0 – 519/666-1599; Fax: 519/666-1599 – Supervisor, Carolyne Walden – Branch of Middlesex County Library (see Arva)

Ingersoll Library, 1 Charles St. East, Ingersoll ON N5C 1J5 – 519/485-2505 – Supervisor, Rosemary Lewis – Branch of Oxford County Library (see Woodstock)

Ingleside Branch Library, PO Box 704, Ingleside ON K0C 1M0 – 613/537-2592 – Supervisor/Branch Head, Joan Magee – Branch of Stormont, Dundas & Glengarry County Library (see Finch)

Inglewood Library, 15825 McLaughlin Rd., Inglewood ON L0N 1K0 – 905/838-3324; Fax: 905/838-3324 – Branch Assistant, Judy Nelson – Branch of Caledon Public Library (see Bolton)

Innerkip Library, PO Box 104, Innerkip ON N0J 1M0 – 519/469-3824 – Branch Supervisor, Irene Priest – Branch of Oxford County Library (see Woodstock)

Inwood Library, 6504 James St., PO Box 41, Inwood ON N0N 1K0 – 519/844-2491 – Librarian, Nola Tait – Branch of Lambton County Library (see Wyoming)

Iron Bridge Public Library, PO Box 339, Iron Bridge ON P0R 1H0 – 705/843-2192 – CEO, Bette C. Size

Iroquois Falls Public Library, 725 Synagogue St., PO Box 860, Iroquois Falls ON P0K 1G0 – 705/232-5722; Fax: 705/232-7166 – CEO, Denise Giroux; Circulation Librarian/ILL, Jeannine Beaudoin

Iroquois Public Library, PO Box 39, Iroquois ON K0E 1K0 – 613/652-4377 – Senior Librarian, Eleanor Pietersma

Jarvis: Nanticoke Public Library Board, 17 Talbot St. East, PO Box 399, Jarvis ON N0A 1J0 – 519/587-4293; Fax: 519/519/587-5569; Email: ERNA; Symbol: NAN – CEO, Katherine Bristol; Reference Librarian, Rosemary Hilton; Children's Librarian, Betty Lee; Technical Services Librarian, Heidi Goodale; Acquisitions Librarian, Patricia Reidy – See also following branches: Jarvis Branch Library, Port Dover Branch Library, Selkirk Branch Library, Waterford Branch Library

Jarvis Branch Library, 37 Main St. North, PO Box 636, Jarvis ON N0A 1J0 – 519/587-4746 – Branch Librarian, Rosemary Hilton – Branch of Nanticoke Public Library Board

Kagawong: Billings Twp. Public Library, Kagawong ON P0P 1J0 – 705/282-2944 – CEO, Lillian Boyd

Kakabeka Falls: Conmee Public Library, Conmee Community Centre, RR#1, Kakabeka Falls ON P0T 1W0 – 807/475-5229 – CEO, Selly Pajamaki

Kanata Public Library, 2500 Campeau Dr., Kanata ON K2K 2W3 – 613/592-1321; Fax: 613/592-0891; Email: as122@freenet.carleton.ca; Symbol: OKAH – CEO, Linda Sherlow Lowdon; Reference Librarian, Pat Skarzinski; Technical Services Librarian, Laura St. Denis – See also following branches: Beaverbrook Branch Library, Hazeldean Branch Library

Kanata: Beaverbrook Branch Library, 2500 Campeau Dr., Kanata ON K2K 2W3 – 613/592-2712; Fax: 613/592-4592 – Branch Manager, Joan Darby – Branch of Kanata Public Library

Kanata: Hazeldean Branch Library, 50 Castlefrank Rd., Kanata ON K2L 2N5 – 613/836-1900; Fax: 613/836-5326 – Branch Manager, Anne Robison – Branch of Kanata Public Library

Kapuskasing Public Library, 24 Mundy Ave., Kapuskasing ON P5N 1P9 – 705/335-3363; Fax: 705/335-2464 – CEO, Louise Boucher

Canadian Almanac & Directory 1997

LIBRARIES — ONTARIO   5-47

Kashechewan First Nation Public Library, c/o St. Andrews School, General Delivery, Kashechewan ON P0L 1S0 – 705/275-4405; Fax: 705/275-4515 – CEO, Lucy Wesley

Kearney & Area Public Library, PO Box 220, Kearney ON P0A 1M0 – 705/636-5849 – CEO/Librarian, Brandi Nolan

Keene: Otonabee Twp. Public Library, PO Box 9, Keene ON K0L 2G0 – 705/295-6814; Fax: 705/295-6814; Symbol: OTO – CEO, Jane Tully – See also following branches: Stewart Hall Branch Library

Keene: Stewart Hall Branch Library, PO Box 9, Keene ON K0L 2G0 – 705/749-5642; Fax: 705/295-6814 – Branch Head, Gail McIntyre – Branch of Otonabee Twp. Public Library

Keewatin Public Library, 812 Ottawa St., PO Box 602, Keewatin ON P0X 1C0 – 807/547-2145; Fax: 807/547-3145; Symbol: OKEE – CEO, Marceline Chagnon; Children's Librarian, Carolyn Heyens; Technical Services Librarian, Shirley Alcock

Kejick: Iskutewisakaygun #39 Independant First Nation Public Library, Kejick PO, Kejick ON P0X 1E0 – 807/733-3772; Fax: 807/733-3773 – CEO, Vernon Fair

Kejick: Shoal Lake #40 First Nation Public Library, Kejick PO, Kejick ON P0X 1E0 – 807/733-3341; Fax: 807/733-3115 – CEO, Ashley Green

Kemptville Public Library, 207 Prescott St., PO Box 538, Kemptville ON K0G 1J0 – 613/258-5577; Email: suehig@kempville.library.on.ca; Symbol: OKEM – CEO/Librarian, Susan Higgins

Kemptville: South Gower Public Library, PO Box 1734, Kemptville ON K0G 1J0 – 613/258-4711 – Librarian, Michelle Stein

Kenora Public Library, 24 Main St. South, Kenora ON P9N 1S7 – 807/467-2081; Fax: 807/467-2085 – CEO, Erin Roussin

Keswick: Georgina Public Libraries, 130 Gwendolyn Blvd., Keswick ON L4P 3W8 – 905/476-7233; Fax: 905/476-8724 – CEO, John McLean – See also following branches: Keswick Branch Library, Pefferlaw Library, Sutton Centennial Library

Keswick Branch Library, 130 Gwendolyn Blvd., Keswick ON L4P 3W8 – 905/476-5762; Fax: 905/476-8724 – Head Librarian, Janice Green – Branch of Georgina Public Libraries

Kilbride Branch Library, 68 Paton Rd., Kilbride ON L0P 1G0 – 905/335-4011; Fax: 905/681-7277 – Branch Head, Sandra Ferris – Branch of Burlington Public Library

Killaloe Public Library, Killaloe ON K0J 2A0 – 613/757-2211 – Librarian, Marnie MacKay

Killarney: Rutherford & George Island Twp. Public Library, 32 Commissioner St., Killarney ON P0M 2A0 – 705/287-2229 – CEO, Susan Tyson

Kimberley: Euphrasia Twp. Public Library, Main St., Kimberley ON N0C 1G0 – 519/599-2589 – Librarian, E. Brooks

Kincardine Branch Library, 727 Queen St., Kincardine ON N2Z 1Z9 – 519/396-3289; Fax: 519/396-3289 – Branch Supervisor, Ann Munn – Branch of Bruce County Public Library (see Port Elgin)

King Twp. Public Library, King Side Rd., PO Box 399, King City ON L7B 1A6 – 905/833-5101; Fax: 905/833-0824 – Chief Librarian, Justin Sainte – See also following branches: Ansnorveldt Branch Library, King City Library, Nobleton Branch Library, Schomberg Library

King City: Ansnorveldt Branch Library, PO Box 399, King City ON L7B 1A6 – 905/775-8717 – Branch Head, Sharon Bentley – Branch of King Twp. Public Library

King City Library, King Side Rd., PO Box 339, King City ON L7B 1A6 – 905/833-5101; Fax: 905/833-0824 – Librarian, Sharon Bentley – Branch of King Twp. Public Library

Kingston: Frontenac County Library, County Court House, Court St., Kingston ON K7L 2N4 – 613/548-8657; Fax: 613/548-8193; Email: mwatkins@frontenac.county.library.on.ca – County Librarian, Marion Watkins; Children's Librarian, Nancy Mohan; Technical Services Librarian, Mary McPhee – See also following branches: Arden Branch Library, Barrie Twp., Cloyne Branch Library, Clarendon Miller Twp., Plevna Branch Library, Howe Island Branch Library, Kingston Twp., Days Rd. Branch Library, Loughborough Twp., Sydenham Branch, Olden Twp., Mountain Grove Branch Library, Oso Twp., Sharbot Lake Branch Library, Palmerston North & South Canonto Twp., Ompah Branch Library, Parham Deposit, Pittsburgh Twp., Barriefield Branch Library, Portland Twp., Hartington Branch Library, Storrington Twp., Sunbury Branch Library, Wolfe Island Twp. - Library

Kingston Public Library, 130 Johnson St., Kingston ON K7L 1X8 – 613/549-8888; Fax: 613/549-8476; Email: jordonl@kingston.library.on.ca – Chief Librarian, Lynne Jordon; Children's Librarian, Mary Beaty; Outreach Contact, Stella Carney; Adult Services Librarian, Deborah Defoe; Technical Services Librarian, Jerome McHenry; Branch Services Librarian, Gail Scala, 613/546-0698; 2582; Systems Contact, Lester Webb – See also following branches: Calvin Park Library, Kingscourt Branch

Kingston: Amherstview Branch Library, 108 Amherst Dr., Kingston ON K7N 1H9 – 613/389-6006; Fax: 613/389-6006 – Branch Head, Anne Taylor – Branch of Lennox & Addington County Library (see Napanee)

Kingston: Calvin Park Library, 88 Wright Cres., Kingston ON K7L 4T9 – 613/546-2582 – Chief Librarian, Lynne Jordon – Branch of Kingston Public Library

Kingscourt Branch, 115 Kirkpatrick St., Kingston ON K7K 2P4 – 613/546-0698 – Chief Librarian, Lynne Jordon – Branch of Kingston Public Library

Kingston Twp., Days Rd. Branch Library, 130 Days Rd., Kingston ON K7M 3P8 – 613/389-2616; Fax: 613/389-4372 – Librarian, A. Black – Branch of Frontenac County Library

Kingston: Pittsburgh Twp., Barriefield Branch Library, 414 Regent St., Kingston ON K7K 5R1 – 613/542-8222 – Lorna Grice – Branch of Frontenac County Library

Kingsville Library, 28 Division St. South, Kingsville ON N9Y 1P3 – 519/733-5620 – Supervisor, Maxene Murdock – Branch of Essex County Library

Kinmount Branch Library, Kinmount ON K0M 2A0 – 705/488-3199 – Branch Head, Ruth Schultz – Branch of Victoria County Public Library (see Lindsay)

Kintore Library, Kintore ON N0M 2C0 – 519/283-6339 – Supervisor, Ruth Sim – Branch of Oxford County Library (see Woodstock)

Kirkfield: Eldon Twp. Branch Library, Kirkfield ON K0M 2B0 – 705/438-3331 – Branch Head, Connie Donovan – Branch of Victoria County Public Library (see Lindsay)

Kirkland Lake Public Library, 10 Kirkland St. East, Kirkland Lake ON P2N 1P1 – 705/567-7966 – CEO, Joyce Allick

Kirkland Lake: Ontario Library Service North - Kirkland Lake, 11 Station Rd. South, Kirkland Lake ON P2N 3H2 – 705/567-3341; Fax: 705/567-9410; Email: ENVOY: OLS.JAMES BAY – Area Director, Brian L. Cahill

Kirkland Lake: Teck Centennial Library, 10 Kirkland St. East, Kirkland Lake ON P2N 1P1 – 705/567-7966; Fax: 705/568-6303; Email: teck@nt.net – Chief Librarian, B. Holmes

Kirkton Branch Library, RR#1, Kirkton ON N0K 1K0 – 519/229-8854 – Branch Supervisor, Joan Francis – Branch of Huron County Library (see Goderich)

Kitchener Public Library, 85 Queen St. North, Kitchener ON N2H 2H1 – 519/743-0271; Fax: 519/743-1261 – CEO, Margaret Y. Walshe; Reference Librarian, Pam Pembroke Leonard; Circulation Librarian, Ann Wood; Children's Librarian, Maureen Sawa; Public Services Manager, Cathy Matyas; Technology Coordinator, Bryan Dunham; Acquisitions Librarian, Cheryl Kaar; Marketing & Community Relations Manager, Harry Froklage – See also following branches: Forest Heights Community Library, Pioneer Park Community Library, Stanley Park Community Library

Kitchener: Waterloo Regional Library, 150 Frederick St., 2nd Fl., Kitchener ON N2G 4J3 – 519/575-4590; Fax: 519/634-5371 – Director of Library Services, Karin Manley; Public Services Librarian, Katherine Seredynska – See also following branches: Ayr Branch Library, Baden Branch Library, Bloomingdale Branch Library, Elmira Branch Library, Linwood Branch Library, New Dundee Branch Library, New Hamburg Branch Library, St. Clements Branch Library, St. Jacobs Branch Library, Wellesley Branch Library

Kitchener: Forest Heights Community Library, 251 Fischer-Hallman Rd., Kitchener ON N2H 2H1 – 519/743-0271; Fax: 519/743-0644 – Branch Head, Sharron Smith – Branch of Kitchener Public Library

Kitchener: Pioneer Park Community Library, 150 Pioneer Dr., Kitchener ON – 519/748-2740; Fax: 519/748-2740 – Branch Head, Maureen Plomske – Branch of Kitchener Public Library

Kitchener: Stanley Park Community Library, 146 Trafalgar Ave., Kitchener ON N2A 1Z7 – 519/896-1736; Fax: 519/896-1736 – Branch Head, Penny Lynn Fielding – Branch of Kitchener Public Library

Kleinburg Library, 10341 Islington Ave. North, Kleinburg ON L0J 1C0 – 905/893-1248; Fax: 905/893-2736 – Manager, Beryl Hall – Branch of Vaughan Public Libraries (see Maple)

Komoka Library, 133 Queen St., Komoka ON N0L 1R0 – 519/657-1461; Fax: 519/657-1461 – Supervisor, June Davis – Branch of Middlesex County Library (see Arva)

Lake Temagami: Temagami First Nation Public Library, Bear Island PO, Lake Temagami ON P0H 1C0 – 705/237-8943; Fax: 705/237-8959 – Librarian, Tammy Birtch

Lakefield Public Library, 1 Bridge St., PO Box 2200, Lakefield ON K0L 2H0 – 705/652-8623 – Librarian, J.C. Warren

Lambeth Library, 7112 Beattie St., Lambeth ON N0L 1A0 – 519/652-2951; Fax: 519/663-6396 – Branch Head, Bonnie Symons – Branch of London Public Library

Lanark Village, Lavant, Dalhousie & North Sherbrooke Twp., & Lanark Twp. Union Public Library, 75 George St., Lanark ON K0G 1K0 – 613/259-3068; Symbol: OLAU – Librarian/CEO, Mary Arnoldi; Librarian, Wanda Proulx

Lancaster Branch Library, PO Box 129, Lancaster ON K0C 1N0 – 613/347-2311 – Supervisor/Branch Head, Donna Parker – Branch of Stormont, Dundas & Glengarry County Library (see Finch)

Lancaster Twp. Branch Library, PO Box 571, Lancaster ON K0C 1N0 – 613/347-1748 – Supervisor/Branch Head, Darlene McKae – Branch of Stormont, Dundas & Glengarry County Library (see Finch)

Lansdowne: Front of Leeds & Lansdowne Public Library, 1B Jessie St., PO Box 219, Lansdowne ON K0E 1L0 – 613/659-3885; Fax: 613/659-3619; Symbol: OLAN – CEO, Yolande LaPointe

Larder Lake Public Library, 29 Godfrey St., PO Box 189, Larder Lake ON P0K 1L0 – 705/643-2222 – Librarian, Cathy Pierce

LaSalle Library, 1301 Front Rd., LaSalle ON N9J 2A9 – 519/734-8111 – Supervisor, Donna Spickett – Branch of Essex County Library

Latchford Public Library, 66 Main St., Latchford ON P0J 1N0 – 705/676-2030 – CEO, Beth Inglis

Leamington Public Library, 1 John St., Leamington ON N8H 1H1 – 519/326-3441; Fax: 519/322-1585 – Chief Librarian, Jill Nicholson

Canadian Almanac & Directory 1997

Lefaivre: Bibliothèque publique du Canton d'Alfred, CP 10, Lefaivre ON K0B 1J0 – 613/679-4470 – Directrice générale, Sr. Hélène Lavoie

Levack Branch Library, 32 School St., PO Box 560, Levack ON P0M 2C0 – 705/966-2140; Fax: 705/966-0710 – Librarian, Anne Matte – Branch of Lionel Rheaume Public Library (see Dowling)

Limoges: Bibliothèque publique de Canton de Cambridge, rue Main, CP 70, Limoges ON K0A 2M0 – 613/443-2310 – Bibliothécaire, Yvette Leduc

Lindsay: Victoria County Public Library, PO Box 9000, Lindsay ON K9V 5R8 – 705/324-9411; Fax: 705/878-1859; Email: vcounty@lindsaycomp.on.ca – County Librarian, Moti Tahiliani – See also following branches: Bobcaygeon Branch Library, Burnt River Branch Library, Cambray Branch Library, Carden Twp. Branch Library, Coboconk Branch Library, Dalton Twp. Branch Library, Downeyville Branch Library, Dunsford Branch Library, Eldon Twp. Branch Library, Fenelon Falls Branch Library, Kinmount Branch Library, Little Britain Branch Library, Manilla Branch Library, Norland Branch Library, Oakwood Branch Library, Omemee Branch Library, Woodville Branch Library

Lindsay: Downeyville Branch Library, RR#5, Lindsay ON K9V 4R5 – 705/799-5265 – Branch Head, Deborah Howe – Branch of Victoria County Public Library

Lindsay Public Library, 190 Kent St. West, Lindsay ON K9V 2Y6 – 705/324-5632; Fax: 705/324-7140; Email: MTahilia@FlemingC.on.ca – Librarian, M. Tahiliani

Linwood Branch Library, 38 Adelaide St., Linwood ON N0B 2A0 – 519/698-2700 – Asst. Branch Supervisor, Helen Sagle – Branch of Waterloo Regional Library (see Kitchener)

Lion's Head & District Branch Library, PO Box 24, Lions Head ON N0H 1W0 – 519/793-3844 – Branch Supervisor, Jacqui Gardiner – Branch of Bruce County Public Library (see Port Elgin)

Listowel Public Library, 260 Main St. West, Listowel ON N4W 1A1 – 519/291-4621; Fax: 519/291-2235 – Chief Librarian, Tom Bentley; Children's Librarian, Gail Clarkson; ILL Librarian, Lorna Wherry

Little Britain Branch Library, Little Britain ON K0M 2C0 – 705/786-2088 – Branch Head, Anne Falconer – Branch of Victoria County Public Library (see Lindsay)

Little Current Public Library, 50 Meredith St., PO Box 790, Little Current ON P0P 1K0 – 705/368-2444 – Librarian, Judith Kift

Little Current: Sucker Creek First Nations Public Library, RR#1, PO Box 21, Little Current ON P0P 1K0 – 705/368-3696; Fax: 705/368-3563 – CEO, Beverly Nahwegahbo

Lively: Walden Public Library, 615 Main St., PO Box 189, Lively ON P3Y 1M3 – 705/692-4749; Fax: 705/692-4261; Email: laframboise@sednet.mcd.on.ca – CEO/Administrator, Margaret LaFramboise; Reference Librarian, Jeanette Laughren, 705/692-4749; Children's Librarian, Mary Woboditsch, 705/692-4238; Technical Services Librarian, Lea Ann Hicks – See also following branches: Beaver Lake Branch Library, Naughton Branch Library, Waters Branch Library, Whitefish Branch Library

Lively: Waters Branch Library, 52 Westview Cres., Lively ON P3Y 1B7 – 705/692-4238 – Branch Head, Mary Woboditsch – Branch of Walden Public Library

Lochlin: Snowdon Twp., Lochlin Library, Lochlin ON K0M 2G0 – Branch Head, Diane Peacock – Branch of Haliburton County Public Library

Lombardy: South Elmsley Twp. Public Library, Lombardy Public School, RR#1, Lombardy ON K0G 1L0 – 613/283-0860; Fax: 613/284-1523 – CEO, Larry Winters

London Public Library, 305 Queens Ave., London ON N6B 3L7 – 519/661-5100; Fax: 519/663-5396 – CEO, Reed Osborne; Director, Public Services, Margaret Mitchell; Director, Technical Support Services, Beth Cada; Director, Community Relations, Carmen Sprovieri; Collection Manager, Susanna Hubbard Krimmer; Coordinator, Lending Services, Nancy Ward; Head, Children's Library, Delilah Deane Cummings – See also following branches: Beacock Branch Library, Byron Memorial Branch Library, Eastwood Centre Branch Library, Fred Landon Branch Library, Glanworth Library, Jalna Branch Library, Lambeth Library, Masonville Branch Library, Northridge Branch Library, Pond Mills Branch Library, Richard E. Crouch Branch Library, Sherwood Forest Branch Library, W.O. Carson Branch Library, Westmount Branch Library, Westown Branch Library

London: Beacock Branch Library, 1280 Huron St., London ON N5Y 1A8 – 519/451-8140; Fax: 519/663-5396 – Branch Head, Frances Huber – Branch of London Public Library

London: Byron Memorial Branch Library, 1295 Commissioners Rd. West, London ON N6K 1C9 – 519/471-4000; Fax: 519/663-5396 – Branch Head, Bonnie Symons – Branch of London Public Library

London: Eastwood Centre Branch Library, Eastwood Centre Plaza, 1920 Dundas St. East, London ON N5V 3P1 – 519/451-7600; Fax: 519/663-5396 – Branch Head, Cheryl Fround; Children's Librarian, Nancy Rastin – Branch of London Public Library

London: Fred Landon Branch Library, 167 Wortley Rd., London ON N6C 3P6 – 519/439-6240; Fax: 519/663-5396 – Branch Head, Gordon Price – Branch of London Public Library

London: Jalna Branch Library, 1119 Jalna Blvd., London ON N6E 3B3 – 519/685-6465; Fax: 519/663-5396 – Branch Head, Arlene Thompson – Branch of London Public Library

London: Masonville Branch Library, 30 North Centre Rd., London ON N5X 3W1 – 519/660-4646 – Branch of London Public Library

London: Northridge Branch Library, 1444 Glenora Dr., London ON N5K 1V2 – 519/439-4331; Fax: 519/663-5396 – Branch Head, Frances Huber – Branch of London Public Library

London: Pond Mills Branch Library, 1166 Commissioners Rd. East, London ON N5Z 4W8 – 519/685-1333; Fax: 519/663-5396 – Branch Head, Judy Shaw – Branch of London Public Library

London: Richard E. Crouch Branch Library, 550 Hamilton Rd., London ON N5Z 1S4 – 519/673-0111; Fax: 519/663-5396 – Branch Head, Regina Patterson – Branch of London Public Library

London: Sherwood Forest Branch Library, Sherwood Forest Mall, 1225 Wonderland Rd. North, London ON N6G 2V9 – 519/473-9965; Fax: 519/663-5396 – Branch Head, Dianne Knoppert – Branch of London Public Library

London: Westmount Branch Library, 507 Village Green Ave., London ON N6J 4G4 – 519/473-4708; Fax: 519/663-5396 – Branch Head, Catherine Morrisey – Branch of London Public Library

London: Westown Branch Library, Westown Plaza Mall, 301 Oxford St. West, London ON N6H 1S6 – 519/439-6456; Fax: 519/663-5396 – Branch Head, Sandra Lang – Branch of London Public Library

London: W.O. Carson Branch Library, 465 Quebec St., London ON N5W 3Y4 – 519/438-4287; Fax: 519/663-5396 – Branch Head, Regina Patterson – Branch of London Public Library

Long Sault Branch Library, PO Box 550, Long Sault ON K0C 1P0 – 613/534-2605 – Supervisor/Branch Head, Lois Smith – Branch of Stormont, Dundas & Glengarry County Library (see Finch)

Longlac Public Library, 168 Kenogami St., PO Box 760, Longlac ON P0T 2A0 – 807/876-4515; Fax: 807/876-4886 – Librarian, Carole McLean

Lucan Library, 183 Main St., PO Box 400, Lucan ON N0M 1J0 – 519/227-4682; Fax: 519/227-4682 – Supervisor, Donna Atkinson – Branch of Middlesex County Library (see Arva)

Lucknow Library, 526 Campbell St., PO Box 130, Lucknow ON N0G 2H0 – 519/528-3011 – Branch Supervisor, Claudia Baskerville – Branch of Bruce County Public Library (see Port Elgin)

Lynden Public Library, Main St., PO Box 9, Lynden ON L0R 1T0 – 519/647-2571; Fax: 519/647-2571 – Branch Head, Cathy Bryden – Branch of Wentworth Libraries (see Hamilton)

Lyndhurst Branch Library, Lyndhurst ON K0E 1N0 – 613/928-2277 – Librarian, Viola McMachen – Branch of Rideau Lakes Union Library (see Elgin)

Lyn: Lyn Branch Library, PO Box 158, Lyn ON K0E 1M0 – 613/345-0033 – Librarian, Beverley LaBrash – Branch of Elizabethtown Twp. Public Library Board

MacDiarmid: Rocky Bay First Nation Public Library, MacDiarmid ON P0T 2B0 – 807/885-3401; Fax: 807/885-3231 – CEO, Roxanne Kowtiash

Mactier: Georgian Bay Twp. Public Library, High St., Mactier ON P0C 1H0 – 705/375-5430; Fax: 705/375-5430 – Librarian, Marilyn Keall – See also following branches: Honey Harbour Branch Library

Mactier: Moose Deer Point Library, PO Box 136, Mactier ON P0C 1H0 – 705/375-5209; Fax: 705/375-2258 – CEO, Gail Russell

Madawaska Local Services Board Public Library, PO Box 59, Madawaska ON K0J 2C0 – 613/637-5533 – CEO, Pamela Aleck

Madoc Public Library, 20 Davidson St., PO Box 6, Madoc ON K0K 2K0 – 613/473-4456 – CEO, Susan Smith

Magnetawan Chapman Public Library, PO Box 130, Magnetawan ON P0A 1P0 – 705/387-4411; Fax: 705/387-0102 – CEO, Lisa Gillette-Haig

Mallorytown: Front of Escott Twp. Public Library, 1348 County Rd. 2, RR#2, Mallorytown ON K0E 1R0 – 613/659-3800; Fax: 613/659-3521 – Librarian, Linda Mallory

Mallorytown: Front of Yonge Twp. Public Library, PO Box 250, Mallorytown ON K0E 1R0 – 613/923-2442 – Librarian, Jack Tennant

Malton Branch Library, 3540 Morningstar Dr., Malton ON L4T 1Y2 – 905/677-5878; Fax: 905/677-0547 – Manager, Ingrid Masterson – Branch of Mississauga Library System

Manilla Branch Library, Manilla ON K0M 2J0 – 705/357-2768 – Branch Supervisor, Cathy Hamill – Branch of Victoria County Public Library (see Lindsay)

Manitoulin Island: Wikwemikong First Nation Public Library, Wikwemikong Reserve, PO Box 112, Manitoulin Island ON P0P 2J0 – 705/859-2692; Fax: 705/859-3851 – CEO, Sheri Mishibinijima

Manitouwadge Twp. Public Library, Community Centre, Manitouwadge ON P0T 2C0 – 807/826-3913; Fax: 807/826-4640 – Librarian, Sheila Durand, 807/826-4789

Manitowaning: Assiginack Public Library, PO Box 280, Manitowaning ON P0P 1N0 – 705/859-2110; Fax: 705/859-3010 Attn:Library – CEO/Librarian, Debbie Robinson

Manotick: Rideau Twp. Public Library Board, PO Box 430, Manotick ON K4M 1A4 – 613/692-3854; Fax: 613/489-2880 – CEO, Verna Preston – See also following branches: Manotick Branch Library, North Gower Branch Library

Manotick Branch Library, PO Box 430, Manotick ON K4M 1A4 – 613/692-3854; Fax: 613/489-2880 – Branch Librarian, Jane McGann – Branch of Rideau Twp. Public Library Board

Maple: Vaughan Public Libraries, 8 Merino Rd., Maple ON L6A 1S9 – 905/832-8515; Fax: 905/832-5207 – CEO, Rosemary Bonanno – See also following branches: Ansley Grove Library, Bathurst Clark Library, Dufferin Clark Library, Kleinburg Library, Maple Library, Woodbridge Library

Maple Library, 10190 Keele St., Maple ON L6A 1S9 – 905/832-2959; Fax: 905/832-4971 – Manager, June Orrell – Branch of Vaughan Public Libraries

Marathon Public Library, PO Box 400, Marathon ON P0T 2E0 – 807/229-0740; Fax: 807/229-3336; Symbol: OMAR – Librarian, Lynn Banks

Marionville Branch Library, 4629, rue Grégoire, PO Box 1141, Marionville ON K4R 1E5 – 613/445-0289 – Branch Head, Francine Dagenais – Branch of Russell Twp. Public Library

Markdale Public Library, 21 Main St. East, PO Box 499, Markdale ON N0C 1H0 – 519/986-3436 – CEO/Acquisitions Librarian, Betty Drummond; Children's Librarian, Beth Kennedy

Markham Public Libraries, #100, 445 Apple Creek Blvd., Markham ON L3R 9X7 – 905/513-7977; Fax: 905/513-7984 – CEO, Gina La Force; Deputy CEO, Catherine Biss; Acquisitions Supervisor, Suraj Sharma; Chief Financial Officer, Bert Rajaram; Technical Services Manager, Bob Henderson; Computer Services Manager, Karina Boenders – See also following branches: Markham Community Library, Milliken Mills Community Library, Thornhill Community Centre Library, Thornhill Village Library, Unionville Branch Library

Markham Community Library, 6031 Hwy. 7, Markham ON L3P 3A7 – 905/294-2782; Fax: 905/294-7586 – Branch Manager, Suzanne White; Reference Librarian, Jellowe Baynit; Circulation Librarian, Wynne Hall; Children's Librarian, Dilys Ward – Branch of Markham Public Libraries

Markham: Unionville Branch Library, 15 Library Lane, Markham ON L3R 5C4 – 905/477-2641; Fax: 905/477-8608; Symbol: UB – Branch Manager, Anita Frank; Children's Librarian, Pat Reid – Branch of Markham Public Libraries

Markstay: Hagar Twp. Public Library, 21 Main St., PO Box 39, Markstay ON P0M 2G0 – 705/853-4536 – Librarian, John Grosshauer

Marmora: Deloro Public Library, RR#2, PO Box 63, Marmora ON K0K 2M0 – 613/472-2172 – Librarian, Bernice Young

Marmora Twp. Public Library, 37 Forsythe St., PO Box 340, Marmora ON K0K 2M0 – 613/472-3122; Symbol: MO – CEO, Sheryl Lewis

Massey & Twp. Public Library, 185 Grove St., PO Box 40, Massey ON P0P 1P0 – 705/865-2641 – CEO, Lilliane Richer

Massey: Sagamok Anishnawbek Public Library, PO Box 610, Massey ON P0P 1P0 – 705/865-2970; Fax: 705/865-3307 – CEO, Colleen Eshkakogan

Matheson: Black River-Matheson Public Library, 352 - 2 St., PO Box 450, Matheson ON P0K 1N0 – 705/273-2760; Fax: 705/273-2760 – CEO, Linda Lougheed – See also following branches: Ramore Branch

Mattawa Public Library, 362 Main St., PO Box 920, Mattawa ON P0H 1V0 – 705/744-5550; Fax: 705/744-1714 – Contact, Lise Moore Asselin

Mattice-Val Côté Public Library, Hwy. 11, PO Box 129, Mattice ON P0L 1T0 – 705/364-5301; Fax: 705/364-6431 – Librarian, Michelle Salonen

Maxville Branch Library, PO Box 58, Maxville ON K0C 1T0 – 613/527-2235 – Supervisor/Branch Head, Nicole Dewar – Branch of Stormont, Dundas & Glengarry County Library (see Finch)

Maynooth: Bangor Wicklow & McClure & Monteagle Union Public Library, Municipal Bldg., Maynooth ON K0L 2S0 – 613/338-2262 – Librarian, C. Browne

McGregor Library, 9532 Walker Rd., McGregor ON N0R 1J0 – 519/726-6311 – Supervisor, Nancy Brown – Branch of Essex County Library

McKellar Twp. Public Library, PO Box 10, McKellar ON P0G 1C0 – 705/389-2611; Fax: 705/389-2611 – Librarian, Joan Ward

Meaford Public Library, 15 Trowbridge St., PO Box 970, Meaford ON N4L 1V4 – 519/538-3500; Fax: 519/538-1808 – CEO, Donna Binsted; Children's Librarian, Marion Mower

Melbourne Library, 7 Queen St., Melbourne ON N0L 1T0 – 519/289-2405 – Supervisor, Donna Wolfe – Branch of Middlesex County Library (see Arva)

Merlin Branch Library, 13 Aberdeen St., Merlin ON N0P 1W0 – 519/689-4944 – Branch Librarian, Dorian Toll – Branch of Kent County Library (see Chatham)

Merrickville Public Library, 111 Main St. East, PO Box 460, Merrickville ON K0G 1N0 – 613/269-3326; Symbol: OMER – Librarian, Mary Kate Laphen

Metcalfe: Osgoode Twp. Public Library Board, PO Box 60, Metcalfe ON K0A 2P0 – 613/821-1330 – See also following branches: Greely Branch Library, Metcalfe Branch Library, Osgoode Branch Library, Vernon Branch Library

Metcalfe Branch Library, 2782 Albert St., PO Box 340, Metcalfe ON K0A 2P0 – 613/821-1330 – Librarian, Shirley Mills – Branch of Osgoode Twp. Public Library Board

Midhurst: Springwater Public Library, 12 Finlay Mill Rd., PO Box 129, Midhurst ON L0L 1X0 – 705/737-5650 – CEO, Lynn Patkau; Technical Services Librarian, Dee-anne Byers – See also following branches: Flos-Elmvale Public Library, Minesing Branch Library

Midhurst: County of Simcoe Library Co-operative, Administration Centre, Midhurst ON L0L 1X0 – 705/726-9300; Fax: 705/721-3991; Symbol: OBAS – CEO, Dianne E. Augustson; Reference Librarian, Gayle Hall

Midland Public Library, 320 King St., Midland ON L4R 3M6 – 705/526-4216; Fax: 705/526-1474 – CEO, Michael V. Saddy; Reference Librarian, Marion Locke; Circulation Librarian, Gail Griffith; Children's Librarian, Bonnie Reynolds; Public Services Librarian, Tina Brophy

Mildmay-Carrick Branch Library, Peter St., PO Box 87, Mildmay ON N0G 2J0 – 519/367-2814 – Branch Supervisor, Pat Markle – Branch of Bruce County Public Library (see Port Elgin)

Milford Bay Public Library, Milford Bay Community Centre, General Delivery, Milford Bay ON P0B 1E0 – 705/764-8912 – Librarian, Nancy Kirkpatrick – Branch of Port Carling Public Library

Milford: South Marysburgh Twp. - Ann Farwell Public Library, King St., Milford ON K0K 2P0 – 613/476-4130 – Librarian, Doris Dance, 613/476-3897

Millbrook: Cavan, Millbrook, South Monaghan Union Library, King St., Millbrook ON L0A 1G0 – 705/932-2919; Fax: 705/932-2595 – See also following branches: Baillieboro Branch Library, Millbrook Public Library, Mount Pleasant Branch Library

Millbrook Public Library, 34 King St. East, Millbrook ON L0G 1G0 – 705/932-2919 – Librarian, Margot Loucks – Branch of Cavan, Millbrook, South Monaghan Union Library

Millgrove Public Library, PO Box 220, Millgrove ON L0R 1V0 – 905/689-6582 – Branch Head, Bev Onufer – Branch of Wentworth Libraries (see Hamilton)

Milton Public Library, 45 Bruce St., Milton ON L9T 2L5 – 905/875-2665; Fax: 905/875-4324 – CEO, Jane Watkins; Information Services, Coordinator, Jane MacDonald; Circulation, Coordinator, Lee Wood; Children's Services Librarian, Janis Marshall; Deputy Chief Librarian, Leslie Fitch; Technical Services Coordinator, Marjorie Bethune

Milverton Public Library, 27 Main St. South, Milverton ON N0K 1M0 – 519/595-8395 – Librarian, S. Ensinger

Mindemoya: Carnarvon Twp. Public Library, King St., PO Box 210, Mindemoya ON P0P 1S0 – 705/377-5334; Fax: 705/377-5585 – Chief Librarian, Claire

Taylor Witt – See also following branches: Providence Bay Branch Library

Minden Branch Library, PO Box 157, Minden ON K0M 2K0 – 705/286-2491 – Branch Head, Bev Wood – Branch of Haliburton County Public Library

Mine Centre: Seine River First Nation Public Library, PO Box 129, Mine Centre ON P0W 1H0 – 807/599-2870; Fax: 807/599-2871

Minesing Branch Library, PO Box 131, Minesing ON L0L 1Y0 – 705/722-6440 – Branch Head, Carol Grenier – Branch of Springwater Public Library (see Midhurst)

Mississauga Library System, 301 Burnhamthorpe Rd. West, Mississauga ON L5B 3Y3 – 905/615-3500; Fax: 905/615-3625 – CEO, Don Mills, 905/615-3601; Public Services, Director, Barbara Quinlan, 905/615-3507; Technical Services, Director, Jenny Lorentowicz, 905/615-3646; Automated Services, Director, Bob Eastman – See also following branches: Burnhamthorpe Branch Library, Clarkson-Lorne Park Branch Library, Erin Mills Branch Library, Lakeview Branch Library, Malton Branch Library, Meadowvale West Branch Library, Mississauga Valley Branch Library, Park Royal Branch Library, Port Credit Branch Library, Sheridan Branch Library, Streetsville Branch Library, Woodlands Branch Library

Mississauga: Burnhamthorpe Branch Library, 1350 Burnhamthorpe Rd. East, Mississauga ON L4Y 3V9 – 905/602-6625; Fax: 905/602-6409 – Manager, Kathy Oakleaf – Branch of Mississauga Library System

Mississauga: Clarkson-Lorne Park Branch Library, 1474 Truscott Dr., Mississauga ON L5J 1Z2 – 905/822-1241; Fax: 905/822-1917 – Manager, Kathy Angus – Branch of Mississauga Library System

Mississauga: Erin Mills Branch Library, 2227 South Millway, Mississauga ON L5L 3R6 – 905/820-5442; Fax: 905/820-6396 – Manager, Ann Jacob – Branch of Mississauga Library System

Mississauga: Lakeview Branch Library, 1110 Atwater Ave., Mississauga ON L5E 1M9 – 905/274-5027 – Manager, Larysa Koshil – Branch of Mississauga Library System

Mississauga: Meadowvale West Branch Library, 6855 Meadowvale Town Centre Circle, Mississauga ON L5N 2Y1 – 905/821-7570; Fax: 905/821-3547 – Manager, Hanne von Bulow – Branch of Mississauga Library System

Mississauga Valley Branch Library, 1275 Mississauga Valley Blvd., Mississauga ON L5A 3R8 – 905/276-6890; Fax: 905/615-3452 – Manager, Patricia Kluge, 905/615-3452 – Branch of Mississauga Library System

Mississauga: Park Royal Branch Library, Park Royal Shopping Plaza, 2425 Truscott Dr., Mississauga ON L5J 2B4 – 905/822-3476; Fax: 905/822-8581 – Manager, Kathy Angus – Branch of Mississauga Library System

Mississauga: Port Credit Branch Library, 20 Lakeshore Rd. East, Mississauga ON L5G 1C8 – 905/278-3437; Fax: 905/278-5099 – Manager, Larysa Koshil – Branch of Mississauga Library System

Mississauga: Sheridan Branch Library, 2225 Erin Mills Pkwy., Mississauga ON L5K 1T9 – 905/823-4106; Fax: 905/823-3499 – Manager, Ann Jacob – Branch of Mississauga Library System

Mississauga: Streetsville Branch Library, 112 Queen St. South, Mississauga ON L5M 1K8 – 905/826-3001; Fax: 905/826-0049 – Manager, Al Stray – Branch of Mississauga Library System

Mississauga: Woodlands Branch Library, 1030 McBride Ave., Mississauga ON L5C 1L6 – 905/275-7087; Fax: 905/615-3453 – Manager, Jo Anne Storen – Branch of Mississauga Library System

Mitchell Public Library, 105 St. Andrew St., Mitchell ON N0K 1N0 – 519/348-9234 – Librarian, J. Thorup

Mobert: Pic Mobert First Nation Public Library, Mobert ON P0M 2J0 – 807/822-2011; Fax: 807/822-2710 – CEO, Cora-Lee Desmoulin

Monetville: Dokis First Nation Library, Monetville PO, Monetville ON P0M 2K0 – 705/763-2211; Fax: 705/763-2087 – Executive Officer, Wanita Dokis; Librarian, Angeline Dokis

Monkton: Elma Twp. Public Library, RR#1, Monkton ON N0K 1P0 – Librarian, Martha Bosch – See also following branches: Atwood Branch Library, Monkton Branch Library

Monkton: Atwood Branch Library, RR#1, Monkton ON N0K 1P0 – 519/356-2371 – Branch Head, Martha Bosch – Branch of Elma Twp. Public Library

Monkton Branch Library, RR#2, Monkton ON N0K 1P0 – Branch Head, Ellen Illman – Branch of Elma Twp. Public Library

Moonbeam: Bibliothèque publique de Moonbeam, 53 St-Aubin St., CP 370, Moonbeam ON P0L 1V0 – 705/367-2462; Téléc: 705/367-2610 – Bibliothécaire, Florence Fortin

Mooretown Library, General Delivery, Mooretown ON N0N 1M0 – 519/867-2823 – Librarian, Pauline Sheriff – Branch of Lambton County Library (see Wyoming)

Moose Creek Branch Library, PO Box 40, Moose Creek ON K0C 1W0 – 613/538-2214 – Supervisor/Branch Head, Janette Atkins – Branch of Stormont, Dundas & Glengarry County Library (see Finch)

Moosonee Public Library, PO Box 130, Moosonee ON P0L 1Y0 – 705/336-2913; Fax: 705/336-2393 – Librarian, Diana Doxtdator

Morewood Branch Library, PO Box 210, Morewood ON K0A 2R0 – 613/448-3822 – Supervisor/Branch Head, Ruth Gilroy – Branch of Stormont, Dundas & Glengarry County Library (see Finch)

Morrisburg Branch Library, PO Box 853, Morrisburg ON K0C 1X0 – 613/543-3384 – Supervisor/Branch Head, Elizabeth Porter – Branch of Stormont, Dundas & Glengarry County Library (see Finch)

Mount Albert Branch Library, 74 Main St., Mount Albert ON L0G 1M0 – 905/473-2472 – Branch Head, Nina Rapon – Branch of East Gwillimbury Public Library (see Holland Landing)

Mount Brydges Library, 23 Bowen St. East, Mount Brydges ON N0L 1W0 – 519/264-1061; Fax: 519/264-1061 – Supervisor, Glenna Smith – Branch of Middlesex County Library (see Arva)

Mount Elgin Library, Mount Elgin ON N0J 1N0 – 519/485-0134 – Supervisor, Lois Kocsis – Branch of Oxford County Library (see Woodstock)

Mount Forest: Egremont Twp. Public Library, PO Box 183, Mount Forest ON N0G 2L0 – 519/334-3480 – Librarian, Debbie Aitken

Mount Forest Branch Library, Mount Forest ON N0G 2L0 – 519/323-4541; Fax: 519/846-2066 – Branch Supervisor, Jean Moore – Branch of Wellington County Library (see Fergus)

Mount Hope Public Library, Mount Hope ON L0R 1W0 – 905/679-6445 – Branch Head, Doris Popper – Branch of Wentworth Libraries (see Hamilton)

Mountain Grove: Olden Twp., Mountain Grove Branch Library, Mountain Grove ON K0H 2E0 – 613/335-5360 – Cindy Cox – Branch of Frontenac County Library (see Kingston)

Muncey: Chippewas of the Thames Library & Resource Centre, RR#1, Muncey ON N0L 1Y0 – 519/797-2781; Fax: 519/264-2203

Muncey: Munsee Deleware Nation Library Services, RR#1, Muncey ON N0L 1Y0 – 519/289-5396; Fax: 519/289-5156 – Library Coordinator, Candy Thomas

Munster Branch Library, 7749 Bleeks Rd., PO Box 470, Munster ON K0A 3P0 – 613/838-2888 – Librarian, Gail Waters – Branch of Goulbourn Twp. Public Library (see Stittsville)

Murillo: Oliver Twp. Public Library, PO Box 26, Murillo ON P0T 2G0 – 807/935-2729; Fax: 807/935-2161 – Librarian, Maxine McCulloch

Nakina Public Library, North St., PO Box 300, Nakina ON P0T 2H0 – 807/329-5906 – Chairman, Jean McHarg; Librarian, Marlene Dowhaniuk

Napanee: Lennox & Addington County Library, 37 Dundas St. West, Napanee ON K7R 1Z5 – 613/354-2585; Fax: 613/354-7527 – Manager, Mary Anne Evans – See also following branches: Amherstview Branch Library, Bath Branch Library, Camden East Branch, Enterprise Branch Library, Napanee Public Library, Newburgh Branch Library, Odessa Branch Library, Sandhurst Branch Library, Stella Branch Library, Tamworth Branch Library, Yarker Branch Library

Napanee Public Library, 37 Dundas St. West, Napanee ON K7R 1Z5 – 613/354-2525 – Branch Head, Jane Vanderzande – Branch of Lennox & Addington County Library (see Napanee)

Naughton Branch Library, PO Box 121, Naughton ON P0M 2M0 – 705/692-3177 – Branch Head, Petrina Lawrie – Branch of Walden Public Library (see Lively)

Naughton: Whitefish Lake First Nation Public Library, PO Box 39, Naughton ON P0M 2M0 – 705/692-9618; Fax: 705/692-5010 – CEO, Connie Brideau

Navan: Cumberland Public Library, 1246 Colonial Rd., PO Box 239, Navan ON K4B 1J4 – 613/835-2665; Fax: 613/835-3677; Email: lindacap@cumberland.canton.library.on.ca – CEO, L. Caporicci; Public Services Librarian, Inta Douglas – See also following branches: Sir Wilfrid Laurier Branch Library

Nepean Public Library, Nepean Civic Square, 101 Centrepointe Dr., Nepean ON K2G 5K7 – 613/727-6637; Fax: 613/727-6677; Email: at058@freenet.carleton.ca – Executive Director, George Skarzynski; Reference Librarian, Peter Loades, 613/727-6659; Circulation Librarian, Ann Marie Madhosingh, 613/727-6660; Children's Librarian, Frank Dimech, 613/727-6649; Coordinator, Community Library Services, Sylvia Teasdale, 613/727-6646; Technical Services Librarian, Catherine Barrette, 613/825-7704; Acquisitions Librarian, Fay Foster, 613/727-6647; Coordinator, Automated & Technical Services, Doris Rankin, 613/727-6647 – See also following branches: Centennial Branch Library, Emerald Plaza Branch Library, Nepean Central Library, Ruth E. Dickinson Branch Library

Nepean: Centennial Branch Library, 3870 Richmond Rd., Nepean ON K2H 5C4 – 613/828-5142; Symbol: ONCB – Branch Library Manager, Linda Daly – Branch of Nepean Public Library

Nepean: Emerald Plaza Branch Library, 1547 Merivale Rd., Nepean ON K2G 4V3 – 613/224-7874 – Branch Library Manager, Josephine Norton – Branch of Nepean Public Library

Nepean Central Library, 101 Centrepointe Dr., Nepean ON K2G 5K7 – 613/727-6646; Fax: 613/727-6677 – Coordinator, Linda Ward – Branch of Nepean Public Library

Nepean: Ruth E. Dickinson Branch Library, Walter Baker Sports Centre, 100 Malvern Dr., Nepean ON K2J 2G5 – 613/825-3508 – Branch Library Manager, Deborah Dearham – Branch of Nepean Public Library

Nephton: Belmont & Methuen Twp. Public Library, PO Box 10, Havelock ON K0L 1Z0 – 705/778-2721; Fax: 705/778-5248 – CEO, Sandra Harris

Neustadt Public Library, 411 Mill St., Neustadt ON N0G 2M0 – 519/799-5830 – Librarian, Merelda Lantz

New Dundee Branch Library, 136 Main St., New Dundee ON N0B 2E0 – 519/696-3041 – Asst. Branch Supervisor, Lynn Weiss – Branch of Waterloo Regional Library (see Kitchener)

New Hamburg Branch Library, 145 Huron St. South, PO Box 179, New Hamburg ON N0B 2G0 – 519/662-1112 – Branch Supervisor, Yvonne Zyma-Stark – Branch of Waterloo Regional Library (see Kitchener)

New Liskeard Public Library, Whitewood Ave., PO Box 668, New Liskeard ON P0J 1P0 – 705/647-4215; Fax: 705/647-4442 – CEO, Carla Drury

New Lowell: Sunnidale Branch, General Delivery, New Lowell ON L0M 1N0 – 705/424-6288; Fax: 705/424-6288; Symbol: SU – Branch Head, M. Joyce Smith – Branch of Clearview Public Library (see Stayner)

Newburgh Branch Library, PO Box 40, Newburgh ON K0K 2S0 – 613/378-2556 – Supervisor, Rika Blakslee – Branch of Lennox & Addington County Library (see Napanee)

Newbury Library, Newbury ON N0L 1Z0 – 519/693-4275 – Supervisor, Sandra Carnegie – Branch of Middlesex County Library (see Arva)

Newcastle Village Branch Library, 50 Mill St. North, Newcastle ON L0A 1H0 – 905/987-4844 – Contact, Andrea MacDonald – Branch of Clarington Public Library

Newmarket Public Library, 438 Park Ave., Newmarket ON L3Y 1W1 – 905/895-5196; Fax: 905/895-7798; Email: lol@god.on.ca; Symbol: ONE – CEO, Pat Wilson; Adult Services Librarian, Marcia Watt; Head, Circulation Department, Linda Peppiatt; Head, Children's Services, Marilyn Read-Stark, 905/895-9056; Head, Adult Services, Judith Bealkowski; Library Systems Librarian, Stephen Whelan; Children's Services Librarian, Wendy Zwaal, 905/895-9056; Head, Audio-Visual Services, Karen Mark, 905/895-5728; Administrative Assistant, Paula Letson

Niagara Falls Public Library, 4848 Victoria Ave., Niagara Falls ON L2E 4C5 – 905/356-8080; Fax: 905/356-7004; Email: nfpl@freenet.niagara.com – Chief Librarian, Joe Longo; Head of Reference & Information Services, Andrew Porteus; Head of Circulation, Connie Dick; Children's Librarian, Colleen Lambert; Public Services Librarian, Claire Beckermann – See also following branches: Chippawa Branch Library, Stamford Centre Branch Library

Niagara Falls: Chippawa Branch Library, 3763 Main St., Niagara Falls ON L2G 6B3 – 905/295-4391 – Branch Head, Mary Joselin – Branch of Niagara Falls Public Library

Niagara Falls: Stamford Centre Branch Library, Town & Country Plaza, 3643 Portage Rd. North, Niagara Falls ON L2J 2K8 – 905/357-0410 – Branch Head, Margaret Ramsay – Branch of Niagara Falls Public Library

Niagara on the Lake Public Library, PO Box 430, Niagara on the Lake ON L0S 1J0 – 905/468-2023; Fax: 905/468-3334; Email: gmolsonl@freenet.niagara.com; Symbol: NL – CEO, Gerda Molson; Children's Librarian, Gerrie Barnim; Technical Services Librarian, Linda Potter

Nipigon Public Library, 25 Third St., PO Box 728, Nipigon ON P0T 2J0 – 807/887-3142; Fax: 807/887-3564; Email: niplib@nipigon.lakeheadu.ca – Librarian/CEO, Karrie Matheson

Nobel: Shawanaga First Nation Public Library, RR#1, Nobel ON P0G 1G0 – 705/366-2526; Fax: 705/366-2740 – CEO, Karen Pawis

Nobleton Branch Library, Sheardown Dr., PO Box 670, Nobleton ON L0G 1N0 – 905/859-4188; Fax: 905/859-4188 – Librarian, Mary Oram – Branch of King Twp. Public Library

Noelville: Cosby, Mason & Martland Twp. Public Library, PO Box 130, Noelville ON P0M 2N0 – 705/898-2965; Fax: 705/898-3481 – CEO, Colette Prévost

Norland Branch Library, Norland ON K0M 2L0 – 705/454-8552 – Branch Head, Grace Graham – Branch of Victoria County Public Library (see Lindsay)

North Bay Public Library, 271 Worthington St. East, North Bay ON P1B 1H1 – 705/474-4830; Fax: 705/495-4010; Email: dbourne@onlink.net; Symbol: VGNX – CEO, Paul Walker; Reference & AV Services Librarian, Donna Bourne-Tyson, 705/474-3332; Children's Librarian, Nora Elliott; Public Services Librarian, Judith Bouman; French Services, Bob Boisvert

North Gower Branch Library, Main St., PO Box 280, North Gower ON K0A 2T0 – 613/489-3909; Fax: 613/489-2880 – Branch Librarian, Karen Craig – Branch of Rideau Twp. Public Library Board (see Manotick)

North York Public Library, 5120 Yonge St., North York ON M2N 5N9 – 416/395-5500; Fax: 416/395-5542; Email: khuntley@nypl.toronto.on.ca – CEO, Josephine Bryant, Email: jbryant@nypl.toronto.on.ca; Deputy CEO, Linda Mackenzie, Email: lmackenz@nypl.toronto.on.ca; Information Technology, Director, Gordon Thomson, Email: gthomson@nypl.toronto.on.ca; Administrative Services, Director, Sid Mowder, Email: smowder@nypl.toronto.on.ca; Public Relations & Planning, Manager, Kim Huntley, 416/395-5511; Public Services, Director, Vickery Bowles, Email: vbowles@nypl.toronto.on.ca – See also following branches: Amesbury Park Community Branch, Armour Heights Community Branch, Barbara Frum Library, Bayview Community Branch, Black Creek Community Branch, Brookbanks Community Branch, Centennial Community Branch, Central Library, Don Mills Regional Branch, Downsview Regional Branch, Fairview Regional Branch, Flemingdon Park Community Branch, Hillcrest Community Branch, Humber Summit Community Branch, Jane/Sheppard Community Branch, Pleasant View Community Branch, Victoria Village Community Branch, Woodview Park Community Branch, York Woods Regional Branch Library

North York: Amesbury Park Community Branch, 1565 Lawrence Ave. West, North York ON M6L 1A8 – 416/395-5420; Fax: 416/395-5432 – Branch of North York Public Library

North York: Armour Heights Community Branch, 2140 Avenue Rd., North York ON M5M 4M7 – 416/395-5430; Fax: 416/395-5433 – Branch of North York Public Library

North York: Barbara Frum Library, 20 Covington Rd., North York ON M6A 3C1 – 416/395-5440; Fax: 416/395-5447 – Branch of North York Public Library

North York: Bayview Community Branch, Bayview Village Shopping Centre, 2901 Bayview Ave., North York ON M2K 1E6 – 416/395-5460; Fax: 416/395-5434 – Branch of North York Public Library

North York: Black Creek Community Branch, 2141 Jane St., North York ON M3M 1A2 – 416/395-5470; Fax: 416/395-5435 – Branch of North York Public Library

North York: Brookbanks Community Branch, 210 Brookbanks Dr., North York ON M3A 2T8 – 416/395-5480; Fax: 416/395-5436 – Branch of North York Public Library

North York: Centennial Community Branch, 578 Finch Ave. West, North York ON M2R 1N7 – 416/395-5490; Fax: 416/395-5437 – Branch of North York Public Library

North York: Central Library, 5120 Yonge St., North York ON M2N 5N9 – 416/395-5700; Fax: 416/395-5668 – Branch of North York Public Library

North York: Don Mills Regional Branch, 888 Lawrence Ave. East, North York ON M3C 1P6 – 416/395-5710; Fax: 416/395-5715 – Branch of North York Public Library

North York: Downsview Regional Branch, 2793 Keele St., North York ON M3M 2G3 – 416/395-5720; Fax: 416/395-5727 – Branch of North York Public Library

North York: Fairview Regional Branch, 35 Fairview Mall Dr., North York ON M2J 4S4 – 416/395-5750; Fax: 416/395-5756 – Branch of North York Public Library

North York: Flemingdon Park Community Branch, 29 St. Dennis Dr., North York ON M3C 3J3 – 416/395-5820; Fax: 416/395-5438 – Branch of North York Public Library

North York: Hillcrest Community Branch, 5801 Leslie St., North York ON M2H 1J8 – 416/395-5830; Fax: 416/395-5439 – Branch of North York Public Library

North York: Humber Summit Community Branch, 2990 Islington Ave., North York ON M9L 2K6 – 416/395-5840; Fax: 416/395-5426 – Branch of North York Public Library

North York: Jane/Sheppard Community Branch, Jane Sheppard Mall, #11, 2721 Jane St., North York ON M3L 1S3 – 416/395-5966; Fax: 416/395-5427 – Branch of North York Public Library

North York: Pleasant View Community Branch, 575 Van Horne Ave., North York ON M2J 4S8 – 416/395-5940; Fax: 416/395-5419 – Branch of North York Public Library

North York: Victoria Village Community Branch, 184 Sloane Ave., North York ON M4A 2C4 – 416/395-5950; Fax: 416/395-5418 – Branch of North York Public Library

North York: Woodview Park Community Branch, 16-18 Bradstock Rd., North York ON M9M 1M8 – 416/395-5960; Fax: 416/395-5417 – Branch of North York Public Library

North York: York Woods Regional Branch Library, 1785 Finch Ave. West, North York ON M3N 1M6 – 416/395-5980; Fax: 416/395-5991 – Branch of North York Public Library

Norwich Library, 21 Stover St., Norwich ON N0J 1P0 – 519/863-3307 – Supervisor, Maureen Baker-Wilkinson – Branch of Oxford County Library (see Woodstock)

Norwood Public Library, 60 Colborne St., PO Box 100, Norwood ON K0L 2V0 – 705/639-2228 – CEO, Mabel Dornan

Oakville Public Library, 120 Navy St., Oakville ON L6J 2Z4 – 905/815-2042; Fax: 905/815-2024; Email: jamese@haltonbc.on.ca – Director, Eleanor James; Deputy Director, Edith Hopkins; Reference Librarian, Florence de Dominicis; Circulation Librarian, Jane Diamanti; Children's Librarian, Daria Sharanewych; Technical Services Manager, Brian Bell; Head, Adult Services, Pam Sadler; Acquisitions Supervisor, Janet Whaley – See also following branches: Glen Abbey Branch Library, White Oaks Branch Library, Woodside Branch Library

Oakville: Glen Abbey Branch Library, 1415 Third Line, Oakville ON L6M 3G2 – 905/815-2039; Fax: 905/815-5951; Email: cravens@haltonbc.on.ca – Branch Head, Suzanne Craven – Branch of Oakville Public Library

Oakville: White Oaks Branch Library, 1070 McCraney St. East, Oakville ON L6H 2R6 – 905/815-2038; Fax: 905/815-2024; Email: kullasj@haltonbc.on.ca – Branch Head, Janice Kullas – Branch of Oakville Public Library

Oakville: Woodside Branch Library, 1274 Rebecca St., Oakville ON L6L 1Z2 – 905/827-3321; Fax: 905/815-5954; Email: mazzak@haltonbc.on.ca – Branch Head, Kathryn Mazza – Branch of Oakville Public Library

Oakwood Branch Library, Oakwood ON K0M 2M0 – 705/953-9060 – Branch Head, Ruth Teel – Branch of Victoria County Public Library (see Lindsay)

Odessa Branch Library, PO Box 250, Odessa ON K0H 2H0 – 613/386-3981 – Supervisor, Mary Lou Fraser – Branch of Lennox & Addington County Library (see Napanee)

Ohsweken: Six Nations Public Library, PO Box 149, Ohsweken ON N0A 1M0 – 519/445-2954 – Librarian, Diana Doxtdator

Oil Springs Library, 4596 Oil Springs Line, PO Box 126, Oil Springs ON N0N 1P0 – 519/834-2670 – Librarian, Nancy Byers – Branch of Lambton County Library (see Wyoming)

Omemee Branch Library, Coronation Hall, Omemee ON K0L 2W0 – 705/799-5711 – Branch Head, Bev McQuade – Branch of Victoria County Public Library (see Lindsay)

Ompah: Palmerston North & South Canonto Twp., Ompah Branch Library, Ompah ON K0H 2J0 – 613/479-2281 – Heather White – Branch of Frontenac County Library (see Kingston)

Onaping: Earle Jarvis Public Library, PO Box 160, Onaping ON P0M 2R0 – 705/966-2740; Fax: 705/966-0711 – Librarian, Marilyn Knoll – Branch of Lionel Rheaume Public Library (see Dowling)

Orangeville Public Library, One Mill St., Orangeville ON L9W 2M2 – 519/941-0610; Fax: 519/941-4698 – CEO, Janice Hindley; Children's Librarian, Lesley McGill; Public Services Librarian, Olive Vousden; Technical Services Librarian, Janet Scheibler

Orillia: Atherley Branch Library, RR#7, Orillia ON L3V 6H7 – 705/325-5776 – Librarian, Louise Duncan – Branch of Mara Twp. Public Library

Orillia Public Library, 36 Mississaga St. West, Orillia ON L3V 3A6 – 705/325-2338; Fax: 705/327-1744 – CEO, Paul E. Blower; Director of Children's & AV Services, Suzanne Campbell; Director of Technical Services, David Rowe

Orleans: Sir Wilfrid Laurier Branch Library, 1515 Tenth Line, Orleans ON K1E 3E8 – 613/830-5422; Fax: 613/834-4511 – Public Services Librarian, I. Douglas – Branch of Cumberland Public Library (see Navan)

Orono: Clarke Branch Library, 127 Church St., Orono ON L0B 1M0 – 905/983-5507 – Contact, Andrea MacDonald – Branch of Clarington Public Library

Osgoode Branch Library, 5630 Main St., PO Box 459, Osgoode ON K0A 2W0 – 613/826-2227 – Librarian, Brenda Porteous – Branch of Osgoode Twp. Public Library Board (see Metcalfe)

Oshawa Public Library, McLaughlin Bldg., 65 Bagot St., Oshawa ON L1H 1N2 – 905/579-6111; Fax: 905/433-8107 – CEO, Brenda Carrigan; Head of Children's Services, Dinah E.W. Gough; Head of Adult Services, Richard Ficek; Head, Technical Services, Kim Pitcher; Manager of Automated Systems, Ian J. Heckford; Acquisitions Librarian, Kim Pitcher – See also following branches: Jess Hann Library, McLaughlin Library, Northview Branch Library

Oshawa: Jess Hann Library, Lake Vista Sq., 199 Wentworth St. West, Oshawa ON L1J 6P4 – 905/728-2441 – Branch Head, Leslie Winston – Branch of Oshawa Public Library

Oshawa: McLaughlin Library, 65 Bagot St., Oshawa ON L1H 1N2 – 905/579-6111; Fax: 905/433-8107 – Librarian, Brenda Carrigan – Branch of Oshawa Public Library

Oshawa: Northview Branch Library, 250 Beatrice St. East, Oshawa ON L1G 7T6 – 905/576-6040 – Branch Head, Jana Schuelke – Branch of Oshawa Public Library

Ottawa Public Library, 120 Metcalfe St., Ottawa ON K1P 5M2 – 613/236-0301; Fax: 613/567-4013; Email: ILL.OOC; Symbol: OOC – Chief Librarian, Barbara Clubb; Reference Librarian, Lynn Legate; Circulation, Valerie Dodge; Children's Librarian, Barbara Herd; Adult Services Librarian, Fernande Arcand; Technical Services Librarian, Karen Smith; Acquisitions, Anna Dooley; Automated Services Librarian, Linnie Kalloo; Financial Services, Jean Martel – See also following branches: Alta Vista Library, Carlingwood Branch Library, Elmvale Acres Library, Rideau Branch Library, South Branch Li-

Canadian Almanac & Directory 1997

brary & Mobile Service, St. Laurent Library, West Branch Library

Ottawa: Alta Vista Library, 2516 Alta Vista Dr., Ottawa ON K1V 7T1 – 613/598-4012; Fax: 613/737-4355 – Librarian, Monique Lavoie – Branch of Ottawa Public Library

Ottawa: Carlingwood Branch Library, 281 Woodroffe Ave., Ottawa ON K2A 3W4 – 613/598-4013; Fax: 613/725-2677 – Librarian, Mabel Hillman – Branch of Ottawa Public Library

Ottawa: Elmvale Acres Library, 1910 St. Laurent Blvd., Ottawa ON K1G 1A4 – 613/598-4014; Fax: 613/738-7534 – Librarian, Gale Hamilton-Murphy – Branch of Ottawa Public Library

Ottawa: Rideau Branch Library, 377 Rideau St., Ottawa ON K1N 5Y6 – 613/598-4015; Fax: 613/241-0358 – Librarian, Monique E. Désormeaux – Branch of Ottawa Public Library

Ottawa: Rockcliffe Park Public Library, 350 Springfield Rd., Ottawa ON K1M 0K7 – 613/745-2562; Fax: 613/749-0127 – Librarian, Barbara Mirsky

Ottawa: St. Laurent Library, 515 Côté St., Ottawa ON K1K 3A7 – 613/598-4016; Fax: 613/748-3546 – Librarian, Suzanne Matte – Branch of Ottawa Public Library

Ottawa: South Branch Library & Mobile Service, 1049 Bank St., Ottawa ON K1S 3W9 – 613/598-4017; Fax: 613/521-4323 – Acting Head, Pamela Rosolen – Branch of Ottawa Public Library

Ottawa: Southern Ontario Library Service - Ottawa, #310, 1900 City Park Dr., Ottawa ON K1J 1A3 – 613/742-0707; Français: 613/742-5640; Fax: 613/742-0712; Symbol: OOEO

Ottawa: West Branch Library, 18 Rosemount Ave., Ottawa ON K1Y 1P4 – 613/598-4018; Fax: 613/729-7945 – Librarian, Joan Weller – Branch of Ottawa Public Library

Otterville Library, John St., Otterville ON N0J 1R0 – 519/879-6984 – Supervisor, Lurene McMullen – Branch of Oxford County Library (*see* Woodstock)

Owen Sound & North Grey Union Public Library, 824 - 1 Ave. West., Owen Sound ON N4K 4K4 – 519/376-6623; Fax: 519/376-7170 – Library Director, Andrew D. Armitage; Assistant Library Director, Judy Beth Armstrong; Reference Librarian, Joan Hull; Children's Librarian, Mary Hopkinson

Oxford Mills Library, Oxford Mills ON K0G 1S0 – 613/258-5040 – Librarian, Elaine Landry – Branch of Oxford-on-Rideau Twp. Public Library (*see* Burritt's Rapids)

Paisley Branch Library, 274 Queen St., PO Box 219, Paisley ON N0G 2N0 – 519/353-7225 – Branch Supervisor, Cheryl Parker – Branch of Bruce County Public Library (*see* Port Elgin)

Pakenham Twp. Public Library, PO Box 59, Pakenham ON K0A 2X0 – 613/624-5306 – CEO, Mary Ellen Jack

Palmerston Branch Library, 265 Bell St., PO Box 340, Palmerston ON N0G 2P0 – 519/343-2142; Fax: 519/846-2066 – Branch Supervisor, Barbara Burrows – Branch of Wellington County Library (*see* Fergus)

Parham Deposit, Long Lake Rd., RR#1, Parham ON K0H 2K0 – Glenda Young – Branch of Frontenac County Library (*see* Kingston)

Paris Public Library, 12 William St., Paris ON N3L 1K7 – 519/442-2433; Fax: 519/442-7582 – Librarian, Werner Mueller

Parkhill Library, 233 Main St., Parkhill ON N0M 2K0 – 519/294-6583; Fax: 519/294-6583 – Supervisor, Karen Woods – Branch of Middlesex County Library (*see* Arva)

Parry Sound: Christie Twp. Public Library, RR#3, Parry Sound ON P2A 2W9 – 705/732-2850; Fax: 705/732-1467 – CEO/Librarian, Liana Bradley

Parry Sound: Humphrey Twp. Public Library, RR#2, Parry Sound ON P2A 2W8 – 705/732-4526 – Librarian, Patricia Coles

Parry Sound Public Library, 29 Mary St., Parry Sound ON P2A 1E3 – 705/746-9601; Fax: 705/746-9601 – Librarian, Laurine Tremaine

Parry Sound: Wasauksing First Nation Public Library, PO Box 253, Parry Sound ON P2A 2X3 – 705/746-2531; Fax: 705/746-5984 – CEO, Carol M. Pegahmagabow

Pawitik: Whitefish Bay First Nation Public Library, c/o BaiBomBeh Anishinabe School, Pawitik ON P0X 1L0 – 807/226-5698; Fax: 807/226-1089 – CEO, Helen Wesley

Pefferlaw Library, PO Box 220, Pefferlaw ON L0E 1N0 – 705/437-1514 – Branch Head, Mary Reddings – Branch of Georgina Public Libraries (*see* Keswick)

Pelee Island Public Library, West Shore Rd., Pelee Island ON N0R 1M0 – 519/724-2028 – Librarian, Debbie Crawford

Pembroke Public Library, 237 Victoria St., Pembroke ON K8A 4K5 – 613/732-8844; Fax: 613/732-1116; Email: pemlib@fox.nstn.ca; Symbol: OPEM – CEO/Chief Librarian, Subhash Mehta; Children's Librarian, Anne Irvine

Penetanguishene Public Library, 24 Simcoe St., Penetanguishene ON L9M 1R6 – 705/549-7164; Fax: 705/549-3932 – CEO, Rosemary Marchand

Perth & District Union Public Library, 30 Herriott St., Perth ON K7H 1T2 – 613/267-1224; Fax: 613/267-7899 – Librarian, Faye Cunningham; Children's Librarian, Susan Snyder

Petawawa Village & Twp. Union Public Library, 16 Civic Centre Rd., Petawawa ON K8H 3H5 – 613/687-2227; Fax: 613/687-2527 – Chief Librarian, Jean Risto; Children's Librarian, Carol Goldsmith; Audio-Visual Librarian, Janet Coulas; Languages & Special Collections, Barbara Collmorgen; Memberships & Statistics, Brenda Meighan; Displays & Special Programs, Eileen Robinson

Peterborough Public Library, 345 Aylmer St. North, Peterborough ON K9H 3V7 – 705/745-5382; Fax: 705/743-8958 – CEO, Wendy Brown; Reference Librarian, Jim Pendergest; Circulation Supervisor, Glenda Underwood; Children's Librarian, Laurie Woollard; Acquisitions Librarian, Cara Peterman; Technical Services Librarian, Ruth Whelham-Umphrey; Deputy CEO, Anne Donnellan – See also following branches: De La Fosse Library

Peterborough: De La Fosse Library, 729 Park St. South, Peterborough ON K9J 3T3 – 705/745-8653 – Jan Ball – Branch of Peterborough Public Library

Petrolia Library, 4200 Petrolia St., PO Box 70, Petrolia ON N0N 1R0 – 519/882-0771 – Librarian, Shirley Banks – Branch of Lambton County Library (*see* Wyoming)

Pickerel: Henvey Inlet First Nation Public Library, Pickerel ON P0G 1J0 – 705/857-2331 – CEO, Fern Panamick

Pickering Public Library, PO Box 368, Pickering ON L1V 2R6 – 905/831-6265; Fax: 905/831-8795 – CEO, Alexander Cameron; Deputy CEO, Valerie Ridgeway; Systems & Technical Services, Head, Elaine Bird; Adult Services Coordinator, Linda Linton; Children's Coordinator, Kathy Williams – See also following branches: Bay Ridges Branch Library, Central Library, Claremont Branch Library, Greenwood Branch Library, Rouge Hill Branch Library, Whitevale Branch Library

Pickering: Bay Ridges Branch Library, PO Box 368, Pickering ON L1V 2R6 – 905/839-3083 – Branch of Pickering Public Library

Pickering: Central Library, One The Esplanade South, Pickering ON L1V 6K7 – 905/831-6265; Fax: 905/831-8795 – Branch of Pickering Public Library

Pickering: Claremont Branch Library, PO Box 368, Pickering ON L1V 2R6 – 905/649-3341 – Branch of Pickering Public Library

Pickering: Greenwood Branch Library, PO Box 368, Pickering ON L1V 2R6 – 905/683-8844 – Branch of Pickering Public Library

Pickering: Rouge Hill Branch Library, PO Box 368, Pickering ON L1V 2R6 – 905/509-2579 – Branch of Pickering Public Library

Pickering: Whitevale Branch Library, PO Box 368, Pickering ON L1V 2R6 – 905/294-0967 – Branch of Pickering Public Library

Pickle Lake: Fort Hope First Nation Public Library, John C. Yesno Education Centre, Eabemet Lake, Pickle Lake ON P0T 1L0 – 807/242-8421; Fax: 807/242-1592 – Librarian, Lucy Slipperjack

Picton Public Library, Main St., PO Box 260, Picton ON K0K 2T0 – 613/476-5962; Fax: 613/476-3325 – Librarian, Valerie Creasy; Children's Librarian, Marie Dawson

Plattsville Library, PO Box 40, Plattsville ON N0J 1S0 – 519/684-7390 – Supervisor, Kathy Hofstetter – Branch of Oxford County Library (*see* Woodstock)

Plevna: Clarendon Miller Twp., Plevna Branch Library, Plevna ON K0H 2M0 – 613/479-2542 – Heather White – Branch of Frontenac County Library (*see* Kingston)

Point Edward Library, 220 Michigan Ave., Point Edward ON N7V 1E8 – 519/336-3291 – Librarian, Margaret Scott – Branch of Lambton County Library (*see* Wyoming)

Port Burwell Library, PO Box 189, Port Burwell ON N0J 1T0 – 519/874-4754; Symbol: PR – Supervisor, Doris Van Den Eeckhout – Branch of Elgin County Library (*see* St. Thomas)

Port Carling Public Library, Port Community Centre, PO Box 189, Port Carling ON P0B 1J0 – 705/765-5650 – Librarian, Elizabeth H. Glen, 705/765-5392 – See also following branches: Bala Public Library, Milford Bay Public Library, Muskoka Lakes Twp. Public Library Board, Ullswater Public Library, Walker's Point Public Library

Port Carling: Muskoka Lakes Twp. Public Library Board, PO Box 189, Port Carling ON P0B 1J0 – 705/765-5650 – CEO, Elizabeth H. Glen – Branch of Port Carling Public Library

Port Colborne Public Library, 310 King St., Port Colborne ON L3K 4H1 – 905/834-6512; Fax: 905/835-5775 – CEO, Mary Karpinchick; Chief Librarian's Assistant, Jennifer Parry; Children's Librarian, Anne Kelly

Port Dover Branch Library, 413 Main St., Port Dover ON N0A 1N0 – 519/583-0622 – Branch Librarian, Betty Lee – Branch of Nanticoke Public Library Board (*see* Jarvis)

Port Elgin: Bruce County Public Library, 1243 Mackenzie Rd., Port Elgin ON N0H 2C2 – 519/832-6935; Fax: 519/832-9000 – Director, Marzio Apolloni; Reference Librarian, Shirley Morningstar – See also following branches: Cargill Branch Library, Chesley Branch Library, Hepworth Branch Library, Kincardine Branch Library, Lion's Head & District Branch Library, Lucknow Library, Mildmay-Carrick Branch Library, Paisley Branch Library, Port Elgin Branch Library, Ripley Branch Library, Sauble Beach Branch Library, Southampton Branch Public Library, Tara Branch Library, Teeswater Branch Library, Tiverton Branch Library, Tobermory Branch Library, Walkerton Branch Library, Wiarton Branch Library

Port Elgin Branch Library, Goderich St., PO Box 609, Port Elgin ON N0H 2C0 – 519/832-2201 – Branch Supervisor, Elizabeth Carter – Branch of Bruce County Public Library

Port Franks Library, 7545 Riverside Dr., PO Box 49, Port Franks ON N0M 2L0 – 519/243-2820 – Librarian, Pat Wells – Branch of Lambton County Library (*see* Wyoming)

Port Hope Public Library, 31 Queen St., Port Hope ON L1A 2Y8 – 905/885-4712; Fax: 905/885-4181 – Chief

Librarian, Patricia Enright; Children's Librarian, Alison Brown
Port Lambton Library, 507 Stoddard St., PO Box 126, Port Lambton ON N0P 2B0 – 519/677-5217 – Librarian, Theresa Lecky – Branch of Lambton County Library (see Wyoming)
Port McNicoll Public Library, 701 Fourth St., PO Box 490, Port McNicoll ON L0K 1R0 – 705/534-3511; Fax: 705/534-3511 – Branch Librarian, Lana Wells-Garrett – Branch of Tay Twp. Public Library (see Waubaushene)
Port Perry: Mississaugas of Scugog Island First Nation Library, RR#5, Port Perry ON L9L 1B6 – 905/935-3337; Fax: 905/985-8828 – CEO, Kelly Ewing
Port Perry: Scugog Memorial Public Library, 231 Water St., PO Box 1049, Port Perry ON L9L 1A8 – 905/985-7686; Fax: 905/985-7210 – CEO, Tom Bonanno
Port Robinson Branch Library, 46 Cross St., Port Robinson ON L0S 1K0 – 905/384-9513 – Branch Head, L. Wronski – Branch of Thorold Public Library
Port Rowan: Norfolk Twp. Public Library Board, 34 Main St., PO Box 130, Port Rowan ON N0E 1M0 – 519/586-3201 – Librarian, Marsha Johnston – See also following branches: Valley Heights Public Library
Port Rowan: Valley Heights Public Library, PO Box 130, Port Rowan ON N0E 1M0 – 519/586-3532 – Librarian, Ben Bailey – Branch of Norfolk Twp. Public Library Board
Port Stanley Public Library, 302 Bridge St., PO Box 280, Port Stanley ON N0L 2A0 – 519/782-4241 – Supervisor, Sue Nemett – Branch of Elgin County Library (see St. Thomas)
Portland Branch Library, Portland ON K0G 1V0 – 613/272-2832 – Librarian, Lois Braidwood – Branch of Rideau Lakes Union Library (see Elgin)
Powassan & District Union Library, 324 Clark St., PO Box 160, Powassan ON P0H 1Z0 – 705/724-3618 – Chief Librarian & CEO, Mary Hall
Prescott Public Library, 360 Dibble St. West, PO Box 430, Prescott ON K0E 1T0 – 613/925-4340; Fax: 613/925-4381 – Chief Librarian, Jane McGuire
Princeton Library, PO Box 99, Princeton ON N0J 1V0 – 519/458-4416 – Supervisor, Margaret Kipp – Branch of Oxford County Library (see Woodstock)
Providence Bay Branch Library, General Delivery, Providence Bay ON P0P 1T0 – 705/377-4503 – Branch of Carnarvon Twp. Public Library (see Mindemoya)
Putnam Library, RR#1, Putnam ON N0L 2B0 – 519/485-4946 – Supervisor, Evelyn Rath – Branch of Middlesex County Library (see Arva)
Rainy River Public Library, 202 - 4 St., PO Box 308, Rainy River ON P0W 1L0 – 807/852-3375 – CEO/Head Librarian, Ruth Bynkoski
Rama: Chippewas of Rama First Nation Public Library, Rama Rd., PO Box 35, Rama ON L0K 1T0 – 705/326-7323; Fax: 705/325-0879 – CEO, Gail Anderson
Ramore Branch, PO Box 250, Ramore ON P0K 1R0 – 705/236-4225 – Branch Head, Lucille Robillard – Branch of Black River-Matheson Public Library
Red Lake Public Library, PO Box 348, Red Lake ON P0V 2M0 – 807/727-2230; Fax: 807/727-3980; Email: remoteinet@lib.lakehead.ca – Librarian/CEO, Darlene Wilson; Reference Librarian, Sherry Boland; Children's Librarian, Tara Brown; Public Services Librarian, Darlene Wilson
Red Rock Public Library, Salls St., PO Box 285, Red Rock ON P0T 2P0 – 807/886-2558; Fax: 807/886-2793 – Chief Librarian, Luella Sumner
Redbridge: Phelps Public Library, RR#1, Redbridge ON P0H 2A0 – 705/663-2720 – CEO, Beverly Reynolds
Renfrew Public Library, 13 Railway Ave., Renfrew ON K7V 3A9 – 613/432-8151 – Chief Librarian, Patricia Eady; Children's Librarian, Susan Klinck
Richards Landing: St. Joseph Twp. Public Library, Richards Landing ON P0R 1J0 – 705/246-2353;

Fax: 705/246-2353 – Librarian/CEO, Karen Van-Sickle
Richmond Hill Public Library, 1 Atkinson St., Richmond Hill ON L4C 0H5 – 905/770-0310; Fax: 905/770-0312 – CEO, Jane Horrocks – See also following branches: Central Library, Oak Ridges Moraine Library, Richvale Library
Richmond Hill: Central Library, 1 Atkinson St., Richmond Hill ON L4C 0H5 – 905/884-9288 – Director of Public Service, Barbara Ransom – Branch of Richmond Hill Public Library
Richmond Hill: Oak Ridges Moraine Library, #12, 13085 Yonge St., Richmond Hill ON L4E 3L2 – 905/773-5533; Fax: 905/773-8107 – Manager of Branch Services, Mary Deciantis – Branch of Richmond Hill Public Library
Richmond Hill: Southern Ontario Library Service, Head Office, #601, 151 Bloor St. West, Toronto ON M5S 1T4 – 416/961-1669; Fax: 416/961-5122 – CEO, Laurey Irvine
Richmond Branch Library, 6240 Perth St., PO Box 1029, Richmond ON K0A 2Z0 – 613/838-2026 – Branch Head, Sharon McMullen – Branch of Goulbourn Twp. Public Library (see Stittsville)
Ridgetown Branch Library, Main St. West, Ridgetown ON N0P 2C0 – 519/674-3121 – Branch Librarian, Mary Lou Wootton – Branch of Kent County Library (see Chatham)
Ripley Branch Library, Jessie St., PO Box 207, Ripley ON N0G 2R0 – 519/395-5919 – Branch Supervisor, Judy Hawrylyshyn – Branch of Bruce County Public Library (see Port Elgin)
Rockland (Bibliothèque publique), 2085, rue Laurier, CP 819, Rockland ON K4K 1L5 – 613/446-5680; Téléc: 613/446-7907 – CEO, Lyne Lapalme
Rockton Public Library, 795 Old Hwy. 8, Rockton PO, Rockton ON L0R 1X0 – 519/647-2272 – Branch Head, Jan Maas – Branch of Wentworth Libraries (see Hamilton)
Rockwood: Eramosa Community Library, PO Box 520, Rockwood ON N0B 2K0 – 519/856-4851; Fax: 519/856-2240 – CEO, Linda Hornick; Children's Librarian, Leanne Clark; Assistant Librarian, Susan Marcoux
Rodney Branch Library, 207 Furnival Rd., PO Box 398, Rodney ON N0L 2C0 – 519/785-2100 – Supervisor, Shelley Fleming – Branch of Elgin County Library (see St. Thomas)
Roseneath: Alderville Library & Resource Centre, PO Box 39, Roseneath ON K0K 2X0 – 905/352-2488; Fax: 905/352-3242 – CEO, Kim Lamothe
Roseneath Branch Library, PO Box 90, Roseneath ON K0K 2X0 – 905/352-1079 – Branch Head, Bronwyn Cochrane – Branch of Northumberland County Public Library (see Hastings)
Rosseau Public Library, PO Box 8, Rosseau ON P0C 1J0 – 705/732-4231 – Librarian, Margaret R. Crawford
Russell Branch Library, 92 Mill St., PO Box 280, Russell ON K4R 1E1 – 613/445-5331 – Branch Head, Jacqueline Lemery – Branch of Russell Twp. Public Library
Ruthven Library, 1695 Elgin St., PO Box 279, Ruthven ON N0P 2G0 – 519/326-8758 – Supervisor, Hilda MacDonald – Branch of Essex County Library
St. Albert: Bibliothèque publique de Cambridge-St-Albert, 201, rue Principale, CP 99, St Albert ON K0A 3C0 – 613/987-2143; Téléc: 613/987-2143 – Directrice générale, Thérèse Piché
St. Andrews West Branch, PO Box 90, St Andrews West ON K0C 2A0 – 613/932-6012 – Supervisor/Branch Head, Mildred Wheeler – Branch of Stormont, Dundas & Glengarry County Library (see Finch)
St Catharines Public Library, 54 Church St., St Catharines ON L2R 7K2 – 905/688-6104; Fax: 905/688-6292; Email: mrossett@scp.st-cath.on.ca – Director, Mady Rossetto; Head, Non-Fiction, Susan Beynon;

Head, Circulation, A. Penfold; Head, Children's Services, B. Rempel; Manager, Acquisitions & Technical Services, K. Cochrane; Head, Fiction & Community Services, D. Andrusko; Head, Audio-Visual Services, P. Errington – See also following branches: Grantham Branch Library, Port Dalhousie Library, William Hamilton Merritt Branch Library
St Catharines: Grantham Branch Library, Scott & Vine Sts., St Catharines ON L2M 3W4 – 905/934-7511; Fax: 905/688-6292 – Head, Branch Library Services, B. Gledhill – Branch of St Catharines Public Library
St Catharines: Port Dalhousie Library, Brock St., St Catharines ON L2N 5E1 – 905/646-0220; Fax: 905/688-6292 – Head, Fiction & Community Services, D. Andrusko – Branch of St Catharines Public Library
St Catharines: William Hamilton Merritt Branch Library, 149 Hartzel Rd., St Catharines ON L2P 1N6 – 905/682-3568; Fax: 905/688-6292 – Head, Branch Library Services, B. Gledhill – Branch of St Catharines Public Library
St Charles: Casimir Jennings & Appleby Twp. Public Library, PO Box 40, St Charles ON P0M 2W0 – 705/867-5332; Fax: 705/867-2511 – CEO, Claudette Pothier
St. Clair Beach Library, 13675 St. Gregory's Rd., St. Clair Beach ON N9N 3E4 – 519/735-3670 – Supervisor, Sheila Eagen – Branch of Essex County Library
St. Clements Branch Library, Main St. North, PO Box 80, St. Clements ON N0B 2M0 – 519/699-4341 – Asst. Branch Supervisor, Annette Gray – Branch of Waterloo Regional Library (see Kitchener)
St. George: South Dumfries Twp. Public Library, 36 Main St. South, PO Box 310, St. George ON N0E 1N0 – 519/448-1300 – CEO, Fiona Clarke – See also following branches: Glen Morris Branch Library, St. George Branch Library
St. George Branch Library, 36 Main St. South, PO Box 310, St. George ON N0E 1N0 – 519/448-1300 – Branch Head, Betty Ames – Branch of South Dumfries Twp. Public Library
St. Isidore & South Plantagenet Union Public Library, Centre Paroissial Joseph Roy, St Isidore de Prescott ON K0C 2B0 – 613/524-2252; Fax: 613/524-2545 – Director, Huguette Bourdon
St. Jacobs Branch Library, 29 Queen St. South, PO Box 507, St Jacobs ON N0B 2N0 – 519/664-3443 – Asst. Branch Supervisor, Helen Biggar – Branch of Waterloo Regional Library (see Kitchener)
St. Marys Public Library, 15 Church St. North, PO Box 700, St. Mary's ON N4X 1B4 – 519/284-3346; Fax: 519/284-2630; Symbol: OSTMY – CEO, Barbara Taylor; Children's Librarian, Vera Symons; Technical Services Librarian, Marlene Weston; Acquisitions Librarian, Barbara Taylor
St-Pascal-Baylon: Succursale de St-Pascal-Baylon, CP 43, St-Pascal-Baylon ON K0A 3N0 – 613/488-2494 – Bibliothécaire, Jocelyne Marton – Branch of Bibliothèque publique de Canton de Clarence (see Bourget)
St. Thomas: Elgin County Library, 450 Sunset Dr., St. Thomas ON N5R 5V1 – 519/631-1460, ext.109; Fax: 519/633-7661 – Manager of Library Services, Cathy Bishop; Public Services Librarian, Frank Clarke; Technical Services Librarian, Cindy Poon; Collection Development, Dorothy Streets – See also following branches: Aylmer Old Town Hall Library, Bayham Twp. Public Library, Belmont Public Library, Dutton Public Library, Port Burwell Library, Port Stanley Public Library, Rodney Branch Library, Shedden Library, Springfield Branch Library, Vienna Branch Library, West Lorne Library
St. Thomas Public Library, 153 Curtis St., St. Thomas ON N5P 3Z7 – 519/631-6050; Fax: 519/631-1987; Email: stpl@ccia.st-thomas.on.ca; Symbol: OSTT – CEO, Carolyn Kneeshaw; Reference Librarian, Peter Bailey; Circulation, Head, Maxine Beleutz;

Canadian Almanac & Directory 1997

Children's Librarian, Julie Siegel; Technical Services, Head, Geri Claridge; Support Services, Stephen Cummings

Sarnia: Chippewas of Sarnia Library, Chippewa Band Community Centre, Marlborough Lane, Sarnia ON N7T 7Y8 – 519/337-7836 – Librarian, Stephanie Williams – Branch of Lambton County Library (see Wyoming)

Sarnia: Mallroad Library, 1652 Lambton Mall Rd., Sarnia ON N7S 5A1 – 519/542-2580 – Librarian, Wendy Washington – Branch of Lambton County Library (see Wyoming)

Sarnia Library, 124 Christina St. South, Sarnia ON N7T 2M6 – 519/337-3291; Fax: 519/337-3041 – Branch Manager, April James – Branch of Lambton County Library (see Wyoming)

Sarnia Reserve Chippewa Library, 1972 Virgil Ave., Sarnia ON N7T 7Y9 – 519/337-7836; Fax: 519/336-0382 – CEO, Stephanie Williams

Sault Ste. Marie Public Library, 50 East St., Sault Ste Marie ON P6A 3C3 – 705/759-5230; Fax: 705/759-8752 – Director, Wilhelm Eisenbichler; Asst. Director & Children's Librarian, Valerie Dawson, 705/759-5244; Head, Technical Services, Robert McWilliam, 705/759-5234; Branch Coordinator, Stephanie Stowe, 705/759-5243; Head of Adult Services, Irma Sauvola – See also following branches: Churchill Branch Library, Korah Library

Sault Ste. Marie: Batchewana First Nation Public Library, 236 Frontenac St., Sault Ste. Marie ON P6A 5K9 – 705/759-0914; Fax: 705/759-9171 – Librarian, Darlene Syrette

Sault Ste. Marie: Churchill Branch Library, 150 Churchill Blvd., Sault Ste. Marie ON P6A 3Z9 – 705/759-5248; Fax: 705/759-8752 – Branch Head, Stephanie Stowe – Branch of Sault Ste. Marie Public Library

Sault Ste. Marie: Garden River First Nation Public Library, RR#4, Site 5, PO Box 7, Sault Ste. Marie ON P6A 5K9 – 705/946-6300; Fax: 705/945-1415 – Librarian, Lisa Cress

Sault Ste. Marie: Korah Library, 496 Second Line West, Sault Ste. Marie ON P6C 2K4 – 705/759-5249; Fax: 705/759-8752 – Branch Head, Stephanie Stowe – Branch of Sault Ste. Marie Public Library

Sault Ste. Marie: Prince Twp. Public Library, 3042 Second Line West, Sault Ste. Marie ON P6A 6K4 – 705/779-3653; Fax: 705/779-2725 – CEO, Elizabeth Papineau

Savant Lake Community Library, General Delivery, Savant Lake ON P0V 2S0 – 807/584-2242; Fax: 807/584-2272

Scarborough Public Library Board, 1076 Ellesmere Rd., Scarborough ON M1P 4P4 – 416/396-8800; Fax: 416/396-8808; Email: ENVOY:SPLB.ADMIN – CEO, Ann Eddie; Deputy CEO, David Reddin; Director, Service Development & Promotion, Michele Topa; Coordinator of Services for Children & Young Adults, Ken Setterington; Coordinator of Multicultural Services, Chryss Mylopoulos; Coordinator of Communications, Marcus Wiseman; Director, Technical Services, Stan Algoo; Head of Acquisitions & Interlibrary Loan, Laurie Saunders; Head of Cataloguing, Ellen Jaaku; Director, Southeastern Division, Donald McKenzie; Director, Northern Division, Vacant; Director, Southwestern Division, Anna Kwan – See also following branches: Agincourt District Library, Albert Campbell District Library, Bendale Neighbourhood Branch Library, Bridlewood Neighbourhood Branch Library, Cedarbrae District Library, Cliffcrest Neighbourhood Branch Library, Eglinton Square Neighbourhood Branch Library, Goldhawk Park Neighbourhood Branch Library, Guildwood Neighbourhood Branch Library, Highland Creek Neighbourhood Branch Library, Kennedy/Eglinton Neighbourhood Branch Library, Malvern Community Library, Maryvale Neighbourhood Branch Library, McGregor Park Neighbourhood Branch Library, Morningside Neighbourhood Branch Library, Port Union Neighbourhood Branch Library, Steeles Neighbourhood Branch Library, Taylor Memorial Neighbourhood Branch Library, Woodside Square Neighbourhood Branch Library

Scarborough: Agincourt District Library, 155 Bonis Ave., c/o 1076 Ellesmere Rd., Scarborough ON M1P 4P4 – 416/396-8943 – Branch Head, Charna Kofsky; Adult Services Librarian, Bill Hamade; Children's Services Librarian, Mee-Shan Lau – Branch of Scarborough Public Library Board

Scarborough: Albert Campbell District Library, 496 Birchmount Rd., c/o 1076 Ellesmere Rd., Scarborough ON M1P 4P4 – 416/396-8890 – Branch Head, Rodger McLennan; Adult Services Librarian, Po-Chung Cheng; Children's Services Librarian, Mary Allen – Branch of Scarborough Public Library Board

Scarborough: Bendale Neighbourhood Branch Library, 1515 Danforth Rd., c/o 1076 Ellesmere Rd., Scarborough ON M1P 4P4 – 416/369-8910 – Branch Supervisor, Carol Ives – Branch of Scarborough Public Library Board

Scarborough: Bridlewood Neighbourhood Branch Library, Bridlewood Mall, c/o 1076 Ellesmere Rd., Scarborough ON M1P 4P4 – 416/396-8960 – Branch Supervisor, Usha Reddy – Branch of Scarborough Public Library Board

Scarborough: Cedarbrae District Library, 545 Markham Rd., Scarborough ON M1H 2A1 – 416/396-8850; Fax: 416/396-8864 – Branch Head, Sylvia King; Adult Services Librarian, Lynne Cuthbert; Children's Services Librarian, Grace Lord – Branch of Scarborough Public Library Board

Scarborough: Cliffcrest Neighbourhood Branch Library, Cliffcrest Plaza, c/o 1076 Ellesmere Rd., Scarborough ON M1P 4P4 – 416/396-8916 – Branch Supervisor, Donna Clifton – Branch of Scarborough Public Library Board

Scarborough: Eglinton Square Neighbourhood Branch Library, Eglinton Square Mall, c/o 1076 Ellesmere Rd., Scarborough ON M1P 4P4 – 416/396-8920 – Branch Supervisor, Roz Mida – Branch of Scarborough Public Library Board

Scarborough: Goldhawk Park Neighbourhood Branch Library, 295 Alton Towers Circle, c/o 1076 Ellesmere Rd., Scarborough ON M1P 4P4 – 416/396-8964 – Branch Head, Paula Smith – Branch of Scarborough Public Library Board

Scarborough: Guildwood Neighbourhood Branch Library, Guildwood Plaza, c/o 1076 Ellesmere Rd., Scarborough ON M1P 4P4 – 416/396-8872 – Branch Supervisor, Barbara More – Branch of Scarborough Public Library Board

Scarborough: Highland Creek Neighbourhood Branch Library, c/o 1076 Ellesmere Rd., Scarborough ON M1P 4P4 – 416/396-8876 – Branch Supervisor, Patricia Green – Branch of Scarborough Public Library Board

Scarborough: Kennedy/Eglinton Neighbourhood Branch Library, Liberty Square Shopping Plaza, c/o 1076 Ellesmere Rd., Scarborough ON M1P 4P4 – 416/396-8924 – Branch Supervisor, Marilyn Sansome – Branch of Scarborough Public Library Board

Scarborough: Malvern Community Library, 30 Sewells Rd., c/o 1076 Ellesmere Rd., Scarborough ON M1P 4P4 – 416/396-8969 – Branch Head, Paul Trumphour – Branch of Scarborough Public Library Board

Scarborough: Maryvale Neighbourhood Branch Library, Parkway Plaza, c/o 1076 Ellesmere Rd., Scarborough ON M1P 4P4 – 416/396-8931 – Branch Supervisor, Sheryl Hyland – Branch of Scarborough Public Library Board

Scarborough: McGregor Park Neighbourhood Branch Library, 2219 Lawrence Ave. East, c/o 1076 Ellesmere Rd., Scarborough ON M1P 4P4 – 416/396-8935 – Branch Supervisor, Gwen Ackerman – Branch of Scarborough Public Library Board

Scarborough: Morningside Neighbourhood Branch Library, Morningside Mall, c/o 1076 Ellesmere Rd., Scarborough ON M1P 4P4 – 416/396-8881 – Branch Head, Linda Martin – Branch of Scarborough Public Library Board

Scarborough: Port Union Neighbourhood Branch Library, 5450 Lawrence Ave. East, c/o 1076 Ellesmere Rd., Scarborough ON M1P 4P4 – 416/396-8885 – Branch Supervisor, Bonnie McAteer – Branch of Scarborough Public Library Board

Scarborough: Steeles Neighbourhood Branch Library, Bamburgh Gardens Shopping Centre, c/o 1076 Ellesmere Rd., Scarborough ON M1P 4P4 – 416/396-8975 – Branch Supervisor, Carol Silverberg – Branch of Scarborough Public Library Board

Scarborough: Taylor Memorial Neighbourhood Branch Library, 1440 Kingston Rd., c/o 1076 Ellesmere Rd., Scarborough ON M1P 4P4 – 416/396-8939 – Branch Supervisor, Linda Flavell – Branch of Scarborough Public Library Board

Scarborough: Woodside Square Neighbourhood Branch Library, Woodside Square Mall, c/o 1076 Ellesmere Rd., Scarborough ON M1P 4P4 – 416/396-8979 – Branch Supervisor, Alice Vaughan – Branch of Scarborough Public Library Board

Schomberg Library, PO Box 9, Schomberg ON L0G 1T0 – 905/939-2102; Fax: 905/939-2102 – Librarian, Linda Chadwick – Branch of King Twp. Public Library

Schreiber Twp. Public Library, PO Box 39, Schreiber ON P0T 2S0 – 807/824-2477; Fax: 807/824-3241; Email: schlib@schreiber.lakeheadu.ca – Librarian, Howard Alexander

Schumacher Memorial Branch Library, 56 First Ave., PO Box 800, Schumacher ON P0N 1G0 – 705/360-1545 – Branch Head, Donna Johnston – Branch of Timmins Public Library

Scotland: Oakland Twp. Public Library, 281 Oakland Rd., PO Box 40, Scotland ON N0E 1R0 – 519/446-0181 – CEO, Linda Zylstra

Seaforth Branch Library, PO Box 490, Seaforth ON N0K 1W0 – 519/527-1430 – Branch Supervisor, Trudy Broome – Branch of Huron County Library (see Goderich)

Sebright: Carden Twp. Branch Library, RR#1, Sebright ON L0K 1W0 – 705/833-2845; Fax: 705/833-2845 – Branch Head, Joyce Townes – Branch of Victoria County Public Library (see Lindsay)

Sebright: Dalton Twp. Branch Library, RR#1, Sebright ON L0K 1W0 – 705/833-2858 – Branch Supervisor, June Hill – Branch of Victoria County Public Library (see Lindsay)

Seeley's Bay Branch, Main St., Seeley's Bay ON K0H 2N0 – 613/387-3909 – Librarian, Hilda Simpson – Branch of Rideau Lakes Union Library (see Elgin)

Selkirk Branch Library, 34 Main St., PO Box 130, Selkirk ON N0A 1P0 – 905/776-2127 – Branch Librarian, Pat Reidy – Branch of Nanticoke Public Library Board (see Jarvis)

Severn Bridge: Morrison Library Outpost, RR#1, Severn Bridge ON P0E 1N0 – Branch Head, Joan Kennedy – Branch of Gravenhurst Public Library

Shannonville: Tyendinaga Twp. Public Library, Queen St., Shannonville ON K0K 3A0 – 613/967-0606 – CEO, Frances Smith

Sharbot Lake: Oso Twp., Sharbot Lake Branch Library, PO Box 251, Sharbot Lake ON K0H 2P0 – 613/279-2583 – Marlin McVeigh – Branch of Frontenac County Library (see Kingston)

Shedden Library, PO Box 10, Shedden ON N0L 2E0 – 519/764-2081 – Supervisor, Cathy Bishop – Branch of Elgin County Library (see St. Thomas)

Sheffield Public Library, 1256 Sheffield Rd., Sheffield ON L0R 1Z0 – 519/623-2681 – Branch Head, Jan

Maas – Branch of Wentworth Libraries (see Hamilton)

Shelburne Public Library, Owen Sound St., PO Box 127, Shelburne ON L0N 1S0 – 519/925-2168; Symbol: SPL – CEO, Mary Lynne Armstrong; Children's Librarian, Jeanne Cruikshank

Simcoe Public Library, 46 Colborne St. South, Simcoe ON N3Y 4H3 – 519/426-3506; Fax: 519/426-0657; Symbol: SIM – CEO, Autar Ganju; Reference Librarian, Carole Henderson; Circulation Librarian, Deborah Verhoeven; Children's Librarian, Wendy Gedy; Technical Services/Acquisitions Librarian, Maryann Armstrong

Sioux Lookout Public Library, PO Box 1028, Sioux Lookout ON P8T 1B3 – 807/737-3660; Fax: 807/737-4046; Email: mwilli@sl.lakeheadu.ca; Symbol: OSI – Chief Librarian, Marianne Williamson

Sioux Narrows Public Library, PO Box 417, Sioux Narrows ON P0X 1N0 – 807/226-5204 – CEO, Allison Motlong

Skead Branch Library, D2-7, Skead ON P0M 2Y0 – 705/969-2416 – Librarian, Rose Rice – Branch of Nickel Centre Public Library (see Garson)

Smiths Falls Public Library, 81 Beckwith St. North, Smiths Falls ON K7A 2B9 – 613/283-2911; Fax: 613/283-9834; Email: sflibrary@falls.igs.net – Librarian, K. Schecter

Smithville: West Lincoln Public Library, PO Box 28, Smithville ON L0R 2A0 – 905/957-3756; Fax: 905/957-3219 – Chief Librarian, Catharine Vaughan – See also following branches: Caistorville Branch Library, Wellandport Branch Library

Smooth Rock Falls Public Library, 120 Ross St., PO Box 670, Smooth Rock Falls ON P0L 2B0 – 705/338-2318; Fax: 705/338-2330 – Librarian, Suzanne Petit

Sombra Library, 3464 St. Clair Parkway, PO Box 39, Sombra ON N0P 2H0 – 519/892-3711 – Librarian, Elizabeth MacDonell – Branch of Lambton County Library (see Wyoming)

South Gillies Community Library, Municipal Bldg., South Gillies ON P0T 2U0 – 807/475-3185; Fax: 807/473-0767 – CEO, Shelbie Brown

South Mountain Branch Library, PO Box 230, South Mountain ON K0E 1W0 – 613/989-2199 – Supervisor/Branch Head, Bonnie Scott – Branch of Stormont, Dundas & Glengarry County Library (see Finch)

South Porcupine: C.M. Shields Centennial Library, 99 Bloor St., PO Box 400, South Porcupine ON P0N 1H0 – 705/235-4974 – Branch Head, Kathi Martin – Branch of Timmins Public Library

South River-Machar Union Public Library, Hwy. 11 North, PO Box 190, South River ON P0A 1X0 – 705/386-0222; Fax: 705/386-0702 – Librarian, Jane Snider; Assistant Librarian, Jeananne Brooks

South Woodslee: Woodslee Library, 118 Malden Rd., PO Box 158, South Woodslee ON N0R 1V0 – 519/975-2433 – Supervisor, Susan Tuck – Branch of Essex County Library

Southampton: Chippewas of Saugeen Library, RR#1, Southampton ON N0H 1H0 – 519/797-2781; Fax: 519/797-2978 – CEO, Chief Richard Kahgee

Southampton Branch Public Library, 215 High St., PO Box 130, Southampton ON N0H 2L0 – 519/797-3586; Fax: 519/797-1221 – Branch Supervisor, Linda Mewhinney – Branch of Bruce County Public Library (see Port Elgin)

Southwold: Onyota'a:ka Language & Cultural Centre, RR#2, Southwold ON N0L 2G0 – 519/652-6227; Fax: 519/652-9287 – Band Librarian, Corey Nicholas; Librarian's Assistant, Judith Cornelius

Spanish Public Library, PO Box 329, Spanish ON P0P 2A0 – 705/844-2555; Fax: 705/844-2550 – Chief/Reference Librarian, Hanne Sauve; Children's Librarian, Christine Grose

Spencerville: Edwardsburg Twp. Public Library, PO Box 130, Spencerville ON K0E 1X0 – 613/658-5575 – Librarian, Marva Sothmann

Springfield Branch Library, 106 Main St., PO Box 9, Springfield ON N0L 2J0 – 519/765-4515 – Supervisor, Maria Smit – Branch of Elgin County Library (see St. Thomas)

Stayner: Clearview Public Library, 201 Huron St., PO Box 160, Stayner ON L0M 1S0 – 705/428-3595; Fax: 705/428-3595; Symbol: OSTA – CEO, Jennifer La Chapelle; Children's Librarian, Amy Bray; Technical Services Librarian, Sandra Squire – See also following branches: Creemore Branch, Sunnidale Branch

Stella Branch Library, Stella ON K0H 2S0 – 613/389-3393 – Supervisor, Karen Fleming – Branch of Lennox & Addington County Library (see Napanee)

Stirling Public Library, 43 Front St., PO Box 730, Stirling ON K0K 3E0 – 613/395-2837; Fax: 613/395-2837 – CEO, Christopher Faiers

Stittsville: Goulbourn Twp. Public Library, 1637 Main St., PO Box 760, Stittsville ON K2S 1A9 – 613/836-4600; Fax: 613/836-7790; Symbol: OSGS – Chief Librarian, Dorothy McGinn – See also following branches: Munster Branch Library, Richmond Branch Library, Stittsville Branch Library

Stittsville Branch Library, 1637 Main St., PO Box 760, Stittsville ON K2S 1A9 – 613/836-3381 – Branch Head, Sharon Ashton – Branch of Goulbourn Twp. Public Library

Stonecliffe: Head, Clara & Maria Twp. Public Library, Stonecliffe ON K0J 2K0 – 613/586-2526; Fax: 613/586-2596 – Sec.-Treas., Diane Beauchamp; Circulation Librarian, Clarence Leach

Stoney Creek: Saltfleet Public Library, 377 Hwy. 8 & Worsley Rd., Stoney Creek ON L8G 1E7 – 905/662-8611; Fax: 905/662-5196 – Branch Head, Nancy Evans – Branch of Wentworth Libraries (see Hamilton)

Stoney Creek Public Library, 10 Second St. North, Stoney Creek ON L8G 1Y6 – 905/662-2211; Fax: 905/662-1340 – Branch Head, Stella Clark – Branch of Wentworth Libraries (see Hamilton)

Stoney Point Library, 6720 Tecumseh Rd., PO Box 14, Stoney Point ON N0R 1N0 – 519/798-3373 – Supervisor, Mary Pardy – Branch of Essex County Library

Stouffville: Whitchurch-Stouffville Public Library, 6240 Main St., Stouffville ON L4A 1E2 – 905/640-2395; Fax: 905/640-1384 – Librarian, M. Ferguson

Straffordville: Bayham Twp. Public Library, PO Box 209, Straffordville ON N0J 1Y0 – 519/866-3584 – Supervisor, Diane Palmer – Branch of Elgin County Library (see St. Thomas)

Stratford Public Library, 19 St. Andrew St., Stratford ON N5A 1A2 – 519/271-0220; Fax: 519/271-3843 – Library Director/CEO, Jane E. Kirkpatrick; Reference Librarian, N. MacPherson; Public Services Librarian, K. Seredynska; Technical Services Librarian, B. Rogers

Strathroy Public Library, 34 Frank St., Strathroy ON N7G 2R4 – 519/245-1290 – Librarian, J. Cummer

Stratton Community Library, PO Box 40, Stratton ON P0W 1N0 – 807/483-5455 – CEO, Anna Boily

Stroud: Innisfil Public Library, PO Box 310, Stroud ON L0L 2M0 – 705/436-1681; Fax: 705/436-7547; Email: sdowns@innisfil.library.on.ca – Chief Librarian/CEO, Susan Downs – See also following branches: Churchill Branch Library, Cookstown Branch Library

Sturgeon Falls: Nipissing First Nation Public Library, 36 Semo Rd., Sturgeon Falls ON P0H 2G0 – 705/753-2050; Fax: 705/753-0207 – CEO, Karen Commanda

Sturgeon Falls Public Library, 225 Holditch St., PO Box 180, Sturgeon Falls ON P0H 2G0 – 705/753-2620; Fax: 705/753-3950 – CEO, Carole Marion

Sudbury Public Library, 74 MacKenzie St., Sudbury ON P3C 4X8 – 705/673-1155; Fax: 705/673-6145 – CEO, Marian F. Ridge; Reference Librarian, Michaele Mueller; Information Services & Systems Librarian, Anne Fabbro; Community Services Librarian, Marg Hardie; Children's Services, Normand Vermette – See also following branches: Copper Cliff Centennial Library, South Branch Library, W. Clarence Sinclair Library

Sudbury: Ontario Library Service North - Sudbury, Administrative Unit, 334 Regent St., Sudbury ON P3C 4E2 – 705/675-6467; Fax: 705/675-6108; Email: OLS.VOYAGEUR – CEO, Alan G. Pepper

Sudbury: South Branch Library, 1991 Regent St. South, Sudbury ON P3E 5V3 – 705/673-1155, ext. 250; Fax: 705/522-7788 – Branch Supervisor, Heini Heinonen-Kari – Branch of Sudbury Public Library

Sudbury: W. Clarence Sinclair Library, New Sudbury Shopping Centre, 1349 LaSalle Blvd., Sudbury ON P3A 1Z2 – 705/673-1155, ext.260; Fax: 705/524-6863 – Branch Supervisor, Connie Lee – Branch of Sudbury Public Library

Sunderland: Brock Twp. Public Library, Church St., PO Box 208, Sunderland ON L0C 1H0 – 705/357-3109 – Librarian, Carole Wetheral – See also following branches: Beaverton Branch, Cannington Branch, Sunderland Branch

Sunderland Branch, Church St., PO Box 208, Sunderland ON L0H 1H0 – 705/357-3109 – Branch Head, Carole Wetheral – Branch of Brock Twp. Public Library

Sundridge-Strong Union Public Library, 110 Main St., PO Box 429, Sundridge ON P0A 1Z0 – 705/384-7311; Fax: 705/384-7311 – CEO, Frances Therrien

Sutton West: Georgina Island First Nation Library, RR#2, Sutton West ON L0E 1R0 – 705/437-4328; Fax: 705/437-4597 – Librarian, Georgina Charles

Sutton Centennial Library, High St., PO Box 338, Sutton West ON L0E 1R0 – 905/722-5702 – Branch Head, Mary Flint – Branch of Georgina Public Libraries (see Keswick)

Sydenham: Loughborough Twp., Sydenham Branch, PO Box 88, Sydenham ON K0H 2T0 – 613/376-3437 – Joan Clark – Branch of Frontenac County Library (see Kingston)

Tamworth Branch Library, PO Box 10, Tamworth ON K0K 3G0 – 613/379-2511 – Supervisor, Joan Larkin – Branch of Lennox & Addington County Library (see Napanee)

Tara Branch Library, Whites Ave., PO Box 59, Tara ON N0H 2N0 – 519/934-2626 – Branch Supervisor, Doreen Hills – Branch of Bruce County Public Library (see Port Elgin)

Tavistock Library, PO Box 190, Tavistock ON N0B 2R0 – 519/655-3013 – Supervisor, Betty Lou Ramseyer – Branch of Oxford County Library (see Woodstock)

Tecumseh Branch Library, 949 Lesperance Rd., Tecumseh ON N8N 1W9 – 519/735-9385 – Supervisor, Kathleen Julien – Branch of Essex County Library

Teeswater Branch Library, Clinton St., PO Box 260, Teeswater ON N0G 2S0 – 519/367-2835 – Branch Supervisor, Lynda Benninger – Branch of Bruce County Public Library (see Port Elgin)

Tehkummah Twp. Public Library, RR#1, Tehkummah ON P0P 2C0 – 705/859-3301; Fax: 705/859-2605 – CEO, Judy McDermid

Temagami First Nations Public Library, Bear Island PO, Temagami ON P0H 1C0 – 705/237-8943; Fax: 705/237-8954 – CEO, Bonnie Turner

Temagami Public Library, PO Box 220, Temagami ON P0H 2H0 – 705/569-2945; Fax: 705/569-2834 – CEO, Paulette Turgeon

Terrace Bay Public Library, PO Box 369, Terrace Bay ON P0T 2W0 – 807/825-3819 – CEO, Jeanne Marcella

Thamesford Library, 165 Dundas St., Thamesford ON N0M 2M0 – 519/285-3219 – Supervisor, Nancy Van Geel – Branch of Oxford County Library (see Woodstock)

Thamesville: Deleware Nation Library, RR#3, Thamesville ON N0P 2K0 – 519/692-3936; Fax: 519/692-5522 – CEO, Darryl Stonefish

Thamesville Branch Library, Town Hall, Thamesville ON N0P 2K0 – 519/692-4251 – Branch Librarian, Debby Kennedy – Branch of Kent County Library (see Chatham)

Thedford Library, #2, 115 Main St., PO Box 204, Thedford ON N0M 2N0 – 519/296-4459 – Librarian, Mary Ellen Anderson – Branch of Lambton County Library (see Wyoming)

Thessalon Union Public Library, PO Box 549, Thessalon ON P0R 1L0 – 705/842-2306; Fax: 705/842-2605 – CEO, Mary Bockman

Thornbury: Leonard E. Shore Memorial Library, 175 Bruce St. South, PO Box 357, Thornbury ON N0H 2P0 – 519/599-3681; Fax: 519/599-7951; Email: leonard@georgian.net – CEO, Ken Haigh

Thorndale: West Nissouri Library, RR#3, PO Box 88, Thorndale ON N0M 2P0 – 519/461-0219; Fax: 519/461-0219 – Supervisor, Reta Young – Branch of Middlesex County Library (see Arva)

Thornhill: Bathurst Clark Library, 900 Clark Ave. West, Thornhill ON L4J 8C1 – 905/709-1103; Fax: 905/709-1099 – Manager, Lilita Stripnieks – Branch of Vaughan Public Libraries (see Maple)

Thornhill: Dufferin Clark Library, 1441 Clark Ave. West, Thornhill ON L4J 7R4 – 905/660-0374; Fax: 905/660-7202 – Manager, Pat Stegenga – Branch of Vaughan Public Libraries (see Maple)

Thornhill: Richvale Library, 40 Pearson Ave., Richmond Hill ON L4C 6T7 – 905/889-2847; Fax: 905/889-2435 – Manager of Branch Services, Mary Deciantis – Branch of Richmond Hill Public Library

Thornhill Community Centre Library, 7755 Bayview Ave., Thornhill ON L3T 4P1 – 905/881-5668; Fax: 905/881-2935 – Branch Manager, Cynthia Teitelman; Children's Librarian, Sharon Philip – Branch of Markham Public Libraries

Thornhill Village Library, 10 Colborne St., Thornhill ON L3T 1Z6 – 905/881-8299; Fax: 905/881-0149 – Branch Manager, Mary Lou Allen – Branch of Markham Public Libraries

Thorold Public Library, 14 Ormond St. North, Thorold ON L2V 1Y8 – 905/227-2581; Fax: 905/227-2311 – Chief Librarian, Patricia Bronson; Reference Librarian, C. Bowman; Children's Services, Lou Anne Wronski – See also following branches: Port Robinson Branch Library

Thunder Bay Public Library, 285 Red River Rd., Thunder Bay ON P7B 1A9 – 807/344-3585; Fax: 807/345-8727; Email: ILL.OTB – CEO, Karen Harrison; Head, Adult Services, Barbara Philp; Head, Children's Services, Angela Meady; Public Services Coordinator, Carole Aitken, 807/623-0925; Head, Automated Services, Larry Joseph – See also following branches: Brodie Resource Library, Mary J.L. Black Branch Library, Victoriaville Branch Library, Waverley Resource Library

Thunder Bay: Brodie Resource Library, 216 South Brodie St., Thunder Bay ON P7E 1C2 – 807/623-0925; Fax: 807/623-0875 – Branch Head, Carole Aitken – Branch of Thunder Bay Public Library

Thunder Bay: Mary J.L. Black Branch Library, 151 West Brock St., Thunder Bay ON P7E 4H9 – 807/475-5906 – Branch Head, Carole Aitken – Branch of Thunder Bay Public Library

Thunder Bay: Ontario Library Service North - Thunder Bay, 910 Victoria Ave. East, Thunder Bay ON P7C 1B4 – 807/623-2794; Fax: 807/623-4623; Email: OLS.NIPIGON – Area Director, Alan G. Pepper

Thunder Bay: Victoriaville Branch Library, 700 Victoria Ave. East, Thunder Bay ON P7C 5P7 – 807/623-4472 – Branch Head, Carole Aitken – Branch of Thunder Bay Public Library

Thunder Bay: Waverley Resource Library, 285 Red River Rd., Thunder Bay ON P7B 1A9 – 807/344-3585; Fax: 807/345-8727 – Branch Head, Carole Aitken – Branch of Thunder Bay Public Library

Tilbury Branch Library, 2 Queen St., PO Box 999, Tilbury ON N0P 2L0 – 519/682-0100 – Branch Librarian, Maxine Gardiner – Branch of Kent County Library (see Chatham)

Tillsonburg Public Library, 2 Library Lane, Tillsonburg ON N4G 4S7 – 519/842-5571; Fax: 519/842-2941 – CEO, Matthew Scholtz; Children's Librarian, Dianne Moore

Timmins Public Library, 236 Algonquin Blvd. East, Timmins ON P4N 1B2 – 705/267-8451; Fax: 705/268-9185 – CEO, Brian Nimeroski; Adult Librarian, Colleen Mares; Children's Librarian, Susan Hoffman; Head, French Services, Colette Proulx; Head, Technical Services, Teresa Woodrow; Systems Administrator, Lucy Gowers – See also following branches: C.M. Shields Centennial Library, Schumacher Memorial Branch Library

Tiverton Branch Library, King St., PO Box 140, Tiverton ON N0G 2T0 – 519/368-5655 – Branch Supervisor, Mary MacKay – Branch of Bruce County Public Library (see Port Elgin)

Tobermory Branch Library, Bay St., PO Box 159, Tobermory ON N0H 2R0 – 519/596-2446 – Branch Supervisor, Kathryn MacLeod – Branch of Bruce County Public Library (see Port Elgin)

Toronto: Metropolitan Toronto Reference Library, 789 Yonge St., Toronto ON M4W 2G8 – 416/393-7000; Fax: 416/393-7229 – CEO, Frances Schwenger; Business & Government Information Centre, Greg Kelner – See also following branches: Metro Urban Affairs Library

Toronto Public Library, 281 Front St. East, Toronto ON M5A 4L2 – 416/393-7500; Fax: 416/393-7782 – CEO, Gabriele Lundeen; Collections Coordinator, Susan Caron; Children's Services Specialist, Katherine Palmer; Public Services, Director, Stephanie Hutcheson; Access & Information Services Coordinator, George Levin; Multicultural Services Specialist, Janice Lavery; Literacy Services Specialist, Brenda Livingston – See also following branches: Annette Library, Beaches Library, Bloor & Gladstone Library, Charles R. Sanderson Library, City Hall Public Library, College/Shaw Library, Danforth/Coxwell Library, Davenport Library, Deer Park Library, Dufferin-St.Clair Library, Forest Hill Library, George H. Locke Branch, Gerrard-Ashdale Library, High Park Library, Jones Ave. Library, Lillian H. Smith Library, Main Street Library, Mount Pleasant Branch, Northern District Library, Palmerston Library, Pape-Danforth Library, Parkdale Library, Parliament Street Library, Perth-Dupont Library, Queen-Saulter Library, Riverdale Library, Runnymede Library, Spadina Rd. Library, St. Clair-Silverthorn Library, St. Lawrence Library/Library on Wheels Branch, Swansea Memorial Branch, Wychwood Library, Yorkville Library

Toronto: Annette Library, 145 Annette St., Toronto ON M6P 1P3 – 416/393-7692 – Branch Head, Marlene Archambeau – Branch of Toronto Public Library

Toronto: Beaches Library, 2161 Queen St. East, Toronto ON M4L 1J1 – 416/393-7703 – Branch Head, Pat Bull – Branch of Toronto Public Library

Toronto: Bloor & Gladstone Library, 1101 Bloor St. West, Toronto ON M6H 1M7 – 416/393-7674; Fax: 416/393-7502 – Branch Head, Brigitte Richter – Branch of Toronto Public Library

Toronto: Charles R. Sanderson Library, 327 Bathurst St., Toronto ON M5T 1J1 – 416/393-7653 – Branch Head, Jim Montgomery – Branch of Toronto Public Library

Toronto: City Hall Public Library, Nathan Phillips Sq., Toronto ON M5H 2N3 – 416/393-7650; Fax: 416/393-7665 – Branch Supervisor, Nancy Jessop – Branch of Toronto Public Library

Toronto: College/Shaw Library, 766 College St. West, Toronto ON M6G 1C4 – 416/393-7668 – Branch Head, Pat O'Sullivan – Branch of Toronto Public Library

Toronto: Danforth/Coxwell Library, 1675 Danforth Ave., Toronto ON M4C 5P2 – 416/393-7783; Symbol: DA – Branch Head, Maggie Gosselin – Branch of Toronto Public Library

Toronto: Davenport Library, 1246 Shaw St., Toronto ON M6G 3P1 – 416/393-7732 – Branch Supervisor, Jean Lee – Branch of Toronto Public Library

Toronto: Deer Park Library, 40 St. Clair Ave. East, Toronto ON M4T 1M9 – 416/393-7657; Fax: 416/393-7696; Symbol: DP – Branch Head, Linda Steinberg – Branch of Toronto Public Library

Toronto: Dufferin-St.Clair Library, 1625 Dufferin St., Toronto ON M6H 3L9 – 416/393-7712 – Branch Head, Ewa Piatkowski – Branch of Toronto Public Library

Toronto: Evelyn Gregory Branch Library, 120 Trowell Ave., Toronto ON M6M 1L7 – 416/394-1006 – Branch Head, B. Warzocha – Branch of City of York Public Library

Toronto: Forest Hill Library, 700 Eglinton Ave. West, Toronto ON M5N 1B9 – 416/393-7706 – Branch Head, Phyllis Malette – Branch of Toronto Public Library

Toronto: George H. Locke Branch, 3083 Yonge St., Toronto ON M4N 2K7 – 416/393-7730; Symbol: LO – Branch Head, Tiiu Kubjas – Branch of Toronto Public Library

Toronto: Gerrard-Ashdale Library, 1432 Gerrard St. East, Toronto ON M4L 1Z6 – 416/393-7717 – Branch Head, Pam Hancock – Branch of Toronto Public Library

Toronto: High Park Library, 228 Roncesvalles Ave., Toronto ON M6R 2L7 – 416/393-7671 – Branch Head, Barrie Gray – Branch of Toronto Public Library

Toronto: Jane-Dundas Branch Library, 620 Jane St., Toronto ON M6S 4A6 – 416/394-1014 – Branch Head, George N. Shirinian – Branch of City of York Public Library

Toronto: Jones Ave. Library, 118 Jones Ave., Toronto ON M4M 2Z9 – 416/393-7715; Symbol: JO – Branch Head, Beverley Howatson – Branch of Toronto Public Library

Toronto: Lillian H. Smith Library, 239 College St., Toronto ON M5T 1R5 – 416/393-7746 – Branch Head, Mary Anne Cree – Branch of Toronto Public Library

Toronto: Main Street Library, 137 Main St., Toronto ON M4E 2V9 – 416/393-7700 – Branch Head, Nancy Harbour – Branch of Toronto Public Library

Toronto: Metro Urban Affairs Library, 55 John St., Toronto ON M5V 3C6 – 416/397-7240; Fax: 416/397-7245; Email: ENVOY: OTMSM – Manager, Berenice Campagne, 416/392-7230 – Branch of Metropolitan Toronto Reference Library

Toronto: Mount Dennis Branch Library, 1123 Weston Rd., Toronto ON M6N 3S3 – 416/394-1008 – Branch Head, B. Warzocha – Branch of City of York Public Library

Toronto: Mount Pleasant Branch, 599 Mount Pleasant Rd., Toronto ON M4S 2M5 – 416/393-7737 – Branch Supervisor, Barbara Forsythe – Branch of Toronto Public Library

Toronto: Northern District Library, 40 Orchard View Blvd., Toronto ON M4R 1B9 – 416/393-7610; Fax: 416/393-7740 – Branch Head, Cheryl Skovronek – Branch of Toronto Public Library

Toronto: Palmerston Library, 560 Palmerston Ave., Toronto ON M6G 2P7 – 416/393-7680; Fax: 416/393-7740 – Branch Head, Rose Marie Spearpoint – Branch of Toronto Public Library

Toronto: Pape-Danforth Library, 701 Pape Ave., Toronto ON M4K 3S6 – 416/393-7727; Fax: 416/393-

7503 – Branch Head, Ann Thoburn – Branch of Toronto Public Library

Toronto: Parkdale Library, 1303 Queen St. West, Toronto ON M6K 1L6 – 416/393-7686 – Branch Head, Linda Karlinsky – Branch of Toronto Public Library

Toronto: Parliament Street Library, 269 Gerrard St. East, Toronto ON M5A 2G3 – 416/393-7663 – Branch Head, Nancy Wade-Stadler – Branch of Toronto Public Library

Toronto: Perth-Dupont Library, 1589 Dupont St., Toronto ON M6P 3S3 – 416/393-7677 – Branch Supervisor, Carmen Martino – Branch of Toronto Public Library

Toronto: Queen-Saulter Library, 765 Queen St. East, Toronto ON M4M 1H3 – 416/393-7723 – Branch Supervisor, Miguelita Costes – Branch of Toronto Public Library

Toronto: Riverdale Library, 370 Broadview Ave., Toronto ON M4P 1X4 – 416/393-7720 – Branch Head, Fidelia Lau – Branch of Toronto Public Library

Toronto: Runnymede Library, 2178 Bloor St. West, Toronto ON M6S 1M8 – 416/393-7697 – Branch Head, Holly Benson – Branch of Toronto Public Library

Toronto: St. Clair-Silverthorn Library, 1748 St. Clair Ave. West, Toronto ON M6N 1J4 – 416/393-7709 – Branch Supervisor, Pat Coulter – Branch of Toronto Public Library

Toronto: St. Lawrence Library/Library on Wheels Branch, 171 Front St. East, Toronto ON M4M 1H3 – 416/393-7655 – Branch Supervisor, Linda Goldman – Branch of Toronto Public Library

Toronto: Spadina Rd. Library, 10 Spadina Rd., Toronto ON M5R 2S7 – 416/393-7666 – Branch Head, Vivienne James – Branch of Toronto Public Library

Toronto: Swansea Memorial Branch, 95 Lavinia Ave., Toronto ON M6S 3H9 – 416/393-7695 – Branch Head, Holly Benson – Branch of Toronto Public Library

Toronto: Weston Branch Library, 2 King St., Toronto ON M9N 1K9 – 416/394-1016; Fax: 416/394-2781 – Branch Head, Linda Davis – Branch of City of York Public Library

Toronto: Wychwood Library, 1431 Bathurst St., Toronto ON M5R 3J2 – 416/393-7683 – Branch Head, Diana Arris – Branch of Toronto Public Library

Toronto: Yorkville Library, 22 Yorkville Ave., Toronto ON M4W 1J4 – 416/393-7660 – Branch Head, Janice Long – Branch of Toronto Public Library

Tottenham Branch Library, 18 Queen St. North, PO Box 339, Tottenham ON L0G 1W0 – 905/936-2291 – Branch of New Tecumseth Public Library (see Alliston)

Trenton: Murray Twp. (Wooler) Branch Library, RR#1, Trenton ON K8V 5P4 – 613/392-4435 – Branch Head, Esther Maples – Branch of Northumberland County Public Library (see Hastings)

Trenton Memorial Public Library, 18 Albert St., Trenton ON K8V 4S3 – 613/394-3381; Symbol: OTRE – Acting CEO, Rosemary Kirby

Trout Creek Public Library, McCarthy St., PO Box 310, Trout Creek ON P0H 2L0 – 705/723-5351 – CEO, Jeannette Schmelefske

Tweed Public Library, 320 Colborne St., PO Box 628, Tweed ON K0K 3J0 – 613/478-1066 – CEO/Librarian, Jane Ferguson

Unionville: Milliken Mills Community Library, 7600 Kennedy Rd., Unit 1, Unionville ON L3R 9S5 – 905/940-8323; Fax: 905/940-8326 – Branch Manager, Larry Pogue – Branch of Markham Public Libraries

Utterson: Ullswater Public Library, Ullswater Community Hall, RR#1, Utterson ON P0B 1M0 – 705/769-3792 – Librarian, Phyllis Olsen – Branch of Port Carling Public Library

Uxbridge Twp. Public Library, 9 Toronto St. South, PO Box 279, Uxbridge ON L9P 1P7 – 905/852-9747; Fax: 905/852-9748 – Chief Librarian, Cathy Thomson; Children's Librarian, Pam Noble – See also following branches: Scott Branch Library

Val Rita-Harty Public Library, Government St., PO Box 69, Val Rita ON P0L 2G0 – 705/335-8700 – CEO, Cecile Lamontagne

Vanier Public Library, 310 Pères Blancs Ave., Vanier ON K1L 7L5 – 613/745-0861; Téléc: 613/747-8795 – Directrice générale, Liliane Pinard

Vankleek Hill Public Library, PO Box 520, Vankleek Hill ON K0B 1R0 – 613/678-2216 – Head Librarian, Margaret Higginson

Verner: Caldwell Twp. Public Library, PO Box 59, Verner ON P0H 2M0 – 705/594-2800; Fax: 705/594-9153 – Librarian, Diane Tellier

Vernon Branch Library, 4082 Dominion St., PO Box 59, Vernon ON K0A 3J0 – 613/821-3389 – Librarian, Kay Porteous – Branch of Osgoode Twp. Public Library Board

Victoria Harbour Public Library, Albert St., Victoria Harbour ON L0K 2A0 – 705/534-3581; Fax: 705/534-3581 – Branch Librarian, Carol Vanderhart – Branch of Tay Twp. Public Library (see Waubaushene)

Vienna Branch Library, PO Box 5, Vienna ON N0J 1Z0 – 519/874-4118 – Librarian, Doris Van Den Eeckhout – Branch of Elgin County Library (see St. Thomas)

Vineland: Moses F. Rittenhouse Branch Library, 4080 John Charles Blvd., Vineland ON L0R 2C0 – 905/562-5711 – Technical Services, Mona McMaster – Branch of Lincoln Public Library (see Beamsville)

Virginiatown: McGarry Public Library, PO Box 250, Virginiatown ON P0K 1X0 – 705/634-2312; Fax: 705/634-2700 – Librarian/CEO, Annie Mino

Wainfleet Twp. Public Library, 19M9 Park St., Wainfleet ON L0S 1V0 – 905/899-1277; Fax: 905/899-2495; Email: mpodolya@freenet.npiec.on.ca; Symbol: WA – CEO/Head Librarian, Mary Podolyak; Reference Librarian/Circulation Librarian, Lorrie Atkinson; Children's Librarian/Public Services Librarian/Acquisitions Librarian, Mary Podolyak; Technical Services Librarian, Lorrie Atkinson

Walkerton Branch Library, 253 Durham St., PO Box 250, Walkerton ON N0G 2V0 – 519/881-3240; Fax: 519/881-3240 – Branch Supervisor, Tracey Knapp – Branch of Bruce County Public Library (see Port Elgin)

Wallaceburg: Bkejwanong First Nations Community Library, RR#3, Wallaceburg ON N8A 4R9 – 519/627-7034; Fax: 519/627-7035 – CEO, Jean Wrightman

Wallaceburg Branch Library, 209 James St., Wallaceburg ON N8A 2N4 – 519/627-5292 – Branch Librarian, Alla Steen – Branch of Kent County Library (see Chatham)

Wardsville Library, Main St., Wardsville ON N0L 2N0 – 519/693-4208 – Supervisor, Janice Moniz – Branch of Middlesex County Library (see Arva)

Warkworth (Percy Twp.) Branch Library, Main & Church Sts., Warkworth ON K0K 3K0 – 705/924-3116 – Branch Head, Claire Jenney – Branch of Northumberland County Public Library (see Hastings)

Warren: Ratter & Dunnet Twp. Public Library, 8 Dyke St., PO Box 250, Warren ON P0H 2N0 – 705/967-2702 – Librarian, Janis Lamothe

Wasaga Beach Public Library, 120 Glenwood Dr., PO Box 530, Wasaga Beach ON L0L 2P0 – 705/429-5481; Fax: 705/429-5481 – CEO/Librarian, Jackie Marshall-Beaudin

Waterdown Public Library, 25 Mill St. North, Waterdown ON L0R 2H0 – 905/689-6269; Fax: 905/689-4684 – Branch Head, Elizabeth Wright – Branch of Wentworth Libraries (see Hamilton)

Waterford Branch Library, 15 Main St., Waterford ON N0E 1Y0 – 519/443-7682 – Branch Librarian, Heidi E. Goodale – Branch of Nanticoke Public Library Board (see Jarvis)

Waterloo Public Library, 35 Albert St., Waterloo ON N2L 5E2 – 519/886-1310; Fax: 519/886-7936; Email: wpl@hookup.net – Chief Librarian, Joanne Tate – See also following branches: McCormick Branch Library

Waterloo: McCormick Branch Library, 500 Parkside Dr., Waterloo ON N2L 5J4 – 519/885-1920 – Branch Supervisor, Doreen Disney – Branch of Waterloo Public Library

Watford: Warwick Library, 6199 First School Rd., RR#5, Watford ON N0M 2S0 – 519/849-5533 – Librarian, Jean O'Neil – Branch of Lambton County Library (see Wyoming)

Watford Library, 5317 Nauvoo Rd., PO Box 9, Watford ON N0M 2S0 – 519/876-2204 – Librarian, Sheryl Mendritzki – Branch of Lambton County Library (see Wyoming)

Waubaushene: Tay Twp. Public Library, Waubaushene Public Library, 9 Maple St., PO Box 280, Waubaushene ON L0K 2C0 – 705/538-1122; Fax: 705/538-1122 – Chief Librarian/CEO, Sheila Hamilton – See also following branches: Port McNicoll Public Library, Victoria Harbour Public Library

Wawa: Michipicoten Twp. Public Library, PO Box 1730, Wawa ON P0S 1K0 – 705/856-2062; Fax: 705/856-2120 – CEO, Sandra Weitzel

Webbwood Public Library, Webbwood ON P0P 2G0 – 705/869-4147; Fax: 705/869-1394 – CEO, Benva Lea Bentley, 705/869-2806

Welland Public Library, 140 King St., Welland ON L3B 3J3 – 905/734-6210; Fax: 905/734-8955; Symbol: WPL – CEO/Chief Librarian, Janet C. Booth; Reference Librarian, Douglas Abbott; Children's Librarian, Janet Hodgkins; Public Services Librarian, Stephen Hanns; Support Services Librarian, Laura Kmety; Audio-Visual Librarian, William Wallis – See also following branches: Northwest Branch Library

Wellandport Branch Library, Wellandport ON L0R 2J0 – 905/386-6792 – Branch Head, Colleen Keizer – Branch of West Lincoln Public Library (see Smithville)

Welland: Northwest Branch Library, 650 South Pelham Rd., Welland ON L3C 3C8 – 905/735-4231 – Branch Head, Shelley Beckett – Branch of Welland Public Library

Wellesley Branch Library, PO Box 190, Wellesley ON N0B 2T0 – 519/656-2001 – Asst. Branch Supervisor, Elizabeth Earle – Branch of Waterloo Regional Library (see Kitchener)

Wellington Public Library, 261 Main St., PO Box 370, Wellington ON K0K 3L0 – 613/399-2023 – Chief Librarian, Dianne Cranshaw

Wendover: Bibliothèque publique du Canton de Plantagenet-Nord, Wendover ON K0A 3K0 – Directrice générale, Denise Bertrand – See also following branches: Succursale Curran, Succursale Wendover

Wendover: Succursale Wendover, Wendover ON K0A 3K0 – Branch of Bibliothèque publique du Canton de Plantagenet-Nord

West Bay First Nations Public Library, Excelsior PO, West Bay ON P0P 1G0 – 705/377-5540 – Librarian, Sandra Bayer

West Lorne Library, 160 Main St., PO Box 10, West Lorne ON N0L 2P0 – 519/768-1150 – Supervisor, Shelley Fleming – Branch of Elgin County Library (see St. Thomas)

Westport-North Crosby Union Public Library, 3 Spring St., PO Box 28, Westport ON K0G 1X0 – 613/273-3223 – Librarian, P. Stuffles

Westwood: Asphodel Public Library, General Delivery, Westwood ON K0L 3B0 – 705/696-2744 – CEO, Nelda Beavis

Wheatley Branch Library, 38 Talbot St. East, Wheatley ON N0P 2P0 – 519/825-7131 – Branch Librarian,

Merle Richmond – Branch of Kent County Library (*see* Chatham)

Whitby Public Library, 405 Dundas St. West, Whitby ON L1N 6A1 – 905/668-6531; Fax: 905/668-7445 – Chief Librarian, Nancy Harsanyi; Reference Librarian, L. Evans; Circulation Supervisor, Pauline Baxter; Children's Librarian, R. Jessup; Public Services Librarian, T. Driesschen; Technical Services Supervisor, Elaine Yatulis – See also following branches: Brooklin Branch Library, Rossland Branch Library

Whitby: Rossland Branch Library, 701 Rossland Rd. East, Whitby ON L1N 8Y9 – 905/668-1886 – Branch Head, Judy McIntosh – Branch of Whitby Public Library

White River Public Library, PO Box 458, White River ON P0M 3G0 – 807/822-2406 – CEO, Mary Lue Constantineau

Whitedog: Islington First Nation Public Library, General Delivery, Whitedog PO, Whitedog ON P0X 1P0 – 807/927-2286 – CEO, Darlene Bunting

Whitefish: Beaver Lake Branch Library, RR#1, Whitefish ON P0M 3E0 – 705/866-2958 – Branch Head, Sharon Krats – Branch of Walden Public Library (*see* Lively)

Whitefish Branch Library, c/o R.H. Murray Public School, 3 Henry St., Whitefish ON P0M 3E0 – 705/866-2651 – Branch Head, Gabrielle Makela – Branch of Walden Public Library (*see* Lively)

Whitney: Airy Twp. Public Library, PO Box 208, Whitney ON K0J 2M0 – 613/637-5471 – CEO, Carol A. Watson

Wiarton: Chippewas of Nawash Public Library, RR#5, Wiarton ON N0H 2T0 – 519/534-1508; Fax: 519/534-2130 – Librarian, Mary Lynne Pedoniquotte

Wiarton Branch Library, 542 Bedford St., PO Box 250, Wiarton ON N0H 2T0 – 519/534-2602; Fax: 519/534-2602 – Branch Supervisor, Clare Drury – Branch of Bruce County Public Library (*see* Port Elgin)

Wilberforce: Monmouth Branch Library, Wilberforce ON K0L 3C0 – 705/448-2510 – Branch Head, Bessie Croft – Branch of Haliburton County Public Library

Wilkesport Library, 1349 Main St., General Delivery, Wilkesport ON N0P 2R0 – 519/846-4000 – Librarian, Shelley Lucier – Branch of Lambton County Library (*see* Wyoming)

Williamsburg Branch Library, PO Box 69, Williamsburg ON K0C 2H0 – 613/535-2185 – Supervisor/Branch Head, Beverly Richmire – Branch of Stormont, Dundas & Glengarry County Library (*see* Finch)

Williamstown Branch Library, PO Box 68, Williamstown ON K0C 2J0 – 613/347-3397 – Supervisor/Branch Head, Sue Harrington – Branch of Stormont, Dundas & Glengarry County Library (*see* Finch)

Wilno: Sherwood Jones & Burns Branch, Wilno ON K0J 2N0 – Branch Head, Angela E. Lorbetskie – Branch of Barry's Bay Public Library

Winchester Branch Library, PO Box 444, Winchester ON K0C 2K0 – 613/774-2612 – Supervisor/Branch Head, Gail Storring – Branch of Stormont, Dundas & Glengarry County Library (*see* Finch)

Windsor Public Library, 850 Ouellette Ave., Windsor ON N9A 4M9 – 519/255-6770; Fax: 519/255-7207 – CEO, Jean Dirksen, 519/255-6750; Deputy CEO, Gail Juris; Technical Services Coordinator, Aziz Chowdhury – See also following branches: Ambassador Library, Forest Glade-Optimist Library, Main Library, Nikola Budimir Library, Remington Park Library, Riverside Library, Seminole Library, South Walkerville Library

Windsor: Ambassador Library, 1564 Huron Church Rd., Windsor ON N9C 2L1 – 519/253-7340; Fax: 519/253-7340 – Librarian, Caroline Taylor – Branch of Windsor Public Library

Windsor: Forest Glade-Optimist Library, 3211 Forest Glade Dr., Windsor ON N8R 1W7 – 519/735-6803; Fax: 519/735-6803 – Librarian, David Eady – Branch of Windsor Public Library

Windsor: Main Library, 850 Ouellette Ave., Windsor ON N9A 4M9 – 519/255-6770; Fax: 519/973-1213 – Manager, Marilyn Scase – Branch of Windsor Public Library

Windsor: Malden Road Library, 5860 Malden Rd., Windsor ON N9H 1S4 – 519/969-0771 – Supervisor, Annette Isaac – Branch of Essex County Library

Windsor: Nikola Budimir Library, 1310 Grand Marais Rd. West, Windsor ON N9E 1E4 – 519/969-5880; Fax: 519/969-5880 – Manager, Shun Shun Soong – Branch of Windsor Public Library

Windsor: Remington Park Library, 2710 Lillian St., Windsor ON N8X 4B5 – 519/966-3441; Fax: 519/966-3441 – Manager, Shun Shun Soong – Branch of Windsor Public Library

Windsor: Riverside Library, 6275 Wyandotte St. East, Windsor ON N8S 1N5 – 519/945-7568; Fax: 519/945-7568 – Manager, David Eady – Branch of Windsor Public Library

Windsor: Seminole Library, 4285 Seminole St., Windsor ON N8Y 1Z5 – 519/945-6467; Fax: 519/945-6467 – Manager, Blodwen Reitz – Branch of Windsor Public Library

Windsor: South Walkerville Library, 1425 Tecumseh Rd. East, Windsor ON N8W 1C2 – 519/253-3600; Fax: 519/253-3600 – Manager, Elizabeth Watson – Branch of Windsor Public Library

Wingham Branch Library, 281 Edward St., PO Box 208, Wingham ON N0G 2W0 – 519/357-3312 – Branch Supervisor, Paula Mackie – Branch of Huron County Library (*see* Goderich)

Winona Public Library, 1304 Hwy. 8, Winona ON L8E 5R1 – 905/643-2912 – Branch Head, Marg Lee – Branch of Wentworth Libraries (*see* Hamilton)

Wolfe Island Twp. - Library, Wolfe Island ON K0H 2Y0 – 613/385-2112 – Brenda MacDonald – Branch of Frontenac County Library (*see* Kingston)

Woodbridge: Ansley Grove Library, 350 Ansley Grove Rd., Woodbridge ON L4L 5C9 – 905/856-6551; Fax: 905/856-6151 – Manager, Jane Salmon – Branch of Vaughan Public Libraries (*see* Maple)

Woodbridge Library, 150 Woodbridge Ave., Woodbridge ON L4L 2S7 – 905/851-1296; Fax: 905/851-2322 – Branch Manager, Beryl Hall – Branch of Vaughan Public Libraries (*see* Maple)

Woodstock: Oxford County Library, 93 Graham St., Woodstock ON N4S 6J8 – 519/421-1700; Fax: 519/537-3024; Symbol: OWOO – Chief Librarian, Sam Coghlan; Reference/Children's/Technical Services Librarian, Gail Jeffrey; Acquisitions Librarian, Judy Johnson – See also following branches: Beachville Library, Brownsville Library, Burgessville Library, Drumbo Library, East Oxford Branch Library, Embro Library, Hickson Library, Ingersoll Library, Innerkip Library, Kintore Library, Mount Elgin Library, Norwich Library, Otterville Library, Plattsville Library, Princeton Library, Tavistock Library, Thamesford Library

Woodstock: East Oxford Branch Library, RR#8, Woodstock ON N4S 7W3 – 519/424-9378 – Supervisor, Heather Taylor – Branch of Oxford County Library

Woodstock Public Library, 445 Hunter St., Woodstock ON N4S 4G7 – 519/539-4801; Fax: 519/539-5246; Symbol: OWO – Chief Librarian, Stephen Nelson; Reference Librarian, Penny Quinn; Children's Librarian, Ursula Benoit; Head of Information Services, Susan Start

Woodville Branch Library, General Delivery, Woodville ON K0M 2T0 – 705/439-2160 – Branch Head, Edith Cameron – Branch of Victoria County Public Library (*see* Lindsay)

Wroxeter: Belmore Community Library, RR#1, Wroxeter ON N0G 2X0 – 519/392-6634 – Supervisor, Jane McQuarrie

Wyoming: Lambton County Library, 787 Broadway St., PO Box 3100, Wyoming ON N0N 1T0 – 519/845-3324; Fax: 519/845-0700; Symbol: LA – Director of Libraries, Museums & Cultural Services, Robert Krieg; Reference Librarian, Darlene LaBelle; Adult Services Librarian, Carol Leckie; Children's Librarian, Paulette Thompson; Public Services Manager, Maureen McKay; Technical Services Manager, Krystyna Stalmach; Manager, Branch Services, Carol Gardiner – See also following branches: Alvinston Library, Arkona Library, Brigden Library, Brights Grove Library, Camlachie Library, Chippewas of Sarnia Library, Corunna Library, Courtright Library, Florence Library, Forest Library, Grand Bend Library, Inwood Library, Mallroad Library, Mandaumin Library, Mooretown Library, Oil Springs Library, Petrolia Library, Point Edward Library, Port Franks Library, Port Lambton Library, Sarnia Library, Shetland Library, Sombra Library, Thedford Library, Warwick Library, Watford Library, Wilkesport Library, Wyoming Library

Wyoming: Mandaumin Library, 3019 Confederation Line, RR#1, Wyoming ON N0N 1T0 – 519/383-8085 – Librarian, Shirley Deelstra – Branch of Lambton County Library

Wyoming Library, 617 Broadway St., Wyoming ON N0N 1T0 – 519/845-0181 – Librarian, Phyllis Brooks – Branch of Lambton County Library

Yarker Branch Library, PO Box 160, Yarker ON K0K 3N0 – 613/377-6698 – Supervisor, Rika Blakslee – Branch of Lennox & Addington County Library (*see* Napanee)

York: City of York Public Library, 1745 Eglinton Ave. West, Toronto ON M6E 2H4 – 416/394-1000; Fax: 416/394-2781 – CEO, Bohus Derer; Branch Head, Maria Shchuka – See also following branches: Evelyn Gregory Branch Library, Jane-Dundas Branch Library, Mount Dennis Branch Library, Weston Branch Library

Zephyr: Scott Branch Library, Zephyr ON L0E 1T0 – 905/473-2375 – Branch Head, Judy Harrison – Branch of Uxbridge Twp. Public Library

Zurich Branch Library, PO Box 201, Zurich ON N0M 2T0 – 519/236-4965 – Branch Supervisor, Helene Ducharme – Branch of Huron County Library (*see* Goderich)

Curran: Succursale Curran, Curran ON K0B 1C0 – Branch of Bibliothèque publique du Canton de Plantagenet-Nord (*see* Wendover)

Special & College Libraries & Resource Centres in Ontario

ALFRED

Alfred College of Agriculture & Food Technology - Library, PO Box 580, Alfred ON K0B 1A0 – 613/679-2443; Fax: 613/679-2430
Chief Librarian, Robert St-Amant
Library Technician, Lyne Gagné-Lalonde

AMHERSTBURG

Fort Malden National Historic Site - Resource Centre, 100 Laird Ave., PO Box 38, Amherstburg ON N9V 2Z2 – 519/736-5416; Fax: 519/736-6603; Symbol: OAMF – Resource Centre Specialist, Bob Garcia, Email: bob_garcia@pch.gc.ca

ANCASTER

Redeemer College - Library, 777 Hwy. 53 East, Ancaster ON L9K 1J4 – 905/648-2131; Fax: 905/648-2134; Email: ENVOY: ILL.OHRC; Symbol: OHRC
Acquisitions, Mavis Hamilton
Cataloguing, Freda Smouter
Circulation, Christina Amis
Reference, Marlene Power

Interlibrary, LoansDiane Proper
Periodicals, Jane Lise

ARKELL
Canadian Tire Coupon Collectors Club – Library, PO Box 1000, Arkell ON N0B 1C0 – 519/822-2910, 823-2646

ARNPRIOR
Canadian Emergency Preparedness College - Library, PO Box 40, Arnprior ON K7S 3H2 – 613/623-7931; Fax: 613/563-9095 – Register, B.F. Robinson

ATIKOKAN
Atikokan Native Friendship Centre – Library, #307, 309 Main St., PO Box 1510, Atikokan ON P0T 1C0 – 807/597-1213

AYLMER
Ontario Police College - Library, PO Box 1190, Aylmer ON N5H 2T2 – 519/773-4266; Fax: 519/773-5762; Symbol: OAWOP – Librarian, Y.P. Chao, 519/773-4264

BARRIE
Barrie & District Rape Crisis Line – Library, 8 Essa Rd., Barrie ON L4N 3K3 – 705/737-0464; Toll Free: 1-800-561-9255
Brereton Field Naturalists' Club Inc. – BFN Library, PO Box 1084, Barrie ON L4N 3S6 – 705/726-8969
Canadian Numismatic Association – Library, PO Box 226, Barrie ON L4M 4T2 – 506/857-9403 – Librarian, Geoffrey G. Bell
County of Simcoe Law Association – Library, Court House, 30 Poyntz St., Barrie ON L4M 1M1 – 705/739-6569 – Patricia L. Henry
Georgian College - Learning Resource Centre, 1 Georgian Dr., Barrie ON L4M 3X9 – 705/722-5139; Fax: 705/722-1584; Email: lrcba@gci.georcoll.on.ca
   Manager, Learning Resource Centre, Michele Beaudoin
   Collection Development, Librarian, Philip Hull
   Film/Video Booking, Head, Marg Ball
   Media Services, Supervisor, Patricia Whyte
   Reference Services, Librarian, Jennifer Varcoe
   Technical Services & Circulation, Head, Carol McNabb
Kenneth P. Kinnear - Law Library, 23 Owen St., PO Box 646, Barrie ON L4M 4V1 – 705/726-6497; Fax: 705/722-4749
Ontario Ministry of the Solicitor General & Correctional Services - Barrie Jail Library, 87 Mulcaster St., PO Box 224, Barrie ON L4M 4T2 – 705/739-6613; Fax: 705/739-6617 – Volunteer Coordinator, Luana Wood
Smith, McLean Law Office - Library, 118 Collier St., PO Box 515, Barrie ON L4M 4T7 – 705/728-5907; Fax: 705/728-1897

BATH
Solicitor General Canada - Millhaven Institution - Library, PO Box 280, Bath ON K0H 1G0 – 613/352-3371; Fax: 613/352-5539; Symbol: OBMI – Librarian, Pat Little

BEAMSVILLE
Literacy Council of Lincoln – Lincoln Public Library, c/o Lincoln Public Library, Flemming Branch, 4996 Beam St., Beamsville ON L0R 1B0 – 905/563-7014 – CEO, Lori Sims

BELLEVILLE
Eastern Ontario Concert Orchestra – Library, PO Box 23087, Belleville ON K8P 5J3 – 613/968-9382 – Music Librarian, Elizabeth Ewashkiw
Hastings County Law Association – Courthouse Library, 235 Pinnacle St., Belleville ON K8N 3A9 – 613/962-2280

Loyalist College - Resource Centre, PO Box 4200, Belleville ON K8N 5B9 – 613/969-1913; Fax: 613/962-1376; Email: LO@LoyalistC.on.ca – Educational Resources, Director, Beatrice Lo
O'Brien & Wright Law Office - Library, 280 Pinnacle St., PO Box 1057, Belleville ON K8N 5E8 – 613/962-5337; Fax: 613/962-6833

BRACEBRIDGE
Muskoka District Law Association – Library, PO Box 1718, Bracebridge ON P1L 1R6 – 705/645-6661 – Mary Anne Kelly

BRAMPTON
Against Drunk Driving – Library, PO Box 397, Brampton ON L6V 2L3 – 905/793-4233 – Office Manager, Kathleen Close
Canadian Air Line Pilots Association (Ind.) – Library, 1300 Steeles Ave. East, Brampton ON L6T 1A2 – 905/453-8210 – Manager, Information Services, Roger Burgess Webb
Ontario Ministry of the Solicitor General & Correctional Services - Ontario Correctional Institute Library, 109 McLaughlin Rd. South, PO Box 1888, Brampton ON L6V 2P1 – 905/457-7050; Fax: 905/452-8606 – Library Technician, Jeanette Fletcher
Vanier Centre for Women Library, 205 McLaughlin Rd. South, PO Box 1150, Brampton ON L6V 2M5 – 905/459-9100, ext.158; Fax: 905/459-5735 – Library Technician, Angie Zanotti
Ontario Provincial Police Academy - Library, PO Box 266, Brampton ON L6V 2L1 – 905/874-3154; Fax: 905/874-4032 – Librarian, Catherine Dowd
Ontario Provinical Police Academy - Library, PO Box 266, Brampton ON L6V 2L1 – 905/459-4193; Fax: 905/324-3688
Peel Law Association – Library, 7755 Hurontario St., Brampton ON L6V 2M7 – 905/451-2924 – Librarian, Marilyn Elkin
Peel Memorial Hospital – Health Sciences Library, 20 Lynch St., Brampton ON L6W 2Z8 – 905/796-4015 – Coordinator, Clare Pirie
Sheridan College - Brampton Campus Library, McLaughlin Rd., PO Box 7500, Brampton ON L6V 1G6 – 905/459-7533; Fax: 905/459-7054; Symbol: OBRASC – Peggy Bram
Spar Aerospace Limited - Spar Space Systems Library/Information Resource Centre, 9445 Airport Rd., Brampton ON L6S 4J3 – 905/790-2800, ext.4108; Fax: 905/790-4423; Email: ENVOY: RMSD.LIB; ttrip@spar.ca; Symbol: OWSA – Library Supervisor, Tim Tripp
Tannahill, Lockhart, Clark & Langlois Law Office - Library, #200, 2 County Court Blvd., Brampton ON L6W 3W8 – 905/453-5770; Fax: 905/453-1313 – Office Manager, Margaret Jamieson
Wanda L. Warren Law Office - Library, 400 Queen St. West, Brampton ON L6X 1B3 – 905/457-3747; Fax: 905/451-9427 – Legal Secretary, Georgia Blancher

BRANTFORD
Brant Historical Society – Library, 57 Charlotte St., Brantford ON N3T 2W6 – 519/752-2483
Canadian Foresters Life Insurance Society – Library, PO Box 850, Brantford ON N3T 5S3 – 905/525-9559 – Personnel Administrator, Gail Newman
Community Information Centre Brantford – Library, 99 Chatham St., Brantford ON N3T 2P3 – 519/753-3171 – Senior Information Consultant, Randa Yacoub
Insulating Glass Manufacturers Association of Canada – Library, PO Box 25013, Brantford ON N3T 6K5 – 519/449-2487
Mohawk College - Brantford Campus Library, 411 Elgin St., Brantford ON N3T 5V2 – 519/758-6019; Fax: 519/758-6043 – Supervisor, Gail Sekine

Brantford General (Nursing) Campus Library, 235 St. Paul Ave., Brantford ON N3R 5Z3 – 519/758-6031 – Library Supervisor, Sandra Arklie
Ontario Ministry of the Solicitor General & Correctional Services - Burtch Correctional Centre Library, PO Box 940, Brantford ON N3T 5S6 – 519/484-2461; Fax: 519/484-2587 – Library Technician, Laurie D'Eon
Woodland Cultural Centre – Library, 184 Mohawk St., PO Box 1506, Brantford ON N3T 5V6 – 519/759-2650 ext.223 – Library Technician, Winnie Jacobs

BROCKVILLE
Leeds & Grenville Law Association - County Courthouse Library, 10 Wall St., Brockville ON K6V 7A8 – 613/342-1832; Fax: 613/342-2462 – Librarian, Florence Atkinson
Ontario Genealogical Society - Leeds & Grenville Branch – Library, PO Box 536, Brockville ON K6V 5V7 – Librarian, Cindy Miller
St. Lawrence College - Learning Resource Centre, 2288 Parkedale Ave., Brockville ON K6V 5X3 – 613/345-0660, ext.3104; Fax: 613/345-2231; Email: staf1277@slcsl.stlawrencec.on.ca; Symbol: OBSL – Group Leader, Sara Manoll

BURLINGTON
The Bible League of Canada – Library, PO Box 5037, Burlington ON L7R 3Y8 – 905/319-9500; Toll Free: 1-800-363-9673
Christian Reformed World Relief Committee of Canada – CRWRC Development Education Library, 3475 Mainway, PO Box 5070, Burlington ON L7R 3Y8 – 905/336-2920; Toll Free: 1-800-730-3490
City of Burlington - Clerk's Department Library, 426 Brant St., Burlington ON L7R 3Z6 – 905/335-7701; Fax: 905/335-7881 – Records Coordinator, Annie Budz, Email: budza@cityhall.city.burlington.on.ca
CUMIS General Insurance Co. - Library, 151 North Service Rd., PO Box 5065, Burlington ON L7R 4C2 – 905/632-1221; Fax: 905/632-9412; Toll Free: 1-800-263-9120 – Librarian, Ann Higgins
Environment Canada - Canada Centre for Inland Waters - Library, 867 Lakeshore Rd., Burlington ON L7R 4A6 – 905/336-4530; Fax: 905/336-4428; Email: eve.dowie@cciw.ca – Head, Library Services, Eve Dowie
Halton Board of Education - J.W. Singleton Education Library, 2050 Guelph Line, PO Box 5005, Burlington ON L7R 3Z2 – 905/335-3665, ext.3312; Fax: 905/335-9802; Email: susan_mickalow@halton.tor.hookup.net
   Supervisor, Media & Libraries, Susan Mickalow
   Technical Services, Library Technician, Bonnie Starr
Joseph Brant Memorial Hospital – Educational Services, 1230 North Shore Blvd., Burlington ON L7R 4C4 – 905/632-3730 – Librarian, Catherine Newman

BURNT RIVER
Toronto & District Square & Round Dance Association – Resource Centre, c/o Ed & Kitty Giles, RR#2, Burnt River ON K0M 1C0 – 705/488-2973 – Ray Quirk

CAMBRIDGE
Gowlings - Library, 19 Thorne St., Cambridge ON N1R 5W1 – 519/621-6910; Fax: 519/621-5028 – Library Technician, Anah Figueiredo
Heritage Baptist College & Heritage Theological Seminary - Library, 175 Holiday Inn Dr., Cambridge ON N3C 3T2 – 519/651-2869; Fax: 519/651-2870; Toll Free: 1-800-465-1961; Symbol: OTCBS – Librarian, Marion E. Meadows

CAMPBELLFORD

Canadian Authors Association – Lionel M. Gelber Canadian Literature Research Library, 27 Doxsee Ave. North, Campbellford ON K0L 1L0 – 705/653-0323

Solicitor General Canada - Warkworth Institution - Library, PO Box 760, Campbellford ON K0L 1L0 – 705/924-2210, ext.2730; Fax: 705/924-3351; Symbol: OCWI – Librarian, Thomas Johnston

CARLETON PLACE

Postal History Society of Canada – Library, 216 Mailey Dr., Carleton Place ON K7C 3X9 – 613/257-5453

CAYUGA

Haldimand Law Library, 55 Munsee St. North, Cayuga ON N0A 1E0 – 905/772-3361 – Betty MacDonald

Ontario Genealogical Society - Haldimand Branch – Library, PO Box 38, Cayuga ON N0A 1E0 – 905/776-2969 – David Runions

CHALK RIVER

Chalk River Laboratories - Information Centre, GPO, Chalk River ON K0J 1J0 – 613/584-8811, ext.3900; Fax: 613/584-1745; Email: refdesk@crl.aecl.ca; Symbol: OCKA
Technical Leader, Monica Lim, Email: limm@crl.aecl.ca
Acquistions Librarian, Linda Crawford

CHATHAM

Rhodes Law Firm Law Office - Library, PO Box 1358, Chatham ON N7M 5W8 – 519/352-4700; Fax: 519/352-5616 – Karen Labadie

St. Clair College - Thames Campus Resource Centre, 1001 Grand Ave. West, PO Box 2017, Chatham ON N7M 5W4 – 519/354-9100, ext.3232, 3273; Fax: 519/354-5496; Email: mtales@sccoll.stclairc.on.ca
Manager, Barry Van Biesbrouck
Library Technician, Linda Grineage
Library Specialist, Matt Tales

St. Joseph's Hospital – Library of the Healing Arts, 519 King St. West, Chatham ON N7M 1G8 – 519/352-2500 – Librarian, Mary Gillies

Union Gas Ltd. - Library Services, 50 Keil Dr. North, Chatham ON N7M 5M1 – 519/352-3100, ext.2495 – Assistant Librarian, Maureen Mason

COBOURG

Ontario Ministry of the Solicitor General & Correctional Services - Brookside Youth Centre Library, 390 King St. East, PO Box 159, Cobourg ON K9A 4K6 – 905/372-5451; Fax: 905/372-7788 – Library Assistant, Gail Cunningham

SHARE INFO Community Information Centre Inc. – Library, 15 Chapel St., Cobourg ON K9A 1J1 – 905/372-8913

CONCORD

CMS Group Inc. – Library, #3, 140 Snow Blvd., Concord ON L4K 4C1 – 905/660-7580 – Administrator, Lynda Bennare

Savage, Bourque, Raffaghello Law Office - Library, #310, 3300 Hwy. 7, Concord ON L4K 4M3 – 905/660-4633; Fax: 905/660-0384

CORNWALL

Canadian Heritage - Parks Canada, Ontario Region Library, 111 Water St. East, Cornwall ON K6H 6S3 – 613/938-5787; Fax: 613/938-5785; Email: ENVOY: PARKS.ILL.OCN; Symbol: OCN – Librarian, Joan Lipscombe

Cornwall & Seaway Valley Tourism – Library, 231 Augustus St., Cornwall ON K6J 3W2 – 613/938-4748; Toll Free: 1-800-937-4748 – Candy Pollard

North American Indian Travelling College – Library, RR#3, Cornwall ON K6H 5R7 – 613/932-9452

Stormont, Dundas & Glengarry Law Association – Courthouse Library, PO Box 35, Cornwall ON K6H 5R9 – 613/932-5411

Transport Canada Training Institute - Library, 1950 Montreal Rd., Cornwall ON K6H 6L2 – 613/936-5018; Fax: 613/936-5044; Symbol: OOTI – Supervisor, Judith Daoust

DEEP RIVER

Deep River Symphony Orchestra – Deep River Symphony Orchestra Library, PO Box 1496, Deep River ON K0J 1P0 – 613/584-3311, x.3743 – Librarian, George Doubt

DELHI

Agriculture & Agri-Food Canada - Canadian Agriculture Library, Pest Management Research Centre, Delhi Farm, Schafer Rd., PO Box 186, Delhi ON N4B 2W9 – 519/582-1950; Fax: 519/582-4223; Symbol: ODEAG – Librarian, Robert Duff

DORSET

Ontario Ministry of Environment & Energy - Dorset Research Station – Library, Bellwood Acres Rd., Dorset ON P0A 1E0 – 705/766-2418; Email: dillonpe@epo.gov.on.ca – Manager, Peter Dillon

Leslie M. Frost Natural Resources Centre - Library, Dorset ON P0A 1E0 – 705/766-2451; Fax: 705/766-9677 – Education Specialist, David Gibson

DUNDAS

Peace Research Institute - Dundas – Peace Research Library, 25 Dundana Ave., Dundas ON L9H 4E5 – 905/628-2356 – Documentation Specialist, Linda Carroll

ELLIOT LAKE

Ontario Ministry of Northern Development & Mines - Departmental Library, 126 Ontario Ave., Elliot Lake ON P5A 1Y2 – 705/670-7341; Fax: 705/670-7108; Symbol: OTNA – Library Coordinator, Linda Davis

EMBRUN

James D. Campbell Law Office - Library, #1, 165 Bay St., Embrun ON K0A 1W1 – 613/443-5683; Fax: 613/443-3285

EXETER

Shared Library Services – Library, South Huron Hospital, 24 Huron St. West, Exeter ON N0M 1S2 – 519/235-2700, ext.249; Fax: 519/235-3405; Email: lwilcox@julian.uwo.ca; Symbol: OESH
Director, Linda Wilcox
Library Assistant, Susan Oke

FERGUS

Information Fergus – Library, Fergus Market Bldg., 100 Queen St. West, Fergus ON N1M 2W7 – 519/843-5020 – Administrator, Patricia Mestern

Wilson, Jack & Grant Law Office - Library, PO Box 128, Fergus ON N1M 2W7 – 519/843-1960; Fax: 519/843-6888 – Partner, Douglas C. Jack

FLAMBOROUGH

Association of Self Employment Developers of Ontario – Library, #200, 7 Innovation Dr., Flamborough ON L9H 7H9 – 905/689-2920 – Coordinator, Douglas Crawford

FORT ERIE

Adult Literacy Council of Greater Fort Erie – Library, #14, 427 Garrison Rd., Fort Erie ON L2A 6E6 – 905/871-6626

FORT FRANCES

United Native Friendship Centre – Library, 516 Portage Ave., PO Box 752, Fort Frances ON P9A 3N1 – 807/274-3207 – Literacy Coordinator, Mike Anderson

GEORGETOWN

Esquesing Historical Society – Halton Hills Public Library, Georgetown Branch, PO Box 51, Georgetown ON L7G 4T1 – 905/873-2681; Fax: 905/873-6118 – Information Services Librarian, Geoffrey Cannon

North Halton Association for the Developmentally Handicapped – Library, 62 Park Ave., Georgetown ON L7G 4Z1 – 905/873-8181 – Executive Assistant, Etta Mills

GLOUCESTER

Federation of Canadian Archers Inc. – Sport Information Resource Centre, #209, 1600 James Naismith Dr., Gloucester ON K1B 5N4 – 613/748-5658; TLX: 053-3660 – Reference Librarian, Ann Romeril

Heraldry Society of Canada – Library, PO Box 8128, Gloucester ON K1G 3H9 – 613/231-0867 – Librarian, Stephen Murray

Ottawa-Carleton Children's Aid Society – Library, 1602 Telesat Court, Gloucester ON K1B 1B1 – 613/747-7800, ext.2750; Fax: 613/742-1607 – Coordinator of Staff Training, Janice Horton

Sport Information Resource Centre, Place R. Tait McKenzie, 1600 James Naismith Dr., Gloucester ON K1B 5N4 – 613/748-5658; Fax: 613/748-5701; Toll Free: 1-800-665-6413; Email: ref@sirc.ca; URL: http://www.sirc.ca/; Symbol: OOFS
President, Gilles Chiasson
Coordinator, Promotion/Marketing, Linda Wheeler
Vice-President, Richard Stark
Head, Technical Services, Christine Lalande

Telesat Canada - Information Resource Centre, 1601 Telesat Ct., Gloucester ON K1B 5P4 – 613/748-0123; Fax: 613/748-8712; Email: ENVOY: TELESAT.LIBRARY; Symbol: OOTEL
Information Services Coordinator, Steven Roby
Library Technician, Suzanne Dion

Transport Canada - Aircraft Services Directorate - Technical Library, 58 Service Rd., Gloucester ON K1V 9B2 – 613/998-8299; Fax: 613/998-8326; Symbol: OOTFS
Head, Technical Library, Jeff White
Acquisitions, Sherry Stewart
Distribution, Jennifer Maguire

GODERICH

Ontario Genealogical Society - Huron County Branch – Library at the Huron County Museum, PO Box 469, Goderich ON N7A 4C7 – 519/887-6989 – Librarian, Anne Clark

GORMLEY

Central Baptist Seminary - W. Gordon Brown Memorial Library, PO Box 28, Gormley ON L0H 1G0 – 905/888-9600; Fax: 905/888-9603; Email: ENVOY 100: Central.Seminary
Librarian, Michael Haykin
Technical Services Librarian, Margaret Everingham

GUELPH

Ontario Ministry of Agriculture, Food & Rural Affairs - Education, Research & Laboratories Division – Library, 95 Stone Rd. West, Zone 2, PO Box 3650, Guelph ON N1H 8J7 – 519/767-6291
Ontario Centre for Soil Resource Evaluation, 52 Royal Rd., PO Box 1030, Guelph ON N1H 6N1 – 519/766-9180

Canadian Botanical Association – Library, Dept. of Botany, University of Guelph, #158, 50 Stone Rd. East, Guelph ON N1G 2W1 – 613/990-6452 – Archivist, Dr. J.F. Gerrath

Christian Farmers Federation of Ontario – Library, 115 Woolwich St., Guelph ON N1H 3V1 – 519/837-1620 – Librarian, Nellie van Donkersgoed

Conestoga College - Guelph Campus Library, 460 Speedvale Ave. West, Guelph ON N1H 6N6 – 519/824-9390, ext.126 – Florence Dumas

Farm Safety Association Inc. – Film Service, #22, 340 Woodlawn Rd. West, Guelph ON N1H 1G8 – 519/823-5600

Fellowship of Evangelical Baptist Churches in Canada – Archives, 679 Southgate Dr., Guelph ON N1G 4S2 – 519/821-4830 – Isabel Freeman

Guelph Correctional Centre - Library, PO Box 3600, Guelph ON N1H 6P3 – 519/822-0020, ext.2313; Fax: 519/822-0591 – Library Technician, Karyn Smith

Guelph International Resource Centre – Resource Centre, #1, 123 Woolwich St., Guelph ON N1H 3V1 – 519/822-3110

Homewood Health Centre – Library, 150 Delhi St., Guelph ON N1E 4J8 – 519/824-1010, ext.148 – Library Technician, Joyce Pharoah

Jubilee Centre for Agricultural Research – Family Farm Stewardship Library, 115 Woolwich St., Guelph ON N1H 3V1 – 519/837-1620 – Librarian, Nellie van Donkersgoed

Moon, Heath Law Office - Library, 164 Norfolk St., PO Box 180, Guelph ON N1H 6K1 – 519/824-2540; Fax: 519/763-6785; Email: moonlaw@sentex.net – Librarian, Pat Breese

Ontario Ministry of Agriculture, Food & Rural Affairs - Audiovisual Library, Visual Communication Services, 52 Royal Rd., Guelph ON N1H 1G3 – 519/767-3622; Fax: 519/824-9521

Ontario Ministry of the Solicitor General & Correctional Services - Guelph Correctional Centre Library, 785 York Rd., PO Box 3600, Guelph ON N1H 6P3 – 519/822-0020, ext.2313/2232; Fax: 519/822-0591 – Library Technician, Vanessa Jabelmann

Rowan Williams Davies & Irwin Inc. – Library, 650 Woodlawn Rd. West, Guelph ON N1K 1B8 – 519/823-1311 – Project Manager, M. Vanderheyden

Stewardship Information Bureau – Library, #104, 150 Research Lane, Guelph ON N1G 4T2 – 519/767-5020; Email: jkerr@uoguelph.ca – Database Manager, John Kerr

Uniroyal Chemical Ltd. - Research Labs Library, 120 Huron St., Guelph ON N1H 6N3 – 519/822-3790, ext.455/458; Fax: 519/837-0523; Email: ENVOY: OGDR.LIB; Symbol: OGDR – Manager of Information Services & Legal Liaison, Lorna Cole

The United Brethren Church in Canada – Library, 501 Whitelaw Rd., Guelph ON N1K 1E7 – 519/836-0180

University of Guelph - Library, #158, 50 Stone Rd. East, Guelph ON N1G 2W1 – 519/824-4120, ext.2181; Fax: 519/824-6931; Email: libloan@uoguelph.ca; URL: http://www.lib.uoguelph.ca; Symbol: OGU
 Chief Librarian, Dr. Michael Ridley
 Administrative & Facilities Support Services, Head, Pat Hock
 Collections Services, Head, Tim Sauer
 Public Services, Head, Ron MacKinnon
 Special Collections & Library Development, Head, Bernard Katz
 Systems Services, Manager, George Loney
 Technical Services, Head, Ellen Tom

Wellington County Board of Education - Terry James Resource Library, 500 Victoria Rd. North, Guelph ON N1E 6K2 – 519/822-4420, ext.226; Fax: 519/763-6870; Email: prowe@hookup.net; Symbol: OGWE – Supervisor, Central Library Services, Paola Rowe, 519/822-4420, ext.270

Wellington County Law Association – Law Library, 74 Woolwich St., Guelph ON N1H 3T9 – 519/763-6365; Symbol: WELN – Librarian, Betty Thiessen

HAGERSVILLE

Grand River Polytechnical Institute - Library Resource Centre, Grand River Territory, Six Nations, PO Box 728, Hagersville ON N0A 1H0 – 905/768-0448; Fax: 905/768-0424 – Diana Doxdator

HAILEYBURY

Northern College of Applied Arts & Technology - Haileybury School of Mines Campus Library, 640 Latchford, Haileybury ON P0J 1K0 – 705/672-3376, ext.806; Fax: 705/672-2014; Toll Free: 1-800-461-5745; Email: libraryh@kirk.northernc.on.ca – Library Technician, Brenda Vaillancourt

HAMILTON

Canadian Academic Accounting Association – Library, Faculty of Management, University of Toronto, #850, 120 King St. West, PO Box 176, Hamilton ON L8N 3C3 – 905/525-1884

Canadian Baptist Archives, McMaster Divinity College, Hamilton ON L8S 4K1 – 905/525-9140, ext.23511 – Archivist, Judith Colwell

Canadian Centre for Occupational Health & Safety – CCOHS Reference Centre, 250 Main St. East, Hamilton ON L8N 1H6 – 905/572-4453; Toll Free: 1-800-668-4284; Symbol: OHOHS – Manager, Documentation, Peter Lukas

Canadian Society of Laboratory Technologists – Library, PO Box 2830, Hamilton ON L8N 3N8 – 905/528-8642 – Continuing Education Director, Ed Hollingham

Centre for Canadian Historical Horticultural Studies, PO Box 399, Hamilton ON L8N 3H8 – 905/527-1158, ext. 259; Fax: 905/577-0375; Symbol: OHRB – Librarian/Curator, Ina Vrugtman

Chedoke-McMaster Hospital – Hospital Library, 1200 Main St. West, PO Box 2000, Hamilton ON L8N 3Z5 – 905/574-5402, ext.7741; Email: wyndham@fhs.csu.mcmaster.ca – Librarian, Lois Wyndham

Community Information Service Hamilton-Wentworth – Library, 55 York Blvd., PO Box 2700, Hamilton ON L8N 4E4 – 905/528-0104

Dofasco Inc. - Library Resource Centre, PO Box 2460, Hamilton ON L8N 3J5 – 905/548-7200, ext.2794; Fax: 905/548-4630; Email: ENVOY: DOF.ISMO – Coordinator, Linda Pauloski

Geoffrey M. Read Law Office - Library, #909, 105 Main St. East, Hamilton ON L8N 1G6 – 905/529-2028; Fax: 905/522-6677

Greater Hamilton Symphony Association – Library, 59 Oxford St., Hamilton ON L8R 2W9 – 905/547-4350 – Librarian, Enid Pottinger

Hamilton & District Chamber of Commerce – Business Reference Library, 555 Bay St. North, Hamilton ON L8L 1H1 – 905/522-1151

Hamilton Board of Education - Dr. Harry Paikin Library, 100 Main St. West, Hamilton ON L8N 3L1 – 905/521-2518; Fax: 905/521-2541; Symbol: OHEC
 Chief Librarian, Ingrid Scott, 905/521-2518, ext.2335
 Research Librarian, Karyn Hogan, 905/527-5092, ext.2308
 Library Technician, Leslie Ferguson, 905/521-2518
 Library Secretary, Sue McCormick, 905/527-5092, ext.2309
 Library Technician, Cherilyn Waterfield, 905/527-5092, ext.2283
 Library Technician, Jane Holbrook, 905/527-5092, ext.2332

Hamilton Law Association – Anthony Pepe Memorial Law Library, 50 Main St. East, Hamilton ON L8N 1E9 – 905/522-1563

Hamilton Psychiatric Hospital – Library Resource Centre, 100 - 5th St. West, PO Box 585, Hamilton ON L8L 2B3 – 905/388-2511; Fax: 905/575-6035; Email: devries@fhs.csu.mcmaster.ca – Librarian, Anne Devries

Hamilton Regional Indian Centre – Resource Library, 712 Main St. East, Hamilton ON L8M 1K8 – 905/548-9593 – Laura Williams

Hamilton Spectator Library, 44 Frid St., Hamilton ON L8N 3G3 – 905/526-3315; Fax: 905/526-3399
 Senior Information Technician, Tammie Danciu, 905/526-3209
 Information Technician, Marilyn McGrory, 905/526-3379

Inch, Easterbrook & Shaker Law Office - Library, 1 King St. West, 15th Fl., Hamilton ON L8P 4X8 – 905/525-4481, ext.31; Fax: 905/525-0031 – Library Technician, Margery Bylsma

McMaster University - Libraries, 1280 Main St. West, Hamilton ON L8S 4L6 – 905/525-9140; Fax: 905/546-0625, 522-1277; Email: ILL.OHM; Symbol: OHM
 University Librarian, Graham R. Hill
 Administrative Services, Head, Mary Ruth Linkert
 Archives & Research Collections, Director, Charlotte Stewart
 Collection Management & Development, Assistant University Librarian, Victor Nunn
 Processing Services, Director, Carol Racheter
 Readers Services, Assistant University Librarian, Sheila Pepper
 Systems Development, Associate University Librarian, Marju Drynan
 Health Sciences Library, Director, Dorothy Fitzgerald
 Innis Library, Business Librarian, Kathryn Ball
 Lloyd Reeds Map Library/Urban Documentation Centre, Documentalist, Cathy Moulder
 Science & Engineering, Librarian, Peggy Findlay

Mohawk College - Resource Centre, 135 Fennell Ave. West, PO Box 2034, Hamilton ON L8N 3T2 – 905/575-2077; Fax: 905/575-2378; Email: hykl@oper-atns.mohawkc.on.ca; Symbol: OHMC
 Director of Learning Resources, Sandra Black
 Acquisition/Cataloguing, Head, Helen Shaver
 Circulation/Reference, Head, Marilyn McDermott

Native Indian/Inuit Photographer's Association – Resource Centre, 134 James St. South, Hamilton ON L8P 2Z4 – 905/529-7477 – Communictions Specialist, Steve Loft

NDE Institute of Canada – Library, 135 Fennell Ave. West, Hamilton ON L8N 3T2 – 905/387-1655

Ontario Cancer Treatment & Research Foundation - Library, 699 Concession St., Hamilton ON L8V 5C2 – 905/387-9711, ext.5100; Fax: 905/575-6317; Email: fraumeni@fhs.csu.mcmaster.ca – Librarian, Michael Fraumeni

Ross & McBride Law Office - Library, 1 King St. West, 10 - 11th Fl., PO Box 907, Hamilton ON L8N 3P6 – 905/526-9800; Fax: 905/526-0732 – Librarian, K. Kennett

Royal Botanical Gardens – Library, PO Box 399, Hamilton ON L8N 3H8 – 905/527-1158; Symbol: OHRB

St. Joseph's Hospital – Library Services, 50 Charlton Ave. East, Hamilton ON L8N 4A6 – 905/522-1155, x.3410; Fax: 905/521-6111; Email: fitzg@fhs.csu.mcmaster.ca – Director, Library Services, Gayle Fitzgerald

SHAIR International Resource Centre – Library, 255 West Ave. North, Hamilton ON L8L 5C8 – 905/528-9055

Simpson, Wigle - Law Library, #1030, 120 King St. West, PO Box 990, Hamilton ON L8N 3R1 – 905/528-8411 – Library Technician, M. Bylsma

Society of Canadian Cine Amateurs – Library, 45 Highcliffe Ave., Hamilton ON L9C 2Y4 – 905/575-1063 – Librarian, Neil Upshall

Stelco Inc. - Research & Development Dept. Technical Information Resources, PO Box 2030, Hamilton ON L8N 3T1 – 905/528-2511, ext.2076; Fax: 905/308-7012; Email: strblib@netaccess.on.ca;

Canadian Almanac & Directory 1997

Symbol: OHSCC – Research Library Technician, Carol Cernile

Thoman, Soule, Gage Law Office - Library, 46 Jackson St. East, PO Box 187, Hamilton ON L8N 3C5 – 905/529-8195; Fax: 905/529-7906 – Managing Lawyer, Stuart Aird

Turkstra Garrod Hodgson - Library, 15 Bold St., Hamilton ON L8P 1T3 – 905/523-1387; Fax: 905/529-3663 – Library Committee Chair, Michael Nash

HARROW

Agriculture & Agri-Food Canada-Harrow Research Centre – Library, Hwy. 18 East, Harrow ON N0R 1G0 – 519/738-2251; Email: lboharag@nc-ccot.agr.ca; Symbol: OHARAG – Research Librarian, Eric Champagne

Harrow Early Immigrant Research Society – Library, PO Box 53, Harrow ON N0R 1G0 – 519/738-4368 – Librarian, J. Ferguson

HEARST

Collège universitaire de Hearst - Bibliothéque Maurice-Saulnier, PO Box 580, Hearst ON P0L 1N0 – 705/372-1781; Fax: 705/362-7518; Email: JM.CORBEIL – Johanne Morin-Corbeil

HULL

Canadian Heritage Information Network – Library, 15, rue Eddy, 4e étage, Hull ON K1A 0M5 – 819/994-1200 – Museum Consultant, Merridy Bradley

Industry Canada - Canadian Intellectual Property Office Library, Place du Portage, Phase 1, 50, rue Victoria, 11e étage, Hull ON K1A 0C9 – 613/997-2964; Fax: 613/997-5585; Email: ENVOY: ILL.OOSP; Symbol: OOSP
 Librarian, Rita Bocar
 Library Technician, Thérèse Renaud

Transportation Safety Board - Library, Place du Centre, 4th Fl., 200 Promenade du Portage, Hull ON K1A 1K8 – 613/994-8020; Fax: 613/994-4330; Symbol: OOTAI – Librarian, Louis Morin

KANATA

Canadian Marconi Co. - Library, 415 Legget Dr., Kanata ON K2K 2B2 – 613/592-6500; Fax: 613/592-7427; URL: http://www.marconi.ca;
 Symbol: OKCM – Chief Librarian, Lois Brimacombe

Fleet Technology Limited – Library, 311 Legget Dr., Kanata ON K2K 1Z8 – 613/592-2830 – Librarian, Faye Bennett

Mitel Corporation - Library, 350 Legget Dr., Kanata ON K2K 1X3 – 613/592-2122; Fax: 613/592-4784 – Librarian, Marie P. Paul, 613/592-2122, ext.4188

KAPUSKASING

Northern College of Applied Arts & Technology - Kapuskasing Campus Library, 3 Aurora Ave., Kapuskasing ON P5N 1J6 – 705/335-8504; Fax: 705/335-8343; Toll Free: 1-800-461-2167; Email: mehta@kirk.northernc.ca – Academic Coordinator, Kishor Mehta

KEMPTVILLE

Kemptville College of Agricultural Technology - Purvis Library, PO Bag 2003, Kemptville ON K0G 1J0 – 613/258-8294; Fax: 613/258-8384; Symbol: OKEMC – Librarian, D. Simpson

KING CITY

Seneca College - King Campus Library Resource Centre, 13990 Dufferin St., King City ON L7B 1B3 – 905/833-3333, ext.5105; Fax: 905/833-1106 – Campus Librarian, Marjorie Hale, 905/833-3333, ext.5106

KINGSTON

Alcan International Ltd. - Kingston Research & Development Centre Technical Library, PO Box 8400, Kingston ON K7L 5L9 – 613/541-2065, 2071; Fax: 613/547-6401; Email: ENVOY: OKA.ILL Coordinator, Brian Chenoweth Specialist, Cindy Cain-Lough

Canadian Association of Social Work Administrators in Health Facilities – Library, Social Work Department, Kingston General Hospital, 76 Stuart St., Kingston ON K7L 2V7 – 613/549-6666, ext.4443 – Chair, Library Committee, M. Jewell

Canadian Land Force Command & Staff College - Fort Frontenac Library, Fort Frontenac, Kingston ON K7K 5L0 – 613/541-5010, ext.5815; Fax: 613/546-0589; Symbol: OKF
 Chief Librarian, Serge Campion, 613/541-5010, ext.5829
 Public Services Librarian, D. Boyd
 Technical Services Librarian, D. Willis

Cunningham, Swan, Carty, Little & Bonham Law Office - Library, Empire Life Bldg., #500, 259 King St. East, PO Box 460, Kingston ON K7L 4W6 – 613/544-0211; Fax: 613/542-9814 – Librarian, Elizabeth A. Marshall

Frontenac Law Association – Frontenac County Courthouse Library, County Courthouse, Court St., Kingston ON K7L 2N4 – 613/542-0034 – Librarian, Jackie Hawkins

Hôtel-Dieu Hospital – Staff Library, 166 Brock St., Kingston ON K7L 5G2 – 613/544-3310 – Director, Lynda Silver

International Centre – Education Abroad Resource Library, Queen's University, John Deutsch University Centre, Kingston ON K7L 3N6 – 613/545-2604 – Senior Secretary, Asha Joneja

Kingston & District Immigrant Services – Library, 315 Johnson St., Kingston ON K7L 1Y6 – 613/548-3302 – Volunteer Librarian, Shirley R. Samuels

Kingston Area Economic Development Commission – Small Business Centre, #200, 181 Wellington St., Kingston ON K7L 3E3 – 613/544-2725 – Administrative Assistant, Sharon Fitch

Kingston District Community Information Centre – Library, St. Paul's Church Hall, 137 Queen St., Kingston ON K7K 1A8 – 613/542-1001 – Database Manager, Jane McDonald

Kingston General Hospital – Library, 76 Stuart St., Kingston ON K7L 2V7 – 613/549-6666, ext.4076; Email: KGHLIB@qucdn.queensu.ca; Symbol: OKGH – Manager, Library Services, Margaret Darling

Kingston Global Community Centre – Library, 461 Princess St., 2nd Fl., Kingston ON K7L 1C3 – 613/530-2105

Kingston Penitentiary - Library, 555 King St., PO Box 22, Kingston ON K7L 4V7 – 613/545-8460, ext.1505; Fax: 613/545-0826; Symbol: OKK – Librarian, N. Rudolph Meier

Kingston Psychiatric Hospital – Staff Library, 752 King St. West, PO Box 603, Kingston ON K7L 4X3 – 613/546-1101, ext.5745; Email: gagnon@qucdn.queensu.ca; Symbol: OKPH – Hospital Librarian, Karen Gagnon

Marine Museum of the Great Lakes at Kingston - Audrey Rushbrook Memorial Library & Archives, 55 Ontario St., Kingston ON K7L 2Y2 – 613/542-2261; Fax: 613/542-0043; Email: CHIN/Trillium: Trill.mmglk – Archivist, Librarian, Earl Moorhead

Queen's University - Libraries, Kingston ON K7L 5C4 – 613/545-2527; Fax: 613/545-6819; Email: ENVOY: ADMIN.QUEENS.LIBRARIES; Symbol: OKQ
 Reference Services, Head, Sheila Johnson
 Chief Librarian, Paul Wiens
 Cataloguing, Head, S. Kalb
 Central Collection Services, Head, David Wang
 Collection Development, Librarian, Dianne Cook
 Documents, Head, J. Offenbeck
 Information & Reference, Head, C. Adamson
 Special Collections, Head, P. Thayer
 Systems, Assistant Librarian, G. W. Clevenger
 Art Library, Librarian, Reinolde Van Weringh
 Biology Library, Library Technician, L. Allen
 Bracken Library (Medicine, Nursing, Health Sciences), Librarian, Vivien Ludwin
 Chemistry, Library Technician, A. Thomson
 Civil Engineering, Library Technician, Jane Walker
 Dupuis Hall Library(Mining Engineering;Chemical Engineering), Library Technician, Mary-Lou Ranger
 Education Library, Librarian, Sandra Casey
 Electrical Engineering, Library Technician, A. Madden
 Geological Sciences Library, Library Technician, Mary Mayson
 Law Library, Chief Law Librarian, Denis Marshall
 Mathematics & Statistics Library, Library Technician, Carol Tennent
 Mechanical Engineering Library, Library Technician, Hilary Richardson
 Music, Librarian, Ann Allen
 Physics Library, Library Technician, Dianne Nuttall
 Psychology Librarian, Library Technician, W. Parks
 Science Librarian, E. Jane Philipps
 Industrial Relations, Library Technician, J. Dee
 Map & Air Photos, Library Technician, S. Harmer

Royal Military College of Canada - Library, Kingston ON K7K 5L0 – 613/541-6000, ext.6004; Fax: 613/542-5055; Symbol: OKR
 Chief Librarian, Samuel O. Alexander, 613/541-6229
 Technical Services & Systems, Head, S.J. Toomey, 613/541-6000, ext.6260
 Massey Library, Head, B. Cameron, 613/541-6000, ext.6674
 Science/Engineering Library, Head, N. Turkington, 613/541-6000, ext.6079

Solicitor General Canada - Collins Bay Institution - Library, 455 Bath Rd., PO Box 190, Kingston ON K7L 4V9 – 613/545-8598, ext.341; Symbol: OKCB
 Joyceville Institution - Library, PO Box 880, Kingston ON K7L 4X9 – 613/542-4554, ext.2491; Symbol: OKJ – Librarian, Lise Maillet
 Prison for Women - Library, 40 Sir John A. MacDonald Blvd., PO Box 515, Kingston ON K7L 4W7 – 613/545-8988; Fax: 613/545-8816; Symbol: OKPW – Librarian, Pat Bender

KIRKLAND LAKE

Northern College of Applied Arts & Technology - Northern College Libraries in South Porcupine & Haileybury, 140 Government Rd. East, Kirkland Lake ON P2N 3L8 – 705/567-9291, ext.700; Fax: 705/568-8186; Toll Free: 1-800-461-4991; Email: libraryk@kirk.northernc.on.ca; Symbol: OKLNC – Library Technician, E. Rose

KITCHENER

AIDS Committee of Cambridge, Kitchener/Waterloo & Area – Library, 123 Duke St., Kitchener ON N2A 1A4 – 519/570-3687

Community Information Centre of Waterloo Region – Library, 25 Frederick St., Lower Level, Kitchener ON N2H 5A5 – 519/579-3800

Conestoga College - Learning Resource Centre, 299 Doon Valley Dr., Kitchener ON N2G 4M4 – 519/748-5220, ext.361; Fax: 519/748-5971
 Manager, Linda Krotz, 519/748-5220, ext.289
 Coordinator, Jill Douglas, 519/748-5220, ext.240

Grand River Hospital Corp. – Health Sciences Library, Kitchener-Waterloo Health Centre, 835 King St. West, Kitchener ON N2G 1G3 – 519/749-4300, ext.2235; Fax: 519/749-4208 – Coordinator, Library Services, Dee Sprung

Freeport Health Centre - Library, 3570 King St. East, Kitchener ON N2A 2W1 – 519/894-8360,

ext.7174; Fax: 519/893-2625 – Librarian, Dawn Bombay
K-W Association for Community Living – Library, 26 College St., Kitchener ON N2H 4Z9 – 519/743-5783
Kitchener Social Planning Council – Library, 10 Water St. North, Kitchener ON N2H 5A5 – 519/578-7430
Kitchener-Waterloo Record - Library, 225 Fairway Rd. South, Kitchener ON N2G 4E5 – 519/894-2231; Fax: 519/894-3829; Email: newsroom@therecord.com
   Acting Librarian, Chris Masterman, 519/894-2231, ext.695
   Library Assistant, Lynn Boland-Richardson
Kitchener-Waterloo Symphony Orchestra Association Inc. – Library, 101 Queen St. North, Kitchener ON N2H 6P7 – 519/745-4711 – Marianne Leach-Hoffer
Ontario Bird Banding Association – Library, 165 Green Valley Dr., Kitchener ON N20 1K3 – 519/748-4853
St. Mary's General Hospital – Library, 911 Queens Blvd., Kitchener ON N2M 1B2 – 519/749-6549; Fax: 519/749-6484 – Medical Librarian, Elaine Baldwin
Waterloo Historical Society – Library, c/o Kitchener Public Library, 85 Queen St. North, Kitchener ON N2H 2H1 – 519/743-0271, ext.252 – Local History Librarian, Susan Hoffman
Waterloo Law Association – Law Library, Court House, 20 Weber St. East, Kitchener ON N2H 1C3 – 519/742-0872 – Librarian, Catherine Whiteman
Waterloo Region Roman Catholic Separate School Board - Resource Centre, 91 Moore Ave., PO Box 1116, Kitchener ON N2G 4G2 – 519/578-3660; Fax: 519/884-0158 – Resource Librarian, Elaine Zink
Waterloo Regional Arts Council Inc. – Resource Centre, 25 Frederick St., Kitchener ON N2H 6M8 – 519/744-4552

KLEINBURG
Canadian Compensation Association – Library, 10435 Islington Ave., PO Box 294, Kleinburg ON L0J 1C0 – 905/893-1689
The McMichael Canadian Art Collection - Library, 10365 Islington Ave., Kleinburg ON L0J 1C0 – 905/893-1121; Fax: 905/893-2588 – Librarian, Linda Morita

LAKEFIELD
Lakefied College - School Library, Lakefield ON K0L 2H0 – 705/652-3324; Fax: 705/652-6320; URL: http://www.lakefieldcs.on.ca/
   Head, Manal Stamboulie, Email: MStamboulie@Lakefieldcs.on.ca
   Library Technician, Friedel Hatje

LEAMINGTON
Climate Control Systems Inc. - Harrow Research Centre – Library, 509 Hwy. 77, RR#5, Leamington ON N8H 3V8 – 519/322-2515
Point Pelee National Park – Library, RR#1, Leamington ON N8H 3V4 – 519/322-2365; Fax: 519/322-1277 – Chief, Lily J. Meleg
South Essex Community Council – Resource Centre, #301, 33 Princess St., Leamington ON N8H 5C5 – 519/326-8629 – Director, Community Education, Debbie Aspinall

LINDSAY
Sir Sandford Fleming College of Applied Arts & Technology - School of Natural Resources, Frost Campus Educational Resource Centre, PO Box 8400, Lindsay ON K9V 5E6 – 705/324-9144; Fax: 705/878-9318; Symbol: OLISF
   Library Supervisor, Gale Butterill, Email: GButteri@flemingc.on.ca
   Director, Joan Webster
   LRC Director, Karen Sjolin

PeriodicalsMaggie Fry
Victoria/Haliburton Law Association – Library, 440 Kent St. West, Lindsay ON K9V 4T7 – 705/324-7114 – Law Librarian, Ann Neale

LION'S HEAD
Bruce Peninsula Environment Group – Library, 30 Main St., PO Box 1119, Lion's Head ON N0H 1W0 – 519/793-4123; Toll Free: 1-800-416-2734 – Librarian, Edith Tompkins

LONDON
3M Canada Inc. - Technical Information Centre, PO Box 5610, London ON N6A 4L6 – 519/451-2500, ext.2486; Fax: 519/452-6142; Email: ENVOY: MMM.TECHINFO; Symbol: OLTMC – Librarian, Cheryl E. Stephenson, Email: cstephenson@mmm.com
Agriculture & Agri-Food Canada - Canadian Agriculture Library, Pest Management Research Centre, 1391 Sandford St., London ON N6V 4T3 – 519/645-4452; Fax: 519/645-5476; Email: lbolag@nc-ccot.agr.ca; Symbol: OLAG – Librarian, Dorothy Drew
Board of Education for the City of London - Education Centre Professional Library, 1250 Dundas St., London ON N5W 5P2 – 519/452-2124; Fax: 519/455-7648; Email: greigpa@epo.gov.on.ca – Librarian, Patricia Grieg
Brescia College - Library, 1285 Western Rd., London ON N6G 1H2 – 519/432-8353; Fax: 519/679-6489; Symbol: OLBR – Librarian, Christine Suokaite
Children's Psychiatric Research Institute – Dr. Joseph Pozonyi Memorial Library, 600 Sanitorium Rd., London ON N6H 3W7 – 519/471-2540 – Library Supervisor, Alexander Lyubechansky
College of Family Physicians of Canada - Canadian Library of Family Medicine, University of Western Ontario, Natural Sciences Centre, Rm. 170C, London ON N6A 5B7 – 519/661-3170; Fax: 519/661-3880; Email: clfm@julian.uwo.ca; Symbol: OLUCL – Director, Library Services, Lynn Dunikowski
Cross Cultural Learner Centre – Resource Library, 617 Dundas St. East, London ON N5W 2Z1 – 519/660-8850; Fax: 519/660-6168 – Librarian, MaryAnn Kennard
Fanshawe College - Library, PO Box 4005, London ON N5W 5H1 – 519/452-4240; Fax: 519/452-4473; URL: http://www.franshawec.on.ca; Symbol: OLFC
   Manager, Library Services, A.K. Frost
   Acquisitions/Cataloguing, Technical Services & Systems Librarian, Vicky Mok
   Circulation/Reference, Public Services Librarian, Suzanne O'Neill, Email: oneills@admin.fanshawec.on.ca
   Media Services, Librarian, Elaine Vitali
Faxon Canada Ltd. - Reference Library, PO Box 2382, London ON N6A 5A7 – 519/472-1005; Fax: 519/472-1072; Email: stuart@faxon.ca – S. Silcox
Fenco MacLaren Inc. - Library, 320 Adelaide St. South, London ON N5Z 3L2 – 519/686-5711; Fax: 519/686-5770 – Library Manager, Jennifer McNenly
Huron College - Silcox Memorial Library, 1349 Western Rd., London ON N6G 1H3 – 519/438-7224, ext.213; Fax: 519/438-3938 – Chief Librarian, Pamela MacKay
King's College - Cardinal Carter Library, 266 Epworth Ave., London ON N6A 2M3 – 519/433-3491, ext.504; Fax: 519/433-0070; Toll Free: 1-800-265-4406; Email: clouston@julian.uwo.ca
   Chief Librarian, Dr. John S. Clouston
   Assistant Librarian/Systems Manager, Linda Whidden, 519/433-3491, ext.506
   Coordinator: Circulation, Toni Barrette, 519/433-3491, ext.505
   Public Services Librarian, Susan Evans, 519/433-3491, ext.327

Labatt Breweries of Canada - Labatt Library Services, PO Box 5050, London ON N6A 4M3 – 519/667-7355; Fax: 519/667-7473
   Manager, Maryanne MacDonald
   Assistant Librarian, Leslee Eden, 519/667-7242
London Chamber of Commerce – Library, 244 Pall Mall St., PO Box 3295, London ON N6A 5P6 – 519/432-7551 – Information Services, Kathy MacIssac
The London Free Press - Editorial Library, 369 York St., PO Box 2280, London ON N6A 4G1 – 519/667-4559 (Reference Library); Fax: 519/667-4528; Email: library@lfpress.com – Librarian, Anita McCallum, 519/679-1111, ext.2097, Email: amccallu@lfpress.com
London Psychiatric Hospital – George E. Jenkins Library, 850 Highbury Ave., PO Box 2532, London ON N6A 4H1 – 519/455-5110, ext.2167; Fax: 519/455-9986; Symbol: OLPH – Librarian, Mai Why
London Regional Resource Centre for Heritage & the Environment – Public Resource Centre, 1017 Western Rd., London ON N6G 1G5 – 519/645-2845 – Librarian, Ann Liberidge
McKenzie Nash Bryant Law Office - Library, 300 Dundas St., PO Box 3120, London ON N6A 4J4 – 519/672-5660; Fax: 519/672-2674 – Librarian, Pat Hodgins
Middlesex Law Association – Library, 80 Dundas St., PO Box 5600, London ON N6A 2P3 – 519/679-7046 – Law Librarian, Cynthia Simpson
Ontario Petroleum Institute Inc. – Library, #104, 555 Southdale Rd. East, London ON N6E 1A2 – 519/680-1620
Orthodox Missionary Church of Canada – Bishop Matthaios Library, Sts. Cyril & Methodius Parish, #514, 186 King St., London ON N6A 1C7 – 519/438-0734
St. Joseph's Health Centre of London - Library Services, 268 Grosvenor St., London ON N6A 4V2 – 519/646-6000, ext.4439; Fax: 519/646-6006; Symbol: OLSJ – Manager, Library Services, Louise Lin
St. Peter's Seminary - A.P. Mahoney Library, 1040 Waterloo St. North, London ON N6A 3Y1 – 519/432-1824, 439-3963; Fax: 519/439-5172; Symbol: OLSP
   Chief Librarian, Lois Côté
   Reference Librarian, Frances Theilade
   Secretary/Library Assistant, Rita Ulrich
University Hospital – Library Services, 339 Windermere Rd., London ON N6A 5A5 – 519/663-3300, ext.5865; Fax: 519/663-3743 – Chief Librarian, Jan Figurski
University of Western Ontario - Library System, The D.B. Weldon Library, London ON N6A 3K7 – 519/679-2111; Fax: 519/661-3911; Email: ENVOY: ADMIN/UWO.LIBRARY
   Director of Libraries, Catherine Quinlan
   Acquisitions, Head, Linda Lutz
   Cataloguing, Head, Wendy Kennedy
   Public Services, Head, Mary Ann Mavrinac
   The J.J. Talman Regional Collection & Special Collections, Head, John Lutman
   Allyn & Betty Taylor Library, Acting Head, Lila Heilbrunn, Email: ENVOY: ILL.SCI.UWO
   Business Library & Information Centre, Head, Jerry Mulcahy
   Education Library, Head, Claire Callaghan
   Engineering Library, Head, Eeva Munoz, Email: ENVOY: ILL.ENG.UWO
   John & Dotsa Bitove Family Law Library, Head, George Robinson
   Music Library, Head, William Guthrie
   Collections Management, Coordinator, Jane Pearce Baldwin
University of Western Ontario Symphony Orchestra – UWO Music Library, Faculty of Music, University of Western Ontario, 1151 Richmond St. North, London ON N6A 3K7 – 519/661-2043 – Betty Tracy

Canadian Almanac & Directory 1997

Westminster Institute for Ethics & Human Values – Library, 361 Windermere Rd., London ON N6G 2K3 – 519/673-0046 – Librarian, Ms. D. Smith

MAPLE

Ahmadiyya Movement in Islam (Canada) – Reference Library, 10610 Jane St., Maple ON L6A 1S1 – 905/832-2669 – Aslam Chaudhary

Anco Chemicals Inc. – Library, 85 Malmo Ct., Box 2, Comp. 13, Maple ON L6A 1R4 – 905/832-2276 – Technical Manager, John Humphrey

Ontario Ministry of Natural Resources - Research Library, 10401 Dufferin St., PO Box 5000, Maple ON L6A 1S9 – 905/832-7145; Fax: 905/832-7149; Email: ENVOY: ILL.OMAPFW; Symbol: OMAPFW

Research Library, Head, Helle Arro

Reference, Technician, Ann Chalk, 905/832-7101

Technical Services, Librarian, Ginnie Galloway, 905/832-7248

Acquisitions, Technician, Judy Kucopy, 905/832-7100

Ontario Public Buyers Association, Inc. – Electronic Library, PO Box 608, Maple ON L6A 1S5 – 905/356-7521, ext.4300; Email: rmiller@city.niagara-falls.on.ca – Director of Technology, Ray Miller

MARKHAM

Evangelical Fellowship of Canada – Library, PO Box 3745, Markham ON L3S 0Y4 – 905/479-5885 – Bruce Clemenger

FinSec Services Inc. - Library, 2820 - 14 St., Markham ON L3R 0S9 – 905/477-4420; Fax: 905/477-4426 – Reference Librarian, Jonathan Corbett

Gartner Lee Limited – Library, #102, 140 Renfrew Dr., Markham ON L3R 6B3 – 905/477-8400 – Librarian, Bev Foss

International Reference & Serials Library, #21, 90 Nolan Ct., Markham ON L3R 4L9 – 905/946-9588; Fax: 905/946-9590 – Librarian, B. Sethi

Superior Propane - Library, 75 Tiverton Ct., Markham ON L3R 9S3 – 905/475-9200; Fax: 905/940-7409 – Librarian, Eva Costa

Vehicle Information Centre of Canada – Library, #220, 175 Commerce Valley Dr. West, Markham ON L3T 7P6 – 905/764-5560

MERRICKVILLE

Canadian Recreational Canoeing Association – Library, 446 Main St. West, PO Box 5000, Merrickville ON K0G 1N0 – 613/269-2910 – Nancy Gough

Ontario Ministry of the Solicitor General & Correctional Services - Rideau Correctional/Treatment Centre Library, RR#3, Merrickville ON K0G 1N0 – 613/269-4771, ext.267; Fax: 613/269-3583 – Library Technician, Elizabeth Smith

MIDLAND

Deacon, Taws, Friend Law Office - Library, 476 Elizabeth St., PO Box 247, Midland ON L4R 4K8 – 705/526-3791; Fax: 705/526-2688 – Paul Marley

Huronia Historical Parks - Resource Centre, PO Box 160, Midland ON L4R 4K8 – 705/526-7838; Fax: 705/526-9193; Symbol: OMIH – Sandra Saddy

Industrial Research & Development Institute – Library, 355 Cranston Cres., PO Box 518, Midland ON L4R 4L3 – 705/526-2163 – Jeannie Tilson

MILLBROOK

Ontario Ministry of the Solicitor General & Correctional Services - Millbrook Correctional Centre Library, PO Box 300, Millbrook ON L0A 1G0 – 705/932-2624; Fax: 705/932-2962 – Library Technician, Margaret Monis

MILTON

Halton County Law Association – Courthouse Library, 491 Steeles Ave. East, Milton ON L9T 1Y7 – 905/878-1272 – Librarian, Betty Dykstra

Information Milton – Library, 311 Commerical St., Milton ON L9T 3Z9 – 905/876-4365 – Coordinator, Sue McCormack

Ontario Ministry of the Solicitor General & Correctional Services - Maplehurst Correctional Centre Library, 661 Martin St., PO Box 10, Milton ON L9T 2Y3 – 905/878-8141, ext.273; Fax: 905/878-1572 – Library Technician, Jutta Legler

MISSISSAUGA

ORTECH Corporation – Business Resource Centre, Sheridan Science & Technology Park, 2395 Speakman Dr., Mississauga ON L5K 1B3 – 905/822-4111 – Suzanne Carlaw

Abitibi-Price Inc. - Technology Centre Library, Sheridan Park, 2240 Speakman Dr., Mississauga ON L5K 1A9 – 905/822-4770, ext.212; Fax: 905/823-9651; Symbol: OMABP – Librarian, Gina Grassi

Allelix Biopharmaceuticals Inc. - Information Centre, 6850 Goreway Dr., Mississauga ON L4V 1V7 – 905/677-0831; Fax: 905/677-9595; Symbol: OMAI

Library Information Specialist, Daphne Bruce, Email: dbruce@ftn.net

Library Technician, Sureena Dhillon

Allergy Asthma Information Association – Library, 30 Eglinton Ave. West, Mississauga ON L5R 3E7 – 905/712-2242

Atomic Energy of Canada Limited-AECL-CANDU - Mississauga Laboratory – Information Resources Centre, 2251 Speakman Dr., Mississauga ON L5K 1B2 – 905/823-9060, ext.5002; Fax: 905/823-8229; Email: scottl@candu.aecl.ca; Symbol: OTAE – Specialist, Information Management, Laurie J. Scott

Canadian International Power Services Inc. – Library, #400, 2233 Argentia Rd., Mississauga ON L5N 2X7 – 905/858-8020 – Head Librarian, Helen Marshall

Canadian Islamic Organization Inc. – Library, 2069 Kempton Park Dr., Mississauga ON L5M 2Z4 – 905/820-4655 – Public Services Librarian, Rayed Abou-Hawtash

Canadian Marfan Association – Resource Centre, 4216 Pheasant Run, Mississauga ON L5L 2B9 – 416/393-7056 – Sharon Gaylor

Canadian Plastics Institute – Technical Information Resource Centre, #515, 5925 Airport Rd., Mississauga ON L4V 1W1 – 905/612-9997 – Librarian, Sally Press

Canadian Society for Nondestructive Testing, Inc. – Library, #7, 966 Pantera Dr., Mississauga ON L4W 2S1 – 905/238-4846 – Office Administrator, Angie Giglio

Canadian Trotting Association – Standardbred Canada Library, 2150 Meadowvale Blvd., Mississauga ON L5N 6R6 – 905/858-3060 – Librarian, Elynne Lewis

CanTox Inc. – Library, #308, 2233 Argentia Rd., Mississauga ON L5N 2X7 – 905/542-2900 – Librarian, Sandra Stewart

College of Family Physicians of Canada – Library, 2630 Skymark Ave., Mississauga ON L4W 5A4 – 905/629-0900 – Librarian, Robert Melrose

Cominco Ltd. Product Technology Centre - Gerald P. Lewis Library, 2380 Speakman Dr., Mississauga ON L5K 1B4 – 905/822-2022; Fax: 905/822-2882; Symbol: OMCS

Technical Information Specialist, Pat Doyle

Library Technician, Vera Rodic

Community Living Mississauga – Knowledge Network, Mississauga Central Library, 2444 Hurontario St., 3rd. Fl., Mississauga ON L5B 2V1 – 905/615-3500

Credit Institute of Canada – Library, #501, 5090 Explorer Dr., Mississauga ON L4W 3T9 – 905/629-9805

The Credit Valley Hospital – Dr. Keith G. MacDonald Health Sciences Library, 2200 Eglinton Ave. West, Mississauga ON L5M 2N1 – 905/820-2411; Fax: 905/820-4101 – Librarian, Alexander Lyubechansky

DuPont Canada Inc. - Central Library, PO Box 2300, Stn Streetsville, Mississauga ON L5M 2J4 – 905/821-5782; Fax: 905/821-5519; Symbol: OMDC – Caren Larner, Email: caren.larner@conoco.dupont.com

Free Methodist Church in Canada – Library, 4315 Village Centre Ct., Mississauga ON L4Z 1S2 – 905/848-2600

General Electric Canada Inc. - Corporate Library, 2300 Meadowvale Blvd., Mail Drop T30, Mississauga ON L5N 5P9 – 905/858-5227; Fax: 905/858-5234 – Head Librarian, Lori Lyle

Glaxo Canada Inc. - Information Centre, 7333 Mississauga Rd. North, Mississauga ON L5N 6L4 – 905/819-3000, ext.6018; Fax: 905/819-3096; Email: ILL.OTGX; Symbol: OTGX

Manager, Helen Kern

Library Technician, Liz Antochin

Information Analyst, Dianna Rodgers

Library Technician, Marion Greer

Golder Associates Ltd. – Library, 2180 Meadowvale Blvd., Mississauga ON L5N 5S3 – 905/567-4444, ext.205; Symbol: OMGA – Librarian, Mira Wrezel

Goodfellow Consultants Inc., #160, 7070 Mississauga Rd., Mississauga ON L5N 7G2 – 905/858-4424; Toll Free: 1-800-649-4424 – Ana Liberatori

Heating, Refrigerating & Air Conditioning Institute of Canada – Library, Bldg. 11, #300, 5045 Orbitor Dr., Mississauga ON L4W 4Y4 – 905/602-4700

Hoffmann-La Roche Ltd. - Corporate Library, 2455 Meadowpine Blvd., Mississauga ON L5N 6L7 – 905/542-5542; Fax: 905/542-7130; Symbol: OMHL

Manager, Corporate Information, Colin Hoare

Circulation Librarian, Nancy Millwood

ICI Forest Products – Research Library, Sheridan Park Research Centre, 2101 Hadwen Rd., Mississauga ON L5K 2L3 – 905/403-2726; Fax: 905/823-0044; Email: morgant@hookup.net; Symbol: OMCILCR – Library Services Coordinator, Tracy Morgan

Inco Limited - J. Roy Gordon Research Laboratory, 2060 Flavelle Blvd., Mississauga ON L5K 1Z9 – 905/403-2487; Fax: 905/403-2401; Symbol: OMIN

Research Librarian, Janet MacLachlan

Library Technologist, Diane Baksa

Mississauga Heritage Foundation Inc. – Library, #1055, 300 City Centre Dr., Mississauga ON L5B 3C9 – 905/272-1432

Northern Telecom Limited - Information Resource Centre, 3 Robert Speck Parkway, Mississauga ON L4Z 3C8 – 905/897-9000; Fax: 905/566-3332 – Jo-Anne Wong

OMF International - Canada – OMF Archives, 5759 Coopers Ave., Mississauga ON L4Z 1R9 – 416/489-4660; Email: dmichell@cproject.com – OMF Ontario Director, Dr. David Michell

Peel Board of Education - J.A. Turner Professional Library, 5650 Hurontario St., Mississauga ON L5R 1C6 – 905/890-1010, ext.2583; Fax: 905/890-4780; Toll Free: 1-800-668-1146

Librarian, Dr. Catherine Wilkins

Information Resources Technician, Marsha Hunt

Petro-Canada - Products/Lubricants Research & Development Library, 2489 North Sheridan Way, Mississauga ON L5K 1A8 – 905/896-6726; Fax: 905/896-6740 – Library Administrator, Jane McAndless

Revenue Canada - Research & Library Services, 77 City Centre Dr., PO Box 6000, Mississauga ON L5A 4E9 – 905/803-7400; Fax: 905/566-6018; Symbol: OMRCT – Librarian, Maureen Reeves

Xerox Research Centre of Canada - Technical Information Centre, 2660 Speakman Dr., Mississauga ON L5K 2L1 – 905/823-7091; Fax: 905/822-7022; Email: sidey.xrcc@xerox.com; Symbol: OMX Manager, Technical Information Centre, Carolyne Sidey

Senior Technical Information Assistant, Gisela Smithson

MOOSONEE

Northern College of Applied Arts & Technology - James Bay Education Centre - Library Resource Centre, PO Box 130, Moosonee ON P0L 1Y0 – 705/336-2913; Fax: 705/336-2393 – Librarian, Diana Doxtdator

MORRISBURG

Upper Canada Village - Reference Library, RR#1, Morrisburg ON K0C 1X0 – 613/543-3704; Fax: 613/543-7847; Symbol: OMUC – Librarian/Archivist, Jack Schecter

NAPANEE

Lennox & Addington Law Association - Courthouse Library, 167 Adelphi St., Napanee ON K7R 1T6 – Librarian, Carol Sirman, 613/354-5469

NEPEAN

Algonquin College - Woodroffe Campus Resource Centre, Nepean ON K2G 1V8 – 613/727-4723, ext.7713; Fax: 613/727-7684 – Jocelyne Chaperon-Beck

Canadian Federation of Humane Societies – Library, #102, 30 Concourse Gate, Nepean ON K2E 7V7 – 613/224-8072 – Gail Dellaire

Carleton Board of Education - Resource Centre, 133 Greenbank Rd., Nepean ON K2H 6L3 – 613/721-1820, ext.432; Fax: 613/820-6968; Symbol: OOCBE – Library Supervisor, Joanne Larocque

Environment Canada - Environmental Conservation Branch - Library, 49 Camelot Dr., Nepean ON K1A 0H3 – 613/952-2406; Fax: 613/952-9027; Symbol: OOECW – Acting Librarian, Carol A. Bentley

Gandalf Canada - Library, 130 Colonnade Rd., Nepean ON K2E 7M4 – 613/274-6500; Fax: 613/274-6501; URL: http://www.gandalf.ca; Symbol: OOGDC – Corporate Librarian, Dawna Kluver, 613/274-6500, ext.8783, Email: dkluver@gandalf.ca

The Naval Officers Association of Canada – Library, 72 Robertson Rd., PO Box 26083, Nepean ON K2H 9R6 – 613/224-7577 – National Archivist, Laurie Farrington

Organization of Military Museums of Canada, Inc. – Canadian War Museum Library, 72 Robertson Rd., PO Box 26106, Nepean ON K2H 9R6 – 613/829-0280 – Librarian, Jean Langdon-Ford

Professional Institute of The Public Service of Canada – Library, 53 Auriga Dr., Nepean ON K2E 8C3 – 613/228-6310; Toll Free: 1-800-267-0446 – Head, Research, Kathryn Brookfield

R.A. Vanier Law Office - Library, 90 Centrepointe Dr., Nepean ON K2G 6B1 – 613/226-3336; Fax: 613/226-8767 – Assistant, Jodi Dean

Russian Literary Association – Library, 19 Homestead St., Nepean ON K2E 7N9 – 613/725-3424 – Office Manager, J. Harris

Shooting Federation of Canada – Library, 45 Shirley Blvd., Nepean ON K2K 2W6 – 613/828-7338 – Technical Director, Jocelyn Langlois

NEW LISKEARD

École St-Michel - Bibliothèque, New Liskeard ON P0J 1P0 – 705/647-6614 – Bibliotechnicienne, Thérèse Benoit

New Liskeard College of Agricultural Technology - Northern Ontario Agricultural Resource Centre, New Liskeard ON P0J 1P0 – 705/647-6738, ext.2538; Fax: 705/647-7008 – Librarian, Corinna Hoogenhoud

NEWMARKET

Toronto Society of Model Engineers – TSME Library, 166 Millard Ave., Newmarket ON L3Y 1Y9 – 416/534-0550 – Librarian, Steve Estok

NIAGARA FALLS

Acres International Limited - Library, 5259 Dorchester Rd., PO Box 1001, Niagara Falls ON L2E 6W1 – 905/374-5200, ext.5247; Fax: 905/374-1157; Symbol: ONFA – Librarian, Marion D'Amboise, Email: mdamboise@nf.acres.com

Arcturus Environmental - Division of Conor Pacific Environmental Technologies Inc. – Library, 7900 Canadian Dr., Niagara Falls ON L2E 6S5 – 905/357-6424

Greater Niagara General Hospital – Health Sciences Library, 5546 Portage Rd., PO Box 1018, Niagara Falls ON L2E 6X2 – 905/358-4937, ext.3470; Email: jdunn@freenet.npiec.on.ca – Library Technician, John Dunn

Martin, Sheppard, Fraser Law Office - Library, 4607 Huron St., PO Box 900, Niagara Falls ON L2E 6V7 – 905/354-1611; Fax: 905/354-5540; Toll Free: 1-800-263-2502 – Debbie Miller

Niagara College - Hospitality & Tourism Centre, 5881 Dunn St., Niagara Falls ON L2J 2N9 – 905/374-7454, ext.3605; Fax: 905/374-1116

Niagara Parks Botanical Gardens - School of Horticulture - C.H. Henning Library, PO Box 150, Niagara Falls ON L2E 6T2 – 905/356-8554; Fax: 905/356-5488 – Library Technician, Ruth Stoner

NIAGARA ON THE LAKE

Niagara Historical Research Centre, c/o Niagara on the Lake Public Library, 26 Queen St., Rear, PO Box 430, Niagara on the Lake ON L0S 1J0 – 905/468-2023; Fax: 905/468-3334; Email: lgula@freenet.niagara.com; Symbol: EBNL
Chief Librarian, Gerda Molson
Local History Librarian, Linda Gula
Reference Librarian, Linda Potter
Circulation Librarian, Gerrie Barnim

NORTH BAY

AIDS Committee of North Bay & Area – Library, #202, 240 Algonquin Ave., North Bay ON P1B 4V9 – 705/497-3560 – Secretary-Receptionist, Kerry Powers

Canadian Centre for Social Justice – Library, #201, 348 Fraser St., North Bay ON P1B 3W7 – 705/495-8887 – Deborah Brewer

Education Centre - Library, PO Box 5002, North Bay ON P1B 8L7 – 705/474-3450, ext.4220; Fax: 705/497-1455; Email: ENVOY: ONBNU or ONBCC
Director, Library Services, Brian Nettlefold
Associate Director, Barbara Lee

Nipissing District Law Association – The Court House Library, 360 Plouffe St., North Bay ON P1B 9L5 – 705/495-3271(am only); Symbol: NIPI

North Bay Literacy Council – Library, 1000 High St., North Bay ON P1B 6S6 – 705/472-2420 – Louise Cicci

North Bay Psychiatric Hospital – Library, PO Box 3010, North Bay ON P1B 8L1 – 705/474-1200

North Bay Symphony Orchestra – Library, #106, 269 Main St. West, North Bay ON P1B 2T8 – 705/494-7744 – Librarian, Judy Statham

The Nugget Newspaper - Library, PO Box 570, North Bay ON P1B 8J6 – 705/472-3200; Fax: 705/472-5128 – Librarian, Allison Barrett

Ontario Ministry of the Solicitor General & Correctional Services - Staff Library, 200 - 1 Ave. West, PO Box 4100, North Bay ON P1B 9M3 – 705/494-3397; Fax: 705/494-3398; Symbol: OTCS
Coordinator of Institutional Library Services, Barry Kendall
Information Clerk, Laura Ranger

Ontario Natural Resources Safety Association – ONRSA Resource Library, 690 McKeown Ave., PO Box 2050, North Bay ON P1B 9P1 – 705/474-7233; Toll Free: 1-800-850-5519 – Customer Service Representative, Jocelyne Leroux

OAKVILLE

Appleby College - Library, 540 Lakeshore Rd. West, Oakville ON L6K 3P1 – 905/845-4681; Fax: 905/845-9828 – Chief Librarian, Isabel Hodge

Canadian Golf Foundation – CGF Reference Library, 1333 Dorval Dr., Oakville ON L6J 4Z3 – 905/849-9700 – Administrative Assistant, Debbie Stohes

Monarchist League of Canada – King George III Memorial Library, PO Box 1057, Oakville ON L6J 5E9 – 905/855-7262; Toll Free: 1-800-465-6925 – Dominion Librarian, Claudia Willetts

O'Connor MacLeod Law Office - Library, 700 Kerr St., Oakville ON L6K 3W5 – 905/842-8030; Fax: 905/842-2460 – Librarian, Ken Watts

Ontario Genealogical Society - Halton-Peel Branch – Library, 2441 Lakeshore Rd. West, PO Box 70030, Oakville ON L6L 6N9 – Librarian, Ruth Holt

Smith Kline Beecham Pharma Inc. – Medical Library, 2030 Bristol Circle, Oakville ON L6H 5V2 – 905/829-2030, ext.291; Fax: 905/829-3907 – Librarian, Jan Hillis

OHSWEKEN

Economic Development for Canadian Aboriginal Women – Resource Centre, PO Box 185, Ohsweken ON N0A 1M0 – 519/445-2912

ORILLIA

Crawford, Worling, McKenzie & Donnelly Law Office - Library, 40 Coldwater St. E., PO Box 520, Orillia ON L3V 6K4 – 705/325-2753; Fax: 705/325-4913 – Karen L. Wilford

Georgian College - Orillia Campus Learning Resources Centre, 825 Memorial Ave., PO Box 2316, Orillia ON L3V 6S2 – 705/325-2705, ext.3051; Fax: 705/325-3690; Email: ENVOY: GEO.ILL.OR; Symbol: OORIGC – Campus/Systems Librarian, Jennifer Varcoe

Ontario Ministry of Community & Social Services - Huronia Regional Centre Library, PO Box 1000, Orillia ON L3V 6L2 – 705/326-7361, ext. 2441; Fax: 705/326-3445; Symbol: OOHUR – Maureen Maguire

Ontario Provincial Police - General Headquarters Library, 777 Memorial Ave., Orillia ON L3V 7V3 – 705/329-6886; Fax: 705/329-6887; Symbol: OOP – Librarian, Sandra Saddy, Email: saddysa@epo.gov.on.ca

Orillia Soldiers' Memorial Hospital – Library, 170 Colborne St. West, Orillia ON L3V 2Z3 – 705/325-2201 – Dir., Devel. & Library Service, Christie Whitman

ORLEANS

Advocacy Group for the Environmentally Sensitive – Library, 1887 Chaine Ct., Orleans ON K1C 2W6 – 613/830-5722 – Librarian, Claudette Guibord

OSHAWA

Christian Record Services Inc. – Lending Library for the Blind, #119, 1300 King St. East, Oshawa ON L1H 8N9 – 905/436-6938

Creighton, Victor, Alexander, Hayward & Morison Law Office - Library, 235 King St. East, PO Box 26010, Oshawa ON L1H 8R4 – 905/723-3446; Fax: 905/432-2323

Durham College - Main Library, 2000 Simcoe St. North, PO Box 385, Oshawa ON L1H 7L7 – 905/721-3082 – Director, Learning Resources, Susan Barclay-Pereira

Information Oshawa – Resource Centre, #204A, 419 King St. West, Oshawa ON L1J 2KS – 905/434-4636

Kingsway College & High School - Library, 1200 Leland Rd., Oshawa ON L1K 2H4 – 905/433-1144, ext.267; Fax: 905/433-1156 – Librarian, Carroll Ryan

Ontario Energy/Environment Caucus of the Ontario Environment Network – Library, PO Box 953, Oshawa ON L1H 7N1 – 905/404-1344

Ontario Ministry of Finance - Library Services - Oshawa, 33 King St. West, PO Box 627, Oshawa ON L1H 8H5 – 905/433-6136; Fax: 905/433-6037; Symbol: OTREV
   Group Leader, Wendy Craig, 905/433-6135, Email: craigw@gov.on.ca
   Senior Library Technician, Penni Lee

Oshawa-Durham Symphony Orchestra – Library, PO Box 444, Oshawa ON L1H 7L5 – 905/683-2680 – Librarian, Mr. Leslie Siklos

Oshawa General Hospital – Library, 24 Alma St., Oshawa ON L1G 2B9 – 905/576-8711, ext.3334/3567; Email: library@hospital.oshawa.on.ca – Director of Library Services, Susan E. Hendricks

OTTAWA

Aboriginal Nurses Association of Canada – Library, #133, 1785 Alta Vista Dr., Ottawa ON K1G 3Y6 – 613/733-1555 – Anna White

Academy of Medicine, Ottawa – Library, #1, 1867 Alta Vista Dr., PO Box 8223, Ottawa ON K1G 3H7 – 613/733-2604

Agriculture & Agri-Food Canada - Canadian Agriculture Library, Sir John Carling Bldg., 930 Carling Ave., Ottawa ON K1A 0C5 – 613/995-7829; Fax: 613/952-3813; Email: ago420492@ncccot.agr.ca; Symbol: OOAG
   Director, Victor Desroches, Email: desrochesv@ncccot.agr.ca
   Systems & Network Services, Librarian, Danielle Jacques
   Acquisition Services, Chief, Janet Stitt
   Technical Services, Chief, Julia Goodman
   Public Services, Chief, Emil Daniel
   Technical Services & Regional Liaison, Assistant Director, Mae Cutler, Email: cutlerm@ncccot.agr.ca
   Canadian Agriculture Library, C.E.F. Research Library, K.W. Neatby Bldg., Rm. 4061, Ottawa ON K1A 0C6 – 613/996-1665; Fax: 613/995-1823; Email: lbooage@ncccot.agr.ca; Symbol: OOAGE – Librarian, Susan Sherman
   Canadian Agriculture Library, Animal Diseases Research Institute, 3851 Fallowfield Rd., Ottawa ON K2H 8P9 – 613/998-9320; Fax: 613/952-2285; Email: lbooaga@ncccot.agr.ca; Symbol: OOAGA – Librarian, Linda Hopson

Agudath Israel Congregation - Malca Pass Library, 1400 Coldrey Ave., Ottawa ON K1Z 7P9 – 613/728-3501 – Librarian, Frieda Lauterman

Algonquin College - Rideau Campus Resource Centre, 200 Lees Ave., Ottawa ON K1S 0C5 – 613/727-4723, ext. 3332 – B. Fraser

Alliance canadienne des responsables et enseignants en français (Langue maternelle) – Bibliothèque, Faculté d'éducation, Université d'Ottawa, 145, rue Jean-Jacques Lussier, CP 415, Ottawa ON K1N 6N5 – 613/562-5800, ext.4144

Alliance of Manufacturers & Exporters Canada - Ottawa Office – Library, #250, 99 Bank St., Ottawa ON K1P 6B9 – 613/238-8888, ext.224; Email: michelle_amyotte@the-alliance.com – Michelle Amyotte

American Research & Documentation Center, United States Embassy, 150 Wellington St., 3rd Fl., Ottawa ON K1P 5A4 – 613/238-4470, ext.391; Fax: 613/563-7701; Email: refott@usia.gov; URL: http://www.usis-canada.usia.gov; Symbol: OOUSI
   Centre Director, Kyle Malone Ward, 613/238-4470, ext.321
   Reference Librarian, Allison Abraszko, 613/238-4470, ext.311
   Reference Librarian, Gail McKeating, 613/238-4470, ext.391

Assembly of First Nations – Resource Centre, #1002, 1 Nicholas St., Ottawa ON K1N 7B7 – 613/241-6789 – Coordinator, Kelly Whiteduck

Association des enseignantes et des enseignants franco-ontariens – Bibliothèque, 681 Belfast Rd., Ottawa ON K1G 0Z4 – 613/244-2336

Association for Baha'i Studies – Library, 34 Copernicus St., Ottawa ON K1N 7K4 – 613/233-1903 – Librarian, Betty Butterill

Association for the Export of Canadian Books – Library, #504, One Nicholas St., Ottawa ON K1N 7B7 – 613/562-2324 – Information Officer, Sue Stewart

Association of Canadian Community Colleges – Information Resource Centre, #200, 1223 Michael St. North, Ottawa ON K1J 7T2 – 613/746-2222 – Contact, Ginette Bourdon

Association of Canadian Distillers – Library, #1100, 90 Sparks St., Ottawa ON K1P 5T8 – 613/238-8444; TLX: 0533783 – Information Specialist, Sandi Bokij

Association of Consulting Engineers of Canada – Library, #616, 130 Albert St., Ottawa ON K1P 5G4 – 613/236-0569

Association of Public Service Financial Administrators (Ind.) – Library, #302, 666 Kirkwood Ave., Ottawa ON K1Z 5X9 – 613/728-0695 – Peter Seguin

Association of Universities & Colleges of Canada – Library, #600, 350 Albert St., Ottawa ON K1R 1B1 – 613/563-1236; TLX: 053-3329; Symbol: OOCU – Reference Librarian, Susan Robert

Atomic Energy Control Board - Library, 280 Slater St., PO Box 1046, Ottawa ON K1P 5S9 – 613/995-7120; Fax: 613/995-5086; Symbol: OOAECB
   Librarian, Jane Naisbitt
   Circulation Technician, Carole Blais, 613/995-1359
   Acquisitions Librarian, Frank Rauterkranz, 613/995-2060
   Proprietary Library, Mary Didyk, 613/992-8292

Atomic Energy of Canada Limited - Library, 344 Slater St., Ottawa ON K1A 0S4 – 613/237-3270, ext.5138; Fax: 613/782-2065; Symbol: OOAECL

Bank of Canada - Library, 234 Wellington St., Ottawa ON K1A 0G9 – 613/782-8466; Fax: 613/782-7387; URL: http://www.bank-banque-canada.ca/library; Symbol: OOB – Chief Librarian, Carly Hunt

Biosystematics Research Centre – Plant Research Library, #219, W.M. Saunders Bldg., Ottawa ON K1A 0C6 – 613/996-1665; Fax: 613/995-1823; Symbol: ODAGB – Librarian, Eva Gavora

Brewers Association of Canada – Library, Heritage Place, #1200, 155 Queen St., Ottawa ON K1P 6L1 – 613/232-9601; Symbol: OOBA – Librarian, Ed Gregory

Buchan, Lawton, Parent Ltd. – Library, 5370 Canotek Rd., Ottawa ON K1J 9E6 – 613/748-3762 – Researcher, Carol Ann Hinde

Bytown Railway Society – Library, PO Box 141, Ottawa ON K1N 8V1 – 613/745-1201 – Archivist, Richard Bonnycastle

CAL Corporation - Information Resource Centre, 1050 Morrison Dr., Ottawa ON K2H 8K7 – 613/820-8280; Fax: 613/820-8314; Email: ENVOY: CAL.IRC; Symbol: 125-OOCAA – Library Administrative Assistant, Sandra Spence, 613/820-8280, ext.1149

The Canada Council - Library, 99 Metcalfe St., PO Box 1047, Ottawa ON K1P 5V8 – 613/598-4308; Fax: 613/566-4390; Symbol: OOCAC – Librarian, Carol Barton

Canada Labour Relations Board - Research & Reference Centre, C.D. Howe Bldg., 240 Sparks St., 4th Fl. West, Ottawa ON K1A 0X8 – 613/947-5404; Fax: 613/947-5407; Email: ENVOY: ILL.OOLRB; Symbol: OOLRB
   Director, Gloria Anderson
   Deputy Director, Joy Patel

Canada Mortgage & Housing Corporation - Canadian Housing Information Centre, 700 Montreal Rd., Ottawa ON K1A 0P7 – 613/748-2367; Fax: 613/748-4069; Email: LLB.CHIC; Symbol: OOCM
   Manager, Leslie Jones, 613/748-2362
   Chief, Reference Librarian, Deanna MacDonald, 613/748-2363
   Technical Services Librarian, Edward Savic, 613/748-2371

Canada Ports Corporation - Business Information Centre & Library, 99 Metcalfe St., Ottawa ON K1A 0N6 – 613/957-6778; Fax: 613/995-3501; Symbol: OOPOR – Librarian, Sylvia Hodel

Canada Post Corporation - Corporate Library, #N0080, 2701 Riverside Dr., Ottawa ON K1A 0B1 – 613/734-7928; Fax: 613/734-7558; Symbol: OOPO – Corporate Librarian, Bruce Moreland

Canadian Association of Chiefs of Police – Library, #1908, 112 Kent St., Ottawa ON K1P 5P2 – 613/233-1106 – Librarian, Laurie Farrell

The Canadian Association of Family Resource Programs – Library, #205, 120 Holland Ave., Ottawa ON K1Y 0X6 – 613/728-3307 – Project Manager, Maureen Kellerman

Canadian Association of Independent Living Centres – Library, #1004, 350 Sparks St., Ottawa ON K1R 7S8 – 613/563-2581 – Services & Development Consultant, Michael Herne

Canadian Association of Occupational Therapists – Library, Carleton Technology & Training Centre, #3400, 1125 Colonel By Dr., Ottawa ON K1S 5R1 – 613/523-2268; Toll Free: 1-800-434-2268 – Executive Director, Anne Strickland

Canadian Association of the Deaf – Library, #205, 2435 Holly Lane, Ottawa ON K1V 7P2 – 613/526-4785

Canadian Association of University Teachers – Library, 2675 Queensview Dr., Ottawa ON K2B 8K2 – 613/820-2270

Canadian Automobile Association – Library, #200, 1145 Hunt Club Rd., Ottawa ON K1V 0Y3 – 613/247-0117 – Rosalinda Weisbrod

Canadian Broadcasting Corporation - Documentation Centre/Centre de documentation, PO Box 3220, Ottawa ON K1Y 1E4 – 613/724-5075; Fax: 613/724-5074 – Responsable, Louise Petitclerc

Canadian Bureau for International Education – Library, #1100, 220 Laurier Ave. West, Ottawa ON K1P 5Z9 – 613/237-4820; TLX: 053-3255 – Editor/Publications Manager, Jennifer Humphries

Canadian Centre for Management Development - Management Resource Centre, PO Box 420, Ottawa ON K1N 8V4 – 819/995-6165; Fax: 819/995-0331; Symbol: OOCCM – Director, Lorraine McQueen

Canadian Centre on Substance Abuse – Library, #300, 75 Albert St., Ottawa ON K1P 5E7 – 613/235-4048 – Margo Hawley

Canadian Chapter of the International Council of Community Churches – Archives, 30 Briermoor Cres., Ottawa ON K1T 3G7 – 613/238-2213 – Bishop, S.A. Thériault

Canadian Child Care Federation – Library, #306, 120 Holland Ave., Ottawa ON K1Y 0X6 – 613/729-5289 – Information Officer, Jennifer Murphy-Hupé

Canadian Co-operative Association – CCA Information Centre, #400, 275 Bank St., Ottawa ON K2P 2L6 – 613/238-6711; Email: carol@coopcca.com – Carol Hunter

Canadian Coalition for High Blood Pressure Prevention & Control – Library, #200, 160 George St., Ottawa ON K1N 9M2 – 613/241-4361, ext.317

Canadian Coast Guard - Fleet Systems Library, Canada Bldg., 344 Slater St., Rm.#737, Ottawa ON K1A 0N7 – 613/998-1801; Fax: 613/993-8659; Symbol: OOTTD – Senior Information Officer, Ginette Dion

Canadian Commercial Corp. - Library, 50 O'Connor St., Ottawa ON K1A 0S6 – 613/996-0034; Fax: 613/995-2121; Email: info@ccc.ca; URL: http://www.ccc.ca – Reference Section, Terry Scott

Canadian Conference of the Arts – Library, 189 Laurier Ave. West, Ottawa ON K1N 6P1 – 613/238-3561; Toll Free: 1-800-463-3561 – Sharon Griffiths

Canadian Conservation Institute – CCI Library, 1030 Innes Rd., Ottawa ON K1A 0M5 – 613/998-3721; Email: alicia.prata@banyan.dgim.doc.c; Symbol: OONMCC – Chief, Library Services, Alicia Prata

Canadian Coordinating Office for Health Technology Assessment – Library, #110, 955 Green Valley Cres., Ottawa ON K2C 3V4 – 613/226-2553 – Librarian, Leigh Ann Topfer

Canadian Council for Multicultural & Intercultural Education – Library, #200, 144 O'Connor St., Ottawa ON K1P 5M9 – 613/233-4916

Canadian Council on Animal Care – Library, Constitution Square, Tower II, #315, 350 Albert St., Ottawa ON K1R 1B1 – 613/238-4031

Canadian Council on International Law – Library, #215, 236 Metcalfe St., Ottawa ON K2P 1R3 – 613/235-0442

Canadian Council on Smoking & Health – National Clearinghouse on Tobacco & Health, #1000, 170 Laurier Ave. West, Ottawa ON K1P 5V5 – 613/567-3050 – Director, John Hamilton

Canadian Criminal Justice Association – Library, #304, 383 Parkdale Ave., Ottawa ON K1Y 4R4 – 613/725-3715

Canadian Dental Association – Library, 1815 Alta Vista Dr., Ottawa ON K1G 3Y6 – 613/523-1770

Canadian Federation of Labour – Library, #300, 107 Sparks St., Ottawa ON K1P 5B5 – 613/234-4141

Canadian Film Institute – Library, 2 Daly Ave., Ottawa ON K1N 6E2 – 613/232-8769 – Film Librarian, Chris Robinson

Canadian General Standards Board – Library, #1402, 222 Queen St., Ottawa ON K1A 1G6 – 613/941-8709, 8703 (Sales Centre); Toll Free: 1-800-665-2472

Canadian Hard of Hearing Association – Clearinghouse, #205, 2435 Holly Lane, Ottawa ON K1V 7P2 – 613/526-1584; Fax: 613/526-4718; Toll Free: 1-800-263-8068 – Special Projects Clerk, Karla Johnston

Canadian Home Care Association – Library, #1005, 350 Sparks St., Ottawa ON K1R 7F8 – 613/569-1585 – Odile Girard

Canadian Home Economics Association – Library, #901, 151 Slater St., Ottawa ON K1P 5H3 – 613/238-8817

Canadian Horticultural Council – Library, #310, 1101 Prince of Wales Dr., Ottawa ON K2C 3W7 – 613/226-4187

Canadian Human Rights Commission - Library, Place de Ville, Tower A, #1413, 320 Queen St., Ottawa ON K1A 1E1 – 613/943-9109; Fax: 613/996-9661; Email: ENVOY: LIBRARY.CHRC; Symbol: OOCHR – Head Librarian, Suzanne Tourigny

Canadian Institute of Financial Accountants – Library, 2380 Holly Lane, 2nd Fl., Ottawa ON K1V 7P2 – 613/521-0620 – Susan Singh

Canadian Institute of Geomatics – Library, #120, 162 Cleopatra Dr., Ottawa ON K2G 5X2 – 613/224-9851 – Susan Pugh

Canadian Intergovernmental Conference Secretariat - Intergovernmental Document Centre, 110 O'Connor St., 10th Fl., PO Box 488, Ottawa ON K1N 8V5 – 613/995-4310; Fax: 613/996-6091; Symbol: OOCIC – Manager, Joan Murphy

Canadian International Trade Tribunal - Library, 333 Laurier Ave. West, Ottawa ON K1A 0G7 – 613/990-2418; Fax: 613/990-2439; Email: ENVOY: SCHULTZ.U; Symbol: OOCITT
Chief Librarian, Ursula Schultz
Library Technician, Marthe Seguin-Muntz

Canadian Labour Congress – Library, 2841 Riverside Dr., Ottawa ON K1V 8X7 – 613/521-3400; TLX: 053-4750; Symbol: OOCLC – Librarian, Nora Lezada Côté

Canadian Livestock Records Corporation – Library, 2417 Holly Lane, Ottawa ON K1V 0M7 – 613/731-7110 – Bruce Hunt

Canadian Meat Council – Library, Dow's Lake Court, #410, 875 Carling Ave., Ottawa ON K1S 5P1 – 613/729-3911

Canadian Medical Association – Library, 1867 Alta Vista Dr., Ottawa ON K1G 3Y6 – 613/731-9331; Toll Free: 1-800-267-9703

Canadian Museum of Nature - Library & Archives, PO Box 3443, Ottawa ON K1P 6P4 – 613/998-3923; Fax: 613/998-1065; Symbol: OONMNS
Chief, Library & Archives, Arch Stewart, 613/998-0092
Reference Librarian, Mireille Boudreau, 613/998-3924
Cataloguer, Patrice Stevenson, 613/998-9517
Archivist, Chantal Dussault, 613/998-1459

Canadian Musical Heritage Society – Library, 50 Rideau St., PO Box 53161, Ottawa ON K1N 1C5 – 613/788-2600, ext.8265 – G. Leclerc

Canadian Nature Federation – Library, #520, One Nicholas St., Ottawa ON K1N 7B7 – 613/562-3447; Toll Free: 1-800-267-4088

Canadian Nurses Association – Helen K. Mussallem Library, 50 Driveway, Ottawa ON K2P 1E2 – 613/237-2133 – Library Manager, Elizabeth Hawkins-Brady

Canadian Organic Growers Inc. – Mail-Lending Library, PO Box 6408, Ottawa ON K2A 3Y6 – 613/256-1848 – Librarian, Brian Woods

Canadian Paediatric Society – Library, Children's Hospital of Eastern Ontario, 401 Smyth Rd., Ottawa ON K1H 8L1 – 613/737-2728 – Publications Coordinator, Louise Painchaud

Canadian Payments Association – Library, #1212, 50 O'Connor St., Ottawa ON K1P 6L2 – 613/238-4173 – Legal Administrator, Debra Dunkerley

Canadian Petroleum Products Institute – Library, #1000, 275 Slater St., Ottawa ON K1P 5H9 – 613/232-3709, ext.217 – Betty Jean Mark

Canadian Pork Council – Library, 75 Albert St., Ottawa ON K1P 5E7 – 613/236-9239 – Executive Secretary, Martin Rice

Canadian Printing Industries Association – Library, #906, 75 Albert St., Ottawa ON K1P 5E7 – 613/236-7208

The Canadian Public Relations Society, Inc. – Library, #720, 220 Laurier Ave. West, Ottawa ON K1P 5Z9 – 613/232-1222 – Pam Bannister

Canadian Radio-Television & Telecommunications Commission - Library, #202, 1, Promenade du Portage, Ottawa ON K1A 0N2 – 819/997-4484; Fax: 819/994-0218
Manager, Library Services, Karla Weys
Acquisitions Librarian, Sheila Roussel, 819/997-4226
Technical Services Librarian, Lorraine Pigeon

The Canadian Red Cross Society – National Office Library, 1800 Alta Vista Dr., Ottawa ON K1G 4J5 – 613/739-2573; TLX: 05-33784 – Ann M. Butryn

Canadian Research Institute for the Advancement of Women – Library, #408, 151 Slater St., Ottawa ON K1P 5H3 – 613/563-0681 – Secretary/Receptionist, Céline Bessette

Canadian Security Intelligence Service - General Information Centre, Ottawa Terminal, PO Box 9732, Ottawa ON K1G 4G4 – 613/782-0021; Fax: 613/782-0705 – Deputy Director General, Mary Joan Dunn

Canadian Society for International Health – Library, #902, 170 Laurier Ave. West, Ottawa ON K1P 5V5 – 613/230-2654, ext.305 – Mary Bridgeo

Canadian Teachers' Federation – George A. Croskery Memorial Library, 110 Argyle Ave., Ottawa ON K2P 1B4 – 613/232-1505 – Program Assistant, Marita Moll

Canadian Tobacco Manufacturers' Council – Information Centre, #701, 99 Bank St., Ottawa ON K1P 6B9 – 613/238-2799; Email: CANTOB.INFO; Symbol: OOCTM – Manager, Information, Philip Gordon

Canadian Tourism Commission - Tourism Reference & Documentation Centre, 235 Queen St., Ottawa ON K1A 0H6 – 613/954-3943; Fax: 613/954-3945; Email: trdc.tsm:ctc@ic.gc.ca; URL: http://www.info.ic.gc.ca; Symbol: OOTB – Chief Librarian, Judith M. Cameron, Email: cameron.judith@ic.gc.ca

Canadian War Museum - Library, 330 Sussex Dr., Ottawa ON K1A 0M8 – 819/776-8609; Fax: 819/776-8623; Symbol: OONMC – Librarian, Jean Langdon-Ford

Canadian Wildlife Federation – Library, 2740 Queensview Dr., Ottawa ON K2B 1A2 – 613/721-2286; Toll Free: 1-800-563-9453 – Education Programs Director, Luba Mycio-Mommers

Canadian Wood Council – Library, #350, 1730 St. Laurent Blvd., Ottawa ON K1G 5L1 – 613/247-7077 – Librarian, Audrey Mattila

Capital Region Centre for the Hearing Impaired – Library, 310 Elmgrove Ave., Ottawa ON K1Z 6V1 – 613/729-1467 (Voice) – Administrative Assistant, Camilla Strickland

Carleton County Law Association – Ottawa Courthouse Library, Ottawa Courthouse, #2004, 161 Elgin St., Ottawa ON K2P 2K1 – 613/233-7386; Symbol: OOCCL

Carleton University - Library, 1125 Colonel By Dr., Ottawa ON K1S 5B6 – 613/788-2735; Fax: 613/788-2750; Email: martin_foss@carleton.ca; Symbol: OOCC
University Librarian, Martin Foss, 613/788-2600, ext.2725
Acquisitions, Head, Gail Catley
Cataloguing, Head, D. Rogers
Circulation, Supervisor, D. Gavin
Documents, Head, S. Jackson
Interlibrary Loans, Head, C. Kelly, 613/788-2732
Map Library, Map Librarian, Barbara Farrell
Reader Services, Head, Elizabeth Knight
Serials, Head, B. Clarke
Special Collections & Archives, Head, Jeremy Palin
Systems & Technical Services, Associate Librarian, T. Clark
Information Services, Associate Librarian, L. Rossman
Administrative Services, Manager, S. Doraty

Catholic Health Association of Canada – Library, 1247 Kilborn Pl., Ottawa ON K1H 6K9 – 613/731-7148 – Technical Services Librarian, Annette Foucault

Child Welfare League of Canada – Canadian Resource Centre on Children & Youth, #312, 180 Argyle Ave., Ottawa ON K2P 1B7 – 613/788-5102 – Elizabeth Bourgue

Children's Hospital of Eastern Ontario – Library Services, 401 Smyth Rd., Ottawa ON K1H 8L1 – 613/737-2206; Fax: 613/738-4806; Email: ENVOY: CHEO.LIB; Symbol: OOCHEO – Library Director, Patricia Johnston

City of Ottawa - Planning & Development Library, 111 Sussex Dr., Ottawa ON K1N 5A1 – 613/564-3095; Fax: 613/564-8077; Symbol: OOCPB
Associate Librarian, Peter McNaughton
Chief Librarian, Evelina Leal

Commissioner of Official Languages - Library, 110 O'Connor St., Ottawa ON K1A 0T8 – 613/995-0403; Fax: 613/993-5082; Email: ac239@frenet.carleton.ca; Symbol: OOCOL – Librarian, Rosemarie Benoit

Commonwealth War Graves Commission - Canadian Agency – Library, #1707, 66 Slater St., Ottawa ON K1A 0P4 – 613/992-3224 – Office Supervisor, Marlene Moffatt

Communications, Energy & Paperworkers Union of Canada (CLC) – Library, 350 Sparks St., 19th Fl., Ottawa ON K1R 1A4 – 613/230-5200, ext.222;

Email: martin@cep.ca – Librarian/Researcher, Martin McGreal

Community Foundation of Ottawa-Carleton – Library, #320, 150 Laurier Ave. West, Ottawa ON K1P 5J4 – 613/236-1616 – Librarian, Anne Ray

Competition Tribunal – Library, 90 Sparks St., 6th Fl., Ottawa ON K1P 5B4 – 613/954-0449; Fax: 613/957-3170; Symbol: OOCOT – Library Manager, Lydia Austin, 613/957-7850

Computing Devices Canada – Technical Library, PO Box 8508, Ottawa ON K1G 3M9 – 613/596-7273; Fax: 613/820-5081; Symbol: OOCDC – Librarian, Elaine Tigges, Email: elaine.tigges@gpo.canada.cdev.com

The Conference Board of Canada – Resource Centre, 255 Smyth Rd., Ottawa ON K1N 6C3 – 613/526-3280; TLX: 053-3343 – Manager, Information Services, Zoë Baxter Buchanan

Conseil de la Coopération de l'Ontario – Bibliothèque, 450 Rideau St., Ottawa ON K1N 5Z4 – 613/789-7777

Consulting & Audit Canada – Information Centre, Place de Ville, Tower B, Room 1736, 112 Kent St., Ottawa ON K1A 0S5 – 613/996-3348; Fax: 613/947-2381; Symbol: OOBMC – Agency Information Centre Officer, Marie-Claire Girouard

Cree Naskapi Commission – Library, Capital Square Bldg., #305, 222 Queen St., Ottawa ON K1P 5V9 – 613/234-4288 – Librarian, Nicole Cheechoo

Defence Research Establishment – Ottawa – Information Services Library, 3701 Carling Ave., Ottawa ON K1A 0Z4 – 613/998-2657; Fax: 613/991-2964; Email: ENVOY: DREO.INFO.SVCS; Symbol: OODRC – Head, Susan G. McIntyre

Dendron Resource Surveys Inc. – Library, #206, 880 Lady Ellen Place, Ottawa ON K1Z 5L9 – 613/725-2971 – Office Manager, Catherine Smyth

Dentistry Canada Fund – Sydney Wood Bradley Library, 1815 Alta Vista Dr., Ottawa ON K1G 3Y6 – 613/523-4770 – Martha Vaughan

Le Droit – Bibliothèque, #222, 47 Clarence St., Ottawa ON K1N 9K1 – 613/562-7747; Fax: 613/562-7539 – Gilles Pilon

E.B. Eddy Forest Products Ltd. – Library, Central Laboratory, 6 Booth St., Ottawa ON K1R 6K8 – 613/782-2645; Fax: 613/782-2515 – Librarian/Secretary, Margaret Jean-Louis

ECS Library, #201, 150 Isabella St., Ottawa ON K1S 5A3 – 613/236-3920; Fax: 613/236-5414

Elections Canada – Library, 1595 Telesat Court, Ottawa ON K1A 0M6 – Fax: 613/954-5880; Toll Free: 1-800-46368683; Symbol: OOELC
 Supervisor, Library, Alain Pelletier
 Assistant to the Supervisor, Library, Tony Coulson

Emergency Preparedness Canada – Library, Jackson Bldg., 122 Bank St., 2nd Fl., Ottawa ON K1A 0W6 – 613/991-7725; Fax: 613/996-0995; Symbol: OOEPC

Federal Court of Canada – Library, Supreme Court Bldg., 90 Sparks St., 12th Fl., Ottawa ON K1A 0H9 – 613/995-1382; Fax: 613/954-7714; Symbol: OOFC
 Head Librarian, Rosalie Fox
 Reference Librarian, Wendy Reynolds, 613/943-0839
 Cataloguing, Systems Librarian, Louise Houston, 613/996-8735
 Collection Development Librarian, Fiona McPherson, 613/947-3906

Fédération des caisses populaires de l'Ontario – Bibliothèque, 450 Rideau St., Ottawa ON K1N 5Z4 – 613/789-7777, poste 622 – Ginette Gagnon

Fédération des communautés francophones et acadienne du Canada – Bibliothèque, #1404, One Nicholas St., Ottawa ON K1N 7B7 – 613/563-0311 – Documentaliste, Micheline Gleixner

Fédération nationale des femmes canadiennes-françaises – Bibliothèque, #525, 325 Dalhousie St., Ottawa ON K1N 7G2 – 613/241-3500

Finance & Treasury Board Canada – Library, 140 O'Connor St., 11th Fl. East, Ottawa ON K1A 0G5 – 613/996-5491; Fax: 613/992-6411; Symbol: OOF – Chief Librarian, Trent Reid

Fisheries & Oceans Canada – Library, 200 Kent St., 10th Fl., Ottawa ON K1A 0E6 – 613/993-2926; Fax: 613/996-9055; Email: ENVOY: DFO.LIB.OTTAWA; Symbol: OOFI – Head, Library Policy & Services, Heather Cameron

Foreign Affairs & International Trade Canada – Legal Library, 125 Sussex Dr., Ottawa ON K1A 0G2 – 613/992-4383; Fax: 613/992-2467; Symbol: OOELB – In Charge, Marilyn McLennan
 Library, Lester B. Pearson Bldg., 125 Sussex Dr., Ottawa ON K1A 0G2 – 613/996-8691; Fax: 613/944-0222; Symbol: OOE

Fresh for Flavour Foundation – Library, #310, 1101 Prince of Wales Dr., Ottawa ON K2C 3W7 – 613/226-4187; Toll Free: 1-800-668-7763 – Administrative Assistant, Jane Proctor

Friends of the Earth – Library, #701, 251 Laurier Ave. West, Ottawa ON K1P 5J6 – 613/230-3352 – Information Officer, Bea Oliver

Fur Institute of Canada – Library, #804, 255 Albert St., Ottawa ON K1P 6A9 – 613/231-7099

Geological Survey of Canada – Canadian Geoscience Information Centre, #350, 601 Booth St., Ottawa ON K1A 0E8 – 613/992-9550; Fax: 613/943-8742; TLX: 053-3117; Email: Library@gsc.emr.ca – Head, Marielle Doyon

Government House – Library, 1 Sussex Dr., Ottawa ON K1A 0A1 – 613/993-5278; Fax: 613/990-7636; Symbol: OOGH – Archivist/Librarian, Sandy Allen

Gowlings – Library, 160 Elgin St., Ottawa ON K1P 1C3 – 613/233-1781; Fax: 613/563-9869, 563-7938 – Librarian, Linda Marchand, 613/233-1781, ext.7335

Health Canada-Environmental Health Directorate – Library, Tunney's Pasture, Environmental Health Centre, Bldg. 8, Ottawa ON K1A 0L2 – 613/957-1725; Symbol: OONHH – Manager, Lorna Adcock

Health Canada-Medical Services Branch – Occupational Health Unit – Library, Tunney's Pasture, Bldg. 17, Ottawa ON K1A 0L3

Health Canada – Health Protection Branch Library Network, Sir Frederick G. Banting Research Centre, Ottawa ON K1A 0L2 – 613/957-1026; Fax: 613/941-6958; Symbol: OONHBR – Chief, Scientific Information & Document Services, Merle McConnell

Heart & Stroke Foundation of Canada – Library, #200, 160 George St., Ottawa ON K1N 9M2 – 237-4361 ext. 225 – Paula Coutts

Hôpital Montfort – Bibliothèque médicale Annie Powers, 713, ch Montréal, Ottawa ON K1K 0T2 – 613/746-4621

Human Rights Institute of Canada – Library, #303, 246 Queen St., Ottawa ON K1P 5E4 – 613/232-2920 – Assistant to the President, Mary Neufeld

Immigration & Refugee Board – Resource Centre, 222 Nepean Rd., Ottawa ON K1A 0K1 – 613/996-0741; Reference: 613/996-0703; Fax: 613/954-1228; Symbol: OOIRB – Coordinator, Katherine Miller

Indian & Northern Affairs Canada – Library, 10 Wellington St., Ottawa ON K1A 0H4 – 613/997-8204; Fax: 613/953-5491; Email: ENVOY: INA.ILL; Symbol: OORD – Departmental Librarian, Sue Hanley

Indian Claims Commission – Library, Enterprise Bldg., #400, 427 Laurier Ave. West, PO Box 1750, Ottawa ON K1P 1A2 – 613/947-0750; Fax: 613/943-0157; Symbol: OOICC – Librarian, Joanne Debassige, Email: JDebassige@IndianClaims.ca

Industry Canada – Communications Research Centre Library, 3701 Carling Ave., PO Box 11490, Ottawa ON K2H 8S2 – 613/998-2202; Fax: 613/998-1216; URL: http://www.crc.doc.ca/library/library.html; Symbol: OORPL
 Manager, Carole Laplante, 613/998-2705
 Circulation & ILL, Jean-Marc Lapointe, 613/998-2202
 Acquisitions Clerk, Miriam Poole, 613/998-2255
 Cataloguer, Ginette Comtois, 613/998-2679
 Journal Towers Library, #1420, 300 Slater St., Ottawa ON K1A 0C8 – 613/941-4943; Fax: 613/990-7016; Symbol: OOCO – Senior Reference Librarian, Monique Perrier
 Library Services, C.D. Howe Library, 235 Queen St., Ottawa ON K1A 0H5 – 613/954-2791; Reference: 613/954-2728; Fax: 613/954-0135; Email: ISTC.LIBRARY; Symbol: OOTC Director, Claire Renaud-Frigon
 Senior Reference Librarian, Nicole Ménard
 Portage Library, Place du Portage, 14th Fl., 50 Victoria St., Ottawa ON K1A 0C9 – 819/997-1632; Fax: 819/997-2378; Email: ENVOY: ILL.OOCI; Symbol: OCI – Senior Reference Librarian, John Marosi

Infertility Awareness Association of Canada – Library, #523, 774 Echo Dr., Ottawa ON K1S 5N8 – 613/730-1322; Toll Free: 1-800-263-2929 – Pamela Lee

Information & Privacy Commissioners of Canada – Library, Place de Ville, Tower B, 112 Kent St., Ottawa ON K1A 1H3 – 613/995-1009; Fax: 613/995-1501; Toll Free: 1-800-267-0441; Symbol: OOIPC
 Head, Library Services, Diane Melski
 Library Technician, Francine Ryan

Institut canadien-français d'Ottawa – Bibliothèque, 316, rue Dalhousie, Ottawa ON K1N 7E7 – 613/241-4469 – Directeur culturel & bibliothécaire, Jean Udvarhelyi

Institute of Speculative Philosophy – Library, PO Box 913, Ottawa ON K1P 5P9 – 613/594-5881

Institute on Governance – Information Resource Centre, 122 Clarence St., Ottawa ON K1N 5P6 – 613/562-0092, ext.229 – Program Officer, Ioanna Sahas

Inter-American Commercial Arbitration Commission – Canadian Section – Library, Canadian Arbitration Centre & Amicable Composition Centre, Inc., Faculty of Law, University of Ottawa, PO Box 450, Ottawa ON K1N 6N5 – 613/564-5939; TLX: 0533338

International Association of Fire Fighters (AFL-CIO/CLC) – Canadian Office – Library, #350, 130 Slater St., Ottawa ON K1P 6E2 – 613/567-8988 – Research Assistant, Donald Mallon

International Council for Canadian Studies – Library, 2 Daly Ave., Ottawa ON K1N 6E2 – 613/789-7834; TLX: 053-3906; Symbol: OOICCS – Librarian, Linda Jones

International Development Research Centre – IDRC Library, 250 Albert St., 10th Fl., PO Box 8500, Ottawa ON K1G 3H9 – 613/236-6163; TLX: 053-3753; Email: reference@idrc.ca; pub@idrc.ca; Symbol: OOID – Director, Carole Joling

International Joint Commission – Library, 100 Metcalfe St., 18th Fl., Ottawa ON K1P 5M1 – 613/995-2984; Fax: 613/993-5583

Islamic Information & Education of Canada – Library, 393 Cooper St., Ottawa ON K2P 0G8 – 613/232-0210 – Hilmi El-Sharief

Jewish Community Council of Ottawa – Library, 151 Chapel St., Ottawa ON K1N 7Y2 – 613/789-1818 – Librarian, Estelle Backman

Jewish Youth Library of Ottawa, 185 Switzer Ave., Ottawa ON K1Z 7H8 – 613/729-7712; Fax: 613/724-3855 – Devora Caytak

Justice Canada – Library Services, Justice Bldg, 239 Wellington St., 8th Fl., Ottawa ON K1A 0H8 – 613/957-4607; Fax: 613/952-5792; Symbol: OOJ – Director, Mireille McCullough

Lapp-Hancock Associates Limited – Library, #904, 280 Albert St., Ottawa ON K1P 5G8 – 613/238-2483 – Library Assistant, Heather McLeod

Learning Disabilities Association of Canada – Library, #200, 323 Chapel St., Ottawa ON K1N 7Z2 – 613/238-5721

Library of Parliament, 111 Wellington St., Ottawa ON K1A 0A9 – 613/992-3122; Fax: 613/992-1269; Email: CN/CP COMO444; Symbol: LP/BP
   Parliamentary Librarian, Richard Paré, 613/992-3122
   Director General, Research Branch, Hugh Finsten, 613/992-1132
   Director General, Information & Technical Services Branch, F. LeMay, 613/996-4934
   Director General, Administration & Personnel, Jean-Jacques Cardinal, 613/996-4477
M.E. Association of Canada – Library, #400, 246 Queen St., Ottawa ON K1P 5E4 – 613/563-1771 – Tina Harvey
Medical Research Council of Canada - Library, Tower B, 1600 Scott St., 5th Fl., Ottawa ON K1A 0W9 – 613/954-1809; Fax: 613/954-1800; Email: mrcinfocrm@hpb.hwc.ca – Special Projects Assistant, Suzane Faltacas
Micro Entrepreneur Support Group – Ventures Resource Centre, 804 Grenon Ave., Ottawa ON K2B 6G2 – 613/596-6262 – Vance MacEwan
National Archives of Canada - Library, 395 Wellington St., Ottawa ON K1A 0N3 – 613/992-6534; Fax: 613/943-8491; Email: library@archives.ca; Symbol: OOA – Acting Director, Alex Delvaux, 613/996-7685
National Association of Friendship Centres – Library, #204, 396 Cooper St., Ottawa ON K2P 2H7 – 613/563-4844 – Monique Godin-Beers
National Aviation Museum - Library, Ottawa Terminal, PO Box 9724, Ottawa ON K1G 5A3 – 613/993-2303; Fax: 613/990-3655; Email: ENVOY: ILL.OONMA; URL: http://www.nmstc.aviation.ca; Symbol: OONMA
   Librarian, Fiona Hale
   Library Assistant, Ian A. Leslie
National Capital Commission - Library, 40 Elgin St., Ottawa ON K1P 1C7 – 613/239-5123; Fax: 613/239-5274; Symbol: OONCC
   Head, Library Services, Gwyneth Hughes
   Library Assistant, Lauretta Bédard
National Clearinghouse on Tobacco & Health – Library, #1000, 170 Laurier Ave. West, Ottawa ON K1P 5V5 – 613/567-3050 – Information/Systems Specialist, Suzanna Gardner
National Defence Headquarters - Directorate Scientific Information Services, 190 O'Connor St., 2nd Fl., Ottawa ON K1A 0K2 – 613/992-2033; Fax: 613/996-0392; Symbol: OODSIS – Director, Mike Schryer
   National Defence Records & Library Services, Major-General George R. Pearkes Bldg., 101 Colonel By Dr., Ottawa ON K1A 0K2 – 613/996-0842; Reference: 613/996-0832; Fax: 613/995-8176; Email: ENVOY: ILL.OOND; Symbol: OOND
   Departmental Librarian, Peter Greig
   Head/NDRLS, Jacques N. Goulet
National Defence Medical Centre – Medical Library, 1745 Alta Vista Dr., Ottawa ON K1A 0K6 – 613/945-6517; Symbol: OONDM – Chief Librarian, Philip B. Allan
National Educational Association of Disabled Students – Library, Carleton University, 4th Level Unicentre, 1125 Colonel By Dr., Ottawa ON K1S 5B6 – 613/526-8008
National Federation of Pakistani Canadians Inc. – Library, #1100, 251 Laurier Ave. West, Ottawa ON K1P 5J6 – 613/232-5346
National Gallery of Canada - Library, 380 Sussex Dr., PO Box 427, Ottawa ON K1N 9N4 – 613/998-8949; Fax: 613/990-9818; Email: ngcref@ngc.chin.gc.ca; URL: http://national.gallery.ca; Symbol: CAOONG
   Chief Librarian, Murray Waddington
   Head, Reader Services, Peter Trepanier
   Technical Services Librarian, Roy Engfield
   Archivist, Cyndie Campbell
   ILL, Bonnie Bates
National Museum of Science & Technology - Library & Information Services, 2380 Lancaster Rd., PO Box 9724, Ottawa ON K1G 5A3 – 613/991-2981; Fax: 613/990-3636; Email: ENVOY: ILL.OONMST; Symbol: OONMS – Chief Librarian, Hilary Perrott
National Research Council Canada - Canada Institute for Scientific & Technical Information, Bldg. M-55, Montréal Rd., Ottawa ON K1A 0S2 – 613/993-1600 (general), 2013 (reference & referral); Fax: 613/952-9112; Toll Free: 1-800-668-1222; Email: cisti.info@nrc.ca; Symbol: OON
   Director General, Margot J. Montgomery
   Acquisitions, Manager, Brenda Hurst
   Communications, Head, Elizabeth Katz
   Construction Research Branch, Head, Scott Mellon, 613/993-2466
   Document Delivery, Manager, Kathryn Mikoski
   Electronic Products & Services, Manager, Cameron Macdonald
   Information Services & Product Development, Director, Mary Jane Maffini
   Information Services, Head, Morna Paterson
   Information Technology & Microstructural Sciences, Head, Jane Dyment, 613/993-2066
   Operations, Director, Bernard Dumouchel
   Biodiagnostics Research Branch, Head, David Colborne
   Biotechnology (Montréal), Head, Sylvie Belzile, 514/496-6119
   Dominion Astrophysical Observatory Branch (Victoria), Head, Eric LeBlanc, 604/388-0020
   Dominion Radio Astrophysical Observatory Branch (Penticton), Contact, B. Jones, 604/497-5321
   Industrial Materials/Matériaux industriels (Boucherville), Head, Louise Venne, 514/641-2280
   Institute for Biodiagnostics (Winnipeg), Head, Vacant
   J.H. Parkin Branch, Head, Kathy Wallace
   Marine Biosciences Branch (Halifax), Head, Vacant, 902/426-8250
   Marine Dynamics Branch (St. John's), Head, David Clark, 709/772-2468
   National Measurements Standards Branch, Head, Ray Jacyna, 613/993-6400
   Plant Biotechnology Branch (Saskatoon), Head, Vacant, 306/975-5256
   Sussex Branch CISTI, Head, Bonnie Bullock, 613/990-6027, Fax: 613/947-2064, Email: library@biologysx.lan.nrc.ca
   Cataloguing & Classification, Manager, Sheila Burvill
   Institute for Research in Construction - Information Service, Bldg. M-20, 1500 Montréal Rd., Ottawa ON K1A 0R6 – 613/993-2466; Fax: 613/952-7671; Symbol: OONBR – Head, Information Services, Scott Mellon
National Revenue Canada - Customs & Excise Library, Connaught Bldg., Sussex Dr., 2nd Fl., Ottawa ON K1A 0L5 – 613/957-9194; Fax: 613/954-1765; Symbol: OONR-C – Dianne L. Parsonage
   Taxation Library, #903, 88 Metcalf St., Ottawa ON K1A 0L8 – 613/957-2275; Fax: 613/957-7476 – Acquisitions Librarian, C. Deeble
Natural Resources Canada-Canada Centre for Remote Sensing – Client Services, 588 Booth St., Ottawa ON K1A 0Y7 – 613/947-1216; Email: jill.marriner@ccrs.nrcan.gc.ca – Jill Marriner
Natural Resources Canada - Canada Centre for Mineral & Energy Technology (CANMET) - Library, 555 Booth St., Ottawa ON K1A 0G1 – 613/995-4132; Fax: 613/995-8730; Symbol: OOM
   Director, Leslie Hamel
   Reference, Lidia Taylor
   Circulation, Larry Fletcher
   Public Services, Margaret Ahearn
   Technical Services, Jeffrey Ho
   Collection Development, Lawrence Wardroper, 613/943-8768
   ILL, Technician, Heather Lindsay, 613/995-4147
   Cataloguing, Technician, José Gelinas, 613/943-8766
   Bells Corners Library, Jean Macaulay, 613/996-1112
   Energy Diversification Research Laboratory Library, Robin Majumdar, 514/652-3210
   Canadian Forest Service - Library, Place Vincent Massey, 351 St. Joseph Blvd., 17th Fl., Ottawa ON K1A 1G5 – 613/997-1107, ext.1741; Fax: 613/997-8697; Email: ENVOY: ILL.OOFR; Symbol: OOFR – Chief, Library Services, Vicki Ritchie
   Earth Science Information Centre Geophysics Collection, One Observatory Cres., Ottawa ON K1A 0Y3 – 613/995-5558; Fax: 613/952-9088; Email: Geophysics_Library@gsc.emr.ca – Coordinator, Louise Simpson
   Headquarters Library, 580 Booth St., Ottawa ON K1A 0E4 – 613/996-8282; Fax: 613/992-7211; Email: ENVOY: ILL.OOMR; URL: http://www.nrcan.gc.ca/hqlib/lib.htm; Symbol: OOMR – Chief Librarian, Sharon Henry, 613/996-0144
   Map Library, 601 Booth St., Room G70, Ottawa ON K1A 0E8 – 613/996-1194; Reference: 613/995-4177; Fax: 613/943-8742; Email: ENVOY: GSC.LIB; Symbol: OOSMM – Librarian, Beverly Chen
   National Air Photo Library, 615 Booth St., Room 180, Ottawa ON K1A 0E9 – 613/996-9369; Fax: 613/995-4568; Symbol: OOMNA – Acting Chief, Marjorie Elwood
Nortel Technology - Information Resource Network - Ottawa, PO Box 3511, Ottawa ON K1Y 4H7 – 613/763-5728; Fax: 613/763-4282; Email: jkealy@bnr.com; Symbol: OONORE – Manager, Bibi Patel
Office of the Auditor General - Information & Library Services, West Tower, C.D. Howe Bldg., 240 Sparks St., 11th Fl., Ottawa ON K1A 0G6 – 613/995-3708; Fax: 613/952-5131; Email: ENVOY: LIBRARY.AGO; Symbol: OOOAG
   Manager, Shayla Mindell
   Head, Client Services, Judy Chamberland
   Reference Assistant, Jim Trigg
   Reference/Cataloguing Librarian, Cathy Ray
   Head, Technical Services, Gail Rawlings
   Acquisitions Clerk, Susan Ames
   Serials Clerk, Diane Morin
Office of the Superintendent of Financial Institutions – Library, 255 Albert St., Ottawa ON K1A 0H2 – 613/990-7729; Symbol: OOIN – Library Technician, Luanne Larose
Ontario Federation of Independent Schools – Library, 2199 Regency Terrace, Ottawa ON K2C 1H2 – 905/596-4013
Ontario Public Interest Research Group - Ottawa – Resource Centre, University of Ottawa, 631 King Edward, 3rd Fl., Ottawa ON K1N 7N8 – 613/230-3076 – Librarian, Leszek Nowosielski
Osler, Hoskin & Harcourt - Library, #1500, 50 O'Connor St., Ottawa ON K1P 6L2 – 613/787-1100; Fax: 613/235-2867; Email: mstenson@osler.com; URL: http://www.osler.com; Symbol: OOOH – Library Technician, Monique Stenson
Ottawa Board of Education - Professional Library, 330 Gilmour St., Ottawa ON K2P 0P9 – 613/239-5958; Fax: 613/239-5940; Symbol: OOBE – Manager, Library Service Centre, Barbara Lance
Ottawa Citizen Library, 1101 Baxter Rd., Ottawa ON K2C 3M4 – 613/596-3742; Fax: 613/726-1198; Email: a1715@freenet.carleton.ca
   Chief Librarian, Ron Tysick, 613/596-3744
   Graphics Librarian, Charlene Ruberry, 613/596-3742
   Photo Librarian, Lois Kirkup, 613/596-3744

Canadian Almanac & Directory 1997

Special Projects, Liisa Tuomenin, 613/596-3744
Ottawa Civic Hospital – Dr. George S. Williamson Health Sciences Library, 1053 Carling Ave., Ottawa ON K1Y 4E9 – 613/761-4459; Fax: 613/761-5292; Email: ifrogley@civich.ottawa.on.ca; Symbol: OOOCH – Manager, Kyungja Shin
Ottawa General Hospital – Library, 501 Smyth Rd., Ottawa ON K1H 8L6 – 613/737-8530; Fax: 613/737-8521; Email: ENVOY: ILL.OGH – Manager, Jessie McGowan
The Parliamentary Centre – Library, 250 Albert St., 4th Fl., Ottawa ON K1P 6M1 – 613/237-0143 – Librarian, Theresa Bruneau
Pauktuutit Inuit Women's Association – Library, 192 Bank St., Ottawa ON K2P 1W8 – 613/238-3977
People, Words & Change – Library, 211 Bronson Ave., Ottawa ON K1R 6H5 – 613/234-2494 – Win Burrows
Perley-Robertson, Panet, Hill & McDougall Law Office - Library, 99 Bank St., Ottawa ON K1P 6C1 – 613/238-2022; Fax: 613/238-8775 – Chief Librarian, Emer Cronin
Potvin Law Office - Library, #1000, 141 Laurier Ave. West, Ottawa ON K1P 5J3 – 613/236-6628; Fax: 613/234-7529
Privy Council Office - Information & Research Centre, #1000, 85 Sparks St., Ottawa ON K1A 0A3 – 613/957-5125; Fax: 613/957-5043; Email: library@pco.gc.ca; Symbol: OOPC – Manager, Jean Weerasinghe
Public Service Commission of Canada - Library, #B1123 West Tower, 300 Laurier Ave. West, Ottawa ON K1A 0M7 – 613/992-4068; Fax: 613/992-4329; Email: ENVOY: ILL.OOCS; Symbol: OOCS – Head, Library Services, Gregory Renaud
Public Service Staff Relations Board - Library, PO Box 1525, Ottawa ON K1P 5V2 – 613/990-1813; Fax: 613/990-1849 – Chief Librarian, Richard Harkin
Public Works & Government Services Canada - Departmental Library, #1E, Phase 3, 11 Laurier St., Ottawa ON K1A 0S5 – 819/956-3460; Fax: 819/997-8909; Symbol: OODP
 Chief Librarian, Henne Kahwa, 819/956-3461
 Acquisitions Librarian, Sylvette Forget-Séguin, 819/956-3462
 Cataloguing Technician, Lois Marcil, 819/956-3441
 Circulation Clerk, Cathy Talbot, 819/956-3460
 Reference Librarian, Elizabeth Kirby, 819/956-3465
 Translation Bureau - Military Terminology Documentation Centre, 390 Laurier St. West, 5th Fl., Ottawa ON K1A 0S5 – 613/990-7964; Fax: 613/990-9020 – Head, M. Drolet
 Translation Bureau - Military Translation Documentation Centre, North Tower, Rm. 168, 101 Colonel By Dr., 18th Fl., Ottawa ON K1A 0M5 – 613/947-7151; Fax: 613/992-8808 – Head, J. Tomlinson
 Translation Bureau - Parliamentary & Interpretation Services Documentation Centre, 171 Slater St., 3rd Fl., Ottawa ON K1A 0S5 – 613/996-7438; Fax: 613/996-8794 – Head, N. Vilandré
 Tupper Library, #B321, Sir Charles Tupper Bldg., 2323 Riverside Dr., Ottawa ON K1A 0M2 – 613/736-2396; Fax: 613/736-2401; Symbol: OOPW – Branch Librarian, Marilyn Dyck
Queen's University of Ottawa - Economic Projects Library, PO Box 1503, Ottawa ON K1P 5R5 – 613/567-7489; Fax: 613/567-7640; Symbol: OOQEP – Librarian, Deborah Scott-Douglas
Regional Municipality of Ottawa-Carleton - Corporate Resource Centre, 111 Lisgar St., Ottawa ON K2P 2L7 – 613/560-2058; Fax: 613/560-1380; Symbol: OORM
 Corporate Librarian, V. El-Zorkany
 Library Technician, M. O'Donnell
 Legal Department Library, 111 Lisgar St., 3rd Fl., Ottawa ON K2P 2L7 – 613/560-2056; Fax: 613/590-1383 – Library Technician, Alice Rabb

The Rehabilitation Centre – Reading Room, 505 Smyth Rd., Ottawa ON K1H 8M2 – 613/737-7350 – Head Librarian, Janet Joyce
RESORS Canada Centre for Remote Sensing - Library, #121, 615 Booth St., Ottawa ON K1A 0Y7 – 613/943-8833; Fax: 613/947-0574; Symbol: OOCCR – Database Manager, Louis Marcotte
Revenue Canada - Departmental Library, Albion Tower, #1100, 25 Nicholas St., Ottawa ON K1A 0L5 – 613/957-2278; Fax: 613/957-9514; Symbol: OONR – Manager, Lorraine Wilkinson
 Scientific & Technical Information Centre, 79 Bentley Ave., Ottawa ON K1A 0L5 – 613/954-9944; Fax: 613/952-7825; Symbol: OOSTI – Head, Ted Racine
Riverside Hospital of Ottawa – Scobie Health Sciences Library, 1967 Riverside Dr., Ottawa ON K1H 7W9 – 613/738-8230; Fax: 613/738-8532; Symbol: OORH – Coordinator, Paula M. Coutts
Royal Canadian Mint - Library, 320 Sussex Dr., Ottawa ON K1A 0G8 – 613/993-3614; Fax: 613/991-2294; Symbol: OOCRM – Manager, Information Systems, Monic Bourgon, 613/991-2028
Royal Canadian Mounted Police - Canadian Police College Library, St. Laurent Blvd. & Sandridge Rd., PO Box 8900, Ottawa ON K1G 3J2 – 613/993-3225; Fax: 613/990-9738; Symbol: OOR
 Manager, Nancy Park, 613/998-0774
 Head of Client Services, Emmett Will
 Head of Technical Services, Margaret Brignell
 Head of Acquisitions, Karyn Morrison
 Scientific Information Centre, Ident Tower, CPS Bldg., #502, 1200 Vanier Pkwy., PO Box 8885, Ottawa ON K1G 3M8 – 613/998-6282; Fax: 613/956-0152; Email: ENVOY: RCMPCPS.LIB; Symbol: OORS
The Royal College of Physicians & Surgeons of Canada – Roddick Room, 774 Echo Dr., Ottawa ON K1S 5N8 – 613/730-8177; Toll Free: 1-800-668-3740 – Jean McQuilliam
Royal Ottawa Health Care Group – Rhodes Chalke Library, 1145 Carling Ave., Ottawa ON K1Z 7K4 – 613/722-6521, ext.6268; Fax: 613/722-5048; Email: jjoyce@rohcg.on.ca; illooro@rohcg.on.ca; Symbol: OORO; OORORR – Manager, Library Services, Janet Joyce
The Royal Society of Canada – Library, #308, 225 Metcalfe St., Ottawa ON K2P 1P9 – 613/991-5760 – Linda Vachon
Saint Paul University - Library, 223 Main St., Ottawa ON K1S 1C4 – 613/236-1393; Fax: 613/782-3005; Symbol: OOSU
 Chief Librarian, Larry Eshelman, 613/236-1393, ext.2314, Email: larrye@spu.stpaul.uottawa.ca
 Principal Cataloguer, Edwin Galipeau
 Acquisitions Librarian, André Paris
Scott & Aylen Law Office - Legal Library, 60 Queen St., Ottawa ON K1P 5Y7 – 613/237-5160; Fax: 613/230-8842
 Librarian, Sherril Nixon
 Library Assistant, Katharine Heney
Scouts Canada – Library, 1345 Baseline Rd., PO Box 5151, LCD Merivale, Ottawa ON K2C 3G7 – 613/224-5131 – Librarian, Valerie Charron
Shipbuilding Association of Canada – Library, #1502, 222 Queen St., Ottawa ON K1P 5V9 – 613/232-7127 – Information Officer, Ellen Radix
Smart & Biggar Law Office - Library, #900, 55 Metcalfe St., Ottawa ON K1P 6L5 – 613/232-2486; Fax: 613/232-8440; Symbol: OOSB – Chief Librarian, Andrea Billingham
Social Sciences & Humanities Research Council - Library, 255 Albert St., PO Box 1610, Ottawa ON K1P 6G4 – 613/992-0638 (morning only); Fax: 613/992-1787; Symbol: OOSSHR – Library Assistant, Diane Séguin

Solar Energy Society of Canada Inc. – Library, #250, 2415 Holly Lane, Ottawa ON K1V 7P2 – 613/523-0974
Solicitor General Canada - Library, 340 Laurier Ave. West, Ottawa ON K1A 0P8 – 613/991-2787; Fax: 613/941-6171; Email: library@sgc.gc.ca; Symbol: OOSG
 Chief Librarian, Heather Moore, 613/991-2779
 Head, Client Services, Leonard Bonavero, 613/991-2780
 ILL/Reference Officer, Noëlla Morvan, 613/991-2787
 Technical Services Librarian, France Grenier, 613/991-2784
Soloway, Wright - Library, #900, 427 Laurier Ave. West, Ottawa ON K1R 7Y2 – 613/236-0111; Fax: 613/238-8507 – Chief Librarian, Norma Vincent
Standards Council of Canada - Document Centre, #1200, 45 O'Connor St., Ottawa ON K1P 6N7 – 613/238-3222; Fax: 613/995-4564; Email: info@scc.ca; URL: http://www.scc.ca; Symbol: OOST
 Manager, Josiane Désilets
 President, Richard LaFontaine
Statistics Canada - Library Services Division, R. H. Coats Bldg., 2nd Fl., Tunney's Pasture, Ottawa ON K1A 0T6 – 613/951-0944; Fax: 613/951-0939; Email: ENVOY: ILL.OOS; Symbol: OOS
 Director, Library Services, Susan Feeney
 Director, Advisory Services, Gail Graser, 613/951-9285
Status of Women Canada - Documentation Centre, #700, 360 Albert St., Ottawa ON K1A 1C3 – 613/995-4008; Fax: 613/957-3359; Symbol: OOSW – Chief, Records & Library Services, Céline Champagne
Supreme Court of Canada - Library, Kent & Wellington Streets, Ottawa ON K1A 0J1 – 613/996-8120; Fax: 613/952-2832; Symbol: OOSC
 Director, F. Diane Teeple, 613/996-8026
 Chief, Reader Services, Judith Rubin, 613/996-8579
 Reference Librarian, Daphne Phillips, 613/943-8879
 Reference Librarian, Alicia Loo, 613/996-7996
 Chief, Technical Services, Ken Lane, 613/996-8183
 Manager, Collection Development, Adela Romero, 613/996-0166
 Chief, Systems & Database Administration, Tara Naraynsingh, 613/947-1636
Tax Court of Canada - Library, 200 Kent St., Ottawa ON K1A 0M1 – 613/992-1704; Fax: 613/943-8449; Symbol: OOTR
 Manager, Library Services, Denis Roussel
 Library Technician, Chantal Beauregard
Traffic Injury Research Foundation of Canada – Resource Centre, #200, 171 Nepean St., Ottawa ON K2P 0B4 – 613/238-5235 – Steve Brown
Transport Canada - Library & Information Services, Place de Ville, Tower C, 15th Fl., 330 Sparks St., Ottawa ON K1A 0N5 – 613/998-5128; Fax: 613/954-4731; Email: ENVOY: ILL.OOT; Symbol: OOT – Director, Gary Brenton
 Road Safety Library, Canada Bldg., Minto Place, #1305, 344 Slater St., Ottawa ON K1A 0N5 – 613/998-1980; Fax: 613/998-4831; Symbol: OOTRS – Librarian, Suzan Zimmerman
Transportation Association of Canada – Technical Information Centre, 2323 St. Laurent Blvd., Ottawa ON K1G 4K6 – 613/736-1350 – Research Program Manager, Chris Hedges
United Nations Association in Canada – Library, #900, 130 Slater St., Ottawa ON K1P 6E2 – 613/232-5751 – Information Officer, Joan Broughton
University of Ottawa - Library Network, 65 University Cres., Ottawa ON K1N 9A5 – 613/564-6892; Fax: 613/564-9886, 5871; Email: ill.oou@acadumi.uottawa.ca; Symbol: OOU
 University Chief Librarian, Richard Greene

Acquisitions Librarian, Raymond Dicaire, 613/564-8118
Collections & Public Services, Librarian, Jean LeBlanc, 613/564-5921
Systems & Technical Services Librarian, Leslie Weir, 613/564-8140
Health Sciences Library, Director, Dianne Kharouba, 613/787-6521
Law Library, Director, Jules Larivière, 613/564-4943
Map Library, Head, Grace Welch, 613/564-6830
Media Library, Head, Guillaume Blais, 613/564-2374
Morisset Library (Humanities & Social Sciences), Head, Michel Theriault, 613/564-4074
Music Library, Head, Debra Begg, 613/564-5717
Teacher Education Library, Head, Jan Kolaczek, 613/564-5986
Vanier Library (Sciences & Engineering), Director, Elizabeth Reicker, 613/564-2324
Administration Studies, Librarian, Angela Kramer, 613/564-8123
Archives & Special Collections Librarian, Christine Banfill, 613/564-8129
Processing Librarian, Pierre Daoust, 613/564-8138
Vietnamese Canadian Federation – Library, 249 Rochester St., Ottawa ON K1R 7M9 – 613/230-8282 – Librarian, Quy Do
World University Service of Canada, PO Box 3000, Ottawa ON K1Y 4M8 – 613/798-7477 – Information Officer, Daun Kennedy

OWEN SOUND

Georgian College - Learning Resource Centre, 1150 - 8 St. East, PO Box 700, Owen Sound ON N4K 5R4 – 519/376-0682, ext.2037; Fax: 519/376-5395; Email: ENVOY: ILL.GEO.OS; Symbol: OOWGC – Supervisor, Karen L. McPhatter
Grey-Bruce Regional Health Centre - Health Sciences Library, 1400 - 8 St. East, PO Box 1400, Owen Sound ON N4K 6M9 – 519/376-2121 ext.2043; Fax: 519/376-1846; Email: ENVOY: GBRHC; Symbol: OOWGM – Health Sciences Librarian, Peggy Binkle
Grey County Law Association – Courthouse Library, 595 - 9 Ave. East, Owen Sound ON N4K 3E3 – 519/371-5495

PEMBROKE

Algonquin College - Pembroke Campus Resource Centre, 315 Pembroke St. East, Pembroke ON K8A 3K2 – 613/735-4707; Fax: 613/735-8801; Symbol: OPEMAC – Library Technician, Jean Lopushanski
Renfrew County Law Association – County Courthouse Library, 283 Pembroke St. East, Pembroke ON K8A 3K2 – 613/732-4880

PENETANGUISHENE

Deacon Taws Friend - Library, 90 Main St., PO Box 869, Penetanguishene ON L0K 1P0 – 705/549-3131; Fax: 705/549-4682 – Midland, Administrator, Phil Marley, CMA, 705/526-3791, Fax: 705/526-2688
Penetanguishene Mental Health Centre - Library, 500 Church St., Penetanguishene ON L9M 1G3 – 705/549-3181, ext.2342; Fax: 705/549-6467; Email: ENVOY 100 ILL.OPENM; Symbol: OPENM – Librarian, Patricia Reid

PERTH

Algonquin College - Lanark County Resource Centre, 7 Craig St., Perth ON K7H 1X7 – 613/267-2859, ext.5607; Fax: 613/267-3950; Symbol: OPAC – Head, Ann L. MacPhail, Email: macphaa@algonquinc.on.ca
Lanark County Law Association - County Courthouse Library, 43 Drummond St. East, Perth ON K7H 1G1 – Iris Nixon

PETERBOROUGH

City of Peterborough - Planning Division Library, City Hall, 500 George St. North, Peterborough ON K9H 3R9 – 705/748-8881; Fax: 705/742-5218 – Secretary, Planning & Economic Development, Judy Reader
Greater Peterborough Chamber of Commerce – Library, 175 George St. North, Peterborough ON K9J 3G6 – 705/748-9771 – Don Frise
H. Girvin Devitt Law Office - Library, 858 Chemong Rd., PO Box 1449, Peterborough ON K9H 7H6 – 705/742-5471 – Bookkeeper, Michelle Towns
Kawartha World Issues Centre – Library, 106 Murray St., Peterborough ON K9H 2S5 – 705/745-1380, 6899; Email: WEB-KWIC – Resource Coordinator, Marisa Kaczmarczyk
Ontario Federation of Anglers & Hunters – Eaton Conservation Resource Library, PO Box 2800, Peterborough ON K9J 8L5 – 705/748-6324 – Freya Long
Ontario Public Interest Research Group - Peterborough – Library, Peter Robinson College, Trent University, Peterborough ON K9J 7B8 – 705/748-1767
Ontario Trails Council – Library, c/o Trail Studies Unit, Trent University, Peterborough ON K9J 7B8 – 709/748-1419
Peterborough Civic Hospital – Hospital Library, 1 Hospital Dr., Peterborough ON K9J 7C6 – 705/876-5005; Fax: 705/743-0188; Email: jmacinto@pch.sjhhc.org; Symbol: OPETCH – Librarian, Judy MacIntosh
Peterborough Law Association – County Courthouse Library, 470 Water St., Peterborough ON K9H 3M3 – 705/742-9341
St. Joseph's General Hospital – Library, 384 Rogers St., Peterborough ON K9H 7B6 – 705/743-4251; Email: envoy: sjhhc.pet.lib.; Symbol: OPETSJ – Librarian, Mary Conchelos
Sir Sandford Fleming College of Applied Arts & Technology - Sutherland Campus, Educational Resources Centre, Brealey Dr., Peterborough ON K9J 7B1 – 705/743-5610; Fax: 705/749-5556; Symbol: OPETSE
Director, Educational Resources, Vacant
Periodicals, Library Technician, D. Sloan
Reference & Acquisition, Library Technician, R. O'Grady
Reference & Acquisition, Library Technician, S. Coones
Interlibrary Loans, Library Technician, P. Moher
Circulation Services, Circulation Clerk, B. McGee
Audiovisual Services, AV Technician, G. Richards
Media Resources, Media Resources Technician, A. Callan
McRae Library, Library Technician, Harriet Knor, 705/743-5610, ext.2283
Survivors of Suicide Support Program – Resource Centre, #301, 349A George St. North, Peterborough ON K9H 3P9 – 705/748-6711 – Administrative Assistant, Anne Cole
Trent University - Thomas J. Bata Library, PO Box 4800, Peterborough ON K9J 7B8 – 705/748-1324; Fax: 705/748-1315; Email: ENVOY 100: ILL.OPET or MW.GENOE; Symbol: OPET
University Librarian, Murray W. Genoe
Information Services, Head, J. Luyben
Monographs (Cat. & Acq.), Head, M.A. Scigliano
Government Publications & Maps, Head, B. Znamirowski
Serials, Microforms & Photoreproduction Services, Head, J. Millard
Collection Development, A. McCalla

PICKERING

Purdue Frederick Inc. - Library, 575 Granite Ct., Pickering ON L1W 3W8 – 905/420-4991; Fax: 905/420-4193 – Librarian, Rebecca Strange

POINT EDWARD

Owens Corning Canada - Technical Information Centre, 704 Mara St., Point Edward ON N7V 1X4 – 519/336-5670; Fax: 519/336-5906 – Information Clerk, Carol Scott

RICHMOND HILL

Canadian Bottled Water Federation – Library, #203-1, 70 East Beaver Creek Rd., Richmond Hill ON L4B 3B2 – 905/886-6928
Environmental Auditors Ltd., #19, 30 Wertheim Ct., Richmond Hill ON L4B 1B9 – 905/886-7965
Helpmate Community Information & Volunteer Bureau – Library, 10100 Yonge St., Richmond Hill ON L4C 1T8 – 905/884-3839; Toll Free: 1-800-363-2412 – Anne Rout
SENES Consultants Limited – Library, #12, 121 Granton Dr., Richmond Hill ON L4B 3N4 – 905/764-9380; Email: hguttman@senes.on.ca; Symbol: OWSCL – Supervisor, Library Services, Henny Guttman
York Central Hospital – Douglas Storms Memorial Library, 10 Trench St., Richmond Hill ON L4C 4Z3 – 905/883-2018; Fax: 905/883-2293

RIDGETOWN

Ridgetown College of Agricultural Technology - Library, Ridgetown ON N0P 2C0 – 519/674-1540; Fax: 519/674-1530; Email: roadhoi@gov.on.ca; Symbol: ORCAT – Librarian, Iona Roadhouse

ST CATHARINES

AIDS Niagara – Library, #200, 50 William St., St Catharines ON L2R 5J2 – 905/984-8684 – Joan Blanchard
Brock University - DeCew Campus Library, St Catharines ON L2S 3A1 – 905/688-5550, ext.3226; Fax: 905/988-5490; Email: ENVOY: ILL.OSTCB; URL: http://www.brocku.ca/library/; Symbol: OSTCB
University Librarian, James W. Hogan, 905/688-5550, ext.3226
Circulation Librarian, Robert Rossini, 905/688-5550, ext.3727
Public Services Librarian, Linda Anderson, 905/688-5550, ext.3230
Technical Services Librarian, Sid Fosdick, 905/688-5550, ext.3181
Acquisitions Librarian, Margaret Grove, 905/688-5550, ext.3198
Serials Librarian, Esther Sleep, 905/688-5550, ext.3266
University Map Library, Map Librarian, Colleen Beard, 905/688-5550, ext.3468
Business Librarian, Douglas Suarez, 905/688-5550, ext.4083
Canadian Canal Society – Canadian Canal Society Library/Archives, 80 King St., PO Box 24102, St Catharines ON L2R 7P7 – 905/688-5550, ext.3264 – John Burtniak
City of St Catharines - Engineering Department, Library, PO Box 3012, St Catharines ON L2R 7C2 – 905/688-5600, ext.644; Fax: 905/641-4450 – Janice Blackmore
Family & Children's Services Niagara – Library, 311 Geneva St., PO Box 24028, St Catharines ON L2R 7P7 – 905/937-7731 – Training Coordinator, Dori Madar
Lincoln County Board of Education - Educational Resource Library, 191 Carlton St., St Catharines ON L2R 7P4 – 905/641-1550, ext.2305; Fax: 905/685-8511
Library Technician, Corrine McKernan
Library Technician, Nicole Kitchen
Niagara College - Mack Nursing Centre - Learning Resource Centre, 178 Queenston St., St Catharines ON L2R 2Z7 – 905/688-5310 ext. 276

Canadian Almanac & Directory 1997

St Catharines Campus Learning Resource Centre, 59 Welland Vale Rd., PO Box 340, St Catharines ON L2R 6V6 – 905/684-4315, ext.2402; Fax: 905/684-3167 – Campus Librarian, Maria Edelman

Niagara Youth Orchestra Association – Library, 600 Ontario St., PO Box 28049, St Catharines ON L2N 7P8 – 905/945-4160 – Librarian, Barbara Bewlay

Ontario Public Interest Research Group - Brock – Library, Brock University, #306, Student Centre, St Catharines ON L2S 3A1 – 905/688-5550, ext.3499 – Karin Perry

Rodman Hall Arts Centre - Library, 109 St. Paul Cres., St Catharines ON L2S 1M3 – 519/684-2925 – Curator of Education & Extensions, Debra Attenborough

Worldwise International Resource Centre – Worldwise Library, 125 Welland Ave., St Catharines ON L2R 2N5 – 905/641-2525

ST MARYS

St Marys & District Association for Community Living – Library, PO Box 1618, St Marys ON N4X 1B9 – 519/284-1424 – Involvement Facilitator, Jennifer Young

ST THOMAS

Elgin County Courthouse - Library, 8 Wellington St., St Thomas ON N5R 2P2 – 519/631-7650; Fax: 519/633-9837

SARNIA

Bayer Rubber Inc. - Information Centre, Sarnia ON N7T 7M2 – 519/337-8251, ext.5711; Fax: 519/339-7748; Symbol: OPS
 Information Services Supervisor, Rosemary O'Donnell
 Reference Librarian, Tina Demars, 519/337-8251, ext. 5388
 Reference Librarian, Sharon Freeman, 519/337-8251, ext.5106

Imperial Oil - Research Technical Information Centre, PO Box 3022, Sarnia ON N7T 7M1 – 519/339-2902; Fax: 519/339-4436; Symbol: OSI
 Information Specialist, Nancy Bourque, 519/339-2617
 Library Assistant, Jackie Baley, 519/339-2626

Lambton College - Resource Centre, PO Box 969, Sarnia ON N7T 7K4 – 519/542-7751, ext.444; Fax: 519/542-1103; Email: leeann@lambton.on.ca; URL: http://www.lambton.on.ca; Symbol: OSLC – Manager, Learning Resources, Margaret Turner

Lambton County Board of Education - Professional Library, 200 Wellington St., PO Box 2019, Sarnia ON N7T 7L2 – 519/336-1500, ext.2422; Fax: 519/383-8937; Email: mccaffd@lambto.lcbe.edu.on.ca – Librarian, Denise McCaffery

Lambton Industrial Society: An Environmental Co-operative – Library, #111, 265 Front St. North, Sarnia ON N7T 7X1 – 519/332-2010 – Administrative Assistant, Christine Facca

SAULT STE MARIE

Algoma University - Arthur A. Wishart Library, Sault Ste Marie ON P6A 2G4 – 705/949-2101; Fax: 705/949-6583; Email: ENVOY: ILL.OSTMA
 Library Director, Patricia V. Burt, 705/949-2301, ext.351
 Technical Services Librarian, Warrick Chin
 Information Services Librarian, Daphne Flanagan

Clean North – Environmental Resource Room, PO Box 1204, Sault Ste Marie ON P6A 6N1 – 705/945-1573

Entomological Society of Ontario – Library, 1219 Queen St. East, PO Box 490, Sault Ste Marie ON P6A 5M7 – 519/824-4120, ext.2479 – Dave Hull

Fisheries & Oceans Canada - Sea Lamprey Control Centre Library, 1 Canal Dr., Sault Ste Marie ON P6A 6W4 – 705/941-3000; Fax: 705/941-3025 – Administrative Officer, Jackie Bassett, 705/941-3002

Natural Resources Canada-Canadian Forest Service: Sault Ste Marie – Library, 1219 Queen St. East, PO Box 490, Sault Ste Marie ON P6A 5M7 – 705/949-9461, ext.2000; Email: ENVOY: OTMF.ILL; Symbol: OSTMF – N.J. Dukes

Ontario Ministry of the Solicitor General & Correctional Services - Northern Treatment Centre Library, 800 Great Northern Rd., Sault Ste Marie ON P6A 5K7 – 705/946-0995, ext.242; Fax: 705/946-2925; Symbol: OSTMNT – Library Technician, Mary Campbell

Plummer Memorial Public Hospital & The Sault Ste. Marie General Hospital – SSMGH/PMPH Hospital Library, 969 Queen St. East, Sault Ste Marie ON P6A 2C4 – 705/759-3434, ext.4368; Fax: 705/759-3847; Email: youkathy@soonet.ca; Symbol: OSTMPH – Librarian, Kathy You

Sault College - Library, 443 Northern Ave., PO Box 60, Sault Ste Marie ON P6A 5L3 – 705/759-2554, ext.711; Fax: 705/759-1319; Email: ENVOY: SAULT.CAATLIB

Sault Community Information & Career Centre – Resource Centre, 8 Albert St. East, Sault Ste Marie ON P6A 2H6 – 705/949-6565; Toll Free: 1-800-461-2259

Sault Symphony Association – Music Library, #2, 121 Brock St., Sault Ste Marie ON P6A 3B6 – 705/945-5337 – Music Librarian, Guy Traficante

SIMCOE

Ontario Ministry of the Solicitor General & Correctional Services - Sprucedale Youth Centre Library, 660 Ireland Rd., PO Box 606, Simcoe ON N3Y 4L8 – 519/426-3561, ext.248; Fax: 519/428-1407 – Library Technician, Ruth Ann Misener

SOUTH PORCUPINE

Northern College of Applied Arts & Technology - Porcupine Campus Learning Resources Centre, Hwy. 101 East, PO Box 3211, South Porcupine ON P4N 8R6 – 705/235-3211, ext.150; Fax: 705/235-7279; Toll Free: 1-800-461-2167; Email: libraryp@kirk.northernc.on.ca; Symbol: OSPNC
 Library Technician, Maire Leigh Sheppard
 Library Technician, Eileen Pope
 Library Technician, Christine Dorval

STONEY CREEK

Contemporary Information Analysis Ltd., 2 Lakeview Dr., Stoney Creek ON L8E 5A5 – 905/643-1094; Fax: 416/927-0427

Mohawk College - Stoney Creek Campus Library, 481 Barton St. East, Stoney Creek ON L8E 2L7 – 905/662-3700, ext.5001; Fax: 905/662-3220
 Library Supervisor, Carol Farr
 Health Sciences Education Centre Library Resource Centre Maureen Price, 905/575-2509, Fax: 905/575-2528
 Highview Campus Library Resource Centre, Library Supervisor, Catherine Walker Hammond, 905/575-2329, Fax: 905/574-5566
 Wentworth Campus Library Resource Centre, Library Supervisor, Iwona Kurek, 905/575-1212, ext.3194, Fax: 905/528-6260

STRATFORD

County of Perth Law Association – Law Library, County Court House, 1 Huron St., Stratford ON N5A 5S4 – 519/271-1871

SUDBURY

Cambrian College - Learning Resources Centre, 1400 Barrydowne Rd., Sudbury ON P3A 3V8 – 705/566-8101, ext.7333; Fax: 705/671-7329; Email: ENVOY: CAM.COLL.LIBRARY; Symbol: OSUC – Head Librarian, Caroline Hallsworth

Centre franco-ontarien de ressources en alphabétisation – Centre FORA, 533, rue Notre-Dame, Sudbury ON P3C 5L1 – 705/673-7033 – Coordonnatrice des ressources et des services, Micheline Trudel

Huntington College - Laurentian Campus, J.W. Tate Library, Sudbury ON P3E 2C6 – 705/673-4148; Fax: 705/673-6917; Email: dmaley@laulibr.laurentian.ca – Librarian, Desmond Maley

Laurentian Hospital – Medical Library, 41 Ramsey Lake Rd., Sudbury ON P3E 5J1 – 705/522-2200; Fax: 705/523-7017; Symbol: OSULH – Director, Library Services, Rannah Brosseau

Laurentian University - J.N. Desmarais Library, 935 Ramsey Lake Rd., Sudbury ON P3E 2C6 – 705/675-1151, ext.3302; Fax: 705/673-6524; Email: ENVOY: ILL.OSUL; URL: http://www.laurentian.ca; Symbol: OSUL
 Director of Library, Joyce C. Garnett
 Technical Services, Chair, Ron Slater
 Public Services, Chair, Ashley Thomson

Miller, Maki Law Office - Library, 176 Elm St., Sudbury ON P3C 1T7 – 705/675-7503; Fax: 705/675-8669

Oldtime Radio-Show Collector's Association – Library, 45 Barry St., Sudbury ON P3B 3H6 – 705/560-2957 – Vice-President/Librarian, Frank Parrick

Ontario Ministry of Northern Development & Mines - Willet Green Miller Centre, Mines Library, 933 Ramsey Lake Rd., Level A3, Sudbury ON P3E 6B5 – 705/670-5615; Fax: 705/670-5622;
 Symbol: CAOTDM – Supervisor, Library Services, Nancy Thurston

Ontario Ministry of the Solicitor General & Correctional Services - Cecil Facer Youth Centre Library, 2500 South Lane Rd., PO Box 850, Sudbury ON P3E 4S3 – 705/522-1250; Fax: 705/522-6017 – Library Technician, Lydia Katulka

Service familial de la région de Sudbury inc. – Bibliothèque, #402, 51 Elm St., Sudbury ON P3C 1S3 – 705/674-5456 – Suzanne Paquin

Sudbury General Hospital – Library, 700 Paris St., Sudbury ON P3B 3B5 – 705/674-3181; Fax: 705/675-4781; Symbol: OSUGH – Librarian, Donald M. Hawryliuk

THORNHILL

The Baha'i Faith in Canada – Library, Baha'i National Centre, 7200 Leslie St., Thornhill ON L3T 6L8 – 905/889-8168; TLX: 06 96413 – Regan Brit

Epilepsy Ontario – Resource Centre, #308, 1 Promenade Circle, Thornhill ON L4J 4P8 – 905/764-5099; Toll Free: 1-800-463-1119 – Communication Officer, John Phair

THOROLD

Donohue Inc. - Library, Allanburg Rd., Thorold ON L2V 3Z5 – 905/227-1121, ext.306; Fax: 905/227-2353; Symbol: OTHOP – Librarian, Isabelle Ridgway, Email: iridgway@niagara.com

THUNDER BAY

Ontario Hydro - Thunder Bay G.S. Laboratory – Library, Mission Island, PO Box 816, Thunder Bay ON P7C 4X7 – 807/625-6455 – Librarian, Impi Sawchuk

Buset & Partners Law Office - Library, 1121 Barton St., Thunder Bay ON P7B 5N3 – 807/623-2500; Fax: 807/622-7808 – Librarian, Carolyn Enns

Confederation College - Challis Resource Centre, PO Box 398, Thunder Bay ON P7C 4W1 – 807/475-6241; Fax: 807/622-3258; Email: tapak@confed.confederationc.on.ca; Symbol: OTBCC – Director, Laraine Tapak

Lakehead Psychiatric Hospital – Northwestern Regional Mental Health Library, 580 Algoma St. North, PO Box 2930, Thunder Bay ON P7B 5G4 – 807/343-4351; Fax: 807/343-4387; Symbol: OTBLP – Library Technician, Helen Hyvarinen

Lakehead University - Library, 855 Oliver Rd., Thunder Bay ON P7B 5E1 – 807/343-8205; Fax: 807/343-8007; URL: http://www.lakeheadu.ca; Symbol: OPAL
Chief Librarian, Fred McIntosh
Reference Librarian, Shirley Boneca, 807/343-8165
Circulation Supervisor, Frank Sebesta, 807/343-8212
Technical Services Librarian, Ian Dew, 807/343-8315
Acquisitions Librarian, Anne Deighton, 807/343-8211
Education Librarian, Jim Arnot, 807/343-8719
Northwestern Ontario Sports Hall of Fame & Museum – Library, 2203 Moodie St. East, Thunder Bay ON P7E 4Z5 – 807/622-2852
Ontario Ministry of the Solicitor General & Correctional Services - Thunder Bay Correctional Centre Library, PO Box 1900, Thunder Bay ON P7B 5G3 – 807/475-8401; Fax: 807/475-9240 – Library Technician, Marjorie Brumwell
Thunder Bay Law Association – District Courthouse Library, 277 Camelot St., Thunder Bay ON P7A 4B3 – 807/344-3481

TILBURY

Tilbury & District Chamber of Commerce – Tilbury Odette Memorial Library, PO Box 1355, Tilbury ON N0P 2L0 – 519/682-1766 – Librarian, Maxine Gardiner

TIMMINS

Ojibway & Cree Cultural Centre – Resource Centre, 152 Third Ave., Timmins ON P4N 1C6 – 705/267-7911 – Supervisor, Dave Trudel
Rape Crisis Centre Timmins – Library, 355 Wilson Ave., Timmins ON P4N 2T7 – 705/268-8381 – Public Education Coordinator, Kathy Dionne

TOBERMORY

Ontario Marine Heritage Committee – Library, PO Box 221, Tobermory ON N0H 2R0 – 519/596-2947 – Joy Buckingham

TORONTO

Ontario Hydro - Ontario Hydro Technologies – Library, 800 Kipling Ave., Toronto ON M8Z 5S4 – 416/207-6706; Fax: 416/231-6738; Email: library@oht.hydro.on.ca – Senior Librarian, Donna Gardner
Ontario Ministry of Environment & Energy - Laboratory Services Branch – Library, 125 Resources Rd., Etobicoke ON M9P 3V6 – 416/235-5751; Fax: 416/235-0189; Email: crawfot@gov.on.ca; Symbol: OTMENL – Interlibrary Loans, Traceyann Crawford
Research & Technology Section, 135 St. Clair Ave. West, 11th Fl., Toronto ON M4V 1P5 – 416/323-4554
ABC CANADA – Library, 1450 Don Mills Rd., North York ON M3B 2X7 – 416/442-2292; Toll Free: 1-800-303-1004 – Caroline Gordon
Academy of Medicine, Toronto - William Boyd Library, c/o The Toronto Hospital Library, 200 Elizabeth St., BW 9th Fl., Toronto ON M5G 2C4 – 416/340-3259; Fax: 416/340-4384; Symbol: OTA
Acres International Limited - Library, 480 University Ave., 13th Fl., Toronto ON M5G 1V2 – 416/595-2000, ext.5247; Fax: 416/595-2004; Symbol: OTAC – Librarian, Marion D'Amboise
Addiction Research Foundation – Library, 33 Russell St., Toronto ON M5S 2S1 – 416/595-6144; Fax: 416/595-6036; Toll Free: 1-800-463-6273; Email: arf@vax.library.utoro – Library Manager, Louise Hamel
Advocacy Resource Centre for the Handicapped – Library, #255, 40 Orchard View Blvd., Toronto ON M4R 1B9 – 416/482-8255

AIDS Committee of Toronto – Library, 399 Church St., 4th Fl., PO Box 55, Toronto ON M4Y 2L4 – 340-2437, ext.223 – Lisa Betel
Aird & Berlis - Law Library, BCE Place, #1800, North Tower, 181 Bay St., PO Box 754, Toronto ON M5J 2T9 – 416/364-1241; Fax: 416/364-4916; Email: library@airdberlis.com – Librarian, Joan Rataic-Lang, 416/865-7756
Al-Anon Family Groups – Library, 1712 Avenue Rd., PO Box 54533, North York ON M5M 4N5 – 416/366-4072; Toll Free: 1-800-443-4525
Albert & Temmy Latner Jewish Public Library, 4600 Bathurst St., North York ON M2R 3V3 – 416/635-2996 – Executive Director, Rabbi Zigmund Wolkenstein
Alexander Consulting Group - Resource Centre, #1900, 20 Bay St., Toronto ON M5J 2N9 – 416/868-5501; Fax: 416/868-5786 – Research Librarian, S. Shapero
Alfa Romeo Club of Canada – Library, PO Box 62, Toronto ON M4T 2L7 – 416/498-6553
Alliance for Canadian New Music Projects – Library, Canadian Music Centre, 20 St. Joseph St., 3rd Fl., Toronto ON M4Y 1J9 – 416/963-5937
AlliedSignal Aerospace Canada - Knowledge Centre, 240 Attwell Dr., Etobicoke ON M9W 6L7 – 416/798-6850; Fax: 416/798-6848; Symbol: OTGAR – Knowledge Centre Principal, M.L. Perrin, Email: perrinl@trtmp003.allied.com
ALPHA Ontario - The Literacy & Language Training Resource Centre, 21 Park Rd., Toronto ON M4W 2N1 – 416/397-5900 (English), 397-5902 (Français); Fax: 416/397-5915; Toll Free: 1-800-363-0007 – Librarian, S. Young
Alzheimer Society for Metropolitan Toronto – Alzheimer Resource Centre, #500, 2323 Yonge St., Toronto ON M4P 2C9 – 416/322-6560 – Telephone Counsellor, Suzanne Sutherland
Alzheimer Society of Canada – Library, #201, 1320 Yonge St., Toronto ON M4T 1X2 – 416/925-3552 – Linda Leduc
Amnesty International, Canadian Section (English Speaking) - Toronto Regional Office – Library, 400 Bloor St. West, 2nd Fl., Toronto ON M5S 1X5 – 416/929-9477
Amyotrophic Lateral Sclerosis Society of Canada – ALS Resource Centre, #220, 6 Adelaide St. East, Toronto ON M5C 1H6 – 416/362-0269; Toll Free: 1-800-267-4257 – Manager of National Services, Helene Vassos
The Anglican Church of Canada – Library, Anglican Church House, 600 Jarvis St., Toronto ON M4Y 2J6 – 416/924-9192; Book Centre: 924-1332 – Karen Evans
Angus Environmental Ltd. – Library, 1127 Leslie St., North York ON M3C 2J6 – 416/443-8360
Anthroposophical Society in Canada – Library, 81 Lawton Blvd., Toronto ON M4V 1Z6 – 416/488-2886 – Helen Cass
Archives of Ontario - Library, #300, 77 Grenville St., Toronto ON M5S 1B3 – 416/327-1553; Fax: 416/327-1999; Toll Free: 1-800-668-9933; Email: vankalf@gov.on.ca; Symbol: OTAR
Librarian, Frank van Kalmthout
Library Technician, Susan Watt
Armstrong, Schiralli, Dunne & Singer Law Office - Library, #1400, 141 Adelaide St. West, Toronto ON M5H 3L5 – 416/868-0180; Fax: 416/863-1814 – Librarian, Cynthia McKeich
Art Gallery of Ontario - Edward P. Taylor Research Library & Archives, 317 Dundas St. West, Toronto ON M5T 1G4 – 416/979-6642; Fax: 416/979-6670; Email: library@ago.on.ca; URL: http://www.ago.on.ca; Symbol: OTAG – Chief Librarian, Karen McKenzie
Arthur Andersen & Co. - Information Centre, Toronto-Dominion Centre, PO Box 29, Stn Toronto-Dominion, Toronto ON M5K 1B9 – 416/947-7898;

Fax: 416/947-7878 – Head, Information Centre, Sean Forbes
Association canadienne-française de l'Ontario – Bibliothèque, #2005, 777 Bay St., Toronto ON M5G 2C8 – 416/595-5585
Association of Canadian Orchestras – Resource Centre, #311, 56 The Esplanade, Toronto ON M5E 1A7 – 416/366-8834 – Information Services Coord., Lois Jackman
Association of Canadian Publishers – Library, #301, 2 Gloucester St., Toronto ON M4Y 1L5 – 416/413-4929
Association of Municipalities of Ontario – Resource Centre, #701, 250 Bloor St. East, Toronto ON M4W 1E6 – 416/929-7573 – Information Officer, S. Vukelic
Association of Ontario Health Centres – Resource Centre, #102, 5233 Dundas St. West, Etobicoke ON M9B 1A6 – 416/236-2539
AT & T Canada Inc. - Market Intelligence Centre (1988), 3650 Victoria Park Ave., North York ON M2H 3P7 – 416/756-5228; Fax: 416/756-5035 – Lucille Slack
AT&T Canada Long Distance Services - Regulatory Information Centre, 200 Wellington St. West, Toronto ON M5V 3C7 – 416/345-2336; Fax: 416/345-2878 – Regulatory Research, Senior Manager, Tracy Tennant
AT&T Global Information Solutions - Marketing Information Retrieval Library, 320 Front St. West, Toronto ON M5V 3C4 – 416/351-2105; Fax: 416/351-2287
Administration Manager, Mary Quattromini
Esther Balevi
Audit Bureau of Circulations – Library of Print Media Circulation Statistics, Canadian Member Service Office, #850, 151 Bloor St. West, Toronto ON M5S 1S4 – 416/962-5840 – Supvr., Cdn. Member Services, Marian C. Robertson
Automobile Journalists Association of Canada – Library, 77 Wembley Dr., Toronto ON M4L 3C9 – 416/463-2658
B'nai Brith Canada – Library, 15 Hove St., North York ON M3H 4Y8 – 416/633-6224 – Sharon Anisman
Baker & McKenzie - Library, #2100, 181 Bay St., PO Box 874, Toronto ON M5J 2T3 – 416/863-1221; Fax: 416/863-6275 – Librarian, Irene Batna
Baker, Schneider, Swartz Law Office, #1000, 120 Adelaide St. West, Toronto ON M5H 3V1 – 416/363-2211; Fax: 416/363-0645 – Howard S. Swartz
Bank of Montreal - Business Information Centre, 100 King St. West, Level B2, Toronto ON M5X 1A1 – 416/867-5833; Fax: 416/867-6951 – Manager, Diane F. James
Bank of Nova Scotia - Library & Business Research, PO Box 7007, Toronto ON M5C 2K7 – 416/866-6257; Fax: 416/866-4036 – Chief Librarian, Marion Miwa, 416/866-4403
Technical Resource Centre, 2201 Eglinton Ave. East, Scarborough ON M1L 4S2 – 416/288-3571; Fax: 416/288-4445 – Manager, Lynda Cavanagh
Bechtel Canada Ltd. – Library Division, #200, 10 Gateway Blvd., Toronto ON M3C 3N8 – 416/467-3100
Bell Canada - Information Resource Centre, F-1N Bell Trinity Square, Toronto ON M5G 2E1 – 416/581-4256; Fax: 416/340-0324; Email: ENVOY: IRC.TORONTO – Rhona Geoyer
Bereaved Families of Ontario – Resource Centre, #204, 214 Merton St., Toronto ON M4S 1A6 – Toll Free: 1-800-236-6364
Bereavement Services & Community Education – Library, 1403 Bayview Ave., Toronto ON M4G 3A8 – 416/485-6415 – Program Co-ordinator, Patricia Corrigall
Beth Tzedec Congregation - Max & Beatrice Wolfe Library, 1700 Bathurst St., Toronto ON M5P 3K3 – 416/781-3511, ext.25; Fax: 416/781-0150

Chief Librarian, Zina Glassman
Children's Librarian, Fagie Goldfarb
Big Sisters Association of Ontario – Resource Centre, 2750 Dufferin St., Toronto ON M6B 3R4 – 416/789-7859 – Serivice Coordinator, Neil Burke
Blake, Cassels & Graydon Law Office - Library, Commerce Court West, PO Box 25, Toronto ON M5L 1A9 – 416/863-2650; Fax: 416/863-4261
Library Manager, Sandra M. Morris
Acquisitions Librarian, Dawn M. Urquhart, 416/863-2701
Technical Services Librarian, Vanessa King, 416/863-2730
Bloorview Macmillan Centre - Bloorview Site – Health Sciences Library, 25 Buchan Court, Willowdale ON M2J 4S9 – 416/494-2222, ext.240; Email: lambert@library.utoronto.ca – Deborah Lambert
Board of Trade of Metropolitan Toronto – Resource Centre, World Trade Centre, One First Canadian Place, PO Box 60, Toronto ON M5X 1C1 – 416/366-6811 – Director, Information Services, Mary de Reus
Bob Rumball Centre for the Deaf – Library Resource Centre, 2395 Bayview Ave., North York ON M2L 1A2 – 416/449-9651 (Voice & TDD); Toll Free: 1-800-841-9663
Borden & Elliot Law Office - Library, Scotia Plaza, #4400, 40 King St. West, Toronto ON M5H 3Y4 – 416/367-6370; Fax: 416/361-2752 – Manager, Information Services, Vivienne Denton, 416/367-6369
British Consulate-General - Library, #2800, 777 Bay St., Toronto ON M5G 2G2 – 416/593-1290 – Valerie Strand
Business Development Centre (Toronto) – Library, 1757 Eglinton Ave. West, 2nd Fl., Toronto ON M6E 2H7 – 416/789-2485
Cadillac Fairview - Records Centre, 20 Queen St. West, 4th Fl., Toronto ON M5H 3R4 – 416/598-8440; Fax: 416/598-8607
Records Librarian, Simonne Nord
Records Clerk, Esther Kim
Calmeadow – Resource Library, #600, 365 Bay St., Toronto ON M5H 2V1 – 416/362-9670
Canada Academy & Association of Chinese Acupuncture/Medicine – Library, #407, 3852 Finch Ave. East, Scarborough ON M1T 3T6 – 416/222-1428 – Dr. Ding
Canada-Caribbean-Central American Policy Alternatives – Library, 947 Queen St. East, Toronto ON M4M 1J9 – 416/469-1123
Canada-Latin America Resource Centre – Library, 603 1/2 Parliament St., Toronto ON M4X 1P9 – 416/921-4424
The Canada Life Assurance Company – Corporate Library Services, 330 University Ave., Toronto ON M5G 1R8 – 416/597-1456, ext.5266; Fax: 416/597-8537 – Nathalie Richard
Canadian Abortion Rights Action League – Video Library, #306, 344 Bloor St. West, Toronto ON M5S 3A7 – 416/961-1507
Canadian Advanced Industrial Materials Forum – Library, 75 International Blvd., 4th Fl., Etobicoke ON M9W 6L9 – 416/798-8055
Canadian Alliance in Solidarity with the Native Peoples – Library, 39 Spadina Rd., PO Box 574, Toronto ON M5R 2S9 – 416/972-1573
The Canadian Art Foundation – Library, 6 Church St., 2nd Fl., Toronto ON M5E 1M1 – 416/368-8854 – Production Manager, Lisa Ghione
Canadian Association for Co-operative Education – Library, 55 Eglinton Ave. East, Toronto ON M4P 1G8 – 416/535-6993
Canadian Association for Community Living – Library, Kinsmen Building, York University Campus, 4700 Keele St., North York ON M3J 1P3 – 416/661-9611; Symbol: OTNIR – Manager, Information Services, Miriam Ticoll

Canadian Association of Food Banks – Library, 530 Lakeshore Blvd. West, Toronto ON M5V 1A5 – 416/203-9241
Canadian Association of Photographers & Illustrators in Communications – Library, #322, 100 Broadview Ave., Toronto ON M4M 2E8 – 416/462-3700 – John Martin
Canadian Aviation Historical Society – Library, PO Box 224, North York ON M2N 5S8 – 416/488-2247 – Bill Turner
Canadian Bankers Association – Library, Commerce Court West, 30th Fl., PO Box 348, Stn Commerce Court, Toronto ON M5L 1G2 – 416/362-6092; Toll Free: 1-800-263-0231
Canadian Bible Society – Library, 10 Carnforth Rd., Toronto ON M4A 2S4 – 416/757-4171; Toll Free: 1-800-465-2425 – Archives/Editor, Connie Stamp
Canadian Bookbinders & Book Artists Guild – Craft Resource Centre, Chalmers Building, #221, 35 McCaul St., Toronto ON M5T 1V7 – 416/581-1071 – Chairperson, Ann Douglas
Canadian Broadcasting Corporation - Reference Library, PO Box 500, Toronto ON M5W 1E6 – 416/205-3244; Fax: 416/205-4707; Symbol: OTBC – Head Librarian, Leone Earls, Email: learls@delphi.com
Canadian Camping Association – Bookstore, #303, 1810 Avenue Rd., Toronto ON M5M 3Z2 – 416/781-4717 – Administrator, Dawn Hunter
Canadian Centre for Victims of Torture – Resource Centre, 25 Merton St., Toronto ON M4S 1A7 – 416/480-0489 – Mulugeta Abai
The Canadian Centre/International P.E.N. – Library, 24 Ryerson Ave., Toronto ON M5T 2P3 – 416/703-8448
The Canadian Children's Book Centre – Library, 35 Spadina Rd., Toronto ON M5R 2S9 – 416/975-0010
Canadian Civil Liberties Association – Library, #403, 229 Yonge St., Toronto ON M5B 1N9 – 416/363-0321 – Research Director, Catherine Gilbert
Canadian Congress for Learning Opportunities for Women – Library, 47 Main St., Toronto ON M4E 2V6 – 416/699-1909
Canadian Copper & Brass Development Association – Library, #375, 10 Gateway Blvd., North York ON M3C 3A1 – 416/421-0788 – Librarian, Sandra J. Knapp
Canadian Copyright Institute – Library, 35 Spadina Rd., Toronto ON M5R 2S9 – 416/975-1756 – Nancy Fleming
Canadian Council for Public-Private Partnerships – Library, #4700, Toronto Dominion Bank Tower, PO Box 48, Stn Toronto Dominion, Toronto ON M5K 1E6 – 416/601-8333
Canadian Council on Rehabilitation & Work – Library, 20 King St. West, 9th Fl., Toronto ON M5H 1C4 – 416/974-2461 – Project Planner, Amy Pike
Canadian Daily Newspaper Association – Library, #1100, 890 Yonge St., Toronto ON M4W 3P4 – 416/923-3567 – Bryan Cantley
Canadian Direct Marketing Association – Library, #607, One Concorde Gate, North York ON M3C 3N6 – 416/391-2362 – Information Officer, Irene Payne
Canadian Drug Manufacturers Association – Library, #606, 4120 Yonge St., Toronto ON M2P 2B8 – 416/223-2333 – Research Director, Julie Tam
Canadian Education Association – Library, #8-200, 252 Bloor St. West, Toronto ON M5S 1V5 – 416/924-7721 – Librarian, Diane Sibbett
Canadian Environmental Law Association – Resource Library for the Environment & the Law, #401, 517 College St., Toronto ON M6G 4A2 – 416/960-2284 – Chief Librarian, Mary Vise
Canadian Federation of Independent Business – Library, #401, 4141 Yonge St., North York ON M2P 2A6 – 416/222-8022 – Katalin Coorsh

Canadian Feed the Children – Library, 174 Bartley Dr., Toronto ON M4A 1E1 – 416/757-1220; Toll Free: 1-800-387-1221
Canadian Film & Television Production Association – Library, #806, 175 Bloor St. East, Toronto ON M4W 3R8 – 416/927-8942 – Cindy Lewis
Canadian Filmmakers Distribution Centre – Library, #220, 37 Hanna Ave., Toronto ON M6K 1W8 – 416/588-0725
Canadian Flag Association – Library, 50 Heathfield Dr., Scarborough ON M1M 3B1 – 416/267-9618
Canadian Forces College - Information Resource Centre, 215 Yonge Blvd., Toronto ON M5M 3H9 – 416/482-6846; Fax: 416/482-6908; Email: ENVOY: CFC.LIBRARY; Symbol: OTRC – Chief Librarian, Cathy Murphy
Canadian Foundation for AIDS Research – Library, #800, 165 University Ave., Toronto ON M5H 3B8 – 416/361-6281
Canadian Foundation for Children, Youth & the Law – Resource Centre, #405, 720 Spadina Ave., Toronto ON M5S 2T9 – 416/920-1633
Canadian Foundation for Economic Education – Library, #501, 2 St. Clair Ave. West, Toronto ON M4V 1L5 – 416/968-2236 – Resource Centre Director, Judith Jackson
Canadian Friends Historical Association – Arthur Garratt Dorland Friends Historical Collection, 60 Lowther Ave., Toronto ON M5R 1C7 – 905/895-1700 – Archivist/Librarian, Jane Zavitz Bond
Canadian Friends of Soviet People – Library, 280 Queen St. West, Toronto ON M5V 2A1 – 416/977-5819 – Secretary, Helen Lucas
Canadian Friends Service Committee – Friends House Library, 60 Lowther Ave., Toronto ON M5R 1C7 – 416/921-0368 – Library Coordinator, Jane Sweet
Canadian Gas Association – Library & Information Services, #1200, 243 Consumers Rd., North York ON M2J 5E3 – 416/498-1994 – Librarian, Barbara Cayley
Canadian German Chamber of Industry & Commerce Inc. – Library, #1410, 480 University Ave., Toronto ON M5G 1V2 – 416/598-3355 – Elisabeth Feil
Canadian Hearing Society – Library, 271 Spadina Rd., Toronto ON M5R 2V3 – 416/964-9595; TTY: 416/964-0023; Toll Free: 1-800-465-4327 – Angela Palmer
Canadian Imperial Bank of Commerce – Business Information, Commerce Court, PO Box 1, Stn Commerce Court, Toronto ON M5L 1A2 – 416/980-3053; Fax: 416/861-3666 – Manager, Cynthea C. Penman
Canadian Institute for Radiation Safety – Resource Centre, #1106, 555 Richmond St. West, Toronto ON M5V 3B1 – 416/504-6565, ext.28 – Information Officer, Tina de Geus
Canadian Institute of Chartered Accountants – Studies & Standards Dept. Library, 277 Wellington St. West, Toronto ON M5V 3H2 – 416/204-3307; Symbol: OTCI – Library Contact, Gerald B. Gerard
Canadian Institute of Chartered Life Underwriters & Chartered Financial Consultants – Library, 41 Lesmill Rd., North York ON M3B 2T3 – 416/444-5251 – Manager/Library Services, Ilse Selwyn
Canadian Institute of Cultural Affairs – Library, 579 Kingston Rd., Toronto ON M4E 1R3 – 416/691-2316 – Jeannette Stanfield
Canadian Institute of International Affairs – The John Holmes Library, 5 Devonshire Pl., Toronto ON M5S 2C8 – 416/979-1851; Email: jen.mcnenly@utoronto.ca – Librarian, Jennifer McNenly
Canadian Institute of Strategic Studies – Library, Box 2321, #402, 2300 Yonge St., Toronto ON M4P 1E4 – 416/322-8128; Toll Free: 1-800-831-5695
Canadian Lesbian & Gay Archives – Library, #201, 56 Temperance St., PO Box 639, Toronto ON M5W 1G2 – 416/777-2755
Canadian Life & Health Insurance Association Inc. – Research & Information Library, #1700, One

Canadian Almanac & Directory 1997

Queen St. East, Toronto ON M5C 2X9 – 416/777-2221; Fax: 416/603-9019; Toll Free: 1-800-268-8099 – Records & Information Manager, Lillian Premovic

Canadian Magazine Publishers Association – Library, #202, 130 Spadina Ave., Toronto ON M5V 2L4 – 416/504-0274

Canadian Management Centre of AMA (American Management Association) International – Library, 150 York St., 5th Fl., Toronto ON M5H 3S5 – 416/214-5678

Canadian Music Centre – Ettore Mazzolini Library, Chalmers House, 20 St. Joseph St., Toronto ON M4Y 1J9 – 416/961-6601 – National Librarian, Mark Hand

The Canadian National Institute for the Blind – CNIB Library for the Blind, 1929 Bayview Ave., Toronto ON M4G 3E8 – 416/480-7520 – Executive Director, Rosemary Kavanagh

Canadian Natural Health Association – Library, #5, 439 Wellington St. West, Toronto ON M5V 1E7 – 416/977-2642 – Book Dept. Coordinator, Michelle Doucette

Canadian Nuclear Society – Library, #475, 144 Front St. West, Toronto ON M5J 2L7 – 416/977-6152; Toll Free: 1-800-387-4477 – A. Laughlin

Canadian Opera Company – Library, 227 Front St. East, Toronto ON M5A 1E8 – 416/363-6671,ext.328 – Archivist, Birthe Joergensen

Canadian Paraplegic Association (Ontario) – Library, 520 Sutherland Dr., Toronto ON M4G 3V9 – 416/422-5644 – Director, Rehabilitation, Michele Mechan

Canadian Physicians for Aid & Relief – Library, #202, 111 Queen St. East, Toronto ON M5C 1S2 – 416/369-0865; Toll Free: 1-800-263-2727; Email: CPAR@WEB 2:254/70 – Administrative Assistant, Sylvia Opena

Canadian Poetry Association – Small Press Reference Library, PO Box 22571, RPO St. George, Toronto ON M5S 1V0 – 905/874-1414; Email: lurc.lspc@onlinesys.com – Librarian, Wayne Ray

Canadian Polish Research Institute – Library, 288 Roncesvalles Ave., Toronto ON M6R 2M4 – 416/274-2021 – Edward Soltys

The Canadian Press – Library, 36 King St. East, Toronto ON M5C 2L9 – 416/364-0321; Broadcast News: 364-3172; Fax: 416/364-0207; TLX: 06-217715; 06-2 – Asma Khan

Canadian Professional Sales Association – Library, #310, 145 Wellington St. West, Toronto ON M5J 1H8 – 416/408-2685; Toll Free: 1-800-268-3794 – Librarian, Anna Fredericks

Canadian Publishers' Council – Library, #203, 250 Merton St., Toronto ON M4S 1B1 – 416/322-7011

Canadian Restaurant & Foodservices Association – CRFA Resource Centre, 316 Bloor St. West, Toronto ON M5S 1W5 – 416/923-8416; Toll Free: 1-800-387-5649 – Information Specialist, Erica Dennis

Canadian Sanitation Supply Association – Library, #G10, 300 Mill Rd., Etobicoke ON M9C 4W7 – 416/620-9320

Canadian Schizophrenia Foundation – Library, 16 Florence Ave., North York ON M2N 1E9 – 416/733-2117 – Secretary, Ollie Chong

The Canadian Society for Mesopotamian Studies – Library, 4 Bancroft Ave., 4th Fl., Toronto ON M5S 1A1 – 416/978-4531 – Archivist, Grant Frame

Canadian Society of Mayflower Descendants – Library, #802, 500 Duplex Ave., Toronto ON M4R 1V6 – Arthur Harris

Canadian Standards Association – Information Centre, 178 Rexdale Blvd., Etobicoke ON M9W 1R3 – 416/747-4007; Toll Free: 1-800-463-6727; TLX: 06-989344; Symbol: OTCSA – Coordinator, Susan Morley

Canadian Sugar Institute – Library, Water Park Place, #620, 10 Bay St., Toronto ON M5J 2R8 – 416/368-8091 – Luana Simpkins

Canadian Union of Educational Workers (Ind.) – Library, #304, 385 Yonge St., Toronto ON M5B 1S1 – 416/979-7394 – Communications Officer, Francois Lachance

Canadian Urban Transit Association – Library, #901, 55 York St., Toronto ON M5J 1R7 – 416/365-9800 – Manager of Research, Brendon Hemily

Candlelighters Childhood Cancer Foundation Canada – Resource Centre, #401, 55 Eglinton Ave. East, Toronto ON M4P 1G8 – 416/489-6440; Toll Free: 1-800-363-1062 – Janet Evans

Cassels, Brock & Blackwell Law Office - Library, #2100, Scotia Plaza, 40 King St. West, Toronto ON M5H 3C2 – 416/869-5436; Fax: 416/360-8877; Symbol: OTCBB
  Library Manager, Clare Lyons, Email: clyons@casselsbrock.com
  Reference Librarian, Elizabeth Baranecki
  Library Technician, Karen Hunter, Email: khunter@casselsbrock.com
  Library Assistant, Allyson Woodward

Catholic Biblical Association of Canada – Resource Centre, 3275 St. Clair Ave. East, Scarborough ON M1L 1W2 – 416/285-9552 – Librarian, Christopher Hay

C.C. Clemmer Health Sciences - Library, 1900 Bayview Ave., Toronto ON M4G 3E6 – 416/482-2340; Fax: 416/482-9745; Symbol: OTCMC
  Director of Library Services, Marilyn E. Schafer, 416/482-2340, ext.159
  Media Services, Head, Margaret Butkovic
  Public Services, Reference Librarian, Andrea Hall
  Technical Services, Head, Claire M. Bowman

C.D. Howe Institute – Library, 125 Adelaide St. East, Toronto ON M5C 1L7 – 416/865-1904 – Librarian, Susan Knapp

Centenary Health Centre – Health Sciences Library, 2867 Ellesmere Rd., Scarborough ON M1E 4B9 – 416/281-7101; Fax: 416/281-7360; Email: poplak@vax.library.utoronto.ca – Librarian, Valda Poplak

Centennial College - Learning & Resource Centres, PO Box 631, Scarborough ON M1K 5E9 – 416/289-5000, ext.2601; Fax: 416/439-5736 – Executive Director, Learning & Resource Centres, Janice Hayes, Email: jhayes@cencol.on.ca

Centre for Christian Studies - Library, 77 Charles St. West, Toronto ON M5S 1K5 – 416/923-1168; Fax: 416/923-5496 – Librarian, Shelagh Telford

Centre for International Studies, University of Toronto – Library, #500, 170 Bloor St. West, Toronto ON M5S 1T9 – 416/978-7293

Centre for Refugee Studies - Andrew Forbes Refugee Resource Centre, York Lanes, York University, #314, 4700 Keele St., North York ON M3J 1P3 – 416/736-5663; Fax: 416/736-5837; Email: lwong@yorku.ca; URL: http://www.yorku.ca/research/crs – Documentalist, Len Wong

Centre for Research on Latin America & The Caribbean – Documentation Centre, 240 York Lanes, York University, 4700 Keele St., North York ON M3J 1P3 – 416/736-5237 – Administrative Assistant, Liddy Gomes

Centre for Spanish Speaking Peoples – Library, 1004 Bathurst St., Toronto ON M5R 3G7 – 416/533-8545 – Telma Meua

The Centre for the Great Lakes – Library, #2408, 77 Harbour Square, Toronto ON M5J 2H2

Centre of Forensic Science - H. Ward Smith Library, 25 Grosvenor St., 2nd Fl., Toronto ON M7A 2G8 – 416/314-3200; Fax: 416/314-3225; Symbol: OTCE – Library Technician, Carolyn Regan

CH2M Gore & Storrie Limited – Library, #401, 255 Consumers Rd., North York ON M2J 5B6 – 416/499-0090; Symbol: OTGS – Librarian, Dianne Sawh

Childbirth By Choice Trust – Library, #306, 344 Bloor St. West, Toronto ON M5S 3A7 – 416/961-1507 – Robin Rowe

The Christian & Missionary Alliance in Canada – Library, #510, 105 Gordon Baker Rd., PO Box 7900, North York ON M2K 2R6 – 416/492-8775 – Director, Communications, Myrna McCombs

The Church Army in Canada – Cowan Memorial Library, Headquarters & College of Evangelism, 397 Brunswick Ave., Toronto ON M5R 2Z2 – 416/924-9279 – Sister, Ruth Wylie

Citizens for Public Justice – Library, #311, 229 College St., Toronto ON M5T 1R4 – 416/979-2443 – Research Clerk, Daniel Kelleher

City of Scarborough - Health Resource Centre, #500, 55 Town Centre Ct., Scarborough ON M1P 4X4 – 416/396-7453; Fax: 416/396-5299 – Resource Librarian, Dianne Beal

City of Toronto - Dept. of Buildings & Inspections Library, City Hall, East Tower, 100 Queen St. West, 17th Fl., Toronto ON M5H 2N2 – 416/392-7608; Fax: 416/392-0677 – Coordinator, Library Services, Irene Moore
  Planning & Development Department - Library, City Hall, East Tower, 100 Queen St. West, 11th Fl., Toronto ON M5H 2N2 – 416/392-1526; Fax: 416/392-0071 – Head Librarian, Deborah Fowler

Civic Garden Centre - Library, 777 Lawrence Ave. East, North York ON M3C 1P2 – 416/397-1340; Fax: 416/397-1354 – Librarian, Roslyn Theodore, 416/397-1353

Clarke Institute of Psychiatry – Farrar Library, 250 College St., Toronto ON M5T 1R8 – 416/979-6824; Fax: 416/979-6817; Email: library@clarke-inst.on.ca; Symbol: OTUDP – Head, Library Services, Diane Thomas

Community AIDS Treatment Information Exchange – CATIE Resources, #420, 517 College St., Toronto ON M6G 4A2 – 416/944-1916; Toll Free: 1-800-263-1638 – Information Manager, Robert MacKay-Melrose

Community Hospice Association of Ontario – Lending Resource Centre, #313, 40 Wynford Dr., North York ON M3C 1J5 – 416/510-3880 – Manager, Membership Services, Jeanette Browne

Community Information Centre of Metropolitan Toronto – Library, 425 Adelaide St. West, 2nd Fl., Toronto ON M5V 3C1 – 416/392-0505 – Charlie Bignell

Community Legal Education Ontario – Library, #600, 119 Spadina Ave., Toronto ON M5V 2L1 – 416/408-4420 – Librarian, Susan Moses

Congregation of St-Basil (Basilian Fathers) – Library, c/o John Kelly Library, 113 St. Joseph St., Toronto ON M5S 1J4 – 416/926-7279 – Archivist, Rev. Kevin Kirley, CSB

Connaught Laboratories Ltd. - Balmer Neilly Library, 1755 Steeles Ave. West, North York ON M2R 3T4 – 416/667-2662; Fax: 416/667-2850; Email: library@toronto.connaught.com; Symbol: OTCL – Library Services Manager, Hugh W. McNaught

Connexions Information Sharing Services – Library, PO Box 158, Toronto ON M6P 3J8 – 416/537-3949 – Ulli Diemer

Conseil des écoles françaises de la communauté urbaine de Toronto – Bibliothéque, #207, One Concorde Gate, North York ON M3C 3N6 – 416/391-1264 – Hélène Amyot

Conseil des organismes francophones du Toronto Métropolitain – Bibliotheque, 20 Lower Spadina Ave., Toronto ON M5V 2Z1 – 416/203-1220

Conservation Council of Ontario – Library, #506, 489 College St., Toronto ON M6G 1A5 – 416/969-9637

Construction Safety Association of Ontario – Information & Systems Group, 74 Victoria St., Toronto ON M5C 2A5 – 416/366-1501

Consumers Gas - Information Resource Centre, 500 Consumers Rd., North York ON M2J 1P8 – 416/495-5490; Fax: 416/495-5402 – Manager, Mirren Hinchley, 416/495-5814

Canadian Almanac & Directory 1997

COSTI – Library, 1710 Dufferin St., Toronto ON M6E 3P2 – 416/658-1600 – Executive Assistant, Mary Pascale

Council of Ontario Universities – Library, #203, 444 Yonge St., Toronto ON M5B 2H4 – 416/979-2165, ext.201 – Research Analyst & Librarian, Arlene Lexine

Counterpoint: A Resource Centre for Global Analyses – Resource Centre, 603 1/2 Parliament St., Toronto ON M4X 1P9 – 416/921-4424

County of York Law Association – Library, 361 University Ave., Toronto ON M5G 1T3 – 416/327-5700 – Library Manager, Anne Matthewman

Cross Cultural Communication Centre – Library, 2909 Dundas St. West, Toronto ON M6P 1Z1 – 416/760-7855 – Resource Librarian, Carmen Alcalde

Cryonics Society of Canada – Library, PO Box 788, Toronto ON M5W 1G3 – 416/534-0967 – Douglas Quinn

CUSO - Toronto Office – Library, #200, 133 Richmond St. West, Toronto ON M5H 2L3 – 416/363-2191 – Secretary, Norma Knuckle

Czech & Slovak Association of Canada – Library, 740 Spadina Ave., Toronto ON M5S 2J2 – 416/925-2241

Dale & Lessmann - Library, #2000, Commercial Union Tower, Box 73, Toronto Dominion Centre, Toronto ON M5K 1E7 – 416/863-1010; Fax: 416/863-1009 – Librarian, Bettina Hakala

de Havilland Inc. - Library Services, Mail Stop N17-09, Garratt Blvd., Downsview ON M3K 1Y5 – 416/375-3365; Fax: 416/375-4533 – Librarian, Cathy Parsons

Delcan Corporation - Division of Delcan Group – Library, 133 Wynford Dr., North York ON M3C 1K1 – 416/441-4111 – Librarian, Gillian Henderson

Deloitte & Touche – National Research Centre, #1300, 95 Wellington St. West, Toronto ON M5J 2P4 – 416/601-5933; Fax: 416/601-5921 – Manager, Suzanne Levasseur
National Tax Resource Centre, BCE Place, #1400, 181 Bay St., Toronto ON M5J 2V1 – 416/601-6286; Fax: 416/601-6151; Email: trc@ftn.net
Manager, Mina Woodruff
Information Specialist, Laurie A. Smith
Administrative Assistant, Michelle Martin

Design Exchange – Resource Centre, Toronto Dominion Centre, 234 Bay St., PO Box 18, Toronto ON M5K 1B2 – 416/216-2125 – Curator, Rachel Gotlieb

Developing Countries Farm Radio Network – Library, Box 12, #227B, 40 Dundas St. West, Toronto ON M5G 2C2 – 416/593-3751 – Librarian, Joan Beckley

DeVry Institute of Technology - Learning Resource Centre, 2201 Finch Ave. West, Weston ON M9M 2Z4 – 416/741-9220; Fax: 416/741-3633
Director, Learning Resource Centre, Susan Heinrich
Library Technician, Hugh Harries-Jones

Dianne Saxe Barrister & Solicitor - Library, 66 Russell Hill Rd., Toronto ON M4V 2T2 – 416/962-5882; Fax: 416/962-8817

Dingwall, McLauchlin, #2100, Commercial Union Tower, Box 69, Toronto Dominion Centre, Toronto ON M5K 1E7 – 416/863-1000; Fax: 416/863-1007 – Librarian, Bettina Hakala

Diversified Research Laboratories Ltd. – Information Resource Centre, 1047 Yonge St., Toronto ON M4W 2L3 – 416/922-5100; Symbol: OTWRC – Manager, Lusi Wong

Doctors Hospital - Health Sciences Library, 340 College St., 6th Fl., Toronto ON M5T 3A9 – 416/963-7677, ext.7464; Email: dh@library.utoronto.ca; Symbol: OTDHS
Health Sciences Librarian, Sharon Virtue
Assistant Librarian, Keith Denny

The Donwood Institute – The Donwood Library, 175 Brentcliffe Rd., Toronto ON M4G 3Z1 – 416/425-3930 – Chris Kirby

East End Literacy - Library, 265 Gerrard St. East, Toronto ON M5A 2G3 – 416/968-6989; Fax: 416/968-0597

The Easter Seal Society (Ontario) – Library, #200, 250 Ferrand Dr., North York ON M3C 3P2 – 416/421-8377; Toll Free: 1-800-668-6252 – Resource Centre Coordinator, Georgina Westdyk

Education Wife Assault – Library, 427 Bloor St. West, Toronto ON M5S 1X7 – 416/968-3422 – Librarian, Tiffany Veinot

Employment & Immigration Canada - Ontario Region Library, #700, 4900 Yonge St., North York ON M2N 6A8 – 416/954-7682; Fax: 416/954-7537; Symbol: OTMIO – Chief Librarian, F.R. Hersom

Energy Probe Research Foundation – Library, 225 Brunswick Ave., Toronto ON M5S 2M6 – 416/964-9223; Toll Free: 1-800-263-2784 – Frank Cianflone

Environment Canada-Atmospheric Environment Service - Climate & Atmospheric Research Directorate – Library, 4905 Dufferin St., Toronto ON M3H 5T4 – 416/739-4995

Environment Canada - Library - Downsview, 4905 Dufferin St., Downsview ON M3H 5T4 – 416/739-4828; Fax: 416/739-4212; Email: ENVOY: ILL.OTM; Symbol: OTM
Head, Maria A. Latyszewskyj
Acquisitions, Clerk, Mary Bozickovic, 416/739-4243
Circulation/Interlibrary Loans, Clerk, Riad Rahal, 416/739-4225
Reference Librarian, Roberta McCarthy, 416/739-5702
Technical Services, Supervisor, Sheila Osborne, 416/739-4831

Environmental Commissioner of Ontario - Library, #605, 1075 Bay St., Toronto ON M5S 2B1 – 416/325-0363 – Librarian, Thérèse Lamie

Ernst & Young - National Tax Library, Toronto-Dominion Centre, 31st Fl., PO Box 251, Stn Toronto Dominion, Toronto ON M5K 1J7 – 416/943-3152; Fax: 416/864-1174
Supervisor, Diane Conwath
Assistant, Lynne Cooper

Estonian Central Council in Canada – Library, #308, 958 Broadview Ave., Toronto ON M4K 2R6 – 416/465-2219 – Contact, Maimu Palumäe

Etobicoke Education Centre - Resource Library, One Civic Centre Ct., Etobicoke ON M9C 2B3 – 416/394-7309; Fax: 416/394-7308 – Coordinator of Media Studies, Alice Churchman

The Etobicoke General Hospital – Library, 101 Humber College Blvd., Etobicoke ON M9V 1R8 – 416/747-3466 – Executive Director, Valery Close

Etobicoke Philharmonic Orchestra, 19 Hilldowntree Rd., Etobicoke ON M9A 2Z4 – 416/233-5665 – Librarian, Mary-Grace Knox

Family Service Association of Metropolitan Toronto – Library, 22 Wellesley St. East, Toronto ON M4Y 1G3 – 416/922-3126 – Theresa Sit

Fasken Campbell Godfrey - Law Library, Toronto-Dominion Centre, PO Box 20, Stn Toronto-Dominion, Toronto ON M5K 1N6 – 416/865-5143; Fax: 416/364-7813 – Head Librarian, Michele L. Miles

Federation of Ontario Naturalists – Library, 355 Lesmill Rd., North York ON M3B 2W8 – 416/444-8419 – Receptionist, Dianne Slyford

The Financial Post - Library, 333 King St. East, Toronto ON M5A 4N2 – 416/350-6690; Fax: 416/350-6301 – Library Manager, Theresa M. Butcher, 416/350-6693

Foodshare Metro Toronto – Library, 238 Queen St. West, Lower Level, Toronto ON M5V 1Z7 – 416/392-1669 – Office Manager, Samantha Dalby

Foundation for International Training – Library, #200, 1262 Don Mills Rd., North York ON M3B 2W7 – 416/449-8838; TLX: 06-986715 FIT T – Development Resources Coord., Rosemary Wolff

Frank Anrep & Associates Ltd. – Library, #200, 515 Consumers Rd., North York ON M2J 4Z2 – 416/502-0540 – Marketing Coordinator, Helen Anrep

Fraser & Beatty Law Office - Library, One First Canadian Place, PO Box 100, Stn First Canadian Place, Toronto ON M5X 1B2 – 416/863-4581; Fax: 416/863-4592; Email: Jan_Barrett@FraserBeatty.ca; URL: http://www.FraserBeatty.ca
Chief Librarian, Jan Barrett, 416/863-4581
Chief Librarian, Linda Boss, 416/863-4581
Reference Librarian, Ian Colvin, 416/862-3489
ILL Technician, Trish Richardson, 416/862-3472
Filing Technician, Marg Goger

George Brown College - Resource Centre, PO Box 1015, Toronto ON M5T 2T9 – 416/415-2676; Email: jhardy@gbrownc.on.ca – Associate Director, Education Resources, John L. Hardy

Giffels Associates Limited – Library, 30 International Blvd., Etobicoke ON M9W 5P3 – 416/675-5950; Toll Free: 1-800-567-8918 – Information Centre Giffels, Desiree Singh

Girl Guides of Canada – Resource Centre, 50 Merton St., Toronto ON M4S 1A3 – 416/487-5281 – Resource Centre Administrator, Lynn Austin

The Globe and Mail Ltd. - Library, 444 Front St. West, Toronto ON M5V 2S9 – 416/585-5076; Fax: 416/585-5085 – Head Librarian, Amanda Valpy

Goethe-Institut Toronto – Library, 1067 Yonge St., Toronto ON M4W 2L2 – 416/924-3327 – Head Librarian, Ulla Habekost

Goodman & Carr Law Office - Library, #2300, 200 King St. West, Toronto ON M5H 3W5 – 416/595-2300; Fax: 416/595-0567; Email: jsimpson@goodman-carr.com
Librarian, Jane Simpson
Assistant Librarian, Gaye Lefebvre

Goodwill Toronto – Library, 234 Adelaide St. East, Toronto ON M5A 1M9 – 416/362-4711 – Life Skills Coordinator, Janet Kerr

Gowlings - Library, #4900, Commerce Court West, PO Box 149, Stn Commerce Court, Toronto ON M5L 1J3 – 416/862-5735; Fax: 416/862-7661
Chief Librarian, Paula Schwindt, 416/862-5735
Assistant Librarian, Joanne Berent, 416/862-4382
Library Technician, Elisabeth Adams-Quan, 416/862-3505
Library Clerk, Ewa Zarska, 862-4383

The Green Brick Road – Library, 8 Dumas Ct., North York ON M3A 2N2 – 905/465-1597

Hay Management Consultants - Information Resource Centre, #700, 121 King St. West, Toronto ON M5H 3X7 – 416/868-1371; Fax: 416/868-6871; Email: haytor@hookup.net – Staff Librarian, Merle Johnson

Health Canada - Health Protection Branch - Regional Library, 2301 Midland Ave., Scarborough ON M1P 4R7 – 416/973-1556; Fax: 416/973-1559; Symbol: OTNHH – Librarian, Sandra Brockhurst

Hemophilia Ontario – Library, #308, 60 St. Clair Ave. East, Toronto ON M4T 1N5 – 416/972-0641 – Administrative Assistant, Marc Laprise

Hewitt Associates - Research Practice, #800, 25 Sheppard Ave. West, Toronto ON M2N 6T1 – 416/225-5001; Fax: 416/225-9790

Hicks Morley Hamilton Stewart Storie Law Office - Library, Toronto Dominion Bank Tower, Toronto-Dominion Centre, 30th Fl., PO Box 371, Toronto ON M5K 1K8 – 416/362-1011; Fax: 416/362-9680; Email: library@hicks.com – Library Technician, Lorenza G. Thompson, 416/362-1011, ext.119

The Hincks Centre for Children's Mental Health - Jackman Library, Silverman Bldg., 114 Maitland St., Toronto ON M4Y 1E1 – 416/972-1935, ext.3308; Fax: 416/924-9808; Symbol: HTC – Librarian, Rita M. Bondi

Holden Day Wilson Law Office - Library, #2400, T-D Bank Tower, T-D Centre, PO Box 52, Toronto ON M5K 1E7 – 416/361-1444; Fax: 416/361-1258

Chief Librarian, James Allan, 416/863-5686
Technician, John Brennan
Technical Services, Diane Rooke
Holocaust Education & Memorial Centre of Toronto – Holocaust Resource Centre, 4600 Bathurst St., North York ON M2R 3V2 – 416/635-2883, ext.144
Hong Fook Mental Health Association – Library, 146 Augusta Ave., 2nd Fl., Toronto ON M5T 2L5 – 416/595-1103 – Administrative Assistant, Theresa Chung
The Hospital for Sick Children – Library, 555 University Ave., Toronto ON M5G 1X8 – 416/813-6693; Fax: 416/813-7523 – Director, Elizabeth Uleryk
Houser, Henry & Syron Law Office - Library, #2000, 145 King St. West, Toronto ON M5H 2B6 – 416/362-3411; Fax: 416/362-3757 – Librarian, Sandra Findlay
The Hugh MacMillan Rehabilitation Centre - Health Sciences Library, 350 Rumsey Rd., Toronto ON M4G 1R8 – 416/425-6220, ext.517; Fax: 416/425-6591 – Librarian, Pui-ying Wong
Hughes, Amys Law Office - Library, North Tower, Royal Bank Plaza, 200 Bay St., 24th Fl., PO Box 45, Toronto ON M5J 2P6 – 416/367-1608; Fax: 416/367-8821; Email: pas@h_amys.mhs.compuserve.com – Librarian, Penny Sheehan
Huguenot Society of Canada – Library, #105, 4936 Yonge St., North York ON M2N 6S3 – Archivist, Paul Litt
Human Resources Development Canada - Ontario Regional Library, #700, 4900 Yonge St., North York ON M2N 6A8 – 416/224-4858; Fax: 416/224-4860; Symbol: OTMIO – Acting Librarian, Flaka Hersom
Humber College of Applied Arts & Technology - Library Services, PO Box 1900, Etobicoke ON M9W 5L7 – 416/675-3111, ext. 4311 – Librarian, Lynne Bentley
IBI Group – Library, 230 Richmond St. West, 5th Fl., Toronto ON M5V 1V6 – 416/596-1930, ext.107 – Librarian, Jennifer Osther
IBM Canada Limited - Information Resource Centre, 844 Don Mills Rd., North York ON M3C 1V7 – 416/448-3555; Fax: 416/448-3545
Librarian, Barbara Wallace, 416/448-3418
Library Assistant, Desiree Lloyd
Immigration & Refugee Board - Documentation Centre, 1 Front St. West, Ground Fl., Toronto ON M5J 1A5 – 416/973-8568; Fax: 416/973-7149; Symbol: OTIR – Chief, Theresa Smith
Documentation Centre, 70 University Ave., 8th Fl., Toronto ON M5J 2M5 – 416/954-1179; Fax: 416/954-1191; Symbol: OTIRB – Chief, Elizabeth Bennett
Imperial Oil Limited - Engineering & Petroleum Information Centre, #4104, 90 Wynford Dr., North York ON M3C 1K5 – 416/441-7858; Fax: 416/441-7926 – Information Specialist, Kathy Wallace
Inco Limited - Records & Information Management, #1500, 145 King St. West, Toronto ON M5H 4B7 – 416/361-7763; Fax: 416/361-7781, 7782
Manager, Records & Information Management, Jennifer Myrie
Librarian, Beverly Langer, 416/361-7518
Industrial Accident Prevention Association Ontario – Information Centre, Eaton Tower, 250 Yonge St., 28th Fl., Toronto ON M5B 2N4 – 416/506-8888; Toll Free: 1-800-669-4939 – Librarian, Delores Harms Penner
Industrial Accident Victims Group of Ontario – Library, #203, 489 College St., Toronto ON M6G 1A5 – 416/924-6477
Information Technology Research Centre – Library, D.L. Pratt Building, #286, 6 King's College Rd., Toronto ON M5S 1A1 – 416/978-7203 – Administrative Assistant, Roseanne Reid
Injured Workers Consultants - Resource Centre, #402, 815 Danforth Ave., Toronto ON M4J 1L2 – 416/461-2411; Fax: 416/461-7138

Institute for Aerospace Studies – Library, University of Toronto, 4925 Dufferin St., North York ON M3H 5T6 – 416/667-7712 – Librarian, Judy Mills
Institute for Policy Analysis – Library, University of Toronto, #707, 140 Saint George St., Toronto ON M5S 1A1 – 416/978-4854 – Ursula Gutenburg
Institute of Canadian Advertising – Library, #500, 2300 Yonge St., PO Box 2350, Toronto ON M4P 1E4 – 416/482-1396; Toll Free: 1-800-567-7422
Institute of Municipal Assessors of Ontario – Library, #303, 109 Railside Rd., North York ON M3A 1B2 – 416/447-7213 – Executive Director, W.J. Lettner
Insurance Bureau of Canada – Library, 181 University Ave., 13th Fl., Toronto ON M5H 3M7 – 416/362-2031, x350; Toll Free: 1-800-387-2880 – Librarian, Sandra Rakovac
Insurance Institute of Canada – Library, 18 King St. East, 6th Fl., Toronto ON M5C 1C4 – 416/591-1572 – Librarian, Nancy MacGillivray
Insurers' Advisory Organization (1989) Inc. – Library, #700, 18 King St. East, Toronto ON M5C 1C4 – 416/368-1801; Toll Free: 1-800-268-8080
Intergovernmental Committee on Urban & Regional Research – Library, #301, 150 Eglinton Ave. East, Toronto ON M4P 1E8 – 416/973-1339 – Senior Information Officer, Vicky Gregor
International Commission for the Co-ordination of Solidarity Among Sugar Workers – Sugar Workers & Industry Education Resource Library, #3, 2084 Danforth Ave., Toronto ON M4C 1J9 – 416/467-8621; Email: Web:iccsasw; Symbol: SWIERL – Librarian, Jennifer Sweeney
International Council for Adult Education – Resource Centre, #500, 720 Bathurst St., Toronto ON M5S 2R4 – 416/588-1211; Email: icae@web.apc.org – Outreach Coordinator, Eva Kupidura
International Relief Agency Inc. – Library, 95 Wood St., Toronto ON M4Y 2Z3 – 416/922-7120 – Office Manager, Eileen Brown
International Society of Toronto for Hungarian Church History – Library, Regis College, 15 St. Mary St., Toronto ON M4Y 2R5 – 416/922-2476
ISM (Information Systems Management) - Corporation Library, 251 Consumers Rd., 10th Fl., North York ON M2J 4R3 – 416/351-6741; Fax: 416/351-6294 – Systems Librarian, Wai Lai
Italian Cultural Institute – Library, 496 Huron St., Toronto ON M5R 2R3 – 416/921-3802 – Administrative Coordinator, Mariolina Franceschetti
Janssen-Ortho Inc. - Information Resource Centre, 19 Green Belt Dr., North York ON M3C 1L9 – 416/442-2500; Fax: 416/449-2520
Manager, Information Resources, Teresa Helik, 416/382-5106, Email: thelik@joica.jnj.com
Information Specialist, Karen Gaggi
Japanese External Trade Organization – Japan Trade Centre, #1600, 181 University Ave., Toronto ON M5H 3M7 – 416/861-0000
The Jesuit Centre for Social Faith & Justice – Library, 947 Queen St. East, Toronto ON M4M 1J9 – 416/469-1123 – JRS/Canada Coordinator, Ezat Mossallanejad
Jewish Genealogical Society of Canada – North York Central Library, Canadiana Room, PO Box 446, North York ON M2N 2T1 – 416/395-5623
Jewish Student Federation – Library, #442, Student Centre, York University, 4700 Keele St., North York ON M3J 1P3 – 416/736-5178
The John Howard Society of Ontario – Library, 6 Jackson Pl., Toronto ON M6P 1T6 – 416/604-8412
John Milton Society for the Blind in Canada – Library, #202, 40 St. Clair Ave. East, Toronto ON M4T 1M9 – 416/960-3953 – Librarian, Rena Riley
Justice Canada - Toronto Regional Office – Library, #3400, 2 First Canadian Place, PO Box 36, Stn First Canadian Place, Toronto ON M5X 1K6 – 416/973-2334; Fax: 416/973-3586; Symbol: OTJ – Librarian, Alison Colvin

Kelly, White & Smith Law Office - Library, #1020, 130 Adelaide St. West, Toronto ON M5H 3P5 – 416/366-5900; Fax: 416/366-1799 – Lori Sangiuliano
Kids Help Phone – Library, 439 University Ave., Toronto ON M5G 1Y8 – 416/586-0100; Toll Free: 1-800-668-6868 – Manager, Information/Grants, Wendy Josberg
Knox College - Caven Library, 59 St. George St., Toronto ON M5S 2E6 – 416/978-4504; Fax: 416/971-2133; Email: tucker@vax.library.utoronto.ca; URL: http://www.utoronto.ca/knox; Symbol: OTK
Readers Services Librarian, Kathleen Gibson
Technical Services Librarian, Chris Tucker
Korean Canadian Cultural Association of Metro Toronto – Library, 20 Mobile Dr., North York ON M4A 1H9 – 416/755-9288
KPMG - John Walker Library, PO Box 31, Toronto ON M5L 1B2 – 416/777-8515; Fax: 416/777-8586; Email: kpmglbry@hookup.net
Manager/Librarian, Cathy Gareau, 416/777-8512
Tax Library, Reference Specialist, M. Ulehla, 416/777-8513
Library Clerk, B. Gravelle, 416/777-8093
Tax Library, Reference, L. Boyko, 416/777-3307
Technical Services Information Specialist, J. Andersen, 416/777-8092
Lang Michener - Library, BCE Pl., #2500, 181 Bay St., PO Box 747, Toronto ON M5J 2T7 – 416/360-8600; Fax: 416/365-1719
Manager, Library Services, Nancy L. Clarke, 416/307-4158
Senior Library Technician, Margaret Harrop, 416/307-4140
Library Technician, Jacquie Gray, 416/360-8611, ext.2083
Library Clerk, Suzanna La Rose, 416/360-8611, ext.2226
Latin American Working Group – Counterpoint Library, 603 1/2 Parliament St., Toronto ON M5S 2T2 – 416/921-4424
Law Society of Upper Canada – Great Library, Osgoode Hall, 130 Queen St. West, Toronto ON M5H 2N6 – 416/947-3300 – Glen W. Howell
League for Human Rights of B'nai Brith Canada – Education & Training Centre, 15 Hove St., Downsview ON M3H 4Y8 – 416/633-6227; Email: bnb@netwave.ca – Manager, Sharon Amsman
The League of Canadian Poets – Poetry Library, The Writers' Centre, 54 Wolseley St., 3rd Fl., Toronto ON M5T 1A5 – 416/504-1657 – Tours Coordinator, Sandie Drzewiecki
Learning Disabilities Association of Ontario – LDAO Resource Library, Box 39, #1004, 365 Bloor St. East, Toronto ON M4W 3L4 – 416/929-4311 – Resource Counsellor, Diane Wagner
Lende & Associates Law Office - Library, #1900, 180 Dundas St. West, Toronto ON M5G 1Z8 – 416/598-7876; Fax: 416/979-0430
Leprosy Mission Canada – Library, #216, 40 Wynford Dr., North York ON M3C 1J5 – 416/441-3618 – Director, Communications, Nicholas Hunter
Life Underwriters Association of Canada, 41 Lesmill Rd., North York ON M3B 2T3 – 416/444-5251 – Librarian, Ilse Selwyn
Lilly, Blott Law Office – Library, Guardian of Canada Tower, #2200, 181 University Ave., Toronto ON M5H 3M7 – 416/365-6300; Fax: 416/365-7429 – Librarian, Micky Wylie
Litton Systems Canada Ltd. - Library, 25 City View Dr., Etobicoke ON M9W 5A7 – 416/249-1231; Fax: 416/246-2016 – Librarian, Jackie Brown
Lyndhurst Hospital – Health Sciences Library, 520 Sutherland Dr., Toronto ON M4G 3V9 – 416/422-5551 – Ann Marie Chin
Maclean's Magazine - Library, 777 Bay St., 7th Fl., Toronto ON M5W 1A7 – 416/596-5340; Fax: 416/596-7730 – Chief Librarian, Basil Guinane

Canadian Almanac & Directory 1997

The Manufacturers Life Insurance Company – Business Library, 200 Bloor St. East, Toronto ON M4W 1E5 – 416/926-5221; Fax: 416/926-5540; Email: fmcmanus@manulife.com – Head Librarian, Frances McManus

Marsh & McLennan Ltd. - Information Centre, Canada Trust Tower, BCE Place, 161 Bay St., PO Box 502, Toronto ON M5J 2S4 – 416/868-2697; Fax: 416/868-2870 – M. Cavers

Massey College - Robertson Davies Library, 4 Devonshire Place, Toronto ON M5S 2E1 – 416/978-2893; Fax: 416/978-1759; Symbol: CoOTMC – Librarian, Marie Korey

McCarthy Tétrault - John J. Robinette Library, #4700, Toronto-Dominion Bank Tower, Toronto-Dominion Centre, Toronto ON M5K 1E6 – 416/601-8200; Fax: 416/868-0673; Email: library@mccarthy.ca – Head Librarian, Mary Percival, 416/601-7843

McLean & Kerr Law Office - Library, #2800, 130 Adelaide St. West, Toronto ON M5H 3P5 – 416/364-5371; Fax: 416/366-8571 – Librarian, Audrey Jessup

McMillan Binch Law Library, Royal Bank Plaza, South Tower, PO Box 38, Toronto ON M5J 2J7 – 416/865-7031; Fax: 416/865-7048; Email: randersen@mcbinch.com
   Manager, Library Services, Ricki Anne Andersen, 416/865-7031
   Reference Librarian, Lenie Ott, 416/865-7269
   Technical Services Technician, Lynn Alvernaz, 416/865-7870
   Acquisitions Clerk, Suzan Walzak, 416/865-7867
   Serials Clerk, Bonnie Brett, 416/865-7161

Meighen Demers Law Office - Library, Merrill Lynch Canada Tower, Box 11, #1100, 200 King St. West, Toronto ON M5H 3T4 – 416/977-8400; Fax: 416/977-5239 – Librarian, Janine Miller

Merrill Lynch Canada Inc. - Corporate Library, 200 King St. West, 5th Fl., Toronto ON M5H 3W3 – 416/586-6016; Fax: 416/586-6419 – Manager, Corporate Library, Susan Bryant

Metropolitan Separate School Board - Catholic Education Centre Library, 80 Sheppard Ave. East, North York ON M2N 6E8 – 416/222-8282, ext.5324; Fax: 416/229-5345 – Program Coordinator, Judy Smith

Metropolitan Toronto Association for Community Living – AV/Reference Services, 20 Spadina Rd., Toronto ON M5R 2S7 – 416/968-0650 – Library Technician, Susan Rawle

Metropolitan Toronto Convention & Visitors Association – Information Centre, Queen's Quay Terminal at Harbourfront, #590, 207 Queen's Quay West, PO Box 126, Toronto ON M5J 1A7 – 416/203-2600; Toll Free: 1-800/363-1990 – Advertising Manager, Ken Gruber

The Michener Institute for Applied Health Sciences – Library, 222 St. Patrick St., Toronto ON M5T 1V4 – 416/596-3101, ext.3123 – Librarian, Ray Banks

Midland Walwyn Capital Inc. - Library, 40 King St. West, 34th Fl., Toronto ON M5H 1B5 – 416/369-7547; Fax: 416/369-2803 – Librarian, Sonia Solomon

Miller Thomson Law Office - Library, #2700, 20 Queen St. West, Toronto ON M5H 3S1 – 416/595-8537; Fax: 416/595-8695 – Librarian, Ines Freeman

Mizrachi-Hapoel Hamizrachi Organization of Canada – Library, #503, 3101 Bathurst St., Toronto ON M6A 2A6 – 416/789-7576 – Rochelle Shulman

M.M. Dillon Ltd. – Library, #300, 100 Sheppard Ave. East, PO Box 1850, Toronto ON M2N 6K7 – 416/229-4646

Molson Breweries - Technical Services Centre, 33 Carlingview Dr., Etobicoke ON M9W 5E4 – 416/798-1786; Fax: 416/798-8390 – TSC Administrator, Sophia A. (Sandi) Lloyd

Morgan Stanley Canada Ltd. - Library, #3700, 181 Bay St., Toronto ON M5J 2T3 – 416/943-8413; Fax: 416/368-0796 – Librarian, Frances Main

Morris, Rose, Ledgett Law Office - Library, Canada Trust Tower, BCE Place, 161 Bay St., Toronto ON M5J 2S1 – 416/981-9400; Fax: 416/863-9500 – Librarian, Helen Hochberg

Morrison Hershfield Ltd. – Library, 4 Lansing Sq., North York ON M2J 1T1 – 416/499-3110 – Manager, Administration, Elaine LaPrarie

Moss Lawson & Co. Ltd. - Library, #410, 1 Toronto St., Toronto ON M5C 2W3 – 416/864-2700; Fax: 416/864-2756 – Librarian, Anne Frelich

Mount Sinai Hospital – Sidney Liswood Library, 600 University Ave., Toronto ON M5G 1X5 – 416/586-4614; Fax: 416/586-4998; Email: msh@library.utoronto.ca – Director, Library Services, Linda Devore

Multicultural History Society of Ontario – Resource Centre, 43 Queen's Park Cres. East, Toronto ON M5S 2C3 – 416/979-2973 – Library Technician, Renée Rogers

Multiple Sclerosis Society of Canada – Information Resource Centre, #1000, 250 Bloor St. East, Toronto ON M4W 3P9 – 416/922-6065; Toll Free: 1-800-268-7582 – Librarian, Nancy Crozier

National Action Committee on the Status of Women – Library, #203, 234 Eglinton Ave. East, Toronto ON M4P 1K5 – 416/932-1718; Toll Free: 1-800-665-5124 – Andrea Ritchie

National Automobile, Aerospace, Transportation & General Workers Union of Canada (CLC) – Library, 205 Placer Ct., North York ON M2H 3H9 – 416/497-4110; Symbol: OWCA – Librarian, Kathy Bennett

National Defence (Canada)-Defence & Civil Institute of Environmental Medicine – Library, 1133 Sheppard Ave. West, PO Box 2000, North York ON M3M 3B9 – 416/635-2070; Email: sic@dciem.dnd.ca; Symbol: OTDR – Head, Information Services, Kathy Sutton

National Eating Disorder Information Centre – Library, College Wing 1-211, 200 Elizabeth St., Toronto ON M5G 2C4 – 416/340-4156

National Trust Mutual Funds – Reference Library, One Financial Place, One Adelaide St. East, Toronto ON M5C 2W8 – 416/361-3863; Toll Free: 1-800-563-4683 – Patricia Greenwell

Native Women's Resource Centre of Toronto – Library, 251 Gerrard St. East, Toronto ON M5A 2G1 – 416/963-9963 – Jackie Alton

Nesbitt Burns - Library, One First Canadian Place, PO Box 150, Stn 1st Cdn Place, Toronto ON M5X 1H3 – 416/359-4587; Fax: 416/365-4417
   Manager of Information Services, Dani Breen
   Library Technician, Karen Nowicki

Nickel Development Institute – Library, #510, 214 King St. West, Toronto ON M5H 3S6 – 416/591-7999; TLX: 06-218565 – Publications Manager, Barbara Fell

Noranda Minerals Inc. - Information Centre, #2700, One Adelaide St. East, Toronto ON M5C 2Z6 – 416/982-7238; Fax: 416/982-7021
   Librarian, Sally A. Goodings
   Assistant, Marjorie Jackson

North York Board of Education - The F.W. Minkler Library, 5050 Yonge St., North York ON M2N 5N8 – 416/395-8289; Fax: 416/395-8292; Email: fwm@hookup.net; Symbol: OTNYE
   Senior Librarian, L.G. Lyons
   Cataloguing, J. Ameline
   Librarian/Archivist, J. Creelman
   Librarian, S. Leclaire

North York General Hospital – W. Keith Welsh Library, 4001 Leslie St., Willowdale ON M2K 1E1 – 416/756-6142; Fax: 416/756-6605 – Director, Library Services, Marjory Morphy

North York Symphony Association – Music Library, #109, 1210 Sheppard Ave. East, North York ON M2K 1E3 – 416/499-2204 – Librarian, Linda Perkins

Northern Miner - Library, 1450 Don Mills Rd., North York ON M3B 2X7 – 416/442-2164; Fax: 416/442-2181 – Administrative Assistant, Mariann Semkin

Ombudsman Ontario - Library, Communications Department, 125 Queen's Park, Toronto ON M5S 2C7 – 416/586-3300; Fax: 416/586-3485; Toll Free: 1-800-263-1830 – Administrative Secretary, Barbara Masukawa, 416/586-3353

The Ontario Archaeological Society Inc. – Library, 126 Willowdale Ave., North York ON M2N 4Y2 – 416/730-0797 – Librarian, Charles Garrad

Ontario Association of Art Galleries – Library, #306, 489 King St. West, Toronto ON M5V 1K4 – 416/598-0714 – Don Stanton

Ontario Association of Distress Centres – Library, #418, 99 Atlantic Ave., Toronto ON M6K 3J8 – 416/537-7373 – Office Manager, Charlotte Redekop

Ontario Association of Volunteer Bureaux/Centres – Library, #203, 2 Dunbloor Rd., Etobicoke ON M9A 2E4 – 416/236-0588 – Iga Jakubowska

Ontario Bible College & Theological Seminary - J. Wm. Horsey Library, 25 Ballyconnor Ct., North York ON M2M 4B3 – 416/226-6380 – Librarian, Hugh Rendle

Ontario Black History Society – Library, Ontario Heritage Centre, #202, 10 Adelaide St. East, Toronto ON M5C 1J3 – 416/867-9420 – Everette Moore

Ontario Cancer Institute – Library, Princess Margaret Hospital, 500 Sherbourne St., Toronto ON M4X 1K9 – 416/926-4482

Ontario Centre for Environmental Technology Advancement – Library, 63 Polson St., 2nd Fl., Toronto ON M5A 1A4 – 416/778-5275 – Information Manager, Nancy Shepherd

Ontario College of Art - Dorothy H. Hoover Library, 100 McCaul St., Toronto ON M5T 1W1 – 416/977-6000; Fax: 416/977-0235; Symbol: OTCA
   Director, Jill Patrick, Email: jpatrick@oca.on.ca
   Head, A/V Services, Angelo Rao
   Head, Technical Support, Jim Forrester
   Media Librarian, Tom Ready
   Circulation Technician, Lee Henderson

Ontario Crafts Council – Library, Chalmer's Building, 35 McCaul St., Toronto ON M5T 1V7 – 416/977-3551 – Information Officer, Jane Moore

Ontario Energy Board - Library, 2300 Yonge St., 26th Fl., PO Box 2319, Toronto ON M4P 1E4 – 416/440-7655; Fax: 416/440-7656 – Librarian, Lina Buccilli

Ontario Environmental Assessment Advisory Committee - Library, 65 St. Clair Ave. East, 7th Fl., Toronto ON M4T 2Y3 – 416/323-2666 – Administrative Assistant, Trish Shayne

Ontario Federation of Agriculture – Library, #500, 491 Eglinton Ave. West, Toronto ON M5N 3A2 – 416/485-3333 – Cecil Bradley

Ontario Federation of Labour – Library, #202, 15 Gervais Dr., North York ON M3C 1Y8 – 416/441-2731 – Secretary-Librarian, Judy Robins

Ontario Genealogical Society – Library, #102, 40 Orchard View Blvd., Toronto ON M4R 1B9 – 416/395-5623 – Coordinator, Library Division, Alison Lobb

Ontario Hydro - Corporate Library, 700 University Ave., Toronto ON M5G 1X6 – 416/592-2716; Fax: 416/592-7532; Symbol: OTH
   Information Resources Supervisor, Kim Cornell
   Reference Librarian, Joanne Collingwood, 416/592-2715

Ontario Institute for Studies in Education - Library, 252 Bloor St. West, Toronto ON M5S 1V6 – 416/923-6641, ext.2206; Fax: 416/926-4745; Email: igibb@oise.on.ca
   Chief Librarian, Malcolm Levin
   Acquisitions & Orders, Valerie Downs
   Audio Visual, Carol Calder
   Public Services, Jan Schmidt
   Reference, Marian Press
   Serials, Valerie Downs
   Systems, Mary Campbell

Technical Services, Ilze Bregzis
Circulation, Kamlesh Sharma
Curriculum Resources, Ruth Marks
ONTERIS, R. McClelland
Special Collections, Jan Schmidt
Ontario Insurance Commission - Library, 5160 Yonge St., PO Box 85, North York ON M2N 6L9 – 416/590-7135; Fax: 416/590-7070; Email: shanfij@gov.on.ca; Symbol: OTOI – Librarian, Joy Shanfield
Ontario Labour Relations Board - Library, 400 University Ave., 4th Fl., Toronto ON M7A 1V4 – 416/326-7468; Fax: 416/326-7531; Symbol: OTOLR
Manager, Kevin Jenkins, 416/326-7467
Reference Technician, Ursula Nocon
Library Assistant, Amy Leung
Ontario Law Reform Commission - Library, 720 Bay St., 11th Fl., Toronto ON M5G 2K1 – 416/326-4199; Fax: 416/326-4693 – Librarian, Carol Frymer
Ontario Legislative Library, Legislative Bldg., Queen's Park, 7 Queens Park Cres. South, Toronto ON M7A 1A4 – 416/325-3900; Fax: 416/325-3925; Email: ONT.LEG.LIB; Symbol: OTL
Executive Director, Mary Dickerson
Information & Reference Services, Donna Burton, 416/325-3945
Collections Development, Brian Tobin, 416/325-3910
Press Clipping Service, Karen Wierucki, 416/314-8534
Technical Services & Systems, Pamela Stoksik, 416/314-8520
Acquisitions Librarian, Deirdre Grimes, 416/314-8525
Legislative Research Service, Cynthia Smith, 416/325-3637
Ontario Lung Association – Environmental Information Centre, #201, 573 King St. East, Toronto ON M5A 4L3 – 416/864-9911; Toll Free: 1-800-668-7682 – Environmental Program Manager, Ian Morton
Ontario Lupus Association – Resource Centre, #901, 250 Bloor St. East, Toronto ON M4W 3P2 – 416/967-1414 – Staff Liaison, Violet Turalba
Ontario Management Board Secretariat - Library & Resource Centre, Ferguson Block, 77 Wellesley St. West, 4th Fl., Toronto ON M7A 1N3 – 416/327-2533; Fax: 416/327-2530; Email: Mackelm@gov.on.ca; Symbol: OTOM
Coordinator, Marilyn MacKellar
Library Assistant, Fabiola Colavizza, 416/327-2534, 0996
Ontario March of Dimes – Resource Centre, 10 Overlea Blvd., Toronto ON M4H 1A4 – 416/425-3463; Toll Free: 1-800-263-3463
Ontario Medical Association – Library, #300, 525 University Ave., Toronto ON M5G 2K7 – 416/340-2914 – Manager, Corporate Info., Jane Buzza
Ontario Ministry of Agriculture & Food - Corporate Library, 801 Bay St., 3rd Fl., Toronto ON M7A 2B2 – 416/326-3138; Fax: 416/325-1152 – Manager, Library Services, Sharon Brown
Ontario Ministry of Citizenship - Resource Centre, 77 Bloor St. West, 9th Fl., Toronto ON M7A 2R9 – 416/314-7499; Fax: 416/314-6543; Symbol: OTCR – Librarian, Angela Vassos
Ontario Ministry of Community & Social Services - Library & Learning Resources, 880 Bay St., 4th Fl., Toronto ON M7A 1E9 – 416/326-6442; Fax: 416/326-6453; Email: ENVOY: ILL.OTPW
Library Manager, Dolly Lyn, 416/326-6446
Reference Librarian, Elizabeth Sharp, 416/326-6448
Technical Services, Sallie Thayer, 416/326-6450
Circulation, Anna DiFelice, 416/326-6442
Acquisitions, Perry Tom, 416/326-6443
Ontario Ministry of Consumer & Commercial Relations - Library, 250 Yonge St., 33rd Fl., Toronto ON M5B 2N5 – 416/326-8561; Fax: 416/326-8387; Symbol: OTFC – Librarian, Mona Arlin

Ontario Ministry of Economic Development, Trade & Tourism - InfoSource, Hearst Block, 900 Bay St., 3rd Fl., Toronto ON M7A 2E1 – 416/325-6626; Fax: 416/325-6635
Information Retrieval Specialist, Lynda Bond, Email: bondl@gov.on.ca
Information Retrieval Specialist, Lindsay Wood Coolidge, Email: coolidl@gov.on.ca
Ontario Ministry of Education & Training - Information Services Unit Library, Mowat Block, 900 Bay St., 13th Fl., Toronto ON M7A 1L2 – 416/325-2640; Fax: 416/325-4235
Chief Librarian, Hilary Roy, 416/325-2653
Reference Librarian, Simon Loban, 416/325-2653
Circulation Librarian, Norman Roxburgh, 416/325-2644
Technical Services Librarian, Joyce Kipps, 416/325-2643
Acquisitions Librarian, Ani Kurdian, 416/325-2640
Ontario Ministry of Environment & Energy - Approvals Branch Library, 250 Davisville Ave., 3rd Fl., Toronto ON M4S 1H2 – 416/440-6985; Fax: 416/440-6973; Symbol: OTMEAB – Library Technician, Peggy Cameron, Email: cameron@gov.on.ca
Energy Board Library, 2300 Yonge St., 26th Fl., Toronto ON M4P 1E4 – 416/440-7666 – Lina Buccilli
Energy Library, 56 Wellesley St. West, 10th Fl., Toronto ON M4S 2S3 – 416/327-1247 – Blake Johnston
Environmental Assessment Library, 250 Davisville Ave., 5th Fl., Toronto ON M4S 1H2 – 416/440-3450 – Peggy Cameron
Environmental Planning & Prevention Division Library, 250 Davisville Ave., 3rd Fl., Toronto ON M4S 1H2 – 416/440-6985; Fax: 416/440-6973 – Library Technician, Peggy Cameron
Legal Services Library, 135 St Clair Ave. West, 10th Fl., Toronto ON M4V 1P5 – 416/323-4309 – Jane Thompson
Program Development Branch Library, 40 St Clair Ave. West, 14th Fl., Toronto ON M4V 1M2 – 416/314-7959 – Maria Nicolescu
Public Information Centre, 135 St. Clair Ave. West, Toronto ON M4V 1P5 – 416/323-4321; Fax: 416/323-4564; Toll Free: 1-800-565-4923 – Researcher/Group Leader, Fania Urbina
Science & Technology Library, 2 St Clair Ave. West, 14th Fl., Toronto ON M4V 1L5 – 416/323-5131; Fax: 416/323-5031; Symbol: OTMEW
Standards Development Branch Library, 2 St Clair Ave. West, 12th Fl., Toronto ON M4V 1L5 – 416/323-5009 – Iraj Rahmani
Ontario Ministry of Finance - Library Services, Frost Bldg. North, 1st Fl., 95 Grosvenor St., Toronto ON M7A 1Y8 – 416/325-1200; Fax: 416/325-1212; Symbol: OTDRE
Coordinator, Library Services, Helen Katz
Information Technician, Ruth Fleming
Ontario Ministry of Health – Laboratory Services Branch, PO Box 9000, Toronto ON M5W 1R5 – 416/235-5935; Symbol: OTDHL – Librarian, Doris Standing
Library, 5700 Yonge St., Ground Fl., North York ON M2M 4K5 – 416/327-8200; Fax: 416/327-8209 – Supervisor, Veronica Brunka
Ontario Ministry of Labour - Library Services, 400 University Ave., 10th Fl., Toronto ON M7A 1T7 – 416/326-7840; Fax: 416/326-7844; Symbol: OTDL – Head, Library Services, Sandra Gold
Ontario Ministry of Municipal Affairs & Housing - Library, 777 Bay St., 2nd Fl., Toronto ON M5G 2E5 – 416/585-6527; Fax: 416/585-7300; Symbol: OTOH
Chief Librarian, Annette Dignan
Information Specialist, Michele Fleet
Ontario Ministry of Natural Resources - Library, 90 Sheppard Ave. East, North York ON M2N 3A1 – 416/314-1206; Fax: 416/314-1210; Email: louets@mnr.gov.on.ca – Manager, Sandra F. Louet

Ontario Ministry of the Attorney General - Law Library, 720 Bay St., 9th Fl., Toronto ON M5G 1K1 – 416/326-4566; Fax: 416/326-4562 – Manager, Maria Cece, 416/326-4563
Ontario Ministry of the Solicitor General & Correctional Services - Mimico Correctional Complex Library, 130 Horner Ave., PO Box 75, Toronto ON M8V 3S9 – 416/314-9684; Fax: 416/314-9698 – Library Technician, Laurie Fenton
Office of the Fire Marshal, Fire Sciences Library, Place Nouveau Bldg., 5775 Yonge St., 7th Fl., North York ON M2M 3T7 – 416/325-3235; Fax: 416/325-3213; Email: chongje@epo.gov.on.ca
Librarian, Jean Chong
Library Technician, Gabrielle Gaedecke
Ontario Ministry of Transportation - MTO Library, Central Bldg., #129, 1201 Wilson Ave., Downsview ON M3M 1J8 – 416/235-4546; Fax: 416/235-4915; Toll Free: 1-800-268-4686; Email: barbergr@epo.gov.on.ca; Symbol: OTDT
Reference Librarian, Greg Barber
Public Services, Judy Martin
Technical Services Librarian, Laila Zvejnieks
Acquisitions, Deanna Clark
Ontario Museum Association – Library, George Brown House, 50 Baldwin St., Toronto ON M5T 1L4 – 416/348-8672 – Librarian, Janet Chessell
Ontario Nurses' Association – Library, #600, 85 Grenville St., Toronto ON M5S 3A2 – 416/964-8833; Toll Free: 1-800-387-5580
Ontario Physical & Health Education Association – Library, #501, 1185 Eglinton Ave. East, North York ON M3C 3C6 – 416/426-7120
Ontario Public Interest Research Group – Library, #201, 455 Spadina Ave., Toronto ON M5S 2G8 – 416/978-7770 – Toronto Coordinator, Andrea Calver
Ontario Public School Boards Association – Library, Phoenix House, 439 University Ave., 18th Fl., Toronto ON M5G 1Y8 – 416/340-2540 – Carol Cohen
Ontario Public Service Employees Union – Library, 100 Lesmill Rd., North York ON M3B 3P8 – 416/443-8888; Fax: 416/448-7454; Toll Free: 1-800-268-7376 – Librarian, Annie Keung
Ontario Recreational Canoeing Association – Library, #104, 1185 Eglinton Ave. East, North York ON M3C 3C6 – 416/426-7170 – Communications Director, Chris Beckett
Ontario Round Table on Environment & Economy - Library, #2502, 1 Dundas St. West, Toronto ON M5G 1Z3 – 416/327-2032 – Secretary, Ruth Meehan
Ontario Safety League – Film Service, #100, 21 Four Seasons Pl., Etobicoke ON M9B 6J8 – 416/620-1720 – Film/Video Librarian, Wendy Cleaver
Ontario Science Centre - Library, 770 Don Mills Rd., North York ON M3C 1T3 – 416/696-3149; Fax: 416/696-3157; Symbol: OTST – Librarian, Valerie Hatten
Ontario Securities Commission - Library, 20 Queen St. West, 8th Fl., Toronto ON M5H 3S8 – 416/593-8268; Fax: 416/593-8240; Email: sinclado@gov.on.ca – Librarian, Donna Sinclair
Ontario Society of Clinical Hypnosis – Library, #402, 200 St. Clair Ave. West, Toronto ON M4V 1R1 – 416/251-2442 – Patricia Derraugh
Ontario Sports & Recreation Centre Inc. – Library, 1185 Eglinton Ave. East, North York ON M3C 3C6 – 416/426-7060 – Heather Stewart
Ontario Teachers' Federation – Library, #700, 1260 Bay St., Toronto ON M5R 2B5 – 416/966-3424 – Elfrieda Young
Ontario Women's Directorate - Resource Centre, 2 Carlton St., 12th Fl., Toronto ON M5B 2M9 – 416/314-0306; Fax: 416/314-0254 – Dr. J. Huie
Ontor Ltd. – Library, 12 Leswyn Rd., Toronto ON M6A 1K3 – 416/781-5286 – Marketing Coordinator, Mary Borg

Canadian Almanac & Directory 1997

Orchestras Ontario – Resource Centre, #311, 56 The Esplanade, Toronto ON M5E 1A7 – 416/366-8834

Orthopaedic & Arthritic Hospital – Health Sciences Library, 43 Wellesley St. East, Toronto ON M4Y 1H1 – 416/967-8545 – Susan Baillie

Osteoporosis Society of Canada – Linda Fraser Library, 33 Laird Dr., Toronto ON M4G 3S9 – 416/696-2663; Toll Free: 1-800-463-6842

Outerbridge, Miller, Sefton, Willms & Shier - Library, #900, 4 King St. West, Toronto ON M5H 1B6 – 416/863-0711; Fax: 416/863-1938 – Librarian, Lesley Rhodes

Packaging Association of Canada – Library, #330, 2255 Sheppard Ave. East, North York ON M2J 4Y1 – 905/490-7860 – Jonathan Wray

Pay Equity Commission - Library, 150 Eglinton Ave. East, 5th Fl., Toronto ON M4P 1E8 – 416/481-4464; Fax: 416/314-8741; Email: walkerc@gov.on.ca; Symbol: OTPE – Librarian, Catherine A. Walker, 416/481-4464, ext.667

Periodical Writers Association of Canada – Library, #203, 54 Wolseley St., Toronto ON M5T 1A5 – 416/504-1645

Photographical Historical Society of Canada – Library, 1512 Avenue Rd., PO Box 54620, Toronto ON M5M 4N5 – 416/691-1555 – Gerry Loban

PLAN International Canada – Library, #1001, 95 St. Clair Ave. West, Toronto ON M4V 3B5 – 416/920-1654; Toll Free: 1-800-268-7174; TLX: 06-367-00847

Playwrights Union of Canada – Drama Reading Room, 54 Wolseley St., 2nd Fl., Toronto ON M5T 1A5 – 416/703-0201; Toll Free: 1-800-561-3318 – Customer Service, Robert Alton

Polten & Hodder Law Office - Library, Guardian of Canada Tower, #2200, 181 University Ave., Toronto ON M5H 3M7 – 416/601-6766; Fax: 416/947-0909 – Acquisitions Librarian, L. Kunzelmann

Price Waterhouse - National/Toronto Office Library, #3300, One First Canadian Place, PO Box 190, Stn First Canadian Place, Toronto ON M5X 1H7 – 416/863-1133; Fax: 416/947-8921
Manager, Nancy Wells
Head of Reference/Public Services, Margaret Ashton
Manager, National Tax Library, H. Kerr, 365-8151

Prospectors & Developers Association of Canada – Library, 34 King St. East, 9th Fl., Toronto ON M5C 2X8 – 416/362-1969 – Saley Lawton

The Prudential Insurance Company of America – Library, 200 Consilium Pl., Scarborough ON M1H 3E6 – 416/296-0777 – Elinor Major

Public Works & Government Services Canada - Translation Bureau - Ontario Regional Library, #210, 55 St Clair Ave. East, Toronto ON M4T 1M2 – 416/973-1154; Fax: 416/973-3325; Email: pwgscth@inforamp.net; Symbol: OTGSC-C – Head, S. Castaneda

The Queen Elizabeth Hospital – Library Services, 550 University Ave., Toronto ON M5G 2A2 – 416/597-3050; Email: qeh@library.utoronto.ca – Manager, Helen Michael

Queen Street Mental Health Centre – Library, 1001 Queen St. West, Toronto ON M6J 1H4 – 416/535-8501 – Mary-Ann Georges

Quetico Foundation – Library, #610, 48 Yonge St., Toronto ON M5E 1G6 – 807/929-2571 – Librarian, Andrea Allison

Real Estate Institute of Canada – Library, #208, 5407 Eglinton Ave. West, Toronto ON M9C 5K6 – 416/695-9000

Recycling Council of Ontario – Library, #504, 489 College St., Toronto ON M6G 1A5 – 416/960-1025; Toll Free: 1-800-263-2849 – Library Coordinator, Irene Fedun

Reed Stenhouse Ltd. - National Resource Centre, 20 Bay St., Toronto ON M5J 2N9 – 416/868-5520; Fax: 416/868-5580; Symbol: OTRS – Research Manager, O. Gil

Retail Council of Canada – Library, #1210, 121 Bloor St. West, Toronto ON M4W 3M5 – 416/922-6678 – Researcher, Irene Fedyushina

Revenue Canada - Research & Library Services, #1000, 5001 Yonge St., North York ON M2N 6R9 – 416/218-4597; Fax: 416/512-2558; Symbol: OTNYR – Librarian, Harinder Guraya
Research & Library Services, 36 Adelaide St. East, Toronto ON M5C 1J7 – 416/973-9359; Fax: 416/954-6015; Symbol: OTRCT – Librarian, Paul Sawa

Richardson Greenshields of Canada Ltd. - Library, #1400, 130 Adelaide St. West, Toronto ON M5H 1T8 – 416/860-3432; Fax: 416/368-2481 – Librarian, Alison Crawley

Right to Life Association of Toronto – Resource Centre, #700, 120 Eglinton Ave. East, Toronto ON M4P 1E2 – 416/483-7869 – June Scandiffio

Rio Algom Ltd. - Information Centre, 120 Adelaide St. West, Toronto ON M5H 1W5 – 416/365-6800; Fax: 416/365-6870; Symbol: OTRAL – Manager, Information Services, Penny Lipman, Email: plipman@rioalgom.com

The Riverdale Hospital – Staff Library, 14 St. Matthews Rd., Toronto ON M4M 2B5 – 416/461-8251 – Librarian, Richard Kopak

The Roeher Institute – Library, Kinsmen Building, York University, 4700 Keele St., North York ON M3J 1P3 – 416/661-9611; Toll Free: 1-800-856-2207; Symbol: OTNIIR – Manager, Information Services, Miriam Ticoll

Rose Technology Group Ltd. - Library, 255 Consumers Rd., North York ON M2J 1R4 – 416/756-4170 – Librarian, Gillian Henderson

Rothmans, Benson & Hedges Inc. – Library, 1500 Don Mills Rd., North York ON M3B 3L1 – 416/449-5525; Fax: 416/449-6142 – Jacqui Clarke

Royal Astronomical Society of Canada – Library, 136 Dupont St., Toronto ON M5R 1V2 – 416/924-7973 – Librarian, W. MacDonald

Royal Bank of Canada - Technical Resource Centre, 315 Front St. West, 2nd Fl., Toronto ON M5V 3A4 – 416/348-5821; Fax: 416/348-5880 – Manager, Susan Reid
Toronto Office, Royal Bank Plaza, Lower Concourse, Toronto ON M5J 2J5 – 416/974-2780; Toll Free: 1-800-263-9191; Symbol: OTRBI – Manager, Sandra Walsh

Royal Canadian Academy of Arts – Library, Office of the Secretary, 163 Queen St. East, PO Box 2, Toronto ON M5A 1S1 – 416/363-9612

Royal Canadian College of Organists – Library, #302, 112 St. Clair Ave. West, Toronto ON M4V 2Y3 – 416/929-6400 – Janice Kerkkamp

Royal Canadian Military Institute – Library, 426 University Ave., Toronto ON M5G 1S9 – 416/597-0286 – Librarian, Anne Melvin

Royal Ontario Museum - Library, 100 Queen's Park, Toronto ON M5S 2C6 – 416/586-5595; Fax: 416/586-5863; Email: matthewsj@vax.library.utoronto.ca – Head, Julia Matthews

The Royal Philatelic Society of Canada – Library, PO Box 929, Toronto ON M4T 2P1

RP Research Foundation – Library, #704, 366 Adelaide St. West, Toronto ON M5V 1R9 – 416/360-4200; Toll Free: 1-800-461-3331

R.V. Anderson Associates Limited – Library, #400, 2001 Sheppard Ave. East, North York ON M2J 4Z8 – 416/497-8600; Email: lindad@rvanderson.com – Librarian, Linda Diener

Ryerson Polytechnic University - Library, 350 Victoria St., Toronto ON M5B 2K3 – 416/979-5144; Fax: 416/979-5215; Email: interlib@acs.ryerson.ca; URL: http://hugo.lib.ryerson.ca; Symbol: CaOTR Chief Librarian, R. Malinski
Access Services, Head, D. Phelan, 416/979-5000, ext.7160
Information Services, Head, O. Cheung, 416/979-5025
Public Services, Associate Librarian, E. Bishop, 416/979-5000, ext.6909
Systems & Technical Support, Associate Librarian, B. Jackson, 416/979-5147
Technical Services, Head, E. Friesen, 416/979-5146

St. Augustine's Seminary - Library, 2661 Kingston Rd., Scarborough ON M1M 1M3 – 416/261-7207, ext.236 – Librarian, Sr. Jean Harris

St. John's Hospital – Beeston Staff Library, 285 Cummer Ave., North York ON M2M 2G1 – 416/226-6790, ext.7350 – Librarian, Sister Margaret Ann

St. Joseph's Health Centre – George Pennal Library, 30 The Queensway, Toronto ON M6R 1B5 – 416/530-6726; Fax: 416/530-6034 – Librarian, Barbara Iwasiuk

St. Michael's Hospital – Health Sciences Library, 30 Bond St., Toronto ON M5B 1W8 – 416/864-5059; Fax: 416/864-5296; Email: OTS.MH; Symbol: OTSM – Director, Anita Wong

St. Vladimir Institute - Resource Centre for Ukrainian Studies, 620 Spadina Ave., Toronto ON M5S 2H4 – 416/923-3318 – Ihor Krut

The Salvation Army - College for Officer Training - Library, 2130 Bayview Ave., Toronto ON M4N 3K6 – 416/481-6131, ext.306; Fax: 416/481-6810 – Librarian, Bill Porter

The Salvation Army in Canada – Library, Territorial Headquarters, Canada & Bermuda, 2 Overlea Blvd., Toronto ON M4H 1P4 – 416/425-2111 – Major Paul Murray

The Salvation Army Scarborough Grace General Hospital – Glenn Gould Memorial Library, 3030 Birchmount Rd., Scarborough ON M1W 3W3 – 416/495-2437 – Manager, Health Sciences Lib., Irene Cameron

Scarborough Board of Education - A.B. Patterson Professional Library, 140 Borough Dr., Level 1, Scarborough ON M1P 4N6 – 416/396-7515; Fax: 416/396-5418; Email: Professional_Library@sbe.scarborough.on.ca – Supervisor, Rowan Amott

Scarborough General Hospital – Health Science Library, 3050 Lawrence Ave. East, Scarborough ON M1P 2V5 – 416/431-8114; Fax: 416/431-8186; Email: sgh@library.utoronto.ca – Library Coordinator, Bonnie Brownstein

Scarborough Historical Society – Library & Archives, PO Box 593, Scarborough ON M1K 5C4 – 416/396-6930 – Archivist, R. Schofield

Schizophrenia Society of Canada – Library, #814, 75 The Donway West, North York ON M3C 2E9 – 416/445-8204 – Office Manager, Toni Lord

Scotia McLeod Inc. - Information Centre, Scotia Plaza, 40 King St. West, PO Box 4085, Toronto ON M5W 2X6 – 416/863-7737; Fax: 416/863-7839; URL: http://wealth.passport.ca/wealth
Associate Director, Angela Devlin
Reference Librarian, Ann Struthers
Technical Services Librarian, Yvonne Rollins
Reference Librarian, Mari Wilson

Sculptor's Society of Canada – Library, Exchange Tower, First Canadian Place, 130 King St. West, PO Box 40, Toronto ON M5X 1B5 – 416/883-3075 – Archivist, Karen Stoskopf Harding

Sears Canada Inc. - Corporate & Marketing Research/Library Resource Centre, 222 Jarvis St., 3rd Fl., Toronto ON M5B 2B8 – 416/941-2544; Fax: 416/941-4514 – Research Assistant, Doris Hamilton

Sedgwick Limited – Library, Commercial Union Tower, Toronto-Dominion Centre, PO Box 439, Toronto ON M5K 1M3 – 416/361-6976 – Barbara Wilson

Self-Help Clearinghouse of Metropolitan Toronto – Library, #219, 40 Orchard View Blvd., Toronto ON M4R 1B9 – 416/487-4355 – Office Manager, Ruth Richardson

Seneca College - Leslie Campus Library, 1255 Sheppard Ave. East, North York ON M2K 1E2 – 416/491-5050, ext.6261; Fax: 416/494-9323 – Campus Librarian, Vinh Le
  Newnham Campus Library, 1750 Finch Ave. East, North York ON M2J 2X5 – 416/491-5050, ext.2100; Fax: 416/491-3349; Symbol: OTSC
  Director, Library Resource Centres, Tanis Fink, 416/491-5050, ext.2096
  Associate Director, Library Resource Centres, Doreen London, 416/491-5050, ext.2097
  Satellite Campus Libraries, Campus Librarian & Manager, Carolyn Lam, 905/833-3333, ext.5105
  Newnham Campus, Campus Librarian, Rhonda Roth
  Public Services, Librarian, Rosalie Walker
  Technical Services, Campus Librarian, Linda Oldham
  Sheppard Campus Library, 43 Sheppard Ave. East, North York ON M2N 2Z8 – 416/491-5050, ext.6444; Fax: 416/733-3855 – Campus Librarian, Joy Muller
Sex Information & Education Council of Canada – Library, 850 Coxwell Ave., East York ON M4C 5R1 – 416/466-5304 – Librarian, Mary Bissell
Shibley Righton Law Office - Library, #1900, 401 Bay St., PO Box 32, Toronto ON M5H 2Z1 – 416/214-5294; Fax: 416/214-5438 – Librarian, Karen Cohen
Sky Works Charitable Foundation – Film Library, 566 Palmerston Ave., Toronto ON M6G 2P7 – 416/536-6581
Smith & Andersen Consulting Engineering – Library, 505 Eglinton Ave. West, Toronto ON M5N 1B1 – 416/487-8151 – Associate, David Vickery
Smith, Lyons, Torrance, Stevenson & Mayer Law Office - Library, #6200, Scotia Plaza, 40 King St. West, Toronto ON M5H 3Z7 – 416/369-7200; Fax: 416/369-7250 – Manager, Library Services, Yvonne MacDonald
SNC-Lavalin Inc. - Ontario Branch Library, Atria North, Phase II, 2235 Sheppard Ave. East, North York ON M2J 5A6 – 416/756-2300, ext.4601; Fax: 416/756-2266; Email: mcnej@snc-lavalin.com; Symbol: OWSNC – Library Manager, Jennifer McNenly, Email: jennifer@passport.ca
Social Investment Organization – Library, #443, 366 Adelaide St. East, Toronto ON M5A 3X9 – 416/360-6047 – Darrell Ross
Society for the Study of Egyptian Antiquities – Library, PO Box 578, Toronto ON M5S 2T1 – 416/586-5632 – Annette Gromow
Southam Business Communications Library, 1450 Don Mills Rd., North York ON M3B 2X7 – 416/445-6641; Fax: 416/442-2200
Spina Bifida & Hydrocephalus Association of Ontario – Resource Lending Library, #310, 35 McCaul St., Toronto ON M5T 1V7 – 416/979-5514; Toll Free: 1-800-387-1575 – Information & Services Director, Joan Booth
Statistics Canada - Ontario Regional Reference Centre, Arthur Meighen Bldg., 25 St. Clair Ave. East, 10th Fl., Toronto ON M4T 1M4 – 416/973-6586; Fax: 416/973-7475; Toll Free: 1-800-263-1136 – Communications Officer, Sandra Lee McIntyre
Sterling Pulp Chemicals Ltd. - Central Library, 2 Gibbs Rd., Toronto ON M9B 1R1 – 416/239-7111, ext.213; Fax: 416/232-2146; Symbol: OIE – Corporate Librarian, Nancy Logan
Stikeman, Elliott - Library, Commerce Court West, PO Box 85, Toronto ON M5L 1B9 – 416/869-5575; Fax: 416/947-0866, 862-8518 – Library Manager, Richard Dubé, Email: duber@stikeman.com
Stone & Webster Canada Limited – Library, 2300 Yonge St., Toronto ON M4P 2W6 – 416/932-4400 – Librarian, Jennifer Webster
Sun Life Assurance Co. of Canada - Research Library, 225 King St. West, Toronto ON M5V 3C5 – 416/408-8840; Fax: 416/359-0346; Email: TMLIB@interlog.com
  Manager, Research Library, Elizabeth Gibson, 416/408-8841
  Reference Librarian, Faye Mitchell
Sunnybrook Health Sciences Centre – Health Sciences Library, 2075 Bayview Ave., North York ON M4N 3M5 – 416/480-6100,ex.4562; Fax: 416/480-6848; Email: ENVOY OTSMC – Chief Librarian, Linda McFarlane
Sus-Ward Editorial Library, 382 Balliol St., Toronto ON M4S 1E2 – Librarian, Emma Ward
Tandem International Inc. - Information Centre, #300, 3625 Dufferin St., Downsview ON M3K 1Z2 – 416/630-8971; Fax: 416/630-9211 – Library Technician, Rita D'Onorio
Thistletown Regional Centre Library, 51 Panorama Ct., Etobicoke ON M9V 4L8 – 416/326-0717; Fax: 416/326-0644 – Acting Supervisor of Libraries, Mary Beth Arrigo
Times Change Women's Employment Service – Access Centre, #1704, 365 Bloor St. East, Toronto ON M4W 3L4 – 416/927-1900
Toronto Board of Education - Education Centre Reference Library, 155 College St., Toronto ON M5T 1P6 – 416/397-3011; Fax: 416/397-3044; Symbol: OTEC – Supervisor, Reference Services, Joan Culley
The Toronto-Dominion Bank – Dept. of Economic Research Library, TD Centre, PO Box 1, Stn Toronto-Dominion, Toronto ON M5K 1A2 – 416/982-8068; Fax: 416/982-6884; Toll Free: 1-800-387-2092 – Patricia Domine
Toronto East General & Orthopaedic Hospital – Health Sciences Library, 825 Coxwell Ave., Toronto ON M4C 3E7 – 416/469-6010 – Librarian, Jennifer Reiswig
Toronto Family History Library, 95 Melbert Rd., PO Box 247, Etobicoke ON M9C 4V3 – 416/621-4607 – Director, E.G. Lansitie
Toronto Historical Board – Library, Administrative Offices, 205 Yonge St., Toronto ON M5B 1N2 – 416/392-6827 – Assistant Curator, John Summers
The Toronto Hospital, Toronto General Division - Fudger Health Sciences Library, 585 University Ave., Toronto ON M5G 2C4 – 416/340-3429; Fax: 416/340-4384 – Library & Information Services, Director, J. Bayne, Email: jbayne@torhosp.toronto.on.ca
The Toronto Hospital, Toronto Western Division - R.C. Laird Health Science Library, 399 Bathurst St., Toronto ON M5T 2S8 – 416/603-5750; Fax: 416/603-5326; Email: ENVOY: OTTWH.LIB; Symbol: OTTWH – Library & Information Services, Director, J. Bayne, Email: jbayne@torhosp.toronto.on.ca
Toronto International Film Festival – Film Reference Library, 2 Carlton St., 16th Fl., Toronto ON M5B 1J3 – 416/967-1517; Fax: 416/967-0628 – Director, Sylvia Frank
Toronto Jewish Media Centre – Library, #252, 4600 Bathurst St., North York ON M2R 3V3 – 416/633-7770
The Toronto Mendelssohn Choir – Library, 60 Simcoe St., Toronto ON M5J 2H5 – 416/598-0422 – Librarian, Roger Hobbs
Toronto PWA Foundation – Treatment Resource Centre, 399 Church St., 2nd Fl., Toronto ON M5B 2J6 – 416/506-1400; Toll Free: 1-800-558-7923 – Treatment Resources Coordinator, Derek Thaczuk
Toronto Real Estate Board – Resource Centre, 1400 Don Mills Rd., North York ON M3B 3N1 – 416/443-8152 – Resource Library Administrator, Michael Murphy
Toronto Star Newspapers Ltd. - Library, One Yonge St., Toronto ON M5E 1E6 – 416/869-4490; Fax: 416/865-3994; Email: snoble@thestar.ca – Chief Librarian, Sonja Noble
Toronto Stock Exchange - Information Resource Centre, Exchange Tower, 2 First Canadian Place, 3rd Fl., PO Box 450, Stn 1st Can Place, Toronto ON M5X 1J2 – 416/947-4653; Fax: 416/947-4662; Email: sfroebel@tse.com – Senior Information Specialist, Shonna Froebel
Toronto Sun - News Research Centre, 333 King St. East, Toronto ON M5A 3X5 – 416/947-2257; Fax: 416/947-2043 – Manager, News Research, Julie Kirsh, Email: jkirsh@sunpub.com
The Toronto Symphony Orchestra – Resource Centre, 212 King St. West, 5th Fl., Toronto ON M5H 1K5 – 416/593-7769, ext.315 – Principal Librarian, Gary Corrin
Toronto Transportation Society – Library, PO Box 5187, Toronto ON M5W 1N5 – 416/883-3322 – Alan Gryfe
Tory Tory DesLauriers & Binnington - Law Library, #3000, IBM Tower, Toronto-Dominion Centre, PO Box 270, Stn Toronto-Dominion, Toronto ON M5K 1N2 – 416/865-8158; Fax: 416/865-7380
  Manager, Library Services, Louis Mirando
  Reference Librarian, Mary Almey
Towers Perrin - Information Centre, #1501, 175 Bloor St. East, Toronto ON M4W 3T6 – 416/960-2600; Fax: 416/960-2819; Email: torinfo@inforamp.net – Information Services Specialist, Lorraine Flanigan
Transport Canada - Ontario Region Library, #300, 4900 Yonge St., North York ON M2N 6A5 – 416/224-3619; Fax: 416/224-3611; Symbol: OTTOA – Librarian, Eng K. Ching
Treasury Management Association of Canada – National Resource Centre, #1010, 8 King St. East, Toronto ON M5C 1B5 – 416/367-8501; Fax: 416/367-3242
TVOntario - Library, 2180 Yonge St., Toronto ON M4S 2C1 – 416/484-2651; Fax: 416/484-7771; Toll Free: 1-800-613-0513; Symbol: OTET – Supervisor, Rechilde Volpatti
Ukrainian National Federation - Library, 297 College St., Toronto ON M5T 1S2 – 416/922-1617; Fax: 416/485-9387 – Director, Nell A. Nakonoczny
United Empire Loyalists' Association of Canada – Reference Library, Dominion Office, The George Brown House, 50 Baldwin St., Toronto ON M5T 1L4 – 416/591-1783
United Steelworkers of America (AFL-CIO/CLC) - Canadian Office – Library, 234 Eglinton Ave. East, 7th Fl., Toronto ON M4P 1K7 – 416/487-1571,ext.214 – Librarian/Researcher, Lesley Stodart
University of Toronto - Business Information Centre, #310, 246 Bloor St. West, Toronto ON M5S 1V4 – 416/978-3421; Fax: 416/978-1920; Toll Free: 1-800-810-8067; Email: bicvlw@fmgmt.mgmt.utoronto.ca – Chief Librarian, Vicki Whitmell, 416/978-1924
  Libraries, 130 Saint George St., Toronto ON M5S 1A5 – 416/978-2294; Fax: 416/978-7653; Email: moore@vax.library.utoronto.ca; Symbol: CAOTU
  John P. Robarts Research Library, Chief Librarian, Carole Moore, 416/978-2292
  Audio Visual Library, Librarian, Liz Avison, 416/978-6520
  University Archives, University Archivist, Garron Wells, 416/978-2277
  Astronomy Library, Librarian, Marlene Cummins, 416/978-4268
  Bora Laskin Law Library, Librarian, Ann Rae, 416/978-8580
  C.H. Best Institute, Medical Research Library, Librarian, Colin Savage, 416/978-2588
  Centre of Criminology Library, Librarian, Catherine Matthews, 416/978-7068
  Chemistry Library (A.D. Allen Memorial Library), Librarian, Mary Power, 416/978-3587

Canadian Almanac & Directory 1997

Computer Science Library, Librarian, Stephanie Johnston, 416/978-2987

Dentistry Library, Faculty Librarian, Susan Goddard, 416/979-4560

East Asian Library, Librarian, Anna U Liang, 416/978-3300

Edward Johnson Music Library, Librarian, Kathleen McMorrow, 416/978-3734

Emmanuel College Library, Librarian, Reverend Douglas Fox, 416/585-4550, Email: fox@library.utoronto.ca

Engineering Library, Librarian, Elaine Granatstein, 416/978-6494

Erindale College Library, College Librarian, Judy Snow, 416/828-5236

Faculty of Education Library, Librarian, Diana George, 416/978-3224

Faculty of Library & Information Science Library, Librarian, Diane Henderson, 416/978-7070

Fine Art Library, Librarian, Andrea Retfalvi, 416/978-5006

Institute for Aerospace Studies Library, Librarian, Judith Mills, 416/667-7712

Institute for Child Study Library, Library Technician, Miriam Herman, 416/978-4897

Institute for Environmental Studies Resource Centre, Library Technician, Judith Eichmanis, 416/978-7429

Institute for Policy Analysis, Librarian, Ursula Gutenburg, 416/978-8623

Knox College, Caven Library, Librarian, C. Tucker, 416/978-4504

Map Library, Map Librarian, Joan Winearls, 416/978-3372

Massey College, Robertson Davies Library, Librarian, Marie Korey, 416/978-2893

Mathematics & Statistics Library, Librarian, C. Graham, 416/978-8624

New College, Donald G. Ivey Library, Librarian, Jeanne Guillaume, 416/978-2493

Newman Industrial Relations Library, Head Librarian, Elizabeth Perry, 416/978-2928

Noranda Earth Sciences Library, Librarian, Jennifer Mendelsohn, 416/978-3024

Occupational & Environmental Health Unit Library, Librarian, Priscilla Wagner, 416/978-4522

Physics Library, Librarian, Barbara Chu, 416/978-5188

Pontifical Institute of Mediaeval Studies Library, Chief Librarian, 416/926-7146

R.D. Hurst Pharmacy Library, Pharmacy Librarian, Sylvia Newman, 416/978-2872

Ramsay Wright Zoology Library, Library Technician, Kim Gallant, 416/978-3515

Scarborough College, Vincent W. Bladen Library, College Librarian, Marla Miller, 416/284-3246

School of Architecture & Landscape Architecture Library, Librarian, Pamela Manson-Smith, 416/978-2649

Science & Medicine Library, Head, Gwynneth T. Heaton, 416/978-7662

Sigmund Samuel Library, Head, Edward Schlauch, 416/978-7685

Thomas Fisher Rare Book Library, Director, Richard Landon, 416/978-6107

Trinity College Library, Librarian, L. Corman, 416/978-2653

University College Library, Librarian, I. Epp, 416/978-8107

Victoria College Library, Librarian, R. Brandeis, 416/585-4470

Wycliffe College Library, Librarian, C. Derrenbacker, 416/979-4870

Centre for Reformation & Renaissance Studies, Curator, Dr. Joseph Black, 416/585-4471

Scarborough College - V.W. Bladen Library, 1265 Military Trail, Scarborough ON M1C 1A4 – 416/287-7508; Fax: 416/287-7507; Email: miller@macpost.scar.utoronto.ca; URL: http://library.scar.utoronto.ca/; Symbol: OTSCC – College Librarian, M. Miller, 416/287-7497

Urban Alliance on Race Relations – Library, #202, 675 King St. West, Toronto ON M5V 1M9 – 416/703-6607 – Randi Lee

VideoFACT, A Foundation to Assist Canadian Talent – Resource Centre, #501, 151 John St., Toronto ON M5V 2T2 – 416/596-8696

Vision Institute of Canada – Bobier-Fisher-Lyle Vision Science Library, York Mills Centre, #110, 16 York Mills Rd., North York ON M2P 2E5 – 416/224-2273

Visual Arts Ontario – Resource Centre, 439 Wellington St. West, 3rd Fl., Toronto ON M5V 1E7 – 416/591-8883

Voice for Hearing Impaired Children – Library, #420, 124 Eglinton Ave. West, Toronto ON M4R 2G8 – 416/487-7719 – Administrative Secretary, Lianne Braun

Warner-Lambert Canada Inc. - Scientific Information Centre, 2200 Eglinton Ave. East, Scarborough ON M1L 2N3 – 416/288-2360; Fax: 416/288-2174 – Library Technician, Kathryn Moore

Waterfront Regeneration Trust - Library, #580, 207 Queens Quay West, Toronto ON M5J 1A7 – 416/314-9490; Fax: 416/314-9497 – Librarian, Janice Hollingsworth

Watts, Griffis & McOuat Ltd. - Library, #400, 8 King St. East, Toronto ON M5C 1B5 – 416/364-6244; Fax: 416/864-1675; Email: wgm@io.org – Librarian, A. Street-Bishop

Weir & Foulds Law Office - Library, Exchange Tower, 2 First Canadian Pl., PO Box 480, Toronto ON M5X 1J5 – 416/947-5057; Fax: 416/365-1876; Symbol: OTWF
Librarian, Jim Spence, Email: spencej@weirfoulds.com
Assistant Librarian, Theresa Kennedy, Email: kennedyt@weirfoulds.com

The Wellesley Central Hospital - Wellesley Site – Library, 160 Wellesley St. East, Toronto ON M4Y 1J3 – 416/926-7071; Email: WELLESLEY.LIBRARY – Manager, Library Services, Verla Empey

West Mississauga Jazz Muddies – Library, 90 Prince George Dr., Etobicoke ON M9B 2X8 – 416/231-4055

William M. Mercer Limited - Information/Research Centre, BCE Place, Box 501, 161 Bay St., Toronto ON M5J 2S5 – 416/868-2005; Fax: 416/868-7002
Manager, Merle J. Ramdial, 416/868-7697
Reference Librarian, Jo-Anne Weiler
Technical Services Librarian, Lise McLeod

Women's Art Resource Centre – Library, #506, 80 Spadina Ave., Toronto ON M5V 2J3 – 416/703-0074

Women's College Hospital – Library, 76 Grenville St., Toronto ON M5S 1B2 – 416/323-6078 – Librarian, Shahida Rashid

Women's Inter-Church Council of Canada, #402, 815 Danforth Ave., Toronto ON M4J 1L2 – 416/462-2528

Women's Legal Education & Action Fund – Library, #1800, 415 Yonge St., Toronto ON M5B 2E7 – 416/595-7170

Wood Gundy Inc. - Library, BCE Place, PO Box 500, Toronto ON M5J 2S8 – 416/594-7716, 7717; Fax: 416/594-7713
Cheif Librarian, Cheryl Dhillon
Acquisitions Librarian, S. Parker

Workers' Compensation Appeals Tribunal - Library, 505 University Ave., 7th Fl., Toronto ON M5G 1X4 – 416/598-4638, ext.203; Fax: 416/326-3558; Symbol: OTWCA – Chief Information Officer, Linda Moskovits

Workers' Compensation Board - Reference Library, 200 Front St. West, Toronto ON M5V 3J1 – 416/927-4972, 3667; Fax: 416/927-4995 – Coordinator, Angela Osterreiche

World Trade Centre Toronto – Resource Centre, 60 Harbour St., Toronto ON M5J 1B7 – 416/863-2008; TLX: 21 06-219666

Wyatt Company - Canadian Research & Information Centre, #1210, 1 Queen St. East, Toronto ON M5C 2Y1 – 416/594-5811; Fax: 416/862-2193 – Librarian, Janice Sipus

Wyeth-Ayerst Canada - Medical Library, PO Box 370, North York ON M3M 3A8 – 416/225-7500; Fax: 416/225-6111; Toll Free: 1-800-268-1946 – Drug Information & Surveillance, Manager, Shamim Jamal-Rajan

York Board of Education - Professional Library, 2 Trethewey Dr., Toronto ON M6M 4A8 – 416/394-2168; Fax: 416/394-3397
Head Librarian, Sheila Moll
Head Librarian, Pat Steenbergen

York-Finch General Hospital – Thomas J. Malcho Memorial Library, 2111 Finch Ave. West, Downsview ON M3N 1N1 – 416/744-2500; Symbol: OTYF – Coordinator, Hospital Library, Mona Frantzke

York Pioneer & Historical Society – Library, 2482 Yonge St., PO Box 45026, Toronto ON M4P 3E3 – 416/489-4188 – Archivist, Paul Litt

York University - Libraries, 4700 Keele St., North York ON M3J 1P3 – 416/736-5601; Fax: 416/736-5451
University Librarian, Ellen Hoffmann, 416/736-5601
Acquisitions, Head, Karen Cassel
Bibliographic Services, Head, Dale Irwin
Circulation, Head, Linda Hansen
Government Documents/Administration Studies Library, Head, Elizabeth Watson, 416/736-5139
Library Computing Services, Director, Robert Thompson, 416/736-5601
Library Computing, Manager, Doug Fenwick
Library Facilities, Head, John Thompson
Public Services, Associate University Librarian, Toni Olshen
Technical Services, Associate University Librarian, Rasma Rugelis
Law Library, Librarian, Balfour J. Halévy, 416/736-5587
Leslie Frost Library, Glendon Campus, Head, Julianna Drexier, 416/487-6729
Steacie Science Library Brian Wilks, 416/736-5639

York University Staff Association – Library, Suite F, East Office Bldg., 4700 Keele St., North York ON M3J 1P3 – 416/736-5109

Youth Assisting Youth – Library, #4080, 3080 Yonge St., Toronto ON M4N 3N1 – 416/932-1919

YWCA of/du Canada – Library, 80 Gerrard St. East, Toronto ON M5B 1G6 – 416/593-9886

Zoological Society of Metropolitan Toronto – Resource Centre, PO Box 370, Scarborough ON M1E 4Y9 – 416/392-9100 – Manager, Education, Caroline Greenland

Zurich Canada - Library, 400 University Ave., 20th Fl., Toronto ON M5G 1S7 – 416/586-2501; Fax: 416/586-2858

UXBRIDGE

Nuclear Awareness Project – Library, PO Box 104, Uxbridge ON L9P 1M6 – 905/852-0571 – Irene Kock

VAL CARON

Sudbury Rock & Lapidary Society – Library, 3171 Romeo St., Val Caron ON P3N 1G5 – 705/522-5140 – Library, R. Debicki

VANIER

Fédération canadienne pour l'alphabétisation en français – Bibliothèque, 235, ch Montréal, Vanier ON K1L 6C7 – 613/749-5333

VERNON

Osgoode Twp. Historical Society – Museum Archives, PO Box 74, Vernon ON K0A 3J0 – 613/821-4062 – Archivist, Donna Bowen

VINELAND STATION

Horticultural Research Institute of Ontario – Library, PO Box 7000, Vineland Station ON L0R 2E0 – 905/562-4141; Email: wannerj@gov.on.ca – Librarian, Judith Wanner

WALKERTON

Bruce Law Association – Courthouse Library, 215 Cayley St., PO Box 818, Walkerton ON N0G 2V0 – 519/881-2384 – Librarian, Laurie McDonald

WATERLOO

Canadian Association for Music Therapy – CAMT Library, Wilfrid Laurier University, Waterloo ON N2L 3C5 – 519/884-1970, ext.6828; Toll Free: 1-800-996-2268 – Administrative Coordinator, Lynda Tracy

Canadian Industrial Innovation Centre – Library, 156 Columbia St. West, Waterloo ON N2L 3L3 – 519/885-5870; Toll Free: 1-800-265-4559

Canadian Water Quality Association – Library, #201A, 151 Frobisher Dr., Waterloo ON N2V 2C9 – 519/885-3854

Conrad Grebel College - Library, Waterloo ON N2L 3G6 – 519/885-0220, ext.239; Fax: 519/885-0014 – Librarian, Sam Steiner, Email: steiner@library.uwaterloo.ca

Ecologistics Ltd. – Library, #A1, 490 Dutton Dr., Waterloo ON N2L 6H7 – 519/886-0522 – Library Manager, Brenda Fansher

Global Community Centre – Library, 89, 91 King St. North, Waterloo ON N2J 2X3 – 519/746-4090 – Resources Coordinator, Louise Murray Gorvett

Kitchener-Waterloo Vegetarian Association – Library, 103 Marshall St., Waterloo ON N2J 2T5 – 519/747-0870 – Librarian, Dianne Meloun

Manulife Securities International Ltd. – Law Library, 500 King St. North, Waterloo ON N2J 4C6 – 519/747-7000, ext.6240; Toll Free: 1-800-265-7401 – Law Librarian, Diana Robertson

Mutual Life of Canada - Business Information Service, 227 King St. South, Waterloo ON N2J 4C5 – 519/888-2262; Fax: 519/888-3899
- Corporate Archivist/Librarian, Nancy Maitland, 519/888-2769, Email: 102232.2046@compuserve.com
- Library Coordinator, Marianna Martisek, 519/888-2262, Email: 102232.2047@compuserve.com

The Network: Interaction for Conflict Resolution – Library, Conrad Grebel College, Waterloo ON N2L 3G6 – 519/885-0880 – Administrative Assistant, Norma Row

Ontario Numismatic Association – Library, PO Box 40033, Stn Waterloo Square, Waterloo ON N2J 4V1 – 519/745-3104 – Librarian, T. Masters

Ontario Public Interest Research Group - Waterloo – Library, University of Waterloo, 200 University Ave. West, Waterloo ON N2L 3G1 – 519/888-4882; 885-1211, ext.2578

Project Ploughshares – Library, Institute of Peace & Conflict Studies, Conrad Grebel College, Waterloo ON N2L 3G6 – 519/888-6541 – Program Associate, Bill Robinson

Renison College - Library, Westmount Rd. North, Waterloo ON N2L 3G4 – 519/884-4404, ext.646; Email: JEGMITCHELL@RENISON.watstar.uwaterloo.ca – Librarian, Jane Mitchell

St. Jerome's College - Library, Waterloo ON N2L 3G3 – 519/884-8110, ext.285; Fax: 519/884-5759; Email: dgdraper@library.uwaterloo.ca – Librarian, Dr. Gary Draper

The Seagram Museum - Library, 57 Erb St. West, Waterloo ON N2L 6C2 – 519/885-1857, ext.19; Fax: 519/746-1673; Email: can-sm@immedia.ca; Symbol: OWSM – Registrar/Researcher, Sean Thomas

University of Waterloo - Library, 200 University Ave. West, Waterloo ON N2L 3G1 – 519/885-1211; Fax: 519/747-4606; Email: liboff09@watserv1.uwaterloo.ca; Symbol: OWTU
- University Librarian, Murray C. Shepherd
- Renison College Library, Librarian, Jane Mitchell, 519/884-4400
- Collections & Cataloguing, Associate Librarian, C. David Emery
- Collections Management, Coordinator, Stuart MacKinnon
- Computer-Assisted Reference Service, Coordinator, Doug Morton
- Dana Porter Reference & Collections Development Dept., Head, Margaret Hendley
- Industrial & Business Information Services, Coordinator, Faye Abrams
- Library Administrative Services, Coordinator, Lorraine Beattie
- Materials Acquisition, Head, Boris Bruder
- Special Collections, Head, Susan Bellingham
- Systems, Associate Librarian, Michael Ridley
- User Services, Coordinator, Susan Routliffe
- Conrad Grebel College Library Sam Sterzer, 519/885-0220
- Davis Centre Library, Associate Librarian, Information, Bruce MacNeil
- Davis Centre Reference & Collections Development Department, Head, Joan MacDonald
- Leisure Studies Data Bank, Coordinator, Dr. R. Mannell, 519/885-1211, ext.6872
- Optometry Learning Resource Centre Susan Morton
- St. Jeromes College Library Dr. Gary Draper, 519/884-8110
- University Map & Design Library, Head, Richard Pinnell

Wilfrid Laurier University - Central Library, 75 University Ave., Waterloo ON N2L 3C5 – 519/884-0710, ext.3380; Fax: 519/884-8023; Email: vgillham@mach2.wlu.ca; URL: http://www.wlu.ca/~wwwhb/; Symbol: OWTL
- University Librarian, Virginia Gillham
- Acquisitions/Bibliographic Searching, Head, John Arndt
- Cataloguing, Head, Brooke Skelton
- Access Services, Head, Vera Fesnak
- Documents & Serials, Head, Linda Cracknell
- Systems, Head, Herbert Schwartz
- Reference Department, Head, Diane Wilkins, 519/884-0710, ext.3417

WELLAND

Niagara College - Welland Campus Learning Resource Centre, PO Box 1005, Welland ON L3B 5S2 – 416/735-2211; Fax: 416/735-5365

Welland County Law Association – Niagara South Courthouse Library, 102 Main St. East, Welland ON L3B 3W6 – 905/734-3174 – Law Librarian, Lorraine Saunders

WHITBY

The Bureau for Excellence in Durham Region – Library, c/o Durham College, Whitby Campus, 1610 Champlain Ave., Whitby ON L1N 6A7 – 905/721-2000; Toll Free: 1-800-263-3845 – Ellen Nolan

Durham Region Law Association – Durham District Courthouse Library, 605 Rossland Rd. East, Whitby ON L1N 5S4 – 905/668-2177 – Libarian, Monica Schjott

Whitby Mental Health Centre – Staff Library, 700 Gordon St., PO Box 613, Whitby ON L1N 5S9 – 905/668-5881; Email: wardc@gov.on.ca – Librarian, Cathy Ward

WINDSOR

Canadian Association of Moldmakers – Library, 424 Tecumseh Rd. East, Windsor ON N8Y 2R6 – 519/255-7863; Toll Free: 1-800-567-2266 – Patricia Pupp

Essex Law Association – County Courthouse Library, 245 Windsor Ave., Windsor ON N9A 1J2 – 519/252-8418 – Doug Hewitt

Glos Engineering Ltd – Library, 3155 Huron Church Rd., Windsor ON N9E 4H6 – 519/966-6750 – Librarian, Jean-Guy Dupuis

Great Lakes United – Library, PO Box 548, Windsor ON N9A 6M6 – 519/255-7141 – Associate Director, Mary Ginnebaugh

Hôtel Dieu Grace Hospital – Library, 1030 Ouellette Ave., Windsor ON N9A 1E1 – 519/255-2245; Fax: 519/255-2458 – Librarian, A. Henshaw

International Joint Commission - Reference Resource Centre, 100 Ouellette Ave., 8th Fl., Windsor ON N9A 6T3 – 519/257-6700; Fax: 519/257-6740; Symbol: OWIJC – Reference Resource Clerk, Mae Carter, 519/257-6702

John XXIII Centre - Library, 2275 Wellesley Ave., Windsor ON N8W 2G1 – 519/254-2090; Fax: 519/254-0330 – Librarian, J.A. Rocheleau

McPherson, Prince & Geddes Law Office - Library, Canada Bldg., #200, 374 Ouellette Ave., Windsor ON N9A 6S5 – 519/258-6600; Fax: 519/258-9669 – Deward J. Postiff

Paroian, Raphael, Courey, Cohen & Houston Law Office - Library, 875 Ouellette Ave., PO Box 970, Windsor ON N9A 6S7 – 519/258-1166; Fax: 519/258-8361 – Clerk, Doye DeLauw

St. Clair College - Library Resource Centre, 2000 Talbot Rd., Windsor ON N9A 6S4 – 519/972-2739; Fax: 519/966-2737

Third World Resource Centre – Library, 125 Tecumseh Rd. West, Windsor ON N8X 1E8 – 519/252-1517 – Contact, Ellen Preuschat

University of Windsor - Leddy Library, 401 Sunset Ave., Windsor ON N9B 3P4 – 519/973-7023; Fax: 519/973-7076, 971-3638; Email: deliver@uwindsor.ca; Symbol: OWA
- Librarian, Madge MacGown
- Access Services, M. Burton, 519/253-4232, ext.3174
- Acquisitions, K. Ball, 519/253-4232, ext.3192
- Cataloguing, Jane Black
- Curriculum Resource Centre, T. Robinson
- Documents & Special Collections, J. McGrath, 519/253-4232, ext.3188
- ILL Librarian, C. Maskell, 519/253-4232, ext.3187
- Public Services, Associate Librarian, P.J. Malone, 519/253-4232, ext.3206
- Reader Services, C. Archer, 519/253-4232, ext.3181
- Systems, Librarian, A. Rhyno, 519/253-4232, ext.3163
- Technical Services, Associate Librarian, J. Foster, 519/253-4232, ext.3185
- Business, Librarian, Ted Venkateswarlu, 519/973-3183
- Paul Martin Law Library, Law Librarian, Prof. Paul Murphy, 519/253-4232, ext.2972

Windsor & District Chamber of Commerce – Library, 2575 Ouellette Place, Windsor ON N8X 1L9 – 519/966-3696

The Windsor Regional Hospital – Health Sciences Library - Metropolitan Campus, 1995 Lens Ave., Windsor ON N8W 1L9 – 519/254-5577, ext.2329; Fax: 519/254-3150 – Coordinator, Loretta Joyce Jewer
- Health Sciences Library - Western Campus, 1453 Prince Rd., Windsor ON N9C 3Z4 – 519/257-5232, 257-2037; Fax: 519/257-5244 – Coordinator, Loretta Joyce Jewer

The Windsor Star - Library, 167 Ferry St., Windsor ON N9A 4M5 – 519/255-5711; Fax: 519/255-5515 – Metro Editor, Bill Hickey, 519/255-5714

LIBRARIES — PRINCE EDWARD ISLAND

WOODSTOCK

Oxford Law Association – Library, PO Box 1029, Woodstock ON N4S 8A4 – 519/539-7711 – Librarian, Doreen Lewis

PRINCE EDWARD ISLAND

PEI Provincial Library System

PEI PROVINCIAL LIBRARY SERVICE

Red Head Rd., PO Box 7500, Morell PE C0A 1S0 – 902/961-7320; Fax: 902/961-7322; Email: plshq@cycor.ca; Symbol: PC
Director of Archives & Libraries, Harry Holman

Alberton Public Library, PO Box 449, Alberton PE C0B 1B0 – 902/853-3049 – Helen Wallace

Borden Public Library, Borden PE C0B 1X0 – 902/855-2225 – Sharon Leard

Breadalbane Public Library, Breadalbane PE C0A 1E0 – 902/964-2446 – Joan Sutton

Carrefour de l'Isle Saint-Jean, 5, rue Acadien, Charlottetown PE C1C 1M2 – 902/368-6092; Fax: 902/368-6092 – Linda Allain

Confederation Centre Public Library, PO Box 7000, Charlottetown PE C1A 8G8 – 902/368-4642; Fax: 902/368-4652; Email: ccpl@cycor.ca – Chief Librarian, Don Scott; Reference Librarian, Gary Ramsay; Children's Librarian, Barbara Kissick

Government Services Library, Basement, Shaw Bldg., PO Box 2000, Charlottetown PE C1A 7N8 – 902/368-4653 – Librarian, Nichola Cleaveland

Cornwall Public Library, Cornwall PE C0A 1H0 – 902/629-8415 – Elmer Power

Crapaud Public Library, PO Box 96, Crapaud PE C0A 1J0 – 902/658-2297 – Luann Molyneaux

Georgetown Public Library, Georgetown PE C0A 1L0 – 902/652-2832 – Brenda Batchilder

Hunter River Public Library, Hunter River PE C0A 1N0 – Pam Wheatley

Kensington Public Library, PO Box 394, Kensington PE C0B 1M0 – 902/836-3721 – Susan Harris

Kinkora Public Library, Kinkora PE C0B 1N0 – 902/887-2868 – Catherine Arsenault

Montague Public Library, PO Box 94, Montague PE C0A 1R0 – 902/838-2528 – Jane Harris

Morell Public Library, PO Box 7500, Morell PE C0A 1S0 – 902/961-7321 – Carol McGrath

Mount Stewart Public Library, Mount Stewart PE C0A 1T0

Murray Harbour Public Library, Murray Harbour PE C0A 1V0 – 902/962-3875 – Kaye MacLean

Murray River Public Library, Murray River PE C0A 1W0 – 902/962-2667 – Ruth Moore

O'Leary Public Library, O'Leary PE C0B 1V0 – 902/859-8788 – Verna Smallman

St. Peter's Public Library, St. Peter's Bay PE C0A 2A0 – 902/961-2268 – Ann MacInnis

Souris Public Library, PO Box 603, Souris PE C0A 2B0 – 902/687-2157 – Tina Davis

Rotary Regional Library, 192 Water St., Summerside PE C1N 1B1 – 902/436-7323; Fax: 902/888-8055 – Librarian, Priscilla Ykelenstam

Tignish Public Library, Tignish PE C0B 2B0 – 902/882-2681 – Dianne McCue

Tyne Valley Public Library, Tyne Valley PE C0B 2C0 – 902/831-2928 – Carolyn Millar

Abram Village Bibliothèque publique, c/o École Evangeline, RR#3, Wellington PE C0B 2E0 – 902/854-3077; Téléc: 902/854-3077 – Judith Arsenault; French Services Librarian, Johanne Jacob

Special & College Libraries & Resource Centres

CHARLOTTETOWN

Agriculture & Agri-Food Canada-Charlottetown Research Centre – Agriculture & Agri-Food Canada Library, 440 University Ave., PO Box 1210, Charlottetown PE C1A 7M8 – 902/566-6861; Email: stanfieldb@em.agr.ca; Symbol: PCAG – Librarian, Barrie Stanfield

Canadian Pension Commission - Policy Reference Library, PO Box 9900, Charlottetown PE C1A 8V6 – 902/566-8870; Fax: 902/566-8879; Symbol: PCCP – Custodian, Kathy Stewart

Community Legal Information Association of Prince Edward Island – Library, Sullivan Building, #158, 20 Fitzroy, PO Box 1207, Stn Central, Charlottetown PE C1A 7M8 – 902/892-0853

Confederation Centre Art Gallery & Museum - Resource Centre, 145 Richmond St., Charlottetown PE C1A 1J1 – 902/628-6111; Fax: 902/566-4648 – Director/Curator, Terry Graff, 902/628-6121

Department of Environmental Resources - Fish & Wildlife Division Library, 3 Queen St., Charlottetown PE C1A 4A2 – 902/368-4688 – E. Long

Farmer & MacLeod, Barristers, Solicitors, Notaries - Library, National Bank Tower, #605, 134 Kent St., PO Box 2500, Charlottetown PE C1A 8C2 – 902/368-3733; Fax: 902/566-4265

Heart & Stroke Foundation of Prince Edward Island – Library, 40 Queen St., PO Box 279, Charlottetown PE C1A 7K4 – 902/892-7441 – Education Director, Donalda Clow

Holland College - Library, Charlottetown Centre, 140 Weymouth St., Charlottetown PE C1A 4Z1 – 902/566-9558; Fax: 902/566-9505; Email: brady@vega.cc.hollandc.pe.ca; Symbol: PCHC – College Librarian, Brenda Brady
Technology Centre Library, 40 Enman Cres., Charlottetown PE C1E 1E6 – 902/566-9358; Fax: 902/566-5670; Email: jmacdonald@victor.rc.hollandc.pe.ca – Manager, Joanne MacDonald

Institute for Bioregional Studies – Library, #126, 449 University Ave., Charlottetown PE C1A 8K3 – 902/892-9578

Law Society of Prince Edward Island – Law Library, 49 Water St., PO Box 128, Charlottetown PE C1A 7K2 – 902/368-6099 – Librarian, Pamela Borden

Medical Society of Prince Edward Island – Library, 559 North River Rd., Charlottetown PE C1E 1J7 – 902/368-7303

PEI Council of the Arts – Library, 151 Richmond St., Charlottetown PE C1A 1H7 – 902/368-4410 – Administrative Assistant, Ferne Taylor

PEI Food Technology Centre - Library, PO Box 2000, Charlottetown PE C1A 7N8 – 902/566-1725; Fax: 902/566-5627; Email: peiftc@peinet.pe.ca; URL: http://www.gov.pe.ca/info/ftc/; Symbol: PCFT
Chief Librarian, Mary Jane Grant
Acquisitions Librarian, Kathy MacEwen

PEI Government - Film Library, Media Centre, 202 Richmond St., Charlottetown PE C1A 1J2 – 902/368-4641, 4644; Fax: 902/368-4621 – Secretary, Rita Sahajpal

Prince Edward Island Museum & Heritage Foundation – Library, 2 Kent St., Charlottetown PE C1A 1M6 – 902/368-6604 – Curator of History, Edward MacDonald

Prince Edward Island Teachers' Federation – Library, PO Box 6000, Charlottetown PE C1A 8B4 – 902/569-4157

Queen Elizabeth Hospital – Frank J. MacDonald Library, PO Box 6600, Charlottetown PE C1A 8T5 – 902/894-2371; Fax: 902/894-2385; Symbol: PCQEH – Librarian, Marion K. MacArthur

University of Prince Edward Island - Robertson Library, 550 University Ave., Charlottetown PE C1A 4P3 – 902/566-0696; Fax: 902/628-4305; Email: ENVOY: ILL.PCU; Symbol: PCU
University Librarian, Daniel A. Savage
Reference, Head, Cathy Callaghan, 902/566-0681
Circulation Librarian, Susanne Manovill, 902/566-0581
Special Collection Librarian, Frank Pigot, 902/566-0536
Systems Librarian, Suzanne Jones, 902/566-0393
Acquisitions Librarian, Meredith Crockett, 902/566-0479
Cataloguing Librarian, Janet Arsenault, 902/566-0741
Reference Librarian, Jennifer Taylor, 902/566-0453
Periodicals Librarian, Cathy Dillon, 902/566-0556

Veterans Affairs Canada - Library, PO Box 7700, Charlottetown PE C1A 8M9 – 902/566-8988; Fax: 902/566-8508; Email: jgaudet@peinet.pe.ca; Symbol: PCV – Librarian, Joyce Gaudet

ELLERSLIE

Prince Edward Island Greens – Library, PO Box 1, Ellerslie PE C0B 1J0 – 902/831-2471 – Research Co-ordinator, Marilyn Sparling

MORELL

Government of PEI - Library, PO Box 7500, Morell PE C0A 1S0 – 902/368-6396; Fax: 902/961-3203 – Director, Library Services, Harry Holman

SHERWOOD

Prince Edward Island Humane Society – Library, PO Box 20022, Sherwood PE C1A 9E3 – 902/892-1190; Toll Free: 1-800-892-1191

SUMMERSIDE

Holland College - Harbourside Centre Library, 298 Water St., Summerside PE C1N 1B8 – 902/888-6452; Fax: 902/888-6401; Email: lykow@harbour.hc.hollandc.pe.ca – Manager, Jean Lykow

Prince County Hospital – Medical Library, 259 Beattie Ave., Summerside PE C1A 2A9 – 902/436-9131 – Health Records Administrator, Joy Jenkins

QUÉBEC

Centres régionaux de services aux bibliothèques publiques (CRSBP)

Abitibi-Témiscamingue: CRSBP d'Abitibi-Témiscamingue, 20, boul Québec, Rouyn-Noranda PQ J9X 2E6 – 819/762-4305; Téléc: 819/797-1161 – Administrateur, Norman Fink

Alma: CRSBP de Saguenay-Lac-St-Jean, 100, rue Price ouest, Alma PQ G8B 4S1 – 418/662-6425; Téléc: 418/662-7593 – Administrateur délégué, Johanne Belley

Charny: CRSPB Régions de Québec-Chaudière-Appalaches, 3189, av Albert-Demers, Charny PQ G6X 3A1 – 418/832-6166; Téléc: 418/832-6168 – Directeur général, Réal Messier; Public Services Librarian, Denis Gravel; Acquisitions Librarian, Lucie Gobeil

Côte-Nord: CRSBP de la Côte-Nord, 59, rue Napoléon, Sept-Îles PQ G4R 5C5 – 418/962-1020; Téléc: 418/962-5124 – Directeur général, Jean-Roch Gagnon

Estrie: CRSBP Estrie, 4155, rue Brodeur, Sherbrooke PQ J1L 1K4 – 819/565-9744 – Administrateur délégué, Normand Bernier

Gaspésie: CRSBP de Gaspésie-Îles-de-la-Madeleine, 31, rue des Écoliers, CP 340, Cap-Chat PQ G0J 1E0 – 418/786-5597; Téléc: 418/786-2024 – Directeur général, Gilles Rochette

Laurentides: CRSBP des Laurentides, 29, rue Brissette, CP 239, Ste-Agathe-des-Monts PQ J8C 3A3 – 819/326-6440; Téléc: 819/326-0885 – Directeur général, Marcel Bouchard

Mauricie: CRSBP de Mauricie, 3125, rue Girard, Trois-Rivières PQ G8Z 2M4 – 819/375-9623; Téléc: 819/375-0132 – Administrateur délégué, Pierre L'Hérault; Public Services Librarian, Judith Dansereau; Technical Services/Acquisitions Librarian, Sonia Loubier

Montérégie: CRSBP de la Montérégie, 275, rue Conrad-Pelletier, La Prairie PQ J5R 4V1 – 514/444-5433; Téléc: 514/659-3364; Courrier électronique: info.biblio@monteregie.crsbp.qc.ca – Administrateur délégué, Richard Boivin; Responsable du développement des bibliothèques affiliées, Claire Dionne; Responsable de la gestion des systèmes d'information, Jacqueline Labelle

Outaouais: CRSBP de l'Outaouais, 736, av Principale, Gatineau PQ J8T 5L8 – 819/561-6008; Téléc: 819/561-6767; Symbol: CRSBPO – Directrice générale, Hélène Arseneau; Technical Services & Acquisitions Librarian, Danielle Sauvé

Portages: CRSBP du Bas-Saint-Laurent, 465, rue St-Pierre, Rivière-du-Loup PQ G5R 4T6 – 418/867-1682; Téléc: 418/867-3434 – Directeur général, Yves Savard

Bibliothèques publiques

Alma: Bibliothèque municipale d'Alma, 500, rue Collard ouest, Alma PQ G8B 1N2 – 418/669-5139; Téléc: 418/669-5089; Symbol: QA – Responsable, Martin Bouchard

Amos: Bibliothèque municipale d'Amos, 222 - 1e avenue est, Amos PQ J9T 1H3 – 819/732-6070; Téléc: 819/732-3242; Courrier électronique: jchabot@ville.amos.qc.ca – Bibliothécaire, Jean Chabot

Amqui: Bibliothèque municipale d'Amqui, 24, promenade de l'Hôtel de Ville, CP 1628, Amqui PQ G0J 1B0 – 418/629-4216; Téléc: 418/629-4090 – Responsable, Marie Côté

Anjou: Bibliothèque municipale d'Anjou, 7500, av Goncourt, Anjou PQ H1K 3X9 – 514/493-8270; Téléc: 514/493-8273; Symbol: QAN – Chef de division/Bibliothèque, Marie-Thérèse Stephen, M. Bibl.; Public Services Librarian, Ivan Filion; Technical Services Librarian, Sylvaine Tétreault – See also following branches: Succursale de la Bibliothèque d'Anjou

Anjou: Succursale de la Bibliothèque d'Anjou, 7070, rue Jarry est, Anjou PQ H1J 1G2 – 514/493-8271 – Branch of Bibliothèque municipale d'Anjou

Arthabaska: Succursale Alcide-Fleury, 841, boul Bois-Francs Sud, Arthabaska PQ G6P 5W3 – 819/357-8240; Téléc: 819/357-2099 Branch of Bibliothèque Charles-Édouard-Mailhot

Asbestos: Bibliothèque municipale d'Asbestos, 187, rue du Roi, CP 117, Asbestos PQ J1T 1S4 – 819/879-4363; Téléc: 819/879-2343 – Responsable, Marie-Hélène Parent

Aylmer: Bibliothèque municipale d'Aylmer, 120, rue Principale, Aylmer PQ J9H 3M3 – 819/685-5005, poste 4700; Téléc: 819/685-5019; Symbol: QAY – Bibliothécaire, Guy Dubois

Baie-Comeau: Bibliothèque municipale de Baie-Comeau, 41, av Mance, Baie-Comeau PQ G4Z 1M6 – 418/296-8305; Téléc: 418/296-3759 – Responsable, Joan Sirois

Baie-d'Urfé: Bibliothèque Baie-d'Urfé Library, 20551, ch Bord du Lac, Baie-d'Urfé PQ H9X 1R3 – 514/457-3274 – President, R. Tunmer; Children's Librarian, M. Spriggs; Technical Services Librarian, J. Collins; Acquisitions Librarian, A. Thompson

Beaconsfield: Bibliothèque municipale de Beaconsfield, 303, boul Beaconsfield, Beaconsfield PQ H9W 4A7 – 514/697-9040; Téléc: 514/697-2064 – Responsable, Linda Burdayron

Beauharnois: Bibliothèque municipale de Beauharnois, 600, rue Ellice, Beauharnois PQ J6N 3P7 – 514/429-4618 – Responsable, Marielle Groulx

Beauport: Bibliothèque municipale de Beauport, 3095, ch Royal, CP 5187, Beauport PQ G1E 6P4 – 418/666-2188; Téléc: 418/666-6173 – Denis Couture – See also following branches: Bibliothèque Étienne-Parent, Bibliothèque Succursale

Beauport: Bibliothèque Étienne-Parent, 3515, Clémenceau, CP 5187, Beauport PQ G1E 6P4 – Branch of Bibliothèque municipale de Beauport

Beauport: Bibliothèque Succursale, 3095, ch Royal, CP 5187, Beauport PQ G1E 6P4 – Branch of Bibliothèque municipale de Beauport

Bécancour: Bibliothèque municipale de Bécancour, 1295, av Nicolas-Perrot, Bécancour PQ G0X 1B0 – 819/294-6500; Téléc: 819/294-6535; Symbol: QBEC – Bibliothécaire, Julie Labrecque – See also following branches: Bibliothèque municipale de Gentilly, Bibliothèque municipale de Précieux-Sang, Bibliothèque municipale de St-Grégoire, Bibliothèque municipale de Ste-Angèle-de-Laval, Bibliothèque municipale de Ste-Gertrude

Bellefeuille: Bibliothèque publique de Bellefeuille, 450, boul La Salette, Bellefeuille PQ J0R 1A0 – 514/432-1226; Téléc: 514/565-2920 – Responsable, Claudine Richer

Beloeil: Bibliothèque municipale de Beloeil, 620, rue Richelieu, Beloeil PQ J3G 5E8 – 514/467-7872; Téléc: 514/467-3257 – Directrice du Service de la bibliothèque, Johanne Guevremont

Black Lake: Bibliothèque publique de Black Lake, 302, rue St-Désiré, Black Lake PQ G0N 1A0 – 418/423-4291 – Responsable, Claude Matte

Blainville: Bibliothèque municipale de Blainville, 980, ch du Plan-Bouchard, Blainville PQ J7C 3S9 – 514/434-5370; Téléc: 514/434-5378 – Directrice, Maud Lefebvre-Roux

Boisbriand: Bibliothèque de Boisbriand, 901, boul de la Grande Allée, Boisbriand PQ J7G 1W6 – 514/435-7466; Téléc: 514/435-0627 – Bibliothécaire, Ghislaine Lauzon

Boucherville: Bibliothèque Montarville-Boucher De la Bruère, 501, ch du Lac, Boucherville PQ J4B 6V6 – 514/449-8209; Téléc: 514/449-6865 – Directeur, Sylvie Provost

Brossard: Bibliothèque municipale Brossard, 3200, boul Lapinière, Brossard PQ J4Z 2L4 – 514/923-7045; Téléc: 514/926-7908; Symbol: QB – Directrice, Danielle Champagne; Reference Librarian, Brigitte Gagnon; Technical Services Librarian, Sylvie Morin; Acquisitions Librarian, Linda Pagé

Buckingham: Bibliothèque municipale de Buckingham, 181, rue Joseph, Buckingham PQ J8L IG6 – 819/986-3351; Téléc: 819/986-8336 – Responsable, Lise Robitaille

Candiac: Bibliothèque municipale Candiac, #100, 4, boul Montcalm nord, Candiac PQ J5R 3M2 – 514/659-7611; Téléc: 514/444-5483 – Responsable, Maryse St-Onge-Hansen

Cap-de-la-Madeleine: Bibliothèque municipale de Cap-de-la-Madeleine, 70, rue Saint-Pierre, CP 368, Cap-de-la-Madeleine PQ G8T 6V8 – 819/378-8206; Téléc: 819/378-5539 – Bibliothécaire, Francine Marcouiller

Cap-Rouge: Bibliothèque municipale de Cap-Rouge, 4705, rue de la Promenade-des-Soeurs, Cap-Rouge PQ G1Y 2W2 – 418/650-7501; Téléc: 418/650-7795 – Responsable, Lucie Dion

Chambly: Bibliothéque municipale Chambly, 1691, rue Bourgogne, Chambly PQ J3L 1Y8 – 514/658-2711; Téléc: 514/447-4525 – Bibliotechnicienne, Carole Mainville-Beriault

Charlesbourg: Bibliothèque municipale de Charlesbourg, 7950, 1e av, Charlesbourg PQ G1H 2Y4 – 418/624-7742; Téléc: 418/624-7886 – Activités culturelles, Chef de division, Constance Grégoire; Services publiques, Chef de section, Lina Rousseau; Services techniques, Technicienne principale, Sylvie Brown

Charny: Bibliothèque municipale de Charny, 2504, av du Viaduc, Charny PQ G6X 2V3 – 418/832-7070; Téléc: 418/832-9286 – Responsable, Jacques Rochette

Châteauguay: Bibliothèque municipale de Châteauguay, 15, boul Maple, Châteauguay PQ J6J 3P7 – 514/691-1934; Téléc: 514/699-4822 – Directeur, René Richer; Public Services Librarian, Marie-France Martel; Technical Services Librarian, Jocelyne Brunet; Acquisitions Librarian, Michel St-Onge; Informatique, Céline Lussier

Chibougamau: Bibliothèque municipale de Chibougamau, 601, 3e rue, Chibougamau PQ G8P 3A2 – 418/748-2497; Téléc: 418/748-6562 – Responsable, Lise Matte

Chicoutimi: Bibliothèque publique de Chicoutimi, 155, rue Racine est, Chicoutimi PQ G7H 5B8 – 418/698-5350; Téléc: 418/698-5359; Courrier électronique: dallaire@chicoutimi.biblio.qc.ca – Régisseur, Andre Y. Duchesne

Coaticook: Bibliothèque publique de Coaticook, 34, rue Main est, Coaticook PQ J1A 1N2 – 819/849-4013; Téléc: 819/849-7918 – Directrice, Ginette Grenier

Contrecoeur: Bibliothèque municipale de Contrecoeur, 4970, rue Marie-Victorin, Contrecoeur PQ J0L 1C0 – 514/587-8145; Téléc: 514/587-5855 – Responsable, Francine Brodeur

Côte-St-Luc: Bibliothèque municipale de Côte-Saint-Luc, 5851, boul Cavendish, Côte-St-Luc PQ H4W 2X8 – 514/485-6900; Téléc: 514/485-6966; Symbol: QMCSL – Director, Eleanor London

Cowansville: Bibliothèque municipale de Cowansville, 220, Place Municipale, Cowansville PQ J2K 1T4 – 514/263-4071; Téléc: 514/263-9357 – Responsable, Anne-Marie Landry

Deux-Montagnes: Bibliothèque municipale de Deux-Montagnes, 200, rue Henri-Dunant, Deux-Montagnes PQ J7R 4W6 – 514/473-2702 – Director, Johanne Chaput

Dolbeau: Bibliothèque municipale de Dolbeau, 1150, boul Wallberg, CP 201, Dolbeau PQ G8L 2R1 – 418/276-5169 – Directrice, Pauline Lapointe

Dollard-des-Ormeaux: Bibliothèque intermunicipale de Dollard-des-Ormeaux, 12001, boul de Salaberry, Dollard-des-Ormeaux PQ H9B 2A7 – 514/684-1496; Téléc: 514/684-9184 – Bibliothécaire, Michèle Dupuy

Dorval: Bibliothèque municipale de Dorval, 1401, ch Bord-du-Lac, Dorval PQ H9S 2E5 – 514/633-4170; Téléc: 514/633-4177; Symbol: QD – Manager, Jill Roberts; Reference Librarian, Cathy Maxwell; Public Services Librarian, Gail Warren; Technical Services Librarian, Roland Guerin; Technical Services Librarian, Roland Guerin – See also following branches: Surrey Branch

Dorval: Surrey Branch, 1945 Parkfield Ave., Dorval PQ H9P 1X5 – 514/633-4072; Fax: 514/633-4165 – Manager, Jill Roberts – Branch of Bibliothèque municipale de Dorval

Drummondville: Centre d'information documentaire Côme-Saint-Germain, 545, rue des Écoles, Drummondville PQ J2B 1J6 – 819/478-6573; Téléc: 819/478-0399; Symbol: CID – Director, Pierre Meunier

Farnham: Bibliothèque publique de Farnham, 479, rue Hôtel-de-Ville nord, Farnham PQ J2N 2H3 – 514/293-3375 – Responsable, Georgette Rahill

Fermont: Bibliothèque publique de Fermont, CP 10, Fermont PQ G0G 1J0 – 418/287-3227; Téléc: 418/287-3274 – Responsable, Rose Vaillancourt

Gatineau: Bibliothèque municipale de Gatineau, 855, boul de la Gappe, Gatineau PQ J8T 8H9 – 819/243-2506; Téléc: 819/243-2527 – Chef de la division, Paule Brochu; Responsable des services techniques, François Gagnon; Responsable des services au public, Nicole Proulx – See also following branches: Succursale de la Riviera, Succursale Docteur-Jean-Lorrain

Gatineau: Succursale de la Riviera, Centre communautaire de la Riviera, 12, rue de Picardie, Gatineau PQ J8T 1N9 – 819/243-2543 – Branch of Bibliothèque municipale de Gatineau

Canadian Almanac & Directory 1997

Gatineau: Succursale Docteur-Jean-Lorrain, 20, boul Lorrain, Gatineau PQ J8T 2C8 – 819/669-5201 – Branch of Bibliothèque municipale de Gatineau

Gentilly: Bibliothèque municipale de Gentilly, 1920, boul Bécancour, Gentilly PQ G0X 1G0 – 819/298-3948 – Bénévole responsable, Lise Emond – Branch of Bibliothèque municipale de Bécancour

Granby: Bibliothèque municipale de Granby, 11, rue Dufferin, Granby PQ J2G 4W5 – 514/776-8310; Téléc: 514/776-8211 – Directrice, Ginette Legault

Grand'Mère: Bibliothèque Hélène-B.-Beauséjour, 650 - 8e rue, Grand'Mère PQ G9T 6K1 – 819/538-5555 – Librarian, Janine Vaugeois-Patry

Greenfield Park: Bibliothèque municipale de Greenfield Park, 225, av Empire, Greenfield Park PQ J4V 1T9 – 514/672-7500; Téléc: 514/671-0517 – Librarian, Linda Travis

Hull: Bibliothèque municipale de Hull, 25, rue Laurier, CP 1970, Succ. B, Hull PQ J8X 3Y9 – 819/595-7460; Téléc: 819/595-7487; Courrier électronique: BMH; Symbol: QH – Librarian, Denis Boyer; Public Services Librarian, Pierre Tessier; Acquisitions, Francine Chevrier – See also following branches: Succursale Aurélien-Doucet, Succursale Lucien-Lalonde

Hull: Succursale Aurélien-Doucet, 207, boul du Mont-Bleu, Hull PQ J8Z 3G3 – 819/595-7490; Téléc: 819/595-7376 – Responsable, Denis Boyer – Branch of Bibliothèque municipale de Hull

Hull: Succursale Lucien-Lalonde, 225, rue Berri, Hull PQ J8Y 4K1 – 819/595-7480; Téléc: 819/595-7479 – Responsable, Denis Boyer – Branch of Bibliothèque municipale de Hull

Île d'Anticosti: Bibliothèque municipale de l'Île d'Anticosti, Île d'Anticosti PQ G0G 2Y0

Joliette: Bibliothèque de la Maison de la culture Bonsecours, 585, rue Archambault, Joliette PQ J6E 2W7 – 514/755-6400; Téléc: 514/755-6426 – Responsable, Chantal Émard

Jonquière: Bibliothèque municipale de Jonquière, 2850, Place Davis, CP 2000, Jonquière PQ G7X 7W7 – 418/699-6068; Téléc: 418/699-6046 – Chef de division bibliothèques, Mireille Boudreault – See also following branches: Succursale Kenogami, Succursale St-Michel

Jonquière: Succursale Kenogami, 3750, boul du Royaume, CP 2000, Jonquière PQ G7X 7W7 – 418/546-2175 – Branch of Bibliothèque municipale de Jonquière

Jonquière: Succursale St-Michel, 3885, boul Harvey, CP 2000, Jonquière PQ G7X 7W7 – 418/546-2173 – Branch of Bibliothèque municipale de Jonquière

Kirkland: Bibliothèque municipale de Kirkland, 17100, boul Hymus, Kirkland PQ H9J 2W2 – 514/630-2726; Téléc: 514/630-2716; Courrier électronique: kirkev@cam.org; Symbol: QK – Bibliothécaire, Claire Clément; Reference Librarian, Beverley Gilbertson; Technical Services Librarian, Gisele Laforce

La Baie: Bibliothèque publique de La Baie, 1911 - 6e av, La Baie PQ G7B 1S1 – 418/544-1151 – Directeur, Anne Lebel

La Malbaie: Bibliothèque publique de La Malbaie, 395, rue St-Etienne, CP 232, La Malbaie PQ G5A 1J7 – 418/665-2483 – Responsable, Roland Gagné

La Plaine: Bibliothèque municipale de La Plaine, 6900, rue Guérin, La Plaine PQ J0N 1B0 – 514/968-2626; Téléc: 514/968-3130 – Directrice, Francine Piché

La Prairie: Bibliothèque municipale de La Prairie, 200, boul Balmoral, La Prairie PQ J5R 4L5 – 514/659-9135; Téléc: 514/444-9133 – Bibliothécaire, Marie-Josée Benoit

La Salle: Bibliothèque L'Octogone, 1080, av Dollard, La Salle PQ H8N 2T9 – 514/367-6488; Téléc: 514/367-6604 – Chef de division, Marie-Andrée Marcoux, 514/367-6488; Reference Librarian, Nicole Cromp, 514/367-6385; Circulation Librarian, France Lecours, 514/367-6372; Children's Librarian, Louise Gagné, 514/367-6379; Technical Services Librarian, Lise Filiatrault, 514/367-6382

La Sarre: Bibliothèque Richelieu de La Sarre, 195, rue Principale sud, La Sarre PQ J9Z 1Y3 – 819/333-2294; Téléc: 819/333-3090 – Responsable, Josée Labbé

La Tuque: Bibliothèque municipale de La Tuque, 575, rue St-Eugène, La Tuque PQ G9X 2T5 – 819/523-3100; Téléc: 819/523-5419 – Bibliothécaire, Alain Michaud

Lac Brome: Bibliothèque Commemorative Pettes, 276, rue Knowlton, CP 177, Lac Brome PQ J0E 1V0 – 514/243-6128 – Head Librarian, Susan Bailey-Godin

Lac-Etchemin: Bibliothèque municipale de Lac-Etchemin, 208 - 2e av, Lac-Etchemin PQ G0R 1S0 – 418/625-8741; Téléc: 418/625-3175 – Responsable, Louise Poulin

Lac-Mégantic: Bibliothèque municipale de Lac-Mégantic, 5086, rue Frontenac, Lac-Mégantic PQ G6B 1H3 – 819/583-0876; Téléc: 819/583-0878 – Directeur, Yves Tanguay; Technical Services Librarian, Nancy Giroux

Lachenaie: Bibliothèque municipale de Lachenaie, 3060, ch Saint-Charles, Lachenaie PQ J6V 1A1 – 514/471-9267; Téléc: 514/471-9872 – Directrice, Céline Paquette

Lachine: Bibliothèque municipale Saul-Bellow, 3100, rue St-Antoine, Lachine PQ H8S 4B8 – 514/634-3471; Téléc: 514/634-8194 – Directrice, JoAnne Turnbull; Adult Services, Andrée Allard; Children's Librarian, Francine Dupuis

Lachute: Bibliothèque municipale de Lachute, 378, rue Principale, Lachute PQ J8H 1Y2 – 514/562-3781; Téléc: 514/562-1431 – Bibliothécaire, Louise Beaulieu-Couture; Bibliotechnicienne, Chantal Belisle

L'Ancienne-Lorette: Bibliothèque Marie-Victorin, 1635, rue Notre-Dame, L'Ancienne-Lorette PQ G2E 3B4 – 418/877-9703; Téléc: 418/872-1962 – Responsable, Camille Deschênes

Laval: Bibliothèque municipale de Laval, 1535, boul Chomedey, Laval PQ H7V 3Z4 – 514/978-5848; Téléc: 514/978-5833 – Directrice, Monique Normandin; Public Services Librarian, Ghislaine Bélanger – See also following branches: Bibliothèque Alain-Grandbois, Bibliothèque Émile-Nelligan, Bibliothèque Gabrielle-Roy, Bibliothèque Germaine-Guèvrement, Bibliothèque Laure-Conan, Bibliothèque Marius-Barbeau, Bibliothèque Multiculturelle, Bibliothèque Philippe-Panneton, Bibliothèque Sylvain-Garneau, Bibliothèque Yves-Thériault

Laval: Bibliothèque Alain-Grandbois, 4300, boul Samson, Laval PQ H7W 2G9 – 514/978-3671; Téléc: 514/686-8270 – Branch of Bibliothèque municipale de Laval

Laval: Bibliothèque Émile-Nelligan, 325, boul Cartier, Laval PQ H7N 2J5 – 514/662-4973; Téléc: 514/668-9374 – Branch of Bibliothèque municipale de Laval

Laval: Bibliothèque Gabrielle-Roy, 3505, boul Dagenais, Laval PQ H7P 4V9 – 514/978-8909; Téléc: 514/628-5992 – Branch of Bibliothèque municipale de Laval

Laval: Bibliothèque Germaine-Guèvrement, 2900, boul de la Concorde, Laval PQ H7E 2B6 – 514/662-4001; Téléc: 514/661-0215 – Branch of Bibliothèque municipale de Laval

Laval: Bibliothèque Laure-Conan, 4660, boul des Laurentides, Laval PQ H7M 2M8 – 514/662-4975; Téléc: 514/628-4674 – Branch of Bibliothèque municipale de Laval

Laval: Bibliothèque Marius-Barbeau, 455, Montée du Moulin, Laval PQ H7A 1Z2 – 514/662-4004; Téléc: 514/665-9889 – Branch of Bibliothèque municipale de Laval

Laval: Bibliothèque Multiculturelle, 1535, boul Chomedey, Laval PQ H7V 3Z4 – 514/978-5995; Téléc: 514/978-5833 – Branch of Bibliothèque municipale de Laval

Laval: Bibliothèque Philippe-Panneton, 4747, boul Arthur-Sauvé, Laval PQ H7N 5P5 – 514/978-8919; Téléc: 514/627-5928 – Branch of Bibliothèque municipale de Laval

Laval: Bibliothèque Sylvain-Garneau, 216, boul Ste-Rose, Laval PQ H7L 1L6 – 514/978-3940; Téléc: 514/963-6002 – Branch of Bibliothèque municipale de Laval

Laval: Bibliothèque Yves-Thériault, 670, Place Publique, Laval PQ H7X 1G1 – 514/978-6599; Téléc: 514/969-3285 – Branch of Bibliothèque municipale de Laval

Le Gardeur: Bibliothèque municipale de Le Gardeur, 1, Montée des Arsenaux, Le Gardeur PQ J5Z 2C1 – 514/582-8288; Téléc: 514/585-5221 – Directrice, Ginette Martin

Lévis: Bibliothèque municipale de Lévis, 17, rue Notre-Dame, Lévis PQ G6V 4A3 – 418/838-4122; Téléc: 418/838-4996 – Régisseur, Suzanne Rochefort; Technical Services Librarian, Carmelle Thériault – See also following branches: Bibliothèque Lauzon, Bibliothèque St-David

Lévis: Bibliothèque Lauzon, 10, rue Giguère, Lévis PQ G6V 1N6 – 418/838-4143; Téléc: 418/838-4948 – Branch of Bibliothèque municipale de Lévis

Lévis: Bibliothèque St-David, 4, rue Olympique, Lévis PQ G6W 6N3 – 418/838-4127; Téléc: 418/838-4955 – Branch of Bibliothèque municipale de Lévis

L'Île-Bizard: Bibliothèque municipale de L'Île-Bizard, 500, rue de l'Église, L'Île-Bizard PQ H9C 1G9 – 514/626-8505; Téléc: 514/620-4153; Symbol: OSTR – Responsable, Hélène Rouette

L'Île-Perrot: Bibliothèque municipale de L'Île-Perrot, 150, boul Perrot, L'Île-Perrot PQ J7V 3G1 – 514/453-3473; Téléc: 514/453-1655 – Bibliothécaire, Chantal Lepage

Longueuil: Bibliothèque municipale de Longueuil, 100, rue St-Laurent ouest, Longueuil PQ J4K 4Y7 – 514/646-8615; Téléc: 514/646-8874; Symbol: PLO – Bibliothécaire en chef, Yves Ouimet; Reference Librarian, Nicole Bourgon, 514/646-8612; Circulation Librarian, Diane Denault, 514/646-8611; Children's Librarian, Sylvie Beaudoin, 514/646-8617; Technical Services Librarian, Christiane Gordon, 514/646-8625; Acquisitions Librarian, Francine L. Boyer, 514/646-8623

Loretteville: Bibliothèque municipale de Loretteville, 307, rue Racine, Loretteville PQ G2B 1E7 – 418/842-1924; Téléc: 418/842-2585 – Directeur, France Lemay

Lorraine: Bibliothèque municipale de Lorraine, 33, boul de Gaulle, Lorraine PQ J6Z 3W9 – 514/621-1071; Téléc: 514/621-6585 – Director, Juanita Sales

Magog: Bibliothèque municipale Memphremagog, 61, rue Merry nord, Magog PQ J1X 2E7 – 819/843-1330; Symbol: QMAGB – Bibliothécaire, Diane Boulé; Technical Services/Acquisitions Librarian, Marie-Renée Saint-Pierre

Malartic: Bibliothèque municipale de Malartic, 870, rue Royale, CP 4170, Malartic PQ J0Y 1Z0 – 819/757-4449 – Responsable, Lucille Mikolajczak

Maniwaki: Bibliothèque municipale de Maniwaki, 8, rue Comeau, Maniwaki PQ J9E 2R8 – 819/449-2738 – Directrice, Jocelyne Leclair

Marieville: Bibliothèque commémorative Desautels, 1801, rue du Pont, Marieville PQ J3M 1J7 – 514/460-4988 – Directeur, Daniel Lalonde, M.Bibl.

Mascouche: Bibliothèque publique de Mascouche, 2685, ch Sainte-Marie, Local P, Mascouche PQ J7K 1M8 – 514/474-4159; Téléc: 514/474-3410 – Directrice, Diane Allard

Matane: Bibliothèque municipale de Matane, 230, av St-Jérôme, Matane PQ G4W 3A2 – 418/562-9233; Téléc: 418/562-4869 – Responsable, Lise Grenier

Mercier: Bibliothèque municipale de Mercier, 16, rue du Parc, Mercier PQ J6R 1E5 – 514/692-6780 – Directeur, Daniel Morin

Mirabel: Bibliothèque municipale de Mirabel, 13908, rte 117, CP 720, Mirabel PQ J0N 1L0 – 514/430-4563; Téléc: 514/430-2868 – Directrice, Claudette Poulin

Mistassini: Bibliothèque municipale de Mistassini, 173, boul St-Michel, Mistassini PQ G0W 2C0 – 418/276-6466; Téléc: 418/276-8164 – Responsable, Carold Sasseville

Mont-Joli: Bibliothèque municipale de Mont-Joli, 1477, boul Jacques-Cartier, CP 576, Mont-Joli PQ G5H 3L3 – 418/775-4106; Téléc: 418/775-6320 – Responsable, Julie Bélanger

Mont-Laurier: Bibliothèque municipale de Mont-Laurier, 485, rue Mercier, Mont-Laurier PQ J9L 3N8 – 819/623-1833; Téléc: 819/623-4840 – Responsable, Edith Whear

Mont-Royal: Bibliothèque Reginald J.P. Dawson, 1967, boul Graham, Mont-Royal PQ H3R 1G9 – 514/734-2967; Téléc: 514/734-3089; Symbol: QMRRD – Head Librarian, Sharon Huffman; Librarian, English Adult Services, Lisa Rasmussen, 514/734-2970; Librarian, French Adult Services, Denis Chouinard, 514/734-2969; Children's Librarian, Julie-Anne Cardella; Children's Librarian, Leanne Bowler; Technical Services Supervisor, Angèle Mailloux; Acquisitions Technician, Elaine Charness; ILL, Chantal Galarneau, 514/734-2971

Mont-St-Hilaire: Bibliothèque municipale de Mont-St-Hilaire, 100, rue du Centre Civique, Mont-St-Hilaire PQ J3H 3M8 – 514/467-6982; Téléc: 514/467-6460 – Responsable de la bibliothèque, Francine Ledoux-Nadeau

Montréal: Bibliothèque de Montréal, #400, 5650, rue d'Iberville, Montréal PQ H2G 3E4 – 514/872-5923, 2900; Téléc: 514/872-4911; Courrier électronique: ENVOY:PEB.QMBM et BVM.DIR; Symbol: QMBM – Bibliothécaire en chef, Jacques Panneton; Division du traitement documentaire, chef de division, Jacques Aird; Division des systèmes et des nouvelles technologies, Isabel Assunçao; Division de la Bibliothèque centrale, chef de division, Michèle Régnier; Division du développement des ressources et services, Hélène Roussel; Section de la préparation matérielle, chef de section, Claire Lahaie; Section des services annexes, chef de section (Div. B. Centrale), Brigitte Raymond – See also following branches: Bibliobus, Bibliothèque Acadie, Bibliothèque Ahuntsic, Bibliothèque Benny, Bibliothèque Centrale, Bibliothèque Centrale-Annexe, Bibliothèque Côte-des-Neiges, Bibliothèque de Rosemont, Bibliothèque Georges-Vanier, Bibliothèque Hochelaga, Bibliothèque la Petite Patrie, Bibliothèque Langelier, Bibliothèque le Prevost, Bibliothèque Maisonneuve, Bibliothèque Marie-Uguay, Bibliothèque Métro McGill, Bibliothèque Mercier, Bibliothèque Mile-End, Bibliothèque Notre-Dame, Bibliothèque Notre-Dame-de-Grace, Bibliothèque Parc Frontenac, Bibliothèque Plateau-Mont-Royal, Bibliothèque Pointe-aux-Trembles, Bibliothèque Rivière-des-Prairies, Bibliothèque Saint-Charles, Bibliothèque Saint-Michel, Bibliothèque Salaberry, Phonothèque

Montréal: Bibliobus, #400, 5650, rue d'Iberville, Montréal PQ H2G 3E4 – 514/872-5690; Téléc: 514/872-4911 – Rachel Boisjoly – Branch of Bibliothèque de Montréal

Montréal: Bibliothèque Acadie, 11833, boul de l'Acadie, Montréal PQ H3M 2T5 – 514/872-6989; Téléc: 514/872-0510 – Louise Jodoin – Branch of Bibliothèque de Montréal

Montréal: Bibliothèque Ahuntsic, 770, boul Henri-Bourassa est, Montréal PQ H2C 1E6 – 514/872-6992 (adultes), 872-6994 (enfants); Téléc: 514/872-0518 – Marie Pilon – Branch of Bibliothèque de Montréal

Montréal: Bibliothèque Benny, 3465, av Benny, Montréal PQ H4B 2R9 – 514/872-4147 (adultes), 872-4636 (enfants); Téléc: 514/872-0515 – Lorraine Guay – Branch of Bibliothèque de Montréal

Montréal: Bibliothèque Centrale, 1210, rue Sherbrooke est, Montréal PQ H2L 1L9 – 514/872-5923 (adultes), 872-1633 (enfants); Téléc: 514/872-1626 – Michèle Régnier – Branch of Bibliothèque de Montréal

Montréal: Bibliothèque Centrale-Annexe, 1160, rue Sherbrooke est, Montréal PQ H2L 1L7 – 514/872-2198; Téléc: 514/872-1626 – Evelyne Caron – Branch of Bibliothèque de Montréal

Montréal: Bibliothèque Côte-des-Neiges, 5290, ch de la Côte-des-Neiges, Montréal PQ H3T 1Y4 – 514/872-6603 (adultes), 872-5118 (enfants); Téléc: 514/872-0516 – Danielle Keable – Branch of Bibliothèque de Montréal

Montréal: Bibliothèque de Rosemont, 3131, boul Rosemont, Montréal PQ H1Y 1M4 – 514/872-4701 (adultes), 872-6139 (enfants); Téléc: 514/872-0527 – Renaud Arcand – Branch of Bibliothèque de Montréal

Montréal: Bibliothèque Georges-Vanier, 530, rue Vinet, Montréal PQ H3J 2E6 – 514/872-2001 (adultes), 872-2002 (enfants); Téléc: 514/872-0511 – Diane Tremblay – Branch of Bibliothèque de Montréal

Montréal: Bibliothèque Hochelaga, 3568, rue Adam, Montréal PQ H1W 1Y9 – 514/872-3555; Téléc: 514/872-0521 – Johanne Petel – Branch of Bibliothèque de Montréal

Montréal: Bibliothèque la Petite Patrie, 6707, av de Lorimier, Montréal PQ H2G 2P8 – 514/872-1733 (adultes), 872-1732 (enfants); Téléc: 514/872-0526 – Lorraine Laberge – Branch of Bibliothèque de Montréal

Montréal: Bibliothèque Langelier, 6473, rue Sherbrooke est, Montréal PQ H1N 1C5 – 514/872-2640 (adultes), 872-4227 (enfants); Téléc: 514/872-0523 – Josée Valiquette – Branch of Bibliothèque de Montréal

Montréal: Bibliothèque le Prevost, 7355, av Christophe-Colomb, Montréal PQ H2R 2S5 – 514/872-1523 (adultes), 872-1526 (enfants); Téléc: 514/872-0529 – Louise Robichaud – Branch of Bibliothèque de Montréal

Montréal: Bibliothèque Maisonneuve, 4120, rue Ontario est, Montréal PQ H1V 1J9 – 514/872-4213 (adultes), 872-4214 (enfants); Téléc: 514/872-0522 – François Séguin – Branch of Bibliothèque de Montréal

Montréal: Bibliothèque Marie-Uguay, 6052, boul Monk, Montréal PQ H4A 1H2 – 514/872-4097 (adultes), 872-4414 (enfants); Téléc: 514/872-0513 – Jean-Pierre Leduc – Branch of Bibliothèque de Montréal

Montréal: Bibliothèque Mercier, 8105, rue Hochelaga, Montréal PQ H1L 2K9 – 514/872-8738 (adultes), 872-8739 (enfants); Téléc: 514/872-0524 – Lucie Beaulac – Branch of Bibliothèque de Montréal

Montréal: Bibliothèque Métro McGill, #310, 2001, rue University, Montréal PQ H3A 2A6 – 514/872-4154; Téléc: 514/872-0530 – Luce Forest-Doyon – Branch of Bibliothèque de Montréal

Montréal: Bibliothèque Mile-End, 5434, av du Parc, Montréal PQ H2V 4G7 – 514/872-2141 (adultes), 872-2142 (enfants); Téléc: 514/872-0531 – Van Be Lam – Branch of Bibliothèque de Montréal

Montréal: Bibliothèque municipale de St-Laurent, 1380, rue de l'Église, St-Laurent PQ H4L 2H2 – 514/855-6130; Téléc: 514/855-6129; Symbol: QSTL – Chef de division, Florian Dubois; Public Services & Reference, Sonia Djevalikian; Technical Services, Head, Josiane Querghi; Special Services, Head, Elaine Sauvé

Montréal: Bibliothèque municipale de St-Léonard, 8420, boul Lacordaire, St-Léonard PQ H1R 3G5 – 514/328-8585; Téléc: 514/328-7002 – Chef de division, France Huvelin; Reference Librarian, Murielle Alary, 514/328-8589; Circulation/Public Services Librarian, Reine Harvey, 514/328-8517; Technical Services/Acquisitions Librarian, Huguette Desmarais, 514/328-8520; Reading Activities Librarian, Claire Séguin

Montréal: Bibliothèque municipale de St-Pierre, 183, rue des Érables, St-Pierre PQ H8R 1B1 – 514/368-5740; Téléc: 514/368-5717 – Responsable, Monique Charette

Montréal: Bibliothèque Notre-Dame, 4700, rue Notre-Dame ouest, Montréal PQ H4C 1S8 – 514/872-2879 (adultes), 872-4698 (enfants); Téléc: 514/872-0512 – Jacques Charbonneau – Branch of Bibliothèque de Montréal

Montréal: Bibliothèque Notre-Dame-de-Grace, 3755, rue Botrel, Montréal PQ H4A 3G8 – 514/872-2398 (adultes), 872-2377 (enfants); Téléc: 514/872-0517 – Michèle Lavigne – Branch of Bibliothèque de Montréal

Montréal: Bibliothèque Parc Frontenac, 2550, rue Ontario est, Montréal PQ H2K 1W7 – 514/872-7888; Téléc: 514/872-0520 – Johanne Prud'Homme – Branch of Bibliothèque de Montréal

Montréal: Bibliothèque Plateau-Mont-Royal, 465, av du Mont-Royal est, Montréal PQ H2J 1W3 – 514/872-2270 (adultes); 872-2271 (enfants); Téléc: 514/872-0532 – Vesna Dell'Olio – Branch of Bibliothèque de Montréal

Montréal: Bibliothèque Pointe-aux-Trembles, 1515, boul du Tricentennaire, Montréal PQ H1B 3A9 – 514/872-6987; Téléc: 514/872-0525 – Nicole St-Vincent – Branch of Bibliothèque de Montréal

Montréal: Bibliothèque Rivière-des-Prairies, 9001, boul Perras, Montréal PQ H1E 3J7 – Gloria Maistrelli – Branch of Bibliothèque de Montréal

Montréal: Bibliothèque Saint-Charles, 2333, rue Mullins, Montréal PQ H3K 3E3 – 514/872-3092 (adultes), 872-3035 (enfants); Téléc: 514/872-0514 – France Machet – Branch of Bibliothèque de Montréal

Montréal: Bibliothèque Saint-Michel, 7601, rue François-Perrault, Montréal PQ H2A 3L6 – 514/872-3899 (adultes), 872-4250 (enfants); Téléc: 514/872-0528 – Suzanne Thibault – Branch of Bibliothèque de Montréal

Montréal: Bibliothèque Salaberry, 4170, rue Salaberry, Montréal PQ H4J 1H1 – 514/872-1521; Téléc: 514/872-0519 – Danièle Bouffard – Branch of Bibliothèque de Montréal

Montréal: La Magnétothèque, #105, 1030, rue Cherrier, Montréal PQ H2L 1H9 – 514/524-6831; Téléc: 514/524-5828; Ligne sans frais: 1-800-361-0635 – Librarian, André Hamel

Montréal: Phonothèque, 880, rue Roy, Montréal PQ H2L 1E6 – 514/872-2862; Téléc: 514/872-7735 – Gérald Forget – Branch of Bibliothèque de Montréal

Montréal: Westmount Public Library, 4574, rue Sherbrooke ouest, Westmount PQ H3Z 1G1 – 514/989-5300; Fax: 514/989-5485; Symbol: QWSMM – Director of Library & Cultural Services, Caroline Thibodeau; Reference Librarian, Ann Moffat; Circulation Librarian, Craig Wright; Children's Librarian, Joanne Stanbridge; Technical Services Librarian, Isabelle Seguin; Adult Services, Brenda Smith; French Services, Lysanne Ferron-Godin

Montréal: Bibliothèque municipale de Montréal-Est, 11370, rue Notre-Dame est, Montréal-Est PQ H1B 2W6 – 514/645-7431; Téléc: 514/645-0107; Symbol: QMEM – Directeur, Jean Ko; Public Services Librarian, Nathalie Joly; Technical Services Librarian, Anne Marie Dufort

Montréal: Centres Biblio-culturels de Montréal-Nord, 5400, boul Henri-Bourassa est, Montréal-Nord PQ H1G 2S9 – 514/328-4128; Téléc: 514/328-4298 – Responsable, Céline Dénommée

Normandin: Bibliothèque municipale de Normandin, 1156, Valois, Normandin PQ G8M 3Z8 – 418/274-

2241; Téléc: 418/274-7171 – Responsable, Denise Morin-Larouche
Notre-Dame-de-l'Île-Perrot: Bibliothèque municipale de Notre-Dame-de-l'Île-Perrot, 21, rue de l'Église, Notre-Dame-de-l'Île-Perrot PQ J7V 8P4 – 514/453-0013; Téléc: 514/453-8961 – Responsable, Guylaine Lauzon
Outremont: Bibliothèque municipale d'Outremont, 544, av Davaar, Outremont PQ H2V 2B9 – 514/495-6209; Téléc: 514/495-6287 – Bibliothécaire, Guy Laverdière
Pierrefonds: Bibliothèque intermunicipale de Pierrefonds, 13555, boul Pierrefonds, Pierrefonds PQ H9A 1A6 – 514/620-4181; Téléc: 514/620-5503; Symbol: QPD – Head Librarian, Michèle Dupuis; Reference/Acquisitions Librarian, Daniel Proulx; Reference Librarian, Louise Zampini; Circulation Librarian, Lise Bertrand; Circulation Librarian, Jennifer Reeves; Children's Librarian, Micheline Patton; Public Services Librarian, Lise Brosseau, 514/684-1496; Technical Services Librarian, Maurice Houle
Pincourt: Bibliothèque municipale de Pincourt, 62, av Mgr. Langlois, Pincourt PQ J7V 5C1 – 514/453-3788; Téléc: 514/453-0934 – Régisseure, Rose-Marie Desjardins
Plessisville: Bibliothèque intermunicipale de Plessisville, 1699, rue St-Calixte, Plessisville PQ G6L 1R2 – 819/362-6628; Téléc: 819/362-6421 – Bibliothécaire, Suzanne Bedard
Pointe-Claire: Bibliothèque publique de Pointe-Claire, 100, av Douglas Shand, Pointe-Claire PQ H9R 4V1 – 514/630-1218; Téléc: 514/630-1261; Symbol: QPOC – Directrice de la bibliothèque et des activités culturelles, Claire Coté; Reference Librarian, Suzanne Lauzier; Children's Librarian, Carole Lanthier-Boiteau; Technical Services Librarian, Céline Laperrière; Programming Librarian, Cristina Segura – See also following branches: Bibliothèque publique de Stewart Hall, Bibliothèque publique de Valois
Pointe-Claire: Bibliothèque publique de Stewart Hall, 176, Bord du Lac, Pointe-Claire PQ H9S 4J7 – 514/630-1221 – Responsable, Gwen Murray – Branch of Bibliothèque publique de Pointe-Claire
Pointe-Claire: Bibliothèque publique de Valois, 68, av Prince Edward, Pointe-Claire PQ H9R 4C7 – 514/630-1219 – Responsable, Mary Pupil – Branch of Bibliothèque publique de Pointe-Claire
Pointe-du-Lac: Bibliothèque Simone-L.-Roy, 101, Grande Allée, Pointe-du-Lac PQ G0X 1Z0 – 819/377-4289 – Responsable, Louise Houle
Port-Cartier: Bibliothèque municipale de Port-Cartier, 40, av Parent, Port-Cartier PQ G5B 2G5 – 418/766-3366; Téléc: 418/766-3561 – Bibliothécaire, Stéphane Harvey; Technical Services Librarian, Chantal Maltais
Précieux-Sang: Bibliothèque municipale de Précieux-Sang, 10995, St-Laurent, Précieux-Sang PQ G0X 2A0 – 819/294-1173 – Bénévole responsable, Louise Labarie – Branch of Bibliothèque municipale de Bécancour
Québec: Bibliothèque de Québec, 350, rue St-Joseph est, Québec PQ G1K 3B2 – 418/529-0924; Téléc: 418/529-1588 – Directeur général, Jean Payeur; Reference Librarian, Sylvie Fournier; Directrice générale adjointe, Marie Goyette; Technical Services Librarian, Julien Marquis; Acquisitions Librarian, Jean-Pierre Germain – See also following branches: Bibliothèque Canardière, Bibliothèque Collège-des-Jésuites, Bibliothèque Les Saules, Bibliothèque Neufchâtel, Bibliothèque Saint-Albert, Bibliothèque Saint-André, Bibliothèque Saint-Charles, Bibliothèque Saint-Jean-Baptiste, Bibliothèque Vieux-Québec, Comptoir Lebourgneuf
Québec: Bibliothèque Canardière, 1601, ch de la Canardière, Québec PQ G1J 2E1 – 418/666-8791 – Bibliothécaire, Hélène Larouche – Branch of Bibliothèque de Québec
Québec: Bibliothèque Collège-des-Jésuites, 1120, boul René-Lévesque ouest, Québec PQ G1S 4W4 – 418/691-6378 – Bibliothécaire, Lise Beaudoin – Branch of Bibliothèque de Québec
Québec: Bibliothèque Les Saules, 2035, boul Masson, Québec PQ G1P 1J3 – 418/872-5086 – Bibliothécaire, Monique Lemieux – Branch of Bibliothèque de Québec
Québec: Bibliothèque Neufchâtel, 4060, rue Blain, Québec PQ G2B 4P3 – 418/843-1395 – Bibliothécaire, Nancy Duscheneau – Branch of Bibliothèque de Québec
Québec: Bibliothèque Saint-Albert, 5, rue des Ormes, Québec PQ G1L 1M5 – 418/623-7996 – Bibliothécaire, Nadia Pizzamiglio – Branch of Bibliothèque de Québec
Québec: Bibliothèque Saint-André, 2155, boul Bastien, Québec PQ G2B 1B8 – 418/843-3263 – Bibliothécaire, Fabienne Labadie – Branch of Bibliothèque de Québec
Québec: Bibliothèque Saint-Charles, 400, 4e av, Québec PQ G1J 2Z9 – 418/691-6358 – Bibliothécaire, Hélène Dufour – Branch of Bibliothèque de Québec
Québec: Bibliothèque Saint-Jean-Baptiste, 755, rue Saint-Jean, Québec PQ G1R 1G1 – 418/691-6492 – Bibliothécaire, Jean Grantham – Branch of Bibliothèque de Québec
Québec: Bibliothèque Vieux-Québec, 37, rue Sainte-Angèle, Québec PQ G1R 4G5 – 418/691-6357 – Bibliothécaire, Isabelle Picard – Branch of Bibliothèque de Québec
Québec: Comptoir Lebourgneuf, 1650, boul La Morille, Québec PQ G2K 2L2 – 418/623-5058 – Fabienne Labadie – Branch of Bibliothèque de Québec
Repentigny: Bibliothèque municipale de Repentigny, 1, place D'Évry, Repentigny PQ J6A 8H7 – 514/654-2346; Téléc: 514/654-2409 – Régisseure, Célyne Ross; Reference Librarian, Maryse Trudeau
Rimouski: Bibliothèque municipale de Rimouski, 110, rue de l'Évéché est, CP 710, Rimouski PQ G5L 7C7 – 418/724-3165; Téléc: 418/724-3180 – Bibiothécaire responsable, Nicole Gagnon
Rivière-du-Loup: Bibliothèque Françoise-Bédard, Maison de la culture, 67, rue du Rocher, Rivière-du-Loup PQ G5R 1J8 – 418/862-4252; Téléc: 418/862-3478; Symbol: QRL – Head Librarian, Marlène Létourneau; Head, Technical Services, Aline Bourgoin
Roberval: Bibliothèque municipale de Roberval, 829, boul St-Joseph, Roberval PQ G8H 2L6 – 418/275-2333 – Responsable, Francine Laflamme-Lachance
Rock Forest: Bibliothèque municipale de Rock Forest, 6630, rue Fontaine, Rock Forest PQ J1N 2T3 – 819/864-6288 – Responsable, Johanne Lavoie
Rosemère: Bibliothèque municipale de Rosemère, 339, ch de la Grande-Côte, Rosemère PQ J7A 1K2 – 514/621-6132; Téléc: 514/621-7601 – Directrice, Carole Trépanier
Rouyn-Noranda: Bibliothèque municipale de Rouyn-Noranda, 201, av Dallaire, Rouyn-Noranda PQ J9X 4T5 – 819/762-0944; Téléc: 819/797-7136 – Responsable, Luc Sigouin
Roxboro: Bibliothèque de Roxboro, 110, rue Cartier, Roxboro PQ H8Y 1G8 – 514/684-8247; Téléc: 514/684-8563 – Directrice, Lesley DesAutels; Reference Librarian, Claudette Fournier; ILL, Monique Conway
Ste-Adèle: Bibliothèque municipale de Ste-Adèle, 1069, boul Ste-Adèle, CP 1046, Ste-Adèle PQ J0R 1L0 – 514/229-2921 – Responsable, Marcia Vaillencourt
Ste-Agathe-des-Monts: Bibliothèque municipale de Ste-Agathe-des-Monts, 10, rue St-Donat, Ste-Agathe-des-Monts PQ J8C 1P5 – 819/326-2848; Téléc: 819/326-5784 – Responsable, France Bélanger
Ste-Angèle-de-Laval: Bibliothèque municipale de Ste-Angèle-de-Laval, 14700, boul Bécancour, Ste-Angèle-de-Laval PQ G0X 2H0 – 819/222-5735 – Bénévole responsable, Pauline Pratt – Branch of Bibliothèque municipale de Bécancour
Ste-Anne-des-Monts: Bibliothèque Blanche-Lamontagne, 120, 7e rue ouest, CP 670, Ste-Anne-des-Monts PQ G0E 2G0 – 418/763-9167; Téléc: 418/763-3473 – Responsable, Yves Bilodeau
Ste-Anne-des-Plaines: Bibliothèque publique de Ste-Anne-des-Plaines, 155, rue des Cèdres, Ste-Anne-des-Plaines PQ J0N 1H0 – 514/478-4337; Téléc: 514/478-6733 – Directrice, Danielle Labelle
St-Antoine: Bibliothèque municipale de St-Antoine, 500, boul des Laurentides, St-Antoine PQ J7Z 4M2 – 514/431-1388; Téléc: 514/431-3684 – Directrice de la bibliothèque, Chantal Paquin
St-Augustin-de-Desmaures: Bibliothèque Alain-Grandbois, 160, rue Jean-Juneau, St-Augustin-de-Desmaures PQ G3A 2P1 – 418/878-4423; Téléc: 418/878-5473; Courrier électronique: biblio@st-augustin.org – Bibliothécaire, Claire Sénéclauze
St-Basile-le-Grand: Bibliothèque municipale de St-Basile-le-Grand, 40, rue Savaria, CP 1010, St-Basile-le-Grand PQ J3N 1M5 – 514/653-0287; Téléc: 514/653-8028 – Directrice, France Goyette
St-Bruno-de-Montarville: Bibliothèque municipale de St-Bruno-de-Montarville, 82, rue Seigneuriale ouest, St-Bruno-de-Montarville PQ J3V 5N7 – 514/653-2443; Téléc: 514/441-0431; Symbol: QSTB – Bibliothécaire en chef, Guylaine Pellerin
Ste-Catherine: Bibliothèque municipale de Ste-Catherine, 5465, boul Marie-Victorin, Ste-Catherine PQ J0L 1E0 – 514/632-9951; Téléc: 514/638-3298 – Librarian, Lise Forcier
St-Constant: Bibliothèque publique de St-Constant, 80, rue Brodeur, St-Constant PQ J5A 1X8 – 514/632-8732; Téléc: 514/635-8414 – Responsable, Nadine Géroli
St-Eustache: Bibliothèque municipale Guy-Bélisle, 80, boul Arthur-Sauvé, St-Eustache PQ J7R 2H7 – 514/472-4440; Téléc: 514/623-6490 – Directrice, Monique Khouzam; Reference Technician, Danielle Touchette; Public Services Librarian, Nicole Grunard
St-Félicien: Bibliothèque municipale de St-Félicien, 1209, boul Sacré-Coeur, St-Félicien PQ G8K 2R5 – 418/679-0251; Téléc: 418/679-1449 – Responable, Johanne Laprise
Ste-Foy: Biliothèque Monique-Corriveau, 999, av Roland-Beaudin, Ste-Foy PQ G1V 4E1 – 418/654-4676; Téléc: 418/654-4172; Symbol: QSF – Responsable/Acquisitions Librarian, Claudette Auger – See also following branches: Succursale Champigny
Ste-Foy: Succursale Champigny, 1465, rue Félix-Antoine-Savard, Ste-Foy PQ – 418/654-4676; Téléc: 418/654-4172 – Branch of Biliothèque Monique-Corriveau
Ste-Geneviève: Bibliothèque municipale de Ste-Geneviève, 35, rue Sainte-Anne, Ste-Geneviève PQ H9H 2Z2 – 514/626-2537; Téléc: 514/626-0312 – Responsable, Cécile Picard
Saint-Georges: Bibliothèque municipale de Saint-Georges, 250, 18e rue, Saint-Georges PQ G5Y 1L3 – 418/226-2271; Téléc: 418/228-1321 – Bibliothécaire, Julie Michaud
Ste-Gertrude: Bibliothèque municipale de Ste-Gertrude, 6095, av des Pins, Ste-Gertrude PQ G0X 2S0 – 819/297-2555 – Bénévole responsable, Lise Montambault – Branch of Bibliothèque municipale de Bécancour
St-Grégoire: Bibliothèque municipale de St-Grégoire, 4000, Port-Royal, St-Grégoire PQ G0X 2T0 – 819/233-4177 – Bénévole responsable, Monique Quellet – Branch of Bibliothèque municipale de Bécancour

St-Hubert: Bibliothèque municipale de St-Hubert, 5900, boul Cousineau, St-Hubert PQ J3Y 7K8 – 514/445-7761; Téléc: 514/445-7836 – Bibliothécaire, Kim Mychau Nguyen; Reference Librarian, Linda Moisan

St-Hyacinthe: Bibliothèque T.A. St-Germain, 2720, rue Dessaulles, St-Hyacinthe PQ J2S 2V7 – 514/773-4865; Téléc: 514/773-3398 – Directeur, Denis Boisvert

St-Jacques-de-Montcalm: Bibliothèque municipale de St-Jacques-de-Montcalm, 16, rue Maréchal, CP 370, St-Jacques-de-Montcalm PQ J0K 2R0 – 514/839-3926; Téléc: 514/839-2387 – Responsable, Francine Roy

St-Jean-Chrysostome: Bibliothèque Francine-McKenzie, 100, Place Centre-Ville, St-Jean-Chrysostome PQ G6Z 3B9 – 418/839-0012; Téléc: 418/839-3102 – Bibliothécaire, Suzanne Fortin

St-Jean-sur-Richelieu: Bibliothèque Adélard-Berger, 180, rue Laurier, CP 1025, St-Jean-sur-Richelieu PQ J3B 7B2 – 514/357-2113; Téléc: 514/357-2055 – Directrice, Camille Bricault; Public Services Librarian, Lise Gosselin

St-Jérôme: Bibliothèque municipale de St-Jérôme, 185, rue du Palais, St-Jérôme PQ J7Z 1X6 – 514/436-1511; Téléc: 514/436-3064 – Directrice, Renée Masse

St-Jovite: Bibliothèque municipale de St-Jovite, 901, rue Ouimet, CP 200, St-Jovite PQ J0T 2H0 – 819/425-2337; Téléc: 819/425-9247 – Responsable, Christiane Langlois

Ste-Julie: Bibliothèque municipale de Ste-Julie, 1580, ch du Fer-à-Cheval, Sainte-Julie PQ J3E 1Y2 – 514/922-7070; Téléc: 514/922-7077 – Responsable, Nicole Perras

St-Lambert: Bibliothèque municipale de St-Lambert, 490, av Mercille, St-Lambert PQ J4P 2L5 – 514/465-4508; Téléc: 514/465-0681; Symbol: QSTLB – Bibliothécaire en chef, Micheline Perreault – See also following branches: Bibliothèque de Préville

Saint-Lambert: Bibliothèque de Préville, 120, rue de Poitou, Saint-Lambert PQ J4S 1E1 – 514/671-2152 – Micheline Perreault – Branch of Bibliothèque municipale de St-Lambert

St-Lazare: Bibliothèque municipale de St-Lazare, 1811, ch Sainte-Angélique, St-Lazare PQ J0P 1V0 – 514/424-6472; Téléc: 514/455-4712 – Responsable, Michel Piché

Saint-Louis-de-France: Bibliothèque municipale de Saint-Louis-de-France, 100, av de la Mairie, Saint-Louis-de-France PQ G8W 1S1 – 819/374-6419; Téléc: 819/374-0659 – Directrice, Lise Thériault

St-Luc: Bibliothèque municipale de St-Luc, 347, boul St-Luc, St-Luc PQ J2W 2A2 – 514/348-4128; Téléc: 514/348-5889 – Directrice, Sylvette Toutant

Ste-Marie: Bibliothèque Honorius-Provost, 80, rue St-Antoine, CP 1750, Ste-Marie PQ G6E 3C7 – 418/387-2240; Téléc: 418/387-2454 – Responsable, Caroline Dion

Ste-Marthe-sur-le-Lac: Bibliothèque municipale de Ste-Marthe-sur-le-Lac, 3075, ch Oka, local 110, Ste-Marthe-sur-le-Lac PQ J0N 1P0 – 514/974-7111; Téléc: 514/472-4283 – Responsable, Brigitte Boiteau, BA, MBSI

Saint-Pierre: Bibliothèque municipale de Saint-Pierre, 183, rue des Érables, Saint-Pierre PQ H8R 1B1 – 514/368-368-5740; Téléc: 514/368-5717 – Responsable, Monique Charette

St-Raphaël-de-l'Île-Bizard: Bibliothèque municipale de St-Raphaël-de-l'Île-Bizard, 500, rue de l'Église, St-Raphaël-de-l'Île-Bizard PQ H9C 1G9 – 514/620-6331; Téléc: 514/620-4153 – Responsable, Hélène Rouette

St-Rémi: Bibliothèque municipale de St-Rémi, 25, rue Saint-Sauveur, CP 578, St-Rémi PQ J0L 2L0 – 514/454-2418; Téléc: 514/454-4083 – Responsable, Nathalie Groulx

St-Romuald: Bibliothèque municipale de St-Romuald, 2161, ch du Fleuve, St-Romuald PQ G6W 5P8 – 418/839-5242; Téléc: 418/839-5323 – Responsable, Martine Boulay

Ste-Thérèse: Bibliothèque municipale de Ste-Thérèse, 150, boul du Séminaire, Ste-Thérèse PQ J7E 1Z2 – 514/434-1442; Téléc: 514/434-6070; Symbol: QMBST – Directeur, Léonard Nadeau; Reference Librarian, Nicole Bouchard

Saint-Timothée: Bibliothèque publique de Saint-Timothée, #400, 5100, boul Hébert, Saint-Timothée PQ J0S 1X0 – 514/371-6854; Téléc: 514/371-7205 – Responsable, Andrée Julien

Salaberry-de-Valleyfield: Bibliothèque municipale de Salaberry-de-Valleyfield, 75, rue St-Jean-Baptiste, Salaberry-de-Valleyfield PQ J6T 1Z6 – 514/370-4321; Téléc: 514/373-5409 – Responsable, Manon Allen

Sept-Îles: Bibliothèque municipale de Sept-Îles, 500, av Jolliet, Sept-Îles PQ G4R 2B4 – 418/964-3355; Téléc: 418/964-3353 – Bibliothécaire en chef, Jocelyne Boudreau

Shawinigan: Bibliothèque municipale de Shawinigan, 550, av de l'Hôtel-de-Ville, CP 400, Shawinigan PQ G9N 6V3 – 819/536-7219; Téléc: 819/536-7255 – Bibliothécaire, Charlotte Lecours-Picard

Sherbrooke: Bibliothèque Eva-Senécal, 450, rue Marquette, Sherbrooke PQ J1H 1M4 – 819/821-5862; Téléc: 819/822-6110; Courrier électronique: bibliotheque@ville.sherbrooke.qc.ca – Directrice, Diane Verville-Caron; Bibliothécaire, Jocelyne Valence; Children's Librarian, Jeanne Desautels; Technical Services Librarian, André Bruneau

Sillery: Bibliothèque Charles-H.-Blais, 1245, av du Chanoine-Morel, Sillery PQ G1S 4B1 – 418/684-2140; Téléc: 418/684-2169 – Bibliothécaire, Francine Pelletier

Sorel: Bibliothèque municipale de Sorel, 145, rue George, Sorel PQ J3P 1C7 – 514/780-5750; Téléc: 514/780-5758 – Symbol: QSO – Directeur, Guy Desjardins

Terrebonne: Bibliothèque André-Guérard, 3425, av Camus, RR#40, Terrebonne PQ J6Y 1L2 – 514/471-4192; Téléc: 514/471-2872 – Directrice, Françoise Martin

Terrebonne: Bibliothèque municipale de l'Île-des-moulins, 855, Place Île-des-Moulins, Terrebonne PQ J6W 4N7 – 514/471-4192; Téléc: 514/471-2872 – Directrice, Françoise Martin

Thetford Mines: Bibliothèque publique de Thetford Mines, 144, rue Notre-Dame sud, CP 489, Thetford Mines PQ G6G 5T3 – 418/335-6111; Téléc: 418/335-7089 – Directeur, Maryse Pomerleau

Tracy: Bibliothèque municipale de Tracy, 3025, boul de la Mairie, Tracy PQ J3R 1C2 – 514/742-8321; Téléc: 514/746-8894 – Responsable, Alain Larouche

Trois-Rivières-Ouest: Bibliothèque municipale de Trois-Rivières-Ouest, 5225, rue Courcelette, Trois-Rivières-Ouest PQ J8Y 4L4 – 819/375-1607; Téléc: 819/375-2815 – Directeur des loisirs, Michel Lemieux

Trois-Rivières: Bibliothèque Gatien-Lapointe, 1225, Place de l'Hôtel-de-Ville, CP 1713, Trois-Rivières PQ G9A 5L9 – 819/374-3521; Téléc: 819/693-1892 – Chef de service, Michel Lacoursière; Technical Services Librarian, Odette Pelletier; Acquisitions Librarian, Madeleine Bessette

Val-Bélair: Bibliothèque Félix-Leclerc, 1130, boul Pie XI nord, CP 8310, Val-Bélair PQ G3K 1Y9 – 418/843-6197; Téléc: 418/842-1945; Symbol: QVBFL – Directeur, Patrice Robitaille, Ph.D.

Val-d'Or: Bibliothèque municipale de Val-d'Or, 600, 7e rue, Val-d'Or PQ J9P 3P3 – 819/824-2666; Téléc: 819/825-3062 – Bibliothécaire, Alain Cloutier

Vanier: Bibliothèque municipale de Vanier, 320, rue Chabot, Vanier PQ G1M 3J5 – 418/683-2908; Téléc: 418/681-9433 – Technicienne en documentation, Martine Caouette

Varennes: Bibliothèque Jacques-Le Moyne-de-Ste-Marie, 2221, boul René-Gaultier, Varennes PQ J3X 1E3 – 514/652-3949; Téléc: 514/652-2349 – Bibliothécaire, Michèle Lamoureux

Vaudreuil-Dorion: Bibliothèque municipale de Vaudreuil-Dorion, 51, rue Jeannotte, Vaudreuil-Dorion PQ J7V 6E6 – 514/455-5588; Téléc: 514/455-5653 – Directrice-adjointe de la bibliothèque et culture, Michelle Dupuy

Verdun: Bibliothèque de Verdun, 5955, av Bannantyne, Verdun PQ H4H 1H6 – 514/765-7170; Téléc: 514/765-7167; Symbol: QVEC – Bibliothécaire en chef, Loïs Ann Clouthier

Victoriaville: Bibliothèque Charles-Édouard-Mailhot, 2, rue de l'Ermitage, CP 370, Victoriaville PQ G6P 6T2 – 819/758-8441; Téléc: 819/357-2099 – Directrice, Sylvie Filiatrault – See also following branches: Succursale Alcide-Fleury

Warwick: Bibliothèque municipale de Warwick, 104, rue St-Louis, CP 577, Warwick PQ J0A 1M0 – 819/358-4325; Téléc: 819/358-4309 – Responsable, Pauline L. Picard

Waterloo: Bibliothèque publique de Waterloo, 650, rue de la Cour, CP 883, Waterloo PQ J0E 2N0 – 514/539-2268 – Bibliothécaire, Gisèle Dupuis

Windsor: Bibliothèque municipale de Windsor, 54, rue St-Georges, Windsor PQ J1S 1J5 – 819/845-7115; Téléc: 819/845-7606 – Responsable, Marie-Pascale Morin

Special & College Libraries & Resource Centres in Québec

ACTON VALE

Société d'histoire des Six Cantons – Bibliothèque, CP 236, Acton Vale PQ J0H 1A0 – 514/546-2093

ALMA

CEGEP d'Alma - Bibliothèque, 675, boul Auger ouest, Alma PQ G8B 2B7 – 418/668-6197; Fax: 418/668-3806 – Bibliothécaire, Janic Trépanier, 418/668-6197, porte 225

Centre locale de services communautaires Le Norois - Centre de documentation, Édifice du complexe J. Gagnon, 100, rue St-Joseph sud, Alma PQ G8B 7A6 – 418/668-4563; Téléc: 418/668-5403 – Isabelle Dufour

Conseil de la culture de la région Saguenay-Lac-St-Jean – Bibliotheque, 414, rue Collard ouest, Alma PQ G8B 1N2 – 418/662-6623 – Secrétaire-comptable, Suzette Villeneuve

Morency, Duchesne & Associé Law Office - Bibliothèque, 521, rue Sacré-Coeur ouest, Alma PQ G8B 1M4 – 418/668-3011; Téléc: 418/668-0209 – Technicienne, Marlene Hudon

Société d'histoire du Lac-St-Jean – Bibliothèque, 54, rue St. Joseph, Alma PQ G8B 3E4 – 418/668-2606

BAIE-COMEAU

CEGEP de Baie-Comeau - Centre de ressources éducatives: documentation, 537, boul Blanche, Baie-Comeau PQ G5C 2B2 – 418/589-5707; Fax: 418/589-9842; Symbol: QHAC – Bibliothécaire en chef, Richard Lachance

Centre hospitalier régional - Pavillon Le Royer – Bibliothèque médicale, 635, boul Joliet, Baie Comeau PQ G5C 1P1 – 418/589-0693 – Technicienne en documentation, Marcelle Vallée

Centre local de services communautaires de l'Aquilon - Centre de documentation, 600, rue Jalbert, Baie-Comeau PQ G5C 1Z9 – 418/589-2191; Téléc: 418/589-7784; Symbol: QBCCL – Technicienne, Anne Côté

Services Myriam Beth-léhem – Bibliothèque Myriam, 105, boul Lasalle, Baie-Comeau PQ G4Z 1R7 – 418/296-6223 – Bibliothécaire, Sylvie Grenier

Canadian Almanac & Directory 1997

BAIE-SAINT-PAUL

Centre hospitalier de Charlevoix – Bibliothèque, 74, rue Ambroise Fafard, CP 5000, Baie-Saint-Paul PQ G0A 1B0 – 418/435-5150 – Louise Leblanc

BEAUCEVILLE

Département de santé communautaire de Beauceville - Centre de documentation, Centre hospitalier régional de la Beauce, 253, 108e rue, Beauceville PQ G0M 1A0 – 418/774-3304; Téléc: 418/774-2304 – Danielle Dumas

BEAUPORT

Association du centre mondial du commerce Québec-Beauport inc. – Bibliothèque, 10, rue de l'Hôtel-de-Ville, Beauport PQ G1E 6P4 – 418/666-6136 – Wayne Tessier

Centre hospitalier Robert Giffard – Bibliothèque professionnelle, 2601, rue de la Canardière, Beauport PQ G1J 2G3 – 418/663-5300; Téléc: 418/666-9416; Symbol: QBRG – Technicienne Documentation, Nicole Drolet

BELLEFEUILLE

Association monnaies des Laurentides – Bibliothèque, 14, ch Raymond, Bellefeuille PQ J0R 1A0 – 819/322-7224 – Directeur, Claude Proulx

BOUCHERVILLE

Canadian Society for Education through Art – Library, 675, Samuel de Champlain, Boucherville PQ J4B 6C4 – 514/655-2435

National Research Council-Industrial Materials Institute – Centre d'information du CNRC, 75, boul de Montagne, Boucherville PQ J4B 6Y4 – 514/641-5131; Fax: 514/641-5133; Email: patrice.dupont@nrc.ca – Spécialiste en information, Patrice Dupont

BRIGHAM

Institut des Érables – Centre de documentation, 278, av des Érables, CP 40, Brigham PQ J0E 1J0 – 514/263-3545 – Technicien, Jean-Yves Dufort

CAP-DE-LA-MADELEINE

Centre hospitalier Cloutier – Bibliothèque, 155, rue Toupin, CP 218, Cap-de-la-Madeleine PQ G8T 7W3 – 819/370-2100 – Lise Caron

René Gervais Inc., Consultants – Library, 303, rue Dessureault, Cap-de-la-Madeleine PQ G8T 2L8 – 819/371-3313 – Technical Director, Réjean Blais

CHARLESBOURG

Jardin zoologique du Québec – Bibliothèque, 8173, av du Zoo, Charlesbourg PQ G1G 4G4 – 418/622-0313 – Personne ressource, Danielle Martel

Ministère des ressources naturelles - Centre de documentation - Énergie, Mines, 5700 - 4e av ouest, #B-208, Charlesbourg PQ G1H 6R1 – 418/643-4624; Téléc: 418/643-5928; TLX: 051-2274; Symbol: QQER – Responsable, Marie-Ève Varin, 418/528-1752, 643-4624

CHÂTEAUGUAY

Centre hospitalier Anna-Laberge – Centre de documentation, 200, boul Brisebois, Châteauguay PQ J6K 4W8 – 514/699-2451 – B. Gagnon

CHELSEA

Historical Society of the Gatineau – Archives, PO Box 485, Chelsea PQ J0X 1N0 – 819/827-1274 – Archivist, Pat Evans

CHIBOUGAMAU

Hôpital Chibougamau Ltée – Centre de documentation, 51, 3e rue, Chibougamau PQ G8P 1N1 – 418/748-2676 – Gracia Vachon

CHICOUTIMI

CEGEP de Chicoutimi - Centre de médias, 534, rue Jacques Cartier est, Chicoutimi PQ G7H 1Z6 – 418/549-9520, poste 330; Téléc: 418/549-1315; Symbol: QCCEC – Référence/Services publiques, Responsable, Louis Gaudreau, 418/549-9520, poste 345

Centre des services sociaux Saguenay-Lac-St-Jean-Chibougamau – Centre de documentation, 520, rue Jacques-Cartier est, CP 158, Chicoutimi PQ G7H 5B7 – 418/549-4853 – Francine Gauthier

Hôpital de Chicoutimi Inc. – Bibliothèque, 305, av Saint-Vallier, CP 5006, Chicoutimi PQ G7H 5H6 – 418/549-2195; Téléc: 418/549-0607 – Marcelle Frigon

Institut Roland-Saucier – Bibliothèque médicale, 150, rue Pinel, CP 2250, Chicoutimi PQ G7G 3W4 – 418/549-5474 – Chef de service, Lorraine Berube

Séminaire de Chicoutimi - Bibliothèque, 679, rue Chabanel, Chicoutimi PQ G7H 1Z7 – 418/549-0190, poste 320 – Technicien en documentation, Lucien Fortin

Société généalogique du Saguenay, inc. – Bibliothèque, CP 814, Chicoutimi PQ G7H 5E8 – 418/674-2487 – Annie Lavoie

Société historique du Saguenay-Lac-Saint-Jean – Bibliothèque, CP 456, Chicoutimi PQ G7H 5C8 – 418/549-2805 – Archiviste, Roland Bélanger

Université du Québec à Chicoutimi - Bibliothèque Paul-Emile-Boulet, 555, boul de l'Université, Chicoutimi PQ G7H 2B1 – 418/545-5031; Téléc: 418/693-5896; Courrier électronique: QCU
Head, Information Services, Gilles Caron
Reference Librarian, Serge Harvey
Circulation Librarian, Réginald Gamache

COATICOOK

Centre hospitalier de Coaticook – Centre de documentation, 138, rue Jeanne-Mance, Coaticook PQ J1A 1W3 – 819/849-2115 – Robert Simard

CONTRECOEUR

Sidbec-Dosco Inc. - Centre de documentation, 3900, route des Aciéries, Contrecoeur PQ J0L 1C0 – 514/392-3200; Téléc: 514/392-3222 – Library Coordinator, Therese Levesque, 514/392-3258

COURCELETTE

Defence Research Establishment - Valcartier - Library, CP 8800, Courcelette PQ G0A 1R0 – 418/844-4262; Téléc: 418/844-4624; Courrier électronique: ENVOY: QQC.LIBRARY; Symbol: QQC – Librarian, Lise Chaillez, 418/844-4244

COWANSVILLE

Hôpital Brôme-Missisquoi-Perkins – Centre de documentation, 950, rue Principale, Cowansville PQ J2K 1K3 – 514/266-4342 – André Marcoux

Solicitor General Canada - Cowansville Establishment - Library, 400 Fordyce St., PO Box 5000, Cowansville PQ J2K 3N7 – 514/263-3073, ext.271; Symbol: QCCE – Librarian, Rose Sybille

DONNACONNA

Solicitor General Canada - Donnaconna Institution - Library, 1538 Hwy. 138, Donnaconna PQ G0A 1T0 – 418/285-2455, ext.2501; Symbol: QDSG – Librarian, Hélène Pellerin

DRUMMONDVILLE

CEGEP de Drummondville - Bibliothèque, 960, rue St-Georges, Drummondville PQ J2C 6A2 – 819/478-4671 – Henriette Dion

Hôpital Ste-Croix – Bibliothèque, 570, rue Heriot, Drummondville PQ J2B 1C1 – 819/478-6464; Symbol: QDHSC – Technicienne, Thérèse Henault

Office des personnes handicapées du Québec - Centre de documentation, 309, rue Brock, CP 820, Drummondville PQ J2B 6X1 – 819/477-7100; Téléc: 819/477-8493 – Responsable, Sophie Janik

Solicitor General Canada - Drummond Establishment - Library, 2025, rue Jean-de-Brébeuf, Drummondville PQ J2B 7Z6 – 819/477-5112, ext.285; Fax: 819/477-5664; Symbol: QDD – Librarian, Mohammed Ben Abdallah

GASPÉ

CEGEP de la Gaspésie - Bibliothèque, 96, rue Jacques-Cartier, CP 590, Gaspé PQ G0C 1R0 – 418/368-2201 – Responsable, Bertrand Beaudry

Ministère de l'agriculture, des pêcheries et de l'alimentation - Centre de documentation, 96, Montée Sandy Beach, CP 1070, Gaspé PQ G0C 1R0 – 418/368-2642; Téléc: 418/368-8400; Symbol: QGAP
Documentalist, Paul Carrier, 418/368-7615
Chef, Services techniques, Jocelyne Anglehart, 418/368-7616
Chef, Service des acquisitions, Louise Lemieux, 418/368-7617
Prêt - PIB - Circulation, Brenda Lapierre, 418/368-7618

GASPÉ-HARBOUR

Centre hospitalier l'Hôtel-Dieu de Gaspé – Centre de documentation, 215, boul York, CP 120, Gaspé-Harbour PQ G0C 1S0 – 418/368-3301 – Mathilda Adams

GATINEAU

Centre hospitalier de Gatineau – Bibliothèque médicale, 909, boul de la Verendrye ouest, CP 2000, Gatineau PQ J8P 7H2 – 819/561-8106; Symbol: QGCH – Michel Turpin

Entraide familiale de l'Outaouais inc. – Bibliothèque, 194, rue Harold, Gatineau PQ J8P 4S4 – 819/643-5711 – Directeur général, Diane Du-Perré

GRANBY

CEGEP de Granby - Bibliothèque, 235, rue St-Jacques, Granby PQ J2G 9H7 – 514/372-6614 – Responsable, Daniel Marquis

Centre hospitalier de Granby – Bibliothèque médicale, 205, boul Leclerc, Granby PQ J2G 1T7 – 514/372-5495, poste 2147; Symbol: QGCHG – Technicienne en documentation, Lise Trudel

Centre local de services communautaires de la Haute Yamaska - Centre de documentation, 294, rue Déragon, Granby PQ J2G 5J5 – 514/375-1442; Téléc: 514/375-5655 – Brigitte Dionne

GREENFIELD PARK

Département de santé communautaire Charles-Lemoyne - Centre de documentation, #200, 25, boul Taschereau, Greenfield Park PQ J4V 2G8 – 514/466-5696; Téléc: 514/465-0816; Symbol: QMHCLC – Sylvie Desbiens

Hôpital Charles Lemoyne – Bibliothèque, 121, boul Taschereau, Greenfield Park PQ J4V 2H1 – 514/466-5410 – Bibliothécaire, Daniel Lamagnère

HULL

Canadian Heritage - Departmental Library, Les Terrasses de la Chaudière, 15, rue Eddy, Hull PQ K1A 0M5 – 819/994-5478; Fax: 819/953-7988; Email: ENVOY:OOSS; Symbol: OOSS
Chief Librarian, Réjean Héroux, 819/997-3981, Email: rejean_heroux_at_TC3@ccmail.chin.doc.ca
Public Services Librarian, Louis Belanger, 819/994-2229
Cataloguing, Zdena Vandoros, 819/994-6588
Acquisitions, Denis Parizeau, 819/997-2345

Wellington Library, Mezzanine Level, 10 Wellington St., Hull PQ K1A 0M5 – 819/997-6679; Fax: 819/953-9312; Symbol: OOPAC

Canadian International Development Agency - Development Information Centre, Place du Centre, 200 Promenade du Portage, 8e étage, Hull PQ K1A 0G4 – 819/953-8168; Fax: 819/953-8132; Symbol: OOCD – Chief, Nicole Sansfaçon

Canadian Museum of Civilization - Information Management Services (IMSD), 100, rue Laurier, PO Box 3100, Hull PQ J8X 4H2 – 819/776-7173 (Ref.Desk); Fax: 819/776-8491; Email: library@cmcc.muse.digital.ca (English); biblio@cmcc.muse.digital.ca (French); Symbol: OONMM
  Director, Manon Guilbert, 819/776-7179, Email: manon.guilbert@cmcc.muse.digital.ca
  Reference Librarian, Brigitte Lafond, 819/776-7151
  Documentation & Technical Services, Head, Margaret McGarry, 819/776-8498
  Acquisitions Assistant, Sam Morgulis, 819/776-8307
  ILL, Sylvie Laflamme, 819/776-7174
  Information Access Services, Head, Geneviève Eustache, 819/776-8183
  Copyright Licensing, Nicole Chamberland, 819/776-8499

Centre hospitalier Pierre Janet – Centre de documentation, 20, rue Pharand, Hull PQ J9A 1K7 – 819/771-7761 – Nguyen Lam

Centre hospitalier régional de l'Outaouais – Bibliothèque, 116, boul Lionel Emond, Hull PQ J8Y 1W7 – 819/595-6050; Téléc: 819/595-6327; Symbol: QHSC – Bibliotechnicienne, Dianne Couture

Collège de l'Outaouais - Bibliothèque Gabrielle Roy, 333, boul Cité des Jeunes, Hull PQ J8Y 6M5 – 819/770-4012; Téléc: 819/770-3855 – Directeur, Marthe Francoeur

Environment Canada-Environmental Protection Service - Technology Development Directorate – Library, Place Cartier, 425, boul St-Joseph, 4e étage, Hull PQ K1A 0H3 – 819/997-1768 – Librarian, Diana Dale

Environment Canada - Departmental Library, 351, St Joseph Blvd., Hull PQ K1A 0H3 – 613/997-7375; Fax: 613/953-7900; Email: librarypvm@ncrsv2.am.doe.ca; URL: http://www.doe.ca/library/libhome.html; Symbol: OOFF – Departmental Librarian, Monica Czanyo

Federal Environmental Assessment Review Office - Reference Centre, Édifice Fontaine, 200, boul Sacré-Coeur, Hull PQ K1A 0H3 – 819/994-2578; Fax: 819/943-2534; Symbol: OOFE – Reference Clerk, Stéphane Parent

Heritage College - Library, 325, boul Cité des Jeunes, Hull PQ J8Y 6T3 – 819/778-2270; Fax: 819/778-7364; Symbol: QHCH
  Librarian, Kate Hughes
  Library Technician, Rachel Patry

Human Resources Development Canada - Branch Library, Place du Portage, Phase II, 7th Fl., 165, rue Hôtel-de-Ville, Hull PQ K1A 0J9 – 819/997-3541; Fax: 819/953-2098; Symbol: OOL – Chief, Client Information Services, Phase II, Michèle Auger, 819/953-0032
  Canadian Clearinghouse on Disability Issues, Status of Disabled Persons Secretariat, #100, 25, rue Eddy, Hull PQ K1A 0M5 – 819/994-7514; Fax: 819/953-4797; Toll Free: 1-800-665-9017; Symbol: OOCCD – Manager, Terri Tomchyshyn
  Main Library, Place du Portage, Phase IV, 1st Fl., 140, Promenade du Portage, Hull PQ K1A 0J9 – 819/944-1683; Fax: 819/953-5482; Symbol: OOMI
  Acting Departmental Librarian, Maryna Nowosielski, 819/994-1683
  Acting Chief, Client Information Services, Phase IV, Martine Patriarcki, 819/953-9134
  Acting Chief, Information Resources & Systems, Helen Apouchtine, 819/997-5616
  Acting Chief, Information Access, Sara Sprague, 819/953-9021

National Transportation Agency of Canada - Library, 15, rue Eddy, 17e étage, Hull PQ K1A 0N9 – 819/997-7160; Fax: 819/953-9815; Email: NTA.LIBRARY; natlib@magi.com; Symbol: OOTT – R. Pareanen

Pavillon Jellinek – Bibliothèque, 25, rue Saint-François, Hull PQ J9A 1B1 – 819/776-5584 – Technicien, Pierre Hamelin

Public Service Commission of Canada - Asticou Centre, 241, boul Cité des Jeunes, Hull PQ J8Y 6L2 – 819/953-7879; Fax: 819/953-2392; Symbol: QHCFP

Public Works & Government Services Canada - Translation Bureau - Documentation Services Division, Place du Portage, Phase II, 165, rue Hôtel-de-Ville, 23e étage, Hull PQ K1A 0S5 – 819/997-4840; Fax: 819/994-3735
  Chief, Lise Sabourin
  Cataloguing & Acquisitions, J. Lalande
  Translation Bureau - Multilingual Documentation Centre, Place du Portage II, West Tower, 165, rue Hotel-de-Ville, 5e étage, Hull PQ K1A 0S5 – 819/997-0258; Fax: 819/994-5900; Symbol: OOSSTM – Head, Martin Tremblay
  Translation Bureau - Terminology Documentation Centre, Place du Portage, Phase II, 165, rue Ho^tel-de-Ville, 4e étage, Hull PQ K1A 0S5 – 819/994-5904; Fax: 819/953-9691; Symbol: OOSSTE – Librarian, Yves Ranger
  Translation Bureau - Translation Services Documentation Centre, Place du Portage, Phase II, 165, rue Hôtel-de-Ville, 23e étage, Hull PQ K1A 0S5 – 819/994-0859; Fax: 819/994-3735 – Head, J. Lachapelle

Régie régionale de la santé et des services sociaux de l'Outaouais – Centre de documentation, 104, rue Lois, Hull PQ J8Y 3R7 – 819/770-7747; Symbol: QHCRS – Bibliotechnicienne, Christiane Boyer

Société de généalogie de l'Outaouais – Bibliothèque, CP 2025, Hull PQ J8X 3Z2 – 819/682-5576

Université du Québec à Hull - Bibliothèque, CP 1250, Hull PQ J8X 3X7 – 819/773-1790; Téléc: 819/773-1699; Courrier électronique: ENVOY: PEB.QHU
  Chief Librarian, Monique Légère
  Public Services Librarian, Danielle Boisvert, 819/595-2374
  Public Services Librarian, Gilles Bergeron, 819/773-1789
  Public Services Librarian, Daniel Pouloit, 819/773-1799
  Technical Services Librarian, Monique Picard, 819/595-3809
  Acquisitions Librarian, Louise Grondines, 819/595-3816

JOLIETTE

CEGEP de Lanaudière - Bibliothèque, 20, rue St-Charles sud, Joliette PQ J6E 4T1 – 514/759-1661; Téléc: 514/759-4468; URL: http://www.collanaud.qc.ca
  Bibliothécaire en chef, Robert Corriveau, 514/759-1661, ext.134
  Bibliotechnicienne, Martine Gagnon, 514/759-1661, ext.288
  Bibliotechnicienne, Francine Grosleau, 514/759-1661, ext.261
  Bibliotechnicienne, Danielle Gagnon, 514/759-1661, ext.160

Centre hospitalier régional de Lanaudière - Bibliothèque, 1000, boul Ste-Anne, Joliette PQ J6E 6J2 – 514/759-8222; Téléc: 514/759-7463; Courrier électronique: ENVOY: ILL.QMJG; Symbol: OSH – Bibliothécaire, Francine Garneau

Département de santé communautaire de Lanaudière - Centre de documentation, Centre hospitalier régional de Lanaudière, 1000, boul Ste-Anne, Joliette PQ J6E 6J2 – 514/759-9900; Téléc: 514/759-5149; Symbol: QJCH – Suzie Desilets

JONQUIÈRE

Alcan International Ltd. - Bibliothèque, CP 1250, Jonquière PQ G7S 4K8 – 418/699-2844; Téléc: 418/699-3996 – Bibliothécaire, P. Leclerc

CEGEP de Jonquière - Centre de ressources éducatives, 2505, rue St-Hubert, Jonquière PQ G7X 7W2 – 418/547-2191; Téléc: 418/547-3359
  Conseiller pédagogique, Jean-Pierre Dufour, 418/547-2191, ext.266
  Reference Librarian, Armande Déry-Allard, 418/547-2191, ext.302
  Circulation Librarian, Rémi Savard, 418/547-2191, ext.268
  Public Services Librarian, Yvon Tremblay, 418/547-2191, ext.302
  Technical Services Librarian, Monique Laforte, 418/547-2191, ext.379
  Acquisitions Librarian, Jacques Fortin, 418/547-2191, ext.269

Centre hospitalier Jonquière – Centre de ressources éducatives, 2230, rue de l'Hôpital, CP 1200, Jonquière PQ G7X 7X2 – 418/695-7700; Téléc: 418/695-4437

Fédération des syndicats du secteur de l'aluminium inc. (ind.) – Bibliothèque, 1924, boul Mellon, Jonquière PQ G7S 3H3 – 418/548-4667 – Odette Murray

KNOWLTON

Brome County Historical Society – Library, 130 Lakeside Rd., PO Box 690, Knowlton PQ J0E 1V0 – 514/243-6782 – Archivist, Marion L. Phelps

L'ASSOMPTION

Collège de l'Assomption - Centre de documentation, 270, boul l'Ange-Gardien, L'Assomption PQ J0K 1G0 – 819/589-5621 – Bibliothécaire, Réjean Oliver

LA MACAZA

Solicitor General Canada - La Macaza Establishment - Library, 321 Airport Rd., La Macaza PQ J0T 1R0 – 819/275-2315, ext.7046; Fax: 819/275-3079; Symbol: QLML – Librarian, Robert Hamelin

LA POCATIÈRE

CEGEP de La Pocatière - Bibliothèque François-Hertel, 140, 4e av, La Pocatière PQ G0R 1Z0 – 418/856-1525; Téléc: 418/856-4589; Courrier électronique: jldem@fedecegeps.qc.ca – Bibliothécaire en chef, Jean-Louis Demers

Collège de Ste-Anne-de-la-Pocatière - Bibliothèque, 100, 4e av, La Pocatière PQ G0R 1Z0 – 418/856-3012; Téléc: 418/856-5611 – Responsable, Marcel Mignault

Institut de technologie agro-alimentaire de La Pocatière - Centre de documentation, 401, rue Poiré, La Pocatière PQ G0R 1Z0 – 418/856-1110, poste 258; Téléc: 418/856-1719; Ligne sans frais: 1-800-463-1351; Symbol: QPES
  Bibliothécaire, Denis Dumont
  Bibliotechnicienne, Ginette Lévesque
  Agente de bureau, Agathe Plante

Société historique de la Côte-du-Sud – Centre de documentation, CP 937, La Pocatière PQ G0R 1Z0 – 418/856-2104

LA SARRE

Centre local de services communautaires des aurores boréales - Centre de documentation, 285, 1re rue est, La Sarre PQ J9Z 3K1 – 819/333-2354; Téléc: 819/333-3111 – Lorraine Carbonneau

Canadian Almanac & Directory 1997

LA TÛQUE

Centre hospitalier Saint-Joseph de La Tuque – Centre de documentation, 885, boul Ducharme, La Tûque PQ G9X 3C1 – 819/523-4581 – Bibliothécaire, Nicole Saint-Pierre

LASALLE

Ligue de sécurité du Québec – Bibliothèque spécialisée en prévention des accidents, 2536, rue Lapierre, Lasalle PQ J4B 6E6 – 514/641-9867 – Bibliotechnicien, Jacques Ratthé

LENNOXVILLE

Agriculture & Agri-Food Canada-Dairy & Swine Research & Development Centre: Lennoxville – Bibliothèque canadienne de l'agriculture, 2000, rte 108 est, CP 90, Lennoxville PQ J1M 1Z3 – 819/565-9171; Téléc: 819/564-5507; Courrier électronique: gagnegigueres@em.agr.ca; Symbol: QLAG – Bibliothécaire, Suzanne Gagné-Giguère

Bishop's University - John Bassett Memorial Library, PO Box 5000, Stn Lennoxville, Lennoxville PQ J1M 1Z7 – 819/822-9605; Fax: 819/822-9644; Email: wcurran@library.ubishops.ca; Symbol: QLB
   University Librarian, William M. Curran, 819/822-9606
   Head, Public Service, Wendy L. Durrant, 819/822-9708
   Head, Technical Services & Systems, Pierre Lafrance, 819/822-9707
   Acquisitions Librarian, Terry Skeats, 819/822-9604
   Reference Librarian, Eckhard Rothe
   Reference Librarian, Gary McCormick, 819/822-9608

LÉVIS

Assurance vie Desjardins-Laurentienne Inc. – Centre de documentation, 200, av des Commandeurs, Lévis PQ G6V 6R2 – 418/838-7619, 7626; Fax: 418/833-7215; Toll Free: 1-800-463-7870 – Technicienne en documentation, Louise Bédard

Cégep de Lévis-Lauzon - Bibliothéque, 205, Mgr Ignace Bourget, Lévis PQ G6V 6Z9 – 418/833-5110; Téléc: 418/833-7323; URL: http://www.clevis-lauzon.qc.ca/
   Responsable des services publics, Alain Gendron, Email: alain.gendron@clevislauzon.qc.ca
   Responsable des services techniques, Jean-Claude Gosselin

Collège de Lévis - Bibliothéque, 9, av Mgr. Gosselin, Lévis PQ G6V 5K1 – 418/833-1249, poste 140 – Responsable, Roger Audet

Confédération des caisses populaires et d'économie desjardins du Québec - Division des ressources informationnelles et documentaires, 100, av des Commandeurs, Lévis PQ G6V 7N5 – 418/835-4593; Téléc: 418/833-5873; Ligne sans frais: 1-800-463-4810; Courrier électronique: GESDOC; Symbol: QLCCP
   Documentaliste, Benjamin Fortin
   Technicienne, Lise Petel
   Technicienne, Jacqueline Dubé

Conseil de la coopération du Québec – Bibliothèque, #304, 4950, boul de la Rive Sud, Lévis PQ G6V 4Z6 – 418/835-3710

Fédération des associations coopérative d'économie familiale du Québec - ACEF Rive-Sud de Québec – Bibliothèque, #2, 11, av Bégin, Lévis PQ G6V 4B6 – 418/835-6633

Hôtel-Dieu – Bibliothèque, 143, rue Wolfe, Lévis PQ G6V 3Z1 – 418/835-7121, ext.3274; Téléc: 418/835-7133; Symbol: QLHD – Secretaire, J. Dufour

LONGUEUIL

Association béton Québec – Bibliothèque, #107, 85, rue St-Charles ouest, Longueuil PQ J4H 1C5 – 514/463-3569 – Diane Morin

Centre hospitalier Pierre-Boucher – Centre de documentation, 1333, boul Jacques-Cartier est, Longueuil PQ J4M 2A5 – 514/468-8111; Téléc: 514/468-4116; Symbol: QLOPB – Dominique Lefrançois

Les Centres jeunesse de la Montérégie – Centre de documentation, 25, boul Lafayette, Longueuil PQ J4K 5C8 – 514/679-0140; Symbol: QLOCSS – Line Marquis

Collège Edouard-Montpetit - Centre des ressources didactiques, 945, ch de Chambly, Longueuil PQ J4H 3M6 – 514/679-2630, poste 609; Fax: 514/677-2945
   Coordonnatrice, Gisèle Laramée
   Responsable de la référence, des services techniques/publiques, Janine Boucher

Conseil culturel de la Montérégie inc. – Bibliothèque, 305, boul Saint-Jean, Longueuil PQ J4H 2X4 – 514/651-0694 – Rita Harvie

La Fédération des producteurs de bois du Québec – Bibliothèque, 555, boul Roland-Therrien, Longueuil PQ J4H 3Y9 – 514/679-0530 – Nicole Pressault

Health Canada - Direction générale de la protection de la santé - Bibliothèque régionale, 1001, boul Saint-Laurent ouest, Longueuil PQ J4K 1C7 – 514/646-1353, poste 312; Téléc: 514/928-4102; Symbol: QMNHH – Library Technician, France Lachapelle

Institut Nazareth et Louis-Braille - Bibliothèque braille, 1111, rue Saint-Charles ouest, Longueuil PQ J4K 5G4 – 514/463-1710; Téléc: 514/463-0243; Ligne sans frais: 1-800-361-7063 – Bibliothécaire, Linda Laberge

Institut Nazareth et Louis Braille - Centre d'information typhlophilique, 1111, rue Saint-Charles ouest, Longueuil PQ J4K 5G4 – 514/463-1710; Téléc: 514/463-0243; Ligne sans frais: 1-800-361-7063; Symbol: QLNLB
   Bibliothécaire, Linda Laberge
   Directeur, André Vincent

Pratt & Whitney Canada Inc. - Library, 1000, rue Marie-Victorin, Longueuil PQ J4G 1A1 – 514/647-7341; Fax: 514/647-7797; TLX: 05-267509; Symbol: QLOU
   Librarian Supervisor, Elizabeth Reader, 514/647-7341, Email: elizabeth.reader@pwc.utc.com
   Reference Librarian, L. St. Amour, 514/647-2607
   Circulation, M. Andrews, 514/647-7342
   Public Services Librarian, B. Pawlowsky, 514/647-7342
   Technical Services, E. Lacombe, 514/647-4694
   Acquisitions, K. Portanier, 514/647-7343
   Circulation, M. Chaput, 514/647-7342

Société historique du Marigot inc. – Centre de documentation, 440, ch de Chambly, Longueuil PQ J4H 3L7 – 514/677-4573; 670-7399

MAGOG

Centre local de services communautaires Alfred-Desrochers - Centre de documentation, 1750, rue Sherbrooke, Magog PQ J1X 2T3 – 819/843-2572; Téléc: 819/843-2940 – Sylvie Morin

MATANE

Collège de Matane - Bibliothèque, 616, rue St-Rédempteur, Matane PQ G4W 1L1 – 418/562-1240, poste 2128; Fax: 418/566-2115 – Bibliothécaire, Colette Côté

Société d'histoire et de généalogie de Matane – Bibliothèque, CP 608, Matane PQ G4W 3P6 – 418/562-9766, 2808 – Secrétaire, J. Bernier

MIRABEL

Bell Helicopter Textron - Library, 12800, rue de l'Avenir, Mirabel PQ J7J 1R4 – 514/437-6041; Fax: 514/437-6382; Email: engineer@bhtc.com; Symbol: QSTTB – Supervisor, Engineering Support, Gerda-Marie Gritzka

MONT-JOLI

Fisheries & Oceans Canada-Institut Maurice-Lamontagne – Bibliothèque, 850, rte de la Mer, CP 1000, Mont-Joli PQ G5H 3Z4 – 418/775-0551; Courrier électronique: ENVOY: DFO.LIB.QUEBEC; biblio@qc.dfo.ca; Symbol: QQPSM – Bibliothécaire, Guy Michaud

Hôpital de Mont-Joli Inc. – Bibliothèque médicale, 800, av du Sanatorium, Mont-Joli PQ G5H 3L6 – 418/775-7261, ext.4323; Téléc: 418/775-8607; Symbol: QMJH – Bibliotechnicienne, Hélène Jean

MONTRÉAL

Québec Ministère des Transports - Service de l'environnement, 35, rue de Port-Royal est, 4e étage, Montréal PQ H3L 3T1 – 514/864-1668 – Bibliothécaire, Vy-Khanh Nguyen

A. Foster Higgins & Cie - Employee Benefit Documentation Centre, #2624, 800 Victoria Sq., Montréal PQ H4Z 1C3 – 514/878-4035; Fax: 514/878-4708 – Coordinator, Documentation Centre, Claire Gendreau

Abbott Laboratories Ltd. - Bibliothèque, 6300, côte de Liesse, CP 6150, Montréal PQ H3C 3K6 – 514/340-7100, ext.3120; Téléc: 514/342-3544; Courrier électronique: ENVOY.HEROUX.GENEVIEVE; Symbol: QMALL – Librarian, Geneviève Héroux

Agence francophone pour l'enseignement supérieur et la recherche – Bibliothèque, Direction générale-Rectorat, CP 400, Succ Côte des Neiges, Montréal PQ H3C 2S7 – 514/343-6630; TLX: 055-60955 – Documentaliste, Céline Brunel

Agriculture & Agri-Food Canada - Bibliothèque canadienne de l'agriculture, #746, 2001, rue University, Montréal PQ H3A 3N2 – 514/283-8888; Téléc: 514/283-3143; Courrier électronique: lbqmtlag@nccot.agr.ca; Symbol: QMPCA – Bibliothécaire, Pierre DiCampo, 514/283-8888, ext.201

Alcan Aluminum Ltd. - Information Centre, 1188, rue Sherbrooke ouest, PO Box 6090, Montréal PQ H3C 3A7 – 514/848-8187; Fax: 514/848-1469; Symbol: QMA – Manager, Information Centre, Lucie Dion, 514/848-8319

Allan Memorial Institute of Psychiatry - Eric D. Wittkower Library, 1025, av des Pins ouest, Montréal PQ H3A 1A1 – 514/842-1231, poste 4528; Symbol: QMAM – Medical Librarian, Barbara Gartner, Email: bgartner@rvhmed.lan.mcgill.ca

Alliance des professeures et professeurs de Montréal – Bibliothèque, 8225, boul Saint-Laurent, Montréal PQ H2P 2M1 – 514/383-4880 – Documentaliste-archiviste, Régent Séguin

Les Amis du Jardin botanique de Montréal – Bibliothèque, 4101, rue Sherbrooke est, Montréal PQ H1X 2B2 – 514/872-1493 – Céline Arsenault

Amnistie internationale, Section canadienne (Francophone) – Bibliothèque, 6250, boul Monk, Montréal PQ H4E 3H7 – 514/766-9766 – Responsable archives, Marguerite Hug

The Asbestos Institute – Library, #1750, 1002, rue Sherbrooke ouest, Montréal PQ H3A 3L6 – 514/844-3956 – John Di Gironimo

Association des auxiliaires bénévoles des établissements de santé du Québec – Bibliothèque, #400, 505, boul de Maisonneuve ouest, Montréal PQ H3A 3C2 – 514/282-4264 – Bibliothécaire, Viera Grmela

Association des collaboratrices et partenaires en affaires – Bibliothèque, 2099, boul Edouard, St-Hubert PQ H2X 2K2 – 514/465-4565 – Farida Chemmakh

Association coopérative d'économie familiale - Montréal (Nord) – Centre de documentation, 7500, av Chateaubriand, Montréal PQ H2R 2M1 – 514/277-7959 – Hélène Talbot

Association féminine d'éducation et d'action sociale – Bibliothèque, 5999, rue de Marseille, Montréal PQ

H1N 1K6 – 514/251-1636 – Documentaliste, Huguette Dalpé

Association for Canadian Studies – Library, c/o UQAM, V-5130, CP 8888, Succ Centre-Ville, Montréal PQ H3C 3P8 – 514/987-7784 – Publications Officer, Nicola Philpott

Association des hôpitaux du Québec – Centre de documentation, #400, 505, boul de Maisonneuve ouest, Montréal PQ H3A 3C2 – 514/842-4861; Symbol: QMAHQ – Virginie Jamet

L'Association des hôteliers du Québec – Bibliothèque, Pavillon Le Rigaud, #0.04, 425, rue Sherbrooke est, Montréal PQ H2L 1J9 – 514/282-5135

Association des ingénieurs-conseils du Québec – Bibliothèque, #1200, 2050, rue Mansfield, Montréal PQ H3A 1Y9 – 514/288-2032 – Adjointe administrative, Joanne Cook

Association des libraires du Québec – Bibliothèque, 1306, rue Logan, Montréal PQ H2L 1X1 – 514/526-3349

Association de manutention du Québec – Bibliothèque, 62A, Labelle, Laval PQ H7N 2S3 – 514/662-3717 – Stephanie Born

Association de Montréal pour la déficience intellectuelle – Centre de documentation multi-média, #100, 633, boul Crémazie est, Montréal PQ H2M 1L9 – 514/381-2307 – Responsable, Michelle Jacques

Association nationale des éditeurs de livres – Bibliothèque, 2514, boul Rosemont, Montréal PQ H1Y 1K4 – 514/273-8130 – Lise Oligny

Association paritaire pour la santé et la sécurité du travail - Affaires municipales – Bibliothèque, #710, 715, carré Victoria, Montréal PQ H2Y 2H7 – 514/849-8373; Toll Free: 1-800-465-1754 – Personne ressource, Jeanne Taussig

Association paritaire pour la santé et la sécurité du travail - Construction – Bibliothèque, #460, 7450, boul Les Galeries d'Anjou, Anjou PQ H1M 3M3 – 514/355-6190; Toll Free: 1-800-361-2061 – Bibliothécaire, Lucie Brunet

Association pour l'éducation interculturelle du Québec – Bibliothèque, #530, 7400, boul Saint-Laurent, Montréal PQ H2R 2Y1 – 514/276-8883

Association professionnelle des technologistes médicaux du Québec (ind.) – Bibliothèque, 1595, rue St-Hubert, 3e étage, Montréal PQ H2L 3Z2 – 514/524-3734; Toll Free: 1-800-361-4306 – Commis-relation de travail, Robert Francine

Association du Québec pour l'intégration sociale – Bibliothèque, 3958, rue Dandurand, Montréal PQ H1X 1P7 – 514/725-7245 – Claude F. Leclair

Association québécoise de loisir pour personnes handicapées – Bibliothèque, 4545, av Pierre de Coubertin, CP 1000, Montréal PQ H1V 3R2 – 514/252-3144 – Marie-Josée Duchesne

Association québécoise des marionnettistes – Centre de documentation, Centre UNIMA au Québec, CP 7, Succ De Lorimier, Montréal PQ H2H 2N6 – 514/499-0875

Association québécoise pour la maîtrise de l'énergie – Bibliothèque, #903, 5, Place Ville-Marie, Montréal PQ H3B 2G2 – 514/866-5584 – Marielle G. Gagné

Association québécoise pour les troubles d'apprentissage – Centre de ressources, #300, 284, rue Notre-Dame ouest, Montréal PQ H2Y 1T7 – 514/847-1324 – Agente d'information, Jeannette Côté

Association québécoise de l'épilepsie - Epilepsie Montréal – Bibliothèque, #115, 3800, rue Radisson, Montréal PQ H1M 1X6 – 514/252-0859

Association québécoise de l'industrie du disque, du spectacle et de la vidéo – Bibliothèque, #706, 3575, boul St-Laurent, Montréal PQ H2X 2T7 – 514/842-5147 – Documentaliste, Marie-Berthe Lefebvre

Association des services de réhabilitation sociale du Québec inc. – Bibliothèque, 1657, boul St-Joseph est, Montréal PQ H2G 1N1 – 514/521-3733 – Chantal Traversy

Association des sexologues du Québec – Bibliothèque, #300, 6915, rue St-Denis, Montréal PQ H2S 2S3 – 514/270-9289 – Sylviane Larose

L'Association de spina-bifida et d'hydrocéphalie du Québec – Bibliothèque, #425, 5757, rue Decelles, Montréal PQ H3S 2C3 – 514/340-9019; Toll Free: 1-800-567-1788 – Adjointe à la direction, Ginette Bélisle

Atelier d'histoire Hochelaga-Maisonneuve – Centre de documentation, 1691, boul Pie IX, Montréal PQ H1V 2C3 – 514/523-5930 – Documentaliste, Mario Laverge

Atomic Energy of Canada Limited-AECL-CANDU - Montréal Laboratory – Information Resources, 1155 Metcalfe St., Montréal PQ H3B 2V6 – 514/871-1116

Atwater Library, 1200, av Atwater, Montréal PQ H3Z 1X4 – 514/935-7344; Fax: 514/935-1960; Symbol: QMMI
Director, Janet Ilavsky
Head of Technical Services, Jana Valasek

Aviation Planning Services Ltd. – Library, #1430, 1100, boul René-Lévesque, Montréal PQ H3B 4N4 – 514/878-4388 – Librarian, Joan Meyer

Bank of Montreal – Business Information Centre, 129, rue St-Jacques ouest, Montréal PQ H2Y 1L6 – 514/877-9383; Fax: 514/877-8189; Toll Free: 1-800-555-3000 – Manager, Sylvia Piggott

Barreau de Montréal – Bibliothèque, Palais de Justice, #980, 1, rue Notre Dame est, Montréal PQ H2Y 1B6 – 514/393-2057; Téléc: 514/879-8592 – Directrice, Celine Amnotte

Batshaw Youth & Family Centre – Centre de documentation, #1010, 2155, rue Guy, Montréal PQ H3H 2R9 – 514/989-1885, poste 274; Symbol: QMVM – Janet Sand

Bell Canada - Bibliothèque du service juridique, #1830, 1800, av McGill College, Montréal PQ H3A 3J6 – 514/870-2683; Fax: 514/288-0717 – Research Assistant, Carolyne Bourgon
Information Resource Centre, #C29, 700, de la Gauchetière ouest, Montréal PQ H3B 4L1 – 514/870-8500; Fax: 514/876-8826;
Email: ENVOY100: IRC.MTL.GENERAL; Symbol: QMB – Associate Director, S. Boyd, 514/870-8922

Bendix Avelex Inc. - Engineering Library, PO Box 2140, Saint-Laurent PQ H4L 4X8 – 514/744-2811, ext.7141; Fax: 514/748-4420 – Rafik Rabbat

Berkowitz Strauber Goldman Law Office - Library, #300, 4141, Sherbrooke ouest, Montréal PQ H3Z 1B8 – 514/931-1788; Téléc: 514/931-3061

Bibliothèque générale C.N.D., Maison-mère, 4873, av Westmount, Westmount PQ H3Y 1X9 – 514/487-2420, poste 251; Courrier électronique: ENVOY: IDEM – Bibliothécaire-responsable, Carmen Brabant

Bibliothèque nationale du Québec, Édifice Marie-Claire-Daveluy, 125, rue Sherbrooke ouest, Montréal PQ H2X 1X4 – 514/873-1100; Téléc: 514/873-4310; Ligne sans frais: 1-800-363-9028; Courrier électronique: web@biblinat.gouv.qc.ca; URL: http://www.biblinat.gouv.qc.ca/
Président/Directeur général, Philippe Sauvageau, 514/873-1100, poste 402
Directeur de la référence, Yvon-André Lacroix, 514/873-1100, poste 441
Directrice des acquisitions, Carole Urbain, 514/873-1100, poste 431
Directeur de l'analyse documentaire, Van Khoa Nguyen, 514/873-1100, poste 447
Directeur de la conservation, Richard Thouin, 514/873-1100, poste 111
Salle de consultation des livres et ouvrages de référence, Édifice Saint-Sulpice, 1700, rue Saint-Denis, Montréal PQ H2X 3K6 – 514/873-1100, poste 441; Téléc: 514/873-4310; Ligne sans frais: 1-800-363-9028 – Directeur de la référence,

Yvon-André Lacroix, Email: ya_lacroix@biblinat.gouv.qc.ca
Salle de consultation des revues, journaux et publications gouvernementales, Édifice Aegidius-Fauteux, 4499, av de l'Esplanade, Montréal PQ H2W 1T2 – 514/873-1100, poste 244; Téléc: 514/873-9933; Ligne sans frais: 1-800-363-9028; Courrier électronique: reference@biblinat.gouv.qc.ca; URL: http://www.biblinat.gouv.qc.ca; Symbol: QMBN – Chef de Division, Louise Tessier

Biothermica International Inc. – Library, #440, 3333, boul Cavendish, Montréal PQ H4B 2M5 – 514/488-3881; Toll Free: 1-800-837-6422 – Technician, Marc Bisson

Bombardier Inc. - Canadair Division, Technical Information Centre, CP 6087, Succ Centre-Ville, Montréal PQ H3C 3G9 – 514/855-5000, ext.6174; Fax: 514/855-7203; Email: ENVOY: ILL.QMCA; Symbol: QMCA – Supervisor, Technical Information & Recordkeeping, Margaret Levesque

Bristol-Myers Squibb Canada - Medical Library, 2365, côte de Liesse, Montréal PQ H4N 2M7 – 514/333-2057; Fax: 514/335-4102; Email: gibson_d@bms.can; Symbol: QMSQC
Medical Librarian, Donna Gibson
Library Assistant, Celine Carriere

Bureau de l'efficacité énergétique - Centre de documentation, #600, 425, av Viger ouest, Montréal PQ H2Z 1W9 – 514/873-5463; Téléc: 514/873-6946; Symbol: QMBE – Bibliothécaire, Marie Viau

Business Development Bank of Canada - Corporate Research Centre, #400, 5, Place Ville Marie, Montréal PQ H4Z 1L4 – 514/283-7632; Fax: 514/283-4039; Symbol: QMFBD
Librarian, Jane Patterson, 514/283-3639
Library Technician, Maria Szulhan

Byers Casgrain - Library, #3900, 1, Place Ville Marie, Montréal PQ H3B 4M7 – 514/878-8800; Fax: 514/866-2241; Symbol: QMBC – Librarian, Sonya Eder

CAE Electronics Ltd. - Reference Library, 8585, Côte de Liesse, Montréal PQ H4T 1D6 – 514/341-6780, ext.2113; Fax: 514/734-5616 – Reference Librarian, Barbara Clement, Email: barbara@cae.ca

Caisse de dépôt et placement du Québec - Bibliothèque, 1981, av McGill College, Montréal PQ H3A 3C7 – 514/842-3261; Fax: 514/842-4833 – Responsable, Pauline Corbeil

Canada Human Resources Development - Québec Regional Library, 1441, rue St-Urbain, Montréal PQ H2X 2M6 – 514/283-4695; Fax: 514/283-3874; Symbol: QMMIQ
Chief Librarian, Jacinthe Castonguay, 514/283-7586
Reference & Technical Services, Angèle Viau, 514/283-4707
Reference & Acquisitions Clerk, Lise Chamberland, 514/283-4695

Canadian Centre for Architecture – Bibliothèque, 1920, rue Baile, Montréal PQ H3H 2S6 – 514/939-7000; Email: RLIN: BM.MOR@RLG.BITNET – Head, Reader Services, Renata Guttman

Canadian Centre for Ecumenism – Library, 2065, rue Sherbrooke ouest, Montréal PQ H3H 1G6 – 514/937-9176 – Coordinator, Bernice Baranowski

Canadian Crossroads International - Group Program Office – Library, 912, rue Sherbrooke est, Montréal PQ H2L 1L2 – 514/528-5363

Canadian Institute for Jewish Research – Library, #550, 5250, boul Decarie, Montréal PQ H3X 2H9 – 514/486-5544 – Guy Mizrachi

Canadian Institute of Hypnotism – Library, 110, rue Greystone, Montréal PQ H9R 5T6 – 514/426-1010

Canadian Institute of Mining, Metallurgy & Petroleum – Library, #1210, 3400, boul de Maisonneuve ouest, Montréal PQ H3Z 3B8 – 514/939-2710

Canadian Jewish Congress – Library, 1590, av Docteur Penfield, Montréal PQ H3G 1C5 – 514/931-7531 – Archivist, Janice Rosen

Canadian Almanac & Directory 1997

Canadian Marconi Co. - Library, 2442, av Trenton, Montréal PQ H3P 1Y9 – 514/341-7630 ext. 4577; Fax: 514/340-3100 – M. Thomson-Oliver

Canadian Psychoanalytic Society – Library, 7000, ch Côte-des-Neiges, Montréal PQ H3S 2C1 – 514/738-6105

Canadian Pulp & Paper Association – Library, Sun Life Building, 1155, rue Metcalfe, 19e étage, Montréal PQ H3B 4T6 – 514/866-6621 – Librarian, Karen Fountain

Canadien National - Dechief Research Library, 1060, rue University, Montréal PQ H3B 3A2 – 514/399-8025; Téléc: 514/399-8258 – G. Martinello

Canatom Inc. - Library, 2020 University St., 22nd Fl., Montréal PQ H3A 2A5 – 514/288-1990; Fax: 514/289-9300 – T. Gellatly

Caron, Bélanger, Ernst & Young - Library, #2400, 1 Place Ville Marie, Montréal PQ H3B 3M9 – 514/875-6060; Fax: 514/871-8713; Symbol: QMCGLI – Librarian, Margaret Cameron

Carrefour des cèdres – Library, 2376, rue Quesnel, Montréal PQ H3J 1G5 – 514/932-3961 – G. Baraghid

CEGEP André Laurendeau - Bibliothèque, 1111 Lapierre, La Salle PQ H8N 2J4 – 514/364-3320; Téléc: 514/364-2627; Courrier électronique: lstp@fedecegeps.qc.ca – Spécialiste en moyens et techniques d'enseignement, Louise St-Pierre

CEGEP Marie-Victorin - Bibliothèque, 7000, rue Marie-Victorin, Montréal PQ H1G 2J6 – 514/325-0150; Téléc: 514/328-3830 – Bibliothécaire, Réjean Charette

CEGEP de Saint Laurent - Bibliothèque, 625, boul Ste-Croix, Saint Laurent PQ H4L 3X7 – 514/747-6521, poste 306 – Paul Martineau

Centraide du Grand Montréal – Bibliothèque, 493, rue Sherbrooke ouest, Montréal PQ H3A 1B6 – 514/288-1261 – Monique Berthiaume

Centre d'accueil Domrémy-Montréal - Centre québécoise de documentation en toxicomanie, 15693, boul Gouin ouest, Sainte-Geneviève PQ H9H 1C3 – 514/626-0220; Téléc: 514/626-7757; Symbol: QMCADM – Monique Gauthier

Centre d'action bénévole de Montréal – Centre de documentation, 235, rue St-Jacques, Montréal PQ H2Y 1M6 – 514/842-3351 – Marisa Gelfusa

Centre d'animation de développement et de recherche en éducation – Bibliothèque, 1940, boul Henri-Bourassa est, Montréal PQ H2B 1S2 – 514/381-8891; Toll Free: 1-888-381-8891 – Documentaliste, Roland Desrosiers

Centre des auteurs dramatiques – Centre de documentation, 3450, rue St. Urbain, Montréal PQ H2X 2N5 – 514/288-3384 – Daniel Gauthier

Centre canadien d'étude et de coopération internationale – Centre de documentation, 180, rue Sainte-Catherine est, Montréal PQ H2X 1K9 – 514/875-9911 – Directeur, Robert Hazel

Centre de caractérisation microscopique des matériaux – École Polytechnique Bibliothèque, CP 6079, Succ Centre Ville, Montréal PQ H3C 3A7 – 514/340-4847

Centre de documentation sur l'éducation des adultes et la condition féminine, #340, 1265, rue Berri, Montréal PQ H2L 4X4 – 514/844-3674; Téléc: 514/844-1598; Symbol: QMICE
Directrice, Rosalie Ndejuru, 514/844-3674, poste 34
Bibliothécaire de référence, Thérèse Leblanc, 514/844-4275

Centre d'éducation interculturelle et de compréhension internationale – Centre de documentation, 3925, rue Villeray, Montréal PQ H2A 1H1 – 514/721-8122 – Bibliothécaire, Michel Craig

Centre d'études et de documentation d'amérique latine – Nouvelles Solidarités, #460, 3680, rue Jeanne-Mance, Montréal PQ H2X 2K5 – 514/982-6664 – Documentaliste, Louise Lavallée

Centre hospitalier Catherine Booth – Bibliothèque du personnel, 4375, av Montclair, Montréal PQ H4B 2J5 – 514/481-0431 – Karen Honegger

Centre hospitalier Côte-des-Neiges – Centre de documentation, 4565, ch de la Reine Marie, Montréal PQ H3W 1W5 – 514/340-1424; Téléc: 514/340-2815; Courrier électronique: bourbonl@ere.umontreal.ca; Symbol: QMQ – Bibliothécaire en chef, Louise Bourbonnais

Centre hospitalier Fleury – Centre de documentation, 2180, rue Fleury est, Montréal PQ H2B 1K3 – 514/381-9311; Symbol: QMHGF – Bibliotechnicienne, Lise Paradis

Centre hospitalier gériatrique Maimonides – Health Information Centre, 5795, av Caldwell, Cote-Saint-Luc PQ H4W 1W3 – 514/483-2121, ext.217; Téléc: 514/483-1086; Symbol: QMMHH – Health Information Officer, D. Scipio

Centre hospitalier Jacques Viger – Centre de documentation, 1051, rue St-Hubert, Montréal PQ H2L 3Y5 – 514/842-7181; Téléc: 514/842-1212; Symbol: QMHM – Technicienne en documentation, Danielle Cayer

Centre hospitalier Nôtre-Dame de la Merci – Centre de documentation, 555, boul Gouin ouest, Montréal PQ H3L 1K5 – 514/331-3020, ext.367; Téléc: 514/331-3358; Symbol: QMNDM – Bibliothécaire, Mario Tessier

Centre Hospitalier Richardson - Bibliothèque médicale, 5425, av Bessborough, Montréal PQ H4V 2S7 – 514/483-1380, local 2125; Téléc: 514/483-4596; Symbol: QMHJR – Manager, Medical Research, Christine Bolduc

Centre hospitalier de St. Mary – Bibliothèque des sciences de la santé, 3830, av Lacombe, Montréal PQ H3T 1M5 – 514/345-3317; Téléc: 514/345-3695; Symbol: QMSMA – Jeannine Lawlor

Centre hospitalier de Verdun – Bibliothèque médicale, 4000, boul Lasalle, Verdun PQ H4G 2A3 – 514/765-8121; Symbol: QMHGC – Marc Lamarre

Centre international de criminologie comparée – Centre de documentation, CP 6128, Montréal PQ H3C 3J7 – 514/343-6534

Centre Justice et Foi - Bibliothèque Édmond Desrochers, 25, rue Jarry ouest, Montréal PQ H2P 1S6 – 514/387-2541; Fax: 514/387-4244 – Directeur, Luc Trépanier, 514/387-2541

Centre local de services communautaires Mercier-est/Anjou - Centre de documentation, 9403, rue Sherbrooke est, Montréal PQ H1L 6P2 – 514/356-2572, poste 3207; Téléc: 514/356-2571 – Isabelle Bonnard

Centre québécois du droit de l'environnement – Bibliothèque, #307, 2360, rue Notre-Dame ouest, Montréal PQ H3G 1N4 – 514/931-9190 – Bibliothécaire, Dora Knez

Centre de réadaptation Constance-Lethbridge – Bibliothèque médicale, 7005, boul de Maisonneuve ouest, Montréal PQ H4B 1T3 – 514/487-1770; Symbol: QMLR – Personne ressource, Jane Petrov

Centre de recherche et développement en économique – Bibliothèque, Pavillon Lionel-Groulx, Université de Montréal, CP 6128, Succ Centre-Ville, Montréal PQ H3C 3J7 – 514/343-6111 – Fethy Mili

Centre de recherche industrielle du Québec - Centre de documentation, 8475, rue Christophe-Colomb, Montréal PQ H2P 2X1 – 514/383-1550; Téléc: 514/383-3238; TLX: 05-827887; Courrier électronique: ENVOY: QMCRI.PEB; Symbol: QMCRI – Carole Lamoureux

Centre de recherche Lionel-Groulx – Bibliothèque, 261, av Bloomfield, Outremont PQ H2V 3R6 – 514/271-4759; Téléc: 514/271-6369 – Bibliothécaire, Jean-Pierre Chalifoux

Centre des services sociaux de Montréal Métropolitain – Centre de documentation, 1001, boul de Maisonneuve est, Montréal PQ H2H 2L5 – 514/527-7261; Symbol: QMCSS – Hélène Neilson

Les Centres jeunesse de Montréal – Centre de documentation, 840, Côte Vertu, Saint-Laurent PQ H4L 1Y4 – 514/855-5055; Symbol: QMMV

Chait Amyot - Law Library, #1900, 1, Place Ville Marie, Montréal PQ H3B 2C3 – 514/879-1353; Fax: 514/879-1460 – Librarian, Pauline Housden

Chambre de commerce du Montréal métropolitain - Information Centre, #12500, Plaza Level, 5, Place Ville Marie, Montréal PQ H3B 4Y2 – 514/871-8000; Téléc: 514/871-1255 – Director, Information Services, Hugues Létourneau

Chambre des notaires du Québec – Bibliothèque, #1700, 630, boul René-Lévesque ouest, Montréal PQ H3B 1T6 – 514/879-1793

La Cinémathèque québécoise – Centre de documentation cinématographique, 335, boul de Maisonneuve est, Montréal PQ H2X 1K1 – 514/842-9763 – Directeur, René Beauclair

Cité de la santé de Laval – Centre de documentation, 1755, boul René-Laennec, CP 440, Laval PQ H7M 3L9 – 514/975-5493; Téléc: 514/975-5572; Courrier électronique: labellel@ere.umontreal.ca; Symbol: QLACS – Bibliothécaire, France Pontbriand

Coalition des organismes communautaires québécois de lutte contre le sida – Bibliothèque, #320, 4205, rue St-Denis, Montréal PQ H2J 2K9 – 514/844-2477 – André Roy

Collège d'Ahuntsic - Bibliothèque, 9155, rue St-Hubert, Montréal PQ H2M 1Y8 – 514/389-5921; Téléc: 514/389-5276
Jean Lortie
Louise Grenier

Collège André-Grasset - Bibliothèque, 1001, boul Crémazie est, Montréal PQ H2M 1M3 – 514/381-4293; Téléc: 514/381-7421 – Jean-Pierre Lussier

Collège de Bois-de-Boulogne - Centre des ressources didactiques et pédagogiques, 10555, av de Bois-de-Boulogne, Montréal PQ H4N 1L4 – 514/332-3000; Téléc: 514/332-0083; Symbol: CRDP
Bibliothécaire en chef, Eduardo Brito
Bibliothécaire, Anne Marie Lachance, 514/332-3000, poste 220

Collège Français - Bibliothèque, 185, av Fairmount ouest, Montréal PQ H2T 2M6 – 514/495-2581, poste 141; Téléc: 514/271-2823 – Responsable de la bibliothèque, Suzanne Howison

Collège Jean-de-Brebeuf - Bibliothèque, 5625, rue Decelles, Montréal PQ H3T 1W4 – 514/342-1320, poste 261; Téléc: 514/342-0130 – Bibliothécaire, Alain Roberge

Collège LaSalle - Centre de documentation, 2000, rue Ste-Catherine ouest, Montréal PQ H3H 2T2 – 514/939-2006; Téléc: 514/939-2015
Bibliothécaire en chef, Madeleine Lambert
Bibliotechnicienne, Josée Berthelette
Bibliotechnicienne, Sylvie Auger

Collège de Maisonneuve - Centre des médias (Bibliothèque), 3800, rue Sherbrooke est, Montréal PQ H1X 2A2 – 514/254-7131; Téléc: 514/254-2517
Coordonnateur, Louis Brunet
Bibliothécaire, Louise Beauregard
Bibliothécaire, Micheline Belleau
Public Services Librarian, Monique Rivard
Acquisitions Librarian, Regine Millaire

Collège des médecins du Québec – Informathèque, 2170, boul René-Lévesque ouest, Montréal PQ H3H 2T8 – poste 254 – Bibliotechnicienne, Hélène Landry

Collège Montmorency - Centre des ressources didactiques, 475, boul de l'Avenir, Laval PQ H7N 5H9 – 514/975-6100; Téléc: 514/975-6153
Directeur, France Bordeleau
Responsable de la référence et des services publics, Gilbert Baillargeon, 514/975-6272

Collège de Montréal - Bibliothèque, 1931, rue Sherbrooke ouest, Montréal PQ H3H 1E3 – 514/933-7397; Téléc: 514/933-3225 – Responsable, Sylvie Caron

College O'Sullivan - Library, 1191, rue de la Montagne, Montréal PQ H3G 1Z2 – 514/866-3124; Fax: 514/866-0668 – Librarian, Krishna Pal, 514-866-4622

Collège de Rosemont - Bibliothèque, 6400, 16e av, Montréal PQ H1X 2S9 – 514/376-1620, poste 261; Téléc: 514/376-8279 – Raymonde Beaudry

Collège St-Jean-Vianney - Bibliothèque, 12630, boul Gouin est, Montréal PQ H1C 1B9 – 514/648-3821; Téléc: 514/648-8401 – Claudine Legault

Collège Stanislas - Bibliothèque, 780, boul Dollard, Outremont PQ H2V 3G5 – 514/273-9521; Fax: 514/273-3409

Comité canadien des électrotechnologies – Bibliothéque, #2075, 630, boul René-Lévesque ouest, Montréal PQ H3B 1S6 – 514/875-2341

Comité des personnes atteintes du VIH – Library, 3600, av Hôtel-de-Ville, Montréal PQ H2X 3B6 – 514/282-6673 – Gilles Picard

Comité sida aide Montréal – Bibliothèque, 3600, av Hôtel-de-Ville, Montréal PQ H2X 3B6 – 514/282-9888; Toll Free: 1-800-463-5656 – Responsable, Patrice Allard

Commission d'appel en matière de lésions professionnelles - Centre de documentation, #350, 1200, av McGill College, Montréal PQ H4A 2K9 – 514/873-1654; Téléc: 514/873-7529; Symbol: QMCAML – Chief Librarian, Monique Desrochers

Commission des droits de la personne - Bibliothèque, 360, rue Saint-Jacques, Montréal PQ H2Y 1P5 – 514/873-5146; Téléc: 514/873-6032;
  Symbol: QMQDP
  Bibliothécaire, Madeleine Beaudoin
  Technicienne, Diane Dupont

Commission des écoles catholiques de Montréal - Bibliothèque centrale, 3737, rue Sherbrooke est, Montréal PQ H1X 3B3 – 514/596-6586

Commission de la construction du Québec - Ressources documentaires, 3530, rue Jean-Talon ouest, Montréal PQ H3R 2G3 – 514/341-7740, poste 355; Téléc: 514/341-6354; Courrier électronique: ENVOY: PEB.QMOC – Chef, section ressources documentaires, Nicole Côté

Commission de la santé et de la sécurité du travail du Québec - Centre de documentation, 1199, rue de Bleury, 4e étage, CP 6067, Montréal PQ H3C 4E2 – 514/873-3160; Téléc: 514/864-2617; Courrier électronique: Envoy: PEB.QMCSST;
  Symbol: QMCSST
  Chef de service, Marc Fournier
  Responsable, Sylvie Lacerte, 514/873-6883
  Bibliothécaire, Carole Bergeron, 514/873-6225

Commission de protection des droits de la jeunesse - Centre de documentation, 505, boul René-Lévesque ouest, 12e étage, Montréal PQ H2Z 1Y7 – 514/873-5435; Téléc: 514/873-2373 – Elisabeth Venne

Commission des services juridiques - Bibliothèque, #1404, 2, Complexe Desjardins, Montréal PQ H5B 1B3 – 514/873-3562; Téléc: 514/873-9263; Symbol: QMJSJ – Documentaliste, Francine Godin

Commission des valeurs mobilières - Bibliothèque, 800 Place Victoria, 17e étage, CP 246, Montréal PQ H4Z 1G3 – 514/873-5326; Téléc: 514/873-3090;
  Symbol: QMCVM
  Chef de service, Jean-François Doutrelepont
  Référence & services publics, Librarian, Lucie Lafrance
  Référence, Gilles Lachance

Communauté Sépharade du Québec – Bibliothèque, 4735, Côte Ste-Catherine, Montréal PQ H3W 1M1 – 514/733-4998 – Elie Benchetrit

Communauté urbaine de Montréal - Service de planification, Bibliothèque, 2580, boul St-Joseph est, Montréal PQ H1Y 2A2 – 514/280-6700; Téléc: 514/280-6744

Concordia University - Libraries, 1455, boul de Maisonneuve ouest, Montréal PQ H3G 1M8 – 514/848-7695; Fax: 514/848-2882; Email: boninr@vax2.concordia.ca
  Chief Librarian, Dr. Roy Bonin, 514/848-7695
  Access Services, Head, Helena Bairos, 514/848-7702
  Government Publications & Special Collections, Head, Louise Carpentier, 514/848-7709
  Information Services, Head, Judy Appleby, 514/848-7769
  Library Personnel, Assistant Director, Lillian Rubinlicht, 514/848-7693
  Planning & Priorities, Assistant Director, Robert Wrightson, 514/848-7742
  User Services, Acting Associate Director, Irene Sendek, 514/848-7699
  User Services, Associate Director & Head, Joseph Princz, 514/848-7699
  Guidance Library, Head, Marlis Hubbard, 514/848-3556
  Special Services, Head, Loren Lerner, 514/848-7712
  Vanier Library, Head, Zuzana Jirkovsky, 514/848-7721
  Collection Services, Assistant Director, Charlotte MacLaurin, 514/848-7742

Confédération québécoise des centres d'hébergement et de réadaptation – Bibliothèque, #1100, 1001, boul de Maisonneuve est, Montréal PQ H2L 4P9 – 514/597-1007 – Responsable, Nicole Tardif

Confédération des syndicats nationaux – Bibliothèque, 1601, av de Lorimier, Montréal PQ H2K 4M5 – 514/598-2121

Conférence des recteurs et des principaux des universités du Québec – Bibliothèque, #1200, 300, Léo Pariseau, CP 952, Succ Place du Parc, Montréal PQ H2W 2N1 – 514/288-8524 – Personne ressource, Roger Charland

Conseil des arts textiles du Québec – Centre de Documentation, 811A, rue Ontario est, Montréal PQ H2L 1P1 – 514/524-6645

Conseil de la Peinture du Québec – Bibliothèque, #913, 460, rue Sainte-Catherine ouest, Montréal PQ H3B 1A7 – 514/279-5600 – Assistante administrative, Reine Coudé

Conseil de la Sculpture du Québec – Bibliothèque, #306, 911, rue Jean-Talon est, Montréal PQ H2R 1V5 – 514/270-7209

Conseil du patronat du Québec – Bibliothèque, #606, 2075 rue Université, Montréal PQ H3A 2L1 – 514/288-5161 – Ginette Bourbonnais

Conservatoire d'art dramatique de Montréal - Bibliothèque, 100, rue Notre Dame est, Montréal PQ H2Y 1C1 – 514/873-3002; Téléc: 514/873-7943; Symbol: QMCADQ – Responsable, Daniel Laflamme

Conservatoire de musique de Montréal - Bibliothèque, 100, rue Notre-Dame est, Montréal PQ H2Y 1C1 – 514/873-7482; Téléc: 514/873-4601;
  Symbol: QMCOM – Directrice, Nicole Boisclair

Coopers & Lybrand - Information Centre, 1170 Peel St., Montréal PQ H3B 4T2 – 514/876-1500; Fax: 514/876-1502, 1527; Symbol: QMCCL – Librarian, Danielle Martin, Email: dmartin@login.net

Corporate-Higher Education Forum – Library, #2501, 1155, boul René-Lévesque ouest, Montréal PQ H3B 2K4 – 514/876-1356 – Louise Brunet Nelson

Corporation des bibliothécaires professionnels du Québec – Bibliothèque, #320, 307, rue Ste-Catherine ouest, Montréal PQ H2X 2A3 – 514/845-3327

Corporation d'Urgences-santé de la région de Montréal métropolitain - Centre de documentation, 3232, rue Bélanger est, Montréal PQ H1Y 3H5 – 514/723-5754; Téléc: 514/723-5790 – Diane Pelletier

CP Rail System - Business Information Services, PO Box 6042, Montréal PQ H3C 3E4 – 514/395-6762; Fax: 514/395-7959; Symbol: QMCP
  Manager, Carole Lacourte, 514/395-6762
  Reference Librarian, Véronique Leblanc, 514/395-7230
  Technical Services Librarian, Heather Berardinucci, 514/395-5562

David M. Stewart Museum at the Fort, Île Sainte-Hélène - Library, PO Box 1200, Montréal PQ H3C 2Y9 – 514/861-6701; Fax: 514/284-0123; Symbol: QMDS – Librarian, Eileen Meillon

Dawson College - Library, 3040 Sherbrooke St. West, Westmount PQ H3Z 1A4 – 514/931-8731; Fax: 514/931-3567; Email: cgilmore@dawsoncollege.qc.ca
  Public Services, Coordinator, Carolyn Gilmore
  Reference Librarian, Beryl Moser
  Reference Librarian, David Jones
  Technical Services, Coordinator, Anne Scott

De Grandpré, Godin Law Office - Bibliothèque, #2900, 1000 rue de la Gauchetière ouest, Montréal PQ H3B 4W5 – 514/878-4311; Téléc: 514/878-4333
  Technicienne en droit, Manon Savoie
  Directeur général, Hélène Schampaert

Département de santé communautaire de l'Hôpital général de Montréal - Centre de documentation, #300, 980, rue Guy, Montréal PQ H3H 2K3 – 514/932-3055; Téléc: 514/932-1502; Symbol: QMGHC – Bibliothécaire, Nora Stamboulieh

DES Action Canada – Library, PO Box 233, Montréal PQ H3X 3T4 – 514/482-3204; Toll Free: 1-800-482-1337 – Librarian, Dawn A. Kiddell

Desjardins Ducharme Stein Monast Law Office - Bibliothèque, Tour de la Banque Nationale, #2400, 600, rue de La Gauchetière ouest, Montréal PQ H3B 4L8 – 514/878-9411; Téléc: 514/878-9092 – Directeur, Jacques Cartier

Le Devoir – Centre de documentation, 2050, rue de Bleury, 9e étage, Montréal PQ H3A 3M9 – 514/985-3423; Téléc: 514/985-3360 – Head Librarian, Gilles Paré

Direction de santé publique - Centre de documentation, 4835, av Christophe-Colomb, Montréal PQ H2J 3G8 – 514/528-2400, poste 3960; Téléc: 514/528-2598; Symbol: QMSPM
  Bibliothécaire, Francine Fiore
  Technicienne en documentation, Raymonde Champagne

Domtar Inc. – Library, 22025, route Transcanada ouest, Senneville PQ H9X 3L7 – 514/457-8208; Fax: 514/457-2983 – Library Assistant, Marilyn Hussey

École des Hautes Études Commerciales - Bibliothèque, 5255, av Decelles, Montréal PQ H3T 1V6 – 514/340-6220; Fax: 514/340-6230 – Directeur, Reference, Gerald Boudreau

École de musique Vincent-d'Indy - Bibliothèque, 628, ch de la Côte Ste-Catherine, Outremont PQ H2V 2C5 – 514/735-5261 – Jeannette Pinard

École Peter Hall inc. - Centre de documentation, 1455, rue Rochon, Saint-Laurent PQ H4L 1W1 – 514/748-6727, local 229; Téléc: 514/748-5122 – Secretary, Louise Leblanc

École polytechnique de Montréal - Bibliothèque, Campus de l'Université de Montréal, CP 6079, Succ Centre-ville, Montréal PQ H3C 3A7 – 514/340-4666; Téléc: 514/340-4026; Courrier électronique: biblio@mailsrv.polymtl.ca;
  Symbol: QMEP
  Directeur de la Bibliothèque, Olivier Paradis, 514/340-4847
  Information Access Services, Richard Dumont, 514/340-4652
  Technical Services & Acquisitions Librarian, Claire Pelletier, 514/340-4641
  Systems Librarian, Minh-Thu Nguyen, 514/340-4993
  Fee-based Services, Marie-Hélène Dupuis, 514/340-4213
  Circulation, Marlène Aubin, 514/340-4659

Ecological Agriculture Projects – Library, Centennial Centre, 21111 Lakeshore Rd., Ste-Anne-de-Bellevue PQ H9X 3V9 – 514/398-7771

Environment Canada - Bibliothèque, 105, rue McGill, Montréal PQ H2Y 2E7 – 514/496-2930; Téléc: 514/283-9451; Courrier électronique: QMEE.PEB; Symbol: QMEE – Library & Records Management, Head, Cécile Morin, 418/648-4768

Canadian Almanac & Directory 1997

Canadian Meteorological Centre - Library, #508, 2121 Trans-Canada Hwy., Dorval PQ H9P 1J3 – 514/421-4754; Fax: 514/421-2106; Symbol: QMEA – Head, Maryse Ferland

Epilepsy Canada – Library, #745, 1470, rue Peel, Montréal PQ H3A 1T1 – 514/845-7855

Equality Party of Québec – Library, #801, 5250 Ferrier St., Montréal PQ H4P 1L4 – 514/733-9131 – Research Director, Tony Kondaks

ERS Youth Development Corporation – Library, #520, 5250 Ferrier St., Montréal PQ H4P 1L4 – 514/731-3419

Facultés de la Compagnie de Jésus - Bibliothèque de théologie, 5605, av Decelles, Montréal PQ H3T 1W4 – 514/737-1465; Symbol: QMFCJ – Directeur, Claude-Roger Nadeau

Fédération acadienne du Québec – Bibliothèque, #102, 2201, rue Sherbrooke est, Montréal PQ H2K 1E2 – 514/527-2127

Fédération des affaires sociales inc. (CSN) – Bibliothèque, 1601, av de Lorimier, Montréal PQ H2K 4M5 – 514/598-2210 – Personne ressource, Lucie Courtemanche

Fédération des associations coopérative d'économie familiale du Québec – Bibliothèque, #305, 5225, rue Berri, Montréal PQ H2J 2S4 – 514/271-7004 – Johanne Groulx

Fédération des cégeps – Bibliothèque, 500, boul Crémazie est, Montréal PQ H2P 1E7 – 514/381-8631 – Lucie Varin

Fédération de gymnastique du Québec – Bibliothèque, 4545, av Pierre-de-Coubertin, CP 1000, Montréal PQ H1V 3R2 – 514/252-3043

Fédération des infirmières et infirmiers du Québec – Bibliothèque, 2050, rue de Bleury, 4e étage, Montréal PQ H3A 2J5 – 514/861-8328, poste 243 – Archiviste, Martine Dubé

Fédération des médecins omnipraticiens du Québec – Centre de documentation, #1000, 1440, rue Ste-Catherine ouest, Montréal PQ H3G 1R8 – 514/878-1911; Toll Free: 1-800-361-8499; Symbol: QMFMO – Technicienne, Ghislaine Lincourt

Fédération nationale des associations de consommateurs du Québec – Bibliothèque, #301, 1212, rue Panet, Montréal PQ H2L 2Y7 – 514/521-6820

Fédération du plongeon amateur du Québec – Bibliothèque, 4545, av Pierre-de-Coubertin, CP 1000, Montréal PQ H1V 3R2 – 514/252-3096 – Donald Normond

Fédération du Québec pour le planning des naissances – Bibliothèque, #302, 4428, boul St-Laurent, Montréal PQ H2W 1Z5 – 514/844-3721 – France Tardif

Fédération des travailleurs et travailleuses du Québec – Centre de documentation de la FTQ, 545, boul Crémazie est, 17e étage, Montréal PQ H2M 2V1 – 514/383-8025 – Documentaliste, Isabelle Reny

Fondation des maladies mentales – Bibliothèque, 212, boul Saint-Joseph ouest, Montréal PQ H2T 2P8 – 514/270-5354 – Secrétaire, Nicole Allard

Fonds de la recherche en santé du Québec - Centre de documentation, 2085, av Union, 19e étage, Montréal PQ H3A 1B9 – 514/873-2114; Téléc: 514/873-8768 – Technicienne, Mme Claude Monast

Forest Engineering Research Institute of Canada – Information Resources, 580, boul Saint-Jean, Pointe Claire PQ H9R 3J9 – 514/694-1140 – Head, Information Resources, Christel Mukhopadhyay

Frank W. Horner Inc. - Research Library, 5485, rue Ferrier, PO Box 959, Montréal PQ H3C 2W6 – 514/731-3931, ext.259; Fax: 514/738-5509 – Librarian, Yvon Dugas

The Fraser-Hickson Institute - Free Library, 4855 Kensington, Montréal PQ H3X 3S6 – 514/489-5301; Fax: 514/489-5302; Email: fratrick@cam.org – Chief Librarian, Frances W. Ackerman

Fraternité nationale des charpentiers-menuisiers, forestiers et travailleurs d'usine (CTC) – Bibliothèque, #205, 3730, boul Crémazie est, Montréal PQ H2A 1B4 – 514/374-5871; Toll Free: 1-800-465-9791 – Directeur du personnel, G. Marois

Gasco, Linteau & Grignon Law Office - Bibliothèque, #2100, 1080, côte du Beaver Hall, Montréal PQ H2Z 1S8 – 514/397-0066; Téléc: 514/397-0393 – Librarian, Pierre-Yves

Grand Séminaire de Montréal - Bibliothèque, 2065, rue Sherbrooke ouest, Montréal PQ H3H 1G6 – 514/935-1169; Téléc: 514/935-5497 – Rev. Paul A. Martin

Groupe d'action pour la prévention du sida – Bibliothèque, #101, 2577A, rue Jean Talon est, Montréal PQ H2A 1T8 – 514/722-5655 – Responsable, Suzon F. Jean-Pierre

Groupe interuniversitaire de recherche en informatique cognitive des organisations – Bibliothèque, #912, 276, rue St-Jacques, Montréal PQ H2Y 1N3 – 514/985-5459 – Jocelyne Gonthier

Groupe de recherche en écologie sociale – Bibliothèque, Dépt. de Soc., Université de Montréal, CP 6128, Montréal PQ H3C 3J7 – 514/343-5959

Groupement des assureurs automobiles – Centre de documentation, #900, 425, boul de Maisonneuve ouest, Montréal PQ H3A 3G5 – 514/288-1537 – Documentaliste, Claude Garceau

Guy & Gilbert Law Office - Bibliothèque, #2300, 770, rue Sherbrooke ouest, Montréal PQ H3A 1G1 – 514/281-1766; Téléc: 514/281-1059, 9948, 5799 – Technical Services & Acquisitions, Librarian, Lise Zaucher

Hébert Denault Law Office - Bibliothèque, 359, Place Royale, Montréal PQ H2Y 2V3 – 514/288-4424; Téléc: 514/288-7859 – Responsable, Colette Bastien

Heenan Blaikie Law Office - Bibliothèque, #2500, 1250, boul René-Lévesque ouest, Montréal PQ H3B 4W8 – 514/281-1212; Téléc: 514/281-1776 – Bibliotecnicienne, Dianne Bellemare

Héritage Montréal – Bibliothèque, 1181, rue de la Montagne, Montréal PQ H3G 1Z2 – 514/875-2985 – Documentaliste, Robert Klein

Historic Theatres' Trust – Library, PO Box 387, Montréal PQ H3Z 2V8 – 514/933-8077

Hoechst Canada Inc. – Library, 4045, Côte Vertu, Montréal PQ H4R 1R6 – 514/333-3500 – Patrick Gregory

L'Hôpital Chinois de Montréal – Bibliothèque, 7500, rue St-Denis, Montréal PQ H2R 2E6 – 514/273-9154; Symbol: QMHCM – Technicienne, Cécile Desjardins

Hôpital Douglas – Staff Library, 6875, boul Lasalle, Verdun PQ H4H 1R3 – 514/762-3029; Téléc: 514/762-3039; Symbol: QMDH – Chief Librarian, Elaine Mancina

Hôpital général Juif Sir Mortimer B. Davis – Library, 3755, ch Côte Ste-Catherine, Montréal PQ H3T 1E2 – 514/340-8222,ext5390; Courrier électronique: envoy: ill.qmjg – Arlene Greenberg

Hôpital général Lasalle – Bibliothèque médicale, 8585, Terrasse Champlain, Lasalle PQ H8P 1C1 – 514/365-8310 – Technicienne, Marie-Noël Chidiac

Hôpital général de Montréal – Nurses' Library, Rm. E6-181, 1650, av Cedar, Montréal PQ H3G 1A4 – 514/937-6011, x4189; Fax: 514/934-8250; Symbol: QMGHN – Nurses' Librarian, Barbara Covington

Hôpital Jean-Talon – Bibliothèque médicale, 1385, rue Jean-Talon est, Montréal PQ H2E 1S6 – 514/495-6767; Téléc: 514/495-6772; Symbol: QMHJT – Pierrette Galarneau

Hôpital Louis-H. Lafontaine – Bibliothèque du personnel, 7401, rue Hochelaga, Montréal PQ H1N 3M5 – 514.251-4000, ext. 2964; Téléc: 514/251-0270; Symbol: QMLHL – Bibliothécaire en chef, Camil Lemire

Hôpital Maisonneuve-Rosemont – Bibliothèque médicale, 5415, boul de l'Assomption, Montréal PQ H1T 2M4 – 514/252-3462; Téléc: 514/252-3574; Courrier électronique: lachaped@ere.umontreal.ca; Symbol: QMHMR – Chef-bibliothécaire, Hélène Lauzon

Hôpital Marie Enfant – Centre de documentation, 5200, rue Belanger est, Montréal PQ H1T 1C9 – 514/374-1710, poste 2033; Téléc: 514/374-6803; Symbol: QMHME – Bibliothécaire, Anca Cojocaru

Hôpital de Montréal pour enfants – Bibliothèque médicale, 2300, rue Tupper, Montréal PQ H3H 1P3 – 514/934-4400; Téléc: 514/934-4345 – Joanne Baird

Hôpital Nôtre-Dame – Bibliothèque, 1560, rue Sherbrooke est, Montréal PQ H2L 4M1 – 514/876-7217; Téléc: 514/876-6748; Symbol: QMHND – Bibliothécaire en chef, André Allard

Hôpital Rivière-des-Prairies – Bibliothèque du personnel, 7070, boul Perras, Montréal PQ H1E 1A4 – 514/323-7260; Courrier électronique: fortinsy@ere.umontréal.ca; Symbol: QMHRP – Head, Robert Aubin

Hôpital Royal Victoria – Bibliothèque du pavillon des femmes, 687, av des Pins ouest, Montréal PQ H3A 1A1 – 514/842-1231; Téléc: 514/843-1678; Symbol: QMRVW – Bibliothécaire, Lynda Dickson

Hôpital du Sacré-Coeur de Montréal – Bibliothèque Norman-Bethune, 5400, boul Gouin ouest, Montréal PQ H4J 1C5 – 514/338-4284 – Bibliothécaire, Jean-Pierre Morissette

Bibliothèque Albert-Prévost, 6555, boul Gouin ouest, Montréal PQ H4K 4M1 – 514/338-2160; Symbol: QMIAP – Bibliothécaire, Jean-Pierre Morissette

Équipe régionale en santé au travail et environnementale - Centre de documentation, #240, 75, rue de Port-Royal Est, Montréal PQ H3L 3T1 – 514/858-7510, poste 267; Téléc: 514/858-5993; Symbol: QMHSCC – Bibliothécaire, Francis Lacasse

L'Hôpital Saint-Luc – Bibliothèque, 1058, rue St-Denis, Montréal PQ H2X 3J4 – 514/281-2121, poste 5867; Téléc: 514/281-2501; Courrier électronique: ENVOY: QMHSL; Symbol: QMHSL – Chef du service de soutien à l'enseignement, Pierre Duchesneau

Hôpital Saint-Luc - Département de santé communautaire - Centre de documentation, 1001, rue Saint-Denis, Montréal PQ H2X 3H9 – 514/281-4076; Téléc: 514/281-4099 – Colette Bérubé

Hôpital Sainte-Anne – Centre de documentation, 305, rue Saint-Pierre, Sainte-Anne-de-Bellevuew PQ H9X 1Y9 – 514/457-2761 – Technicien, Pierre Turcotte

Hôpital Sainte-Jeanne d'Arc de Montréal – Bibliothèque médicale, 3570, rue St-Urbain, Montréal PQ H2X 2N8 – 514/282-6951

Hôpital Sainte-Justine – Centre d'information sur la santé de l'enfant, 3175, ch de la Côte Ste-Catherine, Montréal PQ H3T 1C5 – 514/345-4680; Téléc: 514/345-4806; Courrier électronique: Envoy: QMSTJ; lecomptl@ere.umo; Symbol: QMSTJ – Chef de service, Louis-Luc Lecompte

Hôpital Santa Cabrini – Centre de documentation, 5655, rue St-Zotique est, Montréal PQ H1T 1P7 – 514/252-6488; Téléc: 514/252-6535; Symbol: QMHSCA – Bibliotechnicienne, Diane Séguin

Hôtel-Dieu de Montréal – Centre de documentation, 3840, rue St-Urbain, Montréal PQ H2W 1T8 – 514/843-2611, poste 5355; Téléc: 514/843-2730; Courrier électronique: boyerg@ere.umontreal.ca; Symbol: QMHD – Chef du centre de documentation, Ginette Boyer

Human Resources Development Canada - Regional Library, 1441, rue St-Urbain, CP 7500, Montréal PQ H3C 3L4 – 514/283-7586; Reference: 514/283-4695; Téléc: 514/283-1386; Symbol: QMMIQ – Regional Chief, Jacinthe Castonguay

Hydro-Québec - Bibliothèque, 75, boul René-Lévesque ouest, Montréal PQ H2Z 1A4 – 514/289-2145; Téléc: 514/289-3750; Courrier électronique: se1024@mailgtway.vpi.hydro.qc.ca;

Symbol: QMH – Chef de service, Claude-André Bonin

Immigration & Refugee Board - Documentation Centre, #102, 200, boul René-Lévesque ouest, Montréal PQ H2Z 1X4 – 514/496-6530; Reference: 514/496-6529; Fax: 514/496-1709; Symbol: QMCIS – Chief, Serge Vallée

Imperial Tobacco Ltd. - Corporate Library, 3810, rue Saint-Antoine ouest, PO Box 6500, Montréal PQ H3C 3L6 – 514/932-6161; Fax: 514/932-0383; Symbol: QMIT – Corporate Librarian, Yolande Mukherjee

Industry Canada - Centre for Information Technologies Innovation, 1575, boul Chomedey, Laval PQ H7V 2X2 – 514/973-5740; Fax: 514/973-5757; Email: siri@citi.doc.ca
 Manager, Marcel Simoneau
 Reference Librarian, Marie-Cecile Domeco, 514/973-5748
 Library Technician, Chantal Gasse
 Indexation Librarian, Anne Simard
 Info Entrepreneurs - Documentation Centre, #12500, 5, Place Ville Marie, Niveau Plaza, Montréal PQ H3B 4Y2 – 514/496-4636; Fax: 514/496-5934; Toll Free: 1-800-322-4636; Symbol: QMBFD
 Chief, Documentation Centre, Nicole Beaudry
 Reference Librarian, Sylvie Paquette
 Circulation Librarian, Carole Tousignant
 Technical Services Librarian, Claire Lavoie
 Acquisitions Librarian, Chantal Jetté

Institut du cancer de Montréal – Centre de documentation, 1560, rue Sherbrooke est, Montréal PQ H2L 4M1 – 514/876-7078; Symbol: QMINC – Technicienne, Chantal Corriveau

Institut de cardiologie de Montréal – Bibliothèque, 5000, rue Bélanger est, Montréal PQ H1T 1C8 – 514/376-3330; Symbol: QMICM

Institut d'études médiévales – Bibliothèque, 2715, ch Côte Ste-Catherine, Montréal PQ H3T 1B6 – 514/739-9868

Institut d'histoire de l'Amérique française – Centre de recherches Lionel-Groulx, 261, av Bloomfield, Montréal PQ H2V 3R6 – 514/278-2232

Institut interculturel de Montréal – Centre de documentation, 4917, rue St-Urbain, Montréal PQ H2T 2W1 – 514/288-7229 – Documentaliste, Réal Bathalon

Institut national de la recherche scientifique - Division de santé – Bibliothèque, 245, boul Hymus, Pointe-Claire PQ H9R 1G6 – 514/630-8812; Email: gilbert_leblanc@inrs-sante.uquebec.ca; Symbol: QMUQIS – Bibliothécaire, Gilbert Leblanc

Institut Philippe Pinel de Montréal – Centre de documentation, 10905, boul Henri-Bourassa est, Montréal PQ H1C 1H1 – 514/648-8461; Courrier électronique: beaudetn@ere.umontreal.ca – Normand Beaudet

Institut Raymond-Dewar - Centre de documentation spécialisé en déficience auditive, #034, 3600, rue Berri, Montréal PQ H2L 4G9 – 514/284-2581; Téléc: 514/284-0699; Symbol: QMISM – Chief Librarian, Sylvie Laverdière

Institut de réadaptation de Montréal - Centre de documentation, 6300, av Darlington, Montréal PQ H3S 2J4 – 514/340-2085, poste 2270; Téléc: 514/340-2149; Symbol: QMRI – Head of Library Services, Maryse Boyer

Institut de recherche en santé et en sécurité de travail - Québec – Bibliothèque, 505, boul de Maisonneuve ouest, Montréal PQ H3A 3C2 – 514/288-1551; TLX: 055 61348 – Bibliothécaire, Jacques Blain

Institut de recherches cliniques - Centre de documentation, 110, av des Pins ouest, Montréal PQ H2W 1R7 – 514/987-5599; Téléc: 514/987-5675; Courrier électronique: ENVOY: QMIRC;
Symbol: QMIRC – Bibliothécaire en chef, L.D. Bielmann

Institut Teccart inc. - Bibliothèque, 3155, rue Hochelaga, Montréal PQ H1W 1G4 – 514/526-2501; Fax: 514/526-9192 – Technicienne, Monique Thérien

Institut de tourisme et d'hôtellerie du Québec – Médiathèque, 401, rue de Rigaud, Montréal PQ H2L 4P3 – 514/282-5114; Toll Free: 1-800-361-5111; Symbol: QMTH – Services techniques, Céline Beauchemin

Institute of Community & Family Psychiatry - Library, Sir Mortimer B. Davis Jewish General Hospital, 4333, ch Côte Ste-Catherine, Montréal PQ H3T 1E4 – 514/340-8210, ext.5243; Fax: 514/340-7507; Email: adll@musica.mcgill.ca; Symbol: QMJGI – Librarian, Ruth Stilman

International Civil Aviation Organization – Library, 1000, rue Sherbrooke ouest, Montréal PQ H3A 2R2 – 514/285-8207; TLX: 05-24513; Symbol: QMIC

International Day Committee for the Eradication of Poverty – Library, 6747, rue Drolet, Montréal PQ H2S 2T1 – 514/279-0468 – Claude Dimitroff

International Society of Biometeorology – ISB Archive, Faculty of Agricultural & Environmental Sciences, McGill University, 21111, rue Lakeshore, Ste-Anne-de-Bellevue PQ H9X 3V9 – 514/398-7938; Email: AT28@MUSICA.MCGILL.CA – Secretary, N.W. Barthakur

Italian Chamber of Commerce in Canada – Library, #680, 550, rue Sherbrooke ouest, Montréal PQ H3A 1B9 – 514/844-4249; Toll Free: 1-800-263-4372

Jardin botanique de Montréal - Bibliothèque, 4101, rue Sherbrooke est, Montréal PQ H1X 2B2 – 514/872-1824; Téléc: 514/872-3765 – Botanist/Responsable, Céline Arseneault

Jewish Information Service Montréal – Library, 5151, Côte-Ste-Catherine, Montréal PQ H3W 1M6 – 514/737-2221

Jewish Public Library, 5151, ch Côte-Ste-Catherine, Montréal PQ H3W 1M6 – 514/345-2627; Fax: 514/342-6477
 Executive Director, Zipporah Shnay
 Reference Librarian, Ron Finegold
 Circulation Librarian, Eleanor Steinberg
 Public Services Librarian, Clare Stern
 Technical Services Librarian, Helen Bassal
 Archivist, Carol Katz
 Children's Librarian, Eva Raby

Jewish Rehabilitation Hospital – Health Sciences Information Centre, 3205, Place Alton-Goldbloom, Laval PQ H7V 1R2 – 514/688-9550, ext.226; Courrier électronique: axis@musica.mcgill.ca; Symbol: OCHJC – Librarian, Irene Shanefield

John Abbott College - Library, PO Box 2000, Ste-Anne-de-Bellevue PQ H9X 3L9 – 514/457-6610, ext.331; Fax: 514/457-4730
 Chief Librarian, Janette Wygergangs
 Public Services Librarian, Douglas Armstrong
 Technical Services Librarian, Dale Biteen
 Collections Development Librarian, Sue Evans

Justice Canada - Montréal Regional Office - Library, Guy Favreau Complex, 200, boul René-Lévesque ouest, Montréal PQ H2Z 1X4 – 514/283-6674; Fax: 514/283-9690; Symbol: QMJM – Bibliothécaire en chef, André Archambault, 514/283-8739

Laboratoire de police scientifique/Laboratoire de médecine légale - Centre de documentation, CP 1500, Montréal PQ H2L 4K6 – 514/873-2704; Téléc: 514/873-4847; Symbol: QMJLP – Technicienne, Françoise Pothier

Laboratoire de santé publique du Québec - Centre de documentation, 20045, ch Sainte-Marie, Ste-Anne-de-Bellevue PQ H9X 3R5 – 514/457-2070; Téléc: 514/457-6346; Courrier électronique: lspq@interlink.net; Symbol: QSABS – Technicien, Marc-André Jobin

Lafarge Canada Inc. - Corporate Technical Services Library, 6150 Royalmount Ave., Montréal PQ H4P 2R3 – 514/738-1202; Fax: 514/738-1124; Symbol: QMLC – Head Librarian, Iréne M. Paulmier, 514/738-1202, ext.2274

Langlois Robert Law Office - Bibliothèque, La Tour Scotia, 1002, rue Sherbrooke ouest, 28e étage, Montréal PQ H3A 3L6 – 514/842-9512; Téléc: 514/845-6573; Symbol: QMLR – Chief Librarian, Jacqueline Chan Seng

Loisir littéraire du Québec – Bibliothèque, 4545, av Pierre-de-Coubertin, CP 1000, Montréal PQ H1V 3R2 – 514/252-3033

Lower Canada College - Library, 4090 Royal Ave., Montréal PQ H4A 2M5 – 514/482-9916; Fax: 514/482-0195 – Head Librarian, Maria Varvarikos

Loyola Peace Institute – Library, 2480 West Broadway, Montréal PQ H4B 2A5 – 514/848-7799

Mackenzie Gervais Law Office - Library, #1300, 770 Sherbrooke St. West, Montréal PQ H3A 1G1 – 514/842-9831; Téléc: 514/288-7389 – Librarian, Georges R. Thibaudeau

La Maison Jean Lapointe - Centre de documentation, 111, rue Normand, Montréal PQ H2Y 2K6 – 514/288-26111; Téléc: 514/288-2919 – Bibliothécaire, Claire Simard

Marchand, Magnan, Melançon, Forget Law Office - Bibliothèque, #1640, 600, rue De La Gauchetière ouest, Montréal PQ H3B 4L8 – 514/393-1155; Téléc: 514/861-0727 – Technicienne, Nadine Lemieux

Marius Barbeau - Centre de documentation en arts et traditions populaires, 6560, rue Chambord, Montréal PQ H2G 3B9 – 514/274-5656; Téléc: 514/274-7418

Marsh & McLennan Ltée (Insurance Brokers) - Research & Information Centre, 600, boul de Maisonneuve ouest, Montréal PQ H3A 3J3 – 514/285-5800; Téléc: 514/845-4548 – J. Cabanes

Martineau, Walker - Law Library, #3400, Tour de la Bourse, Carré Victoria, PO Box 242, Montréal PQ H4Z 1E9 – 514/397-4307; Fax: 514/397-7600, 7601; Email: biblio@martineau-walker.com – Librarian, Linda Patry

McCarthy Tétrault - Bibliothèque, 1170, rue Peel, Montréal PQ H3B 4S8 – 514/397-4214; Téléc: 514/875-6246 – Directrice de la bibliothèque, Agathe Bujold

McDougall, Caron - Bibliothèque, #2600, 1000, rue de la Gauchetière ouest, Montréal PQ H3B 4W5 – 514/399-1000; Fax: 514/399-1026 – Bibliothécaire, Stephanie Alyanakian

McGill University - Blacker-Wood Biology Library, Redpath Library Bldg, 3459, rue McTavish, Montréal PQ H3A 1Y1 – 514/398-4744; Fax: 514/398-8231; Email: maclean@lib1.lan.mcgill.ca; Symbol: QMMBZ – Biology Librarian, Eleanor MacLean
 Edward Rosenthall Mathematics & Statistics Library, Burnside Hall, #1105, 805, rue Sherbrooke ouest, Montréal PQ H3A 2K6 – 514/398-4676; Fax: 514/398-3899; Email: Roselib@math.mcgill.ca; Symbol: QMMER
 Librarian, Hanna Waluzyniec
 Library Technician, Mary Morter
 Health Sciences Library, McIntyre Medical Sciences Bldg, 3655, rue Drummond, Montréal PQ H3G 1Y6 – 514/398-4755; Fax: 514/398-3890; Email: Refdesk@healthlib.lan.mcgill.ca; URL: http://www.health.library.mcgill.ca; Symbol: QMMM – Life Sciences Area Librarian, David Crawford, 514/398-4723, Fax: 514/398-3890
 Libraries, 3459, rue McTavish, Montréal PQ H3A 1Y1 – 514/398-4677; Fax: 514/398-7356; URL: http://www.library.mcgill.ca; Symbol: QMM

Director of Libraries, Dr. Eric Ormsby, Email: ormsby@lib1.lan.mcgill.ca
Associate Director, John Hobbins, 514/398-7486
Associate Director, Frances Groen, 514/398-4722
Life Sciences, Librarian, David Crawford, 514/398-4723, Fax: 514/398-3890
McLennan Library of Humanities & Social Sciences, Librarian, Margaret Monks, 514/398-4698
Law Library, Librarian, Patricia Young, 514/398-4712, Fax: 514/398-3585
Branch Services, Librarian, Michael Renshawe, 514/398-7112, Email: renshawe@lib1.lan.mcgill.ca
Blackader-Lauterman Library of Architecture & Art, Head Librarian, Irena Murray, 514/398-4742, Fax: 514/398-6695
Education Library, Head Librarian, Marilyn Cohen, 514/398-4687, Fax: 514/398-2165
Howard Ross Library of Management, Head Librarian, Robert Clarke, 514/398-4691, Fax: 514/398-5046
Islamic Studies Library, Head Librarian, Adam Gacek, 514/398-4688, Fax: 514/398-8189
Marvin Duchow Music Library, Head Librarian, Cynthia Leive, 514/398-4694, Fax: 514/398-8276
Religious Studies Library, Head Librarian, Norma Johnston, 514/398-5043, Fax: 514/398-3903
Macdonald Campus Library, Barton Bldg, 21 111, rue Lakeshore, Ste-Anne-de-Bellevue PQ H9X 3V9 – 514/398-7879; Fax: 514/398-7960; Email: Envoy: PEB.QMAC; Symbol: QMAC
Head Librarian, Janet Finlayson, 514/398-7876, Fax: 514/398-7960
Public Services Librarian, Bruce Grainger
Osler Library (History of Medicine), McIntyre Medical Sciences Bldg, 3655, rue Drummond, 3e étage, Montréal PQ H3G 1Y6 – 514/398-4718; Fax: 514/398-5747; Email: lily@health-lib.lan.mcgill.ca; Symbol: QMMO – History of Medicine Librarian, June Schachter, 514/398-4720
Physical Sciences & Engineering Library, Macdonald Stewart Library Bldg, 809, rue Sherbrooke ouest, Montréal PQ H3A 2K6 – 514/398-4769; Fax: 514/398-3903; Email: pseref@lib1.lan.mcgill.ca; Symbol: QMME – Librarian, Hanna Waluzyniec, 514/398-4763
Walter Hitschfeld Environmental Earth Sciences Library, Burnside Hall, 805, rue Sherbrooke ouest, 5e étage, Montréal PQ H3A 2K6 – 514/398-8095; Symbol: QMM – Librarian, Carol Marley, 514/398-7453, Fax: 514/398-3903
McMaster Meighen Law Office - Library, 630, boul René-Lévesque ouest, Montréal PQ H3B 4H7 – 514/954-3159; Fax: 514/878-0605, 4428 – Librarian, Ronald Charest
Mendelsohn Rosentzveig Shacter Law Office - Bibliothèque, 1000, rue Sherbrooke ouest, 27e étage, Montréal PQ H3A 3G4 – 514/987-5043; Téléc: 514/987-1213 – Bibliothécaire, Marina Bélanger
Merck Frosst Canada Inc. - Research Library & Information Centre, PO Box 1005, Pointe-Claire PQ H9R 4P8 – 514/428-3323; Fax: 514/428-8535; Email: claire.kelly@merck.com; Symbol: QMCF – Manager, Claire B. Kelly
Ministère des Affaires internationales - Centre de documentation, 380, rue Saint-Antoine ouest, 4e étage, Montréal PQ H2Y 3X7 – 514/499-2170; Téléc: 514/873-7825; Symbol: QMCED – Library Technician, Marielle Bernard
Ministère des communautés culturelles et de l'immigration - Centre de documentation, 360, rue McGill, Montréal PQ H2Y 2E9 – 514/873-3255; Téléc: 514/864-2468; Symbol: QMIMM
Bibliothécaire, Denis Robichaud, 514/873-8379
Céline Laquerre, 514/873-3263
Ministère de la santé et des services sociaux - Service de la documentation, 201, rue Crémazie est, R.C. 04, Montréal PQ H2M 1L2 – 514/873-3685;

Symbol: QMSA – Bibliothècaire, Gérard Darlington
Ministère de la Sécurité publique - Direction des expertises judiciaires, Centre de documentation, 1701, rue Parthenais, CP 1500, Montréal PQ H2L 4K6 – 514/873-2704; Téléc: 514/873-4847; Symbol: QMJLP – Bibliotechnicienne, Françoise Pothier
Ministère du loisir, de la chasse et de la pêche - Bibliothèque, 6255, 13e av, Montréal PQ H1X 3E6 – 514/374-5800; Téléc: 514/873-2100; Symbol: QMMLCP – Bibliothécaire, Richard Mathien, 514/374-5840, poste 271
Ministère du revenu - Bibliothèque, 3, Complexe Desjardins, CP 3000, Montréal PQ H5B 1A4 – 514/287-8402 – Responsable, Lisette Desrosiers
Ministère des transports - Centre de documentation, 35, rue de Port-Royal est, 3e étage, Montréal PQ H3L 3T1 – 514/864-1666; Téléc: 514/873-7389; Symbol: QMTRA – Librarian, Vy-Khanh Nguyen
Montréal Gazette - Library, 250, rue St-Antoine ouest, Montréal PQ H2Y 3R7 – 514/987-2583; Fax: 514/987-2433; Symbol: QMGA – Reference Librarian, Donna Machutchin
The Montréal Holocaust Memorial Centre – Library, 5151, ch Côte-Ste-Catherine, Montréal PQ H3W 1M6 – 514/345-2605 – Archivist, Carole Katz
Montréal Neurological Institute - Library, 3801 University St., Montréal PQ H3A 2B4 – 514/398-1980; Fax: 514/398-5077; Email: ENVOY: ILL.QMNIH
Head Librarian, Carol Wiens
Reference Librarian, Avis Antel
Circulation Librarian, Claudia Ugolik
Musée d'art contemporain de Montréal - Médiathèque, 185, rue Ste-Catherine ouest, Montréal PQ H2X 1Z8 – 514/847-6254; Téléc: 514/847-6916; Courrier électronique: ENVOY 100: QMMAC.PEB; Symbol: QMMAC
Bibliothécaire responsable, Michelle Gauthier
Bibliothécaire de référence, Élaine Bégin, 514/847-6257
Technicienne en documentation, Jacqueline Bélanger, 514/847-6260
Technicienne en documentation, Ginette Bujold, 514/847-6259
Technicienne en documentation, Régine Francoeur, 514/847-6256
Technicienne en documentation, Johanne Lefebvre, 514/847-6255
Agente de secrétariat, Manon Garneau, 514/847-6923
Musée des beaux-arts de Montréal - Bibliothèque, CP 3000, Montréal PQ H3G 2T9 – 514/285-1600; Téléc: 514/285-5655; Symbol: QMFA
Bibliothécaire en chef, Joanne Dery
Bibliotechnicienne, Danielle Blanchette
Bibliotechnicienne, Diane Desmarais
Bibliotechnicienne, Silvia Tark
Le Musée Marc-Aurèle Fortin – Bibliothèque, 118, rue St-Pierre, Montréal PQ H2Y 2L7 – 514/845-6108 – Adjointe au directeur, Marcelle Trudeau
Musicaction – Bibliothèque, #209, 455, rue Saint-Antoine ouest, Montréal PQ H2Z 1J1 – 514/861-8444 – Secrétaire, Suzie Champagne
National Bank of Canada – Centre de documentation, 600, rue de La Gauchetière ouest, Montréal PQ H3B 4L2 – 514/394-5000, poste 5470; Fax: 514/394-4167; Symbol: QMBAN – Bibliothécaire, Agathe Sabourin
National Film Board of Canada - Customer Services - Reference Service, PO Box 6100, Montréal PQ H3C 3H5 – 514/283-9045; Fax: 514/283-5729; Toll Free: 1-800-267-7710; URL: http://www.nfb.ca; Symbol: QMNF – Head, Reference Library, Rose-Aimée Todd, Email: r.a.todd@nfb.onf.ca
National Research Council-Biotechnology Research Institute – Library, 6100, av Royalmount, Montréal PQ H4P 2R2 – 514/496-6117; Fax: 514/496-7885;

Email: belzile@biotech.nrc.ca – Librarian, Sylvie Belzile
National Theatre School - Library, 5030 St-Denis, Montréal PQ H2J 2L8 – 514/842-7954; Fax: 514/842-5661
Head Librarian, Wolfgang Noethlichs
Assistant to the Librarian, Monique Forest
Nesbitt Burns - Library, #300, 1501, av McGill College, Montréal PQ H3A 3M8 – 514/286-7200; Fax: 514/282-8104 – Librarian, Nicole Piggott
Noranda Technology Centre - Library, 240, boul Hymus, Pointe Claire PQ H9R 1G5 – 514/630-9524; Fax: 514/630-9379; Symbol: QMNR
Chief Librarian, N. De Brouwer
Reference Librarian, Jean Barrette, 514/630-9300, ext.213
Circulation Librarian, E. Eaton, 514/630-9404
Office des congrès et du tourisme du Grand Montréal – Bibliothèque, #600, 1555, rue Peel, Montréal PQ H3A 1X6 – 514/844-5400 – Personne ressource, Louise Lessard
Office franco-québécois pour la jeunesse - Centre de références, #301, 1441, boul René Lévesque ouest, Montréal PQ H3G 1T7 – 514/873-4255, 1-800-465-4255 (Québec); Téléc: 514/873-0067 – Responsable, Michel Lagacé
Office de la langue française - Service des bibliothèques, 800, place Victoria, 15e étage, CP 316, Montréal PQ H4Z 1G8 – 514/873-2997; Téléc: 514/873-2884; Courrier électronique: OLF.BIBLMTL; Symbol: QMOLF – Bibliothécaire, Chantal Robinson, 514/873-2996
Office des services de garde à l'enfance - Centre de documentation, 100, rue Sherbrooke est, Montréal PQ H2X 1C3 – 514/873-2323; Téléc: 514/873-4250; Ligne sans frais: 1-800-363-0310; Symbol: QMSGE – Responsable, Claire Bergeron
Ogilvy Renault Law Office - Library, #1100, 1981, av McGill College, Montréal PQ H3A 3C1 – 514/847-4747; Téléc: 514/286-5474 – Chief Librarian, Carole Méhul, 514/847-4701
Oratoire St-Joseph - Bibliothèque Sainte-Croix, 3800, ch Reine-Marie, Montréal PQ H3V 1H6 – 514/733-8211, poste 2341; Fax: 514/733-9735 – Directeur, Pierre Germain
Orchestre symphonique de Montréal – Bibliothèque, 85, rue Ste-Catherine ouest, 9e étage, Québec PQ H2X 3P4 – 842-3402, poste 213 – Archiviste, Jean Prévost
Ordre des infirmières et infirmiers auxiliaires du Québec – Bibliothèque, 531, rue Sherbrooke est, Montréal PQ H2L 1K2 – 514/282-9511; Toll Free: 1-800-283-9511 – JoAnne Beaulieu
Ordre des infirmières et infirmiers du Québec – Bibliothèque, 4200, boul Dorchester ouest, Westmount PQ H3Z 1V4 – 514/935-2501; Toll Free: 1-800-363-6048 – Chef de service, Maryse Dumas
Ordre des ingénieurs du Québec – Bibliothèque, 2020, rue University, 18e étage, Montréal PQ H3A 2A5 – 514/845-6141; Toll Free: 1-800-461-6141
Ordre des orthophonistes et audiologistes du Québec – Bibliothèque, #730, 1265, rue Berri, Montréal PQ H2L 4X4 – 514/282-9123
Ordre des pharmaciens du Québec – Bibliothèque, #301, 266, rue Notre Dame ouest, Montréal PQ H2Y 1T5 – 514/284-9588; Toll Free: 1-800-363-0324 – Directrice communications, Elaine Lacaille
Ordre des technologues en radiologie du Québec – Bibliothèque, #420, 7400, boul les Galeries d'Anjou, Anjou PQ H1M 3M2 – 514/351-0052; Toll Free: 1-800-361-8759 – Sec. de direction, Josée Turcotte
Organisation catholique canadienne pour le développement et la paix – Bibliothèque, 5633, rue Sherbrooke est, Montréal PQ H1N 1A3 – 514/257-8711; Courrier électronique: devp@web.apc.org – Documentaliste, Hélène Gobeil
Pfizer Canada Inc. - Medical Library, PO Box 800, Pointe-Claire PQ H9R 4V2 – 514/426-7060;

Fax: 514/426-6824; Email: ENVOY: HAYWARD.M; Symbol: QKPC – Scientific Information Officer, Miriam C. Hayward

Phillips, Friedman, Kotler - Law Library, #900, Place du Canada, Montréal PQ H3B 2P8 – 514/878-3371; Fax: 514/878-3691, 4676 – Librarian, Barbara Shapiro

Polish Institute of Arts & Sciences - Library, 3479, rue Peel, Montréal PQ H3A 1W7 – 514/398-6978; Fax: 514/398-8184; Email: cxsw@musica.mcgill.ca Director, Prof. Hanna M. Pappius Cataloguing Librarian, Sophie Boganski Librarian, Stefan Wladysiuk

Pouliot, Mercure Law Office - Bibliothèque, 1155, boul René-Lévesque ouest, 31e étage, Montréal PQ H3B 3S6 – 514/875-5210

Presbyterian College - Library, 3495 University St., Montréal PQ H3A 2A8 – 514/288-5256 – Librarian, Daniel Shute

La Presse - Centre de documentation, 7, rue St-Jacques, Montréal PQ H2Y 1K9 – 514/285-7019; Téléc: 514/285-6808 – Chef de division, Gérard Monette

Protecteur du Citoyen - Centre de documentation, 505, rue Sherbrooke est, Montréal PQ H2L 1K2 – 514/873-2032; Téléc: 514/873-4640; Ligne sans frais: 1-800-361-5804 – Bibliothécaire, Joanne Sonier

Protestant School Board of Greater Montréal - Professional Library, 6000 Fielding Ave., Montréal PQ H3X 1T4 – 514/483-7269 – Librarian, J. Wrench

Provincial Association of Protestant Teachers of Québec – Library, #1, 17035 Brunswick Blvd., Kirkland PQ H9H 5G6 – 514/694-9777

Public Works & Government Services Canada - Translation Bureau - Montréal Documentation Centre, #307, 200, boul René-Lévesque ouest, Montréal PQ H2Z 1X4 – 514/283-7519; Fax: 514/283-3877 – Head, L. Rebelo

Pulp & Paper Research Institute of Canada – Library, 570, boul St-Jean, Pointe Claire PQ H9R 3J9 – 514/630-4100; Symbol: QMPP – Marilyn McNamee

Québec Community Newspaper Association – Library, Glenaladale House, MacDonald College, 21111, rue Lakeshore, Ste-Anne-de-Bellevue PQ H9X 3V9 – 514/398-7706 – Administrative Assistant, Wendy Ethier

Québec Family History Society – Library, PO Box 1026, Pointe Claire PQ H9S 4H9 – 514/695-1502 – Librarian, Penelope Redmile

Québec Federation of Home & School Associations – Library, #562, 3285, boul Cavendish, Montréal PQ H4B 2L9 – 514/481-5619 – Donna Sauriol

Radio-Québec - Centre des ressources documentaires, 800, rue Fullum, Montréal PQ H2K 3L7 – 514/521-2424, poste 2094; Téléc: 514/873-7464; Symbol: QMRQ – Chef de service, Nicole Charest

Raymond, Chabot, Martin Paré et associés - Bibliothèque, Tour de la Banque nationale, #1900, 600, rue de la Gauchetière ouest, Montréal PQ H3B 4L8 – 514/878-2691; Téléc: 514/878-2127 – Bibliothécaire, Michele Bernard

Reader's Digest Magazines Ltd. - Editorial Library, 215 Redfern, Westmount PQ H3Z 2V9 – 514/934-0751; Fax: 514/934-2357; Symbol: QMRD – Librarian, P. Charlebois

Régie du cinéma du Québec - Centre de documentation, 455, rue Sainte-Hélène, Montréal PQ H2Y 2L3 – 514/873-2371; Téléc: 514/873-8874 – Directrice du classement des films, Carmen Watson

Régie du logement - Centre de documentation, Loc. 11.62, 1, rue Notre-Dame est, Montréal PQ H2Y 1B6 – 514/873-6575; Téléc: 514/873-6805; Symbol: QMRL – Responsable, Denise Barrette

Régie régionale de la santé et des services sociaux de Montréal-Centre – Services documentaires, 3725, rue Saint-Denis, Montréal PQ H2X 3L9 – 514/286-5604; Courrier électronique: CSSSRMM.REF; Symbol: QMCSSS – Responsable des services doc., Louise Bazin

Revenue Canada - Research & Library Services, 3131, boul St-Martin ouest, Laval PQ H7T 2A7 – 514/956-7052; Fax: 514/956-6915 – Library Technician, Claire Rozon
Research & Library Services, 305, boul René-Lévesque ouest, Montréal PQ H2Z 1A6 – 514/283-7725; Téléc: 514/283-6944; Courrier électronique: ENVOY: QMRE.PEB; Symbol: QMRE – Coordonnatrice, Gestion de l'information, Lucie Rebelo, Email: rebellu@cam.org

Robinson Sheppard Shapiro Law Office - Library, Stock Exchange Tower, #4700, 800, Place Victoria, PO Box 322, Montréal PQ H4Z 1H6 – 514/878-2631; Fax: 514/878-1865 – Librarian, Angela Tietolman, 514/393-4009

Rolls-Royce Canada Ltd. - Library, 9500 Côte de Liesse Rd., Lachine PQ H8T 1A2 – 514/631-3541; Fax: 514/636-9969 – Technical Librarian, Juliette Martin

Royal Bank of Canada – Information Resources, Place Ville Marie, CP 6001, Montréal PQ H3C 3A9 – 514/874-2343; Téléc: 514/874-2445 – Librarian, John O'Shaughnessy

Samson Bélair/Deloitte & Touche - Centre de documentation, #3000, 1, Place Ville Marie, Montréal PQ H3B 4T9 – 514/393-5066; Téléc: 514/393-7140 – Librarian, Nancy Bouchard

Sandoz Canada Inc. - Bibliothèque, 385, boul Bouchard, Dorval PQ H9S 1A9 – 514/631-6775; Fax: 514/631-1867; Email: ENVOY: QMSAC; Symbol: QMSAC – Bibliothécaire, Sharon Pipon

Sir Mortimer B. Davis Jewish General Hospital - Library, Institute of Community & Family Psychiatry, 3755, côte Ste-Catherine, Montréal PQ H3T 1E2 – 514/340-8210; Fax: 514/340-7507; Symbol: QMJGI – Ruth Stilman

SNC-Lavalin Environment Inc. – Library, Place Félix-Martin, 455, boul René-Lévesque ouest, Montréal PQ H2Z 1Z3 – 514/393-1000; Téléc: 514/866-6709; Symbol: QMSNC – Manager, Library & Records Management Services, Linda Thivierge

Social Justice Committee of Montréal – Library, 1857, rue de Maisonneuve ouest, Montréal PQ H3H 1J9 – 514/933-6797 – Coordinator, Derek McCuish

Société catholique de la Bible – Bibliothèque, #519, 7400, boul St-Laurent, Montréal PQ H2R 2Y1 – 514/274-4381

Société de criminologie du Québec – Bibliothèque, #620, 425, rue Viger ouest, Montréal PQ H2Z 1X2 – 514/873-4239 – Denise Trottici

Société de développement des entreprises culturelles – Centre de documentation, #200, 1755, boul René-Lévesque est, Montréal PQ H2K 4P6 – 514/873-7768; Symbol: SODEC – Responsable, Micheline Gougeon

Société d'habitation du Québec - Centre de documentation, #2223, 2, Place Desjardins, CP 456, Montréal PQ H5B 1B5 – 514/873-9611; Téléc: 514/873-2849; Symbol: QMSHQ – Responsable, Barbara Maass, 514/873-9611

Société historique de Montréal – Centre de documentation, 460, Place Jacques-Cartier, 2e étage, Montréal PQ H2Y 3B3 – 514/878-9008

La Société des musées québécois – Bibliothèque, CP 8888, Succ Centre-Ville, Montréal PQ H3C 3P8 – 514/987-3264

Société québécoise de développement de la main-d'oeuvre - Région de Montréal - Centre de documentation, 5350, rue Lafond, Montréal PQ H1X 2X2 – 514/725-5221, poste 310; Téléc: 514/725-4311; Symbol: QMCFP – Nicole Dumoulin

Société québécoise d'espéranto – Bibliothèque, 6358A, rue de Bordeaux, Montréal PQ H2G 2R8 – 514/272-0151 – Responsable, Normand Fleury

Société québécoise de spéléologie – Centre de documentation, 4545, av Pierre-de-Coubertin, CP 1000, Montréal PQ H1V 3R2 – 514/252-3006

Société Radio-Canada - Bibliothèque, A74-1, 1400, boul René-Lévesque est, Montréal PQ H2L 2M2 – 514/597-6265; Téléc: 514/597-6236; Symbol: QMCB – Bibliothécaire en chef, Michelle Bachand
Bibliothèque de l'ingénierie, 7925, ch Côte St-Luc, Montréal PQ H4W 1R5 – 514/485-5546; Téléc: 514/485-5885; Courrier électronique: stlauren@srcing.login.qc.ca; Symbol: QMCBE – Technicienne, Lysane St-Laurent
Music Library, 1400, boul René-Lévesque est, CP 6000, Montréal PQ H3C 3A8 – 514/597-6420; Téléc: 514/597-6241; Symbol: QMCBM – Acting Chief, Guy Peloquin

Société de radio-télévision du Québec - Centre de ressources documentaires, 655, rue Parthenais, Montréal PQ J0L 2R0 – 514/521-2424, poste 2091; Téléc: 514/873-5729; Symbol: QMRQ Bibliothécaire, Nicole Charest Technicien, Cécile Brault

Société de transport de la communauté urbaine de Montréal - Bibliothèque, 800, la Gauchetiere ouest, Montréal PQ H5A 1J6 – 514/280-5220; Téléc: 514/280-5631 – Bibliothécaire, Victor Itesco

Sodarcan - Centre de documentation, #804, 1140, boul de Maisonneuve ouest, Montréal PQ H3A 1M8 – 514/288-0100, poste 3704; Fax: 514/282-9405; Symbol: QMGP – Odette Lavoie

Solicitor General Canada - Federal Training Centre - Library, 6099, boul Lévesque est, Laval PQ H7C 1P1 – 514/661-7786, ext.4505; Fax: 514/661-9485; Symbol: QLASGP – Librarian, Claire Jutras
Leclerc Establishment - Library, 400, Montée St-François, Laval PQ H7C 1S7 – 514/664-1320, ext.5505; Symbol: QLL – Librarian, Josée Sauriol

The Spiritual Science Fellowship of Canada – Library, PO Box 1387, Montréal PQ H3G 2N3 – 514/937-8539 – B. Lyman

Statistics Canada - Québec Regional Reference Centre, #412, Complexe Guy-Favreau, Tour Est, 200, boul René-Lévesque ouest, Montréal PQ H2Z 1X4 – 514/283-5725; Fax: 514/283-9350; Toll Free: 1-800-361-2831

Sureté du Québec - Centre de documentation, 1701, rue Parthenais, Montréal PQ H2K 3S7 – 514/598-4330; Téléc: 514/596-3682; Symbol: QMSU Bibliothécaire, Maureen Clapperton Bibliothécaire de référence, France Blackburn Technicienne, Francine Cusson

Tecsult Inc. – Bibliothèque, 85, rue Ste-Catherine ouest, Montréal PQ H2X 3P4 – 514/287-8546; Courrier électronique: biblitec@tecsult.com; Symbol: QMABB – Librarian, Louise Pichet

Teleglobe Canada Inc. - Bibliothèque centrale, 680, rue Sherbrooke ouest, Montréal PQ H3A 2S4 – 514/868-7272; Fax: 514/868-7234 – Lise Gill

Tourisme Québec - Centre de documentation, CP 979, Montréal PQ H3C 2W3 – 514/873-7977; Téléc: 514/873-4537; Symbol: QMTQ – Responsable, France Goyette

Towers Perrin - Information Centre, 1800, av McGill College, 22e étage, Montréal PQ H3A 3J6 – 514/982-9411; Fax: 514/982-9269; Email: tpinfo@lanter.net – Information Specialist, Josée Plamondon

Traditional Chinese Culture Society of Montréal – Library, 1733, Sanguinet, Montréal PQ H2X 3G5

Transportation Development Centre – Judith Nogrady Library, 800, boul René-Lévesque ouest, 6e étage, Montréal PQ H3B 1X9 – 514/283-0007; Fax: 514/283-7158; Email: ludgatg@tc.gc.ca; URL: http://www.tc.gc.ca; Symbol: QMTD – Head Librarian, Georgia Ludgate

Union Carbide/Pétromont - Documentation Centre, PO Box 700, Succ. Pointe-aux-Trembles, Montréal PQ H1B 5K8 – 514/640-6400, ext.1312; Fax: 514/645-8149 – M.C. de Jesus

Union des municipalités du Québec – Bibliothèque, #680, 680, rue Sherbrooke ouest, Montréal PQ H3A 2M7 – 514/282-7700

Union of the Vietnamese Buddhist Churches in Canada – Bibliotheque Tam Bao Som, 4450, av Van Horne, Montréal PQ H3S 1S1 – 819/687-2183 – Secretary & Principal, Pho Tinh

Université écologique internationale – Bibliothèque, #1, 2690, boul Pie IX, Montréal PQ H1V 2E7 – 514/899-5752 – Documentaliste, Claire Gagnon

Université de Montréal - Services des bibliothèques, 2910, boul Édouard-Montpetit, CP 6128, Succ Centre-Ville, Montréal PQ H3C 3J7 – 514/343-6905, 7643; Téléc: 514/343-2252; Courrier électronique: joffe@brise.ere.umontreal.ca; Symbol: QMU
 Directrice générale, Arlette Joffe-Nicodème, 514/343-6905
 Services aux usagers, Directeur, Gilles Picard, 514/343-7643
 Services techniques, Directrice, Ginette Darbon, 514/343-7687
 Bureau des systèmes, Directeur, Paul-Emil Provost, 514/343-2080
 Adjoint général, Jacques Boyer, 514/343-7646
 Banques de donnés, Adjointe, Christiane Robert-Guertin, 514/343-6070
 Développement des collections, Adjointe, Mireille Janeau, 514/343-7653
 Gestion du personnel, Adjoint, Michel Goulet, 514/343-7757
 Service de l'Audiovidéothèque, Chef, Ginette Gagnier, 514/343-7344
 Service de catalogage, Chef, Ginette Grégoire, 514/343-6899
 Service des acquisitions, Chef, Suzanne Simoneau, 514/343-7197
 Services des collections spéciales, Chef, Geneviève Bazin, 514/343-7753
 Service du prêt entre bibliothèques, Chef, Sylvie April, 514/343-6903
 Bibliothèque d'aménagement, Chef, Marc Joanis, 514/343-6009
 Bibliothèque de bibliothéconomie, Chef, Georges Clonda, 514/343-6047
 Bibliothèque de biologie, Chef, Ginette Gagnier, 514/343-7073
 Bibliothèque de chimie, Directrice, Josée Schepper, 514/343-6459
 Bibliothèque d'éducation physique, Chef, Johanne Hopper, 514/343-6765
 Bibliothèque de droit, Directeur, Clément Tremblay, 514/343-7095
 Bibliothèque EPC (Éducation, psychologie, communication), Chef, Robert Gauthier, 514/343-7242
 Bibliothèque de géographie, Directrice, Pâquerette Ranger, 514/343-8063
 Bibliothèque des lettres et des sciences humaines, Directrice, Pâquerette Ranger, 514/343-7430
 Bibliothèque d'optométrie, Chef, Danielle Tardif, 514/343-7674
 Bibliothèque de mathématiques et d'informatique, Chef, Jules Giroux, 514/343-6703
 Bibliothèque de médecine vétérinaire, Chef, Bernard Bédard, 514/773-8521
 Bibliothèque de musique, Chef, Marc Joanis, 514/343-6432
 Bibliothèque para-médicale, Chef, Johanne Hopper, 514/343-6180
 Bibliothèque de physique, Chef, Jules Giroux, 514/343-6613
 Bibliothèque de psycho-éducation, Chef, Tamara Rosenthal, 514/385-2556
 Bibliothèque de la santé, Directrice, Diane Raymond-Clerk, 514/343-6826
 Bibliothèque des sciences de la santé, Directrice, Diane Raymond-Clerk, 514/343-7810
 Bibliothèques scientifiques, Directrice, Josée Schepper, 514/343-5665

Université du Québec - Bibliothèque de l'Institut nationale de la recherche scientifique - Santé, 245, boul Hymus, Pointe-Claire PQ H9R 1G6 – 514/630-8812; Téléc: 514/630-8850; Symbol: QMUQIS – Documentalist, Gilbert Leblanc

Université du Québec à Montréal - Direction des bibliothèques, 455, boul René-Lévesque est, CP 8889, Montréal PQ H3C 3P8 – 514/987-6124; Téléc: 514/987-7787; Symbol: QMUQ
 Directeur général, Jean-Pierre Côté
 Adjointe au Directeur général, Denise Girard
 Dévelopment & exploitation des collections et des services, Directrice, Lisette Dupont
 Bibliothèque des arts, Responsable, Daphné Dufresne
 Bibliothèque centrale, Directeur, Rénald Beaumier
 Bibliothèque des sciences, Directeur, Conrad Corriveau
 Bibliothèque des sciences de l'éducation, Directrice, Lucie Verreault
 Bibliothèque des sciences juridiques, Directrice, Micheline Drapeau
 Services informatisés, Directeur, André Champagne
 Services techniques, Directrice adjointe, Claire Boisvert

Vanier College - Library, 821 Ste-Croix Ave., Saint-Laurent PQ H4L 3X9 – 514/744-7540; Fax: 514/744-7545; Email: ENVOY: VANIER.COLL.LIBRARY; Symbol: QMVC
 Chief Librarian, Beverly Chandler, 514/744-7543
 Collections Librarian, Carol Anne Inglis, 514/744-7538
 Reference Specialist, Michel Starenky, 514/744-7541
 Data Base Manager, Wendy Loucks, 514/744-7551
 Automation Coordinator & Systems Manager, Cheryl Holmes, 514/744-7550

Vidéographe inc. – Centre de documentation, 4550, rue Garnier, Montréal PQ H2J 3S7 – 514/521-2116, 2117 – Vidéothécaire, Laura Lefave

Villa Maria - Bibliothèque, 4245, boul Décarie, Montréal PQ H4A 3K4 – 514/484-4950; Téléc: 514/484-4492 – Irene Wagner

Ville de Montréal - Service de l'urbanisme, Centre de documentation, #5.100, 303, rue Notre-Dame est, Montréal PQ H2Y 3Y8 – 514/872-4119; Téléc: 514/872-0350 – Danielle Fortin, 514/872-4119

William M. Mercer Ltée - Information Centre, #1100, 600, boul de Maisonneuve ouest, Montréal PQ H3A 3J4 – 514/285-1802, ext.418; Fax: 514/285-8831; Email: monique_delorme@mercer.ca
 Manager, Information Centre, Monique Delorme
 Library Technician, Jacqueline Blouin

World Trade Centre - Inforum Montréal – Library, #2100, 380, rue Saint-Antoine ouest, Montréal PQ H2Y 3X7 – 514/849-1999 – Osvaldo Nunez

Wyeth-Ayerst Canada Inc. - Bibliothèque, 1025, boul Marcel Laurin, Montréal PQ H4R 1J6 – 514/744-6771; Téléc: 514/744-0550; Courrier électronique: ENVOY: QMAY.PEB; Symbol: QMAY – Nicole B. Pilon

NICOLET

Institut de police du Québec - Centre de documentation, 350, rue d'Youville, Nicolet PQ J3T 1X4 – 819/293-8631; Téléc: 819/293-8718; Symbol: QNIP – Technicienne en documentation, Dominique Laganière

Séminaire de Nicolet - Bibliothèque, #110, 900, boul Louis-Fréchette, Nicolet PQ J3T 1V5 – 819/293-4838; Téléc: 819/293-4161; Symbol: QNICS – Archiviste, Marie Pelletier

NOTRE-DAME-DU-LAC

Hôpital Notre-Dame-du-Lac – Bibliothèque médicale, 58, rue de l'Eglise, CP 310, Notre-Dame-du-Lac PQ G0L 1X0 – 418/899-6751 – Christine David

PASPÉBIAC

Centre local de services communautaires Chaleurs - Centre de documentation, CP 7000, Paspébiac PQ G0C 2K0 – 418/752-6611; Téléc: 418/752-6734 – Pierre Provost

PORT-CARTIER

Solicitor General Canada - Port-Cartier Establishment - Library, Airport Rd., PO Box 7070, Port-Cartier PQ G5B 2W2 – 418/766-7070; Fax: 418/766-6258; Symbol: QPCP – Librarian, Mick Boucher

QUÉBEC

Assemblée nationale du Québec - Bibliothèque, Hôtel du Parlement, Québec PQ G1A 1A5 – 418/643-4408; Téléc: 418/646-3207; Courrier électronique: ENVOY: PEB.QQL; Symbol: QQL
 Directeur, Gaston Bernier, 418/643-4032, Fax: 418/646-4873
 Reference, Circulation & Public Services, Head, Jean-Luc Fortin, 418/643-2708
 Catalogue, Technical Services & Acquisitions, Head, Clément Lebel, 418/643-1204
 Archives, Head, J.G. Pelletier, 418/646-0695
 Research, Head, Gaston Deschênes, 418/643-4567
 Clipping, Head, Jean-Claude Duval, 418/643-7596

Barreau de Québec - Bibliothèque, Palais de Justice, #5.03, 300, boul Jean-Lesage, Québec PQ G1K 8K6 – 418/649-3536; Téléc: 418/522-4560 – Directrice, Justine Landry, 418/529-0301

Bureau de la statistique du Québec - Centre d'information et de documentation, 200, ch Sainte-Foy, 3e étage, Québec PQ G1R 5T4 – 418/691-2401; Téléc: 418/643-4129; Ligne sans frais: 1-800-463-4090; Symbol: QQBS – Technicienne en documentation, Lorraine Carrier

Carrefour Tiers-Monde – Bibliothèque, 454, rue Caron, Québec PQ G1K 8K8 – 418/647-5853 – Agente d'éducation, Lyse Nadeau

Centrale des syndicats démocratiques – Bibliothèque, 801, 4e rue, 3e étage, Québec PQ G1J 2T7 – 418/529-2956 – Personne ressource, Louis Tremblay

Centrale de l'enseignement du Québec – Centre de documentation, #300, 1170, boul Lebourgneuf, Québec PQ G2K 2G1 – 418/627-8888; Symbol: QSTFCE – Responsable, Guy Duchesne

Centre d'arbitrage commercial national et international du Québec – Bibliothèque, Édifice la Fabrique, #090, 295, boul Charest est, Québec PQ G1K 3G8 – 418/649-1374; Montréal: 519/393-3774 – Céline Vallières

Centre François-Charon – Centre de documentation, 525, boul Wilfrid Hamel, Québec PQ G1M 2S8 – 418/529-9141; Symbol: QQCF – Bibliothécaire, Anne Potvin

Centre hospitalier universitaire de Québec - Pavillon St-François-d'Assise – Bibliothèque médico-administrative, 10, rue de l'Espinay, Québec PQ G1L 3L5 – 418/525-4408 – Coordonnateur administratif, Ulric Lefebvre

Centre local de services communautaire de la Basse-Ville - Centre de documentation, 50, boul St-Joseph est, Québec PQ G1K 3A5 – 418/529-6592, poste 283; Téléc: 418/529-1376; Symbol: QQCBV – Responsable, Ginette Rouleau

Centre local de services communautaires de Matane - Centre de documentation, 349, av St-Jérôme, Québec PQ G4W 3A8 – 418/562-5741; Téléc: 418/562-9236 – Marcel Bélanger

Centre of Entrepreneurship – Library, Faculté des sciences de l'administration, Université Laval, CP 2208, Succ Terminus, Québec PQ G1K 7P4 – 418/656-2490

Centre de prévention du suicide – Centre de documentation, 141, rue St-Jean, Québec PQ G1R 1N4 – 418/525-4588; Symbol: QQCP – Jean-François Sirois

Les Centres jeunesse de Québec – Centre de documentation, 540, boul Charest est, Québec PQ G1K 8L1 – 418/529-0603; Symbol: QQCSSQ – Lydia Chencinska

Collège François-Xavier Garneau - Centre des Médias, 1660, boul de l'Entente, Québec PQ G1S 4S3 – 418/688-8310; Téléc: 418/681-9384, 688-0087
   Service de la référence et choix de la documentation, Bibliothécaire, Andrée Lachance
   Service du Prêt, Bibliotechnicienne, Christiane Lavoie
   Services techniques, Bibliothécaire, Pierre Paré
   Bibliotechnicienne aux acquisitions, Jacqueline Dupont

Collège Jésus-Marie de Sillery - Bibliothèque, 2047, Chemin Saint-Louis, Québec PQ G1T 1P3 – 418/687-9250; Téléc: 418/687-9847 – Bibliothécaire, Jacqueline Lamontagne

Collège Limoilou - Bibliothèque, CP 1400, Québec PQ G1K 7H3 – 418/647-6704; Téléc: 418/647-6796; Courrier électronique: mgod@fedecegeps.qc.ca Bibliothécaire, Francine Pelletier
   Responsable du développement des collections, M. Godin
   Campus de Charlesbourg, Responsable, Centre des médias, Ann Murchison, 418/624-3612

Collège Mérici - Bibliothèque, 755, ch St-Louis, Québec PQ G1S 1C1 – 418/683-1591; Téléc: 418/682-8938; Symbol: QQCM – Bibliothécaire, Maryse Messely, 418/683-1591, poste 253

Commission d'accès à l'information - Centre de documentation, #420, 888, rue St-Jean, Québec PQ G1R 5P1 – 418/529-7741; Téléc: 418/529-3102; Symbol: QCAI – Responsable, Suzanne Plante

Commission d'appel en matière de lésions professionnelles - Centre de documentation, 900, Place d'Youville, 7e étage, Québec PQ G1R 3P7 – 418/644-4618; Symbol: QQCAML – Techniciennne, Monique Boies

Commission de la fonction publique du Québec - Centre de documentation, 8, rue Cook, 4e étage, Québec PQ G1R 5J8 – 418/643-1425; Téléc: 418/643-7264; Symbol: QQCFP – Bibliotechnicienne, Louise Guy

Commission de la santé et de la sécurité du travail du Québec - Centre de documentation, 524, rue Bourdages, CP 1200, Québec PQ G1K 7E2 – 418/643-2362; Symbol: QQCAT – Responsable, Germain Roy

Commission des normes du travail - Centre de documentation, 400, boul Jean-Lesage, 7e étage, CP 18500, Québec PQ G1K 8W1 – 418/646-8713; Téléc: 418/643-5132; Symbol: QQCDT – Responsable, Mireille Barrière

Commission de toponymie du Québec - Bibliothèque, #240, 1245, ch Sainte-Foy, Québec PQ G1S 4P2 – 418/643-8922; Téléc: 418/644-9466; Symbol: QQCT
   Responsable de la documentation, Yolande Morency
   Adjoint au président, Jean Poirier, 418/644-3689

Commission des transports du Québec - Bibliothèque, 5500, boul des Galeries, Québec PQ G2K 2E1 – 418/643-5970; Téléc: 418/643-8368 – Bibliothécaire en chef, Christiane Descarbeaux

Communauté urbaine de Québec - Centre de documentation, 399, rue St-Joseph est, Québec PQ G1K 8E2 – 418/529-8771

Conseil des colleges du Québec - Centre de documentation, 905, Autoroute Dufferin-Montmorency, 3e étage, Québec PQ G1R 5M6 – 418/644-2928; Téléc: 418/643-9019; Symbol: QQCC – Responsable, Micheline Poulin

Conseil de la famille - Centre de documentation, #1.66, 875, Grande Allée est, Québec PQ G1R 4Y8 – 418/646-5865; Téléc: 418/643-9832; Symbol: QQASF – Responsable, Suzanne Lamy

Conseil de la langue française - Centre de documentation, 800, Place d'Youville, 13e étage, Québec PQ G1R 3P4 – 418/646-1127; Téléc: 418/644-7654; Symbol: QQCLF – Responsable, Donald Belley

Conseil de presse du Québec – Centre de documentation, 55 1/2, rue Saint-Louis, Québec PQ G1R 3Z2 – 418/692-3008 – Documentaliste, recherchiste, Lisette Lapointe

Conseil du Statut de la Femme - Centre de documentation, #300, 8, rue Cook, 3e étage, Québec PQ G1R 5J7 – 418/643-4326; Téléc: 418/643-8926; Ligne sans frais: 1-800-463-2851; Courrier électronique: centre.doc@csf.gouv.qc.ca; Symbol: QQCSF – Responsable, Gabrielle Poirier

Conservatoire d'art dramatique de Québec - Bibliothèque, 31, Mont-Carmel, Québec PQ G1R 4A6 – 418/643-9184; Téléc: 418/646-9255; Symbol: QQCADQ – Responsable de la bibliothèque, Denise Gagné

Conservatoire de musique de Québec - Bibliothèque, 270, rue St-Amable, Québec PQ G1R 5G1 – 418/643-2068; Téléc: 418/644-9658; Symbol: QQCMQ – Bibliothécaire, Françoise Ménard

Fisheries and Oceans Canada - Laurentian Region - Documentation Centre, 104, rue Dalhousie, Québec PQ G1K 4B8 – 418/648-5250; Fax: 418/649-6698; Symbol: QQTCG – Regional Librarian, Jean Tremblay

Fondation québécoise du cancer - Centre de documentation, 1675, ch Ste-Foy, Québec PQ G1S 2P7 – 418/681-9989; Fax: 418/681-9947; Toll Free: 1-800-363-0063
   Directrice, Claire Voyer Gosselin
   Documentaliste, France Bélanger

Groupe Conseil Sauger - Bibliothèque, 6499, boul des Gradins, Québec PQ G2J 1E6 – 418/626-2374; Téléc: 418/626-9352 – Denis Maltais

Hôpital du Saint-Sacrement – Bibliothèque Delâge-Couture, 1050, ch Ste-Foy, Québec PQ G1S 4L8 – 418/682-7730; Symbol: QQHSS – Bibliotechnicienne, Diane St-Pierre

Hôpital de l'Enfant-Jesus – Bibliothèque scientifique Charles-Auguste-Gauthier, 1401, 18e rue, Québec PQ G1J 1Z4 – 418/649-5686; Téléc: 418/649-5627; Symbol: QQHEJ – Responsable, Madeleine Dumais

Hôtel-Dieu de Québec - Bibliothèque, 11, côte du Palais, Québec PQ G1R 2J6 – 418/667-9577; Symbol: QQHD – Lizette Germain

Hôtel-Dieu du Sacré-Coeur de Jésus de Québec - Bibliothèque médicale, 1, av du Sacré-Coeur, Québec PQ G1N 2W1 – 418/529-6851, poste 278; Téléc: 418/529-2971; Symbol: QQHDS – Christian Martel

L'Inspecteur général des institutions financières - Bibliothèque, 800, Place d'Youville, Québec PQ G1R 4Y5 – 418/694-5008; Téléc: 418/643-3336; Symbol: QQIF
   Bibliotechnicienne, Sylvie Nadeau
   Ghislaine Gagnon

Institut québécois de recherche sur la culture – Centre de documentation, 14, rue Haldimand, Québec PQ G1R 4N4 – 418/643-4695; Symbol: QQIQRC – Documentaliste, Louise Gauthier-Duguet

Institut de l'Énergie des pays ayant en commun l'usage du français – Bibliothèque, 56, rue St-Pierre, 3e étage, Québec PQ G1K 4A1 – 418/692-5727 – Chef, Service Documentation, Henriette Dumont

Literary & Historical Society of Québec – Library, 44 St-Stanislas, Québec PQ G1R 4H3 – 418/694-9147 – Sylviane Dubois

MFQ Vie, Corporation d'Assurance - Centre de documentation, CP 16040, Québec PQ G1K 7X8 – 418/644-4269; Téléc: 418/646-0370; Ligne sans frais: 1-800-463-5549 – Technicienne en documentation, F. Labrecque

Ministère des Affaires municipales - Centre de documentation, 20, av Chauveau, Québec PQ G1R 4J3 – 418/691-2018; Téléc: 418/646-9266; Symbol: QQAM – Responsable, Ernest-B. Roy

Ministère des Communications - Bibliothèque administrative (Edifice G & H), 1056, rue Conroy, Québec PQ G1R 5E6 – 418/643-1515; Téléc: 418/646-8132, 528-5822; Courrier électronique: PEB.QQMCG; Symbol: QQMC
   Directeur, Jean-Pierre Gagnon, 418/646-0976
   Responsable de la référence et des services publiques (G), Gilbert Plaisance
   Responsable des services techniques, Lise Villeneuve
   Responsable de la référence et des services publiques (H), Lucien Lévesque
   Centre de documentation, #320, 580, Grand Allée est, Québec PQ G1R 2K2 – 418/643-8537; Téléc: 418/643-7853; Symbol: QQCOM – Documentaliste, Michel Gagné

Ministère délégué aux affaires autochtones - Centre de documentation, Édifice H, 875, rue Grande-Allée est, Québec PQ G1R 4Y8 – 418/644-4446; Téléc: 418/646-4918; Symbol: QQSAA – Responsable, Marcel Plourde

Ministère des finances - Bibliothèque, #2.12, 12, rue St-Louis, Québec PQ G1R 5L3 – 418/691-2256; Téléc: 418/646-1631; Symbol: QQMDF – Responsable, Michèle Lavoie

Ministère de la Culture et des Communications - Bibliothèque de l'édifice Guy-Frégault, Bloc B, 225, Grande Allée est, 3e étage, Québec PQ G1R 5G5 – 418/643-3078; Téléc: 418/644-0380; Symbol: QQAC – Bibliothécaire, Hélène Larouche

Ministère de la santé et des services sociaux - Service de la documentation, 845, av Joffre, R.C., Québec PQ G1S 3L8 – 418/643-5572; Téléc: 418/646-2134; Symbol: QQIAS – Chef de service, Yvon Papillion, 418/643-5572

Ministère des ressources naturelles - Centre de documentation - Forêts, Édifice Bois-Fontaine, 880, ch Sainte-Foy, Québec PQ G1S 4X4 – 418/643-2570; Téléc: 418/646-0802; Symbol: QQFO
   Responsable, Marie-Ève Varin
   Référence, PEB, Jacques Hébert
   Acquisitions, Pierrette Labbé
   Traitement, Francine Vachon

Ministère du tourisme - Centre de documentation, #344, 2, Place Québec, Québec PQ G1R 2B5 – 418/643-5090; Téléc: 418/646-8723; Symbol: QQTO – Responsable, François Cantin

Ministère des transports - Centre de documentation, 700, boul René-Lévesque est, 21e étage, Québec PQ G1R 5H1 – 418/643-3578; Téléc: 418/646-2343; Symbol: QQTR – Responsable, Donald Blais
   Centre de documentation, 200, rue Dorchester sud, 3e étage, Québec PQ G1K 5Z1 – 418/643-2256; Téléc: 418/646-6195; Symbol: QQTRD – Bibliothécaire, Nicole Brind Amour

Ministère de l'agriculture, des pêcheries et de l'alimentation - Bibliothèque, 200A, ch Ste-Foy, Québec PQ G1R 4X6 – 418/643-2428; Téléc: 418/646-0829; Symbol: QQAG – Bibliothécaire, Chef de service, Hélène Babineau, 418/644-6244

Ministère de l'Éducation - Centre de documentation, Direction générale des affaires universitaires et scientifiques, 1035, rue de la Chevrotière, 19e étage, Québec PQ G1R 5A5 – 418/643-1572; Symbol: QQESE – Responsable, Claudine Tremblay
   Centre d'information multimédia, 1035, rue de la Chevrotière, 11e étage, Québec PQ G1R 5A5 – 418/643-6363; Téléc: 418/646-6561; Symbol: QQED – Responsable, Solange Cyr

Ministère de l'industrie, du commerce, de la science et de la technologie - Bibliothèque et gestion documentaire, #203, 710, Place d'Youville, Québec PQ

Canadian Almanac & Directory 1997

G1R 4Y4 – 418/691-5972; Téléc: 418/643-9719; Symbol: QQIC – Directeur, Jacques Fournier

Mouvement d'information et d'entraide dans la lutte contre le sida à Québec – Bibliothèque, #200, 175, rue St-Jean, Québec PQ G1R 1N4 – 418/649-1720

Musée de la civilisation - Centre de documentation, 85, rue Dalhousie, CP 155, Québec PQ G1K 7A6 – 418/643-2158; Téléc: 418/646-8779; Symbol: QQMUC – Responsable, Danielle Aubin

Musée du Québec - Bibliothèque, Parc des Champs-de-Bataille, Québec PQ G1R 5H3 – 418/643-7134; Téléc: 418/646-3330
   Bibliothécaire en chef, Louise Allard, 418/644-9908
   Reference, Bibliothécaire, Lucienne Gariepy, 418/643-7134
   Bibliothécaire, Richard St-Gelais, 418/646-4412
   Bibliotechnicienne, Nicole Gastonguay
   Bibliotechnicienne, Lina Doyon

Musée de l'Amérique française - Bibliothèque du Séminaire - Fonds ancien, 9, rue de l'Université, Québec PQ G1R 4R7 – 418/643-2158

Office de la langue française - Bibliothèque, 200, ch Sainte-Foy, Québec PQ G1R 5S4 – 418/643-4575; Téléc: 418/643-3210; Courrier électronique: OLF.BIBLQUE; Symbol: QQOLF – Responsable, Micheline Gagnon

Office de la protection du consommateur - Centre de documentation, #450, 400, boul Jean-Lesage, Québec PQ G1K 8W4 – 418/643-1484; Téléc: 418/643-8686 – Denise Martineau

Office des professions du Québec - Direction de la recherche/Centre de documentation, 320, rue St-Joseph est, Québec PQ G1K 8G5 – 418/643-6912; Téléc: 418/643-0973; Symbol: QQEDOP
   Bibliothécaire, André Contant
   Bibliotechnicienne, Denise Martineau

Patrimoine Canadien - Parcs Canada, Région du Québec, Bibliothèque, 3, rue Buade, CP 6060, Succ Haute-Ville, Québec PQ G1R 4V7 – 418/648-7380; Téléc: 418/648-4234; Courrier électronique: PARCS. QQPCQ.PEB; Symbol: QQPCQ
   Bibliothécaire, Hélène Tardif, 418/649-8259
   Technicienne, Hélène D'Amours

Le Petit Séminaire de Québec - Bibliothèque, Haute-Ville, CP 6100, Québec PQ G1R 4V7 – 418/694-1020; Téléc: 418/694-3363
   Directeur, Louis-J. Lépine
   Services techniques, Georges-Henri De Champlain

Regroupement de Sidac du Québec – Bibliothèque, #402A, 1026, rue St-Jean, CP 862, Québec PQ G1R 4P8 – 418/692-4790

Revenu Canada - Services Fiscaux, Québec - Bibliothèque, 165, rue de la Pointe-aux-Lièvres sud, Québec PQ G1K 7L3 – 418/649-4999, poste 3115; Téléc: 418/649-6765; Symbol: QQRT – Bibliothécaire, Christine Roy

Secrétariat à la condition féminine - Centre de documentation, Édifice H, 875, rue Grande Allée est, 2e étage, Québec PQ G1R 4Y8 – 418/644-4410; Symbol: QQSCF – Responsable, Alfred Letendre

Société d'habitation du Québec - Centre de documentation, 1054, rue Conroy, 3e étage, Québec PQ G1R 5E7 – 418/646-7915; Téléc: 418/643-4059; Symbol: QQSHQ – Technicienne en documentation, Jeanne-Mance Caron

Société historique de Québec – Bibliothèque, 171, rue Grande-Allée ouest, Québec PQ G1R 2H1 – 418/649-0085 – Bibliothécaire, Rev. Honorius Provost

Société de l'assurance automobile du Québec – Bibliothèque, 333, boul Jean-Lesage, CP 19 600, Québec PQ G1K 8J6 – 418/528-4291; Symbol: QQRAA – Bibliothècaire en chef, Michel Dupuis

Le Soleil ltée - Bibliothèque, 925, ch St-Louis, CP 1547, Québec PQ G1K 7J6 – 418/686-3394, poste 2510; Téléc: 418/686-3374 – Responsable de la documentation, Claudine Gagnon

Syndicat de la fonction publique du Québec inc. (ind.) – Centre de documentation, 5100, boul des Gradins, Québec PQ G2J 1N4 – 418/623-2424 – Bibliotechnicienne, Denise Joncas

Union québécoise pour la conservation de la nature – Bibliothèque, 690, Grande Allée est, 4e étage, Québec PQ G1R 2K5 – 418/648-2104 – Diane Neron

Université Laval - Bibliothèque, Pavillon Jean-Charles-Bonenfant, Cité universitaire, Québec PQ G1K 7P4 – 418/656-2008; Téléc: 418/656-7897; Courrier électronique: cbonnelly@bibl.ulaval.ca; URL: gopher://gopher.bibl.ulaval.ca; Symbol: QQLA
   Directeur, Claude Bonnelly
   Acquisitions, Jo-Anne Belair, 418/656-5991
   Adj. Systems, Daniel Prémont, 418/656-3448
   Cataloguing, Rosaire Caron, 418/656-6321
   Circulation, Librarian, N. Deschenes, 418/656-7995
   Collections sciences humaines et sociales, Chef, Claude Busque, 418/656-5196
   Collections scientifiques, Chef, Alain Bourque, 418/656-2948
   Collections spéciales, Chef, Agathe Garon, 418/656-2933
   Directeur adjoint, Philippe Houyoux, 418/656-3918; Email: phouyoux@bibl.ulaval.ca
   Subject Headings, Michel Fournier, 418/656-2871
   Technical Services, Charles H. Pelletier, 418/656-2888

Le Verificateur général du Québec - Centre de documentation, 900, Place d'Youville, 3e étage, Québec PQ G1R 3P7 – 418/691-5931; Téléc: 418/646-1307; Symbol: QQV – Responsable, Bertrand Auger

REPENTIGNY

Centre hospitalier Le Gardeur – Centre de documentation, 135, boul Claude David, Repentigny PQ J6A 1N6 – 514/654-9600 – Michèle Paquette

RICHELAIN

National Defence - CFB Saint-Jean, Richelain PQ J0J 1R0 – 514/358-7509; Fax: 514/358-7800; Symbol: QSTJCF – Library Technician, Réjean Messier

RICHMOND

Centre local de services communautaires du Val Saint-François - Centre de documentation, 110, rue Barlow, CP 890, Richmond PQ J0B 2H0 – 819/826-3781; Symbol: QRVSF – Martha Lemieux

RIMOUSKI

CEGEP de Rimouski - Bibliothèque, 60, rue de l'Eveché ouest, Rimouski PQ G5L 4H6 – 418/723-1880 – Coordonnateur, Carol Amiot

Centre hospitalier Régional de Rimouski – Centre de documentation, 150, av Rouleau, Rimouski PQ G5L 5T1 – 418/724-8394; Téléc: 418/724-8632; Courrier électronique: envoy 100: QRCH.PEB; chrr.doc@sie.qc.ca; Symbol: QRCH – Bibliotechnicienne, Nicole Bélanger

Conseil de la culture de l'Est du Québec – Bibliothèque, 88, rue St-Germain ouest, CP 873, Rimouski PQ G5L 7C9 – 418/722-6246, 6895 – Secrétaire administrative, Renée Poirier

Institut maritime du Québec - Centre de documentation, 53, rue St-Germain ouest, Rimouski PQ G5L 4B4 – 418/724-2822; Téléc: 418/724-0606
   Bibliothécaire, Bruno Lavoie
   Technicienne en documentation, Lise Gagné
   Responsable, Janine Lepage

Société généalogique de l'est du Québec – Bibliothèque, CP 253, Rimouski PQ G5L 7C1 – 418/722-3500 – Archiviste, Donald O'Farrell

Université du Québec à Rimouski - Bibliothèque, 300, Allée des Ursulines, Rimouski PQ G5L 3A1 – 418/724-1476; Téléc: 418/724-1621; Courrier électronique: ENVOY: PEB.QRU **Directeur; Symbol: QRU
   Directeur, Gaston Dumont, 418/723-1986, poste 1470
   Reference Librarian, Christian Bielle, 418/723-1986, poste 1479
   Circulation Librarian, Claude Durocher, 418/723-1986, poste 1474
   Archives Dept., Pierre Collins, 418/723-1986, poste 1669
   Acquisitions Librarian, Gérard Mercure, 418/723-1986, poste 1237

RIVIÈRE-DU-LOUP

Centre hospitalier régional du Grand-Portage – Bibliothèque médicale, 75, rue St-Henri, Rivière-du-Loup PQ G5R 2A4 – 418/868-1000; Téléc: 418/862-5778 – Hadrien Thériault

Collège de Rivière-du-Loup - Bibliothèque, 80, rue Frontenac, Rivière-du-Loup PQ G5R 1R1 – 418/862-6903, poste 238; Téléc: 418/862-4959 – Bibliothécaire, responsable du Centre des ressources didactiques, Marielle Tétreault

ROBERVAL

Claire Fontaine - Centre de documentation, 835, rue Lévesque, Roberval PQ G8H 3J5 – 418/275-1360, poste 144 – Lyne Prince

Hôtel-Dieu de Roberval – Bibliothèque médicale, 450, Brassard, Roberval PQ G8H 1B9 – 418/275-0110; Téléc: 418/275-2322; Symbol: QRHD – Bibliotechnicienne, Lise Laflame

ROUYN-NORANDA

CEGEP de l'Abitibi-Témiscamingue - Bibliothèque, 425 - boul du Collège, CP 8000, Rouyn-Noranda PQ J9X 5M5 – 819/762-0931, poste 1339; Téléc: 819/762-3815; Symbol: QRCN
   Directeur, André Béland
   Secrétaire, Lucie Laprise

Conseil de la culture de L'Abitibi-Témiscamingue – Bibliothèque, 51, Mgr Tessier ouest, Rouyn-Noranda PQ J9X 2S5 – 819/764-9511 – Agente d'information/Recherche, Camille Gauthier

Union des producteurs agricoles - Abitibi/Témiscamingue – Bibliothèque, 970, av Larivière, CP 610, Rouyn-Noranda PQ J9X 4K5 – 819/762-3006 – Marielle Audet

STE-ANNE-DES-MONTS

Société d'histoire et d'archéologie des Monts – Bibliothèque SHAM, 675, ch du Roy, CP 1192, Ste-Anne-des-Monts PQ G0E 2G0 – 418/763-7871 – Directeur, Père Roland Provost

STE-ANNE-DES-PLAINES

Solicitor General Canada - Archambault Institution - Library, 242, Montée Gagnon, Ste-Anne-des-Plaines PQ J0H 1H0 – 514/478-5960, ext.4505; Symbol: QSAA – Librarian, Lise Roy

Regional Reception Centre - Library, 246, Montée Gagnon, Ste-Anne-des-Plaines PQ J0N 1H0 – 514/478-5977, ext.7555; Fax: 514/478-7661; Symbol: QSAS – Bibliotechnicienne, Madeleine Montpetit

ST-AUGUSTIN-DE-DESMAURES

Campus Notre-Dame-de-Foy - Bibliothèque, 5000, rue Clément-Lockquell, St-Augustin-de-Desmaures PQ G3A 1B3 – 418/872-8041; Téléc: 418/872-3448 – Bibliothécaire, Albert Pruneau

Collège St-Augustin - Bibliothèque, 4950, rue Lionel-Groulx, St-Augustin-de-Desmaures PQ G3A 1V2 – 418/872-0954, poste 47; Téléc: 418/872-8249 – Directeur, Yvon Germain

ST-BENOÎT-DU-LAC
Abbaye Saint-Benoît-du-Lac - Bibliothèque, St-Benoît-du-Lac PQ J0B 2M0 – 819/843-4080 – Bibliothécaire, Père Martin Chamberlain

ST-CHARLES-SUR-RICHELIEU
Urgel Delisle & Associés inc. – Library, 426, ch des Patriotes, CP 60, St-Charles-sur-Richelieu PQ J0H 2G0 – 514/584-2207 – Engineer, François Granger

ST-EUSTACHE
Saulnier, Leroux & associés - Bibliothèque, #5070, 430, boul Arthur Sauve, St-Eustache PQ J7R 6V6 – 514/472-0031; Téléc: 514/472-7910 – Mylene Turcotte

ST-FÉLICIEN
CEGEP de St-Félicien - Centre de documentation, CP 7300, St-Félicien PQ G8K 2R8 – 418/679-5412; Téléc: 418/679-8357 – Responsable, Serge Bérubé

STE-FOY
Centre de recherche industrielle du Québec – Centre de documentation, 333, rue Franquet, Ste-Foy PQ G1P 4C7 – 418/652-2210; Fax: 418/652-2225; Email: hbeaumon@criq.qc.ca; Symbol: QSFCR – Chef de groupe, Madeleine Savard

Agriculture & Agri-Food Canada-Soils & Crops Research & Development Centre – Bibliothèque canadienne de l'agriculture, 2560, boul Hochelaga, Ste-Foy PQ G1V 2J3 – 418/657-7980; Courrier électronique: cotes@em.agr.ca; lbqsfag@nccco; Symbol: QSFAG – Spécialiste en information, Suzanne Côté

Archives nationales du Québec - Bibliothèque, 1210, av du Séminaire, CP 10450, Ste-Foy PQ G1V 4N1 – 418/644-4787; Téléc: 418/646-0868; Symbol: QQA – Chef des services au public, Jean-Pierre Therrien

Association professionnelle des meuniers du Québec – Bibliothèque, #115, 2323, boul Versant nord, Ste-Foy PQ G1N 4P4 – 418/688-9227

Association de santé et sécurité des pâtes et papiers du Québec inc. – Bibliothèque, #102, 1200, av Germain-des-Prés, Ste-Foy PQ G1V 3M7 – 418/657-2267 – Secrétaire, Julie Bélanger

Bureau de la coopération et du développement international – Bibliothèque, Université du Québec, 2875, boul Laurier, Ste-Foy PQ G1V 2M3 – 418/657-4378; TLX: 31623 – Guy Gagnon

Centre Cardinal-Villeneuve – Centre de documentation René-Paquet, 2975, ch Saint-Louis, Ste-Foy PQ G1W 1P9 – 418/653-8766

Centre hospitalier de l'Université de Québec – Bibliothèque des sciences de la santé/Centre de recherche, 2705, boul Laurier, Ste-Foy PQ G1V 4G2 – 418/687-1090; Téléc: 418/654-2247, 2714; Courrier électronique: ENVOY 100:BIBLIO.CHUL – Technicienne, Sylvie Bélanger

Centre international de recherche en aménagement linguistique – Bibliothèque, Pavillon Charles-de-Koninck, Université Laval, Ste-Foy PQ G1K 7P4 – 418/656-3232 – Claude Rocheleau

Centre de toxicologie du Québec – Section Information-documentation, Centre hospitalier de l'Université Laval, 2705, boul Laurier, Ste-Foy PQ G1V 4G2 – 418/654-2254; Téléc: 418/654-2148; Courrier électronique: ENVOY: PEB.QQCTO; Symbol: QQCTQ
Director, Albert J. Nantel
Deputy Director, Jean-Philippe Weber

Complexe scientifique - Centre de documentation, 2700, rue Einstein, F2, Ste-Foy PQ G1P 3W8 – 418/643-9730; Téléc: 418/643-3361; Courrier électronique: Michel_Levesque@infopuq.uquebec.CA; Symbol: QQCS – Responsable, Michel Lévesque

Conseil de la science et de la téchnologie du Québec - Centre de documentation, 2050, boul René-Lévesque ouest, 5e étage, Ste-Foy PQ G1V 2K8 – 418/644-4187; Téléc: 418/646-0920; Symbol: QQST – Bibliothécaire, Edith Dubois

Conseil supérieur de l'éducation - Centre de documentation, 2050, boul René-Lévesque ouest, 4e étage, Ste-Foy PQ G1V 2K8 – 418/643-3851; Téléc: 418/644-2530; Symbol: QSFCSE
Bibliotechnicienne, Patricia Réhel
Bibliotechnicienne, Francine Vallée

Directeur général des élections du Québec - Centre de documentation, 3460, rue de la Pérade, Ste-Foy PQ G1X 3Y5 – 418/644-9948; Téléc: 418/643-7291; Symbol: QSFE – Responsable, Jacques Gilbert

Environment Canada - Région du Québec, Bibliothèque, 1141, Rte de l'Église, CP 10100, Ste-Foy PQ G1V 4H5 – 418/649-6545; Téléc: 418/648-4613; Symbol: QQE
Head, Library & Records Management, Cécile Morin, 418/648-4768
Library Technician, Carmen Joseph
Reference, Librarian, Julia Innes, 418/649-6545

Fédération des commissions scolaires du Québec – Bibliothèque, 1001, av Bégon, CP 490, Ste-Foy PQ G1V 4C7 – 418/651-3220 – Clermont Provencher

Fédération québécoise des sociétés de généalogie – Bibliothèque, CP 9454, Ste-Foy PQ G1V 4B8 – 418/653-3940

Forintek Canada Corp. - Eastern Laboratory Library, 319, rue Franquet, Ste-Foy PQ G1P 4R4 – 418/659-2647; Fax: 418/659-2922; Email: doreen.liberty@qc.forintek.ca; Symbol: QSFF
Librarian, Doreen Liberty
Assistant Librarian, Gisele Tellier

Hôpital Laval – Bibliothèque des sciences de la santé, 2725, ch Ste-Foy, Ste-Foy PQ G1V 4G5 – 418/656-4563; Téléc: 418/656-4720; Courrier électronique: PEB.QSFHL – Bibliothécaire, Jocelyne Bellemare

Institut de la technologie du magnésium – Bibliothèque, 357, rue Franquet, Ste-Foy PQ G1P 4N7 – 418/650-3167 – Secrétaire administrative, Johanne Delaunais

Ministère de la justice - Bibliothèque, 1200, Route de l'Église, 4e étage, Ste-Foy PQ G1V 4M1 – 418/643-8409; Téléc: 418/643-9749; Symbol: QQJ
Responsable, Michel Ricard
Martine Boivin
Paulette Landry

Ministère de la sécurité publique - Direction générale de la sécurité civile/Centre de documentation, 2525, boul Laurier, 8e étage, Ste-Foy PQ G1V 2L2 – 418/646-6620; Téléc: 418/646-3564; Symbol: QSFCP – Responsable, Marie José Péan

Ministère du revenu - Bibliothèque, 3800, rue Marly, Ste-Foy PQ G1X 4A5 – 418/652-5765; Téléc: 418/643-4962; Symbol: QQRE – Responsable, Venise L. Roy

Ministère de l'Environnement et de la Faune - Centre de documentation, #57, 3900, rue Marly, 3e étage, Ste-Foy PQ G1X 4E4 – 418/643-5363; Téléc: 418/528-0406; Courrier électronique: ENVOY 100: PEB.QQEN; Symbol: QQEN
Responsable, Gérard Nobréga
Bibliothécaire de référence, Véronique Paré
Technicienne en documentation, Alain Aubin
Technicienne en documentation, Carole Robitaille
Secteur FauneLouise Buisson, 418/643-7522, Fax: 418/643-3330, Email: ENVOY 100: PEB.QQLCP

National Optics Institute – Library, 369, rue Franquet, Ste-Foy PQ G1P 4N8 – 418/657-7006; Email: cbeau@ino.qc.ca – Librarian, Chantal Beauregard

Natural Resources Canada-Canadian Forest Service: Québec Region – Library, 1055, rue du P.E.P.S., CP 3800, Ste-Foy PQ G1V 4C7 – 418/649-6956; Courrier électronique: ENVOY:QQMF.BIB; bizier@am.cfl.forestry.ca; Symbol: QQMF – Librarian, Gilles Bizier

Le Protecteur du citoyen - Centre de documentation, 2875, boul Laurier, Ste-Foy PQ G1V 2M2 – 418/643-2688; Téléc: 418/643-8759; Symbol: QSTFP – Documentaliste, Michèle Désiré, 418/644-6565

Public Works & Government Services Canada - Translation Bureau - Québec Documentation Centre, 1141, rte de l'Église, 3e étage, Ste-Foy PQ G1V 3W5 – 418/648-3906; Fax: 418/648-5700 – Head, M. Guilbault

Québec Geoscience Centre Library - INRS - Georessources, 2535, boul Laurier, PO Box 7500, Ste-Foy PQ G1V 4C7 – 418/654-2677; Fax: 418/654-2615; Email: ENVOY 100: CGQ.BIB; Symbol: QSFIG
Library Coordinator, Sonia Dupuis
Library Technician, Anne Robitaille

Régie des rentes du Québec - Centre de documentation, Place de la Cité, 2635, boul Hochelaga, 2e étage, Ste-Foy PQ G1V 4T3 – 418/644-3003; Téléc: 418/643-9012; Symbol: QQRRQ – Responsable, Nicole Paquin

REXFOR - Centre de documentation, 1195, rue Lavigerie, Ste-Foy PQ G1V 4N3 – 418/659-4530; Téléc: 418/643-4037; Symbol: QSTFR
Directrice des communications, Danielle Dussault
Technicienne en documentation, Réjeanne Fournier

Société de généalogie de Québec – Bibliothèque, CP 9066, Ste-Foy PQ G1V 4A8 – 418/651-9127 – Bibliothécaire, René Doucet

Société québécoise d'exploration minière - Centre de documentation, Tour Belle Cour, 2600, boul Laurier, 5e étage, Ste-Foy PQ G1V 4M6 – 418/658-5400; Téléc: 418/658-5459; Symbol: QSFS – Technicien, Daniel Sauser

ST-GEORGES
CEGEP Beauce-Appalaches - Bibliothèque, 1055, rue 116e, St-Georges PQ G5Y 3G1 – 418/228-8896; Fax: 418/228-0562 – Georges-Henri Goulet

ST-HUBERT
Centre local de services communautaires St-Hubert - Centre de documentation, 6800, boul Cousineau, St-Hubert PQ J3Y 8Z4 – 514/443-7413; Téléc: 514/676-4645 – Technicienne, Hélène Goggin

National Defence - Land Force Command Headquarters - Main Library, St-Hubert PQ J3Y 5T5 – 514/462-7083; Fax: 514/462-8025; Symbol: QSTHUM – Librarian, Mary Finlay

SAINT-HYACINTHE
Agriculture & Agri-Food Canada-Food Research & Development Centre – Bibliothèque canadienne de l'agriculture, 3600, boul Casavant ouest, Saint-Hyacinthe PQ J2S 8E3 – 514/773-1105; Courrier électronique: bernarf@em.agr.ca; Symbol: QSHAG – Librarian, Francine Bernard

Fondation du conseil des gouverneurs du centre de recherche et de développement sur les aliments inc. - CRDA, 3600, boul Casavant ouest, Saint-Hyacinthe PQ J2S 8E3 – 514/773-1105 – Francine Bernard

Hôtel-Dieu – Centre de documentation, 1800, rue Dessaulles, Saint-Hyacinthe PQ J2S 2T2 – 514/774-6495 – Paul-Albert Dufour

Séminaire de St-Hyacinthe - Bibliothèque, 650, rue Girouard est, CP 370, Saint-Hyacinthe PQ J2S 7B7 – 514/774-8977; Téléc: 514/774-7101 – Bibliothécaire, Bernard Auger

ST-JEAN
Collège Militaire Royal de Saint-Jean - Bibliothèque, St-Jean PQ J0J 1R0 – 514/358-6602; Téléc: 514/358-6799; Courrier électronique: cheungg@cmr.ca; Symbol: QSTJ
Directrice, Gretchen Cheung, 514/358-6602
Bibliothécaire, Paul Tremblay, 514/358-6608

Librarian, Léandre Racicot, 514/358-6506
Acquisitions Librarian, Lise Laflèche, 514/358-6607

ST-JEAN-SUR-RICHELIEU

Agriculture & Agri-Food Canada-Horticulture Research & Development Centre – Bibliothèque canadienne de l'agriculture, 430, boul Gouin, CP 457, St-Jean-sur-Richelieu PQ J3B 3E6 – 514/346-4494; Courrier électronique: lbqstjag@ncccot.agr.ca; Symbol: QSTJAG

CEGEP St-Jean-sur-Richelieu - Bibliothèque, 30, boul du Séminaire, CP 1018, St-Jean-sur-Richelieu PQ J3B 7B1 – 514/347-5301; Téléc: 514/347-3329

Bibliothécaire en chef, Michel Robert

Bibliothécaire, Robert Dufort

Chef, Services techniques, Johanne Lorion

Hôpital du Haut-Richelieu – Bibliothèque médicale, 920, boul du Séminaire, St-Jean-sur-Richelieu PQ J3A 1B7 – 514/359-5055; Téléc: 514/359-5064; Symbol: QSTJH – Technicienne, Hélène Héroux-Bouchard

Santé Publique, 485, rue Saint-Jacques, St-Jean-sur-Richelieu PQ J3B 2M1 – 514/346-3220; Téléc: 514/346-8787; Symbol: QSTJC – Technicienne, Hélène Bouchard

Oerlikon Aerospace Inc. - Bibliothèque, 225, boul du Seminaire, St-Jean-sur-Richelieu PQ J3B 8E9 – 514/358-2000; Téléc: 514/358-1744

ST-JÉRÔME

CEGEP St-Jérôme - Bibliothèque, 455, rue Fournier, St-Jérôme PQ J7Z 4V2 – 514/436-1580; Téléc: 514/436-1756

Coordinateur, Claude Riendeau

Bibliothécaire, Daniele Montreuil

Hôtel-Dieu de St-Jérôme – Bibliothèque, 290, rue Montigny, St-Jérôme PQ J7Z 5T3 – 514/431-8200, poste 2157; Symbol: QSJHD – Bibliotechnicienne, Francine Henri

Le Pavillon André Boudreau - Centre de documentation, 910, rue Labelle, St-Jérôme PQ J7Z 5M5 – 514/432-1395; Téléc: 514/432-8654 – Réal Daoust

Société de Jésus - Bibliothèque, 175, boul des Hauteurs, CP 130, St-Jérôme PQ J7Z 5T8 – 514/438-3993, ext.258; Téléc: 514/438-6617

Chief Librarian, Joseph Cossette, 514/438-3593, ext.258

Reference Librarian, Martine Proulx, 514/438-3593, ext.258

ST-LAMBERT

Champlain Regional College - Resource Centre, 900 Riverside Dr., St-Lambert PQ J4P 3P2 – 514/672-7360, ext.221; Fax: 514/672-9299; Email: herling@champlaincollege.qc.ca

Coordinator, Resource Centre, Peggy Herlinger, 514/672-7360, ext.220

Reference Librarian, Dale Huston, 514/672-7360, ext.345

Technical Services Librarian, Teresa Tyszewicz, 514/672-7360, ext.357

STE-THÉRÈSE-DE-BLAINVILLE

Collège Lionel-Groulx - Bibliothèque, 100, rue Duquet, Ste-Thérèse-de-Blainville PQ J7E 3G6 – 514/430-3120; Téléc: 514/430-2783 – Responsable de la bibliothèque, Marcel Paquin

SALABERRY-DE-VALLEYFIELD

Centre hospitalier Régional du Suroît – Centre de documentation, 150, rue St-Thomas, Salaberry-de-Valleyfield PQ J6T 6C1 – 514/371-9925, poste 2121; Téléc: 514/371-7454 – Chef Service Archives, Lise Clovel

SEPT-ÎLES

CEGEP de Sept-Îles - Bibliothèque, 175, rue de la Vérendrye, Sept-Îles PQ G4R 5B7 – 418/962-9848 – Khamsing Sundara

Centre hospitalier régional de Sept-Iles – Bibliothèque, 45, rue Père Divet, Sept-Iles PQ G4R 3N7 – 418/962-9761; Téléc: 418/968-9723 – Bibliothécaire, Brigitte Chiasson

SHAWINIGAN

Centre hospitalier Sainte-Thérèse – Centre de documentation, 1705, av Georges, Shawinigan PQ G9N 2N1 – 819/537-9351, poste 343; Symbol: OSHST – Responsable du Centre de documentation, Lise Gélinas

Collège de Shawinigan - Bibliothèque, 2263, boul du Collège, Shawinigan PQ G9N 6V8 – 819/539-6401; Téléc: 819/539-8819 – Colette Caron

Département de santé communautaire de la Mauricie - Centre de documentation, Centre hospitalier régional de la Mauricie, 550, av Broadway, Shawinigan PQ G9N 1M3 – 819/536-7546; Téléc: 819/537-3518 – Louise Côté

SHAWINIGAN-SUD

Centre hospitalier régional de la Mauricie – Bibliothéque médicale, 50, 118e rue, Shawinigan-Sud PQ G9P 4E7 – 819/536-7665; Téléc: 819/537-7687; Symbol: QSHCH – Responsable de la bibliothèque, Guylaine Vaugeois

SHERBROOKE

College du Sacré-Coeur - Bibliothèque, 155, rue Belvédère nord, Sherbrooke PQ J1H 4A7 – 819/569-9457; Fax: 819/820-0636 – Christine St Martin

Collège de Sherbrooke - Centre des médias, 475, rue Parc, Sherbrooke PQ J1H 5M7 – 819/564-6233; Téléc: 819/564-4025 – Gaétan Roy

Le Groupe Teknika – Bibliothèque, 150, rue de Vimy, Sherbrooke PQ J1J 3M7 – 819/562-3871 – Raymond Demers

Hôpital de St-Vincent de Paul de Sherbrooke – Bibliothèque médicale, 300, rue King est, Sherbrooke PQ J1G 1B1 – 819/563-2366; Courrier électronique: g.poirier@login.net; Symbol: QSHERSV – Responsable, Gilberte Poirier

Hôpital d'Youville – Centre de documentation et d'audio-visuel, 1036, rue Belvedere sud, Sherbrooke PQ J1H 4C4 – 819/821-5100, ext.2237; Téléc: 819/821-2065; Symbol: QSHERY – Technicienne, Louise Routhier

Hôtel-Dieu – Bibliothèque, 580, rue Bowen sud, Sherbrooke PQ J1G 2E8 – 819/569-2551; Téléc: 819/822-6767; Symbol: QSHERHD – Technicienne, Nicole Fontaine

Intervention régionale et information sur le sida en Estrie – Centre de documentation, #204, 6, rue Wellington sud, Sherbrooke PQ J1H 5C7 – 819/823-6704 – Susan Garand

Séminaire de Sherbrooke - Bibliothèque, 195, rue Marquette, Sherbrooke PQ J1H 1L6 – 819/563-2050, ext.46; Téléc: 819/562-8261 – Directrice, Ghislaine Pinard

Société de généalogie des Cantons de l'Est – Bibliothèque, CP 635, Sherbrooke PQ J1H 5K5 – 819/821-5414 – Ginette Arguin

Société d'histoire de Sherbrooke – Bibliothèque, 275, rue Dufferin, Sherbrooke PQ J1H 4M5 – 819/821-5406

Syndicat des professeures et professeurs de l'Université de Sherbrooke – Bibliothèque, 2500, boul Université, Sherbrooke PQ J1K 2R1 – 819/821-7656

Université de Sherbrooke - Services des bibliothèques, 2500, boul Université, Sherbrooke PQ J1K 2R1 – 819/821-7550; Téléc: 819/821-7935; Courrier électronique: chasse@catalo.biblio.usherb.ca; Symbol: QSHERU

Chief Librarian, Jules Chassé

Public Services Librarian, Michel Beaudoin

Acquisitions Librarian, Alain Keroack

Assistant Director, Pierre Gaudette

Bibliothèque des sciences de la santé, Germain Chouinard, 819/564-5297, Fax: 819/564-5378

General Library, Diane Quirion, 819/821-7553

Music Library, Sylvie Bareil, 819/821-8201

Law Library, Guy Tanguay, 819/821-7519

Science Library, Roger B. Bernier, 819/821-7099

Business Librarian, Daniel Beaulyeu

SILLERY

Régie de l'assurance-maladie du Québec - Bibliothèque, 1125, ch Saint-Louis, 7e étage, CP 6600, Sillery PQ G1K 7T3 – 418/682-5118; Téléc: 418/643-7312; Symbol: QQRAMQ – Technicienne de la documentation, Angèle Pouliot

SOREL

Hôtel-Dieu de Sorel – Centre de documentation, 400, av Hôtel-Dieu, Sorel PQ J3P 1N5 – 514/746-6068 – Claudette Laverdiere

STANSTEAD

Stanstead College - Bibliothèque, Stanstead PQ J0B 3E0 – 819/876-5876; Fax: 819/876-5891 – Bibliothécaire, J. Philip

THETFORD MINES

Centre hospitalier de la région de l'Amiante – Bibliothèque, 1717, rue Notre-Dame nord, Thetford Mines PQ G6G 2V4 – 418/338-0976; Téléc: 418/335-7673; Symbol: QTMH – Bibliotechnicienne, Jacinthe Ouellet

Gosselin, Ouellette, Grondin, Houle Law Office - Bibliothèque, 163, Pie XI, CP 667, Thetford Mines PQ G6G 5V1 – 418/335-9151; Téléc: 418/338-4874

Thetford Mines (Succursale Collège de la Région de l'Amiante) - Centre des ressources éducatives, 671, boul Smith sud, Thetford Mines PQ G6G 1N1 – 418/338-8591; Téléc: 418/338-3498 – Responsable, André Gamache

TRACY

CEGEP de Sorel-Tracy - Centre de documentation, 3000, boul de la Mairie, Tracy PQ J3R 5B9 – 514/742-6651 – Bibliothécaire, Jean-Marie Riopel

TROIS-RIVIÈRES

CEGEP de Trois-Rivières - Bibliothèque, 3500, rue de Courval, CP 97, Trois-Rivières PQ G9A 5E6 – 819/376-2059; Téléc: 819/376-4420; Courrier électronique: ldquy@fedecegeps.qc.ca

Coordonnateur, Denis Simard

Bibliothécaire, Daniéle Baillargeon

Bibliothécaire, Monique Paradis

Bibliothécaire, Quy LeDuy

Centre hospitalier St-Joseph – Bibliothèque médicale, 731, rue Ste-Julie, Trois-Rivières PQ G9A 1Y1 – 819/379-8112 – Solange De Rouyn

Centre hospitalier Sainte-Marie – Bibliothèque médicale, 1991, boul du Carmel, Trois-Rivières PQ G8Z 3R9 – 819/378-9878 – Lucie Grondin

Centre de santé publique à Trois-Rivières - Département de santé communautaire - Centre de documentation, 3350, boul Royal, Trois-Rivières PQ G9A 5Z4 – 819/378-9813; Téléc: 819/378-6600; Symbol: OTCRS – Technicienne, Jocelyne Drolet

Comité de solidarité tiers-monde/Trois-Rivières – Bibliothèque, 942, rue Ste-Genevieve, Trois-Rivières PQ G9A 3X6 – 819/373-2598 – Animatrice, Violette Tousignant

Conseil de la culture de la région Mauricie-Bois-Francs – Bibliothèque, 643, rue des Ursulines, Trois-Rivières PQ G9A 5B3 – 819/374-3242

Les Consultants René Gervais inc. - Bibliothèque, 3330, boul Royal, Trois-Rivières PQ G9A 4M3 –

819/371-3313; Téléc: 819/371-2288 – Technical Director, Réjean Blais

Fédération des caisses populaires Desjardins - Centre du Québec – Bibliothèque, 2000, boul des Récollets, CP 1000, Trois-Rivières PQ G9A 5K3 – 819/374-3594, poste 258 – Chef de gestion documentaire, Nicole Garneau

Régie de la sécurité dans les sports du Québec – Bibliothèque, #302, 100, rue Laviolette, Trois-Rivières PQ G9A 5S9 – 819/371-6033 – Responsable, Micheline Denis

Séminaire St-Joseph - Bibliothèque, 858, rue Laviolette, Trois-Rivières PQ G9A 5S3 – 819/376-4459; Téléc: 819/378-0607 – Bibliothécaire, Danielle Cossette

Université du Québec à Trois-Rivières - Service de la bibliothèque, 3351, boul des Forges, Trois-Rivières PQ G9A 5H7 – 819/376-5005; Téléc: 819/376-5144; Symbol: QTU – Directeur, Michel Jacob

VAL-D'OR

Centre hospitalier de Val d'Or – Bibliothèque médicale, 725, 6e rue, Val-d'Or PQ J9P 3Y1 – 819/825-6711 – Janine Desjardins

VALLEYFIELD

CEGEP de Valleyfield - Bibliothèque, 169, rue Champlain, Valleyfield PQ J6T 1X6 – 514/373-9441 – André Deschamps

VARENNES

Natural Resources Canada - Energy Diversification Research Laboratory - Library Services, 1615, boul Lionel-Boulet, PO Box 4800, Varennes PQ J3X 1S6 – 514/652-3210; Fax: 514/652-0999
  Library Services, Robin Majumdar, Email: robin.majumdar@ccsmtp.nrcan.gc.ca
  Administrative Services Manager, Gregory Giannuzzi

VICTORIAVILLE

Association québécoise du théâtre amateur inc. – Bibliothèque, 6, rue de l'Exposition, CP 977, Victoriaville PQ G6P 8Y1 – 819/752-2501 – Joceline Levis

Bureau local d'intervention traitant du sida – Bibliothèque, #110, 59, rue Monfette, Victoriaville PQ G6P 1J8 – 819/758-2662

CEGEP de Victoriaville - Centre de documentation, 475, rue Notre-Dame est, PO Box 68, Victoriaville PQ G6P 4B3 – 819/758-6401; Fax: 819/758-0333; Symbol: QVC – Documentaliste, Hélène Lupien

VILLAGE-DES-HURONS

Institut culturel et éducatif montagnais – Bibliothèque, #7, 40, rue Chef François Gros-Louis, Village-des-Hurons PQ G0A 4V0 – 418/843-0258 – Coordonnatrice de la culture, Marlène Rock

SASKATCHEWAN

Regional Library Systems with Member Libraries

CHINOOK REGIONAL LIBRARY

1240 Chaplin St. West, Swift Current SK S9H 0G8 – 306/773-3186; Fax: 306/773-0434; Symbol: SCR
Director, Michael Keaschuk
Branch Supervisor, Myra Leyshon

Abbey Branch Library, PO Box 185, Abbey SK S0N 0A0 – 306/689-2202 – Librarian, Marilyn Turgeon

Admiral Branch Library, PO Box 152, Admiral SK S0N 0B0 – 306/297-6354 – Librarian, C. Duclos

Burstall Branch Library, PO Box 309, Burstall SK S0N 0H0 – 306/679-2177 – Librarian, Judith Winter

Cabri Branch Library, PO Box 18, Cabri SK S0N 0J0 – 306/587-2500 – Librarian, Ruby Franke

Central Butte Branch Library, PO Box 276, Central Butte SK S0H 0T0 – 306/796-2222 – Librarian, Virginia Hemsworth

Chaplin Branch Library, PO Box 225, Chaplin SK S0H 0V0 – 306/395-2597 – Librarian, Carolyn Walls

Climax Branch Library, PO Box 322, Climax SK S0N 0N0 – 306/293-2006 – Librarian, Sue Smith

Consul Branch Library, PO Box 121, Consul SK S0N 0P0 – 306/299-2118 – Librarian, Linda Brown

Eastend Branch Library, PO Box 91, Eastend SK S0N 0T0 – 306/295-3788 – Librarian, Betty Ann Huhn

Fox Valley Branch Library, PO Box 42, Fox Valley SK S0N 0V0 – 306/666-2045 – Librarian, Valerie Reinboldt

Frontier Branch Library, 1 St. West, Frontier SK S0N 0W0 – 306/296-2147 – Librarian, Cindy Puszkar

Glentworth Branch Library, Main St., Glentworth SK S0H 1V0 – 306/266-2185 – Librarian, Meryle Iwanicki

Gravelbourg Library, PO Box 568, Gravelbourg SK S0H 1X0 – 306/648-3177 – Librarian, Bargara Douglas

Gull Lake Branch Library, Cultural Complex, Conrad St., PO Box 653, Gull Lake SK S0N 1A0 – 306/672-3277 – Librarian, Carol Springer

Hazlet Branch Library, PO Box 73, Hazlet SK S0N 1E0 – 306/678-2155 – Librarian, Linda Kulferst

Herbert Branch Library, PO Box 176, Herbert SK S0H 2A0 – 306/784-2484 – Librarian, Jane Epp

Hodgeville Branch Library, Main St., PO Box 68, Hodgeville SK S0H 2B0 – 306/677-2223 – Librarian, Edna Sauder

Kincaid Branch Library, PO Box 146, Kincaid SK S0H 2J0 – 306/264-3910 – Librarian, Trudy Turgeon

Lafleche Library, 157 Main St., PO Box 132, Lafleche SK S0H 2K0 – 306/472-5466 – Librarian, Diane Clermont

Leader Branch Library, 151 - 1 St. West, Leader SK S0N 1H0 – 306/628-3830 – Librarian, Delores Hudec

Mankota Branch Library, 1st Ave., Mankota SK S0H 2W0 – 306/478-2331 – Librarian, Doreen McCallum

Maple Creek Branch Library, 205 Jasper St., PO Box 760, Maple Creek SK S0N 1N0 – 306/662-3522 – Librarian, Violet Bethel

Morse Branch Library, Main St., Morse SK S0H 3C0 – 306/629-3335 – Librarian, Margaret Ferguson

Pennant Public Library, Standard St., PO Box 219, Pennant SK S0N 1X0 – 306/626-3316 – Librarian, Joanne Heeg-Williams

Piapot Branch Library, McDonald St., Piapot SK S0N 1Y0 – Librarian, Marlene Meacock

Ponteix Library, PO Box 700, Ponteix SK S0N 1Z0 – 306/625-3353 – Librarian, Marie Kouri

Prelate Branch Library, Main St., Drawer 40, Prelate SK S0N 2B0 – 306/673-2340 – Librarian, Darlene Wagner

Sceptre Branch Library, PO Box 128, Sceptre SK S0N 2H0 – 306/623-4244 – Librarian, Sherry Egeland

Shaunavon Branch Library, PO Box 1116, Shaunavon SK S0N 2M0 – 306/297-3844 – Librarian, Pauline James

Simmie Branch Library, PO Box 51, Simmie SK S0N 2N0 – 306/297-6217 – Librarian, Lorna Irish

Stewart Valley Branch Library, Stewart Valley SK S0N 2P0 – Librarian, Kathy King

Swift Current Branch Library, 411 Herbert St. East, Swift Current SK S9H 1M5 – 306/778-2752 – Librarian, Myra Leyshon

Tompkins Library, Main St., Tompkins SK S0N 2S0 – 306/622-2255 – Librarian, Carol Mitchell

Val Marie Branch Library, PO Box 205, Val Marie SK S0N 2T0 – 306/298-2133 – Librarian, Mildred Harbor

Vanguard Branch Library, Main St., Vanguard SK S0N 2V0 – 306/582-2244 – Librarian, Doris Burns

LAKELAND LIBRARY REGION

10023 Thatcher Ave., PO Box 813, North Battleford SK S9A 2Z3 – 306/445-6108; Fax: 306/445-5717; Symbol: SNB
A/Regional Director, Marie Sakon

Battleford Branch Library, PO Box 220, Battleford SK S0M 0E0 – 306/937-2646 – Librarian, Helen MacKay

Borden Branch Library, Borden SK S0K 0N0 – 306/997-2220 – Librarian, Helen Sutherland

Red Pheasant Branch Library, PO Box 155, Cando SK S0K 0V0 – 306/937-7761 – Librarian, Alvena Baptiste

Cut Knife Branch Library, Cut Knife SK S0M 0N0 – 306/398-2342 – Librarian, Shirley Bertoria

Denzil Branch Library, Denzil SK S0L 0S0 – 306/358-2118 – Librarian, Rose Reiniger

Edam Library, PO Box 203, Edam SK S0M 0V0 – 306/397-2223 – Librarian, Trudy McMurphy

Sweet Grass Branch Library, PO Box 80, Gallivan SK S0M 0X0 – 306/937-2974 – Librarian, Johanna Whitecalf

Glaslyn Library, Glaslyn SK S0M 0Y0 – 306/342-4748 – Librarian, Karen Smith

Goodsoil Branch Library, Goodsoil SK S0M 1A0 – 306/238-2155 – Librarian, Collette Himmelsbach

Hafford Branch Library, Hafford SK S0J 1A0 – 306/549-2373 – Librarian, Shelly Hrabia

Lashburn Branch Library, Lashburn SK S0M 1H0 – 306/285-4144 – Librarian, Theresa Coolidge

Lloydminster Public Library, 5010 - 49th St., Lloydminster SK T9V 0K2 – 403/875-0850; Fax: 403/875-6523; Email: ENVOY: ILL.LAL – Librarian, Ronald J. Gillies

Island Lake Library, PO Box 460, Loon Lake SK S0M 1L0 – 306/837-2188; Fax: 306/837-2266 – Librarian, Dorothy Waugh

Loon Lake Branch Library, PO Box 216, Loon Lake SK S0M 1L0 – 306/837-2186 – Librarian, Dorothy Waugh

Macklin Branch Library, Macklin SK S0L 2C0 – 306/753-2933 – Librarian, Hilda Gartner

Maidstone Branch Library, Maidstone SK S0M 1M0 – 306/893-4153 – Librarian, Joyce Weston

Makwa Branch Library, Makwa SK S0M 1N0 – 306/236-3995 – Librarian, Lynda Bertrand

Marsden Branch Library, Marsden SK S0M 1P0 – 306/826-5666 – Librarian, Denise Polkinghorne

Marshall Branch Library, Marshall SK S0M 1R0 – 306/387-6555 – Librarian, Donna Ferguson

Maymont Library, Maymont SK S0M 1T0 – 306/389-2006 – Librarian, Mary Scott

Meadow Lake Branch Library, PO Box 1237, Meadow Lake SK S0M 1V0 – 306/236-5396 – Librarian, Gwyn Breland

Medstead Branch Library, Medstead SK S0M 1W0 – 306/342-4609 – Librarian, Pauline Bovair

Meota Library, Meota SK S0M 1X0 – 306/892-2113 – Librarian, Doreen Griffith

Mervin Branch Library, PO Box 130, Mervin SK S0M 1Y0 – 306/845-2784 – Librarian, Mildred Cormack

Neilburg Branch Library, Neilburg SK S0M 2C0 – 306/823-4234 – Librarian, Sharon Schempp

Mosquito Branch Library, PO Box 368, North Battleford SK S9A 2Z3 – 306/937-2093 – Librarian, Audrey Wahobin

North Battleford Public Library, 1392 - 101st St., North Battleford SK S9A 1A2 – 306/445-3206 – Librarian, Anne Marie Hillson

Saskatchewan Hospital Branch Library, c/o Saskatchewan Hospital, PO Box 39, North Battleford SK S9A 2X8 – 306/446-7913 – Librarian, Dianne Philippon

Paradise Hill Branch Library, Paradise Hill SK S0M 2G0 – 306/344-2206 – Librarian, Dianne Palsich

Little Pine Branch Library, PO Box 327, Paynton SK S0M 2J0 – 306/398-2925 – Librarian, Eileen Frank

Paynton Branch Library, Paynton SK S0M 2J0 – 306/895-2175 – Librarian, Bev Webb

Poundmaker Branch Library, PO Box 329, Paynton SK S0M 0N0 – 306/398-4966 – Librarian, Arlene Chickosis

Joseph Bighead Branch Library, c/o Chief Napayo School, Pierceland SK S0M 2K0 – 306/839-2297 – Librarian, Donna Weinkauf

Pierceland Library, Pierceland SK S0M 2K0 – 306/839-2166 – Librarian, Anita Murphy

Rabbit Lake Branch Library, Rabbit Lake SK S0M 2L0 – 306/824-2089 – Librarian, Laura Ricketts

Radisson Branch Library, Radisson SK S0K 3L0 – 306/827-2118 – Librarian, Linda Brookman

St. Walburg Branch Library, St Walburg SK S0M 2T0 – 306/248-3250 – Librarian, Gen Etcheverry

Speers Branch Library, Speers SK S0M 2V0 – 306/246-4866 – Librarian, Maureen Kachmarski

Thunderchild Branch Library, PO Box 34, Turtleford SK S0M 2Y0 – 306/845-2071 – Librarian, Elaine Standingwater

Turtleford Branch Library, Turtleford SK S0M 2Y0 – 306/845-2074 – Librarian, June Heath

Waterhen Lake Branch Library, Waterhen Lake SK S0M 3B0 – 306/236-4723; Fax: 306/236-6523 – Librarian, Delphine Vincent

PAHKISIMON NUYEAH LIBRARY SYSTEM

PO Box 6600, La Ronge SK S0J 1L0 – 306/425-4525; Fax: 306/425-4572; Email: pnlshq@pnls.lib.sk.ca; Symbol: SLPN

Director, Audrey Mark

Public Library Coordinator, Arlene Kolosky, 306/425-4552

Teacher/Librarian, Harriet Roy, 306/425-4598

Beauval Public Library, Bag Service 9000, Beauval SK S0M 0G0 – 306/288-2022; Fax: 306/288-2202 – Carol Buffin

Wisewood Public Library, PO Box 309, Buffalo Narrows SK S0M 0J0 – 306/235-4240; Fax: 306/235-4452 – Branch Head, Darlene Petit

Cumberland House Library, PO Box 40, Cumberland House SK S0E 0S0 – 306/888-2181; Fax: 306/888-2193 – Elaine Crate

Deschambault Lake Library, General Delivery, Deschambault Lake SK S0P 0C0 – 306/632-4446; Fax: 306/632-4700 – Nicole Ballantyne

Ile a la Crosse Public Library, PO Box 70, Ile a la Crosse SK S0M 1C0 – 306/833-2010; Fax: 306/833-2322 – Myra Gardiner

La Loche Public Library, PO Box 4, La Loche SK S0M 1G0 – 306/822-2151; Fax: 306/822-2280 – Branch Head, Chris Cardinal

La Ronge Public Library, PO Box 5680, La Ronge SK S0J 1L0 – 306/425-2160; Fax: 306/425-3883 – Librarian, Delia Jorgensen

Senator Miles Venne School Public Library, PO Box 328, La Ronge SK S0J 1L0 – 306/425-2478; Fax: 306/425-2815 – Branch Head, Edna Mirasty

Montreal Lake Community Library, General Delivery, Montreal Lake SK S0J 1Y0 – 306/663-5602; Fax: 306/663-5652 – Deidre MacGregor

Tawowikamik Public Library, PO Box 100, Pelican Narrows SK S0P 0E0 – 306/632-2161; Fax: 306/632-2110 – Branch Head, Marilyn Ballantyne

Sandy Bay Public Library, PO Box 150, Sandy Bay SK S0P 0G0 – 306/754-2139; Fax: 306/754-2130 – Geraldine Merasty

Keethanow Public Library, General Delivery, Stanley Mission SK S0J 2P0 – 306/635-2104; Fax: 306/635-2050 – Branch Head, Lucy Ratt

PALLISER REGIONAL LIBRARY

366 Coteau St. West, PO Box 2500, Moose Jaw SK S6H 6Y2 – 306/693-3669; Fax: 306/692-5657; Email: smjp.ill@palliser.lib.sk.ca; ENVOY: ILL.PRL

Director, Cora Greer

Assiniboia Library, 110 - 4 Ave. West, PO Box 940, Assiniboia SK S0H 0B0 – 306/642-3631 – Librarian, Cindy McCarty

Avonlea Library, Main St. West, PO Box 351, Avonlea SK S0H 0C0 – 306/868-2076 – Librarian, Gina Sudom

Bethune Branch Library, Community Hall, Bethune SK S0G 0H0 – 306/638-3046 – Librarian, Mildred Kistner

Briercrest Library, Main St., Briercrest SK S0H 0K0 – 306/799-2137 – Librarian, Eleanor Anderson

Bushell Park Library, Bushell Park SK S0H 0N0 – 306/694-2367 – Librarian, Gayle Kitchen

Caronport Branch Library, Health Care Centre, Caronport SK S0H 0S0 – 306/756-3343 – Librarian, Lorraine Tanner

Coronach Library, Main St., Coronach SK S0H 0Z0 – 306/267-3260 – Librarian, Maxine Thurlow

Craik Library, PO Box 339, Craik SK S0G 0V0 – 306/734-2388; Email: library@dig.craik.sk.ca – Librarian, Linda McMillan

Davidson Library, Garfield St., PO Box 754, Davidson SK S0G 1A0 – 306/567-2022 – Librarian, Sheri Edom

Elbow Branch Library, Main St., Elbow SK S0H 1J0 – 306/845-2277 – Librarian, Wendy Cafferata

Holdfast Branch Library, PO Box 205, Holdfast SK S0G 2H0 – 306/488-2140 – Librarian, Shelley Harms

Imperial Branch Library, Town Office, Main St., Imperial SK S0G 2J0 – 306/963-2272 – Librarian, Donalda MacLellan

Loreburn Branch Library, Village Office, Loreburn SK S0H 2S0 – 306/644-2097 – Librarian, Barbara Kelman

Moose Jaw Public Library, 461 Langdon Cres., Moose Jaw SK S6H 0X6 – 306/692-2787; Fax: 306/692-3368; Email: ENVOY: ILL.MJPL – Head Librarian, Anne Warriner

Mortlach Branch Library, Main St., Mortlach SK S0H 3E0 – 306/355-2202 – Librarian, Phyllis Wolf

Mossbank Public Library, PO Bag Service, 3 St. West, Mossbank SK S0H 3G0 – 306/354-2474 – Librarian, Debbie Sullivan

Riverhurst Library, Main St., Riverhurst SK S0H 3P0 – 306/353-2130 – Librarian, Della Bartzen

Rockglen Library, Main St., Rockglen SK S0H 3R0 – 306/476-2350 – Librarian, Claudette Schnell

Rouleau Library, Main St., Rouleau SK S0G 4H0 – 306/776-2322 – Librarian, Hazel Anaka

Tugaske Branch Library, Main St., Tugaske SK S0H 4B0 – 306/759-2215; Fax: 306/759-2253 – Librarian, Kathy Russell

Willow Bunch Branch Library, PO Box 280, Willow Bunch SK S0H 4K0 – 306/473-2405 – Librarian, Christine Lemieux

Wood Mountain Library, 2nd Ave., Wood Mountain SK S0H 4L0 – 306/266-2110 – Librarian, Edith Klein

PARKLAND REGIONAL LIBRARY

95A Broadway West, Yorkton SK S3N 0L9 – 306/782-2876; Fax: 306/782-2844; Email: ENVOY: ILL.SYP

Acting Regional Librarian, Gladys Stasiuk

Annaheim Branch Library, Annaheim SK S0K 0G0 – 306/598-2155 – Librarian, Joyce Kimmen

Balcarres Branch Library, PO Box 640, Balcarres SK S0G 0C0 – 306/334-2966 – Librarian, Elaine Chatterson

Bredenbury Branch Library, Bredenbury SK S0A 0H0 – 306/898-2299 – Librarian, Lois Smandych

Buchanan Library, Buchanan SK S0A 0J0 – 306/592-2137 – Librarian, Marie Kupchinski

Calder Branch Library, General Delivery, Calder SK S0A 0K0 – Librarian, Margie Mankish

Canora Branch Library, PO Box 694, Canora SK S0A 0L0 – 306/563-6877 – Librarian, Joan Chernoff

Churchbridge Branch Library, PO Box 530, Churchbridge SK S0A 0M0 – 306/896-2322 – Librarian, Jocelyn Mehrer

Cupar Branch Library, Cupar SK S0G 0Y0 – 306/723-4600 – Librarian, Marie Reed

Earl Grey Library, General Delivery, Earl Grey SK S0G 1J0 – 306/939-2212 – Librarian, Lynda Bailey

Elfros Branch Library, PO Box 70, Elfros SK S0A 0V0 – 306/328-2175 – Librarian, Stella Stephanson

Englefeld Branch Library, PO Box 22, Englefeld SK S0K 1N0 – 306/287-3497 – Librarian, Gladys Freriks

Esterhazy Branch Library, Esterhazy SK S0A 0X0 – 306/745-6406 – Librarian, Pamela Knourek

Foam Lake Branch Library, PO Box 181, Foam Lake SK S0A 1A0 – 306/272-3660 – Librarian, Olive Beattie

Govan Branch Library, PO Box 40, Govan SK S0G 1Z0 – 306/484-2122 – Librarian, Gloria Davis

Invermay Branch Library, Invermay SK S0A 1M0 – 306/593-4990 – Librarian, Doreen Johnson

Ituna Library, Ituna SK S0A 1N0 – 306/795-2672 – Librarian, Staffa Renkas

Jansen Branch Library, PO Box 113, Jansen SK S0K 2B0 – 306/364-2122

Kamsack Branch Library, PO Box 1870, Kamsack SK S0A 1S0 – 306/542-3787 – Librarian, Nancy Brunt

Kelliher Library, PO Box 161, Kelliher SK S0A 1V0 – 306/675-2110 – Librarian, Laurel Rugland

Kelvington Branch Library, PO Box 429, Kelvington SK S0A 1W0 – 306/327-4322 – Librarian, Kim Kizlyk

Lake Lenore Branch Library, Lake Lenore SK S0K 2J0 – 306/368-2344 – Librarian, Lucille Eberle

Langenburg Library, PO Box 549, Langenburg SK S0A 2A0 – 306/743-5394 – Librarian, Marlies Nerbas

Lemberg Branch Library, PO Box 339, Lemberg SK S0A 2B0 – 306/335-2267 – Librarian, Barbara Kanciruk

Leroy Branch Library, PO Box 310, Leroy SK S0K 2P0 – 306/286-3356 – Librarian, Tracy Muller

Lintlaw Branch Library, Lintlaw SK S0A 2H0 – 306/325-2166 – Librarian, Georgie Little

Lipton Branch Library, Lipton SK S0G 3B0 – 306/336-2288 – Librarian, Marlene Huber

MacNutt Branch Library, PO Box 150, MacNutt SK S0A 2K0 – Librarian, Cheryl Peppler

Melville Library, PO Box 489, Melville SK S0A 2P0 – 306/728-2171 – Librarian, Evelyn Trost

Muenster Library, Muenster SK S0K 2Y0 – 306/682-5252 – Librarian, Sally Muench

Neudorf Branch Library, Neudorf SK S0A 2T0 – 306/748-2553 – Librarian, Linda Hanowski

Norquay Library, PO Box 460, Norquay SK S0A 2V0 – 306/594-2347; Fax: 306/594-2076 – Librarian, Lori Hudye

Pelly Branch Library, PO Box 40, Pelly SK S0A 2Z0 – 306/595-2243

Punnichy Branch Library, Punnichy SK S0A 3C0 – 306/835-2176 – Librarian, Audrey Brown

Quill Lake Branch Library, PO Box 271, Quill Lake SK S0A 3E0 – 306/383-2242 – Librarian, Kelly Berlinic

Raymore Branch Library, PO Box 244, Raymore SK P0M 1L0 – 306/746-2166

Rose Valley Library, PO Box 384, Rose Valley SK S0E 1M0 – 306/332-2001 – Librarian, Cheryl Holt

Saltcoats Library, Saltcoats SK S0A 3R0 – 306/744-2911 – Librarian, Barbara Straker

Semans Library, PO Box 220, Semans SK S0A 3S0 – 306/524-2224 – Librarian, Donna Oblander

Southey Library, Southey SK S0G 4P0 – 306/726-2907 – Librarian, Sharon Hakl

Spalding Branch Library, Spalding SK S0K 4C0 – 306/872-2184 – Librarian, Olwen Hoffman

Springside Branch Library, Springside SK S0A 3V0 – 306/792-2255 – Librarian, Marion Ockochinski

Spy Hill Branch Library, PO Box 160, Spy Hill SK S0A 3W0 – 306/534-2122 – Librarian, Jeanette Blakley

Stockholm Branch Library, Stockholm SK S0A 3Y0 – 306/793-2102 – Librarian, Carol Closson

Strasbourg Branch Library, PO Box 331, Strasbourg SK S0G 4V0 – 306/725-3239 – Librarian, Patricia Kelln

Sturgis Branch Library, Sturgis SK S0A 4A0 – 306/548-2824 – Librarian, Kathereen Brodu

Theodore Branch Library, Theodore SK S0A 4C0 – 306/647-2369 – Librarian, Darlene Fleming

Wadena Library, PO Box 297, Wadena SK S0A 4J0 – 306/338-2293 – Librarian, Francis Ekstrom

Watson Branch Library, PO Box 489, Watson SK S0K 4V0 – 306/287-3642 – Librarian, Linda Ceaser

Wishart Branch Library, PO Box 58, Wishart SK S0A 4R0 – 306/576-2150 – Librarian, Donna McDougall

Wynyard Library, PO Box 477, Wynyard SK S0A 4T0 – 306/554-3321 – Librarian, Wendy Howie

Yorkton Public Library, 93 Broadway West, Yorkton SK S3N 0L9 – 306/783-3523, 782-2877; Fax: 306/782-2844; Email: ENVOY: ILLSYP – Chief Librarian, Dan Calef

SOUTHEAST REGIONAL LIBRARY

PO Box 550, Weyburn SK S4H 2K7 – 306/842-3432; Fax: 306/842-2665; Email: ENVOY: ILL.SRL
Regional Director, Allan Johnson

Alameda Branch Library, PO Box 144, Alameda SK S0C 0A0 – 306/489-2066 – Librarian, Diane Miller

Arcola Branch Library, 100 Main St., Arcola SK S0C 0G0 – 306/455-2321 – Librarian, Ivy Chandler

Balgonie Branch Library, PO Box 389, Balgonie SK S0G 0E0 – 306/637-2332 – Librarian, Carolyn Selinger

Bengough Branch Library, PO Box 71, Bengough SK S0C 0K0 – 306/268-2022 – Librarian, Maureen Schmaltz

Bienfait Branch Library, PO Box 433, Bienfait SK S0C 0M0 – 306/388-2223 – Librarian, S. Tuchscherer

Broadview Branch Library, 515 Main St., General Delivery, Broadview SK S0G 0K0 – 306/696-2414 – Librarian, Catherine Adams

Carievale Branch Library, Carievale SK S0C 0P0 – 306/928-4619 – Librarian, Diana Cook

Carnduff Branch Library, PO Box 9, Carnduff SK S0C 0S0 – 306/482-3255 – Librarian, Judy Thompson

Estevan Public Library, 1037 - 2 St., Estevan SK S4A 0L8 – 306/634-3237; Fax: 306/634-9790; TLX: 071-2820; Email: SEREG LIB WYBN – City Librarian, Gregory C. Salmers

Fillmore Branch Library, Main St., PO Box 68, Fillmore SK S0G 1N0 – 306/722-3369 – Librarian, Wendy Dionne

Fort Qu'Appelle Branch Library, 148 Company Ave., PO Box 218, Fort Qu'Appelle SK S0G 1S0 – 306/332-6411 – Librarian, Shirley Dryden

Standing Buffalo Branch Library, PO Box 1771, Fort Qu'Appelle SK S0G 1S0 – 306/332-4414 – Librarian, Natalie Yuzicappi

Gainsborough Branch Library, PO Box 57, Gainsborough SK S0C 0Z0 – 306/685-2229 – Library, Marjorie Johnson

Glenavon Branch Library, PO Box 162, Glenavon SK S0G 1Y0 – 306/429-2180 – Librarian, Carol Nyiri

Grenfell Branch Library, Civic Building, Wolseley Ave., Grenfell SK S0G 2B0 – 306/697-2455 – Librarian, Ann Neuls

Indian Head Branch Library, PO Box 986, Indian Head SK S0G 2K0 – 306/695-3922 – Librarian, K. Baydak

Kennedy Branch Library, PO Box 217, Kennedy SK S0G 2R0 – 306/438-2020 – Librarian, Wendy Cancade

Kipling Branch Library, PO Box 608, Kipling SK S0G 2S0 – 306/736-2911 – Librarian, Debbie Toppings

Lake Alma Branch Library, Lake Alma SK S0C 1M0 – 306/447-2061 – Librarian, Bernice Bloor

Lampman Branch Library, Main St., PO Box 9, Lampman SK S0C 1N0 – 306/487-2202 – Librarian, Lee Ann Hutt

Lumsden Branch Library, Centennial Hall, 3rd Ave., Lumsden SK S0G 3C0 – 306/731-2247 – Librarian, Mary Ellen Hengen

Manor Branch Library, Main St., PO Box 115, Manor SK S0C 1R0 – 306/448-2266 – Librarian, Rita Kyle

Maryfield Branch Library, Maryfield SK S0G 3K0 – 306/646-2143 – Librarian, Judy Moore

Midale Branch Library, PO Box 206, Midale SK S0C 1S0 – 306/458-2263 – Librarian, Corrine Sjodin

Milestone Library, 112 Main St., Milestone SK S0G 3L0 – 306/436-2112 – Librarian, Connie Kinvig

Montmartre Regional Library, 133 - 1 Ave. West, Montmartre SK S0G 3M0 – 306/424-2029 – Librarian, Val Perras

Moosomin Branch Library, PO Box 1470, Moosomin SK S0G 3N0 – 306/435-2107 – Librarian, Paulette Green

Odessa Branch Library, Odessa SK S0G 3S0 – 306/957-2020 – Librarian, Sheila Leurer

Ogema Branch Library, Main St., PO Box 185, Ogema SK S0C 1Y0 – 306/459-2985 – Librarian, Valerie Dunn

Oungre Branch Library, PO Box 88, Oungre SK S0C 1Z0 – 306/456-2662 – Librarian, R. Graefer

Oxbow Branch Library, 516 Prospect Ave., Oxbow SK S0C 2B0 – 306/483-5175 – Librarian, Marty James

Pangman Library, Pangman SK S0C 2C0 – 306/442-2119 – Librarian, Carol Colbow

Pilot Butte Branch Library, PO Box 568, Pilot Butte SK S0G 3Z0 – 306/781-4494 – Librarian, Anne Wolfe

Qu'Appelle Branch Library, Walsh & 9 St., PO Box 450, Qu'Appelle SK S0G 4A0 – 306/699-2279 – Librarian, Cindy Duesterbeck

Radville Branch Library, PO Box 791, Radville SK S0C 2G0 – 306/869-2742 – Librarian, Bridget Harder

Redvers Library, 12 Broadway, PO Box 392, Redvers SK S0C 2H0 – 306/452-3255 – Librarian, Janet Dauvin

Regina Beach Branch Library, Main St., PO Box 596, Regina Beach SK S0G 4C0 – 306/729-2062 – Librarian, Karin Bjerke-Lisle

Rocanville Branch Library, PO Box 263, Rocanville SK S0A 3L0 – 306/645-2088 – Librarian, Marcia Birkenshaw

Stoughton Branch Library, PO Box 595, Stoughton SK S0G 4T0 – 306/457-2484 – Librarian, Marjorie Brown

Tribune Branch Library, Rienze St., PO Box 159, Tribune SK S0C 2M0 – 306/456-2200 – Librarian, Amy Pattyson

Vibank Branch Library, 2nd Ave., PO Box 241, Vibank SK S0G 3Y0 – 306/762-2270 – Librarian, S. Fahlman

Wapella Branch Library, 519 Main St., PO Box 130, Wapella SK S0G 4Z0 – 306/532-4419 – Librarian, Sharon Matheson

Wawota Branch Library, 308 Railway, PO Box 65, Wawota SK S0G 5A0 – 306/739-2375 – Librarian, Cheryl Weatherald

Weyburn Public Library, 45 Bison Ave., Weyburn SK S4H 0H9 – 306/842-4352 – Librarian, Marlene Yurkowski

White City Branch Library, PO Box 308, White City SK S0G 5B0 – 306/781-2118 – Librarian, Debi Bruer

Whitewood Branch Library, 731 Lalonde St., PO Box 488, Whitewood SK S0G 5C0 – 306/735-4233 – Librarian, Wendy Paquin

Yellow Grass Branch Library, Main St., PO Box 31, Yellow Grass SK S0G 5J0 – 306/465-2574 – Librarian, Cheryl Watson

WAPITI REGIONAL LIBRARY

145 - 12 St. East, Prince Albert SK S6V 1B7 – 306/764-0712; Fax: 306/922-1516; Email: ILL.SPANC
Regional Director, Kitty Pope
Business Administrator, Anne McLeod

Alvena Public Library, Alvena SK S0K 0E0 – 306/943-2031 – Librarian, Sharon Jungwirth

Arborfield Public Library, Arborfield SK S0E 0A0 – 306/769-8729 – Librarian, Ida Miezianko

Archerwill Public Library, Archerwill SK S0E 0B0 – 306/323-2128 – Librarian, Gwen Wiles

Big River Public Library, PO Box 154, Big River SK S0J 0E0 – 306/469-2152 – Librarian, Joyce Ahearn

Birch Hills Public Library, Civic Centre, PO Box 396, Birch Hills SK S0J 0G0 – 306/749-3281 – Librarian, Bettye Bouchard

Bjorkdale Public Library, Bjorkdale SK S0E 0E0 – 306/886-2135 – Librarian, Trudy Mahussier

Blaine Lake Public Library, Blaine Lake SK S0J 0J0 – 306/497-3130 – Librarian, Lucy Cheveldayoff

Canwood Public Library, Main St., Canwood SK S0J 0K0 – 306/468-2016 – Librarian, H. Butz

Carrot River Public Library, PO Box 10001, Carrot River SK S0E 0L0 – 306/768-2501 – Librarian, Joanne Rempel

Choiceland Public Library, Choiceland SK S0J 0M0 – 306/428-2216 – Librarian, Janice Bakker

Christopher Lake Public Library, RM Building, PO Box 27, Christopher Lake SK S0J 0N0 – 306/982-2010 – Librarian, Gail Anderson

Crystal Springs Public Library, Crystal Springs SK S0K 1A0 – 306/749-2809 – Librarian, Ethel LaRoche

Cudworth Public Library, PO Box 401, Cudworth SK S0K 1B0 – 306/256-3492 – Librarian, Luella Frie

Debden Public Library, PO Box 143, Debden SK S0J 0S0 – 306/724-2240 – Librarian, Priscilla Charpentier

Duck Lake Public Library, Duck Lake SK S0K 1J0 – 306/467-2016 – Librarian, Diane Perrin

Gronid Public Library, PO Box 10, Gronid SK S0E 0W0 – 306/277-4633 – Librarian, Olga Dobrowolsky

Hudson Bay Public Library, PO Box 109, Hudson Bay SK S0E 0Y0 – 204/865-3110 – Librarian, Elly Ferguson

Humboldt Public Library, PO Box 1330, Humboldt SK S0K 2A0 – 306/682-2034 – Librarian, Tina Colistro

Kinistino Public Library, PO Box 774, Kinistino SK S0J 1H0 – 306/864-2537 – Librarian, Evelyn Sjolin

Leask Public Library, PO Box 117, Leask SK S0J 1M0 – 306/466-2000 – Librarian, Irene Bold

Leoville Public Library, Leoville SK S0J 1N0 – 306/984-2057 – Librarian, Anne Marie Laventure

Marcelin Public Library, Marcelin SK S0J 1R0 – 306/226-2110 – Librarian, Julie Bonin

Meath Park Public Library, PO Box 122, Meath SK S0J 1T0 – 306/929-2555 – Librarian, Michele Sachkowski

Melfort Public Library, PO Box 429, Melfort SK S0E 1A0 – 306/752-2022 – Librarian, Bonnie Rogers

Mistatim Public Library, Mistatim SK S0E 1B0 – 306/889-2144 – Librarian, Bethol Kennedy

Naicam Public Library, PO Box 587, Naicam SK S0K 2Z0 – 306/874-2156 – Librarian, Darla Christianson

Nipawin Public Library, PO Box 1720, Nipawin SK S0E 1E0 – 306/862-4867 – Librarian, Nancy Budd

Paddockwood Public Library, Paddockwood SK S0J 1Z0 – 306/989-2033 – Librarian, Rhonda Alland

Pilger Public Library, Pilger SK S0K 3G0 – 306/367-4809 – Librarian, Betty Bregenser

Porcupine Plain Public Library, PO Box 162, Porcupine Plain SK S0E 1H0 – 306/278-2488 – Librarian, Joanne Yacyshyn

Prairie River Public Library, Prairie River SK S0E 1J0 – 306/889-4521 – Librarian, Lorraine Waskouic

Canadian Almanac & Directory 1997

John M. Cuelenaere Library, 125 - 12 St. East, Prince Albert SK S6V 1B7 – 306/763-8496; Fax: 306/922-1516 – Library Director, Eleanor Acorn

Ridgedale Public Library, Ridgedale SK S0E 1L0 – 306/277-2061 – Librarian, Diane Rorke

St. Benedict Public Library, St. Benedict SK S0K 3T0 – 306/289-2072 – Librarian, Rose Mary Reynaud

St. Brieux Public Library, RM Building, St. Brieux SK S0K 3V0 – 306/275-2314 – Librarian, Muriel Lafreniere

St. Louis Public Library, St. Louis SK S0J 2C0 – 306/422-8630 – Librarian, Monique Tremblay

Shell Lake Public Library, PO Box 310, Shell Lake SK S0J 2G0 – 306/427-2272 – Librarian, Joan Ens

Shellbrook Public Library, Shellbrook SK S0J 2E0 – 306/747-3419 – Librarian, Linda Mazurkewich

Sturgeon Lake Public Library, Sturgeon Lake Central School, RR#1, Site 12, Comp. 5, Shellbrook SK S0J 0E0 – 306/764-5506 – Librarian, Sharon Daniels

Smeaton Public Library, Smeaton SK S0J 2J0 – 306/426-2202 – Librarian, Levina Pearson

Spiritwood Public Library, Spiritwood SK S0J 2M0 – 306/883-2337 – Librarian, Joyce Carriere

Star City Public Library, Centennial Recreational Centre, Star City SK S0E 1P0 – 306/863-2545 – Librarian, Pauline Stenzel

Tisdale Public Library, Civic Centre, PO Box 2499, Tisdale SK S0E 1T0 – 306/873-4767 – Librarian, Joan Burroughs

Wakaw Public Library, PO Box 464, Wakaw SK S0K 4P0 – 306/233-5552 – Librarian, Lucille Reynaud

Waskesiu Public Library, Montreal Dr., PO Box 157, Waskesiu SK S0J 2Y0 – 306/663-5999 – Librarian, Deidre MacGregor

Weldon Public Library, Weldon SK S0J 3A0 – Librarian, Myrna Peterson

White Fox Public Library, White Fox SK S0J 3B0 – Librarian, Violet Johnson

Yellow Creek Public Library, Yellow Creek SK S0K 4X0 – 306/279-2191 – Librarian, Sally Wojcicjowsky

Zenon Park Public Library, PO Box 175, Zenon Park SK S0E 1W0 – 306/777-6091 – Librarian, Bev Favreau

WHEATLAND REGIONAL LIBRARY

806 Duchess St., Saskatoon SK S7K 0R3 – 306/652-5077; Fax: 306/931-7611;
Email: ENVOY:ADMIN.WHEATLAND;
Symbol: WRL

Executive Director, Bruce Cameron

Reference Librarian, Paul Hand

Public Services Librarian, Betty Miller

Acquisitions Librarian, Bruce Cameron

Allan Library, PO Box 40, Allan SK S0K 0C0 – 306/257-4222 – Librarian, Rita Beaton

Beechy Library, PO Box 154, Beechy SK S0L 0C0 – 306/859-2032 – Librarian, Ella Holden

Biggar Library, PO Box 157, Biggar SK S0K 0M0 – 306/948-3911 – Librarian, Helen Frantik

Bruno Library, PO Box 2, Bruno SK S0K 0S0 – 306/369-2353 – Librarian, Donna Olchawsk

Coleville Library, PO Box 45, Coleville SK S0L 0K0 – 306/965-2551 – Librarian, Wendy Bahm

Colonsay Library, PO Box 172, Colonsay SK S0K 0Z0 – 306/255-2232 – Librarian, Mrs. Val Pidlisney

Delisle Library, PO Box 340, Delisle SK S0L 0P0 – 306/493-8288 – Librarian, Carole Merkosky

Dinsmore Library, PO Box 369, Dinsmore SK S0L 0T0 – 306/846-2011 – Librarian, Mary McBain

Dodsland Library, PO Box 100, Dodsland SK S0L 0V0 – 306/356-2180 – Librarian, Jan MacDonald

Eatonia Public Library, PO Box 100, Eatonia SK S0L 0Y0 – 306/967-2224 – Librarian, Gisela Steinke

Elrose Library, General Delivery, PO Box 185, Elrose SK S0L 0Z0 – 306/378-2808 – Librarian, Catherine McDonald

Eston Library, PO Box 387, Eston SK S0L 1A0 – 306/962-3513 – Librarian, Nancy Stevenson

Hanley Library, PO Box 263, Hanley SK S0G 2E0 – 306/544-2546 – Librarian, Sonja English

Kenaston Library, PO Box 309, Kenaston SK S0G 2N0 – 306/252-2130 – Librarian, Marion Chugg

Kerrobert Library, PO Box 618, Kerrobert SK S0L 1R0 – 306/834-5211 – Librarian, Heather Wack

Kindersley Plains Library, 104 Princess St., Kindersley SK S0L 1S2 – 306/463-4141 – Librarian, Marilyn Shea

Kyle Public Library, Main St., PO Box 370, Kyle SK S0L 1T0 – 306/375-2566 – Librarian, Shirley Boyer

Landis Library, General Delivery, Landis SK S0K 2K0 – 306/658-2177 – Librarian, Vera Halter

Lanigan Library, Town Office, PO Box 70, Lanigan SK S0K 2M0 – 306/365-2472 – Librarian, Linda Gibney

Lucky Lake Library, PO Box 340, Lucky Lake SK S0L 1Z0 – 306/858-2246 – Librarian, Linda Peters

Luseland Library, PO Box 550, Luseland SK S0L 2A0 – 306/372-4808 – Librarian, Diane Hurford

Nokomis Library, PO Box 38, Nokomis SK S0G 3R0 – 306/528-2251 – Librarian, Irene Proseilo

Osler Library, PO Box 190, Osler SK S0K 3A0 – 306/239-4774 – Librarian, Colleen Rempel

Outlook Library, PO Box 547, Outlook SK S0L 2N0 – 306/867-8823 – Librarian, Susan Jebson

Perdue Library, PO Box 253, Perdue SK S0K 3C0 – 306/237-4227 – Librarian, Marge Featherstone

Plenty Library, PO Box 70, Plenty SK S0L 2R0 – 306/932-2045 – Librarian, Susan McCleod

Rosetown Library, PO Box 1208, Rosetown SK S0L 2V0 – 306/882-3566 – Librarian, Janet Robertson

Rosthern Library, PO Box 27, Rosthern SK S0K 3R0 – 306/232-5377 – Librarian, Andy Lehmann

Sonningdale Library, PO Box 40, Sonningdale SK S0K 4B0 – 306/237-9533 – Librarian, Sharon Farnell

Stranraer Book Deposit, PO Box 34, Stranraer SK S0L 3B0 – 306/377-4845 – Librarian, Linda Ek

Unity Library, General Delivery, Unity SK S0K 4L0 – 306/228-2802 – Librarian, Joan Ballantyne

Viscount Library, 5 Donald St., 3rd Fl., PO Box 117, Viscount SK S0K 4M0 – 306/944-2155 – Librarian, Rose Ward

Waldheim Library, PO Box 265, Waldheim SK S0K 4R0 – 306/945-2221 – Librarian, Irene Balman

Warman Library, PO Box 788, Warman SK S0K 4S0 – 306/933-4387 – Librarian, Kim Cadrain

Watrous Library, PO Box 460, Watrous SK S0K 4T0 – 306/946-2244 – Librarian, Janice Corrigan

Wilkie Library, PO Box 189, Wilkie SK S0K 4W0 – 306/843-2616 – Librarian, Tish Ulrich

Young Branch, PO Box 288, Young SK S0K 4Y0 – 306/259-2227 – Librarian, Helen Weber

Municipal Resource Library Systems

REGINA PUBLIC LIBRARY

2311 - 12 Ave., PO Box 2311, Regina SK S4P 3Z5 – 306/777-6099; Fax: 306/352-5550; Email: kjensen@rpl.regina.sk.ca

Library Director, Ken Jensen

Central Public Services, Head, André Gagnon

Technical Support Services, Head, Vivien Cartmell

Branch Services, Head, Lubbert van der Laan

Finance & Administration, Head, Colleen Schommer

Public Relations, Head, Anne Campbell

Dunlop Art Gallery, Director/Curator, Helen Marzolf

Albert Branch, 1401 Robinson St., Regina SK S4T 2N7 – 306/777-6076; Fax: 306/777-6223 – Branch Head, Wendy Sinclair

Connaught Branch, 3435 - 13 Ave., Regina SK S4T 1P8 – 306/777-6079; Fax: 306/352-5550 – Branch Head, Ann Stuart

George Bothwell Branch, 2965 Gordon Rd., Regina SK S4S 6H7 – 306/777-6091; Fax: 306/777-6213 – Branch Head, Anne James

Glen Elm Branch, 1601 Dewdney Ave. East, Regina SK S4N 4N6 – 306/777-6080; Fax: 306/352-5550 – Branch Head, Charles Ottosen

Interlibrary Loans, 2311 - 12th Ave., PO Box 2311, Regina SK S4P 3Z5 – 306/777-6024; Fax: 306/777-6105; Email: illstaff@rpl.regina.sk.ca – ILLO Supervisor, Janet Craig

Prince of Wales Branch, 2188 Broder St., Regina SK S4N 3S4 – 306/777-6085; Fax: 306/352-5550 – Branch Head, Anna Mann

Regent Place Branch, 107 Albert St., Regina SK S4R 2N3 – 306/777-6086; Fax: 306/777-6215 – Branch Head, Warren James

Sherwood Village Branch, 6121 Rochdale Blvd., Regina SK S4X 2R1 – 306/777-6088; Fax: 306/777-6214 – Branch Head, Bernard Vander Ziel

Sunrise Branch, 3131 East Woodhams Dr., Regina SK S4V 2P9 – 306/777-6095; Fax: 306/777-6212 – Branch Head, Janet Hilderman

SASKATOON PUBLIC LIBRARY SYSTEM

311 - 23 St. East., Saskatoon SK S7K 0J6 – 306/975-7574; Fax: 306/975-7542; Email: ENVOY: ILL.SS

Director, Zenon Zuzak

Reference Librarian, Anne Craggs

Children's Librarian, Judy Buckle

Public Services Librarian, Muriel Dickson

Technical Services Librarian, Diane Vinish

Carlyle King Branch, 3130 Laurier Dr., Saskatoon SK S7L 5J7 – 306/975-7592 – Branch Head, Donna Wells

Cliff Wright Branch, 1635 McKercher Dr., Saskatoon SK S7H 5J9 – 306/975-7550 – Branch Head, Wenda McArthur

J.S. Wood Branch, 1801 Landsowne Ave., Saskatoon SK S7H 2C4 – 306/975-7590 – Branch Head, Josephine Bischoff

Mayfair Branch, 602 - 33 St. West, Saskatoon SK S7L 0W1 – 306/975-7591 – Branch Supervisor, Trudy Harder

Rusty Macdonald Branch, 225 Primrose Dr., Saskatoon SK S7K 5E4 – 306/975-7600; Fax: 306/975-7603 – Branch Head, Bryan Foran

Sutherland Branch, 449 Central Ave., Saskatoon SK S7N 2E9 – 306/975-7593 – Branch Supervisor, Laura Sauffert

Special & College Libraries & Resource Centres

AIR RONGE

Northlands College - Library, PO Box 1000, Air Ronge SK S0J 3G0 – 306/425-4480

CARONPORT

Briercrest Bible College - Archibald Library, 510 College Dr., Caronport SK S0H 0S0 – 306/756-3252; Fax: 306/756-3366; Symbol: SCA – Head Librarian, Laura Klassen, 306/756-3262

CREIGHTON

Northlands College - Eastern Region Library, PO 400, Creighton SK S0P 0A0 – 306/688-3474; Fax: 306/688-7710

FORT QU'APPELLE

Niel Halford Law Office - Library, PO Box 817, Fort Qu'appelle SK S0G 1S0 – 306/332-5661

Canadian Almanac & Directory 1997

HAFFORD

Redberry Pelican Project Inc. – Library, PO Box 221, Hafford SK S0J 1A0 – 306/549-2400 – Eileen Laviolette

HUMBOLDT

Prairie Agricultural Machinery Institute – Library, Hwy. 5 West, PO Box 1900, Humboldt SK S0K 2A0 – 306/682-2555; Symbol: SHPA – Head Librarian, Sharon Deopker

INDIAN HEAD

Indian Head Research Farm - Library, PO Box 760, Indian Head SK S0G 2K0 – 306/695-2274; Fax: 306/695-3445 – Office Manager, B.A. Robb

LLOYDMINSTER

Lloydminster Chamber of Commerce – Library, c/o Lakeland College, PO Bag 6600, Lloydminster SK S9V 1Z3 – 403/871-5736

MOOSE JAW

Moose Jaw Union Hospital – Medical Library, 455 Fairford St. East, Moose Jaw SK S6H 1H3 – 306/694-1515 – Director, Health Records, I. Alraum

Providence Place for Holistic Health – Medical Library, 100 Second Ave. NE, Moose Jaw SK S6H 1B8 – 306/694-8081 – Director, Medical Records, Lori Allcock

Saskatchewan Institute of Applied Science & Technology - Palliser Institute Library, PO Box 1420, Moose Jaw SK S6H 4R4 – 306/694-3256; Fax: 306/694-3427; Email: ENVOY: SMJT; URL: http://www.siast.sk.ca; Symbol: SMJT
 Program Head/Library, Beverley Brooks, 306/694-3255
 Library Technician, Shawna North
 Acquisitions Clerk, Brenda Fallis

Saskatchewan Water Corporation - Library, 111 Fairford St. East, Moose Jaw SK S6H 7X9 – 306/694-3980; Fax: 306/694-3944 – Executive Secretary, Doreen Jerred

Valley View Centre - Harrison Memorial Library, PO Box 1300, Moose Jaw SK S6H 4R2 – 306/694-3096; Fax: 306/694-3003 – Records/Librarian, Diane Gray

MOOSOMIN

Osman, Gardner, Gordon Law Office - Library, Box 280, 626 Carleton St., Moosomin SK S0G 3N0 – 306/435-3851; Fax: 306/435-3962 – Partner, Don Osman

MUENSTER

St. Peter's Abbey & College - Library, PO Box 10, Muenster SK S0K 2Y0 – 306/682-1760; Fax: 306/682-4402; Symbol: SMSP – Managing Librarian, Brenda McNabb

NIPAWIN

Cumberland Regional College - Information Centre, PO Box 2225, Nipawin SK S0E 1E0 – 306/862-9833; Fax: 306/862-4940

NORTH BATTLEFORD

Battlefords Union Hospital – Memorial Library, 1092 - 107 St., North Battleford SK S9A 1Z1 – 306/446-7350

Lojek, Jones & Hudec Law Office - Library, 10211 - 12 Ave., PO Box 1179, North Battleford SK S9A 3X5 – 306/446-2211; Fax: 306/446-3022 – Manager, James G. Burkinshaw

North West Regional College - Career & Educational Information Centre, 1381 - 101 St., North Battleford SK S9A 0Z9 – 306/937-5100; Fax: 306/445-1575
 Coordinator, Michael Brokop
 Receptionist, Judy Caplin

OUTLOOK

Saskatchewan Irrigation Development Centre - Library, PO Box 700, Outlook SK S0L 2N0 – 306/867-5400; Fax: 306/867-9656 – Administrator, Library, Marlene Martinson

PRINCE ALBERT

Harradence, Longworth, Logue & Harradence Law Office - Library, 1102 - 1 Ave. West, PO Box 2080, Prince Albert SK S6V 6V4 – 306/764-4244; Fax: 306/764-4949 – Librarian, Maureen Longworth

Prince Albert Model Forest Association Inc. – PAMF Reference Library, PO Box 2406, Prince Albert SK S6V 7G3 – 306/922-1944 – Communications Director, Ian Monteith

Saskatchewan Environment & Resource Management - Forestry Branch Library, McIntosh Mall, PO Box 3003, Prince Albert SK S6V 6G1 – 306/953-2448; Fax: 306/953-2360 – Library Contact, Andrea Atkinson

Saskatchewan Forestry Association – Library, PO Box 400, Prince Albert SK S6V 5R7 – 306/763-2189 – Carol Adams

Saskatchewan Institute of Applied Science & Technology - Woodland Campus Library Services/Technical Centre, 1100 - 15 St. East, PO Box 3003, Prince Albert SK S6V 6G1 – 306/953-7098, 7108; Fax: 306/953-7099 – Librarian, Martine Morency

Solicitor General Canada - Saskatchewan Penitentiary, PO Box 160, Prince Albert SK S6E 5R6 – 306/953-8500, ext.386; Symbol: SPASP – Librarian, Erin McCrumb

Victoria Union Hospital – Medical Library, 1200 - 24th St. West, Prince Albert SK S6V 5T4 – 306/953-0521; Fax: 306/763-2871 – Coordinator, Health Records, Heather Painchaud

REGINA

Saskatchewan Highways & Transportation - Planning & Coordination – Library & Geotechnical Branch Library, 1855 Victoria Ave., 8th Fl., Regina SK S4P 3V5 – 306/787-2099; Email: basle@explorer.sasknet.sk.ca; Symbol: SRHP – Librarian, Ellen Basler

Agriculture & Agri-Food Canada - Prairie Farm Rehabilitation Administration Information Centre, #603, 1800 Hamilton, Regina SK S4P 0R5 – 306/780-5100; Fax: 306/780-5018; Email: ENVOY: PFRA.LIB; pfrainfo@em.agr.ca; Symbol: SRRE – Manager, Information Centre, Charlene Dusyk

Allan Blair Memorial Clinic - Oncology Library, 4101 Dewdney Ave., Regina SK S4T 7T1 – 306/766-2203; Fax: 306/766-2322; Symbol: SRAB – Medical Secretary/Librarian, Barbara Karchewski

Alzheimer Association of Saskatchewan Inc. – Library, #301, 2550 - 12th Ave., Regina SK S4P 3X1 – 306/949-4141; Toll Free: 1-800-263-3367

Association des juristes d'expression française de la Saskatchewan – Bibliothèque, 2132 Broad St., Regina SK S4P 1Y5 – 306/565-2507

Association of United Ukrainian Canadians - Saskatchewan Provincial Committee – Library, 1809 Toronto St., Regina SK S4P 1M7 – 306/787-9520 – Administrator, Alex Lapchuk

Baha'i Local Spiritual Assembly of Regina - Library, 2900 - 15 Ave., Regina SK S4T 1S7 – 306/584-2771 – Librarian, Joan Prentice-Naqvi

Balfour Moss - Law Library, #700, 2103 - 11 Ave., Regina SK S4P 4G1 – 306/347-8300; Fax: 306/569-2321 – Bonnie Switzer

Basketball Saskatchewan Inc. - Library, 2205 Victoria Ave., Regina SK S4P 0S4 – 306/791-3660 – Roger Bakes

Bertram, Scrivens, Prior & Stradecki Law Office - Library, #1730, 2002 Victoria Ave., Regina SK S4P 0R7 – 306/525-2737; Fax: 306/565-3244 – Robert H. Bertram

Canadian Bible College - Archibald Foundation Library, 4400 - 4 Ave., Regina SK S4T 0H8 – 306/545-1515; Fax: 306/545-0210; Symbol: SRCB – Director of Library Services, H.D. Sandy Ayer, Email: ayerhd@max.cc.uregina.ca

Canadian Plains Research Centre - Library, University of Regina, #100, 3737 Wascana Pkwy., Regina SK S4S 0A2 – 306/585-4758; Fax: 306/585-4699; Email: cprc@leroy.cc.uregina.ca – Secretary, Lorraine Nelson

City of Regina, Planning & Building Department - Library, PO Box 1790, Regina SK S4P 3C8 – 306/777-7556

Cochrane SNC-Lavalin Inc. - Library, #200, 1230 Blackfoot Dr., Regina SK S4S 7G4 – 306/585-1990; Fax: 306/586-9113 – Librarian, Mary Lou Herperger

Community Planning Association of Canada – Saskatchewan – Library, 2837 Dewdney Ave., Regina SK S4T 0X8 – 306/525-0141

Court of Appeal - Library, Courthouse, 2425 Victoria Ave., Regina SK S4P 3V7 – 306/787-7399; Fax: 306/787-0505 – Librarian, Shirley A. Hurnard

Crown Life Insurance Co. - Crown Life Library, 1901 Scarth St., Regina SK S4P 4L4 – 306/751-6078; Fax: 306/751-7070; Email: sprid@sasknet.sk.ca – Librarian, Darlene Springer

Law Library, 1901 Scarth St., 8th Fl., Regina SK S4P 3B1 – 306/751-6108; Fax: 306/751-6100 – Reference Librarian, Mari White

Early Childhood Intervention Program - Regina Region – Toy & Reference Libraries, 2180 - 23 Ave., Regina SK S4S 0A5 – 306/359-5300 – Toy Library Coordinator, Marlene Cabylis

Environment Canada - Atmospheric & Hydrobiological Sciences Division - Library, PO Box 4800, Regina SK S4P 3Y4 – 306/780-5739; Fax: 306/780-7588; Symbol: SREAE – Officer-in-Charge, Ronald F. Hopkinson
 Prairie & Northern Region - Library, #300, 2365 Albert St., Regina SK S4P 4K1 – 306/780-5306; Fax: 306/780-5311; Symbol: SREIW – In Charge, Priya Montgomery

Gabriel Dumont Institute of Native Studies & Applied Research – Metis Management Training Program Library, 121 Broadway Ave. East, Regina SK S4N 0Z6 – 306/522-5691; Fax: 306/565-0809; Symbol: SRGD

Indian & Northern Affairs Canada - Resource Centre, 2110 Hamilton St., Regina SK S4P 4K4 – 306/780-5945; Fax: 306/780-5733; Symbol: SRIN – Information Assistant, Marilyn Hill

Law Society of Saskatchewan - Library, Courthouse, 2425 Victoria Ave., PO Box 5032, Regina SK S4P 3M3 – 306/569-8020; Fax: 306/569-0155 – Reference Librarian, M. Seeley

Leader-Post Ltd. - Library, 1964 Park St., PO Box 2020, Regina SK S4P 3G4 – 306/565-8234

Luther College - Library, University of Regina, #100, 3737 Wascana Pkwy., Regina SK S4S 0A2 – 306/585-5030; Fax: 306/585-5267; Email: halliday@max.cc.uregina.ca – Library Coordinator, Judith L. Halliday

Museums Association of Saskatchewan – Library, 1808 Smith St., Regina SK S4P 2N4 – 306/780-9279 – Museums Advisor, Wendy Fitch

Pasqua Hospital – Health Sciences Library, 4101 Dewdney Ave., Regina SK S4T 1A5 – 306/359-2370 – Director, Leona Lang

Plains Health Centre – Health Sciences Library, Regina Health District, 4500 Wascana Pkwy., Regina SK S4S 5W9 – 306/766-6211; Email: ENVOY 100: SRHS; esilzer@cableregina.com; Symbol: SRHS – Director, Beth Silzer

Prairie Farm Rehabilitation Administration - Library, CIBC Tower, #603, 1800 Hamilton St., Regina SK S4P 4L2 – 306/780-5070; Fax: 306/780-5018 – Librarian, Charlene Dusyk

Canadian Almanac & Directory 1997

LIBRARIES — SASKATCHEWAN

Provincial Auditor Saskatchewan - Library, #1500, 1920 Broad St., Regina SK S4P 3V7 – 306/787-6398; Fax: 306/787-6383; Symbol: SRPA – Librarian, Rita Schiller

Randall, McCannell & Wellsch Law Office - Library, #300, 2445 - 13 Ave., Regina SK S4P 0W1 – 306/569-1530; Fax: 306/569-0121

Regina General Hospital – Health Sciences Library, 1440 - 14 Ave., Regina SK S4P 0W5 – 306/359-4314; Fax: 306/359-4723; Email: envoy: ill.srg. – Coordinator, T. Bouchard

Regina Humane Society Inc. – Library, PO Box 3143, Regina SK S4P 3G7 – 306/543-6363

Regina Police Service - Resource Centre, 1717 Osler St., PO Box 196, Regina SK S4P 2Z8 – 306/777-8614; Fax: 306/757-5461 – Planning & Research Analyst, Lois Wallace

Regina School Division #4 - Alex Robb Resource Centre, 1600 - 4 Ave., Regina SK S4R 8C8 – 306/791-8261, 8272; Fax: 306/352-2898
 Learning Resources Consultant, Dianna Dushinski
 Resource Centre Assistant, Yvette Ast

Regina Symphony – Library, 200 Lakeshore Dr., Regina SK S4P 3V7 – 306/586-9555 – James Fitzpatrick

Resource Centre for Sport, Culture & Recreation, #224, 1942 Hamilton St., Regina SK S4P 3V7 – 306/791-3666; Fax: 306/525-6775; Toll Free: 1-800-563-2555; Email: SASK.SPRC; Symbol: SRCR – Roger Bakes

Royal Canadian Mounted Police - Training Academy Resource Centre, PO Box 6500, Regina SK S4P 3J7 – 306/780-5824; Fax: 306/780-7599; Symbol: IS – Manager, Resource Centre, Ruth Hoffart

Saskatchewan Agriculture & Food - Library, #B33, 3085 Albert St., Regina SK S4S 0B1 – 306/787-5151; Fax: 306/787-0216; Email: ENVOY: SK.AG.LIB; Symbol: SRAG – Librarian, Hélène Stewart

Saskatchewan Archives Board - Resource Centre, University of Regina, 3303 Hillsdale St., Regina SK S4S 0A2 – 306/787-4066; Fax: 306/787-1975 – Provincial Archivist, Trevor J.D. Powell

Saskatchewan Association for Multicultural Education – Library, #201, 2205 Victoria Ave., Regina SK S4P 0S4 – 306/780-9428

Saskatchewan Association of Licensed Practical Nurses – Library, 2310 Smith St., Regina SK S4P 2P6 – 306/525-1436 – Ede Leeson

Saskatchewan Association of Rural Municipalities – Library, 2075 Hamilton St., Regina SK S4P 2E1 – 306/757-3577; Toll Free: 1-800-667-3604

Saskatchewan Bureau of Statistics - Library, 2350 Albert St., 5th Fl., Regina SK S4P 4A6 – 306/787-6333; Fax: 306/787-6311 – Statistical Clerk, Yvonne Small

Saskatchewan Choral Federation – Library, 1860 Lorne St., Regina SK S4P 2L7 – 306/780-9230; Email: ylozow@unibase.unibase.com – Librarian, Merle Bintner

Saskatchewan Council for International Co-operation – Library, 2138 McIntyre St., Regina SK S4P 2R7 – 306/757-4669

Saskatchewan Department of Education & Department of Post-Secondary Education & Skills Training - Resource Centre, 2220 College Ave., Regina SK S4P 3V7 – 306/787-2262; Fax: 306/787-2223; Email: ENVOY: ILL.SRED; URL: http://www.sasked.gov.sk.ca/resources/lib4_hom.html; Symbol: SRED – Head Librarian, Charlene Kramer, 306/787-2262

Saskatchewan Drama Association – Library, #203, 2135 Albert St., Regina SK S4P 2V1 – 306/525-0151

Saskatchewan Energy & Mines - Marketing & Publications, 1914 Hamilton St., Regina SK S4P 4V4 – 306/787-2528; Fax: 306/787-2527 – Terry Theiss, 306/787-7643

Saskatchewan Environment & Resource Management - Resource Library, #238, 3211 Albert St., Regina SK S4S 5W6 – 306/787-6114, 0902; Fax: 306/787-3941; Email: ENVOY: SPRC; Symbol: SRE – Librarian, Janice Szuch

Saskatchewan Genealogical Society – Library, 1870 Lorne St., Regina SK S4P 2L7 – 306/780-9207 – Librarian, Laura M. Hanowski

Saskatchewan Government Insurance - Library, 2260 - 11 Ave., 10th Fl., Regina SK S4P 0J9 – 306/751-1830; Fax: 306/359-7333

Saskatchewan Health - Resource Centre, 3475 Albert St., Regina SK S4S 6X6 – 306/787-3090; Fax: 306/787-0218; Email: ENVOY: ILL.SRPH; Symbol: SRPH – Manager, Lynn Kozun

Saskatchewan History & Folklore Society Inc. – Library, 1860 Lorne St., Regina SK S4P 2L7 – 306/780-9204; Toll Free: 1-800-919-9437

Saskatchewan Indian Federated College - Library, University of Regina, 188 College St. West, Regina SK S4S 0A2 – 306/779-6299; Fax: 306/584-0955
 Head Librarian, Phyllis G. Lerat, Email: plerat@tansi.sifc.sk.ca
 Assistant Librarian, Rob Nestor, Email: rnestor@tanis.sifc.sk.ca
 Administration, Suzanne Pelletier

Saskatchewan Institute of Applied Science & Technology - Wascana Insitute, Library Services, Parkway Centre, 4635 Wascana Pkwy., PO Box 556, Regina SK S4P 3A3 – 306/787-4323; Fax: 306/787-0560; Email: waslib@siast.sk.ca; Symbol: SRRI
 Learning Centre, Coordinator, Colleen Warren, 306/787-4321
 Technical Services, Duane Meyers, 306/787-4277
 Parkway Centre Library, Library Technician, Ruth Prentice, 306/787-4323, 0564
 St. John Centre Library, Library Technician, Chris Ast, 306/787-4344
 Albert South Library, Public Services Librarian, Sean O'Hara, 306/787-4005
 8 Ave. North Library, Library Technician, Charlotte Ewert, 306/787-6036
 Maxwell Cres. Library, Library Technician, Anand Vaid, 306/787-4713
 Winnipeg North Library, Public Services Library, Heather West, 306/787-0728
 Interlibrary Loans, Laureen Marchuk, 306/787-4323

Saskatchewan Justice - Library, 1874 Scarth St., 9th Fl., Regina SK S4P 3V7 – 306/787-7281; Fax: 306/787-0581; Symbol: SRJC – Librarian, Andrew Stirling

Saskatchewan Labour - Resource Centre, 1870 Albert St., Regina SK S4P 3V7 – 306/787-3662; Fax: 306/787-1064; Email: sklab@sasknet.sk.ca; Symbol: SRDL

Saskatchewan Legislative Library, #234, Legislative Bldg., Regina SK S4S 0B3 – 306/787-2276; Fax: 306/787-1772; Email: ENVOY: SASKLEG.LIBR
 Legislative Librarian, Marian Powell, 306/787-2277
 Secretary to the Legislative Librarian, Sandra M. Gardner, 306/787-1824
 Reference Librarian, Marilyn Nykiforuk, 306/787-2276

Saskatchewan Municipal Government - Housing Division, Library, 1855 Victoria Ave., 6th Fl., Regina SK S4P 3V7 – 306/787-0226; Fax: 306/787-5166
 Librarian, Eileen Badiuk
 Secretary/Assistant Librarian, Ann Kaytor

Saskatchewan Music Festival Association Inc. – Library & Archives, #201, 1819 Cornwall St., Regina SK S4P 2K4 – 306/757-1722

Saskatchewan Palliative Care Association Inc. – Resource Library, #332, 845 Broad St., Regina SK S4R 8G9 – 306/359-7484

Saskatchewan Parks & Recreation Association – Library, #210, 3303 Hillsdale St., Regina SK S4S 6W9 – 306/791-3666 – Roger Bakes

Saskatchewan Piping Industry - Joint Training Board Library, 1366 Cornwall St., Regina SK S4R 2H5 – 306/522-4237; Fax: 306/789-7949 – Darlene Pellerin

Saskatchewan Property Management Corporation - Photographic Services Agency Image Bank, #314, 3085 Albert St., Regina SK S4S 0B1 – 306/787-6298; Fax: 306/787-0600
 Director, Ray Christensen
 Image Library, Coordinator, Alan Mills, 306/787-6298

Saskatchewan Registered Nurses Association – L. Jane Knox Resource Centre, 2066 Retallack St., Regina SK S4T 7X5 – 306/757-4643; Toll Free: 1-800-667-9945; Symbol: SRN – Librarian, Alice Lalonde

Saskatchewan Securities Commission Library, 1914 Hamilton St., 8th Fl., Regina SK S4P 3V7 – 306/787-5645; Fax: 306/787-5899 – Deputy Director, Legal, Dean Murrison

Saskatchewan Social Services - Resource Centre, 1920 Broad St., Regina SK S4P 3V6 – 306/787-3680; Fax: 306/787-3441; Symbol: SRSS – Library Technician, Muriel Griffiths

Saskatchewan Society for the Autistic Inc. – Library, 3510 - 25 Ave., Regina SK S4S 1L8 – 306/569-0858

Saskatchewan Sports Hall of Fame & Museum – Library, 2205 Victoria Ave., Regina SK S4P 0S4 – 306/780-9200 – Curator, Nancy Noble

Saskatchewan Wheat Pool - Corporate Library, 2625 Victoria Ave., Regina SK S4T 7T9 – 306/569-4480; Fax: 306/569-4885; Symbol: SRW
 Corporate Librarian, Diana Behrns, Email: dbehrns@swp.com
 Public Serives Librarian, Shannon Ponsford, 306/569-4753

Saskatchewan Writers Guild Inc. – Library, PO Box 3986, Regina SK S4P 3R9 – 306/757-6310 – Communications Officer, April Davies

SaskPower - Technical Services & Research Library, 2025 Victoria Ave., Regina SK S4P 0S1 – 306/566-3333; Fax: 306/566-3348; Symbol: SRPCRD – Librarian/Private Secretary, D.A. Tsakires

SaskTel - Corporate Library, 2121 Saskatchewan Dr., 7th Fl., Regina SK S4P 3Y2 – 306/347-2249; Fax: 306/359-9022; Symbol: SRST – Manager, Information Resources, Basil Pogue, 306/777-2004

Sheppard, Braun & Muma Law Office - Library, #204, 3988 Albert St., PO Box 4228, Regina SK S4S 3R1 – 306/586-6020; Fax: 306/586-8525 – D.D. Muma

Statistics Canada - Prairie Regional Reference Centre, Avord Tower, 2002 Victoria Ave., 9th Fl., Regina SK S4P 0R7 – 306/780-5405; Fax: 306/780-5403; Toll Free: 1-800-563-7828

University of Regina - Library, #100, 3737 Wascana Pkwy., Regina SK S4S 0A2 – 306/585-4134; Fax: 306/585-4878, 586-9862; Toll Free: 1-800-667-6014; Email: wmaes@max.cc.uregina.ca; Symbol: SRU
 Director of Libraries & Information Services, William R. Maes, 306/585-4132
 Acquisitions, Manager, E. Magee, 306/585-4398
 Cataloguing, Head, Bibliographic Services, B. Browne, 306/585-5101
 Circulation/Reference, Associate Librarian/Client Services, C.L. Adams, 306/585-4289
 Resources, Associate Librarian/Resources, Margaret A. Hammond, 306/585-4283
 Campion College Library, Librarian, Myfanwy Truscott, 306/359-1234
 Education Branch Library, Education Librarian, Del Affleck, 306/585-4642
 Fine Arts Branch Library, Library Supervisor, Margaret Steffensen, 306/779-4826
 Luther College Library, Librarian, Judith Halliday, 306/585-5030
 Language Institute Library, Librarian, Richard Lapointe, 306/585-5241

Wascana Rehabilitation Centre – Health Sciences Library, 2180 - 23 Ave., Regina SK S4S 0A5 – 306/359-5441; Fax: 306/359-5554;
 Email: SRSH.WASCANA; Symbol: SRSH – Library Technician, Lily Walter-Smith

Woloshyn Mattison Law Office - Library, Saskatchewan Pl., #200, 1870 Albert St., Regina SK

Canadian Almanac & Directory 1997

S4P 4B7 – 306/352-9676; Fax: 306/569-8411 – Dirk Silversides

Workers' Compensation Board - Resource Centre, #200, 1881 Scarth St., Regina SK S4P 4L1 – 306/787-2112; Fax: 306/787-3915; Toll Free: 1-800-667-7590; Email: wcbrc@ucomnet.unibase.com; Symbol: SRWCB – Library Technician, Nick Langshaw

SASKATOON

Saskatchewan Energy Conservation & Development Authority – Library, #109, 15 Innovation Blvd., Saskatoon SK S7N 2X8 – 306/933-5310

Ag-West Biotech Inc. – Library, #230, 111 Research Dr., Saskatoon SK S7N 3R2 – 306/975-1939 – Chief Librarian, Toni Clendening

Agriculture & Agri-Food Canada-Saskatoon Research Centre – Canadian Agriculture Library, 107 Science Place, Saskatoon SK S7N 0X2 – 306/956-7222; Fax: 306/956-7247; Email: lbssagr@ncccot.agr.ca; Symbol: SSAGR – Librarian, Van Keane

Canadian Institute for Radiation Safety - National Laboratory & Centre for Public Education – Library, #102, 110 Research Dr., Saskatoon SK S7N 3R3 – 306/975-0566 – Administrative Assistant, Colette LePoudre

Catholic Health Association of Saskatchewan – Library, 1702 - 20 St. West, Saskatoon SK S7M 0Z9 – 306/655-5330 – Secretary, Marilyn Ellis

Certified General Accountants Association of Saskatchewan – Library, 4 - 2345 Ave. C North, Saskatoon SK S7L 5Z5 – 306/955-4622; Toll Free: 1-800-667-5745

Cogema Resources Inc. Library, #817, 825 - 45 St. West, PO Box 9204, Saskatoon SK S7K 3X5 – 306/343-4530; Fax: 306/343-4632 – Professional Librarian, Cathy Padfield, 306/343-4530

College of Emmanuel & St. Chad - Library, 1337 College Dr., Saskatoon SK S7N 0W6 – 306/975-1554; Fax: 306/934-2683 – Librarian, Judith Postle

Dance Saskatchewan – Library, 225 - 23rd St. East, PO Box 8789, Saskatoon SK S7K 6S6 – 306/931-8480; Toll Free: 1-800-667-8480 – Librarian, Maria Theresa Colambani

Entomological Society of Saskatchewan – Library, Agriculture Canada Research Stn., 107 Science Pl., Saskatoon SK S7N 0X2 – 306/975-7014

Environment Canada - Canadian Wildlife Service, Prairie & Northern Wildlife Research Centre - Library, 115 Perimeter Rd., Saskatoon SK S7N 0X4 – 306/975-4096; Fax: 306/975-4089; Symbol: SSECW – Library Technician, Patricia Yeudall, Email: yeudallp@desoto.wxe.doe.ca

   National Hydrology Research Centre Library, 11 Innovation Blvd., Saskatoon SK S7N 3H5 – 306/975-5559; Fax: 306/975-5143; Symbol: SSEH – Library Technician, Heather Popoff

H.O.P.E. for Autism – Library, #202, 310 Idylwyld Dr. North, Saskatoon SK S7L 0Z2 – 306/665-7013 – Bonnie Stewart

Industry Canada - Business Service Centre, #401, 119 - 4 Ave. South, Saskatoon SK S7K 5X2 – 306/975-4682; Fax: 306/975-5334 – Information Officer, Carol Tanner

Law Society of Saskatchewan - Library, Courthouse, 520 Spadina Cres. East, Saskatoon SK S7K 3G7 – 306/933-5141; Fax: 306/933-5166 – Librarian, Peta J. Bates

Learning Disabilities Association of Saskatchewan – Kinsmen Resource Centre, Albert Community Centre, #26, 610 Clarence Ave. South, Saskatoon SK S7H 2E2 – 306/652-4114 – Administrative Assistant, Sheri Gavin

Mendel Art Gallery - Library, 950 Spadina Cres. East, PO Box 569, Saskatoon SK S7K 3L6 – 306/975-7611; Fax: 306/975-7670 – Librarian, Frances Daw Bergles, 306/975-8058

National Research Council-Plant Biotechnology Institute – Library, 110 Gymnasium Place, Saskatoon SK S7N 0W9 – 306/975-5256; Fax: 306/975-6144; Email: faxil@pbi.nrc.ca – Acting Head, Marilee Fazil

Nutana Collegiate Institute - Memorial Library & Art Gallery, 411 - 11 St. East, Saskatoon SK S7N 0E9 – 306/683-7593; Fax: 306/683-7587 – Librarian, Ron Berntson, Email: berntson@duke.usask.ca

One Sky, The Saskatchewan Cross Cultural Centre Inc. – Resource Centre, 259A - 3 Ave. South, Saskatoon SK S7K 1M3 – 306/652-1571

Persons Living with AIDS Network of Saskatchewan Inc. – Library, PO Box 7123, Saskatoon SK S7K 4J1 – 306/373-7766 – Tracie Wood

Photographers Gallery Society Inc. – Library, 12 - 23 St. East, 2nd Fl., Saskatoon SK S7K 0H5 – 306/244-8018

POS Information Services – Library, 118 Veterinary Rd., Saskatoon SK S7N 2R4 – 306/975-7066; Fax: 306/975-3766; Symbol: SSPP – Manager, Information Services, Betty Vankoughnett

Potash Corporation of Saskatchewan Inc. - Library, #500, 122 - 1 Ave. South, Saskatoon SK S7K 7G3 – 306/933-8501; Fax: 306/652-2699; Toll Free: 1-800-667-0403; Email: pcsinc@sasknet.sk.ca; Symbol: SSPCT – Library Coordinator, Marybelle White

Public Health Services - Resource Centre, 101 - 310 Idylwyld Dr. North, Saskatoon SK S7L 0Z2 – 306/655-4600; Fax: 306/655-4718; Symbol: SSCHE – Resource Coordinator, Helen Beaven

Public Legal Education Association of Saskatchewan, Inc. – Library, #115, 701 Cynthia St., Saskatoon SK S7L 6B7 – 306/653-1868

Robertson Stromberg Law Office - Library, #600, 105 - 21 St. East, Saskatoon SK S7K 0B3 – 306/652-7575; Fax: 306/652-2445; Email: robertson.stromberg@sasknet.sk.ca – Library Technician, Ann Marie Melvie

St. Andrew's College - Library, 1121 College Dr., Saskatoon SK S7N 0W3 – 306/966-8983; Fax: 306/966-6575; Email: bergerman@sklib.usask.ca; Symbol: SSLL – Librarian, Joe Bergerman

St. Paul's Hospital – Library, 1702 - 20 St. West, Saskatoon SK S7M 0Z9 – 306/664-5224; Symbol: SSS – Library Technician, Colleen Haichert

St. Thomas More College - Shannon Library, 1437 College Dr., Saskatoon SK S7N 0W6 – 306/966-8962; Fax: 306/966-8904; Symbol: SSM – Librarian, Jane Morris

Saskatchewan Abilities Council – Library, 2310 Louise Ave., Saskatoon SK S7J 2C7 – 306/374-4448 – Library Clerk, Anne Cox

Saskatchewan Archaeological Society – Resource Centre, #5, 816 - 1 Ave. North, Saskatoon SK S7K 1Y3 – 306/664-4124

Saskatchewan Archives Board - Resource Centre, University of Saskatchewan, 3 Campus Dr., Saskatoon SK S7N 5A4 – 306/933-5832; Fax: 306/933-7305; Symbol: SSA – Director, D'Arcy Hande

Saskatchewan Association for Community Living – John Dolan Library, 3031 Louise St., Saskatoon SK S7J 3L1 – 306/955-3344 – Margie Inglehart

Saskatchewan Early Childhood Intervention Program Incorporated – John Dolan Resource Library, 3031 Louise St., Saskatoon SK S7J 3L1 – Margie Inglehart

Saskatchewan Environmental Society – Library, PO Box 1372, Saskatoon SK S7K 3N9 – 306/665-1915 – Office Manager, Larry Morris

Saskatchewan Indian Cultural Centre – Library & Information Services, 120 - 33rd St. East, Saskatoon SK S7K 0S2 – 306/244-1146

Saskatchewan Indian Federated College - Saskatoon Campus Library, 310 - 20 St. East, Saskatoon SK S7K 0A7 – 306/931-1825; Fax: 306/665-0175 – Library Technician, April Chiefcalf Assistant, Yvonne Littlecrow

Saskatchewan Institute of Applied Science & Technology - Kelsey Institute Learning Resources Centre, PO Box 1520, Saskatoon SK S7K 3R5 – 306/933-6417; Fax: 306/933-6490; Email: ENVOY: ILL.SSSI; Symbol: SSSI
Librarian, T.K. Harrison
A/V Librarian, Ethel Crosthwaite

Saskatchewan Institute on Prevention of Handicaps - Library, Royal University Hospital, PO Box 81, Saskatoon SK S7N 4J9 – 306/966-2512 – Research Officer, Rosemary Bolaria

Saskatchewan Real Estate Association – Library, 231 Robin Cres., Saskatoon SK S7L 6M8 – 306/373-3350 – Ede Hirsch

Saskatchewan Research Council - Library, 15 Innovation Blvd., Saskatoon SK S7N 2X8 – 306/933-5400; Fax: 306/933-7446; Email: macleod@src.sk.ca; URL: http://library.usask.ca; Symbol: SSR – Library Coordinator, Colleen MacLeod

Saskatchewan Teachers' Federation – Stewart Resource Centre, 2317 Arlington Ave., PO Box 1108, Saskatoon SK S7K 3N3 – 306/373-1660; Fax: 306/374-1122 – Coordinator, Jean Nahachewsky

Saskatchewan Women's Institutes – Library, #137, Kirk Hall, University of Saskatchewan, 117 Science Pl., Saskatoon SK S7N 0W0 – 306/966-5566

Saskatoon City Hospital – Medical Library, 701 Queen St., Saskatoon SK S7K 0M7 – 306/655-8228; Fax: 306/655-8727 – Library Technician, Shirley Blanchette

Saskatoon Society for Autism Inc. – Library, #202, 310 Idylwyld Dr. North, Saskatoon SK S7L 0Z2 – 306/665-7013, 7011 – Administrative Assistant, Denise Rollheiser

SED Systems Inc. - Library, 18 Innovation Blvd., PO Box 1464, Saskatoon SK S7K 3P7 – 306/933-1672; Fax: 306/933-1486; Symbol: SSSED – DM Coordinator, Lynn Kennedy

Solicitor General Canada - Regional Psychiatric Centre (Prairies) - Library, PO Box 9243, Saskatoon SK S7K 3X5 – 306/975-5442; Fax: 306/975-6024; Symbol: SSRP – Library Technician, Rose Brandt

Star-Phoenix Newspaper - Library, 204 - 5 Ave. North, Saskatoon SK S7K 2P1 – 306/664-8242; Fax: 306/664-0437 – Librarian, Miriam Clemence

Ukrainian Canadian Congress – Saskatchewan Provincial Council – Library, #203, 611 University Dr., Saskatoon SK S7N 0H8 – 306/652-5850 – Computer/Resource Officer, Ihor Kodak

University of Saskatchewan - Libraries, Murray Bldg., Room 103 Main Library, 3 Campus Dr., Saskatoon SK S7N 5A4 – 306/966-5927; Fax: 306/966-6040; Symbol: CASSU
Director of Libraries, Frank Winter
Education Library, Education Librarian, Debbie McGugan, 306/966-5975
Engineering Library, Head, David Salt, 306/966-5976
Geology/Physics Library, Science Librarian, Vacant, 306/966-6049
Health Sciences Library, Librarian, Wilma Sweaney, 306/966-5991
Law Library, Law Librarian, Edward Stanek, 306/966-5999
Thorvaldson Library, Librarian, Vacant, 306/966-6038
Veterinary Medicine Library, Librarian, Ken Ladd, 306/966-7205
Reference Librarian, Linda Fritz, 306/966-6003
Public Services Librarian, Margaret Baldock, 306/966-5927
Technical Services Librarian, Marian Dworaczek, 306/966-5049
Acquisitions Librarian, Diana Kichuk

Western Development Museum - George Shepherd Library, 2935 Melville St., Saskatoon SK S7J 5A6 – 306/934-1400; Fax: 306/934-4467 – Exhibits Curator, Warren Clubb, 306/934-1400

SWIFT CURRENT

Agriculture & Agri-Food Canada-Semiarid Prairie Agricultural Research Centre – Canadian Agriculture Library, Airport Rd., PO Box 1030, Swift Current SK S9H 3X2 – 306/773-4621; Email: lbsscag@nc-ccot.agr.ca; Symbol: SSCAG – Regl. Librarian, Man./Sask., Karen Wilton

Canadian Feed Information Centre – Library, PO Box 1251, Swift Current SK S9H 3X4 – 306/773-5401 – Librarian, K. Wilton

Douglas J. Heinricks Law Office - Library, 327 Central Ave. North, PO Box 1327, Swift Current SK S9H 3X4 – 306/773-7226; Fax: 306/773-5696

MacBean Tessem Law Office - Library, Box 550, 151 First Ave. NE., Swift Current SK S9H 3W4 – 306/773-9343; Fax: 306/773-3828 – Librarian, Robert J. Hale

WEYBURN

Souris Valley Regional Care Centre - Health Sciences Library, PO Box 2003, Weyburn SK S4H 2Z9 – 306/842-8706; Fax: 306/842-7710; Symbol: SWSVC – Librarian, Melva Cooke

Weyburn & Area Early Childhood Intervention Program Inc. – Library, 415 Souris Ave., Weyburn SK S4H 0C9 – 306/842-2686

Weyburn Mental Health Centre - Library, PO Box 1056, Weyburn SK S4H 2L4 – 306/848-2800; Fax: 306/848-2835 – Shirley Biliak

WILCOX

Athol Murray College of Notre Dame - Lane Hall Memorial Library, PO Box 220, Wilcox SK S0G 5E0 – 306/732-2080, ext.137 – Chief Librarian, James Williams

YORKTON

East Central Health District – Information Resource Centre, 270 Bradbrooke Dr., Yorkton SK S3N 2K6 – 306/786-3170; Fax: 306/782-3359; Symbol: SYU – Information Technician, Callie Pickering

Parkland Regional College - University Program & Resource Centre, 72 Melrose Ave., Yorkton SK S3N 1Z2 – 306/783-6566; Fax: 306/786-7866 – University Coordinator, Christine Hudy

St. Gerard's Roman Catholic Parish - Library, 125 - 3 Ave. North, Yorkton SK S3N 1C4 – 306/782-2449

Wrubell Tourney Law Office - Library, 18 - 1 Ave. North, Yorkton SK S3N 1J4 – 306/783-6509; Fax: 306/786-6404

YUKON TERRITORY

Public Libraries

Carcross: Isabelle Pringle Library, PO Box 93, Carcross YT Y0B 1B0 – 403/821-3801; Symbol: YCL – Librarian, Jennifer Stephens

Carmacks Community Library, PO Box 131, Carmacks YT Y0B 1C0 – 403/863-5901

Dawson City Community Library, PO Box 1410, Dawson City YT Y0B 1G0 – 403/993-5571; Fax: 403/993-6112; Email: dpublic@mariposa.whfip.yknet.yk.ca – Librarian, Vicki McCollum; Librarian, Jennifer Docken

Faro Community Library, PO Box 279, Faro YT Y0B 1K0 – 403/994-2684

Haines Junction Community Library, PO Box 5350, Haines Junction YT Y0B 1L0 – 403/634-2215

Mayo Community Library, PO Box 158, Mayo YT Y0B 1M0 – 403/995-2541

Pelly Crossing Community Library, Pelly Crossing YT Y0B 1P0 – 403/537-3711

Ross River Library, General Delivery, Ross River YT Y0B 1S0 – 403/969-2909

Teslin Community Library, PO Box 161, Teslin YT Y0A 1B0 – 403/390-2802 – Librarian, Brenda Oziewicz

Watson Lake Community Library, PO Box 390, Watson Lake YT Y0A 1C0 – 403/536-7517; Fax: 403/536-7515; Email: wlpublib@ynet.yk.ca – Librarian, Ursula Fedorak

Whitehorse Public Library, PO Box 2703, Whitehorse YT Y1A 2C6 – 403/667-5239; Email: ILLYUKON.GOVT

Special & College Libraries & Resource Centres

WHITEHORSE

Anton, Campion, Macdonald & Phillips Law Office - Library, #200, 204 Lambert St., Whitehorse YT Y1A 3T2 – 403/667-7885; Fax: 403/667-7600 – Librarian, Karen St. Pierre

Canadian Heritage - Parks Canada, Yukon National Historic Sites Library, #205, 300 Main St., Whitehorse YT Y1A 2B5 – 403/667-3910; Fax: 403/668-3780 – Manager, Program Services, Ernest Depatie, 403/667-3912

Environment Canada - Pacific & Yukon Region - Library, Mile 917.6 Alaska Hwy., Whitehorse YT Y1A 5X7 – 403/667-3407; Fax: 403/667-7962; Email: library@ywc.yk.doe.ca; Symbol: YWEEP – Librarian, Mary Martin

Indian & Northern Affairs Canada - Yukon Region Library, #345, 300 Main St., Whitehorse YT Y1A 2B5 – 403/667-3111; Fax: 403/667-3196; Email: dyrlib@yknet.yk.ca; Symbol: YWIN
 Manager, Library Services, Brenda Oziewicz
 Reference Librarian, Donna McBee

Law Society of Yukon – Library, #201, 302 Steele St., Whitehorse YT Y1A 2C5 – 403/667-3086 – Librarian, Jenny Nesbitt-Dufort

Learning Disabilities Association of Yukon Territory – Resource Centre, #205, 4133 - 4 Ave., PO Box 4853, Whitehorse YT Y1A 4N6 – 403/668-5167

Public Service Alliance of Canada (CLC) - Yukon Employees Union/Syndicat des employés du Yukon – Library, 208 Strickland St., Whitehorse YT Y1A 2J8 – 403/667-2332 – Administrations Assistant, Carolyn Booker

Tourism Industry Association of the Yukon – Library, 1109 - 1st Ave., Whitehorse YT Y1A 2A9 – 403/668-3331

Yukon Archives, PO Box 2703, Whitehorse YT Y1A 2C6 – 403/667-5321; Fax: 403/667-4253; Symbol: YWA
 Assistant Territorial Archivist, Diane Chisholm, 403/667-5641
 Archives Librarian, Peggy D'Orsay, 403/667-5625
 Accession Archivist, Clara Rutherford, 403/667-5333
 Government Records Archivist, Blair Taylor, 403/667-5926
 Reference Coordinator, Fay Tangermann, 403/667-8064
 Reference Coordinator, Heather Jones

Yukon Chamber of Mines – Library, PO Box 4427, Whitehorse YT Y1A 3T5 – 403/667-2090 – Office Manager, R.M. Hanlin

Yukon College - Resource Centre, PO Box 2799, Whitehorse YT Y1A 5K4 – 403/668-8870; Fax: 403/668-8808; Symbol: YCLIB
 Manager, Rob Sutherland, Email: rsuther@yknet.yk.ca
 Reference Librarian, Sally Bremner
 Public Services Librarian, Maureen Long
 Technical Services Librarian, Eileen Edmunds
 AV/Computers, Richard Klassen

Yukon Conservation Society – Library, 302 Hawkins St., PO Box 4163, Whitehorse YT Y1A 3T3 – 403/668-5678

Yukon Economic Development - Library, PO Box 2703, Whitehorse YT Y1A 2C6 – 403/667-5818; Fax: 403/667-8601; Email: ENVOY: ILL.YWED; Symbol: YWED
 Librarian, Margaret Donnelly, Email: donnelly@yknet.yk.ca
 Oil & Gas Library, Monica Woelfel, 403/667-3427
 Geoscience Library, Diane Carruthers, 403/667-8808
 Energy Library, Cathy Cottrell-Tribes, 403/667-5387

Yukon Family Services Association – Library, 210 Elliott St., Whitehorse YT Y1A 2A2 – 403/667-2970 – Office Supervisor, Haley Argen

Yukon Health & Social Services - Library, PO Box 2703, Whitehorse YT Y1A 2C6 – 403/667-5919; Fax: 403/667-3096; Toll Free: 1-800-661-0408; Email: jpelchat@gov.yk.ca; Symbol: ywhhr
 Librarian, Judy Pelchat
 Alchohol & Drug Services Collection, J. Gauthier, 403/667-5777
 Biblio-Santé, J. Wackett, 403/667-8949
 Child Care Services Division, C. Smith, 403/667-5405

Yukon Law Library, PO Box 2703, Whitehorse YT Y1A 2C6 – 403/667-3086; Fax: 403/667-4116; Email: lawlib@gov.yk.ca; Symbol: YWL
 Librarian, Tanya Astika
 Librarian, Jenny Nesbitt-Dufort

Yukon Public Legal Education Association – Library, Yukon College, PO Box 2799, Whitehorse YT Y1A 5K4 – 403/668-5297; Toll Free: 1-800-668-5297

Yukon Renewable Resources - Library, PO Box 2703, Whitehorse YT Y1A 2C6 – 403/667-3029 – Contact, Kate Moylan-Smith, Email: moylan@yknet.yk.ca

Yukon Workers' Compensation Board - Library, 401 Strickland St., Whitehorse YT Y1A 5N8 – 403/667-8209; Fax: 403/668-2079 – Nina Sutherland

ARCHIVES

National Archives of Canada/Archives nationales du Canada

395 Wellington St., Ottawa ON K1A 0N3
613/992-3884; Fax: 613/995-6274
URL: http://www.archives.ca
Private papers, public records, machine-readable archives, maps, paintings, photographs, films, sound recordings & books on Canadian History & other subjects. Research services & facilities.
National Archivist, J.P. Wallot – 613/992-2473
Assistant National Archivist, M. Swift – 613/992-7445

ALBERTA

Calgary: Canadian Architectural Archives, University of Calgary Libraries, 2500 University Dr. NW, Calgary AB T2N 1N4 – 403/220-7420 – Curator, Kathy Zimon – Open year round

Calgary: Diocese of Calgary Archives, 602 - 1 St. SE, 2nd Fl., Calgary AB T2G 4W4 – 403/284-5972 – Diocesan Archivist, David Carter – Open year round

Calgary: University of Calgary Archives, 2500 University Dr. NW, Calgary AB T2N 1N4 – 403/220-7271; Fax: 403/282-6837; Email: jgafuik@ucdasvm1.admin.ucalgary.ca – University Archivist, Jo-Ann Munn Gafuik

Edmonton: Archives of the Sisters of Charity of Montréal-Grey Nuns, c/o Grey Nuns Regional Centre, 9810 - 165 St., Edmonton AB T5P 3S7 – 403/484-5611; Fax: 403/484-7145 – Archiviste, Soeur Fernande Champagne

Edmonton: City of Edmonton Archives, PO Box 2359, Edmonton AB T5J 2R7 – 403/496-8710; Fax: 403/496-8732 – City Archivist, Bruce Ibsen

Edmonton: Lutheran Historical Institute, 7100 Ada Blvd., Edmonton AB T5B 4E4 – 403/474-8156;

Fax: 403/477-9829 – Director, Norman J. Threinen; Archivist, Karen Baron – Open year round

Edmonton: Provincial Archives of Alberta/Archives provinciales d'Alberta (PAA), 12845 - 102 Ave., Edmonton AB T5N 0M6 – 403/427-1750; Fax: 403/427-4646; Email: SThomson@mcd.gov.ab.ca; URL: http://www.ab.ca/~mcd/archives/index.htm – Director & Provincial Archivist, Dr. Sandra Thomson

Edmonton: University of Alberta Archives, University of Alberta, Ring House #1, Edmonton AB T6G 2E2 – 403/492-0531; Fax: 403/492-6185; Email: archives@library.ualberta.ca – Chief Archivist, Bryan Corbett, Email: bcorbett@library.ualberta.ca; Associate Archivist, Brian Hobbs, 403/466-6123; Archives Assistant, Kevan Warner, 403/466-6118

Lethbridge: City of Lethbridge Archives, 910 - 4 Ave. South, Lethbridge AB T1J 0P6 – 403/329-7302; Fax: 403/329-4958; Email: archives@city.lethbridge.ab.ca – City Archivist, Greg Ellis

St. Albert: Oblate Archives - Grandin Province/Archives Oblates - Province Grandin, 3 St. Vital Ave., St. Albert AB T8N 1K1 – 403/459-5072 – Archivist, Dr. Gaston J. Montmigny., O.M.I.

BRITISH COLUMBIA

Burnaby: BC Telephone Company Archives, c/o Business Library, BC Tel., #5, 3777 Kingsway, Burnaby BC V5H 3Z7 – 604/432-2671 – Curator, Donna Serviss

Castlegar: Selkirk College Archives & Local History Collection, PO Box 1200, Castlegar BC V1N 3J1 – 250/365-7292; Fax: 250/365-7259; Email: johnmans@selkirk.bc.ca – Chief Librarian, John Mansbridge – West Kootenay area & the Doukhobors

Chilliwack Archives, 9291 Corbould St., Chilliwack BC V2P 4A6 – 604/795-5210 – Archivist, Jim Bowman – Open year round

Gold River: Nootka Sound Historical Society Archives, PO Box 748, Gold River BC V0P 1G0

Kaslo: Kootenay Lake Archives, PO Box 537, Kaslo BC V0G 1M0 – Director, Elizabeth Scarlett

Nanaimo Community Archives, 100 Cameron Rd., Nanaimo BC V9R 2X1 – 250/753-4462; Fax: 250/753-1777; Email: nca@nanaimo.ark.com – Community Archivist, Diane Foster

Nelson: David Thompson Archives, 1402 Fell St., Nelson BC V1L 3C7 – 250/352-5188 – Librarian, Roberta Griffiths

Trail: Cristoforo Colombo Lodge Archives, 3995 Woodland Dr., Trail BC V1R 2V6 – 250/368-8921 – Curator, Sergio Freschi – Italians in Trail

Victoria: BC Archives & Records Service (BCARS), 655 Belleville St., Victoria BC V8V 1X4 – 250/387-5885; Fax: 250/387-2072; Email: access@bcars.gs.gov.bc.ca; URL: http://www.bcars.gs.gov.bc.ca/bcars.html – Provincial Archivist, John A. Bovey; Deputy Provincial Archivist, Gary A. Mitchell, CRM

Victoria: City of Victoria Archives & Records Division (CVARD), 1 Centennial Sq., Victoria BC V8W 1P6 – 250/361-0375; Fax: 250/361-0348; Email: Archives@ch.city.victoria.bc.ca – Archives Manager, James Burrows

Williams Lake: Cariboo Chilcotin Archives, Williams Lake Library, 110 Oliver St., Williams Lake BC V2G 1L8 – 250/392-3630; Fax: 250/392-3518 – Librarian, Lillian Mack

MANITOBA

Brandon: S.J. McKee Archives, c/o Brandon University, #270, 18th St., Brandon MB R7A 6A9 – 204/727-9634

Winnipeg: Jewish Historical Society of Western Canada Archives, #404, 365 Hargrave St., Winnipeg MB R3B 2K3 – 204/942-4822; Fax: 204/942-9299 – Executive Secretary, Esther Slater; President, Harry Gutkin; Archivist, Bonnie Tregobov

Winnipeg: Mennonite Heritage Centre Gallery & Archives, 600 Shaftesbury Blvd., Winnipeg MB R3P 0M4 – 204/888-6781; Fax: 204/831-5675; Email: lkippen@mbnet.mb.ca – Historian/Archivist, Lawrence Klippenstein; Assistant Archivist, Alf Redekopp – Western Canadian, Russian & Prussian Mennonite manuscripts, documents, photographs, etc.; open Mon. - Fri., 8:30 am - 5 pm

Winnipeg: Provincial Archives of Manitoba, 200 Vaughan St., Winnipeg MB R3C 1T5 – 204/945-3971 – Provincial Archivist, Peter Bower

NEW BRUNSWICK

Fredericton: Provincial Archives of New Brunswick/Archives provinciales du Nouveau-Brunswick (PANB), PO Box 6000, Fredericton NB E3B 5H1 – 506/453-2122; Fax: 506/453-3288; Email: mbeyea@gov.nb.ca – Director, Marion Beyea

St. Andrews: Charlotte County Archives, 123 Frederick St., General Delivery, St. Andrews NB E0G 2X0 – 506/529-4248 – Archivist, Charlotte McAdam

NEWFOUNDLAND

St. John's: Maritime History Archive, Henrietta Harvey Bldg., Memorial Univieristy, St. John's NF A1C 5S7 – 709/737-8428; Fax: 709/737-4569 – Archivist, Heather Wareham

St. John's: Memorial University of Newfoundland Folklore & Language Archive (MUNFLA), Dept. of Folklore, Memorial University, St. John's NF A1B 3X8 – 709/737-8401; Fax: 709/737-2345; Email: munfla@kean.ucs.mun.ca – Director, Martin Lovelace; Archivist, Philip Hiscock – Collections of folklore/folklife, oral history & popular culture, primarily pertaining to Newfoundland & Labrador

St. John's: Provincial Archives of Newfoundland & Labrador, Colonial Bldg., Military Rd., St. John's NF A1C 2C9 – 709/729-3065; Fax: 709/729-0578 – Provincial Archivist, David J. Davis

NOVA SCOTIA

Halifax: Dalhousie University Archives, Killam Memorial Library, Dalhousie University, Halifax NS B3H 4H8 – 902/494-6490; Fax: 902/494-2062; Email: charles.armour@dal.ca – University Archivist, Dr. Charles Armour

Halifax: Public Archives of Nova Scotia, 6016 University Ave., Halifax NS B3H 1W4 – 902/424-6060 – Provincial Archivist, Carman Carroll – Open year round

Sydney: Beaton Institute of Cape Breton Studies, PO Box 5300, Sydney NS B1P 6L2 – 902/563-1329; Fax: 902/562-8899; Email: cmacleod@caper2.uccb.ns.ca – Archivist, Dr. R. Morgan

Tusket: Argyle Township Court House, Archives & Gaol, PO Box 101, Tusket NS B0W 3M0 – 902/648-2493; Fax: 902/648-0367 – Archivist, Peter Crowell – Canada's oldest standing courthouse, 1805

ONTARIO

Fonthill: Pelham Historical Resource Centre, PO Box 903, Fonthill ON L0S 1E0 – Collection Coordinator, Mary Lamb

Haileybury: Archives de les Soeurs de l'Assomption de la Sainte-Vierge, PO Box 1420, Haileybury ON P0J 1K0 – 705/672-3033

Hamilton: Canadian Baptist Archives, c/o McMaster Divinity College, McMaster University, Hamilton ON L8S 4K1 – 905/525-9140, ext.3511 – Archivist, Judith Colwell

Kingston: Anglican Diocese of Ontario Archives, 90 Johnson St., Kingston ON K7L 1X7 – 613/544-4774; Fax: 613/547-3745 – Diocesan Archivist, Paul Banfield

Kingston: Queen's University Archives, Kathleen Ryan Hall, Queen's University, Kingston ON K7L 3N6 – 613/545-2378; Fax: 613/545-6403; Email: richand@qucdn.queensu.ca – University Archivist, Donald S. Richan

Maple: City of Vaughan Archives, 2141 Major Mackenzie Dr., Maple ON L6A 1T1 – 905/832-2281; Fax: 905/832-8535

Minesing: Simcoe County Archives, RR#2, Minesing ON L0L 1Y0 – 705/726-9300, ext.287; Fax: 705/725-5341 – County Archivist, Bruce Beacock

North York: Archives of the Sisters of St. Joseph of Toronto, 3377 Bayview Ave., North York ON M2M 3S4 – 416/222-1101 – Archivist, Sr. Mary Trimble

North York: The Ontario Jewish Archives, 4600 Bathurst St., North York ON M2R 3V2 – 416/635-2883, ext.170; Fax: 416/635-1408 – Director, Dr. Stephen Speisman

North York: York University Archives, Scott Library, #305, 4700 Keele St., North York ON M3J 1P3 – 416/736-5442 – Archivist, Barbara Craig

Orillia: Huronia Regional Centre Archives/Museum, Ontario Ministry of Community & Social Services, 700 Memorial Ave., PO Box 1000, Orillia ON L3V 6L2 – 705/326-7361, ext.2441; Fax: 705/326-3445 – Librarian, William Land; Chair, HRC Archives/Museum Committee, Hugh Duncan

Oshawa Community Archives, 1450 Simcoe St. South, Oshawa ON L1H 8S8 – 905/436-7624; Fax: 905/436-7625 – Archivist, Tammy Robinson

Ottawa: Archives de l'Université d'Ottawa/University of Ottawa Archives, 100 Marie-Curie, salle 012, Ottawa ON K1N 6N5 – 613/562-5750; Fax: 613/562-5198 – Archiviste en chef de l'Université, Michel Prévost, Email: prevost@uottawa.ca

Ottawa: Archives de l'Université Saint-Paul, Edifice Deschâtelets, 175 Main St., Ottawa ON K1S 1C3 – 613/237-0580 – Pére Roland Trudeau

Ottawa: Canadian Postal Archives, 365 Laurier Ave. West, Ottawa ON K1A 0N3 – 613/995-8085 – Chief, Cimon Morin

Ottawa: City of Ottawa Archives/Archives municipales d'Ottawa, 174 Stanley Ave., Ottawa ON K1M 1P1 – 613/742-5014; Fax: 613/742-5113 – City Archivist, Louise Roy-Brochu; Assistant Archivist, David Bullock

Ottawa: Department of National Defence - Directorate of History/Service historique de la défense nationale, Major-General George R. Pearkes Bldg., 101 Colonel By Dr., Ottawa ON K1A 0K2 – 613/998-7058; Fax: 613/990-8579 – Acting Director, Dr. Serge Bernier

Peterborough: Trent University Archives, Peterborough ON K9J 7B8 – 705/748-1413; Fax: 705/748-1315; Email: bdodge@trentu.ca – University Archivist, Bernadine Dodge

Scarborough Archives & Historical Collection, 730 Scarborough Golf Club Rd., Scarborough ON M1G 1H7 – 416/396-6930 – Archivist, Richard Schofield – Research material about Scarborough & education in Scarborough

Stratford Festival Archives, PO Box 520, Stratford ON N5A 6V2 – 519/271-4040, ext. 278 – Archivist, Lisa Brant

Stratford-Perth Archives, 24 St. Andrew St., Stratford ON N5A 1A3 – 519/273-0399; Fax: 519/271-6265 – Archivist-Administrator, Lutzen Riedstra

Sudbury: Archives de l'Université de Sudbury, Ramsey Lake Rd., Sudbury ON P3E 2C6 – 705/673-5661, ext.64 – Responsable, Pére Robert Toupin

Sudbury: Northeastern Ontario Labour Industrial Archives, Laurentian University Library, Ramsay Lake Rd., Sudbury ON P3E 2C6 – 705/675-1151, ext.251 – Archivist, Prof. A. Mrozewski

Toronto: Academy of Medicine Archives, 288 Bloor St. West, Toronto ON M5S 1V8 – 416/964-7088 – Archivist, S. Swanson

Toronto: Alternative Community History Archives, PO Box 158, Stn D, Toronto ON M6P 3J8 – 416/537-3949

Toronto: Anglican Church of Canada General Synod Archives, 600 Jarvis St., Toronto ON M4Y 2J6 – 416/924-9192; Fax: 416/968-7983 – Director, Terry Thompson

Toronto: Anglican Diocese of Toronto Archives, Synod Office, 135 Adelaide St. East, Toronto ON M5C 1L8 – 416/363-6021; Fax: 416/363-7678 – Archivist, Mary-Anne Nicholls

Toronto: Archives of the Institute of the Blessed Virgin Mary in North America (ANA-ibvm), 101 Mason Blvd., Toronto ON M5M 3E2 – 416/487-5543; Fax: 416/485-9884 – General Archivist, Sr. M. Esther Hanley

Toronto: Archives of Ontario, Queen's Park, 77 Grenville St., Toronto ON M7A 2R9 – 416/327-1600 – Archivist of Ontario, Ian E. Wilson

Toronto: Archives of the Roman Catholic Archdiocese of Toronto, 355 Church St., Toronto ON M5B 1Z8 – 416/977-1500, ext.141; Fax: 416/977-6063 – Archivist, Sr. Marc F. Lerman

Toronto: Archives Society of Jesus, Upper Canada (ASJUC), 15 St. Mary St., Toronto ON M4Y 2R5 – 416/922-5474; Fax: 416/922-2898 – Director, Rev. P. Boyle, S.J.

Toronto: Canadian Lesbian & Gay Archives, #201, 56 Temperance St., PO Box 639, Stn A, Toronto ON M5W 1G2 – 416/921-6310; Fax: 416/777-2755 – President, Ray Brillinger

Toronto: Canadian Women's Movement Archives/Archives canadiennes du mouvement des femmes, PO Box 128, Stn P, Toronto ON M5S 2S7 – 416/597-8865 – Archivist, J. Pelletier

Toronto: City of Toronto Archives, City Hall, 100 Queen St. West, Toronto ON M5H 2N2 – 416/392-7483 – City Archivist, Robert A. Halifax

Toronto: Dance Collection Danse, 145 George St., Toronto ON M5A 2M6 – 416/365-3233; Fax: 416/365-3169 – Co-Director, Lawrence Adams; Co-Director, Miriam Adams – Canadian dance history; database; publishing; education

Toronto: General Archives of the Basilian Fathers (GABF), 81 St. Mary St., Toronto ON M5S 1J4 – 416/926-7279; Fax: 416/920-3413 – Archivist, Rev. Kevin Kirley

Toronto: The Joan Baillie Archives of the Canadian Opera Company, 227 Front St. East, Toronto ON M5A 1E8 – 416/363-6671; Fax: 416/363-5584 – Archivist, Birthe Joergensen

Toronto: Mariposa Archives, c/o Mariposa Folk Foundation, 786 Dundas St. East, Toronto ON M4M 1R1 – 416/778-9063; Fax: 416/469-2120 – Executive Director, Michael Greenspoon

Toronto: Metropolitan Toronto Archives & Records Centre, 255 Spadina Rd., Toronto ON M5R 2V3 – 416/397-5000; Fax: 416/392-9685; Email: archives@metrodesk.metrotor.on.ca; URL: http://www.metrotor.on.ca/services/departments/clerk.html#archives – Manager, Archives & Outreach, Michael Moir

Toronto: National Ballet of Canada Archives, 470 Queens Quay West, Toronto ON M5V 3K4 – 416/345-9686; Fax: 416/345-8323; Email: info@national.ballet.ca; URL: http://www.national.ballet.ca – Archivist, Sharon Vanderlinde

Toronto: Ontario Hydro Archives, 800 Kipling Ave., Rm. KD-170, Toronto ON M8Z 5S4 – 416/231-4111 ext.7102

Toronto: The Presbyterian Church in Canada Archives, #104, 11 Soho St., Toronto ON M5T 1Z6 – 416/595-1277 – Archivist/Records Administrator, Kim Arnold

Toronto: Ryerson Polytechnic University Archives, 350 Victoria St., Toronto ON M5B 2K3 – 416/979-5000, ext.7027; Fax: 416/979-5215; Email: cdoucet@acs.ryerson.ca – Archivist, Claude Doucet

Toronto Harbour Commission Archives, 60 Harbour St., Toronto ON M5J 1B7 – 416/863-2008; Fax: 416/863-4830; Email: torport@io.org – Archivist, Michele Dale

Toronto: Trinity College Archives, 6 Hoskin Ave., Toronto ON M5S 1H8 – 416/978-2019; Fax: 416/978-2797; Email: Pilon@epas.utoronto.ca – Archivist, Henri Pilon

Toronto: Trinity Square Video Archives, 172 John St., 4th Fl., Toronto ON M5T 1X5 – 416/593-1332; Fax: 416/593-0958; Email: tsv@magic.ca; http://www.magic.ca/tsv

Toronto: United Church of Canada/Victoria University Archives, 73 Queen's Park Cres. East, Toronto ON M5S 1K7 – 416/585-4563; Fax: 416/585-4584 – Chief Archivist, Jean Dryden

Toronto: University College Archives, University of Toronto, Toronto ON M5S 1A1 – 416/978-8601

Toronto: University of St. Michael's College Archives, 113 St. Jospeh St., Toronto ON M5S 1J4 – 416/926-1300 ext.3405 – Archivist, Rev. Frederick Black

Toronto: University of Toronto Archives, Thomas Fisher Rare Book Library, 120 Saint George St., Toronto ON M5S 1A5 – 416/978-7656 – University Archivist, Garron Wells

Waterloo: Evangelical Lutheran Church in Canada Archives, Eastern Synod, Wilfrid Laurier University, 75 University Ave. West, Waterloo ON N2L 3C5 – 519/884-1710, ext.3380; Fax: 519/884-8023; Email: vgillham@mach2.wlu.ca – Archivist, Erich Schultz

Waterloo: Mennonite Archives of Ontario, Conrad Grebel College, Waterloo ON N2L 3G6 – 519/885-0220, ext.242 – Archivist, Samuel Steiner

Waterloo: Wilfrid Laurier University Archives, 75 University Ave. West, Waterloo ON N2L 3C5 – 519/884-1970, ext.2380 – University Librarian, Virginia Gillham

PRINCE EDWARD ISLAND

Charlottetown: Public Archives & Records Office (PARO), PO Box 1000, Charlottetown PE C1A 7M4 – 902/368-4290; Fax: 902/368-5544; Email: htholman@gov.pe.ca – Provincial Archivist, H.T. Holman; Historic Records Archivist, Marilyn Bell

QUÉBEC

Beauport: Archives de la Maison Généralice des Soeurs de la Charité de Québec, 2655, rue Le Pelletier, Beauport PQ G1C 3X7 – 418/628-8860; Fax: 418/628-6052 – Archiviste, Gemma Gastonguay

Chicoutimi: Archives de la Société historique du Saguenay, CP 456, Chicoutimi PQ G7H 5C8 – 418/549-2805; Fax: 418/545-8240 – Archiviste, Roland Bélanger

L'Assomption: Archives du Collège de L'Assomption, 270, boul Ange-Gardien, L'Assomption PQ J0K 1G0 – 514/589-5621 – Archiviste, Fernand Boulet

La Pocatière: Archives de la Côte-du-Sud et du Collège de Sainte-Anne, 100, av Painchaud, CP 937, La Pocatière PQ G0R 1Z0 – 418/856-2104 – Archiviste, François Taillon

Montréal: Archives de la Province du Canada: Oblats de Marie-Immaculée, 3456, av du Musée, Montréal PQ H3G 2C7 – 514/844-3064; Fax: 514/285-2248 – Archiviste, Normand Martel

Montréal: Archives de la Société historique de Montréal, 329, rue de la Commune ouest, Montréal PQ H2Y 2E1 – 514/844-0309 – Présidente, Lise Cadotte

Montréal: Archives de la Société Saint-Jean Baptiste de Montréal, 82, rue Sherbrooke ouest, Montréal PQ H2X 1X3 – 514/843-8851 – Archiviste, Gérard Turcotte

Montréal: Archives de l'Archevêché de Montréal/Archives of the Archdiocese of Montréal, 2000, rue Sherbrooke ouest, Montréal PQ H3H 1G4 – 514/931-7311; Fax: 514/931-3432 – Archivist, Mgr Michel Parent

Montréal: Archives gaies du Québec, PO Box 395, Stn Place-du-Parc, Montréal PQ H2W 2N9

Montréal: Archives of the Canadian National Ralways, PO Box 8100, Montréal PQ H3C 3N4 – 514/399-5027 – Historical Research Officer, J. Norman Lowe

Montréal: Bell Canada Telephone Historical Collection/Le service de la documentation historique de Bell Canada, #820, 1050, Côte du Beaver Hall, Montréal PQ H2Z 1S4 – 514/870-5214; Fax: 514/875-2537 – Director, Historical/IRC, Stephanie Sykes

Montréal: Canadian Jewish Congress National Archives, 1590, av Dr. Penfield, Montréal PQ H3G 1C5 – 514/931-7531 – A/Director, Janice Rosen

Montréal: Canadian Pacific Archives/Archives Canadien Pacifique, PO Box 6042, Stn Centre-Ville, Montréal PQ H3C 3E4 – 514/395-5135; Fax: 514/395-5132 – Archivist, Judith L. Nefsky

Montréal: Concordia University Archives/Service des archives de l'Université Concordia, 1455, boul de Maisonneuve ouest, Montréal PQ H3G 1M8 – 514/848-7775; Fax: 514/848-2857; Email: archive@vax2.concordia.ca – Director, Nancy Marrelli

Montréal: Corporate Archives, Royal Bank of Canada, Mezzinine-2, 1, Place Ville-Marie, PO Box 6001, Montréal PQ H3C 3A9 – 514/874-2104; Fax: 514/874-2445 – Corporate Archivist, Gordon Rabchuk

Montréal: McGill University Archives (MUA), 3459, rue McTavish, Montréal PQ H3A 1Y1 – 514/398-3772; Fax: 514/398.8456; Email: gordie@archive.lan.mcgill.ca; URL: http://www.archives.mcgill.ca – University Archivist, Gordon Burr

Montréal: Service des archives de l'Université de Montréal, 2700, boul Édouard-Montpetit, CP 6128, Succ Centre-Ville, Montréal PQ H3C 3J7 – 514/343-6023; Fax: 514/343-2239 – Directeur, Jean-Yves Rousseau

Montréal: Service des archives et de gestion des documents, Université du Québec à Montréal, 1430, rue Saint-Denis, CP 8888, Succ Centre-Ville, Montréal PQ H3C 3P8 – 514/987-6130; Fax: 514/987-8487 – Directrice, Christine Huot

Montréal: Ville de Montréal - Gestion de documents et des archives, #16, 275, rue Notre-Dame est, Montréal PQ H2Y 1C6 – 514/872-2678; Fax: 514/872-3475 – Chef de division, Diane Charland

Québec: Archives de la Ville de Québec, 350, rue Saint-Joseph est, 4e étage, Québec PQ G1K 3B2 – 418/691-6371; Fax: 418/691-7894 – Archiviste, Ginette Noël

Rigaud: Archives du Collège Bourget, 65, rue Saint-Pierre, Rigaud PQ J0P 1P0 – 514/451-4718 – Archiviste, Frère Desjardins

Ste-Foy: Archives nationales du Québec, 1210, av du Séminaire, CP 10450, Ste-Foy PQ G1V 4N1 – 418/

644-3906; Fax: 418/646-0868; URL: http://www.anq.gouv.qc.ca – Conservateur, Robert Garon

Centre d'archives de Montréal, de Laval, de Lanaudière, des Laurentides et de la Montérégie, 145, rue Mullins, Montréal PQ H3K 1N9 – 514/873-3065; Fax: 514/873-2980 – Conservateur adjoint, Normand Gouger

Centre d'archives de Québec et de Chaudière-Appalaches, 1210, av du Séminaire, PO Box 10450, Ste-Foy PQ G1V 4N1 – 418/643-8904; Fax: 418/646-0868 – Conservateur adjoint, Robert Garon

Centre d'archives de l'Abitibi-Témiscamingue et du Nord-du-Québec, 27, rue du Terminus ouest, Rouyn-Noranda PQ J9X 2P3 – 819/762-4484; Fax: 819/764-6480 – Archiviste régionale, Louise-Hélène Audet

Centre d'archives de l'Estrie, 740, rue Galt ouest, rez-de-chaussée, Sherbrooke PQ J1H 1Z3 – 819/820-3010; Fax: 819/820-3930 – Archiviste régional, Gilles Durand

Centre d'archives de l'Outaouais, 170, rue de l'Hôtel-de-Ville, Hull PQ J8X 4C2 – 819/772-3010; Fax: 819/772-3950 – Archiviste régionale, Hélène Cadieux

Centre d'archives de la Côte-Nord, #190, 700, boul Laure, Sept-Îles PQ G4R 1Y1 – 418/962-3434; Fax: 418/962-6500

Centre d'archives de la Mauricie - Bois-Francs, #208, 225, rue des Forges, Trois-Rivières PQ G9A 2G7 – 819/371-6015; Fax: 819/371-6999 – Archiviste régional, Yvon Martin

Centre d'archives du Bas-Saint-Laurent et de la Gaspésie - Îles-de-la-Madeleine, 337, rue Moreault (sous-sol), Rimouski PQ G5L 1P4 – 418/727-3500; Fax: 418/727-3824 – Archiviste régional, Donald O'Farrell

Centre d'archives du Saguenay - Lac-Saint-Jean, 930, rue Jacques-Cartier est, local C-103, Chicoutimi PQ G7H 2A9 – 418/698-3516; Fax: 418/698-3522 – Archiviste régional, Jacques Thibeault

Trois-Rivières: Archives de la Collection Robert-Lionel Séguin, rue de l'Université, Trois-Rivières PQ G9A 5H7 – 819/376-5030 – Archiviste, Claude Lessard

Trois-Rivières: Archives de la Société d'histoire régionale de Trois-Rivières, 190, rue Bonaventure, Trois-Rivières PQ G9A 2B1 – 819/374-8466 – Président, Conrad Godin

SASKATCHEWAN

Regina: City of Regina Archives (CORA), 3303 Hillsdale St., Regina SK S4S 6W9 – 306/787-3399; Fax: 306/787-1975 – City Archivist, Ivan J. Saunders

Saskatchewan Archives Board, Murray Bldg., University of Saskatchewan, 3, Campus Dr., Saskatoon SK S7N 5A4 – 306/933-5832; Fax: 306/933-7305 – Director, D'Arcy Hande

BOOK PUBLISHERS

Includes Book Publishers, Distributors, Publishers' Representatives, with ISBN (International Standard Book Number) & SAN (Standard Address Number) where available.

Les 400 Coups
   474, rue Hervé, Laval PQ H7P 3M8
   514/622-8028; Fax: 514/622-8028
   ISBN: 2-921620

49th Avenue Press
   100 West 49th Ave., Vancouver BC V5Y 2Z6
   604/323-5374; Fax: 604/323-5597
   ISBN: 0-921218

Aardvark Enterprises (Div. of Speers Investments Ltd.)
   204 Millbank Dr. SW, Calgary AB T2Y 2H9
   403/256-4639
   ISBN: 0-921057; ISSN: 0831-1919

Abbeyfield Publishers
   33 Springbank Ave., Scarborough ON M1N 1G3
   416/698-8687; Fax: 416/698-8687; Email: caamtb@inforamp.net
   ISBN: 0-9680045

Academic Printing & Publishing
   PO Box 4218, Edmonton AB T6E 4T2
   403/435-5898; Fax: 403/435-5852
   ISBN: 0-920980

Acadiensis Press
   Campus House, University of New Brunswick, PO Box 4400, Stn A, Fredericton NB E3B 5A3
   506/453-4978; Fax: 506/453-4599; Email: acadnsis@unb.ca
   ISBN: 0-919107; SAN: 115-2386

Actualisation
   #705, 300, av Léo-Parizeau, CP 1142, Succ Place du Parc, Montréal PQ H2W 2P4
   514/284-2622; Fax: 514/284-2625; Email: formatio@actualisation.com; URL: http://www.actualisation.com
   ISBN: 2-920007, 2-921547

Actuel Inc. Livres Français
   492 Hurontario St., Collingwood ON L9Y 2N1
   705/444-2424; Fax: 705/445-8600; Toll Free: 1-800-461-9177

Ad Astra Books
   PO Box 53081, Stn Dorval, Dorval PQ H9S 5W4
   514/636-6080; Email: adastra@hexonx.com
   ISBN: 0-9691416

Addiction Research Foundation
   33 Russell St., Toronto ON M5S 2S1
   416/595-6059; Fax: 416/593-4694; Toll Free: 1-800-661-1111; Email: mktg@arf.org
   ISBN: 0-88868; SAN 115-0081

Addison-Wesley Publishers Ltd.
   26 Prince Andrew Pl., PO Box 580, North York ON M3C 2T8
   416/447-5101, 6489 (customer service); Fax: 416/443-0948; URL: gopher://aw.com/
   ISBN: 0-201; SAN 115-0022

Agence de Distribution Populaire
   1261A, rue Shearer, Montréal PQ H3K 3G4
   514/523-1182; Fax: 514/521-4434; Toll Free: 1-800-603-0433

Ages Publications
   #153, 1054-2 Centre St., Thornhill ON L4J 8E5
   905/709-3929; Fax: 905/731-1778
   ISBN: 1-896280, 1-886508; SAN: 117-3103

Aggie Blinkhorn Organization Inc.
   #101, 13753 - 72nd Ave., PO Box 88549, Surrey BC V3W 0X1
   604/594-7607; Fax: 604/594-7289
   ISBN: 0-9696248; SAN: 118-5039

Alcuin Society
   PO Box 3216, Vancouver BC V6B 3X8
   604/872-2376
   ISBN: 0-919026

Alexis Press
   PO Box 755, Guelph ON N1H 6L8
   519/821-7653; Fax: 519/836-3369; Email: rlcent@sentex.net
   ISBN: 0-9694159

Alive Books
   Canadian Health Reform Products Ltd., 7436 Fraser Park Dr., Burnaby BC V5J 5B9
   604/438-1919; Fax: 604/435-4888; Toll Free: 1-800-663-6513
   ISBN: 0-920470; SAN: 115-7078

Alliage Éditeur
   30, rue Palmerston, Mont Royal PQ H3P 1V2
   514/277-5456; Fax: 514/277-2934
   ISBN: 2-9800671, 2-921327

Almark & Co. - Booksellers
   PO Box 7, Thornhill ON L3T 3N1
   905/764-2665; Fax: 905/764-2665

Alpel Publishing
   PO Box 203, Chambly PQ J3L 4B3
   514/658-6205; Fax: 514/658-3514
   ISBN: 0-9691932, 0-921993

Alter Ego Editions
   3447, av Hôtel-de-Ville, Montréal PQ H2X 3B5
   514/849-9886

The Alternate Press
   272 Hwy. 5, RR#1, St. George ON N0E 1N0
   519/448-4001; Fax: 519/448-4001; Email: altpress@netroute.net

Althouse Press
   University of Western Ontario, 1137 Western Rd., London ON N6G 1G7
   519/661-2096; Fax: 519/661-3833; Email: press@edu.uwo.ca
   ISBN: 0-920354; SAN: 115-2440

Altitude Publishing Ltd.
   1408 Railway Ave., PO Box 1410, Canmore AB T0L 0M0
   403/678-6888; Fax: 403/678-6951
   ISBN: 1-55153; SAN 115-0049

Ampersand Communications Inc.
   5606 Scobie Cr., Manotick ON K4M 1B7
   613/692-2080; Fax: 613/692-1419; Email: editors@magi.com
   ISBN: 0-920262

And All That/AAT Publishing
   1801 Lakeshore Rd. West, PO Box 52614, Mississauga ON L5J 4S6
   905/820-6160; Fax: 905/820-6409; Toll Free: 1-800-461-2752
   ISBN: 1-895698

Angel Publications
   #123, 3691 Albion Rd. South, Gloucester ON K1T 1P2

Anglican Book Centre
   600 Jarvis St., Toronto ON M4Y 2J6
   416/924-9192; Fax: 416/924-2760; Toll Free: 1-800-268-1168
   ISBN: 0-919030, 0-919891, 0-921846, 1-55126

Annick Press Ltd.
   15 Patricia Ave., North York ON M2M 1H9
   416/221-4802; Fax: 416/221-8400
   ISBN: 0-920236, 920303, 1-55037; SAN: 115-0065

Annron Sales Ltd.
   #4, 5155 Spectrum Way, Mississauga ON L4W 5A1
   905/624-1009; Fax: 905/624-5499; Toll Free: 1-800-668-0492

Anson-Cartwright Editions
   229 College St., Toronto ON M5T 1R4
   416/979-2441; Fax: 416/979-2441
   ISBN: 0-919974

Antioch Inc.
   125 Harry Walker Pkwy., Unit A, Newmarket ON L3Y 7B3
   905/836-9686; Fax: 905/836-9409; Toll Free: 1-800-268-8002
   ISBN: 0-89954; SAN: 115-2475

Anvil Press
   #204A, 175 East Broadway, Vancouver BC V5T 1W2
   604/876-8710; Fax: 604/879-2667; Email: suber@pinc.com
   ISBN: 1-895636

Apple Press Publishing
   #9, 57 Glen Cameron Rd., Thornhill ON L3T 1P3
   905/882-0988; Fax: 905/881-8770
   ISBN: 0-919972

Aquila Communications Ltd.
   2646 Diab St., St. Laurent PQ H4S 1E8
   514/338-1065; Fax: 514/338-1948; Toll Free: 1-800-667-7071
   ISBN: 0-88510, 2-89054; SAN: 115-2483, 115-8295

Canadian Almanac & Directory 1997

BOOK PUBLISHERS

Argenta Friends Press
Argenta BC V0G 1B0
250/366-4314; Fax: 250/366-4314

Ariane Publications
#110, 1209, av Bernard ouest, Outremont PQ H2V 1V7
514/276-2949; Fax: 514/276-2141
ISBN: 2-920987

Arion
10570, rue Elisabeth-II, Québec PQ G2A 1Y3
418/842-4622; Fax: 418/842-4622
ISBN: 2-921493

Arnold Publishing Ltd.
#101, 10301 - 104 St., Edmonton AB T5J 1B9
403/426-2998; Fax: 403/426-4607; Toll Free: 1-800-563-2665
ISBN: 0-919913

Arsenal Pulp Press Ltd.
#103, 1014 Homer St., Vancouver BC V6B 2W9
604/687-4233; Fax: 604/669-8250
ISBN: 0-88978, 1-55152; SAN: 115-0847

Art Global
384, av Laurier ouest, Montréal PQ H2V 2K7
514/272-6111; Fax: 514/272-8609
ISBN: 2-920718

Art Metropole
788 King St. West, Toronto ON M5V 1N6
416/367-2304; Fax: 416/365-9208;
Email: art_metropole@inagg.web.net
ISBN: 0-920956; SAN: 156-9902

Artel Educational Resources Ltd.
5528 Kingsway, Burnaby BC V5H 2G2
604/435-4949; Fax: 604/435-1955; Toll Free: 1-800-665-9255
SAN: 116-029X

Artemis Enterprises
578 Ofield Rd. North, RR#2, PO Box 54, Dundas ON L9H 5E2
905/628-0596; Fax: 905/628-0596; Email: artemis@icom.ca
ISBN: 1-895247

Artery Enterprises Ltd.
#102, 1037 West Broadway, Vancouver BC V6H 1E3
604/730-2520; Fax: 604/730-7959
ISBN: 0-920431; SAN: 117-0198

Artexte Information Centre
#103, 3575, boul Saint-Laurent, Montréal PQ H2X 2T7
514/845-2759; Fax: 514/845-4345
ISBN: 2-98006

Ascension Books
3 Iolanta Ct., Etobicoke ON M9W 6H2
416/798-1731; Fax: 416/798-1731
ISBN: 0-929431; SAN: 117-0198

Asclépiade
3436, rue Archambault, Longueuil PQ J4M 2W8
514/448-5049; Fax: 514/448-9898
ISBN: 2-9801115

Asquith House Limited/Michael Preston Associates
94 Asquith Ave., Toronto ON M4W 1J8
416/925-3577; Fax: 416/925-8823

Athabasca University
PO Box 10,000, Athabasca AB T9S 1A1
403/675-5864

Athena Publisher's Agency
2146 - 17 Ave. SW, Calgary AB T2T 0G3
403/245-2087; Fax: 403/245-2098

Atlantic Book Ltd.
35 Cobequid Dr., PO Box 1910, Truro NS B2N 5R1
902/895-6666; Fax: 902/893-1464
SAN: 111-0608

Augsburg Fortress Canada
#1, 216 - 40 Ave. NE, Calgary AB T2E 8C6
403/276-7000; Fax: 403/230-1165; Toll Free: 1-800-661-8379
Ontario Office: 500 Trillium Dr., PO Box 940, Kitchener ON N2G 4E3

519/748-2200; Fax: 519/748-9835; Toll Free: 1-800-265-8922

Aurora Editions
1184 Garfield St. North, Winnipeg MB R3E 2P1
204/783-7113; Fax: 204/831-5675
ISBN: 0-9697590

Aviation Publishers Co. Ltd.
PO Box 1361, Stn B, Ottawa ON K1P 5R4
613/745-2943; Fax: 613/745-9851;
Email: aviationpub@igs.net
ISBN: 0-9690054

Avon Books of Canada
#210, 2061 McCowan Rd., Scarborough ON M1S 3Y6
416/293-9404; Fax: 416/293-8401; Toll Free: 1-800-268-3531
ISBN: 0-380; SAN: 115-1460

Aya Press see The Mercury Press

B & B Publishing
#115, 4823, rue Sherbrooke ouest, Westmount PQ H3Z 1G7
514/932-9466; Fax: 514/932-5929
ISBN: 2-7615

B. Broughton Co. Ltd.
2105 Danforth Ave., Toronto ON M4C 1K1
416/690-4777; Fax: 416/690-5357; Toll Free: 1-800-268-4449
SAN: 168-4213

Bacon & Hughes
13 Deerlane Ave., Nepean ON K2E 6W7
613/226-8136; Fax: 613/226-8121

Ballantine-Fawcett Books see Random House of Canada Ltd.

Balmuir Book Publishing Ltd.
128 Manning Ave., Toronto ON M6J 2K5
416/861-9129; Fax: 416/861-8702
ISBN: 0-919511; SAN: 115-6551

Banff Centre Press
The Banff Centre, PO Box 102050, Banff AB T0L 0C0
403/762-6697; Fax: 403/762-6238; Email: press@banffcentre.ab.ca
ISBN: 0-929159

Bantam Books Canada Inc.
105 Bond St., 4th Fl., Toronto ON M5B 1Y3
416/340-0777; Fax: 416/340-1069; Toll Free: 1-800-387-5621
ISBN: 0-553; SAN: 115-1479

Bare Bones Publishing
#305, 4625 Varsity Dr. NW, PO Box 355, Calgary AB T3A 0Z9
403/239-7555; Fax: 403/239-0563;
Email: barebones@cadvision.com
ISBN: 0-9696095, 1-896865

Barron's Educational Series Inc.
34 Armstrong Ave., Georgetown ON L7G 4R9
905/458-5506; Fax: 905/877-5575; Toll Free: 1-800-247-7160
ISBN: 0-8120; SAN: 115-2033

Beach Holme Publishers Limited
4252 Commerce Circle, Victoria BC V8Z 4M2
250/727-6522; Fax: 250/727-6418; Toll Free: 1-800-663-7560; Email: bhp@softwords.bc.ca
ISBN: 0-88878; SAN: 115-0812

Beacon Distributing/Cook Communications
55 Woodslee Ave., PO Box 98, Paris ON N3L 3E5
519/442-7853; Fax: 519/442-1303; Toll Free: 1-800-263-2664
ISBN: 0-89693; SAN: 170-0197

BeJo Sales Ltd.
#52, 7050B Bramalea Rd., Mississauga ON L5S 1S9
905/677-0730; Fax: 905/677-0905; Toll Free: 1-800-668-7932
SAN: 115-2602

Bella Flor Enterprises
#3, 2250 Leckie Rd., Kelowna BC V1X 7K1
250/860-3377; Fax: 250/860-0833; Toll Free: 1-800-667-1902

Ben-Simon Publications
PO Box 318, Brentwood Bay BC V0S 1A0
250/652-6332; Fax: 250/652-6332;
Email: bensimon@pinc.com; URL: http://www.simon-sez.com
ISBN: 0-920808; SAN: 115-2637

Benben Publications
1483 Carmen Dr., Mississauga ON L5G 3Z2
905/274-4380
ISBN: 0-920808

Bendall Books
PO Box 115, Mill Ray BC V0R 2P0
250/743-2946; Fax: 250/743-2910;
Email: bendallbooks@islandnet.com;
URL: http://www.islandnet.com/bendallbooks
ISBN: 0-9696985

The Best of Bridge Publishing Ltd.
6037 - 6 St. SE, Calgary AB T2H 1L8
403/252-0119; Fax: 403/252-0206
ISBN: 0-9690425

Betelgeuse Books
#193, 55 McCaul St., Toronto ON M5T 2W7
ISBN: 0-9690783

Between the Lines
#404, 720 Bathurst St., Toronto ON M5S 2R4
416/535-9914; Fax: 416/535-1484;
Email: mamorris@web.apc.org
ISBN: 0-919946, 0-921284; SAN: 115-0189

Black Moss Press
2450 Byng Rd., PO Box 143, Stn A, Windsor ON N9A 6K1
519/252-2551; Fax: 519/253-7809
ISBN: 0-88753; SAN: 115-2645

Black Rose Books Ltd.
#888, 3981, boul Saint-Laurent, PO Box 1258, Stn Pl du Parc, Montréal PQ H2W 2R3
514/844-4076; Fax: 514/849-1956; Email: info@blakrose@web.apc.org
ISBN: 0-919, 0-920, 0-921; SAN: 115-2653

Blizzard Publishing Ltd.
73 Furby St., Winnipeg MB R3B 2C2
204/775-2923; Fax: 204/775-2947; Email: atwood@blizzard.mb.ca; URL: http://www.blizzard.mb.ca/catalog/
ISBN: 0-921368

Blue Nun Press
3226 Midland Pl., Duncan BC V9L 4H7
250/748-4545

Blue Ribbon Bookhouse
PO Box 158, Shakespeare ON N0B 2P0
519/655-3360; Fax: 519/655-3167
ISBN: 0-895; SAN: 115-1878

Boardwalk Books
#301, 2181 Queen St. East, Toronto ON M4E 1E5
416/698-0454; Fax: 416/698-1102; Toll Free: 1-800-391-1653
ISBN: 1-895681

Book Express
8680 Cambie St., Vancouver BC V6P 6M9
604/323-7106; Fax: 604/323-7109; Toll Free: 1-800-663-5714; Email: info@raincoast.com
SAN: 115-0871

The Book Room
1546 Barrington St., PO Box 272, Halifax NS B3J 2N7
902/423-8271; Fax: 902/423-0398; Toll Free: 1-800-387-2665
ISBN: 0-9690177; SAN: 168-020X

Bookfellows
3404 Connorton Lane, Victoria BC V8P 3K1
250/380-2665; Fax: 250/380-2664

Bookworm Literary Productions
PO Box 2095, Kingston ON K7L 5J8

Borealis/Tecumseh Presses Ltd.
9 Ashburn Dr., Ottawa ON K2E 6N4
613/224-6837; Fax: 613/829-7783
ISBN: 0-919594, 0-88887

Boston Mills Press
132 Main St., Erin ON N0B 1T0
519/833-2407; Fax: 519/833-2195; Toll Free: 1-800-565-3111
ISBN: 0-919822, 0-919783, 1-55046; SAN: 115-0138

Bow-Dell Publishing Ltd.
PO Box 40620, Stn UpperBrant, Burlington ON L7P 4W1
905/333-9049; Fax: 905/333-6780
SAN: 115-270X

Bradley Publications
2352 Smith St., Regina SK S4P 2P6
306/525-3305; Fax: 306/757-1810

Braun & Braun Educational Enterprise Ltd.
PO Box 84129, Stn Market Mall, Calgary AB T2A 5C4
403/282-1584; Fax: 403/282-1584
ISBN: 0-9690605

Breakwater Books Ltd.
100 Water St., PO Box 2188, St. John's NF A1C 6E6
709/722-6680; Fax: 709/753-0708; Toll Free: 1-800-563-3333; Email: breakwater@nfld.com
ISBN: 0-919519, 0-920911, 1-55081; SAN 115-0154

Breton Books
RR#1, Wreck Cove, Victoria County, Englishtown NS B0C 1H0
902/539-3817; Fax: 902/539-9117
ISBN: 1-895415

Brick Books
431 Boler Rd., PO Box 20081, London ON N6K 4G6
519/657-8579; Fax: 519/657-8579
ISBN: 0-919626; SAN: 115-0162

Broadview Press
PO Box 1243, Peterborough ON K9J 7H5
705/743-8990; Fax: 705/743-8353; Email: 75322.44@compuserve.com
ISBN: 0-921149; SAN: 115-6772

Broken Jaw Press/Maritimes Arts Projects Productions
PO Box 596, Stn A, Fredericton NB E3B 5A6
506/454-5127; Fax: 506/452-8568; Email: jblades@nbnet.nb.ca
ISBN: 0-921411; SAN: 117-1437

Bungalo Books
#100, 17 Elk Ct., Kingston ON K7M 7A4
613/389-2494; Fax: 613/389-2351; Email: bungalohq@sol.com
ISBN: 0-921285

Bunker to Bunker Books
34 Blue Spruce Cres., Winnipeg MB R2M 4C2
204/255-5843; Fax: 204/255-8537
ISBN: 0-9699039

Butterfly Books Ltd.
PO Box 294, Maple Creek SK S0N 1N0

Butterworths Canada Ltd.
75 Clegg Rd., Markham ON L6G 1A1
905/479-2665; Fax: 905/479-2826; Toll Free: 1-800-461-3275; Email: info@butterworths.ca; URL: http://www.butterworths.ca
Western Office: #1721, 808 Nelson St., Vancouver BC V6Z 2H2
604/684-4116; Fax: 604/682-5779
ISBN: 0-409; SAN: 115-2750

C. Kirkness Press
93B Woodbridge Ave., PO Box 56510, Woodbridge ON L4L 8V3
905/851-4660; Fax: 905/851-5507
ISBN: 0-86596, 0-04150

Caboodle & Co.
217 Pickering St., Toronto ON M4E 3J9
416/699-0669; Fax: 416/699-2651
ISBN: 0-9694654

Cacanadadada Press see Ronsdale Press

The Caitlin Press
PO Box 2387, Stn B, Prince George BC V2N 2S6
250/964-4953; Fax: 250/964-4953
ISBN: 0-920576; SAN: 115-2793

Callawind Publications Inc.
#205, 3383, boul Sources, Dollard-des-Ormeaux PQ H9B 1Z8
514/685-9109; Fax: 514/685-7055; Email: info@callawind.com; URL: http://www.callawind.com
ISBN: 1-896511

Camden House Publishing
Harrowsmith Country Life, #100, 25 Sheppard Ave. West, Toronto ON M2N 6S7
416/733-7600; Fax: 416/733-7981; Toll Free: 1-800-267-7833
ISBN: 0-920656, 0-921820; SAN: 115-7086

Campbell Communications Inc.
1218 Langley St., 3rd Fl., Victoria BC V8W 1W2
250/388-7231; Fax: 250/383-1140
ISBN: 1-895297

Can-Ed Media Ltd.
43 Moccasin Trail, North York ON M3C 1Y5
416/445-3900
ISBN: 0-920102

Canada Communications Group Publishing/Groupe Communication Canada - Édition
Dept. of Public Works & Government Services Canada, #D2200, 45, boul Sacre-Coeur, Hull PQ K1A 0S9
819/956-4800; Fax: 819/994-1498; Email: publishing@ccg-gcc.ca; URL: http://www.ccg.gcc.ca
ISBN: 0-662, 0-660; SAN: 115-2882

Canada Law Book Inc.
240 Edward St., Aurora ON L4G 3S9
905/841-6472; Fax: 905/841-5085; Toll Free: 1-800-263-2037
ISBN: 0-88804

Canada Publishing Corporation
164 Commander Blvd., Agincourt ON M1S 3C7
416/293-8141; Fax: 416/293-9009
ISBN: 0-7715, 7705

Canadian Almanac & Directory Publishing Company
200 Adelaide St. West, 3rd Fl., Toronto, ON M5H 1W7
416/597-1616; Fax: 416/597-1617; Toll Free: 1-800-815-9417; Email: info@mail.CanadaInfo.com; URL: http://www.CanadaInfo.com

Canadian Book Review Annual
#3205, 44 Charles St. West, Toronto ON M4Y 1R8
416/961-8537; Fax: 416/961-1855; Email: cbra@interlog.com; URL: http://www.interlog.com/~cbra
ISBN: 0-969996

Canadian Caboose Press see Good Medicine Books

Canadian Educators' Press
1230 White Clover Way, Mississauga ON L5V 1K7
905/826-0578; Fax: 905/826-0578
ISBN: 1-896191

Canadian Manda Group
#105, One Atlantic Ave., Toronto ON M6K 3E7
416/516-0911; Fax: 416/516-0917; Email: manda@sympatico.ca

Canadian MasterAthlete Federation, Book Division
#8, 100 West Beaver Creek, Richmond Hill ON L4B 1H4
905/707-8464; Fax: 905/707-8464; Toll Free: 1-800-363-9709; Email: sports@passport.ca

Canadian News
1530 Erin St., Winnipeg MB R3E 3K5
204/786-3465; Fax: 204/772-1316

Canadian Paperbacks Publishing Ltd.
17 Gwynne Ave., Ottawa ON K1Y 1X1
613/722-1171
ISBN: 0-919554

Canadian Professional Information Centre Ltd.
#108, 6200 Dixie Rd., Mississauga ON L5T 2E1
905/670-1250; Fax: 905/670-1252; Email: web@idirect.com

Canadian Scholars' Press Inc.
#402, 180 Bloor St. West, Toronto ON M5S 2V6
416/929-2774; Fax: 416/929-1926; Email: info@cspi.org
ISBN: 0-921627, 1-55130

Canadian Stage and Arts Publications Limited
104 Glenrose Ave., Toronto ON M4T 1K8
416/484-4534; Fax: 416/484-6214
ISBN: 0-919952

CANAV Books
51 Balsam Ave., Toronto ON M4E 3B6
416/698-7559; Fax: 416/693-4344
ISBN: 0-9690703

Canbook Distribution Services
1220 Nicholson Rd., Newmarket ON L3Y 7B1
905/713-3852; Fax: 1-800-363-2665; Toll Free: 1-800-399-6858

Cannon Book Distribution Ltd.
3710 Nashua Dr., Mississauga ON L4V 1M5
905/678-7668; Fax: 905/678-6303
ISBN: 0-9695251; SAN: 170-009X

Captus Press
York University Campus, 4700 Keele St., North York ON M3J 1P3
416/736-5537; Fax: 416/736-5103; Email: captpres@io.org; URL: http://www.io.org/~captpres
ISBN: 0-921801, 1-895712

Caravan Books Co. Ltd.
121 Lee Ave., Toronto ON M4E 2P2
416/298-9540, 9541; Fax: 416/298-9541
Warehouse & Showroom: #1, 70 Weybright Ct., Scarborough ON M1S 4E4
416/298-9540, 9541; Fax: 416/298-9541
SAN: 115-3048

Cariad Ltd.
#1103, 89 Isabella St., Toronto ON M4Y 1N8
416/924-1918

Carib-Can Communications Inc.
555 Bloor St. W., 2nd Fl., Toronto ON M5S 1Y6
416/531-3414; Fax: 416/531-3197; Email: ccrc@ccrc.org
ISBN: 0-920997

Carleton University Press Inc.
Carleton University, #1400, 1125 Colonel By Dr., Ottawa ON K1S 5B6
613/788-3740; Fax: 613/788-2893; Email: cu_press@carleton.ca
ISBN: 0-88629; SAN: 115-3056

Carraig Books/Livres Carraig
PO Box 8733, Ste. Foy PQ G1V 4N6
418/651-5918
ISBN: 0-9690805

Carswell
Corporate Plaza, 2075 Kennedy Rd., Scarborough ON M1T 3V4
416/609-8000; Fax: 416/298-5094; URL: http://www.carswell.com/carswell.home
Distribution Centre: 245 Bartley Dr., Toronto ON M4A 2V8
416/759-4411; Fax: 416/759-5415; Toll Free: 1-800-387-5164
ISBN: 0-459, 0-88820; SAN: 115-0316

Castlefield Press
892 Castlefield Ave., Toronto ON M6B 1C8
416/782-3116; Fax: 416/782-3116; Email: 75533.3202@compuserve.com
ISBN: 0-9632554; SAN: 119-6251

Cavendish Books Inc.
#5, 801 West 1st St., North Vancouver BC V7P 1A4
604/985-2969; Fax: 604/985-2955; Toll Free: 1-800-665-3166
ISBN: 0-929050; SAN: 115-0944

CCH Canadian Limited
6 Garamond Ct., North York ON M3C 1Z5
416/441-2992; Fax: 416/441-9011; Toll Free: 1-800-268-4522; URL: http://www.ca.cch.com/
ISBN: 0-88796; SAN: 115-2785

C.D. Howe Institute
125 Adelaide St. East, Toronto ON M5C 1L7

Canadian Almanac & Directory 1997

416/865-1904; Fax: 416/865-1866; Email: cdhowe@cdhowe.org
ISBN: 0-88806; SAN: 115-0502

Cedar Cave Publishing
PO Box 867, Stn F, Toronto ON M4Y 2N7
416/657-8621; Fax: 416/658-0327; Email: iw@io.org
ISBN: 0-929403

Centax Books & Distribution
1150 - 8th Ave., Regina SK S4R 1C9
306/525-2304; Fax: 306/757-2439
ISBN: 0-919845, 1-895292; SAN: 115-1630

Centre Éducatif et Culturel Inc.
8101, boul Métropolitain, Anjou PQ H1J 1J9
514/351-6010; Fax: 514/351-3534
ISBN: 2-7617

Chapters Inc.
90 Ronson Dr., Etobicoke ON M9W 1C1
416/243-3138; Fax: 416/243-8964
ISBN: 0-7740; SAN: 115-3102

Charlemagne Press
1384 Hope Rd., North Vancouver BC V7P 1W7
604/988-7724; Fax: 604/984-7718
ISBN: 0-921845

The Charlton Press
2010 Yonge St., Toronto ON M4S 1Z9
416/488-4653; Fax: 416/488-4656
ISBN: 0-88968; SAN: 115-0235

Chenelière/McGraw Hill
215, rue Jean-Talon est, Montréal PQ H2R 1S9
514/273-1066; Fax: 514/276-0324
ISBN: 2-89310

Cherev Canada Inc.
RR#3, PO Box 698, Markdale ON N0C 1H0
519/986-4353; Fax: 519/986-3103; Toll Free: 1-800-263-2408

The Chessnut Press/Éditions Fou des Échecs
PO Box 117, Stn Victoria, Montréal PQ H3Z 2V4
514/489-6733; Fax: 514/485-3828; Email: drknight@odyssee.net
ISBN: 0-919848

Child's Play
#5, 120 Watline Ave., Mississauga ON L4Z 2C1
905/890-8111; Fax: 905/890-3149
ISBN: 0-85953

Childe Thursday
29 Sussex Ave., Toronto ON M5S 1J6
416/979-2544
ISBN: 0-920459

The Children's Book Store
2532 Yonge St., Toronto ON M4P 2H7
416/480-0233; Fax: 416/480-9345; Toll Free: 1-800-265-5622

Christie & Christie Associates
261 Alice St., Kincardine ON N2Z 2P9
519/396-9553; Fax: 519/396-9554; Toll Free: 1-800-263-1991

Claude M. Diffusion Ltd.
1544, rue Villeray, Montréal PQ H2E 1H1
514/376-9723; Fax: 514/727-0899

CMC Distribution
590 York Rd., Niagara-on-the-Lake ON L0S 1J0
905/641-0631; Fax: 905/641-8824; Toll Free: 1-800-387-6950

CMD
1544, rue Villeray, Montréal PQ H2E 1H1
514/376-9723; Fax: 514/727-0899

Coles Publishing see Chapters Inc.

Colombo & Company
42 Dell Park Ave., Toronto ON M6B 2T6
416/782-6853; Fax: 416/782-0285; Email: jrc@inforamp.net; URL: http://www.inforamp.net/~JRC
ISBN: 1-896308

Commoners' Publishing Society Inc.
73 Eccles St., Ottawa ON K1R 6S5
613/238-3699; Fax: 613/238-3491
ISBN: 0-88970; SAN: 115-0243

Commonwealth Publications Inc.
9764 - 45th Ave., Edmonton AB T6E 5C5
403/465-7316; Fax: 403/432-9409; Email: cpub@worldgate.com; URL: http://www.commonwealthpub.com

Company's Coming Publishing Limited
PO Box 8037, Stn F, Edmonton AB T6H 4N9
403/450-6223; Fax: 403/450-1857
ISBN: 0-9690695, 1-895444; SAN: 115-3129

Computofacts
209 Sheppard Ave. East, North York ON M2N 5W2
416/222-4361
ISBN: 0-919640; SAN: 115-3137

Conîcidence/Jeunesse
60, rue Lorrain, CP 143, Iberville PQ J2X 4J5
514/346-6958; Fax: 514/347-6727
ISBN: 2-89397

Continental Records Co. Ltd.
PO Box 2604, Brampton ON L6T 5M6
905/450-6660; Fax: 905/457-9417; Email: conrecs@gocontinental.com; URL: http://www.gocontinental.com

Copp Clark Professional
200 Adelaide St. West, 3rd Fl., Toronto ON M5H 1W7
416/597-1616; Fax: 416/597-1617, 8941; Toll Free: 1-800-815-9417; Email: info@mail.CanadaInfo.com; URL: http://www.CanadaInfo.com
ISBN: 1-895021

Cordillera Publishing Co.
8415 Granville St., PO Box 46, Vancouver BC V6P 4Z9
604/261-1695; Fax: 604/266-4469
ISBN: 1-895590

Cormorant Books Inc.
RR#1, Dunvegan ON K0C 1J0
613/527-3348; Fax: 613/527-2262; Email: cormoran@flen-net.ca
ISBN: 0-920953; SAN: 115-4176

Coteau Books/Thunder Creek Publishing Cooperative
#401, 2206 Dewdney Ave., Regina SK S4R 1H3
306/777-0170; Fax: 306/522-5152; Email: coteau@coteau.unibase.com; URL: http://www.coteau.unibase.com
ISBN: 0-919926, 0-55050; SAN: 115-0391

Cottage Life Books
#408, 111 Queen St. East, Toronto ON M5C 1S2
416/360-6880; Fax: 416/360-6814
ISBN: 0-9696922

La Courte Échelle
5243, boul Saint-Laurent, Montréal PQ H2T 1S4
514/274-2004; Fax: 514/270-4160
ISBN: 2-89021, 2-7625; SAN: 116-0249

Coyote Books
PO Box 3397, Canmore AB T0L 0M0
403/678-4978; Fax: 403/522-3842
ISBN: 0-9692457, 0-9698939

Crabtree Publishing Co. Ltd.
360 York St., RR#4, Niagara on the Lake ON L0S 1J0
905/682-5221; Fax: 905/682-7166; Email: marketing@crabtreee~pub.com
ISBN: 0-86505; SAN: 115-1436

Crane Editions
PO Box 460, Dundurn SK S0K 1K0
306/492-2128; Fax: 306/492-2202
ISBN: 1-895285

Creative Book Publishing Ltd.
PO Box 8660, St. John's NF A1B 3T7
709/722-8500; Fax: 709/722-2228
ISBN: 0-920021, 1-895387

Creative Bound Inc.
151 Tansley Dr., PO Box 424, Carp ON K0A 1L0
613/831-3641; Fax: 613/831-3643
ISBN: 0-921165; SAN: 116-7413

Cross Canada Books
354 Wellesley St. East, PO Box 550, Stn P, Toronto ON M5S 2T1

416/925-7807; Fax: 416/925-7807

Crown Publications Inc.
521 Fort St., Victoria BC V8W 1E7
250/386-4636; Fax: 250/386-0221; Email: crown@pinc.com
ISBN: 0-9696417

Culture Concepts Inc.
5 Darlingbrook Cres., Toronto ON M9A 3H4
416/231-1692; Fax: 416/237-1832
ISBN: 0-921472

Daillac Éditeur
99, rue Beaumont ouest, Saint-Bruno PQ J3V 2P3
514/653-7226
ISBN: 2-9801025

Dance Collection Danse Press/es
145 George St., Toronto ON M5A 2M6
416/365-3233; Fax: 416/365-3169; Toll Free: 1-800-665-5320
ISBN: 0-929003

David C. Cook Publishing (Canada) Ltd. see Beacon Distributing/Cook Communications

Davis Press
6060 Doulton Ave., Richmond BC V7C 4Y4
604/277-6003; Fax: 604/277-6003
ISBN: 0-895209; SAN: 115-7588

D.C. Books/Livres DC
1495, rue de l'Église, PO Box 662, Montréal PQ H4L 4V9
514/843-8130
ISBN: 0-919688; SAN: 115-8988

D.C. Heath Canada Ltd. see ITP Nelson

Décarie Éditeur inc.
233, av Dunbar, Mont-Royal PQ H3P 2H4
514/343-8500; Fax: 514/342-3982
ISBN: 2-89137

Dempsey - Your Distributor Inc.
#200, 1396 Richards St., Vancouver BC V6B 3G6
604/683-5541; Fax: 604/683-5521; Toll Free: 1-800-667-3399

Detselig Enterprises Ltd.
#210, 1220 Kensington Rd. NW, Calgary AB T2N 3P5
403/283-0900; Fax: 403/283-6947
ISBN: 0-920490, 1-55059; SAN: 115-0324

Development Press
5096 Catalina Terrace, Victoria BC V8Y 2A5
250/658-1323; Fax: 250/658-8110; Email: connor@islandnet.com; URL: http://www.islandnet.com/~connor
ISBN: 0-929136

Didacta Inc.
1228, rue St-Mathieu, Montréal PQ H3H 2H7
514/931-0707; Fax: 514/931-0708
ISBN: 2-89199; SAN: 115-3269

Diffulivre Inc.
817, rue McCaffrey, St-Laurent PQ H4T 1N3
514/738-2911; Fax: 514/738-8512; Email: mlaberge@interlink.net

Le Diffuseur G. Vermette Inc.
151A, boul de Mortagne, PO Box 85, Boucherville PQ J4B 5E6
514/641-1334; Fax: 514/641-2002
ISBN: 2-920653, 2-89416; SAN: 115-8694

Diffusion Dimedia Inc.
539, boul Lebeau, Montréal PQ H4N 1S2
514/336-3941; Fax: 514/331-3916

Diffusion Inter-livres enr.
1703, av Belleville, Lemoyne PQ J4P 3M2
514/465-0037; Fax: 514/923-8966

Diffusion du Livre Mirabel
5757, rue Cypihot, St-Laurent PQ H4S 1X4
514/334-2690; Fax: 514/334-4720
ISBN: 0-88527

Diffusion Prologue
1650, boul Lionel-Bertrand, Boisbriand PQ G7E 4H4
514/434-0306; Fax: 514/434-2627; Toll Free: 1-800-363-2864

Diffusion et Promotion du Livre Universitaire Inc. (DPLU)
  #112, 5165, rue Sherbrooke ouest, Montréal PQ H4A 1T6
  514/484-3940; Fax: 514/484-9325
Diffusion Raffin, inc.
  7870, rue Fleuricourt, St-Léonard PQ H1R 2L3
  514/325-5553; Fax: 514/325-7329; Toll Free: 1-800-361-4293
Diffusion Rive-nord
  1977, boul Industriel, Laval PQ H7S 1P6
  514/662-1975; Fax: 514/662-2125
Diffusion Soussan Edilivre Inc.
  5740, rue Ferrier, Ville Mont-Royal PQ H4P 1H7
  514/738-0202; Fax: 514/738-5102
  ISBN: 2-89393
Distican Inc.
  35 Fulton Way, Richmond Hill ON L4B 2N4
  905/764-0073; Fax: 905/764-0086; Toll Free: 1-800-268-3216; Email: postmaster@distican.com
  ISBN: 0-7701; SAN: 115-4788
DMR Distribution Inc.
  3700A, boul St-Laurent, Montréal PQ
  514/499-0072; Fax: 514/499-0851
Doubleday Canada Ltd.
  105 Bond St., Toronto ON M5B 1Y3
  416/340-0777; Fax: 416/340-1069; Toll Free: 1-800-387-5621
  ISBN: 0-385; SAN: 115-0340
Douglas & McIntyre Ltd.
  Adult Trade Division, 1615 Venables St., Vancouver BC V5L 2H1
  604/254-7191; Fax: 604/254-9099; Toll Free: 1-800-667-6902
  ISBN: 0-88894, 1-55054; SAN: 115-1886, 115-2270
Doutre et Vandal, éditeurs
  CP 159, Succ C, Montréal PQ H2T 3A7
  514/495-8968; Fax: 514/272-6058
  ISBN: 2-89410
Dovehouse Editions Inc.
  1890 Fairmeadow Cres., Ottawa ON K1H 7B9
  613/731-7601
  ISBN: 0-919473, 1-895537
Dragon Hill Publishing
  5541 - 39th Ave., Edmonton AB T6L 1B7
  403/465-5279; Fax: 403/466-3999; Email: dragon@superiway.net
  ISBN: 1-896124
Dundurn Press Ltd.
  #301, 2181 Queen St. East, Toronto ON M4E 1E5
  416/698-0454; Fax: 416/698-1102; Toll Free: 1-800-391-1653; Email: orders@dundurn.com
  ISBN: 0-919670, 1-55002, 0-88924
Durkin Hayes Publishing Ltd.
  3375 North Service Rd., #B7, Burlington ON L7N 3G2
  905/335-0393; Fax: 905/332-3008; Toll Free: 1-800-263-5224
  ISBN: 0-88625, 0-88646; SAN: 115-3765
Earthscan Canada
  225 Brunswick Ave., Toronto ON M5S 2M6
  416/978-5602; Fax: 416/978-3824
  ISBN: 185383; SAN: 116-838X
Ecrits des Forges
  PO Box 335, Trois-Rivières PQ G9A 5G4
  819/379-9813; Fax: 819/376-0774
  ISBN: 2-89046
ECW Press
  #200, 2120 Queen St. East, Toronto ON M4E 1E2
  416/694-3348; Fax: 416/698-9906
  ISBN: 1-55022; SAN: 115-1274
Éd-Archambault-Inc.
  500, rue Sainte-Catherine est, Montréal PQ H2L 2C6
  514/849-6201; Fax: 514/849-0764
EDIMAG inc.
  CP 325, Succ Rosemont, Montréal PQ H1X 3B8
  514/522-2244; Fax: 514/522-6301; Email: pnadeau@edimag.qc.com; URL: http://www.edimag.com
  ISBN: 2-921207
Edipress inc.
  945, av Beaumont, Montréal PQ H3N 1W3
  514/272-6141; Fax: 514/273-7021
Edisem Inc.
  2475, av Sylva-Clapin, CP 295, Saint-Hyacinthe PQ J2S 7B6
  514/774-8118; Fax: 514/774-3017
  ISBN: 2-89130
Les Éditions d'Acadie Ltée
  236, rue St-Georges, PO Box 885, Moncton NB E1C 8N8
  506/857-8490; Fax: 506/855-3130; Email: edacadie@nbnet.nb.ca
  ISBN: 2-7600
Éditions Adage
  12306, boul O'Brien, Montréal PQ H4J 1Z4
  514/336-2938; Fax: 514/336-0614
  ISBN: 2-9801053
Éditions Agence d'Arc
  955, rue Bergar, Laval PQ H7L 4Z7
  514/334-8466; Fax: 514/334-8387
  ISBN: 0-88586, 0-289022
Éditions Anne Sigier inc.
  1073, boul René-Lévesque ouest, Sillery PQ G1S 4R5
  418/687-6086; Fax: 418/687-3565; Toll Free: 1-800-463-6846; Email: sigier@megatoon.com
  ISBN: 2-89129
Éditions Arts, Lettres et Techniques Inc.
  901, boul Ste-Croix, Montréal PQ H4L 3Y5
  514/747-4784, 747-4785; Fax: 514/747-5366
  ISBN: 0-9211137
Éditions Autres Rives
  #7516, 1260, rue Richmond, Montréal PQ H3K 1H2
  514/939-4189; Fax: 514/939-2661
Éditions Beauchemin Ltée
  3281, av Jean Béraud, Chomedey PQ H7T 2L2
  514/334-5912; Fax: 514/688-6269; Toll Free: 1-800-361-4504; Email: gfrenet@beauchemic.qc.ca; URL: http://www.beauchemin.qc.ca
  ISBN: 2-7616
Éditions Behaviora
  151, ch Bellevue, CP 91, Eastman PQ J0E 1P0
  514/297-0515; Fax: 514/297-0516
  ISBN: 2-7629
Éditions Bellarmin
  165, rue Deslauriers, Saint-Laurent PQ H4N 2S4
  514/745-4290; Fax: 514/745-4299
  ISBN: 0-88502, 2-89007
Éditions Bibi et Geneviève
  3409, rue Saint-Antoine, Westmount PQ H3Z 1X1
  514/931-6190; Fax: 514/939-2034
  ISBN: 2-921577
Les Éditions du Blé
  CP 31, Saint-Boniface MB R3H 3B4
  204/237-8200; Fax: 204/233-2373; Email: alexis@magic.mb.ca; URL: http://www.magic.mb.ca/~alexis
  ISBN: 0-920640, 2-921347
Éditions Bo-Pré
  817, rue McCaffrey, St-Laurent PQ H4T 1N3
  514/738-2911; Fax: 514/738-8512
  ISBN: 2-89315
Éditions du Bois-de-Coulogne
  1140, av de Montigny, Sillery PQ G1S 3T7
  418/683-6332; Fax: 418/683-6332; Email: acces@ebc.qc.ca; URL: http://www.ebc.qc.ca
  ISBN: 2-9801397
Éditions du Boréal
  4447, rue St-Denis, Montréal PQ H2J 2L2
  514/287-7401; Fax: 514/287-7664
  ISBN: 2-89052
Les Éditions Brault et Bouthillier
  #115, 4823, rue Sherbrooke ouest, Westmount PQ H3Z 1G7
  514/932-9466; Fax: 514/932-5929
  ISBN: 0-88537, 2-7615
Éditions Brimar Inc.
  338, rue Saint-Antoine est, Montréal PQ H2Y 1A3
  514/954-1441; Fax: 514/954-1443
  ISBN: 2-920845
Éditions Broquet Inc./Broquet Publishing Company Inc.
  418, ch des Frênes, L'Acadie PQ J2Y 1J1
  514/357-9626; Fax: 514/357-9625
  ISBN: 2-89000
Éditions Centre Flora
  533, rue Notre-Dame, Sudbury ON P3C 5L1
  705/673-7033; Fax: 705/673-5520
  ISBN 2-921706
Éditions Ceres
  CP 1386, Succ Place Bonaventure, Montréal PQ H5A 1H3
  514/937-7138; Fax: 514/937-7138
  ISBN: 0-919089
Éditions de la Chenelière inc. see Chenelière/McGraw Hill
Éditions Chouette inc.
  CP 509, Succ Pierrefonds, Pierrefonds PQ H9H 4M6
  514/624-3996; Fax: 514/624-4344
  ISBN: 2-9800909, 2-921198
Les Éditions Compton
  #110, 55, rue Belvédère nord, Sherbrooke PQ J1H 6B2
  819/562-9082
  ISBN: 2-920482
Éditions Doberman inc.
  CP 2021, Saint-Nicholas est PQ G0S 3L0
  418/831-1304; Fax: 418/836-3645; Email: pgerrits@qui.qc.ca
  ISBN: 2-921204; music publishers
Éditions École Active
  2244, rue de Rouen, Montréal PQ H2K 1L5
  514/527-3425; Fax: 514/527-6713
  ISBN: 2-89069
Éditions Fides
  165, rue Deslauriers, Saint-Laurent PQ H4N 2S4
  514/745-4290; Fax: 514/745-4299; Email: editions@fides.qc.ca
  ISBN: 2-7621, 2-89007
Les Éditions Flammarion Ltée
  375, av Laurier ouest, Montréal PQ H2V 2K3
  514/277-8807; Fax: 514/278-2085
  ISBN: 2-89077
Éditions FM
  1113, av Desnoyers, Laval PQ H7C 1Y6
  514/324-0712; Fax: 514/664-1521
  ISBN: 2-89047, 0-88519
Les Éditions Françaises Inc.
  1411, rue Amère, Boucherville PQ J4B 5Z5
  514/641-0514; Fax: 514/641-4893; Toll Free: 1-800-361-9635
  ISBN: 0-7756; SAN: 115-7756
Éditions La Frégate Inc.
  CP 157, Succ H, Montréal PQ H3G 2K7
  514/481-6368; Fax: 514/683-5014
  ISBN: 2-920047
Les Éditions Ganesha inc.
  CP 484, Succ Youville, Montréal PQ H2P 2W1
  514/641-2395; Fax: 514/641-2989
  ISBN: 2-89145
Les Éditions le Griffon d'argile
  7649, boul Wilfrid-Hamel, Ste-Foy PQ G2G 1C3
  418/871-6898; Fax: 418/871-6818
  ISBN: 2-920210, 2-920922, 2-89443
Éditions Grosvenor Inc.
  Passage Du Musée, 1456, rue Sherbrooke ouest, Montréal PQ H3G 1K4
  514/284-1138; Fax: 514/284-0415
  ISBN: 0-919959
Éditions les Herbes rouges
  #304, 3575, boul St-Laurent, Montréal PQ H2X 2T7

Canadian Almanac & Directory 1997

514/845-4039; Fax: 514/845-3629
ISBN: 2-89419

Les Éditions Heritage
300, rue Arran, Saint-Lambert PQ J4R 1K5
514/672-6710; Fax: 514/672-1481
ISBN: 2-7625, 0-7773

Les Éditions de l'Hexagone
1010, rue de la Gauchetière est, Montréal PQ H2L 2N5
514/523-1182; Fax: 514/282-7530
ISBN: 2-89006, 2-89295

Éditions de l'Homme see Sogides Ltée

Éditions HRW see Groupe Éducalivres inc. - Éditions Études Vivantes

Éditions Hurtubise HMH Ltée
7360, boul Newman, La Salle PQ H8N 1X2
514/364-0323; Fax: 514/364-7435; Toll Free: 1-800-361-1664
Services editoriaux: 3140, rue Allard, Montréal PQ H4E 2M7
514/364-0323; Fax: 514/761-0239
ISBN: 2-89045, 2-89428

Les Éditions l'Image de l'art
#304, 6300, av du Parc, Montréal PQ H2V 4H8
514/495-1222; Fax: 514/272-6058
ISBN: 2-920822, 2-9211370, 2-921580

Éditions de L'instant même
865, av Moncton, Québec PQ G1S 2Y4
418/527-8690; Fax: 418/681-6780
ISBN: 2-921197

Les Éditions internationales Alain Stanké Ltée
1212, rue St-Mathieu, Montréal PQ H3H 2H7
514/935-7452; Fax: 514/931-1627
ISBN: 2-7604, 0-88566

Les Éditions JCL inc.
930, rue Jacques-Cartier est, Chicoutimi PQ G7H 2A9
418/696-0536; Fax: 418/696-3132; Email: jlc@saglac.qc.ca
ISBN: 2-89431, 2-920176

Les Éditions La Liberté Inc.
3020, ch Ste-Foy, Ste-Foy PQ G1X 3V6
418/658-3763; Fax: 418/658-3763; Toll Free: 1-800-567-5449
ISBN: 2-89084

Les Éditions Libre expression ltée
2016, rue St-Hubert, Motnréal PQ H2L 3Z5
514/849-5259; Fax: 514/849-1388
ISBN: 2-89111

Éditions Logiques
1225, rue de Condé, Montréal PQ H3K 2E4
514/933-2225; Fax: 514/933-2182
ISBN: 2-89381

Les Éditions Louis Riel Coopérative ltée
#218, 514 Victoria Ave. East, Regina SK S4N 0N7
306/352-7435; Fax: 306/565-2922

Les Éditions le Loup de Gouttière
347, rue Saint-Paul, Québec PQ G1K 3X1
418/694-2224; Fax: 418/694-2225
ISBN: 2-921310

Éditions Marie-France Ltée
3688, rue Fleury est, Montréal PQ H1H 2S6
514/329-3700, 329-3701; Fax: 514/329-0630; Toll Free: 1-800-563-6644
ISBN: 2-89168

Éditions Médiaspaul
3965, boul Henri-Bourassa est, Montréal PQ H1H 1L1
514/322-7341; Fax: 514/322-4281
ISBN: 0-88840, 2-89039, 2-89420

Éditions du Meridien
#870, 550, rue Sherbrooke ouest, Montréal PQ H3A 1B9
514/845-5445; Fax: 514/843-9491
ISBN: 2-920417

Les Éditions Modus vivendi inc.
(Presses Aventure)
CP 213, Succ Ste-Dorothée, Laval PQ H7X 2T4

514/627-7093; Fax: 514/962-6577
ISBN: 2-92155, 2-922148 (Presses Aventure)

Éditions du Mortagne
#100, 250, boul Industriel, Boucherville PQ J4B 2X4
514/641-2387; Fax: 514/655-6092
ISBN: 2-89074

Éditions Multimondes
930, rue Pouliot, Ste-Foy PQ G1V 3N9
418/651-3885; Fax: 418/651-6822;
 Email: multimondes@maltim.com; URL: http://multim.com
ISBN: 2-921146

Éditions du Nordir
17, rue Berville, CP 580, Hearst ON P0L 1N0
705/362-8964; Fax: 705/362-8964
ISBN: 2-921365

Les Éditions du Norôit
CP 156, Succ de Lorimier, Montréal PQ H2H 2N6
514/563-1644; Fax: 514/563-1644
ISBN: 2-89018

Les Éditions d'Orphée
2770, rue Darling, Montréal PQ H1W 2X5
514/523-5307
ISBN: 2-89418

Éditions de la paix
125, rue Lussier, Saint-Alphonse-de-Granby PQ J0E 2A0
514/375-4765; Fax: 514/375-4765
ISBN: 2-921255

Éditions Papyrus
745, av Eymard, Québec PQ G1S 3Z9
418/688-9694
ISBN: 2-9800941

Éditions la Pensée inc.
#1, 4243, rue Beaubien est, Montréal PQ H1T 1S5
514/593-1144; Fax: 514/593-6380
ISBN: 2-921187

Éditions Phidal inc.
5740, rue Ferrier, Mount-Royal PQ H4P 1M7
514/738-0202; Fax: 514/738-5102; Toll Free: 1-800-738-7349
ISBN: 2-89393

Éditions Pierre Tisseyre
5757, rue Cypihot, Montréal PQ H4S 1X4
514/334-2690; Fax: 514/334-8809
ISBN: 2-89041

Les Éditions des Plaines
202, boul Provencher, CP 123, Saint-Boniface MB R2H 3B4
204/235-0078; Fax: 204/233-7741
ISBN: 0-920944, 1-895173

Les Éditions de la Pleine Lune
#223, 34e av, Lachine PQ H8T 1Z4
514/637-6366; Fax: 514/637-6366
ISBN: 2-89024

Éditions Québec-Amérique
425, rue Saint-Jean-Baptiste, Montréal PQ H2Y 2Z7
514/393-1450; Fax: 514/866-2430; Email: montreal@editionsqa.qc.ca
ISBN: 0-88552, 2-89037

Éditions Quebecor
7, ch Bates, Outremont PQ H2V 1A6
514/270-1746; Fax: 514/270-5313
ISBN: 2-89089, 2-7640

Éditions Quinze
1010, rue de la Gauchetière, Montréal PQ H2L 2N5
514/523-1182; Fax: 514/282-7530
ISBN: 2-98026

Les Éditions du Remue-Ménage inc.
#404, 4428, boul St-Laurent, Montréal PQ H2W 1Z5
514/982-0730
ISBN: 2-89091

Les Éditions le Renouveau Charlesbourg inc.
870, Carré de Tracy est, CP 7605, Charlesbourg PQ G1G 5W6
418/628-3445; Fax: 418/624-2277

ISBN: 2-89254

Éditions du Renouveau Pédagogique inc.
5757, rue Cypihot, Saint-Laurent PQ H4S 1R3
514/334-2690; Fax: 514/334-4720; Email: erpidlm@odyssee.net
ISBN: 2-7613

Éditions Reynald Goulet
40, rue Mireault, Repentigny PQ J6A 1M1
514/654-2626; Fax: 514/654-5433
ISBN: 2-89377

Éditions du Roseau
6521, rue Louis Hémon, Montréal PQ H2G 2L1
514/725-7772; Fax: 514/725-5889
ISBN: 2-920083

Éditions Saint-Martin
#3203, 5000, rue Iberville, Montréal PQ H2H 2S6
514/529-0920; Fax: 514/529-8384
ISBN: 2-89035

Éditions Saint-Yves
CP 9638, Ste-Foy PQ G1V 4C2
418/657-4399; Fax: 418/657-2096
ISBN: 2-89034

Éditions Sciences et Culture Inc.
5090, rue de Bellechasse, Montréal PQ H1T 2A2
514/253-0403; Fax: 514/256-5078
ISBN: 2-89092, 2-920052

Les Éditions Sedes
755, rue Robitaille, Saint-Lambert PQ J4P 1C5
514/465-1077; Fax: 514/465-0328
ISBN: 2-921140

Éditions du Septentrion
1300, av Maguire, CP 430, Sillery PQ G1T 2R8
418/688-3556; Fax: 418/527-4978
ISBN: 2-921114

Les Éditions du Sphinx
CP 8742, Ste-Foy PQ G1V 4N6
418/656-2493
ISBN: 2-920123

Les Éditions Thémis
Faculté de droit, Université de Montréal, CP 6128, Succ A, Montréal PQ H3C 3J7
514/739-9945; Fax: 514/343-2199
ISBN 2-920376

Éditions Tormont
#300, 338, rue Saint-Antoine est, Montréal PQ H2Y 1A3
514/954-1441; Fax: 514/954-1443
ISBN: 2-89429

Les Éditions Transcontinental inc.
1247, rue de Condé, Montréal PQ H3K 2E4
514/933-2225; Fax: 514/933-2182; Toll Free: 1-800-361-5479
ISBN: 2-921030, 2-89472

Éditions du Trécarré
817, rue McCaffrey, St Laurent PQ H4T 1N3
514/738-2911; Fax: 514/738-8512; Email: mlaberge@interlink.net
ISBN: 2-89249

Éditions Trois
2033, av Jessop, Laval PQ H7S 1X3
514/663-4028; Fax: 514/663-1639; Email: ed3ama@contact.net
ISBN: 2-920887

Les éditions Un monde différenet ltée
3925, boul Grane-Allée, Saint-Hubert PQ J4T 2V8
514/656-2660; Fax: 514/445-9098
ISBN: 2-92000, 2-89225

Éditions Vents d'ouest
99, rue Montcalm, Hull PQ J8X 2L9
819/770-6377 Fax: 819/770-0559
ISBN: 2-921603

Les Éditions Villes Nouvelles - Villes Anciennes
CP 192, Succ Côte-des-Neiges, Montréal PQ H3S 2S5
514/733-6689; Fax: 514/733-6689
ISBN: 2-9801943

Les Éditions Yvon Blais inc.
CP 180, Cowansville PQ J2K 3H6

514/266-1086; Fax: 514/263-9256; Toll Free: 1-800-363-3047; Email: cowansvillw@editionsyvonblais.qc.ca
ISBN: 0-89073, 0-89451

Ekstasis Editions
PO Box 8474, Stn Main, Victoria BC V8W 3S1
250/385-3378; Fax: 250/385-3378
ISBN: 0-921215

Elan Publishing Inc.
PO Box 21009, Stn Dominion SW, Calgary AB T2P 4H5
403/293-1030; Fax: 403/280-1400
ISBN: 0-9694626

Emond Montgomery Publications Ltd.
58 Shaftesbury Ave., Toronto ON M4T 1A3
416/975-3925; Fax: 416/975-3924; Email: emplaw@io.org; URL: http://www.io.org/~emplaw
ISBN: 0-920722

Empyreal Press
PO Box 1746, Stn Place du Parc, Montréal PQ H2W 2R7
ISBN: 0-921852

Encyclopaedia Britannica Publications Ltd.
186 Shoemaker St., PO Box 9055, Kitchener ON N2G 4X1
519/893-0499; Fax: 519/893-7106; Toll Free: 1-800-465-9439
ISBN: 0-7738; SAN: 115-1363

English Literary Studies
Dept. of English, University of Victoria, PO Box 3045, Victoria BC V8W 3P4
250/721-7239; Fax: 250/721-6498
ISBN: 0-920604; SAN: 115-3366

Ergo Productions
PO Box 4460, London ON N5W 5J2
519/432-4357
ISBN: 0-920516; SAN: 115-3374

Erin Publications
82 Edenstone View NW, Calgary AB T3A 4T5
403/239-4318; Fax: 403/239-6044
ISBN: 0-9690609

Escart Press *see* Upney Editions

L'Etincelle Éditeur Inc.
#311, 4999, rue St-Catharine ouest, Westmount PQ H3Z 1T3
514/481-2440; Fax: 514/481-9973; Email: rdppub@vir.com
ISBN: 2-89019

Evangelical Tract Distributors
PO Box 146, Edmonton AB T5J 2G9
403/477-1538

Everyday Publications Inc.
#2, 421 Nugget Ave., Scarborough ON M1S 4L8
416/291-9411; Fax: 416/291-9411; Email: 102604.1530compuserve.com
ISBN: 0-88873, 0-919586; SAN: 115-3398

Exile Editions Ltd.
20 Dale Ave., Toronto ON M4W 1K4
416/969-8877; Fax: 416/969-9556
ISBN: 1-55096, 0-920428; SAN: 115-3404

Exportlivre
PO Box 307, Saint-Lambert PQ J4P 3P8
514/671-3888; Fax: 514/671-2121

Fairmount Books Ltd.
120 Duffield Dr., Markham ON L6G 1B5
905/475-0988; Fax: 905/475-1072
ISBN: 0-921372; SAN: 106-7886

Fernwood Publishing Co. Ltd.
PO Box 9409, Stn A, Halifax NS B3K 5S3
902/422-3302; Fax: 902/422-3179; Email: esharpe@bbs.mmcs.com
ISBN: 1-895686

Fiddlehead Poetry Books *see* Goose Lane Editions

Fifth House Publishers
#201, 165 - 3rd Ave. South, Saskatoon SK S7K 1L8
306/242-4936; Fax: 306/242-7667
ISBN: 0-920079, 1-895618; SAN: 115-141X

Firefly Books Ltd.
3680 Victoria Park Ave., North York ON M2H 3K1
416/499-8412; Fax: 416/499-8313; Toll Free: 1-800-387-6192
ISBN: 0-920668; SAN: 115-3439

First Avenue Publications
1328 Avenue Rd., Toronto ON M5N 2G9
416/483-1564; Fax: 416/481-4721
ISBN: 0-9695315

Fischer Presses inc.
1228, av Rousseau, Sillery PQ G2S 4H1
418/687-5679; Fax: 418/683-0531
ISBN: 2-921225

Fitzhenry & Whiteside Limited
195 Allstate Pkwy., Markham ON L3R 4T8
905/477-9700; Fax: 905/477-9179; Toll Free: 1-800-387-9776
ISBN: 0-55041; SAN: 115-1444

Fleurbec
198, ch de la Grande-Grillade, St-Henri-de-Lévis PQ G0R 3E0
418/882-0843; Fax: 418/882-6133; Email: floraqca@versicolores.ca
ISBN: 2-920174

Forest Press
6053 Wyandotte East, Windsor ON N8S 1N3
519/944-7155; Fax: 519/945-1524
ISBN: 0-9696249

Formac Publishing Ltd.
5502 Atlantic St., Halifax NS B3H 1G4
902/421-7022; Fax: 902/425-0166; Toll Free: 1-800-565-1975
ISBN: 0-88780; SAN: 115-1371

Fortress Publications
221 Barton St. East, Unit B, Stoney Creek ON L8E 2K3
905/662-3505; Fax: 905/662-3855
ISBN: 0-9690486, 0-9191945; SAN: 115-3455

Foxwood International Ltd.
PO Box 523, Milton ON L9T 4Z1
905/875-4040; Fax: 905/875-1668
ISBN: 0-921854; SAN: 116-0206

The Fraser Institute
626 Bute St., 2nd Fl., Vancouver BC V6E 3M1
604/688-0221; Fax: 604/688-8539
ISBN: 0-88975; SAN: 115-3498

Frederick Harris Music Co. Ltd.
#1, 5865 McLaughlin Rd., Mississauga ON L5R 1B8
905/501-1595; Fax: 905/501-0929; Toll Free: 1-800-387-4013

Gaëtan Morin Éditeur Ltée
171, boul de Mortagne, Boucherville PQ J4B 6G4
514/449-2369; Fax: 514/449-1096
ISBN: 2-89105

Gage Educational Publishing
Division of Canada Publishing Corporation
164 Commander Blvd., Scarborough ON M1S 3C7
416/293-8141; Fax: 416/293-9009; Toll Free: 1-800-667-1115
ISBN: 0-7715, 7705; SAN: 115-0375

Gallerie Publications
2901 Panorama Dr., North Vancouver BC V7G 2A4
604/929-8706
ISBN: 1-895640, 0-969336

Garamond Press
#403, 77 Mowat Ave., Toronto ON M6K 3E3
416/516-2709; Fax: 416/533-5652; Email: garamond@web.apc.org; URL: http://www.garamond.ca/garamond
ISBN: 0-920059; SAN: 115-1339

GB Publishing
PO Box 6292, Stn D, Calgary AB T2P 2C9
403/228-6897

General Publishing Co. Limited
30 Lesmill Rd., North York ON M3B 2T6
416/445-3333; Fax: 416/445-5967
ISBN: 0-7736, 0-7737; SAN: 115-0391

General Store Publishing House Inc.
One Main St., Burnstown ON K0J 1G0
613/432-7697; Fax: 613/432-7184; Toll Free: 1-800-465-6072
ISBN: 0-919431; SAN: 115-6853

Gesture Press
68 Tyrrel Ave., Toronto ON M6G 2G4
416/654-9094
ISBN: 0-920585; SAN: 115-8279

Get a Life Publishing
#127, 2255B Queen St. East, Toronto ON M4E 1G3
416/699-6070; Fax: 416/536-9101
ISBN 0-9697755

Gilpin Publishing
PO Box 597, Alliston ON L0M 1A0
705/424-6507; Fax: 705/424-6507
ISBN: 0-921046

Ginn Publishing Canada Inc. *see* Prentice-Hall Canada Inc.

Global Press *see* Macmillan Canada

Globe Information Services
444 Front St. West, Toronto ON M5V 2S9
416/585-5250; Fax: 416/585-5249; Toll Free: 1-800-268-9128
ISBN: 0-921925

Godwin Books
PO Box 4781, Vancouver BC V6B 4A4
604/988-2407; Fax: 604/984-9821; Email: thomsonr@direct.ca
ISBN: 0-9696774

Golden Books Publishing
200 Sheldon Dr., Cambridge ON N1R 5X2
519/623-3590; Fax: 519/623-3598; Email: goldenbk@sentex.net
ISBN: 0-307; SAN: 115-5598

The Golden Dog Press
409 Oxford St. East, PO Box 393, Kemptville ON K0G 1J0
613/258-3882; Fax: 613/258-3882
ISBN: 0-919614

Good Medicine Books
(Canadian Caboose Press)
PO Box 844, Skookumchuck BC V0B 2E0
250/427-7014 (orders)
ISBN: 0-920698

Goodread Biographies
5502 Atlantic St., Halifax NS B3H 1G4
902/421-7022; Fax: 902/425-0166
ISBN: 0-88780; SAN: 115-1371

Goose Lane Editions
469 King St., Fredericton NB E3B 1E5
506/450-4251; Fax: 506/459-4991; URL: http://www.cygnus.nb.ca/bookstr/glane.glogo.html
ISBN: 0-919197, 0-86492, 0-920110; SAN: 115-3420

Gordon Soules Book Publishers Ltd.
1352B Marine Dr., West Vancouver BC V7T 1B5
604/922-6588; Fax: 604/688-5442
ISBN: 0-919574; SAN: 115-0987

Gordon V. Thompson Music
85 Scarsdale Rd., Toronto ON M3B 2R2
416/445-3131; Fax: 416/445-2473; Toll Free: 1-800-268-7736
ISBN: 1-55122; SAN: 115-7159

Gospel Publishing House
6745 Century Ave., Mississauga ON L5N 6P7
905/542-8340; Fax: 905/542-1624; Toll Free: 1-800-567-2420
SAN: 115-3528

Great Pacific News
2500 Vauxhall Pl., Richmond BC V6V 1Y8
604/278-4841; Fax: 604/278-5642; Email: gpn@direct.ca

Greey de Pencier Books *see* Owl Books

Grolier Limited
12 Banigan Dr., Toronto ON M4H 1A6
416/425-1924; Fax: 416/425-8858; Toll Free: 1-800-563-3231

Grolier Limitée: 45, rue Montpellier, Saint-Laurent PQ H4N 3H6
514/747-5000; Fax: 514/747-0444
ISBN: 0-7172; SAN 115-3668
Grosvenor Books Canada *see* MRA Books
Grosvenor House Press Inc./Éditions Grosvenor inc.
1456, rue Sherbrooke ouest, Montréal PQ H3G 1K4
514/284-1138; Fax: 514/284-0415
Toronto office: #203, 2 Pardee Ave., Toronto ON M6K 3H5
416/532-3211; Fax: 416/532-9277
ISBN: 0-919959; SAN: 115-3684
Groundwood Books
Division of Douglas & McIntyre Ltd.
Juvenile Trade Division, 585 Bloor St. West, 2nd Fl., Toronto ON M6G 1K5
250/537-2501; Fax: 250/537-4647
ISBN: 0-88899; SAN 115-2270
Groupe Communication Canada - Édition *see* Canada Communications Group Publishing
Groupe Éducalivres inc. - Éditions Études Vivantes
955, rue Bergar, Laval PQ H7L 4Z7
514/334-8466; Fax: 514/334-8387
ISBN: 2-7607
Guérin Éditeur Ltée
4501, rue Drolet, Montréal PQ H2T 2G2
514/842-3481; Fax: 514/842-4923
ISBN: 2-7601, 0-7764
Guernica Editions Inc.
PO Box 117, Stn D, Toronto ON M5S 2S6
416/657-8885; Fax: 416/657-8885;
Email: 102026.1331@compuserve.com
ISBN: 0-919349, 2-89135, 0-920717; SAN: 115-0421
Guidance Centre
712 Gordon Baker Rd., Toronto ON M2H 3R7
416/502-1262; Fax: 416/502-1101; Toll Free: 1-800-668-6247
ISBN: 0-7713; SAN: 110-2818
Gutter Press
109 Manning Ave., Toronto ON M6J 2K6
416/603-3181; Fax: 416/861-8802; Email: shiyate@alias.com; URL: http://www.io.org/~gutter/
ISBN: 0-9696520
Guy Saint-Jean Éditeur
#200B, 674, Place Publique, Laval PQ H7X 1G1
514/689-6402; Fax: 514/689-9393; Email: jacques@mlink.net
ISBN: 2-920340, 2-89455
gynergy books *see* Ragweed Press Inc./gynergy books
Hancock House Publishers Ltd.
19313 Zero Ave., Surrey BC V4P 1M7
604/538-1114; Fax: 604/538-2262; Toll Free: 1-800-938-1114; Email: hancock@uniserve.com
ISBN: 0-88839, 0-919654; SAN: 115-3730
Hans Schaffler & Co. Ltd.
#2, 1252 Speers Rd., Oakville ON L6L 5N9
905/825-2185; Fax: 905/825-2130
Harbour Publishing Co. Ltd.
PO Box 219, Madeira Park BC V0N 2H0
604/883-2730; Fax: 604/883-9451;
Email: harbour_publishing@sunshine.net
ISBN: 0-920080, 1-55017; SAN: 115-1231
Harcourt Brace & Co. Canada Ltd.
55 Horner Ave., Toronto ON M8Z 4X6
416/255-4491; Fax: 416/255-4046; Email: hbc_can@harcourtbrace.com
ISBN: 0-7747, 0-7216; SAN: 115-1754
Hargreaves, Fuller & Company
#13, 4335 West 10th Ave., Vancouver BC V6R 2H6
604/222-2955; Fax: 604/222-2965
Harlequin Enterprises Ltd.
225 Duncan Mill Rd., Toronto ON M3B 3K9
416/445-5860; Fax: 416/445-8655, 8736; Toll Free: 1-800-387-0112; Email: http://www.romance.net
ISBN: 0-373; SAN: 115-3749
Harry Cuff Publications Ltd.
94 LeMarchant Rd., St. John's NF A1C 2H2
709/726-6590; Fax: 709/726-0902; Email: hcp@public.comusult.nf.ca
ISBN: 0-919095, 0-921191
Hartley & Marks Publishers
3661 Broadway West, Vancouver BC V6R 2B8
604/738-0644; Fax: 604/738-1913
ISBN: 0-88179; SAN: 115-3757
Harvest House Ltd.
#1, 1200, av Atwater, Montréal PQ H3Z 1X4
514/932-0666; Fax: 514/489-4287
ISBN: 0-88772; SAN: 115-0456
Havelock House
5211 Landsdowne Dr., Edmonton AB T6H 4L2
403/434-7504; Fax: 403/436-7976
ISBN: 0-920805
H.B. Fenn and Company Ltd.
1090 Lorimar Dr., Mississauga ON L5S 1R7
905/670-3366; Fax: 905/670-3422; Toll Free: 1-800-267-3366
ISBN: 0-919768; SAN: 115-1746
Heirloom Publishing Inc.
6509B Mississauga Rd., Mississauga ON L5N 1A6
905/821-1152; Fax: 905/821-1158
ISBN: 0-9692182, 0-9694247
Hemlock Press
#201, 89 Colborne St. East, Orillia ON L3V 1T8
705/484-1096
ISBN: 0-829066; SAN: 116-0931
Herald Press
490 Dutton Dr., Waterloo ON N2L 6H7
519/747-5722; Fax: 519/747-5721; Toll Free: 1-800-245-7894; Email: mpcan%5904477@mcimail.com
ISBN: 0-8361; SAN: 116-0931
Heritage House Publishing Co. Ltd.
#8, 17921 - 55th Ave., Surrey BC V3S V3S
604/574-7067; Fax: 604/574-9992; Toll Free: 1-800-665-3302
ISBN: 0-919214; SAN: 115-8287
H.H. Marshall Ltd.
6371 Lady Hammond Rd., PO Box 9301, Stn A, Halifax NS B3K 5N5
902/454-8381; Fax: 902/455-3652; Toll Free: 1-800-456-7881
Highway Book Shop
Hwy. 11, Cobalt ON P0J 1C0
705/679-8375; Fax: 705/679-8511; Toll Free: 1-800-461-2062; Email: bookshop@onlink.net; URL: http://www.onlink.net/cybermail/bookshop/index.htm
ISBN 0-88954; SAN 115-0464
HMS Press
PO Box 340, Stn B, London ON N6A 4W1
519/433-8994; Fax: 519/432-6299;
Email: resource.centre@onlinesys.com
ISBN: 0-919957, 1-895700, 1-57105; SAN: 115-0480
Hogrefe & Huber Publishers
12 Bruce Park Ave., Toronto ON M4P 2S3
416/482-6339; Fax: 416/484-4200
ISBN: 0-88937, 0-920887; SAN: 115-379X
Holt, Rinehart & Winston of Canada Ltd. *see* Harcourt Brace & Co. Canada Ltd.
Homo House Publishing
#101, 1001 West Broadway, PO Box 180, Vancouver BC V6H 4B1
604/879-1583; Fax: 604/879-4352; Email: homohse@eyecon.com
Hornblower Books Ltd.
#201, 4001 Berri St., Montréal PQ H2L 4H2
514/843-7410; Fax: 514/843-7798
Horsdal & Schubart Publishers Ltd.
#623, 425 Simcoe St., PO Box 1, Victoria BC V8V 4T3
250/360-2031; Fax: 250/360-0829
ISBN: 0-920663; SAN: 115-7094
Hounslow Press
Division of Dundurn Press Ltd.
#301, 2181 Queen St. East, Toronto ON M4E 1E5
416/698-0454; Fax: 416/698-1102
ISBN: 0-88882; SAN: 115-1223
House of Anansi Press
1800 Steeles Ave. West, Concord ON L4K 2P3
905/660-0611; Fax: 905/660-0676; Email: anansi@irwin-pub.com; URL: http://www.irwin-pub.com/irwin/anansi/
ISBN: 0-88784; SAN: 115-0391
Humanica Press
#110, 186 Sutton Place, Beaconsfield PQ H9W 5S3
514/695-0834; Fax: 514/694-2059
ISBN: 0-9693115
Humanitas
5780, av Decelles, Montréal PQ H3S 2C7
514/737-1332; Fax: 514/737-1332
ISBN: 2-89396, 2-9800950
Hume Publishing Company Limited
#515, 4100 Yonge St., North York ON M2P 2B9
416/221-4596; Fax: 416/221-4968
ISBN: 0-919255
Hushion House Publishing Ltd.
36 Northline Rd., Toronto ON M4B 3E2
416/285-6100; Fax: 416/285-1777
Hyperion Press Ltd.
300 Wales Ave., Winnipeg MB R2M 2S9
204/256-9204; Fax: 204/255-7845
ISBN: 0-920534; SAN: 115-124X
D'Ici et d'ailleurs
343, 4e av, CP 314, Val-d'Or PQ J9P 4P4
819/824-4248; Fax: 819/825-8953
ISBN: 2-921055
ICURR Press/Les Presses du CIRUR
#301, 150 Eglinton Ave. East, Toronto ON M4P 1E8
416/973-5629; Fax: 416/973-1375; Email: awxler@icurr.org; URL: http://www.icurr.org/icurr/
ISBN: 1-895469
IDRC Books/Les Éditions du CRDI
PO Box 8500, Ottawa ON K1G 3H9
613/236-6163; Email: order@idrc.ca
ISBN: 0-88936
Imp Press
PO Box 32066, Cambridge ON N3H 5M2
519/653-4813; Fax: 519/653-4813
ISBN: 0-9694385
Inclusion Press International
24 Thorne Cres., Toronto ON M6H 2S5
416/658-5363; Fax: 416/658-5067;
Email: 74640.1124@compuserve
ISBN: 1-895418
Inner City Books
PO Box 1271, Stn Q, Toronto ON M4T 2P4
416/927-0355; Fax: 416/924-1814; Email: icb@inforamp.net
ISBN: 0-919123; SAN: 115-3870
Insomniac Press
378 Delaware Ave., Toronto ON M6H 2T8
416/536-4308; Fax: 416/588-4198; Email: insomna@pathcom.com
ISBN: 0-895837
The Institute for Research on Public Policy/L'Institut de recherches politiques
#200, 1470, rue Peel, Montréal PQ H3A 1T1
514/985-2461; Fax: 514/985-2559
ISBN: 0-920380, 0-88645; SAN: 115-3889, 115-0537
International Press Publications Inc.
#23, 90 Nolan Ct., Markham ON L3R 4L9
905/946-9588; Fax: 905/946-9590
I.P.I. Publishing Ltd.
#708, 50 Prince Arthur Ave., Toronto ON M5R 1B5
416/944-1141; Fax: 416/944-1153
ISBN: 0-920702; SAN: 115-3854
Iris Diffusion *see* Éditions Sciences et Culture Inc.
Iroquois Publishing & Crafts Supplies Ltd.
RR#2, Ohsweken ON N0A 1M0
905/765-4206; Fax: 905/765-5633
ISBN: 0-919645; SAN: 159-236X
Irwin Publishing
Division of General Publishing Co. Limited

1800 Steeles Ave. West, Concord ON L4K 2P3
905/660-0611; Fax: 905/660-0676; Toll Free: 1-800-263-7824; Email: irwin@irwin-pub.com
ISBN: 0-7725; SAN: 115-0391

Is Five Press
#4, 400 Mount Pleasant Rd., Toronto ON M4S 2L6
416/480-2408; Fax: 416/480-2546
ISBN: 0-920934; SAN: 115-3943

ISER Books (Institute of Social & Economic Research)
Memorial University of Newfoundland, PO Box 4200, Stn C, St. John's NF A1C 5S7
709/737-7450; Fax: 709/737-7560; Email: jgleeson@morgan.ucs.mun.ca
ISBN: 0-919666; SAN: 115-3897

ISM Library Information Services
3300 Bloor St. West, 16th Fl., Toronto ON M8X 2X2
416/236-7171; Fax: 416/236-7541; Toll Free: 1-800-268-0982
ISBN: 0-920748; SAN: 115-5423

Israel's The Judaica Centre
897 Eglinton Ave. West, Toronto ON M6C 2C1
416/256-2858; Fax: 416/256-2750
SAN: 115-396X

ITMB Publishing Ltd.
736A Granville St., Vancouver BC V6Z 1G3
604/687-3320; Fax: 604/687-5925
ISBN: 0-921463

ITP Nelson
1120 Birchmount Rd., Scarborough ON M1K 5G4
416/752-9100; Fax: 416/752-9646; Toll Free: 1-800-268-2222; URL: http://www.nelson.com/nelson.html
ISBN: 0-17; SAN: 115-0669

J. Gordon Shillingford Ltd.
905 Corydon Ave., PO Box 86, Winnipeg MB R3M 3S3
204/284-0985; Fax: 204/453-8320
ISBN: 1-896239, 0-919754, 0-969761

J & L Macpherson Educational Services Ltd.
3030 Collens Hill Rd., Kelowna BC V1Z 1P5
250/769-4321; Fax: 250/769-3297

Jack The Bookman Ltd.
#16, 10 Newkirk Rd. South, Richmond Hill ON L4C 5S3
905/884-6177; Fax: 905/884-2411; Toll Free: 1-800-563-5168

Jam Ink Publishing
261 Alice St., Kincardine ON N2Z 2P9
519/396-9553; Fax: 519/396-9554; Toll Free: 1-800-263-1991
ISBN: 1-895268

James Lorimer & Co. Publishers
35 Britain St., Toronto ON M5A 1R7
416/362-4762; Fax: 416/362-3939; Toll Free: 1-800-565-1975
Sales & Marketing Offices: 5502 Atlantic St., Halifax NS B3H 1G4
902/421-7022 (customer service); Fax: 902/425-0166; Toll Free: 1-800-565-1975
ISBN: 0-88862, 1-55028; SAN: 115-1134

J.C. George Enterprises Ltd.
577 Mt. Pleasant Rd., Toronto ON M4S 2M5
416/483-4353; Fax: 416/483-4353
ISBN: 0-921369

J.E.S.L. Educational Products
58 Glen Park Ave., Toronto ON M6B 2C2
416/785-7941; Fax: 416/785-7941
ISBN: 0-9691264

Jesperson Press
39 James Lane, St. John's NF A1E 3H3
709/753-0633; Fax: 709/753-5507
ISBN: 0-920502, 0-921692; SAN: 115-1320

Jeux de mots
6256, rue Saint-Denis, Montréal PQ H2S 2R7
514/272-5389; Fax: 514/279-4768
ISBN: 2-9209867

J.L.H. Law Books Ltd.
#8, 166 Bullock Dr., Markham ON L3P 1W2
905/472-0219; Fax: 905/472-5578; Email: lawbook@io.org; URL: http://www.airlink.org/lawbook

J.M. LeBel Enterprises Ltd.
10335 - 61 Ave., Edmonton AB T6H 1K9
403/436-8205; Fax: 403/437-5256; Toll Free: 1-800-882-0667
ISBN: 0-920008; SAN: 115-1282

JMC Press Ltd./Les Presses JMC Ltée
34, rue Fleury ouest, Montréal PQ H3L 1S9
514/382-3000; Fax: 514/382-3007; Toll Free: 1-800-363-7800

John Coutts Library Services Ltd.
6900 Kinsmen Ct., PO Box 1000, Niagara Falls ON L2E 7E7
905/356-6382; Fax: 905/356-5064; Toll Free: 1-800-263-1686
SAN: 169-5401

John Markham & Associates
11210 Elderberry Way, Sidney BC V8L 5J6
250/655-1823; Fax: 250/655-1826
ISBN: 0-903001

John Wiley & Sons Canada Ltd.
5353 Dundas St. West, 4th Fl., Etobicoke ON M9B 6H8
416/236-4433; Fax: 416/236-4448; Toll Free: 1-800-567-4797
Customer Service Dept.: 22 Worcester Rd., Etobicoke ON M9W 1L1
416/675-3580, 236-4433 (sales & marketing); Fax: 416/675-6599; Toll Free: 1-800-567-4797
ISBN: 0-471; SAN: 115-1185

Johnson Gorman Publishers
3669 - 41 Ave., Red Deer AB T4N 2X7
403/342-0917; Fax: 403/342-0917
ISBN 0-921835

Juno Press
PO Box 502, Port Hope ON L1A 3Z4
905/885-9653; Fax: 905/372-5847
ISBN: 0-921516

Karver Distributors
85 Linden Ave., Winnipeg MB R2K 0M7
800/563-3290; Fax: 800/567-2908

Kate Walker & Co. Ltd.
8660 Cambie St., Vancouver BC V6P 6M9
604/323-7111; Fax: 604/323-7118
SAN: 115-7213

Kellington & Associates
#202, 88 Mutual St., Toronto ON M5B 2N3
416/368-3737; Fax: 416/368-3380

Keng Seng Enterprises
#227, 4030, rue St-Ambroise, Montréal PQ H4C 2C7
514/939-3971; Fax: 514/989-1922
ISBN: 1-895494

Key Porter Books Limited
70 The Esplanade, Toronto ON M5E 1R2
416/862-7777; Fax: 416/862-2304
ISBN: 0-919493, 1-55013; SAN: 115-0561

Kids Can Press Ltd.
29 Birch Ave., Toronto ON M4V 1E2
416/925-5437; Fax: 416/960-5437
ISBN: 0-919964, 0-921103, 1-55074; SAN: 115-4001

Kinbridge Publications
PO Box 89065, RPO Westdale, Hamilton ON L8S 4R5
ISBN 0-9693233

Kindred Productions
#4, 169 Riverton Ave., Winnipeg MB R2L 2E5
204/669-6575; Fax: 204/654-1865
ISBN: 0-919797, 0-921788

Kirkton Press Ltd.
RR#1, Kirkton ON N0K 1K0
519/229-6795; Fax: 519/229-6969
ISBN: 0-9693768

Kitchener News Company Ltd.
455 Dutton Dr., PO Box 274, Stn Waterloo, Waterloo ON N2J 4A4
519/884-3710; Fax: 519/885-4640; Toll Free: 1-800-265-8839; Email: cosgrove@nic.wat.hookup,net; URL: http://www.kitnews.com
ISBN 0-394

Knopf Canada
#210, 33 Yonge St., Toronto ON M5E 1G4
416/777-9477; Fax: 416/777-9470
Orders & Customer Service: 1265 Aerowood Dr., Mississauga ON L4W 1B9
905/624-0672; Fax: 905/624-6217; Toll Free: 1-800-668-4247
ISBN: 0-394

Knowbuddy Resources
PO Box 37, Collingwood ON L9Y 3Z7
Fax: 705/444-0274; Toll Free: 1-800-667-1121

Koala Books of Canada Ltd.
14327 - 95A Ave., Edmonton AB T5N 0B6
403/452-5149; Fax: 403/452-5149
SAN: 169-9385

Kosoy Travel Guides
112 Fairholme Ave., Toronto ON M6B 2W9
416/256-0974; Fax: 416/256-1216
ISBN: 0-919632; SAN: 115-8724

Kylix Media Inc.
5165, rue Sherbrooke ouest, Montréal PQ H4A 1T6
514/481-6606; Fax: 514/481-9699
ISBN: 0-9191632

Lambrecht Publications
1763 Maple Bay Rd., Duncan BC V9L 4T6
250/748-8722; Fax: 250/748-8722
ISBN: 0-919383; SAN: 115-057X

Lancelot Press Ltd.
PO Box 425, Hantsport NS B0P 1P0
902/684-9129; Fax: 902/684-3685; Email: lancelot@atcon.com; URL: http://www.atcon.com/lancelot
ISBN: 0-88999; SAN: 115-4052

Laurier Books Ltd.
PO Box 2694, Stn D, Ottawa ON K1P 5W6
613/738-2163; Fax: 613/247-0256; Email: laurierbooks@intertel.net
ISBN: 1-895959; SAN: 168-2806

Lawson-Falle Ltd.
1245 Franklin Blvd., PO Box 940, Cambridge ON N1R 5X9
519/622-1941; Fax: 519/622-2755
SAN: 115-4052

Lazara Press
PO Box 2269, Stn Main, Vancouver BC V6B 3W2
604/872-1134; Fax: 604/874-6661
ISBN 0-920999

Learnxs Press
155 College St., Toronto ON M5T 1P6
416/397-3911; Fax: 416/397-3044
ISBN: 0-920020; SAN: 115-4060

Leméac Éditeur Inc.
1124, rue Marie-Anne est, Montréal PQ H2J 2B7
514/524-5558; Fax: 514/524-3145
ISBN: 2-7609, 0-7761

Lester Publishing Ltd.
#507A, 56 The Esplanade, Toronto ON M5E 1A7
416/362-1032; Fax: 416/362-1647
ISBN: 1-895555

Librairie Champlain
468 Queen St. East, Toronto ON M5A 1T7
416/364-4345; Fax: 416/364-8843
ISBN: 0-9209

Librairie Raffin, Inc.
7870, rue Fleuricourt, St-Léonard PQ H1R 2L3
514/325-5553, 5555; Fax: 514/325-7329; Toll Free: 1-800-361-4293

Librairie Scolaire Canadienne
2244, rue de Rouen, Montréal PQ H2K 1L5
514/527-3425; Fax: 514/527-6713
ISBN 2-89069

Librairie Wilson & Lafleur Ltée
  40, rue Notre-Dame est, Montréal PQ H2Y 1B9
  514/875-6326; Fax: 514/875-8356; Toll Free: 1-800-363-2327
  ISBN: 2-89127
Librarie du Soleil
  434, boul St-Joseph, Hull PQ J8Y 3Y7
  819/595-2414; Fax: 819/595-3672
Library Bound
  200C Frobisher Dr., Waterloo ON N2V 2A2
  519/885-3233; Fax: 519/885-2662; Toll Free: 1-800-363-4783; Email: cpmlbi@nic.boojup.net
  SAN: 116-9203
The Library Services Centre
  141 Dearborn Pl., Waterloo ON N2J 4N5
  519/746-4420; Fax: 519/746-4425; Toll Free: 1-800-265-3360; Email: mckim@lsc.on.ca
  ISBN: 0-921830; SAN: 319-2024
Lidec Inc.
  4350, av de l'Hôtel-de-Ville, Montréal PQ H2W 2H5
  514/843-5991; Fax: 514/843-5252
  ISBN: 2-7608
Life Cycle Books Ltd.
  2205 Danforth Ave., Toronto ON M4C 1K4
  416/690-5860; Fax: 416/690-8532
  ISBN: 0-919225; SAN: 115-8417
Lifestyle Books
  6 Dawe Cres., Grand Falls NF A2A 2T2
  709/489-6796; Fax: 709/489-6796
  ISBN: 0-9691126
Lilmur Publishing
  147 Brooke Ave., Toronto ON M5M 2K3
  416/486-0145; Fax: 416/486-5380
  ISBN: 0-9692729; SAN: 115-7035
The Literary Press Group of Canada Inc.
  #301, 2 Gloucester St., Toronto ON M4Y 1L5
  416/413-4929; Fax: 416/413-4920
  ISBN 0-316
Little Brick Schoolhouse Inc.
  1235 Trafalgar Rd., PO Box 84001, Oakville ON L6H 3J0
  905/844-4669; Fax: 905/844-4669
  ISBN: 0-919788
Little Brown & Co.
  148 Yorkville Ave., Toronto ON M5R 1C2
  416/967-3888; Fax: 416/967-4591; Toll Free: 1-800-387-6922
  ISBN: 0-316; SAN: 115-4109, 115-0499
Livres Mercier Ltée
  RR#2, Tara ON N0H 2N0
  519/934-0262; Fax: 519/934-0262
Log House Publishing Co. Ltd.
  RR#1, Pender Island BC V0N 2M0
  250/629-6521; Fax: 250/629-2010
  ISBN: 0-920270; SAN: 115-0588
Logidisque inc.
  CP 10, Succ D, Montréal PQ H3K 3B9
  514/933-2225; Fax: 514/933-2182
  ISBN: 2-89381
Login Brothers Canada
  324 Saulteaux Cres., Winnipeg MB R3J 3T2
  204/837-2987; Fax: 204/837-3116; Toll Free: 1-800-665-0103
  SAN: 119-6049
Lone Pine Publishing
  #206, 10426 - 81 Ave., Edmonton AB T6E 1X5
  403/433-9333; Fax: 403/433-9646
  ISBN: 0-919433, 1-55105; SAN: 115-4125
Lorraine Greey Publications Limited
  #303, 56 The Esplanade, Toronto ON M5E 1A7
  416/422-3995; Fax: 416/422-3995
Lost Moose, The Yukon Publishers
  58 Kluane Cres., Whitehorse YT Y1A 3G7
  403/688-3441, 5076; Fax: 403/668-6223
  ISBN: 0-9694612

Louise Courteau, éditrice inc.
  1, Lac St-Louis est, CP 481, Saint-Zénon PQ J0K 3N0
  514/884-5958; Fax: 514/884-5913; URL: http://club-culture.com/club/
  ISBN: 2-89239
Loyal Colonies Press
  304 Olympus Ave., Kingston ON K7M 4T9
  613/389-0866
  ISBN: 0-929832
Lugus Publications
  48 Falcon St., Toronto ON M4S 2P5
  416/322-5113; Fax: 416/484-9512; Email: lugust@tvo.org
  ISBN: 0-921633
Lynn McClory
  215 Ashworth Ave., Toronto ON M6G 2A6
  416/535-6494; Fax: 416/535-6599
Lynx Images Releasing
  #606, 174 Spadina Ave., Toronto ON M5T 2C2
  416/504-9333; Fax: 416/504-5404; Email: lynximag@interlog.com
  ISBN: 0-9698427
Macfarlane Walter & Ross
  37A Hazelton Ave., Toronto ON M5R 2E3
  416/924-7595; Fax: 416/924-4254
  ISBN: 0-921912
Macmillan Canada
  Division of Canada Publishing Corporation
  29 Birch Ave., Toronto ON M4V 1E2
  416/963-8830; 293-8141 (customer service); Fax: 416/923-4821; Toll Free: 1-800-667-1115
  ISBN: 0-7715, 0-7705; SAN: 115-0375
MacNeill Library Service
  1701 West 3rd Ave., Vancouver BC V6J 1K7
  604/732-1335; Fax: 604/732-3765; Toll Free: 1-800-663-1174; Email: macneill@literascape.com
Madison Press Books
  40 Madison Ave., Toronto ON M5R 2S1
  416/923-5027; Fax: 416/923-9708
Magra Publishing
  44 Tally-Ho Dr., Hamilton ON L9H 3M6
  905/628-4388; Fax: 905/628-4388
  ISBN: 0-9693817
La Maison de l'Education
  10485, boul Saint-Laurent, Montréal PQ H3L 2P1
  514/384-4401; Fax: 514/384-4844
Malin Head Press
  PO Box 72172, Stn Kanata North, Kanata ON K2K 2P4
  613/592-4453; Fax: 613/592-7078; Email: shearoni@magi.com
  ISBN: 0-9698039
Mandragore
  127A Castlerock Dr., Richmond Hill ON L4C 6A1
  905/770-0183; Fax: 905/881-6710
Marcus Books
  PO Box 327, Queensville ON L0G 1R0
  905/478-2201; Fax: 905/478-8338
  ISBN: 0-919951; SAN: 115-4249
Marginal Distribution
  #103 Lower Mall, 277 George St. North, Peterborough ON K9J 3G9
  705/745-2326; Fax: 705/745-2326; Email: marginal@ptbo.igs.net
  SAN: 115-4257
Marine Press of Canada Ltd.
  295, rue de la Montagne, Montréal PQ H3C 4K4
  514/932-8342; Fax: 514/931-3711
Marshall Cavendish
  93B Woodbridge Ave., PO Box 56510, Woodbridge ON L4L 8V3
  905/851-4660; Fax: 905/851-5507
  ISBN: 1-85435
Martin & Ziegler Ltd.
  6958 Laburnum St., Vancouver BC V6P 5M9
  604/261-4615; Fax: 604/266-6472

Marvin Melnyk Associates Ltd
  PO Box 220, Queenston ON L0S 1L0
  905/262-4964; Fax: 905/262-4974; Toll Free: 1-800-682-0029
  ISBN: 0-919803; SAN: 115-4281
McBeth of Canada
  #2, 110 Morton Ave. East, Brantford ON N3S 7J7
  519/753-1903; Fax: 519/753-4811
  SAN: 169-9717
McClelland & Stewart Inc.
  #900, 481 University Ave., Toronto ON M5G 2E9
  416/598-1114; Fax: 416/598-7764; Toll Free: 1-800-788-1074
  ISBN: 0-7710; SAN: 115-4192
McGill-Queen's University Press
  3430 McTavish St., Montréal PQ H3A 1X9
  514/398-3750; Fax: 514/398-4333; Toll Free: 1-800-565-9523; Email: mqup@printing.lan.mcgill.ca
  Queen's University: 184 Union St., Kingston ON K7L 2P6
  613/545-2155; Fax: 613/545-6822
  ISBN: 0-7735
McGilligan Books
  859 Dundas St. West, PO Box 16024, Toronto ON M6J 1V6
  416/603-0994; Fax: 416/603-4385
  ISBN: 0-9698064
McGraw-Hill Ryerson Ltd.
  300 Water St., Whitby ON L1N 9B6
  905/430-5000; Fax: 905/430-5020; Email: johnd@mcgrawhill.ca
  ISBN: 0-07; SAN: 115-060X
Meakin and Associates
  #17, 81 Auriga Dr., Nepean ON K2E 7Y5
  613/226-4381; Fax: 613/226-1687
  ISBN: 1-895195; SAN: 115-7183
The Mercury Press
  137 Birmingham St., PO Box 446, Stratford ON N5A 2T1
  519/273-7083; Fax: 519/273-7932
  ISBN: 0-920544, 1-55128; SAN: 115-009X
Meridian Press
  50 Main St., Ottawa ON K1S 1B2
  613/237-5577; Fax: 613/230-1762; Toll Free: 1-800-265-0375
  ISBN: 2-929058, 2-920417, 1-895771
Michael Reynolds & Associates
  #202, 1224 Hamilton St., Vancouver BC V6B 2S8
  604/688-6918; Fax: 604/687-4624
Michelin North America (Canada) Inc.
  Maps & Guides Division, 2450, boul Daniel Johnson, Laval PQ H7T 2T9
  514/856-8855; Fax: 514/856-0551; Toll Free: 1-800-361-8236
  ISBN: 2-06; SAN: 115-0618
Michi-Mook Enterprises
  664 Queen St. East, Sault Ste Marie ON P6A 2A4
  705/946-5746, 253-8543
Micromedia Limited
  20 Victoria St., Toronto ON M5C 2N8
  416/362-5211; Fax: 416/362-6161; Toll Free: 1-800-387-2689; Email: info@mmltd.com; URL: http://www.mmltd.com
  ISBN: 0-88892; SAN: 115-4303
Midwestern News Agency
  344 Portage Ave., Saskatoon SK S7J 4C6
  306/934-4414; Fax: 306/934-3515
Mika Publishing Co.
  200 Stanley St., PO Box 536, Belleville ON K8N 5B2
  613/962-4022
  ISBN: 0-919302, 0-919303
Mile Oak Publishing
  #81, 20 Mineola Rd. East, Mississauga ON L5G 4N9
  905/274-4356; Fax: 905/274-8656; Email: 102535.312@compuserve.com
  ISBN: 0-9696376
Milestone Publications Inc.
  3284 Heather St., Vancouver BC V5Z 3K5

604/875-0611; Fax: 604/738-5135
SAN: 115-169X

Mind Resources Inc.
PO Box 126, Kitchener ON N2G 3W9
519/895-0330; Fax: 519/895-0331
SAN: 115-3986

Mini Mocho Press
PO Box 57424, Stn Jackson, Hamilton ON L8P 4X2
905/523-1518

Minnow Books Inc.
1251 Northside Rd., Burlington ON L7M 1H7
905/336-4003; Fax: 905/336-3766; Toll Free: 1-800-262-5210

MLR Editions Canada
Dept. of English, Wilfrid Laurier University, Waterloo ON N2L 3C5
519/884-1970; Email: ptiessen@machi1.wlu.ca
ISBN: 0-9692539

Modulo Publisher Inc./Modulo Éditeur Inc.
#300, 233, av Dunbar, Montréal PQ H3P 2H4
514/738-9818; Fax: 514/738-5838
ISBN: 2-89113

Monarch Books of Canada
5000 Dufferin St., Downsview ON M3H 5T5
416/663-8231; Fax: 416/736-1702; Toll Free: 1-800-404-7404
SAN: 111-171X

Mondia Éditeurs inc.
1977, boul Industriel, Laval PQ H7S 1P6
514/667-9221; Fax: 514/667-8658
ISBN: 0-88556, 2-89114

Moneyjar Publishing
#1711, 642 Sheppard Ave. East, North York ON M2K 1B9
416/223-7312; Fax: 416/223-3348; Email: millyard@tvo.org
ISBN: 0-9695889

moonprint
PO Box 293, Winnipeg MB R3C 2G9

Moonstone Press
167 Delaware St., London ON N5Z 2N6
519/659-5784; Fax: 519/659-6278
ISBN: 0-920259; SAN: 115-4354

Mosaic Press
1252 Speers Rd., Unit 1, Oakville ON L6L 5N9
905/825-2130; Fax: 905/825-2130
ISBN: 0-88962

Mosby Yearbook see Times Mirror Professional Publishing

Moulin Publishing Ltd.
PO Box 560, Norval ON L0P 1K0
905/877-3555; Fax: 905/877-3555
ISBN: 0-9697079

Moving Publications Ltd.
#100, 44 Upjohn Rd., North York ON M2B 2W1
416/441-1168; Fax: 416/441-1641; Email: movingto@idirect.com
ISBN: 1-895020

MRA Books
#500, 251 Bank St., Ottawa ON K2P 1X3
613/230-7197; Fax: 613/230-4233; Email: mra@web.net
ISBN: 0-85239, 0-901269; SAN: 115-7515

Multicultural Books
2384 Yonge St., PO Box 1279, Stn K, Toronto ON M4P 3E5
416/488-9997; Fax: 416/488-4831; Email: mul@io.org
ISBN: 0-9694933

Munsey Music
PO Box 511, Richmond Hill ON L4C 4Y8
905/737-0208; Fax: 905/737-0208
ISBN: 0-9697066; SAN: 116-967X

The Muses' Company see J. Gordon Shillingford Ltd.
Musson Publishing see General Publishing Co. Limited

Napoleon Publishing Inc.
#1005, 3266 Yonge St., Toronto ON M4N 3P6

416/730-9052; Fax: 416/226-9975; Toll Free: 1-800-387-8028
ISBN: 0-929141; SAN: 115-0022

National Book Service
25 Kodiak Cres., North York ON M3J 3E5
416/630-2950; Fax: 416/630-0274; Toll Free: 1-800-263-8738
SAN: 108-0830

National News Co. Ltd.
2655 Lancaster Rd., Ottawa ON K1B 4L5
613/731-2840; Fax: 613/731-2320

Natural Heritage/Natural History Inc.
PO Box 95, Stn O, Toronto ON M4A 2M8
416/694-7907; Fax: 416/690-0819
ISBN: 0-920474; SAN: 115-4559

NC Press Limited
#400, 345 Adelaide St. West, Toronto ON M5V 1R5
416/593-6284; Fax: 416/593-6204; Email: ncpress@fox.nstn.ca
ISBN: 0-919, 0-920, 1-55021; SAN: 115-0650

Negev Importing Co. Ltd. House of Judaica
3509 Bathurst St., Toronto ON M6A 2C5
416/781-9356; Fax: 416/781-0071
SAN: 170-0154

Nelson/Word Communications Ltd.
7720 Alderbridge Way, Richmond BC V6X 2A2
604/270-7231; Fax: 604/270-0821; Toll Free: 1-800-663-3133

Netherlandic Press
PO Box 396, Stn A, Windsor ON N9A 6S9
519/944-2171
ISBN: 0-919417

New Magazine Publishing Co. Ltd.
PO Box 390, Stn A, Ottawa ON K1N 8V4
613/230-1644; Fax: 613/234-6662
ISBN: 0-921032

New Society Publishers
PO Box 189, Gabriola Island BC V0R 1X0
250/247-9737; Fax: 250/247-7471; Toll Free: 1-800-567-6772; Email: nspc@epaus.island.net
ISBN: 1-55092

New Star Books Ltd.
2504 York Ave., Vancouver BC V6K 1E3
604/738-9429; Fax: 604/738-9332; Email: newstar@pinc.com
ISBN: 0-919888, 0-919573, 0-921586; SAN: 115-1908

New World Perspectives
3652, av Laval, Montréal PQ H2X 3C9
514/282-9298; Fax: 514/987-9724
ISBN: 0-920393; SAN: 116-0273

NeWest Publishers Ltd.
(NeWest Press)
#310, 10359 - 82 Ave., Edmonton AB T6E 1Z9
403/432-9427; Fax: 403/432-9429; Email: newest@planet.eon.net
ISBN: 0-920316, 0-920897; SAN: 115-0677

Newport Bay Publishing
356 Cyril Owen Place, RR#3, Victoria BC V8X 3X1
250/479-4616; Fax: 250/479-3836
ISBN: 0-921513

Next Century Books
PO Box 43093, Burnaby BC V5G 4S2
604/521-6524; Fax: 604/299-4020
ISBN: 0-9694734

Nicholas Hoare Ltd.
2165, av Madison, Montréal PQ H4B 2T2
514/489-9341; Fax: 514/489-1784
SAN: 170-0332

Nightwood Editions
#13, RR#2, Site 26, Gibson BC V0N 1V0
604/885-0212; Fax: 604/885-0212
ISBN: 0-88971; SAN: 115-2661

Nimbus Publishing Ltd.
PO Box 9301, Stn A, Halifax NS B3K 5N5
902/454-8381; Fax: 902/455-3652; Toll Free: 1-800-646-2879
ISBN: 0-920852, 0-921054, 1-55109; SAN: 115-0685

Nine Pines Publishing
1128 Church St., Manotick ON K4M 1A5
613/692-1601; Fax: 613/692-1602; Toll Free: 1-800-465-3287; Email: unity_arts/nine_pines@bcon.com
ISBN: 1-895456

Non-Entity Press Ltd./New Ireland Press
217 Aberdeen St., Fredericton NB E3B 1R6
506/454-1153
ISBN: 0-9690215

Norris-Whitney Communications Inc.
#7, 23 Hannover St., St. Catharines ON L2W 1A3
905/641-3471641-1648; Toll Free: 1-800-265-8481; Email: order@nor.com
ISBN: 0-9691272

North 49 Books
193 Bartley Dr., Toronto ON M4A 1E6
416/750-7777; Fax: 416/750-2049; Toll Free: 1-800-490-4049; Email: north49@terraport.net
SAN: 117-2689

Northstone Publishing
#330, 1980 Cooper Rd., Kelowna BC V1Y 9G8
250/766-2926; Fax: 250/766-1201

Les Nouvelles Éditions de l'Arc
5844, rue Duquesne, Montréal PQ H1M 2K4
514/251-7625; Fax: 514/483-3810
ISBN: 2-89016

Novalis
6255, rue Hutchison, Montréal PQ H2V 4C7
514/278-3020; Fax: 514/278-3030; Toll Free: 1-800-668-2547
Toronto Office: 49 Front St. East, 2nd Fl., Toronto ON M5E 1B3
416/363-3303; Fax: 416/363-9409; Toll Free: 1-800-387-7164
ISBN: 2-89088

Nuage Editions
PO Box 8, Stn E, Montréal PQ H2T 3A5
514/272-5226; Fax: 514/271-5722
ISBN: 0-921833

Oberon Press
#400, 350 Sparks St., Ottawa ON K1R 7S8
613/238-3275; Fax: 613/238-3275
ISBN: 0-88750; SAN: 115-0723

Ocapt Publications
27 Donna Marie Dr., Welland ON L3C 2X7
905/735-2967; Fax: 905/788-0839

OISE Press
(Ontario Institute for Studies in Education Press)
252 Bloor St. West, Toronto ON M5S 1V5
416/926-4707; Fax: 416/926-4725
ISBN: 0-7744; SAN: 115-2818

Ontario Outdoor Publications
1431 Stavebank Rd., Mississauga ON L5G 2V5
905/891-1714; Fax: 905/891-2352
ISBN: 0-9690474; SAN: 115-4672

Oolichan Books
PO Box 10, Lantzville BC V0R 2H0
250/390-4839; Fax: 250/390-4839
ISBN: 0-88982; SAN: 115-4680

Orca Book Publishers Ltd.
PO Box 5626, Stn B, Victoria BC V8R 6S4
250/380-1229; Fax: 250/380-1892; Toll Free: 1-800-210-5277; Email: orca@pinc.com; URL: http://www.swifty.com/orca/index.htm
ISBN: 0-920501, 1-55143; SAN: 115-7485

Orchard Press Inc.
55 Lismer, PO Box 72144, Stn Kanata North, Kanata ON K2K 2P4
613/592-6226; Fax: 613/592-9315
ISBN: 0-919741

Otter Press
81 Albert St., Waterloo ON N2L 3S6
519/885-4130
ISBN: 0-9690963

Our Schools/Our Selves
107 Earl Grey Rd., Toronto ON M4J 3L6

416/463-6978; Fax: 416/463-6978; Toll Free: 1-800-565-1975
ISBN: 0-921908

Outcrop, The Northern Publishers
PO Box 1350, Yellowknife NT X1A 2N9
403/920-4652; Fax: 403/873-2844
ISBN: 0-919315; SAN: 115-4710

Outport Publishing
PO Box 1072, Lewisporte NF A0G 3A0
709/535-8464; Fax: 709/535-0382
ISBN: 0-9696544

Owl Books
#500, 179 John St., Toronto ON M5T 3G5
416/971-5275; Fax: 416/971-5294
ISBN: 0-919872, 0-920775, 1-895688; SAN: 115-4044

Owl's Head Press
PO Box 57, Alma NB E0A 1B0
506/887-2073; Fax: 506/887-2074
ISBN: 0-929635

Oxford University Press
70 Wynford Drive, North York ON M3C 1J9
416/441-2941; Fax: 416/444-0427; Toll Free: 1-800-387-8020
ISBN: 0-19; SAN: 115-731

OZ New Media
10050 - 117 St., Edmonton AB T5K 1X2
403/482-2171; Fax: 403/488-5834; Email: jscrimger@planet.eon.net
ISBN: 1-896295

Pacesetter Press
236 Sunset Cres., PO Box 326, Stroud ON L0L 2M0
705/431-6898; Fax: 705/431-6898; Toll Free: 1-800-813-7223
ISBN: 0-9697317

Pacific Edge Publishing
Comp. 50, Site 21, Gabriola BC V0R 1X0
250/247-8806; Fax: 250/247-8299; Email: pacedge@island.net; URL: http://www.schoolnet.ca/vp/cdncont/
ISBN: 1-895110

Pacific Educational Press
The Faculty of Education, U.B.C., 2173 East Mall, Vancouver BC V6T 1Z4
604/822-5385; Fax: 604/822-6603
ISBN 0-88865; SAN 115-1266

Pacific-Rim Publishers
Comp. 7, Site 28, RR#1, Gabriola BC V0R 1X0
250/247-0014; Fax: 250/247-0015; Email: prp@island.net
ISBN: 0-921358

Paideia Press Ltd.
PO Box 1000, Jordan Station ON L0R 1S0
905/562-5719; Fax: 905/562-7828
ISBN: 0-88815; SAN: 115-4761

Paje Éditeur
CP 897, Succ C, Montréal PQ H2L 4L6
514/849-3379; Fax: 514/849-6445
ISBN: 2-9801495

Palmerston Press
822 Manning Ave., Toronto ON M6G 2W8
416/516-9056; Fax: 416/5160282

Pannonia Books - The Hungarian Bookstore
PO Box 1017, Stn B, Toronto ON M5T 2T8
416/966-5156; Fax: 416/966-5156
ISBN: 0-919368; SAN: 168-5104

paperplates books
19 Kenwood Ave., Toronto ON M6C 2RB
416/651-2551

Parchment Press
90 Charlton Blvd., North York ON M2M 1B9
ISBN: 0-9695504

Pathway Publishers
RR#4, Aylmer ON N5H 2R3
ISBN: 0-919374

Paulines Books & Media
3022 Dufferin St., Toronto ON M6B 3T5

416/781-9131; Fax: 416/783-1615; Email: pauline@netrover.com; URL: http://www.netrover.com/~pauline
ISBN: 0-8198

P.D. Meany Publishers
PO Box 18, Streetsville ON L5M 2R7
905/567-5803; Fax: 905/567-1687
ISBN: 0-88835; SAN: 115-4273

Pegasus Publishing
Causeway Rd., Site 19, PO Box 26, Seaforth NS B0J 1N0
902/827-3204; Email: aj401@ccn.cs.dal.ca
ISBN 0-9692552

Peguis Publishers Limited
#100, 318 McVermot Ave., Winnipeg MB R3A 0A2
204/987-3500; Fax: 204/947-0080; Email: peguis@peguis.mb.ca
ISBN: 0-920541, 1-895411; SAN: 115-480X

Pembroke Publishers Limited
528 Hood Rd., Markham ON L3R 3K9
905/477-0650; Fax: 905/477-3691; Toll Free: 1-800-997-9807
ISBN: 0-921217

Pemmican Publications
#2, 1635 Burrows Ave., Winnipeg MB R2X 0T1
204/589-4351; Fax: 204/947-1816
ISBN: 0-921827; SAN: 115-1657

Pendas Press
32 Hammersmith Ave., Toronto ON M4E 2W4
416/699-5338
ISBN: 0-920820

Pendragon House Ltd.
PO Box 338, Stn Port Credit, Mississauga ON L5G 4L8
905/823-0222; Fax: 905/823-9931; Toll Free: 1-800-727-2751
ISBN: 0-88761; SAN: 156-7764

Penguin Books Canada Ltd.
#300, 10 Alcorn Ave., Toronto ON M4V 3B2
416/925-2249; Fax: 416/925-0068
ISBN: 0-14; SAN: 115-4826, 115-074X

Penlan Publishing
743 View St., Victoria BC V8W 1J9
250/383-3983; Fax: 250/383-1580; Email: penlan@penlan.com; URL: http://www.penlancom/penlan
ISBN: 0-9692032

Penumbra Press
PO Box 40062, Ottawa ON K1V 0W8
613/526-3232; Fax: 613/526-3244; Toll Free: 1-800-567-6591
ISBN: 0-921254, 0-929806; SAN: 115-0774

Petheric Press Ltd. see Nimbus Publishing Ltd.

Phoenix Publishing Inc.
821 - 254 St., Langley BC V4W 2R8
604/878-0248; Toll Free: 1-800-563-6050
ISBN: 0-91345

Pippin Publishing Ltd.
481 University Ave., Toronto ON M5G 2E9
416/598-1866; Fax: 416/598-1565; Toll Free: 1-800-524-5428
ISBN: 0-88751; SAN: 115-3293

Plains Publishing Inc.
17340 - 106A Ave., Edmonton AB T5S 1E6
403/451-0871; Fax: 403/455-1388; Toll Free: 1-800-661-5967
ISBN 0-920985; SAN 115-8716

Playwrights Canada Press
54 Wolseley St., 2nd Fl., Toronto ON M5T 1A5
416/947-0201; Fax: 416/947-0159; Toll Free: 1-800-561-3318; Email: cdplays@interlog.com; URL: http://www.puc.ca
ISBN: 0-88754, 0-919834; SAN: 115-0766

Point-to-Point
PO Box 133, Stn B, Ottawa ON K1P 6C3
613/237-4658; Email: cz173@freenet.carleton.ca
ISBN: 0-9695731

Polestar Press Ltd.
1011 Commercial Dr., 2nd Fl., Vancouver BC V5L 3X1
604/251-9718; Fax: 604/251-9718
ISBN: 0-919591; SAN 115-4931

Polyscience Publications Inc.
44 Seize Arpents, PO Box 148, Morin Heights PQ J0R 1H0
514/226-5870; Fax: 514/226-5866
ISBN: 0-921317; SAN: 115-4419

Porcepic Books see Beach Holme Publishers Limited

Porcupine's Quill Inc.
68 Main St., Erin ON N0B 1T0
519/833-9158; Fax: 519/833-9158
ISBN: 0-88984; SAN: 115-0820

Porphry Press
148 McComber Cres., Thunder Bay ON P7A 7E8
807/767-2705
ISBN: 0-9693138

Porthole Press Ltd.
2082 Neptune Rd., RR#3, Sidney BC V8L 3X9
250/656-7902; Fax: 250/652-1521
ISBN: 0-919931

Potentials Within
161 Franklin Ave., North York ON M2N 1C6
416/512-1168; Fax: 416/512-1168
ISBN: 0-9695781; SAN: 118-413X

Potlatch Publications Limited
30 Berry Hill, Waterdown ON L0R 2H4
905/689-1632
ISBN: 0-919676; SAN: 115-1355

Pottersfield Press
RR#2, Porters Lake NS B0J 2S0
902/827-4517; Fax: 902/455-3652 (orders)
ISBN: 0-919001; SAN: 115-0790

Power Engineering Books Ltd.
7 Perron St., St Albert AB T8N 1E3
403/459-2525; Fax: 403/460-2530; Toll Free: 1-800-667-3155
SAN: 115-4850

Prairie House Books
PO Box 84007, Stn MarketMall, Calgary AB T3A 5C4
403/229-2040; Fax: 403/247-3675
ISBN: 1-895012

Prairie Lily Books
PO Box 1673, Saskatoon SK S7K 3R8
306/955-4238

The Prairie Publishing Co.
PO Box 2997, Winnipeg MB R3C 4B5
204/885-6496; Fax: 204/775-3277
ISBN: 0-919576; SAN: 115-4869

Prentice-Hall Canada Inc.
1870 Birchmount Rd., Scarborough ON M1P 2J7
416/293-3621; Fax: 416/299-2540; Telex: 065-25184; URL: http://prenhall.com/
ISBN: 0-13; SAN; 115-0839

Press Gang Publishers Feminist Co-operative
#101, 225 - 17th Ave. East, Vancouver BC V5V 1A6
604/876-7787; Fax: 604/876-7892
ISBN: 0-88974; SAN: 115-4893

Presses d'Amérique
#100, 50, rue Saint-Paul ouest, Montréal PQ H2Y 1Y8
514/847-1953; Fax: 514/847-1647
ISBN: 2-921378

Presses d'Or
#105, 7875, boul Louis-H-Lafontaine, Anjou PQ H1K 4E4
514/355-7703; Fax: 514/354-3144
ISBN: 2-920903

Les Presses de l'Université Laval
Edifice Jean Durand, 2336, ch Ste-Foy, 2e étage, Ste-Foy PQ G1K 7P4
418/656-7381; Fax: 418/656-3305
ISBN 2-7637

Les Presses de l'Université de Montréal
CP 6128, Succ A, Montréal PQ H3C 3J7

514/343-6929; Fax: 514/343-2232
ISBN: 2-7606
Presses de l'Université du Québec
2875, boul Laurier, Sainte-Foy PQ G1V 2M3
418/657-3551; Fax: 418/657-2096;
Email: marketing@puq.uquebec.ca
ISBN 0-7770, 2-7605, 2-920073
Primary Press
PO Box 372, Peterborough ON K9J 6Z3
705/749-9276; Fax: 705/742-7651
ISBN: 0-919895; SAN: 118-4113
Prime Books Inc.
166 Bayview Fairways Dr., Thornhill ON L3T 2Y8
905/881-2853; Fax: 905/881-4334
ISBN: 0-920814, 0-921573, 2-89423
Prise de Parole Inc.
111 Elm St., PO Box 550, Stn B, Sudbury ON P3E 4R2
705/675-6491; Fax: 705/673-1817; Email: pdp550dt@vianet.on.ca
ISBN: 0-920814, 0-921573, 2-89423
Productions Boule de neige
1175, rue Notre-Dame ouest, Victoriaville PQ G6P 7L1
819/758-5073; Fax: 819/758-4787; Toll Free: 1-800-567-2531
ISBN: 2-921380
Productive Publications
PO Box 7200, Stn A, Toronto ON M5W 1X8
416/483-0634; Fax: 416/322-7434
ISBN: 0-920847
Promotional Book Company
36 Northline Rd., Toronto ON M4B 3E2
416/759-2226; Fax: 416/759-2150;
Email: 75030.1713@compuserve.com
Prosveta Inc.
1565, Montée Masson, Laval PQ H7E 4P2
514/661-4242; Fax: 514/661-4984; Toll Free: 1-800-667-2665; Email: prosveta@pop.generation.net
Vancouver Office: #202, 141 West 7th Ave., Vancouver BC V5Y 1L8
604/872-7292; Fax: 604/872-7292
ISBN: 1-895978, 2-920344, 2-85566; SAN 115-6896
Provincial News Co.
16504 - 121A Ave., Edmonton AB T5V 1J9
403/454-0306; Fax: 403/453-3687
P.S.A. Ventures Inc
#408, 11 Cooperage Pl., Victoria BC V9A 1J9
250/360-0306; Fax: 250/360-0710
ISBN: 0-9691999, 0-9695386
Ptarmigan Press Ltd.
1372 - 18th Ave., Campbell River BC V9W 2E1
250/286-0878; Fax: 250/286-9749
ISBN: 0-919537; SAN: 116-0281
Publications Chant de mon pays
860, ch de la Montagne, CP 28, Beloeil PQ J3S 4S8
514/464-1837; Fax: 514/464-2146
ISBN: 2-921124
Les Publications Graficor
175, boul de Mortagne, Boucherville PQ J4B 6G4
514/449-2369; Fax: 514/449-7808
ISBN: 2-89242
Publications Ontario
50 Grosvenor St., Toronto ON M7A 1N8
416/326-5300; Fax: 416/326-5317; Toll Free: 1-800-668-9938
ISBN: 0-7743, 0-7729, 0-7778
Les Publications du Québec
1500D, boul Charest ouest, 1er étage, Ste-Foy PQ G1N 2E5
418/643-5150; Fax: 418/643-6177; Toll Free: 1-800-463-2100
ISBN: 2-551
Publishers Group West
#223, 543 Richmond St. West, PO Box 106, Toronto ON M5V 1Y6
416/504-3900; Fax: 416/504-3902; Toll Free: 1-800-747-8147; Email: alan.zweig@pgw.com

SAN: 117-0171
Purich Publishing
PO Box 23032, Stn Market Mall, Saskatoon SK S7J 5H3
306/373-5311; Fax: 306/373-5315
ISBN: 1-895830
Purpleville Publishing
#5, 3405 American Dr., Mississauga ON L4V 1T6
905/678-2855; Fax: 905/678-6036
ISBN: 0-9695306
Quarry Press
PO Box 1061, Kingston ON K7L 4Y5
613/548-8429; Fax: 613/548-1556
ISBN: 0-919627; SAN: 115-4958
Québec dans le Monde
#302, 1001, rte de l'Eglise, CP 8503, Ste-Foy PQ G1V 4N5
418/659-5540; Fax: 418/659-4143
ISBN: 2-921309
Québec Livres
2185, autoroute des Laurentide, Laval PQ H7S 1Z6
514/687-1210; Fax: 514/687-1331
ISBN: 2-920596
Québec Science Éditeur
2875, boul Laurier, Ste-Foy PQ G1V 2M3
418/657-4390; Fax: 418/657-2096
ISBN: 2-920073
Quintin Publishers/Éditions Michel Quintin
PO Box 340, Waterloo PQ J0E 2N0
514/539-3774; Fax: 514/539-4905
ISBN: 2-920438, 2-89435; SAN: 116-5356
Quon Éditions
10103 - 97A Ave., Edmonton AB T5K 2T3
403/428-3333; Fax: 403/428-3966; Toll Free: 1-800-565-9398
ISBN: 0-9694432, 0-9695539, 0-9696831
Ragweed Press Inc./gynergy books
PO Box 2023, Charlottetown PE C1A 7N7
902/566-5750; Fax: 902/566-4473; Email: gb@gynergy.com
ISBN:0-920304, 0-921556, 0-921881; SAN: 115-0863
Rainbird Press
3456 Dunbar St., PO Box 206, Vancouver BC V6S 2C2
604/224-4756; Fax: 604/731-3511
ISBN: 0-9690504
Rainbow House Distributors
#10, 160 Frobisher Dr., Waterloo ON N2V 2B1
519/746-8921; Fax: 519/746-5244; Toll Free: 1-800-265-8887
Raincoast Books
8680 Cambie St., Vancouver BC V6P 6M9
604/323-7100; Fax: 604/323-2600; Toll Free: 1-800-663-5714; Email: info@raincoast.com
ISBN: 0-920417, 1-895714; SAN 115-087
Random House of Canada Ltd.
1265 Aerowood Dr., Mississauga ON L4W 1B9
905/624-0672; Fax: 905/624-6217; Toll Free: 1-800-668-2427; URL: http://www.randomhouse.com
Editorial & Publicity Offices: #210, 33 Yonge St., Toronto ON M5E 1G4
416/777-9477; Fax: 416/777-9470
ISBN: 0-394, 0-679; SAN: 115-088X
Reader's Digest Association (Canada) Ltd.
215, av Redfern, Montréal PQ H3Z 2V9
514/934-0751; Fax: 514/934-6177
Warehouse & Customer Service: 300 Orenda Rd. East, Brampton ON L6T 1G2
905/793-8221; Fax: 905/793-0846; Toll Free: 1-800-363-6259
ISBN: 0-88850; SAN 115-0898, 115-4974
Rebel Publishing
PO Box 2294, Peterborough ON K9J 7Y8
705/742-4831
Red Deer College Press
PO Box 5005, Red Deer AB T4N 5H5
403/342-3321; Fax: 403/340-8940
ISBN 0-88995; SAN 115-1819

Reed Books Canada
Division of Butterworths Canada Ltd.
#300, 204 Richmond St. West, Toronto ON M5V 1V6
416/598-0045; Fax: 416/598-0358; Toll Free: 1-800-450-2236
ISBN: 0-408, 0-409, 0-433; SAN 115-2750
Reference Press
PO Box 70, Teeswater ON N0G 2S0
519/392-6634; Fax: 519/392-8043
ISBN: 0-919981; SAN: 115-687X
Reference West
2450 Central Ave., Victoria BC V8S 2S8
250/598-0096
ISBN: 1-895362
Reflections
PO Box 178, Gabriola BC V0R 1X0
250/247-8685; Fax: 250/247-8116
ISBN: 0-9692570
Regina News Ltd.
1201 Lorne St., Regina SK S4R 2J9
306/525-3757; Fax: 306/569-9899; Toll Free: 1-800-665-8135
Reid Publishing Ltd.
109 Thomas St., PO Box 69559, Oakville ON L6J 7R4
905/842-4428; Fax: 905/842-9327; Toll Free: 1-800-4464797
ISBN: 0-921601; SAN: 116-0478
Reidmore Books
#1200, 10109 - 106 St., Edmonton AB T2J 3L7
403/488-5091; Fax: 403/482-7213; Toll Free: 1-800-661-2859; Email: reidmore@compusmart.ab.ca
ISBN: 0-919091, 1-895073
Renewable Energy in Canada
15010 Yonge St., Aurora ON L4G 1M6
905/841-5551; Fax: 905/841-6744
ISBN: 0-920456; SAN: 115-4990
Renouf Publishing Co. Ltd.
5369 Canotek Rd., Ottawa ON K1J 9J3
613/745-2665; Fax: 613/745-7660; URL: http://fox.nstn.ca/~renouf/
ISBN: 0-88852; SAN: 170-8066
Repository Press
Comp. 8, Site 29, RR#7, Prince George BC V2N 2J5
250/562-7074; Fax: 250/561-7094
ISBN: 0-920104; SAN: 115-5016
Research Press
60 Rankin St., Waterloo ON N2V 1V9
519/747-2477; Fax: 519/747-0062; Toll Free: 1-800-265-3375
ISBN: 0-87822; SAN: 115-5024
The Resource Centre Inc.
PO Box 190, Waterloo ON N2J 3Z9
519/885-0826; Fax: 519/747-5629
ISBN: 0-920701; SAN: 115-5032
Revue Cap-aux-Diamants
1, Côte de la Fabrique, CP 609, Succ HauteVille, Québec PQ G1R 4S2
418/656-5040; Fax: 418/656-7282
ISBN: 2-920069
R.G. Mitchell Family Books Inc.
565 Gordon Baker Rd., North York ON M2H 2W2
416/499-4615; Fax: 416/499-6340; Toll Free: 1-800-268-3445; Email: 10214.131@compuserve.com
ISBN: 0-9293201; SAN: 115-8511
The Riverbank Press
369 Shuter St., Toronto ON M5A 1X2
416/955-0866
Riverwood Publishers Ltd.
6 Donlands Ave., PO Box 70, Sharon ON L0G 1V0
905/478-8396; Fax: 905/478-8380; Email: rwpub@interlog.com
ISBN: 1-895121; SAN: 116-1288
Robert Davies Publishing
Division of L'Etincelle Éditeur Inc.
#311, 4999, rue Ste-Catherine ouest, Westmount PQ H3Z 1T3

514/481-2440; Fax: 514/481-9973; Email: rdppub@vir.com
ISBN: 1-895854

Robert Rose Inc.
#12, 156 Duncan Mill Rd., Don Mills ON M3B 3N2
416/449-3535; Fax: 416/449-9887
ISBN: 1-896503

Robert S. Ing Publishers
#102, 1170 Bay St., Toronto ON M5S 2B4
416/580-7508; Fax: 416/928-0243
ISBN: 0-9692707, 1-895377; SAN: 115-6934

Rockland Press
c/o Ken Haycock & Associates Inc., #284, 810 Broadway West, Vancouver BC V5Z 4C9
604/925-0266; Fax: 604/925-0566
ISBN: 0-920175

Rocky Mountain Books
4 Spruce Centre SW, Calgary AB T3C 3B3
403/249-9490; Fax: 403/249-2968; Email: tonyd@cadvision.com; URL: http://www.ffa.ucalgary.ca/rmb/
ISBN: 0-9690038, 0-921102; SAN: 115-5040

Ron Belanger & Associates Inc.
217 Fairview Ave., Toronto ON M6P 3A6
416/763-0101; Fax: 416/763-0508

Ronald P. Frye & Company (Publisher)
55 Lismer, Kanata ON K2K 1A5
613/592-6226; Fax: 613/592-9315
ISBN: 0-919741; SAN: 115-351X

Ronsdale Press
3350 - 21st Ave. West, Vancouver BC V6S 1G7
604/738-1195; Fax: 604/731-4548; Email: ronhatch@pinc.com
ISBN: 0-921870; SAN: 116-2454

A Room of One's Own Press
PO Box 5215, Stn B, Victoria BC V8R 6N4
250/598-8458; Fax: 250/598-8458
ISBN: 0-919998

Roseway Publishing Co.
RR#1, Lockeport NS B0T 1L0
902/656-2223; Fax: 902/656-2223; Email: ktudor@atcon.com
ISBN: 0-9694180

Roussan Publishers Inc./Roussan éditeur inc.
#100, 2110, boul Decarie, Montréal PQ H4A 3J3
514/487-2895; Fax: 514/487-2899; URL: http://www.magnet.ca/roussan
ISBN: 1-896184, 2-921212

Rowland & Jacob Inc.
PO Box 545, Stn p, Toronto ON M5S 2T1
416/921-9557; Fax: 416/921-0408
ISBN: 0-921430

Rubicon Publishing Inc.
#1, 116 Thomas St., Oakville ON L6J 3A8
905/849-8777; Fax: 905/849-7579; Email: rubicon@pathway1.pathcom.com
ISBN: 0-921156; SAN 115-432X49-7579

S & B Books Ltd.
3043 Universal Dr., Mississauga ON L4X 2E2
905/629-5055; Fax: 905/629-5054
SAN: 119-6014

S & B Large Print & Special Lines Ltd.
4132 Dundas St. West, Toronto ON M8X 1X3
416/234-5015; Fax: 416/234-8781
SAN: 170-7736

S. Rosoph Publishers & Representatives
631, av Smart, Montréal PQ H4X 1T2
514/488-3395
ISBN: 0-920341; SAN: 115-0936

Sage Books Canada
335 Catharine St., Ottawa ON K1R 5T4
613/333-7243; Fax: 613/233-8626; Toll Free: 1-800-363-2845

Sandhill Book Marketing
#99, 1270 Ellis St., Kelowna BC V1Y 1Z4
250/763-1406; Fax: 250/763-5211; Email: sandhill@awinc.com
ISBN: 0-920923; SAN: 115-2181

Sara Jordon/Jordon Music Productions Inc.
PO Box 160, Stn M, Toronto ON M6S 4T3
416/760-7664; Fax: 416/762-2770; Toll Free: 1-800-567-7733
ISBN: 1-895523

Saturn Distributing Inc.
25 Bodrington Ct., Markham ON L6G 1B6
905/470-2666; Fax: 905/470-2672

Saunders Book Co.
199 Campbell St., PO Box 308, Collingwood ON L9Y 3Z7
705/445-4777; Fax: 705/445-9569; Toll Free: 1-800-461-9120; Email: sunders@saundersbook.ca
ISBN: 1-89505; SAN: 169-9768

SBF Media Limited
2201 Dunwin Dr., Mississauga ON L5L 1A3
905/828-6620; Fax: 905/828-2761; Toll Free: 1-800-268-4557; Email: sbfmedia@idrect.com
ISBN: 0-921932; SAN: 115-5083

Scholar's Choice
2323 Trafalgar St., PO Box 4214, London ON N5W 5W3
519/453-7470; Fax: 519/455-2214; Toll Free: 1-800-265-1095
ISBN: 0-88809; SAN: 170-0014

Scholarly Book Services Inc.
#403, 77 Mowat Ave., Toronto ON M6K 3E3
416/533-5490; Fax: 416/533-5652; Toll Free: 1-800-847-9736
SAN: 115-1339

Scholars' Books International Ltd.
PO Box 5218, Stn B, Victoria BC V8R 6W4
250/383-3215; Fax: 250/382-5512
SAN: 115-5148

Scholastic Canada Ltd.
123 Newkirk Rd., Richmond Hill ON L4C 3G5
905/883-5300; Fax: 905/883-4113; Email: 102234.3707@compuserve.com
ISBN: 0-590; SAN: 115-5164

School Book Fairs Limited
2201 Dunwin Dr., Mississauga ON L5L 1A3
905/828-6620; Fax: 905/828-2761; Toll Free: 1-800-268-4557; Email: sbfmedia@idirect.com
SAN: 169-9881

Script Publishing Inc.
#200, 839 - 5 Ave. SW, Calgary AB T2P 3C8
403/290-0800; Fax: 403/241-8575; Toll Free: 1-800-661-1096; Email: scriptbk@cadvision.com
ISBN: 0-9694287, 1-896015

Seal Books
105 Bond St., Toronto ON M5B 1Y3
416/340-0777; Fax: 416/340-1069
ISBN: 0-7704; SAN 115-5210

Second Story Press
#301, 720 Bathurst St., Toronto ON M5S 1R4
416/537-7850; Fax: 416/537-7850; Email: secstory@fox.nstn.ca
ISBN: 0-929005

SeeMore Information Systems see Reidmore Books

Self-Counsel Press Ltd.
1481 Charlotte Rd., North Vancouver BC V7J 1H1
604/986-3366; Fax: 604/986-3947; Toll Free: 1-800-663-3007; URL: http://www.swifty.com/scp
Toronto Office: 4 Bram Ct., Brampton ON L6W 3R6
905/450-0336; Fax: 905/450-7626; Toll Free: 1-800-387-3362
ISBN: 0-88908; SAN: 115-0545

Services Documentaires Multimedia Inc.
#300, 75, Port-Royal est, Montréal PQ H3L 3T1
514/382-0895; Fax: 514/384-9139; Email: info@sdm.qc.ca; URL: http://www.sdm.qc.ca

Servidec
50 Main St., Ottawa ON K1S 1B2
613/237-5577; Fax: 613/230-1762; Toll Free: 1-800-265-0375

Sheltus & Picard Inc.
CP 1321, Bedford PQ J0J 1A0

514/248-7319
ISBN: 0-9696296

Shirley Lewis Information Services
3081A Universal Dr., Mississauga ON L4X 2E2
905/626-9119; Fax: 905/629-8001; Toll Free: 1-800-665-9464; Email: slid@flexnet.com
ISBN: 0-920493

Shoreline/Littoral
23, rue Sainte-Anne, Sainte-Anne-de-Bellevue PQ H9X 1L1
514/457-5733; Fax: 514/457-5733
ISBN: 0-9695180; SAN 116-9564

Siddall & Associates
#200, 1168 Hamilton St., Vancouver BC V6B 2S2
604/662-3511; Fax: 604/683-7540; Email: siddall@axionet.com

Simon & Pierre Publishing Co. Ltd. see Dundurn Press Ltd.

Sister Vision Press
PO Box 217, Stn E, Toronto ON M6H 4E2
416/595-5033; Fax: 416/595-0627
ISBN: 0-929813

Slavuta Publishers
72 Westbrook Dr., Edmonton AB T6J 2E1
403/434-2449
ISBN: 0-919452

Snowapple Press
PO Box 66024, Stn Heritage, Edmonton AB T6J 6T4
403/437-0191
ISBN: 1-895592

Socadis Inc.
350, boul Lebeau, Ville St-Laurent PQ H4N 1W6
514/331-3300; Fax: 514/745-3282; Toll Free: 1-800-361-2847

Sogides Ltée
955, rue Amherst, Montréal PQ H2L 3K4
514/523-1182; Fax: 514/521-4434; Toll Free: 1-800-361-4806
ISBN: 2-7619

Somabec Ltée
2475, av Sylva-Clapin, Saint-Hyacinthe PQ J2S 7B6
514/774-8118; Fax: 514/774-3017

Somerset Books Ltd.
RR#2, PO Box 1500, Stayner ON L0M 1S0
705/428-0378; Fax: 705/428-0310
SAN: 115-8260

Somerville House Books Ltd.
#5000, 3080 Yonge St., Toronto ON M4N 3N1
416/488-5938; Fax: 416/488-5506
ISBN: 0-921051

Sono Nis Press
1725 Blanshard St., Victoria BC V8W 2J8
250/382-1024; Fax: 250/382-0775
ISBN: 0-919462, 0-919203, 1-55039; SAN: 115-1398

The Sound Post
130 Harbord St., Toronto ON M5S 1G8
416/323-1839; Fax: 416/324-9435
SAN: 118-3656

Sound And Vision Publishing Ltd.
359 Riverdale Ave., Toronto ON M4J 1A4
416/465-8184; Fax: 416/465-4163
ISBN: 0-920151; SAN: 115-0979

Southam Magazine & Information Group
1450 Don Mills Rd., North York ON M3B 2X7
416/445-6641; Fax: 416/442-2077; Toll Free: 1-800-268-7742; Email: irhind@southam.ca; URL: hhtp://www.southam.com
SAN: 115-5253

Southwest Québec Publishing (Dialogue)
27, rue Prince, PO Box 2004, Huntingdon PQ J0S 1H0
514/264-9149; Fax: 514/264-5387; Toll Free: 1-800-665-9841
ISBN: 1-895656

Spectrum Educational Supplies Ltd.
125 Mary St., Aurora ON L4G 1G3

905/841-0600; Fax: 905/727-6265; Toll Free: 1-800-668-0600
SAN: 116-0311

Spindrift Publishing
PO Box 50, Barrington NS B0W 1E0
902/637-2569
ISBN: 0-9691458

Springbank Publishing
5425 Elbow Dr. SW, Calgary AB T2V 1H7
403/640-9137; Fax: 403/640-9138
ISBN: 1-895653

Stanton & MacDougall see Kate Walker & Co. Ltd.

Statistics Canada
c/o Marketing Dept., 120 Parkdale Ave., Ottawa ON K1A 9Z9
613/951-7277; Fax: 613/951-1584; Toll Free: 1-800-267-6677; Email: order@statcan.ca
ISBN: 0-660, 0-662

Stewart House
c/o Canbook Distribution Services, 1220 Nicholson Rd., Newmarket ON L3Y 7B1
800/399-6858; Fax: 800/363-2665
ISBN: 1-895246; SAN: 115-4192

Stoddart Publishing Co. Limited
34 Lesmill Rd., Toronto ON M3B 2T6
416/445-3333; Fax: 416/445-5967; URL: http://www.genpub.com
ISBN: 0-7737; SAN: 115-0391

Storytrain
2255 Dunwin Dr., Mississauga ON L5L 1A3
905/607-2255; Fax: 905/607-7234
ISBN: 1-895617

Summerhill Books see Breakwater Books Ltd.

Summerthought Ltd.
PO Box 1420, Banff AB T0L 0C0
403/762-3919; Fax: 403/762-4126
ISBN: 0-919934; SAN: 115-2149

Summit Educational Services
PO Box 149, Richmond Hill ON L4C 4X9
905/883-9427; Fax: 905/770-8576; Toll Free: 1-800-741-5956
ISBN: 1-895187

Sun-Scape Enterprises Ltd.
PO Box 793, Stn F, Toronto ON M4Y 2N7
905/470-8634; Fax: 905/470-1632;
Email: 74601.2021@compuserve.com
ISBN: 0-919842

Synaxis Press
37323 Hawkins Rd., Dewdney BC V0M 1H0
604/826-9336; Fax: 604/820-9758
ISBN: 0-919672; SAN: 115-532

Talmage Book Centre
1260 Lakeshore Rd. East, Mississauga ON L5E 3B8
905/271-7173; Fax: 905/274-1843; Email: tbc@terraport.net; URL: http://www.terraport.net/tbc/tbc.htm
SAN: 118-1327

Talon Books Ltd.
#104, 3100 Production Way, Burnaby BC V5A 4R4
604/444-4889; Fax: 604/444-4119; Email: talon@pinc.com
ISBN: 0-88922; SAN: 115-5334; Telebook: S1150391

Tanager Press
145 Troy St., Mississauga ON L5G 1S8
905/891-2502; Fax: 905/891-6884
ISBN: 1-895410

Tantalas Books
PO Box 255, Gander NF A1V 1W6
709/651-3136; Fax: 709/651-3849
ISBN: 0-9695519

Temeron Books Inc.
#210, 1220 Kensington Rd. NW, Calgary AB T2N 3P5
403/283-0900; Fax: 403/283-6947
ISBN: 1-895510

Terrific Titles for Young Readers
PO Box 545, Stn P, Toronto ON M5S 2T1
416/921-9557; Fax: 416/921-0408

Theytus Books
PO Box 20040, Penticton BC V2A 6K3
250/493-7181; Fax: 250/493-5302
ISBN: 0-919441; SAN: 115-1517

Thistledown Press Ltd.
633 Main St., Saskatoon SK S7H 0J8
306/244-1722; Fax: 306/244-1762
ISBN: 0-920066, 0-920633, 1-895449; SAN: 115-1061

Thomas Allen & Son Ltd./Saunders of Toronto
390 Steelcase Rd. East, Markham ON L3R 1G2
905/475-9126; Fax: 905/475-6747
ISBN: 0-919028; SAN: 115-1762

Thompson Educational Publishing, Inc.
#105, 14 Ripley Ave., Toronto ON M6S 3N9
416/766-2763; Fax: 416/766-0398;
Email: thompson@canadabooks.ingenia.com
ISBN: 1-55077, 1-921332

Tikka Books
PO Box 242, Chambly PQ J3L 4B3
514/658-6205; Fax: 514/658-3514
ISBN: 1-896106

Times Mirror Professional Publishing
130 Flaska Dr., Markham ON L6G 1B8
905/470-6739; Fax: 905/470-6780; Toll Free: 1-800-268-4178
ISBN: 0-8016; SAN: 115-4389

Tralco Educational Services Inc.
297 Brucedale Ave. East, Hamilton ON L9A 1R2
905/575-5717; Fax: 905/575-1783; Email: tralco@binatech.on.ca
ISBN: 0-921376

Trans-Canada Press see Who's Who Publications

Tree Frog Press Ltd.
10144 - 89 St., Edmonton AB T5H 1P7
403/429-1947; Fax: 403/425-8760
ISBN: 0-88967; SAN: 115-1053

Tree House Press Inc.
85 Lansing Dr., Unit O, Hamilton ON L8W 2Z9
905/574-3399; Fax: 905/574-0228; Toll Free: 1-800-776-8733
ISBN 1-895165

Tri-Fold Books (Distributor)
55 Wyndham St. North, PO Box 29078, Guelph ON N1H 8J4
519/821-9901; Fax: 519/821-5333
SAN: 106-4320

Trifolium Books Inc.
#28, 238 Davenport Rd., Toronto ON M5R 1J6
416/925-0765; Fax: 416/485-5563; Email: trising@io.org
ISBN: 1-895579

Trilobyte Press
1486 Willowdown Rd., Oakville ON L6L 1X3
905/847-7366; Fax: 905/847-3258
ISBN: 1-895482

True Remainders Ltd.
PO Box 500, Jordan Station ON L0R 1S0
905/562-5719; Fax: 905/562-7828
ISBN: 0-88815

TSAR Publications
PO Box 6996, Stn A, Toronto ON M5W 1X7
416/483-7191; Fax: 416/486-0706
ISBN: 0-929661

Tundra Books Inc. see McClelland & Stewart Inc.

TUNS Press
Faculty of Architecture, Technical University of NS, PO Box 1000, Halifax NS B3J 2X4
902/420-7641; Fax: 902/423-6672; Email: press@tuns.ca; URL: http://tuns.ca/architecture/press/html
ISBN: 0-929112

Turner-Warwick Publications Inc.
PO Box 1029, North Battleford SK S9A 3E6
306/445-7261; Fax: 306/445-3223
ISBN: 0-919899

Turnstone Press
#607, 100 Arthur St., Winnipeg MB R3B 1H3
204/947-1555, 1556; Fax: 204/942-1555

ISBN: 0-88801; SAN: 115-1096

Two Views Press Inc.
89 Northview, Montréal PQ H4X 1C9
514/489-3071; Fax: 514/489-3495
ISBN: 0-9699069

Ulverscroft Large Print (Canada) Ltd.
PO Box 80038, Burlington ON L7L 6B1
905/637-8734; Fax: 905/333-6788; Email: ulpbcan@worldchat.com; URL: http://dspace.dial.pipex.com/town/plaza/hfss/
ISBN: 0-7089

Ulysses Books & Maps Distribution/Éditions Ulysse
4176, rue Saint-Denis, Montréal PQ H2W 2M5
514/843-9882; Fax: 514/843-9448
ISBN: 2-921444; SAN: 115-7167

Umbrella Press
56 Rivercourt Blvd., Toronto ON M4J 3A4
416/696-6665; Fax: 416/696-9189
ISBN: 1-895642

United Church Publishing House
3250 Bloor St. West, 4th Fl., Etobicoke ON M8X 2Y4
416/231-7680, ext.4113; Fax: 416/232-6004
ISBN: 0-919000, 1-55134; SAN: 115-3013

United Library Services
7140 Fairmount Dr. SE, Calgary AB T2H 0X4
403/252-4426; Fax: 403/258-3426
SAN: 169-9342

United News (Wholesalers) Ltd.
5716 Burbank Rd. SE, Calgary AB T2H 1Z4
403/253-8856; Fax: 403/252-8360

The Unitrade Press
(Unitrade Associates)
95 Floral Pkwy., Toronto ON M6L 2C4
416/242-5900; Fax: 416/242-6115
ISBN: 0-919801, 0-895909; SAN: 115-544X

University of Alberta Press
141 Athabasca Hall, University of Alberta, 26 University Campus NW, Edmonton AB T6G 2E8
403/492-3662; Fax: 403/492-0719; Email: uap@gpu.srv.ualberta.ca
ISBN: 0-88864; SAN: 115-110X

University of British Columbia Press
UBC, 6344 Memorial Rd., Vancouver BC V6T 1Z2
604/822-3259; Fax: 604/822-6083; Toll Free: 1-800-668-0821; Email: orders@ubcpress.ubc.ca; URL: gopher://gopher.ubc.ca:70/11/libraries/ubc-press
ISBN: 0-7748; SAN: 115-1118

University of Calgary Press
2500 University Dr. NW, Calgary AB T2N 1N4
403/220-7578; Fax: 403/282-0085; Toll Free: 1-800-668-0821; Email: 75001@ucdasvml.admin.ucalgary.ca
ISBN: 0-919813, 1-895176; Telebook: S115-1118

University College of Cape Breton Press
PO Box 5300, Stn A, Sydney NS B1P 6L2
902/539-5300; Fax: 902/562-0119;
Email: pmarshall@caper2.uccb.ns.ca
ISBN 0-920336; SAN: 115-5458

University Extension Press
Rm. 118, Kirk Hall, University of Saskatchewan, 117 Science Pl., Saskatoon SK S7N 5C8
306/966-5558; Fax: 306/966-5567

University of Guelph Publications
The Library, Guelph University, #158, 50 Stone Rd. East, Guelph ON N1G 2W1
519/824-4120, ext.2079; Fax: 519/824-6931
ISBN: 0-88955; SAN: 115-7345

University of Manitoba Press
#244, 15 Gilson St., Winnipeg MB R3T 5V6
204/474-9495; Fax: 204/275-2270
ISBN: 0-88755; SAN: 115-5474

University of Ottawa Press/Presses de l'Université d'Ottawa
542 King Edward St., Ottawa ON K1N 6N5
613/562-5246; Fax: 613/562-5247
ISBN: 0-7766, 2-7603; SAN: 115-5482

University of Saskatchewan
   Office of Public Relations, Administration Bldg., E280, Saskatoon SK S7N 0W0
   306/966-6607; Fax: 306/966-6815
   ISBN 0-88880
University of Toronto Press
   #700, 10 St. Mary St., Toronto ON M4Y 2W8
   416/978-2239; Fax: 416/978-4738; Email: utpbooks@gpu.utcc.utoronto.ca
   Order Department & Distribution: 5201 Dufferin St., North York ON M3H 5T8
   416/667-7791; Fax: 416/667-7832; Toll Free: 1-800-565-9523
   ISBN: 0-8020; SAN: 115-1134
Upney Editions
   19 Appalachian Cres., Kitchener ON N2E 1A3
Vanwell Publishing Limited
   1 Northrup Cres., PO Box 2131, St. Catharines ON L2M 6P5
   905/937-3100; Fax: 905/937-1760; Toll Free: 1-800-661-6136
   ISBN: 0-92027, 1-55068
Véhicule Press
   PO Box 125, Stn Place du Parc, Montréal PQ H2W 2M9
   514/844-6073; Fax: 514/844-7543; Email: vpress@cam.org
   ISBN: 0-919890, 1-55065; SAN: 115-1150
Vesta Publications Ltd.
   PO Box 1641, Cornwall ON K6H 5V6
   613/932-2135; Fax: 613/932-7735
   ISBN: 0-919806, 1-55065; SAN: 115-5520
VLB Éditeur
   1010, rue de la Gauchetière est, Montréal PQ H2L 2N5
   514/523-1182; Fax: 514/282-7530
   ISBN: 2-89295
Voyageur Publishing
   Maple Pond, Maple Ave., RR#2, Prescott ON K0E 1T0
   613/925-2111; Fax: 613/925-0029
   ISBN: 0-921842
Wall & Emerson, Inc.
   (Wall & Thompson)
   6 O'Connor Dr., Toronto ON M4K 2K1
   416/467-8685; Fax: 416/696-2460; Email: wall@maple.net
   ISBN: 1-895131, 0-921332; SAN: 116-0486
Warwick Publishing
   #200, 24 Mercer St., Toronto ON M5V 1H3
   416/596-1555; Fax: 416/596-1520
   ISBN: 1-895629
Waterloo Music Co. Ltd.
   3 Regina St. North, Waterloo ON N2J 4A5
   519/886-4990; Fax: 519/886-4999
   ISBN: 0-88909; SAN: 157-9363
Watson & Dwyer Publishing Ltd.
   905 Corydon Ave., PO Box 86, Winnipeg MB R3M 3S3
   204/284-0985; Fax: 204/453-8320
   ISBN: 0-920480; SAN: 115-7175
Weigl Educational Publishers
   1900 - 11th St. SE, Calgary AB T2G 3G2
   403/233-7747; Fax: 403/233-7769; Toll Free: 1-800-668-0766
   ISBN: 0-9690637, 0-919879; SAN: 115-1312, 115-5536
West Coast Paradise Publishing
   #5, 9060 Tronson Rd., Vernon BC V1T 6L7
   250/545-4186; Fax: 250/545-4194
   ISBN: 0-9697494, 1-896779
Western Extension College Publishers
   PO Box 110, Saskatoon SK S7K 3K1
   306/373-6399; Fax: 306/892-2046
Western Publishing (Canada) Inc. *see* Golden Books Publishing
Whitecap Books Ltd.
   351 Lynn Ave., North Vancouver BC V7J 2C4

604/980-9852; Fax: 604/980-8197
   Toronto Office: 602 Richmond St. West, Toronto ON M5Y 1Y9
   416/777-0929
   ISBN: 1-895099; SAN: 115-1290
Whitehots Inc.
   #2, 2 Vata Ct., Aurora ON L4G 4B6
   905/727-9188; Fax: 905/727-8756; Toll Free: 1-800-567-9188; Email: whitehot@idirect.com
Who's Who Publications
   777 Bay St., 5th Fl., Toronto ON M5W 1A7
   416/595-5100; Fax: 416/596-5155
   ISBN: 0-920966; SAN: 115-1045
Wilfrid Laurier University Press
   75 University Ave. West, Waterloo ON N2L 3C5
   519/884-0710, ext.6124; Fax: 519/725-1399; Email: press@machi.wlu.ca
   ISBN: 0-88920; SAN: 115-1525
William Street Press
   PO Box 21114, Stratford ON N5A 7X4
   519/263-5973; Fax: 519/263-5973
   ISBN: 0-9691075, 0-9695097
Williams Books
   3007 Granville St., Vancouver BC V6H 3J9
   604/733-1326; Fax: 604/733-1326
Wilson et Lafleur
   40, rue Notre-Dame, Montréal PQ H2Y 1B9
   514/875-6326; Fax: 514/875-8356
   ISBN: 2-89127
Windflower Communications
   844K McLeod Ave., Winnipeg MB R2G 2T7
   204/668-7475; Fax: 204/661-8530; Toll Free: 1-800-465-6564; Email: 74114.470@compuserve.com
   ISBN: 1-895308
Windsor News Educational Division
   3350 North Talbot Rd., Oldcastle ON N0R 1L0
   519/737-6923; Fax: 519/737-1612; Toll Free: 1-800-265-2892
Wolsak & Wynn Publishers Ltd.
   PO Box 316, Stn Don Mills, Don Mills ON M3C 2S7
   416/445-7498; Fax: 416/445-1816
   ISBN: 0-919897; SAN: 115-749
Women's Press
   #233, 517 College St., Toronto ON M6G 4A2
   416/921-2425; Fax: 416/921-4428; Email: wompress@web.apc.org
   ISBN: 0-88961; SAN: 115-5628
Wood Lake Books, Inc.
   10162 Newene Rd., Winfield BC V4V 1R2
   250/766-2778; Fax: 250/766-2736; Toll Free: 1-800-663-2775; Email: woodlake@awinc.com
   ISBN: 0-919599, 0-929032; SAN: 115-5636
Word Alive
   60 Cedar St., Niverville MB R0A 1E0
   Fax: 204/388-9999; Toll Free: 1-800-665-1468
Word Communications Ltd. *see* Nelson/Word Communications Ltd.
World Book Childcraft of Canada Ltd.
   #240, 4411 East Hastings St., Burnaby BC V5C 2K1
   604/298-3915; Fax: 604/298-8273
   ISBN: 0-7166; SAN: 115-5644, 115-5662
Wuerz Publishing Ltd.
   895 McMillan Ave., Winnipeg MB R3M 0T2
   204/453-7429; Fax: 204/453-6598
   ISBN: 0-929963
Wyman & Son Publishers
   866 Campbell Ave., Ottawa ON K2A 2C5
   613/729-8495; Fax: 613/729-9230; Toll Free: 1-800-668-3283
XYZ Éditeur
   1781, rue Saint-Hubert, Montréal PQ H2L 3Z1
   514/525-2170; Fax: 514/525-7537
   ISBN: 2-89261
York Press Ltd.
   PO Box 1172, Fredericton NB E3B 5C8
   506/458-8748; Fax: 506/458-8748
   ISBN: 0-919966; SAN: 115-5687

Young Alberta Book Society
   Percy Page Ctr., 2nd Fl., 11759 Groat Rd., Edmonton AB T5M 3K8
   403/422-8232; Fax: 403/422-2663
   ISBN: 0-9693147
Young Readers Ltd.
   11 Banington Cres., Brampton ON L7A 1G4
   905/840-1765; Fax: 905/840-0463

NEWSPAPERS

Alberta Daily Newspapers

CALGARY:

Calgary Herald, Southam Inc., 215 - 16 St. SE, PO Box 2400, Stn M, Calgary AB T2P 0W8 – 403/235-7100; Fax: 403/235-7113; Telex: 038-22793 – Circ.: 140,000; Morning – Publisher, Ken King; Editor, Crosbie Cotton

The Calgary Sun, 2615 - 12 St. NE, Calgary AB T2E 7W9 – 403/250-4200; Fax: 403/491-4116; URL: http://www.canoe.ca/CalgarySun/home.html – Circ.: 67,526, Mon.-Sat.; 98,480, Sun.; Morning – Editor-in-Chief, Chris Nelson

EDMONTON:

The Edmonton Journal, Southam Inc., 10006 - 101 St., PO Box 2421, Edmonton AB T5J 2S6 – 403/429-5100; Fax: 403/498-5677; URL: http://www.southam.com/edmontonjournal/ – Circ.: 150,500; Morning – Publisher, Linda Hughes; Editor, Murdoch Davis; Reader Sales & Service, Dave Reidie

The Edmonton Sun, #250, 4990 - 92 Ave., Edmonton AB T6B 3A1 – 403/468-0100; Fax: 403/468-0139; Email: sun.letters@ccinet.ab.ca – Circ.: 73,036, Mon.-Sat.; 113,297, Sun.; Morning – Publisher, Craig Martin; Editor, Paul Stanway

FORT MCMURRAY:

Fort McMurray Today, Bowes Publishers Ltd., 8550 Franklin Ave., Fort McMurray AB T9H 3G1 – 403/743-8186; Fax: 403/790-1006; Email: today@ccinet.ab.ca – Circ.: 4,909, Mon.-Thur.; 7,248, Fri.; Afternoon/evening, Mon.-Fri. – Publisher, Tim O'Rouke; Managing Editor, Darrell Skidnuk; Circulation Manager, Juliet Normand

GRANDE PRAIRIE:

Daily Herald-Tribune, Bowes Publishers Ltd., 10604 - 100 St., PO Box 3000, Grande Prairie AB T8V 6V4 – 403/532-1110; Fax: 403/532-2120 – Circ.: 8,500, Mon.-Thur.; 12,130 Fri.; Afternoon – Publisher, Peter J. Woolsey; Managing Editor, David Lassner

LETHBRIDGE:

The Lethbridge Herald, Thomson Newspapers Co. Ltd., 504 - 7th St. South, Lethbridge AB T1J 3Z7 – 403/328-4411; Fax: 403/328-4536; URL: http://www.lis.ab.ca/lhearld/ – Circ.: 22,370, Mon.-Sat.; 20,416, Sun.; Evening – Publisher, Don Doram; Managing Editor, Bill Whitelaw; Circulation Manager, Shannon Simpson

MEDICINE HAT:

Medicine Hat News, Southam Inc., 3257 Dunmore Rd. SE, PO Box 10, Medicine Hat AB T1A 7E6 – 403/527-1101; Fax: 403/527-6029 – Circ.: 14,500; Evening – Acting Publisher, Jim Struthers; Managing Editor, Gordon Wright

Other Newspapers in Alberta

Airdrie & District Echo, PO Box 3820, Airdrie AB T4B 2B9 – 403/948-7280 – Wed.

NEWSPAPERS 5-131

Athabasca: The Advocate, 4917B - 49 St., Athabasca AB T9S 1C5 – 403/675-9222; Fax: 403/675-3143 – Circ.: 5,000; Tue. – Publisher & Editor, Donny Rajoo

Banff Crag & Canyon, 201 Bear St., 2nd Fl., PO Box 129, Banff AB T0L 0C0 – 403/762-2453; Fax: 403/762-5274 – Circ.: 3,993; Wed. – Publisher, Sandra Santa Lucia; Editor, David Rodney; Circulation Manager, Anne Bosma

Barrhead Leader, PO Box 4520, Barrhead AB T7N 1A4 – 403/674-3823; Fax: 403/674-6337; Email: leader@west-teq.net – Circ.: 3,959; Tue. – Publisher, Carol Farnalls; Editor, John Ollerenshaw

Bashaw Star, PO Box 188, Bashaw AB T0B 0H0 – 403/372-3608; Fax: 403/372-4445 – Tue.

Bassano Times, PO Box 780, Bassano AB T0J 0B0 – 403/641-3636; Fax: 403/641-3952 – Circ.: 749; Mon. – Publisher & Editor-in-Chief, Mary Lou Brooks

Beaumont La Nouvelle, 5021B - 52nd Ave., Beaumont AB T4X 1E5 – 403/929-5552; Fax: 403/929-5553 – Circ.: 1,800; Mon.; English & French – Publisher, Hugh Johnston; Editor, Kimberly Carr

Beaverlodge & District Advertiser, PO Box 300, Beaverlodge AB T0H 0C0 – 403/354-2460 – Wed.

Bentley Bugle, PO Box 380, Rimbey AB T0C 2J0 – 403/843-2231; Fax: 403/843-2990 – Circ.: 1,850; Monthly – Publisher, Ed Moller; Editor, John Roberts; Circulation Manager, E. Archer

Blairmore: The Crowsnest Pass Promoter, PO Box 1019, Blairmore AB T0K 0E0 – 403/562-8884; Fax: 403/562-2242 – Circ.: 2,500; Tue. – Publisher, Jim Prentice; Editor, Ross Purnell

Blairmore: The Pass Herald, PO Box 960, Blairmore AB T0K 0E0 – 403/562-2248; Fax: 403/562-2242 – Tue.

Bonnyville Nouvelle, PO Box 8174, Bonnyville AB T9N 2J5 – 403/826-3876 – Tue.; English & French

Bow Island: The 40-Mile County Commentator, PO Box 580, Bow Island AB T0K 0G0 – 403/545-2258; Fax: 403/545-6886 – Tue.

Bowden: The Voice of Bowden, PO Box 209, Bowden AB T0M 0K0 – 403/224-2288; Fax: 403/224-3010 – Circ.: 1,000; Tues. – Publisher & Editor, Wray Hutchinson

Brooks Bulletin, 124 - 3rd St. West, PO Box 1450, Brooks AB T1R 1C3 – 403/362-5571; Fax: 403/362-5080 – Wed.

Calgary Community Digest, #453, 3545 - 32nd Ave. NE, Calgary AB T1Y 6M6 – 403/275-8275 – Circ.: 25,000; Fri.

Calgary Herald Neighbors, PO Box 2400, Stn M, Calgary AB T2P 0W8 – 403/235-8680; Fax: 403/235-7379 – Thur.; 6 city area editions

Calgary Mirror, 2080 - 39 Ave. NE, Calgary AB T2E 6P7 – 403/250-1042; Fax: 403/291-3028 – Sun.; 4 city area editions

Calgary Rural Times, 315 First St. East, Cochrane AB T0L 0W1 – 403/932-3000; Fax: 403/932-3935 – Circ.: 12,063; Tue. – Publisher, Linda Ryan; Editor, Ardith Finnegan

Calgary: Le Chinook, 4 Hunterhorn Rd. NE, Calgary AB T2K 6E8 – 403/274-7320 – Tirage: 9,000; Mensuel; français – Rédacteur, Richard Belanger

Camrose Booster, 4925 - 48 St., Camrose AB T4V 1L7 – 403/672-3142; Fax: 403/672-2518 – Circ.: 12,357; Tue. – Publisher, Blain Fowler; Editor, Berdie Fowler; Circulation Manager, Doug Schwartz

Camrose Canadian, 4903 - 49 Ave., Camrose AB T4V 0M9 – 403/672-4421; Fax: 403/672-5323 – Circ.: 3,875; Wed.; also Camrose Canadian Extra (Mon.) – Publisher, Lynne Cherntn; Editor, Douglas Stinson; Circulation Manager, Karen Olsen

Canmore: The Canmore Leader, PO Box 1320, Canmore AB T0L 0M0 – 403/678-2365; Fax: 403/678-2996 – Tue.

Cardston Chronicle, PO Box 1800, Cardston AB T0K 0K0 – 403/653-2222; Fax: 403/653-1935 – Tue.

Carstairs Courier, PO Box 40, Irricana AB T0M 1B0 – 403/935-4688 – Circ.: 3,100; Tue. – Publisher, Fred Denishuk; Editor, Leanne Rekiel

Castor Advance, PO Box 120, Castor AB T0C 0X0 – 403/882-4044; Fax: 403/882-2010 – Thur.

Claresholm Local Press, PO Box 520, Claresholm AB T0L 0T0 – 403/4474; Fax: 403/625-2828 – Wed.

Coaldale: Sunny South News, PO Box 30, Coaldale AB T1M 1M2 – 403/345-3081; Fax: 403/345-5408 – Circ.: 4,025; Tue. – Publisher, Coleen Campbell, 403/223-9659; Editor, Harley Richards; Circulation Manager, Valerie Wiebe

Cochrane This Week, 315 First St. East, Cochrane AB T0L 0W1 – 403/932-3000; Fax: 403/932-3935 – Circ.: 2,284; Tue. – Publisher, Linda Ryan; Editor, Ardith Finnegan

Consort Enterprise, PO Box 129, Consort AB T0C 1B0 – 403/577-3611; Fax: 403/577-3611; Email: consort_entrprise@awnet.net – Circ.: 1,201; Tue. – Publisher, Wm. J. Readman; Editor, Mary K. Readman; Circulation Manager, Carol Readman

Coronation Review, PO Box 70, Coronation AB T0C 1C0 – 403/578-4111; Fax: 403/578-2088 – Tue.

Devon Dispatch, PO Box 479, Devon AB T0C 1E0 – 403/987-2522 – Tue.

Didsbury Review, PO Box 760, Didsbury AB T0M 0W0 – 403/335-3301; Fax: 403/335-8143 – Circ.: 1,782; Tue. – Publisher, Gene Hartmann; Editor-in-Chief, Janice Harrington

Drayton Valley Western Review, PO Box 6960, Drayton Valley AB T7A 1SE – 403/542-5380; Fax: 403/542-9200 – Tue. – Editor, Mark Mellott

Drumheller Mail, PO Box 1629, Drumheller AB T0J 0Y0 – 403/823-2580 – Wed.

Eckville Examiner, PO Box 380, Rimbey AB T0C 2J0 – 403/843-2231; Fax: 403/843-2990; Email: eckville_examiner@awnet.net – Circ.: 1,000; Tue. – Publisher, Ed Moller; Editor, John Roberts; Circulation Manager, E. Archer

Edmonton City News, Alberta Business Research Ltd., #800, 10179 - 105 St., Edmonton AB T5J 3N1 – 403/424-0190; Fax: 403/421-7677 – Circ.: 40,000; Monthly – Publisher, Lorne Silverstein; Editor, Colin Smith

Edmonton Examiner, 17533 - 106 Ave., Edmonton AB T5S 1E7 – 403/483-6000, 487-9691 (editorial); Fax: 403/483-2000 – Circ.: 153,000; 7 city area editions – Publisher, Bob Pearce; Editor-in-Chief, Maurice Tougas; Circulation Manager, Kent Verlick

Edmonton Jewish Life, #107, 10342 0 107 St., Edmonton AB T5J 1K2 – 403/488-7276 – Monthly

Edmonton: Le Franco Albertain, ACFA, 8923 - 82 Ave., Edmonton AB T6C 0Z2 – 403/465-6581; Fax: 403/465-3647; Email: lefranco@compusmart.ab.ca – Circ.: 3,000; Vendredi; français – Rédacteur, François V. Pageau

Edmonton: SeaLandAir, CFB Edmonton, PO Box 10500, Edmonton AB T5J 4J5 – 403/473-7764; Fax: 403/457-8481 – Every other Thur.

Edmonton: Windspeaker, 15001 - 112 Ave., Edmonton AB T5M 2V6 – 403/455-2700; Fax: 403/455-7639 – Circ.: 15,000; Monthly – Publisher, Bert Crowfoot; Managing Editor, Linda Caldwell

Edson: The Anchor, PO Box 6870, Edson AB T7E 1V2 – 403/723-5787; Fax: 403/723-5725 – Circ.: 5,500; Every other Mon. – Publisher, Craig McArthur

Edson Leader, PO Box 6330, Edson AB T7E 1T8 – 403/723-3301 – Tue.

Elk Point Review, PO Box 309, Elk Point AB T0A 1A0 – 403/724-4087; Fax: 403/724-4211 – Tue.

Fairview Post, PO Box 1900, Fairview AB T0H 1L0 – 403/835-4925; Fax: 403/835-4227; Email: Fairview_Post@awnet.net – Circ.: 3,800; Tue. – Publisher, Bob Doornenbal; Editor-in-Chief, Erikki Pohjolainen

Falher: Smoky River Express, PO Box 644, Falher AB T0H 1M0 – 403/837-2585; Fax: 403/837-2102 – Circ.: 2,500; Wed., English with some French – Publisher, Jeff Burgar; Editor, Shari Maertens-Poole

Fort Macleod: Macleod Gazette, PO Box 720, Fort Macleod AB T0L 0Z0 – 403/553-3391; Fax: 403/553-2961 – Circ.: 1,591; Wed. – Publisher & Editor, Jack Murphy

Fort Saskatchewan Record, 9804B - 104 St., Fort Saskatchewan AB T8L 2E6 – 403/998-7070; Fax: 403/998-5515 – Tue.

Fort Saskatchewan This Week, 10109 - 99 Ave., Fort Saskatchewan AB T8L 1X7 – 403/998-1638; Fax: 403/998-3258 – Fri.

Gibbons: The Free Press, PO Box 330, Gibbons AB T0A 1N0 – Circ.: 4,648; Mon.

Grande Cache Mountaineer, PO Box 660, Grande Cache AB T0E 0Y0 – 403/827-3539; Fax: 403/827-3530; Email: grande.cache.mountaineer@awnet.net – Circ.: 1,462; Tue. – Publisher, Noel Edey; Editor, Arthur Veitch

Grande Centre: Cold Lake Sun, PO Box 268, Grande Centre AB T0A 1T0 – 403/594-5881; Fax: 403/594-2120 – Tue.

Grande Prairie: Peace Country Extra, 10604 - 100 St., PO Box 3000, Grande Prairie AB T8V 2M5 – 403/532-1110 – Circ.: 12,123; bi-weekly; also Peace Country Farmer (circ. 29,190)

Grimshaw: The Mile Zero News, PO Box 1010, Grimshaw AB T0H 1W0 – 403/332-2215; Fax: 403/332-4380 – Wed.

Hanna Herald, PO Box 790, Hanna AB T0J 1P0 – 403/854-3366; Fax: 403/854-3256 – Wed.

High Level Echo, PO Box 240, High Level AB T0H 1Z0 – 403/926-2000; Fax: 403/926-2001 – Wed.

High Prairie: The Mirror, 4732 - 53 Ave., PO Box 269, High Prairie AB T0G 1E0 – 403/523-3706 – Circ.: 2,061; Monthly

High Prairie: South Peace News, PO Box 1000, High Prairie AB T0G 1E0 – 403/523-4484 – Wed.

High River Times, 618 Centre St. South, High River AB T1V 1E9 – 403/652-2034; Fax: 403/652-3962 – Tue.

Hinton Parklander, 104 McLeod Ave., Hinton AB T7V 2A9 – 403/865-3115; Fax: 403/865-1252 – Circ.: 3,061; Mon. – Publisher, Neil Sutcliffe; Editor, Rod Kelley; Circulation Manager, Merna Strawson

Hythe Headliner, Hythe Family & Community Support Services, 10011A - 100 St., PO Box 622, Hythe AB T0H 2C0 – 403/356-2000; Fax: 403/356-2009 – Circ.: 1,000; Bi-weekly – Editor, Bonnie Joyes

Innisfail Booster, 4932 - 49th St., Innisfail AB T4G 1N2 – 403/227-3477; Fax: 403/227-3330 – Circ.: 7,500; Tue. – Publisher & Editor, Ray Brinson

Innisfail Province, PO Box 9, Innisfail AB T0M 1A0 – 403/227-3612; Fax: 403/222-1570 – Mon.

Irricana/Rocky View/Five Village Weekly, PO Box 40, Irricana AB T0M 1B0 – 403/935-4688 – Circ.: 9,992; Mon.

Jasper Booster, PO Box 940, Jasper AB T0E 1E0 – 403/852-3620; Fax: 403/852-3384 – Circ.: 1,980; Wed. – Publisher, Don Traplin; Editor, David Berezowski; Circulation Manager, Karen Young

La Crete: The Northern Pioneer, PO Box 571, La Crete AB T0H 2H0 – 403/928-3800 – Wed.

Lac La Biche Post, PO Box 508, Lac La Biche AB T0A 2C0 – 403/623-4221 – Tue.

Lacombe Globe, PO Box 519, Lacome AB T0C 1S0 – 403/782-3498 – Tue.

Lamont: Lifestyle Regional News, 5028 - 50 Ave., PO Box 182, Lamont AB T0B 2R0 – 403/895-2063; Fax: 403/895-2063 – Circ.: 4,000; Thur.

Leduc & County This Week, 4712 - 50 Ave., Leduc AB T9E 6Y6 – 403/986-0860; Fax: 403/986-8870; Email: thisweek@compusmart.ab.ca/thisweek; URL: http://www.compusmart.ab.ca/thisweek – Circ.: 15,336; Fri. – Publisher, Maureen Klatt; Editor, Kimberly Carr

Leduc Representative, 4504 - 61 Ave., Leduc AB T9E 3Z1 – 403/986-2271; Fax: 403/986-6397 – Circ.: 2,808,

Canadian Almanac & Directory 1997

Wed.; 10,717, Sun.; Sun. – Publisher, Brent Spilak; Managing Editor, Susan Blackman

Leslieville: The Western Star, PO Box 100, Leslieville AB T0M 1H0 – 403/729-3000 – Wed.

Lethbridge Shopper, 234 - 12B St. North, Lethbridge AB T1H 2K7 – 403/329-8225; Fax: 403/329-8211 – Circ.: 32,500; Sat., supplement to West Lethbridge Sun – Publisher & Editor, Ted Ominski; Circulation Manager, John Sheer

Manning Banner Post, PO Box 686, Manning AB T0H 2M0 – 403/836-3588 – Wed.

Mayerthorpe: The Freelancer, PO Box 599, Mayerthorpe AB T0E 1N0 – 403/786-2602; Fax: 403/786-2663 – Circ.: 1,738; Wed. – Publisher, Jim Gray; Editor, Kevin Laliberte

Medicine Hat Shopper, 922 Allowance Ave. SE, Medicine Hat AB T1A 3G7 – 403/527-5777; Fax: 403/526-7352 – Circ.: 23,500; Sat. – Publisher, Ted Ominski

Medley: Cold Lake Courier, CFB Cold Lake, PO Box 3190, Medley AB T0A 2M0 – 403/594-5206; Fax: 403/594-2139 – Wed.

Morinville Gazette, PO Box 263, St. Albert AB T8N 1N3 – 403/459-2240; Fax: 403/460-8220 – Tue.; supplement, Homestyle

Morinville Mirror, 10205 - 100 Ave., Morinville AB T8R 1P9 – 403/939-2133; Fax: 403/939-2425 – Circ.: 5,355; Tue.

Nanton News, PO Box 429, Nanton AB T0L 1R0 – 403/646-2023; Fax: 403/646-2848 – Wed.

Okotoks: The Western Wheel, PO Bag 9, Okotoks AB T0L 1T0 – 403/938-6397 – Wed.

Olds: Mountain View County News, PO Box 3870, Olds AB T4H 1P6 – 403/556-3351; Fax: 403/556-3464 – Every other Fri. – Editor, M.J. Harper

Olds: The Olds Albertan, 5018 - 57th Ave., Olds AB T4H 1J1 – 403/556-7510 – Circ.: 8,200; Wed.

Olds Gazette, PO Box 3870, Olds AB T4H 1P6 – 403/556-3351; Fax: 403/556-3464 – Wed. – Editor, M.J. Harper

Onoway Community Voice, A.F. Keller & Associates Ltd., PO Box 6000, Spruce Grove AB T7X 2Z5 – 403/962-9228; Fax: 403/962-1021 – Circ.: 4,600; Every other Tue. – Editor, Al Keller

Oyen Echo, PO Box 420, Oyen AB T0J 2J0 – 403/664-3622; Fax: 403/664-3622; Email: oyenecho@agt.net; URL: http://www.inter.ab.ca/oyen – Circ.: 1,411; Wed. – Publisher, Ronald Holmes; Editor, Diana Walker; Co-Editor, H.E. Ball

Peace River Record-Gazette, PO Box 6870, Peace River AB T8S 1S6 – 403/624-2591; Fax: 403/624-8600; Email: rgazette@agt.net – Circ.: 4,097; Wed. – Publisher, Shaun Jessome; Editor, Irene Chomokovski; Circulation Manager, Penny Ashdown

Pincher Creek Echo, PO Box 1000, Pincher Creek AB T0K 1W0 – 403/627-3252; Fax: 403/627-3949 – Tue.

Ponoka Herald, PO Box 4308, Ponoka AB T0C 2H0 – 403/783-3074; Fax: 403/783-5350; Email: ponoka_herald@awnet.net – Circ.: 6,300; Mon. – Publisher, Ed Moller; Editor, Tara Ennis-Reddick; Circulation Manager, Sandra Klinger

Ponoka News & Advertiser, PO Box 4217, Ponoka AB T0C 2H0 – 403/783-3311; Fax: 403/783-3311 – Mon.

Provost News, PO Box 180, Provost AB T0B 3S0 – 403/753-2564; Fax: 403/753-6117 – Wed.

Raymond: The County Review, PO Box 315, Raymond AB T0K 2S0 – 403/752-3635 – Tue.

Red Deer Express, PO Bag 5012, Red Deer AB T4N 6R4 – 403/346-3356; Fax: 403/347-6620; Email: RDPUB@cnnet.com – Circ.: 24,277; Wed. – Publisher, Cal Dallas; Editor, Glen Werkman; Circulation Manager, Murray Wieting

Redwater Tribune, PO Box 1180, Redwater AB T0A 2W0 – 403/942-4535; Fax: 403/939-2425 – Tue.

Redwater: The Review, PO Box 850, Redwater AB R0A 2W0 – 403/942-2023 – Mon.

Rimbey Record, PO Box 380, Rimbey AB T0C 2J0 – 403/843-2231; Fax: 403/843-2990;

Email: rimbey_record@awnet.net – Circ.: 2,060; Tue. – Publisher, Ed Moller; Editor, John Roberts; Circulation Manager, E. Archer

Rocky Mountain House: The Mountaineer, 4814 - 49 St., Rocky Mountain House AB T0M 1T1 – 403/845-3334; Fax: 403/845-5570 – Wed.

Rycroft: The Central Peace Signal, PO Box 250, Rycroft AB T0H 3A0 – 403/765-3604; Fax: 403/765-2188 – Tue.

St. Albert Gazette, PO Box 263, St. Albert AB T8N 1N3 – 403/459-2240; Fax: 403/460-8220 – Wed. & Sat.; supplement Homestyle (Wed.)

St. Albert This Week, #150, 44 Riel Dr., St. Albert AB T8N 5C4 – 403/459-5446; Fax: 403/460-2437 – Circ.: 17,620; Fri.; also Edmonton Suburban This Week (Fri., circ. 75,000)

St. Michael: Elk Island Triangle, PO Box 170, St. Michael AB T0B 4B0 – 403/896-2223; Fax: 403/896-2281 – Circ.: 1,600; Every other week – Publisher, Joanne Paltzat

St. Paul Journal, PO Box 159, St. Paul AB T0A 3A0 – 403/645-3342; Fax: 403/645-2346 – Tue.

Sedgewick: The Community Press, PO Box 99, Sedgewick AB T0B 4C0 – 403/384-3641; Fax: 403/384-2244 – Tue.

Sherwood Park: The News, 168 Kaska Rd., Sherwood Park AB T8A 4G7 – 403/464-0033; Fax: 403/464-2117 – Circ.: 18,648; Wed.

Sherwood Park This Week, #112A, 101 Granada Blvd., Sherwood Park AB T8A 4W2 – 403/464-5176; Fax: 403/467-4125; Email: thisweek@compusmart.ab.ca; URL: http://www.compusmart.ab.ca/thisweek – Circ.: 20,600; Fri. – Publisher, John Putters; Editor, Jackie Bibby; Circulation Manager, Paul Percival

Slave Lake: Lakeside Leader, PO Box 849, Slave Lake AB T0G 2A0 – 403/849-4380; Fax: 403/849-3903 – Wed.

Slave Lake Scope, PO Box 1130, Slave Lake AB T0G 2A0 – 403/849-4350; Fax: 403/849-2433 – Circ.: 2,000; Wed. – Bruce D. Thomas

Smoky Lake Signal, PO Box 328, Smoky Lake AB T0A 2A0 – 403/656-4114 – Wed.

Spruce Grove: Calmar Community Voice, A.F. Keller & Associates Ltd., PO Box 6000, Spruce Grove AB T7X 2Z5 – 403/962-9228; Fax: 403/962-1021 – Circ.: 4,600; Every other Tue. – Editor, Al Keller

Spruce Grove: The Examiner, PO Box 4206, Spruce Grove AB T7X 3B4 – 403/962-4257; Fax: 403/962-0658; Email: spruce_grove_examiner@awnet.net – Circ.: 5,120; Sun. – Publisher, Inez Scheideman; Editor, Rich Gossen; Circulation Manager, Lyle Martin

Spruce Grove This Week, 322 McLeod Ave., PO Box 3006, Spruce Grove AB T7X 3A4 – 403/962-8457; Fax: 403/962-2902 – Fri.

Stettler Independent, 5006 - 50th Ave., PO Box 310, Stettler AB T0C 2L0 – 403/742-2395; Fax: 403/742-8050 – Circ.: 4,200; Wed.

Stony Plain Reporter, PO Box 780, Stony Plain AB T0E 2G0 – 403/963-2291; Fax: 403/963-9716 – Tue.

Stony Plain This Week, #7 Heritage Market, 5009 - 50 St., Stony Plain AB T7Z 1T3 – 403/963-0453 – Circ.: 11,900; Fri.

Strathmore Standard, 136 Main St., PO Box 2250, Strathmore AB T1P 1K2 – 403/934-3021; Fax: 403/934-5011 – Circ.: 3,671; Tue. – Publisher, Lori Jurawsky; Editor, Jim Greer

Sundre Round-Up, PO Box 599, Sundre AB T0M 1X0 – 403/638-3577; Fax: 403/638-3077 – Circ.: 2,245; Wed. – Publisher, Monica Leatherdale; Editor, Dan Singleton

Swan Hills Grizzly Gazette, PO Box 1000, Swan Hills AB T0G 2C0 – 403/333-2100; Fax: 403/333-2111 – Circ.: 637; Tue. – Publisher, Carol Webster; Editor, Marla Prochozka

Sylvan Lake News, 5020 - 50A St., Sylvan Lake AB T4S 1R2 – 403/887-2331; Fax: 403/887-2081 – Circ.: 1,220; Wed.

Taber Times, 5403 - 48 Ave., Taber AB T1G 1S6 – 403/223-2266; Fax: 403/223-1408 – Circ.: 3,365; Wed. – Publisher, Coleen Campbell; Editor, Harley Richards

Three Hills Capital, PO Box 158, Three Hills AB T0M 2A0 – 403/443-5133; Fax: 403/443-7331 – Circ.: 3,900; Wed. – Publisher & Editor, Timothy J. Sherlaw; Circulation Manager, Denean Denis

Tofield Mercury, PO Box 150, Tofield AB T0B 4J0 – 403/662-4046; Fax: 403/662-3735 – Tue.

Trochu: Highway 21 News, PO Box 665, Trochu AB T0M 2C0 – 403/442-2711; Fax: 403/442-2633; Email: trochu_highway_21_news@awest.net – Circ.: 6,100; Tue. – Publisher, Ed Moller; Editor, Frank Ryan

Two Hills Times, PO Box 430, Two Hills AB T0B 4K0 – 403/657-2530; Fax: 403/657-2721 – Tue.

Valley Views, Valleyviews Publishing Ltd., PO Box 787, Valleyview AB T0H 3N0 – 403/524-3490; Fax: 403/524-4545; Email: valley_views@awnet.net – Circ.: 1,538; Wed. – Co-Publisher, Wayne Plaxton; Co-Publisher & Editor, Joan Plaxton; Circulation Manager, Betty Kobe

Vauxhall Advance, PO Box 302, Vauxhall AB T0K 2K0 – 403/654-2122 – Thur.

Vegreville News Advertiser, PO Box 810, Vegreville AB T9C 1R9 – 403/632-2861; Fax: 403/632-7981 – Circ.: 10,700; Mon. – Publisher, Arthur Beaudrette; Editor, Dan Beaudrette

Vegreville Times Observer, 4910 - 50th St., PO Box 160, Vegreville AB T0B 4L0 – 403/632-2353 – Circ.: 3,840; Tue.

Vermilion News Advertiser, PO Box 810, Vegreville AB T9C 1R9 – 403/853-6397; Fax: 403/853-6526 – Circ.: 6,800; Mon. – Editor, Dan Beaudrette

Vermilion Standard, 4917 - 50 Ave., Vermilion AB T9X 1A6 – 403/853-5344; Fax: 403/853-5203 – Circ.: 3,400; Tue.

Veteran Eagle, PO Box 462, Veteran AB T0C 2S0 – 403/575-3892; Fax: 403/575-3938 – Circ.: 550 – Publisher, Les Hainer

Viking: The Weekly Review, PO Box 240, Viking AB T0B 4N0 – 403/336-3422; Fax: 403/336-2550 – Tue.

Vulcan Advocate, PO Box 389, Vulcan AB T0L 2B0 – 403/485-2036; Fax: 403/485-2911 – Wed.

Wabamun Community Voice, A.F. Keller & Associates Ltd., PO Box 6000, Spruce Grove AB T7X 2Z5 – 403/962-9228; Fax: 403/962-1021 – Circ.: 4,600; Every other Tue. – Editor, Al Keller

Wainwright Star-Chronicle, 414 - 10 St., Wainwright AB T9W 1P5 – 403/842-4465; Fax: 403/842-2760 – Circ.: 1,920; Wed.; also Wainwright Star Regional

Westlock News, PO Box 40, Westlock AB T0G 2L0 – 403/349-3033; Fax: 403/349-3677 – Mon. – Editor, Town & Country Section, Les Dunford

Wetaskiwin Times Advertiser, PO Box 6900, Wetaskiwin AB T9A 2G5 – 403/352-2231; Fax: 403/352-4333 – Circ.: 12,625; Mon. – Publisher, Doug Hare; Editor, George Brown

Whitecourt Star, PO Box 630, Whitecourt AB T7S 1N7 – 403/778-3977; Fax: 403/778-6459 – Wed.

British Columbia Daily Newspapers

CRANBROOK:

Daily Townsman, E. Kootenay Newspapers Ltd., 822 Cranbrook St. North, Cranbrook BC V1C 3R9 – 250/426-5201; Fax: 250/426-5003 – Circ.: 4,300 – Publisher, Carol Murray; Editor, David Sands

DAWSON CREEK:

Peace River Block News, Sterling Newspapers Ltd., 901 - 100th Ave., PO Box 180, Dawson Creek BC V1G 4G6 – 250/782-4888; Fax: 250/782-6770; Email: PRBNEWS@PRIS.BC.CA; URL: http://www.sterlingnews.com/peace – Circ.: 2,572; Mon.-

Fri; also Peace River Block News Regional Weekly (Sun., circ. 10,788) – Publisher, Margaret Forbes; Editor, Jeremy Hainsworth; Circulation Manager, Tiffany Lewis

FORT ST. JOHN:
Alaska Highway News, 9916 - 98th St., Fort St. John BC V1J 3T8 – 250/785-5631; Fax: 250/785-3522; Email: ahnews@awinc.com; URL: http://sterling-news.com/alaska – Circ.: 3,100; Mon.-Fri. – Publisher, Bruce Lantz; Editor, Tom Wilkinson; Circulation Manager, Tawny Schultz

KAMLOOPS:
The Kamloops Daily News, Southam Inc., 393 Seymour St., Kamloops BC V2C 6P6 – 250/372-2331; Fax: 250/374-3884 – Circ.: 16,900; Morning – Publisher, Brian Butters; Editor, Mel Rothenburger; Circulation Manager, Dale Brin

KELOWNA:
Daily Courier, Thomson Newspapers Co. Ltd., 550 Doyle Ave., Kelowna BC V1Y 7V1 – 250/762-4445; Fax: 250/762-3866 – Circ.: 17,002, Mon.-Sat.; 16,205, Sun.; Morning – Publisher & General Manager, Jonathan Franklin

KIMBERLEY:
The Daily Bulletin, E. Kootenay Newspapers Ltd., 335 Spokane St., Kimberley BC V1A 1Y9 – 250/427-5333; Fax: 250/427-5336; Email: Bulletin@cyberlink.bc.ca – Circ.: 8,200; Afternoon – Publisher, Michelle Jaques; Editor, Christalee Davan; Circulation Manager, Laura Butler

NANAIMO:
Daily Free Press, Thomson Newspapers Co. Ltd., 223 Commercial St., PO Box 69, Nanaimo BC V9R 5K5 – 250/753-3451; Fax: 250/753-2426 – Circ.: 12,700; Morning, Mon.-Sat. – Publisher & General Manager, Jim Rice

NELSON:
Daily News, News Publishing Co., 266 Baker St., Nelson BC V1L 4H3 – 250/352-3552; Fax: 250/352-2418 – Circ.: 4,345; Afternoon – Publisher, Verne Shaull; Editor, David Howe

PENTICTON:
Herald, Thomson Newspapers Co. Ltd., 186 Nanaimo Ave. West, Penticton BC V2A 1N4 – 250/492-4002; Fax: 250/492-2403 – Circ.: 8,600; Morning, Mon.-Sat. – Publisher, Jane Howard; Managing Editor, Michael Turner; Circulation Manager, Dave Hamilton

PORT ALBERNI:
Alberni Valley Times, Sterling Newspapers Ltd., 4918 Napier St., PO Box 400, Port Alberni BC V9Y 7N1 – 250/723-8171; Fax: 250/723-0586; Email: avtimes@cedar.alberni.net; URL: http://www.alberni.net/~avtimes/index.html – Circ.: 6,500; Evening – Publisher, N.E. Hannaford; Managing Editor, Rob Diotte; Circulation Manager, John Richardson

PRINCE GEORGE:
The Citizen, Southam Inc., 150 Brunswick St., PO Box 5700, Prince George BC V2L 5K9 – 250/562-2441; Fax: 250/562-7453 – Circ.: 17,679, Mon.-Thur., Sat.; 20,273, Fri.; Morning – Publisher, Bill Peterson; Editor, Roy K. Nagel

PRINCE RUPERT:
Daily News, Sterling Newspapers Ltd., 801 - 2nd Ave. West, Prince Rupert BC V8J 1H6 – 250/624-6781; Fax: 250/624-2851; Email: prdnews@kaien.awinc.com; URL: http://www.sterling-news.com – Circ.: 3,612; Evening, Mon.-Fri. – Publisher, Peter Godfrey; Editor, Scott Crowson; Circulation Manager, Margaret Bob

TRAIL:
Times, 1163 Cedar Ave., Trail BC V1R 4B8 – 250/364-1416; Fax: 250/368-8550; Email: trailtimes@awinc.com; URL: http://haven.uniserve.com/~swise – Circ.: 6,200; Afternoon – Publisher, Raymon D. Picco; Editor, Tracy Konschuk; Circulation Manager, Terry Finlay

VANCOUVER:
The Province, Pacific Press Ltd., 2250 Granville St., Vancouver BC V6H 3G2 – 604/732-2478; Fax: 604/732-2704 – Circ.: 158,490, 192,271 Sun.; Morning, Sun.-Fri. – Managing Editor, Neil Graham

The Vancouver Sun, Pacific Press Ltd., 2250 Granville St., Vancouver BC V6H 3G2 – 604/732-2111; Fax: 604/732-2323 – Circ.: 192,300 Mon.-Thur., 252,000 Fri., 253,900 Sat.; Morning – Editor-in-Chief, Ian Haysom

VICTORIA:
Times Colonist, Thomson Newspapers Co. Ltd., 2621 Douglas St., PO Box 300, Victoria BC V8T 4M2 – 250/380-5211; Fax: 250/380-5353; Email: times@interlink.bc.ca – Circ.: 79,000; Morning – Publisher, Peter Baillie; Editor, Jody Paterson; Circulation Manager, Jerry Jackson

Other Newspapers in British Columbia

Abbotsford Clearbrook Times, #1, 30887 Peardonville Rd., Abbotsford BC V2T 6K2 – 604/854-5244; Fax: 604/854-1140; Email: abbotsford_times@mindunk.bc.ca – Circ.: 37,000; Wed., Sat. – Publisher, Rod Thomson; Editor, Phil Melnychuk

Abbotsford News, 34375 Cyril St., Abbotsford BC V2S 2H5 – 604/856-9543; Fax: 604/853-9808 – Circ.: 15,000, 40,000 Sat.; Tue., Thur., Sat.; also Sumas & Matsqui Times

Agassiz-Harrison Observer, PO Box 129, Agassiz BC V0M 1A0 – 604/796-2022 – Wed.

Aldergrove Star, 3089 - 272 St., Aldergrove BC V4W 3R9 – 604/856-8303; Fax: 604/856-5212 – Wed.

Armstrong Advertiser, PO Box 610, Armstrong BC V0E 1B0 – 250/546-3121 – Wed.

Ashcroft Journal, PO Box 190, Ashcroft BC V0K 1A0 – 250/453-2261, 2655; Fax: 250/453-9625 – Tue. – Publisher, Judy Van Allen; Editor, Barry Tait; Circulation Manager, Linda Koster

Barriere: North Thompson Star/Journal, PO Box 1020, Barriere BC V0E 1E0 – 250/672-5611; Fax: 250/672-9900 – Mon.

Burnaby News Leader, 6569 Kingsway, Burnaby BC V5E 1E1 – 604/526-9696 – Circ.: 46,300; Wed., Sun.

Burnaby Now, #205A - 3430 Brighton Ave., Burnaby BC V5A 3H4 – 604/444-3451; Fax: 604/444-3460 – Sun., Wed.

Burns Lake: Lakes District News, PO Box 309, Burns Lake BC V0J 1E0 – 250/692-7526 – Wed.

Campbell River Courier-Islander, PO Box 310, Campbell River BC V9W 5B5 – 250/287-7464 – Circ.: 7,500; Wed., Fri.

Campbell River Mirror, #104 - 250 Dogwood St., Campbell River BC V9W 2X9 – 250/287-9227; Fax: 250/287-3238 – Circ.: 7,980; Wed.; also North Island Weekender (Sat., circ. 21,000)

Campbell River: The Wrap, 1040 Cedar St., Campbell River BC V9W 5B5 – 250/287-7464 – Circ.: 21,000; Sat.

Castlegar Sun, 233 Columbia Ave., Castlegar BC V1N 1G3 – 250/365-2278; Fax: 250/365-7762 – Circ.: 3,600; Wed. – Publisher, Marilyn Strong; Editor, Sharlene Imhoff, 250/365-5266

Chetwynd Echo, #215, 5021 - 49th Ave., PO Box 750, Chetwynd BC V0C 1J0 – 250/788-2246; Fax: 250/788-9988; Email: chetecho@pris.bc.ca – Circ.: 1,900; Tues. – Publisher, Margaret Mouold; Editor, Rick Davison

Chilliwack Progress, 45860 Spadina Ave., Chilliwack BC V2P 6H9 – 604/792-1931; Fax: 604/792-4936 – Wed., Fri. – Publisher, Julian Galbecka; Editor, Paul Bucci; Circulation Manager, Kellee Taylor

Chilliwack Times, #102 - 45951 Tretheway Ave., Chilliwack BC V2P 1K4 – 604/792-9117; Fax: 604/792-9300 – Circ.: 25,400; Tue., Fri.

Chilliwack: The Mountaineer, CFB Chilliwack, Chilliwack BC V0X 2E0 – 604/858-1157 – Every other Tue.

Clearwater: North Thompson Times, RR#1, PO Box 1102, Clearwater BC V0E 1N0 – 250/674-3343; Fax: 250/674-3777; Email: nttimes@netshop.net – Circ.: 3,822; Tue. – Publisher, Bruce Chappell; Editor, Nancy Chappell

Coquitlam: Now, #1, 2700 Barnet Hwy., Coquitlam BC V3B 1B8 – 604/942-4192 – Circ.: 47,784; Wed., Sun.

Courtenay: Comox Valley Echo, 407D Fifth St., Courtenay BC V9N 1J7 – 250/334-4722 – Circ.: 19,000; Tue., Fri.

Courtenay: Comox Valley Record, PO Box 3729, Courtenay BC V9N 7P1 – 250/338-5811; Fax: 250/338-5568 – Circ.: 18,200; Wed., Fri. – Publisher, Grant Lawrence; Editor, Bruce Winfield; Circulation Manager, Vicky Butters

Cranbrook: East Kootenay Weekly, 822 Cranbrook St. North, Cranbrook BC V1C 3R9 – 250/426-5201; Fax: 250/426-5003 – Circ.: 15,000; Wed. – Publisher, Carol Murray; Editor, David Sands

Cranbrook: The Kootenay Advertiser, Koocanusa Publications Inc., 1510 - 2nd St. North, Cranbrook BC V1C 3L2 – 250/426-7253; Fax: 250/489-3743; Email: advertiser@cyberlink.bc.ca – Circ.: 31,260; Mon.; TV listing supplement, 7 Days Magazine (Mon.) – Publisher & Editor, Daryl D. Shellborn

Cranbrook: The Rocky Mountain Weekender, 19 Ninth Ave. South, Cranbrook BC V1C 2L9 – 603/426-6119; Fax: 603/426-6070 – Circ.: 25,500; Sat. – Publisher, Melba Hanson; Editor, Deb Saffin

Creston Valley Advance, 115 - 10th Ave., PO Box 1279, Creston Valley BC V0B 1G0 – 250/428-2266; Fax: 250/428-3320; Email: advance@kootenay.awinc.com – Circ.: 4,086; Mon., Thur. – Publisher, Helena E. White; Editor, Brain Bell; Circulation Manager, Dianne Audette

Dawson Creek Mirror, 10224 - 10th St., Dawson Creek BC V1G 3T4 – 250/782-9424 – Sat.

Delta Optimist, 5485 - 48 Ave., Delta BC V4K 1X2 – 604/946-4451; Fax: 604/946-5680 – Circ.: 15,700; Wed., Sat.

Delta: North Delta Sentinel, 10680 - 84 Ave., Delta BC V4C 2L2 – 604/589-2233; Fax: 604/581-1519 – Every other Tue.

Duncan: The Citizen, 469 Whistler St., Duncan BC V9L 4X5 – 250/748-2666; Fax: 250/748-1552 – Circ.: 20,200; Sun., Wed.

Duncan: Cowichan News Leader, 2742 James St., PO Box 910, Duncan BC V9L 2X9 – 250/746-4471; Fax: 250/746-8529 – Circ.: 19,000; Wed., also Cowichan Pictorial (Sun.)

Enderby Commoner, PO Box 190, Enderby BC V0E 1V0 – 250/838-7229 – Wed.

Esquimalt News, 538 Fraser St., Victoria BC V9A 6H7 – 250/381-5664; Fax: 250/361-9283 – Circ.: 7,500; Wed. – Publisher, Marilyn Cowie; Editor, Alanna Jorde

Esquimalt: Lookout, c/o CFB Esquimalt, Victoria BC V0S 1B0 – 250/385-0313; Fax: 250/361-3512; Email: lookout@horizon.bc.ca – Circ.: 5,000; Wed.; English & French – Managing Editor, Corina DeGuire

Fernie: Elk Valley Extra, 342 - 2nd Ave., PO Box 500, Fernie BC V0B 1M0 – 250/423-4666 – Circ.: 6,700; Fri.

Fernie Free Press, PO Bag 5000, Fernie BC V0B 1M0 – 250/423-4666; Fax: 250/423-3110 – Wed.

Canadian Almanac & Directory 1997

5-134 NEWSPAPERS

Fort Nelson News, Site 3, Sikanni Bldg., Liard St. North, PO Box 600, Fort Nelson BC V0C 1R0 – 250/774-2357; Fax: 250/774-3612 – Wed.

Fort St. James Caledonia Courier, PO Box 1007, Vanderhoof BC V0J 3A0 – 250/567-9258; Fax: 250/567-2070 – Circ.: 1,100; Wed. – Publisher, Wayne Stolz; Editor, Leah Blain

Fort St. John: The Northerner, 9824 - 98A Ave., Fort St. John BC V1J 1S2 – 250/785-2890; Fax: 250/785-1638; Email: cclovis@awinc.com – Circ.: 4,000; Tues. – Publisher, Cindy Cloris; Editor, Wendy Cloris; Circulation Manager, Sarah Brown

Fort St. John: North Peace Express, Sterling Newspapers Ltd., 9916 - 98 St., Fort St. John BC V1J 3T8 – 250/785-5631; Fax: 250/785-3522; Email: ahnews@awinc.com; URL: http://sterlingnews.com/alaska – Circ.: 10,800; Sun. – Publisher, Bruce Lantz; Editor, Janelle Lake

Gabriola Sounder, Box 56, Site 17, RR#1, Gabriola BC V0R 1X0 – 250/247-9337; Fax: 250/247-8147; Email: sounder@island.net – Circ.: 3,500; Every other Fri. – Publisher, Bill de Carteret; Editor, Sue de Carteret; Circulation Manager, Terri Hawkins

Gibsons: The Coast Outlook, PO Box 567, Gibsons BC V0N 1V0 – 604/885-5121 – Thur.

Gibsons/Sechelt Coast Independent, PO Box 125Y, Gibsons BC V0N 1V0 – 604/886-4003 – Circ.: 12,990; Mon.

Gold River: The Record, PO Box 279, Gold River BC V0P 1G0 – 250/283-2324; Fax: 250/283-2527; Email: record@goldrvr.island.net – Circ.: 1,500; Twice monthly – Publisher, Jerry West

Golden News, PO Box 4114, Golden BC V0A 1H0 – 250/344-6333 – Wed.

Golden Star, PO Box 149, Golden BC V0A 1H0 – 250/344-5251; Fax: 250/344-7344 – Circ.: 2,302; Wed.; also Columbia Valley This Week (Wed.) – Publisher, Holly Magoon; Editor, Bill Costello; Circulation Manager, Patti Roberts

Golden: Windermere Valley Shoppers Guide, PO Box 4114, Golden BC V0A 1H0 – 250/344-6333 – Mon.

Grand Forks: Boundary Bulletin, PO Box 700, Grand Forks BC V0H 1H0 – 250/442-2191; Fax: 250/442-3336 – Circ.: 5,195; Mon. – Publisher, Sandra. Watts; Editor, Mia Thomas; Circulation Manager, Shirley Larsen

Grand Forks Gazette, 7330 - 2nd St., PO Box 700, Grand Forks BC V0H 1H0 – 250/442-2191; Fax: 250/442-3336 – Circ.: 3,076; Wed. – Publisher, Sandra Watts; Editor, Mia Thomas; Circulation Manager, Shirley Larsen

Greenwood: Boundary Creek Times, PO Box 99, Greenwood BC V0H 1J0 – 250/445-2233; Fax: 250/445-2240 – Wed.

Hagensborg: Coast Mountain News, PO Box 250, Hagensborg BC V0T 1H0 – 250/982-2696; Fax: 250/982-2512 – Circ.: 3,500; Every other Thur. – Publisher & Editor, Angela Hall

Hope Standard, 895 - 3rd Ave., Unit 3, PO Box 1090, Hope BC V0X 1L0 – 604/869-2421; Fax: 604/869-7351 – Circ.: 2,372; Thur.

Houston Today, PO Box 899, Houston BC V0J 1Z0 – 250/845-2890; Fax: 250/845-7893 – Wed.

Invermere: The Valley Echo, PO Box 70, Invermere BC V0A 1K0 – 250/342-9216; Fax: 250/342-3930 – Circ.: 3,500; Wed. – Publisher, Sheila Tutty; Editor, Ian Cobb, 250/342-3223

Kamloops This Week, 1365B Dalhousie Dr., Kamloops BC V2C 5P6 – 250/374-7467; Fax: 250/374-1033 – Sun., Wed., Fri. – Publisher, Linda Hooton; Editor, Gene Laverty

Kaslo-Kootenay Lake Pennywise, PO Box 430, Kaslo BC V0G 1M0 – 250/353-2602 – Wed.; also Nelson Pennywise, New Denver/Winlaw/Slocan Valley Pennywise, Salmo-Fruitvale Pennywise

Kelowna: Capital News, 2495 Enterprise Way, Kelowna BC V1X 7K2 – 250/763-3212; Fax: 250/763-8469 – Sun., Wed., Fri; supplement TV Week (Fri.)

Keremeos: Gazette of the Similkameen, PO Box 299, Keremeos BC V0X 1N0 – 250/499-2920 – Wed.

Kitimat: Northern Sentinel, 626 Enterprise Ave., Kitimat BC V8C 2E4 – 250/632-6144; Fax: 250/639-9373; Email: mbaxter@sno.net – Circ.: 2,600; Wed; supplement, TV & Video Scanner (Wed); also Weekend Advertiser (Sat., circ. 15,800) – Publisher, Sandra Dugdale; Editor, Malcolm Baxter

Ladysmith-Chemainus Chronicle, PO Box 400, Ladysmith BC V0R 2E0 – 250/245-2277; Fax: 250/245-2260 – Circ.: 3,000; Tue. – Publisher, Bobby Cloke; Editor, John McKinley

Lake Cowichan Gazette, PO Box 2500, Lake Cowichan BC V0R 2G0 – 604/749-4383 – Circ.: 2,500; Wed.

Lake Cowichan: The Lake News, PO Box 962, Lake Cowichan BC V0R 2G0 – 250/749-3143 – Wed.

Langley Advance News, #111, 20353 - 6th Ave., Langley BC V2Y 1N5 – 604/534-8641; Fax: 604/534-3383 – Circ.: 37,900; Wed., Fri.

Langley Times, PO Box 3097, Langley BC V3A 4R3 – 604/533-4157; Fax: 604/533-0219 – Wed., Sat.

Lantzville: The Lantzville Log, Lantzville Log Society, PO Box 268, Lantzville BC V0R 2H0 – 250/390-2847 – Circ.: 3,075; Monthly – Editor, Lynn Reeve

Lazo: Comox Totem Times, CFB Comox, Lazo BC V0R 2K0 – 250/339-2541; Fax: 250/339-8673 – Circ.: 2,300; Monthly – Editor, Joel Clarkson

Lillooet: Bridge River-Lillooet News, 979 Main St., PO Box 709, Lillooet BC V0K 1V0 – 250/256-4219; Fax: 250/256-4210 – Wed.

Lumby Valley Times, #3, 1879 Vernon St., PO Box 408, Lumby BC V0E 2G0 – 604/547-6990 – Wed.

Mackenzie: The Times, PO Box 609, Mackenzie BC V0J 2C0 – 250/997-6675 – Tue.

Maple Ridge-Pitt Meadows Times, 22334 Selkirk Ave., Maple Ridge BC V2X 2X5 – 604/463-2281; Fax: 604/463-9943 – Circ.: 23,000; Wed. & Sun. – Publisher, Lois Lee; Editor, Chris Campbell

Merritt Herald, PO Box 9, Merritt BC V0N 2B0 – 250/378-4241 – Wed.

Merritt: The Merritt News, PO Box 939, Merritt BC V0K 2B0 – 250/378-8876; Fax: 250/378-8853 – Wed.

Merritt: Nicola-Thompson Today, PO Box 9, Merritt BC V0K 2B0 – 250/378-4241 – Mon.

Mission: Record, 33047 First Ave., Mission BC V2V 1G2 – 604/826-6221; Fax: 604/826-8266 – Circ.: 4,986; Thur.

Nakusp: Arrow Lakes News, PO Box 189, Nakusp BC V0G 1R0 – 250/265-3823; Fax: 250/265-3841 – Circ.: 2,200; Wed. – Publisher & Editor, Chuck Bennett; Circulation Manager, Linda McInnis

Nanaimo: The Bulletin, 777B Poplar St., Nanaimo BC V9S 2H7 – 250/753-3707; Fax: 250/753-0788 – Circ.: 28,900; Mon., Thur.

Nanaimo Times, PO Box 486, Nanaimo BC V9R 5L5 – 250/753-1102 – Tue.,Thur.,Sat.

Nelson: Kootenay Weekly Express, 554 Ward St., Nelson BC V1L 1S9 – 250/354-3910; Fax: 250/352-5075; Email: express@netidea.com – Circ.: 12,814; Wed. – Publisher & Editor, Nelson Becker

Nelson: West Kootenay Weekender & TV Today, 266 Baker St., Nelson BC V1L 4H3 – 250/352-3552; Fax: 250/352-2418 – Circ.: 29,230; Fri; supplement to Nelson Daily News, Trail Daily Times, & Castlegar Sun

New Westminster Now/Royal City Record, 418 - 6th St., New Westminster BC V3L 3B2 – 604/525-6306 – Circ.: 16,219; Sat., Wed.

North Shore News, 1139 Lonsdale Ave., North Vancouver BC V7M 2H4 – 604/985-2131; Fax: 604/985-2104; URL: http://www.nsnews.com – Circ.: 58,000; Wed., Fri., Sun. – Publisher, Peter Speck; Managing Editor, Timothy Renshaw

Oliver Chronicle, PO Box 880, Oliver BC V0H 1T0 – 250/498-3711; Fax: 250/498-3966; Email: mnewman@ftcnet.com; URL: http://www.ftcnet.com/~mnewman – Circ.: 3,380; Wed. – Publisher, Michael Newman; Editor, Kathleen Connolly

One Hundred Mile House Free Press, PO Box 459, One Hundred Mile House BC V0K 2E0 – 250/395-2219; Fax: 250/395-3939 – Wed.

Osoyoos Times, PO Box 359, Osoyoos BC V0H 1V0 – 250/495-7225; Fax: 250/495-6616; Email: pturner@ftcnet.com – Circ.: 2,637; Wed. – Co-Publisher, C. Stodola; Editor & Co-Publisher, Patrick Turner

Parksville: The Morning Sun, 114 East Hirst Ave., PO Box 45, Parksville BC V9P 2G3 – 250/954-0600 – Circ.: 15,000; Wed.

Parksville-Qualicum News, PO Box 1180, Parksville BC V9P 2H2 – 250/248-4341; Fax: 250/248-4655 – Circ.: 16,117; Tue., Thurs., Sat. – Publisher, Judi Thompson; Editor, Jeff H. Vircoe; Circulation Manager, Bernice Kenney

Pender Island: Island Tides, Island Tides Publishing Ltd., RR#1, Pender Island BC V0N 2M0 – 250/629-3660; Fax: 250/629-3838 – Circ.: 8,500; Every other Thur. – President & Editor, Christa Grace-Warrick

Penticton: Western News Advertiser, 2250 Camrose St., Penticton BC V2A 8R1 – 250/492-0444; Fax: 250/492-9843 – Circ.: 21,260; Wed., Fri.

Port Alberni: Pennyworth, 3017 - 3rd Ave., Port Alberni BC V9Y 2A5 – 250/723-3709 – Wed.

Port Coquitlam: The Tri-City News, 1405 Broadway, Port Coquitlam BC V3C 5W9 – 604/526-9696 – Sun., Wed.

Port Hardy: North Island Gazette, PO Box 458, Port Hardy BC V0N 2P0 – 250/949-6225; Fax: 250/949-7655 – Circ.: 3,382; Wed. – Publisher, Rod A. Sluggett; Editor, Rob Giblak; Circulation Manager, Sandy Haydamack

Port Hardy: The View, PO Box 458, Port Hardy BC V0N 2P0 – 250/949-6225 – Wed.

Powell River News, 7030 Alberni St., Powell River BC V8A 2C3 – 604/485-4255; Fax: 604/485-5832; Email: prnews@thecentre.com – Circ.: 5,600; Wed. – Publisher, Pam Krompocker; Editor, Terry Kruger

Powell River Peak, 4312A Franklin Ave., Powell River BC V8A 5L7 – 604/485-5313 – Circ.: 8,700; Thur.

Powell River Town Crier, 7030 Alberni St., Powell River BC V8A 2C3 – 604/485-4255; Fax: 604/485-5832; Email: prnews@thecentre.com – Circ.: 5,600; Mon. – Publisher, Pam Krompocker; Editor, Terry Kruger

Prince George Free Press, #200, 1515 - 2nd Ave., Prince George BC V2L 3B8 – 250/564-0005 – Circ.: 29,500; Thur.

Prince George This Week, 190 Victoria St., Prince George BC V2L 2J2 – 250/563-9988; Fax: 250/562-5012 – Sun.

Prince Rupert This Week, 413 - 3rd Ave. East, Prince Rupert BC V8J 1K7 – 250/627-8482 – Sun.

Princeton: Similkameen Spotlight, PO Box 340, Princeton BC V0X 1W0 – 250/295-3535 – Wed.

Queen Charlotte Islands Observer, PO Box 205, Queen Charlotte BC V0T 1S0 – 250/559-4680 – Thur.

Quesnel: Cariboo Observer, 188 Carson Ave., Quesnel BC V2J 2A8 – 250/992-2121; Fax: 250/992-5229 – Wed., Sun.

Revelstoke Times Review, 402 Third St. West, PO Box 20, Revelstoke BC V0E 2S0 – 250/837-4667; Fax: 250/837-3070 – Wed.

Richmond News, 5731 No. 3 Rd., Richmond BC V6X 2C9 – 604/270-8031; Fax: 604/270-2248 – Wed. & Sun.

Richmond Review, #120, 5851 #3 Rd., Richmond BC V6X 2C9 – 604/526-9696 – Sat.

Rossland: The Summit, 2207 Columbia Ave., Rossland BC V0G 1Y0 – 604/362-7210 – Wed.

Saanich News, 1824 Store St., Victoria BC V8T 4R4 – 250/920-2090; Fax: 250/920-7352 – Circ.: 32,800; Wed. – Publisher, Trevor Flatman; Editor, Jennifer Blyth; Circulation Manager, Susan Glover

Salmon Arm Observer, PO Box 550, Salmon Arm BC V1E 4N7 – 250/832-2131; Fax: 250/832-5140 –

Canadian Almanac & Directory 1997

Circ.: 5,200; Wed. – Publisher, Ron Lovestone; Editor, Gordon Priestman; Circulation Manager, Liz Smith

Salmon Arm Shoppers' Guide, PO Box 1270, Salmon Arm BC V1E 4P4 – 250/832-9461; Fax: 250/832-5246 – Circ.: 15,000; Mon. – Publisher, Sally Scales; Editor, G. Paul Skelhorne

Salmon Arm: The Shuswap Market News, PO Box 550, Salmon Arm BC V1E 4N7 – 250/832-2131; Fax: 250/832-5140 – Circ.: 17,000; Sat. – Publisher, Ron Lovestone; Editor, Lorne Reimer

Salmon Arm: The Shuswap Sun, PO Box 729, Salmon Arm BC V1E 4N8 – 250/832-6364; Fax: 250/832-2206; Email: writeon@jetstream.com – Circ.: 15,800; Thur. – Publisher, Robin Campbell; Editor, Chris Ladd

Salt Spring Island: Gulf Islands Driftwood, Driftwood Publishing Ltd., 328 Lower Ganges Rd., Salt Spring Island BC V8K 2V3 – 250/537-9933; Fax: 250/537-2613; Email: trichards@saltspring.com – Circ.: 4,700; Wed. – Publisher & Editor, Tony Richards; Circulation, Linda Pickell

Sechelt: The Sunshine Press, PO Box 519, Sechelt BC V0N 3A0 – 604/885-5121; Fax: 604/885-5399 – Circ.: 13,500; Mon.

Sicamous: Eagle Valley News, 1133 Parksville St., PO Box 113, Sicamous BC V0E 2V0 – 250/836-2570 – Wed.

Sidney: Peninsula News Review, PO Box 2070, Sidney BC V8L 3S5 – 250/656-1151 – Wed.

Smithers: Interior News, PO Box 2560, Smithers BC V0J 2N0 – 250/847-3266; Fax: 250/847-2995; Email: swan@stargazer.netshop.net – Circ.: 4,398; Wed. – Publisher, Vic Swan; Editor, John Young

Sooke News Mirror, PO Box 339, Sooke BC V0S 1N0 – 250/642-5752; Fax: 250/642-4767 – Wed.

Sparwood: The Elk Valley Miner, PO Box 820, Sparwood BC V0B 2G0 – 250/425-6411; Fax: 250/425-6201 – Circ.: 2,803; Tue. – Publisher, Fritz Brockel; Editor, Richard Collicutte; Circulation Manager, Wendy Fitzmaurice

Squamish Chief, PO Box 3500, Squamish BC V0N 3G0 – 604/892-9161 – Tue.

Summerland/Peachland Bulletin, PO Box 309, Summerland BC V0H 1Z0 – 250/494-5406; Fax: 250/494-5453; Email: slandreview@img.net – Circ.: 5,500; Mon.; also Summerland Review (Thur., circ. 2,850) – Publisher, Juanita Gibney; Editor, Bill Hodgson; Circulation Manager, Sonja Waller

Surrey: The Leader, PO Box 276, Surrey BC V3T 4W8 – 604/588-4313; Fax: 604/588-1863 – Wed., Sun.

Surrey-North Delta Now, #201, 7889 - 132nd St., Surrey BC V3W 4N2 – 604/572-0064; Fax: 604/572-6438 – Circ.: 105,000; Wed., Sat. – Publisher, Frank Teskey; Editor, Jeff Beamish

Terrace: Skeena Messenger, 4663 Lazelle Ave., Terrace BC V8G 1S4 – 250/638-1681; Fax: 250/638-1606 – Monthly – Publisher/Editor, Mike Kelly

Terrace: The Terrace Standard, 3210 Clinton Ave., Terrace BC V8G 5R2 – 250/638-7283; Fax: 250/638-8432 – Circ.: 8,200; Wed.; also The Skeena Marketplace (Sat., circ. 14,100) – Publisher & Editor, Rod Link

Terrace Times, #4, 3240 Kalum St., Terrace BC V8G 2N4 – Wed.

Tumbler Ridge Observer, 901 - 100 Ave., Dawson Creek BC V1G 1W2 – 250/782-4888; Fax: 250/782-6770 – Circ.: 1,808; Tue. – Publisher, Margaret Forbes; Editor, Kathleen Couturier

Ucluelet: The Westerly News, PO Box 317, Ucluelet BC V0R 3A0 – 250/726-7029 – Wed.

Valemount: The Valley Sentinel, PO Box 688, Valemount BC V0E 2Z0 – 250/566-4425; Fax: 250/566-4528 – Circ.: 1,324; Wed.

Vancouver: East Side Revue, 1736 - 33rd Ave. East, Vancouver BC V5N 3E2 – 604/327-0221; Fax: 604/327-0221 – Circ.: 5,600; Every other Thur.; English, Chinese & Punjabi; also West Side Revue (every other Sun.) – Publisher & Editor, Rod Raglin

Vancouver: Jewish Western Bulletin, #203, 873 Beatty St., Vancouver BC V6B 2M6 – 604/689-1520; Email: abuerger@mindlink.bc.ca – Thur.

Vancouver: The Link, #201, 225 - 17th Ave. East, Vancouver BC V5V 1A6 – 604/876-9300; Email: Indolink@mindlink.bc.ca – Circ.: 10,000; Wed., Sat. – Publisher & Editor, Promod Puri

Vancouver: Le Soleil de Colombie, 1645 - 5th Ave. West, Vancouver BC V6J 1N4 – 604/730-9575; Fax: 604/730-9576 – Tirage: 3,000; Vendredi; français – Éditeur, Jacques Baillout; Rédactrice, Hélène Péronny

Vancouver/False Creek News, 661A Market Hill, Leg-in-Boot Sq., False Creek South, Vancouver BC V5Z 4B5 – 604/876-6770 – Fri.

Vancouver: The Vancouver Courier, 1574 - West Sixth Ave., Vancouver BC V6J 1R2 – 604/738-1411; Fax: 604/731-1474 – Circ.: 61,500, Wed.; 124,500, Sun.; Wed., Sun. – Publisher, Peter Ballard; Editor, Mick Maloney; General Manager, J. Davis

Vancouver Echo, 3355 Grandview Hwy., Vancouver BC V5M 1Z5 – 604/439-2671; Email: rshore@vanecho.com; URL: http://www.vannet.com/vanecho – Circ.: 47,000; Wed. – Publisher, R. Mark Walker; Editor, Randy Shore; Circulation Manager, Linda Caravatta

Vancouver: West Ender/Kitsilano News, #103, 2145 West Broadway, Vancouver BC V6K 4L3 – 604/733-6397; Fax: 604/733-6398 – Circ.: 60,000; Thur., West Ender; Wed., Kitsilano News; also Undercurrent (Fri.) – Publisher, Ken Wood; Editor, Ted Townsend

Vancouver: West End Times, #501, 68 Water St., Vancouver BC V6B 1A4 – 604/682-1424 – Fri.

Vanderhoof: Omineca Express Bugle, PO Box 1007, Vanderhoof BC V0J 3A0 – 250/567-9258; Fax: 250/567-2070 – Circ.: 2,300; Wed. – Publisher, Wayne Stolz; Editor, Mark Nielsen

Vernon: The Morning Star, 4407 - 25th St., Vernon BC V1T 1P5 – 250/545-3322; Fax: 250/542-1510 – Sun., Wed., Fri.

Victoria: Goldstream News Gazette, PO Box 7310, Stn D, Victoria BC V9B 5B7 – 250/478-9552 – Wed. – Publisher, Jane Norman; Editor, Keith Norbury; Circulation, Ev Melanson

Victoria: Oak Bay News, #219 - 2187 Oak Bay Ave., Victoria BC V8R 1G1 – 250/598-4123; Fax: 250/598-1896 – Circ.: 9,400; Wed., Fri. – Publisher, Carol Bailey; Editor, David Lennam; Circulation Manager, Sharon Tiffin

Victoria's Monday Magazine, 1609 Blanshard St., Victoria BC V8W 5J5 – 250/382-6188 – Circ.: 40,000; Thur.

Victoria News, 1824 Shore St., Victoria BC V8T 4R4 – 250/360-0817 – Circ.: 25,127; Wed.

Victoria Pennysaver & CoverSTORY, 4210 Commerce Circle, Victoria BC V8Z 6N6 – 250/479-2331 – Tue.

Westside Weekly, #140, 2300 Carrington Rd., Westbank BC V4T 2E6 – 604/768-5030 – Circ.: 11,604; Wed., Fri.

Whistler: The Whistler Question, #238, 4370 Lorimer Rd., Whistler BC V0N 1B7 – 604/932-5131; Fax: 604/932-2862; Email: question@#whistler.net – Mon. (circ. 3,457), Thur. (circ. 4,611) – Publisher, Claire Macdonald; Editor, Jacqueline Waldorf; Circulation Manager, Henry Lacroix

White Rock: The Peace Arch News, #101, 1440 George St., White Rock BC V4B 4A3 – 604/531-1711; Fax: 604/531-7977; Email: pa_news@deepcove.com – Circ.: 28,000; Wed., Sun. – Publisher, Fred Gorman; Editor, Diane Strandberg

Williams Lake: The Tribune, 188 - 1st Ave. North, Williams Lake BC V2G 1Y8 – 250/392-2331; Fax: 250/392-7253; Email: bphillip@awinc.com – Circ.: 6,600; Tue., Thur; also the Weekender (circ. 10,300) – Publisher, Gary Crosina; Editor, Bill Phillips; Circulation Manager, Ramona Strombom

Winfield: The Calendar, PO Box 54, Winfield BC V0H 2C0 – 250/766-4688 – Wed.

Manitoba Daily Newspapers

BRANDON:

Brandon Sun, Thomson Newspapers Co. Ltd., 501 Rosser Ave., Brandon MB R7A 5Z6 – 204/727-2451; Fax: 204/725-0976, editorial 727-0385 – Circ.: 18,980; Evening; supplement - CoverSTORY (Sun., circ. 23,000) – Publisher, Rob Forbes; Managing Editor, Brian D. Marshall

FLIN FLON:

The Reminder, Eagles Printers, 10 North Ave., Flin Flon MB R8A 0T2 – 204/687-3454; Fax: 204/687-4473 – Circ.: 3,800; Evening – Publisher, Randy Daneliuk

PORTAGE LA PRAIRIE:

The Daily Graphic, Bowes Publishers Ltd., 1941 Saskatchewan Ave. West, PO Box 130, Portage La Prairie MB R1N 3B4 – 204/857-3427; Fax: 204/239-1270 – Circ.: 4,148; Evening – Publisher, Tom Tenszen; Editor, Simon Blake; Circulation Manager, Carolyn Miller

WINNIPEG:

Winnipeg Free Press, Thomson Newspapers Co. Ltd., 1355 Mountain Ave., Winnipeg MB R2X 3B6 – 204/697-7000; Fax: 204/697-7412 – Circ.: 133,530 Mon.-Fri., 207,720 Sat., 141,131 Sun.; Morning – Publisher, H.R. Redekop; Editor, Duncan McMonagle

The Winnipeg Sun, 1700 Church Ave., Winnipeg MB R2X 3A2 – 204/694-2022; Fax: 204/697-0759 – Circ.: 47,214 Mon.-Sat., 62,822 Sun.; Morning – Publisher, John Cochrane

Other Newspapers in Manitoba

Altona Red River Valley Echo, Interlake Publishing, PO Box 700, Altona, MB R0G 0B0 – 204/324-5001; Fax: 204/324-1402 – Circ.: 2,400; Tue.; monthly special issues – Editor & Business Manager, Liz Wieler

Baldur Gazette, PO Box 280, Baldur MB R0K 0B0 – 204/535-2127; Fax: 204/535-2350 – Tue.

Birtle Eye-Witness, PO Box 160, Shoal Lake MB R0J 1Z0 – 204/759-2644; Fax: 204/759-2521 – Circ.: 1,100; Mon.; supplement Crossroads (circ. 4,400) – Publisher & Editor, Greg Nesbitt

Boissevain Recorder, PO Box 220, Boissevain MB R0K 0E0 – 204/534-6479; Fax: 204/534-2977 – Circ.: 1,624; Wed. – Publisher & Editor, Miles G. Phillips

Brandon: Westman Review, 501 Rosser Ave., Brandon MB R7A 0K4 – 204/727-2451 – Circ.: 20,000; Tue.

Carberry News-Express, PO Box 220, Carberry MB R0K 0H0 – 204/834-2153; Fax: 204/834-2714; Email: newsexpress@mail.techplus.com – Circ.: 1,377; Wed. – Editor & Publisher, John W.H. Lupton; Circulation Manager, Diana Fisher

Carman: The Valley Leader, 70 Main St. South, PO Box 70, Carman MB R0G 0J0 – 204/745-2051; Fax: 204/745-3976 – Circ.: 7,300; Mon.

Cartwright: Southern Manitoba Review, PO Box 249, Cartwright MB R0K 0L0 – 204/529-2342 – Tue.

Dauphin Herald, PO Box 548, Dauphin MB R7N 2V4 – 204/638-4420; Fax: 204/638-8760 – Tue.

Deloraine Times & Star, PO Box 407, Deloraine MB R0M 0M0 – 204/747-2249 – Wed.

Gimli: The Interlake Spectator, 70 - 2nd Ave., PO Box 450, Gimli MB R0C 1B0 – 204/467-2421 – Circ.: 13,316; Mon.

Gladstone Enterprise, Sundance Publications Ltd., PO Box 939, Neepawa MB R0J 1H0 – 204/476-2309; Fax: 204/476-5802; Email: neepress@mts.net –

Canadian Almanac & Directory 1997

Circ.: 2,200; Tue. – Publisher, Ewan Pow; Editor, Jack Gibson

Glenboro Gazette, PO Box 10, Glenboro MB R0K 0X0 – 204/827-2343; Fax: 204/827-2207 – Tue. – Co-Publisher, Travis Johnson; Co-Publisher & Editor, Michael Johnson; Circulation Manager, Agnes Witherspoon

Grandview Exponent, PO Box 39, Grandview MB R0L 0Y0 – 204/546-2555; Fax: 204/546-3081 – Circ.: 1,506; Wed. – Publisher & Editor, Jim Chaloner

Hamiota Echo, PO Box 160, Shoal Lake MB R0J 1Z0 – 204/759-2644; Fax: 204/759-2521 – Circ.: 1,250; Mon.; supplement Crossroads – Publisher, Greg Nesbitt

Killarney Guide, PO Box 670, Killarney MB R0K 1G0 – 204/523-4611 – Tue.

Lac du Bonnet Leader, PO Box 910, Lac du Bonnet MB R0E 1A0 – 204/345-8611; Fax: 204/345-6344 – Tue.

Manitou Western Canadian, PO Box 190, Manitou MB R0G 1G0 – 204/242-2555; Fax: 204/242-3137 – Circ.: 1,850; Tue. – Publisher & Editor, Bryan Klippenstein

Melita New Era, 149 Main St., PO Box 820, Melita MB R0M 1L0 – 204/522-3491 – Tue.

Minnedosa Tribune, PO Box 930, Minnedosa MB R0J 1E0 – 204/867-3816; Fax: 204/867-5171; Email: tribune@mail.techplus.com; URL: http://www.techplus.com/trib/index.htm – Tues. – Publisher & Editor, R.M. Mummery

Morden: The Morden Times, PO Box 1356, Winkler MB R6W 4B3 – 204/325-4771 – Mon.

Morris: Crow Wing Warrior, PO Box 578, Morris MB R0G 1K0 – Circ.: 728; Mon.

Morris: The Scratching River Post, PO Box 160, Morris MB R0G 1K0 – 204/746-2823 – Circ.: 2,957; Mon; 4 local area editions – Publisher & Editor, Doug Penner; Circulation Manager, Joyce Penner

Neepawa Banner, PO Box 699, Neepawa MB R0J 1H0 – 204/476-3401; Fax: 204/476-5073 – Mon. – Publisher, Ken Waddell; Editor, Rod Nickel; Circulation Manager, Chris Waddell

Neepawa Press, Sundance Publications Ltd., PO Box 939, Neepawa MB R0J 1H0 – 204/476-2309; Fax: 204/476-5802; Email: neepress@mts.net – Circ.: 3,000; Tue. – Publisher, Ewan Pow; Editor, Jack Gibson

Pilot Mound: The Sentinel Courier, PO Box 179, Pilot Mound MB R0G 1P0 – 204/825-2772; Fax: 204/825-2772 – Circ.: 1,400; Tue. – Publisher, Jeff Howell; Editor, Sheila Howell

Portage La Prairie: Herald Leader Press, 1941 Saskatchewan Ave. West, Portage La Prairie MB R1N 2B4 – 204/857-3427; Fax: 204/239-1270 – Circ.: 6,500; Tue. – Publisher, Tom Tenszen; Editor, Simon Blake; Circulation Manager, Carolyn Miller

Reston Recorder, PO Box 10, Reston MB R0M 1X0 – 204/877-3321; Fax: 204/877-3331 – Mon.

Rivers: The Rivers Banner, PO Box 70, Rivers MB R0K 1X0 – 204/328-7494; Fax: 204/328-5212 – Circ.: 650; Mon. – Publisher, Ken Waddell; Managing Editor, Sheila Szapko; Circulation Manager, Audrey Mackay

Roblin Review, PO Box 938, Roblin MB R0L 1P0 – 204/937-8377; Fax: 204/937-8212 – Tue.

Rossburn Review, PO Box 160, Shoal Lake MB R0J 1Z0 – 204/759-2644; Fax: 204/759-2521 – Circ.: 1,100; Mon.; supplement Crossroads – Publisher & Editor, Greg Nesbitt

Russell Banner, PO Box 100, Russell Banner MB R0J 1W0 – 204/773-2069; Fax: 204/773-2645 – Tue. – Publisher & Editor, Clayton G. Chaloner

St. Boniface: La Liberté, CP 190, St. Boniface MB R2H 3B4 – 204/237-4823; Fax: 204/231-1998; Email: la_liberte@presse-ouest.mb.ca; URL: http://www.presse.ouest.mb.ca – Tirage: 4,000; Vendredi; français – Éditeur, Jean-François Lacerte; Rédactrice, Sylviane Lanthier

Selkirk Journal, 217 Clandeboye Ave., Selkirk MB R1A 0X2 – 204/482-7402 – Mon.

Shilo Stag, CFB Shilo, Shilo MB R0K 2A0 – 204/765-3013 – Every other Tue.

Shoal Lake Star, PO Box 160, Shoal Lake MB R0Z 1Z0 – 204/759-2644; Fax: 204/759-2521 – Circ.: 1,100; Mon.; supplement Crossroads – Publisher & Editor, Greg Nesbitt

Souris Plaindealer, PO Box 488, Souris MB R0K 2C0 – 204/483-2070; Fax: 204/483-3866 – Circ.: 1,400; Mon.

Steinbach: The Carillon, 377 Main St., Steinbach MB R0A 2A0 – 204/326-3421; Fax: 204/326-4860 – Circ.: 14,100; Wed. – Publisher, Rick Derksem; Editor, Peter Dyck

Stonewall Argus & Teulon Times, 410 Main St., PO Box 190, Stonewall MB R0C 2Z0 – 204/467-2421 – Circ.: 4,689; Mon.

Swan River Star & Times, PO Box 670, Swan River MB R0L 1Z0 – 204/734-3858; Fax: 204/734-4935 – Wed. – Manager/Owner, Bob Gilroy

The Pas: Opasquia Times, PO Box 750, The Pas MB R9A 1K8 – 204/623-3435; Fax: 204/623-5601 – Wed., Fri.

Thompson: The Citizen, PO Box 887, Thompson MB R8N 1N8 – 204/677-4534; Fax: 204/677-3681 – Mon., Wed., Fri. – Grant Wright

Thompson Nickel Belt News, PO Box 887, Thompson MB R8N 1N8 – 204/677-4534; Fax: 204/677-3681 – Circ.: 6,921; Mon. – Publisher, Joan Wright

Treherne: The Times, PO Box 50, Treherne MB R0G 2V0 – 204/723-2542 – Mon.

Virden Empire Advance, 300 Nelson St. West, PO Box 250, Virden MB R0M 2C0 – 204/748-3931; Fax: 204/748-1816; Email: empire@mail.techplus.com – Circ.: 2,128; Tues. – Publisher, J.H. McLachlan; Editor, B. Griffith

Westwin: Winnipeg Voxair, CFB Winnipeg, Westwin MB R3J 0T0 – 204/889-3963; Fax: 204/885-4176 – Circ.: 4,000; Every other Wed.; English & French – Editor-in-Chief, Lt.-Col. S. Marcott; Circulation Manager, Maureen Walls

Winkler: The Winkler Times, PO Box 1356, Winkler MB R6W 4B3 – 204/325-4771; Fax: 204/325-5059 – Tue.

Winnipeg: Canadian Publishers, 1465 St. James St., Winnipeg MB R3H 0W9 – 204/949-6100; Fax: 204/949-6122 – Publishers of: The Herald (Tue., circ. 38,579), The Lance (Tue., circ. 49,862), The Metro (Tue., circ. 52,928), The Times (Tue., circ. 33,757)

Winnipeg: The Jewish Post & News, 117 Hutchings St., Winnipeg MB R2X 2V4 – 204/694-3332; Fax: 204/694-3916; Email: jewishpost@pangee.ca; URL: http://www.jewishpost.mb.ca – Circ.: 5,500; Wed.; supplement, Lifestyles (6 times a year; circ. 30,000) – Editor, Matt Bellan; Co-Publisher, Bernie Bellan; Circulation Manager, Bernie Bellan

New Brunswick Daily Newspapers

CARAQUET:
L'Acadie Nouvelle, 476, boul St-Pierre ouest, Caraquet NB E0B 1K0 – 506/727-4444; Fax: 506/727-4277 – Tirage: 17,761; Matin; français

FREDERICTON:
Daily Gleaner, PO Box 3370, Fredericton NB E3B 5A2 – 506/452-6671; Fax: 506/452-7405 – Circ.: 29,828; Evening, Mon.-Sat. – Publisher, Tom Crowther; Editorial Page Editor, Steven Benteau; Circulation Manager, Robert MacFarlane

MONCTON:
The Times-Transcript, 939 Main St., PO Box 1001, Moncton NB E1C 8P3 – 506/859-4900; Fax: 506/859-4904 – Circ.: 42,234 Mon.-Fri., 55,946 Sat.; Evening – Publisher & General Manager, T.M. Bembridge

SAINT JOHN:
Telegraph-Journal/Times-Globe, 210 Crown St., PO Box 2350, Saint John NB E2L 3V8 – 506/632-8888; Fax: 506/648-2652; Email: tjetg@nbnet.nb.ca; URL: http://www.nubpub.nb.ca – Circ.: 28,000 morning, 28,000 evening; Telegraph-Journal morning; Times-Globe evening – Publisher & Editor, Neil Reynolds

Other Newspapers in New Brunswick

Bathurst: Northern Light, PO Box N, Bathurst NB E2A 3Z3 – 506/546-4491; Fax: 506/546-1491 – Wed., includes Marketplace (Fri.)

Campbellton: L'Aviron, CP 637, Campbellton NB E3N 3H1 – 506/753-7637; Fax: 506/759-7738 – Mercredi; français – Éditrice-deleguée, France Senéchal

Campbellton Tribune, PO Box 486, Campbellton NB E3N 3G9 – 506/753-4413; Fax: 506/759-9595 – Circ.: 8,000; Wed.; English & French – Publisher & Editor, Terrence Raymond; Circulation Manager, Nancy Cook

Edmundston: Le Madawaska, 20 St. François, Edmundston NB E3V 1E3 – 506/735-5575; Fax: 506/735-8086 – Tirage: 7,600; Mercredi; français – Éditeur, J.P. Boucher

Grand Falls: Cataract, PO Box 2756, Grand Falls NB E0J 1M0 – 506/473-3083; Fax: 506/473-3083 – Circ.: 3,084; Wed., English & French

Hartland Observer, 65 Jane St., PO Box 330, Hartland NB E0J 1N0 – 506/375-4458 – Wed.

Miramichi Leader, 65 Jane St., PO Box 500, Miramichi NB E1V 3M6 – 506/622-1600; Fax: 506/622-7422 – Circ.: 7,734; Tue.

Miramichi Weekend, 371 Water St., PO Box 250, Miramichi NB E1N 3A6 – 506/622-1600 – Circ.: 7,989; Fri.

Oromocto Post, 101 Hersey St., Oromocto NB E2V 1J4 – 506/357-9813; Fax: 506/357-6440 – Wed.

Perth: Victoria County Record, PO Box 990, Perth NB E0J 1V0 – 506/273-2285 – Wed.

Richibucto: Pro-Kent, PO Box 280, Richibucto NB E0A 2M0 – 506/523-9148; Fax: 506/523-7556 – Circ.: 11,000; Wed. English & French – Éditeur, Raymond Beaudouin; Rédacteur, Mario Tardif

Sackville Tribune-Post, PO Box 1530, Sackville NB E0A 3C0 – 506/536-2500; Fax: 506/536-4024; Email: sackville.tribune.post@ocna.org – Circ.: 3,800; Wed. – Publisher, Vince Arbing; Editor, Lourdes Ann Richard; Circulation Manager, Mary Estabrooks

St. Croix Courier, Courier Newspapers Ltd., PO Box 250, St. Stephen NB E3L 2X2 – 506/466-3220; Fax: 506/466-9950; Email: stcroixcourier@ocna.org – Circ.: 5,700; Tue; also Courier Weekend – Editor, Laura Harley

Shediac: Le Moniteur Acadien, C.P. 1807, Shediac NB E0A 3G0 – 506/532-6680; Fax: 506/532-6681 – Mercredi; français – Rédacteur en chef, Daniel DeGrâce

Sussex: Kings County Record, Cadogan Publishing Ltd., PO Box 40, Sussex NB E0E 1P0 – 506/433-1070; Fax: 506/432-3532 – Circ.: 5,500; Tue. – Editor, Jamie Roach; Circulation Manager, Teresa Perry

Woodstock: The Bugle, PO Box 130, Woodstock NB E0J 2B0 – 506/328-8863; Fax: 506/328-3208 – Wed.

Newfoundland Daily Newspapers

CORNER BROOK:
The Western Star, Thomson Newspapers Co. Ltd., PO Box 460, Corner Brook NF A2H 6E7 – 709/634-4348; Fax: 709/634-9824 – Circ.: 11,590; Evening, Mon.-Sat. – Publisher, Ian Baird; Editor, Richard Williams

ST JOHN'S:
Telegram, Thomson Newspapers Co. Ltd., Columbus Dr., PO Box 5970, St John's NF A1C 5X7 – 709/364-6300; Fax: 709/364-9333 – Circ.: 40,649 Mon.-Fri., 62,807 Sat., 40,211 Sun.; Evening – Publisher, Miller H. Ayre; Managing Editor, Joe Walsh

Other Newspapers in Newfoundland
Bay Roberts: The Compass, PO Box 530, Bay Roberts NF A0A 1G0 – 709/786-7014; Fax: 709/786-0666 – Circ.: 8,778; Tues. – Editor, Heather May

Channel-Port aux Basques: The Gulf News, PO Box 129, Grand Falls NF A2A 2J4 – 709/722-8500 – Circ.: 3,342; Mon.

Clarenville: The Packet, PO Box 129, Grand Falls NF A2A 2J4 – 709/722-8500 – Circ.: 6,347; Mon.

Corner Brook: Humber Log, PO Box 129, Grand Falls NF A2A 2J4 – 709/722-8500 – Circ.: 3,422; Wed.

Gander: Beacon, PO Box 129, Gander NF A2A 2J4 – 709/722-8500 – Circ.: 6,072; Wed.

Grand Falls: Advertiser, PO Box 129, Grand Falls NF A2A 2J4 – 709/489-2162; Fax: 709/489-4817 – Circ.: 4,309; Wed.

Happy Valley/Goose Bay: The Labradorian, PO Box 39, Stn B, Happy Valley/Goose Bay NF A0P 1E0 – 709/896-3341; Fax: 709/896-8781 – Circ.: 3,500; Mon. – Publisher, Robinson Blackmore; Editor, Bert Pomeroy

Harbour-Breton-Bay d'Espoir: The Coaster, PO Box 129, Grand Falls NF A2A 2J4 – 709/722-8500 – Circ.: 1,822; Thur.

Labrador City: The Aurora, Labrador Mall, 500 Vanier Ave., PO Box 423, Labrador City NF A2V 2K7 – 709/944-2957; Fax: 709/944-2958 – Circ.: 3,600; Mon. – Publisher, Robinson Blackmore; Editor, Gordon Parsons; Circulation Manager, Wilson Hiscock

Lewisporte: The Pilot, PO Box 129, Grand Falls NF A2A 2J4 – 709/722-8500 – Circ.: 4,759; Wed.

Marystowns: Southern Gazette, PO Box 1116, Marystowns NF A0G 2M0 – 709/279-3188 – Tue.

Paradise: The Shoreline News, PO Box 850, Paradise NF A1L 1E2 – 709/834-2169; Fax: 709/834-4364 – Tue.

St. Anthony: The Northern Pen, PO Box 520, St. Anthony NF A0K 4S0 – 709/454-2191; Fax: 709/454-3718 – Wed. – Publisher, Bernard Bromley; Editor, Allan Bock; Circulation, Frances Reardon

St. John's: The Express, PO Box 8660, St. John's NF A1B 3T7 – 709/579-1312 – Wed.

Springdale: The Nor-Wester, PO Box 129, Grand Falls NF A2A 2J4 – 709/722-8500 – Circ.: 933; Wed.

Stephenville: Le Gaboteur, 41, rue Main, Stephenville NF A2N 1H5 – 709/643-9585; Fax: 709/643-9586; Email: gaboteur@atcon.com – Tirage: 1,000; Bi-mensuel; français – Éditeur, Robinson Blackmore; Éditrice, Jacinthe Lafrance

Stephenville: The Georgian, PO Box 129, Grand Falls NF A2A 2J4 – 709/643-4531; Fax: 709/643-5041 – Circ.: 3,016; Tue.

Newspapers in Northwest Territories
Fort Smith: Slave River Journal, PO Box 990, Fort Smith NT X0E 0P0 – 403/872-2734; Fax: 403/872-2754; Email: slaveriver@aol.com; URL: http://www.auroranet.nt.ca.srj – Circ.: 2,193; Tues. – Publisher, Don Jaque; Editor-in-Chief, James Carroll; Circulation Manager, Dinesh Deonarian

Hay River: The Hub, PO Box 1250, Hay River NT X0E 0R0 – 403/874-6577; Fax: 403/874-2679 – Tue. – Publisher & Editor, Chris Brodeur

Inuvik: The Drum, PO Box 2820, Yellowknife NT X1A 2R1 – 403/873-4031 – Circ.: 1,436; Thur.

Iqaluit: Nunatsiaq News, PO Box 8, Iqaluit NT X0A 0H0 – 819/979-5357; Fax: 819/979-4763; Email: nunat@nunanet.com; URL: http://www.nunanet.com/~nunat – Circ.: 6,500; Fri.;

English & Inukitut – Publisher, Steven Roberts; Editor, Todd Phillips; Circulation Manager, Doug Hawey

Yellowknife: L'Aquilon, CP 1325, Yellowknife NT X1A 2N9 – 403/873-6603; Fax: 403/873-2158; Email: aquilon@internorth.com – Vendredi; français

Yellowknife: News/North, PO Box 2820, Yellowknife NT X1A 2R1 – 403/873-8109 – Circ.: 9,581; Mon.

Yellowknifer, 5108 - 50th St., PO Box 2820, Yellowknife NT X1A 2R1 – 403/873-4031 – Circ.: 5,375; Wed., Fri.

Nova Scotia Daily Newspapers

AMHERST:
Daily News, Cumberland Publishing Ltd., PO Box 280, Amherst NS B4H 3Z2 – 902/667-5102; Fax: 902/667-0419 – Circ.: 4,071 Mon.-Fri., 6,225 Sat.; Morning, Mon.-Sat. – President & Publisher, Earl J. Gouchie; Editor, John Conrad

HALIFAX:
The Chronicle-Herald and The Mail-Star, 1650 Argyle St., Halifax NS B3J 2T2 – 902/426-2811; Fax: 902/426-3014; Email: sarahd@herald.ns.ca; URL: http://www.herald.ns.ca – Circ.: 96,744 morning, 45,817 evening; The Chronicle-Herald morning, The Mail-Star evening – Publisher, G.W. Dennis; Managing Editor, Jane Purves; Circulation Manager, Scott Bayle

The Daily News, NewCap Inc., PO Box 8330, Stn A, Halifax NS B3K 5M1 – 902/465-1222; Fax: 902/468-2645 news, 468-3609 adv.; Email: dnews@fox.nstn.ns.ca – Circ.: 26,400 Mon.-Sat., 43,200 Sun.; Morning; also Sunday Daily News (Circ. 45,408) – Publisher, Mark Richardson; Editor-in-Chief, Douglas MacKay

NEW GLASGOW:
The Evening News, Thomson Newspapers Co. Ltd., 352 East River Rd., New Glasgow NS B2H 5E2 – 902/752-3000; Fax: 902/752-1945 – Circ.: 10,695; Evening – Publisher & General Manager, Lee Ballantyne; Managing Editor, Doug MacNeil

SYDNEY:
Cape Breton Post, Thomson Newspapers Co. Ltd., 255 George St., PO Box 1500, Sydney NS B1P 6K6 – 902/564-5451; Fax: 902/562-7077 – Circ.: 31,398; Morning – Publisher & General Manager, Peter Kapyrka; Managing Editor, Fred Jackson

TRURO:
The Daily News, Thomson Newspapers Co. Ltd., 6 Louise St., PO Box 220, Truro NS B2N 5C3 – 902/893-9405; Fax: 902/893-0518 – Circ.: 8,809 Mon.-Fri., 10,498 Sat.; Evening, Sat. morning – Publisher, Leith Orr; Managing Editor, Bill McGuire

Other Newspapers in Nova Scotia
Amherst: The Citizen, PO Box 280, Amherst NS B4H 3Z2 – 902/667-5116; Fax: 902/667-0419 – Sat.

Annapolis: The Royal Spectator, PO Box 250, Bridgetown NS B0S 1C0 – 902/665-4441; Fax: 902/665-4014 – Tue.

Antigonish: The Casket, PO Box 1300, Antigonish NS B2G 2L6 – 902/863-4370; Fax: 902/863-5808 – Tue.

Berwick Register, PO Box 640, Berwick NS B0P 1E0 – 902/538-3189; Fax: 902/538-8583 – Wed.

Bible HIll: The Light, 228 Main St., Bible HIll NS B2N 4H2 – 902/895-7946; Fax: 902/893-1427 – Monthly; also TV This Week (Wed.)

Bridgetown Monitor, PO Box 250, Bridgetown NS B0S 1C0 – 902/665-4441; Fax: 902/665-4014 – Circ.: 1,445; Tue.; also Mirror-Examiner (Wed.)

Bridgewater: Progress Enterprise, 353 York St., Bridgewater NS B4V 3K2 – 902/543-2457; Fax: 902/543-2228; Email: lighthse@fox.nstn.ca – Circ.: 4,500; Wed.; also South Shore Living (Wed.) & Lighhouse Log (Mon.)

Dartmouth: Metro Weekly & Telecaster, 565 Windmill Rd., Dartmouth NS B3B 1B4 – 902/468-6688; Fax: 902/468-8838 – Circ.: 16,000; Thur. – Publisher, R.B. Cameron; Editor-in-Chief, Jeremy Akerman

Digby Courier, PO Box 670, Digby NS B0V 1A0 – 902/245-4715; Fax: 902/245-4715 – Wed. – Editor, John DeMings

Enfield: The Laker, PO Box 98, Enfield NS B0N 1G2 – 902/883-3181 – Tue.

Enfield: The Weekly Press, 287 Hwy. 2, Enfield NS B2T 1C9 – 902/883-3181; Fax: 902/420-0524 – Circ.: 2,620; Wed.

Glace Bay: The Coastal Courier, 15 MacLean St., PO Box 113, Glace Bay NS B1A 5V1 – 902/849-1830 – Circ.: 3,000; Wed. – Publisher, Ken Cotter

Greenwood: The Aurora, CFB Greenwood, PO Box 99, Greenwood NS B0P 1N0 – 902/765-3391 – Mon.; English & French

Halifax: Maritime Command Trident, Trident Military Newspaper, PO Box 3308, Halifax NS B3J 3J1 – 902/427-0550, ext.2347; Fax: 902/427-2539 – Circ.: 10,500; Every other Thur; English & French – Publisher, Sheila Fournier; Editor, Dan Bedell; Circulation Manager, Kim Cameron

Inverness: The Oran, PO Box 100, Inverness NS B0E 1N0 – 902/258-2253 – Wed.

Kentville: The Advertiser, PO Box 430, Kentville NS B4N 3X4 – 902/681-2121; Fax: 902/681-0830 – Tue., Fri; also Kentville Teleguide (Wed.)

Liverpool Advance, PO Box 10, Liverpool NS B0T 1K0 – 902/354-3441; Fax: 902/354-2455 – Wed.

Northside Tribune, 205 Commercial St., PO Box 144, North Sydney NS B2A 1B7 – 902/794-8253; Fax: 902/794-2104; Email: North Sydney – Wed.

Oxford Journal, PO Box 10, Oxford NS B0M 1P0 – 902/447-2051 – Wed.

Pictou Advocate, PO Box 1000, Pictou NS B0K 1H0 – 902/485-8014; Fax: 902/752-4816 – Circ.: 6,000; Wed. – Publisher, George Bellefontaine; Editor, Gordon Stiles; General Manager, Andrew Robertson

Port Hawkesbury: The Reporter, PO Box 3300, Port Hawkesbury NS B0E 2V0 – 902/625-3300; Fax: 902/625-2369 – Circ.: 4,525; Tue.

Port Hawkesbury: The Scotia Sun, PO Box 599, Port Hawkesbury NS B0E 2V0 – 902/625-1900 – Thur.

Shearwater: The Warrior, PO Box 190, Shearwater NS B0J 3A0 – 902/460-1013; Fax: 902/460-1796 – Circ.: 6,500; Bi-weekly; English & French – Managing Editor, Jon Houston

Sheet Harbour: The Eastern Shore Sandpiper, PO Box 136, Sheet Harbour NS B0J 3B0 – 902/885-2146; Fax: 902/885-3424 – Circ.: 13,500; Monthly – Co-Publisher, Heather Robinson; Co-Publisher, James Robinson

Shelburne: The Coast Guard, PO Box 100, Shelburne NS B0T 1W0 – 902/875-3244; Fax: 902/875-3545 – Tue.

Springhill & Parrsboro Record, PO Box 670, Springhill NS B0M 1X0 – 902/597-3731; Fax: 902/667-1402 – Wed.

Truro: The Weekly Record, 615 Prince St., Truro NS B2N 1G2 – 902/895-7946 – Circ.: 4,978; Wed.

Windsor: Hants Journal, PO Box 550, Windsor NS B0N 2T0 – 902/798-8371; Fax: 902/798-5451 – Wed.

Yarmouth: Le Courrier de la Nouvelle-Ecosse, 4 Alma St., PO Box 402, Yarmouth NS B5A 4B3 – 902/742-9119; Fax: 902/742-9110 – Vendredi; français

Yarmouth: The Vanguard, PO Box 128, Yarmouth NS B5A 4B1 – 902/742-7111; Fax: 902/742-2311 – Tue., Fri; also Telecaster (Tue.)

Ontario Daily Newspapers

BARRIE:
Barrie Examiner, Hollinger Inc., 16 Bayfield St., Barrie ON L4M 4T6 – 705/726-6537; Fax: 705/726-7245 – Circ.: 44,353; Evening – Publisher, Ron Laurin

BELLEVILLE:
The Intelligencer, 45 Bridge St. East, PO Box 5600, Belleville ON K8N 5C7 – 613/962-9171; Fax: 613/962-9652; Email: intel@intranet.ca.on – Circ.: 18,670 Mon.-Sat., 16,998 Sun.; Afternoon – Publisher & General Manager, Peter E. Leichnitz; Managing Editor, Nick Palmer; Circulation Manager, Ron Prins

BRANTFORD:
The Expositor, Southam Inc., 53 Dalhousie St., Brantford ON N3T 5S8 – 519/756-2020; Fax: 519/756-9481 – Circ.: 26,593; Morning – Publisher, William R. Findlay; Managing Editor, David Schultz; Reader Sales Manager, Susan Azzopardi

BROCKVILLE:
Recorder and Times, 23 King St. West, PO Box 10, Brockville ON K6V 5T8 – 613/342-4441; Fax: 613/342-4456 – Circ.: 17,001, 18,300 Fri.; Evening – Co-Publisher, Hunter S. Grant; Co-Publisher & Editor, Perry S. Beverley, 613/342-4443

CAMBRIDGE:
Cambridge Reporter, Hollinger Corp., 26 Ainslie St. South, Cambridge ON N1R 3K1 – 519/621-3810; Fax: 519/621-8239 – Circ.: 10,070; Evening – Publisher, Verne Shaull; Managing Editor, Christina Jonas; Circulation Manager, Sue Wood

CHATHAM:
Chatham Daily News, Thomson Newspapers Co. Ltd., 45 Fourth St., PO Box 2007, Chatham ON N7M 2G4 – 519/354-2000; Fax: 519/436-0949 – Circ.: 16,273; Evening – Publisher & General Manager, John Cheek; Managing Editor, Jim Blake

COBOURG:
Daily Star, Northumberland Publishers Ltd., 415 King St. West, PO Box 400, Cobourg ON K9A 4L1 – 905/372-0131; Fax: 905/372-4966 – Circ.: 5,813; Evening; also Guide (evening; circ. 3,345) – Publisher, C. Burke; Editor, J.T. Grossmith

CORNWALL:
Standard-Freeholder, 44 Pitt St., Cornwall ON K6J 3P3 – 613/933-3160; Fax: 613/933-7521 – Circ.: 18,497; Morning – Publisher, Milton Ellis; Managing Editor, Craig Elson; Circulation Manager, Arnold Jesmer

FORT FRANCES:
Daily Bulletin, PO Box 339, Fort Frances ON P9A 3M7 – 807/274-5373; Fax: 807/274-7286 – Circ.: 2,778; Afternoon – Publisher, J.R. Cumming; Editor, Mike Behan

GUELPH:
The Guelph Mercury, Hollinger Inc., 8-14 Macdonell St., PO Box 3604, Guelph ON N1H 6P7 – 519/822-4310; Fax: 519/767-1681 – Circ.: 16,655 Mon.-Sat., 15,521 Sun.; Evening – Publisher & General Manager, Stephen Rhodes; Editor, Ed Cassavoy

HAMILTON:
The Spectator, Southam Inc., 44 Frid St., Hamilton ON L8N 3G3 – 905/526-3333; Fax: 905/522-1696; Toronto line: 416/825-0111; Telex: 06-18390; URL: http://www.southam.com/hamiltonspector – Circ.: 110,611, 132,091 Sat.; Evening – Publisher, Patrick J. Collins; Acting Editor, Rob Austin, 905/526-3203; Reader Sales & Serv. Dir., Terry Willows

KENORA:
Daily Miner & News, Bowes Publishers Ltd., 33 Main St. South, PO Box 1620, Kenora ON P9N 3X7 – 807/468-5555; Fax: 807/468-4318; Email: kendmn@awinc.com – Circ.: 4,792; Evening – Publisher, Mitch Wolfe; Circulation Manager, Bob Stewart

KINGSTON:
The Kingston Whig-Standard, 306 King St. East, Kingston ON K7L 4Z7 – 613/544-5000; Fax: 613/544-6994 – Circ.: 28,127 Mon.-Fri., 36,176 Sat.; Morning & evening – Publisher, Bill Peterson; Editor, Lynn Messerschmidt

KIRKLAND LAKE:
Northern Daily News, Thomson Newspapers Co. Ltd., 8 Duncan Ave., Kirkland Lake ON P2N 3L4 – 705/567-5321; Fax: 705/567-6162 – Circ.: 5,319; Evening – Publisher & Manager, Syl Belisle; Editor, Tim Kelly

KITCHENER:
Kitchener-Waterloo Record, Southam Inc., 225 Fairway Rd. South, Kitchener ON N2G 4E5 – 519/894-2231; Fax: 519/894-3912; Toronto line: 416/826-9182 – Circ.: 74,000; Afternoon, 6 days a week – Publisher, Wayne MacDonald; Editor, Carolyne Rittinger

LINDSAY:
The Lindsay Daily Post, Hollinger Inc., 15 William St. North, Lindsay ON K9V 3Z8 – 705/324-2114; Fax: 705/324-0174 – Circ.: 8,066; Morning – Publisher & General Manger, F.M. (Mac) Dundas; Editor, Joe Hornyak

LONDON:
The London Free Press, 369 York St., PO Box 2280, London ON N6A 4G1 – 519/679-1111; Fax: 519/667-4523; Email: letters@lfpress.com; URL: http://www.lfpress.com – Circ.: 108,501 Mon.-Fri., 137,725 Sat.; Morning – President & Publisher, Sandy Green; Editor, Phil McLeod; Customer Service Manager, Michelle Grantham

NIAGARA FALLS:
Review, Hollinger Inc., 4801 Valley Way, PO Box 270, Niagara Falls ON L2E 6T6 – 905/358-5711; Fax: 905/356-0785 – Circ.: 46,500; Evening – Publisher, John VanKooten; Editor, Michael Brown

NORTH BAY:
North Bay Nugget, 259 Worthington St. West, PO Box 570, North Bay ON P1B 8J6 – 705/472-3200; Fax: 705/472-5128 – Circ.: 22,500; Evening, Mon.-Fri.; morning, Sat. – Publisher, Robert Hull; Editor, David McLennan; Circulation Manager, Ron Bean

ORILLIA:
Packet and Times, Hollinger Inc., 31 Colborne St. East, Orillia ON L3V 1T4 – 705/325-1355; Fax: 705/325-7691 – Circ.: 9,628; Evening – General Manager, Bruce MacIntyre; Managing Editor, Jeff Day

OTTAWA:
Le Droit, #222, 47 Clarence St., CP 8860, Succ T, Ottawa ON K1G 3J9 – 613/560-2747; Fax: 613/560-2572 – Tirage: 35,020 Lundi.-Ven., 42,490 Samedi.; Matin; français – Éditeur, Pierre Bergeron; Rédacteur, Claude Beauregard

The Ottawa Citizen, Southam Inc., 1101 Baxter Rd., PO Box 5020, Ottawa ON K2C 3M4 – 613/829-9100; Fax: 613/829-5032 – Circ.: 152,751 Mon.-Fri., 210,256 Sat., 139,745 Sun.; All day – Publisher, Russ Mills; Editor, James Travers; Circulation Manager, Harold Lundy

Ottawa Sun and Sunday Sun, 380 Hunt Club Rd., PO Box 9729, Stn T, Ottawa ON K1G 5H7 – 613/739-7000; Fax: 613/739-8043 – Circ.: 51,035 Mon.-Fri., 60,063 Sun.; Morning – Publisher, John Paton

OWEN SOUND:
Sun Times, Southam Inc., 290 - 9th St. East, PO Box 200, Owen Sound ON N4K 5P2 – 519/376-2250; Fax: 519/376-7190 – Circ.: 22,000; Evening – Publisher, Clyde Wicks; Editor, Jim Merriam; Circulation Manager, Dan Patterson

PEMBROKE:
Daily News, Runge Newspapers, Inc., 86 Pembroke St. West, PO Box 10, Pembroke ON K8A 6X1 – 613/735-3141; Fax: 613/732-7214 – Morning – General Manager, Jim Badgley

Pembroke Observer, Hollinger Inc., 186 Alexander St., Pembroke ON K8A 4L9 – 613/732-3691; Fax: 613/732-2645 – Circ.: 8,000; Evening – Publisher, Lois Hornby; Editor, Peter Lapinskie; Circulation Manager, David Bell

PETERBOROUGH:
Examiner, Hollinger Inc., 400 Water St., PO Box 3890, Peterborough ON K9J 8L4 – 705/745-4641; Fax: 705/743-4581 – Circ.: 25,453 Mon.-Sat., 23,367 Sun.; Morning – Publisher & General Manager, Mac Dundas; Managing Editor, Ed Arnold

ST. CATHARINES:
The St. Catharines Standard, 17 Queen St., St. Catharines ON L2R 5G5 – 905/684-7251; Fax: 905/684-8011 – Circ.: 38,720 Mon.-Fri., 47,047 Sat.; Afternoon – Publisher, J.A. Lehnen

ST. THOMAS:
Times-Journal, Bowes Publishers Ltd., 16 Hincks St., St. Thomas ON N5R 5Z2 – 519/631-2790; Fax: 519/631-5653 – Circ.: 9,154; Evening – Publisher, Terry Carroll; Managing Editor, Ross Porter

SARNIA:
Observer, Thomson Newspapers Co. Ltd., 140 South Front St., PO Box 3009, Sarnia ON N7T 7M8 – 519/344-3641; Fax: 519/332-2951 – Circ.: 24,000; Evening – Publisher, Daryl Smith; Circulation Manager, Terry Pimlatt

SAULT STE. MARIE:
Star, Southam Inc., 145 Old Garden Rd., PO Box 460, Sault Ste. Marie ON P6A 5M5 – 705/759-3030; Fax: 705/942-8690, 759-0102 – Circ.: 24,500, Mon. - Sat.; Evening – Publisher, Robert Richardson; Editor-in-Chief, John Halucha; Circulation Manager, Lou Maulucci

SIMCOE:
Reformer, Southwestern Ontario Publishing Ltd., 105 Donly Dr. South, PO Box 370, Simcoe ON N3Y 4L2 – 519/426-5710; Fax: 519/426-9255 – Circ.: 9,584; Evening – Publisher, Michael Fredericks; Managing Editor, Kim Novak

STRATFORD:
The Beacon-Herald, 108 Ontario St., PO Box 430, Stratford ON N5A 6T6 – 519/271-2220; Fax: 519/271-1026 – Circ.: 13,283; Evening – Co-Publisher, Charles W. Dingman; Co-Publisher & Editor, Stanford H. Dingman

SUDBURY:
The Sudbury Star, Thomson Newspapers Co. Ltd., 33 MacKenzie St., Sudbury ON P3C 4Y1 – 705/674-5271; Fax: 705/674-0624; Email: ss-publisher@cw-connect.ca; URL: http://sudbury.siteseet.ca –

Circ.: 26,333 Mon.-Sat., 23,960 Sun.; Morning – Publisher, Ken Sequin; Editor, Roger Cazabon; Circulation Manager, Dave Paquette

THUNDER BAY:
The Chronicle-Journal, Thomson Newspapers Co. Ltd., 75 South Cumberland St., Thunder Bay ON P7B 1A3 – 807/343-6200; Fax: 807/345-5991; Email: cj-editorial@cwconnect.ca; URL: http://netreader.com/tbay/index2.html – Circ.: 7,058 morning, 28,306 evening, 40,918 Sat., 33,843 Sun. – Publisher & General Manager, Colin Bruce; Editor, Peter Haggert; Circulation Manager, Mike Keating

TIMMINS:
Daily Press, Thomson Newspapers Co. Ltd., 187 Cedar St. South, Timmins ON P4N 2G9 – 705/268-5050; Fax: 705/268-7373 – Circ.: 12,000; Evening – Publisher, John A. Farrington; Editor, David McGee

TORONTO:
Daily Racing Form, 47 Voyageur Ct. North, Etobicoke ON M9W 4Y6 – 416/798-1911; Fax: 416/798-1921 – Circ.: 3,570 Mon., 5,529 Tue.-Fri., 9,558 Sat., 8,465 Sun.; Morning – Editor, Bill Tallon

The Financial Post, 333 King St. East, Toronto ON M5A 4N2 – 416/350-6300; Fax: 416/350-6301; Email: letters@finpost.com; URL: http://www.canoe.ca/FP – Circ.: 78,463 Tue.-Fri., 170,380 Sat.; Morning – Publisher, Doug Knight, 416/350-6161; Editor, Diane Francis, 416/350-6350

The Globe and Mail, 444 Front St. West, Toronto ON M5V 2S9 – 416/585-5000; Fax: 416/585-5085; URL: http://www.globeandmail.ca/ – Circ.: 313,747; Morning, Mon. to Sat.; also Report on Business & Broadcast Week – Publisher & CEO, Roger P. Parkinson; Editor-in-chief, William Thorsell

The Toronto Star, One Yonge St., Toronto ON M5E 1E6 – 416/367-2000; Fax: 416/869-4328 editorial, 869-4155 advtg.; Email: newsroom@webramp.net; URL: http://www.t-o.com – Circ.: 463,218 Mon.-Fri., 712,873 Sat., 469,738 Sun.; Morning, 2 editions – Publisher, John Honderich

The Toronto Sun, The Toronto Sun Publishing Corp., 333 King St. East, Toronto ON M5A 3X5 – 416/947-2222; Fax: 416/947-1664; Email: sun@inforamp.net – Circ.: 247,187, daily; 430,140, Sunday; Morning – Publisher, Hartley Steward; Executive Editor, Peter O'Sullivan; Manager, News Research, Julie Kirsh, 416/947-2257

WELLAND:
Welland-Port Colborne Tribune, Hollinger Inc., 228 East Main St., Welland ON L3B 5P5 – 905/732-2411; Fax: 905/732-4883; Email: tribune@iaw.on.ca – Circ.: 18,000; Morning, Mon. to Sat. – Publisher, David A. Beattie; Managing Editor, Gary W. Manning; Circulation Manager, Karin Vanderzee

WINDSOR:
The Windsor Star, Southam Inc., 167 Ferry St., Windsor ON N9A 4M5 – 519/255-5711; Fax: 519/255-5778 – Circ.: 82,077 Mon.-Fri., 94,849 Sat.; Evening – Publisher, James Bruce

WOODSTOCK:
Woodstock-Ingersoll Daily Sentinel Review, Southwestern Ontario Publishing Ltd., 16 Brock St., PO Box 1000, Woodstock ON N4S 8A5 – 519/537-2341; Fax: 519/537-3049 – Circ.: 10,049; Evening; supplement - CoverStory (weekly, circ. 15,200) – Publisher, Pat Logan; City Editor, Alison Downie; Circulation Manager, Andy Clifford

Other Newspapers in Ontario

Ajax/Pickering News Advertiser, Metroland Printing Publishing & Distribution, 130 Commercial Ave., Ajax ON L1S 2H5 – 905/683-5110; Fax: 905/683-7363 – Circ.: 39,555; Wed., Fri., Sun. - Tim Whittaker

Alexandria: Glengarry News, PO Box 10, Alexandria ON K0C 1A0 – 613/525-2020; Fax: 613/525-3824 – Wed.

Alliston Herald, Metroland Printing Publishing & Distribution, 169 Dufferin St. South, Unit 22, Alliston ON L9R 1E6 – 705/435-6228; Fax: 705/435-3342 – Circ.: 4,709; Wed; also The Herald Courier (Sat., circ. 18,791) – Publisher, Joe Anderson

Almonte Gazette, PO Box 130, Almonte ON K0A 1A0 – 613/256-1311; Fax: 613/256-5168 – Wed.

Amherstburg Echo Community News, 238 Dalhousie St., Amherstburg ON N9V 1W4 – 519/736-2147; Fax: 519/736-8384 – Circ.: 2,611; Wed.

Ancaster News, 311 Wilson St. East, Ancaster ON L9G 2B8 – 905/628-6313; Fax: 905/648-7458 – Circ.: 8,172; Wed.

Angus Star, 3 Caroline St. West, PO Box 70, Creemore ON L0M 1G0 – Wed.; also publishes: Clearview Star (Wed.), Elmvale Lance (Wed.), & Wasaga Star Times (Wed.)

Arnprior Chronicle Guide, 116 John St. North, Arnprior ON K7S 2N6 – 613/623-6571; Fax: 613/623-7518 – Circ.: 4,783; Wed.; also The Arnprior Weekend Chronicle (circ. 13,000) – Publisher, Marjory McBride; News Editor, Rita Racicot; Circulation Manager, Beverly Quattrocchi

Arnprior News, 98 John St. North, Arnprior ON K7S 2N3 – 613/623-5064 – Sun.

Arthur Enterprise-News, 106 Charles St. East, PO Box 310, Arthur ON N0G 1A0 – 519/848-2410; Fax: 519/848-3665 – Circ.: 1,443; Wed. – Publisher, Clive Williams; Editor, Mike Robinson

Astra: Contact, 8 Wing, PO Box 40, Astra ON K0K 1B0 – 613/965-7248; Fax: 613/965-7490 – Circ.: 3,500; Wed.; English & French – Editor, Capt. Charlene Fawcett; Circulation Manager, Keith Cleaton

Atikokan Progress, PO Box 220, Atikokan ON P0T 1C0 – 807/597-2731; Fax: 807/597-6103 – Circ.: 1,769; Mon. – Publisher, Eve Shine; Editor, Michael P. McKinnon; Circulation Manager, Marie Cornell

Aurora Weekly, 237 Romina Dr., Unit 2, Concord ON L4K 4V3 – 905/660-9556 – Wed.

Aurora: Newmarket/Aurora Era Banner, Metroland Printing Publishing & Distribution, 580 Steven Ct., Bldg. B, PO Box 236, Aurora ON L3Y 4X1 – 905/493-1300; Fax: 905/853-4629 – Wed., Fri., Sun. – Publisher, Bruce Annan

Aylmer Express, 390 Talbot St. East, PO Box 160, Aylmer ON N5H 2R9 – 519/773-3126; Fax: 519/773-3147 – Wed.

Ayr News, 40 Piper St., Ayr ON N0B 1E0 – 519/632-7432; Fax: 519/632-7743 – Circ.: 4,350; Wed. – Publisher, James W. Schmidt; Editor, John P. Schmidt

Bancroft Times, 93 Hastings St. North, Bancroft ON K0L 1C0 – 613/332-2300 – Wed.

Barrie Advance, Metroland Printing Publishing & Distribution, 21 Patterson Rd., Barrie ON L4N 7W6 – 705/726-0573; Fax: 705/726-9350 – Circ.: 28,000 Fri., 45,500 Sat,; Wed., Fri., Sun. – Publisher, Joe Anderson

Barrie: Super Shopper, Buy, Trade & Sell, 124 Brock St., Barrie ON L4N 2M2 – 705/726-6015; Fax: 705/726-6015; Email: tyler@bconnex.net – Circ.: 15,000; Thur.

Barry's Bay This Week, PO Box 220, Barry's Bay ON K0J 1B0 – 613/756-2944; Fax: 613/756-2994 – Circ.: 5,500; Tue. – Publisher, Phil Conway; Editor, Helen Conway

Beamsville: Lincoln Post Express, 4309 Central Ave., PO Box 400, Beamsville ON L0R 1B0 – 905/563-5393; Fax: 905/563-7977 – Wed.

Beaverton: Brock Citizen, 384 Simcoe St., PO Box 10, Beaverton ON L0K 1A0 – 705/426-7443; Fax: 705/426-5953 – Circ.: 2,800; Tue. – Publisher, Mark Skelton; Editor, Louise Middleton

Beeton Record Sentinel, PO Box 310, Beeton, ON L0G 1A0 – 905/729-2287 – Circ.: 1,450; Wed.

Beeton: Schomberg Record Sentinel, PO Box 310, Beeton ON L0G 1A0 – 905/939-5008 – Wed.

Belle River: North Essex News, c/o Phoenix Media Group Inc., PO Box 429, Belle River ON N0R 1A0 – 519/728-1082; Fax: 519/728-4551 – Circ.: 2,500; Wed. – Editor, Karen Fallon

Belleville Shopper's Market, 366 North Front St., Belleville ON K8P 5E6 – 613/962-3422 – Sun.

Blenheim News-Tribune, 62 Talbot St. West, PO Box 160, Blenheim ON N0P 1A0 – 519/676-3321; Fax: 519/676-5454 – Wed.

Blyth: The Citizen, 136 Queen St., PO Box 429, Blyth ON N0M 1H0 – 519/523-4792; Fax: 519/523-9140 – Circ.: 2,191; Wed. – Publishers, Keith Roulston; Editor, Bonnie Grupp; Circulation Manager, Jill Roulston

Bobcaygeon Independent, 49 Main St., PO Box 220, Bobcaygeon ON K0M 1A0 – 705/738-2212; Fax: 705/738-4332 – Wed.

Bolton Enterprise, 2 Marconi Ct., Unit 13, Bolton ON L7E 1E5 – 905/857-3433; Fax: 905/857-5002 – Circ.: 10,000; Sun. – Publisher, Bill Anderson; Editor, Bill Whitbread

Borden: The Borden Citizen, CFB Borden, Borden ON L0M 1C0 – 705/423-2567 – Wed., English & French

Bothwell Times, PO Box 40, Bothwell ON N0P 1C0 – 519/692-3105 – Wed.

Bracebridge Examiner, 16 Manitoba St., PO Box 1049, Bracebridge ON P0B 1C0 – 705/645-1718 – Wed.

Bracebridge: The Muskokan, 16 Manitoba St., PO Box 1049, Bracebridge ON P1L 1S1 – 705/645-8771 – Thur. – Editor, Susan Pryle

Bracebridge: Muskoka Advance, #103, 175 Manitoba St., PO Box 1600, Bracebridge ON P1L 1V6 – 705/645-4463 – Sun.

Bracebridge: Muskoka Sun, PO Box 1600, Bracebridge ON P1L 1V6 – 705/645-4463 – Thur.

Bradford West Gwillimbury Times, 32 Holland St. East, PO Box 1570, Bradford ON L3Z 2B8 – 905/775-4471; Fax: 905/775-4489; Email: rfonger@times.net – Circ.: 7,800; Wed. – Publisher, Richard Fonger; Editor, Miriam King

Brampton Guardian, Metroland Printing Publishing & Distribution, 685 Queen St. West, RR#2, Brampton ON L6V 1A1 – 905/454-4344; Fax: 905/454-4385 – Circ.: 60,000; Wed., Fri., Sun. – Publisher, Ken Nugent; Editor-in-Chief, Lorne Drury

Brampton Pennysaver, 56 Bramsteele Rd., Unit 1, Brampton ON L6W 3M7 – 905/454-0854 – Sun.; also publish: Caledon Pennysaver, Malton Pennysaver, Mississauga Pennysaver, & Rexdale Pennysaver

Brantford/Tekawennake-6 Nations-New Credit Reporter, PO Box 130, Ohsweken ON N0A 1M0 – 519/753-0077; Fax: 519/753-0011 – Wed.

Brantford Pennysaver, 61 Dalkeith Dr., Unit 5, Brantford ON N3P 1M1 – 519/756-0076 – Sat.

Brant News, #301-446 Grey St., Brantford ON N3S 7L6 – 519/759-5550; Fax: 519/759-8425 – Circ.: 35,000; Tue. – Publisher, Dianne Geerlinks; Editor, Sue Gage

Brighton Independent, 1 Young St., PO Box 1030, Brighton ON K0K 1H0 – 613/475-0255; Fax: 613/475-4546 – Tue., also Brighton Independent East Northumberland (Tue.)

Burford Times, 115 King St., Burford ON N0E 1A0 – 519/449-5478; Fax: 519/449-5478 – Circ.: 2,000; Wed. – Publisher & Editor, Bill Johnston

Burks Falls: Almaguin News, PO Box 518, Burks Falls ON P0A 1C0 – 705/382-3843; Fax: 705/382-3440; Email: aldennis@onlink.com – Circ.: 7,200; Wed. – Publisher, Peter Barr; Editor, Allan Dennis

Burks Falls Marketplace, 183 Ontario St., PO Box 518, Burks Falls ON P0A 1C0 – 705/382-3842 – Mon.

Burlington Post, 2317 Fairview St., Burlington ON L7R 2E3 – 905/632-4444; Fax: 905/632-6604 – Wed., Fri., Sun. – Publisher, Ian Oliver

Canadian Almanac & Directory 1997

NEWSPAPERS

Caledon Citizen, 25 Queen St. North, Bolton ON L7E 1C1 – 905/857-6626; Fax: 905/857-6363 – Circ.: 7,800; Wed. – Publisher, Bruce Haire; Editor, Mark Pavilona

Caledonia: Grand River Sachem, PO Box 160, Caledonia ON N0A 1A0 – 905/765-4441; Fax: 905/765-3651; Email: grand.river.sachem@ocna.org – Circ.: 2,400; Thur. – Publisher, Neil Dring; Editor, Kim Huson; Circulation Manager, Lynda Dunn

Cambridge Times, 240 Holiday Inn Dr., Units B & C, Cambridge ON N3C 3X4 – 519/651-2390 – Circ.: 31,567; Wed., Sat.

Campbellford Herald, PO Box 400, Cobourg ON K9A 4L1 – 905/372-0131 – Tue.

Campbellville: Nassagaweya News & Rockwood Area, PO Box 478, Campbellville ON L0P 1B0 – Monthly

Cardiff Courier, PO Box 99, Cardiff ON K0L 1M0 – 613/332-3889 – Circ.: 1,000; Every other Tue.

Carleton Place: The Canadian, PO Box 430, Carleton Place ON K7C 3P5 – 613/257-1303; Fax: 613/257-7373 – Wed.

Cayuga: The Haldimand Press, PO Box 100, Cayuga ON N0A 1E0 – 905/772-3852; Fax: 905/772-5465 – Circ.: 4,313; Wed.

Chapleau Sentinel, PO Box 158, Chapleau ON P0M 1K0 – 705/864-0640; Fax: 705/864-2317 – Circ.: 1,400; Weds.; French & English – Editor, Rene C. Decosse

Chatham Pennysaver, 930 Richmond St., Unit 7, Chatham ON N7M 5L1 – 519/351-4362 – Sun.

Chatham Shopper, 55 St. Clair St., PO Box 758, Chatham ON N7M 5L1 – 519/351-8360 – Circ.: 24,000; Wed.

Chatham This Week, 930 Richmond St., Unit 7, Chatham ON N7M 5J5 – 519/351-7331 – Wed.

Chesterville Record, PO Box 368, Chesterville ON K0C 1H0 – 613/448-2321; Fax: 613/448-3260 – Wed.

Clarington/Courtice Independent, PO Box 190, Bowmanville ON L1C 3K9 – 905/623-3303; Fax: 905/623-6161; Email: statesman@ocna.org – Circ.: 18,865; Wed.; also Canadian Statesman (Wed., circ. 6,256) – Publisher, John M. James; Editor, Peter Parrett; Circulation Manager, Angela Luscher

Clinton News-Record, 53 Albert St., PO Box 39, Clinton ON N0M 1L0 – 519/482-3443; Fax: 519/482-7341 – Wed.

Cobden Sun, 36 Crawford St., PO Box 100, Cobden ON K0J 1K0 – 613/646-2380; Fax: 613/628-3291 – Wed.

Cobourg: Northumberland News, Metroland Printing, Publishing & Distributing Ltd., 180 Tremaine St., PO Box 967, Cobourg ON K9A 2Z3 – 905/373-7355 – Sun. – Publisher, Tim Whittaker

Cochrane Northland Post, PO Box 10, Cochrane ON P0L 1C0 – 705/272-4363; Fax: 705/272-2935 – Wed.

Colborne Chronicle, 11 King St. East, PO Box 208, Colborne ON K0K 1S0 – 905/355-2843; Fax: 905/355-1639 – Circ.: 1,760; Wed. – Publisher, Cheryl McMenemy; Editor, Eileen Argyris

Collingwood Connection, Metroland Printing, Publishing & Distributing Ltd., 25 Second St., Collingwood ON L9Y 1E4 – 705/444-1875 – Wed., Sun. – Joe Anderson

Collingwood Enterprise-Bulletin, 77 Marie St., PO Box 98, Collingwood ON L9Y 3Z4 – 705/445-4611; Fax: 705/444-6477; Email: publisher@eb.georgian.net; URL: http://www.eb.georgian.net – Circ.: 5,600; Wed.; also Huron Saver (Sat., circ. 12,900) – Publisher, Michael Walsh; Editor, Ian Chadwick; Circulation Manager, Linda McCoy

Cornwall: Le Journal, 113 Montréal Rd., Cornwall ON K6H 1B2 – 613/938-1433; Fax: 613/938-2798 – Tirage: 2,300; Jeudi; français – President, Roger Duplantie

Cornwall: Seaway News, 329 - 2nd St. West, Cornwall ON K6J 1G8 – 613/933-0014; Fax: 613/933-0024 – Circ.: 31,499; Mon. – Publisher & Editor, R.N. Aubry

Courtice/Bowmanville News, 2651 Trulls Rd. South, Unit 3, Courtice ON L1E 2N3 – 905/433-1629, 5546; Fax: 905/433-7050 – Circ.: 30,000; Wed. – Publisher, Sandra McDowell; Editor, Greg McDowell; Circulation Manager, Dave Cole

Deep River: North Renfrew Times, 25A Champlain St., PO Box 310, Deep River ON K0J 1P0 – 613/584-4161 – Wed.

Delhi News-Record, 222 Argyle St., Delhi ON N4B 2Y1 – 519/582-2510; Fax: 519/582-4040 – Circ.: 3,500; Wed. – Publisher, Cam McKnight; Editor, Jeff Helsdon

Dorchester Signpost, 15 Brydge St., Dorchester ON N0L 1G02 – 519/268-7337 – Circ.: 2,128; Wed.

Drayton: The Community News, PO Box 189, Drayton ON N0G 1P0 – 519/638-3066 – Wed.

Dresden: North Kent Leader, PO Box 490, Dresden ON N0P 1M0 – 519/683-4485 – Wed.

Dryden Observer, Coldstream Ltd., PO Box 3009, Dryden ON P8N 2Y9 – 807/223-2390; Fax: 807/223-2907; Email: editor.observer@awcoldstream.on.ca; URL: http://www.awc/on.ca.observer – Circ.: 6,200; Wed. – Publisher, Alex Wilson; Editor, Sylvia Veal

Dryden: Local Express, 22 King St., Dryden ON P8N 1B3 – 807/223-3600; Fax: 807/223-3599 – Wed.

Dundalk Herald, Herald Publishing Co., PO Box 280, Dundalk ON N0C 1B0 – 519/923-2203; Fax: 519/923-2747 – Circ.: 3,400; Wed. – Publisher, Matthew Walls; Editor, Melodee Lovering; Circulation Manager, Cathy Walls

Dundas-Ancaster Recorder, 264 East 22nd St., PO Box 68041, Stn Blakely PO, Hamilton ON L8M 3M7 – 905/385-7192 – Tue.

Dundas Star, 47 Cootes Dr., Dundas ON L9H 1B5 – 905/628-6313; Fax: 905/628-5485 – Circ.: 10,477; Wed.

Dunnville Chronicle, 131 Lock St. East, PO Box 216, Dunnville ON N1A 2X5 – 905/774-5855 – Circ.: 4,275; Wed.; also CoverStory (Sat.)

Durham Chronicle, PO Box 230, Durham ON N0G 1R0 – 519/369-2504 – Wed.

Dutton Advance, PO Box 220, Dutton ON N0L 1J0 – 519/762-2310 – Circ.: 1,700; Wed. – Publisher, D.W. Moore; Editor, Marlene Moore

Eganville Leader, 154 John St., PO Box 310, Eganville ON K0J 1T0 – 613/628-2332 – Circ.: 6,500; Wed. – Co-Publisher, Ron Tracey; Editor & Co-Publisher, Gerald Tracey

Elgin: The Rideau Review, PO Box 220, Elgin ON K0G 1E0 – 613/359-5544 – Wed. – Publisher, David Morris; Circulation Manager, Penny Griffin

Elliot Lake/North Shore Market Place, 14 Hillside Dr. South, Elliot Lake, ON P5A 2G9 – 705/848-6397 – Sat.

Elliot Lake Standard, 14 Hillsdale Dr. South, Elliot Lake ON P5A 1M6 – 705/848-7195 – Wed.

Elmira Independent, 15 King St., Elmira ON N3B 2R1 – 519/669-5155; Fax: 519/669-5928; Email: enews@realm.tdkcs.waterloo.on.ca – Circ.: 8,611; Mon; also National Edition – Editor, J. Robert Verdun

Elmira: K.W. Real Estate News, 15 King St., Elmira ON N3B 2R1 – 519/749-1400; Fax: 519/749-0488 – Circ.: 9,000; Fri. – Publisher & Editor, Bob Verdun

Embrun: Le Reflet, #3, 793 Notre-Dame St., Embrun ON K0A 1W1 – 613/443-2741 – Mercredi; français

Erin Advocate, PO Box 160, Erin ON N0B 1T0 – 519/833-9603 – Wed.

Espanola: Mid-North Monitor, 407 Station Rd., PO Box 1629, Espanola ON P0P 1C0 – 705/869-2860; Fax: 705/869-5140 – Wed., English & French

Essex Free Press, 16 Centre St., Essex ON N8M 1N9 – 519/776-4268; Fax: 519/776-4014 – Circ.: 4,300; Wed. – Editor, W.R. Brett

Etobicoke Guardian, Metroland Printing, Publishing & Distributing Ltd., 260 Galaxy Blvd., Etobicoke ON M9W 5R8 – 416/675-4390; Fax: 416/675-9296 – Circ.: 64,998 Wed., 6,011 Sun.; Wed., Sun; also Monthly Business – Publisher, Betty Carr

Etobicoke Life, 3874 Bloor St. West, Etobicoke ON M9B 1L3 – 416/231-6809; Fax: 416/231-2035; Email: etobicoke_life@ocna.org – Circ.: 30,000; Wed. – Publisher, W. Domanski; Editor, Patrick McConnell; Circulation Manager, Karyn Haystead

Exeter Times-Advocate, PO Box 850, Exeter ON N0M 1S6 – 519/235-1331; Fax: 519/235-0766 – Wed.

Fenelon Falls Gazette, PO Box 340, Fenelon Falls ON K0M 1N0 – 705/887-2940 – Wed.

Fergus-Elora News-Express, 390 Tower St. South, PO Box 130, Fergus, ON N1M 2W7 – 519/843-1310 – Circ.: 3,971; Wed.

Fergus: The Wellington Advertiser, 180 St. Andrews St. East, PO Box 252, Fergus ON N1M 2W8 – 519/843-5410 – Mon.

Flesherton Advance, Herald Publishing Co. Ltd., PO Box 280, Dundalk ON 0C 1B0 – 519/923-2203; Fax: 519/923-2747

Forest Standard, PO Box 220, Forest ON N0N 1J0 – 519/786-5242; Fax: 519/786-4884 – Wed.

Fort Erie: The Times, 450 Garrison Rd., Unit 5, PO Box 1219, Fort Erie ON L2A 5Y2 – 905/871-3100; Fax: 905/871-5243; Email: mrobinson@rannie.com; URL: http://www.rannie.com – Tue. (circ. 10,900), Sat. (circ. 11,500) – Publisher, Tim Dundas; Editor, Mike Robinson; Circulation Manager, Petrina Richardson

Fort Frances Times, PO Box 339, Fort Frances ON P9A 3M7 – 807/274-5373; Fax: 807/274-7286 – Wed.

Foxoboro: The Real Estate Weekender, PO Box 171, Foxoboro ON K0K 2B0 – 613/969-8896; Fax: 613/969-1836 – Circ.: 35,000; Fri. – Owner, P. Kell

Gananoque Reporter, 79 King St. East, Gananoque ON K7G 1E8 – 613/382-2156 – Wed.

Georgetown Independent/Acton Free Press, Metroland Printing, Publishing & Distributing Ltd., 211 Armstrong Ave., Georgetown ON L7G 4X5 – 905/873-0301; Fax: 905/877-0442 – Wed., Sun; also Acton Free Press – Publisher, Ken Nugent

Geraldton: Times Star, 401 Main St., PO Box 490, Geraldton ON P0T 1M0 – 807/854-1919; Fax: 807/854-1682 – Wed.

Glencoe: Transcript & Free Press, 243 Main St., PO Box 400, Glencoe ON N0L 1M0 – 519/287-2615 – Circ.: 2,810; Wed. – Publisher & Editor, Walter Vanderkwaak

Goderich Signal-Star, Industrial Park, PO Box 220, Goderich ON N7A 4B6 – 519/524-2614; Fax: 519/524-5145 – Circ.: 5,600; Wed; also Focus (every other Tues.) – Publisher, John Buchanan; Editor, Dave Sykes; Circulation Manager, Irene Ott

Gore Bay: Manitoulin Recorder, PO Box 235, Gore Bay ON P0P 1H0 – 705/282-2003; Fax: 705/282-2432 – Circ.: 4,178; Wed. – Publisher & Editor, Margaret E. Robinson; Circulation Manager, Nancy Noland

Grand Valley Star & Vidette, PO Box 119, Grand Valley ON L0N 1G0 – 519/928-2822 – Wed.

Gravenhurst Banner, 140 Muskoka Rd. South, PO Box 849, Gravenhurst ON P0C 1G0 – 705/687-6674 – Wed.

Grimsby Independent, 19 Adelaide St., PO Box 310, Grimsby ON L3M 4G5 – 905/945-9264; Fax: 905/945-0540 – Wed.

Guelph Pennysaver, Netmar Inc., 86 Dawson Rd., Guelph ON N1H 1A8 – 519/823-5070; Fax: 519/823-2161 – Sat.

Guelph: The Guelph Tribune, 650 Woodlawn Rd. W., Unit 11 & 12, Guelph ON N1K 1B8 – 519/763-3333; Fax: 519/763-4814 – Wed.

Haliburton County Echo, PO Box 360, Haliburton ON K0M 1S0 – 705/457-1037; Fax: 705/457-3275 – Circ.: 5,000; Tue. – Publisher, Len Pizzey; Editor, Martha Perkins

Hamilton Recorder, PO Box 68041, Stn Blakely, Hamilton ON L8M 3M7 – 905/561-1090 – Wed.

Hamilton: New Hamilton Weekly, #203, 131 John St. South, Hamilton ON L8N 2C3 – 905/527-0070 – Fri.

Canadian Almanac & Directory 1997

Hanover Post & District Advertisers News, 413 - 18th Ave., Hanover ON N4N 3S5 – 519/364-2001; Fax: 519/364-6950 – Tue; also The Hanover Post (Tue.) & The Hanover Post Postscripts (Fri.) – Publisher, Marie David

Hanover: The Saugeen City News, 414 - 10th St., PO Box 69, Hanover ON N4N 1P6 – 519/364-4597 – Tue.

Harriston Review, PO Box 370, Harriston ON N0G 1Z0 – 519/338-2341 – Circ.: 1,068; Tue. – Publisher, Clive Williams, 519/848-2410

Harrow & Colchester South This Week, 72 King St. East, Harrow, ON N0R 1G0 – 519/738-2000 – Wed.

Harrow News, PO Box 310, Harrow ON N0R 1G0 – 519/738-2542; Fax: 519/738-3874 – Wed.

Hastings Star, Cembal Publications Ltd, PO Box 250, Marmora ON K0K 2M0 – 613/472-2431; Fax: 613/472-5026 – Circ.: 1,400; Wed. – Editor, Bill Freeman

Havelock Citizen, Cembal Publications Ltd, PO Box 250, Marmora ON K0K 2M0 – 613/472-2431; Fax: 613/472-5026 – Circ.: 2,280; Wed. – Editor, Nancy Powers

Hawkesbury: Le Carillon, CP 1000, Hawkesbury ON K6A 3H1 – 613/632-4155; Fax: 613/632-6122 – Tirage: 10,000; Mercredi; français

Hawkesbury Tribune/Express, 299, rue Principale est, Hawkesbury ON K6A 3H1 – 613/632-4605 – Circ.: 23,000; Sat., English & French

Hawkesbury: Le/The Regional, 124, rue Principale est, Hawkesbury ON K6A 1A8 – 613/632-0112 – Circ.: 30,000; Fri.; English & French

Hearst: Le Nord, 905, rue Georges, CP 2320, Hearst ON P0L 1N0 – 705/372-1233; Fax: 705/362-5954; Email: lenord@nt.net – Tirage: 3,500; Mercredi; français – Éditeur & Rédacteur, Omer Cantin

Hornell Heights PO: North Bay Shield, CFB North Bay, Hornell Heights PO ON P0H 1P0 – 705/474-9292 – Mon.; English & French

Hornepayne: The Bear News, 79 Front St., PO Box 660, Hornepayne ON P0M 1Z0 – 807/868-2701; Fax: 807/868-3337 – Wed.

Huntsville Forester, PO Box 940, Huntsville ON P0A 1K0 – 705/789-5541; Fax: 705/789-9381 – Wed.

Ignace Driftwood, PO Box 989, Ignace ON P0T 1T0 – 807/934-6482 – Wed.

Ingersoll Times, 19 King St. West, Ingersoll ON N5C 2J2 – 519/485-3631; Fax: 519/485-6652 – Circ.: 3,600; Wed. – Publisher, Pat Logan; Editor, Geoff Dale; Circulation Manager, Mary Pinney

Innisfil Scope, PO Box 310, Beeton ON L0G 1A0 – 905/458-4434 – Wed.

Iroquois: The Chieftain, PO Box 529, Iroquois ON K0E 1K0 – 613/652-4395; Fax: 613/652-2508 – Circ.: 2,000; Wed. – Publisher, Brian Crawford; Editor, Rebecca van Noppen; Circulation Manager, Karen Cooke

Iroquois Falls A: Le Boîte à Nouvelles, PO Box 1268, Iroquois Falls A ON P0K 1G0 – 705/232-5222; Fax: 705/232-7755 – Mercredi; français

Iroquois Falls A: The Enterprise, PO Box 834, Iroquois Falls A ON P0K 1G0 – 705/232-4081 – Wed.; English & French

Kanata Kourier-Standard, 3 Beaverbrook Rd., Kanata ON K2K 1L2 – 613/591-3060; Fax: 613/591-8503 – Circ.: 16,781; Fri.

Kapuskasing Northern Times, 51 Riverside Dr., Kapuskasing ON P5N 1A7 – 705/335-2283; Fax: 705/337-1222 – Circ.: 5,300; Wed.; English & French – Publisher, Rene Piché; Editor, Wayne Major, 705/335-8032

Kemptville Weekly Advance, PO Box 669, Kemptville ON K0G 1J0 – 613/258-3451; Fax: 613/258-7734 – Wed; also Kemptville Accent Magazine (monthly)

Keswick: Georgina Advocate, 204 Simcoe Ave., Keswick ON L4P 3S6 – 905/476-7753; Fax: 905/476-5785 – Circ.: 14,000; Mon. – Publisher, Mark Skelton; Editor, John Slyknuis

Kincardine: The Independent, PO Box 1240, Kincardine ON N2Z 2Z4 – 519/396-3111; Fax: 519/396-3899 – Circ.: 3,100; Wed. – Editor, Eric Howard

Kincardine News, 708 Queen St., Kincardine ON N2Z 2A3 – 519/396-2963; Fax: 519/396-3790 – Wed.

King Weekly, 237 Romina Dr., Unit 2, Concord ON L4K 4V3 – 905/660-9556 – Wed.

King/Vaughan Weekly, PO Box 1036, King City ON L0G 1K0 – 905/660-9556; Fax: 905/660-9558 – Wed.

Kingston: The Heritage Newspaper, 784 Bath Rd., Kingston ON K7M 4Y2 – 613/389-8884; Fax: 613/389-1870 – Circ.: 29,600; Tue.

Kingston This Week, Metroland Printing, Publishing & Distributing Ltd., 677 Gardiners Rd., Kingston ON K7M 3Y4 – 613/389-7400; Fax: 613/389-7507 – Circ.: 46,200; Wed., Sat. – Publisher, Cam Inglis; Editor, Dan Donohue; Circulation Manager, Margaret Amsun

Kingsville Reporter, 17 Chestnut St., Kingsville ON N9Y 1J9 – 519/733-2211; Fax: 519/733-6464 – Tue.

Kitchener: Cambridge Pennysaver, 685 Wabanaki Dr., Kitchener ON N2C 2G3 – 519/894-1400 – Sat.; also Kitchener-Waterloo Pennysaver (Sat.)

Kitchener This Week, #112, 22 Frederick St., Kitchener ON N2H 6M6 – 519/576-5300 – Circ.: 58,000; Wed.

Lakefield: Katchewanooka Herald, 112 Queen St., PO Box 1000, Lakefield ON K0L 2H0 – 705/652-6594; Fax: 705/652-6912; Email: The_Herald@ocna.org – Circ.: 2,200; Mon. – Publisher, June K. Helwig; Editor, Neil Boughen; Circulation Manager, Eva Smith

Lambeth News-Star, PO Box 490, Lambeth ON N0L 1S0 – 519/652-3421 – Thur.

Leamington Pennysaver, NETMAR, 60 Oak St. East, Leamington ON N8H 2C2 – 519/322-0400; Fax: 519/322-0405 – Circ.: 18,500; Sun. – Publications Manager, Kanita Thiessen; Editor, Shelley Fellows

Leamington Post & News, Bowes Publishers Ltd., 27 Princess St., Leamington ON N8H 2X8 – 519/326-4434; Fax: 519/326-2171; Email: lempost@wincom.net – Circ.: 6,000; Wed.; also Leamington Shopper (Tues., circ. 16,491) – Publisher, Don Gage; Editor, Mike Thibodeau, 519/326-4434; Circulation Manager, John Patterson

Lindsay Performer, 15 William St. North, Lindsay ON K9V 3Z8 – 705/324-2114 – Fri. – Publisher, F.M. Dundas

Lindsay This Week, Metroland Printing, Publishing & Distributing Ltd., 96 Albert St. South, Lindsay ON K9V 3H7 – 705/324-8600 – Wed.

Listowel: The Independent, 128 Wallace Ave. North, Listowel ON N4W 1K7 – 519/291-5220 – Mon.

Listowel: The Independent Plus, 188 Wallace Ave. North, PO Box 97, Listowel ON N4W 3H2 – 519/291-1660 – Mon.

Listowel Banner, 185 Wallace Ave. North, PO Box 97, Listowel ON N4W 3H2 – 519/291-1660; Fax: 519/291-3771 – Circ.: 5,000; Wed.; also Independent Plus (Mon.) – Publisher, Paul Teahen; Editor, Marion Duke

Little Current: The Manitoulin Expositor, PO Box 369, Little Current ON P0P 1K0 – 705/368-2744; Fax: 705/368-3822; Email: expositor@msdcorp.com – Circ.: 5,800; Wed. – Publisher, R.L. McCutcheon; Editor, Ross Muir

London Pennysaver, 244 Adelaide St. South, London ON N5Z 3L1 – 519/685-2020; Fax: 519/649-0908 – Circ.: 144,000; Sun. – General Manager, Marj Bastow

Lucknow Sentinel, Bowes Publishers, PO Box 400, Lucknow ON N0G 2H0 – 519/528-2822; Fax: 519/528-3529 – Circ.: 2,000; Wed. – Editor, Pat Livingstone; Circulation Manager, Phyllis Matthews Helm

Madoc Review, Cembal Publications Ltd, PO Box 250, Marmora ON K0K 2M0 – 613/472-2431; Fax: 613/472-5026 – Circ.: 2,680; Wed. – Editor, Jeff Wilson

Manitouwadge: The Echo, PO Box 550, Manitouwadge ON P0T 2C0 – 807/826-3788; Fax: 807/826-3910 – Circ.: 1,750; Wed. – Publisher & Editor, B.J. Schermann

Marathon Mercury, PO Box 369, Marathon ON P0T 2E0 – 807/229-1520; Fax: 807/229-1595 – Wed.

Markdale Standard, PO Box 465, Markdale ON N0C 1H0 – 519/986-3151 – Wed.

Markham Economist & Sun, 9 Heritage Rd., Markham ON L3P 1M3 – 905/294-2200; Fax: 905/294-1538; Toronto line: 416/798-7624 – Circ.: 45,000; Wed. & Sat. – Publisher, Patricia Pappas; Editor-in-Chief, Jo Ann Stevenson; Editor, Alan Shackleton

Marmora: Land O'Lakes Sun, PO Box 250, Marmora ON K0K 2M0 – 613/472-2431 – Circ.: 6,755; Tue.

Marmora Herald, Cembal Publications Ltd, PO Box 250, Marmora ON K0K 2M0 – 613/472-2431; Fax: 613/472-5026 – Circ.: 1,880; Tue. – Editor, Nancy Powers

Mattawa Recorder, 341 McConnell St., PO Box 67, Mattawa ON P0H 1V0 – 705/744-5361; Fax: 705/744-5361 – Circ.: 1,050; Wed. – Publisher, Carole Edwards

Meaford: The Courier Herald, 68 Sykes St. North, Meaford ON N4L 1R2 – 519/599-3760; Fax: 519/599-3214 – Wed.; also Meaford Express (Wed., circ. 2,521)

Midland/Penetanguishene Mirror, Metroland Printing, Publishing & Distributing Ltd., RR#2, Mountainview Mall, PO Box 77, Midland ON L4R 4R4 – 705/527-5500 – Wed., Sun. – Publisher, Joe Anderson

Midland: Penetanguishene Free Press, 248 First St., Midland ON L4R 4K6 – 705/526-5431; Fax: 705/526-1771 – Wed., Fri.

Mildmay Town & Country Crier, PO Box 190, Mildmay ON N0G 2J0 – 519/367-2681; Fax: 519/367-5417 – Every other Tue.

Millbrook Times, 28 King St. East, Millbrook ON L0A 1G0 – 705/932-3001; Fax: 705/932-3377 – Circ.: 2,000; Mon. – Publisher & Editor, Lynda Todd

Milton Canadian Champion, Metroland Printing, Publishing & Distributing Ltd., 191 Main St, Milton ON L9T 1N7 – 905/878-2341; Fax: 905/878-4943 – Wed., Fri. – Publisher, Ian Oliver

Minden: The Times, PO Box 97, Minden ON K0M 2K0 – 705/286-1288; Fax: 705/286-4768 – Mon. – Editor, Jack B. Rezina

Mississauga Booster, 24 Falconer Dr., Mississauga ON L5N 1B1 – 905/826-3672; Fax: 905/567-7299 – Every other Wed.

Mississauga News, Metroland Printing, Publishing & Distributing Ltd., 3145 Wolfedale Rd., Mississauga ON L5C 3A9 – 905/273-8118 – Tue., Thur., Sun; supplement, Community News (Wed.) – Publisher, Ron Lenyk

Mitchell Advocate, PO Box 669, Mitchell ON N0K 1N0 – 519/348-8431; Fax: 519/348-8836 – Wed.

Morrisburg Leader, PO Box 891, Morrisburg ON K0C 1X0 – 613/543-2987 – Circ.: 2,850; Wed. – Publisher & Editor, Arthur Laurin

Mount Forest Confederate, PO Box 130, Mount Forest ON N0G 2L0 – 519/323-1550; Fax: 519/323-4548 – Wed.

Napanee Beaver, 72 Dundas St. East, Napanee ON K7R 1H9 – 613/354-6641; Fax: 613/354-2622 – Wed.

Napanee Weekly Guide, 41 Dundas St. East, Napanee ON K7R 1H1 – 613/354-6648; Fax: 613/354-6708 – Tue.

Nepean Clarion, 25B Northside Rd., Nepean ON K2H 8S1 – 613/820-3126; Fax: 613/820-6147 – Sun.

New Hamburg Independent, 91 Peel St., PO Box 670, New Hamburg ON N0B 2G0 – 519/662-1240; Fax: 519/662-3521 – Wed; also The Advertiser (Wed.)

New Liskeard/Temiskaming Speaker, PO Box 580, New Liskeard ON P0J 1P0 – 705/647-6791; Toll free: 1-800-461-8751 – Wed.

Newmarket: Aurora/Newmarket Town Crier, 16700 Bayview Ave., Unit 27, Newmarket ON L4P 3B2 – 416/853-5056 – Wed.

Canadian Almanac & Directory 1997

Niagara on Lake Review Weekly, 4801 Valley Way, Niagara Falls ON L2E 6T6 – 905/358-5711 – Circ.: 5,600; Wed.; also Fort Erie Review Weekly (Tue., circ. 11,000)

Niagara Shopping News, 4949 Victoria Ave., Niagara Falls ON L2E 4C7 – 905/357-2440 – Wed., Sat.

Nipigon-Red Rock Gazette, PO Box 1057, Nipigon ON P0T 2J0 – 807/887-3583 – Tue.

North York: Hi-Rise, 95 Leewad Glenway, Unit 121, North York ON M3C 2Z6 – 416/424-1393 – Monthly

Norwich Gazette, 46 Main St. West, PO Box 459, Norwich ON N0J 1P0 – 519/863-2262; Fax: 519/863-3229 – Circ.: 2,000; Wed. – Publisher, Pat Logan; Editor, John Tapley; Circulation Manager, Deb Clifford

Oakville: Abbey Oaks News, PO Box 306, Oakville ON L6J 5A2 – 905/825-2229 – Circ.: 15,000; Thur.

Oakville: Milton Shopping News, 1158 South Service Rd. West, Oakville ON L6L 5T7 – 905/827-2244; Fax: 905/827-2308 – Circ.: 16,865; Tue. – Bill Whitaker Sr.

Oakville Beaver, Metroland Printing, Publishing & Distributing Ltd., 467 Speers Rd., Oakville ON L6K 3S4 – 905/845-3824; Fax: 905/845-3085 – Circ.: 21,000; Wed., Fri., Sun.; also North News (Fri.), & Oakville Marketplace (Tue.) – Publisher, Ian Oliver; Editor, Norm Alexander; Circulation Manager, Martin Doherty

Oakville Free Press Journal, 1158 South Service Rd. West, Oakville ON L6L 5T7 – 905/827-2596; Fax: 905/827-2308 – Circ.: 37,000; Tue. – Publisher, Arnold L. Huffman; Editor, Peter West

Oakville North News, 467 Speers Rd., Oakville ON L6K 3S4 – 905/845-3824 – Circ.: 17,500; Fri.; also Oakville Marketplace (Tue., circ. 39,000)

Oakville Shopping News, 1158 South Service Rd. West, Oakville ON L6L 5T7 – 905/827-2244; Fax: 905/827-2308 – Circ.: 37,000; Tue., Fri. – Bill Whitaker Sr.

Orangeville Banner, 37 Mill St., Orangeville ON L9W 2M4 – 519/941-1350; Fax: 519/941-9600 – Circ.: 6,305; Wed., Fri; supplement, Orangeville & District Shopping News (Fri.) – Publisher, David J. Mitchell; Editor, Steve Harron; Circulation Manager, Patricia Mahrle

Orangeville Citizen, 14 Mill St., Orangeville ON L9W 2M3 – 519/941-2230; Fax: 519/941-9361; Email: editor@headwaters.com; URL: http://www.headwaters.com/citizen/citizen.html – Circ.: 10,700; Wed. – Publisher, Pamela Claridge; Editor, Sheila Duncan; Circulation Manager, Sandi Jovic

Orillia Today, Metroland Printing, Publishing & Distributing Ltd., 425 West St. North, Unit 10, Orillia ON L3V 7R2 – 705/329-2058 – Sun., Wed. – Publisher, Joe Anderson

Orleans Community Weekly Journal, #205, 815 Taylor Creek Dr., Orleans ON K1C 1T1 – 613/830-3005 – Circ.: 30,965; Sat.

Orleans Express, #209-1455 Youville Dr., Orleans ON K1C 4R1 – 613/830-2000; Fax: 613/830-9338 – Tirage.: 36,500; Mardi; français

Orleans: The Star, #209-1455 Youville Dr., Orleans ON K1C 4R1 – 613/830-7827; Fax: 613/830-1116 – Circ.: 44,000; Wed. – Publisher, Derek Walter; Editor, Michael Curran

Orono Weekly Times, PO Box 209, Orono ON L0B 1M0 – 905/983-5301; Fax: 905/983-5301 – Wed. – Publisher & Editor, Troy Young; Circulation Manager, Christine Faulkner

Oshawa: Break Time, PO Box 481, Oshawa ON L1J 7L5 – 905/434-6400 – Thur.

Oshawa/Whitby This Week, 865 Farewell Ave., PO Box 481, Oshawa ON L1H 7L5 – 905/579-4400; Fax: 905/579-2238; Toronto line: 416-798-7672 – Wed., Fri., Sun. – Publisher, Tim Whittaker

Oshawa News, 2651 Trullis Rd. South, Unit 3, Courtice ON L1E 2N3 – 905/433-1629, 5546; Fax: 905/433-7050 – Circ.: 17,000; Wed. – Publisher, Sandra McDowell; Editor, Greg McDowell

Ottawa: The Alta Vista News (Ottawa), Ottawa News Publishing, 15 Antares Dr., Unit 3B, Nepean ON K2E 7Y9 – 613/723-5970; Fax: 613/723-1862 – Circ.: 12,000; Every other Wed.; also Greenboro Hunt Club Park News (every other Wed., circ. 12,000) – Publisher, Michael Wollock; Editor, Patrick Uguccioni

Ottawa: The Hill Times, 69 Sparks St., Ottawa ON K1P 5A5 – 613/232-5952; Fax: 613/232-9055; URL: http://resudox.net/paper/hill.html – Circ.: 15,000; Thur. – Co-Publisher, Ross Dickson; Co-Publisher & Editor, Jim Creskey

Ottawa-Carleton This Month, PO Box 102, Manotick ON K4M 1A2 – 613/692-2436; Fax: 613/258-7736 & 692-2456 – Circ.: 13,500; Every 3rd Wed. – Publisher, Ann Marie Crawford; Editor, Pat Hitsman

Ottawa/Centretown News, c/o Carleton University School of Journalism, Colonel By Dr., Ottawa ON K1S 5B6 – 613/564-6388 – Every other Fri.

Ottawa Pennysaver, 48 Colonnade Rd., Nepean ON K2E 7J6 – 613/723-1707 – Sat.

Palmerston Observer, PO Box 757, Palmerston ON N0G 2P0 – 519/343-2440; Fax: 519/343-2267 – Wed.

Paris Star, 59 Grand River St. North, Paris ON N3L 2M3 – 519/442-7866; Fax: 519/442-3100 – Wed.

Parkhill Gazette, PO Box 400, Parkhill ON N0M 2K0 – 519/294-6264; Fax: 519/294-6391 – Wed.

Parry Sound Beacon/Star, 67 James St., Parry Sound ON P2A 1T6 – 705/746-4228; Fax: 705/746-8369 – Sun.

Parry Sound North Star, PO Box 370, Parry Sound ON P2A 2X4 – 705/746-2104; Fax: 705/746-8369 – Wed.

Pelham Herald, 1477 Pelham St. South, Pelham ON L0S 1E0 – 905/892-6022; Fax: 905/892-0502 – Circ.: 7,400; Wed. – Publisher, Martha Cepuch; Editor, Carolyn Mullin

Penetanguishene: Le Goût de Vivre, CP 58, Penetanguishene ON L0K 1P0 – 705/549-3116; Fax: 705/549-4925 – Tous les deux jeudi; français

Perth Courier, PO Box 156, Perth ON K7H 3E3 – 613/267-1100; Fax: 613/267-3986 – Wed.

Petawawa Messenger, 35A Highway St., Petawawa ON K8H 1Z3 – 613/687-1440 – Circ.: 7,600; Thur.

Petawawa Post, Bldg. G-1, Petawawa ON K8H 2X3 – 613/687-5386; Fax: 613/588-6996 – Wed.; English & French – Editor, W. Fowler

Peterborough This Week, 884 Ford St., Peterborough ON K9J 5V3 – 705/749-3383; Fax: 705/749-0074 – Circ.: 42,500; Wed., Sat. – Publisher, Hugh Nicholson

Petrolia: The Petrolia Topic, 4182 Petrolia Line, PO Box 40, Petrolia ON N0N 1R0 – 519/882-1770; Fax: 519/882-3212 – Circ.: 3,300; Wed. – Publisher, Denise Thibeault; Editor, David Pattenaude

Pickering/Ajax Bay News, 1730 McPherson Crt., Unit 18, Pickering ON L1W 3E6 – 905/839-8087; Fax: 905/839-8135 – Wed.

Picton: The County Guide, 281 Main St., Picton ON K0K 2T0 – 613/476-5838 – Circ.: 9,825; Sun.

Picton Gazette, PO Box 80, Picton ON K0K 2T0 – 613/476-3201; Fax: 613/476-3464; Email: gazette@connect.reach.net – Circ.: 4,400; Wed., Sat.; also Piction Gazette Regional (Sat. circ., 12,000) – Publisher, Jean M. Morrison; Editor, Kevin Wood; Circulation Manager, David Fabius

Port Dover Maple Leaf, 351 Main St., Port Dover ON N0A 1N0 – 519/583-0112 – Wed.

Port Elgin: The Beacon Times, PO Box 580, Port Elgin ON N0H 2C0 – 519/832-9001; Fax: 519/389-4793 – Wed.

Port Elgin: Chesley Enterprise, PO Box 580, Port Elgin ON N0H 2C0 – 519/363-2414; Fax: 519/363-2726 – Wed.

Port Elgin: Shoreline News, 685 Goderich St., Port Elgin ON N0H 2C0 – 519/389-4733 – Wed.

Port Perry Star, 188 Mary St., PO Box 90, Port Perry ON L9L 1B7 – 905/985-7383; Fax: 905/985-3708 – Circ.: 5,000; Tue; supplement, Port Perry Weekend Star (Fri., circ. 17,000) – Publisher, Peter Huidsten; Editor, Jeff Mitchell; Circulation Manager, Gayle Stapley

Prescott Journal, PO Box 549, Prescott ON K0E 1T0 – 613/925-4265; Fax: 613/925-3472 – Wed.

Rainy River Record, PO Box 280, Rainy River ON P0W 1L0 – 807/852-3366; Fax: 807/852-4434; Email: Rainy_River_Record@ocna.org – Circ.: 1,500; Wed. – Publisher, J.R. Cumming; Editor, Ken Johnston

Rainy River: The Westend Weekly, PO Box 188, Rainy River ON P0W 1L0 – 807/852-3815 – Circ.: 8,050; Fri.

Red Lake District News, PO Box 425, Red Lake ON P0V 2M0 – 807/727-2618; Fax: 807/727-3717 – Circ.: 2,800; Wed. – Publisher, Rick Smit; Circulation Manager, Wendy Beidler

Renfrew Mercury, PO Box 400, Renfrew ON K7V 4A8 – 613/432-3655 – Circ.: 7,000; Wed.; also Weekender (Sat., circ. 14,000) – Publisher, Fred Runge; Editor, Elaine Dick

Renfrew News, 250 Raglan St. South, Renfrew ON K7V 1R4 – 613/432-7544 – Circ.: 13,186; Sun.

Richmond Hill Liberal, Metroland Printing, Publishing & Distributing Ltd., 9350 Yonge St., PO Box 390, Richmond Hill ON L4C 4Y6 – 905/881-3373; Fax: 905/881-9924; Toronto line: 416/661-0047 – Circ.: 68,000; Wed., Sun. – Publisher, Bruce Annan; Editor, Debra Kelly

Richmond Hill Weekly, 237 Romina Dr., Unit 2, Concord ON L4K 4V3 – 905/660-9556 – Wed.

Rodney: The Chronicle, 246 Furnival Rd., PO Box 400, Rodney ON N0L 2C0 – 519/785-2455 – Circ.: 4,800; Weekly

Russell Villager, PO Box 550, Russell ON K4R 1E1 – 613/445-3805 – Circ.: 1,265; Thur.

St. Catharines Shopping News, 140 Welland Ave., Unit 1, St. Catharines ON L2R 2N6 – 905/688-4332 – Wed.

St. Marys Journal-Argus, PO Box 1030, St. Marys ON N4X 1B7 – 519/284-2440; Fax: 519/284-3650 – Wed.

St. Thomas: Our Community Press, 4 Curtis St., St. Thomas ON N5P 1H4 – 519/631-3782 – Circ.: 8,564; Wed.; also Elgin County Market (Tue.)

Sarnia: This Week, 1383 Confederation St., PO Box 99, Sarnia ON N7S 5P1 – 519/336-1100; Fax: 519/336-1833 – Circ.: 21,500; Wed. – Editor, Jim Connelly

Sault Ste. Marie This Week, PO Box 188, Sault Ste. Marie ON P6A 2T9 – 705/949-6111 – Wed.

Scarborough: Bluffs Monitor-Birch Cliff News, 14 Lynn Rd., Scarborough ON M1N 2A3 – 416/691-4085 – Circ.: 20,000; Monthly, Sept.-July – Publisher, L. Graves

Scarborough: Toronto East End Express, 80 Nashdene Rd., Unit 15, Scarborough ON M1V 5E4 – 416/463-4634 – Wed.

Seaforth Huron Expositor, 100 Main St., PO Box 69, Seaforth ON N0K 1W0 – 519/527-0240; Fax: 519/527-2858 – Circ.: 2,782; Wed. – Publisher, Tom Flynn; Editor, Tim Cumming

Shelburne Free Press & Economist, PO Box 100, Shelburne ON L0N 1S0 – 519/925-2832; Fax: 519/925-5500 – Wed.

Simcoe: Tuesday Times-Reformer, 105 Donly Dr. South, PO Box 370, Simcoe ON N3Y 4L2 – 519/426-5710; Fax: 519/426-9504; Email: refedit@nornet.on.ca; URL: http://www.nornet.on.ca/reformer/refmain.html – Circ.: 17,200; Tue. – Publisher, Michael Fredericks; Editor, Kimberley Novak; Circulation Manager, Steve Smithson

Sioux Lookout Bulletin, 40 Front St., PO Box 1389, Sioux Lookout ON P8T 1B7 – 807/737-3209, advtg. 737-4207; Fax: 807/737-3084 – Circ.: 4,717; Wed. – Editor, Jason van Rassel

Sioux Lookout: Wawatay News, Wataway Native Communications Society, PO Box 1180, Sioux Lookout ON P8T 1B7 – 807/737-2951; Fax: 807/737-3224 –

Circ.: 8,000; Every other Thur.; English & Ojibwe – Editor-in-Chief, Bryan Phelan

Smiths Falls Record News, PO Box 158, Smith Falls ON K7A 4T1 – 613/283-3182; Fax: 613/283-7480 – Circ.: 4,402; Wed; supplement, Record News EMC (Sun., circ. 35,727) – Publisher, Chuck Hudson; Editor, Michael Hayes

Stayner Sun, PO Box 80, Stayner ON L0M 1S0 – 705/428-2638; Fax: 705/428-6909 – Circ.: 1,056; Wed.; also Wasaga Sun (Wed., circ. 3,900)

Stirling: The Community Press, PO Box 88, Stirling ON K0K 3E0 – 613/395-3015; Fax: 613/395-2992 – Circ.: 54,937; Sat. – Publisher, John Seckar; Editor, Alan Coxwell; Circulation Manager, Dan Kennedy

Stittsville News, PO Box 610, Stittsville ON K2S 1A7 – 613/836-1357; Fax: 613/836-5621 – Circ.: 4,400; Wed. – Publisher & Editor, John Curry

Stoney Creek: Hamilton News, Mountain Edition, 333 Arvin Ave., Stoney Creek ON L8E 2M6 – 905/523-5800 – Circ.: 44,369; Wed.

Stoney Creek News, 333 Arvin Ave., Stoney Creek ON L8E 2M6 – 905/561-1090; Fax: 905/664-3102 – Circ.: 25,000; Wed.; also The Real Estate News & Buyer's Guide (Wed.) – Publisher, Dave O'Reilly, 905/523-5800; Editor, Stephen Beecroft, 905/523-5800; Circulation Manager, Dave Settle

Stouffville Sun, 6306 Main St., PO Box 154, Stouffville ON L4A 7Z5 – 905/640-2612; Fax: 905/640-8778 – Wed.

Stouffville Tribune, Metroland Printing, Publishing & Distributing Ltd., 6244 Main St., Stouffville ON L4A 1E2 – 905/640-2100; Toronto line: 416/798-7625 – Wed. – Publisher, Patricia Pappas

Stratford This Week, 108 Ontario St., PO Box 430, Stratford ON N5A 6T6 – 519/271-2220; Fax: 519/271-1026 – Circ.: 14,604; Wed. – Publisher, Charles W. Dingman

Strathroy Age-Dispatch, 8 Front St. East, Strathroy ON N7G 1Y4 – 519/245-2370 – Wed.

Sturgeon Falls Tribune, PO Box 900, Sturgeon Falls ON P0H 2G0 – 705/753-2930 – Tue.; English & French

Sudbury: Northern Life, 158 Elgin St., Sudbury ON P3E 3N5 – 705/673-5667; Fax: 705/673-4652 – Wed.

Sudbury: South Side Story, #204, 469 Bouchard St., Sudbury ON P3E 2K8 – 705/523-2339

Sudbury: Le Voyageur, 20 St. Anne St., Sudbury ON P3A 5N4 – 705/673-3377; Fax: 705/673-5854; Email: voyageur@vianet.on.ca – Tirage: 3,900; Mercredi; français – Éditeur, Guy Lemieux; Rédacteur, Jacques des Bacquers

Tavistock Gazette, PO Box 70, Tavistock ON N0B 2R0 – 519/655-2341 – Wed.

Tecumseh: Le Rempart, 7515 Forest Glade, Tecumseh ON N8N 2M1 – 519/234-6735 – Mercredi; français

Tecumseh: Shoreline Week, 1614 Lesperance Rd., Tecumseh ON N8N 1Y3 – Wed.

Teeswater: The Clifford News, 13 Clinton St., PO Box 250, Teeswater ON N0G 2S0 – 519/327-8668 – Wed.

Teeswater News, PO Box 250, Teeswater ON N0G 2S0 – 519/392-6175 – Wed.

Terrace Bay Schreiber News, PO Box 730, Schreiber ON P0T 2S0 – 807/824-2021 – Tue.

Thamesville Herald, 65 London Rd., Thamesville ON N0P 2K0 – 519/692-3825 – Wed.

Thessalon: The North Shore Sentinel, PO Box 640, Thessalon ON P0R 1L0 – 705/842-2504; Fax: 705/842-2679 – Circ.: 3,500; Tue. – Publisher, Randy Rankin; Editor, D. Brent Rankin; Circulation Manager, Jackie Dauphin

Thorold News, 13 Front St., Thorold ON L2V 1X3 – 905/227-1141; Fax: 905/227-0222 – Tue.

Thunder Bay Post, 1126 Roland St., Thunder Bay ON P7B 5M4 – 807/622-8588 – Tue.

Tilbury Times, PO Box 490, Tilbury ON N0P 2L0 – 519/682-0411; Fax: 519/682-3633 – Wed.

Tillsonburg: Simcoe/Tillsonbury Lake Shore Shopper, 25 Town Line Rd., Tillsonburg ON N4G 4H6 – 519/688-1177 – Circ.: 35,977; Sat.

Tillsonburg Independent, 25 Townline Rd., Tillsonburg ON N4G 2R5 – 519/688-6892 – Circ.: 9,909; Mon., also Lakeshore Shopper (Sat., circ. 35,977)

Tillsonburg News, PO Box 190, Tillsonburg ON K4G 4H6 – 519/688-6397; Fax: 519/842-3511 – Circ.: 5,746; Wed., Fri.

Timmins: The Freighter, 550 Lamminen, Timmins ON P4N 4R3 – 705/268-4282 – Wed.

Timmins Times, The 101 Mall, 38 Pine St. North, PO Box 1006, Timmins ON P4N 6K6 – 705/628-6252; Fax: 705/268-2255 – Circ.: 19,157; Sat.; English & French – Publisher & Editor, Kevin Vincent; Circulation Manager, Mike Lemieux

Tobermory: The Bruce Peninsula Press, PO Box 89, Tobermory ON N0H 2R0 – 519/596-2658 – Circ.: 3,000; Every other Wed.

Toronto: Beach Metro Community News, Ward Nine Community News Inc., 2196 Gerrard St. East, Toronto ON M4E 2G7 – 416/698-1164; Fax: 416/698-1253 – Circ.: 30,000; Every other Tue. except 1 issue only in Aug. – Editor, Carole Stimmell; Circulation Manager, Sheila Blinoff

Toronto: Beach Town Crier, 1834A Queen St. East, Toronto ON M4L 1H2 – 416/690-9166 – Circ.: 30,000; Monthly – Owner, Julie Morris

Toronto: East Toronto Advocate, Toronto WenDay Publishing Ltd., #307, 146 Laird Ave., Toronto ON M4G 3V7 – 416/467-7037; Fax: 416/467-6700 – Thur.; also publishes: East York Times (Thur.,); Forest Hill Journal (every other Thur.); Leaside Advertiser (Thur.); North Toronto Free Press (every other Thur.); North Toronto Herald (every other Thur.); The St. Clair Examiner (every other Thur.)

Toronto: L'Express, 17 Carlaw Ave., Toronto ON M4M 2R6 – 416/465-2107 – Mardi; français; also publishes: L'Observateur, London; L'Information, Hamilton/Burlington, & Le Courrier d'Oshawa

Toronto: North Toronto Post, Post Newspapers Inc., 340 Sheppard Ave. East, Toronto ON M2N 3B4 – 416/250-7979 – Monthly; also publishes: Bayview Post, Thornhill Post, The Village Post

Toronto: Nouveau Canada, #1506, 141 Adelaide St. West, Toronto ON M5H 3L5 – 416/481-7793 – Vendredi; français

Toronto: The Times, #213, 2323 Bloor St. West, Toronto ON M6S 4W1 – 416/763-6397 – 24 times a year

Toronto etc...News, 201 Leslie St., Toronto ON M4M 3C6 – 416/465-7554; Fax: 416/465-8190 – Circ.: 25,000; Monthly – Publisher, Bruce Brackett; Editor, Terry Brackett

Toronto Jewish Press, PO Box 142, Downsview ON M3M 3A3 – 416/633-0202 – Fri.; English & Hebrew

Toronto: The Toronto Voice, 249 Sherbourne St., Toronto ON M5A 2R9 – 416/927-0150 – Circ.: 32,500; Monthly – Publisher & Editor-in-Chief, Barbara Neyedly

Toronto: Town Crier, #303-1560 Bayview Ave., Toronto ON M4G 3B8 – 416/488-4779; Fax: 416/488-4918 – Monthly; four separate newspapers: Leaside-Rosedale Town Crier (circ. 25,000); North Toronto Town Crier (circ. 27,000); Forest Hill Town Crier (circ. 26,000); Bayview Mills Town Crier (circ. 25,000) – Publisher, Harry Goldhar; Editor, Kate Robertson

Toronto: Villager, 2259 Bloor St. West, Toronto ON M6S 1N8 – 416/767-3644; Fax: 416/767-4880 – Circ.: 42,000; Monthly – Publisher, George Longo; Editor, Ian McMillan

Tottenham Times, PO Box 310, Beeton ON L0G 1A0 – 905/729-2287 – Wed.

Trenton Trentonian, PO Box 130, Trenton ON K8V 5R3 – 613/392-6501 – Circ.: 7,677; Mon., Wed., Fri.; also CoverStory (Fri.)

Tweed News, PO Box 550, Tweed ON K0K 3J0 – 613/478-2017; Fax: 613/478-2749 – Circ.: 2,100; Wed. – Publisher & Editor, Ivy Hanna; Circulation Manager, Roseann Turcotte

Uxbridge Times Journal, 8 Church St., PO Box 459, Uxbridge ON L9P 1M9 – 905/852-9141; Fax: 905/852-9341 – Circ.: 5,000; Wed. – Publisher, Don MacLeod; Managing Editor, Jim Belyea

Vankleek Hill Review, PO Box 160, Vankleek Hill ON K0B 1R0 – 613/678-3327; Fax: 613/678-2700; Email: review@hawknet.ca – Circ.: 4,500; Wed.; English & French – Publisher, Louise Sproule; Editor, Richard Mahoney

Virgil: Niagara Advance, PO Box 430, Virgil ON L0S 1T0 – 905/468-3283; Fax: 905/468-3137 – Circ.: 5,750; Tue. – Publisher, Tim Dundas; Editor, Doug Morton

Walkerton Herald-Times, 110 Durham St. East, PO Box 190, Walkerton ON N0G 2V0 – 519/881-1600; Fax: 519/881-0276 – Wed.

Wallaceburg Courier-Press, PO Box 86, Wallaceburg ON N8A 4L5 – 519/627-1488 – Wed.

Wallaceburg News, 222 Wellington St., Wallaceburg ON N8A 2X9 – 519/627-2243 – Wed.

Warkworth Journal, PO Box 400, Cobourg ON K9A 4L1 – 905/372-0131 – Wed.

Waterdown Flamborough Review, 30 Main St. North, PO Box 20, Waterdown ON L0R 2H0 – 905/689-4841 – Wed.

Waterloo Chronicle, 75 King St. South, 2nd Fl., Waterloo ON N2J 1P2 – 519/886-2830; Fax: 519/886-9383; Email: Editor@waterloo-chronicle.com – Circ.: 25,000; Wed. – Publisher, Rick Campbell; Editor, Melodee Martinik; Circulation Manager, Andrew Pearen

Watford Guide-Advocate, 5292 Nauvoo Rd., Watford ON N0M 2S0 – 519/876-2809; Fax: 519/876-2322 – Circ.: 1,408; Wed.

Wawa/Algoma News Review, PO Box 528, Wawa ON P0S 1K0 – 705/856-2267; Fax: 705/856-4952 – Circ.: 1,850; Wed. – Publisher & Editor, W. Robert Avis; Circulation Manager, Nancy Pavlic

Welland Regional Shopping News, 440 Niagara St., Unit 7, Welland ON L3C 1L5 – 905/735-9222 – Wed.

West Lincoln Review, PO Box 40, Smithville ON L0R 2A0 – 905/957-3315 – Wed.

Westport & Rideau Valley Mirror, PO Box 130, Westport ON K0G 1X0 – Circ.: 2,511; Wed.

Wheatley Journal, PO Box 10, Wheatley ON N0P 2P0 – 519/825-4541 – Wed.

Whitby Free Press, PO Box 206, Whitby ON L1N 5S1 – 905/668-6111; Fax: 905/668-0594 – Circ.: 28,500; Wed. – Publisher, Doug Anderson; Editor, Maurice Pifher

Wiarton Echo, PO Box 220, Wiarton ON N0H 2T0 – 519/534-1560; Fax: 519/534-4616 – Wed.

Willowdale: Scarborough/North York Mirror, Metroland Printing, Publishing & Distributing Ltd., 10 Tempo Ave., Willowdale ON M2H 2N8 – 416/493-4400; Fax: 416/493-4703 – Circ.: 106,000; Wed., Sun. – Publisher, Betty Carr; Editor, Tracy Kibble

Winchester Press, 2woMor Publications Inc., PO Box 399, Winchester ON K0C 2K0 – 613/774-2524; Fax: 613/774-3967 – Circ.: 4,300; Wed. – Publisher, John Morris; Editor, Liz Edwards; Circulation Manager, Connie Hart

Windsor Pennysaver, 2610 Pillette Rd., Windsor ON N8T 1R1 – 519/944-7070 – Sun.

Wingham Advance-Times, PO Box 390, Wingham ON N0G 2W0 – 519/357-2320 – Circ.: 2,010; Wed.

Woodbridge Advertiser, RR#1, Palgrave ON L0N 1P0 – 905/729-4501 – Tue.

Woodstock: Oxford Shopping News, 809 Dundas St., Woodstock ON N4S 1G2 – 519/537-6657 – Circ.: 27,800; Tue., Fri.

Wyoming: Lambton-Sarnia Shopping News, PO Box 695, Wyoming ON N0N 1T0 – 519/845-3366; Fax: 519/845-3110 – Sat. – Publisher, Peter Wilpstra

Zurich: The Lakeshore Advance, PO Box 190, Zurich ON N0M 2T0 – 519/236-4312; Fax: 519/236-7558 – Wed.

Canadian Almanac & Directory 1997

Prince Edward Island Daily Newspapers

CHARLOTTETOWN:
The Guardian, Thomson Newspapers Co. Ltd., 165 Prince St., Charlottetown PE C1A 4R7 – 902/629-6000; Fax: 902/566-3808 – Circ.: 23,225 morning; Morning – Publisher & General Manager, Don Brander; Editor, Jim Palmateer; Circulation Manager, Julie Murtha

SUMMERSIDE:
Journal Pioneer, 4 Queen St., PO Box 2480, Summerside PE C1N 4K5 – 902/436-2121; Fax: 902/436-3027 – Circ.: 10,891; Evening – Publisher, Steen O. Jorgensen

Other Newspapers in Prince Edward Island
Alberton: West Prince Graphic, PO Box 790, Montague PE C0A 1R0 – 902/838-2515; Fax: 902/838-4392; Email: wgrakphic@cycor.ca – Circ.: 2,149; Wed. – Publisher & Editor, Jim MacNeill; Circulation Manager, Hazel Easter
Montague: The Eastern Graphic, PO Box 790, Montague PQ C0A 1R0 – 902/838-2515; Fax: 902/838-4392 – Circ.: 5,789; Wed.
Summerside: La Voix Acadienne, 340, rue Court, CP 1420, Summerside PE C1N 4K2 – 902/436-6005; Fax: 902/888-3976 – Mercredi; français

Québec Daily Newspapers

CHICOUTIMI:
Le Quotidien, 1051, boul Talbot, Chicoutimi PQ G7H 5C1 – 418/545-4474; Fax: 418/690-8824 – Tirage: 30,562; Matin; français – Éditeur & Rédacteur, Claude Gagnon; Directeur de tirage, Jean-Louis Lavoie

GRANBY:
La Voix de L'Est, 76, rue Dufferin, Granby PQ J2G 9L4 – 514/375-4555; Fax: 514/777-7221 – Tirage: 15,324 lun.-ven., 19,151 sam.; Matin; français – Éditeur & Rédacteur, Pierre Gobeil

MONTRÉAL:
Le Devoir, 2050, rue de Bleury, Montréal PQ H3A 3M9 – 514/985-3399; Fax: 514/985-3390; URL: http://www.vir.com/~wily/intoronto/chrnint.htm – Tirage: 29,534 lun.-ven., 34,948 sam.; Matin; français – Éditrice, Lise Bissonnette
The Gazette, 250, rue St-Antoine ouest, Montréal PQ H2Y 3R7 – 514/987-2222; Fax: 514/987-2323; URL: http://www.montrealgazette.com – Circ.: 148,092 Mon.-Fri., 217,456 Sat., 138,204 Sun.; Morning; also South Shore Edition (Thur., circ. 21,747), West End Edition (Thur., circ. 35,512), West Island Edition (Thur., circ. 40,000) – Publisher, Michael Goldbloom; Editor-in-Chief, Joan Fraser; Reader Sales & Service VP, Cathy Hamilton Lambie
Le Journal de Montréal, Groupe Québécor Inc., 4545, rue Frontenac, Montréal PQ H2H 2R7 – 514/521-4545; Fax: 514/521-5442 – Tirage: 277,383 lun.-ven., 336,294 sam., 292,691 dim.; Matin; français – Éditeur, Pierre Francoeur
La Presse, 7, rue St-Jacques, Montréal PQ H2Y 1K9 – 514/285-7306; Fax: 514/845-8129 – Tirage: 190,623 lun.-ven., 331,082 sam., 192,552 dim.; Matin; français – Éditeur, Roger D. Landry

QUÉBEC:
Le Soleil, 925, chemin Saint-Louis, CP 1547, Succ Terminus, Québec PQ G1K 7J6 – 418/686-3233; Fax: 418/686-3374 & 686-3260 – Matin; français – Éditeur, Gilbert Lacasse

RIMOUSKI:
Le Journal le Fleuve, Société du Fleuve d'information, 24, rue St-Pierre, Rimouski PQ G5L 1T3 – 418/721-3538; Fax: 418/721-3580 – Tirage: 14,000; Matin, mardi-samedi – Rédacteur, Robert Maltais

SHERBROOKE:
Record, Groupe Québécor Inc., 2850, rue Delorme, Sherbrooke PQ J1K 1A1 – 819/569-9525; Fax: 819/569-3945 – Circ.: 5,500; Morning, five days a week – Publisher, Randy Kinnear; Editor-in-Chief, Charles Bury
La Tribune, 1950, rue Roy, Sherbrooke PQ J1K 2X8 – 819/564-5450; Fax: 819/564-5455 – Tirage: 32,246 lun.-ven., 43,557 sam.; Matin; français – Éditeur, Raymond Tardif

TROIS-RIVIÈRES:
Le Nouvelliste, 1920, rue Bellefeuille, Trois-Rivières PQ G9A 3Y2 – 819/376-2501; Fax: 819/376-0946 – Tirage: 49,347; Matin; français – Rédacteur, Jean Sisto

VANIER:
Le Journal de Québec, Groupe Québécor Inc., 450, rue Bechard, Vanier PQ G1M 2E9 – 418/683-1573; Fax: 418/683-1027 – Tirage: 102,701 lun.-ven., 122,079 sam., 99,905 dim.; Matin; français – Éditeur, Jean-Claude L'Abbée; Rédacteur, Serge Côté; Directeur de tirage, Marc Couture

Other Newspapers in Québec
Alma: L'Echo, 525, av du Pont sud, Alma PQ G8B 2T9 – 819/523-6141 – Dimanche; aussi L'Etoile du Lac (mardi)
Alma: Le Lac Saint-Jean, 525, av du Pont, Alma PQ G8B 2T9 – 418/668-4545 – Tirage: 19 716; Dimanche
Amqui: L'Avant-Poste Gaspesien, CP 410, Rimouski PQ G5L 7C4 – 418/723-4800; Fax: 418/722-4078 – Dimanche
Arthabaska: L'Union, 43, rue Notre-Dame est, PO Box 130, Arthabaska PQ G6P 3Z4 – 514/357-8232; Fax: 514/357-3623 – Circ.: 25,150; Mercredi
Asbestos: Les Actualités, 78, rue St-Jean, Asbestos PQ J1T 3R3 – 819/879-6681; Fax: 819/879-2355 – Lundi
Aylmer Bulletin d'Aylmer, 9, av Principale, Aylmer PQ J9H 3K9 – 819/684-4755; Fax: 819/684-6428 – Wed.; English & French
Aylmer: The Outaouais Informer, #26, 210 Aylmer Rd., Aylmer PQ J9H 1A2 – 819/682-6397; Fax: 819/682-4348 – Circ.: 72,992; Wed. – Publisher, Colin Clarke; Editor-in-Chief, Ken James; Circulation Manager, Paul Sabourin
Baie-Comeau Objectif-Plein-Jour, Rive-Nord médias inc., 896, rue de Puyjalon, Baie-Comeau PQ G5C 1N1 – 418/589-5900; Fax: 418/589-5263 – Samedi; aussi Plein jour sur la Manicouagan (mercredi, tirage 15 687) – Rédactrice, Thérèse Lepebure
Baie-Commeau: Le Plein-Jour en Haute Côte-Nord, Rive Nord média, inc., 896, rue de Puyjalon, Baie-Commeau PQ J5C 1N5 – 418/589-5900; Fax: 418/589-5263 – Lundi – Rédactrice, Thérèse Lefebvre
Beauport Express, Groupe Quebecor inc., 597 av Royale, Beauport PQ G1E 1Y6 – 418/663-6131; Fax: 418/663-3469 – Tirage: 40,000; Hebdomadaire – Directeur Général, Paul Lessard
Bedford: Journal des Rivières, CP 960, Bedford PQ J0J 1A0 – 514/248-3303; Fax: 514/248-7540 – Tirage: 6,562; Samedi – Rédacteur, Richard Hamel
Beloeil: L'Oeil Régional, 393 av Laurier, Beloeil PQ J3G 4H6 – 514/467-1821; Fax: 514/467-3087 – Tirage: 27,000; Samedi – Rédacteur, Guy Gilbert
Boucherville: Journal La Relève, 528, rue St-Charles, Boucherville PQ J4B 3M5 – Tirage: 16 000; Samedi
Boucherville: La Seigneurie, 391, boul de Montagne, Boucherville PQ J4B 1B7 – 514/641-3360; Fax: 514/655-9752 – Tirage: 30 000; Samedi – Rédacteur, S. Landry

Bromont: Ici maintenant Bromont, a/s Imprimerie Désourdy, 30, rue Pacifique est, Bromont PQ J0E 1L0 – 514/534-2823 – Marianik Gagnon
Brossard-Eclair Extra, #A105, 7900, boul Taschereau, Brossard PQ J4X 1C2 – 514/466-3344; Fax: 514/466-9019 – Circ.: 23 800; Sun.; French & English
Buckingham: Le Bulletin, 435, rue Principale, Buckingham PQ J8L 2G8 – 819/986-5089; Fax: 819/986-2073 – Tirage: 10 200; Mercredi
Buckingham: La Vie à Buckingham Life, #203, 585 James St., PO Box 180, Buckingham PQ J8L 2R7 – 819/986-8557; Fax: 819/986-8167 – Circ.: 7,000; Wed.
Cabano: Témis nouvelles, 1639, rue Commerciale, Cabano PQ G0L 1E0 – Dimanche
Cabano: Le Touladi, CP 430, Cabano PQ G0L 1E0 – 418/854-2766; Fax: 418/854-2830 – Tirage: 9 800; Dimanche
Cacouna: Journal Epik de Cacouna, 245, rue Principale, Cacouna PQ G0L 1G0 – Circ.: 770
Cap-de-la-Madeleine: L'Hebdo-Journal, 44, rue de la Fonderie, Cap-de-la-Madeleine PQ G8T 2E8 – 819/379-1490; Fax: 819/379-0705 – Tirage: 44 500; Dimanche
Chambly: Le Journal de Chambly, 1685 Bourgogne, CP 175, Chambly PQ J3L 1Y8 – 514/658-6516; Fax: 514/658-3785 – Tirage: 20,725; Mardi – Rédacteur, Daniel Noiseux
Chandler: Le Havre, PO Box 410, Rimouski PQ G5L 7C4 – 418/723-4800; Fax: 418/722-4078 – Tirage: 8 035; Dimanche
Charlesbourg Express, 1380, boul René-Lévesque ouest, Charlesbourg PQ G1S 1W6 – 418/681-3454; Fax: 418/682-5910 – Dimanche – Directeur-General, L. Béchette
Châteauguay: L'Information Regional, #202, 243, boul d'Anjou, Châteauguay PQ J6J 2R3 – 514/691-3863; Fax: 514/691-3883 – Tirage: 27 105; Mercredi – Rédacteur, André Gendron
Châteauguay: Le Soleil du St-Laurent, Hebdos Montérégiens, 82, boul Salaberry sud, Châteauguay PQ J6J 4J6 – 514/692-8555; Fax: 514/692-3460 – Tirage: 25 250; Samedi – Rédacteur, Jeanne D'Arc Germain, 514/692-8552
Chelsea: The Low Down to Hull & Back News, PO Box 99, Wakefield PQ J0X 3G0 – 819/459-2222; Email: wakefield_news@ocna.org – Circ.: 2,500; Mon. – Publisher, K.J. Mantell; Editor, Arthur Mantell
Chibougamau: La Sentinelle, CP 250, Chibougamau PQ G8P 2K7 – 819/748-6406 – Tirage: 3 200; Mardi
Chicoutimi: Le Progrès Dimanche, 1051, boul Talbot, Chicoutimi PQ G7H 5C1 – 418/545-4474; Fax: 418/690-8824 – Tirage: 30 610; Dimanche
Chicoutimi: Le Réveil à Chicoutimi, 3388, boul St-François, Jonquière PQ G7X 2W9 – 418/695-2601 – Tirage: 30 610; Dimanche
Coaticook: Le Progrès, CP 150, Coaticook PQ J1A 2S9 – 819/849-3616 – Tirage: 7 585; Samedi
Cookshire: Le Haut St-François, 80, rue Principale est, CP 292, Cookshire PQ J0B 1M0 – 819/875-5501; Fax: 819/875-3135 – Tirage: 9 500; Mensuel – Pierre Hébert
Côte-Saint-Luc: The Suburban, 8170, ch Wavell, Côte-Saint-Luc PQ H4W 1M3 – 514/484-1107; Fax: 514/484-7284 – Wed., 8 area editions: Cote-des-Neiges/Snowdon, Côte-Saint-Luc, Hampstead, Chomedy/St-Laurent, Montréal-ouest, Town of Mount Royal, Westmount, The West Island
Cowansville: Le Citoyen, 352, rue Principale, St-Alphonse-de-Granby PQ J0E 2A0 – 514/777-1636 – Lundi
Cowansville: Le Guide, 245, rue Principale, Cowansville PQ J2K 1J4 – 514/263-5288; Fax: 514/263-9435 – Tirage: 16 000; Samedi
Delson: Le Reflet, 54, boul Marie-Victorin, Delson PQ J0L 1E0 – Tirage: 26 500; Samedi
Donnacona: Le Courrier de Portneuf, 274, rue Notre-Dame, CP 1030, Donnacona PQ G0A 1T0 – 418/285-

0211; Fax: 418/285-2441 – Tirage: 29,700; Samedi – Rédacteur, Maurice Marcotte

Dorion: L'Etoile de l'Outaouais St-Laurent, 123, rue Dumont, CP 160, Dorion PQ J7V 5W1 – 514/455-6111 – Tirage: 30 750; Mercredi; aussi 1ére Édition du Sud-ouest (samedi)

Drummondville: L'Express, 1050, Cormier, Drummondville PQ J2C 2N6 – 819/477-3773; Email: unimedia@9bit.qc.ca – Tirage: 40 600; Dimanche – Rédacteur, Real Brodeur

Drummondville: La Parole, 1050, rue Cormier, Drummondville PQ J2C 2N6 – 819/478-8171; Fax: 819/478-4306; Email: unimedia@9bit.qc.ca – Tirage: 35 835; Mercredi – Rédacteur, Real Brodeur

Farnham: L'Avenir, 322A, rue Principale est, Farnham PQ J2N 1L7 – 514/293-3138; Fax: 514/293-2093 – Tirage: 41 398; Samedi

Fermont: Le Trait d'Union du Nord, Ctr. L.J. Patterson, CP 561, Fermont PQ G0G 1J0 – Tirage: 1 500

Fort Coulonge/Pontiac Journal, 184, rue Principale, PO Box 893, Fort Coulonge PQ J0X 1V0 – 819/683-3582; Fax: 819/683-2977 – Circ.: 9,855; Every other Tue.; English & French – Publisher & Editor, Fred Ryan; Circulation Manager, Peter L. Smith

Gaspé Peninsula Spec, 128 Main St., PO Box 99, New Carlisle PQ G0C 1Z0 – 418/752-5400, 5070; Fax: 418/752-6932; Email: SPEC@OCNA.org – Circ.: 3,200; Sun. – Publisher, Sharon Farrell; Editor, Cynthia Dow

Gaspé: Le Pharillon, CP 410, Rimouski PQ G5L 7C4 – 418/723-4800; Fax: 418/722-4078 – Tirage: 8 470; Dimanche

Gatineau: La Revue de Gatineau, #106, 430, boul de l'Hôpital, Gatineau PQ J8V 1T7 – 819/568-7736; Fax: 819/568-7038 – Tirage: 36,947; Mercredi – Éditeur, Yves Blondin; Rédacteur, Sylvain Dupras

Gatineau: Week-end Outaouais, 418, ch du Golf, Gatineau PQ J8P 6K3 – Tirage: 64 700; Dimanche

Granby: L'Hebdo Granbyen, #102, 11, boul Montagne, Granby PQ J2G 9M5 – Samedi

Granby: Le Nouvelle Revue, #2A, 45, rue Centre, PO Box 369, Granby PQ J2G 5B4 – 514/372-3605; Fax: 514/375-1249 – Dimanche

Granby: Samedi Express, /3201, 460 rue Principale, Granby PQ J2G 2X1 – 514/777-4515 – Circ.: 36 000; Samedi

Granby: La Voix de l'est plus dimanche, 76, rue Dufferin, Granby PQ J2G 9L4 – 514/375-6993 – Tirage: 40 142; Dimanche

Grosse Île, Magdalen Islands: First Informer, PO Box 148, Grosse Île, Magdalen Islands PQ G0B 1M0 – 418/985-2100; Fax: 418/985-2274 – Fri. – Publisher & Editor, Norma Jean Clarke

Hudson: Lake of Two Mountains Gazette, PO Box 70, Hudson PQ J0P 1H0 – 514/458-5482; Fax: 514/458-3337 – Circ.: 3,500; Wed. – Publisher & Editor, J. Jones

Hull: Bonjour Dimanche, 825, boul de la Carrière, Hull PQ J8Y 6T7 – 819/770-2205 – Tirage: 77 000; Dimanche

Hull: Le Régional Aylmer, 141, rue Jean-Proulx, Hull PQ J8Z 1T4 – 514/844-3131 – Tirage: 10 650; Mercredi

Hull: Le Regional Hull, 141, rue Jean-Proulx, Hull PQ J8Z 1T4 – 819/776-1063; Fax: 819/776-1668 – Tirage: 26 352; Mercredi

Huntingdon: The Gleaner/La Source, PO Box 130, Huntingdon PQ J0S 1H0 – 514/264-5364; Fax: 514/264-9521 – Circ.: 4,230; Wed.; English & French – Publisher, Jocelyn Ranger; Editor, Judith Taylor

Iles-de-la-Madeleine: Le Radar, L'Hebos des Iles-de-la-Madeleine, CP 580, Iles-de-la-Madeleine PQ G0B 1B0 – 418/986-2345; Fax: 418/986-6358 – Tirage: 3,000; Vendredi; français – Éditeur, Achille Hubert; Rédactrice, Isabelle Cummings; Directeur de tirage, Daniel La Pierre

Joliette: L'Expression de Lanaudière, 342, Beaudry nord, Joliette PQ J6E 6A6 – 514/752-0447 – Tirage: 43 500; Tous les deux lundi

Joliette: Le Régional de Lanaudière, 262, boul l'Industrie, Joliette PQ J6E 3Z1 – Tirage: 20 965; Mercredi

Joliettte: L'Action, 262, boul l'Industrie, Joliettte PQ J8E 3Z1 – 514/759-3664; Fax: 514/759-9828 – Tirage: 44 000; Dimanche

Jonquière: Le Réveil à Jonquière, 3388, boul St-François, Jonquière PQ G7X 2W9 – 418/695-2601 – Tirage: 26 992; Dimanche; aussi Le Point (dimanche), Le Réveil à la Baie (dimanche)

Knowlton: Brome County News, 88 Lakeside, Knowlton PQ J0E 1V0 – Wed.

La Malbaie: L'Hebdo Charlevoisien, 176, boul de Comporte, La Malbaie PQ G5A 1P7 – 418/665-1299 – Tirage: 13 033; Dimanche

La Malbaie: Le Plein Jour Charlevoix, #110, 249, rue Nairn, La Malbaie PQ G5A 1M4 – 418/665-6121; Fax: 418/665-3105 – Tirage: 12 118; Samedi

La Plaine: Journal le Plainois, #205, 1456A, Montée Major, La Plaine PQ J0N 1B0 – 514/964-4444 – Tirage: 19 000; Mercredi

Lac Etchemin: La Voix du Sud, CP 789, Lac Etchemin PQ G0R 1S0 – 418/625-7471; Fax: 418/625-5200 – Tirage: 19 400; Dimanche

Lac-Mégantic: L'Echo de Frontenac, 5040, boul des Vétérans, Lac-Mégantic PQ G6B 2G5 – 819/583-1630; Fax: 819/583-1124 – Tirage: 9,050; Dimanche – Éditeur, Gaétan Poulin; Rédacteur en chef, Rémi Tremblay; Directrice de tirage, Suzanne Poulin

Lachine: Le Messager de Lachine, 1015, rue Notre-Dame, Lachine PQ H8S 2C3 – 514/637-2381; Fax: 514/637-8273 – Tirage: 18 100; Wed.; English & French

Lachute: L'Argenteuil, 52, rue Principale, Lachute PQ J8H 3A8 – 514/562-2494; Fax: 514/562-1434 – Tirage: 12,900; Mercredi; français – Éditeur, André Paquette; Rédacteur, François Legault; Directeur de tirage, Alain Morris

Lachute: Tribune/Express, 52, rue Principale, Lachute PQ J8H 3A8 – 514/562-8593; Fax: 514/562-1434 – Email: watchman@ocna.org – Circ.: 12.900; Sat.; English & French – Publisher, André Paquette; Editor, François Legault; Circulation Manager, Alain Morris

LaSalle: Le Messenger de LaSalle, 9216, ch Boivin, LaSalle PQ H8R 2E7 – 514/363-5656; Fax: 514/363-3151 – Circ.: 26,600; Sun.; English & French

Laurier Station: Le Peuple de Lotbinière, 1000, ch St-Joseph, CP 130, Laurier Station PQ G0S 1N0 – 418/728-2131; Fax: 418/728-4819 – Tirage: 10 971; Dimanche

Laval: Nouvelles Chomedey News, #200, 1530, boul Curé Labelle, Laval PQ H7V 2W2 – 514/978-9999 – Tirage: 40 000; Samedi

Laval-des-Rapides: Contact Laval, 189, rue Laval, Laval-des-Rapides PQ H7N 3V8 – 514/667-4360; Fax: 514/667-9498 – Tirage: 98 158; Mercredi; aussi Courrier Laval (dimanche; tirage 90 200) – Éditeur & Rédacteur, Jacques Dion; Directrice de tirage, Lynn Fortin

Lennoxville: The Townships Sun, 7 Conley St., PO Box 28, Lennoxville PQ J1M 1Z3 – 819/566-7424; Fax: 819/566-7424 – Circ.: 1,000; Monthly – Editor, Patricia Ball

Levis-Lauzon: Le Peuple-Tribune, 45, rue Desjardins, Levis-Lauzon PQ G6V 5V3 – 418/833-9398; Fax: 418/833-8177 – Tirage: 27 705; Samedi

Longueuil: Le Courrier du Sud, 267, rue St-Charles ouest, Longueuil PQ J4H 1E3 – 514/646-3333 – Tirage: 118 000; Dimanche; aussi Longueuil Extra (dimanche, tirage 53 000)

Loretteville: L'Actuel, 1380, boul René Lévesque ouest, Québec PQ G1S 1W6 – 418/681-3454; Fax: 418/682-5910 – Tirage: 44 133; Dimanche – Directeur-General, L. Béchette

Louiseville: L'Echo de Louiseville/Berthier, 50, rue St-Aimé, Louiseville PQ J5V 2Y7 – 819/228-2766 – Tirage: 8 745; Mercredi; aussi Salut Dimanche (dimanche, tirage 17 599)

Magog: Le Progres de Magog, 355, rue Principale ouest, Magog PQ J1X 2B1 – 819/843-2000; Fax: 819/843-2608 – Samedi

Magog: Le Reflect du Lac, 106, Place du Commerce, Magog PQ J1X 5G6 – 819/843-3500; Fax: 819/843-3085 – Dimanche

Malartic: Le Courrier de Malartic, CP 4020, Malartic PQ J0Y 1Z0 – 819/757-4712; Fax: 819/757-4712 – Tirage: 1,200; Mardi – Éditeur, Pierre Routhier; Rédactrice, Denyse Roberge

Maniwaki: La Gatineau, 93, rue de la Ferme, Maniwaki PQ J9E 2H5 – 819/449-1725; Fax: 819/449-5108 – Mardi

Maniwaki: La Gazette de Maniwaki, 93, rue Notre-Dame, Maniwaki PQ J9E 2H5 – 819/449-2233; Fax: 819/449-7067 – Tirage: 10,200; Dimanche; français – Éditrice, Denise Carrière

Mascouche: Le Trait d'Union, 2522, boul Ste-Marie, Mascouche PQ J7K 1M5 – Tirage: 42 245; Dimanche

Matane: La Voix Gaspesienne, #107, 305, rue de la Gare, Matane PQ G4W 3M5 – 418/562-4040; Fax: 418/562-4607 – Tirage: 4 938; Mercredi; aussi La Voix du dimanche (dimanche)

Mont Joli: L'Information, 135, rue Doucet, Mont Joli PQ G5H 1R6 – 418/775-4381 – Tirage: 12 000; Dimanche

Mont-Laurier: Le Choix, 501, boul Paquette, Mont-Laurier PQ J9L 1K8 – Tirage: 14 624; Vendredi

Mont-Laurier: L'Echo de la Lievre, 500, rue de la Madonne, Mont-Laurier PQ J9L 1S5 – 819/623-5250 – Tirage: 11 610; Dimanche

Montmagny: L'Oie Blanche, #401, 1, Place de l'Eglise, CP 40, Montmagny PQ G5V 3S3 – Tirage: 19 027; Samedi

Montmagny: Le Peuple de la Côte-du-Sud, CP 430, Montmagny PQ G5V 3S7 – 418/248-0415 – Tirage: 19 200; Vendredi

Montréal: Afiya, #605, 180, rue Ste-Catherine est, Montréal PQ H2X 1K9 – 514/876-8940 – Ibrahima Sory Baldé

Montréal: Canadian Jewish News, #341, 6900, boul Decarie, Montréal PQ H3X 2T8 – 514/735-2612; Fax: 514/735-9090; Email: 102574.1304@compuserve.com – Circ.: 20,000; Thur.; English with some French – Editor, Mordechai Ben-Dat

Montréal: Le Citoyen de Saint-Lambert, #902, 1550, rue Metcalfe, Montréal PQ H3A 1X6 – 514/845-8724 – Tue.; English & French

Montréal: Échos du Vieux-Montréal, 230, rue St-Paul ouest, Montréal PQ H2Y 1Z9 – 514/844-2133 – Vincent Di Candido

Montréal: L'Express d'Outremont, 230, av Laurier ouest, Montréal PQ H2T 2N8 – 514/276-9615; Fax: 514/274-5564 – Tirage: 16 000; Vendredi, tous les deux semaines; français – Éditeur, Jean Lessard; Éditeur & Rédacteur, Alain Tittley

Montréal: Les Hebdos Metropolitains de Montréal, #202, 6424, rue Jean Talon est, Montréal PQ H1S 1M8 – 514/899-5888; Fax: 514/899-5001 – Mardi; publie: Le Flambeau de l'Est, Anjou (tirage 45 908), Nouvelles de l'Est (tirage 27 031), Le Guide Mont-Royal (tirage 16 900), La Petite Patrie (tirage 18 097), Le Journal de Rosemont (tirage 35 570), Nouveau Journal de St-Michel (dimanche, tirage 22 400), Le Progres de Villeray (tirage 21 630), Le Guide de Montréal-Nord (tirage 32 388), L'Avenir de l'Est (tirage 40 815), L'Informateur (mercredi, tirage 16 811), Le Progres de st-Léonard (tirage 34 668)

Montréal: Journal St-Louis et Mile-End, 4181, rue Saint-Dominique, Montréal PQ H2W 2A7 – Dimanche

Montréal: Messager de Verdun Messenger, 1735, av de l'Eglise, Montréal PQ H4E 1G6 – 514/768-2544 – Mon.; English & French

Canadian Almanac & Directory 1997

Montréal: Le Monde, CP 7, Succ St-Michel, Montréal PQ H2A 7L8 – 514/722-7708 – Vendredi – Éditeur, Normand Lalonde; Rédacteur, Guy Jolicoeur

Montréal: The Monitor, 5925, av Monkland, Montréal PQ H4A 1G7 – 514/481-7510; Fax: 514/481-3492 – Circ.: 30,000; Wed.; English & French – Publisher, Robert Fisher; Editor, Leonard J. Gervais; Circulation Manager, Amy Miller

Montréal: Nouvelles Parc-Extension News, #403, 7000, av Parc, Montréal PQ H3N 1X1 – 514/272-0252 – Wed.; English & French

Montréal: La Voix Populaire, 1735, rue de l'Église, Montréal PQ H4E 1G6 – 514/678-4777 – Tirage: 25 000; Dimanche

Montréal/Ahuntsic: Courrier Ahuntsic, 189, rue Laval, Laval-des-Rapides PQ H7N 3V8 – 514/667-4360; Fax: 514/667-9498 – Tirage: 33 366; Dimanche – Rédacteur, Jacques Dion

Mount-Royal: Le Journal de Ville Mont-Royal, CP 697, Succ Mont-Royal, Mount-Royal PQ H3P 3G4 – 514/739-5839 – Mensuel; aussi Town of Mount Royal Journal (English)

Mount-Royal: Weekly Post/L'Hebdo de Ville Mount-Royal, #280, 1255, boul Laird, Mount-Royal PQ H3P 2T1 – 514/739-3302; Fax: 514/739-3304 – Thur.; English & French

Napierville: Coup D'Oeil, 350, rue St-Jacques, Napierville PQ J0J 1L0 – 514/245-3344; Fax: 514/245-7419 – Tirage: 12,270; Samedi

New Richmond: L'Écho de la Baie, 140, boul Perron ouest, CP 129, New Richmond PQ G0C 2B0 – 418/392-5083; Fax: 418/392-6605 – Mardi

New Richmond: Le Journal Le Chaleur, CP 410, Rimouski PQ G5L 7C4 – 418/723-4800; Fax: 418/722-4078 – Dimanche

Nicolet Courrier-Sud, Les Publications J.T.C. inc., 3255, rue Marie Victorin, Nicolet PQ J3T 1X5 – 819/293-4551; Fax: 819/293-8758 – Tirage: 21,544; Dimanche – Rédacteur, Jean Blanchette

Nun's Island Magazine, #320, 1, Place du Commerce, Nun's Island PQ H3E 1A4 – 514/767-7154 – Wed.; English & French

Outremont: Le Journal d'Outremont, 812, av Davaar, CP 727, Succ Outremont, Outremont PQ H2V 3B5 – 514/276-6671; Fax: 514/276-1011 – Tirage: 16,000; Mensuel – Éditrice, Patrice Dauzet; Éditrice, Louise Perron

Pierrefonds: Le Reflet de L'Ouest-de-l'Ile, 15650, boul Pierrefonds, Pierrefonds PQ H9H 2G2 – Vendredi

Plessisville: La Feuille d'Erable, CP 160, Plessisville PQ G6L 2Y7 – 819/362-7049; Fax: 819/362-2216 – Tirage: 5 000; Mardi

Pointe-aux-Trembles: Journal PAT, 13630, rue Sherbrooke ouest, Pointe-aux-Trembles PQ H1A 4B2 – Tirage: 19 653; Mardi

Pointe-Claire: The Chronicle, 15 Cartier Ave., Pointe-Claire PQ H9S 4R7 – 514/630-6688; Fax: 514/630-7340 – Tirage: 19,049; Wed.

Québec: Droit de parole, 301, rue Carillon, Québec PQ G1K 5B3 – 418/648-8043 – Denis Cusson

Québec: Journal le Carrefour, 155, boul Charest est, Québec PQ G1K 3G6 – 418/649-0775 – Tirage: 30 000; Dimanche

Repentigny: L'Artisan, 1004, rue Notre-Dame, Repentigny PQ J5Y 1S9 – 514/581-5120; Fax: 514/581-6509 – Tirage: 43 680; Mardi; aussi Hebdo Rive-Nord (dimanche, tirage 39 900) – Helenè Ouellette

Repentigny: Hebdo Rive-Nord, 1004, rue Notre-Dame, Repentigny PQ J5Y 1S9 – 514/581-5120; Fax: 514/581-6509 – Tirage: 40 240; Dimanche – Helenè Ouellette

Rimouski: Le Progrès Echo Dimanche, CP 410, Rimouski PQ G5L 7C4 – 418/723-4800; Fax: 418/722-4078 – Tirage: 28 244; Jeudi

Rimouski: Le Rimouskois, 156, Lepage, Rimouski PQ G5L 3H2 – 418/723-2571; Fax: 418/722-4078 – Tirage: 23 317; Mardi

Rivière-du-Loup: Info Dimanche, 72, rue Fraser, Rivière-du-Loup PQ G5R 1C6 – 418/862-1911; Fax: 418/862-6165 – Tirage: 20,350; Dimanche – Éditeur & Rédacteur, Michel Chalifour

Rivière-du-Loup: Le Portage, 16, rue du Domaine, Rivière-du-Loup PQ G5R 2R2 – 418/862-1774; Fax: 418/862-4387 – Dimanche

Rouyn-Noranda: Le Citoyen, CP 490, Rouyn-Noranda PQ J9X 5C4 – 819/797-2450; Fax: 819/762-4361 – Tirage: 57,000; Dimanche; supplement, Journal du Nord-Ouest – Directeur, Andre Renaud, 819/762-4361

Rouyn-Noranda: La Frontière, 25, rue Gamble est, CP 490, Rouyn-Noranda PQ J9X 4F9 – 819/762-4361 – Tirage: 13 681; Mercredi

Rouyn-Noranda: Rouanda Express, 26, rue Gambles, Rouyn-Noranda PQ J9X 3B7 – Dimanche

Ste-Adèle: Le Journal du Pays D'en Haut, c/o Quebecor, CP 1890, Ste-Adèle PQ J0R 1L0 – 514/229-6664; Fax: 514/229-6063 – Tirage: 17,000; Mercredi – Directeur-General, Michel Gareau

Ste-Agathe: L'Information du Nord, 1107, rue Ouimet, CP 1480, Ste-Agathe PQ J0T 2H0 – 418/425-8658 – Tirage: 11 499; Samedi

St-Andre-Avelin: La Revue Mensuelde la Petite Nation, Publications Dumont inc., 70, Principale, CP 440, St-Andre-Avelin PQ J0V 1W0 – 819/983-2725; Fax: 819/983-6844 – Tirage: 8 150; Lundi – Rédacteur, Michel Blais

Saint-Bruno: L'Écho de Saint-Bruno, 1688, Place Seigneuriale, Saint-Bruno PQ J3V 4E4 – 514/653-5295 – Tirage: 10 000; Mensuel – Faouzi Majeri

Saint-Bruno: Le Journal de Saint-Bruno, 1507, rue Roberval, Saint-Bruno PQ J3V 3P8 – Tirage: 14 900; Samedi

St-Donat: Journal Altitude, CP 1350, St-Donat PQ J0T 2C0 – 819/424-2610; Fax: 819/424-3615 – Tirage: 4,000; Vendredi – Directrice de tirage, Marthe Lafortune; Rédacteur, Jean Lafortune

St-Eustache: La Concorde, 53, rue St-Eustache, St-Eustache PQ J7R 2L2 – 514/473-1700 – Tirage: 37 500; Mercredi; aussi L'Eveil (dimanche; tirage 37 400)

St-Eustache: Courrier Deux-Montagnes, 189, rue Laval, Laval-des-Rapides PQ H7N 1X1 – 514/667-4360; Fax: 514/667-9498 – Tirage: 33 366; Dimanche – Éditeur & Rédacteur, Jacques Dion; Directrice de tirage, Lynn Fortin

Sainte-Foy: L'Appel, 1380, boul René-Lévesque ouest, Sainte-Foy PQ G1S 1W6 – 418/681-3454; Fax: 418/682-5910 – Tirage: 51 959; Dimanche – Directeur-general, L. Béchette

Sainte-Foy: Québec Chronicle-Telegraph, 3484, ch Ste-Foy, Sainte-Foy PQ G1X 1S8 – 418/650-1764; Fax: 418/650-1764; Email: QUEBEC_Chron-Telegraph@ocna.org – Circ.: 2,000; Wed. – Publisher & Editor, Karen Macdonald

Sainte-Geneviève: Cités Nouvelles, 15716, boul Gouin ouest, Sainte-Geneviève PQ H9H 1C4 – Circ.: 55 000; Sun.; English & French

Saint-Georges: L'Impact, 225, rue 125, Saint-Georges PQ G5Y 2Y3 – 418/227-7700; Fax: 418/227-7711 – Tirage: 24,700; Vendredi – Rédacteur, Paul-André Parent

St-Georges-Est: L'Eclaireur Progrès-Nouvelle, 12625, av 1e, St-Georges-Est PQ G5Y 2E8 – 418/228-8858 – Tirage: 26 850; Mercredi, samedi

Saint-Hubert: Journal Servir, Base des Forces canadiennes Montréal, Saint-Hubert PQ J3Y 4T5 – 418/358-7099, ext.7426; Fax: 418/358-7423; Email: servir@aei.ca – Circ.: 4,000; English & French – Rédacteur, J.H.R. Gauthier

Saint-Hubert: Le Journal de St-Hubert Extra, 5863, boul Cousineau, Saint-Hubert PQ J3Y 7P5 – Tirage: 27 500; Dimanche

Saint-Hyacinthe: Le Clairon, CP 276, Saint-Hyacinthe PQ J2S 7B6 – 514/774-5375 – Tirage: 22 107; Mercredi

Saint-Hyacinthe: Le Courrier de Saint-Hyacinthe, 655, rue Ste-Anne, CP 340, Saint-Hyacinthe PQ J2S 7B6 – 514/773-6028; Fax: 514/773-3115 – Tirage: 14 500; Mardi; français – Rédacteur, Denis Lacasse

Saint-Hyacinthe: Le Regional Maskoutain, 592, av Ste-Marie, Saint-Hyacinthe PQ J2S 4R5 – 514/778-1045; Fax: 514/773-3115 – Tirage: 30 900; Dimanche

St-Jean-sur-Richelieu: Le Canada Français, 84, rue Richelieu, St-Jean-sur-Richelieu PQ J3B 6X3 – 514/347-0323; Fax: 514/347-4539 – Tirage: 18 000; Mercredi; aussi Le Richelieu Dimanche (dimanche)

St-Jérôme: L'Annonceur, #1, 287, rue Labelle, St-Jérôme PQ J7Z 5L2 – Tirage: 33 406; Mercredi

St-Jérôme: L'Echo du Nord, 225, rue de Palais, St-Jérôme PQ J7Z 1X7 – 514/436-5381; Fax: 514/436-5904 – Tirage: 12,000; Mercredi – Directeur de la Rédaction, Charles Michaud, 514/436-5887

St-Jérôme: Journal Le Mirabel, 225, du Palais, St-Jérôme PQ J7Z 1X7 – 514/436-8200; Fax: 514/436-8912 – Tirage: 7 999; Dimanche

St-Jovite: L'Information du Nord, 1107, rue Ouimet, CP 1480, St-Jovite PQ J0T 2H0 – 819/425-8658; Fax: 819/425-7713 – Tirage: 7 999; Samedi

Sainte-Julie: L'Information, 500, rue Jules Choquet, Sainte-Julie PQ J3E 1W6 – Dimanche

Sainte-Julie: Le Montagnard, #218, 461, boul St-Joseph, Sainte-Julie PQ J3E 1W8 – 514/649-0632 – Tirage: 18 000; Samedi

Saint-Lambert: Nun's Island Journal, 574 Victoria St., Saint-Lambert PQ J4P 2J5 – 514/932-1454 – Thur.; English & French

Saint-Lambert Journal, 574, rue Victoria, Saint-Lambert PQ J4P 2J5 – 514/671-0014 – Circ.: 10,800; Wed.; English & French

Saint-Lambert: South Shore/Greenfield Park Journal, 574 Victoria St., Saint-Lambert PQ J4P 2J5 – 514/932-1454 – Wed.

Saint-Laurent: Nouvelles Saint-Laurent, 1963, Place Thimens, Saint-Laurent PQ H4R 1K8 – 514/339-1292; Fax: 514/339-5304 – Circ.: 25 650; Tue.; English & French

St-Léonard: L'Édition Commerciale, 6885, rue Jarry est, 2e étage, St-Léonard PQ – 514/321-7000 – Tirage: 29 700; Mensuel

Sainte-Marie: Beauce Media, CP 400, Sainte-Marie PQ G0S 2Y0 – 418/387-8000; Fax: 418/387-4495 – Tirage: 16 807; Lundi

Sainte-Marie: Beauce Week-End, 450, 2e av, Sainte-Marie PQ G6E 1B6 – 418/387-6969 – Tirage: 15 200; Lundi

Sainte-Martine: Le Regional, 290, rue St. Joseph, Sainte-Martine PQ J0S 1V0 – 514/427-2306; Fax: 514/427-0120 – Circ.: 13,500; Wed.; English & French – Directeur, Pierre Doré

St-Pascal: Le Placoteux, 491, rue d'Anjou, CP 1199, St-Pascal PQ G0L 3Y0 – 418/492-2706; Fax: 418/492-9706 – Tirage: 16,623; Dimanche – Directeur-général, Raymond Freve

St-Sauveur-des-Monts: Le Journal de la Vallée, 43, rue Filion, CP 2100, St-Sauveur-des-Monts PQ J0R 1R0 – Tirage: 27 500; Jeudi

St-Siméon: Le Goéland, 127, boul Perron ouest, CP 250, St-Siméon PQ G0C 3A0 – 418/534-2026 – Micheline Babin

Ste-Thérèse/Blainville: Courrier de Groulx, 189, rue Laval, Laval-des-Rapides PQ H7N 3V8 – 514/667-4360; Fax: 514/667-9498 – Tirage: 34 816; Dimanche – Éditeur & Rédacteur, Jacques Dion; Directrice de tirage, Lynn Fortin

Ste-Thérèse/Blainville: Le Nord Info, 53, rue St-Eustache, St-Eustache PQ J7R 2L3 – 514/473-1700 – Tirage: 47 100; Dimanche

Sept-Îles: Le Nord-Est, 365, boul Laure, Sept-Îles PQ G4R 1X2 – 418/962-4100; Fax: 418/962-0439 – Tirage: 12 305; Dimanche; aussi Le Nord-Est Plus (mercredi)

Sept-Îles: Le Port-Cartois, 8, boul des Iles, Sept-Îles PQ G5B 2N1 – 418/766-5322; Fax: 418/766-5329 – Tirage: 3 600; Dimanche

Shawinigan: Hebdo du St-Maurice, CP 10, Shawinigan PQ G9N 6T8 – 819/537-5111; Fax: 819/537-5471 – Lundi

Shawville: The Equity, PO Box 430, Shawville PQ J0X 2Y0 – 819/647-2204; Fax: 819/647-2206 – Circ.: 4,523; Wed.; English & French – Publisher, Heather Dickson; Editor, Richard Wills

Sherbrooke: Entrée Libre, #317, 187, rue Laurier, Sherbrooke PQ J1H 4Z4 – 819/821-2270 – Normand Gilbert

Sherbrooke: La Nouvelle de Sherbrooke, 716, rue Short, Sherbrooke PQ J1H 2E8 – 819/566-8022; Fax: 819/563-1977 – Tirage: 43,500; Dimanche – Éditeur, Cèline Maheu; Rédacteur, Richard Gendron

Sorel: Les 2 Rives, 77, rue George, Sorel PQ J3P 1B9 – 514/742-9409 – Tirage: 28 000; Mardi

Sorel: Journal La Voix, 38, rue Augusta, Sorel PQ J3P 1A3 – 514/743-8466; Fax: 514/742-8567 – Tirage: 27,850; Dimanche – Directeur, Johanne Berthiaume; Rédactrice, Hélène Goulet

Stanstead Journal, 25A Dufferin St., CP 30, Stanstead PQ J0B 3E0 – 819/876-7514; Fax: 819/876-7515 – Wed.

Terrebonne: Le Courrier des Moulins, 790, boul des Seigneurs, Terrebonne PQ J6W 1T7 – 514/964-2655; Fax: 514/964-1692 – Dimanche; aussi Le Courrier des Moulins Mascouche/Lplaine – Éditeur & Rédacteur, Serge Lemuire; Directrice de tirage, Lynn Fortin

Terrebonne: La Revue de Terrebonne, 231, rue Ste-Marie, Terrebonne PQ J6W 3E4 – 514/964-4444; Fax: 514/471-1023 – Tirage: 39 850; Mardi – Éditeur, Marie-France Despatis; Rédacteur, Gilles Bordonado

Thetford Mines: Le Courrier Frontenac, 541, boul Smith nord, CP 789, Thetford Mines PQ G6G 5V3 – 418/338-5181; Fax: 418/338-5482 – Tirage: 19,530; Dimanche; aussi Le Flect du Lac Aylmer (Mensuel) – Rédacteur, Carol Isabel

Trois-Pistoles: Le Courrier de Trois-Pistoles, CP 759, Trois-Pistoles PQ G0L 4K0 – 418/851-3644 – Tirage: 8 901; Dimanche

Trois-Rivières: La Gazette Populaire, 952, rue Ste-Geneviève, Trois-Rivières PQ G9A 3X6 – 819/375-4012 – Dimanche – Rédacteur, Jean Martineau

Val-David: Ski-se-dit, 1280, rue Dion, CP 1080, Val-David PQ J0T 2N0 – Mensuel

Val d'Or: Les Echos Abitibiens, CP 100, Val d'Or PQ J9P 4P2 – 819/825-3755; Fax: 819/825-0361 – Tirage: 17 700; Mercredi; (Amos, Lasarre, Malartic, Matagami)

Valleyfield: Le St-François Journal, 55, rue Jacques-Cartier, Valleyfield PQ J6T 4R4 – 514/371-6222; Fax: 514/371-7254 – Tirage: 30,000; Mardi – Rédacteur, Andre Pomerleau

Vaudreuil: 1ere Édition du Sud-Ouest, 123, rue Dumont, Vaudreuil PQ J7V 1W9 – 514/455-7955; Fax: 514/455-1050 – Circ.: 34 982; Sat.; English & French

Victoriaville: La Nouvelle, PO Box 130, Victoriaville PQ G6P 3Z4 – 819/752-6718; Fax: 819/758-2759 – Circ.: 38 000; Dimanche

Ville-Marie: Le Journal Témiscamien, CP 219, Ville-Marie PQ J0Z 3W0 – 819/629-2618 – Tirage: 8 500; Mercredi

Ville-Marie: Le Reflet, Le Reflet Témiscamein inc., CP 877, Ville-Marie PQ J0Z 3W0 – 819/622-1313; Fax: 819/622-1333 – Tirage: 8,500; Mardi – Rédacteur en chef, Monic Ray

Westmount Examiner, 210 Victoria Ave., Westmount PQ H3Z 2M4 – 514/932-3157; Fax: 514/932-5700 – Thur.

Windsor: L'Etincelle, 193, rue St-Georges, Windsor PQ J1S 1J7 – 819/845-2705; Fax: 819/845-5520 – Mardi

Saskatchewan Daily Newspapers

MOOSE JAW:

Times-Herald, Hollinger Corp., 44 Fairford St. West, Moose Jaw SK S6H 6E4 – 306/692-6441; Fax: 306/692-2101; Email: moose.jaw.times@sasknet.sk.ca – Circ.: 10,261; Evening – Publisher, Bob Calvert; Editor, Carl DeGurse; Circulation Manager, Dave Mak

PRINCE ALBERT:

Daily Herald, Hollinger Inc., 30 - 10th St. East, Prince Albert SK S6V 5R9 – 306/764-4276; Fax: 306/763-3331 – Circ.: 10,036; Evening – Publisher & General Manager, Robert W. Gibb; Managing Editor, Barb Gustafson

REGINA:

The Leader-Post, 1964 Park St., Regina SK S4P 3G4 – 306/565-8211; Fax: 306/565-8350 – Circ.: 67,958; Afternoon – Publisher, Robert Hughes; Editor, John Swan, 306/565-8242

SASKATOON:

Star-Phoenix, 204 - 5th Ave. North, Saskatoon SK S7K 2P1 – 306/664-8340; Fax: 306/664-8208 – Circ.: 58,866 Mon.-Thur., 76,154 Fri., 65,594 Sat.; Morning – Exec. VP, Lyle Sinkewicz; Editor, Steve K. Gibb

Other Newspapers in Saskatchewan

Assiniboia Times, PO Box 910, Assiniboia SK S0H 0B0 – 306/642-5901; Fax: 306/642-4519 – Tue.

Biggar Independent, PO Box 40, Biggar SK S0K 0M0 – 306/948-3344 – Mon.

Canora Courier, PO Box 746, Canora SK S0A 0L0 – 306/563-5131; Fax: 306/563-6144 – Circ.: 2,240; Wed.

Carlyle Observer, PO Box 160, Carlyle SK S0C 0R0 – 306/453-2525; Fax: 306/453-2938; also The Prairie Progress(Wed.) – Tue.

Carnduff Gazette-Post News, PO Box 220, Carnduff SK S0C 0S0 – 306/482-3252; Fax: 306/482-3373 – Wed.

Coronach: Triangle News, PO Box 689, Coronach SK S0H 0Z0 – 306/267-3381 – Wed.

Craik Weekly News, PO Box 360, Craik SK S0G 0V0 – 306/734-2313 – Wed.

Creighton: The Gold Belt Gazette, PO Box 900, Creighton SK S0P 0A0 – 306/688-3999 – Wed.

Cut Knife: Highway 40 Courier, PO Box 400, Cut Knife SK S0M 0N0 – 306/398-4901; Fax: 306/398-4909 – Circ.: 700; Wed. – Publisher & Editor, Roger Manegre

Davidson Leader, PO Box 786, Davidson SK S0G 1A0 – 306/567-2047 – Mon.

Esterhazy Potashville Miner-Journal, PO Box 1000, Esterhazy SK S0A 0X0 – 306/745-6669; Fax: 306/745-2699 – Circ.: 1,700; Wed. – Publisher & Editor, Robert Koskie

Estevan Mercury, PO Box 730, Estevan SK S4A 2A6 – 306/634-2654; Fax: 306/634-3934 – Wed.

Estevan This Week, 1330 - 4th St., Estevan SK S4A 0T6 – 306/634-6088; Fax: 306/634-4964 – Sat. – Publisher, Andrea Heath; Editor, P. Glenn Froh

Estevan: The Southeast Trader Express, 814 - 4th St., PO Box 730, Estevan SK S4A 2A6 – 306/634-2654; Fax: 306/634-3934 – Circ.: 11,484; Mon. – Publisher, Peter Ng; Editor, Jonas Weinraueh

Eston: The Press Review, PO Box 787, Eston SK S0L 1A0 – 306/962-3221; Fax: 306/962-4445 – Tue. – Publisher, Verna Thompson

Foam Lake Review, PO Box 550, Foam Lake SK S0A 1A0 – 306/272-3262; Fax: 306/272-4521 – Mon. – Publisher, Bob Johnson

Fort Qu'Appelle Times, PO Box 940, Fort Qu'Appelle SK S0G 1S0 – 306/332-5526 – Tue.

Gravelbourg: Tribune, PO Box 1017, Gravelbourg SK S0H 1X0 – 306/648-3479; Fax: 306/648-2520 – Circ.: 1,552; Tues.; English & French – Editor, Paul Boisvert

Grenfell: Broadview Express, PO Box 189, Grenfell SK S0G 2B0 – 306/697-2722; Fax: 306/697-2689 – Wed.

Grenfell Sun, PO Box 189, Grenfell SK S0G 2B0 – 306/697-2722; Fax: 306/697-2689 – Tue.

Gull Lake Advance, PO Box 628, Gull Lake SK S0N 1A0 – 306/672-3373 – Tue.

Hafford: The Riverbend Review, PO Box 1029, North Battleford SK S9A 3E6 – 306/445-7261 – Wed.

Herbert Herald, PO Box 399, Herbert SK S0H 2A0 – 306/784-2422; Fax: 306/784-3246 – Circ.: 1,700; Tue. – Publisher, Rhonda Ens; Editor, Cynthia Firus

Hudson Bay Post-Review, PO Box 10, Hudson Bay SK S0E 0Y0 – 306/865-2771; Fax: 306/865-2340 – Circ.: 1,800; Tue. – Publisher, Bob Gilroy; Editor, Bruce Paproske

Humboldt Journal, PO Box 970, Humboldt SK S0K 2A0 – 306/682-2561; Fax: 306/682-3322 – Circ.: 3,865; Mon. & Wed; also, Humboldt Trader Regional (Mon.) – Publisher, Chad Charbonneau; Editor, Sharon Domotor

Indian Head-Wolseley News, PO Box 70, Indian Head SK S0G 2K0 – 306/695-3565 – Tue.

Ituna: The Ituna News, PO Box 413, Ituna SK S0A 1N0 – 306/795-2412; Fax: 306/795-3621 – Circ.: 1,033; Mon. – Editor, Susan Antonishyn

Kamsack Times, PO Box 746, Canora SK S0A 0L0 – 306/563-5131; Fax: 306/563-6144 – Circ.: 1,700; Thur.

Kelvington Radio, PO Box 100, Wadena SK S0A 4J0 – 306/338-2231 – Circ.: 1,395; Weds. – Publisher & Editor, James R. Headington

Kerrobert Citizen, PO Box 1150, Kindersley SK S0L 1S0 – 306/463-4611; Fax: 306/463-6505 – Wed.

Kindersley Clarion, PO Box 1150, Kindersley SK S0L 1S0 – 306/463-4611; Fax: 306/463-6505 – Wed.

Kindersley: Leader News, PO Box 1150, Kindersley SK S0L 1S0 – 306/463-4611; Fax: 306/463-6505 – Wed.

Kindersley: West Central Crossroads, PO Box 1150, Kindersley SK S0L 1S0 – 306/463-4611 – Wed.

Kinistino: Birch Hills Post Gazette, PO Box 340, Kinistino SK S0J 1H0 – 306/864-2266; Fax: 306/752-5358 – Wed.

Kipling Citizen, PO Box 329, Kipling SK S0J 2S0 – 306/736-2535; Fax: 306/736-8445 – Sun.

La Ronge: The Northerner, PO Box 1350, La Ronge SK S0J 1L0 – 306/425-3344; Fax: 306/425-2827 – Wed.

Langenburg: The Four-Town Journal, PO Box 68, Langenburg SK S0A 2A0 – 306/743-2617; Fax: 306/743-2299 – Circ.: 1,966; Wed. – Publisher & Editor, Bill Johnston

Lanigan Advisor, PO Box 1029, Lanigan SK S0K 2M0 – 306/365-2010; Fax: 306/365-3388 – Mon.

Lloydminster: CCA Rodeo News, Canadian Cowboys Association, PO Box 1877, Lloydminster SK S9V 1N4 – 306/825-7116; Fax: 306/825-7762 – Circ.: 2,000; 10 times a year – Editor, Julie Nolin-Grant

Lloydminster Meridian Booster, PO Box 830, Lloydminster SK S9V 1C2 – 403/875-3362; Fax: 403/875-3423 – Circ.: 14,600; Sun., Wed.

Lloydminster Times, 4828 - 44th St., Lloydminster SK S9V 0G8 – 306/825-5522; Fax: 306/825-3207 – Wed.; Sun.

Lumsden: Waterfront Press, PO Box 507, Lumsden SK S0G 3C0 – 306/731-3143; Fax: 306/731-2277; Email: watpress@eagle.wbm.ca – Circ.: 1,602; Thur. – Co-Publisher, Lucien Chouinard; Co-Publisher, Jacqueline Chouinard

Macklin Mirror, PO Box 100, Macklin SK S0L 2C0 – 306/753-2424; Fax: 306/753-2424 – Wed.

Maidstone Mirror, PO Box 308, Maidstone SK S0M 1M0 – 306/893-2251; Fax: 306/893-4707 – Thur.

Maple Creek News, PO Box 1360, Maple Creek SK S0N 1N0 – 306/662-2133; Fax: 306/662-3092 – Tue.

Meadow Lake Progress, 311 Centre St., Meadow Lake SK S9X 1L7 – 306/236-5265; Fax: 306/236-3130; Email: meadow.lake.progress@sk.sympatico.ca – Circ.: 4,500; Tue. – Publisher, Al Guthro; Editor, Dan McPherson

Meadow Lake: Northern Pride, 205A - 3rd Ave. East, Meadow Lake SK S9X 1L7 – 306/236-5353; Fax: 306/236-5962 – Mon. – Publisher, Terry Villeneuve

Melfort Journal, Phillips Publishers Ltd., PO Box 1300, Melfort SK S0E 1A0 – 306/752-5737; Fax: 306/752-5358; supplement – Circ.: 4,215; Tue. – Editor, Ron Phillips

Melville Advance, PO Box 1420, Melville SK S0A 2P0 – 306/728-5448; Fax: 306/728-4004 – Circ.: 4,000; Wed. – Publisher, Mark Orosz; Editor, Lin Orosz

Moose Jaw This Week, 44 Fairford St. West, Moose Jaw SK S6H 6E4 – 306/692-6441; Fax: 306/692-2101 – Tue.

Moosomin World-Spectator, PO Box 250, Moosomin SK S0G 3N0 – 306/435-2445; Fax: 306/435-3969; Email: world.spectator@sk.sympatico.ca; URL: http://www.sasknet.com/~world – Circ.: 3,350; Tues. – Co-Publisher, Bruce Penton; Co-Publisher, Barb Penton; Editor, Kevin Weedmark

Naicam: The Naicam News, PO Box 507, Watson SK S0K 4V0 – 306/287-4388; Fax: 306/287-3308 – Circ.: 540; Mon. – Publisher, Debbie Schueller; Editor, Linda Griffith

Nipawin Journal, PO Box 2014, Nipawin SK S0E 1E0 – 306/862-4618; Fax: 306/862-4566 – Circ.: 4,700; Wed. – Publisher, Donna Bohnen; Editor, Dennis Hegland

Nipawin N.E. Region Community Booster, PO Box 2014, Nipawin SK S0E 1E0 – 306/862-4618; Fax: 306/862-4566 – Circ.: 18,750; Every other Mon. – Publisher & Editor, Ken Nelson

Nokomis: Last Mountain Times, PO Box 340, Nokomis SK S0G 3R0 – 306/528-2020; Fax: 306/528-2090 – Tue. – Publisher, Lyle Emmons

Norquay North Star, PO Box 746, Canora SK S0A 0L0 – 306/563-5131; Fax: 306/563-6144 – Circ.: 841; Thur.

North Battleford: Regional Optimist/Advertiser-Post, PO Box 1029, North Battleford SK S9A 3E6 – 306/445-7261; Fax: 306/445-3223 – Circ.: 20,000; Mon.; also: The Telegraph (Fri., circ. 3,444); Northwest Neighbours, Turtleford (Wed., circ. 693) – Publisher, Steven Dills; Editor, Lorne Cooper

Outlook: The Outlook, PO Box 399, Outlook SK S0L 2N0 – 306/867-8262; Fax: 306/867-9556; Email: the_outlook@awnet.net – Circ.: 2,431; Mon. – Publisher, Roland Jenson; Editor, Debra Murphy; Circulation Manager, Denise Jenson

Oxbow Herald, PO Box 420, Oxbow SK S0C 2B0 – 306/483-2323; Fax: 306/483-5258 – Circ.: 1,402; Tue. – Publisher & Editor, J.K. Pedlar

Pierceland: The Beaver River Banner, General Delivery, Pierceland SK S0M 2K0 – 306/839-4496 – Circ.: 1.780; Mon.

Preeceville Progress, PO Box 746, Canora SK S0A 0L0 – 306/563-5131; Fax: 306/563-6144 – Circ.: 1,636; Thur.

Radville Star, PO Box 370, Radville SK S0C 2G0 – 306/869-2202 – Thur.

Redvers: The Optimist, PO Box 490, Redvers SK S0C 2H0 – 306/452-3363 – Tue.

Regina: Journal L'Eau Vive, 2606, rue Centrale, Regina SK S4N 2N9 – 306/347-0481; Fax: 306/565-3450 – Jeudi; français

Regina Sun, 1964 Park St., PO Box 2020, Regina SK S4P 3G4 – 306/565-8250 – Wed.

Rose Valley: The View from Here, PO Box 307, Rose Valley SK S0E 1M0 – 306/322-2051 – Wed.

Rosetown Eagle, PO Box 130, Rosetown SK S0L 2V0 – 306/882-4202; Fax: 306/882-4204 – Circ.: 2,638; Mon. – Publisher & Editor, Dan Page

Rosthern: Saskatchewan Valley News, PO Box 10, Rosthern SK S0K 3R0 – 306/232-4865 – Thur.

Saskatoon Sun, 204 - 5th Ave., North, Saskatoon SK S7K 2P1 – 306/664-8340 – Sun.

Shaunavon Standard, PO Box 729, Shaunavon SK S0N 2M0 – 306/297-4144; Fax: 306/297-3357 – Tue.

Shellbrook Chronicle, PO Box 10, Shellbrook SK S0J 2E0 – 306/747-2442; Fax: 306/747-3000 – Tue.

Shellbrook: Spiritwood Herald, PO Box 10, Shellbrook SK S0J 2E0 – 306/747-2442; Fax: 306/747-3000 – Wed.

Swift Current: The Southwest Booster, PO Box 1330, Swift Current SK S9H 3X4 – 306/773-9321; Fax: 306/773-9136 – Circ.: 19,000; Mon. – Publisher, Bill Mann; Editor, Katherine Wasiak

Swift Current Sun, PO Box 670, Swift Current SK S9H 3W7 – 306/773-3116; Fax: 306/773-2653 – Circ.: 19,685; Sun. – Publisher, Mike Hertz; Editor, Scott Anderson

Tisdale Recorder, PO Box 1660, Tisdale SK S0E 1T0 – 306/873-4515; Fax: 306/873-4712 – Circ.: 2,200; Mon. – Publisher, Larry Mitchell; Editor, Peggy Todd

Unity: The Northwest Herald, 304 Main St., PO Box 309, Unity SK S0K 4L0 – 306/228-2267; Fax: 306/228-2767 – Mon.

Wadena News, PO Box 100, Wadena SK S0A 4J0 – 306/338-2231 – Circ.: 3,500; Wed. – Publisher & Editor, James R. Headington

Wakaw Recorder, PO Box 9, Wakaw SK S0K 4P0 – 306/233-4325; Fax: 306/233-4386 – Circ.: 1,900; Thur. – Editor, D. Biccum

Watrous Manitou, PO Box 100, Watrous SK S0K 4T0 – 306/946-3343 – Mon.

Watson Witness, PO Box 746, Canora SK S0A 0L0 – 306/287-3245; Fax: 306/287-4333 – Circ.: 600; Wed.

Weyburn Review, PO Box 400, Weyburn SK S4H 2K4 – 306/842-7487; Fax: 306/842-0282 – Circ.: 5,800; Wed.; also Weyburn Booster (Mon.), & Southern Form Guide – Publisher, Darryl Ward; Editor-in-Chief, Patricia Ward

Weyburn This Week, 19 - 11th St., Weyburn SK S4H 1J1 – 306/842-3900; Fax: 306/842-2515 – Circ.: 9,819; Sat. & Tue. – Publisher, Andrea L. Heath; Editor, P. Glenn Froh; Circulation Manager, Margaret Medwed

Whitewood Herald, 3rd St., PO Box 160, Whitewood SK S0G 5C0 – 306/735-2230 – Mon.

Wilkie Press, PO Box 309, Unity SK S0K 4L0 – 306/228-2267; Fax: 306/228-2767 – Mon.

Wolseley: The Wolseley Bulletin, PO Box 89, Wolseley SK S0G 5H0 – 306/698-2369 – Fri.

Wynyard Advance/Gazette, PO Box 10, Wynyard SK S0A 4T0 – 306/554-2224; Fax: 306/554-3226 – Mon. – Ray Lachambre

Yorkton: The News, 29 - 2nd Ave. North, Yorkton SK S3N 1G1 – 306/783-7355 – Mon.

Yorkton This Week & Enterprise, Hollinger Inc., PO Box 1300, Yorkton SK S3N 2X3 – 306/782-2465; Fax: 306/786-1898 – Circ.: 7,941; Wed. & Sat; also Marketplace (Fri., circ. 39,900) – Editor, Girard Hengen

Yukon Daily Newspapers

WHITEHORSE:

The Whitehorse Star, 2149 - 2nd Ave., Whitehorse YT Y1A 1C5 – 403/668-2063; Fax: 403/668-7130 – Circ.: 5,000; Daily, weekdays – Publisher, Bob Erlam; Editor, Jim Butler, 403/667-4481

Newspapers in Yukon

Whitehorse: L'Aurore Boréale, PO Box 5205, Whitehorse YT Y1A 4Z1 – 403/667-2931; Fax: 403/668-3511 – Circ.: 1,000; Mensuel; français

Whitehorse: Yukon News, 211 Wood St., Whitehorse YT Y1A 2E4 – 403/667-6285; Fax: 403/668-3755; Email: STEVEROB@YKNET.YK.CA; URL: http://www.yukonweb.com/community/yukon-news – Circ.: 7,447 Wed., 8,893 Fri.; Wed., Fri. – Publisher, Doug Bell; Editor, Peter Lesniak

MAGAZINE INDEX

18th Century Fiction / Scholarly (Scholarly Publication)
2 x 4 / Business (Woodworking)
7 Jours / Consumer (News)
A.A.R.N Newsletter / Business (Nursing)
Aawaz / Ethnic (Pakistani)
Abaka / Ethnic (Armenian)
L'Abattoir / University
Abilities: Canada's Lifestyle Magazine for People with Disabilities / Consumer (General Interest)
Ability Network / Consumer (Health, Medical)
Aboriginal Voices / Ethnic (Aboriginal)
Above & Beyond / Consumer (Airline Inflight, Train & Bus In-transit)
absinthe / Consumer (Literary)
Acadiensis: Journal of the History of the Atlantic Region / Scholarly (Scholarly Publication)
Access / Business (Books, Stationery)
Access Magazine / Consumer (Music)
Accident Prevention / Business (Industrial Safety)
Achieving a Healthy Environment / Consumer (Environment & Nature)
Acontece / Ethnic (Portuguese)
Acropolis / Ethnic (Greek)
Actif / Consumer (General Interest)
L'Actif / University
L'Action / University
Action Now / Consumer (Women's & Feminist)
L'Actualité / Consumer (News)
Actualité Canada / Business (Journalism)
L'Actualité Médicale / Business (Medical)
L'Actualité Pharmaceutique / Business (Drugs)
L'Actuel / Consumer (Women's & Feminist)
The Ad-Viser / Farm (Farm Publication)
Adnews / Business (Advertising, Marketing, Sales)
The Advocate / Business (Legal)
Les Affaires / Business (Business)
AfriCan Access Magazine / Business (Business)
African Identity / Consumer (General Interest)
Aftermarket Canada / Business (Automotive & Accessories)
Agri-book: Beans in Canada / Farm (Farm Publication)
Agri-book: Corn in Canada / Farm (Farm Publication)
Agri-book: Drainage Contractor / Farm (Farm Publication)
Agri-book: Potatoes in Canada / Farm (Farm Publication)
Agri-book: Top Crop Manager / Farm (Farm Publication)
Agricom / Farm (Farm Publication)
AgWorld news / Farm (Farm Publication)
Airforce / Business (Aviation & Aerospace)
Airports North America / Business (Aviation & Aerospace)
Alberta/Western Report / Consumer (News)
Alberta Beef / Farm (Farm Publication)
Alberta Business / Business (Business)
Alberta Construction / Business (Construction)
Alberta Dairyman, see Western Dairy Farmer
The Alberta Doctors' Digest / Business (Medical)
Alberta FarmLIFE / Farm (Farm Publication)
Alberta Fishing Guide / Consumer (Fishing & Hunting)

Alberta Insurance Directory / Business (Insurance)
Alberta Italian Times / Ethnic (Italian)
Alberta Oil & Gas Directory / Business (Petroleum, Oil & Gas)
Alberta Woman / Consumer (Women's & Feminist)
Alderlea Magazine / Consumer (City Magazine)
Algonquin Times / University
L'Alimentation / Business (Grocery Trade)
L'Alinéa / University
alive magazine - The Canadian Journal of Health & Nutrition / Consumer (Health, Medical)
Almanach de L'Auto / Consumer (Automobile & Cycle)
Almanach du Peuple / Consumer (Directories & Almanacs)
L'Almanach Québec en santé / Consumer (Health, Medical)
Alternatives: Perspectives on Society, Technology & Environment / Consumer (Environment & Nature)
Alumni-News/Bulletin des Anciens / University
Alumni Chronicle / University
Alumni Gazette / University
Alumni Journal / University
Alumni Magazine / University
Alumni News / University
Angles / Consumer (General Interest)
The Anglican / Consumer (Religious & Denominational)
Anglican Journal / Consumer (Religious & Denominational)
Annals of Air & Space Law / Scholarly (Scholarly Publication)
Annals of the Royal College of Physicians & Surgeons of Canada / Business (Medical)
Annuaire Téléphonique de la Construction du Québec / Business (Engineering)
Anthropologica / Scholarly (Scholarly Publication)
The Antigonish Review / Consumer (Literary)
Antiques / Consumer (Arts, Art & Antiques)
Antique Showcase / Consumer (Arts, Art & Antiques)
L'Apercu Révue / Business (Construction)
Apparel / Business (Clothing & Accessories)
Applied Arts / Business (Graphic Arts)
Aquinian / University
Arab News International / Ethnic (Arabic)
ARC: A Magazine of Poetry & Poetry Criticism / Consumer (Literary)
Arch-Type / Consumer (General Interest)
Arctic / Scholarly (Scholarly Publication)
Argosy Weekly / University
The Argus / University
ARIEL -- A Review of International English Literature / Scholarly (Scholarly Publication)
ARN Messager / University
ARQ/La Revue d'Architecture / Business (Architecture)
Artère / Business (Hospitals, Health Care)
Artfocus / Consumer (Arts, Art & Antiques)
Arthritis News / Consumer (Health, Medical)
Arthroexpress / Consumer (Health, Medical)
Arthur / University
Artichoke / Consumer (Arts, Art & Antiques)
Art Impressions / Consumer (Arts, Art & Antiques)
ArtsAtlantic / Consumer (Arts, Art & Antiques)
Association / Business (Conventions & Meetings)
The ATA Magazine / Business (Education)
The Athenaeum / University
Athletics: Canada's National Track & Field/Running Magazine / Consumer (Sports & Recreation)
Atkinsonian / University
The Atlantic Baptist / Consumer (Religious & Denominational)
Atlantic Beef / Farm (Farm Publication)
Atlantic Chamber Journal / Business (Business)
The Atlantic Co-Operator / Business (Credit)
Atlantic Construction Journal / Business (Construction)
Atlantic Firefighter / Business (Fire Protection)

Atlantic Fisherman / Business (Fisheries)
Atlantic Fishfarming / Business (Fisheries)
Atlantic Horse & Pony / Consumer (Horses, Riding & Breeding)
Atlantic Progress / Business (Business)
Atlantic Region Aviation Business Directory / Business (Aviation & Aerospace)
The Atlantic Salmon Journal / Consumer (Fishing & Hunting)
Atlantic Transportation Journal / Business (Transportation, Shipping & Distribution)
Atlantic Trucking / Business (Motor Trucks & Buses)
Audaces / University
AutoCAD User / Business (Computer-aided Design)
L'Automobile / Business (Automotive & Accessories)
Automotive Retailer / Business (Automotive & Accessories)
Automotive Service Data Book / Business (Automotive & Accessories)
L'Autonome / Business (Business & Finance)
Autopinion Annual / Consumer (Automobile & Cycle)
AutoRoute / Consumer (Travel)
Avantages / Business (Business)
Avenir - formation, compétences / Business (Human Resources)
Avenue / Consumer (City Magazine)
Award Magazine / Business (Architecture)
Azure / Business (Interior Design & Decor)
The Baby & Child Care Encyclopedia / Consumer (Babies & Mothers)
Backspin: Manitoba's Golf Newspaper / Consumer (Sports & Recreation)
Bakers Journal / Business (Baking & Bakers' Supplies)
Bandersnatch / University
Le Banquier / Business (Business)
Barley Country / Farm (Farm Publication)
The Baron / University
La Barrique / Business (Hotels & Restaurants)
Bâtiment / Business (Construction)
B.C. Agri Digest / Farm (Farm Publication)
The BC Broker / Business (Insurance)
BC Business Magazine / Business (Business)
BC Business Service / Business (Business)
B.C. Dairy Directory / Farm (Farm Publication)
BC Fishing Directory & Atlas / Consumer (Fishing & Hunting)
BCIT Link / University
BC Municipal Yearbook: Redbook / Business (Government)
B.C. Orchardist / Farm (Farm Publication)
B.C. Outdoors / Consumer (Fishing & Hunting)
The B.C. Professional Engineer / Business (Engineering)
B.C. Simmental News / Farm (Farm Publication)
B.C. Sport Fishing Magazine / Consumer (Fishing & Hunting)
BC Studies: The British Columbian Quarterly / Scholarly (Scholarly Publication)
B.C. Wine Trails / Consumer (Food & Beverage)
BC Woman / Consumer (Women's & Feminist)
Beautiful British Columbia Magazine / Consumer (General Interest)
The Beaver Magazine: Exploring Canada's History / Consumer (General Interest)
Beef in B.C. Inc. / Farm (Farm Publication)
Le Bel Age / Consumer (Senior Citizens)
Benefits Canada / Business (Business)
Benefits & Pensions Monitor / Business (Business)
Best Wishes / Consumer (Babies & Mothers)
Better Health Magazine / Consumer (Health, Medical)
Bharat Darshan / Ethnic (East Indian)
Bienvenue en Nouvelle-Écosse / Consumer (Travel)
Bike Trade Canada / Business (Automobile & Cycle)
Bilan / Business (Business)
Bilan / University
Bingo News & Gaming Hi-Lites / Consumer (Entertainment)

Biochemistry & Cell Biology / Business (Science, Research & Development)
Biz-Hamilton/Halton Business Report / Business (Business)
Blackflash / Consumer (Photography)
Blood & Aphorisms / Consumer (Literary)
Bluegrass Canada Magazine / Consumer (Music)
Blue Line Magazine / Business (Police)
Boat Guide / Consumer (Boating & Yachting)
Boating Business / Business (Boating & Yachting)
Boating East Ports & Cruising Guide / Consumer (Boating & Yachting)
Bodyshop / Business (Automotive & Accessories)
Books in Canada / Consumer (Literary)
Border/Lines / Consumer (Culture, Current Events)
Border Crossings / Consumer (Arts, Art & Antiques)
The Bottom Line / Business (Business)
Boudoir Noir / Consumer (Sports & Recreation)
bout de papier / Consumer (Political)
Bow Valley This Week / Consumer (Television, Radio, Video & Home Appliances)
The Brandon Sun TV Book / Consumer (Television, Radio, Video & Home Appliances)
Briarpatch / Consumer (Political)
Brick: A Literary Journal / Consumer (Literary)
Bricklayer / University
La Brise / University
British Columbia Commercial Marine Directory & Buyers Guide / Business (Shipping, Marine)
British Columbia Insurance Directory / Business (Insurance)
British Columbia Medical Journal / Business (Medical)
British Columbia Report / Consumer (News)
Broadcaster / Business (Broadcasting)
Broadcast Technology / Business (Broadcasting)
Brock Press / University
The Bruce County Marketplace / Business (Business)
The Brunswick Business Journal / Business (Business)
The Brunswickian / University
Buildcore Product Source / Business (Architecture)
Build & Green / Consumer (Homes)
Building & Construction Trades Today / Business (Construction)
Building Magazine / Business (Building)
The Bulletin / University
Le Bulletin des Agriculteurs / Farm (Farm Publication)
Bulletin Voyages / Business (Travel)
The Business Advocate / Business (Business)
The Business Annual / Business (Business)
Business Bulletin / Business (Business)
Business Examiner - Mid/North Island Edition / Business (Business)
Business Examiner - South Island Edition / Business (Business)
The Business Executive / Business (Business)
Business Farmer / Business (Forest & Lumber Industries)
Business in Vancouver / Business (Business)
The Business Logger / Business (Forest & Lumber Industries)
Business People Magazine / Business (Business)
The Business & Professional Woman / Business (Business)
Business Quarterly / Business (Business)
The Business Times / Business (Business)
Business Today / Business (Business)
Businest / Business (Business)
CAAR Communicator / Business (Farm Implements & Supplies)
Cablecaster / Business (Broadcasting)
Cable Communications Magazine / Business (Broadcasting)
CAD Systems / Business (Computer-aided Design)
Le Caducée / University
CAEP/ACMU Communiqué / Business (Medical)
Calgary & Area Airport Business Directory / Business (Aviation & Aerospace)
Calgary Cityscope / Consumer (City Magazine)

Canadian Almanac & Directory 1997

CA Magazine / Business (Business)
Camera Canada / Consumer (Photography)
Camionneurs / Business (Motor Trucks & Buses)
Camping Canada / Consumer (Camping & Outdoor Recreation)
Camping Canada Dealer News / Business (Sporting Goods & Recreational Equipment)
Camping Caravaning / Consumer (Camping & Outdoor Recreation)
Camping in Ontario / Consumer (Camping & Outdoor Recreation)
The Campus / University
Campus Canada / University (Student Guides)
Campus Reel / Consumer (Entertainment)
Canada-Z Oil Gas Mining Directory / Business (Petroleum, Oil & Gas)
Canada Computes!, see Toronto COmputes!
Canada Japan Business Journal / Business (Business)
Canada Journal / Business (Business)
Canada Lutheran / Consumer (Religious & Denominational)
Canada on Location / Business (Broadcasting)
Canada Poultryman / Farm (Farm Publication)
Canada Quilts Magazine / Consumer (Arts, Art & Antiques)
Canadan Uutiset / Ethnic (Finnish)
Canada's The Latin Trade Report / Business (Business)
Canada's Who's Who Of The Poultry Industry / Farm (Farm Publication)
Canadian / Consumer (Airline Inflight, Train & Bus Intransit)
Canadian Advertising Rates & Data / Business (Advertising, Marketing, Sales)
Canadian Aggregates & Roadbuilding Contractor / Business (Engineering)
Canadian Amateur / Consumer (Hobbies)
Canadian Antique Power: An Adventure into Canada's Agricultural Heritage / Consumer (Hobbies)
Canadian Arabian News / Consumer (Horses, Riding & Breeding)
Canadian Architect / Business (Architecture)
Canadian Architectural Directory / Business (Architecture)
Canadian Art / Consumer (Arts, Art & Antiques)
Canadian Association of Radiologists Journal / Business (Medical)
Canadian Author / Business (Books, Stationery)
Canadian Automotive Fleet / Business (Automotive & Accessories)
Canadian Auto World / Business (Automotive & Accessories)
Canadian Aviation & Aircraft for Sale / Business (Aviation & Aerospace)
Canadian Aviation Historical Society Journal / Consumer (Aviation & Aerospace)
Canadian Ayrshire Review / Farm (Farm Publication)
The Canadian Banker / Business (Business)
The Canadian Baptist / Consumer (Religious & Denominational)
Canadian Bar Review / Business (Legal)
Canadian Biker / Consumer (Automobile & Cycle)
Canadian Bookseller / Business (Books, Stationery)
Canadian Business / Business (Business)
Canadian Business Economics / Consumer (Business & Finance)
Canadian Business Life Magazine / Business (Business)
Canadian Ceramics Quarterly / Business (Ceramics)
Canadian Chemical News / Business (Chemicals & Chemical Process Industries)
Canadian Children's Literature / Scholarly (Scholarly Publication)
Canadian Cleaner & Launderer, see Fabricare Canada
Canadian Coin Box Magazine / Business (Vending & Vending Equipment)
Canadian Coin News / Consumer (Hobbies)

Canadian Collectibles Retailer / Business (Art & Antiques)
Canadian Communications Network Letter / Business (Telecommunications)
Canadian Communications Reports / Business (Telecommunications)
Canadian Computer Reseller / Business (Computing & Technology)
Canadian Computer Wholesaler / Business (Computers)
Canadian Construction Service & Supply Directory - Alberta / Business (Construction)
Canadian Consulting Engineer / Business (Engineering)
Canadian Curling News / Consumer (Sports & Recreation)
Canadian Customs Guide / Business (Transportation, Shipping & Distribution)
Canadian Cyclist / Consumer (Sports & Recreation)
Canadian Dairy / Business (Dairy Products)
Canadian Defence Quarterly / Business (Military)
Canadian Defence Review / Business (Military)
Canadian Dimension / Consumer (Social Welfare)
Canadian Direct Marketing News / Business (Advertising, Marketing, Sales)
Canadian Directory of Professional Photographers, see Professional Photographers
Canadian Electronics / Business (Electronics)
Canadian Emergency News / Business (Emergency Services)
Canadian Environmental Protection / Business (Water & Wastes Treatment)
Canadian Ethnic Studies / Scholarly (Scholarly Publication)
Canadian Exporters Association Membership Directory / Business (Import, Export)
Canadian Facility Management & Design / Business (Interior Design & Decor)
Canadian Family Physician / Business (Medical)
Canadian Fiction Magazine / Consumer (Literary)
The Canadian Firefighter / Business (Fire Protection)
Canadian Flight / Business (Aviation & Aerospace)
Canadian Florist, Greenhouse & Nursery / Business (Florists)
Canadian Folk Music Journal / Scholarly (Scholarly Publication)
Canadian Football Journal / Consumer (Sports & Recreation)
Canadian Footwear Journal / Business (Footwear)
Canadian Forces Base Kingston Official Directory / Consumer (Directories & Almanacs)
Canadian Foreign Policy / Scholarly (Scholarly Publication)
Canadian Forest Industries / Business (Forest & Lumber Industries)
The Canadian Forum / Consumer (General Interest)
Canadian Fruitgrower / Farm (Farm Publication)
Canadian Funeral Director / Business (Funeral Service)
Canadian Funeral News / Business (Funeral Service)
Canadian Gaming & Fundraising Magazine / Business (Sports & Recreation)
Canadian Gardening / Consumer (Gardening)
Canadian Geographic / Consumer (General Interest)
Canadian Geotechnical Journal / Business (Science, Research & Development)
Canadian German Trade / Business (Business)
Canadian Grocer / Business (Grocery Trade)
Canadian Guernsey Journal / Farm (Farm Publication)
Canadian Guider / Consumer (Women's & Feminist)
Canadian Healthcare Manager / Business (Hospitals, Health Care)
Canadian Heavy Equipment Guide / Business (Engineering)
Canadian Hereford Digest / Farm (Farm Publication)
The Canadian Historical Review / Scholarly (Scholarly Publication)

Canadian Homebuilder & Renovation Contractor / Business (Building)
Canadian Homebuilt Aircraft News / Consumer (Aviation & Aerospace)
Canadian Home Economics Journal / Business (Institutions)
The Canadian Home Planner / Consumer (Homes)
Canadian Homestyle Magazine / Business (Housewares)
Canadian Horseman / Consumer (Horses, Riding & Breeding)
Canadian Hotel & Restaurant Product News, see Foodservice & Hospitality
Canadian House & Home / Consumer (Homes)
Canadian HR Reporter / Business (Human Resources)
Canadian Industrial Equipment News / Business (Industrial & Industrial Automation)
Canadian Insurance / Business (Insurance)
Canadian Insurance Claims Directory / Business (Insurance)
Canadian Interiors / Business (Interior Design & Decor)
Canadian Investment Review / Business (Business & Finance)
Canadian Jersey Breeder / Farm (Farm Publication)
Canadian Jeweller / Business (Jewellery & Giftware)
Canadian Jewish News / Consumer (Religious & Denominational)
Canadian Journal of Allergy & Immunology / Business (Medical)
Canadian Journal of Anaesthesia / Business (Medical)
Canadian Journal of Analytical Sciences & Spectroscopy / Business (Science, Research & Development)
Canadian Journal of Botany / Business (Science, Research & Development)
Canadian Journal of Cardiology / Business (Medical)
Canadian Journal of Cardiovascular Nursing / Business (Nursing)
Canadian Journal of Chemistry / Business (Science, Research & Development)
Canadian Journal of Civil Engineering / Business (Science, Research & Development)
The Canadian Journal of Clinical Pharmacology / Business (Medical)
Canadian Journal of Continuing Medical Education / Business (Medical)
Canadian Journal of Dermatology / Business (Medical)
Canadian Journal of Development Studies / Scholarly (Scholarly Publication)
The Canadian Journal of Diagnosis / Business (Medical)
Canadian Journal of Earth Sciences / Business (Science, Research & Development)
Canadian Journal of Economics / Scholarly (Scholarly Publication)
Canadian Journal of Forest Research / Business (Science, Research & Development)
Canadian Journal of Gastroenterology / Business (Medical)
Canadian Journal of Higher Education / Scholarly (Scholarly Publication)
Canadian Journal of History / Scholarly (Scholarly Publication)
The Canadian Journal of Hospital Pharmacy / Business (Drugs)
Canadian Journal of Infection Control / Business (Hospitals, Health Care)
Canadian Journal of Infectious Diseases / Business (Medical)
The Canadian Journal of Information & Library Science / Scholarly (Scholarly Publication)
Canadian Journal of Italian Studies / Scholarly (Scholarly Publication)
Canadian Journal of Law & Society / Scholarly (Scholarly Publication)
Canadian Journal of Linguistics / Scholarly (Scholarly Publication)

Canadian Journal of Mathematics / Scholarly (Scholarly Publication)
Canadian Journal of Medical Laboratory Science / Business (Medical)
Canadian Journal of Medical Radiation Technology / Business (Medical)
Canadian Journal of Microbiology / Business (Science, Research & Development)
Canadian Journal of Neurological Sciences / Business (Medical)
The Canadian Journal of Occupational Therapy / Business (Medical)
Canadian Journal of Ophthalmology / Business (Medical)
Canadian Journal of Optometry / Business (Optical)
Canadian Journal of Pediatrics / Business (Medical)
Canadian Journal of Philosophy / Scholarly (Scholarly Publication)
Canadian Journal of Physics / Business (Science, Research & Development)
Canadian Journal of Physiology & Pharmacology / Business (Science, Research & Development)
The Canadian Journal of Plastic Surgery / Business (Medical)
Canadian Journal of Political & Social Theory / Scholarly (Scholarly Publication)
Canadian Journal of Program Evaluation / Scholarly (Scholarly Publication)
Canadian Journal of Psychiatry / Business (Medical)
Canadian Journal of Psychoanalysis / Scholarly
Canadian Journal of Public Health / Business (Medical)
Canadian Journal of Rehabilitation / Business (Medical)
Canadian Journal of Respiratory Therapy / Business (Medical)
Canadian Journal of Sociology / Scholarly (Scholarly Publication)
Canadian Journal of Surgery / Business (Medical)
Canadian Journal of Women & The Law / Scholarly (Scholarly Publication)
Canadian Journal of Women's Health Care / Business (Medical)
Canadian Journal of Zoology / Business (Science, Research & Development)
Canadian Journal on Aging / Scholarly (Scholarly Publication)
Canadian Lawyer / Business (Legal)
The Canadian Leader / Consumer (Youth)
Canadian Literature / Scholarly (Scholarly Publication)
Canadian Living / Consumer (Homes)
Canadian Machinery & Metalworking / Business (Metalworking)
The Canadian Manager / Business (Business)
Canadian Masonry Contractor / Business (Building)
Canadian Mathematical Bulletin / Scholarly (Scholarly Publication)
Canadian Medical Association Journal / Business (Medical)
The Canadian Messenger / Consumer (Religious & Denominational)
Canadian Mines Handbook / Business (Mining)
Canadian Mining Journal / Business (Mining)
Canadian Modern Language Review / Scholarly (Scholarly Publication)
Canadian MoneySaver / Consumer (Business & Finance)
The Canadian Music Educator / Business (Music & Music Trades)
Canadian Musician / Consumer (Music)
Canadian Music Trade / Business (Music & Music Trades)
The Canadian Nurse / Business (Nursing)
Canadian Nursing Home / Business (Hospitals, Health Care)
Canadian Occupational Safety / Business (Industrial Safety)

Canadian Oilfield Gas Plant Atlas / Business (Petroleum, Oil & Gas)
Canadian Oilfield Service & Supply Directory / Business (Petroleum, Oil & Gas)
Canadian Oil Register / Business (Petroleum, Oil & Gas)
Canadian Oncology Nursing Journal / Business (Nursing)
Canadian Operating Room Nursing Journal / Business (Nursing)
Canadian Orthodox Missionary / Consumer (Religious & Denominational)
Canadian Ostrich / Farm (Farm Publication)
Canadian Packaging / Business (Packaging)
Canadian Papermaker / Business (Pulp & Paper)
Canadian Pharmaceutical Journal / Business (Drugs)
Canadian Pizza Magazine / Business (Food & Food Processing)
Canadian Plastics / Business (Plastics)
Canadian Plastics Directory & Buyer's Guide / Business (Plastics)
Canadian Poetry: Studies, Documents, Reviews / Scholarly (Scholarly Publication)
Canadian Printer / Business (Printing & Publishing)
Canadian Process Equipment & Control News / Business (Chemicals & Chemical Process Industries)
Canadian Property Management / Business (Building)
Canadian Public Administration / Scholarly (Scholarly Publication)
Canadian Public Policy / Scholarly (Scholarly Publication)
Canadian Purchaser / Business (Purchasing)
Canadian Railway Modeller / Consumer (Hobbies)
Canadian Realtor News / Business (Real Estate)
Canadian Rental Service / Business (Rental Equipment & Leasing Equipment)
Canadian Resources / Business (Petroleum, Oil & Gas)
Canadian Respiratory Journal / Business (Medical)
Canadian Retailer / Business (Retailing)
The Canadian Review of American Studies / Scholarly (Scholarly Publication)
Canadian Review of Comparative Literature / Scholarly (Scholarly Publication)
Canadian Review of Sociology & Anthropology / Scholarly (Scholarly Publication)
Canadian Rodeo News / Consumer (Sports & Recreation)
Canadian Roofing Contractor / Business (Building)
Canadian RV & Light Truck Dealer, see Camping Canada Dealer News
Canadian Sailings incorporating Seaports and the Shipping World / Business (Shipping, Marine)
The Canadian School Executive / Business (Education)
Canadian Security / Business (Security)
Canadian Select Homes / Consumer (Homes)
Canadian Shareowner / Consumer (Business & Finance)
Canadian Shipper / Business (Transportation, Shipping & Distribution)
Canadian Speeches: Issues of the Day / Consumer (Political)
Canadian Sportfishing / Consumer (Fishing & Hunting)
Canadian Sportscard Collector / Consumer (Hobbies)
The Canadian Sportsman / Consumer (Horses, Riding & Breeding)
Canadian Stamp News / Consumer (Hobbies)
Canadian Telecom / Business (Telecommunications)
Canadian Textile Journal / Business (Textiles)
Canadian Theatre Review / Consumer (Entertainment)
Canadian Thoroughbred / Consumer (Horses, Riding & Breeding)
The Canadian Tobacco Grower / Farm (Farm Publication)
Canadian Trade Index / Business (Purchasing)
Canadian Transportation Logistics / Business (Transportation, Shipping & Distribution)

The Canadian Trapper / Business (Fur Trade)
Canadian Traveller / Business (Travel)
Canadian Travel Press / Business (Travel)
Canadian Treasurer / Business (Business & Finance)
Canadian Ultralight News / Business (Aviation & Aerospace)
Canadian Underwriter / Business (Insurance)
Canadian University Music Review / Scholarly (Scholarly Publication)
Canadian Vending / Business (Vending & Vending Equipment)
The Canadian Veterinary Journal / Business (Veterinary)
Canadian Vocational Journal / Business (Education)
Canadian Water Well / Business (Water & Wastes Treatment)
Canadian Wildlife / Consumer (Environment & Nature)
Canadian Window & Door Manufacturer / Business (Building)
Canadian Woman Studies / Consumer (Women's & Feminist)
Canadian Wood Products / Business (Forest & Lumber Industries)
Canadian Workshop / Consumer (Hobbies)
Canadian Yachting / Consumer (Boating & Yachting)
Le Canard Déchaîne / University
Canine Review / Consumer (Animals)
Canola Country / Farm (Farm Publication)
Canola Guide / Farm (Farm Publication)
Cape Breton's Magazine / Consumer (General Interest)
Caper Times / University
Capilano Courier / University
The Capilano Review / Consumer (Literary)
The Capital Chinese News / Ethnic (Chinese)
Captain Lillie's Coast Guide & Radiotelephone Directory / Business (Shipping, Marine)
The Care Connection / Business (Nursing)
Carguide/Le Magazine Carguide / Consumer (Automobile & Cycle)
The Carillon / University
Carousel / Consumer (Literary)
CARP News / Consumer (Senior Citizens)
Cartographica / Scholarly (Scholarly Publication)
Catholic New Times / Consumer (Religious & Denominational)
The Catholic Register / Consumer (Religious & Denominational)
Cattlemen Magazine / Farm (Farm Publication)
CAUT Bulletin ACPU / Business (Education)
CCHSE Members Directory / Business (Hospitals, Health Care)
CD Plus Compact Disk Catalogue / Consumer (Music)
CEDA Current Annual, see Electrical Supply & Distribution Annual
Celtic Heritage / Ethnic (Celtic)
Central Alberta Adviser / Farm (Farm Publication)
Central Alberta Farmer / Farm (Farm Publication)
Central Alberta Life / Farm (Farm Publication)
Central Nova Business News / Business (Business)
Centre Magazine / Business (Hardware Trade)
Century Home / Consumer (Homes)
C'est Pour Quand? / Consumer (Babies & Mothers)
CGA Magazine / Business (Business)
CGTA Retail News / Business (Gifts)
CHAC Review / Business (Hospitals, Health Care)
Champlain Bugle / University
Charhdi Kala / Ethnic (East Indian)
The Charlatan / University
Charolais Banner / Farm (Farm Publication)
Charolais Connection / Farm (Farm Publication)
Chart / Consumer (Music)
Chatelaine / Consumer (Women's & Feminist)
Châtelaine / Consumer (Women's & Feminist)
Chatelaine Gardens / Consumer (Gardening)
Le Chef du service alimentaire / Business (Hotels & Restaurants)

Canadian Almanac & Directory 1997

The Chesterton Review / Consumer (Literary)
Chickadee / Consumer (Children's)
Chinacity / Ethnic (Chinese)
Chinese News / Ethnic (Chinese)
Choices After 50 / Consumer (Senior Citizens)
Christian Courier / Consumer (Religious & Denominational)
Christian Info News / Consumer (Religious & Denominational)
ChristianWeek / Consumer (Religious & Denominational)
The Chronicle / University
The Chronicle of Skin & Allergy / Business (Medical)
The Chronicle of Urology & Sexual Medicine / Business (Medical)
Church Business Magazine / Business (Church Administration)
CIAO Magazine / Ethnic (Italian)
CIM Bulletin / Business (Mining)
CIM Directory / Business (Mining)
CIM Reporter / Business (Mining)
Cineaction: Radical Film Criticism & Theory / Consumer (Entertainment)
CIO Canada / Business (Computing & Technology)
CISM Journal, see Geomatica
Cité Universitaire / University
Il Cittadino Canadese / Ethnic (Italian)
City & Country HOmes, see Chatelaine Gardens
City Parent / Consumer (Families)
Cityscope, see Calgary Cityscope
Cityside / University
The Clansman, see Celtic Heritage
Le Clap / University
The Claremont Review / Consumer (Literary)
Classical Music Magazine / Consumer (Music)
Classic Home / Consumer (Homes)
Clin d'oeil / Consumer (Women's & Feminist)
Clinical and Investigative Medicine / Business (Medical)
Le Clinicien / Business (Medical)
C Magazine / Consumer (Arts, Art & Antiques)
CMA Magazine / Business (Business)
CMA News / Business (Medical)
CM Magazine / Business (Books, Stationery)
The Coastal Grower Magazine / Consumer (Gardening)
Coast the outdoor recreation magazine / Consumer (Sports & Recreation)
Coatings / Business (Paint, Finishes, Coatings)
Coda Magazine / Consumer (Music)
Collectibles Canada / Consumer (Arts, Art & Antiques)
Le Collectif / University
Commerce News / Business (Business)
Common Ground / Consumer (General Interest)
Community Action: Canada's Community Service Newspaper / Consumer (Social Welfare)
Community Digest / Ethnic (Multicultural)
Community Resource Directory / Consumer (Senior Citizens)
Compass: A Jesuit Journal / Consumer (Religious & Denominational)
The Compleat Mother / Consumer (Babies & Mothers)
CompuSource / Consumer (Computers)
Computer Dealer News / Business (Computing & Technology)
Computer & Entertainment Retailing / Business (Computers)
Computer Freelancer / Business (Computers)
The Computer Paper / Business (Computers)
The Computer Post / Business (Computers)
Computer World / Business (Computing & Technology)
Computing Canada / Business (Computing & Technology)
Le Concept / University
Concern / Business (Nursing)
The Concordian / University

Concordia University Magazine / University
Condominium Magazine / Business (Building)
The Condominium Manager / Business (Building)
Condos de Rêves / Consumer (Homes)
Congrès Mensuel / Business (Conventions & Meetings)
Il Congresso / Ethnic (Italian)
Connections Northwest / Consumer (Airline Inflight, Train & Bus In-transit)
Construction Alberta News / Business (Engineering)
Construction Canada / Business (Architecture)
Construction Comment / Business (Construction)
Construire / Business (Construction)
Contact / Business (Hospitals, Health Care)
Contact / Consumer (General Interest)
Contact / Consumer (Arts, Art & Antiques)
Contemporary Verse 2 / Consumer (Women's & Feminist)
Continuité / Consumer (General Interest)
Conventions & Meetings Canada / Business (Conventions & Meetings)
Le Coopérateur Agricole / Farm (Farm Publication)
Le Coopérateur forestier / Business (Forest & Lumber Industries)
COPA Conversation / Business (Office Equipment)
The Cord Weekly / University
Corn-Soy Guide / Farm (Farm Publication)
Corporate Fleet Management / Business (Automotive & Accessories)
Correio Português / Ethnic (Portuguese)
Correo Latinoamericano / Ethnic (Spanish)
Corriere Canadese / Ethnic (Italian)
Corriere Illustrato, see Tandem
Corriere Italiano / Ethnic (Italian)
Cosmetics / Business (Cosmetics)
Cottage Life / Consumer (General Interest)
Cottage News / Consumer (General Interest)
Coulicou / Consumer (Children's)
Country / Consumer (Music)
The Country Connection / Consumer (General Interest)
Country Guide / Farm (Farm Publication)
Country Life in B.C. / Farm (Farm Publication)
Country Music News / Consumer (Music)
Coup d'oeil / Business (Optical)
Coup d'oeil / Consumer (Travel)
Coup de Pouce / Consumer (Women's & Feminist)
Coup de Pouce Extra Cuisine / Consumer (Food & Beverage)
Le Coureur des Neiges / Consumer (Sports & Recreation)
Courrier Grec / Ethnic (Greek)
Le Courrier Hippique / Consumer (Horses, Riding & Breeding)
Coven / University
The Covenant, see The Jewish Tribune
Coverings: Floors, Windows & Walls / Business (Floor Coverings)
CraftNews / Consumer (Hobbies)
Crafts Plus / Consumer (Hobbies)
Crescendo / Consumer (Music)
La Criée / University
La Crise / University
Croatian Voice / Ethnic (Croatian)
Croissance / Consumer (Health, Medical)
Cut & Dried / Business (Florists)
CV Photo / Consumer (Photography)
Cycle Canada / Consumer (Automobile & Cycle)
Daily Commercial News & Construction Record / Business (Construction)
Dairy Contact / Farm (Farm Publication)
Dairy Guide / Farm (Farm Publication)
Dalhousie Review / Consumer (Literary)
Dance International / Consumer (Arts, Art & Antiques)
Dandelion / Consumer (Literary)
DC Magazine / Business (Barbers & Beauticians)
Debit Memo / University
Les Débrouillards / Consumer (Children's)

Décoration Chez-Soi / Consumer (Homes)
Décormag / Consumer (Homes)
Défi-Sciences / University
Del Condominium Life / Consumer (Homes)
Dental Practice Management / Business (Dentistry)
Dentist's Guide / Business (Dentistry)
Dermatology Times of Canada / Business (Medical)
Descant / Consumer (Literary)
Design Engineering / Business (Product Engineering & Design)
Designers' Best Home Plans / Consumer (Homes)
Design Product News / Business (Product Engineering & Design)
Destinations Canada/USA / Business (Travel)
Deutsche Presse / Ethnic (German)
Deutsche Presse / Ethnic (German)
Diabetes News / Consumer (Health, Medical)
Dialogue: A Forum for the Exchange of Ideas / Consumer (General Interest)
Diététique en Action / Business (Hospitals, Health Care)
Digest Business & Law Journal / Business (Legal)
The Diocesan Times / Consumer (Religious & Denominational)
Les Diplômés / University
Direction Informatique / Business (Computing & Technology)
Directory of Ontario Lumber & Building Materials Retailers, Buyers' Guide & Product Directory / Business (Forest & Lumber Industries)
Disability International / Business (Hospitals, Health Care)
Disability Today / Consumer (General Interest)
Discorder - Student Radio Society of U.B.C / University
Diva / Consumer (Women's & Feminist)
Diver Magazine / Consumer (Sports & Recreation)
DIY Boat Owner / Consumer (Boating & Yachting)
Doctor's Review / Business (Medical)
Dogs, Dogs, Dogs / Consumer (Animals)
Dogs in Canada / Consumer (Animals)
Durham Business News / Business (Business)
Earthkeeper Magazine, see Natural Life Magazine
Eastern News / Ethnic (Pakistani)
Eastern Woods & Waters / Consumer (Fishing & Hunting)
ÉCHEC+ / Consumer (Hobbies)
L'Echo du Transport / Business (Motor Trucks & Buses)
Echoes / Consumer (Fraternal, Service Clubs, Associations)
L'Echorché / University
Echos du Monde Classique / Scholarly (Scholarly Publication)
Eclairage Plus / Business (Lighting)
Eclosion / University
Ecodecision / Consumer (Environment & Nature)
L'Eco D'Italia / Ethnic (Italian)
Economic Planning in Free Sociétés / Farm (Farm Publication)
Economics Working Papers / Scholarly (Scholarly Publication)
L'Économique / Business (Business)
Edges: New Planetary Patterns / Consumer (Culture, Current Events)
Edmonton & Area Airport Business Directory / Business (Aviation & Aerospace)
Edmonton Commerce & Industry / Business (Business)
The Edmonton Senior / Consumer (Senior Citizens)
Edmonton Woman / Consumer (Women's & Feminist)
Educational Digest / Business (Education)
Education Forum / Business (Education)
Education Today / Business (Education)
L'Éffronté / University
EIC (Electronique, industrielle et commerciale) / Business (Electronics)
Electique / University

Electrical Bluebook / Business (Electrical Equipment)
Electrical Business / Business (Electrical Equipment)
Electrical Equipment News - The Industrial Buyer / Business (Electrical Equipment)
Electrical Line Advertiser / Business (Electrical Equipment)
Electrical Supply & Distribution Annual / Business (Electrical Equipment)
Électricité Québec / Business (Electrical Equipment)
Electricity Today / Business (Electrical Equipment)
Electronic Composition & Imaging / Business (Computing & Technology)
Electronic Link, see Applied Arts
The Electronics Communicator / Business (Electronics)
Elle Québec / Consumer (Women's & Feminist)
Ellipse / Scholarly (Scholarly Publication)
Elm Street / Consumer (Women's & Feminist)
El Popular / Ethnic (Spanish)
Emergency Librarian / Business (Books, Stationery)
Emergency Prepardness Direct / Business (Emergency Services)
The Emery Weal / University
Energy Manager / Business (Engineering)
Energy Processing/Canada / Business (Petroleum, Oil & Gas)
Energy Studies Review / Scholarly (Scholarly Publication)
Engineering Dimensions / Business (Engineering)
Enoteca Wine & Food Magazine / Business (Food & Food Processing)
En Primeur Jeunesse / Consumer (Children's)
enRoute / Consumer (Airline Inflight, Train & Bus In-transit)
En Tete / University
L'Entremetteur / University
Entreprendre / Business (Business)
L'Envers du décor / Business (Interior Design & Decor)
Environmental Science & Engineering / Business (Water & Wastes Treatment)
Environments: A Journal of Interdisciplinary Studies / Scholarly (Scholarly Publication)
Environment Views / Consumer (Environment & Nature)
Envirotech / Business (Water & Wastes Treatment)
EP&T Electronic Products & Technology / Business (Electronics)
Equality News / Ethnic (Caribbean)
Equinox / Consumer (General Interest)
Equipment Journal / Business (Engineering)
L'Escale Nautique / Consumer (Boating & Yachting)
Espace / Consumer (Arts, Art & Antiques)
Espaces Verts / Business (Landscaping)
Essays on Canadian Writing / Scholarly (Scholarly Publication)
L'Essentiel / Consumer (Women's & Feminist)
Estimators' & Buyers' Guide / Business (Printing & Publishing)
ETC Montréal / Consumer (Arts, Art & Antiques)
Eté Contact / Business (Sporting Goods & Recreational Equipment)
Event / Scholarly (Scholarly Publication)
Events Planner / Consumer (City Magazine)
Excalibur / University
Exceptionality Education Canada / Scholarly (Scholarly Publication)
Exchange: Magazine for Business / Business (Business)
Excursions en Autocar / Business (Travel)
Executive's Guide, see The Professional's Guide to Luxury Cars
L'Exemplaire / University
L'Exhibitioniste / University
Exile / Consumer (Literary)
Expecting / Consumer (Babies & Mothers)
L'Expéditeur / Business (Transportation, Shipping & Distribution)
Explore / Consumer (Camping & Outdoor Recreation)

Export is Our Business / Business (Import, Export)
Express / Consumer (Entertainment)
Eye / Consumer (City Magazine)
The Eyeopener / University
Fabricare Canada / Business (Laundry & Dry Cleaning)
Faith Today / Consumer (Religious & Denominational)
Family & Education / Consumer (Women's & Feminist)
Family Health / Consumer (Health, Medical)
Family Practice / Business (Medical)
Farm & Country / Farm (Farm Publication)
Farm Focus / Farm (Farm Publication)
The Farm Gate / Farm (Farm Publication)
Farm Light & Power / Farm (Farm Publication)
Farm Review / Farm (Farm Publication)
Farmers' Choice / Farm (Farm Publication)
FarmLIFE / Farm (Farm Publication)
Farmwoman / Farm
Fashion femme / Business (Clothing & Accessories)
The Faucet / University
FCM Forum / Business (Government)
Feather Fancier / Farm (Farm Publication)
Feature (Your Premium Entertainment Magazine) / Consumer (Television, Radio, Video & Home Appliances)
Feliciter / Business (Books, Stationery)
Femme Plus / Consumer (Women's & Feminist)
The Fiddlehead / Consumer (Literary)
Fifty-Five Plus / Consumer (Senior Citizens)
Au Fil des Evénements / University
Filipino Journal / Ethnic (Filipino)
Filles d'aujourd'hui / Consumer (Women's & Feminist)
The Financial Post 500 / Business (Business)
The Financial Post Magazine Canada / Consumer (Business & Finance)
The Financial Post Survey of Industrials / Business (Business)
The Financial Post Survey of Mines & Energy Resources / Business (Mining)
Fire Fighting in Canada / Business (Fire Protection)
Fireweed: A Feminist Quarterly of Writing, Politics, Art & Culture / Consumer (Women's & Feminist)
First Home Buyer's Guide / Consumer (Homes)
The Fisherman / Business (Fisheries)
Fittingly Yours / Consumer (Sports & Recreation)
The Flag & Banner / Consumer (General Interest)
Flare / Consumer (Fashion)
Fleet Management Journal / Business (Automotive & Accessories)
Fleur Design / Business (Florists)
Fleurs, plantes et jardins / Consumer (Gardening)
Floor Coverings / Business (Floor Coverings)
FMWC Newsletter / Business (Medical)
Focus / Business (Government)
Focus on Women / Consumer (Women's & Feminist)
Food & Drink / Consumer (Food & Beverage)
Food in Canada / Business (Food & Food Processing)
Foodservice & Hospitality / Business (Hotels & Restaurants)
Footwear Forum, see Canadian Footwear Journal
The Forestry Chronicle / Business (Forest & Lumber Industries)
Forêt Conservation / Business (Pulp & Paper)
Fortnightly Universal News / Ethnic (Pakistani)
Forum / University
La Fournée / Business (Baking & Bakers' Supplies)
Franc-Vert / Consumer (Environment & Nature)
Fraser's Canadian Trade Directory / Business (Purchasing)
Le Front / University
The Fulcrum / University
Fuse / Consumer (Culture, Current Events)
Fusion / Consumer (Arts, Art & Antiques)
Future Health / Consumer (Health, Medical)
Futur présent / Business (Business)
Gallery Impressions / Business (Art & Antiques)

Gam on Yachting / Consumer (Boating & Yachting)
Gardening Life / Consumer (Gardening)
Gardens West / Consumer (Gardening)
Gargoyle / University
Garrison / Business (Military)
Gateway / University
The Gauntlet / University
Gazeta Montrealska / Ethnic (Polish)
Gazette / University
The Gazette / University
La Gazzetta / Ethnic (Italian)
Geist / Consumer (Literary)
General Insurance Register / Business (Insurance)
Genome / Business (Science, Research & Development)
Geomatica / Business (Engineering)
Geo Plein Air / Consumer (Travel)
The Georgian / University
Georgian Bay Today / Consumer (General Interest)
The Georgia Straight / Consumer (City Magazine)
German American Trade / Business (Business)
Germs & Ideas / Business (Medical)
Gestion / Business (Business)
Gestion et Technologie Agricoles / Farm (Farm Publication)
La Giffle / University
Gifts & Tablewares / Business (Gifts)
Il Giornale Italiano del Manitoba / Ethnic (Italian)
Glasnik Hrvatske Seljacke Stranke / Ethnic (Croatian)
Glass Canada / Business (Glass)
The Gleaner / University
Global Biodiversity / Consumer (Environment & Nature)
Globe Magazine / Consumer (General Interest)
The Globe and Mail Broadcast Week / Consumer (Television, Radio, Video & Home Appliances)
Going Natural / Consumer (General Interest)
Golden Words / University
Golf Albatros / Consumer (Sports & Recreation)
Golf Canada / Consumer (Sports & Recreation)
Golf Course Ranking Magazine / Consumer (Sports & Recreation)
Golf Guide / Consumer (Sports & Recreation)
Golf International / Consumer (Sports & Recreation)
Golf the West / Consumer (Sports & Recreation)
Good Times / Consumer (Senior Citizens)
Gospel Herald / Consumer (Religious & Denominational)
Government Business / Business (Government)
Government Business Opportunities / Business (Government)
Government Computing Digest / Business (Computing & Technology)
Government Purchasing Guide / Business (Government)
Le Grafitti / University
Grail: An Ecumenical Journal / Consumer (Religious & Denominational)
Grain / Consumer (Literary)
Grainews / Farm (Farm Publication)
The Graphic Exchange / Business (Graphic Arts)
The Graphic Monthly / Business (Printing & Publishing)
Great Expectations / Consumer (Babies & Mothers)
Great Lakes Liberty Press / Consumer (News)
Great Lakes Navigation / Business (Shipping, Marine)
Greek Canadian Action / Ethnic (Greek)
Greek Canadian Reportage / Ethnic (Greek)
Greek Canadian Tribune / Ethnic (Greek)
Greenhouse Canada / Business (Garden Supplies & Equipment)
GreenMaster / Business (Landscaping)
Green Teacher: Education for Planet Earth / Business (Education)
The Green and White / University
La Grenouille / University
Grocer Today / Business (Grocery Trade)
The Grower / Farm (Farm Publication)

GSA: The Travel Magazine for Western Canada / Business (Travel)
Guelph Peak / University
Le Gugusse / University
Le Guide de l'Agriculture du Québec / Farm (Farm Publication)
Le Guide Cuisine / Consumer (Food & Beverage)
Le Guide des fournisseurs des centres de rénovation et des quincailleries du Québec / Business (Hardware Trade)
Guide du Transport par Camion / Business (Transportation, Shipping & Distribution)
Le Guide Prestige Montréal / Consumer (City Magazine)
Guide Ressources / Consumer (Health, Medical)
Guide to Canadian Healthcare Facilities / Business (Hospitals, Health Care)
Gujarat Vartman / Ethnic (East Indian)
Habitabec Plus / Consumer (Homes)
HAC News / Consumer (General Interest)
Hallelujah / Consumer (Religious & Denominational)
Hamilton Business Report, see Biz-Hamilton/Halton Business Report
Hamilton This Month / Consumer (City Magazine)
Harbour & Shipping / Business (Shipping, Marine)
Hardware Merchandising / Business (Hardware Trade)
Harrowsmith Country Life / Consumer (General Interest)
Hazardous Materials Directory / Business (Water & Wastes Treatment)
Hazardous Materials Management / Business (Water & Wastes Treatment)
Head Office at Home / Business (Business)
Health Economics / Business (Medical)
The Health Journal: Canada's Authorative Health Forum / Consumer (Health, Medical)
Health Naturally / Consumer (Health, Medical)
Healthcare Management FORUM / Business (Hospitals, Health Care)
HealthWatch Canada / Consumer (Health, Medical)
Heart of the Country / Consumer (Music)
Heating-Plumbing-Air Conditioning / Business (Heating, Plumbing, Air Conditioning)
Heavy Construction News / Business (Engineering)
Helicopters / Business (Aviation & Aerospace)
Hellenic-Canadian Chronicles / Ethnic (Greek)
Hellenic Hamilton News / Ethnic (Greek)
The Hellenic News / Ethnic (Greek)
Heritage Canada / Consumer (Environment & Nature)
Heritage News / Consumer (General Interest)
Herizons / Consumer (Women's & Feminist)
L'Hermes / University
Hi-Rise / Consumer (City Magazine)
Hiballer Forest Magazine / Business (Forest & Lumber Industries)
Hibou / Consumer (Children's)
The Hockey News / Consumer (Sports & Recreation)
De Hollandse Krant / Ethnic (Dutch)
Holstein Journal / Farm (Farm Publication)
Home Builder Magazine / Business (Building)
Home Computing & Entertainment / Consumer (Computers)
Home Improvement Retailing / Business (Hardware Trade)
Home & School, see Family & Education
Homemaker's / Consumer (Women's & Feminist)
Home & School / Consumer (Women's & Feminist)
Homes & Cottages / Consumer (Homes)
Homes Magazine / Consumer (Homes)
Homin Ukrayiny / Ethnic (Ukrainian)
Horse Action International / Consumer (Horses, Riding & Breeding)
The Horse Chronicle / Consumer (Horses, Riding & Breeding)
Horse & Country Canada / Consumer (Horses, Riding & Breeding)
Horsepower: Magazine for Young Horse Lovers / Consumer (Horses, Riding & Breeding)

Horses All / Consumer (Horses, Riding & Breeding)
Horse Sport / Consumer (Horses, Riding & Breeding)
Horticulture Review: The Voice of Landscape Ontario / Business (Landscaping)
Hortwest / Business (Landscaping)
Hospital Business / Business (Hospitals, Health Care)
Hospital News / Business (Hospitals, Health Care)
Hospital Pharmacy Practice / Business (Drugs)
Hotelier / Business (Hotels & Restaurants)
Hour / Consumer (City Magazine)
Hum - The Government Computer Magazine / Business (Computing & Technology)
Humanist in Canada / Consumer (General Interest)
Human Resources Professional / Business (Human Resources)
Hunter's Guide to Professional Outfitters / Consumer (Fishing & Hunting)
Huron Soil & Crop News / Farm (Farm Publication)
Huronia Business Times / Business (Business)
ICAO Journal / Business (Aviation & Aerospace)
Les Idées de ma Maison / Consumer (Homes)
id magazine / Consumer (Culture, Current Events)
Image de la Mauricie / Consumer (Entertainment)
Images / Consumer (Women's & Feminist)
iMPACT / Consumer (Music)
Impact Campus / University
L'Important / Consumer (City Magazine)
Imprint / University
The Independent Senior / Consumer (Senior Citizens)
India Calling / Ethnic (East Indian)
Indo-Canadian Times / Ethnic (East Indian)
Indo Canadian Phulwari / Ethnic (East Indian)
Indo Pak Community Voice, see The South Asian Voice
Industrial Process Products & Technology / Business (Chemicals & Chemical Process Industries)
L'Infirmière auxiliaire, voir Santé Québec
L'Infirmière du Québec / Business (Nursing)
Inflight/En vol / Consumer (Airline Inflight, Train & Bus In-transit)
Influence / Consumer (Fashion)
Info-affaires / Business (Business)
Info-tech Magazine / Business (Computing & Technology)
Info Canada / Business (Computing & Technology)
Info Presse Communications / Business (Advertising, Marketing, Sales)
L'Infomane / University
Infor / Scholarly (Scholarly Publication)
INFORMATION highways: The Magazine for Users of Electronic Information / Consumer (Computers)
In Montréal / Consumer (City Magazine)
The Inner Ear Report / Consumer (Television, Radio, Video & Home Appliances)
Insieme / Ethnic (Italian)
Insight on Collectibles, see Collectibles Canada
Insite / Business (Architecture)
Insurance West / Business (Insurance)
Inter / Consumer (Arts, Art & Antiques)
Inter-Canadian, see Globe Magazine
Inter-mécanique du bâtiment / Business (Heating, Plumbing, Air Conditioning)
Interculture / Consumer (Literary)
L'Interdit / University
L'Interêt / University
Interface / Business (Business)
Interlog Magazine / Business (Forest & Lumber Industries)
International Guide / Consumer (City Magazine)
Internet Marketing Report / Business (Computing & Technology)
The Interpreter / University
Inuit Art Quarterly / Consumer (Arts, Art & Antiques)
Investment Executive / Business (Business)
Investor's Digest of Canada / Business (Business)
Island Farmer / Farm (Farm Publication)
The Island Grower, see The Coastal Grower Magazine
Island Parent Magazine / Consumer (Families)

Italcommerce / Business (Business)
Italian Link / Ethnic (Italian)
Italy Canada Trade / Business (Business)
J'Aime Lire / Consumer (Children's)
The Jamaican Weekly Gleaner / Ethnic (Caribbean)
Jewish Free Press / Consumer (Religious & Denominational)
The Jewish Tribune / Consumer (Religious & Denominational)
Jobber News / Business (Automotive & Accessories)
The Journal / Business (Hospitals, Health Care)
The Journal / University
Le Journal de l'Assurance / Business (Insurance)
Le Journal Barreau / Business (Legal)
Journal Constructo / Business (Construction)
Journal Dentaire du Québec / Business (Dentistry)
Journal des pâtes et papiers / Business (Pulp & Paper)
Journal les Enseignants / Business (Education)
Le Journal Industriel du Québec / Business (Industrial & Industrial Automation)
Journal of Baha'i Studies / Scholarly (Scholarly Publication)
Journal of Canadian Art History / Scholarly (Scholarly Publication)
Journal of the Canadian Chiropractic Association / Business (Medical)
Journal of the Canadian Dental Association / Business (Dentistry)
Journal of the Canadian Dietetic Association / Business (Hospitals, Health Care)
The Journal of Canadian Petroleum Technology / Business (Petroleum, Oil & Gas)
Journal of Canadian Poetry / Scholarly (Scholarly Publication)
Journal of Canadian Studies / Scholarly (Scholarly Publication)
Journal of Child & Youth Care / Scholarly (Scholarly Publication)
Journal of Commerce / Business (Construction)
Journal of Law and Social Policy / Scholarly (Scholarly Publication)
Journal of Otolaryngology / Business (Medical)
Journal of Psychiatry & Neuroscience / Business (Medical)
Journal of Rheumatology / Business (Medical)
Journal of Scholarly Publishing / Scholarly (Scholarly Publication)
Le Journal Québec Quilles / Consumer (Sports & Recreation)
Journal SOGC / Business (Medical)
Journal Sports Nature Plein Air Chasse - Pêche / Consumer (Fishing & Hunting)
Journal U.Q.A.M / University
JourneyWoman / Consumer (Women's & Feminist)
Junior / Consumer (Families)
Kahtou News / Ethnic (Aboriginal)
Kanada Kurier / Ethnic (German)
Kanadai Magyarsag / Ethnic (Hungarian)
Kanadske Listy / Ethnic (Slovak, Czech)
Kanadski Srbobran / Ethnic (Serbian)
Kanawa: Canada's Canoeing & Kayaking Magazine / Consumer (Camping & Outdoor Recreation)
Kerala Express / Ethnic (East Indian)
Key to Kingston / Consumer (City Magazine)
Kick it Over / Consumer (Political)
Kids Creations / Business (Clothing & Accessories)
Kids Tribute / Consumer (Children's)
Kids World Magazine / Consumer (Children's)
KIN Magazine / Consumer (Fraternal, Service Clubs, Associations)
Kindred Spirits of PEI / Consumer (General Interest)
Kinesis / Consumer (Women's & Feminist)
Kootenay Business Magazine / Business (Business)
Kootenay Visitor's Magazine / Consumer (City Magazine)
The Korea Times Daily / Ethnic (Korean)
Kulisy Polonii / Ethnic (Polish)

LAB Business / Business (Science, Research & Development)
Laboratory Buyers Guide / Business (Science, Research & Development)
Laboratory Product News / Business (Science, Research & Development)
Labour / Scholarly (Scholarly Publication)
Labour, Capital & Society: A Journal on the Third World / Scholarly (Scholarly Publication)
Lambda / University
The Lance / University
Landmark / Business (Landscaping)
Landscape Trades / Business (Landscaping)
Latitudes / Consumer (Travel)
Latvija-Amerika / Ethnic (Latvian)
The Laurentians Tourist Guide / Consumer (Travel)
Law Now / Business (Legal)
Law Times / Business (Legal)
The Lawyers Weekly / Business (Legal)
LBMAO Reporter / Business (Building)
Leadership in Health Services / Business (Hospitals, Health Care)
Legion / Consumer (Fraternal, Service Clubs, Associations)
Leisurability / Scholarly (Scholarly Publication)
Leisureways/Westworld/Going Places Magazine / Consumer (General Interest)
Leisure World / Consumer (General Interest)
Lemon-Aid Magazine / Consumer (Automobile & Cycle)
Lethbridge Living / Consumer (City Magazine)
Lexicon / University
Liaison / Business (Insurance)
Liaison / University
Lifestyles 5755 / Consumer (General Interest)
Lighting Magazine / Business (Lighting)
The Limousin Leader / Farm (Farm Publication)
The Link / University
Literary Review of Canada / Consumer (Literary)
Living Safety / Consumer (General Interest)
Local Women / Consumer (Women's & Feminist)
Locator / Consumer (Directories & Almanacs)
Logberg-Heimskringla / Ethnic (Icelandic)
Logging & Sawmilling Journal / Business (Forest & Lumber Industries)
London / Consumer (City Magazine)
London Business Monthly Magazine / Business (Business)
London & District Construction Association Magazine / Business (Construction)
Long Term Care / Business (Hospitals, Health Care)
LOOKwest Magazine / Consumer (Women's & Feminist)
Lo Specchio/Vaughan / Ethnic (Italian)
The Loyalist Gazette / Consumer (History & Genealogy)
LUAC Forum / Business (Insurance)
Luggage, Leathergoods & Accessories / Business (Leather)
Le Lundi / Consumer (General Interest)
Luxe / Consumer (Fashion)
Macedonia / Ethnic (Macedonian)
The Macedonian Link / Ethnic (Macedonian)
The MacEwan Journalist / University
Machinery & Equipment MRO / Business (Machinery Maintenance)
Maclean's / Consumer (News)
Madison's Canadian Lumber Directory / Business (Forest & Lumber Industries)
Magazine Affaires Plus / Consumer (Business & Finance)
Le Magazine L'agent de voyages inc. / Business (Travel)
Magazine Le Clap / Consumer (Entertainment)
Le Magazine Enfants Québec / Consumer (Families)
Le Magazine FADOQ / Consumer (Senior Citizens)
Le Magazine Jeunesse / Consumer (Youth)
Magazine Québec International / Business (Business)

Magyar Elet / Ethnic (Hungarian)
Mainly for Seniors Lambton-Kent / Consumer (Senior Citizens)
Maître d'Oeuvre / Consumer (Homes)
Le Maître Electricien, voir Électricité Québec
Le Maître Imprimeur / Business (Printing & Publishing)
The Malahat Review / Consumer (Literary)
Manitoba Business / Business (Business)
The Manitoba Co-Operator / Farm (Farm Publication)
Manitoba Farm Life / Farm (Farm Publication)
Manitoba Living Guide / Consumer (Homes)
Manitoba Medicine, see Prairie Medical Journal
Manitoba Ship-by-Truck Directory / Business (Motor Trucks & Buses)
The Manitoba Teacher / Business (Education)
The Manitoban / University
Manufacturing & Process Automation / Business (Industrial & Industrial Automation)
Ma Revue de Machinerie Agricole / Farm (Farm Publication)
Mariage Québec / Consumer (Brides, Bridal)
Marina News / Business (Boating & Yachting)
Maritime Magazine / Business (Transportation, Shipping & Distribution)
Maritime Provinces Water & Wastewater Report / Business (Water & Wastes Treatment)
Marketing / Business (Advertising, Marketing, Sales)
Marketnews / Business (Radio, TV, Appliances & Video)
Marquee / Consumer (Entertainment)
The Martlet / University
Master Builder / Consumer (Homes)
Masthead / Business (Publishing)
Material History Review / Scholarly (Scholarly Publication)
Materials Management & Distribution / Business (Materials Handling & Distribution)
Mathematics Reports / Scholarly (Scholarly Publication)
Matriart / Consumer (Women's & Feminist)
Matricule Zéro / University
Matrix / Consumer (Literary)
Le Matulu / University
Mature Lifestyles / Consumer (Senior Citizens)
Maturity / Consumer (Senior Citizens)
McGill Daily / University
McGill French / University
McGill Journal of Education / Scholarly (Scholarly Publication)
McGill Law Journal / Business (Legal)
The McGill News / University
McGill Reporter / University
McGill Tribune / University
The McMaster Courier / University
McMaster Journal of Theology & Ministry / Scholarly (Scholarly Publication)
Mechanical Buyer & Specifier: HVAC/Refrigeration Magazine / Business (Heating, Plumbing, Air Conditioning)
Mechanical Buyer & Specifier: Plumbing, Piping & Heating Magazine / Business (Heating, Plumbing, Air Conditioning)
Le Médecin du Québec / Business (Medical)
Le Médecin Vétérinaire du Québec / Business (Veterinary)
Media / Business (Journalism)
The Media Book / Business (Advertising, Marketing, Sales)
Media Wave Magazine / Business (Advertising, Marketing, Sales)
The Medical Post / Business (Medical)
Medical Scope Monthly Journal / Business (Medical)
Medical Society of Nova Scotia News / Business (Medical)
Medicine North America / Business (Medical)
Mediscan / Business (Medical)
Medium II / University

Meetings & Incentive Travel / Business (Conventions & Meetings)
Meetings Monthly / Business (Conventions & Meetings)
Mehfil Magazine / Ethnic (East Indian)
Meie Elu / Ethnic (Estonian)
The Meliorist / University
Mémo - le gout des régions / Business (Business)
Mennonite Brethren Herald / Consumer (Religious & Denominational)
Mennonite Reporter / Consumer (Religious & Denominational)
Die Mennonitische Post / Ethnic (German)
Mennonitische Rundschau / Ethnic (German)
Menorah-Egyenloseg / Ethnic (Hungarian)
Mensa Canada Communications / Consumer (Fraternal, Service Clubs, Associations)
Menz / Consumer (General Interest)
Mère Nouvelle / Consumer (Babies & Mothers)
The Messenger / Ethnic (Pakistani)
Metalworking Production & Purchasing / Business (Metalworking)
Le Meunier / Farm (Farm Publication)
Micmac Business Finder / Consumer (Directories & Almanacs)
Micmac-Maliseet Nation News / Ethnic (Aboriginal)
Micro-Gazette / Business (Computing & Technology)
The Microscopical Society of Canada Bulletin / Business (Science, Research & Development)
Mid-Canada & Area Airport Business Directory / Business (Aviation & Aerospace)
The Mike / University
Mill Product News / Business (Pulp & Paper)
La Minerve / University
Ming Pao Daily News / Ethnic (Chinese)
Mining Review / Business (Mining)
Mining Sourcebook / Business (Mining)
Le Misanthrope / University
Mississauga Business Times / Business (Business)
MIX / Consumer (Culture, Current Events)
Model Aviation Canada / Consumer (Hobbies)
Modern Dairy, see Canadian Dairy
Modern Drama / Scholarly (Scholarly Publication)
Modern Purchasing / Business (Purchasing)
Modern Woman / Consumer (Women's & Feminist)
Moloda Ukraina / Ethnic (Ukrainian)
Monarchy Canada / Consumer (General Interest)
Mon Bébé / Consumer (Babies & Mothers)
Le Monde de l'Auto / Consumer (Automobile & Cycle)
Le Monde de L'Electricité / Business (Electrical Equipment)
Le Monde Juridique / Business (Legal)
Mon Enfant / Consumer (Babies & Mothers)
The Monograph - Journal of the Ont. Assn. for Geographical & Environmental Education / Scholarly (Scholarly Publication)
Monographs in Education / Scholarly (Scholarly Publication)
Montréal & Area Aviation Business Directory / Business (Aviation & Aerospace)
Montréal Business Magazine / Business (Business)
Montréal Campus / University
Montréal Mirror / Consumer (City Magazine)
Montréal Plus / Business (Business)
Montréal Port Guide & Transportation Register / Business (Shipping, Marine)
Montréal Scope / Consumer (City Magazine)
Mosaic: A Journal for the Interdisciplinary Study of Literature / Scholarly (Scholarly Publication)
Le Motdit / University
Moto Journal / Consumer (Automobile & Cycle)
Motoneige Québec / Consumer (Sports & Recreation)
Motor Fleet Management / Business (Automotive & Accessories)
Motor Truck / Business (Motor Trucks & Buses)
Motorsport Dealer & Trade / Business (Sporting Goods & Recreational Equipment)

Canadian Almanac & Directory 1997

Mouton Noir / University
Moving to & Around... / Consumer (City Magazine)
MSOS Journal / Consumer (Senior Citizens)
Multi-Cultural Magazine / Ethnic (Multicultural)
Municipal Business Canada / Business (Government)
Municipal Monitor / Business (Government)
Municipal World / Business (Government)
Muse / Consumer (Arts, Art & Antiques)
The Muse / University
Music in our Lives / Consumer (Music)
Musicien Québécois / Consumer (Music)
Musicworks: The Journal of Sound Explorations / Consumer (Music)
Muskoka Life / Consumer (General Interest)
Muskoka Real Estate Guide / Consumer (Homes)
The Mystery Review / Consumer (Literary)
The Nation: The News & Cultural Magazine of the James Bay Cree / Consumer (Culture, Current Events)
National / Business (Legal)
National Industrial / Business (Industrial & Industrial Automation)
The National List of Advertisers / Business (Advertising, Marketing, Sales)
The National Radio Guide / Consumer (Television, Radio, Video & Home Appliances)
National Rugby Post / Consumer (Sports & Recreation)
Native Network News / Ethnic (Aboriginal)
Natural Life Magazine / Consumer (Environment & Nature)
Nature Canada / Consumer (Environment & Nature)
Navigator / University
De Nederlandse Courant / Ethnic (Dutch)
Nepriklausoma Lietuva / Ethnic (Lithuanian)
The Network / Business (Hotels & Restaurants)
Network / Business (Funeral Service)
Network / Consumer (Entertainment)
Network World Canada / Business (Computing & Technology)
The New Brunswick Anglican / Consumer (Religious & Denominational)
New Canada Weekly / Ethnic (Multicultural)
The New Canadian / Ethnic (Japanese)
New City Magazine / Consumer (City Magazine)
New Clarion / Consumer (Senior Citizens)
New Edition / University
New Equipment News / Business (Industrial & Industrial Automation)
The New Freeman / Consumer (Religious & Denominational)
New Maritimes / Consumer (General Interest)
New Mother / Consumer (Babies & Mothers)
The New Quarterly / Consumer (Literary)
New Trail / University
NeWest Review / Consumer (Culture, Current Events)
The Newfoundland Herald / Consumer (Television, Radio, Video & Home Appliances)
Newfoundland Sportsman / Consumer (Fishing & Hunting)
Newfoundland Studies / Scholarly (Scholarly Publication)
Newhomes / Consumer (Homes)
News Canada / Business (Journalism)
The Newspaper / University
News & Views / Business (Police)
The Next City / Consumer (General Interest)
Niagara Anglican / Consumer (Religious & Denominational)
Niagara Business Report / Business (Business)
Niagara Farmers' Monthly / Farm (Farm Publication)
Niagara Magazine / Consumer (City Magazine)
Niagara News / University
Northern Aquaculture / Business (Fisheries)
The Northern Horizon / Farm (Farm Publication)
Northern Horse Review / Farm (Farm Publication)
The Northern Miner / Business (Mining)
Northern Ontario Business / Business (Business)

Northern Woman Journal: An Analysis of Feminist Issues / Consumer (Women's & Feminist)
Northpoint / Business (Engineering)
Northwest Business / Business (Business)
Northwest Farmer/Rancher / Farm (Farm Publication)
Northwestern Ontario Snowmobile News / Consumer (Sports & Recreation)
Nouveau-Quartier / University
Nouvelles CEQ / Consumer (General Interest)
Nova Scotia Business Journal / Business (Business)
Nova Scotia Historical Review / Scholarly (Scholarly Publication)
Novy Domov / Ethnic (Slovak, Czech)
Novy Shliakh / Ethnic (Ukrainian)
Now / Consumer (City Magazine)
Nowi Dni / Ethnic (Ukrainian)
Nuclear Canada Yearbook / Business (Power & Power Plants)
Nuit Blanche / Consumer (Literary)
Il Nuovo Mondo / Ethnic (Italian)
Nursing B.C. / Business (Nursing)
Nursing Québec, see L'Infirmière du Québec
The Nutrition Post / Business (Medical)
Obiter Dicta (Osgood Hall) / University
Occupational Health & Safety Canada / Business (Industrial Safety)
Octane / Business (Automotive & Accessories)
OHS Bulletin / Consumer (General Interest)
Oil & Gas Inquirer / Business (Petroleum, Oil & Gas)
Oil Patch Magazine / Business (Petroleum, Oil & Gas)
Oilweek / Business (Petroleum, Oil & Gas)
Okanagan Business Magazine / Business (Business)
Okanagan Life Magazine / Consumer (City Magazine)
OK Phoenix / University
Old Autos / Consumer (Automobile & Cycle)
Oldtimers' Hockey News / Consumer (Sports & Recreation)
L'Omnipraticien / Business (Medical)
On Spec: The Canadian Magazine of Speculative Writing / Consumer (Literary)
Ontario Beef / Farm (Farm Publication)
Ontario Beef Farmer / Farm (Farm Publication)
Ontario Business Report / Business (Business)
The Ontario Camping & Recreational Guide / Consumer (Camping & Outdoor Recreation)
Ontario Corn Producer / Farm (Farm Publication)
Ontario Craft / Consumer (Arts, Art & Antiques)
Ontario Dairy Farmer / Farm (Farm Publication)
Ontario Dentist / Business (Dentistry)
Ontario Design / Business (Interior Design & Decor)
Ontario Farmer / Farm (Farm Publication)
Ontario Fisherman / Consumer (Fishing & Hunting)
Ontario General Contractors' Association Membership Directory / Business (Construction)
Ontario Golf News / Consumer (Sports & Recreation)
Ontario History / Scholarly (Scholarly Publication)
Ontario Hog Farmer / Farm (Farm Publication)
Ontario Home Builder / Business (Building)
Ontario Insurance Directory / Business (Insurance)
The Ontario Land Surveyor Quarterly / Business (Engineering)
Ontario Medical Review / Business (Medical)
Ontario Milk Producer / Farm (Farm Publication)
Ontario Out of Doors / Consumer (Fishing & Hunting)
The Ontario Psychologist / Business (Medical)
The Ontario Reports / Business (Legal)
Ontario Restaurant Association Membership Directory & Buyers' Guide / Business (Hotels & Restaurants)
Ontario Restaurant News / Business (Hotels & Restaurants)
Ontario Snowmobiler / Consumer (Sports & Recreation)
Ontario Technologist / Business (Engineering)
Ontario Tennis / Consumer (Sports & Recreation)
Ontario Woman / Consumer (Women's & Feminist)
Ontario's Common Ground Magazine / Consumer (Health, Medical)

The Ontarion / University
Open Letter / Scholarly (Scholarly Publication)
Opera Canada / Consumer (Music)
Opérations Forestières et de Scierie / Business (Forest & Lumber Industries)
Ophthalmic Practice / Business (Medical)
Opportunities Canada / Business (Business)
Optical Prism / Business (Optical)
L'Optométriste / Business (Medical)
L'Ora Di Ottawa / Ethnic (Italian)
Orah Magazine / Consumer (Women's & Feminist)
Oral Health / Business (Dentistry)
L'Oratoire / Consumer (Religious & Denominational)
L'Original déchaîné / University
Osgoode Hall Law Journal / Business (Legal)
OSMT Advocate / Business (Science, Research & Development)
Other Press / University
Ottawa Business Journal / Business (Business)
Ottawa Magazine / Consumer (City Magazine)
The Ottawa X Press / Consumer (City Magazine)
Our Computer Player / Consumer (Computers)
Our Schools/Our Selves / Consumer (Social Welfare)
Our Times / Consumer (Labour, Trade Unions)
Outdoor Canada / Consumer (Fishing & Hunting)
The Outdoor Edge / Consumer (Fishing & Hunting)
Outlook / Consumer (Culture, Current Events)
Outside Guide / Consumer (Sports & Recreation)
Owl Magazine / Consumer (Children's)
Pacific Affairs / Scholarly (Scholarly Publication)
Pacific Current / Consumer (Political)
Pacific Golf Magazine / Consumer (Sports & Recreation)
Pacific Horse Journal / Consumer (Horses, Riding & Breeding)
The Pacific Hosteller / Consumer (Travel)
Pacific Yachting / Consumer (Boating & Yachting)
Paediatrics & Child Health / Business (Medical)
Pain Research Management / Business (Medical)
Pakeeza International / Ethnic (Pakistani)
paperplates / Consumer (Literary)
Les Papetières du Québec / Business (Pulp & Paper)
Papyrus / Consumer (Fraternal, Service Clubs, Associations)
Parachute Contemporary Art Magazine / Consumer (Arts, Art & Antiques)
Paragraph: The Canadian Fiction Review / Consumer (Literary)
Parallélogramme, see MIX
Parent-To-Parent / Consumer (Families)
The Parkhurst Exchange / Business (Medical)
Parks Companion / Consumer (Travel)
Parks and Recreation Canada / Consumer (Sports & Recreation)
Parlons Affaires Beauce/Etchemin / Business (Business)
Parlons Affaires Laurentides / Business (Business)
Pars ailleurs / University
Patient Care / Business (Medical)
Pazifische Rundschau / Ethnic (German)
Peace Magazine / Consumer (Political)
The Peak / University
Pedal Magazine / Consumer (Automobile & Cycle)
The PEGG / Business (Engineering)
PEM: Plant Engineering & Maintenance / Business (Industrial & Industrial Automation)
Peninsula Magazine / Consumer (General Interest)
The Pentecostal Testimony / Consumer (Religious & Denominational)
Perception / Consumer (Social Welfare)
Perdesi Panjab / Ethnic (East Indian)
Performance Racing News / Consumer (Automobile & Cycle)
Performing Arts & Entertainment in Canada / Consumer (Entertainment)
Persil-Parlant / University
Personnel Guide to Canada's Travel Industry / Business (Travel)

Perspectives in Cardiology / Business (Medical)
The Peterborough Review / Consumer (Literary)
La Petite Caisse / University
Pets Magazine / Consumer (Animals)
Pets Quarterly Magazine / Consumer (Animals)
Pharmacist News / Business (Drugs)
Le Pharmactuel / Business (Drugs)
Pharmacy Post / Business (Drugs)
Pharmacy Practice / Business (Drugs)
The Philantropist / Scholarly (Scholarly Publication)
Philatélie Québec / Consumer (Hobbies)
The Philippine Reporter / Ethnic (Filipino)
Philosophia Mathematica / Scholarly (Scholarly Publication)
Photo Life / Consumer (Photography)
Photo Retailer / Business (Photography)
Photo Sélection / Consumer (Photography)
Photonews & Electronic Imaging / Business (Photography)
Physical Education Digest / Consumer (Sports & Recreation)
Physics in Canada / Business (Science, Research & Development)
Physiotherapy Canada / Business (Medical)
Picaro / University
La Pige / University
Pigeon Dissident / University
Pioneer Christian Monthly / Consumer (Religious & Denominational)
Pique Newsmagazine / Consumer (City Magazine)
Les Plaisanciers / Consumer (Boating & Yachting)
Plan / Business (Engineering)
Plans de Maisons du Québec / Consumer (Homes)
Plant / Business (Industrial & Industrial Automation)
Plant / University
Plant & Garden / Consumer (Gardening)
Plastics Business / Business (Plastics)
Plastics in Canada Magazine / Business (Plastics)
Plastics Industry Reference Guide & Sourcebook / Business (Plastics)
Playback / Business (Broadcasting)
Playboard / Consumer (Entertainment)
PME (Le Magazine PME) / Business (Business)
Pocket Pro / Consumer (Sports & Recreation)
Poetry Canada / Consumer (Literary)
The Point / University
Point of View / Consumer (Women's & Feminist)
Polar Press / University
The Police Governor / Business (Police)
Policy Options / Scholarly (Scholarly Publication)
The Polish Canadian Courier / Ethnic (Polish)
Le Polyscope / University
Pomme d'Api Québec / Consumer (Families)
Pool & Spa Marketing / Business (Sporting Goods & Recreational Equipment)
Pop Life/Info Pop / Consumer (Youth)
Porc Québec / Farm (Farm Publication)
Pork Producer / Farm (Farm Publication)
Le Portefeuille d'assurances / Business (Insurance)
Port Hole / Consumer (Boating & Yachting)
Ports Annual / Business (Shipping, Marine)
Portugal Ilustrado / Ethnic (Portuguese)
Pottersfield Portfolio / Consumer (Literary)
Pouponnière / Consumer (Babies & Mothers)
Power Boating Canada / Consumer (Boating & Yachting)
Practical Allergy & Immunology, see Canadian Journal of Allergy & Immunology
Practical Homes Home Plans / Consumer (Homes)
Practical Optometry / Business (Medical)
The Prairie Agricultural Newspaper / Farm (Farm Publication)
Prairie Fire / Consumer (Literary)
Prairie Forum: Journal of the Canadian Plains Research Centre / Scholarly (Scholarly Publication)
Prairie Journal / Consumer (Literary)
Prairie Landscape Magazine / Business (Landscaping)
Prairie Medical Journal / Business (Medical)

Prairie Messenger / Consumer (Religious & Denominational)
Première: Video Magazine / Business (Radio, TV, Appliances & Video)
Pre & Post Natal News / Business (Nursing)
Presbyterian Record / Consumer (Religious & Denominational)
Press Review / Business (Journalism)
La Pression / University
Preview/Review / Business (Construction)
PrimeTime / Consumer (Television, Radio, Video & Home Appliances)
Prime Time / Consumer (Senior Citizens)
Primeurs / Consumer (Television, Radio, Video & Home Appliances)
PrintAction / Business (Printing & Publishing)
Prism International / Consumer (Literary)
Pro-farm / Farm (Farm Publication)
Probe / Business (Dentistry)
Le Producteur de lait québécois / Farm (Farm Publication)
Producteur Plus / Farm (Farm Publication)
Production Imprimée / Business (Printing & Publishing)
Produits Pour L'Industrie Québécoise / Business (Industrial & Industrial Automation)
Professional Farm Magazine / Farm (Farm Publication)
Professional Photographers of Canada / Business (Photography)
Professional Photographers of Canada Directory / Business (Photography)
Professional Renovation Magazine, see Renovation Magazine
Professional Sound / Business (Music & Music Trades)
The Professional's Guide to Luxury Cars / Consumer (Automobile & Cycle)
Profile Kingston / Consumer (City Magazine)
Profiles / Business (Business)
Profit: The Magazine for Canadian Entrepreneurs / Business (Business)
Project Magazine / University
The Projector / University
Promin / Ethnic (Ukrainian)
Propane-Canada / Business (Petroleum, Oil & Gas)
Property Management News / Business (Building)
Prospective / Business (Insurance)
The Prospector Exploration & Investment Bulletin / Business (Mining)
The Pro Tem (Glendon College) / University
Proven & Popular Home Plans / Consumer (Homes)
Provincial Building Trades Yearbook / Business (Building)
Psycause / University
Publication Profiles / Business (Advertising, Marketing, Sales)
Public Sector Management et Secteur Public / Scholarly (Scholarly Publication)
Publiquip/Roucam / Business (Engineering)
The Publisher / Business (Printing & Publishing)
Pulp & Paper Canada / Business (Pulp & Paper)
Qalam / Consumer (Religious & Denominational)
Quarry / Consumer (Literary)
Qubec Construction, voir Bâtiment
Quartier Libre / University
Quart de rond / Business (Hardware Trade)
Québec Enterprise / Business (Business)
Québec Farmers' Advocate / Farm (Farm Publication)
Québec Habitation / Business (Construction)
Quebec Home & School News / Business (Education)
Québec Pharmacie / Business (Drugs)
Québec Science / Consumer (Science & Technology)
Québec Soccer / Consumer (Sports & Recreation)
Québec Vert / Business (Landscaping)
Québec Yachting Voile & Moteur / Consumer (Boating & Yachting)
Queen's Alumni Review / University
Queen's Journal / University
Queen's Quarterly / Scholarly (Scholarly Publication)

Quill / University
Quill & Quire / Business (Books, Stationery)
Quincaillerie-Matériaux / Business (Hardware Trade)
Raddle Moon / Consumer (Literary)
Reader's Digest / Consumer (General Interest)
The Readers Showcase / Consumer (Literary)
Real Estate News / Consumer (Homes)
Real Estate Victoria / Consumer (Homes)
Real Outdoors / Consumer (Sports & Recreation)
Recycling Product News / Business (Water & Wastes Treatment)
Red Deer Advocate Plus, see Central Alberta Life
Reflector / University
The Registered Nurse / Business (Nursing)
Rehab & Community Care Management / Business (Hospitals, Health Care)
Rehabilitation Digest / Consumer (Social Welfare)
REM: Canada's Magazine for Real Estate Professionals / Business (Real Estate)
Renaissance & Reformation / Scholarly (Scholarly Publication)
Rendez-Vous / Business (Travel)
Rénovation Bricolage / Consumer (Homes)
Renovation Magazine / Consumer (Homes)
La Répliqué / University
The Reporter / Business (Education)
The Reporter / University
Report on Business Magazine / Business (Business)
Le Republique / University
Le Resam forestier / Business (Forest & Lumber Industries)
Research Money / Business (Science, Research & Development)
Réseau/U.Q. Network / University
Résidences Plaisirs de Vivre/Living in Style / Consumer (Homes)
Resolution / Scholarly (Scholarly Publication)
Resort Weekly / Consumer (Travel)
Resources for Feminist Research / Scholarly (Scholarly Publication)
Revue Commerce / Business (Business)
Revue juridique la femme et la droit, voir Canadian Journal of Women & the Law
La Revue des Sports / Consumer (Sports & Recreation)
La Revue Municipale / Business (Government)
La Revue Occasions d'Affaires / Business (Business)
Revue de l'Université de Moncton / Scholarly (Scholarly Publication)
Richmond Hill Month / Consumer (City Magazine)
The Rider / Consumer (Horses, Riding & Breeding)
Il Rincontro / Ethnic (Italian)
The Road Explorer / Business (Travel)
Room of One's Own / Consumer (Women's & Feminist)
La Rotonde / University
Rotunda / Consumer (Arts, Art & Antiques)
The Roughneck / Business (Petroleum, Oil & Gas)
Routes et Transports / Business (Transportation, Shipping & Distribution)
RPM Weekly / Business (Music & Music Trades)
Rural Roots / Farm (Farm Publication)
The Rural Voice / Farm (Farm Publication)
Russell: The Journal of the Bertrand Russell Archives / Scholarly (Scholarly Publication)
The Ryerson Rambler / University
Ryerson Review of Journalism / Business (Journalism)
Ryersonian / University
Safarir / Consumer (General Interest)
The Saint / University
Salon Beauté / Consumer (Barbers & Beauticians)
Salon Magazine / Business (Barbers & Beauticians)
Sanitation Canada / Business (Building)
Santé / Consumer (Health, Medical)
Santé Québec / Business (Nursing)
Saskatchewan Business / Business (Business)
The Saskatchewan Educator / Business (Education)
Saskatchewan Farm Life / Farm (Farm Publication)
The Satellite / University

Canadian Almanac & Directory 1997

Satellite Entertainment Guide / Consumer (Television, Radio, Video & Home Appliances)
Saturday Night / Consumer (General Interest)
Scarlet & Gold / Business (Police)
Scene / Consumer (Entertainment)
School Business Magazine / Business (Education)
Science-Fiction Studies / Scholarly (Scholarly Publication)
Scientia Canadensis - Journal of the History of Cdn. Science, Technology & Medicine / Scholarly (Scholarly Publication)
SCORE / Consumer (Sports & Recreation)
Scoreguide / Consumer (Sports & Recreation)
Scrivener / Scholarly (Scholarly Publication)
Seasons / Consumer (Environment & Nature)
Second Impressions / Business (Printing & Publishing)
Second Wind / Consumer (Health, Medical)
SEE Magazine / Consumer (City Magazine)
Sei Ping Monthly / Ethnic (Chinese)
Select Home Designs / Consumer (Homes)
Select Homes & Food, see Canadian Select Homes
Seminar / Scholarly (Scholarly Publication)
Seneca Impact / University
The Senior Times / Consumer (Senior Citizens)
The Seniors Choice / Consumer (Senior Citizens)
SeniorsPlus Newspaper / Consumer (Senior Citizens)
The Seniors Review / Consumer (Senior Citizens)
Seniors Today / Consumer (Senior Citizens)
Sentier Chasse-Pêche / Consumer (Fishing & Hunting)
The Sentinel / Consumer (Fraternal, Service Clubs, Associations)
Service Station & Garage Management / Business (Automotive & Accessories)
Shalom / Consumer (Religious & Denominational)
Shama / Ethnic (Pakistani)
Share / Ethnic (Black Community)
The Sheaf / University
Sheep Canada / Farm (Farm Publication)
The Sheridan Sun / University
The Shield / University
Shift Magazine / Consumer (Entertainment)
Shing Wah News / Ethnic (Chinese)
Short Courses & Seminars / Business (Education)
Show Guide / Business (Hardware Trade)
Shows & Exhibitions / Business (Shows & Exhibitions)
Siding Windows & Remodelling / Business (Building)
Signal / Consumer (Television, Radio, Video & Home Appliances)
Signals / Business (Advertising, Marketing, Sales)
Signs Canada / Business (Advertising, Marketing, Sales)
The Silhouette / University
Silicon Valley North / Business (Business)
The Silver Pages / Consumer (Senior Citizens)
Simmental Country / Farm (Farm Publication)
Siren / University
Le Ski / Consumer (Sports & Recreation)
Ski Canada Magazine / Consumer (Sports & Recreation)
Ski Presse / Consumer (Sports & Recreation)
SkiTrax Magazine / Consumer (Sports & Recreation)
Ski The West / Consumer (Sports & Recreation)
Sky News / Consumer (General Interest)
Slate / Consumer (Arts, Art & Antiques)
Sno Riders West / Consumer (Sports & Recreation)
Snow Goer / Consumer (Sports & Recreation)
Social History / Scholarly (Scholarly Publication)
Socialist Alternatives / Scholarly (Scholarly Publication)
Socialist Worker / Consumer (Labour, Trade Unions)
The Social Worker / Consumer (Social Welfare)
Solid Waste Management / Business (Water & Wastes Treatment)
Sommets / University
Son Hi-Fi Video / Consumer (Television, Radio, Video & Home Appliances)
Sounding Board / Business (Business)

Sound & Vision / Consumer (Television, Radio, Video & Home Appliances)
Sources / Business (Journalism)
The South Asian Voice / Ethnic (Pakistani)
Southern Africa Report / Consumer (News)
Southern Farm Guide / Farm (Farm Publication)
The Sou'Wester / Business (Fisheries)
Spa Destinations / Business (Travel)
Spa Management / Business (Cosmetics)
Speciality & Performance Magazine / Business (Automotive & Accessories)
Sporting Scene / Consumer (Sports & Recreation)
Sports Business / Business (Sporting Goods & Recreational Equipment)
Sposa Magazine / Consumer (Brides, Bridal)
Squash Life / Consumer (Sports & Recreation)
StarWeek Magazine / Consumer (Television, Radio, Video & Home Appliances)
The Sting / University
Stitches: The Journal of Medical Humour / Business (Medical)
Storefront Paper / Consumer (City Magazine)
Strand / University
Strategy / Business (Advertising, Marketing, Sales)
Strategy / Business (Medical)
Studies in Canadian Literature / Scholarly (Scholarly Publication)
Studies in Political Economy / Scholarly (Scholarly Publication)
Studies in Religion / Consumer (Religious & Denominational)
Studio Magazine / Business (Graphic Arts)
Style / Business (Clothing & Accessories)
sub-TERRAIN Magazine / Consumer (Literary)
Sunday Sun Television Magazine / Consumer (Television, Radio, Video & Home Appliances)
Sunsports, see Outside Guide
Supertrax Int'l / Consumer (Sports & Recreation)
Supply Post / Business (Engineering)
Surface / Business (Floor Coverings)
Swedish Press / Ethnic (Swedish)
Sweet's Canadian Construction Catalogue File / Business (Architecture)
Sympatico NetLife / Business (Computing & Technology)
Tandem / Ethnic (Italian)
Taxi News / Business (Automotive & Accessories)
The Teacher / Business (Education)
Teach Magazine / Business (Education)
Techno: Le journal des technologies á domicile / Consumer (Computers)
Technology in Government / Business (Computing & Technology)
Télé+ / Consumer (Television, Radio, Video & Home Appliances)
Télé Horaire / Consumer (Television, Radio, Video & Home Appliances)
Télé Horaire (Québec) / Consumer (Television, Radio, Video & Home Appliances)
Téléromans / Consumer (Television, Radio, Video & Home Appliances)
Télé Soleil / Consumer (Television, Radio, Video & Home Appliances)
Le Temporel / University
Temps Libre / University (Student Guides)
La Terre de chez-nous / Farm (Farm Publication)
Tessera / Scholarly (Scholarly Publication)
Teviskes Ziburiai / Ethnic (Lithuanian)
Texte / Scholarly (Scholarly Publication)
TG: Voices of Today's Generation / Consumer (Youth)
Theatre Research in Canada / Scholarly (Scholarly Publication)
This Country Canada / Consumer (General Interest)
This Magazine / Consumer (Culture, Current Events)
This Week in Business / Business (Business)
Thornhill Month / Consumer (City Magazine)
The Three Penny Beaver / University
Thunder Bay Business / Business (Business)

Thunder Bay Car & Truck News / Business (Automotive & Accessories)
Thunder Bay Guest / Consumer (City Magazine)
Thunder Bay Guide / Consumer (Television, Radio, Video & Home Appliances)
Thunder Bay Life / Consumer (City Magazine)
Thunder Bay Magazine / Consumer (City Magazine)
Thunder Bay Real Estate News / Consumer (Homes)
Thunderbird Sports Magazine / University
Thursday Report / University
TickleAce / Consumer (Literary)
Time / Consumer (News)
The Tocqueville Review / Scholarly (Scholarly Publication)
Today's Boating / Consumer (Boating & Yachting)
Today's Bride / Consumer (Brides, Bridal)
Today's Choices / Consumer (Senior Citizens)
Today's Corporate Investor / Business (Business)
Today's Parent / Consumer (Families)
Today's Parent Prenatal Class Guide / Consumer (Babies & Mothers)
Today's Seniors / Consumer (Senior Citizens)
Today's Times / Consumer (Senior Citizens)
Today's Trucking / Business (Motor Trucks & Buses)
Today's Woman in Business / Business (Business)
Top Forty Focus / Consumer (Music)
Toronto & Area Aviation Business Directory / Business (Aviation & Aerospace)
Toronto Computes / Consumer (Computers)
Toronto Construction News / Business (Construction)
Toronto Events Planner / Consumer (City Magazine)
Toronto Gardens / Consumer (Gardening)
Toronto Legal Directory / Business (Legal)
Toronto Life / Consumer (City Magazine)
Toronto Life Fashion Magazine / Consumer (Fashion)
Toronto Life Gardens / Consumer (Gardening)
The Toronto Review of Contemporary Writing Abroad / Consumer (Literary)
Toronto's Original Jewish Pages / Consumer (Religious & Denominational)
Toronto Special Events / Consumer (City Magazine)
The Toronto Stock Exchange Review / Business (Business)
Toronto This Season / Consumer (City Magazine)
Touchez-Dubois / Consumer (Homes)
Touring: The Car & Travel Magazine / Consumer (General Interest)
Tourisme + / Business (Travel)
Tours on Motorcoach / Business (Travel)
Toys & Games / Business (Toys)
Trade & Commerce / Business (Business)
Le Trait d'Union / University
Transactions / University
Transcultural Psychiatric Research Review / Scholarly (Scholarly Publication)
Travail et santé / Business (Industrial Safety)
Travel à la carte / Consumer (Travel)
Travel Courier / Business (Travel)
Travelweek Bulletin / Business (Travel)
Travelworld / Consumer (Travel)
Tree House Family / Consumer (Families)
Tribute Magazine / Consumer (Entertainment)
Trot / Consumer (Horses, Riding & Breeding)
Truck Logger Magazine / Business (Forest & Lumber Industries)
Truck News / Business (Motor Trucks & Buses)
Truck West / Business (Motor Trucks & Buses)
Truck World / Business (Motor Trucks & Buses)
True North Volleyball Magazine / Consumer (Sports & Recreation)
Turf & Recreation / Business (Landscaping)
TV 7 Jours / Consumer (Television, Radio, Video & Home Appliances)
TV Guide / Consumer (Television, Radio, Video & Home Appliances)
TV Hebdo / Consumer (Television, Radio, Video & Home Appliances)

TV Magazine (Central B.C.) / Consumer (Television, Radio, Video & Home Appliances)
TV Scene / Consumer (Television, Radio, Video & Home Appliances)
TV Times / Consumer (Television, Radio, Video & Home Appliances)
TV Week Magazine (Vancouver & Victoria) / Consumer (Television, Radio, Video & Home Appliances)
TV Week Stratford / Consumer (Television, Radio, Video & Home Appliances)
U-Choose: A Student's Guide to Financial Survival / University (Student Guides)
The Ubyssey / University
Ukrainian News / Ethnic (Ukrainian)
Ukrainsky Holos / Ethnic (Ukrainian)
L'Ulcère / University
Ultimate Reality & Meaning / Scholarly (Scholarly Publication)
Underground / University
Union Farmer / Farm (Farm Publication)
Unité / University
The United Church Observer / Consumer (Religious & Denominational)
University Affairs / Business (Education)
University Manager / Business (Education)
University of Toronto Law Journal / Scholarly (Scholarly Publication)
University of Toronto Magazine / Consumer (General Interest)
The University of Toronto Medical Journal / Business (Medical)
University of Toronto Quarterly / Scholarly (Scholarly Publication)
Up Here: Life in Canada's North / Consumer (General Interest)
Uptown Magazine / Consumer (City Magazine)
U.Q.A.R. Information / University
Uquam / University
Uquarium / University
Urba / Business (Government)
Urban History Review / Scholarly (Scholarly Publication)
Urology Times of Canada / Business (Medical)
L'Usine / Business (Industrial & Industrial Automation)
The UVic Torch / University
Vaba Eestlane / Ethnic (Estonian)
Vacances pour Tous / Consumer (Travel)
The Valley Circle / Consumer (Music)
Value Plus Magazine, see Alderlea Magazine
Vancouver & Area Aviation Business Directory / Business (Aviation & Aerospace)
Vancouver Home Buyers Guide / Consumer (Homes)
Vancouver Magazine / Consumer (City Magazine)
Vanier Phoenix / University
The Vanier Vandoo / University
Vapaa Sana / Ethnic (Finnish)
Varsity / University
V.C.C. Voice / University
Vecteur envrionnement / Business (Water & Wastes Treatment)
Vélo Mag / Consumer (Automobile & Cycle)
Ven'd'est / Consumer (News)
Le Vétérinarius / Business (Veterinary)
Victoria Today, see Where Victoria
Video News & Reviews / Consumer (Television, Radio, Video & Home Appliances)
Vie des Arts / Consumer (Arts, Art & Antiques)
Vie en Plein Air / Consumer (Camping & Outdoor Recreation)
Vie Etudiante / University (Student Guides)
Vision Magazine / Business (Optical)
Vision Mode / Consumer (Fashion)
Visitor / Consumer (City Magazine)
Visitor's Choice / Consumer (City Magazine)
Vitalité Québec / Consumer (Health, Medical)
Vitality Magazine / Consumer (Health, Medical)

Vitality Newsmagazine / Consumer (Senior Citizens)
La Voce degli Italo Canadesi / Ethnic (Italian)
The Voice of Canadian Serbs / Ethnic (Serbian)
Voice of the Essex Farmer / Farm (Farm Publication)
The Voice of Montréal / Consumer (Culture, Current Events)
Voilà Québec / Consumer (City Magazine)
Voir / Consumer (City Magazine)
La Voix du vrac / Business (Motor Trucks & Buses)
La Voix Sépharade / Consumer (Religious & Denominational)
Vox / Consumer (Entertainment)
Vox-Populi / University
Voyage en Groupe / Business (Travel)
Le Voyeur / University
La Voz de Montréal / Ethnic (Slovak, Czech)
A Voz de Portugal / Ethnic (Portuguese)
Waste Business West, see Hazardous Materials Directory
Watch / University
Watch Magazine / Consumer (Youth)
Water Goer / Consumer (Sports & Recreation)
Water & Pollution Control / Business (Water & Wastes Treatment)
Watershed Sentinel / Consumer (Environment & Nature)
Web World / Business (Computers)
We Compute / Consumer (Computers)
Wedding Bells / Consumer (Brides, Bridal)
The Wedding Pages Planner & Pocket Guide / Consumer (Brides, Bridal)
Weddings & Honeymoons / Consumer (Brides, Bridal)
Welcome Back Student Guide / University (Student Guides)
Welcome Home / Consumer (Homes)
Welding Canada / Business (Welding)
Wellness MD / Business (Medical)
Westbridge Art Market Report / Business (Art & Antiques)
West Coast Aviator Magazine / Business (Aviation & Aerospace)
West Coast Line / Consumer (Literary)
The Westcoast Fisherman / Business (Fisheries)
Westcoast Logger, see Business Farmer
The Westcoast Mariner / Business (Boating & Yachting)
Westcoast Reflections / Consumer (Senior Citizens)
Western Alumni Gazette / University
Western Automotive Repair / Business (Automotive & Accessories)
Western Canada Highway News / Business (Motor Trucks & Buses)
Western Catholic Reporter / Consumer (Religious & Denominational)
Western Collision Repair / Business (Automotive & Accessories)
Western Commerce & Industry / Business (Business)
Western Dairy Farmer / Farm (Farm Publication)
Western Dairy Farmer Magazine / Farm (Farm Publication)
Western Grocer / Business (Grocery Trade)
Western Hog Journal / Farm (Farm Publication)
Western Homebuilder & Renovation Contractor / Business (Building)
Western Hospitality News / Business (Hotels & Restaurants)
The Western Investor / Business (Real Estate)
Western Living / Consumer (General Interest)
Western News / University
The Western Producer / Farm (Farm Publication)
Western Restaurant News / Business (Hotels & Restaurants)
Western Skier / Consumer (Sports & Recreation)
Western Sportsman / Consumer (Fishing & Hunting)
Westworld, see Leisureways/Westworld/Going Places Magazine
WFCD Communicator, see CAAR Communicator
What! A Magazine / Consumer (Youth)

What's Happening Magazine / Consumer (City Magazine)
What's New in Welding, see Welding Canada
Where Calgary / Consumer (City Magazine)
Where Edmonton / Consumer (City Magazine)
Where Halifax / Consumer (City Magazine)
Where Ottawa-Hull / Consumer (City Magazine)
Where Rocky Mountains / Consumer (City Magazine)
Where Toronto / Consumer (City Magazine)
Where Vancouver / Consumer (City Magazine)
Where Vancouver Island / Consumer (City Magazine)
Where Victoria / Consumer (City Magazine)
Where Winnipeg / Consumer (City Magazine)
Whetstone / Consumer (Literary)
White Wall Review / Consumer (Literary)
Why: A Magazine About Life / Consumer (General Interest)
WhyNot Magazine / Consumer (Sports & Recreation)
Wildflower / Consumer (Environment & Nature)
Windspeaker / Consumer (General Interest)
Windsport / Consumer (Boating & Yachting)
WineTidings / Consumer (Food & Beverage)
Wings / Business (Aviation & Aerospace)
Winnipeg Homes & Lifestyles / Consumer (Homes)
The Winnipeg Sun TV Preview / Consumer (Television, Radio, Video & Home Appliances)
Wireless Telecom / Business (Telecommunications)
Women & Environments / Consumer (Environment & Nature)
Women's Education des femmes / Consumer (Women's & Feminist)
Woodworking / Business (Woodworking)
World: Toronto's Black Culture Magazine / Ethnic
World Journal (Toronto) / Ethnic (Chinese)
World Journal (Vancouver) / Ethnic (Chinese)
World of Chabad / Consumer (Religious & Denominational)
World of Wheels / Consumer (Automobile & Cycle)
X-Press / University
Xaverian / University
Yardstick / Business (Forest & Lumber Industries)
You / Consumer (Women's & Feminist)
Your Baby / Consumer (Babies & Mothers)
Your Office / Business (Business)
Youth Culture Unleased / Consumer (Youth)
Youth Today / Consumer (Youth)
Die Zeit / Ethnic (German)
Le Zèle / University
Zhinochy Svit / Ethnic (Ukrainian)
Zone Outaouais / Consumer (City Magazine)

MAGAZINES

BUSINESS PUBLICATIONS

ADVERTISING, MARKETING, SALES

Adnews, #212, 80 Park Lawn Rd., Etobicoke ON M8Y 3H8 – 416/252-9400; Fax: 416/252-8002; Email: adnews@io.org; URL: http://www.io.org~adnews/ – Weekly – Publisher, Rob Bale; Managing Editor, Mike Deibert

Canadian Advertising Rates & Data (Published by Maclean Hunter Publishing), 777 Bay St., Toronto ON M5W 1A7 – 416/596-6044; Fax: 416/596-5158; Email: bmason@inforamp.net; URL: http://www.cardmedia.com – Circ.: 2,197; Monthly – Publisher, Gloria Gallagher; Editor, Beth Mason; Circulation Manager, Victoria Newland

Canadian Direct Marketing News, c/o Lloydmedia Inc., #301, 1200 Markham Rd., Scarborough ON M1H 3C3 – 416/439-4083; Fax: 416/439-4086; Email: 75130.2016@compusearch; URL: http://www.mainstay.on.ca/dmn – Circ.: 7,000; Monthly,

Canadian Almanac & Directory 1997

plus annual directory of suppliers – Publisher, Stephen P. Lloyd
Info Presse Communications, #400, 4316, boul St-Laurent, Montréal PQ H2W 1Z3 – 514/842-5873; Fax: 514/842-2422 – 10 fois par an – Éditeur, Bruno Gautier; Rédacteur, Bruno Boutot
Marketing (Published by Maclean Hunter Publishing), 777 Bay St., Toronto ON M5W 1A7 – 416/596-5835; Fax: 416/593-3170; Email: marketmh@aol.com; Telex: 06-219547; URL: http://www.marketingmag.ca – Circ.: 14,200; Weekly – Publisher, Cameron Gardner; Editor, Stan Sutter; Circulation Manager, Victoria Newland
The Media Book, #415, 204 Richmond St. West, Toronto ON M5V 1V6 – 416/599-3737; Fax: 416/599-5730; Email: staff@mediastop.com; URL: http://www.mediastop.com – Circ.: 27,000; 2 times a year – Publisher, Tom Monson; Editor, Janet Forbes
Media Wave Magazine, #580, 916 West Broadway, Vancouver BC V5Z 1K7 – 604/875-1942; Fax: 604/875-1942; Email: Sniffy@mindlink.bc.ca; URL: http://www.media-wave.com – Circ.: 10,000; 6 times a year; ISSN 0228-1544 – Publisher & Editor, John Shinnick, Email: Shinnick@media-wave.com; Circulation Manager, Debra McNiven
The National List of Advertisers (Published by Maclean Hunter Publishing), 777 Bay St., Toronto ON M5W 1A7 – 416/596-5000; Fax: 416/596-5158 – Circ.: 3,000; Annually, Dec. – Publisher, Gloria Gallagher; Editor, Beth Mason; Circulation Manager, Victoria Newland
Publication Profiles (Published by Maclean Hunter Publishing), 777 Bay St., Toronto ON M5W 1A7 – 416/596-5000; Fax: 416/596-5158; Email: bmason@inforamp.net – Circ.: 4,400; Annually, Sept. – Publisher, Gloria Gallagher; Publisher, Beth Mason; Circulation Manager, Victoria Newland
Signals, Northworthy Communications, 39 Bedford Park Ave., Richmond Hill ON L4C 2N9 – 905/508-7374; Fax: 905/508-7376 – Circ.: 7,200; 11 times a year – Publisher, Steve Brown; Editor, Kevin Press
Signs Canada (Published by Kenilworth Publishing), #201, 27 West Beaver Creek, Richmond Hill ON L4B 1M8 – 905/771-7333; Fax: 905/771-7336 – Publisher, Jim Davidson
Strategy, #500, 366 Adelaide St. West, Toronto ON M5V 1R9 – 416/408-2300; Fax: 416/408-0870; URL: http://www.bulldog.ca/burnico/ – Circ.: 18,000; 25 times a year – President & Executive Publisher, James Shenkman; Editor, Mark Smyka

ARCHITECTURE

ARQ/La Revue d'Architecture, 1463, rue Préfontaine, Montréal PQ H1W 2N6 – 514/523-6832 – Circ.: 5,000; 6 times a year; English & French – Admin.-Director, Pierre Boyer-Mercier
Award Magazine (Published by Canada Wide Magazines & Communications Ltd.), 4180 Lougheed Hwy., 4th Fl., Burnaby BC V5C 6A7 – 604/299-7311; Fax: 604/299-9188 – Circ.: 7,500; 6 times a year – Publisher, Peter Legge; Editor, Marisa Paterson; Circulation Manager, Mark Weeks
Buildcore Product Source, 280 Yorkland Blvd., North York ON M2J 4Z6 – 416/494-4990; Fax: 416/756-2767; Email: BROWNP@SOUTHAM.CA – Circ.: 8,515; Annually – Publisher, Susan Steele; Editor, Nigel Heseltine
Canadian Architect (Published by Southam Magazine Group), 1450 Don Mills Rd., Don Mills ON M3B 2X7 – 416/445-6641; Fax: 416/442-2077 – Circ.: 13,000; Monthly – Publisher, Gord Carley; Managing Editor, Bronwen Ledger
Canadian Architectural Directory (Published by Crailer Communications), 360 Dupont St., Toronto ON M5R 1V9 – 416/966-9944; Fax: 416/966-9946 – Circ.: 7,500; Annually, Nov./Dec. – Publisher, Sheri Craig
Construction Canada, 316 Adelaide St. West, Toronto ON M5V 1R1 – 416/977-8104; Fax: 416/598-0658 – Circ.: 6,671; 6 times a year – Publisher, Frank Spangenberg; Editor, Jim Tobros
Insite, #217, 312 Dolomite Dr., Downsview ON M3J 2N2 – 416/667-9609; Fax: 416/667-9715 – Circ.: 11,180; 6 times a year – Publisher, Orly Sibilia; Editor, Adele Weder
Sweet's Canadian Construction Catalogue File, 270 Yorkland Blvd., North York ON M2J 1R8 – 416/496-3100; Fax: 416/496-3123 – Circ.: 6,660; Annually – Director, Finance & Admin., Eve L. Brown

ART & ANTIQUES

Canadian Collectibles Retailer (Published by Trajan Publishing Corp.), #292, 103 Lakeshore Rd., St Catharines ON L2N 2T6 – 905/646-7744; Fax: 905/646-0995; URL: http://www.trajan.com/collectibles/default.ehtml – Circ.: 8,000; 7 times a year – Publisher, Paul Fiocca; Editor, Bret Evans; Circulation Manager, Tammy Kruck
Gallery Impressions, 344 Edgeley Blvd., Unit 16, Concord ON L4K 4B7 – 905/738-2310; Fax: 905/738-4994 – 6 times a year – Editor, Michael Knell
Westbridge Art Market Report, 2339 Granville St., Vancouver BC V6H 3G4 – 604/736-1014; Fax: 604/734-4944 – 6 times a year – Publisher & Editor, Anthony R. Westbridge

AUTOMOBILE & CYCLE

Bike Trade Canada, #204, 2 Pardee Ave., Toronto ON M6K 3H5 – 416/530-1350; Fax: 416/530-4155; Email: pedal@passport.ca; URL: http://www.pedal.com – Circ.: 4,000; 3 times a year – Publisher & Editor, Benjamin A. Sadavoy

AUTOMOTIVE & ACCESSORIES

Aftermarket Canada, 2050 Speers Rd., Unit 1, Oakville ON L6L 2X8 – 905/847-0277; Fax: 905/847-7752 – Circ.: 11,000; Monthly – President/Publisher, Shirley G. Brown; Editor, Steve Manning
L'Automobile, #410, 3300, Place Côte Vertu, Saint-Laurent PQ H4R 2B7 – 514/339-1399; Fax: 514/339-1396; URL: http://www.southam.com/b1-1-1.html – Tirage: 11,804; 6 fois par an; français – Éditeur, Richard Thornton; Rédacteur, Marc Beauchamp
Automotive Retailer, #1, 8980 Fraserwood Ct., Burnaby BC V5J 5H7 – 604/432-7987; Fax: 604/432-1756; Email: rromero@axionet.com – Circ.: 10,000; 6 times a year – Publisher & Editor, Reg Romero; Circulation Manager, Angela Cook
Automotive Service Data Book (Published by Southam Magazine Group), 1450 Don Mills Rd., Don Mills ON M3B 2X7 – 416/445-6641; Fax: 416/442-2261 – Annually, Dec. – Editor, David Booth
Bodyshop (Published by Southam Magazine Group), 1450 Don Mills Rd., Don Mills ON M3B 2X7 – 416/445-6641; Fax: 416/442-2213; URL: http://www.southam.com/b1-1-2.html – Circ.: 12,863; 6 times a year – Group Publisher, Paul Wilson; Editor, Brian Harper
Canadian Automotive Fleet, Bobit Publishing, #207, 95 Barber Greene Rd., Don Mills ON M3C 3E9 – 416/383-0302; Fax: 416/383-0313 – Circ.: 12,350; 6 times a year – Publisher, Jake McLaughlin; Managing Editor, Kevin Sheehy
Canadian Auto World (Published by World of Wheels Publishing Inc.), #220, 1200 Markham Rd., Scarborough ON M1H 3C3 – 416/438-7777; Fax: 416/438-5333 – Circ.: 5,700; 12 times a year – Publisher, Lynn R. Helpard; Executive Editor, Joe Knycha; Circulation Manager, Susan Brown
Corporate Fleet Management (Published by Maclean Hunter Publishing), 777 Bay St., Toronto ON M5W 1A7 – 416/596-5086, 595-5704; Fax: 416/593-3201 – 4 times a year – Publisher, Tim Dimopoulos; Editor in Chief, Joe Terrett
Fleet Management Journal, Powershift Communications Inc., #308, 245 Fairview Mall Dr., North York ON M2J 4T1 – 416/494-1066; Fax: 416/491-2757 – Circ.: 11,990; 4 times a year – Publisher, John L. McLaine; Managing Editor, Tony Whitney
Jobber News (Published by Southam Magazine Group), 1450 Don Mills Rd., Don Mills ON M3B 2X7 – 416/445-6641; Fax: 416/442-2077; URL: http://www.southam.com/b1-1-3.html – Circ.: 11,000; Monthly – Group Publisher, Paul D. Wilson; Editor, Bob Blans
Motor Fleet Management (Published by Toro Communications), #209B, 1450 Midland Ave., Scarborough ON M1P 4Z8 – 416/757-6080; Fax: 416/757-6288 – Circ.: 12,300 – Publisher & Editor, Dan Radulescu
Octane (Published by Maclean Hunter Publishing Ltd.), #2450, 101 - 6th Ave. SW, Calgary AB T2P 3P4 – 403/266-8700; Fax: 403/266-6634; 1-800-561-1294 Toll Free – Circ.: 6,863; 4 times a year – Publisher, Phil Boyd; Editor, Dave Coll; Circulation Manager, Christine Madioni
Service Station & Garage Management (Published by Southam Magazine Group), 1450 Don Mills Rd., Don Mills ON M3B 2X7 – 416/445-6641; Fax: 416/442-2077; Email: hostmaster@southam.com; URL: http://www.southam.com/b1-1-4.html – Circ.: 25,000; Monthly – Publisher, Rob Wilkins; Editor, Gary Kenez
Speciality & Performance Magazine (Published by Southam Magazine Group), 1450 Don Mills Rd., Don Mills ON M3B 2X7 – 416/445-6641; Fax: 416/442-2213 – Circ.: 10,000; 4 times a year – Publisher, Robert Lauder; Editor, Andrew Ross
Taxi News, 38 Fairmount Cres., Toronto ON M4L 2H4 – 416/466-2328; Fax: 416/466-4220 – Circ.: 10,200; Monthly – Publisher, John Duffy; Editor, William McOuat; Circulation Manager, Barb Whitehurst
Thunder Bay Car & Truck News (Published by North Superior Publishing Inc.), 1145 Barton St., Thunder Bay ON P7B 5N3 – 807/623-2348; Fax: 807/623-7515 – Circ.: 30,000; 24 times a year – Publisher/Editor, Scott Sumner
Western Automotive Repair (Published by New Horizons West Ltd.), PO Box 64011, Winnipeg MB R2K 4K6 – 204/654-3573; Fax: 204/667-8922 – Circ.: 10,757; 6 times a year – Publisher, Ilan Moyle; Editor, Dan Proudley
Western Collision Repair (Published by New Horizons West Ltd.), PO Box 64011, Winnipeg MB R2K 4K6 – 204/654-3573; Fax: 204/667-8922 – Circ.: 5,781; 5 times a year – Publisher, Ilan Moyle; Editor, Dan Proudley

AVIATION & AEROSPACE

Airforce, c/o Airforce Productions Ltd., 100 Metcalfe St., PO Box 2460, Stn D, Ottawa ON K1P 5W6 – 613/992-2355; Fax: 613/995-2196 – Circ.: 20,200; 4 times a year – Publisher, Bob Tracy; Editor, Vic Johnson
Airports North America (Published by Baum International Media), #203, 2323 Boundary Rd., Vancouver BC V5M 4V8 – 604/298-3004; Fax: 604/291-3966 – Circ.: 15,000; 4 times a year – Publisher, Heri R. Baum; Editor, Toni Dabbs
Atlantic Region Aviation Business Directory (Published by OP Publishing), 1132 Hamilton St., Vancouver BC V6B 2S2 – 604/687-1581 – Annually – Publisher, Rex Armstead
Calgary & Area Airport Business Directory (Published by OP Publishing), 1132 Hamilton St., Vancouver BC V6B 2S2 – 604/687-1581 – Annually – Publisher, Rex Armstead
Canadian Aviation & Aircraft for Sale, PO Box 4755, Hamilton ON L8H 7S7 – 800/567-5966 – 6 times a year – Publisher, Gerry Boyar
Canadian Flight (Published by Canadian Flight Publishing Co.), PO Box 734, Stn B, Ottawa ON K1P 5P7 – 613/565-0881; Fax: 613/236-8646; Email: copa@magi.com – Circ.: 20,000; Monthly;

also Canadian Flight Annual, Canadian Plane Trade (monthly), & Canadian Warplane Heritage Museum News (4 times a year) – Publisher, Garth Wallace; Editor, Doris Ohlmann

Canadian Ultralight News (Published by Canadian Flight Publishing Co.), PO Box 734, Stn B, Ottawa ON K1P 5P7 – 613/565-0881; Fax: 613/236-8646 – Circ.: 20,000; Monthly – Publisher, Garth Wallace; Editor, Doris Ohlmann

Edmonton & Area Airport Business Directory (Published by OP Publishing), 1132 Hamilton St., Vancouver BC V6B 2S2 – 604/687-1581 – Annually – Publisher, Rex Armstead

Helicopters (Published by Corvus Publishing Group), #320, 3115 - 12 St. NE, Calgary AB T2E 7J2 – 403/735-5000; Fax: 403/735-0537 – Circ.: 5,750; 4 times a year – Publisher/Editor, Paul J. Skinner

ICAO Journal, International Civil Aviation Organization, #652, 1000 Sherbrooke St. West, Montréal PQ H3A 2R2 – 514/285-8222; Fax: 514/288-4772; Telex: 05-24513 ICAO – Circ.: 66,758; 10 issues a year; English, French & Spanish Editions – Editor-in-Chief, Eric MacBurnie

Mid-Canada & Area Airport Business Directory (Published by OP Publishing), 1132 Hamilton St., Vancouver BC V6B 2S2 – 604/687-1581 – Annually – Publisher, Rex Armstead

Montréal & Area Aviation Business Directory (Published by OP Publishing), 1132 Hamilton St., Vancouver BC V6B 2S2 – 604/687-1581 – Annually

Toronto & Area Aviation Business Directory (Published by OP Publishing), 1132 Hamilton St., Vancouver BC V6B 2S2 – 604/687-1581 – Annually

Vancouver & Area Aviation Business Directory (Published by OP Publishing), 1132 Hamilton St., Vancouver BC V6B 2S2 – 604/687-1581 – Annually

West Coast Aviator Magazine, PO Box 2065, Sidney BC V8L 3S3 – 604/656-7598; Fax: 604/655-4090 – Circ.: 20,000; 6 times a year – Publisher, Colleen Sinclair

Wings (Published by Corvus Publishing Group), #320, 3115 - 12 St. NE, Calgary AB T2E 7J2 – 403/735-5000; Fax: 403/735-0537 – Circ.: 11,000; 6 times a year – Publisher/Editor, Paul J. Skinner

BAKING & BAKERS' SUPPLIES

Bakers Journal (Published by NCC Publishing), 222 Argyle Ave., Delhi ON N4B 2Y2 – 905/271-1366; Fax: 905/271-6373 – Circ.: 6,160; 10 times a year – Publisher, Anna Spencer; Editor, Blair Adams; Circulation Manager, Florence Jacques

La Fournée (Published by Les Éditions du monde alimentaires), #102, 200, rue MacDonald, Saint-Jacques-sur-Richelieu PQ J3B 8J6 – 514/349-0107; Fax: 514/349-6923 – Tirage: 4 718; 4 fois par an; français – Rédacteur, Johanne Latour

BARBERS & BEAUTICIANS

DC Magazine, PO Box 50536, North York ON M3J 1L5 – 416/633-5360; Fax: 416/633-5717 – 12 times a year – Editor in Chief, Patrick Matishak

Salon Beauté (Published by Salon Communications Inc.), #300, 411 Richmond St. East, Toronto ON M5A 3S5 – 416/869-3131; Fax: 416/869-3808; Email: salon@beautynet.com; URL: http://www.salon-line.com – Tirage: 14,000; 8 fois par an – Éditrice, Christine Daviault

Salon Magazine (Published by Salon Communications Inc.), #300, 411 Richmond St. East, Toronto ON M5A 3S5 – 416/869-3131; Fax: 416/869-3008; Email: salon@beautynet.com; URL: http://www.sa-lonline.com – Circ.: 28,000; 8 times a year – Co-Publisher, Gregory Robins; Editor, Alison Wood; Circulation Manager, Keith Fulford

BOATING & YACHTING

Boating Business (Published by Formula Publications Ltd.), #4, 446 Speers Rd., Oakville ON L6K 3S7 – 905/842-6591; Fax: 905/842-6843 – 6 times a year – Publisher, Scott Robinson; Editor, Lizanne Madigan; Circulation Manager, Deadra Worth

Marina News, #211, 4 Cataraqui St., Kingston ON K7K 1Z7 – 613/547-6662; Fax: 613/547-6813 – Circ.: 700; 8 times a year – Editor, Michael Shaw

The Westcoast Mariner (Published by Westcoast Publishing Ltd), 1496 - 72nd Ave. West, Vancouver BC V6P 3C8 – 604/266-7433; Fax: 604/263-8620; Email: wcoast@wimsey.com – Circ.: 10,500; Monthly – Publisher, David Rahn; Editor, Rob Morris

BOOKS, STATIONERY

Access, c/o Ontario Library Association, #303, 100 Lombard St., Toronto ON M5C 1M3 – 416/363-3388; Fax: 416/941-9581; Email: jgilbert@interlog.com; 1-800-387-1181 Toll Free; URL: http://www.OLA.ca.dyna.com – Circ.: 4,000; 3 times a year – Publisher, Jefferson Gilbert; Editor, Lawrence Moore

Canadian Author, Canadian Authors Association, 27 Doxsee Ave. North, Campbellford ON K0L 1L0 – 705/653-0323; Fax: 705/653-0593 – Circ.: 2,914; 4 times a year – Managing Editor, Welwyn Wilton Katz, 519/641-6768

Canadian Bookseller, Canadian Booksellers Association, 301 Donlands Ave., Toronto ON M4J 3R8 – 416/467-7883; Fax: 416/467-7886; Email: enquiries@cbabook.org; URL: http://www.cbabook.org – Circ.: 2,000; 10 times a year – Editor, Margo Beggs

CM Magazine, Manitoba Library Association, #208, 100 Arthur St., Winnipeg MB R3B 1H3 – 204/943-4567; Fax: 204/942-1555; Email: camera@mbnet.mb.ca; URL: http://www.mbnet.mb.ca/cm/index.html – Circ.: 1,000; Weekly

Emergency Librarian, #101, 1001 West Broadway, Vancouver BC V6H 4E4 – 604/925-0266; Fax: 604/925-0566; Email: eml@rockland.com – Circ.: 10,000; 5 times a year – Editor, Ken Haycock; Editor, Karin Paul; Circulation Manager, Millie Watson

Feliciter, c/o Canadian Library Association, #602, 200 Elgin St., Ottawa ON K2P 1L5 – 613/232-9625, ext.321; Fax: 613/563-9895; Email: azo57@freenet.carleton.ca; URL: http://www.uccb.ns.ca/c/a96 – Circ.: 3,700; 10 times a year – Editor, Mary J. Moore

Quill & Quire, #210, 70 The Esplanade, Toronto ON M5E 1R2 – 416/360-0044; Fax: 416/955-0794; Email: quill@hookup.net – Circ.: 7,200; Monthly; supplement, Canadian Publishers' Directory (June & Dec.) – Publisher, Sharon McAuley; Editor, Scott Anderson

BROADCASTING

Broadcaster (Published by Southam Magazine Group), 1450 Don Mills Rd., Don Mills ON M3B 2X7 – 416/510-6835; Fax: 416/442-2213; Email: jbugailiskis@southam.ca; URL: http://www.southam.com/b1-2-1.html – Circ.: 8,000; 10 times a year – Publisher, James A. Cook; Editor, John Bugailiskis; Circulation Manager, Hasina Ahmed

Broadcast Technology, PO Box 420, Bolton ON L7E 5T3 – 905/857-6076; Fax: 905/857-6045 – Circ.: 7,000; 10 times a year, plus July/August Annual Buyers' Guide – Editor & Publisher, Doug Loney

Cablecaster (Published by Southam Magazine Group), 1450 Don Mills Rd., Don Mills ON M3B 2X7 – 416/445-6641; Fax: 416/442-2213 – Circ.: 6,075; 8 times a year – Publisher, James A. Cook; Editor, Steve Pawlett

Cable Communications Magazine, 57 Peachwood Ct., Kitchener ON N2B 1S7 – 519/744-4111; Fax: 519/744-1261 – Circ.: 6,900; 6 times a year – Publisher/Editor, Udo Salwsky

Canada on Location (Published by Brunico Communications), #500, 366 Adelaide St. West, Toronto ON M5V 1R9 – 416/408-2300; Fax: 416/408-0860 – Circ.: 3,523; 2 times a year – Publisher, James Shenkman; Editor, Mary Maddever

Playback (Published by Brunico Communications), #500, 366 Adelaide St. West, Toronto ON M5V 1R9 – 416/408-2300; Fax: 416/408-0870 – Circ.: 10,000; 25 times a year; also Playback International (2 times a year; circ. 2,162) – Publisher, James Shenkman; Editor, Mary Madderer

BUILDING

Building Magazine (Published by Crailer Communications), 360 Dupont St., Toronto ON M5R 1V9 – 416/966-9944; Fax: 416/966-9946 – Circ.: 14,500; 6 times a year; includes Real Estate Development Annual Directory – Publisher, Sheri Craig; Editor, John Fennell; Circulation Manager, Beata Olechnowicz

Canadian Homebuilder & Renovation Contractor, #403, 1230 Quayside Dr., New Westminster BC V3M 6H1 – 604/522-6033 – General Manager, Mark Bowen

Canadian Masonry Contractor (Published by Perks Publications Ltd.), #7A, 1735 Bayly St., Pickering ON L1W 3G7 – 905/831-4711 – 4 times a year – E. Brian Perks; Editor, Tanja Nowotny

Canadian Property Management (Published by Media Edge Communications), #208, 33 Fraser Ave., Toronto ON M6K 3J9 – 416/588-6220; Fax: 416/588-5217 – Circ.: 14,500; 8 times a year – Editor, Kim Morningstar, 416/588-6220, ext.226

Canadian Roofing Contractor (Published by Perks Publications Ltd.), #7A, 1735 Bayly St., Pickering ON L1W 3G7 – 905/831-4711 – 4 times a year – Publisher, E.B. Perks; Editor, Tanja Nowotny

Canadian Window & Door Manufacturer (Published by Bryarhouse Publishing Ltd.), 10893 Old River Rd., Komoka ON N0L 1R0 – 519/657-2088; Fax: 519/657-2796 – Circ.: 2,077; 2 times a year – Editor, Bruce Munro

Condominium Magazine (Published by Media Edge Communications), #208, 33 Fraser Ave., Toronto ON M6K 3J9 – 416/588-6220; Fax: 416/588-5217 – Circ.: 2,500; 12 times a year – Managing Editor, Kim Morningstar

The Condominium Manager, #1105, 191 The West Mall, Etobicoke ON M9C 5K8 – 416/626-7895; Fax: 416/620-5392; Email: bbandc@enterprise.ca; URL: http://www.bbandc.com – Circ.: 7,016; 4 times a year – Publisher, Don Braden; Editor, Denis Olorenshaw

Home Builder Magazine, 4819 St. Charles Blvd., Pierrefonds PQ H9H 3C7 – 514/620-2200; Fax: 514/620-6300 – Circ.: 17,400; 6 times a year – Associate Publisher, Ady Artzy; Circulation Manager, Joyce Crandall

LBMAO Reporter (Published by Perks Publications Ltd.), #7A, 1735 Bayly St., Pickering ON L1W 3G7 – 905/831-4711; Fax: 905/831-4725 – Bi-monthly – Managing Editor, Lumber & Bldg. Materials Assn. of Ont., Steve Johns, 416/298-1731, 1-800-465-5270; Fax: 416/298-4865

Ontario Home Builder, 1455 Lakeshore Rd., Burlington ON L7S 2J1 – 905/634-5770; Fax: 905/634-8335 – Circ.: 8,000; 6 times a year – Publisher, Mary Anne Crooker

Property Management News, K-Rey Publishing Inc., #720, 789 West Pender St., Vancouver BC V6C 1H2 – 604/669-7671; Fax: 604/681-9535 – Circ.: 5,000; 6 times a year – Publisher, Steve Munday; Editor, Margaret Munday; Circulation Manager, Andria Preiss

Provincial Building Trades Yearbook (Published by Naylor Communications Ltd.), 920 Yonge St., 6th Fl., Toronto ON M4W 3C7 – 416/961-1028; Fax: 416/924-4408 – Annually, Oct. – Publisher, Robert Thompson; Editor, Kim Laudrum

Sanitation Canada (Published by Perks Publications Ltd.), #7A, 1735 Bayly St., Pickering ON L1W 3G7

– 905/831-4711; Fax: 905/831-4725 – Circ.: 4,500; 6 times a year – Editor, Tanja Nowotny

Siding Windows & Remodelling (Published by Bryarhouse Publishing Ltd.), 10893 Old River Rd., Komoka ON N0L 1R0 – 519/657-2088; Fax: 519/657-2796 – 5 times a year – Publisher/Editor, R.B. Munro

Western Homebuilder & Renovation Contractor (Published by Bowen Communications), #403, 1230 Quayside Dr., New Westminster BC V3M 6H1 – 604/522-6033

BUSINESS

Les Affaires (Published by Transcontinental Publications Inc.), 1100, boul René-Levesque ouest, 24e étage, Montréal PQ H3B 4X9 – 514/392-9000; Fax: 514/392-1586 – Tirage: 86 500; 50 fois par an; français; aussi Les Affaires 500, Les Affaires plus (10 fois par an, 93 288) – Rédacteur en chef, Jean-Paul Gagné

AfriCan Access Magazine, #201, 1290 Broad St., Vancouver BC V8W 2A5 – 604/598-4940; Fax: 604/598-4977; Email: editor@AfriCanAccess.com – Circ.: 6,000; 4 times a year

Alberta Business (Published by Sunrise Publishing), 2213C Hanselman Ct., Saskatoon SK S7L 6A8 – 306/244-5668; Fax: 306/653-4515 – Circ.: 11,000; 6 times a year – Publisher, Twila Reddekopp

Atlantic Chamber Journal, EastCan Publications Inc., 309 Amirault St., Dieppe NB E1A 1G1 – 506/858-8710; Fax: 506/858-1707; Email: eastpub@nbnet.nb.ca – 6 times a year – Publisher, Elie J. Richard

Atlantic Progress, #212, 57 Portland, PO Box 428, Dartmouth NS B2Y 3Y5 – 902/461-1631; Fax: 902/469-0126; Email: PROGRESS@ISTAR.CA – Circ.: 25,000; 8 times a year – Publisher, Neville Gilfoy; Editor, David Holt; Circulation Manager, Pamela Scott-Grace

Avantages (Published by Maclean Hunter Publishing), 777 Bay St., Toronto ON M5W 1A7 – 416/596-5070; Fax: 416/596-5071; Email: 74227.2473@compuserve.com – Tirage: 5,000; 6 fois par an; français – Éditeur, Paul Williams

Le Banquier, Canadian Bankers Assn., Tour Scotia, 1002, rue Sherbrooke ouest, Montréal PQ H3A 3M5 – 514/840-8732; Fax: 514/282-7551 – Tirage: 8,500; 6 fois par an; français – Rédacteur, Jacques Hébert

BC Business Magazine (Published by Canada Wide Magazines & Communications Ltd.), 4180 Lougheed Hwy., 4th Fl., Burnaby BC V5C 6A7 – 604/299-7311; Fax: 604/299-9188 – Circ.: 21,572; Monthly – Publisher, Peter Legge; Editor, Bonnie Irving; Circulation Manager, Mark Weeks

BC Business Service, Merrick Enterprises, #310, 1122 Mainland St., Vancouver BC V6B 5L1 – Circ.: 10,500; 4 times a year – Publisher, John Merrick

Benefits Canada (Published by Maclean Hunter Publishing), 777 Bay St., Toronto ON M5W 1A7 – 416/596-5959; Fax: 416/596-5071; Email: 74227.2743@compuserve.com – Circ.: 15,400; 11 times a year; English & French – Publisher, Paul Williams; Editor, Lori Bak; Circulation Manager, Donna Singh

Benefits & Pensions Monitor, c/o Powershift Communications Inc., #308, 245 Fairview Mall Dr., North York ON M2J 4T1 – 416/491-1066; Fax: 416/494-2536; Email: pwrshift@idirect.com – Circ.: 15,670; 6 times a year – Publisher, John L. McLaine; Managing Editor, Patricia McCullagh; Circulation Manager, D. Brian McKerchar

Bilan, c/o Ordre des compatables agréés du Québec, 680 Sherbrooke St. West, 7th Fl., Montréal PQ H3A 2S3 – 514/288-3256; Fax: 514/843-8375; Email: m.parant@ocaq.qc.ca; URL: http://www.ocaq.qc.ca – Circ.: 19,000; 6 times a year; English & French – Editor, Maryse Parant; Circulation Manager, Paul-Marcel Adam

Biz-Hamilton/Halton Business Report (Published by Town Publishing Inc), 875 Main St., Hamilton ON L8S 4R1 – 905/522-6117; Fax: 905/529-2242 – Circ.: 20,000; 4 times a year – Publisher & Editor, Wayne Narciso; Circulation Manager, Laurie Ann Raynor

The Bottom Line (Published by Butterworths), 75 Clegg Rd., Markham ON L6G 1A7 – 905/479-2665; Fax: 905/474-9803; Email: tbl@butterworths.ca; URL: http://www.butterworths.ca – Circ.: 24,000; Monthly – Publisher, Don Brillinger, 905-415-5801; Editor, Michael Lewis; Circulation Controller, Kim Rattray

The Bruce County Marketplace, 910 Queen St., Kincardine ON N2Z 2Y9 – 519/396-9142; Fax: 519/396-3555 – Circ.: 13,000; 12 times a year – Publisher, James Pannell; Editor, Charles Whipp

The Brunswick Business Journal, ABJ Publishing Inc., #203, 599 Main St., Moncton NB E1E 1C8 – 506/857-9696; Fax: 506/859-7395 – Monthly – Publisher, Dalton Jensen; Editor, Suzanne MacDonald-Boyce

The Business Advocate, 244 Pall Mall St., PO Box 3295, London ON N6A 5P6 – 519/432-7551; Fax: 519/432-8063 – Monthly – Publisher, Jack Mann; Editor & Co-Publisher, John Redmond

The Business Annual, #203, 231 Dundas St., London ON N6A 1H1 – 519/679-4901; Fax: 519/434-7842 – Annually, Aug. – Publisher, Carol Kehoe; Editor, Nadia Shousher

Business Bulletin, Mississauga Board of Trade, 100-3 Robert Speck Pkwy., Mississauga ON L4Z 2G5 – 905/273-6151; Fax: 905/273-4937 – Circ.: 22,000; 11 times a year

Business Examiner - Mid/North Island Edition, Island Publishers, 777 Poplar St., Nanaimo BC V9S 2H7 – 250/754-8344; Fax: 250/753-0788 – Circ.: 10,400; Monthly – Publisher, Mark A. MacDonald

Business Examiner - South Island Edition, Island Publishers, 1824 Shore St., Victoria BC V8T 4R4 – 250/381-3926; Fax: 250/381-5606 – Circ.: 14,000; Monthly – Publisher, Woodrow Turnquist

The Business Executive, #220, 466 Speers Rd., Oakville ON L6K 2G3 – 905/845-8300; Fax: 905/845-9086; URL: http://cybersquare.com/executive/ – Circ.: 21,000; Monthly – Publisher, Thomas Peters; Editor, Wendy Peters; Circulation Manager, Brenda Jefferies

Business in Vancouver, #500, 1155 West Pender St., Vancouver BC V6E 2P4 – 604/688-2398; Fax: 604/688-1963; Email: biv@mindlink.bc.ca – Circ.: 9,447; Weekly, Mon. – Editor & Publisher, Peter Ladner

Business People Magazine (Published by McCaine-Davis Communications Ltd.), 232 Henderson Hwy., Winnipeg MB R2L 1L9 – 204/982-4002; Fax: 204/982-4001 – Circ.: 11,000; 4 times a year – Publisher & Editor, Heather McCaine-Davies

The Business & Professional Woman, Val Publications Ltd., 95 Leeward Glenway, Unit 121, Don Mills ON M3C 2Z6 – 416/467-1393; Fax: 416/467-8262 – Circ.: 5,000; 4 times a year – Editor, Valerie Dunn

Business Quarterly, c/o Richard Ivey School of Business, University of Western Ontario, 1151 Richmond St. North, London ON N6A 3K7 – 519/661-3309; Fax: 519/661-3838; Email: asmith@ivey.uwo.ca; URL: http://www.ivey.uwo.ca – Circ.: 10,000; 4 times a year – Publisher & Editor, Angela Smith; Circulation Manager, Agnes Bellegris

The Business Times, #203, 231 Dundas St., London ON N6A 1H1 – 519/679-4901; Fax: 519/434-7842 – Monthly – General Manager, Carol Kehoe; Managing Editor, Nadia Shousher

Business Today, Saskatoon Today Inc., 2241 Henselman Ave., PO Box 54, Stn Main, Saskatoon SK S7K 3K1 – 306/242-9922; Fax: 306/242-6888 – Circ.: 10,000; Monthly – General Manager, Gerald Rekue

Businest, CP 410, Rimouski PQ G5L 7C4 – 418/723-4800; Fax: 418/722-4078 – Mensuel; français – Éditeur, Claude Bellavance

CA Magazine, 277 Wellington St. West, Toronto ON M5V 3H2 – 416/977-3222; Fax: 416/204-3409; Email: nelson.luscombe@cica.ca; URL: http://www.cic.ca/cica/camag/e_camag.htm – Circ.: 67,000; 10 times a year; English & French – Publisher & Editor, Nelson Luscombe; Circulation Manager, Coleen Schoonhoven

Canada Japan Business Journal, Van Network Ltd., #370, 220 Cambie St., Vancouver BC V6B 2M9 – 604/688-2486; Fax: 604/688-1487; Email: janpan@helix.net – Monthly – Editor, Taka Aoki

Canada Journal (Published by Ruland Communications), 12 Lawton Blvd., Toronto ON M4V 1Z4 – 416/927-9129; Fax: 416/927-9118 – Circ.: 14,250; 6 times a year – Publisher/Editor, Joseph F. Ruland; Publisher/Editor, Ulli Nadine Ruland

Canada's The Latin Trade Report, #204, 35 The Links Rd., North York ON M2P 1T8 – 416/223-6944; Fax: 416/223-5927 – 6 times a year

The Canadian Banker, Canadian Bankers Assn., #3000, Commerce Ct. West, 199 Bay St., PO Box 348, Toronto ON M5L 1G2 – 416/362-6092; Fax: 416/362-8465; URL: http://www.cba.ca – Circ.: 33,400; 6 times a year – President & CEO, Raymond J. Protti; Editor, Simon Hally; Circulation Manager, Karen Bentley

Canadian Business (Published by Maclean Hunter Publishing), 777 Bay St., Toronto ON M5W 1A7 – 416/596-5151; Fax: 416/596-5152; Email: peterm@cbmedia.ca – Circ.: 82,000; Monthly with quarterly technology supplements – Publisher, Paul Jones; Editor, Arthur Johnson; Circulation Manager, Sarah Watt

Canadian Business Life Magazine, Better Business Bureau of Metro Toronto, #501, 1 St. Johns Rd., Toronto ON M6P 4C7 – 416/766-5744; Fax: 416/766-1970 – Circ.: 50,000; 4 times a year – Publisher, Paul Tuz

Canadian German Trade (Published by Ruland Communications), 12 Lawton Blvd., Toronto ON M4V 1Z4 – 416/927-9129; Fax: 416/929-9118 – Circ.: 1,500; 10 times a year – Publisher, Ulli N. Ruland

The Canadian Manager, #310, 2175 Sheppard Ave. East, Willowdale ON M2J 1W8 – 416/493-0155; Fax: 416/491-1670 – 4 times a year – Editor, Ruth Max

Central Nova Business News, 228 Main St., Bible Hill NS B2N 4H2 – 902/895-7948; Fax: 902/893-1427 – Monthly – Publisher, Tom Maclean; Editor, Mary-Ann Archibald

CGA Magazine, #700, 1188 Georgia St. West, Vancouver BC V6E 4E2 – 604/669-3555, 1-800-663-1529; Fax: 604/689-5845 – Circ.: 47,000; Monthly; English & French – Publisher & Editor, Lesley A. Wood

CMA Magazine, c/o Society of Management Accountants, #850, 120 King St. West, PO Box 1, Hamilton ON L8N 3C3 – 905/525-4100; Fax: 905/525-4533; Email: smac.cma@resonet.com; URL: http://www.cma-canada.org – Circ.: 75,000; 10 times a year; English & French – Publisher, Dan R. Hicks; Circulation Manager, Claire Keane

Commerce News, #600, 10213 - 99 St., Edmonton AB T5J 3G9 – 403/426-4620; Fax: 403/424-7946; Email: ecc@tns.com – Circ.: 15,000; 8 times a year – Publisher, Martin Sabhoum; Editor, Gretchen M. Ziegler

Durham Business News, PO Box 206, Whitby ON L1N 5S1 – 905/668-6111; Fax: 905/668-0594 – Circ.: 12,500; Monthly – Publisher, Doug Anderson; Editor, Garrett Dunne

L'Économique, #3030, 1000, de la Gauchetiere ouest, Montréal PQ H3B 4W5 – 514/856-2214 – Circ.: 45,040; 6 times a year – Publisher, Ian Dobson

Edmonton Commerce & Industry, #215, 11802 - 124 St., Edmonton AB T5L 0M3 – 403/454-5540; Fax: 403/453-2553 – Monthly – Publisher, D. Homersham

Entreprendre, Éditions Qualité performante inc., #630, 1600, boul St-Martin est, Laval PQ H7G 4S7 – 514/669-8373; Fax: 514/669-9078 – Tirage: 50,000; 6 fois par an; français – Rédacteur en chef, Edmond Bourque

Exchange: Magazine for Business, 75 King St. South, Waterloo ON N2J 1P2 – 519/886-2831; Fax: 519/886-9383 – Circ.: 15,000; Monthly – Publisher, Jon Rohr; Executive Editor, Rick Campbell

The Financial Post 500 (Published by Financial Post Co. Ltd.), 333 King St. East, Toronto ON M5A 4N2 – 416/350-6000; Fax: 416/350-6301 – Circ.: 100,000; Annually, May – Publisher, Douglas W. Knight; Editor, Diane Francis

The Financial Post Survey of Industrials (Published by Financial Post Co. Ltd.), 333 King St. East, Toronto ON M5A 4N2 – 416/350-6500; Fax: 416/350-6501 – Editor, Robert Pearson, 416/350-6452

Futur présent, Publi-Relais, 119, boul St-Joseph ouest, Montréal PQ H2T 2P7 – 514/278-3344; Fax: 514/278-1543 – Tirage: 10 000; 6 fois par an; français – Rédactrice en chef, Pierrette Gagné

German American Trade (Published by Ruland Communications), 12 Lawton Blvd., Toronto ON M4V 1Z4 – 416/927-9129; Fax: 416/927-9118 – Circ.: 2,600; 10 times a year – Publisher, Ulli N. Ruland

Gestion, 3000, ch de la Côte-Sainte-Catherine, Montréal PQ H3T 2A7 – 514/340-6677; Fax: 514/340-6382; Email: Revue-gestion@heg.ca – 4 fois par an; français – Rédacteur, Laurent Lapierre

Head Office at Home, Abaco Communications Ltd., 44 Carlton Rd., Unionville ON L3R 1Z5 – 905/477-4349; Fax: 905/477-0412 – Circ.: 50,000; 6 times a year – Publisher/Editor, Elizabeth Harris

Huronia Business Times, 24 Dunlop St. East, 2nd Fl., Barrie ON L4M 1A3 – 705/721-1450; Fax: 705/721-1449 – Circ.: 7,500; 10 times a year – Publisher, Alexander Donald; Editor, Eric Skelton

Info-affaires, Bell Productions inc., CP 399, Richibucto NB E0A 2M0 – 506/523-1123; Fax: 506/523-1122 – Mensuel; français – Éditeur, Gilles Belleau

Interface, 425, rue de la Gauchetière est, Montréal PQ H2L 2M7 – 514/849-0045; Fax: 514/849-5558; Email: interface@acfas.ca; URL: http://www.acfas.ca/ – Tirage: 9,000; 6 fois par an; français – Éditrice & Rédactrice, Sophie Malavoy

Investment Executive, #202, 90 Richmond St. East, Toronto ON M5C 1P1 – 416/366-4200; Fax: 416/366-7844 – Circ.: 23,950; 11 times a year – Editor, Tessa Wilmott

Investor's Digest of Canada, #700, 133 Richmond St. West, Toronto ON M5H 3M8 – 416/869-1177; Fax: 416/869-0616 – Circ.: 20,500; 24 times a year – Editor, Rick Morrison

Italcommerce, #680, 550 Sherbrooke St. West, Montréal PQ H3A 1B9 – 514/844-4249; Fax: 514/844-4875 – 5 times a year; French, English & Italian – Editor in Chief, Giuseppe Mancini

Italy Canada Trade, Italian Chamber of Commerce of Toronto, #306, 901 Lawrence Ave. West, Toronto ON M6A 1C3 – 416/789-7169; Fax: 416/789-7160 – 4 times a year – Editor-in-Chief, Arturo Pelliccione

Kootenay Business Magazine (Published by Koocanusa Publications Inc.), 1510 - 2nd St. North, Cranbrook BC V1C 3L2 – 250/426-7253; Fax: 250/489-3743 – Circ.: 8,000; Monthly – Publisher, Daryl D. Shellborn; Editor, Stacey Curry

London Business Monthly Magazine (Published by Bowes Publishers Ltd.), PO Box 7400, London ON N5Y 4X3 – 519/472-7601; Fax: 519/473-2256 – Circ.: 12,176; Monthly – Publisher, Robert Way; Managing Editor, Janine Foster

Magazine Québec International, Ministère des Relations internationales, 525, boul René Lévesque est, Montréal PQ G1R 5R9 – 418/649-2345; Fax: 418/649-2656; Email: communication@mri.gouv.qc.ca – Circ.: 30,000; 3 times a year; French, English & Spanish – Editor, Céline Coulombe; Circulation Manager, France Dupont

Manitoba Business, Canada Wide Magazines, 4180 Lougheed Hwy., 4th Fl., Burnaby BC V5C 6A7 – 604/299-7311; Fax: 604/299-9188 – Circ.: 6,600; 10 times a year – President/Publisher, Peter Legge; Editor, Ritchie Gage

Mémo - le gout des régions, #200, 3715, av Lacombe, Montréal PQ H3T 1M3 – 514/341-7916; Fax: 514/341-2644 – 6 fois par an; français; 8-page English supplement in June-July issue – Éditeur, Marie Claire Dupré; Rédacteur, Michel Guénard

Mississauga Business Times (Published by North Island Sound Ltd.), #8, 1606 Sedlescomb Dr., Mississauga ON L4X 1M6 – 905/625-7070; Fax: 905/625-4856 – Circ.: 19,000; 10 times a year – Publisher, Alexander Donald; Managing Editor, Adam Gutteridge

Montréal Business Magazine, #43, 275, rue St-Jacques, Montréal PQ H2Y 1M9 – 514/286-8038 – Circ.: 17,700; 6 times a year – Publisher, Mark Weller; Associate Publisher, Ian Dobson

Montréal Plus, Board of Trade of Metropolitan Montréal, #12500, 5, Place Ville Marie, Plaza Level, Montréal PQ H3B 4Y2 – 514/871-4000; Fax: 514/871-1255 – Circ.: 10,000; 7 times a year; English & French – Editor, Joëlle Ganguillet

Niagara Business Report, Southam Community Newspapers Inc., 4309 Central Ave., PO Box 400, Beamsville ON L0R 1B0 – 905/563-1629; Fax: 905/563-7977 – Circ.: 15,000; 4 times a year – Publisher, Tom Haire; Circulation Manager, Pattie Corsini

Northern Ontario Business, 158 Elgin St., Sudbury ON P3E 3N5 – 705/673-5705; Fax: 705/673-9542 – Monthly – Publisher/Editor, Mark Sandford

Northwest Business, Sylvester Publicatins Ltd., 16 Palmer Close, Sylvan Lake AB T4S 1K3 – 403/887-4781; Fax: 403/887-4717 – Circ.: 25,000; 6 times a year – Publisher/Editor, Donald C. Sylvester

Nova Scotia Business Journal (Published by NCC Specialty Publications), #107, 900 Windmill Rd., Dartmouth NS B3B 1P7 – 902/468-8027; Fax: 902/468-2425 – Circ.: 13,600; Monthly – Publisher, Peter Steele; Editor, Ken Partridge

Okanagan Business Magazine (Published by Byrne Publishing Group Inc), PO Box 1479, Stn A, Kelowna BC V1Y 7V8 – 250/861-5399; Fax: 250/868-3040; Email: oklife@awinc.com – Circ.: 11,000; 8 times a year – Editor, Mike Haines; Circulation Manager, Tammy Tomiye

Ontario Business Report, Business Communications Inc., #370, 135 Queens Plate Dr., Etobicoke ON M9W 6V7 – 416/746-6531; Fax: 416/746-7775; Email: obr@arcos.org; 1-800-494-6397 – Circ.: 12,000; 12 times a year – Publisher, Jeffrey Phipps

Opportunities Canada, The Type People Inc., 1293 Matheson Blvd. East, Mississauga ON L4W 1R1 – 905/238-3320; Fax: 905/238-3301 – Circ.: 15,000; 3 times a year – Publisher, Robert Sinclair

Ottawa Business Journal, The Business Press Group Inc., #319, 126 York St., Ottawa ON K1N 5T5 – 613/789-0403; Fax: 613/789-0227 – Circ.: 40,000; 52 times a year – Editor, Mark Sutcliffe

Parlons Affaires Beauce/Etchemin, 12625, av 1e est, St-Georges PQ G5Y 2E4 – 418/228-8858; Fax: 418/228-0268 – Tirage: 4 300; Mensuel; français

Parlons Affaires Laurentides, Les Éditions Hebcor inc., 801, rue Sherbrook est, 4e étage, Montréal PQ H2L 4X9 – 514/523-5800; Fax: 514/523-5944 – Tirage: 15 000; Mensuel; français – Directrice, Diane Bougie

PME (Le Magazine PME) (Published by Transcontinental Publications Inc.), 1100, boul René-Levesque ouest, 24e étage, Montréal PQ H3B 4X9 – 514/392-9000; Fax: 514/392-4726; Email: PME@mail.transc.com – Tirage: 35,000; 10 fois par an; français – Éditeur, Alain Guilbert; Rédacteur en chef, Denis Dubé; Directeur de tirage, François Blondin

Profiles, York University, #280, York Lanes, 4700 Keele St., North York ON M3J 1P3 – 416/736-2100, ext.33160; Fax: 416/736-5681 – Circ.: 98,807; 4 times a year – Publisher, Jessie-May Rowntree

Profit: The Magazine for Canadian Entrepreneurs (Published by Maclean Hunter Publishing), 777 Bay St., Toronto ON M5W 1A7 – 416/596-5100; Fax: 416/596-5152; Email: peterm@cbmedia.ca – Circ.: 100,000; 6 times a year – Publisher, Paul Jones; Editor, Rick Spence; Circulation Manager, Sarah Watt

Québec Enterprise, #507, 715, Square Victoria, Montréal PQ H2Y 2H7 – 514/842-5492; Fax: 514/842-5375 – Tirage: 25,000; 6 fois par an; français – Rédacteur, Daniel Boisvert

Report on Business Magazine, c/o The Globe and Mail, 444 Front St. West, Toronto ON M5V 2S9 – 416/585-5411; Fax: 416/585-5275; Email: robmag@globeandmail.ca; URL: http://www.GlobeAndMail.ca – Circ.: 300,000; 12 times a year – Publisher, Stephen Petherbridge; Editor, David Olive

Revue Commerce (Published by Transcontinental Publications Inc.), 1100, boul René-Levesque ouest, 24e étage, Montréal PQ H3B 4X9 – 514/392-9000; Fax: 514/392-4726 – Tirage: 39,800; Mensuel; français – Éditeur, Alain Guilbert

La Revue Occasions d'Affaires, #145, 425, rue St-Amable, Québec PQ G1R 5E4 – 418/640-1686, 1-800-361-1686; Fax: 418/640-1687; Email: revueroa@aniq.com; URL: http://www.roa-mag.com; http://www.rda.net – Tirage: 150,000; 6 fois par an; français – Éditeur, Michel Bédard; Rédacteur, Pierre Bhérer; Directrice de tirage, Marie-Claude Lachance

Saskatchewan Business (Published by Sunrise Publishing), 2213C Hanselman Ct., Saskatoon SK S7L 6A8 – 306/244-5668; Fax: 306/653-4515 – Circ.: 9,000; 6 times a year – Publisher, Twila Reddekopp; Editor, Heather Sterling

Silicon Valley North, Silvan Communications Inc., #605, 45 Rideau St., Ottawa ON K1N 5W8 – 613/562-3648; Fax: 613/562-2649; Email: mailroom@silvan.com – Circ.: 30,000; Monthly – Publisher & Editor, Tony Patterson

Sounding Board, The Vancouver Board of Trade, #400, 999 Canada Place, Vancouver BC V6C 3C1 – 604/681-2111; Fax: 604/681-0437; Email: contactus@vancouver.boardoftrade.com – Circ.: 12,000; 10 times a year – Editor, Darcy Rezac

This Week in Business, The Gazette, 250, rue Saint-Antoine ouest, Montréal PQ H2Y 3R7 – 514/987-2512; Fax: 514/987-2433 – Weekly – Publisher, Michael Goldbloom

Thunder Bay Business (Published by North Superior Publishing Inc.), 1145 Barton St., Thunder Bay ON P7B 5N3 – 807/623-2348; Fax: 807/623-7515 – Circ.: 6,000; Monthly – Publisher/Editor, Scott Sumner

Today's Corporate Investor (Published by Toro Communications), #209B, 1450 Midland Ave., Scarborough ON M1P 4Z8 – 416/757-6080; Fax: 416/757-6288 – Circ.: 15,278; 6 times a year – Publisher, Dan Radulescu

Today's Woman in Business, 113 Old Black River Rd., PO Box 1291, Saint John NB E2L 4H8 – 506/658-0754; Fax: 506/633-0868 – 4 times a year – Publisher/Editor, Carol Maber

The Toronto Stock Exchange Review, 2 First Canadian Place, Exchange Tower, 8th Fl., Toronto ON M5X 1J2 – 416/947-4681; Fax: 416/814-8811 – Circ.: 2,500; 12 times a year – Publisher, Chris Matthews; Manager, Peter Traynor, 416/947-4660

Trade & Commerce, 1700 Church Ave., PO Box 6900, Winnipeg MB R3C 3B1 – 204/632-2606; Fax: 204/

694-3040 – 5 times a year – Managing Director, George Mitchell; Editor, Laura Jean Stewart

Western Commerce & Industry (Published by Mercury Publications Ltd.), 945 King Edward St., Winnipeg MB R3H 0P8 – 204/775-0387; Fax: 204/775-7830 – Circ.: 12,610; 6 times a year – Publisher, Gren R. Yeo; Editor, Kelly Gray; Circulation Manager, Juanita Unrau

Your Office (Published by Canadian Office Products Association), #911, 1243 Islington Ave., Toronto ON M8X 1X9 – 416/239-2737; Fax: 416/239-1553 – Circ.: 70,000; 4 times a year – Publisher, James Pearce

BUSINESS & FINANCE

L'Autonome, 907, rue Rachel est, Montréal PQ H2J 2J2 – 514/528-7671; Fax: 514/879-3495; Email: autonome@poinnet.com – Tirage: 12 150; 6 fois par an – Éditeur, Pierre Bertucat

Canadian Investment Review (Published by Maclean Hunter Publishing), 777 Bay St., Toronto ON M5W 1A7 – 416/596-5959; Fax: 416/596-5071; Email: 74227.2743@compuserve.com – Circ.: 8,000 – Publisher & Editor, Paul Williams; Circulation Manager, Donna Singh

Canadian Treasurer, c/o Treasury Management Association of Canada, #1010, 8 King St. East, Toronto ON M5C 1B5 – 416/367-8500; Fax: 416/367-3240; Email: tmac@inforamp.net; URL: http://www.tmac.ca – Circ.: 4,500; 6 times a year – Editor, Bruce McDougall; Circulation Manager, Eileen Leung

CERAMICS

Canadian Ceramics Quarterly, Macking Graphics, #310, 2175 Sheppard Ave. East, Willowdale ON M2J 1W8 – 416/491-2886; Fax: 416/491-1670 – 4 times a year – Editor, Dr. M. Sayer; Circulation Manager, B. Howell

CHEMICALS & CHEMICAL PROCESS INDUSTRIES

Canadian Chemical News, c/o Chemcan Publishers Ltd., #550, 130 Slater St., Ottawa ON K1P 6E2 – 613/232-6252; Fax: 613/232-5862; Email: cic_publ@fox.nstn.ca – Circ.: 6,500; 10 times a year – Editor, Nola Haddadian; Circulation Manager, Allison McLean

Canadian Process Equipment & Control News, 343 Eglinton Ave. East, Toronto ON M4P 1L7 – 416/481-6483; Fax: 416/481-6436 – Circ.: 25,000; 6 times a year – Publisher, J.P. Birchard; Editor, V.J. Sharp; Circulation Manager, L. Bargh

Industrial Process Products & Technology (Published by Swan Erickson Publishing Inc.), #1235, 1011 Upper Middle Rd. East, Oakville ON L6H 5Z9 – 905/475-4231; Fax: 905/475-3512 – Circ.: 23,500; 6 times a year – Publisher, M.H. Swan; Editor in Chief, Bob Erickson, 905/845-1347

CHURCH ADMINISTRATION

Church Business Magazine (Published by Sawmill Creek Communications), #11, 4040 Creditview Rd., PO Box 1800, Mississauga ON L5C 3Y8 – 905/569-1800; Fax: 905/569-1818 – 6 times a year – Publisher & Editor, Hugh Parkinson

CLOTHING & ACCESSORIES

Apparel (Published by CTJ-Inc.), 1, rue Pacifique, Ste-Anne-de-Bellevue PQ H9X 1C5 – 514/457-2347; Fax: 514/457-2147 – Publisher & Editor, Gillian Crosby; Circulation Manager, S. Vallée

Fashion femme (Published by McLeish Communications Inc.), 1, rue Pacifique, Ste-Anne-de-Bellevue PQ H9X 1C5 – 514/457-2423; Fax: 514/457-2577 – Circ.: 7,584; 6 times a year; English & French – Editor, Babara McLeish

Kids Creations, c/o Children's Apparel Manufacturers' Association, #3110, 6900 Decarie Blvd., Montréal PQ H3X 2T8 – 514/731-7774; Fax: 514/731-7459 – Circ.: 6,000; 4 times a year; English & French – Editor, Lisa Peters; Circulation Manager, Della Druick

Style, #302, 1448 Lawrence Ave. East, Toronto ON M4A 2V6 – 416/755-5199; Fax: 416/755-9123 – 16 times a year – Publisher, John Peters; Editor, Marsha Ross

COMPUTER-AIDED DESIGN

AutoCAD User (Published by Swan Erickson Publishing Inc.), #1235, 1011 Upper Middle Rd. East, Oakville ON L6H 5Z9 – 905/475-4231; Fax: 905/475-3512 – Circ.: 15,000; 4 times a year – Publisher, R.A. Erickson, 905/845-1347; Editor-in-Chief, K. Pashuk

CAD Systems (Published by Kerrwil Publications Ltd.), 395 Matheson Blvd. East, Mississauga ON L4Z 2H2 – 905/890-1846; Fax: 905/890-5769; Email: kdalton@cadsystems.com; URL: http://www.cadsystems.com – Circ.: 16,200; 6 times a year – Publisher & Editor, Karen Dalton; Circulation Manager, Jean Bilkey

COMPUTERS

Canadian Computer Wholesaler, #900, 1788 West Broadway, Vancouver BC V6J 1Y1 – 604/739-8266; Fax: 604/739-3589 – Circ.: 11,900; 6 times a year – Publisher, Li Qin Chen

Computer & Entertainment Retailing (Published by Plesman Publications Ltd.), 2005 Sheppard Ave. East, 4th Fl., Willowdale ON M2J 5B1 – 416/497-9562; Fax: 416/497-9427; Email: ceredit@plesman.com; URL: http://www.plesman.com – Circ.: 6,133 – Publisher, George Soltys; Editor, Pamela Addo

Computer Freelancer, 1800 Sheppard Ave. East, North York ON M2J 5B9 – 416/493-6752; Fax: 416/493-7093 – Circ.: 11,839; 8 times a year – Publisher, Jayanti Parmar

The Computer Paper, #503, 425 Carrall St., Vancouver BC V6B 6E3 – 604/688-2120; Fax: 604/688-4270; URL: http://tcp.ca – Circ.: 92,700; Monthly – Publisher, Douglas Alder; Editor, David Tanaka

The Computer Post, #660, 125 Garry St., Winnipeg MB R3C 3P2 – 204/947-9766; Fax: 204/947-9767; Email: jstrause@cpost.mb.ca; URL: http://www.cpost.mb.ca – Circ.: 12,000; Monthly – Publisher, Jonathan Strauss

Web World (Published by Laurentian Technomedia Inc./Laurentian Media), 501 Oakdale Rd., North York ON M3N 1W7 – 416/746-7360; Fax: 416/746-1421 – 4 times a year – Publisher, Andrew White; Editor-in-Chief, John Pickett; Circulation Manager, Pauline White

COMPUTING & TECHNOLOGY

Canadian Computer Reseller (Published by Maclean Hunter Publishing), 777 Bay St., Toronto ON M5W 1A7 – 416/596-2668; Fax: 416/593-3166; Email: ccrcinforamp.net – Circ.: 15,000; 24 times a year – Publisher, Kathryn Swan; Editor, Steve McHale; Circulation Manager, Donna Singh

CIO Canada (Published by Laurentian Technomedia Inc./Laurentian Media), 501 Oakdale Rd., North York ON M3N 1W7 – 416/746-7360; Fax: 416/746-1421 – Circ.: 7,500; 10 times a year – Publisher, Andrew White; Managing Editor, David Charey; Circulation Director, Pauline White

Computer Dealer News (Published by Plesman Publications Ltd.), 2005 Sheppard Ave. East, 4th Fl., Willowdale ON M2J 5B1 – 416/497-9562; Fax: 416/497-9427; Email: cdnedit@plesman.com; USA Toll Free 1-800-387-5012; URL: http://www.pleasman.com/cdn – Circ.: 14,883; 26 times a year – Publisher, George Soltys; Editor, James Bouchok

Computer World (Published by Laurentian Technomedia Inc./Laurentian Media), 501 Oakdale Rd., North York ON M3N 1W7 – 416/746-7360; Fax: 416/746-1421 – Circ.: 40,000; 25 times a year – Publisher, Andrew White; Editor, Ron Glen

Computing Canada (Published by Plesman Publications Ltd.), 2005 Sheppard Ave. East, 4th Fl., Willowdale ON M2J 5B1 – 416/497-9562; Fax: 416/497-9427; Email: ccedit@plesman.com; USA Toll Free 1-800-387-5012 – Circ.: 35,465; 26 times a year – Publisher, George Soltys; Editor, Martin Slopstra

Direction Informatique (Published by Plesman Publications Ltd.), 2005 Sheppard Ave. East, 4th Fl., Willowdale ON M2J 5B1 – 416/497-9562; Fax: 416/497-9427; USA Toll Free 1-800-387-5017; URL: http://www.direction-informatique.qc.ca – Tirage: 18,837; Mensuel; français – Éditeur, George Soltys; Rédacteur, Guy Martin

Electronic Composition & Imaging (Published by Youngblood Publishing), #1204, 2240 Midland Ave., Scarborough ON M1R 4R8 – 416/299-6007; Fax: 416/299-6674 – Circ.: 9,000; 6 times a year – Publisher, Sara Young

Government Computing Digest (Published by Synergistic Publications), 132 Adrian Cres., Markham ON L3P 7B3 – 905/472-2801; Fax: 905/472-3091 – Circ.: 9,329; 6 times a year – Publisher, Peter Kitchens; Editor, Gabriel Oak; Circulation Manager, Dianne Osadchuk

Hum - The Government Computer Magazine, #202, 557 Cambridge St. South, Ottawa ON K1S 4J4 – 613/237-4862; Fax: 613/237-4232; Email: lee.hunter@hum.com; URL: http://www.hum.com – Circ.: 14,000; 11 times a year; supplements - Official Show Guide for Technology in Government Week/Government Technology Exhibition – Publisher, Lee Hunter; Editor, Tim Lougheed; Circulation Manager, Loriel Langille

Info-tech Magazine (Published by Transcontinental Publications Inc.), 1100, boul René-Levesque ouest, 24e étage, Montréal PQ H3B 4X9 – 514/392-9000; Fax: 514/392-2088 – Tirage: 19,600; 11 fois par an; français – Éditeur, Alain Thibault

Info Canada (Published by Laurentian Technomedia Inc./Laurentian Media), 501 Oakdale Rd., North York ON M3N 1W7 – 416/746-7360; Fax: 416/746-1421 – Circ.: 30,000; Monthly – Publisher, Andrew White; Editor, Dan McLean; Circulation Manager, Pauline White

Internet Marketing Report, #303, 170 Evans Ave., Etobicoke ON M8Z 5Y6 – 416/255-5679; Fax: 416/255-3070 – Circ.: 10,000; 4 times a year – Publisher, Precana Thompson

Micro-Gazette, #117, 785, av Plymouth, Ville Mont-Royal PQ H4P 1B3 – 514/735-2992; Fax: 514/735-1269; Email: ggauthier@micro-gazette.com; URL: http://www.micro-gazette.com – Tirage: 12,000; 10 fois par an; français – Éditeur & Rédacteur, Gérald Gauthier

Network World Canada (Published by Laurentian Technomedia Inc./Laurentian Media), 501 Oakdale Rd., North York ON M3N 1W7 – 416/746-7360; Fax: 416/746-1421 – Circ.: 12,000; 24 times a year – Publisher, Andrew White; Editor, Dan McLean; Circulation Manager, Pauline White

Sympatico NetLife (Published by Telemedia Publishing), #100, 25 Sheppard Ave. West, North York ON M2N 6S7 – 416/733-7600; Fax: 416/733-8272 – Circ.: 80,000; 6 times a year – Publisher, Graham Morris; Editor, Paul Sullivan

Technology in Government (Published by Plesman Publications Ltd.), 2005 Sheppard Ave. East, 4th Fl., Willowdale ON M2J 5B1 – 416/497-9562; Fax: 416/497-9427; Email: tigedit@plesman.com; URL: http://www.plesman.com – Circ.: 24,202; Monthly – Publisher, George Soltys; Editor, Alison Eastwood

CONSTRUCTION

Alberta Construction, Naylor Communications, 100 Sutherland Ave., Winnipeg MB R2W 3C7 – 204/947-0222; Fax: 204/947-2047 – 4 times a year; also

Alberta Constuction Association Membership Roster & Buyers' Guide (annual, May) – Editor, Wendy Melanson

L'Apercu Révue (Published by Naylor Communications Ltd.), 920 Yonge St., 6th Fl., Toronto ON M4W 3C7 – 416/961-1028; Fax: 416/924-4408 – Annuellement; français – Éditeur, Robert Thompson; Rédactrice, Kim Laudrum

Atlantic Construction Journal (Published by NCC Specialty Publications), #107, 900 Windmill Rd., Dartmouth NS B3B 1P7 – 902/468-8027; Fax: 902/468-2425 – 4 times a year – Publisher, Reg Prest; Editor, Ken Partridge

Bâtiment, #200, 1500, boul Jules-Poitras, St-Laurent PQ H4N 1X7 – 514/745-5720, 1-800-363-0910; Fax: 514/339-2267 – 7 fois par an; français; aussi, Québec construction grands travaux – Éditeur, Guy Choinère; Rédacteur, Johanne Rouleau

Building & Construction Trades Today, c/o 29 Bernard Ave., Toronto ON M5R 1R3 – 416/944-1217; Fax: 416/944-0133; Email: 103727.2265@compuserve.com – Circ.: 4,000; 8 times a year – Publisher, Alan Heisey; Editor, Laura Kosterski; Circulation Manager, Alexandra Irving

Canadian Construction Service & Supply Directory - Alberta (Published by June Warren Publishing Ltd.), 9915 - 56 Ave., Edmonton AB T6E 5L7 – 403/944-9333; Fax: 403/944-9500 – Circ.: 16,112; Annually – Publisher, Colin Eicher

Construction Comment (Published by Naylor Communications Ltd.), 920 Yonge St., 6th Fl., Toronto ON M4W 3C7 – 416/961-1028; Fax: 416/924-4408 – 2 times a year – Publisher, Robert Thompson; Editor, Kim Laudrum

Construire, Québec Construction Assn., #200, 4970, Place de la Savane, Montréal PQ H4P 1Z6 – 514/739-2381; Fax: 514/341-1216 – Tirage: 20,000; 6 fois par an; français – Rédactrice, Christiane Rioux

Daily Commercial News & Construction Record, 280 Yorkland Blvd., Willowdale ON M2J 4Z6 – 416/494-4990; Fax: 416/756-2767 – Circ.: 4,758; Daily – Publisher, Ian Hardy; Editor, Scott Button

Journal Constructo, #200, 1500, boul Jules-Poitras, St-Laurent PQ H4N 1X7 – 514/745-5720; Fax: 514/339-2267; 1-800-363-0910 Toll free – 2 fois par an; français – Éditeur, Guy Coinière; Rédacteur, Johanne Rouleau

Journal of Commerce, 4285 Canada Way, PO Box 82230, Burnaby BC V5C 6E7 – 604/433-8164; Fax: 604/433-9549 – Circ.: 5,300; 2 times a week – President/Publisher, Brian Martin; Editor, Frank Lillquist

London & District Construction Association Magazine (Published by Naylor Communications Ltd.), 920 Yonge St., 6th Fl., Toronto ON M4W 3C7 – 416/961-1028; Fax: 416/924-4408 – Annually – Publisher, Robert Thompson; Editor, Kim Laudrum

Ontario General Contractors' Association Membership Directory, #703, 6299 Airport Rd., Mississauga ON L4V 1N3 – 905/671-3969; Fax: 905/671-8212; Email: ogca@sympatico.ca – Annually – Editor, M. Lim

Preview/Review (Published by Naylor Communications Ltd.), 920 Yonge St., 6th Fl., Toronto ON M4W 3C7 – 416/961-1028; Fax: 416/924-4408 – Annually – Publisher, Robert Thompson; Editor, Kim Laudrum

Québec Habitation, 5930, boul Louis-H.-Lafontaine, Anjou PQ H1M 1S7 – 514/353-9960; Fax: 514/353-4825; Email: quebec-hab@apchq.com – Tirage: 15,000; 6 fois par an; français – Rédacteur, Martin Viau; Directrice de tirage, Nathalie Renauld

Toronto Construction News (Published by Southam Information & Technology Group Inc.), 280 Yorkland Blvd., Willowdale ON M2J 4Z6 – 416/494-4990; Fax: 416/756-2767 – Circ.: 3,900; 4 times a year – Managing Editor, Randy Threndyle

CONVENTIONS & MEETINGS

Association (Published by August Communications Ltd.), #200, 388 Donald St., Winnipeg MB R3B 2J4 – 204/957-0265; Fax: 204/957-0217; Email: august@inforamp.net – Circ.: 3,000; 6 times a year; English & French – Publisher, Gladwyn Nickel; Editor, Andrea Kuch

Congrès Mensuel (Published by Publicom inc.), #400, 1055, côte du Beaver Hall, CP 365, Montréal PQ H2Y 3H1 – 514/274-0004; Fax: 514/274-5884 – Tirage: 5,500; 10 fois par an; français – Rédacteur en chef, Guy Jonkman

Conventions & Meetings Canada, #207, 5762 Hwy. 7, Markham ON L3P 1A8 – 905/471-1550; Fax: 905/471-1552 – Annually, Aug. – Publisher & Editor, James Nuttall; Circulation Manager, Marylan Nuttall

Meetings & Incentive Travel (Published by Maclean Hunter Publishing), 777 Bay St., Toronto ON M5W 1A7 – 416/596-5165, 2697; Fax: 416/596-5810 – Circ.: 10,000; 8 times a year – Editor, Julie Charles, 416/596-2697

Meetings Monthly (Published by Publicom inc.), #400, 1055, côte du Beaver Hall, CP 365, Montréal PQ H2Y 3H1 – 514/274-0004; Fax: 514/274-5884 – Circ.: 12,600; 10 times a year – Editor-in-Chief, Guy J. Jonkman

COSMETICS

Cosmetics (Published by Maclean Hunter Publishing), 777 Bay St., Toronto ON M5W 1A7 – 416/596-5817; Fax: 416/596-5179 – Circ.: 13,000; 6 times a year; supplement - Men'sline, for consumer market; also Cosmetiques (2 fois par an; français) – Publisher, Jim Hicks, 416/596-5246; Editor, Ronald A. Wood

Spa Management (Published by Publicom inc.), #400, 1055, côte du Beaver Hall, CP 365, Montréal PQ H2Y 3H1 – 514/274-0004; Fax: 514/274-5884 – Circ.: 13,200; 6 times a year – Publisher, Guy J. Jonkman

CREDIT

The Atlantic Co-Operator, Atlantic Co-operative Publishers, PO Box 1386, Antigonish NS B2G 2L7 – 902/863-2776; Fax: 902/863-8077; Email: atlcoop@atcon.com.ca – Circ.: 60,000; Bi-monthly – Editor, Brenda MacKinnon; Circulation Manager, Jerome D'Eon

DAIRY PRODUCTS

Canadian Dairy, #205, 3269 Bloor St. West, Toronto ON M8X 1E2 – 416/239-8423; URL: http://www.inforamp.net/~dbattler – Circ.: 2,027; 5 times a year – Publisher & Editor, Iain Macnab

DENTISTRY

Dental Practice Management (Published by Southam Magazine Group), 1450 Don Mills Rd., Don Mills ON M3B 2X7 – 416/442-2046; Fax: 416/442-2214 – Circ.: 16,500; 4 times a year – Publisher & Editor, Erla May; Managing Editor, Janet Bonellie, 416/442-2193

Dentist's Guide (Published by Stitches Publishing Inc.), 16787 Warden Ave., Newmarket ON L3Y 4W1 – 905/853-1884; Fax: 905/853-6565; Email: jcocker@medhumor.com – Circ.: 16,000; 4 times a year – Publisher, Dr. John Cocker; Editor, Simon Hally; Circulation Manager, Kathy Nyenhuis

Journal Dentaire du Québec, Ordre des dentistes du Québec, 625, boul René Lévesque ouest, 15e étage, Montréal PQ H3B 1R2 – 514/875-8511; Fax: 514/875-9412 – Circ.: 4,800; 10 times a year; English & French – Editor, Dr. Denis Forest

Journal of the Canadian Dental Association, 1815 Alta Vista Dr., Ottawa ON K1G 3Y6 – 613/523-1770; Fax: 613/523-7736 – Circ.: 18,600; Monthly; English & French – Publisher, Jardine Neilson; Editor, Dr. P. Ralph Crawford

Ontario Dentist, 4 New St., Toronto ON M5R 1P6 – 416/922-3900; Fax: 416/922-9005 – Circ.: 6,000; 10 times a year – Publisher, Peter James; Editor-in-Chief, James Shosenberg; Managing Editor, Nadine Hubert

Oral Health (Published by Southam Magazine Group), 1450 Don Mills Rd., Don Mills ON M3B 2X7 – 416/442-2046; Fax: 416/442-2214; URL: http://www.southam.com/b1-3-1.html – Circ.: 16,500; Monthly – Publisher & Editor, Erla Kay; Managing Editor, Janet Bonellie, 416/442-2193

Probe, c/o Canadian Dental Hygienists' Assn., 96 Centrepointe Dr., Nepean ON K2G 6B1 – 613/224-5515; Fax: 613/224-7283 – Circ.: 6,800; 6 times a year – Manager, Publications & Conferences, Janice Edgar

DRUGS

L'Actualité Pharmaceutique (Published by Maclean Hunter Publishing), 1001, boul de Maisonneuve ouest, Montréal PQ H3A 3E1 – 514/843-2542; Fax: 514/845-2063 – Éditeur, Jacques Lafontaine; Rédacteur, Danièle Rudel-Tessier

The Canadian Journal of Hospital Pharmacy, The Cdn. Society of Hospital Pharmacists, #350, 1145 Hunt Club Rd., Ottawa ON K1V 0Y3 – 613/736-9733; Fax: 613/736-5660 – Circ.: 3,600; 6 times a year; English & French – Editor, Scott Walker; Circulation Manager, Sue Dohuchie

Canadian Pharmaceutical Journal, Clifford K. Goodman Inc., 1382 Hurontario St., Mississauga ON L5G 3H4 – 905/278-6700, 1-800-661-5004; Fax: 905/278-4850 – Circ.: 15,000; 10 times a year – Editor, Andrew Reinboldt

Hospital Pharmacy Practice (Published by Thomson Healthcare Communications), #200, 1120 Birchmount Rd., Scarborough ON M1K 5G4 – 416/750-8900; Fax: 416/751-8126; Email: pharmacy@mednews.com – 5 times a year – Publisher, Peter Craig; Editor, Ruth Hanley

Pharmacist News (Published by Maclean Hunter Publishing), 777 Bay St., Toronto ON M5W 1A7 – 416/596-2662; Fax: 416/596-2589; Email: phnews@cycor.ca – Circ.: 20,000; 10 times a year – Publisher, Robyn Brooking; Editor, Gary Sands; Circulation Manager, Monica Idrovo

Le Pharmactuel, #900, 1470, rue Peel, Montréal PQ H3A 1T1 – 514/286-0776; Fax: 514/286-1081 – Tirage: 1,300; 6 times a year – Rédacteur, Denis Lebel

Pharmacy Post (Published by Thomson Healthcare Communications), #200, 1120 Birchmount Rd., Scarborough ON M1K 5G4 – 416/750-8900; Fax: 416/751-8126 – Circ.: 17,000; 12 times a year; Health & Beauty supplement – Editorial Director, Pharmacy Publications, Anne Bokma; Managing Editor, Karen Welds

Pharmacy Practice (Published by Thomson Healthcare Communications), #200, 1120 Birchmount Rd., Scarborough ON M1K 5G4 – 416/750-8900; Fax: 416/751-8126 – Circ.: 17,435; 10 times a year; supplement - The Industry Pharmacy Relations Directory – Publisher, Frank Lederer; Editorial Director, Pharmacy Publications, Anne Bokma; Circulation Manager, Denise Brearley

Québec Pharmacie, 4375, av Pierre-de-Coubertin, Montréal PQ H1V 1A6 – 514/254-0346; Fax: 514/254-1288 – Tirage: 6,700; 10 fois par an; français – Éditrice, Jacqueline Racicot; Rédactrice, Monique Richer

EDUCATION

The ATA Magazine, 11010 - 142 St., Edmonton AB T5N 2R1 – 403/453-2411; Fax: 403/455-6481 – Circ.: 39,500; 4 times a year – Editor, Timothy Johnston

The Canadian School Executive, Bentall Centre, PO Box 48265, Vancouver BC V7X 1A1 – 604/739-8600; Fax: 604/739-8200 – 10 times a year – Publisher & Editor-in-Chief, Dr. James Balderson

Canadian Almanac & Directory 1997

Canadian Vocational Journal, Association Canadienne de la formation professionnelle, PO Box 3435, Stn D, Ottawa ON K1P 6L4 – 613/722-7696; Fax: 613/722-7696 – Circ.: 1,000; 4 times a year; English & French – Editor, B. Louks

CAUT Bulletin ACPU, 2675 Queensview Dr., Ottawa ON K2B 8K2 – 613/820-2270; Fax: 613/820-2417; Email: caut@carleton.ca – Circ.: 34,000; 10 times a year; English & French; supplements - Income Tax Guide (Feb.), Status of Women in Academe (April), Status of Librarians in Academe (May) – Publications Officer, Liza R. Duhaime

Educational Digest (Published by Zanny Ltd.), 11966 Woodbine Ave., Gormley ON L0H 1G0 – 905/887-5048; Fax: 905/887-0764 – Circ.: 17,000; 4 times a year – Publisher, Janet Gardiner

Education Forum, c/o Ontario Secondary School Teachers' Federation, 60 Mobile Dr., Toronto ON M4A 2P3 – 416/751-8300; Fax: 416/751-3394; Email: walkern@osstfon.ca – Circ.: 46,000; 3 times a year – Editor, Neil Walker; Circulation Manager, June Pariaug

Education Today, Ontario Public School Board's Assn., 439 University Ave. 18th Fl., Toronto ON M5G 1Y8 – 416/340-2540; Fax: 416/340-7571; Email: admin@opsba.org; URL: http://www.opsba.org – Circ.: 4,000; 5 times a year – Editor, Heather Ropseveare Dion; Circulation Manager, Elsa Moura

Green Teacher: Education for Planet Earth, 95 Robert St., Toronto ON M5S 2K5 – 416/960-1244; Fax: 416/925-3474; Email: greentea@web.ca; URL: http://www.web.ca/~greentea/ – Circ.: 5,700; 5 times a year – Co-Publisher, Tim Grant; Co-Publisher, Gail Littlejohn

Journal les Enseignants, 1316 Domaine du Moulin, L'Ancienne-Lorette PQ G2E 4N1 – 418/872-6966 – Tirage: 5 000; 10 fois par an; français; ISSN: 1196-7838 – Éditeur & Rédacteur, Jean-Louis Jobin, Ph.D.

The Manitoba Teacher, The Manitoba Teachers' Society, 191 Harcourt St., Winnipeg MB R3J 3H2 – 204/888-7961; Fax: 204/831-0877 – Circ.: 17,000; 9 times a year – Managing Editor, Raman Job

Quebec Home & School News, Québec Federation of Home & School Associations, #562, 3285 Cavendish Blvd., Montréal PQ H4B 2L9 – 514/481-5619; Fax: 514/481-5619 – Circ.: 7,750; 5 times a year – Editor, Dorothy Nixon

The Reporter, c/o Ontario English Catholic Teachers' Association, 65 St. Clair Ave. East, Toronto ON M4T 2Y8 – 416/925-2493; Fax: 416/925-7764; URL: http://www.oecta.library@sympatico.ca – Circ.: 40,000; 3 times a year – Editor-in-Chief, Aleda O'Connor

The Saskatchewan Educator, EdVisor Communications, 2366 Ave. C North, Saskatoon SK S7L 5X5 – 306/244-1307; Fax: 306/244-1308; Email: edvisor@eagle.wbm.ca – Circ.: 13,000; 14 times a year; ISSN 1205-9889 – Editor, Lawrence McMahen

School Business Magazine (Published by Sawmill Creek Communications), #11, 4040 Creditview Rd., PO Box 1800, Mississauga ON L5C 3Y8 – 905/569-1800; Fax: 905/569-1818 – 6 times a year – Publisher, Hugh Parkinson

Short Courses & Seminars, Development Publications, 152 Carlton St., PO Box 92530, Toronto ON M5A 2K0 – 416/972-1027; Fax: 416/972-1027 – Circ.: 3,000; 2 times a year – Circulation Manager, Detchena Bowler

The Teacher, c/o Nova Scotia Teachers Union, 3106 Dutch Village Rd., Halifax NS B3L 4L7 – 902/477-5621; Fax: 902/477-3517; Email: theteacher@nstu.ns.ca; URL: http://Fox.nstn.ca/~nstu – Circ.: 15,000; Every other Fri., Sept. to June, 17 times a year – Editor, Paul R. McCormick; Circulation & Advertising Manager, Patricia Crowdis

Teach Magazine, Quadrant Educational Media Services Inc., #206, 258 Wallace Ave., Toronto ON M6P 3M9 – 416/537-2103; Fax: 416/537-3491 – Circ.: 22,000; 5 times a year – Publisher & Editor, Wili Liberman

University Affairs, c/o Assn. of Universities & Colleges of Canada, #600, 350 Albert St., Ottawa ON K1R 1B1 – 613/563-1236; Fax: 613/563-9745; Email: ctausig@aucc.ca; URL: http://www.aucc.ca – Circ.: 31,000; 10 times a year; English & French – Editor, Christine Tausig Ford; Coordinator, Advertising & Circulation, Colleen LaPlante

University Manager (Published by August Communications Ltd.), #200, 388 Donald St., Winnipeg MB R3B 2J4 – 204/957-0265; Fax: 204/957-0217; Email: august@inforamp.net – Circ.: 3,000; 4 times a year; English & French – Publisher, Gladwyn Nickel; Editor, Andrea Kuch

ELECTRICAL EQUIPMENT

Electrical Bluebook (Published by Kerrwil Publications Ltd.), 395 Matheson Blvd. East, Mississauga ON L4Z 2H2 – 905/890-1846; Fax: 905/890-5769; Email: rbm@inforamp.net – Circ.: 18,000; Annually, Jan. – Publisher, Janet Small; Editor, Roger Burford Mason; Circulation Manager, Jean Bilkey

Electrical Business (Published by Kerrwil Publications Ltd.), 395 Matheson Blvd. East, Mississauga ON L4Z 2H2 – 905/890-1846; Fax: 905/890-5769; Email: ibm@inforamp.net – Circ.: 19,500; Monthly – Publisher, Janet Small; Editor, Roger Burford Mason; Circulation Manager, Jean Bilkey

Electrical Equipment News - The Industrial Buyer (Published by Southam Magazine Group), 1450 Don Mills Rd., Don Mills ON M3B 2X7 1450 Don Mills Rd., Don Mills ON M3B 2X7 – 416/445-6641; Fax: 416/442-2214 – Circ.: 24,202; 6 times a year – Publisher, Alex Papanov; Editor, Olga Markovich

Electrical Line Advertiser, 3105 Benbow Rd., West Vancouver BC V7V 3E1 – 604/922-5516; Fax: 604/922-5312; Email: e-line@vkool.com – Circ.: 7,200; 6 times a year – Publisher & Editor, Kevin Buhr; Circulation Manager, Sheila Wilson

Electrical Supply & Distribution Annual (Published by Kerrwil Publications Ltd.), 395 Matheson Blvd. East, Mississauga ON L4Z 2H2 – 905/890-1846; Fax: 905/890-5769; Email: rbm@inforamp.net – Circ.: 12,500; Annually, May – Publisher, Janet Small; Editor, Roger Burford Mason; Circulation Manager, Jean Bilkey

Électricité Québec, 5925, boul Decarie, Montréal PQ H3W 3C9 – 514/738-2184; Fax: 514/738-2192 – Tirage: 9,301; 9 fois par an – Éditrice & Rédactrice, Suzanne Desrosiers; Directrice de tirage, Louisette Broussean

Electricity Today, Hurst Communications, #101, 345 Kingston Rd., Pickering ON L1V 1A1 – 905/509-4448; Fax: 905/509-4451; Email: hq@ELECTRICITYFORM.com; URL: http://www.electricity-forum.com – Circ.: 12,000; 10 times a year – Publisher, Randolph Hurst; Editor, Richard Douglas; Circulaton Manager, Colleen Hurst

Le Monde de L'Electricité (Published by Groupe Constructo), #200, 1500, boul Jules-Poitras, Saint-Laurent PQ H4N 1X7 – 514/745-5720; Fax: 514/339-2267 – Tirage: 7,649; 10 fois par an; français – Éditeur, Guy Choinicke; Rédacteur, Johanne Rouleau

ELECTRONICS

Canadian Electronics (Published by Action Communications Inc.), 135 Spy Ct., Markham ON L3R 5H6 135 Spy Ct., Markham ON L3R 5H6 – 905/447-3222; Fax: 905/477-4320 – Circ.: 22,000; Monthly – Publisher, Tony Chisholm

EIC (Electronique, industrielle et commerciale), 8735, rue Lucien-Plante, Montréal PQ H2M 2M7 – 514/383-7700; Fax: 514/383-7691 – Tirage: 9,019; 5 fois par an; français – Éditeur, Ernest Bourgault; Rédacteur, J.J. Pierre Tremblay

The Electronics Communicator (Published by Evert Communications Ltd.), 1296 Carling Ave., 2nd Fl., Ottawa ON K1Z 7K8 – 613/728-4621; Fax: 613/728-0385 – 40 times a year – Publisher/Editor, Gordon D. Hutchison; Circulation Manager, Carole Jeffrey

EP&T Electronic Products & Technology, Lakeview Publications, 1200 Aerowood Dr., Unit 27, Mississauga ON L4W 2S7 – 905/624-8100; Fax: 905/624-1760; Email: info@ept.ca; URL: http://www.ept.ca – Circ.: 23,786; 8 times a year; also EP&T's Electrosource Product Reference Guide & Telephone Directory (annually, Jan.) – Publisher, Robert C. Luton; Editor, David Kerfoot

EMERGENCY SERVICES

Canadian Emergency News, Pendragon Publishing, 7750 Ranchview Dr. NW, PO Box 68010, Calgary AB T3G 3N8 – 403/547-5748, 1-800-567-0911; Fax: 403/547-5749 – Circ.: 5,000; 6 times a year – Publisher/Editor, Lyle Blumhagen

Emergency Prepardness Direct (Published by Canada Communications Group), #A-2411, 45, boul Sacre-Coeur, Hull PQ K1A 0S9 – 819/956-7864; Fax: 819/956-5134; Email: cominfo@x400.gc.ca – Circ.: 3,300; 4 times a year; English & French – Editor, Anne-Marie Demeres; Circulation Manager, 819-956-4802

ENGINEERING

Annuaire Téléphonique de la Construction du Québec, 22, rue St-Charles, CP 590, Ste-Thérèse PQ J7E 2A4 – 514/437-1600; Fax: 514/437-0723; Email: optilog@optilog.com; URL: http://www.optilog.com – Annuellement; français – Éditeur & Rédacteur, Michel Vaudrin

The B.C. Professional Engineer, c/o Assn. of Professional Engineers & Geoscientists of BC, #200, 4010 Regent St., Burnaby BC V5C 6NZ – 604/929-6733; Fax: 604/929-6753; Email: apegomfp@apeg.bc.ca; http://www.apeg.bc.ca – Circ.: 17,080; 10 times a year – Editor, Wayne Gibson, P.Eng.

Canadian Aggregates & Roadbuilding Contractor, Franmore Communications Inc., #215, 4999 Ste-Catherine St. West, Westmount PQ H3Z 1T3 – 514/487-9868; Fax: 514/487-9276 – Circ.: 7,627; 8 times a year – Publisher & Editor, Robert L. Consedine

Canadian Consulting Engineer (Published by Southam Magazine Group), 1450 Don Mills Rd., Don Mills ON M3B 2X7 – 416/445-6641; Fax: 416/442-2214 – Circ.: 8,900; 6 times a year – Publisher, Jack Meli; Editor, Sophie Kneisel

Canadian Heavy Equipment Guide (Published by Baum International Media), #203, 2323 Boundary Rd., Vancouver BC V5M 4V8 – 604/291-9900; Fax: 604/291-1906 – Circ.: 30,000; 10 times a year – Publisher, Englebert Baum; Editor, Len Webster

Construction Alberta News, 10536 - 106 St., Edmonton AB T5H 2X6 – 403/424-1146; Fax: 403/425-5886 – Circ.: 4,030; Mon. & Thur – Editor, D. Coates

Energy Manager (Published by Kerrwil Publications Ltd.), 395 Matheson Blvd. East, Mississauga ON L4Z 2H2 – 905/890-1846; Fax: 905/890-5769 – Circ.: 11,000; 6 times a year – Publisher, Gary A. Dugan; Editor, Bryan S. Rogers; Circulation Manager, Jean Bilkey

Engineering Dimensions, #1000, 25 Sheppard Ave. West, North York ON M2N 6S9 – 416/224-1100; Fax: 416/224-8168; URL: http://www.peo.on.ca – Circ.: 60,000; 6 times a year – Publisher, David Fletcher; Managing Editor, Connie Mucklestone

Equipment Journal, Page Publishing Limited, #36, 150 Lakeshore West, Mississauga ON L5H 3R2 – 905/274-4883; Fax: 905/274-8686 – Circ.: 18,000; 17 issues a year, every 3 weeks – Publisher & Editor, E.E. Abel; Managing Editor, Michael Anderson; Associate Publisher, John Baker

Geomatica, c/o Canadian Institute of Geomatics, PO Box 5378, Stn F, Ottawa ON K2C 3J1 – 613/224-9851; Fax: 613/224-9577; Email: editgeo@magi.com – Circ.: 1,600; 4 times a year; English & French – Editor, G. Yeaton

Heavy Construction News (Published by Maclean Hunter Publishing), 777 Bay St., Toronto ON M5W 1A7 – 416/596-5848; Fax: 416/593-3193; URL: http://www.io.org/~hcn – Circ.: 25,442; Monthly – Publisher, David J. Fidler

Northpoint (Published by Ontario Association of Certified Engineering Technicians & Technologists), #404, 10 Four Seasons Pl., Etobicoke ON M6B 6H7 – 416/621-9621; Fax: 416/621-8694 – Circ.: 1,300; 4 times a year – Director, Publications & Communications, R.M. Klein, 416/621-9621, ext.237; Editor, Robert Fowler

The Ontario Land Surveyor Quarterly, 1043 McNicoll Ave., Scarborough ON M1W 3W6 – 416/491-9020; Fax: 416/491-2576; Email: aols@interlog.com; URL: http://www/interlog.com/~aols – Circ.: 1,600; 4 times a year – Editor, Brian Munday

Ontario Technologist (Published by Ontario Association of Certified Engineering Technicians & Technologists), #404, 10 Four Seasons Pl., Etobicoke ON M6B 6H7 – 416/621-9621; Fax: 416/621-8694 – Circ.: 21,000; 6 times a year – Editor, Ruth M. Klein

The PEGG, APEGGA, Tower One, 15th Fl., 10060 Jasper Ave., Edmonton AB T5J 4A2 – 403/426-3990; Fax: 403/426-1877; Email: email@appega.com; URL: http://www.appega.com – Circ.: 33,000; 10 times a year – Managing Editor, Trevor Maine, P.Eng.

Plan, #1800, 2020 University St., Montréal PQ H3A 2A5 – 514/845-6141; Fax: 514/845-1833 – Tirage: 40,000; 10 fois par an; français – Rédacteur, Jean-Marc Papineau

Publiquip/Roucam, #202, 582 - 90th Ave., LaSalle PQ H8R 2Z7 – 514/367-0882, 1-800-361-5295; Fax: 514/367-3655 – Tirage: 27,000; Mensuel; français

Supply Post, #108, 19329 Enterprise Way, Surrey BC V3S 6J8 – 604/533-5577; Fax: 604/533-9533; 1-800-663-4802 Toll Free (BC & Alta) – Circ.: 14,900; 11 times a year – Managing Editor, T.R.C. Kenward

FARM IMPLEMENTS & SUPPLIES

CAAR Communicator, Canadian Association of Agricultural Retailers, #107, 1090 Waverly St., PO Box 13, Winnipeg MB R3T 0P4 – 204/989-9300; Fax: 204/989-9306; Email: robeva@freenet.mb.ca – Circ.: 3,300; 4 times a year – R. Anderson

FIRE PROTECTION

Atlantic Firefighter, Hilden Publishing Ltd., 34 Spring St., PO Box 919, Amherst NS B4H 4E1 – 902/667-3009; Fax: 902/667-2868 – Circ.: 9,073; 12 times a year – Publisher, Earl Gouchie; Editor, Doug Harkness

The Canadian Firefighter, PO Box 95, Stn D, Etobicoke ON M9A 4X1 – 416/233-2516; Fax: 416/233-2051; Email: cdnff@interhop.net; URL: http://www.interhop.net/cdnff/cdnff.html – Circ.: 11,607; 6 times a year – Publisher & Editor, Lorne Campbell; Circulation Manager, R.V. Mullen

Fire Fighting in Canada (Published by NCC Publishing), 222 Argyle Ave., Delhi ON N4B 2Y2 – 519/582-2513; Fax: 519/582-4040; Email: 102704.3531@compuserve.com – Circ.: 7,500; 10 times a year – Publisher, David Douglas; Editor, James Haley

FISHERIES

Atlantic Fisherman, Graphic Advocate Co. Ltd., #107, 1127 Barrington St., Halifax NS B3J 1S9 – 902/422-4990; Fax: 902/422-4278 – Circ.: 4,486; Monthly – Editor, Karen Futton

Atlantic Fishfarming, PO Box 790, Montague PE C0A 1R0 – 902/838-2515; Fax: 902/838-4392 – Publisher, Jim MacNeill

The Fisherman, #160, 111 Victoria Dr., Vancouver BC V5L 4C4 – 604/255-1366; Fax: 604/255-3162 – Circ.: 7,700; Monthly – Editor, Sean Griffin

Northern Aquaculture, RR#4, Site 465, C-37, Courtenay BC V9N 7J3 – 250/338-2455, 1-800-661-0368; Fax: 250/338-2466; Email: naqua@mars.ark.com; URL: http://www.naqua.com/ – Circ.: 4,200; 12 times a year – Editor (West Coast), Peter Chettleburgh, Email: chet@islandnet.com; Business Manager, Catherine Egan; Editor (East Coast), John Gracey, Email: jgracey@cycor.ca

The Sou'Wester, Cameron Publishing, PO Box 128, Yarmouth NS B5A 4B1 – 902/742-7111; Fax: 902/742-2311 – Circ.: 10,500; 24 times a year – Editor, Alain Meuse

The Westcoast Fisherman (Published by Westcoast Publishing Ltd), 1496 - 72nd Ave. West, Vancouver BC V6P 3C8 – 604/266-7433; Fax: 604/263-8620; Email: fish@west_coast.com – Circ.: 10,000; Monthly – Publisher, David Rahn

FLOOR COVERINGS

Coverings: Floors, Windows & Walls, Mayville Publishing (Canada) Ltd., RR#1, Picton K0 K0K 2T0 – 613/476-4244; Fax: 613/476-5233 – Circ.: 8,229; 7 times a year – Publisher, Peter Spragg

Floor Coverings, #302, 1448 Lawrence Ave. East, Toronto ON M4A 2V6 – 416/755-5199; Fax: 416/755-9123 – Publisher, John Peters, 514/739-7766; Editor, Jill Sawyer

Surface, 1475 Maisonneuve, Val-David PQ J0T 2N0 – 819/322-7940; Fax: 819/322-1789 – Tirage: 6,325; 8 fois par an; français – Rédacteur, Richard Boiduc

FLORISTS

Canadian Florist, Greenhouse & Nursery, Horticulture Publications Ltd., 1090 Aerowood Dr., Unit #1, Mississauga ON L4W 1Y5 – 905/625-2730; Fax: 905/625-1355 – Monthly – Publisher/Editor, Peter Heywood

Cut & Dried, 2 Highview Dr., Simcoe ON N3Y 2K2 – 519/428-8020; Fax: 519/428-1122 – Publisher, Sue Fredericks

Fleur Design (Published by Éditions Versicolores inc.), 1320, boul St-Joseph, Québec PQ G2K 1G2 – 418/628-8690; Fax: 418/628-0524; 1-800-463-1576 Toll Free – 6 fois par an; français – Éditeur, François Bernatchez; Rédacteur en chef, Caty Bérubé

FOOD & FOOD PROCESSING

Canadian Pizza Magazine (Published by NCC Publishing), 222 Argyle Ave., Delhi ON N4B 2Y2 – 519/582-2513; Fax: 519/582-4040 – Circ.: 12,250; 4 times a year – Publisher, David W. Douglas

Enoteca Wine & Food Magazine, PO Box 37, Concord ON L4K 1B2 – 905/850-9463; Fax: 905/850-8099 – Circ.: 10,000; 4 times a year – Editor, W. Cavalière

Food in Canada (Published by Maclean Hunter Publishing), 777 Bay St., Toronto ON M5W 1A7 – 416/596-5192; Fax: 416/593-3189 – Circ.: 8,384; 9 times a year – Publisher, Heather Oliver

FOOTWEAR

Canadian Footwear Journal (Published by McLeish Communications Inc.), 1, rue Pacifique, Ste-Anne-de-Bellevue PQ H9X 1C5 – 514/457-2423; Fax: 514/457-2577 – Circ.: 7,000; 8 times a year; plus Retail Buyers' Guide (annual), Shoemaking Buyers' Guide (annual) – Publisher, George McLeish; Editor, Peter Matz; Circulation Manager, Ruth Gardiner

FOREST & LUMBER INDUSTRIES

Business Farmer (Published by Westcoast Publishing Ltd), 1496 - 72nd Ave. West, Vancouver BC V6P 3C8 – 604/266-7433; Fax: 604/263-8620 – Circ.: 9,000; Monthly – Publisher, David Rahn

The Business Logger (Published by Westcoast Publishing Ltd), 1496 - 72nd Ave. West, Vancouver BC V6P 3C8 – 604/266-7433; Fax: 604/263-8620; Email: wcoast@wimsey.com – Circ.: 9,000; Monthly – Publisher, David Rahn

Canadian Forest Industries (Published by JCFT Forest Communications Inc.), 1, rue Pacifique, Ste-Anne-de-Bellevue PQ H9X 1C5 – 514/457-2211; Fax: 514/457-2558 – Circ.: 13,000; 8 times a year – Publisher, Tim Tolton; Editor, Scott Jamieson; Circulation Manager, Carol Nixon

Canadian Wood Products (Published by JCFT Forest Communications Inc.), 1, rue Pacifique, Ste-Anne-de-Bellevue PQ H9X 1C5 – 514/457-2211; Fax: 514/457-2558 – Circ.: 7,500; 6 times a year – Publisher, Tim Tolton; Editor, Scott Jamieson; Circulation Manager, Carol Nixon

Le Coopérateur forestier (Published by Les Éditions forestières), 520, rue des Méandres, Québec PQ G2E 5N4 – 418/877-4583; Fax: 418/877-6449 – Tirage: 5,500; 10 fois par an; français – Rédacteur en chef, Alain Castonguay; Circulation Manager, Sylvie Julien

Directory of Ontario Lumber & Building Materials Retailers, Buyers' Guide & Product Directory (Published by Naylor Communications Ltd.), 920 Yonge St. 6th Fl., Toronto ON M4W 3C7 920 Yonge St., 6th Fl., Toronto ON M4W 3C7 – 416/961-1028; Fax: 416/924-4408 – Annually, Oct. – Editor, Lori Knowles

The Forestry Chronicle, Canadian Institute of Forestry, #606, 151 Slater St., Ottawa ON K1P 5H3 – 613/234-2242; Fax: 613/234-6181; Email: 103741.553@compuserve.com; URL: http://www.cif-ifc.org – Circ.: 2,822; 6 times a year – Editor, D. Burgess; Editor, V.J. Nordin

Hiballer Forest Magazine, HB Publishers, #11, 106 - 14th St. East, North Vancouver BC V7L 2N3 – 604/984-2002; Fax: 604/984-2820 – 6 times a year – Publisher/Managing Editor, Paul Young

Interlog Magazine, PO Box 601, Stn A, Vancouver BC V8C 2N5 – 604/683-1515; Fax: 604/683-4142 – Circ.: 4,497; 4 times a year – Publisher/Managing Editor, Bob Beattie

Logging & Sawmilling Journal, 622 - 22nd St. West, North Vancouver BC V7L 4L2 – 604/990-9970; Fax: 604/990-9971 – Circ.: 15,900; 9 times a year – Publisher, Robert Stanhope; Editor, Norm Poole, 604/944-6146

Madison's Canadian Lumber Directory, PO Box 2486, Vancouver BC V6B 3W7 – 604/681-6838; Fax: 604/681-6585; Email: madisons@dowco.com; URL: http://www.dowco.com/cmd/madisons – Circ.: 1,200; Annually, Spring – Publisher, Laurence Cater; Editor, Leah McNutt

Opérations Forestières et de Scierie, JCFT Forest Communications, 1, rue Pacifique, Ste-Anne-de-Bellevue PQ H9X 1C5 – 514/457-2211; Fax: 514/457-2558 – Tirage: 5,500; 4 fois par an; français – Éditeur/Rédacteur, Guy Fortin

Le Resam forestier (Published by Les Éditions forestières), 520, rue des Méandres, Québec PQ G2E 5N4 – 418/877-4583; Fax: 418/877-6449 – Tirage: 11,700; 10 fois par an; français – Rédacteur, Alain Castonguay; Directrice de tirage, Sylvie Julien

Truck Logger Magazine, #725, 815 West Hastings St., Vancouver BC V6C 1B4 – 604/682-4080; Fax: 604/682-3775 – 6 times a year – Publisher/Editor, David Webster; Circulation, Rita Conte

Yardstick, Craig Kelman & Assoc., #3C, 2020 Portage Ave., Winnipeg MB R3J 0K4 – 204/885-7798; Fax: 204/889-3576 – Circ.: 1,600; 6 times a year; also WRLA Directory & Buyers' Guide (annually, Jan.) – Editor, Jim E. Watson

FUNERAL SERVICE

Canadian Funeral Director, Halket Publishing Ltd., #206, 174 Harwood Ave. South, Ajax ON L1S 2H7 – 905/427-6121; Fax: 905/427-1660 – Monthly – Publisher, Ray Halket; Editor, Scott Hillier

Canadian Almanac & Directory 1997

Canadian Funeral News (Published by OT Communications), #600, 237 - 8th Ave. SE, Calgary AB T2G 5C3 – 403/264-3270; Fax: 403/264-3276 – Monthly – Publisher, Patrick Ottmann; Editor, Natika Sunstrum

Network (Published by OT Communications), #600, 237 - 8th Ave. SE, Calgary AB T2G 5C3 – 403/569-9520; Fax: 403/569-9590 – 6 times a year – Editor, Richard Bronstein

FUR TRADE

The Canadian Trapper, M2 Publications Ltd., 9936 - 100th Ave., Grand Prairie AB T8V 0T9 – 403/539-7870; Fax: 403/539-7919 – 6 times a year – Publisher, Becky McIntosh McDonald

GARDEN SUPPLIES & EQUIPMENT

Greenhouse Canada (Published by NCC Publishing), 222 Argyle Ave., Delhi ON N4B 2Y2 – 519/582-2513; Fax: 519/582-4040 – Circ.: 4,500; Monthly – Publisher, Dave Douglas

GIFTS

CGTA Retail News, Canadian Gift & Tableware Association, #301, 265 Yorkland Blvd., North York ON M2J 1S5 – 416/497-5771; Fax: 416/497-3448 – Circ.: 33,380; 4 times a year – Editor, Diana Daniels

Gifts & Tablewares (Published by Southam Magazine Group), 1450 Don Mills Rd., Don Mills ON M3B 2X7 – 416/445-6641; Fax: 416/442-2213; Email: lsmith@southam.ca; URL: http://www.southam.com/b1-9-1/html – Circ.: 14,000; 7 times a year – Editor/Publisher, Dawn Dickinson, 416/442-2996

GLASS

Glass Canada (Published by AIS Communications Ltd.), 145 Thames Rd. West, Exeter ON N0M 1S3 – 519/235-2400; Fax: 519/235-0798 – Circ.: 5,144; 6 times a year – Publisher, Peter Phillips; Editor, Peter Darbishire; Circulation Manager, Jan Jeffery

GOVERNMENT

BC Municipal Yearbook: Redbook, PO Box 82230, Burnaby BC V5G 1H2 – 604/433-8164; Fax: 604/433-9549 – Circ.: 2,000 – Publisher, Judy Sirett; Editor, Anne Crittenden

FCM Forum, Federation of Canadian Municipalities, 24 Clarence St., Ottawa ON K1N 5P3 – 613/241-5221; Fax: 613/241-7440 – Circ.: 7,000; 6 times a year – Editor, Sheila Keating-Nause

Focus, The Government Source, 1025 Richmond Rd., Unit 107, Ottawa ON K2B 8G8 – 613/820-3272; Fax: 613/820-3646 – Circ.: 12,700; 11 times a year; English & French – Publisher, Ken Lagasse; Editor, Richard Newport

Government Business (Published by Sawmill Creek Communications), #11, 4040 Creditview Rd., PO Box 1800, Mississauga ON L5C 3Y8 – 905/813-7100; Fax: 905/813-7117 – Circ.: 19,000; 6 times a year – Publisher, Hugh Parkinson

Government Business Opportunities (Published by Canada Communications Group), #A-2411, 45, boul Sacre-Coeur, Hull PQ K1A 0S9 – 819/956-7864; Fax: 819/956-5134 – Circ.: 2,000; 3 issues per week; English & French – Editor, Carole Kennedy

Government Purchasing Guide (Published by Moorshead Magazines Ltd.), #490, 10 Gateway Blvd., Toronto ON M3C 3T4 – 416/696-5488; Fax: 416/696-7395; Email: gpg@moorshead.com – Circ.: 17,000; Monthly – Publisher, Halvor Moorshead; Editor, John Dujay; Circulation Manager, Rick Cree

Municipal Business Canada, #277, 200 Rivercrest Dr. SE, Calgary AB T2C 2X5 – 403/279-5151; Fax: 403/236-7298 – 10 times a year – Jerry Skinner

Municipal Monitor (Published by Kenilworth Publishing), #201, 27 West Beaver Creek, Richmond Hill ON L4B 1M8 – 905/771-7333; Fax: 905/771-7336 – Circ.: 2,486; 6 times a year – Publisher, James Davidson

Municipal World, PO Box 399, Stn Main, St. Thomas ON N5P 3V3 – 519/633-0031; Fax: 519/633-1001; Email: mwadmin@municipalworld.com; URL: http://www.municipalworld.com – Circ.: 7,400; Monthly – Publisher & Editor, Michael J. Smither; Circulation Manager, Wanda Tully

La Revue Municipale, Publigam, 10595, Louis-H.-Lafonatine, Anjou PQ H1J 2E8 – 514/353-3434; Fax: 514/353-3848 – Tirage: 7,332; Mensuel; français – Éditeur, Gilles P. Verronneau; Rédacteur, Robert Bastin

Urba, L'Union des municipalitiés de Québec, #680, 680, rue Sherbrooke ouest, Montréal PQ H3A 2M7 – 514/282-7700; Fax: 514/282-7711 – Tirage: 8,000; 10 fois par an; français – Rédacteur, Martin Lasalle

GRAPHIC ARTS

Applied Arts, #324, 885 Don Mills Rd., Don Mills ON M3C 1V9 – 416/510-0909; Fax: 416/510-0913; Email: app-arts@interlog.com – Circ.: 11,000; 6 times a year – Publisher, George Haroutiun; Managing Editor, Joanna Pachner

The Graphic Exchange, Brill Communications Inc., #65090, 358 Danforth Ave., Toronto ON M4K 3Z2 – 416/961-1325; Fax: 416/961-0941 – 6 times a year – Publisher & Editor, Dan Brill

Studio Magazine, Roger Murray & Associates Inc., 124 Galaxy Blvd., Toronto ON M9W 4Y6 – 416/675-1999; Fax: 416/675-6093 – Circ.: 9,000; 6 times a year – Group Publisher/Designer, Roger E. Murray; Executive Editor, Barbara J. Murray

GROCERY TRADE

L'Alimentation, Les Éditions du marchand Québécois, 1298, rue St-Zotique est, Montréal PQ H2S 1N7 – 514/271-6922; Fax: 514/283-3170 – Tirage: 14,500; 11 fois par an; français – Rédactrice, Françoise Pitt

Canadian Grocer (Published by Maclean Hunter Publishing), 777 Bay St., Toronto ON M5W 1A7 – 416/596-5191; Fax: 416/593-3162; Email: emasters@cycor.ca – Circ.: 18,000; Monthly; supplements - The Excecutive Report, Food Brokers Issue, Directory of Non-Food Suppliers – Publisher, Karen James; Editor, George H. Condon, 416/596-5772; Circulation Manager, Monica Idrovo

Grocer Today (Published by Canada Wide Magazines & Communications Ltd.), 4180 Lougheed Hwy., 4th Fl., Burnaby BC V5C 6A7 – 604/299-7311; Fax: 604/299-9188 – Circ.: 11,500; 10 times a year – Publisher, Peter Legge; Editor, Marisa Paterson; Circulation Manager, Mark Weeks

Western Grocer (Published by Mercury Publications Ltd.), 945 King Edward St., Winnipeg MB R3H 0P8 – 204/775-0387; Fax: 204/775-7830 – Circ.: 11,986; 6 times a year – Publisher, Gren R. Yeo; Editor, Kelly Gray; Circulation Manager, Juanita Unrau

HARDWARE TRADE

Centre Magazine (Published by Southam Magazine Group), 1450 Don Mills Rd., Don Mills ON M3B 2X7 – 416/445-6641; Fax: 416/442-2077; URL: http://www.southam.com/b1-9-2.html – Circ.: 14,960; 8 times a year – Publisher, Hugh Clemence; Editor, Elena Opasini

Le Guide des fournisseurs des centres de rénovation et des quincailleries du Québec (Published by Publiédition inc.), 620, boul Industriel, St-Jean-sur-Richelieu PQ J3B 7X4 – 514/856-7821; Fax: 514/359-0836 – Annuellement – Éditeur, Yves Bégnoche

Hardware Merchandising (Published by Maclean Hunter Publishing), 777 Bay St., Toronto ON M5W 1A7 – 416/596-5094, 5259; Fax: 416/593-3201 – Circ.: 14,943; 9 times a year – Publisher, Hélène Chevrette

Home Improvement Retailing, Powershift Communications Inc., #308, 245 Fairview Mall Dr., North York ON M2J 4T1 – 416/494-1066; Fax: 416/494-2536 – Circ.: 15,600; 6 times a year – Publisher, Dante Piccinin

Quart de rond, Assn des détaillants de matériaux de construction du Québec, 474, Place Trans-Canada, Longueuil PQ J4G 1N8 – 514/646-5842; Fax: 514/646-6171; Email: admcq@accent.net – Tirage: 4,400; 8 fois par an; français – Rédacteur, Gabriel Pollender; Directrice de tirage, Lisette Leduc

Quincaillerie-Matériaux (Published by Maclean Hunter Publishing), 777 Bay St., Toronto ON M5W 1A7 – 416/596-5259; Fax: 416/596-5553; URL: http://www.cyberplex.com/quincaillerie – Tirage: 4,900; 6 fois par an; français – Rédacteur, Benoit Bisson

Show Guide (Published by Maclean Hunter Publishing), 777 Bay St., Toronto ON M5W 1A7 – 416/596-5094; Fax: 416/593-3201 – Annually, Feb. – Publisher, Hélène Chevrette, 416/596-5284

HEATING, PLUMBING, AIR CONDITIONING

Heating-Plumbing-Air Conditioning, Cowgate Communications, #300, 1370 Don Mills Rd., Don Mills ON M3B 3N7 – 416/759-2500; Fax: 416/759-6979 – Circ.: 16,300; 7 times a year; also Buyers Guide (annually, Aug.) – Publisher, W. Bruce Meacock; Editor, Lynne Erskine-Chelo

Inter-mécanique du bâtiment, 8175, boul St-Laurent, Montréal PQ H2P 2M1 – 514/382-2668; Fax: 514/382-1566 – Tirage: 5,500; 10 fois par an; français – Rédacteur, André Dupuis, 1-800-465-2668; Directrice de tirage, Sonia Audet

Mechanical Buyer & Specifier: HVAC/Refrigeration Magazine (Published by Nytek Publishing Inc), 130 Belfield Rd., Etobicoke ON M9W 1G1 – 416/242-8088; Fax: 416/242-8085 – Circ.: 8,100; 7 times a year – Publisher, Don Beaulieu; Editor, Ron Shuker; Circulation Manager, Pat Glionna

Mechanical Buyer & Specifier: Plumbing, Piping & Heating Magazine (Published by Nytek Publishing Inc), 130 Belfield Rd., Etobicoke ON M9W 1G1 – 416/242-8088; Fax: 416/242-8085 – Circ.: 13,100; 6 times a year – Publisher, Don Beaulieu; Editor, Ron Shuker; Circulation Manager, Pat Glionna

HOSPITALS, HEALTH CARE

Artère, c/o L'Assn des Hôpitaux du Québec, #400, 505, boul de Maisonneuve ouest, Montréal PQ H3A 3C2 – 514/842-4861; Fax: 514/282-4271; Email: 2009mtl@accent.net – Tirage: 6,865; 10 fois par an; français – Éditeur, Robert Nadon; Rédacteur, Louis-Pierre Coté

Canadian Healthcare Manager (Published by Maclean Hunter Publishing), 777 Bay St., Toronto ON M5W 1A7 – 416/596-5794; Fax: 416/596-5071 – Circ.: 20,000; 4 times a year 6 – Publisher, John Milne; Editor, Celia Milne; Circulation Manager, Donna Singh

Canadian Journal of Infection Control (Published by Pulsus Group Inc.), 2902 South Sheridan Way, Oakville ON L6J 7L6 – 905/829-4770; Fax: 905/829-4799 – Circ.: 3,000; 4 times a year – Publisher, Robert B. Kalina; Editor, Marilyn Jacks

Canadian Nursing Home, c/o Health Media, 14453 - 29A Ave., White Rock BC V4P 1P7 – 604/535-7933; Fax: 604/535-9000 – Circ.: 2,800; 4 times a year – Publisher & Adv. Manager, Ron Forster; Editor, Frank Fagan

CCHSE Members Directory, #402, 350 Sparks St., Ottawa ON K1R 7S8 – 613/235-7218; Fax: 613/235-5451; 1-800-363-9056 Toll Free – Circ.: 3,387; Annually, June – Luc Vaugeois

CHAC Review, c/o Catholic Health Association of Canada, 1247 Kilborn Ave., Ottawa ON K1H 6K9 – 613/731-7148; Fax: 613/731-7797; Email: chac@neb.net – Circ.: 2,000; 3 times a year – Editor, Maryse Blouin

Contact, #402, 350 Sparks St., Ottawa ON K1R 7S8 – 613/235-7218, 1-800-363-9056; Fax: 613/235-5451 –

Circ.: 3,387; 4 times a year; English & French – Editor, Daniel Sarazin

Diététique en Action, #703, 1425, boul René-Lévesque ouest, Montréal PQ H3G 1T7 – 514/393-3733; Fax: 514/393-3582 – Circ.: 2,500; 3 times a year; English & French – President, Micheline Seguin Bernier

Disability International, #309, 175 Hargrave St., Winnipeg MB R3C 3R8 – 204/982-6777; Fax: 204/982-6789 – Circ.: 12,000; 4 times a year – Editor, R.H. Johnson

Guide to Canadian Healthcare Facilities, c/o Canadian Healthcare Association, 17 York St., Ottawa ON K1N 9J6 – 613/241-8005; Fax: 613/241-5055 – Editor, Eleanor Sawyer

Healthcare Management FORUM, Canadian College of Health Service Executives, #402, 350 Sparks St., Ottawa ON K1R 7S8 – 613/235-7218; Fax: 613/235-5451; Email: CCHSE@hpb/hurc.ca; URL: http://www.hurc.ca:8080/cchse/ – Circ.: 3,560; 4 times a year – Managing Editor, Randall R. Steffan

Hospital Business (Published by Sawmill Creek Communications), #11, 4040 Creditview Rd., PO Box 1800, Mississauga ON L5C 3Y8 – 905/813-7000; Fax: 905/813-7117 – Circ.: 10,100; 6 times a year – Publisher, Hugh Parkinson; Editor, Jay Barwell

Hospital News, Auto Mart Magazines Ltd., 23 Apex Rd., Toronto ON M6A 2V6 – 416/781-5516; Fax: 416/781-5499 – Circ.: 46,000; Monthly – Editor, Cindy Woods

The Journal, Addiction Research Foundation, 33 Russell St., Toronto ON M5S 2S1 – 416/595-6714; Fax: 416/595-6892; Email: adubey@arf.org; URL: http://www.intropage.html – Circ.: 11,000; 6 times a year; English & French – Publisher, Perry Kendall; Editor, Anita Dubey

Journal of the Canadian Dietetic Association, #601, 480 University Ave., Toronto ON M5G 1V2 – 416/596-0857; Fax: 416/596-0603 – Circ.: 5,000; 4 times a year; French & English – Editor, Eunice Chao

Leadership in Health Services, Canadian Healthcare Assn., 17 York St., Ottawa ON K1N 9J6 – 613/241-8005; Fax: 613/241-5055 – Circ.: 5,218; 6 times a year; English with some French – Editor, Michelle Albagli; Circulation Manager, Lyne Sauvé

Long Term Care, Ontario Nursing Home Association, #202, 345 Renfrew Dr., Markham ON L3R 9S9 – 905/470-8995; Fax: 905/470-9595 – Circ.: 4,200; 4 times a year – Editor, Heather Lang-Runtz

Rehab & Community Care Management, BCS Communications Ltd., 101 Thorncliffe Park Dr., Toronto ON M4H 1M2 – 416/421-7944; Fax: 416/421-0966 – Circ.: 20,000; 4 times a year – Publisher, Caroline Tapp-McDougall

HOTELS & RESTAURANTS

La Barrique (Published by Kylix Media Inc), #414, 5165 Sherbrooke St. West, Montréal PQ H4A 1T6 – 514/481-5892; Fax: 514/481-9699; URL: http://www.magnet.ca/wine – Tirage: 8,332; 6 fois par an; français – Éditrice, Judy Rochester; Rédactrice, Nicole Barrette-Ryan; Tirage, Veronica Gumilar

Le Chef du service alimentaire, 252, rte 171, CP 1010, St-Etienne-de-Lauzon PQ G6J 1S2 – 418/831-5317; Fax: 418/831-5172 – Tirage: 18,500; 6 fois par an; français – Éditeur, Maurice LeBlanc; Rédactrice, Ann Labrecque

Foodservice & Hospitality (Published by Kostuch Publications Ltd.), #101, 23 Lesmill Rd., Don Mills ON M3B 3P6 – 416/447-0888; Fax: 416/447-5333; Email: mkostuch@foodservice.ca; URL: http://www.foodservice.ca – Circ.: 24,475; Monthly; supplement - Ontario Headlines – President/Publisher, Mitch Kostuch; Editor, Rosanna Caira; Circulation Manager, Rosetta Austin

Hotelier (Published by Kostuch Publications Ltd.), #101, 23 Lesmill Rd., Don Mills ON M3B 3P6 – 416/447-0888; Fax: 416/447-5333; Email: rcaira@foodservice.ca; URL: http://www.foodservice.ca – Circ.: 8,000; 6 times a year – Publisher, Mitch Kostuch; Editor, Rosanna Caira; Circulation Manager, Rosetta Austin

The Network (Published by Naylor Communications Ltd.), 920 Yonge St., 6th Fl., Toronto ON M4W 3C7 – 416/961-1028; Fax: 416/924-4408 – Annually – Publisher, Robert Thompson; Editor, Kim Laudrum

Ontario Restaurant Association Membership Directory & Buyers' Guide (Published by Naylor Communications Ltd.), 920 Yonge St., 6th Fl., Toronto ON M4W 3C7 – 416/961-1028; Fax: 416/924-4408 – Annually – Publisher, Robert Thompson; Editor, Kim Laudrum

Ontario Restaurant News (Published by Ishcom Publications Ltd.), #101, 2065 Dundas St. East, Mississauga ON L4X 2W1 – 905/206-0150; Fax: 905/206-9972 – 12 times a year – Publisher, Stephen Isherwood; Editor, Stephen Law

Western Hospitality News (Published by Ishcom Publications Ltd.), #101, 2065 Dundas St. East, Mississauga ON L4X 2W1 – 905/206-0150; Fax: 905/206-9972 – Circ.: 13,500; 6 times a year – Publisher, Steve Isherwood; Managing Editor, Susan Jedrzejek

Western Restaurant News (Published by Mercury Publications Ltd.), 945 King Edward St., Winnipeg MB R3H 0P8 – 204/775-0387; Fax: 204/775-7830 – Circ.: 11,996; 4 times a year – Publisher, Gren R. Yeo; Editor, Kelly Gray; Circulation Manager, Juanita Unrau

HOUSEWARES

Canadian Homestyle Magazine, Lorell Communications, 598 Stillwater Ct., Burlington ON L7T 4G7 – 905/681-7932; Fax: 905/681-2141 – Circ.: 6,800; 7 times a year – Publisher & Editor, Laurie O'Halloran

HUMAN RESOURCES

Avenir - formation, compétences, #200, 3715, av Lacombe, Montréal PQ H3T 1M3 – 514/341-7916; Fax: 514/341-2644 – 6 fois par an; français – Éditeur, Marie-Claire Dupré; Rédacteur, Michel Guénard

Canadian HR Reporter, MPL Communications, #700, 133 Richmond St. West, Toronto ON M5H 3M8 – 416/869-1177; Fax: 416/869-0616; Email: chrr@cycor.ca – Circ.: 7,700; 22 times a year – Publisher & Editor, George Pearson; Circulation Manager, David Berger

Human Resources Professional, Human Resources Professionals Assn. of Ontario (HRPAO), #1902, 2 Bloor St. West, Toronto ON M4W 3E2 – 416/923-2324; Fax: 416/923-7264; 1-800-387-1311 Toll Free – Circ.: 8,100; 9 times a year – Editor, Ruta Lovett; Circulation Manager, Farah Allen-Goldson

IMPORT, EXPORT

Canadian Exporters Association Membership Directory (Published by Naylor Communications Ltd.), 920 Yonge St., 6th Fl., Toronto ON M4W 3C7 – 416/961-1028; Fax: 416/924-4408 – Annually – Publisher, Robert Thompson; Editor, Kim Laudrum

Export is Our Business (Published by Naylor Communications Ltd.), 920 Yonge St., 6th Fl., Toronto ON M4W 3C7 – 416/961-1028; Fax: 416/924-4408 – 2 times a year; English & French – Publisher, Robert Thompson; Editor, Kim Laudrum

INDUSTRIAL & INDUSTRIAL AUTOMATION

Canadian Industrial Equipment News (Published by Southam Magazine Group), 1450 Don Mills Rd., Don Mills ON M3B 2X7 – 416/445-6641; Fax: 416/442-2214; URL: http://www.southam.com/b1-5-1.html – Circ.: 23,500; Monthly – Publisher, Alex Papanov; Editor, Olga Markovich

Le Journal Industriel du Québec, Info-industriel inc., 2370, boul Henri-Bourassa est, Montréal PQ H2B 1T6 – 514/388-8801; Fax: 514/388-7871 – Tirage: 20,900; 10 fois par an; français – Rédacteur, Yvan Gauthier

Manufacturing & Process Automation (Published by Kerrwil Publications Ltd.), 395 Matheson Blvd. East, Mississauga ON L4Z 2H2 – 905/890-1846; Fax: 905/890-5769; Email: mpa@inforamp.net – Circ.: 15,400; 6 times a year – Publisher, Klaus Pirker; Editor, Meg Mathur; Circulation Manager, Jean Bilkey

National Industrial, Brymell Publications Inc., #201, 801 York Mills Rd., Don Mills ON M3B 1X7 – 416/446-1404; Fax: 416/446-0502 – Circ.: 25,500; Monthly – Publisher/Editor, W.R. Bryson

New Equipment News, c/o Canadian Engineering Publications Ltd., 204 Richmond St. West, Toronto ON M5V 1V6 – 416/599-3737; Fax: 416/599-3730 – Circ.: 22,500; 10 times a year – Publisher, Tom Monson; Editor, D. Barrie Lehman; Circulation Manager, Maureen Wheeler

PEM: Plant Engineering & Maintenance (Published by Clifford Elliott & Associates Ltd.), #209, 277 Lakeshore Rd. East, Oakville ON L6J 6J3 – 905/842-2884; Fax: 905/842-8226 – Circ.: 21,300; 5 times a year; also Sourcebook (2 times a year) – Publisher, Julie Clifford; Editor, Rae Robb; Circulation Manager, Janice Armbrust

Plant (Published by Maclean Hunter Publishing), 777 Bay St., Toronto ON M5W 1A7 – 416/596-5777; Fax: 416/596-5552 – Circ.: 34,000; 18 times a year – Publisher, Dan Bordun; Editor, Wayne Karl, 416/596-5761

Produits Pour L'Industrie Québécoise, Action communications inc., CP 357, Pointe Claire PQ H9R 4P4 – 514/337-2177; Fax: 514/477-4320 – Tirage: 15,000; 6 fois par an; français – Éditeur, Michael L. Doody; Rédacteur, David Terhune

L'Usine (Published by Maclean Hunter Publishing), 1001, boul de Maisonneuve ouest, Montréal PQ H3A 3E1 – 514/845-5141; Fax: 514/845-4393 – Tirage: 15,400; 4 fois par an – Éditeur, Dan Bordun; Rédacteur, Pierre Deschamps

INDUSTRIAL SAFETY

Accident Prevention, 250 Yonge St., 28th Fl., Toronto ON M5B 2N4 – 416/506-8888, 1-800-669-4939 – Circ.: 16,388; 6 times a year – Editor, Susan Stanton

Canadian Occupational Safety (Published by Clifford Elliott & Associates Ltd.), #209, 277 Lakeshore Rd. East, Oakville ON L6J 6J3 – 905/842-2884; Fax: 905/842-8226 – Circ.: 12,100; 6 times a year – Publisher, Ralph Elliot; Editor, Jackie Roth; Circulation Manager, Janice Armbrust

Occupational Health & Safety Canada (Published by Southam Magazine Group), 1450 Don Mills Rd., Don Mills ON M3B 2X7 – 416/445-6641; Fax: 416/442-2200; Email: gpeck@southam.ca – Circ.: 10,000; 7 times a year – Publisher, Gregory Peek; Editor, David Dewaas

Travail et santé, CP 1089, Napierville PQ J0J 1L0 – 514/245-7285; Fax: 514/245-0593 – Tirage: 2,400; 4 fois par an; français – Rédacteur, Robert Richards

INSTITUTIONS

Canadian Home Economics Journal, Canadian Home Economics Association, #307, 151 Slater St., Ottawa ON K1P 5H3 – 613/238-8817; Fax: 613/238-8972 – Circ.: 2,600; 4 times a year; English & French – Editor, J. Estelle Reddin

INSURANCE

Alberta Insurance Directory (Published by Arbutus Publications Ltd.), PO Box 3311, Stn MPO, Vancouver BC V6B 3Y3 – 604/874-1001; Fax: 604/874-3922 – Circ.: 1,050; Annually, Jan. – Publisher & Editor, Bill Earle

The BC Broker (Published by Arbutus Publications Ltd.), PO Box 3311, Stn MPO, Vancouver BC V6B 3Y3 – 604/874-1001; Fax: 604/874-3922 –

Circ.: 2,500; 6 times a year – Publisher & Managing Editor, Bill Earle

British Columbia Insurance Directory (Published by Arbutus Publications Ltd.), PO Box 3311, Stn MPO, Vancouver BC V6B 3Y3 – 604/874-1001; Fax: 604/874-3922 – Circ.: 2,095; Annually, April – Editor & Publisher, Bill Earle

Canadian Insurance (Published by Stone & Cox Ltd.), #202, 111 Peter St., Toronto ON M5V 2H1 – 416/599-0772; Fax: 416/599-0867; Email: canadian_insurance@stonecox.com – Monthly – Publisher, J. Kent Chisholm; Editor, Craig Harris

Canadian Insurance Claims Directory, University of Toronto Press, #700, 10 St. Mary St., Toronto ON M4Y 2W8 – 416/978-2239, ext.245; Fax: 416/978-4738 – Circ.: 2,000; Annually, July – Editor, Elizabeth Lumley

Canadian Underwriter (Published by Southam Magazine Group), 1450 Don Mills Rd., Don Mills ON M3B 2X7 – 416/445-6641; Fax: 416/442-2213; Email: ndunlop@southam.ca; URL: http://www.cdnunderwriter.com – Circ.: 6,250; Monthly; also Rehabilitation Services Guide, Guide to Legal Firms, Insurance Marketer & annual statistical issue – Publisher, Steve Wilson; Managing Editor, Larry Welsh

General Insurance Register (Published by Stone & Cox Ltd.), #202, 111 Peter St., Toronto ON M5V 2H1 – 416/599-0772; Fax: 416/599-0867; Email: gir@stonecox.com – Annually, Jan. – Editor, J. Wyndham

Insurance West (Published by Arbutus Publications Ltd.), PO Box 3311, Stn MPO, Vancouver BC V6B 3Y3 – 604/874-1001; Fax: 604/874-3922 – 4 times a year – Publisher, Bill Earle; Associate Publisher, Jim Bensley

Le Journal de l'Assurance, #4, 353, rue St-Nicholas, Montréal PQ H2Y 2P1 – 514/289-9595; Fax: 514/289-9527; Email: journass@interlink.net – Tirage: 18,000; 10 fois par an; français; aussi The Insurance Journal (circ. 7,500, English) – Éditeur/Rédacteur, Serge Therrien; Directrice de tirage, Daniel Campeau

Liaison, #139, 955, rue d'Assigny, Longueuil PQ J4K 5C3 – 514/674-6258; Fax: 514/674-3609 – Tirage: 3,000; 6 fois par an – Directrice-générale, Claudette Carrier

LUAC Forum, c/o Life Underwriters Association, 41 Lesmill Rd., Don Mills ON M3B 2T3 – 416/444-5251, 1-800-563-5822; Fax: 416/444-8031 – Circ.: 18,100; 10 times a year – Director, Val Osborne

Ontario Insurance Directory (Published by Southam Magazine Group), 1450 Don Mills Rd., Don Mills ON M3B 2X7 – 416/445-6641; Fax: 416/442-2213; Email: s.wilson@netcom.ca; URL: http://cdnunderwriter.com – Circ.: 5,500; Annually, Jan. – Publisher, Steve Wilson; Editor, Nancy V. Campbell, 416/510-6840

Le Portefeuille d'assurances, L. Chaput, files et cie ltée, #114, 3328, av Troie, Montréal PQ H3V 1B1 – 514/739-2230; Fax: 514/739-1422 – Mensuel – Éditeur, Pierre M Chaput

Prospective, Life Underwriters Association of Québec, #500, 1 Westmount Sq., Montréal PQ H3Z 2P9 – 514/932-4277; Fax: 514/932-6400 – Circ.: 13,000; 9 times a year; English & French – Editor-in-Chief, Louis Garneau

INTERIOR DESIGN & DECOR

Azure, 2 Silver Ave., Toronto ON M6R 3A2 – 416/588-2588; Fax: 416/588-2357 – Circ.: 14,000; 6 times a year – Publisher, Sergio Sgaramella; Editor, Nelda Rodger

Canadian Facility Management & Design, 62 Olsen Dr., Don Mills ON M3A 3J3 – 416/447-3417; Fax: 416/447-4410 – Circ.: 6,156; 6 times a year – Publisher, Arvid B. Stonkus; Editor, Victor von Buchstab

Canadian Interiors (Published by Crailer Communications), 360 Dupont St., Toronto ON M5R 1V9 – 416/966-9944; Fax: 416/966-9946 – Circ.: 12,000; 6 times a year; includes Annual Sources Directory for Products & Services – Publisher & Editor, Sheri Craig; Circulation Manager, Beata Olechnowicz

L'Envers du décor, Groupe Inter data inc., #102, 491, boul Lebeau, Ville St-Laurent PQ H4N 1S2 – 514/745-0080; Fax: 514/745-0993 – Tirage: 6,000; 6 fois par an

Ontario Design, 905/479-4663; Fax: 905/479-4482 – Circ.: 12,000; Annually – Publisher, Michael Rosset

JEWELLERY & GIFTWARE

Canadian Jeweller, Style Communications, #302, 1448 Lawrence Ave. East, Toronto ON M4A 2V6 – 416/755-5199; Fax: 416/755-9123 – Monthly – Publisher, John Peters; Editor, Carol Besler

JOURNALISM

Actualité Canada (Published by News Canada Inc.), #606, 366 Adelaide St. West, Toronto ON M5V 1R9 – 416/599-9900; Fax: 416/599-9700 – Mensuel; français – Éditeur, Rodney N. Morris; Rédactrice, Linda Kroboth

Media, Carleton University, St. Patrick's Bldg., Rm. 316B, 1125 Colonel By Drive, Ottawa ON K1S 5B6 – 613/233-2801; Fax: 613/233-3904; Email: cf408@freenet.carleton.ca – Publisher, Robert Roth; Editor, David McKie

News Canada (Published by News Canada Inc.), #606, 366 Adelaide St. West, Toronto ON M5V 1R9 – 416/599-9900; Fax: 416/599-9700 – Monthly – Publisher, Rodney Morris; Editor, Linda Kroboth

Press Review, PO Box 368, Stn A, Toronto ON M5W 1C2 – 416/368-0512; Fax: 416/366-0104 – Circ.: 15,000; 4 times a year – Publisher & Editor, B.M. Cassidy

Ryerson Review of Journalism, School of Journalism, Ryerson Polytechnic University, 350 Victoria St., Toronto ON M5B 2K3 – 416/979-5319 – 2 times a year – Editor, Lynn Cunningham

Sources, #109, 4 Phipps St., Toronto ON M4Y 1J5 – 416/964-7799; Fax: 416/964-8763; Email: sources@sources.com; URL: Http://www.sources.com – Circ.: 14,000; 2 times a year – Publisher, Barrie Zwicker; Editor, Kate MacDougall

LANDSCAPING

Espaces Verts, 1320, boul St-Joseph, Québec PQ G2K 1G2 – 418/628-8690; Fax: 418/628-0524; 1-800-463-1576 Toll Free – 7 fois par an; français – Éditeur, François Bernatchez; Rédacteur en chef, François Bertrand

GreenMaster (Published by Kenilworth Publishing), #201, 27 West Beaver Creek, Richmond Hill ON L4B 1M8 – 905/771-7333; Fax: 905/771-7336 – 6 times a year – Publisher, Jim Davidson

Horticulture Review: The Voice of Landscape Ontario (Published by Landscape Ontario Horticultural Trades Association), 7856 Fifth Line South, RR#4, Stn Main, Milton ON L9T 2X8 – 905/875-1805; Fax: 905/875-0183 – Monthly – Publisher, Rita Weedenburg; Editor, Linda Erskine; Circulation Manager, Crispin Co

Hortwest, c/o British Columbia Nursery Trades Association, #101, 5830 - 176A St., Surrey BC V3S 4E3 – 604/574-7772; Fax: 604/574-7773; Email: info@bcnta.nwave.com – Circ.: 1,250; 6 times a year – Managing Editor, Jane Stock

Landmark (Published by Charlton Communications), #1000, 1777 Victoria Ave., Regina SK S4P 4K5 – 306/584-1000; Fax: 306/584-2824 – Circ.: 15,680; 6 times a year – Publisher, Mary-Lynn Charlton; Editor, Tom Steve

Landscape Trades (Published by Landscape Ontario Horticultural Trades Association), 7856 Fifth Line South, RR#4, Stn Main, Milton ON L9T 2X8 – 905/875-1805; Fax: 905/875-0183 – Circ.: 7,890; 9 times a year – Publisher, Rita Weedenburg; Editor, Linda Erskine; Circulation Manager, Crispin Co

Prairie Landscape Magazine (Published by OT Communications), #600, 237 - 8th Ave. SE, Calgary AB T2G 5C3 – 403/264-3270; Fax: 403/264-3276; Email: biclions.com – Circ.: 1,100; 6 times a year – Editor, Nigel Bowles

Québec Vert (Published by Éditions Versicolores inc.), 1320, boul St-Joseph, Québec PQ G2K 1G2 – 418/628-8690; Fax: 418/628-0524; 1-800-463-1576 Toll Free – 8 fois par an; français – Éditeur, François Bernatchez

Turf & Recreation, 123B King St., Delhi ON N4B 1X9 – 519/582-8873; Fax: 519/582-8877 – Circ.: 14,000; 7 times a year – Publisher, Bart Crandon; Editor, Michael Jiggens

LAUNDRY & DRY CLEANING

Fabricare Canada (Published by CTJ-Inc.), 1, rue Pacifique, Ste-Anne-de-Bellevue PQ H9X 1C5 – 514/457-2347; Fax: 514/457-2147 – 6 times a year – Publisher, Gillian Crosby; Editor, Marcia Todd

LEATHER

Luggage, Leathergoods & Accessories (Published by Laurentian Technomedia Inc./Laurentian Media), 501 Oakdale Rd., North York ON M3N 1W7 – 416/746-7360; Fax: 416/746-1421; Email: lmi@inforamp.net – Circ.: 5,100; 4 times a year – Publisher, Tony Muccilli; Editor, Bruce Etheridge; Circulation Manager, Pauline White

LEGAL

The Advocate, Vancouver Bar Association, 4765 Pilot House Rd., West Vancouver BC V7W 1J2 – 604/925-2122; Fax: 604/925-2065 – Circ.: 9,900; 6 times a year – Editor, Thomas S. Woods, QC; Circulation Manager, Gillian Roberts

Canadian Bar Review, c/o Canadian Bar Association, #902, 50 O'Connor St., Ottawa ON K1P 6L2 – 613/237-2925; Fax: 613/237-0185; Email: info@cba.org, editor.cba@anb.ca – Circ.: 35,525; Quarterly; English & French – Editor-in-Chief, Prof. Edward Veitch; Circulation Manager, Monique Cassidy

Canadian Lawyer, 240 Edward St., Aurora ON L4G 3S9 – 905/841-6480; Fax: 905/841-5078 – Circ.: 28,300; 10 times a year – Publisher, Stuart Morrison; Executive Editor, D. Michael Fitz-James

Digest Business & Law Journal, 826 Erin St., Winnipeg MB R3G 2W4 – 204/775-8918; Fax: 204/788-4322 – Circ.: 1,600; Weekly – Publisher, Walter Bowden; Editor, Frank Chalmers

Le Journal Barreau, 445, boul St-Laurent, Montréal PQ H2Y 3T8 – 514/954-3439; Fax: 514/954-3451 – 20 fois par an; français – Éditeur, Léon Bébard; Rédacteur, Jocelyne Duverger

Law Now, 11019 - 90 Ave., Edmonton AB T6G 1A6 – 403/492-1751; Fax: 403/492-6180; Email: pmagnan@gpu.srv.ualberta.ca; URL: http://www.extension.ualberta.ca/lawnow/ – Circ.: 3,000; 6 times a year – Publisher, Lois Gander; Editor, Marsha Mildon

Law Times, 240 Edward St., Aurora ON L4G 3S9 – 905/841-6481; Fax: 905/841-5078 – Circ.: 14,000; 43 times a year – Stuart Morrison; Managing Editor, Beth Marlin

The Lawyers Weekly (Published by Butterworths), 75 Clegg Rd., Markham ON L6G 1A7 – 905/479-2665, 1-800-668-6481; Fax: 905/479-3758; Email: tlw@butterworths.ca – Circ.: 7,000; 48 times a year – Publisher, Don Brillinger; Managing Editor, Beverley Spencer; Circulation Controller, Kim Rattray

McGill Law Journal, McGill Law Journal Inc., c/o Faculty of Law, McGill University, 3644 Peel St., Montréal PQ H3A 1W9 – 514/874-9038; Fax: 514/874-0679; Email: mlj@lsa.lan.mcgill.ca – Circ.: 1,468; 4 times a year; English & French – Managing Editor,

Michael F.E. Akkani; Editor-in-Chief, Mary-Pat Cornier

Le Monde Juridique, 7423, de Fougeray, Anjou PQ H1K 3K2 – 514/353-3549; Fax: 514/353-4159 – 12 fois par an; français – Éditeur/Rédacteur, André Gagnon

National, c/o Canadian Bar Association, #902, 50 O'Connor St., Ottawa ON K1P 6L2 – 613/237-2925; Fax: 613/237-0185; Email: info@cba.org; URL: http://cba.org/abc – Circ.: 35,500; 7 times a year; English & French – Publisher, Jim Hall; Editor, J. Stuart Langford; Circulation Manager, Monique Cassidy

The Ontario Reports (Published by Butterworths), 75 Clegg Rd., Markham ON L6G 1A7 – 905/479-2665; Fax: 905/479-3758 – Circ.: 27,000; Weekly – Editor, Anne Eichenberg

Osgoode Hall Law Journal, c/o York University, 4700 Keele St., North York ON M3J 1P3 – 416/736-5354; Fax: 416/736-5736; URL: http://www.yorku.ca/faculty/osgoode/ohlj/ohljhome.htm – Circ.: 1,500; 4 times a year, plus index; English or French – Editor, John D. McCamus

Toronto Legal Directory, University of Toronto Press, 10 St. Mary St., Toronto ON M4Y 2W8 – 416/978-2239, ext.245; Fax: 416/978-4738 – Circ.: 6,500; Annually, Feb. – Editor, Elizabeth Lumley

LIGHTING

Eclairage Plus (Published by Groupe Constructo), #200, 1500, boul Jules-Poitras, Saint-Laurent PQ H4N 1X7 – 514/745-5720; Fax: 514/339-2267 – 4 fois par an; français – Éditeur, Guy Choinière; Rédacteur, Johanne Rouleau

Lighting Magazine (Published by Kerrwil Publications Ltd.), 395 Matheson Blvd. East, Mississauga ON L4Z 2H2 – 905/890-1846; Fax: 905/890-5769 – Circ.: 7,488; 6 times a year – Publisher, Gary A. Dugan; Editor, Bryan S. Rogers

MACHINERY MAINTENANCE

Machinery & Equipment MRO (Published by Southam Magazine Group), 1450 Don Mills Rd., Don Mills ON M3B 2X7 – 416/445-6641; Fax: 416/442-2214; Email: broebuck@southam.ca; URL: http://www.southam.com/b1-5-4.html – Circ.: 22,000; 6 times a year – Publisher, Peter Helston; Editor, William Roebuck; Circulation Manager, Diane Rakoff

MATERIALS HANDLING & DISTRIBUTION

Materials Management & Distribution (Published by Maclean Hunter Publishing), 777 Bay St., Toronto ON M5W 1A7 – 416/596-5000; Fax: 416/596-5554 – Circ.: 19,000; Monthly – Editor, Robert Robertson

MEDICAL

L'Actualité Médicale (Published by Maclean Hunter Publishing), 1001, boul de Maisonneuve ouest, Montréal PQ H3A 3E1 – 514/843-2542; Fax: 514/845-2063 – 44 fois par an; français – Éditeur, Jacques Lafontaine; Rédactrice en chef, Danièle Rudel-Tessier

The Alberta Doctors' Digest, Alberta Medical Association, 12230 - 106 Ave. NW, Edmonton AB T5N 3Z1 – 403/482-2626; Fax: 403/482-5445; Email: dms@amda.ab.ca; URL: http://www.amda.ab.ca – Circ.: 5,600; 10 times a year – Editor, Dr. Gerald L. Higgins

Annals of the Royal College of Physicians & Surgeons of Canada, Royal College of Physicians & Surgeons of Canada, 774 Promenade Echo Dr., Ottawa ON K1S 5N8 – 613/730-6200; Fax: 613/730-8830; Email: john.last@rcpsc.edu – Circ.: 29,000; 8 times a year; English & French – Editor, Dr. John Last, 613/730-6236; Associate Editor, Lynne Quon-Mak

British Columbia Medical Journal, c/o BC Medical Association, #115, 1665 West Broadway, Vancouver BC V6J 5A4 – 604/736-5551; Fax: 604/733-7317; Email: cupton@bcma.bc.ca; 1-800-972-2262 Toll Free (BC) – Circ.: 8,000; Monthly – Editor, James A. Wilson, M.D.; Kashmira Suraliwalla

CAEP/ACMU Communiqué (Published by Canadian Medical Association), 1867 Alta Vista Dr., Ottawa ON K1G 3Y6 – 613/731-9331; Fax: 613/523-0937; Email: pubs@cma.ca – Circ.: 1,800; 4 times a year – Editor, Robert Street, M.D.

Canadian Association of Radiologists Journal (Published by Canadian Medical Association), 1867 Alta Vista Dr., Ottawa ON K1G 3Y6 – 613/731-9331; Fax: 613/523-0937; Email: pubs@cma.ca; URL: http://www.cma.ca/journals/carj – Circ.: 1,800; Bi-monthly; English & French – Editor, Dr. A. Dale Vellet

Canadian Family Physician, College of Family Physicians of Canada, 2630 Skymark Ave., Mississauga ON L4W 5A4 – 905/629-0900; Fax: 905/629-0893; Email: national postoffice pek@cfpc.attmail.com – Circ.: 33,000; Monthly – Editor-in-Chief, Dr. Tony Reid; Managing Editor, Primrose Ketchum

Canadian Journal of Allergy & Immunology (Published by Medicopea International Inc.), #300, 3333, boul Cote-Vertu, Saint-Laurent PQ H4R 2N1 – 514/331-4561; Fax: 514/336-1129 – Circ.: 3,600; 6 times a year – Publisher, Lawrence Goldstein; Circulation Manager, Mary Di Lemme

Canadian Journal of Anaesthesia, c/o Canadian Anaestists' Society, #208, 1 Eglinton Ave. East, Toronto ON M4P 3A1 – 416/480-0602; Fax: 416/480-0320; Email: cas@multinet.org – Circ.: 5,000; Monthly – Editor, Dr. David R. Bevan; Circulation Manager, Lisa McNeill

Canadian Journal of Cardiology (Published by Pulsus Group Inc.), 2902 South Sheridan Way, Oakville ON L6J 7L6 – 905/829-4770; Fax: 905/829-4799; Email: pulsus@pulsus.com; URL: http://www.pulsus.com.home.htm – Circ.: 16,000; Monthly – Publisher, Robert B. Kalina; Editor, Dr. R. Beamish

The Canadian Journal of Clinical Pharmacology (Published by Pulsus Group Inc.), 2902 South Sheridan Way, Oakville ON L6J 7L6 – 905/829-4770; Fax: 905/829-4799 – Circ.: 20,000; 4 times a year; English with French abstracts – Publisher, Robert J. Kalina; Editor, Dr. Neil Shear

Canadian Journal of Continuing Medical Education (Published by STA Communications Inc.), #306, 955, boul Saint-Jean, Pointe-Claire PQ H9R 5K3 – 514/695-7623; Fax: 514/695-8554 – Circ.: 35,065; Monthly – Publisher, Robert E. Passaretti; Editor, Monica Matys; Circulation Manager, Gail Gafka

Canadian Journal of Dermatology (Published by Rodar International Inc.), 47 Hymus Blvd., Pointe-Claire PQ H9R 4T2 – 514/697-7738; Fax: 514/697-4114 – Circ.: 9,300; 6 times a year – Publisher, Bob Fauteux; Managing Editor, Terry O'Shaughnessy

The Canadian Journal of Diagnosis (Published by STA Communications Inc.), #306, 955, boul Saint-Jean, Pointe-Claire PQ H9R 5K3 – 514/695-7623; Fax: 514/695-8554 – Circ.: 34,270; Monthly – Publisher, Robert Passaretti; Editor, Tracy Schuppli; Circulation Manager, Gail Gafka

Canadian Journal of Gastroenterology (Published by Pulsus Group Inc.), 2902 South Sheridan Way, Oakville ON L6J 7L6 – 905/829-4770; Fax: 905/829-4799 – Circ.: 17,000; 8 times a year – Publisher, Robert B. Kalina; Co-Editor, Dr. A.B.R. Thomson; Co-Editor, Dr. C.N. Williams

Canadian Journal of Infectious Diseases (Published by Pulsus Group Inc.), 2902 South Sheridan Way, Oakville ON L6J 7L6 – 905/829-4770; Fax: 905/829-4799; Email: pulsus@pulsus.com; URL: http://www.plusus.com.home.htm – Circ.: 7,500; 6 times a year – Publisher, Robert B. Kalina; Editor, Dr. L.E. Nicolle

Canadian Journal of Medical Laboratory Science, Cdn. Society of Laboratory Technologists, PO Box 2830, Stn LCD 1, Hamilton ON L8N 3N8 – 905/528-8642; Fax: 905/528-4968 – Circ.: 18,500; 4 times a year; English & French editions – Publisher, Kurt H. Davis

Canadian Journal of Medical Radiation Technology, Canadian Assn. of Medical Radiation Technologists, #601, 294 Albert St., Ottawa ON K1P 6E6 – 613/234-0012; Fax: 613/234-1097 – Circ.: 10,000; 4 times a year; English & French – Director of Communications, Steven Brasier; Registrar, Norma Saunders

Canadian Journal of Neurological Sciences, #810, 906 - 12 Ave. SW, Calgary AB T2R 1K7 – 403/229-9575; Fax: 403/229-1661; Email: cjns@canjhe.ugo.sci.org – Circ.: 1,600; 4 times a year; English & French – Publisher, Sally Gregg; Editor, James A. Sharpe, M.D.; Circulation Manager, Pam Edwards

The Canadian Journal of Occupational Therapy, Carleton Technology & Training Ctr., Carleton University Campus, #3400, 1125 Colonel By Dr., Ottawa ON K1S 5R1 – 613/523-2268; Fax: 613/523-2552 – Circ.: 6,000; 5 times a year plus Feb. conference supplement; English & French – Editor, Geraldine Moore

Canadian Journal of Ophthalmology, Canadian Ophthalmological Society, #610, 1525 Carling Ave., Ottawa ON K1Z 8R9 – 8 times a year – Editor, Dr. B.J. MacInnis

Canadian Journal of Pediatrics (Published by Rodar International Inc.), 47 Hymus Blvd., Pointe-Claire PQ H9R 4T2 – 514/697-7738; Fax: 514/697-4114; Email: cjo.cancer.ctrl@sympatico.ca – 10 times a year – Publisher, Bob Fauteux; Managing Editor, Jefferey Price

The Canadian Journal of Plastic Surgery (Published by Pulsus Group Inc.), 2902 South Sheridan Way, Oakville ON L6J 7L6 – 905/829-4770; Fax: 905/829-4799 – Circ.: 5,000; 4 times a year; English with French abstracts – Publisher, Robert B. Kalina; Editor, Dr. P. Wyshynski

Canadian Journal of Psychiatry, Cdn. Psychiatric Assn., #200, 237 Argyle St., Ottawa ON K2P 1B8 – 613/234-2815; Fax: 613/234-9857; URL: http://www.medical.org – Circ.: 3,300; 10 times a year – Editor, Dr. Q. Rae-Grant; Circulation Manager, Christy Bradnock Paddick

Canadian Journal of Public Health, Canadian Public Health Association, #400, 1565 Carling Ave., Ottawa ON K1Z 8R1 – 613/725-3769; Fax: 613/725-9826 – Circ.: 3,000; Bi-monthly; English & French – Editor, Dr. Richard Mathias; Circulation Manager, Ellan McWeeny

Canadian Journal of Rehabilitation, University of Alberta, Faculty of Rehabilitation Medicine, Edmonton AB T6G 2G4 – 403/492-1734; Fax: 403/492-1626; Email: cjrehab@gpu.srv.ualberta.ca – Circ.: 350; 4 times a year; ISSN 0828-0827 – Editor, Dr. Hy Day

Canadian Journal of Respiratory Therapy (Published by Canadian Medical Association), 1867 Alta Vista Dr., Ottawa ON K1G 3Y6 – 613/731-9331; Fax: 613/523-0937; Email: pubs@cma.ca; URL: http://www.cma.ca/journals/cjrt – Circ.: 2,800; 4 times a year – Editor, Dr Norman Tiffin

Canadian Journal of Surgery (Published by Canadian Medical Association), 1867 Alta Vista Dr., Ottawa ON K1G 3Y6 – 613/731-9331; Fax: 613/523-0937; Email: pubs@cma.ca; URL: http://www.cma.ca/journals/cjs – Circ.: 3,100; 6 times a year; English & French – Co-Editor, R.G. Keith; Co-Editor, J.L. Meakins

Canadian Journal of Women's Health Care (Published by Rodar International Inc.), 47 Hymus Blvd., Pointe-Claire PQ H9R 4T2 – 514/697-7738; Fax: 514/697-4114; Email: cjo.cancer.ctrl@sympatico.ca – Circ.: 17,000; 6 times a year – Publisher, Bob Fauteux; Managing Editor, Terry O'Shaughnessy

Canadian Medical Association Journal (Published by Canadian Medical Association), 1867 Alta Vista Dr., Ottawa ON K1G 3Y6 – 613/731-9331; Fax: 613/523-0937; Email: pubs@cma.ca; URL: http://www.cma.ca/journals/cmaj – Circ.: 58,500; 24 times a year; English & French – Editor, John Hoey, M.D.

Canadian Respiratory Journal (Published by Pulsus Group Inc.), 2902 South Sheridan Way, Oakville ON L6J 7L6 – 905/829-4770; Fax: 905/829-4799 – Circ.: 15,000 – Publisher, Robert B. Kalina; Editor, Dr. N. James

The Chronicle of Skin & Allergy (Published by Chronicle Information Research Ltd.), 1270 The Queensway, Toronto ON M8Z 1S3 – 416/503-3957; Fax: 416/503-4118 – Circ.: 6,119; 9 times a year – Publisher, Mitchell Shannon

The Chronicle of Urology & Sexual Medicine (Published by Chronicle Information Research Ltd.), 1270 The Queensway, Toronto ON M8Z 1S3 – 416/503-3957; Fax: 416/503-4118 – Circ.: 3,860; 6 times a year – Publisher, Mitchell Shannon

Clinical and Investigative Medicine (Published by Canadian Medical Association), 1867 Alta Vista Dr., Ottawa ON K1G 3Y6 – 613/731-9331; Fax: 613/523-0937; Email: pubs@cma.ca; URL: http://www.cma.ca/journals/cim – Circ.: 1,000; 6 times a year – Acting Editor, David S. Rosenblatt, M.D.

Le Clinicien (Published by STA Communications Inc.), #306, 955, boul Saint-Jean, Pointe-Claire PQ H9R 5K3 – 514/695-7623; Fax: 514/695-8554 – Tirage: 12,984; Mensuel; français – Éditeur, Robert Passaretti; Rédactrice, Anne Jamez; Directrice de tirage, Gail Gafka

CMA News (Published by Canadian Medical Association), 1867 Alta Vista Dr., Ottawa ON K1G 3Y6 – 613/731-9331; Fax: 613/523-0937; Email: pubs@cma.ca; URL: http://www.cma.ca/news/menu.htm – Circ.: 46,000; Monthly; English & French – Publisher, Jill Rafuse; Editor, Patrick Sullivan

Dermatology Times of Canada (Published by CTC Communications Corp.), 1382 Hurontario St., Mississauga ON L5G 3H4 – 905/278-6700; Fax: 905/278-4850 – Circ.: 5,313; 9 times a year – Managing Editor, Ian J.S. Moore

Doctor's Review (Published by Parkhurst Publishing), 400 McGill St., 3rd Fl., Montréal PQ H2Y 2G1 – 514/397-8833; Fax: 514/397-0228 – Circ.: 37,370; Monthly – Publisher, David Elkins; Editor, Madeleine Partous; Circulation Manager, Yvonne MacKinder

Family Practice (Published by Thomson Healthcare Communications), #200, 1120 Birchmount Rd., Scarborough ON M1K 5G4 – 416/750-8900; Fax: 416/751-8126 – Circ.: 24,800; 32 times a year – Publisher, Frank B. Lederer; Editor, John Shaughnessy

FMWC Newsletter (Published by Canadian Medical Association), 1867 Alta Vista Dr., Ottawa ON K1G 3Y6 – 613/731-9331; Fax: 613/523-0937; Email: pubs@cma.ca – Circ.: 750; 4 times a year – Editor, Catherine Younger-Lewis, M.D.

Germs & Ideas (Published by Pulsus Group Inc.), 2902 South Sheridan Way, Oakville ON L6J 7L6 – 905/829-4770; Fax: 905/829-4700 – Circ.: 3,200; 4 times a year – Publisher, Robert Kalina

Health Economics, #200, 1120 Birchmount Rd., Scarborough ON M1K 5G4 – 416/750-8900; Fax: 416/751-8126 – 6 times a year – Publisher, Frank B. Lederer

Journal of the Canadian Chiropractic Association, 1396 Eglinton Ave. West, Toronto ON M6C 2E4 – 416/781-5656; Fax: 416/781-7344 – Circ.: 4,500; 4 times a year – Editor, Dr. Allan Gotlib

Journal of Otolaryngology, Decker Periodicals, 4 Hughson Ct. South, 4th Fl., Hamilton ON L8N 3J1 – 905/522-7017; Fax: 905/522-7839 – Circ.: 1,191; 6 times a year – Publisher, Brian Decker; Editor, Dr. Peter Alberti

Journal of Psychiatry & Neuroscience, Canadian Psychiatric Assn., #200, 237 Argyle Ave., Ottawa ON K2P 1B8 – 613/234-2815; Fax: 613/234-9857; URL: http://www.medical.org – Circ.: 2,439; 5 times a year – Editor, Y.D. Lapierre

Journal of Rheumatology, Journal of Rheumatology Publishing Co. Ltd., #115, 920 Yonge St., Toronto ON M4W 3C7 – 416/967-5155; Fax: 416/967-7556; Email: jrheum@inforamp.net; URL: http://biginc.on.ca/jrheum – Circ.: 3,500; Monthly – Editor-in-Chief, Duncan A. Gordon

Journal SOGC, Ribsome Communications, 50A Hillholm Rd., Toronto ON M5P 1N5 – 416/322-5510; Fax: 416/322-5263; Email: ribosome@inforamp.net – Circ.: 14,000; Monthly; English with French abstracts – Publisher, Adrian Stein; Editor, Dr. Patrick J. Taylor; Circulation Manager, Kismet Goodbaum

Le Médecin du Québec, Quebec Federation of General Practitioners, #1000, 1440 St. Catherine St. West, Montréal PQ H3G 1R8 – 514/878-1911; Fax: 514/878-4455; Email: med.que@fmoq.org – Tirage: 17,800; Mensuel; français – Rédactuer, Georges Boileau, M.D.; Circulation Manager, Marie-Hélène Wolford

The Medical Post (Published by Maclean Hunter Publishing), 777 Bay St., Toronto ON M5W 1A7 – 416/596-5748; Fax: 416/593-3177; Email: dmarston@hookup.net; URL: http://www.io.org/~cjaimet/outlook/outlook.html – 44 times a year; also The Medical Post Outlook (7 times a year; URL: http://www.mdlink.com/mdlink) – Editor in Chief, Derek Cassels

Medical Scope Monthly Journal, 1015 Hooke Rd., Edmonton AB T5A 4K5 – 403/456-9547; Fax: 403/476-1363; Email: medial@planet.con.net – Editor, Patrick McLaughlin

Medical Society of Nova Scotia News, Medical Society of Nova Scotia, 5 Spectacle Lake Dr., Dartmouth NS B3B 1X7 – 902/468-1866; Fax: 902/468-6578 – Circ.: 2,400; Monthly – Editor, Camille Sobrian

Medicine North America (Published by Parkhurst Publishing), 400 McGill St., 3rd Fl., Montréal PQ H2Y 2G1 – 514/397-9393; Fax: 514/397-0228 – Circ.: 30,000; Monthly – Publisher, David Elkins; Editor, Catherine Addleman; Circulation Manager, Yvonne MacKinder

Mediscan (Published by Canadian Medical Association), 1867 Alta Vista Dr., Ottawa ON K1G 3Y6 – 613/731-9331; Fax: 613/523-0937; Email: pubs@cma.ca; URL: http://www.ualberta.ca/~cfms/ – Circ.: 5,500; 3 times a year – Editor, Toni Barnes; Editor, Sanjeev Dutta; Editor, Jeff Pasenau

The Nutrition Post (Published by Maclean Hunter Publishing), 777 Bay St., Toronto ON M5W 1A7 – 416/596-5726; Fax: 416/593-3177 – Circ.: 40,000; 4 times a year – Publisher, John Milne; Editor, Diana Swift

L'Omnipraticien, Thomas Healthcare Communications, #906, 1425, boul René-Lévesque ouest, Montréal PQ H3G 1T7 – 514/878-2595; Fax: 514/878-8270 – Tirage: 10,600; 24 fois par an – Éditeur, Marc Thibodeau; Rédactrice, Lyse Savard

Ontario Medical Review, Ontario Medical Assn., #300, 525 University Ave., Toronto ON M5G 2K7 – 416/599-2580; Fax: 416/599-9309; Email: kim-secord@oma.org; URL: http://www.oma.org – Circ.: 26,000; Monthly – Editor, Jeff Henry; Circulation Manager, Kim Secord

The Ontario Psychologist, #221, 730 Yonge St., Toronto ON M4Y 2B7 – 416/961-5552; Fax: 416/961-5516 – Circ.: 1,500; 6 times a year – Editor, Dr. Donald Rudzinski; Publication Manager, Sandra Traub

Ophthalmic Practice (Published by Medicopea International Inc.), #300, 3333, boul Cote-Vertu, Saint-Laurent PQ H4R 2N1 – 514/331-4561; Fax: 514/336-1129 – Circ.: 1,200; 6 times a year – Publisher, Lawrence Golstein; Editor, Dr. Leon Solomon; Circulation Manager, Mary Di Lemme

L'Optométriste, #740, 1265, rue Berri, Montréal PQ H2L 4X4 – 514/288-6272; Fax: 514/288-7071 – 6 fois par an; français – Jean-Pierre Lagacé

Paediatrics & Child Health (Published by Pulsus Group Inc.), 2902 South Sheridan Way, Oakville ON L6J 7L6 – 905/829-4770; Fax: 905/829-4799 – Circ.: 16,500; 4 times a year – Publisher, Robert Kalina

Pain Research Management (Published by Pulsus Group Inc.), 2902 South Sheridan Way, Oakville ON L6J 7L6 – 905/829-4770; Fax: 905/829-4799 – Circ.: 20,000; 4 times a year – Publisher, Robert Kalina

The Parkhurst Exchange (Published by Parkhurst Publishing), 400 McGill St., 3rd Fl., Montréal PQ H2Y 2G1 – 514/397-8833; Fax: 514/397-0228 – Circ.: 37,000 – Publisher, David Elkins; Editor, Catherine Addleman; Circulation Manager, Yvonne MacKinder

Patient Care (Published by Thomson Healthcare Communications), #200, 1120 Birchmount Rd., Scarborough ON M1K 5G4 – 416/750-8900; Fax: 416/751-8126 – Circ.: 27,000; 10 times a year – Publisher, Peter Craig; Editor, Vil Meere; Circulation Manager, Denise Brearley

Perspectives in Cardiology (Published by STA Communications Inc.), #306, 955, boul Saint-Jean, Pointe-Claire PQ H9R 5K3 – 514/695-7623; Fax: 514/695-8554 – Circ.: 15,269; 9 times a year – Editor, Keff Alexander; Circulation Manager, Gail Gafka

Physiotherapy Canada, 890 Yonge St., 9th Fl., Toronto ON M4W 3P4 – 416/924-5312; Fax: 416/924-7335 – 4 times a year – Editor, Diane Charter

Practical Optometry (Published by Medicopea International Inc.), #300, 3333, boul Cote-Vertu, Saint-Laurent PQ H4R 2N1 – 514/331-4561; Fax: 514/336-1129; Email: Medicopea@NETAXIS.qc.ca – Circ.: 2,700; 6 times a year – Publisher, Lawrence Goldstein; Editor, Dr. John Jantzi; Circulation Manager, Mary Di Lemme

Prairie Medical Journal, Rm S105, Faculty of Medicine, University of Manitoba, 750 Bannatyne Ave., Winnipeg MB R3E 0W3 – 204/789-3660; Fax: 204/774-4120 – Circ.: 2,500; 4 times a year – Editor, Dr. I. Carr

Stitches: The Journal of Medical Humour (Published by Stitches Publishing Inc.), 16787 Warden Ave., Newmarket ON L3Y 4W1 – 905/853-1884; Fax: 905/853-6565; Email: jcocker@medhumor.com – Circ.: 43,000; 11 times a year – Publisher, Dr. John Cocker; Editor/Associate Publisher, Simon Hally

Strategy (Published by Canadian Medical Association), 1867 Alta Vista Dr., Ottawa ON K1G 3Y6 – 613/731-9331; Fax: 613/523-0937; Email: pubs@cma.ca – Circ.: 46,000; Monthly – Managing Editor, Matthew Bonsall

The University of Toronto Medical Journal, Medical Science Bldg., #2141, 1 King's College Circle, Toronto ON M5S 1A8 – 416/978-8730; Fax: 416/971-2163 – 3 times a year – Co-Editor, Mark Korman; Co-Editor, Mary Nagai

Urology Times of Canada, CTC Communications Corp., 1382 Hurontario St., Mississauga ON L5G 3H4 – 905/278-6700; Fax: 905/278-4850; Email: derm.urol@sympatico.ca – Circ.: 4,800; 6 times a year – Associate Publisher, Marg Churchill; Editor, Ian Moore; Circulation Manager, Olga Murphy

Wellness MD, 344 Edgeley Blvd., Unit 16-17, Concord ON L4K 4B7 – 905/738-9086; Fax: 905/738-4994 – 6 times a year – Executive Publisher, Peter Calluori; Editor, Gordon Bagley

METALWORKING

Canadian Machinery & Metalworking (Published by Maclean Hunter Publishing), 777 Bay St., Toronto ON M5W 1A7 – 416/596-2667, 5714; Fax: 416/596-

5881 – Circ.: 16,600; 8 times a year – Publisher, Glen Alton; Editor, Mike Overment

Metalworking Production & Purchasing (Published by Action Communications Inc.), 135 Spy Ct., Markham ON L3R 5H6 – 905/477-3222; Fax: 905/477-4320; Email: MPP@ACTIONCOM.COM – Circ.: 18,200; 6 times a year – Publisher, Michael L. Doody

MILITARY

Canadian Defence Quarterly (Published by Baxter Publishing Co), 310 Dupont St., Toronto ON M5R 1V9 – 416/968-7252; Fax: 416/968-2377; URL: http://www/baxter.net – Circ.: 5,958; 4 times a year; English & French – Publisher, David McClung; Editor, Alex Morrison

Canadian Defence Review (Published by Synergistic Publications), 132 Adrian Cres., Markham ON L3P 7B3 – 905/472-2801; Fax: 905/472-3091 – Circ.: 11,000; 4 times a year – Publisher, Peter A. Kitchen; Editor, Nick Stephens; Circulation Manager, Dianne Osadchuk

Garrison, HQ LFCA, 5775 Yonge St., PO Box 17, North York ON M2M 4J7 – 416/733-4681; Fax: 416/363-3944 – Circ.: 11,000; 8 times a year – Editor-in-Chief, Col. G.B. Mitchell; Editor, Capt. R.N. Kennedy, 416/733-4681, ext.5501

MINING

Canadian Mines Handbook (Published by Southam Magazine Group), 1450 Don Mills Rd., Don Mills ON M3B 2X7 – 416/445-6641; Fax: 416/442-2272 – Annually, July – Publisher, Doug Donnelly; Editor, Diane Giancola; Circulation Manager, Aileen Manganaro

Canadian Mining Journal (Published by Southam Magazine Group), 1450 Don Mills Rd., Don Mills ON M3B 2X7 – 416/445-6641; Fax: 416/442-2181; URL: http://www.southam.co.b1-6-1.html – Circ.: 8,513; 6 times a year – Publisher, Craig Coulter; Editor, Patrick Whiteway; Circulation Manager, Cindi Holder

CIM Bulletin (Published by Canadian Inst. of Mining, Metallurgy & Petroleum), #1210, 3400, boul de Maisonneuve ouest, Montréal PQ H3Z 3B8 – 514/939-2710; Fax: 514/939-2714 – Circ.: 11,000; 10 times a year – Publisher, Yvan Jacques; Editor, Perla Gantz; Circulation Manager, Lynda Battista

CIM Directory (Published by Canadian Inst. of Mining, Metallurgy & Petroleum), #1210, 3400, boul de Maisonneuve ouest, Montréal PQ H3Z 3B8 – 514/939-2710; Fax: 514/939-2714; Email: Publications@osinet.net – Circ.: 10,531 – Publisher, Yvan Jacques; Editor, Perla Gantz; Circulation Manager, Lynda Battista

CIM Reporter (Published by Canadian Inst. of Mining, Metallurgy & Petroleum), #1210, 3400, boul de Maisonneuve ouest, Montréal PQ H3Z 3B8 – 514/939-2710; Fax: 514/939-2714 – Circ.: 6,583 – Publisher, Yvan Jacques; Editor, Perla Gantz; Circulation Manager, Lynda Battista

The Financial Post Survey of Mines & Energy Resources (Published by Financial Post Co. Ltd.), 333 King St. East, Toronto ON M5A 4N2 – 416/350-6500, 1-800-661-7678; Fax: 416/350-6501; Email: fpdg@fpdata.finpost.com – Circ.: 4,300; Annually, Aug. – Editor, Robert Pearson

Mining Review, Naylor Communications, 100 Sutherland Ave., Winnipeg MB R2W 3C7 – 204/947-0222; Fax: 204/204-947-2047 – 4 times a year – Editor, Wendy Melanson

Mining Sourcebook (Published by Southam Magazine Group), 1450 Don Mills Rd., Don Mills ON M3B 2X7 – 416/445-6641; Fax: 416/442-2272 – Annually, Nov. – Associate Publisher, Craig Coulter; Group Publisher, Doug Donnelly

The Northern Miner (Published by Southam Magazine Group), 1450 Don Mills Rd., Don Mills ON M3B 2X7 – 416/445-6641; Fax: 416/442-2175; Email: tnm@southam.ca; URL: http://www.northernminer.com/ – Circ.: 25,000; Weekly – Publisher, Doug Donnelly; Executive Publisher, John Cooke; Circulation Manager, Aileen Manganaro

The Prospector Exploration & Investment Bulletin, K.W. Publishing Ltd., 1268 West Pender St., Vancouver BC V6E 2S8 – 604/688-2271; Fax: 604/688-2038; Email: prospector@info_mine.com; URL: http://www.info_mine.com/daily.news/ – Circ.: 25,000; 6 times a year – Publisher, Darlene Liboiron; Editor, A. Leonard

MOTOR TRUCKS & BUSES

Atlantic Trucking (Published by Naylor Communications Ltd.), 920 Yonge St., 6th Fl., Toronto ON M4W 3C7 – 416/961-1028; Fax: 416/924-4408 – 4 times a year – Publisher, Robert Thompson; Editor, Kim Laudrum

Camionneurs, Publications media plus inc., #114, 4058, rue Mouselet, Montréal-Nord PQ H1H 2C5 – 514/328-3485; Fax: 514/328-3131; Email: ccqi@camionquevec.com – Tirage: 12,186; 8 fois par an; français – Éditeur, Jean Raymond

L'Echo du Transport (Published by Les Éditions Bomart ltée), #103, 7493 Trans Canada Hwy., St-Laurent PQ H4T 1T3 – 514/337-9043; Fax: 514/337-1862 – Tirage: 19,517; 10 fois par an; français – Rédacteur, Steve Bouchard; Directrice de tirage, Linette Marsolais

Manitoba Ship-by-Truck Directory (Published by Craig Kelman & Associates Ltd.), #3C, 2020 Portage Ave., Winnipeg MB R3J 0K4 – 204/885-7798; Fax: 204/889-3576 – Circ.: 1,000; Annually – Editor, Al Harris

Motor Truck (Published by Southam Magazine Group), 1450 Don Mills Rd., Don Mills ON M3B 2X7 – 416/445-6641; Fax: 416/442-2213; URL: http://www.southam.com/b1-10-1.html – Circ.: 29,000; Monthly – Publisher, John T. McClung; Executive Editor, Barry Holmes

Today's Trucking, New Communications Group Inc., 130 Belfield Rd., Etobicoke ON M9W 1G1 – 416/614-2200; Fax: 416/614-8861 – Circ.: 29,400; 10 times a year – Publisher, James B. Glionna; Editor, Rolf Lockwood

Truck News (Published by Southam Magazine Group), 1450 Don Mills Rd., Don Mills ON M3B 2X7 – 416/442-2062; Fax: 416/442-2092; Email: jsmith@southam.ca; URL: http://www.southam.com/b1-10-2.html – Circ.: 39,872; Monthly – Publisher, Ted Light; Editor, John G. Smith; Circulation Manager, Keith Fulford

Truck West, c/o Southam Business Communications Inc., #9, 1555 Dublin Ave., Winnipeg MB R3E 3M8 – 204/831-8814; Fax: 204/888-3853; URL: http://www.southam.com/b1-10-3/html – Circ.: 20,300; Monthly – Publisher, Patrick Munro

Truck World, HB Publishers Ltd., #11, 106 - 14th St. East, North Vancouver BC V7L 2N3 – 604/984-2002; Fax: 604/984-2820 – Circ.: 14,600; 6 times a year – Publisher/Editor, Paul Young; Managing Editor, Ken Barnsohn

La Voix du vrac, #215, 710, rue Bouvier, Québec PQ G2J 1C2 – 418/623-7923; Fax: 418/623-0448 – Tirage: 9,000; 6 fois par an; français – Éditeur, André Lavoie

Western Canada Highway News (Published by Craig Kelman & Associates Ltd.), #3C, 2020 Portage Ave., Winnipeg MB R3J 0K4 – 204/885-7798; Fax: 204/889-3576 – Circ.: 4,000; 4 times a year – Publisher, Craig Kelman; Editor, T. Ross

MUSIC & MUSIC TRADES

The Canadian Music Educator, Canadian Music Educators' Assn., 43 Victoria Hill, Sydney NS B1R 1N9 – 902/567-2398; Fax: 902/564-0123; Email: efavaro@fox.nstn.ca; URL: http://www.stemnet.nf.ca/~barobert/.cmea/cmea.html – Circ.: 2,000; 5-7 times a year; includes the CMEA Newsletter – Editor, Dr. Brian Roberts

Canadian Music Trade (Published by Norris-Whitney Communications Inc.), #7, 23 Hannover Dr., St Catharines ON L2W 1A3 – 905/641-3471; Fax: 905/641-1648 – Circ.: 3,516; 6 times a year – Publisher, Jim Norris

Professional Sound (Published by Norris-Whitney Communications Inc.), #7, 23 Hannover Dr., St Catharines ON L2W 1A3 – 905/641-1512; Fax: 905/641-1648 – Circ.: 12,700; 4 times a year – Publisher, Jim Norris

RPM Weekly, 6 Brentcliffe Rd., Toronto ON M4G 3Y2 – 416/425-0257; Fax: 416/425-8629 – Weekly – Publisher, Walt Grealis

NURSING

A.A.R.N Newsletter, Alberta Association of Registered Nurses, 11620 - 168 St., Edmonton AB T5M 4A6 – 403/451-0043; Fax: 403/452-3276; Email: jalberta@mail.compusmart.ab.ca – Circ.: 26,000; 11 times a year – Editor/Information Officer, Evelyn Henderson

Canadian Journal of Cardiovascular Nursing, c/o Canadian Council of Cardiovascular Nurses, #200, 160 George St., Ottawa ON K1N 9M2 – 613/241-4361; Fax: 613/241-3278 – Annual

The Canadian Nurse, Canadian Nurses' Assn., 50 Driveway, Ottawa ON K2P 1E2 – 613/237-2133; Fax: 613/237-3520 – Circ.: 110,000; 11 times a year; English & French – Editor-in-Chief, Heather Broughton

Canadian Oncology Nursing Journal, Pappin Communications, 84 Isabella St., Pembroke ON K8A 5S5 – 613/735-0952; Fax: 613/735-7983 – Circ.: 1,000; 4 times a year – Editor, Beverley Page

Canadian Operating Room Nursing Journal, c/o Health Media, 14453 - 29A Ave., Surrey BC V4A 9K8 – 604/535-7933; Fax: 604/535-9000 – Circ.: 2,800; 4 times a year – Publisher, Ronald Forster; Executive Editor, Agnes Forster

The Care Connection, Bldg. 4, #200, 5025 Orbitor Dr., Mississauga ON L4W 4Y5 – 905/602-4664; Fax: 905/602-4666 – Circ.: 5,500; 4 times a year – Editor, Kelly Goodine

Concern, 2066 Retallack St., Regina SK S4T 7X5 – 306/757-4643; Fax: 306/525-0849 – Circ.: 10,000; 6 times a year – Editor, J. Johnson

L'Infirmière du Québec, 4200, boul Dorchester ouest, Montréal PQ H3Z 1V4 – 514/935-2501; Fax: 514/935-2055 – Tirage: 67,186; 6 fois par an; français – Rédactrice, Diane Iezzi

Nursing B.C., 2855 Arbutus St., Vancouver BC V6J 3Y8 – 604/736-7331; Fax: 604/738-2272 – Circ.: 36,000; 5 times a year – Editor, Bruce Wells

Pre & Post Natal News (Published by Professional Publishing), 269 Richmond St. West, Toronto ON M5V 1X1 – 416/596-8680; Fax: 416/596-1991 – 3 times a year – Editor, Beverly Topping

The Registered Nurse (Published by Kenilworth Publishing), #201, 27 West Beaver Creek, Richmond Hill ON L4B 1M8 – 905/771-7333; Fax: 905/771-7336 – Circ.: 24,600; 6 times a year – Editor, Jeannine Pitt-Clark

Santé Québec, Ordre des infirmières & infirmiers auxiliaires du Québec, 531, rue Sherbrooke est, Montréal PQ H2L 1K2 – 514/282-9511; Fax: 514/282-0631 – Tirage: 23,000; 3 fois par an; français – Rédactrice, Madeleine Pelletier

OFFICE EQUIPMENT

COPA Conversation (Published by Canadian Office Products Association), #911, 1243 Islington Ave., Toronto ON M8X 1X9 – 416/239-2737; Fax: 416/239-1553 – 4 times a year – Publisher, James H. Preece; Editor, Darrell O. Townson

Canadian Almanac & Directory 1997

OPTICAL

Canadian Journal of Optometry, #301, 1785 Alta Vista Dr., Ottawa ON K1G 3Y6 – 613/738-4412; Fax: 613/738-7161 – 4 times a year – Medical Editor, Dr. Mitch Samek

Coup d'oeil, Martine Breton Communications, #206, 6955, boul Taschereau, Brossard PQ J4Z 1A7 – 514/462-2112; Fax: 514/462-3352 – Tirage: 2,737; 6 fois par an

Optical Prism, Vezcom Inc., 31 Hastings Dr., Unionville ON L3R 4Y5 – 905/475-9343; Fax: 905/477-2821; Email: vezina@hookup.net – Circ.: 7,500; 9 times a year – Editor, Allan K. Vezina

Vision Magazine (Published by August Communications Ltd.), #200, 388 Donald St., Winnipeg MB R3B 2J4 – 204/957-0265; Fax: 204/957-0217; Email: august@inforamp.net – Circ.: 3,000; 6 times a year; English & French – Publisher, Gladwyn Nickel; Editor, JoAnne Sommers

PACKAGING

Canadian Packaging (Published by Maclean Hunter Publishing), 777 Bay St., Toronto ON M5W 1A7 – 416/596-5744; Fax: 416/596-5810 – Circ.: 12,200; 11 times a year – Publisher, Stephen Dean; Editor, Douglas W. Faulkner, 416/596-5746

PAINT, FINISHES, COATINGS

Coatings (Published by Kay Publishing), #1, 406 North Service Rd. East, Oakville ON L6H 5R2 – 905/844-9773; Fax: 905/844-5672 – Circ.: 7,200; 6 times a year – Publisher & Editor, G. Barry Kay

PETROLEUM, OIL & GAS

Alberta Oil & Gas Directory (Published by Armadale Publications Inc.), PO Box 1193, Stn Main PO, Edmonton AB T5J 2M4 – 403/429-1073; Fax: 403/425-5844 – Annually – Editor, Cal Kelly

Canada-Z Oil Gas Mining Directory (Published by Armadale Publications Inc.), PO Box 1193, Stn Main PO, Edmonton AB T5J 2M4 – 403/429-1073; Fax: 403/425-5844 – Annually – Editor, Cal Kelly

Canadian Oilfield Gas Plant Atlas (Published by June Warren Publishing Ltd.), 9915 - 56 Ave., Edmonton AB T6E 5L7 – 403/944-9333; Fax: 403/944-9500 – Circ.: 1,547; Annually – Publisher, Colin Either

Canadian Oilfield Service & Supply Directory (Published by June Warren Publishing Ltd.), 9915 - 56 Ave., Edmonton AB T6E 5L7 – 403/944-9333; Fax: 403/944-9500 – Annually – Publisher, Colin Either

Canadian Oil Register, #300, 999 - 8 St. SW, Calgary AB T2R 1N7 – 403/244-6111; Fax: 403/245-8666 – Annually, Sept. – Doreen McArthur

Canadian Resources (published by Charlton Communications), #1000, 1777 Victoria Ave., Regina SK S4P 4K5 – 306/584-1000; Fax: 306/584-2824 – Circ.: 6,000; 4 times a year – Publisher, Mary-Lynn Charlton

Energy Processing/Canada (Published by Northern Star Communications Ltd.), 900 - 6 Ave. SW, 5th Fl., Calgary AB T2P 3K2 – 403/263-6881; Fax: 403/263-6886; Email: nstar@cadvision.com – Circ.: 6,420; 6 times a year – Publisher, Scott Jeffrey; Editor, Alister Thomas; Circulation Manager, Kim Glonnie

The Journal of Canadian Petroleum Technology, The Petroleum Society, #320, 101 - 6th Ave. SW, Calgary AB T2KP 3P4 – 403/237-5112; Fax: 403/262-4792; Email: petsoc@canpic.ca; URL: http://www.canpic.ca/PETSOC – Circ.: 5,600; 10 times a year – Editor, Catherine Buchanan; Circulation Manager, Wes Scott

Oil & Gas Inquirer (Published by June Warren Publishing Ltd.), 9915 - 56 Ave., Edmonton AB T6E 5L7 – 403/944-9333; Fax: 403/944-9500 – Monthly – Publisher, Colin Either

Oil Patch Magazine, Master Publications, 17560 - 107 Ave., 2nd Fl., Edmonton AB T5S 1E9 – 403/486-1295; Fax: 403/484-0884 – 6 times a year – Publisher/Senior Editor, L.M. Hyman

Oilweek (Published by Maclean Hunter Publishing Ltd.), #2450, 101 - 6th Ave. SW, Calgary AB T2P 3P4 – 403/266-8700; Fax: 403/266-6634 – Circ.: 7,500; Weekly – Publisher, Philip J. Boyd; Editor, David Coll

Propane-Canada (Published by Northern Star Communications Ltd.), 900 - 6 Ave. SW, 5th Fl., Calgary AB T2P 3K2 – 403/263-6881; Fax: 403/263-6886 – Circ.: 5,500; 6 times a year – Publisher, Scott Jeffrey; Editor, Alister Thomas; Circulation Manager, Eric Anderson

The Roughneck (Published by Northern Star Communications Ltd.), 900 - 6 Ave. SW, 5th Fl., Calgary AB T2P 3K2 – 403/263-6881; Fax: 403/263-6886 – Circ.: 5,700; Monthly – Publisher, Scott Jeffrey; Editor, Alister Thomas; Circulation Manager, Eric Anderson

PHOTOGRAPHY

Photonews & Electronic Imaging, BCS Communications Ltd., 101 Thorncliffe Park Dr., Toronto ON M4H 1M2 – 416/421-7944; Fax: 416/421-0966; Email: gunter.ott@canrem.com – Circ.: 30,500 – Editor, Gunter Ott

Photo Retailer (Published by Les Publications Apex inc.), 185, rue St-Paul, Québec PQ G1K 3W2 – 418/692-2110; Fax: 418/692-3392 – Circ.: 5,000; 3 times a year – Publisher, Curtis J. Sommerville; Editor, Don Long; Circulation Manager, Jeffery A. Sommerville

Professional Photographers of Canada (Published by Craig Kelman & Associates Ltd.), #3C, 2020 Portage Ave., Winnipeg MB R3J 0K4 – 204/885-7798; Fax: 204/889-3576 – Circ.: 1,600; 6 times a year; English & French – Editor, Jim E. Watson

Professional Photographers of Canada Directory (Published by Craig Kelman & Associates Ltd.), #3C, 2020 Portage Ave., Winnipeg MB R3J 0K4 – 204/885-7798; Fax: 204/889-3576 – Circ.: 3,500; Annually, April – Editor, Jim E. Watson

PLASTICS

Canadian Plastics (Published by Southam Magazine Group), 1450 Don Mills Rd., Don Mills ON M3B 2X7 – 416/445-6641; Fax: 416/442-2213; Email: cmacdonald@southam.ca; URL: http://www.southam.com/magazines/plastics.html – Circ.: 10,100; 8 times a year – Publisher, Judith Nancekivell, 416/442-2067; Editor, Michael LeGault

Canadian Plastics Directory & Buyer's Guide (Published by Southam Magazine Group), 1450 Don Mills Rd., Don Mills ON M3B 2X7 – 416/445-6641; Fax: 416/442-2213; Email: cmacdonald@southam.ca; URL: http://www.southam.com/magazines/plastics.html – Circ.: 10,100 – Publisher, Judith Nancekivell; Editor, Cindy Macdonald; Circulation Manager, Diane Rakoff

Plastics Business (Published by Southam Magazine Group), 1450 Don Mills Rd., Don Mills ON M3B 2X7 – 416/445-6641; Fax: 416/442-2213; Email: cmacdonald@southam.ca; URL: http://www.southam.com/magazines/plastics.html – Circ.: 10,900; 4 times a year – Publisher, Judith Nancekivell; Editor, Michael LeGault; Circulation Manager, Diane Rakoff

Plastics in Canada Magazine (Published by Kay Publishing), #1, 406 North Service Rd. East, Oakville ON L6H 5R2 – 905/844-9773; Fax: 905/844-5672 – Circ.: 10,145; 6 times a year – Publisher, Larry Bonikowsky

Plastics Industry Reference Guide & Sourcebook (Published by Kenilworth Publishing), #201, 27 West Beaver Creek, Richmond Hill ON L4B 1M8 – 905/771-7333; Fax: 905/771-7336 – Circ.: 1,020; Annually, July – Publisher, James Davidson

POLICE

Blue Line Magazine, Unit 12A, Hwy. 7 East, Markham ON L3R 1N1 – 905/640-3048; Fax: 905/640-7547 – Circ.: 10,000; 10 times a year – Publisher, Morley S. Lymburner

News & Views, Metropolitan Toronto Police Assn., 180 Yorkland Blvd., North York ON M2J 1R5 – 416/491-4301; Fax: 416/494-4948 – Circ.: 9,245; Monthly – Editor, Elizabeth Alexander

The Police Governor (Published by Naylor Communications Ltd.), 920 Yonge St., 6th Fl., Toronto ON M4W 3C7 – 416/961-1028; Fax: 416/924-4408 – 2 times a year – Publisher, Robert Thompson; Editor, Kim Laudrum

Scarlet & Gold, 1215 Alder Bay Walk, Vancouver BC V6H 3T6 – 604/738-4423; Fax: 604/681-5230 – Circ.: 2,000; Annually – Editor & Publisher, J. Murphy

POWER & POWER PLANTS

Nuclear Canada Yearbook, #725, 144 Front St., Toronto ON M5J 2L7 – 416/977-6152; Fax: 416/979-8356 – Circ.: 3,000; Annually, May – Publications Editor, Colin Hunt

PRINTING

Canadian Printer (Published by Maclean Hunter Publishing), 777 Bay St., Toronto ON M5W 1A7 – 416/596-5781; Fax: 416/596-5965 – Circ.: 13,000; 10 times a year – Publisher, Susan Leggat; Editor, Stephen Forbes

Estimators' & Buyers' Guide (Published by North Island Sound Ltd.), #8, 1606 Sedlescomb Dr., Mississauga ON L4X 1M6 – 905/625-7070; Fax: 905/625-4856 – Annually, Feb. – Publisher/Owner, Sandy Alexander Donald

The Graphic Monthly (Published by North Island Sound Ltd.), #8, 1606 Sedlescomb Dr., Mississauga ON L4X 1M6 – 905/625-7070; Fax: 905/625-4856 – Circ.: 10,088; 6 times a year – Publisher/Owner, Sandy Alexander Donald; Managing Editor, Nancy Clark

Le Maître Imprimeur, #13, 255, Montée Seraphin, Ste-Adèle PQ J0R 1L0 – 514/227-7300; Fax: 514/229-4710 – Tirage: 4,100; Mensuel; français – Éditeur, Jules Côte; Rédacteur, Gerard Thérien

Masthead (Published by North Island Sound Ltd.), #8, 1606 Sedlescomb Dr., Mississauga ON L4X 1M6 – 905/625-7070; Fax: 905/625-4856; Email: the-editor@biginc.ca; URL: http://www.the-wire.com/bishop/biginc.html – Circ.: 4,300; 10 times a year; ISSN 0832-512X – Publisher, Alexander Donald; Acting Editor, Kirsteen MacLeod

PrintAction (Published by Youngblood Publishing), #1204, 2240 Midland Ave., Scarborough ON M1R 4R8 – 416/299-6007; Fax: 416/299-6674 – Circ.: 11,500; Monthly – Publisher, John Galbraith; Editor, Julian Mills

Production Imprimée, Éditions info presse inc., #400, 4316, boul St-Laurent, Montréal PQ H2W 1Z3 – 514/842-5873; Fax: 514/842-2422 – 6 fois par an – Éditeur, Bruno Gautier; Rédacteur, Patrick Pierra

The Publisher, #206, 90 Eglinton Ave. East, Toronto ON M4P 2Y3 – 416/482-1090; Fax: 416/482-1908; Email: ccna@sentex.net; URL: http://www.sentex.net/~ccna/ – Circ.: 2,100; 10 times a year – Publisher, Michael Anderson; Editor, Dave De Jong, 905/336-3801

Second Impressions, 35 Mill Dr., St. Albert AB T8N 1J5 – 403/458-9889; Fax: 403/458-9839; Email: simttm@supernet.ab.ca – Circ.: 6,650; 6 times a year – Publisher, Loretta Puckrin

PRODUCT ENGINEERING & DESIGN

Design Engineering (Published by Maclean Hunter Publishing), 777 Bay St., Toronto ON M5W 1A7 – 416/596-5819; Fax: 416/593-3193 – Circ.: 19,000; 8

times a year – Publisher, Frank Ragan; Editor, James Barnes

Design Product News (Published by Action Communications Inc.), 135 Spy Ct., Markham ON L3R 5H6 – 905/477-3222; Fax: 905/477-4320; Email: DPN@ACTIONCOM.COM – Circ.: 19,158; 6 times a year – Publisher, Michael Doody; Editor, Mike Edwards; Circulation Manager, Carole Halse

PULP & PAPER

Canadian Papermaker (Published by Maclean Hunter Publishing), 777 Bay St., Toronto ON M5W 1A7 – 416/596-5787; Fax: 416/593-3193 – Circ.: 38,490; 12 times a year – Publishers, Philip J. Boyd, 416/596-5518

Forêt Conservation, 175, rue St-Jean, 4 étage, Québec PQ G1R 1N4 – 418/529-2542; Fax: 418/529-3021 – Tirage: 6,500; 6 fois par an; français – Rédacteur, Pierre Dubois

Journal des pâtes et papiers, #1000, 1001, boul de Maisonneuve ouest, Montréal PQ H3A 3E1 – 514/845-5141; Fax: 514/845-4393 – 4 fois par an; français

Mill Product News (Published by Baum International Media), #203, 2323 Boundary Rd., Vancouver BC V5M 4V8 – 604/298-3004; Fax: 604/298-3966 – Circ.: 18,000; 6 times a year – Publisher, Heri R. Baum; Editor, Toni Dabbs

Les Papetières du Québec (Published by Southam Magazine Group), #410, 3300, boul Côte Vertu, Saint-Laurent PQ H4R 2B7 – 514/339-1399, 1-800-363-1327; Fax: 514/339-1396; URL: http://www.southam.com/b1-7-1.html – Tirage: 3,733; 4 fois par an; français – President, W. Mann; Rédacteur, Jaclin Ouellet

Pulp & Paper Canada (Published by Southam Magazine Group), #410, 3300, boul Côte Vertu, Saint-Laurent PQ H4R 2B7 – 514/339-1399; Fax: 514/339-1396; URL: http://www.southam.com/b1-7-2.html – Circ.: 9,600; Monthly; aslo Annual Directory (Nov.) – Publisher, Mark Yerbury; Editor, Graeme Rodden

PURCHASING

Canadian Purchaser (Published by Canadian Office Products Association), #911, 1243 Islington Ave., Toronto ON M8X 1X9 – 416/239-2737; Fax: 416/239-1553 – Circ.: 20,000; 4 times a year – Publisher, James H. Preece

Canadian Trade Index, c/o Alliance of Manufacturers & Exporters Canada, 75 International Blvd., 4th Fl., Etobicoke ON M9W 6L9 – 416/798-8000; Fax: 416/798-8050; Email: orders@allianceonline.com – Annually, March – Editor, Fran Chung

Fraser's Canadian Trade Directory (Published by Maclean Hunter Publishing), 777 Bay St., Toronto ON M5W 1A7 – 416/596-5086; Fax: 416/593-3201 – Circ.: 8,000; Annually, May – Publisher, Bert Bauer

Modern Purchasing (Published by Maclean Hunter Publishing), 777 Bay St., Toronto ON M5W 1A7 – 416/596-5792, 5704; Fax: 416/596-5866 – Circ.: 20,000; 10 times a year – Publisher, Tim Dimopoulos; Editor, Joe Terrett

RADIO, TV, APPLIANCES & VIDEO

Marketnews, Bomar Publishing Inc., 364 Supertest Rd., 2nd Fl., North York ON M3J 2M2 – 416/667-9945; Fax: 416/667-0609; Email: rfranner@lcan.net – Circ.: 9,800; Monthly – Publisher, Bob Grierson; Editor, Robert Franner; Circulation Manager, Elizabeth Solara

Première: Video Magazine, 1314 Britannia Rd. East, Mississauga ON L4W 1C8 – 905/564-1033; Fax: 905/564-3398 – Circ.: 7,900; 12 times a year – Editor, Salah Bachir

REAL ESTATE

Canadian Realtor News, Canadian Real Estate Association, #1600. 344 Slater St., Ottawa ON K1R 7Y3 – 613/237-7111; Fax: 613/234-2567; Email: info@crea.ca; URL: Http://www.crea.ca – Circ.: 72,000; Monthly; separate English & French editions – Editor, Jim McCarthy

REM: Canada's Magazine for Real Estate Professionals, House Magazine Inc., 115 Thorncliffe Park Dr., Toronto ON M4H 1M1 – 416/425-3509 – Circ.: 33,000; 12 times a year – Publisher, Heino Molls; Editor, Jim Adair

The Western Investor, Westward Publications, #1200, 609 Granville St., Vancouver BC V7Y 1G5 – 604/669-8500, 1-800-661-6988; Fax: 604/669-2154 – Circ.: 12,000; Monthly – Publisher, Tracy Chysik; Editor, Susan MacDonald; Circulation Manager, Pam Withers

RENTAL EQUIPMENT & LEASING EQUIPMENT

Canadian Rental Service (Published by AIS Communications Ltd.), 145 Thames Rd. West, Exeter ON NOM 1S3 – 519/235-2400; Fax: 519/235-0798 – Circ.: 3,830; 8 times a year – Publisher, Peter Phillips; Editor, Peter Darbishire; Circulation Manager, Jan Jeffery

RETAILING

Canadian Retailer, Retail Council of Canada, 121 Bloor St. East, 12th Fl., Toronto ON M4W 3M5 – 416/922-6678; Fax: 416/922-8011 – Circ.: 9,500; 6 times a year – Publisher, Diane J. Brisebois

SCIENCE, RESEARCH & DEVELOPMENT

Biochemistry & Cell Biology (Published by National Research Council of Canada - Research Journals), Montréal Rd., Ottawa ON K1A 0R6 – 613/993-9085; Fax: 613/952-7656; Email: Hoda.Jabbour@NRC.CA; URL: http://www.cisti.nrc.ca/cisti/journals.rj.html – Circ.: 1.085; Bi-monthly; English & French – Editor, D.L. Brown; Editor, M. Tenniswood

Canadian Geotechnical Journal (Published by National Research Council of Canada - Research Journals), Montréal Rd., Ottawa ON K1A 0R6 – 613/993-9085; Fax: 613/952-7656; Email: Hoda.Jabbour@NRC.ca; URL: http://www/nrc.ca/cisti/journals/ – Circ.: 2,553; 6 times a year; English & French – Editor, Dr. R.J. Mitchell

Canadian Journal of Analytical Sciences & Spectroscopy (Published by Polyscience Publications Inc.), 44 Seize Arpents, PO Box 148, Morin-Heights PQ J0R 1H0 – 514/226-5870; Fax: 514/226-5866; URL: http://www.ietc.ca/polysci/ – Circ.: 1,000; 6 times a year; English & French – Editor, Dr. Ian Butler

Canadian Journal of Botany (Published by National Research Council of Canada - Research Journals), Montréal Rd., Ottawa ON K1A 0R6 – 613/993-9085; Fax: 613/952-7656; Email: Hoda.Jabbour@NRC.CA; URL: http://www.cisti.nrc.ca/cisti/journals/rj.html – Circ.: 1,460; Monthly; English & French – Editor, Dr. B.P. Dancik

Canadian Journal of Chemistry (Published by National Research Council of Canada - Research Journals), Montréal Rd., Ottawa ON K1A 0R6 – 613/993-9085; Fax: 613/953-7656 – Monthly; English & French – Editor, T. Chivers

Canadian Journal of Civil Engineering (Published by National Research Council of Canada - Research Journals), Montréal Rd., Ottawa ON K1A 0R6 – 613/993-9085; Fax: 613/953-7656 – 6 times a year; English & French – Editor, Dr. M. Isaacson

Canadian Journal of Earth Sciences (Published by National Research Council of Canada - Research Journals), Montréal Rd., Ottawa ON K1A 0R6 – 613/993-9085; Fax: 613/953-7656; Email: Hoda.Jabbour@NRC.CA; URL: http://www.cisti.nrc.ca/cisti/journals/rj.html – Circ.: 1,830; Monthly; English & French – Editor, Dr. B.P. Dancik

Canadian Journal of Forest Research (Published by National Research Council of Canada - Research Journals), Montréal Rd., Ottawa ON K1A 0R6 – 613/993-9085; Fax: 613/953-7656 – Monthly; English & French – Editor, Dr. W.M. Cheliak

Canadian Journal of Microbiology (Published by National Research Council of Canada - Research Journals), Montréal Rd., Ottawa ON K1A 0R6 – 613/993-9085; Fax: 613/953-7656 – Monthly; English & French – Co-Editor, L.M. Nelson

Canadian Journal of Physics (Published by National Research Council of Canada - Research Journals), Montréal Rd., Ottawa ON K1A 0R6 – 613/993-9085; Fax: 613/953-7656 – Monthly; English & French – Editor, Dr. Donald Betts

Canadian Journal of Physiology & Pharmacology (Published by National Research Council of Canada - Research Journals), Montréal Rd., Ottawa ON K1A 0R6 – 613/993-9085; Fax: 613/953-7656; Email: Hoda.Jabbour@NRC.CA; URL: http://www.cisti.nrc.ca/cisti/journals/rj.html – Circ.: 980; Monthly; English & French – Editor, Dr. B.P. Dancik

Canadian Journal of Zoology (Published by National Research Council of Canada - Research Journals), Montréal Rd., Ottawa ON K1A 0R6 – 613/993-9085; Fax: 613/953-7656 – Monthly; English & French – Editor, Dr. K.G. Davey; Editor, Dr. A.S.M. Saleuddin

Genome (Published by National Research Council of Canada - Research Journals), Montréal Rd., Ottawa ON K1A 0R6 – 613/993-9085; Fax: 613/953-7656; Email: Hoda.Jabbour@NRC.CA; URL: http://www.cisti.nrc.ca/cisti/journals.rj.html – Circ.: 1,270; 6 times a year; English & French – Editor, Dr. Peter Moens

LAB Business, #202, 30 East Beaver Creek Rd., Richmond Hill ON L4B 1J2 – 905/886-5040; Fax: 905/886-6615 – Circ.: 43,303; 4 times a year – Publisher, Christopher Forbes

Laboratory Buyers Guide (Published by Southam Magazine Group), 1450 Don Mills Rd., Don Mills ON M3B 2X7 – 416/445-6641; Fax: 416/442-2201 – Annually – Publisher/Editor, Rita Tate, 416/442-2052

Laboratory Product News (Published by Southam Magazine Group), 1450 Don Mills Rd., Don Mills ON M3B 2X7 – 416/445-6641; Fax: 416/442-2201; URL: http://www.southam.com/b1-5-3.html – Circ.: 18,000; 6 times a year – Publisher/Editor, Rita Tate, 416/442-2052

The Microscopical Society of Canada Bulletin, Microscopical Society of Canada, Dept. of Pathology, McMaster Univ., 1200 Main St., Hamilton ON L8N 3Z5 – 905/525-9140, ext.22496; Email: cemerson@kean.ucs.mun.ca – Circ.: 650; 4 times a year; ISSN 0383-1825 – Editor, Carolyn J. Emerson, 709/737-7515

OSMT Advocate, #600, 234 Eglinton Ave. East, Toronto ON M4P 1K5 – 416/485-6768; Fax: 416/672-0244 – Circ.: 4,000; 4 times a year – Executive Editor, Sam Laldin

Physics in Canada, #112, McDonald Bldg., 150 Louis Pasteur Ave., Ottawa ON K1N 6N5 – 613/237-3392; Fax: 613/238-1677; Email: cap@physics.uottawa.ca – Circ.: 2,000; 6 times a year; French & English – Publisher, F.M. Ford; Editor, J.S.C. McKee

Research Money (Published by Evert Communications Ltd.), 1296 Carling Ave., 2nd Fl., Ottawa ON K1Z 7K8 – 613/728-4621; Fax: 613/728-0385 – 20 times a year – Publisher, Gordon D. Hutchison; Editor, Mark Henderson; Circulation Manager, Carole Jeffrey

SECURITY

Canadian Security, c/o Security Publishing, 46 Crockford Blvd., Scarborough ON M1R 3C3 – 416/755-4343; Fax: 416/755-7487 – Circ.: 11,900; 7 times a year – Publisher, Maureen Percival; Editor, Robert R. Robinson; Circulation Manager, Lisa Drummond

SHIPPING, MARINE

British Columbia Commercial Marine Directory & Buyers Guide (Published by Westcoast Publishing Ltd), 1496 - 72nd Ave. West, Vancouver BC V6P 3C8 – 602/266-7433; Fax: 602/263-8620; Email: marinedir@west-coast.com – Annually (Nov.)

Canadian Sailings incorporating Seaports and the Shipping World, 4634 St. Catherine St. West, Montréal PQ H3Z 1S3 – 514/934-0373; Fax: 514/934-4708 – Circ.: 10,000; Weekly – Publisher, Brian O'N. Gallery; Editor, Leo Ryan; Circulation Manager, Diane Lazar

Captain Lillie's Coast Guide & Radiotelephone Directory (Published by Progress Publishing Co Ltd.), #200, 1865 Marine Dr., West Vancouver BC V7V 1J7 – 604/922-6717; Fax: 604/922-1739 – Biennially – Publisher, M.D. McLellan

Great Lakes Navigation (Published by Canadian Marine Publications), #512, 1434, rue Ste-Catherine ouest, Montréal PQ H3G 1R4 – 514/861-6715; Fax: 514/861-0966 – Annually, March – Publisher, John W. McManus; Editor, Megan D. Perkins; Circulation Manager, Marilyn Bélanger

Harbour & Shipping (Published by Progress Publishing Co Ltd.), #200, 1865 Marine Dr., West Vancouver BC V7V 1J7 – 604/922-6717; Fax: 604/922-1739 – Monthly – President/Publisher, M.D. McLellan; Editor, Liz Bennett

Montréal Port Guide & Transportation Register, 1056, ch du Golf, Nun's Island, Verdun PQ H3E 1H4 – 514/766-8650; Fax: 514/766-5559 – Annually, May

Ports Annual (Published by Canadian Marine Publications), #512, 1434, rue Ste-Catherine ouest, Montréal PQ H3G 1R4 – 514/861-6715; Fax: 514/861-0966 – Annually, Aug. – Editor, Megan D. Perkins

SHOWS & EXHIBITIONS

Shows & Exhibitions (Published by Maclean Hunter Publishing), 777 Bay St., Toronto ON M5W 1A7 – 416/596-5862; Fax: 416/596-5158 – Circ.: 6,000; 2 times a year – Senior Group Publisher, Henry Beckman; Associate Publisher, Bruce D. Richards

SPORTING GOODS & RECREATIONAL EQUIPMENT

Camping Canada Dealer News, #306, 2585 Skymark Ave., Mississauga ON L4W 4L5 – 905/624-8218; Fax: 905/624-6764 – 4 times a year – Publisher, William E. Taylor; Editor, Diane Batten

Eté Contact (Published by Éditions Versicolores inc.), 1320, boul St-Joseph, Québec PQ G2K 1G2 – 418/628-8690; Fax: 418/628-0524 – 4 fois par an – Éditeur, François Bernatchez; Rédacteur, Caty Bérubé

Motorsport Dealer & Trade (Published by Turbopress Inc.), #3B, 86 Parliament St., Toronto ON M5A 2Y6 – 416/362-7966; Fax: 416/362-3950; Email: cyclecan@aol.com – Circ.: 3,500; 6 times a year – Publisher, Jean-Pierre Belmonte; Editor, David Martin

Pool & Spa Marketing, Hubbard Marketing & Publishing Ltd., 270 Esna Park Dr., Unit 12, Markham ON L3R 1H3 – 905/513-0090; Fax: 905/513-1377 – Circ.: 9,000; 7 times a year – Publisher, Richard Hubbard; Editor, David Barnsley

Sports Business (Published by Laurentian Technomedia Inc./Laurentian Media), 501 Oakdale Rd., North York ON M3N 1W7 – 416/746-7360; Fax: 416/746-1421; Email: lmi@inforamp.net – Circ.: 9,100; 5 times a year – Publisher, Tony Muccilli; Editor, Bruce Etheridge; Circulation Manager, Pauline White

SPORTS & RECREATION

Canadian Gaming & Fundraising Magazine, #10, 6 Nanne Walk, Elliot Lake ON P5A 1Z5 – 705/ 848-2832; Fax: 705/949-3079 – Circ.: 7,800; Monthly – Publisher/Editor, Thomas J. Turner

TELECOMMUNICATIONS

Canadian Communications Network Letter (Published by Evert Communications Ltd.), 1296 Carling Ave., 2nd Fl., Ottawa ON K1Z 7K8 – 613/728-4621; Fax: 613/728-0385 – 40 times a year – Publisher, Gordon D. Hutchison; Editor, Brant Scott; Circulation Manager, Carol Jeffrey

Canadian Communications Reports (Published by Evert Communications Ltd.), 1296 Carling Ave., 2nd Fl., Ottawa ON K1Z 7K8 – 613/728-4621; Fax: 613/728-0385 – 20 times a year – Publisher, Gordon D. Hutchison; Editor, Debbie Lawes; Circulation Manager, Carole Jeffrey

Canadian Telecom, The ABY Group, #1160, 36 Toronto St., Toronto ON M5C 2C5 – 416/359-2911; Fax: 416/359-9909 – Circ.: 5,520; 6 times a year – Publisher, John Burry

Wireless Telecom, #2004, 275 Slater St., Ottawa ON K1P 5H9 – 613/233-4888; Fax: 613/233-2032; Email: chopwood@cwta.ca; URL: http://www.cwta.ca – Circ.: 5,000 – Managing Editor, Catherine Hopwood

TEXTILES

Canadian Textile Journal (Published by CTJ-Inc.), 1, rue Pacifique, Ste-Anne-de-Bellevue PQ H9X 1C5 – 514/457-2347; Fax: 514/457-2147 – 7 times a year – Publisher, Gillian Crosby; Editor, Réginald Marchand

TOYS

Toys & Games (Published by Laurentian Technomedia Inc./Laurentian Media), 501 Oakdale Rd., Downsview ON M3N 1W7501 Oakdale Rd., North York ON M3N 1W7 – 416/746-7360; Fax: 416/746-1421 – Circ.: 6,300; 6 times a year – Publisher, Graham Kennedy; Editor, Lynn Winston

TRANSPORTATION, SHIPPING & DISTRIBUTION

Atlantic Transportation Journal (Published by NCC Specialty Publications), #107, 900 Windmill Rd., Dartmouth NS B3B 1P7 – 902/468-8027; Fax: 902/468-2425 – 4 times a year – Managing Editor, Ken Partridge

Canadian Customs Guide, Les Éditions adequate inc, #717, 117, rue Ste-Catherine ouest, Montréal PQ H3B 1H9 – 514/843-7660; Fax: 514/843-7174 – Circ.: 14,369; 6 times a year; English & French – Editor, Djamel Lazreg

Canadian Shipper (Published by Maclean Hunter Publishing), 777 Bay St., Toronto ON M5W 1A7 – 416/586-5000; Fax: 416/596-5158 – Circ.: 4,890; 6 times a year – Publisher, Warren Patterson, 416/596-5708; Editor, Robert Robertson

Canadian Transportation Logistics (Published by Southam Magazine Group), 1450 Don Mills Rd., Don Mills ON M3B 2X7 – 416/445-6641; Fax: 416/442-2214; URL: http://www.southam.com/b1-5-2.html – Circ.: 15,280; Monthly – Publisher, Ted McKnight, 416/442-2050; Editor, Bonnie Toews, 416/442-2228

L'Expéditeur (Published by Les Éditions Bomart ltée), H4T 1T3#103, 7493 Trans Canada Hwy., St-Laurent PQ H4T 1T3 – 514/337-9043; Fax: 514/337-1862 – Tirage: 10,828; 10 fois par an; français – Éditrice, Sophie Beaudoin; Directrice de tirage, Linette Marsolais

Guide du Transport par Camion (Published by Les Éditions Bomart ltée), #103, 7493 Trans Canada Hwy., St-Laurent PQ H4T 1T3 – 514/337-9043; Fax: 514/337-1862 – Annually, Nov.; French & English – Directrice de tirage, Linette Marsolais

Maritime Magazine (Published by Productions Maritimes), 175, rue Saint-Paul, Québec PQ G1K 3W2 – 418/692-3779; Fax: 418/692-5198 – Tirage: 5,700; 4 fois par an; français et anglais – Rédacteur, Pierre Terrien

Routes et Transports, A.Q.T.R., #100, 1595, rue Saint-Hubert, Montréal PQ H2L 3Z2 – 514/523-6444; Fax: 514/523-2666 – Tirage: 1,500; 4 fois par an; français – Directeur, Gérard Chagnon

TRAVEL

Bulletin Voyages, Distribution ACRA ltée, 78, boul St-Joseph ouest, Montréal PQ H2T 2P4 – 514/287-9773; Fax: 514/842-6180 – Tirage: 8,095; Hebdomadaire; français – Éditeur, Etienne Ozan-Groulx

Canadian Traveller, Altracs Publishing Inc., #157, 10551 Shellbridge Way, Richmond BC V6X 2W9 – 604/276-0818; Fax: 604/276-0843 – Circ.: 15,000; Monthly – Publisher, Susan Youle; Co-Editor, Ursula Retief

Canadian Travel Press (Published by Baxter Publishing Co), 310 Dupont St., Toronto ON M5R 1V9 – 416/968-7252; Fax: 416/968-2377; Email: ctp@baxter.net; URL: http://www.baxter.net – Circ.: 13,097; 46 times a year – Publisher, David McClung; Editor, Edith Baxter; Circulation Manager, Susan Bedder

Destinations Canada/USA (Published by Ruland Communications), 12 Lawton Blvd., Toronto ON M4V 1Z4 – 416/927-9129; Fax: 416/927-9118 – 5 times a year – Publisher, Joseph F. Ruland; Editor, Ulli Nadine Ruland

Excursions en Autocar (Published by Publicom inc.), #400, 1055, côte du Beaver Hall, CP 365, Montréal PQ H2Y 3H1 – 514/274-0004; Fax: 514/274-5884 – Tirage: 5,500; 10 fois par an; français – Éditeur, Guy J. Jonkman

GSA: The Travel Magazine for Western Canada, #209, 1015 Burrard St., Vancouver BC V6Z 1Y5 – 604/689-2909; Fax: 604/689-2989 – Circ.: 4,500; 24 times a year – Publisher, Frank Cumming; Editor, Lynda Cumming

Le Magazine L'agent de voyages inc., CP 38, Ville d'Anjou PQ H1K 4G5 – 514/881-9637; Fax: 514/881-2578; Email: plani@monde.com – Tirage: 7,000; 26 fois par an; français – Rédacteur en chef, Michel Villeneuve

Personnel Guide to Canada's Travel Industry (Published by Baxter Publishing Co), 310 Dupont St., Toronto ON M5R 1V9 – 416/968-7252; Fax: 416/968-2377 – Circ.: 4,500; 2 times a year

Rendez-Vous (Published by Baxter Publishing Co), 310 Dupont St., Toronto ON M5R 1V9 – 416/968-7252; Fax: 416/968-2377 – Annually, May

The Road Explorer (Published by Naylor Communications Ltd.), 920 Yonge St., 6th Fl., Toronto ON M4W 3C7 – 416/961-1028; Fax: 416/924-4408 – 2 times a year – Publisher, Robert Thompson; Editor, Kim Laudrum

Spa Destinations (Published by Publicom inc.), #400, 1055, côte du Beaver Hall, CP 365, Montréal PQ H2Y 3H1 – 514/274-0004; Fax: 514/274-5884 – Circ.: 20,500; Annually – Publisher, Guy J. Jonkman

Tourisme + (Published by Groupe Constructo), #200, 1500, boul Jules-Poitras, Saint-Laurent PQ H4N 1X7 – 514/745-5720; Fax: 514/339-2267 – Tirage: 6,882; 47 fois par an; français – Rédacteur en chef, Michel Villeneuve

Tours on Motorcoach (Published by Publicom inc.), #400, 1055, côte du Beaver Hall, CP 365, Montréal PQ H2Y 3H1 – 514/274-0004; Fax: 514/274-5884 – Circ.: 12,000; 10 times a year – Publisher, Guy J. Jonkman

Travel Courier (Published by Moving Publications Ltd.), 40 Upjohn Rd., Don Mills ON M3B 2W1 – 416/968-7252; Fax: 416/968-2377 – Circ.: 7,100; Weekly – Editor in Chief, Edith Baxter

Travelweek Bulletin, Concepts Travel Media Ltd., 282 Richmond St. East, Toronto ON M5A 1P4 – 416/365-1500; Fax: 416/365-1504; Email: travelwk@astral.magic.ca – Circ.: 10,000; 2 times a week – Publisher, Elga Mannik; Editor, Patrick Dineen

Voyage en Groupe, 425, rue Harris, Saint-Laurent PQ H4N 2G8 – 514/744-3867 – Tirage: 13,000; 6 fois par an; français – Éditeur & Rédacteur, Andre Quesnel

VENDING & VENDING EQUIPMENT

Canadian Coin Box Magazine (Published by NCC Publishing), 222 Argyle Ave., Delhi ON N4B 2Y2 – 519/582-2513; Fax: 519/582-4040 – Circ.: 1,921; 9 times a year – Publisher, David Douglas; Editor, Sandra L. Anderson-Lloy; Circulation Manager, Flo Jacques

Canadian Vending (Published by NCC Publishing), 222 Argyle Ave., Delhi ON N4B 2Y2 – 519/582-1513; Fax: 519/582-4040; URL: http://www.vendnet.com – Circ.: 2,108; 7 times a year – Publisher, David Douglas; Editor, Sandra L. Anderson-Lloy; Circulation Manager, Flo Jacques

VETERINARY

The Canadian Veterinary Journal, c/o Canadian Veterinary Medical Association, 339 Booth St., Ottawa ON K1R 7K1 – 613/236-1162; Fax: 613/236-9681; Email: jnlscuma@magi.com – Circ.: 5,000; Monthly; English & French – Editor, Dr. W.C.D. Hare; Manager, Journals, Kimberley Allen-McGill

Le Médecin Vétérinaire du Québec, Ordre des médecins vétérinaires du Québec, #200, 795, av du Palais, St-Hyacinthe PQ J2S 5C6 – 514/774-1427; Fax: 514/774-7635 – Tirage: 2,500; 4 fois par an; français – Rédacteur, Guy-Pierre Martineau, d.m.v.

Le Vétérinarius, #200, 795, av du Palais, St-Hyacinthe PQ J2S 5C6 – 514/774-1427; Fax: 514/774-7635 – 6 fois par an; français – Dr. Marcel Bouvier

WATER & WASTES TREATMENT

Canadian Environmental Protection (Published by Baum International Media), #203, 2323 Boundary Rd., Vancouver BC V5M 4V8 – 604/291-9900; Fax: 604/291-1906 – Circ.: 22,097; 9 times a year – Publisher, Englebert Baum; Editor, Dan Kennedy

Canadian Water Well (Published by AIS Communications Ltd.), 145 Thames Rd. West, Exeter ON N0M 1S3 – 519/235-2400; Fax: 519/235-0798 – Circ.: 4,040; 4 times a year – Publisher, Peter Phillips; Editor, Peter Darbishire; Circulation Manager, Jan Jeffery

Environmental Science & Engineering, Environmental Science & Engineering Publications Inc., 220 Industrial Pkwy. South, Unit 30, Aurora ON L4G 3V6 – 905/727-4666; Fax: 905/841-7271; Email: esemag@istar.ca; URL: http://www.ese.mag.com – Circ.: 19,062; 6 times a year; ISSN 0835-605X – Publisher & Editor, Tom Davey

Envirotech, Société Ecropolis inc., #200, 640, rue St-Paul ouest, Montréal PQ H3C 1L9 – 514/393-8862; Fax: 514/393-3568; Email: envirotec@citenet.net; URL: http://www.citenet.net/envirotech/ – Tirage: 9,000; 6 fois par an; français; supplement - Québec Environmental Industry Source Book – Éditeur & Rédacteur, Perry Nino

Hazardous Materials Directory, #200, 85 Somerset Ave., Toronto ON M6H 2R3 – 416/658-7519; Fax: 416/658-9708 – Circ.: 40,400; 2 times a year – Publisher/Editor, Matthew Keegan

Hazardous Materials Management (Published by CHMM Inc.), #4, 951 Denison St., Markham ON L3R 3W9 – 905/305-6155; Fax: 905/305-6255; Email: hazmatmg@inforamp.com; URL: http://www.hazmatmag.com – Circ.: 20,000; Bi-monthly - also annual Québec regional supplement in French; ISSN 0843-9303 – Publisher, Todd Latham; Editor, Guy Crittenden; Circulation Manager, Karen Bell

Maritime Provinces Water & Wastewater Report (Published by NCC Specialty Publications), #107, 900 Windmill Rd., Dartmouth NS B3B 1P7 – 902/468-8027; Fax: 902/468-2425 – 4 times a year

Recycling Product News, Baum Publications, 1625 Ingleton Ave., Burnaby BC V5C 4L8 – 604/291-9900; Fax: 604/291-1906 – Circ.: 14,700; 6 times a year – Publisher, Engelbert J. Baum; Editor, Dan Kennedy

Solid Waste Management (Published by CHMM Inc.), #4, 951 Denison St., Markham ON L3R 3W9 – 905/305-6155; Fax: 905/305-6255 – Circ.: 10,000; 6 times a year – Publisher, Todd Latham

Vecteur envrionnement, #220, 911, rue Jean-Talon est, Montréal PQ H2R 1V5 – 514/864-8085 – 6 fois par an; français – Éditeur, Christian Scott; Rédacteur en chef, Guy Giasson

Water & Pollution Control (Published by Zanny Ltd.), 11966 Woodbine Ave., Gormley ON L0H 1G0 – 905/887-5048; Fax: 905/887-0764 – 6 times a year

WELDING

Welding Canada (Published by Maclean Hunter Publishing), 777 Bay St., Toronto ON M5W 1A7 – 416/596-5713; Fax: 416/596-5881 – 6 times a year – Publisher, Glen Alton, 416/596-5000

WOODWORKING

2 x 4, Editions C.R. Inc., PO Box 1010, Victoriaville PQ G6P 8Y1 – 819/752-4243; Fax: 819/758-8812 – Circ.: 8,000; 5 times a year; English & French – Editor & Publisher, Claude Roy

Woodworking (Published by Action Communications Inc.), 135 Spy Ct., Markham ON L3R 5H6 – 905/477-3222; Fax: 905/477-4320; Email: WOO@ACTIONCOM.COM – Circ.: 11,000; 6 times a year; also Woodworking Sourcer (annually) – Publisher, R. Blair Tullis; Editor, Maurice Holtham; Circulation Manager, Connie Warren

CONSUMER MAGAZINES

AIRLINE INFLIGHT, TRAIN & BUS IN-TRANSIT

Above & Beyond, PO Box 2348, Yellowknife NT X1A 2P7 – 403/873-2299; Fax: 403/873-2295 – Circ.: 30,000; 4 times a year – Publisher & Editor, Annelies Pool

Canadian, Transcontinental Publications Inc., #2700, 777 Bay St., PO Box 148, Toronto ON M5G 2N1 – 416/340-8000; Fax: 416/977-0566 – Circ.: 75,000; Monthly – Publisher, Tim Goodman

Connections Northwest, #209, 1015 Burrard St., Vancouver BC V6Z 1Y5 – 604/689-2909; Fax: 604/689-2989 – Circ.: 4,500; 4 times a year – Publisher, Frank Cumming; Editor, Richard Williams

enRoute (Published by Publicor), 7, ch Bates, Outremont PQ H2V 1A6 – 514/270-1100, ext.260; Fax: 514/270-9618; Email: info@enroute.quebecor.com – Circ.: 113,409; Monthly – Editor, Lise Ravary

Inflight/En vol, Melaine Communications Group Inc., #3120, 3300 Bloor St. West, Etobicoke ON M8X 2X3 – 416/233-4348; Fax: 416/233-9367 – Circ.: 87,750; 2 times a year – Editor, Susan Melnyk

ANIMALS

Canine Review, SS2, Site 4, Comp. 22, Beaton Rd., Kamloops BC V2C 6C3 – 250/828-1978; Fax: 250/828-0052 – Circ.: 1,500; 10 times a year – Publisher/Editor, Helen W. Lee

Dogs, Dogs, Dogs, Kodiak Cycle Ltd., 2424 Danforth Ave., PO Box 101, Toronto ON M4C 1K9 – 416/465-4406; Fax: 416/465-1513; Email: jenny@netcom.ca – Circ.: 18,430; 6 times a year – Publisher & Editor, Jackie Lindsay

Dogs in Canada, Apex Publishers, #200, 89 Skyway Ave., Etobicoke ON M9W 6R4 – 416/675-5511; Fax: 416/675-6506 – Monthly

Pets Magazine (Published by Moorshead Magazines Ltd.), #490, 10 Gateway Blvd., Toronto ON M3C 3T4 – 416/696-5488; Fax: 416/696-7395; Email: pets@moorshead.com – Circ.: 48,500; 6 times a year – Publisher, Halvor Moorshead; Editor, Ed Zapletal; Circulation Manager, Rick Cree

Pets Quarterly Magazine, Omnicom Publications Inc., #300, 512 King St. East, Toronto ON M5A 1M1 – 416/955-1550; Fax: 416/955-1391 – Circ.: 70,000; 4 times a year – Publisher, Robert W. Oates; Editor, Valerie Wilson

ARTS, ART & ANTIQUES

Antiques, 20 Bloor St. East, PO Box 75114, Toronto ON M4W 3T3 – 416/944-3880; Email: marnia@msn.com – Circ.: 5,000; 6 times a year – Publisher & Editor, Marni Andrews

Antique Showcase (Published by Trajan Publishing Corp.), #292, 103 Lakeshore Rd., St Catharines ON L2N 2T6 – 905/646-7744; Fax: 905/646-0995 – 9 times a year – Publisher, Paul Fiocca; Editor, Barbara Sutton-Smith; Circulation Manager, Tammy Kruck

Artfocus, PO Box 1063, Stn F, Toronto ON M4Y 2T7 – 416/925-5564; Fax: 416/925-2972; Email: pfleisher@artfocus.com; URL: http://www.artfocus.com – Circ.: 8,000; 4 times a year – Editor, Pat Fleisher

Artichoke, #210, 901 Jervis St., Vancouver BC V6E 2B6 – 604/683-1941; Fax: 604/683-1941 – Circ.: 1,000; 3 times a year – Editor, Paula Gustafson

Art Impressions, 344 Edgeley Blvd., Unit 16, Concord ON L4K 4B7 – 905/738-2310; Fax: 905/738-4994 – Circ.: 3,500; 4 times a year & 2 annual supplements – Editor, Michael Knell

ArtsAtlantic, 145 Richmond St., Charlottetown PE C1A 1J1 – 902/628-6138; Fax: 902/566-4648; Email: artsatlantic@isn.net – Circ.: 2,500; 3 times a year – Editor, Joseph Sherman; Circulation Manager, Ellen MacPhail

Border Crossings, #300, 393 Portage Ave., Winnipeg MB R3B 3H6 – 204/942-5778; Fax: 204/949-0793 – 4 times a year

Canada Quilts Magazine, PO Box 39, Stn A, Hamilton ON L8N 3A2 – 905/523-5828; Fax: 905/523-1200 – Circ.: 3,200; 5 times a year – Publisher & Editor, Deborrah Sherman

Canadian Art, 70 The Esplanade, 2nd Fl., Toronto ON M5E 1R2 – 416/368-8854; Fax: 416/594-3375 – Circ.: 20,000; 4 times a year – Publisher, Debbie Gibson; Editor, Richard Rhodes

C Magazine, 988 Queen St. West, Stn B, Toronto ON M6J 1H1 – 416/539-9495; Fax: 416/539-9903 – Circ.: 4,500; 4 times a year – Publisher & Editor, Joyce Mason

Collectibles Canada, #202, 103 Lakeshore Rd., St. Catharines ON L2N 2T6 – 905/646-7744; Fax: 905/646-0095; Email: bret@trajan.com; URL: http://www.trajan.com/collectibles/default.ehtml – 7 times a year – Publisher, Paul Fiocca; Editor, Bret Evans

Contact, c/o Alberta Potters' Association, #400, 119 - 14th St., Calgary AB T2N 1Z6 – 403/270-3759 – 4 times a year

Dance International, The Vancouver Ballet Society, 1415 Barclay St., Vancouver BC V6G 1J6 – 604/681-1525 – Circ.: 3,800; 4 times a year – Editor, Maureen Riches

Espace, Succ. C, PO Box 878, Montréal PQ H2L 4L6 – 514/598-8982 – 4 times a year

ETC Montréal, #806, 1435, rue de Bleury, Montréal PQ H3A 2H7 – 514/848-1125; Fax: 514/843-4749; Email: alainparadis@babylon.montreal.qc.ca – Circ.: 2,000; 4 times a year; English & French – Editor, Isabelle Lelarge

Fusion, The Gardener's Cottage, 225 Conferation Dr., Scarborough ON M1G 1B2 – 416/438-8946; Fax: 416/438-0192 – Circ.: 700; 4 times a year – Editor, Elizabeth Dingman

Canadian Almanac & Directory 1997

Inter, Les Éditions Intervention, PO Box 227, Haute-Ville PQ G1R 4P8 – 418/529-9680; Fax: 418/529-6933; Email: revueinter@accent.net – Circ.: 1,200; 3 times a year – Directrice de tirage, Lise Bourassa

Inuit Art Quarterly, Inuit Art Foundation, 2081 Merivale Rd., Nepean ON K2G 1G9 – 613/224-8189; Fax: 613/224-2907 – Circ.: 3,500; 4 times a year – Editor, Marybelle Mitchell; Circulation Manager, Matthew Fox

Muse, Canadian Museums Assn., #400, 280 Metcalfe St., Ottawa ON K2P 1R7 – 613/567-0099; Fax: 613/233-5438; Email: can_cma@immedia.ca – 4 times a year; English & French – Editor, Aline Michaud

Ontario Craft, Ontario Crafts Council, 35 McCaul St., Toronto ON M5T 1V7 – 416/977-3551; Fax: 416/977-3552 – Circ.: 4,500; 6 times a year – Editor, Anne McPherson

Parachute Contemporary Art Magazine, #501, 4060, boul St-Laurent, Montréal PQ H2W 1Y9 – 514/842-9805; Fax: 514/287-7146 – 4 times a year – Rédacteur, C. Pontbriand

Rotunda, c/o Royal Ontario Museum, 100 Queen's Park, Toronto ON M5S 2C6 – 416/586-5590; Fax: 416/586-5827; Email: sandras@rom.on.ca – Circ.: 25,000; 4 times a year – Editor-in-Chief, Sandra Shaul

Slate, 155 King St. East, Kingston ON K7L 2Z9 – 613/542-3717; Fax: 613/542-1447 – 8 times a year – Editor, Sonya Dodich

Vie des Arts, #600, 200, rue Saint-Jacques, Montréal PQ H2Y 1M1 – 514/282-0205; Fax: 514/282-0235 – Tirage: 6,600; 4 fois par an; français – Rédacteur en chef, Bernard Lévy

AUTOMOBILE & CYCLE

Almanach de L'Auto (Published by Publicor), 7, ch Bates, Outremont PQ H2V 1A6 – 514/270-1100; Fax: 514/270-6900 – Annuellement; français – Lyane D. Blackman

Autopinion Annual, Canadian Automobile Association, #200, 1145 Hunt Club Rd., Ottawa ON K1V 0Y3 – 613/247-0117; Fax: 613/247-0018; Email: dsteventon@caa.ca; URL: http://www.caa.ca – Circ.: 56,414; Annually – Editor, David Steventon

Canadian Biker, PO Box 4122, Victoria BC V8X 3X4 – 250/384-0333; Fax: 250/384-1832; Email: canbike@islandnet.com; URL: http://canadianbiker.com – Circ.: 25,000; 8 times a year – Editor & Publisher, Len Creed; Circulation Manager, Chris Creed

Carguide/Le Magazine Carguide (Published by Formula Publications Ltd.), #4, 446 Speers Rd., Oakville ON L6K 3S7 – 905/842-6591; Fax: 905/842-6843 – 6 times a year, English; 4 fois par an, français – Publisher, J. Scott Robinson; Editor, Graham Fletcher; Circulation Manager, Deadra Worth

Cycle Canada, #3B, 86 Parliament St., Toronto ON M5A 2Y6 – 416/362-7966; Fax: 416/362-3950 – Circ.: 20,000; 10 issues a year – Publisher, Jean-Pierre Belmonte; Editor, Bruce Reeve

Lemon-Aid Magazine, c/o Automobile Protection Association, 292, boul St-Joseph ouest, Montréal PQ H2V 2N7 – 514/272-5555; Fax: 514/273-0797 – Circ.: 12,000; 4 times a year – Co-Editor, Antoinette Greco, 514/273-1662; Co-Editor, George Iny

Le Monde de l'Auto, World of Wheels Publishing Inc., #401, 7575 Trans Canada Hwy., St-Laurent PQ H4T 1V6 – 514/958-1361; Fax: 514/956-1461 – 6 fois par an; français – Rédacteur, Luc Gagné

Moto Journal (Published by Turbopress Inc.), #3B, 86 Parliament St., Toronto ON M5A 2Y6 – 416/362-7966; Fax: 416/362-3950 – Tirage: 7,000; 10 fois par an – Éditeur, Jean-Pierre Belmonte; Rédacteur, Claude Leonard

Old Autos, 348 Main St., PO Box 419, Bothwell ON N0P 1C0 – 519/695-2303; Fax: 519/695-3716 – Circ.: 14,000; 24 times a year – Publisher/Editor, Murray McEwan

Pedal Magazine, #204, 2 Pardee Ave., Toronto ON M6K 3H5 – 416/530-1350; Fax: 416/530-4155 – Circ.: 18,000; 8 times a year – Publisher & Editor, Benjamin Sadavoy

Performance Racing News, Buy & Sell Newspaper Ltd., 593 Yonge St., PO Box 5, Toronto ON M4Y 1Z4 – 416/922-7223; Fax: 416/922-8001; Email: greggo@io.org – Circ.: 10,060; 12 times a year – Editor, John Hopkins

The Professional's Guide to Luxury Cars, 3 Ainsley Gardens, Etobicoke ON M9A 1M5 – 416/233-2171; Fax: 416/233-2171 – 2 times a year – Publisher, John D. Duncan; Editor, Bob English, 519/833-2089

Vélo Mag (Published by Les Éditions Tricycle inc.), 1251, rue Rachel est, Montréal PQ H2J 2J9 – 514/521-8356; Fax: 514/521-5711; Email: velo_mag@velo.qc.ca – Tirage: 20,000; 6 fois par an; français – Éditeur & Rédacteur, Pierre Hamel

World of Wheels (Published by World of Wheels Publishing Inc.), #220, 1200 Markham Rd., Scarborough ON M1H 3C3 – 416/438-7777; Fax: 416/438-5333 – Circ.: 125,000; 6 times a year – Publisher, Lynn R. Helpard; Executive Editor, Joe Knycha; Circulation Manager, Susan Brown

AVIATION & AEROSPACE

Canadian Aviation Historical Society Journal, PO Box 224, Stn A, Willowdale ON M2N 5S8 – 416/488-2247; Fax: 416/488-2247 – Circ.: 1,300; 4 times a year – Editor, W. Wheeler

Canadian Homebuilt Aircraft News, PO Box 563, Stn B, Ottawa ON K1P 5P7 – 613/545-0881; Fax: 613/236-8646 – Circ.: 20,000; Monthly – Publisher, Garth Wallace; Editor, Doris Ohlmann

BABIES & MOTHERS

The Baby & Child Care Encyclopedia (Published by Family Communications Inc.), #1, 37 Hanna Ave., Toronto ON M6K 1X1 – 416/537-2604; Fax: 416/538-1794 – Circ.: 100,000; 2 times a year (May & Nov.). – Publisher, Donald Swinburne; Editor-in-Chief, Bettie Bradley

Best Wishes (Published by Family Communications Inc.), #1, 37 Hanna Ave., Toronto ON M6K 1X1 – 416/537-2604; Fax: 416/538-1794 – Circ.: 170,012; 2 times a year (March & Sept.) – Publisher, Donald Swinburne; Editor-in-Chief, Bettie Bradley

C'est Pour Quand? (Published by Family Communications Inc.), 2260, rue des Patriotes, Sainte-Rose PQ H7L 3K8 – 514/622-0091; Fax: 514/622-0099 – Tirage: 51,228; 2 fois par an; français – Éditeur, Manon Le Moyne

The Compleat Mother, RR#2, Chesley ON N0G 1L0 – 519/363-3778 – Circ.: 15,000; 4 times a year – Editor, Catherine Young

Expecting (Published by Family Communications Inc.), #1, 37 Hanna Ave., Toronto ON M6K 1X1 – 416/537-2604; Fax: 416/538-1794 – President, Donald G. Swinburne

Great Expectations (Published by Professional Publishing), 269 Richmond St. West, Toronto ON M5V 1X1 – 416/596-6680; Fax: 416/596-1991 – Circ.: 200,000; 3 times a year – Publisher, Mitchell Dent; Editor-in-Chief, Fran Fearnley

Mère Nouvelle (Published by Professional Publishing), 269 Richmond St. West, Toronto ON M5V 1X1 – 416/596-6680; Fax: 416/596-1991 – Publisher, Beverly Topping; Editor in Chief, Fran Fearnley

Mon Bébé (Published by Family Communications Inc.), 2260, rue des Patriotes, Sainte-Rose PQ H7L 3K8 – 514/622-0091; Fax: 514/622-0099 – Tirage: 51,770; 2 fois par an; français – Éditeur, Manon Le Moyne

Mon Enfant (Published by Professional Publishing), 269 Richmond St. West, Toronto ON M5V 1X1 – 416/596-6680; Fax: 416/596-1991 – Tirage: 62,500; 2 fois par an; français – Éditrice, Beverly Topping; Rédactrice, Fran Fearnley

New Mother (Published by Professional Publishing), 269 Richmond St. West, Toronto ON M5V 1X1 – 416/596-6680; Fax: 416/596-1991 – Circ.: 165,000; 2 times a year; English & French editions – Publisher, Beverly Topping; Editor-in-Chief, Fran Fearnley

Pouponnière (Published by Professional Publishing), 269 Richmond St. West, Toronto ON M5V 1X1 – 416/596-6680; Fax: 416/596-1991 – Tirage: 90,000; Annuellement; français – Éditrice, Beverly Topping; Rédactrice, Fran Fearnley

Today's Parent Prenatal Class Guide (Published by Professional Publishing), 269 Richmond St. West, Toronto ON M5V 1X1 – 416/596-6680; Fax: 416/596-1991 – Circ.: 200,000; Annually – Publisher, Beverly Topping; Editor-in-Chief, Fran Fearnley

Your Baby (Published by Professional Publishing), 269 Richmond St. West, Toronto ON M5V 1X1 – 416/596-6680; Fax: 416/596-1991 – Circ.: 187,500; 3 times a year – Publisher, Beverly Topping; Editor-in-Chief, Fran Fearnley

BOATING & YACHTING

Boat Guide (Published by Formula Publications Ltd.), #4, 446 Speers Rd., Oakville ON L6K 3S7 – 905/842-6591; Fax: 905/842-6843 – 2 times a year – Publisher, Scott Robinson; Editor, Lizanne Madigan; Circulation Manager, Deadra Worth

Boating East Ports & Cruising Guide, Marble Rock Rd., RR#2, Gananoque ON K7G 2V4 – 613/382-5735 – Annually, May

Canadian Yachting (Published by Kerrwil Publications Ltd.), 395 Matheson Blvd. East, Mississauga ON L4Z 2H2 – 905/890-1846; Fax: 905/890-5769 – 6 times a year (April to Oct.) – Editor, Graham Jones

DIY Boat Owner, JM Publishing, #515, 2511 Lakeshore Rd. West, Oakville ON L6L 6L9 – 905/847-3009; Fax: 905/847-3590; Email: diy@diy-boat.com – Circ.: 15,000; 4 times a year – Publisher & Editor, Jan Mundy

L'Escale Nautique (Published by Productions Maritimes), 175, rue Saint-Paul, Québec PQ G1K 3W2 – 418/692-3779; Fax: 418/692-5198 – Tirage: 6,700; 5 fois par an; français – Redacteur en chef, Michel Sacco

Gam on Yachting, #202, 250 The Esplanade, Toronto ON M5A 1J2 – 416/368-1559; Fax: 416/368-2831 – 8 times a year – Editor, Karin Larson

Pacific Yachting (Published by OP Publishing), 1132 Hamilton St., Vancouver BC V6B 2S2 – 604/687-1581; Fax: 604/687-1925; Email: op@mindlink.bc.ca – Circ.: 19,126; Monthly – Publisher, Rex Armstead; Editor, Duart Snow

Les Plaisanciers, #310, 970, Montee de Liesse, St-Laurent PQ H4T 1W7 – 514/856-0788; Fax: 514/856-0790 – Tirage: 20,000; 5 fois par an; français – Éditeur, William E. Taylor; Rédacteur, Claude Leonard; Directrice de tirage, Marlene Jolicover

Port Hole, c/o Canadian Power & Sail Squadrons, 26 Golden Gate Ct., Scarborough ON M1P 3A5 – 416/293-2438; Fax: 416/293-2445 – Circ.: 28,000; 4 times a year; English & French – Editor-in-Chief, Herb Henderson; Managing Editor, D. Zonnenberg

Power Boating Canada, #306, 2585 Skymark Ave., Mississauga ON L4W 4L5 – 905/624-8218; Fax: 905/624-6764 – Circ.: 50,000; 6 times a year – Publisher, William Taylor; Editor, Pam Cottrell

Québec Yachting Voile & Moteur (Published by Transcontinental Publications Inc.), 1100, boul René-Levesque ouest, 24e étage, Montréal PQ H3B 4X9 – 514/392-9000; Fax: 514/392-4726 – Tirage: 8,000; 6 fois par an; français – Éditeur, Alain Guilbert; Rédacteur en chef, Henri René de Cotret

Today's Boating, Ranmore Publishing Inc., 3#606, 366 Adelaide St. West, Toronto ON M5V 1R9 – 416/595-6439; Fax: 416/599-9700 – Circ.: 25,500; 5 times a year; English & French

Windsport, True Wind Corp. Ltd., #3266, 2255B Queen St. East, Toronto ON M4E 1G3 – 416/698-0138;

Fax: 416/698-8080; Email: infro@windsport.com; URL: http://www.windsport.com – 4 times a year – Editor, Steve Jarrett; Circulation Manager, Duncan O'Brien

BRIDES, BRIDAL

Mariage Québec, #780, 740, rue Notre-Dame ouest, Montréal PQ H3C 3X6 – 514/392-9030; Fax: 514/392-0328 – Tirage: 22,500; 2 fois par an; français – Rédacteur, Janine Salne

Sposa Magazine, #410, 77 Mowat Ave., Toronto ON M6K 3E3 – 416/534-1851; Fax: 416/534-0262 – Circ.: 32,000; 2 times a year – Publisher, Gulshan Sippy; Editor, Ross Skoggard

Today's Bride (Published by Family Communications Inc.), #1, 37 Hanna Ave., Toronto ON M6K 1X1 – 416/537-2604; Fax: 416/538-1794 – Circ.: 101,000; 2 times a year – President/Publisher, Don Swinburne; Corporate Editor, Bettie Bradley

Wedding Bells, 50 Wellington St. East, 2nd Fl., Toronto ON M5E 1C8 – 416/862-8479; Fax: 416/862-2184; Email: editor@weddingbells.com; URL: http://www.weddingbells.com – 2 times a year – Publisher, Diane Hall; Editor-in-Chief, Crys Stewart; Circulation Manager, Marlene Semple

The Wedding Pages Planner & Pocket Guide, 30 Relroy Ct., Scarborough ON M1W 2Y7 – 416/498-4996; Fax: 416/498-5997 – Circ.: 23,400; Annually, Sept – Publisher, Brandon Jones; Publisher, Chris Jones

Weddings & Honeymoons, 65 Helena Ave., Toronto ON M6G 2H3 – 416/653-4986; Fax: 416/653-2291; Email: wedhon@to.org – Circ.: 50,000; 2 times a year; ISSN: 1192-764X – Publisher & Editor, Joyce Barshow; Circulation Manager, Beverley Colbourne

BUSINESS & FINANCE

Canadian Business Economics, PO Box 828, Stn B, Ottawa ON K1P 5P9 – 613/234-0505 – 4 times a year; ISSN 0705-8330

Canadian MoneySaver, PO Box 370, Bath ON K0H 1G0 – 613/352-7448 – 11 times a year – President & Publisher, Dale Ennis

Canadian Shareowner, #202, 1090 University Ave., Windsor ON N9A 5S4 – 519/252-9965; Fax: 519/252-9570 – Circ.: 12,000; 6 times a year – Publisher & Editor, John T. Bart

The Financial Post Magazine Canada (Published by Financial Post Co. Ltd.), 333 King St. East, Toronto ON M5A 4N2 – 416/350-6170; Fax: 416/350-6171 – 11 times a year – Publisher, David Bailey, 416/350-6198; Editor, Wayne Gooding

Magazine Affaires Plus, 1100, boul René-Lévesque, Montréal PQ H3B 4X9 – 514/392-9000; Fax: 514/392-4726 – Tirage: 93,000; 10 fois par an; français – Éditrice, Suzanne Paquet; Rédacteur, Pierre Duhamel; Directeur de tirage, François Blondin

CAMPING & OUTDOOR RECREATION

Camping Canada, #306, 2585 Skymark Ave., Mississauga ON L4W 4L5 – 905/624-8218; Fax: 905/624-6764 – 7 times a year – Publisher, William E. Taylor; Editor, Diane Batten

Camping Caravaning, Communication Camping Caravaning, 4545, av Pierre de Coubertin, CP 1000, Succ M, Montréal PQ H1V 3R2 – 514/252-3003; Fax: 514/254-0694 – Tirage: 13,482; 8 fois par an – Rédacteur en chef, Robert Aubin

Camping in Ontario, Ontario Private Campground Assn., RR#5, Owen Sound ON N4K 5N7 – 519/371-3393; Fax: 519/371-5315 – Circ.: 125,000; annually, Feb. – Managing Director, Marcel Gobeil

Explore, Thompson & Gordon Publishing Co. Ltd., #420, 301 - 14 St. NW, Calgary AB T2N 2A1 – 403/270-8890; Fax: 403/270-7922; Email: explore@cadvision.com – Circ.: 35,000; 6 times a year – Publisher,

Peter Thompson; Editor, Marion Harrison, 403/270-8911; Circulation Manager, Brigitte Clarke

Kanawa: Canada's Canoeing & Kayaking Magazine, PO Box 398, Merrickville ON K0G 1N0 – 613/269-2910; Fax: 613/269-2908; Email: staff@craca.ca; URL: http://www.crca.ca/ – Circ.: 20,000; 4 times a year – Publisher & Editor, Joseph Agnew; Circulation Manager, Nancy Gough

The Ontario Camping & Recreational Guide, #1116, 40 University Ave., Toronto ON M5J 1T1 – 416/977-8610; Fax: 416/977-3299 – Circ.: 100,000; Annually, Jan. – Publisher, J.F.H. Gray

Vie en Plein Air, #310, 970 Montée de Liesse, Ville St-Laurent PQ H4T 1W7 – 514/856-0787; Fax: 514/856-0790 – Tirage: 30,000; 1 fois par an; français – Éditeur, William E. Taylor; Rédacteur, Claude Leonard

CHILDREN'S

Chickadee, #500, 179 John St., Toronto ON M5T 3G5 – 416/971-5275; Fax: 416/971-5294; Email: owlcom@owl.on.ca; URL: http://www.owl.on.ca – Circ.: 100,000; 9 times a year – Publisher, Diane Davy; Editor, Nyla Ahmad; Circulation Manager, Deanna Kennedy

Coulicou (Published by Les Éditions Héritage), 300, rue Arran, Saint-Laurent PQ J4R 1K5 – 514/875-0327; Fax: 514/672-5448 – 10 fois par an; français – Éditeur, Luc Payette

Les Débrouillards, 3995, rue Ste-Catherine est, Montréal PQ H1W 2G7 – 514/522-1304; Fax: 514/522-1761 – Tirage: 31,000; 10 fois par an; français – Éditeur, Felix Maltais; Rédactrice, Sarah Perreault

En Primeur Jeunesse (Published by Tribute Publishing Inc.), #1000, 900A Don Mills Rd., Don Mills ON M3C 1V6 – 416/4445-0544; Fax: 416/445-2894 – Tirage: 50,000; 4 fois par an; français – Éditeur, Brian Stewart; Rédactrice, Sandra Stewart; Directeur de triage, Guy Murnaghan

Hibou (Published by Les Éditions Héritage), 300, rue Arran, Saint-Laurent PQ J4R 1K5 – 514/875-0327; Fax: 514/672-1481 – 10 fois par an; français – Éditeur, Luc Payette

J'Aime Lire (Published by Bayard Presse Canada Inc.), 3995, rue Ste-Catherine est, Montréal PQ H1W 2G7 – 514/522-3936; Fax: 514/522-1761 – Tirage: 16,000 – Éditrice & Rédactrice, Suzanne Spino

Kids Tribute (Published by Tribute Publishing Inc.), #1000, 900A Don Mills Rd., Don Mills ON M3C 1V6 – 416/445-0544; Fax: 416/445-2894 – Circ.: 300,000; 4 times a year – Publisher, Brian Stewart; Editor, Sandra Stewart; Circulation Manager, Guy Murnaghan

Kids World Magazine, #108, 93 Lombard Ave., Winnipeg MB R3B 3B1 – 204/942-2214; Fax: 204/943-8991; Email: kidsworld@kidsworld-online.com; URL: http://www.kidsworld-online.com – Circ.: 225,000; 6 times a year – Publisher, Nancy Moore; Editor, Stuart Slayen; Circulation Manager, Sherry Jones

Owl Magazine, #500, 179 John St., Toronto ON M5T 3G5 – 416/971-5275; Fax: 416/971-5294; Email: owlcom@owl-on.ca; URL: http://www.owl.on.ca – Circ.: 110,000; 9 times a year – Publisher, Diane Davy; Editor, Nyla Ahmad; Circulation Manager, Deanna Kennedy

CITY MAGAZINES

Alderlea Magazine, 105 Kenneth St., Duncan BC V9L 1N5 – 250/746-6463; Fax: 250/746-7745 – Circ.: 12,700; 12 times a year – Publisher, George E. Spong; Editor, Frank Hird-Rutter

Avenue, 625 - 14th St. NW, Calgary AB T2N 2A1 – 403/283-8260; Fax: 403/283-6026 – Circ.: 40,000; 10 times a year – Publisher, Daniel Bowman; Editor, Valerie Fortney

Calgary Cityscope, I.E. Publications Inc., #300, 1324 - 11 Ave. SW, Calgary AB T3C 0M6 – 403/228-7020; Fax: 403/228-7193; Email: editor@city-scopemag.com; URL: http://www.city-scopemag.com – Circ.: 60,000; 6 times a year; ISSN 1188-4835; also publishes a Chinese edition – Publisher, Larry Jones; Editor, Gary Davies

Events Planner, Pearl Publishing, 99 Kimbark Blvd., Toronto ON M5N 2Y3 – 416/782-3322; Fax: 416/787-9299 – Circ.: 2,000; 3 times a year – Publisher, Sybil Levine; Editor, R.S. Diamond

Eye, #207, 57 Spadina Ave., Toronto ON M5V 2J2 – 416/971-8421; Fax: 416/971-9697; URL: http://www.interlog.com:80/eye/ – Circ.: 100,000; Weekly – Publisher, Andrew V. Go; Managing Editor, Bill Reynolds

The Georgia Straight, 1770 Burrard St., 2nd Fl., Vancouver BC V6J 3G7 – 604/730-7000; Fax: 604/730-7010; Email: info@straight.com – Circ.: 99,253; Weekly – Publisher, Dan McLeod, 604/730-7088; Managing Editor, Charles Campbell; Circulation Manager, Nick Collier

Le Guide Prestige Montréal, #1401, 1115, rue Sherbrooke ouest, Montréal PQ H3A 1H3 – 514/982-9823; Fax: 514/289-9160 – Circ.: 150,000; 4 times a year; English & French – Publisher, Peter Weiss; Editor, André Ducharme

Hamilton This Month (Published by Town Publishing Inc), 875 Main St., Hamilton ON L8S 4R1 – 905/522-6117; Fax: 905/529-2242 – Circ.: 40,000; 7 times a year – Publisher, Wayne Narciso; Editor, Elizabeth Kelly; Circulation Manager, Laurie Ann Raynor

Hi-Rise, #121, 95 Leeward Glenway, Don Mills ON M3C 2Z6 – 416/424-1393; Fax: 416/467-8262 – Circ.: 30,000; 11 times a year – Editor & Publisher, Valerie Dunn

Hour, Communications Voir Inc., #302, 4126, rue St-Denis, Montréal PQ H2W 2M5 – 514/848-0777; Fax: 514/848-0360; Email: hour@eureka.qc.ca – Circ.: 46,000; 52 times a year – Publisher, Pierre Paquet

L'Important (Published by Groupe Magazines S.A. Inc.), #300, 275, boul des Braves, Terrebonne PQ J6W 3H6 – 514/964-7590; Fax: 514/964-2327 – 4 fois par an; français – Éditeur, Denis Clermont; Rédacteur, Louise Bourbonnais

In Montréal, 5151, ch Côte St-Catherine, Montréal PQ H3W 1M6 – 514/345-2624; Fax: 514/345-2643; Email: in_mtl@aed.net – Circ.: 30,000; 9 times a year – Editor-in-Chief, Susan Levine; Editor, Robin Charney

International Guide (Published by I.G. Publications Ltd.), #222, 999 - 8 St. SW, Calgary AB T2R 1J5 – 403/244-7343 – Circ.: 16,000; Annually, June – Publisher, Wayne R. Kehoe; Editor, Sharon Komori

Key to Kingston, c/o Kingston Publications, 11 Princess St., PO Box 1352, Kingston ON K7L 5C6 – 613/549-8442; Fax: 613/549-4333 – Circ.: 17,000; 8 times a year – Publisher, Dan Bedford; Editor, Mary Owens

Kootenay Visitor's Magazine (Published by Koocanusa Publications Inc.), 1510 - 2nd St. North, Cranbrook BC V1C 3L2 – 250/426-7253; Fax: 250/489-3743 – Circ.: 40,000; Annually, June – Publisher, Daryl D. Shellborn; Editor, Stacey Curry

Lethbridge Living (Published by Robins Southern Printing (1990) Ltd.), 1320 - 36 St. North, Lethbridge AB T1H 5H8 – 403/328-5114; Fax: 403/328-5443 – Circ.: 17,200; 4 times a year – Editor, Rick Gillis; Circulation Manager, Leona Milford

London, Blackburn Magazine Group, #203, 231 Dundas St., London ON N6B 1R5 – 519/679-4901; Fax: 519/434-7842 – Circ.: 35,000; 8 times a year – Publisher, C. Kehoe; Editor, J. Skender

Montréal Mirror, Communications Gratte-Ciel ltée, 400 McGill St. 1st Fl., Montréal PQ H2Y 2G1 – 514/393-1010; Fax: 514/393-3173, 3756; Email: mirror@babylon.montreal.qc.ca – Circ.: 75,000; Weekly, Thur – Catherine Leconte

Montréal Scope, #232, 1253 McGill College, Montréal PQ H3B 2Y5 – 514/933-3333; Fax: 514/931-9581 –

Circ.: 40,800; 11 times a year – Editor/Publisher, N. Evreinow

Moving to & Around... (Published by Moving Publications Ltd.), 40 Upjohn Rd., Don Mills ON M3B 2W1 – 416/441-1168; Fax: 416/441-1641 – Circ.: 220,000; Annually, or bi-annual issues cover all major Canadian cities & areas; 2 bilingual issues - Montréal, Ottawa/Hull – Publisher, Anita Wood; Editor, Lorraine Hunter; Circulation Manager, Paula Muzzin

New City Magazine, PO Box 26083, Winnipeg MB R3C 4K9 – 204/775-9327; Fax: 204/788-0109 – Circ.: 1,000; 4 times a year – Publisher, Ross Dobson

Niagara Magazine, #B2, 11 Bond St., St. Catharines ON L2R 4Z4 – 905/641-3505; Fax: 905/687-6911 – Circ.: 30,000; 6 times a year – Publisher, Ted Szymanski; Editor, Wendy Luce

Now, 150 Danforth Ave., Toronto ON M4K 1N1 – 416/461-0871; Fax: 416/461-2886 – Circ.: 100,000; Weekly – Editor/Publisher, Michael Hollett

Okanagan Life Magazine (Published by Byrne Publishing Group Inc), PO Box 1479, Stn A, Kelowna BC V1Y 7V8 – 250/861-5399; Fax: 250/868-3040 – Circ.: 18,000; 6 times a year – Publisher, Paul Byrne; Circulation Manager, Tammy Tomiye

Ottawa Magazine, Pegasus Publishing Inc., 1312 Bank St., Ottawa ON K1S 3Y4 – 613/731-9194; Fax: 613/731-9884 – Circ.: 37,999; 6 times a year – Publisher, Peter Ginsberg; Editor, Mark Sutcliffe

The Ottawa X Press, 69 Sparks St., Ottawa ON K1P 5A5 – 613/237-8226; Fax: 613/232-9055 – Publisher, Ross Dickson; Managing Editor, Derek Raymaker

Pique Newsmagazine, #5, 1050 Millar Creek Rd., Whistler BC V0N 1B1 – 604/938-0202; Fax: 604/938-0201 – Circ.: 6,840; Weekly, Tues. – Publisher & Editor, Kathy Bernett

Profile Kingston, PO Box 91, Kingston ON K7L 4V6 – 613/546-6723; Fax: 613/546-0707 – Publisher, Bonnie H. Golomb

Richmond Hill Month, #16, 7780 Woodbine Ave., Markham ON L3R 2N7 – 905/475-1743 – Publisher, P.G. Grosskurth; Editor, Deborah Smith

SEE Magazine, 10310 - 102 Ave., Edmonton AB T5J 2X6 – 403/428-9354; Fax: 403/428-9349 – Weekly, Thur.

Storefront Paper, Abacaxi Network, PO Box 619, Stn C, Toronto ON M6J 3R9 – 416/533-7799; Fax: 416/533-7799 – Monthly – Editor, Leon Kaplan

Thornhill Month, 7780 Woodbine Ave., Unit 16, Markham ON L3R 2N7 – 905/475-1743 – Monthly – Publisher, P.G. Grosskurth; Editor, Deborah Smith

Thunder Bay Guest, 1126 Roland St., Thunder Bay ON P7B 5M4 – 807/623-4424; Fax: 807/622-3140 – Circ.: 14,000; Monthly – Publisher, G. Dougall; Editor, Lorraine Deck

Thunder Bay Life (Published by North Superior Publishing Inc.), 1145 Barton St., Thunder Bay ON P7B 5N3 – 807/623-2348; Fax: 807/623-7515 – Circ.: 30,000; Bi-monthly – Publisher & Editor, Scott A. Sumnor

Thunder Bay Magazine, 1184 Roland St., Thunder Bay ON P7B 5M4 – 807/623-8545; Fax: 807/623-7110 – Circ.: 31,000; 6 times a year – Editor/Publisher, John P. Mallon; Associate Editor, Michael Thompson

Toronto Events Planner, 99 Kimbark Blvd., Toronto ON M5N 2Y3 – 416/782-3322; Fax: 416/787-9299 – 3 times a year, Jan., May, Sept. – Publisher, Sybil Levine

Toronto Life (Published by Key Publishers), 59 Front St. East, 2nd Fl., Toronto 0N M5E 1B3 – 416/364-3333; Fax: 416/861-1169; URL: http://www.tor-lifeline.com/tl – Circ.: 93,500; Monthly; also monthly Chinese edition co-published with Ming Pao Daily – Publisher, William M. Duron; Editor, John MacFarlane

Toronto Special Events (Published by Maclean Hunter Publishing), 777 Bay St., Toronto ON M5W 1A7 – 416/596-5165 – Publisher, Richard Elliott; Editor, Karen Orme

Toronto This Season, Tele-Direct, #402, 60 St. Clair Ave. East, Toronto ON M4T 1N5 – 416/924-3292; Fax: 416/924-5765 – Circ.: 150,000; 2 times a year

Uptown Magazine, Canadian Publishers, #101, 457 Main St., Winnipeg MB R3B 1B5 – 204/949-8680; Fax: 204/957-0795; Email: uptown@copcomm.mb.ca; URL: http://www.pangea.ca/~uptown – Circ.: 25,000; Weekly – Publisher, Gerald L. Dorge; Editor, Nancy Westaway

Vancouver Magazine, Telemedia Publishing Inc., #300, 555 - 12th Ave. West, Vancouver BC V5Z 4L4 – 604/877-7732; Fax: 604/877-4848 – Circ.: 70,000; 8 times a year – Publisher, Greg Hryhorchuk; Editor, Jim Sutherland

Visitor, 75 King St. South, Waterloo ON N2J 1P2 – 519/886-2831; Fax: 519/886-9383; Email: Editor@Visitor-Infozine – Circ.: 50,000; 5 times a year – Publisher, Jon Rour; Circulation Manager, Heather Mitchell

Visitor's Choice (Published by I.G. Publications Ltd.), #222, 999 - 8 St. SW, Calgary AB T2R 1J5 – 403/244-7343 – Annually; also editions for: Banff & Lake Louise, Vancouver, & Victoria – Publisher, Wayne Kehoe; Editor, Sharon Komori

Voilà Québec, 185, rue St-Paul, Québec PQ G1K 3W2 – 418/694-1272; Fax: 418/694-0083 – Circ.: 225,000; 4 times a year; English & French – Publisher, Curtis J. Sommerville; Editor, Jo Ouellet

Voir, 4130, rue St-Denis, Montréal PQ H2W 2M5 – 514/848-0805; Fax: 514/848-9004 – Tirage: 84,600; Hebdomadaire; français, aussi Voir Québec City – Éditeur, Pierre Paquet

What's Happening Magazine, 135-137 Main St., PO Box 171, Foxboro ON K0K 2B0 – 613/989-8896 – Circ.: 15,000; 6 times a year – Publisher, Susan Kell

Where Calgary, Keywest Publishers, #250, 125 - 9 Ave. SE, Calgary AB T2G 0P6 – 403/299-1888; Fax: 403/299-1899 – Circ.: 25,000; Monthly – Publisher, Thomas Tait; Editor, Jennifer MacLeod

Where Edmonton, Tanner Publishing Ltd., #4, 9343 - 50 St., Edmonton AB T6B 2L5 – 403/465-3362; Fax: 403/448-0424 – Circ.: 48,000; 4 times a year – Publisher, Rob Tanner

Where Halifax, 5475 Spring Garden Rd., PO Box 14, Halifax NS B3J 3T2 – 902/420-9943; Fax: 902/429-9058 – Circ.: 25,000; 10 times a year – Publisher, Sheila Pottie; Editor, Karen Janik; Circulation Manager, Patricia Baxter

Where Ottawa-Hull, 400 Cumberland St., Ottawa ON K1N 8X3 – 613/241-7888; Fax: 613/241-3112 – Circ.: 32,000; Monthly; English with one section in French – Publisher, Stephen Ball; Editor, Marc Choma

Where Rocky Mountains, #250, 125 - 9 Ave. SE, Calgary AB T2G 0P6 – 403/299-1888; Fax: 403/299-1899; URL: http://www.wheremags.com/world – Circ.: 125,000 summer, 150,000 winter; 2 times a year; English with some Japanese – Publisher, Jack Newton, 403/299-1885

Where Toronto, 6 Church St., 2nd Fl., Toronto ON M5E 1M1 – 416/364-3333; Fax: 416/594-3375; Email: 102216.1067@compuserve; URL: http://www.wheremags.com/world – Circ.: 80,000; Monthly; supplements - Where Toronto West, Heart of the City – Publisher, Giorgina Bigioni; Editor, Jacquelyn Waller-Vintar; Communications Manager, Marilou Cruz

Where Vancouver, 2208 Spruce St., Vancouver BC V6H 2P3 – 604/736-5586; Fax: 604/736-3465 – Circ.: 32,000; Monthly – Publisher, Peggie Terry; Editor, Louise Whitney

Where Vancouver Island (Published by Key Pacific Publishers Co. Ltd.), 1001 Wharf St., 3rd Fl., Victoria BC V8W 1T6 – 250/388-4324; Fax: 250/388-6166 – Circ.: 60,000; Annually, May – Publisher, Randy Rochefort

Where Victoria (Published by Key Pacific Publishers Co. Ltd.), 1001 Wharf St., 3rd Fl., Victoria BC V8W 1T6 – 250/388-4324; Fax: 250/388-6166 – Circ.: 22,000; Monthly – Publisher, Randy Rochefort; Editor & Associate Publisher, Kirsten Meincke

Where Winnipeg, #300, 128 James Ave., Winnipeg MB R3B 0N8 – 204/943-4439; Fax: 204/947-5463 – Monthly – Publisher, Brad Hughes; Editor, Alison Kirkland

Zone Outaouais, 35, rue Gamelin, Hull PQ J8Y 1V4 – 819/777-5538; Fax: 819/777-8525 – Tirage: 17,000; Mensuel; français – Éditeur, Nicolas Cazelais; Rédacteur, Marie-Josée Prince

COMPUTERS

CompuSource, 128 Queen St. South, PO Box 42136, Mississauga ON L5M 4Z0 – 905/542-8570; Fax: 905/542-1960; Email: info@compusource.org. – Circ.: 9,260; 2 times a year – Publisher & Editor, Alan Arthur

Home Computing & Entertainment (Published by Plesman Publications Ltd.), 2005 Sheppard Ave. East, 4th Fl., Willowdale ON M2J 5B1 – 416/497-9562; Fax: 416/497-9427; Email: hceedit@plesman.com; URL: http://www.plesman.com/hce – Circ.: 136,947; 10 times a year – Publisher, George Soltys; Editor, Gordon Brockhouse

INFORMATION highways: The Magazine for Users of Electronic Information, c/o TCE Information Group Ltd., 162 Joicey Blvd., Toronto ON M5M 2V2 – 416/488-7372; Fax: 416/488-7078; Email: info@tce.on.ca; URL: http://www.flexnet cp,/~infohiwy/ – Circ.: 5,000; 6 times a year – Publisher, David Shinwell; Editor, Beverley Watters; Circulation Manager, Toula Zootis

Our Computer Player, #602, 1788 West Broadway, Vancouver BC V6J 1Y1 – 604/739-8266; Fax: 604/739-3589 – Circ.: 65,000 – Publisher, Li Qin Chen; Managing Editor, Chow Yen Chong

Techno: Le journal des technologies á domicile (Published by Transcontinental Publications Inc.), 1100, boul René-Levesque ouest, 24e étage, Montréal PQ H3B 4X9 – 514/392-9000; Fax: 514/392-2088 – 11 fois par an; français – Éditeur & Rédacteur, Alain Thibault

Toronto Computes, #408, 99 Atlantic Ave., Toronto ON M6K 3J8 – 416/588-6818; Fax: 416/588-4110; URL: http://www.canadacomputes.com – Circ.: 100,000; Monthly; also publish: Canada Computes BC (60,000 circ.), Canada Computes Alberta (30,000 circ.) & Québec Micro (85,000 circ.) – Publisher, Douglas Alder; Editor, Mara Gulens

We Compute, Read/Write Media Inc., #302A, 1560 Bayview Ave., Toronto ON M4G 3B8 – 416/481-1955; Fax: 416/481-2819 – Circ.: 80,000; 10 times a year – Editor, Eric McMillan

CULTURE, CURRENT EVENTS

Border/Lines, #301, 183 Bathurst St., Toronto ON M5T 2R7 – 4 times a year

Edges: New Planetary Patterns, #1, 577 Kingston Rd., Toronto ON M4E 1R3 – 416/691-2316; Fax: 416/691-2491 – 4 times a year – Editor, Brian Stanfield

Fuse, #454, 401 Richmond St. West, Toronto ON M5V 3A8 – 416/340-8026; Fax: 416/340-8458; Email: fuse@intacc.web.net – Circ.: 3,300; 5 times a year – Editorial Coordinator, Tom Folland

id magazine, #211, 69 Wyndham St. North, Guelph ON N1H 4E7 – 519/766-9853, 9336 editorial; Fax: 519/766-9336; Email: jpetrie@idmagazine.com – Circ.: 15,000; Bi-weekly – Publisher, Michael McLarnon; Editor-in-Chief, Nate Hendley

MIX, Parallélogramme Artist-Run Culture & Publishing, #446, 401 Richmond St. West, Toronto ON M5V 3A8 – 416/506-1012; Fax: 416/340-8458; Email: mix@web.net; URL: http://www.mix.web.net/mix/ – 4 times a year; English &

French – Editor, Margaret Christakos; Circulation Manager, Lorne Fromer

The Nation: The News & Cultural Magazine of the James Bay Cree, 5678 Park Ave., PO Box 48036, Montréal PQ H2V 4S8 – 514/272-3077; Fax: 514/278-9914 – 24 times a year

NeWest Review, Sub PO 6, PO Box 394, Saskatoon SK S7N 0W0 – 306/934-1444; Fax: 306/242-5004 – 6 times a year

Outlook, #3, 6184 Ash St., Vancouver BC V5Z 3G9 – 604/324-5101; Fax: 604/325-2470 – 8 times a year

This Magazine, Red Maple Foundation, #396, 401 Richmond St. West, Toronto ON M5V 3A8 – 416/979-9429; Fax: 416/979-1143; Email: this_magazine@intacc.web.net – Circ.: 8,000; 6 times a year – Editor, Clive Thompson

The Voice of Montréal, Interimages Communications, 275, rue St-Jacques, Montréal PQ H2Y 1M9 – 514/842-7127; Fax: 514/842-5647 – Circ.: 35,000; Monthly – Editor, Suroosh Allie; Co-Publisher, Alix Laurent; Co-Publisher, Dominique Olivier

DIRECTORIES & ALMANACS

Almanach du Peuple (Published by Le Groupe Polygone editeurs inc.), 11450, boul Albert-Hudon, Montréal-Nord PQ H1G 3J9 – 514/327-4464; Fax: 514/327-0602 – Tirage: 150,000; Annuellement; français – Éditeur, Luc Lemay; Directeur de tirage, Robert Ferlaud

Canadian Forces Base Kingston Official Directory, PO Box 1352, Kingston ON K7L 5C6 – 613/549-8442 – Annually, March; English & French – Editor, Danny Bedford

Locator, #202, 8400 Jane St., Concord ON L4K 4L8 – 905/669-3737; Fax: 905/771-9144; 1-800-265-9199 Toll Free – Annually, 31 editions – Publisher, Paul Moroney

Micmac Business Finder, Abenaki Rd., PO Box 1320, Truro NS B2N 5N2 – 902/893-7115; Fax: 902/895-0024 – Annually, April

ENTERTAINMENT

Bingo News & Gaming Hi-Lites, 10171 Saskatchewan Dr., PO Box 106, Edmonton AB T6E 4R5 – 403/433-9740; Fax: 403/433-9842 – Circ.: 25,000; 11 times a year – Editor & Publisher, Lorraine B. Kramer Kalmbach

Campus Reel, #1000, 900A Don Mills Rd., Don Mills ON M3C 1V6 – 416/445-0544; Fax: 416/445-2894 – Circ.: 270,000; 4 times a year – Publisher & Editor, Sandra Stewart

Canadian Theatre Review, University of Toronto Press, 5201 Dufferin St., Downsview ON M3H 5T8 – 416/667-7781; Email: journals@gpu.utcc.utoronto.ca; URL: library.utoronto.ca/www/utpress.depthome.htm – Circ.: 1,000; 4 times a year – Co-Editor, Alan Filewod; Co-Editor, Natalie Rewa

Cineaction: Radical Film Criticism & Theory, #705, 40 Alexander St., Toronto ON M4Y 1B5 – 416/323-9083 – 3 times a year

Express, 167 Ferry St., Windsor ON N9A 4M5 – 519/255-5741; Fax: 519/255-5515; Email: star.express@mnsi.net; URL: http://www.southam.com/windsorstar/ – Circ.: 89,000; Weekly, Thurs. – Publisher, Andre Prefontaine; Editor, Lisa Monforton; Circulation Manager, James Bruce

Image de la Mauricie, 564, boul des Prairies, Cap-de-la-Madeleine PQ G8T 1K9 – 819/378-2176; Fax: 819/374-2263 – Mensuel; français – Rédacteur, Gilles Mercier

Magazine Le Clap, 2360, ch Ste-Foy, Ste-Foy PQ G1V 4H2 – 418/653-2470; Fax: 418/653-6018 – Tirage: 98,000; 8 fois par an; français – Éditeur, Michel Aubé

Marquee, #621, 77 Mowat Ave., Toronto ON M6K 3E3 – 416/538-1000; Fax: 416/538-0201 – Circ.: 633,296; 9 times a year – Publisher, David Haslam

Network, 287 MacPherson Ave., Toronto ON M4V 1A4 – 416/928-2909; Fax: 416/928-1357 –

Circ.: 146,000; 6 times a year – Managing Editor, Stephen Hubbard

Performing Arts & Entertainment in Canada, 104 Glenrose Ave., Toronto ON M4T 1K8 – 416/484-4534; Fax: 416/484-6214 – Circ.: 44,000; 4 times a year – Publisher, George Hencz; Editor, Karen Bell; Circulation Manager, Margaret Kennedy

Playboard, Arch-Way Publishers Ltd., 7560 Lawrence Dr., Burnaby BC V5A 1T6 – 604/420-6115; Fax: 604/420-6115 – Circ.: 44,360; Monthly – Publisher, Harold Schiel; Editor, Chuck Davis

Scene, 398 Clarence St., PO Box 2302, London ON N6A 4E3 – 519/642-4780; Fax: 519/433-1284 – Circ.: 20,000; 48 times a year – Editor, Herman Goodden

Shift Magazine, #407, 174 Spadina Ave., Toronto ON M5T 2C2 – 416/504-1887; Fax: 416/504-1889; URL: http://www.shift.com/shift.home – Circ.: 30,000; 6 times a year – Publisher, Andrew Heintzman; Editor, Evan Solomon

Tribute Magazine (Published by Tribute Publishing Inc.), #1000, 900A Don Mills Rd., Don Mills ON M3C 1V6 – 416/445-0544; Fax: 416/445-2894 – Circ.: 656,000; 7 times a year – Publisher & Editor, Sandra Stewart

Vox, #127 MacEwan Hall, University of Calgary, 2500 University Dr. NW, Calgary AB T2N 1N4 – 403/220-5165 – Monthly

ENVIRONMENT & NATURE

Achieving a Healthy Environment, #200, 311 Richmond Rd., Ottawa ON K1Z 6X3 – 613/233-8863 – 4 times a year

Alternatives: Perspectives on Society, Technology & Environment, c/o Faculty of Environmental Studies, University of Waterloo, 200 University Ave. West, Waterloo ON N2L 3G1 – 519/885-1211, ext.6783; Fax: 519/746-2031; Email: alternat@fes.uwaterloo.ca; URL: http://www.fes.uwaterloo.ca/Research/Alternatives – 4 times a year

Canadian Wildlife, Canadian Wildlife Federation, 2740 Queensview Dr., Ottawa ON K2B 1A2 – 613/721-2286, 1-800-563-9453; Fax: 613/721-2902; Email: infor@cwf-fcf.org; URL: http://www.toucan.ca/cwf-fcf/cwfhome.html – Circ.: 50,000; 5 times a year – Editor, Martin Silverstone; Circulation Manager, Paola Cernicchi

Ecodecision, #924, 276, rue St-Jacques, Montréal PQ H2Y 1N3 – 514/284-3043; URL: http://www.ecodec.org – 4 times a year

Environment Views, PO Box 53038, Stn Glenora, Edmonton AB T5N 2L0 – 403/439-8922; Email: enviews@ccinet.ab.ca; URL: http://www.ccinet.ab.ca/enviews/ – Circ.: 3,500; 4 times a year – Publisher, David Dodge, Email: ddodge@ccinet.ab.ca; Editor, Lynn Zwicky; Circulation Manager, Marlene Dodge

Franc-Vert, c/o Union Québecoise pour la conservation de la nature, 690, Grande-Allée est, 4e étage, Québec PQ G1R 2K5 – 418/648-2014; Fax: 418/648-0991; Email: evert@uqcn.qc.ca – Tirage: 8,000; 6 fois par an; français – Rédactrice, Louise Desautels

Global Biodiversity, c/o Canadian Museum of Nature, PO Box 3443, Stn D, Ottawa ON K1P 6P4 – 613/990-6671; Fax: 613/990-0318; Email: sswan@mus-nature.ca – Circ.: 1,200; 4 times a year; separate English & French editions (La biodiversité mondiale) – Publisher, Dawn Arnold, 613/993-5908; Email: darnold@mus-nature.ca; Editor, Catherine Ripley, 613/990-0319; Email: cripley@mus-nature.ca; Circulation Manager, Susan Swan, Email: sswan@mus-nature.ca

Heritage Canada, 412 Maclaren St., Ottawa ON K2P 0M8 – 613/237-1066, ext.1238; Fax: 613/237-5987 – 4 times a year; ISSN 1195-5899

Natural Life Magazine, 272 Highway 5, RR#1, St. George ON N0E 1N0 – 519/448-4001; Fax: 519/448-4001; Email: natlife@netroute.net; URL: http://www/netroute.net/natlife – Circ.: 25,000; 6 times a year; includes "Earthkeeper" & "Growth Spurts" sections – Publisher & Editor, Wendy Priesnitz

Nature Canada, c/o Canadian Nature Federation, #520, 1 Nicholas St., Ottawa ON K1N 7B7 – 613/562-3447; Fax: 613/562-3371; Email: cnf@web.net; URL: http://www.web.apc.org/~cnf – Circ.: 22,000; 4 times a year – Editor, Barbara Stevenson

Seasons, Federation of Ontario Naturalists, 355 Lesmill Rd., Don Mills ON M3B 2W8 – 416/444-8419; Fax: 416/444-9866; Email: fon@web.net; URL: http://www.web.net/fon – Circ.: 15,775; 4 times a year – Editor, Gail Muir

Watershed Sentinel, PO Box 39, Whaletown BC V0P 1Z0 – 250/935-6992; Email: dbroten@oberon.ark.com – Circ.: 3,000; 6 times a year – Publisher & Editor, Delores Broten

Wildflower, c/o Canadian Wildflower Society, 4981 Highway 7 East, Unit 12A, #228, Markham ON L3R 1N1 – 4 times a year

Women & Environments, 736 Bathurst St., Toronto ON M5S 2R4 – 416/516-2600; Fax: 416/531-6214; Email: weed@web.apc.org. – Circ.: 1,200; 4 times a year – Magazine Co-ordinator, Lisa Dale

FAMILIES

City Parent, Metroland Printing, Publishing & Distributing Ltd., 467 Speers Rd., Oakville ON L6K 3S4 – 905/815-0017; Fax: 905/815-0511 – Circ.: 274,500; 12 times a year – Publisher, Ian Oliver; Editor-in-Chief, Jane Muller; Circulation, Geoff Hill

Island Parent Magazine, 941 Kings Rd., Victoria BC V8T 1W7 – 250/388-6905; Fax: 250/388-4391 – Circ.: 25,000; Monthly – Publisher/Editor, Selinde Krayehoff

Junior, c/o Les Éditions Multi-concept inc., #425, 1600, boul Henri Bourassa, Montréal PQ H3M 3E2 – 514/331-0661; Fax: 514/331-8821 – Tirage: 40 000; 4 fois par an; français – Éditeur, Michel Choinière; Rédacteur, Ronald Lapierre

Le Magazine Enfants Québec (Published by Les Éditions Héritage), 300, rue Arran, Saint-Laurent PQ J4R 1K5 – 514/672-7027; Fax: 514/672-5448 – Tirage: 43,755 – Éditrice, Sylvie Payette; Rédactrice, Claire Chabot

Parent-To-Parent, PO Box 85324, Burlington ON L7R 2G6 – 905/335-3549; Fax: 905/336-0761 – Circ.: 60,000; 6 times a year – Publisher, B. Burrows; Editor, A. Greenway

Pomme d'Api Québec (Published by Bayard Presse Canada Inc.), 3995, rue Ste-Catherine est, Montréal PQ H1W 2G7 – 514/522-3936; Fax: 514/522-1761 – Tirage: 9,000 – Éditeur, Suzanne Spino; Rédacteur, Paule Brière

Today's Parent (Published by Professional Publishing), 269 Richmond St. West, Toronto ON M5V 1X1 – 416/596-8680; Fax: 416/596-1991 – Circ.: 160,000; 9 times a year – Publisher, Mitchell B. Dent; Editor-in-Chief, Fran Fearnley

Tree House Family, Multi-Vision Publishing, #1100, 655 Bay St., Toronto ON M5G 2K4 – 416/595-9944; Fax: 416/595-7217 – Circ.: 210,000; 6 times a year – Publisher, Greg MacNeil; Editor, Kristin Jenkins; Circulation Manager, Terry De Rose; Managing Editor, J. Weeks

FASHION

Flare (Published by Maclean Hunter Publishing), 777 Bay St., Toronto ON M5W 1A7 – 416/596-5462, 5453; Fax: 416/596-5799; URL: http://www.flare.com – Circ.: 182,000; Monthly

Influence (Published by Groupe Magazines S.A. Inc.), #300, 275, boul des Braves, Terrebonne PQ J6W 3H6 – 514/964-7590; Fax: 514/964-2327 – 3 times a year; English & French – Publisher, Denis Clermont; Editor, Sophie Bertrand

Luxe, Style Communications Inc., #302, 1448 Lawrence Ave. West, Toronto ON M4A 2V6 – 416/755-5199;

MAGAZINES — CONSUMER MAGAZINES

Fax: 416/755-9123; Email: stylcom@cycor.ca – Circ.: 100,000 – Publisher, John Peters; Editor, Pat MacLean; Circulation Manager, Johnathan Hill

Toronto Life Fashion Magazine (Published by Key Publishers), 59 Front St. East, 2nd Fl., Toronto 0N M5E 1B3 – 416/364-3334; Fax: 416/594-3374 – Circ.: 129,000; 6 times a year – Publisher, Shelagh Tarleton; Editor, Joan Harting Barham; Circulation Director, Scott Bullock

Vision Mode (Published by Groupe Magazines S.A. Inc.), #300, 275, boul des Braves, Terrebonne PQ J6W 3H6 – 514/964-7590; Fax: 514/964-2327 – 3 fois par an; français – Éditeur, Denis Clermont; Rédactrice, Sophie Bertrand

FISHING & HUNTING

Alberta Fishing Guide, #6C, 5571 - 45 St., Red Deer AB T4N 1L2 – 403/347-5079; Fax: 403/341-5454 – Circ.: 24,269; Annually, March – Publisher, Barry Mitchell; Editor, Ann Mitchell

The Atlantic Salmon Journal, Atlantic Salmon Federation, PO Box 429, St. Andrews NB E0G 2X0 – 506/529-4581; Fax: 506/529-4438 – 4 times a year – Editor, Harry Bruce

BC Fishing Directory & Atlas, OP Publishing Ltd., #202, 1132 Hamilton St., Vancouver BC V6B 2S2 – 604/687-1581; Fax: 604/687-1925; Email: OP@mindlink – Annually - Saltwater (March, circ. 14,000), Freshwater (Jan., circ. 17,000) – Publisher, Rex Armstead; Editor, Karl Brahn; Circulation Director, Janet Genders

B.C. Outdoors (Published by OP Publishing), 1132 Hamilton St., Vancouver BC V6B 2S2 – 604/687-1581; Fax: 604/687-1925 – Circ.: 34,868; 8 times a year – Editor, Karl Bruhn

B.C. Sport Fishing Magazine, 909 Jackson Cres., New Westminster BC V3L 4S1 – 604/683-4871 – Circ.: 21,000; 6 times a year – Publisher & Editor, Rikk Taylor

Canadian Sportfishing, #2020, 937 Centre Rd., Waterdown ON L0R 2H0 – 905/689-1112; Fax: 905/689-2065 – 6 times a year – Publisher, Henry Waszczuk; Editor, Kerry Knudsen; Circulation Co-ordinator, Elaine Lauzon

Eastern Woods & Waters, Land & Sea Events Ltd., 44 Wildwood Blvd., Dartmouth NS B2W 2L8 – 902/435-4576; Fax: 902/435-4576 – Circ.: 15,600; 6 times a year – Publisher & Editor, Jim Gourlay; Circulation Manager, Faith Drinnan

Hunter's Guide to Professional Outfitters, #1009, 50 Eglinton Ave. West, Mississauga ON L5R 3P5 – 416/967-4319; Fax: 416/964-1553 – Publisher/Editor, Sherman Hines

Journal Sports Nature Plein Air Chasse - Pêche (Published by Le Groupe Polygone editeurs inc.), 11450, boul Albert-Hudon, Montréal-Nord PQ H1G 3J9 – 514/327-4464; Fax: 514/327-0602 – Rédacteur, Jean Pagé

Newfoundland Sportsman, 803 Water St. West, PO Box 13754, Stn A, St. John's NF A1B 4G5 – 709/754-3515; Fax: 709/754-2490 – 6 times a year – Publisher, Dwight J. Blackwood; Editor, Gordon Follet

Ontario Fisherman, Transcontinental Sports Publications, #2700, 777 Bay St., PO Box 148, Toronto ON M5G 2C8 – 416/340-8000; Fax: 416/340-2786 – Circ.: 22,000; 6 times a year – Publisher, Ed Pearce; Editor, Matt Nicholls

Ontario Out of Doors (Published by Maclean Hunter Publishing), 777 Bay St., Toronto ON M5W 1A7 – 416/596-5908; Fax: 416/596-2517; Email: 102677.1125@compuserve.com; URL: http:/ /www.cyberplex.com/fishontario – Circ.: 89,000; 10 times a year – Publisher, Ron Goodman; Editor, Burton J. Myers; Circulation Manager, Linda Chick

Outdoor Canada, #202, 703 Evans Ave., Toronto ON M9C 5E9 – 416/695-0311; Fax: 416/695-0382 – Circ.: 93,000; 8 times a year – Publisher, Ildiko Marshall; Editor, James Little; Circulation Manager, Terry Gray

The Outdoor Edge, Keywest Marketing Ltd., 5829 - 97 St., Edmonton AB T6E 3J2 – 403/448-0381; Fax: 403/438-3244 – Circ.: 55,000; 6 times a year – Publisher, Kevin Rolfe

Sentier Chasse-Pêche (Published by Le Groupe Polygone editeurs inc.), 11450, boul Albert-Hudon, Montréal-Nord PQ H1G 3J9 – 514/327-4464; Fax: 514/327-0602 – Tirage: 90,000; 11 fois par an; français – Éditeur, Luc Lemay; Rédactrice, Jeannot Ruel; Directeur de tirage, Robert Ferlaud

Western Sportsman, Canadian Outdoor Publications Inc., 140 Ave. F North, Saskatoon SK S7L 1V8 – 306/665-6302; Fax: 306/244-8859; Email: copi@sasknet.sk.ca – Circ.: 22,000; 6 times a year – Editor, George Gruenefeld

FOOD & BEVERAGE

B.C. Wine Trails, PO Box 1077, Summerland BC V0H 1Z0 – 250/494-7733; Fax: 250/494-7737 – Circ.: 17,500; 4 times a year – Publisher/Editor, Dave Gamble

Coup de Pouce Extra Cuisine (Published by Les Éditions Télémédia), #900, 2001, rue University, Montréal PQ H3A 2A6 – 514/499-0561; Fax: 514/499-1844 – 4 fois par an; français – Éditrice, Michèle Cyr

Food & Drink, Liquor Control Board of Ontario, 55 Lakeshore Blvd. East, Toronto ON M5E 1A4 – 416/864-6630; Fax: 416/365-5935 – 4 times a year – Editor, Michelle Oosterman

Le Guide Cuisine, Communication Duocom Inc., #203, 90, rue Sainte-Anne, Sainte-Anne-de-Bellevue PQ H9X 1L8 – 514/457-0144; Fax: 514/457-0226 – Tirage: 19,200; 5 fois par an – Éditeur, Nicolas Vallée; Rédacteur, Claude Gervais

WineTidings (Published by Kylix Media Inc), #414, 5165 Sherbrooke St. West, Montréal PQ H4A 1T6 – 514/481-5892; Fax: 514/481-9699; URL: http://www.cmpa.ca/ – Circ.: 13,391; 8 times a year – Publisher, Judy Rochester; Executive Editor, Tony Aspler; Circulation, Veronica Gumilar

FRATERNAL, SERVICE CLUBS, ASSOCIATIONS

Echoes, IODE, #254, 40 Orchard View Blvd., Toronto ON M4R 1B9 – 416/487-4416; Fax: 416/487-4417 – 3 times a year

KIN Magazine, c/o Kinsmen & Kinette Clubs of Canada, Cambridge ON N3H 5C6 – 519/653-1920; Fax: 519/650-1091 – Circ.: 16,000; 4 times a year – Publications Manager, David Brown, 1-800-742-5546

Legion, Canvet Publications, #407, 359 Kent St., Ottawa ON K2P 0R6 – 613/235-8741 – Circ.: 458,919; 10 times a year – Editor, Mac Johnston; Advertising & Circulation Director, Jan Buchanan-Redden

Mensa Canada Communications, Mensa Canada Society, PO Box 1025, Stn O, Toronto ON M4A 2V4 – 416/431-4314; Fax: 416/289-6951; Email: bn628@freenet.toronto.on.ca; URL: http://www.canada.mensa.org/mensa – Circ.: 2,100; 10 times a year – Editor, Peggi Warner-Lalonde; Circulation Manager, Karen Lechner

Papyrus, c/o Rameses Temple, A.A.O.N.M.S., 3100 Keele St., Downsview ON M3M 2H4 – 416/633-6317; Fax: 416/633-6345 – Circ.: 7,200; 6 times a year – Editor, Otto Yoworski

The Sentinel, c/o Loyal Orange Association, 94 Sheppard Ave. West, Willowdale ON M2N 1M5 – 416/223-1690; Fax: 416/223-1324 – Circ.: 2,229; 6 times a year – Editor, Norman R. Ritchie

GARDENING

Canadian Gardening (Published by Camar Publications), 130 Spy Ct., Markham ON L3R 5H6 – 905/475-8440; Fax: 905/475-9246, 9560 – Circ.: 135,000; 7 times a year – Publisher, Phil Whalen; Editor, Liz Primeau; Circulation Manager, Randy Lamming

Chatelaine Gardens (Published by Maclean Hunter Publishing), 777 Bay St., Toronto ON M5W 1A7 – 416/596-5936; Fax: 416/593-3197 – Circ.: 115,000; Annually, Feb. – Publisher, Lee Simpson; Editor-in-Chief, Anita Draycott; Editorial & Administrative Manager, Holly Lee

The Coastal Grower Magazine, c/o Greenheart Publications Ltd., 1075 Alston St., Victoria BC V9A 3S8 – 250/360-0709; Fax: 250/360-1709; Email: grower@islandnet.com – Circ.: 10,000; 9 times a year – Publisher/Editor, Mary Mills; Circulation Manager, John Bryant

Fleurs, plantes et jardins (Published by Éditions Versicolores inc.), 1320, boul St-Joseph, Québec PQ G2K 1G2 – 418/628-8690; Fax: 418/628-0524 – Tirage: 53,131; 8 fois par an; français – Éditeur, François Bernatchez; Rédacteur, Bertrand Dumont

Gardening Life (Published by Canadian Home Publishers), #120, 511 King St. West, Toronto ON M5V 2Z4 – 416/593-0204; Fax: 416/591-1630; Email: home.pub@inforamp.net – Circ.: 100,000; 4 times a year – Publisher, Jennifer McLean; Editor, Nancy Jane Hastings; Circulation Manager, Alexandra Cooper

Gardens West, Cornwall Publishing Co. Ltd., PO Box 2680, Vancouver BC V6B 3W8 – 604/879-4991; Fax: 604/879-5110 – 9 times a year – Publisher/Editor, Dorothy Horton

Plant & Garden, Gardenvale Publishing Co. Ltd., 1, rue Pacifique, Ste-Anne-de-Bellevue PQ H9X 1C5 – 514/457-2744; Fax: 514/457-6255; Email: p@gmag@lanzen.net – Circ.: 35,000 – Publisher, Barbara Paul; Editor, Robert Paul; Circulation Manager, Gloria Waschke

Toronto Gardens, Bayview Media Inc., #302A, 1560 Bayview Ave., Toronto ON M4G 3B8 – 416/481-1955; Fax: 416/481-2819 – Circ.: 50,000; 6 times a year; ISSN 1198-8649 – Publisher/Editor, Eric McMillan

Toronto Life Gardens (Published by Key Publishers), 59 Front St. East, 2nd Fl., Toronto 0N M5E 1B3 – 416/364-3333; Fax: 416/955-4982; URL: http://www.tcr-lifeline.com – Circ.: 50,000; 4 times a year – Publisher, Donna Murphy; Co-Editor, Mary Anne Brinckman; Co-Editor, Marjorie Harris; Circulation Manager, Scott Bullock

GENERAL INTEREST

Abilities: Canada's Lifestyle Magazine for People with Disabilities, Canadian Abilities Foundation, College Park, 444 Yonge St., Toronto ON M5S 2T1 – 416/977-5185; Fax: 416/977-5098 – 4 times a year – Publisher & Editor, Raymond D. Cohen

Actif, Édibec inc., 2251, boul Shervchenko, Lasalle PQ H8N 2Y8 – 514/366-4436; Fax: 514/366-4495 – 5 fois par an; français – Éditeur, Stéphane Leroy

African Identity, #1910, 236 Albion Rd., Rexdale ON M9W 6A6 – 416/743-1900; Fax: 416/923-1599 – 12 times a year – Publisher, Kingsley Marfo

Angles, Lavender Publishing Society of BC, 1170 Bute St., Vancouver BC V6E 1Z2 – 604/688-0265; Fax: 604/688-5405 – Circ.: 17,800; Monthly

Arch-Type, #255, 40 Orchard View Blvd., Toronto ON M4R 1B9 – 416/482-8255; Fax: 416/482-2981 – 6 times a year

Beautiful British Columbia Magazine, 929 Ellery St., Victoria BC V9A 7B4 – 250/384-5456; Fax: 250/384-2812; Email: ed@bbcmag.bc.ca – Circ.: 255,000; 4 times a year; also Traveller – Publisher, John Thomson; Editor-in-Chief, Bryan McGill

The Beaver Magazine: Exploring Canada's History, Canada's National History Society, #478, 167 Lombard Ave., Winnipeg MB R3B 0T6 – 204/988-9300; Fax: 204/988-9309; Email: beaver@cyberspc.mb.ca; URL: http://www.cyberspc.mb.ca/~otwm/chns/cnhs.html – Circ.: 44,560; 6 times a year – Publisher, A.R. Huband; Editor, Christopher Dafoe

The Canadian Forum, #804, 251 Laurier Ave. West, Ottawa ON K1P 5J6 – 613/230-3078; Fax: 613/233-1458 – Circ.: 10,000; 10 times a year – Publisher, James Lorimer; Editor, Duncan Cameron

Canadian Geographic, c/o Royal Canadian Geographical Society, 39 McArthur Ave., Vanier ON K1L 8L7 – 613/745-4629; Fax: 613/744-0947; Email: editorial@cangeo.ca; URL: http://www.cangeo.ca/ – Circ.: 245,000; 6 times a year – Publisher, Edwin O'Dacre; Editor, Rick Boychuk; Circulation Manager, Maureen Ogilvie

Cape Breton's Magazine, Wreck Cove NS B0C 1H0 – 902/539-3817; Fax: 902/539-9117; Email: sirwin@fox.nstn.ca – Circ.: 7,500; 3 times a year – Publisher & Editor, Ronald Caplan

Common Ground, PO Box 34090, Stn D, Vancouver BC V6J 4M1 – 604/733-2215; Fax: 604/733-4415 – Circ.: 88,000; 10 times a year – Publisher & Editor, Joseph Roberts

Contact, Cité Universitaire, Université Laval, 77, Pavillon Alphonse-Desjardins, Québec PQ G1K 7P4 – 418/656-2571; Fax: 418/656-2809; Email: contact@scom.ulaval.ca – Tirage: 115,000; 3 fois par an; français – Rédactrice en chef, Diane Dontigny

Continuité, 82, Grande-Allée ouest, Québec PQ G1R 2G6 – 418/647-4525; Fax: 418/647-6483 – Tirage: 5,000; 4 fois par an – Rédactrice, Micheline Piché

Cottage Life, #408, 111 Queen St. East, Toronto ON M5C 1S2 – 416/360-6880; Fax: 416/360-6814; Email: cottage_life@magic.ca – Circ.: 70,000; 6 times a year – Publisher, Al Zikovitz; Editor, Ann Vanderhoof

Cottage News, Hwy. 11 North, Gravenhurst ON P1P 1R1 – 705/687-7788; Fax: 705/687-7789 – Circ.: 30,000; 7 times a year – Publisher, Bruce Clark; Editor, Margaret Bellamy

The Country Connection, PO Box 100, Boulter ON K0L 1G0 – 613/332-3651; Fax: 613/332-5183 – Circ.: 15,000; 2 times a year – Editor & Publisher, Gus Zylstra; Circulation Manager, Nancy Zylstra

Dialogue: A Forum for the Exchange of Ideas, Gabriel Communications, 19383 Kenyon Rd., Apple Hill ON K0C 1B0 – Email: dialogue@rocler.qc.ca – Circ.: 8,000; Monthly – Publisher, Maurice J. King; Editor, Janet Hicks

Disability Today, Disability Today Publishing Group Inc., #203, 627 Lyons Lane, Oakville ON L6J 5Z7 – 905/338-6894; Fax: 905/338-1836 – Circ.: 45,000; 4 times a year, plus Disability Today's Buyers' Guide Product & Service Directory (annual) – Publisher, Jeffrey Tiessen; Editor, Hilda Hoch; Circulation Manager, Karen Penner

Equinox (Published by Malcolm Publishing), #1450, 450, boul Albert-Hudon, Montréal-Nord PQ H1G 3J9 – 514/323-6800, 372-4464; Fax: 514/327-7592; URL: http://www.equinox.ca – Circ.: 140,296; 6 times a year – Publisher, Michele Paradis

The Flag & Banner, J. Braverman Inc., 1755 - 4th Ave. West, Vancouver BC V6J 1M2 – 604/732-7586; Fax: 604/736-6439; Email: doreen@flagshop.ca – Circ.: 18,000; 4 times a year – Editor, Doreen Braveman; Circulation Manager, Dennis Dong

Georgian Bay Today, 29 Bernard Ave., Toronto ON M5R 1R3 – 416/944-1217; Fax: 416/944-0133; Email: 103727.2265@compuserve.com – Circ.: 3,500; 4 times a year – Publisher, Alan Heisey; Editor, Andrea Stenberg; Circulation Manager, Alexandra Irving

Globe Magazine, 422, ch du Roy, St-Augustin-de-Desmaures PQ G3A 1W8 – 418/878-1800; Fax: 418/878-4506 – Tirage: 23,719; 6 fois par an; français – Éditeur/Rédacteur, Florian Chassé

Going Natural, Federation of Canadian Naturists, PO Box 186, Islington ON M9A 4X2 – 416/410-6833; Fax: 416/723-5531 – Circ.: 630; 4 times a year – Editor, Doug Beckett

HAC News, 393 Main St., Hamilton ON L8N 3T7 – 905/525-1210; Fax: 905/525-1654 – 6 times a year – Editor, Mark Fenton, 905/312-1612

Harrowsmith Country Life (Published by Malcolm Publishing), #1450, 450, boul Albert-Hudon, Montréal-Nord PQ H1G 3J9 – 514/323-6800; Fax: 514/327-7592 – Circ.: 140,146; 6 times a year – Publisher, Michele Paradis

Heritage News, PO Box 81076, Stn Fiddlers Green, Ancaster ON L9G 4X1 – Fax: 905/648-8799 – Bi-monthly

Humanist in Canada, PO Box 3769, Stn C, Ottawa ON K1Y 4J8 – 613/749-8929; Fax: 613/749-8929 – Circ.: 1,500; 4 times a year – Editor, J.E. Piercy

Kindred Spirits of PEI, PO Box 491, Kensington PE C0B 1M0 – 902/436-7329; Fax: 902/436-1787 – Circ.: 5,000; 4 times a year; English & Japanese – Publisher & Editor, George Campbell

Leisureways/Westworld/Going Places Magazine (Published by Canada Wide Magazines & Communications Ltd.), 4180 Lougheed Hwy., 4th Fl., Burnaby BC V5C 6A7 – 604/299-7311; Fax: 604/299-9188 – Circ.: 465,000; 4 times a year; also Westworld Saskatchewan (circ. 110,000, 4 times a year), Westworld Alberta (circ. 320,000, 6 times a year) & Going Places in Manitoba (circ. 95,000, 6 times a year) – Publisher, Peter Legge; Editor, Robin Roberts

Leisure World, 1253 Ouellette Ave., Windsor ON N8X 1J3 – 519/971-3207; Fax: 519/977-1197 – Circ.: 338,400; 6 times a year – Editor, Douglas O'Neil

Lifestyles 5755, A.T.E. Publishing Co. Ltd., 155 East Beaver Creek Rd., Unit 25, PO Box 1000, Richmond Hill ON L4B 2N1 – 905/881-3070; Fax: 905/731-6000 – 6 times a year – Publisher, Gabriel Erem; Editor, Jeannette Friedman

Living Safety, c/o Canada Safety Council, 1020 Thomas Spratt Place, Ottawa ON K1G 5L5 – 613/739-1535; Fax: 613/739-1566; Email: csu@safety-council.org; URL: http://www.safety-council.org – 4 times a year – General Manager, Jack A. Smith, 613/739-1535, ext.225

Le Lundi (Published by Trustar Ltd.), #2000, 2020, rue University, Montréal PQ H5A 2A5 – 514/848-7000; Fax: 514/848-9854 – Tirage: 82,000; Hebdomadaire; français – Rédactrice, Michèle Lemieux

Menz, #610, 4150, rue St-Catharine ouest, Montréal PQ H3Z 2X7 – 514/937-3131; Fax: 514/937-3515 – Circ.: 85,000; 6 times a year – Publisher, Bhaskar Patel; Editor-in-Chief, Vanessa Berkling

Monarchy Canada, PO Box 1057, Oakville ON L5J 5E9 – 905/975-2608; Fax: 905/975-2608 – 4 times a year

Muskoka Life, #103, 175 Manitoba St., PO Box 1600, Bracebridge ON P1L 1V6 – 705/645-4463; Fax: 705/645-3928 – Annually

New Maritimes, PO Box 31269, Halifax NS B3K 5Y5 – 902/425-6622 – 6 times a year

The Next City, PEMA & Energy Probe Research Foundation, 225 Brunswick Ave., Toronto ON M5S 2M6 – 416/964-9223, ext.236; Fax: 416/964-8239; Email: letters@nextcity.com; URL: http://www.nextcity.com – Circ.: 10,000; 4 times a year – Publisher, Lawrence Solomon; Email: LawrenceSolomon@nextcity.com; Managing Editor, Cecily Ross

Nouvelles CEQ, Centrale de l'enseignement du Québec, 9405, rue Sherbrooke est, Montréal PQ H1L 6P3 – 514/356-8888; Fax: 514/356-9999 – Tirage: 99,000; 5 fois par an; français – Directeur, Guy Brouillette

OHS Bulletin (Published by Ontario Historical Society), 34 Parkview Ave., Willowdale ON M2N 3Y2 – 416/226-9011; Fax: 416/226-2740 – Circ.: 2,500; 6 times a year – Circulation Manager, Barbara Truax; Editor, Meribeth Clow

Peninsula Magazine, The Peace Arch News, #101, 1440 George St., PO Box 75149, White Rock BC V4B 4A3 – 604/531-1711; Fax: 604/531-7977 – Monthly – Publisher, Fred Gorman; Editor, Diane Strandberg

Reader's Digest, 215 Redfern Ave., Montréal PQ H3Z 2V9 – 514/934-0751; Fax: 514/932-3637 – Circ.: 1,537,200; Monthly; English & French editions – Editor, R. Aubin

Safarir, 549, av Grande-Allée est, Québec PQ G1R 2J5 – 418/522-1062; Fax: 418/522-3592 – 12 fois par an; français – Éditeur, Sylvain Bolduc; Rédacteur, Claude Desrocher

Saturday Night, Hollinger Inc., #400, 184 Front St. East, Toronto ON M5A 4N3 – 416/368-7237; Fax: 416/368-5112 – Circ.: 330,000; 10 times a year – Publisher, Jeffrey W. Shearer; Editor, Ken Whyte; Managing Editor, Anne Collins

Sky News, National Museum of Science & Technology Corp., 2421 Lancaster Rd., PO Box 9724, Stn T, Ottawa ON K1G 5A3 – Fax: 613/990-3635; 1-800-267-3999 – Publisher, Wendy McPeake; Editor, Terence Dickinson

This Country Canada, One Mill St., PO Box 39, Pakenham ON K0A 2X0 – 613/524-5000; Fax: 613/624-5952 – Circ.: 100,000; 4 times a year; ISSN 1188-8261 – Publisher, Corrie Pugh; Editor, Judith Haines; Circulation Manager, Barbara Norton

Touring: The Car & Travel Magazine, c/o Consultants CGEI inc., 3281, av Jean-Béraud, Chomedey, Laval PQ H7T 2L2 – 514/334-5912; Fax: 514/688-6269 – Circ.: 474,000; 4 times a year; English & French – Delegate Publisher, Ginette St-Pierre; Editor, André Ducharme

University of Toronto Magazine, University of Toronto, Dept. of Public Affairs, 21 King's College Circle, Toronto ON M5S 1A1 – 416/978-2106; Fax: 416/978-7430 – Circ.: 196,400; 4 times a year – Editor, George Cook

Up Here: Life in Canada's North, Outcrop Ltd., PO Box 1350, Yellowknife NT X1A 2N9 – 403/920-4652; Fax: 403/873-2844; Email: outrcop@inter-north.com – Circ.: 35,000; Bi-monthly – Publisher, Marion LaVigne; Editor, Mike Vlessidos

Western Living, Telemedia, #300, South East Tower, 555 - 12th Ave. West, Vancouver BC V5Z 4L4 – 604/877-7732; Fax: 604/877-4848 – Monthly – Editor, Carolann Rule

Why: A Magazine About Life, RAZ Communications, #217, 312 Dolomite Dr., Downsview ON M3J 2N2 – 416/667-9609; Fax: 416/667-9715 – Circ.: 55,000; 6 times a year – Publisher, Orly Sibilia; Editor, Diane Stivak; Circulation Manager, Esther Abbou

Windspeaker, 15001 - 112 Ave., Edmonton AB T5M 2V6 – 403/455-2700; Fax: 403/455-7639 – 6 times a year

HEALTH, MEDICAL

Ability Network, 19 Mount Pleasant Ave., Dartmouth NS B3A 3T3 – 902/461-9009; Fax: 902/461-9484 – Circ.: 24,000; 4 times a year – Spencer Bevan-John

alive magazine - The Canadian Journal of Health & Nutrition, Canadian Health Reform Products Ltd., 7436 Fraser Park Dr., Burnaby BC V5J 5B9 – 604/435-1919; Fax: 604/435-4888 – Circ.: 173,000; 12 times a year – Publisher, Siegfried Gursche; Managing Editor, Rhody Lake

L'Almanach Québec en santé, #210, 630, rue Sherbrooke ouest, Montréal PQ H3A 1E2 – 514/990-0872; Fax: 514/990-0872 – Circ.: 25,000; Annually; English & French – Editor, Dominique Rouleau

Arthritis News, The Arthritis Society, #901, 250 Bloor St. East, Toronto ON M4W 3P2 – 416/967-1414; Fax: 416/967-7171 – Circ.: 14,000; 4 times a year – Editor, Rod Tamer

Arthroexpress, c/o The Arthritis Society, #901, 250 Bloor St. East, Toronto ON M4W 3P2 – 416/967-1414; Fax: 416/967-7171 – Tirage: 5,000; 4 fois par an; français – Rédacteur, Rod Tamer

Better Health Magazine, The Harvard Publishing Co., #406, 220 Duncan Mill Rd., North York ON

M3B 3J5 – 416/443-0875; Fax: 416/447-0059 – Circ.: 498,000; 2 times a year; English & French – Editor, Frances Litwin; Circulation Manager, Chaya Glezerman

Croissance, Les Publication Neomag inc., CP 339, Bellefeuille PQ J0R 1A0 – 514/565-9256; Fax: 514/565-2797 – Tirage: 21,000; 10 fois par an – Éditeur & Rédacteur, François Charron; Directrice de tirage, Nathalie Lebersan

Diabetes News, #500, 15 Toronto St., Toronto ON M5C 2E3 – 416/363-3373; Fax: 416/363-3393 – 4 times a year – Editor, Alison Wynd

Family Health, PO Box 2421, Edmonton AB T5J 2S6 – 403/429-5189; Fax: 403/498-5661 – 4 times a year; ISSN 0830-0305

Future Health, c/o Canadians for Health Research, PO Box 126, Westmount PQ H3Z 2T1 – 514/398-7478; Fax: 514/398-8361 – Circ.: 2,000; 4 times a year – Editor, Heather Pengelley; Assistant Editor, Linda Bazinet

Guide Ressources, SWAA Communication Inc., #305, 4388, rue St-Denis, Montréal PQ H2J 2L1 – 514/847-0060; Fax: 514/847-0062; Email: swaa@vir.com – Tirage: 15,000; 10 fois par an; français – Éditeur, Christian Lamontagne; Rédactrice, Lucie Dumoulin

The Health Journal: Canada's Authoritative Health Forum, Gemini Communications, 113 Mildenhall Rd., North York ON M4N 3H4 – 416/488-1513; Fax: 416/484-9377 – Circ.: 200,000; 6 times a year – Co-Publisher, Chantal Goudreau; Co-Publisher, Donnalyn Manitni

Health Naturally, PO Box 580, Parry Sound ON P2A 2X5 – 705/746-7839; Fax: 705/746-7893 – Circ.: 43,000; 6 times a year – Co-Publisher, David Rowland; Editor, Lorrie Imbert; Office Manager, Gloria Marshall

HealthWatch Canada (Published by Multi-Vision Publishing), #1000, 655 Bay St., Toronto ON M5G 2K4 – 416/595-9944; Fax: 416/595-7217 – Circ.: 520,000; 4 times a year – Publisher, Ashley Harvey

Ontario's Common Ground Magazine (Published by New Age Times Ink.), 356 Dupont St., Toronto ON M5R 1V9 – 416/964-0528 – Circ.: 52,000; 4 times a year – Editor, Julia Woodford

Santé (Published by Les Éditions du Feu vert), 5148, boul St-Laurent, Montréal PQ H2T 1R8 – 514/273-9773; Fax: 514/273-9034 – Tirage: 65,000; 10 fois par an; français – Éditeur, Francine Tremblay; Rédactrice, Hélène Matteau; Directrice de tirage, Sylvie Hamel

Second Wind, The Alberta Lung Assn., 11402 University Ave., 3rd Fl., PO Box 4500, Edmonton AB T6E 6K2 – 403/492-0354; Fax: 403/492-0362 – 4 times a year – Editor, Robin Telasky

Vitalité Québec, 99, rue Laurel, Baie d'Urfé PQ H9X 3M6 – 514/990-6040; Fax: 514/457-0385 – Tirage: 40,000; 6 fois par an' français – Rédacteur, Daniel Crisfai

Vitality Magazine (Published by New Age Times Ink.), 356 Dupont St., Toronto ON M5R 1V9 – 416/964-0528 – Circ.: 38,000; 10 times a year – Editor & Publisher, Julia Woodford

HISTORY & GENEALOGY

The Loyalist Gazette, U.E.L. Association of Canada, 50 Baldwin St., Toronto ON M5T 1L4 – 416/591-1783; Fax: 416/591-1783 – Circ.: 3,000; 2 times a year – Editor, David K. Dorward

HOBBIES

Canadian Amateur, C.A.R.F. Publications, #114, 535 Canteval Terrace, Orleans ON K4A 2E4 – 613/837-4477; Fax: 613/837-5723; Email: RDL2@IGS.NET; URL: http://www.cac.ca – Circ.: 8,500; 11 times a year – Editor, Robin Ludlow; Circulation Manager, Deborah Norman

Canadian Antique Power: An Adventure into Canada's Agricultural Heritage, PO Box 120, Teeswater ON N0G 2S0 – 519/392-6733; Fax: 519/392-6731 – 6 times a year; ISSN 1198-5011

Canadian Coin News (Published by Trajan Publishing Corp.), #292, 103 Lakeshore Rd., St Catharines ON L2N 2T6 – 905/646-7744; Fax: 905/646-0995; URL: http://www.trajan.com/coin.default.ehtml – 26 times a year – Publisher, Paul Fiocca; Editor, Bret Evans; Circulation Manager, Tammy Kruck

Canadian Railway Modeller, c/o North Kildonan Publications, 1453 Henderson Hwy, PO Box 28006, Winnipeg MB R2G 4E9 – 204/668-0168; Fax: 204/668-0168 – Circ.: 24,000; 6 times a year – Editor, Morgan B. Turney; Circulation Manager, Dianne Williams

Canadian Sportscard Collector (Published by Trajan Publishing Corp.), #292, 103 Lakeshore Rd., St Catharines ON L2N 2T6 – 905/646-7744; Fax: 905/646-0995 – Circ.: 25,000; Monthly – Editor, Jeffrey Morris

Canadian Stamp News (Published by Trajan Publishing Corp.), #292, 103 Lakeshore Rd., St Catharines ON L2N 2T6 – 905/646-7744; Fax: 905/646-0995; URL: http://www.trajan.com/stamp/default.ehtml – 26 times a year – Publisher, Paul Fiocca; Editor, Ellen Rodger; Circulation Manager, Tammy Kruck

Canadian Workshop (Published by Camar Publications), 130 Spy Ct., Markham ON L3R 5H6 – 905/475-8440; Fax: 905/475-9246; Email: nstn.4303@fox.nstn.ca – Circ.: 113,000; 11 times a year – Editor, Tom Hopkins

CraftNews, c/o Ontario Crafts Council, 35 McCaul St., Toronto ON M5T 1V7 – 416/977-3551; Fax: 416/977-3552 – Circ.: 4,500; 4 times a year – Editor, Anne McPherson

Crafts Plus (Published by Camar Publications), 130 Spy Ct., Markham ON L3R 5H6 130 Spy Ct., Markham ON L3R 5H6 – 905/475-8440; Fax: 905/475-9246 – Circ.: 105,000; 8 times a year

ÉCHEC+, c/o La Fédération Québécoise des Échecs, CP 640, Succ C, Montréal PQ H2L 4L5 – 514/252-3034; Fax: 514/251-8038; Email: gh191873@merlin.si.uqam.ca; URL: http://www.er.uqam.ca/merlingh/191873/fge.htm – Tirage: 1,800; 6 fois par an; français – Rédacteur, Jean Hébert; Directeur de tirage, Richard Bérubé

Model Aviation Canada, 5100 South Service Rd., Unit 9, Burlington ON L7L 6A5 – 905/632-9808; Fax: 905/632-3304; URL: http://www.maac.ca – Circ.: 12,600; 6 times a year – Publisher, Linda Patrick; Editor, Peter Perry, 416/269-8747; Circulation Manager, Karen Franks

Philatélie Québec, Les Éditions Phibec inc., CP 1000, Succ M, Montréal PQ H1V 3R2 – 514/252-3035; Fax: 514/251-8038 – Tirage: 1,500; 10 fois par an; français – Rédacteur, Jean-Pierre Durard

HOMES

Build & Green, #D, 2922 West 6th Ave., Vancouver BC V6K 1X3 – 604/730-1940; Fax: 604/730-7860 – Circ.: 29,000; 10 times a year – Publisher & Editor, Leonard Wexler

The Canadian Home Planner (Published by Family Communications Inc.), #1, 37 Hanna Ave., Toronto ON M6K 1X1 – 416/537-2604; Fax: 416/538-1794 – Circ.: 100,000; Annual – Publisher, Donald Swimburne

Canadian House & Home (Published by Canadian Home Publishers), #120, 511 King St. West, Toronto ON M5V 2Z4 – 416/593-0204; Fax: 416/591-1630; Email: homepub@inforamp.net – Circ.: 140,000; 8 times a year – Publisher, Lynda Reeves; Editor, Cobi Ladner; Circulation Manager, Alexandra Cooper

Canadian Living (Published by Telemedia Publishing), #100, 25 Sheppard Ave. West, North York ON M2N 6S7 – 416/733-7600; Fax: 416/733-3398; Email: canadianliving@telemedia.org; URL: http://www.canadianliving.com – Circ.: 563,000; 12 times a year – Publisher, Caren King; Editor, Bonnie Baker Cowan; Circulation Manager, Darlene Storey

Canadian Select Homes (Published by Telemedia Publishing), #100, 25 Sheppard Ave. West, North York ON M2N 6S7 – 416/733-7600; Fax: 416/218-3632 – Circ.: 145,000; 8 times a year – Publisher, Maureen Cavan; Editor, Barbara Dixon; Circulation Manager, Darlene Storey

Century Home, Bluestone House Inc., 12 Mill St. South, Port Hope ON L1A 2S5 – 905/885-2449; Fax: 905/885-5355 – Circ.: 35,000; 7 times a year – Publisher & Editor, J. Rumgay

Classic Home (Published by Giroux Publishing), 102 Ellis St., Penticton BC V2A 4L5 – 250/493-0942; Fax: 250/493-7526; Email: cgiroux@awinc.com; 1-800-361-7526 – Circ.: 10,000; Annually – Publisher, G.T. Giroux; Editor, Michael A. Giroux

Condos de Rêves (Published by Groupe Magazines S.A. Inc.), #300, 275, boul des Braves, Terrebonne PQ J6W 3H6 – 514/964-7590; Fax: 514/964-2327 – Annuellement – Éditeur, Denis Clermont

Décoration Chez-Soi (Published by Publicor), 7, ch Bates, Outremont PQ H2V 1A6 – 514/270-1100; Fax: 514/270-9618 – Tirage: 63,000; 10 fois par an; français – Directeur, Pierre Deschènes

Décormag (Published by Les Éditions du Feu vert), 5148, boul St-Laurent, Montréal PQ H2T 1R8 – 514/273-9773; Fax: 514/273-9034 – Tirage: 60,000; 10 fois par an; français – Éditrice, Michèle Dubreuil; Rédactrice, Michèle Deraîche; Directrice de tirage, Sylvie Hamel

Del Condominium Life, 4800 Dufferin St., Downsview ON M3H 5S9 – 416/661-3640; Fax: 416/661-8653 – Circ.: 25,000; 3 times a year – Editor in Chief, Andre Pilish

Designers' Best Home Plans (Published by Giroux Publishing), 102 Ellis St., Penticton BC V2A 4L5 – 250/493-0942; Fax: 250/493-7526; Email: cgiroux@awinc.com; 1-800-361-7526 – Circ.: 10,000; Annually – Publisher, G.T. Giroux; Editor-in-Chief, Michael A. Giroux

First Home Buyer's Guide (Published by Homes for Sale Magazine Ltd.), 178 Main St., Unionville ON L3R 2G9 – 905/479-4663; Fax: 905/479-4482 – Circ.: 300,000; 2 times a year – Publisher, Michael Rosset; Editor, Risë Levy; Circulation Manager, Natalie Armstrong

Habitabec Plus, 8620, rue Berri, Montréal PQ H2P 2G4 – 514/389-5943; Fax: 514/385-5982 – 48 times a year; English & French – President & Executive Editor, Jacques Dery

Homes & Cottages, The In-Home Show, #D, 6557 Mississauga Rd., Mississauga ON L5N 1A6 – 905/567-1440; Fax: 905/567-1442; Email: janhre@pathcom.com – Circ.: 55,000; 8 times a year – Publisher, Steven Griffin; Editor, Janice Naisbly; Circulation, Louise Berridge

Homes Magazine (Published by Homes for Sale Magazine Ltd.), 178 Main St., Unionville ON L3R 2G9 – 905/479-4663; Fax: 905/479-4482 – Circ.: 100,000; 8 times a year – Publisher, Michael Rosset; Editor, Risë Levy; Circulation Manager, Natalie Armstrong

Les Idées de ma Maison (Published by Publicor), 7, ch Bates, Outremont PQ H2V 1A6 – 514/270-1100; Fax: 514/270-6900 – Tirage: 68,000; 10 fois par an; français – Rédactrice, Béatrix Marik

Maître d'Oeuvre, 1250, rue Nobel, Boucherville PQ J4B 5K1 – 514/599-5106; Fax: 514/599-5161 – 3 fois par an; français; 1 English issue – Rédacteur en chef, Marcel Soucy

Manitoba Living Guide, 826 Erin St., Winnipeg MB R3G 2W4 – 204/775-8918 – Annually, Sept – Publisher, Walter G. Bowden; Editor, Frank Chalmers

Master Builder, 1250, rue Nobel, Boucherville PQ J4B 5K1 – 514/599-5106; Fax: 514/599-5157 – Éditeur/Rédacteur, Marcel Soucy

Muskoka Real Estate Guide, Muskoka Publications Group Inc., PO Box 1600, Bracebridge ON P1L 1V6

– 705/645-4463; Fax: 705/645-3928 – Circ.: 8,713, winter; 22,274, summer; Weekly – Publisher, Donald F. Smith

Newhomes (Published by Canadian Publishers), 1465 St. James St., Winnipeg MB R3H 0W9 – 204/949-6100; Fax: 204/949-6122 – Circ.: 40,000; 18 times a year – Publisher, Gerald L. Dorge; Editor, Bruce Nairn

Plans de Maisons du Québec (Published by Publicor), 7, ch Bates, Outremont PQ H2V 1A6 – 514/270-1100; Fax: 514/270-6900 – Tirage: 27,000; 4 fois par an; français – Rédacteur, Claude Leclerc

Practical Homes Home Plans (Published by Giroux Publishing), 102 Ellis St., Penticton BC V2A 4L5 – 250/493-0942; Fax: 250/493-7526; Email: cgiroux@awinc.com; 1-800-361-7526 – Circ.: 10,000; Annually – Publisher, G.T. Giroux; Editor-in-Chief, Michael A. Giroux

Proven & Popular Home Plans (Published by Giroux Publishing), 102 Ellis St., Penticton BC V2A 4L5 – 250/493-0942; Fax: 250/493-7526; Email: cgiroux@awinc.com; 1-800-361-7526 – Circ.: 10,000; Annually – Publisher, G.T. Giroux; Editor-in-Chief, Michael A. Giroux

Real Estate News, c/o Toronto Real Estate Board, 1400 Don Mills Rd., Don Mills ON M3B 3N1 – 416/443-8113; Fax: 416/443-9185 – Circ.: 74,000; Weekly – Editorial Coordinator, Dan O'Reilly

Real Estate Victoria, Monday Publications, 1609 Blanshard St., Victoria BC V8W 2J5 – 250/382-9171; Fax: 250/382-9172 – Circ.: 25,000; Weekly – Publisher, Andrew Lynch; Editor, Glenda Turner

Rénovation Bricolage (Published by Publicor), 7, ch Bates, Outremont PQ H2V 1A6 – 514/270-1100; Fax: 514/270-6900 – Tirage: 34,886; 9 fois par an; français – Rédacteur, Claude LeClerc

Renovation Magazine (Published by Homes for Sale Magazine Ltd.), 178 Main St., Unionville ON L3R 2G9 – 905/479-4663; Fax: 905/479-4482; Email: house@homesmag.com – Circ.: 50,000; 2 times a year – Publisher, Michael Rosset; Editor, Risë Levy; Circulation Manager, Natalie Armstrong

Résidences Plaisirs de Vivre/Living in Style, 554 Grosvenor Ave., Westmount PQ H3Y 2S4 – 514/935-1171; Fax: 514/935-4504 – Circ.: 70,500; 5 times a year; English & French – Éditeur, Danièle Adam; Rédactrice, Martine Demange

Select Home Designs, #301, 611 Alexander St., Vancouver BC V6A 1E1 – 604/879-4144; Fax: 604/251-3212; Email: selecthomedesigns@msn.com; URL: http://www.select-online.com – Circ.: 150,000; Annually – Publisher, Brian Thorn; Editor, Brant Furdyk

Thunder Bay Real Estate News (Published by North Superior Publishing Inc.), 1145 Barton St., Thunder Bay ON P7B 5N3 – 807/623-2348; Fax: 807/623-7515 – Circ.: 30,000; Weekly – Scott A. Sumnor

Touchez-Dubois, 1001, Bromont, Longueuil PQ J4M 2P9 – 514/674-6668; Fax: 514/674-6658 – Tirage: 30,000; 10 fois par an – Rédacteur, Robert Dubois

Vancouver Home Buyers Guide, Read Publishing Inc., 2225 Folkestone Way, West Vancouver BC V7S 2Y6 – 604/683-4663; Fax: 604/922-7201 – Circ.: 25,000; 6 times a year; also Vancouver's Home Handbook (annual, circ. 40,000) – Publisher, Robert Read

Welcome Home (Published by Maclean Hunter Publishing), 777 Bay St., Toronto ON M5W 1A7 – 416/596-5425; Fax: 416/593-3197 – Circ.: 150,000; Annually, April – Publisher, Lee Simpson; Editor, Anita Draycott

Winnipeg Homes & Lifestyles, 444 Brooklyn St., Winnipeg MB M3J 1M7 – 204/885-5577; Fax: 204/889-2015 – 4 times a year – Publisher, Fred H. Glazerman

HORSES, RIDING & BREEDING

Atlantic Horse & Pony, PO Box 1509, Liverpool NS B0T 1K0 – 902/354-3321 – 6 times a year – Editor, Dirk van Loon

Canadian Arabian News, Canadian Arabian Horse Registry, #801 Terrace Plaza, 4445 Calgary Trail, Edmonton AB T6H 4R7 – 403/436-4244; Fax: 403/438-2971 – Circ.: 2,200; 6 times a year – Editor, Peggy Arthurs

Canadian Horseman (Published by Corinthian Publishing Co. Ltd.), 225 Industrial Pkwy. South, PO Box 670, Aurora ON L4G 4J9 – 905/727-0107; Fax: 905/841-1530 – 6 times a year – Publisher, Susan Jane Anstey; Editor, Lee Benson

The Canadian Sportsman, 25 Old Plank Rd., PO Box 129, Straffordville ON N0J 1Y0 – 519/866-5558; Fax: 519/866-5596; Email: cdnsport@nornet.on.ca – 26 times a year – Editor, Gary Foerster

Canadian Thoroughbred (Published by Corinthian Publishing Co. Ltd.), 225 Industrial Pkwy. South, PO Box 670, Aurora ON L4G 4J9 – 905/727-0107; Fax: 905/841-1530 – 6 times a year – Publisher, Susan Jane Anstey; Editor, Lee Benson

Le Courrier Hippique, Sportam Inc., 4545, av Pierre-de-Coubertin, CP 1000, Succ M, Montréal PQ H1V 3R2 – 514/252-3053; Fax: 514/252-3165 – 6 fois par an; français – Rédacteur, Richard Mongeau

Horse Action International, PO Box 1778, Vernon BC V1T 8C3 – 250/545-9896; Fax: 250/545-9896 – Circ.: 20,000 – Publisher/Editor, Dr. B.J. (Jan) White

The Horse Chronicle, Grace Publishing, RR#1, Orillia ON L3V 6H1 – Fax: 705/325-6639; 1-800-410-PONY – 6 times a year – Publisher/Editor, John D. Kennedy

Horse & Country Canada, Equine Communications & Publications, 8b Sweetnam Dr., Stittsville ON K2S 1A2 – 613/831-2928; Fax: 613/831-0240 – Circ.: 9,000; 6 times a year – Publisher & Editor, Judith H. McCartney

Horsepower: Magazine for Young Horse Lovers (Published by Corinthian Publishing Co. Ltd.), 225 Industrial Pkwy. South, PO Box 670, Aurora ON L4G 4J9 – 905/727-0107; Fax: 905/841-1530; Email: 74273.3167@compuserve.com – Circ.: 20,000; 6 times a year – Publisher, Susan Jane Anstey; Editor, Susan Stafford; Circulation Manager, Karin Appel

Horses All, 4000 - 19th St. NE, Calgary AB T2E 6P8 – 403/250-6633; Fax: 403/291-0703 – Circ.: 10,000; Monthly – Publisher, Steven Mark; Editor, Cindy Dickson; Circulation Manager, Michella Treiber

Horse Sport (Published by Corinthian Publishing Co. Ltd.), 225 Industrial Pkwy. South, PO Box 670, Aurora ON L4G 4J9 – 905/727-0107; Fax: 905/841-1530 – Circ.: 10,000; 12 times a year – Publisher, Susan Jane Anstey; Editor, Susan Stafford; Circulation Manager, Karin Appel

Pacific Horse Journal, 10148 Bowerbank Rd., Sidney BC V8L 3T9 – 250/655-8883; Fax: 250/655-8883; Email: pachorse@nanaimo.ark.com; URL: http://www.ibnd.com/horsejnl – Circ.: 20,000; 10 times a year – Co-Publisher, Marina Sacht; Editor & Co-Publisher, Kathy Smith

The Rider, 491 Book Rd. West, Ancaster ON L9G 3L1 – 905/648-2035; Fax: 905/648-6977 – Circ.: 9,000; 10 times a year – Publisher, Aidan Finn; Editor, Barry Finn

Trot, c/o Canadian Trotting Association, 2150 Meadowvale Blvd., Mississauga ON L5N 6R6 – 905/858-3060; Fax: 905/858-3111 – Monthly – Editor, Harold Howe

LABOUR, TRADE UNIONS

Our Times, 390 Dufferin St., Toronto ON M6K 2A3 – 416/531-5762; Fax: 416/533-2397 – 6 times a year – Editor, Lorraine Endicott

Socialist Worker, PO Box 339, Stn E, Toronto ON M6H 4E3 – 416/972-6391; Fax: 416/464-5930 – 24 times a year; ISSN 0836-7094

LITERARY

absinthe, PO Box 61113, Stn Kensington PO, Calgary AB T2N 4S6; URL: http://www.ucalgary.ca/~amathur/absinthe.html – 2 times a year

The Antigonish Review, St. Francis Xavier University, PO Box 5000, Antigonish NS B2G 2W5 – 902/867-3962; Fax: 902/867-5153; Email: tar@stfx.ca – Circ.: 800; 4 times a year – Editor, George Sanderson

ARC: A Magazine of Poetry & Poetry Criticism, PO Box 7368, Ottawa ON K1L 8E4 – Circ.: 680; 2 times a year – Co-Editor, John Barton; Co-Editor, Rita Donovan

Blood & Aphorisms, PO Box 702, Stn P, Toronto ON M5S 2Y4 – 416/535-1233; Email: blood@io.org; URL: http://www.io.org/~blood – Circ.: 2,500; 4 times a year – Publisher, Tim Paleczny

Books in Canada, 427 Mount Pleasant Rd., Toronto ON M4S 2L8 – 416/489-4755; Fax: 416/489-6045; Email: BinC@intacc.web.net – Circ.: 8,000; 9 times a year; ISSN: 0045-2564 – Co-Publisher, Adrian Stein; Editor, Norman Doidge; Managing Editor, Gerald Owen

Brick: A Literary Journal, PO Box 537, Stn Q, Toronto ON M4T 2M5 – 3 times a year

Canadian Fiction Magazine, Quarry Press, PO Box 1061, Kingston ON L7L 4Y5 – 613/548-8429; Fax: 613/548-1556 – Circ.: 2,000; 4 times a year – Editor, Geoff Hancock

The Capilano Review, 2055 Purcell Way, North Vancouver BC V7J 3H5 – 604/984-1712; Fax: 604/984-4985; Email: erains@capcollege.bc.ca; URL: http://www.capcollege.bc.ca/departments.tcr/tcr.html – Circ.: 900; 3 times a year – Editor, Robert Sherrin; Circulation Manager, Elizabeth Rains

Carousel, c/o University of Guelph, #217, University Centre, Guelph ON N1G 2W1 – 519/824-4120, ext.6748; Fax: 519/673-9603; Email: daniel@uoguelph.ca – Circ.: 600; Annually – Editor, Daniel Evans

The Chesterton Review, c/o STM College, 1437 College Dr., Saskatoon SK S7N 0W6 – 306/966-8917; Fax: 306/966-8917; Email: morrisj@duke.usask.ca – Circ.: 1,700; 4 times a year – Editor, Rev. J. Ian Boyd, C.S.B.; Circulation Manager, Jane Morris

The Claremont Review, c/o Claremont Review Publishers, 4980 Wesley Rd., Victoria BC V8Y 1Y9 – 250/658-5221; Fax: 250/658-5387; Email: aurora@IslandNet.com; URL: http://206.12.151.25.3 – Circ.: 1,500; 2 times a year – Circulation Manager, Bill Stenson

Dalhousie Review, c/o Dalhousie University, #314, Sir James Dunn Bldg., Halifax NS B3H 3J5 – 902/494-2541; Fax: 902/494-1665; Email: DALREV@AC.DAL.CA – 3 times a year – Editor, Dr. Alan R. Andrews; Circulation Manager, Debbie Hills

Dandelion, 992 - 9 Ave. SE, Calgary AB T2G 0S4 – 403/265-0524 – 2 times a year; ISSN 0383-9275

Descant, Descant Arts & Letters Foundation, PO Box 314, Stn P, Toronto ON M5S 2S8 – 416/593-2557 – Circ.: 1,100; 4 times a year – Editor, Karen Mulhallen

Exile, PO Box 67, Stn B, Toronto ON M5T 2C0 – 416/969-9556 – Circ.: 1,200; 4 times a year – Publisher & Editor, Barry Callaghan

The Fiddlehead, Campus House, University of New Brunswick, PO Box 4400, Stn A, Fredericton NB E3B 5A3 – 506/453-3501; Fax: 506/453-4599 – Circ.: 1,000; 4 times a year – Editor, Don McKay; Circulation Manager, S. Campbell

Geist, #103, 1014 Homer St., Vancouver BC V6B 2W9 – 604/681-9161; Fax: 604/669-8250; Email: geist@geist.com – Circ.: 5,000; 4 times a year – Publisher, Stephen Osborne; Editor, Kevin Barefoot

Canadian Almanac & Directory 1997

Grain, Saskatchewan Writers Guild, PO Box 1154, Regina SK S4P 3B4 – 306/244-2828; Fax: 306/244-0255; Email: grain.mag@sasknet.sk.ca; URL: http://www.sasknet.com/corporate/skwriter – Circ.: 1,500; 4 times a year – Editor, J.Jill Robinson

Interculture, 4917, rue Saint-Urbain, Montréal PQ H2T 2W1 – 514/288-7229; Fax: 514/844-6800 – Circ.: 1,000; 2 times a year; English & French editions – Publisher & Editor, Robert Vachon; Circulation Manager, André Giguere

Literary Review of Canada, 3266 Yonge St., PO Box 1830, Toronto ON M4N 3P6 – Fax: 416/322-4852 – Circ.: 2,000; 11 times a year – Publisher & Editor, P.A. Dutil

The Malahat Review, University of Victoria, PO Box 3045, Victoria BC V8W 3P4 – 250/721-8524; Fax: 250/721-8653 – Circ.: 2,000; 4 times a year – Editor, Derk Wynand

Matrix, #LB509-7, 1400, boul de Maisonneuve ouest, Montréal PQ H3G 1M8 – 514/848-2340; Fax: 514/848-4501 – 2 times a year; ISSN 0318-3610

The Mystery Review, PO Box 233, Colborne ON K0K 1S0 – 613/475-4440; Fax: 613/475-3400; Email: 71554.551@compuserve.com – Circ.: 2.500; 4 times a year – Publisher, Christian von Hessert; Editor, Barbara Davey

The New Quarterly, c/o English Language Proficiency Programme, PAS 2082, U of Waterloo, 200 University Ave. West, Waterloo ON N2L 3G1 – 519/885-1211, ext.2837; Email: mmerikle@watarts.uwaterloo.ca – Circ.: 400; 4 times a year – Managing Editor, Mary Merikle

Nuit Blanche, #403, 1026, rue St-Jean, Québec PQ G1R 1R7 – 418/692-1354; Fax: 418/692-1355; URL: http://www.qbc.clic.net/~carl/nuit/nuit.html – Tirage: 5,000; 4 fois par an; français – Rédacteur, Alain Lessard

On Spec: The Canadian Magazine of Speculative Writing, The Copper Pig Writers' Society, PO Box 4727, Edmonton AB T6E 5G6 – 403/413-0215; Fax: 403/413-0215; Email: onspec@freenet.edmonton.ab.ca; URL: http://www.greenwoods.com/onspec/ – Circ.: 2,000; 4 times a year – Publisher's Assistant, Karen Desgane

paperplates, 19 Kenwood Ave., Toronto ON M6C 2R8 – 416/651-2551; Fax: 416/651-2910; Email: beekelly@perkolator.com; URL: http://www.perkolator.com – 2/3 issues a year – Publisher & Editor, Bernard Kelly; Circulation Manager, Dan Yashinsky

Paragraph: The Canadian Fiction Review, The Mercury Press, 137 Birmingham St., Stratford ON N5A 2T1 – 519/273-7932; Fax: 519/273-7932 – Circ.: 1,200; 3 times a year – Editor, Beverley Daurio

The Peterborough Review, PO Box 1684, Peterborough ON K9J 7S4 – 705/748-1500; Email: jrouse@trentu.ca – 4 times a year – Co-Publisher & Co-Editor, George Kirkpatrick; Co-Publisher & Co-Editor, Julie Rouse

Poetry Canada, PO Box 1061, Kingston ON K7L 4Y5 – 613/548-8429; Fax: 613/548-1556 – Circ.: 1.750; 4 times a year – Publisher, Bob Hilderley; Editor, Barry Dempster

Pottersfield Portfolio, The Gatsby Press, 5280 Green St., PO Box 27094, Halifax NS B3H 4M8 – 902/443-9178; Email: icolford@is.dal.ca – Circ.: 500; 3 times a year – Editor, Ian Colford

Prairie Fire, Prairie Fire Press Inc., #423, 100 Arthur St., Winnipeg MB R3B 1H3 – 204/943-9066; Fax: 204/942-1555 – Circ.: 1,400; 4 times a year – Editor, Andris Taskand; Circulation Manager, Heidi Harms

Prairie Journal, Prairie Journal Press, PO Box 61203, Stn Brentwood, Calgary AB T2L 2K6 – Circ.: 600; 2 times a year – Editor, A. Burke

Prism International, #E462, Dept. of Creative Writing, UBC, 1866 Main Mall, Vancouver BC V6T 1Z1 – 604/822-2514; Email: prism@unixg.ubc.ca; URL: http://www.arts.ubc.ca/crwr/prism/prism.html – 4 times a year – Executive Editor, Tim Mitchell

Quarry, PO Box 1061, Kingston ON K7L 4Y5 – 613/548-8429; Fax: 613/548-1556 – Circ.: 1,200; 4 times a year – Publisher, Bob Hilderley; Editor, Mary Cameron

Raddle Moon, 2239 Stephens St., Upper, Vancouver BC V6K 3W5 – 2 times a year

The Readers Showcase (Published by Suggitt Publishing Ltd.), 10608 - 172 St., Edmonton AB T5S 1H8 – 403/486-5802; Fax: 403/481-9276; Email: suggitt@planet.eon.net – Circ.: 300,000; 12 times a year – Publisher, Thomas J. Suggitt; Editor, Tanis Nessler

sub-TERRAIN Magazine, sub-TERRAIN Literary Collective Society, PO Box 1575, Stn Bentall Ctr., Vancouver BC V6C 2P7 – 604/876-8710; Fax: 604/879-2667; Email: subter@pinc.com – Circ.: 3,000; 4 issues a year – Managing Editor, Brian Kaufman

TickleAce, PO Box 5353, St. John's NF A1C 5W2 – 709/754-6610; Fax: 709/754-5579 – Circ.: 1,000; 2 times a year – Editor, Bruce Porter

The Toronto Review of Contemporary Writing Abroad, PO Box 6996, Stn A, Toronto ON M5W 1X7 – 416/483-7191; Fax: 416/486-0706 – 3 times a year – Editor, M.C. Vassanji

West Coast Line, West Coast Review Publishing Society, 2027 East Academic Annex, Simon Fraser University, Burnaby BC V5A 1S6 – 604/291-4287; Fax: 604/291-5737 – Circ.: 600; 3 times a year – Editor, Roy Miki; Managing Editor, Jacqueline Larson

Whetstone, c/o University of Lethbridge, 4401 University Dr., Lethbridge AB T1K 3M4 – 403/329-2367; Fax: 403/329-5130 – Circ.: 1,000; 2 times a year – Editor, TheresaMarie Tougas

White Wall Review, 63 Gould St., Toronto ON M5B 1E9 – 416/977-1045; Fax: 416/977-7709 – Annually

MUSIC

Access Magazine, Trafalgar Publications, 109 Morse St., Toronto ON M4M 2P7 – 416/465-9718; Fax: 416/465-6876 – Circ.: 88,000; 10 times a year – Publisher/Editor, Keith Sharp

Bluegrass Canada Magazine, #1, 231 Victoria St., Kamloops BC V2C 2A1 – 250/374-3313; Fax: 250/374-0304 – 6 times a year; Circ.: 4,000; ISSN 0035-8495

Canadian Musician (Published by Norris-Whitney Communications Inc.), #7, 23 Hannover Dr., St Catharines ON L2W 1A3 – 905/641-3471; Fax: 905/641-1648; Email: info@nor.com – Circ.: 30,000; 6 times a year – Publisher, Jim Norris; Managing Editor, Shauna Kennedy

CD Plus Compact Disk Catalogue, 766 Gordon Baker Rd., Willowdale ON M2H 3B4 – 416/490-8850; Fax: 416/490-9662; 1-800-263-4020 Toll free – 2 times a year – Publisher, David Cubitt

Chart, Chart Communications Inc., PO Box 332, Stn A Willowdale, North York ON M2N 5S9 – 416/363-3101; Fax: 416/363-3109; Email: chart@chartnet.com; URL: http://www.chartnet.com – Circ.: 20,000; Monthly – Co-Publisher, Edward Skira; Co-Publisher, Nada Laskovski

Classical Music Magazine, 81 Lakeshore Rd. East, PO Box 45045, Mississauga ON L5G 4S7 – 905/271-0339; Fax: 905/271-9748; Email: music@inforamp.net – 4 times a year – Publisher, Anthony D. Copperthwaite; Editor, Derek Deroy

Coda Magazine, PO Box 1002, Stn D, Toronto ON M4A 2N4 – 416/593-7230; Fax: 416/593-7230; Email: codawest@mars.ark.com – Circ.: 3,000; 6 times a year – Publisher, John Norris; Editor, William E. Smith

Country, RR#1, Holstein ON N0G 2A0 – 519/334-3246; Fax: 519/334-3366 – Circ.: 25,000; 6 times a year – Editor/Publisher, Jim Baine

Country Music News, PO Box 7323, Stn Vanier Terminal, Ottawa ON K1L 8E4 – 613/745-6006; Fax: 613/745-0576 – Circ.: 12,500; Monthly – Editor/Publisher, Larry Delaney

Crescendo, Toronto Musicians' Assn., 101 Thorncliffe Park Dr., Toronto ON M4H 1M2 – 416/421-1020; Fax: 416/421-7011 – Circ.: 4,000; 4 times a year – Circulation Manager, Tina Bagno; Editor, Kevan McKenzie

Heart of the Country, 56A Brybeck Circle, Kitchener ON N2M 2C6 – 519/745-9124; Fax: 519/886-2283; Email: hotc@golden.net – Circ.: 9,500; Monthly – Editor, Jim Cornall

iMPACT, Roll Magazines Inc., 880 Queen St. West, Toronto ON M6J 1G3 – 416/531-8040; Fax: 416/531-2388; Email: impact@inforamp.net; URL: http://www.impactmag.com – Circ.: 85,000; 10 times a year – Editor, Mary Dickie

Musicien Québécois, 439, rue Ste-Hélène, Longueuil PQ J4K 3R3 – 514/928-1726; Fax: 514/670-8683 – Tirage: 13,000; 6 fois par an – Éditeur et Rédacteur, Ralph Angelillo; Directeur de tirage, Serge Gamache

Music in our Lives, The Royal Conservatory of Music, 273 Bloor St. West, Toronto ON M5S 1W2 – 416/408-2824; Fax: 416/698-7081 – Circ.: 40,000; 4 times a year – Publisher, Ann Francis Oakes; Editor, Louise Yearwood; Director of Circulation, Deborah Wood

Musicworks: The Journal of Sound Explorations, 179 Richmond St. West, 3rd Fl., Toronto ON M5V 1V3 – 416/977-3546; Fax: 416/204-1084 – Circ.: 2,000; 3 times a year; English & French – Editor, Gayle Young

Opera Canada, Foundation for Coast to Coast Opera Publication, #434, 366 Adelaide St. East, Toronto ON M5A 3X9 – 416/363-0395; Fax: 416/363-0395 – 4 times a year

Top Forty Focus (Published by Suggitt Publishing Ltd.), 10608 - 172 St., Edmonton AB T5S 1H8 – 403/486-5802; Fax: 403/481-9276; Email: suggitt@planet.eon.net – Circ.: 50,000; 6 times a year – Publisher, Thomas J. Suggitt; Editor, Tanis Nessler

The Valley Circle, c/o Fraser Valley Square & Round Dance Association, 13665 - 88th Ave., Surrey BC V3W 6H1 – 604/594-6415 – Circ.: 2,500; 9 times a year – Editor, Alex Galbraith; Editor, Jean Galbraith

NEWS

7 Jours (Published by Trustar Ltd.), #2000, 2020, rue University, Montréal PQ H5A 2A5 – 514/848-7000; Fax: 514/848-9854 – Tirage: 166,366; Hebdomadaire – Publisher, Claude J. Charron

L'Actualité (Published by Maclean Hunter Publishing), 1001, boul de Maisonneuve ouest, Montréal PQ H3A 3E1 – 514/843-2567; Fax: 514/845-3879 – Tirage: 205,514; 20 fois par an; français – Éditeur, Jean Paré

Alberta/Western Report, 17327 - 106A Ave., Edmonton AB T5S 1M7 – 403/486-2277; Fax: 403/489-3280 – Circ.: 43,603; Weekly – Publisher/Editor, Link Byfield

British Columbia Report, #600, 535 Thurlow St., Vancouver BC V6E 3L2 – 604/682-8202; Fax: 604/682-0963; Email: bcreport@axionet.com; URL: http://www.axionet.com/bcreport – Circ.: 27,000; Weekly – Publisher, Ted Byfield; Editor-in-Chief, Terry O'Neill

Great Lakes Liberty Press, PO Box 7482, Windsor ON N9C 4G1 – Circ.: 8,500 – Co-Publisher, Dan Burr; Co-Publisher, Brett Skinner

Maclean's (Published by Maclean Hunter Publishing), 777 Bay St., Toronto ON M5W 1A7 – 416/596-5311, 5386; Fax: 416/596-6001; Email: 76702.2251@compuserve.com – Circ.: 510,000; Weekly; also Chinese edition co-published six times a year with Sing Tao Daily – Publisher, Brian Segal

Southern Africa Report, 603 1/2 Parliament St., Toronto ON M4X 1P9 – 416/967-5562; Fax: 416/978-1547; Email: tclsac@web.apg.org; vise@physics.utoronto.ca – 5 times a year

Time, Time Canada Ltd., #602, 175 Bloor St. East, Toronto ON M4W 3R8 – 416/929-1115; Fax: 416/929-0019 – Circ.: 327,000; Weekly – Managing Director, Sandra F. Berry

Ven'd'est, L'Éditions coopératives du ven'd'est ltée, 725, rue de Collège, CP 266, Bathurst NB E2A 3Z2 – 506/548-4097; Fax: 506/545-6299 – Tirage: 4,500; 6 fois par an; français – Rédacteur, Michel St-Onge

PHOTOGRAPHY

Blackflash, P.G. Press, 12 - 23rd St. East, 2nd Fl., Saskatoon SK S7K 0H5 – 306/244-8018; Fax: 306/665-6568 – Circ.: 1,300; 4 times a year – Editor, Wallace Polsom

Camera Canada, National Association for Photographic Art, 1120 South Dyke Rd., New Westminster BC V3M 5A2 – 604/524-5039 – Circ.: 6,000; Semi-annually – Editor, Marilyn McEwen

CV Photo, Productions Ciel Variable, #301, 4060, boul Saint-Laurent, Montréal PQ H2W 1Y9 – 514/849-0508; Fax: 514/284-6775; Email: vpopuli@cam.org; URL: http://www.cam.org/~vpopuli – Circ.: 900; 4 times a year; English & French – Publisher, Marcel Blouin; Editor, Franck Michel

Photo Life, Apex Publications, Toronto-Dominion Ctr., PO Box 77, Toronto ON M5K 1E7 – 416/287-6357; Fax: 416/287-6359; Email: 76743.3210@compuserve.com; 1-800-905-7468; URL: http://www.photolife.com – Circ.: 40,500; 6 times a year – Publisher, Curtis J. Sommerville; Editor, Jacques Thibault; Circulation Manager, Jeffrey A. Sommerville

Photo Sélection (Published by Les Publications Apex inc.), 185, rue St-Paul, Québec PQ G1K 3W2 – 418/692-2110; Fax: 418/692-3392 – Tirage: 17,000; 6 fois par an; français, – Éditeur, Curtis J. Sommerville; Rédacteur, Jacques Thibault

POLITICAL

bout de papier, #412, 47 Clarence St., Ottawa ON K1N 9K1 – 613/241-1391; Fax: 613/241-5911 – 4 times a year; English & French

Briarpatch, 2138 McIntyre St., Regina SK S4P 2R7 – 306/525-2949; Fax: 306/565-3430 – Circ.: 2,000; 10 times a year – Managing Editor, George Martin Manz

Canadian Speeches: Issues of the Day, 194 King St., PO Box 250, Woodville ON K0M 2T0 – 705/439-2580; Fax: 705/439-1208 – 10 times a year – Publisher & Editor, Earle Grey

Kick it Over, PO Box 5811, Stn A, Toronto ON M5W 1P2 – 416/766-0972; Email: kio@web.apc.ord – Circ.: 1,600 – Editor, Bob Melcombe

Pacific Current, Pacific New Directions Publishing Society, PO Box 34279, Stn D, Vancouver BC V6J 4P2 – 604/873-1739; Fax: 604/873-6379 – Circ.: 2,000; 8 times a year – Editor, Geoff Meggs

Peace Magazine, 736 Bathurst St., Toronto ON M5S 2R4 – 416/533-7581; Fax: 416/531-6214; Email: msoebcer@apc.org – Circ.: 3,000; 6 times a year – Publisher & Editor, Metta Spencer; Circulation Manager, Brian Burch

RELIGIOUS & DENOMINATIONAL

The Anglican, 135 Adelaide St. East, Toronto ON M5C 1L8 – 416/604-0082; Fax: 416/604-9409 – Monthly – Editor, Stuart Mann

Anglican Journal, c/o Anglican Church of Canada, 600 Jarvis St., Toronto ON M4Y 2J6 – 416/924-9199; Fax: 416/921-4452; Email: anglican_journal@ecunet.org – Circ.: 255,000; 10 times a year – Editor, Rev. David Harris; Circulation Manager, Beverley Murphy

The Atlantic Baptist, PO Box 756, Kentville NS B4N 3X9 – 902/678-6868; Fax: 902/681-0315 – Circ.: 7,000; Monthly – Editor & Manager, Rev. Michael A. Lipe

Canada Lutheran, 1512 St. James St., Winnipeg MB R3H 0L2 – 204/786-6707; Fax: 204/783-7548 – Circ.: 22,000; Monthly – Kenn Ward

The Canadian Baptist, #414, 195 The West Mall, Etobicoke ON M9C 5K1 – 416/622-8600; Fax: 416/622-0780; Email: canbap@user.rose.com – Circ.: 12,000; 10 times a year – Editor, Dr. Larry Matthews; Circulation Manager, Carol Gouveia

Canadian Jewish News, #420, 10 Gateway Blvd., Don Mills ON M3C 3A1 – 416/422-2331; Fax: 416/422-3790 – Circ.: 50,000; Weekly – President, Don Carr, Q.C.; Editor, Mordecai Ben-Dat; General Manager, Gary Laforet

The Canadian Messenger, c/o Jesuit Fathers, 661 Greenwood Ave., Toronto ON M4J 4B3 – 416/466-1195 – Circ.: 16,500; 11 times a year – Editor, Rev. F.J. Power

Canadian Orthodox Missionary, 37323 Hawkins Rd., Dewdney BC V0M 1H0 – 604/826-9336; Fax: 604/820-9758 – Bi-monthly – Editor, Fr. Moses Armstrong

Catholic New Times, 80 Sackville St., Toronto ON M5A 3E5 – 416/361-0761; Fax: 416/251-8191 – Bi-weekly – Editor, Sister Anne O'Brien

The Catholic Register, #303, 67 Bond St., Toronto ON M5B 1X6 – 416/362-6822; Fax: 416/362-8652 – Weekly – Editor, Joe Sinesac

Christian Courier, c/o Calvinist Contact Publishing Ltd., 261 Martindale Rd., Unit 4, St. Catharines ON L2W 1A1 – 905/682-8311; Fax: 905/682-8313 – Circ.: 5,000; Weekly – Publisher, Stan de Jong; Editor, Bert Witvoet

Christian Info News, #200, 20316 - 56th Ave., Langley BC V3A 3Y7 – 604/534-1444; Fax: 604/534-2970 – Circ.: 31,000; Monthly – Publisher, Allan Stanchi; Editor, Flyn Ritchie

ChristianWeek, #300, 228 Notre Dame Ave., Winnipeg MB R3B 1N7 – 204/943-1147; Fax: 204/947-5632; Email: c.week@awnet.com – Circ.: 11,000; Every other Tues., except every 3 weeks in July & Aug. – Publisher, Doug McLeod; Editor-in-Chief, Doug Koop

Compass: A Jesuit Journal, 50 Charles St. East, PO Box 400, Stn F, Toronto ON M4Y 2L8 – 416/921-0653; Fax: 416/921-1864; Email: 74163.2472@compuserve.com; URL: http://www.io.org/~gvanv/compass/comphome.html – Circ.: 3,700; 6 times a year – Publisher, William Addley; Editor, Robert Chodos; Circulation Manager, Barbara Barrett

The Diocesan Times, 5732 College St., Halifax NS B3H 1X3 – Monthly – Editor, Lawrin Armstrong

Faith Today, c/o The Evangelical Fellowship of Canada, #300, 600 Alden Rd., Markham ON L3R 0Y4 – 905/479-5885; Fax: 905/479-4742; Email: ft@efc-canada.com – Circ.: 22,000; 6 times a year – Editor, Dr. Brian C. Stiller; Circulation Manager, Juanita Sternbergh

Gospel Herald, c/o Gospel Herald Foundation, 4904 King St., Beamsville ON L0R 1B6 – 905/563-7503; Fax: 905/563-7503; Email: eperry@freenet.npsic.on.ca – Circ.: 1,400; Monthly – Editor, Wayne Turner; Managing Editor, Eugene C. Perry

Grail: An Ecumenical Journal, c/o Novalis, Saint Paul University, 223 Main St., Ottawa ON K1S 1C4 – 613/236-1393; Fax: 613/782-3004; Email: humphrey@spu.stpaul.uottawa.ca – Circ.: 700; 4 times a year – Co-Editor, Michael Higgins; Co-Editor, Christopher Humphrey

Hallelujah, #0116, 65 Front St. West, PO Box 25, Toronto ON M5J 1E6 – 416/778-8042 – Circ.: 2,000; 4 times a year – Publisher, D.Bruce Arnold

Jewish Free Press, 8411 Elbow Dr. SW, Calgary AB T2V 1K8 – 403/252-9423; Fax: 403/255-5640 – Circ.: 2,000; Semi-monthly – Editor, Judy Shapiro

The Jewish Tribune, 15 Hove St., Downsview ON M3H 4Y8 – 416/633-6224; Fax: 416/630-2159; URL: http://www.canada_ibm.net/bnaibrith/ – Circ.: 65,000;

24 times a year – Publisher, Frank Dimant; Editor, Len Butcher

Mennonite Brethren Herald, Canadian Mennonite Brethern Conference, #3, 169 Riverton Ave., Winnipeg MB R2L 2G5 – 204/669-6575; Fax: 204/654-1865; Email: mbherald@cdnmbconf.ca; URL: http://www.cdnmbconf.ca/mb/mbherald.htm – Circ.: 15,100; Bi-weekly – Managing Editor, Susan Brandt; Editor, Jim Coggins

Mennonite Reporter, #3, 312 Marsland Dr., Waterloo ON N2J 3Z1 – 519/884-3810; Fax: 519/884-3331 – Circ.: 10,300; Every other week – Editor, Ron Rempel

The New Brunswick Anglican, 773 Glengarry Place, Fredericton NB E3B 5Z8 – 506/459-5358 – Monthly exc. July & Aug. – Editor/Production Manager, Ana Watts

The New Freeman, 1 Bayard Dr., Saint John NB E2L 3L5 – 506/632-9226 – Circ.: 6,850; Weekly – Editor, W.L. Donovan

Niagara Anglican, c/o Anglican Diocese of Niagara, Cathedral Place, 252 James St. North, Hamilton ON L8R 2L3 – 905/521-9598; Fax: 905/521-9598 – Circ.: 18,000; Monthly exc. July & Aug. – Editor, Larry Perks; Circulation Manager, Beverley Murphy

L'Oratoire, 3800, ch Queen Mary, Montréal PQ H3V 1H6 – 514/733-8211; Fax: 514/733-9735 – Circ.: 8,500 English; 58,000 French; 6 fois par an; français – Rédacteur en chef, Thérèse Baron

The Pentecostal Testimony, The Penetecostal Assemblies of Canada, 6745 Century Ave., Mississauga ON L5N 6P7 – 905/542-7400; Fax: 905/542-7313 – Circ.: 23,700; Monthly – Editor, Rick Hiebert

Pioneer Christian Monthly, Reformed Church in Canada, RR#4, Cambridge ON N1R 5S5 – 519/622-1777; Fax: 519/622-1993 – Circ.: 2,000; Monthly – Editorial Committee Chairman, Jeff Kingswood, 519/537-6422

Prairie Messenger, Benedictine Monks of St. Peter's Abbey, PO Box 190, Muenster SK S0K 2Y0 – 306/682-1772; Fax: 306/682-5285; Email: ccnpm@explorer.sasknet.sk.ca – Circ.: 7,600; 46 times a year – Editor-in-Chief, Rev. Andrew M. Britz; Circulation Manager, Gail Kleefeld

Presbyterian Record, 50 Wynford Dr., North York ON M3C 1J7 – 416/441-1111; Fax: 416/441-2825 – Circ.: 58,000; Monthly exc. Aug. – Editor, John Congram

Qalam, Qalam International Inc., 150 Main St., PO Box 74013, Brampton ON L6V 1M0 – 905/840-6778; Fax: 905/840-6778 – Circ.: 10,000; 4 times a year – Editor, Khizar Hayat

Shalom, The Printer, #30, 1515 South Park St., Halifax NS B3J 2L2 – 902/422-7491; Fax: 902/425-3722; Email: ai993@ccn.cs.dal.ca – Circ.: 1,200; 4 times a year – Editor, Jon M. Goldberg

Studies in Religion, c/o Prof. Peter Richardson, University College, University of Toronto, Toronto ON M5S 1A1 – 416/978-7149; Fax: 416/325-1399 – Circ.: 1,400; 4 times a year – Editor-in-Chief, John Sandys-Wunsch; Managing Editor, Peter Richardson

Toronto's Original Jewish Pages, Market Solutions Inc., #100, 1118 Centre St., Thornhill ON L4J 7R9 – 905/709-2988; Fax: 905/709-3099 – Circ.: 50,000; 2 times a year

The United Church Observer, c/o United Church of Canada, 478 Huron St., Toronto ON M5R 2R3 – 416/960-8500; Fax: 416/960-8477 – Circ.: 134,600; Monthly – Editor, Muriel Duncan

La Voix Sépharade, 4735, ch de la Côte Ste-Catherine, Montréal PQ H3W 1M1 – 514/733-4998; Fax: 514/733-3158 – Circ.: 5,000; 5 times a year – Publisher, Elie Benchetrit; Editor, Judah Castiel

Western Catholic Reporter, 8421 - 101 Ave., Edmonton AB T6A 0L1 – 403/465-8030; Fax: 403/465-8031; Email: wer@supernet.ab.ca – Circ.: 38,000;

Canadian Almanac & Directory 1997

43 times a year – Managing Editor, Glen Argan; Circulation Manager, Sharon Bly

World of Chabad, c/o Lubavitch, British Columbia, 5750 Oak St., Vancouver BC V6M 2V9 – 604/266-1313; Fax: 604/263-7934 – Circ.: 6,000; 8 times a year – Editor, Yoseph Thomson

SCIENCE & TECHNOLOGY

Québec Science, 425, rue de la Gauchetière est, Montréal PQ H2L 2M7 – 514/843-6888; Fax: 514/843-4897; Email: courrier@QuebecScience.qc.ca; URL: http://www.QuebecScience.qc.ca – Tirage: 15,971; 10 fois par an; français – Éditeur, Michel Gauquelin; Rédacteur en chef, Raymond Lemieux

SENIOR CITIZENS

Le Bel Age (Published by Les Éditions du Feu vert), 5148, boul St-Laurent, Montréal PQ H2T 1R8 – 514/273-9773; Fax: 514/273-9034 – Tirage: 145,000; 11 fois par an; français – Éditrice, Francine Tremblay; Rédactrice, Lucie Deaulniers

CARP News, #702, 27 Queen St. East, Toronto ON M5C 2M6 – 416/363-5562; Fax: 416/363-7394 – Circ.: 180,000; 6 times a year – Publisher & Editor, David Tafler

Choices After 50, EMC Marketing Associates Ltd., PO Box 1291, Saint John NB E2L 4H8 – 506/658-0754; Fax: 506/633-0868 – Editor, Carol Maber

Community Resource Directory (Published by Egress Enterprises Inc.), PO Box 1094, Stn A, Kelowna BC V1Y 7P8 – 250/765-6065; Fax: 250/765-7346 – 8 editions covering different BC regions – Publisher, Joel A. Rickard

The Edmonton Senior (Published by Alberta Business Research Ltd), #800, 10179 - 105 St., Edmonton AB T5J 3N1 – 403/425-1185; Fax: 403/421-7677 – Circ.: 45,000; 10 times a year – Publisher, Lorne Silverstein, 403/429-1610; Editor, Colin Smith

Fifty-Five Plus, c/o Limestone City Publications, PO Box 47, Battersea ON K0H 1H0 – 613/353-2060; Fax: 613/353-7681 – Circ.: 40,000; Bi-monthly – Co-Publisher, Pat MacAulay; Editor & Co-Publisher, Sharon Freeman

Good Times, Senior Publications, 5148, boul St-Laurent, Montréal PQ H2T 1R8 – 514/273-9773; Fax: 514/273-3408 – Circ.: 100,000; 10 times a year – Editor, Denise B. Crawford

The Independent Senior, K.W. Publishing Ltd., 1268 West Pender St., Vancouver BC V6E 2S8 – 604/688-2271; Fax: 604/688-2038 – Circ.: 48,900; 10 times a year – Publisher, Darlene Liboiron; Editor, Adrian Leonard

Le Magazine FADOQ, Editador, 4545, av Pierre-de-Coubertin, CP 1000, Succ M, Montréal PQ H1V 3R2 – 514/252-3017; Fax: 514/252-3154 – Tirage: 108,000; 5 fois par an; français – Directeur, Lyne Rémillard

Mainly for Seniors Lambton-Kent, 4182 Petrolia Line, PO Box 40, Petrolia ON N0N 1R0 – 519/882-1770; Fax: 519/882-3212 – Circ.: 10,000; Monthly – Publisher, Denise Thibeault; Editor, David Pattenaude

Mature Lifestyles, RobJay Holdings Ltd., 6 Trumpourt Ct., Markham ON L3R 1Y9 – 905/475-0586; Fax: 905/474-9851 – Circ.: 25,000; 10 times a year – Publisher, Diane Peterson

Maturity, CYN Investments Ltd., PO Box 397, New Westminster BC V3L 4Y7 – 604/540-7911; Fax: 604/540-7912

MSOS Journal, c/o Manitoba Society of Seniors, 697B Carter Ave., Winnipeg MB R3M 2C3 – 204/453-8502; Fax: 204/475-6853 – Monthly – Editor, Irv Kroeker

New Clarion, PO Box 3151, Stn B, Saint John NB E2M 4X8 – 506/674-2439; Fax: 506/672-1537 – Publisher, Karen Wilson

Prime Time, c/o Canterbury Publishing, 298 Prince St., Peterborough ON K9J 2A5 – 705/749-1895; Fax: 705/749-1105 – Circ.: 8,100; Monthly – Editorial Manager, Leanne Lavender; Circulation Manager, Brian Lavender

The Seniors Choice (Published by Egress Enterprises Inc), PO Box 1094, Stn A, Kelowna BC V1Y 7P8 – 250/765-6065; Fax: 250/765-7346 – Monthly – Publisher, Joel A. Rickard

SeniorsPlus Newspaper, PO Box 1112, Barrie ON L4M 4Y6 – 705/725-9269; Fax: 705/725-9684 – Circ.: 17,000; Monthly – Publisher, W. Moran

The Seniors Review, 11 Bond St., #B2, St. Catharines ON L2R 4Z4 – 905/687-9861; Fax: 905/687-6911; 1-800-627-3111 – Circ.: 40,000 – Publisher, David Irwin; Editor, Elaine Irwin

Seniors Today (Published by McCaine-Davis Communications Ltd.), 232 Henderson Hwy., Winnipeg MB R2L 1L9 – 204/982-4000; Fax: 204/982-4001 – 24 times a year – President, Heather McCaine-Davis

The Senior Times, 4077 Decarie Blvd., Montréal PQ H4A 3J8 – 514/484-5033; Fax: 514/484-8254 – 22 times a year – Publisher/Editor, Barbara Moser

The Silver Pages, Silver Pages International Corporation, #1200, 111 Elizabeth St., Toronto ON M5G 1P7 – 416/977-5911, 8382; Fax: 416/977-4951 – Circ.: 250,000 – Publisher & Editor, Joanna M. Bickus

Today's Choices, 17533 - 106 Ave., Edmonton AB T5S 1E7 – 403/489-5898; Fax: 403/483-2000 – Circ.: 35,000; Monthly – Publisher, Bob Pearce; Associate Publisher/Editor, Elsie Rose

Today's Seniors, Metroland Printing, Publishing & Distributing Ltd., 467 Speers Rd., Oakville ON L6K 3S4 – 905/815-0017, 0045; Fax: 905/815-0026 – Circ.: 567,000; 12 times a year – Publisher, Ian Oliver; Editor in Chief, Don Wall

Today's Times, #13, 12240 Horseshoe Way, Stn A, Richmond BC V7A 4X9 – 604/277-2295; Fax: 604/277-2295 – 10 times a year – Publisher, Brian Scharf

Vitality Newsmagazine, Gold Quill Enterprises Ltd., 208 Princess, 2nd Fl., Winnipeg MB R3B 1L4 – 204/949-9355; Fax: 204/956-0030 – Circ.: 21,000; 10 times a year – Editor, Evelyn Seida; Circulation Manager, Gale Whiteside

Westcoast Reflections, 2604 Quadra St., Victoria BC V8T 4E4 – 250/383-1149; Fax: 250/388-4479; Email: magazine@islandnet.com; URL: http://www.islandnet.com/~magazine/ – Circ.: 20,000; Monthly – Publisher, Jim Bisakowski; Editor, Jane Kezar

SOCIAL WELFARE

Canadian Dimension, #401, 228 Notre Dame Ave., Winnipeg MB R3B 1N7 – 204/957-1519; Fax: 204/943-4617; Email: info@canadiandimension.mb.ca; URL: http://www.canadiandimension.mb.ca/cd/index.htm – Circ.: 3,500; 6 times a year – Office Manager, Michelle Torrres

Community Action: Canada's Community Service Newspaper, 41 Marbury Cres., PO Box 444, Don Mills ON M3C 2T2 – 416/449-6766; Fax: 416/444-5850; Email: comact@interlog.com; URL: http://www.comact@interlog.com – Circ.: 12,000; 22 times a year – Publisher & Editor, Leon Kumove

Our Schools/Our Selves, 107 Earl Grey Rd., Toronto ON M4J 3L6 – 6 times a year; ISSN 0840-7339

Perception, Canadian Council on Social Development, 441 MacLaren, 4th Fl., Stn C, Ottawa ON K2P 2H3 – 613/236-8977; Fax: 613/236-2750; Email: council@ccsd.ca; URL: http://www.achilles.net/~council/ – Circ.: 2,000; 4 times a year; English & French – Editor, Ellen Adelberg; Circulation Manager, Louise Clarke

Rehabilitation Digest, Easter Seals/March of Dimes National Council, #511, 90 Eglinton Ave. East, Toronto ON M4P 2Y3 – 416/932-8382; Fax: 416/932-9844 – Circ.: 2,000; 4 times a year – Editor, Heather Stonehouse

The Social Worker, Myropen Publications Ltd., #402, 383 Parkdale Ave., Ottawa ON K1Y 4R4 – 613/729-6668; Fax: 613/729-9608; Email: casw@casw-acts.ca – Circ.: 14,500; English/French; 4 times a year – Co-ordination, Penny Sipkes

SPORTS & RECREATION

Athletics: Canada's National Track & Field/Running Magazine, #601, 1185 Eglinton Ave. East, North York ON M3C 3C6 – 416/426-7215; Fax: 416/426-7358; Email: ontrack@io.org; URL: http://www.io.org/~ontrack – Circ.: 6,000; 9 times a year; ISSN 0229-4966 – Publisher & Editor, Cecil Smith; Circulation Manager, Bernie Eckler

Backspin: Manitoba's Golf Newspaper (Published by Canadian Publishers), 1465 St. James St., Winnipeg MB R3H 0W9 – 204/949-6100; Fax: 204/949-6122 – Circ.: 15,000; 6 times a year – Publisher, Gerald A. Dorge

Boudoir Noir, PO Box 5, Stn F, Toronto ON M4Y 2L4 – 416/591-2387; Fax: 416/591-1572; Email: boudoir@boudoir-noir.com; URL: http://www.boudoir-noir.com – Circ.: 10,000; 4 times a year – Co-Publisher, Mary Dante; Co-Publisher, Robert Dante

Canadian Curling News, #100, 75 The East Mall, Etobicoke ON M8Z 5W3 – 416/253-0022; Fax: 416/253-9356 – Monthly from Sept. to April – Publisher, Brian Cooke; Editor, George Karrys

Canadian Cyclist, Les Éditions Tricycle Inc., 1251, rue Rachel est, Montréal PQ H2J 2J9 – 514/521-8356; Fax: 514/521-5711 – Annually

Canadian Football Journal, Lark Promotions, 708 Francis Rd., Burlington ON L7T 3X7 – 905/681-1126; Fax: 905/681-1126 – Circ.: 50,000; 4 times a year – Publisher, Larry Robertson

Canadian Rodeo News, #223, 2116 - 27 Ave. NE, Calgary AB T2E 7A6 – 403/250-7292; Fax: 403/250-6926; Email: rodeonews@awinc.com – Circ.: 4,000; Monthly – Editor, P. Kirby Meston; Circulation Manager, Vicki Mowat

Coast the outdoor recreation magazine, PO Box 65837, Stn A, Vancouver BC V5N 5L3 – 604/876-1473; Fax: 604/876-1474; Email: coastmag@mindlink.net – Circ.: 40,000; 10 times a year – Publisher, Allan Main; Editor, Steven Threndyle

Le Coureur des Neiges (Published by Camar Publications), 130 Spy Ct., Markham ON L3R 5H6130 Spy Ct., Markham ON L3R 5H6 – 905/475-8440; Fax: 905/475-9246 – Tirage: 39,400; Annuellement; français – Éditeur, Jacqueline Howe; Rédacteur, Chris Knowles

Diver Magazine, #230, 11780 Hammersmith Way, Richmond BC V7A 5E3 – 604/274-4333; Fax: 604/274-4366; Email: divermag@axionet.com – 9 times a year – Publisher, Peter Vassilopoulos; Editor, Stephanie Bold

Fittingly Yours, #184, 1857 West 4th Ave., Vancouver BC V6J 1M4 – 604/878-1297; Fax: 604/582-7382 – Circ.: 40,000; 6 times a year – Publisher & Editor, Karen Zaitchik

Golf Albatros, CP 115, Succ Cte-des-Neiges, Montréal PQ H3S 2S4 – 514/737-4050; Fax: 514/343-4653 – Tirage: 30,000; 2 fois par an; français – Éditeur, Vivian Mardelli

Golf Canada, Laurel Oak Marketing, #205, 1455 Lakeshore Rd. South, Burlington ON L7S 2J1 – 905/634-5770; Fax: 905/634-8335 – Circ.: 118,720; 4 times a year – Publisher, Wayne Narcisco

Golf Course Ranking Magazine, Longhurst Golf Corp., #14, 85 West Wilmot St., Richmond Hill ON L4B 1K7 – 905/764-5409; Fax: 905/764-5462 – Circ.: 125,000; Annually – Publisher, Bruce Longhurst

Golf Guide, 16410 - 137 Ave., Edmonton AB T5L 4H8 – 403/447-2128; Fax: 403/447-1933 – Annually, April – Editor/Publisher, Paul McCracken

Golf International, 798, boul Arthur Sauvé, CP 91022, St-Eustache PQ J7R 6V9 – 514/386-2927; Fax: 514/974-2212 – Tirage: 28,000; 6 fois par an; français – Éditeur/Rédacteur, Jacques Landry

Golf the West (Published by Koocanusa Publications Inc.), 1510 - 2nd St. North, Cranbrook BC V1C 3L2 – 250/426-7253; Fax: 250/489-3743 – Circ.: 35,000; Annually, April – Publisher, Daryl D. Shellborn; Editor, Stacey Curry

The Hockey News, Transcontinental Publications Inc., #2700, 777 Bay St., Toronto ON M5G 2C8 – 416/340-8000; Fax: 416/340-2786 – Circ.: 112,837; 42 times a year – Publisher, Ed Pearce; Editor, Steve Dryden

Le Journal Québec Quilles, CP 126, Succ Anjou, Montréal PQ H1L 4N7 – 514/351-5224; Fax: 514/351-6818 – Tirage: 26,000; 7 fois par an; français – Éditeur, Yves Larocque; Rédacteur, Gilles Poulin

Motoneige Québec, 99, rue Brouillard, Vaudreuil PQ J7V 6T5 – 514/252-3163; Fax: 514/254-2066 – Tirage: 59,000; 6 fois par an; français – Rédacteur en chef, Pierre Vaillancourt

National Rugby Post, 13228 - 76 St., Edmonton AB T5C 1B6 – 403/476-0268; Fax: 403/473-1066 – Circ.: 6,000; 6 times a year – Publisher, David C. Graham; Editor, Don Whidden

Northwestern Ontario Snowmobile News (Published by North Superior Publishing Inc.), 1145 Barton St., Thunder Bay ON P7B 5N3 – 807/623-2348; Fax: 807/623-7515 – Circ.: 5,000; 6 times a year – Publisher & Editor, Scott A. Summer

Oldtimers' Hockey News, 640 Christopher Rd., PO Box 951, Peterborough ON K9J 7A5 – 705/743-2679; Fax: 705/748-3470 – Circ.: 15,000; 8 times a year – Publisher & Editor, David E. Tatham; Circulation Manager, Deborah Tatham

Ontario Golf News, #400, 2 Billingham Rd., Toronto ON M9B 6E1 – 416/232-2380; Fax: 416/232-9291 – Circ.: 30,000; 5 times a year – Publisher, Ken McKenzie; Editor, Charles Halpin

Ontario Snowmobiler, Centre Rd., RR#3, Mount Albert ON L1G 1M0 – 905/473-7009; Fax: 905/473-5217 – Circ.: 80,000; 5 times a year – Publisher, Terrence D. Kehoe; Editor, Kent Lester; Circulation Manager, D.B. Stevens

Ontario Tennis, Ontario Tennis Association, 1185 Eglinton Ave. East, North York ON M3C 3C6 – 416/426-7135; Fax: 416/426-7370 – Circ.: 16,500; 5 times a year – Executive Director, Peter Budreo

Outside Guide (Published by Solstice Publishing Inc.), 47 Soho Sq., Toronto ON M5T 2Z2 – 416/595-1252; Fax: 416/595-7255 – Circ.: 60,000; 2 times a year – Publisher, Paul Green; Editor, Iain MacMillan; Circulation Manager, Jon Spencer

Pacific Golf Magazine (Published by Canada Wide Magazines & Communications Ltd.), 4180 Lougheed Hwy., 4th Fl., Burnaby BC V5C 6A7 – 604/299-7311; Fax: 604/299-9188 – Publisher, Peter Legge; Editor, Bonnie Irving; Circulation Manager, Mark Weeks

Parks and Recreation Canada, Canadian Parks/Recreation Association, #306, 1600 James Naismith Dr., Ottawa ON K1B 5N4 – 613/748-5651; Fax: 613/748-5854; Email: cpra@cdnsport.ca – Circ.: 1,200; 5 times a year – Editor, Tom Steve; Circulation Manager, Kathleen Luten

Physical Education Digest, 111 Kingsmount Blvd., Sudbury ON P3E 1K8 – Fax: 705/675-5539; Email: pedigest@cyberbeach.net; 1-800-455-8782; URL: http://www.cyberbeach.net/pedigest – Circ.: 3,600; 4 times a year – Publisher & Editor, Dick Moss

Pocket Pro, 85 West Wilmont St., Unit 14, Richmond Hill ON L4B 1K7 – 905/764-5409; Fax: 905/764-5462 – Annually – Publisher, Bruce Longhurst

Québec Soccer, 4545, av Pierre-de-Coubertin, CP 1000, Succ M, Montréal PQ H1V 3R2 – 514/252-3070; Fax: 514/252-3162 – Mensuel; français

Real Outdoors, 940 Sheldon Ct., Burlington ON L7L 5K6 – 905/632-8679 – 6 times a year – Publisher, Fred Delsey; Editor, Craig Ritchie

La Revue des Sports, #353, 1205, rue Papineau, Montréal PQ H2K 4R2 – 514/521-8228; Fax: 514/521-0102 – Tirage: 65,000; Mensuel; français – Éditeur, Guy J. Letourneau

SCORE, 287 MacPherson Ave., Toronto ON M4V 1A4 – 416/928-2909; Fax: 416/928-1357; Email: weeksy@idirect.com – Circ.: 115,900; 6 times a year – Publisher, Randy McDonald; Editor, Bob Weeks

Scoreguide, 3645 Beaverdale Rd., Cambridge ON N3H 4R7 – 519/658-4126; Fax: 519/654-0041 – Publisher/Editor, Bob Zarzycki

Le Ski, 8 Winnifred Ave., Toronto ON M4M 2X3 – 416/462-0611; Fax: 416/462-9419 – Tirage: 22,500; 4 fois par an; français – Éditeur, Paul Green, 416/595-1252; Rédacteur en chef, Robert Choquette

Ski Canada Magazine (Published by Solstice Publishing Inc.), 47 Soho Sq., Toronto ON M5T 2Z2 – 416/595-1252; Fax: 416/595-7255; Email: skicanada@shift.com; URL: http://www.softnc.com/waveworks/skicanada.html – Circ.: 48,500; 6 times a year – Publisher, Paul Green; Editor, Iain MacMillan; Circulation Manager, Jon Spencer

Ski Presse, 850, rue Bernard-Pilon, McMasterville PQ J3G 5X7 – 514/464-3121; Fax: 514/464-9210 – Éditeur, Jean Marc Blais; Rédacteur, Maxime Tremblay

SkiTrax Magazine, #204, 2 Pardee Ave., Toronto ON M6K 3H5 – 416/530-1350; Fax: 416/530-4155; Email: medal@passport.ca; URL: http://www.pedal.com – Circ.: 18,000; 4 times a year – Publisher & Editor, Benjamin Sadavoy

Ski The West (Published by Koocanusa Publications Inc.), 1510 - 2nd St. North, Cranbrook BC V1C 3L2 – 250/426-7253; Fax: 250/489-3743 – Circ.: 40,000; Annually, Oct. – Publisher, Daryl D. Shellborn; Editor, Stacey Curry

Sno Riders West (Published by Koocanusa Publications Inc.), 1510 - 2nd St. North, Cranbrook BC V1C 3L2 – 250/426-7253; Fax: 250/489-3743 – Circ.: 35,000; 4 times a year – Publisher, Daryl Shellborn; Editor, Stacey Curry

Snow Goer (Published by Camar Publications), 130 Spy Ct., Markham ON L3R 5H6 130 Spy Ct., Markham ON L3R 5H6 – 905/475-8440; Fax: 905/475-9246 – Circ.: 99,000; 4 times a year – Publisher, Jacqueline Howe; Editor, Chris Knowles

Sporting Scene, 22 Maberley Cres., West Hill ON M1C 3K8 – 416/284-0304; Fax: 416/284-1299 – Circ.: 24,000; Monthly Sept. to May – Publisher & Editor, Peter Martens

Squash Life, c/o Squash Ontario, 1185 Eglinton Ave. East, North York ON M3C 3C6 – 416/426-7201; Fax: 416/426-7393; Email: squash.ontario@sympatico.ca – 3 times a year – Editor, Sherry Funston

Supertrax Int'l, 856 Upper James St., PO Box 20219, Hamilton ON L9C 7M8 – 905/473-7009; Fax: 905/473-5217; Email: supertrax@aol.com – Circ.: 160,000; 4 times a year; English & French – Publisher, Terrence D. Kehoe; Editor, Kent Lester; Circulation, Kathy Hildebrandt; Circulation Manager, Kathy Hildebrandt

True North Volleyball Magazine, 416 Cranbrook Ave., North York ON M5M 1N5 – 416/780-9686; Email: 4ewg@qlink.queensv.ca – Circ.: 15,000; 6 times a year – Publisher, Ted Graham; Editor, Tony Martins; Circulation Manager, Paul Brownstein

Water Goer (Published by Camar Publications), 130 Spy Ct., Markham ON L3R 5H6 130 Spy Ct., Markham ON L3R 5H6 – 905/475-8440; Fax: 905/475-9246 – Annually – Publisher, Jacqueline Howe

Western Skier (Published by Battleford Publishing Ltd.), PO Box 1029, North Battleford SK S9A 3E6 – 306/445-4401; Fax: 306/445-1977 – 5 times a year – Publisher, Rod McDonald

WhyNot Magazine, Canadian Foundation for Physically Disabled Persons, 731 Runnymede Ave., Toronto ON M6N 3V7 – 416/760-7351; Fax: 416/760-9405 – 6 times a year – Publisher, Vim Kochlar; Editor, Marsha Stall

TELEVISION, RADIO, VIDEO & HOME APPLIANCES

Bow Valley This Week, 201 Bear St., 2nd Fl., PO Box 129, Banff AB T0L 0C0 – 403/762-2453; Fax: 403/762-5274 – Circ.: 12,249; Weekly – Publisher, Sandra Santa Lucia; Editor, David Rodney; Circulation Manager, Anne Bosma

The Brandon Sun TV Book, 501 Rosser Ave., Brandon MB R7A 5Z6 – 204/727-2451; Fax: 204/725-0976, 0385 (ed.) – Circ.: 24,785; Weekly – Publisher, Rob Forbes; Editor, Cathy Arthur

Feature (Your Premium Entertainment Magazine) (Published by Les Publications Feature ltée), 2100, rue Ste-Catherine ouest, 9e étage, Montréal PQ H3H 2T3 – 514/939-5024; Fax: 514/939-1515 – Circ.: 650,000; Monthly – Publisher, Marvin Boisvert; Editor, David Sherman; Circulation Manager, Nathalie Abitbul

The Globe and Mail Broadcast Week, 444 Front St. West, Toronto ON M5V 2S9 – 416/585-5608, 5045; Fax: 416/585-5275, 5085 – Weekly

The Inner Ear Report, 85 Moorehouse Dr., Scarborough ON M1V 2E2 – 416/297-7968; Fax: 416/297-7968; Email: tier@terraport.net – Circ.: 16,000 – Editor, Ernie Fisher

The National Radio Guide, Bentall Centre, PO Box 48417, Vancouver BC V7X 1A2 – 604/688-0382; Fax: 604/688-3105 – Circ.: 8,000; Monthly – Publisher, Catherine Robertson; Managing Editor, Jane McIvor

The Newfoundland Herald, PO Box 2015, St. John's NF A1C 5R7 – 709/726-7060; Fax: 709/726-8227 – Weekly – Publisher, Geoff W. Stirling

PrimeTime, Riviera Plaza, 5308 Calgary Trail, Edmonton AB T6H 4J8 – 403/434-7424; Fax: 403/437-0123 – Circ.: 298,000; 12 times a year – Publisher, Harold Roozen; Editor, Ruth Kelly

Primeurs (Published by Les Publications Feature ltée), 2100, rue Ste-Catherine ouest, 9e étage, Montréal PQ H3H 2T3 – 514/939-5036; Fax: 514/939-1515 – Tirage: 280,000; Mensuel; français – Éditeur, Marvin Boisvert; Rédactrice, Marielle Duhamel; Directrice de tirage, Nathalie Abitbul

Satellite Entertainment Guide, #1109 TD Tower, 10205 - 101 St., Edmonton AB T5J 2Z1 – 403/424-6222; Fax: 403/425-8392 – Circ.: 82,600; Monthly – Publisher, Steven R. Vogel

Signal, TV Ontario, 2190 Yonge St., 4th Fl., Toronto ON M4T 2Z4 – 416/484-2898; Fax: 416/484-2896 – Circ.: 45,243; 10 times a year

Son Hi-Fi Video (Published by Les Éditions du Feu vert), 5148, boul St-Laurent, Montréal PQ H2T 1R8 – 514/273-9773; Fax: 514/273-9034 – 6 fois par an; français – Éditrice, Francine Tremblay; Rédacteur, Claude Corbeil; Directrice de tirage, Sylvie Hamel

Sound & Vision, #302, 99 Atlantic Ave., Toronto ON M6K 3J8 – 416/535-7611; Fax: 416/535-6325 – Circ.: 35,000; 6 times a year – Publisher, Michael H. Briant

StarWeek Magazine, c/o Toronto Star, One Yonge St., 5th Fl., Toronto ON M5E 1E6 – 416/869-4244, 4936; Fax: 416/869-4103 – Circ.: 740,000; Weekly – Publisher, John Honderich; Editor, Jim Atkins, 416/869-4870

Sunday Sun Television Magazine, Calgary Sun, 2615 - 12 St. NE, Calgary AB T2E 7W9 – 403/250-4200; Fax: 403/250-4180; URL: http://www.canoe.ca – Circ.: 100,000; Weekly – Publisher, Les Pyette; Editor, Chris Nelson; Circulation Manager, Joe King

Sunday Sun Television Magazine, c/o Edmonton Sun, #250, 4990 - 92 Ave., Edmonton AB T6B 3A1 – 403/468-0100; Fax: 403/468-0128; Email: edmonton.sun@ccinet.ab.ca – Circ.: 121,800; Weekly – Publisher, Craig Martin

Sunday Sun Television Magazine, c/o Ottawa Sun, 380 Hunt Club Rd., Ottawa ON K1G 3N3 – 613/739-

7000; Fax: 613/739-8043 – Circ.: 55,108 Mon.-Fri., 62,025 Sun.; Weekly – Publisher, John Paton; Editor, Rick Vansickle

Sunday Sun Television Magazine, c/o Toronto Sun, 333 King St. East, Toronto ON M5A 3X5 – 416/947-2333; Fax: 416/947-3139; Telex: 06-217688 – Circ.: 445,600; Weekly – General Manager, Mark Stevens

Télé+, 7, rue St-Jacques, Montréal PQ H2Y 1K9 – 514/285-7306; Fax: 514/845-8129 – Hebdomadaire; français – Éditeur, Roger D. Landry

Télé Horaire, c/o Le Journal, 4545 Frontenac, Montréal PQ H2H 2R7 – 514/521-4545 – Tirage: 331,000; Hebdomadaire; français – Éditeur, Yvon Lamarre

Télé Horaire (Québec) (Published by Groupe Québécor Inc.), c/o Le Journal de Québec, 450, rue Bechard, Vanier PQ G1M 2E9 – 418/683-1573; Fax: 418/683-1027 – Tirage: 122,000; Hebdomadaire; français – Éditeur, Jean-Claude L'Abbée; Rédacteur, Serge Côté; Directeur de tirage, Marc Couture

Téléromans, #900, 2001, rue Université, Montréal PQ H3A 2A6 – 514/499-0561; Fax: 514/843-3529 – Tirage: 70,000; 4 fois par an; français – Éditeur, Michel Trudeau; Rédacteur, Thérèse Parisien

Télé Soleil, c/o Le Soleil, 925, ch Saint-Louis, CP 1547, Succ Terminus, Québec PQ G1K 7J6 – 418/686-3270; Fax: 418/686-3260 – Hebdomadaire; français – Rédacteur, Gilbert Lacasse

Thunder Bay Guide, 1126 Roland St., Thunder Bay ON P7B 5M4 – 807/623-5788; Fax: 807/622-3140 – Circ.: 10,000; Weekly – Editor, Debbie Junnila

TV 7 Jours (Published by Trustar Ltd.), #2000, 2020, rue University, Montréal PQ H5A 2A5 – 514/848-7000; Fax: 514/848-9854 – Tirage: 170,000; Hebdomadaire; français – Éditeur, Claude J. Charron

TV Guide (Published by Telemedia Publishing), #100, 25 Sheppard Ave. West, North York ON M2N 6S7 – 416/733-7600; Fax: 416/218-3632; Email: tvguide@telemedia.org – Circ.: 838,000; Weekly – Publisher, Graham Morris; Editor, Nicholas Hirst

TV Hebdo (Published by Trustar Ltd.), #2000, 2020, rue University, Montréal PQ H5A 2A5 – 514/499-0561; Fax: 514/499-1844 – Tirage: 234,000; Hebdomadaire – Éditeur, François de Gaspé-Beaubien; Rédacteur en chef, Jean-Louis Podlesak

TV Magazine (Central B.C.), Spartan Printing & Advertising Ltd., 101 Marsh Dr., Quesnel BC V2J 3K3 – 250/992-2713; Fax: 250/992-3902 – Circ.: 4,600; Weekly; also TV Guide Style (weekly) – Co-Editor, J.P. Hartnett; Co-Editor, G. Seale

TV Scene, c/o Thunder Bay Times, 75 South Cumberland St., Thunder Bay ON P7B 1A3 – 807/343-6200; Fax: 807/345-5991; Email: cj-editorial@cwconnect.ca; URL: http://netreader.com/tbay/index2.html – Circ.: 40,900; Weekly – Publisher, Colin Bruce; Editor, Peter Haggert; Circulation Manager, Mike Keating

TV Scene, c/o Times Colonist, 2621 Douglas St., Victoria BC V8W 2N4 – 250/380-5211; Fax: 250/380-5255 – Circ.: 83,700; Weekly

TV Scene, c/o Winnipeg Free Press, 1355 Mountain Ave., Winnipeg MB R2X 3B6 – 204/697-7000; Fax: 204/697-7412 – Weekly

TV Scene Around, 922 - 102nd Ave., Dawson Creek BC V1G 2B7 – 250/782-3190 – Weekly – Publisher, Retta Pitt

TV Times (Published by Southam Magazine Group), 1450 Don Mills Rd., Don Mills ON M3B 2X7 – 416/442-3444; Fax: 416/442-2088 – Circ.: 1.8 million; Weekly – Publisher, Liz Martin; Editor, Barbara Righton

TV Week Magazine (Vancouver & Victoria) (Published by Canada Wide Magazines & Communications Ltd.), 4180 Lougheed Hwy., 4th Fl., Burnaby BC V5C 6A7 – 604/299-7311; Fax: 604/299-9188 – Weekly – Publisher, Peter Legge; Editor, Hardip Randhawa; Circulation Manager, Mark Weeks

TV Week Stratford, c/o The Beacon Herald of Stratford, PO Box 430, Stratford ON N5A 6T6 – 519/271-2220; Fax: 519/271-1026 – Circ.: 13,283; Weekly – Co-Publisher, Charles Dingman; Editor, Ron Carson

Video News & Reviews (Published by Suggitt Publishing Ltd.), 10608 - 172 St., Edmonton AB T5S 1H8 – 403/486-5802; Fax: 403/481-9276; Email: suggitt@planet.eon.net – Circ.: 40,000; 12 times a year – Publisher, Thomas J. Suggitt; Editor, Tanis Nessler

The Winnipeg Sun TV Preview, 1700 Church Ave., Winnipeg MB R2X 3A2 – 204/694-2022; Fax: 204/632-8709 – Circ.: 52,000; Weekly – Publisher, John Cochrane

TRAVEL

AutoRoute, #606, 366 Adelaide St. West, Toronto ON M5V 1R9 – 416/599-9900; Fax: 416/599-9700 – Circ.: 285,000; 4 times a year; English & French – Publisher, Rod Morris; Managing Editor, John Terauds

Bienvenue en Nouvelle-Écosse, Mardelli Publishing, PO Box 811, Yarmouth NS B5K 4K4 – 902/742-4653; Fax: 902/742-2460 – Circ.: 150,000; Annually – Publisher, Bill Mardelli

Coup d'oeil, Les Éditions M.C.C. ltée, 1048, d'Avangour, Chicoutimi PQ G7H 2T1 – 418/696-4805 – Tirage: 30,000; 4 fois par an; français – Éditeur, Chantal Tremblay

Geo Plein Air (Published by Les Éditions Tricycle inc.), 1251, rue Rachel est, Montréal PQ H2J 2J9 – 514/521-8356; Fax: 514/521-5711; Email: geo_pleinair@ve;p/qc/ca – Tirage: 25,000; 7 fois par an; français – Éditeur, Pierre Hamel; Rédacteur, Simon Kretz

Latitudes, Plan B Strategies Inc., #217, 45 Sheppard Ave. East, Toronto ON M2N 5W9 – 416/226-1700; Fax: 416/226-2566 – Circ.: 200,000; 4 times a year; English & French – Publisher, Eve Howse; Editor in Chief, Louis Gauthier

The Laurentians Tourist Guide, RR#1, St-Jérôme PQ J7Z 5T4 – 514/436-8532 – Circ.: 50,000; Annually; English & French editions – General Manager, André Goyer

The Pacific Hosteller, c/o Canadian Hostelling Association, #402, 134 Abbott St., Vancouver BC V6B 4K4 – 604/684-7101; Fax: 604/684-7181 – 4 times a year – Publisher, Morris Jenkinson

Parks Companion (Published by Koocanusa Publications Inc.), 1510 - 2nd St. North, Cranbrook BC V1C 3L21510 - 2nd St. North, Cranbrook BC V1C 3L2 – 250/426-7253; Fax: 250/489-3743 – Circ.: 110,000; Infrequent – Publisher, Daryl D. Shellborn

Resort Weekly, South East Press Ltd., 521 Main St., PO Box 329, Kipling SK S0G 2S0 – 306/736-2535; Fax: 306/736-8445 – Circ.: 2,700; 13 times a year, weekly beginning May 24 – Editor, Scott Kearns

Travel à la carte, 136 Walton St., Port Hope ON L1A 1N5 – 905/885-7948; Fax: 905/885-7202 – 6 times a year – Publisher, Paul Rumgay; Editor, Donna Carter

Travelworld, Gemini International Inc., #490, 10 Gateway Blvd., North York ON M3C 3T4 – 416/221-0288; Fax: 416/221-0287 – Circ.: 165,000 – Editor, James A. Bruce Sr.

Vacances pour Tous, #110, 455, rue Marais, Vanier PQ G1M 3A2 – 418/686-1940; Fax: 418/686-1942 – Tirage: 40,000; 6 fois par an; français – Éditeur, Eric Sohier; Rédactrice, Marie-Christine Magnan

WOMEN'S & FEMINIST

Action Now, National Action Committee on the Status of Women, #203, 234 Eglinton Ave. West, Toronto ON M4P 1K5 – 416/932-1718; Fax: 416/932-0646; Email: nac@web.net – Circ.: 1,400; 8 times a year – Editor, Laurie Kinston; Circulation Manager, Michele Havens

L'Actuel, 1043, Tiffin, Longueuil PQ J4P 3G7 – 514/442-3983; Fax: 514/442-4363 – 7 fois par an; français – Éditeur, Renel Bouchard; Rédactrice, Suzanne G. Paquin

Alberta Woman, Merrick Enterprises, 101 - 6th Ave. SW, Calgary AB T2P 3P4 – Circ.: 79,000; 4 times a year – Publisher, John Merrick

BC Woman, 704 Clarkson St., New Westminster BC V3M 1E2 – 604/540-8448; Fax: 604/524-0041 – Circ.: 35,000; Monthly – Publisher, Rosemarie Nakamura; Editor, Nikki Groocock

Canadian Guider, c/o Girl Guides of Canada, 50 Merton St., Toronto ON M4S 1A3 – 416/487-5281; Fax: 416/487-5570; URL: http://www.girlguides.ca – Circ.: 45,000; 5 times a year – Editor, Sharon Pruner

Canadian Woman Studies, 212 Founders College, York University, 4700 Keele St., Downsview ON M3J 1P3 – 416/736-5356; Fax: 416/736-5765; Email: cwscf@yorku.ca – Circ.: 5,000; 4 times a year – Editor, Luciana Ricciutelli; Circulation Manager, Rosemary Moore

Chatelaine (Published by Maclean Hunter Publishing), 777 Bay St., Toronto ON M5W 1A7 – 416/596-5425; Fax: 416/596-5516; Email: ishapiro@interlog.com – Circ.: 1,100,000; Monthly; also Welcome Home (annually), Chatelaine Renovates (annually); ISSN 0009-1995 – Publisher, Lee Simpson; Editor-in-Chief, Rona Maynard

Châtelaine (Published by Maclean Hunter Publishing), 1001, boul de Maisonneuve ouest, Montréal PQ H3A 3E1 – 514/845-5141; Fax: 514/845-4302 – Tirage: 188,000; Mensuel; français – Éditeur, Jean-François Douville; Rédactrice, Catherine Elie

Clin d'oeil (Published by Publicor), 7, ch Bates, Outremont PQ H2V 1A6 – 514/270-1100; Fax: 514/270-6900 – Tirage: 100,000; Mensuel; français – Rédactrice en chef, Dominique Betrand

Contemporary Verse 2, PO Box 3062, Winnipeg MB R3C 4E5 – 204/949-1365 – Circ.: 650; 4 times a year – Editor, Janine Tschuncky

Coup de Pouce (Published by Les Éditions Télémedia), #900, 2001, rue University, Montréal PQ H3A 2A6 – 514/499-0561; Fax: 514/499-1844 – Tirage: 155,000; 12 times a year – Éditrice, Michéle Cyr; Rédactrice, Sandra Cliche

Diva, 364 Coxwell Ave., Toronto ON M4L 3B7 – 416/461-2744; Fax: 416/461-3315 – 4 times a year; ISSN 0842-4330

Edmonton Woman (Published by Alberta Business Research Ltd), #800, 10179 - 105 St., Edmonton AB T5J 3N1 – 403/424-1221; Fax: 403/421-7677 – Circ.: 40,000; 10 times a year – Publisher, Lorne Silverstein, 403/429-1610; Editor, Colin Smith

Elle Québec (Published by Les Éditions Télémedia), #900, 2001, rue University, Montréal PQ H3A 2A6 – 514/499-0561; Fax: 514/499-1844 – Tirage: 80,000; Mensuel; français – Éditeur, Michéle Cyr

Elm Street (Published by Multi-Vision Publishing), #1000, 655 Bay St., Toronto ON M5G 2K4 – 416/595-9944 – Circ.: 700,000; 6 times a year – Editor-in-Chief, Stevie Cameron

L'Essentiel (Published by Publicor), 7, ch Bates, Outremont PQ H2V 1A6 – 514/270-1100; Fax: 514/270-6900 – Tirage: 94,750; Mensuel; français – Rédacteur, Sylvie Laplante

Family & Education, #2, 105 West Beaver Creek, Richmond Hill ON L4B 1C6 – 905/886-1212; Fax: 905/886-6868; Email: educan@idirect.com – Circ.: 16,000 – Publisher & Editor, Alawn Lai; Circulation Manager, Anita Lai

Femme Plus (Published by Publicor), 7, ch Bates, Outremont PQ H2V 1A6 – 514/270-1100; Fax: 514/270-6900 – Tirage: 57,790; Mensuel; français – Rédacteur, Jean-Louis Maubois

Filles d'aujourd'hui (Published by Publicor), 7, ch Bates, Outremont PQ H2V 1A6 – 514/270-1100; Fax: 514/270-6900 – Tirage: 54,211; Mensuel; français – Rédacteur, Francine Trudeau

Fireweed: A Feminist Quarterly of Writing, Politics, Art & Culture, PO Box 279, Stn B, Toronto ON

M5T 2W2 – 416/504-1339 – Circ.: 2,000; 4 times a year – Co-ordinating Editor, Sandra Haar

Focus on Women, Campbell Communicatons Inc., 1218 Langley St. 3rd Fl., Victoria BC V8W 1W2 – 250/388-7231; Fax: 250/383-1140; Email: uc698@freenet.victoria.bc.ca – Circ.: 30,000; Monthly – Publisher, Leslie Campbell; Editor, Kerry Slavens

Herizons, Herizons Magazine Inc., PO Box 128, Stn Main, Winnipeg MB R3C 2G1 – 204/783-1312; Fax: 204/786-8038 – 4 times a year; ISSN 0711-7485 – Business Manager, Yvonne Block; Editor, Penni Mitchell

Homemaker's (Published by Telemedia Publishing), #100, 25 Sheppard Ave. West, North York ON M2N 6S7 – 416/733-7600; Fax: 416/733-8683 – Circ.: 1,600,000; 8 times a year – Publisher, Barrie Pykes; Editor, Sally Armstrong; Circulation Manager, Lisa Rivers

Home & School, Home & School International Inc., 105 West Beaver Creek, Unit 2, Richmond Hill ON L4B 1C6 – 905/886-1212; Fax: 905/886-6868; Email: educan@idirect.com – Circ.: 99,000; 8 times a year – Publisher, Allan Lai

Images (Published by Multi-Vision Publishing), #1000, 655 Bay St., Toronto ON M5G 2K4 – 416/595-9944; Fax: 416/595-7217 – Circ.: 411,000; 4 times a year – Editor, Kate MacDonald

JourneyWoman, #1703, 50 Prince Arthur Ave., Toronto ON M5R 1B5 – 416/929-7654; Fax: 416/929-1433; Email: jwoman@web.net; URL: http://www.web.net/~jwoman/ – Circ.: 6,000; 4 times a year – Publisher, C. Eve; Editor, Evelyn Hannon; Circulation Manager, L. Hannon

Kinesis, c/o Vancouver Status of Women, #301, 1720 Grant St., Vancouver BC V5L 2Y6 – 604/255-5499; Fax: 604/255-5511 – Circ.: 3,000; 10 times a year – Editor, Agnes Huang

Local Women, JR Publishing, 6826 - 135A St., Surrey BC V3W 4X3 – 604/760-7607; Fax: 604/591-6557 – 10 times a year – Editor, Sharon Whiting

LOOKwest Magazine, #2850, 350 - 7th Ave. SW, Calgary AB T2P 3N9 – 403/571-5665; Fax: 403/571-5667 – Circ.: 50,000; 6 times a year – Publisher, Jeff Hunter

Matriart, Women's Art Resource Centre, #506, 80 Spadina Ave., Toronto ON M5V 2J3 – 416/703-0074, 1920; Fax: 416/703-0441; Email: warc@intacc.web net – Circ.: 2,000; 4 times a year – Editor, Linda Abrahams

Modern Woman (Published by Maclean Hunter Publishing), 777 Bay St., Toronto ON M5W 1A7 – 416/596-5425; Fax: 416/593-3197 – Circ.: 500,000; Monthly – Publisher, Lee Simpson; Editor, Charlotte Empey

Northern Woman Journal: An Analysis of Feminist Issues, PO Box 144, Thunder Bay ON P7C 4V5 – 807/346-8809 – 4 times a year

Ontario Woman, Merrick Enterprises, 20 Edgevalley Dr., Islington ON M9A 4N7 – Circ.: 35,500; 4 times a year – Publisher, John Merrick

Orah Magazine, Canadian Hadassah-WIZO, #900, 1310 Greene Ave., Westmount PQ H3Z 2B2 – 514/937-9431; Fax: 514/933-6483 – Circ.: 14,000; 4 times a year – Editor, Judy Mandleman

Point of View, c/o Holt Renfrew, 50 Bloor St. West, Toronto ON M4W 1A1 – 416/960-2917; Fax: 416/922-3240 – Circ.: 132,000; 2 times a year; English & French – Managing Editor, Nancy Moore

Room of One's Own, Growing Room Collective, PO Box 46160, Stn G, Vancouver BC V6R 4G5 – 4 times a year

Women's Education des femmes, Cdn. Congress for Learning Opportunities for Women, 47 Main St., Toronto ON M4E 2V6 – 416/699-1909; Fax: 416/699-2145; Email: cclow@web.apc.org – Circ.: 1,200; 4 times a year; English & French – Editor, Christina Starr; Circulation Manager, Dianne Palachik

You (Published by Family Communications Inc.), #1, 37 Hanna Ave., Toronto ON M6K 1X1 – 416/537-2604; Fax: 416/538-1794 – Circ.: 221,000; 4 times a year – Editor, Bettie Bradley

YOUTH

The Canadian Leader, PO Box 5112, Stn F, Ottawa ON K2C 3H4 – 613/224-5131; Fax: 613/224-3571; Email: leader@scouts.ca; URL: http://www/scouts.ca – Circ.: 44,000; 10 times a year – Publisher, Andy McLaughlin

Le Magazine Jeunesse, 7383, rue de la Roche, Montréal PQ H2R 2T4 – 514/274-6124; Fax: 514/272-5939 – Tirage: 60,000; 4 fois par an; français – Rédacteur, Yves Daigle

Pop Life/Info Pop, 256 Adelaide St. East, Toronto ON M5A 1N1 – 416/777-1124; Fax: 416/777-0060 – Circ.: 500,000; Annually – Publisher, Tony Chapman

TG: Voices of Today's Generation, #1050, 70 University Ave., Toronto ON M5J 2M4 – 416/597-8297 – Circ.: 150,000; 4 times a year; English & French – Publisher, Stoney McCart

Watch Magazine, #245, 401 Richmond St. West, Toronto ON M5V 1X3 – 416/595-1313; Fax: 416/595-1312 – Circ.: 75,000; 12 times a year – Publisher, Doug Stewart; Managing Editor, Paul Anderson

What! A Magazine, #108, 93 Lombard Ave., Winnipeg MB R3B 3B1 – 204/942-2214; Fax: 204/943-8991; Email: waht@fox.nstn.ca – Circ.: 200,000; 5 times a year – Publisher, Nancy Moore; Editor, Stuart Slayen; Circulation Manager, Sherry Jones

Youth Culture Unleased, Watch Magazines Inc., #245, 401 Richmond St. West, Toronto ON M5V 1X3 – 416/595-1313; Fax: 416/595-1312 – Circ.: 75,000; 10 times a year – Publisher, Doug Stewart

Youth Today, PO Box 390, Stn A, Ottawa ON K1N 8V4 – 819/771-5591; Fax: 819/595-6838

ETHNIC PUBLICATIONS

ABORIGINAL

Aboriginal Voices, #201, 116 Spadina Ave., Toronto ON M5V 2K6 – 416/703-4577; Fax: 416/703-4581; Email: abvoices@inforamp.net; URL: http://www.vli.ca/clients/abc/cmall/abvoices – Circ.: 15,000; 4 times a year – Editor-in-Chief, Gary Farmer; Circulation Manager, David Shilling

Kahtou News, 5526 Sinku Dr., PO Box 192, Sechelt BC V0N 3A0 – 604/885-7391; Fax: 604/885-7397 – Circ.: 11,000; Monthly – Editor, Stan Dixon

Micmac-Maliseet Nation News, 840 Willow St., PO Box 1590, Truro NS B2N 5V3 – 902/895-6385; Fax: 902/893-1520; Email: nstn2436@fox.nstn.ca – Circ.: 2,000; Monthly – Publisher, Donald Julien; Editor, Tim Bernard

Native Network News, Alberta Native Information Network Ltd., 13140 St. Albert Trail, Edmonton AB T5L 4R8 – 403/454-7076; Fax: 403/452-3468 – Circ.: 13,000; 12 times a year – Editor, Mark McCallum

ARABIC

Arab News International, 368 Queen St. East, Toronto ON M5A 1T1 – 416/362-0304; Telex: 06-52629 – Weekly

ARMENIAN

Abaka, 825, rue Manoogian, St-Laurent PQ H4N 1Z5 – 514/747-6680; Fax: 514/747-6162 – Weekly

BLACK COMMUNITY

Share, 658 Vaughan Rd., Toronto ON M6E 2Y5 – 416/656-3400; Fax: 416/656-0691 – Circ.: 43,500; Weekly – Publisher, Arnold Auguste; Managing Editor, Jules Elder

CARIBBEAN

Equality News, #2500, 2500 Eglinton Ave. East, Scarborough ON M1K 2R5 – 416/266-9711; Fax: 416/282-6534 – Circ.: 37,000; Weekly – Publisher & Editor, Bhaskar Sharma

The Jamaican Weekly Gleaner, 1390 Eglinton Ave. West, Toronto ON M6C 2E4 – 416/784-3002, 1-800-565-3961; Fax: 416/784-5719 – Circ.: 120,000; Weekly – Publisher, John Hudson; Editor, Gail Scala

CELTIC

Celtic Heritage, PO Box 8805, Stn A, Halifax NS B3K 5M4 – 902/835-6244; Fax: 902/835-0080; Email: celtic@fox.nstn.ns.ca; URL: http://fox.nstn.ca/~celtic – Circ.: 10,000; 6 times a year – Publisher, Angus M. MacQuarrie; Editor, Alexa Thompson; Circulation Manager, Cabrini Macquarrie

CHINESE

The Capital Chinese News, 695 Somerset St. West, Ottawa ON K1R 6P5 – 613/837-3564 – Monthly

Chinacity, 17916 - 93 Ave. NW, Edmonton AB T5T 1V6 – 403/487-3536; Fax: 403/439-5604; Email: kendagee@freenet.edmonton.ab.ca – Circ.: 6,000; 12 times a year – Publisher & Editor-in-Chief, Kenda D. Gee

Chinese News, c/o Chinese Financial News, #415, 192 Spadina Ave., Toronto ON M5T 2C2 – 416/362-5670; Fax: 416/865-0366 – Weekly

Ming Pao Daily News, 1355 Huntingwood Dr., Scarborough ON M1S 3J1 – 416/321-0088; Fax: 416/321-6339 – Circ.: 25,803, Mon.-Wed.; 31.353, Thur.-Fri.; 42,653, Sat.; 51,453, Sun.; Daily; Chinese – Editor-in-Chief, H.Y. Chan; Assist. General Manager, Angela Ahmed

Sei Ping Monthly, #505, 13231 Delf Pl., Richmond BC V6V 2A2 – 604/273-7744; Fax: 604/273-5272 – Monthly

Shing Wah News, 793 Gerrard St. East, Toronto ON M4M 1Y5 – 416/778-1854; Fax: 416/778-8108 – Monthly

World Journal (Toronto), 415 Eastern Ave., Toronto ON M4M 1B7 – 416/778-0888; Fax: 416/778-1037 – Daily

World Journal (Vancouver), 2288 Clark Dr., Vancouver BC V5N 3G8 – 604/876-1338; Fax: 604/876-3728 – Circ.: 30,000; Daily; Chinese – Publisher, Wang Shaw Lan; Editor, John Hsu

CROATIAN

Croatian Voice, PO Box 596, Nanaimo BC V9R 5L5 – 250/754-8282; Fax: 250/753-4303 – Circ.: 2,500; 12 times a year – Publisher, Dr. Mladen G. Zorkin

Glasnik Hrvatske Seljacke Stranke, PO Box 82187, North Burnaby BC V5C 5P2 – 604/524-2813; Fax: 604/521-0030 – Monthly

DUTCH

De Hollandse Krant, #201, 20408 Douglas Cres., Langley BC V3A 4B4 – 604/530-9446; Fax: 604/530-9766; Email: holkrant@awinc.com – Circ.: 7,800; Monthly; Dutch – Editor, Gerald Bonekamp

De Nederlandse Courant, 3019 Harvester Rd., Burlington ON L7N 3G4 – 905/333-3615; Fax: 905/333-5958; Email: Dutch@inforamp.net – Circ.: 6,000; 26 times a year – Publisher, Theo Luykenaar; Editor, Rebecca Saager; Circulation Manager, Mark Luykenaar

EAST INDIAN

Bharat Darshan, 3127 Purnell Ct., Mississauga ON L4T 2J7 – 905/612-0107; Fax: 905/612-0108 – Semimonthly; Hindi

Charhdi Kala, #6, 7743 - 128th St., Surrey BC V3W 4E6 – 604/590-6397; Fax: 604/591-6397 – Weekly; Punjabi

Gujarat Vartman, Gujarat Vartman Ltd., 250 Norfinch Dr., North York ON M3N 1Y4 – 416/736-9699; Fax: 416/736-1640 – Circ.: 3,000; Monthly; Gujarti – Editor, J.D. Shah

India Calling, 1693 Pengilley Place, Mississauga ON L5J 4P4 – 905/823-2541 – Bi-monthly

Indo-Canadian Times, PO Box 2296, Vancouver BC V6B 3W5 – 604/599-5408; Fax: 604/599-5415 – Weekly; Punjabi

Indo Canadian Phulwari, Indo Canadian Phulwari Publications Inc., 14891 Spenser Dr., Surrey BC V3S 7K7 – 604/599-6400; Fax: 604/599-6400 – Monthly; English & Punjabi – Gurjit Singh Sangra

Kerala Express, 1565 Jane St., PO Box 34556, Toronto ON M9N 2R3 – 416/654-0431 – Weekly; Malayalam – Publisher, J.P. George

Mehfil Magazine, 2050 Clark Dr., Vancouver BC V5N 3G7 – 604/254-9015; Fax: 604/420-0626 – 6 times a year; Indo-Canadian

Perdesi Panjab, 3127 Purnell Ct., Mississauga ON L4T 2J7 – 905/612-0107; Fax: 905/612-0108 – Weekly; Punjabi

ESTONIAN

Meie Elu, 958 Broadview Ave., Toronto ON M4K 2R6 – 416/466-8404; Fax: 416/466-4339 – Weekly

Vaba Eestlane, c/o Free Estonian Publishers, 120A Willowdale Ave., Willowdale ON M2N 4Y2 – 416/733-4551; Fax: 416/733-4550 – Circ.: 2,500; Bi-weekly; Estonian – Editor-in-Chief, Arvi E. Tinits

FILIPINO

Filipino Journal, 483 Bannatyne Ave., Winnipeg MB R3A 0G2 – 204/943-4512; Fax: 204/943-4512 – Monthly

The Philippine Reporter, Byword Media, #405B, 815 Danforth Ave., Toronto ON M4J 1L2 – 416/461-8694; Fax: 416/461-7399 – Circ.: 8,000; 24 times a year – Editor, Hermie Garcia

FINNISH

Canadan Uutiset, Finnews Ltd., 31 North Court St., Thunder Bay ON P7A 4T4 – 807/344-1611; Fax: 807/344-1879; Email: canuutiset@aol.com – Circ.: 1,800; Weekly; English & Finnish – Editor, Sakri A. Viklund

Vapaa Sana, #22, 50 Weybright Ct., Scarborough ON M1S 5A8 – 416/321-0808; Fax: 416/321-0811 – Weekly

GERMAN

Deutsche Presse, #303, 455 Spadina Ave., Toronto ON M5S 2G8 – 416/595-9714; Fax: 416/595-9716 – Weekly

Deutsche Presse, #7, 707 East 21st Ave., Vancouver BC V5V 1R9 – 604/877-0305; Fax: 604/877-0308 – Circ.: 7,500; Weekly; German – Erhard Matthaes

Kanada Kurier, 955 Alexander Ave., Winnipeg MB R3C 2X8 – 204/774-1883; Fax: 204/783-5740 – Weekly

Die Mennonitische Post, PO Box 1120, Steinbach MB R0A 2A0 – 204/326-6790 – 24 times a year

Mennonitische Rundschau, c/o Bd. of Commun. of the Cdn. Conference of the M.B. Churches, #3, 169 Riverton Ave., Winnipeg MB R2L 2E5 – 204/669-6575; Fax: 204/654-1865 – Circ.: 3,000; Monthly; German – Editor, Lorina Marsch; Circulation Manager, Helga Kosdorf

Pazifische Rundschau, 4551 Northey Rd., PO Box 88047, Richmond BC V6X 3T6 – 604/270-2923; Fax: 604/273-9365 – Every other week

Die Zeit, 29 Coldwater Rd., Toronto ON M3B 1Y8 – 416/391-4196 – Weekly

GREEK

Acropolis, 2122 - 47th St. West, Vancouver BC V6M 2M7 – 604/266-6137; Fax: 604/266-3595 – 24 times a year

Courrier Grec, 5700B St. Lawrence Blvd., Montréal PQ H2T 1S8 – 514/278-9299; Fax: 514/278-4572 – Weekly

Greek Canadian Action, 4879 Faulkner St., Chomedey PQ H7W 1H9 – 514/272-4000; Fax: 514/687-6330 – Circ.: 44,000; 24 times a year – Publisher, George Guzmas

Greek Canadian Reportage, 7438, rue Durocher, Montréal PQ H3N 2A3 – 514/279-7772 – Weekly

Greek Canadian Tribune, 897, rue Jean-Talon ouest, Montréal PQ H3N 1S7 – 514/272-6873; Fax: 514/272-3157 – Weekly

Hellenic-Canadian Chronicles, Ledra Publishing Ltd., 437 Danforth Ave., Toronto ON M4K 1P1 – 416/465-4628; Fax: 416/465-6592 – Weekly; English & Greek – Editor, Peter Maniatakos

Hellenic Hamilton News, #2, 8 Morris Ave., Hamilton ON L8L 1X7 – 905/549-9208; Fax: 905/549-7935 – Circ.: 2,000; Monthly – Publisher & Editor, Panos Andronidis

The Hellenic News, 37 Hillsmount Rd., London ON N6K 1W1 – 519/472-4807 – Monthly

HUNGARIAN

Kanadai Magyarsag, 74 Advance Rd., Etobicoke ON M8Z 2T7 – 416/233-3131 – Weekly

Magyar Elet, 313 Sheppard Ave. East, North York ON M2N 3B3 – 416/221-6195; Fax: 416/221-6358 – Weekly

Menorah-Egyenloseg, 87 Searle Ave., Downsview ON M3H 4A6 – 416/398-2870 – Weekly

ICELANDIC

Logberg-Heimskringla, 699 Carter Ave., Winnipeg MB R3M 2C3 – 204/284-5686; Fax: 204/284-3870 – Circ.: 2,000; Weekly; English & Icelandic – Publisher, Kevin Johnson; Editor, Tom Oleson; Circulation Manager, Sandra Duma

ITALIAN

Alberta Italian Times, 504 Alder Ave., Sherwood Park AB T8A 1S9 – 403/472-6397; Fax: 403/478-5493 – Weekly – Publisher, Josephine Sicoli

CIAO Magazine, 1081, Bas de L'Assomption Nord, L'Assomption PQ J0K 1G0 – 514/589-7195; Fax: 514/589-4485 – Monthly

Il Cittadino Canadese, #600, 6020, rue Jean Talon est, Montréal PQ H1S 3B1 – 514/253-2332; Fax: 514/253-6574 – Weekly

Il Congresso, 10865 - 96 St., Edmonton AB T5H 2K2 – 403/424-3010 – Monthly

Corriere Canadese, 890 Caledonia Rd., Toronto ON M6B 3Y1 – 416/785-4300; Fax: 416/785-4329; Email: corriere@hookup.net – Circ.: 28,500; Daily Mon. to Fri. – Founder, Daniel Iannuzzi; Editor, Elena Caprice; Circulation Manager, Salvatore Barbieri

Corriere Italiano, 6900, rue St-Denis, Montréal PQ H2S 2S2 – 514/279-4536; Fax: 514/376-4260 – Weekly

L'Eco D'Italia, Zone Publishing, 3849 Hastings St. East, Burnaby BC V5C 2H7 – 604/294-8707; Fax: 604/291-1707 – Circ.: 5,900; Weekly – Editor, Rino Vultaggio

La Gazzetta, 909 Howard Ave., Windsor ON N9A 1S3 – 519/253-8883; Fax: 519/253-3280 – Weekly

Il Giornale Italiano del Manitoba, 520 Corydon Ave., Winnipeg MB R3L 0P1 – 204/477-1221; Fax: 204/453-8244 – Monthly

Insieme, 4358, rue Charleroi, Montréal PQ H1H 1T3 – 514/328-2062; Fax: 514/328-6562 – Circ.: 38,000; Weekly; Italian – Publisher, P. Giuseppe De Rossi; Editor, Mimmo Forte

Italian Link, 8720 - 137 Ave., Edmonton AB T5E 1X4 – 403/472-6397; Fax: 403/478-5493 – Monthly

Lo Specchio/Vaughan, #100, 166 Woodbridge Ave., Woodbridge ON L4L 2S7 – 905/856-2823; Fax: 905/856-2825 – Circ.: 16,000; Weekly – Editor, Sergio Tagliavini

Il Nuovo Mondo, 8720 - 137 Ave., Edmonton AB T5E 1X4 – 403/472-6397; Fax: 403/478-5493 – 24 times a year

L'Ora Di Ottawa, 203 Louisa St., Ottawa ON K1R 6Y9 – 613/232-5689; Fax: 613/563-2573 – Weekly

Il Rincontro, 6675 Winderton Ave., Montréal PQ H3S 2L8 – 514/739-4213; Fax: 514/344-8238 – Circ.: 11,500; Monthly; Italian – Editor, Tony Vellone

Tandem, 890 Caledonia Rd., Toronto ON M6B 3Y1 – 416/785-4300; Fax: 416/785-4329 – Circ.: 35,000; Weekly, Sat. – Editor, Elena Caprice

La Voce degli Italo Canadesi, 6736, boul Monk, Montréal PQ H4E 3J1 – 514/769-5711; Fax: 514/366-4783 – 24 times a year

JAPANESE

The New Canadian, 524 Front St. West, Toronto ON M5V 1B8 – 416/593-6118; Fax: 416/593-1871 – Circ.: 4,000; Thur.; English & Japanese – Publisher, Shin Kawai; Editor, Sakura Torizuka

KOREAN

The Korea Times Daily, 287 Bridgeland Ave., North York ON M6A 1Z6 – 416/787-1111; Fax: 416/781-7777 – 5 times a week – Publisher, W.Y. Kim

LATVIAN

Latvija-Amerika, 125 Broadview Ave., Toronto ON M4M 2E9 – 416/465-7902; Fax: 416/465-7902 – Weekly

LITHUANIAN

Nepriklausoma Lietuva, 7722, rue George, LaSalle PQ H8P 1C4 – 514/366-6220 – Bi-weekly

Teviskes Ziburiai, 2185 Stavebank Rd., Mississauga ON L5C 1T3 – 905/275-4672; Fax: 905/275-1336 – Weekly; Lithuanian – Editor-in-Chief, Dr. P. Gaida

MACEDONIAN

Macedonia, 364 Old Kingston Rd., PO Box 97589, Scarborough ON M1C 4Z1 – 416/286-7673 – Monthly

The Macedonian Link, West Hill Stn, PO Box 291, Scarborough ON M1E 4R5 – 416/286-7673 – Monthly

MULTICULTURAL

Community Digest, #216, 1755 Robson St., Vancouver BC V6G 3B7 – 604/875-8313; Fax: 604/875-0336 – Weekly

Multi-Cultural Magazine, 20 Edge Valley Dr., Islington ON M9A 4N7 – Monthly

New Canada Weekly, PO Box 994, Stn Q, Toronto ON M4T 2P1 – 416/481-7793; Fax: 416/481-7793 – Circ.: 10,000; Weekly; English & Urdu & French – Publisher & Editor, Hasanat Ahmad Syed

PAKISTANI

Aawaz, 2 Middleport Cres., Scarborough ON M1B 4L5 – 416/283-7255 – 24 times a year; Urdu

Eastern News, PO Box 1061, Stn B, Mississauga ON L4Y 2E0 – 905/858-7525; Fax: 905/858-7951 – Circ.: 5,000; 24 times a year – Publisher, Alia Sultana; Editor, Masood Khan

Fortnightly Universal News, PO Box 21051, Stn Bridgeview, Windsor ON N9B 3T4 – 519/253-5851; Fax: 519/253-8658 – Twice monthly; Urdu

The Messenger, 2 Middleport Cres., Scarborough ON M1B 3L1 – 416/283-7255 – Twice monthly; Urdu

Pakeeza International, 17 Burnhope Dr., Brampton ON L6X 3R9 – 905/455-9839; Fax: 905/452-8133; Email: pakvoice@inforamp.net – Circ.: 4,000; Wed.; Urdu – Publisher & Editor, Sabih Mansoor; Circulation Manager, Umber Mansoor

Shama, PO Box 1304, Stn B, Mississauga ON L4Y 3W4 – 905/858-7525; Fax: 905/823-2312 – Monthly; Urdu

MAGAZINES — FARM PUBLICATIONS 5-193

The South Asian Voice, 370 Main St. North, PO Box 44007, Brampton ON L6V 4H5 – 905/455-9839; Fax: 905/452-8133; Email: pakvoice@inforamp.net – Circ.: 4,000; Wed.; English & Urdu – Publisher & Managing Editor, Sabih Mansoor; Circulation Manager, Umber Mansoor

POLISH

Gazeta Montrealska, #202, 665, rue Principale, Laval PQ H7X 1E2 – 514/748-2666; Fax: 514/748-8109 – Monthly

Kulisy Polonii, 10806 - 81 Ave., Edmonton AB T6E 1Y4 – 403/439-0806, 2215; Fax: 403/439-0806 – Circ.: 4,500; 24 times a year – Editor, Mary Carlton

The Polish Canadian Courier, PO Box 161, Stn P, Toronto ON M5S 2S7 – 416/259-4353; Fax: 416/259-4353 – Weekly

PORTUGUESE

Acontece, 102 Atlantic Ave., PO Box 614, Stn C, Toronto ON M6J 3R9 – 416/533-7799; Fax: 416/533-2410 – 24 times a year

Correio Português, 793 Ossington Ave., Toronto ON M6G 3T8 – 416/532-9894; Fax: 416/532-1475 – 24 times a year

Portugal Ilustrado, 60 Hanson Rd., Unit 138, Mississauga ON L5B 2P6 – 905/279-8368; Fax: 905/279-8368 – Circ.: 8,000; Weekly – Editor, Manuel Neto

A Voz de Portugal, 4181, rue Saint-Dominique, Montréal PQ H2W 2A7 – 514/844-0388; Fax: 514/844-6283 – Circ.: 10,000; Weekly – Editor, Armando Barquairo

SERBIAN

Kanadski Srbobran, Serbian League of Canada, 335 Britannia Ave., Hamilton ON L3H 1Y4 – 905/549-4079 – Circ.: 1,000; 3 times a month – Administrator, M. Marijan

The Voice of Canadian Serbs, c/o Serbian National Shield Society of Canada, 1900 Sheppard Ave. East, PO Box 303, Willowdale ON M2J 4T4 – 416/496-7881; Fax: 416/493-0335 – Circ.: 2,000; Monthly; Serbian & English – Editor, Bora Dragasevich

SLOVAK, CZECH

Kanadske Listy, 388 Atwater Ave., Mississauga ON L5G 2A3 – 905/278-4116 – Circ.: 2,500; Monthly; Czech – Publisher & Editor, M. Janecek

Novy Domov, Masaryk Memorial Institute Inc., 450 Scarborough Golf Club Rd., Scarborough ON M1G 1H1 – 416/439-9557; Email: novydom@interlog.com – Circ.: 3,000; Bi-weekly; Czech, Slovak & English – Editor, Vera M. Roller

La Voz de Montréal, #600, 6020, rue Jean Talon est, Montréal PQ H1S 3B1 – 514/253-2332; Fax: 514/253-6574 – 50 times a year

SPANISH

Correo Latinoamericano, 2413 Dundas St. West, Toronto ON M6P 1X3 – 416/538-0588; Fax: 416/531-7187 – Weekly – Publisher, Eduardo Uruena

El Popular, 2413 Dundas St. West, Toronto ON M6P 1X3 – 416/531-2495; Fax: 416/531-7187 – Daily – Publisher, Eduardo Uruena; Editor, Walter Seminario; Circulation Manager, Mayde Mauianda

SWEDISH

Swedish Press, 1294 - 7th Ave. West, Vancouver BC V6H 1B6 – 604/731-6381; Fax: 604/731-6361; Email: swedress@unix.info.serve.net – Circ.: 6,000; Monthly; English & Swedish; also Scandinavian Press (4 times a year; English) covers all Nordic countries – Publisher & Editor, Anders Neumuller

UKRAINIAN

Homin Ukrainy, 140 Bathurst St., Toronto ON M5V 2R3 – 416/504-3443; Fax: 416/703-0687 –
Circ.: 15,000; Weekly; Ukrainian & English – Publisher, W. Okipniuk; Editor, O. Romanyshyn

Moloda Ukraina, c/o Walentina Rodak, 12 Minstrel Dr., Toronto ON M8Y 3H4 – 416/255-8604; Fax: 905/238-9821 – Circ.: 1,050; Monthly – Executive Publisher, P. Rodak; Editor, L. Lishchyna

Novy Shliakh, 297 College St., Toronto ON M5T 1S2 – 416/960-3424 – Weekly

Nowi Dni, Nowi Dni Co. Ltd., PO Box 400, Stn D, Toronto ON M6P 3J9 – 416/767-8440 – Circ.: 1,500; Monthly; Ukrainian – Editor, Marjan Horhota-Dalney

Promin, 842 Main St., Winnipeg MB R2W 3N8 – 204/589-5101; Fax: 204/586-3618 – Monthly

Ukrainian News, c/o Edmonton Lasergraphics, #1, 12227 - 107 Ave., Edmonton AB T5M 1Y9 – 403/488-3693; Fax: 403/488-3859; Email: 75030.1537@compuserve.com – Circ.: 6,500; Bi-weekly; English & Ukrainian – Editor, Marco Levytsky; Circulation Manager, Alexandra Cybulsky

Ukrainsky Holos, 842 Main St., Winnipeg MB R2W 3N8 – 204/589-5101; Fax: 204/586-3618 – Weekly

Zhinochy Svit, Ukrainian Women's Organization of Canada, 937 Main St., Winnipeg MB R2W 3P2 – 204/943-8230; Fax: 204/943-8230 – Circ.: 2,500; 10 issues a year; English & Ukrainian – Managing Editor, Anne Wach

FARM PUBLICATIONS

The Ad-Viser (Published by Robins Southern Printing (1990) Ltd.), 1320 - 36 St. North, Lethbridge AB T1H 5H8 – 403/328-5114; Fax: 403/328-5443 – Circ.: 20,159; Every other Thurs. – Editor, Rick Gillis; Circulation Manager, Leona Milford

Agri-book: Beans in Canada (Published by AIS Communications Ltd.), 145 Thames Rd. West, Exeter ON N0M 1S3 – 519/235-2400; Fax: 519/235-0798 – Circ.: 22,897; Annually – Publisher, Peter Phillips; Editor, Peter Darbishire; Circulation Manager, Jan Jeffery

Agri-book: Corn in Canada (Published by AIS Communications Ltd.), 145 Thames Rd. West, Exeter ON N0M 1S3 – 519/235-2400; Fax: 519/235-0798 – Circ.: 21,360; Annually – Publisher, Peter Phillips; Editor, Peter Darbishire; Circulation Manager, Jan Jeffery

Agri-book: Drainage Contractor (Published by AIS Communications Ltd.), 145 Thames Rd. West, Exeter ON N0M 1S3 – 519/235-2400; Fax: 519/235-0798 – Circ.: 8,425; Annually – Publisher, Peter Phillips; Editor, Peter Darbishire; Circulation Manager, Jan Jeffery

Agri-book: Potatoes in Canada (Published by AIS Communications Ltd.), 145 Thames Rd. West, Exeter ON N0M 1S3 – 519/235-2400; Fax: 519/235-0798 – Circ.: 3,363; Annually – Publisher, Peter Phillips; Editor, Peter Darbishire; Circulation Manager, Jan Jeffery

Agri-book: Top Crop Manager (Published by AIS Communications Ltd.), 145 Thames Rd. West, Exeter ON N0M 1S3 – 519/235-2400; Fax: 519/235-0798 – Circ.: 31,397; 4 times a year – Publisher, Peter Phillips; Editor, Peter Darbishire; Circulation Manager, Jan Jeffery

Agricom, 2474 Champlain St., CP 220, Clarence Creek ON K0A 1N0 – 613/488-2651; Fax: 613/488-2541 – 22 times a year – Editor, Pierre Glaude

AgWorld news, The StarPhoenix, 204 - 5th Ave. North, Saskatoon SK S7K 2P1 – 306/664-8340; Fax: 306/664-8208 – Circ.: 67,206; 4 times a year

Alberta Beef, #202, 2915 - 19 St. NE, Calgary AB T2E 7A2 – 403/250-1090; Fax: 403/291-9546 – Circ.: 13,400; 12 times a year – Publisher/Editor, Garth McClintock

Alberta FarmLIFE, #200, 4850 - 51 St., Red Deer AB T2N 2A5 – 403/343-2769; Fax: 403/343-2736 –
Circ.: 168,000; 24 times a year – Manager, Keith Rideout

Atlantic Beef, PO Box 1509, Liverpool NS B0T 1K0 – 902/354-3321 – 4 times a year – Editor, Dirk van Loon

Barley Country, c/o Alberta Barley Commission, #237, 2116 - 27 Ave. NE, Calgary AB T2E 7A6 – 403/291-9111; Fax: 403/291-0190; Email: abbarley@cadvision.com – Circ.: 40,936; 4 times a year – Editor, Shannon Park

B.C. Agri Digest, RR#2, Chase BC V0E 1M0 – 250/679-5362; Fax: 250/679-5362; Email: frankay@netshop.net; URL: http://www.shuswap.bc.ca/sunny/fkay-mg.htm – Circ.: 11,862; 12 times a year; Aug. issue - BC Agri Directory (annual) – Publisher & Editor, Fran Kay; Circulation Manager, Delores Barkman

B.C. Dairy Directory, #108, 10721 - 139 St., Surrey BC V3T 4L8 – 604/582-7288; Fax: 604/583-3000 – Circ.: 1,400; Annually, June – Publisher, Lloyd Mackey; Editor, Edna Mackey

B.C. Orchardist, Growers Publishing, PO Box 423, Salmon Arm BC V1E 4N6 – 250/833-0071; Fax: 250/833-0622 – Monthly – Publisher, Jim Hayward; Editor, E.W. Noonan

B.C. Simmental News, 1860 - 232nd Ave., RR#9, Langley BC V3A 6H5 – 604/533-1054 – 4 times a year

Beef in B.C. Inc., c/o B.C. Cattlemen's Association, #4, 10145 Durango Rd., Kamloops BC V2C 6T4 – 250/573-3611; Fax: 250/573-5155 – Circ.: 3,000; 7 times a year – Editor, A.L. Leach

Le Bulletin des Agriculteurs, 514/843-2100; Fax: 514/845-6261; Email: bulletin@maclean-hunter-quebec.qc.ca; URL: http://www.cyberplex.com/bulletin – Tirage: 30,000; Mensuel; français – Éditeur, Simon M. Guertin; Rédacteur, Marc-Alain Soucy

Canada Poultryman, Farm Papers Ltd., #105B, 9547 - 152 St., Surrey BC V3R 5Y5 – 604/585-3131; Fax: 604/585-1504; Email: tgreaves@wimsey.com – Circ.: 7,734; Monthly; English & French – Editor, Tony Greaves; Circulation Manager, Irene Trueman

Canada's Who's Who Of The Poultry Industry, Farm Papers Ltd., #105B, 9547 - 152 St., Surrey BC V3R 5Y5 – 604/585-3131; Fax: 604/585-1504; Email: tgreavers@wimsey.com – Circ.: 4,993; Annually, June – Editor, Tony Greaves; Circulation Manager, Irene Trueman

Canadian Ayrshire Review, PO Box 188, Ste-Anne-de-Bellevue PQ H9X 1C0 – 514/398-7970 – Monthly; English & French – Business Manager, Linda Ness

Canadian Fruitgrower (Published by NCC Publishing), 222 Argyle Ave., Delhi ON N4B 2Y2 – 519/582-2513; Fax: 519/582-4040 – Circ.: 3,200; 9 times a year – Publisher, Dave Douglas; Editor, Dave Harrison

Canadian Guernsey Journal, Canadian Guernsey Assn., 368 Woolwich St., Guelph ON N1H 3W6 – 519/836-2141; Fax: 519/824-9250 – 2 times a year – Editor, V.M. Macdonald

Canadian Hereford Digest, 5160 Skyline Way NE, Calgary AB T2E 6V1 – 403/274-1734 – Monthly, except July; English & French – Publisher & Editor, Kurt Gilmore

Canadian Jersey Breeder, 350 Speedvale Ave. West, Unit 9, Guelph ON N1H 7M7 – 519/821-9150; Fax: 519/821-2723 – 10 times a year – Editor, Betty Clements

Canadian Ostrich (Published by Dakota Design & Advertising Ltd.), #201, 2915 - 19th St. NE, Calgary AB T2E 7A2 – 403/250-1128; Fax: 403/250-1194 – Circ.: 2,600; Monthly – Co-Publisher, Ruth Dunbar; Co-Publisher & Editor, Ingrid Schulz

The Canadian Tobacco Grower (Published by NCC Publishing), 222 Argyle Ave., Delhi ON N4B 2Y2 – 519/582-2513; Fax: 519/582-4040 – Circ.: 2,800; 4 times a year – Publisher, David Douglas; Editor, Marlene Opdecam

Canadian Almanac & Directory 1997

MAGAZINES — FARM PUBLICATIONS

Canola Country, Saskatchewan Canola Growers Association, #210, 111 Research Dr., Saskatoon SK S7N 3R2 – 306/668-2380; Fax: 306/975-1126 – Circ.: 1,100; 6 times a year – Editor, Holly Rask

Canola Guide (Published by Farm Business Communications), #2500, 201 Portage Ave., PO Box 6600, Winnipeg MB R3C 3A7 – 204/944-2254; Fax: 204/944-5416; Email: bstrautman@fbc.unitedgrain.ca – Circ.: 26,000; 9 times a year – Managing Director, Palmer Anderson; Editor, Bill Strautman; Circulation Manager, Heather Anderson

Cattlemen Magazine (Published by Farm Business Communications), #2500, 201 Portage Ave., PO Box 6600, Winnipeg MB R3C 3A7 – 204/944-5750; Fax: 204/942-8463; Email: gwinslow@fbc.unitedgrain.ca – Circ.: 27,200; Monthly – Editor, Gren Winslow; Circulation Manager, Andy Sirski

Central Alberta Adviser, Red Deer Publications, 5929 - 48th Ave., PO Box 5023, Stn MPO, Red Deer AB T4N 6R4 – 403/346-3356; Fax: 403/347-6620; Email: RDPUB@cnnet.com – Circ.: 27,327; Weekly – Publisher, Cal Dallas; Editor, Glen Werkman

Central Alberta Farmer, Bowes Publishers, 4504 - 61 Ave., Leduc AB T9E 3Z1 – 403/986-2271; Fax: 403/986-6397; Email: leduc_rep@awnet.net – Circ.: 26,428; 12 times a year – Publisher, Neil Sutcliffe

Central Alberta Life (Published by Red Deer Advocate), 2950 Bremner Ave., PO Box 5200, Red Deer AB T4N 5G3 – 403/343-2400; Fax: 403/342-4051 – Circ.: 38,500; Weekly – Publisher, Howard Jenzen; Editor, Joe McLaughlin; Circulation Manager, Allan Melbourne

Charolais Banner (Published by Charolais Banner Ltd.), #205, 3016 - 19 St. NE, Calgary AB T2E 6Y9 – 403/291-1420; Fax: 403/291-0081; URL: http://www.charolaisbanner.com – Circ.: 3,000; 10 times a year – Managing Editor, Rob Pek; Circulation Manager, Sharon Degner

Charolais Connection (Published by Charolais Banner Ltd.), #205, 3016 - 19 St. NE, Calgary AB T2E 6Y9 – 403/291-1420; Fax: 403/291-0081 – Circ.: 30,000; 2 times a year – Managing Editor, Rob Pek

Le Coopérateur Agricole, #200, 9001, boul de l'Acadie, CP 500, Montréal PQ H4N 3H7 – 514/384-6450; Fax: 514/858-2025 – Tirage: 25,439; 9 fois par an; français – Rédacteur, Patrick Dupuis

Corn-Soy Guide (Published by Farm Business Communications), #2500, 201 Portage Ave., PO Box 6600, Winnipeg MB R3C 3A7 – 204/944-5760; Fax: 204/942-8463; Email: dwreford@fbc.unitedgrain.ca – Circ.: 22,500; 10 times a year – Editor, Dave Wreford; Circulation Manager, Andy Sirski

Country Guide (Published by Farm Business Communications), #2500, 201 Portage Ave., PO Box 6600, Winnipeg MB R3C 3A7 – 204/944-5761; Fax: 204/942-8463; Email: dwreford@fbc.unitedgrain.ca; URL: http://www.agriculture.com – Circ.: 69,000; 11 times a year – Managing Director, Palmer Anderson; Managing Editor, Dave Wreford; Circulation Manager, Heather Anderson

Country Life in B.C., 3308 King George Hwy., Surrey BC V4P 1A8 – 604/536-7622; Fax: 604/536-5677; Email: countrylife@bc.sympatico.ca – Circ.: 8,176; Monthly – Publisher & Editor, Malcolm Young; Circulation Manager, L.A. Noonan

Dairy Contact, PO Box 549, Onoway AB T0E 1V0 – 403/967-2929; Fax: 403/967-2930 – Monthly – Editor, Allen Parr

Dairy Guide (Published by Farm Business Communications), #2500, 201 Portage Ave., PO Box 6600, Winnipeg MB R3C 3A7 – 204/944-5750; Fax: 204/942-8463; Email: gwinslow@fbc.unitedgrain.ca; URL: http://www.mbnet.mb.ca/~wilkins – Circ.: 18,100; 5 times a year – Editor, Gren Winslow; Circulation Manager, Andy Sirski, 204/944-5762

Economic Planning in Free Societies, Academic Publishing Co., PO Box 145, Mount Royal PQ H3P 3B9 – 514/738-5255; Fax: 514/738-5255, 305/463-7020, Nov.-May – Circ.: 1,200; 6 times a year – Editor, Dr. Peter Harsany; Circulation Manager, A. Graul

Farm & Country (Published by Agricultural Publishing Co Ltd.), #1504, One Yonge St., Toronto ON M5E 1E5 – 416/364-5324; Fax: 416/364-5857 – Circ.: 51,870; 18 times a year; also Farm Power Today (monthly supplement) – Managing Editor, John Muggeridge

Farmers' Choice (Published by Red Deer Advocate), 2950 Bremner Ave., PO Box 5200, Red Deer AB T4N 5G3 – 403/343-2400; Fax: 403/342-4051 – Circ.: 83,600; Monthly – Publisher, Howard Jenzen; Editor, Joe McLaughlin; Circulation Manager, Allan Melbourne

Farm Focus, Cameron Publishing, PO Box 128, Yarmouth NS B5A 4B1 – 902/742-7111; Fax: 902/742-2311 – Circ.: 7,982; 24 times a year

The Farm Gate, North Waterlook Publishing Ltd., 15 King St., Elmira ON N3B 2R1 – 519/669-5155 – Circ.: 21,000; Monthly

FarmLIFE, #4, 75 Lenore Dr., Saskatoon SK S7K 7Y1 – 306/242-5723; Fax: 306/668-6164 – Circ.: 168,000; 24 times a year – Editor, Larry Hiatt

Farm Light & Power, 2352 Smith St., Regina SK S4P 2P6 – 800/668-3300; Fax: 800/213-9999 – Circ.: 70,363; Monthly – Publisher, Tom Bradley

Farm Review, 41 Dundas St. East, Napanee ON K7R 1H7 – 613/354-6648; Fax: 613/354-6708 – Publisher, Victor Mlodecki; Editor, Kathleen Clark

Feather Fancier, 4094 Ross St., RR#5, Forest ON N0N 1J0 – 519/899-2364; Fax: 519/899-2364 – Circ.: 2,800; 11 times a year – Co-Publisher, Linda Gryner; Co-Publisher & Editor, James Gryner

Gestion et Technologie Agricoles, 655, av Sainte-Anne, St-Hyacinthe PQ J2S 5G4 – 514/773-6028; Fax: 514/773-3115 – Tirage: 20,000; 8 fois par an; français – Rédacteur, Louis A. Bernard

Grainews (Published by Farm Business Communications), #2500, 201 Portage Ave., PO Box 6600, Winnipeg MB R3C 3A7 – 204/944-5587; Fax: 204/944-5416; Email: jham@fbc.unitedgrain.ca – Circ.: 52,000; 16 times a year – Managing Director, Palmer Anderson; Editor, Andy Sirski; Circulation Manager, Heather Anderson

The Grower, c/o Ontario Fruit & Vegetable Growers Assn., #103, 355 Elmira Rd., Guelph ON N1K 1S5 – 519/763-6160; Fax: 519/763-6604 – Circ.: 8,000; Monthly – Editor, Gayle Anderson, 519/763-8728

Le Guide de l'Agriculture du Québec (Published by Publiédition inc.), 620, boul Industriel, St-Jean-sur-Richelieu PQ J3B 7X4 – 514/856-7821; Fax: 514/359-0836 – Tirage: 5,000; Annuellement – Éditeur, Yves Bégnoche

Holstein Journal, 9120 Leslie St., Unit 105, Richmond Hill ON L4B 3J9 – 905/886-4222; Fax: 905/866-0037 – Circ.: 9,577; Monthly; English & French – Publisher, Peter English; Editor, Bonnie Cooper

Huron Soil & Crop News, c/o Exeter Times-Advocate, 424 Main St., Exeter ON N0M 1S0 – 519/235-1331; Fax: 519/235-0766 – Circ.: 7,000; Annually, March – Editor, Ross Haugh

Island Farmer, PO Box 790, Montague PE C0A 1R0 – 902/838-2515; Fax: 902/838-4392 – Circ.: 2,000; 26 times a year – Publisher, J. MacNeill

The Limousin Leader, Bollum Marketing, #253, 1935 - 32 Ave. NE, Calgary AB T2E 7C8 – 403/291-6770; Fax: 403/291-6744 – 11 times a year – Editor, Randy Bollum

The Manitoba Co-Operator, 220 Portage Ave., PO Box 9800, Winnipeg MB R3C 3K7 – 204/934-0401; Fax: 204/934-0480 – Circ.: 23,600; Weekly – Publisher/Editor, John W. Morriss

Manitoba Farm Life, Deversa Group, #1, 217 - 10th St., Brandon MB R7A 4E9 – 204/727-5459; Fax: 204/729-8965 – 24 times a year – Editor, Craig Laursen

Ma Revue de Machinerie Agricole, Rubricor inc., CP 454, Drummondville PQ J2B 6W4 – 819/478-2136; Fax: 819/478-4819 – Tirage: 35,000; 11 fois par an; français – Rédacteur, Jean-Marc Beland

Le Meunier, #115, 2323, boul du Versant Nord, Ste-Foy PQ G1N 4P4 – 418/688-9227; Fax: 418/688-3575 – 4 fois par an; français – Directeur, Andre J. Pilon

Niagara Farmers' Monthly, 131 College St., PO Box 52, Smithville ON L0R 2A0 – 905/957-3751; Fax: 905/957-0088 – Circ.: 18,000; 11 times a year – Publisher & Editor, I.G. Carruthers; Circulation Manager, Rob Shepherd

The Northern Horizon, 901 - 100th Ave., Dawson Creek BC V1G 1W2 – 250/782-4888; Fax: 250/782-6770 – Circ.: 28,055; 25 times a year – Publisher, Margaret Forbes; Editor, Reg Minall; Circulation Manager, Tiffany Lewis

Northern Horse Review (Published by Dakota Design & Advertising Ltd.), #201, 2915 - 19th St. NE, Calgary AB T2E 7A2 – 403/250-1128; Fax: 403/250-1194; Email: dakota@supernet.ab.ca – Circ.: 10,000; 10 times a year – Co-Publisher, Ruth Dunbar; Co-Publisher & Editor, Ingrid Schulz

Northwest Farmer/Rancher (Published by Battleford Publishing Ltd.), PO Box 1029, North Battleford SK S9A 3E6 – 306/445-7261; Fax: 306/445-3223 – Circ.: 15,000; 4 times a year – Publisher, Steven Dills; Editor, Lorne Cooper

Ontario Beef, Ontario Cattlemen's Assn., 130 Malcolm Rd., Guelph ON N1K 1B1 – 519/824-0334; Fax: 519/824-9101; Email: ontbeef@cattle.guelph.on.ca; URL: http://www.cattle.guelph.on.ca – Circ.: 21,000; 5 times a year – Publisher, Sandra Eby; Circulation Manager, Donna Corbet

Ontario Beef Farmer (Published by Bowes Publishers Ltd.), PO Box 7400, London ON N5Y 4X3 – 519/471-8520; Fax: 519/473-2256 – Circ.: 12,800; 4 times a year – Publisher, Mervyn J. Hawkins; Editor, Paul Mahon; Circulation Manager, Arland Klein

Ontario Corn Producer, c/o Ontario Corn Producers Assn., 90 Woodlawn Rd. West, Guelph ON N1H 1B2 – 519/837-1660; Fax: 519/837-1674; Email: ontcorn@ontariocorn.org; http://www.ontariocron.org – Circ.: 21,000; 10 times a year – Editor, Terry Boland

Ontario Dairy Farmer (Published by Bowes Publishers Ltd.), PO Box 7400, London ON N5Y 4X3 – 519/473-0010; Fax: 519/473-2256; Email: ontariofarmer@online.sys.com – Circ.: 13,900; 6 times a year – Publisher, Mervyn J. Hawkins; Editor, Paul Mahon

Ontario Farmer (Published by Bowes Publishers Ltd.), PO Box 7400, London ON N5Y 4X3 – 519/473-0010; Fax: 519/473-2256 – Circ.: 33,800; Weekly, Tues. – Publisher, Mervyn J. Hawkins; Editor, Paul Mahon; Circulation Manager, Arland Klein

Ontario Hog Farmer (Published by Bowes Publishers Ltd.), PO Box 7400, London ON N5Y 4X3 – 519/473-0010; Fax: 519/473-2256 – Circ.: 8,500; 6 times a year – Publisher, Mervyn J. Hawkins; Editor, Paul Mahon; Circulation Manager, Arland Klein

Ontario Milk Producer, Dairy Farmers of Ontario, 6780 Campobello Rd., Mississauga ON L5N 2L8 – 905/821-8970; Fax: 905/821-3160; Email: bdimmick@milk.ong – Circ.: 11,500; Monthly – Editor, Bill Dimmick, 905/821-8035

Porc Québec, 555, boul Roland Therrien, Longueuil PQ J4H 3Y9 – 514/679-0530, ext.276; Fax: 514/670-4788; Email: publicite@tcn.upa.qc.ca – Tirage: 3,700; 5 times a year – Hélène Perrault

Pork Producer (Published by Agricultural Publishing Co Ltd.), #1504, One Yonge St., Toronto ON M5E 1E5 – 416/364-5324; Fax: 416/364-5857 – Circ.: 7,300; 4 times a year – Managing Editor, Bernard Tobin

The Prairie Agricultural Newspaper, L & L Communications Inc., PO Box 1623, Rosetown SK S0L 2V0 – 306/882-2221; Fax: 306/882-2217 – Circ.: 65,400; 20 times a year – Editor, Kevin Hursh

Pro-farm, 1836 Victoria Ave., Regina SK S4N 7K3 – 306/586-5866; Fax: 306/586-2707 – Circ.: 9,000; 6

Canadian Almanac & Directory 1997

times a year – Publisher, Chris Dodd; Editor, Alanna Koch; Circulation Manager, Glenys Fox

Le Producteur de lait québécois, Fédération des producteurs de lait du Québec, 555, boul Roland Thérrien, Longueuil PQ J4H 3Y9 – 514/679-0530; Fax: 514/670-4788; Email: publicite@tcn.upa.qc.ca – Tirage: 14,099; Mensuel; français – Rédacteur en chef, Jean Vigneault

Producteur Plus, 455A, rue St-Hilaire, CP 147, Farnham PQ J2N 2R4 – 514/293-8282; Fax: 514/293-8554 – Tirage: 22,000; 10 fois par an; français – Directeur, Bertrand Beaumont; Rédacteur, Leonard Pigeon

Professional Farm Magazine, 41 West 1st Ave. South, Magrath AB T0K 1J0 – 403/758-3661; Fax: 403/758-3818; Email: pfmag@agt.net – Circ.: 11,500; 6 times a year – Pubisher, Duane Thomson

Québec Farmers' Advocate, CP 80, Ste-Anne-de-Bellevue PQ H9X 3L4 – 514/457-2010; Fax: 514/398-7972 – Tirage: 4,000; 11 times a year – Publisher, Hugh Maynard; Managing Editor, Susanne Brown

Rural Roots, 30 - 10th Ave. East, PO Box 550, Prince Albert SK S6V 5R9 – 306/764-4276; Fax: 306/763-3331 – Circ.: 35,000; 50 times a year – Publisher, Bob Gibb; Editor, Barb Gustafson

The Rural Voice (Published by North Huron Publishing Ltd.), 136 Queen St., PO Box 429, Blyth ON N0M 1H0 – 519/523-4311; Fax: 519/523-9140 – Circ.: 15,100; Monthly – Publisher & Editor, Keith Roulston; Circulation Manager, Joan Caldwell

Saskatchewan Farm Life, #4, 75 Lenore Dr., Saskatoon SK S7K 7Y1 – 306/242-5723; Fax: 306/244-6656 – 25 times a year

Sheep Canada, #600, 237 - 8th Ave. SE, Calgary AB T2G 5C3 – 403/264-3270; Fax: 403/264-3276 – 4 times a year – Publisher, Patrick Ottmann

Simmental Country, Pritchett Publications, #13, 4101 - 19 St. NE, Calgary AB T2E 7C4 – 403/250-5255; Fax: 403/250-5279 – Monthly – Publisher/Editor, Ted Pritchett

Southern Farm Guide, The Weyburn Review, 904 East Ave., PO Box 400, Weyburn SK S4H 2K4 – 306/842-7487; Fax: 306/842-0282 – Circ.: 17,675; 12 times a year – Publisher, Darryl Ward; Editor, Patricia Ward

La Terre de chez-nous, Agricultural Producers Union, 555, boul Roland Thérrien, Longueuil PQ J4H 3Y9 – 514/679-0530; Fax: 514/670-4788; Email: publicite@tcn.upa.qc.ca – Tirage: 39,500; Hebdomadaire; français – Rédacteur en chef, France Groulx

Union Farmer, National Farmers Union, 250C - 2nd Ave. South, Saskatoon SK S7K 2M1 – 306/652-9465; Fax: 306/664-6226 – Circ.: 4,300; 4 times a year – Editor, Carla Roppel

Voice of the Essex Farmer, 254 Main St., PO Box 490, Dresden ON N0P 1M0 – 519/683-4485; Fax: 519/683-4355 – Circ.: 35,000; Bi-weekly; also - Voice of the Huron Farmer, Voice of the Kent Farmer, Voice of the Lambton Farmer, Voice of the Middlesex Farmer, Voice of the Elgin Farmer, Voice of the Perth Farmer, Voice of the Oxford Farmer, & Voice of the Waterloo Farmer – Publisher, Denise Thibeault; Editor, Peter Epp; Circulation Manager, Marilyn Leitch

Western Dairy Farmer (Published by Bowes Publishers Ltd.), 4504 - 61 Ave., Leduc AB T9E 3Z1 – 403/986-2271; Fax: 403/986-6397; Email: Leduc_Rep@AWNET.Net – Circ.: 6,500; 5 times a year – Publisher, Neil Sutcliffe; Editor, Ken M. Nelson

Western Dairy Farmer Magazine (Published by Bowes Publishers Ltd.), 4504 - 61 Ave., Leduc AB T9E 3Z1 – 403/986-2271; Fax: 403/986-6397; Email: wdfarmer@ccinet.ab.ca – Circ.: 6,400; 5 times a year – Publisher, Neil Sutcliffe; Editor, Ken Nelson; Circulation Manager, Karen Clayton

Western Hog Journal, Alberta Pork Producers Development Corp., 10319 Princess Elizabeth Ave., Edmonton AB T5G 0Y5 – 403/474-8288; Fax: 403/471-8065 – Circ.: 7,723; 4 times a year – Editorial Director, Ward Toma

The Western Producer, PO Box 2500, Saskatoon SK S7K 2C4 – 306/665-3500, 1-800-667-7776; Fax: 306/653-1255; Email: newsroom@producer.com; URL: http://www.producer.com/ – Circ.: 98,000; Weekly – Publisher, Allan Laughland; Editor, Garry Fairbairn, 306/665-3577; Circulation Manager, Glenn Caleval

SCHOLARLY PUBLICATIONS

18th Century Fiction (Published by University of Toronto Press), Journals Division, 5201 Dufferin St., North York ON M3H 5T8 – 416/667-7810; Fax: 416/667-7881 – Circ.: 560; 4 times a year – Editor, David Blewett; Circulation Manager, Wendy Thornton

Acadiensis: Journal of the History of the Atlantic Region, Campus House, University of New Brunswick, PO Box 4400, Stn A, Fredericton NB E3B 5A3 – 506/453-4978; Fax: 506/453-4599; Email: Acadnsis@UNB.ca – Circ.: 900; 2 times a year; English & French – Editor, Gail Campbell

Annals of Air & Space Law, Institute & Centre of Air & Space Law, McGill University, 3661 Peel St., Montréal PQ H3A 1X1 – 514/398-3544; Fax: 514/398-8197; Email: annals@falaw.lan.mcgill.ca; URL: http://www.iasl.mcgill.ca – Circ.: 1,000; 2 times a year – Editor, Dr. Michael Milde; Circulation Manager, Melissa Knock

Anthropologica, c/o Dr. Mathias Guenther, Dept. of Sociology & Anthropology, Wilfred Laurier University, Waterloo ON N2L 3C5 – 519/884-1970; Fax: 519/884-8854 – 2 times a year

Arctic, c/o Arctic Institute of North America, University of Calgary, 2500 University Dr. NW, Calgary AB T2N 1N4 – 403/220-7515; Fax: 403/282-4609; Email: kmccullo@acs.ucalgary.ca – Circ.: 2,200; 4 times a year – Editor, Karen McCullough, 403/220-4049

ARIEL -- A Review of International English Literature, Department of English, Univ. of Calgary, 2500 University Dr. NW, Calgary AB T2N 1N4 – 403/220-7578; Fax: 403/282-0848; Email: ariel@acs.ucalgary.ca – Circ.: 1,000; 4 times a year – Editor, Victor J. Ramraj, 403/220-4657

BC Studies: The British Columbian Quarterly, c/o University of British Columbia, #165, 1855 West Mall, Vancouver BC V6T 1Z2 – 604/822-3727; Fax: 604/822-9452; Email: bcstudies@unixg.ubc.ca; URL: http://www.swifty.com/bcamp/directors/humansci/bcs.html – Circ.: 650; 4 times a year – Co-Editor, Jean Barman; Co-Editor, R. Cole Harris

Canadian Children's Literature, c/o Dept. of English, University of Guelph, Guelph ON N1G 2W1 – 519/824-4120, ext.3189; Fax: 519/837-1315; Email: ccl@uoguelph.ca; URL: http://www.uoguelph.ca/englit/ccl/ – Circ.: 900; 4 times a year; English & French; ISSN 0319-0080 – Co-Editor, Mary Rubio; Co-Editor, Daniel Chouinard

Canadian Ethnic Studies, Cdn. Ethnic Studies Assn., Centre for Ukrainian Canadian Studies, 424 University Centre, Winnipeg MB R2T 2N2 – 204/474-8906 – 3 times a year

Canadian Folk Music Journal (Published by Becker Associates), PO Box 507, Stn Q, Toronto ON M4T 2M5 – 416/483-7282; Fax: 416/489-1713 – Annually; ISSN 0318-2568 – Editor, Prof. Jay Rahn

Canadian Foreign Policy, PO Box 70030, Ottawa ON K2P 2M3 – 613/241-1391; Fax: 613/241-5911; Email: epotter@gsro.carleton.ca – 3 times a year

The Canadian Historical Review (Published by University of Toronto Press), Journals Division, 5201 Dufferin St., North York ON M3H 5T8 – 416/667-7781; Fax: 416/667-7881; Email: chr@gpu.utcc.utoronto.ca – Circ.: 2,200; 4 times a year; English & French – Editor, Linda Kealey; Circulation Manager, Wendy Thornton

Canadian Journal of Development Studies, c/o University of Ottawa, 5550 Cumberland, Room 160B, Ottawa ON K1N 6N5 – 613/564-5459; Fax: 613/564-9525 – 3 times a year

Canadian Journal of Economics, University of Toronto Press, #700, 10 St. Mary St., Toronto ON M4Y 2W8 – 416/978-6739; Email: journals@gpw.utcc.utoronto.ca – Circ.: 3,200; 4 times a year – Editor, B. Curtis Eaton, 604/291-5825

Canadian Journal of Higher Education, c/o Canadian Society for the Study of Higher Education, Secretariat, 151 Slater St., Ottawa ON K1P 1B1 – 613/563-1236; Fax: 613/563-7739; Email: kclements@aucc.ca – Circ.: 550; 3 times a year – Executive Secretary, Ken Clements

Canadian Journal of History, Dept. of History, University of Saskatchewan, 9 Campus Dr., Saskatoon SK S7N 5A5 – 306/966-5794; Fax: 306/966-5852; Email: cjh@duke.usask.ca; URL: http://www.usask.ca/history/cjh – Circ.: 725; 3 times a year – Editor-in-Chief, C.A. Kent; Managing Editor, Jacqueline Fraser

The Canadian Journal of Information & Library Science (Published by University of Toronto Press), Journals Division, 5201 Dufferin St., North York ON M3H 5T8 – 416/667-7810; Fax: 416/667-7881 – Circ.: 615; 4 times a year – Editor, Lynne Howarth; Circulation Manager, Wendy Thornton

Canadian Journal of Italian Studies, McMaster University, Main St. West, Hamilton ON L8S 4M2 – 905/525-9140, ext.23761 – 2 times a year

Canadian Journal of Law & Society, Dept des sciences jurigiques, UQAM, PO Box 8888, Stn Centre-Ville, Montréal PQ H3C 3P8 – 514/987-3000, ext.4712; Fax: 514/987-6548; Email: benoist@canelle.telecom.uquam.ca; URL: http://www.juris.uquam.ca/rcds/index_en.htm – Circ.: 400; Biennially; English & French – Editor-in-Chief, Roderick Macdonald

Canadian Journal of Linguistics (Published by University of Toronto Press), Journals Division, 5201 Dufferin St., North York ON M3H 5T8 – 416/667-7810; Fax: 416/667-7881 – Circ.: 900; 4 times a year – Editor, Anne Rochette; Circulation Manager, Wendy Thornton

Canadian Journal of Mathematics (Published by University of Toronto Press), Journals Division, 5201 Dufferin St., North York ON M3H 5T8 – 416/667-7810; Fax: 416/667-7881 – Circ.: 1,225; 6 times a year – Editor, Dr. Graham Wright; Circulation Manager, Wendy Thornton

Canadian Journal of Philosophy (Published by University of Calgary Press), 2500 University Dr. NW, Calgary AB T2N 1N4 – 403/220-7578; Fax: 403/282-0085 – Circ.: 1,150; 4 times a year – Editorial Board Coordinator, Dr. T. Hurka; Circulation Manager, Leslie Moore

Canadian Journal of Political & Social Theory, c/o Concordia University, 1455, boul de Maisonneuve ouest, Montréal PQ H3G 1M8 – 514/848-2119; Fax: 514/848-3494; Email: ctheory@vax2.concordia.ca; URL: http://english-server.hss.cmu.edu/ctheory.html – Circ.: 2,500; Weekly – Co-Publisher, Arthur Kroker; Co-Publisher & Editor, Marilouise Kroker, 514/282-9298

Canadian Journal of Program Evaluation (Published by University of Calgary Press), 2500 University Dr. NW, Calgary AB T2N 1N4 – 403/220-7578; Fax: 403/282-0085 – Circ.: 1,300; Bi-annually; English & French – Editor, Dr. Robert Segsworth

Canadian Journal of Psychoanalysis (Published by Becker Associates), PO Box 507, Toronto ON M4T 2M5 – 416/483-7282; Fax: 416/489-1713; Email: 72124-1360@compuserve.com – Annually; ISSN 0829-3929 – Editor, Dr. Eva P. Lester

Canadian Journal of Sociology, 5-21 Tory Bldg., Dept. of Sociology, University of Alberta, Edmonton AB T6G 2H4 – 403/492-5941; Fax: 403/492-5941; Email: cjscopy@gpu.srv.ualberta.ca – Circ.: 750; 4 times a year; English with French abstracts – Editor, Susan A. McDaniel

Canadian Journal of Women & The Law, 575 King Edward, PO Box 450, Ottawa ON K1N 6N5 – 613/562-5800, ext.3473; Fax: 613/562-5129; Email: sullivan@admin.comlaw.uottawa.ca – Circ.: 1,000; 2 times a year; English & French – Editor, Martha Jackman; Circulation Manager, Lucille Béland

Canadian Journal on Aging, Rm. 039, MacKinnon Bldg., University of Guelph, Guelph ON N1G 2W1 – 519/824-4120, ext.6925; Fax: 519/837-9953; Email: rvanderk@uoguelph.ca – Circ.: 1,800; 4 times a year; English & French – Editor, François Béland; Circulation Manager, Rosemary Vanderkamp

Canadian Literature, c/o University of British Columbia, #167, 1855 West Mall, Vancouver BC V6T 1Z2 – 604/822-2780; Fax: 604/822-9452; URL: http://www.swifty.com/cdn_lit – Circ.: 1,500; 4 times a year – Editor, E.M. Kröller; Sandra Christensen

Canadian Mathematical Bulletin (Published by University of Toronto Press), Journals Division, 5201 Dufferin St., North York ON M3H 5T8 – 416/667-7810; Fax: 416/667-7881 – Circ.: 775; 4 times a year – Editor, Dr. Graham Wright; Circulation Manager, Wendy Thornton

Canadian Modern Language Review (Published by University of Toronto Press), Journals Division, 5201 Dufferin St., North York ON M3H 5T8 – 416/667-7810; Fax: 416/667-7881; Email: cmlr@gpu.utcc.utoronto.ca – Circ.: 1,600; 4 times a year – Editor, Sharon Lapkin; Circulation Manager, Wendy Thornton

Canadian Poetry: Studies, Documents, Reviews, Dept. of English, University of Western Ontario, Richmond St. North, London ON N6A 3K7 – 519/673-1164; Fax: 519/661-3776 – Circ.: 400; 2 times a year – Editor, D.M.R. Bentley

Canadian Public Administration, #305, 150 Eglinton Ave. East, Toronto ON M4P 1E7 – 416/932-3666; Fax: 416/932-3667 – Circ.: 4,000; 4 times a year – Editor, Paul G. Thomas

Canadian Public Policy, Rm.409, School of Policy Studies, Queen's University, Kingston ON K7L 3N6 – 613/545-6644; Fax: 613/545-6960; Email: constant@qed.econ.queensu.ca; URL: http://wwwqed.econ.queensu.ca/pub/cpp/ – Circ.: 1,500; 4 times a year; English & French – Editor, Charles M. Beach

The Canadian Review of American Studies (Published by University of Calgary Press), 2500 University Dr. NW, Calgary AB T2N 1N4 – 403/220-7578; Fax: 403/282-0085 – Circ.: 500; 3 times a year; English & French – Editor-in-Chief, Dr. S. Randall; Circulation Manager, Leslie Moore

Canadian Review of Comparative Literature (Published by University of Toronto Press), Journals Division, 5201 Dufferin St., North York ON M3H 5T8 – 416/667-7810; Fax: 416/667-7881 – Circ.: 260; 4 times a year – Editor, M.V. Dimic; Circulation Manager, Wendy Thornton

Canadian Review of Sociology & Anthropology, #LB-615, 1455 de Maisonneuve West, Montréal PQ H3G 1M8 – 514/848-8780; Fax: 514/848-4539; Email: csaa@vax2.concordia.ca – Circ.: 1,700; 4 times a year; French & English – Editor, Rosalind Sydie

Canadian University Music Review, PO Box 507, Stn Q, Toronto ON M4T 2M5 – 416/483-7282; Fax: 416/489-1713; Email: 72124.1360@compuserve.com – Circ.: 400; 2 times a year; ISSN 0710-0353; English & French – Editor, Prof. William R. Bowen; Rédacteur, Marc-André Roberge

Cartographica (Published by University of Toronto Press), Journals Division, 5201 Dufferin St., North York ON M3H 5T8 – 416/667-7810; Fax: 416/667-7881 – Circ.: 1,000; 4 times a year – Editor, Michael Coulson; Circulation Manager, Wendy Thornton

Echos du Monde Classique (Published by University of Calgary Press), 2500 University Dr. NW, Calgary AB T2N 1N4 – 403/220-7578; Fax: 403/282-0085 – Circ.: 750; 3 times a year; English & French – Dr. Mark Joyal; Circulation Manager, Leslie Moore

Economics Working Papers, Dept. of Economics, McMaster University, Hamilton ON L8S 4M4 – 905/525-9140, ext.22765; Fax: 905/521-8232; Email: econ@mcmaster.ca; URL: http://socserv2.socsci.mcmaster.ca/~econ/ – Circ.: 75; 4 times a year – Editor, Lonnie Magee, Email: magee@mcmaster.ca; Circulation Manager, Rosalie Goodwin

Ellipse, Faculté des Lettres et sciences humaines, Université de Sherbrooke, Sherbrooke PQ J1K 2R1 – 819/821-7238; Fax: 819/821-7285 – Circ.: 750; 2 times a year; English & French – Director, Charly Bouchara, 514/821-7000, ext.3268

Energy Studies Review, McMaster University, Hamilton ON L8S 4M4 – 905/525-9140, ext.4527; Fax: 905/521-8232 – 3 times a year

Environments: A Journal of Interdisciplinary Studies, ES1, Rm. 107J, Environmental Studies, University of Waterloo, 200 University Ave. West, Waterloo ON N2L 3G1 – 519/885-1211, ext.3586; Fax: 519/746-2031; Email: hrc@fes.uwaterloo.ca – 3 times a year – Editor, J. Gordon Nelson; Circulation Manager, Lisa Weber

Essays on Canadian Writing, #200, 2120 Queen St. East, Toronto ON M4E 1E2 – 416/694-3348; Fax: 416/698-9906; Email: ecw@sympatico.ca – Circ.: 1,200; 3 times a year – Publisher & Editor, Robert Lecker

Event, c/o Douglas College, PO Box 2503, New Westminster BC V3L 5B2 – 604/527-5293; Fax: 604/527-5095; URL: http://www.douglas.ca/Event/homepage.html – 3 times a year – Editor, Calvin Wharton; Assistant Editor, Bonnie Bauder

Exceptionality Education Canada (Published by University of Calgary Press), 2500 University Dr. NW, Calgary AB T2N 1N4 – 403/220-7578; Fax: 403/282-0085 – Circ.: 250; 4 times a year – Editor, Dr. J. Goldberg; Circulation Manager, Leslie Moore

Infor (Published by University of Toronto Press), Journals Division, 5201 Dufferin St., North York ON M3H 5T8 – 416/667-7810; Fax: 416/667-7881 – Circ.: 1,700; 4 times a year – Editor, David Wright; Circulation Manager, Wendy Thornton

Journal of Baha'i Studies, 34 Copernicus St., Ottawa ON K1N 7K4 – 613/233-1903; Fax: 613/233-3644; Email: as929freenet.carleton.ca – Circ.: 2,000; 4 times a year; English, French & Spanish – Executive Officer & Editor, Christine Zerbinis

Journal of Canadian Art History, c/o VA-432, Concordia University, 1455, boul de Maisonneuve ouest, Montréal PQ H3G 1M8 – 514/848-4699; Fax: 514/848-8627; Email: sparik@vax2.concordia.ca – 2 times a year – Sandra Paikowski

Journal of Canadian Poetry, Dept. of English, University of Ottawa, 175 Waller St., PO Box 450, Stn A, Ottawa ON K1N 6N5 – 613/562-5972; Fax: 613/562-5975 – Circ.: 350; Annually – Editor, David Staines

Journal of Canadian Studies, c/o Trent University, PO Box 4800, Peterborough ON K9J 7B8 – 705/748-1279; Fax: 705/748-1655; Email: jcs_rec@trentu.ca – Circ.: 1,300; 4 times a year – Editor-in-Chief, Michèle Lacombe; Managing Editor, Joy Manson

Journal of Child & Youth Care, Dept. of Human Services, Malaspina University College, 900 Fifth St., Nanaimo BC V9R 5S5 – Circ.: 450; 4 times a year – Co-Editor, Dr. G. Fewster; Co-Editor, Dr. T. Garfat

Journal of Law and Social Policy (Published by Becker Associates), PO Box 507, Stn Q, Toronto ON M4T 2M5 – 416/483-7282; Fax: 416/489-1713 – Annually; ISSN 0829-3929 – Editor, Paul Dusome

Journal of Scholarly Publishing (Published by University of Toronto Press), Journals Division, 5201 Dufferin St., North York ON M3H 5T8 – 416/667-7810; Fax: 416/667-7881 – Circ.: 1,560; 4 times a year – Editor, Sandra Meadow; Circulation Manager, Wendy Thornton

Labour, c/o Dept. of History, Memorial University, St. John's NF A1C 5S7 – 709/737-2144; Fax: 709/737-4342; Email: joanb@plato.ucs.mun.ca; URL: http://www.mun.ca/cclh/ – Circ.: 1,000; 2 times a year; English & French – Editor-in-Chief, Gregory S. Keahley; Managing Editor, Irene Whitfield, 709/737-3453

Labour, Capital & Society: A Journal on the Third World, Centre for Developing Area Studies, McGill University, 3715 Peel St., Montréal PQ H3A 1X1 – 514/398-3508; Fax: 514/398-8432; Email: ed10@musica.mcgill.ca – Circ.: 700; 2 times a year; English & French – Editor, Dr. Rosalind Boyd

Leisurability (Published by Becker Associates), PO Box 507, Stn Q, Toronto ON M4T 2M5 – 416/483-7282; Fax: 416/489-1713 – 4 times a year; ISSN 0711-222X – Editor, Dr. Peggy Hutchison

Material History Review, c/o National Museum of Science & Technology, PO Box 9724, Stn T, Ottawa ON K1G 5A3 – 613/991-3081; Fax: 613/990-3636 – 2 times a year – Managing Editor, Geoffrey Rider

Mathematics Reports, McMaster University, Main St. West, Hamilton ON L8S 4K1 – 905/525-9140, ext.24841; Fax: 905/522-0935 – 12 times a year

McGill Journal of Education, c/o Faculty of Education, McGill University, 3700 McTavish St., Montréal PQ H3A 1Y2 – 514/398-4246; Fax: 514/398-6968; Email: keenana@education.mcgill.ca – Circ.: 500; 3 times a year; English & French – Editor, William M. Talley; Editorial Assistant, Ann Keenan

McMaster Journal of Theology & Ministry, c/o Divinity College, McMaster University, Main St. West, Hamilton ON L8S 4K1 – 905/525-9140, ext.24401; Fax: 905/577-4782; Email: bellousk@mcmaster.ca; URL: http://www.mcmaster.ca/divinity – 2 times a year – Editor, Kenneth W. Bellous

Modern Drama, University of Toronto Press, 5201 Dufferin St., Toronto ON M3H 5T8 – 416/667-7781; Fax: 416/667-7832; Email: journals@gpu.utcc.utoronto.ca; editorial office email: moddram@epas.utoronto.ca; URL: http://www/utpress/depthome.htm – Circ.: 2,223; 4 times a year – Editor, Dorothy Parker

The Monograph - Journal of the Ont. Assn. for Geographical & Environmental Education (Published by Becker Associates), PO Box 507, Stn Q, Toronto ON M4T 2M5 – 416/483-7282; Fax: 416/489-1713 – 4 times a year; ISSN 0048-1973 – Editor, Gary Birchall

Monographs in Education, Rm 230, Education Bldg., University of Manitoba, Winnipeg MB R3T 2N2 – 204/474-8309; Fax: 204/275-5962 – Annual – Editor, Dr. A.D. Gregor

Mosaic: A Journal for the Interdisciplinary Study of Literature, Room 208, Tier Bldg., University of Manitoba, Winnipeg MB R3T 2N2 – 204/474-9763; Fax: 204/261-9086; Email: ejhinz@bldgarts.lan1.umanitoba.ca; URL: http://www.umanitoba.ca/publications/mosaic – Circ.: 900; 4 times a year – Editor, Evelyn J. Hinz; Circulation Manager, Donna Derenchuk

Newfoundland Studies, c/o English Dept., Memorial University, St. John's NF A1C 5S7 – 709/737-3453; Fax: 709/737-4342; Email: irenew@plato.ucs.mun.ca – Circ.: 250; 2 times a year – Editor-in-Chief, Mary Dalton; Circulation Manager, Irene Whitfield

Nova Scotia Historical Review, c/o Public Archives of NS, 6016 University Ave., Halifax NS B3H 1W4 – 902/424-6085; Fax: 902/424-0628 – Circ.: 500; 2 times a year – Editor, Barry Cahill; Circulation Manager, Stephen Crowell

Canadian Almanac & Directory 1997

Ontario History (Published by Ontario Historical Society), 34 Parkview Ave., Willowdale ON M2N 3Y2 – 416/226-9011; Fax: 416/226-2740 – Circ.: 1,200; 4 times a year – Editor, Dr. Terry Crowley; Circulation Manager, Barbara Truax

Open Letter, 499 Dufferin Ave., London ON N6B 2A1 – 519/673-5732; Email: fdavey@uwo.ca – 3 times a year

Pacific Affairs, c/o University of British Columbia, #164, 1855 West Mall, Vancouver BC V6T 1Z2 – 604/822-6508; Fax: 604/822-5207 – 4 times a year – Editor, Dr. Ian Slater

The Philantropist (Published by Becker Associates), PO Box 507, Stn Q, Toronto ON M4T 2M5 – 416/483-7282; Fax: 416/489-1713 – 4 times a year – Editor, John D. Gregory

Philosophia Mathematica (Published by University of Toronto Press), Journals Division, 5201 Dufferin St., North York ON M3H 5T8 – 416/667-7810; Fax: 416/667-7881 – Circ.: 250; 3 times a year – Editor, Robert S.D. Thomas; Circulation Manager, Wendy Thomas

Policy Options, Inst. for Research on Public Policy, #200, 1470, rue Peel, Montréal PQ H3A 1T1 – 514/985-2461; Fax: 514/985-2559; Email: policyop@odyssee.net – 10 times a year – Editor, Alfred Leblanc

Prairie Forum: Journal of the Canadian Plains Research Centre, Canadian Plains Research Centre, University of Regina, Regina SK S4S 0A2 – 306/585-4758; Fax: 306/585-4699; Email: canadian.plains@uregina.ca; URL: http://www.cas.uregina.ca/~cprc/ – Circ.: 300; 2 times a year – Editor, Dr. Patrick Douaud; Circulation Manager, Lorraine Nelson

Public Sector Management et Secteur Public, #305, 150 Eglinton Ave. East, Toronto ON M4P 1E8 – 416/932-3666; Fax: 416/932-3667 – Circ.: 4,000 – Editor, Joseph Galimberti

Queen's Quarterly, c/o Queen's University, 184 Union St., Kingston ON K7L 3N6 – 613/545-2667; Fax: 613/545-6822; Email: qquartly@qucd.queensu.ca; URL: http://www.info.queensu.ca/quarterly – Circ.: 3,000; 4 times a year – Editor, Dr. Boris Castel; Business Manager, Penny Roantree

Renaissance & Reformation (Published by Becker Associates), PO Box 507, Stn Q, Toronto ON M4T 2M5 – 416/483-7282; Fax: 416/489-1713 – 4 times a year; ISSN 0034-429X – Editor, Prof. Francois Paré

Resolution, c/o Maritime Museum of British Columbia, 28 Bastion Sq, Victoria BC V8W 1H9 – 250/385-4222, ext.10; Fax: 250/382-2867 – 4 times a year – Editor, H. Keenan

Resources for Feminist Research, 252 Bloor St. West, Toronto ON M5S 1V6 – 416/923-6641, ext. 2278; Fax: 416/926-4725; Email: rfr@oise.on.ca – Circ.: 2,000; 4 times a year – Coordinating Editor, Philinda Masters

Revue de l'Université de Moncton, Université de Moncton, Moncton NB E1A 3E9 – 506/858-4062; Fax: 506/858-4103 – Circ.: 700; 2 times a year – Editor, James de Finney

Russell: The Journal of the Bertrand Russell Archives, c/o McMaster University, Main St. West, Hamilton ON L8S 4L6 – 905/525-9140, ext.24738; Fax: 905/546-0625; Email: blackwk@mcmaster.ca – Circ.: 500 – Russell Archivist & Editor, Kenneth Blackwell

Science-Fiction Studies, Arts Bldg., McGill University, 853 Sherbrooke St. West, Montréal PQ H3A 2T6 – 514/848-2332; Fax: 514/848-3492 – 3 times a year

Scientia Canadensis - Journal of the History of Cdn. Science, Technology & Medicine (Published by Becker Associates), PO Box 507, Stn Q, Toronto ON M4T 2M5 – 416/483-7282; Fax: 416/489-1713 – 2 times a year; ISSN 0829-2507 – Editor, Prof. Yves Gingras

Scrivener, c/o McGill University, 853 Sherbrooke St. West, Montréal PQ H3A 2T6 – 514/398-6588 – Annually – Editor, Ursula Hines

Seminar (Published by University of Toronto Press), Journals Division, 5201 Dufferin St., North York ON M3H 5T8 – 416/667-7810; Fax: 416/667-7881 – Circ.: 770; 4 times a year – Editor, Rodney Symington; Circulation Manager, Wendy Thornton

Social History (Published by University of Toronto Press), Journals Division, 5201 Dufferin St., North York ON M3H 5T8 – 416/667-7810; Fax: 416/667-7881 – Circ.: 560; 2 times a year – Editor, Chad Gaffield; Circulation Manager, Wendy Thornton

Socialist Alternatives, Centre for Developing Area Studies, McGill University, 3715, rue Peel, Montréal PQ H3A 1X1 – 514/987-4165; Fax: 514/987-4749 – 4 times a year

Studies in Canadian Literature, Hut 5, University of New Brunswick, PO Box 4400, Stn Stn A, Fredericton NB E3B 5A3 – 506/453-4598; Fax: 506/453-4995 – Circ.: 500; 2 times a year – Editor, K. Scherf; Managing Editor, S. Campbell, 506/453-3501

Studies in Political Economy, PO Box 4729, Stn E, Ottawa ON K1S 5H9 – 613/788-2600, ext.6625 – 3 times a year

Tessera, c/o 350 Stong College, York University, 4700 Keele St., North York ON M3J 1P3 – 416/736-5412; Email: jennifer@yorku.ca – Circ.: 500; 2 times a year – Co-Editor, Jennifer Henderson

Texte (Published by University of Toronto Press), Journals Division, 5201 Dufferin St., North York ON M3H 5T8 – 416/667-7810; Fax: 416/667-7881 – Circ.: 150; Annually – Editor, Andrew Oliver; Circulation Manager, Wendy Thornton

Theatre Research in Canada, Graduate Centre for Study of Drama, Koffler Student Centre, 214 College St., Toronto ON M5S 2Z9 – 416/978-7984; Fax: 416/971-1378; Email: trican@epas.utoronto.ca – 2 times a year; English & French – Co-Editor, Hélène Beauchamp; Co-Editor, Stephen Johnson; Co-Editor, Rob Nunn

The Tocqueville Review (Published by University of Toronto Press), Journals Division, 5201 Dufferin St., North York ON M3H 5T8 – 416/667-7781 – Circ.: 800; 2 times a year; English & French – Editor, Henri Mendras

Transcultural Psychiatric Research Review, Psychiatry Dept., McGill University, 1033 Pine Ave. West, Montréal PQ H3A 1A1 – 514/398-7302; Fax: 514/398-4370; Email: cylk@musica.mcgill.ca; URL: http://www.mcgill.ca/psychiatry – Circ.: 500; 4 times a year – Editor, Laurence J. Kirmayer, M.D.; Circulation Manager, Margie Gabriel

Ultimate Reality & Meaning (Published by University of Toronto Press), Journals Division, 5201 Dufferin St., North York ON M3H 5T8 – 416/667-7810; Fax: 416/667-7881 – Circ.: 380; 4 times a year – Editor, Tibor Horvath; Circulation Manager, Wendy Thornton

University of Toronto Law Journal (Published by University of Toronto Press), Journals Division, 5201 Dufferin St., North York ON M3H 5T8 – 416/667-7810; Fax: 416/667-7881 – Circ.: 700; 4 times a year – Editor, Bruce Chapman; Circulation Manager, Wendy Thornton

University of Toronto Quarterly (Published by University of Toronto Press), Journals Division, 5201 Dufferin St., North York ON M3H 5T8 – 416/667-7810; Fax: 416/667-7881 – Circ.: 940; 4 times a year – Editor, Alan Bewell; Circulation Manager, Wendy Thornton

Urban History Review (Published by Becker Associates), PO Box 507, Stn Q, Toronto ON M4T 2M5 – 416/483-7282; Fax: 416/489-1713 – Circ.: 500; 2 times a year; ISSN 0703-0428 – Editor, Prof. Richard Harris

STUDENT GUIDES

STUDENT GUIDES

Campus Canada, 287 MacPherson Ave., Toronto ON M4V 1A4 – 416/928-2909; Fax: 416/928-1357 – Circ.: 125,000 – Publisher, Harvey Wolfe; Editor, Sarah Moore

Temps Libre, 4545, Pierre-de-Coubertin, CP 1000, Succ M, Montréal PQ H1V 3R2 – 514/252-3117; Fax: 514/252-3119

U-Choose: A Student's Guide to Financial Survival (Published by Moving Publications Ltd.), 40 Upjohn Rd., Don Mills ON M3B 2W1 – 416/441-1168; Fax: 416/441-1641 – Circ.: 305,000 – Publisher, Anita Wood; Editor, Lorraine Hunter; Circulation Manager, Paula Muzzin

Vie Etudiante, 539, rue Ontario est, Montréal PQ H2L 1N8 – 514/848-1750; Fax: 514/848-9610

Welcome Back Student Guide, PO Box 1352, Kingston ON K7L 5C6 – 613/549-8442 – Annually – Publisher, Danny Bedford; Editor, Mary Owens

UNIVERSITY & SCHOOL PUBLICATIONS

Contact the publication, c/o the school, for editorial purposes. Addresses of the schools are given in the Education Section of the Almanac

L'Abattoir — Cégep de Lévis-Lauzon
L'Actif — Cégep de Trois-Rivières
L'Action — Université du Québec à Montréal
Algonquin Times — Algonquin College
L'Alinéa — Cégep Joliette-De Lanaudière
Alumni-News/Bulletin des Anciens — Univ. of Ottawa
Alumni Chronicle — University of British Columbia
Alumni Gazette — University of Western Ontario
Alumni Journal — University of Manitoba
Alumni Journal — Simon Fraser University
Alumni Magazine — The University of Calgary
Alumni News — Carleton University
Aquinian — St. Thomas University
Argosy Weekly — Mount Allison University
The Argus — Lakehead University
ARN Messager — Université de Montréal
Arthur — Trent University
The Athenaeum — Acadia University
Atkinsonian — York University
Audaces — Cégep Joliette-De Lanaudière
Bandersnatch — John Abbott College
The Baron — University of New Brunswick
BCIT Link — BC Institute of Technology
Bilan — Université de Sherbrooke
Bricklayer — Red Deer College
La Brise — Cégep de l'Outaouais
Brock Press — Brock University
The Brunswickian — University of New Brunswick
The Bulletin — University of Toronto
Le Caducée — École des Hautes Études Commerciales
The Campus — Bishop's University
Le Canard Déchaine — Université du Québec à Hull
Caper Times — University College of Cape Breton
Capilano Courier — Capilano College
The Carillon — The University of Regina
Champlain Bugle — Champlain Regional College
The Charlatan — Carleton University
The Chronicle — Durham College
Cité Universitaire — Université de Montréal
Cityside — The University of Regina
Le Clap — Cégep de La Pocatière
Le Collectif — Université de Sherbrooke
Le Concept — Cégep de Rimouski
The Concordian — Concordia University
Concordia University Magazine — Concordia University
The Cord Weekly — Wilfrid Laurier University
Coven — Humber College
La Criée — Cégep de Matane

La Crise — Cégep François-Xavier-Garneau
Debit Memo — McGill University
Défi-Sciences — Université Laval
Les Diplômés — Université de Montréal
Discorder - Student Radio Society of U.B.C — University of British Columbia
L'Echorché — Cégep Lionel-Groulx
Eclosion — Cégep de Ste-Foy
L'Éffronté — Cégep de Rimouski
Electique — Cégep de St-Hyacinthe
The Emery Weal — The Southern Alberta Institute of Technology
En Tete — Université du Québec à Trois-Rivières
L'Entremetteur — Cégep de l'Outaouais
Excalibur — York University
L'Exemplaire — Cégep de Sorel-Tracy
L'Exhibitioniste — Cégep de Granby-Haute-Yamaska
The Eyeopener — Ryerson Polytechnic University
The Faucet — McGill University
Au Fil des Evénements — Université Laval
Forum — Université de Montréal
Le Front — Université de Moncton
The Fulcrum — University of Ottawa
Gargoyle — University College
Gateway — University of Alberta
The Gauntlet — The University of Calgary
Gazette — Dalhousie University
The Gazette — University of Western Ontario
The Georgian — Georgian College
La Giffle — Cégep de Trois-Rivières
The Gleaner — Vancouver Community College
Golden Words — Queen's University
Le Grafitti — Collège Jean-de-Brebeuf Inc.
The Green and White — University of Saskatchewan
La Grenouille — Cégep de Chicoutimi
Guelph Peak — University of Guelph
Le Gugusse — Cégep de Shawinigan
L'Hermes — Cégep St-Jean-sur-Richelieu
Impact Campus — Université Laval
Imprint — University of Waterloo
L'Infomane — Cégep de Bois-de-Boulogne
L'Interdit — Cégep de Limoilou
L'Interêt — École des Hautes Études Commerciales
The Interpreter — Grant MacEwan Community College
The Journal — Saint Mary's University
Journal U.Q.A.M — Université du Québec à Montréal
Lambda — Laurentian University of Sudbury
The Lance — University of Windsor
Lexicon — York University
Liaison — Université de Sherbrooke
The Link — Concordia University
The MacEwan Journalist — Grant MacEwan Community College
The Manitoban — University of Manitoba
The Martlet — University of Victoria
Matricule Zéro — Cégep de Sherbrooke
Le Matulu — École Secondaire Marie-Victorin
McGill Daily — McGill University
McGill French — McGill University
The McGill News — McGill University
McGill Reporter — McGill University
McGill Tribune — McGill University
The McMaster Courier — McMaster University
Medium II — Erindale College
The Meliorist — University of Lethbridge
The Mike — St. Michael's College
La Minerve — Cégep de Saint-Laurent
Le Misanthrope — Cégep Ahuntsic
Montréal Campus — Université du Québec à Montréal
Le Motdit — Cégep Édouard-Montpetit
Mouton Noir — Cégep de Drummondville
The Muse — Memorial University of Newfoundland
Navigator — Malaspina University College
New Edition — New College
The Newspaper — University of Toronto
New Trail — University of Alberta
Niagara News — Niagara College

Nouveau-Quartier — Cégep de Rosemont
Obiter Dicta (Osgood Hall) — York University
OK Phoenix — Okanagan University College
The Ontarion — University of Guelph
L'Original déchainé — Laurentian University of Sudbury
Other Press — Douglas College
Pars ailleurs — Cégep de Valleyfield
The Peak — Simon Fraser University
Persil-Parlant — Cégep de Baie-Comeau
La Petite Caisse — Université du Québec à Chicoutimi
Picaro — Mount Saint Vincent University
La Pige — Cégep de Jonquière
Pigeon Dissident — Université de Montréal
Plant — Dawson College
The Point — University of British Columbia
Polar Press — Confederation College
Le Polyscope — École Polytechnique
La Pression — Cégep de Lévis-Lauzon
Project Magazine — McMaster University
The Projector — Red River Community College
The Pro Tem (Glendon College) — York University
Psycause — Université de Montréal
Quartier Libre — Université de Montréal
Queen's Alumni Review — Queen's University
Queen's Journal — Queen's University
Quill — Brandon University
Reflector — Mount Royal College
La Répliqué — Cégep de Victoriaville
The Reporter — McGill University
Le Republique — Cégep du Vieux-Montréal
Réseau/U.Q. Network — Université du Québec
La Rotonde — University of Ottawa
Ryersonian — Ryerson Polytechnic University
The Ryerson Rambler — Ryerson Polytechnic University
The Saint — St. Clair College
The Satellite — Mohawk College
Seneca Impact — Seneca College
The Sheaf — University of Saskatchewan
The Sheridan Sun — Sheridan College
The Shield — Cambrian College
The Silhouette — McMaster University
Siren — Centennial College
Sommets — Université de Sherbrooke
The Sting — Concordia University
Strand — Victoria College
Le Temporel — Université du Québec à Montréal
The Three Penny Beaver — Sir Sandford Fleming College
Thunderbird Sports Magazine — University of BC
Thursday Report — Concordia University
Le Trait d'Union — Cégep de Maisonneuve
Transactions — Université du Québec à Montréal
The Ubyssey — University of British Columbia
L'Ulcère — Cégep de Rivière-du-Loup
Underground — Scarborough College
Unité — Université du Québec à Montréal
University of Toronto Magazine — University of Toronto
U.Q.A.R. Information — Université du Québec à Rimouski
Uquam — Université du Québec à Montréal
Uquarium — Université du Québec à Rimouski
The UVic Torch — University of Victoria
Vanier Phoenix — Vanier College
The Vanier Vandoo — Vanier College
Varsity — University of Toronto
V.C.C. Voice — Vancouver Community College
Vox-Populi — Cégep André-Laurendeau
Le Voyeur — Université du Québec à Trois-Rivières
Watch — University of King's College
Western Alumni Gazette — University of Western Ontario
Western News — University of Western Ontario
X-Press — University of Prince Edward Island
Xaverian — St. Francis Xavier University
Le Zèle — Cégep Montmorency

BROADCASTING STATIONS

BROADCASTING NETWORK HEAD OFFICES

Astral Entertainment Group, Maison Astral, #900, 2100, rue Ste-Catherine ouest, Montréal PQ H3N 2T3 – 514/939-5000; Fax: 514/939-1515

Atlantic Television System (ATV), PO Box 1653, Halifax NS B3J 2Z4 – 902/453-4000; Fax: 902/454-3302

Baton Broadcasting Inc., PO Box 9, Stn O, Toronto ON M4A 2M9 – 416/299-2000; Fax: 416/299-2220

The Blackburn Group Inc, 369 York St., PO Box 2280, London ON N6A 4G1 – 519/667-4545; Fax: 519/667-4530

British Columbia Television (BCTV), 7850 Enterprise St., PO Box 4700, Burnaby BC V6B 4A3 – 604/420-2288; Fax: 604/421-9427

Cablecasting Ltd., #900, 1200 Bay St., Toronto ON M5R 2A5 – 416/964-6411; Fax: 416/964-9206

Canadian Broadcasting Corporation (CBC/SRC), 1500 Bronson Ave., PO Box 8478, Ottawa ON K1G 3J5 – 613/724-1200; TDD: 613/738-6686

    Canadian Broadcasting Corporation - English Network (CBC), PO Box 500, Stn A, Toronto ON M5W 1E6 – 416/205-3311; TDD: 416/205-6688

    Radio Canada International, 1055, boul René-Lévesque est, CP 6000, Montréal PQ H3C 3A8 – 514/597-7555; Fax: 514/284-0891

    Société Radio-Canada - French Network, 1400, boul René-Lévesque est, CP 6000, Montréal PQ H3C 3A8 – 514/597-5970; Fax: 514/597-5970; TDD: 514/597-6013

Canadian Radio Networks Inc., 61 James St., St. Catharines ON L2R 5B9 – 905/687-8595

Canadian Satellite Communications Inc. (CANCOM), 50 Burnhamthorpe Rd. West, 10th Fl., Mississauga ON L5B 3C2 – 905/272-4960; Fax: 905/272-3399; Email: pdumas@cancom.ca

Canwest Broadcasting Ltd., 603 St. Mary's Rd., Winnipeg MB R2M 3L8 – 204/233-3304; Fax: 204/233-5615

CHUM Limited, 1331 Yonge St., Toronto ON M4T 1Y1 – 416/925-6666; Fax: 416/926-4042

Cogeco Cable inc., #200, 1630 - 6e rue, Trois-Rivières PQ G8Y 5B8 – 819/372-9292; Fax: 819/372-3318

Craig Broadcast Systems Inc., 2940 Victoria Ave., Brandon MB R7B 0N2 – 204/728-1150; Fax: 204/728-1838

CUC Broadcasting Ltd., #600, 1530 Markham Rd., Scarborough ON M1B 3G4 – 416/296-7373; Fax: 416/296-7377

Fawcett Broadcasting Ltd., 242 Scott St., Fort Frances ON P9A 1G7 – 807/274-5341; Fax: 807/274-8746

Forvest Broadcasting Corp., 345 - 4 Ave. South, Saskatoon SK S7K 5S5 – 306/244-1975; Fax: 306/665-8484

Fraser Valley Radio Group, 45715 Hocking Ave., PO Box 386, Chilliwack BC V2P 6J7 – 604/795-5711; Fax: 604/795-6643

Global Television Network, 81 Barber Greene Rd., Don Mills ON M3C 2A2 – 416/446-5311; Fax: 416/446-5447

Golden West Broadcasting Ltd., PO Box 950, Altona MB R0G 0B0 – 204/324-6464; Fax: 204/324-8918

Groupe Videotron Lteé, 300, rue Viger est, Montréal PQ H2X 3W4 – 514/281-1232; Fax: 514/985-8425

Humber Valley Broadcasting Co. Ltd., 345 O'Connell Dr., PO Box 570, Corner Brook NF A2H 6H5 – 709/634-3111; Fax: 709/634-4081

Inuit Broadcasting Corporation (IBC), #703, 251 Laurier Avenue, Ottawa ON K1P 5J6 – 613/235-1892; Fax: 613/230-8824; Email: ibcicsl@sonetis.com

Knowledge Network, Service of the Open Learning Agency (KN), 4355 Mathissi Place, Burnaby BC V5B 4S8 – 604/431-3000; Fax: 604/525-5511; Email: knowline@ola.bc.ca

Learning Skills Television of Alberta (ACCESS - The Education Station), 3720 - 76 Ave., Edmonton AB T6B 2N9 – 403/440-7777; Fax: 403/440-8899

MCTV-TV, 699 Frood Rd., Sudbury ON P3C 5A3 – 705/674-8301; Fax: 705/671-2444

Metro Marketing West, 680C, Leg-in-Boot-Sq., Vancouver BC V5Z 4B5 – 604/874-8463; Fax: 604/874-9300

Moffat Communications Ltd., CKY Bldg., Polo Park, PO Box 220, Stn L, Winnipeg MB R3H 0Z5 – 204/788-3440; Fax: 204/956-2710

Monarch Communications, 361 - 1 St. SE, Medicine Hat AB T1A 0A5 – 403/526-4529; Fax: 403/526-4000

Northern Cable Holdings Ltd., #15 - 500 Barrydowne Rd., PO Box 4500, Sudbury ON P3A 5W1 – 705/560-1560; Fax: 705/560-4752

NTV Network, 446 Logy Bay Rd., PO Box 2020, St. John's NF A1C 5S2 – 709/722-5015; Fax: 709/726-5107

Okalakatiget Society, PO Box 160, Nain NF A0P 1L0 – 709/922-2955; Fax: 709/922-2293

Pelmorex Radio Inc., #200, 186 Robert Speck Pkwy., Mississauga ON L4Z 3G1 – 905/566-9511; Fax: 905/566-9696

  Pelmorex Infomedia/Weather (PIW), #200, 186 Robert Speck Pkwy., Mississauga ON L4Z 3G1 – 905/566-9511; Fax: 905/566-9696

  Pelmorex Radio Network (PRN), #200, 186 Robert Speck Pkwy., Mississauga ON L4Z 3G1 – 905/566-9511; Fax: 905/566-9696

Quatre Saisons (Le réseau de télévision), 405, av Ogilvy, Montréal PQ H3N 2Y4 – 514/271-3535; Fax: 514/271-6231

Radio Corp. Inc. (Oldies 1290 CJBK), 743 Wellington Rd. South, London ON N6C 4R5 – 519/686-2525; Fax: 519/686-9067; Email: oldies1290.cjbk@odyssey.on.ca

Radio Futura Ltée, 211, av Gordon, Verdun PQ H4G 2R2 – 514/766-2311; Fax: 514/761-2122

Radio Nord inc., 380, rue Murdoch, Rouyn-Noranda PQ J9P 1G5 – 819/762-0741; Fax: 819/762-2280

Radio-Québec, 1000, rue Fullum, Montréal PQ H2K 3L7 – 514/521-2424; Fax: 514/525-5511

Radiomutuel inc., #405, 1717, boul René-Lévesque est, Montréal PQ H2L 4E8 – 514/529-3210; Fax: 514/529-3219

RAWLCO Communications Ltd., 2723 - 37 Ave. NE, Calgary AB T1Y 5R8 – 403/291-0000; Fax: 403/291-0037

Réseau des Appalaches, 327, av Labbé, CP 69, Thetford Mines PQ G6S 5S3 – 418/335-7533; Fax: 418/335-9009

Rogers Broadcasting Ltd., 25 Adelaide St. East, 10th Fl., Toronto ON M5C 1H3 – 416/864-2000; Fax: 416/864-2002

  Satellite Radio Network, 2440 Ash St., Vancouver BC V5Z 4J6 – 604/873-9583; Fax: 604/873-5305

Rogers Cablesystems Ltd., 1 Valleybrook Dr., 5th Fl., North York ON M3B 2S7 – 416/447-5500; Fax: 416/391-7247

Rogers Communications Inc., Scotia Plaza, #6400, 40 King St. West, PO Box 1007, Toronto ON M5H 3Y2 – 416/864-2373; Fax: 416/864-2385

Shaw Communications Inc., 7605 - 50 St., Edmonton AB T6B 2W9 – 403/468-1230; Fax: 403/466-4544

Skeena Broadcasters, Division of Okanagan Skeena Group Ltd., 4625 Lazelle Ave., Terrace BC V8G 1S4 – 250/635-6316; Fax: 250/638-6320; Email: info@osg.net

Slaight Communications Inc., 2 St. Clair Ave. West, 11th Fl., Toronto ON M4V 1L6 – 416/960-9911; Fax: 416/323-6828

Standard Broadcasting Corp. Ltd., 2 St. Clair Ave. West, 11th Fl., Toronto ON M4V 1L6 – 416/960-9911; Fax: 416/323-6828

Stentor Telecom Policy Inc., #1800, 45 O'Connor St., Ottawa ON K1P 1A4 – 613/567-7000; Fax: 613/567-7001

SupeRadio, #2400 - 250 Yonge St., Toronto ON M5B 2M6 – 416/599-3949; Fax: 416/599-3958

Taqramiut Nipingat Inc. (Voice of the North) (TNI), #501, 185, av Dorval, Dorval PQ H9S 5J9 – 514/631-1394; Fax: 514/631-6258

Télémédia Communications inc., 1411, rue Peel, 5e étage, Montréal PQ H3A 1S5 – 514/845-6291; Fax: 514/845-3628

Telesat Canada, 1601 Telesat Ct., Gloucester ON K1B 5P4 – 613/748-0123; Fax: 613/748-8784

Television Northern Canada (TVNC), PO Box 1630, Iqaluit NT X0A 0H0 – 819/979-1707; Fax: 819/979-1708

TVA inc. (Le réseau de télévision), 1600, boul de Maisonneuve est, Montréal PQ H2L 4P2 – 514/526-9251; Fax: 514/598-6085

TVOntario (Ontario Educational Communications Authority) (CICA), PO Box 200, Stn Q, Toronto ON M4T 2T1 – 416/484-2600; Fax: 416/484-6285

Videotron Communications Ltd., 10450 - 178 St., Edmonton AB T5S 1S2 – 403/486-6500; Fax: 403/486-6506

Wawatay Native Communications Society, PO Box 1180, Sioux Lookout ON P8T 1B7 – 807/737-2951; Fax: 807/737-3224

WIC Western International Communications Ltd., #1960, 505 Burrard St., Vancouver BC V7X 1M6 – 604/687-2844; Fax: 604/687-4118

AM BROADCASTING STATIONS

LOCATION	CALL	*CBC Stations/Affiliates †French Language Stations	FREQ.
Abbotsford, BC	CKMA	Fraser Valley Broadcasters Ltd., 2722 Allwood St., Abbotsford BC V2T 3R8 – 604/859-5277; Fax: 604/859-9907; Email: alpen@uniserve.com	850
Alma, PQ	†CFGT	3100 0185 Québec Inc., #200, 460, Pl. Sacré-Coeur ouest, Alma PQ G8B 1L9 – 418/662-6673; Fax: 418/662-6070	1270
Altona, MB	CFAM	Golden West Broadcasting Ltd., PO Box 950, Altona MB R0G 0B0 – 204/324-6464; Fax: 204/324-8918	950
Altona, MB	CKMW	Golden West Broadcasting Ltd., PO Box 950, Altona MB R0G 0B0 – 204/324-6464; Fax: 204/324-8918	1570
Amherst, NS	CKDH	Maritime Broadcasting System Ltd., 32 Church St., PO Box 670, Amherst NS B4H 4B8 – 902/667-3875; Fax: 902/667-4490; Email: am90@atcon.com; URL: http://www.atcon.com/~am90/	900
Amos, PQ	†CHAD	Radio Nord Inc., 751, 1re av ouest, Amos PQ J9T 1V7 – 819/762-0741; Fax: 819/732-6310	1340
Amqui, PQ	†CFVM	Power Broadcasting Inc./Diffusion Power Inc., 111, rue de l'Hopital, CP 1840, Amqui PQ G0J 1B0 – 418/629-2025; Fax: 418/629-2599	1220
Anse-a-Valleau, PQ	†CJRV	See Gaspé (CJRG-FM)	
Antigonish, NS	CIGO	See Port Hawkesbury (CIGO)	
Antigonish, NS	CJFX	Atlantic Broadcasters Ltd., PO Box 5800, Antigonish NS B2G 2R9 – 902/863-4580; Fax: 902/863-6300	580
Antigonish, NS	CFXU	St. Francis Xavier University, PO Box 948, Antigonish NS B2G 1C0 – 902/867-2410; Fax: 902/867-5138	690
Arnprior, ON	CHVR-2	Pelmorex Radio, 490 Didak St., Arnprior ON K7S 3R1 – 613/623-7711; Fax: 613/623-7748	1490
Asbestos, PQ	†CJAN	Radio Plus BMD Inc., 185, rue du Roi, Asbestos PQ J1T 1S4 – 819/879-5439; Fax: 819/879-7922	1340
Athabasca, AB	CKBA	Nor-Net Communications Ltd., #1, 4818 - 49 St., Athabasca AB T9S 1C3 – 403/675-5301; Fax: 403/675-4938	850
Atikokan, ON	CKDR-6	See Dryden (CKDR)	1240
Baie-Comeau, PQ	†CHLC	Radio Côte-Nord inc., 399, rue de Puyjalon, Baie-Comeau PQ J5C 2Z7 – 418/589-3771; Fax: 418/589-9086	580
Baie-Comeau, PQ	CFRP	See Baie-Comeau (CHLC-FM)	620
Baie Verte, NF	CKIM	See Grand Falls-Windsor (CKCM)	1240
Bancroft, ON	CJNH	Quinte Broadcasting Co. Ltd., PO Box 1240, Bancroft ON K0L 1C0 – 613/332-1423; Fax: 613/332-0841	1240
Banff, AB	CFHC-1	See Canmore (CFHC)	1340
Barrie, ON	CKBB	Power Broadcasting Inc., PO Box 950, Barrie ON L4M 4V1 – 705/726-9500; Fax: 705/726-0022	950
Bathurst, NB	CKBC	Radio Atlantic (CKBC) Ltd., 176 Main St., PO Box 1360, Bathurst NB E2A 4J1 – 506/547-1360; Fax: 506/547-1367	1360
Beaver Creek, YT	*CBDM	See Whitehorse (CFWH)	690
Bedford, NS	CFDR	NewCap Broadcasting Inc., #800, 1550 Bedford Hwy., Bedford NS B4A 1E6 – 902/835-6100; Fax: 902/835-1511	780
Belleville, ON	CJBQ	Quinte Broadcasting Co. Ltd., 10 Front St. South, PO Box 488, Belleville ON K8N 5B2 – 613/969-5555; Fax: 613/969-0288	800
Blairmore, AB	CJPR	Lethbridge Broadcasting, PO Box 840, Blairmore AB T0K 0E0 – 403/562-2200; Fax: 403/562-8114	1490
Blind River, ON	CJNR	See Elliot Lake (CJNR)	730
Boissevain, MB	CJRB	Golden West Broadcasting Ltd., PO Box 1220, Boissevain MB R0K 0E0 – 204/324-6464; Fax: 204/324-8918	1220
Brampton, ON	CIAO	CKMW Radio Ltd., 50 Kennedy Rd. South, Unit 20, Brampton ON L6W 3R7 – 905/798-4888; Fax: 905/453-4788	530
Brandon, MB	CKLQ	Riding Mountain Broadcasting Ltd., PO Box 880, Brandon MB R7A 6N6 – 204/726-8888; Fax: 204/726-1270	880
Brandon, MB	CKX	Craig Broadcasting Systems Inc., 2940 Victoria Ave., Brandon MB R7B 0N2 – 204/728-1150; Fax: 204/727-2505	1150
Brantford, ON	CKPC	Telephone City Broadcast Ltd., 571 West St., Brantford ON N3T 5P8 – 519/759-1000; Fax: 519/753-1470	1380

Canadian Almanac & Directory 1997

5-200 AM BROADCASTING STATIONS

LOCATION	CALL	*CBC Stations/Affiliates †French Language Stations	FREQ.
Bridgewater, NS	CKBW	Acadia Broadcasting Co. Ltd., 215 Dominion St., Bridgewater NS B4V 2G8 – 902/543-2401; Fax: 902/543-1208; Email: ckbw@ckbw.com	1000
Brockville, ON	CFJR	St. Lawrence Broadcasting Co. Ltd., PO Box 666, Brockville ON K6V 5V9 – 613/345-1666; Fax: 613/342-2438; Email: cfjr@cfjr.brockville.com	830
Brooks, AB	CIBQ	NorNet Broadcasting, #7, 403 - 2nd Ave. West, PO Box 180, Brooks AB T1R 1B3 – 03/362-3418; Fax: 403/362-8168.	1340
Burnaby, BC	CJSF	Simon Fraser Campus Radio Society, TC 216, Simon Fraser University, Burnaby BC V5A 1S6 – 604/291-3727; Fax: 604/291-3695; Email: cjsf@sfu.ca; URL: http://www.sfu.ca/~cjsf.	940
Burns Lake, BC	CFLD	PO Box 600, Burns Lake BC V0J 1E0 – 250/692-3414; Fax: 250/692-3020	760
Cabano, PQ	†CJAF	See Rivière-du-Loup (CJFP)	1340
Cache Creek, BC	CHNL-2	See Kamloops (CHNL)	610
Calgary, AB	CHQR	Westcom Radio Group Ltd., #1900, 125 - 9 Ave. SE, Calgary AB T2G 0P6 – 403/233-0770; Fax: 403/266-4040.	770
Calgary, AB	CKMX	Standard Broadcasting Inc., PO Box 2750, Stn M, Calgary AB T2P 4P8 – 403/240-5800; Fax: 403/240-5801	1060
Calgary, AB	CMRC	Mount Royal College, 4825 Richard Rd. SW, Calgary AB T3E 6K6 – 403/240-6119; Fax: 403/240-6563	closed circuit
Calgary, AB	CFAC	Rogers Broadcasting Ltd., 3320 - 17 Ave. SW, Calgary AB T3E 6X6 – 403/246-9696; Fax: 403/246-6660	960
Calgary, AB	CFFR	RAWLCO Communications Ltd., #220, 2723 - 37 Ave. NE, Calgary AB T1Y 5R8 – 403/291-0000; Fax: 403/252-6690.	660
Calgary, AB	CFXL	Golden West Broadcasting Ltd., 804 - 16 Ave. SW, Calgary AB T2R 0S9 – 403/228-1140; Fax: 403/244-3343	1140
Calgary, AB	*CBR	CBC, PO Box 2640, Calgary AB T2P 2M7 – 403/521-6000; Fax: 403/521-6007.	1010
Cambridge, ON	CIAM	Power Broadcasting Inc., 46 Main St., Cambridge ON N1R 1V4 – 519/621-7510; Fax: 519/621-0165	960
Campbell River, BC	CFWB	CFCP Radio Ltd., 909 Ironwood St., Campbell River BC V9W 3E5 – 250/287-7106; Fax: 250/287-7170	1490
Campbellton, NB	CKNB	Maritime Broadcasting System Ltd., 100 Water St., PO Box 340, Campbellton NB E3N 3G7 – 506/753-4415; Fax: 506/789-9505.	950
Camrose, AB	CFCW	See Edmonton (CFCW)	
Canmore, AB	CFHC	Rogers Broadcasting Ltd., PO Box 1450, Canmore AB T0L 0M0 – 403/678-2222; Fax: 403/678-6844	1450
Caraquet, NB	†CJVA	Radio Acadie Ltée, CP 5694, Caraquet NB E1W 1B7 – 506/727-4426; Fax: 506/727-6707	810
Carbonear, NF	CHVO	VOCM Radio Newfoundland Ltd., 1 CHVO Dr., Carbonear NF A1Y 1A2 – 709/596-7144; Fax: 709/596-8626	560
Castlegar, BC	CKQR	Valley Broadcasters Ltd., 525 - 11 Ave., Castlegar BC V1N 1J6 – 250/365-7600; Fax: 250/365-8480	760
Charlottetown, PE	CFCY	Maritime Broadcasting Ltd., 141 Kent St., PO Box 1060, Charlottetown PE C1A 7M7 – 902/892-1066; Fax: 902/566-1338.	630
Charlottetown, PE	CHTN	NewCap Broadcasting Ltd., 141 Kent St., PO Box 1060, Charlottetown PE C1A 7M7 – 902/892-8591; Fax: 902/566-1338.	720
Charlottetown, PE	CIMN	University of P.E.I., Student Union Bldg., 550 University Ave., Charlottetown PE C1A 4P3 – 902/566-0417; Fax: 902/566-0979.	700
Chatham, ON	CFCO	Blackburn Radio Ltd., 21 Keil Dr., PO Box 630, Chatham ON N7M 5K9 – 519/352-3000; Fax: 519/352-9690.	630
Chetwynd, BC	CHET	See Dawson Creek (CJDC)	1450
Chibougamau, PQ	†CJMD	Groupe Radio Antenne 6, 568, boul St-Joseph, Chibougamau PQ G8H 2K6 – 418/275-1831; Fax: 418/275-2475	1240
Chicoutimi, PQ	†CKRS	Radiomutuel inc., 121, rue Racine est, Chicoutimi PQ G7H 5G4 – 418/545-2577; Fax: 418/695-2654	590
Chicoutimi, PQ	*†CBJ	Société Radio-Canada, 500, rue des Sagueneens, CP 790, Chicoutimi PQ G7H 5E7 – 418/696-6600; Fax: 418/696-6689.	1580
Chilliwack, BC	CHWK	Fraser Valley Broadcasters Ltd., PO Box 386, Chilliwack BC V2P 6J7 – 604/795-5711; Fax: 604/795-6643	1270
Clearwater, BC	CHNL-1	See Kamloops (CHNL)	1400
Cobourg, ON	CHUC	Pineridge Broadcasting, PO Box 520, Cobourg ON K9A 4L3 – 905/372-5401; Fax: 905/372-6280; Email: dconway@eagle.ca.	1450
Corner Brook, NF	CFCB	Humber Valley Broadcasting Co. Ltd., PO Box 570, Corner Brook NF A2H 6H5 – 709/634-3111; Fax: 709/634-4081.	570
Corner Brook, NF	CKXX	Newcap Broadcasting Ltd., PO Box 1340, Corner Brook NF A2H 7B2 – 709/634-1340; Fax: 709/634-6397	1340
Corner Brook, NF	*CBY	CBC, 162 Premier Dr., PO Box 610, Corner Brook NF A2H 6G1 – 709/634-3141; Fax: 709/634-8506	990
Cornwall, ON	CJSS	Tri-Co Broadcasting Ltd., 237 Water St. East, PO Box 969, Cornwall ON K6H 5V1 – 613/932-5180; Fax: 613/938-0355; Email: cjssradiocornwall@cnwl.igs.net.	1220
Courtenay, BC	CFCP	CFCP Radio Ltd., 1595 Cliffe Ave., Courtenay BC V9N 2K6 – 250/334-2421; Fax: 250/334-1977	1440
Cranbrook, BC	CKEK	Columbia Kootenay Broadcasting Co. Ltd., 19 - 9 Ave. South, Cranbrook BC V1C 2L9 – 250/426-2224; Fax: 250/426-5520.	570
Cross Lake, MB	CFNC	Native Communications Inc., PO Box 129, Cross Lake MB R0B 0J0 – 204/676-2457; Fax: 204/676-2911	1490
Crowsnest Pass, AB	CJPR	Lethbridge Broadcasting Ltd., 13213 - 20th Ave., PO Box 840, Crowsnest Pass AB T0K 0E0 – 403/562-2806; Fax: 403/562-8114.	1490
Dauphin, MB	CKDM	Dauphin Broadcasting Co. Ltd., 27 - 3 Ave. NE, Dauphin MB R7N 0Y5 – 204/638-3230; Fax: 204/638-8257	730
Dawson Creek, BC	CJDC	MEGA Communications Ltd., 901 - 102 Ave., Dawson Creek BC V1G 2B6 – 250/782-3341; Fax: 250/782-3154; URL: http://www.pris.bc.ca/CJDC/CJDC.html.	890
Dégelis, PQ	†CFVD	Radio Dégelis inc., 654 - 6e rue, CP 670, Dégelis PQ G0L 1H0 – 514/853-3370; Fax: 514/853-3321	1370
Digby, NS	CKDY	See Kentville (CKEN)	1420
Disraeli, PQ	†CJLP	See Thetford-Mines (CKLD)	1230
Dolbeau, PQ	†CHVD	Radio CHVD Inc., 1975, boul Wallberg, Dolbeau PQ G8L 1J5 – 418/276-3333; Fax: 418/276-6755	1230
Drumheller, AB	CKDQ	Nor-Net Broadcasting Ltd., PO Box 1480, Drumheller AB T0J 0Y0 – 403/823-3384; Fax: 403/823-7241	910
Drummondville, PQ	†CHRD	Radio Drummond (1993) Inc., 2070, St-Georges, Drummondville PQ J2C 5G6 – 819/478-1480; Fax: 819/478-8361	1480
Dryden, ON	CKDR	Fawcett Broadcasting Ltd., PO Box 580, Dryden ON P8N 2Z3 – 807/223-2355; Fax: 807/223-5090	800
Duncan, BC	CKAY	CKAY Radio (1979) Inc., #205, 2700 Beverly St., Duncan BC V9L 5C7 – 250/748-1500; Fax: 250/748-1517	1500
Ear Falls, ON	CKEF-4	See Dryden (CKDR)	1450
Edmonton, AB	CFCW	NewCap Broadcasting Inc., 4752 - 99 St., Edmonton AB T6E 5H5 – 403/437-7879; Fax: 403/436-9803	790
Edmonton, AB	CFRN	Standard Radio Inc., #100, 18520 Stony Plain Rd., Edmonton AB T5S 2E2 – 403/486-2800; Fax: 403/489-6927; Email: mforbes@worldgate.com	1260
Edmonton, AB	CHED	Westcom Radio Group Ltd., 5204 - 84 St., Edmonton AB T6E 5N8 – 403/440-6300; Fax: 403/468-5937	630
Edmonton, AB	CHQT	Shaw Radio Ltd., 10550 - 105 St., Edmonton AB T5H 2T3 – 403/424-8800; Fax: 403/426-6502	880
Edmonton, AB	CJCA	CJCA Limited Partnership, 10250 - 108 St., Edmonton AB T5J 2X3 – 403/423-4930; Fax: 403/426-2171; Email: dmain@supernet.ab.ca	930

Canadian Almanac & Directory 1997

AM BROADCASTING STATIONS 5-201

LOCATION	CALL	*CBC Stations/Affiliates †French Language Stations	FREQ.
Edmonton, AB	CKUA	CKUA Radio Foundation, 10526 Jasper Ave., 4th Fl., Edmonton AB T5J 1Z7 – 403/428-7595; Fax: 403/428-7624; Email: ckua@freenet.edmonton.ab.ca	580
Edmonton, AB	*CBX	CBC, 7909 - 51 Ave., Edmonton AB T6E 5L9 – 403/468-7500; Fax: 403/468-7471	740
Edmonton, AB	*†CHFA	Société Radio-Canada, 7909 - 51 Ave., CP 555, Edmonton AB T5J 2P4 – 403/468-7800; Fax: 403/468-7812	680
Edmundston, NB	†CJEM	Edmundston Radio Ltd., 174, rue de l'Église, CP 188, Edmundston NB E3V 3K8 – 506/735-3351; Fax: 506/739-5803	570
Edson, AB	CJYR	Yellowhead Broadcasting Ltd., PO Box 6600, Edson AB T7E 1T9 – 403/723-4461; Fax: 403/723-3765	970
Elkford, BC	CJEV	See Crowsnest Pass (CJPR)	1340
Elliot Lake, ON	CKNR	Pelmorex Radio, 15 Charles Walk, Elliot Lake ON P5A 2A2 – 705/848-3608; Fax: 705/848-1378	1340
Elliot Lake, ON	CJNR	Pelmorex Broadcasting Inc., 15 Charles Walk, Elliot Lake ON P5A 2A2 – 705/356-2209	730
Espanola, ON	CKNS	Pelmorex Radio, 46 Mead Blvd., Espanola ON P0P 1C0 – 705/869-4930; Fax: 705/869-3764	930
Estevan, SK	CJSL	Golden West Broadcasting Ltd., 1132 - 5 St., PO Box 1280, Estevan SK S4A 2H8 – 306/634-1280; Fax: 306/634-6364	1280
Fernie, BC	CFEK	Columbia Kootenay Broadcasting Co. Ltd., 441 - 2nd Ave., PO Box 1170, Fernie BC V0B 1M0 – 250/423-4449; Fax: 250/423-6009	1240
Flin Flon, MB	CFAR	Arctic Radio (1982) Ltd., PO Box 430, Flin Flon MB R8A 1N3 – 204/687-3469; Fax: 204/687-6786	590
Forestville, PQ	†CFRP	See Baie-Comeau (CHLC)	620
Fort Frances, ON	CFOB	Fawcett Broadcasting Ltd., 242 Scott St., Fort Frances ON P9A 1G7 – 807/274-5341; Fax: 807/274-2033	640
Fort McMurray, AB	CJOK	OK Radio Group Ltd., 9912 Franklin Ave., Fort McMurray AB T9H 2K5 – 403/743-2246; Fax: 403/791-7250	1230
Fort Nelson, BC	CFNL	Nor-Net Communications Ltd., PO Box 880, Fort Nelson BC V0C 1R0 – 250/774-2525; Fax: 250/774-2577	590
Fort St. John, BC	CKNL	Nor-Net Broadcasting Ltd., 10532 Alaska Rd., Fort St. John BC V1J 1B3 – 250/785-6634; Fax: 250/785-4544	560
Fraser Lake, BC	CIFL	See Vanderhoof (CIVH)	1450
Fredericton, NB	CIHI	Radio One Ltd., 206 Rookwood Ave., Fredericton NB E3B 2M2 – 506/454-2444; Fax: 506/452-2345	1260
Fredericton, NB	*CBZ	CBC, 1160 Regent St., PO Box 2200, Fredericton NB E3B 2M2 – 506/452-8974	970
Gander, NF	CKXD	NewCap Inc., 78 Elizabeth Dr., Gander NF A1V 1G7 – 709/651-2787; Fax: 709/651-2780	1010
Gander, NF	CKGA	VOCM Radio Newfoundland Ltd., PO Box 650, Gander NF A1V 1X2 – 709/651-3650; Fax: 709/651-2542	650
Gander, NF	*CBG	CBC, 98 Sullivan Ave., PO Box 369, Gander NF A1V 1W7 – 709/256-4311; Fax: 709/651-2021	1400
Gaspé, PQ	†CHGM	See New Carlisle (CHNC)	1150
Gatineau, PQ	†CJRC	Radiomutuel inc., 22, rue St-Louis, Gatineau PQ J8T 2R9 – 819/561-8801; Fax: 819/561-9439; Email: cjrc@rheodatum.ca	1150
Gold River, BC	CJGR	See Campbell River (CFWB)	
Golden, BC	CKGR	Copper Island Broadcasting Ltd., PO Box 1403, Golden BC V0A 1H0 – 250/344-7177; Fax: 250/344-7233	1400
Goose Bay, NF	CFLN	Humber Valley Broadcasting Co. Ltd., PO Box 4000, Stn C, Goose Bay NF A0P 1C0 – 709/896-2968; Fax: 709/896-8708	1230
Granby, PQ	†CHEF	Power Corp., 76, rue Dufferin, Granby PQ J2G 9L4v514/375-1450; Fax: 514/777-1450	1450
Grand Cache, AB	CKYR	See Edson (CJYR)	1230
Grand Centre, AB	CJCM	Nor-Net Communications, 5418 - 55 St., PO Box 433, Grand Centre AB T0A 1T1 – 403/594-2459; Fax: 403/594-3001	1340
Grand Falls, NB	†CKMV	See Edmundston (CJEM)	1490
Grand Falls-Windsor, NF	CKCM	VOCM Radio Newfoundland Ltd., PO Box 620, Grand Falls-Windsor NF A2A 2K2 – 709/489-2192; Fax: 709/489-8626	620
Grand Falls-Windsor, NF	CKXG	NewCap Inc., PO Box 810, Grand Falls-Windsor NF A2A 2M4 – 709/489-9663; Fax: 709/489-1081	680
Grand Falls-Windsor, NF	*CBT	CBC, 2 Harris Ave., PO Box 218, Grand Falls-Windsor NF A2A 2J7 – 709/489-1055	540
Grand Forks, BC	CKGF	Boundary Broadcasting Ltd., PO Box 1570, Grand Forks BC V0H 1H0 – 250/442-5844; Fax: 250/442-3340	1340
Grande Prairie, AB	CJXX	Monarch Broadcasting Ltd., #202, 9817 - 101 Ave., Grande Prairie AB T8V 0X6 – 403/532-0840; Fax: 403/538-1266	840
Grande Prairie, AB	CKUA	See Edmonton (CKUA-FM)	1280
Granisle, BC	CHLD	See Smithers (CFBV)	1480
Gravelbourg, SK	*†CBRG-1	See Regina (CBKF-FM)	690
Guelph, ON	CJOY	Power Broadcasting Inc., 75 Speedvale Ave. East, Guelph ON N1E 6M3 – 519/824-7000; Fax: 519/824-4118; Email: power@in.on.ca	1460
Halifax, NS	CFSM	Saint Mary's University, 5th Fl., Student Union Bldg., Halifax NS B3H 3C3 – 902/423-1739; Fax: 902/425-4636	550
Halifax, NS	CHNS	Maritime Broadcasting System, 1313 Barrington St., PO Box 400, Halifax NS B3J 2R2 – 902/422-1651; Fax: 902/422-5330	960
Halifax, NS	CJCH	CHUM Ltd., 2900 Agricola St., PO Box 1653, Halifax NS B3J 2Z4 – 902/453-2524; Fax: 902/453-3132; URL: http://www.newedge.ca/cjch	920
Halifax, NS	CFDR	See Bedford (CFDR)	780
Hamilton, ON	CHAM	Golden West Broadcasting Ltd., 151 York Blvd., Hamilton ON L8R 3M2 – 905/526-8200; Fax: 905/525-1416	820
Hamilton, ON	CHML	Westcom Radio Group Ltd., #900, 875 Main St. West, Hamilton ON L8S 4R1 – 905/521-9900; Fax: 905/521-2306	900
Hamilton, ON	CKOC	Radio Corp. Inc., 883 Upper Wentworth St., PO Box 1150, Hamilton ON L8N 3P5 – 905/574-1150; Fax: 905/575-6429	1150
Hauterive, PQ	CHLC	See Baie-Comeau (CHLC)	580
Hazelton, BC	CKBV	See Smithers (CFBV)	1490
Hearst, ON	†CHOH	See Timmins (CKOY)	1340
High Level, AB	CKYL	See Peace River (CKYL)	530
High Prairie, AB	CKVH	Nor-Net Broadcasting Ltd., PO Box 2219, High Prairie AB T0G 1E0 – 403/523-5111; Fax: 403/523-3360	1020
High River, AB	CHRB	Golden West Broadcasting Ltd., 11 - 5th Ave. SE, High River AB T1V 1G2 – 403/652-2472; Fax: 403/652-7861	1280
Hinton, AB	CIYR	PO Box 3140, Hinton AB T7V 1Y3 – 403/865-8804; Fax: 403/865-7792	1230
Hope, BC	CKGO	Fraser Valley Broadcasters Ltd., PO Box 1600, Hope BC V0X 1L0 – 604/869-9313; Fax: 604/869-2454	1240
Houston, BC	CHBV	See Smithers (CFBV)	1450
Hudson, ON	CKDR-3	See Dryden (CKDR)	1400
Hull, PQ	*†CBOF	See Ottawa (CBOF-FM)	1250
Ignace, ON	CKIG	See Dryden (CKDR)	1340
Inuvik, NT	*CHAK	CBC, 155 MacKenzie Rd., Bag Service No. 8, Inuvik NT X0E 0T0 – 403/979-9411	860
Invermere, BC	CKIR	See Golden (CKGR)	870
Iqaluit, NT	*CFFB	CBC, PO Box 490, Iqaluit NT X0A 0H0 – 819/979-6100; Fax: 819/979-6147	1230
Jasper, AB	CKYR	See Edson (CJYR)	1450
Kamloops, BC	CFJC	Jim Pattison Group, 460 Pemberton Terrace, Kamloops BC V2C 1T5 – 250/372-3322; Fax: 250/374-0445	550

Canadian Almanac & Directory 1997

5-202 AM BROADCASTING STATIONS

LOCATION	CALL	*CBC Stations/Affiliates †French Language Stations	FREQ.
Kamloops, BC	CHNL	NL Broadcasting Ltd., PO Box 610, Kamloops BC V2C 1Y6 – 250/372-2292; Fax: 250/372-0682	610
Kamloops, BC	CMMD	Cariboo College, PO Box 3010, Kamloops BC V2C 5N3 – 250/828-5000; Fax: 250/828-5086	
Kapuskasing, ON	†CHYK	See Timmins (CKOY)	1230
Kapuskasing, ON	CKAP	Pelmorex Radio, 52 Riverside Dr., Kapuskasing ON P5N 1A8 – 705/335-2379; Fax: 705/337-6391	580
Kelowna, BC	CKIQ	Four Seasons Radio Ltd., 2419 Hwy. 97 North, Kelowna BC V1X 4J2 – 250/860-8600; Fax: 250/886-8856	1150
Kelowna, BC	CKOV	Seacoast Communications Group Inc., 3805 Lakeshore Rd., Kelowna BC V1W 3K6 – 250/762-3331; Fax: 250/762-2141; Email: ckov@awinc.com	630
Kenora, ON	CJRL	Fawcett Broadcasting Ltd., 128 Main St. South, Kenora ON P9N 1S9 – 807/468-3181; Fax: 807/468-4188	1220
Kentville, NS	CKEN	Annapolis Valley Radio Ltd., 29 Oakdene Ave., PO Box 310, Kentville NS B4N 1H5 – 902/678-2111; Fax: 902/678-9894	1490
Kimberley, BC	CKKI	See Cranbrook (CKEK)	
Kindersley, SK	CFYM	See Rosetown (CJYM/CFYM)	1210
Kingston, ON	CFFX	Power Broadcasting Inc., 479 Counter St., Kingston ON K7M 7J3 – 613/549-1911; Fax: 613/549-7974	960
Kingston, ON	CKLC	St. Lawrence Broadcasting Co. Ltd., 99 Brock St., PO Box 1380, Kingston ON K7L 4Y5 – 613/544-1380; Fax: 613/546-9751	1380
Kirkland Lake, ON	*CJKL	Connelly Communications Corp., 5 Kirkland St., PO Box 430, Kirkland Lake ON P2N 3J4 – 705/567-3366; Fax: 705/567-6101	560
Kitchener, ON	CKGL	Rogers Broadcasting Ltd., 305 King St. West, Kitchener ON N2G 4E4 – 519/743-2611; Fax: 519/743-7510	570
Kitchener, ON	CXLR	Conestoga College, 299 Doon Valley Dr., Kitchener ON N2G 4M4 – 519/748-5220, ext.310; Fax: 519/748-3505	closed circuit
Kitchener, ON	CIAM	See Cambridge (CIAM)	
Kitchener, ON	CKKW	See Waterloo (CKKW)	1090
Kitimat, BC	CKTK	Skeena Broadcasters, Division of Okanagan Skeena Group Ltd., 350 City Centre, Kitimat BC V8C 1T6 – 250/632-2102	1230
La Pocatière, PQ	†CHGB	Radio La Pocatière ltée, 1000 - 6e av, CP 550, La Pocatière PQ G0R 1Z0 – 418/856-1310; Fax: 418/856-3747	1310
La Sarre, PQ	†CKLS	Radio La Sarre inc., 122, 52e rue est, La Sarre PQ J9Z 2Y1 – 819/333-5505; Fax: 819/333-2066	1240
La Tûque, PQ	*†CFLM	Radio Haute-Mauricie inc., 529, rue St-Louis, CP 850, La Tûque PQ G9X 3P6 – 819/523-4575; Fax: 819/676-8000	1240
Labrador City, NF	*CBDQ	CBC, PO Box 576, Labrador City NF A2V 2L3 – 709/944-3616	1490
Lac-Etchemin, PQ	†CIRB	See St-Georges-de-Beauce (CKRB)	1240
Lac-Mégantic, PQ	†CKFL	Radio PLUS Lac-Mégantic inc., 5088, rue Frontenac, Lac-Mégantic PQ G6B 1H3 – 819/583-0663; Fax: 819/583-0665	1400
Lennoxville, PQ	CJMQ	Radio Bishop's University, 112, Mountain House, CP 2135, Lennoxville PQ J1M 1Z7 – 819/822-9689; Fax: 819/822-9747; URL: http://www.cyniska.vbishops.ca/cjmo/	550
Lethbridge, AB	CJOC	Rogers Broadcasting Ltd., PO Box 820, Lethbridge AB T1J 3Z9 – 403/320-1220; Fax: 403/327-5879	1220
Lethbridge, AB	CKRX	Monarch Broadcasting Ltd., 401 Mayor McGrath Dr. South, Lethbridge AB T1J 4A3 – 403/329-1090; Fax: 403/329-0195; Email: ckrxckta@agt.net	1090
Lethbridge, AB	CLCC	Lethbridge Community College, Student Service Centre, 3000 College Dr. South, Lethbridge AB T1K 1L6 – 403/320-3256; Fax: 403/320-1461	730; closed circuit
Lethbridge, AB	CKTA	Monarch Broadcasting Ltd., 401 Mayor McGrath Dr. South, Lethbridge AB T1J 4A3 – 403/329-1090; Fax: 403/329-0195; Email: ckrxckta@agt.net	1570
Lindsay, ON	CKLY	Centario Communications Inc., 249 Kent St. West, Lindsay ON K9V 2Z3 – 705/324-9103; Fax: 705/324-4149	910
Lloydminster, AB	CKSA	Saskatchewan-Alberta Broadcasters Ltd., 5026 - 50 St., Lloydminster AB T9V 1P3 – 403/875-3321; Fax: 403/875-4704	1080
London, ON	CFPL	Blackburn Radio Inc., 369 York St., PO Box 2580, London ON N6A 4H3 – 519/438-8391; Fax: 519/438-2415	980
London, ON	CJBK	London Communications Ltd., 743 Wellington Rd. South, London ON N6C 4R5 – 519/686-2525; Fax: 519/686-3658; Email: oldies1290.cjbc@odyssey.on.ca	1290
London, ON	CKSL	Telemedia Communications Ontario Inc., 380 Wellington St. South, PO Box 1410, London ON N6A 5J2 – 519/667-1410; Fax: 519/667-2175	1410
Mackenzie, BC	CKMK	Monarch Broadcasting Ltd., PO Box 1210, Mackenzie BC V0J 2C0 – 250/997-3400; Fax: 250/997-4818	1240
Mackenzie, NT	*CFYK-1	See Yellowknife (CFYK)	1340
Marystown, NF	CHCM	VOCM Radio Newfoundland Ltd., PO Box 560, Marystown NF A0E 2M0 – 709/279-2560; Fax: 709/279-3538	740
Matane, PQ	†CHRM	Les Communications Matane inc., 800, av du Phare ouest, CP 605, Matane PQ G4W 1V7 – 418/562-4141; Fax: 418/562-0778	1290
Matane, PQ	*†CBGA	Société Radio-Canada, 155, rue St-Sacrament, Matane PQ G4W 1Y9 – 418/562-0290; Fax: 418/562-5555	1250
Meadow Lake, SK	CJNS	Northwestern Radio Partnership Ltd., PO Box 1660, Meadow Lake SK S0M 1V0 – 306/236-6494; Fax: 306/236-6141	1240
Medicine Hat, AB	CHAT	Monarch Broadcasting Ltd., PO Box 1270, Medicine Hat AB T1A 7H5 – 403/529-1270; Fax: 403/529-1292; Email: ddietric@mlc.awinc.com	1270
Medicine Hat, AB	CJCY	Medicine Hat Broadcasting Ltd., 457 - 3 St. SE, 2nd Fl., Medicine Hat AB T1A 0G8 – 403/529-1390; Fax: 403/527-5971	1390
Medley, AB	CHCL	CHCL, PO Box 1220, Medley AB T0A 2M0 – 403/594-1450	1450
Melfort, SK	CJVR	Radio CJVR Ltd., 611 Main St., PO Box 750, Melfort SK S0E 1A0 – 306/752-2587; Fax: 306/752-5932	1420
Merritt, BC	CJNL	Merritt Broadcasting, 1970 Quilchena Ave., Merritt BC V1K 1B8 – 250/378-4288; Fax: 250/378-6979	1230
Middleton, NS	CKAD	Annapolis Valley Radio Inc., 90 Commercial St., Middleton NS B0S 1P0 – 902/825-3429; Fax: 902/825-6009	1350
Miramichi, NB	CFAN	Maritime Broadcasting Co. Ltd., 245 Pleasant St., PO Box 338, Miramichi NB E1V 1Y6 – 506/622-3311; Fax: 506/627-0335	790
Moncton, NB	CKCW	Maritime Broadcasting System Ltd., 1000 St. George Blvd., Moncton NB E1E 4M7 – 506/858-1220; Fax: 506/858-1209	1220
Moncton, NB	*CBA	CBC, 250 Archibald St., PO Box 950, Moncton NB E1C 8N8 – 506/853-6666; Fax: 506/853-6409	1070
Mont Laurier, PQ	CFLO	Sonème inc., 332, rue de la Madone, Mont Laurier PQ J9L 1R9 – 819/623-6610; Fax: 819/623-7406	610
Montréal, PQ	CFMB	Radio Montréal, 35, rue York, Montréal PQ H3Z 2Z5 – 514/483-2362; Fax: 514/483-1362; Email: admin@cfmb.ca; URL: http://www.cfmb.ca	1410
Montréal, PQ	CIQC	Mount Royal Broadcasting Inc., #300, 1200, av McGill College, Montréal PQ H3B 4G7 – 514/874-4040; Fax: 514/393-4659	600
Montréal, PQ	CFLI	Concordia University, 6931, rue Sherbrooke ouest, Montréal PQ H4B 1R6 – 514/848-7470; Fax: 514/848-7450	closed circuit

Canadian Almanac & Directory 1997

LOCATION	CALL	*CBC Stations/Affiliates †French Language Stations	FREQ.
Montréal, PQ	CJAD	Standard Radio Inc., 1411, rue du Fort, Montréal PQ H3H 2R1 – 514/989-2523; Fax: 514/989-3868	800
Montréal, PQ	†CKAC	Radio Média, #300, 1411, rue Peel, Montréal PQ H3A 3L5 – 514/845-5151; Fax: 514/845-2229	730
Montréal, PQ	CKIS	CHUM Ltd., 1310, av Greene, Montréal PQ H3Z 2B5 – 514/931-4487; Fax: 514/931-4057	990
Montréal, PQ	†CKVL	Métromédia CMR inc., 211, av Gordon, Montréal PQ H4G 2R2 – 514/766-2311; Fax: 514/766-2474	850
Montréal, PQ	*†CBF	Société Radio-Canada, CP 6000, Succ A, Montréal PQ H3C 3A8 – 514/597-5970; Fax: 514/597-5551	690
Montréal, PQ	*CBM	CBC, CP 6000, Succ A, Montréal PQ H3C 3A8 – 514/597-4444; Fax: 514/597-4511	940
Moose Jaw, SK	CHAB	Golden West Broadcasting, 1704 Main St. North, PO Box 800, Moose Jaw SK S6H 4P5 – 306/694-0800; Fax: 306/692-8880	800
Moosonee, ON	CHMO	James Bay Broadcasting Corp. Inc., PO Box 400, Moosonee ON P0L 1Y0 – 705/336-2466; Fax: 705/336-3689	1450
Mount Pearl, NF	VOAR	VOAR Christian Radio, PO Box 2520, Mount Pearl NF A1N 4M7 – 709/745-8627; Fax: 709/745-1600	1210
Murdochville, PQ	†CHNC	See New Carlisle (CHNC)	1450
Musgravetown, NF	CKVB	See St. John's (CJYQ)	670
Nanaimo, BC	CKEG	Central Island Broadcasting Ltd., 4550 Wellington Rd., Nanaimo BC V9T 2H3 – 250/758-1131; Fax: 250/758-4644	1570
New Carlisle, PQ	†CHNC	Radio CHNC Ltée, 153, rue Principale, CP 610, New Carlisle PQ G0C 1Z0 – 418/752-2215; Fax: 418/752-6939	610
New Glasgow, NS	CKEC	Hector Broadcasting Co. Ltd., 84 Provost St., PO Box 519, New Glasgow NS B2H 5E7 – 902/752-4200; Fax: 902/755-2468	1320
New Liskeard, ON	*CJTT	Connelly Communications Corp., 55 Whitewood Ave., PO Box 1058, New Liskeard ON P0J 1P0 – 705/647-7334; Fax: 705/647-8660; Email: cjtt@nt.net; URL: http://www.nt.net/1230cjtt.com	1230
New Westminster, BC	CKNW	Westcom Radio Group Ltd., #2600, 700 West Georgia St., New Westminster BC V7Y 1K9 – 604/331-2711; Fax: 604/331-2722; URL: http://www.cknw.com	980
Niagara Falls, ON	CJRN	CJRN 710 Inc., PO Box 710, Niagara Falls ON L2E 6X7 – 905/356-6710; Fax: 905/356-0696; Email: rock@theplanet.com	710
North Battleford, SK	CJNB	Northwestern Radio Partnership, PO Box 1460, North Battleford SK S9A 2Z5 – 306/445-2477; Fax: 306/445-4599	1050
North Bay, ON	CFCH	Telemedia Communications Ontario Inc., 743 Main St. East, PO Box 3000, North Bay ON P1B 8K8 – 705/474-2000; Fax: 705/474-7761	600
North Bay, ON	CHUR	Pelmorex Broadcasting Inc., 215 Oak St. East, North Bay ON P1B 8P8 – 705/472-1110; Fax: 705/476-8400	840
North River, PE	CFCY	See Charlottetown (CFCY)	
North York, ON	CRSC	Seneca College, 1750 Finch Ave. East, North York ON M2J 2X5 – 416/491-5050, ext.2994; Fax: 416/756-2765	closed circuit
Norway House, MB	CJNC	Norway House Communications Inc., PO Box 250, Norway House MB R0B 1B0 – 204/359-4683; Fax: 204/359-6191	1340
Oakville, ON	CJMR	CJMR 1320 Radio Ltd., 284 Church St., Oakville ON L6J 7N2 – 905/271-1320; Fax: 905/842-1250	1320
Oakville, ON	CHWO	CHWO Radio Ltd., 284 Church St., Oakville ON L6J 7N2 – 905/845-2821; Fax: 905/842-1250	1250
100 Mile House, BC	CKBX	Cariboo Broadcasters Ltd., 260 - 3rd St., PO Box 939, 100 Mile House BC V0K 2E0 – 250/395-3848; Fax: 250/395-4147	840
Oshawa, ON	CKDO	Power Broadcasting Inc., 360 King St. West, Oshawa ON L1J 2K2 – 905/571-1350; Fax: 905/571-1150	1350
Osoyoos, BC	CJOR	Okanagan Radio Ltd., PO Box 539, Osoyoos BC V0H 1V0 – 250/495-7226; Fax: 250/495-7228	1240
Ottawa, ON	CFGO	RAWLCO Communications Ltd., 1575 Carling Ave., Ottawa ON K1Z 7M3 – 613/729-1200; Fax: 613/729-9829	1200
Ottawa, ON	CFRA	CHUM Ltd., 1900 Walkley Rd., Ottawa ON K1H 8P4 – 613/738-2372; Fax: 613/523-6423	580
Ottawa, ON	CIWW	Rogers Broadcasting Ltd., #1900, Tower B, Place de Ville, 112 Kent St., Ottawa ON K1P 6J1 – 613/238-7482; Fax: 613/236-5382; Email: oldies-1310@ottawa.net; URL: http://www.ottawa.net/~oldies-1310/	1310
Owen Sound, ON	CFOS	Bayshore Broadcasting Corp., 270 - 9 St. East, PO Box 280, Owen Sound ON N4K 5P5 – 519/376-2030; Fax: 519/371-9683	560
Parksville, ON	CHPQ	Central Island Broadcasting Ltd., #4, 182 Harrison Ave., PO Box 1370, Parksville ON V0R 2S0 – 250/248-4211; Fax: 250/248-4210	1370
Peace River, AB	CKYL	Peace River Broadcasting Corp., Bag 300, Peace River AB T8S 1T5 – 403/624-2535; Fax: 403/624-5424	610
Penticton, BC	CKOR	Okanagan Radio Ltd., 33 Carmi Ave., Penticton BC V2A 3G4 – 250/492-2800; Fax: 250/493-0370	800
Perth-Andover, NS	CJCJ	See Woodstock (CJCJ)	1140
Peterborough, ON	CKPT	CHUM Ltd., PO Box 177, Peterborough ON K9J 6Y8 – 705/742-8844; Fax: 705/742-1417	1420
Peterborough, ON	CKRU	Power Broadcasting Inc., 1925 Television Rd., PO Box 4150, Peterborough ON K9J 6Z9 – 705/742-7708; Fax: 705/742-7274	980
Plaster Rock, NS	CJCJ	See Woodstock (CJCJ)	990
Plessisville, PQ	†CKTL	Radio Média ltée, CP 142, Plessisville PQ G6L 2Y6 – 819/362-3737; Fax: 819/362-3414	1420
Pohenegamook, PQ	†CHRT	See Rivière-du-Loup (CJFP)	1450
Port Alberni, BC	CJAV	CJAV Radio Ltd., 2970 - 3 Ave. South, Port Alberni BC V9Y 7N4 – 250/723-2455; Fax: 250/723-0797; Email: cjav@cedar.alberni.net; URL: http://www.alberni.net/~cjav/cjav.htm	1240
Port au Choix, NF	CFNW	See Corner Brook (CFCB)	790
Port aux Basques, NF	CFGN	Humber Valley Broadcasting Co. Ltd., PO Box 1230, Port aux Basques NF A0M 1C0 – 709/695-2183; Fax: 709/695-9614	1230
Port Elgin, ON	CFPS	See Owen Sound (CFOS)	1490
Port Hardy, BC	CFNI	CFCP Radio Ltd., PO Box 1240, Port Hardy BC V0N 2P0 – 250/949-6500; Fax: 250/949-6580	1240
Port Hawkesbury, NS	CIGO	MacEachern Broadcasting Ltd., Business Park, PO Box 1410, Port Hawkesbury NS B0E 2V0 – 902/625-1220; Fax: 902/625-2664	1410
Port Hawkesbury, NS	CJFX	See Antigonish (CJFX)	
Port Hope, ON	CHUC	See Cobourg (CHUC)	
Portage La Prairie, MB	CFRY	Portage-Delta Broadcasting Co. Ltd., 1500 Saskatchewan Ave. West, Portage La Prairie MB R1N 0N6 – 204/239-5111; Fax: 204/857-3456	920
Powell River, BC	CHQB	Sunshine Coast Broadcasting Co. Ltd., 6816 Courtenay St., Powell River BC V8A 1X1 – 604/485-4207; Fax: 604/485-4210	1280
Prince Albert, SK	CKBI	Central Broadcasting Co. Ltd., PO Box 900, Prince Albert SK S6V 7R4 – 306/763-7421; Fax: 306/764-1850900	
Prince George, BC	CJCI	Cariboo Central Interior Radio Inc., 1940 - 3 Ave., Prince George BC V2M 1G7 – 250/564-2524; Fax: 250/562-6611; URL: http://www.cjci.com	620
Prince George, BC	*CKPG	Monarch Broadcasting Ltd., 1220 - 6 Ave., Prince George BC V2L 3M8 – 250/564-8861; Fax: 250/562-8768; Email: benny@mindlink.net; http://pgonline.com/benny	550

5-204 AM BROADCASTING STATIONS

LOCATION	CALL	*CBC Stations/Affiliates †French Language Stations	FREQ.
Prince Rupert, BC	CHTK	Skeena Broadcasting Group Ltd., Division of Okanagan Skeena Group Ltd., 346 Stiles Pl., Prince Rupert BC V8J 3S5 – 250/624-9111; Fax: 250/624-3100.	560
Prince Rupert, BC	*CFPR	CBC, #1, 222 - 3 Ave. West, Prince Rupert BC V8J 1L1250/624-2161; Fax: 250/627-8594; Email: daybreak@kaien.awinc.com.	860
Princeton, BC	CIOR	Princeton Broadcasting Ltd., PO Box 1400, Princeton BC V0X 1W0 – 250/295-6991; Fax: 250/295-6628	1400
Québec, PQ	*†CBV	Société Radio-Canada, 2505, boul Laurier, CP 10400, Québec PQ G1V 2X2 – 418/654-1341; Fax: 418/656-8225	980
Québec, PQ	*†CHRC	Radiomédia inc., CP 8080, Québec PQ G1V 1R8 – 418/688-8080; Fax: 418/682-8429	800
Quesnel, BC	CKCQ	Cariboo Central Interior Radio Inc., 160 Front St., Quesnel BC V2J 2K1 – 250/992-7046; Fax: 250/992-2354	920
Radium, BC	CKIR	See Golden (CKGR)	870
Red Deer, AB	CKGY	Shaw Radio Ltd., PO Bag 5339, Red Deer AB T4N 6W1 – 403/343-1170; Fax: 403/346-1230	1170
Red Deer, AB	CKRD	Monarch Broadcasting Ltd., PO Box 5700, Red Deer AB T4N 6V5 – 403/343-0700; Fax: 403/343-2573	700
Red Lake, ON	CKDR-5	See Dryden (CKDR)	1340
Regina, SK	CJME	RAWLCO Communications Ltd., #210, 2401 Saskatchewan Dr., Regina SK S4P 4H8 – 306/569-1300; Fax: 306/347-8557	1300
Regina, SK	CKCK	Western World Communications Corp., 1922 Park St., Regina SK S4N 7M4 – 306/569-6200; Fax: 306/936-8329	620
Regina, SK	CKRM	Harvard Developments Ltd., 2060 Halifax St, PO Box 9800, Regina SK S4P 1T7 – 306/566-9800; Fax: 306/781-7338	980
Regina, SK	CKUR	University of Regina, Student Service Centre, Regina SK S4S 0A2 – 306/588-8812	closed circuit; 760
Regina, SK	CHAB	See Moose Jaw (CHAB)	
Regina, SK	*CBK	CBC, 2440 Broad St., PO Box 540, Regina SK S4P 4A1 – 306/347-9540; Fax: 306/347-9493	540
Regina, SK	*†CBKF	Société Radio-Canada, 2440 Broad St., Regina SK S4P 4A1 – 306/347-9540; Fax: 306/347-9493	
Renfrew, ON	CHVR-1	Pelmorex Broadcasting Inc., 595 Pembroke St. East, Renfrew ON K8A 3L7 – 613/432-6428; Fax: 613/432-8236	1400
Revelstoke, BC	CKCR	See Salmon Arm (CKXR)	1340
Richmond, BC	CISL	Standard Radio Inc., #20, 11151 Horseshoe Way, Richmond BC V7A 4S5 – 604/272-6500; Fax: 604/272-0917; Email: cisl@uniserve.com	650
Rimouski, PQ	†CAJT	CEGEP de Rimouski, a/s Agecor inc., 60, rue de l'Éveché ouest, Rimouski PQ G5L 4H6 – 418/723-1880, ext.2265	closed circuit
Rimouski, PQ	†CFLP	Power Broadcasting Inc./Diffusion Power Inc., 875, boul St-Germain ouest, CP 3875, Rimouski PQ G5L 7P3 – 418/723-2323; Fax: 418/722-7508	1000
Rimouski, PQ	*†CJBR	Société Radio-Canada, 273, rue St-Jean Baptiste ouest, Rimouski PQ G5L 4J8 – 418/723-2217; Fax: 418/723-4730	900
Rivière-du-Loup, PQ	†CJFP	Radio CJFP (1986) ltée, 1, rue Frontenac, Rivière-du-Loup PQ G5R 1R7 – 418/862-8241; Fax: 418/862-7704	1400
Roberval, PQ	†CHRL	Radio Roberval inc., 568, boul St-Joseph, Roberval PQ G8H 2K6 – 418/275-1831; Fax: 418/275-2475	910
Roberval, PQ	*CJMD	See Chibougamau (CJMD)	
Roberval, PQ	CFED	Groupe Radio Antenne 6 inc., 568, boul St-Joseph, Roberval PQ G8H 2K6 – 418/275-1831; Fax: 418/275-2475	1340
Rosetown, SK	CJYM/CFYM	Dace Broadcasting Corp., PO Box 490, Rosetown SK S0L 2V0 – 306/882-2686; Fax: 306/882-3037	1300
Rouyn-Noranda, PQ	†CKRN	Radio Nord inc., 380, av Murdoch, CP 70, Rouyn-Noranda PQ J9X 1G5 – 819/762-0741; Fax: 819/762-2280	1400
Ste-Anne-des-Monts, PQ	†CJMC	Radio du Golfe inc., 170, boul Ste-Anne est, CP 820, Ste-Anne-des-Monts PQ G0E 2G0 – 418/763-5522; Fax: 418/763-7211	1490
St. Catharines, ON	CHSC	Coultis Broadcasting Ltd., 36 Queenston St., St. Catharines ON L2R 2Y9 – 905/682-6691; Fax: 905/682-9434	1220
St. Catharines, ON	CKTB	Standard Radio Inc., PO Box 610, St. Catharines ON L2R 6X7 – 905/684-1174; Fax: 905/684-4800; URL: http://www.htzfm.com	610
St-Eleuthère, PQ	CHRT	See Rivière-du-Loup (CJFP)	1450
Ste-Foy, PQ	CHRC	See Québec (CHRC)	800
St-Georges-de-Beauce, PQ	†CKRB	Radio Beauce inc., 170, rue 120, St-Georges-de-Beauce PQ G5Y 5C4 – 418/228-1460; Fax: 418/228-0096	1460
St-Hyacinthe, PQ	†CKBS	Radio St-Hyacinthe (1978) ltée, 855, rue Ste-Marie, St-Hyacinthe PQ J2S 4R9 – 514/774-6486; Fax: 514/774-7785	1240
St-Jean-sur-Richelieu, PQ	†CFZZ	Diffusion Power inc., 104, rue Richelieu, St-Jean-sur-Richelieu PQ J3B 6X3 – 514/346-0104; Fax: 514/348-2274	1040
Saint John, NB	CFBC	Fundy Cable Ltd./Ltée, PO Box 930, Saint John NB E2L 4E2 – 506/658-2330; Fax: 506/658-2320	930
Saint John, NB	CHSJ	New Brunswick Broadcasting Ltd., 335 Union St., PO Box 2000, Saint John NB E2L 3T4 – 506/632-2222; Fax: 506/632-3485	700
St. John's, NF	CKVO	VOCM Radio Newfoundland Ltd., PO Box 8590, St. John's NF A1B 3P5 – 709/726-5590; Fax: 709/726-4633	710
St. John's, NF	CJYQ	NewCap Broadcasting, 208 Kenmount Rd., PO Box 8010, Stn A, St. John's NF A1B 3M7 – 709/753-4040; Fax: 709/753-4420	930
St. John's, NF	VOCM	VOCM Radio Newfoundland Ltd., PO Box 80590, Stn A, St. John's NF A1B 3P5 – 709/726-5590; Fax: 709/726-4633	590
St. John's, NF	VOWR	VOWR Radio Board, PO Box 7430, St. John's NF A1E 3Y5 – 709/579-9233; Fax: 709/579-9232	800
St. John's, NF	*CBN	CBC, 344 Duckworth St., PO Box 12010, Stn A, St. John's NF A1B 3T8 – 709/576-5000; Fax: 709/576-5234	640
Ste-Marie-de-Beauce, PQ	†CJVL	Radio Beauce inc., 1360, rue Notre-Dame sud, Ste-Marie-de-Beauce PQ G6E 2W9 – 418/387-1360; Fax: 418/387-37571360	
St-Pamphile, PQ	†CHAL	See La Pocatière (CHGB)	1350
St. Paul, AB	CHLW	Nor-Net Broadcasting Ltd., #201, 4341 - 50 Ave., St. Paul AB T0A 3A3 – 403/645-4425; Fax: 403/645-2383	1310
St. Stephen, NB	WQDY	International Radio, PO Box 305, St. Stephen NB E3L 2X2 – 506/465-0989; Fax: 207/454-3062	1230
St. Thomas, ON	CHLO	CHLO Radio Ltd., 133 Curtis St., St. Thomas ON N5P 3T8 – 519/637-1572; Fax: 519/631-4693	
Salmon Arm, BC	CKXR	Copper Island Broadcasting Co., PO Box 69, Salmon Arm BC V1E 4N2 – 250/832-2161; Fax: 250/832-2240	580
Sarnia, ON	CHOK	Sarnia Broadcasters (1993) Ltd., 148 North Front St., PO Box 1070, Sarnia ON N7T 7K5 – 519/336-1070; Fax: 519/336-7523	1070
Sarnia, ON	CKTY	Bluewater Broadcasting Ltd., 1415 London Rd., Sarnia ON N7S 1P6 – 519/332-5500; Fax: 519/542-1520	1110
Saskatoon, SK	CJWW	Radio One (Saskatoon) Corp., 345 - 4 Ave. South, Saskatoon SK S7K 5S5 – 306/244-1975; Fax: 306/665-7730; Email: cjww.radio@sasknet.sk.ca; URL: http://www.sasknet.com/cjww/	600
Saskatoon, SK	CKOM	RAWLCO Communications Ltd., 3333 - 8 St. East, Saskatoon SK S7H 0W3 – 306/955-6595; Fax: 306/373-7587	650
Saskatoon, SK	†CBKF-2	See Regina (CBKF)	860
Saskatoon, SK	*CBK	CBC, CN Tower, 5th Fl., Saskatoon SK S7K 1J5 – 306/956-7400; Fax: 306/956-7488	540
Sault Ste. Marie, ON	CFYN	Telemedia Communications Ontario Inc., 426 Bruce St., PO Box 1050, Sault Ste. Marie ON P6A 5N5 – 705/942-1050; Fax: 705/942-8246	1050
Scarborough, ON	CKCC	Centennial College, 651 Warden Ave., Scarborough ON M1L 3Z6 – 416/694-3033; Fax: 416/694-2664	closed circuit
Sechelt, BC	CISE	See Squamish (CISQ-FM)	
Sept-Îles, PQ	†CKCN	Radio Sept-Îles inc., 437, av Arnaud, Sept-Îles PQ G4R 3B3 – 418/962-3838; Fax: 418/968-6662	560

Canadian Almanac & Directory 1997

AM BROADCASTING STATIONS 5-205

LOCATION	CALL	*CBC Stations/Affiliates †French Language Stations	FREQ.
Shawinigan, PQ	†CKSM	Radiomutuel inc., 550, rue de l'Hôtel de Ville, CP 578, Shawinigan PQ G9N 6V6 – 819/537-8824; Fax: 819/537-8827	1220
Sherbrooke, PQ	†CHLT	Télémedia Communications inc., 25, rue Bryant, Sherbrooke PQ J1J 3Z5 – 819/563-6363; Fax: 819/566-4222	630
Sherbrooke, PQ	CKTS	See Montréal (CJAD)	900
Sherbrooke, PQ	†CFLX	Radio Communautaire de l'Estrie, #400, 244, rue Dufferin, Sherbrooke PQ J1H 4M4 – 819/566-2787; Fax: 819/566-7331	1300
Simcoe, ON	CHNR	Redmond Broadcasting Inc., 600 Norfolk St. North, PO Box 1600, Simcoe ON N3Y 4K8 – 519/426-7700; Fax: 519/426-8574	1600
Sioux Lookout, ON	CKSI	See Dryden (CKDR)	1400
Slave Lake, AB	CKWA	Nor-Net Communications Ltd., PO Box 2470, Slave Lake AB T0G 2A0 – 403/849-2577; Fax: 403/849-4833	1210
Smithers, BC	CFBV	Cariboo Central Interior Radio Inc., PO Box 335, Smithers BC V0J 2N0 – 250/847-2277; Fax: 250/847-9411	870
Smiths Falls, ON	CJET	Rideau Broadcasting, PO Box 630, Smiths Falls ON K7A 4T4 – 613/562-4630; Fax: 613/283-7243	630
Sparwood, BC	CJEK	See Fernie (CFEK)	1400
Steinbach, MB	CHSM	Golden West Broadcasting Ltd., 250 Main St., Steinbach MB R0A 2A0 – 204/326-3737; Fax: 204/324-8918	1250
Stephenville, NF	CFSX	Humber Valley Broadcasting Co. Ltd., 30 Oregon Dr., Stephenville NF A2N 2XZ9 – 709/643-2191; Fax: 709/643-5025	870
Stettler, AB	CKSQ	Nor-Net Broadcasting Ltd., 4703 - 58 St., Stettler AB T0C 2L1 – 403/742-2930; Fax: 403/742-0660	1400
Stratford, ON	CJCS	Telemedia Communications Ontario Inc., 178 Ontario St., PO Box 904, Stratford ON N5A 6W3 – 519/271-2450; Fax: 519/271-3102	1240
Sudbury, ON	CHNO	Pelmorex Radio, 295 Victoria St., Sudbury ON P3C 1K5 – 705/674-6401; Fax: 705/674-7322	550
Sudbury, ON	†CHYC	Pelmorex Radio, 295 Victoria St., Sudbury ON P3C 1K5 – 705/674-6401; Fax: 705/674-7322	900
Sudbury, ON	CIGM	Telemedia Communications Ontario Inc., 880 LaSalle Blvd., Sudbury ON P3A 1X5 – 705/566-4480; Fax: 705/560-7232	790
Summerland, BC	CHOR	Okanagan Radio Ltd., PO Box 1170, Summerland BC V0H 1Z0 – 250/494-0333; Fax: 250/494-0333	1450
Summerside, PE	CJRW	Gulf Broadcasting Co. Ltd., 763 Water St. East, Summerside PE C1N 4J3 – 902/436-2201; Fax: 902/436-8573	1240
Sussex, NB	CJCW	Maritime Broadcasting System Ltd., PO Box 5900, Sussex NB E0E 1P0 – 506/432-2529; Fax: 506/433-4900	590
Swift Current, SK	CKSW	Frontier City Broadcasting Co. Ltd., 134 Central Ave. North, Swift Current SK S9H 0L1 – 306/773-4605; Fax: 306/773-6390	570
Swift Current, SK	CJSN	Frontier City Broadcasting Co. Ltd., 134 Central Ave. North, Swift Current SK S9H 0L1 – 306/773-4605; Fax: 306/773-6390	1490
Sydney, NS	CJCB	Celtic Broadcasting Ltd., Radio Bldg., 318 Charlotte St., Sydney NS B1P 6K2 – 902/564-5596; Fax: 902/564-1057	1270
Sydney, NS	CHER	Bras d'Or Broadcasting Ltd., PO Box 1201, Sydney NS B1P 6J9 – 902/539-8500; Fax: 902/562-5720	950
Sydney, NS	*CBI	CBC, 285 Alexandra St., Sydney NS B1S 2E8 – 902/539-5050; Fax: 902/562-7547	1140
Taber, AB	CKTA	See Lethbridge (CKTA)	1570
Terrace, BC	CFTK	Okanagan Skeena Group Ltd., 4625 Lazelle Ave., Terrace BC V8G 1S4 – 250/635-6316; Fax: 250/638-6320; Email: info@osg.net; URL: http://www.osg.net	590
The Pas, MB	CJAR	Arctic Radio (1982) Ltd., PO Box 2980, The Pas MB R9A 1R7 – 204/623-5307; Fax: 204/623-5337	1240
Thetford-Mines, PQ	†CKLD	Radio-Mégantic ltée, CP 69, Thetford-Mines PQ G6G 5S3 – 418/335-7533; Fax: 418/335-9009	1330
Thompson, MB	CHTM	Arctic Radio (1982) Ltd., 201 Hayes Rd., Thompson MB R8N 1M5 – 204/778-7361; Fax: 204/778-5252	610
Thunder Bay, ON	CJLB	NewCap Broadcasting Inc., 87 North Hill St., Thunder Bay ON P7A 5V6 – 807/346-2660; Fax: 807/345-6814	1230
Thunder Bay, ON	CKPR	CJSD Inc., 87 North Hill St., Thunder Bay ON P7A 5V6 – 807/346-2580; Fax: 807/345-4671	580
Tillsonburg, ON.	CKOT	Tillsonburg Broadcasting Co. Ltd., PO Box 10, Tillsonburg ON N4G 4H3 – 519/842-4284; Fax: 519/842-4284	1510
Timmins, ON	CKGB	Telemedia Communications Ontario Inc., PO Box 1046, Timmins ON P4N 7H8 – 705/264-2351; Fax: 705/264-2984	750
Timmins, ON	†CKOY	Pelmorex Radio, CP 1340, Timmins ON P4N 7J8 – 705/267-6070; Fax: 705/267-6095	620
Toronto, ON	CFRB	Standard Radio Inc., 2 St. Clair Ave. West, Toronto ON M4V 1L6 – 416/924-5711; Fax: 416/323-6830	1010
Toronto, ON	CFTR	Rogers Broadcasting Ltd., 25 Adelaide St., 11th Fl., Toronto ON M5C 1H3 – 416/864-2000; Fax: 416/864-2116	680
Toronto, ON	CHIN	Radio 1540 Ltd., 622 College St., Toronto ON M6G 1B6 – 416/531-9991; Fax: 416/531-5274; Email: chin@istar.ca; URL: http://www.chinradio.com	1540
Toronto, ON	CHOG	Westcom Radio Group Ltd., #1400, 5255 Yonge St., Toronto ON M2N 6P4 – 416/221-6400; Fax: 416/512-4810	640
Toronto, ON	CHUM	CHUM Ltd., 1331 Yonge St., Toronto ON M4T 1Y1 – 416/925-6666; Fax: 416/926-4026; Email: chumam@1050chum.com	1050
Toronto, ON	CJCL	Telemedia Communications Ontario Inc., 40 Holly St., 9th Fl., Toronto ON M4S 3C3 – 416/482-0590; Fax: 416/488-1845	590
Toronto, ON	CKYC	Telemedia Communciations Ontario Inc., One Yonge St., 25th Fl., Toronto ON M5E 1G1 – 416/361-1281; Fax: 416/361-9529	590
Toronto, ON	CHWO	See Oakville (CHWO)	
Toronto, ON	CIAO	See Brampton (CIAO)	
Toronto, ON	CKCC	See Scarborough (CKCC)	
Toronto, ON	CRSC	See North York (CRSC)	
Toronto, ON	*CBL	CBC, PO Box 500, Stn A, Toronto ON M5W 1E6 – 416/205-3311; Fax: 416/205-6336	740
Toronto, ON	*†CJBC	Société Radio-Canada, CP 500, Succ A, Toronto ON M5W 1E6 – 416/205-2522; Fax: 416/205-5622	860
Trail, BC	CJAT	Four Seasons Radio Ltd., 1560 Second Ave., Trail BC V1R 1M4 – 250/368-5510; Fax: 250/368-8471	610
Trail, BC	CFKC	Four Seasons Radio Inc., 1560 Second Ave., Trail BC V1R 1M4 – 250/428-5311; Fax: 250/368-8471	1340
Trail, BC	CKKC	Four Seasons Radio Inc., 1560 Second Ave., Trail BC V1R 1M4 – 250/352-5510; Fax: 250/368-8471	880
Trenton, ON	CJTN	Quinte Broadcasting Co. Ltd., 31 Quinte St., PO Box 9, Trenton ON K8V 5R1 – 613/392-1237; Fax: 613/394-6430	1270
Trois-Rivières, PQ	†CHLN	Télémedia Communications inc., 1500, rue Royal, Trois-Rivières PQ G9A 6J4 – 819/374-3556; Fax: 819/374-3222	550
Truro, NS	CKCL	Radio Atlantic (CKCL) Ltd., 187 Industrial Ave., Truro NS B2N 6V3 – 902/893-6060; Fax: 902/893-7771; Email: ckcl@atcon.com; URL: http://www.truroradio.ca	600
Val-d'Or, PQ	†CKVD	Radio Nord inc., 1729 - 3e av, Val-d'Or PQ J9P 1W3 – 819/825-9994; Fax: 819/825-6741	900
Vancouver, BC	CFUN	CHUM Ltd., #300, 380 West 2nd Ave., Vancouver BC V5Y 1C8 – 604/871-9000; Fax: 604/871-2901	1410
Vancouver, BC	CHMB	Mainstream Braodcasting Corp., #100, 1200 West 73 Ave., Vancouver BC V6P 6G5 – 604/263-1320; Fax: 604/263-0320; Email: chmb@am1320.com; http://www.am1320.com	1320
Vancouver, BC	CIMA	Monarch Broadcasting Ltd., #101, 1199 West Pender St., Vancouver BC V6E 2R1 – 604/669-1040; Fax: 604/684-7911	1040
Vancouver, BC	CJVB	YBC Holdings Ltd., #101, 814 Richards St., Vancouver BC V6B 3A7 – 604/688-9931; Fax: 604/688-6559	1470
Vancouver, BC	CKBD	Great Pacific Industries Inc., 1401 - 8 Ave. West, Vancouver BC V6H 1C9 – 604/731-6111; Fax: 604/731-0493	600

Canadian Almanac & Directory 1997

5-206 FM BROADCASTING STATIONS

LOCATION	CALL	*CBC Stations/Affiliates †French Language Stations	FREQ.
Vancouver, BC	CKLG	Shaw Radio Ltd., 1006 Richards St., Vancouver BC V6B 1S8 – 604/681-7511; Fax: 604/681-9134.	730
Vancouver, BC	CKST	#100, 856 Homer St., Vancouver BC V6B 2W5 – 604/669-1040; Fax: 604/684-6949.	1040
Vancouver, BC	CKWX	Rogers Broadcasting Ltd., 2440 Ash St., Vancouver BC V5Z 4J6 – 604/873-2599; Fax: 604/877-4494.	1130
Vancouver, BC	CISL	See Richmond (CISL).	650
Vancouver, BC	*CBU	CBC, 700 Hamilton St., PO Box 4600, Vancouver BC V6B 4A2 – 604/662-6920; Fax: 604/662-6088.	690
Vanderhoof, BC	CIVH	Cariboo Central Interior Radio Inc., 150 West Columbia St., PO Box 1370, Vanderhoof BC V0J 3A0 – 250/567-4914; Fax: 250/567-4982.	1340
Vernon, BC	CICF	Okanagan Radio Ltd., 2800 - 31 St., Vernon BC V1T 5H4 – 250/545-9222; Fax: 250/549-8375; URL: http://www.mix105.com.	1050
Vernon, BC	CJIB	Rogers Broadcasting Ltd., 3313 - 32 Ave., Vernon BC V1T 2E1 – 250/545-2141; Fax: 250/545-9008.	940
Victoria, BC	CFAX	Seacoast Communications Group Inc., 825 Broughton St., Victoria BC V8W 1E5 – 250/386-1070; Fax: 250/386-5775; Email: cfax@islandnet.com; URL: http://www.cfax1070.com	1070
Victoria, BC	CJVI	Rogers Broadcasting Ltd., 817 Fort St., Victoria BC V8W 1H6 – 250/382-0900; Fax: 250/382-4358; Email: asimpson@rci.rogers.com.	900
Victoria, BC	CKXM	OK Radio Group Ltd., 3795 Carey Rd., Victoria BC V8Z 6T8 – 250/475-6611; Fax: 250/475-6626; URL: http://www.ckxm.com.	1200
Victoriaville, PQ	†CFDA	Les Réseau des Appalaches, 55, rue St-Jean Baptiste, CP 490, Victoriaville PQ G6P 6T3 – 819/752-5545; Fax: 819/752-7552.	1380
Ville-Marie, PQ	*†CKVM	Radio-Témiscamingue inc., CP 3000, Ville-Marie PQ J0Z 3W0 – 819/629-2710; Fax: 819/622-0716.	710
Wainwright, AB	CKKY	Nor-Net Communications Ltd., 1037 - 2nd Ave., Wainwright AB T9W 1K7 – 403/875-9153; Fax: 403/842-4636.	830
Ward Creek, NB	CJCW	See Sussex (CJCW).	950
Waterloo, ON	CKKW	CHUM Ltd., 255 King St. North, Waterloo ON N2J 4V2 – 519/884-4470; Fax: 519/884-6482.	1090
Wawa, ON	CJWA	Pelmorex Radio, 55 Broadway Ave., Wawa ON P0S 1K0 – 705/856-4555; Fax: 705/856-1520.	1240
Welland, ON	CHOW	R.B. Communications, RR#23, Welland ON L3B 5R6 – 905/732-4433; Fax: 905/372-4780.	1470
Welland, ON	CRNC	Niagara College, PO Box 1005, Welland ON L3B 5S2 – 905/735-2211, ext.7434; Fax: 905/735-7987.	closed circuit
Westlock, AB	CFOK	Nor-Net Communications Ltd., 9701 - 99 St., PO Box 1800, Westlock AB T0G 2L0 – 403/349-4421; Fax: 403/349-6259.	1370
Wetaskiwin, AB	CKJR	Nor-Net Communications Ltd., 5220 - 51 Ave., Wetaskiwin AB T9A 3A2 – 403/352-0144; Fax: 403/352-0606.	1440
Weyburn, SK	CFSL	Golden West Broadcasting Ltd., PO Box 340, Weyburn SK S4H 2K2 – 306/848-1190; Fax: 306/842-2720.	1190
White Rock, BC	KARI	Birch Bay Broadcasting Co. Ltd., PO Box 75150, White Rock BC V4A 9M4 – 604/536-7733; Fax: 360/371-7617.	550
Whitecourt, AB	CFYR	See Edson (CJYR).	1400
Whitehorse, YT	CKRW	Klondike Broadcasting Co. Ltd., #203, 4103 - 4 Ave., Whitehorse YT Y1A 1H6 – 403/668-6100; Fax: 403/668-4209.	610
Whitehorse, YT	*CFWH	CBC, 210 Elliott St., Whitehorse YT Y1A 2A2 – 403/668-8400; Fax: 403/668-8408.	570
Williams Lake, BC	CKWL	Cariboo Central Interior Radio Inc., 83 South 1 Ave., Williams Lake BC V2G 1H4 – 250/392-6551; Fax: 250/392-4142.	570
Windsor, NS	CFAB	See Kentville (CKEN).	1450
Windsor, ON	CKLW	CHUM Ltd., 1640 Ouellette Ave., Windsor ON N8X 1L1 – 519/258-8888; Fax: 519/258-0182.	800
Windsor, ON	CKWW	CHUM Ltd., 1640 Ouellette Ave., Windsor ON N8X 1L1 – 519/258-8888; Fax: 519/258-0182.	580
Windsor, ON	*CBE	CBC, 825 Riverside Dr. West, Windsor ON N9A 5K9 – 519/255-3411; Fax: 519/255-3443.	1550
Windsor, ON	*†CBEF	Société Radio-Canada, 825 Riverside Dr. West, Windsor ON N9A 5K9 – 519/255-3411; Fax: 519/255-3573.	540
Wingham, ON	CKNX	Blackburn Radio Inc., 215 Carling Terrace, Wingham ON N0G 2W0 – 519/357-1310; Fax: 519/357-1897.	920
Winnipeg, MB	CIFX	CHUM Ltd., 1445 Pembina Hwy., Winnipeg MB R3T 5C2 – 204/477-5120; Fax: 204/453-8777.	1290
Winnipeg, MB	CJOB	Westcom Radio Group Ltd., 930 Portage Ave., Winnipeg MB R3G 0P8 – 204/786-2471; Fax: 204/783-4512.	680
Winnipeg, MB	CKJS	CKJS Ltd., 520 Corydon Ave., Winnipeg MB R3L 0P1 – 204/477-1221; Fax: 204/453-8244.	810
Winnipeg, MB	CKY	Rogers Broadcasting, Polo Park, Winnipeg MB R3G 0L7 – 204/788-3400; Fax: 204/788-3401.	580
Winnipeg, MB	CMOR	Red River Community College, #DM20, 2055 Notre Dame Ave., Winnipeg MB R3H 0J9 – 204/632-2475, 7896.	closed circuit
Winnipeg, MB	CFQX	See Selkirk (CFQX-FM)	
Winnipeg, MB	*†CKSB	Société Radio-Canada, CP 160, Winnipeg MB R3C 2H1 – 204/788-3236; Fax: 204/788-3245.	1050
Winnipeg, MB	*CBW	CBC, 541 Portage Ave., PO Box 160, Winnipeg MB R3C 2H1 – 204/788-3222; Fax: 204/788-3225.	990
Woodstock, NB	CJCJ	Carleton-Victoria Broadcasting Co. Ltd., 131 Queen St., PO Box 920, Woodstock NB E0J 2B0 – 506/325-3030; Fax: 506/325-3031.	920
Yarmouth, NS	CJLS	Radio CJLS Ltd., #201, 328 Main St., Yarmouth NS B5A 1E4 – 902/742-7175; Fax: 902/742-3143.	1340
Yellowknife, NT	CJCD	CJCD Radio Ltd., PO Box 218, Yellowknife NT X1A 2N2 – 403/920-4636; Fax: 403/920-4033.	1240
Yellowknife, NT	*CFYK	CBC, PO Box 160, Yellowknife NT X1A 2N2 – 403/920-5400; Fax: 403/920-5440.	1340
Yorkton, SK	CJGX	Yorkton Broadcasting Co. Ltd., 120 Smith St. East, PO Box 9400, Yorkton SK S3N 3V3 – 306/782-2256; Fax: 306/783-4994.	940

FM BROADCASTING STATIONS

Abbotsford, BC	CKSR-FM	See Chilliwack (CKSR-FM).	104.9/107.5
Ajax, ON	CJKX-FM	Durham Radio Inc., #201, 339 Westney Rd. South, Ajax ON L1S 7J6 – 905/428-9600; Fax: 905/686-2444; Email: kx96fm@hazel.com; URL: http://www.hazel.com/kx96fm.	95.9
Alma, PQ	CKYK-FM	Groupe Radio Antenne 6, 460, Sacré-Coeur ouest, Alma PQ G8B 1L9 – 418/662-6888; Fax: 418/662-6070.	95.5
Argentia, NF	CFOZ-FM	See St. John's (CHOZ-FM).	100.3
Armstrong, BC	CKAL-FM	See Vernon (CICF).	98.7
Athabasca, AB	CKUA-FM-10	See Edmonton (CKUA-FM).	98.3
Baie-Comeau, PQ	CHLC-FM	COGECO Radio-Télévision Inc., 399, de Puyjalon, Baie-Comeau PQ G5C 2Z7 – 418/589-3771; Fax: 418/589-9086.	97.1
Barrie, ON	CFJB-FM	Rock 95 (Barrie Orillia Ltd.), #205, 400 Bayfield St., PO Box 95, Barrie ON L4M 5A1 – 705/721-1291; Fax: 705/721-7842.	95.7
Barrie, ON	CHAY-FM	Shaw Radio Ltd., PO Box 937, Barrie ON L4M 4Y6 – 705/737-3511; Fax: 705/737-0603; Email: chayinfo@chayfm.com.	93.1
Barrie, ON	CIQB-FM	Power Broadcasting Inc., 129 Ferris Lane, PO Box 101, Barrie ON L4M 4V1 – 705/726-1011; Fax: 705/726-0022; Email: talkback@b101fm.com; URL: http://www.b101fm.com.	101.1
Belleville, ON	CJLX-FM	Loyalist College Radio Inc., PO Box 4200, Belleville ON K8N 5B9 – 613/969-0923; Fax: 613/966-1993; Email: cjix@loyalistc.on.ca.	closed circuit; 92.3

Canadian Almanac & Directory 1997

FM BROADCASTING STATIONS 5-207

LOCATION	CALL	*CBC Stations/Affiliates †French Language Stations	FREQ.
Belleville, ON	CIGL-FM	Quinte Broadcasting Co. Ltd., 10 Front St. South, PO Box 488, Belleville ON K8N 5B2 – 613/969-5555; Fax: 613/969-0288	97.1
Belleville, ON	CJOJ-FM	354 Pinnacle St., Belleville ON K8N 3B4 – 613/966-0955; Fax: 613/967-2565	95.5
Big White Village, BC	CKIQ-FM-1	See Kelowna (CKIQ)	98.1
Boston Bar, BC	CKGO-FM-1	See Hope (CKGO)	106.1
Bracebridge, ON	CFBG-FM	Telemedia Communications Ontario Inc., 50 Balls Dr., Bracebridge ON P1L 1T5 – 705/645-2218; Fax: 705/645-6957	100.9
Brandon, MB	CKX-FM	Craig Broadcast Systems Inc., 2940 Victoria Ave., Brandon MB R7B 0N2 – 204/728-1150; Fax: 204/727-2505	96.1
Brantford, ON	CKPC-FM	Telephone City Broadcast Ltd., 571 West St., Brantford ON N3T 5P8 – 519/759-1000; Fax: 519/753-1470	92.1
Brockville, ON	CHXL-FM	St. Lawrence Broadcasting Co. Ltd., PO Box 666, Brockville ON K6V 5V9 – 613/345-1666; Fax: 613/342-2438; Email: river@theriverrolls.com; URL: http://www.theriverrolls.com	103.7
Burlington, ON	CING-FM	Burlington Broadcasting Inc., 4144 South Service Rd., Burlington ON L7L 4X5 – 905/681-1079; Fax: 905/681-1758; Email: energy108@cdx.net; URL: http://www.cdx.net/energy108/	107.9
Burnaby, BC	CJSF-FM	Simon Fraser Campus Radio, TC216, Simon Fraser University, Burnaby BC V5A 1S6 – 604/291-3727; Fax: 604/291-3695	93.9
Burnaby, BC	CFML-FM	BC Institute of Technology, 2700 Willingdon Ave., Burnaby BC V5G 3H2 – 604/432-8510; Fax: 604/432-1792; Email: bcitbcst@bcit.bc.ca; URL: http://www.bcit.bc.ca	104.5;cable
Burns Lake, BC	CJFW-FM	See Terrace (CJFW-FM)	92.9
Cabano, PQ	†CFVD-FM-1	See Dégelis (CFVD)	102.7
Cache Creek, BC	CFFM-FM	See Kamloops (CFJC)	95.3
Calgary, AB	CBR-FM	See Calgary (CBR)	102.1
Calgary, AB	CHFM-FM	Rogers Broadcasting Ltd., 3320 - 17 Ave. SW, Calgary AB T3E 6X6 – 403/246-9696; Fax: 403/246-6660	95.9
Calgary, AB	CJAY-FM	Standard Radio Inc., PO Box 2750, Stn M, Calgary AB T2P 4P8 – 403/240-5850; Fax: 403/240-5801; URL: http://www.cjay92.com	92.1
Calgary, AB	CJSW-FM	University of Calgary, #127, MacEwan Hall, Calgary AB T2N 1N4 – 403/220-3904	90.9
Calgary, AB	CKIK-FM	CKIK-FM Ltd., 1107 - 17 Ave. SW, Calgary AB T2P 1B2 – 403/264-0107; Fax: 403/232-6492	107.3
Calgary, AB	CKRY-FM	Redmond Broadcasting Ltd., #500, 1121 Centre St. North, Calgary AB T2E 7K6 – 403/276-6105; Fax: 403/230-4343; Email: feedback@country105.com; URL: http://www.country105.com	105.1
Calgary, AB	CKUA-FM	Alberta Educational Communications Corp., 4825 Richard Rd. South, Calgary AB T33 6K6 – 403/428-7595; Fax: 403/452-7233	93.7
Camrose, AB	CLCR	Augustana University College, 4901 - 46 Ave., Camrose AB T4V 2R3 – 403/672-2999	closed circuit
Cap-aux-Meules, PQ	†CFIM-FM	Diffusion Communautaire des Îles inc., CP 490, Cap-aux-Meules PQ G0B 1K0 – 418/986-5233; Fax: 418/986-5319	92.7
Carleton, PQ	†CIEU-FM	Diffusion Communautaire-Baie des Chaleurs inc., 1645, boul Perron est, CP 3000, Carleton PQ G0C 1J0 – 418/364-7094; Fax: 418/364-3150	94.9
Centreville, ON	CKNX-FM	See Wingham (CKNX-FM)	104.9
Charlevoix, PQ	†CIHO-FM	See St-Hilarion (CIHO-FM)	96.3
Charlottetown, PE	CHLQ-FM	Maritime Broadcasting Ltd., 141 Kent St., Charlottetown PE C1A 7M7 – 902/566-5550; Fax: 902/566-1338	93.1
Charlottetown, PE	*†CBCT-FM	CBC, 430 University Ave., CP 2230, Charlottetown PE C1A 8B9 – 902/629-6400; Fax: 902/629-6518; URL: http://www.isn.net/cbc/	96.1
Chatham, ON	CKSY-FM	Bea-Ver Communications Inc., 117 Keil Dr., PO Box 100, Chatham ON N7M 5K1 – 519/354-2200; Fax: 519/354-2880; Email: cksyfm@mnsi.net; URL: http://www.mnsi.net~cksyfm	95.1
Chicoutimi, PQ	†CFIX-FM	Télémédia Communications inc., CP 1506, Chicoutimi PQ G7H 5K3 – 418/543-9797; Fax: 418/543-7968	96.9
Chicoutimi, PQ	†CJAB-FM	Radiomutuel inc., 121, rue Racine est, CP 1090, Chicoutimi PQ G7H 5G4 – 418/545-9450; Fax: 418/545-9186	94.5
Chicoutimi, PQ	*†CBJ-FM	See Chicoutimi (CBJ)	100.9
Chilliwack, BC	CKSR-FM	Star-FM Radio Inc., PO Box 386, Chilliwack BC V2P 6J7 – 604/795-7827; Fax: 604/795-6643	104.9/107.5
Clarenville, NF	CHOZ-FM	See St. John's (CHOZ-FM)	105.3
Clearwater, BC	CFJC-FM-1	See Kamloops (CFJC)	102.9
Cobourg, ON	CFMX-FM	See Toronto (CFMX-FM)	96.3
Collingwood, ON	CKCB	Power Broadcasting Inc., 1400 Hwy. 26 East, Collingwood ON L9Y 4W2 – 705/444-1400; Fax: 705/444-6776	95.1
Corner Brook, NF	CKOZ-FM	See St. John's (CHOZ-FM)	92.3
Cornwall, ON	CFLG-FM	Tri-Co Broadcasting Ltd., 237 Water St. East, PO Box 969, Cornwall ON K6H 5V1 – 613/932-5180; Fax: 613/938-0355; Email: cflgradio@cnwl.igs.net	104.5
Cornwall, ON	CKON-FM	Akwesasne Communications Society, PO Box 1496, Cornwall ON K6H 5V5 – 613/575-2100; Fax: 613/575-2935	97.3
Cornwall, ON	†CHOD-FM	Radio communautaire Cornwall-Alexandria inc., #202, 1111 Montreal Rd., Cornwall ON K6H 1E1 – 613/936-2463; Fax: 613/936-2568	92.1
Cranbrook, BC	CKKR-FM	Columbia Kootenay Broadcasting Co. Ltd., 19 - 9 Ave. South, Cranbrook BC V1C 2L9 – 250/426-2224; Fax: 250/426-5520	104.7
Dartmouth, NS	CFRQ-FM	NewCap Broadcasting, 45 Alderney Dr., PO Box 1007, Dartmouth NS B2Y 3Z7 – 902/835-6100; Fax: 902/835-1511	104.3
Deer Lake, NF	CFDL-FM	See Corner Brook (CFCB)	97.9
Digby, NS	CJLS-FM-2	See Yarmouth (CJLS)	93.5
Dolbeau, PQ	†CHVD-FM	See Dolbeau (CHVD)	92.1
Drayton Valley, AB	CIBW-FM	Big West Communications Corp., #3, 5606 - 55 St., PO Box 929, Drayton Valley AB T7A 1V3 – 403/542-9290; Fax: 403/542-9319	92.9
Drumheller, AB	CKUA-FM	See Edmonton (CKUA)	91.3
Drummondville, PQ	†CJDM-FM	Diffusion Power inc., #203, 412, rue Hériot, Drummondville PQ J2B 1B5 – 819/474-1892; Fax: 819/474-6610	92.1
Edmonton, AB	CKER	CKER Radio Ltd., 6005 - 103 St., Edmonton AB T6H 2H3 – 403/438-1480; Fax: 403/437-5129	101.9
Edmonton, AB	CFBR-FM	Standard Radio Inc., #100, 18520 Stony Plain Rd., Edmonton AB T5S 2E2 – 403/486-2800; Fax: 403/444-6927	100.3
Edmonton, AB	CIRK-FM	Radio One Edmonton Corp., 10250 - 108 St., Edmonton AB T5J 2X3 – 403/428-8597; Fax: 403/428-7168	97.3
Edmonton, AB	CISN-FM	Shaw Radio Ltd., 10550 - 102 St., Edmonton AB T5H 2T3 – 403/428-1104; Fax: 403/426-6502	103.9
Edmonton, AB	CKNG-FM	Westcom Radio Group Ltd., 5204 - 84 St., Edmonton AB T6E 5N8 – 403/469-6992; Fax: 403/469-5937	92.5
Edmonton, AB	CKRA-FM	NewCap Inc., 4752 - 99 St., Edmonton AB T6E 5H5 – 403/437-4996; Fax: 403/436-9803	96.3
Edmonton, AB	CJSR-FM	First Alberta Campus Radio Association, #224 SUB, Edmonton AB T6G 2J7 – 403/492-5244; Fax: 403/492-3121; Email: cjsrfm@gpu.scv.ualberta.ca; URL: http://www.ualberta.ca/~cjcrfm/	
Edmonton, AB	CKUA-FM	CKUA Radio Foundation, 10526 Jasper Ave., 4th Fl., Edmonton AB T5J 1Z5 – 403/428-7595; Fax: 403/728-7624; Email: ckua@freenet.edmonton.ab.ca; URL: http://www.ckua.cadvision.com/ckua	94.9

Canadian Almanac & Directory 1997

5-208 FM BROADCASTING STATIONS

LOCATION	CALL	*CBC Stations/Affiliates †French Language Stations	FREQ.
Edmonton, AB	*CBX-FM	See Edmonton (CBX)	90.9
Edson, AB	CKUA-FM-8	See Edmonton (CKUA-FM)	103.7
Egmont, BC	CIEG-FM	See Squamish (CISQ-FM)	107.5
Etobicoke, ON	CKHC-FM	Humber College, 205 Humber College Blvd., Etobicoke ON M9W 5L7 – 416/675-5046	closed circuit
Fermont, PQ	†CFMF-FM	Radio Communautaire Fermont inc., 20, Place Daviault, CP 280, Fermont PQ G0G 1J0 – 418/287-3147; Fax: 418/287-5776	103.1
Fort-Coulonge, PQ	†CHIP-FM	La Radio du Pontiac inc., 33, rue Romain, CP 820, Fort-Coulonge PQ J0X 1V0 – 819/683-3155; Fax: 819/683-3211	94.5
Fort McMurray, AB	CKYX-FM	OK Radio Group Ltd., 9912 Franklin Ave., Fort McMurray AB T9H 2K5 – 403/743-2246; Fax: 403/791-7250	97.9
Fort McMurray, AB	CKUA-FM-11	See Edmonton (CKUA-FM)	96.7
Fort McMurray, AB	CJOK-FM	See Fort McMurray (CJOK)	95.7
Fredericton, NB	CKHJ-FM	Radio One Ltd., 206 Rookwood Ave., Fredericton NB E3B 2M2 – 506/451-9111; Fax: 506/452-2345	105.3
Fredericton, NB	CHSR-FM	CHSR Broadcasting Inc., PO Box 4400, Fredericton NB E3B 5A3 – 506/453-4985; Fax: 506/453-4958; Email: chsr@mi.net; URL: http://www.unb.ca/web/chsr	97.9
Fredericton, NB	CIBX-FM	Radio One Ltd., 206 Rookwood Ave., Fredericton NB E3B 2M2 – 506/455-1069; Fax: 506/452-2345	106.9
Fredericton, NB	*CBZ-FM	See Fredericton (CBZ)	101.5
Fredericton, NB	*†CBAF-FM-14	See Moncton (CBAF-FM)	101.5
Gaspé, PQ	†CJRG-FM	Radio Gaspé inc., 162, rue Jacques Cartier, CP 380, Gaspé PQ G0C 1R0 – 418/368-3511; Fax: 418/368-1663	94.5
Gatineau, PQ	†CKTF-FM	Radio-Média inc., #200, 105, rue Bellehumeur, Gatineau PQ J8T 6K5 – 819/243-5555; Fax: 819/243-6828	104.1
Geraldton, ON	CFNO-FM	See Marathon (CFNO-FM)	107.1
Gold River, BC	CJGR-FM	See Campbell River (CFWB)	101.1
Grand Falls, NF	CHOZ-FM	See St. John's (CHOZ-FM)	95.9
Grand Manan, NB	*†CBZA-FM	See Moncton (CBAF-FM)	103.7
Grande Prairie, AB	CFGP	CFGP Radio, Division of OK Radio Group Ltd., #200, 9835 - 101 Ave., Grande Prairie AB T8V 5V4 – 403/532-9700; Fax: 403/532-1600; Email: cfgp@ccinet.ab.ca; http://www.terranet.ab.ca/sunfm	97.7
Grande Prairie, AB	*†CHFA-FM-5	See Edmonton (CHFA)	90.5
Grande Vallée, PQ	†CJMC-FM-3	See Ste-Anne-des-Monts (CJMC)	
Guelph, ON	CFRU-FM	Radio Gryphon, University Centre, Level 2, University of Guelph, Guelph ON N1G 2W1 – 519/824-4120, ext.6919; Fax: 519/763-9603; Email: cfru@tdg.uoguelph.ca; URL: http://tdg.uoguelph.ca/~cfru9	3.3
Guelph, ON	CIMJ-FM	Power Broadcasting Inc., 75 Speedvale Ave. East, Guelph ON N1E 6M3 – 519/824-7000; Fax: 519/824-4118; Email: power@in.on.ca	106.1
Halifax, NS	CHFX-FM	Maritime Broadcasting Co. Ltd., PO Box 400, Halifax NS B3J 2R2 – 902/422-1651; Fax: 902/422-5330	101.9
Halifax, NS	CIEZ-FM	Sun Radio Ltd., #800, 1550 Bedford Hwy., Halifax NS B4A 1E6 – 902/835-6100; Fax: 902/835-1511	96.5
Halifax, NS	CIOO-FM	CHUM Ltd., 2900 Agricola St., PO Box 1653, Halifax NS B3J 2Z4 – 902/453-2524; Fax: 902/453-3132; Email: c100@newedge.ca; URL: http://www.newedge.ca/c100	100.1
Halifax, NS	CKDU-FM	Dalhousie University, Student Union Bldg., 6136 University Ave., Halifax NS B3H 4J2 – 902/494-6479	97.5
Halifax, NS	CFRQ-FM	See Dartmouth (CFRQ-FM)	104.3
Halifax, NS	*CBH-FM	CBC, 5600 Sackville St., PO Box 3000, Halifax NS B3J 3E9 – 902/420-8311; Fax: 902/420-4429	102.7
Halifax, NS	*CBHA-FM	CBC, 5600 Sackville St., PO Box 3000, Halifax NS B3J 3E9 – 902/420-8311; Fax: 902/420-4429	90.5
Hamilton, ON	CFMU-FM	McMaster University, Room 301, Hamilton Hall, McMaster University, Hamilton ON L8S 4K1 – 905/525-9140, ext.27208; Fax: 905/529-3208; Email: cfmu@freenet.hamilton.on.ca; URL: http://www.freenet.hamilton.on.ca/~ip007/cfmu.html	93.3
Hamilton, ON	CHMR-FM	Mohawk College, 135 Fennell Ave., PO Box 2034, Hamilton ON L8N 3T2 – 905/575-2175; Fax: 905/575-2385	closed circuit/cable; 91.7
Hamilton, ON	CJXY-FM	Western Radio Group Ltd., #900, 875 Main St. West, Hamilton ON L8S 4R1 – 905/521-9900; Fax: 905/521-2306	95.3
Hamilton, ON	CKLH-FM	Radiocorp Inc., #401, 883 Upper Wentworth St., Hamilton ON L9A 4Y6 – 905/574-1150; Fax: 905/574-6429; Email: klite@radiocorp.ca; URL: http://www.radiocorp.ca	102.9
Happy Valley, NF	*CFGB-FM	CBC, PO Box 1270, Happy Valley NF A0P 1E0 – 709/896-2911; Fax: 709/896-8900	89.5
Hawkesbury, ON	†CHPR-FM	Radio Nord Inc., #101, 115 Main St. East, Hawkesbury ON K6A 1A1 – 613/632-1000; Fax: 613/632-1110	102.1
Hay River, NT	CKHR-FM	Hay River Broadcasting Society, PO Box 36, Hay River NT X0E 0R0 – 403/874-2547	107.3
Hay River, NT	CFYK-FM	See Yellowknife (CFYK)	93.7
Hay River, NT	CJCD-FM-1	See Yellowknife (CJCD)	100.1
Hearst, ON	†CINN-FM	Radio de l'Epinette Noire inc., CP 2648, Hearst ON P0L 1N0 – 705/372-1011; Fax: 705/362-7411; Email: cinn@nt.net	94.1
Hinton, AB	CKUA-FM-7	See Edmonton (CKUA-FM)	102.5
Houston, BC	CFJW-FM	See Terrace (CJFW-FM)	105.5
Hull, PQ	†CIMF-FM	Télémédia Communications inc., 150, rue Edmonton, Hull PQ J8Y 3S6 – 819/770-2463; Fax: 819/770-9338	94.9
Huntsville, ON	CFBK-FM	Muskoka-Parry Sound Broadcasting, 15 Main St. East, PO Box 1055, Huntsville ON P0A 1K0 – 705/789-4461; Fax: 705/789-1269	105.5
Joliette, PQ	CJLM-FM	Coopérative de Radiodiffusion MF 103,5 de Lanaudière, 540, rue St-Thomas, Joliette PQ J6E 3R4 – 514/756-1035; Fax: 514/756-8097	103.5
Jonquière, PQ	†CHOC-FM	Radio Communautaire du Saguenay inc., CP 306, Jonquière PQ G7X 5M4 – 418/542-2265; Fax: 418/547-5356	92.5
Kahnawake, PQ	CKRK-FM	Kahnawake Broadcasting Service, PO Box 1050, Kahnawake PQ J0L 1B0 – 514/638-1313; Fax: 514/638-4009	103.7
Kamloops, BC	CIFM-FM	Jim Pattison Group, 460 Pemberton Terrace, Kamloops BC V2C 1T5 – 250/372-3322; Fax: 250/374-0445; URL: http://www.cifm.com	98.3
Kamloops, BC	CKRV-FM	NL Broadcasting, 611 Lansdowne St., Kamloops BC V2C 1Y6 – 250/372-2197; Fax: 250/372-0682	97.5
Kamloops, BC	CFJC-FM	See Kamloops (CFJC)	99.5
Kaslo, BC	CICF-FM-3	See Trail (CKKC)	95.3
Kelowna, BC	CILK-FM	SILK-FM Broadcasting Ltd., 1598 Pandosy St., Kelowna BC V1Y 1P4 – 250/860-1010; Fax: 250/860-0505	101.5
Kelowna, BC	CKLZ-FM	Seacoast Communications Group Inc., 3805 Lakeshore Rd., Kelowna BC V1W 3K6 – 250/763-1047; Fax: 250/762-2141; Email: cklz-fm@awmc.com; URL: http://www.cklz.com	104.7
Kelowna, BC	CKBL-FM	Four Seasons Radio Ltd., 2419 Hwy. 97 North, Kelowna BC V1X 4J2 – 250/763-9099; Fax: 250/860-8856	99.9
Kelowna, BC	*CBTK-FM	CBC, 243 Lawrence Ave., Kelowna BC V1Y 6L2 – 250/861-3781; Fax: 250/861-6644	88.9
Kentville, NS	CKWM-FM	Annapolis Valley Radio, PO Box 310, Kentville NS B4N 1H5 – 902/678-2111; Fax: 902/678-9894	97.7
Keremeos-Cawston, BC	CIGV-FM-1	See Penticton (CIGV-FM)	98.9
Kingston, ON	CFLY-FM	St. Lawrence Broadcasting Co. Ltd., 99 Brock St., PO Box 1380, Kingston ON K7L 4Y5 – 613/544-1380; Fax: 613/546-9751	98.3

Canadian Almanac & Directory 1997

FM BROADCASTING STATIONS

LOCATION	CALL	*CBC Stations/Affiliates †French Language Stations	FREQ.
Kingston, ON	CFMK-FM	Power Broadcasting Inc., 479 Counter St., Kingston ON K7M 7J3 – 613/549-1911; Fax: 613/549-7974; URL: http://www.spiritofkingston.com	96.3
Kingston, ON	CFRC-FM	Queen's University, Carruthers Hall, Kingston ON K7L 3N6 – 613/545-2121; Fax: 613/545-6049	101.9
Kingston, ON	*†CJBC-FM-2	See Toronto (CJBC)	99.5
Kitchener, ON	CHYM-FM	Rogers Broadcasting Ltd., 305 King St. West, Kitchener ON N2G 4E4 – 519/743-2611; Fax: 519/743-7510	96.7
Kitchener, ON	CFCA-FM	See Waterloo (CFCA-FM)	105.3
Kitimat, BC	*†CJFW-FM-1	See Terrace (CJFW-FM)	92.9
Kivalliq, NT	*CBQR-FM	CBC, Kivalliq NT X0C 0G0 – 819/645-2632	105.1
Kootenay Lake, BC	CKKC-FM-1	See Trail (CJAT)	120.0
La Pocatière, PQ	†CHOX-FM	CIBM-FM Mont-Bleu ltée, 1000 - 6 av, CP 550, La Pocatière PQ G0R 1Z0 – 418/856-1310; Fax: 418/856-3747	97.5
La Ronge, SK	*CBKA-FM	CBC, PO Box 959, La Ronge SK S0J 1L0 – 306/425-3324; Fax: 306/425-2270	105.9
Lac-Mégantic, PQ	†CFJO-FM	See Thetford-Mines (CFJO-FM)	101.7
Lachute, PQ	†CJLA-FM	Radio Fusion inc., 385, rue Principale, Lachute PQ J8H 1Y1 – 514/562-8862; Fax: 514/562-1902	104.9
Laval, PQ	†CFGL-FM	Cogeco Radio-Télévision inc., 2830, boul St-Martin est, Laval PQ H7E 5A9 – 514/381-5903; Fax: 514/664-1651	105.7
Leamington, ON	CHYR	The Blackburn Group, 100 Talbot St. East, Leamington ON N8H 1L3 – 519/326-6171; Fax: 519/322-1110	96.7
Leamington, ON	CHYR-FM	KEY Radio, 100 Talbot St. East, Leamington ON N8H 1L3 – 519/326-6171; Fax: 519/322-1110	96.7
Lethbridge, AB	CFRV-FM	Rogers Broadcasting Ltd., PO Box 820, Lethbridge AB T1J 3Z9 – 403/328-1077; Fax: 403/327-5879	107.7
Lethbridge, AB	CKUA-FM-2	See Edmonton (CKUA-FM)	99.3
Lethbridge, AB	*†CHFA-1-FM	See Edmonton (CHFA)	104.3
Lévis, PQ	†CFLS-FM	Radio Etchemin inc., 5, boul de la Rive sud, Lévis PQ G6V 4Y5 – 418/833-2151; Fax: 418/833-4462	102.9
Liverpool, NS	CKBW-FM-1	See Bridgewater (CKBW)	94.5
London, ON	CFPL-FM	Blackburn Radio Inc., 369 York St., PO Box 2580, London ON N6A 4H3 – 519/438-8391; Fax: 519/438-2415; Email: daubrey@cfplradio.com; URL: http://www.mediawb.com	95.9
London, ON	CHRW-FM	University of Western Ontario, #250, UCC Bldg., London ON N6A 3K7 – 519/661-3601; Fax: 519/661-3816	94.7
London, ON	CIQM-FM	Telemedia Communications Ontario Inc., 380 Wellington Rd., PO Box 1410, London ON N6A 5J2 – 519/661-2000; Fax: 519/667-2175	97.5
London, ON	CIXX-FM	Radio Fanshawe Inc., Fanshawe College, 1460 Oxford St. East, London ON N5B 5H1 – 519/453-2810; Fax: 519/452-3139	106.9
London, ON	CJBX-FM	Radio Corp., 743 Wellington Rd. South, London ON N6C 4R5 – 519/686-2525; Fax: 519/686-9067; Email: bx93@odyssey.on.ca	92.7
London, ON	CFRL-FM	Fanshawe College, 1460 Oxford St. East, London ON N5W 5H1 – 519/453-2810; Fax: 519/452-3570	closed circuit
Longueuil, PQ	†CIEL-FM	Radio MF CIEL (1981) inc., 89, St-Charles ouest, Longueuil PQ J4H 1C5 – 514/527-8321; Fax: 514/646-9405	98.5
Longueuil, PQ	CIME-FM	See Ste-Adèle (CIME-FM)	
Lytton, BC	CIAK-FM	See Kamloops (CFJC)	106.1
Magog, PQ	†CIMO-FM	Radio-Média, #100, 1750 rue Sherbrooke, Magog PQ J1X 2T3 – 819/843-1414; Fax: 819/843-7769	106.1
Maniwaki, PQ	†CHGA-FM	Radio communautaire FM de la Haute Gatineau, 163, rue Laurier, Maniwaki PQ J9E 2K6 – 819/449-3959; Fax: 819/449-7331	97.3
Maniwaki, PQ	†CKMG-FM	161, rue Commerciale, Maniwaki PQ J9E 1P1 – 819/449-1211; Fax: 819/449-7457	99.3
Marathon, ON	CFNO-FM	North Superior Broadcasting Ltd., 93 Evergreen Dr., PO Box 1000, Marathon ON P0T 2E0 – 807/229-1010; Fax: 807/229-1686; Email: sbell@marathon.lakeheadu.ca	93.1
Marystown, NF	CIOZ-FM	See St. John's (CHOZ-FM)	96.3
Massett, BC	CJFW-FM-4	See Terrace (CJFW-FM)	92.9
Matane, PQ	†CHOE-FM	Communications Matane inc., 800, av du Phare ouest, CP 605, Matane PQ G4W 1V7 – 418/562-4141; Fax: 418/562-0778	95.3
Medicine Hat, AB	CKUA-FM	See Edmonton (CKUA-FM)	97.3
Merritt, BC	CFJC-FM	See Kamloops (CFJC)	99.5
Merritt, BC	CFFM-FM-3	See Kamloops (CIFM-FM)	103.9
Midland, ON	KICX-FM	Telemedia Communications Ontario Inc., 355 Cranston Cres., PO Box 609, Midland ON L4R 4L3 – 705/526-2268; Fax: 705/526-3060	104.1
Mirabel, PQ	†CJLA-FM	See Lachute (CJLA-FM)	
Mississauga, ON	CFRE-FM	Erindale College, University of Toronto, 3359 Missisauga Rd., Mississauga ON L5L 1C6 – 905/828-5310	
Moncton, NB	CFQM-FM	Maritime Broadcasting System, 1000 St. George Blvd., Moncton NB E1E 4M7 – 506/858-1039; Fax: 506/858-1209	103.9
Moncton, NB	CJMO-FM	Atlantic Stereo Ltd., 27 Arsenault Court, Moncton NB E1E 4J8 – 506/858-5525; Fax: 506/858-5539	103.1
Moncton, NB	†CKUM-FM	Université de Moncton, 159, av Massey, Moncton NB E1A 3E9 – 506/858-4485; Fax: 506/858-4524	105.7
Moncton, NB	*CBA-FM	See Moncton (CBA)	95.5
Moncton, NB	*†CBAF-FM	Société Radio-Canada, 250 Archibald St., CP 950, Moncton NB E1C 8N8 – 506/853-6666; Fax: 506/853-6618	88.5, 98.3
Mont Joli, PQ	†CKMN-FM	See Rimouski (CKMN-FM)	
Montmagny, PQ	†CFEL-FM	Diffusion Power Inc., 191, ch des Poirier, Montmagny PQ G5V 4L2 – 514/248-1122; Fax: 514/248-1951	102.1
Montréal, PQ	CFQR-FM	Mount Royal Broadcasting Inc., #300, 1200, av McGill College, Montréal PQ H3B 4G7 – 514/874-4040; Fax: 514/393-4659	92.5
Montréal, PQ	CHOM-FM	CHUM Ltd., 1310, av Greene, Montréal PQ H3Z 2B5 – 514/937-2466; Fax: 514/931-3977	97.7
Montréal, PQ	†CIBL-FM	Radio communautaire francophone de Montréal, #201, 1691, boul Pie-IX, Montréal PQ H1V 2C3 – 514/526-2581; Fax: 514/526-3583; Email: cibl@generation.net	101.5
Montréal, PQ	CINQ-FM	Radio Centre-Ville St-Louis, 5212, boul St-Laurent, 2e étage, Montréal PQ H2T 1S1 – 514/495-2597; Fax: 514/495-2429	102.3
Montréal, PQ	CITE-FM	Télémedia Communications inc., #602, 1411, rue Peel, Montréal PQ H3A 1S5 – 514/845-2483; Fax: 514/288-1073	107.3
Montréal, PQ	CJFM-FM	Standard Radio Inc., 1411, rue du Fort, Montréal PQ H3H 2R1 – 514/989-2536; Fax: 514/989-2525	95.9
Montréal, PQ	†CKMF-FM	Radiomutuel inc., #120, 1717, boul René-Lévesque est, Montréal PQ H2L 4T9 – 514/529-3229; Fax: 514/529-9308	94.3
Montréal, PQ	CKUT-FM	Radio McGill, 3647, rue University, Montréal PQ H3A 2B3 – 514/398-6787; Fax: 514/398-8261	90.3
Montréal, PQ	CRSG	Concordia University, #647, 1455, boul de Maisonneuve ouest, Montréal PQ H3G 1M8 – 514/848-7401; Fax: 514/848-7450	88.9
Montréal, PQ	†CFGL-FM	See Laval (CFGL-FM)	105.7
Montréal, PQ	CFZZ-FM	See St-Jean-sur-Richelieu (CFZZ)	104.1
Montréal, PQ	CHCR-FM	Canadian Hellenic Cable Radio, 5899 Park Ave., Montréal PQ H2V 4H4 – 514/273-2481; Fax: 514/273-3707	106.5
Montréal, PQ	CKOI-FM	See Verdun (CKOI-FM)	96.9
Montréal, PQ	*†CBF-FM	See Montréal (CBF)	100.7

Canadian Almanac & Directory 1997

5-210 FM BROADCASTING STATIONS

LOCATION	CALL	*CBC Stations/Affiliates †French Language Stations	FREQ.
Montréal, PQ	*CBM-FM	See Montréal (CBM)	93.5
Nakusp, BC	CKAL-FM-1	See Vernon (CICF)	103.1
Nanaimo, BC	CKWV-FM	Central Island Broadcasting Ltd., 4550 Wellington Rd., Nanaimo BC V9T 2H3 – 250/758-1131; Fax: 250/758-4644	
Nelson, BC	CKQR-FM-1	See Castlegar (CKQR)	102.5
Nepean, ON	CKDJ-FM	Radio Algonquin, Algonquin College, 1385 Woodroffe Ave., Nepean ON K2G 1V8 – 613/727-4723, ext.7740; Fax: 613/727-7689; URL: http://www.ckdj.comnet.ca	96.9; closed circuit
New Denver, BC	CICF-FM-2	See Trail (CKKC)	93.5
New Westminster, BC	CFMI-FM	Westcom Radio Group Ltd., 815 McBride Plaza, New Westminster BC V3L 2C1 – 604/521-4808; Fax: 604/522-4168	101.1
Newmarket, ON	CKDX-FM	1093641 Ontario Ltd., #402, 465 Davis Dr., Newmarket ON L3Y 2P1 – 905/898-1100; Fax: 905/853-4433; Email: ckdx@idirect.com	88.5
Niagara Falls, ON	CKEY-FM	CJRN 710 Inc., PO Box 710, Niagara Falls ON L2E 6X7 – 905/356-6710; Fax: 905/356-0696	101.1
Niagara Falls, ON	CJRN-FM	CJRN 710 Inc., PO Box 710, Niagara Falls ON L2E 6X7 – 905/356-6710; Fax: 905/356-0696	101.0
North Bay, ON	CKAT-FM	Telemedia Communications Ontario Inc., 743 Main St. East, PO Box 3000, North Bay ON P1B 8K8 – 705/474-2000; Fax: 705/474-7761	101.9
North Bay, ON	CRFM-FM	Canadore Radio, Canadore College, 100 College Dr., PO Box 5001, North Bay ON P1B 8K9 – 705/474-7601; Fax: 705/474-2384	89.9
Oakville, ON	CORS	CORS Radio Sheridan, Sheridan College, 1430 Trafalgar Rd., Oakville ON L6H 2L1 – 905/845-9430, ext.2302; Fax: 905/815-4043	closed circuit
100 Mile House, BC	CFFM-FM-5	See Williams Lake (CFFM-FM)	95.9
Orangeville, ON	CIDC-FM	Dufferin Communications Inc., 287 Broadway Ave., Orangeville ON L9W 1L2 – 519/942-1030; Fax: 519/942-2550	103.5
Orillia, ON	CICX-FM	Telemedia Communications Ontario Inc., 7 Progress Dr., Orillia ON L3V 5C9 – 705/326-3511; Fax: 705/326-1816	105.9
Oshawa, ON	CKGE-FM	Power Broadcasting Inc., 360 King St. West, Oshawa ON L1J 2K2 – 905/571-1350; Fax: 905/571-1150	94.9
Ottawa, ON	CHEZ-FM	CHEZ-FM Inc., #509, 126 York St., Ottawa ON K1N 5T5 – 613/562-1061; Fax: 613/562-1515	106.1
Ottawa, ON	CHUO-FM	Radio Ottawa Inc., University of Ottawa, #227, 85 University Ave., Ottawa ON K1N 6N5 – 613/562-5965; Fax: 613/562-5848	89.1
Ottawa, ON	CJMJ-FM	RAWLCO Communications Ltd., 1575 Carling Ave., Ottawa ON K1Z 7M3 – 613/798-2565; Fax: 613/729-9829	100.3
Ottawa, ON	CKQB-FM	Standard Radio Inc., 1504 Merivale Rd., Ottawa ON K2E 6Z5 – 613/225-1069; Fax: 613/226-3381; Email: thebear@magi.com; URL: http://www.thebear.net	106.9
Ottawa, ON	CKBY-FM	Rogers Broadcasting Ltd., #1900, Tower B, Place de Ville, 112 Kent St., Ottawa ON K1P 6J1 – 613/238-7482; Fax: 613/236-5382; Email: y105@ottawa.net; URL: http://www.ottawa.net/~105/	105.3
Ottawa, ON	CKCU-FM	Radio Carleton, Unicentre, Carleton University, #517, 1125 Colonel By Dr., Ottawa ON K1S 5B6 – 613/520-2898; Fax: 613/520-4060	93.1
Ottawa, ON	CKKL-FM	CHUM Ltd., 1900 Walkley Rd., Ottawa ON K1H 8P4 – 613/526-9393; Fax: 613/523-6423	93.9
Ottawa, ON	†CIMF-FM	See Hull (CIMF-FM)	94.9
Ottawa, ON	CBRT-FM	See Nepean (CKDJ-FM)	
Ottawa, ON	†CBOX-FM	See Ottawa (CBOF-FM)	102.5
Ottawa, ON	*CBO	CBC, PO Box 3220, Stn C, Ottawa ON K1Y 1E4 – 613/562-8400; Fax: 613/562-8408	91.5
Ottawa, ON	*†CBOF-FM	Société Radio-Canada, CP 3220, Succ C, Ottawa ON K1Y 1E4 – 613/724-1200; Fax: 613/562-8447	90.7
Ottawa, ON	*CBOQ-FM	See Ottawa (CBO)	103.3
Ottawa, ON	*†CBOX-FM	See Ottawa (CBOF-FM)	102.5
Owen Sound, ON	CIXK-FM	Bayshore Broadcasting Corp., 270 - 9 St. East, PO Box 280, Owen Sound ON N4K 5P5 – 519/376-2030; Fax: 519/371-9683	106.5
Parksville, BC	CKWV-FM-1	See Nanaimo (CKWV-FM)	99.9
Parry Sound, ON	CKLP-FM	Playland Broadcasting Ltd., 4 Miller St., Parry Sound ON P2A 1S8 – 705/746-2163; Fax: 705/746-4292	103.3
Peace River, AB	CKUA-FM-5	See Edmonton (CKUA-FM)	96.9
Pemberton, BC	CISP-FM	See Squamish (CISQ-FM)	104.5
Pembroke, ON	CHVR	Pelmorex Radio, 595 Pembroke St. East, Pembroke ON K8A 3L7 – 613/735-9670; Fax: 613/735-7748; Email: star96@fox.nstn.ca	96.7
Pender Harbour, BC	CIPN-FM	See Squamish (CISQ-FM)	104.7
Penetanguishene, ON	†CFRH-FM	Radio-Huronie CFRM-FM Communautaire Inc., 63 Main St., CP 1270, Penetanguishene ON L0K 1P0 – 705/549-8288; Fax: 705/549-3121	101.9, 96.5
Penticton, BC	CIGV-FM	Great Valleys Radio Ltd., 125 Nanaimo Ave. West, Penticton BC V2A 1N7 – 250/493-6767; Fax: 250/493-0098; Email: rhopson@mail.awinc.com; URL: http://www.pentonline.com	100.7
Penticton, BC	CJMG-FM	Okanagan Radio Ltd., 33 Carmi Ave., Penticton BC V2A 3G4 – 250/492-2800; Fax: 250/493-0370	97.1
Peterborough, ON	CFFF-FM	Trent Radio, Trent University, Peterborough ON K9J 7B8 – 705/748-1777; Fax: 705/748-1795	96.3
Peterborough, ON	CKQM-FM	CHUM Ltd., PO Box 177, Peterborough ON K9J 6Y8 – 705/742-8844; Fax: 705/742-1417	105.1
Peterborough, ON	CKWF-FM	Power Broadcasting Inc., 1925 Television Rd., PO Box 4150, Peterborough ON K9J 6Z9 – 705/742-6101; Fax: 705/742-7274	101.5
Pincher Creek, AB	CKIZ-FM	PO Box 2092, Pincher Creek AB T0K 1W0 – 403/627-3844; Fax: 403/627-3859	90.5
Pohénégamook, PQ	†CFVD-FM-2	See Dégelis (CFVD)	104.9
Port-Cartier, PQ	†CIPC-FM	Radio Port-Cartier inc., 52, Elie-Rochefort, Port-Cartier PQ G5B 1N2 – 418/766-6868; Fax: 418/766-6870	
Prince Albert, SK	CFMM-FM	Central Broadcasting Co. Ltd., PO Box 900, Prince Albert SK S6V 7R4 – 306/763-7421; Fax: 306/764-1850	99.1
Prince George, BC	CKKN-FM	Monarch Broadcasting Ltd., 1220 - 6 Ave., Prince George BC V2L 3M8 – 250/564-8861; Fax: 250/562-8768; Email: benny@mindlink.net; http://www.pgonline.com/benny	101.3
Prince George, BC	CIRX-FM	Cariboo Central Interior Radio Inc., 1940 - 3 Ave., Prince George BC V2M 1G7 – 250/564-2524; Fax: 250/562-6611	94.3
Prince George, BC	*CBYG-FM	CBC, 1268 - 5 Ave., Prince George BC V2L 3L2 – 250/562-6701; Fax: 250/562-4777; Email: daybreak@netbistro.com	91.5
Prince Rupert, BC	CJFW-FM-2	See Terrace (CJFW-FM)	109.9
Princeton, BC	CIGV-FM-2	See Penticton (CIGV-FM)	98.1
Québec, PQ	†CHIK-FM	Radio-Média inc., #105, 1245, ch Ste-Foy, Québec PQ G1S 4P2 – 418/687-9900; Fax: 418/687-3106	98.9
Québec, PQ	†CHOI-FM	Radio-Média inc., 2136, ch Ste-Foy, Québec PQ G1V 1R8 – 418/687-9810; Fax: 418/682-8427	98.1
Québec, PQ	†CITF-FM	Radio-Média inc., #250, 580, Grande-Allée est, Québec PQ G1R 2K2 – 418/525-4545; Fax: 418/525-6399	107.5
Québec, PQ	†CJMF-FM	COGECO Radio-Télévision inc., 600, rue Belvédère, Québec PQ G1S 3E5 – 418/687-9330; Fax: 418/687-0211	93.3
Québec, PQ	†CKIA-FM	Radio Basse-Ville Inc., 600, côte d'Abraham, Québec PQ G1R 1A1 – 418/529-9026; Fax: 418/529-4156	96.1
Québec, PQ	†CKRL-FM	Laval Campus, 47, rue Ste-Ursule, Québec PQ G1R 4E4 – 418/692-2575; Fax: 418/692-5581	89.1

Canadian Almanac & Directory 1997

LOCATION	CALL	*CBC Stations/Affiliates †French Language Stations	FREQ.
Québec, PQ	*†CBV-FM	See Québec (CBV)	95.3
Québec, PQ	*CBVE-FM	CBC, #100, 900, Place d'Youville, Québec PQ G1R 3P7 – 418/691-3620; Fax: 418/691-3610	104.7
Quesnel, BC	CFFM-FM	See Williams Lake (CFFM-FM)	94.9
Red Deer, AB	CIZZ-FM	Shaw Radio Ltd., PO Bag 5339, Red Deer AB T4P 2N7 – 403/342-7655; Fax: 403/346-1230	98.9
Red Deer, AB	CKUA-FM	See Edmonton (CKUA)	101.3
Regina, SK	CHMX-FM	Harvard Developments Ltd., 2060 Halifax St., PO Box 9200, Regina SK S4P 1T7 – 306/525-9195; Fax: 306/781-7338	92.1
Regina, SK	CIZL-FM	RAWLCO Communications Ltd., #210, 2401 Saskatchewan Dr., Regina SK S4P 4H8 – 306/359-9936; Fax: 306/347-8557	98.9
Regina, SK	CKIT-FM	Craig Broadcast Systems Inc., 1922 Park St., PO Box 6200, Regina SK S4N 7M4 – 306/569-6200; Fax: 306/936-8329	104.9
Regina, SK	*CBK-FM	See Québec (CBV)	96.9
Regina, SK	*†CBKF-FM	Société Radio-Canada, 2440 Broad St., CP 540, Regina SK S4P 4A1 – 306/347-9540; Fax: 306/347-9493	97.7
Richmond, BC	CKZZ-FM	Standard Radio Inc., #20, 11151 Horseshoe Way, Richmond BC V7A 4S5 – 604/241-0953; Fax: 604/272-0917; Email: zinfo@z95.com; URL: http://www.z95.com	95.3
Rimouski, PQ	†CIKI-FM	Diffusion Power Inc., 875, boul St-Germain ouest, Rimouski PQ G5L 3T9 – 418/724-8833; Fax: 418/722-7508	98.7
Rimouski, PQ	CKMN-FM	Radio Communautaire du Comté, 570, boul St-Germaine ouest, Rimouski PQ G5L 3R2 – 418/725-7137; Fax: 418/725-2137	96.5
Rimouski, PQ	*†CJBR-FM	See Rimouski (CJBR)	101.5
Rivière-au-Rinard, PQ	†CJRE-FM	See Gaspé (CJRG-FM)	97.9
Rivière-du-Loup, PQ	†CIBM-FM	64, rue Hôtel-de-Ville, Rivière-du-Loup PQ G5R 1L5 – 418/867-1071; Fax: 418/862-7704	107.1
Rivière-du-Loup, PQ	CFFP-FM	See Rivière-du-Loup (CJFP)	103.7
Rouyn-Noranda, PQ	†CHOA-FM	Radio Nord inc., CP 70, Rouyn-Noranda PQ J9X 5A5 – 819/762-0741; Fax: 819/762-2280; URL: http://www.rock-detente.com	
Rouyn-Noranda, PQ	†CHLM-FM	See Rouyn-Noranda (CKRN)	90.7
Sackville, NB	CHMA-FM	Mount Allison University, #315, University Centre, Sackville NB E0A 3C0 – 506/364-2221; Fax: 506/364-2233; Email: cradio@bigmac.mta.ca; URL: http://www.aci.mta.ca/theumbrella/chma	106.9
Ste-Adèle, PQ	†CIME-FM	Diffusion Laurentides inc., CP 1260, Ste-Adèle PQ J0R 1L0 – 514/229-2995; Fax: 514/229-7557	99.5
St. Albert, AB	CFMG-FM	Balsa Broadcasting Corp., #602, 22 Sir Winston Churchill Ave., St. Albert AB T8N 1B4 – 403/458-1200; Fax: 403/460-9671; Email: cfmg@plant.cor.net	104.9
St. Andrews, NF	CFCV-FM	See Port aux Basques (CFGN)	97.7
Ste-Anne-des-Monts, PQ	CJMC-FM	See Ste-Anne-des-Monts (CJMC)	92.7, 92.9
St. Anthony, NF	CFNN-FM	See Corner Brook (CFCB)	97.9
St. Catharines, ON	CHRE-FM	Redmond Broadcasting Inc., 80 King St., St. Catharines ON L2R 7G1 – 905/688-1057; Fax: 905/688-3377; Email: light.fm@vaxxine.com; URL: http://www.lightfm.com/rock	105.7
St. Catharines, ON	CHTZ-FM	Standard Radio Inc., PO Box 610, St. Catharines ON L2R 6X7 – 905/688-0977; Fax: 905/684-4800	97.7
St. Felicien, PQ	†CHVD-FM	See Dolbeau (CHVD)	92.1
St-Gabriel-de-Brandon, PQ	CFNJ-FM	Radio Nord-Joli Inc., 30, rue des Écoles, CP 120, St-Gabriel-de-Brandon PQ J0K 2N0 – 514/835-3437; Fax: 514/835-3581	99.1
St-Georges-de-Beauce, PQ	†CIRO-FM	Radio Beauce Inc., 170, rue 120 est, St-Georges-de-Beauce PQ G5Y 5C4 – 418/227-0997; Fax: 418/228-0096	99.7
St-Hilarion, PQ	†CIHO-FM	Radio MF Charlevoix Inc., 315, ch Cartier nord, CP 160, St-Hilarion PQ G0A 3V0 – 418/457-3333; Fax: 418/457-3518	96.3
St-Hyacinthe, PQ	†CFEI-FM	COGECO Radio-Télévision inc., 855, rue Ste-Marie, St-Hyacinthe PQ J2S 4R9 – 514/774-6486; Fax: 514/774-7785	106.5
Saint John, NB	CIOK-FM	Maritime Broadcasting Ltd., 400 Main St. East, Saint John NB E2K 1J4 – 506/658-5100; Fax: 506/658-5116	100.5
Saint John, NB	CJYC-FM	Fundy Broadcasting Co. Ltd., PO Box 930, Saint John NB E2L 4E2 – 506/658-2330; Fax: 506/658-2320; Email: info@radio.mi.net; URL: http://www.mi.net/radio	98.9
Saint John, NB	*CBD-FM	CBC, 560 Main St., PO Box 2358, Saint John NB E2L 3V6 – 506/632-7710; Fax: 506/632-7761	91.3
Saint John, NB	*†CBZF-FM	See Moncton (CBAF-FM)	102.3
St. John's, NF	CHOZ-FM	Newfoundland Broadcasting Co. Ltd., 446 Logy Bay Rd., PO Box 2050, St. John's NF A1C 5R6 – 709/726-2922; Fax: 709/726-3300	94.7
St. John's, NF	CKIX-FM	NewCap Broadcasting, PO Box 8010, St. John's NF A1B 3M7 – 709/753-4040; Fax: 709/753-6984	99.1
St. John's, NF	VOCM-FM	VOCM Radio Newfoundland Ltd., PO Box 8-590, Stn A, St. John's NF A1B 3P5 – 709/726-5590; Fax: 709/726-8636	97.5
St. John's, NF	*CBN-FM	See St. John's (CBN)	106.9
St. Stephen, NB	WQDY	PO Box 305, St. Stephen NB E3L 2X2 – 506/465-0989	92.7
St. Thomas, ON	CFHK-FM	CFHK Radio Ltd., 133 Curtis St., St. Thomas ON N5P 4H5 – 519/637-1572; Fax: 519/631-4693	103.0
Salmon Arm, BC	CKXR-FM	Copper Island Broadcasting Ltd., PO Box 69, Salmon Arm BC V1E 4N2 – 250/832-2161; Fax: 250/832-2240	
Sarnia, ON	CFGX-FM	Blackburn Radio, 1415 London Rd., Sarnia ON N7S 1P6 – 519/332-5500; Fax: 519/542-1520	99.9
Saskatoon, SK	CFCR-FM	Community Radio Society of Saskatoon Inc., PO Box 7544, Saskatoon SK S7K 4L4 – 306/664-6678; Fax: 306/933-0038	90.5
Saskatoon, SK	CFMC-FM	RAWLCO Communications Ltd., 3333 - 8 St. East, Saskatoon SK S7H 0W3 – 306/955-9500; Fax: 306/373-7587	95.1
Saskatoon, SK	CHSN-FM	High-Line Broadcasting, #219, 3501 - 8th St. East, Saskatoon SK S7H 0W5 – 306/668-1021; Fax: 306/664-2090	102.1
Saskatoon, SK	CFQC-FM	Forvest Broadcasting Corp., 345 - th Ave. South, Saskatoon SK S7K 5S5 – 306/244-1975; Fax: 306/665-7730; Email: cjww.radio@sasknet.sk.ca; URL: http://www.sasknet.com/cjww/	92.9
Saskatoon, SK	*CBKS-FM	CBC, CN Tower, Midtown Plaza, 5th Fl., Saskatoon SK S7K 1J5 – 306/956-7400; Fax: 306/956-7417	105.5
Sault Ste. Marie, ON	CHAS-FM	Telemedia Communications Ontario Inc., 642 Great Northern Rd., Sault Ste. Marie ON P6B 4Z9 – 705/759-9200; Fax: 705/942-6549; Email: mix100@soonet.ca	100.5
Sault Ste. Marie, ON	CJQM-FM	Pelmorex Radio, 642 Great Northern Rd., Sault Ste. Marie ON P6B 4Z9 – 705/759-9200; Fax: 705/942-6549	104.3
Scarborough, ON	CSCR-FM	Scarborough College, University of Toronto, 1265 Military Trail, Scarborough ON M1C 1A4 – 416/287-7051; Fax: 416/287-7041; Email: cscr@wave.scar.utoronto.ca	cable; 90.5
Sechelt, BC	CISE-FM	See Squamish (CISQ-FM)	104.7
Selkirk, MB	CFQX-FM	Forvest Broadcasting, 701 Greenwood Ave., PO Box 400, Selkirk MB R1A 2B3 – 204/785-2929; Fax: 204/482-7853	104.1
Senneterre, PQ	†CIBO-FM	Radio Communautaire de Senneterre, 121, rue Première est, CP 1150, Senneterre PQ J0Y 2M0 – 819/737-2222; Fax: 819/737-2221	100.5
Sept-Îles, PQ	*†CBSI-FM	Société Radio-Canada, #30, 350, rue Smith, Sept-Îles PQ G4R 3X2 – 418/968-0720; Fax: 418/968-9219	98.1
Shelburne, NS	CJLS-FM-1	See Yarmouth (CJLS)	96.3

Canadian Almanac & Directory 1997

5-212 FM BROADCASTING STATIONS

LOCATION	CALL	*CBC Stations/Affiliates †French Language Stations	FREQ.
Shelburne, NS	CKBW-FM-2	See Bridgewater (CKBW)	93.1
Sherbrooke, PQ	†CITE-FM	Télémedia Communications Inc., 25, rue Bryant, Sherbrooke PQ J1J 3Z5 – 819/563-6363; Fax: 819/566-1011	102.7
Sherbrooke, PQ	†CIMO-FM	See Magog (CIMO-FM)	106.9
Sioux Lookout, ON	WRN-FM	Wawatay Radio Network, 16 - 5 Ave., PO Box 1180, Sioux Lookout ON P8T 1B7 – 807/737-2951; Fax: 807/737-3224.	89.1, 106.7
Smithers, BC	CJFW-FM	See Terrace (CJFW-FM)	92.9
Smiths Falls, ON	CFMO-FM	Rideau Broadcasting, PO Box 630, Smiths Falls ON K7A 4T4 – 613/283-4630; Fax: 613/283-7243	101.1
Sorel, PQ	†CJSO-FM	Radio Diffusion Sorel-Tracy Inc., 100, boul Couillard Després, Sorel PQ J3P 5C1 – 514/743-2772; Fax: 514/743-0293.	101.7
Sorrento, BC	CKIR-FM	See Salmon Arm (CKXR)	102.1
Spirit River, AB	CKUA-FM-12	See Edmonton (CKUA-FM)	99.5
Squamish, BC	CISQ-FM	Rogers Broadcasting Ltd., PO Box 1068, Squamish BC V0N 3G0 – 604/892-1021; Fax: 604/892-6383; Email: mountainfm@mountain-inter.net	107.1
Stephenville, NF	CIOS-FM	See St. John's (CHOZ-FM)	98.5
Sudbury, ON	CFLR	Laurentian Student & Community Radio Corp., Laurentian University, 935 Ramsey Rd., Sudbury ON P3E 2C6 – 705/675-1151, ext.2405; Fax: 705/675-4878; Email: mail@cflr.isys.ca; URL: http://www.cflr.isys.ca	cable; 106.7
Sudbury, ON	CJMX-FM	Pelmorex Radio, 295 Victoria St., Sudbury ON P3C 1K5 – 705/674-6401; Fax: 705/674-7322.	105.3
Sudbury, ON	CJRQ-FM	Telemedia Communications Ontario Inc., 880 Lasalle Blvd., Sudbury ON P3A 1X5 – 705/566-4480; Fax: 705/560-7232; Email: q92@cwconnect.com	92.7
Sudbury, ON	*CBCS-FM	CBC Northern Ontario Radio, 15 MacKenzie St., Sudbury ON P3C 4Y1 – 705/688-3200; Fax: 705/688-3220	99.9
Sudbury, ON	*†CBON-FM	Société Radio-Canada, 15 MacKenzie St., Sudbury ON P3C 4Y1 – 705/688-3200; Fax: 705/688-3220	98.1
Swift Current, SK	CIMG-FM	Frontier City Broadcasting Co. Ltd., 28 - 4th Ave. NW, PO Box 1590, Swift Current SK S9H 4G5 – 306/773-1505; Fax: 306/778-3737.	94.1
Sydney, NS	CKPE-FM	Celtic Broadcasting Ltd., 318 Charlotte St., Sydney NS B1P 6K2 – 902/564-5596; Fax: 902/564-1057	94.9
Sydney, NS	*†CBI-FM	See Sydney (CBI).	91.3
Sydney, NS	*†CBAF-FM	See Moncton (CBAF-FM)	95.9
Temiscaming, PQ	†CKVM-FM	See Ville-Marie (CKVM)	92.1
Terrace, BC	CJFW-FM	Skeena Broadcasters, Division of Okanagan Skeena Group Ltd., 4625 Lazelle Ave., Terrace BC V8G 1S4 – 250/635-6316; Fax: 250/638-6320; Email: info@osg.net; URL: http://www.osg.net.	103.1
Thetford-Mines, PQ	†CFJO-FM	Réseau des Appalaches (FM) Ltée, 327, rue Labbé, CP 69, Thetford-Mines PQ G6P 6T3 – 418/338-1009; Fax: 418/338-0386; Email: cfjo@ivic.qc.ca	103.3
Thompson, MB	CINC-FM	Native Communications Inc., 76 Severn Cres., Thompson MB R8N 1M6 – 204/778-8343; Fax: 204/778-6559	96.3
Thompson, MB	*CBWK-FM	CBC, 7 Selkirk St., Thompson MB R8N 0M4 – 204/677-2307; Fax: 204/677-9517	100.9
Thunder Bay, ON	CCSR-FM	Confederation College, PO Box 398, Thunder Bay ON P7C 4W1 – 807/475-6226; Fax: 807/623-6230	
Thunder Bay, ON	CJSD-FM	CJSD Inc., 87 North Hill St., Thunder Bay ON P7A 5V6 – 807/346-2594; Fax: 807/345-4671	94.3
Thunder Bay, ON	*CBQ-FM	CBC, 213 Miles St. East, Thunder Bay ON P7C 1J5 – 807/625-5000; Fax: 807/625-5035	88.3
Tillsonburg, ON	CKOT-FM	Tillsonburg Broadcasting Co. Ltd., PO Box 10, Tillsonburg ON N4G 4H3 – 519/842-4281; Fax: 519/842-4284	101.3
Timmins, ON	CJQQ-FM	Telemedia Communications Ontario Inc., 260 Second Ave., PO Box 1046, Timmins ON P4N 7H8 – 705/264-1316; Fax: 705/264-2984.	92.1
Toronto, ON	CFMX-FM	#101, 468 Queen St. East, Toronto ON M5A 1T7 – 416/367-5353; Fax: 416/367-1742	96.3/103.1
Toronto, ON	CFNY-FM	KEY Radio CFNY Ltd., #1600, 1 Dundas St. West, PO Box 14, Toronto ON M5G 1Z3 – 416/966-3343; Email: edge@passport.ca; URL: http://www.edge.passport.ca	102.1
Toronto, ON	CHFI-FM	Rogers Broadcasting Ltd., 25 Adelaide St. East, 11th Fl., Toronto ON M5C 1H3 – 416/864-2070; Fax: 416/864-2002	98.1
Toronto, ON	CHIN-FM	Radio 1540 Ltd., 622 College St., Toronto ON M6G 1B6 – 416/531-9991; Fax: 416/531-5274; Email: chin@istar.ca; URL: http://www.chinradio.com	100.7
Toronto, ON	CHRY-FM	CHRY Community Radio Inc., York University, 258A Vanier College, 4700 Keele St., Toronto ON M3J 1P3 – 416/736-5293; Fax: 416/736-5700	105.5
Toronto, ON	CHUM-FM	CHUM Ltd., 1331 Yonge St., Toronto ON M4T 1Y1 – 416/925-6666; Fax: 416/926-4026	104.5
Toronto, ON	CILQ-FM	Westcom Radio Group, #1400, 5255 Yonge St., Toronto ON M2N 6P4 – 416/221-0107; Fax: 416/512-4810	107.1
Toronto, ON	CIRV-FM	CIRC Radio Inc., 1087 Dundas St. West, Toronto ON M6J 1W9 – 416/537-1088; Fax: 416/537-2463	88.9
Toronto, ON	CISS-FM	RAWLCO Communications, 49 Ontario St., 4th Fl., Toronto ON M5A 2V1 – 416/368-2000; Fax: 416/368-1036	92.5
Toronto, ON	CIUT-FM	University of Toronto Community Radio, 91 St. George St., Toronto ON M5S 2E8 – 416/595-0909; Fax: 416/978-8182.	89.5
Toronto, ON	CJEZ-FM	Telemedia Communications Ontario Inc., 40 Eglinton Ave. East, 6th Fl., Toronto ON M4P 3B6 – 416/480-2097; Fax: 416/480-0688	97.3
Toronto, ON	CJRT-FM	CJRT-FM INC., 150 Mutual St., Toronto ON M5B 2M1 – 416/595-0404; Fax: 416/595-9413	91.1
Toronto, ON	CKFM-FM	Standard Radio Inc., 2 St. Clair Ave. West, Toronto ON M4V 1L6 – 416/922-9999; Fax: 416/323-6800	99.9
Toronto, ON	CKLN-FM	CKLN Radio Inc., Ryerson Polytechnical Institute, 380 Victoria St., Toronto ON M5B 1W7 – 416/595-1477	88.1
Toronto, ON	CBFM-FM	George Brown College, 200 King St. East, Toronto ON M5A 3W8 – 416/867-2455; Fax: 416/867-2302	closed circuit
Toronto, ON	CSCR-FM	See Scarborough (CSCR-FM)	
Toronto, ON	CFRE-FM	See Mississauga (CFRE-FM)	
Toronto, ON	*CBL-FM	See Toronto (CBL)	94.1
Trois-Pistoles, PQ	†CJFP-FM	See Rivière-du-Loup (CJFP)	93.9
Trois-Rivières, PQ	†CHEY-FM	See Trois-Rivières (CHLN)	94.7
Trois-Rivières, PQ	†CIGB-FM	Radio-Média Inc., 1350, rue Royal, 12e étage, Trois-Rivières PQ G9A 4J4 – 819/378-1023; Fax: 819/378-1360	102.3
Truro, NS	CKTO-FM	Radio Atlantic (CKCL) Ltd., 187 Industrial Ave., PO Box 788, Truro NS B2N 5E8 – 902/893-6060; Fax: 902/893-7771.	100.9
Tumbler Ridge, BC	CJDC-FM	See Dawson Creek (CJDC)	92.7
Ucluelet, BC	CKKS-FM-1	See Vancouver (CKKS-FM).	102.7
Val d'Or, PQ	†CJMV-FM	Radiomutuel inc., 173, rue Perreault, Val d'Or PQ J9P 2H3 – 819/825-2568; Fax: 819/825-2840	102.7
Valleyfield, PQ	†CKOD-FM	Radio Express Inc., 249, rue Victoria, Valleyfield PQ J6T 1A9 – 514/373-0103; Fax: 514/373-4297.	103.1
Vancouver, BC	CFOX-FM	Shaw Radio Ltd., 1006 Richards St., Vancouver BC V6B 1S8 – 604/684-7221; Fax: 604/681-9134.	99.3
Vancouver, BC	CFRO-FM	Vancouver Co-operative Radio, 337 Carrall St., Vancouver BC V6B 2J4 – 604/684-8494; URL: http://vcr.bc.ca/cfro/welcome.html	102.7
Vancouver, BC	CHQM-FM	CHUM Ltd., #300, 380 West 2nd Ave., Vancouver BC V5Y 1C8 – 604/871-9000; Fax: 604/871-2901	103.5

Canadian Almanac & Directory 1997

LOCATION	CALL	*CBC Stations/Affiliates †French Language Stations	FREQ.
Vancouver, BC	CITR-FM	UBC, #233, 6138 Sub Blvd., Vancouver BC V6T 1Z1 – 604/882-3017; Fax: 604/882-9364; Email: citr@unixg.ubc.ca; URL: http://www.ans.ubc.ca/citr/citr.htm	101.9
Vancouver, BC	CJJR-FM	Great Pacific Industries Inc., 1401 West 8 Ave., Vancouver BC V6H 1C9 – 604/731-7772; Fax: 604/731-0493	93.7
Vancouver, BC	CKKS-FM	Rogers Broadcasting Ltd., 2440 Ash St., Vancouver BC V5Z 4J6 – 604/872-2557; Fax: 604/877-4494	96.9
Vancouver, BC	*CBU-FM	See Vancouver (CBU)	105.7
Vancouver, BC	*†CBUF-FM	Société Radio-Canada, 700 Hamilton St., CP 4600, Vancouver BC V6B 2R5 – 604/662-6135; Fax: 604/662-6161	97.7
Vanderhoof, BC	CIRX-FM-1	See Prince George (CIRX-FM)	95.9
Verdun, PQ	†CKOI-FM	Metromédia CMR inc., 211, av Gordon, Verdun PQ H4G 2R2 – 514/766-2311; Fax: 514/761-2122	96.9
Victoria, BC	CFMS-FM	Capital Broadcasting System Ltd., 1450 Douglas St., PO Box 1200, Stn E, Victoria BC V8W 2G1 – 250/384-9311; Fax: 250/384-1213	98.5
Victoria, BC	CFUV-FM	University of Victoria Student Radio Society, PO Box 3035, Victoria BC V8W 3P3 – 250/721-8702; Fax: 250/721-7111	101.9
Victoria, BC	CKKQ-FM	OK Radio Group Ltd., 3795 Carey Rd., Victoria BC V8Z 6T8 – 250/475-0100; Fax: 250/475-3299; URL: http://www.100.3theq.com/q	100.3
Victoria, BC	CKMO-FM	Camosun College, 3100 Foul Bay Rd., Victoria BC V8P 5J2 – 250/370-3658; Fax: 250/370-3660; Email: lalonde@camosun.bc.ca	
Victoriaville, PQ	†CFJO-FM	Réseau des Appalaches (FM) Ltée, 55, rue St-Jean-Baptiste, Victoriaville PQ G6P 6T3 – 819/752-2785; Fax: 819/752-3182; Email: cfjo@ivic.qc.ca	103.3
Ville-Marie, PQ	†CKVM-FM	Radio Témiscamingue inc., CP 3000, Ville-Marie PQ J0Z 3W0 – 819/629-2710; Fax: 819/622-0716	
Waterloo, ON	CFCA-FM	CHUM Ltd., 255 King St. North, Waterloo ON N2J 4V2 – 519/884-4470; Fax: 519/884-6482	105.3
Waterloo, ON	CKMS-FM	Radio Waterloo Inc., University of Waterloo, Bauer Warehouse, 200 University Ave. West, Waterloo ON N2L 3G1 – 519/886-2567; Fax: 519/884-3530	100.3
Waterloo, ON	CKWR-FM	Wired World Inc., 56 Regina St., Waterloo ON N2J 3A3 – 519/886-9870; Fax: 519/886-0090; Email: ckwr@worldchat.com	98.7
Weymouth, NS	CKDY-FM	See Kentville (CKEN)	103.3
Whistler, BC	CISW-FM	See Squamish (CISQ-FM)	102.1
Whitecourt, AB	CKUA-FM	See Edmonton (CKUA-FM)	107.1
Whitehorse, YT	CHON-FM	Northern Native Broadcasting, 4228A - 4 Ave., Whitehorse YT Y1A 1K1 – 403/668-6629; Fax: 403/668-6612	98.1
Williams Lake, BC	CFFM-FM	Cariboo Central Interior Radio, 83 South First Ave., Williams Lake BC V2G 1H4 – 250/398-2336; Fax: 250/392-4184	97.5, 94.9
Windsor, ON	CIMX-FM	CHUM Ltd., 1640 Ouellette Ave., Windsor ON N8X 1L1 – 519/258-8888; Fax: 519/258-0182	88.7
Windsor, ON	CJAM-FM	University of Windsor, 401 Sunset Ave., Windsor ON N9B 3P4 – 519/971-3606; Fax: 519/971-7050	91.5
Windsor, ON	CIDR-FM	CHUM Ltd., 1640 Ouellette Ave., Windsor ON N8X 1L1 – 519/258-8888; Fax: 519/258-0182	93.9
Windsor, ON	*CBE-FM	See Windsor (CBE)	89.9
Wingham, ON	CKNX-FM	Blackburn Radio Group, 215 Carling Terrace, Wingham ON N0G 2W0 – 519/357-1310; Fax: 519/357-1897	101.7
Winnipeg, MB	CKRC	Celtic Communications, #1630, 155 Carlton St., Winnipeg MB R3C 3H8 – 204/988-9999; Fax: 204/988-2118	99.9
Winnipeg, MB	CFQX-FM	QX-FM Ltd., 701 Greenwood Ave., Winnipeg MB R1A 2B1 – 204/785-2929; Fax: 204/482-7853	
Winnipeg, MB	CHIQ-FM	CHUM Ltd., 1445 Pembina Hwy., Winnipeg MB R3T 5C2 – 204/477-5120; Fax: 204/453-0815	94.3
Winnipeg, MB	CITI-FM	Rogers Broadcasting Ltd., Polo Park, Winnipeg MB R3G 0L7 – 204/788-3400; Fax: 204/788-3401	92.1
Winnipeg, MB	CJKR-FM	Westcom Radio Group Ltd., 930 Portage Ave., Winnipeg MB R3G 0P8v204/786-2471; Fax: 204/783-4512	87.5
Winnipeg, MB	CKMM-FM	Craig Broadcast Systems Inc., #1700, 155 Carlton St., Winnipeg MB R3C 3H8 – 204/942-1031; Fax: 204/943-7687; URL: http://www.star103.com	103.1
Winnipeg, MB	*CBW-FM	See Winnipeg (CBW)	98.3
Woodstock, ON	CKDK-FM	Shaw Radio Ltd., 290 Dundas St., PO Box 100, Woodstock ON N4S 7W7 – 519/539-1040; Fax: 519/539-7479; Email: k104@saturn.execulink.com; http://www.saturn.execulink.com/~k104	103.9
Yellowknife, NT	CKLB-FM	Native Communications Society of Western N.W.T., 5120 - 49 St., PO Box 1919, Yellowknife NT X1A 2P4 – 403/920-2277; Fax: 403/920-4205	101.9

TELEVISION STATIONS

LOCATION	CALL	*CBC Stations/Affiliates †French Language Stations	CHANNEL
100 Mile House, BC	CFJC-TV-6	See Kamloops (CFJC-TV)	5
16 Mile House, BC	CHCS-TV-1	See Burnaby (CHAN-TV)	7
Alert Bay, BC	CBUT-TV-16	See Vancouver (CBUT-TV)	11
Alexis Creek, BC	CHIL-TV-1	See Kamloops (CFJC-TV)	8
Alexis Creek, BC	CIAC-TV	See Burnaby (CHAN-TV)	11
Alma, PQ	CBJET-TV-1	See Montréal (CBMT-TV)	32
Alta Lake, BC	CHWM-TV-1	See Victoria (CHEK-TV)	7
Anahim Lake, BC	CIAL-TV-1	See Burnaby (CHAN-TV)	5
Annapolis Valley, NS	CJCH-TV-1	See Halifax (CJCH-TV)	10
Anse-aux-Gascons, PQ	CIVK-TV	See Montréal (CIVM-TV)	32
Antigonish, NS	CJCB-TV-2	See Sydney (CJCB-TV)	9
Argentia, NF	CJAP-TV	See St. John's (CJON-TV)	3
Ashcroft, BC	CHAC-TV-2	See Burnaby (CHAN-TV)	2
Ashcroft, BC	CJAC-TV-2	See Kamloops (CFJC-TV)	5
Ashmont, AB	CFRN-TV-4	See Edmonton (CFRN-TV)	12
Athabasca, AB	CBXT-TV-1	See Edmonton (CBXT-TV)	8
Atikokan, ON	CBWCT-TV-1	See Winnipeg (CBWT-TV)	7
Avola, BC	CJVO-TV	See Burnaby (CHAN-TV)	13
Baie-Comeau, PQ	CBMIT-TV	See Montréal (CBMT-TV)	28
Baie-Trinité, PQ	CIVF-TV	See Montréal (CIVM-TV)	12
Baie Verte, NF	CBNAT-TV-1	See St. John's (CBNT-TV)	3, 12
Banff, AB	CFCN-TV-2	See Calgary (CFCN-TV)	7
Banff, AB	CBRT-TV-1	See Calgary (CBRT-TV)	5
Barrie, ON	CKVR-TV	CKVR Channel 3, Division of CHUM Ltd., PO Box 519, Barrie ON L4M 4T9 – 705/734-3300; Fax: 705/733-0302	3

TELEVISION STATIONS

LOCATION	CALL	*CBC Stations/Affiliates †French Language Stations	CHANNEL
Barriere, BC	CKTV-TV-1	See Kamloops (CFJC-TV)	12
Barriere, BC	CKTV-TV-2	See Burnaby (CHAN-TV)	7
Bassano, AB	CFCN-TV-7	See Calgary (CFCN-TV)	10
Battle River, AB	CBXAT-TV-6	See Edmonton (CBXT-TV)	9
Bay Bulls, NF	CJON-TV	See St. John's (CJON-TV)	10
Bay L'Argent, NF	CBNT-TV-27	See St. John's (CBNT-TV)	8
Bay St. Lawrence, NS	CBIT-TV-17	See Sydney (CBIT-TV)	13
Bay St. Lawrence, NS	CJCB-TV-5	See Sydney (CJCB-TV)	7
Beaton, BC	CHBC-TV	See Kelowna (CHBC-TV)	8
Beauval, SK	CBKBT-TV	See Saskatoon (CBKST-TV)	7
Bellegarde, NF	†CBKFT-TV-9	See St. John's (CBNT-TV)	7
Bellevue, AB	CBRT-TV-10	See Calgary (CBRT-TV)	57
Big River, SK	CKBI-TV-5	See Prince Albert (CKBI-TV)	9
Big Trout Lake, ON	CBWT-TV-1	See Winnipeg (CBWT-TV)	13
Blackville, NB	CKAM-TV-3	See Moncton (CKCW-TV)	9
Blanc Sablon, PQ	CBMAST-TV	See Montréal (CBMT-TV)	5
Boiestown, NB	CHSJ-TV-3	See Saint John (CHSJ-TV)	13
Bonavista, NF	CJWB-TV	See St. John's (CJON-TV)	10
Bonnington, BC	CBUDT-TV	See Vancouver (CBUT-TV)	13
Bonnyville, AB	CKSA-TV-2	See Lloydminster (CKSA-TV)	9
Boston Bar, BC	CFJC-TV-1	See Kamloops (CFJC-TV)	5
Bowen Island, BC	CBUT-TV-4	See Vancouver (CBUT-TV)	13
Bowen Island, BC	CHAN-TV-2	See Burnaby (CHAN-TV)	3
Brackendale, BC	CBUT-TV-34	See Vancouver (CBUT-TV)	35
Brackendale, BC	CHAN-TV-5	See Burnaby (CHAN-TV)	9
Brandon, MB	CKX-TV	Craig Broadcast Systems Inc., 2940 Victoria Ave., PO Box 1180, Brandon MB R7B 0N2 – 204/728-1150; Fax: 204/727-2505	5, 9, 11
Brandon, MB	CKYB-TV	See Winnipeg (CKY-TV)	4
Brent's Cove, NF	CBNAT-TV-18	See St. John's (CBNT-TV)	10
Bridgetown, NS	CJCH-TV-4	See Halifax (CJCH-TV)	13
Bridgewater, NS	CIHF-TV-6	See Dartmouth (CIHF-TV)	9
Brighton, ON	CKWS-TV-2	See Kingston (CKWS-TV)	66
Brooks, AB	CFCN-TV-3	See Calgary (CFCN-TV)	9
Buchans, NF	CBNAT-TV-2	See St. John's (CBNT-TV)	13
Buffalo Narrows, SK	CBKDT-TV	See Saskatoon (CBKST-TV)	11
Bullhead Mountain, BC	CJDC-TV-2	See Dawson Creek (CJDC-TV)	8
Burmis, AB	CBRT-TV-8	See Calgary (CBRT-TV)	47
Burmis, AB	CFCN-TV-4	See Calgary (CFCN-TV)	5
Burnaby, BC	CHAN-TV	Western International Communications Inc., 7850 Enterprise St., PO Box 4700, Burnaby BC V5A 1V7 – 604/420-2288; Fax: 604/421-9427	7
Burns Lake, BC	CBCH-TV-2	See Terrace (CFTK-TV)	4
Burns Lake, BC	CKHS-TV	See Burnaby (CHAN-TV)	13
Cache Creek, BC	CHAC-TV-1	See Burnaby (CHAN-TV)	12
Cache Creek, BC	CJAC-TV-1	See Kamloops (CFJC-TV)	10
Calgary, AB	CICT-TV	Calgary Television Ltd., Division of Westcom Television Group Ltd., 222 - 23 St. NE, Calgary AB T2E 7N2 – 403/235-7727; Fax: 403/248-0252; URL: http://www.cict.com	2
Calgary, AB	CFCN-TV	CFCN Communications Ltd., PO Box 7060, Stn E, Calgary AB T3C 3L9 – 403/240-5600; Fax: 403/240-5773; Email: channel3promo@cfcn.ca; URL: http://www.cfcn.ca	3
Calgary, AB	†CBRFT-TV	See Edmonton (CBXFT-TV)	16
Calgary, AB	*CBRT-TV	CBC, 1724 Westmount Blvd. NW, PO Box 2640, Calgary AB T2P 2M7 – 403/521-6000; Fax: 403/521-6007	9
Campbell River, BC	CBUT-TV-8	See Vancouver (CBUT-TV)	3, 82
Campbellton, NB	CKCD-TV	See Moncton (CKCW-TV)	7
Canal Flats, BC	CBUBT-TV-1	See Vancouver (CBUT-TV)	12
Canoe, BC	CHBC-TV-8	See Kelowna (CHBC-TV)	6
Cape Broyle, NF	CJBL-TV-13	See St. John's (CJON-TV)	13
Cardston, AB	CBRT-TV-12	See Calgary (CBRT-TV)	2
Carleton, PQ	†CHAU-TV	Diffusion Power Inc., CP 100, Carleton PQ G0C 1J0 – 418/364-3344; Fax: 418/364-7168	5
Carleton, PQ	†CIVK-TV	See Montréal (CIVM-TV)	15
Cartwright, NF	CBNT-TV-21	See St. John's (CBNT-TV)	9
Castlegar, BC	CBUAT-TV-2	See Vancouver (CBUT-TV)	3
Castlegar, BC	CKTN-TV-1	See Burnaby (CHAN-TV)	5
Causapscal, PQ	†CBGAT-TV-5	See Matane (CBGA-TV)	9
Celista, BC	CHBC-TV-6	See Kelowna (CHBC-TV)	3
Chapais, PQ	†CBFAT-TV-1	See Montréal (CBFT-TV)	12
Chapeau, PQ	†CIVP-TV	See Montréal (CIVM-TV)	23
Charlottetown, PE	CKCW-TV-1	See Moncton (CKCW-TV)	8
Charlottetown, PE	*CBCT-TV	CBC, 430 University Ave., PO Box 2230, Charlottetown PE C1A 8B9 – 902/629-6400; Fax: 902/629-6518	13
Charlottettetown, PE	†CBAFT-TV-5	See Moncton (CBAFT-TV)	31
Chase, BC	CHSH-TV-2	See Burnaby (CHAN-TV)	13
Chase, BC	CHSH-TV-1	See Burnaby (CHAN-TV)	7
Chase, BC	CFJC-TV-8	See Kamloops (CFJC-TV)	11
Chateh, AB	CBXAT-TV-7	See Edmonton (CBXT-TV)	5
Chatham, NB	CKAM-TV-2	See Moncton (CKCW-TV)	10
Chatham, ON	CBLN-TV-3	See Toronto (CBLT-TV)	64
Cherryville, BC	CJCC-TV	See Burnaby (CHAN-TV)	13
Cherryville, BC	CJWR-TV-1	See Kelowna (CHBC-TV)	10

Canadian Almanac & Directory 1997

TELEVISION STATIONS   5-215

LOCATION	CALL	*CBC Stations/Affiliates †French Language Stations	CHANNEL
Cheticamp, NS	CBIT-TV-2	See Sydney (CBIT-TV)	2
Chetwynd, BC	CBCD-TV-2	See Dawson Creek (CJDC-TV)	7
Chibougamau, PQ	†CBFAT-TV	See Montréal (CBFT-TV)	5
Chibougamau, PQ	CBMCT-TV	See Montréal (CBMT-TV)	4
Chicoutimi, PQ	†CJPM-TV	Télé-Metropole inc., CP 600, Chicoutimi PQ G7H 5G3 – 418/549-2576; Fax: 418/549-1130.	6
Chicoutimi, PQ	CBJET-TV	See Montréal (CBMT-TV)	58
Chilliwack, BC	CBUT-TV-2	See Vancouver (CBUT-TV)	3
Chilliwack, BC	CHAN-TV-1	See Burnaby (CHAN-TV)	11
Christina Lake, BC	CBUAT-TV-7	See Vancouver (CBUT-TV)	13
Churchill, MB	CHFC-TV	See Winnipeg (CBWT-TV)	8
Clarenville, NF	CBNT-TV-10	See St. John's (CBNT-TV)	7
Clarenville, NF	CJCN-TV-10	See St. John's (CJON-TV)	10
Clearwater, BC	CHCW-TV-1	See Kamloops (CFJC-TV)	2
Clearwater, BC	CHCW-TV-2	See Burnaby (CHAN-TV)	10
Clinton, BC	CFJC-TV-4	See Kamloops (CFJC-TV)	9
Clinton, BC	CHTS-TV-1	See Burnaby (CHAN-TV)	13
Coachman's Cove, NF	CBNAT-TV-16	See St. John's (CBNT-TV)	8
Coal Harbour, BC	CBUT-TV-20	See Vancouver (CBUT-TV)	8
Coleman, AB	CBRT-TV-11	See Calgary (CBRT-TV)	17
Conche, NF	CBNAT-TV-8	See St. John's (CBNT-TV)	13
Corner Brook, NF	CJWN-TV	See St. John's (CJON-TV)	10
Corner Brook, NF	*CBYT-TV	CBC, 162 Premier Dr., PO Box 610, Corner Brook NF A2H 6G1 – 709/634-3141; Fax: 709/634-8506	5
Courtenay, BC	CHAN-TV-4	See Burnaby (CHAN-TV)	13
Courtenay, BC	CBUT-TV-1	See Vancouver (CBUT-TV)	9
Coutts, AB	CBRT-TV-16	See Calgary (CBRT-TV)	4
Cowley, AB	CBRT-TV-15	See Calgary (CBRT-TV)	27
Cranbrook, BC	CBUBT-TV-7	See Vancouver (CBUT-TV)	65
Crawford Bay, BC	CBUCT-TV-1	See Vancouver (CBUT-TV)	5
Crescent Valley, BC	CBUCT-TV-4	See Vancouver (CBUT-TV)	33
Creston, BC	CBUCT-TV-2	See Vancouver (CBUT-TV)	3
Creston, BC	CKTN-TV-4	See Burnaby (CHAN-TV)	12
Cross Lake, MB	CBWNT-TV	See Winnipeg (CBWT-TV)	12
Cumberland House, SK	CBWIT-TV	See Winnipeg (CBWT-TV)	9
Cypress Hills, SK	*CBCP-TV-2	See Swift Current (CJFB-TV)	2
Dartmouth, NS	CIHF-TV	Global Communications Ltd., 14 Akerley Blvd., Dartmouth NS B3B 1J3 – 902/481-7400; Fax: 902/468-2154	20, 9, 18, 8, 45, 10, 34, 11, 6
Dauphin, MB	CKYD-TV	Craig Broadcast Systems Inc., 28 Second Ave. NE, PO Box 628, Dauphin MB R7N 3B3 – 204/638-3116; Fax: 204/638-4071	12
Dawson Creek, BC	CJDC-TV	Mega Communications Ltd., 901 - 102 Ave., Dawson Creek BC V1G 2B6 – 250/782-3341; Fax: 250/782-1809; Email: cjdctv@pris.bc.ca	5
Deer Lake, NF	CJLW-TV-7	See St. John's (CJON-TV)	7
Digby, NS	CBHT	See Halifax (CBHT-TV)	52
Dingwall, NS	CBIT-TV-16	See Sydney (CBIT-TV)	12
Dingwall, NS	CJCB-TV-3	See Sydney (CJCB-TV)	9
Doaktown, NB	CHSJ-TV-2	See Saint John (CHSJ-TV)	8
Doaktown, NB	CKAM-TV-4	See Moncton (CKCW-TV)	10
Donald Station, BC	CBUBT-TV-4	See Vancouver (CBUT-TV)	3
Drumheller, AB	CFCN-TV-6	See Calgary (CFCN-TV)	10
Dryden, ON	CBWDT-TV	See Winnipeg (CBWT-TV)	8
Ear Falls, ON	CBWJT-TV	See Winnipeg (CBWT-TV)	13
Eastend, SK	CJFB-TV-1	See Swift Current (CJFB-TV)	2
Easterville, MB	CBWHT-TV-2	See Winnipeg (CBWT-TV)	11
Edmonton, AB	†CBXFT-TV	Société Radio-Canada, 8861 - 75 St., CP 660, Edmonton AB T5J 2P4 – 403/468-7500; Fax: 403/468-7792	11
Edmonton, AB	CFRN-TV	Sunwapta Broadcasting, Division of Electrohome Ltd., 18520 Stony Plain Rd., PO Box 5030, Stn E, Edmonton AB T5S 1A8 – 403/483-3311; Fax: 403/486-5121; Email: cfrntv@worldgate.com	3
Edmonton, AB	CITV-TV	ITV, A Division of Westcom TV Group Ltd., 5325 Allard Way, Edmonton AB T6H 5B8 – 403/436-1250; Fax: 403/438-8448; Email: itv@ccinet.ab.ca; URL: http://www.itv.ca	13
Edmonton, AB	*CBXT-TV	CBC, 8861 - 75 St., PO Box 555, Edmonton AB T5J 2P4 – 403/468-7000; Fax: 403/468-7897	5
Edmundston, NB	CBAFT-TV-2	See Moncton (CBAFT-TV)	13
Edmundston, NB	CHCN-TV	See Saint John (CHSJ-TV)	6
Elliston, NF	CBNT-TV-7	See St. John's (CBNT-TV)	4
Elrose, SK	CKEL-TV-1	See Swift Current (CJFB-TV)	7
Enderby, BC	CFEN-TV-2	See Burnaby (CHAN-TV)	11
Enderby, BC	CFEN-TV-1	See Kelowna (CHBC-TV)	4
Erie, BC	CBUAT-TV-4	See Vancouver (CBUT-TV)	13
Etzikom, AB	CHAT-TV-5	See Medicine Hat (CHAT-TV)	12
Exshaw, AB	CBRT-TV	See Calgary (CBRT-TV)	6, 34
Fairford, MB	CBWGT-TV-2	See Winnipeg (CBWT-TV)	7
Falkland, BC	CFAW-TV	See Burnaby (CHAN-TV)	12
Falkland, BC	CFWS-TV-1	See Kelowna (CHBC-TV)	10
Fermeuse, NF	CBNT-TV-5	See St. John's (CBNT-TV)	11
Fermeuse, NF	CJFR-TV-12	See St. John's (CJON-TV)	12
Fernie, BC	CBUBT-TV-9	See Vancouver (CBUT-TV)	8
Ferryland, NF	CBNT-TV-38	See St. John's (CBNT-TV)	4
Field, BC	CBUBT-TV-13	See Vancouver (CBUT-TV)	11
Fisher Branch, MB	CBWGT-TV	See Winnipeg (CBWT-TV)	10

Canadian Almanac & Directory 1997

TELEVISION STATIONS

LOCATION	CALL	*CBC Stations/Affiliates †French Language Stations	CHANNEL
Fisher Branch, MB	CKYA-TV	See Winnipeg (CKY-TV)	8
Fleur-de-Lys, NF	CBNAT-TV-20	See St. John's (CBNT-TV)	5
Flin Flon, MB	CBWBT-TV	See Winnipeg (CBWT-TV)	10
Flin Flon, MB	CKYF-TV	See Winnipeg (CKY-TV)	13
Fogo Island, NF	CBNAT-TV-6	See St. John's (CBNT-TV)	2
Fort Frances, ON	CBWCT-TV	See Winnipeg (CBWT-TV)	5
Fort Fraser, BC	CBCB-TV-2	See Prince George (CKPG-TV)	6
Fort McMurray, AB	CBXT-TV-6	See Edmonton (CBXT-TV)	9
Fort Nelson, BC	CBUGT-TV	See Vancouver (CBUT-TV)	8
Fort Qu'Appelle, SK	CBKT-TV-3	See Regina (CBKT-TV)	4
Fort St. James, BC	CFFS-TV	See Burnaby (CHAN-TV)	10
Fort St. James, BC	CBCB-TV-3	See Prince George (CKPG-TV)	8
Fort St. John, BC	CBCD-TV-3	See Dawson Creek (CJDC-TV)	9
Fort Vermilion, AB	CBXAT-TV-5	See Edmonton (CBXT-TV)	11
Fortune, NF	CBNT-TV-33	See St. John's (CBNT-TV)	9
Fountain, BC	CFDF-TV-1	See Burnaby (CHAN-TV)	5
Fox Creek, AB	CBXT-TV-7	See Edmonton (CBXT-TV)	5
Fox Harbour, NF	CBNAT-TV-10	See St. John's (CBNT-TV)	7
Fox Lake, AB	CBXAT-TV-10	See Edmonton (CBXT-TV)	9
Foxwarren, MB	CKX-TV-1	See Brandon (CKX-TV)	
Fraser Lake, BC	CFFL-TV-1	See Burnaby (CHAN-TV)	9
Fraser Lake, BC	CFFL-TV-2	See Prince George (CKPG-TV)	6
Fredericton, NB	†CBAFT-TV-10	See Moncton (CBAFT-TV)	19
Fredericton, NB	*CBAT-TV	CBC, 1160 Regent St., PO Box 2200, Fredericton NB E3B 5G4 – 506/451-4000; Fax: 506/451-4003	4
Fruitvale/Montrose, BC	CBUAT-TV-3	See Vancouver (CBUT-TV)	9
Gillam, MB	CBWLT-TV	See Winnipeg (CBWT-TV)	8
Glovertown, NF	CBNT-TV-13	See St. John's (CBNT-TV)	3
Gods Lake Narrows, MB	CBWXT-TV	See Winnipeg (CBWT-TV)	13
Gold Bridge, BC	CJGB-TV-1	See Burnaby (CHAN-TV)	6
Gold River, BC	CBUT-TV-12	See Vancouver (CBUT-TV)	7
Golden, BC	CBUBT-TV-2	See Vancouver (CBUT-TV)	13
Goose Bay, NF	*CFLA-TV	CBC, 171 Hamilton River Rd., PO Box 1270, Goose Bay NF A0P 1E0 – 709/896-2911; Fax: 709/896-8900	8
Grand Bank, NF	CJOX-TV	See St. John's (CJON-TV)	2
Grand Falls, NB	†CBAFT-TV-4	See Moncton (CBAFT-TV)	12
Grand Falls, NF	CBNAT-TV	See St. John's (CBNT-TV)	11
Grand Falls, NF	CJCN-TV	See St. John's (CJON-TV)	4
Grand-Fonds, PQ	†CIVB-TV	See Montréal (CIVM-TV)	31
Grand Forks, BC	CKSR-TV-1	See Burnaby (CHAN-TV)	7
Grand Forks, BC	CBUT-TV-37	See Vancouver (CBUT-TV)	5
Grand Rapids, MB	CBWHT-TV	See Winnipeg (CBWT-TV)	8
Grande Prairie, AB	CBXAT-TV	See Edmonton (CBXT-TV)	10
Grande Prairie, AB	CFRN-TV-1	See Edmonton (CFRN-TV)	13
Grande Vallée, PQ	†CBGAT-TV-3	See Matane (CBGA-TV)	6
Granisle, BC	CIGR-TV-1	See Burnaby (CHAN-TV)	7
Gravelbourg, SK	†CBKFT-TV-6	See Winnipeg (CBWFT-TV)	39
Gravelbourg, SK	CKGT-TV	See Regina (CBKT-TV)	
Greenwater Lake, SK	CKBI-TV-3	See Prince Albert (CKBI-TV)	4
Greenwood, BC	CBUT-TV-31	See Vancouver (CBUT-TV)	13
Grinrod, BC	CHBC-TV	See Kelowna (CHBC-TV)	72
Gros Morne, PQ	†CBGAT-TV-9	See Matane (CBGA-TV)	4
Hagensborg, BC	CBUIT-TV-4	See Vancouver (CBUT-TV)	11
Halifax, NS	CJCH-TV	Atlantic Television System, PO Box 1653, Halifax NS B3J 2Z4 – 902/453-4000; Fax: 902/454-3302; URL: http://www.atv.ca	5
Halifax, NS	CIHF-TV	See Dartmouth (CIHF-TV)	8
Halifax, NS	*CBHT-TV	CBC, 1840 Bell St., PO Box 3000, Halifax NS B3J 3E9 – 902/420-8311; Fax: 902/420-4010	3
Hamilton, ON	CHCH-TV	Niagara Television Ltd., 163 Jackson St. West, PO Box 2230, Stn A, Hamilton ON L8N 3A6 – 905/522-1101; Fax: 905/523-8011; URL: http://www.chch.com	11
Hampden, NF	CBNAT-TV-23	See St. John's (CBNT-TV)	13
Hand Hills, AB	CFCN-TV-1	See Calgary (CFCN-TV)	12
Harbour Breton, NF	CBNT-TV-22	See St. John's (CBNT-TV)	13
Harbour Breton, NF	CBNT-TV	See St. John's (CBNT-TV)	13
Harbour Mile, NF	CBNT-TV-29	See St. John's (CBNT-TV)	13
Harbour Round, NF	CBNAT-TV-19	See St. John's (CBNT-TV)	12
Harrington Harbour, BC	CBMUT-TV	See Montréal (CBMT-TV)	8
Harrison Hot Springs, BC	CBUT-TV-23	See Vancouver (CBUT-TV)	13
Harvie Heights, AB	CBRT-TV-13	See Calgary (CBRT-TV)	61
Hazelton, BC	CFTK-TV	See Terrace (CFTK-TV)	9
Hendrix Lake, BC	CIHL-TV	See Burnaby (CHAN-TV)	12
Hermitage, NF	CBNT-TV-24	See St. John's (CBNT-TV)	4
Hickman's Harbour, NF	CBNT-TV-18	See St. John's (CBNT-TV)	4
High Level, AB	CBXAT-TV-4	See Edmonton (CBXT-TV)	8
High Prairie, AB	CBXAT-TV-2	See Edmonton (CBXT-TV)	2
Hinton, AB	CBXT-TV-3	See Edmonton (CBXT-TV)	8
Hixon, BC	CKPG-TV-1	See Prince George (CKPG-TV)	10
Holberg, BC	CBUT-TV-21	See Vancouver (CBUT-TV)	2
Hope, BC	CBUT-TV-6	See Vancouver (CBUT-TV)	9

Canadian Almanac & Directory 1997

LOCATION	CALL	*CBC Stations/Affiliates †French Language Stations	CHANNEL
Houston, BC	CFHO-TV	See Burnaby (CHAN-TV)	8
Houston, BC	CBCH-TV-1	See Terrace (CFTK-TV)	2
Hudson Bay, SK	CKOS	See Yorkton (CKOS-TV)	9
Hudson Hope, BC	CJDC	See Dawson Creek (CJDC-TV)	11
Hull, PQ	†CFGS-TV	Radio Nord Inc., 171, rue Jean-Proulx, Hull PQ J8Z 1W5 – 819/776-4949; Fax: 819/770-0272	49
Hull, PQ	†CHOT-TV	Radio Nord Inc., 171, rue Jean-Proulx, Hull PQ J8Z 1W5 – 819/770-1040; Fax: 819/770-0272	40
Hull, PQ	CBOT-TV	See Ottawa (CBOT-TV)	4
Hull, PQ	CIVO-TV	See Montréal (CIVM-TV)	30
Ignace, ON	CBWDT-TV-2	See Winnipeg (CBWT-TV)	13
Ile a la Crosse, SK	CBKCT-TV	See Saskatoon (CBKST-TV)	9
Ingonish, NS	CBIT-TV-15	See Sydney (CBIT-TV)	2
Invermere, BC	CBUBT-TV-3	See Vancouver (CBUT-TV)	2
Inverness, NS	CJCB-TV-1	See Sydney (CJCB-TV)	6
Island Falls, SK	CBWBT-TV-2	See Winnipeg (CBWT-TV)	7
Jackhead, MB	CBWGT-TV-1	See Winnipeg (CBWT-TV)	5
Jasper, AB	CBXT-TV-4	See Edmonton (CBXT-TV)	5
Jean Cote, AB	CBXAT-TV-13	See Edmonton (CBXT-TV)	31
Jean D'Or, AB	CBXAT-TV-9	See Edmonton (CBXT-TV)	13
Jonquière, PQ	†CFRS-TV	Radio Saguenay Ltée, 2303, rue Sir Wilfrid Laurier, Jonquière PQ G7X 7X3 – 418/542-4551; Fax: 418/542-7217	4
Jonquière, PQ	†CJPM-TV	See Chicoutimi (CJPM-TV)	
Jonquière, PQ	†CIVO-TV	See Montréal (CIVM-TV)	
Jonquière, PQ	†CIVV-TV	Société de Radio-Télévision du Québec, CP 23041, Jonquière PQ G7X 9Z8 – 418/695-8152; Fax: 418/695-8155	8
Kamloops, BC	CFJC-TV	Jim Pattison Group, 460 Pemberton Terrace, Kamloops BC V2C 1T5 – 250/372-3322; Fax: 250/374-0445	4
Kamloops, BC	CHKM-TV	See Burnaby (CHAN-TV)	6
Kedgwick, NB	†CBAFT-TV-9	See Moncton (CBAFT-TV)	44
Kelowna, BC	CHBC-TV	Okanagan Valley Television, Division of Westcom TV Group Ltd., 342 Leon Ave., Kelowna BC V1Y 6J2 – 250/762-4535; Fax: 250/860-2422	2
Kelowna, BC	CHKL-TV	See Burnaby (CHAN-TV)	5
Kemano, BC	CFTK-TV	See Terrace (CFTK-TV)	
Kenora, ON	CJBN-TV	Norcom Telecommunications Ltd., PO Box 1810, Kenora ON P9N 3X8 – 807/547-2852; Fax: 807/547-2236	13
Kenora, ON	CBWT-TV-7	See Winnipeg (CBWT-TV)	8
Keremeos, BC	CHBC-TV	See Kelowna (CHBC-TV)	4
Kildala, BC	CFTK-TV	See Terrace (CFTK-TV)	5
Kingston, ON	CKWS-TV	Power Broadcasting Inc., 170 Queen St., Kingston ON K7K 1B2 – 613/544-2340; Fax: 613/544-5508	11
Kitchener, ON	CKCO-TV	CAP Communications, 864 King St. West, Kitchener ON N2G 4E9 – 519/578-1313; Fax: 519/578-8375	13
Kitchener, ON	CBLN-TV-1	See Toronto (CBLT-TV)	56
Kitwanga, BC	CFTK-TV	See Terrace (CFTK-TV)	13
La Loche, SK	CBKDT-TV-2	See Saskatoon (CBKST-TV)	13
La Ronge, SK	CBKST-TV-2	See Saskatoon (CBKST-TV)	12
La Scie, NF	CBNAT-TV-21	See St. John's (CBNT-TV)	9
La Tabatière, PQ	CBMLT-TV	See Montréal (CBMT-TV)	10
La Tûque, PQ	CBMET-TV	See Montréal (CBMT-TV)	9
Labrador City, NF	*CBNLT-TV	CBC, PO Box 576, Labrador City NF A2V 2L3 – 709/944-3616; Fax: 709/944-5472	13
Lac-Bonnet, MB	CBWT-TV-2	See Winnipeg (CBWT-TV)	4
Lac La Biche, AB	CFRN-TV-5	See Edmonton (CFRN-TV)	2
Lac La Biche, AB	CBXT-TV-5	See Edmonton (CBXT-TV)	10
Lake Louise, AB	CBRT-TV-4	See Calgary (CBRT-TV)	
Lake Louise, AB	CFLL-TV-1	See Calgary (CFCN-TV)	6
Lamaline, NF	CBNT-TV-35	See St. John's (CBNT-TV)	18
Lawn, NF	CBNT-TV-36	See St. John's (CBNT-TV)	6
Lawn, NF	CJLN-TV	See St. John's (CJON-TV)	10
Leaf Rapids, MB	CBWQT-TV	See Winnipeg (CBWT-TV)	13
Leoville, SK	CBKST-TV-3	See Saskatoon (CBKST-TV)	12
Lethbridge, AB	CISA-TV	Lethbridge Television, Division of Westcom TV Group Ltd., PO Box 1120, Lethbridge AB T1J 4A4 – 403/327-1521; Fax: 403/320-2620; Email: cisa@leth.sas.ab.ca; http://www.cisatv.com	7
Lethbridge, AB	CBRT-TV-6	See Calgary (CBRT-TV)	85
Lethbridge, AB	CFCN-TV-5	See Calgary (CFCN-TV)	13
Lillooet, BC	CFMZ-TV-1	See Kamloops (CFJC-TV)	2
Lillooet, BC	CDFD-TV-2	See Burnaby (CHAN-TV)	13
Little Fort, BC	CKTV-TV-1	See Kamloops (CFJC-TV)	12
Liverpool, NS	CBHT-TV-1	See Halifax (CBHT-TV)	12
Lloydminster, AB	CITL-TV	MidWest Television Ltd., 5026 - 50th St., Lloydminster AB T9V 1P3 – 403/875-3321; Fax: 403/875-4704	4
Lloydminster, AB	CKSA-TV	MidWest Television Ltd., 5026 - 50th St., Lloydminster AB T9V 1P3 – 403/875-3321; Fax: 403/875-4704	2
Lochaber, NS	CBLT-TV-12	See Sydney (CBIT-TV)	33
Logan Lake, BC	CHLK-TV-2	See Burnaby (CHAN-TV)	13
Logan Lake, BC	CFJC-TV	See Kamloops (CFJC-TV)	11
London, ON	CFPL-TV	Baton Broadcasting Inc., PO Box 2880, Stn A, London ON N6A 4H9 – 519/686-8810; Fax: 519/668-3288	10
Loos, BC	CBUHT-TV-2	See Vancouver (CBUT-TV)	6
Lord's Cove, NF	CBNT-TV-34	See St. John's (CBNT-TV)	9
Lougheed, AB	CFRN-TV-7	See Edmonton (CFRN-TV)	7
Lumby, BC	CHID-TV-2	See Burnaby (CHAN-TV)	9
Lumsden, NF	CBNT-TV-20	See St. John's (CBNT-TV)	12
Lynn Lake, MB	CBWRT-TV	See Winnipeg (CBWT-TV)	6
Lytton, BC	CHWS-TV-1	See Kamloops (CFJC-TV)	11
Lytton, BC	CILY-TV-2	See Burnaby (CHAN-TV)	8
Mabel Lake, BC	CHPL-TV-1	See Burnaby (CHAN-TV)	13

TELEVISION STATIONS

LOCATION	CALL	*CBC Stations/Affiliates †French Language Stations	CHANNEL
Mabel Lake, BC	CHPP-TV-1	See Kelowna (CHBC-TV)	8
Mabou, NS	CBIT-TV-4	See Sydney (CBIT-TV)	10
Mackenzie, BC	CKPG-TV-4	See Prince George (CKPG-TV)	6
Mackenzie, BC	CIMK-TV-1	See Burnaby (CHAN-TV)	9
Mafeking, MB	CBWYT-TV	See Winnipeg (CBWT-TV)	2
Malakwa, BC	CFFI-TV-1	See Kelowna (CHBC-TV)	4
Malakwa, BC	CFFI-TV-2	See Burnaby (CHAN-TV)	11
Manigotagan, MB	CBWGT-TV-3	See Winnipeg (CBWT-TV)	22
Manning, AB	CBXAT-TV-3	See Edmonton (CBXT-TV)	12
Maple Creek, SK	CHAT-TV-2	See Medicine Hat (CHAT-TV)	
Margaree, NS	CBIT-TV-5	See Sydney (CBIT-TV)	8
Marinette, NS	CJCH-TV-8	See Halifax (CJCH-TV)	23
Marsoui, PQ	†CBGAT-TV-8	See Matane (CBGA-TV)	12
Marten Mtn./Slave Lake, AB	CBXAT-TV-11	See Edmonton (CBXT-TV)	11
Marystown, NF	CBNT-TV-3	See St. John's (CBNT-TV)	5
Marystown, NF	CJMA-TV-11	See St. John's (CJON-TV)	11
Masset, BC	CHMH-TV-1	See Terrace (CFTK-TV)	8
Matane, PQ	CBGA-TV	Société Radio-Canada, 155, rue St-Sacrement, CP 2000, Matane PQ G4W 3P7 – 418/562-0290; Fax: 418/562-3555	6
McBride, BC	CBUHT-TV-3	See Vancouver (CBUT-TV)	2
McCreary, MB	CKX-TV-3	See Brandon (CKX-TV)	11
McCusker Lake, MB	CBWUT-TV	See Winnipeg (CBWT-TV)	10
Meadow Lake, SK	CBCS-TV-1	See Lloydminster (CKSA-TV)	8
Medicine Hat, AB	CHAT-TV	Monarch Broadcasting Co. Ltd., PO Box 1270, Medicine Hat AB T1A 7H5 – 403/529-1270; Fax: 403/529-1292; Email: ddietric@mlc.awinc.com	6
Medicine Hat, AB	CFCN-TV-8	See Calgary (CFCN-TV)	8
Melfort, SK	CKBQ-TV	See Prince Albert (CKBI-TV)	
Melita, MB	CKX-TV-2	See Brandon (CKX-TV)	
Merritt, BC	CFJC-TV-3	See Kamloops (CFJC-TV)	8
Middleton, NS	CBHT-TV-6	See Halifax (CBHT-TV)	8
Midway, BC	CBUT-TV-32	See Vancouver (CBUT-TV)	7
Millertown, NF	CBNAT-TV-5	See St. John's (CBNT-TV)	9
Ming's Bight, NF	CBNAT-TV-14	See St. John's (CBNT-TV)	10
Minnedosa, MB	CKND-TV-2	See Winnipeg (CKND-TV)	
Minto, BC	CFMT-TV-3	See Kamloops (CFJC-TV)	3
Moncton, NB	CKCW-TV	CKCW-TV, Division of CHUM Ltd., 191 Halifax St., Moncton NB E1C 8R6 – 506/857-2600; Fax: 506/857-2618; URL: http://www.atv.ca	2
Moncton, NB	CHMT-TV	See Saint John (CHSJ-TV)	7
Moncton, NB	CIHF-TV-3	See Dartmouth (CIHF-TV)	27
Moncton, NB	*CBAFT-TV	CBC, 250 Archibald St., Moncton NB E1C 8N8 – 506/853-6666; Fax: 506/853-6739	7
Mont-Climont, PQ	†CBGAT-TV-1	See Matane (CBGA-TV)	13
Mont-Laurier, PQ	†CBFT-TV-2	See Montréal (CBFT-TV)	3
Mont-Louis, PQ	†CBGAT-TV-4	See Matane (CBGA-TV)	2
Mont-Louis-Haut, PQ	†CBGAT-TV-10	See Matane (CBGA-TV)	19
Mont St-Michel, PQ	†CBFT-TV-9	See Montréal (CBFT-TV)	16
Mont-Tremblant, PQ	†CBFT-TV-1	See Montréal (CBFT-TV)	11
Montréal, PQ	†CBFT-TV	Société Radio-Canada, 1400, boul René-Lévesque est, CP 6000, Montréal PQ H3C 3A8 – 514/597-5970; Fax: 514/597-5551	2
Montréal, PQ	CFCF-TV	CFCF Inc., 405, av Ogilvy, Montréal PQ H3N 1M4 – 514/273-6311; Fax: 514/276-9399	12
Montréal, PQ	†CFJP-TV	Télévision Quatre Saisons Inc., 405, av Ogilvy, Montréal PQ H3N 2Y4 – 514/271-3535; Fax: 514/271-6047	35
Montréal, PQ	†CFTM-TV	Télé-Métropole Inc., 1600, boul de Maisonneuve est, Montréal PQ H2L 4P2 – 514/526-9251; Fax: 514/526-4857	10
Montréal, PQ	†CIVM-TV	Radio-Québec, 800, rue Fullum, Montréal PQ H2K 3L7 – 514/521-2424; Fax: 514/873-7464	17
Montréal, PQ	*CBMT-TV	CBC, 1400, boul René-Lévesque est, CP 6000, Montréal PQ H3C 3A8 – 514/597-5970; Fax: 514/597-4596	6
Montreal Lake, SK	CBKST-TV	See Saskatoon (CBKST-TV)	11
Moose Jaw, SK	CBKT-TV-1	See Regina (CBKT-TV)	4
Moose Lake, MB	CBWIT-TV-1	See Winnipeg (CBWT-TV)	10
Mount Hamilton, BC	CFHM-TV-1	See Kamloops (CFJC-TV)	7
Mount McDonald, BC	CBUT-TV-27	See Vancouver (CBUT-TV)	59
Moyie, BC	CBUBT-TV-14	See Vancouver (CBUT-TV)	6
Mulgrave, NS	CBHT-TV-11	See Sydney (CBIT-TV)	12
Murdochville, PQ	†CBGAT-TV-2	See Matane (CBGA-TV)	10
Murdochville, PQ	CBMMT-TV	See Montréal (CBMT-TV)	21
Musgrave Harbour, NF	CBNAT-TV-11	See St. John's (CBNT-TV)	9
Musgravetown, NF	CBNT-TV-17	See St. John's (CBNT-TV)	9
Nakusp, BC	CJNP-TV-1	See Kelowna (CHBC-TV)	2
Nakusp, BC	CJNP-TV-3	See Burnaby (CHAN-TV)	7
Narrows Inlet, BC	CHNI-TV	See Victoria (CHEK-TV)	10
Natal, BC	CBUBT-TV-10	See Vancouver (CBUT-TV)	11
Nelson, BC	CKTN-TV-3	See Burnaby (CHAN-TV)	3
Nelson, BC	CBUCT-TV	See Vancouver (CBUT-TV)	
Nelson House, MB	CBWPT-TV	See Winnipeg (CBWT-TV)	11
New Denver, BC	CHJV-TV	See Burnaby (CHAN-TV)	13
New Denver, BC	CBUCT-TV-6	See Vancouver (CBUT-TV)	17
New Glasgow, NS	CBHT-TV-5	See Halifax (CBHT-TV)	4
New Glasgow, NS	CJCB-TV-4	See Sydney (CJCB-TV)	2

LOCATION	CALL	*CBC Stations/Affiliates †French Language Stations	CHANNEL
Newcastle, NB	CKAM-TV-1	*See* Moncton (CKCW-TV)	10
Newcastle Ridge, BC	CFKB-TV-1	*See* Victoria (CHEK-TV)	7
Nicola Valley, BC	CFJC-TV-12	*See* Kamloops (CFJC-TV)	10
Nimpkish, BC	CFNV-TV-2	*See* Victoria (CHEK-TV)	6
Noranda Mines, BC	CFJC-TV	*See* Kamloops (CFJC-TV)	7
Norquay, SK	CKOS-TV-1	*See* Yorkton (CKOS-TV)	13
North Battleford, SK	CKBI-TV-2	*See* Prince Albert (CKBI-TV)	7
North Bay, ON	CHNB-TV	MCTV-Mid Canada Communications Corp., 245 Oak St. East, PO Box 3220, North Bay ON P1B 8P8 – 705/476-3111; Fax: 705/495-4474	4
North Bay, ON	CKNY-TV	MCTV-Mid Canada Communications Corp., 245 Oak St. East, PO Box 3220, North Bay ON P1B 8P8 – 705/476-3111; Fax: 705/495-4474	10
Northeast Margaree, NS	CBIT-TV-6	*See* Sydney (CBIT-TV)	13
Northwest Brook, NF	CBNT-TV-11	*See* St. John's (CBNT-TV)	4
Norway House, MB	CBWOT-TV	*See* Winnipeg (CBWT-TV)	9
Notre-Dame-Laus, PQ	†CBOFT-TV-3	*See* Montréal (CBFT-TV)	10
Olalla, BC	CHKC-TV-5	*See* Burnaby (CHAN-TV)	11
Old Fort Bay, PQ	CBMVT-TV	*See* Montréal (CBMT-TV)	13
Oliver, BC	CHBC-TV-3	*See* Kelowna (CHBC-TV)	8
Osnaburgh, ON	CBWDT-TV-4	*See* Winnipeg (CBWT-TV)	13
Ottawa, ON	CHOT-TV	*See* Hull (CHOT-TV)	
Ottawa, ON	†CBOFT-TV	Société Radio-Canada, CP 3220, Succ C, Ottawa ON K1Y 1E4 – 613/724-1200; Fax: 613/724-5233	9
Ottawa, ON	CHRO-TV	Baton Broadcasting Inc., 10 Kimway Cres., Ottawa ON K2E 6Z6 – 613/236-2476	5
Ottawa, ON	CJOH-TV	Baton Broadcasting Inc., PO Box 5813, Stn Merivale, Ottawa ON K2C 3G6 – 613/224-1313; Fax: 613/224-7998	13
Ottawa, ON	*CBOT-TV	CBC, PO Box 3220, Stn C, Ottawa ON K1Y 1E4 – 613/724-1200; Fax: 613/724-5512	4
Oxford House, MB	CBWVT-TV	*See* Winnipeg (CBWT-TV)	8
Oyen, AB	CFON-TV-1	*See* Calgary (CFCN-TV)	2
Oyen, AB	CHAT-TV-3, -4	*See* Medicine Hat (CHAT-TV)	4,6
Pacquet, NF	CBNAT-TV-17	*See* St. John's (CBNT-TV)	6
Palmbere Lake, SK	CBKDT-TV-1	*See* Saskatoon (CBKST-TV)	8
Peace River, AB	CBXAT-TV-1	*See* Edmonton (CBXT-TV)	7
Peace River, AB	CFRN-TV-2	*See* Edmonton (CFRN-TV)	3
Peachland, BC	CHPT-TV-1	*See* Kelowna (CHBC-TV)	4
Peachland, BC	CIPL-TV	*See* Burnaby (CHAN-TV)	9
Pelican Narrows, SK	CBWBT-TV-3	*See* Winnipeg (CBWT-TV)	5
Pemberton, BC	CBUPT-TV	*See* Vancouver (CBUT-TV)	4
Pemberton, BC	CHPV-TV-1	*See* Victoria (CHEK-TV)	9
Pembroke, ON	CHRO-TV	Baton Broadcasting Inc., PO Box 1010, Pembroke ON K8A 7T3 – 613/735-1036; Fax: 613/735-0022	5
Penticton, BC	CHBC-TV-1	*See* Kelowna (CHBC-TV)	13
Penticton, BC	CHKL-TV-1	*See* Burnaby (CHAN-TV)	10
Percé, PQ	CIVK-TV-2	*See* Montréal (CIVM-TV)	40
Peterborough, ON	CHEX-TV	Power Broadcasting Inc., 1925 Television Rd., PO Box 4150, Peterborough ON K9J 6Z9 – 705/742-0451; Fax: 705/742-7274	12
Petty Harbour, NF	CBNT-TV-37	*See* St. John's (CBNT-TV)	13
Phoenix, BC	CBUT-TV-30	*See* Vancouver (CBUT-TV)	15
Pickle Lake, ON	CBWDT-TV-5	*See* Winnipeg (CBWT-TV)	9
Pikangikum, ON	CBWDT-TV-6	*See* Winnipeg (CBWT-TV)	7
Pincher Creek, AB	CBRT-TV-9	*See* Calgary (CBRT-TV)	15
Pincher Creek, AB	CHPC-TV-2	*See* Calgary (CFCN-TV)	11
Pinehouse Lake, SK	CBKST-TV-6	*See* Saskatoon (CBKST-TV)	10
Pitt River, BC	CIPT-TV	*See* Victoria (CHEK-TV)	10
Placentia, NF	CBNT-TV-2	*See* St. John's (CBNT-TV)	12
Pleasant Bay, NS	CBIT-TV-3	*See* Sydney (CBIT-TV)	8
Pointe-au-Père, PQ	CFER-TV	TéléMétropole Multi-Regions Inc., 465, boul Ste-Anne, Pointe-au-Père PQ G5M 1G1 – 418/722-6011; Fax: 418/724-7810	11
Ponteix, SK	*CBCP-TV-3	*See* Swift Current (CJFB-TV)	3
Port Alberni, BC	CHEK-TV-3	*See* Victoria (CHEK-TV)	11
Port Alberni, BC	CBUT-TV-3	*See* Vancouver (CBUT-TV)	4
Port Alice, BC	CBUT-TV-17	*See* Vancouver (CBUT-TV)	10
Port Blandford, NF	CBNT-TV-32	*See* St. John's (CBNT-TV)	6
Port Hardy, BC	CBUT-TV-19	*See* Vancouver (CBUT-TV)	6
Port Hope Simpson, NF	CBNAT-TV-12	*See* St. John's (CBNT-TV)	12
Port McNeill, BC	CBUT-TV-18	*See* Vancouver (CBUT-TV)	2
Port Renfrew, BC	CJTV-TV-1	*See* Burnaby (CHAN-TV)	11
Port Rexton, NF	CBNT-TV-1	*See* St. John's (CBNT-TV)	13
Portage La Prairie, MB	CHMI-TV	Craig Broadcast Systems Inc., 350 River Rd., PO Box 13000, Portage La Prairie MB R1N 3V3 – 204/239-1113; Fax: 204/239-5794; Email: promo@opnet.net	13
Pouce Coupe, BC	CBCD-TV-1	*See* Dawson Creek (CJDC-TV)	7
Prince Albert, SK	CIPA-TV	Shamrock Television System Inc., Prince Albert Division, 22 - 10 St. West, Prince Albert SK S6V 3A5 – 306/922-6066; Fax: 306/763-3041	9
Prince Albert, SK	CKBI-TV	Shamrock Television System Inc., Prince Albert Division, 22 - 10 St. West, Prince Albert SK S6V 3A5 – 306/922-6066; Fax: 306/763-3041	5
Prince George, BC	CKPG-TV	Monarch Broadcasting Ltd., 1220 - 6th Ave., Prince George BC V2L 3M8 – 250/564-8861; Fax: 250/562-8768; Email: benny@mindlink.net; URL: http://www.pgonline.com/benny	2
Prince George, BC	CIFG-TV	*See* Burnaby (CHAN-TV)	12
Prince Rupert, BC	CFTK-TV-1	*See* Terrace (CFTK-TV)	6

Canadian Almanac & Directory 1997

LOCATION	CALL	*CBC Stations/Affiliates †French Language Stations	CHANNEL
Princeton, BC	CHNJ-TV-1	See Burnaby (CHAN-TV)	11
Pritchard, BC	CFJC-TV-19	See Kamloops (CFJC-TV)	5
Pritchard, BC	CHKM-TV-1	See Burnaby (CHAN-TV)	9
Provost, AB	CKSA-TV-4	See Lloydminster (CKSA-TV)	12
Pukatawagan, MB	CBWBT-TV-1	See Winnipeg (CBWT-TV)	11
Purden, BC	CBUHT-TV-1	See Vancouver (CBUT-TV)	10
Québec, PQ	†CFAP-TV	Télévision Quatre Saisons inc., 500, rue Bouvier, CP 17500, Succ Terminus, Québec PQ G1K 7X2 – 418/624-2222; Fax: 418/624-3099	2
Québec, PQ	†CFER-TV-2	See Pointe-au-Père (CFER-TV)	5
Québec, PQ	†CIVQ-TV	See Montréal (CIVM-TV)	15
Queen Charlotte City, BC	CFTK-TV	See Terrace (CFTK-TV)	4
Quesnel, BC	CFJC-TV-11	See Kamloops (CFJC-TV)	7
Quesnel, BC	CKPG-TV-5	See Prince George (CKPG-TV)	13
Quesnel, BC	CITM-TV-2	See Burnaby (CHAN-TV)	8
Radium Hot Springs, BC	CBUBT-TV-5	See Vancouver (CBUT-TV)	77
Rainbow Lake, AB	CBXAT-TV-8	See Edmonton (CBXT-TV)	11
Ramea, NF	CBNT-TV-25	See St. John's (CBNT-TV)	13
Random Island, NF	CBNT-TV-19	See St. John's (CBNT-TV)	43
Rapides-des-Joachims, PQ	†CBOFT-TV-2	See Ottawa (CBOFT-TV)	31
Red Deer, AB	CKRD-TV	RDTV, Division of Westcom TV Group Ltd., 2840 Bremner Ave., Red Deer AB T4R 1M9 – 403/346-2573; Fax: 403/346-9980; URL: http://www.rdtv.com	6
Red Deer, AB	CFRN-TV-6	See Edmonton (CFRN-TV)	8
Red Lake, ON	CBWET-TV	See Winnipeg (CBWT-TV)	10
Red Rocks, NF	CJRF-TV-11	See St. John's (CJON-TV)	11
Regina, SK	CKCK-TV	BBS Saskatchewan Inc., PO Box 2000, Regina SK S4P 3E5 – 306/569-2000; Fax: 306/522-0090	2
Regina, SK	CFSS-TV	See Yorkton (CKOS-TV)	3
Regina, SK	CFRE-TV	CanWest Television Inc., 370 Hoffer Dr., Regina SK S4N 7A4 – 306/721-2211; Fax: 306/721-4817	11
Regina, SK	*†CBKFT-TV	Société Radio-Canada, 2440 Broad St., Regina SK S4P 4A1 – 306/347-9540; Fax: 306/347-9493	13
Regina, SK	*CBKT-TV	CBC, 2440 Broad St., PO Box 540, Regina SK S4P 4A1 – 306/347-9540; Fax: 306/347-9493	9
Revelstoke, BC	CHRP-TV-2	See Burnaby (CHAN-TV)	
Revelstoke, BC	CHRP-TV-1	See Kelowna (CHBC-TV)	7
Rimouski, PQ	†CIVB-TV	Radio-Télévision du Québec, 79, rue de l'Évêché est, Rimouski PQ G5L 1X7 – 418/727-3743; Fax: 418/727-3814	22
Rimouski, PQ	†CJPC-TV	See Montréal (CFJP-TV)	18
Rimrock, BC	CKRR-TV-1	See Kamloops (CFJC-TV)	9
Rimrock, BC	CKRN-TV-2	See Burnaby (CHAN-TV)	11
Riverhurst, SK	CJFB-TV-3	See Swift Current (CJFB-TV)	10
Rivière-du-Loup, PQ	†CFTF-TV	Télévision MBS, #100, 1298, boul Thériault, Rivière-du-Loup PQ 418 – 418/867-1341; Fax: 418/867-4710	29
Rivière-du-Loup, PQ	†CIMT-TV	Télé Inter-Rives Ltée, 15, rue de la Chute, Rivière-du-Loup PQ G5R 2V1 – 418/867-1341; Fax: 418/867-4710	9
Rivière-du-Loup, PQ	†CKRT-TV	Télé Inter-Rives Ltée, 15, rue de la Chute, Rivière-du-Loup PQ G5R 5B7 – 418/867-1341; Fax: 418/867-4710	7
Rivière-Paul, PQ	CBMPT-TV	See Montréal (CBMT-TV)	11
Rock Creek, BC	CBUT-TV-33	See Vancouver (CBUT-TV)	33
Rocky Mountain House, AB	CFMH-TV-2	See Edmonton (CFRN-TV)	12
Roddickton, NF	CBNAT-TV-22	See St. John's (CBNT-TV)	11
Rosemary, AB	CBRT-TV-5	See Calgary (CBRT-TV)	11
Rouyn-Noranda, PQ	†CFEM-TV	Radio Nord Inc., 380, rue Murdoch, CP 70, Rouyn-Noranda PQ J9X 5C2 – 819/762-0741; Fax: 819/762-2280	13
Rouyn-Noranda, PQ	†CKRN-TV	Radio Nord inc., 380, rue Murdoch, CP 70, Rouyn-Noranda PQ J9X 5C2 – 819/762-0741; Fax: 819/762-2280	4
Rouyn-Noranda, PQ	†CIVN-TV	See Montréal (CIVM-TV)	8
Ruby Creek, BC	CBUT-TV-26	See Vancouver (CBUT-TV)	25
St. Albans, NF	CBNT-TV-4	See St. John's (CBNT-TV)	9
St. Albans, NF	CJST-TV-13	See St. John's (CJON-TV)	13
Ste-Anne-des-Monts, PQ	†CBGAT-TV-11	See Matane (CBGA-TV)	8
St. Anthony, NF	CBNAT-TV-4	See St. John's (CBNT-TV)	6
St-Augustin-Saguenay, PQ	CBMXT-TV	See Montréal (CBMT-TV)	7
St. Bernards, NF	CBNT-TV-30	See St. John's (CBNT-TV)	6
St. Edward, PE	†CBAFT-TV-6	See Moncton (CBAFT-TV)	9
Ste-Foy, PQ	†CFCM-TV	Télé-Métropole Inc., 1000, av Myrand, CP 2026, Ste-Foy PQ G1V 2W3 – 418/688-9330; Fax: 418/681-4239	4
Ste-Foy, PQ	CKMI-TV	Télé-Métropole Inc., 1000, av Myrand, CP 2026, Ste-Foy PQ G1V 2W3 – 418/688-9330; Fax: 418/681-4239	5
Ste-Foy, PQ	*†CBVT-TV	Société Radio-Canada, 2505, boul Laurier, Ste-Foy PQ G1V 2X2 – 418/654-1341; Fax: 418/654-3299	11
Saint John, NB	CHSJ-TV	N.B. Broadcasting Co. Ltd., 335 Union St., PO Box 2000, Saint John NB E2L 3T4 – 506/632-2222; Fax: 506/632-3485	4
Saint John, NB	CKLT-TV	ATV, Division of CHUM Ltd., 251 Bayside Dr., Saint John NB E2J 1A7 – 506/658-0100; Fax: 506/658-1208	9
Saint John, NB	†CBAFT-TV-1	See Moncton (CBAFT-TV)	5
Saint John, NB	CIHF-TV-2	See Dartmouth (CIHF-TV)	12
Saint John, NB	*CBAT-TV	CBC, 560 Main St., PO Box 2358, Saint John NB E2L 3V6 – 506/632-7710; Fax: 506/632-7761	4
St. John's, NF	CJON-TV	Newfoundland Broadcasting Co. Ltd., 446 Logy Bay Rd., PO Box 2020, St. John's NF A1C 5S2 – 709/722-5015; Fax: 709/726-5107	6
St. John's, NF	*CBNT-TV	CBC, 95 University Ave., PO Box 12010, Stn A, St. John's NF A1B 3T8 – 709/576-5000; Fax: 709/576-5144	8
St. Jones Within, NF	CBNT-TV-12	See St. John's (CBNT-TV)	9
St. Lawrence, NF	CBNT-TV-28	See St. John's (CBNT-TV)	12
St. Lawrence, NF	CJXL-TV-10	See St. John's (CJON-TV)	10
St. Mary's, NF	CBNT-TV-6	See St. John's (CBNT-TV)	10
St-Michel-des-Saints, PQ	†CBFT-TV-3	See Montréal (CBFT-TV)	7
St. Quentin, NB	†CBAFT-TV-8	See Moncton (CBAFT-TV)	21
St. Vincent's, NF	CBNT-TV-26	See St. John's (CBNT-TV)	7
Salmo, BC	CBUAT-TV-5	See Vancouver (CBUT-TV)	10

LOCATION	CALL	*CBC Stations/Affiliates　　†French Language Stations	CHANNEL
Salmon Arm, BC	CHBC-TV-4	See Kelowna (CHBC-TV)	9
Salmon Arm, BC	CFSA-TV-1	See Burnaby (CHAN-TV)	13
Sandy Lake, ON	CBWDT-TV-7	See Winnipeg (CBWT-TV)	10
Santa Rosa, BC	CKSR-TV	See Burnaby (CHAN-TV)	83
Sarnia, ON	CBLN-TV-2	See Toronto (CBLT-TV)	34
Saskatoon, SK	CFQC-TV	STN Television Network Inc., 216 - 1 Ave. North, Saskatoon SK S7K 3W3 – 306/665-8600; Fax: 306/664-0450	8
Saskatoon, SK	CFSK-TV	CanWest Television Inc., 218 Robin Cres., Saskatoon SK S7L 7C3 – 306/665-6969; Fax: 306/665-6069	4
Saskatoon, SK	†CBKFT-TV	See Regina (CBKFT-TV)	13
Saskatoon, SK	*CBKST-TV	CBC, CN Tower, Midtown Plaza, 5th Fl., Saskatoon SK S7K 1J5 – 306/956-7400; Fax: 306/956-7417	11
Sault Ste. Marie, ON	CHBX-TV	Baton Broadcasting Inc., 119 East St., PO Box 370, Sault Ste. Marie ON P6A 5M2 – 705/254-7111; Fax: 705/759-7782	
Sault Ste. Marie, ON	CJIC-TV	Baton Broadcasting Inc., 119 East St., PO Box 370, Sault Ste. Marie ON P6A 5M2 – 705/759-8232; Fax: 705/759-7783	5
Savant Lake, ON	CBWDT-TV-3	See Winnipeg (CBWT-TV)	8
Savona, BC	CFSC-TV-2	See Burnaby (CHAN-TV)	13
Savona, BC	CFSC-TV-1	See Kamloops (CFJC-TV)	8
Sayward, BC	CBUT-TV-10	See Vancouver (CBUT-TV)	4
Scarborough, ON	CFTO-TV	Baton Broadcasting Inc., PO Box 9, Stn O, Scarborough ON M4A 2M9 – 416/299-2000; Fax: 416/299-2386	9
Seal Cove, NF	CBNAT-TV-15	See St. John's (CBNT-TV)	7
Sept-Îles, PQ	†CIVG-TV	See Montréal (CIVM-TV)	9
Sept-Îles, PQ	CBSET-TV	See Montréal (CBMT-TV)	3
Shalalth, BC	CJBT-TV-2	See Burnaby (CHAN-TV)	11
Shalalth, BC	CJBT-TV-1	See Kamloops (CFJC-TV)	5
Shaunavon, SK	*CBCP-TV-1	See Swift Current (CJFB-TV)	7
Sheet Harbour, NS	CBHT-TV-4	See Halifax (CBHT-TV)	11
Sheet Harbour, NS	CJCH-TV-5	See Halifax (CJCH-TV)	2
Shelburne, NS	CBHT-TV-2	See Halifax (CBHT-TV)	7
Sherbrooke, NS	CBHT-TV-16	See Sydney (CBIT-TV)	4
Sherbrooke, PQ	CFKS-TV	COGECO Inc., 3720, boul Industriel, Sherbrooke PQ J1L 1Z9 – 819/565-9999; Fax: 819/822-4205	30
Sherbrooke, PQ	†CHLT-TV	Reseau TVA Inc., 3330, rue King ouest, Sherbrooke PQ J1L 1C9 – 819/565-7777; Fax: 819/563-0141	7
Sherbrooke, PQ	†CKSH-TV	COGECO Inc., 3720 boul Industriel, Sherbrooke PQ J1L 1Z9 – 819/565-9999; Fax: 819/822-4205	9
Sherbrooke, PQ	†CIVS-TV	See Montréal (CIVM-TV)	24
Sherbrooke, PQ	CBMT-TV-3	See Montréal (CBMT-TV)	50
Shoulder Mtn., BC	CFTK-TV	See Terrace (CFTK-TV)	9
Sioux Lookout, ON	CBWDT-TV-1	See Winnipeg (CBWT-TV)	12
Sioux Narrows, ON	CBWAT-TV-1	See Winnipeg (CBWT-TV)	4
Skaha Lake, BC	CHBC-TV-7	See Kelowna (CHBC-TV)	7
Slave Lake, AB	CKHP-TV-1	See Edmonton (CFRN-TV)	4
Slocan, BC	CBUCT-TV-5	See Vancouver (CBUT-TV)	39
Smithers, BC	CFHO-TV-1	See Burnaby (CHAN-TV)	13
Snow Lake, MB	CKYS-TV	See Winnipeg (CKY-TV)	11
Snow Lake, MB	CBWKT-TV	See Winnipeg (CBWT-TV)	8
Soda Creek, BC	CKSC-TV-1	See Kamloops (CFJC-TV)	4
Soda Creek, BC	CKSC-TV-2	See Burnaby (CHAN-TV)	2
Sooke, BC	CBUT-TV-28	See Vancouver (CBUT-TV)	3
Southend, SK	CBKST-TV-8	See Saskatoon (CBKST-TV)	13
Spencerville, ON	CKWS-TV-2	See Kingston (CKWS-TV)	26
Spence's Bridge, BC	CJNA-TV-1	See Kamloops (CFJC-TV)	3
Spence's Bridge, BC	CJNA-TV-2	See Burnaby (CHAN-TV)	7
Spillimacheen, BC	CBUBT-TV-6	See Vancouver (CBUT-TV)	69
Spiritwood, SK	CKBI-TV-6	See Prince Albert (CKBI-TV)	2
Springdale, NF	CBNAT-TV-13	See St. John's (CBNT-TV)	13
Squamish, BC	CHAN-TV-3	See Burnaby (CHAN-TV)	7
Squamish, BC	CBUT-TV-5	See Vancouver (CBUT-TV)	11
Stanley Mission, SK	CBKST-TV-4	See Saskatoon (CBKST-TV)	8
Stewart, BC	CFTK-TV	See Terrace (CFTK-TV)	11
Stranraer, SK	CBKST-TV-1	See Saskatoon (CBKST-TV)	9
Sudbury, ON	CICI-TV	Mid Canada Television, 699 Frood Rd., Sudbury ON P3C 5A3 – 705/674-8301	5
Sudbury, ON	CKNC-TV	Baton Broadcasting Inc., 699 Frood Rd., Sudbury ON P3C 5A3 – 705/674-8301	9
Sunnybrae, NS	CBHT-TV-17	See Sydney (CBIT-TV)	6
Swift Current, NF	CBNT-TV-31	See St. John's (CBNT-TV)	5
Swift Current, NF	CJSC-TV-10	See St. John's (CJON-TV)	10
Swift Current, SK	CJFB-TV	Swift Current Telecasting Co. Ltd., PO Box 160, Swift Current SK S9H 3V7 – 306/773-7266; Fax: 306/773-0123	5
Sydney, NS	CJCB-TV	ATV, Division of CHUM Ltd., PO Box 4691, Sydney NS B1P 6H5 – 902/562-5511; Fax: 902/564-0495	4
Sydney, NS	*CBIT-TV	CBC, 285 Alexandra St., Sydney NS B1S 2E8 – 902/539-5050; Fax: 902/562-7547	5
Tabor Mountain, BC	CBUHT-TV	See Vancouver (CBUT-TV)	78
Taghum, BC	CKTN-TV-2	See Burnaby (CHAN-TV)	23
Tahsis, BC	CBUT-TV-14	See Vancouver (CBUT-TV)	9
Tasu, BC	CFTK-TV	See Prince George (CKPG-TV)	11
Tatla Lake, BC	CIAL-TV-2	See Burnaby (CHAN-TV)	9
Taylor, BC	*CBCD-TV-4	See Dawson Creek (CJDC-TV)	7
Telkwa, BC	CFTK-TV-2	See Terrace (CFTK-TV)	7
Temiscaming, PQ	CIVK-TV	See Montréal (CIVM-TV)	8
Terrace, BC	CFTK-TV	Skeena Broadcasters, Division of Okanagan Skeena Group, 4625 Lazelle Ave., Terrace BC V2L 2M8 – 250/635-6316; Fax: 250/638-6320; Email: info@osg.net; URL: http://www.osg.net	3
Tête Jaune, BC	CBUHT-TV-4	See Vancouver (CBUT-TV)	10
The Pas, MB	CKYP-TV	See Winnipeg (CKY-TV)	12

Canadian Almanac & Directory 1997

TELEVISION STATIONS

LOCATION	CALL	*CBC Stations/Affiliates †French Language Stations	CHANNEL
Thetford Mines, PQ	CBMT-TV-4	See Montréal (CBMT-TV)	32
Thompson, MB	CKYT-TV	See Winnipeg (CKY-TV)	9
Thunder Bay, ON	CKPR-TV	Thunder Bay Electronics Ltd., 87 North Hill St., Thunder Bay ON P7A 5V6 – 807/346-2600; Fax: 807/345-0932	2
Thunder Bay, ON	CHFD-TV	Thunder Bay Electronics Ltd., 87 North Hill St., Thunder Bay ON P7A 5V6 – 807/346-2600; Fax: 807/345-0932	4
Timmins, ON	CFCL-TV	Baton Broadcasting Inc., PO Box 620, Timmins ON P4N 7G3 – 705/264-4211; Fax: 705/264-3266	6
Timmins, ON	CITO-TV	Baton Broadcasting Inc., PO Box 620, Timmins ON P4N 7G3 – 705/264-4211; Fax: 705/264-3266	3
Tisdale, SK	CKBI-TV-6	See Prince Albert (CKBI-TV)	13
Tofino, BC	CBUT-TV-22	See Vancouver (CBUT-TV)	10
Topley Landing, BC	CHAN-TV	See Burnaby (CHAN-TV)	
Toronto, ON	CFMT-TV	Baton Broadcasting Inc., 545 Lakeshore Blvd. West, Toronto ON M5V 1A3 – 416/260-0047; Fax: 416/260-3621; Email: cfmt@rci.rogers.com	47
Toronto, ON	CICA-TV	TVOntario, 2180 Yonge St., PO Box 200, Stn Q, Toronto ON M4T 2T1 – 416/484-2600; Fax: 416/484-2725, 2867	19
Toronto, ON	CIII-TV	Global Television Network, 81 Barber Greene Rd., Toronto ON M3C 2A2 – 416/446-5311; Fax: 416/446-5371	41
Toronto, ON	CITY-TV	City TV, Division of CHUM Ltd., 299 Queen St. West, Toronto ON M5V 2Z5 – 416/591-5757; URL: www.citytv.com	57
Toronto, ON	CFTO-TV	See Scarborough (CFTO-TV)	9
Toronto, ON	*CBLT-TV	CBC, PO Box 500, Stn A, Toronto ON M5W 1E6 – 416/205-3311; Fax: 416/205-3453	5
Toronto, ON	*†CBLFT-TV	Société Radio-Canada, CP 500, Succ A, Toronto ON M5W 1E6 – 416/205-3311; Fax: 416/205-5622	25
Tors Cove, NF	CJON-TV-5	See St. John's (CJON-TV)	2
Trail, BC	CBUAT-TV-6	See Vancouver (CBUT-TV)	11
Trail, BC	CKTN-TV	See Burnaby (CHAN-TV)	8
Trepassey, NF	CJTP-TV-10	See St. John's (CJON-TV)	10
Trinity-Wareham, NF	CBNT-TV-16	See St. John's (CBNT-TV)	2
Trois-Rivières, PQ	†CHEM-TV	TéléMétropole Multi-Régions inc., 3625, boul Chanoine-Moreau, Trois-Rivières PQ G8Y 5N6 – 819/376-8880; Fax: 819/376-2906	8
Trois-Rivières, PQ	†CKTM-TV	COGECO Inc., 4141, boul St-Jean, CP 277, Trois-Rivières PQ G9A 5G3 – 819/377-1441; Fax: 819/377-1109	13
Trois-Rivières, PQ	CFKM-TV	See Trois-Rivières (CKTM-TV)	29
Trois-Rivières, PQ	CBMT-TV-1	See Montréal (CBMT-TV)	28
Truro, NS	CBHT-TV-8	See Halifax (CBHT-TV)	55
Truro, NS	CJCH-TV-2	See Halifax (CJCH-TV)	12
Ucluelet, BC	CBUT-FM-7	See Vancouver (CBUT-TV)	7
Ucluelet, BC	CKUP-TV-1	See Burnaby (CHAN-TV)	6
Val-d'Or, PQ	†CFVS-TV	Radio Nord Inc., 1729, av 3, Val-d'Or PQ J9P 1W3 – 819/825-0010; Fax: 819/825-6741	29
Val-d'Or, PQ	CJDG-TV	See Rouyn-Noranda (CFEM-TV)	10
Val d'Or, PQ	†CFVS-TV-1	Radio Nord Inc., 1729, 3e av, Val d'Or PQ J9P 1W3 – 819/825-9994; Fax: 819/825-6741	20
Val d'Or, PQ	†CIVA-TV	Société de Radio-Télévision du Québec, 689, 3e av, Val d'Or PQ J9P 1S7 – 819/874-5132; Fax: 819/824-2431	8
Val Marie, SK	CJFB-TV-2	See Swift Current (CJFB-TV)	2
Valemount, BC	CBUHT-TV-5	See Vancouver (CBUT-TV)	6
Vancouver, BC	CKVU-TV	Canwest Pacific Television Inc., 180 West 2nd St., Vancouver BC V5Y 3T9 – 604/876-1344; Fax: 604/874-8225	10
Vancouver, BC	KVOS-TV	KVOS-TV Inc., 1764 West 7th Ave., Vancouver BC V6J 5A3 – 604/681-1212; Fax: 604/738-4510	12
Vancouver, BC	*†CBUFT-TV	Société Radio-Canada, 700 Hamilton St., CP 4600, Vancouver BC V6B 4A2 – 604/662-6168; Fax: 604/662-6161	26
Vancouver, BC	*CBUT-TV	CBC, 700 Hamilton St., PO Box 4600, Vancouver BC V6B 4A2 – 604/662-6000; Fax: 604/662-6414	2
Vanderhoof, BC	CBCB-TV-1	See Prince George (CKPG-TV)	18
Vanderhoof, BC	CKIN-TV-1	See Burnaby (CHAN-TV)	8
Vavenby, BC	CKVA-TV-1	See Burnaby (CHAN-TV)	8
Vernon, BC	CHBC-TV-2	See Kelowna (CHBC-TV)	7
Vernon, BC	CHKL-TV-2	See Burnaby (CHAN-TV)	12
Victoria, BC	CHEK-TV	CHEK, Division of Westcom TV Group Ltd., 780 Kings Rd., Victoria BC V8T 5A2 – 250/383-2435; Fax: 250/384-7766; URL: http://www.chek6.com	6
Wabasca, AB	CBXAT-TV-12	See Edmonton (CBXT-TV)	7
Wabowden, MB	CBWMT-TV	See Winnipeg (CBWT-TV)	10
Wainwright, AB	CKSA-TV-3	See Lloydminster (CKSA-TV)	8
Wakeman Sound, BC	CJWS-TV	See Victoria (CHEK-TV)	7
Waterton Park, AB	CBRT-TV-7	See Calgary (CBRT-TV)	4
Waterton Park, AB	CJWP-TV-2	See Calgary (CFCN-TV)	6
Wellington/Hare Bay, NF	CBNT-TV-15	See St. John's (CBNT-TV)	24
Wells/Barkerville, BC	CKWB-TV	See Burnaby (CHAN-TV)	11
Wesleyville, NF	CBNT-TV-9	See St. John's (CBNT-TV)	5
Westwold, BC	CHBC-TV	See Kelowna (CHBC-TV)	12
Whistler, BC	CBUWT-TV	See Vancouver (CBUT-TV)	13
Whitecourt, AB	CFRN-TV-3	See Edmonton (CFRN-TV)	12
Whitecourt, AB	CBXT-TV-2	See Edmonton (CBXT-TV)	8
Wiarton, ON	CBLN-TV-5	See Toronto (CBLT-TV)	20
Williams Lake, BC	CFJC-TV-5	See Kamloops (CFJC-TV)	8
Williams Lake, BC	CITM-TV-1	See Burnaby (CHAN-TV)	13
Willow Bunch, SK	CBKT-TV-2	See Regina (CBKT-TV)	10
Windsor, ON	CHWI-TV	Baton Broadcasting Inc., 75 Riverside Dr. West, Windsor ON N9A 7C4 – 519/977-7432; Fax: 519/977-0564	16
Windsor, ON	CKCO-TV	See Kitchener (CKCO-TV)	42
Windsor, ON	*CBET-TV	CBC, 825 Riverside Dr. West, PO Box 1609, Windsor ON N9A 1K7 – 519/255-3411; Fax: 519/255-3403	9
Windsor, ON	*†CBEFT-TV	Société Radio-Canada, 825 Riverside Dr. West, CP 1609, Windsor ON N9A 1K7 – 519/255-3411; Fax: 519/255-3573	54
Wingham, ON	CBLN-TV-4	See Toronto (CBLT-TV)	45
Wingham, ON	CKNX-TV	Baton Broadcasting Inc., 215 Carling Terrace, PO Box 100, Wingham ON N0G 1W0 – 519/357-4438; Fax: 519/357-4398	8
Winlaw, BC	CBUCT-TV-3	See Vancouver (CBUT-TV)	12
Winnipeg, MB	†CBWFT-TV	Société Radio-Canada, 541 Portage Ave., CP 160, Winnipeg MB R3C 2H1 – 204/788-3141; Fax: 204/788-3639	3

LOCATION	CALL	*CBC Stations/Affiliates †French Language Stations	CHANNEL
Winnipeg, MB	CKND-TV	CanWest Television Inc., 603 St. Mary's Rd., Winnipeg MB R2M 3L8 – 204/233-3304; Fax: 204/233-5615	9
Winnipeg, MB	CKY-TV	Moffat Communications Ltd., Polo Park, Winnipeg MB R3G 0L7 – 204/788-3300; Fax: 204/788-3399	7
Winnipeg, MB	CHMI-TV	Craig Broadcast Systems Inc., #100, 167 Lombard Ave., Winnipeg MB R3B 0T6 – 204/947-9613; Fax: 204/956-0811	13
Winnipeg, MB	*CBWT-TV	CBC, 541 Portage Ave., PO Box 160, Winnipeg MB R3C 2H1 – 204/788-3222; Fax: 204/788-3167	6
Wynyard, SK	CHSS-TV	See Yorkton (CKOS-TV)	6
Yarmouth, NS	CJCH-TV-7	See Halifax (CJCH-TV)	40
Yarmouth, NS	CBHT-TV-3	See Halifax (CBHT-TV)	11
Yellowknife, NT	CABL-TV	Mackenzie Media Ltd., PO Box 1469, Yellowknife NT X1A 2P1 – 403/920-2929; Fax: 403/920-2331	2
Yellowknife, NT	*CFYK-TV	CBC, PO Box 160, Yellowknife NT X1A 2N2 – 403/920-5400; Fax: 403/920-5489	8
Yorkton, SK	CKOS-TV	Baton Broadcasting Inc., 95 East Broadway, Yorkton SK S3N 0L1 – 306/783-3685; Fax: 306/782-3433	5
Yorkton, SK	CICC-TV	Baton Broadcasting Inc., 95 East Broadway, Yorkton SK S3N 0L1 – 306/783-3685; Fax: 306/782-3433	10

SPECIALTY & PAY SERVICES

A&E Television Networks, 235 East 45 St., New York NY 10017 USA – 212/210-9104; Fax: 212/210-1303
Arts et Divertissement, 2100, rue Ste-Catherine ouest, Montréal PQ H3H 2T3 – 514/939-3150; Fax: 514/939-3151
Bravo!, The New Style Arts Channel, 299 Queen St. West, Toronto ON M5V 2Z5 – 416/591-5757; Email: bravospeakers@bravo.ca; URL: http://www.bravo.ca/bravo.html
Broadcast News Ltd., 36 King St. East, Toronto ON M5C 2L9 – 416/364-3172; Fax: 416/364-8896
C-SPAN (National Cable Satellite Corporation), #650, 400 North Capitol St. NW, Washington DC 20001 USA – 202/737-3220; Fax: 202/737-7323; Email: CSPANviewr@aol.com
Canadian Home Shopping Network (CHSN), 1400 Castlefield Ave., Toronto ON M6B 4H8 – 416/785-3500; Fax: 416/785-1300
Canadian Satellite Communications Ltd. (CANCOM), 50 Burnhamthorpe Rd. West, 10th Fl., Mississauga ON L5B 3C2 – 416/272-4960; Fax: 416/272-3399; Email: pdumas@cancom.ca; URL: http://www.cancom.ca
Canal D, #800, 2100, rue Sainte-Catherine ouest, Montréal PQ H3H 2T3 – 514/939-3150; Fax: 514/939-3151; Email: rpc@rpchoix.com
Canal Famille, #800, 2100, rue Ste-Catherine ouest, Montréal PQ H3H 2T3 – 514/939-3150; Fax: 514/939-3151; Email: rpc@rpchoix.com
CBC Newsworld, PO Box 500, Stn A, Toronto ON M5W 1E6 – 416/205-2950; Fax: 416/205-6080
The Classic Channel, BCE Place, #100, 181 Bay St., PO Box 707, Toronto ON M5J 2T3 – 416/965-2010; Fax: 416/965-2015
CNN (Cable News Network), 1 CNN Center, Atlanta GA 30348-5366 USA – 404/827-2039; Fax: 404/827-2478; http://www.cnn.com
Country Music Television, 49 Ontario St., 5th Fl, Toronto ON M5A 2V1 – 416/360-4626; Fax: 416/360-6263
The Discovery Channel, #100, 2225 Sheppard Ave. East, North York ON M2J 5C2 – 416/494-2929; Fax: 416/490-7067; Email: comments@discovery.ca; URL: http://www.discovery.ca
Fairchild Television Ltd., 35 East Beaver Creek Rd., Richmond Hill ON L4B 1B3 – 905/889-8090; Fax: 905/882-7120
Family Channel Inc., BCE Place, 181 Bay St., PO Box 787, Toronto ON M5J 2T3 – 416/956-2030; Fax: 416/956-2035; Email: info@familychannel.ca
Kaledioscope - America's Disability Channel, #300, 1777 NE Loop 410, San Antonio TX 78217 USA – 210/824-7446; Fax: 210/829-1388; TDD: 210/824-1666
Le Reseau des Sports (RDS), #300, 1755, boul René-Lévesque est, Montréal PQ H2X 4P6 – 514/599-2244; Fax: 514/599-2299
The Learning Channel, 7700 Wisconsin Ave., Bethesda MD 20814 USA – 301/986-0444; Fax: 301/986-4829
Les Réseaux Premier Choix, #800, 2100, rue Ste-Catherine ouest, Montréal PQ H3H 2T3 – 514/939-3150; Fax: 514/939-3151; Email: rpc@rpchoix.xom
Life Network, 1155 Leslie St., Toronto ON M3C 2J6 – 416/444-9494; Fax: 416/444-0018; Email: info@lifenet.ca
MovieMax, Division of Allarcom Pay Television Ltd., #200, 5324 Calgary Trail, Edmonton AB T6H 4J8 – 403/430-2800; Fax: 403/437-3188
MOVIEPIX (TMN Networks Inc.), 181 Bay St., PO Box 787, Toronto ON M5J 2T3 – 416/956-2010; Fax: 416/956-2012; Email: tmnpix@tmn.ca
MuchMusic Network, 299 Queen St. West, Toronto ON M5V 2Z5 – 416/591-5757; Fax: 416/591-9317; URL: http://www.muchmusic.com
Musiqueplus, 209, rue Ste-Catherine est, Montréal PQ H2X 1L2 – 514/284-7587; Fax: 514/284-1889
The Nashville Network (TNN), c/o Group Satellite Communications, 250 Harbor Dr., Stamford CT 06904-2210 USA – 203/965-6000; Fax: 203/965-6315
Ontario Parliament Network Broadcast & Recording Service, Legislative Assembly, Queen's Park, Toronto ON M7A 1A2 – 416/325-7900; Fax: 416/325-7916
Premier Choix, 2100, rue Ste-Catherine ouest, Montréal PQ H3H 2T3 – 514/939-3150; Fax: 514/939-3151
RadioTélévision des débats de l'Assemblée nationale, #2.14, Édifice Pamphile-Le May, Québec PQ G1A 1A3 – 418/643-9448; Fax: 418/646-8498
Réseau de l'information (RDI), Société Radio-Canada, Maison de Radio-Canada, CP 6000, Montréal PQ H3C 3A8 – 514/597-5700; Fax: 514/597-5749
Saskatchewan Legislative Assembly Broadcast Services, #123 Legislative Bldg., Regina SK S4S 0B3 – 306/787-2181; Fax: 306/787-1558
Showcase Television Inc., #1000, 160 Bloor St. East, Toronto ON M4W 1B9 – 416/967-0022; Fax: 416/967-0044; Email: drama@showcase.ca; URL: www.screen.com/showcase
The Sports Network (TSN), 1155 Leslie St., North York ON M3C 2T6 – 416/449-2244; Fax: 416/391-8210
Sportscope Television Network, #104, 590 Alden Rd., Markham ON L3R 8N2 – 905/477-6787; Fax: 905/477-5547
Super Écran, #800, 2100, rue Sainte-Catherine ouest, Montréal PQ H3H 2T3 – 514/939-3150; Fax: 514/939-3151; Email: rpc@rpchoix.com
Superchannel, Division of Allarcom Pay Television Ltd., #200, 5324 Calgary Trail, Edmonton AB T6H 4J8 – 403/430-2800; Fax: 403/437-3188
Talentvision TV Ltd., #138, 525 West Broadway, Vancouver BC V5Z 4K5 – 604/708-1328; Fax: 604/708-1333
Telelatino Network Inc., 5125 Steeles Ave. West, North York ON M9L 1R5 – 416/744-8200; Fax: 416/744-0966
TMN The Movie Network (TMN Networks Inc.), 181 Bay St., PO Box 787, Toronto ON M5J 2T3 – 416/956-2010; Fax: 416/956-2018; Email: tmnpix@tmn.ca
TV5, La Télévision Internationale, #101, 1755, boul René-Lévesque est, Montréal PQ H2K 4P6 – 514/522-5322; Fax: 514/522-6572; Email: tv5@tv5.org
Viewer's Choice Canada, BCE Place, #100, 181 Bay St., PO Box 707, Toronto ON M5J 2T3 – 416/956-2050; Fax: 416/956-2055
Vision TV (Canada's Faith Network), 80 Bond St., Toronto ON M5B 1X2 – 416/368-3194; Fax: 416/368-9774
The Weather Network, 1755, boul René-Lévesque est, Montréal PQ H2K 4P6 – 514/597-1700; Fax: 514/597-1591
Women's Television Network, #300, 1661 Portage Ave., Winnipeg MB R3J 3T7 – 204/783-5116; Fax: 204/774-3227; Email: wtn@web.apc.org
YTV Canada Inc., #18, 64 Jefferson Ave., Toronto ON M6K 3H3 – 416/534-1191; Fax: 416/533-0346; Email: info@ytv.ca

CABLE STATIONS

BY TRANSMITTING LOCATION

Abbotsford, BC . . . . Rogers Cablesystems, 31450 Marshall Rd., PO Box 2125, Stn Clearbrook, Abbotsford BC V2T 3X8 – 604/858-0776; Fax: 604/850-2517
Acadieville, NB . . . . See Fundy Cable TV Ltd./ltée, Newcastle
Acton, ON . . . . Halton Cable Systems, 21 Main St. North, Acton ON L7J 1V9 – 519/853-1270; Fax: 519/853-1731
Albanel, PQ . . . . Télécâble Albanel inc., 95, rue Industrielle, Albanel PQ G0W 1A0 – 418/279-5702; Fax: 418/279-3113
Albert Bridge, NS . . . . See Seaside Cable TV (1984) Ltd., Glace Bay
Alberton, PE . . . . See Island Cablevision Ltd., Charlottetown
Alexandria, ON . . . . See Rogers Cablesystems Ottawa, Ottawa
Alfred, ON . . . . See Rogers Cablesystems Ottawa, Ottawa
Allan, SK . . . . See Shaw Cable Saskatoon, Saskatoon

Canadian Almanac & Directory 1997

5-224 CABLE STATIONS

Allanburg, ON . . . . *See* Rogers Cablesystems Niagara Partnership, Niagara Falls
Allardville, NB . . . . *See* Cable 2000 Inc., Bathurst
Allenford, ON . . . . *See* Trillium Communications Ltd., Port Elgin
Alma, PQ . . . . Câblovision Alma inc., 590, rue Collard ouest, Alma PQ G8B 1N2 – 418/668-3310; Fax: 418/668-0938
Alouette, PQ . . . . CFB Bagotville, Alouette PQ G0V 1A0 – 418/693-2513; Fax: 418/693-2185
Altona, MB . . . . *See* Valley Cable Vision Ltd., Selkirk
Amos, PQ . . . . Télédistribution Amos inc., 27, rue Principale nord, Amos PQ J9T 2K7 – 819/732-5570; Fax: 819/732-9282; Email: dufresne@leiro.com
Angers/Masson, PQ . . . . *See* Télécâble Laurentien inc., Hull
Arnprior, ON . . . . *See* Rogers Cablesystems Ottawa, Ottawa
Assiniboia, SK . . . . *See* Prairie Co-Ax TV Ltd., Moose Jaw
Atikokan, ON . . . . Videon, 120 Marks St., PO Box 1840, Atikokan ON P0T 1C0 – 807/597-6050; Fax: 807/597-4554
Aurora, ON . . . . Aurora Cable TV Ltd., 350 Industrial Pkwy. South, PO Box 547, Aurora ON L4G 3H3 – 905/727-1981; Fax: 905/727-7407
Aylmer, ON . . . . Clearview Cable TV, c/o AGI Cablevision Inc., 121 Donly Dr. South, PO Box 327, Simcoe ON N3Y 4L2 – 519/426-7360; Fax: 519/426-7360; Email: agicable@kanservu.ca
Ayton, ON . . . . *See* Saugeen Telecable Ltd., Hanover
Baddeck, NS . . . . *See* Seaside Cable TV (1984) Ltd., Glace Bay
Baie-St-Paul, PQ . . . . *See* Vidéo Dery ltée, La Baie
Baie-Ste-Anne, NB . . . . *See* Fundy Cable TV Ltd./ltée, Newcastle
Bancroft, ON . . . . *See* Shaw Cable, Smiths Falls
Banff, AB . . . . *See* Monarch Cable TV, Canmore
Barrys Bay, ON . . . . *See* Shaw Cable, Smiths Falls
Bathurst, NB . . . . Cable 2000 Inc., PO Box 2000, Bathurst NB E2A 4W4 – 506/547-8877; Fax: 506/548-3208
Beachburg, ON . . . . *See* Rogers Cablesystems Ottawa, Ottawa
Bearn, PQ . . . . *See* Câblotem inc., Ville-Marie
Beausejour, MB . . . . *See* Interlake Cable TV Ltd., Selkirk
Beaverbank, NB . . . . *See* Fundy Cable TV Ltd./ltée, Newcastle
Beaverlodge, AB . . . . Small Community TV Inc., PO Box 510, Beaverlodge AB T0H 0C0 – 403/354-2510; Fax: 403/354-8780
Beebe, PQ . . . . *See* Vidéotron ltée, Sherbrooke
Belgrave, ON . . . . *See* Kincardine Cable TV Ltd., Kincardine
Bellevue, AB . . . . Shaw Cable, PO Box 400, Bellevue AB T0H 0C0 – 403/250-8080; Fax: 403/426-8900
Bellfond, NB . . . . *See* Fundy Cable TV Ltd./ltée, Newcastle
Benito, MB . . . . *See* Westman Cable TV, Brandon
Big Cove, NB . . . . *See* Fundy Cable TV Ltd./ltée, Newcastle
Binscarth, MB . . . . *See* Westman Cable TV, Brandon
Birch River, MB . . . . *See* Westman Cable TV, Brandon
Birtle, MB . . . . *See* Westman Cable TV, Brandon
Blackville, NB . . . . *See* Fundy Cable TV Ltd./ltée, Newcastle
Block House, NS . . . . Bragg Communications Inc., PO Box 84, Block House NS B0J 1E0 – 902/624-8305; Fax: 902/543-6582
Blyth, ON . . . . *See* Mitchell-Seaforth Cable TV Ltd., Dryden
Boissevain, MB . . . . *See* Westman Cable TV, Brandon
Borden, PE . . . . *See* Island Cablevision Ltd., Charlottetown
Botwood, NF . . . . *See* Cable Atlantic Inc., St. John's
Bourget, ON . . . . *See* Rogers Cablesystems Ottawa, Ottawa
Bowsman, MB . . . . *See* Westman Cable TV, Brandon
Brampton, ON . . . . Rogers Community 10, 13 Hansen Rd. South, Brampton ON L6W 3H6 – 905/457-3270; Fax: 905/456-1067
Brandon, MB . . . . Westman Cable TV, 1906 Park Ave., Brandon MB R7B 0R9 – 204/725-4300; Fax: 204/728-9288; Email: cathcart@wmcl.com
Brantford, ON . . . . *See* Rogers Cablesystems, Oshawa
Brechin, ON . . . . Bayshore Village Association Cable TV, Hayloft Lane, RR#3, Brechin ON L0K 1B0 – 705/484-0754
Bredenbury, SK . . . . *See* North Eastern Cablevision Ltd., Yorkton
Brockville, ON . . . . Brockville Cable, 205 King St. West, Brockville ON K6V 3R7 – 613/342-2640
Bruno, SK . . . . *See* Shaw Cable Saskatoon, Saskatoon
Brussels, ON . . . . *See* Mitchell-Seaforth Cable TV Ltd., Dryden
Buckingham, PQ . . . . *See* Télécâble Laurentien inc., Hull
Buctouche, NB . . . . *See* Fundy Cable TV Ltd./ltée, Newcastle
Burnaby, BC . . . . West Coast Cablevision Ltd., 6665 Hastings St. East, Burnaby BC V5B 1S4 – 604/291-6691; Fax: 604/291-2944
Burnt Islands, NF . . . . *See* Cable Atlantic Inc., St. John's
Caledon, ON . . . . *See* Shaw Cable, Orangeville
Calgary, AB . . . . Rogers Cable TV, 3003 MacLeod Trail SW, Calgary AB T2G 2P8 – 403/261-4200; Fax: 403/263-6076
Cambridge, NS . . . . *See* Cross Country TV Ltd., Canning
Campbell River, BC . . . . Campbell River TV Association, 500 Robron Rd., Campbell River BC V9W 5Z2 – 250/923-8899; Fax: 250/923-7796; Email: forsyth@cr.iscanv.net
Campbell's Bay, PQ . . . . Pontiac Cable Co. Inc., CP 217, Campbell's Bay PQ J0X 1W7 – 819/648-2005; Fax: 819/648-5778
Canmore, AB . . . . Monarch Cable TV, 715 Railway Ave., PO Box 1989, Canmore AB T0L 0M0 – 403/678-5973; Fax: 403/678-5286
Canning, NS . . . . Cross Country TV Ltd., PO Box 310, Canning NS B0P 1H0 – 902/582-3328; Fax: 902/582-7499
Canora, SK . . . . *See* North Eastern Cablevision Ltd., Yorkton
Cap-de-la-Madeleine, PQ . . . . Vidéotron ltée, #101, 190, rue Fusey, Cap-de-la-Madeleine PQ G8T 2V8 – 819/375-7742; Fax: 819/375-8950
Cap-Lumière, NB . . . . *See* Fundy Cable TV Ltd./ltée, Newcastle
Carberry, MB . . . . *See* Westman Cable TV, Brandon
Cardiff, ON . . . . *See* Village Cablesystems Ltd., Tweed
Carman, MB . . . . *See* Valley Cable Vision Ltd., Selkirk
Carmanville, NF . . . . *See* Cable Atlantic Inc., St. John's
Caroline, AB . . . . *See* Monarch Cable TV, Canmore
Carp, ON . . . . *See* Rogers Cablesystems Ottawa, Ottawa
Carstairs, AB . . . . *See* Monarch Cable TV, Canmore
Casselman, ON . . . . Casselman Cable Co. Inc., PO Box 499, Casselman ON K0A 1M0 – 613/764-3420; Fax: 613/764-5631
Castlegar, BC . . . . Castlegar Shaw Cable Systems (B.C.) Ltd., 1951 Columbia Ave., Castlegar BC V1N 2W8 – 250/365-3122; Fax: 250/365-2676
Catalone, NS . . . . *See* Seaside Cable TV (1984) Ltd., Glace Bay
Chapais, PQ . . . . *See* Vidéotron ltée, Chicoutimi
Charlesbourg, PQ . . . . Coopérative de Câblodistribution de l'Arrière-pays, 860, av Notre-Dame, Charlesbourg PQ G2N 1P7 – 819/849-7125; Fax: 819/849-7128

Canadian Almanac & Directory 1997

Charlottetown, PE	Island Cablevision Ltd., 100 Cable Ct., Charlottetown PE C1B 1A9 – 902/569-4101; Fax: 902/569-4731
Chatham, ON	Trillium Cable Communications Ltd., 491 Richmond St., Chatham ON N7M 1R2 – 519/352-8270; Fax: 519/352-8274
Chesley, ON	*See* Saugeen Telecable Ltd., Hanover
Cheticamp, NS	Acadian Communications Ltd., PO Box 308, Cheticamp NS B0E 1H0 – 902/224-3204; Fax: 902/224-3000
Chibougamau, PQ	*See* Vidéotron ltée, Chicoutimi
Chicoutimi, PQ	Vidéotron ltée, 21, rue Racine ouest, CP 700, Chicoutimi PQ G7H 5E1 – 418/693-9366; Fax: 418/545-6455
Chilliwack, BC	*See* Lethbridge Cablenet, Lethbridge
Chilliwack, BC	Chilliwack Cablenet, 9275 Nowell St., Chilliwack BC V2P 7G7 – 604/793-9944; Fax: 604/792-0966
Chipman, NB	*See* Fundy Cable Ltd. ltée, Fredericton
Churchbridge, SK	*See* North Eastern Cablevision Ltd., Yorkton
Chute-aux-Outardes, PQ	Télécâble Côte-Nord inc., 113, Vallilee, Chute-aux-Outardes PQ G0H 1C0 – 418/567-8404; Fax: 418/567-2106
Clarence Creek, ON	*See* Rogers Cablesystems Ottawa, Ottawa
Clinton, ON	Bluewater TV Cable, RR#2, Clinton ON N0M 1L0 – 519/482-9233; Fax: 519/482-7098
Cobbs Hill, PE	*See* Island Cablevision Ltd., Charlottetown
Cobden, ON	*See* Rogers Cablesystems Ottawa, Ottawa
Cobourg, ON	Northumberland Cable TV, 9 Albert St., Cobourg ON K9A 2P7 – 905/372-2274; Fax: 905/372-2472
Collingwood, ON	Rogers Cablesystems, 4 Sandford Fleming Dr., PO Box 520, Collingwood ON L9Y 4V9 – 705/445-3400; Fax: 705/445-9949
Comox, BC	*See* Lethbridge Cablenet, Lethbridge
Consort, AB	Progressive Cable Television Ltd., PO Box 250, Consort AB T0C 1B0 – 403/577-3550; Fax: 403/577-3503
Corner Brook, NF	*See* Cable Atlantic Inc., St. John's
Cornwall, ON	Rogers Cablesystems, 517 Pitt St., Cornwall ON K6J 3R4 – 613/932-5966; Fax: 613/932-3176
Courtenay, BC	Comox Valley Cablenet Ltd., 1591 McPhee Ave., Courtenay BC V9N 3A6 – 250/334-0888; Fax: 250/334-3640
Cranberry, MB	*See* Romik Communications Ltd., Flin Flon
Cranbrook, BC	Shaw Cable, 133 - 8 Ave. South, Cranbrook BC V1C 2K6 – 250/426-3341; Fax: 250/334-8900
Crapaud, PE	*See* Island Cablevision Ltd., Charlottetown
Cremona, AB	*See* Monarch Cable TV, Canmore
Creston, BC	*See* Shaw Cable, Cranbrook
Crossfield, AB	*See* Rogers Cable TV, Calgary
Crystal Beach, ON	*See* Rogers Cablesystems Niagara Partnership, Niagara Falls
Cudworth, SK	*See* Shaw Cable Saskatoon, Saskatoon
Dalmeny, SK	*See* Shaw Cable Saskatoon, Saskatoon
Dauphin, MB	*See* Westman Cable TV, Brandon
Deer Lake, NF	*See* Cable Atlantic Inc., St. John's
Delisle, SK	*See* Shaw Cable Saskatoon, Saskatoon
Deloraine, MB	*See* Westman Cable TV, Brandon
Delta, BC	Delta Cable Television Ltd., 5381 - 48 Ave., Delta BC V4K 1W7 – 604/946-1144; Fax: 604/946-5627
Digby, NS	Access Cable Television Ltd., 88 Warwick St., Digby NS B0V 1A0 – 902/245-2519; Fax: 902/245-6511
Doaktown, NB	*See* Fundy Cable Ltd. ltée, Fredericton
Dolbeau, PQ	*See* Vidéotron ltée, Chicoutimi
Drayton, ON	*See* Saugeen Telecable Ltd., Hanover
Drummondville, PQ	Drummondville Câblestrie inc., 1960, boul Lemire, Drummondville PQ J2B 6X5 – 819/477-8687; Fax: 819/474-5313
Dryden, ON	*See* Videon, Atikokan
Dryden, ON	Dryden Cable TV Ltd., 75 Queen St., Dryden ON P8N 1A1 – 807/223-5525; Fax: 807/223-4445
Dublin, ON	Mitchell-Seaforth Cable TV Ltd., 123 Ontario St., Dryden ON N0K 1E0 – 519/345-2341; Fax: 519/345-2873
Durham, ON	*See* Saugeen Telecable Ltd., Hanover
Dysart, SK	Cable Dysart, PO Box 70, Dysart SK S0G 1H0 – 306/432-2100
Earlton, ON	Earlton Cable Vision Ltd., 7 - 12th Ave. South, Earlton ON P0J 1E0 – 705/563-2698
Edmonton, AB	Regional Cable TV (Western) Inc., 3552 - 78th Ave., Edmonton AB T6B 2X9 – 403/440-2525; Fax: 403/440-2828
Edmonton, AB	Shaw Cablesystems (Alberta) Ltd., 7633 - 50 St., Edmonton AB T6B 2W9 – 403/468-7115; Fax: 403/465-6405
Edmonton, AB	Videotron Communications Ltd., 10450 - 178 St., Edmonton AB T5S 1S2 – Fax: 403/483-1732
Elkhorn, MB	*See* Westman Cable TV, Brandon
Elmsdale, PE	*See* Island Cablevision Ltd., Charlottetown
Elmwood, ON	*See* Saugeen Telecable Ltd., Hanover
Erickson, MB	*See* Westman Cable TV, Brandon
Esterhazy, SK	*See* North Eastern Cablevision Ltd., Yorkton
Estevan, SK	*See* Lethbridge Cablenet, Lethbridge
Exshaw, AB	*See* Monarch Cable TV, Canmore
Fabre, PQ	*See* Câblotem inc., Ville-Marie
Faro, YT	*See* Northern Television Systems Ltd., Whitehorse
Fenelon Falls, ON	Cable Cable Inc., RR#3, Fenelon Falls ON K0M 1M0 – 705/887-4563; Fax: 705/887-2580
Fenelon Falls, ON	Bobcaygeon Cable Inc., RR#3, Fenelon Falls ON K0M 1N0 – 705/887-2580
Fenwick, ON	*See* Rogers Cablesystems Niagara Partnership, Niagara Falls
Fergus, ON	Fergus-Elora Cable TV Ltd., 475 St. Patrick St. West, Fergus ON N1M 1M2 – 519/843-3700; Fax: 519/843-2312
Fermont, PQ	La Coopérative de la télévision communautaire de Fermont, 850, Le Carrefour, CP 1379, Fermont PQ G0G 1J0 – 418/287-5443; Fax: 418/287-3477
Fleurimont, PQ	Transvision Paré inc., 2175, ch Champigny, Fleurimont PQ J1H 5H2 – 819/821-2021; Fax: 819/821-0231
Flin Flon, MB	Romik Communications Ltd., 35 - 3 Ave., PO Box 5, Flin Flon MB R8A 1M6 – 204/687-3375; Fax: 204/687-3341
Fonthill, ON	*See* Rogers Cablesystems Niagara Partnership, Niagara Falls
Fort Erie, ON	*See* Rogers Cablesystems Niagara Partnership, Niagara Falls
Fort McMurray, AB	ABC Cable TV, #200, 208 Beaconhill Dr., Fort McMurray AB T9H 2R1 – 403/743-3717; Fax: 403/790-1193
Fredericton, NB	Fundy Cable Ltd. ltée, PO Box 1569, Fredericton NB E3B 5B1 – 506/453-1000; Fax: 506/452-2846
Gander, NF	*See* Cable Atlantic Inc., St. John's
Ganges, BC	Saltspring Cablevision (1981) Ltd., PO Box 300, RPO Ganges, Salt Spring Island BC V8K 2V9 – 250/537-5550
Gaspé, PQ	Câblo Distribution G. inc., 494, montée Wakeham, CP 1720, Gaspé PQ G0C 1R0 – 418/368-3636; Fax: 418/368-7759
Georgetown, ON	*See* Halton Cable Systems, Acton
Georgetown, PE	*See* Island Cablevision Ltd., Charlottetown
Geraldton, ON	Astrocom Cablevision Inc., 112 - 3 Ave. NE, PO Box 910, Geraldton ON P0T 1M0 – 807/854-1569; Fax: 807/854-2169
Gibsons, BC	Coast Cable Communications Ltd., PO Box 218, Sechelt BC V0N 3A0 – 604/885-3224; Fax: 604/885-3203
Gilbert Plains, MB	*See* Westman Cable TV, Brandon

Canadian Almanac & Directory 1997

CABLE STATIONS

Glace Bay, NS . . . . Seaside Cable TV (1984) Ltd., 1318 Grand Lake Rd., PO Box 279, Glace Bay NS B1A 5V4 – 902/539-6250; Fax: 902/539-2597; Email: hwoodman@highlander.cbnet.ns.ca
Gladstone, MB . . . . *See* Westman Cable TV, Brandon
Glenboro, MB . . . . *See* Westman Cable TV, Brandon
Glovertown, NF . . . . Glovertown Cable TV Ltd., PO Box 131, Glovertown NF A0G 2L0 – 709/533-2377; Fax: 709/533-2702
Golden Valley, PE . . . . *See* Island Cablevision Ltd., Charlottetown
Gorrie, ON . . . . *See* Kincardine Cable TV Ltd., Kincardine
Granby, PQ . . . . Maxi Transvision inc., 210, St-Urbain, CP 10000, Granby PQ J2G 9H7 – 514/378-5133; Fax: 514/372-5464
Grand Bend, ON . . . . *See* Mitchell-Seaforth Cable TV Ltd., Dryden
Grand Falls-Windsor, NF . . . . . *See* Cable Atlantic Inc., St. John's
Grandview, MB . . . . *See* Westman Cable TV, Brandon
Gravenhurst, ON . . . . Gravenhurst Cable System Ltd., 205 Jones Rd., Gravenhurst ON P1P 1M8 – 705/687-2256; Fax: 705/687-4789
Greenville, BC . . . . Greenville Television Association, General Delivery, Greenville BC V0J 1X0 – 250/621-3212; 621-3320
Grimsby, ON . . . . *See* Western Co-Axial Ltd., Hamilton
Guigues, PQ . . . . *See* Câblotem inc., Ville-Marie
Halifax, NS . . . . Halifax Cable Ltd., PO Box 8660, Stn A, Halifax NS B3K 5M3 – 902/453-2800; Fax: 902/454-9159
Hamilton, ON. . . . . Rogers Cablesystems, #105, 135 James St. South, Hamilton ON L8P 2Z6 – 905/522-0123; Fax: 905/522-2420
Hamilton, ON. . . . . Mountain Cablevision Ltd., 141 Hester St., Hamilton ON L9A 2N9 – 905/389-1347; Fax: 905/574-6330
Hamilton, ON. . . . . Northgate Cable TV Ltd., 1603 Main St. West, Hamilton ON L8S 4R4 – 905/522-1400; Fax: 905/522-1044
Hamilton, ON. . . . . Rogers Cablesystems, 695 Lawrence Rd., Hamilton ON L8K 6P1 – 905/547-7836; Fax: 905/547-5237
Hamilton, ON. . . . . TV Hamilton, Cable 14, 150 Dundurn St. South, Hamilton ON L8P 4K3 – 905/523-1414; Fax: 905/645-3234
Hamilton, ON. . . . . Western Co-Axial Ltd., 1603 Main St. West, Hamilton ON L8S 1E6 – 905/522-3012; Fax: 905/522-1044
Hamiota, MB . . . . *See* Westman Cable TV, Brandon
Hanover, ON . . . . Saugeen Telecable Ltd., 111 - 7 Ave., Hanover ON N4N 2G8 – 519/364-2131; Fax: 519/364-4380
Happy Valley-Goose Bay, NF . Northern Television Services Ltd., PO Box 879, Stn B, Happy Valley-Goose Bay NF A0P 1E0 – 709/896-5519; Fax: 709/896-0239
Happy Valley-Goose Bay, NF . CF Cable, PO Box 148, Stn A, Happy Valley-Goose Bay NF A0P 1S0 – 709/896-2888; Fax: 709/989-7371
Harbour Grace, NF . . . . Andromeda Cablevision Ltd., PO Box 500, Harbour Grace NF A0A 2M0 – 709/596-7302; Fax: 709/596-2440
Harbour Grace, NF . . . . Community Cable Ltd., 410 Harvey St., PO Box 500, Harbour Grace NF A0A 2M0 – 709/596-7302; Fax: 709/596-2440
Harmony Junction, PE . . . . *See* Island Cablevision Ltd., Charlottetown
Hawkesbury, ON . . . . Rogers Cablesystems Ltd., 1444 Aberdeen St., Hawkesbury ON K6A 1K7 – 613/632-2514; Fax: 613/632-8531
Hazelton, BC . . . . *See* Skeena Cablevision, Terrace
Hensall, ON . . . . *See* Mitchell-Seaforth Cable TV Ltd., Dryden
High Prairie, AB . . . . KBS TV, PO Box 1222, High Prairie AB T0G 1E0 – 403/523-3223; Fax: 403/523-3411
Hillsburgh, ON. . . . . *See* Shaw Cable, Orangeville
Holland Gardens, MB . . . . *See* Valley Cable Vision Ltd., Selkirk
Hope, BC . . . . Hope Cable Television, 380 Wallace St., PO Box 489, Hope BC V0X 1L0 – 604/869-2616; Fax: 604/869-9393
Houston, BC. . . . . *See* Skeena Cablevision, Terrace
Hull, PQ . . . . Télécâble Laurentien inc., 190, rue Edmonton, Hull PQ J8Y 3S6 – 819/771-7717; Fax: 819/770-6112
Hunter River, PE . . . . *See* Island Cablevision Ltd., Charlottetown
Huntsville, ON . . . . Rogers Cablesystems, 20 West St. South, Huntsville ON P0A 1K0 – 705/789-2731
Ile a la Crosse, SK . . . . Bellanger Communications Inc., PO Box 304, Ile a la Crosse SK S0M 1C0 – 306/833-2173; Fax: 306/833-2132
Ile des Chenes, MB . . . . *See* Valley Cable Vision Ltd., Selkirk
Imperial, SK . . . . Imperial Cable System, PO Box 90, Imperial SK S0G 2J0 – 306/963-2220
Inuvik, NT. . . . . Inuvik TV Ltd., PO Box 2338, Inuvik NT X0E 0T0 – 403/979-2111; Fax: 403/979-3412
Isles-aux-Morts, NF . . . . *See* Cable Atlantic Inc., St. John's
Kamloops, BC . . . . Kamloops Cablenet, 180 Briar Ave., Kamloops BC V2B 1C1 – 250/376-8888; Fax: 250/376-2544
Kamsack, SK. . . . . *See* North Eastern Cablevision Ltd., Yorkton
Kaslo, BC . . . . Kaslo Cable Ltd., PO Box 637, Kaslo BC V0G 1M0 – 250/353-2547
Kelowna, BC. . . . . Shaw Cablesystems (B.C.) Ltd., 2350 Hunter Rd., Kelowna BC V1X 7H6 – 250/762-4433; Fax: 250/762-7997
Kemptville, ON . . . . *See* Shaw Cable, Smiths Falls
Kenora, ON . . . . Norcom Telecommunications Ltd., PO Box 1810, Kenora ON P9N 3X8 – 807/547-2853; Fax: 807/547-2236
Killarney, MB. . . . . *See* Westman Cable TV, Brandon
Kincardine, ON . . . . Kincardine Cable TV Ltd., 223 Bruce Ave., Kincardine ON N2Z 2P2 – 519/396-7802; Fax: 519/396-2599
Kingston, ON . . . . Kingston Cablenet, 170 Colborne St., PO Bag 5500, Kingston ON K7L 5M7 – 613/544-6311; Fax: 613/545-0169
Kinistino, SK. . . . . Kinistino Cable TV Ltd., PO Box 10, Kinistino SK S0J 1H0 – 306/864-2461; Fax: 306/864-2880
Kitchener, ON . . . . Rogers Cable TV - Grand River, 85 Grand Crest Pl., PO Box 488, Kitchener ON N2G 4A8 – 519/893-2101; Fax: 519/893-5861
Kitimat, BC. . . . . *See* Skeena Cablevision, Terrace
La Baie, PQ . . . . Vidéo Dery ltée, 524, rue Albert, La Baie PQ G7B 3P3 – 418/544-3358; Fax: 418/544-0187
La Dore, PQ . . . . *See* Vidéotron ltée, Chicoutimi
La Patrie, PQ . . . . La Patrie Video inc., 23, rue Notre-Dame ouest, CP 210, La Patrie PQ J0B 1Y0 – 819/888-2468; Fax: 819/888-2468
La Pocatière, PQ . . . . Câblodistribution de la Côte du Sud inc., 88, av 11e, CP 500, La Pocatière PQ G0R 1Z0 – 418/856-2253; Fax: 418/856-4772
La Ronge, SK . . . . Cable Ronge Inc., PO Box 1397, La Ronge SK S0J 1L0 – 306/425-2276; Fax: 306/425-2042
La Tûque, PQ. . . . . Electro-Vision (La Tûque) inc., 333, rue St-Joseph, La Tûque PQ G9X 1L3 – 819/523-3737; Fax: 819/523-3506
Labrador City, NF . . . . Community Recreation Rebroadcasting Service Association/CRRS TV, Carol Lake Shopping Centre, Labrador City NF A2V 1L1 – 709/944-7676; Fax: 709/944-7675
Lac Megantic, PQ . . . . Megantic Transvision inc., 5084, rue Frontenac, Lac Megantic PQ G6B 1H3 – 819/583-0432; Fax: 819/583-0454
Lachenaie, PQ . . . . Télécâble des Mille-Îles inc., 940, montée Masson, Lachenaie PQ J6W 2C9 – 514/471-2710; Fax: 514/471-5811
Lachute, PQ . . . . Communi-Cable inc., 330, rue Bethany, Lachute PQ J8H 2N2 – 514/562-4059; Fax: 514/562-2213
Lakefield, ON. . . . . *See* Shaw Cable, Smiths Falls
Lanark, ON. . . . . *See* Shaw Cable, Smiths Falls
Lancaster, ON . . . . *See* Rogers Cablesystems Ottawa, Ottawa
Langley, BC . . . . *See* Shaw Cable (NW Vancouver), North Vancouver
L'Ardoise, NS. . . . . *See* Seaside Cable TV (1984) Ltd., Glace Bay
Leamington, ON . . . . Trillium Cable Communications, 94 Talbot St. East, Leamington ON N8H 1L3 – 519/326-4423; Fax: 519/326-5666
Lethbridge, AB . . . . Lethbridge Cablenet, 1232 - 3 Ave. South, Lethbridge AB T1J 0J9 – 403/328-2002; Fax: 403/329-4482
Limoges, ON. . . . . *See* Rogers Cablesystems Ottawa, Ottawa
Lindsay, ON . . . . Lindsay Comcable, 55 George St. West, Lindsay ON K9V 4V6 – 705/878-9000; Fax: 705/328-2511; Email: comcable@lindsaytown.org
Lion's Bay, BC . . . . *See* Shaw Cable (NW Vancouver), North Vancouver

Lion's Head, ON . . . . *See* Trillium Communications Ltd., Port Elgin
Liverpool, NS. . . . . Able Cablevision Ltd., 212 Main St., PO Box 449, Liverpool NS B0T 1K0 – 902/354-3424; Fax: 902/354-2246
London, ON. . . . . Rogers Cablesystems, 499 MacGregor Ave., London ON N6J 2K9 – 519/433-0141; Fax: 519/433-0157
London, ON. . . . . *See* Rogers Cablesystems, Oshawa
London, ON. . . . . *See* Rogers Cablesystems, Oshawa
Lorette, MB . . . . *See* Valley Cable Vision Ltd., Selkirk
Louisbourg, NS . . . . *See* Seaside Cable TV (1984) Ltd., Glace Bay
Lucknow, ON . . . . *See* Kincardine Cable TV Ltd., Kincardine
Madoc, ON. . . . . Hastings Cable Vision Ltd., 37 Durham St. South, Madoc ON K0K 2K0 – 613/473-2839; Fax: 613/473-4853
Main-à-Dieu, NS . . . . *See* Seaside Cable TV (1984) Ltd., Glace Bay
Manitou, MB . . . . *See* Valley Cable Vision Ltd., Selkirk
Marion Bridge, NS . . . . *See* Seaside Cable TV (1984) Ltd., Glace Bay
Masset, BC. . . . . Masset Haida Television Society, 1686 Main St., PO Box 602, Masset BC V0T 1M0 – 250/626-3997; Fax: 250/626-3968
Maxville, ON . . . . *See* Rogers Cablesystems Ottawa, Ottawa
McCreary, MB. . . . . *See* Westman Cable TV, Brandon
McLennan, AB . . . . *See* Small Community TV Inc., Beaverlodge
Medicine Hat, AB. . . . . Ralston Community Cable System, CFB Suffield, PO Box 6000, Medicine Hat AB T1A 8K8 – 403/544-4405; Fax: 403/544-4433
Melfort, SK . . . . *See* Image Cable Systems Ltd., Yorkton
Melita, MB . . . . *See* Westman Cable TV, Brandon
Melville, SK . . . . *See* North Eastern Cablevision Ltd., Yorkton
Merritt, BC. . . . . Shaw Cablesystems (B.C.) Ltd., 2350 Hunter Rd., Kelowna BC V1X 7H6 – 250/762-4433; Fax: 250/762-7997
Miami, MB . . . . *See* Valley Cable Vision Ltd., Selkirk
Midland, ON . . . . Rogers Cablesystems Georgian Bay Ltd., PO Box 489, Midland ON L4R 4L3 – 705/526-5031; Fax: 705/526-0682
Millbrook, ON. . . . . *See* Shaw Cable, Smiths Falls
Milton, ON. . . . . *See* Halton Cable Systems, Acton
Milverton, ON . . . . *See* Saugeen Telecable Ltd., Hanover
Miminigash, PE . . . . *See* Island Cablevision Ltd., Charlottetown
Minden, ON. . . . . Haliburton/Minden Cable TV, PO Box 10, Minden ON K0M 2K0 – 613/767-2675; Fax: 613/694-4006
Minitonas, MB. . . . . *See* Westman Cable TV, Brandon
Minnedosa, MB. . . . . *See* Westman Cable TV, Brandon
Minto, NB . . . . *See* Fundy Cable Ltd. ltée, Fredericton
Mississauga, ON . . . . Rogers Cablesystems, 3573 Wolfedale Rd., Mississauga ON L5C 1V8 – 905/273-8000; Fax: 905/273-9661
Mistassini, PQ . . . . *See* Vidéotron ltée, Chicoutimi
Moncton, NB . . . . Fundy Cable Ltd./ltée, 90 Driscoll Cres., Moncton NB E1E 3R8 – 506/857-8700; Fax: 506/857-8406
Montague, PE . . . . *See* Island Cablevision Ltd., Charlottetown
Montréal, PQ. . . . . CF CABLE TV inc., #200, 405, av Ogilvy, Montréal PQ H3N 2Y1 – 514/277-7133; Fax: 514/277-1823
Montréal, PQ. . . . . Sorel-O-Vision, #500, 1420, rue Sherbrooke ouest, Montréal PQ H3G 1K5 – 514/849-3711; Fax: 514/849-1855
Montréal, PQ. . . . . Vidéotron ltée, 2000, rue Berri, Montréal PQ H2L 4V7 – 514/281-1232; Fax: 514/985-8794; Email: communic@videotron.ca
Moose Jaw, SK . . . . Prairie Co-Ax TV Ltd., 201 Manitoba St. East, PO Box 760, Moose Jaw SK S6H 4P5 – 306/693-8585; Fax: 306/692-4859
Morden, MB . . . . *See* Valley Cable Vision Ltd., Selkirk
Morell, PE . . . . *See* Island Cablevision Ltd., Charlottetown
Morris, MB. . . . . *See* Valley Cable Vision Ltd., Selkirk
Mount Stewart, PE . . . . *See* Island Cablevision Ltd., Charlottetown
Murray River, PE . . . . *See* Island Cablevision Ltd., Charlottetown
Musgrave Harbour, NF . . . . . . *See* Cable Atlantic Inc., St. John's
Musgravetown, NF . . . . BMC Cablevision Co. Ltd., PO Box 16, Musgravetown NF A0C 1Z0 – 709/467-5306; Fax: 709/467-2489
Mynarski Park, AB . . . . CFB Penhold CATV, 636 Maple Cres., PO Box 35, Mynarski Park AB T0M 1N0 – 403/886-2729; Fax: 403/346-5158
Nanaimo, BC. . . . . Shaw Cablesystems (B.C.) Ltd., 711 Poplar St., Nanaimo BC V9S 5L8 – 250/754-5571; Fax: 250/754-3504
Nanticoke, ON. . . . . *See* Nor-Del Cablevision Ltd., Norwich
Neepawa, MB . . . . *See* Westman Cable TV, Brandon
Nelson, BC. . . . . *See* Shaw Cable, Cranbrook
Neustadt, ON. . . . . *See* Saugeen Telecable Ltd., Hanover
New Germany, NS . . . . New Germany Cablevision Ltd., RR#2, New Germany NS B0R 1E0 – 902/644-2358
New Glasgow, NS . . . . Shaw Cable, PO Box 157, New Glasgow NS B2H 5E2 – 902/752-0310; Fax: 902/755-2236
Newcastle, NB . . . . Fundy Cable TV Ltd./ltée, 454 King George Hwy., Newcastle NB E1V 1M1 – 506/622-9120; Fax: 506/622-3712
Newmarket, ON . . . . Rogers Cable TV Ltd., 20 Gladman Ave., Newmarket ON L3Y 2N2 – 905/895-1604; Fax: 905/898-7577
Niagara Falls, ON . . . . Rogers Cablesystems Niagara Partnership, 7170 McLeod Rd., Niagara Falls ON L2G 3H2 – 905/374-5570; Fax: 905/374-2398
Niagara Falls, ON . . . . *See* Rogers Cablesystems Niagara Partnership, Niagara Falls
Niagara on the Lake, ON. . . . . *See* Rogers Cablesystems Niagara Partnership, Niagara Falls
Niverville, MB. . . . . *See* Valley Cable Television Ltd., Selkirk
Norquay, SK . . . . *See* North Eastern Cablevision Ltd., Yorkton
North Rustico, PE . . . . *See* Island Cablevision Ltd., Charlottetown
North Vancouver, BC. . . . . Shaw Cable (NW Vancouver), 1471 Pemberton Ave., North Vancouver BC V7P 2R9 – 604/985-2151; Fax: 604/985-7495
Norwich, ON . . . . Nor Del Cablcvision Ltd., PO Box 340, Norwich ON N0J 1P0 – 519/468-3116
Notre Dame de Lourdes, MB . *See* Valley Cable Vision Ltd., Selkirk
Oakville, ON . . . . O1 Cablesystems Inc., 1173 North Service Rd. West, Unit 6, Oakville ON L6M 1V9 – 905/847-1132; Fax: 905/847-1139
O'Leary, PE. . . . . *See* Island Cablevision Ltd., Charlottetown
Oliver, BC. . . . . OTV Cablevision, 9502 - 348th Ave., PO Box 790, Oliver BC V0H 1T0 – 250/498-3630; Fax: 250/498-8810
100 Mile House, BC . . . . *See* Shaw Cablesystems (B.C.) Ltd., Prince George
Orangeville, ON . . . . Shaw Cable, 70 C-Line Rd., PO Box 56, Orangeville ON L9W 2Z5 – 519/941-4030; Fax: 519/941-6091
Oshawa, ON. . . . . Rogers Cablesystems, 301 Marwood Dr., Oshawa ON L1H 1J4 – 905/579-1601; Fax: 905/579-5559
Ottawa, ON . . . . Rogers Cablesystems Ottawa, 475 Richmond Rd., PO Box 6315, Stn J, Ottawa ON K2A 3Y8 – 613/722-1111; Fax: 613/725-2223
Owen Sound, ON . . . . Rogers Cablesystems, 1040 - 20 St. East, PO Box 440, Owen Sound ON N4K 5P7 – 519/376-5195; Fax: 519/376-5216
Oxford Mills, ON . . . . *See* Shaw Cable, Smiths Falls
Paisley, ON . . . . *See* Trillium Communications Ltd., Port Elgin
Pakenham, ON . . . . *See* Rogers Cablesystems Ottawa, Ottawa
Pangnirtung, NT . . . . Pangnirtung Cable Television Ltd., PO Box 304, Pangnirtung NT X0A 0R0 – 819/473-8743
Panorama, BC. . . . . *See* Shaw Cable, Cranbrook

Canadian Almanac & Directory 1997

Paradise River, NF..........Paradise River Communications, 1 Sternpost Cove, Paradise River NF A0K 3Y8 – 709/845-5238; Fax: 709/845-5238
Parksville, BC...............Shaw Cablesystems (B.C.) Ltd., PO Box 880, Parksville BC V7P 2G9 – 250/248-3444; Fax: 250/754-3504
Pasadena, NF...............See Cable Atlantic Inc., St. John's
Pembroke, ON..............Rogers Cablesystems, 185 Lake St., Pembroke ON K8A 5M1 – 613/735-6819; Fax: 613/735-6177
Pender Harbour, BC........See Coast Cable Communications Ltd., Sechelt
Penetanguishene, ON.......See Rogers Cablesystems Georgian Bay Ltd., Midland
Perkinsfield, ON............See Rogers Cablesystems Ottawa, Ottawa
Perth, ON..................See Shaw Cable, Smiths Falls
Peterborough, ON..........Rogers Cablesystems, 685 Queensway, PO Box 2290, Peterborough ON K9J 7Y8 – 705/742-9264; Fax: 705/742-3563
Pine Falls, MB..............Winnipeg River CATV, PO Box 659, Pine Falls MB R0E 1M0 – 204/367-2858; Fax: 204/367-4991
Plum Coulee, MB...........See Valley Cable Vision Ltd., Selkirk
Pointe-Sapin, NB...........See Fundy Cable TV Ltd./ltée, Newcastle
Pond Inlet, NT.............P.I. Cable TV, 4367 - 11 Ave. North, Pond Inlet NT X0A 0S0 – 819/899-8887; Fax: 819/899-8849
Port Alberni, BC............Ucluelet Video Services, PO Box 546, Port Alberni BC V9Y 7M9 – 250/726-7792; Fax: 250/726-4373
Port Alberni, BC............Shaw Cable, 3744 - 3 Ave., Port Alberni BC V9Y 4G1 – 250/723-6295; Fax: 250/723-4024
Port-aux-Basques, NF.......See Cable Atlantic Inc., St. John's
Port Colborne, ON..........See Rogers Cablesystems Niagara Partnership, Niagara Falls
Port Elgin, ON..............Trillium Communications Ltd., 1119 Goderich St. North, PO Box 1330, Port Elgin ON N0H 2C0 – 519/832-6297; Fax: 519/389-4096
Port McNicoll, ON..........See Rogers Cablesystems Georgian Bay Ltd., Midland
Port Perry, ON.............Compton Cable TV Ltd., Lot 7, Con. 5, PO Box 73, Port Perry ON L9L 1A2 – 905/985-8171; Fax: 905/985-0010
Port Robinson, ON.........See Rogers Cablesystems Niagara Partnership, Niagara Falls
Portage La Prairie, MB......See Romik Communications Ltd., Flin Flon
Portage la Prairie, MB......Portage Community Cablevision Ltd., PO Box 146, Portage La Prairie MB R1N 3B2 – 204/857-6623; Fax: 204/857-6665
Powell River, BC...........Powell River Cablenet, 4706 Ewing Place, Powell River BC V8A 2N5 – 604/485-4410; Fax: 604/485-6030
Prince Albert, SK...........Shaw Cable Prince Albert, 2290 Second Ave. West, Prince Albert SK S6V 7E9 – 306/922-0202; Fax: 306/922-7122
Prince George, BC..........Shaw Cablesystems (B.C.) Ltd., 470 - 3rd Ave., Prince George BC V2L 3B9 – 250/562-1345; Fax: 250/563-9222
Queenston, ON............See Rogers Cablesystems Niagara Partnership, Niagara Falls
Quesnel, BC...............See Shaw Cablesystems (B.C.) Ltd., Prince George
Ramea, NF................Ramea Broadcasting Co., PO Box 23, Ramea NF A0M 1N0 – 709/625-2618; Fax: 709/625-2151
Red Deer, AB.............Shaw Cablesystems, 6123 - 48th Ave., Red Deer AB T4N 5Z9 – 403/346-6633; Fax: 403/346-3962
Reef's Harbour, NF.........Clearview Cable Ltd., PO Box 10, Reef's Harbour NF A0K 4L0 – 709/847-7441; Fax: 709/847-7100
Regina, SK................Regina Cablevision Co-operative, 2250 Park St., Regina SK S4N 7K7 – 306/569-3510; Fax: 306/757-3262
Regina Beach, SK..........Regina Beach District TV Co-operative, PO Box 245, Regina Beach SK S0G 4C0 – 306/729-2666; Fax: 306/729-4898
Renfrew, ON..............See Rogers Cablesystems Ottawa, Ottawa
Resolute Bay, NT...........Narwhal Arctic Services Ltd., PO Box 88, Resolute Bay NT X0A 0V0 – 819/252-3968; Fax: 819/252-3960
Revelstoke, BC.............Revelstoke Cable TV Ltd., 309 MacKenzie Ave., PO Box 651, Revelstoke BC V0E 2S0 – 250/837-5246; Fax: 250/837-2900
Richibucto, NB.............See Fundy Cable TV Ltd./ltée, Newcastle
Richmond Hill, ON.........Classic Communications Ltd., 244 Newkirk Rd., Richmond Hill ON L4C 3S5 – 905/884-8111; Fax: 905/884-8151
Ridgeville, ON..............See Rogers Cablesystems Niagara Partnership, Niagara Falls
Ridgeway, ON.............See Rogers Cablesystems Niagara Partnership, Niagara Falls
Rimouski, PQ..............Compagnie de Télévision de Sept-Îles ltée, 384, av de la Cathédrale, Rimouski PQ G5L 5L1 – 418/724-7230; Fax: 418/724-7167
Riondel, BC...............Riondel Community Cable & Video Society, PO Box 59, Riondel BC V0B 2B0
River Bourgeois, NS........See Seaside Cable TV (1984) Ltd., Glace Bay
Rivers, MB.................See Westman Cable TV, Brandon
Rivière-du-Loup, PQ........Le Cable de Rivière-du-Loup ltée, 279A, rue Lafontaine, CP 1390, Rivière-du-Loup PQ G5R 4L9 – 418/867-1478; Fax: 418/867-2829
Rivière-du-Loup, PQ........Télédistribution Cablouis inc., 279A, rue Lafontaine, CP 1390, Rivière-du-Loup PQ G5R 4L9 – 418/854-2453; Fax: 418/867-2829
Robe Blanche, NF..........See Cable Atlantic Inc., St. John's
Roblin, MB................See Westman Cable TV, Brandon
Rock Island, PQ............See Vidéotron ltée, Sherbrooke
Rockwood, ON............See Halton Cable Systems, Acton
Rocky Mountain House, AB..Anderson Cable Contractors Ltd., PO Box 2010, Rocky Mountain House AB T0M 1T0 – 403/845-2940
Rocky Mountain House, AB..Ram River Cable TV Ltd., 4712 - 49 Ave., PO Box 2010, Rocky Mountain House AB T0M 1T0 – 403/845-4940; Fax: 403/845-4797
Rocky Point, PE............See Island Cablevision Ltd., Charlottetown
Rogersville, NB.............See Fundy Cable TV Ltd./ltée, Newcastle
Rossburn, MB..............See Westman Cable TV, Brandon
Rouleau, SK...............Rouleau Cable TV Association Inc., PO Box 250, Rouleau SK S0G 4H0 – 306/776-2270; Fax: 306/776-2270
Rupert, BC................See Skeena Cablevision, Terrace
Russell, MB................See Westman Cable TV, Brandon
Rycroft, AB................See Small Community TV Inc., Beaverlodge
Ste-Adèle, PQ..............Télédiffusion Ste-Adèle inc., 605, ch Ste-Marguerite, CP 1375, Ste-Adèle PQ J0R 1L0 – 514/229-7666; Fax: 514/229-7910
St. Adolphe, MB...........See Valley Cable Vision Ltd., Selkirk
Ste-Agathe-des-Monts, PQ...Cable Laurentides ltée, 5, rue Laroque, CP 265, Ste-Agathe-des-Monts PQ J8C 3A3 – 819/326-5572
Ste. Anne, MB.............See Valley Cable Vision Ltd., Selkirk
Ste-Anne-de-Kent, NB......See Fundy Cable TV Ltd./ltée, Newcastle
St-Antoine, NB.............See Fundy Cable TV Ltd./ltée, Newcastle
St Catharines, ON..........See Rogers Cablesystems Niagara Partnership, Niagara Falls
St. Claude, MB.............See Valley Cable Vision Ltd., Selkirk
St-Cyrille-de-Wendover, PQ..Transvision Weedon, 235, rue Nathalie, St-Cyrille-de-Wendover PQ J1Z 2V8 – 819/477-4305; Fax: 819/477-4305
St. David's, ON............See Rogers Cablesystems Niagara Partnership, Niagara Falls
St-Édouard, NB............See Fundy Cable TV Ltd./ltée, Newcastle
St-Évariste, PQ.............La Gaudeloupe Télévision inc., 430, rue Principale, St-Évariste PQ G0M 1S0 – 418/459-6844
St-Évariste, PQ.............Télé-Câble Labonté inc., 430, rue Principale, St-Évariste PQ G0M 1S0 – 418/459-6844
St-Felicien, PQ.............See Vidéotron ltée, Chicoutimi
St-Georges-de-Beauce, PQ...Beauce Vidéo ltée, 11197 - 2e av, St-Georges-de-Beauce PQ G5Y 1VP – 418/228-2755; Fax: 418/228-3015
St-Ignace, NB..............See Fundy Cable TV Ltd./ltée, Newcastle
St. Isidore, ON.............See Rogers Cablesystems Ottawa, Ottawa
St. Jean Baptiste, MB.......See Valley Cable Vision Ltd., Selkirk
St. John's, NF..............Cable Atlantic Inc., PO Box 8596, St. John's NF A1B 3P2 – 709/753-7583; Fax: 709/722-8384

Canadian Almanac & Directory 1997

St. John's, NF	Regional Cable TV (Atlantic) Inc., PO Box 12155, Stn A, St. John's NF A1B 4L1 – 709/754-3775; Fax: 709/754-3883
St. Lazare, MB	*See* Westman Cable TV, Brandon
St-Marc-des-Carrière, PQ	Télé-Câble St-Marc-des-Carrières inc., 448, rue Sauvageau, St-Marc-des-Carrière PQ G0A 4B0 – 418/268-5453; Fax: 418/268-5131
Ste-Marie-de-Beauce, PQ	Télécâble Lac-Etchemin inc., 166, rue Notre-Dame nord, CP 1570, Ste-Marie-de-Beauce PQ G6E 3C6 – 418/464-4416; Fax: 418/387-6915
Ste-Marie-de-Kent, NB	*See* Fundy Cable TV Ltd./ltée, Newcastle
St. Peters, PE	*See* Island Cablevision Ltd., Charlottetown
St. Peter's, NS	*See* Seaside Cable TV (1984) Ltd., Glace Bay
St. Pierre Jolys, MB	*See* Valley Cable Vision Ltd., Selkirk
St-Prime, PQ	*See* Vidéotron ltée, Chicoutimi
St-Raymond, PQ	*See* Vidéo Dery ltée, La Baie
Ste-Rose-du-Lac, MB	*See* Westman Cable TV, Brandon
Ste-Thérèse-de-Colombier, PQ	*See* Télécâble Côte-Nord inc., Chute-aux-Outardes
St. Thomas, ON	Till Cable TV Ltd., PO Box 582, St. Thomas ON N5P 4B1 – 519/842-5242; Fax: 519/631-3253
St. Thomas, ON	Shaw Cable, PO Box 582, St. Thomas ON N5P 4B1 – 519/631-5060; Fax: 519/631-3253
Salmon Arm, BC	Mascom Communications, PO Box 3386, Salmon Arm BC V1E 4S2 – 250/832-6000; Fax: 250/832-5575
Saltcoats, SK	*See* North Eastern Cablevision Ltd., Yorkton
Sandy Lake, MB	*See* Westman Cable TV, Brandon
Sarnia, ON	Rogers Cablesystems, 1421 Confederation St., PO Box 218, Sarnia ON N7T 7J1 – 519/332-8439
Saskatoon, SK	Shaw Cable Saskatoon, 2326 Hanselman Ave., PO Box 1950, Saskatoon SK S7K 3S5 – 306/664-1007; Fax: 306/244-0105
Sauble Beach, ON	*See* Trillium Communications Ltd., Port Elgin
Schreiber, ON	Morrill's Cable TV Ltd., 224 Park St., Schreiber ON P0T 2S0 – 807/824-2619
Selkirk, MB	Interlake Cable TV Ltd., PO Box 243, Selkirk MB R1A 2B2 – 204/785-8701; Fax: 204/785-8749
Selkirk, MB	Valley Cable Vision Ltd., 186 Main St., PO Box 243, Selkirk MB R1A 2B2 – 204/785-8701; Fax: 204/785-8749
Shannon, PQ	Shannon Vision inc., 75, ch Gosford, Shannon PQ G0A 4N0 – 418/844-3849; Fax: 418/844-2111
Shediac, NB	Cable 2000 Inc., 79 Sackville St., PO Box 1317, Shediac NB E0A 3G0 – 506/532-6215
Shelburne, NS	Seabreeze Cablevision Ltd., PO Box 1090, Shelburne NS B0T 1W0 – 902/875-4438; Fax: 902/875-4219
Sherbrooke, PQ	Vidéotron ltée, 2830, rue Galt ouest, Sherbrooke PQ J1K 2V8 – 819/822-6812; Fax: 819/822-6821
Shilo, MB	Shilo Cable TV, PO Box 40, Stn CFB, Shilo MB R0K 2A0 – 204/765-2586; Fax: 204/765-3093
Shoal Lake, MB	*See* Westman Cable TV, Brandon
Smithers, BC	*See* Skeena Cablevision, Terrace
Smiths Falls, ON	Shaw Cable, 207 Brockville St., Smiths Falls ON K7A 3Z3 – 613/283-6150; Fax: 613/283-1526
Snow Lake, MB	*See* Romik Communications Ltd., Flin Flon
Souris, MB	*See* Westman Cable TV, Brandon
Southampton, ON	*See* Trillium Communications Ltd., Port Elgin
Southern Kings, PE	*See* Island Cablevision Ltd., Charlottetown
Southey, SK	Southey Cable, PO Box 248, Southey SK S0G 4P0 – 306/726-2202; Fax: 306/726-2202
Spirit River, AB	*See* Small Community TV Inc., Beaverlodge
Springhill, PE	*See* Island Cablevision Ltd., Charlottetown
Springside, SK	*See* North Eastern Cablevision Ltd., Yorkton
Stanstead, PQ	*See* Vidéotron ltée, Chicoutimi
Steinbach, MB	*See* Valley Cable Vision Ltd., Selkirk
Stewart, BC	*See* Skeena Cablevision, Terrace
Stonewall, MB	*See* Interlake Cable TV Ltd., Selkirk
Strathclair, MB	*See* Westman Cable TV, Brandon
Sudbury, ON	Northern Cable Holdings Ltd., #15, 500 Barrydowne Rd., PO Box 4500, Sudbury ON P3A 5W1 – 705/560-1560; Fax: 705/560-4752
Sundre, AB	*See* Monarch Cable TV, Canmore
Surrey, BC	*See* Shaw Cable (NW Vancouver), North Vancouver
Surrey, BC	Rogers Cablesystems Ltd., 10445 - 138 St., Surrey BC V3T 4X3 – 604/588-1229; Fax: 604/588-3404
Sussex, NB	Kings County Cable Ltd., 500 Main St., PO Box 1428, Sussex NB E0E 1P0 – 506/432-1000; Fax: 506/432-6330
Swan River, MB	*See* Westman Cable TV, Brandon
Swift Current, SK	*See* Prairie Co-Ax TV Ltd., Moose Jaw
Swift Current, SK	Shaw Cablesystems, 15 Dufferin St. West, Swift Current SK S9H 5A1 – 306/773-7218; Fax: 306/773-6421
Sydney, NS	Cape Breton Cablevision Ltd., 61 Melody Lane, Sydney NS B1P 3K4 – 902/562-5600; Fax: 902/564-5428
Taber, AB	Monarch Cable TV Ltd., PO Box 1448, Taber AB T0K 2G0 – 403/223-3331; Fax: 403/527-4770
Tara, ON	*See* Trillium Communications Ltd., Port Elgin
Teeswater, ON	*See* Kincardine Cable TV Ltd., Kincardine
Terrace, BC	Skeena Cablevision, 4625 Lazelle Ave., Terrace BC V8G 1S4 – 250/635-6316; Fax: 250/638-6320; Email: info@osg.net
Teulon, MB	*See* Interlake Cable TV Ltd., Selkirk
The Rapids, NB	*See* Fundy Cable TV Ltd./ltée, Newcastle
Theodore, SK	*See* North Eastern Cablevision Ltd., Yorkton
Thetford-Mines, PQ	Appareils Electroniques Bérubé, 37, rue St-Joseph ouest, CP 274, Thetford-Mines PQ G6G 5T1 – 418/335-6620; Fax: 418/335-9125
Thetford-Mines, PQ	Thetford Vidéo inc. 37, rue St-Joseph ouest, CP 274, Thetford-Mines PQ G6G 5T1 – 418/335-6622; Fax: 418/335-9125
Thompson, MB	Videon Cable TV, 50 Selkirk Ave., Thompson MB R8N 0M7 – 204/778-7321; Fax: 204/677-9953
Thompson, MB	Native Communications Inc., 76 Severn Cres., Thompson MB R8N 1M6 – 204/778-8343; Fax: 204/778-6559
Thorold, ON	*See* Rogers Cablesystems Niagara Partnership, Niagara Falls
Thunder Bay, ON	Rogers Cablesystems, 1635 Paquette Rd., PO Box 3450, Thunder Bay ON P7B 5J9 – 807/767-4422; Fax: 807/767-7211
Toronto, ON	Shaw Cable, 35 Scarlett Rd., Toronto ON M6N 4J8 – 416/762-3622; Fax: 416/762-0380
Toronto, ON	Rogers Cablesystems, 47 Lisgar St., Toronto ON M6J 3T4 – 416/534-2948; Fax: 416/534-3367
Toronto, ON	Rogers Community 10 Etobicoke, 80 Worcester Rd., Etobicoke ON M9W 1K7 – 416/675-5930, ext.297; Fax: 416/675-4254
Toronto, ON	Newton Cable Communications Ltd., 78 Martin Ross Ave., North York ON M3J 2L4 – 416/661-5000; Fax: 416/661-7892
Toronto, ON	Rogers Cable TV, 855 York Mills Rd., Don Mills ON M3B 1Z1 – 416/446-6500; Fax: 416/446-6003
Toronto, ON	Shaw Cablesystems Ltd., #1, 700 Progress Ave., Scarborough ON M1H 2Z7 – 416/290-6222; Fax: 416/439-9978
Trail, BC	*See* Shaw Cable, Cranbrook
Treherne, MB	*See* Valley Cable Vision Ltd., Selkirk
Trois-Rivières, PQ	COGECO Câble inc., #200, 1630 - 6e rue, Trois-Rivières PQ G8V 5B8 – 819/372-9292; Fax: 819/372-3318
Truro, NS	North Nova Cable Ltd., 361 Prince St., Truro NS B2N 1E4 – 902/895-1515; Fax: 902/893-2256
Tumbler Ridge, BC	North East Cable TV Ltd., PO Box 2050, Tumbler Ridge BC V0C 2W0 – 250/242-4300; Fax: 250/242-4840
Tweed, ON	Village Cablesystems Ltd., 36 Metcalfe St., PO Box 616, Tweed ON K0K 3J0 – 613/478-5766; Fax: 613/478-2192; Email: tgr@blvl.igs.net

Canadian Almanac & Directory 1997

Val-d'Or, PQ . . . . Cablevision du Nord de Québec inc., 45, boul Hôtel de Ville, Val-d'Or PQ J9P 2M5 – 819/825-5133; Fax: 819/825-8710
Valleyfield, PQ . . . . Valleyfield Transvision inc., 135, rue Alexandre, Valleyfield PQ J6S 3K5 – 514/373-6616; Fax: 514/373-7234
Vananda, BC . . . . Texada Community TV Association, PO Box 158, Vananda BC V0N 3K0 – 604/486-7640
Vancouver, BC . . . . *See* Shaw Cable (NW Vancouver), North Vancouver
Vernon, BC . . . . Shaw Cable, 2924 - 28 Ave., Vernon BC V1T 8W6 – 250/542-4007; Fax: 250/542-2928
Victoria, BC . . . . Rogers Cablesystems, 861 Cloverdale Ave., Victoria BC V8X 4S7 – 250/381-5050; Fax: 250/381-4190
Victoria, BC . . . . Royal Oak Cablevision Ltd., 4500 West Saanich Rd., Victoria BC V8Z 3G2 – 250/479-8611; Fax: 250/479-8421
Victoria, BC . . . . Shaw Cablesystems (B.C.) Ltd., 2614 Sooke Rd., Victoria BC V9B 1Y2 – 250/474-2111; Fax: 250/474-5005
Victoria Harbour, ON . . . . *See* Rogers Cablesystems Georgian Bay Ltd., Midland
Ville-Marie, PQ . . . . Câblotem inc., 981, rte 101 nord, CP 9, Ville-Marie PQ J0Z 3W0 – 819/629-3458; Fax: 819/622-0044
Virden, MB . . . . *See* Westman Cable TV, Brandon
Virgil, ON . . . . *See* Rogers Cablesystems Niagara Partnership, Niagara Falls
Wallaceburg, ON . . . . *See* Rogers Cablesystems, Sarnia
Watson Lake, YT . . . . Liard River Indian Reserve #3, PO Box 489, Watson Lake YT Y0A 1C0 – 250/779-3161; Fax: 250/779-3371
Weirdale, SK . . . . J.L.R. Systems, PO Box 1000, Weirdale SK S0J 2Z0 – 306/929-4851; Fax: 306/929-3104
Welland, ON . . . . *See* Rogers Cablesystems Niagara Partnership, Niagara Falls
Welland, ON . . . . *See* Rogers Cablesystems, Sarnia
Wembley, AB . . . . *See* Small Community TV Inc., Beaverlodge
Wesleyville, NF . . . . *See* Cable Atlantic Inc., St. John's
Wetaskiwin, AB . . . . Cable TV of Wetaskiwin Inc., 5001A - 51 Ave., Wetaskiwin AB T9A 0T9 – 403/352-3666; Fax: 403/352-7755
Weyburn, SK . . . . Weyburn Cablenet, PO Box 1210, Weyburn SK S4H 2L5 – 306/842-0032; Fax: 306/842-3465
Whale Cove, NT . . . . Hamlet of Whale Cove, Whale Cove NT X0C 0J0 – 819/896-9961; Fax: 819/896-9709
Whistler, BC . . . . Whistler Cable Television Ltd., PO Box 630, Whistler BC V0N 1B0 – 604/932-1111; Fax: 604/932-1852
White City, SK . . . . *See* Prairie Co-Ax TV Ltd., Moose Jaw
White Rock, BC . . . . *See* Shaw Cable (NW Vancouver), North Vancouver
Whitehorse, YT . . . . Northern Television Systems Ltd., #203, 4103 - 4 Ave., Whitehorse YT Y1A 1H6 – 403/667-4247; Fax: 403/667-4217
Whitney, ON . . . . *See* Shaw Cable, Smiths Falls
Wiarton, ON . . . . *See* Trillium Communications Ltd., Port Elgin
Williams Lake, BC . . . . *See* Shaw Cablesystems (B.C.) Ltd., Prince George
Windsor, NS . . . . Windsor Cable, 19 Nelson St., PO Box 640, Windsor NS B0N 2T0 – 902/798-8313; Fax: 902/798-4426
Windsor, ON . . . . Shaw Cable, 2525 Dougall Ave., Windsor ON N8X 5A7 – 519/972-6677; Fax: 519/972-6688; Email: windsorcable11@wincom.net
Winkler, MB . . . . *See* Valley Cable Vision Ltd., Selkirk
Winnipeg, MB . . . . Hughes Aircraft of Canada Ltd., 260 Saulteaux Cres., Winnipeg MB R3J 3T2 – 204/949-2400; Fax: 204/889-1268
Winnipeg, MB . . . . Winnipeg Videon Inc., 22 Scurfield Blvd., Winnipeg MB R3Y 1S7 – 204/287-4536; Fax: 204/287-8068
Witless Bay, NF . . . . *See* Cable Atlantic Inc., St. John's
Woodlawn, ON . . . . Constance Bay Cable Television Ltd., PO Box 310, Woodlawn ON K0A 3M0 – 613/832-3470; Fax: 613/832-2889
Woodstock, ON . . . . Shaw Cablesystems (Ontario) Ltd., 21 Ridgeway Circle, PO Box 1208, Woodstock ON N4S 8P6 – 519/539-8101; Fax: 519/539-7731
Wynndel, BC . . . . Wynndel Community TV Society, PO Box 5, Wynndel BC V0B 2N0 – 250/866-5542
Yarmouth, NS . . . . *See* Halifax Cable Ltd., Halifax
Yellowknife, NT . . . . Mackenzie Media Ltd., PO Box 1469, Yellowknife NT X1A 2P1 – 403/920-2929; Fax: 403/920-2331
Yorkton, SK . . . . Image Cable Systems Ltd., PO Box 280, Yorkton SK S3N 2V9 – 306/783-1322; Fax: 306/786-7686
Yorkton, SK . . . . North Eastern Cablevision Ltd., PO Box 550, Yorkton SK S3N 0X5 – 306/783-1566; Fax: 306/782-1952
Young, SK . . . . Village of Young, PO Box 359, Young SK S0K 4Y0 – 306/259-2242
Zurich, ON . . . . *See* Mitchell-Seaforth Cable TV Ltd., Dryden

ONLINE SERVICE PROVIDERS

The following listings include information on connection speeds, phone lines and number of users for online service providers. Many of the companies that responded to our request for information pointed out that the industry is changing rapidly; access, in terms of connection speed, number of users, etc. changes with demand. Contact the company directly for up-to-date information.

ALBERTA

Alberta Supernet
   Pacific Plaza, #1660, 10020 - 101A Ave., Edmonton AB T5J 2G3
   403/441-3663; Fax: 403/424-0743; Email: info@supernet.ab.ca
   Technical Sales Manager, Kelly Marples
   Connection speed to Internet: T1
   Users' top connection speed: 256K
   Number of phone lines: 250
   Number of users: 3,000

SmartNet Internet Services
   16810 - 104A Ave., Edmonton AB T5P 4J6
   403/429-4388; Fax: 403/426-7110; Email: support@compusmart.ab.ca

Spots InterConnect Inc.
   #807, 100 - 4th Ave. SW, Calgary AB T2P 3N2
   403/571-7768; Fax: 403/237-7380; Email: info@spots.ab.ca
   Vice-President, Operations, Jason Marshall
   Connection speed to Internet: T1
   Users' top connection speed: 128K
   Number of phone lines: 10:1 user/modem

Super I-Way Internet Services.
   #100, 10620 - 178 St., Edmonton AB T5S 2E3
   403/413-9111; Fax: 403/413-9150; Email: sales@superiway.net
   General, Manager, Ken Darby

T-8000 Information Systems
   #36001, 6449 Crowchild Trail SW, Calgary AB T3E 3Y3
   403/686-1169; Fax: 403/686-1193; Email: brian.simpson@t8000.com
   President, Brian Simpson
   Connection speed to Internet: Dual T1
   Users' top connection speed: 128K
   Number of phone lines: 32
   Number of users: 100

TELUS PLAnet
   #20E, 10020 - 100 St., Edmonton AB T5J 0N5
   403/423-4638; Fax: 403/493-4277; Email: webmaster@planet.eon.net
   Product Manager, Gemini Waghmare
   Users' top connection speed: 128K

TIC Internet
   PO Box 4041, Edmonton AB T6E 4S8
   403/944-6941; Fax: 403/944-6942; Email: info@tic.ab.ca
   Web Administrator/Internet Technician, Kris Dlouhy
   Users' top connection speed: 33.6K
   Number of phone lines: 16
   Number of users: 190

TNC The Network Centre Ltd.
   #212, 10509 - 81 Ave., Edmonton AB T6E 1X7
   403/448-1290; Fax: 403/944-0233; Email: info@tnc.com
   General Manager, Ralph Playdon
   Connection speed to Internet: T1
   Users' top connection speed: T1

BRITISH COLUMBIA

Fairview Technology Centre Ltd.
   Route 1, Site 24, Conc. 9, Oliver BC V0H 1T0
   250/498-4316; Fax: 250/498-3214; Email: bwklatt@ftcnet.com
   Partner, Bernard Klatt
   Connection speed to Internet: 256K
   Users' top connection speed: 33.6K
   Number of phone lines: 16
   Number of users: 175

ICE Online
   #208, 2465 Beta Ave., Burnaby BC V5C 5N1
   604/482-7575; Fax: 604/482-7599; Email: krish@iceonline.com
   Contact, Corporate Relations, Buz Ried

Connection speed to Internet: T1
Users' top connection speed: 33.6K
Number of phone lines: 100
Number of users: 1,000+
Internet Portal Services Inc.
#201, 2525 Manitoba St., Vancouver BC V5Y 3A7
604/257-9400; Fax: 604/257-9401; Email: info@portal.ca
President, Larry Tolton
Connection speed to Internet: T1
Users' top connection speed: 128K
Number of phone lines: 82
Number of users: 1,625
MIND LINK! Communications Corp.
#230, 435 Columbia St., New Westminster BC V3L 5N8
604/668-5000; Fax: 604/668-5028; Email: info@mindlink.net
General Manager, Carla Dubé
Connection speed to Internet: Ethernet
Users' top connection speed: 28.8K
World Tel
#810, 675 West Hastings St., Vancouver BC V6B 1N2
604/685-3877; Fax: 604/687-0688; Email: info@worldtel.com
President, Barclay Hambrook
Connection speed to Internet: T1
Users' top connection speed: 33.6K
Number of phone lines: 14:1

MANITOBA

Cyberspace Online Information Systems
#18, 794 Sargent Ave., Winnipeg MB R3E 0B7
204/775-3650; Fax: 204/775-3501; Email: info@cyberspc.mb.ca
Account, Manager, Steven Fingold
Connection speed to Internet: T1
Users' top connection speed: 28.8K
Number of phone lines: 101
Number of users: 790
Escape Communications Corp.
#206, 1383 Pembina Hwy., Winnipeg MB R3T 2B9
204/925-4290; Fax: 204/925-4291; Email: info@escape.ca
Connection speed to Internet: T1
Users' top connection speed: 33.6K
InfoHighway OnRamp Centre Inc.
375 York Ave., Winnipeg MB R3C 3J3
204/925-7200; Fax: 204/925-7260; Email: info@wpg.ramp.net
President/CEO, Orest Serwylo
Connection speed to Internet: T1
Users' top connection speed: T1
Number of users: 4,000
Internet Solutions Inc.
490 Des Meurons St., 2nd Fl., Winnipeg MB R2H 2P5
204/982-1060; Fax: 204/982-1070; Email: info@solutions.net
Director, Jason L.M. Remillard
Connection speed to Internet: T1
Users' top connection speed: 128K
Number of phone lines: 10:1 user/modem ratio
Number of users: 10:1 user/modem ratio
MBnet
Univ. of Manitoba, Computer Services, 603 Engineering Bldg., 15 Gilson St., Winnipeg MB R3T 5V6
204/474-7325; Fax: 204/275-5420; Email: info@mbnet.mb.ca
Manager, Ron Dallmeier
Connection speed to Internet: ATM
Users' top connection speed: 28.8K
Number of phone lines: 120
Number of users: 16,000+
Technology Plus Ltd.
244 Hamilton St., Neepawa MB R0J 1H0
204/476-3389; Fax: 204/476-3479; Email: mark@techplus.com
Manager, Mark Anderson
Connection speed to Internet: T1
Users' top connection speed: 33.6K
Number of phone lines: 140
Number of users: 2,000

NOVA SCOTIA

Internet Services & Information Systems Inc.
#1501, 1505 Barrington St., Halifax NS B3J 3K5
902/429-4747; Fax: 902/429-9003; Email: lineinfo@ra.isisnet.com

ONTARIO

Achilles Internet Ltd.
#260, 14 Colonnade Rd., Nepean ON K2E 7M6
613/723-6624; Fax: 613/723-8583; Email: office@achilles.net
Manager, Richard Stephens
Users' top connection speed: 128K
Barrie Connex Inc.
#606, 55 Cedar Pointe Dr., Barrie ON L4N 5R7
705/725-0819; Fax: 705/725-1287; Email: info@bconnex.net; Toll Free: 1-800-461-8883
Connection speed to Internet: T1
Users' top connection speed: 128K
Number of phone lines: 250
Burlington Network Services
140 Plains Rd. East, Burlington ON L7T 2C3
905/632-3977; Fax: 905/632-3536; Email: webmaster@bserv.com; Toll Free: 1-800-263-8433
Cyberlink Online
#211, 464 Yonge St., Toronto ON M5G 1Y6
416/410-0111; Fax: 416/921-7934; Email: info@clo.com
Vice-President, Customer Service & Support, Peter Van Leeuwen
Connection speed to Internet: T1
Users' top connection speed: 128K
Number of phone lines: 55+
Number of users: 500
CyberPlus Technologies Inc.
PO Box 27011, Gloucester ON K1J 9L9
613/749-8598; Fax: 613/749-7108; Email: info@cyberplus.ca
Durham.Net Inc.
306 King St. West, Oshawa ON L1J 2J9
905/427-5330; Fax: 905/728-7918; Email: sales@durham.net
President, Dean Forester
Connection speed to Internet: T1
Users' top connection speed: 28.8K
Number of phone lines: 100
Number of users: 1,000
Electro-Byte Technologies
559B Exmouth St., Sarnia ON N7T 5P6
519/332-8235; Fax: 519/332-8307; Email: info@ebtech.net
Owner, Bernie Brockelhurst
Connection speed to Internet: 1.7 Mbps
Users' top connection speed: 33.6K
Number of phone lines: 155
Number of users: 1,500
Ezenet Inc.
#300, 1992 Yonge St., Toronto ON M4S 1Z7
416/482-5250; Email: info@ezenet.com
Vice-President, Kasra Meshkin
Connection speed to Internet: T1
Users' top connection speed: 128K, 28.8K
Number of phone lines: 200
Number of users: 300
Globalserve Communications Inc.
#323, 466 Speers Rd., Oakville ON L6K 3W9
905/337-0152; Fax: 905/337-1063; Email: info@globalserve.net
CEO, Robin Dua
Connection speed to Internet: T3
Users' top connection speed: 33.6K, 128K
Number of phone lines: 900
HookUp Communications
#207, 1075 North Service Rd., Oakville ON L6M 2G2
905/847-8000; Fax: 905/847-8420; Email: info@hookup.net; accounts@hookup.net
Regional Sales Administrator, Sara Mansell
Connection speed to Internet: T1
Users' top connection speed: 128K
iCOM Internet Services
#200, 7 Mary St., Hamilton ON L8R 1J6
905/522-1220; Email: sales@icom.ca
Manager, Denise Zammit
Connection speed to Internet: T1
Users' top connection speed: 28.8
Number of phone lines: 5:1 user/modem
Information Gateway Services Belleville
#209, 199 Front St., Belleville ON K8N 5H5
613/962-9299; Fax: 613/962-0877; Email: info@blvl.igs.net
President, Ivan (Ike) Csaszar
Connection speed to Internet: T1
Users' top connection speed: 128K
Information Gateway Services Cobourg
#21, 609 William St., Cobourg ON K9A 3A6
905/377-1066; Fax: 905/377-1289; Email: info@phc.igs.net
President, Ivan (Ike) Csaszar
Connection speed to Internet: T1
Users' top connection speed: 28.8K
Information Gateway Services Oshawa
#2N, 57 Simcoe St. South, Oshawa ON L1H 4G4
905/723-2750; Fax: 905/723-2199; Email: info@osha.igs.net
President, Ivan (Ike) Csaszar
Connection speed to Internet: T1
Users' top connection speed: 128K
Interhop Network Services Inc.
#500, 150 Consumers Rd., Toronto ON M2J 1P9
416/494-1603; Fax: 416/494-3788; Email: postmaster@interhop.net
President, David Granic
Connection speed to Internet: T1
Users' top connection speed: 28.8K
Number of phone lines: 160
Number of users: 2,000
Interhop Network Services Inc.
#500, 150 Consumers Rd., North York ON M2J 1P9
416/494-1603; Fax: 416/494-3788; Email: sales@interhop.net
Manager, Operations, Jordi McLaughlin
Connection speed to Internet: 2 x T1
Users' top connection speed: 128 - 384K, 28.8K
InterLog Internet Services
#510, 1075 Bay St., Toronto ON M7A 2B1
416/975-2655; Fax: 416/975-9639; Email: sales@interlog.com
Support, Manager, Scott Allan
Connection speed to Internet: 3 x T1
Users' top connection speed: 28.8K
Number of phone lines: 1,000
Number of users: 14,000
InterNet Kingston
#302, 177 Wellington St., Kingston ON K7L 3E3
613/547-6939; Fax: 613/547-5436; Email: info@adan.kingston.net
CEO, Margaret Row
Connection speed to Internet: T1
Users' top connection speed: 28.8K, 33.6K, 64K, 128K
Number of phone lines: 101
Number of users: 1,200
Intranet Technologies Inc.
#330, 220 Laurier Ave. West, Ottawa ON K1P 5Z9
613/233-7455; Fax: 613/233-7535; Email: info@intranet.on.ca

Account Executive, Robert Menzies
Connection speed to Internet: 3 x T1
Users' top connection speed: 128K
Number of users: 5,000
Kingston Online Services
#309, 303 Bagot St., Kingston ON K7K 5W7
613/549-8667; Fax: 613/549-0642; Email: support@kos.net
Administrator, Steve Cole
Connection speed to Internet: Dual T1
Users' top connection speed: 64K
Number of users: 4,500+
Magma Communications Ltd.
#201, 52 Antares Dr., Nepean ON K2E 7Z1
613/228-3565; Fax: 613/228-8313; Email: sales@magmacom.com
Vice-President, Sales, David Cobey
Connection speed to Internet: T1
Users' top connection speed: 128K
Number of phone lines: 200
Number of users: 1,700
Managed Network Systems Inc.
870 University Ave. West, Windsor ON N9A 5R9
519/258-2333; Fax: 519/258-3009; Email: info@mnsi.net
Contact, Clayton Zekelman
Connection speed to Internet: 2 x T1
Users' top connection speed: 33.6K, dedicated T1
Number of phone lines: 336+
Number of users: 3,000+
NetCore
360 Victoria Ave., Windsor ON N9A 4M6
519/258-0004; Fax: 519/258-9601; Email: help@netcore.ca
Pathway Communications Inc.
#2205, 1 Yonge St., Toronto ON M5E 1E5
416/214-6363; Fax: 416/214-6238; Email: info@pathcom.com
Connection speed to Internet: T1
Users' top connection speed: 28.8K
Number of phone lines: 496
Number of users: 7,000
Qnetix Computer Consultants Inc.
95 King St. East, 4th Fl., Toronto ON M5C 1G4
416/861-0423; Fax: 416/861-1838; Email: paul@qnetix.ca
Senior Account Manager, Paul Baron
Connection speed to Internet: T3
Number of phone lines: 100+
Sentex Communications Corp.
240D Holiday Inn Dr., Cambridge ON N3C 3X4
519/651-3400; Fax: 519/651-2903; Email: support@sentex.net
Owner, Keith Winter
Connection speed to Internet: T1
Users' top connection speed: 128K
Number of phone lines: fewer than 100
Span Information Technology Inc.
110 Hunt St., Ajax ON L1S 1T5
905/619-7726; Fax: 905/619-6819; Email: info@spanit.com
Manager, Nabila Malik
Connection speed to Internet: Fractional T1
Users' top connection speed: 128K
Weslink Datalink Corporation
1603 Main St. West, Hamilton ON L8S 1E6
905/522-4101; Fax: 905/522-2123; Email: info@weslink.ca
Manager, Marketing/Development, Randy Bastarache
Connection speed to Internet: 3Mbps
Users' top connection speed: 128K
Number of phone lines: 300
WINCOM (Windsor Information Network Company)
#905, 4510 Rhodes Dr., Windsor ON N8W 5K5
519/945-9462; Fax: 519/945-9777; Email: sales@wincom.net

Vice-President, Customer Services, Morris Whatmore
Connection speed to Internet: T1
Users' top connection speed: 128K

QUÉBEC
Accès au Noeud Internet Québec
#086, 3930, boul Hamel ouest, Québec PQ G1P 2J2
418/872-6008; Fax: 418/872-6750; Email: info@aniq.com
Contact, Christian Bacon
Connection speed to Internet: 512K, 128K
Users' top connection speed: 28.8K
Number of phone lines: 10
Number of users: 80
Axess Communications
CP 4822, St-Laurent PQ H4L 1G9
514/337-2002; Fax: 514/337-2061; Email: support@axess.com
Office Manager, Susan Tress
Connection speed to Internet: T1
Users' top connection speed: 28.8K
Number of phone lines: 8:1 ratio
CitéNet Telecom Inc.
1155, rue René-Lévesque ouest, Montréal PQ H3B 3T6
514/861-5050; Fax: 514/861-5953; Email: info@citenet.net; http://www.citenet.net
Connection speed to Internet: T3
Users' top connection speed: 28.8K
Internet Login
#916, 500, boul René-Lévesque ouest, Montréal PQ H2Z 1W7
514/875-6446; Fax: 514/875-8596; Email: info@login.net
Contact, Catherine Zegray
Internet Montréal
#2821, 1 Place Ville-Marie, Montréal PQ H3B 4R4
514/393-1014; Fax: 514/527-4066; Email: info@mtl.net
Manager, Business Services, Daniel Gaucher
Multi-Médias Québec
#200, 40, boul Queen sud, Sherbrooke PQ J1H 3P3
819/563-4311; Fax: 819/563-5833; Email: mike@multi-medias.ca
Contact, Internet Solution, Mike Savoy
Connection speed to Internet: T1
Users' top connection speed: 128K
Number of phone lines: 150
Number of users: 1,600
NetAxis Inc.
#511, 5253, boul Decarie, Montréal PQ H3W 3C3
514/482-8989; Fax: 514/483-6718; Email: info@netaxis.qc.ca
Coordinator, Helda Belik
Connection speed to Internet: T1
PubNIX Montréal
CP 147, Côte-St-Luc PQ H4V 2Y3
514/990-5911; Fax: 514/990-9443; Email: info@pubnix.net
Contact, Customer Service, Shelagh Webster
Connection speed to Internet: 128K
Users' top connection speed: 28.8K
Number of phone lines: 20
Number of users: 200
Réseau Interordinateurs Scientifique Québécois
#800, 1801, rue McGill College, Montréal PQ H3A 2N4
514/398-1234; Fax: 514/398-1244; Email: info-cir-risq@risq.qc.ca
Liaison, Officer, Aline Artinian
Connection speed to Internet: Ethernet scalable to 35MB
Users' top connection speed: Ethernet
TotalNet
750, côte de la Pente-Douce, Québec PQ G1N 2M1
418/481-2585; Fax: 418/481-2785; Email: support@total.net

Contact, Support Team, Sylvain Naud
Zercom Technologies Inc.
1594, rue Beaulac, St-Laurent PQ H4R 1W8
514/956-8337; Fax: 514/956-8329; Email: info@zercom.net
President, Ronald Ziernicki
Connection speed to Internet: T1
Users' top connection speed: 28.8K

SASKATCHEWAN
Data Link Canada
12 Gardiner Ave., Regina SK S4P 4P6
306/585-0362; Fax: 306/352-6450; Email: jim.nickel@dlcwest.com
President, Jim Nickel
Connection speed to Internet: T1
Users' top connection speed: 33.6K
Number of phone lines: 104
Number of users: 1,000
WBM Office Systems
414 McDonald St., Regina SK S4N 6E1
306/721-2560; Fax: 306/721-2498; Email: webmaster@eagle.wbm.ca
Vice-President/General Manager, Jeff Persic
Connection speed to Internet: T1
Users' top connection speed: 128K

UNITED STATES
America On-Line
8619 Westwood Center Dr., Vienna VA 22185-2285
Toll Free: 1-800-827-6364
CompuServe Inc.
5000 Arlington Center Blvd., PO Box 20212, Columbus OH 43220
Toll Free: 1-800-848-8199

FREENETS

Community Access Canada (Cnet) = Programme d'accÈs communautaire, (Industry Canada = Industrie Canada) - http://cnet.unb.ca/
CivicNet(tm) Municipal Index (Union of BC Municipalities) - http://www.civicnet.gov.bc.ca/muni/muni.html

ALBERTA
Calgary Free-Net (AB) - http://www.freenet.calgary.ab.ca/
Edmonton Free-Net (AB) - http://www.freenet.edmonton.ab.ca/

BRITISH COLUMBIA
Canada Home Town Page (Valemount, BC) - http://netbistro.com/~jgrogan/
Campbell River Community Network (BC) - http://www.cn.camriv.bc.ca/
CIAO! (Community Information Access Organization) (Trail, BC) - http://www.ciao.trail.bc.ca/
Mount Arrowsmith Community Network (BC) - http://macn.bc.ca/ Serving Central Vancouver Island
Nanaimo SchoolsNET (BC) - http://www.sd68.nanaimo.bc.ca
NANO (Nechako Access Network Organization) (Vanderhoof, BC) - http://www.nano.bc.ca
Sea to Sky Free-Net (BC) - http://www.mountain-inter.net/~freenet/
Sunshine Coast Community Network (BC) - http://www.sunshine.net/sunshine.html
Valley Net (Abbotsford, BC) - http://mindlink.net/paul_kurucz/vnet.htm
Vancouver CommunityNet (BC) - http://www.vcn.bc.ca
Victoria Telecommunity Network (BC) - http://freenet.victoria.bc.ca/vifa.html

MANITOBA
Blue Sky Freenet (Winnipeg, MB) - http://www.freenet.mb.ca/
EASTMAN FreeNet (MB) - http://wtp1.eastman.freenet.mb.ca/

NEW BRUNSWICK
Fredericton Area Network (FAN) (NB) - http://fan1.csd.unb.ca/cfn/info/Home.html

NEWFOUNDLAND
St. John's InfoNET (NF) - http://www.InfoNET.st-johns.nf.ca/

NOVA SCOTIA
Antigonish Community Network (NS) - http://www.grassroots.ns.ca/

Cape Breton Community Network (CBNet) - http://highlander.cbnet.ns.ca/cbnet/mainmenu.html
Chebucto FreeNet (Halifax, NS) - http://www.ccn.cs.dal.ca/

ONTARIO
Brant FreeNet (Brantford, ON) - http://www.bfree.on.ca/
Durham Free-Net (Durham Region, ON) - http://www.freenet.durham.org/
FLORA Community Web (Ottawa, ON) - http://www.flora.ottawa.on.ca
Hamilton-Wentworth FreeNet (ON) - http://www.freenet.hamilton.on.ca
HOMEtown Community Network (SW Ontario) - http://www.hometown.on.ca/
National Capital Free-Net (Ottawa, ON) - http://www.ncf.carleton.ca

Niagara Peninsula Free-Net (ON) - http://freenet.npiec.on.ca/
Social Development Network (ON) - http://www.web.apc.org/sdn/
Toronto Free-Net (ON) - http://www.torfree.net
Wellington FreeSpace (ON) - http://www.freespace.net

QUÉBEC
Libertel Montréal (PQ) - http://www.libertel.mont-real.qc.ca

SASKATCHEWAN
Great Plains Free-Net (Regina, SK) - http://www.gpfn.sk.ca
Saskatoon Free-Net (SK) - http://www.sfn.saskatoon.sk.ca/

WEBSITE DIRECTORY

ARTS & CULTURE

ABC CANADA	http://www.abc-canada.org
absinthe	http://www.ucalgary.ca/~amathur/absinthe.html
Academy of Canadian Cinema & Television	http://www.academy.ca
Agnes Etherington Art Centre	http://www.queensu.ca/ageth/
Ajax Public Library	http://www.io.org/~bruin/
Alberta Playwrights' Network	http://www.nucleus.com/~apn
Anne Murray Centre	http://www.grtplaces.com/ac/anne
Antigonish Heritage Museum	http://www.grassroots.ns.ca/tour/ahm.htm
Antigonish Highland Society	http://www.grassroots.ns.ca/tour/ahs.htm
Antiquarian Booksellers' Association of Canada	http://206.217.21.64/ca/index.html
Archives Association of British Columbia	http://www.harbour.com/AABC/
Archives nationales du Québec	http://www.anq.gouv.qc.ca
Art Gallery of Newfoundland & Labrador	http://www.ucs.mun.ca/~agnl/
Art Gallery of Ontario	http://www.AGO.on.ca
Art Gallery of York University	http://www.yorku.ca/admin/agyu
Art Libraries Society of North America	http://caroline.eastlib.ufl.edu/arlis/
Artfocus	http://www.artfocus.com
Associated Designers of Canada	http://www.ffa.ucalgary.ca/adc/indexadc.htm
Association des archivistes du Québec	http://www.libertel.montreal.qc.ca/info/aaq
Association for Canadian Theatre Research	http://www.athabascan.ca
Association for the Export of Canadian Books	http://infoweb.magi.com/~aecb/
Association of Canadian Orchestras	http://www.terraport.net/aco
Association of Canadian Publishers	http://www.can.net/marketplace/pub/acp/acp.htm
Association québécoise des marionnettistes	http://www.aei.ca/~aqm/
BC Archives & Records Service	http://www.bcars.gs.gov.bc.ca/bcars.html
Bata Shoe Museum	http://www.hype.com/toronto/attractions/bata.htm
Bibliographical Society of Canada	http://www.library.utoronto.ca/~bsc
Black Cultural Centre for Nova Scotia	http://www.nstn.ca/bccns/bcc.html
Blood & Aphorisms	http://www.io.org/~blood
Boudoir Noir	http://www.boudoir-noir.com
British Columbia Library Association	http://www.interchg.ubc.ca/bcla
British Columbia Museums Association	http://www.MuseumsAssn.bc.ca/~bcma/
Bruce County Museum & Archives	http://www.swbi.net/bruce_county_museum.htm
Burlington Art Centre	http://www.burlingtonartcentre.on.ca
CV Photo	http://www.cam.org/~vpopuli
Calgary Opera Association	http://www.lexicom.ab.ca/~calopera
Camosun College - Library	http://www.camosun.bc.ca/~library
Canada Asia Accord Association	http://www.lights.com/caaa/
Canada's National History Society	http://www.cyberspc.mb.ca/~otmw/cnhs/cnhs-ind.html
Canadian Antique Phonograph Society	http://www.rose.com/~caps/index.htm
Canadian Arts Presenting Association	http://www.ffa.ucalgary.ca/capacoa/
Canadian Association of Journalists	http://freenet.carleton.ca/freeport/prof.assoc/caj/menu;
	http://www.ncf.carleton.ca/freeport/prof.assoc/caj/menu
Canadian Association of Music Libraries, Archives & Documentation Centres Inc.	http://www.caml.yorku.ca
Canadian Bookbinders & Book Artists Guild	http://knet.flemingc.on.ca/~rmiller/cbbag/CBBAGhome.html
Canadian Centre for Architecture	http://cca.qc.ca/
Canadian Children's Book Centre	http://www.lglobal.com/~ccbc/
Canadian Children's Literature	http://www.uoguelph.ca/englit/ccl/
Canadian Collectibles Retailer	http://www.trajan.com/collectibles/default.ehtml
Canadian Esperanto Youth	http://www.engcorp.com/kea/jek.html
Canadian Film Centre	http://www.hype.com/cfc/home.htm
Canadian Heritage - Fortress of Louisbourg - Library	http://fortress.uccb.ns.ca
Canadian Heritage Information Network	http://www.chin.gc.ca
Canadian Institute for Theatre Technology	http://www.ffa.ucalgary.ca/citt/index.html

Canadian Institute of the Arts for Young Audiences	http://www.wimsey.com/Youngarts/
Canadian Literature	http://www.swifty.com/cdn_lit
Canadian Museum of Civilization	http://www.cmcc.muse.digital.ca/
Canadian Music Centre	http://www.culturenet.ca/cmc
Canadian Music Educator	http://www.stemnet.nf.ca/~barobert/.cmea/cmea.html
Canadian Music Educators' Association	http://www.stemnet.nf.ca/~barobert/cmea/cmea.html
Canadian National Aboriginal Tourism Association	http://www.v1i.ca/clients/abc/cnata/cnata3.htm
Canadian Publishers' Council	http://www.pubcouncil.ca
Canadian Quilters Association	http://www.nt.net/~giselef/cqaacc1.htm
Canadian Science Writers' Association	http://www.interlog.com/~cswa
Capilano Review	http://www.capcollege.bc.ca/departments.tcr/tcr.html
The Capitol Foundation	http://www.eagle.ca/~capitol/
Chart	http://www.chartnet.com
Claremont Review	http://206.12.151.25.3
Classical Guitar Society of Calgary	http://www.freenet.calgary.ab.ca/art/cgsc/contact.html
Coastal Jazz & Blues Society	http://euphony.com/music/JazzFest/
Collectibles Canada	http://www.trajan.com/collectibles/default.ehtml
Conseil de la culture de L'Abitibi-Témiscamingue	http://lino.com/~crcat
Contemporary Dancers Canada	http://www.escape.ca/~cesmb/wcd/wcdhome.htm
The Crime Writers of Canada	http://www.swifty.com/cwc/cwchome.htm
Currency Museum of the Bank of Canada	http://www.bank-banque-canada.ca
Dancemakers	http://www.interlog.com/~dncemkrs
Doon Heritage Crossroads	http://www.oceta.on.ca/region.waterloo/doon
Early Music Vancouver	http://mindlink.net/earlymusic
Earth Sciences Museum	http://www.science.uwaterloo.ca/earth/museum/museum.html
Editors' Association of Canada	http://www.web.net/eac-acr
Edmonton Chinese Bilingual Education Association	http://www.alvin.org/acr/ecbea.htm#organ
Edmonton Jazz Society	http://www.ualberta.ca/edmonton/jazz
Edmonton Space & Science Centre	http://www.ee.ualberta.ca/essc
Embroiderers' Association of Canada, Inc.	http://www.antibe.com/westview/eac.html
Emily Carr Institute of Art & Design - Library	http://www.eciad.bc.ca/
Esperanto Association of Canada	http://www.engcorp.com/kea/
Feliciter	http://www.uccb.ns.ca/c/a96
Festival du cinéma international en Abitibi-Témiscamingue	http://www.telebec.qc.ca/fciat/
Festival International de Jazz de Montréal	http://www.montrealjazzfestival.worldlinx.com/
Festival of Festivals	http://www.bell.ca/toronto/filmfest
Film Studies Association of Canada	http://www.film.queensu.ca/FSAC/Home.html
Foothills Library Association	http://www.ucalgary.ca
Friends of the Mounted Police Museum	http://www.cs.uregina.ca/~mcintyre/rcmp_museum/rcmp.html
The Friends of the National Library of Canada	http://www.nlc-bnc.ca/friends/efriends.htm; http://www.nlc-bnc.ca/friends/ffriends.htm
Galerie d'art de L'Université de Moncton	http://www.umoncton.ca/gaum/hp_luc8.html
Gallery 1.1.1	http://www.umanitoba.ca/schools/art/info/gallery.html
Gallery Gachet	http://www.info-mine.com/gachet
George R. Gardiner Museum of Ceramic Art	http://www.rom.on.ca
Glenbow Museum, Art Gallery, Library & Archives	http://www.lexicon.ab.ca/~glenbow
Grain	http://www.sasknet.com/corporate/skwriter
Grand Forks Art Gallery	http://www.islandnet.com/~bcma/museums/gfag/gfag.html
Greater Vancouver International Film Festival Society	http://viff.org/viff/
Gros Morne National Park Visitor Reception Centre	http://www.stemnet.nf.ca/~amorceau/gmnp.html
Huntsman Marine Science Centre	http://www.unb.ca/web/huntsman
Images Festival of Independent Film & Video	http://www.interlog.com/~images/
iMPACT	http://www.impactmag.com
Independent Film & Video Alliance	http://www.ffa.ucalgary.ca/
Interior Designers Institute of British Columbia	http://www.designsource.bc.ca
International Centre	http://quic.queensu.ca
International Committee for Documentation	http://www.icom.nrm.se/icom/cidoc
International Council on Monuments & Sites	http://icomos.org/
International Council on Monuments & Sites Canada	http://www.icomos.org/canada
International Federation of Library Associations & Institutions	http://www.nlc-bnc.ca/ifla/
Inverarden Regency Cottage Museum	http://www.cnwl.igs.net/~slm/index.html
Jackson Park Queen Elizabeth II Garden	http://www.city.windsor.on.ca
Kings Landing Historical Settlement	http://www.grtplaces.com/ac/landing/
L'Opéra de Montréal	http://www.stria.ca/opera-mtl
La La La Human Steps	http://www.bart.nl/~xipe/lalala.htm
Lieu historique national du Parc-de-L'Artillerie	http://www.upc.qc.ca/pch/artillerie
	http://www.upc.qc.ca/pch/artillery
Lord Strathcona's Horse (Royal Canadians) Regimental Museum	http://www.nucleus.com/~rdennis/
MIX	http://www.mix.web.net/mix/
MacLachlan Woodworking Museum	http://mal.rmc.ca/museum/home.html
Maltwood Art Museum & Gallery	http://kafka.uvic.ca/~maltwood
Manitoba Association of Architects	http://cad9.cadlab.umanitoba.ca/MAA.html
Manitoba Library Association	http://www.mbnet.mb.ca/cm
Manitoba Museum of Man & Nature	http://www.mbnet.mb.ca/manitobamuseum
Manitoba Sports Hall of Fame & Museum Inc.	http://www.sport.mb.ca
Mariposa Folk Foundation	http://www.eagle.ca/mariposa
Maritime Museum of the Atlantic	http://www.ednet.ns.ca/educ/museum/mma.html
Mayworks Festival Society	http://www.artworld.com/mayworks/
McGill University - Libraries	http://www.library.mcgill.ca

McGill University Archives	http://www.archives.mcgill.ca
McMichael Canadian Art Collection	http://www.mcmichael.com
Metropolitan Toronto Archives & Records Centre	http://www.metrotor.on.ca/services/departments/clerk.html#archives
Miller Museum of Mineralogy & Geology	http://geol.queensu.ca/museum/museum.html
Modern Drama	http://www.utpress/depthome.htm
Morris & Helen Belkin Art Gallery	http://edziza.arts.ubc.ca/finearts/gallery.html
Musée J. Armand Bombardier	http://www.ucctech.com/museejab
Musée d'art contemporain de Montréal	http://Media.MACM.qc.ca
Musée de l'Amerique française	http://www.mcq.org
Musée de la civilisation	http://www.mcq.org
Musée des beaux arts de Montréal	http://www.interax.net/tcenter/tour/mba.html
Musée du Québec	http://www.mdq.org
Museum for Textiles	http://www.interlog.com/~gwhite/ttt/tttintro.html
Music for Young Children	http://www.myc.com
Muskoka Pioneer Village & Museum	http://www.muskoka.net/village.html
National Archives of Canada	http://www.archives.ca
National Aviation Museum - Library	http://www.nmstc.aviation.ca
National Ballet of Canada	http://www.national.ballet.ca
National Ballet of Canada Archives	http://www.national.ballet.ca
National Gallery of Canada	http://national.gallery.ca; http://musee.beaux.arts.ca
The National Library of Canada	http://www.nlc-bnc.ca/
National Museum of Science & Technology	http://www.science-tech.nmstc.ca; http://www.sciences-tech.smnst.ca
Native Earth Performing Arts Inc.	http://www.io.org/~naterth/naterth.htm
New Westminster Public Library	http://www.nwpl.new-westminster.bc.ca
Newfoundland Museum	http://calvin.stemnet.nf.ca/~cshea/
Next City	http://www.nextcity.com
Nickle Arts Museum	http://www.ucalgary.ca
Nova Scotia Highland Village	http://www.ednet.ns.ca/educ/museum/other_ns/highland_village/
Nova Scotia Museum	http://www.ednet.ns.ca/educ/museum/
Nuit Blanche	http://www.qbc.clic.net/~carl/nuit/nuit.html
On Spec: The Canadian Magazine of Speculative Writing	http://www.greenwoods.com/onspec/
Ontario Association of Art Galleries	http://www.culturenet.ca/oaag/
Ontario Folk Dance Association	http://www.web.net/~ofda
Ontario Museum Association	http://www.museum.assn.on.ca
Ontario Science Centre	http://www.osc.on.ca
Orchestra London Canada Inc.	http://www.icis.on.ca/orchestra
Orchestras Ontario	http://www.terraport.net/aco
PACT Communications Centre	http://www.culturenet.ucalgary.ca/pact
Pacific Opera Victoria	http://www.islandnet.com/~opera/POVhome.html
Pacific Space Centre	http://pacific-space-centre.bc.ca
paperplates	http://www.perkolator.com
Parkdale-Maplewood Community Museum	http://www.ednet.ns.ca/educ/museum/other_ns/parkdale/museum1.html
Parkland Regional Library System	http://www.rtt.ab.ca/rtt/prl
Photo Life	http://www.photolife.com
Photo Marketing Association International - Canada	http://www.pmai.org
Photographical Historical Society of Canada	http://web.onramp.ca/phsc
Power Plant	http://www.culturenet.ca/powerplant
Prince Edward Island Crafts Council	http://www.crafts-council.pe.ca/index.html
Prince of Wales Northern Heritage Centre	http://tailpipe.learnNet.nt.ca/pwnhc
Prism International	http://www.arts.ubc.ca/crwr/prism/prism.html
Professional Association of Canadian Theatres	http://www.culturenet.ucalgary.ca/pact
Provincial Archives of Alberta	http://www.ab.ca/~mcd/archives/index.htm
Queens County Museum	http://www.geocities.com/Paris/2669/
Red Deer Public Library	http://www.rdpl.red-deer.ab.ca
Redpath Museum	http://www.mcgill.ca/Redpath
Richmond Public Library	http://www.rpl.richmond.bc.ca
Riding Mountain National Park Visitor Centre	http://parkscanada.pch.gc.ca/parks/manitoba/riding_mountain/riding_mountain.htm
Right Hon. John G. Diefenbaker Centre for the Study of Canada	http://library.usask.ca/remate.html
Royal Architectural Institute of Canada	http://www.aecinfo.com/raic/index.html
Royal British Columbia Museum	http://rbcm1.rbcm.gov.bc.ca/index.html
Royal Canadian College of Organists	http://magi.com/~rjewell/rcco.html
Royal Canadian Mounted Police Centennial Museum	http://rbcm1.rbcm.gov.bc.ca
Royal London Wax Museum	http://www.victoriabc.com/guide/vicat4.html
Royal Ontario Museum	http://www.rom.on.ca
Royal Roads University - Library & Learning Resources Centre	http://www.royalroads.ca/docs/library/home.html
Royal Saskatchewan Museum	http://www.gov.sk.ca/govt/munigov/cult&rec/rsm/
The Royal Society of Canada	http://library.utoronto.ca/www/rsc/
Royal Tyrrell Museum of Palaeontology	http://tyrrell.magtech.ab.ca
Saskatchewan Community Theatre Inc.	http://www.ffa.ucalgary.ca/scco/scti.html
Saskatchewan Council of Cultural Organizations	http://www.sasknet.sk.ca/scco/
Saskatchewan Crafts Council	http://www.ffa.ucalgary.ca/scco/scc.html; http://www.sasknet.sk.ca/SCCO/SCC.html
Saskatchewan Jazz Festival	http://www.sasknet.com/jazz/
Saskatchewan Motion Picture Association	http://midxpress.com/midxpress/smpia/main.htm
Saskatchewan Music Festival Association Inc.	http://www.ffa.ucalgary.ca/scco/smea.html
Saskatchewan Playwrights Centre	http://bailey2.unibase.com/~grain/SPC_Homepage.html
Saskatchewan Provincial Library	http://www.lib.sk.ca/provlib/; http://www.lib.sk.ca/pleis/
Saskatchewan Society for Education through Art	http://www.ffa.ucalgary.ca/scco/ssea.html
Saskatchewan Writers Guild Inc.	http://bailey2.unibase.com/~grain/SWG_Homepage.html

Science World British Columbia	http://www.scienceworld.bc.ca
Shift Magazine	http://www.shift.com/shift.home
Simon Fraser University Museum of Archaeology & Ethnology	http://www.sfu.ca/archaeology
Sir Wilfred Grenfell College Art Gallery	http://www.swgc.mun.ca
La Société Historique de la Mer Rouge	http://www.rbmulti.nb.ca/shmr/shmr.htm
La Société des musées québécois	http://www.uqam.ca/musees/
Société Pro Musica Inc.	http://www.apexdigital.com/promusica
Songwriters Association of Canada	http://www.goodmedia.com/sac/
Springhill Miners Museum	http://www.grtplaces.com/ac/mine
Stratford Festival	http://www.ffa.ucalgary.ca/stratford/home.htm
Tafelmusik Baroque Orchestra	http://www.hype.com/tafel/
Toronto International Film Festival	http://www.bell.ca/toronto/filmfest
Tuxedo Junction Orchestra	http://www.glide.com/tuxedo
Two Turtle Iroquois Fine Art Gallery	http://wchat.on.ca/tom/2turtle.htm
U'Mista Cultural Centre & Society	http://www.swifty.com/umista/
Univers Maurice Rocket Richard Universe	http://www.Rocket9.org
VU centre de diffusion et de production de la photographie	http://www2.zone.ca/~vuphoto
Vancouver Art Gallery	http://www.vanartgallery.bc.ca
Vancouver Cultural Alliance	http://www.culturenet.ca/vca
Vancouver Folk Music Festival	http://www.ffa.ucalgary.ca/vca/canfol.htm
Vancouver International Film Festival	http://www.viff.org.viff
Vancouver International Writers Festival	http://www.ffa.ucalgary.ca/vca/vanwri.htm
Vancouver Symphony Society	http://www.worldtel.com/vancouver/symphony.html
Victoria Guitar Society	http://kafka.uvic.ca/~adunn/
Visual Arts Ontario	http://vao.on.ca
Walter Phillips Gallery	http://www-nmr.banffcentre.ab.ca/WPG
Westfield Heritage Centre	http://www.worldchat.com/public/westfield/westfl.htm
Whyte Museum of the Canadian Rockies	http://www.cadvision.com/db/wmer
Winnipeg Art Gallery	http://www.umanitoba.ca/schools/art/gallery/hpgs/wag/
Winnipeg Folk Festival	http://www.magic.mb.ca/~wff/
Winnipeg Jazz Festival	http://www.xpressnet.com/~cohenm/jazzwpg/
Women in View	http://www.ffa.ucalgary.ca/vca/wmnvie.htm
Woodland Cultural Centre	http://microplacement.com/woodland/languages.html
Word on the Street	http://www.ffa.ucalgary.ca/vca/wordon.htm
The Writers' Union of Canada	http://www.swifty.com/twuc

BUSINESS & FINANCE

AGF Management Limited	http://www.agf.com/
Admax Regent International Management Ltd.	http://www.admaxregent.com
Adnews	http://www.io.org~adnews/
Aetna Life Insurance Company of Canada	http://www.aetna.ca
Alberta Association of the Appraisal Institute of Canada	http://www.cyberpage.com/appraisal/alberta/appraisal.html
Alberta Stock Exchange	http://www.alberta.net/
Alberta Treasury Branches	http://www.atb.com
Altamira Investment Services Inc.	http://www.altamira.com
American Society of Association Executives	http://www.asaenet.org/
Assurances Générales des Caisses Desjardins Inc.	http://www.insurance_canada.ca/insurcan/desjard.nt
Bank of Canada - Library	http://www.bank-banque-canada.ca/library
Bank of Montreal	http://www.bmo.com
Bank of Montreal Investment Management Ltd.	http://www.fcfunds.bomil.ca/
Bank of Nova Scotia	http://www.scotiabank.com
Bay Area Business Women's Network	http://www.freenet.hamilton.on.ca/Information/business/BABWN/index.html
Bayshore Trust Company	http://www.bayshoretrust.com
Better Business Bureau of Windsor & Southern Ontario	http://www.wincom.net/wbbb/
Bike Trade Canada	http://www.pedal.com
Bilan	http://www.ocaq.qc.ca
Bottom Line	http://www.butterworths.ca
British Columbia Real Estate Association	http://www.bcrea.bc.ca
Burlington Chamber of Commerce	http://wchat.on.ca/commerce/index.html
Burnaby Chamber of Commerce	http://www.bendtech.com/communities/burnabycofc.html
Business Executive	http://cybersquare.com/executive/
Business Quarterly	http://www.ivey.uwo.ca
C.D. Howe Institute	http://www.cdhowe.org
CA Magazine	http://www.cic.ca/cica/camag/e_camag.htm
CMA Magazine	http://www.cma-canada.org
Canaccord Capital Corporation	http://www.canaccord.com
Canada Asia Accord Association	http://www.lights.com/caaa/
Canada Life Assurance Company	http://www.canadalife.com
Canada Taiwan Trade Association	http://www.jurock.com/ctta/
Canada Trust Company	http://www.canadatrust.com
Canada West Foundation	http://www.freenet.calgary.ab.ca/populati/communit/cwf/cwf.html
Canadian Advertising Rates & Data	http://www.cardmedia.com
Canadian Association of Career Educators & Employers	http://www.cacee.com/workweb
Canadian Banker	http://www.cba.ca
Canadian Bankers Association	http://www.cba.ca/
Canadian Board of Marine Underwriters	http://www.webcom.com/cbmu
Canadian Commercial Corp. - Library	http://www.ccc.ca

Canadian Almanac & Directory 1997

Canadian Council for Public-Private Partnerships	http://www.inforamp.net/~partners
Canadian Direct Marketing Association	http://www.cdma.org
Canadian Direct Marketing News	http://www.mainstay.on.ca/dmn
Canadian Federation of Independent Business	http://www.cfib.ca
Canadian Finance & Leasing Association	http://www.inforamp.net/~mreid/cfla.html
Canadian Imperial Bank of Commerce	http://www.cibc.com
Canadian Importers Association Inc.	http://www.importers.ca
Canadian Institute of Actuaries	http://www.actuaries.ca/CIA/CIA.html
Canadian Institute of Chartered Accountants	http://www.cica.ca/
Canadian Institute of Management	http://www.interlog.com/~consult/cimhp1.html
Canadian International Mutual Funds	http://www.fundlib.com/ci.html
Canadian Law & Economics Association	http://www.epas.utoronto.ca:5680/clea/clea.html
Canadian Life & Health Insurance Association Inc.	http://www.inforamp.net/~clhia/
Canadian Marconi Co. - Library	http://www.marconi.ca
Canadian Meat Importers Committee	http://www.importers.ca
Canadian Payroll Association	http://www.payroll.ca/
Canadian Professional Sales Association	http://www.cpsa.com
Canadian Real Estate Association	http://www.mls.ca/crea.ca
Canadian Realtor News	Http://www.crea.ca
Canadian Standards Association	http://www.csa.ca/isotes
Canadian Treasurer	http://www.tmac.ca
Canadian Underwriter	http://www.cdnunderwriter.com
Certified General Accountants Association of Canada	http://www.cga-canada.org
Chambre de Commerce de St-Laurent	http://www.cibus.ca/stlaurent
Chambre de Commerce du Québec	http://www.ccq.ca
Chambre de Commerce et d'industrie du Québec métropolitain	http://cciqm.megatoon.com
Chambre de Commerce régionale de Ste-Foy	http://www.riq.qc.ca/ccrsf
Chatham & District Chamber of Commerce	http://www.ciaccess.com/~pmartin/cdccatog.htm
Chubb Insurance Company of Canada	http://www.chubbinsurance.ca
Citizens Trust Company	http://www.citizenstrust.ca
Cobourg & District Chamber of Commerce	http://www.eagle.ca.cobourg.chamber
Comox Valley Chamber of Commerce	http://www.ark.com/valley/chamber.html
Conseil des assurances de dommages	http://wure.montrealnet.ca/conseilad
Cornwall Chamber of Commerce	http://www.busitech.com/cornwall/
Cranbrook Chamber of Commerce	http://www.cyberlink.bc.ca/chamber/cranbrook/index.html
Credit Union Central of Canada	http://www.cucentral.ca
Currency Museum of the Bank of Canada	http://www.bank-banque-canada.ca
Dynamic Mutual Funds	http://www.dynamic.ca
Economics Working Papers	http://socserv2.socsci.mcmaster.ca/~econ/
Edmonton Chamber of Commerce	http://www.tnc.com/ecc/
Electronic Commerce Canada	http://www.globalx.net/eca/
Electronic Commerce Council of Canada	http://www.edicc.ca/edicc
Elliott & Page Limited	http://www.fundlib.com/ellpag.html
Federal Insurance Company	http://www.chubbinsurance.ca
Fidelity Investments Canada Limited	http://www.fid-inv.com
First American Title Insurance Company	http://www.firstam.com
Fort Frances Chamber of Commerce	http://www.tradenet.ca/Fort_Frances
Fort McMurray Chamber of Commerce	http://www.tnc.com/tncn/fmcc/index.html
Fraser Institute	http://www.fraserinstitute.ca/
Fredericton Chamber of Commerce	http://www.discribe.ca/chamber/
Friends of the Environment Foundation	http://www.fef.ca/
G.T. Global Canada	http://www.fundlib.com/gt.html
Gandalf Canada - Library	http://www.gandalf.ca
General Accident Assurance Company of Canada	http://www.genacc.ca/
General American Life Insurance Company	http://www.genam.com
Great-West Life Assurance Company	http://www.gwl.ca
Greater Kingston Chamber of Commerce	http://www.kosone.com/chamber
Greater Peterborough Chamber of Commerce	http://www.ptbo.igs.net/~chamber
Greater Victoria Chamber of Commerce	http://vvv.com/Chamber
Guelph Chamber of Commerce	http://www.mgl.ca/~gchamber
Hamilton & District Chamber of Commerce	http://www.jmg.on.ca/chamber/home.htm
Hartford Insurance Company of Canada	http://www.itthartford.com
Institute for Canadian Studies	http://www.instcanstudies.mb.ca
Institute of Canadian Advertising	http://www1.goodmedia.com/ica/
Institute of Certified Management Consultants of Canada	http://www.cmc-consult.org
Institute of Chartered Accountants of British Columbia	http://www.ica.bc.ca
Institute of Chartered Accountants of Ontario	http://www.icao.on.ca
Insurance Bureau of Canada	http://www.ibc.ca
Insurance Institute of Canada	http://insurance-canada.ca/iic/
Interface	http://www.acfas.ca/
International Special Events Society - Toronto Chapter	http://www.ndgphoenix.com/ises.html
Investment Funds Institute of Canada	http://www.mutfunds.com/ific
Japanese External Trade Organization	http://www.jetro.go.jp
La Revue Occasions d'Affaires	http://www.roa-mag.com; http://www.rda.net
Laurentian Bank of Canada	http://www.mortgagestore.com/laurent/laurent.html
Le publicité club de Montréal	http://www.pcm.montreal.qc.ca/
Leduc & District Chamber of Commerce	http://www.tnc.com/commerce
Mackenzie Financial Corporation	http://www.fundlib.com/mackenzie.html

Canadian Almanac & Directory 1997

Manitoba Taxpayers Association.	http://www.freenet.mb.ca/community/bscn/iphome/m/mta/index.html
Manufacturers Life Insurance Company	http://www.manulife.com
Marketing	http://www.marketingmag.ca
Media Book	http://www.mediastop.com
Media Wave Magazine	http://www.media-wave.com
Mississauga Board of Trade	http://www.mbot.com
Montréal Exchange	http://www.bdm.org; http://www.me.org
Motor Dealers' Association of Alberta.	http://www.compusmart.ab.ca/mdaalta
NN Life Insurance Company of Canada.	http://www.ingfin.com
Napanee & District Chamber of Commerce	http://chamber.napanee.on.ca
National Advertising Benevolent Society.	http://www.partnersweb.com/NABS
National Quality Institute	http://www.nqi.com
Neepawa & District Chamber of Commerce	http://www.techplus.com/neep.htm
Niagara on the Lake Chamber of Commerce	http://www.niagara.com/chamber.no1
North American Association for Export to Eastern Europe	http://www.ijs.com/naafetee
North Bay & District Chamber of Commerce	http://www.city.north-bay.on.ca/chamber.htm
Ontario Insurance Directory	http://cdnunderwriter.com
Ontario Public Buyers Association, Inc.	http://vaxxine.com/opba
Ontario Society for Training & Development	http://www.ncf.carleton.ca/freeport/prof.assoc/ostd/menu
Ordre des comptables agréés du Québec	http://www.uquebec.ca/comptables/agrees
Organisation for Economic Cooperation & Development	http://www.oecd.org/
Ottawa-Carleton Board of Trade	http://www.board-of-trade.org
PARTNERS.	http://www.ocri.ca/partners/partners.html
Penticton Chamber of Commerce	http://www.penticton.org
Peoples Trust Company	http://www.peoplestrust.com
Petroleum Accountants Society of Canada	http://www.cadvision.com/pasc
Port Dover Board of Trade	http://www.nornet.on.ca/portdover/
Powell River Chamber of Commerce	http://www.coc.powell-river.bc.ca/index.html
Project Management Institute	http://www.pmi.org
Real Estate Board of Ottawa-Carleton.	http://www.ottawarealestate.org
Report on Business Magazine	http://www.GlobeAndMail.ca
Revelstoke Chamber of Commerce	http://www.revelstokecc.bc.ca/mountns
Richmond Chamber of Commerce	http://www.rpl.richmond.bc.ca/community/chamber/index.html
Royal Bank of Canada	http://www.royalbank.com
Royal Mutual Funds Inc..	http://www.royalbank.com/english/fund/index.html
SMART Toronto	http://www.canada.hp.com/smarttoronto
Saanich Peninsula Chamber of Commerce.	http://www.octonet.com/saanpcoc
Sagit Investment Management Ltd..	http://www.fundlib.com/specbull.html
Scotia McLeod Inc. - Information Centre.	http://wealth.passport.ca/wealth
Scotia Securities Inc.	http://www.scotiabank.ca
ScotiaMcLeod Inc.	http://www.scotiacapital.com
Scudder Canada Investor Services Ltd.	http://www.scudder.ca
Scugog Chamber of Commerce	http://web.idirect.com/~haertel/chamber/chamber.html
Simcoe & District Chamber of Commerce.	http://www.kwic.com:80/~chamber
Society of Management Accountants of Ontario	http://www.cma-ontario.org
Sooke-Jordan River Chamber of Commerce.	http://www.sookenet.com/sooke/chamber/homepage.html
South Cariboo Chamber of Commerce.	http://www.netshop.net/~100mile/sccofc.html
Spectrum United Mutual Funds Inc.	http://www.fundlib.com/specbull.html
Spruce Grove & District Chamber of Commerce	http://www.tnc.com/sgcc
St Catharines & District Chamber of Commerce	http://www.niagara.com/stc-chamber
St Thomas & District Chamber of Commerce.	http://www.mts-inc.com/chamber/
Strategy	http://www.bulldog.ca/burnico/
Surrey Regional Chamber of Commerce	http://www.surreycoc.com/cip/CHAMBER.HTML
TD Asset Management	http://www.tdbank.ca/tdbank/mutual/index.html
TD Trust Company	http://www.tdbank.ca
Talvest Fund Management Inc.	http://www.talvest.com
Templeton Management Limited	http://www.templeton.ca
Toronto-Dominion Bank	http://www.tdbank.ca
Tradex Management Inc.	http://www.tradex.ca
Treasury Management Association of Canada	http://www.tmac.ca/
Trimark Investment Management Inc.	http://www.trimark.com/
Vancouver Stock Exchange	http://www.vse.com
Vermilion & District Chamber of Commerce	http://www.agt.net/public/townvrml/index.htm
Whistler Chamber of Commerce	http://www.whistler.net/coc/index.html
Winnipeg Chamber of Commerce	http://www.winnipegchmbr.mb.ca
Winnipeg Real Estate Board	http://www.mls.ca

CANADIANS & SOCIETY

Alberta Family History Society	http://www.freenet.calgary.ab.ca/science/afhs.html
Amnistie internationale, Section canadienne (Francophone)	http://www.amnistie.qc.ca
B'nai Brith Canada	http://www.canada.ibm.net/bnaibrith
Bangladesh Awami League of Canada.	http://www.interlog.com/~fkhan/; http://www.ica.net/pages/fkhan420
Canada's National History Society	http://www.cyberspc.mb.ca/~otmw/cnhs/cnhs-ind.html
Canadian Foundation for the Americas	http://www.focal.ca
Canadian Grey Panthers Advocacy Network	http://www.panthers.net
Canadian Heritage Information Network	http://www.chin.gc.ca
Canadian Institute	http://www.io.org/~cicomm

Canadian Almanac & Directory 1997

Canadian Institute of International Affairs	http://www.trinity.utoronto.ca/ciia/intro.html
Canadian Lesbian & Gay Archives	http://www.clga.ca/archives
Centre for Refugee Studies - Andrew Forbes Refugee Resource Centre	http://www.yorku.ca/research/crs
Citizens for Safe Cycling	http://www.ncf.carleton.ca/freeport/community.associations/cfsc/menu
Communist Party of Canada (Marxist-Leninist)	http://fox.nstn.ca/~cpc-ml/index.html
Equality for Gays & Lesbians Everywhere	http://www.netfinder.com/egale/
Fédération de la jeunesse canadienne-française inc.	http://franco.ca/fjcf/index
Genealogical Association of Nova Scotia	http://www.ccn.cs.dal.ca/Recreation/GANS/gans_homepage.html
Goethe-Institut Toronto	http://www.goethe.de/uk/tor
History of Canada Music Society	http://www.ffa.ucalgary.ca/hcms/contact_info.html
Icelandic National League	http://www.helix.net/~rasgeirs/
Infant/Maternal Nutrition Education Association	http://www.io.org/~infacto
Institut québécois des hautes études internationales	http://www.ulaval.ca/iqhei
International Council on Monuments & Sites Canada	http://www.icomos.org/canada
International Development Education Resource Association	http://www.vcn.bc.ca/idera
Makivik Corporation	http://www.accent.net/adst/MakWeb/Index.html
Missing Children Society of Canada	http://www.childcybersearch.org
Ontario Genealogical Society	htpp://www.interlog.com/~dreed/ogs_home.htm
Operation Go Home	http://www.maracomm.com/ccsc/opgohome
Ottawa-Carleton Immigrant Services Organization	http://www.ncf.carleton.ca/freeport/social.services/cis/ociso/menu
Peace & Environment Resource Centre	http://www.ncf.carleton.ca/freeport/community.associations/perc/menu
Pearson-Shoyama Institute	http://www.cyberpages.com/db/~pearson-shoyama
Physicians for Global Survival (Canada)	http://www.web.apc.org/~pgs/
Project Ploughshares	http://watserv1.uwaterloo.ca/~plough/
Québec Family History Society	http://www.cam.org/~qfhs/index.html
Royal Society of Canada	http://library.utoronto.ca/www/rsc/
Saskatchewan Genealogical Society	http://www.regina.ism.ca/orgs/sgs/index.htm
Save Ontario Shipwrecks	http://yoda.sscl.uwo.ca/assoc/sos/
Science for Peace	http://www.math.yorku.ca/sfp/
Société des Acadiens et Acadiennes du Nouveau-Brunswick	http://www.rbmulti.nb.ca/saanb/saanb.htm
Société franco-manitobaine	http://www.franco-manitobain.org
United Synagogue of Conservative Judaism, Ontario Region	http://www.uscj.org
Urban Native Indian Education Society	gopher://gopher.native-ed.bc.ca/
World University Service of Canada	http://www.wusc.ca

COMMUNICATION

ACCESS - Media Resource Centre	http://www.ccinet.ab.ca/access
Aboriginal Voices	http://www.vli.ca/clients/abc/cmall/abvoices
Actualisation	http://www.actualisation.com
Addison-Wesley Publishers Ltd.	http://www.aw.com
Alaska Highway News	http://sterlingnews.com/alaska
Alberni Valley Times	http://www.alberni.net/~avtimes/index.html
Association des journalistes indépendants du Québec	http://www.cam.org/~paslap/ajiq.html
Association for the Export of Canadian Books	http://infoweb.magi.com/~aecb/
Association of Canadian Publishers	http://www.can.net/marketplace/pub/acp/acp.htm
Association of Competitive Telecommunications Suppliers	http://www.bbande.com
Association pour l'avancement des sciences et des techniques de la documentation	http://www.asted.org
Atlantic Television System	http://www.atv.ca
BBM Bureau of Measurement	http://www.bbm.ca/
BC Advanced Systems Institute	http://www.asi.bc.ca/asi/
Ben-Simon Publications	http://www.simon-sez.com
Bendall Books	http://www.islandnet.com/bendallbooks
Blizzard Publishing Ltd.	http://www.blizzard.mb.ca/catalog/
Bowes Publishers Ltd.	http://www.bowes.net.com
Bravo!, The New Style Arts Channel	http://www.bravo.ca/bravo.html
British Columbia Association of Broadcasters	http://www.bcab.org
British Columbia Report	http://www.axionet.com/bcreport
Broadcaster	http://www.southam.com/b1-2-1.html
Butterworths Canada Ltd.	http://www.butterworths.ca
CAD Systems	http://www.cadsystems.com
CANARIE Inc.	http://www.canarie.ca/
CCH Canadian Limited	http://www.ca.cch.com/
CM Magazine	http://www.mbnet.mb.ca/cm/index.html
Calgary Sun	http://www.canoe.ca/CalgarySun/home.html
Callawind Publications Inc.	http://www.callawind.com
Canada Communications Group Publishing	http://www.ccg.gcc.ca
Canadian Association of Broadcasters	http://www.cab-acr.ca
Canadian Association of Ethnic (Radio) Broadcasters	http://www.chinradio.com
Canadian Book Review Annual	http://www.interlog.com/~cbra
Canadian Booksellers Association	http://www.cbabook.org
Canadian Broadcasting Corporation	http://www.cbc.ca; http://www.radio.cbc.ca
Canadian Business Telecommunications Alliance	http://www.telecon.ca
Canadian Community Newspapers Association	http://www.sentex.net/~ccna
Canadian Daily Newspaper Association	http://fox.nstn.ca/~bcantley/cdna.html
Canadian Farm Writers' Federation	http://www.uoguelph.ca/Research/cfwf
Canadian Heritage Information Network	http://www.chin.gc.ca
Canadian Information Processing Society	http://cips.ca

Canadian Almanac & Directory 1997

Canadian Information Processing Society - Calgary	http://www.agt.net/public/cipsweb/cips.info.html
Canadian Information Processing Society - Edmonton	http://www.planet.eon.net/~cips/
Canadian Information Processing Society - Ottawa	http://infoweb.magi.com/~interimg/cips/
Canadian Information Processing Society - Regina	http://leroy.cc.uregina.ca/~cipsnews/
Canadian Information Processing Society - Vancouver	http://unixg.ubc.ca:780/~cips
Canadian Information Processing Society - Winnipeg	http://www.mbnet.mb.ca/~cipsinfo
Canadian Institute for Historical Microreproductions	http://www.nlc-bnc.ca/cihm/cihm.html
Canadian Institute for Telecommunications Research	http://www.citr.ee.mcgill.ca
Canadian Internet Awards	http://enterprise.ic.gc.ca/~will/net95
Canadian Magazine Publishers Association	http://www.cmpa.ca/
Canadian Press	http://www.xe.com/canpress/
Canadian Publishers' Council	http://www.pubcouncil.ca
Canadian Satellite Communications Inc.	http://www.cancom.ca
Canadian Satellite Users Association	http://www.bbande.com
Canadian Society for Computational Studies of Intelligence	http://ai.iit.nrc.ca/cscsi_point.html
Canadian Telecommunications Consultants Association	http://www.ctca.ca
Canadian Wireless Telecommunications Association	http://www.cwta.ca
Captus Press	http://www.io.org/~captpres
Carswell	http://www.carswell.com/carswell.home
Chronicle-Herald and The Mail-Star	http://www.herald.ns.ca
Chronicle-Journal	http://netreader.com/tbay/index2.html
Cogeco Cable inc.	www.cgocable.ca
Collingwood Enterprise-Bulletin	http://www.eb.georgian.net
Colombo & Company	http://www.inforamp.net/~JRC
Commonwealth Publications Inc.	http://www.commonwealthpub.com
Communications, Energy & Paperworkers Union of Canada (CLC)	http://www.cep.ca/cep/
Computer & Entertainment Retailing	http://www.plesman.com
Computer Dealer News	http://www.pleasman.com/cdn
Computer Paper	http://tcp.ca/
Computer Post	http://www.cpost.mb.ca
Continental Records Co. Ltd.	http://www.gocontinental.com
Copp Clark Professional	http://www.CanadaInfo.com
Corporation des maîtres photographes du Québec inc.	http://www.intertower.com/rimage/cmpq.html
Coteau Books/Thunder Creek Publishing Cooperative	http://www.coteau.unibase.com
Daily News	http://www.sterlingnews.com
Development Press	http://www.islandnet.com/~connor
Direction Informatique	http://www.direction-informatique.qc.ca
Discovery Channel	http://www.discovery.ca
Dryden Observer	http://www.awc/on.ca.observer
Éditions Beauchemin Ltée	http://www.beauchemin.qc.ca
Éditions Multimondes	http://multim.com
EDIMAG inc.	http://www.edimag.com
Editions du Bois-de-Coulogne	http://www.ebc.qc.ca
Edmonton Journal	http://www.southam.com/edmontonjournal/
Electronic Frontier Canada Inc.	http://insight.mcmaster.ca/org/efc/efc.html
Emond Montgomery Publications Ltd.	http://www.io.org/~emplaw
Express	http://www.southam.com/windsorstar/
Financial Post	http://www.canoe.ca/FP
Fraser Valley Community Information Society	http://mindlink.net/paul_kurucz/vnet.htm
Fraser Valley Radio Group	http://www.fraservalley.com
Garamond Press	http://www.garamond.ca/garamond
Gazette	http://www.montrealgazette.com
Globe and Mail	http://www.globeandmail.ca/
Goose Lane Editions	http://www.cygnus.nb.ca/bookstr/glane.glogo.html
Gutter Press	http://www.io.org/~gutter/
HarperCollins Canada Ltd.	http://www.harpercollins.com
Hazardous Materials Management	http://www.hazmatmag.com
Highway Book Shop	http://www.onlink.net/cybermail/bookshop/index.htm
Hill Times	http://resudox.net/paper/hill.html
Home Computing & Entertainment	http://www.plesman.com/hce
House of Anansi Press	http://www.irwin-pub.com/irwin/anansi/
Hum - The Government Computer Magazine	http://www.hum.com
ICURR Press	http://www.icurr.org/icurr/
INFORMATION highways: The Magazine for Users of Electronic Information	http://www.flexnet/cp,/~infohiwy/
ITP Nelson	http://www.nelson.com/nelson.html
Industry Canada - Communications Research Centre Library	http://www.crc.doc.ca/library/library.html
Information Resource Management Association of Canada	http://www.io.org/~irmac/
Information Technology Association of Canada	http://www.itac.ca/ITAC.home
Information Technology Research Centre	http://www.itrc.on.ca/
Interactive Multimedia Arts & Technologies Association	http://www.goodmedia.com/imat
International Interactive Communications Society - Toronto Chapter	http://toronto.ark.com/~iics
International Special Events Society - Toronto Chapter	http://www.ndgphoenix.com/ises.html
J.L.H. Law Books Ltd.	http://www.airlink.org/lawbook
Jewish Post & News	http://www.jewishpost.mb.ca
JourneyWoman	http://www.web.net/~jwoman/
Kitchener News Company Ltd.	http://www.kitnews.com
Knowledge Network, Service of the Open Learning Agency	http://www.ola.bc.ca
La Liberté	http://www.presse.ouest.mb.ca

Lancelot Press Ltd.	http://www.atcon.com/lancelot
Le Devoir	http://www.vir.com/~wily/intoronte/chrnint.htm
Learning Skills Television of Alberta	http://www.ccinet.ab.ca/access
Leduc & County This Week	http://www.compusmart.ab.ca/thisweek
Les Éditions du Blé	http://www.magic.mb.ca/~alexis
Lethbridge Herald	http://www.lis.ab.ca/lherald/
London Free Press	http://www.lfpress.com
Louise Courteau, éditrice inc.	http://club-culture.com/club/
Micro-Gazette	http://www.micro-gazette.com
Micromedia Limited	http://www.mmltd.com
Minnedosa Tribune	http://www.techplus.com/trib/index.htm
Moosomin World-Spectator	http://www/sasknet.com/~world
MuchMusic Network	http://www.muchmusic.com
National Advertising Benevolent Society	http://www.partnersweb.com/NABS
National Capital FreeNet	http://www.ncf.carleton.ca/
National Film Board of Canada	http://www.nfb.ca
North Peace Express	http://sterlingnews.com/alaska
North Shore News	http://www.nsnews.com
Nunatsiaq News	http://www.nunanet.com/~nunat
Oliver Chronicle	http://www.ftcnet.com/~mnewman
Ontario Community Newspapers Association	http://www.ocna.org
Orangeville Citizen	http://www.headwaters.com/citizen/citizen.html
Orca Book Publishers Ltd.	http://www.swifty.com/orca/index.htm
Oyen Echo	http://www.inter.ab.ca/oyen
Pacific Edge Publishing	http://www.schoolnet.ca/vp/cdncont/
Paulines Books & Media	http://www.netrover.com/~pauline
Peace River Block News	http://www.sterlingnews.com/peace
Penlan Publishing	http://www.penlancom/penlan
Photo Marketing Association International - Canada	http://www.pmai.org
Playwrights Canada Press	http://www.puc.ca
Prentice-Hall Canada Inc.	http://prenhall.com/
Radio Amateurs of Canada	http://www.rac.ca/
Radio Television News Directors' Association (Canada)	http://www.vvv.com/~rtnda
Random House of Canada Ltd.	http://www.randomhouse.com
Regroupement québécois pour le sous-titrage inc.	http://www.surdite.org/
Renouf Publishing Co. Ltd.	http://fox.nstn.ca/~renouf/
Rocky Mountain Books	http://www.ffa.ucalgary.ca/rmb/
Rogers Communications Inc.	http://www.rogers.com
Roussan Publishers Inc./Roussan éditeur inc.	http://www.magnet.ca/roussan
Routledge	http://www.routledge.com/routledge.html
SF Canada	http://helios.physics.utoronto.ca:8080/sfchome.html
SchoolNet National Advisory Board	http://www.schoolnet.ca/snab; http://www.rescol.ca/ccnr
Sea to Sky Free-Net Association	http://www.mountain-inter.net/~freenet/html
Self-Counsel Press Ltd.	http://www.swifty.com/scp
Services Documentaires Multimedia Inc.	http://www.sdm.qc.ca
Sherwood Park This Week	http://www.compusmart.ab.ca/thisweek
Showcase Television Inc.	http://www.screen.com/showcase
Skeena Broadcasters, Division of Okanagan Skeena Group Ltd.	http://www.osg.net
Slave River Journal	http://www.auroranet.nt.casrj
Sources	http://www.sources.com
Southam Magazine & Information Group	hhtp://www.southam.com
Spectator	http://www.southam.com/hamiltonspector
Star Phoenix	http://www.wbm.ca/users/sphoenix
Stoddart Publishing Co. Limited	http://www.genpub.com
Sudbury Star	http://sudbury.siteseet.ca
TUNS Press	http://tuns.ca/architecture/press/html
TVOntario	http://www.tvo.org/
Talmage Book Centre	http://www.terraport.net/tbc/tbc.htm
Technology in Government	http://www.plesman.com
Telecommunications Research Institute of Ontario	http://www.trio.ca/trio/
Telegraph-Journal/Times-Globe	http://www.nubpub.nb.ca
Telesat Canada	http://www.telesat.ca
Television Northern Canada	http://www.silksik.learnet.nt.ca/tvnc/main.html
Toronto Computes!	http://www.canadacomputes.com
Toronto Star	http://www.t-o.com
Tuesday Times-Reformer	http://www.nornet.on.ca/reformer/refmain.html
Ulverscroft Large Print (Canada) Ltd.	http://dspace.dial.pipex.com/town/plaza/hfss/
University of British Columbia Press	gopher://gopher.ubc.ca:70/11/libraries/ubc-press
University of Toronto Press	http://www.library.utoronto.ca/www/utpress/depthome.htm
Vancouver Echo	http://www.vannet.com/vanecho
Vancouver Regional FreeNet Association	http://freenet.vancouver.bc.ca/
Videotron Communications Ltd.	http://www.videotron.ab.ca
Wireless Telecom	http://www.cwta.ca
Women in Film & Television - Toronto	http://www.goodmedia.com/wift
Yukon News	http://www.yukonweb.com/community/yukon-news

Canadian Almanac & Directory 1997

EDUCATION

Acadia University	http://www.acadiau.ca
Agence francophone pour l'enseignement supérieur et la recherche	http://www.refer.qc.ca
Albert College	http://www.telos.ca/quinta/albertc
Alberta Association of Courseware Producers	http://www.sas.ab.ca/aacp/
Algonquin College	http://algonquinc.on.ca/
Annals of Air & Space Law	http://www.iasl.mcgill.ca
Architectural Institute of British Columbia	http://www.aibc.bc.ca/home.html
Assiniboine Community College	http://www.assiniboinec.mb.ca
Association canadienne d'éducation de langue française	http://www.acelf.ca
Association for Canadian Theatre Research	http://www.athabascan.ca
Association for Jewish Studies - USA	gopher://gopher.brandeis.edu:70/11/campusinfo/ajs
Association for Media & Technology in Education in Canada	http://www.camosun.bc.ca/~amtec/
Association for the Promotion & Advancement of Science Education	http://www.swifty.com/apase/charlotte/apase!.html
Association francophone internationale des directeurs d'établissements scolaires	http://grics.qc.ca/afides
Association of Canadian Community Colleges	http://www.accc.ca/index.html
Association of Colleges of Applied Arts & Technology of Ontario	gopher://info.senecac.on.ca:2000/
Association of English-German Bilingual Education of Edmonton	http://www.tgx.com/german
Association of Universities & Colleges of Canada	http://www.aucc.ca/
Association pour l'avancement des sciences et des techniques de la documentation	http://www.asted.org
Athabasca University	http://www.athabascau.ca
Atlantic School of Theology - Library	http://novanet.ns.ca/ast/homepage.html
Augustana University College	gopher://gopher/augustana.ab.ca:70/1
BC Institute of Technology	http://www.bcit.bc.ca/
BC School District 63 - District Resource Centre	http://www.sd63.bc.ca/
BC Studies: The British Columbian Quarterly	http://www.swifty.com/bcamp/directors/humansci/bcs.html
Banff Centre for the Arts & Centre for Management & Centre for Conferences	http://www-nmr.banffcentre.ab.ca
Banff Centre for the Arts - Library	http://www.banffcentre.ab.ca
Bishop's University	http://www.ubishops.ca
Brandon University	http://www.brandonu.ca
British Columbia Teachers' Federation	http://www.bctf.bc.ca
Brock University	http://www.brocku.ca
CEGEP de Lanaudière - Bibliothèque	http://www.collanaud.qc.ca
Cambrian College	http://www.cambrianc.on.ca/
Camosun College	http://www.camosun.bc.ca
Campion College	http://www.uregina.ca/calendar/fedcoll/html#camp
Canadian Alliance for Lifelong Learning Inc.	http://gcll.carleton.ca/
Canadian Association for University Continuing Education	http://www.tile.net/tile/listserv/caucel.html
Canadian Association of Career Educators & Employers	http://www.cacee.com/workweb
Canadian Association of Second Language Teachers	http://www2.tvo.org/education/caslt
Canadian Association of University Teachers	http://www.caut.ca
Canadian Children's Literature	http://www.uoguelph.ca/englit/ccl/
Canadian Coast Guard College - Library	http://www.cgc.ns.ca
Canadian Federation for the Humanities	http://137.122.12.15/HumCanada.html
Canadian Federation of Students	http://www.cfs-fcee.ca
Canadian Home & School Federation	http://cnet.unb.ca/cap/partners/chsptf/
Canadian Institute of Strategic Studies	http://www.ciss.ca
Canadian Institutional Research & Planning Association	http://www.usask.ca/cirpa/index.html
Canadian Journal of History	http://www.usask.ca/history/cjh
Canadian Journal of Law & Society	http://www.juris.uqam.ca/rcds/index_en.htm
Canadian Journal of Political & Social Theory	http://english-server.hss.cmu.edu/ctheory.html
Canadian Literature	http://www.swifty.com/cdn_lit
Canadian Mathematical Society	http://camel.cecm.sfu.ca/index.html
Canadian Memorial Chiropractic College	http://www.cmcc.ca
Canadian Music Educators' Association	http://www.stemnet.nf.ca/~barobert/cmea/cmea.html
Canadian Network for the Advancement of Research, Industry & Education	http://www.canarie.ca
Canadian Philosophical Association	http://www.uwindsor.ca/cpa
Canadian Public Policy	http://wwwqed.econ.queensu.ca/pub/cpp/
Canadian Teachers' Federation	http://www.ctf-fce.ca
Canadian Vocational Association	http://www.cva.ca
Canadore College	http://canadorec.on.ca/
Capilano College	http://www.capcollege.bc.ca/
Carleton University	http://www.carleton.ca
Cégep de Lévis-Lauzon - Bibliothéque	http://www.clevislauzon.qc.ca/
Centennial College	gopher://cenvmc.cencol.on.ca
Centre for Refugee Studies - Andrew Forbes Refugee Resource Centre	http://www.yorku.ca/research/crs
Classical Association of Canada	http://137.122.12.15/Docs/Societies/ClassAc/Classic.Assoc.html
Collège Boréal	http://www.borealc.on.ca
Commonwealth of Learning	http://www.col.org
Concordia University	http://www.concordia.ca
Conestoga College	http://www.conestogac.on.ca/
Conférence des recteurs et des principaux des universités du Québec	http://www.crepuq.qc.ca
Confederation College	http://spider-web.confederationc.on.ca/
Council of Ontario Universities	http://www.cou.on.ca
Council of Prairie & Pacific University Libraries	http://library.usask.ca/coppul
Dalhousie University	http://www.da.ca
Department of Education, Culture & Employment	http://siksik.learnnet.nt.ca
Douglas College	http://www.douglas.bc.ca/

Canadian Almanac & Directory 1997

Durham College	http://durham.durhamc.on.ca/index.html
École Polytechnique	http://www.polymtl.ca
Economics Working Papers	http://socserv2.socsci.mcmaster.ca/~econ/
Edmonton Chinese Bilingual Education Association	http://www.alvin.org/acr/ecbea.htm#organ
Education Today	http://www.opsba.org
Emily Carr Institute of Art & Design	http://www.eciad.bc.ca/
Erindale College	http://www.erin.utoronto.ca/
Event	http://www.douglas.ca/Event/homepage.html
Fanshawe College	http://www.fanshawec.on.ca/
Fédération des commissions scolaires du Québec	http://grics.qc.ca/fcsq/accueil.htm
Foundation for Educational Exchange Between Canada & the United States	http://www.usis.canada.usia.gov/fulbrigh.htm
George Brown College	http://www.gbrownc.on.ca/
Georgian College	http://www.georcoll.on.ca
Grant MacEwan Community College	http://www.gmcc.ab.ca/
Green Teacher: Education for Planet Earth	http://www.web.ca/~greentea/
Herbert Marshall McLuhan Foundation	http://www.mcluhan.ca/mcluhan/foundation.html
Humanist Association of Canada	http://magi.com/~hac/hac.html
Humber College	http://www.humberc.on.ca/
Infant/Maternal Nutrition Education Association	http://www.io.org/~infacto
Institut National de la Recherche Scientifique (INRS)	http://www.inrds-urb.uquebec.ca
Interactive Multimedia Arts & Technologies Association	http://www.goodmedia.com/imat/
International Academy of Merchandising & Design Ltd.	http://www.iaod.com
International Centre	http://quic.queensu.ca
International Development Education Resource Association	http://www.vcn.bc.ca/idera
International Federation of Institutes for Advanced Study	http://www.ifias.ca/
Keewatin Community College	http://www.keewatincc.mb.ca
King's College	http://www.kingsu.ab.ca
Knox College - Caven Library	http://www.utoronto.ca/knox
Kwantlen University College	http://www.kwantlen.bc.ca/
La Cité Collégiale	http://www.lacitec.on.ca
Labour	http://www.mun.ca/cclh/
Lakefied College - School Library	http://www.lakefieldcs.on.ca/
Lakehead University	http://www.lakeheadu.ca
Lambton College	http://www.lambton.on.ca/
Langara College	http://www.langara.bc.ca
Laurentian University of Sudbury	http://www.laurentian.ca/
Lethbridge Community College	http://www.lethbridgec.ab.ca
London, Board of Education for the City of	http://www.lbe.edu.on.ca
Malaspina University College	http://www.mala.bc.ca
McGill University	http://www.mcgill.ca
McGill University - Health Sciences Library	http://www.health.library.mcgill.ca
McGill University - Libraries	http://www.library.mcgill.ca
McGill University Archives	http://www.archives.mcgill.ca
McMaster University	http://www.mcmaster.ca; gopher://gopher.mcmaster.ca
Memorial University of Newfoundland	http://www.mun.ca; gopher://gopher.mun.ca
Mensa Canada Society	http://www.rohcg.on.ca/mensa/mensa.html
Modern Drama	http://www/utpress/depthome.htm
Mohawk College	http://www.mohawkc.on.ca/
Mosaic: A Journal for the Interdisciplinary Study of Literature	http://www.umanitoba.ca/publications/mosaic
Mount Allison University	http://www/mta.ca/
Mount Royal College	http://www.mtroyal.ab.ca/
Mount Saint Bernard College	http://www.stfx.ca/msbresid/
Mount Saint Vincent University	http://www.msvu.ca/
Niagara College	http://www.niagarac.on.ca/
Niagara Parks Botanical Gardens & School of Horticulture	http://www.niagara.com/~;shoup/botanic_gardens.html
North American Association for Environmental Education	http://www.nceet.snre.umich.edu/naacc.html
North Island College	http://www.nic.bc.ca
Northern Alberta Institute of Technology	http://www.schoolfinder.com/profiles/colleges/nait.htm
Northern College	http://www.northernc.on.ca/
Northern Lights College	http://www.nlc.bc.ca
Nova Scotia Agricultural College	gopher://gopher.nsac.ns.ca
Nova Scotia Teachers College	http://fox.nstn.ca:89/~ptiwana/nstc.html
Nova Scotia Teachers Union	http://fox.nstn.ca/~nstu/
Okanagan University College	http://www.okanagan.bc.ca/
Ottawa School of Art	http://infoweb.magi.com/~osa/
PARTNERS	http://www.ocri.ca/partners/partners.html
Post-secondary Application Service of BC	http://www.pas.bc.ca
Prairie Forum: Journal of the Canadian Plains Research Centre	http://www.cas.uregina.ca/~cprc/
Providence College & Seminary	http://www.providence.mb.ca
Public School Boards Association of Alberta	http://www.planet.eon.net/~psbaa
Queen's Quarterly	http://www.info.queensu.ca/quarterly
Queen's University	http://info.queensu.ca/
Ready to Learn Association	http://www.nald.ca/homep.htm
Reporter	http://www.oecta.library@sympatico.ca
Royal Canadian Institute	http://www.psych.utoronto.ca/people/vislab/rci.html
Royal Military College of Canada	http://www.rmc.ca/
Royal Roads University	http://www.royalroads.ca
Ryerson Polytechnic University	http://www.ryerson.ca/

Ryerson Polytechnic University - Library . . . . http://hugo.lib.ryerson.ca
Saint Mary's University. . . . . http://www.stmarys.ca
Saskatchewan Indian Federated College . . . . http://www.uregina.ca/calendar/fedcoll.html#sifc
Sask. Institute of Applied Science & Technology - Palliser Institute Library . . . . http://www.siast.sk.ca
Sault College. . . . . http://www.saultc.on.ca/
Scarborough College . . . . http://www.scar.utoronto.ca/
School Counsellors Association of Newfoundland . . . . http://www.stemnet.nf.ca/Organizations/SCAN/
SchoolNet National Advisory Board. . . . . http://www.schoolnet.ca/snab; http://www.rescol.ca/ccnr
Selkirk College . . . . http://www.selkirk.bc.ca/
Seneca College . . . . http://www.senecac.on.ca/
Sheridan College . . . . http://www.sheridanc.on.ca
Simon Fraser University . . . . http://www.sfu.ca/
Simon Fraser University - W.A.C. Bennett Library . . . . http://www.lib.sfu.ca/
Sir Sandford Fleming College . . . . http://www.flemingc.on.ca/
Société pour la promotion de l'enseignement de l'anglais (langue seconde) au Québec . http://cyberscol.qc.ca/partenaires/speaq/speaq.htm
Southern Alberta Institute of Technology . . . . http://www.sait.ab.ca/
St. Clair College . . . . http://www.stclairc.on.ca/
St. Francis Xavier University . . . . http://www.stfx.ca/
St. Lawrence College . . . . http://www.stlawrencec.on.ca/
St. Thomas University . . . . http://www.stthomasu.ca
Syndicat des professeures et professeurs de l'Université de Sherbrooke. http://132.210.12.120/
TESL Canada Federation . . . . http://raven.ritslab.ubc.ca/teslcanada.html
Télé-Université. . . . . http://www.teluq.uquebec.ca/
Teacher . . . . http://Fox.nstn.ca/~nstu
Technical University of Nova Scotia . . . . http://www.tuns.ca/index.html
TeleLearning Research Network. . . . . http://fas.sfu.ca/telelearn
Toronto Baptist Seminary & Bible College . . . . http://www.io.org/~tbsedu/
Toronto Institute of Pharmaceutical Technology . . . . http://www.tipt.on.ca/tipt.html
Transcultural Psychiatric Research Review . . . . http://www.mcgill.ca/psychiatry
Trent University . . . . http://www.trentu.ca
Trinity Western University . . . . http://www.twu.ca
Université Laval . . . . http://www.ulaval.ca/index.html
Université Sainte Anne . . . . http://www.isisnet.com/ustanne
Université de Moncton . . . . gopher://gopher.umoncton.ca
Université de Montréal . . . . http://www.umontreal.ca
Université du Québec . . . . http://www.uquebec.ca
Université du Québec à Chicoutimi . . . . http://www.uqac.uquebec.ca/
Université du Québec à Hull . . . . http://www.uqah.uquebec.ca/
Université du Québec à Montréal . . . . http://www.uqam.ca
Université du Québec à Rimouski . . . . http://www.uqar.uquebec.ca
Université du Québec en Abitibi-Témiscamingue . . . . http://www.uqat.uquebec.ca/
University College of Cape Breton . . . . http://www.uccb.ns.ca
University College of the Cariboo . . . . http://www.cariboo.bc.ca/
University College of the Fraser Valley . . . . gopher://gopher.ucfv.bc.ca/
University of Alberta . . . . http://web.cs.ualberta.ca/UAlberta.html
University of Alberta - Libraries . . . . http://www.library.ualberta.ca/library.html
University of British Columbia http://view.ubc.ca:80/
University of Calgary . . . . http://www.ucalgary.ca/
University of Guelph . . . . http://www.uoguelph.ca/
University of Guelph - Library . . . . http://www.lib.uoguelph.ca
University of King's College . . . . http://www.ukings.ns.ca
University of Lethbridge . . . . http://www.uleth.ca
University of Manitoba . . . . http://www.umanitoba.ca; gopher://gopher.cc.umanitoba.ca
University of Manitoba - Libraries . . . . http://www.cc.umanitoba.ca/academic_support/libraries/
University of New Brunswick . . . . http://degaulle.hil.unb.ca
University of Northern British Columbia . . . . http://www.unbc.edu; http://quarles.unbc.edu/keen/welcome.html
University of Ottawa . . . . http://www.uottawa.ca; gopher://gopher.uottawa.ca
University of Prince Edward Island . . . . http://www.upei.ca
University of Saskatchewan . . . . http://www.usask.ca/
University of Toronto . . . . http://www.utoronto.ca/
University of Toronto - Scarborough College - V.W. Bladen Library . . . . http://library.scar.utoronto.ca/
University of Victoria . . . . http://www.uvic.ca
University of Waterloo . . . . http://www.uwaterloo.ca/
University of Western Ontario . . . . http://www.uwo.ca/
University of Windsor . . . . http://www.cs.uwindsor.ca/index.html; gopher://access/cs.uwindsor.ca70/1
Vancouver Island Advanced Technology Centre . . . . http://vvv.com/VIATeC/
Waterloo County Roman Catholic Separate School Board . . . . http://www.watrc.edu.on.ca
Wilfrid Laurier University - Central Library . . . . http://www.wlu.ca/~wwwhb/
World University Service of Canada . . . . http://www.wusc.ca
York University . . . . http://www.yorku.ca

GOVERNMENT & PUBLIC ADMINISTRATION

Government of Canada
Canadian Government Site . . . . http://canada.gc.ca
InfoCan URL: . . . . http://www.infocan.gc.ca/
Office of the Prime Minister . . . . http://canada.gc.ca/english/pmo/index.htm

Canadian Almanac & Directory 1997

Prime Minister's Correspondence Page	http://canada.gc.ca/english/pmo/e_corres.htm
Office of the Leader, Opposition (BQ)	http://www.ncf.carleton.ca/freeport/government/fedelect/nat/bq/menu
Office of the Leader, Reform Party (Ref.)	http://www.reform.ca/english/
Office of the Leader, New Democratic Party (NDP)	http://www.fed.ndp.ca/ndp
Office of the Leader, Progressive Conservative Party (PC)	http://www.ncf.carleton.ca/freeport/government/fedelect/nat/pc/menu
Privy Council Office	http://canada.gc.ca/depts/agencies/pcoind_e.html
Senate of Canada	http://www.parl.gc.ca/english/emember.html
The Canadian Ministry (Cabinet)	http://canada.gc.ca/howgoc/cab/cabind_e.html
House of Commons, Canada	http://www.parl.gc.ca/english/index.html
Agriculture & Agri-Food Canada	http://aceis.agr.ca
Atlantic Canada Opportunities Agency	http://www.acoa.ca/
Atomic Energy Control Board	http://www.gc.ca/aecb/
Atomic Energy of Canada Limited	http://www.aecl.ca
Auditor General of Canada	http://www.oag-bvg.gc.ca
Bank of Canada	http://www.bank-banque-canada.ca/english/intro-e.htm
Bayfield Institute for Marine Science & Surveys	http://www.cciw.ca/dfo/dfo-home.html
Bedford Institute of Oceanography	http://biome.bio.dfo.ca
Business Development Bank of Canada	http://www.bdc.ca/
Canada Centre for Remote Sensing	http://www.ccrs.nrcan.gc.ca/
Canada Council	http://www.culturenet.ca/cc
Canada Deposit Insurance Corporation	http://canada.gc.ca/depts/agencies/cdiind_e.html
Canada Mortgage & Housing Corporation	http://www.cmhc-schl.gc.ca
Canada Ports Corporation	http://canada.gc.ca/depts/agencies/cpoind_e.html
Canada Post Corporation	http://www.canpost.ca/
Canadian Artists & Producers Professional Relations Tribunal	http://info.ic.gc.ca/opengov/capprt
Canadian Broadcasting Corporation	http://www.cbc.ca/
Canadian Centre for Management Development	http://www.infoshare.ca/ccmd/mainpage.html
Canadian Centre for Occupational Health & Safety	http://www.ccohs.ca
Canadian Centre on Substance Abuse	http://www.ccsa.ca
Canadian Commercial Corporation	http://www.ccc.ca
Canadian Dairy Commission	http://www.agr.ca/cdc
Canadian Environmental Assessment Agency	http://www.ceaa.gc.ca/
Canadian Forest Service	http://mf.ncr.forestry.ca
Canadian Heritage	http://www.pch.gc.ca/
Canadian Heritage - Fortress of Louisbourg	http://fortress.uccb.ns.ca
Canadian Heritage -Parks Canada Sector	http://parkscanada.pch.gc.ca/
Canadian Human Rights Commission	http://www.chrc.ca/chrc.html
Canadian International Development Agency	http://www.acdi.cida.gc.ca
Canadian International Trade Tribunal	http://canada.gc.ca/depts/agencies/cttind_e.html
Canadian Polar Commission	http://www.polarcom.gc.ca/
Canadian Radio-Television & Telecommunications Commission	http://www.crtc.gc.ca/
Canadian Security Intelligence Service (CSIS)	http://www.csis-scrs.gc.ca/eng/menu/menue.html
Canadian Space Agency	http://www.space.gc.ca/welcomee.html
Canadian Transportation Agency	http://www.cta-otc.gc.ca
Canadian Wheat Board	http://canada.gc.ca/depts/agencies/cwbind_e.html
Citizenship & Immigration Canada	http://cicnet.ingenia.com/english/index.html
Correctional Service Canada	http://www.csc-scc.gc.ca/csce.htm
Defence Construction Canada	http://canada.gc.ca/depts/agencies/dccind_e.html
Elections Canada	http://www.elections.ca/
Emergency Preparedness Canada	http://hoshi.cic.sfu.ca/epc
Environment Canada	http://www.ec.gc.ca
Export Development Corporation	http://www.edc.ca
Federal Office of Regional Development (Québec)	http://canada.gc.ca/depts/agencies/frqind_e.html
Finance Canada	http://www.fin.gc.ca/fin-eng.html
Fisheries & Oceans Canada	http://www.ncr.dfo.ca/home_e.htm
Foreign Affairs & International Trade Canada	http://www.dfait-maeci.gc.ca
Foreign Affairs & International Trade Canada-Passport Office	http://www.dfait-maeci.gc.ca/passport/passport.htm
Geological Survey of Canada	http://www.emr.ca/gsc/
Geomatics Canada	http://www.geocan.nrcan.gc.ca/
Government Purchasing - Public Works & Government Services Canada	http://www.pwgsc.gc.ca
Government Purchasing - Open Bidding Service	http://www.obs.ism.ca/eginfo.html
Governor General & Commander-in-Chief of Canada	http://canada.gc.ca/howgoc/govgen/ggind_e.html
Hazardous Materials Information Review Commission	http://canada.gc.ca/depts/agencies/hmiind_e.html
Health Canada	http://www.hwc.ca/links/english.html
Human Resources Development Canada	http://www.hrdc-drhc.gc.ca/hrdc/menu-en.html
Immigration & Refugee Board	http://www.ncf.carleton.ca/freeport/government/federal/irb/menu
Indian & Northern Affairs Canada	http://www.inac.gc.ca/
Industry Canada	http://info.ic.gc.ca/ic-data/index.html; Strategis URL: http://strategis.ic.gc.ca
Information Commissioner of Canada	http://infoweb.magi.com/~accessca/oic.html
Institute for Marine Biosciences	http://www.corpserv.nrc.ca/corpserv/imd.html
Institute for Marine Dynamics	http://www.corpserv.nrc.ca/corpserv/imd.html
Institute of Ocean Sciences	http://www.ios.bc.ca/
International Development Research Centre	http://www.idrc.ca
Justice Canada	http://canada.justice.gc.ca/
Maurice Lamontagne Institute	http://www.ncr.dfo.ca/communic/offices/iml/iml_e.htm
Medical Research Council of Canada	http://hpb1.hwc.ca:8100/
National Advisory Council on Aging	http://hpb1.hwc.ca/datahpsb/seniors/senpage.html
National Advisory Council on Science & Technology	http://info.ic.gc.ca/opengov/nabst/nabst.html

Canadian Almanac & Directory 1997

National Archives of Canada . . . . http://www.archives.ca/
National Capital Commission. . . . . http://canada.gc.ca/depts/agencies/nccind_e.html
National Defence (Canada) . . . . http://www.debbs.ndhq.dnd.ca/dnd.htm
National Energy Board. . . . . http://canada.gc.ca/depts/agencies/nebind_e.html
National Farm Products Council . . . . http://www.aceis.agr.ca/./nfpce.html
National Film Board of Canada. . . . . http://www.nfb.ca/
National Parole Board. . . . . http://canada.gc.ca/depts/agencies/npbind_e.html
National Research Council (Canada) . . . . http://www.nrc.ca/
National Search & Rescue Secretariat . . . . http://www.synapse.net/~nss/nss/nsshome.htm
Natural Resources Canada . . . . http://www.NRCan.gc.ca/
Natural Sciences & Engineering Research Council . . . . http://www.nserc.ca
Northern Pipeline Agency Canada . . . . http://canada.gc.ca/depts/agencies/npaind_e.html
Privacy Commissioner of Canada . . . . http://infoweb.magi.com/~privcan/
Public Service Commission of Canada . . . . http://www.psc-cfp.gc.ca
Public Works & Government Services Canada . . . . http://www.pwgsc.gc.ca
Revenue Canada . . . . http://www.revcan.ca/menue.html
Royal Canadian Mint . . . . http://www.rcmint.ca
Royal Canadian Mounted Police. http://www.rcmp-grc.gc.ca/html/rcmp2.htm
Security Intelligence Review Committee . . . . http://canada.gc.ca/depts/agencies/sirind_e.html
Solicitor General Canada . . . . http://www.sgc.gc.ca
St. Lawrence Seaway Authority. . . . . http://www.seaway.ca/english/seaway/index.html
Standards Council of Canada. . . . . http://www.scc.ca/indexe.html
Statistics Canada . . . . http://www.statcan.ca
Status of Women Canada . . . . http://canada.gc.ca/depts/agencies/swcind_e.html
Transport Canada . . . . http://www.tc.gc.ca
Treasury Board of Canada . . . . http://www.tbs-sct.gc.ca
Western Economic Diversification Canada . . . . http://www.myriadgate.net/wd/

Government of Alberta
Alberta Governement Site . . . . http://www.gov.ab.ca/
Office of the Premier. . . . . http://www.gov.ab.ca/gov/prem/premier.html
Legislative Assembly. . . . . http://www.assembly.ab.ca/
Alberta Advanced Education & Career Development . . . . http://www.gov.ab.ca/dept/aecd.html
Alberta Agriculture, Food & Rural Development . . . . http://www.gov.ab.ca/dept/agric.html
Alberta Community Development . . . . http://www.gov.ab.ca/dept/mcd.html
Alberta Economic Development & Tourism. . . . . http://www.edt.gov.ab.ca/
Alberta Education. . . . . http://ednet.edc.gov.ab.ca
Alberta Energy. . . . . http://www.gov.ab.ca/dept/enr.html
Alberta Energy & Utilities Board . . . . http://www.eub.gov.ab.ca
Alberta Environmental Protection . . . . http://www.gov.ab.ca/~env/
Alberta Family & Social Services . . . . http://www.gov.ab.ca/dept/fss.html
Alberta Federal & Intergovernmental Affairs. . . . . http://www.gov.ab.ca/dept/figa.html
Alberta Health . . . . http://www.gov.ab.ca/dept/health.html
Alberta Justice . . . . http://www.gov.ab.ca/dept/just.html
Alberta Labour . . . . http://www.gov.ab.ca/dept/lbr.html
Alberta Municipal Affairs. . . . . http://www.gov.ab.ca/dept/ma.html
Alberta Natural Resources Conservation Board. . . . . http://www.gov.ab.ca/~NRCB/index.html
Alberta Office of the Auditor General . . . . http://www.assembly.ab.ca/auditor.gen/auditor.htm
Alberta Public Works, Supply & Services . . . . http://www.gov.ab.ca/dept.pwss.html
Alberta Research Council. . . . . http://www.arc.ab.ca
Alberta Science & Research Authority . . . . http://www.gov.ab.ca/gov/agency/sara.html
Alberta Transportation & Utilities . . . . http://www.gov.ab.ca/dept/tu.html

Government of British Columbia
British Columbia Government Site. . . . . http://www.gov.bc.ca/
Legislative Assembly. . . . . http://www.legis.gov.bc.ca/
British Columbia Hydro & Power Authority. . . . . http://www.bchydro.bc.ca
British Columbia Provincial Emergency Program. . . . . http://hoshi.cic.sfu.ca/~pep/
British Columbia Securities Commission . . . . http://www.bcsc.bc.ca/
Elections British Columbia. . . . . http://vvv.com/~electionsbc/
Government Purchasing - British Columbia Buildings Corporation . . . . http://www.bcbc.gov.bc.ca
Government Purchasing - Ministry of Government Services. http://www.pc.gov.bc.ca
Ministry of Aboriginal Affairs . . . . http://www.aaf.gov.bc.ca/aaf/
Ministry of Agriculture, Fisheries & Food . . . . http://bbs.qp.gov.bc.ca/bcmaff/bcagweb.htm
Ministry of the Attorney General-Consumer Services Division . . . . http://www.lcs.gov.bc.ca/
Ministry of Education, Skills & Training . . . . http://www.educ.gov.bc.ca/
Ministry of Employment & Investment . . . . http://www.ei.gov.bc.ca/
Ministry of Environment, Lands & Parks. . . . . http://www.env.gov.bc.ca/
Ministry of Finance & Corporate Relations. . . . . http://www.fin.gov.bc.ca/
Ministry of Forests. . . . . http://mofwww.for.gov.bc.ca
Ministry of Government Services . . . . http://brahma.gs.gov.bc.ca/
Ministry of Health . . . . http://www.hlth.gov.bc.ca
Ministry of Housing, Recreation & Consumer Services. . . . . http://nt_server3.lcs.gov.bc.ca/homepage.htn
Ministry of Labour. . . . . http://www.labour.gov.bc.ca/welcome.htm
Ministry of Municipal Affairs & Housing. . . . . http://www.marh.gov.bc.ca/
Ministry of Small Business, Tourism & Culture . . . . http://www.tbc.gov.bc.ca/homepage.html
Ministry of Women's Equality . . . . http:www.weq.gov.bc.ca/
Office of the Auditor General . . . . http://www.aud.gov.bc.ca/

Canadian Almanac & Directory 1997

Office of the Ombudsman . . . . http://www.ombud.gov.bc.ca/
Science Council of British Columbia . . . . http://www.scbc.org/

Government of Manitoba
Manitoba Government Site . . . . http://www.gov.mb.ca/
Office of the Premier http://www.gov.mb.ca/text/quotepg1.html
Legislative Assembly http://www.gov.mb.ca/leg-asmb/index1.html
Manitoba Culture, Heritage & Citizenship . . . . http://www.gov.mb.ca/manitoba/chc/immsettl/citz_hom.html
Manitoba Economic Development Board. . . . . http://www.gov.mb.ca/manitoba/board/board.html
Manitoba Economic Innovation & Technology Council . . . . http://www.eitc.mb.ca/eitc.html
Manitoba Education & Training . . . . http://www.gov.mb.ca/educate/main/index.html
Manitoba Energy & Mines . . . . http://www.gov.mb.ca/em/index.html
Manitoba Environment . . . . http://www.gov.mb.ca/manitoba/environ/index.html
Manitoba Family Services . . . . http://www.gov.mb.ca/fs/first/ffindex.html
Manitoba Finance . . . . http://www.gov.mb.ca/finance/
Manitoba Health . . . . http://www.gov.mb.ca/health/index.html
Manitoba Industry, Trade & Tourism-Tourism Initiative . . . . http://www.gov.mb.ca/manitoba/itt/travel/explore/
Manitoba Labour . . . . http://www.gov.mb.ca/labour/
Manitoba Natural Resources . . . . http://www.gov.mb.ca/natres/index.html

Government of New Brunswick
New Brunswick Government Site . . . . http://www.gov.nb.ca/
Legislative Assembly . . . . http://www.gov.nb.ca/legis/index.htm
Department of Advanced Education & Labour . . . . http://www.gov.nb.ca/ael/index.htm
Department of Agriculture & Rural Development . . . . http//www.gov.nb.ca/agricult/index.htm
Department of Economic Development & Tourism . . . . http://www.gov.nb.ca/edt/index.htm
Department of Education . . . . http://www.gov.nb.ca/education/index.htm
Department of Finance . . . . http://www.gov.nb.ca/finance/index.htm
Department of Fisheries & Aquaculture . . . . http://www.gov.nb.ca/dfa/index.htm
Department of Health & Community Services . . . . http://www.gov.nb.ca/hcs/
Department of Intergovernmental & Aboriginal Affairs . . . . http://www.gov.nb.ca/iga/home1_e.htm
Department of Justice . . . . http://www.gov.nb.ca/justice/index.htm
Department of Municipalities, Culture & Housing . . . . http://www.gov.nb.ca/mch/index.htm
Department of Natural Resources & Energy . . . . http://www.gov.nb.ca/dnre/index.htm
Department of Supply & Services . . . . http://www.gov.nb.ca/supply/index.htm
Department of the Environment . . . . http://www.gov.nb.ca/environ/index.htm
Department of the Solicitor General . . . . http://www.gov.nb.ca/solgen/index.htm
Government Purchasing - BIDS System Tendering . . . . http://www.bids.ca
Government Purchasing - Department of Supply & Services . . . . http://www.gov.nb.ca/supply/index.htm
Information Highway Secretariat . . . . http://www.gov.nb.ca/edt/infohigh/index.htm
New Brunswick Emergency Measures Organization . . . . http://www.gov.nb.ca/pss/emo.htm
New Brunswick Research & Productivity Council . . . . http://www.rpc.unb.ca
Workplace Health, Safety & Compensation Commission of New Brunswick . . . . http://www.gov.nb.ca/whscc/index.htm

Government of Newfoundland & Labrador
Newfoundland & Labrador Government Site . . . . http://www.gov.nf.ca/
Office of the Premier . . . . http://www.gov.nf.ca/exec/premier/premier.htm
Executive Council . . . . http://www.gov.nf.ca/exec/start.htm
House of Assembly . . . . http://www.gov.nf.ca/house/hoa_ovr.htm
Department of Development & Rural Renewal . . . . http://www.gov.nf.ca/dev.htm
Department of Education . . . . http://www.gov.nf.ca/edu/startedu.htm
Department of Environment & Labour . . . . http://www.gov.nf.ca/envlab.htm
Department of Finance & Treasury Board . . . . http://www.gov.nf.ca/fin/startfin.htm
Department of Fisheries & Aquaculture . . . . http://www.gov.nf.ca/fishaq.htm
Department of Forest Resources & Agrifoods . . . . http://www.gov.nf.ca/forest.htm
Department of Government Services & Lands . . . . http://www.gov.nf.ca/govtsrv.htm
Department of Health . . . . http://www.gov.nf.ca/health/starthel.htm
Department of Industry, Trade & Technology . . . . http://www.gov.nf.ca/itt/startitt.htm
Department of Justice & Attorney General . . . . http://www.gov.nf.ca/just/startjus.htm
Department of Mines & Energy . . . . http://www.gov.nf.ca/mines.htm
Department of Municipal & Provincial Affairs . . . . http://www.gov.nf.ca/mpa/startmpa.htm
Department of Social Services . . . . http://www.gov.nf.ca/doss/startdos.htm
Department of Tourism, Culture & Recreation . . . . http://www.gov.nf.ca/tcr/starttcr.htm
Department of Works, Services & Transportation . . . . http://www.gov.nf.ca/wststart.htm
Economic Recovery Commission . . . . http://www.gov.nf.ca/erc/
Newfoundland & Labrador Housing Corporation . . . . http://www.gov.nf.ca/nlhc/nlhc.htm
Newfoundland Offshore Petroleum Board . . . . http://canada.gc.ca/depts/agencies/cnpind_e.html
Provincial Advisory Council on the Status of Women . . . . http://www.gov.nf.ca/exec/wpo/info.htm
Treasury Board Secretariat . . . . http://www.gov.nf.ca/exec/Presiden/presiden.htm

Government of the Northwest Territories
Northwest Territories Government Site . . . . http://www.ssmicro.com/~xpsognwt/Net/index.html
Legislative Assembly . . . . http://www.ssimicro.com/~epsognwt/Net/departments/assembly/Gov.html
Department of Education, Culture & Employment . . . . http://siksik.learnnet.nt.ca
Department of Finance . . . . http://www.fin.gov.nt.ca
Department of Health & Social Services . . . . http://www.hltnss.gov.nt.ca/
Department of Justice . . . . http://pingo.gov.nt.ca/Phone/Dept/dep0013.htm#Il
Department of Municipal & Community Affairs . . . . http://www.maca.gov.nt.ca

Department of Public Works & Services . . . . http://www.ssimicro.com/~xpsognwt/Net/departments/Dept-PublicWorks.HTML
Department of Resources, Wildlife & Economic Development . . . . http://www.edt.gov.nt.ca/
Department of Safety & Public Services. . . . . http://www.ssimicro.com/~epsognwt/Net/departments/dept-Safety.HTML
Department of Transportation. . . . . http://www.ssimicro.com/~xpsognwt/Net//departments/Dept-Transport.HTML
Department of the Executive . . . . http://www.ssimirro.com/~xpsognwt/Net/departments/Dept-Executive.HTML

Government of Nova Scotia
Nova Scotia Government Site . . . . http://www.gov.ns.ca/
Office of the Premier. . . . . http://www.gov.ns.ca/govt/prem/
Legislative House of Assembly . . . . http://www.gov.ns.ca/legi/house.htm
Canada-Nova Scotia Offshore Petroleum Board. . . . . http://Fox.nstn.ca:80/~cnsopb/
Department of Agriculture & Marketing. . . . . http://www.nsac.ns.ca/nsdam/
Department of Business & Consumer Services . . . . http://www.gov.ns.ca/bacs/
Department of Education & Culture . . . . http://www.ednet.ns.ca/
Department of Finance. . . . . http://www.gov.ns.ca/fina/
Department of Fisheries . . . . http://www.gov.ns.ca/fish/
Department of Housing & Municipal Affairs . . . . http://www.gov.ns.ca/homa/
Department of Human Resources. . . . . http://www.gov.ns.ca/humr/
Department of Justice . . . . http://www.gov.ns.ca/just/
Department of Labour . . . . http://www.gov.ns.ca/labr/
Department of Natural Resources. . . . . http://www.gov.ns.ca/natr/
Department of the Environment . . . . http://www.gov.ns.ca/envi/
Government Purchasing - Public Tenders Office . . . . http://www.gov.ns.ca/fina/ptns/index.htm
Innovation Corporation (InNOVAcorp) . . . . http:www.innovacorp.ns.ca
Nova Scotia Advisory Council on the Status of Women . . . . http://www.gov.ns.ca/govt/staw/
Nova Scotia Economic Renewal Agency . . . . http://www.gov.ns.ca/ecor/
Nova Scotia Film Development Corporation. . . . . http://fox.nstn.ca/~nsfdc/
Nova Scotia Human Rights Commission . . . . http://www.gov.ns.ca/just/humanrts/
Nova Scotia Police Commission. . . . . http://www.gov.ns.ca/just/services.htm#POLCOM
Nova Scotia Research Foundation Corporation . . . . http://www.nsrfc.ns.ca
Nova Scotia Technology & Science Secretariat. . . . . http://www.gov.ns.ca/tss/
Office of the Auditor General . . . . http://www.gov.ns.ca/legi/audg/
Office of the Ombudsman . . . . http://www.gov.ns.ca/govt/ombu/
Waterfront Development Corporation. . . . . http://www.gov.ns.ca/ecor/cpr/aagagi.htm#wdc
Workers' Compensation Board of Nova Scotia. . . . . http://www.pixelmotion.ns.ca/wcb/

Government of Ontario
Ontario Government Site. . . . . http://www.gov.on.ca/
Office of the Premier. . . . . http://www.gov.on.ca/premier/office/html
Government Caucus Services. . . . . http://ontariopc.on.ca
Office of the Official Opposition (Lib.) . . . . http://www.io.org/~liberal
Office of the New Democratic Party (NDP) . . . . http://www.ndp.on.ca
Executive Council . . . . http://ontla.on.ca/members/exec.htm
Legislative Assembly. . . . . http://www.ontla.on.ca
Information & Privacy Commissioner of Ontario. . . . . http://www.ipc.on.ca
Ministry of Agriculture, Food & Rural Affairs . . . . http://tdg.uoguelph.ca/omafra/start.html
Ministry of Community & Social Services . . . . http://www.gov.on.ca/CSS/
Ministry of Economic Development, Trade & Tourism. gopher://govonca.gov.on.ca:70/11/medt/english
Ministry of Education & Training . . . . http://www.edu.gov.on.ca
Ministry of Environment & Energy. . . . . http://www.ene.gov.on.ca/
Ministry of Finance . . . . http://www.gov.ca/FIN/hmpage.html
Ministry of Municipal Affairs & Housing. . . . . http://nrserv.mmah.gov.on.ca/
Ministry of Natural Resources . . . . http://www.mnr.gov.on.ca/mnr/
Ministry of Transportation . . . . http://www.gov.on.ca/MTO/
Office of the Lieutenant Governor . . . . http://ontla.on.ca/assemsrv/lg.htm
Ontario Arts Council. . . . . http://www.ffa.ucalgary.ca/oac/index.html
Ontario Film Development Corporation . . . . http://www.to-ontfilm.com/
Ontario Hydro . . . . http://www.hydro.on.ca/
Ontario Provincial Police . . . . http://www.gov.on.ca/opp/
Ontario Science Centre . . . . http://www.osc.on.ca/
Workers' Compensation Board . . . . http://www.wcb.on.ca/

Government of Prince Edward Island
Prince Edward Island Government Site . . . . http://www.gov.pe.ca/
Office of the Premier. . . . . http://www.gov.pe.ca/premier/index.html
Executive Council . . . . http://www.gov.pe.ca/ec/index.html
Legislative Assembly. . . . . http://www.gov.pe.ca/leg.index.html
Department of Agriculture, Fisheries & Forestry. . . . . http://www.gov.pe.ca/daff/index.html
Department of Economic Development & Tourism. . . . . http://www.gov.pe.ca/edt/index.html
Department of Education. . . . . http://www.gov.pe.ca/educ/index.html
Department of Environmental Resources . . . . http://www.gov.pe.ca/env/index.html
Department of Health & Social Services . . . . http://www.gov.pe.ca/hss/index.html
Department of Provincial Affairs & Attorney General . . . . http://www.gov.pe.ca/paag/index.html
Department of Transportation & Public Works . . . . http://www.gov.pe.ca/tpw/index.html
Department of the Provincial Treasury . . . . http://www.gov.pe.ca/pt/index.html
Enterprise PEI . . . . http://www.gov.pe.ca/edt/epei.html
Food Technology Centre . . . . http://www.gov.pe.ca/ftc/index.html

Office of Higher Education, Training & Adult Learning . . . . http://www.gov.pe.ca/ohet/index.html
Office of the Lieutenant Governor. . . . . http://www.gov.pe.ca/lg/index.html

Government of Québec
Québec Government Site. . . . . http://www.gouv.qc.ca/
Assemblée nationale. . . . . http://www.assnat.qc.ca/assnat
Cabinet du premier ministre . . . . http://www.gouv.qc.ca/anglais/premin/premin_intro.html
Conseil exécutif. . . . . http://www.gouv.qc.ca/francais/minorg/mcex/mcex_intro.html
Conseil de la science et de la technologie . . . . http://www.cst.gouv.qc.ca/cst/cst_mandatE.html
Conseil du trésor. . . . . http://www.riq.qc.ca/scthtml/sct.htm
L'Inspecteur général des Institutions financières . . . . http://www.igif.gouv.qc.ca/igif
Ministère de l'Agriculture, des Pêcheries et de l'Alimentation . . . . http://www.agr.gouv.qc.ca/mapaq/
Ministère de l'Éducation . . . . http://www.gouv.qc.ca/francais/minorg/medu/medu_intro.html
Ministère de l'Environnement et de la Faune. . . . . http://www.mef.gouv.qc.ca
Ministère de l'Industrie, du commerce, de la Science et de la technologie . . . . http://www.gouv.qc.ca/francais/minorg/micst/micst_intro.html
Ministère de la Culture et des Communications. . . . . http://www.gouv.qc.ca/francais/minorg/mccq/mccq_intro.html
Ministère de la Justice . . . . http://www.gouv.qc.ca/francais/minorg/mjust/mjust_intro.html
Ministère de la Santé et des services sociaux. . . . . http://www.gouv.qc.ca/francais/minorg/msss/msss_intro.html
Ministère de la Sécurité du revenu . . . . http://www.gouv.qc.ca/francais/minorg/msp/msp_intro.html
Ministère de la Sécurité publique . . . . http://www.secpub.bouv.qc.ca/secpub/index.html
Ministère des Affaires Municipales . . . . http://www.mam.gouv.qc.ca/mam/annuaire.html
Ministère des Finances . . . . http://www.finances.gouv.qc.ca/
Ministère des Relations Internationales . . . . http://www.mri.gouv.qc.ca/introan.htm
Ministère des Ressources Naturelles . . . . http://www.mrn.gouv.qc.ca
Ministère des Transports . . . . http://www.gouv.qc.ca/francais/minorg/mtrans/mtrans_intro.html
Ministère du Travail. . . . . http://www.travail.gouv.qc.ca/
Protecteur du Citoyen . . . . http://www.ombuds.gouv.qc.ca
Secrétariat à la famille . . . . http://www.gouv.qc.ca/gouv/francais/minorg/sfamille/const.html
Secrétariat aux affaires autochtones. . . . . http://www.gouv.qc.ca/gouv/francais/minorg/saa/index.html
Secrétariat aux affaires intergouvernementales canadiennes . . . . http://www.bouv.qc.ca/francais/minorg/maig/maig_intro.html
Tourisme Québec . . . . http://www.gouv.qc.ca/francais/minorg/mto/mto_intro.html

Government of Saskatchewan
Saskatchewan Government Site . . . . http://www.gov.sk.ca/
Office of the Premier . . . . http://www.sasknet.sk.ca
Government Caucus Office (NDP) . . . . http://www.sasknet.com/~ndpmla/
Office of the Third Party (PC) . . . . http://www.wbm.ca/actionet/pc/
Executive Council. . . . . http://www.gov.sk.ca/execcoun/cabinet.htm#nillson
Legislative Assembly . . . . http://www.gov.sk.ca/members.htm
Saskatchewan Agriculture & Food. . . . . http://www.gov.sk.ca/agfood/
Saskatchewan Crown Investments Corporation . . . . http://www.gov.sk.ca/govt/crowninv/
Saskatchewan Economic Development . . . . http://www.gov.sk.ca/govt/econdev/
Saskatchewan Education . . . . http://www.sasked.gov.sk.ca
Saskatchewan Energy Conservation & Development Authority http://www.innovplace.saskatoon.sk.ca:80/SECDA/
Saskatchewan Energy & Mines. . . . . http://www.gov.sk.ca/govt/enermine/
Saskatchewan Environment & Resource Management. . . . . http://www.gov.sk.ca/govt/environ/
Saskatchewan Finance . . . . http://www.gov.sk.ca/govt/finance/
Saskatchewan Health . . . . http://www.gov.sk.ca/govt/health/
Saskatchewan Highways & Transportation. . . . . http://www.gov.sk.ca/govt/highways/
Saskatchewan Human Rights Commission . . . . http://www.gov.sk.ca/govt/hrc/
Saskatchewan Indian & Metis Affairs Secretariat . . . . http://www.gov.sk.ca/govt/indmet/
Saskatchewan Intergovernmental Affairs . . . . http://www.gov.sk.ca/govt/intergov/
Saskatchewan Justice . . . . http://www.gov.sk.ca/govt/justice/
Saskatchewan Labour. . . . . http://www.gov.sk.ca/govt/labour/
Saskatchewan Municipal Board . . . . http://www.gov.sk.ca/govt/munibrd/
Saskatchewan Municipal Government. . . . . http://www.gov.sk.ca/govt/munigov/
Saskatchewan Opportunities Corporation. . . . . http://www.gov.sk.ca/soco/
Saskatchewan Post-Secondary Education & Skills Training . . . . http://www.gov.sk.ca/govt/pseduc/
Saskatchewan Research Council. . . . . http://www.src.sk.ca
Saskatchewan Social Services . . . . http://www.gov.sk.ca/govt/socserv/
Saskatchewan Telecommunications (SaskTel) . . . . http://www.sasktel.com/
Saskatchewan Wetland Conservation Corporation . . . . http://www.wetland.sk.ca/
Saskatchewan Women's Secretariat . . . . http://www.gov.sk.ca/govt/womsec/

Municipal & Regional Government
Annapolis County . . . . http://www.munofann@clan.tartannet.ns.ca/
Barrie . . . . http://www.city.barrie.on.ca/citymin.htm
Brockville. . . . . http://www.brockville.com
Burlington . . . . http://worldchat.com/cob
Capital Regional District . . . . http://vvv.com/crd/
Chilliwack. . . . . http://www.gov.chilliwack.bc.ca/
Coquitlam. . . . . http://www.gov.coquitlam.bc.ca/
Cornwall . . . . http://www.city.cornwall.on.ca
Cranbrook . . . . http://cyberlink.bc.ca/~pthiessen/cranb1.htm
Cumberland . . . . http://www.municipality.cumberland.on.ca
Edmonton . . . . http://www.gov.edmonton.ab.ca/city/
Gatineau. . . . . http://gamma.omnimage.ca/clients/gatineau/
Gloucester . . . . http://www.city.gloucester.on.ca/

Grande Prairie	http://www.ccinet.ab.ca/city-of-gp/homepage.html
Halifax	http://www.ccn.cs.dal.ca/Government/HRM/HRMHome.html/
Kitchener	http://www.oceta.on.ca/city.kitchener
Lachine	http://www/cum.qc.ca/LACHINE
Lanark County	http://www.county.lanark.on.ca
Lethbridge	http://www.city.lethbridge.ab.ca
Metropolitan Montréal	http://www.cum.qc.ca/
Metropolitan Toronto	http://www.metrotor.on.ca/
Mississauga	http://www.city.mississauga.on.ca
Montréal	http://www.ville.montreal.qc.ca/
Nanaimo	http://www.sd68.nanaimo.bc.ca/nol/welcome.html
Niagara Falls	http://www.niagara.com:80/city.niagara_falls/
Niagara	http://www.regional.niagara.on.ca/niagara/
North Vancouver	http://www.district.north-van.bc.ca/
Peel	http://www.region.peel.on.ca
Saint John	http://www.city.saint-john.nb.ca
Sherbrooke	http://ville.sherbrooke.qc.ca
Slave Lake	http://www.supernet.ab.ca/Communities/slavelake.html
St. Albert	http://www.city.st-albert.ab.ca
Surrey	http://www.city.surrey.bc.ca/
Tillsonburg	http://oxford.net/~tburg
Toronto	http://www.city.toronto.on.ca/
Vancouver Regional District	http://www.gvrd.bc.ca/index.html
Vaughan	http://www.city.vaughan.on.ca/
Victoria	http://www.city.victoria.bc.ca/
Waterloo	http://www.oceta.on.ca/region.waterloo/gov/
Yellowknife	http://www.city.yellowknife.nt.ca

Miscellaneous Government

Alberta Urban Municipalities Association	http://www.auma.ab.ca
American Research & Documentation Center	http://www.usis-canada.usia.gov
Archives nationales du Québec	http://www.anq.gouv.qc.ca
BC Archives & Records Service	http://www.bcars.gs.gov.bc.ca/bcars.html
Bibliothèque nationale du Québec	http://www.biblinat.gouv.qc.ca/
Canadian Council on Social Development	http://www.achilles.net/~council/
Canadian Defence Quarterly	http://www/baxter.net
Canadian Foundation for the Americas	http://www.focal.ca
Canadian Institute of International Affairs	http://www.trinity.utoronto.ca/ciia/intro.html
Canadian Institute of Planners	http://infoweb.magi.com/~cip/cip.html
Canadian Institute of Strategic Studies	http://www.ciss.ca
Canadian Public Policy	http://wwwqed.econ.queensu.ca/pub/cpp/
Canadian Tourism Commission - Tourism Reference & Documentation Centre	http://www.info.ic.gc.ca
Communist Party of Canada (Marxist-Leninist)	http://fox.nstn.ca/~cpc-ml/index.html
Economic Innovation & Technology Council - Industrial Technology Library	http://itc.mb.ca
Friends of the Mounted Police Museum	http://www.cs.uregina.ca/~mcintyre/rcmp_museum/rcmp.html
Green Party Political Association of British Columbia	http://www.islandnet.com/~bcgreens/
Green Party USA	http://www.greens.org/
Huntsman Marine Science Centre	http://www.unb.ca/web/huntsman
Institut québécois des hautes études internationales	http://www.ulaval.ca/iqhei
Intergovernmental Committee on Urban & Regional Research	http://www.icurr.org/icurr
International Labour Organisation	http://www.unicc.org/ilo
Liberal Party of Canada	http://www.liberal.ca/
Manitoba Legislative Assembly - Library	http://www.gov.mb.ca/leg-lib/contents.html
Municipal World	http://www.municipalworld.com
National Archives of Canada	http://www.archives.ca
National Film Board of Canada - Customer Services - Reference Service	http://www.nfb.ca
National Gallery of Canada - Library	http://national.gallery.ca
New Democratic Party	http://www.ncf.carleton.ca/freeport/government/fedelect/nat/ndp/menu
Ontario Professional Planners Institute	http://www.interlog.com/~oppi
Progressive Conservative Association of Alberta	http://www.albertapc.ab.ca
Progressive Conservative Party of Canada	http://www.pcparty.ca/
Provincial Archives of Alberta	http://www.ab.ca/~mcd/archives/index.htm
Recreation Association of the Public Service of Canada	http://www.magi.com/~racentre
Royal Canadian Regiment Association	http://www.anadas.com/rcr/f-association.html
Saskatchewan Provincial Library	http://www.lib.sk.ca/provlib/
Science for Peace	http://www.math.yorku.ca/sfp/
Sport Information Resource Centre	http://www.sirc.ca/
Standards Council of Canada - Document Centre	http://www.scc.ca
TeleLearning Research Network	http://fas.sfu.ca/telelearn
United Nations Development Programme	http://www.undp.org/
United Nations Environment Program	http://unep.unep.no/
Urban Development Institute of Canada	http://www.udi.bc.ca

HEALTH & MEDICAL

Acupuncture Foundation of Canada Institute	http://www.afcinstitute.com/afc.html
Addiction Research Foundation	http://www.arf.org
Alberta Doctors' Digest	http://www.amda.ab.ca

Alzheimer Society of Ottawa-Carleton	http://www.ncf.carleton.ca/freeport/social.services/alzheimer/menu
Amyotrophic Lateral Sclerosis Society of Canada	http://www.als.ca
Association of Ontario Health Centres	http://www.aohc.org
Breast Cancer Action	http://infoweb.magi.com/~bcanet/
British Columbia Naturopathic Association	http://www.infoserve.net:80/selene/bcna/
CMA News	http://www.cma.ca/news/menu.htm
Canadian Abortion Rights Action League	http://www.io.org/~caral
Canadian Association for Quality in Health Care	http://www.hwc.ca:8080/caqhc/
Canadian Association for Williams Syndrome	http://www.sos.on.ca/~pmackay/williams.html
Canadian Association of Emergency Physicians	http://unixg.ubc.ca:780/~grunfeld/caep.html
Canadian Association for Music Therapy	http://www.sos.cn.ca/~smacnay/camt/camt.html
Canadian Association of Optometrists	http://fox.nstn.ca/~eyedocs/caoorg.html
Canadian Association of Radiologists Journal	http://www.cma.ca/journals/carj
Canadian Bacterial Diseases Network	http://www.cbdn.ca/
Canadian Centre for Occupational Health & Safety	http://www.ccohs.ca/
Canadian Centre on Substance Abuse	http://www.ccsa.ca/default.htm
Canadian Coordinating Office for Health Technology Assessment	http://www.ccohta.ca
Canadian Diabetes Association	http://www.diabetes.ca/
Canadian Foundation for the Study of Infant Deaths	http://www.sidscanada.org/sids.html
Canadian Genetic Diseases Network	http://www.bc.irap.nrc.ca/ctn/cgdn/cgdn-e.html
Canadian HIV Trials Network	http://unixg.ubc.ca:780/~fortin/marcel.htm
Canadian HIV/AIDS Legal Network	http://www.odyssee.net/~jujube
Canadian Institute for Barrier-Free Design	http://cad9.cadlab.umanitoba.ca/uofm/cibfd.html
Canadian Intravenous Nurses Association	http://web.idirect.com/~csotcina
Canadian Journal of Cardiology	http://www.pulsus.com.home.htm
Canadian Journal of Infectious Diseases	http://www.plusus.com.home.htm
Canadian Journal of Psychiatry	http://www.medical.org
Canadian Journal of Respiratory Therapy	http://www.cma.ca/journals/cjrt
Canadian Journal of Rural Medicine	http://www.cma.ca/journals/cjrm
Canadian Journal of Surgery	http://www.cma.ca/journals/cjs
Canadian Medical Association Journal	http://www.cma.ca/journals/cmaj
Canadian Mental Health Association	http://www.io.org/~cmhator/
Canadian Organization for Advancement of Computers in Health	http://www.agt.net/public/coachorg
Canadian Play Therapy Institute	http://www.playtherapy.org/
Canadian Psychiatric Association	http://medical.org
Canadian Psychological Association	http://www.phoenix.ca/cpa/
Canadian Society for International Health	http://hpb1.hwc.ca:8500/default.html
Canadian Society of Hospital Pharmacists	http://www.cshp.ca/~cshp
Canadian Society of Laboratory Technologists	http://cslt.com/
Canadian Society of Orthopaedic Technologists	http://web.idirect.com/~scotcina
Candlelighters Childhood Cancer Foundation Canada	http://www.candlelighters.ca
Centre for Studies of Aging	http://library.utoronto.ca/www/aging/depthome.html
Centre for Toxicology	http://www.uoguelph.ca/cntc/
Centre hospitalier régional du Suroît	http://www.rocler.qc.ca/chrs/chrs.html
Clinical and Investigative Medicine	http://www.cma.ca/journals/cim
Community AIDS Treatment Information Exchange	http://www.catie.ca
Deer Lodge Centre Inc.	http://www.mbnet.mb.ca/cvm/health/deerlod2.html
Dept. of Health & Community Services - Communications	http://www.gov.nb.ca/hcs/
Epilepsy Canada	http://www.generation.net/~epilepsy/
Epilepsy Ontario	http://www.epilepsy.org
Health Action Network Society	http://www.hans.org/
Healthcare Management FORUM	http://www.hurc.ca:8080/cchse/
Human Life International	http://hli.org
Infant Feeding Action Coalition	http://www.io.org/~infacto
Infant/Maternal Nutrition Education Association	http://www.io.org/~infacto
International Association for Medical Assistance to Travellers	http://www.sentex.net/~iamat
International Council of AIDS Service Organizations	http://www.web.apc.org/~icaso/webpage.html
Journal of Psychiatry & Neuroscience	http://www.medical.org
Journal of Rheumatology	http://biginc.on.ca/jrheum
Kaiser Youth Foundation	http://www.tether.com/KYF
ME Support Network	http://www.freenet.mb.ca/community/bscn/iphome/m/mesn/index.html
McGill University - Health Sciences Library	http://www.health.library.mcgill.ca
Medical Post	http://www.io.org/~cjaimet/outlook/outlook.html
Medical Research Council of Canada	http://www.hwc.ca:8100/
Mediscan	http://www.ualberta.ca/~cfms/
Michener Institute for Applied Health Sciences	http://www.michener.on.ca
Multiple Sclerosis Society of Canada	http://www.mssoc.ca
Muscular Dystrophy Association of Canada	http://www.trends.ca/MDAC
Mycological Society of Toronto	http://www.id.org/mst.htm
National Institute of Nutrition	http://www.hwc.ca:8080/nin
Ontario Lung Association	http://www.on.lung.ca
Ontario Medical Review	http://www.oma.org
Oral Health	http://www.southam.com/b1-3-1.html
Ordre des dentistes du Québec	http://odq.qc.ca
Ordre professionnel des diététistes du Québec	http://www.opdq.org
Physicians for Global Survival (Canada)	http://www.web.apc.org/~pgs/
Physiotherapy Association of BC	http://www.interchg.ubc.ca/pmacgreg/index.htm
Protein Engineering Network of Centres of Excellence	http://diadem.biochem.ualberta.ca/pence.html

Society of Obstetricians & Gynaecologists of Canada	http://www.medical.org/sogc_docs/SOGC.html
St. Boniface General Hospital	http://bison.umanitoba.ca
Thyroid Foundation of Canada	http://www.io.org/~thyroid/canada.html
Toronto PWA Foundation	http://www.io.org/~pwa
Toronto Vegetarian Association	http://www.interlog.com/~tva
Transcultural Psychiatric Research Review	http://www.mcgill.ca/psychiatry
University of Manitoba - Neil John Maclean Health Sciences Library	http://www.cc.umanitoba.ca/libraries/medical/main.html
Winnipeg Vegetarian Association	http://www.mbnet.mb.ca/~wva/index.html

INDUSTRY

Aboriginal Tourism Authority Inc.	http://www.aboriginalnet.com/tourism
Access	http://www.OLA.ca.dyna.com
Agents immobiliers du Québec	http://www.prospection.qc.ca/agents/
Alberta Association of Courseware Producers	http://www.sas.ab.ca/aacp/
Alberta Hotel Association	http://www.albertahotels.ab.ca
Alberta Tourism Partnership Corporation	http://www.atp.ab.ca/
Alberta Wheat Pool	http://fis.awp.com
American Society of Association Executives	http://www.asaenet.org/
Annuaire Téléphonique de la Construction du Québec	http://www.optilog.com
Applied Science Technologists & Technicians of British Columbia	http://www.imaginet.ca/asttbc/
Architectural Institute of British Columbia	http://www.aibc.bc.ca/home.html
Associated Designers of Canada	http://www.ffa.ucalgary.ca/adc/indexadc.htm
Association des agences de publicité du Québec	http://www.aapq.qc.ca
Association for the Export of Canadian Books	http://infoweb.magi.com/~aecb/
Association of Architectural Technologists of Ontario	http://aecinfo.com/assoc/aato/index.htm
Association of Canadian Publishers	http://www.can.net/marketplace/pub/acp/acp.htm
Association of Consulting Engineers of Canada	http://buildingweb.com/acec
Association of Consulting Engineers of Manitoba Inc.	http://www.tetres.ca/acem/index.html
Association of Engineering Technicians & Technologists of Newfoundland	http://www.cabot.nf.ca/CCTT/aettn/index.html
Association of Exploration Geochemists	http://aeg.org/aeg/aeghome.htm/
Association of Independent Consultants	http://www.io.org/~duke/Files/AIC/AIC-home.html
Association of Professional Engineers of Nova Scotia	www.cfn.cs.dal.ca/technology/apens/apenspg.html
Association of Professional Engineers, Geologists & Geophysicists of Alberta	http://www.apegga.com
Association of Women in Engineering & Science	gopher://freenet.edmonton.ab.ca:70/11/i/awes
Association touristique de l'Outaouais	http://www.achilles.net/~ato/
Automotive Industries Association of Canada	http://www.aftmkt.com
B.C. Agri Digest	http://www.shuswap.bc.ca/sunny/fkay-mg.htm
BBM Bureau of Measurement	http://www.bbm.ca/
Bay Area Business Women's Network	http://www.freenet.hamilton.on.ca/Information/business/BABWN/index.html
Bodyshop	http://www.southam.com/b1-1-2.html
British Columbia & Yukon Hotels Association	http://www.fleethouse.com/fhcanada/bc-acco.htm
British Columbia Technology Industries Association	http://technet.org
Building Owners & Managers Association International	http://www.boma.org
CANARIE Inc.	http://www.canarie.ca/
Calgary Construction Association	http://www.logicnet.com/calgary.const.association
Calgary Convention & Visitors Bureau	http://www.visitor.calgary.ab.ca/
Canadian Advanced Technology Association	http://www.cata.ca/
Canadian Alarm & Security Association	http://www.canasa.com
Canadian Association of Career Educators & Employers	http://www.cacee.com/workweb
Canadian Association of Drilling Engineers	http://www.lexicom.ab.ca/~cade
Canadian Association of Home Inspectors	http://www.bconnex.net/~jmlueck/cahi.html
Canadian Association of Internet Providers	http://www.caip.ca/
Canadian Association of Mining Equipment & Services for Export	http://www.info-mine.com/camese
Canadian Association of Petroleum Producers	http://www.capp.ca
Canadian Association of Senior Travellers	http://www.seniorsnet.com/cast.htm
Canadian Booksellers Association	http://www.cbabook.org
Canadian Centre for Creative Technology	http://www.ccct.ca
Canadian Centre for Occupational Health & Safety	http://www.ccohs.ca/
Canadian Chemical Producers' Association	http://www.ccpa.ca
Canadian Council for Human Resources in the Environment Industry	http://www.chatsubo.com/cchrei
Canadian Council of Technicians & Technologists	http://www.cabot.nf.ca/CCTT/index.html
Canadian Dairy	http://www.inforamp.net/~dbattler
Canadian Energy Pipeline Association	http://www.cepa.com
Canadian Environment Industry Association	http://www.ceia.org
Canadian Environment Industry Association - British Columbia	http://www.ceia-bc.com/
Canadian Food Brokers Association	http://web.idirect.com/~cfba
Canadian Independent Record Production Association	http://www.cmrra.ca/cirpa
Canadian Industrial Equipment News	http://www.southam.com/b1-5-1.html
Canadian Industrial Innovation Centre	http://www.innovationcentre.ca
Canadian Institute for Barrier-Free Design	http://cad9.cadlab.umanitoba.ca/uofm/cibfd.html
Canadian Institute of Forestry	http://www.episet/cif
Canadian Institute of Gemmology	http://deepcove.com/cig
Canadian Magazine Publishers Association	http://www.cmpa.ca/
Canadian Meat Importers Committee	http://www.importers.ca
Canadian Mineral Analysts	http://www.info-mine.com/assoc-inst/cma/
Canadian Mining Journal	http://www.southam.com.b1-6-1.html
Canadian Morgan Horse Association Inc.	http://www.osha.igs.net/~cmha/index.htm

Canadian Almanac & Directory 1997

Canadian National Aboriginal Tourism Association	http://www.v1i.ca/clients/abc/cnata/cnata3.htm
Canadian Network for the Advancement of Research, Industry & Education	http://www.canarie.ca
Canadian Oil Scouts Association	http://www.canpic.ca/COSA
Canadian Plastics	http://www.southam.com/magazines/plastics.html
Canadian Plastics Directory & Buyer's Guide	http://www.southam.com/magazines/plastics.html
Canadian Port & Harbour Association	http://www.newswire.ca/cpha.
Canadian Prestressed Concrete Institute	http://www.buildingweb.com/cpci/
Canadian Publishers' Council	http://www.pubcouncil.ca
Canadian Society for Chemical Engineering	http://fox.nstn.ca/~cic_adm/csche.html
Canadian Society for Chemical Technology	http://fox.nstn.ca/~cic_adm/csct.html
Canadian Society for Chemistry	http://fox.nstn.ca/~cic_adm/csc.html
Canadian Society of Agricultural Engineering	http://www.engr.usask.ca/societies/csae/
Canadian Society of Petroleum Geologists	http://www.cspg.org
Canadian Society of Safety Engineering, Inc.	http://www.csse.org
Canadian Soft Drink Association	http://www.softdrink.ca
Canadian Sphagnum Peat Moss Association	http://www.peatmoss.com
Canadian Standardbred Horse Society	http://home.ican.net/~troton
Canadian Standards Association	http://www.csa.ca/isotes
Canadian Tourism Commission - Tourism Reference & Documentation Centre	http://www.info.ic.gc.ca
Canadian Travel Press	http://www.baxter.net
Canadian Turkey Marketing Agency	http://www.canturk.ca
Canadian Vending	http://www.vendnet.com
Canadian Well Logging Society	http://www.canpic.ca/CWLS
Canadian Western Agribition Association	http://www.sasknet.com/corporate/Agribition/
Canadian Wood Council	http://www.cwc.metrics.com/
Certified Technicians & Technologists Association of Manitoba	http://www.rots.net/~cttam
Charolais Banner	http://www.charolaisbanner.com
Christmas Tree Growers' Association of Ontario Inc.	http://www.christmastree.on.ca
Condominium Manager	http://www.bbandc.com
Conseil de l'enveloppe du bâtiment du Québec	http://www.aecinfo.com/qbec/index.html
Consultative Group on International Agricultural Research	http://www.worldbank.org/html/cgiar/HomePage.html
Cornwall & Seaway Valley Tourism	http://www.visit.cornwall.on.ca
Country Guide	http://www.agriculture.com
Crop Protection Institute of Canada	http://www.cropro.org
Dairy Farmers of Ontario	http://www.milk.org/
Dairy Guide	http://www.mbnet.mb.ca/~wilkins
EP&T Electronic Products & Technology	http://www/ept.ca
EcoDesign Resource Society	http://www.ecodesign.bc.ca
Economic Innovation & Technology Council - Industrial Technology Library	http://itc.mb.ca
Edmonton Construction Association	http://www.planet.eon.net/~tonto/eca.html
Electricity Today	http://www.electricityforum.com
Electronic Commerce Canada	http://www.globalx.net/eca/
Engineering Dimensions	http://www.peo.on.ca
Environmental Services Association of Alberta	http://www.ccinet.ab.ca/esaa/home.html
Food Institute of Canada	http://foodnet.fic.ca
Foodservice & Hospitality	http://www.foodservice.ca
Forestry Chronicle	http://www.cif-ifc.org
Gifts & Tablewares	http://www.southam.com/b1-9-1/html
Globe Foundation of Canada	http://www.globe.ca
Greater Toronto Homebuilders' Association	http://www.aecinfo.com/gthba/index.html
Green Building Information Council	http://greenbuilding.ca
Heavy Construction News	http://www.io.org/~hcn
Holstein Association of Canada	http://www.holstein.ca/index.htm
Hotelier	http://www.foodservice.ca
Independent Power Producers Society of Ontario	http://www.newenergy.org/newenergy
Industry Canada - Technology Partnerships Canada	http://info.ic.gc.ca/ic-data/industry/tpc/broche.html
Information Technology Association of Canada	http://www.itac.ca/ITAC.home
Institute of Electrical & Electronics Engineers Canada	http://www.ieee.ca
Interior Designers Institute of British Columbia	http://www.designsource.bc.ca
International Institute for Sustainable Development	http://www.iisd.ca/linkages/
Jobber News	http://www.southam.com/b1-1-3.html
Journal of Canadian Petroleum Technology	http://www.canpic.ca/PETSOC
Kingston Area Economic Development Commission	http://www.kingstonarea.on.ca
Kootenay Country Tourist Association	http://travel.bc.ca.kootenay
L'Automobile	http://www.southam.com/b1-1-1.html
La Barrique	http://www.magnet.ca/wine
Laboratory Product News	http://www.southam.com/b1-5-3.html
Le Bulletin des Agriculteurs	http://www.cyberplex.com/bulletin
Les Papetières du Québec	http://www.southam.com/b1-7-1.html
MacLachlan Woodworking Museum	http://mal.rmc.ca/museum/home.html
Machinery & Equipment MRO	http://www.southam.com/b1-5-4.html
Madison's Canadian Lumber Directory	http://www.dowco.com/cmd/madisons
Manitoba Association of Architects	http://cad9.cadlab.umanitoba.ca/MAA.html
Manitoba Labour - Workplace Safety & Health Library	http://www.gov.mb.ca/manitoba/safety
Manufacturing Research Corporation of Ontario	http://network.admin.ists.ca/OCE/mrco.html
Masthead	http://www.the-wire.com/bishop/biginc.html

Mining Association of Canada	http://www.mining.ca
Motor Dealers' Association of Alberta	http://www.compusmart.ab.ca/mdaalta
National Agri-Food Technology Centre	http://www.eitc.mb.ca/naf/
National Farmers Union	http://www.wbm.ca/users/farmers
Newfoundland Environmental Industry Association	http://enterprise.newcomm.net/webpage/neia
Northern Aquaculture	http://www.naqua.com/
Northern Miner	http://www.northernminer.com/
Northern Ontario Tourist Outfitters Association	http://virtualnorth.com/noto/
Nova Scotia Environmental Industry Association	http://www.nseia.ns.ca/nseia
Nunavut Tourism	http://nunanet.com/~nunanet.com
Office des congrès et du tourisme du Grand Montréal	http://www.cum.qc.ca/octgm/Welcome.html
Ontario Association of Certified Engineering Technicians & Technologists	http://www.onramp.ca/business/oacett/
Ontario Beef	http://www.cattle.guelph.on.ca
Ontario Centre for Materials Research	http://www.queensu.ca/ocmr
Ontario Community Newspapers Association	http://www.ocna.org
Ontario Land Surveyor Quarterly	http://www/interlog.com/~aols
Ontario Milk Marketing Board	http://www.milk.org/
Ontario Professional Planners Institute	http://www.interlog.com/~oppi
Pacific Music Industry Association	http://www.nextlevel.com/pmia/
Pacific Rim Institute of Tourism	http://www.fleethouse.com/fhcanada/western/bc/pit-home.htm
Petroleum Communication Foundation	http://www.pcf.ab.ca
Petroleum Services Association of Canada	http://www.psac.ca
Petroleum Services Trading Association of Canada	http://www.petro-trade.ab.ca
Petroleum Society of CIM	http://www.canpic.ca/PETSOC/
Plastics Business	http://www.southam.com/magazines/plastics.html
Prairie Implement Manufacturers Association	http://www.pima.ca
Professional Association of Canadian Theatres	http://www.culturenet.ucalgary.ca/pact
Professional Engineers Ontario	http://www.peo.on.ca
Prospector Exploration & Investment Bulletin	http://www.info_mine.com/daily.news/
Publisher	http://www.sentex.net/~ccna/
Pulp & Paper Canada	http://www.southam.com/b1-7-2.html
Quincaillerie-Matériaux	http://www.cyberplex.com/quincaillerie
Restaurant & Foodservices Association of British Columbia & the Yukon	http://www.yes.net/RFABCY/
Roofing Contractors Association of British Columbia	http://www.rcabc.org
Royal Agricultural Winter Fair Association	http://www.royalfair.org
Royal Architectural Institute of Canada	http://www.aecinfo.com/raic/index.html
SMART Toronto	http://www.canada.hp.com/smarttoronto
Salon Beauté	http://www.salonline.com
Salon Magazine	http://www.salonline.com
Saskatchewan Applied Science Technologists & Technicians	http://www.siast.sk.ca/~wasect/sastt.html
Saskatchewan Motion Picture Association	http://midxpress.com/midxpress/smpia/main.htm
Saskatchewan Recording Industry Association	http://www.ffa.ucalgary.ca/scco/sria.html
Service Station & Garage Management	http://www.southam.com/b1-1-4.html
Ship Stamp Society	http://www.sron.ruu.nl/~erikp/sss.html
Society of Graphic Designers of Canada	http://www.swifty.com/gdc/
Springhill Miners Museum	http://www.grtplaces.com/ac/mine
Standards Council of Canada - Document Centre	http://www.scc.ca
Structural Board Association	http://www.sba_osb.ca
TeleLearning Research Network	http://fas.sfu.ca/telelearn
Tourism Industry Association of Canada	http://www.achilles.net/~tiac/homepage.html
Tourism Industry Association of PEI	http://www.gov.pe.ca/conv/tiapei.html
Tourism Victoria/Greater Victoria Visitors & Convention Bureau	http://travel.victoria.bc.ca/
Tourism Winnipeg	http://www.tourism.winnipeg.mb.ca/tourismw/
Trout Unlimited Canada	http://www.freenet.calgary.ab.ca/populati/community/trout.html
Union des producteurs agricoles	http://www.upa.qc.ca/
Urban Development Institute of Canada	http://www.udi.bc.ca
Vancouver Coast & Mountains Tourism Region	http://travel.bc.ca
Western Producer	http://www.producer.com/
Women's Entrepreneurship Program	http://www.mgmt.utoronto.ca
Wool Bureau of Canada	http://www.woolmark.com

LABOUR & TRADES

Association des propriétaires d'autobus du Québec	http://www.apaq.qc.ca
British Columbia Teachers' Federation	http://www.bctf.bc.ca
Canadian Centre for Occupational Health & Safety	http://www.ccohs.ca/
Canadian Council for Human Resources in the Environment Industry	http://www.chatsubo.com/cchrei
Communications, Energy & Paperworkers Union of Canada (CLC)	http://www.cep.ca/cep/
Edmonton Construction Association	http://www.planet.eon.net/~tonto/eca.html
International Labour Organisation	http://www.unicc.org/ilo
L'Ordre professionnel des conseillers en relations industrielles du Québec	http://www.opcriq.qc.ca
Labour	http://www.mun.ca/cclh/
Manitoba Labour - Workplace Safety & Health Library	http://www.gov.mb.ca/manitoba/safety
Ontario Society for Training & Development	http://www.ncf.carleton.ca/freeport/prof.assoc/ostd/menu
Public Service Alliance of Canada (CLC)	http://www.psac.com/
Roofing Contractors Association of British Columbia	http://www.rcabc.org

Canadian Almanac & Directory 1997

LAW & JUSTICE

Andriessen & Associate	http://ourworld.compuserve.com/homepages/andriessen_and_associates
Baker, Newby & Company	http://www.bakernewby.com
Balfour Moss	http://saskweb.com/~balfourmoss
Blaney, McMurtry, Stapells, Friedman	http://www.blaney.com
Borden & Elliot	http://www.borden.com
Braithwaite Boyle	http://www.edmonton.com/web/injurylaw/
Bratty & Partners	http://www.bratty.com
Brent & Greenhorn	http://broadwaynet.com/~bandglaw
C.N. Karbaliotis	http://www.techne.com
Calvin Martin, Q.C.	http://fox.nstn.ca/~duc14/law.html
Canadian Association of Law Libraries	http://www.kingston.net/iknet/call
Canadian Association of Law Teachers	http://www.droit.umontreal.ca/acpd/liste/
Canadian Bar Association	http://cba.org/abc
Canadian Copyright Licensing Agency	http://cancopy.com/
Canadian HIV/AIDS Legal Network	http://www.odyssee.net/~jujube
Canadian Law & Economics Association	http://www.epas.utoronto.ca:5680/clea/clea.html
Canadian Society for the Advancement of Legal Technology	http://www.io.org/~csalt/csalt.htm
Chown, Cairns	http://www.chown-cairns.com/northland/cc
Cohen Highley Vogel & Dawson	http://www.icis.on.ca/chvd
Dianne Saxe	http://www.magic.ca/saxe/
Durocher Simpson	http://www.tgx.com/durocher
Eric P. Polten	http://www.poltenhodder.com/~ph
Farano, Green	http://www.inforamp.net/~goldfarb/
Ferguson Gifford	http://www.fergif.com
Filion, Wakely & Thorup	http://www.filion.on.ca
Fraser & Beatty	http://www.fraserbeatty.ca
Friends of the Mounted Police Museum	http://www.cs.uregina.ca/~mcintyre/rcmp_museum/rcmp.html
Goodman & Carr	http://www.goodmancarr.com
Gowlings	http://www.gowlings.com
Guberman, Garson	http://www.gubermangarson.com
Hughes, Amys	http://www.hughes-amys.on.ca/h-amys
Institut québécois des hautes études internationales	http://www.ulaval.ca/iqhei
International Environmental Liability Management Association	http://www.magic.ca/ielma/IELMA.html
Irvin H. Sherman, Q.C.	http://www.teraport.net/sherman/shermanl.html
Jamieson Bains	http://www.jblawyers.com
Karas & Associates	http://www.karas.ca
Kershman & Warren	http://www.bankruptlaw.com
Keyser Mason Ball	http://www.kmblaw.com
Koskie & Company	http://www.wbm.ca/koskie/
Koskie & Minsky	http://www.koskieminsky.com
L.S. Jackson	http://web.idirect.com/~kid
Labour	http://www.mun.ca/cclh/
Ladner Downs	http://www.ladner.com/ladner
Lancaster, Mix & Welch	http://www.lmw.com
Law Society of Alberta	http://www.law.ualberta.ca/lawsociety
Legal Education Society of Alberta	http://www.law.ualberta.ca/lesa/
Levine Associates	http://www.interlog.com/~levlaw/
Linda H. Kolyn	http://www.pathcom.com/~dadey/homepage.htm
Lindsay Kenney Law Office - Library	http://www.lindsaykenney.bc.ca
Lon Hall Attorneys	http://ourworld.compuserve.com/homepages/lha_ent_law
Low, Glenn & Card	http://www.canfind.com/index.html
MacTavish, de Lint, Hamersfeld	http://www.inforamp.net/~mdlh
Major, Caron	majorcaron.com
McCarthy Tétrault	http://www.mccarthy.ca
McDonald & Hayden	http://www.mchayden.on.ca
McInnes Cooper & Robertson	http://fox.nstn.ca/~mcrhfx/
Milner Fenerty	http://www.milfen.com
Murphy Collette Murphy	http://www.discribe.ca/marco
Osler, Hoskin & Harcourt	http://www.osler.com
Paul E. Harte	http://www.hartelaw.com
Pitblado & Hoskin	http://www.mts.net/~lawyers/text/pitblado.html
Poole Milligan	http://www.poolemilligan.ca
Poole, A.F.N., Q.C.	http://web.idirect.com/~poole/
Public Legal Education Association of Saskatchewan, Inc.	http://www.sfn.saskatoon.sk.ca.education/pleasask/index.html
Reid, McNaughton	http://reidlaw.com/lawyers
Reynolds, Mirth, Richards & Farmer	http://www.ualberta.ca/~law/firms/reynolds/
Robertson Stromberg	http://www.robertsonstromberg.com
Russell & DuMoulin	http://rdcounsel.com/rd
Shtabsky & Tussman	http://www.stlaw.com
Singleton Urquhart Scott Law Office - Library	http://www.singleton.com
Smith Lyons	http://www.smithlyons.ca
Stephen J. Lautens	http://beachnet.org/sjl
Stewart McKelvey Stirling Scales	http://www.nstn.ca/smss
Stringam Denecky	http://www.agt.net/public.lethlaw/sd.htm
Weir & Foulds	http://www.weirfoulds.com
West Coast Environmental Law Research Foundation	http://freenet.vancouver.bc.ca/local/wcel

William B. Horkins ... http://www.interlog.com/~horkins
Zalapski & Pahl ... http://www.tnc.com/zap/

PUBLIC SERVICES
Air Cadet League of Canada ... http://www.isisnet.com/smacdouga/rcac.html
Alberta Association for Community Living ... http://www.ccinet.ab.ca//aacl/
Association of Community Information Centres in Ontario ... http://www.web.apc.org/acico/
BC Council for the Family ... http://familyforum.com/
Bereaved Families of Ontario ... http://www.inforamp.net/~bfo
Big Brothers of Canada ... http://www.bbsc.ca
Boys & Girls Clubs of Canada - Boys & Girls Clubs of Newfoundland & Labrador ... http://www.stemnnet.nf.ca/~jpollard/
Canadian Association of Elizabeth Fry Societies ... http://www.web.apc.org/~kpate
Canadian Association of Senior Travellers ... http://www.seniorsnet.com/cast.htm
Canadian Avalanche Association ... http://www.avalanche.ca/snow
Canadian Career Development Foundation ... http://infoweb.magi.com/~ccdffcac
Canadian Council on Rehabilitation & Work ... http://www.ccrw.org
Canadian Dimension ... http://www.canadiandimension.mb.ca/cd/index.htm
Canadian Firefighter ... http://www.interhop.net/cdnff/cdnff.html
Canadian Grey Panthers Advocacy Network ... http://www.panthers.net
Canadian Hearing Society ... http://www.chs.ca
Canadian Home Builders' Association ... http://www.chba.ca
Child Find Canada Inc. ... http://www.discribe.ca/childfind/cfhome.htm
Community Action: Canada's Community Service Newspaper ... http://www.comact@interlog.com
Confédération des organismes familiaux du Québec inc. ... http://www.odyssee.net/~cofaq3ci/cofaq
Consumers' Association of Canada ... http://www.cfn.cs.dal.ca/Commerce/CAC/cacscript.html
Dying with Dignity ... http://www.web.apc.org/dwd
Independent Power Producers Society of Ontario ... http://www.newenergy.org/newenergy
International Development Research Centre ... http://www.idrc.ca/index.html
Kinsmen Rehabilitation Foundation of British Columbia ... http://mindlink.net/kinsmen_rehab/
Mensa Canada Communications ... http://www.canada.mensa.org/mensa
Missing Children Society of Canada ... http://www.childcybersearch.org
North America Missing Children Association Inc. ... http://namca.isisnet.com
Ontario Association for Community Living ... http://www.acl.on.ca
Ontario Association for Marriage & Family Therapy ... http://www.inforamp.net/~mbehar/index.htm
Ontario March of Dimes ... http://www.omod.org
Operation Go Home ... http://www.maracomm.com/ccsc/opgohome
Ottawa South Community Association ... http://www.ncf.carleton.ca/freeport/community.associations/osca/menu
Perception ... http://www.achilles.net/~council/
Prince George United Way ... http://www.pgonline.com/unitedway
Right to Die Society of Canada ... http://www.islandnet.com/~deathnet
Royal Life Saving Society Canada ... http://www.interlog.com/~jlogan/rlss/rlssc.html
School Counsellors Association of Newfoundland ... http://www.stemnet.nf.ca/Organizations/SCAN/
Scouts Canada ... http://www.scouts.ca
Suicide Information & Education Centre ... http://www.siec.ca
United Way of Barrie/South Simcoe ... http://www.bconnex.net/~uwbss
War Amputations of Canada ... http://www.waramps.ca
WaterCan ... http://ottawa.public.net/watercan/watercan.html

RECREATION
Active Living Alliance for Canadians with a Disability ... http://www.activeliving.ca/activeliving/alliance/alliance.html
Alberta Hotel Association ... http://www.albertahotels.ab.ca
Alberta Tourism Partnership Corporation ... http://www.atp.ab.ca/
Alpine Club of Canada ... http://www.culturenet.ucalgary.ca/acc/
Athletics: Canada's National Track & Field/Running Magazine ... http://www.io.org/~ontrack
Atlantic Film Festival ... http://www.ccn.cs.dal.ca/Culture/AFF/AFF-Home.html
Autopinion Annual ... http://www.caa.ca
BMW Club of Canada ... http://www.istgec.com/bmw/
Banff Festival of Mountain Films ... http://www.banffcentre.ab.ca/MFF/index.html
Barrow Bay & District Sports Fishing Association ... http://www.bltg.com/bbdsfa/
Baseball Canada ... http://www.cdnsport.ca/baseball
Basketball Canada ... http://www.cdnsport.ca/basketball/
Bluenose Soaring Club ... http://www.ccn.cs.dal.ca/Recreation/BSC/homebsc.html
Bobsleigh Canada ... http://www.cdnsport.ca/bobcan
British Columbia & Yukon Hotels Association ... http://www.fleethouse.com/fhcanada/bc-acco.htm
British Columbia Automobile Association ... http://www.bcaa.bc.ca
British North America Philatelic Society Ltd. ... http://www.composmart.ab.ca/stalbert/bnaps/htm
Bruce Trail Association ... http://www.brucetrail.org/
Canadian Amateur ... http://www.cac.ca
Canadian Amateur Diving Association Inc. ... http://www.diving.ca/diving/cada.html
Canadian Amateur Wrestling Association ... http://www.cdnsport.ca/~kellyd
Canadian Association for Health, Physical Education, Recreation & Dance ... http://www.cdnsport.ca/activeliving/cahperd/index.html
Canadian Automobile Association ... http://www.caa.ca
Canadian Biker ... http://canadianbiker.com
Canadian Bridge Federation ... http://www.cbf.ca/query/CBFHome.html
Canadian Canoe Association ... http://www.openface.ca/paddle/
Canadian Coin News ... http://www.trajan.com/coin.default.ehtml

Canadian Curling Association	http://www.cdnsport.ca/curling
Canadian Fencing Federation	http://www.fencing.ca/
Canadian Figure Skating Association	http://www.cfsa.ca/
Canadian Fitness & Lifestyle Research Institute	http://activeliving.ca/activeliving/cflri.html
Canadian Football League	http://www.cfl.ca/
Canadian Hockey Association	http://www.cadnsport.ca/hockey
Canadian In-Line & Roller Skating Association	http://www.io.org/~cirsa/cirsa.html
Canadian Intramural Recreation Association	http://www.cdnsport.ca/activeliving/cira.html
Canadian Living	http://www.canadianliving.com
Canadian Parks & Wilderness Society	http://web.idirect.com/~wildland
Canadian Parks/Recreation Association	http://www.cdnsport.ca/activeliving/cpra.html
Canadian Quilters Association	http://www.nt.net/~giselef/cqaacc1.htm
Canadian Recreational Canoeing Association	http://www.crca.ca/
Canadian Ski Council	http://www.skican.org
Canadian Special Olympics Inc.	http://www.incontext.ca/cso/index.html
Canadian Sport & Fitness Administration Centre	http://www.cdnsport.ca/
Canadian Sport Council	http://cansport.magi.com/cansport
Canadian Sport Parachuting Association	http://www.islandnet.com/~murrays/cspa.html
Canadian Sporting Arms & Ammunition Association	http://www.eagle.ca/showgun
Canadian Stamp News	http://www.trajan.com/stamp/default.ehtml
Canadian Tennis Association	http://www.tenniscanada.com
Canadian Volkssport Federation	http://www.teleport.com/~walking/canada.htm
Canadian Wheelchair Basketball Association	http://www.cwba.ca/
Canadian Yachting Association	http://www.cdnsport.ca/~smorrow
Canadian Youth Bridge Organization	http://jeeves.uwaterloo.ca/~esutherl/cyborg/cyborg.html
Cantrav West Services Ltd.	http://www.cantrav.com
Central Ontario Soaring Association	http://www.idirect.com/users/bobleger.html
Chess Federation of Canada	http://www.globalx.net/cfc/
Chickadee	http://www.owl.on.ca
Citizens for Safe Cycling	http://www.ncf.carleton.ca/freeport/community.associations/cfsc/menu
Coaching Association of Canada	http://www.coach.ca/
ÉCHEC+	http://www.er.uqam.ca/merlingh/191873/fge.htm
Embroiderers' Association of Canada, Inc.	http://www.antibe.com/westview/eac.html
Erin Soaring Society	http://watarts.uwaterloo.ca/~cemaclea/ess.html
Fédération du plongeon amateur du Québec	http://www.cigp.com/atlanta/federati/plongeon/
Field Hockey Canada	http://www.cdnsport.ca/~snichols/1fhc.html
Gatineau Gliding Club	http://www.PubNIX.Net/~rmacpher/ggc.html
Guelph Gliding & Soaring Association	http://www.thinkage.on.ca/~GG&SA/
Hang Gliding & Paragliding Association of Canada	http://www.cadvision.com/Home_Pages/accounts/midtoad/hpac.html
Hike Ontario	http://www.freenet.durham.org/hikeon/
International Curling Information Network Group	http://netaccess.on.ca/icing/icehome.htm
Just for Laughs Festival	http://www.hahaha.com
Kanawa: Canada's Canoeing & Kayaking Magazine	http://www.crca.ca/
Kids World Magazine	http://www.kidsworld-online.com
Kitchener-Waterloo Oktoberfest	http://www.sentex.net/oktoberfest
Living Safety	http://www.safety-council.org
London International Airshow	http://www.airshow.org/lias.html
MW Productions	http://www.mwprod.com
Making Scenes Film & Video Festival	http://fox.nstn.ca/~scenes/
Manitoba Recreational Canoeing Association	http://kohlrabi.cs.umanitoba.ca/mrca/mrca.html
Manitoba Sports Hall of Fame & Museum Inc.	http://www.sport.mb.ca
Masters Swimming Canada	http://www.unb.ca/web/Masters_swimming/index.html
McGill University Conference Office	http://www.mcgill.ca/mco
Meteor Show Productions Inc.	http://www.meteorshows.com
Model Aeronautics Association of Canada Inc.	http://www.maac.ca
Model Aviation Canada	http://www.maac.ca
Montréal World Film Festival	http://www.ffm-montreal.org/
National Hockey League Players' Association (Ind.)	http://www.nhlpa.com
National Tae Kwon-Do Federation	gopher://freenet.edmonton.ab.ca:70/11/i/taek
New Brunswick Outfitters Association	http://www.discribe.ca/nboa/nboahome.htm
Northern Ontario Tourist Outfitters Association	http://virtualnorth.com/noto/
Nunavut Tourism	http://nunanet.com/~nunanet.com
Office des congrès et du tourisme du Grand Montréal	http://www.cum.qc.ca/octgm/Welcome.html
Ontario Camping Association	http://www.ontcamp.on.ca
Ontario Federation of Snowmobile Clubs	http://www.transdata.ca/ofsc/index.html
Ontario Horticultural Association	http://www.interlog.com/~onthort
Ontario Motor Coach Association	http://www.omca.com/
Ontario Out of Doors	http://www.cyberplex.com/fishontario
Ontario Parks Association	http://www.hookup.net/~opa
Ontario Soaring Association	http://www.interlog.com/~kwithrow/osa.html
Ontario Trails Council	http://www.csp.trentu.ca/gomrm/otc.html
Ottawalk	http://www.ncf.carleton.ca/freeport/community.associations/ottawalk/menu
Outdoor Recreation Council of British Columbia	http://mindlink.net/outrec_council/outrec.htm
Pacific Horse Journal	http://www.ibnd.com/horsejnl
Physical Education Digest	http://www.cyberbeach.net/pedigest
Prince Edward Island Crafts Council	http://www.crafts-council.pe.ca/index.html
Radio Amateurs of Canada	http://www.rac.ca/
Régie de la sécurité dans les sports du Québec	http://www.rssq.gouv.qc.ca

Recreation Association of the Public Service of Canada . . . . http://www.magi.com/~racentre
Regina Folk Festival http://bfsmedia.com/RBCS/rff96/
Ringette Canada . . . . http://www.cdnsport.ca/~anikd
Royal Canadian Golf Association . . . . http://www.rcga.org
SOSA Gliding Club . . . . http://psych.utoronto.ca/~sosa/
Saskatchewan Crafts Council . . . . http://www.ffa.ucalgary.ca/scco/scc.html
Ship Stamp Society . . . . http://www.sron.ruu.nl/~erikp/sss.html
Ski Canada Magazine . . . . http://www.softnc.com/waveworks/skicanada.html
Ski Jumping Canada . . . . http://www.cdnsport.ca/jump
SkiTrax Magazine . . . . http://www.pedal.com
Softball Canada . . . . http://www.cdnsport.ca/softball/
Southex Exhibitions . . . . http://www.southex.com
Sport BC . . . . http://www.sport.bc.ca/SportBC/
Sport Information Resource Centre . . . . http://www.sirc.ca/
Squash Canada http://symphony.eecg.toronto.edu:8888/danv/
Swim Ontario . . . . http://www.interlog.com/~colburn
Trail Riders of the Canadian Rockies . . . . http://www.canuck.com/~trcr
Vancouver Soaring Association . . . . http://www.sd69.bc.ca/~vsoaring/vsa.html
Where Rocky Mountains . . . . http://www.wheremags.com/world
Where Toronto . . . . http://www.wheremags.com/world
Windsport . . . . http://www.windsport.com
WineTidings . . . . http://www.cmpa.ca/
York Soaring Association . . . . http://www.agile-graphics.com/york/

RELIGION
Atlantic School of Theology - Library . . . . http://novanet.ns.ca/ast/homepage.html
Canadian Baptist Ministries . . . . http://www.inforamp.net/~cbmcomp
Canadian Chapter of the International Council of Community Churches http://www.geocities.com/Heartland/3285
Canadian Conference of Catholic Bishops . . . . http://www.cam.org/~cccb/
Canadian Council of Christians & Jews . . . . http://www.interlog.com/~cccj/
Christian Aid Mission . . . . http://www.christianaid.ca
Compass: A Jesuit Journal . . . . http://www.io.org/~gvanv/compass/comphome.html
Evangelical Fellowship of Canada . . . . http://www.efc-canada.com
Jewish Tribune . . . . http://www.canada_ibm.net/bnaibrith/
McMaster Journal of Theology & Ministry . . . . http://www.mcmaster.ca/divinity
Mennonite Brethren Herald . . . . http://www.cdnmbconf.ca/mb/mbherald.htm
Mennonite Central Committee Canada . . . . http://www.mennonitecc.ca/mcc
Missionary Union of the Clergy & Religious . . . . http://www.eda.net~missions
Ontario Centre for Religious Tolerance . . . . http://www.kosone.com/people/ocrt/ocrt_hp.htm
Orthodox Missionary Church of Canada . . . . http://phobos.astro.uwo.ca/~arenburg/omcc.html
Providence College & Seminary - Library . . . . http://www.providence.mb.ca
Society for the Propagation of the Faith for Canada . . . . http://www.eda.net~missions
Society of Saint Peter the Apostle . . . . http://www.eda.net~mission
United Synagogue of Conservative Judaism, Ontario Region . . . . http://www.uscj.org

SCIENCE & NATURE
100 Mile House Demonstration Forest . . . . http://www.netshop.net/~100mile/sccofc/html
Aerospace Industries Association of Canada . . . . http://www.aiac.ca
African Lion Safari & Game Farm . . . . http://www.lionsafari.com/
Alberta Association of Courseware Producers . . . . http://www.sas.ab.ca/aacp/
Alberta Bottle Depot Association http://recycle.net/Associations/rs000024.htm
Alberta Research Council . . . . http://www.arc.ab.ca
Alberta Society of Professional Biologists . . . . http://www.ccinet.ab.ca/aspb
Alternatives: Perspectives on Society, Technology & Environment . . . . http://www.fes.uwaterloo.ca/Research/Alternatives
American Research & Documentation Center . . . . http://www.usis-canada.usia.gov
American Society of Landscape Architects . . . . http://www.asla.orglasla/
Applied Science Technologists & Technicians of British Columbia . . . . http://www.imaginet.ca/asttbc/
Aquatic Conservation Network . . . . http://www.achilles.net/holiday/acn/acnhome.html
Assiniboine Park . . . . http://www.mbnet.mb.ca/city/parks/
Association for the Promotion & Advancement of Science Education . . . . http://www.swifty.com/apase/charlotte/apase!.html
Association of Exploration Geochemists . . . . http://aeg.org./aeg/aeghome.htm/
Association of Personal Computer Users Groups . . . . http://www.apcug.org
Association of Professional Engineers, Geologists & Geophysicists of Alberta . . . . http://www.apegga.com
Association of Women in Engineering & Science gopher://freenet.edmonton.ab.ca:70/11/i/awes
Association of the Chemical Profession of Ontario . . . . http://www.acpo.on.ca/
Atlantic Salmon Federation . . . . http://www.flyfishing.com/asf/
Avicultural Advancement Council of Canada . . . . http://www.islandnet.com/~aacc
BC Advanced Systems Institute . . . . http://www.asi.bc.ca/asi/
BC Biotechnology Alliance . . . . http://www.asi.bc.ca/bcba/
BC Environmental Network . . . . http://www.earthcare.org/bcen/bcen.html
Biochemistry & Cell Biology . . . . http://www.cisti.nrc.ca/cisti/journals.rj.html
British Columbia Humane Education Society . . . . http://bcyellowpages.com/BCHES/
Bruce Peninsula Environment Group . . . . http://ourworld.compuserve.com/homepages/Hoita_BPEG
Bruce Trail Association . . . . http://www.brucetrail.org/
Burke-Gaffney Observatory . . . . http://apworld.stmarys.ca/bgo/bgo.html
Butchart Gardens Ltd. . . . . http://butchartgardens.bc.ca/butchart/

Calgary Rainforest Action Group	http://www.freenet.calgary.ab.ca/populati/communit/crag/crag.html
Calgary Zoo, Botanical Garden & Prehistoric Park	http://www.cadvision.com/Home_Pages/accounts/calzoo/
Canadian Advanced Technology Association	http://www.cata.ca/
Canadian Association of Internet Providers	http://www.caip.ca/
Canadian Association of Palynologists	http://gpu.srv.ualberta.ca/~abeaudoi/cap/cap.html
Canadian Association of Petroleum Producers	http://www.capp.ca
Canadian Avalanche Association	http://www.avalanche.ca/snow
Canadian Bacterial Diseases Network	http://www.cbdn.ca/
Canadian Centre for Creative Technology	http://www.ccct.ca
Canadian Coast Guard College - Library	http://www.cgc.ns.ca
Canadian Council of Technicians & Technologists	http://www.cabot.nf.ca/CCTT/index.html
Canadian Earth Energy Association	http://www.earthenergy.org
Canadian Energy Pipeline Association	http://www.cepa.com
Canadian Environment Industry Association	http://www.ceia.org
Canadian Environment Industry Association - British Columbia	http://www.ceia-bc.com/
Canadian Farm Writers' Federation	http://www.uoguelph.ca/Research/cfwf
Canadian Gas Association	http://iplace.com/cga
Canadian Gas Research Institute	http://www.hookup.net/~cgri/
Canadian Genetic Diseases Network	http://www.bc.irap.nrc.ca/ctn/cgdn/cgdn-e.html
Canadian Geographic	http://www.cangeo.ca/
Canadian Geophysical Union	http://www.cg.nrcan.gc.ca/cgu/cgu.html
Canadian Geoscience Council	http://www.science.uwaterloo.ca/earth/cgc/cgc.html
Canadian Geotechnical Journal	http://www/nrc.ca/cisti/journals/
Canadian Hydrographic Association	http://www.cciw.ca/dfo/chs/cha/cha-home.html
Canadian Institute for Environmental Law & Policy	http://www.web.net/cielap
Canadian Institute of Biotechnology	http://www.biotech.ca/
Canadian Institute of Forestry	http://www.episet/cif
Canadian Institute of International Affairs	http://www.trinity.utoronto.ca/ciia/intro.html
Canadian Institute of Resources Law	http://www.ucalgary.ca/~cirl/
Canadian Institutional Research & Planning Association	http://www.usask.ca/cirpa/index.html
Canadian Journal of Analytical Sciences & Spectroscopy	http://www.ietc.ca/polysci/
Canadian Journal of Botany	http://www.cisti.nrc.ca/cisti/journals/rj.html
Canadian Journal of Earth Sciences	http://www.cisti.nrc.ca/cisti/journals/rj.html
Canadian Journal of Physiology & Pharmacology	http://www.cisti.nrc.ca/cisti/journals/rj.html
Canadian Kennel Club	http://www.ncf.carleton.ca/freeport/community.associations/kennel-club/menu
Canadian Mathematical Society	http://camel.cecm.sfu.ca/index.html
Canadian Morgan Horse Association Inc.	http://www.osha.igs.net/~cmha/index.htm
Canadian Nature Federation	http://www.web.apc.org~cnf
Canadian Operational Research Society	http://www.ncf.carleton.ca/freeport/prof.assoc/cors/menu
Canadian Parks & Wilderness Society	http://web.idirect.com/~wildland
Canadian Renewable Fuels Association	http://www.greenfuels.org
Canadian Science & Technology Historical Association	http://www.physics.uoguelph.ca/hist/CSTHA.html
Canadian Science Writers' Association	http://www.interlog.com/~cswa
Canadian Society for Chemical Engineering	http://fox.nstn.ca/~cic_adm/csche.html
Canadian Society for Chemical Technology	http://fox.nstn.ca/~cic_adm/csct.html
Canadian Society for Chemistry	http://fox.nstn.ca/~cic_adm/csc.html
Canadian Society of Agricultural Engineering	http://www.engr.usask.ca/societies/csae/
Canadian Society of Exploration Geophysicists	http://www.geo.ucalgary.ca:80/cseg
Canadian Society of Laboratory Technologists	http://cslt.com/
Canadian Society of Landscape Architects	http://www.clr.utoronto.ca/ORG/CSLA/
Canadian Society of Petroleum Geologists	http://www.cspg.org
Canadian Society of Safety Engineering, Inc.	http://www.csse.org
Canadian Solar Industries Association Inc.	http://www.newenergy.org/newenergy/sesci.html
Canadian Sphagnum Peat Moss Association	http://www.peatmoss.com
Canadian Standardbred Horse Society	http://home.ican.net/~troton
Canadian Water Resources Association	http://www.cwra.org/cwra
Canadian Well Logging Society	http://www.canpic.ca/CWLS
Canadian Wildlife	http://www.toucan.net/cwf-fcf/cwfhome.html
Canadian Wood Council	http://www.cwc.metrics.com/
Capilano College - Library	http://www.capcollege.bc.ca
Centre for Engineering Research	http://www.cfer.ualberta.ca
Centre for Toxicology	http://www.uoguelph.ca/cntc/
Chemical Institute of Canada	http://fox.nstn.ca/~cic_adm/
City Farmer - Canada's Office of Urban Agriculture	http://www.cityfarmer.org
Clean Air Strategic Alliance	http://www.ccinet.ab.ca/casa
Climenhaga Observatory	http://astrowww.phys.uvic.ca
Coalition to Save the Elms	http://iisd1.iisd.ca/comm/saveelms.htm
Composting Council of Canada	http://www.compost.org/
Consultative Group on International Agricultural Research	http://www.worldbank.org/html/cgiar/HomePage.html
Crop Protection Institute of Canada	http://www.cropro.org
Dairy Farmers of Ontario	http://www.milk.org/
David Dunlap Observatory	http://www.astro.utoronto.ca
Dominion Astrophysical Observatory	http://www.hia.nrc.ca
Doran Planetarium	http://ALUMNI.LAURENTIAN.CA/
Earth Island Institute	http://www.earthisland.org/ei/
Earth Sciences Museum	http://www.science.uwaterloo.ca/earth/museum/museum.html
EcoDesign Resource Society	http://www.ecodesign.bc.ca
Ecodecision	http://www.ecodec.org

Ecological Society of America	http://www.sdsc.eta/SDSC/Research/Comp_Bio/ESA/ESA.html
Economic Innovation & Technology Council - National Agri-Food Technology Centre	http://www.eitc.mb.ca/naf/
Edmonton Space & Science Centre	http://www.ee.ualberta.ca/essc
Energy Pathways Inc.	http://www.epi.ca/home.htm
Enviro-Accès Inc.	http://www.enviroaccess.ca
Environment Canada - Departmental Library	http://www.doe.ca/library/libhome.html
Environment Views	http://www.ccinet.ab.ca/enviews/
Environmental Data Research Institute	http://www.envirolink.org/products/edri/
Environmental Research Institute of Michigan	http://www.erim.org
Environmental Science & Engineering	http://www.ese.mag.com
Environmental Services Association of Alberta	http://www.ccinet.ab.ca/esaa/home.html
Envirotech	http://www.citenet.net/envirotech/
Equinox	http://www.equinox.ca
Evergreen Foundation	http://www.evergreen.ca/
Fanshawe College - Library	http://www.franshawec.on.ca
Federation of BC Naturalists	http://edie.cprost.sfu.ca/~jacsen7/land4nature.html
Federation of Nova Scotia Naturalists	http://ccn.cs.dal.ca/Environment/FNSN/hp-fnsn.html
Federation of Ontario Naturalists	http://www.web.net/fon
Food Institute of Canada	http://foodnet.fic.ca
Forest Alliance of British Columbia	http://www.forest.org
Friends of the Environment Foundation	http://www.fef.ca/
Gandalf Canada - Library	http://www.gandalf.ca
Genome	http://www.cisti.nrc.ca/cisti/journals.rj.html
Gordon MacMillan Southam Observatory	http://pacific-space-centre.bc.ca
Green Building Information Council	http://greenbuilding.ca
Green Party USA	http://www.greens.org/
Greenpeace Austria	http://greenpeace.or.at/greenpeace/
Greenpeace Canada	http://rs560.cl.msu.edu/weather/interactiv.html
Greenpeace Germany	http://www.icf.de/greenpeace-berlin
Greenpeace International HQ	http://www.greenpeace.org/
Greenpeace USA	http://www.greenpeace.org/~usa/
Gros Morne National Park Visitor Reception Centre	http://www.stemnet.nf.ca/~amorceau/gmnp.html
Halifax Field Naturalists	http://www.cfn.cs.dal.ca/Recreation/FieldNaturalists/fieldnat.html
Hazardous Materials Management	http://www.hazmatmag.com
Hike Ontario	http://www.freenet.durham.org/hikeon/
Holstein Association of Canada	http://www.holstein.ca/index.htm
Humanist Association of Canada	http://magi.com/~hac/hac.html
Hume Cronyn Observatory	http://phobos.astro.uwo.ca
Huntsman Marine Science Centre	http://www.unb.ca/web/huntsman
Hydrographic Society	http://hydrography.ims.plym.ac.uk/hydsoc.htm
Industrial Biotechnology Association of Canada	http://www.biotech.ca/members/ibac.htm
Industry Canada - Communications Research Centre Library	http://www.crc.doc.ca/library/library.html
Information Technology Research Centre	http://www.itrc.on.ca/
Institute for Aerospace Studies	http://www.utias.utoronto.ca/
Institute for Risk Research	http://sail.uwaterloo.ca/~irr.home.html
Institute for Robotics & Intelligent Systems	http://www.precarn.ca
Institute for Space & Terrestrial Science	http://www.ists.ca/
Institute of Industrial Engineers	http://www.iienet.org
International Arctic Science Committee	http://www.npolar.no/iasc
International Association for Great Lakes Research	http://www.geog.buffalo.edu/glp/iaglr/iaglr.html
International Association of Science & Technology for Development	http://www.curg.ab.ca:8001/~warwodad/iasted.html
International Development Research Centre	http://www.idrc.ca/index.html
International Environmental Liability Management Association	http://www.magic.ca/ielma/IELMA.html
International Institute for Energy Conservation	http://solstice.crest.org/clients/iiec/iiec.html
International Institute for Sustainable Development	http://www.iisd.ca/linkages/
International Society of Arboriculture	http://www.ag.uiuc.edu/~isa
International Society of Indoor Air Quality & Climate	http://www.cyberus.ca/~dsw/
Inventors Association of Ottawa	http://www.ncf.carleton.ca/freeport/community.associations/inventors/menu
Jackson Park Queen Elizabeth II Garden	http://www.city.windsor.on.ca
Kortright Centre for Conservation	http://www.kortright.on.ca/
Laboratory Product News	http://www.southam.com/b1-5-3.html
Lakehead University - Library	http://www.lakeheadu.ca
Lambton College - Resource Centre	http://www.lambton.on.ca
Laurentian University - J.N. Desmarais Library	http://www.laurentian.ca
Manitoba Animal Rights Coalition	http://envirolink.org/arrs/marc/marc.htlm
Manitoba Environment - Resource Centre	http://www.gov.mb.ca/manitoba/environ/
Manitoba UNIX User Group	http://www.muug.mb.ca
Manufacturing Research Corporation of Ontario	http://network.admin.ists.ca/OCE/mrco.html
Microelectronic Devices, Circuits & Systems for Ultra Large Scale Integration	http://www.utoronto.ca/micronet
Miller Museum of Mineralogy & Geology	http://geol.queensu.ca/museum/museum.html
Mining Association of Canada	http://www.mining.ca
National Computer Security Association	http://www.ncsa.com
National Farmers Union	http://www.wbm.ca/users/farmers
National Museum of Science & Technology	http://www.science-tech.nmstc.ca; http://www.sciences-tech.smnst.ca
Natural Life Magazine	http://www/netroute.net/natlife
Nature Canada	http://www.web.apc.org/~cnf
Nature Saskatchewan	http://www.unibase.com/~naturesk
NeuroScience Network	http://www.cns.ucalgary.ca/nce

Newfoundland & Labrador Dept. of Mines & Energy - Geological Survey Library	http://www.geosurv.gov.nf.ca
Newfoundland Environmental Industry Association	http://enterprise.newcomm.net/webpage/neia
Niagara Parks Botanical Gardens & School of Horticulture	http://www.niagara.com/~; shoup/botanic_gardens.html
Northern Aquaculture	http://www.naqua.com/
Nova Scotia Environmental Industry Association	http://www.nseia.ns.ca/nseia
Ocean Voice International, Inc.	http://www.ovi.ca
Ontario Association of Landscape Architects	http://www.clr.utoronto.ca/org/oala
Ontario Camping Association	http://www.ontcamp.on.ca
Ontario Centre for Environmental Technology Advancement	http://www.oceta.on.ca
Ontario Centre for Materials Research	http://www.queensu.ca/ocmr
Ontario Environmental Network	http://www.web.net/~oen
Ontario Horticultural Association	http://www.interlog.com/~onthort
Ontario Laser & Lightwave Research Centre	http://network.admin.ists.ca/OCE/ollrc.html
Ontario Parks Association	http://www.hookup.net/~opa
Ontario Science Centre	http://www.osc.on.ca
Ontario Trails Council	http://www.csp.trentu.ca/gomrm/otc.html
PEI Food Technology Centre - Library	http://www.gov.pe.ca/info/ftc/
Pacific Space Centre	http://pacific-space-centre.bc.ca
Parrot Association of Canada	http://wchat.on.ca/parrot/pac.htm
Peace & Environment Resource Centre	http://www.ncf.carleton.ca/freeport/community.associations/perc/menu
People for the Ethical Treatment of Animals	http://envirolink.org/arrs/peta
Pesticide Action Network North America	http://www.panna.org/panna/
Petroleum Communication Foundation	http://www.pcf.ab.ca
Petroleum Services Association of Canada	http://www.psac.ca
Petroleum Society of CIM	http://www.canpic.ca/PETSOC/
Planétarium de Montréal	http://www.planetarium.montreal.qc.ca
Protein Engineering Network of Centres of Excellence	http://diadem.biochem.ualberta.ca/pence.html
Québec Science	http://QuebecScience.qc.ca
Rainforest Action Network	http://www.ran.org/ran/
reBOOT Canada	http://www.reboot.on.ca
Recycling Council of Ontario	http://www.web.apc.org/rco
Riding Mountain National Park Visitor Centre	http://parkscanada.pch.gc.ca/parks/manitoba/riding_mountain/riding_mountain.htm
Rothney Astrophysical Observatory	http://www.ucalgary.ca/~milone/rao.html
Royal Agricultural Winter Fair Association	http://www.royalfair.org
Royal British Columbia Museum	http://rbcm1.rbcm.gov.bc.ca/index.html
Royal Tyrrell Museum of Palaeontology	http://tyrrell.magtech.ab.ca
Ryerson Polytechnic University - Library	http://hugo.lib.ryerson.ca
SMART Toronto	http://www.canada.hp.com/smarttoronto
Saskatchewan Applied Science Technologists & Technicians	http://www.siast.sk.ca/~wasect/sastt.html
Sask. Institute of Applied Science & Technology - Palliser Institute Library	http://www.siast.sk.ca
Saskatchewan Research Council - Library	http://library.usask.ca
Science Alberta Foundation	http://www.FreeNet.Calgary.ab.ca/science/sciencab.html
Science World British Columbia	http://www.scienceworld.bc.ca
Science for Peace	http://www.math.yorku.ca/sfp/
Scotia McLeod Inc. - Information Centre	http://wealth.passport.ca/wealth
Seasons	http://www.web.net/fon
Sierra Club	http://www.sierraclub.org/
Simon Fraser University - W.A.C. Bennett Library	http://www.lib.sfu.ca/
Society of Canadian Office Automation Professionals	http://www.ncf.carleton.ca/freeport/prof.assoc/scoap/menu
Soil & Water Conservation Society	http://www.netins.net/showcase/swcs/
Soil & Water Conservation Society of Metro Halifax	http://www.ccn.cs.dal.ca/Science/SWCS/SWCS.html
Solar Energy Society of Canada Inc.	http://www.newenergy.org/newenergy/sesci.html
Statistical Society of Canada	http://www.mast.queensu.ca/~ssc
Stewardship Information Bureau	http://sib.lrs.uoguelph.ca/sib3.htm
Stockholm Environment Institute	http://nn.apc.org/sei/
Tellus Institute	http://www.tellus.com
Toronto Atari Federation	http://www.io.org/~schrist/taf.html
Toronto Biotechnology Initiative	http://www.biotech.ca/members/tbi.htm
Toronto Life Gardens	http://www.tcr-lifeline.com
Union des producteurs agricoles	http://www.upa.qc.ca/
United Nations Development Programme	http://www.undp.org/
Université Laval - Bibliothèque	gopher://gopher.bibl.ulaval.ca
University of Alberta - Libraries	http://www.library.ualberta.ca/library.html
University of British Columbia Observatory	http://www.astro.ubc.ca/
University of Guelph - Library	http://www.lib.uoguelph.ca
University of Manitoba - Libraries	http://www.cc.umanitoba.ca/academic_support/libraries/
University of Western Ontario Astronomical Observatory	http://phobos.astro.uwo.ca/~dfgray/
Vancouver Island Rock & Alpine Garden Society	http://freenet.victoria.bc.ca/virags/virags.html
Victoria FreeNet	http://freenet.victoria.bc.ca/vifa.html
WaterCan	http://ottawa.public.net/watercan/watercan.html
Waterloo Centre for Groundwater Research	http://darcy.uwaterloo.ca/home.html
Western Canada Wilderness Committee	http://www.web.apc.org/wcwild/welcome.htm
Wilfrid Laurier University - Central Library	http://www.wlu.ca/~wwwhb/

TRANSPORTATION

Aerospace Industries Association of Canada	http://www.aiac.ca
Air Canada	http://www.aircanada.ca

Air Transport Association of Canada	http://www.atac.ca
Algoma Central Railway Inc.	http://www.mcs.net/~dsdawdy/Canpass/acr/soo_her.html
American Airlines Inc.	http://www.amrcorp.com
Annals of Air & Space Law	http://www.iasl.mcgill.ca
BC Rail Ltd.	http://www.mcs.net/~dsdawdy/Canpass/bcr/bcr.html
British Columbia Automobile Association	http://www.bcaa.bc.ca
Canadian Aeronautics & Space Institute	http://www.ncf.carleton.ca/freeport/prof.assoc/casi/menu
Canadian Airlines International Ltd.	http://www.cdnair.ca
Canadian Automobile Association	http://www.caa.ca
Canadian International Freight Forwarders Association, Inc.	http://www.webcom.com.ciffa/
Canadian Port & Harbour Association	http://www.newswire.ca/cpha.
Canadian Transportation Logistics	http://www.southam.com/b1-5-2.html
Chartered Institute of Transport in North America	http://www.worldlink.ca/~cit
Czech Airlines	http://www.baxter.net/csa
GO Transit	http://www.mcs.net/~dsdawdy/Canpass/go/go_top.html
Institute for Aerospace Studies	http://www.utias.utoronto.ca/
International Institute for Energy Conservation	http://solstice.crest.org/clients/iiec/iiec.html
Maritime Museum of the Atlantic	http://www.ednet.ns.ca/educ/museum/mma.html
Metropolitan Toronto Archives & Records Centre	http://www.metrotor.on.ca/services/departments/clerk.html#archives
Motor Truck	http://www.southam.com/b1-10-1.html
Northwest Airlines	http://www.nwa.com
Ontario Northland Transportation Commission	http://www.mcs.net/~dsdawdy/Canpass/onr/onr.html
Ontario Trucking Association	http://www.ontruck.org
Québec North Shore & Labrador Railway Company	http://www.mcs.net/~dsdawdy/Canpass/qnsl/qnsl.html
SEDS - Canada	http://www.seds.ca
Transportation Development Centre - Judith Nogrady Library	http://www.tc.gc.ca
Truck News	http://www.southam.com/b1-10-2.html
Truck West	http://www.southam.com/b1-10-3/html
Via Rail Canada Inc.	http://www.mcs.net/~dsdawdy/Canpass/via/via.html

Canadian Almanac & Directory 1997

SECTION 6

ARTS & CULTURE DIRECTORY

MUSEUMS & SCIENCE CENTRES	1
ART GALLERIES	29
PERFORMING ARTS	35
THEATRE	35
MUSIC	37
DANCE	41
FLORA & FAUNA	44
WILDLIFE, ZOOS & OUTDOOR EDUCATION CENTRES	44
AQUARIA	45
BOTANICAL GARDENS	45

See ADDENDA at the back of this book for late changes & additional information.

MUSEUMS & SCIENCE CENTRES

The Canadian Museum of Civilization/Musée canadien des civilisations (CMC)
100 Laurier St., PO Box 3100, Stn B, Hull PQ J8X 4H2
819/776-7000; Fax: 819/776-8300
URL: http://www.cmcc.muse.digital.ca/
The Canadian Museum of Civilization conducts research in Canadian studies & collects, preserves & displays objects which reflect Canada's cultural heritage. Its activities extend across the country through field research programs, publications & loans to various groups & institutions. Through permanent & changing exhibitions, public programs, film & theatre programs, the museum unfolds the stories of Canada's prehistory, native cultures, explorers, settlers & multicultural heritage. The Canadian War Museum, an affiliated museum of the Canadian Museum of Civilization, houses an extensive collection depicting Canada's military history; The National Postal Museum, a division of CMC, is responsible for a collection depicting postal history.
President & Executive Director, Dr. George MacDonald
Vice-President, Public Affairs, Pierre Pontbriand

CANADIAN WAR MUSEUM/MUSÉE CANADIEN DE LA GUERRE
350 Sussex Dr., Ottawa ON K1A 0M8
URL: http://www.cmcc.muse.digital.ca/cwm/cwmeng/cwmeng.html

Canadian Museum of Contemporary Photography/Musée canadien de la photographie contemporaine (CMCP/MCPC)
1 Rideau Canal, PO Box 465, Stn A, Ottawa ON K1N 9N6
613/990-8257; Fax: 613/990-6542
The CMCP collects, interprets & disseminates contemporary Canadian photography as an art form & as a form of social documentation. Thematic & solo exhibitions are organized & presented quarterly at the museum's galleries & circulated across Canada & abroad through travelling exhibitions. Education programs & publications; boutique; theatre; collection storage; an affiliate of the National Gallery of Canada.
Director, Martha Hanna
Manager, Exhibitions, Publications & Communications, Maureen McEvoy

Canadian Museum of Nature/Musée canadien de la nature
PO Box 3443, Stn D, Ottawa ON K1P 6P4
613/566-4700; Fax: 613/954-5958
The CMN conducts research, maintains collections & presents educational programs across Canada. At the Victoria Memorial Museum Bldg. in Ottawa there are seven permanent exhibit halls on the Earth, Life Through the Ages, Birds in Canada, Mammals in Canada, Animals in Nature, Plant Life & the Viola MacMillan Mineral Gallery as well as three special exhibits areas. The Museum is the repository of some eight million specimens, with approximately 100,000 new items being added every year. These collections, although used in exhibits, are more for research than display & are open to study by qualified students & others. Museum expertise is available for consultation or project co-ordination.
Interim President, Colin Eades
Executive Vice-President, Dr. Patrick Colgan – 613/953-5357
Vice-President, Public Programs, Leslie Patten – 613/998-4972
Director, Capital Projects, Colin Eades – 613/991-2264
Director, Arctic Program, Mark Araham – 613/998-0247
Director, Origins Program, Gerald Fitzgerald – 613/954-0358
Director, Biodiversity Program, Robert McFetridge – 613/998-9486
Director, Business Initiatives Bureau, Maryse Brunet-Lalonde – 613/998-5673

Currency Museum of the Bank of Canada/Musée de la monnaie
245 Sparks St., Ottawa ON K1A 0G9
613/782-8914; Fax: 613/782-8874
URL: http://www.bank-banque-canada.ca
The most complete collection of Canadian notes & coins in the world, plus representative collections of world coins & paper money, including whales' teeth, glass pearls, elephant-hair bracelets, shells & copper axes.
Chief Curator & Head of Museum, J. Graham Esler
Director, Museum Programming, Louise O'Neill
Coordinator, Public Relations, Laurette Bergeron

National Aviation Museum/Musée national de l'aviation
Rockcliffe Airport, PO Box 9724, Stn T, Ottawa ON K1G 5A3
613/993-2010; Fax: 613/990-3655; Email: kinsella@fox.nstn.ca; TDD: 613/990-7530; 1-800-463-2038
Forty-nine airplanes on display (out of a total collection of 118 aircraft) tell the story of aviation from Canada's first powered flight in 1909 to the jet age; stars include the A.E.G. G.IV, the only WWI German twin-engine aircraft in existence; the Lancaster Bomber, built & flown by Canadians; the 1947 prototype of the world famous bush plane, the Beaver; the only remains of the controversial Avro Arrow; the Messerschmitt Me 163B, the first rocket airplane; the Museum also sponsors & displays Artflight, an annual nation-wide competition in aviation art.
Director, Public Programmes, Victoria Dickenson
Communications Officer, Daniel Kinsella – 613/993-4243
Director, Collection & Research, A.J. Shortt
Director General, Christopher Terry

National Museum of Science & Technology/Musée national des sciences et de la technologie (NMST/MNST)
1867 St. Laurent Blvd., PO Box 9724, Ottawa ON K1G 5A3
613/991-3044; Fax: 613/990-3654; TTY: 613/991-9207
URL: http://www.science-tech.nmstc.ca; http://www.sciences-tech.smnst.ca
Hands-on exhibits in the areas of ground transportation, marine technology, communications, space, agriculture, industrial & domestic technologies, physics, computer science, printing & astronomy, from early

Canadian Almanac & Directory 1997

times to the present. Automobiles, locomotives, music boxes & telephones make up some of the museum's many collections. The National Aviation Museum, located at Rockcliffe Airport, is affiliated with the National Museum of Science & Technology. Public programs at the Central Experimental Farm include farm animals, "A Barn of the 1920s" & "The Amazing Potato" exhibits, horse-drawn wagon rides, the Sheep Shearing Festival in May & the Fall Harvest Celebration in Oct.

Director, NMST Corporation, Dr. Geneviève Sainte-Marie
Director General, National Aviation Museum, Christopher Terry
Director General, Public Programmes, Dr. Paul Donahue
Director General, Collection & Research, David Richeson
Director General, Management Services, Graham Parsons
Director, Curatorial Services, Geoff Rider
Senior Curator, Communications, E.A. DeCoste
Senior Curator, Industrial & Domestic Technology, Thierry Ruddel
Senior Curator, Energy, Louise Trottier
Senior Curator, Physical Sciences & Space, Randall Brooks
Curator, Land Transportation, David Monaghan
Curator, Marine Transportation, Garth Wilson
Director, Collection & Research, NAM, A.J. Short
Director, Agriculture Museum, Michelle Dondo-Tardiff
Coordinator, Public Programming (Agric. Museum), Tamara Tarasoff
Director, Exhibit Development & Production, Ginette Bériault
Director, Interpretation & Visitor Services Division, Claude Faubert
Director, Communications & Promotion, Marion Grobb
Advertising & Promotion Officer, Elizabeth McCrea
Senior Communications Officer, Jean-Guy Monette

ALBERTA

Glenbow Museum, Art Gallery, Library & Archives

130 - 9 Ave. SE, Calgary AB T2G 0P3
403/268-4100; Fax: 403/265-9769
URL: http://www.lexicon.ab.ca/~glenbow
Glenbow documents the settlement of Western Canada with exhibits tracing the lives & traditions of native peoples, the development of the railway, ranching, farming & growing up in the West. A large art gallery highlights historical & contemporary art from Glenbow's own collections as well as from national & international collections. Books, maps, photographs & manuscripts relating to southern Alberta history are available for study in the extensive Library & Archives.
President & CEO, Dr. Robert Janes
Chief Financial Officer & Vice-President, Central Services, Joe Konrad
Vice-President, Program & Exhibit Development, Donna Livingstone

Provincial Museum of Alberta

12845 - 102 Ave., Edmonton AB T5N 0M6
403/453-9100; Fax: 403/454-6629
Major collections & exhibits of Alberta's natural & human history, including habitat groups, geology, palaeontology, native cultures, archaeology & western Canadian history; presentations from major museums around the world & an annual natural history exhibition; museum shop, cafeteria, publications information service, films, lectures, live demonstrations & cultural performances; special programs for schools & other groups; discovery room.

Director, Dr. Philip H.R. Stepney
Manager, Operations, Tim Willis
Manager, Exhibits & Visitor Services, Don Clevett
Manager, Archaeology & Ethnology, Dr. J.W. Ives
Manager, Curatorial & Collections Administration, Dr. Bruce McGillivray
Communications Co-ordinator, Kathleen Thurber

Royal Tyrrell Museum of Palaeontology

c/o Midland Provincial Park, PO Box 7500, Drumheller AB T0J 0Y0
403/823-7707; Fax: 403/823-7131; Email: rtmp@dns.magtech.ab.ca
URL: http://tyrrell.magtech.ab.ca
Operated by Alberta Community Development; the 11,200 sq.m. facility includes a public gallery which features dramatic murals, interactive displays, computer games, mini-theatres & some 800 fossil specimens, including more than 35 complete dinosaur skeletons & 100s of fossil reptiles. A Paleoconservatory houses semi-tropical plants, aquaria, interpreted trails, a cafeteria & giftshop. The museum conducts major field based research in Western Canada & abroad.
Director, Dr. Bruce Naylor

FIELD STATION

Dinosaur Provincial Park, PO Box 60, Patricia AB T0J 0Y0
403/378-4342; Fax: 403/378-4247
The satellite Field Station exhibits the knowledge of local ancient environments & contains on-site preparation & research facilities to support annual fieldwork programs.

Other Museums & Science Centres in Alberta

Airdrie: Nose Creek Valley Museum, PO Box 3351, Airdrie AB T4B 2B6 – 403/948-6685 – Curator, Julian Fell – Open year round
Alberta Beach: Garden Park Farm Museum, PO Box 639, Alberta Beach AB T0E 0A0 – 403/924-3391 – David Oselies
Alix Wagon Wheel Regional Museum, PO Box 157, Alix AB T0C 0B0 – 403/747-2708 – Curator, Alice Whitfield – Local history; open year round
Alliance & District Museum, PO Box 101, Alliance AB T0B 0A0 – President, Rose Barnes – Pioneer & farm life; open year round
Andrew & District Local History Museum, PO Box 180, Andrew AB T0B 0C0 – 403/365-3606 – Verna Topolinsky – Open year round
Banff Park Museum, PO Box 900, Banff AB T0L 0C0 – 403/762-1558; Fax: 403/762-3380; Email: hsmanager@pksbnp.dots.ddg.ca – Historic Sites Manager, Maureen Peniuk – Open year round; winter closed Tues. & Wed.
Banff: Luxton Museum of the Plains Indian, c/o Buffalo Nations Cultural Society, PO Box 850, Banff AB T0L 0C0 – 403/762-2388; Fax: 403/762-2388 – Executive Director, Pete Brewster – Plains Indians artifacts; open year round
Banff: Whyte Museum of the Canadian Rockies, PO Box 160, Banff AB T0L 0C0 – 403/762-2291; Fax: 403/762-8919; Email: wmcr@banff.net; URL: http://www.cadvision.com/db/wmer – Director, Edward J. Hart – Open year round
Barrhead & District Centennial Museum, PO Box 4122, Barrhead AB T7N 1A1 – 403/674-5203 – Curator, Mabel Gravel – Open daily in summer; winter by appt.
Beaverlodge: South Peace Centennial Museum, PO Box 493, Beaverlodge AB T0H 0C0 – 403/354-8869 – President, Gordon McLean – Pioneer equipment & buildings; open mid-May - Oct. 1
Blairmore: The Frank Slide Interpretive Centre (FSIC), PO Box 959, Blairmore AB T0K 0E0 – 403/562-7388; Fax: 403/562-8635 – Acting Facility Supervisor, Monica Field – Site of the 1903 rockslide avalanche; open May 15 - Labour Day, 9 am - 8 pm; 10 am - 4 pm remainder of year
Blairmore: Leitch Collieries Provincial Historic Site, PO Box 959, Blairmore AB T0K 0E0 – 403/562-7388; Fax: 403/562-8635 – Acting Facility Supervisor, Monica Field – Open May 15 - Labour Day
Bowden Pioneer Museum, PO Box 576, Bowden AB T0M 0K0 – 403/224-2122 – Curator, Bill Henderson
Brooks & District Museum, PO Box 2078, Brooks AB T1R 1C7 – 403/362-5073 – Open May 1 - Aug. 31
Calgary: Aerospace Museum of Calgary, Hangar #10, 4629 McCall Way NE, Calgary AB T2E 7H1 – 403/250-3752; Fax: 403/250-8399 – Executive Director, Everett L. Bunnell – Open year round
Calgary: Alberta Sports Hall of Fame & Museum, #100, 635 - 6 Ave. SW, Calgary AB T2P 0T5 – 403/269-6000; Fax: 403/297-6669 – Curator, Janice Smith – Open year round
Calgary Chinese Cultural Centre, 197 - 1 St. SW, Calgary AB T2P 4M4 – 403/262-5071; Fax: 403/232-6387 – Administrator, Stephen Lee – Open year round
Calgary Police Service Interpretive Centre & Archives, 133 - 6 Ave. SE, Calgary AB T2G 4Z1 – 403/268-4565; Fax: 403/974-0508 – Curator/Administrator, Janet Pieschel – Open year round
Calgary Science Centre (CSC), #73, 701 - 11 St. SW, PO Box 2100, Stn M, Calgary AB T2P 2M5 – 403/221-3700; Fax: 403/237-0186; Email: discover@calgaryscience.ca – Executive Director, William T. Peters – Open year round.
Calgary: Canadian Western Natural Gas Museum & Archives, 909 - 11 Ave. SW, Calgary AB T2R 1L8 – 403/245-7611
Calgary: Energeum, 640 - 5 Ave. SW, Calgary AB T2P 3G4 – 403/297-4293; Fax: 403/297-2882 – Curator, Andrea Main – Energy resources; open year round
Calgary: Fort Calgary, #106, 750 - 9th Ave. SE, PO Box 2100, Stn M, Calgary AB T2P 2M5 – 403/290-1875; Fax: 403/265-6534 – Supt., Don S. Hardy – 40 acre park; interpretive centre; 1875 fort reconstruction project; guided tours; open May 1 - Oct. 9
Calgary: Heritage Park Historical Village, 1900 Heritage Dr. SW, Calgary AB T2V 2X3 – 403/259-1900; Fax: 403/252-3528 – Manager, Historical Operations, W.D. Parama; General Manager, R.R. Smith – Pre-1914 western Canadian history in an authentic life setting; open May - Oct.
Calgary: Lord Strathcona's Horse (Royal Canadians) Regimental Museum, 4520 Crowchild Trail SW, Calgary AB T3E 1T8 – 403/242-6610; Fax: 403/974-2854; Email: rdennis@nucleus.com; URL: http://www.nucleus.com/~rdennis/ – Curator, Rick Dennis – Open year round
Calgary: Museum of Movie Art, #9, 3600 - 21 St. NE, Calgary AB T2E 6V6 – 403/250-7588 – Open Tues. - Sat.
Calgary: Museum of the Regiments, CFB Calgary, 4520 Crowchild Trail SW, Calgary AB T3E 1Y8 – 403/240-7057; Fax: 403/240-7190; Email: regiments@lexicom.ab.ca – Depicts the history of the four regiments of Calgary; art gallery
Calgary: The Nickle Arts Museum (NAM), c/o The University of Calgary, 2500 University Dr. NW, Calgary AB T2N 1N4 – 403/220-7234; Fax: 403/282-4742; Email: nickle@acs.ucalgary.ca; URL: http://www.ucalgary.ca – Director, Dr. Ann Davis – Founded in 1979 through a donation from Sam Nickle & a Province of Alberta grant; champions contemporary Western Canadian art & numismatics; changing exhibitions & programs
Calgary: Olympic Hall of Fame & Museum/Temple Olympique de la Renommée, Canada Olympic Park, 88 Canada Olympic Rd. SW, Calgary AB T3B 5R5 – 403/247-5454; Fax: 403/286-7213 – Curator, J. Thomas West – Three floors of exhibits on Winter Olympic history & the XV Olympic Winter Games in Calgary; Olympic Volunteer Theatre; Bobsleigh & Ski Jump simulators

Calgary: Princess Patricia's Canadian Light Infantry Regimental Museum & Archives, Currie Barracks, CFB Calgary, Calgary AB T3E 1T8 – 403/240-7525 – Curator, Capt. R. Raidt, MMM, CD – Artifacts relating to history & traditions of the PPCLI; PPCLI primary source documents, letters & papers; also a small, unique library

Calgary: Sam Livingston Fish Hatchery & Rearing Station, 1440 - 17A St. SE, Calgary AB T2G 4T9 – 403/297-6561; Fax: 403/297-2839 – Superintendent, W. Schenk – Open year round

Calgary: Sarcee People's Museum, 3700 Anderson Rd. SW, Calgary AB T2W 3C4 – 403/238-2677

Calgary: University of Calgary Museum of Zoology, 2500 University Dr., Calgary AB T2N 1N4 – 403/220-5269 – Curator, Dr. H.I. Rosenberg

Camrose & District Centennial Museum, PO Box 1622, Camrose AB T4V 1X6 – 403/672-3298 – Volunteer Curator, Della Robson – Open May - Sept., otherwise by appt.

Canmore: Centennial Museum of Canmore, PO Box 2131, Canmore AB T0L 0M0 – President, Vi Sandford

Cardston: Brooks Aqueduct Provincial/National Historic Site, c/o Remington Alberta Carriage Centre, PO Box 1649, Cardston AB T0K 0K0 – 403/653-5139; Summer: 362-4451; Fax: 403/653-5160 – Aqueduct Supervisor, Heather MacAulay

Cardston: C.O. Card Home & Court House Museum, PO Box 1830, Cardston AB T0K 0K0 – 403/653-4322 – Curator, Leo S. Stutz – Open June 1-Aug. 31, Mon.-Sat.; archives open year round on Wed. or by appt.

Cardston: Remington-Alberta Carriage Centre, 339 Main St., PO Box 1649, Cardston AB T0K 0K0 – 403/653-5139; Fax: 403/653-5160 – Manager, Chris Williams

Carstairs: Roulston Museum, PO Box 1067, Carstairs AB T0M 0N0 – Curator, Betty Ayers

Castor & District Museum, PO Box 864, Castor AB T0C 0X0 – 403/882-3409 – President, Marjorie Marshall

Cereal Prairie Pioneer Museum, PO Box 131, Cereal AB T0J 0N0 – 403/326-3899 – Director, F. Adams

Claresholm Museum, PO Box 397, Claresholm AB T0L 0T0 – 403/625-3131 – Curator, Mae Weber

Cochrane Ranch Historic Site, PO Box 1522, Cochrane AB T0L 0W0 – 403/932-2902; Fax: 403/932-2578 – Area Manager, Ken Carson – Alberta's first large-scale ranch; open May 15 - Labour Day; hiking & picnic areas open year round

Cochrane: Riding Mountain Historical Society & Pinewood Museum, PO Box 339, Cochrane AB T0L 0W0 – President, Marilyn Whittle

Cochrane: Stephansson House Provincial Historic Site, c/o Historic Sites & Archives Service, PO Box 1522, Cochrane AB T0W 0W0 – 403/935-2902 – Area Manager, Frank Milligan – Icelandic poet's pioneer home; open May 15 - Labour Day

Coleman: Crowsnest Museum, PO Box 306, Coleman AB T0K 0M0 – 403/563-5434 – Curator, Laura Johnston – Open year round

Coutts: Belmore's Museum, PO Box 176, Coutts AB T0K 0N0 – 403/344-3888 – Director, Belmore Schultz – Open summer

Czar: Prairie Panorama Museum, PO Box 60, Czar AB T0B 0Z0 – 403/857-2155 – Curator, Irene Brown; Curator, Helena Lawrason

DeBolt & District Pioneer Museum, PO Box 447, DeBolt AB T0H 1B0 – 403/957-3957; Fax: 403/957-2934 – Curator, Fran Moore – Open summer

Delburne: Anthony Henday Museum, PO Box 374, Delburne AB T0M 0V0 – 403/749-2711 – President, Audrey Nicholson

Donalda & District Museum, PO Box 40, Donalda AB T0B 1H0 – 403/883-2345 – Director, Georgina Brown

Drumheller Dinosaur & Fossil Museum, PO Box 2135, Drumheller AB T0J 0Y0 – 403/823-2593 – Curator, Dorothy Farmer

Drumheller: Homestead Antique Museum, PO Box 3154, Drumheller AB T0J 0Y0 – 403/823-2600 – Curator, Robert Llewellyn – Open summer

East Coulee School Museum, PO Box 539, East Coulee AB T0J 1B0 – 403/822-3970 – Manager, Ann Sarsfield – Open year round

Edmonton: 408 Tactical Helicopter Squadron Museum, CFB Edmonton, Edmonton AB T0A 2H0 – 403/973-4381

Edmonton: AGT Vista 33: View Gallery & Museum, 10020 - 100 St., 33rd Fl., Edmonton AB T5J 0N5 – 403/493-3333; Fax: 403/493-3006 – Technician/Restoration & Fabrication Specialist, R. Foster – Telephone industry artifacts; open year round

Edmonton: Alberta Railroad Museum, PO Box 6102, Stn C, Edmonton AB T5B 4K5 – 403/472-6229 – General Manager, Herb Dixon – Open summer

Edmonton: Beaver House, c/o Alberta Culture & Multiculturalism, 10158 - 103 St., 3rd Fl., Edmonton AB T5J 0X6 – 403/427-2031; Fax: 403/422-9132

Edmonton Police Museum & Archives, 9620 - 103A Ave., Edmonton AB T5H 0H7 – 403/421-2274; Fax: 403/421-2341; Email: EPS@whet.gov.edmonton.ab.ca – Curator/Director, Anne Lindsay – Open Mon. - Sat., 9 am - 3 pm

Edmonton Public Schools Archives & Museum, 10425 - 99 Ave., Edmonton AB T5K 0E5 – 403/422-1970 – Supervisor, Catherine Luck

Edmonton Radial Railway Society, PO Box 8337, Stn F, Edmonton AB T6H 4W6 – 403/457-1269 – President, Harvey Bradley – Restored streetcar rides for visitors to Fort Edmonton Park

Edmonton Space & Science Centre, 11211 - 142 St. NW, Edmonton AB T5M 4A1 – 403/452-9100; Fax: 403/455-5882; Email: essc@freenet.edmonton.ab.ca; URL: http://www.ee.ualberta.ca/essc – Director, Les G. Young; Director, Development, George Smith – IMAX theatre; planetarium; exhibit galleries; challenger Centre; observatory; giftshop; café; Amateur Radio Station

Edmonton: Father Lacombe Chapel/La Chapelle du Père Lacombe, c/o Historic Sites Service, 8820 -112 St., Edmonton AB T6G 2P8 – 403/427-3995; Fax: 403/422-4288 – Area Manager, Catherine Whalley – Located on St. Vital Ave., St. Albert; open May 15 - Labour Day

Edmonton: Fort Edmonton Park, c/o Edmonton Parks & Recreation, PO Box 2359, Edmonton AB T5J 2R7 – 403/496-8787; Fax: 403/496-8797 – Director, Bryan Monaghan – Canada's largest living history park; more than 70 period buildings set in four time eras; steam train & street car; giftshops & restaurants

Edmonton: John Janzen Nature Centre, Edmonton Parks & Recreation, PO Box 2359, Edmonton AB T5J 2R7 – 403/496-2939; Fax: 403/496-4701 – Director, Linda Cochrane

Edmonton: John Walter Museum, Edmonton Parks & Recreation, PO Box 2359, Edmonton AB T5J 2R7 – 403/428-3033 – Director, Gary Dewar

Edmonton: Old Strathcona Model & Toy Museum, 8603 - 104 St., Edmonton AB T6E 4G6 – 403/433-4512 – Director, Gerry Bell; Director, Bob Bell

Edmonton: Rutherford House Provincial Historic Site, c/o Historic Sites Service, 8820 - 112 St., Edmonton AB T6G 2P8 – 403/427-3995; Fax: 403/422-4288 – Area Manager, Catherine Whalley – Home of Alberta's first premier; gift shop, tea room, tours & special events; open year round

Edmonton: Strathcona Archaeological Centre in Strathcona Science Park, c/o Historic Sites & Archives Service, 8820 - 112 St., Edmonton AB T6G 2P8

Edmonton: The Telephone Historical Centre (THC), 10437 - 83 Ave., PO Box 4962, Edmonton AB T6E 4T5 – 403/441-2077; Fax: 403/433-4068 – Executive Director, Bert Yeudall – Open year round

Edmonton: Ukrainian Canadian Archives & Museum, 9543 - 110 Ave., Edmonton AB T5H 1H3 – 403/424-7580 – Director, Harry Yopyk

Edmonton: Ukrainian Catholic Women's League of Canada Arts & Crafts Museum, 10825 - 97th St., Edmonton AB T5H 2M4 – 403/466-7210 – President, Vera Kunda – Open year round

Edmonton: Ukrainian Cultural Heritage Village, c/o Historic Sites & Archives Service, 8820 - 112 St., Edmonton AB T6G 2P8 – 403/662-3640; Fax: 403/662-3273 – Manager, Barry Manchak – Open May 15 - Thanksgiving

Edmonton: Ukrainian Museum of Canada (Alberta Branch), 10611 - 110 Ave., Edmonton AB T5H 1H7 – 403/483-5932; Fax: 403/423-6738 – President, N. Seniw

Edmonton: University of Alberta - Museums & Collections Services, Ring House #1, Edmonton AB T6G 2E2 – 403/492-5834; Fax: 403/492-6185 – Director, Janine Andrews, Email: Janine.Andrews@ualberta.ca; Exhibition & Art Program Coordinator, Jim Corrigan, Email: j.corrigan@ualberta.ca; Collections Management Coordinator, Leslie Latta-Guthrie, Email: l.latta-guthrie@ualberta.ca; Public Information Coordinator, Frannie Blondheim, Email: Frannie.Blondheim@ualberta.ca – A central service & coordinating unit for the University of Alberta's 40 teaching & research collections, which include natural & applied science, human history & art

Edmonton: University of Alberta Dental Museum, Dentistry Pharmacy Centre, University of Alberta, Edmonton AB T6G 2N8 – 403/492-5194; Fax: 403/492-1624; Email: gsperber@gpu.srv.ualberta.ca – Curator, Dr. G. Sperber

Edmonton: University of Alberta Museum of Geology, Dept. of Geology, University of Alberta, Saskatchewan Dr., Edmonton AB T6G 2E3 – 403/492-3265; Fax: 403/492-2030 – Director, B.D. Chatterton

Elk Point: Fort George Museum, PO Box 66, Elk Point AB T0A 1A0 – 403/724-3654 – Director, Steve Andrishak – Open May 15 - Labour Day

Evansburg: Pembina Lobstick Historical Museum, PO Box 85, Evansburg AB T0E 0T0 – 403/727-3861; Fax: 403/727-3861 – President, Hazel B. Fausak; Secretary, Lois M. Jenkins

Fairview: RCMP Centennial Celebration Museum, PO Box 326, Fairview AB T0H 1L0 – 403/835-2467 – Curator, Viola Evans – Original barracks; open summer

Fort Chipewyan: Wood Buffalo National Park, c/o Visitor Reception Centre, PO Box 38, Fort Chipewyan AB T0P 1B0 – 403/697-3662; Fax: 403/697-3560 – Supt., Doug Stewart

Fort Museum, PO Box 776, Fort Macleod AB T0L 0Z0 – 403/553-4703 – Manager, Carla Niers – NWMP & RCMP fort

Fort Macleod: Head-Smashed-In Buffalo Jump, PO Box 1977, Fort Macleod AB T0L 0Z0 – 403/553-2731; Fax: 403/553-3141; Calgary line: 403/265-0048 – Facility Manager, Chris Williams – Designated World Heritage Site; open year round

Fort McMurray Heritage Park, 1 Tolen Dr., Fort McMurray AB T9H 1G7 – 403/791-7575; Fax: 403/790-6489 – Curator, Rose Bendfeld – Open May - June, Mon. - Fri.; July - Aug., daily; in winter by appt.

Fort McMurray Oil Sands Interpretive Centre, 515 MacKenzie Blvd., Fort McMurray AB T9H 4X3 – 403/743-7166; Fax: 403/791-0710 – Manager, Marsha Regensburg – Open year round

Fort McMurray: Historic Dunvegan, c/o Oil Sands Interpretive Centre, 515 MacKenzie Blvd., Fort McMurray AB T9H 4X3 – 403/743-7147 – Manager, Marsha Regensburg – Fur & provision post; open May 15 - Labour Day

Canadian Almanac & Directory 1997

Fort Saskatchewan Museum, 10104 - 101 St., Fort Saskatchewan AB T8L 1V9 – 403/998-1750 – Curator, Kris Nygren

Fort Vermilion: Rocky Lane School Museum, PO Box 9000, Fort Vermilion AB T0H 1N0 – 403/927-3297 – Director, M. Nugent

Girouxville: Musée Girouxville Museum, PO Box 276, Girouxville AB T0H 1S0 – 403/323-4252 – Administrator, Estelle Girard

Grande Prairie Museum, Pioneer Museum Society of Grande Prairie & District, PO Box 687, Grande Prairie AB T8V 3A8 – 403/532-5482; Fax: 403/532-5488 – Administrator/Curator, Peter Goertzen

Hanna Pioneer Village Archives & Museum, PO Box 1528, Hanna AB T0J 1P0 – 403/854-4244; Fax: 403/854-3279 – President, Bill McFalls; Curator, George Patzer

High Prairie & District Museum & Historical Society, PO Box 1442, High Prairie AB T0G 1E0 – 403/523-2601 – Curator, Jean Perritt

High River: Museum of the Highwood, 129 - 3rd Ave. SW, High River AB T1V 1M9 – 403/652-7156; Fax: 403/652-2396 – Director, Lynn Cartwright

Hines Creek: End of Steel Heritage Museum & Park, PO Box 686, Hines Creek AB T0H 2A0 – 403/494-3522 – President, Wilson Coon – Northern Alberta Railway

Hinton: Alberta Forest Service Museum, 1176 Switzer Dr., Hinton AB T7V 1V3 – 403/865-8200; Fax: 403/865-8266 – Director, Terry Smith

Iddesleigh: Rainy Hills Historical Society Pioneer Exhibits, Iddesleigh AB T0J 1T0 – 403/898-2443 – Sec.-Treas., Michele Olson

Innisfail Historical Village, 52nd Ave. & 42nd St., Innisfail AB T0M 1A0 – 403/227-2906 – Curator, L. Boyd

Irvine: Prairie Memories Museum, Irvine AB T0J 1V0 – 403/834-3923

Islay: Morrison Museum of the Country School, PO Box 120, Islay AB T0B 2J0 – Director, Allen Ronaghan

Jasper-Yellowhead Museum & Archives, PO Box 42, Jasper AB T0E 1E0 – 403/852-3013 – Museum Manager, Wendy deCandole – Open year round

Leduc: Dr. Woods House Museum, PO Box 5201, Leduc AB T9E 6L6 – 403/986-1517 – Open year round

Lethbridge: Fort Whoop-Up, PO Box 1074, Lethbridge AB T1J 4A2 – 403/329-0444; Fax: 403/329-0645 – Director, Richard Shockley – Located in Indian Battle Park, west end of 3rd Ave. South; open year round

Lethbridge: Sir Alexander Galt Museum, c/o Community Services Dept., 910 - 4 Ave. South, Lethbridge AB T1J 0P6 – 403/320-3898; Fax: 403/329-4958 – Coordinator/Curator, Cecile McCleary

Lougheed: Iron Creek Museum, PO Box 294, Lougheed AB T0B 2V0 – 403/386-3747 – Secretary, William Dolany

Medicine Hat Museum & Art Gallery, 1302 Bomford Cres. SW, Medicine Hat AB T1A 5E6 – 403/527-6266; Fax: 403/528-2464 – Director, T.A. Willock

Mirror & District Museum, PO Box 246, Mirror AB T0B 3C0 – 403/788-3828 – President, G.W. Neis

Mundare: Basilian Fathers Museum, PO Box 379, Mundare AB T0B 3H0 – 403/764-3887 – Administrator, Rev. Larry Huculak – Ukrainian culture & religion

Olds: Mountain View Museum, PO Box 63, Olds AB T0M 1P0 – 403/556-8464 – Director, Betty M. Caskey

Oyen: Crossroads Museum, PO Box 477, Oyen AB T0J 2J0 – 403/664-3850 – President, Nellie Eaton

Peace River Centennial Museum & Archives, 10302 - 99 St., Peace River AB T8S 1K1 – 403/624-4261; Fax: 403/624-4270 – Executive Director, Victoria Barsalou; Executive Assistant/Curator, Albert Kilkenny

Pincher Creek Museum & Kootenai Brown Historical Park, PO Box 1226, Pincher Creek AB T0K 1W0 – 403/627-3684 – President, Ernie Kettles – Open year round

Plamondon & District Museum, PO Box 75, Plamondon AB T0A 2T0 – 403/798-3883 – Director, Marie Bourassa

Ponoka: Alberta Hospital Museum, PO Box 296, Ponoka AB T0C 2H0 – 403/783-3290 – Director, Barb Greshner

Ponoka: Fort Ostell Museum, PO Box 2192, Ponoka AB T0C 2H0 – 403/783-5224 – Director, Connie Pugh

Red Deer: Fort Normandeau Historic Site & Interpretive Centre, 6300 - 45 Ave., Red Deer AB T4N 3M4 – 403/347-7550; Fax: 403/347-2550 – Head of Interpretation, J. Robertson

Red Deer & District Museum & Exhibition Centre, PO Box 800, Red Deer AB T4N 5H2 – 403/343-6844; Fax: 403/342-6644 – Director, Morris Flewwelling

Redcliff Historical & Museum Society, PO Box 758, Redcliff AB T0J 2P0 – 403/548-6260 – President, Chuck Watkins; Vice-President, Dwight Kilpatrick

Redwater & District Museum, PO Box 114, Redwater AB T0A 2W0 – 403/942-3552 – Anne Key

Rimbey: Pas-Ka-Poo Historical Park, Rimbey AB T0C 2J0 – 403/843-2084 – Secretary, Charles F. Plank

Rocky Mountain House National Historic Park, PO Box 2130, Rocky Mountain House AB T0M 1T0 – 403/845-2412; Fax: 403/845-5320 – Area Supt., Dan Gaudet – Site of fur trading posts; open spring & summer

Rosebud Centennial Museum, PO Box 601, Rosebud AB T0J 2T0 – 403/677-2284 – Director, Terry Schlinker

Rowley: Yester-Year Artifacts Museum, Rowley AB T0J 2X0 – 403/368-3816 – President, Heather McKee

Sangudo: Lac Ste-Anne Pioneer Museum, PO Box 525, Sangudo AB T0E 2A0 – 403/785-2398 – Archivist, Marian Dinwoodie

Seba Beach: All Saints Heritage Place, Seba Beach AB T0E 2B0 – 403/420-6704 – Lorna Cowley

St. Albert: Musée Héritage Museum, 5 Ste-Anne St., St. Albert AB T8N 3Z9 – 403/459-1528; Fax: 403/460-2394; Email: museum@compusmart.ab.ca – Director/Curator, James Tirrul-Jones

St. Paul: Fort George & Buckingham House Provincial Historic Site (FGBH), Provincial Bldg., #316, 5025 - 49 Ave., St. Paul AB T0A 3A4 – 403/645-6256; Fax: 403/645-4760 – Facility Manager, Karen L. Doyle – Archaeological remains of 2 fur trade forts; interpretive centre

St. Paul: Musée Historique de St. Paul, PO Box 1925, St. Paul AB T0A 3A0 – 403/645-4800 – Présidente, Germaine Champagne

St. Paul: Victoria Settlement Provincial Historic Site, Provinical Bldg., #316, 5025 - 49 Ave., St. Paul AB T0A 3A4 – 403/645-6256; Fax: 403/645-4760 – Facility Manager, Karen L. Doyle – Hudson Bay Company post & settlement; open May 15-Labour Day

Stettler Town & Country Museum, PO Box 2118, Stettler AB T0C 2L0 – 403/742-4534 – Curator, Catherine Anderson

Stony Plain: Multicultural Heritage Centre, PO Box 2188, Stony Plain AB T7Z 1X7 – 403/963-2777; Fax: 403/963-0935 – Executive Director, Judy Unterschultz

Strome: Sodbuster Archives Museum, PO Box 151, Strome AB T0B 4H0 – 403/376-3688 – Sec.-Treas., Joan Brockhoff

Sundre Historical Museum & Pioneer Village, PO Box 314, Sundre AB T0M 1X0 – 403/638-3233 – Manager, Sheilagh MacGregor – Open summer

Three Hills: Kneehill Historical Museum, PO Box 653, Three Hills AB T0M 2A0 – 403/443-5348 – Muriel Park

Tofield Historical Museum, Tofield AB T0B 4J0 – 403/662-2542 – President, Harold Schultz

Trochu & District Museum, PO Box 538, Trochu AB T0M 2C0 – 403/442-2334 – Curator, George O. Braham

Viking Historical Museum, PO Box 270, Viking AB T0B 4N0 – 403/336-3066 – Director, J.H. Roddick – Open summer

Wainwright Museum, PO Box 2294, Wainwright AB T0B 4P0 – 403/842-3115 – President, Battle River Historical Society, Thelma Congdon

Wanham: Grizzly Bear Prairie Museum, PO Box 68, Wanham AB T0H 3P0 – 403/694-3933 – Curator, Stanley Sather

Wetaskiwin: Alberta Central Railway Museum, RR#2, Wetaskiwin AB T9A 1W9 – 403/352-2257; Fax: 403/352-2257 – Operations Manager, W.G. Wilson; Curatorial Manager, Ellen Wilson – CPR rolling stock

Wetaskiwin: Canada's Aviation Hall of Fame, PO Box 6360, Wetaskiwin AB T9A 2G1 – 403/361-1351; Fax: 403/361-1239; Toll Free: 1-800-661-4726 – Curator, Jennifer Romanko

Wetaskiwin: Reynolds-Alberta Museum, PO Box 6360, Wetaskiwin AB T9A 2G1 – 403/361-1351; Fax: 403/361-1239; Email: ram.library@ccinet.ab.ca – Facility Manager, Bill Casey – Museum of transportation, agriculture & industry; home to Canada's Aviation Hall of Fame; open year round

Wetaskiwin: Reynolds Aviation Museum, c/o Reynolds Museum, 4118 - 57 St., Wetaskiwin AB T9A 2B6 – 403/352-5201; Fax: 403/352-4666 – President, Stanley G. Reynolds; Curator, Byron Reynolds – Antique & military aircraft & related articles

Wetaskiwin & District Museum, 5010 - 53 Ave., Wetaskiwin AB T9A 0Y7 – 403/352-0227 – Director, Sylvia Larson

Willingdon: Historic Village & Pioneer Museum, PO Box 102, Willingdon AB T0B 4R0 – 403/367-2445 – Curator, Nancy Hawrelak; President, Nick P. Hawrelak – Ukrainian & Romanian artifacts; open summer

BRITISH COLUMBIA

Museum of Anthropology
University of British Columbia, 6393 Marine Dr. NW, Vancouver BC V6T 1Z2
604/822-5087; Fax: 604/822-2974; Email: jenwebb@unixg.ubc.ca
Art & objects from around the world, with emphasis on First Nations cultures of the Northwest Coast; displayed in architect Arthur Erickson's award-winning building overlooking Howe Sound.
Director, Dr. Michael M. Ames

Royal British Columbia Museum
Heritage Court, 675 Belleville St., Victoria BC V8V 1X4
250/356-8197; Toll Free: 1-800-661-5411
URL: http://rbcm1.rbcm.gov.bc.ca/index.html
Founded in 1886, the RBCM specializes in the natural and human history of British Columbia.
Executive Director, Bill Barkley
Director, Curatorial Services, Grant Hughes
Director, Operations, Pauline Rafferty
Director, Public Programmes, Brent Cooke
Manager, Policy & Planning, Gayle Tomlinson
Chief, Marketing Services, Vacant
Chief, Publishing, Gerry Truscott
Chief, Exhibits, Doug Sage
Chief, Biological Collections, Jim Cosgrove
Chief, Conservation Services, Val Thorp
Chief, Anthropological Collections, Vacant
Manager, History, Jim Wardrop
Chief, Library Services, Frederike Verspoor
Manager, Natural History Research, Rob Cannings

Section Chief, Botany, Richard Hebda
Head, Vertebrate Zoology, Alex Peden
Head, Invertebrate Zoology, Phil Lambert
Manager, Anthropology, Alan Hoover
Head, History, Bob Griffin

The Vancouver Museum
1100 Chestnut St., Vancouver BC V6J 3J9
604/736-4431; Fax: 604/736-5417
Established in 1894. Collections include Vancouver civic history, First Nations, Asian decorative arts. Special programming, gift shop; open year round.
Acting Director, Hendrik Slegtenhorst

Other Museums & Science Centres in British Columbia

Abbotsford: Matsqui-Sumas-Abbotsford Museum - Trethewey House, 2313 Ware St., Abbotsford BC V2S 3C6 – 604/853-0313 – Director, Lynne Wright

Agassiz-Harrison Historical Society, PO Box 313, Agassiz BC V0M 1A0 – 604/796-3545 – President, Ro Walley – Open daily May - Labour Day

Ainsworth Hot Springs: Silver Ledge Hotel, Ainsworth Hot Springs BC V0G 1A0 – 250/229-4640 – Director, L. Duff – Open summer

Alert Bay Museum & Library, PO Box 208, Alert Bay BC V0N 1A0 – 250/974-5721 – Curator, Joyce Wilby

Alert Bay: U'Mista Cultural Centre & Society, PO Box 253, Alert Bay BC V0N 1A0 – 250/974-5403; Fax: 250/974-5499; Email: umista@north.island.net; URL: http://www.swifty.com/umista/ – Administrator, Linda Manz – Kwakwaka'wakw museum contains potlach collection returned by the National Museum of Man & the Royal Ontario Museum

Armstrong-Spallumcheen Museum & Art Society, PO Box 308, Armstrong BC V0E 1B0 – 250/546-8318

Ashcroft Museum & Archives, PO Box 129, Ashcroft BC V0K 1A0 – 250/453-9232; Fax: 250/453-9664 – Curator, Helen Forster – Open 5 days a week, April - Nov.

Atlin Historical Museum & Society, PO Box 111, Atlin BC V0W 1A0 – 250/651-7522; Fax: 250/651-7721 – President, Carrie Knickerbocker – Open daily June - Aug. & by appt.

Barkerville Historic Town, PO Box 19, Barkerville BC V0K 1B0 – 250/994-3332; Fax: 250/994-3435; Email: can-bht@immedia.ca – Manager, Jim Worton; Curator, William Quackenbush – Restored Cariboo Gold Rush town; Cottonwood House Historic Site; Blessing's Grave; McLeod Lake Post; Richfield Court House; open year round

Barriere: North Thompson Museum, PO Box 228, Barriere BC V0E 1E0 – 250/672-5583; Fax: 250/672-9311 – President, Heritage Society, Fran Wagstaff

Bella Coola Museum, PO Box 726, Bella Coola BC V0T 1C0 – 250/799-5537

Black Creek: Miracle Beach Provincial Park Nature House, RR#1, Site 11, PO Box 1, Black Creek BC V0R 1C0 – 250/337-5121 – Manager, John Kelch

Britannia Beach: British Columbia Museum of Mining, PO Box 188, Britannia Beach BC V0N 1J0 – 604/688-8735, 896-2233; Fax: 604/896-2260 – Executive Director, Marilyn Mullan; Curator/Manager, Sherry Elchuk – Open May - Oct. & by appt.

Burnaby Village Museum, 6501 Deer Lake Ave., Burnaby BC V5G 3T6 – 604/293-6500; Fax: 604/293-6525 – Manager, Cultural Services, Denis Nokony – Open daily Apr. - Sept. & Christmas

Burnaby: Simon Fraser University Museum of Archaeology & Ethnology, c/o Dept. of Archaeology, Simon Fraser University, Burnaby BC V5A 1S6 – 604/291-3325; Fax: 604/291-4727; URL: http://www.sfu.ca/archaeology – Curator, Barbara Winter – Major emphasis on the Pacific Northwest coast; open year round

Burns Lake: Lakes District Museum Society, PO Box 266, Burns Lake BC V0J 1E0 – 250/692-7450 – President, Ronnice Gelz

Cache Creek: Historic Hat Creek Ranch, PO Box 878, Cache Creek BC V0K 1H0 – 250/457-9722; Fax: 250/457-9311 – General Manager, D.W. Scott – Early ranching & transportation history; grounds open year round; visitor services open mid-May - mid-Oct.

Campbell River Museum, 470 Island Hwy., PO Box 70, Stn A, Campbell River BC V9W 4Z9 – 250/287-3103; Fax: 250/286-0109 – Acting Director, Jeanette Taylor – Exhibits include First Nations ceremonial masks & regalia, coastal logging history & settler development; Archives & Research Centre; gift shop

Campbell River Optical Maritime Museum, #102, 250 Dogwood St., Campbell River BC V9W 2X9 – 250/287-2052 – Curator, Robert Somerville – Open year round

Castlegar: Doukhobor Village Museum, PO Box 3081, Castlegar BC V1N 3H4 – 250/365-6622 – President, John Foster – Open daily May -Sept.

Castlegar: Railroad Station, 400 - 13th Ave., Castlegar BC V1N 1G2 – 250/365-6440 – Local history museum built in 1907; open daily Apr. - Oct.

Castlegar: Zuckerberg Island Heritage Park, c/o Castlegar & District Heritage Society, 400 - 13 Ave., Castlegar BC V1N 1G2 – 250/365-6440 – Russian Orthodox chapel house; Indian band Kukuli houses; open daily, Apr. - Oct.

Chase: Shuswap Lake Provincial Park Nature House, RR#1, Chase BC V0E 1M0 – 250/955-2217 – Zone Manager, P.V. Rathbone

Chetwynd Caboose Museum, 5217 North Access Rd., PO Box 1000, Chetwynd BC V0C 1J0 – 250/788-3345, 3655; Fax: 250/788-7843 – Open July & Aug.

Chetwynd: Little Prairie Heritage Museum, PO Box 1777, Chetwynd BC V0C 1J0 – 250/788-3358 – President, Shirley Weeks; Sec.-Treas., Bobbie Larsen – Open July & Aug.

Chilliwack: Canadian Military Engineers Museum, c/o CFB Chilliwack, MPO 612, Chilliwack BC V0X 2E0 – 604/858-1462; Fax: 604/858-1686 – Maj. T.C. Duffin

Chilliwack Museum, 45820 Spadina Ave., Chilliwack BC V2P 1T3 – 604/795-5210; Fax: 604/795-5291 – Director, Ron Denman – Open year round

Clearbrook: Fraser Valley Antique Farm Machinery Association, PO Box 2234, Clearbrook BC V2T 3X8 – 604/859-4979 – President, Jake Woelk

Clearbrook: Mennonite Historical Society Museum of BC, PO Box 2032, Clearbrook BC V2T 3T8 – Curator, Anna Wiens

Clearwater: Yellowhead Museum, RR#1, PO Box 1778, Clearwater BC V0E 1N0 – 250/674-3660 – Curator, Ida Dekelver

Clinton: South Cariboo Historical Museum Society, 1419 Cariboo Hwy., Clinton BC V0K 1K0 – 250/459-2442 – President, Loraine Huestis – Open daily May - Oct.

Courtenay & District Museum, c/o Cultural & Natural Heritage of the Comox Valley, 360 Cliffe Ave., Courtenay BC V9N 2H9 – 250/334-3611 – Curator, Deborah Griffiths – Includes archives; open year round

Cranbrook: Aasland Museum Taxidermy, 220 Kimberley Hwy. NE, Cranbrook BC V1C 4H4 – 250/426-3566 – Director, Odd Aasland

Cranbrook: Canadian Museum of Rail Travel - Cranbook, 1 Van Horne St., PO Box 400, Cranbrook BC V1C 4H9 – 250/489-3918; Fax: 250/489-5744; Email: camal@cyberlink.bc.ca – Executive Director, Garry W. Anderson; Associate Director, Mark McDonald

Cranbrook: St. Eugene Mission Development Project, Site 15, SS#3, Comp. 14, Cranbrook BC V1C 6H3 – 250/489-2372; Fax: 250/489-5760 – Manager, Helder Ponte – Open June - Labour Day, Mon.-Fri.

Creston Valley Museum, PO Box 1123, Creston BC V0B 1G0 – 250/428-9262 – President, Cyril Colonel – Open spring, summer, fall; in winter by appt.

Creston Valley Wildlife Centre (CVWC), PO Box 640, Creston BC V0B 1G0 – 250/428-3259; Fax: 250/428-3276 – Area Manager, Brian Stushnoff

Crofton: Old Crofton School Museum Society, PO Box 159, Crofton BC V0R 1R0 – 250/246-3804 – President, John Fransen

Cumberland Museum & Archives, 2680 Dunsmuir Ave., PO Box 258, Cumberland BC V0R 1S0 – 250/336-2445; Fax: 250/336-2321 – Curator, Barbara Lemky – Open year round

Dawson Creek Station Museum & Walter Wright Pioneer Village, 900 Alaska Ave., Dawson Creek BC V1G 4T6 – 250/782-9595, 9538 – President, Day Roberts – Open year round

Delta Museum & Archives, 4858 Delta St., Delta BC V4K 2T8 – 604/946-9322; Fax: 604/946-5791 – Director/Curator, Donna Bryman; Archivist, Christine O'Donnell

Denman Island Museum, PO Box 28, Denman Island BC V0R 1T0 – 250/335-0880 – Curator, Jean Brooks

Duncan: British Columbia Forest Museum, RR#4, Trans Canada Hwy., Duncan BC V9L 3W8 – 250/746-1251; Fax: 250/746-1487 – Manager, Michael Osborn – Also contains BC Forest Service Museum

Duncan: Cowichan & Chemainus Valleys Ecomuseum, PO Box 491, Duncan BC V9L 3X8 – 250/746-1611 – Executive Director, Wilma Wood

Duncan: Cowichan Bay Maritime Centre, PO Box 787, Duncan BC V9L 3Y1 – 250/746-4955; Fax: 250/746-4955 – Executive Director, Cowichan Wooden Boat Society, Paul Mitchell; Curator, Eric Sandilands

Duncan: Cowichan Valley Museum, PO Box 1014, Duncan BC V9L 2W3 – 250/746-6612; Fax: 250/748-4818; Email: cvm@islandnet.com – Curator/Manager, Priscilla Davis – Includes archives; open year round

Enderby & District Museum Society, PO Box 367, Enderby BC V0E 1V0 – 250/838-7170; Fax: 250/838-0123 – Curator, Joan Cowan – Open year round

Fernie & District Historical Society Museum, PO Box 1527, Fernie BC V0B 1M0 – 250/423-7016 – Sec.-Treas., Ella A. Verkerk – Coal mining history museum

Fort Langley: BC Farm Machinery & Agricultural Museum Association, PO Box 279, Fort Langley BC V1M 2R8 – 604/888-2273 – President, Tom Burton – Open daily mid-Mar. - Thanksgiving; in winter by appt.

Fort Langley National Historic Site/Lieu historique national Fort-Langley (FLNHS), PO Box 129, Fort Langley BC V1M 2R5 – 604/888-4424; Fax: 604/888-2577 – Area Supt., Janet Weatherston; Chief, Heritage Communications, Terence McCalmont – Birthplace of British Columbia; partially reconstructed Hudson's Bay Co. trading post, c.1858; open year round

Fort Langley: Langley Centennial Museum & National Exhibition Centre, PO Box 800, Fort Langley BC V1M 2S2 – 604/888-3922; Fax: 604/888-7291; Email: can-lconnec@immedia.ca – Arts & Heritage Supervisor, Sue Morhun – Open year round

Fort Nelson Heritage Museum, PO Box 716, Fort Nelson BC V0C 1R0 – 250/774-3536; Fax: 250/774-3536 – Curator, Marlin Brown – Artifacts related to the construction of the Alaska Highway; open mid-May - mid-Sept.

Fort St. James National Historic Site, PO Box 1148, Fort St. James BC V0J 1P0 – 250/996-7191; Fax: 250/966-8566 – Superintendent, Steve Langdon – Historic buildings from 1890s fur trading era; open mid-May - Aug.

Fort St. James: Kitwanga Fort National Historic Site, c/o Fort St. James National Historic Park, PO Box 1148, Fort St. James BC V0J 1P0 – 250/996-7191; Fax: 250/996-8566 – First major western Canadian native site commemorated by Parks Canada; open summer

Canadian Almanac & Directory 1997

Fort St. John-North Peace Museum, 9323 - 100 St., Fort St. John BC V1J 4N4 – 250/787-0430; Fax: 250/787-0405 – President, Larry Evans – Open year round

Fort Steele Heritage Town, Fort Steele BC V0B 1N0 – 489/489-3351; Fax: 489/489-2624 – Regional Manager, Martin J.E. Ross – Restored 1890's mining boom town of the East Kootenay; open year round

Fraser Lake Museum, PO Box 430, Fraser Lake BC V0J 1S0 – 250/699-6257; Fax: 250/699-6469 – Municipal Clerk, Angus Davis – Open summer

Ganges: Salt Spring Island Farmer's Institute & Museum, PO Box 961, Ganges BC V0S 1E0 – 250/537-9567 – President, Perry Booth

Garibaldi Heights: Squamish Valley Museum, PO Box 166, Garibaldi Heights BC V0N 1T0 – 604/898-3273 – President, Doug Fenton – Open summer

Gibsons: Elphinstone Pioneer Museum & Society, PO Box 766, Gibsons BC V0N 1V0 – 604/886-8232 – President, Lola Westell

Gold Bridge: Bralorne Pioneer Museum, SS#1 - Bralorne, Gold Bridge BC V0K 1P0 – 250/238-2240, 2519 – Director, Gail Goudry – Open summer

Golden & District Museum, 1302 - 11 Ave., PO Box 992, Golden BC V0A 1H0 – 250/344-5169 – Curator, Colleen Torrence – Open Apr. - Sept.

Grand Forks: Boundary Museum Society, 7370 - 5th St., PO Box 817, Grand Forks BC V0H 1H0 – 250/442-3737 – Manager, Joan Miller – Open year round

Grand Forks: Chain Saw Museum, PO Box 1180, Grand Forks BC V0H 1H0 – 250/442-3518 – Director, Michael Acres

Grand Forks: Mountain View Doukhobor Museum, Hardy Mountain Rd., PO Box 1235, Grand Forks BC V0H 1H0 – 250/442-8855 – Open June-Sept.

Greenwood Museum, PO Box 399, Greenwood BC V0H 1J0 – 250/445-6355; Fax: 250/445-6166 – Chairman, Wally Duerksen – Old jail, supreme court

Groundbirch: Bruce Groner Museum, PO Box 149, Groundbirch BC V0C 1T0 – 250/780-2383; Fax: 250/780-2248 – Director, Olga Lineham – Open summer

Harrison Mills: Kilby Historic Store & Farm, 215 Kilby Rd., PO Box 48, Harrison Mills BC V0M 1L0 – 604/796-9576; Fax: 604/796-9592 – General Manager, Kevin Logan – Open May - Oct., Thurs. - Mon., 10 am - 5 pm, & by appt.

Hazelton: 'Ksan Indian Village & Museum, PO Box 326, Hazelton BC V0J 1Y0 – 250/842-5544 – Manager, Darlene Hockman – Reconstructed Gitskan Indian Village; open year round

Hope Museum, 919 Water Ave., PO Box 26, Hope BC V0X 1L0 – 604/869-7322; Fax: 604/869-2160 – Manager, Inge Wilson – Open summer; off-season tours by request

Hope: John Weaver Sculpture Museum, PO Box 1723, Hope BC V0X 1L0 – 604/869-5312; Fax: 604/869-5117 – Curator, Henry Weaver

Hope: Remember When Doll Museum, RR#2, PO Box 6, Hope BC V0X 1L0 – 604/869-2923

Horsefly: Jack Lynn Memorial Museum, c/o Horsefly Historical Society, PO Box 148, Horsefly BC V0L 1L0 – 250/620-3304 – Curator, Harriette Erickson

Hudson's Hope Museum & Historical Society, PO Box 98, Hudson's Hope BC V0C 1V0 – 250/783-5769 – Curator, Jan McCarthy

Invermere: Windermere Valley Museum, PO Box 2315, Invermere BC V0A 1K0 – 250/342-9769 – Archivist, Jaryl McIsaac; Curator, Anne Newhouse – Open June - Sept.

Kamloops Museum Association & Archives, 207 Seymour St., Kamloops BC V2C 2E7 – 250/828-3576; Fax: 250/828-3578 – Archivist/Curator, Elisabeth Duckworth – Open year round

Kamloops: Rocky Mountain Rangers Museum & Archives, 1221 McGill Rd., PO Box 3250, Kamloops BC V2C 6B8 – 604/327-7424; Fax: 604/374-1063 – W.C. Robertson

Kamloops: Secwepemc Cultural Education Society & Native Heritage Park, 355 Yellowhead Hwy., Kamloops BC V2H 1H1 – 250/828-9801; Fax: 250/372-1127 – Executive Director, Stephen Conway – Traditional culture of the Shuswap people; open year round

Kaslo City Hall, 413 - 4th St., PO Box 576, Kaslo BC V0G 1M0 – 250/353-2311; Fax: 250/353-7767 – Designated National Historic Site; open Mon. - Fri.

Kaslo: S.S. Moyie National Historic Site, PO Box 537, Kaslo BC V0G 1M0 – 250/353-2525; Fax: 250/353-2525 – President, Gordon Gaskell; Manager, Visitor Services, Lucille Busse – Oldest intact passenger sternwheeler in the world; open daily mid-May to mid-Sept.

Kelowna: BC Orchard Industry Museum, 1304 Ellis St., Kelowna BC V1Y 1Z8 – 250/763-0433; Fax: 250/763-5722; Email: kelowna.museum@cyberstore.ca – Director, U. Surtees; Curator, W. Wilson

Kelowna: Benvoulin Heritage Church, 2279 Benvoulin Rd., Kelowna BC V1W 2C8 – 250/762-6911 – Open daily in summer; in winter by appt.

Kelowna: Father Pandosy Mission, 3685 Benvoulin Rd., Kelowna BC V1Y 8R3 – 250/763-4590 – Caretaker/Manager, Judy Toms – Oblate Mission, 1859; open daily Easter - Thanksgiving

Kelowna: Guisachan House, 1060 Cameron Ave., PO Box 1055, Stn A, Kelowna BC V1Y 7P7 – 250/862-9368

Kelowna Centennial Museum & National Exhibition Centre, 470 Queensway, Kelowna BC V1Y 6S7 – 250/763-2417; Fax: 250/763-5722; Email: kelowna.museum@cyberstore.ca – Curator/Director, Kelowna Museum Association, Ursula Surtees; Assistant Director, Dan Bruce; Assistant Curator, Wayne Wilson

Kelowna: Silver Lake Forestry Centre, #105 - 2417 Hwy. 97 North, Kelowna BC V1X 4J2 – 250/860-6410; Fax: 250/604/860-8856 – Regional Manager, Heather Rice – Logging artifacts

Keremeos: The Grist Mill at Keremeos, Upper Bench Rd., RR#1, Keremeos BC V0X 1N0 – 250/499-2888; Fax: 250/499-2434 – Designated British Columbia Heritage Site; open May - Oct.

Keremeos: South Similkameen Museum, PO Box 135, Keremeos BC V0X 1N0 – 250/499-5445 – Custodian, Doreen Smith – Open May - Aug.

Kimberley Heritage Musuem, PO Box 144, Kimberley BC V1A 2Y5 – 250/427-7510 – Curator, Marie Stang – Early mining; North Star schoolhouse; open year round

Kitimat Centennial Museum, 293 City Centre, Kitimat BC V8C 1T6 – 250/632-7022; Fax: 250/632-4995 – Curator, Montserrat Gonzalez – Natural history; homesteader & Haisla histories; Kemano-Kitimat Project history; temporary exhibitions; giftshop; open year round

Kitwanga: Meanskinisht Village Historical Association & Museum, PO Box 183, Kitwanga BC V0J 2A0 – 250/849-5732 – Director, Mary G. Dalen

Ladysmith: Black Nugget Museum, 12 Gatacre St., PO Box 1449, Ladysmith BC V0R 2E0 – 250/245-4846; Fax: 250/246-2441 – Curator, Kurt Guilbride – Open daily May - Sept.

Ladysmith Railway Historical Society & Museum, PO Box 777, Ladysmith BC V0R 2E0 – 250/245-4454 – President, Vincent J. Herkel

Lake Cowichan: Kaatza Station Museum & Archives, PO Box 135, Lake Cowichan BC V0R 2G0 – 250/749-6142; Fax: 250/749-3900 – Curator, Barbara Simkins – Open year round

Langley: Canadian Museum of Flight & Transportation (CMFT), #200, 5333 - 216th St., Langley BC V3A 4R1 – 604/532-0035; Fax: 604/532-0056 – Curator, George Proulx – Historic aircraft & other artifacts; research library & photo collections; open daily, year round

Lazo: Comox Air Museum, CFB Comox, 19 Wing, Lazo BC V0R 2K0 – 250/339-8162; Fax: 250/339-8162

Lazo: Comox Airforce Museum, CFB Comox, Lazo BC V0R 2K0 – 250/339-8635; Fax: 250/339-8673 – Coordinator, John F. Logan

Lillooet District Historical Society & Museum, PO Box 441, Lillooet BC V0K 1V0 – 250/256-4308; Fax: 250/256-4288 – Curator, Hilda Bryson – Open daily May - Oct.

Mackenzie Museum, PO Box 934, Mackenzie BC V0J 2C0 – 250/997-4323 – President, Christopher Johansen

Manning Park Visitor Centre, PO Box 3, Manning Park BC V0X 1H0 – 250/804-8836 – Area Supervisor, Jim Wiebe

Manson Creek: Omenica Museum, PO Box 100, Manson Creek BC V0J 2H0 – Curator, Stan Evans; Curator, Joan Evans – Mining, logging and trapping artifacts

Maple Ridge Museum & Archives, 22520 - 116th Ave., Maple Ridge BC V2X 0S4 – 604/463-5311; Email: valerie_patenaude@mindlink.bc.ca – Curator, Val Patenaude – Open year round

Maple Ridge: Thomas Haney House, 11612 - 224 St., Maple Ridge BC V2X 5Z7 – Curator, Rona Kelleway

Masset: Ed Jones Haida Museum, PO Box 186, Masset BC V0T 1M0 – 250/626-5159 – Open year round

Mayne Island Agricultural Society & Museum, Mayne Island BC V0N 2J0 – 250/539-2283 – Director, M.W. Haggart

McBride: Valley Museum & Archives Society, PO Box 775, McBride BC V0J 2E0 – 250/569-2411 – Trustee, Matthew Wheeler – Displays within McBride & District Public Library

Merritt: Nicola Valley Museum & Archives, 2202 Jackson Ave., PO Box 1262, Merritt BC V0K 2B0 – 250/378-4145 – Office Manager, Bette Sulz – Craigmont, ranching & mining displays; open year round

Midway: Kettle River Museum, PO Box 149, Midway BC V0H 1M0 – 250/449-2618; Fax: 250/449-2614 – CPR Station, courthouse & school

Mission: Fraser River Heritage Park, 7494 Mary St., PO Box 3341, Mission BC V2V 4J5 – 604/826-0277 – Former site of St. Mary's Mission & Indian Residential School; open daily Victoria Day - Labour Day

Mission District Historical Society & Museum, 33201 - 2nd Ave., Mission BC V2V 1J9 – 604/826-1011 – Curator, Dorothy Crosby – Local & Native Indian history

Nakusp Museum, c/o Arrow Lakes Historical Society, PO Box 584, Nakusp BC V0G 1R0 – 250/265-3323 – Curator, Milton Parent – Open June - Sept.

Nanaimo: The Bastion, #211, 450 Stewart Ave., Nanaimo BC V9S 4C6 – 250/754-6195 – Director, W. Stannard – 1853 Hudson's Bay Co. log fortification

Nanaimo District Museum (NDM), 100 Cameron Rd., Nanaimo BC V9R 2X1 – 250/753-1821; Fax: 250/753-1777; Email: ndmuseum@island.net – Director/Curator, Debra Bodner – Open year round

Naramata Museum, S5, C41, RR#1, Naramata BC V0H 1N0 – 250/496-5567 – Director, Phil Rounds

Nelson: Chamber of Mines of Eastern BC Museum, 215 Hall St., Nelson BC V1L 5X4 – 250/352-5242

Nelson Museum, 402 Anderson St., Nelson BC V1L 3Y3 – 250/352-9813; Fax: 250/352-5721 – Director, Mrs. Shawn Lamb; President, Alan R. Ramsden – Small boats; archives - extensive local newspapers, Notre Dame University Collection; Doukhobor & Kooteniana Collection; local artists in Mildred Erb Gallery

New Denver: Sandon Museum, PO Box 52, New Denver BC V0G 1S0 – 250/358-2247; Fax: 250/358-2607 – President, Hal Wright – Historic site & silver mining history; open daily May 20 - Oct. 15; in winter by appt.

Canadian Almanac & Directory 1997

New Denver: Silvery Slocan Museum, 202 Main St., PO Box 301, New Denver BC V0G 1S0 – 250/358-2201; Fax: 250/358-7251 – Open daily June - Thanksgiving

New Westminster: BC Transportation Heritage Centre Society, 224 Front St., New Westminster BC V3L 1A2 – 604/525-7707 – President, G. Hall Mackenzie

New Westminster: Canadian Lacrosse Hall of Fame, PO Box 308, New Westminster BC V3L 1H7 – 604/521-7656 – Curator, Archie W. Miller

New Westminster: Irving House Historic Centre & New Westminster Museum & Archives, 302 Royal Ave., New Westminster BC V3L 1H7 – 604/521-7656; Fax: 604/521-2079; Email: can-nwm@im-media.ca – Curator, Archie W. Miller – Open year round

New Westminster: Museum of the Royal Westminster Regiment Historical Society, The Armouries, 530 Queens Ave., New Westminster BC V3L 1K3 – 604/526-5116; Fax: 604/666-4042 – Curator, Lt.Col. B.V. Morgan

New Westminster: Samson V Maritime Museum, 302 Royal Ave., New Westminster BC V3L 1H7 – 604/521-1425 – Curator, Archie W. Miller – Moored on the Fraser River at the Westminster Quay Public Market

North Vancouver: Deep Cove & Area Heritage Association, 1204 Caledonia Ave., North Vancouver BC V7G 2A6 – President, Damian Inwood – Archives; open year round

North Vancouver: Lynn Canyon Ecology Centre, 3663 Park Rd., North Vancouver BC V7J 3G3 – 604/981-3103; Fax: 604/981-3154 – Chief Naturalist, Kevin M. Bell

North Vancouver Museum & Archives, 209 West 4th St., North Vancouver BC V7M 1H8 – 604/987-5618; Fax: 604/987-5600 – Director, Robin Inglis

Okanagan Falls: Bassett House Museum, 1145 Main St., Okanagan Falls BC V0H 1R0 – 250/497-5308; Fax: 250/497-5358 – Open May - Sept.

Okanagan Falls Heritage Place, c/o Okanagan Falls Heritage & Museum Society, PO Box 323, Okanagan Falls BC V0H 1R0 – 250/497-8734 – President, Paul Mallory

Oliver Heritage Society Museum & Archives, PO Box 847, Oliver BC V0H 1T0 – 250/498-4027 – Curator, C.M. Pinske – Open year round

Osoyoos Museum & Archives, PO Box 791, Osoyoos BC V0H 1V0 – 250/495-6723 – President, F. Western Smith – Wide range of displays, including dioramas & murals; open daily July - Sept.

Parksville: Craig Park & Museum, PO Box 1452, Parksville BC V0R 2S0 – 250/248-6966 – Museum Manager, M. Leffler; Archives, P. Cardwell – Open mid-May - Labour Day

Peachland Museum, 5890 Beach Ave., Peachland BC V0H 1X0 – 250/767-3441 – Open June - Aug.

Pemberton Museum, PO Box 267, Pemberton BC V0N 2L0 – 604/894-6274 – Curator, Margaret Fougberg

Penticton (R.N. Atkinson) Museum & Archives, 785 Main St., Penticton BC V2A 5E3 – 250/490-2451; Fax: 250/492-0440; Historic Ships: 604/492-0403 – Curator/Director, R.S. Manuel; Administrator, Marlene Trenholm – The historic CPR steamships S.S. Sicamous & S.S. Naramata are part of the museum; open Mon. - Sat. year round

Pitt Meadows Heritage & Museum Society, 19235 Davison Rd., Pitt Meadows BC V3Y 1A2 – 604/465-5238 – President, Sandra Caddo

Port Clements Museum, PO Box 417, Port Clements BC V0T 1R0 – 250/557-4576 – Historical Coordinator, Kathleen E. Dalzell – Logging, mining, marine & pioneering artifacts; open year round, reduced hours in winter

Port Alberni: Alberni Valley Museum, 4255 Wallace St., Port Alberni BC V9Y 3Y6 – 250/723-2181; Fax: 250/723-1035 – Director, Jean McIntosh; Education/Extension, Shelley Harding; Curator, Charlene Garvey

Port Edward: North Pacific Cannery Museum, 1889 Skeena Dr., Port Edward BC V0V 1G0 – 250/628-3538 – Manager, Dr. Nancy Oliver – Open year round

Port Hardy Museum & Archives, PO Box 2126, Port Hardy BC V0N 2P0 – 250/949-8143 – Curator, William F. Reeve

Port Moody Station Museum, 2734 Murray St., Port Moody BC V3H 1X2 – 604/939-1648 – Director, Al Sholund; President, A. McNeil

Pouce Coupe Museum, 5006 - 49th Ave., PO Box 293, Pouce Coupe BC V0C 2C0 – 250/786-5555; Fax: 250/786-5257 – Open May 15 - Sept. 15

Powell River Historical Museum & Archives Association, PO Box 42, Powell River BC V8A 4Z5 – 604/485-2222 – Coordinator, Teedie Kagume – Open year round

Prince George: Fraser-Fort George Regional Museum (FFGRM), PO Box 1779, Prince George BC V2L 4V7 – 250/562-1612; Fax: 250/562-6395; Email: ffgrmuseum@solutions-4u.com – Director, George Phillips – Natural history, transportation, town development, photo archives; McGregor Model Forest Info Centre; hands-on science & technology exhibit; open year round

Prince George Railway & Forest Industry Museum, PO Box 2408, Prince George BC V2N 2S6 – 250/563-7351; Fax: 250/561-1776 – President, Roy Smith

Prince Rupert: Kwinitsa Station Railway Museum, PO Box 669, Prince Rupert BC V8J 3S1 – 250/627-1915 (summer), 627-3207 (winter); Fax: 250/627-8009; Email: smarsden@citytel.net – Director, Susan Marsden – Railway & early Prince Rupert history; museum is a restored train station; open June - Sept.

Prince Rupert: Museum of Northern British Columbia, & Ruth Harvey Art Gallery, PO Box 669, Prince Rupert BC V8J 3S1 – 250/624-3207; Fax: 250/627-0999 – Curator, Elaine Moore – Northwest coast native artifacts; open year round

Prince Rupert Fire Museum, 200 - 1st Ave. West, Prince Rupert BC V8J 1A8 – 250/624-2211; 627-4475; Fax: 250/624-3407 – Director, Brian Hadland; President, Marvin Kristoff – Firefighting in Prince Rupert since 1908; restored 1925 fire engine; BC Police display; open year round

Princeton & District Museum & Archives Society, 167 Vermillion Ave., PO Box 281, Princeton BC V0X 1W0 – 250/295-7588 – Director, Margaret Stoneberg – Museum open mid-June - Aug.; archives open year round

Quathiaski Cove: Kwagiulth Museum & Cultural Centre, PO Box 8, Quathiaski Cove BC V0P 1N0 – 250/285-3733; Fax: 250/285-2400 – Director, Gina Robertson – Potlatch collection of Kwagiulth ceremonial artifacts

Quesnel & District Museum & Archives (QDMA), 405 Barlow Ave., Quesnel BC V2J 2C3 – 250/992-9580; Fax: 250/992-9680; Email: can-qdm@immedia.ca – Curator, Ruth Stubbs – Open year round

Revelstoke Court House, 1100 - 2nd St. West, Revelstoke BC V0E 2S0 – 250/837-7636; Fax: 250/836-7640

Revelstoke Museum & Archives, PO Box 1908, Revelstoke BC V0E 2S0 – 250/837-3067, 2898 – Curator, Anne Catto – Open year round

Revelstoke Railway Museum, 719 Track St. West, PO Box 3018, Revelstoke BC V0E 2S0 – 250/837-6060; Fax: 250/837-3732 – Director, Wilma Wood

Revelstoke: Rogers Pass Centre, Glacier National Park, PO Box 350, Revelstoke BC V0E 2S0 – 250/837-6274; Fax: 250/837-9696 – Superintendent, Roger Beardmore – Open daily in summer; contact for winter hours

Revelstoke: Three Valley Gap, PO Box 860, Revelstoke BC V0E 2S0 – 250/837-2109 – Historic frontier ghost town

Richmond Museum, #180, 7700 Minoru Gate, Richmond BC V6Y 1R9 – 604/231-6440; Fax: 604/231-6423; Email: museum@city.richmond.bc.ca – Curator/Director, Lana Panko – Holdings include archaeology, ethnology, textiles, furnishings & items significant to agriculture, fishing, transportation, recreation, communications, business & technology; public & education programs; art gallery, library & archives also form part of the Centre

Richmond: Steveston Museum, 3811 Moncton St., Richmond BC V7E 3A0 – 604/271-6868 – Chairman, N. Peterson – Open Mon. - Sat.

Richmond: The Trev Deeley Motorcycle Museum, 13500 Verdun Pl., Richmond BC V6V 1V4 – 604/273-5421; Fax: 604/273-2029 – Over 240 antique motorcycles; open Mon. - Fri., 10 am - 4 pm

Rossland: BC Firefighters Museum, PO Box 789, Rossland BC V0G 1Y0 – 250/362-5514 (summer); 362-9531 (winter) – President, M. Pickering; Manager, K. Thatcher – Open June -Sept.

Rossland Historical Museum, PO Box 26, Rossland BC V0G 1Y0 – 250/362-7722; Fax: 250/362-5379 – Manager, Joyce Austin – Local pioneer & mining history; Western Canada Ski Hall of Fame; open daily mid-May - mid-Sept.; in winter by appt.

Saanich Pioneer's Museum & Archives, 7910 Saanich Rd. East, RR#1, Saanichton BC V0S 1M0 – 250/656-7861 – Curator, Alice Ritchie

Saanichton Historical Artifacts Society, 7321 Lochside Dr., RR#3, Saanichton BC V0S 1M0 – 250/652-5522 – Curator, Robert Norwood

Salmo Museum, 104 - 4th St., PO Box 69, Salmo BC V0G 1Z0 – 250/357-2200 – Curator, Gloria Currie

Salmon Arm Museum Heritage Association, PO Box 1642, Salmon Arm BC V1E 4P7 – 250/832-5243; Fax: 250/832-5291 – Curator, Deborah Chapman; Manager, Ted McTaggart – Open June - Sept.

Sayward: Link & Pin Logging Museum, Sayward BC V0P 1R0 – 250/287-9421 – Director, Frances Duncan – Open June-Sept.

Shawnigan Lake Historical Society Museum, PO Box 331, Shawnigan Lake BC V0R 2W0 – 250/743-4811; Fax: 250/383-7833 – Open daily July & Aug., weekends in winter

Sicamous: Eagle Valley Museum & Heritage Society, PO Box 944, Sicamous BC V0E 2V0 – 250/836-4635 – President, Adelaide Simpson – Open July - Aug., Wed. - Sun., 10 am - 5 pm

Sidney: A.N.A.F. Vets Sidney No. 302 Museum Unit, PO Box 2051, Sidney BC V8L 3S3 – 250/656-9004 – Director, J.H. Nunn – Military artifacts

Sidney: BC Aviation Museum, Victoria Airport, 1910 Norseman Rd., Sidney BC V8L 4R1 – 250/655-3300

Sidney: James Island Museum, #3, 10084 - 3rd St., Sidney BC V8L 3B3 – 250/656-1868 – President, S. Beatrice Bond

Sidney Marine Mammal & Historical Museum, 9801 Seaport Pl., Sidney BC V8L 1Y2 – 250/656-1322; Fax: 250/655-4508; Email: can-smmhm@im-media.ca – Manager, Calvor Palmateer – Open May - Sept. 1, 10 am - 5 pm; Sept. 1 - April 30, 10 am - 4 pm

Sidney: West Coast Museum of Flying, 10137 West Saanich Rd., Sidney BC V8L 5T6 – 250/656-9339; Fax: 250/655-3993

Skidegate: Queen Charlotte Islands Museum, PO Box 1373, Skidegate BC V0T 1S1 – 250/559-4643; Fax: 250/559-4662; Email: muse@island.net – Curator, Nathalie Macfarlane

Smithers: Adams Igloo Wildlife Museum, Site 9, Comp. 1, RR#1, Smithers BC V0J 2N0 – 250/847-3188

Smithers: Bulkley Valley Museum, PO Box 2615, Smithers BC V0J 2N0 – 250/847-5322; Fax: 250/847-3337 – Curator, Lillian Weedmark – Open year round

Sooke Region Museum, Art Gallery & Historic Moss Cottage, PO Box 774, Sooke BC V0S 1N0 – 250/642-6351; Fax: 250/642-7089 – Executive Director, Terry Malone – Open year round

Canadian Almanac & Directory 1997

Stewart Historical Museum, PO Box 402, Stewart BC V0T 1W0 – 250/636-2568; Fax: 250/636-2568 – President, Karin Hanhart

Summerland Museum & Heritage Society, 9521 Wharton St., PO Box 1491, Summerland BC V0H 1Z0 – 250/494-9395 – Curator, Ursula Richardson – Open year round

Surrey: Historic Stewart Farmhouse, 13723 Crescent Rd., Surrey BC V4A 2W3 – 604/574-5744; Fax: 604/574-7338 – Director, B.A. Sommer – 1894 historic farm; open mid-Feb. - mid-Dec.

Surrey Museum & Archives, 6022 - 176 St., Surrey BC V3S 4E7 – 604/574-5744 – Manager, Heritage Services, Beverly Sommer – Community history; open Tues. - Sun. year round

Terrace Heritage Park Museum, PO Box 246, Terrace BC V8G 4A6 – 250/635-2508 – President, Mamie Kerby – Open April - Sept. & by appt.

Tofino: West Coast Maritime Museum, PO Box 249, Tofino BC V0R 2Z0 – 250/725-3346 – Curator, Olivia Mal

Trail Museum, 1051 Victoria St., PO Box 405, Trail BC V1R 4L7 – 250/364-1262; Fax: 250/364-0830 – Curator, Jamie Forbes – Open June - Aug.

Valemount & Area Museum, PO Box 850, Valemount BC V0E 2Z0 – 250/566-4177, 4324; Fax: 250/566-9832 – Open May - Oct.

Vancouver: 15th Field Artillery Regiment Museum & Archives Society, 2025 - 11th Ave. West, Vancouver BC V6J 2C7 – 604/666-4370; Fax: 604/666-4083 – Director, Victor Stevenson

Vancouver: BC Medical Association Archives & Museum, 1665 Broadway West, Vancouver BC V6J 1X1 – 604/736-5551 – C.W. Fraser

Vancouver: BC Sugar Museum, 123 Rogers St., PO Box 2150, Vancouver BC V6B 3V2 – 604/253-1131; Fax: 604/253-2517 – Museum Co-ordinator, Joanne Denton – Open year round; closed weekends & holidays

Vancouver: Beatles Museum, 498 Seymour St., Vancouver BC V6B 3H1 – 604/685-8841 – Open year round

Vancouver: Biblical Museum of Canada, 5800 University Blvd., PO Box 27090, Stn Collingwood, Vancouver BC V5R 6A8 – 604/432-6122; Fax: 604/435-8181 – Curator, Rev. Frederick W. Metzger

Vancouver: British Columbia Museum of Medicine, Academy of Medicine Bldg., 1807 - 10 Ave. West, Vancouver BC V6J 2A9 – Director, Dr. C. McDonnel

Vancouver: British Columbia Regiment Museum & Society, 620 Beatty St., Vancouver BC V6B 2L9 – 604/666-4368 – Curator, W.D. Edgar

Vancouver: British Columbia Sports Hall of Fame & Museum, BC Place Stadium, 777 Pacific Blvd. South, Vancouver BC V6B 4Y8 – 604/687-5520; Fax: 604/687-5510 – Executive Director, Bob Graham; General Manager, Sue Lewis; Curator, Patricia Armstrong

Vancouver: Canadian Craft Museum, 639 Hornby St., Vancouver BC V6C 2G3 – 604/687-8266; Fax: 604/687-7174 – Administrative Director, Giovanni Festa

Vancouver: Cowan Vertebrate Museum, Dept. of Zoology, University of British Columbia, 6270 University Blvd., Vancouver BC V6T 2A9 – 604/228-4665 – Director, G. Scudder

Vancouver: M.Y. Williams Geological Museum, Dept. of Geological Sciences, University of British Columbia, 6339 Stores Rd., Vancouver BC V6T 1Z4 – 604/228-5586; Fax: 604/228-6088 – Curator, Joe Nagel – Includes mounted dinosaur

Vancouver: Old Hastings Mill Store Museum, 1575 Alma Rd., Vancouver BC V6R 3P3 – 604/228-1213 – Open daily June 1 - Sept. 15, 11 am - 4 pm; Sept. - May, Sat. & Sun. only, 1 pm - 4 pm

Vancouver: Pacific Space Centre (PSC), 1100 Chestnut St., Vancouver BC V6J 3J9 – 604/738-7827; Fax: 604/736-5665; Email: ddodge@pacific-space-centre.bc.ca; URL: http://pacific-space-centre.bc.ca – Managing Director, John Dickenson; Programme Director, Paul Deans – Open year round; observatory open Fri., Sat., Sun. & statutory holidays, weather and volunteer staff permitting

Vancouver: Science World British Columbia, 1455 Quebec St., Vancouver BC V6A 3Z7 – 604/268-6363; 443-7440 (Admin.); Fax: 604/682-2923; Email: mcotic@scienceworld.bc.ca; URL: http://www.scienceworld.bc.ca – Executive Director, Dr. Sid Katz; Managing Director, Pauline Thompson

Vancouver: Seaforth Highlanders Regimental Museum, Seaforth Armoury, 1650 Burrard St., Vancouver BC V6J 3G4 – 604/738-9510

Vancouver: Spencer Entomological Museum, Dept. of Zoology, University of British Columbia, 6270 University Blvd., Vancouver BC V6T 2A9 – 604/228-3379; Fax: 604/228-2416 – Curator, S. Cannings

Vancouver: The Station Museum, c/o Mahon Park, 209 -14th St. West, Vancouver BC V7M 1H8

Vancouver: The Vancouver Maritime Museum Society (VMM), 1905 Ogden Ave., Vancouver BC V6J 1A3 – 604/257-8300; Fax: 604/737-2621 – Executive Director, James P. Delgado – Includes National Historic Site St. Roch, RCMP Schooner

Vancouver Police Historical Society & Centennial Museum, 240 Cordova St. East, Vancouver BC V6A 1L3 – 604/665-3346; Fax: 604/665-5078 – Curator, Udcon Rhymer – Open daily year round

Vanderhoof Community Museum, c/o Nechako Valley Historical Society, PO Box 1515, Vanderhoof BC V0J 3A0 – 250/567-2991 – President, Jay Sherwood

Vernon: Greater Vernon Museum & Archives, 3009 - 32 Ave., Vernon BC V1T 2L8 – 250/542-3142; Fax: 250/545-7876 – Curator, Ron Candy – Open year round

Vernon: O'Keefe Ranch & Interior Heritage Society, PO Box 955, Vernon BC V1T 6M8 – 250/542-7868; Email: can-orihs@immedia.ca – Manager/Curator, Ken Mather; Visitor Services Manager, Dave Sayer – Open May - Thanksgiving

Victoria: Canadian Scottish (Princess Mary's) Regimental Museum, Bay Street Armoury, #231, 715 Bay St., Victoria BC V8T 1R1 – 250/388-3897 – Director, Col. Michael Allen

Victoria: Canadiana Costume Museum & Archives of BC, 2818 Aldwynd Rd., Victoria BC V9B 3S7 – 250/478-7564 – President, Sherrie McIvor Wade

Victoria: Carr House, c/o Ministry of Small Business, Tourism & Culture, 1117 Wharf St., Victoria BC V8W 2Z2 – 250/356-6363; Fax: 250/356-8248 – Manager, John D. Adams – Birthplace of Emily Carr

Victoria: CFB Esquimalt Naval Museum, FMO, Victoria BC V0S 1B0 – 250/380-4395; Fax: 250/380-5665 – Director, E.W. Colwell – Open year round

Victoria: The Craigdarroch Castle Historical Museum Society, 1050 Joan Cres., Victoria BC V8S 3L5 – 250/592-5323; Fax: 250/592-1099 – Executive Director, Bruce W. Davies

Victoria: Craigflower Heritage Site, 110 Island Hwy., Victoria BC V9B 1E9 – 250/387-3067 – Director, Colin K. Campbell

Victoria: Fort Rood Hill & Fisgard Lighthouse National Historic Sites, 501 Belmont Rd., Victoria BC V9C 1B5 – 250/380-4662 – Turn of the century coastal defence gun batteries & first permanent lighthouse on Canada's west coast; open daily

Victoria: Goldstream Region Museum Society, #2, 697 Goldstream Ave., Victoria BC V9B 2X2 – 250/474-6113 – President, Phyllis Griffiths

Victoria: Helmcken House Pioneer Doctor's Residence, 638 Elliott St., Victoria BC V8V 1W1 – 250/387-4697; Fax: 250/387-5129 – Manager, John D. Adams – Open June - Sept.

Victoria: Maritime Museum of British Columbia, 28 Bastion Sq., Victoria BC V8W 1H9 – 250/385-4222; Fax: 250/382-2869 – Director, John MacFarlane – Open daily

Victoria: Metchosin School Museum, 4475 Happy Valley Rd., RR#1, Victoria BC V8X 3W9 – 250/478-2804 – Curator, Julian Rapps – Open mid-Apr. - mid-Oct.

Victoria: Point Ellice House Museum, 2616 Pleasant St., Victoria BC V8T 4V3 – 250/385-3837 – Curator, Michael Zarb – Open June - Sept.

Victoria: Royal London Wax Museum, 470 Belleville St., Victoria BC V8V 1W9 – 250/388-4461; Fax: 250/388-4493; URL: http://www.victoriabc.com/guide/vicat4.html – President, Dr. Arne H. Lane; Managing Director, Ken H. Lane – Open daily

Wells Museum, Wells Historical Society, PO Box 244, Wells BC V0K 2R0 – 250/994-3422 – Curator, Judy Campbell – Open May - Labour Day

White Rock Museum/Archives, 15322 Buena Vista Ave., White Rock BC V4B 1Y6 – Curator, Lorraine M. Ellenwood

Williams Lake Museum, RR#2, Williams Lake BC V2G 2C8 – 250/392-5573 – Director, Reg Beck – Open June - Sept.

Yale: Historic Yale Museum, 31179 Douglas St., PO Box 74, Yale BC V0K 2S0 – 604/863-2324 – President, Verna Shilson

Ymir Arts & Museum Society, PO Box 65, Ymir BC V0G 2K0 – 250/357-9600 – Chairperson, Kay Boyes

MANITOBA

Manitoba Museum of Man & Nature/Musée de l'homme et de la nature du Manitoba

190 Rupert Ave., Winnipeg MB R3B 0N2
204/956-2830; Fax: 204/942-3679; Email: info@manitobamuseum; 204/943-3139 (Info line)
URL: http://www.mbnet.mb.ca/manitobamuseum
Seven permanent galleries & Alloway Hall which houses temporary & travelling exhibitions. Permanent galleries are: Orientation (in which the main theme of the Museum is expounded), Earth History, Grasslands, Urban (a section of Winnipeg, reconstructed as it might have been in 1920), Nonsuch (a replica of the 17th-century Hudson Bay ship), Arctic-Subarctic & Boreal Forest. The Planetarium provides educational & entertaining programs for the general public & school groups in the 287-seat Star Theatre; feature presentations touch all aspects of astronomy, science fact/science fiction, as well as present day space programs & technology. "Touch the Universe" is a hands-on science & education centre dealing with the ways in which the universe is perceived by the five senses. The Education & Programs Departments provide special activities for schools & other groups. Live demonstrations & performances; films; lectures.
Executive Director, Joanne DiCosimo
Director, Programs, G. Wurtak
Director, Operations, T. Nickle
Chief, Marketing, K. Roos Pavlik
Assistant Executive Director, D. Leonard
Head, Natural History, K. Johnson
Producer, Planetarium, E. Barker
Communications Officer, Joyce Moroz

Other Museums & Science Centres in Manitoba

Alonsa: Alex Robertson Museum, Alonsa MB R0H 0A0 – 204/767-2095, 2101

Anola & District Museum, PO Box 153, Anola MB R0E 0A0 – 204/866-2922, 3009 – Treasurer, J.F. Mavins – Open May - Sept., Sun. or by appt.

Arrow River: Clegg's Museum of Horse-Drawn Vehicles, Arrow River MB R0M 2H0 – 204/562-3648 – Director, R.E. Clegg – Open by appointment

Ashern Pioneer Museum, PO Box 642, Ashern MB R0C 0E0 – 204/768-3147 – Chairperson, Emma Geisler – Open July & Aug.

Austin: Manitoba Agricultural Museum, PO Box 10, Austin MB R0H 0C0 – 204/637-2354; Fax: 204/637-

2395 – Administrator, Terry Farley – Pioneer artifacts; homesteaders' village, annual Thresherman's Reunion & Stampede; Open Victoria Day - Oct. 1

Beausejour: Pioneer Village Museum, PO Box 310, Beausejour MB R0E 0C0 – 204/268-3048 – President, Peter H. Kozyra – Open July & Aug.

Belmont & District Museum, PO Box 69, Belmont MB R0K 0C0 – 204/537-2252, 2430

Belmont: Evergreen Firearms Museum Inc., Belmont MB R0K 0C0 – 204/537-2647 – Military & sporting firearms; open by appt.

Birtle: Birdtail Country Museum, PO Box 508, Birtle MB R0M 0C0 – 204/842-3363, 5219 – President, G. Huberdeau – Open May 23 - Sept. & by appt.

Boissevain: Beckoning Hills Museum Inc., 425 Mill Rd. South, PO Box 389, Boissevain MB R0K 0E0 – 204/534-6544 – President, Ken Patterson; Secretary, E. Brake – Pioneer & native artifacts; Open end of May - Sept.

Boissevain: Moncur Gallery, Civic Centre, Boissevain MB R0K 0E0 – 204/534-2433, 6478; Fax: 204/534-6085 – Sec.-Treas., Gerald May – Open Mon. - Sat.; Sun. by appt.

Bowsman: McKay's Museum, Lenswood Rd., Bowsman MB R0L 0H0 – 204/238-4412 – Open Mon. - Sat.; Sun. by appt.

Brandon: 26th Field Artillery Regiment Museum, PO Box 730, Brandon MB R7A 5Z8 – 204/728-2559 – President, Col. J.A. Brerton – Open Sun.

Brandon: B.J. Hales Museum of Natural History, McMaster Hall Concourse, Brandon University, #270 - 18th St., Brandon MB R7A 6A9 – 204/727-7307; Fax: 204/728-7346 – Curator, Maureen Rodgers

Brandon Mental Health Centre Museum & Archives, PO Box 420, Brandon MB R7A 5Z5 – 204/726-2725; Fax: 204/726-4157 – Curator, Jessie Little

Brandon: Chapman Museum, RR#2, PO Box 43, Brandon MB R7A 5Y2 – 204/728-7396 – Director, A.T. Chapman – 16 historic buildings

Brandon: Commonwealth Air Training Plan Museum, Group 520, PO Box 3, RR#5, Brandon MB R7A 5Y5 – 204/727-2444 – President, Archie Londry

Brandon: Daly House Museum & Steve Magnacca Research Centre, 122 - 18 St., Brandon MB R7A 5A4 – 204/727-1722 – Curator, Sandra Head – Period home of the 1890s; 1903 grocery store; 1882 council chambers; open daily in the summer; Wed. to Sun. winter

Brandon: Manitoba Amateur Radio Museum Inc. (MARM), 25 Queens Cres., Brandon MB R7B 1G1 – 204/728-2463 – Curator, Dave Snydal – Canada's only amateur radio museum

Carberry Plains Museum, 520 - 4 Ave., PO Box 130, Carberry MB R0K 0H0 – 204/834-2195, 3295 – Chairman, Marjorie Baron – Open mid-June - mid-Sept.

Carberry: The Seton Centre, 116 Main St., PO Box 508, Carberry MB R0K 0H0 – 204/834-2059 – Materials by & about Ernest Thompson Seton; open June - Thanksgiving

Carberry: Spruce Woods Provincial Heritage Park, Visitor Services Information Centre & Museum, PO Box 900, Carberry MB R0K 0H0 – 204/827-2543; Fax: 204/834-2614 – Interpreter, Lisa Mandziak – Northwest Co. fur-trading artifacts

Carman: Dufferin Historical Museum, PO Box 426, Carman MB R0G 0J0 – Chairman, L.G. Budd – Open Victoria Day - Labour Day

Carman: Heaman's Antique Autorama, Hwy. 3, PO Box 105, Carman MB R0G 0J0 – 204/745-2981

Cartwright: Badger Creek Museum, MTS Bldg., Cartwright MB R0K 0L0 – 204/529-2339 – A. Thompson – Open summer

Cartwright Museum, PO Box 9, Cartwright MB R0K 0L0 – 204/529-2263; Fax: 204/529-2288 – Colleen Mullin

Churchill: Eskimo Museum, PO Box 10, Churchill MB R0B 0E0 – 204/675-2030; Fax: 204/675-2140 – Curator, Lorraine Brandson – Open Mon. - Sat.

Churchill: Fort Prince of Wales National Historic Site, PO Box 127, Churchill MB R0B 0E0 – 204/675-8863 – Area Superintendent, Peter Lamb

Churchill: Prince of Wales Fort & Cape Merry National Historic Site, PO Box 127, Churchill MB R0B 0E0 – 204/675-8863

Crystal City Community Museum, 218 Broadway, Crystal City MB R0K 0N0 – 204/873-2293

Darlingford School Heritage Museum, Darlingford MB R0G 0L0 – 204/246-2026, 2137

Dauphin: Cross of Freedom Historical Site & Museum, 121 - 7 Ave. SE, Dauphin MB R7N 2E3 – 204/638-9641, 9607 – President, John Slobodzian

Dauphin: Fort Dauphin Museum, 140 Jackson Ave., PO Box 181, Dauphin MB R7N 2V1 – 204/638-6630 – Executive Director, Gladys Hendick; Administrator, Nell Roy – Replica of Northwest Co. Trading Post, plus numerous artifacts & an archaeological lab; open mid-May - mid-Sept. & by appt.

Dufresne: Aunt Margaret's Museum of Childhood Inc., Trans-Canada Hwy., Dufresne MB R0A 0J0 – 204/422-8426

Dugald: Cook's Creek Heritage Museum, RR#2, Dugald MB R0E 0N0 – 204/853-2166 – Curator, Candace Daher – Open Daily May - Oct. & by appt.

Dugald Costume Museum & Pioneer Home, PO Box 38, Dugald MB R0E 0K0 – 204/853-2166

Eddystone: Village Site Museum, Eddystone MB R0L 0S0 – 204/448-2040

Elkhorn: Manitoba Automobile Museum Foundation, PO Box 477, Elkhorn MB R0M 0N0 – 204/845-2604 – Sec.-Treas., Garth Mitchell – 70 restored antique automobiles 1908-1930, pioneer & Indian artifacts; open May - Sept.

Erickson: The Parsonage & Nedrob School, Erickson MB R0J 0P0 – 204/636-2431

Eriksdale Museum, PO Box 71, Eriksdale MB R0C 0W0 – 204/739-2621, 5273 – Chair, Donna Smith; Secretary, Eileen McLelland – Open mid-May - Sept., 1:30 pm - 4:30 pm, excluding Thurs. & Sun.

Flin Flon Museum, PO Box 100, Flin Flon MB R8A 1M6 – 204/687-7511; Fax: 204/687-5133 – Director, Brenda Russell – Mining, transportation & culture; open daily May - mid-Sept.

Gardenton: Ukrainian Museum, Park & Village, Gardenton MB R0A 0M0 – 204/425-3501 – President, Linda Shewchuk

Gimli Historical Museum, PO Box 1197, Gimli MB R0C 1B0 – 204/642-5317

Gladstone & District Museum, PO Box 651, Gladstone MB R0J 0T0 – 204/385-2551 – President, O.E. Whitten

Grandview: The Watson Crossley Community Museum, PO Box 396, Grandview MB R0L 0Y0 – 204/546-2661 – President, Gerald Morran – Historical, agricultural & antique cars; open daily mid-June - Labour Day

Hamiota Pioneer Club Museum, PO Box 577, Hamiota MB R0M 0T0 – 204/764-2222, 2434 – President, John L. Rankin – Open Sundays in July & Aug. & by appt.

Hartney: Hart-Cam Museum, PO Box 323, Hartney MB R0M 0X0

Inglis: St. Elie 1908 Pioneer Church Museum, Inglis MB R0J 0X0 – 204/564-2228, 2276 – President, Barry Sawchuk – Designated provincial historic site

Killarney: J.A. Victor David Municipal Museum, 414 Williams Ave., PO Box 584, Killarney MB R0K 1G0 – 204/523-7325 – Director, Gwen Powell

La Broquerie: Musée Saint Joachim, PO Box 66, La Broquerie MB R0A 0W0 – 204/424-5232 – Directrice, Laura Gallant

La Rivière: Archibald Historical Museum, PO Box 97, La Rivière MB R0G 1A0 – 204/242-2825, 2554 – President, R.K. Wallcraft – 1878 log house furnished as it was during Nellie McClung's residency; open mid-May - Labour Day

Ladywood: Atelier Ladywood Museum, RR#3, PO Box 14, Ladywood MB R0E 0C0 – 204/265-3226 – Director, Lenard Anthony

Lundar Museum Society, PO Box 265, Lundar MB R0C 1Y0 – 204/762-5689 – Director, Sigfus Johannson – Open mid-June - Sept.

Melita: Antler River Historical Society Museum, PO Box 155, Melita MB R0M 1L0 – 204/522-8289 – President, J. McRae – Open June 15 - Sept. 15

Miami Museum, PO Box 38, Miami MB R0G 1H0 – 204/435-2245 – President, John Andrews

Miniota Municipal Museum Inc., PO Box 189, Miniota MB R0M 1M0 – 204/567-3675, 3789 – Chairman, Vernon Rollo – Open May - Oct.

Minnedosa & District Co-operative Museum, 49 - 2 Ave. NW, PO Box 1453, Minnedosa MB R0J 1E0 – 204/867-3444; Fax: 204/867-5171 – President, Margret Shorrock – Open July 1 - Labour Day

Moosehorn Heritage Museum Inc., PO Box 2066, Moosehorn MB R0C 2E0 – 204/768-2087 – Director, Lois Metner; President, Elsie Kiesman, 204/768-2066 – May 15 - Aug. 30 & by appt.

Morden & District Museum of Palaeontology & Pioneer Artifacts, c/o Morden Recreation Centre, PO Box 728, Morden MB R0G 1J0 – 204/822-3406 – Director, Henry Isaak

Morris & District Centennial Museum Inc., PO Box 344, Morris MB R0G 1K0 – 204/746-2528 – Director, W.M. Schellenberg

Neepawa: Beautiful Plains Museum, PO Box 1732, Neepawa MB R0J 1H0 – 204/476-3896 – Secretary, M. McKenzie – Open daily in summer

Neepawa: The Margaret Laurence Home, 312 First Ave., PO Box 2099, Neepawa MB R0J 1H0 – Open Daily May - Sept.; open weekends in winter

Notre Dame de Lourdes: Museum Dom Benoît & Chapel Ste. Thérèse, Notre Dame de Lourdes MB R0G 1M0 – 204/248-2372, 2105 – 1,000 artifacts on pioneer life; open daily May 15 - Oct. 15

Pilot Mound: Marringhurst Pioneer Park Museum, RR#2, Pilot Mound MB R0G 1P0 – 204/825-2697 – Jeannie Neustaedter

Pilot Mound Centennial Museum, Centennial Bldg., Broadway St., Pilot Mound MB R0G 1P0

Plum Coulee & District Museum, PO Box 36, Plum Coulee MB R0G 1R0 – 204/829-3419; Fax: 204/829-3436 – Director, Kim Porte – Mennonite pioneer artifacts

Portage la Prairie: The Fort-La-Reine Museum & Pioneer Village, PO Box 744, Portage la Prairie MB R2Y 0A9 – 204/857-3259 – Manager, Chris Leslie

Rapid City Museum, PO Box 271, Rapid City MB R0K 1W0 – 204/826-2597 – Curator, J.W. Northam – Open July & Aug.

Reston & District Museum, PO Box 292, Reston MB R0M 1X0 – 204/877-3960 – Curator, Art Smith – Open July - Aug.

Rivers: The Clack Bros. Museum, Rivers MB R0K 1X0 – Open May - Nov.

Riverton: Hecla Island Heritage Home Museum, c/o Hecla Provincial Park, PO Box 70, Riverton MB R0C 2R0 – 204/279-2056, 378-2945 – Icelandic homestead

Roblin: Keystone Pioneer Museum, Hwy. 5, PO Box 10, Roblin MB R0L 1P0 – 204/937-2935 – President, Art McIntyre

Sainte-Anne des Chênes: Musée Pointe des Chênes, PO Box 280, Sainte-Anne des Chênes MB R0A 1R0 – 204/422-5624; Fax: 204/422-5842 – Executive Directeur, Francis M. Labossière

Sandy Lake: Ukrainian Cultural Heritage Museum, Sandy Lake MB R0J 1X0 – 204/585-2168, 2636 – 1899 Ukrainian settlement; open daily in summer & by appointment

Selkirk: Kennedy House, 1 Keystone Dr., Selkirk MB R1A 2H5 – 204/334-2498 (Summer); 204/785-5080

Canadian Almanac & Directory 1997

(Off-Season) – 19th-century home owned by Hudson Bay Co. fur trader & Arctic explorer
Selkirk: Lower Fort Garry National Historic Site, Group 343, RR#3, PO Box 37, Selkirk MB R1A 2A8 – 204/785-6050; Fax: 204/482-5887; Visitor Info: 204/949-3600 – Site Coordinator, Bob Andrews; Elena Vandale – 1830s Hudson's Bay Co.; open mid-May - Labour Day
Selkirk: Marine Museum of Manitoba Inc., PO Box 7, Selkirk MB R1A 2B1 – 204/482-7761; Fax: 204/785-2452 – Chairperson, Ted Francis – Open May - Sept.
Selkirk: St. Andrews' Rectory National Historic Park, Group 343, RR#3, PO Box 37, Selkirk MB R1A 2A8 – 204/949-3600; Fax: 204/482-5887; 1-800-442-0600 – Open daily mid-May - Labour Day & weekends in Sept.
Seven Sisters Falls: Nutimik Lake Museum, c/o Whiteshell Provincial Park, Seven Sisters Falls MB R0E 1Y0 – 204/348-2203
Seven Sisters Falls: Whiteshell Natural History Museum, c/o Dept. of Natural Resources, Seven Sisters Falls MB R0E 1Y0 – 204/348-2846; Fax: 204/348-7141 – Park Manager, Mark Clarke
Shilo: Royal Canadian Artillery Museum, CFB Shilo, Shilo MB R0K 2A0 – 204/765-3534; Fax: 204/765-3095 – Curator, J.A. Eskritt – Two permanent galleries & one hall; research library; archives; war diary rooms; outdoor display area; over 150 major pieces of equipment; over 10,000 military articles; open year round
Shoal Lake: Police & Pioneer Museum, PO Box 315, Shoal Lake MB R0J 1Z0 – 1870s & 1880s NWMP & pioneer artifacts; open by appt.
Snowflake: Star Mound School Museum Park, Snowflake MB R0G 2K0 – 204/876-4749 – President, Alvin Findlay – One-room country school c. 1886
Souris: Hillcrest Museum, PO Box 1287, Souris MB R0K 2C0 – 204/483-2008, 3245 – President, Anne Rose – Includes agricultural museum & CPR caboose; open May - Sept.
St-Georges: Musée St-Georges, CP 171, St-Georges MB R0E 1V0 – 204/367-8801, 2927 – Conservateur, Jean Dupont – Open May - Sept.
St-Joseph: Musée St-Joseph Museum Inc., PO Box 47, St-Joseph MB R0G 2C0 – 204/737-2241 – Président, Jean-Louis Perron – Domestic & agricultural artifacts; open May 15 - Sept. 15
St-Malo: Musée Le Pionnier, St-Malo MB R0A 1T0 – 204/347-5767 – Director, Maurice Comeault
St-Pierre-Jolys: Musée de St-Pierre-Jolys Inc., 432, rue Joubert, CP 321, St-Pierre-Jolys MB R0A 1V0 – 204/433-7226; Fax: 204/433-7181 – President, Gerald Fontaine – Religious & early settlement artifacts; tea room; open July & Aug. & by appt.
St. Claude Museum, PO Box 131, St. Claude MB R0G 1Z0 – 204/379-2405 – President, Henri Bellec – 1,500 artifacts relating to French history of the area; open summer & by request
Steinbach: Mennonite Heritage Village, PO Box 1136, Steinbach MB R0A 2A0 – 204/326-9661 – Executive Director, Peter Goertzen – Includes J.J. Reimer Historical Library & Archives; open year round
Stonewall Quarry Park, PO Box 250, Stonewall MB R0C 2Z0 – 204/467-5354; Fax: 204/467-9129 – Manager, Carl Martin
Strathclair Museum, Strathclair MB R0J 2C0 – 204/365-5202, 5201 – Sec.-Treas., Helga Gerrard – Open mid-May - mid-Sept.
Swan Valley Museum, PO Box 2078, Swan River MB R0L 1Z0 – 204/734-3585 – President, Glynn Donaldson; Curator, Debbie Holland – Open mid-May - mid-Sept.
Teulon & District Museum, PO Box 197, Teulon MB R0C 3B0 – 204/886-2792 – Secretary, Mary Revel
The Pas: The Sam Waller Museum, 306 Fischer Ave., PO Box 185, The Pas MB R9A 1K4 – 204/623-3802; Fax: 204/623-5506 – Director, Laura MacLean

Thompson: Heritage North Museum, 162 Princeton Dr., Thompson MB R8N 2A4 – 204/677-2216; Fax: 204/677-3434 – Curator, Paul Legault – Geology, natural history, archaeology, community history, travelling exhibits, pioneer artifacts; open year round
Treherne Museum, PO Box 30, Treherne MB R0G 2V0 – 204/723-2621 (Museum), 2044 (Civic Centre) – Chairperson, Lorraine Darling
Victoria Beach: Ateah Homestead, Victoria Beach MB R0E 2C0 – 204/754-2357 – Director, Sam Ateah
Virden: Currahee Military Museum, PO Box 729, Virden MB R0M 2C0 – 204/748-2454; Fax: 204/748-1805 – Director, John Hipwell – Open year round
Virden: Pioneer Home Museum of Virden & District, 390 King St. West, PO Box 2001, Virden MB R0M 2C0 – 204/748-1659 – President, Ruth Craik – Open summer
Virden: River Valley School Museum, PO Box 729, Virden MB R0M 2C0 – 204/748-2454 – President, Pat Hipwell
Wabowden Historical Museum Inc., Wabowden MB R0B 1S0 – 204/689-2362, 2269 – Open in summer & by appt.
Wasagaming: Pinewood Museum, 154 Wasagaming Dr., Wasagaming MB R0J 2H0 – 204/735-2205, 848-7622 – Open daily June - Labour Day
Wasagaming: Riding Mountain National Park Visitor Centre, Wasagaming MB R0J 2H0 – 204/848-7275; Fax: 204/848-2596; 1-800-707-8480; URL: http://parkscanada.pch.gc.ca/parks/manitoba/riding_mountain/riding_mountain.htm – Chief Interpreter, C. Davar
Waskada Museum, Waskada MB R0M 2E0 – 204/673-2533 – Sec.-Treas., E.V. Dow – Open summer
Wawanesa: Sipiweske Museum, Wawanesa MB R0K 2J0 – 204/824-2244
Whitemouth Municipal Museum, PO Box 294, Whitemouth MB R0E 2G0 – 204/348-2576 – President, Harvey Pischke – Open June 1 - Sept. 30
Winkler: Pembina Threshermen's Museum Inc., PO Box 1103, Winkler MB R6W 4B2 – 204/822-5369, 325-7497; Fax: 204/325-7938 – John C. Heide
Winnipeg: Aquatic Hall of Fame & Museum of Canada Inc., #300, 360 Main St., Winnipeg MB R3C 3Z3 – 204/957-1700; Fax: 204/942-2325 – Director, Vaughan L. Baird – Open daily year round
Winnipeg: Clothing & Textiles Museum, Human Ecology Bldg., University of Manitoba., 35 Chancellor's Circle, Winnipeg MB R3T 2N2 – 204/474-8137; Fax: 204/275-5299 – Dr. Susan Turnbull Caton
Winnipeg: Crafts Museum at the Crafts Guild of Manitoba, 183 Kennedy St., Winnipeg MB R3C 1S6 – 204/943-1190
Winnipeg: Dalnavert, 61 Carlton St., Winnipeg MB R3C 1N7 – 204/943-2835 – Curator, Tim Worth – 1895 restored Victorian home of Hugh John Macdonald, son of Sir John A. Macdonald
Winnipeg: Forest Sandilands Centre & Museum, c/o Manitoba Forestry Association, 900 Corydon Ave., Winnipeg MB R3M 0Y4 – 204/453-3182 – Program Director, William Baker
Winnipeg: Fort Garry Horse Regimental Museum & Archives Inc., c/o McGregor Armoury, 551 Machray Ave., Winnipeg MB R2W 1A8 – 204/586-6298; Fax: 204/582-0370 – Chairman, L. Lajeunesse
Winnipeg: Fort Whyte Centre for Environmental Education, 1961 McCreary Rd., PO Box 124, Winnipeg MB R3Y 1G5 – 204/989-8350
Winnipeg: Grant's Old Mill, PO Box 344, Stn A, Winnipeg MB R3K 2C2 – 204/837-5761 – Miller, Archibald McLachlan – Open June - Aug.
Winnipeg: Historical Museum of St. James-Assiniboia, 3180 Portage Ave., Winnipeg MB R3K 0Y5 – 204/888-8706 – Curator, Grant Tyler – Open year round
Winnipeg: Ivan Franko Museum, 595 Pritchard Ave., Winnipeg MB R2W 2K4 – 204/589-4397; Fax: 204/589-3404 – Director, Anthony Bilecki

Winnipeg: J.B. Wallis Museum of Entomology, Dept. of Entomology, Entomology Bldg., University of Manitoba, 424 University Centre, Winnipeg MB R3T 2N2 – 204/474-6023, 6024; Fax: 204/275-0402 – Curator, Dr. R.E. Roughley – 250,000 species of insects
Winnipeg: Le Musée de St-Boniface Museum, 494, av Taché, Winnipeg MB R2H 2B2 – 204/237-4500; Fax: 204/231-2657 – Curator, Pierrette Boily; Administrator, Dr. Philippe R. Mailhot – Open year round
Winnipeg: Living Prairie Museum, 2795 Ness Ave., Winnipeg MB R3J 3S4 – 204/832-0167; Fax: 204/986-4172; Email: prairie@mbnet.mb.ca – Nature centre & one of the last remaining examples of Tall Grass Prairie in a 12-hectare outdoor museum
Winnipeg: Manitoba Children's Museum, The Forks, 45 Forks Market Rd., Winnipeg MB R3C 4T6 – 204/956-1888 – Executive Director, Jane Eisbrenner – Hands-on exhibits; open daily year round
Winnipeg: Manitoba Sports Hall of Fame & Museum Inc. (MSHOF), Offices, #210, 200 Main St., Winnipeg MB R3C 4M2 – 204/925-5735; Fax: 204/925-5792; URL: http://www.sport.mb.ca – Executive Director, Rick D. Brownlee
Winnipeg: Miami Station Museum, PO Box 1855, Winnipeg MB R3C 3R1 – 204/942-4632 – Director, Peter Lacey – National historic site; 1889 Northern Pacific & Manitoba Railway station; open weekends & holidays during summer & by appt.
Winnipeg: Ogniwo Polish Museum, 205 Cathedral Ave., Winnipeg MB R2W 0X2 – 204/582-2966 – Chairperson, Genowefa Kuzia
Winnipeg: Oseredok Ukrainian Cultural & Educational Centre, Art Gallery & Museum, 184 Alexander Ave. East, Winnipeg MB R3B 0L6 – 204/942-0218 – Curator, Shawna Balas – Open Tues. - Sat.
Winnipeg: Queen's Own Cameron Highlanders of Canada Regimental Museum Inc., Rm. 230, Minto Armoury, 969 St. Matthew's Ave., Winnipeg MB R3G 0J7 – 204/786-4330 – Curator, Sgt. Grant Tyler
Winnipeg: Riel House National Historic Site/Lieu historique national de la Maison-Riel, 330 River Rd., Winnipeg MB R2M 3Z8 – 204/257-1783 (summer), 233-4888 (winter); Fax: 204/233-4888 – Directrice, Janelle Reynolds – Open daily mid-May - Labour Day
Winnipeg: Ross House Museum, 61 Carlton St., Winnipeg MB R3C 1N7 – 204/943-2835, off-season; 204/943-3958, summer – Curator, Tim Worth – Western Canada's first post office, built 1854; open summer
Winnipeg: Royal Canadian Mint, 520 Lagimodiere Blvd., Winnipeg MB R2J 3E7 – 204/257-3359 – Open May - Sept.
Winnipeg: Royal Winnipeg Rifles Regimental Museum, Minto Armoury, #208, 969 St. Matthews Ave., Winnipeg MB R3G 0J7 – 204/786-4350 (Orderly Room) – Curator, MWO Max M. Abrams, CD – Open Tues. & Sat. & by appt.
Winnipeg: Seven Oaks House Museum, 1760 Main St., Winnipeg MB R2V 4C8 – 204/339-7429 – M. Johnson – Home of John Inkster, c.1851; open mid-May - Labour Day
Winnipeg: St. Volodymyr Ukranian Catholic Centre Museum, 418 Aberdeen Ave., Winnipeg MB R2W 1V7 – 204/582-1940 – Chairperson, Jean Michalishyn
Winnipeg: Ukrainian Museum of Canada, Manitoba Branch, 1175 Main St., Winnipeg MB R2W 3S4 – 204/334-6531, 582-7345 – Curator, Nellie Pawlik
Winnipeg: University of Manitoba Museums, c/o Fort Garry Campus, 424 University Centre, Winnipeg MB R3T 2N2 – Director, Dale Amundson – Gallery III; Janet Ian Gallery; Mineralogy Museum; Zoology Museum; Planetarium
Winnipeg: UVAN Historical Museum & Archives, #205, 456 Main St., Winnipeg MB R3B 1B6 – 204/942-5095 – Curator, Dr. Sophia Kachor

Winnipeg: Vintage Locomotive Society Inc., 1485 Portage Ave., PO Box 33021, Stn Polo Park, Winnipeg MB R3G 3N4 – 204/832-5259 – Treasurer, K.G. Younger – Operates "Prairie Dog Central" steam train

Winnipeg: Western Canada Aviation Museum Inc./ Musée de l'aviation de l'ouest du Canada (WCAM), Hangar T-2, 958 Ferry Rd., Winnipeg MB R3H 0Y8 – 204/786-5503; Fax: 204/775-4761 – Executive Director, George W. Elliott

Winnipeg Police Department Museum, 10 Vermillion Rd., Winnipeg MB R2J 2T1 – 204/256-7381 – Staff Sgt., Jack Templeman

Winnipeg Beach Ukranian Homestead, PO Box 396, Winnipeg Beach MB R0C 3G0 – 204/389-4079 – F. Domitruk

Winnipegosis Museum, Winnipegosis MB R0L 2G0 – 204/656-4791

Woodlands Pioneer Museum, Woodlands MB R0C 3H0 – 204/383-5584 – Director, Opal Langrell – Open mid-May - August or by appt.

NEW BRUNSWICK

Kings Landing Historical Settlement
Transcanada, Exit 259, Prince William NB E0H 1S0
506/363-5090; Fax: 506/363-5757
URL: http://www.grtplaces.com/ac/landing/
Vibrant historical settlement along the banks of the St. John River, depicting rural life from the Loyalist to the Victorian eras (1784-1890).

Le Musée Acadien/Acadian Historical Village
15, boul St-Pierre est, CP 420, Caraquet NB E0B 1K0
506/727-1713; Fax: 506/727-7719
1780 to early 1900's recreated Acadian settlement.
Président-directeur, Léopold Chaisson

New Brunswick Museum/Musée du Nouveau-Brunswick
277 Douglas Ave., Saint John NB E2K 1E5
506/643-2300; Fax: 506/643-2360
Collections include human history, marine & technology, prints, fine & decorative arts, botany, zoology, geology; provincial museum of New Brunswick, established in 1842; full range of exhibitions & programs offered daily; closed Christmas Day and Good Friday.
Director, Frank Milligan

Other Museums & Science Centres in New Brunswick

Bathurst: Herman J. Good V.C. Memorial Museum, c/o Royal Canadian Legion Branch 18, 575 St. Peters Ave., Bathurst NB E2A 2Y5 – 506/546-3135 – Director, Cy Comeau

Blackville Historical Society Museum, Rte. 8, Blackville NB E0C 1C0 – 506/843-7761

Boiestown: Central New Brunswick Woodmen's Museum, PO Box 7, Boiestown NB E0H 1A0 – 506/369-7214; Fax: 506/369-9081 – Museum Manager, Jane Gibson

Chatham: Miramichi Natural History Museum, 149 Wellington St., PO Box 162, Chatham NB E1N 3A5 – 506/773-7305 – Curator, Carl Landry

Chatham: St. Michael's Historical Museum, 12 Alexandra St., Chatham NB E1N 1V2 – 506/773-3277 – Curator, John Connell

Chatham: W.S. Loggie Cultural Centre & Loggie House, 222 Wellington St., Chatham NB E1N 1M9 – 506/773-7645 – President, Joan Cripps

Clair: Le Petit Musée, PO Box 401, Clair NB E0L 1B0 – 506/992-3637 – Présidente, Blanche Long

Clifton Royal: John Fisher Memorial Museum, c/o Peninsula Heritage Inc., RR#1, Clifton Royal NB E0G 1N0 – 506/763-2101 – Director, Judith Baxter

Dalhousie: Musée Restigouche Regional Museum, 437 George St., PO Box 1717, Dalhousie NB E0K 1B0 – 506/684-4685 – Manager, Andrew Blackadar

Doaktown: Doak Historic Park & Doak House, Rte. 8, Doaktown NB E0C 1G0 – 506/365-4363

Doaktown: Miramichi Atlantic Salmon Museum, PO Box 38, Doaktown NB E0C 1G0 – 506/365-7787; Fax: 506/365-7359 – General Manager, Isabelle Loughead

Dorchester Properties Committee, c/o Westmorland Historical Society, PO Box 166, Dorchester NB E0A 1M0 – 506/379-6633 – Chair, Sylvia Yeoman – Operating: The Keillor House (Westmorland Centennial Museum, c. 1813), 506/379-6633; open June - Sept. or by appt.; Bell Inn (c.1811), 506/379-6633; open April - Dec.; St. James Presbyterian Church Museum, 506/379-2580; Beachkirk Collection (c. 1884); open June-Sept. or by appt.; The Maritime Penetentiary Museum, 506/379-6633; open June-Sept.

Douglastown: MacDonald Farm Historic Park, Douglastown NB E0C 1H0 – 506/778-6693 – Charles Alain – c. 1815-20

Douglastown: Rankin House Museum, Rte. 8, Douglastown NB E0C 1H0 – 506/773-3448 – Archivist, Edith MacAllister

Edmundston: Musée Historique du Madawaska, 165, boul Hébert, Edmundston NB E3V 2S8 – 506/735-8804; Fax: 506/739-5373 – Curator, Richard Therrien

Fredericton: Brydone Jack Observatory Museum, c/o University of New Brunswick, PO Box 4400, Fredericton NB E3B 5A3 – 506/453-4723

Fredericton: Electrical Engineering Museum, University of New Brunswick, Dept. of Electrical Engineering, PO Box 4400, Fredericton NB E3B 5A3 – 506/453-4561; Fax: 506/453-3589 – Chair, Dr. Eugene Lewis

Fredericton: Guard House & Soldier's Barracks, Fredericton Military Compound, PO Box 6000, Fredericton NB E3B 5H1 – 506/453-3747; Fax: 506/459-0481; Email: cynthiaw@gov.nb.ca – Manager, Cynthia Wallace-Casey

Fredericton: House of International Dolls, 214 Cedar Ave., Fredericton NB E3A 2C6 – 902/658-2449 – D.J. Sparling – Open mid-June - Labour Day

Fredericton: New Brunswick Power Electricity Museum, 515 Queen St., PO Box 2000, Fredericton NB E3B 1B9 – 506/458-6805; Fax: 506/458-3060

Fredericton: New Brunswick Sports Hall of Fame/ Temple de la renommée sportive du Nouveau-Brunswick, 503 Queen St., PO Box 6000, Fredericton NB E3B 5H1 – 506/453- 3747; Fax: 506/459-0481; Email: deborahw@gov.nb – Executive Director, Kathy Meagher

Fredericton: York-Sunbury Historical Society Museum, PO Box 1312, Fredericton NB E3B 5C8 – 506/455-6041 – Assistant Curator, Bruce Lynch; Administrator/Program Officer, Lynn Frizzell – Military & local history

Fredericton Junction: Currie House, Fredericton Junction NB E0G 1T0 – 506/368-2818 – President, Arline Landry

Gagetown: Queens County Museum, The Tilley House, Gagetown NB E0G 1V0 – 506/488-2966 – Curator, Jean Shannon – Birthplace of Sir Leonard Tilley, Father of Confederation

Grand Falls Museum/Musée de Grand-Sault, PO Box 1572, Grand Falls NB E0J 1M0 – 506/473-5265; Fax: 506/473-7160 – Director, Patrick McCooey

Grand Manan Museum & Walter B. McLaughlin Marine Gallery, PO Box 66, Grand Harbour NB E0G 1X0 – 506/662-3524 – Curator, Wendy Dathan – Open June - Sept.; in winter by appt.

Grand-Anse: Musée des Papes, 184 Acadie St., PO Box 60, Grand-Anse NB E0B 1R0 – 506/732-3003; Fax: 506/732-5491 – Directeur, Edmond Landry

Hampton: Kings County Historical Society Museum, c/o Kings County Historical & Archival Society Inc., Hampton NB E0G 1Z0 – 506/832-6009 – Archives Curator, Ernest Friars

Hillsborough Railway Museum, PO Box 70, Hillsborough NB E0A 1X0 – 506/734-3195 – Director, John N. Whitmore

Hillsborough: Hon. William Henry Steeves House, 24 Mill St., PO Box 148, Hillsborough NB E0A 1X0 – 506/734-3102 – Director, Dawna Crew

Hopewell Cape: Albert County Museum, PO Box 3, Hopewell Cape NB E0A 1Y0 – 506/734-2003 – President, Dawn Kinnie – County Jail, c.1846; County Court House, c.1904; Agricultural Exhibit Building; open June 15-Sept. 15

Kedgwick Heritage Lumber Camp, Rte. 17, Kedgwick NB E0K 1C0 – 506/284-3138

Madawaska: Connors Museum, Connors, Madawaska NB E0L 1J0 – 506/992-2500 – Director, Suzie Bernier

Masionnette: Oyster Museum, Rte. 303, Masionnette NB E0B 1X0 – 506/727-2004

Minto Museum, 71 Main St., Minto NB E0E 1J0 – 506/327-3383

Moncton: Free Meeting House, c/o Moncton Museum, 20 Mountain Rd., Moncton NB E1C 2J8 – 506/853-3003 – Director, Jim Roper – Open summer

Moncton: Lutz Mountain Meeting House, 3030 Mountain Rd., RR#8, Moncton NB E1C 8K2 – 506/384-7719 – President, Eleanor Weldon – Museum located at 3143 Mountain Rd.

Moncton Museum/Musée de Moncton, 20 Mountain Rd., Moncton NB E1C 2J8 – 506/853-3003; Fax: 506/853-7558 – Director, Jim Roper – Open year round

Moncton: Musée Acadien, c/o Université de Moncton, Moncton NB E1A 3E9 – 506/858-4088; Fax: 506/858-4043 – Directeur, Bernard LeBlanc – Toute l'année

New Denmark Memorial Museum, c/o New Denmark Historical Society, New Denmark NB E0J 1T0 – 506/553-6464 – President, Sterling Jensen

Oromocto: CFB Gagetown Military Museum/Musée militaire de la BFC Gagetown, CFB Gagetown, Oromocto NB E0G 2P0 – 506/422-2630; Fax: 506/422-3325 – Curator, M. Richard – Open year round

Oromocto: Fort Hughes Military Blockhouse, PO Box 37, Oromocto NB E2V 2G4 – 506/357-3333 – Programme Director, B. Dermer-Norris

Perth-Andover: Southern Victoria Historical Society Museum, Main St., Perth-Andover NB E0J 1V0 – 506/273-6750

Petit-Rocher: New Brunswick Mining & Mineral Interpretation Centre, Rte. 134, Petit-Rocher NB E0B 2E0 – 506/783-8714

Plaster Rock Museum, Rte. 109, Plaster Rock NB E0J 1W0 – 506/356-8834

Rexton: Richibucto River Historical Society & Museum, PO Box 211, Rexton NB E0A 2L0 – 506/523-4408 – President, Dr. John McCleave

Riverside: Old Bank of New Brunswick Museum, Rte. 114, Riverside NB E0A 2R0 – 506/882-2015, 2100

Robichaud: Sportsmans Museum Reg'd., PO Box 9, Robichaud NB E0A 2S0 – 506/532-4750 – Owner/Operator, Clorice Landry

Sackville: Acadian Odyssey National Historic Site/Lieu historique national de l'odyssée acadienne, c/o Fort Beauséjour National Historic Site, RR#3, Sackville NB E0A 3C0 – 506/758-9783; Fax: 506/536-4399 – Officer-in-Charge, Steve Ridlington

Sackville: Fort Beauséjour National Historic Site, RR#3, Sackville NB E0A 3C0 – 506/536-0720; Fax: 506/536-4399 – Officer-in-Charge, Steve Ridlington

Sackville: Struts Centre, 5 Willow Place, Sackville NB E0A 3C0 – 506/536-1211 – Director, Christopher Lawlor

Saint John: Barbour's General Store, PO Box 1971, Saint John NB E2L 4L1 – 506/658-2939; Fax: 506/632-6118 – Tourist Officer, Shirley Elliott
Saint John: Carleton Martello Tower National Historic Site, Canadian Parks Service, PO Box 3946, Stn B, Saint John NB E2M 5E6 – 506/648-4957 – Area Supt., Claude DeGrâce
Saint John: Loyalist House Museum, 120 Union St., Saint John NB E2L 1A3 – 506/652-3590 – Supvr., Willard Merritt – Open year round
Saint John: Partridge Island Museum, PO Box 6326, Saint John NB E2L 4R7 – 506/693-2598; Fax: 506/693-2598; Email: hew@mi.net – Executive Director, Harold E. Wright; President, Michael H. Bamford
Saint John Firefighters Association Museum, 24 Sydney St., Saint John NB E2L 2L3 – 506/633-1840
Saint John Jewish Historical Museum, 29 Wellington Row, Saint John NB E2L 3H4 – 506/633-1833 – Director, Marcia Koven – To collect, display & preserve articles related specifically to the Saint John Jewish community, & to educate; to provide a research facility for genealogists, historians & religious scholars
Saint John Sports Hall of Fame, PO Box 1971, Saint John NB E2L 4L1 – 506/658-2909 – Chair, Betty MacMillan
Saint John: St. Andrews Blockhouse National Historic Site, Canadian Parks Service, PO Box 3946, Saint John NB E2M 5E6 – 506/648-4957 – Area Supt., Claude DeGrâce
Saint John: Tel & Telephone Pioneer Museum, Saint John NB E2L 4K2 – Community Relations Officer, D.E. Trueman
Shediac: Maison Pascal-Poirier, 259, rue Principale, Shediac NB E0A 3G0 – 506/532-9726
Shippagan: Historic Society Nicolas-Denys Documentation Centre, Rte. 113, Shippagan NB E0B 2P0 – 506/336-2346
St-Basile Chapel Museum, PO Box 150, St-Basile NB E0L 1H0 – 506/266-5971 – Director, Rev. Napoléon Michaud
St-Isidore Museum Inc., Rte. 160, St-Isidore NB E0B 2L0 – 506/358-6344
St-Jacques: Musée Automobile Museum, PO Box 180, St-Jacques NB E0L 1K0 – 506/735-2525; Fax: 506/735-7262 – Conservateur, Jean Pelletier
St. Andrews: The Henry Phipps Ross & Sarah Juliette Ross Memorial Museum, 188 Montague St., PO Box 603, St. Andrews NB E0G 2X0 – 506/529-1824; Fax: 506/529-3383 – Director, Margot Magee Sackett – Decorative arts museum is one of St. Andrews' finest early houses; open June - Oct.
St. Andrews: Huntsman Marine Science Centre, Brandy Cove Road, St. Andrews NB E0G 2X0 – 506/529-1200; Fax: 506/529-1212; Email: huntsman@nbnet.nb.ca; URL: http://www.unb.ca/web/huntsman – Executive Director, Dr. John H. Allen – Includes a public aquarium/museum with local flora & fauna, & the Atlantic Reference Centre which houses a zoological & botanical museum reference collection
St. Martins: Quaco Museum & Library, Rte. 111, St. Martins NB E0G 2Z0 – 506/833-4740 (July & Aug.), 833-4768 (off-season) – Curator, Barbara McIntyre; Librarian, Elizabeth Thibodeau
St. Stephen: Charlotte County Museum, 443 Milltown Blvd., St. Stephen NB E3L 1J9 – 506/466-3295; Fax: 506/466-6588 – Curator, Jane MacLeod – James Murchie Memorial Home
Sussex: Agricultural Museum of New Brunswick, Rte. 1, Sussex NB E0E 1P0 – 506/433-6799
Tabusintac Centennial Memorial Library & Museum, Rte. 11, Tabusintac NB E0C 2A0 – 506/779-9261 – Bertha Stymiest; Bertha Wishart
Tracadie-Sheila: Musée Historique de Tracadie, #399, 222, rue du Couvent, Tracadie-Sheila NB E1X 1E1 – 506/395-1500; Fax: 506/395-1504 – S. Dorina Frigault

Village de Barachois: L'Église historique Saint-Henri-de Barachois, RR#1, Village de Barachois NB E0A 2S0 – 506/532-2976 – Contremaître, Armand Landry
Welshpool: Campobello Island Public Library & Museum, Welshpool NB E0G 3H0 – 506/752-2268 – President, Dale Calder
Welshpool: Roosevelt Campobello International Park, PO Box 9, Welshpool NB E0G 3H0 – 506/752-2922 – A/Executive Secretary & Superintendent, Henry W. Stevens – Summer home of Franklin Delano Roosevelt
Woodstock: Old Carleton County Court House, c/o Carleton County Historical Society, 128 Connell St., PO Box 898, Woodstock NB E0J 2B0 – 506/328-9706 – President, John Glass

NEWFOUNDLAND

Newfoundland Museum/Musée de Terra Nova
285 Duckworth St., PO Box 8700, St. John's NF A1B 4J6
709/729-2329; Fax: 709/729-2179
URL: http://calvin.stemnet.nf.ca/~cshea/
Holdings include artifacts, prints & watercolours relating to the province in the areas of Archaeology, Ethnology, Natural History & History (large collection of folk furniture & military artifacts).
Director, Michael Clair
Chief Curator, Dr. Bernard Ransom
Curator, Museum Education Services, Allan Clarke

Other Museums & Science Centres in Newfoundland
Baie Verte Peninsula Miners' Museum, PO Box 122, Baie Verte NF A0K 1B0 – 709/532-8090 – Yvonne Bradbury-Wiseman
Bonavista Museum, PO Box 882, Bonavista NF A0C 1B0 – 709/468-2575, 2880 – Curator, Marguerite Linthorne – Open daily in summer & in winter by appt.
Bonne Bay: Wiltondale Pioneer Village, c/o Bonne Bay Development Association, Woody Point, PO Box 86, Bonne Bay NF A0K 1P0 – 709/453-2470 – Curator, Colleen Howell
Botwood Heritage Centre, PO Box 490, Botwood NF A0H 1E0 – 709/257-2839; Fax: 709/257-3330 – Director, Ed Evans
Burin Heritage House, PO Box 326, Burin NF A0E 1E0 – 709/891-2217 – President, Jessie Shave
Carbonear Railway Station, PO Box 64, Carbonear NF A0A 1T0 – 709/596-2267 – President, Bobbie Hatch
Carbonear: Shades of the Past, PO Box 496, Carbonear NF A0A 1T0 – 709/596-1977 – Director, Stan Deering
Channel-Port-aux-Basques Museum, 118 Main St., PO Box 1299, Channel-Port-aux-Basques NF A0M 1C0 – 709/695-7604, 2460 – Maitland Strangemore – Maritime artifacts; open daily in summer
Corner Brook: Humber-Bay of Islands Museum Society, 65 Central St., Corner Brook NF A2H 2M7 – 709/634-7907; Fax: 709/634-7907 – Acting President, Philip Greenacre; Sec.-Treas., George Rose
Corner Brook: Royal Newfoundland Constabulary Museum, University Dr., Corner Brook NF A2H 6C3 – 709/634-4222 – Open year round
Corner Brook: Sticks & Stones House, 12 Riverhead Rd., Corner Brook NF A2H 1J6 – 709/634-3275 – Director, Ruby MacDonald
Cow Head: Tête de Vache Community Museum, PO Box 40, Cow Head NF A0K 2A0 – 709/243-2446 – Curator, Phyllis Caines; Curator, Elsie Payne
Deer Lake: Humber Valley Heritage Museum, c/o Humber Valley Development Association, PO Box 989, Deer Lake NF A0K 2E0 – 709/635-3861 – Coordinator, Glenda Garnier – Open June-Aug. & by appt.

Durrell Museum, Durrell NF A0G 1Y0 – 709/884-2613 – Curator, David Burton – Open Summer
Ferryland: Historic Ferryland Museum & Shoreline Crafts, Ferryland NF A0A 2H0 – 709/432-2711 – Curator, Maxine Dunne
Flat Rock Museum, c/o Site 10, PO Box 10, Flat Rock NF A0A 3Z0 – 709/437-1473 – Curator, Randall Russell – Open July - Sept. or by appt.
Fogo Island: Bleakhouse Museum, Fogo, Fogo Island NF A0G 2B0 – 709/266-2237 – c.1816; Schoolhouse Museum, c.1888; open July - Aug.
Gander: North Atlantic Aviation Museum, PO Box 234, Gander NF A1V 1W6 – 709/256-2923; Fax: 709/256-2124
Glovertown: Terra Nova National Park/Parc national Terra-Nova (TNNP), Glovertown NF A0G 2L0 – 709/533-2801; Fax: 709/533-2706; Email: christine_pike@pch.gc.ca – Supt., A.C. Bird
Goose Bay: Northern Lights Military Museum, PO Box 188, Goose Bay NF A0P 1C0 – 709/896-5939 – Curator, Bruce Haynes
Grand Bank: Southern Newfoundland Seamen's Museum (SNSM), Marine Dr., PO Box 1109, Grand Bank NF A0E 1W0 – 709/832-1484; Fax: 709/832-2053 – Museum Curator, Gerald Crews
Grand Falls-Windsor: Beothuck Village, St. Catherine St., Grand Falls-Windsor NF A2A 1W9 – 709/489-9629 – Open June - Sept.
Grand Falls-Windsor: Mary March Regional Museum, 22 St. Catherine St., Grand Falls-Windsor NF A2A 1W9 – 709/292-4523; Fax: 709/292-4526 – Curator, Clifford O. Evans
Greenspond Museum, PO Box 100, Greenspond NF A0G 2N0 – 709/269-4111 – Director, Derrick Bragg – Open July & Aug.
Griquet: Port aux Choix National Historic Park, PO Box 70, Griquet NF A0K 2X0 – 709/623-2608, 861-3522 – Supt., Bruce Bradbury
Happy Valley: Labrador Heritage Society & Museum, Main Branch, PO Box 719, Stn B, Happy Valley NF A0P 1E0 – 709/896-2762 – Director, Elsie Johnson – Open summer
Happy Valley: Them Days, PO Box 939, Stn B, Happy Valley NF A0P 1E0 – Archivist & Business Manager, Gilliam H. Brown
Harbour Grace: Conception Bay Museum, PO Box 298, Harbour Grace NF A0A 2M0 – 709/596-5465, 596-1309 (winter) – Curator, Peggy Fahey – Open June - Aug.
Jerseyside: Castle Hill National Historic Park, PO Box 10, Jerseyside NF A0B 2G0 – 709/227-2401; Fax: 709/227-2452 – Officer-in-Charge, Ann Smith – 17th & 18th century remains of French & English fortifications
L'Anse au Loup: Labrador Straits Museum, PO Box 98, L'Anse au Loup NF A0K 3L0 – 709/927-5659 – President, Margaret Buckle
Lewisporte: Bye the Bay Museum, Women's Institute Bldg., PO Box 291, Lewisporte NF A0G 3A0 – 709/535-2844, 8787 – Committee Secretary, Joy Freake – Open year round
Marystown Museum, PO Box 688, Marystown NF A0E 2M0 – 709/279-1507, 1462 – Chairman, Albert Dober – Open daily mid-June - Aug.
Moreton's Harbour Museum, PO Box 28, Moreton's Harbour NF A0G 3H0 – 709/684-2355 – Chair, Women's Institute, Margaret Knight – Open in summer & by appt.
Musgrave Harbour: Fishermen's Museum, 4 Marine Dr., Musgrave Harbour NF A0G 3J0 – 709/655-2162 – Curator, Roland W. Abbott – Open daily in summer
Nain: Piulimatsivik - Nain Museum, PO Box 247, Nain NF A0P 1L0 – 709/922-2821 – Supervisor, Rev. Renatus Hunter – Inuit & Moravian artifacts
Old Perlican: Howard House of Artifacts, PO Box 100, Old Perlican NF A0A 3G0 – 709/587-2022 – Owner, Jerome Howard

Placentia Area Museum, O'Reilly House, 48 Riverside Dr., PO Box 233, Placentia NF A0B 2Y0 – 709/227-5568 – Chairperson, Barbara Bailey – Restored to 1902

Placentia Bay: St. Bartholomew's Church, c/o Mt. Arlington Hts., PO Box 25, Placentia Bay NF A0B 2L0 – 709/228-2394 – Supervisor, Mary Jane Keating

Port Union Museum, PO Box 98, Port Union NF A0C 2J0 – 709/464-3315, 469-2728 – Manager, Linda Clarke – Open summer

Port aux Basques: Gulf Museum, c/o South West Coast Historical Society, PO Box 1299, Port aux Basques NF A0M 1C0 – 709/695-7604 – President, Simeon Barter

Port de Grave: Fishermen's Museum & Porter House, Port de Grave NF A0A 3J0 – 709/786-3912 – Curator, Herman Porter

Pouch Cove Museum, PO Box 59, Pouch Cove NF A0A 3L0 – 709/335-2848 – Curator, Agatha Walsh

Red Bay Interpretation Centre, Red Bay NF A0K 4K0 – 709/920-2197 – Community Clerk, Josie Moore – Archaeological remains of world's largest 16th-century whaling port; open June 15 - Sept. & by request

Rocky Harbour: Gros Morne National Park Visitor Reception Centre, PO Box 130, Rocky Harbour NF A0K 4N0 – 709/458-2417; Fax: 709/458-2059; URL: http://www.stemnet.nf.ca/~amorceau/gmnp.html

Salvage Fishermens' Museum, Salvage NF A0G 3X0 – 709/677-2137 – Marion Heffern – Open in summer

Springdale: Harvey Grant Heritage Centre Community Museum, PO Box 57, Springdale NF A0J 1T0 – 709/673-4313; Fax: 709/673-4969 – Greg Hillier – Open Tues.-Sat. in summer

St. Anthony: Grenfell House Museum, PO Box 93, St. Anthony NF A0K 4S0 – 709/454-3333; Fax: 709/454-3171 – Sir Wilfred Grenfell Home; open May - Sept.

St. John's: Anglican Cathedral Museum, 68 Queen's Rd., St. John's NF A1C 2N8 – 709/726-5677; Fax: 709/726-2053 – Parish Archivist, Clarence Dewling

St. John's: Beothuck Provincial Park, Dept. of Tourism, Culture & Recreation, Parks & Natural Areas, PO Box 8700, St. John's NF A1B 4J6 – 709/489-9832; Fax: 709/729-1100; Email: dhustins@tourism.gov.nf.ca – Director, D. Hustins

St. John's: Boyd's Cove Beothuk Interpretation Centre, Newfoundland Historic Resources Division, PO Box 8700, St. John's NF A1B 4J6 – 709/729-0592; Fax: 709/729-0870; Email: lbadcock@tourism.gov.nf.ca; Interpretation Centre: 709/656-3114 – Historic Sites Officer, Linda Badcock – Exhibits on Beothuk life c. 1700; preserved archaeological site; walking trails; open daily in summer

St. John's: Cape Bonavista Lighthouse Provincial Historic Site, Newfoundland Historic Resources Division, PO Box 8700, St. John's NF A1B 4J6 – 709/729-0592; Fax: 709/729-0870; Email: lbadcock@tourism.gov.nf.ca; Lighthouse: 709/468-7444 – Historic Sites Officer, Linda Badcock – Restored to 1870 period; open daily in summer & in winter by appt.

St. John's: Cape Spear National Historic Site/Lieu historique national du Cap-Spear, PO Box 1268, St. John's NF A1C 5M9 – 709/772-5367; Fax: 709/772-6302; Operational Season: 709/772-4210; Fax: 709/772-6302 – Head, Client Services, Robert Sheldon – 1835 lighthouse; most Easterly point North America

St. John's: CBC Radio Museum, 344 Duckworth St., St. John's NF A1B 3T8 – 709/737-4207; Fax: 709/737-4954 – Director, John F. O'Mara

St. John's: Commissariat House Provincial Historic Site, c/o Newfoundland Historic Resources Division, PO Box 8700, St. John's NF A1B 4J6 – 709/729-0592; House: 709/729-6730; Fax: 709/729-0820; Email: lbadcock@tourism.gov.nf.ca – Historic Sites Officer, Linda Badcock – Restored to 1830; open daily in summer & in winter by appt.

St. John's: Heart's Content Cable Station Provincial Historic Site, Newfoundland Historic Resources Division, PO Box 8700, St. John's NF A1B 4J6 – 709/729-0592; Site: 709/583-2160; Fax: 709/729-0870; Email: lbadcock@tourism.gov.nf.ca – Historic Sites Officer, Linda Badcock – Site of the first successful transatlantic telegraph cable landing, 1866; open daily in summer

St. John's: Hiscock House Provincial Historic Site, c/o Newfoundland Historic Resources Division, PO Box 8700, St. John's NF A1B 4J6 – 709/729-0592; Fax: 709/729-0870; Email: lbadcock@tourism.gov.nf.ca; Historic Site: 709/464-2042 – Historic Sites Officer, Linda Badcock – Restored to 1910; open daily mid-June to mid-Oct.

St. John's: James J. O'Mara Pharmacy Museum, Apothecary Hall, 488 Water St., St. John's NF A1E 1B3 – 709/753-5877 – Secretary-Registrar, Nelson F. Stowe – Drug store c.1895; open mid-June - mid-Sept. or by appt.

St. John's: Lester-Garland Premises Provincial Historic Site, c/o Newfoundland Historic Resources Division, PO Box 8700, St. John's NF A1B 4J6 – 709/729-0592; Fax: 709/729-0870; Email: lbadcock@tourism.gov.nf.ca; Historic Site: 709/464-2042 – Historic Sites Officer, Linda Badcock – Mercantile bldg. including counting house restored to 1820 & retail shop restored to 1910; open daily mid-June to mid-Oct.

St. John's: MockBeggar Property Provincial Historic Site, c/o Newfoundland Historic Resources Division, PO Box 8700, St. John's NF A1B 4J6 – 709/729-0592; Fax: 709/729-0870; Email: lbadcock@tourism.gov.nf.ca; Historic Site: 709/468-7300; Fax: 709/468-7444 – Historic Sites Officer, Linda Badcock – Home of Newfoundland statesman, Senator F. Gordon Bradley; restored to 1939; open daily mid-June to mid-Oct.

St. John's: Newfoundland & Labrador Sports Hall of Fame, c/o Sport Newfoundland & Labrador, Bldg. 25, Torbay, PO Box 8700, St. John's NF A1B 4J6 – 709/576-4932; Fax: 709/576-7493 – General Manager, Glenn Normore

St. John's: Newfoundland Freshwater Resource Centre, PO Box 5, St. John's NF A1B 2Z2 – 709/754-3474; Fax: 709/754-5947 – Executive Director, Patricia Buchanan

St. John's: Newfoundland Transport Museum in Pippy Park, 212 Mount Scio Rd., PO Box 21059, St. John's NF A1A 5B2 – Chairman, Clement Durachko – Series of exhibits on transport themes of historic importance; open Canada Day to Labour Day

St. John's: Point Amour Lighthouse Provincial Historic Site, Newfoundland Historic Resources Division, PO Box 8700, St. John's NF A1B 4J6 – 709/729-0592; Fax: 709/729-0870; Email: lbadcock@tourism.gov.nf.ca; Lighthouse: 709/927-5825; Fax: 709/927-5833 – Historic Sites Officer, Linda Badcock – Exhibits on the history of the Labrador Straits & on lighthouses; open daily in the summer

St. John's: Quidi Vidi Battery Provincial Historic Site, Newfoundland Historic Resources Division, PO Box 8700, St. John's NF A1B 4J6 – 709/729-0592; Battery: 709/729-2977; Fax: 709/729-0870; Email: lbadcock@tourism.gov.nf.ca – Historic Sites Officer, Linda Badcock – Restored to 1812; open daily in summer

St. John's: Regatta Museum, PO Box 214, St. John's NF A1C 5J3 – 709/753-9448 – Director, Gail Malone

St. John's: Royal Newfoundland Constabulary Museum, PO Box 7247, St. John's NF A1E 3Y4 – 709/729-8151 – Curator, Paul Kenny – North America's oldest police force

St. John's: Signal Hill National Historic Site, PO Box 1268, St. John's NF A1C 5M9 – 709/772-5367; Fax: 709/772-2940 – Area Interpretive Officer, Ray Troke

St. John's: St. Thomas' Old Garrison Church Museum, 8 Military Rd., St. John's NF A1C 2C4 – 709/722-2632 – Curator, Dr. John Netten – c.1836

St. John's: Trinity Interpretation Centre, Newfoundland Historic Resources Division, PO Box 8700, St. John's NF A1B 4J6 – 709/729-0592; Fax: 709/729-0870; Email: lbadcock@tourism.gov.nf.ca; Interpretation Centre: 709/464-2042 – Historic Sites Officer, Linda Badcock – Exhibits on the commercial & social history of Trinity; open daily in summer

St. John's: Victoria Hydro Electric Plant, 55 Kenmount Rd., St. John's NF A1B 3P6 – 709/737-5614; Fax: 709/737-5832 – Director, R.F. Gosine – 1904 hydro electric plant

St. Lawrence Miner's Museum, PO Box 128, St. Lawrence NF A0E 2V0 – 709/873-2222; Fax: 709/873-3352 – Curator, Leo Slaney – Open daily in summer

St. Lunaire-Griquest: Hopedale Mission, c/o Area Supt., Canadian Parks Service, PO Box 70, St. Lunaire-Griquest NF A0K 2X0 – 709/623-2601 – Collection spans 200+ years of European Moravian Mission as well as artifacts from early Inuit/Eskimo cultures

St. Lunaire-Griquest: L'Anse aux Meadows National Historic Site, Canadian Parks Service, PO Box 70, St. Lunaire-Griquest NF A0K 2X0 – 709/623-2601 – Park Supt., Bruce Bradbury – UNESCO World Heritage Site depicting first authenticated European presence in North America; Visitor centre open mid-June - Labour Day

Stephenville: Port au Bay/Bay St. George Heritage Association, PO Box 314, Stephenville NF A2N 2Z5 – 709/643-9042 – Chair, Gilbert Higgins – Regional archive & exhibition centre

Stephenville: Sandy Point Museum, PO Box 154, Stephenville NF A2N 2Y9 – 709/643-5653 – Manager, Sylvia Walsh – Sandy Point artifacts dating to early 1800s; open June-Aug.

Torbay Museum, PO Box 190, Torbay NF A1K 1E3 – 709/437-6571 – Curator, Jerri Pellegrinetti – Open daily in summer & in winter by appt.

Trepassey Area Museum, PO Box 13, Trepassey NF A0A 4B0 – 709/438-2465 – President, Stella Devereaux – Open July & Aug.

Trinity Museum & Archives, PO Box 54, Trinity NF A0C 2S0 – 709/464-3720 – Curator, Rupert Morris – Open daily mid-June - mid-Sept. Operates: The Green Family Forge Blacksmith Museum

Twillingate Museum, General Delivery, Twillingate NF A0G 4M0 – 709/884-2825 – Curator, Lorna Stuckless – Open mid-June - mid-Sept.

Wesleyville: Bonavista North Regional Museum, PO Box 48, Wesleyville NF A0G 4R0 – 709/536-2402 – Curator, Rev. Naboth Winsor – Open daily in summer

Whitbourne Museum, Whitbourne NF A0B 3K0 – 709/759-2345 – Curator, Judy Gosse – Open July - Labour Day

NOVA SCOTIA

Fisheries Museum of the Atlantic
Lunenburg Waterfront, PO Box 1363, Lunenburg NS B0J 2C0
902/634-4794; Fax: 902/634-8990
Fishing heritage of the Atlantic coast; includes fishing vessels, aquarium, theatre & reference library; part of the Nova Scotia Museum.
Curator, Heather Getson
Curator, Education, Ralph Getson
General Manager, Jim Tupper

Maritime Museum of the Atlantic/Musée Maritime d'Atlantique (MMA)
1675 Lower Water St., Halifax NS B3J 1S3

Canadian Almanac & Directory 1997

902/429-7490; Fax: 902/424-0612
URL: http://www.ednet.ns.ca/educ/museum/mma.html
Marine history branch of the Nova Scotia Museum; on waterfront; marine artifacts, memorabilia from the Titanic, Halifax explosion exhibit, restored ship chandlery, extensive small craft collection; library & gift shop; Vessel CSS Acadia at museum wharf along with schooner Bluenose II.
Director, David B. Flemming

Nova Scotia Museum
1747 Summer St., Halifax NS B3H 3A6
902/424-6471; Fax: 902/424-0560
URL: http://www.ednet.ns.ca/educ/museum/
Established in 1868, the Nova Scotia Museum consists of 25 museums across the province: Nova Scotia Museum of Natural History, Halifax; Maritime Museum of the Atlantic, Halifax; Haliburton House, Windsor; Uniacke Estate Park Museum, Mount Uniacke; Prescott House, Starr's Point; Lawrence House, Maitland; Balmoral Grist Mill, Balmoral; Sutherland Steam Mill, Denmark; Fishermen's Life Museum, Jeddore; Shand House, Windsor; Nova Scotia Museum of Industry, Stellarton; Fisheries Museum of the Atlantic, Lunenburg; Wile Carding Mill, Bridgewater; Perkins House, Liverpool; Ross-Thomson House, Shelburne; Dory Shop, Shelburne; Old Meeting House, Barrington; Barrington Woolen Mill, Barrington; Firefighters' Museum of Nova Scotia, Yarmouth; North Hills Museum, Granville Ferry; McCulloch House, Pictou; Sherbrooke Village, Sherbrooke; Cossit House, Sydney; Ross Farm, New Ross; Fundy Geological Museum, Parrsboro.

Other Museums & Science Centres in Nova Scotia
Amherst: Cumberland County Museum & Archives, 150 Church St., Amherst NS B4H 3C3 – 902/667-2561 – Director/Curator, Kim M. Gorveatt – Exhibits on natural, social & industrial heritage of Cumberland County; open year round

Annapolis Royal: Fort Anne National Historic Site, PO Box 9, Annapolis Royal NS B0S 1A0 – 902/532-2397 – Area Supt., Lillian Stewart – French & English period fortifications, 1606-1854; open May 15 -Oct. 15

Annapolis Royal: Habitation National Historic Site, c/o Fort Anne National Historic Site, PO Box 503, Annapolis Royal NS B0S 1A0 – 902/532-2898 – 1605 French fur-trading post founded by Champlain; open May 15 - Oct. 15

Annapolis Royal: Historic Restoration Society of Annapolis County, PO Box 503, Annapolis Royal NS B0S 1A0 – 902/532-7754

Annapolis Royal: Port Royal National Historic Site, PO Box 9, Annapolis Royal NS B0S 1A0 – 902/532-5197 – Area Supt., Lilian Stewart

Antigonish Heritage Museum, 20 East Main St., Antigonish NS B2G 2B2 – 902/863-6160; URL: http://www.grassroots.ns.ca/tour/ahm.htm – Manager, Jocelyn Gillis

Arichat: Le Noir Forge, PO Box 305, Arichat NS B0E 1A0 – 902/226-3776 – Curator, Marshall Bourinot

Baddeck: Alexander Graham Bell National Historic Site, PO Box 159, Baddeck NS B0E 1B0 – 902/295-2069; Fax: 902/295-3496 – District Director, B. Villeneuve; Chief, Visitor Activities, Aynsley MacFarlane – Collection concentrates on Bell's work in Baddeck

Baddeck: Grassy Island National Historic Site/Lieu historique national de l'Île-Grassy, c/o Supt., Alexander Graham Bell National Historic Site, PO Box 159, Baddeck NS B0E 1B0 – 902/295-2069; Fax: 902/295-3496 – District Director, B. Villeneuve; Chief, Visitor Activities, Aynsley MacFarlane – Open June 1 - Sept. 15

Baddeck: The Great Hall of the Clans, Highland Pioneers Museum, PO Box 9, Baddeck NS B0E 1B0 – 902/295-3411 – Executive Director, Jim MacAulay

Baddeck: Marconi National Historic Site/Lieu historique national Marconi, c/o Alexander Graham Bell National Historic Site, PO Box 159, Baddeck NS B0E 1B0 – 902/295-2069; Fax: 902/295-3496 – District Director, B. Villeneuve; Chief, Visitor Activities, Aynsley MacFarlane

Baddeck: Victoria County Archives & Museum, PO Box 75, Baddeck NS B0E 1B0 – 902/295-3397 – Curator, Margot MacAulay; Curator, Donald MacAulay – Open summer

Barrington: Cape Sable Historical Society Centre, Barrington NS B0W 1E0 – 902/637-2185 – Executive Director, Candace Stevenson – Local history & archives; operates: Old Meeting House, c.1765, oldest nonconformist church in Canada, open June - Sept.; Woolen Mill, c.1884, open June - Sept.; Seal Island Lighthouse Museum, open June 15 - Sept.

Barss Corner: Parkdale-Maplewood Community Museum, 3005 Barss Corner Rd., RR#1, Barss Corner NS B0R 1A0 – 902/644-3288; Fax: 902/644-3422; Email: rosmith@fox.nstn.ns.ca; URL: http://www.ednet.ns.ca/educ/museum/other_ns/parkdale/museum1.html – Administrator, Donna M. Smith; Curator, Barbara Veinot; Sec.-Treas., Wendy Looke

Bear River: Riverview Ethnographic Museum, 18 Chute Rd., RR#1, Box 3, Bear River NS B0S 1B0 – 902/467-3762; Fax: 902/467-3762 – Owner & Curator, Sarah Elizabeth Glover – Folk costumes & early Americana, open year round

Bedford: Atlantic Canada Aviation Museum, 1658 Bedford Hwy., PO Box 44006, Bedford NS B4A 4J7 – 902/873-3773 – Curator, Carl Gilbert

Bridgetown: James House Museum, c/o Bridgetown & Area Historical Society, PO Box 373, Bridgetown NS B0S 1C0 – 902/665-4530, 4215 – President, Ken Nye

Bridgetown: Tupperville School Museum, RR#3, Bridgetown NS B0S 1C0 – 902/665-2004 – Chairperson, Marion Inglis – Open daily mid-May - mid-Sept.

Bridgewater: DesBrisay Museum & Exhibition Centre, PO Box 353, Bridgewater NS B4V 2W9 – 902/543-4033; Fax: 902/543-6876 – Director, Gary Selig – Home of famed porcupine quill-decorated cradle; parkland & trails; open year round

Bridgewater: Wile Carding Mill, PO Box 353, Bridgewater NS B4V 2W9 – 902/543-8233; Fax: 902/543-6876 – Director, Gary Selig – Last surviving plant of a 19th century water-powered industrial park; part of Nova Scotia Museum; open June - Sept.

Canso Museum/Whitman House, Union St., Canso NS B0H 1H0 – 902/366-2170 – Chairman, Joseph Walsh; Martha, Kavanaugh, Curator Dollard – c.1885

Cheticamp: Musée Acadien, CP 98, Cheticamp NS B0E 1H0 – 902/224-2170 – Directrice, Diane Poirier

Church Point: Le Musée Sainte-Marie, PO Box 28, Church Point NS B0W 1M0 – 902/769-2832 – Présidente, Marguerite Leblanc – Largest wooden church in North America; open June - Oct.

Church Point: Musée du centre Acadien de L'Université Sainte-Anne, Church Point NS B0W 1M0 – 902/769-2114, poste 159 – Directeur, Neil Boucher

Clark's Harbour: Archelaus Smith Museum & Historical Society, PO Box 190, Clark's Harbour NS B0W 1P0 – 902/745-3361 – President, Heather Atkinson

Cole Harbour Heritage Farm Museum, 471 Poplar Dr., Cole Harbour NS B2W 4L2 – 902/434-0222 – Open year round

Dartmouth: Evergreen Historic House, 26 Newcastle St., Dartmouth NS B2Y 3M5 – 902/421-2300 – Curator, Betty-Ann Aaboe-Milligan – Open July & Aug.

Dartmouth: Quaker Whalers House, c/o Dartmouth Museum Society, 57-50 Ochterloney St., Dartmouth NS B2Y 1C3 – 902/464-2300 – President, G.S. Gosley – c.1785; Nantucket whalers; open June - Sept.

Dartmouth: Shubenacadie Canal Commission, Fairbanks Centre, 54 Locks Rd., Dartmouth NS B2X 2W7 – 902/462-1826; Fax: 902/434-6787 – General Manager, Peter Latta

Deep Brook: Old St. Edwards Loyalist Church, Clementsport, Nova Scotia, Deep Brook NS B0S 1J0 – 902/638-8554 – Contact, Kathleen Cox – Original Loyalist church consecrated 1797; open summer afternoons or by appt.

Digby: Admiral Digby Museum, 95 Montague Row, PO Box 1644, Digby NS B0V 1A0 – 902/245-6322 – President, Capt. Archer Turnbull – Open June - Sept. & by appt.

Dingwall: North Highland Community Museum, RR#1, Dingwall NS B0C 1G0 – 902/383-2051 – Director, Heather Morrison

Glace Bay: Cape Breton Miners' Museum, 42 Birkley St., Glace Bay NS B1A 5T8 – 902/849-4522; Fax: 902/849-8022 – Curator, Tom Miller

Grand Pré: Fort Edward National Historic Site, c/o Grand Pré National Historic Site, PO Box 150, Grand Pré NS B0P 1M0 – 902/542-3631

Grand-Pré National Historic Site, PO Box 150, Grand Pré NS B0P 1M0 – 902/542-3631 – Superintendent, Barbara LeBlanc – Bilingual guides interpret history of the Acadians; open daily May 15 - Oct. 15

Granville Ferry: North Hills Museum, PO Box 109, Granville Ferry NS B0S 1K0 – 902/532-2168 – Curator, Ken Gilmour

Guysborough: Old Court House Museum, PO Box 232, Guysborough NS B0H 1N0 – 902/533-4008 – Curator, Ila Dort – Open June - Sept.

Halifax: Army Museum/The Citadel, PO Box 3666, Halifax NS B3J 3K6 – 902/422-5979 – Curator, Bruce F. Ellis – Citadel fortifications date to 1749; open May 15 - Nov. & by appt.

Halifax: Fisherman's Life Museum, c/o Curator, Branch Museums, Nova Scotia Museum, 1747 Summer St., Halifax NS B3H 3A6 – Open June-October 15

Halifax Citadel National Historic Site, PO Box 9080, Stn A, Halifax NS B3K 5M7 – 902/426-5080; Fax: 902/426-4228

Halifax Police Museum, 1975 Gottingen St., Halifax NS B3J 2H1 – 902/421-6840; Email: hpd@atcon.com – Curator, Sgt. Dan Young

Halifax: HMCS Sackville, 1675 Lower Water St., Halifax NS B3K 3B4 – 902/429-5600 – World War II ship & interpretation centre; open summer

Halifax: Lawrence House, c/o Curator, Branch Museums, Nova Scotia Museum, 1747 Summer St., Halifax NS B3H 3A6 – c.1865 home of William D. Lawrence, shipwright; open daily May 15 - Oct.

Halifax: Maritime Command Museum/Musée du Commandement Maritime, Admiralty House, CFB Halifax, FMO, Halifax NS B3K 2X0 – 902/427-8250; Fax: 902/427-8541 – Director, Marilyn Gurney – Open year round

Halifax: Nova Scotia Sport Heritage Centre, World Trade & Convention Centre, #403, 1800 Argyle St., Halifax NS B3J 3N8 – 902/421-1266; Fax: 902/425-1148 – Executive Director, Bill Robinson – Open year round

Halifax: Perkins House, 105 Main St., PO Box 1078, Halifax NS B3H 3A6 – 902/354-4058 – Curator, Linda Rafuse – Connecticut style cottage built by merchant & diarist Simeon Perkins; open June - Oct. 15

Halifax: Prescott House, c/o Curator, Branch Museums, Nova Scotia Museum, 1747 Summer St., Halifax NS B3H 3A6 – 902/542-3984 – c.1814, open June - Oct. 15

Halifax: Prince of Wales Martello Tower National Historic Site, PO Box 9080, Stn A, Halifax NS B3K 5M7 – 902/426-5080; Fax: 902/426-4228

Halifax: Sutherland Steam Mill, c/o Curator, Branch Museums, Nova Scotia Museum, 1747 Summer St., Halifax NS B3H 3A6 – 902/657-3365

Halifax: Thomas McCulloch Museum, Biology Dept., Dalhousie University, Henry St., Halifax NS B3H 4J1 – 902/424-3530 – Chief Curator, Stephen Fry

Halifax: Uniacke House, c/o Curator, Branch Museums, Nova Scotia Museum, 1747 Summer St., Halifax NS B3H 3A6 – c.1813; open June - Oct. 15

Halifax: York Redoubt National Historic Site, PO Box 9080, Stn A, Halifax NS B3K 5M7 – 902/426-5080

Hantsport: Churchill House & Marine Memorial Room Museum, PO Box 399, Hantsport NS B0P 1P0 – 902/684-3461 – Administrator, Norma MacLeod

Inverness Miners Museum, PO Box 161, Inverness NS B0E 1N0 – 902/258-2097 – Director, T. MacDonald

Iona: Nova Scotia Highland Village, PO Box 58, Iona NS B0A 1L0 – 902/725-2272; Fax: 902/725-2227; Email: nshviona@fox.nstn.ca; URL: http://www.ednet.ns.ca/educ/museum/other_ns/highland_village/ – Manager, Rodney Chaisson

Kentville: Blair House Museum, Kentville Agricultural Centre, Kentville NS B4N 1J5 – 902/678-1093; Fax: 902/678-1567 – Manager, Janice Lutz

Kentville: Old Kings Courthouse Museum, 37 Cornwalllis St., Kentville NS B4N 2E2 – 902/678-6237; Fax: 902/679-0066; Email: vlad@iol.ns.ca – Curator, Bria Stokesbury; Assistant-Curator, Cathy Margeson – Social & natural history of Kings County; Parks Canada commemorative exhibit to the New England Planters

La Have: Fort Point Museum, c/o Lunenburg County Historical Society, PO Box 99, La Have NS B0R 1C0 – 902/688-2696 (summer) – President, Jean Gaudet – On site of Fort Ste. Marie de Grâce, 1632

La Have Island Marine Museum, Bell's Island, La Have Island NS B0R 1C0 – 902/688-2565 – President, Eric Hirtie

Liverpool: Milton Heritage Society & Blacksmith Shop Museum, PO Box 10, Liverpool NS B0T 1K0 – 902/354-5663 – Curator, Christine Tupper

Liverpool: Queens County Museum, PO Box 1078, Liverpool NS B0T 1K0 – 902/354-4058; URL: http://www.geocities.com/Paris/2669/ – Curator, Linda Rafuse

Lockeport: Little School Museum, Lockeport NS B0T 1L0 – 902/656-2238 – Secretary, Lorna Laing

Louisbourg: Atlantic Statiquarium Marine Museum, PO Box 316, Louisbourg NS B0A 1M0 – 902/733-2721 – Director, Alex Storm

Louisbourg: The Fortress of Louisbourg National Historic Site/Forteresse-de-Louisourg, Lieu historique nationale, PO Box 160, Louisbourg NS B0A 1M0 – 902/733-2280; Fax: 902/733-2362; Email: krasuee@pkslhs.dots.doe.ca – Director, Parks Canada, Cape Breton District, Bernard Villeneuve

Louisbourg: The Rectory, PO Box 396, Louisbourg NS B0Z 1M0 – President, William O'Shea – Open year round

Louisbourg: S&L (Sydney & Louisburg) Railway Museum, PO Box 225, Louisbourg NS B0A 1M0 – 902/733-2720 – President, William Bussy – Open June 1 - Oct. 15.

Mabou: An Drochaid/The Bridge, PO Box 175, Mabou NS B0E 1X0 – 902/945-2311

Mahone Bay: Settlers' Museum & Culture Centre, 578 Main St., PO Box 583, Mahone Bay NS B0J 2E0 – 902/624-6263 – Curator, Wilma Stewart – Open May 15 - Sept.

Mahone Bay: Titanic Memorial Museum of the Atlantic, Mader's Wharf, 613 Main St., PO Box 479, Mahone Bay NS B0J 2E0 – Director, Steve Santini

Maitland: East Hants Historical Museum, RR#1, Maitland NS B0N 1T0 – 902/261-2627 – President, Roy Rhyno

Meteghan: La Vieille Maison, CP 10, Meteghan NS B0W 2J0 – 902/645-2322; Fax: 902/645-3032 – Director, Eddie Comeau

Middleton: Annapolis Valley Macdonald Museum, 21 School St., PO Box 925, Middleton NS B0S 1P0 – 902/825-6116 – Executive Director, Cathy Bezanson – Open year round

Mount Uniacke: South Rawdon Museum, RR#1, Mount Uniacke NS B0N 1Z0 – 902/757-2344 – Curator, Helen Haley

Musquodoboit Railway Museum, PO Box 303, Musquodoboit Harbour NS B0J 2L0 – 902/889-2689 – Director, Ena Rowlings – Open May 16 - Oct.

New Glasgow: MacPherson's Mill & Farm Homestead, PO Box 403, New Glasgow NS B2H 5E5 – 902/752-7828 – Director, Dr. H. Locke – c. 1857

New Glasgow: Pictou County Historical Museum, 86 Temperance St., New Glasgow NS B2H 3A7 – 902/752-5583 – President, Graham Holman – Open July & Aug.

New Ross: Ross Farm Museum, New Ross NS B0J 2M0 – 902/689-2210 – Branch Director, A. Hiltz – Ross family farm 1817; open daily June 1 - Oct. 31, Jan. 2 - Mar. 15

North East Margaree: Margaree Salmon Museum, North East Margaree NS B0E 2H0 – 902/248-2848 – Curator, Frances Hart

North East Margaree: Museum of Cape Breton Heritage, North East Margaree NS B0E 2H0 – 902/248-2551

Parrsboro: Fundy Geological Museum, PO Box 640, Parrsboro NS B0M 1S0 – 902/254-3814; Fax: 902/254-3666 – Director/Curator, Kenneth Admans – Open daily June 1 - Oct. 15.

Parrsboro: Mineral & Gem Geological Museum, PO Box 297, Parrsboro NS B0M 1S0 – 902/254-2627 – Curator, Marilyn Smith

Pictou: Loch Broom Log Church, RR#2, Pictou NS B0K 1H0 – 902/925-2178

Pictou: Northumberland Fisheries Museum, PO Box 1210, Pictou NS B0K 1H0 – 902/485-4563 – Administrator, Caroline Fraser

Pictou: Presbyterian Church Museum, c/o First Presbyterian Church, 9 Prince St., PO Box 1003, Pictou NS B0K 1H0 – 902/485-4298

Pictou: Thomas McCulloch Historic House, Old Haliburton Rd., PO Box 1210, Pictou NS B0K 1H0 – 902/485-4563 – Administrator, Caroline Fraser – Open May 15 - Oct.

Port Hastings Museum & Archives, PO Box 115, Port Hastings NS B0E 2T0 – 902/625-1295 – Curator, Beryl MacDonald

Port Hood: Chestico Museum & Historical Society, PO Box 144, Port Hood NS B0E 2W0 – 902/787-2244 – President, Susan Mailette

River Hebert: King Seaman School Museum, c/o Minudie Tourist Council, RR#2, River Hebert NS B0L 1G0 – 902/251-2041 – Open daily July - Labour Day

Riverport: Ovens Natural Park & Museum, PO Box 38, Riverport NS B0J 2W0 – 902/766-4621; Fax: 902/766-4344 – Director, Nancy Sherwood

Sackville: Fultz Corner Restoration Society, Fultz House Museum, PO Box 124, Sackville NS B0J 2S0 – 902/865-3794 – Director, A. Ruth Auld

Shag Harbour: Chapel Hill Museum, Shag Harbour NS B0W 3B0 – 902/723-2830 – President, Eric Shand; Secretary, Cindy Nickerson; Treasurer, Kaye Ross

Shearwater Aviation Museum, CFB Shearwater, Shearwater NS B0J 3A0 – 902/460-1083; Fax: 902/460-1449 – Director, Lt.-Col. J. Hincke; Curator, Gordon McLauchlan – Open May - Oct.

Shelburne: John C. Williams Dory Shop, PO Box 39, Shelburne NS B0T 1W0 – 902/875-3219 – Restored dory factory, est. 1880; open June 15 - Sept. 15

Shelburne: Ross Thomson House, c/o Chief Guide, PO Box 39, Shelburne NS B0T 1W0 – 902/875-3141

Shelburne County Museum, Dock St. & Maiden Lane, PO Box 39, Shelburne NS B0T 1W0 – 902/875-3219 – Curator, Finn Bower – Open year round

Sherbrooke Restoration, PO Box 295, Sherbrooke NS B0J 3C0 – 902/522-2400 – Project Director, Craig MacDonald – 20 buildings, 1860-1890, on original sites; open June - Oct. 15

Smith's Cove Historical Museum, RR#1, Smith's Cove NS B0S 1S0 – President, Dorothy Gray

Springhill: The Anne Murray Centre, Main St., PO Box 610, Springhill NS B0M 1X0 – 902/597-8614; Fax: 902/597-2001; URL: http://www.grtplaces.com/ac/anne – Executive Director, Shelagh F. Rayworth – Pays tribute to the achievements of Springhill's internationally acclaimed singing superstar; Open May - Oct., otherwise by appt.

Springhill Miners Museum, Black River Rd., PO Box 610, Springhill NS B0M 1X0 – 902/597-3449 (summer); 902/597-8614; Fax: 902/597-2001; URL: http://www.grtplaces.com/ac/mine – Acting Director, Shelagh Rayworth – Tours of the Springhill coal mine, famous in song & legend; gift shop & picnic area; open May - Oct.

St. Peter's: Nicolas Denys Museum, PO Box 249, St. Peter's NS B0E 3B0 – 902/535-2175 – Curator, Jessie MacDonald – Micmac, Acadien, Scottish & Irish artifacts

Stellarton: The Museum of Industry, PO Box 2590, Stellarton NS B0K 1S0 – 902/755-5425 – Branch Director, John Hault

Sydney: Cape Breton Centre for Heritage & Science, 225 George St., Sydney NS B1P 1J5 – 902/539-1572 – Curator, Janet Maltby – Operates Cossit House, c.1787, open June - Oct. 15; St. Patrick's Church Museum, open summer & fall

Tatamagouche: Balmoral Grist Mill, RR#4, Tatamagouche NS B0K 1V0 – 902/657-3016 – Supt., John E. Taylor

Tatamagouche: Sunrise Trail Museum, Main St., Tatamagouche NS B0K 1V0 – 902/657-2433 – Director, Ellen Millard – Open daily mid-June - mid-Sept.

Truro: Colchester Historical Society Museum, 29 Young St., PO Box 412, Truro NS B2N 5C5 – 902/895-6284 – Curator, Ira E. Creelman; Archivist, Nan Harvey – Open year round

Truro: The Little White Schoolhouse, c/o Nova Scotia Teachers College, PO Box 810, Truro NS B2N 5G5 – 902/895-5347; Fax: 902/893-5610 – President, Dr. Jane Norman; Curator, Harvey W. MacPhee

West Bay: Marble Mountain Community Museum, RR#1, West Bay NS B0E 3K0 – 902/756-2638 – Curator, Jean McNicol

West Pubnico: Musée acadien de Pubnico-Ouest, CP 92, West Pubnico NS B0W 3S0 – 902/762-2039 – Président, Elaine Surette

Westphal: Black Cultural Centre for Nova Scotia, 1149 Main St., Westphal NS B2Z 1A8 – 902/434-6223; Fax: 902/434-2306; Toll Free (in NS): 1-800-465-0767; URL: http://www.nstn.ca/bccns/bcc.html – Executive Director, Wayne Adams – History & culture dating back to the 1600s; open year round

Windsor: Shand House, Clifton Ave., PO Box 2683, Windsor NS B0N 2T0 – 902/798-8213

Windsor: Thomas Chandler Haliburton House, PO Box 2683, Windsor NS B0N 2T0 – 902/798-2915 – Open June 1 - Oct. 15

Windsor: West Hants Historical Society, 281 King St., Windsor NS B0N 2T0 – 902/798-5265 – President, Veronica Connelly – June - Sept 30

Wolfville: Randall House Museum, 171 Main St., PO Box 38, Wolfville NS B0P 1X0 – 902/542-9775 – Director, Heather A. Davidson – c.1808; open daily June 15 - Sept. 15

Yarmouth: Firefighters' Museum of Nova Scotia & National Exhibition Centre, Nova Scotia Museum Complex, 451 Main St., Yarmouth NS B5A 1G9 – 902/742-5525; Fax: 902/742-5525 – Curator, David Darby – Artifacts date to the early 1800s; open year round

Yarmouth County Museum & Historical Research Archives, c/o Yarmouth County Historical Society, 22 Collins St., Yarmouth NS B5A 3C8 – 902/742-5539

Canadian Almanac & Directory 1997

– Director/Curator, E.J. Ruff; Archivist, Laura Bradley – Open year round

NORTHWEST TERRITORIES

Prince of Wales Northern Heritage Centre (PWNHC)
PO Box 1320, Yellowknife NT X1A 2L9
403/873-7551; Fax: 403/873-0205
URL: http://tailpipe.learnNet.nt.ca/pwnhc
Archeological, ethnological, historical & fine arts collections from the Arctic & Subarctic regions of the NWT; comparative faunal collections of indigenous animals; NWT Archives contain 7,000 books, newspapers & periodicals; historical photo collection; research centre.
Director, Charles D. Arnold
Territorial Achivist, Richard Valpy
Curator, Joanne Bird

Other Museums & Science Centres in Northwest Territories
Eskimo Point: Inuit Cultural Institute, Eskimo Point NT X1A 0E0 – 819/857-2803 – Director, Roy Goose
Fort Good Hope: Dene Museum/Archives, General Delivery, Fort Good Hope NT X0E 0H0 – 403/598-2331
Fort Smith: Northern Life Museum & National Exhibition Centre, PO Box 420, Fort Smith NT X0E 0P0 – 403/872-2349; Fax: 403/872-4345 – Director, Boris Atamanenko; Curator, Gina Sydenham – Collection, preservation & presentation of NWT culture & history - Open year round
Fort Smith: Wood Buffalo National Park Visitor Reception Centre, PO Box 750, Fort Smith NT X0E 0P0 – 403/872-2349; Fax: 403/872-4345 – Community Liaison Officer, Tamar Vandenberghe
Hamlet of Arctic Bay: Sod House Museum, c/o Innumarit Committee, Hamlet of Arctic Bay NT X0E 0A0 – 819/439-9918
Holman Museum, General Delivery, Holman NT X0A 0S0 – 403/396-3141 – Curator, Alan Sim
Iqaluit: Nuantta Sunaqutangit Museum, PO Box 605, Iqaluit NT X0A 0H0 – 819/979-5537; Fax: 819/979-4533 – Curator, Denise Kekkema
Norman Wells: Colville Lake Museum, Norman Wells NT X0E 0V0 – Curator, Bern Will Brown
Norman Wells Historical Centre, PO Box 56, Norman Wells NT X0E 0V0 – 403/587-2415; Fax: 403/587-2469 – Manager, Warren Schmitke
Pangnirtung: Auyuittuq National Park Reserve, Parks Canada, Eastern Arctic District, PO Box 353e, Pangnirtung NT X0A 0R0 – 819/473-8828
Pangnirtung: Sipalaseequtt Museum Society, Angmarlik Centre, Pangnirtung NT X0E 0R0 – 819/473-8756 – Manager, Simeonie Akpalialuk
Sachs Harbour Museum, c/o Hamlet Council, Sachs Harbour NT X0E 0Z0 – 403/690-4361

ONTARIO

Canadian Football Hall of Fame & Museum
58 Jackson St. West, Hamilton ON L8P 1L4
905/528-7566; Fax: 905/528-9781
Exhibits profile the history & progression of football in Canada; interactive education programs, unique collections, a library/archives & the Grey Cup trophy; gift shop & mail order.
Managing Director, Janice Smith

Hockey Hall of Fame/Le Temple de la Renommée du Hockey
BCE Place, 30 Yonge St., Toronto ON M5E 1X8
416/360-7765; Fax: 416/360-1501

Opened in June 1993. Films, photos, memorabilia.
Chairman, Board of Directors, Scotty (Ian) Morrison

Ontario Science Centre/Centre des sciences de l'Ontario
770 Don Mills Rd., North York ON M3C 1T3
416/429-4100; Fax: 416/696-3124
URL: http://www.osc.on.ca
Over 600 interactive exhibits on the environment, technology, food, chemistry, communications, sport & space; exhibits, programs, demonstrations, workshops & films for the public; special programs for school groups, children, adults & senior citizens; gift shops & restaurant; open year round.
Director General, Dr. Emlyn Koster

Royal Ontario Museum
100 Queen's Park, Toronto ON M5S 2C6
416/586-5549; Fax: 416/586-5863; Info Line: 416/586-8000
URL: http://www.rom.on.ca
The Royal Ontario Museum is Canada's largest museum & is a major research institution consisting of curatorial departments in the fields of art, archaeology & science & a number of other departments dealing with education, communication & administration. The ROM continues to develop new galleries after completing an extensive renovation & expansion project. On display are Far Eastern, Greek, Roman & Egyptian artifacts & textiles, European art, life science specimens, invertebrate fossils & dinosaurs. Also featured are special exhibitions. Notable galleries include the S.R. Perfen Gem & Gold Room, which showcases nearly 1,000 gems & 70 gold specimens, the Dinosaur Gallery, the Bat Cave Gallery & a hands-on Gallery, the Discovery Centre; the Canadian Heritage Floor, which includes the Sigmund Samuel Canadiana Gallery, shows the fine & decorative art achievements of early French & English settlers. The museum offers a variety of programs & activities including special exhibitions, concerts, lectures, film, & gallery tours & field trips. The George R. Gardiner Museum of Ceramic Art houses one of the great collections of European ceramic art from the early 15th century to the turn of the 19th century. Education Services: The department organizes school tours, produces learning resource materials, & provides professional development courses for Ontario teachers. For school bookings, call 416/586-5801. Outreach Services: The department offers circulating & modular exhibitions to local museums, libraries, shopping centres, schools & service organizations throughout the province & the country (416/586-5682). Public Services: Free guided gallery tours; walking tours during summer.
Director, John McNeill

Other Museums & Science Centres in Ontario
Alexandria: Glengarry Sports Hall of Fame, PO Box 833, Alexandria ON K0C 1A0 – Curator, Angus H. McDonnell
Alliston: South Simcoe Pioneer Museum, PO Box 910, Alliston ON L9R 1A1 – 705/435-6219; Fax: 705/435-7019; Museum: 705/435-0167 – Curator, Parks, Recreation & Culture, Rachelle Clayton
Almonte: Mill of Kintail, RR#1, Almonte ON K0A 1A0 – 613/256-3610; Fax: 613/259-3468 – Curator, Carol Munden
Almonte: Mississippi Valley Textile Museum, PO Box 784, Almonte ON K0A 1A0 – 613/256-3754
Almonte: North Lanark Regional Museum, PO Box 218, Almonte ON K0A 1A0 – 613/257-3756 – Curator, Dawn Leduc
Ameliasburgh Historical Museum, PO Box 67, Ameliasburgh ON K0K 1A0 – 613/968-9678; Fax: 613/962-1514 – Curator, Marion Casson
Amherstburg: Fort Malden National Historic Site/Lieu historique national du Fort-Malden (FMNHS), 100 Laird Ave., PO Box 38, Amherstburg ON N9V 2Z2

– 519/736-5416; Fax: 519/736-6603;
Email: Bob_Garcia@pch.gc.ca – Site Manager, Bruce Horan
Amherstburg: North American Black Historical Museum Inc., PO Box 12, Amherstburg ON N9V 2Z2 – 519/736-5433; Fax: 519/736-5433 – Curator, Mary E. Baruth – Open April - Nov.
Amherstburg: Park House Museum, 214 Dalhousie St., Amherstburg ON N9V 1W4 – 519/736-2511 – Curator, Valerie Buckle
Ancaster: Fieldcote Memorial Park & Museum, 64 Sulphur Springs Rd., PO Box 81123, Ancaster ON L9G 4X1 – 905/648-8144; Fax: 905/648-4622
Ancaster: Hermitage Gatehouse Museum, Hamilton Region Conservation Authority, PO Box 7099, Ancaster ON L9G 3L3 – 905/648-4427; Fax: 905/648-4622 – Director, Community Relations, Joan Bell
Ancaster: Ingledale, c/o Hamilton Region Conservation Authority, PO Box 7099, Ancaster ON L9G 3L3 – 416/643-2103 – Superintendent, Bruce Mackenzie – c.1812 home of Inglehart family
Ancaster: Sulpher Springs Station/Dundas Valley Trail Centre, c/o Hamilton Region Conservation Authority, PO Box 7099, Ancaster ON L9G 3L3 – 905/648-4427 – Supt., Paul Piett
Ancaster: Valens Log Cabin/Valens Conservation Area, c/o Hamilton Region Conservation Authority, PO Box 7099, Ancaster ON L9G 3L3 – 905/659-7715 – Curator, Scott Hanville
Appin: Ekfrid Township Museum, Appin ON N0L 1A0 – 519/289-2016 – President, Margot Dargatz
Arnprior & District Museum, 35 Madawaska St., Arnprior ON K7S 1R6 – 613/623-4902 – Curator, Helen Anglin – Open Tues. - Fri., mid-June - mid-September
Atikokan Centennial Museum, Civic Centre, PO Box 849, Atikokan ON P0T 1C0 – 807/597-6585 – Manager/Curator, Lorraine Stromberg
Aurora Museum, 22 Church St., Aurora ON L4G 1G4 – 905/727-8991 – Curator, Jacqueline Stuart
Aurora: Hillary House & the Koffler Museum of Medicine, PO Box 356, Aurora ON L4G 3H4
Aylmer & District Museum, 14 East St., Aylmer ON N5H 1W2 – 519/773-9723 – Curator, Patricia Zimmer – Changing historical exhibits, local archives, tourist centre
Aylmer: Ontario Police College Museum, PO Box 1190, Aylmer ON N5H 2T2 – 519/773-5361; Fax: 519/773-5762 – Curator, M. Brown
Bancroft Mineral Museum, c/o Bancroft & District Chamber of Commerce, PO Box 539, Bancroft ON K0L 1C0 – 613/332-1513; Fax: 613/332-2119 – 350 locally collected mineral specimens; mineral collecting field trips; open year round
Bancroft: North Hastings Heritage Museum, PO Box 239, Bancroft ON K0L 1C0 – 613/332-1884 – Chair, Vilma Walker
Bath Museum, c/o Helen Talbot, PO Box 376, Bath ON K0H 1G0
Bath: Loyalist Cultural Centre, Adolphustown Park, Bath ON K0H 1G0 – 613/373-2196 – Katherine Staples
Beachville District Museum, 236 Main St. West, PO Box 6, Beachville ON N0J 1A0 – 519/423-6497; Fax: 519/423-6126 – Coordinator, Shirley Riddick
Beaver River Museum, 284 Simcoe St., PO Box 314, Beaverton ON L0K 1A0 – 705/426-9641 – Curator, Julienne Everett
Belleville: Hastings County Museum, 257 Bridge St. East, Belleville ON K8N 1P4 – 613/962-2329; Fax: 613/962-6340 – Curator/Manager, Rona Rustige
Belleville: O'Hara Mill Museum, c/o Moira River Conservation Authority, PO Box 698, Belleville ON K8N 5B3 – 613/968-8240
Blind River: Timber Village Museum, PO Box 628, Blind River ON P0R 1B0 – 705/356-7544; Fax: 705/962-6340 – Secretary, Linda Rainville

MUSEUMS & SCIENCE CENTRES — ONTARIO 6-17

Bloomfield: Quinte Educational Museum & Archives, 1 Stanley St., PO Box 220, Bloomfield ON K0K 1G0 – 613/393-3166, ext.254 – Curator, Lisa Sarles

Bobcaygeon: Kawartha Settlers' Village, 85 Dunn St., Bobcaygeon ON K0M 1A0 – 705/738-6163

Bothwell: Fairfield Museum, RR#3, Bothwell ON N0P 1C0 – 519/692-4397 – Curator, Archie McIntyre – Site of Moravian Delaware mission, est. 1792, destroyed 1813 by US soldiers; artifacts from burnt village

Bowmanville Museum, 37 Silver St., PO Box 188, Bowmanville ON L1C 3K9 – 905/623-2734 – Curator, Charles Taws

Bracebridge: Woodchester Villa, PO Box 2231, Bracebridge ON P1L 1W1 – 705/645-8111 – Curator, Elene J. Freer – Open July - Labour Day, Tues. - Sun.

Bracebridge: Woodmere Logging Museum, PO Box 2001, Bracebridge ON P0B 1C0 – 705/767-3303 – Jim Wood – Open July - Aug.

Brampton: Lorne Scots PD&H Regimental Museum, #201, 58 Church St. East, Brampton ON L6V 1G3 – 416/451-5724 – Curator, G. Wilkinson

Brampton: Region of Peel Archives & Museum, 9 Wellington St. East, Brampton ON L6W 1Y1 – 905/451-9051; Fax: 905/451-9051 – Curator, William Barber; Regional Archivist, Sharon Larade

Brantford: Bell Homestead & Henderson Home, 94 Tutela Heights Rd., Brantford ON N3T 1A1 – 519/756-6220; Fax: 519/759-5975 – Curator, Brian Wood – Family home of Alexander Graham Bell. Open daily, Tues. - Sun., year round

Brant County Museum, 57 Charlotte St., Brantford ON N3T 2W6 – 519/752-2483; Email: can-bcma-b@immedia.ca – Curator, Susan Twist

Brantford: Myrtleville House Museum, 34 Myrtleville Dr., Brantford ON N3V 1C2 – 519/752-3216; Fax: 519/752-9550; Tourism Brantford: 1-800-265-6299 – Executive Director/Curator, Susan E. Sager

Brantford: Woodland Cultural Centre, 184 Mohawk St., PO Box 1506, Brantford ON N3T 5V6 – 519/759-2650; Fax: 519/759-8912; URL: http://microplacement.com/woodland/languages.html – Museum Director, Tom Hill; Executive Director, Joanna Bedard

Brighton: Presqu'ile Provincial Park Museum, RR#4, Brighton ON K0K 1H0 – 613/475-2204 – Park Supt, Brian R. Peck

Brighton: Proctor House Museum (SOHO), 96 Young St., PO Box 578, Brighton ON K0K 1H0 – 613/475-2144 – President, Tom Cunningham

Brockville Museum, 5 Henry St., Brockville ON K6V 6M4 – 613/342-4397 – Director, Deborah Emerton

Bruce Mines Museum, Taylor St., Hwy. #17, Bruce Mines ON P0R 1C0 – 705/785-3426 – Curator, Arthur M. Henderson

Burgessville: Oxford County Museum School, PO Box 40, Burgessville ON N0J 1C0 – 519/424-9964 – Director, W.F. Brown

Burlington: Ireland House Museum, 2168 Guelph Line, Burlington ON L7P 4M3 – 905/332-9888

Burlington: Joseph Brant Museum, 1240 North Shore Blvd. East, Burlington ON L7S 1C5 – 905/634-3556; Fax: 905/634-4498 – Collection housed in reconstruction of Chief Brant's home

Burlington: Spruce Lane Farm, 1219 Burloak Dr., Burlington ON L7R 3X5 – Farm Manager, John McKinnon

CFB Borden: Borden Military Museum & Archives/Musée commémoratif et archives de la Borden, CFB Borden ON L0M 1C0 – 705/423-3531; Fax: 705/423-3531 – Curator, Keith Lawson; Asst. Curator, Jim Sadlier

Caledonia: Edinburgh Square Heritage & Cultural Centre, 80 Caithness St. East, PO Box 2056, Caledonia ON N3W 2G6 – 416/765-3134 – Director/Curator, Barbra Lang Walker

Callander: North Himsworth Twp. Museum, PO Box 100, Callander ON P0H 1H0 – 705/752-2282 – Curator, Monique Yerke

Cambellcroft: Dorothy's House Museum, 3632 Ganaraska Rd., Cambellcroft ON L0A 1B0

Campbellford-Seymour Heritage Centre, 113 Front St. North, PO Box 300, Campbellford ON K0L 1L0 – 705/653-3656 – Margaret Macmillan

Cannington & Area Historical Society, Centennial Museum, PO Box 196, Cannington ON L0E 1E0 – 705/432-2558 – Curator, Edna Eastman

Carleton Place: Victoria School Museum, 267 Edmund St., Carleton Place ON K7C 3E8 – 613/253-1395

Cayuga: Haldimand County Museum, 8 Echo St., PO Box 38, Cayuga ON N0A 1E0 – 905/772-5880 – Curator, Merle Knight

Chapleau Centennial Museum, PO Box 129, Chapleau ON P0M 1K0 – 705/864-1330; Fax: 705/864-0761 – Open May 15 - Oct. 15

Chatham-Kent Museum, 75 William St. North, Chatham ON N7M 4L4 – 519/354-8338; Fax: 519/354-4170; Email: can-ccg@immedia.ca – Curator, David Benson – Open Tues.- Sun.; researchers by appt. only

Chatham Railroad Museum, PO Box 434, Chatham ON N7M 5K5 – 519/352-3097 – Gary Shurgold

Chatham: Firefighting Museum, c/o Chatham Fire Department,, 5 Second St., Chatham ON K7M 5X2

Chatham: Milner Heritage House, c/o Chatham-Kent Museum, 75 William St. North, Chatham ON N7M 4L4 – 519/354-8338; Fax: 519/354-4170; Email: can-ccc@immedia.ca – Curator, David Benson – Open by appt. only

Cheltenham: The Great War Flying Museum, Brampton Airport, RR#1, Cheltenham ON L0P 1C0 – 905/838-1400

Clarksburg: Beaver Valley Military Museum, Marsh St., PO Box 40, Clarksburg ON N0H 1J0 – 519/599-3031; Fax: 519/599-2474 – Curator, Muriel Hewgill – WWI & WWII; open summer

Cloyne Pioneer Museum, PO Box 228, Cloyne ON K0H 1K0 – 613/336-8712 – Curator, Frances Watt – Open July - Sept.

Cobalt's Northern Ontario Mining Museum, 24 Silver St., PO Box 215, Cobalt ON P0J 1C0 – 705/679-8301; Fax: 705/679-5050 – Sec.-Treas., Anne Fraboni

Cochrane Railway & Pioneer Museum, 210 Railway St., PO Box 490, Cochrane ON P0L 1C0 – 705/272-4361; Fax: 705/272-6068 – Curator, Paul Latondress

Coldwater Canadiana Museum, PO Box 125, Coldwater ON L0K 1E0 – 705/835-5032 – Curator, Arthur Gray

Collingwood: The Collingwood Museum, Hwy. 26 & St. Paul St., PO Box 556, Collingwood ON L9Y 4B2 – 705/445-4811; Fax: 705/445-9004; Email: can-cm@immedia – Curator, Tracy Marsh

Comber: Tilbury West Agricultural Museum, PO Box 158, Comber ON N0P 1J0 – 519/687-2240 – Curator, Myrtle Frankfurth

Combermere: Madonna House Pioneer Museum, Combermere ON K0J 1L0 – 613/756-0103 – Director, Linda Lambeth

Commanda General Store Museum, Commanda ON P0H 1J0 – 705/729-2113 – Chair, Richard Jeffrey

Cornwall: Inverarden Regency Cottage Museum, 3332 Montréal Rd., PO Box 773, Cornwall ON K6H 5T5 – 613/938-9585; Fax: 613/938-9585; Email: slm@cnwl.igs.net; URL: http://www.cnwl.igs.net/~slm/index.html – Curator, Ian Bowering – Open daily Apr. - Nov.; closed Monday

Cornwall: United Counties Museum, 731 Second St. West, PO Box 773, Cornwall ON K6H 5T5 – 613/932-2381; Fax: 613/830-8741 – Curator, Marie Lacabanne – Open daily Apr. - Oct.

Cornwall Island: Museum of the North American Indian Travelling College, RR#3, Cornwall Island ON K6H 5R7 – 613/932-9454 – Executive Director, Barbara Barnes

Cumberland Township Museum, PO Box 159, Cumberland ON K0A 1S0 – 613/833-3059; Fax: 613/830-8741 – Curator, Elmer Pilon

Delhi: The Ontario Tobacco Museum & Heritage Centre, 200 Talbot Rd., PO Box 182, Delhi ON N4B 2W9 – 519/582-0278 – Curator/Director, Myles G. Cowan – Open daily mid-May - mid-Oct.; Mon.-Fri. in fall & winter

Delhi: Windham Township Pioneer Museum, 117 Henry St., Delhi ON N4B 2G1 – Curator, Yates Eaker

Delta: The Delta Mill, PO Box 172, Delta ON K0E 1G0 – 613/924-2658 – President, A. Shaw – Stone mill c. 1810; open daily Victoria Day - Labour Day, weekends until Thanksgiving

Dresden: Uncle Tom's Cabin Historic Site, RR#5, Dresden ON N0P 1M0 – 519/683-2978; Fax: 519/683-1256 – Curator, Barbara Carter – Original home of the Rev. Josiah Henson

Dryden & District Museum, 15 Van Horne Ave., Dryden ON P8N 2A5 – 807/223-4671; Fax: 807/223-3999 – Director/Curator, Edna Libbus Boon

Dundas Historical Society Museum, 139 Park St. West, Dundas ON L9H 5G1 – 905/627-7412; Fax: 905/223-3999 – Curator, Olive Newcombe

Dunvegan: The Glengarry Pioneer Museum, PO Box 27, Dunvegan ON K0C 1J0 – 613/527-5230 – Curator, Ruth McIntosh

Ear Falls District Museum, PO Box 309, Ear Falls ON P0V 1T0 – 807/222-3198 – Curator, J. Appel

Elgin: Jones Falls Defensible Lockmaster's House & Blacksmith Shop, PO Box 10, Elgin ON K0G 1E0 – 613/359-5377; Fax: 613/354-6042 – Area Interpreter, Kevin Fox – Lockmaster's house c.1841; blacksmith shop produces hardware c.1843

Elgin: Kingston Mills Blockhouse, PO Box 10, Elgin ON K0G 1E0 – 613/359-5377; Fax: 613/359-6042; 1-800-815-9417 – Sector Supervisor, A.J. "Sandy" Haining – 1840s animated militia barracks

Elk Lake Museum & Heritage Centre, c/o Corporation of Township of James, Elk Lake ON P0J 1G0 – 705/678-2237 – Chairman, M.D. Giles

Elliot Lake Nuclear & Mining Museum, Municipal Offices, 45 Hillside Dr. North, Elliot Lake ON P5A 1X5 – 705/461-7233; Fax: 705/461-7244 – Curator, Robert E. Manuel – Logging & wildlife display, art gallery; open year round

Emo: Rainy River District Women's Institute Museum, PO Box 511, Emo ON P0W 1E0 – 807/482-2792 – Curator, Tina Visser – Small pioneer museum

Englehart & Area Historical Museum, PO Box 444, Englehart ON P0J 1H0 – 705/544-2400 – Curator, Berdina Beaven – Open May 1 - Dec. 1

Essex: Bicentennial Museum, Township of Maidstone & Area, 1095 Puce Rd., RR#3, Essex ON N8M 2X7 – 519/727-6668, ext.39 – President, Sue Sylvester

Essex: John R. Park Homestead, c/o Essex Region Conservation Authority, 360 Fairview Ave. West, Essex ON N8M 1Y6 – 519/738-2029; Fax: 519/776-8688 – Curator, Janet Cobban – Open year round

Etobicoke: The Canadian Business Hall of Fame/Le Temple de la renommée de l'entreprise canadienne, c/o Junior Achievement of Canada, 1 Westside Dr., Etobicoke ON M9C 1B2 – 416/622-4602; Fax: 416/622-6861 – President & CEO, Colin P. Campbell – Located in The Galleria, BCE Place

Etobicoke: Montgomery's Inn, 4709 Dundas St. West, Etobicoke ON M9A 1A8 – 416/394-8113; Fax: 416/394-6027 – Heritage Coordinator/Director, U. Ernest Buchner

Exeter: Arkona Lion's Museum & Information Centre, Ausable-Bayfield Conservation Authority, RR#3, Exeter ON N0M 1S5 – 519/828-3071 – Native artifacts, fossils & minerals

Fenelon Falls Museum, 50 Oak St., PO Box 667, Fenelon Falls ON K0M 1N0 – 705/887-1044; Fax: 705/887-4337 – Chairman of Museum Board,

Canadian Almanac & Directory 1997

Malcolm Fleck; Sec.-Treas., Evelyn Fleck; Curator, Naomi Struik
Fergus: Wellington County Museum & Archives, RR#1, Fergus ON N1M 2W3 – 519/846-0916; Fax: 519/846-9630 – Director, Ellen Langlands – English, Irish & Scottish heritage of the area; museum housed in an 1877 limestone House of Industry & Refuge; open year round
Flesherton: Archie Bernards Pioneer Village, Flesherton ON N0C 1E0 – 519/924-2002
Flesherton: South Grey Museum & Historical Library, PO Box 299, Flesherton ON N0C 1E0 – 519/924-2843 – Curator, Catherine Carmichael – Open daily
Forest-Lambton Museum, 59 Broadway Ave., RR#1, Forest ON N0N 1J0 – 519/786-5884 – Curator, E.M. Powell
Fort Erie: Mildred M. Mahoney Silver Jubilee Dolls' House Gallery, 657 Niagara Blvd., Fort Erie ON L2A 3H9 – 905/262-5676 – Curator, June Spear – Open year round
Fort Frances Museum & Cultural Centre, 259 Scott St., Fort Frances ON P9A 1G8 – 807/274-7891 – Curator, Darryl Allan – Operates: Logging Tugboat Hallett; Tower Lookout Historical Museum & Fort St. Pierre, Pither's Point Park; open summer
Frankford: Orval Berry Museum, 22 Belleville St., Frankford ON K0K 2C0 – 613/398-6531 – Open year round, Sat., Sun. & holidays
Frankville: Montgomery House, Kitley Historical Association, RR#1, Frankville ON K0E 1H0 – 613/275-2025 – President, Grant Montgomery
Gananoque Historical Museum, 10 King St. East, PO Box 158, Gananoque ON K7G 2T7 – 613/382-4024; Fax: 613/382-8587 – Curator, Lynette McLellan – Open mid-June - mid-Sept., Mon. - Sat.
Glenburnie: Polliwog Castle/Antique Doll & Toy Museum, Division St. North, RR#1, Glenburnie ON K0H 1S0 – 613/548-4702 – Open daily Victoria Day - Labour Day & weekends in winter
Gloucester: Canadian Basketball Hall of Fame, c/o Basketball Canada, 1600 James Naismith Dr., Gloucester ON K1B 5N4
Gloucester: Curling Hall of Fame & Museum of Canada Inc., 1600 James Naismith Dr., Gloucester ON K1B 5N4 – Curator, Tom Fisher
Gloucester Museum, 4550 Bank St., RR#6, Gloucester ON K1G 3N4 – 613/822-2076
Goderich: Huron County Museum & Archives, 110 North St., Goderich ON N7A 2T8 – 519/524-2686; Fax: 519/524-5677 – Director, Claus Breede – Operates the Marine Museum, South Harbour
Huron Historical Gaol, 181 Victoria St., Goderich ON N7A 2S9 – 524-2686; Fax: 524-5677 – Curator, Harold Erb
Goderich: The Livery, 35 South St., Goderich ON N7A 3L4 – 519/524-4376 – Executive Director, Dennis Little
Golden Lake Algonquin Museum, PO Box 28, Golden Lake ON K0J 1X0 – 613/625-2027 – Curator, Philip Commanda
Gore Bay Museum, Western Manitoulin Historical Society, c/o Town Clerk, PO Box 298, Gore Bay ON P0P 1H0 – 705/282-2420
Gore Bay: Mississagi Strait Lighthouse Museum, PO Box 10, Gore Bay ON P0P 1H0 – Riet Wilson
Gormley: Whitchurch-Stouffville Museum, 14732 Woodbine Ave., Gormley ON L0H 1G0 – 905/727-8954; Fax: 905/640-7957 – Curator, Dorie Billich
Gowganda & Area Museum, Gowganda ON P0J 1J0 – 705//624-3171 – Director, David Ford – Open mid-May - mid-Sept.
Grafton: Barnum House Museum, PO Box 161, Grafton ON K0K 2G0 – 416/349-2656; Fax: 416/349-2656 – Curator, Cyndie Paul-Girdwood – Open year round
Grand Bend: Lambton Heritage Museum, RR#2, Grand Bend ON N0M 1T0 – 519/243-2600 – Curator, Robert Tremain

Gravenhurst: Bethune Memorial House, 235 John St. North, Gravenhurst ON P1P 1G4 – 705/687-4261; Fax: 705/687-4935 – Chief, Visitor Activities, Maryellen Corcelli – Birthplace of Dr. Norman Bethune; tours of restored 1890 Presbyterian mansion; open year round
Gravenhurst: Muskoka Steamship & Historical Society, PO Box 1283, Gravenhurst ON P0C 1G0
Grimsby: The Grimsby Museum, 6 Murray St., PO Box 244, Grimsby ON L3M 4G5 – 905/945-5292; Fax: 905/945-0715 – Curator, Janet Cannon
Guelph Civic Museum, Guelph Museums, 6 Dublin St. South, Guelph ON N1H 4L5 – 519/836-1221; Fax: 519/836-5280 – Director, Laurence Grant; Curator, Bev Dietrich; Program Co-ordinator, Tali Laurenson
Guelph: McCrae House, c/o Guelph Museums, 6 Dublin St. South, Guelph ON N1H 4L5 – 519/836-1482; Fax: 519/836-5280 – Director, Laurence Grant; Curator, Bev Dietrich – 1872 birthplace of John McCrae, author of "In Flanders Fields"; located at 108 Water St.
Haliburton Highlands Museum, PO Box 535, Haliburton ON K0M 1S0 – 705/457-2760 – Director, Thomas Ballantine
Hamilton: Dundurn Castle, Dundurn Park, York Blvd., Hamilton ON L8R 3H1 – 905/522-5313; Fax: 905/522-4535 – Curator, Bill Nesbitt
Hamilton: Greater Hamilton Health Sciences Museum, 312 Bay St. South, Hamilton ON L8P 3J8 – Peter L. Hill
Hamilton Children's Museum, 1072 Main St. East, Hamilton ON L8M 1N6 – 905/546-4848; Fax: 905/546-4851 – Curator, Diane Collins
Hamilton Military Museum/Le musée militaire de Hamilton, Dundurn Park, York Blvd., Hamilton ON L8R 3H1 – 905/546-4974; Fax: 905/546-2016; Email: can-hmm@immedia.ca – Curator, Brenda Brownlee
Hamilton: The Hamilton Museum of Steam & Technology, 900 Woodward Ave., Hamilton ON L8H 7N2 – 905/549-5225; Fax: 905/549-1156 – Curator, Ian Kerr-Wilson – Two Gartshore steam powered beam engines housed in 1859 Hamilton Pumping Station
Hamilton Psychiatric Hospital Museum, PO Box 585, Hamilton ON L8N 3K7 – 905/575-6022
Hamilton-Scourge Project, City Hall, 71 Main St. West, Hamilton ON L8N 3T4 – 905/546-4601; Fax: 905/546-2058 – Research & Coordinating Officer, Emily Cain
Hamilton: McMaster Museum of Art (MMA), 1280 Main St. West, Hamilton ON L8S 4L6 – 905/525-9140, ext.23081; Fax: 905/527-4548; Email: nesskg@mcmaster.ca – Director & Curator, Kim G. Ness; Registrar/Operations Manager, Gerrie Loveys; Assistant to the Director/Special Projects Officer, Jane Zatylyn
Hamilton: Mohawk Trail School Museum, 141 Reno Ave., Hamilton ON L8T 2S6 – 905/527-5092 – Director, Walter Moir – 1882 schoolhouse
Hamilton: Royal Hamilton Light Infantry Heritage Museum, John Weir Foote VC Armoury, 200 James St. North, Hamilton ON L8R 2L1 – 905/572-2742; Fax: 905/528-5443 – Curator, D. Wentworth
Hamilton: Whitehern, McQuesten Residence, 41 Jackson St. West, Hamilton ON L8P 1L3 – 905/522-5664; Fax: 905/522-1666 – Curator, Ania Latoszek
Harrow: Southwestern Ontario Heritage Village, PO Box 221, Harrow ON N0R 1G0 – 519/776-6909 – Administrator, Georgia Klym-Skeates – Open daily July - Aug.; April - Nov., Wed. - Sun.
Holland Centre: Comber Pioneer Village, Rte. 3, Holland Centre ON N0H 1R0 – 519/794-3467 – Director, Robert James Comber
Huntsville: Muskoka Pioneer Village & Museum, 88 Brunel Rd., Huntsville ON P1H 1R1 – 705/789-7576; Fax: 705/789-6169; Email: village@vianet.on.ca;

URL: http://www.muskoka.net/village.html – General Manager, John Finley
Ignace Heritage Centre, 36 Hwy. #17 West, PO Box 480, Ignace ON P0T 1T0 – 807/934-2280; Fax: 807/934-6452 – CEO, C. Penney – Open year round
Ingersoll Cheese Factory Museum/Musée de la fabrique de fromage d'Ingersol, PO Box 340, Ingersoll ON N5C 3V3 – 519/485-0120, 485-5510 (summer); Fax: 519/485-3543 – Curator, Shirley Lovell – 5 buildings including cheese factory museum, blacksmith shop, barn & community museum; Ingersoll Sports Hall of Fame houses Harold Wilson's Miss Canada IV Speedboat; open daily July - Aug; weekends May - Labour Day
Iron Bridge Historical Museum, PO Box 460, Iron Bridge ON P0R 1H0
Iroquois: Carman House Museum, c/o Municipal Clerk, Carman Rd. South, PO Box 249, Iroquois ON K0E 1K0 – 613/-652-4422; Fax: 613/652-4636
Iroquois Falls Pioneer Museum, PO Box 448, Iroquois Falls ON P0K 1E0 – 705/258-3730 – Curator, Debbie Arsenault – Open June 15 - Aug. 31
Jordan: Ball's Falls Historical Park & Conservation, 6th Ave., RR#1, Jordan ON L0R 1S0 – 905/562-5235; Fax: 905/227-2998; Site Fax: 905/562-7051 – Curator, Christine Hayward
Jordan Historical Museum of the Twenty, PO Box 39, Jordan ON L0R 1S0 – 905/562-5242 – Curator/Director, Diane O'Neill
Kakabeka Falls: Hymers Museum, RR#1, Kakabeka Falls ON P0T 1W0 – Curator, M. Petryshyn
Kapuskasing: Ron Morel Memorial Museum, 88 Riverside Dr., Kapuskasing ON P5N 1B3 – 705/335-5443, 2341; Fax: 705/337-1741 – Open Victoria Day - Labour Day, 7 days per week, 9 am - 5 pm
Kenora: Lake of the Woods Museum, 300 Main St. South, PO Box 497, Kenora ON P9N 3X5 – 807/467-2105 – Director, Reg Reeve
Keswick: Georgina Village Museum, Civic Centre Rd., RR#2, Keswick ON L4P 3E9 – 905/476-4301 – Open June - Labour Day
Killarney Centennial Museum, 32 Commissioners St., Killarney ON P0M 2A0 – 705/287-2424; Fax: 705/287-2660 – Howard Beauvais; Mark Wilson
King Township Historical Society Museum, PO Box 136, King City ON L0G 1K0 – 905/727-6322 – Director, Helen Poulis
Kingston: Bellevue House National Historic Site/La Villa-Bellevue (BHNHS), 35 Centre St., Kingston ON K7L 4E5 – 613/545-8666; Fax: 613/545-8721; Email: Ont_Bellvue@pch.gc.ca – Supt., John H. Grenville – Home of Sir John A. Macdonald, restored to late 1840s period
Kingston: Canadian Forces Communications & Electronics Museum, CFB Kingston, Stn Vimy, Kingston ON K7K 5L0 – 613/541-5395; Fax: 613/546-0908 – Director, Capt. J.A. MacKenzie
Kingston: Correctional Service of Canada Museum/Musée du service correctionnel du Canada (CSCM/MSCC), 555 King St. West, PO Box 22, Kingston ON K7L 4V7 – 613/530-3122; Fax: 613/545-8698 – Curator, Dave St. Onge – Open mid-May - Sept., Wed. - Sun.
Kingston: Fort Henry, PO Box 213, Kingston ON K7L 4V8 – 613/542-7388; Fax: 613/542-3054; Email: can-fh@immedia.ca; 1-800-437-2233 – Manager, John Robertson – The Citadel of Upper Canada, brought to life by the Fort Henry Guard; restaurant; gift stores; children's muster parades; open Victoria Day to Sept. 29
Kingston: Frontenac County Schools Museum, 5 Clergy St. East, Kingston ON K7L 3H7 – 613/544-9113 – Curator, Beth Hogan; Association President, Gwendolyn Thorburn
Kingston: International Hockey Hall of Fame & Museum Inc., PO Box 82, Kingston ON K7L 4V6 – 613/544-2355, 546-5687 – Executive Director, Doug

Nichols – Hockey from its organized beginning in Kingston, 1855, to now; Bobby Hull collection

Kingston Archaeological Centre, c/o Cataraqui Archaeological Research Foundation, 370 King St. West, Kingston ON K7L 2X4

Kingston Fire Department Museum, 271 Brock St., Kingston ON K7L 1S5 – 613/542-9727

Kingston: MacLachlan Woodworking Museum, Grass Creek Park, 2993 Hwy. 2, PO Box 966, Kingston ON K7L 4X8 – 613/542-0543; Fax: 613/546-0908; URL: http://mal.rmc.ca/museum/home.html – Director, Matthew Turner

Kingston: Marine Museum of the Great Lakes at Kingston, 55 Ontario St., Kingston ON K7L 2Y2 – 613/542-2261 – Executive Director, Maurice D. Smith – Includes library & archives; open year round

Kingston: Miller Museum of Mineralogy & Geology, Miller Hall, Queen's University, Kingston ON K7L 3N6 – 613/545-6767; Fax: 613/545-6592; Email: badham@geolserv.geol.queensu.ca; URL: http://geol.queensu.ca/museum/museum.html – Curator, Mark Badham

Kingston: Murney Tower Museum, PO Box 54, Kingston ON K7L 4V6 – 613/544-9925 – c. 1846 Martello Tower; open daily Victoria Day - Labour Day

Kingston: Pump House Steam Museum, 23 Ontario St., Kingston ON K7L 2Y2 – 613/546-4696 – Director, R. York

Kingston: The Royal Military College Museum/Le musée du Collège militaire royal du Canada, Kingston ON K7K 5L0 – 613/541-6000, ext.6664; Fax: 613/542-3565 – Committee Chair, Dr. J.G. Pike; Curator, Ross McKenzie – Open daily July - Labour Day

Kingsville: Jack Miner Museum, c/o The Jack Miner Migratory Bird Foundation, Kingsville ON N9Y 2E8 – 519/733-4034 – Curator, Beth Shaughnessy

Kirkland Lake: Museum of Northern History at the Sir Harry Oakes Chateau, 2 Chateau Dr., PO Box 1148, Kirkland Lake ON P2N 3M7 – 705/568-8800; Fax: 705/567-6611; Email: museumkl@nt.net – Director/Curator, Lydia Alexander

Kitchener: Doon Heritage Crossroads, RR#2, Kitchener ON N2G 3W5 – 519/748-1914; URL: http://www.oceta.on.ca/region.waterloo/doon – Curator, Interpretations & Programmes, Wendy Connell; Curator/Manager, Thomas A. Reitz – Turn of the century living history village; open daily May - Dec.

Kitchener: Joseph Schneider Haus Museum, 466 Queen St. South, Kitchener ON N2G 1W7 – 519/742-7752; Fax: 519/885-1436 – Manager/Curator, Susan Burke

Kitchener: Woodside National Historic Site/Lieu historique nationale de Woodside, 528 Wellington St. North, Kitchener ON N2H 5L5 – 519/742-5273; Fax: 519/742-0561; TTY: 519/742-5273 – Supt., Kim Seward-Hannam – Boyhood home of William Lyon Mackenzie King, 1891; open May - Dec.

Kleinburg Doll Museum, 10489 Islington Ave. North, Kleinburg ON L0J 1C0 – 905/893-1358 – Open year round

Komoka Railway Museum Inc., 133 Queen St., PO Box 22, Komoka ON N0L 1R0 – 519/657-1912 – President, John Kanakos; Curator, Ron Davis

Lakefield: Christ Church Museum, 33 Colborne St., PO Box 926, Lakefield ON K0L 2H0 – 705/652-3614 – Chairman, Charles McDermott

Lambeth: Bygone Babies Doll & Bear Museum, Lambeth ON N0L 1S0 – 519/652-9240 – Open year round

Lanark: Middleville Museum, RR#2, Lanark ON K0G 1K0 – 613/259-5462 – Chairperson, Alice Borrowman

Latchford: House of Memories, PO Box 82, Latchford ON P0J 1N0 – 705/676-2417; Fax: 705/676-2121 – Curator, Helen LaRose

Leamington: Point Pelee National Park Visitor Centre (Natural History Museum), RR#1, Leamington ON N8H 3V4 – 519/322-2365; Fax: 519/322-1277 – Chief, Visitor Activities, Lily J. Meleg

Limehouse: Canadian Military Studies Museum, RR#1, Limehouse ON L0P 1H0 – 905/877-6522 – Director, Frank F. Grant

Lindsay: Victoria County Historical Society Museum, 435 Kent St. West, PO Box 74, Lindsay ON K9V 4R8 – 705/324-6756 – Director, Tammy Robinson – May - Oct., Wed. - Sun., 1 pm - 5 pm

Lively: Anderson Farm Museum, 25 Black Lake Rd., Lively ON P3Y 1J3 – 705/692-4448; Fax: 705/692-3225 – Curator, James Fortin – Open year round

London: Fanshawe Pioneer Village (FPV), 2609 Fanshawe Park Rd. East, London ON N5X 4A1 – 519/457-1296; Fax: 519/457-3364 – Executive Director, Dr. William Finlayson; Manager, Luanne Ollivier

London: First Hussars: Citizen Soldiers Museum, 399 Ridout St. North, London ON N6A 2P1 – 519/471-1538 – Director, Alastair Neely

London: Grosvenor Lodge, 1017 Western Rd., London ON N6G 1G5 – 519/645-2845; Fax: 519/645-0981

London: Guy Lombardo Museum, 205 Wonderland Rd. South, London ON N6K 2T3 – 519/473-9003; Fax: 519/473-9003 – Managing-Director, John Noubarian; Chairman, Gino Nicodemo – Open May - Sept., 11 am - 5 pm daily; Sept. - May, call in advance

London Museum of Archaeology, Lawson-Jury Bldg., University of Western Ontario, 1600 Attawandaron Rd., London ON N6G 3M6 – 519/473-1360; Fax: 519/473-1363 – Director General, Dr. William Finlayson; Manager, B. Rigutto – Wilfrid Jury collection

London Regional Art & Historical Museums (LRAHM), 421 Ridout St. North, London ON N6A 5H4 – 519/672-4580; Fax: 519/660-8397 – Executive Director, Ted Fraser; Director, Finance, Shelagh Parg; Chief Curator, Lynne DiStefano – Operates: Eldon House

Eldon House, 481 Ridout St. North, London ON N6A 2P8 – 672-4580; Fax: 660-8397 – House & contents exemplify family life in the London area from 1834 to the present

London Regional Children's Museum (LRCM), 21 Wharncliffe Rd. South, London ON N6J 4G5 – 519/434-5726; Fax: 519/434-1443 – Executive Director, Leigh-Anne Stradeski

London: The Royal Canadian Regiment Museum, Wolseley Barracks, London ON N5Y 4T7 – 519/660-5102; Fax: 519/660-5344; Email: rhq.thercr@onlinesys.com – Curator, Maj. A.F. Butlers; Asst. Curator, M.Cpl. G.H. Johnson

Magnetawan Historical Museum, PO Box 130, Magnetawan ON P0A 1P0 – 705/387-3947 – Curator, Marilyn Raaflaub

Mallorytown: Interpretive Centre & Brown's Bay Wreck/Centre d'acceuil & l'Épave de la baie Brown, St. Lawrence Islands National Park, RR#3, 2 Country Rd. 5, Mallorytown ON K0E 1R0 – 613/923-5261; Fax: 613/923-2229 – Chief, Visitor Activities, Ken Robinson – Natural & human history of 1,000 Islands; 1812 gunboat raised from the river

Manitowaning: Assiginack Museum, Mill Complex & SS Norisle Heritage Park, PO Box 238, Manitowaning ON P0P 1N0 – 705/859-3905 – Curator, Jeanette Allen

Manotick: Silversides Tool Museum, c/o Rideau Valley Conservation Authority, PO Box 599, Manotick ON K0A 2N0 – 613/692-3571

Manotick: Swords & Ploughshares Museum, PO Box 520, Manotick ON K0A 2N0 – 613/837-0149

Manotick: Watson's Mill, c/o Dickinson Square Conservation Area, PO Box 599, Manotick ON K4M 1A5 – 613/692-3571; Fax: 613/692-0831 – General Manager, Dell Hallett

Markham District Historical Museum, 9350 Hwy. 48, Markham ON L3P 3J3 – 905/294-4576; Fax: 905/294-4590 – Manager, Birgitta MacLeod – Open year round

Marten River Logging Museum, c/o Marten River Provincial Park, Marten River ON P0H 1T0 – 705/892-2200 – Park Supt., C.J. Osborne

Massey Area Pioneer Museum, PO Box 237, Massey ON P0P 1P0 – 705/865-2266 – Curator, Francis Goyetche

Matheson: Thelma Miles Museum, PO Box 329, Matheson ON P0K 1N0 – 705/273-2325; Fax: 705/273-2140 – Director/Curator, Karen Barber

Mattawa & District Museum, PO Box 9, Mattawa ON P0H 1V0 – 705/744-5495 – Curator, Joan Kilner – Open May - Oct.

Mattawa: Voyageur Heritage Centre, Samuel de Champlain Provincial Park, PO Box 147, Mattawa ON P0H 1V0 – 705/744-2276 – Park Supt., J. Drechsler

Meaford Museum, PO Box 1633, Meaford ON N0H 1Y0 – 519/538-1060 – Curator, Loretta McNally – Open daily May -Sept.

Meldrum Bay: The Net Shed Museum, Water St., Meldrum Bay ON P0P 1R0 – 705/283-3385 – Director, Dawn McKinlay – Open June - Labour Day

Merrickville: The Blockhouse Museum, c/o Secretary, Merrickville & District Historical Society, PO Box 29, Merrickville ON K0G 1N0 – 613/269-3614

Midland: Huronia Museum, PO Box 638, Midland ON L4R 4P4 – 705/526-2844; Fax: 705/527-6622; Email: can-hm@immedia.ca – Director/Curator, Jamie Hunter – Recreated Huron Village represents one of hundreds that existed in the Georgian Bay area, representing a unique & sophisticated society which lasted nearly 1,000 years; Canada's first recreated Native village

Midland: Martyrs' Shrine, Midland ON L4R 4K5 – 705/526-3788; Fax: 705/526-1546 – Director, Rev. James J. Farrell, S.J.

Midland: Sainte-Marie among the Hurons/Sainte-Marie-au-Pays-des-Hurons (SMATH), c/o Economic Development, Trade & Tourism, Huronia Historical Parks, PO Box 160, Midland ON L4R 4K8 – 705/526-7838; Fax: 705/526-9193 – General Manager, John Barrett-Hamilton; Site Manager, Pierre Lafaive

Midland: Wye Marsh Wildlife Centre, PO Box 100, Midland ON L4R 4K6 – 705/526-7809 – Executive Director, Robert Whittam

Milford: Mariners' Park Museum, PO Box 54, Milford ON K0K 2P0 – 613/476-4695; Fax: 613/476-8392 – Chair, Judy Zeleny

Milton: Halton Region Museum, RR#3, Milton ON L9T 2X7 – 905/875-2200; Fax: 905/876-4322 – Manager, Heritage Services, Paul H. Attack

Milton: Ontario Agricultural Museum, PO Box 38, Milton ON L9T 2Y3 – 905/878-8151, 876-4530 – General Manager, John Wiley

Minden: Kanawa International Museum of Canoes, Kayaks & Rowing Craft, RR#2, Minden ON K0M 2K0 – 705/489-2644 – Curator, Michael Ketemer

Minesing: Simcoe County Museum, RR#2, Minesing ON L0L 1Y0 – 705/728-3721; Fax: 705/726-3991 – Curator, Gloria Crawford

Mississauga: Benares Historic House & Visitor Centre, 1507 Clarkson Rd. North, Mississauga ON L5J 2W8 – 905/615-3277; 822-2061 – Restored to reflect the way the Harris family of Benares, Clarkson, lived in 1918

Mississauga: Bradley Museum, 1620 Orr Rd., Mississauga ON L5J 4T2 – 905/822-1569, 4884; Fax: 905/822-1569 – Curator, Scott Gillies – Restored 1830s Loyalist farmhouse; period gardens; display galleries in 1830s Regency cottage; Sunday Tea Room; special events throughout the year

Moore Museum, 94 Moore Line, Mooretown ON N0N 1M0 – 519/867-2020 – Curator, Laurie Mason – Open year round; Jan. - Feb. by appt.

Canadian Almanac & Directory 1997

Moosonee: Revillon Frères Museum, c/o Moosonee Development Area Board, PO Box 127, Moosonee ON P0L 1Y0 – 705/336-2933, 2497 – Recreation Director, Robin Langille – Open June - Labour Day

Morpeth: Rondeau Provincial Park Visitor Centre, c/o Ministry of Natural Resources, RR#1, Morpeth ON N0P 1X0 – 519/674-1772; Fax: 519/674-1755 – Director, Pamela E. Burns

Morrisburg: Upper Canada Village, RR#1, Morrisburg ON K0C 1X0 – 613/543-3704; Fax: 613/543-4098 – Manager, Paul Deault – Representation of 1860s riverfront community with over 30 homes, shops & operating mills; children's activities; open daily from Victoria Day weekend to Thanksgiving Monday

Mount Brydges: Ska-Nah-Doht Indian Village, RR#1, Mount Brydges ON N0L 1W0 – 519/264-2420 – Curator, Andrea French

Mount Hope: Canadian Warplane Heritage Museum, Hamilton Airport, 9280 Airport Rd., Mount Hope ON L0R 1W0 – 905/679-4183; Fax: 905/679-4186; Email: museum@warplane.com – Executive Director, A.L. Lutchin

Napanee: Allan Macpherson House, 180 Elizabeth St., PO Box 183, Napanee ON K7R 3M3 – 613/354-5982 – Director/Curator, Elizabeth Hunter

Napanee: Lennox & Addington County Museum & Archives, 97 Thomas St. East, PO Bag 1000, Napanee ON K7R 3S9 – 613/354-3027; Fax: 613/354-3112; Email: museum@fox.nstn.ca – Manager, Jane Foster; Archivist, Jennifer Bunting

Napanee: Old Hay Bay Church, RR#2, Napanee ON K7R 3K7 – 613/373-2232 – Secretary, K.J. Crawford; D. Hough – Circa 1792, oldest exisiting Methodist Church in Canada; open daily July 1 - Labour Day & by appt.

Nepean: Algonquin College Museum, Museum Technology Program, Algonquin College, 1385 Woodroffe Ave., Nepean ON K2G 1V8 – 613/727-7612; Fax: 613/727-7684 – Director, Patrick Wohler

Nepean: The Log Farm/La Vieille Ferme, RR#7, Nepean ON K2H 7V2 – 613/825-4352, 239-5188

Nepean Museum Inc., 16 Rowley Ave., Nepean ON K2G 1L9 – 613/723-7936; Fax: 613/723-7936 – Director, Dan Hoffman

New Liskeard: Little Claybelt Homesteaders Museum, PO Box 1718, New Liskeard ON P0J 1P0 – 705/647-9575 – Chairperson, Dorothy Greenwood

Newmarket: Elman W. Campbell Museum, #31, 543 Timothy St., Newmarket ON L3Y 1R1 – 905/895-4679; Fax: 905/895-6004 – Curator, Elizabeth Sinyard

Niagara Falls: Guinness Museum of World Records, 4943 Clifton Hill, Niagara Falls ON L2G 3N5 – 905/356-2299 – Open year round

Niagara Falls: Louis Tussaud's Waxworks, 4915 Clifton Hill, Niagara Falls ON L2G 3N5 – 905/374-6601 – General Manager, Rick Blanchard

Niagara Falls: Lundy's Lane Historical Museum, 5810 Ferry St., Niagara Falls ON L2G 1S9 – 905/358-5082 – Curator, Margaret Anne Tabaka

Niagara Falls: McFarland House, c/o Niagara Parks Commission, PO Box 150, Niagara Falls ON L2E 6T2 – 905/356-2241; Fax: 905/354-6041 – Community Services Officer, April Petrie – Early 1800s Loyalist home

Niagara Falls: Movieland Wax Museum, 4950 Clifton Hill, Niagara Falls ON L2G 3N4 – 905/358-3061; Fax: 905/358-9456 – General Manager, Guy Paone – Open year round

Niagara Falls Museum, Est. 1827, 5651 River Rd., PO Box 960, Niagara Falls ON L2E 6V8 – 905/356-2151; USA tel: 716/285-4898 – Director, Jacob Sherman

Niagara Falls: Oak Hall, PO Box 150, Niagara Falls ON L2E 6T2 – 905/356-2241; Fax: 905/354-6041 – Administrative offices for the Niagara Parks Commission

Niagara Falls: Old Fort Erie, Niagara Parks Commission, PO Box 150, Niagara Falls ON L2E 6T2 – 905/871-0540 – Manager, J. Saunders

Niagara Falls: Ripley's Believe It or Not Museum, 4960 Clifton Hill, Niagara Falls ON L2G 3N4 – 905/356-2238 – General Manager, Rick Blanchard

Niagara Falls: Willoughby Twp. Historical Museum, 9935 Niagara Pkwy., RR#3, Niagara Falls ON L2E 6S6 – 905/295-4036 – Curator, Emma Chambers

Niagara on the Lake: The French Perfume Factory & Museum, 393 York Rd., Niagara on the Lake ON L0S 1J0 – 905/685-6666; Fax: 905/984-8226 – Eddie Youssoufian – Open Feb. - Dec.

Niagara Fire Museum, PO Box 498, Niagara on the Lake ON L0S 1J0 – 905/468-7279 – Asst. Curator, Michele Stewart

Niagara Historical Society Museum, 43 Castlereagh St., PO Box 208, Niagara on the Lake ON L0S 1J0 – 905/468-3912 – Curator/Director, William Severin

Niagara National Historic Sites, Parks Canada, PO Box 787, Niagara on the Lake ON L0S 1J0 – 905/468-4257; 905/468-4638; Fax: 905/468-4638; Email: daler@pksnia.dots.doe.ca – Supt., R. Dale; Chief, Visitor Activities, D. Webb; Chief, Historic Resource Conservation, D. Greenall – Includes Fort George, Navy Hall, Brock's Monument & Butler's Barracks

Niagara Apothecary, 5 Queen St., Niagara-on-the-Lake ON L0S 1J0 – 905/468-3845, 962-4861 (off-season) – Curator, Ernst Stieb

Nipigon Museum, PO Box 208, Nipigon ON P0T 2J0 – 807/887-2727 – Curator, Roland Choiselat

Nipissing Twp. Museum, Twp. of Nipissing Office, Nipissing ON P0H 1W0 – 705/724-2938 – Curator, Lela Daub

North Bay: Dionne Homestead Museum, c/o Chamber of Commerce, PO Box 747, North Bay ON P1B 8J8 – 705/472-8480; Fax: 705/472-8027 – Director, Sharon Clark-Bedard – Open Victoria Day - Thanksgiving

North Bay & Area Museum, 171 Main St. West, PO Box 628, North Bay ON P1B 8J5 – 705/476-2323 – Curator, Pamela Handley – Exhibits on local history as well as special exhibits from the Royal Ontario Museum & other national & provinical museums

North Bay: Ontario Northland Transportation Commission Archives & Museum, 555 Oak St. East, North Bay ON P1B 8L3 – 705/472-4500 – Archivist, Janet Calcaterra

North Bay: Trappers Museum, PO Box 705, North Bay ON P1B 8J8 – 705/472-5850, ext.212 – Curator, Bob Groves

North Buxton: Raleigh Township Centennial Museum, PO Box 53, North Buxton ON N0P 1Y0 – 519/352-4799 – Curator, Alice Newby

North York: Black Creek Pioneer Village, 1000 Murray Ross Pkwy., North York ON M3J 2P3 – 416/736-1733; Fax: 416/661-6610 – Manager, Marty Brent

North York: Gibson House Museum, 5172 Yonge St., North York ON M2N 5P6 – 416/395-7432; Fax: 416/395-7886 – Curator, Beth Hanna

North York: History of Contraception Museum, c/o Ortho Pharmaceutical (Canada) Ltd., 19 Green Belt Dr., North York ON M3C 1L9 – 416/449-9444 – Curator, Heather Bennett

North York: Irving E. & Ray Kanner Heritage Museum, 3560 Bathurst St., North York ON M6A 2E1 – 416/789-5131, ext.2802; Fax: 416/785-2378 – Coordinator, Pat Dickinson

North York: The Roberta Bondar Earth & Space Centre, 1750 Finch Ave. East, North York ON M2J 2X5 – 416/491-5050

Norwich & District Museum & Archives, RR#3, Norwich ON N0J 1P0 – 519/863-3101 (Museum); 863-3638 (Archives) – Curator, Ian Bell; Archivist, Lisa Miettinen – 1889 Quaker Meeting House

Oakville Museum, 8 Navy St., Oakville ON L6J 2Y5 – 905/845-3541; Fax: 905/845-3955 – Manager/Curator, Irene Knight – Museum buildings: Custom House, Chisholm Family Home & Old Post Office

Oakville: Royal Canadian Golf Association Museum & Library, Canadian Golf Hall of Fame, 1333 Dorval Dr., Oakville ON L6J 4Z3 – 905/849-9700; Fax: 905/845-7040 – Curator, Karen E. Hewson

Odessa: Historic Babcock Mill, 100 Bridge St., PO Box 70, Odessa ON K0H 2H0 – 613/389-8314

Ohsweken: Chiefswood Museum, PO Box 5000, Ohsweken ON N0A 1M0 – 519/752-5005; Fax: 519/752-9578 – Curator, Paula Whitlow – Birthplace of poet E. Pauline Johnson; plans to open fully restored for summer, 1996

Oil Springs: Oil Museum of Canada, PO Box 16, Oil Springs ON N0N 1P0 – 519/834-2840; Fax: 519/834-2840 – Manager, Donna McGuire – Open daily May - Oct. 31; Nov. - Apr., Mon. - Fri.

Orillia: Stephen Leacock Museum, PO Box 625, Orillia ON L3V 6K5 – 705/326-9357; Fax: 705/326-9357 – Director/Curator, Daphne Mainprize

Orono: Clarke Museum & Archives, Municipality of Clarington, PO Box 152, Orono ON L0B 1M0 – 905/983-9243; Email: can-cma-mc@immedia.ca – Curator, Mark Jackman

Oshawa: Canadian Automotive Museum, 99 Simcoe St. South, Oshawa ON L1H 4G7 – 905/576-1222 – Curator/Manager, Michael Foley

Oshawa Sydenham Museum, Lakeview Park, 7 Henry St., PO Box 2303, Oshawa ON L1H 7V5 – 905/436-7624 – Director, Laura Suchan – Henry House; Robinson House; Guy House

Oshawa: Parkwood Estate, 270 Simcoe St. North, Oshawa ON L1G 4T5 – 905/579-1311 – Curator, Brian Malcolm

Ottawa: Agricultural Museum/Musée de l'Agriculture, Bldg. 88, Central Experimental Farm, PO Box 9724, Stn T, Ottawa ON K1G 5A3 – 613/991-3044; Fax: 613/947-2374 – Director, Michelle Dondo-Tardiff; Head, Interpretation & School Services, Tamara Tarasoff

Ottawa: The Billings Estate Museum/Musée du domaine Billings, 2100 Cabot St., Ottawa ON K1H 6K1 – 613/247-4830; Fax: 613/247-4832 – Curator/Manager, Lynn Villeneuve – Home & property of Braddish & Lamira Billings, two of Ottawa's earliest settlers, c. 1828; exhibits highlight 5 generations of family & community history; open May 1 - Oct. 31, Sun. - Thurs., 12 pm - 5 pm; otherwise by appt.

Ottawa: Bytown Historical Museum/Musée Bytown, PO Box 523, Stn B, Ottawa ON K1P 5P6 – 613/234-4570; Fax: 613/234-4846; Email: ah294@freenet.carleton.ca – Director/Curator, Lana Shaw

Ottawa: Canadian Ski Museum Inc., 457A Sussex Dr., Ottawa ON K1N 6Z4 – 613/233-5832; Fax: 613/230-2054 – Chairman, W.P. Tindale

Ottawa: Governor General's Foot Guards Museum, Drill Hall, Cartier Sq., Ottawa ON K1A 0K2 – 613/992-3771 – Curator, Martin J. Lane, CD

Ottawa: Laurier House National Historic Site, 335 Laurier Ave. East, Ottawa ON K1N 6R4 – 613/992-8142

Ottawa: Mackenzie King Estate, National Capital Commission, 40 Elgin St., Ottawa ON K1P 1C7 – 613/239-5555; Fax: 613/239-5188 – Coordinator, Denis Messier – Located in Gatineau Park; Open May 15-Thanksgiving.

Ottawa: Museum of Canadian Scouting, 1345 Baseline Rd., PO Box 5151, Stn F, Ottawa ON K2C 3G7 – 613/224-5131; Fax: 613/224-3571 – Executive Director, Bob Hallett

Ottawa Sports Hall of Fame/Temple de la renomée des sports d'Ottawa, Civic Centre, 1015 Bank St., Ottawa ON K1S 3W7 – 613/564-1485; Fax: 613/564-1619 – Chairman, James A. Durrell

Owen Sound: Billy Bishop Heritage Museum, 948 - 3rd Ave. West, Owen Sound ON N4K 4P6 – 519/371-0031 – Childhood home of Canada's most-decorated serviceman, William Avery Bishop, VC ; photographs, documents & artifacts

Owen Sound: County of Grey-Owen Sound Museum, 975 - 6th St. East, Owen Sound ON N4K 1G9 – 519/376-3690 – Director, A.W. Landen

Owen Sound Marine-Rail Museum, 1165 First Ave. West, Owen Sound ON N4K 4K8 – 519/371-3333 – Acting Curator, Orris Hull

Parry Sound: West Parry Sound District Museum (WPSDM), 17 George St., PO Box 337, Parry Sound ON P2A 2X4 – 705/746-5365; Fax: 705/746-8775; Email: can-wpsdm@immedia.ca – Director/Curator, Craig E. D'Arcy

Pelee Island Heritage Centre, c/o Pelee Island Municipal Office, Pelee Island ON N0R 1M0

Pembroke: Champlain Trail Museum, 1032 Pembroke St. East, PO Box 985, Pembroke ON K8A 7M5 – 613/735-0517 – Curator, Sharon E. Adams

Penetanguishene: Discovery Harbour/Havre de la Découverte, PO Box 1800, Penetanguishene ON L0K 1P0 – 705/549-8064; Fax: 705/549-4858 – General Manager, John Barrett-Hamilton

Penetanguishene Centennial Museum, 8 Burke St., Penetanguishene ON L0K 1P0 – 705/549-2150 – Curator, Donna Beauvais

Perth: Innisville & District Museum, c/o Willard Shaw, RR#6, Perth ON K7H 3C8 – 613/257-1527

Perth: The Perth Museum, 80 Gore St. East, Perth ON K7H 1H9 – 613/267-1947; Fax: 613/267-7351 – Curator, Douglas M. McNichol – 1840 stone home of Senator Matheson; open year round

Petawawa: Canadian Forces Base Petawawa Military Museum, Canadian Forces Base Petawawa, Petawawa ON K8H 2X3 – 613/588-5239 – Base Museologist, Dennis Lavoie

Peterborough: Hope Water Powered Saw Mill, c/o Otonabee Region Conservation Authority, #200, 380 Armour Rd., Time Sq., Peterborough ON K9H 7L7 – 705/745-5791; Fax: 705/745-7488 – General Manager, Dan White

Peterborough: Hutchison House Museum, 270 Brock St., Peterborough ON K9H 2P9 – 705/743-9710 – Curator, Stephanie Ford Forrester

Peterborough: Lang Pioneer Village, 470 Water St., Peterborough ON K9H 3M3 – 705/295-6694; Fax: 705/876-1730 – Manager, Angela Chittick

Peterborough: Lang Water Powered Grist Mill, c/o Otonabee Region Conservation Authority, #200, Time Sq., 380 Armour Rd., Peterborough ON K9H 7L7 – 705/745-5791; Fax: 705/745-7488 – General Manager, Dan White

Peterborough Centennial Museum & Archives, PO Box 143, Peterborough ON K9J 6Y5 – 705/743-5180 – Manager, Ken Doherty

Peterborough Lift Lock Visitor Centre, c/o Trent Severn Waterway, PO Box 567, Peterborough ON K9J 6Z6 – 705/745-8389; Fax: 705/742-3515 – Manager, F. Irons – Open year round

Peterborough: Trent-Severn Waterway/Voie navigable Trent-Severn (TSW), PO Box 567, Peterborough ON K9J 6Z6 – 705/742-9267; Fax: 705/742-9644 – Supt., John Lewis; Director of Canal Operations, Fred Alyea; Chief Engineer, Wayne Pacey

Pickering Museum Village, c/o Town of Pickering, One The Esplanade, Pickering ON L1V 6K7 – 905/420-4620 (winter), 683-8401 (summer); Fax: 905/420-0515 – Manager, Lynn Winterstein

Picton: Macaulay Heritage Park, PO Box 2150, Picton ON K0K 2T0 – 613/476-3833; Fax: 613/476-8356 – Curator, Tom Kuglin – Administers Prince Edward County Museum; Macaulay House, County Court House & Jail

Picton: Mariners' Museum Lighthouse Park, RR#3, Picton ON K0K 2T0 – 613/476-4695

Picton: North Marysburgh Museum, The Rose House, Prince Edward County, RR#4, Picton ON K0K 2T0 – 613/476-4436 (winter), 5439 (summer) – Curator, Kimmberley L. Hart – Early settlers home furnished with 19th-century artifacts.

Port Carling: Muskoka Lakes Museum, PO Box 432, Port Carling ON P0B 1J0 – 705/765-5367; Fax: 705/765-6271; Email: musklake@muskoka.com – Director, Lindsay Hill

Port Colborne Historical & Marine Museum, 280 King St., PO Box 572, Port Colborne ON L3K 5X8 – 905/834-7604 – Director/Curator, Virginia Anger

Port Dover: City of Nanticoke Museum Board, Clerk's Department, 230 Main St., Port Dover ON N0A 1N0

Port Dover Harbour Museum, 44 Harbour St., PO Box 1298, Port Dover ON N0A 1N0 – 519/583-2660; Email: RNET: can-pdhm@immedia.ca – Curator, Sylvia Crossland

Port Perry: Scugog Shores Historical Museum, 16210 Island Rd., RR#3, Port Perry ON L9L 1B4 – 905/985-3589; Fax: 905/985-3492; Email: can-sshm@immedia.ca – Curator/Director, Daniel Robert

Prescott: Fort Wellington National Historic Site/Lieu historique national du Fort-Wellington, PO Box 479, Prescott ON K0E 1T0 – 613/925-2896; Fax: 613/925-1536 – Area Supt., D.J. Delaney

Prescott: The Forwarders' Museum, PO Box 2179, Prescott ON K0E 1T0 – 613/925-5788 – Curator, Harg Solomatenko

Prescott: Homewood Museum, PO Box 982, Prescott ON K0E 1T0 – 613/348-3560

Queenston: Laura Secord Homestead, PO Box 1812, Queenston ON L0S 1L0 – 905/357-4020, 262-4851 – District Manager, Sandra Theal

Queenston,: Mackenzie House, Heritage Printery, PO Box 1824, Queenston, ON L0S 1L0 – 905/262-5676

Red Lake Museum, PO Box 64, Red Lake ON P0V 2M0 – 807/727-3006

Renfrew: McDougall Mill Museum, PO Box 544, Renfrew ON K7V 4B1 – 613/432-2129 – Curator, Marie Henderson

Richards Landing: Fort St. Joseph National Historic Site, PO Box 220, Richards Landing ON P0R 1J0 – 705/246-2664(summer); 942-6262 (winter) – Winter mailing: c/o Ken B. McMillan, Soo Ship Canal, 1 Canal Dr., Sault Ste. Marie, ON P6A 6W4.

Richards Landing: St. Joseph Island Museum Complex, RR#2, Richards Landing ON P0R 1J0 – 705/246-2672; Winter: 705/246-2482 – Curator, Gayle Tisdall

Richmond: Goulbourn Museum, PO Box 1065, Richmond ON K0A 2Z0 – 613/831-2393

Ridge House Museum, 53 Erie St. South, Ridgetown ON N0P 2C0 – 519/674-2223; Fax: 519/674-0660 – Director, Elsie Reynolds – Open May - Dec.

Ridgeway: Fort Erie Historical Museum, c/o Fort Erie Museum Board, 402 Ridge Rd., PO Box 339, Ridgeway ON L0S 1N0 – 905/894-5322; Fax: 905/894-6851 – Curator, Jane Davies – Open daily mid-June - Labour Day; otherwise by appt.

Ridgeway: Fort Erie Historical Railroad Museum, PO Box 339, Ridgeway ON L0S 1N0 – 905/871-1412 – Curator, Jane Davies – Located on Central Ave.; open daily Victoria Day - Labour Day

Ridgeway Battlefield Park, c/o Fort Erie Museum Board, PO Box 339, Ridgeway ON L0S 1N0 – 905/894-5322 – Curator, Jane Davies – Open daily, 12:30 pm - 5 pm, mid-June - Labour Day

Rockton: Westfield Heritage Centre, Rockton ON L0R 1X0 – 519/621-8851; Fax: 519/621-6897; Email: westfld@worldchat.com; URL: http://www.worldchat.com/public/westfield/westfl.htm – Manager, Rondalyn Brown – 33 historic buildings; special programs include Christmas, Maple Syrup, American Civil War Re-enactment & Anne of Green Gables Day; educational programs & guided tours

Rockwood: Halton County Radial Railway Museum, RR#2, Rockwood ON N0B 2K0 – 519/856-9802 – Curator, Joan Johns

Rockwood: Ontario Electric Railway Museum, RR#2, Rockwood ON N0B 2K0 – 519/886-0258 – Curator, Joan Johns

Rosemont: Dufferin County Museum, PO Box 120, Rosemont ON L0N 1R0 – 519/435-1881; Fax: 705/435-9876 – Curator, Wayne Townsend

Sarnia: Pilot House Museum, 2012 Wayne Ave. South, RR#4, Sarnia ON N7T 7H5 – 519/344-6136 – Director, Malcolm McRae – Centre castle of Great Lakes tanker SS Imperial Hamilton

Sault Ste. Marie: Ermatinger Old Stone House, c/o Historic Sites Board, PO Box 580, Sault Ste. Marie ON P6A 5N1 – 705/759-5443; Fax: 705/759-6605; Email: can-eosh@immedia.ca – Curator, Daphne Poirier

Sault Ste. Marie: Moose Factory Centennial Museum, c/o Ministry of Northern Affairs, 421 Bay St., Sault Ste. Marie ON P6A 1X2 – 705/472-4500 – Director, Roy Thompson – Located at 521 Government Rd. West, Kirkland Lake; open June - Labour Day

Sault Ste. Marie Canal National Historic Site, Sault Ste. Marie ON P6A 6W4 – 705/941-6262; Fax: 705/941-6206; Email: pkssc.dots.doe.ca@igw – Acting Supt., Fred Howe

Sault Ste. Marie Museum, 690 Queen St. East, Sault Ste. Marie ON P6A 2A4 – 705/759-7278; Fax: 705/759-3058 – Curator/Administrator, Judy McGonigal

Sault Ste. Marie: St. Mary's River Marine Centre, PO Box 23099, Stn Mall, Sault Ste. Marie ON P6A 6W6 – 705/942-2919; Fax: 705/942-6368; Seasonal Tel. on board Norgoma: 705/253-74474680 – President, Udo Rauk

Scarborough Historical Museum, Thomson Memorial Park, 1007 Brimley Rd., Scarborough ON M1P 3E8 – 416/431-3441; Fax: 416/431-3441 – Manager/Curator, Madeleine Callaghan – Includes Cornell House, McCowan Log Cabin & Hough Carriage Works

Schomberg: Canadian Museum of Animal Art, 14290 Concession 11, RR#3, Schomberg ON L0G 1T0 – Judith, James,

Seaforth: The Van Egmond House, PO Box 1033, Seaforth ON N0K 1W0 – 519/522-0413 – Curator, Jayne Cardno

Selkirk: Wilson P. MacDonald Memorial School Museum, Selkirk ON N0A 1P0 – 416/776-3319 – Curator, Dana B. Stavinga

Sharon Temple Museum, 18974 Leslie St., PO Box 331, Sharon ON L0G 1V0 – 905/478-2389 – Site Director, Ruth Mahoney

Sheguiandah: Little Current-Howland Centennial Museum, Sheguiandah ON P0P 1W0 – 705/368-2367 – Curator, Eva Skipper

Shelburne: Dufferin County Historical Society Museum, PO Box 957, Shelburne ON L0N 1S0 – 519/925-5565 – Director, Harold Doan

Simcoe: Backus Heritage Village & Conservation Education Centre, RR#3, Simcoe ON N3Y 4K2 – 519/586-2201; Fax: 519/586-7333 – Curator, Mary E. Baruth-Walsh

Simcoe: Eva Brook Donly Museum, 109 Norfolk St. South, Simcoe ON N3Y 2W3 – 519/426-1583 – Curator, William Yeager

Sioux Lookout Museum, PO Box 158, Sioux Lookout ON P0V 2T0 – 807/737-1562

Smiths Falls: Heritage House Museum, a Victorian restoration, c.1867/Musée de la maison du patrimoine, Old Slys Rd., PO Box 695, Smiths Falls ON K7A 4T6 – 613/283-8560; Fax: 613/283-4764 – Curator, Susan McNichol – Open year round, 11 am - 4:30 pm

Smiths Falls: Industrial Heritage Complex, Merrickville Lockstation, 34A Beckwith St. South, Smiths Falls ON K7A 2A8 – 613/283-5170; Fax: 613/283-0677 – Chief of Interpretation, Judy Sutherland – 19th century development of Rideau Canal at Merrickville

Smiths Falls Railway Museum Association Inc. - Rideau Valley Division, PO Box 962, Smiths Falls ON K7A 5A5 – 613/283-5696 – President, Ross Robinson; Archivist, Bill Lesurf; Curator, Julia Brady – Former CNoR/CNR Station

Canadian Almanac & Directory 1997

MUSEUMS & SCIENCE CENTRES — ONTARIO

Sombra Township Museum, PO Box 76, Sombra ON N0P 2H0 – 519/892-3982, 3631 – Curator, Sandy Broad

Southampton: Bruce County Museum & Archives, 33 Victoria St. North, PO Box 180, Southampton ON N0H 2L0 – 519/797-3644, 2080; Fax: 519/797-2191; Email: museum@swbi.net; URL: http://www.swbi.net/bruce_county_museum.htm – Director/Curator, Barbara Ribey

St Catharines: Mountain Mills Museum, c/o Parks & Recreation Dept., City of St Catharines, PO Box 3012, St Catharines ON L2R 7C2

St Catharines: St. Catharines Museum, 1932 Government Rd., PO Box 3012, St Catharines ON L2R 7C2 – 905/984-8880; Fax: 905/984-6910; Email: muslk3@niagara.com – Chief Museum Complex Officer, Virginia Hatch Stewart

St. George: Adelaide Hunter-Hoodless Homestead, 359 Blue Lake Rd., RR#1, St. George ON N0E 1N0 – 519/448-1130 – Curator, Suzanne Doiron

St. Jacobs: The Maple Syrup Museum, Princess St., St. Jacobs ON N0B 2N0 – 519/664-3626 – Open year round

St. Marys Museum, 177 Church St. South, PO Box 98, St. Marys ON N4X 1A9 – 519/284-3556; Fax: 519/284-2881; Email: can-stmm@immedia.ca – Curator, Mary Smith

St. Thomas: Elgin County Pioneer Museum, 32 Talbot St., St. Thomas ON N5P 1A3 – 519/631-6537 – Curator/Director, Deborah Herkimer

St. Thomas: The Elgin Military Museum, 30 Talbot St., St. Thomas ON N5P 1A3 – 519/633-7641 – Curator, Sterling Ince

Stoney Creek: Battlefield House Museum, 77 King St. West, PO Box 66561, Stoney Creek ON L8G 5E5 – 905/662-8458, 643-6161 – Curator, Susan Ramsay

Stoney Creek: Erland Lee (Museum) Home, 552 Ridge Rd., Stoney Creek ON L8J 2Y6 – 905/662-2691; Fax: 905/662-2691 – Curator, Mary Kneebone – Open April - Nov., M - F, 10 am - 4 pm; Dec. - March by appt.

Stratford: Brocksden Country School Museum, 87 Nile St., Stratford ON N5A 4C7

Stratford: Fryfogel Inn, PO Box 462, Stratford ON N5A 5S4 – 1850s country inn

Stratford: Minnie Thomson Memorial Museum, 138 Vivian St., Stratford ON N5A 5E1 – 519/271-1138

Stratford: Perth Regiment Museum, c/o Stratford Armoury, 80 Waterloo St. South, Stratford ON N5A 4A9 – Curator, John Blue

Strathroy: A.W. Campbell House Museum, c/o St. Clair Region Conservation Authority, 205 Mill Pond Cres., Strathroy ON N7G 3P9 – 519/245-3710 – Community Relations Supervisor, Rick Battson

Strathroy Middlesex Museum, 84 Oxford St., Strathroy ON N7G 3A5 – 519/245-0492 – Director, Muriel Kew

Sturgeon Falls: Musée Sturgeon River House Museum, PO Box 1390, Sturgeon Falls ON P0H 2G0 – 705/753-4716; Fax: 705/753-5476 – Chief Officer, Denis Arseneau

Sudbury: Centre franco-ontarien de folklore (CFOF), Maison d'Youville, 38, rue Xavier, Sudbury ON P3C 2B9 – 705/675-8986; Fax: 705/675-5809 – Directeur de la recherche, folkloriste, Rév. P. Germain Lemieux, S.J.

Sudbury: Copper Cliff Museum, Leisure Services Dept., PO Bag 5000, Stn A, Sudbury ON P3A 5P3 – 705/674-3141, ext.457; Fax: 705/671-8145 – Rick Sleaver

Sudbury: Flour Mill Museum, 514 Notre Dame St., Bag 5000, Stn A, Sudbury ON P3A 5P3 – 705/674-2391; Fax: 705/671-8145 – Curator, Peter Philipon

Sudbury: Laurentian University Museum & Art Centre/Musée et Centre artistique de l'Université Laurentienne (LUMAC), c/o Dept. of Cultural Affairs, 251 John St., Sudbury ON P3E 2C6 – 705/675-1151, ext. 1400; Fax: 705/674-3065

Sudbury: Science North, 100 Ramsey Lake Rd., Sudbury ON P3E 5S9 – 705/522-3701; Fax: 705/522-4954 – CEO, Jim Marchbank; Marketing Manager, Leslie Standford – Includes Solar Observatory; open daily except Christmas Day, Boxing Day & New Year's Day

Sundridge Maple Sugar House & Museum, Art Gallery, & Pioneer Home, Sundridge ON P0A 1Z0 – 705/384-7764 – Open year round

Sutton West: Georgina Village Museum, PO Box 495, Sutton West ON L0E 1R0 – 905/476-4301; Fax: 905/476-8100 – President, Eric Lamaus; Treasurer, Marg Godfrey

Sutton West: Eildon Hall Sibbald Memorial Museum, Sibbald Point Provincial Park, RR#2, Sutton West ON L0E 1R0 – 905/722-3268 – Chief Volunteer, Mary Brown

Tehkummah Township Little Schoolhouse and Museum, c/o Municipal Office, Tehkummah ON P0P 2C0 – 705/859-3293 – Curator, John Novak

Thunder Bay: 1910 Logging Museum, Centennial Park, 950 Memorial Ave., Thunder Bay ON P7B 4A2 – 807/625-2351 – Custodian, Mary Dohan

Thunder Bay: Northwestern Ontario Sports Hall of Fame, 2203 Moodie St. East, Thunder Bay ON P7C 5N4 – 807/622-2852; Fax: 807/622-2736 – Executive Director, Diane Imrie

Thunder Bay: Old Fort William, Vickers Heights PO, Thunder Bay ON P0T 2Z0 – 807/577-8461; Fax: 807/473-2327 – General Manager, Ronald D. Zizman

Thunder Bay: Paipoonge Historical Museum, RR#6, Thunder Bay ON P7C 5N5 – 807/939-1262; Fax: 807/939-1550 – Curator, Phyllis Kite

Thunder Bay Museum, 425 East Donald St., Thunder Bay ON P7E 5V1 – 807/623-0801; Fax: 807/622-6880 – Curator, Tory Tronrud

Tillsonburg Museum, 30 Tillson Ave., Tillsonburg ON N4G 2Z8 – 519/842-2294; Fax: 519/842-9431 – Curator, Rita Corner

Timmins Museum: National Exhibition Centre/Musée de Timmins: Centre national d'exposition, City of Timmins, 220 Algonquin Blvd. East, Timmins ON P4N 1B3 – 705/235-5066; Fax: 705/235-9631; Email: can-tmnec@immedia.ca – Director/Curator, Karen Bachmann

Timmins: Ukrainian Historical & Cultural Museum, 98 Mountjoy St. South, Timmins ON P4N 1S7 – 705/364-3393 – Curator/Director, Nancy Perger – Open year round

Tobermory: The Peninsula & St. Edmunds Township Museum, PO Box 70, Tobermory ON N0H 2R0 – 519/596-2479 – Curator, Marjorie Munn

Toronto: The Bata Shoe Museum (BSM), 327 Bloor St. West, Toronto ON M5S 1W7 – 416/979-7799; Fax: 416/979-0078; URL: http://www.hype.com/toronto/attractions/bata.htm – Chair, Sonja Bata; Director, Edward Maeder

Toronto: Beth Tzedec Reuben & Helene Dennis Museum, 1700 Bathurst St., Toronto ON M5P 3K3 – 416/781-3511; Fax: 416/781-0150 – Curator, Dorion Liebgett

Toronto: Campbell House, 160 Queen St. West, Toronto ON M5H 3H3 – 416/597-0227; Fax: 416/597-1588 – Senior Interpreter, Michael Franklin; Chair, Tim Bates

Toronto: Canada's Sports Hall of Fame/Temple de la Rénommée des Sports du Canada, Exhibition Place, Toronto ON M6K 3C3 – 416/595-1046; Fax: 416/595-1228 – Executive Director, Allan Stewart

Toronto: Canadian Baseball Hall of Fame, c/o Ontario Place, 955 Lake Shore Blvd. West, Toronto ON M6K 3B9 – 416/965-7917; Fax: 416/598-0056 – Open May - Labour Day

Toronto: Canadian Museum of Photography, 176 Balmoral Ave., Toronto ON M4V 1J6

Toronto: Casa Loma, 1 Austin Terrace, Toronto ON M5R 1X8 – 416/923-1171; Fax: 416/923-5734 – General Manager, Virginia Cooper – Former home of industrialist Sir Henry Pellatt; open for tours daily

Toronto: CBC Museum, 250 Front St. West, PO Box 500, Stn A, Toronto ON M5W 1E6 – 416/205-5574; Fax: 416/205-7583 – Curator, Ivan Harris; Coordinator, Faye Blum

Toronto: Century Schoolhouse, East York Board of Education, 840 Coxwell Ave., Toronto ON M4C 2V3 – 416/396-2074

Toronto: City of York Museum, c/o City Clerk, 2700 Eglinton Ave. West, Toronto ON M6M 1V1 – 416/394-2513; Fax: 416/394-2803 – Curator, Bernard J. Thompson

Toronto: Colborne Lodge, c/o Toronto Historical Board, 205 Yonge St., Toronto ON M5B 1N2 – 416/392-6827; Fax: 416/392-0375 – Assistant Curator, Betty Roodhart

Toronto: The Enoch Turner Schoolhouse (1848), 106 Trinity St., Toronto ON M5A 3C6 – 416/863-0010 – Executive Officer, Dean Mallory

Toronto: Fire Fighting Museum, Toronto Fire Academy, 895 Eastern Ave., Toronto ON M4L 1A2

Toronto: George R. Gardiner Museum of Ceramic Art, 111 Queen's Park, Toronto ON M5S 2C7 – 416/586-8000; Fax: 416/586-8085; Email: maryf@rom.on.ca; URL: http://www.rom.on.ca – Director, John McNeill

Toronto: The Grange, Art Gallery of Ontario, 317 Dundas St. West, Toronto ON M5T 1G4 – 416/977-0414

Toronto: Historic Fort York, c/o Toronto Historical Board, 205 Yonge St., Toronto ON M5B 1N2 – 416/392-6907; Fax: 416/392-6917 – Site Supervisor, Ken Purvis – Accessible at Strachan & Fleet Sts., on Garrison Rd., or by TTC on Bathurst south of Front

Toronto: HMCS Haida Naval Museum/NCSM Haida Musée Navale, Ontario Place, 955 Lakeshore Blvd. West, Toronto ON M6K 3B9 – 416/314-9755; Fax: 416/314-9878 – Manager, Cdr. R.A. Willson, RCN (Ret'd)

Toronto: Latvian History Museum, 125 Broadview Ave., Toronto ON M4M 2E9 – 416/889-0472 – Curator, Andrew Brumelis

Toronto: Mackenzie House, c/o Toronto Historical Board, 205 Yonge St., Toronto ON M5B 1N2 – 416/392-6827; Fax: 416/392-6834 – Curator, Gabriella Karadi – Located at: 82 Bond St., Toronto

Toronto: Marine Museum of Upper Canada, c/o Toronto Historical Board, 205 Yonge St., Toronto ON M5B 1N2 – 416/392-1765; Fax: 416/392-1767 – Curator, John Summers – Located in Exhibition Place, next to the Automotive Bldg.

Toronto: Metropolitan Toronto Police Museum & Discovery Centre, 40 College St., Toronto ON M5G 2J3 – 416/808-7020; Fax: 416/808-7052 – Curator, Sharon McDonald – Interactive displays portray the diverse aspects of policing, past & present; open 9 am - 9 pm, Mon. - Sun.; gift shop open 10 am - 3:30 pm weekdays; wheelchair accessible; free

Toronto: Museum for Textiles, 55 Centre Ave., Toronto ON M5G 2H5 – 416/599-5321; Fax: 416/599-2911; URL: http://www.interlog.com/~gwhite/ttt/tt-tintro.html – Executive Director, Sarah Holland

Toronto: Museum of the History of Medicine, 288 Bloor St. West, Toronto ON M5S 1V8 – 416/922-0564; Fax: 416/964-9668 – Curator, Felicity Pope

Toronto: Museum of Mental Health Services, 1001 Queen St. West, Toronto ON M6J 1H4 – 416/535-8501

Toronto: Museum of Promotional Arts, Toronto, PO Box 400, Stn Adelaide, Toronto ON M5C 2J5 – President/CEO, Frances E.M. Johnston

Toronto: Museum of the Ukrainian Catholic Women's League, 278 Bathurst St., 3rd Fl., Toronto ON M5T 2S3

Toronto: The Queen's Own Rifles of Canada Regimental Museum, Casa Loma, 1 Austin Terrace, Tor-

onto ON M5R 1X8 – 416/923-1171 – Curator, Capt. Peter Simundson, CD
Toronto: Queen's York Rangers Museum, 660 Fleet St., Toronto ON M5V 1A9 – 416/973-3265 – Acting Curator, Maj. S.H. Bull
Toronto: Redpath Sugar Museum, 95 Queen's Quay East, Toronto ON M5E 1A3 – 416/366-3561; Fax: 416/366-7550 – Corporate Archivist, Richard Feltoe
Toronto: Royal Canadian Military Institute Museum, 426 University Ave., Toronto ON M5G 1S9 – 416/597-0286 – Curator, Gregory Loughton
Toronto: Royals Museum, Fort York Armoury, c/o W. Bennett, 54 Meighen Ave., Toronto ON M4B 2G9 – 416/757-3955; 369-3677 – Curator, Capt. W. Bennett
Toronto: The Salvation Army George Scott Railton Heritage Centre, 2130 Bayview Ave., Toronto ON M4N 3K6 – 416/481-4441; Fax: 416/481-6096 – Director, Major Paul Murray
Toronto: Scadding Cabin, PO Box 481, Stn K, Toronto ON M6K 3C3
Toronto: Sesquicentennial Museum, Records & Archives, Toronto Board of Education, 155 College St., Toronto ON M5T 1P6 – 416/591-8202; Fax: 416/591-8375 – Curator, Gail Gregory
Toronto: Spadina Historic House Museum, c/o Toronto Historical Board, 205 Yonge St., Toronto ON M5B 1N2 – 416/392-6827; Fax: 416/392-6834 – Curator, Gabriella Karadi – Located at: 285 Spadina Rd., Toronto
Toronto: Taras H. Shevchenko Museum, 962 Bloor St. West, Toronto ON M6H 1L6 – 416/535-1063 – President, Wm. Harasym
Toronto: Todmorden Mills Heritage Museum & Art Centre, 850 Coxwell Ave., Toronto ON M4C 5R1 – 416/396-2819; Fax: 416/466-4170 – Curator/Administrator, Susan Hughes – Located at 67 Pottery Rd.
Toronto Museum of Childhood, 121 Brunswick Ave., Toronto ON M5S 2M3 – 416/964-8255 – President, Loet Vos
Toronto Scottish Regimental Museum, Fort York Armoury, 660 Fleet St., Toronto ON M5V 1A9
Toronto's First Post Office, 260 Adelaide St. East, Toronto ON M5A 1N1 – 416/865-1833; Fax: 416/865-9414 – Curator, Victoria von Schilling
Toronto: Ukrainian Heritage Association & Museum of Canada, 1 Austin Terrace, Toronto ON M5R 1X8 – 416/925-0924 – Curator, V. Luczkiw
Toronto: Ukrainian Museum of Canada, Ukrainian Women's Association of Canada, Eastern Branch, 620 Spadina, Toronto ON M5S 2H4 – 416/923-3318 – Curator, Halya Kluchko
Trenton: RCAF Memorial Museum/ARC Musée Commémoratif, CFB Trenton Astra, Trenton ON K0K 1B0 – 613/965-2140; 2208; Fax: 613/965-7532 – Executive Director, Ken Kee; Curator, Earl Hewison
Tweed & Area Heritage Centre, 40 Victoria St. North, PO Box 665, Tweed ON K0K 3J0 – 613/478-3989; Fax: 613/478-6457 – Curator, E. Morton
Uxbridge: Thomas Foster Memorial Temple, c/o Uxbridge-Scott Historical Society, PO Box 1301, Uxbridge ON L9P 1N5 – 905/852-5854 – Curator, Allan McGillivray
Uxbridge-Scott Museum, PO Box 1301, Uxbridge ON L9P 1N5 – 905/852-5854 – Curator, Allan McGillivray
Vernon: Osgoode Twp. Historical Society & Museum, PO Box 74, Vernon ON K0A 3J0 – 613/821-4062 – Archivist, Donna Bowen; Curator, Ann Leighton-Kyle
Verona: Bell Rock Mill Museum, Verona ON K0H 2W0 – 705/277-2766; Mill: 613/374-1458 – Owner/Curator, Richard Tosswill – Working milling technology

Wasaga Beach: Nancy Island Historic Site, c/o Wasaga Beach Provincial Park, PO Box 183, Wasaga Beach ON L0L 2P0 – 705/429-2728; Fax: 705/429-7983
Waterford: Spruce Row Museum, 159 Nichol St., Waterford ON N0E 1Y0 – 519/443-4211; Fax: 519/443-4211 – Curator, Priscilla Ivey
Waterloo: Brubacher House Museum, c/o Conrad Grebel College, Waterloo ON N2L 3G6 – 519/886-3855 – Director, Nelson Scheifele
Waterloo: Earth Sciences Museum, Biology Bldg., University of Waterloo, Waterloo ON N2L 3G1 – 519/888-4567, ext.2469; Fax: 519/746-7484; Email: esmuseum@sciborg.uwaterloo.ca; URL: http://www.science.uwaterloo.ca/earth/museum/museum.html – Director, Dr. Jocelyne Legault; Curator, Peter Russell
Waterloo: Museum & Archive of Games, Burt Matthews Hall, University of Waterloo, Waterloo ON N2L 3G1 – 519/888-4424; Fax: 519/746-6776; Email: GAMES@WATDCS.UWaterloo.ca – Curator, Dr. Ronald Johnson
Waterloo: Museum of Visual Science & Optometry, University of Waterloo, Waterloo ON N2L 3G1 – 519/885-1211, ext.3405; Fax: 519/725-0784 – Curator, Prof. E. Fisher
Waterloo: The Seagram Museum, 57 Erb St. W., Waterloo ON N2L 6C2 – 519/885-1857; Fax: 519/746-1673 – Executive Director, T.G. Tyssen
Welland Historical Museum, 65 Hooker St., Welland ON L3C 5G9 – 905/732-2215 – Curator/Director, Mac Swackhammer
Wellington Community Historical Museum, Main St., PO Box 55, Wellington ON K0K 3L0 – 613/399-3041 – Curator, Ruth Armstrong
Westport: Rideau District Museum, PO Box 305, Westport ON K0G 1X0 – 613/273-2502 – Curator, Janice Chornohus
Whitby Museum, 960 Dundas St. West, PO Box 281, Whitby ON L1N 5S1 – 416/668-4401 – Curator/Director, Deseree Rowley
White Lake: Waba Cottage Museum, PO Box 167, White Lake ON K0A 3L0 – 613/623-4341 – Chairperson, V. Miller
Whitney: Algonquin Park Museum & Algonquin Logging Museum, PO Box 219, Whitney ON K0J 2M0 – 613/637-2828; Fax: 613/637-2138 – Park Naturalist, Ron Tozer
Williamstown: The Nor'Westers & Loyalist Museum, PO Box 69, Williamstown ON K0C 2J0 – 613/347-3547 – Chair, Joan P. MacDonald
Windsor: Ojibway Nature Centre, c/o Dept. of Parks & Recreation, 2450 McDougall, Windsor ON N8X 3N6 – 519/966-5852; Fax: 519/255-7990 – Director, Paul Pratt
Windsor: Serbian Heritage Museum of Windsor (SHM), 6770 Tecumseh Rd. East, Windsor ON N8T 1E6 – 519/944-4884; Fax: 519/974-3963 – Director, Svetlana Miskovic
Windsor: Willistead Manor, 1899 Niagara St., Windsor ON N8Y 1K3 – 519/255-6545
Windsor's Community Museum, 254 Pitt St. West, Windsor ON N9A 5L5 – 519/253-1812; Fax: 519/253-0919 – Curator, Janet Cobban; Assistant Curator, Madelyn Della Valle
Wingham & District Historical Museum, 275 Josephine St., PO Box 1522, Wingham ON N0G 2W0 – 519/357-3550
Woodstock Museum, 466 Dundas St., City Square, Woodstock ON N4S 1C4 – 519/537-8411; Fax: 519/539-3275 – Curator, Sheila A. Johnson

PRINCE EDWARD ISLAND

Prince Edward Island Museum & Heritage Foundation
2 Kent St., Charlottetown PE C1A 1M6
902/368-6600; Fax: 902/368-6608; Email: peimhf@cycor.ca
The Foundation operates 7 museum sites across the country: Basin Head Fisheries Museum, 902/357-2966; Beaconsfield Historic House, 902/368-6600; Elmira Railway Museum, 902/357-2481; Eptek National Exhibition Centre, 902/888-8373; Green Park Shipbuilding Museum, 902/831-2206; Le Musée acadien, 902/436-6237; Orwell Corner Historical Village, 902/651-2013
Executive Director, Christopher Severance

Other Museums & Science Centres in Prince Edward Island

Alberton Museum, PO Box 285, Alberton PE C0B 1B0 – 902/853-4048 – Curator, Dr. Allan J. MacRae – Genealogy room, old photo collection, history of fox industry; Micmac Indian display & displays of antique furniture, glassware, textiles & toys; open July - Labour Day
Charlottetown: Beaconsfield Historic House, 2 Kent St., Charlottetown PE C1A 1M6 – 902/892-9127 – Open year round
Charlottetown: Car Life Museum, 45 Oak Dr., Charlottetown PE C1A 6T6 – 902/892-1754 – Director, Ken MacKay – Open mid-June - mid-Sept.
Charlottetown: Fort Amherst/Port La Joye National Historic Site, c/o Canadian Parks Service, PO Box 487, Charlottetown PE C1A 7L1 – 902/675-2220 – First European settlement on the Island; open June - Labour Day
Charlottetown: Green Gables House, PEI National Park, PO Box 487, Charlottetown PE C1A 7L1 – 902/672-2211; Fax: 902/672-3154 – District Chief, Visitor Activities, Philip Michael – Open May 14 - Oct. 31
Charlottetown: Province House National Historic Site, c/o Canadian Heritage, 165 Richmond St., Charlottetown PE C1A 1J1 – 902/566-7626; Fax: 902/566-7226 – Provincial Director, Carmen Comeau-Anderson – Includes Confederation Chamber, the site of historic discussions regarding union of the BNA colonies; remains the Legislative Bldg. for PEI; open year round
Charlottetown: Spoke Wheel Car Museum, RR#3, Charlottetown PE C1A 7J7 – Director, Clarence Foster
Hunter River: Farmers' Bank Museum, RR#3, Hunter River PE C0A 1N0 – 902/963-2304 – P. Edward Blanchard – Open June 26 - Labour Day
Hunter River: Royal Atlantic Wax Museum, c/o Allan & Marjoria Evans, Rte. 6, Canvendish Beach, Hunter River PE C0A 1N0 – 902/963-2350
Kensington: Anne of Green Gables Museum at Silver Bush, PO Box 491, Kensington PE C0B 1M0 – 902/436-1787; Fax: 902/436-7329 – Director, George Campbell – Open June, Sept. & Oct.
Kensington: The Keir Memorial Museum, PO Box 56, Kensington PE C0B 1M0 – 902/836-3054 – Curator, Bill Auld – Open July - Sept.
Kensington: Lucy Maud Montgomery Birthplace, RR#6, Kensington PE C0B 1M0 – 902/886-2596 – Curator, Merle Cole – Open May - Thanksgiving
Kensington: Veterans' Memorial Military Museum, Legion Branch 9, Kensington PE C0B 1M0 – 902/836-3600 – Col. E.W. Johnstone – Open June 15 - Sept. 15
Miscouche: Le Musée Acadien de l'Ile-du-Prince-Édouard, 23 Main Dr. East, CP 159, Miscouche PE C0B 1T0 – 902/436-6237 – Directrice, Cécile Gallant
Montague: Garden of the Gulf Museum, PO Box 1237, Montague PE C0A 1R0 – 902/838-2460 – Curator, Mary Brydon – Pioneer history; open mid-June - Sept.
Murray Harbour: Log Cabin Museum, Murray Harbour PE C0A 1V0 – 902/962-2201 – Director, Preston Robertson – Open July - Labour Day

Canadian Almanac & Directory 1997

Murray River: Northumberland Mill & Museum, Murray River PE C0A 1W0 – President, Linda Lidstone-Reynolds

O'Leary: Prince Edward Island Potato Museum, 22 Parkview Dr., PO Box 602, O'Leary PE C0B 1V0 – 902/859-2039 – President, Dr. L. George Dewar – Community museum, little red schoolhouse, a heritage chapel & log barn; open June 1 - Oct. 15

O'Leary: West Point Lighthouse Museum, RR#2, O'Leary PE C0B 1V0 – 902/859-3605; Fax: 902/859-3117; 1-800-764-6854 – Manager, Carol Livingstone

Richmond: Les Maisons de Bouteilles/The Bottle Houses, CP 72, Richmond PE C0B 1Y0 – 902/854-2987 – Rejeanne Arsenault – Three fantasy-like buildings made of over 25,000 vari-coloured bottles, creating a symphony of light and colour within; located in Cape Egmont

Summerside: International Fox Hall of Fame Museum, 286 Fitzroy St., Summerside PE C1N 1J2 – 902/436-2400 – Curator, Robynn Quinn

Tyne Valley: Ellerslie Shellfish Museum Association, PO Box 24, Tyne Valley PE C0B 2C0 – 902/831-2933 – Director, Nan Kernaghan

Wellington: Musée d'Art religieux, Rte 11, 802 Water St. East, Wellington PE C1N 4J6 – 902/854-2260 – Director, Ulric Poirier

Wood Islands: Ripley's Believe It or Not Museum, c/o Thomas MacMillan, Rte. 6, PO Belle River, Wood Islands PE C0A 1B0 – 902/963-3444 – Open June & Sept.

QUÉBEC

Canadian Centre for Architecture/Centre Canadien d'Architecture (CCA)
1920, rue Baile, Montréal PQ H3H 2S6
514/939-7000; Fax: 514/939-7020; Email: ref@cca.qc.ca
URL: http://cca.qc.ca/
Museum & study centre devoted to the art of architecture & its history. Four major research collections: (Library of over 160,000 vols.); prints & drawings (some 22,000 works); archives (over 250,000) items; photographs (some 50,000 images); Facilities include seven main galleries, octagonal gallery, theatre, library, scholars' wing, bookstore, meeting & reception area, park & garden.
Director, Phyllis Lambert
Associate Director, Robert Spickler
Chief Curator, Nicholas Olsberg
Associate Librarian, Rosemary Haddad
Assistant Director, Museum Services, Wendy Owens
Head, Communications, Hélène Panaiote

McCord Museum of Canadian History/Musée McCord d'histoire canadienne
690, rue Sherbrooke ouest, Montréal PQ H3A 1E9
514/398-7100; Fax: 514/398-5045
Costumes & textiles; ethnology & archaeology; photographic archives; decorative arts; paintings, prints & drawings; archives & library. Open year round.
Executive Director, Claude Benoit
Director, Communications, Wanda Palma
Director, Development, Elizabeth Kennell
Director, Marketing, Michel Pelletier
Director, Finance & Administration, Philip Leduc
Director, Curatorial & Research Services, Moira McCaffrey
Director, Collection Management & Access Services, Nicole Vallières
Director, Building & Security, William Misuirak

Musée de la civilisation
85, rue Dalhousie, CP 155, Succ B, Québec PQ G1K 7A6
418/643-2158; Fax: 418/646-9705; Email: mcqweb@riq.qc.ca
URL: http://www.mcq.org
Located in Quebec City's Old Port, near Place Royale; the Museum offers more than ten theme-oriented exhibitions simultaneously, of which three are permanent: Memoirs (The history of Québec); Objects of Civilization; LaBarque (a 250 year-old boat, found on the site of the Museum); temporary & international exhibitions reflect human adventure & experiences from societies around the world; French & English texts; tours in French & English. Open June 24 - Labour Day, 10 am - 7 pm; Sept. 3 - June 23, Tues-Sun., 10 am - 5 pm & Wed., 10 am - 7 pm; closed Mondays.
Directeur général, Roland Arpin
Director, Communications, Julie Gagnon

Musée de l'Amerique française (MAF)
9, rue de l'Université, CP 460, Succ Haute-Ville, Québec PQ G1R 4R7
418/643-2158; Fax: 418/692-5206; Email: mcqweb@rig.qc.ca
URL: http://www.mcq.org
Collections of paintings by European & Canadian artists, scientific works, rare & ancient books, works of gold & silver; numismatic collection; ethnological collection; historical archives; open year round.
Directeur, Roland Arpin
Director, Communications, Julie Gagnon

Musée des arts décoratifs
2929, av Jeanne-d'Arc, Montréal PQ H1W 3W2
514/259-2575; Fax: 514/284-0123
Founded in 1979, collections date from 1935 to the present; the Lilliane & David M. Stewart Collection is considered one of the foremost collections of decorative arts & industrial design in North America; international exhibitions on furniture, glass, textiles, ceramics, graphic arts; open year round.
Directeur, Luc d'Iberville-Moreau
Information Officer, Suzanne Taylor

Musée du Québec
Parc des Champs-de-Bataille, Québec PQ G1R 5H3
418/643-2150; Fax: 418/646-3330; Email: webmdq@mdq.org
URL: http://www.mdq.org
Prestigious collections of 17th-, 18th- & 19th-century art; collection of contemporary art; library, bookstore & educational service; varied temporary exhibitions; situated on the Plains of Abraham; open year round.
Director, Dr. John R. Porter
Chief Librarian, Louise Allard

Pointe-à-Callière, Museum of Archaeology & History
350, place Royale, Montréal PQ H2Y 3Y5
514/872-9150; Fax: 514/872-9151
Overlooking the St-Lawrence River, this museum is a key attraction in the historical quarter of Old Montréal; collection comprises artifacts & architectural remains relating to the founding of the city; includes the Old Customs House (150, rue Saint-Paul); program activities can be adapted to the needs of the general public, school groups, students or anyone with an interest in archaeology or history; multimedia show, permanent & temporary exhibits; open July-Aug., 10 am - 8 pm; Sept. - June, 10 am - 5 pm; closed Mondays; children under 5 free.
Directrice générale, Francine Lelièvre
Directrice, Communications/Marketing, TBA
Directrice, Recherche/Conservation/Diffusion, Sylvie Dufresne
Directrice, Animation/Éducation, Ginette Cloutier
Directeur, Commercialisation, Guy Brisebois
Directrice, Administration Finances, Johane Freenette

Other Museums & Science Centres in Québec

Angliers: Site historique T.E. Draper, 11, rue du T.E. Draper, PO Box 82, Angliers PQ J0Z 1A0 – 819/949-4431 – Directeur touristique, André Raymond

Anse-au-Griffon: Site historique Manoir Leboutillier, CP 37, Anse-au-Griffon PQ G0E 1A0 – 418/892-5150; Fax: 418/892-5189 – Directrice générale, Johanne Murray

Asbestos: Musée minéralogique d'Asbestos, 104, rue Letendre, Asbestos PQ J1T 1E3 – 819/879-6444, 5308 – Directeur, A.J. Millen

Aylmer: The Canadian Golf Museum & Historical Institute, The Kingsway Golf & Country Club, 1461 Mountain Rd., RR#2, Aylmer PQ J9H 5E1 – 819/827-0330 – Director, W. Lyn Stewart

Aylmer: Musée d'Aymer Museum Inc., PO Box 311, Aylmer PQ J9H 5E6 – 819/682-0291 – Curator, Paul George

Baie Comeau: La Musée de Baie-Comeau, 43, rue Mance, PO Box 273, Baie Comeau PQ G4Z 2H1 – 418/296-9690 – Président, Raphael Hovington

Batiscan: Musée, Vieux Presbytère de Batiscan, 340, rue Principale, PO Box 76, Batiscan PQ G0X 1A0 – 418/362-2051 – Responsable, Claire Grandbois

Beaumont: Moulin de Beaumont, 2, route du Fleuve, Beaumont PQ G0R 1C0 – 418/833-1867 – Directeur, Gilles Sheedy

Berthierville: Musée Gilles-Villeneuve, Formule No. 27, Berthierville PQ J0K 1A0 – 514/836-2714 – Superviseur, Alain Bellehumeur

Berthierville: Village du Défricheur, 1497, Grande Côte, Route 138, Berthierville PQ J0K 1A0 – 514/836-4539

Bonaventure: Musée acadien du Québec, 95, av Port-Royal, CP 730, Bonaventure PQ G0C 1E0 – 418/534-4000; Fax: 418/534-4105 – Directeur, Jean-Claude Cyr

Boucherville: Maison Louis-Hippolyte Lafontaine, 566, Marie Victorin, Boucherville PQ J4B 1X1 – 514/449-8347; Fax: 514/449-4709 – Directeur, Daniel Marineau

Château-Richer: Musée de l'Abeille, 8862, boul Sainte-Anne, Château-Richer PQ G0A 1N0 – 418/824-4411; Fax: 418/824-4411 – Vice-President, Redmond Hayes – Bee museum

Chambly: Lieu historique du Fort-Chambly, 2, rue Richelieu, PO Box 115, Chambly PQ J3L 2B9 – 514/658-1585 – Régisseur, Claude Picher

Chicoutimi: La Musée du Saguenay-Lac-St-Jean et Musée de site de la Pulperie, 300, rue Dubuc, Chicoutimi PQ G7J 4M1 – 418/698-3100; Fax: 418/698-3158 – Louis Jalbert

Coaticook: Musée Beaulne, 96, rue Union, Coaticook PQ J1A 1Y9 – 819/849-6560; Fax: 819/849-9519 – Directeur, Pierre Jean

Cookshire: Compton County Historical Museum Society, Cookshire PQ J0B 1M0 – 819/875-5256 – Curator, M. Owens

Coteau-du-Lac: Lieu historique national de Coteau-du-Lac, 308a, ch du Fleuve, CP 550, Coteau-du-Lac PQ J0P 1B0 – 514/763-5631; Fax: 514/763-1654

Desbiens: Centre d'interpretation de la Métabetchouane, 243, rue Hébert, CP 266, Desbiens PQ G0W 1N0 – 418/346-5341 – Présidente, Gisèle Gagnon-Plourde

Drummondville: Le Village Québecois d'Antan, 1425, rue Montplaisir, Drummondville PQ J2B 7T5 – 819/478-1441; Fax: 819/478-8155 – Reconstitution d'un village canadien-français du siècle dernier (1810-1910).

Gaspé: Centre d'interpretation du Parc National Forillon/Forillon National Park Interpretation Centre, CP 1220, Gaspé PQ G0C 1R0 – 418/892-5572; Fax: 418/368-6837 – Chef, section de l'interpretation, Maxime St-Amour

Gaspé: Musée de la Gaspésie, 80, boul Gaspé, CP 680, Gaspé PQ G0C 1R0 – 418/368-5710; Fax: 418/368-5715 – Directeur général, Jean-Marie Fallu

Guérin: Musée plein air régional, Guérin PQ J0Z 2E0 – 819/784-4321 – Directrice, Laurette Rivard

Havre-Aubert, Îles-de-la-Madeleine: Musée de la Mer Inc., CP 69, Havre-Aubert, Îles-de-la-Madeleine PQ G0B 1J0 – 418/937-5711 – Directeur, Frédéric Landry

Hull: National Postal Museum/Musée national de la Poste, Canadian Museum of Civilization, 100 Laurier St., PO Box 3100, Stn B, Hull PQ J8X 4H2 – 819/776-8200; Fax: 819/776-8300

Joliette: Musée d'art de Joliette, 145, rue Wilfrid-Corbeil, Joliette PQ J6E 4T4 – 514/756-0311; Fax: 514/756-6511 – Directrice, France Gascon

Kahnawake: Musée Kateri Tekakwitha, PO Box 70, Kahnawake PQ J0L 1B0 – 514/632-6030 – Directeur/Conservateur, Léon Lajoie

Kamouraska: Musée de Kamouraska, 69, av Morel, PO Box 99, Kamouraska PQ G0L 1M0 – 418/492-3144, 9783 – Directrice générale, Yvette Raymond

Knowlton: Brome County Historical Museum, Archives & Historical Society (BCHS), PO Box 690, Knowlton PQ J0E 1V0 – 514/243-6782 – Archivist, Marion L. Phelps – Museum open mid-May - mid-Sept.; archives by appt.

La Baie: Musée du Fjord, 3346, boul de la Grande-Baie sud, La Baie PQ G7B 1G2 – 418/544-7394; Fax: 418/544-1764 – Directrice, Guylaine Simard

La Guadeloupe: Écomusée de la Haute-Beauce, Musée Territoire, 325, rue Principale, rte 108, St-Evariste, PO Box 595, La Guadeloupe PQ G0M 1G0 – 418/459-3195; Fax: 418/459-3122 – Directrice, Nicole Lamontagne

La Pocatière: Musée François-Pilote, 100, av Painchaud, La Pocatière PQ G0R 1Z0 – 418/856-3145; Fax: 418/856-5611 – Directeur général, Paul-André Leclerc

La Prairie: Société historique de la Prairie de la Magdeleine, 249, rue Sainte-Marie, CP 131, La Prairie PQ J5R 3Y2 – 514/659-1393 – Président, Jean L'Heureux

La Sarre: Musée d'histoire et d'Archéologie, av Principale, CP 115, La Sarre PQ J9X 2X4 – 514/333-2512 – Directeur, Dominique Godbout

Lac-à-la-Croix: Musée Jules Lamy de Lac-à-la-Croix, 301, av du Musée, CP 40, Lac-à-la-Croix PQ G0W 1W0 – 418/349-3633; Fax: 418/349-8724

Lac-à-la-Tortue: Aviation Museum, Lac-à-la-Tortue PQ G0X 1L0 – Open May - Oct.

Lachine: Lieu historique national de commerce de la fourrure à Lachine, 1255, St-Joseph, Lachine PQ H8S 2M2 – 514/637-7433

Lachine: Musée de la Ville de Lachine, 110, ch de La-Salle, Lachine PQ H8S 2X1 – 514/634-3471; Fax: 514/634-8164 – Directeur, Jacques Toupin

Lachine: Musée des Soeurs de Sainte-Anne, 1950, rue Provost, Lachine PQ H8S 1P7 – 514/637-3783; Fax: 514/637-5400 – Conservatrice, Sr. Colette Masson

Lachute: Musée régional d'Argenteuil, 50, rue Principale, PO Box 5, Lachute PQ J8H 3X2 – 514/387-3861 – Conservateur, Stéphane Chagnon

Laurentides: Lieu historique national Sir Wilfrid Laurier, PO Box 70, Laurentides PQ J0R 1C0 – 514/439-3702 – Directrice, Lorraine Neault

Laval: Maison André-Benjamin-Papineau, 5475, boul St-Martin ouest, Laval PQ H7T 1C6 – 514/681-1157

Laval: Musée Écologique - (C.J.N.) Vanier, 3995, boul Lévesque, Laval PQ H7E 2R3 – 514/661-9320 – Directeur, Alfred Rioux

Lévis: La Société historique Alphonse-Desjardins (SHAD), 6, rue du Mont-Marie, Lévis PQ G6V 1V9 – 418/835-2090; Fax: 418/835-9173; 1-800-463-4810, poste 2090 – Administrative Assistant, Esther Normand – Résidence du fondateur de la première caisse populaire en Amérique du Nord (c 1882); ouverte à l'année; entrée gratuite

Lévis: Musée du College de Lévis, 9, rue Mgr Gosselin, Lévis PQ G6V 5K1 – 418/837-8600 – Directeur/conservateur, Loic Bernard

Longueuil: Musée historique Charles Le Moyne, 4, rue St-Charles est, Longueuil PQ J4H 1A9

Longueuil: Musée Marie-Rose Durocher/Lieux historiques S.N.J.M., a/s 80, rue St-Charles est, Longueuil PQ J4H 1A9 – 514/651-8104; Fax: 514/651-8636; Email: SNJMGA@connectino.com – Directrice, Stella Plante – Congregation des Soeurs des Saints Noms de Jésus et de Marie

Loretteville: Musée Kio-Warini, Village Huron, Loretteville PQ G2B 3W5 – 418/843-5515 – Directeur, François Vincent

Malartic: Musée régional des Mines et des arts de Malartic, 650, rue de la Paix, PO Box 4227, Malartic PQ J0Y 1Z0 – 819/757-4677 – Directeur, Jean Massiscotte

Maniwaki: Château Logue, 8, rue Comeau, Maniwaki PQ J9E 2R8 – 819/449-7999, 5102; Fax: 819/449-7078 – Director, François Ledoux – Interpretative centre focusing on the history & evolution of fire prevention; open May - Oct.

Matane: Musée du Vieux-Phare, 968, av du Phare ouest, CP 608, Matane PQ G4W 1V7 – 418/562-9766 – Directeur, Dr. Robert Fournier

Melbourne: Richmond County Historical Society Museum, PO Box 280, Melbourne PQ J0B 2B0 – 819/845-2303 – President, Agnes Keenan

Mont St-Hilaire Nature Conservation Centre, 422, rue des Moulins, Mont St-Hilaire PQ J3G 4S6 – 514/467-1755 – Michel Drew

Montebello: Manoir Louis-Joseph Papineau, Le Château Montebello, 392, rue Notre-Dame, Montebello PQ J0V 1L0 – 819/423-6341 – Directeur général, Armand A. Agabab – 1846 Papineau family home restored to period style; open May - Oct.

Montmagny: Maison de l'accordéon, 301, boul Taché est, CP 71, Montmagny PQ G5V 3S3 – 418/248-9196 – Research centre & collection of accordians; open June 24 - Labour Day

Montréal: Alcan Museum & Archives, 1188, rue Sherbrooke ouest, Montréal PQ H3A 3G2 – 514/848-8187; Fax: 514/848-8116 – Chief Librarian, Lucie Dion

Montréal: Art Gallery of the Saidye Bronfman Centre, 5170, Côte Sainte-Catherine, Montréal PQ H3W 1M7 – 514/739-2301; Fax: 514/739-9340 – Curator/Director, David Liss

Montréal: Biodôme de Montréal, 4777, av Pierre-de-Coubertin, Montréal PQ H1V 1B3 – 514/872-3034; Fax: 514/872-3066 – Directeur adjoint, Jean-Pierre Doyon – Écosystemes: forêt tropicale, forêt laurentienne, Saint-Laurent marine, monde polaire

Montréal: Black Watch of Canada Regimental Memorial Museum, 2067, Bleury St., Montréal PQ H3A 2K2 – 514/842-5045; Fax: 514/496-2759 – Curator, Johanna Douglas-O'Neill

Montréal: Canadian Olympic Hall of Fame/Temple de la renommée olympique du Canada, c/o Canadian Olympic Association, 2380, av Pierre Dupuy, Montréal PQ H3C 3R4 – 514/861-3371; Fax: 514/861-2896 – Director, Corporate Affairs, Kathleen Giguère

Montréal: Dinosaurium, Québec Pavillion, Parc des Îles, Île Notre-Dame, Montréal PQ H3C 1A9

Montréal: Écomusée de la Maison du Fier Monde, 2349, rue de Rouen, PO Box 1048, Stn C, Montréal PQ H2L 4V3 – 514/598-8185; Fax: 514/598-8185 – Coordinnateur de muséologie, René Binette

Montréal: Insectarium de Montréal, 4581, rue Sherbrooke est, Montréal PQ H1X 2B1 – 514/872-0663; Fax: 514/872-0662 – Curator, Georges Brossard

Montréal: International Museum of Cartoon Art/Le Musée international de la caricature (IMOCA), 5788, rue Notre Dame de Grace, Montréal PQ H4A 1M4 – 514/489-0527 – President, Peter Adamakos

Montréal: Le Musée David M. Stewart au Fort de l'Île Sainte-Hélène/The David M. Stewart Museum at the Fort Île Sainte-Hélène, CP 1200, Succ A, Montréal PQ H3C 2Y9 – 514/861-6701; Fax: 514/284-0123 – Directeur, Bruce D. Bolton; Conservateur, Guy Vadeboncoeur

Montréal: Maison de la poste/Post Office Houe, 1035, rue St-Jacques, Montréal PQ H3C 1H0 – 514/283-4602

Montréal: Maison Saint-Gabriel, 2146, Place Dublin, Montréal PQ H3K 2A2 – 514/935-8136; Fax: 514/935-5692 – Directrice, Thérèse Cloutier, CND

Montréal: Marguerite d'Youville Museum, 1185, rue St-Mathieu, Montréal PQ H3H 2H6 – 514/932-7724

Montréal History Centre/Centre d'histoire de Montréal, 335, Place d'Youville, Montréal PQ H2Y 3T1 – 514/872-3207; Fax: 514/872-9645 – Anne Marie Collins

Montréal: The Montréal Holocaust Memorial Centre/Le Centre Commémoratif de l'Holocauste à Montréal, 5151, Côte Sainte-Catherine, Montréal PQ H3W 1M6 – 514/345-2605; Fax: 514/344-2651; Email: mhmc@accent.net – Executive Director, Bill A. Surkis

Montréal: Musée de la Banque de Montréal/Bank of Montreal Museum, 129, rue St-Jacques, CP 6002, Montréal PQ H2Y 1L6 – 514/877-6892; Fax: 514/877-1140 – Archivist, Yolaine Toussaint

Montréal: Musée de l'Église Notre-Dame, 426, rue Saint-Sulpice, Montréal PQ H2Y 2V5 – 514/842-2925

Montréal: Musée de l'Oratoire Saint-Joseph/Saint Joseph Oratory Museum, 3800, ch Reine-Marie, Montréal PQ H3V 1H6 – 514/733-8211; Fax: 514/733-9735 – Directeur, André Bergeron

Montréal: Musée des Soeurs Grises de Montréal, 1185, rue Saint-Mathieu, Montréal PQ H3H 2H6 – 514/937-9501, ext.222; Fax: 514/937-0503 – Directrice, Sr. Jeanne Laporte

Montréal: Musée du Château Ramezay/Château Ramezay Museum, 280, rue Notre-Dame est, Montréal PQ H2Y 1C5 – 514/861-7182; Fax: 514/861-8317 – Directeur, André J. Delisle

Montréal: Musée du Cinéma/cinémathèque québécoise, 335, boul de la Maisonneuve ouest, Montréal PQ H2X 1K1 – 514/842-9763 – Directeur, Robert Daudelin

Montréal: Musée itinérant d'art Byzantin, 10025, boul l'Acadie, Montréal PQ H4N 2S1 – Directrice, Rosette Mociornitza

Montréal: Musée Juste pour rire, 2111, boul St-Laurent, Montréal PQ H2X 2T5 – 514/845-4000; Fax: 514/845-4140

Montréal: Musée Marc-Aurèle Fortin, 118, rue St-Pierre, Montréal PQ H2Y 2L7 – 514/845-6108 – Directeur, René Buisson

Montréal: Musée Marguerite Bourgeoys, 400, rue St-Paul est, Montréal PQ H2Y 1H4 – 514/845-9991 – Chapelain, PSS Bernard Amyot

Montréal: Parc historique national Sir George-Etienne Cartier, 458, Notre-Dame est, Montréal PQ H2Y 1C8 – 514/283-2282 – Régisseur, Lorraine Neault

Montréal: Redpath Museum/Musée Redpath, McGill University, 859, rue Sherbrooke ouest, Montréal PQ H3A 2K6 – 514/398-4086; Fax: 514/398-3185; URL: http://www.mcgill.ca/Redpath – Director, Dr. Graham Bell

Montréal: Royal Canadian Ordnance Corps Museum/Le Musée du Corps des Magasins Militaires Royal Canadien, 6560, rue Hochlega, CP 4000, Succ K, Montréal PQ H1N 3R9 – 514/252-2241 – Curator, Maj. Ivan Burch, (Ret'd)

Montréal: Saint-Laurent Art Museum, 615, boul Ste-Croix, Montréal PQ H4L 3X6 – 514/747-7367

Montréal: Univers Maurice Rocket Richard Universe, 2800, rue Viau, Montréal PQ H1V 3J3 – 514/251-9930; URL: http://www.Rocket9.org

Canadian Almanac & Directory 1997

New Richmond: Gaspesian British Heritage Centre, 351, boul Perron ouest, New Richmond PQ G0C 2B0 – 418/392-4487 – Loyalist era from 1760 to 1900s; June - Sept.

Nicolet: Musée des religions, 900, boul Louis-Fréchette, Nicolet PQ J3T 1V5 – 819/293-6148; Fax: 819/293-4161; Email: Musée_des_Religions@itr.qc.ca – Directrice, Michèle Paradis

Odanak: Musée des Abénakis d'Odanak, Société historique d'Odanak, 108, Waban-Aki, Odanak PQ J0G 1H0 – 514/568-2600; Fax: 514/568-5959 – Directrice, Nicole O'Bomsawin

Paspébiac: Site historique du Banc-de-Paspébiac, rte du Banc, CP 430, Paspébiac PQ G0C 2K0 – 418/752-6229; Fax: 418/752-6408 – Directrice générale, Sylvie Bond – Sea heritage & traditional trades; open June - Oct.

Péribonka: Musée Louis-Hémon, 700, Maria-Chapdelaine, Péribonka PQ G0W 2G0 – 418/374-2177; Fax: 418/374-2516 – Directrice, Lynn Boisselle

Percé: Centre d'interprétation du Parc de l'Île-Bonaventure-et-du-rocher-Percé, CP 310, Percé PQ G0C 2L0 – 418/782-2721 – Natural heritage & history; saltwater aquariums; open June - mid-Oct.

Percé: Musée Le Chafaud, 145, rte 132, Percé PQ G0C 2L0 – 418/782-5100 – Open June - mid-Oct.

Pointe-au-Père: Musée de la Mer de Rimouski, 1034, du Phare, Pointe-au-Père PQ G5M 1L8 – 418/724-6214 – Directeur, Serge Guay

Pointe-au-Pic: Musée de Charlevoix, 1, ch du Hâvre, CP 549, Pointe-au-Pic PQ G0T 1M0 – 418/665-4411 – Directrice, Nicole Desjardins

Québec: Centre d'interprétation du Vieux-Port-de-Québec/Old Port of Québec Interpretation Centre, 2, rue d'Auteuil, CP 2474, Succ Terminus, Québec PQ G1K 7R3 – 418/648-3300; Fax: 418/648-3678 – Régisseure, Nicole Ouellet

Québec: Lieu historique national Cartier-Brébeuf, 2, rue d'Auteuil, CP 2474, Succ Terminus, Québec PQ G1L 7R3 – 418/648-4038 – Régisseure, Eve Bardou – Reproduction grandeur nature du vaisseau amiral de Jacques Cartier, "La Grande Hermine"

Québec: Lieu historique national des Fortifications-de-Québec/Fortifications of Québec National Historic Site, 2, rue d'Auteuil, CP 2474, Succ Terminus, Québec PQ G1K 7R3 – 418/648-7016; Fax: 418/648-4825 – Supt., Pierre-Denis Cloutier

Québec: Lieu historique national du Fort-Numéro-Un/Fort No. 1 at Pointe-de-Lévy National Historic Site, 41, ch du Gouvernement, a/s 2, rue d'Auteuil, CP 2474, Succ Terminus, Québec PQ G1K 7R3 – 418/835-5182; Fax: 418/835-5443 – Interpretive Technician, Gabriel Laliberté

Québec: Lieu historique national du Parc-de-L'Artillerie/Artillery Park National Historic Site, 2, rue d'Auteuil, CP 2474, Succ Terminus, Québec PQ G1K 7R3 – 418/648-4205; Fax: 418/648-4825; URL: http://www.upc.qc.ca/pch/artillerie (Français); http://www.upc.qc.ca/pch/artillery (English) – Supt., Pierre-Denis Cloutier

Québec: Musée des Augustines de l'Hôpital général de Québec, Monastère des Augustines, 260, boul Langelier, Québec PQ G1K 5N1 – 418/529-0931 – Responsable, S. Corinne Cloutier

Québec: Musée des Augustines de l'Hôtel-Dieu de Québec, 32, rue Charlevoix, Québec PQ G1R 5C4 – 418/692-2492; Fax: 418/692-2668 – Directrice du Musée, S. Nicole Perron, AMJ – A rich patrimony of art and ethnology gathered by the Augustines three & a half centuries; open year round

Québec: Musée des Ursulines de Québec, 12, rue Donnacona, PO Box 760, Stn Haute-Ville, Québec PQ G1R 4T1 – 418/694-0694 – Directrice, Soeur Gabrielle Dagnault, o.s.u. – Ursuline heritage under the French regime (1639 - 1759), art gallery, chapel; open Jan. - Nov.

Québec: Musée du Royal 22e Régiment, La Citadelle, CP 6020, Succ Haute-Ville, Québec PQ G1R 4V7 – 418/648-3563 – Conservateur, Maj. Robert Girard

Québec: Place-Royale, a/s Ministère des Affaires culturelles, Secteur Place-Royale, 225, Grande-Allée est, Bloc C, Québec PQ G1R 5K5 – 418/643-9314 – Directeur, André Couture – Grande concentration de bâtiments des XVII et XVIIIe siècles

Rimouski: Musée régional de Rimouski, 35, rue Saint-Germain ouest, Rimouski PQ G5L 4B4 – 418/724-2272 – Directeur général, François Lachapelle

Rimouski: Site historique de la Maison Lamontagne, 540, rue St-Germain est, Rimouski PQ G5L 1E9 – 418/722-4038; Fax: 418/722-0226 – Directeur, Robert Malenfant

Rivière-Du-Loup: Musée du Bas-St-Laurent, 300, rue Saint-Pierre, Rivière-Du-Loup PQ G5R 3V3 – 418/862-7547; Fax: 418/862-3019 – Directeur, Pierre Rastoul

Roberval: Village Historique de Val-Jalbert, PO Box 34, Roberval PQ G8H 2N4 – 418/275-3132; Fax: 418/275-5875 – Directeur, Philippe Auguste Morin

Rouyn-Noranda: La Maison Dumulon, CP 242, Rouyn-Noranda PQ J9X 5C3 – 819/797-7125; Fax: 819/762-3367 – Directrice, Diane Tremblay

Saint-Constant: Canadian Railway Museum/Musée ferroviaire canadien, 120, rue St-Pierre, Saint-Constant PQ J5A 2G9 – 514/638-1522; Fax: 514/638-1563 – Françine St-Jean

Saint-Hyacinthe: Musée du Séminaire de Saint-Hyacinthe, 650, rue Girouard est, CP 370, Saint-Hyacinthe PQ J2S 7B7 – 514/774-0203 – Directeur, Joseph-Hector Lemieux

Saint-Jean-sur-Richelieu: Musée du Fort Saint-Jean, Collège Militaire Royal Saint-Jean, Saint-Jean-sur-Richelieu PQ J0J 1R0 – 514/346-2131 – Directeur, Capt. D. Landry – Histoire du Fort Saint-Jean de 1666 à aujourd'hui

Saint-Jean-sur-Richelieu: Musée régional du Haut-Richelieu, 182, Jacques-Cartier nord, Saint-Jean-sur-Richelieu PQ J3B 7W3 – 514/347-0649; Fax: 514/357-2285 – Directeur, Michel Roy

Saint-Joseph-de-Beauce: Musée Marius Barbeau, PO Box 1081, Saint-Joseph-de-Beauce PQ G0S 2V0 – 418/397-4039 – Animatrice, Johanne Lessard

Saint-Lambert: Musée Marsil/Marsil Museum, 349, Riverside, Saint-Lambert PQ J4P 1A8 – 514/671-3098; Fax: 514/465-8694 – Directrice, Louise Séguin; Curator of Costume, Cynthia Cooper – Original exhibitions exploring costume, textiles & fibre; permanent collection of costumes (19th & 20th century) & textiles

Sept-Îles: Centre d'interpretation Le Vieux-Poste, CP 725, Sept-Îles PQ G4R 1X7 – 418/968-2070 – Directeur, Guy Tremblay

Sept-Îles: Musée Régional de la Côte-Nord, 500, boul Laure, PO Box 725, Sept-Îles PQ G4R 4K9 – 418/968-2070 – Directeur, Guy Tremblay

Sherbrooke: Centre d'interpretation de l'histoire de Sherbrooke, 275, rue Dufferin, Sherbrooke PQ J1H 4M5 – 819/821-5406; Fax: 819/821-5417 – Directrice, Johanne Lacasse – Heritage of Sherbrooke & the Eastern Townships; open year round

Sherbrooke: Musée de Séminaire de Sherbrooke, Musée de la Tour, Centre d'exposition Léon Marcotte, 222, rue Frontenac, Sherbrooke PQ J1H 1J9 – 819/564-3200; Fax: 819/564-7388 – Directeur général, Charles Farrar; Directeur, Marketing, Michel Rodrigue

Sherbrooke: Musée des beaux-arts de Sherbrooke, 174, rue Palais, Sherbrooke PQ J1H 4P9 – 819/821-2115 – Directeur/conservateur, Michel Forest

Sillery: Domaine Cataraqui, 2141, ch Saint-Louis, Sillery PQ G1T 1P9 – 418/681-3031; Fax: 418/681-3865 – Conservateur, Yves Goudreau – Exhibition centre & historic gardens

Sillery: Maison des Jésuites, 2320, ch du Foulon, Sillery PQ G1T 1X4 – 418/654-0259; Fax: 418/681-3865 – Conservateur, Eric Lord – Exhibition centre, garden & traditional Amerindian campsite

St-Eustache: Moulin Légaré, 232, rue St-Eustache, St-Eustache PQ J7R 2L7 – 514/472-4440, poste 433 – 1762 flour mill; open mid-April - mid-Dec.

St-Eustache: Musée Jean-Hotte, 405, Grande-Côte, St-Eustache PQ J7P 1H6 – 514/473-4370 – 15,000 artifacts; toys, antique cars, trains; open March 15 - Nov.

St-Jean-Port-Joli: Musée des Anciens Canadiens, 332, av de Gaspé ouest, St-Jean-Port-Joli PQ G0R 3G0 – 418/598-3392 – Woodcarving, arts & crafts traditions; open year round

St-Jean-Port-Joli: Musée les Retrouvailles, 248, av de Gaspé est, St-Jean-Port-Joli PQ G0R 3G0 – 418/598-3531 – Weaving looms, spinning wheels, agricultural & domestic artifacts; open June 24 - Labour Day

St-Ulric: Le Musée La Gare de Rivière Blanche, 235, boul Joseph Roy, PO Box 57, St-Ulric PQ G0J 3H0 – 418/737-4708 – Responsable, Chantal Frégeot

Stanbridge East: Missisquoi Museum/Musée de Missisquoi, PO Box 186, Stanbridge East PQ J0J 2H0 – 514/248-3153 – Curator, Heather Darch; Archivist, Judy Antle – Cornell Mill, Hodge's Store & Bill's Barn.; UEL Archives

Stanstead Historical Society, 35, rue Dufferin, PO Box 268, Stanstead PQ J0B 3E0 – 819/876-7322 – Director/Curator, Sylvia Bertolini – Operates the Colby Curtis Museum & Carrollcroft Property

Ste-Foy: Le Centre muséographique de l'Université Laval, Pavillon Louis-Jacques-Casault, Université Laval, Ste-Foy PQ G1K 7P4 – 418/656-7111; Fax: 418/656-7925 – Directrice, Nicole Brindle

Ste-Foy: Maison Hamel-Bruneau, 2608, ch St-Louis, CP 218, Ste-Foy PQ G1V 4E1 – 418/654-4325

Ste-Foy: Musée d'anthropologie, Université Laval, Ste-Foy PQ G1K 7P4 – 418/656-5867 – Professeur, Nancy Schmitz

Ste-Foy: Musée de Géologie, Université Laval, Pavillon Pouliot, 4e étage, Ste-Foy PQ G1K 7P4 – 418/656-2193 – Conservateur, André Lévesque

Sutton: Eberdt Museum of Communications, PO Box 430, Sutton PQ J0E 2K0 – 514/538-2649 – Director/Curator, E. Eberdt

Tadoussac: Chapelle des Indiens, CP 69, Tadoussac PQ G0T 2A0 – 418/235-4324 – Curé, Yvon Cholette

Thetford Mines: Musée minéralogique et minier de Thetford Mines, PO Box 462, Thetford Mines PQ G6G 5T3 – 418/335-2123; Fax: 418/335-5605 – Directeur, François Cinq-Mars

Tourelle: Halte touristique Menoum, 22, boul Perron ouest, Tourelle PQ G0E 2J0 – 418/763-7446 – Traditional fishery methods; open June-Sept.

Trois-Rivières: Lieu historique national des forges du Saint-Maurice/Forges du Saint-Maurice National Historic Site, 10 000, boul des Forges, Trois-Rivières PQ G9C 1B1 – 819/378-5116; Fax: 819/378-0887 – Régisseure, Carmen Desfossés LePage

Trois-Rivières: Musée d'archaéologie de l'Université du Québec à Trois-Rivières, 3351, boul des Forges, Trois-Rivières PQ G9A 5H7 – 819/376-5032 – Conservateur, René Ribes

Trois-Rivières: Musée Pierre Boucher, Séminaire Saint-Joseph, 858, rue Laviolette, Trois-Rivières PQ G9A 5S3 – 819/376-4459; Fax: 819/378-0607 – Directrice, Françoise Chainé

Val d'Or: Village Minier de Bourlamaque, 90, av Perreault, CP 212, Val d'Or PQ J9P 4P3 – 819/825-7616; Fax: 819/825-9853 – Directeur, Pierre Dufour

Valcourt: Musée J. Armand Bombardier, 1001, av J.A. Bombardier, CP 370, Valcourt PQ J0E 2L0 – 514/532-5300; Fax: 514/532-2260; URL: http://www.ucctech.com/museejab – Directrice générale, France Bissonnette; Conservateur, Carl F. Eisan

Valleyfield: Écomusée des deux-rives, 111, rue Ellice, Valleyfield PQ J6T 1E7 – 514/371-6772 – Présidente, Yolande Latour

Vaudreuil: Musée régional de Vaudreuil-Soulanges (MRVS), 431, av St-Charles, Vaudreuil PQ J7V 2N3

– 514/455-2092; Fax: 514/455-6782 – Directeur, Daniel Bissonnette
Victoriaville: Musée Laurier, 16, rue Laurier ouest, Victoriaville PQ G6P 6P3 – 819/357-8655; Fax: 819/357-8655 – Directeur/Conservateur, Richard Pedneault – Résidence de Sir et Lady Laurier.
Wendake: Musée Arouane, 10, rue Alexandre-Duchesneau, Wendake PQ G0A 4V0 – 418/845-1241
l'Islet-sur-Mer: Musée maritime Bernier, 55, rue des Pionniers est, l'Islet-sur-Mer PQ G0R 2B0 – 418/247-5001; Fax: 418/247-5002 – Directrice générale, Sonia Chassé

SASKATCHEWAN

Royal Saskatchewan Museum
Wascana Park, College & Albert, Regina SK S4P 3V7
306/787-2815, 2810; Fax: 306/787-2820
URL: http://www.gov.sk.ca/govt/munigov/cult&rec/rsm/
Major collections & exhibits of Saskatchewan's natural & human history, including archaeology, entomology, botany, natural history, paleontology & geology. First Nations Gallery opened June 1993. Life Sciences Gallery under development. Earth Sciences Gallery, Paleo Pit interactive gallery for children & Megamunch, a half-size robotic Tyrannosaurus. Publication of informational booklets & nature notes, giftshop, research library, information services, films, teachers' workshops, educational programs.
Director, Ron Borden
Curator, Life Sciences, David Baron
Curator, Aboriginal History, Margaret Hanna
Curator, Entomology, Keith Roney
Curator, Archaeology, Ian Brace
Supervisor, Exhibits, Ron Tillie
Supervisor, Education & Extension, Paula Hill

Western Development Museum
Curatorial Centre, 2935 Melville St., Saskatoon SK S7J 5A6
306/934-1400; Fax: 306/934-4467
Executive Director, David Klatt
Marketing Director, Jan Krystyniak

1910 BOOMTOWN
2610 Lorne Ave. South, Saskatoon SK S7J 0S6
306/931-1910; Fax: 306/934-0525
Manager, Tom Waiser

HERITAGE FARM & VILLAGE
PO Box 183, North Battleford SK S9A 2Y1
306/445-8033; Fax: 306/445-7211
Manager, Wayne Fennig

HISTORY OF TRANSPORTATION
50 Diefenbaker Dr., PO Box 185, Moose Jaw SK S6H 4N8
306/693-6556; Fax: 306/691-0511
Manager, Lyn Johnson

STORY OF PEOPLE
Hwy. #16 West, PO Box 98, Yorkton SK S3N 2V6
306/783-8361; Fax: 306/782-1027
Manager, Susan Manziuk

Other Museums & Science Centres in Saskatchewan
Abernethy Nature Heritage Museum, PO Box 125, Abernethy SK S0A 0A0 – 306/333-2113 – Secretary/Manager, Joy McKen
Abernethy: Motherwell Homestead Natural Historic Site, PO Box 247, Abernethy SK S0A 0A0 – 306/333-2116 – Operations Manager, Greg Prynne – Open May - Oct.
Alida: Gervais Wheels Museum, PO Box 40, Alida SK S0C 0B0 – 306/443-2303 – Director, Alex Gervais
Arcola Museum, PO Box 279, Arcola SK S0C 0G0 – 306/455-2480 – President, JoAnne Martin
Assiniboia & District Historical Museum, Assiniboia SK S0H 0B0 – 306/642-3003, 4216 – 1912 stores & offices; open year round
Avonlea: Heritage House & Avonlea District Museum, PO Box 401, Avonlea SK S0H 0C0 – 306/868-2200 – President, Kathleen Geisler
Battleford: Fort Battleford National Historic Site, PO Box 70, Battleford SK S0M 0E0 – 306/937-2621; Fax: 306/937-3370 – A/Supt., Glen Ebert – NWMP post, c. 1886; open May - Oct.
Battleford: Fred Light Museum, PO Box 40, Battleford SK S0M 0E0 – 306/937-7111; Fax: 306/937-2450 – Supervisor, Bernadette Leslie – Pioneer artifacts, gun collection, military artifacts; open May - Sept.
Beauval: Frazer's Museum, PO Box 64, Beauval SK S0M 0G0 – Director, John Frazer
Big Beaver Nature Centre & Museum, c/o Big Muddy Guided Tour Association, Big Beaver SK S0H 0G0 – 306/267-6017
Biggar Museum & Gallery, 202 - 3rd Ave. West, PO Box 1598, Biggar SK S0K 0M0 – 306/948-3451 – Curator, Diane LaRouche
Biggar: Homestead Museum, PO Box 542, Biggar SK S0K 0M0 – 306/948-3427 – Director, Roger Martin
Blaine Lake Museum, PO Box 10, Blaine Lake SK S0J 0J0 – Town Administrator, Eleanora Boyko
Bracken Community Museum, PO Box 35, Bracken SK S0N 0G0 – 306/293-2878 – Laura Wright
Broadview Museum, c/o Broadview Historical & Museum Association Inc., PO Box 556, Broadview SK S0G 0K0 – 306/696-2612 – Archivist, Iva Galbraith – Pioneer buildings, CPR Station & caboose, Indian & military artifacts; open summer
Bulyea: Lakeside Museum, PO Box 101, Bulyea SK S0G 0L0 – 306/725-4558 – Director, Robert Swanston
Cadillac Historical Society & Museum, Cadillac SK S0N 0K0 – 306/785-2128 – Sec.-Treas., Alta Legros
Canwood Museum, Canwood SK S0J 0K0 – 306/468-2338
Carlyle: Rusty Relics Museum Inc., PO Box 840, Carlyle SK S0C 0R0 – 306/453-2266 – President, Sheila Andrews
Climax Community Museum, PO Box 59, Climax SK S0N 0N0 – 306/293-2135 – President/Curator, Victor Van Allen
Coronach District Museum, PO Box 449, Coronach SK S0H 0Z0 – 306/267-2132 – Chairman, Judy Greenwood
Craik: Prairie Pioneer Museum, PO Box 157, Craik SK S0G 0V0 – 306/734-2480 – Director, R. Meshke
Cut Knife: Clayton McLain Memorial Museum, PO Box 335, Cut Knife SK S0M 0N0 – 306/398-2590
Denare Beach: Northern Gateway Museum, PO Box 70, Denare Beach SK S0P 0B0 – 306/362-2054 – Director, Brenda Avison; Director, Maxine Gunn
Dinsmore: Yester-Years Community Museum, PO Box 216, Dinsmore SK S0L 0T0 – 306/846-4613 – President, Garry Blackwell
Dodsland Museum, Dodsland SK S0L 0V0 – Director, Jocelyn Sipley
Duck Lake Regional Interpretive Centre, PO Box 328, Duck Lake SK S0K 1J0 – 306/467-2057; Fax: 306/467-2257 – Executive Director, Chris M. Patenaude; President, Denis Poirier
Duff Community Heritage Museum, PO Box 57, Duff SK S0A 0S0 – 306/728-3592 – Sec.-Treas., Norman Schick
Earl Grey Centennial Museum, PO Box 100, Earl Grey SK S0G 1J0 – 306/939-2062 – Helene Huber
Eastend Museum & Cultural Centre, PO Box 214, Eastend SK S0N 0T0 – 306/295-3819 – Secretary, Jean Bascom – Open May - Sept.
Edam: Harry S. Washbrook Museum, PO Box 182, Edam SK S0M 0V0 – 306/397-2260 – Director, Harry Washbrook
Elbow Museum & Historical Society, PO Box 207, Elbow SK S0H 1J0 – 306/854-2285 – President, Lewis Webster
Elrose Heritage Society, PO Box 556, Elrose SK S0L 0Z0 – 306/378-2213 – President, Betty Rudd
Esterhazy Community Museum, Esterhazy SK S0A 0X0 – 306/745-6761, 2988 – A.M. Provick – Potash mine; fall-out shelter; first Bohemian Band instruments
Esterhazy: Kaposvar Historic Site, PO Box 115, Esterhazy SK S0A 0X0 – 306/745-6761 – Secretary, Jean Pask
Estevan National Exhibition Centre, 118 - 4th St., Estevan SK S4A 0T4 – 306/634-7644 – NWMP barracks, local artifacts, travelling exhibitions; open year round
Eston: Prairie West Historical Centre & Society, PO Box 910, Eston SK S0L 1A0 – 306/962-3772 – Programme Coordinator, Pat Rooke
Foam Lake Museum, PO Box 1041, Foam Lake SK S0A 1A0 – 306/272-4292 – Sec.-Treas., Inge Helgason
Fort Qu'Appelle Museum, PO Box 544, Fort Qu'Appelle SK S0G 1S0 – 306/332-6033 – Secretary, Nellie Hiebert – 1864 Hudson Bay Co. post; open July - Sept.
Frenchman Butte Museum, PO Box 114, Frenchman Butte SK S0M 0W0 – 306/344-4478 – President, Gordon Howard; Curator, Gwen Zweifel
Frobisher Threshermen's Museum, PO Box 194, Frobisher SK S0C 0Y0 – 306/486-2162 – Sec.-Treas., S. Stobart
Glen Ewen Community Antique Centre, Glen Ewen SK S0C 1C0 – 306/925-2221 – Director, Arne Hansen
Glentworth Museum, PO Box 174, Glentworth SK S0H 1V0 – Secretary, Sonia Falconer
Goodsoil Historical Museum, PO Box 57, Goodsoil SK S0M 1A0 – 306/238-2084 – Secretary, Minnie Hofer
Grenfell Community Museum, PO Box 1156, Grenfell SK S0G 2B0 – 306/697-2431; Fax: 306/697-2500 – Secretary, Jean Kerr
Hague: Saskatchewan River Valley Museum, PO Box 630, Hague SK S0K 1X0 – Receptionist, Shirley Fisher
Hazenmore: Heritage Hazenmore Inc., PO Box 6, Hazenmore SK S0N 1C0 – 306/264-3651 – President, Britta Lovely
Herbert: Klassen's Homestead Museum, PO Box 28, Herbert SK S0H 2A0 – 306/784-2915 – Director, Peter Klassen
Herbert: Main Centre Heritage Museum, PO Box 308, Herbert SK S0H 2A0 – 306/784-3272 – Chairman, Dora Wall
Hodgeville Community Museum, Hodgeville SK S0H 2B0 – 306/677-2673 – President, Faye Rister
Hudson Bay Museum, PO Box 931, Hudson Bay SK S0E 0Y0 – 306/865-2170 – Curator, Barbara Demasson
Humboldt & District Museum & Gallery, PO Box 2349, Humboldt SK S0K 2A0 – 306/682-5226; Fax: 306/682-3144 – Curator, J. Hoesgen
Imperial & District Museum, PO Box 269, Imperial SK S0G 2J0 – 306/963-2280 – Chairman, Fred Grigg
Imperial: Nels Berggren Museum, PO Box 125, Imperial SK S0G 2J0 – 306/963-2033 – Director, Nels Berggren
Indian Head Museum, PO Box 566, Indian Head SK S0G 2K0 – 306/695-2556 – President, Lloyd Pearon
Ituna Cultural & Historical Museum, PO Box 282, Ituna SK S0A 1N0
Kamsack & District Museum, PO Box 991, Kamsack SK S0A 1S0 – 306/542-4415 – President, John Barisow – Open May - Sept.
Kerrobert & District Museum, PO Box 401, Kerrobert SK S0L 1R0 – 306/834-2744 – Secretary, Mary Andrews

Kincaid Museum, PO Box 177, Kincaid SK S0H 2J0 – 306/264-3910 – Chairperson, Val Wurmlinger

Kindersley Plains Museum Inc., 903 - 11th Ave. East, PO Box 599, Kindersley SK S0L 1S0 – 306/463-6620 – Curator, Kathie Chandler – Open year round

Kinistino District Pioneer Museum Inc., PO Box 10, Kinistino SK S0J 1H0 – 306/864-2474; Fax: 306/864-3465 – Treasurer, Shirley Jackson

Kipling District Museum, Kipling SK S0G 2S0 – 306/736-2488 – Treasurer, Alvin Cunningham

Kisbey Museum, 291 Ross St., PO Box 117, Kisbey SK S0C 1L0 – 306/462-2027 – Secretary, Charlotte Hookenson

La Ronge: Mistasinihk Place Interpretive Centre, c/o Saskatchewan Family Foundation, PO Box 5000, La Ronge SK S0J 1L0 – 306/425-4350; Fax: 306/425-2580 – Sport & Recreation Consultant, Dennis Moore

Lancer Centennial Museum, PO Box 3, Lancer SK S0N 1G0 – 306/689-2925; Fax: 306/689-2890 – Cliff Murch

Lashburn Centennial Museum, PO Box 343, Lashburn SK S0M 1H0 – 306/285-3860

Lloydminster: Barr Colony Heritage Cultural Centre, 5011 - 49 Ave., Lloydminster SK S9V 0T8 – 306/825-5655; Fax: 306/825-7170 – Includes Barr Colony Museum, Imhoff & Berghammer Art Collections, Fuch's Wildlife

Loon Lake: Big Bear Trails Museum, PO Box 219, Loon Lake SK S0M 1L0 – 306/837-2070 – Director, John W. Simpson

Lumsden Heritage Museum, Qu'Appelle Dr., Lumsden SK S0G 3C0 – 306/731-2905 – President, B. McGill – Qu'Appelle Valley history; John Deere tractor display, town history & picnic area; open May - Sept.

Maple Creek: Antique Tractor Museum & Frontier Village, Maple Creek SK S0N 1N0 – 306/667-2964 – Director, John Stewart

Maple Creek: Fort Walsh National Historic Park, PO Box 278, Maple Creek SK S0N 1N0 – 306/662-2645 – Operations Manager, Tom Kynman – NWMP & trading post; open May - Oct.

Maple Creek: Old Timers Museum Inc., PO Box 1540, Maple Creek SK S0N 1N0 – 306/662-2474 – Treasurer, Cindy Drury – Open year round

Maryfield Museum, PO Box 262, Maryfield SK S0G 3K0 – 306/646-2201

McCord & District Museum, PO Box 30, McCord SK S0H 2T0 – 306/478-2522 – Secretary, Audrey J. Wilson – CPR station bldg., caboose & historic church tell of prairie pioneers & the rise & decline of a railway prairie town

Meadow Lake Museum, PO Box 610, Meadow Lake SK S0M 1V0 – 306/236-3622 – Director, Vincent Huffman

Melfort & District Museum, 401 Melfort St. West, PO Box 3222, Melfort SK S0E 1A0 – 306/752-5870 – Curator, Frances Westlund – Open Victoria Day - Labour Day

Melville Heritage Museum Inc., PO Box 2528, Melville SK S0A 2P0 – 306/728-2070 – Curator, Marj Redenbach; President, Joe Miller

Melville Railway Museum, PO Box 2863, Melville SK S0A 2P0 – 306/728-4205; Fax: 306/728-5911 – Chairman, Mark Orosz

Middle Lake Museum, PO Box 157, Middle Lake SK S0K 2X0 – Curator, Susan Bauer

Milden Community Museum, Milden SK S0L 2L0 – 306/935-4722 – President, G.H. Bailey

Moose Jaw Art Museum & National Exhibition Centre, Crescent Park, Moose Jaw SK S6H 0X6 – 306/692-4471; Fax: 306/694-8016 – Curator, Heather Smith – Art, history & science exhibits; 3,000 artifacts; open year round

Moose Jaw: Sukanen Ship Pioneer Village & Museum of Saskatchewan, PO Box 2071, Moose Jaw SK S6H 7T2 – 306/693-3506 – President, R. Jones; Secretary, A. Giesbretch

Moosomin: Jamieson Museum, 306 Gertie St. North, PO Box 236, Moosomin SK S0G 3N0 – 306/435-3156 – President, Tim Jamieson – Open May - Oct.

Morse Museum & Cultural Centre, PO Box 308, Morse SK S0H 3C0 – 306/629-3230; Fax: 306/629-3230 – President, Darlene Nicholson

Mossbank & District Museum Inc., PO Box 278, Mossbank SK S0H 3G0 – 306/354-2889 – President, Roy Tollefson

Muenster: St. Peter's College Museum, PO Box 10, Muenster SK S0K 2Y6 – 306/682-3373 – Curator, Rev. Rudolph Novecosky

Naicam Museum, PO Box 62, Naicam SK S0K 2Z0 – 306/874-2173 – Sec.-Treas., Nora Nelson

Neudorf Historical Museum, PO Box 12, Neudorf SK S0A 2T0 – 306/748-2519 – Curator, Norman Miller

Nipawin & District Living Forestry Museum, Hwy. 35 West, PO Box 1917, Nipawin SK S0E 1E0 – 306/862-9299; Fax: 306/862-4717 – Curator, Mike Mochoruk – Open May - Sept.

Nokomis & District Museum & Heritage Co-op, PO Box 56, Nokomis SK S0G 3R0 – 306/528-2080 – Director, R.F. Edwards

North Battleford: Saskatchewan Baseball Hall of Fame & Museum, 121 - 20th St., PO Box 1388, North Battleford SK S0M 0E0 – 306/445-8485; Fax: 306/446-0509 – President, David W. Shury, Q.C.

Oxbow: Ralph Allen Memorial Museum, 802 Railway Ave., Oxbow SK S0C 2B0 – 306/483-2400, 5065 – President, N. Black – Open May - Sept.

Paynton: Bresaylor Heritage Museum Association Inc., PO Box 33, Paynton SK S0M 2J0 – 306/895-4813 – Curator, Velma Foster

Pelly: Fort Pelly & Livingston Museum, PO Box 363, Pelly SK S0A 2Z0 – 306/595-2030 – President, Mabel Campbell

Plenty: Carscadden's Museum, PO Box 149, Plenty SK S0L 2R0 – 306/932-2226 – Director, William Olson

Porcupine Plain & District Museum, PO Box 148, Porcupine Plain SK S0E 1H0 – 306/278-2317 – Curator/Director, Joyce Logan

Prairie River Museum, PO Box 9, Prairie River SK S0E 1J0 – 306/889-4220 – President, Edward G. Suwinski

Prelate: St. Angela's Museum & Archives, PO Box 220, Prelate SK S0N 2B0 – 306/673-2200; Fax: 306/673-2635 – Director, Sister Philomena

Prince Albert: John & Olive Diefenbaker House, 246 - 19th St. West, Prince Albert SK S6V 4C6 – 306/922-9641 – Director, Stan Hanson – Open May - Sept.

Prince Albert: Lund Wildlife Exhibit, 839 - 4th St. East, Prince Albert SK S6V 0K6 – 306/764-2860 – Open June - Sept.

Prince Albert Historical Museum, PO Box 531, Prince Albert SK S6V 4V5 – 306/764-2992, 1394 – Manager/Curator, R.E.G. Smith – Photos, documents & artifacts on the history of Prince Albert; open May 15 - Sept. 5

Raymore Pioneer Museum Inc., PO Box 453, Raymore SK S0A 3J0 – 306/746-2264 – Sec.-Treas., Jean Grymaloski

Regina: Diefenbaker Homestead, c/o Wascana Centre Authority, 2900 Wascana Dr., PO Box 7111, Regina SK S4P 3S7 – 306/522-3661; Fax: 306/565-2742; Email: wca@sasknet.sk.ca – Public Relations Officer, Irene Pisula – Open May - Sept.

Regina: Fort Carlton Historic Park, c/o Parks & Protected Areas, 3211 Albert St., Regina SK S4S 5W6 – 306/467-4512 (summer)

Regina: Government House Historic Property, 4607 Dewdney Ave., Regina SK S4P 3V7 – 306/787-5726 – Manager, Garth Pugh – Open year round

Regina Plains Museum, 1801 Scarth St., 4th Fl., Regina SK S4P 2G9 – 306/352-0844 – Curator, Sandra Massey

Regina: Royal Canadian Mounted Police Centennial Museum/Musée de la GRC, PO Box 6500, Regina SK S4P 3J7 – 306/780-5838; Fax: 306/780-6349; URL: http://rbcm1.rbcm.gov.bc.ca – Director, M.J.H. Wake

Regina: Saskatchewan Pharmacy Museum, #301, 2531 - 28 Ave., Regina SK S4S 6X3 – 306/584-2292 – President, C. Choplan

Regina: Saskatchewan Science Centre, Wascana Centre, College & Albert, Regina SK S4P 3V7 – 306/791-7900 – Over 70 hands-on exhibits; open year-round

Regina: Wood Mountain Historic Park, c/o Parks & Protected Areas, 3211 Albert St., Regina SK S4K 5W6 – 306/266-4322

Riverhurst: F.T. Hill Museum, Riverhurst SK S0H 3P0 – 306/353-2112 – Curator, Winnie Hockman – Gun collection, Indian artifacts, pioneer items; open June - Sept. & by appt.

Rocanville & District Museum Society Inc., PO Box 490, Rocanville SK S0A 3L0 – 306/645-2113, 4308 – Sec.-Treas., Phyllis Ore

Rockglen: Rolling Hills Historical Society, PO Box 136, Rockglen SK S0H 3R0 – Secretary, Bernice Belbeck

Rose Valley & District Heritage Museum, PO Box 232, Rose Valley SK S0E 1M0 – 306/322-2034 – Sec.-Treas., Irene Martinson

Rosetown Museum & Art Centre, Centennial Library, Rosetown SK S0L 2V0 – 306/882-3566 – Director, Frank Glass

Rosthern: Batoche National Historic Park/Lieu national historique Batoche (BNHS), PO Box 999, Rosthern SK S0K 3R0 – 306/423-6227; Fax: 306/423-5400

Rosthern: Mennonite Heritage Museum, PO Box 546, Rosthern SK S0K 3R0 – 306/232-5353; Fax: 306/232-5518 – Chairman, Ed Roth

Saskatoon: Geological Museum, Dept. of Geological Sciences, University of Saskatchewan, Saskatoon SK S7N 0W0 – 306/966-5683; Fax: 306/966-8593 – Head/Geological Sciences, J. Oliphant

Saskatoon: Meewasin Valley Authority, 402 - 3rd Ave. South, Saskatoon SK S7K 3G5 – 306/665-6888; Fax: 306/665-6117 – Chief Interpreter, Brenda Jansen

Saskatoon: Musée Ukraina Museum, 202 Ave. M South, Saskatoon SK S7M 2K4 – 306/244-4212 – Director, Emilia Panamaroff; Curator, Judy Jurdyga

Saskatoon: Museum of Antiquities, University of Saskatchewan, Murray Bldg., Rm. 237, 3 Campus Dr., Saskatoon SK S7N 5A4 – 306/966-7818 – Administrator, Catherine F. Gunderson

Saskatoon: Natural Science Museum, Dept. of Biology & Natural Science, University of Saskatchewan, Saskatoon SK S7N 0W0 – 306/966-4400 (bio); 966-5684 (geo); Fax: 306/966-4461 – Head/Biology Dept., Dr. R.J.F. Smith

Saskatoon: Right Hon. John G. Diefenbaker Centre for the Study of Canada, University of Saskatchewan, 101 Diefenbaker Place, Saskatoon SK S7N 5B8 – 306/966-8382; Fax: 306/966-6207; Email: aikenhead@admin.usask.ca; URL: http://library.usask.ca/remate.html – Director, R. Bruce Shepard – Public museum, archives & centre for Canadian Studies

Saskatoon: Ukrainian Museum of Canada, 910 Spadina Cres. East, Saskatoon SK S7K 3H5 – 306/244-3800; Fax: 306/652-7620 – Acting Director, Marie Kishchuk; Curator, Rose Marie Fedorak

Sceptre: Great Sandhills Museum, PO Box 29, Sceptre SK S0N 2H0 – 306/623-4345; Fax: 306/623-4612 – President, Gertrude Hale

Shaunavon: Grand Coteau Heritage & Cultural Centre, Centre St., PO Box 966, Shaunavon SK S0N 2M0 – 306/297-3882 – Curator, Ingrid Cazakoff – Natural history museum, heritage museum, art gallery, public library; open year round

Spalding: Reynold Rapp Museum, PO Box 308, Spalding SK S0K 4C0 – 306/872-2164 – President, Ruth Briggs; Secretary, Garth Ulrich

Spruce Home: Buckland Heritage Museum, Hwy. 2, Spruce Home SK S0J 2N0 – 306/764-8470 – Open June - Sept.

Spy Hill: Wolverine Hobby & Historical Society Museum, PO Box 191, Spy Hill SK S0A 3W0 – 306/534-4534 – Secretary, Jean Olson

St. Brieux: Musée St. Brieux Museum, 300 Barbier Dr., CP 224, St. Brieux SK S0K 3V0 – 306/275-2123 – Curator, Lilianne Leray – Documentation au sujet de la vie des pionniers, de leurs origines, des missions environnantes et de l'église catholique pré-Vatican II; des tournées en français ou en anglais sont offertes

St. Victor: McGillis Pioneer Home, St. Victor SK S0H 3T0 – 306/642-3155 – Co-Director, L. Bissonnette

St. Walburg & District Historical Museum Inc., PO Box 336, St. Walburg SK S0M 2T0 – 306/248-3359 – President, J.F. Schmitz

Star City: Our Heritage Museum, PO Box 38, Star City SK S0E 1P0 – 306/863-2309 – Sec.-Treas., Jean Jacklin

Stoughton & District Museum, 327 Main St., PO Box 381, Stoughton SK S0G 4T0 – 306/457-2662 – Committee Chairperson, Betty Wright

Strasbourg & District Museum, PO Box 446, Strasbourg SK S0G 4V0 – 306/725-3372 – Director, Albert Keyser

Sturgis Station House Museum, PO Box 255, Sturgis SK S0A 4A0 – 306/548-5565 – Chairperson, Tom Smith

Swift Current: Canadian Country Music Hall of Fame, 1100 - 5th Ave. NE, Swift Current SK S9H 5A6 – Portraits, memorabilia & artifacts; open year round

Swift Current Museum, 105 Chaplin St. East, Swift Current SK S9H 1H9 – 306/778-2775; Fax: 306/778-2194 – Director, Hugh Henry – Natural & human history museum; open year round

Swift Current: Wright Historical Museum, PO Box 712, Swift Current SK S9H 3W7 – 306/773-8733 – Director, Andrew Wright

Tompkins Museum, PO Box 393, Tompkins SK S0N 2S0 – 306/622-2024 – Owner, Stanley A. Dimmock

Unity & District Heritage Museum, PO Box 591, Unity SK S0K 4L0 – 306/228-3864 – President, Bev Smith – Open May 20 - Sept. 5

Val Marie: Perrault's Museum, PO Box 216, Val Marie SK S0N 2T0 – 306/298-2241 – Directrice, Lise Perrault

Vanguard Centennial Museum, Vanguard SK S0N 2V0 – 306/582-2244 – Librarian, Doris Burns

Verigin: National Doukhobour Heritage Village, PO Box 99, Verigin SK S0A 4H0 – 306/542-4441 – Manager, Philip Perepelkin

Verwood Community Museum, Verwood SK S0H 4G0 – 306/642-5767 – Secretary, Helen Domes

Wakaw: John G. Diefenbaker Replica Law Office, PO Box 760, Wakaw SK S0K 4P0 – 306/233-5157 – Curator, William Kindrachuk

Wakaw Heritage Society Museum, PO Box 475, Wakaw SK S0K 4P0 – 306/233-4257 – President, Celestine Boehm

Waskesiu Lake: Prince Albert National Park Nature Centre, Waskesiu Lake SK S0J 2Y0 – 306/663-5322; Fax: 306/663-5424 – Chief Client Services, Don Bronson – Participatory exhibits & displays

Wawota & District Museum, Wawota SK S0G 5A0 – 306/739-2110 – Chairman, Tom Wayling

Webb: Prairie Wildlife Interpretation Centre, PO Box 10, Webb SK S0N 2X0 – 306/674-2287 – Manager, Russell Wall

Weekes: Dunwell & Community Museum, Weekes Recreation Centre, PO Box 120, Weekes SK S0E 1V0 – 306/278-2906

Weyburn: Soo Line Historical Museum, 411 Industrial Lane, PO Box 1016, Weyburn SK S4H 2L2 – 306/842-2922 – Curator/Manager, Lavine Stepp – Old power house

Weyburn: Turner Curling Museum, PO Box 370, Weyburn SK S4H 2K6 – 306/848-3217; Fax: 306/842-2001 – Don Turner – Open Sat. & Sun., 2-5 pm, year round; tours by appt.

White Fox Museum, PO Box 68, White Fox SK S0J 3B0 – 306/276-2170

Whitewood: Chopping Museum, PO Box 118, Whitewood SK S0G 5C0 – 306/735-2255 – Owner/Curator, George C. Chopping

Whitewood Historical Museum, PO Box 752, Whitewood SK S0G 5C0 – 306/735-4388 – Sec.-Treas., Carole Armstrong

Wilkie & District Museum, PO Box 868, Wilkie SK S0K 4W0 – 306/843-2717 – Sec.-Treas., Frances Lowe

Willow Bunch Museum, 8 - 5th St. East, Willow Bunch SK S0H 4K0 – 306/473-2806; Fax: 306/473-2245 – President, Marguerite Campagne; Secretary, Louise Boisvert

Wolseley & District Museum, Wolseley SK S0G 5H0 – Director, Harold Olive

Wood Mountain Rodeo-Ranch Museum, PO Box 53, Wood Mountain SK S0H 4L0 – 306/266-4539 – President, Pat Fitzpatrick; Coordinator, Lois Todd

Wynard & District Museum, PO Box 743, Wynard SK S0A 4T0 – 306/554-2898; Fax: 306/554-3224 – Director, Dave Cross

YUKON

MacBride Museum
1st Ave. & Wood St., PO Box 4037, Whitehorse YT Y1A 3S9
403/667-2709; Fax: 403/633-6607
Museum of cultural & natural history. Yukon heritage from pre-history to present. Natural history, archeological & paleontological specimens; ethnographic artifacts, historic artifacts, photographs & archival materials; large industrial & transportation artifacts. Includes outdoor displays, two heritage buildings, 450 sq. m. of exhibits. Open May 15 to Sept. 15 & by appointment.
Director/Curator, Clifford Evans

Other Museums & Science Centres in Yukon
Dawson City Museum, PO Box 303, Dawson City YT Y0B 1G0 – 403/993-5839 – Acting Director, Daintry Chapple – Klondike era, native history; open June - Labour Day

Dawson City: Klondike National Historic Sites, PO Box 390, Dawson City YT Y0B 1G0 – 403/993-5462; Fax: 403/993-5683 – Supt., A.N. Fisk

Destruction Bay: Kluane Museum of Natural History, Mile 1093, Alaska Hwy., General Delivery, Destruction Bay YT Y0B 1H0 – 403/841-4541 – Manager, Iris Wilson – Wildlife display, native handicrafts; open Victoria Day - Labour Day

Haines Junction: Klukshu National Park, PO Box 5309, Haines Junction YT Y0B 1L0 – 403/634-2251; Fax: 403/634-2686 – Traditional salmon fishing & processing as done by Southern Tutchone people; open mid-May - Sept.

Keno City Mining Museum, General Delivery, Keno City YT Y0B 1J0 – 403/995-2792 summer, 995-3103 winter; Fax: 403/995-2730 – Mike Mancini – Open Victoria Day - Labour Day

Teslin: George Johnston Tingit Indian Museum, Mile 84, Alaska Hwy., PO Box 146, Teslin YT Y0A 1B0 – 403/390-2550; Fax: 403/390-2828 – Manager/Curator, Kelly Boutilier – Open Victoria Day - Labour Day

Whitehorse: Fort Selkirk, c/o Tourism Yukon, Heritage Branch, PO Box 2703, Whitehorse YT Y1A 2C6 – 403/667-5386; Fax: 403/667-3546 – Historic Sites Coordinator, Yukon Heritage Branch, Doug Olynyk – Accessible only by boat or plane; contact Selkirk First Nation, Pelly Crossing, YK Y0B 1P0; 403/537-3331; Fax: 403/537-3902; Attn: Chief Pat Van Bibber; open mid-May - mid-Sept.

Whitehorse: LePage Park, c/o Yukon Historical & Museums Association, PO Box 4357, Whitehorse YT Y1A 3T5 – 403/667-4704; Fax: 403/667-4506 – President, Brent Slobodin – Open year round

Whitehorse: Old Log Church Museum, 3rd Ave. & Elliot St., PO Box 5956, Whitehorse YT Y1A 5L7 – 403/668-2555; Fax: 403/668-2555 – Curator, Clare McDowell – Open May - Labour Day

Whitehorse: Yukon Transportation Museum, PO Box 5867, Whitehorse YT Y1A 5L6 – 403/668-4792; Fax: 403/633-5547; Email: ytranmus@yknet.yk.ca – Curator, Dale Perry; President, Bill Stuart – Transporation displays depicting the first commercial aircraft in the Yukon; construction of the Alaska Highway, the White Pass & Yukon Route Railway; open daily, Victoria Day - mid-Sept.

ART GALLERIES

National Gallery of Canada/Musée des beaux-arts du Canada (NGC/MBAC)
380 Sussex Dr., PO Box 427, Stn A, Ottawa ON K1N 9N4
613/990-1985; Fax: 613/993-4385
URL: http://national.gallery.ca; http://musee.beaux.arts.ca

The permanent collection of the National Gallery comprises paintings, sculpture, prints & drawings, photographs, film & video art from the Canadian, European, American & Asian schools. Special exhibitions as well as permanent installations of the gallery's collections are on display. The gallery also sends its exhibitions on tour across the country & participates in international exhibitions. Services provided to the public include lectures, talks, tours, films, workshops, concerts & a bookstore.

Director, Dr. Shirley Thomson
Deputy Director, Yves Dagenais
Chief Librarian, Murray Waddington
Assistant Director, Exhibitions & Installations, Daniel Amadei
Head, Restoration & Conservation Laboratory, Marian Barclay
Registrar, Delphine Bishop
Curator, Prints & Drawings, Mimi Cazort
Chief, Education, Mary Ellen Herbert
Curator, Canadian Art, Charles Hill
Curator, European Art, Catherine Johnston
Assistant Director, Communications & Marketing, Helen Murphy
Curator, Contemporary Art, Diana Nemiroff
Assistant Director, CCVA, G.V. Shepherd
Chief, Publications, Serge Thériault
Acting Curator, Photographs, Anne Thomas

ALBERTA

The Edmonton Art Gallery (EAG)
2 Sir Winston Churchill Sq., Edmonton AB T5J 2C1
403/422-6223; Fax: 403/426-3105
Collections include: Canadian & international contemporary & historical paintings, sculpture, photography & graphic art. Research fields: western Canadian art, historical & contemporary art; painting; sculpture; photography; graphics. Activities: Guided tours; lectures; films; gallery talks; art rental & sales gallery; studio art classes for children & adults; docent program workshops & seminars; tour exhibitions across Canada. Facilities: 10 exhibition areas; 158-seat auditorium; classrooms; members' lounge. Art books; handicrafts; ceramics, prints & reproductions for sale in gallery shop.

Director, Alf Bogusky
Communications Co-ordinator, John Tuckwell

Other Art Galleries in Alberta
Banff: Walter Phillips Gallery (WPG), PO Box 1020, Banff AB T0L 0C0 – 403/762-6281; Fax: 403/762-6659; URL: http://www.nmr.banffcentre.ab.ca/WPG – Director/Curator, Catherine Crowston – Contemporary, fine & decorative arts; open year round, closed Mondays
Brocket: Oldman River Cultural Centre, PO Box 70, Brocket AB T0K 0H0 – 403/965-3939 – Director, Jo-Ann Yellow Horn – Open year round
Calgary: Illingworth Kerr Gallery, Alberta College of Art, 1407 - 14 Ave. NW, Calgary AB T2N 4R3 – 403/284-7632; Fax: 403/289-6682 – Director/Curator, Ron Moppett – Contemporary exhibitions
Calgary: Mount Royal College Gallery, 4825 Richard Rd. SW, Calgary AB T3E 6K6 – 403/246-6344
Calgary: Muttart Public Art Gallery, 1221 - 2nd St. SW, Calgary AB T2R 0W5 – 403/266-2764; Fax: 403/264-8077 – Director/Curator, Kathryn Burns; Assistant Director, Marilyn L. Horne; President, Board of Directors, Thomas E. Lester
Edmonton: Canadiana Galleries, 12306 Jasper Ave., Edmonton AB T5N 3K5 – 403/482-5471
Edmonton: Front Gallery, 12306 Jasper Ave., Edmonton AB T5N 3K5 – 403/488-2952
Edmonton: Horizon Art Galleries, 10114 - 123 St., Edmonton AB T5N 1N2 – 403/482-2011
Edmonton: West End Gallery, 12308 Jasper Ave., Edmonton AB T5N 3K5 – 403/488-4892
Grande Prairie: Prairie Gallery, 10209 - 99 St., Grande Prairie AB T8V 2H3 – 403/532-8111; Fax: 403/539-1991 – Director/Curator, Elizabeth Ginn
Lethbridge: Southern Alberta Art Gallery (SAAG), 601 - 3 Ave. South, Lethbridge AB T1J 0H4 – 403/327-8770; Fax: 403/328-3913; Email: SAAG@upanet.uleth.ca – Director/Curator, Joan Stebbins
Lethbridge: University of Lethbridge Art Gallery, 4401 University Dr., Lethbridge AB T1K 3M4 – 403/329-2690; Fax: 403/329-2022 – Director, Jeffrey Spalding

BRITISH COLUMBIA

The Vancouver Art Gallery
750 Hornby St., Vancouver BC V6Z 2H7
604/662-4719; Fax: 604/682-1086; Admin. tel.: 604/682-4668
URL: http://www.vanartgallery.bc.ca
Interim Director, Daina Augaitis
Public Relations, Donna Call

Other Art Galleries in British Columbia
Brackendale Art Gallery Theatre Teahouse, PO Box 100, Brackendale BC V0N 1H0 – 604/898-3333 – Director, Michael Malcolm
Burnaby Art Gallery, 6344 Deer Lake Ave., Burnaby BC V5G 2J3 – 604/291-9441; Fax: 604/291-6776; Email: can-bag-bb@immedia.can – Director/Curator, Karen Henry
Burnaby: The Simon Fraser Gallery, AQ 3004, Simon Fraser University, Burnaby BC V5A 1S6 – 604/291-4266; Fax: 604/291-3029 – Director, Dr. E.M. Gibson; Registrar of the Collection, Janet Menzies
Canyon: The Alfoldy Gallery, PO Box 57, Canyon BC V0B 1C0 – 250/428-7473 – Elaine & Andy Alfoldy – Open Wed., Fri. - Sun.; July, Aug. & Sept. open daily
Castlegar: West Kootenay National Exhibition Centre, RR#1, Site 2, Comp. 10, Castlegar BC V1N 3H7 – 250/365-3337; Fax: 250/354-1450 – Director, Myrna Cobb – Exhibits on art, history & science, from international to local sources; open year round, Tues. - Sun.; open Mondays July - Aug.
Dawson Creek Art Gallery, #101, 816 Alaska Ave., Dawson Creek BC V1G 4T6 – 250/782-2601; Fax: 250/782-3352 – Manager, Loris Martin – Open year round
Grand Forks Art Gallery, PO Box 2140, Grand Forks BC V0H 1H0 – 250/442-2211; Fax: 250/442-0099; Email: can-gfag@immedia.ca; URL: http://www.islandnet.com/~bcma/museums/gfag/gfag.html – Director, Richard Reid – Historical & contemporary works by established & emerging regional, national & international artists
Hazelton: Northwestern National Exhibition Centre, PO Box 333, Hazelton BC V0J 1Y0 – 250/842-5723 – Director, Eve Hope – 'Ksan permanent collection of artifacts; art, history displays; open year round
Kamloops Art Gallery Society, 207 Seymour St., Kamloops BC V2C 2E7 – 250/828-3543; Fax: 250/828-0662; Email: can-kag-kl@immedia.ca – Director/Curator, Jann L.M. Bailey
Kaslo: The Artery Gallery of Photography, PO Box 1102, Kaslo BC V0G 1M0 – 250/353-2575
Kaslo: Langham Cultural Centre Galleries, PO Box 1000, Kaslo BC V0G 1M0 – 250/353-2661
Kelowna Art Gallery, 1315 Water St., Kelowna BC V1Y 9P4 – 250/762-2226 – Director, Carolyn Vesely – Historical & contemporary fine art; gift shop; open year round
Maple Ridge Art Gallery Society, 11995 Haney Pl., Maple Ridge BC V2X 6G2 – 604/467-5855 – President, Jo Moncur
Nakusp: Bonnington Arts Centre, 6th Ave. West & 4th St. North, Nakusp BC V0G 1R0 – 250/265-4234; Fax: 250/265-3808 – Open Sept. -Jun.
Nanaimo Art Gallery & Exhibition Centre, c/o Malaspina College, 900 - 5 St., Nanaimo BC V9R 5S5 – 250/755-8790; Fax: 250/755-8725 – Director, Jane Cole
New Westminster: Amelia Douglas Gallery, PO Box 2503, New Westminster BC V3L 5B2 – 604/527-5528 – Representative, Ulrike Ebeling
North Vancouver: Bernadette's Galleries, #103, 1200 Lonsdale Ave., North Vancouver BC V7M 3H6 – 604/980-7216
North Vancouver: Presentation House Gallery, 333 Chesterfield Ave., North Vancouver BC V7M 3G9 – 604/986-1351; Fax: 604/986-5380 – Gallery Director/Curator, Karen Love
North Vancouver: Sharli Galleries, 53 Lonsdale Ave., North Vancouver BC V7M 2E3 – 604/985-1731
Oliver: Vaseaux Lake Galleries, Hwy. 97 North, RR#2, Oliver BC V0H 1T0 – 250/498-3522; Fax: 250/498-3546
Osoyoos Art Gallery, 89 St. & Main, Osoyoos BC V0H 1V0 – 250/495-2800
Penticton: Art Gallery of the South Okanagan, 11 Ellis St., Penticton BC V2A 7X9 – 250/493-2928 – Director, Brenda Fredrick
Port Alberni: Rollin Art Centre, 3061 - 8th Ave., Port Alberni BC V9Y 2K5 – 250/724-3412; Fax: 250/724-3472 – Administrator, Margi Kristensen
Port Moody: Mountain View Gallery, 2720 St. Johns St., Port Moody BC V3H 2B7 – 604/936-3472 – Chief Officer, Noreen De Jong
Prince George Art Gallery, 2820 - 15th Ave., Prince George BC V2M 1T1 – 250/563-6447; Fax: 250/563-3211; Email: pgag@vortex.netbistro.com – Director/Curator, George Harris – Open Tues. - Sun.
Qualicum Beach: The Old School House Gallery & Arts Centre (TOSH), 122 Fern Rd. West, PO Box 1791, Qualicum Beach BC V0R 2T0 – 250/752-6133; Fax: 250/752-2600 – President, Brad Wylie
Smithers Gallery Association & Public Art Gallery, Central Park Bldg., PO Box 122, Smithers BC V0J 2N0 – 250/847-3898, 2996 – President, Marjory Then – Open summer
Surrey Art Gallery, Surrey Arts Centre, 13750 - 88 Ave., Surrey BC V3W 3L1 – 250/501-5566; Fax: 250/501-5581; Email: artgallery@city.surrey.bc.ca; http://www.surreyartgallery.com – Curator, Exhibitions, Liane Davison; Curator, Visual Arts Programs, Ingrid Kolt – Promotes contemporary BC & Canadian artists; exhibitions & public programs encourage community appreciation of contemporary visual art; open year round
Vancouver: Butler Galleries, 341 Pender St. West, Vancouver BC V6B 1T3 – 604/681-6537
Vancouver: Charles H. Scott Gallery, Emily Carr College of Art & Design, 1399 Johnston St., Granville Island, Vancouver BC V6H 3R9 – 604/844-3809; Fax: 604/844-3801 – Curator, Greg Bellerby
Vancouver: Circle Craft Gallery, #1, 1666 Johnston St., Vancouver BC V6H 3S2 – 604/669-8021; Fax: 604/669-8585 – Contact, Helen Wennerstrom
Vancouver: Contemporary Art Gallery, 555 Hamilton St., Vancouver BC V6B 2R1 – 604/681-2700; Fax: 604/681-2710 – Director/Curator, Keith Wallace
Vancouver: Exposure Gallery, 851 Beatty St., Vancouver BC V6B 2M6 – 604/688-6853
Vancouver: Gallery Gachet, 88 East Cordova St., Vancouver BC V6A 1K2 – 604/687-2468; Fax: 604/687-1196; Email: gachet@cafe.net; URL: http://www.info-mine.com/gachet – General Manager, Mary Ann Anderson; Promotions Director, April Porter
Vancouver: Gallery of BC Ceramics, 1359 Cartwright St., Vancouver BC V6H 3R7 – 604/669-5645; Fax: 604/669-5627
Vancouver: grunt gallery, 209 East 6th Ave., Vancouver BC V5T 1J7 – 604/875-9516 – Director, Glenn Alteen
Vancouver: Heffel Gallery Limited, 2247 Granville St., Vancouver BC V6H 3G1 – 604/732-6505; Fax: 604/732-4245
Vancouver: Marion Scott Gallery, 481 Howe St., Vancouver BC V6C 2X6 – 604/685-1934; Fax: 604/685-1890 – Director, Judy Kardosh
Vancouver: Morris & Helen Belkin Art Gallery, 1825 Main Mall, Vancouver BC V6T 1Z2 – 604/822-2759; Fax: 604/822-6689; URL: http://edziza.arts.ubc.ca/finearts/gallery.html – Director/Curator, Scott Watson; Program Coordinator, Mary Williams
Vancouver: Raymond Chow Art Gallery, 770 Pacific Blvd. South, Vancouver BC V6B 5E7 – 604/681-7930
Vancouver: Sidney & Gertrude Zack Gallery, 950 West 41st Ave., Vancouver BC V5Z 2N7 – 604/257-5111; Fax: 604/257-5121 – Cultural/Arts Coordinator, Jeannie Kamins
Vancouver: Terra Cotta Gallery, 3610 - 4th Ave. West, Vancouver BC V6R 1P1 – 604/733-9181
Vancouver: Wickaninnish Gallery, #14, 1166 Johnston Rd., Vancouver BC V6H 3S2 – 604/681-1057
Vernon Public Art Gallery (VPAG), 3228 - 31st Ave., Vernon BC V1T 2H3 – 250/545-3173; Fax: 250/545-9096 – Director, Susan Brandoli – Community programming; local, regional, national & international exhibitions; gift shop; art & video rentals; group tours
Victoria: Art Gallery of Greater Victoria (AGGV), 1040 Moss St., Victoria BC V8V 4P1 – 250/384-4101; Fax: 250/361-3995 – Director, Patricia E. Bovey – Canadiana 1860 to present; permanent exhibition of work of Emily Carr
Victoria: Maltwood Art Museum & Gallery (MAMAG), PO Box 3025, Victoria BC V8W 3P2 – 250/721-8298; Fax: 250/721-8997; Email: msegger@uvic.ca; URL: http://kafka.uvic.ca/~maltwood – Director, Martin Segger
Victoria: Open Space, 510 Fort St., Victoria BC V8W 1E6 – 250/383-8833; Email: openarc@islandnet.com – Director, Sue Donaldson
Wells: Island Mountain Gallery, PO Box 65, Wells BC V0K 2R0 – 250/994-3466; 1-800-442-2787 – Executive Director, Dorothea Funk; Treasurer, Marilyn Rummel

West Vancouver: Ferry Building Gallery, 1414 Argyle Ave., West Vancouver BC V7T 1C2 – 604/925-7290; Fax: 604/925-5913

White Rock: Arnold Mikelson Mind & Matter Gallery, 13743 -16 Ave., White Rock BC V4A 1P7 – 604/536-6460; Fax: 604/536-7117 – Mary Mikelson

Williams Lake: Image Gallery, #3, 85 South 3rd Ave., Williams Lake BC V2G 1J1 – 250/392-6360; Fax: 250/392-6188; Toll Free: 1-800-661-5520

Williams Lake: Stationhouse Gallery, BC Rail Station, 1 North Mackenzie Ave., Williams Lake BC V2G 1N4 – 250/392-6113 – Open year round

MANITOBA

The Winnipeg Art Gallery/Le beaux art de Winnipeg (WAG)
300 Memorial Blvd., Winnipeg MB R3C 1V1
204/786-6641; Fax: 204/788-4998; 204/775-7297 (24hr.)
URL: http://www.umanitoba.ca/schools/art/gallery/hpgs/wag/
Founded in 1912 & opened in its present location in 1971. A permanent collection of almost 20,000 works of art with emphasis on Canadian & Manitoba artists. Also includes traditional & contemporary decorative arts, photography & European art. Highlights include the largest collection of contemporary Inuit art in the world, & the Gort Collection or Northern Gothic & late Renaissance paintings & altar panels. Facilities: 120,000 sq. ft. building with 9 major galleries; 25,000 sq. ft. rooftop sculpture garden; 325 seat Muriel Richardson Auditorium; 8,000 sq. ft. rooftop restaurant; 12,000 sq. ft. studio bldg.; gift shop, art rental & sales; lecture & seminar rooms; Clara Lander Library (24,000 volumes, 100 subscriptions, 10,000 artist biographies, 20,000 slides, misc. archives).
Director, Michel V. Cheff
Deputy Director & Head of Curatorial, Kate Davis
Associate Director, Education & Public Programs, Claudette Lagimodière
Finance & Administration Manager, Judy Murphy
Marketing & Communications Manager, Chris Brown

Other Art Galleries in Manitoba
Brandon: The Art Gallery of Southwestern Manitoba, 638 Princess Ave., Brandon MB R7A 0P3 – 204/727-1036 – Director/Curator, Glenn Allison; Art Educator, Linda Carreiro; Gallery Assistant/Technician, Lei Anne Sharratt – Approximately 32 exhibitions a year; open year round

Leaf Rapids National Exhibition Centre, PO Box 220, Leaf Rapids MB R0B 1W0 – 204/473-8682 – Director, Denise Desjarlais

Portage & District Arts Council (PDAC), 160 Saskatchewan Ave. West, Portage la Prairie MB R1N 0M1 – 204/239-6029; Fax: 204/239-1472; Email: pdac@portage.net – Executive Director, Eveline Mauws – Tues. - Sat., 11 am - 5 pm; new gallery exhibition each month; gift shop

Winnipeg: Ace Art Inc., 290 McDermot Ave., Winnipeg MB R3B 2A2 – 204/944-9763

Winnipeg: Centre culturel franco-manitobain (CCFM), 340, boul Provencher, Winnipeg MB R2H 0G7 – 204/233-8972; Fax: 204/233-3324 – Directeur, Alain Boucher

Winnipeg: The Floating Gallery, #218, 100 Arthur St., Winnipeg MB R3B 1H3 – 204/942-8183

Winnipeg: Gallery 1.1.1., 211 FitzGerald Bldg., School of Art, University of Manitoba, Winnipeg MB R3T 2N2 – 204/474-9322; Fax: 204/275-3148; URL: http://www.umanitoba.ca/schools/art/info/gallery.html – Gallery Director, Prof. Dale Amundson, Email: amundsn@bldgumsu.lan1.umanitoba.ca; Gallery Assistant, Donalda Johnson, Email: djohnso@bldgumsu.lan1.umanitoba.ca

Winnipeg: Site Gallery, 250 McDermot Ave., 2nd Fl., Winnipeg MB R3B 0S5 – 204/942-1618 – President, Don Reichert – T-D, 11 am - 4 pm; R, 11 am - 8 pm & by appt.

Winnipeg: Upstairs Gallery, 266 Edmonton St., Winnipeg MB R3C 1R9 – 204/943-2734; Fax: 204/949-0793 – Director, Faye Settler

NEW BRUNSWICK

Owens Art Gallery
c/o Mount Allison University, York St., Sackville NB E0A 3C0
506/364-2574; Fax: 506/364-2575; Email: gkelly@mta.ca
Permanent collection of over 2500 works, dating from the 18th century; 30 exhibitions yearly.
Director, Gemey Kelly

Other Art Galleries in New Brunswick
Edmundston: Gallerie Colline, 165, boul Hébert, Edmundston NB E3V 2S8 – 506/737-5050 – Président, Jacques Martin

Florenceville: Andrew & Laura McCain Gallery, PO Box 270, Florenceville NB E0J 1K0 – 506/392-5249; Fax: 506/392-6143 – Exhibition Coordinator, Bernice Beaulieu

Fredericton: Beaverbrook Art Gallery/La galerie d'art Beaverbrook, 703 Queen St., PO Box 605, Fredericton NB E3B 5A6 – 506/458-8545, 8546; Fax: 506/459-7450; Email: bag@nbnet.nb.ca – Director, Ian G. Lumsden

Fredericton: Gallery Connexion, PO Box 696, Fredericton NB E3B 5B4 – 506/454-1433; Fax: 506/454-1401; Email: connex@nbnet.nb.ca – Coordinator, Sarah Maloney

Fredericton: National Exhibition Centre, John Thurston Clark Memorial Building, 503 Queen St., Fredericton NB E3B 5H1 – 506/453-3747; Fax: 506/459-0481; Email: cynthiaw@gov.nb.ca – Exhibits Director, Cynthia Wallace-Casey

Fredericton: UNB Art Centre, Memorial Hall, University of New Brunswick, PO Box 4400, Fredericton NB E3B 5A3 – 506/453-4623; Fax: 506/453-4599; Email: mem@unb.ca – Director, Marie Maltais

Moncton: Atelier IMAGO, 140 Botsford St., Moncton NB E1C 4X5 – 506/388-1431

Moncton: Galerie d'art de L'Université de Moncton (GAUM), Édifice Clément-Cormier, Université de Moncton, Moncton NB E1A 3E9 – 506/858-4088; Fax: 506/858-4043; Email: charetl@umoncton.ca; URL: http://www.umoncton.ca/gaum/hp_luc8.html – Directeur-conservateur, Luc A. Charette

Moncton: Galerie Sans Nom Coop Ltée, #16, 140 Botsford St., Moncton NB E1C 4X4 – 506/854-5381; Fax: 506/857-2064

Moncton: Mini Galerie/Radio Canada, 250 Archibald St., Moncton NB E1C 5K3 – 506/853-6790

Saint John: City of Saint John Gallery, Aitken Bicentennial Exhibition Centre, 20 Hazen Ave., Saint John NB E2L 3G8 – 506/633-4870

St. Andrews: Sunbury Shores Arts & Nature Centre, 139 Water St., PO Box 100, St. Andrews NB E0G 2X0 – 506/529-3386 – Director, Ray Peterson

St. Stephen: St. Croix Library Gallery, 1 Budd Ave., St. Stephen NB E3L 1E8 – 506/466-4781

NEWFOUNDLAND

Art Gallery of Newfoundland & Labrador
Arts and Cultural Centre, Memorial University of Newfoundland, PO Box 4200, St. John's NF A1C 5S7
709/737-8210; Fax: 709/737-2007; Email: agnl@morgan.ucs.mun.ca; Info Line: 709/737-8209
URL: http://www.ucs.mun.ca/~agnl/
Regularly changing exhibitions of all media, chiefly contemporary Canadian, with some international, historic Canadian & Newfoundland folk art & traditional crafts; permanent collection of contemporary Canadian art in many media, with strong holdings of Newfoundland work; art slide library. Extensive public programming & special projects with emphasis on collaboration with professional artists & performers; education activities; travelling exhibitions organized & circulated nationally & through APAGA; open year round.
Director, Patricia Grattan

Other Art Galleries in Newfoundland
Corner Brook: Sir Wilfred Grenfell College Art Gallery (SWGC), Memorial University of Newfoundland, Corner Brook NF A2H 6P9 – 709/637-6357; Fax: 709/637-6383; Email: coneill@beothuk.swgc.mun.ca; URL: http://www.swgc.mun.ca – Director/Curator, Colleen O'Neill

Grand Falls-Windsor: Central Newfoundland Visual Arts Society, PO Box 898, Grand Falls-Windsor NF A2A 2P7 – President, Alice Dicks

St. John's: Eastern Edge Art Gallery, PO Box 2641, Stn C, St. John's NF A1C 6K1 – 709/739-1882; Fax: 709/579-1636 – Bonnie Leyton

NOVA SCOTIA

Art Gallery of Nova Scotia (AGNS)
1741 Hollis St., PO Box 2262, Halifax NS B3J 3C8
902/424-7542; Fax: 902/424-7359
Housed in 1868 heritage building.
Director, Bernard Riordon

Other Art Galleries in Nova Scotia
Cheticamp: Galerie Elizabeth LeFort, La Société St-Pierre, Les Trois Pignons, CP 430, Cheticamp NS B0E 1H0 – 902/224-2642; Fax: 902/224-1579 – Directrice, Sandra LeFort – Les tapisseries du Dr. Elizabeth LeFort ainsi que d'autres tapis historiques de la région

Halifax: Anna Leonowens Gallery, Nova Scotia College of Art & Design, 5163 Duke St., Halifax NS B3J 3J6 – 902/494-8184; Fax: 902/425-3997; Email: jessica@nscad.ns.ca – Administrative Director, Jessica Kerrin

Halifax: The Art Gallery, Mount Saint Vincent University, Seton Academic Centre, Mount Saint Vincent University, Halifax NS B3M 2J6 – 902/457-6160; Fax: 902/445-3960; Email: ingrid.jenkner@msvu.ca – Director, Ingrid Jenkner – Open daily except Mondays; exhibition program emphasizes women as cultural subjects & producers

Halifax: Centre for Art Tapes, c/o Alexandra Community Centre, 2156 Brunswick St., Halifax NS B3K 2Y8 – 902/429-7299 – Managing Director, Fran Shuebrook-Gallagher

Halifax: Dalhousie Art Gallery (DAG), 6101 University Ave., Halifax NS B3H 3J5 – 902/424-2403; Fax: 902/494-2890 – Director, Mern O'Brien – Open year round

Halifax: Eye Level Gallery, 1672 Barrington St., Halifax NS B3J 2A2 – 902/425-6412; Fax: 902/425-6412; Email: ak593@ccn.cs.dal.ca – Gallery Coordinator, Moritz Gaede

Halifax: Nova Scotia Centre for Craft & Design (NSCCD), J.W. Johston Bldg., 1683 Barrington St., Halifax NS B3J 1Z9 – 902/424-4062; Fax: 902/424-0670; Email: hlfxjohn.coms.tylercd@gov.ns.ca – Head, C.D. Tyler – Open year round

Canadian Almanac & Directory 1997

Halifax: Nova Scotia Photo Gallery Co-op, 2182 Gottingen St., Halifax NS B3K 3B4 – 902/429-8348 – Open year round

Halifax: Saint Mary's University Art Gallery, Saint Mary's University, Halifax NS B3H 3C3 – 902/420-5445, ext.5444 – Director/Curator, J.R. Leighton Davis

Halifax: Seniors' Art Gallery, c/o Senior Citizen's Secretariat, World Trade & Convention Centre, 1800 Argyle St., Halifax NS B3J 2Z1

Lunenburg Art Gallery, 19 Pelham St., PO Box 1418, Lunenburg NS B0J 2C0 – 902/634-3305 – President, Ann Hebb – Meldrum collection by the late Earl Bailly; open year round

Pictou: Hector National Exhibit Centre, PO Box 1210, Pictou NS B0K 1H0 – 902/485-4563 – Administrator, Caroline Fraser

Sydney: University College of Cape Breton Art Gallery, PO Box 5300, Sydney NS B1P 6L2 – 902/539-5300, ext.311 – Director, Barry Gabriel

Wolfville: Acadia University Art Gallery, Wolfville NS B0P 1X0 – 902/542-2201, ext.1373; Fax: 902/542-4727; Email: fran.kruschen@acadiau.ca – Director, Franziska Kruschen – Open year round

ONTARIO

Art Gallery of Hamilton (AGH)
123 King St. West, Hamilton ON L8P 4S8
905/527-6610; Fax: 905/577-6940
Director, Ted Pietrzak

Art Gallery of Ontario
317 Dundas St. West, Toronto ON M5T 1G4
416/979-6648; Fax: 416/204-2713
URL: http://www.AGO.on.ca
One of the largest art museums in North America, with 50 new & renovated galleries. Collection of more than 16,000 works, from 15th-century European to contemporary, reflects 600 years of creativity; more than half of the collection comprises Canadian & Inuit art. The Gallery's Henry Moore Sculpture Centre contains the world's largest public collection of Moore's work. Other services include the Anne Tannenbaum Gallery School, the Edward P. Taylor Audio-Visual Centre, Reference Library & Archives, the Marvin Gelber Print & Drawing Study Centre, the Dr. Mariano Elia Hands-On Centre, the Gallery Shop, restaurant & café. A visit to The Grange, an historic home restored to the 1830s, is included with admission.
Director, Dr. Maxwell Anderson

Art Gallery of Windsor
3100 Howard Ave., Windsor ON N8X 3Y8
519/969-4494; Fax: 519/969-3732
One of the larger, non-government run galleries in Ontario; focus is on Canadian art in an international context; permanent collection of 2,500 paintings & sculptures; resource centre & gift shop; closed Mondays.
Director, Nataley Nagy
Curator, Contemporary Art, Helga Pakasaar
Curator, Historical Art, Robert McKaskell
Curator, Education, Christine Goodchild

The McMichael Canadian Art Collection
10365 Islington Ave., Kleinburg ON L0J 1C0
905/893-1121; Fax: 905/893-2588; Email: info@mcmichael.com
URL: http://www.mcmichael.com
The collection features works of art created by First Nations & Inuit artists, the artists of the Group of Seven & their contemporaries, & other artists who have contributed to the development of Canadian art. Comprehensive education program at kindergarten, elementary & secondary school levels; guided group tours by appointment; extension program & temporary exhibition program. Also programs for adults & special interest groups.
Executive Director/CEO, Barbara A. Tyler
Chief Curator, Jean Blodgett
Chairman, Board of Trustees, G. Joan Goldfarb
Manager, Marketing, Neil Beaudry
Director, Marketing & Visitor Services, Vicki Lymburner
Librarian/Archivist, Linda Morita

Other Art Galleries in Ontario

Bancroft: The Art Gallery of Bancroft, PO Box 1360, Bancroft ON K0L 1C0 – 613/332-1542; Fax: 613/332-2119; Email: aac@wownet.kosone.com – Director, Heather Rennie; Asst. Director, John Keith; Curator, David Paulsen – Local & other Ontario artists; gift shop for area artists only; open year round

Barrie: MacLaren Art Centre, 147 Toronto St., Barrie ON L4N 1V3 – 705/721-9696 – Open year round

Bolton: Yaneff Gallery, 12295 Hwy. 50, Bolton ON L7E 1M2 – 905/951-3535; Fax: 905/951-3537

Bracebridge: Chapel Gallery, c/o Muskoka Arts & Crafts Inc., 15 King St., PO Box 376, Bracebridge ON P1L 1T7 – 705/645-5501; Fax: 705/645-0385 – Curator, Elene J. Freer – Open Tues. - Sat.

Bracebridge: Ziska Gallery - Muskoka, Ziska Rd., RR#1, Bracebridge ON P1L 1W8 – 705/645-2587 – Curator, Anne MacCallum; Curator, Jack MacCallum

Brampton: Art Gallery of Peel, 9 Wellington St. East, Brampton ON L6W 1Y1 – 905/454-5441 – Curator, David Somers

Brantford: Glenhyrst Art Gallery of Brant, 20 Ava Rd., Brantford ON N3T 5G9 – 519/756-5932; Fax: 519/756-5910 – Gallery Director, Stephen Robinson

Buckhorn: The Gallery On the Lake ... Buckhorn, Hwy. #36, PO Box 10, Buckhorn ON K0L 1J0 – 705/657-3296; Fax: 705/657-8766 – President & CEO, Edwin H. Matthews; Vice-President, Barbara J. Matthews – Largest privately owned gallery in Canada; open daily, 9 am - 5 pm, year round

Burlington Art Centre (BAC), 1333 Lakeshore Rd., Burlington ON L7S 1A9 – 905/632-7796; Fax: 905/632-0278; Email: infobac@burlingtonart-centre.on.ca; URL: http://www.burlingtonart-centre.on.ca – Executive Director, Ian D. Ross; Curator of Collection, Jonathan Smith; Associate Curator, Theresa Morin; Curator of Programs, George Wale

Cambridge: The Library & Gallery, 20 Grand Ave. North, Cambridge ON N1S 2K6 – 519/621-0460 – Gallery Director, Mary Misner

Chatham: Thames Art Gallery, Chatham Cultural Centre, 75 William St. North, Chatham ON N7M 4L4 – 519/354-8338; Fax: 519/436-3237 – Curator, Leonard A. Jubenville

Cobourg: Art Gallery of Northumberland, 55 King St. West, Cobourg ON K9A 2M2 – 416/372-0333; Fax: 416/372-1587 – Director/Curator, Heather Ardies

Cornwall Regional Art Gallery/Galerie régionale des arts de Cornwall (CRAG), 164 Pitt St., PO Box 1822, Cornwall ON K6H 6N6 – 613/938-7387; Fax: 613/937-3399 – Executive Director, Sylvie Lizotte

Curve Lake: Whetung Craft Centre & Art Gallery, Curve Lake ON K0L 1R0 – 705/657-3661; Fax: 705/657-3412 – Owner, Michael Whetung – Open year round

Durham Art Gallery, PO Box 1021, Durham ON N0G 1R0 – 519/369-3692 – Director, Bear Epp

Etobicoke: The Art Gallery, Neilson Park Creative Centre, 56 Neilson Dr., Etobicoke ON M9C 1V7 – 416/622-5294

Grimsby Public Art Gallery, 25 Adelaide St., Grimsby ON L3M 1X2 – 905/945-3246 – Director, Mary A. Rashleigh

Guelph: Macdonald Stewart Art Centre (MSAC), 358 Gordon St., Guelph ON N1G 1Y1 – 519/837-0010; Fax: 519/767-2661 – Curator, Nancy Campbell, Email: Ngcampbe@uoguelph.ca; Director, Judith Nasby, Email: Jnasby@uoguelph.ca

Haileybury: Temiskaming Art Gallery, 545 Lakeshore Rd., PO Box 1090, Haileybury ON P0J 1K0 – 705/672-3707 – Director/Curator, Karen Davidson

Haliburton: Rails' End Gallery, PO Box 912, Haliburton ON K0M 1S0 – 705/457-2330 – Open year round

Hamilton Place Gallery, PO Box 2080, Stn A, Hamilton ON L8N 3Y7 – 905/525-3100

Kingston: Agnes Etherington Art Centre/Centre d'art Agnes Etherington (AEAC), Queen's University, Kingston ON K7L 3N6 – 613/545-2190; Fax: 613/545-6765; Email: agnes@post.queensu.ca; URL: http://www.queensu.ca/ageth/ – Director, David McTavish – Contemporary & historical art exhibitions; open year round

Kingston: Edward Day Gallery, 253 Ontario St., Kingston ON K7L 2Z4 – 613/547-0774; Fax: 613/547-2757

Kingston: St. Lawrence College Art Gallery, Portsmouth Ave., Kingston ON K7L 5A6 – Director, D. Gordon

Kitchener: Canadian Clay & Glass Gallery, 25 Caroline St. North, Kitchener ON N2L 2Y5 – 519/746-1882 – Director, Suzanne E. Greening

Kitchener: Homer Watson House & Gallery, 1754 Old Mill Rd., Kitchener ON N2P 1H7 – 519/748-4377 – Curator, Gretchen McCulloch – Open Apr. - Dec.

Kitchener-Waterloo Art Gallery (KWAG), 101 Queen St. North, Kitchener ON N2H 6P7 – 519/579-5860; Fax: 519/578-0740 – Director, Brad Blain – Open year round

Lakefield: Village House Gallery Inc., 60 Queen St., Lakefield ON K0L 2H0 – 705/652-6363 – Open Apr. - Aug. & Oct. - Dec.

Leamington Regional Art Gallery, 11 Queen's Ave., PO Box 148, Leamington ON N8H 3W1 – 519/326-3634 – Open year round

Lindsay: The Lindsay Gallery, 8 Victoria Ave. North, Lindsay ON K9V 4E5 – 705/324-1780 – Director, Rodney Malham

London: Gibson Gallery, 181 King St., London ON N6A 1C9 – 519/439-0451

London: McIntosh Gallery, University of Western Ontario, London ON N6A 3K7 – 519/661-3181; Fax: 519/661-3059; Email: mciamk@uwoadmin.uwo.ca – Director, Arlene Kennedy

Minden: Agnes Jamieson Gallery, PO Box 648, Minden ON K0M 2K0 – 705/286-3763 – Administrator, Alice Don

Mississauga: Art Gallery of Mississauga, 300 City Centre Dr., Mississauga ON L5B 3C9 – 905/896-5088

Mississauga: Blackwood Gallery, Erindale College, University of Toronto, Mississauga ON L5L 1C6 – 905/828-3789; Fax: 905/828-5474; Email: nhazelgrove@credit.erin.utoronto.ca – Curator, Nancy Hazelgrove; Administrator, Maryann Wells

Mississauga: The Gallery, 1900 Dundas St. West, Mississauga ON L5K 1P9 – 905/823-7323

Mississauga: Harbour Gallery, 1697 Lakeshore Rd. West, Mississauga ON L5J 1J4 – 905/822-5495; Fax: 905/822-5578 – Director, Jacqueline Bryant; Assistant Director, Indira Roy Choudhury

Mississauga: Springbank Visual Arts Centre, c/o Mississauga Visual Arts, 3057 Mississauga Rd. North, Mississauga ON L5L 1C8 – 905/828-9151 – President, Norm Reid

Morrow: Olga Korper Gallery, 17 Morrow Ave., Morrow ON M6R 2H9 – 416/538-8220

Niagara Falls Art Gallery, Kurelek Collection, 8058 Oakwood Dr., RR#2, Niagara Falls ON L2E 6S5 – 905/356-1514 – Director/Curator, Brian Smylski

ART GALLERIES — ONTARIO

Niagara on the Lake: Samuel E. Weir Collection & Library of Art, RR#1, Niagara on the Lake ON L0S 1J0 – 905/262-4510; Fax: 905/262-4477 – Curator, Shiava Alwis – Open Victoria Day - Thanksgiving

North Bay: White Water Gallery, 226 Main St. West, PO Box 1491, North Bay ON P1B 8K6 – 705/476-2444 – Director, Martin Karch-Ackerman; Director, Michele Karch-Ackerman

North Bay: W.K.P. Kennedy Gallery of the North Bay Arts Centre, 150 Main St. East, PO Box 911, North Bay ON P1B 8K1 – 705/474-1944; Fax: 705/474-8431 – Director/Curator, Dennis Geden

North York: Art Gallery of North York, Ford Centre for the Performing Arts, 5040 Yonge St., North York ON M2N 6R8 – 416/395-0067

North York: Art Gallery of York University (AGYU), Ross Bldg. N145, 4700 Keele St., North York ON M3J 1P3 – 416/736-5169; Fax: 416/736-5985; Email: AGYU@yorku.ca; URL: http://www.yorku.ca/admin/agyu – Director/Curator, Loretta Yarlow

North York: Glendon Gallery, Glendon College, York University, 2275 Bayview Ave., North York ON M4N 3M6 – 416/487-6721 – Director/Curator, Sylviane de Roquebrune

North York: Knight Galleries International, 476 Bedford Park Ave., North York ON M5M 1K1 – 416/781-9940; Fax: 416/787-7750

North York: Koffler Gallery, 4588 Bathurst St., North York ON M2R 1W6 – 416/636-2145; Fax: 416/636-1536 – Director, Jane Mahuth

Oakville Galleries, Gairloch Gallery, 1306 Lakeshore Rd. East, Oakville ON L6L 1G2 – 905/844-4402 – Director, Steven Pozel
 Centennial Gallery, 120 Navy St., Oakville ON L6J 2Z4

Ohsweken: Two Turtle Iroquois Fine Art Gallery, RR#1, Ohsweken ON N0A 1M0 – 519/751-2774; Email: twoturtl@wchat.on.ca; URL: http://wchat.on.ca/tom/2turtle.htm

Orton: Burdette Gallery Ltd., RR#2, Orton ON L0N 1N0 – 519/928-5547 – Open year round

Oshawa: The Robert McLaughlin Gallery, Civic Centre, Oshawa ON L1H 3Z3 – 905/576-3000; Fax: 905/576-9774 – Director, Joan Murray

Ottawa: Artists' Centre d'Artistes Ottawa Inc., (Gallery 101), 319 Lisgar St., Ottawa ON K2P 0E1 – 613/230-2799 – Managing Director, Diane Shantz

Ottawa: The Canadian Wildlife & Wilderness Art Museum/Musée canadien d'art naturaliste (CWWAM), 150 MacLaren St., Ottawa ON K2P 0C2 – 613/237-1581 – Director, Gary Slimon

Ottawa: Carleton University Art Gallery, Carleton University, St. Patrick's Bldg., Ottawa ON K1S 5B6 – 613/788-2120; Fax: 613/788-4409

Ottawa: Galerie SAW Video, 67 Nicholas St., Ottawa ON K1N 7B9 – 613/236-6181; Fax: 613/564-4428; Video: 613/238-7648 – Garry Mainprize

Ottawa: Gallery 101 Centre d'Artistes, An Artist-Run Centre for Contemporary Visual Art, 319 Lisgar St., Ottawa ON K2P 0E1 – 613/230-2799; Fax: 613/230-3253; Email: oneooone@web.net – Artistic Director, Tim Dallett; Managing Director, Kevin Aaron Gibbs

Ottawa: Heritage Ottawa Gallery, PO Box 510, Stn B, Ottawa ON K1P 5P6 – 613/745-0551 – President, Marc Denhez

Owen Sound: Tom Thomson Memorial Art Gallery, 840 - 1 Ave. West, Owen Sound ON N4K 4K4 – 519/376-1932; Fax: 519/376-3037; Email: tthomson@log.on.ca – Director, Brian Meehan

Peterborough: Art Gallery of Peterborough, 2 Crescent St., Peterborough ON K9J 2G1 – 705/743-9179; Fax: 705/743-8168 – Director, Illi-Maria Tamplin

Peterborough: Artspace Strike 3 Gallery, 129A Hunter St. West, PO Box 1748, Peterborough ON K9J 7X6 – 705/748-3883; Fax: 705/748-3224 – Artistic Director, Andrea Fatona

Peterborough: Hunter West Gallery, 131 Hunter St. West, Peterborough ON K9H 2K7 – 705/876-9623

Peterborough: The Russell Gallery of Fine Art, 138 Simcoe St., Peterborough ON K9H 2H5 – 705/743-0151; Fax: 705/743-8010 – Bruce Rapp; Sally Rapp

Sarnia: Gallery Lambton, 124 South Christina St., Sarnia ON N7T 2M6 – 519/337-3291 – Director, Howard Ford

Sault Ste. Marie: The Art Gallery of Algoma, 10 East St., Sault Ste. Marie ON P6A 3C3 – 705/949-9067; Fax: 705/949-6261 – Director, Michael Burtch

Simcoe: Lynnwood Arts Centre, 21 Lynnwood Ave., PO Box 67, Simcoe ON N3Y 4K8 – 519/428-0540; Fax: 519/428-0787 – Director, Susan J. Lowery

St Catharines: Rodman Hall Arts Centre, 109 St. Paul Cres., St Catharines ON L2S 1M3 – 905/684-2925; Fax: 905/682-4733 – Director, David Aurandt

St. Thomas: Art Gallery St. Thomas-Elgin, 301 Talbot St., St. Thomas ON N5P 1B5 – 519/631-4040; Fax: 519/631-4040 – Executive Director, Rick Nixon; Administrator, Diane Dobson

Stouffville: The Latcham Gallery, 6240 Main St., Stouffville ON L4A 1E2 – 905/640-2395 – Art Director, D. Vanessa Perry

Stratford: The Gallery/Stratford, 54 Romeo St., Stratford ON N5A 4S9 – 519/271-5271 – Director, Robert Freeman

Thunder Bay Art Gallery, 1080 Keewatin St., PO Box 1193, Stn F, Thunder Bay ON P7C 4X9 – 807/577-6427; Fax: 807/577-3781 – Director, Sharon Godwin; Curator, Janet Clark

Toronto: A Space, 183 Bathurst St., Toronto ON M5T 2R7 – 416/504-3227 – Coordinator, Michael Banger

Toronto: Annex Art Centre Gallery, 1073 Bathurst St., Toronto ON M5R 3G8 – 416/516-0110

Toronto: Art at 80, #313, 80 Spadina Ave., Toronto ON M5V 2J3 – 416/366-3690; Fax: 416/348-9058

Toronto: Art Metropole, 788 King St. West, Toronto ON M5V 1N6 – 416/703-4400; Fax: 416/703-4404; Email: ART_Metropole@intacc.web.net – Director, Stella Kyriakakis; President, A.A. Bronson; Manager, Bookstore, Ann Dean

Toronto: Artia Russian Fine Art, 620 Richmond St. West, Toronto ON M5V 1Y9 – 416/703-1255

Toronto: Bau-Xi Gallery, 340 Dundas St. West, Toronto ON M5T 1G5 – 416/977-0600

Toronto: Burdett-Coutts Gallery, 61 Adelaide St. East, Toronto ON M5C 2K5 – 416/361-9901

Toronto: Christopher Cutts Gallery, #204, 23 Morrow Ave., Toronto ON M6R 2H9 – 416/532-5566

Toronto: Cold City Gallery, 686 Richmond St. West, Toronto ON M6J 1C3 – 416/504-6681

Toronto: Costin & Klintworth, 80 Spadina Ave., 4th Fl., Toronto ON M5V 2J4 – 416/504-7800

Toronto: Cygnet Gallery, 80 Scollard St., Toronto ON M5R 1G2 – 416/923-5695

Toronto: Drabinsky Gallery, 86 Scollard St., Toronto ON M5R 1G2 – 416/324-5766

Toronto: Galerie Dresdnere, 12 Hazelton Ave., Toronto ON M5R 2E2 – 416/923-4662

Toronto: Gallery 44, Centre for Contemporary Photography, 183 Bathurst St., 1st Fl., Toronto ON M5T 2R7 – 416/504-5187

Toronto: Gallery 7, 33 Hazelton Ave., Toronto ON M5R 2E3 – 416/968-6247; Fax: 416/968-7231

Toronto: Gallery Gabor Ltd., 587 Markham St., Toronto ON M6G 2L7 – 416/534-1839

Toronto: Gallery Louise Smith, 33 Prince Arthur Ave., Toronto ON M5R 1B2 – 416/924-1096; Fax: 416/924-3918

Toronto: Gallery Moos Ltd., 622 Richmond St. West, Toronto ON M5V 1Y9 – 416/504-5445; Fax: 416/504-5446

Toronto: Gallery One, 121 Scollard St., Toronto ON M5R 1G4 – 416/929-3103

Toronto: Gallery Phillip, 939 Lawrence Ave. East, Toronto ON M3C 1P8 – 416/447-1301

Toronto: Gallery Sheila Roth, 276 Avenue Rd., Toronto ON M4V 2G7 – 416/920-0112

Toronto: Gallery TPW, #310, 80 Spadina Ave., Toronto ON M5V 2J4 – 416/504-4242

Toronto: Garnet Press, 580 Richmond St. West, Toronto ON M5V 1Y9 – 416/504-5012

Toronto: Group of Ten Artists Gallery, Queen's Quay Terminal, 207 Queen's Quay West, 2nd Level, Toronto ON M5J 1A7 – 416/203-6940

Toronto: The Isaacs/Innuit Gallery, 9 Prince Arthur Ave., Toronto ON M5R 1B2 – 416/921-9985

Toronto: Jane Corkin Gallery, 179 John St., Toronto ON M5T 1X4 – 416/979-1980

Toronto: John B. Aird Gallery, MacDonald Block, 900 Bay St., Main Fl., Toronto ON M7A 1Y5 – 416/928-6772

Toronto: Joseph D. Carrier Art Gallery, 901 Lawrence Ave. West, Toronto ON M6A 1C3 – 416/789-7011

Toronto: The Justina M. Barnicke Gallery, Hart House, University of Toronto, 7 Hart House Circle, Toronto ON M5S 3H3 – 416/978-8398; Fax: 416/978-8387 – Director/Curator, Judith Schwartz

Toronto: Kaspar Gallery, 27 Prince Arthur Ave., Toronto ON M5R 1B2 – 416/968-2536

Toronto: La Parete Gallery, 1086 Bathurst St., Toronto ON M5R 3G9 – 416/533-8292; Fax: 416/533-4632

Toronto: Linda Genereux Gallery, 21 Morrow Ave., Toronto ON M6R 2H9 – 416/588-0430; Fax: 416/588-6843

Toronto: Marianne Friedland Gallery, 122 Scollard St., Toronto ON M5R 1G2 – 416/961-4900; Fax: 416/968-3401

Toronto: The Market Gallery, 95 Front St. East, Toronto ON M5E 1C2 – 416/392-7604 – Curator, Pamela Wachna

Toronto: Maslak-McLeod Gallery, 25 Prince Arthur Ave., Toronto ON M5R 1B2 – 416/944-2577

Toronto: Mercer Union, A Centre for Contemporary Visual Art, 439 King St. West, Toronto ON M5V 1R5 – 416/977-1412; Fax: 416/977-8622 – Co-Director, Anette Larsson; Co-Director, Kelly McCray

Toronto: Mira Godard Gallery, 22 Hazelton Ave., Toronto ON M5R 2E2 – 416/964-8197

Toronto: The Mitchell Gallery, 112 Scollard St., Toronto ON M5R 1G2 – 416/515-7246; Fax: 416/515-7568

Toronto: Odon Wagner Gallery, 194 Davenport Rd., Toronto ON M5R 1J2 – 416/962-0438; Fax: 416/962-1581

Toronto: Open Studio, 520 King St. West, 3rd Fl., Toronto ON M5V 1L7 – 416/504-8238

Toronto: The Power Plant, 231 Queen's Quay West, Toronto ON M5J 2G8 – 416/973-4949; Fax: 416/973-4933; Email: powerplant@harbourfront.on.ca; URL: http://www.culturenet.ca/powerplant – Director, Steven Pozel

Toronto: Prime Gallery, 52 McCaul St., Toronto ON M5T 1V9 – 416/593-5750

Toronto: The Red Head, The Darling Bldg., 96 Spadina Ave., 8th Fl., Toronto ON M5V 2J6 – 416/504-5654

Toronto: Sable-Castelli Gallery, 33 Hazelton Ave., Toronto ON M5R 2E3 – 416/961-0011

Toronto: S.L. Simpson Gallery, 515 Queen St. West, Toronto ON M5V 2B4 – 416/504-3738

Toronto: Stephen Bulger Gallery, 700 Queen St. West, Toronto ON M6J 1E7 – 416/504-0575

Toronto: Susan Hobbs Gallery, 137 Tecumseth St., Toronto ON M6J 2H2 – 416/504-3699; Fax: 416/504-8064 – Susan Hobbs

Toronto: Teodora Art Gallery, 45 Avenue Rd., Toronto ON M5R 2G3 – 416/515-0450

Toronto: Thebes Gallery, 613 King St. West, Toronto ON M5V 1M5 – 416/504-3956

Toronto Centre for Contemporary Art, 155A Roncesvalles Ave., Toronto ON M6R 2L3 – 416/536-6220 – Director, Kazimir Glaz

Canadian Almanac & Directory 1997

6-34 ART GALLERIES — PRINCE EDWARD ISLAND

Toronto Dominion Gallery of Inuit Art, Aetna Tower, Ground Level, T-D Centre, PO Box 1, Stn Toronto Dom, Toronto ON M5K 1A2 – 416/982-8473

Toronto: Twist, #313, 80 Spadina Ave., Toronto ON M5V 2J4 – 416/960-1140

Toronto: The Upper Canada Brewing Company - Art Gallery, 2 Atlantic Ave., Toronto ON M6K 1X8 – 416/534-9281

Toronto: Wellington-Cooke Gallery Ltd., 40 Wellington St. East, Toronto ON M5E 1C7 – 416/214-4969

Toronto: Wynick/Tuck Gallery, 80 Spadina Ave., 4th Fl., Toronto ON M5V 2J4 – 416/504-8716

Toronto: Ydessa Hendeles Art Foundation (YHAF), PO Box 757, Stn F, Toronto ON M4Y 2N6 – 416/413-9400; Fax: 416/969-9889 – Ydessa Hendeles – Located at 778 King St. West

Toronto: YYZ Artists' Outlet, 1087 Queen St. West, Toronto ON M6J 1H3 – 416/531-7869; Fax: 416/531-6839; Email: yyz@intacc.web.net – Co-Director, Melinda Sato

Waterloo: Arts Centre Gallery, University of Waterloo, Waterloo ON N2L 3G1 – 519/885-1211, ext.2442 – Curator, Earl W. Stieler

Waterloo: Enook Galleries, 29 Young St. East, PO Box 335, Waterloo ON N2J 4A4 – 519/884-3221 – Curator, L. Napran

Waterloo: Robert Langen Gallery, Wilfrid Laurier University, Waterloo ON N2L 3C5 – 519/884-1970, ext.3801; Email: thranka@mach1.wlu.ca – Curator/Art Gallery Coordinator, Teri Hranka

Whitby Arts Incorporated "The Station Gallery", PO Box 124, Whitby ON L1N 5R7 – 905/668-4185 – Director/Curator, Linda Paulocik

Woodstock Art Gallery, 445 Hunter St., Woodstock ON N4S 4G7 – 519/539-6761; Fax: 519/539-2564 – Director/Curator, Anna-Marie Larsen

PRINCE EDWARD ISLAND

Confederation Centre Art Gallery & Museum/Le Musée d'Art du Centre de la Confédération (CCAG&M)
145 Richmond St., Charlottetown PE C1A 1J1
902/628-6111; Fax: 902/566-4648
Critical inquiry into 200 years of Canadian art; 28 annual exhibitions; 15,000 work collection.
Director, Terry Graff

Other Art Galleries in Prince Edward Island
Charlottetown: Great George Street Gallery, 132 Richmond St., Charlottetown PE C1A 7N3 – 902/892-8168 – Coordinator, Myrna Germaine-Brown

QUÉBEC

Musée d'art contemporain de Montréal
185, rue Ste-Catherine ouest, Montréal PQ H2X 1Z8
514/847-6226; Fax: 514/847-6290
URL: http://Media.MACM.qc.ca
Collection of over 5,000 works dating from 1939 by artists from Québec, Canada & around the world; a specialized reference centre is available for research; various performances, lectures & educational programs are offered by the museum throughout the year; restaurant, boutique & bookstore.
Directeur, Marcel Brisebois
Curator-in-Chief, Paulette Gagnon

Musée des beaux arts de Montréal/Montréal Museum of Fine Arts
1379-1380, rue Sherbrooke ouest, PO Box 3000, Stn H, Montréal PQ H3G 2T9
514/285-1600; Fax: 514/844-6042

URL: http://www.interax.net/tcenter/tour/mba.html
Oldest art museum in Canada (1860); 65 rooms house important collections of engravings, drawings, sculptures, paintings, furniture, silverware & porcelain; open year round.
Directeur, Pierre Théberge
Head, Public Relations, Marie-Josée LeBlanc

Other Art Galleries in Québec
Alma: Langage Plus, 750, rue Scott ouest, CP 518, Alma PQ G8B 5W1 – 418/668-6635

Amos: Centre d'exposition d'Amos, 222, 1ère av est, Amos PQ J9T 1H3 – 819/732-6070; Fax: 819/732-3242 – Directrice, Marianne Trudel

Aylmer: Centre d'exposition l'imagier, 9, rue Front, Aylmer PQ J9H 4W8 – 819/684-1445 – Directrice, Yvette Debain

Baie-Saint-Paul: Centre d'Art, 4, boul Fafard, CP 789, Baie-Saint-Paul PQ G0A 1B0 – 418/435-3681

Beauport: Galerie des Sculptures, 907, boul Rochette, Beauport PQ G1C 1C7

Carleton: Centre d'Artistes Vaste et Vague, 756, boul Perron, CP 877, Carleton PQ G0C 1J0 – 418/364-3123

Château-Richer: Atelier Pomme de Pin, 8698, rue Royale, Château-Richer PQ G0A 1N0 – 418/824-3349

Chicoutimi: Espace Virtuel, 534, rue Jacques-Cartier, Chicoutimi PQ G7H 5B7 – 418/549-3618 – Présidente, Diane Landry

Drummondville: Galerie d'art du Centre culturel, 175, rue Ringuet, Drummondville PQ J2C 2P7 – 819/477-5416; Fax: 819/477-5723 – Directeur, Normand Blanchette

Hull: Axe Néo-7 Art Contemporain, 205, rue Montcalm, Hull PQ J8Y 3B7 – 819/771-2122 – Coordonnateur, Jean-Yves Vigneau

Hull: Galerie Montcalm, Maison du Citoyen, 25, rue Laurier, Hull PQ J8X 4C8 – 819/595-7488; Fax: 819/595-7425 – Directrice, Jacqueline Tardiff

Jonquière: Centre national d'exposition, 4160, rue du Vieux Pont, CP 605, Succ A, Jonquière PQ G7X 7W4 – 418/546-2177; Fax: 418/546-2180 – Directrice, Jacqueline Caron

Laval: Cercle d'Art, Complexe Alfred Dallaire, 2159, boul St-Martin est, Laval PQ H7E 4X6 – 514/384-2551

Laval: Galerie d'art Mayfair, 1550, boul des Laurentides, Laval PQ H7M 2N8 – 514/662-0555

Laval: Galerie de l'Atelier, 74, av du Pacifique, Laval PQ H7N 3X7 – 514/662-1513

Laval: Salle Alfred Pellan, Maison des arts de Laval, 1395, boul de la Concorde ouest, Laval PQ H7N 5W1 – 514/662-4440

Lévis: Centre d'Art de Lévis, 33, rue Wolfe, Lévis PQ G6V 8T2 – 418/833-8831

Lennoxville: Bishop's University Artists' Centre/Centre d'Artistes de l'Université Bishop's, Bishop's University, Lennoxville PQ J1M 1Z7 – 819/822-9687; Fax: 819/822-9661 – Gallery Coordinator, Christine Ljungkull, Email: cljungku@admin.ubishops.ca

Matane: Galerie d'art de Matane, 616, rue St-Rédempteur, Matane PQ G4W 1L1 – 418/562-1240, poste 2250; Fax: 418/566-2115 – Président, Delphis Bélanger

Mont-Laurier: Centre d'exposition Mont-Laurier, 385, rue Du Pont, PO Box 323, Mont-Laurier PQ J9L 3N7 – 819/623-2441; Fax: 819/623-7262 – Directrice, Reine Charbonneau

Montréal: Atelier d'historie Hochelaga-Maisonneuve, 1691, boul Pie IX, Montréal PQ H1V 2C3 – 514/523-5930 – Directeur, Ghyslaine Teller

Montréal: Galerie de l'UQAM, 1400, rue Berri, CP 8888, Succ Centre-ville, Montréal PQ H3C 3P8 – 514/987-6150; Fax: 514/987-3009 – Directrice par intérim, Chantal Bouthat

Montréal: Galerie Dominion, 1438, rue Sherbrooke ouest, Montréal PQ H3G 1K4 – 514/845-7833

Montréal: Galerie l'Industrielle-alliance, 680, rue Sherbrooke ouest, Montréal PQ H3A 2S6 – 514/499-3768; Fax: 514/284-2655 – Directrice, Danielle Brunelle

Montréal: La Centrale (Galerie Powerhouse), #311D, 279, rue Sherbrooke ouest, Montréal PQ H2X 1Y2 – 514/844-3489 – Coordinator, Elaine Frigon

Montréal: Leonard & Bina Ellen Art Gallery/Galerie d'art Leonard & Bina Ellen, Concordia University, 1400, boul de Maisonneuve ouest, Montréal PQ H3G 1M8 – 514/848-4750; Fax: 514/848-4751 – Director/Curator, Karen Antaki

Pointe-Claire: Stewart Hall Art Gallery, 176, rue Lakeshore, Pointe-Claire PQ H9S 4J7 – 514/630-1254

Québec: Galerie Municipale au Palais Montcalm, Bureau des arts et de la culture, Palais Montcalm, 995, place D'Youville, Québec PQ G1R 3P1 – Chargée d'interpretation, Henriette Thériault

Québec: VU centre de diffusion et de production de la photographie, 523, Saint-Vallier est, Québec PQ G1K 3P9 – 418/640-2585; Fax: 418/640-2586; Email: vuphoto@microtec.ca; URL: http://www2.zone.ca/~vuphoto – Directeur, Gaétan Gosselin

Rouyn-Noranda: Centre d'exposition de Rouyn-Noranda inc., 425, boul du Collège, CP 415, Rouyn-Noranda PQ J9X 5C4 – 819/762-6600 – Directrice, Céline Rivard

Saint-Georges: Centre d'Art de St-Georges, 250, 18e rue ouest, Saint-Georges PQ G5Y 4S9 – 418/228-2027 – Jacqueline Ferland – Open year round

Saint-Hyacinthe: Expression, Centre d'exposition de Saint-Hyacinthe, 405, av Saint-Simon, Saint-Hyacinthe PQ J2S 5C3 – 514/773-4209 – Directeur, Michel Groleau

Saint-Lambert: Galarie du Centre, 250, rue Saint-Laurent, CP 555, Saint-Lambert PQ J4P 3R8 – 514/672-4772 – Directrice, Jacqueline Beaudry Dion

Saint-Léonard: Galerie Port-Maurice, 8420, boul Lacordaire, Saint-Léonard PQ H1R 3G5 – 514/328-8585 – Coordonnatrice, Louise Cayer

Shawinigan: Centre d'exposition de Shawinigan, 2100, boul Des Hêtres, PO Box 400, Shawinigan PQ G9N 6V3 – 819/539-1888; Fax: 819/536-7255 – Directeur, Robert Y. Desjardins

St-Laurent: Musée d'Art de St-Laurent (MASL), 615, av Ste-Croix, St-Laurent PQ H4L 3X6 – 514/747-7367; Fax: 514/747-8892 – Directrice, Louise Ethier

Trois-Rivières: Galerie d'art du Parc Inc., Manoir de Tonnancour, 864, rue des Ursulines, CP 871, Trois-Rivières PQ G9A 5J9 – 819/374-2355; Fax: 819/374-1758 – Directrice, Christiane Simoneau

Val d'Or: Centre d'exposition de Val d'Or inc., 600, 7e rue, Val d'Or PQ J9P 3P3 – 819/825-0942 – Directrice, Lise Gagné

Verdun: Centre culturel de Verdun, 5955, rue Bannantyne, Verdun PQ H4H 1H6 – 514/765-7170; Fax: 514/765-7167 – Directeur, Claude Vadeboncoeur

SASKATCHEWAN

MacKenzie Art Gallery
3475 Albert St. South, Regina SK S4S 6X6
306/522-4242; Fax: 306/569-8191

Historical & contemporary Canadian, American & European works; special emphasis on western Canadian art; major touring exhibits; facilities include learning centre, studios, theatre, gift shop; open daily year round.
Director, Vacant
Communications & Development, Bonnie Schaffer

Canadian Almanac & Directory 1997

Mendel Art Gallery & Civic Conservatory
950 Spadina Cres. East, PO Box 569, Saskatoon SK S7K 3L6
306/975-7610; Fax: 306/975-7670
Historical & contemporary Canadian & international art; 3,500 works; open daily year round.
Director, Terry Fenton

Other Art Galleries in Saskatchewan
North Battleford: Allen Sapp Gallery, 1091 - 100th St., PO Box 460, North Battleford SK S9A 2Y6 – 306/445-1760; Fax: 306/445-0411 – Curator, Dean Bauche – Cree art & interpretive centre; open year round
North Battleford: The Chapel Gallery, PO Box 460, North Battleford SK S9A 2Y6 – 306/445-7266 – Curator, Unafred Ann Shiplett
Prince Albert: Grace Campbell Gallery, c/o John M. Cuelenaere Public Library, 125 - 12 St. East, Prince Albert SK S6V 1B7 – 306/763-8496; Fax: 306/763-3816 – Gallery Coordinator, Janet Gray, Email: gray@panet.panet.pa.sk.ca; Library Director, Eleanor Acorn
Regina: Assiniboia Gallery, 2429 - 11th Ave., Regina SK S4P 0K4 – 306/522-0997 – Contemporary Canadian art; open year round
Regina: Dunlop Art Gallery, 2311 - 12th Ave., PO Box 2311, Regina SK S4P 3Z5 – 306/777-6040; Fax: 306/352-5550; Email: hmarzolf@rpl.regina.sk.ca – Director, Helen Marzolf; Curator, Vera Lemecha
Regina: Gallery on the Roof, Saskatchewan Power Corp., 2025 Victoria Ave., Regina SK S4P 0S1 – 306/566-3176 – Curator, Dale Kilbride
Regina: McIntyre Street Gallery, 2347 McIntyre St., Regina SK S4P 2S3 – 306/757-4323 – Contemporary Saskatchewan art; open year round
Regina: Rosemont Art Gallery, 2420 Elphinstone St., PO Box 1790, Regina SK S4P 3C8 – 306/522-5940 – Director/Curator, Karen Schoonover
Saskatchewan Craft Gallery, 813 Broadway Ave., Saskatchewan SK S7N 1B5 – 306/653-3616; Fax: 306/244-2711 – Executive Director, Terry Schwalm
Saskatoon: A.K.A. Gallery, 12 - 23rd St. East, 3rd Fl., Saskatoon SK S7K 0H5 – 306/652-0044; Fax: 306/652-9924; Email: aa/82@SFN.Saskatoon.sk.ca – Administrative Co-ordinator, Susan Bustin
Saskatoon: Gordon Snelgrove Art Gallery, 191 Murray Bldg., University of Saskatchewan, Saskatoon SK S7N 5A4 – 306/966-4196, 4208 – Coordinator, Don Foulds
Saskatoon: Photographers Gallery, 12 - 23rd St. East, 2nd Fl., Saskatoon SK S7K 0H5 – 306/244-8018; Fax: 306/665-6568 – Director, Monte Greenshields
Saskatoon: St. Thomas Moore Art Gallery, 1437 College Dr., Saskatoon SK S7N 0W6 – 306/966-8900 – Director, Colleen Fitzgerald
Swift Current National Exhibition Centre, 411 Hebert St. East, Swift Current SK S9H 1M5 – 306/778-2736; Fax: 306/778-2198 – Director, David Humphries
Weyburn: Allie Griffin Art Gallery (AGAG), PO Box 1178, Weyburn SK S4H 0H9 – 306/848-3278; Fax: 306/848-3220 – Arts Director, Alice Neufeld – Located at 45 Bison Ave.
Weyburn: Prairie Gallery, Signal Hill Arts Centre, 424 - 10th Ave. South, 2nd Fl., Weyburn SK S4H 2A1
Yorkton: Geoffrey Dean Cultural Centre, Yorkton Arts Council, 49 Smith St. East, Yorkton SK S3N 0H4 – 306/783-8722; Fax: 306/786-7667 – President, Eileen Boryski

PERFORMING ARTS

THEATRE

The Actors' Fund of Canada/La Caisse des acteurs du Canada inc. (1957)
#860, 10 Saint Mary St., Toronto, ON M4Y 1P9
416/975-0304, Fax: 416/975-0306
President, V. Harwood

Alberta Playwrights' Network (APN) (1985)
1134 - 8 Ave. SW, 2nd Fl., Calgary, AB T2P 1J5
403/269-8564, Fax: 403/269-8564, Toll Free: 1-800-268-8564, Email: apn@nucleus.com, URL: http://www.nucleus.com/~apn
President, Sherring Amsden
Administrator, Diane Wild
Publications: Rave Review, bi-m.
Affiliates: Theatre Alberta

Association for Canadian Theatre Research/ Association de recherches théâtrales au Canada (ACTR) (1976)
90 Beauvista Dr., Sherwood Park, AB T8A 3X1
403/464-0703, Fax: 403/467-6731, Toll Free: 1-800-269-7037, Email: annen@cs.athabascan.ca, URL: http://www.athabascan.ca
President, Richard Plant
Treasurer, Anne Nothof
Secretary, Louise Forsyth
Publications: ACTR/ARTC Newsletter, s-a.; Theatre Research in Canada

Association québécoise des critiques de théâtre (AQCT) (1984)
54, av Helmwood, Montréal, PQ H2V 2E4
514/278-5764
Président, Michel Vais

Association québécoise des marionnettistes (AQM) (1981)
Union internationale de la marionnette - Canada
Centre UNIMA au Québec, CP 7, Succ De Lorimier, Montréal, PQ H2H 2N6
514/499-0875, Courrier électronique: aqm@aei.ca, URL: http://www.aei.ca/~aqm/
Président, Benoît Dubois
Publications: La Marionnette en manchette, 5 fois par an

Association québécoise du théâtre amateur inc. (AQTA) (1988)
6, rue de l'Exposition, CP 977, Victoriaville, PQ G6P 8Y1
819/752-2501, Téléc: 819/758-4466
Directrice générale, Jocelyne Lévis
Publications: Trac, 10 fois par an

Association of Summer Theatres 'Round Ontario (ASTRO)
#1500, 415 Yonge St., Toronto, ON M5B 2E7
416/408-4556, Fax: 416/408-3402
Diana Belshaw

Bard on the Beach Shakespeare Festival
1101 West Broadway, Vancouver, BC V6H 1G2
604/737-0625; Box Office: 604/739-0559, Fax: 604/737-0425
Artistic Director, Christopher Gaze
General Manager, Marilyn Navarro Leiton

British Columbia Drama Association (1933)
Theatre BC
#307, 1005 Broad St., Victoria, BC V8W 2A1
250/381-2443, Fax: 250/381-4419

Executive Director, Jim Harding
Publications: Theatre BC Newsletter, q.

Buddies in Bad Times Theatre
12 Alexander St., Toronto, ON M4Y 1B4
416/975-9130; Box Office: 416/975-8555, Fax: 416/975-9293
Artistic Director, Sky Gilbert
General Manager, Tim Jones

Canadian Institute for Theatre Technology (CITT) (1989)
2500 University Dr. NW, Calgary, AB T2N 1N4
403/220-4905, Fax: 403/282-7751, Email: citt@cnet-mail.ffa.ucalgary.ca, URL: http://www.ffa.ucalgary.ca/citt/index.html
Office Manager, Kathy Watson
Publications: Sightlines, 10 pa; Theatre Design & Technology
Affiliates: United States Institute for Theatre Technology

Canadian Popular Theatre Alliance (CPTA)
c/o Concrete Theatre, 10920 - 88 Ave., Edmonton, AB T6G 0Z1
403/439-3905, Fax: 403/439-9677
Coordinator, Caroline Howarth

The Canadian Stage Company
26 Berkeley St., Toronto, ON M5A 2W3
416/367-8243; Box Office: 416/368-3110, Fax: 416/367-1768, Email: canthe@idirect.com
Managing Director & Producer, Martin Bragg
Artistic Director, Bob Baker
Director of Communications & Development, Celia Smith

Canadian Theatre Critics Association/ Association des critiques de théâtre du Canada (CTCA) (1979)
#2100, 181 University Ave., Toronto, ON M5H 3M7
416/367-8896, Fax: 416/367-8896
Founding President, Jeniva Berger
Publications: CTCA Newsletter, q.
Affiliates: Toronto Drama Bench; Capital Critics Association; Association québécoise des critiques de théâtre

Caravan Stage Society
349 Wellington St., PO Box 1995, Kingston, ON K7K 6E1
613/531-8390, Fax: 613/531-8391
Artistic Director, Paul Kirby
Administrator, Ted Worth

Centre des auteurs dramatiques (CEAD) (1965)
3450, rue St. Urbain, Montréal, PQ H2X 2N5
514/288-3384, Téléc: 514/288-7043
Directrice général, Jacques Vézina
Présidente, Carole Fréchette
Publications: Dramaturgies/Nouvelles, semi-annuel; Théâtre Québec

Le Cercle Molière (1925)
340, boul Provencher, CP 1, Winnipeg, MB R2H 3B4
204/233-8053; Box Office: 204/233-8972, Téléc: 204/233-2373
Directeur artistique, Roland Mahé

Coconut Theatre Society
984 West Broadway, PO Box 53541, Vancouver, BC V5Z 1K7
604/876-4200, Fax: 604/876-4200
Artistic Manager, Patricia Andrew-Keith

Conseil québécois du théâtre (CQT)
#4120, 5505, boul Saint-Laurent, Montréal, PQ H2T 1S6

514/278-9208, Téléc: 514/278-9239, Courrier électronique: cqt@cam.org
Directrice générale, Dominique Violette

Council of Drama in Education (CODE)
#1106, 360 Watson St., Whitby, ON L1N 9G2
905/666-4408, Fax: 905/723-7024
Liaison Officer, Lisa Taylor
Publications: CODE Journal, a.; CODE Newsletter

First Vancouver Theatrespace Society
18 - 2414 Main St., Vancouver, BC V5T 3E3
604/873-3646, Fax: 604/873-4231
Executive Director, Joanna Maratta

Fringe of Toronto Festival
#303, 720 Bathurst St., Toronto, ON M5S 2R4
416/534-5919, Fax: 416/534-6021
Producer, Nancy Webster
General Manager, Linda Keyworth

Globe Theatre Society (1966)
1801 Scarth St., Regina, SK S4P 2G9
306/525-9553, Fax: 306/352-4194
Artistic Director, Susan Ferley
Affiliates: Canadian Actors' Equity

Gryphon Theatre Foundation (1969)
PO Box 454, Barrie, ON L4M 4T7
705/728-4634; Box Office: 705/728-4613, Fax: 705/728-4623
Producer, Uwe Meyer
Administrator, Barbara Aoki

Harbourfront Centre
#100, 410 Queens Quay West, Toronto, ON M5V 2Z3
416/973-4600, Fax: 416/973-8729
Artistic Director, Don Shipley
General Manager, Bill Boyle
Director of Communications, Ellen T. Cole

International Theatre Institute - Canadian Centre (1979)
Canadian Centre of the ITI
Acadia University, PO Box 1441, Wolfville, NS B0P 1X0
902/542-1932, Fax: 902/542-1526
Administrator, Andria Hill
Publications: ITI Newsletter, q.
Affiliates: Organisation internationale des scenographes, architectes et techniciens de théâtre

Intrepid Theatre Co. Society
#511, 620 View St., Victoria, BC V8W 1V6
250/383-2663, Fax: 250/380-1999, Email: vicfring@pinc.com
General Manager, Janet Munsil

Manitoba Association of Playwrights (MAP) (1979)
#503, 100 Arthur St., Winnipeg, MB R3B 1H3
204/942-8941, Fax: 204/942-1555
Coordinator, Rory Runnells
Publications: Ellipsis, 4-5 pa

Manitoba Theatre Centre (MTC) (1957)
174 Market Ave., Winnipeg, MB R3B 0P8
204/956-1340, Fax: 204/947-3741
Artistic Director, Steven Schipper
General Manager, Zaz Bajon
Publications: Ovation, bi-m.

Native Earth Performing Arts Inc. (NEPA) (1983)
#302, 720 Bathurst St., Toronto, ON M5S 2R4
416/531-1402, Fax: 416/531-6377, URL: http://www.io.org/~naterth/naterth.htm
Artistic Director, Drew Hayden Taylor

General Manager, Eva Nell Harin
Publications: Native Earth Performing Arts Newsletter, q.

Neptune Theatre Foundation
#B24, 1903 Barrington St., Halifax, NS B3J 3L7
902/429-7300, Fax: 902/429-1211
General Manager, Bruce Klinger
Artistic Director, Linda Moore

New West Theatre Society
c/o Yates Centre, 910 - 4th Ave. South, Lethbridge, AB T1J 0P6
403/381-9378; Box Office: 403/329-7328, Fax: 403/380-4694, Email: parkinson@uleth.ca
Artistic/Managing Director, Brian C. Parkinson

Nova Scotia Drama League
#901, 1809 Barrington St., Halifax, NS B3J 3K8
902/425-3876, Fax: 902/422-0881
Executive Director, Eva Moore

Nova Scotia Professional Theatre Alliance (NSPTA)
c/o Two Planks & a Passion Theatre, PO Box 413, Canning, NS B0P 1H0
902/582-3073, Fax: 902/582-7943, Email: twoplanx@atcon.com
President, Ken Schwartz

Ontario Puppetry Association
Box 180, #0116, 65 Front St. West, Toronto, ON M5J 1E6
General Manager, Sara Meurling
President, Tom Vandenberg
Publications: Opal, bi-m.
Affiliates: UNIMA International; Theatre Ontario; North York Arts Council
Office: #306, 56 The Esplanade, Toronto, ON M5E 1A7, 416/861-0202
Ontario Centre for Puppetry Arts: 116 Cornelius Pkwy., North York, ON M6L 2K5, 416/246-9222, Fax: 416/246-0922 (call first)

PACT Communications Centre (PCC) (1985)
#1500, 415 Yonge St., Toronto, ON M5B 2E7
416/595-6455, Fax: 416/595-6450, Toll Free: 1-800-263-7228, Email: pact@mail.culturenet.ca, URL: http://www.culturenet.ucalgary.ca/pact
Executive Director, Pat Bradley
Chair, Duval Lang
Publications: Canada On Stage; Artsboard
Affiliates: Charitable Wing of Professional Association of Canadian Theatres

Performing Arts Sponsors Organization of Nova Scotia (PASONS)
PO Box 3150, Windsor, NS B0N 2T0
902/798-3893, Fax: 902/798-0557
Executive Director, Pamela Kinsman

Phoenix Theatre Society
10330 - 84 Ave., Edmonton, AB T6E 2G9
403/434-4015, Fax: 403/438-4016, Email: phoenix@freenet.edm.ab.ca
General Manager, Laurie Blakeman

Playwrights Theatre Centre
1405 Anderson St., Vancouver, BC V6H 3R5
604/685-6228, Fax: 604/685-7451, Email: ptcplays@cyberstore.ca
General Manager, Jan Carley

Playwrights Union of Canada (PUC) (1972)
54 Wolseley St., 2nd Fl., Toronto, ON M5T 1A5
416/703-0201, Fax: 416/703-0059, Toll Free: 1-800-561-3318, Email: cdplay@interlog.com

Executive Director, Angela Rebeiro
Publications: CanPlay, bi-m.; Directory of Members

Popular Theatre Alliance of Manitoba (PTAM) (1984)
413 Selkirk Ave., 2nd Fl., Winnipeg, MB R2W 2M4
204/589-8408, Fax: 204/586-0486
Artistic Director, Debbie Patterson
Publications: PTAM News, bi-a.

Prairie Theatre Exchange (PTE) (1972)
Portage Place, #Y300, 393 Portage Ave., Winnipeg, MB R3B 3H6
204/942-7291, Fax: 204/942-1774
General Manager, Cherry Karpyshin
President, Janice Penner

Professional Association of Canadian Theatres/Association professionnelle des théâtres canadiens (PACT) (1976)
#1500, 415 Yonge St., Toronto, ON M5B 2E7
416/595-6455, Fax: 416/595-6450, Toll Free: 1-800-263-7228, Email: pact@mail.culturenet.com, URL: http://www.culturenet.ucalgary.ca/pact
Executive Director, Pat Bradley
President, Jerry Doiron
Publications: Impact, q.; The Theatre Listing
Affiliates: PACT Communications Centre; Canadian Centre of the International Theatre Institute; Canadian Conference of the Arts

Saskatchewan Drama Association
#203, 2135 Albert St., Regina, SK S4P 2V1
306/525-0151, Fax: 306/525-6277
Executive Director, Catherine Anderson

Saskatchewan Playwrights Centre (SPC)
PO Box 3092, Saskatoon, SK S7K 3S9
306/665-7707, Fax: 306/665-7707, Email: spc@bailey2.unibase.com, URL: http://bailey2.unibase.com/~grain/SPC_Homepage.html
Dramaturge, Patti Shedden

Shaw Festival
PO Box 774, Niagara on the Lake, ON L0S 1J0
905/468-2153, Fax: 905/468-5438, Toll Free: 1-800-511-7429
Artistic Director, Christopher Newton
Administrative Director, Colleen Blake

Société québécoise d'études théâtrales (SQET) (1976)
CP 459, Succ. Outremont, Montréal, PQ H2V 4N3
514/237-7466
Contact, Claude Larouche
Publications: L'Annuaire théâtral, semi-annuel

Stratford Festival (1952)
PO Box 520, Stratford, ON N5A 6V2
705/271-4040; Box Office: 273-1600, Fax: 705/271-2734, Toll Free: 1-800-567-1600, Email: dprosser@stratford_festival.on.ca, URL: http://www.ffa.ucalgary.ca/stratford/home.htm
Artistic Director, Richard Monette
General Manager, Mary Hofstetter

Theatre Alberta Society
11759 Groat Rd., 3rd Fl., Edmonton, AB T5M 3K6
403/422-8162, Fax: 403/422-2663
Executive Director, Kathy Classen

Theatre Calgary
220 - 9 Ave. SE, Calgary, AB T2G 5C4
403/294-7440; Box Office: 403/294-7447, Fax: 403/294-7493, Email: schniedm@cadvision.com
Executive Producer, Brian Rintoul
Production/Facility Manager, Monty Schnieder

Théâtre français de Toronto
#303, 219 Dufferin St., Toronto, ON M6K 1Y9
416/534-7303; Box Office: 416/534-6604, Téléc: 416/534-9087
Administrative Director, Greg Brown

Theatre Network (1975) Society (1975)
10708 - 124 St., Edmonton, AB T5M 0H1
403/453-2440, Fax: 403/453-2596
Artistic Director, Ben Henderson
General Manager, David Hennessey

Theatre New Brunswick (TNB) (1967)
The Playhouse, PO Box 566, Fredericton, NB E3B 5A6
506/458-8345, Fax: 506/459-6206
Executive Producer, Walter Learning
General Manager, Nancy Coy

Theatre Newfoundland Labrador
PO Box 655, Corner Brook, NF A2H 6G1
709/639-7238, Fax: 709/639-1006
Artistic Director, Jerry Etienne
Administrator, Gaylene Buckle

Theatre Ontario (1971)
#1500, 415 Yonge St., Toronto, ON M5B 2E7
416/408-4556, Fax: 416/408-3402
Executive Director, Sandra Tulloch
Publications: Theatre Ontario News, 5 pa.

Theatre Prince Edward Island (1980)
550 University Ave., Charlottetown, PE C1A 4P3
902/566-0321, Fax: 902/566-0420
Administrator, Daphne Harker
Artistic Director, Ron Irving
Associate Artistic Director, Rob MacLean
Publications: Newsletter
Affiliates: PEI Council of the Arts

Theatre Terrific Society
4397 West 2nd Ave., Vancouver, BC V6R 1K4
604/222-4020, Fax: 604/222-4024
General Manager, Dean McMillan

Théâtres associés inc. (TAI)
1501, rue Jeanne-Mance, Montréal, PQ H2X 1Z9
514/842-6361, Téléc: 514/842-9730
Secrétaire général, Jacques Cousineau

Théâtres unis enfance jeunesse (TUEJ) (1986)
CP 627, Succ. Desjardins, Montréal, PQ H5B 1B7
514/446-4863, Téléc: 514/467-1982
Président, Stéphane Lavoie
Coordonnatrice, Andrée Garon
Organisation(s) affiliée(s): Conseil québécois du Théâtre

Toronto Theatre Alliance (TTA)
#403, 720 Bathurst St., Toronto, ON M5S 2R4
416/536-6468, Fax: 416/536-3463, Email: tta@idirect.com
Executive Director, Jessica Fraser

Vancouver Professional Theatre Alliance (VPTA)
#2, 2414 Main St., Vancouver, BC V5T 3E3
604/879-2999, Fax: 604/876-5114
Administrator, Amanda Spottiswoode

Vancouver Youth Theatre Society
#200, 275 East 8th Ave., Vancouver, BC V5T 1R9
604/877-0678, Fax: 604/876-7100
Artistic Director, Judith Hogan
Business Manager, Craig Laven

Women in View
314 Powell St., Vancouver, BC V6A 1G4

604/685-6684, Fax: 604/685-6649, URL: http://www.ffa.ucalgary.ca/vca/wmnvie.htm
Executive Director, Dawn Brennan

Young People's Theatre (YPT)
165 Front St. East, Toronto, ON M5A 3Z4
416/363-5131; Box Office: 416/862-2222, Fax: 416/363-5136
Artistic Director, Maja Ardal
General Manager, Catherine Smalley

MUSIC

Alberta Choral Federation (ACF) (1972)
#209, 14218 Stony Plain Rd., Edmonton, AB T5N 3R3
403/488-7464, Fax: 403/488-4132
Executive Director, Robin John King
Publications: Quires, q.

Alberta Recording Industries Association (ARIA) (1984)
#208, 10136 - 100 St., Edmonton, AB T5J 0P1
403/428-3372, Fax: 403/426-0188, Toll Free: 1-800-465-3117
President, R. Harlan Smith
Publications: Notes, m.

Alliance for Canadian New Music Projects/ Alliance pour des projets de musique canadienne nouvelle (ACNMP) (1978)
Contemporary Showcase
Canadian Music Centre, 20 St. Joseph St., 3rd Fl., Toronto, ON M4Y 1J9
416/963-5937, Fax: 416/961-7198
General Manager, Colleen Perrin
President, Jill Kelman
Publications: Contempo, q.; Contemporary Showcase Syllabus

Alliance Chorale Manitoba
340 Provencher Blvd., Winnipeg, MB R2H 0G7
204/233-8972, Téléc: 204/233-3324
Contact, Gilles Landry

Alliance des chorales du Québec (ACQ)
4545, av Pierre-de-Coubertin, CP 1000, Succ. M, Montréal, PQ H1V 3R2
514/252-3020, Téléc: 514/252-3222
Directrice générale, Christine Dumas

Association of Canadian Choral Conductors/ Association des chefs de choeur canadiens (ACCC) (1980)
49, rue de Tracy, Blainville, PQ J7C 4B7
514/430-5573, Fax: 514/430-4999
Executive Director, Patricia Abbott
President, Dr. Malcolm V. Edwards
Publications: Anacrusis, q.; Membership/Professional Directory; Repertoire Lists
Affiliates: Canadian Conference of the Arts; International Federation for Choral Music

Association of Canadian Orchestras/Association des orchestres canadiens (ACO) (1972)
#311, 56 The Esplanade, Toronto, ON M5E 1A7
416/366-8834, Fax: 416/366-1780, Email: assoc@terraport.net, URL: http://www.terraport.net/aco
Executive Director, Betty Webster
Publications: Orchestra Canada/Orchestres Canada, bi-m.; The Directory of Canadian Orchestras & Youth Orchestras
Affiliates: American Symphony Orchestra League; International Alliance of Orchestra Associations
Member Orchestras
Brandon University Orchestra: Director, Nándor Szederkényi; Dr. Earl Davey, School of Music, Brandon University, 270 - 18th St., Brandon, MB R7A 6A9, 204/728-9520, Fax: 204/728-6839, Email: music@brandonu.ca
Brantford Symphony Orchestra Association Inc.: General Manager, Michael French, 185 King George Rd., PO Box 24012, Brantford, ON N3R 7X3, 519/759-8781
Calgary Philharmonic Society: Executive Director, Leonard D. Stone; Executive Assistant, Joyce Van Halderen, 205 - 8 Ave. SE, Calgary, AB T2G 0K9, 403/571-0270, Fax: 403/294-7424
Calgary Youth Orchestra: Mount Royal College, 4825 Richard Rd. SW, Calgary, AB T3E 6K6, 403/240-5978, Fax: 403/240-6594
Cathedral Bluffs Symphony Orchestra of Scarborough: President, Neil Blair, 4410 Kingston Rd., PO Box 53539, Scarborough, ON M1E 5G2, 905/509-5857, Fax: 905/509-5883
Concerts symphoniques de Sherbrooke inc.: Directeur administrative, Louise Deslongchamps; Président, Claude Métras; Directeur artistique, Marc David, 14, rue Alexandre, Sherbrooke, PQ J1H 4S6, 819/821-0227
Deep River Symphony Orchestra: President, Blair Smith, PO Box 1496, Deep River, ON K0J 1P0
East York Symphony Orchestra (1972) Inc.: Chairperson, Heather Anderson; Music Director, Douglas Sanford, 110 Rumsey Rd., East York, ON M4G 1P2, 416/467-7142, Fax: 416/467-7142
Eastern Ontario Concert Orchestra: President, Sister Barbara Thiffault, PO Box 23087, Belleville, ON K8P 5J3, 613/962-2153
Edmonton Symphony Society: General Manager, W.R. McPhee, 10160 - 103 St., Edmonton, AB T5J 0X6, 403/428-1108, Fax: 403/425-0167
Edmonton Youth Orchestra Association: General Manager, Eileen Lee, PO Box 66041, RPO Heritage, Edmonton, AB T6J 6T4, 403/436-7932, Fax: 403/436-7932
Etobicoke Philharmonic Orchestra: President, Peggy Pinkerton, 19 Hilldowntree Rd., Etobicoke, ON M9A 2Z4, 416/233-5665
Fraser Valley Symphony Society: House Manager, Martin Vander Schans, PO Box 122, Abbotsford, BC V2S 4N8, 604/859-8728
Georgian Bay Symphony: General Manager, Bert Hood; President, Trevor Burns, PO Box 133, Owen Sound, ON N4K 5P1, 519/371-4065, Info Line: 519/376-2847
Greater Hamilton Symphony Association: Manager, Sandra E. Motta; President, Sandi Sherk, 59 Oxford St., Hamilton, ON L8R 2W9, 905/526-6690, Fax: 905/526-1050
Greater Victoria Youth Orchestra: Associate Manager, Diana MacDonald; Associate Manager, Susan MacRae; President, Dr. John Money, 1611 Quadra St., Victoria, BC V8W 2L5, 250/360-1121, Fax: 250/381-3573, Info Line: 250/360-1121
Guelph Youth Orchestra Association: President, James Bruder, PO Box 1604, Guelph, ON N1H 6R7, 519/824-1642
Halton Youth Symphony: President, Wayne Jones; Manager, Sharon Johnston, PO Box 494, Stn Main, Oakville, ON L6J 5A8, 905/847-7578
Hamilton Philharmonic Society Inc.: Managing Director, John F. Shaw; President, Mary Ann Simpson, Hamilton Place, 25 Main St. West, 8th Fl., Hamilton, ON L8P 1H1, 905/526-8800, Fax: 905/526-6569
Hamilton Philharmonic Youth Orchestra: Conductor/Founder, Glenn Mallory, PO Box 2080, Stn A, Hamilton, ON L8N 3Y7, 905/526-8800, Fax: 905/526-6569
Hart House Orchestra: Conductor, Errol Gay, Hart House, University of Toronto, Toronto, ON M5S 1A1, 416/978-5362, Fax: 416/978-0893
Huronia Symphony: Business Manager, Sandra Martin, PO Box 904, Barrie, ON L4M 4Y6, 705/721-4752, Fax: 705/721-5192

Canadian Almanac & Directory 1997

PERFORMING ARTS — MUSIC

International Symphony Orchestra of Sarnia & Port Huron: Executive Director, Anne M. Brown; President, Thomas Awdison, 774C London Rd., Sarnia, ON N7T 4Y1, 519/337-7775

Kamloops Symphony Society: General Manager, Kathy Humphreys, PO Box 57, Kamloops, BC V2C 5K3, 250/372-5000, Fax: 250/372-5089

Kingston Symphony Association: General Manager, Tricia Baldwin; President, James Coles, PO Box 1616, Kingston, ON K7L 5C8, 613/546-9729, Fax: 613/546-8580

Kitchener-Waterloo Symphony Orchestra Association Inc.: Acting Managing Director, George Lange, 101 Queen St. North, Kitchener, ON N2H 6P7, 519/745-4711, Fax: 519/745-4474, Email: kwsymph@worldchat.com

Kitchener-Waterloo Symphony Youth Orchestra: Manager, Heather Bean, 101 Queen St. North, Kitchener, ON N2H 6P7, 519/745-4711, Fax: 519/745-4474

Lethbridge Symphony Association: General Manager, Alan S. Young, Yates Memorial Theatre, PO Box 1101, Lethbridge, AB T1J 4A2, 403/328-6808, Fax: 403/380-4418

London Community Orchestra: President, Malcolm Morham; Music Director, Mariusz Debich; Manager, Margaret Whitby, 1551 Ryersie Rd., London, ON N6G 2S2, 519/432-4461, Fax: 519/858-4982

London Youth Symphony: General Manager, P. Austin, PO Box 553, Stn B, London, ON N6A 4W8, 519/472-2606

Manitoba Chamber Orchestra: General Manager, Rita Menzies, #202, 1317A Portage Ave., Winnipeg, MB R3G 0V3, 204/783-7377

Medicine Hat Symphonic Society: President, James Vandersloot, PO Box 1295, Medicine Hat, AB T1A 7N1, 403/529-6813

Mississauga Chamber Players: Director, Megan Pallett, 7781 Tremaine Rd., RR#6, Milton, ON L9T 2Y1, 905/878-1041

Mississauga Symphonic Association: Executive Director, Richard Solomon, 161 Lakeshore Rd. West, Mississauga, ON L5H 1G3, 905/274-1571, Fax: 905/274-7770

National Arts Centre Orchestra of Canada: Contact, Christopher Deacon, PO Box 1534, Stn B, Ottawa, ON K1P 5W1, 613/947-7000, ext. 361, Fax: 613/943-1400

National Youth Orchestra Association of Canada: General Manager, Hubert C. Meyer, 1032 Bathurst St., Toronto, ON M5R 3G7, 416/532-4470, Fax: 416/532-6879

New Brunswick Youth Orchestra: Administrator, Don Rayment, Email: Rayment@nbnet.nb.ca, 38 Cliff St., Saint John, NB E2L 3A7, 506/657-1498

Newfoundland Symphony Orchestra Association: President, Keith Wellon; Office Manager, Wendy Stevenson, Arts & Culture Centre, Prince Philip Dr., St. John's, NF A1C 5P9, 709/753-6492, Fax: 709/753-0561

Niagara Symphony Association: President, David R. Penney, #104, 73 Ontario St., St Catharines, ON L2R 5J5, 905/687-4993, Fax: 905/687-1149

Niagara Youth Orchestra Association: President, John Lekx; Executive Secretary, Arlene Brice, 600 Ontario St., PO Box 28049, St Catharines, ON L2N 7P8, 905/934-3314, Fax: 905/934-2323

North Bay Symphony Orchestra: General Manager, Rex Hiscock; President, Nori Sugimoto; Music Director, Victor Sawa, #106, 269 Main St. West, North Bay, ON P1B 2T8, 705/494-7744, Fax: 705/494-7663

North York Symphony Association: Executive Director, Al Kowalenko, CAE; President, Harry Cogill, #109, 1210 Sheppard Ave. East, North York, ON M2K 1E3, 416/499-2204, Fax: 416/490-9739

Northumberland Orchestra Society: President, Starr Olsen, PO Box 1012, Cobourg, ON K9A 4W4, 905/372-8025

Nova Scotia Youth Orchestra: President, Ian Mann; Music Director, Gregory Burton; Managing Director, Carolyn Davies, #200, 1541 Barrington St., Halifax, NS B3J 1Z5, 902/423-5984, Fax: 902/423-5984

Oakville Symphony Orchestra Inc.: General Manager, Kim Hall, 297 Lakeshore Rd. East, Oakville, ON L6J 1J3, 905/844-7984, Fax: 905/844-0823

Okanagan Symphony Society: Executive Director, Bill Woodward; President, Fred Miles, PO Box 1120, Stn A, Kelowna, BC V1Y 7P8, 250/763-7544, Fax: 250/763-3553

Orchestra London Canada Inc.: General Manager, Patricia McLaughlin, 520 Wellington St., London, ON N6A 3R1, 519/679-8558, Fax: 519/679-8914, Email: orchestra.london@icis.on.ca, URL: http://www.icis.on.ca/orchestra

Orchestre de chambre de Montréal: Music Director, Wanda Kaluzny, #1100, 1200, av McGill College, Montréal, PQ H3B 4G7, 514/871-1224, Téléc: 514/393-9069

Orchestre de jeunes de la Montérégie: President, Jean Martel, 496, Pierre Germain, St-Hilaire, PQ G3H 5L2, 514/460-7101, Téléc: 514/464-2794

Orchestre symphonique des jeunes du West Island: Présidente, Aline Blain; Trésorière, Claire Cote; Secrétaire, Lise Lockwell, 100, av Douglas Shand, Pointe Claire, PQ H9R 4V1, 514/630-1218, Téléc: 514/630-1261

Orchestre symphonique de Laval: Présidente, Thérèse Spénard-Pilon, 4, Place Laval, Laval, PQ H7N 5Y3, 514/662-7222, Téléc: 514/629-2972

Orchestre symphonique de Montréal: Directrice générale, Louise Laplante; Musicothécaire, Gjiulio Masella; Directeur artistique, Charles Dutoit, 85, rue Ste-Catherine ouest, 9e étage, Québec, PQ H2X 3P4, 514/842-3402

Orchestre symphonique de Québec: Directeur général, Gilles Moisan, 130, av Grande-Allée ouest, Québec, PQ G1R 2G7, 418/643-5598, Téléc: 418/646-9665

Orchestre symphonique de Trois-Rivières: Président, Pierre Kirouac, CP 1281, Trois-Rivières, PQ G9A 5K8, 819/373-5340, Téléc: 819/373-6693

Orillia Youth Symphony Orchestra: Manager, Grace Miller, 52 Elmer Ave., Orillia, ON L3V 2S7, 705/326-7548; 325-3209

Oshawa-Durham Symphony Orchestra: Executive Director, Bob Johnston; Chairman, Alice Sheffield, PO Box 444, Oshawa, ON L1H 7L5, 905/579-6711, Fax: 905/576-0833, Email: 70244.1652@compuserve.com

Ottawa Symphony Orchestra Inc.: General Manager, Marian Pickering; Music Director, David Currie, #309, 1390 Prince of Wales Dr., Ottawa, ON K2C 3N6, 613/224-4982, Fax: 613/224-4982

Ottawa Youth Orchestra: Music Director, John Gomez, 604 Queen Elizabeth Driveway, Ottawa, ON K1S 3N5, 613/238-7270

Peterborough Symphony Orchestra: General Manager, Sigrid Rishor, PO Box 1135, Peterborough, ON K9J 7H4, 705/742-1992, Fax: 705/742-2077

Prince Edward Island Symphony Society: General Manager, John Clement; Executive Secretary, Maryanne E. Palmer, PO Box 185, Charlottetown, PE C1A 7K4, 902/894-3566, Fax: 902/892-5637

Prince George Symphony Orchestra Society: General Manager, Wendy Dawson; President, Les Waldie; Music Director, Paul Andreas Mahr, 2880 - 15 Ave., Prince George, BC V2M 1T1, 250/562-0800, Fax: 250/562-0844

Pro Arte Orchestra: President, Joseph Macerollo; Music Director, Victor Di Bello, 1692 Danforth Ave., Toronto, ON M4C 1H8, 416/466-4515

Regina Symphony: Executive Director, Pat Middleton; President, W. Douglas Keam, 200 Lakeshore Dr., Regina, SK S4P 3V7, 306/586-9555, Fax: 306/586-2133

Royal Conservatory Orchestra: Director, Rennie Regehr, 273 Bloor St. West, Toronto, ON M5S 1W2, 416/408-2824, Fax: 416/408-3096

Saskatchewan Orchestral Association: Administrator, Kathy Butler; President, Lola Mae Crawley, 23 Quincy Dr., Regina, SK S4S 6L7, 306/586-6879, Fax: 306/585-3701

Saskatoon Symphony Society: General Manager, Sigrid-Ann Thors, 703 Delta Bessborough, PO Box 1361, Saskatoon, SK S7K 3N9, 306/665-6414, Fax: 306/652-3364

Sault Symphony Association: Conductor/Director, John Wilkinson; Chairman, T.F. Baxter, #2, 121 Brock St., Sault Ste Marie, ON P6A 3B6, 705/945-5337, Fax: 705/949-6583

Scarborough Philharmonic Orchestra: General Manager, Ann Brokelman, 128 Sylvan Ave., Scarborough, ON M1M 1K3, 416/261-0380, Fax: 416/261-0652

Scotia Chamber Players: Managing & Artistic Director, Christopher Wilcox, #317, 1541 Barrington St., Halifax, NS B3J 1Z5, 902/429-9467, Fax: 902/425-6785

Sudbury Symphony Orchestra Association Inc.: Executive Director, Marg Barry; Artistic Director, Dr. Metro Kozak, St. Andrew's Place, 111 Larch St., 3rd Fl., Sudbury, ON P3E 4T5, 705/673-1280

Sudbury Youth Orchestra Inc.: Philip Candelaria, PO Box 2241, Stn A, Sudbury, ON P3A 4S1

Surrey Youth Orchestra: Music Director, Lucille Lewis, 14636 - 55A Ave., Surrey, BC V3S 1B1, 604/599-6731

Symphony of the Kootenays: General Manager, Ronald Edinger, PO Box 512, Cranbrook, BC V1C 4J1, 250/426-2924, Fax: 250/489-2101

Symphony New Brunswick: General Manager, Marje Harrison, 32 King St., Saint John, NB E2L 1G3, 506/634-8379, Fax: 506/634-0843, Toll Free: 1-800-848-3311, Email: symphony@nbnet.nb.ca

Symphony Nova Scotia: General Manager, Michael La Leune, Park Lane, #301, 5657 Spring Garden Rd., PO Box 218, Halifax, NS B3J 3R4, 902/421-1300, Fax: 902/422-1209

Tafelmusik Baroque Orchestra: Managing Director, Ottie Lockey, 427 Bloor St. West, Toronto, ON M5S 1X7, 416/964-6337, Fax: 416/964-2782, Email: info@tafelmusik.org, URL: http://www.hype.com/tafel

Te Deum Orchestra & Singers: Artistic Director, Dr. Richard Birney-Smith, 105 Victoria St., Dundas, ON L9H 2C1, 905/628-4533; Box Office: 416/205-5555, Fax: 905/628-9204, Toll Free: 1-800-263-0320

Thunder Bay Symphony Orchestra Association: Administrative Assistant, Brenda Gilham, PO Box 24036, Thunder Bay, ON P7A 7A9, 807/345-4331, Fax: 807/345-8915

Thunder Bay Symphony Youth Orchestra: Conductor, Diane Garrett, 1431 Cuthbertson Pl., Thunder Bay, ON P7E 5L3, 807/622-4220

Timmins Symphony Orchestra: Manager, Susan Huggins, PO Box 1365, Timmins, ON P4N 7N2, 705/267-1006, Fax: 705/267-1006

The Toronto Symphony Orchestra: Managing Director, Stan Shortt; President, Robert Martin; Music Director, Jukka-Pekka Saraste, 212 King St. West, 5th Fl., Toronto, ON M5H 1K5, 416/593-7769, Fax: 416/977-2912

Toronto Symphony Youth Orchestra: Manager, Colin Clarke, #550, 212 King St. West, Toronto, ON M5H 1K5, 416/593-7769, ext.372, Fax: 416/593-6788

University of Toronto Symphony Orchestra: Conductor, Dwight Bennett, Faculty of Music, Edward Johnson Bldg., University of Toronto, Toronto, ON M5S 1A1, 416/978-3750, Fax: 416/978-5771

University of Western Ontario Symphony Orchestra: Director, Jerome David Summers, Faculty of Music, University of Western Ontario, 1151 Richmond St. North, London, ON N6A 3K7, 519/661-2043, Fax: 519/661-3531

Canadian Almanac & Directory 1997

Vancouver Symphony Society: Acting General Manager, Michael Wall; Artistic Administrator, Michael Aze, 601 Smithe St., Vancouver, BC V6B 5G1, 604/684-9100, Fax: 604/684-9264, URL: http://www.worldtel.com/vancouver/symphony.html

Vancouver Youth Symphony Orchestra: Administrator, Charlotte Epp, #204, 3737 Oak St., Vancouver, BC V6H 2M4, 604/737-0714, Fax: 604/738-5161

Victoria Symphony: General Manager, C. Stephen Smith; Administrative Assistant, Lynn Mesher; President, Joan Banister, 846 Broughton St., Victoria, BC V8W 1E4, 250/385-9771, Fax: 250/385-7767

Wilfrid Laurier University Symphony Orchestra: Music Director, Paul Pulford, Faculty of Music, 75 University Ave. West, Waterloo, ON N2L 3C5, 519/884-1970, ext.2692

Windsor Symphony Society: Executive Director, T. Dawkins, 198 Pitt St. West., Windsor, ON N9A 5L4, 519/973-1238, Fax: 519/973-0764

Winnipeg Symphony Orchestra Inc.: Executive Director, Max Tappet; Artistic Director, Bramwell Tovey, #101, 555 Main St., Winnipeg, MB R3B 1C3, 204/949-3950; Box Office: 949-3999, Fax: 204/956-4271

York Symphony Orchestra Inc.: General Manager, Norma Thomas; Music Director, Roberto De Clara, PO Box 355, Richmond Hill, ON L4C 4Y6, 416/460-0860

Bach Elgar Choral Society (1905)
Bach Elgar Choir
10 MacNab St. South, Hamilton, ON L8P 4Y3
905/527-5995, Fax: 905/527-5088
Administrator, Susan Worthington
Publications: Voice of the City, q.
Affiliates: Ontario Choral Federation; Hamilton & Region Arts Council; Council for Business & the Arts in Canada; Canadian Conference of the Arts

Calgary Early Music Society (CEMS) (1976)
PO Box 157, Stn M, Calgary, AB T2P 2H6
403/286-0023
President, Alan Jessop
Publications: Newsletter, q.

Calgary Opera Association (1972)
The Burns Bldg., #601, 237 - 8th Ave. SE, Calgary, AB T2G 5C3
403/262-7286, Fax: 403/263-5428, Email: calopera@lexicom.ab.ca, URL: http://www.lexicom.ab.ca/~calopera
General Director, David Speers
Publications: Bravo, q.
Affiliates: Actors Equity Association

Canadian Academy of Recording Arts & Sciences/Académie canadienne des arts et des sciences de l'enregistrement (CARAS) (1975)
124 Merton St., 3rd Fl., Toronto, ON M4S 2Z2
416/485-3135, Fax: 416/485-4978
Executive Director, Daisy C. Falle
Publications: CARAS News, q.

Canadian Amateur Musicians/Musiciens amateurs du Canada (CAMMAC) (1953)
#2509, 1751, rue Richardson, Montréal, PQ H3K 1G6
514/932-8755, Fax: 514/932-9811
Executive Director, Danièle Rhéaume
Publications: The Amateur Musician/Le musicien amateur, s-a.

Canadian Association for Music Therapy/Association de Musicothérapie du Canada (CAMT) (1974)
Wilfrid Laurier University, Waterloo, ON N2L 3C5
519/884-1970, ext.6828, Fax: 519/884-8853, Toll Free: 1-800-996-2268, Email: ltracy@mach1.wlu.ca, URL: http://www.sos.cn.ca/~smacnay/camt/camt.html
President, Dr. Johanne Brodeur
Administrative Coordinator, Lynda Tracy
Publications: CAMT Newsletter, 3 pa; Canadian Journal of Music Therapy

Canadian Band Association/Association canadienne des harmonies (CBA) (1934)
2345 Orchard Dr., Abbotsford, BC V3G 2B5
604/850-1413, Fax: 604/888-4324
President, Allan Hicks
Publications: The Canadian Band Journal, q.; Canadian Band Association Directory

ALBERTA BAND ASSOCIATION (ABA)
#808, 10136 - 100 St., Edmonton, AB T5J 0P1
403/429-0482, Fax: 403/429-0559
Executive Director, Raymond Baril
Publications: Musicom, q.

BRITISH COLUMBIA BAND ASSOCIATION
PO Box 100, Sardis, BC V2R 1A5
604/858-0263, Fax: 604/837-7164
Secretary, Dale Warr

FÉDÉRATION DES HARMONIES DU QUÉBEC (FHQ) (1927)
4545, av Pierre-de-Coubertin, CP 1000, Succ. M, Montréal, PQ H1V 3R2
514/252-3026, Téléc: 514/251-8038
Coordonnatrice, Chantal Isabelle
Président, Claude St-Amand
Publications: Harmonie-Québec, trimestriel
Organisation(s) affiliée(s): Fédération des associations de musiciens éducateurs du Québec

MANITOBA BAND ASSOCIATION (1987)
15 Pinecrest Bay, Winnipeg, MB R2G 1W2
204/663-1226
Executive Director, Ken Epp
Publications: BandNews, 3 pa

NEW BRUNSWICK BAND ASSOCIATION
PO Box 32, Florenceville, NB E3B 6J6
506/392-5115
Secretary, Sonja Sproull

NOVA SCOTIA BAND ASSOCIATION
210 Kaulback St., Truro, NS B2N 3T9
902/895-1015, Fax: 902/328-6220
Secretary, Jean McKenzie

ONTARIO BAND ASSOCIATION (1934)
Canadian Forces, School of Music, CFB Borden, Borden, ON L0M 1C0
613/993-2016
Executive Secretary, Benjamin Trowell
Publications: CBA Newsletter, q.

SASKATCHEWAN BAND ASSOCIATION (SBA) (1983)
1840 McIntyre St., Regina, SK S4P 2P9
306/522-2263, Fax: 306/656-2177
Executive Director, Holly Wildeman
Publications: SBA Journal, q.
Affiliates: Saskatchewan Pipe Band Association

Canadian Bureau for the Advancement of Music (CBAM) (1917)
Exhibition Place, Toronto, ON M6K 3C3
416/260-6451; 7795
CAO, Nancy Manning

Canadian Children's Opera Chorus (CCOC) (1968)
Opera Centre, #215, 227 Front St. East, Toronto, ON M5A 1E8
416/366-0467, Fax: 416/363-5584

Manager, Ann Hartford Marshall
Publications: Keynotes, s-a.

Canadian Country Music Association/Association de la musique country canadienne (CCMA) (1976)
#127, 3800 Steeles Ave. West, Woodbridge, ON L4L 4G9
905/850-1144, Fax: 905/856-1633
Executive Director, Sheila Hamilton
Assistant Executive Director, Donna Martens
Publications: Canada Country, q.

Canadian Disc Jockey Association (CDJA) (1977)
#300, 3148 Kingston Rd., Scarborough, ON M1M 1P4
416/755-3898, Fax: 416/287-8817
Executive Director, Dennis E. Hampson
National Vice-President, James Griffin
National Membership Director, Blain Davis
National Secretary, Dan Shantz
Publications: CDJA Newsletter, m.
Affiliates: American DJ Association

Canadian Independent Record Production Association (CIRPA) (1975)
#614, 214 King St. West, Toronto, ON M5H 3S6
416/593-1665, Fax: 416/593-7563, Email: cirpa@interlog.com, URL: http://www.cmrra.ca/cirpa
President, Brian Chater
Program Coordinator, Mary Vrantsidis
Membership, Sharon Hookway
Publications: CIRPA Newsletter, m.

Canadian League of Composers
c/o Canadian Music Centre, 20 St. Joseph St., Toronto, ON M4Y 1J9
416/964-1364
President, Dr. Rodney Sharman

Canadian Music Centre/Centre de musique canadienne (CMC) (1959)
Chalmers House, 20 St. Joseph St., Toronto, ON M4Y 1J9
416/961-6601, Fax: 416/961-7198, Email: cmc@interlog.com, URL: http://www.culturenet.ca/cmc
Executive Director, Simone Auger
President, Timothy Maloney
Publications: Directory of Associate Composers; Acquisitions; CMCDS Catalogue; Canadian Choral Music Catalogue; Canadian Orchestral Music Catalogue
Affiliates: International Association of Music Information Centres; Canadian Music Libraries Association

Canadian Music Competitions Inc./Concours de musique du Canada inc.
#705, 1030, rue Saint-Alexandra, Montréal, PQ H2Z 1P3
514/879-1959, Fax: 514/979-1835
Founder, Claude Deschamps
Acting General Director, Louis Dallaire

Canadian Music Educators' Association/Association canadienne des éducateurs de musique (CMEA) (1959)
43 Victoria Hill, Sydney, NS B1R 1N9
902/567-2398, Fax: 902/564-0123, Email: efavaro@fox.nstn.ca, URL: http://www.stemnet.nf.ca/~barobert/cmea/cmea.html
President, Eric Favaro
Publications: Canadian Music Educator, Newsletter Edition, 3 pa; Canadian Music Educator
Affiliates: International Society for Music Education

Canadian Music Festival Adjudicators' Association (1960)
1671 Lakeshore Rd., RR#5, Sarnia, ON N7T 7H6
519/542-4572, Fax: 519/542-4854

President, Gwen Beamish
Vice-President, Kathleen Keple
Vice-President, Ireneus Zuk
Publications: CMFAA Newsletter, 3 pa

Canadian Musical Heritage Society/Société pour le patrimoine musical canadien (CMHS) (1982)
50 Rideau St., PO Box 53161, Ottawa, ON K1N 1C5
613/788-2600, ext.8265, Email: cford@ccs.carleton.ca
Executive Secretary, Clifford Ford
Publications: News from the Canadian Musical Heritage/Nouvelles de la société pour le patrimoine musical canadien

Canadian Opera Company/Compagnie d'opéra canadienne (COC) (1950)
227 Front St. East, Toronto, ON M5A 1E8
416/363-6671, Fax: 416/363-5584, Email: hweide@interlog.com
Artistic Director, Richard Bradshaw
General Manager, Elaine Calder
Publications: Prelude, 2-3 pa
Affiliates: The Canadian Opera Foundation; Canadian Opera Women's Committee

Canadian Recording Industry Association/Association de l'industrie canadienne de l'enregistrement (CRIA)
#400, 1250 Bay St., Toronto, ON M5R 2B1
416/967-7272, Fax: 416/967-9415
President, W. Brian Robertson
Office Manager, Brenda Gaze

Canadian Society for Traditional Music (CSTM) (1956)
PO Box 4232, Stn C, Calgary, AB T2T 5N1
403/230-0340
Director, John Leeder
Publications: Canadian Folk Music Journal; Canadian Folk Music Bulletin

Canadian University Music Society/Société de musique des universités canadiennes (CUMS) (1979)
c/o Faculty of Music, Wilfrid Laurier University, Waterloo, ON N2L 3C5
519/253-4232, Fax: 519/973-7050
President, Dr. Anne C. Hall
Secretary, Prof. Martin Waltz
Treasurer, Dr. James Deaville
Publications: Canadian University Music Review, s-a.; CUMS Newsletter; CUMS Directory
Affiliates: Social Sciences & Humanities Research Council of Canada

Country Music Foundation of Canada Inc. (1987)
8607 - 128 Ave., Edmonton, AB T5E 0G3
403/476-8230, Fax: 403/472-2584
Chairman, William Maxim

Early Music Vancouver (1970)
Vancouver Society for Early Music
1254 - 7 Ave. West, Vancouver, BC V6H 1B6
604/732-1610, Fax: 604/732-1602, Email: earlymusic@mindlink.bc.ca, URL: http://mindlink.net/early-music
Executive Director, José Verstappen
Publications: Musick, q.

Edmonton Jazz Society (EJS) (1973)
Yardbird Suite
10203 - 86 Ave., Edmonton, AB T6E 2M2
403/432-0428, Fax: 403/433-3773, Email: yardbird@istar.ca, URL: http://www.ualberta.ca/edmonton/jazz
Publications: Newsletter, 5-6 pa

Edmonton Opera Association (1963)
#320, 10232 - 112 St., Edmonton, AB T5K 1M4
403/424-4040; Box Office: 429-1000, Fax: 403/429-0600
Artistic Director, Irving Guttman, C.M.
General Manager, Nejolla B. Korris
Publications: About Opera, 3 pa

Festival Chorus of Calgary
The Calgary Centre for Performing Arts, 205 - 8 Ave. SE, Calgary, AB T2G 0K9
403/294-7400

Foundation to Assist Canadian Talent on Records (FACTOR) (1982)
125 George St., 2nd Fl., Toronto, ON M5A 2N4
416/368-8678
Executive Director, Heather Ostertag
Publications: Canadian Record Catalogue/de disques canadiens

Friends of Chamber Music (1948)
PO Box 74636, RPO Kits, Vancouver, BC V6K 4P4
604/437-5716, Fax: 604/437-4769
Program Chairman, Eric Wilson

Kiwanis Music Festival Association of Greater Toronto
#501, 100 Adelaide St. West, Toronto, ON M5H 1S3
416/363-3238, Fax: 416/363-2657
General Manager, Jane Craig

Manitoba Composers' Association Inc. (MCA) (1982)
#407, 100 Arthur St., Winnipeg, MB R3B 1H3
204/942-6152, Fax: 204/942-1555
President, Paul Sparling

Manitoba Opera Association Inc. (1969)
Portage Place, #393, Portage Ave., PO Box 31027, Winnipeg, MB R3B 3K9
204/942-7479, Fax: 204/949-0377
President, James Astwood
Publications: House Programs, 3 pa
Affiliates: Opera America; Canadian Actor's Equity

Mariposa Folk Foundation (1961)
1436 Queen St. West, PO Box 90026, Toronto, ON M6K 1L0
416/924-4839, Fax: 416/536-4021, URL: http://www.eagle.ca/mariposa
President, Lynne Hurry
Publications: Mariposa Notes, bi-m.

Music & Entertainment Industry Educators Association (MEIEA) (1978)
c/o Trebas Institute, 451, rue St-Jean, Montréal, PQ H2Y 2R5
514/845-4141
Director, David P. Leonard
Publications: MEIEA Notes, q.

Music Industries Association of Canada/Association canadienne des industries de la musique (MIAC) (1971)
#109, 1210 Sheppard Ave. East, North York, ON M2K 1E3
416/490-1871, Fax: 416/490-9739
Executive Director, Al Kowalenko, CAE
Publications: MIAC Statistics Report, a.; MIAC Newsletter
Affiliates: Music Distributors Association - USA; National Association of Music Merchants - USA

Music for Young Children/Musique pour les jeunes enfants (MYC) (1980)
39 Leacock Way, Kanata, ON K2K 1T1
613/592-7565, Fax: 613/592-9353, Toll Free: 1-800-561-1692, Email: myc@myc.com, URL: http://www.myc.com
International Director, Frances M. Balodis, M.Ed., A.R.C.T.
Business Manager, Gunars Balodis
Administrator, Dianne Markle
Publications: MYC from C to C/Gofrit, m.; MY YOU Communicate

Musicaction (1985)
#209, 455, rue Saint-Antoine ouest, Montréal, PQ H2Z 1J1
514/861-8444, Téléc: 514/861-4423
Directrice générale, Nicole Payette

The National Music Festival/Festival national de musique (1972)
1034 Chestnut Ave., Moose Jaw, SK S6H 1A6
306/693-7087, Fax: 306/693-7087
Executive Director, Sharon L. Penner
Chairman, J. Alexander Clark
Publications: Official Regulations & Syllabus, a.
Affiliates: Federation of Canadian Music Festivals

National Shevchenko Musical Ensemble Guild of Canada (1972)
626 Bathurst St., Toronto, ON M5S 2R1
416/533-2725, Fax: 416/533-6348
Administrator, Ginger Kautto
Publications: Bulletin, s-a.

New Brunswick Competitive Festival of Music Inc. (1936)
PO Box 2022, Saint John, NB E2L 3T5
506/652-8581
President, Shirley Dysart
Executive Secretary, Colleen Arseneau
Affiliates: New Brunswick Federation of Music Festivals; Canadian Federation of Music Festivals

Nova Scotia Kiwanis Music Festival (1935)
PO Box 1623, Stn Central Halifax, Halifax, NS B3J 2Z1
902/423-6147, Fax: 902/423-6147
Executive Director, Sharon Harland
Publications: Syllabus, a.; Program
Affiliates: Federation of Music Festivals of Nova Scotia; Federation of Canadian Music Festivals; CIBC National Festival of Music

Ontario Choral Federation
100 Richmond St. East, Toronto, ON M5C 1P9
416/363-7488, Fax: 416/363-8236
Executive Director, Bev Jahnke

Opera Canada (1960)
#434, 366 Adelaide St. East, Toronto, ON M5A 3X9
416/363-0395, Fax: 416/363-0396, Toll Free: 1-800-331-6014
Executive Director, Ric Amis
Publications: Opera Canada, q.
Affiliates: Professional Opera Companies of Canada

L'Opéra de Montréal (L'OdM) (1980)
260, boul de Maisonneuve ouest, Montréal, PQ H2X 1Y9
514/985-2222, Téléc: 514/985-2219, Infoligne: 514/282-6732, Courrier électronique: opera@mtl@stria.ca, URL: http://www.stria.ca/opera-mtl
Directeur général et artistique, Bernard Uzan
Adjoint au directeur artistique, Michel Beaulac
Directeur, Communications et marketing, Patrick-Jean Poirier
Directrice, Développement et financement, Elise Côté
Directrice, Atelier Lyrique, Chantal Lambert, 514/596-0223
Directeur, Production, Michel Gagnon

Directeur, Technique, Olivier Gascon
Président, Conseil d'administration, Roger D. Landry

Opera Ontario (1980)
Kitchener Waterloo Opera; Opera Hamilton
Stelco Tower, #200, 100 King St. West, Hamilton, ON L8P 1A2
905/527-7627, Box Office: 526-6556, Fax: 905/527-0014
General Director, Kenneth D. Freeman
Publications: High Notes, q.; Kudos

Orchestras Ontario (1955)
#311, 56 The Esplanade, Toronto, ON M5E 1A7
416/366-8834, Fax: 416/366-1780, Email: assoc@terraport.net/aco, URL: http://www.terraport.net/aco
Executive Director, Betty Webster
Publications: Orchestra Canada, bi-m.

Orchestre symphonique des jeunes de Montréal (OSJM) (1976)
CP 418, Succ. Youville, Montréal, PQ H2P 2V6
514/385-0064, Téléc: 514/385-5879
Président, Jean-Paul Jacques
Vice-présidente, Marguerite Schabas
Trésorier, Jean-Claude Lamontagne
Secrétaire, Marielle Wertheimer
Directeur artistique, Louis Lavigueur

Organization of Canadian Symphony Musicians/ L'Organisation des musiciens d'orchestres symphonique du Canada (OCSM) (1981)
#6, 445, rue Gerard-Morrisset, Québec, PQ G1S 4V5
418/688-0801
President, Evelyne Robitaille
Publications: Una Voce, q.
Affiliates: Association of Canadian Orchestras; Canadian Conference of the Arts

Pacific Opera Victoria (POV) (1975)
1316B Government St., Victoria, BC V8W 1Y8
250/385-0222, Fax: 250/382-4944, Info Line: 250/382-1641, URL: http://www.islandnet.com/~opera/POVhome.html
General Manager, Jeffrey Ouellette
Manager, Ticket Services & Artistic Administration, Barbara Newton
Marketing & Development Coordinator, Susan Kerschbaum
Administrative Assistant, Kathy Allison

Professional Opera Companies of Canada (1980)
c/o L'Opéra de Montréal, 260, boul de Maisonneuve ouest, Montréal, PQ H2X 1Y9
514/985-2222, Fax: 514/985-2219
General Artistic Director, Bernard Uzan

Raag-Mala Music Society of Toronto
63 Cassis Dr., Etobicoke, ON M9V 4Z4
905/472-0937
President, Dinesh Gandhi

Royal Canadian College of Organists/Collège royal canadien des organistes (RCCO) (1909)
#302, 112 St. Clair Ave. West, Toronto, ON M4V 2Y3
416/929-6400, Fax: 416/929-6400, URL: http://magi.com/~rjewell/rcco.html
Executive Director, Peter Nikiforuk
Publications: Yearbook; The College Newsletter; The American Organist

Saskatoon Opera Association (1977)
PO Box 414, Stn Sub 6, Saskatoon, SK S7N 0W0
306/374-1630
General Manager, Marilyn Harrison
Publications: Newsletter

Société Pro Musica Inc./Pro Musica Society Inc. (1948)
3450, rue St-Urbain, Montréal, PQ H2X 2N5
514/845-0532, Téléc: 514/845-1500, URL: http://www.apexdigital.com/promusica
Directeur général, Monique Dubé
Directeur artistique, Pierre Rolland

Society for the Preservation & Encouragement of Barber Shop Quartet Singing in America Inc. (1938)
c/o Harmony Hall, 6315 Third Ave., Kenosha, WI 53140 USA
414/654-9111, 653-8440, Fax: 414/654-4048
Executive Director, Joe Liles
Publications: The Harmonizer, bi-m.

Songwriters Association of Canada/Association des auteurs-compositeurs canadiens
#400, 1235 Bay St., Toronto, ON M5R 3K4
416/924-7664, Fax: 416/924-5228, Email: sac@goodmedia.com, URL: http://www.goodmedia.com/sac/
Executive Director, Donna Murphy
Publications: The Bridge, q.

The Toronto Mendelssohn Choir (1894)
60 Simcoe St., Toronto, ON M5J 2H5
416/598-0422, Fax: 416/598-2992
General Manager, Donna White

Vancouver New Music Society (VNMS) (1973)
#400, 873 Beatty St., Vancouver, BC V6B 2M6
604/606-6440, Fax: 604/606-6442
General Manager, Randy Smith
President, Michael Shea
Artistic Director, Owen Underhill
Affiliates: Canadian Music Centre

Vancouver Opera (VO) (1958)
Vancouver Opera Association
#500, 845 Cambie St., Vancouver, BC V6B 4Z9
604/682-2871; Box Office: 604/683-0222, Fax: 604/682-3981, Telex: 04-352848 VCR
General Director, Robert J. Hallam
Director, Marketing & Communications, Tricia Baldwin
Affiliates: Canadian Actors' Equity Association; IATSE; AFM

Western Board of Music (WBM) (1934)
11044 - 90 Ave., Edmonton, AB T6G 1A7
403/492-3264, Fax: 403/492-0200, Toll Free: 1-800-263-9738
Executive Director, Leslie Vermeer
Publications: WB News/Bulletin, 3-4 pa

Winnipeg Music Competition Festival
#206, 180 Market Ave. East, Winnipeg, MB R3B 0P7
204/947-0184, Fax: 204/957-1132
Executive Director, Bill Muir

Youth & Music Canada/Jeunesses musicales du Canada (YMC)
305, av Mont-Royal est, Montréal, PQ H2T 1P8
514/845-4108; Toronto: 416/535-0660
Executive Director, Nicolas Desjardins

DANCE

Alberta Ballet (1966)
Nat Christie Centre, 141 - 18 Ave. SW, Calgary, AB T2S 0B8
403/245-4222, Fax: 403/245-6573
Artistic Director, Ali Pourfarrokh
Executive Director, Greg Epton
Publications: Balletin, q.

Alberta Ballet School of Dance: West Annex, 2nd Fl., 906 - 12th Ave. SW, Calgary, AB T2R 1K7, 403/245-2274, Fax: 403/245-2293
Edmonton Branch Office: #201, 10310 Jasper Ave., Edmonton, AB T5J 2W4, 403/428-6839, Fax: 403/428-4589

Alberta Dance Alliance
11759 Groat Rd., 2nd Fl., Edmonton, AB T5M 3K6
403/422-8107, Fax: 403/422-8161, Email: abdance@ccinet.ab.ca
Executive Director, Bobbi Westman

Anjali Cultural Horizons Inc.
#174, 11 Dufferin Rd., Ottawa, ON K1M 2A6
613/745-1368, Fax: 613/745-0299
Artistic Director, Anne-Marie Gaston

Ballet British Columbia (1986)
#102, 1101 West Broadway, Vancouver, BC V6H 1G2
604/732-5003, Fax: 604/732-4417
Artistic Director, John Alleyne
General Manager, Howard R. Jang
Publications: Back Stage with the Ballet, s-a.

Ballet Creole
428C Queen St. East, Toronto, ON M5A 1T4
416/861-3048, Fax: 416/214-0620
Artistic Director, Patrick Parson

Ballet Jörgen
213B Glebeholme Blvd., Toronto, ON M4J 1S8
416/461-5045, Fax: 416/751-8388
Artistic Director, Bengt Jörgen
Administrator, Susan Bodie

Ballet North
12245 - 131 St., Edmonton, AB T5L 1M8
403/455-8407, Fax: 403/454-0137
Artistic Director, Paula Groulx
General Manager, Paul Reich

Ballet Ouest
CP 85, Beaconsfield, PQ H9W 5T6
514/990-7729, Téléc: 514/398-8241
Artistic Director, Margaret Mehuys
Secretary, Suzanne Watt

Les Ballets Jazz de Montréal (1972)
3450, rue St-Urbain, Montréal, PQ H2X 2N5
514/982-6771, Téléc: 514/982-9145
Directeur artistique, Yvan Michaud
Directrice administrative, Caroline Salbaing

birtz & co dance institute
579 - 3rd St. SE, Medicine Hat, AB T1A 0H2
403/526-4485, Email: jbirtz@mlc.awinc.com
Artistic Director, Joanne Birtz
General Manager, Louise Plante

Brian Webb Dance Co.
c/o Grant MacEwan College, PO Box 1796, Edmonton, AB T5J 2P2
403/497-4416, Fax: 403/497-4330
Artistic Director, Brian Webb
Administrative Assistant, Daisy Kaiser

Brouhaha danse
5277, rue St-Denis, Montréal, PQ H2J 2M4
514/273-8221, Téléc: 514/528-5842
Directrice artistique, Hélène Langevin

Canadian Association of Professional Dance Organizations/Association canadienne des organisations professionnelles de danse (CAPDO) (1978)
3790 Farmview Rd., RR#1, Kinburn, ON K0A 2H0

Canadian Almanac & Directory 1997

613/832-0397, Fax: 613/832-1321, Email: capdo@magi.com; ay8_8@freenet.carleton.ca
Executive Director, Ellen Busby
Publications: Membership Directory; Fax News Bulletin
Affiliates: Member Companies: Alberta Ballet Company, Edmonton; Anna Wyman Dance Theatre, Vancouver; Ballet British Columbia, Vancouver; Contemporary Dancers, Winnipeg; Dancemakers, Toronto; Dancevision/Dansevision, Toronto; Danny Grossman Dance Company, Toronto; Les Grands Ballets Canadiens, Montréal; Le Groupe de la Place Royale, Ottawa; The National Ballet of Canada, Toronto; The National Ballet School, Toronto; Royal Winnipeg Ballet, Winnipeg; Theatre Ballet of Canada, Ottawa; Toronto Dance Theatre, Toronto

Canadian Children's Dance Theatre
509 Parliament St., Toronto, ON M4X 1P3
416/924-5657, Fax: 416/924-4141
Artistic Director, Deborah Lundmark
Managing Director, Michael Smith

Canadian Dance Teachers Association/ Association canadienne des professeurs de danse (CDTA) (1949)
#38, 6033 Shawson Dr., Mississauga, ON L5T 1H8
905/564-2139
President, Irene Collins
Office Manager, Joan Amodeo
Publications: Newsletter, s-a.

Carousel Theatre Society
1411 Cartwright St., Vancouver, BC V6H 3R7
604/669-3410; Box Office: 604/685-6217, Fax: 604/669-3817
Managing Artistic Director, Elizabeth Ball
General Manager, Kimberly Dossett

Carré des Lombes
#514, 3575, boul St-Laurent, Montréal, PQ H2X 2T7
514/287-9339, Téléc: 514/287-9415
Directrice artistique, Danièle Desnoyers

Cash & Company Dance
925 Longfellow Ave., Mississauga, ON L5H 2X9
416/274-5057
Artistic Director, Susan Cash

Catalyst Theatre Society of Alberta
10943 - 84 Ave., Edmonton, AB T6G 0V5
403/431-1750, Fax: 403/433-3060
Co-Artistic Director, Jonathan Christenson
Co-Artistic Director, Joey Tremblay

Cercle d'expression artistique Nyata Nyata
4374, boul St-Laurent, 3e étage, Montréal, PQ H2W 1Z5
514/849-9781, Téléc: 514/849-9781
Directeur artistique, Zab Maboungou
Directeur général, Paul Miller

Cercle virtueux dansethéâtre
3772, rue de Bullion, Montréal, PQ H2W 2C8
514/499-0678
Directrice artistique, Dulcinea Langfelder

Compagnie de Brune
CP 656, Succ. Desjardins, Montréal, PQ H5B 1B7
514/525-0663, Téléc: 514/525-2052
Directrice artistique, Lynda Gaudreau

Compagnie de Danse ethnique Migrations
CP 8892, Ste-Foy, PQ G1V 4N7
418/522-0539
Directeur artistique, Richard Turcotte
Directrice générale, Yvette Michelin

La Compagnie Danse Partout
#214, 310, boul Langelier, Québec, PQ G1K 5N3
418/649-8312, Téléc: 418/649-4702
Directeur artistique, Luc Tremblay
Responsable, Administration, Jean-Pierre Parent

Compagnie Marie Chouinard
#615, 3981, boul St-Laurent, Montréal, PQ H2W 1Y5
514/843-9036, Téléc: 514/849-7616
Directrice artistique, Marie Chouinard
Directeur général, Pierre Des Marais

Contemporary Dancers Canada (1964)
Winnipeg's Contemporary Dancers
109 Pulford St., Winnipeg, MB R3L 1X8
204/452-0229, Fax: 204/287-8618, Email: mwq250@freenet.mb.ca, URL: http://www.escape.ca/~cesmb/wcd/wcdhome.htm
Artistic Director, Tom Stroud
General Manager, Alanna M. Keefe

Création Isis
760, av Walker, Montréal, PQ H4C 2H4
514/933-4571, Fax: 514/933-2680
Co-Artistic Director, Jo Lechay
Co-Artistic Director, Eugene Lion
Administrator, Robert Byron Hutchings

Dance Collective
671 Walker Ave., Winnipeg, MB R3L 1C6
204/284-4886
Artistic Director, Ruth Cansfield
General Manager, Hugh Conacher

Dance Manitoba Inc.
#204, 180 Market Ave. East, Winnipeg, MB R3B 0P7
204/943-7116, Fax: 204/986-4400
Administrator, Heather Guest

Dance Nova Scotia (DANS)
#901, 1809 Barrington St., Halifax, NS B3J 3K8
902/422-1749, Fax: 902/422-0881
Executive Director, Dianne Milligan
Publications: DANS News, q.; Quarterly Report

Dance Ontario Association
179 Richmond St. West, Toronto, ON M5V 1V3
416/204-1083, Fax: 416/204-1085, Email: danceont@io.org
Executive Director, Mimi Beck
General Manager, Rosslyn Jacob-Edwards

Dance Oremus Danse
#6, 510 Jarvis St., Toronto, ON M4Y 2H6
416/928-0208, Fax: 416/927-0042
Artistic Director, Paul Dwyer
General Manager, Peter Stadnyk

Dance Saskatchewan (1979)
225 - 23rd St. East, PO Box 8789, Saskatoon, SK S7K 6S6
306/931-8480, Fax: 306/244-1520, Toll Free: 1-800-667-8480, Email: ac355@sfn.saskatoon.sk.ca
Executive Director, Jill Reid
Publications: Footnotes, 5 pa; Youthline; Dance Directory

Dance Umbrella of Ontario
#201, 490 Adelaide St. West, Toronto, ON M5V 1Y2
416/504-6429, Fax: 416/504-8702, Email: duodance@interlog.com
Executive Director, Myles Warren

Dancecorps
399 West 5th Ave., Vancouver, BC V5Y 1J6
604/877-1910, Fax: 604/877-1910
Co-Artistic Director, Harvey Meller

Co-Artistic Director, Cornelius Fisher-Credo
General Manager, Jim Smith

Dancemakers (1974)
927 Dupont St., Toronto, ON M6H 1Z1
416/535-8880, Fax: 416/535-8929, Email: dncemkrs@interlog.com, URL: http://www.interlog.com/~dncemkrs
Artistic Director, Serge Bennathan
General Manager, K. George Wolf
Administrative Assistant, Lisanne Gavigan
Publications: Dancemakers News, s-a.

Dancer Transition Resource Centre/Centre de Ressources pour Danseurs en Transition (1985)
#202, 66 Gerrard St. East, Toronto, ON M4Y 2R3
416/595-5655, Fax: 416/595-0009
Executive Director, Joysanne Sidimus
President, Karen Kain
Administrator, Jennifer Spencer
Publications: Dancer Transition Resource Centre Newsletter; Connections: Networking Directory; Dance Life
Affiliates: Canadian Association of Professional Dance Organizations; The Ontario Dance Network; Le Regroupement québécois de la Danse

Dancer's Studio West
2007 - 10th Ave. SW, Calgary, AB T3C 0K4
403/244-0950, Fax: 403/243-5178
Artistic Director, Elaine Bowman
Director General, Peter Hoff

Danny Grossman Dance Company
511 Bloor St. West, Toronto, ON M5S 1Y4
416/531-8350, Fax: 416/531-1791, Email: dgdance@interlog.com
Artistic Director, Danny Grossman
General Manager, Jane Marsland

Danse actuelle Martine Époque
986, rue Fabre, Longueuil, PQ J4J 5A8
514/282-7063
Directrice artistique, Martine Époque

Danse-Cite inc.
#2220, 840, rue Cherrier est, Montréal, PQ H2L 1H4
514/525-3595, Téléc: 514/525-6632
Directeur artistique, Daniel Soulières

Danse Imédia
1204, Mont-Royal est, Montréal, PQ H2J 1Y1
514/526-2201
Directeur artistique, Rafik Sabbagh

Danse Kalashas
#27, 6186, av Notre-Dame de Grâce, Montréal, PQ H4B 1K8
514/484-3508
Chorégraphe, Richard Tremblay

Danse Trielle
CP 1433, Succ. St-Martin, Laval, PQ H7V 3P7
514/629-4514
Directrice artistique, Sylvie Samson
Administrateur, Richard Beaupré

Danstabat
2456 Pandora St., Vancouver, BC V5K 1V6
604/255-2930
Artistic Director, Chick Snipper
General Manager, Louise Bentall

Decidedly Jazz Danceworks
1514 - 4 St. SW, Calgary, AB T2R 0Y4
403/245-3533, Fax: 403/245-3584
Artistic Director, Vicki Adams Willis
General Manager, Kathi Sundstrom

Desrosiers Dance Theatre
#103, 219 Broadview Ave., Toronto, ON M4M 2G3
416/463-5341, Fax: 416/463-4770
Artistic Director, Robert Desrosiers

EDAM Performing Arts Society (EDAM)
303 East 8th Ave., Vancouver, BC V5T 1S1
604/876-9559, Fax: 604/876-4099
Artistic Director, Peter Bingham
General Manager, Mona Hamill
Affiliates: Canadian Association of Professional Dance Organizations

Fijiwara Dance Inventions
66 Humewood Dr., Toronto, ON M6C 2W5
416/654-8426
Artistic Director, Denise Fujiwara

Fondation Jean-Pierre Perreault
2022, rue Sherbrooke est, Montréal, PQ H2K 1B9
514/525-2464, Téléc: 514/525-0172
Directeur artistique et chorégraphe, Jean-Pierre Perreault
Directrice générale, Louise Laplante

Formation de danse Howard Richard
551, Mont-Royal est, 3e étage, Montréal, PQ H2J 1W6
514/527-7770, Téléc: 514/527-7621
Directeur artistique, Howard Richard
Directeur administratif, Charles St-Onge

Fortier Danse-Création
CP 605, Succ. C, Montréal, PQ H2L 4L5
514/529-8158, Téléc: 514/525-0172
Directeur artistique, Paul-André Fortier
Directeur administratif, Gilles Savary

Gina Lori Riley Dance Enterprises
3277 Sandwich St., Windsor, ON N9C 1A9
519/977-5438, Fax: 519/977-8218
Artistic Director, Gina Lori Riley
General Manager, Patricia Wilson

Goh Ballet Society
2345 Main St., Vancouver, BC V5T 3C9
604/872-4014, Fax: 604/872-4011
Artistic Director, Choo Chiat Goh

Les Grands Ballets Canadiens (1958)
Maison de la Danse, 4816, rue Rivard, Montréal, PQ H2J 2N6
514/849-8681, Téléc: 514/849-0098
Directeur artistique, Lawrence Rhodes
Directrice générale intérimaire, Suzanne Thomas

Le Groupe de la Place Royale
#2, 2 Daly St., Ottawa, ON K1N 6E2
613/235-1492, Fax: 613/235-1651, Email: bj581@freenet.carleton.ca
Artistic Director, Peter Boneham
General Manager & Associate Director, Katherine Watson

Intempco
New Dance Horizons
#202, 1808 Smith St., Regina, SK S4P 2N4
306/525-5393, Fax: 306/569-4649
Artistic Director, Robin Poitras
Administrative/Production Coordinator, Michael Toppings

Jocelyne Montpetit Danse
a/s Gestion artistique Badeaux, 4387, av Christophe-Colomb, Montréal, PQ H2J 3G4
514/521-5850, Téléc: 514/521-7157
Directrice artistique, Jocelyne Montpetit

Judith Marcuse Dance Projects
#402, 873 Beatty St., Vancouver, BC V6B 2M6
604/606-6425, Fax: 604/606-6432
Artistic Director, Judith Marcuse
Executive Director, Andrew Wilhelm-Boyles

Julie West Dance Foundation
#3, 88 MacLaren St., Ottawa, ON K2P 0K6
613/234-4310, Fax: 613/594-8705
Artistic Director, Julie West

Jumpstart Performance Society
6450 Deer Lake Ave., Burnaby, BC V5G 2J3
604/299-4522, Fax: 604/299-7635
Artistic Director, Lee Eisler
General Manager, Sarah Stewart

Karen Jamieson Dance Company
221 East 16th Ave., Vancouver, BC V5T 2T5
604/872-5658, Fax: 604/872-7932
Artistic Director, Karen Jamieson
Managing Director, Jay Rankin, Email: jay_rankin@mindlink.bc.ca

Kinesis Dance Society
1773 East 4th Ave., Vancouver, BC V5N 1J9
604/872-0233
Artistic Director, Paras Terezakis

Kokora Dance Theatre Society
314 Powell St., Vancouver, BC V6A 1G4
604/662-7441, Fax: 604/683-6649
Artistic Director, Barbara Bourget
Executive Director, Jay Hirabayashi

Kompany Dance
#810, 10136 - 100 St., Edmonton, AB T5J 0P1
403/944-9115
Artistic Director, Darold Roles
Artistic Director, Ron Schuster
General Manager, Colette Switzer

La La La Human Steps
#206, 5655, av du Parc, Montréal, PQ H2V 4H2
514/277-9090, Téléc: 514/277-0862, URL: http://www.bart.nl/~xipe/lalala.htm
Directeur artistique, Édouard Lock
Directeur général, Paul Tanguay

Lola MacLaughlin Dance
#103, 1014 Homer St., Vancouver, BC V6B 2W9
604/683-8240
Artistic Director, Lola MacLaughlin

Louise Bédard Danse
a/s de La Femme 100 Têtes, #304, 150, rue Grant, Longueuil, PQ J4H 3H6
514/646-6248, Téléc: 514/646-7619
Directrice artistique, Louise Bédard
Directrice générale, Yolaine Gervais

Lucie Grégoire Danse
a/s de Diagramme gestion culturelle, #4140, 5505, boul St-Laurent, Montréal, PQ H2T 1S6
514/273-7785, Fax: 514/273-8051
Directrice artistique, Lucie Grégoire

Manitoba Independent Choreographers Association
131 Salme Dr., Winnipeg, MB R2M 1Y9
204/255-1048, Fax: 204/255-6499
Gail Petursson-Hiley
Patti Caplette

Margie Gillis Dance Foundation
#502, 3575 boul St-Laurent, Montréal, PQ H2X 2T7
514/845-3115, Fax: 514/845-3424, Email: nicholas@mgdf.interax.net
Artistic Director, Margie Gillis
Administrative Director, Linda Foy

Mascall Dance
1130 Jervis St., Vancouver, BC V6E 2C7
604/689-9339, Fax: 604/689-9399
Artistic Director, Jennifer Mascall
General Manager, Jim Smith, Email: jgsmith@wimsey.com

Menaka Thakkar & Company
c/o DUO, #201, 490 Adelaide St. West, Toronto, ON M5V 1T2
416/360-6429, Fax: 416/363-8702
Artistic Director, Menaka Thakkar

Mile Zero Dance Company
#112, 2315 - 119 St., Edmonton, AB T6G 4E2
403/437-5907, Fax: 403/437-5907
Artistic Director, Deborah Shantz

Montanaro Dance
#601, 24, Mont-Royal ouest, Montréal, PQ H2T 2S2
514/281-6510, Fax: 514/281-6588, Email: montandangp@babylon.montreal.qc.ca
Artistic Director, Michael Montanaro
Managing Director, Gregg Parks

Montréal Danse
300, boul de Maisonneuve est, Montréal, PQ H2X 3X6
514/845-2031, Téléc: 514/845-5376
Directrice artistique, Kathy Casey
Directrice générale, Raymonde Gazaille

Movements
10053 - 111 St., 6th Fl., Edmonton, AB T5K 2H8
403/488-6745, Fax: 403/488-8713
Artistic Director, Sharlene Thomas
Administrator, Gail Graham

National Ballet of Canada
Walter Carsen Centre, 470 Queens Quay West, Toronto, ON M5V 3K4
416/345-9686, Fax: 416/345-8323, Email: info@national.ballet.ca, URL: http://www.national.ballet.ca
Artistic Director, James Kudelka
Executive Director, Valerie Wilder
General Manager, Robert Johnston

O Vertigo Danse
4455, de Rouen, Montréal, PQ H1V 1H1
514/251-9177, Téléc: 514/251-7358
Directrice artistique, Ginette Laurin
Directrice administrative, Mireille Martin

Ontario Ballet Theatre
1133 St. Clair Ave. West, Toronto, ON M6E 1B1
416/656-9568, Fax: 416/651-4803
Artistic Director, Sarah Lockett
General Manager, Diana Southern

Ontario Folk Dance Association (OFDA) (1969)
22 Latimer Ave., Toronto, ON M5N 2L8
416/489-3566, Info Line: 416/489-1621, Email: kbudd@web.net, URL: http://www.web.net/~ofda
President, Diane Gladstone
Publications: Ontario Folkdancer, 7 pa

Opéra Atelier
Upper Concourse, Cumberland Terrace, 2 Bloor St. West, Toronto, ON M4W 3E2
416/925-3767, Fax: 416/925-4895
Co-Artistic Director, Marshall Pynkoski
Co-Artistic Director, Jeannette Zingg
General Manager, Joan Bosworth

Paula Moreno Spanish Dance Co.
c/o DUO, #201, 490 Adelaide St. West, Toronto, ON M5V 1T2
416/504-6429, Fax: 416/504-8702
Artistic Director, Paula Moreno

Les Productions DancEncorps
#13, 140, rue Botsford, Moncton, NB E1C 4X4
506/855-0998, Téléc: 506/852-3401
Directrice artistique, Chantal Cadieux
Directrice exécutive, Louise Olivier

Red Thunder Cultural Society
Chadi K'Azi Company
3700 Anderson Rd. SW, PO Box 81, Calgary, AB T2W 3C4
403/281-8410, Fax: 403/281-8460
Artistic Director, Lee Crowchild

Regroupement québécois de la Danse (RQD) (1984)
#818, 3575, boul St-Laurent, Montréal, PQ H2X 2T7
514/849-4003, Téléc: 514/849-3288
Directeur général, Gaétan Patenaude
Publications: Bulletin, semi-annuel; Bulletin Express
Organisation(s) affiliée(s): Agora de la danse; Regroupement québécois des créateurs professionnels

Royal Academy of Dancing/Canada
#404, 3284 Yonge St., Toronto, ON M4N 2L6
416/489-2813, Fax: 416/489-3222
Administrator, Jan Garvey

The Royal Scottish Country Dance Society (RSCDS)
12 Coates Cres., Edinburgh EH3 7AF Scotland
031/225-3854, Fax: 031/225-7783
Secretary, G.S. Parker
Office Manager, E. Watt

Royal Winnipeg Ballet (1939)
380 Graham Ave., Winnipeg, MB R3C 4K2
204/956-0183, Fax: 204/943-1994
Executive Director, Jeffrey J. Bentley
President, Terrance Wright
School Director, David Moroni
Artistic Director, William Whitener
Publications: Warm-Up, q.; Ballet-Hoo; Souvenir Program
Affiliates: Canadian Association of Professional Dance Organizations; Association of Performing Arts Presenters; International Society of Performing Arts Administrators

Les Sortilèges
6560, rue Chambord, Montréal, PQ H2G 3B9
514/274-5655, Téléc: 514/274-7418
Directeur artistique, Jimmy Di Genova
Administratrice, Carmen Millette

Split Second Dance Collective
c/o Halifax Dance Association, PO Box 302, Halifax, NS B3J 2N7
902/422-2006, Fax: 902/423-2057, Email: prichard@is.dal.ca
Leica Hardy
Pat Richards

Springboard Dance Collective
#1420, 700 - 4 Ave. SW, Calgary, AB T2P 3J4
403/237-7452, Fax: 403/237-7452
Artistic Director, Alison Bonney-Gregson
General Manager, Laurie Montemurro

Square & Round Dance Federation of Nova Scotia (1983)
RR#1, Cambridge Station, NS B0P 1G0
902/538-9513, Email: buttons@fox.nstn.ca

Publicity, Harold Redden
Publications: Between Tips, irreg.; Newsletter
Affiliates: Dance Nova Scotia

Sun Ergos
#2205, 700 - 9th St. SW, Calgary, AB T2P 2B5
403/264-4621, Fax: 403/245-5613
Artistic Director, Robert Greenwood
Artistic Director, Dana Luebke

Sursaut inc.
CP 1591, Sherbrooke, PQ J1H 5M4
819/822-8912
Directrice artistique, Francine Châteauvert
Administratrice, Lucie Boulay

Sylvain Émard Danse
a/s Diagramme gestion culturelle, #4140, 5505, boul St-Laurent, Montréal, PQ H2T 1S6
514/273-7785, Téléc: 514/273-8051
Directeur artistique, Sylvain Émard

Toronto Dance Theatre (TDT) (1969)
80 Winchester St., Toronto, ON M4X 1B2
416/967-1365, Fax: 416/963-4379
Artistic Director, Christopher House
General Manager, Jini Stolk
Publications: Toronto Dance Theatre Newsletter, q.

Toronto & District Square & Round Dance Association (1951)
c/o Ed & Kitty Giles, RR#2, Burnt River, ON K0M 1C0
705/488-2973, Info Line: 416/510-1811
President, Ed Calhoun
Secretary, Ed Giles
Publications: Topics, 10 pa
Affiliates: Canadian Square & Round Dance Society

Vancouver Independent Dance Agency
Dance Centre
#400, 873 Beatty St., Vancouver, BC V6B 2M6
604/606-6413, Fax: 604/606-6401
Coordinator, Ruth Norgaard
Executive Director, Marlin Clapson

Vancouver Moving Theatre
PO Box 88270, Vancouver, BC V5T 3E2
604/876-5114, Fax: 604/876-5114
Artistic Director, Savannah Walling
General Manager, Terry Hunter

Vinok Folkdance Ensemble
PO Box 4867, Edmonton, AB T6E 5G7
403/454-3739, Fax: 403/454-3436
Artistic Director, Doyle Marko
Artistic Director, Leanne Koziak Marko

Wild Excursions Movement Theatre
#1, 1306 East 18th Ave., Vancouver, BC V5N 1H6
604/873-1631
Artistic Director, Conrad Alexandrowicz

Zone animée
5426, rue Casgrain, Montréal, PQ H2T 1X2
514/274-3721
Chorégraphe, Nathalie Lamarche
Chorégraphe, Danielle Lecourtois
Chorégraphe, Daniel Éthier

FLORA & FAUNA

WILDLIFE, ZOOS & OUTDOOR EDUCATION CENTRES

Alberta
Calgary Zoo, Botanical Garden & Prehistoric Park, St. George's Island, 13 Zoo Rd. NE, PO Box 3036, Stn B, Calgary AB T2M 4R8 – 403/232-9300; Fax: 403/237-7582, URL: http://www.cadvision.com/Home_Pages/accounts/calzoo/ – Associate Director, Zoological Operations, Greg Tarry – Open year round

Edmonton: Valley Zoo, PO Box 2359, Edmonton AB T5J 2R7 – 403/496-6912; Fax: 403/944-7529 – Director, Linda D.M. Cochrane

Rocky Mountain House: Sleepy Valley Game Farm, RR#1, Rocky Mountain House AB T0M 1T0 – 403/845-6357 – Open July & Aug.

British Columbia
Aldergrove: Vancouver Game Farm, 5048 - 264th St., Aldergrove BC V4W 1N7 – 604/856-6825; Fax: 604/857-9008; Info Line: 604/857-9005 – C. Kwon

Kamloops Wildlife Park, PO Box 698, Kamloops BC V2C 5L7 – 250/573-3242; Fax: 250/573-2406 – General Manager, Rob Purdy – Vertebrate collection; conservation, education & recreation

Kelowna: Speedwell Bird Sanctuary, PO Box 144, Kelowna BC V1Y 7N3 – 250/766-2081; Fax: 250/766-0617 – Dan Bruce

Penticton: Okanagan Game Farm, PO Box 100, Penticton BC V2A 6J9 – 250/497-5405; Fax: 250/497-6145

Vancouver: Stanley Park Wildlife Services Dept., 2099 Beach Ave., Vancouver BC V6G 1Z4 – 604/257-8528; Fax: 604/257-8378 – Manager, Wildlife Services, Mike Mackintosh

Manitoba
Rennie: Alfred Hole Goose Sanctuary, Rennie MB R0E 1R0 – 204/369-5470 (summer); 369-5258 (winter); Fax: 204/369-5341 – Park Manager, Mark Clarke – Visitor Centre interprets the history of the site as well as the biology of geese

Thompson Recreation Zoo, 275 Thompson Dr. North, Thompson MB R8N 0C3 – 204/677-7982; Fax: 204/677-4854 – Ray Johnson – Open year round

Winnipeg: Assiniboine Park Zoo, 2355 Corydon Ave., Winnipeg MB R3P 0R5 – 204/986-6921; Fax: 204/832-5420, URL: http://www.mbnet.mb.ca/city/parks/envserv/zoo/zoo.html – Director, Douglas Ross

New Brunswick
Edmundston: Ferme Aqua Zoo, St-Jacques, RR#3, Edmundston NB E3V 3K5 – 506/739-9149

Fredericton: Woolastook Wildlife Park, Faunatlantic Ltd., RR#6, Fredericton NB E3B 4X7 – 506/363-5410

Lamèque Zoo, Lamèque NB E0B 1V0 – 506/344-7214, 7343

Moncton: Magnetic Hill Zoo, c/o City of Moncton, Community Services Dept., 655 Main St., Moncton NB E1C 1E8 – 506/384-9381; Fax: 506/853-3569; Email: bruce.dougan@moncton.org – Manager, Bruce Dougan

Saint John: Cherry Brook Zoo, Sandy Point Rd., RR#1, Saint John NB E2L 3W2 – 506/634-1440; Fax: 506/634-0717

Newfoundland
Holyrood: Salmonier Nature Park, PO Box 190, Holyrood NF A0A 2R0 – 709/729-6974; Fax: 709/229-7888

Canadian Almanac & Directory 1997

Nova Scotia
Aylesford: Oaklawn Farm, Aylesford NS B0P 1C0 – 902/847-9790 – Open Easter - autumn

Ontario
Bowmanville Zoological Park, 340 King St. East, Bowmanville ON L1C 3K5 – 905/623-5655; Fax: 905/623-9675 – Co-Director, Leslie Pon Tell – Canada's oldest operating zoo, featuring Animal Kingdom shows, elephant rides, restaurant & gift shop; open May - Sept.

Cambridge: African Lion Safari & Game Farm, RR#1, Cambridge ON N1R 5S2 – 519/623-2620; Fax: 519/623-9542; Toll Free: 1-800-461-9453, URL: http://www.lionsafari.com/ – General Manager, Mike Takacs – Open Apr. - Oct.

Earlton Zoo, PO Box 430, Earlton ON P0J 1E0 – 705/563-8300; Fax: 705/563-2200 – Pierre Belanger – Open May - Oct.

Elmvale Jungle Zoo, PO Box 460, Elmvale ON L0L 1P0 – 705/322-1112

Gananoque: 1000 Islands Wild Kingdom, 855 Stone St. North, Gananoque ON K7G 1Z6 – 613/382-7141

Grand Bend: Pineridge Zoo, RR#2, Grand Bend ON N0M 1T0 – 519/238-2769

Guelph: Kortright Waterfowl Park, 305 Niska Rd., Guelph ON N1H 6J3 – 519/824-6729 – Open March - Oct. on weekends & statutory holidays

Kingsville: Jack Miner's Bird Sanctuary, PO Box 39, Kingsville ON N9Y 2E8 – 519/733-4034

Marlbank: Philoxia Zoo, c/o Lilah Chickalo, The Philoxians, Marlbank ON K0K 2L0 – 613/478-6070

Morrisburg: Upper Canada Migratory Bird Sanctuary, Parks of the St. Lawrence, RR#1, Morrisburg ON K0C 1X0 – 613/543-3704; Fax: 613/543-2847 – Parks Operations Coordinator, Rod Davidson

North York: Kortright Centre for Conservation, c/o Metro Region Conservation Authority, 5 Shoreham Dr., North York ON M3N 1S4 – 416/661-6600; Email: kcc@interlog.com, URL: http://www.kortright.on.ca/

Orono: Jungle Cat World Inc., 3667 Conc. 6, RR#1, Orono ON L0B 1M0 – 905/983-5016; Fax: 905/983-9858; Email: jungle@netrover.com – President, Wolfram H. Klose

Peterborough: Riverview Park & Zoo, Peterborough Utilities Commission, PO Box 4125, Peterborough ON K9J 6Z5 – 705/748-9300, ext.303; Fax: 705/745-6866

Picton: The Exotarium, c/o The Reptile Breeding Foundation, PO Box 1450, Picton ON K0K 2T0 – 613/476-7710 (May - Oct.), 613/476-3351 (all year) – Rare & endangered reptiles, amphibians & invertebrates

Scarborough: Metro Toronto Zoo, 361A Old Finch Ave., Scarborough ON M1B 5K7 – 416/392-5900; Fax: 416/392-5934 – General Manager, Calvin J. White – Open year round

St Catharines: Happy Rolph Bird Sanctuary & Children's Farm, c/o St Catharines Parks & Recreation Dept., PO Box 3012, St Catharines ON L2R 7C2 – 905/937-7210

Thunder Bay: Chippewa Park Zoo, c/o Parks & Recreation Dept., 950 Memorial Ave., Thunder Bay ON P7B 4A2 – 807/623-3463, 625-2351

Toronto: High Park Menagerie, c/o Parks & Recreation, City Hall, Toronto ON M5H 2N2 – 416/392-7251

Toronto: Riverdale Farm, Riverdale Park, c/o Dept. of Parks & Recreation, City Hall, 201 Winchester St., Toronto ON M5H 2N2 – 416/392-7251

Toronto Islands Park Farm, c/o Metro Toronto Parks & Property Dept., 8th Fl., 365 Bay St., Toronto ON M5H 2V1 – 416/392-8193, 863-2212

Wasaga Beach Wildlife Park, Wasaga Beach ON L0L 2P0 – 416/429-5522 – President, Julio Orsatti

Québec
Bonaventure: Jardin Zoologique de Bonaventure, PO Box 428, Bonaventure PQ G0C 1E0 – 418/534-3410 – Director, Bernard Arsenault

Charlesbourg: Jardin Zoologique du Québec, 8191, av du Zoo, Charlesbourg PQ G1G 4G4 – 418/622-0312; Fax: 418/646-9239 – Biologiste, Christian Potvin – Open year round

Granby: Jardin Zoologique de Granby, 347, rue Bourget ouest, Granby PQ J2G 1E8 – 514/372-9113; Fax: 514/372-5531; Email: zoo@granby.mtl.net – Directeur Général, Pierre G. Cartier – Open mid-May - Oct. (Thanksgiving Day)

Hemmingford: Parc Safari Africain (Québec) Inc., 850, rte 202, Hemmingford PQ J0L 1H0 – 514/247-2727; Toll-Free: 1-800-465-8724

Maskinongé: Zoo de St. Édouard-Maskinongé, 3381, rte 248 ouest, Maskinongé PQ J0K 2H0 – 819/268-5150; Fax: 819/268-5150

Sherbrooke: Parc Plateau, av du Parc/Terrill, PO Box 610, Sherbrooke PQ J1H 5H9 – 819/821-5500

St-Félicien: Jardin Zoologique de St-Félicien, 2230, boul du Jardin, PO Box 90, St-Félicien PQ G8K 2P8 – 418/679-0543; Fax: 418/679-3647 – Directeur général, Martin Laforge

St-Georges-Ouest: Parc des Sept-Chutes, a/s 1500, 6e av, St-Georges-Ouest PQ G5Y 3W1

Ste-Anne-de-Bellevue: Ecomuseum, 21125, ch Sainte-Marie, Ste-Anne-de-Bellevue PQ H9X 1C0 – 514/457-9449 – Open mid-April - mid-Nov.

Saskatchewan
Moose Jaw Zoo & Recreation, 7th Ave. SW, Moose Jaw SK S6H 5W5 – 306/691-0111 – Open May 1 - Oct.

Regina: Ipsco Wild Life Park & Pool, PO Box 1670, Regina SK S4P 3C7 – 306/949-4360 – Park Manager, Fred Hannah

Regina: Wascana Waterfowl Park, Wascana Centre, Lakeshore Dr., PO Box 7111, Regina SK S4P 3S7 – 306/522-3661; Fax: 306/565-2742 – Executive Director, J.B. Paterson

Saskatoon: Forestry Farm Park & Zoo, 1903 Forest Dr., Saskatoon SK S7S 1G9 – 306/975-3382 – Open year round

AQUARIA

British Columbia
Vancouver Aquarium, Stanley Park, PO Box 3232, Vancouver BC V6B 3X8 – 604/685-3364; Fax: 604/631-2529; Info Line: 604/682-1118 – Executive Director, Dr. John Nightingale

Victoria: Pacific Undersea Gardens, 490 Belleville St., Victoria BC V8V 1W9 – 250/382-5717; Fax: 250/382-5210 – Manager, Maxine Becker

Victoria: Undersea Gardens of Victoria, Inner Harbour, 490 Belleville St., Victoria BC V8V 1W9 – 250/382-5717; Fax: 250/598-1361

Manitoba
Winnipeg: Resolute Bay Aquarium, c/o H. Welch, Fisheries & Oceans Canada, 501 University Cres., Winnipeg MB R3T 2N6 – 204/983-5132; Fax: 204/984-2404 – Open summers

New Brunswick
Shippigan: Aquarium et Centre Marin de Shippagan, CP 1010, Shippigan NB E0B 2P0 – 506/336-4771; Fax: 506/336-3057 – Directeur, Clarence LeBreton

Newfoundland
St. John's: The Fluvarium, Nagle's Place, Box 5, St. John's NF A1B 2Z2 – 709/754-FISH; Fax: 709/754-5947 – Executive Director, Pamela Karasek

Ontario
Niagara Falls: Marineland, 7657 Portage Rd., Niagara Falls ON L2E 6X8 – 905/356-8250; Fax: 905/374-6652 – Open April 1 - Oct. 15

Prince Edward Island
Charlottetown: PEI Marine Aquarium Ltd., 68 Queen St., Charlottetown PE C1A 7K7 – 902/892-2203 – V.E. Williams – Open June - Sept.

Québec
Ste-Flavie: Centre d'Interpretation du Saumon Atlantique, 900, rte de la Mer, Ste-Flavie PQ G0J 2L0 – 418/775-2969; Fax: 418/775-9466 – Jean Marc Vincent – Open June - mid-Oct.

Ste-Foy: Aquarium du Québec, 1675, av des Hôtels, Ste-Foy PQ G1W 4S3 – 418/659-5266; Fax: 418/646-9238 – Directeur, André Martel – Open year round

Ste-Foy: Pointe-Noire, Parc Marin du Saguenay, a/s Société Linnéenne du Québec Inc., #219, 2095, boul Charest ouest, Ste-Foy PQ G1N 4L8 – 418/237-4348; Fax: 418/683-2893 – Président, Daniel Banville – Open year round

Saskatchewan
Fort Qu'Appelle: Fish Culture Station, PO Box 190, Fort Qu'Appelle SK S0G 1S0 – 306/332-3200 – R. Kidd

BOTANICAL GARDENS

Alberta
Brooks: Golden Prairie Arboretum, Alberta Agriculture, Food & Rural Development, SS#4, Brooks AB T1R 1E6 – ; Email: murray@agric.gov.ab.ca – Dr., Christine Murray

Calgary Zoo, Botanical Garden & Prehistoric Park, PO Box 3036, Stn B, Calgary AB T2M 4R8 – 403/232-9300; Fax: 403/237-7582 – Associate Director, Botanical Operations, Keith Scott

Calgary: Devonian Gardens, Level 4, Toronto-Dominion Square, 317 - 7 Ave. SW, Calgary AB T2P 2Y9 – 403/269-5217; Fax: 403/221-4581 – Supervisor, David Kroeker – 2.5 acre indoor park; 138 varieties of greenery; available for private functions; open daily 9 am - 9 pm; admission free

Edmonton: Devonian Botanic Garden of the University of Alberta, University of Alberta, Edmonton AB T6G 2E1 – 403/987-3054; Fax: 403/987-4141 – Director, Dr. Dale Vitt – 80 acres of cultivated gardens & 110 acres of natural area; native & alpine plants, ecological reserves, the Kurimoto Japanese Garden & a Butterfly House; picnic area, concession & gift shop; open daily May - mid-Oct.

Edmonton: McCalla Orchard & Arboretum, Alberta Tree Nursery & Horticultural Centre, RR#6, Edmonton AB T5B 4K3

Edmonton: Muttart Conservatory, 98 Ave. & 96A St., Edmonton AB T6C 3Z8 – 403/496-8755; Fax: 403/496-8747 – Director, David Schneider – Four pyramids house flora of different climates; 2,000 species of orchids

Glenevis: George Pegg Botanic Garden, General Delivery, Glenevis AB T0E 0X0 – 403/785-2421 – President, R. Peterson

High Level: Boreal Botanic Garden, PO Box 1106, High Level AB T0H 1Z0 – 403/926-4697 – Jorden Johnston

Lethbridge Brewery & Gardens, c/o Lethbridge City Hall, 910 - 4 Ave. South, Lethbridge AB T1J 0P6 – 403/320-3000

Lethbridge: Nikka Yuko Japanese Gardens, c/o Lethbridge & District Japanese Garden Society, PO Box 751, Lethbridge AB T1J 3Z6 – 403/328-3511 – Manager, Jack Welch – Open spring, summer, fall

Olds College Arboretum, Olds College, Olds AB T0M 1P0

Canadian Almanac & Directory 1997

Trochu Arboretum & Gardens, PO Box 340, Trochu AB T0M 2C0 – 403/442-2111; Fax: 403/442-2528 – President, Brenda Cunningham – Weekends only

British Columbia

100 Mile House Demonstration Forest, c/o South Cariboo Chamber of Commerce, 422 Cariboo Hwy. 97 South, PO Box 2312, 100 Mile House BC V0K 2E0 – 250/395-5353; Fax: 250/395-4085; Email: sccofc@netshop.net, URL: http://www.netshop.net/~100mile/sccofc/html – Manager, Kathy McKenzie

Burnaby: Simon Fraser University Arboretum, Dept. of Biological Sciences, Simon Fraser University, Burnaby BC V5A 1S6

Chilliwack: Minter Gardens, 52892 Bunker Rd., Rosedale, PO Box 40, Chilliwack BC V2P 6H7 – 604/794-7191; Fax: 604/792-8893; 1-800-661-3919 – Brian & Faye Minter – Open Apr. - Oct.

Kimberley: Cominco Gardens, PO Box 144, Kimberley BC V1A 2Y5 – 250/428-5311; Fax: 250/427-5252

Nanaimo: Grant Ainscough Arboretum & Tree Improvement Centre, 65 Front St., Nanaimo BC V9R 5H9 – 250/755-3467; Fax: 250/755-3464 – Open year round

North Vancouver: Park & Tilford Gardens, Park & Tilford Centre, #440, 333 Brookbank Ave., North Vancouver BC V7J 3S8 – 604/984-8200; Fax: 604/984-6099 – Garden Director, Todd Major

Prince George: David Douglas Botanical Garden Society, PO Box 1305, Prince George BC V2M 2S3

Richmond: Fantasy Garden World, 10800 No. 5 Rd., Richmond BC V7A 4E5

Vancouver: Bloedel Conservatory, Queen Elizabeth Park, c/o Sunset Nursery, 290 - 51 Ave. East, Vancouver BC V5X 1C5 – 604/257-8584; Fax: 604/257-8636 – Manager, Alex M. Downie

Vancouver: Dr. Sun Yat-Sen Classical Chinese Garden, 578 Carrall St., Vancouver BC V6B 5K2 – 604/662-3207; Fax: 604/682-4008 – Executive Director, Heather O'Hagan

Vancouver: Nitobe Memorial Garden, University of British Columbia, 1903 West Mall, Vancouver BC V6T 1Z4 – 604/822-6038; Fax: 604/822-2016; Email: blaine@unixg.ubc.ca – Director, Bruce Macdonald

Vancouver: Queen Elizabeth & Bloedel Conservatory, 2099 Beach Ave., Vancouver BC V6G 1Z4 – 604/874-9411 – Trades Foreman, T. Mathot

Vancouver: UBC Botanical Garden, University of British Columbia, 6804 Southwest Marine Dr., Vancouver BC V6T 1W5 – 604/822-4208, 6038; Fax: 604/822-2016; Email: blaine@unixg.ubc.ca – Director, Bruce Macdonald

Vancouver: VanDusen Botanical Garden, 5251 Oak St., Vancouver BC V6M 4H1 – 604/878-9274; Fax: 604/266-4326 – Curator, Roy Forster – Open year round

Victoria: The Butchart Gardens Ltd., PO Box 4010, Victoria BC V8X 3X4 – 250/652-4422; Fax: 250/652-3883; Email: email@butchartgardens.bc.ca; Info line: 604/652-2422, URL: http://butchartgardens.bc.ca/butchart/ – Director, R. Ian Ross – Open year round

Victoria: The Crystal Garden, 713 Douglas St., Victoria BC V8W 2B4 – 250/381-1213, 1277; Fax: 250/383-1218 – Open year round

Victoria: Douglas Fir Arboretum, c/o Research Division, BC Forest Service, Victoria BC V8V 1X5

Victoria: Fable Cottage Estate & World Class Gardens, 5187 Cordova Bay Rd., Victoria BC V8Y 2K7 – 250/658-5741 – Open Mar. - Oct.

Victoria: Horticulture Centre of the Pacific, 505 Quayle Rd., Victoria BC V8X 3X1

Manitoba

Boisevain: International Peace Garden, PO Box 419, Boisevain MB R0K 0E0

Morden Arboretum, Agriculture Canada Research Centre, Unit 100-101, Rte. 100, Morden MB R6M 1Y5 – 204/822-4471; Fax: 204/822-6841; Email: cdavidson@em.agr.ca – Dr. Campbell G. Davidson

Portage La Prairie: Island Park Arboretum, Parks Division, 97 Saskatchewan Ave. East, Portage La Prairie MB R1N 0L8

Winnipeg: Assiniboine Park, 2799 Roblin Blvd., Winnipeg MB R3R 0B8 – 204/986-2675; Fax: 204/832-7134, URL: http://www.mbnet.mb.ca/city/parks/ – Manager of Park & Open Space, City of Winnipeg Parks & Recreation, Don Budinsky – Includes Conservatory, English Garden, 280 ha forest

Winnipeg: Woody Plant Test Arboretum, Dept. of Plant Science, University of Manitoba, Winnipeg MB R3T 2N2

New Brunswick

Fredericton Botanic Garden, PO Box 57, Stn A, Fredericton NB E3B 4Y2

Saint-Jacques: New Brunswick Botanical Gardens, Main St., Saint-Jacques NB E0L 1K0 – 506/739-6335 – Opened 1993; 22 acres

Newfoundland

St. John's: The Memorial University Botanical Garden at Oxen Pond, c/o Memorial Univeristy, St. John's NF A1C 5S7 – 709/737-8590; Fax: 709/737-4569 – Director, Dr. Peter J. Scott – Open May - Nov.

Nova Scotia

Annapolis Royal Historic Gardens, 441 Saint George St., PO Box 278, Annapolis Royal NS B0S 1A0 – 902/532-7018 – Theme gardens, collections & displays reflect historical periods - Open May - Oct.

Halifax Public Gardens, c/o Parks & Grounds Division, Engineering & Works, City of Halifax., PO Box 812, Stn Armdale, Halifax NS B3L 4K5 – 902/421-6551 – Formal Victorian Garden, located at Summer St. & Spring Garden Rd.

Ontario

Brampton: J.A. Carol Arboretum, 74 McCaule St., Brampton ON L6V 1J3

Guelph: The Arboretum, University of Guelph, Guelph ON N1G 2W1 – 519/824-4120, ext. 2113; Fax: 519/763-9598; Email: agallina@uoguelph.ca – Director, Prof. Alan Watson Email: awatson@uoguelph.ca

Hamilton: Centre for Canadian Historical Horticultural Studies, Royal Botanical Gardens, PO Box 399, Hamilton ON L8N 3H8 – 905/527-1158; Fax: 905/577-0375; Toll Free: 1-800-668-9449 – Contact, Linda Brownlee 905/527-1158, ext.246

Hamilton: Royal Botanical Gardens, PO Box 399, Hamilton ON L8N 3H8 – 905/527-1158; Fax: 905/577-0375 – Director, Sharilyn Ingram

Kakabeka Falls: Plum Grove Arboretum, RR#1, Kakabeka Falls ON P0T 1W0

London: Sherwood Fox Arboretum, University of Western Ontario, Richmond St. North, London ON N6A 5B7 – 519/679-2111, ext. 6506

Miller Lake: Larkwhistle Garden, RR#1, Miller Lake ON N0H 1Z0

Mississauga: Eridale College Arboretum, Erindale College, Mississauga Rd. North, Mississauga ON L5L 1C6

Mississauga Public Garden, 2038 Lorelei Rd., Mississauga ON L5A 1C2

New Liskeard: Becky Hughes Arboretum, New Liskeard College of Agriculture, New Liskeard ON P0J 1P0

Niagara Parks Botanical Gardens & School of Horticulture, c/o Niagara Parks Commission, PO Box 150, Niagara Falls ON L2E 6T2 – 905/356-8554; Fax: 905/356-5488, URL: http://www.niagara.com/~;shoup/botanic_gardens.html – Director, Deborah Whitehouse

North York: Edwards Gardens, Civic Garden Centre, 777 Lawrence Ave. E, North York ON M3C 1P2 – 416/392-2556

Ottawa: Dominion Arboretum, Research Branch, Agriculture Canada, Ottawa Research Station Bldg. 50, Ottawa ON K1A 0C6 – 613/995-3700

Rexdale: Humber Arboretum, 205 Humber College Blvd., Rexdale ON M9W 5L7 – 416/675-6622, ext.4661; Fax: 416/675-9730; Email: bodwort@admin.humberc.on.ca – Director, Stephen Bodsworth

Ridgetown: J.J. Neilson Arboretum, Ridgetown College of Agricultural Technology, Ridgetown ON N0P 2C0

Ruthven: Colasanti Tropical Gardens & Petting Farm, PO Box 40, Ruthven ON N0P 2G0 – 519/326-3287; Fax: 519/322-2302

Sault Ste Marie: Great Lakes Forestry Centre Arboretum, Canadian Forest Service, PO Box 490, Sault Ste Marie ON P6A 5M7 – 705/949-9461; Fax: 705/759-5700; Email: dkennington@fcor.glfc.forestry.ca – Arboretum Manager, D.J. Kennington

Sebringville: Brickman Botanical Garden, RR#1, Sebringville ON N0K 1X0

St Catharines: Walker Botanic Garden, Rodman Hall Arts Centre, 109 St. Paul Cres., St Catharines ON L2S 1M3

Sudbury: Laurentian University Arboretum, Ramsey Lake Rd., Sudbury ON P3E 2C6

Thunder Bay: Centennial Conservatory, c/o Parks & Recreation Dept., 1601 Dease St. North, Thunder Bay ON P7B 4A2 – 807/625-2351; Fax: 807/622-7036 – Open year round

Thunder Bay: International Friendship Garden, Parks Division, City of Thunder Bay, 111 South Syndicate Ave., Thunder Bay ON P7E 6S4

Thunder Bay: Lakehead University Arboretum, c/o Lakehead University, 955 Oliver Rd., Thunder Bay ON P7B 5E1 – 807/343-8624; Fax: 807/343-8116 – Nancy Luckai – Open year round

Toronto: Allan Gardens Conservatory, 19 Horticultural Ave., Toronto ON M5A 2P2 – 416/392-7288; Fax: 416/392-0318 – Supt., Tom Powers – At Carlton & Jarvis Sts., Open year round, M-F 9 am - 4 pm, weekends & holidays 10 am - 5 pm; admission free

Whitby: Cullen Gardens, RR #2, 300 Taunton Rd. West, Whitby ON L1N 5R5 – 416/294-7965, 668-6606; Toll-Free: 1-800-461-1821

Windsor: Fogolar Furlan Botanic Garden, 1800 E.C. Row, North Service Rd., Windsor ON N8W 1Y3

Windsor: Jackson Park Queen Elizabeth II Garden, c/o Parks & Recreation Dept., 2450 McDougall Rd., Windsor ON N8X 3N6 – 519/255-6276; Fax: 519/255-7990, URL: http://www.city.windsor.on.ca – Commissioner, Lloyd Burridge

Prince Edward Island

Kensington: Malpeque Gardens, RR#1, Blue Heron Dr., Kensington PE C0B 1M0 – George MacKay – Open June 15 - Aug. 15

Québec

Mont-Joli: Les Jardins de Métis, PO Box 242, Mont-Joli PQ G5H 3L1 – 418/775-2221; Fax: 418/775-6201 – Directeur, Alexander Reford

Montréal: Jardin botanique de Montréal, 4101, rue Sherbrooke est, Montréal PQ H1X 2B2

Otter Lake: Belle Terre Botanic Garden & Arboretum, Otter Lake PQ J0X 2P0

Ste-Anne-de-Bellevue: Morgan Arboretum, Macdonald College, McGill University, PO Box 500, Ste-Anne-de-Bellevue PQ H8X 3Z9 – 514/398-7811 – Director, Eric R. Thompson

Ste-Foy: Jardin Roger-Van den Hende, Universite Laval, Pavillon de L'Envirotron, Ste-Foy PQ G1K 7P4 – 418/656-3410; Fax: 418/656-7871 – Open April - Oct.

Saskatchewan

Estevan: Shand Greenhouse, PO Box 280, Estevan SK S4A 2A3 – 306/634-5413; Fax: 306/634-6682; Email: shand.greenhouse@awinc.com – Manager, Debbie Nielsen – Greenhouse, shade houses, nursery, display area; uses by-products of energy generation from the Shand Power Station - Open year round

Indian Head: Prairie Farm Rehabilitation Administration, Hwys. 1 & 56, PO Box 940, Indian Head SK S0G 2K0 – 306/695-2284; Fax: 306/695-2568; Email: pf21802@pfra.gc.ca – Manager, Dr. J.A.G. Howe – Arboretum, nursery, horticultural displays - Open daily

Saskatoon: Patterson Garden, Dept. of Horticulture Science, University of Saskatchewan, 51 Campus Dr., Saskatoon SK S7N 5M8 – 306/966-5855; Fax: 306/966-8106; Email: harvey@duke.usask.ca – B.L. Harvey

SECTION 7

BUSINESS & FINANCE DIRECTORY

DOMESTIC BANKS	1
TRUST COMPANIES	3
MORTGAGE & LOAN COMPANIES	4
INVESTMENT FUND MANAGERS	4
STOCK EXCHANGES	9
INSURANCE COMPANIES	13
BOARDS OF TRADE & CHAMBERS OF COMMERCE	23
CONSULTANT LOBBYISTS	35
MAJOR CANADIAN COMPANIES	40

See ADDENDA at the back of this book for late changes & additional information.

DOMESTIC BANKS

See Index for Bank of Canada, and the Federal Business Development Bank, which are Crown Corporations, listed in the Government Section.

Chartered banks in Canada are incorporated by letters patent and are governed by the Bank Act which establishes the legislative framework for Canada's banking system.

The Bank Act provides for the incorporation of two classes of banks. Schedule I banks are those banks in which no one shareholder or group of associated shareholders owns more than 10 per cent of any class of shares of the bank. Schedule II banks are closely held by foreign banks or other eligible financial institutions. Schedule I and Schedule II banks have the same general powers, restrictions and obligations under the Bank Act.

Foreign banks are permitted to incorporate "foreign bank subsidiaries" under the Bank Act, and to commence business in Canada on the basis of reciprocal treatment for Canadian banks. Foreign bank subsidiaries are Schedule II banks under the Bank Act.

The Bank Act provides that banks have the power of a natural person and may engage in or carry on the business of banking, including the authority to provide any financial service; lend money, and make advances, with or without security; issue subordinated debentures, subject to terms and conditions; hold and deal with real property; take and set conditions for realization on security; pay interest on a debt payable to a bank and charge interest on a loan, advance or any debt or liability of the bank; and subject to terms and conditions, engage in financial leasing and factoring, venture capital and data processing.

The Bank Act embodies many provisions designed for the protection of creditors and shareholders including requirements related to minimum capital adequacy, shareholders' audits by public accountants and government inspection.

Office of the Superintendent of Financial Institutions/Bureau du Surintendant des Institutions Financières
255 Albert St., Ottawa ON K1A 0H2
613/990-7788; Fax: 613/952-8219; Toll Free: 1-800-385-8647
Superintendent, John Palmer

Canadian Banking Ombudsman
#1602, 4950 Yonge St., North York ON M2N 6K1
416/362-0560; Fax: 416/225-4722
Ombudsman, Michael Lauber

SCHEDULE I BANKS

Bank of Montreal/Banque de Montréal
   129, rue St-Jacques ouest, Montréal PQ H2Y 1L6
   514/877-1285; Fax: 514/877-6922; Toll Free: 1-800-555-3000; URL: http://www.bmo.com
   Chairman/CEO, Matthew W. Barrett
   Toronto Office: 1 First Canadian Place, PO Box 1, Stn 1st Can Place, Toronto ON M5X 1A1
   416/867-5000; Fax: 416/927-2710; Email: info@bmo.com
   Capital & Reserves: $7,476,000,000 (31-7-96)
   Number of Branches: Alta. 125; Atlantic Canada 87; BC 150; Man./Sask. 116; Ont. 475; Qué. 198

The Bank of Nova Scotia/La Banque de Nouvelle-Écosse
   (Scotiabank)
   Scotia Plaza, 44 King St. West, Toronto ON M5H 1H1
   416/866-6161; Fax: 416/866-3750; URL: http://www.scotiabank.com
   Chair, President & CEO, Peter Godsoe
   Capital & Reserves: $6,764,399,000 (31-5-95)
   Number of Branches: Alta. 118; BC 114; Man. 37; NB 54; Nfld. 63; NS 74; NWT 1; Ont. 471; PEI 9; Qué. 96; Sask. 51; Yukon 1

Canadian Imperial Bank of Commerce/Banque de commerce canadienne imperiale
   Commerce Court, PO Box 1, Stn Commerce Court, Toronto ON M5L 1A2
   416/980-2211; Fax: 416/368-8843; URL: http://www.cibc.com
   Chairman/CEO, A.L. Flood
   Total Capital Funds: $11,800,000,000 (6-5-95)
   Number of Branches: Alta. 157; BC 186; Man. 71; NB 21; Nfld 16; NWT 6; NS 34; Ont. 618; PEI 7; Qué. 171; Sask. 75; Yukon 10

Canadian Western Bank
   #2300, 10303 Jasper Ave., Edmonton AB T5J 3X6
   403/423-8888; Fax: 403/423-8897
   President/CEO, Larry M. Pollock
   Capital & Reserves: $92,299,000 (31-10-95)

National Bank of Canada/Banque Nationale du Canada
   600, rue de La Gauchetière ouest, Montréal PQ H3B 4L2
   514/394-4000; Fax: 514/394-8434
   Chairman/CEO, André Bérard
   Toronto Office: #300, 150 York St., Toronto ON M5H 3A9
   416/351-4000
   Capital & Reserves: $2,372,361,000 (30-4-95)
   Number of Branches: Alta. 2; BC 1; Man. 4; NB 28; Nfld. 1; NS 4; Ont. 87; PEI 2; Qué. 499; Sask. 2

Royal Bank of Canada
   Place Ville Marie, CP 6001, Succ A, Montréal PQ H3C 3A9
   514/874-2110; Fax: 514/874-6582; URL: http://www.royalbank.com
   Chair/CEO, John Cleghorn
   Toronto Office: Royal Bank Plaza, Lower Concourse, Toronto ON M5J 2J5
   416/974-5151; Fax: 416/974-0135; Toll Free: 1-800-263-9191
   Shareholder Equity: $9,387,060,000 (30-6-96)
   Number of Branches: Alta. (inc. NWT) 128; Atlantic Canada 128; BC (inc. Yukon) 164; Man. 88; Ont. 497; Qué. 192; Sask. 79

The Toronto-Dominion Bank
   (TD Bank)
   TD Centre, PO Box 1, Stn Toronto-Dominion, Toronto ON M5K 1A2
   416/982-8222; Toll Free: 1-800-387-2092; URL: http://www.tdbank.ca
   Chair & CEO, R.M. Thomson
   Capital & Reserves: $6,053,000,000

Canadian Almanac & Directory 1997

7-2 DOMESTIC BANKS

Number of Branches: Alta. 105; Pacific 105; Man./Sask. 99; Atlantic Canada 45; Ont. 517; Qué. 71

SCHEDULE II BANKS

Laurentian Bank of Canada/Banque Laurentienne du Canada
#1585, 1981, av McGill College, Montréal PQ H3A 3K3
514/284-3911; URL: http://www.mortgagestore.com/laurent/laurent.html
Chairman, Claude Castonguay
Capital & Reserves: $417,909,000 (31-5-95)
Number of Branches: Alta. 2; BC 5; Man. 1; NS 2; Ont. 48; Qué. 175; Sask. 1

Manulife Bank of Canada
500 King St., Waterloo ON N2J 4C6
519/747-7000; Fax: 519/747-2112

FOREIGN BANK SUBSIDIARIES IN CANADA

Address shown is that of the Canadian head office.

ABN AMRO Bank Canada
IBM Tower, Toronto-Dominion Centre, 15th Fl., PO Box 114, Stn Toronto-Dominion, Toronto ON M5K 1G8
416/367-0850; Fax: 416/367-1485; Telex: 06-524016
President/CEO, W. Veger
Capital & Reserves: $103,528,000 (31-5-95)

Amex Bank of Canada
American Express Place, 101 McNabb St., Markham ON L3R 4H8
905/474-8000; Fax: 905/474-8363, 1515
President/General Manager, A. Stark
Capital & Reserves: $123,729,000 (31-5-95)

Banca Commerciale Italiana of Canada
#1800, 130 Adelaide St. West, PO Box 100, Toronto ON M5H 3P5
416/366-8101; Fax: 416/366-2577; Telex: 06-22977
President/CEO, G. Stammati
Capital & Reserves: $107,900,000 (30-6-95)
Number of Branches: BC 1; Ont. 8; Qué. 3

Banco Central Hispano-Canada
330 Bay St., Toronto ON M5H 2S8
416/365-7070; Fax: 416/365-7850; Telex: 06-218904
Executive Vice-President & CEO, Fernando Bustamante
Capital & Reserves: $14,555,662 (31-5-95)

Bank of America Canada
4 King St. West, 18th Fl., Toronto ON M5H 1B6
416/863-5400; Fax: 416/863-2350; Telex: 06-219707
Chairman/President/CEO, Alfred P. Buhler
Capital & Reserves: $175,266,000 (31-5-95)

Bank of China (Canada)
Canada Trust Tower, BCE Place, Box 612, #3740, 161 Bay St., Toronto ON M5J 2S1
416/362-2991, 4958; Fax: 416/362-3047
President/CEO, Y. Chen
Capital & Reserves: $24,411,000 (31-3-95)

The Bank of East Asia (Canada)
East Asia Center, #102-103, 350 Hwy. 7 East, Richmond Hill ON L4B 3N2
905/882-8182; Fax: 905/882-0253
CEO & General Manager, Cedric C.K. Ng
Capital & Reserves: $13,752,764 (30-4-96)

Bank of Tokyo-Mitsubishi (Canada)
#2100, Royal Bank Plaza, South Tower, PO Box 42, Stn Royal Bank, Toronto ON M5J 2J1
416/865-0220; Fax: 416/865-9511, 0196; Telex: 06-524440
President/CEO, Seiji Adachi
Capital & Reserves: $157,200,000 (30-4-96)

Banque Nationale de Paris (Canada)
1981, av McGill College, Montréal PQ H3A 2W8
514/285-6000; Fax: 514/285-6278; Telex: 05-25241
President/CEO, André Chaffringeon
Toronto Office: #750, 36 Toronto St., Toronto ON M5C 2C5
416/360-8040; Fax: 416/947-3541

Capital & Reserves: $164,529,000 (31-7-96)

Barclays Bank of Canada
304 Bay St., 5th Fl., PO Box 1, Toronto ON M5H 4A5
416/359-8000; Fax: 416/359-8230
President/CEO, Graeme P. Hensen
Capital & Reserves: $84,121,000 (31-5-95)

BT Bank of Canada
#1700, North Tower, Royal Bank Plaza, PO Box 100, Stn Royal Bank, Toronto ON M5J 2J2
416/865-0770; Fax: 416/941-9587; Telex: 06-217524
President/CEO, Harvey Naglie
Capital & Reserves: $95,518,000 (31-5-95)

Chemical Bank of Canada see The Chase Manhattan Bank of Canada

Cho Hung Bank of Canada
#1100, 2 Sheppard Ave. East, North York ON M2N 5Y7
416/590-9500; Fax: 416/590-9550
President/CEO, Chee Kwan
Capital & Reserves: $13,015,000 (31-5-95)

Citibank Canada
#1900, 123 Front St. West, Toronto ON M5J 2M3
416/947-5500; Fax: 416/947-5813
Chair/CEO, R.E. Lint
Capital & Reserves: $371,854,000 (31-5-95)

Crédit Lyonnais Canada
Centre ManuVie, 2000, rue Mansfield, 18e étage, Montréal PQ H3A 3A6
514/288-4848; Fax: 514/288-5679; Telex: 05-25245
Président, André Froissant
Toronto Office: One Financial Place, Box 190, #2505, One Adelaide St. East, Toronto ON M5C 2V9
416/947-9355; Fax: 416/947-9471
Capital & Reserves: $150,707,177 (31-8-96)

Crédit Suisse Canada
#1300, 525 University Ave., Toronto ON M5G 2K6
416/351-3500; Fax: 416/351-3630; Telex: 06-23620
President/CEO, K.P. Kuebel
Capital & Reserves: $173,044,000 (31-5-95)

Dai-Ichi Kangyo Bank (Canada)
#5025, Commerce Court West, PO Box 295, Stn Commerce Court, Toronto ON M5L 1H9
416/365-9666; Fax: 416/365-7314
Chair, President & CEO, Toshiro Motohashi
Capital & Reserves: $54,952,000 (31-5-95)

Daiwa Bank Canada
Sun Life Tower, Sun Life Centre, #2509, 150 King St. West, PO Box 95, Toronto ON M5H 1J9
416/979-7177; Fax: 416/979-7176
President/CEO, G. Watanabe
Capital & Reserves: $45,005,000 (31-5-95)

Deutsche Bank Canada
#1200, 222 Bay St., PO Box 196, Toronto ON M5K 1H6
416/682-8400; Fax: 416/682-8484; Telex: 06-218479
President/CEO, Stephen von Romberg-Droste
Capital & Reserves: $160,174,000 (31-12-95)

Dresdner Bank Canada
#1700, 2 First Canadian Place, PO Box 430, Stn 1st Can Place, Toronto ON M5X 1E3
416/369-8300; Fax: 416/369-8362; Telex: 06-524503
President/CEO, David N. Brandt
Capital & Reserves: $53,121,000 (31-5-95)

First Chicago NBD Bank, Canada
BCEE Place, Box 613, #4240, 161 Bay St., Toronto ON M5J 2S1
416/865-0466; Fax: 416/363-7574; Telex: 06-218425
President/CEO, William J. Buchanan
Capital & Reserves: $64,367,000 (31-12-95)

Fuji Bank Canada
Canada Trust Tower, BCE Place, #2800, 161 Bay St., PO Box 609, Toronto ON M5H 2S1
416/865-1020; Fax: 416/865-9618; Telex: 06-22094
President/CEO, Koji Hayashi
Capital & Reserves: $67,893,000 (31-5-95)

Hanil Bank Canada
36 Lombard St., Toronto ON M5C 2X3
416/214-1111; Fax: 416/214-1112
President/CEO, C.K. Choe
Capital & Reserves: $12,203,000 (31-5-95)

Hongkong Bank of Canada
#300, 885 Georgia St. West, Vancouver BC V6C 3E9
604/685-1000; Fax: 604/641-1909; Telex: 04-507750
President & CEO, W.R.P. Dalton
Capital & Reserves: $586,793,000 (31-5-95)

The Industrial Bank of Japan (Canada)
(IBJ Canada)
#1102, 100 Yonge St., PO Box 29, Toronto ON M5C 2W1
416/365-9550; Fax: 416/367-3452
President/CEO, Katsuhiko Otaki
Capital & Reserves: $59,464,000 (31-7-96)

International Commercial Bank of Cathay (Canada)
#910, 150 York St., PO Box 4037, Toronto ON M5H 3S5
416/947-2800; Fax: 416/947-9964; Telex: 06-218002 ICBC
President/CEO, H.H.B. Tai
Capital & Reserves: $17,190,000 (31-5-95)

Israel Discount Bank of Canada
#M100, 150 Bloor St. West, Toronto ON M5S 2Y5
416/926-7200; Fax: 416/926-0090; Telex: 06-218920 SCONT
CEO/Chief General Manager, Manfred H. Gerstung
Capital & Reserves: $13,689,000 (31-5-95)

Korea Exchange Bank of Canada
#600, 2345 Yonge St., Toronto ON M4P 2E5
416/932-1234; Fax: 416/932-1235
President/CEO, Jai Hak Roh
Capital & Reserves: $23,140,000 (30-4-95)

Mellon Bank Canada
Toronto Dominion Centre, #3200, Royal Trust Tower, Toronto ON M5K 1K2
416/860-0777; Telex: 06-218291
President, Tom Macmillan
Capital & Reserves: $51,144,000 (31-5-95)

Morgan Bank of Canada
#2200, Royal Bank Plaza, South Tower, PO Box 80, Stn Royal Bank, Toronto ON M5J 2J2
416/981-9200; Fax: 416/865-1641
President/CEO, Geoff Gouinlock
Capital & Reserves: $51,336,000 (31-5-95)

National Bank of Greece (Canada)/Banque Nationale de Grèce (Canada)
1170, Place du Frère André, Montréal PQ H3B 3C6
514/954-1522; Fax: 514/954-1224; Telex: 05-24196
CEO, C.P. Zissis
Capital & Reserves: $24,562,000 (31-7-96)

National Westminster Bank of Canada
(NatWest Markets)
#2060, Royal Bank Plaza, South Tower, PO Box 10, Stn Royal Bank, Toronto ON M5J 2J1
416/865-0170; Fax: 416/865-0934; Telex: 06-22572
President/CEO, Alex Constandse
Capital & Reserves: $104,998,000 (31-7-96)

Paribas Bank of Canada
#4100, Toronto-Dominion Centre, Royal Trust Tower, PO Box 31, Stn Toronto-Dominion, Toronto ON M5K 1N8
416/365-9600; Fax: 416/947-0086; Telex: 06-218608
President/CEO, Pascal Notté
Capital & Reserves: $47,700,000 (31-5-96)

Republic National Bank of New York (Canada)
1981, av McGill College, Montréal PQ H3A 3A9
514/288-5551; 416/367-1710 (Toronto); Fax: 514/286-4577
President/CEO, Allan Schouela
Capital & Reserves: $67,977,000 (31-12-95)

Sakura Bank (Canada)
#3601, Commerce Court West, PO Box 59, Stn Commerce Court, Toronto ON M5L 1B9
416/369-8531; Fax: 416/369-0268; Telex: 06-23400

Canadian Almanac & Directory 1997

President/CEO, Naoaki Yokota
Capital & Reserves: $70,679,000 (31-5-95)
Sanwa Bank Canada
Canada Trust Tower, BCE Place, Box 525, #4400, 161 Bay St., Toronto ON M5J 2S1
416/366-2583; Fax: 416/366-8599; Telex: 06-219585
President/CEO, K. Sakurai
Capital & Reserves: $63,103,000 (31-5-95)
Société Générale (Canada)
#1800, 1501, av McGill College, Montréal PQ H3A 3M8
514/841-6000
Président, Alain Clot
Toronto Office: Scotia Plaza, #1002, 100 Yonge St., Toronto ON M5C 2W1
416/364-2864; Fax: 416/364-9996
Capital & Reserves: $151,783,000 (31-5-95)
Sottomayor Bank Canada
1102 Dundas St. West, Toronto ON M6J 1X2
416/588-9819; Fax: 416/588-8564
President, Cesar De Morais
Capital & Reserves: $11,474,000 (31-5-95)
State Bank of India (Canada)
#800, Royal Bank Plaza, North Tower, PO Box 81, Stn Royal Bank, Toronto ON M5J 2J2
416/865-0414; Fax: 416/865-1735; Toll Free: 1-800-668-8947
President/CEO, N. Krishnan
Capital & Reserves: $7,795,000 (31-5-95)
The Sumitomo Bank of Canada
#1400, Ernst & Young Tower, Toronto-Dominion Centre, PO Box 172, Stn Toronto Dominion, Toronto ON M5K 1H6
416/368-4766; Fax: 416/367-3565
President/CEO, Osamu Okahashi
Capital & Reserves: $64,280,000 (31-10-95)
Swiss Bank Corporation (Canada)/Société de Banque Suisse (Canada)
#780, 207 Queen's Quay West, PO Box 103, Toronto ON M5J 1A7
416/203-2180; Fax: 416/203-4303
President/CEO, Joseph H.. Wright
Capital & Reserves: $72,071,000 (31-7-96)
Tokai Bank Canada
Sun Life Centre, #2401, 150 King St. West, PO Box 84, Toronto ON M5H 1J9
416/597-2210; Fax: 416/591-7415
President/CEO, H. Osada
Capital & Reserves: $37,061,000 (31-5-95)
Union Bank of Switzerland (Canada)
154 University Ave., Toronto ON M5H 3Z4
416/343-1800; Fax: 416/343-1900
President/CEO, Max P. Strebel
Capital & Reserves: $108,022,000 (31-5-95)
United Overseas Bank (Canada)
Vancouver Centre, #310, 650 Georgia St. West, PO Box 11616, Vancouver BC V6B 4N9
604/662-7055; Fax: 604/662-3356; Telex: 04-507520
Director/General Manager, Terence Tong
Capital & Reserves: $16,331,000 (31-12-95)

SAVINGS BANKS IN CANADA

Alberta Treasury Branches
ATB Plaza, #1200, 9925 - 109 St., PO Box 1440, Edmonton AB T5J 2N6
403/493-7300; Fax: 403/422-4178; Telex: 03-743122; URL: http://www.atb.com
CEO & Superintendent, P.G. Haggis
147 branches & 130 agencies in Alberta
Province of Ontario Savings Office
33 King St. West, 2nd Fl., Oshawa ON L1H 8H5
905/433-5788; Fax: 905/433-6519
Director, Qaid Silk
23 branches & five agencies in Ontario

TRUST COMPANIES

Trust companies are incorporated under the federal Trust and Loan Companies Act and/or corresponding provincial legislation. The business of trust companies falls into two distinct activities - financial intermediary (banking) and fiduciary functions. As a financial intermediary, a trust company borrows funds from the public in the form of guaranteed investment certificates or savings deposits and invests them in mortgages, securities and other loans.

The fiduciary or trustee functions are unique to trust companies. In their fiduciary functions, trust companies serve as administrators of estates, trusts and agencies and do not have ownership of the assets under their administration. The estate, trust and agency activities of trust companies are governed by provincial legislation. Trust companies also act as agents and registrars for various types of stocks and as trustees for corporate bond issues; real estate managers and real estate agents; investment managers or counsellors; managers of sinking funds; custodians; and agents for personal services.

Aetna Trust Company
Park Place, #2230, 666 Burrard St., Vancouver BC V6C 2X8
604/685-1208; Fax: 604/685-9997
President, Arnold E. Miles-Pickup
AGF Trust Company
Toronto-Dominion Centre, #2006, 77 King St. West, Toronto ON M5K 1E9
416/216-5353; Fax: 416/216-5350
President/COO, D.R. Doherty
The Bank of Nova Scotia Trust Company (Scotiatrust)
44 King St. West, Toronto ON M5H 1H1
416/866-6161
President/CEO, J. Rory MacDonald
Bayshore Trust Company
BCE Place, #2810, 181 Bay St., PO Box 784, Toronto ON M5J 2T3
416/364-9499; Fax: 416/364-0625; Toll Free: 1-800-387-4553; Email: webmaster@bayshoretrust.com; URL: http://www.bayshoretrust.com
President, Harry Enchin
Bonaventure Trust Inc.
#200, 1245, rue Sherbrooke ouest, Montréal PQ H3G 1G3
514/879-9257; Fax: 514/879-0663; Toll Free: 1-800-363-6337
President, Claude A. Garcia
Canada Trust Company
Canada Trust Tower, BCE Place, 161 Bay St., 35th Fl., Toronto ON M5J 2T2
416/361-8000; Fax: 416/361-8253; Toll Free: 1-800-668-8888; URL: http://www.canadatrust.com
President/CEO, Edmund Clark
Canadian Italian Trust Company/Fiducie Canadienne Italienne
6999, boul St-Laurent, Montréal PQ H2S 3E1
514/270-4124; Fax: 514/270-2247
President, Giuseppe Di Battista
Capital Trust Corporation
600, boul René-Lévesque, Montréal PQ H3B 1N4
514/393-7233
President, Samuel Luft
CIBC Trust Corporation
#900, 55 Yonge St., Toronto ON M5E 1S4
416/861-7000; Fax: 416/862-2272; Toll Free: 1-800-668-7389
President/CEO, P. Jane Bazarkewich
Citizens Trust Company
#401, 815 Hastings St. West, Vancouver BC V6C 1B4
604/682-7171; Fax: 604/708-7790; URL: http://www.citizenstrust.ca

President, Peter Cook
Co-Operative Trust Company of Canada
333 - 3rd Ave. North, Saskatoon SK S7K 2M2
306/956-1800; Fax: 306/652-7614
President/CEO, Edward J. Gebert
Community Trust Company Ltd.
2271 Bloor St. West, 3rd Fl., Toronto ON M6S 1P1
416/763-2291; Fax: 416/763-2444; Toll Free: 1-800-268-1576
Executive Vice-President/General Manager, Michael N. Wytiuk
The Effort Trust Company
242 Main St. East, Hamilton ON L8N 1H5
905/528-8956; Fax: 905/528-8182
President, Thomas J. Weisz
The Equitable Trust Company
#700, 30 St. Clair Ave. West, Toronto ON M4V 3A1
416/515-7000
Evangeline Trust Company/Société de Fiducie Évangeline
535 Albert St., Windsor NS B0N 2T0
902/798-8326; Fax: 902/798-3656
Chair & CEO, Barbara D. Hughes, Q.C.
Family Trust Corporation
5954 Hwy. 7 East, Markham ON L3P 1A2
905/471-1111; Fax: 905/471-3767
President & CEO, G.L. Jed Purcell
Fiducie Desjardins Inc./Desjardins Trust Inc.
1, Complexe Desjardins, CP 34, Montréal PQ H5B 1E4
514/286-9441; Fax: 514/286-3184; Toll Free: 1-800-361-6840
President & CEO, Marc Lemieux, FCA
FirstLine Trust Company
#700, 33 Yonge St., Toronto ON M5E 1G4
416/865-1511; Fax: 416/865-1566
President, Brendan Calder
Fortis Trust Corporation
139 Water St., PO Box 767, St. John's NF A1E 3Y3
709/726-7992; Fax: 709/726-1839
President, Stanley Marshall
Household Trust Company
#1000, 100 Sheppard Ave. East, North York ON M2N 6N7
416/250-3400; Fax: 416/250-9146
Chair, President & CEO, Tom Kimble
Inland Trust & Savings Corporation Ltd.
#201, One Forks Market Rd., Winnipeg MB R3C 4L9
204/949-4800; Fax: 204/949-4848; Toll Free: 1-800-665-8897
President, Ken Cooper
Investors Group Trust Co. Ltd./La Compagnie de Fiducie du Groupe Investors Ltée
One Canada Centre, 447 Portage Ave., Winnipeg MB R3C 3B6
204/943-0361; Fax: 204/949-1340
President, R.E. Archer
London Trust & Savings Corporation
#200, 4950 Yonge St., North York ON M2N 6K1
416/229-6700; Fax: 416/229-2478
President, S. Goldfarb
The Merchant Private Trust Company
Scotia Plaza #4714, 40 King St. West, Toronto ON M5H 3Y2
416/360-4115
Vice-President, Finance, Mark Damelin
Metropolitan Trust Company of Canada
#2700, 10303 Jasper Ave., Edmonton AB T5J 3N6
403/421-2020; Fax: 403/421-2022
President/CEO, Robert J. Kallir
Montreal Trust
(Montreal Trustco Inc.)
Place Montréal Trust, 1800, av McGill College, 15e étage, CP 1900, Succ B, Montréal PQ H3A 3K9
514/982-7000; Fax: 514/982-7069
President/CEO, Robert W. Chisholm

Canadian Almanac & Directory 1997

MRS Trust Company
#520, 150 Bloor St. West, Toronto ON M5S 2X9
416/926-0221
President, Tim Conway

The Municipal Trust Company
70 Collier St., PO Box 147, Barrie ON L4M 4S9
705/734-7500; Fax: 705/734-7600; Telex: 06-875524
Chair/CEO, Maxwell L. Rotstein

Mutual Trust Company
#400, 70 University Ave., PO Box 17, Toronto ON M5J 2M4
416/591-2710; Fax: 416/598-7837
President/CEO, R. Dore

Natcan Trust Company/Société de Fiducie Natcan
National Bank Bldg., 600, rue de la Gauchetière ouest, Montréal PQ H3B 4L2
514/394-8494; Fax: 514/394-6987
President, Richard Carter

National Trust Company
1 Adelaide St. East, Toronto ON M5C 2W8
416/361-3918
Chairman & CEO, Paul Cantor

Northern Trust Company Canada
BCE Place, #4540, 161 Bay St., Toronto ON M5J 2S1
416/365-7161; Fax: 416/365-9484

Oxford Trust Company Ltd.
First Alberta Place, #1500, 777 - 8 Ave. SW, Calgary AB T2P 3R5
403/262-9889
President, Carl Cheverie

Pacific Corporate Trust
#830, 625 Howe St., Vancouver BC V6C 3B8
604/689-9853; Fax: 604/689-8144
President, John Andrew Halse

Pacific & Western Trust Corporation
#950, 410 - 22nd St. East, Saskatoon SK S7K 5T6
306/244-1868; Fax: 306/244-4649
President, David R. Taylor

Peace Hills Trust Company
Kensington Place, 10011 - 109 St., 10th Fl., Edmonton AB T5J 3S8
403/421-1606; Fax: 403/426-6568
President/CEO, W.W. Hannay

Peoples Trust Company
888 Dunsmuir St., 14th Fl., Vancouver BC V6C 3K4
604/683-2881; Fax: 604/683-8798; Email: people@peoplestrust.com; URL: http://www.peoplestrust.com
President/CEO, Frank A. Renou

RBC Trust
Royal Bank Plaza, 14th Fl., North Tower, Toronto ON M5J 2J2
416/865-0515

RM Trust Company
393 University Ave., 5th Fl., Toronto ON M5C 2W9
416/813-4500
President/CEO, Julian Clark

Royal Trust Corporation of Canada
(Royal Trust)
Royal Trust Tower, PO Box 7500, Stn A, Toronto ON M5W 1Y2
416/981-7000; Fax: 416/861-9658; Telex: TORB 0652437
President, Anthony A. Webb
Montréal Office: 630, boul René-Lévesque ouest, Montréal PQ H3B 1S6
514/876-2525; Fax: 514/876-7604

Sherbrooke Trust
75, rue Wellington nord, CP 250, Sherbrooke PQ J1H 5J2
819/563-4011
Executive Vice-President/Managing Director, Michel Lavoie

Sun Life Trust Company
225 King St. West, 5th Fl., Toronto ON M5V 3C5
416/943-6532
President, Gary Corsi

TD Trust Company
(TD Bank & Trust)
Commercial Union Tower, 4th Fl., Toronto ON M5K 1A2
416/982-2638; Fax: 416/345-5227; Toll Free: 1-800-268-7878; URL: http://www.tdbank.ca
President, Charles Macfarlane

The Trust Company of Bank of Montreal
302 Bay St., 7th Fl., Toronto ON M5X 1A1
416/867-5688; Fax: 416/956-2363
President, A. Donald C. Mutch

Trust Général du Canada
1100, rue University, 12e étage, Montréal PQ H3B 2G7
514/871-7180; Fax: 514/871-7525
President/CEO, Michel W. Petit

Trust La Laurentienne du Canada Inc./Laurentian Trust of Canada Inc.
425, boul de Maisonneuve ouest, Montréal PQ H3A 3G5
514/284-7000; Fax: 514/284-3210; Toll Free: 1-800-363-9560
Vice-President/COO, Philippe Visintini

Trust Prêt et Revenu/Savings & Investment Trust
#700, 850, Place d'Youville, Québec PQ G1K 7P3
418/692-1221; Fax: 418/692-1675
Chair, President & CEO, Paul Tardif

MORTGAGE & LOAN COMPANIES

Loan companies are incorporated under the federal Trust and Loan Companies Act and/or corresponding provincial legislation. Loan companies raise funds through the acceptance of deposits and issuance of short-term and long-term debentures or other debt instruments. In practice, a majority of the funds are invested in mortgages secured by real estate.

Canada Trustco Mortgage Company
Canada Trust Tower, BCE Place, 161 Bay St., 35th Fl., Toronto ON M5J 2T2
Toll Free: 1-800-668-8888
President/CEO, Edmund Clark

Granville Savings & Mortgage Corporation
Grosvenor Bldg., #290, 1040 Georgia St. West, Vancouver BC V6E 6H1
Chair/CEO, Sidney J. Mendelson

Home Savings & Loans Corporation
#1910, 145 King St. West, Toronto ON M5H 1J8
416/360-4663; Fax: 416/363-7611
Chair, President & CEO, Gerald M. Soloway

League Savings & Mortgage Company
6074 Lady Hammond Rd., PO Box 8900, Stn A, Halifax NS B3K 5N3
CEO/General Manager, Robert J. Mowbrey

Municipal Savings & Loan Corporation
(Municipal Trust)
70 Collier St., Barrie ON L4M 4S9
705/734-7500; Fax: 705/734-7605
Chair/CEO, Maxwell L. Rotstein

NAL Mortgage Company
#1800, 151 Yonge St., Toronto ON M5C 2W7
President, Alan Hibben

Security Home Mortgage Investment Corporation
Victoria Tower, #1510, 25 Adelaide St. East, Toronto ON M5C 1Y2
416/366-2254
CEO, Russell Kalmacoff

Seel Mortgage Investment Corporation
#400, 70 University Ave., Toronto ON M5J 2M4
Executive Vice-President/COO, Ian Sutherland

Sun Life Savings & Mortgage Corp.
225 King St. West, 5th Fl., Toronto ON M5V 3C5
416/408-7283; Fax: 416/974-9407
President, Gary Corsi

TD Mortgage Corporation
Toronto-Dominion Centre, 55 King St. West, PO Box 191, Toronto ON M5K 1H6
416/982-6744; Fax: 416/944-5853
President, Bruce Shireff

INVESTMENT FUND MANAGERS IN CANADA

Funds marked with an * are RRSP eligible; ** are 20% RRSP eligible.

20/20 Funds Inc.
#700, 690 Dorval Dr., Oakville ON L6K 3X9
905/339-2020; Fax: 905/339-3863; Toll Free: 1-800-268-8690
CEO, John Wood
Mutual Funds: 20/20 Aggressive Global Fund; 20/20 Aggressive Growth Fund; 20/20 American Tactical Asset Allocation Fund; 20/20 Asia Pacific Fund; *20/20 Canadian Asset Allocation Fund; *20/20 Canadian Growth Fund; *20/20 Dividend Fund; 20/20 European Asset Allocation Fund; *20/20 Foreign RSP Bond Fund; *20/20 Income Fund; 20/20 India Fund; 20/20 International Value Fund; 20/20 Latin American Fund; *Managed Futures Value Fund; *20/20 Money Market Fund; 20/20 MultiManager Emerging Markets Fund; *20/20 RSP Agressive Equity Fund; *20/20 RSP International Equity Allocation Fund; 20/20 Aggressive Smaller Companies Fund; 20/20 U.S. Short-Term High Yield Fund; 20/20 World Bond Fund; 20/20 World Fund

20/20 Group Financial Inc. *see* 20/20 Funds Inc.

ABC Funds
#500, 8 King St. East, Toronto ON M5C 1B5
416/365-9696; Fax: 416/365-9705
President, Irwin Michael
Mutual Funds: *ABC Fully-Managed Fund; *ABC Fundamental-Value Fund

Admax Regent International Management Ltd.
#1802, 150 King St. West, PO Box 80, Toronto ON M5H 1J9
416/408-2222; Fax: 416/408-1228; Toll Free: 1-800-667-2369; Email: admax@terraport.net; URL: http://www.admaxregent.com
CEO, Lou Voticky
Mutual Funds: Admax American Performance Fund; Admax American Select Growth Fund; *Admax Asset Allocation Fund; *Admax Canadian Performance Fund; *Admax Canadian Select Growth Fund; *Admax Cash Performance Fund; Admax Global Health Sciences Fund; Regent Dragon 888 Fund; Regent Europa Performance Fund; *Regent International Fund; Regent Korea Fund; *Regent Nippon Fund; *Regent Tiger Fund; *Regent World Income Fund

AGF Management Limited
Toronto-Dominion Centre, Toronto-Dominion Tower, 31st Fl., PO Box 50, Stn Toronto-Dominion, Toronto ON M5K 1E9
416/367-1900; Fax: 416/865-4197; Toll Free: 1-800-268-8583; Email: tiger@agf.com; URL: http://www.agf.com/
Mutual Funds: AGF American Growth Fund Ltd.; AGF Asian Growth Fund; *AGF Canadian Bond Fund; *AGF Canadian Equity Fund; *AGF Canadian Resources Fund; AGF China Focus Fund; AGF European Growth Fund; AGF Germany Fund; AGF Global Government Bond Fund; AGF Growth & Income Fund; *AGF Growth Equity Fund; AGF High Income Fund; AGF International Short-Term Income Fund; AGF Japan Fund; *AGF Money Market Account; AGF Resources Capital Fund; AGF Special Fund Ltd.; AGF Strategic Income Fund;

AGF U.S. Dollar Money Market Fund; AGF U.S. Income Fund; AGF World Equity Fund

AIC Limited
1 Markland St., Hamilton ON L8P 2J5
905/529-5500; Fax: 905/529-0966; Toll Free: 1-800-263-2144
Assistant to President, Terry Levely
Mutual Funds: *AIC Advantage Fund; *AIC Diversified Canada Fund; AIC Emerging Markets Fund; *AIC Money Market Fund; AIC Value Fund; AIC World Equity Fund

All-Canadian Funds
PO Box 7320, Ancaster ON L9G 3N6
905/648-2025; Fax: 905/648-5422
Chairman, Paul A. Gratton
Mutual Funds: *All-Canadian Capital Fund; *All-Canadian Compound Fund; *All-Canadian Consumer Fund; *All-Canadian Resources Corp.

Altamira Investment Services Inc.
#200, 250 Bloor St. East, Toronto ON M4W 1E6
416/925-1623; Fax: 416/925-5352; URL: http://www.altamira.com
Mutual Funds: *AltaFund Investment Corp.; **Altamira Asia Pacific Fund; *Altamira Balanced Fund; *Altamira Bond Fund; *Altamira Capital Growth Fund Limited; *Altamira Dividend Fund Inc.; *Altamira Equity Fund; **Altamira European Equity Fund; *Altamira Global Bond Fund; Altamira Global Discovery Fund; **Altamira Global Diversified Fund; *Altamira Growth & Income Fund; *Altamira Income Fund; **Altamira Japanese Opportunity Fund; *Altamira North American Recovery Fund; *Altamira Precious & Strategic Metal Fund; *Altamira Resource Fund; **Altamira Select American Fund; *Altamira Short-term Global Income Fund; *Altamira Short Term Government Bond Fund; *Altamira Special Growth Fund; **Altamira Speculative High Yield Bond Fund; **Altamira US Larger Company Fund; **Altamira Science & Technology Fund; **Altamira Global Small Company Fund

AMI Private Capital
#900, 26 Wellington St. East, Toronto ON M5E 1S2
416/865-1985; Fax: 416/865-9241
Mutual Funds: *AMI Private Capital Equity Fund; *AMI Private Capital Income Fund; *AMI Private Capital Money Market Fund; *AMI Private Capital Optimix Fund

Atlas Asset Management Inc.
BCE Place, #400, 181 Bay St., Toronto ON M5J 2V8
416/369-4525; Fax: 416/369-8176; Toll Free: 1-800-463-2857
Executive Vice-President, Dan Geraci
Mutual Funds: Atlas American Advantage Fund; Atlas American Emerging Value Fund; Atlas American Large Cap Growth Fund; Atlas American Money Market Fund; Atlas American Opportunity Fund; Atlas American Large Cap Value Fund; *Atlas Canadian Balanced Fund; *Atlas Canadian Bond Fund; *Atlas Canadian Diversified Fund; *Atlas Canadian Emerging Growth Fund; *Atlas Canadian Emerging Value Fund; *Atlas Canadian High Yield Bond Fund; *Atlas Canadian Large Cap Value Fund; *Atlas Canadian Money Market Fund; *Atlas Canadian T-Bill Fund; *Atlas Global Equity Fund; Atlas Managed Futures Fund; Atlas NAFTA Fund; Hercules Emerging Market Debt Fund; Hercules European Value Fund; Hercules Global Short-Term Fund; Hercules Latin American Fund; Hercules Pacific Basin Value Fund; *Hercules World Bond Fund

Atlas Capital Group see Atlas Asset Management Inc.

Bank of Montreal Investment Management Ltd.
55 Bloor St. West, 15th Fl., Toronto ON M4W 3N5
416/867-5000; Fax: 416/956-2363; Toll Free: 1-800-387-1342; URL: http://www.fcfunds.bomil.ca/
Mutual Funds: *First Canadian Asset Allocation Fund; *First Canadian Bond Fund; First Canadian Dividend Income Fund; First Canadian Emerging Markets Fund; *First Canadian Equity Index Fund; First Canadian European Growth Fund; First Canadian Far East Growth Fund; *First Canadian Growth Fund; First Canadian International Bond Fund; First Canadian International Growth Fund; First Canadian Japanese Growth Fund; *First Canadian Money Market Fund; *First Canadian Mortgage Fund; First Canadian NAFTA Advantage Fund; *First Canadian Resource Fund; *First Canadian Special Growth Fund; *First Canadian T-Bill Fund; First Canadian US Growth Fund

Bissett & Associates Investment Management Ltd.
#1120, 500 - 4 Ave. SW, Calgary AB T2P 2V6
403/266-4664; Fax: 403/237-2334; Toll Free: 1-800-267-3862
Mutual Funds: Bissett American Equity Fund; *Bissett Bond Fund; *Bissett Canadian Equity Fund; Bissett Dividend Income Fund; *Bissett Money Market Fund; *Bissett Multinational Growth Fund; *Bissett Small Cap Fund

BNP (Canada) Valeurs Mobilières Inc.
1981, av McGill College, 5e étage, Montréal PQ H3A 2W8
514/285-7597; Fax: 514/285-7598
Mutual Funds: *Fonds marché monétaire BNP (Canada); *Fonds d'obligations BNP (Canada)

Bolton Tremblay Funds Inc. see BPI Capital Management Corporation

BPI Capital Management Corporation
Canada Trust Tower, BCE Place, #3900, 161 Bay St., Toronto ON M5J 2S1
416/861-9811; Fax: 416/861-9415; Toll Free: 1-800-263-2427
President/CEO, Mark S. Bonham
Mutual Funds: BPI American Equity Value Fund; BPI American Small Companies Fund; *BPI Canadian Balanced Fund; *BPI Canadian Bond Fund; *BPI Canadian Equity Value Fund; *BPI Canadian Opportunities RSP Fund; *BPI Canadian Resource Fund Inc.; BPI Canadian Small Companies Fund; BPI Global Balanced RSP Fund; BPI Global Equity Fund; BPI Global Opportunities Fund; BPI Global RSP Bond Fund; BPI Global Small Companies Fund; *BPI Income Fund; BPI International Equity Fund; *BPI North American TAA RSP Fund; *BPI T-Bill Fund

Burgeonvest Investment Counsel Ltd.
Commerce Place, 1 King St. West, 11th Fl., Hamilton ON L8N 3P6
905/528-6505; Fax: 905/528-3540
Mutual Funds: *Dolphin Growth Fund; *Dolphin Income Fund; Marlborough Canadian Balanced Fund; Marlborough International Balanced Fund

Caldwell Securities Ltd.
#340, 55 University Ave., Toronto ON M5J 2H7
416/862-7755; Fax: 416/862-2498; Toll Free: 1-800-387-0859
President, T.S. Caldwell
Mutual Funds: *Caldwell Securities Associate Fund; Caldwell Securities International Fund

Canada Trust Fund Services Inc.
(CT Fund Services)
BCE Place, 161 Bay St., 3rd Fl., Toronto ON M5J 2T2
416/361-8268; Fax: 416/361-5333
Mutual Funds: *Everest Amerigrowth Fund; *Everest Asiagrowth Fund; *Everest Balanced Fund; *Everest Bond Fund; *Everest Dividend Income Fund; Everest Emerging Markets Fund; *Everest Eurogrowth Fund; *Everest International Bond Fund; Everest International Equity Fund; *Everest Money Market Fund; *Everest Mortgage Fund; Everest North American Fund; *Everest Special Equity Fund; *Everest Stock Fund; Everest US Equity Fund

Canadian International Mutual Funds
(C.I. Mutual Funds)
151 Yonge St., 8th Fl., Toronto ON M5C 2Y1
416/364-1145; Fax: 416/364-2969; Toll Free: 1-800-563-5181; URL: http://www.fundlib.com/ci.html
Mutual Funds: C.I. American Fund; *C.I. American RSP Fund; *C.I. Canadian Balanced Fund; *C.I. Canadian Bond Fund; *C.I. Canadian Growth Fund; C.I. Canadian Income Fund; *C.I. Emerging Asian Fund; C.I. Emerging Markets Fund; C.I. European Fund; *C.I. Global Bond RSP Fund; *C.I. Global Equity RSP Fund; C.I. Global Fund; C.I. International Balanced Fund; C.I. International Balanced RSP Fund; C.I. Latin American Fund; *C.I. Money Market Fund; C.I. New World Income Fund; C.I. Pacific Fund; C.I. Sector American Shares; C.I. Sector Canadian Shares; C.I. Sector Emerging Market Shares; C.I. Sector European Shares; C.I. Sector Global Shares; C.I. Sector Latin American Shares; C.I. Sector Pacific Shares; C.I. Sector Short Term Shares; C.I. US Money Market Fund; C.I. World Bond Fund

Century DJ Fund
819 Belhaven Cres., Burlington ON L7T 2J7
905/608-0727
Mutual Funds: Century DJ Mutual Fund

Chou Associates Management Inc.
70 Dragoon Cres., Scarborough ON M1V 1N4
416/299-6749; Fax: 416/299-6749
Mutual Funds: Chou Associates Fund; *Chou RRSP Fund

CIBC Securities Inc.
200 King St. West, 7th Fl., Toronto ON M5H 4A8
416/351-4444; Fax: 416/351-4455; Toll Free: 1-800-465-3863
President/CEO, Keith Sjogren
Mutual Funds: *CIBC Balanced Income & Growth Fund; *CIBC Canadian Bond Fund: *CIBC Canadian Equity Fund; *CIBC Canadian Income Fund; *CIBC Canadian Resources Fund; *CIBC Canadian T-Bill Fund; CIBC Capital Appreciation Fund; CIBC Emerging Economies Fund; *CIBC Equity Income Fund; CIBC Far East Prosperity Fund; CIBC Global Bond Fund; CIBC Global Equity Fund; CIBC Global Technology Fund; CIBC Japanese Equity Fund; *CIBC Money Market Fund; *CIBC Mortgage Investment Fund; *CIBC Premium Canadian T-Bill Fund; CIBC US Dollar Money Market Fund; CIBC US Opportunity Fund; CIBC US Equity Fund

Clean Environment Mutual Funds
#1800, 65 Queen St. West, Toronto ON M5H 2M5
416/366-9933; Fax: 416/366-2568; Toll Free: 1-800-461-4570
Mutual Funds: *Clean Environment Balanced Fund; *Clean Environment Equity Fund; *Clean Environment Income Fund; *Clean Environment International Equity Fund

Confederation Funds Management (Canada) Limited
321 Bloor St. East, 8th Fl., Toronto ON M4W 1H1
416/323-8999; Fax: 416/323-4100
President/Investment Officer, Barry Graham
Mutual Funds: *Confed Growth Fund; *Confed Mortgage Fund

Dominion Equity Resource Fund Inc.
Bow Valley Square II, #1710, 205 - 5 Ave. SW, Calgary AB T2P 2V7
403/531-2657; Fax: 403/264-5844
President, R.B. Coleman
Mutual Fund: *Dominion Equity Resource Fund Inc.

Dynamic Mutual Funds/Fonds d'Investissement Dynamique

Canadian Almanac & Directory 1997

Scotia Plaza, 40 King St. West, 55th Fl., Toronto ON M5H 4A9
416/363-5621; Fax: 416/365-2558; Toll Free: 1-800-268-8186; Email: invest@dynamic.ca; URL: http://www.dynamic.ca
Chairman, Ned Goodman
Mutual Funds: Dynamic Americas Fund; *Dynamic Canadian Growth Fund; *Dynamic Dividend Fund; *Dynamic Dividend Growth Fund; Dynamic Europe Fund; Dynamic Far East Fund; *Dynamic Fund of Canada Ltd.; *Dynamic Global Bond Fund; Dynamic Global Millennia Fund; Dynamic Global Partners Fund; Dynamic Global Precious Metals Fund; Dynamic Global Resource Fund; *Dynamic Government Income Fund; *Dynamic Income Fund; Dynamic International Fund; *Dynamic Money Market Fund; *Dynamic Partners Fund; *Dynamic Precious Metals Fund; *Dynamic Real Estate Equity Fund; *Dynamic Team Fund

Elliott & Page Limited
#1120, 120 Adelaide St. West, Toronto ON M5H 1V1
416/365-8300; Fax: 416/365-2143, 2156; URL: http://www.fundlib.com/ellpag.html
Mutual Funds: *Elliott & Page American Growth Fund; Elliott & Page Asian Growth Fund; *Elliott & Page Balanced Fund; *Elliott & Page Bond Fund; Elliott & Page Emerging Markets Fund; *Elliott & Page Equity Fund; Elliott & Page Global Balanced Fund; Elliott & Page Global Bond Fund; Elliott & Page Global Equity Fund; *Elliott & Page Money Fund; Elliott & Page T-Bill Fund

Ethical Funds Inc.
#510, 815 West Hastings St., Vancouver BC V6C 1B4
604/331-8350; Fax: 604/331-8399; Toll Free: 1-800-267-5019
President, John A. Linthwaite
Mutual Funds: *Ethical Balanced Fund; Ethical Global Bond Fund; *Ethical Growth Fund; *Ethical Income Fund; *Ethical Money Market Fund; Ethical North American Equity Fund, Ethical Pacific Rim Fund; *Ethical Special Equity Fund

Fidelity Investments Canada Limited
Ernst & Young Tower, #900, 222 Bay St., PO Box 90, Toronto ON M5K 1P1
416/307-5300; Fax: 416/307-5523; Toll Free: 1-800-263-4077; URL: http://www.fid-inv.com
CEO, John H. Simpson
Mutual Funds: Fidelity Asset Manager Fund (Cdn $); Fidelity Canadian Asset Allocation Fund; *Fidelity Canadian Bond Fund; *Fidelity Canadian Growth Company Fund; Fidelity Canadian Income Fund; *Fidelity Canadian Short-Term Asset Fund; *Fidelity Capital Builder Fund; Fidelity Emerging Markets Bond Fund; Fidelity Emerging Markets Portfolio Fund; Fidelity European Growth Fund (Cdn $); Fidelity Far East Fund; *Fidelity Growth America Fund; Fidelity International Portfolio Fund; Fidelity Japanese Growth Fund; Fidelity Latin American Growth Fund; Fidelity North American Income Fund (Cdn $); Fidelity RSP Global Bond Fund; Fidelity Small Cap America Fund; Fidelity US Money Market Fund

Fiducie Desjardins
#1422, 1, Complexe Desjardins, PO Box 34, Montréal PQ H5B 1E4
514/286-9441; Fax: 514/286-3472; Toll Free: 1-800-361-6840; Email: chayerd@interlink.net
Desjardins Money Market Fund*; Desjardins Mortgage Fund*; Desjardins Bond Fund*; Desjardins Balanced Fund*; Desjardins Diversified Secure Fund*; Desjardins Diversfied Moderate Fund*; Desjardins Diversified Audacious Fund*; Desjardins Dividend Fund*; Desjardins Equity Fund*; Desjardins Environment Fund*; Desjardins Growth Fund*; Desjardins Worldwide Balanced Fund*; Desjardins American Market Fund*; Desjardins International Fund

First Marathon Securities Limited
The Exchange Tower, #3200, 2 First Canadian Place, PO Box 21, Toronto ON M5X 1J9
416/869-3707; Fax: 416/869-0089; Toll Free: 1-800-661-3863
Mutual Funds: *Marathon Equity Fund

Fonds Ficadre/Ficadre Fund
625, rue Saint-Amable, Québec PQ G1R 2G5
418/643-3884; Fax: 418/528-0457; Toll Free: 1-800-667-7643
Directrice, Vivianne Drolet, 418/692-1221
Mutual Funds: *Fonds Ficadre d'actions; *Fonds Ficadre d'obligations; *Fonds Ficadre équilibré; *Fonds Ficadre marché monetaire

Fonds de Placement Acadie Inc./Acadia Investment Funds Inc.
295 St. Pierre Blvd. West, PO Box 5554, Caraquet NB E1W 1B7
506/727-1345; Fax: 506/727-1344; Toll Free: 1-800-461-1318
President/CEO, Amédée Haché
Mutual Funds: *Acadia Balanced Fund; *Acadia Bond Fund; *Acadia Money Market Fund; *Acadia Mortgage Fund

Global Strategy Financial Inc.
#1600, 33 Bloor St. East, Toronto ON M4W 3T8
416/966-3676; Fax: 416/927-9168; Toll Free: 1-800-387-1229
Mutual Funds: Global Strategy Asia Fund; *Global Strategy Bond Fund; *Global Strategy Canada Growth Fund; Global Strategy Canadian Small Cap Fund; *Global Strategy Diversified Americas Fund; *Global Strategy Diversified Asia Fund; *Global Strategy Diversified Bond Fund; *Global Strategy Diversified Europe Fund; *Global Strategy Diversified Foreign Bond Fund; *Global Strategy Diversified Gold Plus Fund; *Global Strategy Diversified Growth Fund; Global Strategy Diversified Japan Plus Fund; *Global Strategy Diversified Latin American Fund; *Global Strategy Diversified Short-Term Income Fund; *Global Strategy Diversified World Equity; Global Strategy Europe Plus Fund; Global Strategy Foreign Bond Fund; *Global Strategy Income Plus Fund; *Global Strategy Japan Fund; Global Strategy Latin American Fund; Global Strategy Real Estate Securities Fund; *Global Strategy T-Bill Savings Fund; *Global Strategy US Equity Fund; Global Strategy US Growth Fund; Global Strategy US Savings Fund; Global Strategy World Funds

Groupe Financier Concorde
850, Place d'Youville, Québec PQ G1R 3P6
418/694-0000; Fax: 418/692-1679; Toll Free: 1-800-363-0598
President/CEO, Michel Fragasso
Mutual Funds: *Concorde Balanced Fund; *Concorde Fonds Dividende; Concorde International Fund; *Fonds d'hypothèques Concorde; *Fonds de croissance Concorde; *Fonds de revenu Concorde; Fonds du marché monetaire Concorde

G.T. Global Canada
Royal Trust Tower, TD Centre, #4001, 77 King St. West, PO Box 297, Toronto ON M5K 1K2
416/594-4300; Fax: 416/594-0656; Toll Free: 1-800-588-4880; Email: glbcan@inforamp.net; URL: http://www.fundlib.com/gt.html
President, Joseph Canavan
Mutual Funds: G.T. Canada Worldwide RSP Class; G.T. Global Fund Inc. American Growth; G.T. Global Fund Inc. Global Infrastructure; G.T. Global Fund Inc. Global Natural Resources; G.T. Global Fund Inc. Global Telecommunications; G.T. Global Fund Inc. Latin America Growth; G.T. Global Fund Inc. Pacific Growth; G.T. Global Growth & Income Fund; G.T. Global Short-Term Income; G.T. Global Strategic Income Fund; G.T. World Wide Bond Fund

The Guardian Group of Funds Limited
#3100, Commerce Court West, PO Box 201, Toronto ON M5L 1E8
416/947-4099; Fax: 416/369-6758; Toll Free: 1-800-668-5613
President/COO, Harold Hillier
Mutual Funds: Guardian American Equity Fund Ltd.; Guardian Asia Pacific Fund; *Guardian Canadian Balanced Fund; *Guardian Canadian Income Fund; *Guardian Canadian Money Market Fund; Guardian Emerging Markets Fund; *Guardian Enterprise Fund; *Guardian Foreign Income Fund; Guardian Global Equity Fund; *Guardian Growth Equity Fund; *Guardian International Balanced Fund; *Guardian International Income Fund; *Guardian US Money Market Fund; *Guardian Monthly Dividend Fund Ltd.

Hercules International Management
c/o Midland Walwyn Capital Inc., #400, 181 Bay St., Toronto ON M5J 2V8
416/369-7672; Fax: 416/369-7756
Mutual Funds: Hercules Emerging Market Debt US$ (Cdn $); Hercules Emerging Market Debt US$ Fund; *Hercules European Value Fund; Hercules Global Short-Term Fund; Hercules Latin American Fund; Hercules Money Market Fund; Hercules Money Market US$ Fund; Hercules North American Growth & Income Fund; Hercules Basin Value Fund; Hercules World Bond Fund; Hercules World Bond US$ Fund

Hodgson Roberton Laing
#1920, 1 Queen St. East, Toronto ON M5C 2Y5
416/368-1428; Fax: 416/869-1653; Toll Free: 1-800-268-9622
Mutual Funds: *Hodgson Roberton Laing Balanced Fund; *Hodgson Roberton Laing Bond Fund; *Hodgson Roberton Laing Canadian Fund; *Hodgson Roberton Laing Instant $$ Fund; Hodgson Roberton Laing Overseas Growth Fund

Hongkong Bank Securities Inc.
1066 West Hastings St., 25th Fl., Vancouver BC V6E 3X1
604/257-4841; Fax: 604/257-4867; Toll Free: 1-800-565-3883
President, Steve Wilson
Mutual Funds: Hongkong Bank Americas Fund; Hongkong Bank Emerging Markets Fund; Hongkong Bank European Growth Fund; Hongkong Bank Global Fund; Hongkong Bank Asian Growth Fund; Hongkong Bank Balanced Fund; Hongkong Bank Canadian Bond Fund; Hongkong Bank Dividend Income Fund; *Hongkong Bank Equity Fund; *Hongkong Bank Money Market Fund; *Hongkong Bank Mortgage Fund; Hongkong Bank Small Cap Growth Fund

Investors Group
One Canada Centre, 447 Portage Ave., PO Box 5000, Winnipeg MB R3C 3B6
204/943-0361; Fax: 204/949-1340
President & CEO, H. Sanford Riley
Mutual Funds: *Investors Asset Allocation Fund; *Investors Canadian Equity Fund; *Investors Corporate Bond Fund; Investors Dividend Fund Ltd.; Investors European Growth Fund; Investors Global Bond Fund; Investors Global Fund Ltd.; *Investors Government Bond Fund; Investors Growth Plus Portfolio Fund; Investors Growth Portfolio Fund; *Investors Income Plus Portfolio Fund; *Investors Income Portfolio Fund; Investors Japanese Growth Fund Ltd.; *Investors Money Market Fund; *Investors

Mortgage Fund; Investors Mutual of Canada Ltd.; Investors North American Growth Fund Ltd.; Investors Pacific International Fund; *Investors Real Property Fund; *Investors Retirement Growth Portfolio Fund; *Investors Retirement Mutual Fund; *Investors Retirement Plus Portfolio Fund; Investors Special Fund Ltd.; *Investors Summa Fund Ltd.; Investors US Growth Fund Ltd.; Investors World Growth Portfolio; Merrill Lynch Canadian Equity Fund; Merrill Lynch World Bond Fund; Merrill Lynch Capital Asset Fund; Merrill Lynch Emerging Markets

Jones Heward Investment Management Inc.
#4200, 77 King St. West, Toronto ON M5K 1J5
416/359-5019; Fax: 416/359-5040; Toll Free: 1-800-361-1392
President/CEO, John P. Donnelly
Mutual Funds: Jones Heward American Fund; *Jones Heward Bond Fund; *Jones Heward Canadian Balanced Fund; *Jones Heward Fund; *Jones Heward Money Market Fund

Laurentian Funds Management Inc./Gestion de Fonds la Laurentienne Inc.
95 St. Clair Ave. West, 7th Fl., Toronto ON M4V 1N7
416/324-1617; Fax: 416/324-1670
President/COO, Peter N. Dabbikeh
Mutual Funds: Laurentian American Equity Fund Ltd.; Laurentian Asia Pacific Fund; *Laurentian Canadian Balanced Fund; *Laurentian Canadian Equity Fund Ltd.; Laurentian Commonwealth Fund Ltd.; *Laurentian Dividend Fund Ltd.; Laurentian Emerging Markets Fund; Laurentian Europe Fund; Laurentian Global Balanced Fund; *Laurentian Government Bond Fund; *Laurentian Income Fund; Laurentian International Fund Ltd.; *Laurentian Money Market Fund; *Laurentian Special Equity Fund

Leon Frazer & Associates Ltd.
#2001, 8 King St. East, Toronto ON M5C 1B6
416/864-1120; Fax: 416/864-1491
President, W.G. Tynkaluk
Mutual Funds: *Associate Investors Limited

Mackenzie Financial Corporation
#400, 150 Bloor St. West, Toronto ON M5S 2X9
416/922-5322; Fax: 416/922-9194; Toll Free: 1-800-387-0614; Email: 74404.3443@compuserve.com; URL: http://www.fundlib.com/mackenzie.html
Mutual Funds: Industrial American Fund; *Industrial Balanced Fund; *Industrial Bond Fund; *Industrial Cash Management Fund; *Industrial Dividend Fund Limited; *Industrial Equity Fund Limited; *Industrial Future Fund; *Industrial Growth Fund; *Industrial Horizon Fund; *Industrial Income Fund; *Industrial Mortgage Securities Fund; *Industrial Pension Fund; *Industrial Short Term Fund; *Mackenzie Sentinel Canada Equity Fund; Mackenzie Sentinel Global Fund; Universal Americas Fund; *Universal Canadian Growth Fund Limited; *Universal Canadian Resource Fund; Universal European Opportunities Fund; Universal Far East Fund; Universal Growth Fund; Universal Japan Fund; Universal US Emerging Growth Fund; Universal US Money Market Fund; *Universal World Asset Allocation Fund; *Universal World Balanced RRSP Fund; *Universal World Emerging Growth Fund; Universal World Equity Fund; Universal World Growth RRSP Fund; Universal World Income RRSP Fund; Universal World Precious Metals Fund; Universal World Tactical Bond Fund; Ivy Funds: *Ivy Canadian Fund; *Ivy Enterprise Fund; *Ivy Foreign Equity Fund; *Ivy Growth & Income Fund; *Ivy Mortgage Fund

Majendie Securities Inc.
Waterfront Centre, #320, 200 Burrard St., Vancouver BC V6C 3L6
604/682-6446; Fax: 604/662-8594; Toll Free: 1-800-665-6669
President/CEO, Nick Majendie
Mutual Funds: *Top 50 Equity Fund; *Top 50 T-Bill/Bond Fund; Top 50 US Equity Fund

Manulife Securities International Ltd./Placements Manuvie Internationale Ltée
500 King St. North, Waterloo ON N2J 4C6
519/747-7000; Fax: 519/747-6325; Toll Free: 1-800-265-7401
President & CEO, J.A. Vivash
Mutual Funds: *Manulife Cabot Blue Chip Fund; *Manulife Cabot Canadian Equity Fund; *Manulife Cabot Canadian Growth Fund; *Manulife Cabot Diversified Bond Fund; *Manulife Cabot Emerging Growth Fund; Manulife Cabot Global Equity Fund; *Manulife Cabot Money Market Fund

MD Management Limited/Gestion MD Limitée
1867 Alta Vista Dr., Ottawa ON K1G 5W8
613/731-4552; Fax: 613/526-1352; Toll Free: 1-800-267-4022
President/CEO, R.B. Breton
Mutual Funds: *MD Balanced Fund; *MD Bond Fund; *MD Bond & Mortgage Fund; *MD Dividend Fund; MD Emerging Markets Fund; *MD Equity Fund; MD Global Bond Fund; MD Growth Fund Ltd.; *MD Money Fund; *MD Realty Fund; *MD Select Fund; MD US Equity Fund

M.K. Wong & Associates Ltd.
#2520, 1066 Hastings St. West, Vancouver BC V6E 3X1
604/257-1000; Fax: 604/669-8420; Toll Free: 1-800-665-9360; Email: pryan@cyberstore.ca
CEO, Milton Wong
Mutual Funds: *Lotus Group - Balanced; *Lotus Group Bond Fund; *Lotus Group Canadian Equity Fund; *Lotus Group Income Fund; *Lotus Group International Bond Fund; Lotus International Equity Fund

MOF Management Ltd.
Pacific Centre, #2020, 609 Granville St., PO Box 10379, Vancouver BC V7Y 1G6
604/643-7414; Fax: 604/643-7733; Toll Free: 1-800-663-6370
CEO, Donald D. MacFayden
Mutual Funds: *Multiple Opportunities Fund; Special Opportunities Fund Ltd.

The Mutual Group
227 King St. South, Waterloo ON N2J 4C5
519/888-3900; Fax: 519/888-3480
Mutual Funds: Mutual Amerifund; *Mutual Bond Fund; *Mutual Diversifund 40; *Mutual Equifund; *Mutual Money Market Fund; Mutual Premier American Fund; *Mutual Premier Blue Chip Fund; *Mutual Premier Bond Fund; *Mutual Premier Diversified Fund; Mutual Premier Emerging Markets Fund; *Mutual Premier Growth Fund; *Mutual Premier International Fund; *Mutual Premier Mortgage Fund

National Bank Securities Inc./Placements banque nationale inc.
1100, rue University, 7e étage, Montréal PQ H3B 2G7
514/394-9937; Fax: 514/394-4013; Toll Free: 1-800-280-3088
CEO, Jacques Daoust
Mutual Funds: InvesNat Blue Chip American Equity; *InvesNat Canadian Bond Fund; *InvesNat Canadian Equity Fund; *InvesNat Corporate Cash Management Fund; *InvesNat Dividend Fund; InvesNat European Equity Fund; InvesNat Far East Equity Fund; *InvesNat International RSP Bond Fund; InvesNat Japanese Equity Fund; *InvesNat Money Market Fund; *InvesNat Mortgage Fund; *InvesNat Retirement Balanced Fund; *InvesNat Short-Term Government Bond Fund; *InvesNat Treasury Bill Plus Fund; InvesNat US Money Market Fund; *General Trust of Canada - Balanced Fund; *General Trust of Canada - Bond Fund; *General Trust of Canada - Canadian Equity Fund; *General Trust of Canada - Growth Fund; *General Trust of Canada - International Fund; *General Trust of Canada - Money Market Fund; *General Trust of Canada - Mortgage Fund; *General Trust of Canada - US Equity Fund

National Trust Mutual Funds
One Financial Place, One Adelaide St. East, Toronto ON M5C 2W8
416/361-3863; Fax: 416/361-5563; Toll Free: 1-800-563-4683
Mutual Funds: National Trust American Equity Fund; *National Trust Balanced Fund; *National Trust Canadian Bond Fund; *National Trust Canadian Equity Fund; *National Trust Dividend Fund; National Trust Emerging Markets Fund; National Trust International Equity Fund; National Trust International RSP Bond Fund; *National Trust Money Market Fund; *National Trust Mortgage Fund; *National Trust Special Equity Fund

Navigator Fund Company Ltd.
#1500, 444 St. Mary Ave., Winnipeg MB R3C 3T1
204/942-7788; Fax: 204/942-5100; Toll Free: 1-800-665-1667
Mutual Funds: Navigator American Value Investment Fund; Navigator Asia-Pacific Fund; *Navigator Canadian Income Fund; Navigator Latin-American Fund; *Navigator Value Investment Retirement Fund

North American Trust
Yonge-Richmond Centre, 151 Yonge St., 4th Fl., Toronto ON M5C 2W7
416/947-5100; Fax: 416/947-5116; Toll Free: 1-800-387-9805
Marketing Analyst, Paul Saunders
Mutual Funds: Cornerstone Balanced Fund; *Cornerstone Bond Fund; *Cornerstone Canadian Growth Fund; Cornerstone Global Fund; *Cornerstone Government Money Fund; Cornerstone U.S. Fund

O'Donnell Investment Management Corporation
Exchange Tower, #1010, 2 First Canadian Place, PO Box 447, Toronto ON M5X 1E4
416/214-2214; Fax: 416/214-1244
Mutual Funds: *O'Donnell American Sector Growth Fund; *O'Donnell Canadian Emerging Growth Fund; *O'Donnell Growth Fund; *O'Donnell High Income Fund; *O'Donnell Money Market Fund; *O'Donnell Short Term Fund

OHA Investment Management Limited
150 Ferrand Dr., North York ON M3C 1H6
416/429-2661; Fax: 416/429-9198; Toll Free: 1-800-268-9597
President, R. Hutcheon
Mutual Funds: *OHA Balanced Fund; *OHA Bond Fund; *OHA Canadian Equity Fund; *OHA Foreign Equity Fund; *OHA Short-Term Fund

Ontario Teachers' Group Investment Fund
57 Mobile Dr., Toronto ON M4A 1H5
416/752-9410; Fax: 416/752-6649; Toll Free: 1-800-263-9541
Mutual Funds: OTG Investment Fund: *Balanced Section; *Diversified Section; *Fixed Value Section; *Growth Section; *Mortgage Income Section; Ontario Teachers' Group Global Value Fund

Peter Cundill & Associates Ltd.
Sun Life Plaza, #1200, 1100 Melville St., Vancouver BC V6E 4A6
604/685-4231; Fax: 604/689-9532; Toll Free: 1-800-663-0156
President/CEO, Mark C. Stevens

Canadian Almanac & Directory 1997

Mutual Funds: *Cundill Security Fund; Cundill Value Fund

Phillips, Hager & North Investment Management Ltd.
#1700, 1055 Hastings St. West, Vancouver BC V6E 2H3
604/691-6781; Fax: 604/685-5712; Toll Free: 1-800-661-6141
President, Tony Gage
Mutual Funds: *Phillips, Hager & North Balanced Fund; *Phillips, Hager & North Bond Fund; *Phillips, Hager & North Canadian Equity Fund; *Phillips, Hager & North Canadian Money Market Fund; Phillips, Hager & North Dividend Income Fund; *Phillips, Hager & North International Equity Fund; PH&N North American Equity Fund; *Phillips, Hager & North RSP/RIF Equity Fund; Phillips, Hager & North U.S. Equity Fund; Phillips, Hager & North Short-Term Bond & Mortgage Fund; *Phillips, Hager & North Vintage Fund

Prudential Fund Management Canada Ltd.
200 Consilium Pl., 6th Fl., Scarborough ON M1H 3E6
416/296-3395; Fax: 416/296-3186; Toll Free: 1-800-463-6778
President, Robert C. Wallace
Mutual Funds: Prudential American Equity Fund; *Prudential Diversified Investment Fund of Canada; *Prudential Dividend Fund of Canada; Prudential Global Equity Fund; *Prudential Growth Fund Canada Limited; *Prudential Income Fund of Canada; *Prudential Money Market Fund of Canada; *Prudential Natural Resources Fund of Canada; *Prudential Precious Metals Fund of Canada

Pursuit Financial Management Corp.
#402, 1200 Sheppard Ave. East, North York ON M2K 2S5
416/502-9300; Fax: 416/502-9394; Toll Free: 1-800-253-9619
Mutual Funds: Pursuit American Fund; *Pursuit Canadian Equity Fund; Pursuit Global Bond Fund; Pursuit Global Equity Fund; *Pursuit Income Fund; Pursuit Money Market Fund

Royal Mutual Funds Inc.
Royal Trust Tower, TD Centre, 5th Fl., PO Box 7500, Stn A, Toronto ON M5W 1P9
800/463-3863; Email: funds@www.royalbank.com; URL: http://www.royalbank.com/english/fund/index.html
President/CEO, Simon Lewis
Mutual Funds: Royal Asian Growth Fund; Royal Balanced Fund; Royal Canadian Growth Fund; *Royal Canadian Small Cap Fund; *Royal Energy Fund; *Royal European Growth Fund; Royal International Equity Fund; Royal Japanese Stock Fund; *Royal Latin American Fund; Royal Life Science & Technology Fund; Royal Precious Metals Fund; *Royal Trust Advantage Balanced Fund; *Royal Trust Advantage Income Fund; *Royal Trust Advantage Growth Fund; Royal Trust American Stock Fund; *Royal Trust Bond Fund; *Royal Trust Canadian Money Market Fund; *Royal Trust Canadian Stock Fund; *Royal Trust Canadian T-Bill Fund; Royal Trust Growth & Income Fund; *Royal Trust International Bond Fund; *Royal Trust Mortgage Fund; Royal Trust US Money Market Fund; *RoyFund Bond Fund; *RoyFund Canadian Equity Fund; RoyFund Canadian Money Market Fund; *RoyFund Cdn T-Bill Fund; *RoyFund Dividend Fund; *RoyFund International Income Fund; *RoyFund Mortgage Fund; *RoyFund US Dollar Money Market Fund; RoyFund US Equity Fund; Zweig Global Managed Assets; Zweig Strategic Growth Fund

Roycom Securities Limited
#2101, 1969 Upper Water St., Halifax NS B3J 3R7
902/421-1222; Fax: 902/420-0559
President, John Roy
Toronto Office: #700, 10 Bay St., Toronto ON M5J 2R8
416/363-3730; Fax: 416/363-4972; Toll Free: 1-800-565-1979
Mutual Funds: *Roycom-Summit Realty Fund; *Roycom-Summit TDF Fund

Sagit Investment Management Ltd.
#900, 789 Pender St. West, Vancouver BC V6C 1H2
604/685-3193; Fax: 604/681-7536; Toll Free: 1-800-663-1003; Email: client@sagit.com; URL: http://www.fundlib.com/specbull.html
Mutual Funds: Cambridge Americas Fund; Cambridge American Growth Fund; *Cambridge Balanced Fund; Cambridge China Fund; Cambridge Global Fund; *Cambridge Growth Fund; Cambridge Pacific Fund; *Cambridge Resource Fund; *Cambridge Special Equity Fund; *Trans-Canada Bond Fund; *Trans-Canada Equity Fund; *Trans-Canada Income Fund; *Trans-Canada Money Market Fund; *Trans-Canada Pension Fund

Saxon Group of Funds
Cadillac Fairview Tower, #1904, 20 Queen St. West, PO Box 95, Toronto ON M5H 3R3
416/979-1818; Fax: 416/979-7424
Mutual Funds: *Saxon Balanced Fund; *Saxon Small Cap Fund; *Saxon Stock Fund; Saxon World Growth Fund

Sceptre Investment Council Limited
#1200, 26 Wellington St. East, Toronto ON M5E 1W4
416/367-9898; Fax: 416/367-5938; Toll Free: 1-800-265-1888
Mutual Funds: Sceptre Asian Growth Fund; *Sceptre Balanced Growth Fund; *Sceptre Bond Fund; *Sceptre Equity Growth Fund; Sceptre International Fund; *Sceptre Money Market Fund

Scotia Securities Inc.
Scotia Plaza, 40 King St., 5th Fl., Toronto ON M5H 1H1
416/866-2014; Fax: 416/866-2018; Toll Free: 1-800-268-9269; URL: http://www.scotiabank.ca
President/CEO, A. Scipio del Campo
Mutual Funds: *Scotia CanAm Growth Fund; *Scotia CanAm Income Fund; Scotia Excelsior American Equity Growth Fund; *Scotia Excelsior Balanced Fund; *Scotia Excelsior Canadian Blue Chip Fund; *Scotia Excelsior Canadian Growth Fund; *Scotia Excelsior Defensive Income Fund; *Scotia Excelsior Dividend Fund; Scotia Global Bond Fund; Scotia Excelsior Government of Canada T-Bill Fund; *Scotia Excelsior Income Fund; Scotia Excelsior International Fund; Scotia Excelsior Latin American Fund; *Scotia Excelsior Money Market Fund; *Scotia Excelsior Mortgage Fund; Scotia Excelsior Pacific Rim Fund; *Scotia Excelsior Precious Metals Fund; *Scotia Excelsior Premium T-Bill Fund; *Scotia Excelsior Total Return Fund

Scudder Canada Investor Services Ltd.
BCE Place, 161 Bay St., PO Box 712, Toronto ON M5J 2S1
416/941-9393; Fax: 416/350-2018; Toll Free: 1-800-850-3863; Email: canada_mail@scudder.com; URL: http://www.scudder.ca
President & CEO, Gale K. Caruso
Mutual Funds: *Scudder Canadian Equity Fund; *Scudder Canadian Short Term Bond Fund; **Scudder Emerging Markets Fund; **Scudder Global Fund; **Scudder Great Europe Fund; **Scudder Pacific Fund; **Scudder US Growth & Income Fund

Spectrum United Mutual Funds Inc.
145 King St. West, 3rd Fl., Toronto ON M5H 1J8
416/352-3100; Fax: 416/352-3239; Toll Free: 1-800-263-1851; URL: http://www.fundlib.com/specbull.html
President, Allen C. Marple
Mutual Funds: Bullock American Fund; Bullock Asian Dynasty Fund; Bullock Asset Strategy Fund; Bullock European Enterprise Fund; Bullock Emerging Markets Fund; Bullock Global Bond Fund; Bullock Growth Fund; Bullock Optimax USA Fund; *Canadian Investment Fund; *Spectrum Canadian Equity Fund; *Spectrum Cash Reserve Fund; *Spectrum Diversifed Fund; *Spectrum Dividend Fund; *Spectrum Government Bond Fund; *Spectrum Interest Fund; *Spectrum International Bond Fund; *Spectrum International Equity Fund; Spectrum Savings Fund; United American Equity Fund Ltd.; United American Growth Fund Ltd.; *United Canadian Bond Fund; *United Canadian Equity Fund; *United Canadian Growth Fund; *United Canadian Interest Fund; *United Canadian Mortgage Fund; *United Canadian Portfolio of Funds; United Global Telecommunication Fund; United US Dollar Money Market Fund

Standard Life Mutual Funds Ltd.
1245, rue Sherbrooke ouest, Montréal PQ H3G 1G3
514/499-4188; Fax: 514/499-4466
President, Canadian Operations, Claude Gaveau
Mutual Funds: *Standard Life Balanced Mutual Fund; *Standard Life Bond Mutual Fund; *Standard Life Canadian Dividend Mutual Fund; *Standard Life Equity Mutual Fund; *Standard Life Growth Equity Mutual Fund; *Standard International Bond Mutual Fund; *Standard International Equity Mutual Fund; *Standard Life Money Market Mutual Fund; *Standard Life Natural Resource Mutual Fund; *Standard Life US Equity Mutual Fund

Stone & Co. Limited
#710, 155 University Ave., Toronto ON M5H 3B7
416/364-9188; Fax: 416/364-8456; Toll Free: 1-800-336-9528
Mutual Funds: *Flagship Stock Fund Canada

Strata Mutual Funds Limited
Scott Tower, 101 Frederick St., Kitchener ON N2G 4R8
519/888-5096; Fax: 519/888-5925
Mutual Funds: *StrataFund 40; *StrataFund 60; *Strata Canadian Fund; *Strata Government Bond Fund; *Strata Growth Fund; *Strata Income Fund; *Strata Money Market Fund; *Strata Tactical Fund

Talvest Fund Management Inc./Gestion financière Talvest Inc.
#3200, 1000, rue de la Gauchetière ouest, Montréal PQ H3B 4W5
514/875-9090; Fax: 514/875-9304; Toll Free: 1-800-268-8258; Email: talvest@marketing.com; URL: http://www.talvest.com
Chairman, Jean-Guy Desjardins
Toronto Office: The Exchange Tower, #2200, 130 King St. West, Toronto ON M5X 1B1
416/364-5620; Fax: 416/364-4472; Toll Free: 1-800-268-8258
Vancouver Office: Oceanic Plaza, #2600, 1066 West Hastings St., Vancouver BC V6E 3X1
604/689-8688; Fax: 604/689-8612; Toll Free: 1-800-465-1657
Mutual Funds: *Talvest Bond Fund; *Talvest Diversified Fund; *Talvest Dividend Fund; *Talvest Foreign Pay Cdn. Bond Fund; Talvest Global Diversified Fund; *Talvest Global RRSP Fund; *Talvest Growth Fund; *Talvest Income Fund; *Talvest Money Fund; *Talvest New Economy Fund; Talvest US Diversified Fund; Talvest US Growth Fund Inc.; Hyperion Funds: Hyperion Asian Fund; *Hyperion Aurora Fund; Hyperion

European Fund; Hyperion Value Line Equity Fund

TD Asset Management
Toronto-Dominion Tower, Toronto-Dominion Centre, PO Box 100, Stn Toronto-Dominion, Toronto ON M5K 1G8
416/982-6432; Fax: 416/982-6625; Toll Free: 1-800-268-8166; Email: infoline@tdbank.ca; URL: http://www.tdbank.ca/tdbank/mutual/index.html
Mutual Funds: Green Line Asian Growth Fund; *Green Line Balanced Growth Fund; *Green Line Balanced Income Fund; *Green Line Blue Chip Equity Fund; *Green Line Canadian Bond Fund; *Green Line Canadian Equity Fund; *Green Line Canadian Government Bond Fund; *Green Line Canadian Index Fund; *Green Line Canadian Money Market Fund; Green Line Canadian T-Bill Fund; Green Line Dividend Fund; Green Line Emerging Markets Fund; *Green Line Energy Fund; *Green Line European Growth Fund; Green Line Global Government Bond Fund; *Green Line Global RSP Bond Fund; Green Line Global Select Fund; Green Line International Equity Fund; *Green Line Japanese Growth Fund; Green Line Latin American Growth Fund; *Green Line Mortgage Fund; *Green Line Mortgage-Backed Fund; Green Line North American Growth Fund; *Green Line Precious Metal Fund; *Green Line Real Return Bond Fund; *Green Line Resource Fund; Green Line Science & Technology Fund; *Green Line Short-Term Income Fund; Green Line US Index Fund; Green Line US Money Market Fund; *Green Line Value Fund

Templeton Management Limited
4 King St. West, 19th Fl., PO Box 4070, Stn A, Toronto ON M5W 1M3
416/364-4672; Fax: 416/364-1163; Toll Free: 1-800-387-0830; URL: http://www.templeton.ca
President/CEO, Donald F. Reed
Mutual Funds: *Templeton Balanced Fund; *Templeton Canadian Asset Allocation Fund; *Templeton Canadian Bond Fund; *Templeton Canadian Stock Fund; *Templeton Emerging Markets Fund; *Templeton Global Balanced Fund; *Templeton Global Bond Fund; *Templeton Global Smaller Companies Fund; *Templeton Growth Fund, Ltd.; *Templeton International Balanced Fund; *Templeton International Stock Fund; *Templeton Treasury Bill Fund

Total Return Management Inc.
#2305, 1 Place Ville Marie, Montréal PQ H3B 3M5
514/875-6755; Fax: 514/875-2940; Toll Free: 1-800-267-6021
Mutual Funds: CIS Commax Hedge Fund; *CIS Global Telecommunications Fund; Total Return Fund Inc.

Tradex Management Inc./Gestion Tradex Inc.
#1860, 45 O'Connor St., Ottawa ON K1P 1A4
613/233-3394; Fax: 613/233-8191; Toll Free: 1-800-567-3863; Email: tradex@fox.nstn.ca; URL: http://www.tradex.ca
President, Andrew Billingsley
Mutual Funds: *Tradex Bond Fund; Tradex Emerging Markets Country Fund; *Tradex Equity Fund Limited

Trimark Investment Management Inc.
#5600, One First Canadian Place, PO Box 487, Toronto ON M5X 1E5
416/362-7181; Fax: 416/362-8515; Toll Free: 1-800-387-9841; URL: http://www.trimark.com/
President, Arthur S. Labatt
Mutual Funds: The Americas Fund; *Trimark Advantage Bond Fund; *Trimark Canadian Fund; Trimark Canadian Bond Fund; *Trimark Government Income Fund; *Trimark Income Growth Fund; Trimark Indo-Pacific Fund; *Trimark Interest Fund; *Trimark RSP Equity Fund; *Trimark Select Balanced Fund; *Trimark Select Canadian Growth Fund; Trimark Select Growth Fund

Trust Général du Canada
1100, rue University, Montréal PQ H3B 2G7
514/871-7100; Fax: 514/871-8525
Toronto Office: #200, 120 Adelaide St. West, Toronto ON M5H 3Y3
416/867-3200; Fax: 416/364-2670
Mutual Funds: Trust Général fonds équilibre; *Trust Général fonds international; *Trust Général fonds marché monétaire; Trust Général d'actions Americaines; *Trust Général fonds d'actions Canadiennes; Trust Général fonds d'hypothèques; *Trust Général fonds d'obligations; *Trust Général fonds de croissance

University Avenue Group of Funds
40 University Ave., Toronto ON M5J 1T1
416/351-1617; Fax: 416/351-8225; Toll Free: 1-800-465-1812
President/CEO, Andrew M. Roblin
Mutual Funds: *University Avenue Bond Fund; *University Avenue Canadian Fund; *University Avenue Growth Fund

STOCK EXCHANGES

The Alberta Stock Exchange
Stock Exchange Tower, 300 - 5 Ave. SW, 21st Fl., Calgary AB T2P 3C4
403/974-7400; Fax: 403/237-0450; URL: http://www.alberta.net/
1994 Volume: 2,236,066,664 shares ($2,226,739,339)
Chairman, M.G. Prew
President/CEO, T.A. Cumming
Executive Vice-President, G.A. Romanzin

MEMBER FIRMS & CORPORATIONS
with member seatholder

HSBC James Capel Canada Inc., Home Oil Tower, #702, 324 - 8 Ave. SW, Calgary AB T2P 2Z2 – 403/531-0545; Fax: 403/531-0540 – J.M. Romanchuk

Brink, Hudson & Lefever Ltd., Bentall Centre, #1200, 595 Burrard St., PO Box 49135, Vancouver BC V7X 1J1 – 604/688-0133; Fax: 604/682-2574 – P.J. Jennings

Bunting Warburg Inc., BCE Place, #4100, 161 Bay St., PO Box 617, Toronto ON M5J 2S1 – 416/364-3293; Fax: 416/364-1976 – P.D. Ayriss

Canaccord Capital Corporation, Stock Exchange Tower, #2200, 609 Granville St., PO Box 10337, Vancouver BC V7Y 1H2 – 604/643-7300; Fax: 604/643-7620 – D.N. Burdett

Charlton Securities Limited, #2710, 140 - 4 Ave. SW, Calgary AB T2P 3N3 – 403/262-5542; Fax: 403/265-9655 – W.W. Charlton

C.M. Oliver & Company Limited, #1205, 855 - 2nd St. SW, Calgary AB T2P 3N4 – 403/263-6133; Fax: 403/233-8835 – J. Ross

CT Securities Services Inc., 70 York St., 8th Fl., Toronto ON M5J 1S9 – 416/981-5000; Fax: 416/947-7190 – R.A. Cosburn

DFI Securities Inc., #1814, 150 York St., Toronto ON M5H 3S5 – 416/362-7747; Fax: 416/362-4924 – E.A. Pennock

First Marathon Securities Limited, #4100, 855 - 2 St. SW, Calgary AB T2P 4J8 – 403/290-0809; Fax: 403/269-7099 – C.M. Stuart

FirstEnergy Capital Corp., #400, 404 - 6 Ave. SW, Calgary AB T2P 0R9 – 403/262-0600; Fax: 403/262-0644 – W. B. Wilson

Georgia Pacific Securities Corporation, Two Bentall Centre, 555 Burrard St., 16th Fl., Vancouver BC V7X 1S6 – 604/668-1800; Fax: 604/668-1816 – R.B. Ashton

Global Securities Corporation, Royal Centre, #2900, 1055 West Georgia St., PO Box 11190, Vancouver BC V6E 3R5 – 604/689-5400; Fax: 604/689-5401 – D.S. Chernoff

Goepel Shields & Partners Inc., Canada Place, #730, 407 - 2 St. SW, Calgary AB T2P 2Y3 – 403/297-0434; Fax: 403/297-0430 – T.A. Budd

Golden Capital Securities Limited, #168, 1177 West Hastings St., Vancouver BC V6B 2K3 – 604/688-1898; Fax: 604/682-8874

Gordon Capital Corporation, Bankers Hall, #3450, 855 - 2 St. SW, Calgary AB T2P 4J8 – 403/261-3790; Fax: 403/269-5897 – J. Lloyd-Price

Haywood Securities Inc., Commerce Place, #1100, 400 Burrard St., Vancouver BC V6C 3A6 – 604/643-1100; Fax: 604/643-1199 – J.P.P. Tognetti

Jennings Capital Inc., #2600, 520 - 5 Ave. SW, Calgary AB T2P 3R7 – 403/292-0970; Fax: 403/292-0979 – R.G. Jennings

Jones, Gable & Company Limited, #600, 110 Yonge St., Toronto ON M5C 1T6 – 416/362-5454; Fax: 416/365-8037 – D.M. Ross

Lévesque Beaubien Geoffrion Inc., #2150, 421 - 7 Ave. SW, Calgary AB T2P 4K9 – 403/531-8400; Fax: 403/531-8413 – K. Bannister

Loewen, Ondaatje, McCutcheon Limited, #200, 30A Hazelton Ave., Toronto ON M5R 2E2 – 416/964-4455; Fax: 416/964-4429 – G. Herman

McDermid St. Lawrence Securities Ltd., #2600, 700 - 9 Ave. SW, Calgary AB T2P 3V4 – 403/221-0333; Fax: 403/221-0350 – I.S. Brown

Merit Investment Corporation, #1000, 55 University Ave., Toronto ON M5J 2P8 – 416/867-6000; Fax: 416/867-6137 – L. Kieselstein

Merrill Lynch Canada Inc., Merrill Lynch Canada Tower, 200 King St. West, Toronto ON M5H 3W3 – 416/586-6000; Fax: 416/586-6076, 6616 – G.B. Dunn

Midland Walwyn Capital Inc., #900, 350 - 7 Ave. SW, Calgary AB T2P 3N9 – 403/266-0123; Fax: 403/264-1030 – B.J. Geisler

Nesbitt Burns Inc., Bankers Hall East, #4000, 855 - 2 St. SW, Calgary AB T2P 4N2 – 403/260-9300; Fax: 403/260-9356 – G.E. Perron

Odlum Brown Limited, Pacific Centre, #1800, 609 Granville St., PO Box 10012, Vancouver BC V7Y 1A3 – 604/669-1600; Fax: 604/681-8310 – S.R. Sherwood

Pacific International Securities Inc., Pacific Centre, #1500, 700 Georgia St. West, PO Box 10015, Vancouver BC V7Y 1J1 – 604/664-2900; Fax: 604/664-2666 – L.H. McQuid

Perry Securities Ltd., 10135 - 101 Ave., Grande Prairie AB T8V 0Y4 – 403/532-7717; Fax: 403/538-0600 – K.G. Perry

Peters & Co. Limited, #2500, 350 - 7 Ave. SW, Calgary AB T2P 4N1 – 403/261-4850; Fax: 403/266-4116 – H.F. Osler

RBC Dominion Securities Inc., 707 - 7 Ave. SW, 3rd Fl., Calgary AB T2P 3H6 – 403/299-7000; Fax: 403/298-1601 – I.D. Beddis

Research Capital Corporation, #1330, 140 - 4 Ave. SW, Calgary AB T2P 3M3 – 403/265-7400; Fax: 403/237-5951 – I.G. Griffin

Richardson Greenshields of Canada Limited, 421 - 7 Ave. SW, 16th Fl., Calgary AB T2P 4K9 – 403/266-9600; Fax: 403/266-9686 – D.W. Milligan

Rogers & Partners Securities Inc., Plus 15, First Alberta Place, 777 - 8 Ave. SW, Calgary AB T2P 3R5 – Fax: 403/265-6039; Toll Free: 1-800-430-6999 – J.V. Rogers

ScotiaMcLeod Inc., #920, 401 - 9 Ave. SW, Calgary AB T2P 3C5 – 403/298-4000; Fax: 403/298-4099 – J.W. Cranston

Sprott Securities Limited, #2300, South Tower, Royal Bank Plaza, 200 Bay St., PO Box 63, Stn Royal Bank,

Canadian Almanac & Directory 1997

Toronto ON M5J 2J2 – 416/362-7485; Fax: 416/943-6499 – E.S. Sprott
Stephen Avenue Securities Inc., Lancaster Bldg., #701, 304 - 8th Ave. SW., Calgary AB T2P 1C2 – 403/777-2442; Fax: 403/777-2469 – P.E. Pullam
TD Securities Inc., Toronto Dominion Tower, 18th Fl., PO Box 100, Toronto ON M5K 1G8 – 416/982-5900; Fax: 416/944-6932 – W.K. Gray
Union Securities Inc., Pacific Centre, #900, 609 Granville St., PO Box 10341, Vancouver BC V7Y 1H4 – 604/687-2201; Fax: 604/684-6307 – N.F. Thompson
W.D. Latimer Co. Limited, #2508, Toronto-Dominion Centre, PO Box 96, Stn Toronto-Dominion, Toronto ON M5K 1G8 – 416/363-5631; Fax: 416/363-8022 – C.M. Bracken
Wolverton Securities Ltd., #1750, 701 Georgia West St., PO Box 10115, Vancouver BC V7Y 1J5 – 604/688-3477; Fax: 604/662-5205 – B.N. Wolverton
Wood Gundy Inc., Bankers Hall, 808 - 8 Ave. SW, 2nd Level, Calgary AB T2P 1C4 – 403/260-0400; Fax: 403/260-0410 – I.G. McLeod
Yorkton Securities Inc., #4400, 400 - 3 Ave. SW, Calgary AB T2P 4H2 – 403/260-8400; Fax: 403/269-7870 – M.G. Prew

Montréal Exchange/Bourse de Montréal

Tour de la Bourse, 800, Victoria Sq., PO Box 61, Montréal PQ H4Z 1A9
514/871-2424; Fax: 514/871-3553; Email: info@me.org; URL: http://www.bdm.org; http://www.me.org
1995 Volume: 2,876,483,704 shares ($38,590,875,482)
Chair, Governing Committee, Claude Bédard
President/CEO, Gérald A. Lacoste
Senior Vice-President, Derivative Products, John S. Ballard
Senior Vice-President, Information Technologies, Pierre Vinet
Senior Vice-President, Equities, Elaine C. Phénix
Senior Vice-President, Corporate Affairs & General Secretary, Sylvain Perreault
Senior Vice-President, Finance & Administration, Joan S. Paiement

MEMBER FIRMS & CORPORATIONS
with member seatholder

Altamira Securities, #301, 250 Bloor St. East, Toronto ON M4W 1E6 – 416/925-2512; Fax: 416/925-5352
Beacon Securities Limited, 1707 Grafton St., Halifax NS B3J 2C6 – 902/423-1260; Fax: 902/425-5237
BLC Rousseau inc., #1985, 1981, av McGill College, Montréal PQ H3A 3K3 – 514/284-5333; Fax: 514/284-6224
Brockhouse & Cooper Inc., #4025, 1250, boul René-Lévesque ouest, Montréal PQ H3B 4W8 – 514/932-7171; Fax: 514/932-8288
Bunting Warburg Inc., BCE Place, #4100, 161 Bay St., PO Box 617, Toronto ON M5J 2S1 – 416/364-3293; Fax: 416/364-1976
Canaccord Capital Corporation, Stock Exchange Tower, #2200, 609 Granville St., PO Box 10337, Vancouver BC V7Y 1H2 – 604/643-7300; Fax: 604/643-7620
Casgrain & Compagnie Limitée, #1625, 500, boul René-Lévesque ouest, Montréal PQ H2Z 1W7 – 514/871-8080; Fax: 514/871-1943
Chouinard, McNamara Inc., #1300, 1100, boul René-Lévesque ouest, Montréal PQ H3B 4N4 – 514/393-3430; Fax: 514/393-1110
CIBC Wood Gundy Inc., BCE Place, 161 Bay St., PO Box 500, Toronto ON M5J 2S8 – 416/594-7000; Fax: 416/594-7618
C.M. Oliver & Company Limited, 750 West Pender St., 2nd Fl., Vancouver BC V6C 1B5 – 604/668-6700; Fax: 604/681-8964

Commission Direct Inc., #1010, 121 King St. West, PO Box 11, Toronto ON M5H 3T9 – 416/941-5622; Fax: 416/941-5626
Credifinance Securities Limited, #3303, 130 Adelaide St. West, Toronto ON M5H 3P5 – 416/955-0159; Fax: 416/364-1522
CS First Boston (Canada), Inc., Standard Life Centre, #2500, 121 King St. West, PO Box 111, Toronto ON M5H 3T9 – 416/947-2600; Fax: 416/947-2607
CT Securities Services Inc., 70 York St., 8th Fl., Toronto ON M5J 1S9 – 416/981-5000; Fax: 416/947-7190
CTI Capital inc., #1635, 1, Place Ville-Marie, Montréal PQ H3B 2B6 – 514/861-3500; Fax: 514/861-3230
D&B Internat Securities Inc., #1702, 1115, rue Sherbrooke ouest, Montréal PQ H3A 1H3 – 514/842-4111; Fax: 514/842-3600
Deacon Capital Corp., 320 Bay St., 9th Fl., PO Box 3, Toronto ON M5H 4A6 – 416/350-3250; Fax: 416/350-3252
Demers Conseil inc., #1120, 615, boul René-Lévesque ouest, Montréal PQ H3B 1P5 – 514/879-1702; Fax: 514/879-5977
Desjardins Securities Inc./Valeurs mobilières Desjardins inc., Tour de l'Est, 2, complexe Desjardins, 15e étage, CP 394, Montréal PQ H5B 1J2 – 514/987-1749; Fax: 514/842-3137
Deutsche Morgan Grenfell Canada Ltd., Ernst & Young Tower, TD Centre, #1100, 222 Bay St., PO Box 64, Toronto ON M5K 1E7 – 416/682-8000; Fax: 416/368-6676
DFI Securities Inc., #1814, 150 York St., Toronto ON M5H 3S5 – 416/362-7747; Fax: 416/362-4924
Dlouhy Investments Inc./Investissments Dlouhy inc, #1200, 1350, rue Sherbrooke ouest, Montréal PQ H3G 1J1 – 514/845-8111; Fax: 514/845-0200
DPM Securities Inc., #602, 755, boul St-Jean, Pointe-Claire PQ H9R 5M9 – 514/630-7500; Fax: 514/630-7347
Dubeau Capital & Compagnie ltée, #530, 5600, boul des Galeries, Québec PQ G2K 2H6 – 418/628-5533; Fax: 418/628-7844
Edward D. Jones & Co., #902, 90 Burnhampthorpe Rd. West, Mississauga ON L5B 3C3 – 905/273-8400; Fax: 905/273-8424
Fairvest Securities Corporation, #700, 8 King St. East, Toronto ON M5C 1B5 – 416/364-9000; Fax: 416/364-6710
F.C.G. Securities Corporation, #2750, 145 King St. West, Toronto ON M5H 1J8 – 416/364-8600; Fax: 416/364-3581
Fimat Produits Dérivés Canada Inc., #1800, 1501 av McGill College, Montréal PQ H3A 3M8 – 514/841-6200; Fax: 514/841-6254
First Marathon Securities Limited, #3200, The Stock Exchange Tower, 2 First Canadian Place, Toronto ON M5X 1J9 – 416/869-3707; Fax: 416/869-0089
Fortune Financial Corporation, One Corporate Plaza, #608, 2075 Kennedy Rd., Scarborough ON M1T 3V3 – 416/291-4400; Fax: 416/291-4457
Friedberg Mercantile Group, BCE Place, #250, 181 Bay St., PO Box 866, Toronto ON M5J 2T3 – 416/364-2700; Fax: 416/364-5385
Georgia Pacific Securities Corporation, Two Bentall Centre, 555 Burrard St., 16th Fl., Vancouver BC V7X 1S6 – 604/668-1800; Fax: 604/668-1816
Goepel Shields & Partners Inc., Pacific Centre, #1100, 701 Georgia St. West, PO Box 10111, Vancouver BC V7Y 1C6 – 604/661-1777; Fax: 604/684-0475
Golden Capital Securities Limited, #168, 1177 West Hastings St., Vancouver BC V6B 2K3 – 604/688-1898; Fax: 604/682-8874
Goldman Sachs Canada, #1201, 150 King St. West, Toronto ON M5H 1J9 – 416/343-8900; Fax: 416/593-8506
Gordon Capital Corporation, #5300, Toronto-Dominion Centre, PO Box 67, Stn Toronto-Dominion, Toronto ON M5K 1E7 – 416/868-7800; Fax: 416/868-5450

Great Pacific Management Co. Limited, 1125 Howe St., 4th Fl., Vancouver BC V6Z 2K8 – 604/669-1143; Fax: 604/669-1979
HSBC James Capel Canada Inc., One Financial Place, #2420, One Adelaide St. East, Toronto ON M5C 2V9 – 416/947-2700; Fax: 416/947-2730
John Pasztor & Associates Inc., 19 Shorncliffe Ave., Toronto ON M4V 1S9 – 416/922-1326; Fax: 416/922-1110
Lafferty, Harwood & Partners Limited/Lafferty, Harwood & Associés limitée, #1920, 2020, rue University, Montréal PQ H3A 2A5 – 514/287-7306; Fax: 514/287-7123
Le Groupe Option Retraite inc., #201, 455, rue St-Antoine, Montréal PQ H2Z 1J1 – 514/861-0777; Fax: 514/861-1976
Leduc & Associés valeurs mobilières inc., #2300, 2020, rue University, Montréal PQ H3A 2L4 – 514/499-1066; Fax: 514/499-1071
Lévesque Beaubien Geoffrion Inc., Édifice Sun Life, 1155, rue Metcalfe, 5e étage, Montréal PQ H3B 4S9 – 514/879-2222; Fax: 514/879-5142
Loewen, Ondaatje, McCutcheon Limited, #200, 30A Hazelton Ave., Toronto ON M5R 2E2 – 416/964-4455; Fax: 416/964-4429
MacDougall, MacDougall & MacTier Inc., #2000, Place du Canada, Montréal PQ H3B 4J1 – 514/394-3000; Fax: 514/871-1481
MacDougall, Meyer inc., #1500, 2050, rue Mansfield, Montréal PQ H3A 1Y9 – 514/288-8823; Fax: 514/288-3272
Maison Placements Canada Inc., #906, 130 Adelaide St. West, PO Box 99, Toronto ON M5H 3P5 – 416/947-6040; Fax: 416/947-6046
Marleau, Lemire Securities Inc., #2400, 150 King St. West, Toronto ON M5H 1J9 – 416/591-5500; Fax: 416/595-0996
Maxima Capital inc., 266, rue St-Paul est, Montréal PQ H2Y 1G9 – 514/878-2525; Fax: 514/878-2393
Merit Investment Corporation, #1000, 55 University Ave., Toronto ON M5J 2P8 – 416/867-6000; Fax: 416/867-6137
Merrill Lynch Canada Inc., Merrill Lynch Canada Tower, 200 King St. West, Toronto ON M5H 3W3 – 416/586-6000; Fax: 416/586-6076, 6616
Midland Walwyn Capital Inc., Bay Wellington Tower, BCE Place, #400, 181 Bay St., Toronto ON M5J 2V8 – 416/369-7400; Fax: 416/369-7760
Morgan Stanley Canada Ltd., #3700, 181 Bay St., PO Box 776, Toronto ON M5J 2T3 – 416/943-8400; Fax: 416/368-0796
National Bank Securities Inc./Placements Banque Nationale inc., 1100, rue University, 7e étage, Montréal PQ H3B 2G7 – 514/394-5000; Fax: 514/394-6610
Nesbitt Burns Ltd., #5000, 1 First Canadian Place, PO Box 150, Toronto ON M5X 1H3 – 416/359-4000; Fax: 416/359-4311
Newcrest Capital Inc., #1200, 55 Yonge St., Toronto ON M5E 1J4 – 416/862-9160; Fax: 416/862-2224
Odlum Brown Limited, Pacific Centre, #1800, 609 Granville St., PO Box 10012, Vancouver BC V7Y 1A3 – 604/669-1600; Fax: 604/681-8310
Pensec Inc., #860, 55 Metcalfe St., Ottawa ON K1P 6L5 – 613/724-5434; Fax: 613/724-5489
Pictet (Canada) & Company Limited/Pictet (Canada), société en commandite, #2900, 1800, av McGill College, Montréal PQ H3A 3J6 – 514/288-8161; Fax: 514/288-5472
Pollitt & Co. Inc., Commerce Court North, #1101, 25 King St. West, PO Box 94, Stn Commerce Court, Toronto ON M5L 1B9 – 416/365-3313; Fax: 416/368-0141
RBC Dominion Securities Inc., Commerce Court South, PO Box 21, Stn Commerce Court, Toronto ON M5L 1A7 – 416/864-4000; Fax: 416/941-5418
Refco Futures (Canada) Limited/Refco valeurs mobilières (Canada) ltée, #4110, 800, place Victoria, PO

STOCK EXCHANGES 7-11

Box 313, Montréal PQ H4Z 1G8 – 514/866-1000; Fax: 514/866-1161
Research Capital Corporation, Ernst & Young Tower, TD Centre, 15th Fl., PO Box 265, Toronto ON M5K 1J5 – 416/860-7600; Fax: 416/860-7674
Richardson Greenshields of Canada Limited, #1200, 130 Adelaide St. West, Toronto ON M5H 1T8 – 416/860-3400; Fax: 416/866-7350
ScotiaMcLeod Inc., Scotia Plaza, 40 King St. West, PO Box 4085, Stn A, Toronto ON M5W 2X6 – 416/863-7411; Fax: 416/863-7751
Société Générale Securities Inc./Société générale valeurs mobilières inc., #1800, 1501, av McGill College, Montréal PQ H3A 3M8 – 514/841-6150; Fax: 514/841-6250
Sprott Securities Limited, #2300, South Tower, Royal Bank Plaza, 200 Bay St., PO Box 63, Stn Royal Bank, Toronto ON M5J 2J2 – 416/362-7485; Fax: 416/943-6499
Tassé & Associés, limitée, #1200, 630, boul René-Lévesque ouest, Montréal PQ H3B 1S6 – 514/879-2100; Fax: 514/879-3903
TD Securities Inc., Toronto Dominion Tower, 18th Fl., PO Box 100, Toronto ON M5K 1G8 – 416/982-5900; Fax: 416/944-6932
Thomson Kernaghan & Co. Ltd., 365 Bay St., 2nd Fl., Toronto ON M5H 2V2 – 416/860-8800; Fax: 416/367-8055
Versus Brokerage Services Inc., BCE Place, #3810, 181 Bay St., PO Box 751, Toronto ON M5J 2T3 – 416/214-1960; Fax: 416/864-3918
W.D. Latimer Co. Limited, #2508, Toronto-Dominion Centre, PO Box 96, Stn Toronto-Dominion, Toronto ON M5K 1G8 – 416/363-5631; Fax: 416/363-8022
Whalen, Béliveau & Associates Inc., #600, 1010, rue Sherbrooke ouest, Montréal PQ H3A 2R7 – 514/844-5443; Fax: 514/844-5216
Yamaichi International (Canada) Limited, #2300, 600, boul de Maisonneuve ouest, Montréal PQ H3A 3J2 – 514/499-1110; Fax: 514/499-1113
Yorkton Securities Inc., Bentall Centre, #1000, 1055 Dunsmuir St., PO Box 49333, Vancouver BC V7X 1L4 – 604/640-0400; Fax: 604/640-0300

The Toronto Stock Exchange

The Exchange Tower, 2 First Canadian Place, Toronto ON M5X 1J2
416/947-4700; Fax: 416/947-4585
1995 Volume: 15,757,820,395 shares ($207,665,152,647)
President & CEO, Rowland W. Fleming
Senior Vice-President, Member & Market Regulation, John Carson
Vice-President, Finance & Administration, D.H. Page
Vice-President, Corporate Affairs, L.P. Petrillo
Senior Vice-President, Equities & Derivative Markets, Susan E. Crocker
Senior Vice-President, Information Systems & Trading Services, Brian C. Harding
Vice-President, External Affairs, Keith Boast, Q.C.

MEMBER FIRMS & CORPORATIONS
with member seatholder

Brant Securities Limited, #1000, 2200 Yonge St., Toronto ON M4S 2C6 – 416/486-2200; Fax: 416/486-3907 – R. Brant
Brawley Cathers Limited, #600, 141 Adelaide St. West, Toronto ON M5H 3L9 – 416/363-5821 – D.M. Stovel
Brenark Securities Ltd., 1100 Burloak Dr., 6th Fl., Burlington ON L7L 6B2 – 905/332-5222 – Ronald W. Smith
Brink, Hudson & Lefever Ltd., Bentall Centre, #1200, 595 Burrard St., PO Box 49135, Vancouver BC V7X 1J1 – 604/688-0133; Fax: 604/682-2574 – B.D. Graves
Brockhouse & Cooper Inc., #4025, 1250, boul René-Lévesque ouest, Montréal PQ H3B 4W8 – 514/932-7171; Fax: 514/932-8288 – R.L. Cooper

Bunting Warburg Inc., BCE Place, #4100, 161 Bay St., PO Box 617, Toronto ON M5J 2S1 – 416/364-3293; Fax: 416/364-1976 – J.M. Estey
BZW Canada Limited, 304 Bay St., 9th Fl., Toronto ON M5H 4A5 – 416/350-3200; Fax: 416/350-3201 – J.L. Easson
Caldwell Securities Ltd., #340, 55 University Ave., Toronto ON M5J 2H7 – 416/862-7755; Fax: 416/862-2498 – T.S. Caldwell
Canaccord Capital Corporation, #1200, 320 Bay St., PO Box 6, Toronto ON M5H 4A6 – 416/869-7368; Fax: 416/869-7356 – B.D. Harwood
Cassels Blaikie & Co. Limited, #1200, 1 Adelaide St. East, Toronto ON M5C 2W8 – 416/941-7500; Fax: 416/867-9821 – J.A. Brown
CIBC Wood Gundy Inc., BCE Place, 161 Bay St., PO Box 500, Toronto ON M5J 2S8 – 416/594-7000; Fax: 416/594-7618 – W.C. Fox
C.M. Oliver & Company Limited, 750 West Pender St., 2nd Fl., Vancouver BC V6C 1B5 – 604/668-6700; Fax: 604/681-8964 – C.M. O'Brian
Commission Direct Inc., #1010, 121 King St. West, PO Box 11, Toronto ON M5H 3T9 – 416/941-5622; Fax: 416/941-5626 – T.R. Green
Connor, Clark & Company Ltd., Scotia Plaza, #5110, 40 King St. West, PO Box 125, Toronto ON M5H 3Y2 – 416/360-0006; Fax: 416/360-8380 – J.C. Clark
Correspondent Network, The Exchange Tower, #3100, 2 First Canadian Place, PO Box 470, Toronto ON M5X 1J9 – 416/869-6410; Fax: 416/869-7400 – L.S. Bloomberg
Credifinance Securities Limited, #3303, 130 Adelaide St. West, Toronto ON M5H 3P5 – 416/955-0159; Fax: 416/364-1522 – G. Benarroch
CS First Boston (Canada), Inc., Standard Life Centre, #2500, 121 King St. West, PO Box 111, Toronto ON M5H 3T9 – 416/947-2600; Fax: 416/947-2607 – K.W. Redpath
CT Securities Services Inc., 70 York St., 8th Fl., Toronto ON M5J 1S9 – 416/981-5000; Fax: 416/947-7190 – O.V. Dwyer
Daiwa Securities Canada Limited, #904, 105 Adelaide St. West, Toronto ON M5H 1P9 – 416/863-6560; Fax: 416/364-2445 – H. Mashimo
Deacon Capital Corp., 320 Bay St., 9th Fl., PO Box 3, Toronto ON M5H 4A6 – 416/350-3250; Fax: 416/350-3252 – J.L. Easson
Desjardins Securities Inc./Valeurs mobilières Desjardins inc., Tour de l'Est, 2, complexe Desjardins, 15e étage, CP 394, Montréal PQ H5B 1J2 – 514/987-1749; Fax: 514/842-3137 – R. Perreault
Deutsche Morgan Grenfell Canada Ltd., Ernst & Young Tower, TD Centre, #1100, 222 Bay St., PO Box 64, Toronto ON M5K 1E7 – 416/682-8000; Fax: 416/368-6676 – M.J.H. Brown
DFI Securities Inc., #1814, 150 York St., Toronto ON M5H 3S5 – 416/362-7747; Fax: 416/362-4924
Dominick & Dominick Securities Inc., #1714, 150 York St., Toronto ON M5H 3S5 – 416/363-0201; Fax: 416/366-8279 – J.S. Jenkins
Eagle & Partners Inc., Scotia Plaza, #3912, 40 King St. West, PO Box 506, Toronto ON M5H 3Z7 – 416/365-2440; Fax: 416/365-2449 – B.S. Gordon
Edward D. Jones & Co., #902, 90 Burnhamphtorpe Rd. West, Mississauga ON L5B 3C3 – 905/273-8400; Fax: 905/273-8424 – G.D. Reamey
Equion Securities Canada Limited, #1100, 320 Bay St., PO Box 15, Toronto ON M5H 4A6 – 416/216-6500; Fax: 416/216-6510 – Michael Nairne
Fairvest Securities Corporation, #700, 8 King St. East, Toronto ON M5C 1B5 – 416/364-9000; Fax: 416/364-6710 – William R. Riedl
First Marathon Securities Limited, #3200, The Stock Exchange Tower, 2 First Canadian Place, Toronto ON M5X 1J9 – 416/869-3707; Fax: 416/869-0089 – L.S. Bloomberg

FirstEnergy Capital Corp., #400, 404 - 6 Ave. SW, Calgary AB T2P 0R9 – 403/262-0600; Fax: 403/262-0644 – W. B. Wilson
Forbes & Walker Securities Limited, #400, 30A Hazelton Ave., Toronto ON M5R 2E2 – 416/925-3555; Fax: 416/925-5633 – J.D. Hamilton
Foster & Associates Financial Services Inc., #500, 10 King St. East, Toronto ON M5C 1C3 – 416/369-1980; Fax: 416/369-1070 – W.G.L. Foster
Friedberg Mercantile Group, BCE Place, #250, 181 Bay St., PO Box 866, Toronto ON M5J 2T3 – 416/364-2700; Fax: 416/364-5385 – A.D. Friedberg
Georgia Pacific Securities Corporation, Two Bentall Centre, 555 Burrard St., 16th Fl., Vancouver BC V7X 1S6 – 604/668-1800; Fax: 604/668-1816 – R.B. Ashton
Global Securities Corporation, Royal Centre, #2900, 1055 West Georgia St., PO Box 11190, Vancouver BC V6E 3R5 – 604/689-5400; Fax: 604/689-5401 – D.S. Chernoff
Goepel Shields & Partners Inc., #1600, 150 York St., Toronto ON M5H 3S5 – 416/594-1000; Fax: 416/594-1008 – D.E. Roberts
Golden Capital Securities Limited, #168, 1177 West Hastings St., Vancouver BC V6B 2K3 – 604/688-1898; Fax: 604/682-8874
Gordon Capital Corporation, #5300, Toronto-Dominion Centre, PO Box 67, Stn Toronto-Dominion, Toronto ON M5K 1E7 – 416/868-7800; Fax: 416/868-5450 – P.A. Bailey
Griffiths McBurney & Partners, #500, 90 Adelaide St. West, Toronto ON M5H 3V9 – 416/367-8600; Fax: 416/367-2756 – B.D. Griffiths
G.W. Welkin Capital Corp. of Canada, #312, 15 Wertheim Ct., Richmond Hill ON L4B 3H7 – 905/886-0312; Fax: 905/886-0200 – G.T.H. Wong
Haywood Securities Inc., Commerce Place, #1100, 400 Burrard St., Vancouver BC V6C 3A6 – 604/643-1100; Fax: 604/643-1199 – J.P.P. Tognetti
HSBC James Capel Canada Inc., One Financial Place, #2420, One Adelaide St. East, Toronto ON M5C 2V9 – 416/947-2700; Fax: 416/947-2730 – D.C. Pangman
Independent Trading Group, The Exchange Tower, 2 First Canadian Place, 3rd Fl., PO Box 84, Toronto ON M5X 1J2 – 416/365-2225 – J.F. Taugher
Instinet Canada Limited, #2100, 2 First Canadian Place, Toronto ON M5Y 1E3 – 416/367-2100; Fax: 416/594-1452 – J.P. Watts
Jones, Gable & Company Limited, #600, 110 Yonge St., Toronto ON M5C 1T6 – 416/362-5454; Fax: 416/365-8037 – D.M. Ross
Kearns Capital Limited, #1604, 141 Adelaide St. West, Toronto ON M5H 3L9 – 416/361-6032; Fax: 416/361-6050 – H.M. Kearns
Kingwest and Company, 86 Avenue Rd., Toronto ON M5R 2H2 – 416/927-7740; Fax: 416/927-9264 – R.L. Fogler
Lafferty, Harwood & Partners Limited/Lafferty, Harwood & Associés limitée, #1920, 2020, rue University, Montréal PQ H3A 2A5 – 514/287-7306; Fax: 514/287-7123 – N. Trudeau
Lévesque Beaubien Geoffrion Inc., #600, 121 King St. West, Toronto ON M5H 3T9 – 416/865-7400; Fax: 416/865-7605 – P. Brunet
Lévesque Securities Inc., #600, 121 King St. West, Toronto ON M5H 3T9 – 416/865-7400; Fax: 416/865-7605 – P. Brunet
Loewen, Ondaatje, McCutcheon Limited, #200, 30A Hazelton Ave., Toronto ON M5R 2E2 – 416/964-4455; Fax: 416/964-4429 – G. Herman
MacDougall, MacDougall & MacTier Inc., #2510, 150 King St. West, PO Box 13, Toronto ON M5H 1J9 – 416/977-0663; Fax: 416/596-7453 – B.H. MacDougall
Maison Placements Canada Inc., #906, 130 Adelaide St. West, PO Box 99, Toronto ON M5H 3P5 – 416/947-6040; Fax: 416/947-6046 – J.R. Ing

Canadian Almanac & Directory 1997

Majendie Securities Ltd., #1112, 150 York St., Toronto ON M5H 3S5 – 416/366-1980; Fax: 416/366-0656 – N.L. Majendie

Marleau, Lemire Securities Inc., #2400, 150 King St. West, Toronto ON M5H 1J9 – 416/591-5500; Fax: 416/595-0996 – M.S. Eisen

McDermid St. Lawrence Securities, #1300, 151 Yonge St., Toronto ON M5C 3A2 – 416/777-7000; Fax: 416/777-7020 – J.A. Chisholm

Merit Investment Corporation, #1000, 55 University Ave., Toronto ON M5J 2P8 – 416/867-6000; Fax: 416/867-6137 – D.A. Doiran

Merrill Lynch Canada Inc., Merrill Lynch Canada Tower, 200 King St. West, Toronto ON M5H 3W3 – 416/586-6000; Fax: 416/586-6076, 6616 – G.B. Dunn

Midland Walwyn Capital Inc., Bay Wellington Tower, BCE Place, #400, 181 Bay St., Toronto ON M5J 2V8 – 416/369-7400; Fax: 416/369-7760 – L. Rodney Sim

MMI Group Inc., 135 King St. East, 2nd Fl., Toronto ON M5C 1G6 – 416/363-3050; Fax: 416/368-4330 – C.H. Bayles

Morgan Stanley Canada Ltd., #3700, 181 Bay St., PO Box 776, Toronto ON M5J 2T3 – 416/943-8400; Fax: 416/368-0796 – Peter J. Dey

Moss, Lawson & Co. Limited, #410, One Toronto St., Toronto ON M5C 2W3 – 416/864-2700; Fax: 416/864-2756 – B.H. Pryce

NBC Clearing Services Inc., 1155, rue Metcalfe, 5e étage, Montréal PQ H3B 4S9 – 514/879-5363; Fax: 514/879-2520 – G. Ostiguy

Nesbitt Burns Ltd., #5000, 1 First Canadian Place, PO Box 150, Toronto ON M5X 1H3 – 416/359-4000; Fax: 416/359-4311 – P.E. Norris

Newcrest Capital Inc., #1200, 55 Yonge St., Toronto ON M5E 1J4 – 416/862-9160; Fax: 416/862-2224 – R.J. O'Leary

The Nikko Securities Co. Canada, Ltd., #3808, Toronto-Dominion Bank Tower, Toronto-Dominion Centre, PO Box 84, Stn Toronto-Dominion, Toronto ON M5K 1G8 – 416/366-2600; Fax: 416/364-4110 – K. Nii

Nomura Canada Inc., #5830, One First Canadian Place, PO Box 434, Toronto ON M5X 1E3 – 416/868-1683; Fax: 416/368-0857 – T.K. Wu

Octagon Capital Canada Corporation, Guardian of Canada Tower, #406, 181 University Ave., Toronto ON M5H 3M7 – 416/368-3322; Fax: 416/368-3811 – L.P. Haughton

Odlum Brown Limited, 8 King St. East, Toronto ON M5C 1B5 – 416/363-8443; Fax: 416/363-6776 – R.G. Sutherland

Pacific International Securities Inc., Pacific Centre, #1500, 700 Georgia St. West, PO Box 10015, Vancouver BC V7Y 1J1 – 604/664-2900; Fax: 604/664-2666 – M. Meier

Pensec Inc., #860, 55 Metcalfe St., Ottawa ON K1P 6L5 – 613/724-5434; Fax: 613/724-5489 – A.E. Smith

Peters & Co. Limited, #2500, 350 - 7 Ave. SW, Calgary AB T2P 4N1 – 403/261-4850; Fax: 403/266-4116 – R.G. Peters

Polar Securities Inc., 350 Bay St., 13th Fl., Toronto ON M5H 2S6 – 416/367-4364; Fax: 416/367-0564 – J.P. Sabourin

Pollitt & Co. Inc., Commerce Court North, #1101, 25 King St. West, PO Box 94, Stn Commerce Court, Toronto ON M5L 1B9 – 416/365-3313; Fax: 416/368-0141 – M.H. Pollitt

Pope & Company, 15 Duncan St., Toronto ON M5H 3P9 – 416/593-5535; Fax: 416/593-5099 – J. Pope

Porthmeor Securities Inc., Aetna Tower, #1207, Toronto-Dominion Centre, PO Box 183, Toronto ON M5K 1H6 – 416/361-1511; Fax: 416/361-1099 – Paul K. Bates

Puccetti Farrell Capital Partners, #1604, 141 Adelaide St. West, Toronto ON M5H 3L9 – 416/361-6030; Fax: 416/361-6050 – L.G. Farrell

RBC Dominion Securities Inc., Commerce Court South, PO Box 21, Stn Commerce Court, Toronto ON M5L 1A7 – 416/864-4000; Fax: 416/941-5418 – P.W. Hand

Research Capital Corporation, Ernst & Young Tower, TD Centre, 15th Fl., PO Box 265, Toronto ON M5K 1J5 – 416/860-7600; Fax: 416/860-7674 – D.C. Hetherington

Richardson Greenshields of Canada Limited, #1200, 130 Adelaide St. West, Toronto ON M5H 1T8 – 416/860-3400; Fax: 416/866-7350 – K.M. Edwards

Salman Partners Inc., Bentall Centre, #2393, 595 Burrard St., PO Box 49062, Vancouver BC V7X 1C4 – 604/685-2450; Fax: 604/685-2471 – T.K. Salman

ScotiaMcLeod Inc., Scotia Plaza, 40 King St. West, PO Box 4085, Stn A, Toronto ON M5W 2X6 – 416/863-7411; Fax: 416/863-7751 – F.M. Ketchen

Sprott Securities Limited, #2300, South Tower, Royal Bank Plaza, 200 Bay St., PO Box 63, Stn Royal Bank, Toronto ON M5J 2J2 – 416/362-7485; Fax: 416/943-6499 – E.S. Sprott

Standard Securities Capital Corporation, 35A Hazelton Ave., Toronto ON M5R 2E3 – 416/515-0505; Fax: 416/515-0477 – G.R. Winthrope

Tassé & Associates, Limited, #1118, 181 University Ave., Toronto ON M5H 3M7 – 416/868-6200; Fax: 416/868-1566 – J.L. Tassé

Taurus Capital Markets Ltd., Scotia Plaza, #3000, 40 King St. West, Toronto ON M5H 3Y2 – 416/361-2000; Fax: 416/364-0971 – L.J. Levy

TD Securities Inc., Toronto Dominion Tower, 18th Fl., PO Box 100, Toronto ON M5K 1G8 – 416/982-5900; Fax: 416/944-6932 – W.K. Gray

Thomson Kernaghan & Co. Ltd., 365 Bay St., 2nd Fl., Toronto ON M5H 2V2 – 416/860-8800; Fax: 416/367-8055 – E.J. Kernaghan

Union Securities Ltd., Pacific Centre, #900, 609 Granville St., PO Box 10341, Vancouver BC V7Y 1H4 – 604/687-2201; Fax: 604/684-6307 – N.F. Thompson

Versus Brokerage Services Inc., BCE Place, #3810, 181 Bay St., PO Box 751, Toronto ON M5J 2T3 – 416/214-1960; Fax: 416/864-3918 – D.E. Steiner

Wallace Dewan & Partners Inc., #4300, Royal Trust Tower, TD Centre, PO Box 47, Toronto ON M5K 1B7 – 416/350-2828; Fax: 416/359-2820 – P.L. Wallace

Watt Carmichael Inc., Commercial Union Tower, #1402, Toronto-Dominion Centre, PO Box 60, Toronto ON M5K 1E7 – 416/864-1500; Fax: 416/864-0883 – H.J.W. Carmichael

W.D. Latimer Co. Limited, #2508, Toronto-Dominion Centre, PO Box 96, Stn Toronto-Dominion, Toronto ON M5K 1G8 – 416/363-5631; Fax: 416/363-8022 – C.M. Bracken

Whalen, Béliveau & Associates Inc., #901, 141 Adelaide St. West, Toronto ON M5H 3L5 – 416/362-2813; Fax: 416/362-5908 – W.R. Whalen

Wolverton Securities Ltd., #1750, 701 Georgia West St., PO Box 10115, Vancouver BC V7Y 1J5 – 604/688-3477; Fax: 604/662-5205 – E.C. Paterson

Yamaichi International (Canada) Limited, #2300, 600, boul de Maisonneuve ouest, Montréal PQ H3A 3J2 – 514/499-1110; Fax: 514/499-1113 – T. Shoji

Yorkton Securities Inc., Exchange Tower, #3640, 2 First Canadian Place, PO Box 379, Toronto ON M5X 1J8 – 416/864-3500 – G.S. Paterson

The Vancouver Stock Exchange

Stock Exchange Tower, 609 Granville St., PO Box 10333, Vancouver BC V7Y 1H1
604/689-3334; Fax: 604/688-6051; URL: http://www.vse.com
1995 Volume: 6,142,187,348 shares ($6,422,256,855)
President & CEO, Michael E. Johnson
Vice-President, Compliance, Mary K. Beck
Vice-President, Marketing, John E. Boddie
Vice-President & CFO, Lloyd Costley
Vice-President, Human Resources, Heather Dalcourt
Vice-President, Corporate Affairs & Secretary, John M. Forbes
Vice-President, Trading & Market Information Services, Marc A. Foreman
Vice-President, Corporate Finance Services, Warren H. Funt
Director, Depository, Clearing & Settlement Services, Glenn Knowles
Vice-President, Technology, Dave D. Ross

MEMBER FIRMS & CORPORATIONS
with member seatholder

Asia Pacific Securities Corp., #368, 666 Burrard St., Vancouver BC V6C 2X8 – 604/688-3808 – T.J.L. McKinney

Brink, Hudson & Lefever Ltd., Bentall Centre, #1200, 595 Burrard St., PO Box 49135, Vancouver BC V7X 1J1 – 604/688-0133; Fax: 604/682-2574 – J.L. Mathers

Bunting Warburg Inc., Bentall Centre, #3314, 1055 Dunsmuir St., PO Box 49332, Vancouver BC V7X 1L4 – 604/682-0791; Fax: 604/681-4220 – P.D. Ayriss

Canaccord Capital Corporation, Stock Exchange Tower, #2200, 609 Granville St., PO Box 10337, Vancouver BC V7Y 1H2 – 604/643-7300; Fax: 604/643-7620 – P.M. Brown

CIBC Wood Gundy Inc., #2100, 885 Georgia St. West, Vancouver BC V6C 3E8 – 604/687-2699; Fax: 604/689-8437 – J.C. Lay

C.M. Oliver & Company Limited, 750 West Pender St., 2nd Fl., Vancouver BC V6C 1B5 – 604/668-6700; Fax: 604/681-8964 – C.M. O'Brian

Connor, Clark & Company Ltd., Cathedral Place, #1100, 925 Georgia St. West, Vancouver BC V6C 3L2 – 604/689-0006; Fax: 604/688-1406 – G.P. Reid

Correspondent Network, The Exchange Tower, #3100, 2 First Canadian Place, PO Box 470, Toronto ON M5X 1J9 – 416/869-6410; Fax: 416/869-7400 – L.S. Bloomberg

CT Securities International Inc., Oceanic Plaza, #1980, 1066 West Hastings St., Vancouver BC V6E 3X1 – 604/685-3809; Fax: 604/681-1722 – G.J. Handley

CT Securities Services Inc., 70 York St., 8th Fl., Toronto ON M5J 1S9 – 416/981-5000; Fax: 416/947-7190 – R.A. Cosburn

Davrey Securities Inc., #536, 999 Canada Place, Vancouver BC V6C 3E1 – 604/662-7866; Fax: 604/844-2828

Deacon Capital Corp., 320 Bay St., 9th Fl., PO Box 3, Toronto ON M5H 4A6 – 416/350-3250; Fax: 416/350-3252

Dominick & Dominick Securities Inc., #1714, 150 York St., Toronto ON M5H 3S5 – 416/363-0201; Fax: 416/366-8279

Eagle & Partners Inc., Scotia Plaza, #3912, 40 King St. West, PO Box 506, Toronto ON M5H 3Z7 – 416/365-2440; Fax: 416/365-2449 – B.S. Gordon

First Marathon Securities Limited, Commerce Place, #2000, 400 Burrard St., Vancouver BC V6C 3A6 – 604/682-6351; Fax: 604/681-7538 – R.J. Disbrow

Friedberg Mercantile Group, BCE Place, #250, 181 Bay St., PO Box 866, Toronto ON M5J 2T3 – 416/364-2700; Fax: 416/364-5385

Georgia Pacific Securities Corporation, Two Bentall Centre, 555 Burrard St., 16th Fl., Vancouver BC V7X 1S6 – 604/668-1800; Fax: 604/668-1816 – R.B. Ashton

Global Securities Corporation, Royal Centre, #2900, 1055 West Georgia St., PO Box 11190, Vancouver BC V6E 0R5 – 604/689-5400; Fax: 604/689-5401 – D.S. Chernoff

Goepel Shields & Partners Inc., Pacific Centre, #1100, 701 Georgia St. West, PO Box 10111, Vancouver BC V7Y 1C6 – 604/661-1777; Fax: 604/684-0475 – R.E.T. Goepel

Golden Capital Securities Limited, #168, 1177 Hastings St. West, Vancouver BC V6E 2K3 – 604/688-1898; Fax: 604/682-8874 – D.Y.H. Siu

Gordon Capital Corporation, Commerce Place, #2100, 400 Burrard St., Vancouver BC V6C 3A6 – 604/669-9555; Fax: 604/669-8848 – D.C. Gordon

Grafton Global Management Ltd., #6, 3045 Tutt St., Kelowna BC V1Y 2H4 – 250/860-2092; Fax: 250/860-3246 – G.M. Grafton

Great Pacific Management Co. Ltd., 1125 Howe St., 4th Fl., Vancouver BC V6Z 2K8 – 604/669-1143; Fax: 604/669-0310 – S.R. Isaac

Haywood Securities Inc., Commerce Place, #1100, 400 Burrard St., Vancouver BC V6C 3A6 – 604/643-1100; Fax: 604/643-1199 – J.P.P. Tognetti

HSBC James Capel Canada Inc., #1620, 885 West Georgia St., Vancouver BC V6C 3E8 – 604/687-8557; Fax: 604/687-8566 – A.M.B. Olivier

Jones, Gable & Company Limited, #400, 700 Pender St. West, Vancouver BC V6C 1C1 – 604/685-1481; Fax: 604/685-3761 – J.D. Gunther

Lévesque Beaubien Geoffrion Inc., Montreal Trust Centre, 510 Burrard St., 7th Fl., Vancouver BC V6C 3A8 – 604/643-2820; Fax: 604/643-2792 – P. Brunet

Lévesque Securities Inc., Montreal Trust Centre, 510 Burrard St., 7th Fl., Vancouver BC V6C 3A8 – 604/643-2800; Fax: 604/643-2792 – P. Brunet

Loewen Ondaatje McCutcheon Limited, Grosvenor Bldg., #3133, 595 Burrard St., Vancouver BC V7X 1G4 – 604/683-3545; Fax: 604/683-3547 – G. Herman

Majendie Securities Ltd., Waterfront Centre, #320, 200 Burrard St., Vancouver BC V6C 3L6 – 604/682-6446; Fax: 604/662-8594 – N.L. Majendie

Marleau Lemire Securities Inc., #500, 999 Hastings St. West, Vancouver BC V6C 2W7 – 604/668-7900; Fax: 604/683-7127 – H. Eisen

McDermid St. Lawrence Chisholm Ltd., #1000, 601 Hastings St. West, Vancouver BC V6B 5E2 – 604/654-1111; Fax: 604/654-1224 – K.N. Aune

Merit Investment Corporation, #1000, 55 University Ave., Toronto ON M5J 2P8 – 416/867-6000; Fax: 416/867-6137 – L. Kieselstein

Merrill Lynch Canada Inc., #2080, 200 Burrard St., Vancouver BC V6C 3L6 – 604/687-2663; Fax: 604/687-3663 – G.B. Dunn

Midland Walwyn Capital Inc., 11th Fl., Three Bentall Centre, 595 Burrard St., PO Box 49020, Vancouver BC V7X 1C3 – 604/688-2111; Fax: 604/661-7700 – G.G. Fabbro

Moss, Lawson & Co. Limited, #410, One Toronto St., Toronto ON M5C 2W3 – 416/864-2700; Fax: 416/864-2756 – B.H. Pryce

Nesbitt Burns Inc., Park Place, #2500, 666 Burrard St., Vancouver BC V6C 2X8 – 604/669-7424; Fax: 604/631-2658 – P.J. Powell

Odlum Brown Limited, Pacific Centre, #1800, 609 Granville St., PO Box 10012, Vancouver BC V7Y 1A3 – 604/669-1600; Fax: 604/681-8310 – S.R. Sherwood

Pacific International Securities Inc., Pacific Centre, #1500, 700 Georgia St. West, PO Box 10015, Vancouver BC V7Y 1J1 – 604/664-2900; Fax: 604/664-2666 – M. Meier

Peters & Co. Limited, #2500, 350 - 7 Ave. SW, Calgary AB T2P 4N1 – 403/261-4850; Fax: 403/266-4116 – R.G. Peters

RBC Dominion Securities Inc., Park Place, #2100, 666 Burrard St., Vancouver BC V6C 3B1 – 604/257-7000; Fax: 604/257-7138 – M.L. Cullen

Research Capital Corp., Bentall Centre, #564, 1055 Dunsmuir St., PO Box 49356, Vancouver BC V7X 1L4 – 604/669-7122; Fax: 604/669-5034

Richardson Greenshields of Canada Limited, Park Place, #1800, 666 Burrard St., Vancouver BC V6C 2X8 – 250/602-2000; Fax: 250/602-2004 – D.L. Motion

Salman Partners Inc., Bentall Centre, #2393, 595 Burrard St., PO Box 49062, Vancouver BC V7X 1C4 – 604/685-2450; Fax: 604/685-2471 – T.K. Salman

ScotiaMcLeod Inc., #1100, 609 Granville St., PO Box 10342, Vancouver BC V7Y 1H6 – 604/661-7400; Fax: 604/661-7432 – D.M. Rodger

Sprott Securities Limited, #1560, 200 Burrard St., Vancouver BC V6C 3L6 – 604/681-7344; Fax: 604/681-7322 – E.S. Sprott

Taurus Capital Markets Ltd., Scotia Plaza, #3000, 40 King St. West, Toronto ON M5H 3Y2 – 416/361-2000; Fax: 416/364-0971

TD Securities Inc., Pacific Centre, #1800, 700 Georgia St. West, PO Box 10001, Vancouver BC V7Y 1A2 – 604/654-3700; Fax: 604/654-3757 – W.K. Gray

Thomson Kernaghan & Co. Ltd., 365 Bay St., 2nd Fl., Toronto ON M5H 2V2 – 416/860-8800; Fax: 416/367-8055 – E.J. Kernaghan

UCC United Capital Corp., Pacific Centre, #2701, 1055 West Georgia St., Vancouver BC V6E 3R5 – 250/602-0218; Fax: 250/602-0219

Union Securities Ltd., Pacific Centre, #900, 609 Granville St., PO Box 10341, Vancouver BC V7Y 1H4 – 604/687-2201; Fax: 604/684-6307 – N.N. Thompson

Versus Brokerage Services Inc., Park Place, #730, 666 Burrard St., Vancouver BC V6C 2X8 – 604/257-7676; Fax: 604/257-7699 – D.E. Steiner

W.D. Latimer Co. Limited, #2508, Toronto-Dominion Centre, PO Box 96, Stn Toronto-Dominion, Toronto ON M5K 1G8 – 416/363-5631; Fax: 416/363-8022 – C.M. Bracken

West Coast Securities Ltd., #509, 700 Pender St. West, Vancouver BC V6C 1G8 – 604/681-1286; Fax: 604/688-7145 – J.D. Thomas

Whalen, Beliveau & Associates, #3210, 666 Burrard St., Vancouver BC V6C 2X8 – 604/683-1887; Fax: 604/683-8891 – J. Beliveau

Wolverton Securities Ltd., #1750, 701 Georgia West St., PO Box 10115, Vancouver BC V7Y 1J5 – 604/688-3477; Fax: 604/662-5205 – B.N. Wolverton

Yorkton Securities Inc., Bentall Centre, #1000, 1055 Dunsmuir St., PO Box 49333, Vancouver BC V7X 1L4 – 604/640-0400; Fax: 604/640-0300 – F. Giustra

The Winnipeg Stock Exchange

#620, One Lombard Place, Winnipeg MB R3B 0X3
204/987-7070; Fax: 204/987-7079
1995 Volume: Industrials - 42,182 shares ($523,364); Mines & Oils - 14,500 shares ($725)
Governor, Ronald L. Coke
Governor, Patrick M. Cooney
Governor, Duncan D. Jessiman
Governor, Edward G.A. Percival
Governor, Harvey R.G. Scrivener
Governor, Richard H. Shantz
Governor, Charles D. Spiring
Governor, Philip A. Taylor
Chairman of the Board, Thomas D.A. Waitt
Vice-Chairman of the Board, Gordon J. Wimble
President, Vincent W. Catalano
Corporate Secretary, Joyce C. Fieting

MEMBER FIRMS & CORPORATIONS
with member seatholder

Bank of Montréal Investor Services, First Canadian Place, 20th Fl., Toronto ON M5X 1A1 – 416/867-5503; Fax: 416/867-4728 – Alan C. Joudrey

Bieber Securities Inc., #801, 400 St. Mary Ave., Winnipeg MB R3C 0A5 – 204/946-0297; Fax: 204/956-0747 – Guy N. Bieber

CIBC Investor Services Inc., 200 King St. West, 7th Fl., PO Box 51, Toronto ON M5L 1A2 – 416/351-4331; Fax: 416/351-4333 – Jack Verkruysse

CIBC Wood Gundy Securities Inc., #2600, 360 Main St., Winnipeg MB R3C 3Z3 – 204/958-4300; Fax: 204/958-4361 – Gordon J. Wimble

Correspondent Network, The Exchange Tower, #3100, 2 First Canadian Place, PO Box 470, Toronto ON M5X 1J9 – 416/869-6410; Fax: 416/869-7400 – B. David Burnes

Hongkong Bank Discount Trading Inc., 70 York St., 3rd Fl., Toronto ON M5J 1S9 – 416/868-6800; Fax: 416/868-6249 – Peter J.H. Bacon

Investors Group Securities Inc., 444 Portage Ave., 2nd Fl., Winnipeg MB R3C 3B6 – 204/956-8783; Fax: 204/944-8985 – Mark A. Koley

Lévesque Securities Inc., #1498, 360 Main St., Winnipeg MB R3C 3Z3 – 204/942-8942; Fax: 204/942-1597 – Edward G.A. Percival

Majendie Securities Ltd., Waterfront Centre, #320, 200 Burrard St., Vancouver BC V6C 3L6 – 604/682-6446; Fax: 604/662-8594 – N.L. Majendie

Merrill Lynch Canada Inc., Merrill Lynch Canada Tower, 200 King St. West, Toronto ON M5H 3W3 – 416/586-6000; Fax: 416/586-6076, 6616 – G.B. Dunn

Midland Walwyn Capital Inc., #3003, 201 Portage Ave., Winnipeg MB R3B 3K6 – 204/942-0311; Fax: 204/943-2350 – Patrick M. Cooney

Nesbitt Burns Inc., #1300, 360 Main St., Winnipeg MB R3C 3Z3 – 204/949-2500; Fax: 204/947-3415 – Thomas D.A. Waitt

RBC Dominion Securities, #900, 360 Main St., PO Box 278, Winnipeg MB R3C 2T5 – 204/988-2600; Fax: 204/947-9540 – Harvey R.G. Scrivener

Richardson Greenshields of Canada Limited, #2900, One Lombard Place, Winnipeg MB R3B 0Y2 – 204/934-5311; Fax: 204/942-8276 – Richard M. Shantz

Royal Bank Action Direct Inc., Mezzanine Floor, 220 Portage Ave., Winnipeg MB R3C 3A6 – 204/988-4492; Fax: 204/988-4494 – Jack Di Santo

Scotia Discount Brokerage Inc., 1 Richmond St. West, 7th Fl., Toronto ON M5H 3W4 – 416/866-2021; Fax: 416/866-2018 – Andrew H. Scipio del Campo

ScotiaMcLeod Inc., #501, 200 Portage Ave., Winnipeg MB R3C 3X2 – 204/944-0025; Fax: 204/946-9236 – Edward R. Griffith

TD Securities Inc., #1709, 201 Portage Ave., Winnipeg MB R3C 3E7 – 204/988-2200; Fax: 204/988-2875 – James A. Coldwell

Wellington West Capital Inc., #3106, 201 Portage Ave., Winnipeg MB R3B 3K6 – 204/925-2250; Fax: 204/942-6194 – Walter N. Silicz

INSURANCE COMPANIES

Insurance companies are registered to conduct business under the federal Insurance Companies Act and/or corresponding provincial legislation. Life insurance companies are registered to underwrite life insurance, accident and sickness insurance and annuity business. Property and casualty insurance companies are registered to provide insurance other than life insurance. The companies may either be stock companies owned by shareholders, or mutual companies which are owned by their policyholders.

For provincially incorporated companies (marked *) not listed below, contact the Superintendent of Insurance, each province (see "Insurance" in the Government Quick Reference, Section 4).

CLASSES OF INSURANCE

Classes of insurance indicated below may be one or more of the following: Automobile; Fire; Life; Accident & Sickness; Property (in some classification systems may include fire); Miscellaneous (includes one or more of the following: aircraft, boiler & machinery, credit, fidelity, hail, legal expense, liability, marine, mortgage, surety or title)

INSURANCE COMPANIES

*Acadie Vie/Acadia Life
   295, boul St. Pierre ouest, CP 5554, Caraquet NB
     E1W 1B7
   506/727-1300; Fax: 506/727-1338
   Contact, Amédée Haché
   Classes of insurance: Life, Accident & Sickness
*Additional Municipal Hail Ltd.
   2100 Cornwall St., Regina SK S4P 2K7
   306/569-1852
Aetna Casualty & Surety Company of Canada
   Aetna Tower, TD Centre, 79 Wellington St. West,
     PO Box 120, Toronto ON M5K 1N9
   416/864-8660; Fax: 416/864-3888
   President/CEO, Gordon J. Henderson
   Classes of insurance: Auto, Property, Misc
Aetna Life Insurance Company
   Aetna Tower, TD Centre, 79 Wellington St. West,
     PO Box 120, Toronto ON M5K 1N9
   416/864-8000; Fax: 416/864-8189
   Chief Agent, Gordon J. Henderson
   Classes of insurance: Life, Accident & Sickness
Aetna Life Insurance Company of Canada
   (Aetna Canada)
   Aetna Tower, TD Centre, 79 Wellington St. West,
     PO Box 120, Toronto ON M5K 1N9
   416/864-8000; Fax: 416/864-1270; Toll Free: 1-800-
     361-7979; URL: http://www.aetna.ca
   President/CEO, Nick Villani
   Classes of insurance: Life, Accident & Sickness
Affiliated FM Insurance Company
   #202, 155 Gordon Baker Rd., North York ON
     M2H 3N7
   416/494-7111; Fax: 416/494-7598
   Chief Agent, Perry Brazeau
   Classes of insurance: Property
*AFLAC Insurance Company of Canada
   (AFLAC Canada)
   #300, 5915 Airport Rd., Mississauga ON L4V 1T1
   905/678-7800; Fax: 905/673-8598; Toll Free: 1-800-
     263-6188
   President, Denis R. Scodellaro
   Classes of insurance: Life, Accident & Sickness
*Alberta Motor Association Insurance Co.
   10310 G.A. MacDonald Ave., PO Box 8180,
     Stn South, Edmonton AB T6J 6R7
   403/430-5600; Fax: 403/430-5599
   General Manager, Gord Wentworth
   Classes of insurance: Auto, Fire, Accident & Sick-
     ness, Property
Alexander Hamilton Life Insurance Company of
   America
   #1000, 100 Sheppard Ave. East, North York ON
     M2N 6N7
   416/250-8154
   Chief Agent, Paul F. Palmer
   Classes of insurance: Life, Accident & Sickness
Allendale Mutual Insurance Company
   #202, 155 Gordon Baker Rd., North York ON
     M2H 3N7
   416/494-7111; Fax: 416/494-7598
   Chief Agent, Perry Brazeau
   Classes of insurance: Property
Allianz Insurance Company of Canada
   #100, 425 Bloor St. East, Toronto ON M4W 3R5
   416/961-5015; Fax: 416/961-8874; Toll Free: 1-800-
     387-5601
   Vice-President, Marketing, Don Harder
   Classes of insurance: Auto, Fire, Property
Allianz Life Insurance Company of North America
   2005 Sheppard Ave. East, 7th Fl., North York ON
     M2J 5B4
   416/502-2500; Fax: 416/502-2555
   Chief Agent, Doreen Johnston
   Classes of insurance: Life, Accident & Sickness
Allstate Insurance Company of Canada
   10 Allstate Pkwy., Markham ON L3R 5P8
   905/477-6900; Fax: 905/475-4991
   President & COO, Bruce I. MacDonald

Classes of insurance: Auto, Property
Allstate Life Insurance Company
   10 Allstate Pkwy., Markham ON L3R 5P8
   905/477-6900; Fax: 905/475-4991
   President/COO, Bruce I. MacDonald
   Classes of insurance: Life, Accident & Sickness
*L'Alpha, Compagnie d'Assurances Inc.
   430, rue Saint-Georges, Drummondville PQ
     J2C 4H4
   819/474-7958; Fax: 819/478-1736
   Directeur général, Michel Verrier
Alpina Insurance Company Ltd.
   400 University Ave., Toronto ON M5G 1S7
   416/586-3000; Fax: 416/586-2858
   Chief Agent, Stephen R. Smith
   Classes of insurance: Auto, Property, Misc
American Bankers Insurance Company of Florida
   #1700, 5001 Yonge St., North York ON M2N 6T7
   416/733-3360; Fax: 416/733-7826
   Vice-President/Chief Agent, John Leslie
   Classes of insurance: Accident & Sickness, Property
American Bankers Life Assurance Company of
   Florida
   #1700, 5001 Yonge St., North York ON M2N 6T7
   416/733-3360; Fax: 416/733-7826
   Vice-President/Chief Agent, John Leslie
   Classes of insurance: Life, Accident & Sickness
American Credit Indemnity Company
   #800, 1010, rue De Serigny, Longueuil PQ J4K 5G7
   514/646-1515; Fax: 514/646-4170; Toll Free: 1-800-
     361-3367
   Chief Agent, R. Labelle
   Classes of insurance: Misc
American Home Assurance Company
   145 Wellington St. West, 14th Fl., Toronto ON
     M5J 1H8
   416/596-3000; Fax: 416/977-2743
   Chief Agent, Gary A. McMillan
   Classes of insurance: Auto, Accident & Sickness,
     Property, Misc
American Income Life Insurance Company
   c/o McLean & Kerr, #2800, 130 Adelaide St. West,
     Toronto ON M5H 3P5
   416/364-5371; Fax: 416/366-8571
   Chief Agent, R.B. Cumine, Q.C.
   Classes of insurance: Life, Accident & Sickness
American Insurance Company
   425 Bloor St. East, Toronto ON M4W 3R5
   Chief Agent, Jill Field
   Classes of insurance: Auto, Property, Misc
American International Assurance Life Company Ltd.
   145 Wellington St. West, Toronto ON M5J 1H8
   President/CEO, James C.K. Wong
   Classes of insurance: Life, Accident & Sickness
American National Fire Insurance Company
   Scotia Plaza, #2100, 40 King St. West, Toronto ON
     M5H 3C2
   Chief Agent, J. Brian Reeve
   Classes of insurance: Auto, Fire, Accident & Sick-
     ness, Property, Misc
American Re-Insurance Company
   #1902, 20 Queen St. West, PO Box 65, Toronto ON
     M5H 3R3
   416/591-8668; Fax: 416/591-8830
   Chief Agent, Stephen Halfpenny
   Classes of insurance: Auto, Accident & Sickness,
     Property, Misc
The American Road Insurance Company
   #4, 1101 Nicholson Rd., Newmarket ON L3Y 7V1
   Chief Agent, Colleen Sexsmith
   Classes of insurance: Auto, Property
AMEX Life Assurance Company
   #403, 60 Bloor St. West, Toronto ON M4W 3L8
   416/969-9216; Fax: 416/926-9434
   Chief Agent, Judy Ha
   Classes of insurance: Life, Accident & Sickness
*Anglo-Canada General Insurance Company
   #1400, 5700 Yonge St., North York ON M2M 4K2

416/250-1992; Fax: 416/218-4175
   President/COO, Robert M. Fitzgerald
   Classes of insurance: Auto, Fire, Life, Accident &
     Sickness, Property
Antigonish Farmers' Mutual Fire Insurance Company
   PO Box 1535, Antigonish NS B2G 2L8
   902/863-3544; Fax: 902/863-0664
   Treasurer/Manager, W.J. Chisholm
   Classes of insurance: Fire, Misc
Arkwright Mutual Insurance Company
   #4, 1101 Nicholson Rd., Newmarket ON L3Y 7V1
   Chief Agent, Alan R. Hayes
   Classes of insurance: Property, Misc
Assicurazioni Generali S.P.A.
   #500, 1000, rue de la Gauchetière ouest, Montréal
     PQ H3B 4W5
   Chief Agent, W.J. Green
   Classes of insurance: Auto, Property, Misc
*Assumption Mutual Life Insurance Company/As-
   somption Compagnie Mutuelle d'Assurance-Vie
   (Assumption Life)
   770 Main St., PO Box 160, Moncton NB E1C 1E7
   506/853-6040; Fax: 506/853-5421
   Contact, Denis Losier
   Classes of insurance: Life, Accident & Sickness
*L'Assurance Mutuelle des Fabriques de Montréal
   1071, rue de la Cathédrale, Montréal PQ H3B 2V4
   514/395-4969; Fax: 514/861-8921; Toll Free: 1-800-
     567-6586
   Directeur général, Serge Léonard
   Classes of insurance: Property
*L'Assurance Mutuelle des Fabriques de Québec
   Archevêché de Québec, 2, rue Port Dauphin,
     Québec PQ G1R 5K5
   418/687-2564; Fax: 418/687-1056
   Directeur général, Jean-Guy Dupont
   Classes of insurance: Fire, Property
*Assurance-Vie Banque Nationale, Compagnie d'As-
   surance-Vie
   600, rue de la Gauchetière ouest, 4e étage, Montréal
     PQ H3B 4L2
   514/394-6080; Fax: 514/394-6601
   Directeur général, Pierre Desbins
*Assurance vie Desjardins-Laurentienne Inc./Desjar-
   dins Life Assurance Company Inc.
   (Desjardins Life)
   200, av des Commandeurs, Lévis PQ G6V 6R2
   418/838-7701; Fax: 418/833-5985; Toll Free: 1-800-
     463-7870
   President/CEO, Michel Thérien
   Classes of insurance: Life, Accident & Sickness
*Assurances Générales des Caisses Desjardins Inc.
   6300, boul de la Rive-Sud, Lévis PQ G6V 6P9
   418/835-4771; Fax: 418/835-5599; URL: http://
     www.insurance_canada.ca/insurcan/desjard.nt
   Président, Jude Martineau
   Classes of insurance: Auto, Fire, Property
*Atlantic Insurance Company Ltd.
   64 Commonwealth Ave., Mount Pearl NF A1N 1W8
   709/364-5209
   President, David Woolley
Avemco Insurance Company
   #600, 133 Richmond St. West, Toronto ON
     M5H 2L3
   416/363-6103; Fax: 416/363-7454
   Chief Agent, Donald G. Smith
   Classes of insurance: Accident & Sickness, Misc
Aviation & General Insurance Company Limited
   c/o British Aviation Insurance Group (Canada)
     Ltd., #100, 100 Renfrew Dr., Markham ON
     L3R 9R6
   905/479-2244; Fax: 905/479-0751
   Chief Agent, Peter S. May
   Classes of insurance: Misc
*AXA Assurances
   #600, 2020, rue University, Montréal PQ H3A 2A5
   514/282-1914; Fax: 514/982-6152

Canadian Almanac & Directory 1997

INSURANCE COMPANIES 7-15

Classes of insurance: Auto, Life, Accident & Sickness, Property, Misc
*AXA Insurance (Canada)
#1400, 5700 Yonge St., North York ON M2M 4K2
416/250-1992; Fax: 416/218-4175
President/COO, Robert M. Fitzgerald
Classes of insurance: Auto, Fire, Life, Accident & Sickness, Property
AXA Réassurances
#910, 70 York St., Toronto ON M5J 1S9
416/368-8191; Fax: 416/368-8983
Toronto Branch Office Manager, Didier Bellec
Classes of insurance: Auto, Fire, Life, Accident & Sickness, Property
Balboa Insurance Company
201 Queens Ave., PO Box 5071, Stn A, London ON N6A 4M5
Chief Agent, Anthony W. Miles
Classes of insurance: Accident & Sickness, Property
Balboa Life Insurance Company
201 Queens Ave., PO Box 5071, Stn A, London ON N6A 4M5
519/672-1070; Fax: 519/672-2623
Chief Agent, A. Miles
Classes of insurance: Life, Accident & Sickness
The Baloise Insurance Company Ltd./La Baloîse, Compagnie d'Assurances
#1703, 155 University Ave., Toronto ON M5H 3B6
416/366-3012; Fax: 416/366-3465
Chief Agent, Jack G. Dovey
Classes of insurance: Auto, Accident & Sickness, Property, Misc
Bankers Life & Casualty Company
Scotia Plaza, #2100, 40 King St. West, Toronto ON M5H 3C2
416/869-5300; Fax: 416/360-8877
Chief Agent, J. Brian Reeve
Classes of insurance: Life, Accident & Sickness
*BCAA Insurance Corporation
4567 Canada Way, Vancouver BC V5G 4T1
604/268-5000; Fax: 604/268-5023
Vice-President/COO, Len Kelsey
Classes of insurance: Accident & Sickness, Property
*Blue Cross of Atlantic Canada
644 Main St., PO Box 220, Moncton NB E1C 8L3
506/853-1811; Fax: 506/853-4651
President, L.R. Furlong
Classes of insurance: Life, Accident & Sickness
Blue Cross Life Insurance Company of Canada/La Compagnie d'Assurance-vie Croix Bleue du Canada
644 Main St., PO Box 220, Moncton NB E1C 8L3
506/853-1811; Fax: 506/853-4651
Contact, L.R. Furlong
Classes of insurance: Life, Accident & Sickness
The Boiler Inspection and Insurance Company of Canada
18 King St. East, Toronto ON M5C 1C4
416/363-5491; Fax: 416/363-0538
President, Normand Mercier
Classes of insurance: Property, Misc
*Boréal Assurances Agricoles Inc./Boreal Farm Insurance Inc.
1100, boul René-Lévesque ouest, 25e étage, Montréal PQ H3B 4P4
514/392-6366; Fax: 514/392-6328; Toll Free: 1-800-361-1594
Directeur général, Jacques A. Drouin
Classes of insurance: Auto, Accident & Sickness, Property, Misc
*Boréal Assurances Inc./Boreal Insurance Inc.
1100, boul René-Lévesque ouest, 25e étage, Montréal PQ H3B 4P4
514/392-6366; Fax: 514/392-6328; Toll Free: 1-800-361-1594
Directeur général, Jacques A. Drouin
Classes of insurance: Auto, Fire, Accident & Sickness, Property

British Aviation Insurance Group (Canada) Ltd.
#200, 100 Renfrew Dr., Markham ON L3R 9R6
905/479-2244; Fax: 905/479-0751
President, Peter May
Classes of insurance: Misc
*British Columbia Insurance Company
#1800, 777 Hornby St., Vancouver BC V6Z 1S4
604/688-1541; Fax: 604/688-5978; Toll Free: 1-800-663-0597
Vice-President, Operations, Clifford Quesnel
Classes of insurance: Auto, Fire, Property, Misc
*British Columbia Life & Casualty Company
2025 Broadway West, PO Box 9300, Vancouver BC V6B 4G3
Classes of insurance: Life, Accident & Sickness
Business Men's Assurance Company of America
c/o McLean & Kerr, #2800, 130 Adelaide St. West, Toronto ON M5H 3P5
416/364-5371; Fax: 416/366-8571
Chief Agent, R.B. Cumine, Q.C.
Classes of insurance: Life, Accident & Sickness
*CAA Insurance Company (Ontario)
60 Commerce Valley Dr. East, Thornhill ON L3T 7P9
905/771-3000; Fax: 905/771-3410
COO, Nicholas J. Parks
Classes of insurance: Auto, Accident & Sickness, Property
*Cabot Insurance Company
PO Box 5937, St. John's NF A1C 5X5
President, John Nolan
Calvert Insurance Company
#500, 36 King St. East, Toronto ON M5C 1E5
416/361-1728; Fax: 416/361-6113
Chief Agent, Philip H. Cook
Classes of insurance: Auto, Fire, Property
The Canada Life Assurance Company/La Compagnie d'Assurance du Canada sur la Vie
330 University Ave., Toronto ON M5G 1R8
416/597-1456; Fax: 416/597-6215; Email: info@canadalife.com; URL: http://www.canadalife.com
President/CEO, David A. Nield
Classes of insurance: Life, Accident & Sickness
Canada Life Casualty Insurance Company
330 University Ave., Toronto ON M5G 1R8
416/597-1456; Fax: 416/597-6825; Toll Free: 1-800-387-2640
President/COO, D.V. Newton
Classes of insurance: Auto, Accident & Sickness, Property, Misc
*Canada West Insurance Company
Canada Place, #400, 9777 - 102 Ave. NW, PO Box 1520, Edmonton AB T5J 2N7
403/497-3000; Fax: 403/429-4659; Toll Free: 1-800-661-5636
President/CEO, Jean-Charles Freimuller
Classes of insurance: Auto, Fire, Property
Canadian Direct Insurance Company
#217, 610 - 6th St., New Westminster BC V3L 3C2
President/CEO, Guy Cloutier
Classes of insurance: Auto, Property, Misc
Canadian General Insurance Company
#500, 2206 Eglinton Ave. East, Scarborough ON M1L 4S8
416/288-1800; Fax: 416/288-9756
President/CEO, Lewis Dunn
Classes of insurance: Auto, Accident & Sickness, Property, Misc
Canadian Group Underwriters Insurance Company
#300, 6733 Mississauga Rd., Mississauga ON L5N 6J5
905/819-2030
President, J.P. McCarthy
Classes of insurance: Auto, Accident & Sickness, Property, Misc
*Canadian Lawyers Insurance Association
#600, 919 - 11th Ave. SW, Calgary AB T2R 1P3
403/229-4716; Fax: 403/228-1728

Chair, Daniel Campbell
Classes of insurance: Misc
*Canadian Millers' Mutual Insurance Company
40 George St. North, Cambridge ON N1S 2M8
519/621-4060; Fax: 519/740-3490
President, David Sparling
Classes of insurance: Fire, Property
Canadian Northern Shield Insurance Company
#1900, 555 Hastings St. West, PO Box 12133, Vancouver BC V6B 4N6
604/662-2911; Fax: 604/662-5698; Toll Free: 1-800-663-1953
President/CEO, R.J. Ferguson
Classes of insurance: Auto, Accident & Sickness, Property, Misc
Canadian Premier Life Insurance Company
#500, 80 Tiverton Ct., Markham ON L3R 0G4
905/479-7500
Vice-President/CEO, Aaron Hill
Classes of insurance: Life, Accident & Sickness
Canadian Reassurance Company see Swiss RE Life
The Canadian Surety Company
#1200, 2200 Yonge St., Toronto ON M4S 2C6
416/487-7195; Fax: 416/482-6176
President/CEO, Jean-Charles Freimuller
Classes of insurance: Auto, Accident & Sickness, Property, Misc
*Canadian Trinity Life Insurance Company
288 Lakeshore Rd. East, Oakville ON L6J 1J2
905/844-9413; Fax: 905/844-5274
President, Richard G. Bruce
Classes of insurance: Life, Accident & Sickness
*Canassurance, Compagnie d'Assurance-Vie Inc.
#160, 550, rue Sherbrooke ouest, Montréal PQ H3A 1B9
514/286-8400; Fax: 514/286-8475
Directeur général, Claude Ferron
Classes of insurance: Life
*Canassurance, Compagnie d'Assurances Générales Inc./Canassurance General Insurance Company Inc.
#160, 550, rue Sherbrooke ouest, Montréal PQ H3A 1B9
514/286-8400; Fax: 514/286-8475
Directeur général, Pierre Julien
Classes of insurance: Property
*La Capitale, Compagnie d'Assurance Générale
525, boul René-Lévesque est, 6e étage, Québec PQ G1K 7X2
418/528-5525; Fax: 418/646-5960; Toll Free: 1-800-561-7279
Directeur général, André Pilon
Classes of insurance: Auto, Fire, Property, Misc
*Carleton Mutual Fire Insurance Company
PO Box 154, Florenceville NB E0J 1K0
506/392-6041
Contact, Elaine Hunter
Classes of insurance: Property
Centennial Insurance Company
c/o Focus Group Inc., #500, 36 King St. East, Toronto ON M5C 1E5
416/361-1728; Fax: 416/361-6113
Chief Agent, Philip H. Cook
Classes of insurance: Auto, Fire, Accident & Sickness, Property, Misc
*Chambre des Notaires du Québec
#2650, 630, boul René-Lévesque ouest, Montréal PQ H3B 1T6
514/879-1793
Contact, Michel A. Charland
Classes of insurance: Misc
Chicago Title Insurance Company
c/o McLean & Kerr, #2800, 130 Adelaide St. West, Toronto ON M5H 3P5
416/364-5371; Fax: 416/366-8571
Chief Agent, R.B. Cumine, Q.C.
Classes of insurance: Misc

Canadian Almanac & Directory 1997

Christiania General Insurance Corporation (Canadian Branch)
#1202, 80 Bloor St. West, Toronto ON M5S 2V1
416/961-0400; Fax: 416/961-5797
Chief Agent, Jim M. Willis
Classes of insurance: Auto, Accident & Sickness, Property, Misc

Chrysler Insurance Company
#308, 390 Brant St., Burlington ON L7R 2E9
905/333-8770; Fax: 905/333-2741, 2722
Chief Agent, Richard Wong
Classes of insurance: Auto, Property, Misc

Chubb Insurance Company of Canada/Chubb du Canada Compagnie d'Assurance
One Financial Place, One Adelaide St. East, Toronto ON M5C 2V9
416/863-0550; Fax: 416/863-5010; URL: http://www.chubbinsurance.ca
President, Janice M. Tomlinson
Classes of insurance: Auto, Fire, Accident & Sickness, Property

CIBC General Insurance Company Limited
5150 Spectrum Way, Mississauga ON L4W 5G8
President/COO, Kevin McNeil
Classes of insurance: Auto, Property, Misc

CIBC Life Insurance Company Limited
5150 Spectrum Way, Mississauga ON L4W 5G8
905/206-6000; Toll Free: 1-800-565-6010
President/COO, Gabor Kalmar
Classes of insurance: Life, Accident & Sickness

CIGNA Insurance Company of Canada
2 First Canadian Place, PO Box 185, Stn 1st Can Pl, Toronto ON M5X 1A8
416/368-2911; Fax: 416/368-6336
President/CEO, Samuel B. Cupp
Classes of insurance: Auto, Accident & Sickness, Property, Misc

CIGNA Life Insurance Company of Canada
#1400, 250 Yonge St., Toronto ON M5B 2L7
416/591-1225; Fax: 416/591-7488
President, Brendan McCormick
Classes of insurance: Life, Accident & Sickness

The Citadel General Assurance Company
1075 Bay St., Toronto ON M5S 2W5
416/928-8500; Fax: 416/928-1553
President/CEO, William H. Gleed
Classes of insurance: Auto, Accident & Sickness, Property, Misc

Clare Mutual Insurance Company
Belliveau Cove NS B0W 1J0
902/837-4597
President, Aldaige Comeau
Classes of insurance: Fire

*Co-operative Hail Insurance Company Ltd.
2709 - 13th Ave., PO Box 777, Regina SK S4P 3A8
306/522-8691; Fax: 306/352-9130
CEO, Denis D. Stumph
Classes of insurance: Misc

Co-operators General Insurance Company
Priory Square, Guelph ON N1H 6P8
519/824-4400; Fax: 519/822-4173
President/CEO, Terry Squire
Classes of insurance: Auto, Accident & Sickness, Property, Misc

Co-operators Life Insurance Company
Priory Square, Guelph ON N1H 6P8
519/824-4400; Fax: 519/822-4173
President/CEO, Terry Squire
Classes of insurance: Life, Accident & Sickness

*Coachman Insurance Company
802 The Queensway, PO Box 157, Stn U, Toronto ON M8Z 5P1
416/255-3417; Fax: 416/255-1454
President, David Rooney
Classes of insurance: Auto

Cologne Life Reinsurance Company
2 St. Clair Ave. East, 6th Fl., Toronto ON M4T 2V6
416/960-3601; Fax: 416/960-5291
Chief Agent, John M. Kosiancic
Classes of insurance: Life, Accident & Sickness

Cologne Reinsurance Company (Koelnische Rueck-versicherungs-Gesellschaft Ag)
#201, 3650 Victoria Park Ave., Scarborough ON M2H 3P7
Chief Agent, V. Lorraine Williams
Classes of insurance: Auto, Property, Misc

COLONIA Life Insurance Company
2 St. Clair Ave. East, 6th Fl., Toronto ON M4T 2V6
416/960-3601; Fax: 416/960-5291
President/CEO, J.M. Kosiancic
Classes of insurance: Life, Accident & Sickness

*Colonial Fire & General Insurance Company Ltd.
PO Box 13370, St. John's NF A1B 4B7
709/753-3069
President & CEO, Godfrey J. Wedgwood

Combined Insurance Company of America/Compagnie d'Assurance Combined d'Amerique
PO Box 4081, Stn A, Toronto ON M5W 1W7
416/922-1922; Fax: 416/922-1914
Chief Agent, Dan C. Evans
Classes of insurance: Life, Accident & Sickness

The Commerce Group Insurance Company/Le Groupe Commerce Compagnie d'Assurances
2450, rue Girouard ouest, CP 1000, St-Hyacinthe PQ J2S 7C4
President/CEO, Yves Brouillette
Classes of insurance: Auto, Accident & Sickness, Property, Misc

*Commerce & Industry Insurance Company of Canada
145 Wellington St. West, 14th Fl., Toronto ON M5J 1H8
416/596-3000; Fax: 416/977-2743
Vice-President & General Manager, Gary A. McMillan
Classes of insurance: Accident & Sickness, Property, Misc

Commercial Union Assurance Company of Canada
PO Box 441, Stn Toronto-Dominion, Toronto ON M5K 1L9
416/361-2500; Fax: 416/361-2522
President & CEO, G.S. Stafford
Classes of insurance: Auto, Accident & Sickness, Property, Misc

Commercial Union Assurance Company plc
c/o Encon Management Services Inc., #700, 99 Metcalfe St., Ottawa ON K1P 6L7
613/238-6373; Fax: 613/238-7448
Chief Agent, D. Shillington
Classes of insurance: Property, Misc

Commercial Union Life Assurance Company of Canada
#300, Consilium Place, PO Box 370, Stn A, Scarborough ON M1K 5C3
416/296-0700; Fax: 416/296-1705
President/CEO, Frank J. Crowley
Classes of insurance: Life, Accident & Sickness

Commonwealth Insurance Company
Bentall Three, #1500, 595 Burrard St., PO Box 49115, Vancouver BC V7X 1G4
604/683-5511; Fax: 604/683-8968
President, John Watson
Classes of insurance: Auto, Accident & Sickness, Property, Misc

*La Compagnie d'Assurance Belair Inc./Belair Insurance Company Inc.
5455, rue St-André, Montréal PQ H2J 4A9
514/270-1700; Fax: 514/270-9809
Président, Jacques Valotaire
Classes of insurance: Auto, Property

Compagnie Transcontinentale de Réassurance
1080, côte de Beaver Hall, 19e étage, Montréal PQ H2Z 1S8
514/878-2600; Fax: 514/866-6860
Chief Agent, Jacques Mailloux
Classes of insurance: Auto, Fire, Accident & Sickness, Property

CompCorp Life Insurance Company
#1700, One Queen St. East, Toronto ON M5C 2X9
President/CEO, Alan E. Morson
Classes of insurance: Life, Accident & Sickness

Connecticut General Life Insurance Company
#1400, 250 Yonge St., PO Box 14, Toronto ON M5B 2L7
416/591-1225; Fax: 416/591-7488
Chief Agent, Eman Hassan
Classes of insurance: Life, Accident & Sickness

Consolidated General Insurance Company Limited
#510, 154 University Ave., Toronto ON M5H 3Y9
President/CEO, Ian Wright
Classes of insurance: Property

Continental Assurance Company
105 Adelaide St. West, Toronto ON M5H 1P9
Chief Agent, Byron G. Messier
Classes of insurance: Life, Accident & Sickness

Continental Casualty Company
105 Adelaide St. West, Toronto ON M5H 1P9
Chief Agent, Byron G. Messier
Classes of insurance: Auto, Accident & Sickness, Property, Misc

The Continental Insurance Company
105 Adelaide St. West, Toronto ON M5H 1P9
Chief Agent, Byron G. Messier
Classes of insurance: Auto, Property, Misc

*Les Cooperants, Compagnie d'Assurance Generale
2475, boul Laurier, Sillery PQ G1T 1C4
418/651-3551; Fax: 418/651-9301

*Coronation Insurance Company, Limited
Royal Trust Tower, #3426, 77 King St. West, PO Box 284, Toronto ON M5K 1K2
416/360-8183; Fax: 416/360-8267
President, Robert E. Taylor
Classes of insurance: Property, Misc

*La Corporation d'Assurance de Personnes la Laurentienne
500, rue Grande Allée est, Québec PQ G1R 7E3
418/647-5222; Fax: 418/647-5119
Directeur général, Humberto Santos

Coseco Insurance Company
Priory Square, Guelph ON N1H 6P8
519/824-4400; Fax: 519/822-4173
President/CEO, Terry Squire
Classes of insurance: Auto, Property, Misc

Crown Life Insurance Company
1901 Scarth St., PO Box 827, Regina SK S4P 3B1
306/751-6000; Fax: 306/751-6001
Vice-President/General Counsel, Robert W. Bell
Classes of insurance: Life, Accident & Sickness

*CUMBA
562 Eglinton Ave. East, Toronto ON M4P 1B9
416/487-5451; Fax: 416/487-3379
General Manager, D. Tripp
Classes of insurance: Accident & Sickness

CUMIS General Insurance Company
PO Box 5065, Burlington ON L7R 4C2
905/632-1221; Fax: 905/632-9412; Toll Free: 1-800-263-9120
President/CEO, Robert J. Ferguson
Classes of insurance: Auto, Fire, Property

CUMIS Insurance Society, Inc.
PO Box 5065, Burlington ON L7R 4C2
905/632-1221; Fax: 905/632-9412; Toll Free: 1-800-263-9120
Chief Agent, Robert J. Ferguson
Classes of insurance: Life, Accident & Sickness

CUMIS Life Insurance Co.
PO Box 5065, Burlington ON L7R 4C2
905/632-1221; Fax: 905/632-9412; Toll Free: 1-800-263-9122
President/CEO, Robert J. Ferguson
Classes of insurance: Life, Accident & Sickness

Cuna Mutual Insurance Society
PO Box 5065, Burlington ON L7R 4C2
905/632-1221; Fax: 905/632-9412
Chief Agent, Robert J. Ferguson

INSURANCE COMPANIES 7-17

Classes of insurance: Life, Accident & Sickness
*Dome Insurance Corp. Ltd.
#800, 240 Graham Ave., Winnipeg MB R3C 0J7
204/947-2835
Chief Agent, Richard R. Bracken
Classes of insurance: Auto, Fire, Misc
The Dominion of Canada General Insurance Company/Compagnie d'assurance générale dominion du Canada
165 University Ave., Toronto ON M5H 3B9
416/362-7231; Fax: 416/362-9918
President/CEO, George L. Cooke
Classes of insurance: Auto, Property
Eagle Star Insurance Company Ltd.
c/o Focus Group Inc., #500, 36 King St. East, Toronto ON M5C 1E5
416/361-1728; Fax: 416/361-6113
Chief Agent, P.H. Cook
Classes of insurance: Auto, Accident & Sickness, Property, Misc
Ecclesiastical Insurance Office plc/Société des Assurances Écclésiastiques
#502, 2300 Yonge St., PO Box 2401, Toronto ON M4P 1E4
416/484-4555; Fax: 416/484-6352
Chief Agent, W.T. Breckles
Classes of insurance: Auto, Property, Misc
Economical Mutual Insurance Company
111 Westmount Rd. South, PO Box 2000, Waterloo ON N2J 4S4
519/570-8200; Fax: 519/570-8389
President/CEO, N.G. Walpole
Classes of insurance: Auto, Accident & Sickness, Property
Elite Insurance Company
649 North Service Rd. West, Burlington ON L7R 4L5
905/333-4400; Fax: 905/681-4951; Toll Free: 1-800-565-7090
President, R.J. Lever
Classes of insurance: Auto, Accident & Sickness, Property, Misc
The Empire Life Insurance Company/L'Empire Compagnie d'Assurance-Vie
(Empire Financial Group)
259 King St. East, Kingston ON K7L 3A8
613/548-1881; Fax: 613/548-4584
President & CEO, Christopher H. McElvaine
Classes of insurance: Life, Accident & Sickness
Employers Insurance of Wausau - a Mutual Company/Société d'Assurance Mutuelle des Employeurs de Wausau
c/o D.M. Williams & Associates Ltd., #201, 3650 Victoria Park Ave., North York ON M2H 3P7
416/496-1148; Fax: 416/496-1089
Chief Agent, V.L. Williams
Classes of insurance: Auto, Accident & Sickness, Property, Misc
Employers Reinsurance Corporation
#1402, Toronto-Dominion Centre, PO Box 311, Stn Toronto-Dominion, Toronto ON M5K 1K2
416/362-6527; Fax: 416/362-9303
Chief Agent, Peter Borst
Classes of insurance: Auto, Accident & Sickness, Property, Misc
The Equitable Life Assurance Society of the United States
#1400, 250 Yonge St., PO Box 14, Toronto ON M5B 2L7
Chief Agent, M.E. Hassan
Classes of insurance: Life, Accident & Sickness
The Equitable Life Insurance Company of Canada
One Westmount Rd. North, Waterloo ON N2J 4C7
519/886-5110; Fax: 519/886-5314
President/CEO, Ron Beaubien
Classes of insurance: Life, Accident & Sickness
Everest Reinsurance Company
Scotia Plaza, #5001, 40 King St. West, Toronto ON M5H 3Y2
416/862-1228; Fax: 416/366-5899
Chief Agent, T.D. MacKenzie
Classes of insurance: Auto, Accident & Sickness, Property, Misc
*L'Excellence Compagnie d'Assurance-Vie
#202, 5055, boul Métropolitain est, Montréal PQ H1R 1Z7
514/327-0020; Fax: 514/327-6242
Directeur général, Louis Gosselin
Classes of insurance: Life, Accident & Sickness
*Family Insurance Corporation
#450, 1040 Georgia St. West, Vancouver BC V6E 2H1
Classes of insurance: Auto, Property, Misc
Federal Insurance Company/Compagnie d'Assurances Federale
One Financial Place, One Adelaide St. East, Toronto ON M5C 2V9
416/863-0550; Fax: 416/863-5010; URL: http://www.chubbinsurance.ca
Chief Agent, Janice M. Tomlinson
Classes of insurance: Auto, Fire, Accident & Sickness, Property
Federated Insurance Company of Canada
717 Portage Ave., PO Box 5800, Winnipeg MB R3C 3C9
204/786-6431; Fax: 204/783-6913; Toll Free: 1-800-665-1934
President, John Paisley
Classes of insurance: Auto, Fire, Property
Federated Life Insurance Company of Canada
717 Portage Ave., PO Box 5800, Winnipeg MB R3C 3C9
204/786-6431; Fax: 204/783-6913; Toll Free: 1-800-665-1934
President, John Paisley
Classes of insurance: Life, Accident & Sickness
Federation Insurance Company of Canada/La Fédération Compagnie d'Assurances du Canada
#500, 1000, de la Gauchetière ouest, Montréal PQ H3B 4W5
514/875-5790; Fax: 514/875-9769
President, W.J. Green
Classes of insurance: Auto, Fire, Property
Financial Life Assurance Company of Canada
10 Four Seasons Pl., 10th Fl., PO Box 335, Etobicoke ON M9C 4V3
416/626-7002; Fax: 416/626-0657
President, Hugh D. Haney
Classes of insurance: Life, Accident & Sickness
Fireman's Fund Insurance Company
425 Bloor St. East, Toronto ON M4W 3R5
416/966-8119; Fax: 416/961-3088
Chief Agent, Jill Field
Classes of insurance: Auto, Property, Misc
First American Title Insurance Company
#801, 1290 Central Parkway West, Mississauga ON L5C 4R3
905/566-8675; Fax: 905/566-8676; Toll Free: 1-800-663-6777; Email: ddavies@firstam.com; URL: http://www.firstam.com
Regional Vice-President, International Operations, Thomas H. Grifferty
Classes of insurance: Property
*First Canadian Insurance Corporation
10727 - 82 Ave., Edmonton AB T6E 2B1
Classes of insurance: Life, Accident & Sickness
First North American Insurance Company
5650 Yonge St., North York ON M2M 4G4
President/CEO, Domenic D'Alessandro
Classes of insurance: Auto, Accident & Sickness, Property, Misc
Folksamerica National Reinsurance Company
c/o Focus Group Inc., #500, 36 King St. East, Toronto ON M5C 1E5
Chief Agent, Philip H. Cook
Classes of insurance: Auto, Accident & Sickness, Property, Misc
Folksamerica Reinsurance Company
c/o Focus Group Inc., #500, 36 King St. East, Toronto ON M5C 1E5
Chief Agent, Philip H. Cook
Classes of insurance: Property, Misc
Forethought Life Insurance Company
#2100, Scotia Plaza, 40 King St. West, Toronto ON M5H 3C2
Chief Agent, J. Brian Reeve
Classes of insurance: Life
The Franklin Life Insurance Company
#2100, Scotia Plaza, 40 King St. West, Toronto ON M5H 3C2
Chief Agent, J. Brian Reeve
Classes of insurance: Life, Accident & Sickness
Frankona Ruckversicherungs -- Aktien -- Gesellschaft
#330, 20 Richmond St. East, Toronto ON M5C 2R9
416/777-0066; Fax: 416/777-0365
Chief Agent, David E. Wilmot
Classes of insurance: Auto, Fire, Life, Accident & Sickness, Property
*Fundy Mutual Fire Insurance Company
700 Main St., PO Box 730, Sussex NB E0E 1P0
506/433-1535; Fax: 506/433-6788
Contact, Gail Scovil
Classes of insurance: Property, Misc
GAN General Insurance Company
649 North Service Rd. West, PO Box 5012, Burlington ON L7R 4L5
905/681-4901; Fax: 905/681-4944; Toll Free: 1-800-565-7090
President, Robert Lever
Classes of insurance: Auto, Accident & Sickness, Property, Misc
GAN VIE (Compagnie Française d'Assurances sur la Vie)
#1200, 425, boul de Maisonneuve ouest, Montréal PQ H3A 3G5
514/938-1313
Chief Agent, Eric L. Clark
Classes of insurance: Life
GE Capital Mortgage Insurance Company (Canada)
2300 Meadowvale Blvd., Mississauga ON L5N 5P9
President/CEO, Brian L. Hurley
Classes of insurance: Misc
The General Accident Assurance Company of Canada
#2600, 2 First Canadian Place, PO Box 410, Stn 1st Can Place, Toronto ON M5X 1J1
416/368-4733; Fax: 416/368-7055; URL: http://www.genacc.ca/
President/CEO, Howard Moran
Classes of insurance: Auto, Accident & Sickness, Property, Misc
General American Life Insurance Company
c/o RGA Life Reinsurance Company of Canada, #2220, 1501, av McGill College, Montréal PQ H3A 3M8
514/985-5260; Fax: 514/985-3066; Toll Free: 1-800-985-GEAM; Email: mail@rga-reinsurance.com; URL: http://www.genam.com
Chief Agent, André St-Amour
Classes of insurance: Life, Accident & Sickness
General American Life Reinsurance Company of Canada/General American, Compagnie de Réassurance-Vie du Canada
(RGA)
#2220, 1501, av McGill College, Montréal PQ H3A 3M8
514/985-5260; Fax: 514/985-3066; Toll Free: 1-800-985-GEAM; Email: mail@rga-reinsurance.com
President/CEO, André St-Amour
Classes of insurance: Life, Accident & Sickness
General Reinsurance Corporation
#700, 95 Wellington St. West, PO Box 26, Toronto ON M5J 2N7
416/869-0490; Fax: 416/360-2020

Canadian Almanac & Directory 1997

7-18 INSURANCE COMPANIES

Chief Agent, Gerald A. Wolfe
Classes of insurance: Auto, Accident & Sickness, Property, Misc
*Gerling Global General Insurance Company
480 University Ave., Toronto ON M5G 1V6
416/598-4688; Fax: 416/598-9507
President, Andreas H. Henke, M.A., F.I.I.C.
Classes of insurance: Fire, Property, Misc
*Gerling Global Life Insurance Company/La Gerling Globale, Compagnie d'Assurance-Vie
480 University Ave., 15th Fl., Toronto ON M5G 1V6
416/598-4677; Fax: 416/598-3901
President, Peter Schaefer
Classes of insurance: Life, Accident & Sickness
*Gerling Global Reinsurance Company
480 University Ave., Toronto ON M5G 1V6
416/598-4688; Fax: 416/598-9507
President, Andreas H. Henke, M.A., F.I.I.C.
Classes of insurance: Auto, Fire, Life, Property, Misc
*Germania Mutual Insurance Company
217 Kaiser William Ave., PO Box 40, Langenburg SK S0A 2A0
306/743-5363
Gore Mutual Insurance Company
252 Dundas St., Cambridge ON N1R 5T3
519/623-1910; Fax: 519/623-4411; Toll Free: 1-800-265-8600
Chairman of the Board/CEO, Robert J. Collins-Wright
Classes of insurance: Auto, Fire, Accident & Sickness, Property, Misc
Grain Insurance & Guarantee Company
#1240, One Lombard Pl., Winnipeg MB R3B 0P6
204/943-0721; Fax: 204/943-6419
President/General Manager, Ralph N. Jackson
Classes of insurance: Property, Misc
Great American Insurance Company
#2100, 40 King St. West, Toronto ON M5H 3C2
Chief Agent, J. Brian Reeve
Classes of insurance: Auto, Accident & Sickness, Property, Misc
The Great Lakes Reinsurance Company
390 Bay St., 21st Fl., Toronto ON M5H 2Y2
416/364-2851; Fax: 416/361-1163
President, Ian P. Emblin
Classes of insurance: Auto, Life, Accident & Sickness, Property, Misc
*Le Groupe Estrie-Richelieu, Compagnie d'Assurance
770, rue Principale, Granby PQ J2G 2Y7
514/378-0101; Fax: 514/378-5189
Président, Michel Prévost
Classes of insurance: Auto, Fire, Property
The Guarantee Company of North America/La Garantie, Compagnie d'Assurance de l'Amérique du Nord
Place du Canada, #1560, 1010, rue de la Gauchetière ouest, Montréal PQ H3B 2R4
514/866-6351; Fax: 514/866-0157
President/CEO, Jules Quenneville, C.A.
Classes of insurance: Auto, Accident & Sickness, Property, Misc
Guardian Insurance Company of Canada
181 University Ave., Toronto ON M5W 3M7
416/941-5050; Fax: 416/941-9791
President, Henry J. Curtis
Classes of insurance: Auto, Accident & Sickness, Property, Misc
The Halifax Insurance Company
75 Eglinton Ave. East, Toronto ON M4P 3A4
416/440-1000; Fax: 416/440-0799
President, Donald K. Lough
Classes of insurance: Auto, Accident & Sickness, Property, Misc
Hannover Ruckversicherungs -- Aktiengesellschaft
c/o D.M. Williams & Assoc. Ltd., #201, 3650 Victoria Park Ave., North York ON M2H 3P7

416/496-1148; Fax: 416/496-1089
Chief Agent, V.L. Williams
Classes of insurance: Auto, Accident & Sickness, Property, Misc
The Hartford Fire Insurance Company
20 York Mills Rd., Willowdale ON M2P 2C2
President/CEO, Gray G. Davis
Classes of insurance: Auto, Fire, Accident & Sickness, Misc
Hartford Insurance Company of Canada
20 York Mills Rd., North York ON M2P 2C2
416/733-1777; Fax: 416/733-1463;
Email: 103455.2225@compuserve.com;
URL: http://www.itthartford.com
President/CEO, Gray G. Davis
Classes of insurance: Auto, Fire, Accident & Sickness, Property, Misc
Hartford Life Insurance Company
3027 Harvester Rd., Burlington ON L7N 3G9
Chief Agent, Mark A. Sylvia
Helvetia Swiss Insurance Company Limited/Helvetia Compagnie Suisse d'Assurances
#500, 1000, rue de la Gauchetière ouest, Montréal PQ H3B 4W5
514/875-5790; Fax: 514/875-9769
Chief Agent, W.J. Green
Classes of insurance: Auto, Fire, Property
*Heritage General Insurance Company
#M101, 401 Bay St., Toronto ON M5H 2Y4
416/861-6991; Fax: 416/861-6989
President, Robert N.D. Hogan
Classes of insurance: Accident & Sickness
The Home Insurance Company
c/o The Focus Group Inc., #500, 36 King St. East, Toronto ON M5C 1E5
416/361-1728; Fax: 416/361-6113
Chief Agent, Philip H. Cook
Classes of insurance: Auto, Accident & Sickness, Property, Misc
*Hutterian Brethren Mutual Insurance Corporation
c/o H.B. Farm Agencies Ltd., #208, 62 Hargrave St., Winnipeg MB R3C 1N1
204/943-9042; Fax: 204/947-3876
Chief Agent, David M. Miller
Classes of insurance: Property
The Imperial Life Assurance Company of Canada (Imperial Life)
95 St. Clair Ave. West, Toronto ON M4V 1N7
416/926-2600; Fax: 416/923-1599
President, Robert E. Ferguson
Classes of insurance: Life, Accident & Sickness
*L'Industrielle-Alliance Compagnie d'Assurance Generales
#100, 2475, boul Laurier, Sillery PQ G1T 1C4
418/651-3551; Fax: 418/651-9301
Directeur général, Gilles Duchesneau
*L'Industrielle-Alliance Compagnie d'Assurance sur la Vie/Industrial-Alliance Life Insurance Company
1080, ch Saint-Louis, Sillery PQ G1K 7M3
418/684-5000; Fax: 418/683-5663
Directeur général, Raymond Garneau
Classes of insurance: Life, Accident & Sickness
*Insurance Company of Prince Edward Island
125 Pownal St., PO Box 666, Charlottetown PE C1A 7L3
902/566-5666
President, Charles C. Cooke
Classes of insurance: Auto, Property
*Insurance Corporation of British Columbia
151 Esplanade West, North Vancouver BC V7M 3H9
604/661-2800; Fax: 604/661-2244; Toll Free: 1-800-663-3051
President/CEO, Thom M. Thompson
Classes of insurance: Auto
*Insurance Corporation of Newfoundland Ltd.
187 Kenmount Rd., PO Box 8485, St. John's NF A1B 3N9

President, David Anthony
*L'Internationale, Compagnie d'Assurance-Vie/The International Life Insurance Company
#2002, 1010, rue Sherbrooke ouest, Montréal PQ H3A 2R7
514/842-3905; Fax: 514/287-9457
Directeur général, Yolande Blouin
Classes of insurance: Life, Accident & Sickness
ITT Hartford Life Insurance Company of Canada/ITT Hartford du Canada, Compagnie d'Assurance Vie
3027 Harvester Rd., Burlington ON L7N 3G9
905/639-6200; Fax: 905/639-7763; Email: hartford@ftn.net
President & CEO, Mark Sylvia
Classes of insurance: Life, Accident & Sickness
J.C. Penney Life Insurance Company
#500, 80 Tiverton Ct., Markham ON L3R 0G4
Chief Agent, Aaron Hill
Classes of insurance: Life, Accident & Sickness
Jevco Insurance Company/La Compagnie d'Assurances Jevco
#1150, 2021, rue Union, Montréal PQ H3A 2S9
514/284-9340/50; Fax: 514/289-9257
Chief Agent, Raymond David
Classes of insurance: Auto, Property, Misc
John Deere Insurance Company of Canada
PO Box 1000, Grimsby ON L3M 4H5
905/945-7478
President, G.J. Clark
Classes of insurance: Auto, Accident & Sickness, Property, Misc
Kemper Reinsurance Company
#201, 3650 Victoria Park Ave., North York ON M2H 3P7
416/496-1148; Fax: 416/496-1089
Chief Agent, V.L. Williams
Classes of insurance: Auto, Accident & Sickness, Property, Misc
The Kings Mutual Insurance Company
PO Box 10, Berwick NS B0P 1E0
902/538-3187; Fax: 902/538-7271
Manager, D.C. Cook
Classes of insurance: Property, Misc
*Kingsway General Insurance Company
175 Traders Blvd., Mississauga ON L4Z 3S8
905/890-7616; Fax: 905/890-2535; Toll Free: 1-800-265-5458
President/General Manager, William G. Star
Classes of insurance: Auto, Accident & Sickness, Property, Misc
*La Laurentienne Vie Inc./Laurentian Life Inc.
500, Grande Allée est, Québec PQ G1R 5M4
418/647-5151; Fax: 418/647-5118
Classes of insurance: Life, Accident & Sickness
Laurier Life Insurance Company
304 The East Mall, 9th Fl., Etobicoke ON M9B 6E2
416/234-9700; Fax: 416/234-9764
President, Van M. Campbell
Classes of insurance: Life, Accident & Sickness
Lawyers Title Insurance Corporation
65 Queen St. West, 17th Fl., Toronto ON M5H 2M5
416/368-4611; Fax: 416/367-2502
Chief Agent, David L. Gibson
Classes of insurance: Misc
*Lawyers' Professional Indemnity Company
Osgoode Hall, 130 Queen St. West, Toronto ON M5H 2N6
416/947-3431; Fax: 416/599-8341
President, Edwin J. Anderson
Legacy General Insurance Company
#500, 80 Tiverton Ct., Markham ON L3R 0G4
Vice-President/CEO, Aaron Hill
Classes of insurance: Accident & Sickness, Property
*Liberty Health
150 Ferrand Dr., North York ON M3C 1H6
416/429-2670; Fax: 416/429-8179; Toll Free: 1-800-668-6262
President, Brian C. Johnston

Canadian Almanac & Directory 1997

INSURANCE COMPANIES 7-19

Classes of insurance: Life, Accident & Sickness, Misc
Liberty Life Assurance Company of Boston
#3320, 181 Bay St., Toronto ON M5J 2T3
416/365-7587; Fax: 416/365-9302
Chief Agent, B.G. Johnston
Classes of insurance: Life, Accident & Sickness
Liberty Mutual Fire Insurance Company
#3320, 181 Bay St., Toronto ON M5J 2T3
416/365-7587; Fax: 416/365-9302
Chief Agent, B.G. Johnston
Classes of insurance: Auto, Accident & Sickness, Property, Misc
Liberty Mutual Insurance Company
#3320, 181 Bay St., Toronto ON M5J 2T3
416/365-7587; Fax: 416/365-9302
Vice-President/Chief Agent, B.G. Johnston
Classes of insurance: Auto, Fire, Accident & Sickness, Property
Life Insurance Company of North America
#1400, 250 Yonge St., PO Box 14, Toronto ON M5B 2L7
416/591-1225; Fax: 416/591-7488
Chief Agent, Eman Hassan
Classes of insurance: Life, Accident & Sickness
Life Investors Insurance Company of America
c/o John Milnes & Associates, 68 Scollard St., 2nd Fl., Toronto ON M5R 1G2
Chief Agent, John R. Milnes
Classes of insurance: Life, Accident & Sickness
Life Reassurance Corporation of America
c/o Deloitte & Touche, #1400, 181 Bay St., PO Box 12, Toronto ON M5J 2V1
Chief Agent, Wayne Musselman
Classes of insurance: Life, Accident & Sickness
The Lincoln National Life Insurance Company
#1450, One Queen St. East, PO Box 101, Toronto ON M5C 2W5
416/777-2500
Chief Agent, James A. Faichnie, Q.C.
Classes of insurance: Life, Accident & Sickness
Lombard General Insurance Company of Canada
105 Adelaide St. West, Toronto ON M5H 1P9
416/350-4400; Fax: 416/350-4412
CEO, Byron G. Messier
Classes of insurance: Auto, Fire, Property, Misc
Lombard Insurance Company
105 Adelaide St. West, Toronto ON M5H 1P9
Vice-President/General Manager, A.W. Miles
The London Assurance
#630, 48 Yonge St., Toronto ON M5E 1G6
416/363-0814; Fax: 416/363-0459
Chief Agent, E.A. Richards
Classes of insurance: Fire, Property, Misc
London Gurantee Insurance Company
#342B, 77 King St. West, PO Box 284, Toronto ON M5K 1K2
President, R.E. Taylor
Classes of insurance: Auto, Accident & Sickness, Property, Misc
London Life Insurance Company/London Life, Compagnie d'Assurance-Vie
255 Dufferin Ave., London ON N6A 4K1
519/432-5281; Fax: 519/432-7781
President, Gordon R. Cunningham
Classes of insurance: Life, Accident & Sickness
London & Midland General Insurance Company
201 Queens Ave., PO Box 5071, London ON N6A 4M5
519/672-1070; Fax: 519/672-2623
Sr. Vice-President/General Manager, A.J. Smith-Windsor
Classes of insurance: Auto, Accident & Sickness, Property
*The Loyalist Insurance Company
#106, 911 Golf Links Rd., Ancaster ON L9K 1H9
905/648-1722; Fax: 905/648-7399
Chair, James D. Coon

Lumbermen's Underwriting Alliance
#500, 185, av Dorval, Dorval PQ H9S 5J9
514/631-2710; Fax: 514/631-9788
Chief Agent, Maurice R. Piché
Classes of insurance: Property
Lumbermens Mutual Casualty Company
(Kemper National Insurance Companies)
320 Front St. West, 6th Fl., Toronto ON M5V 3B6
416/593-6626; Fax: 416/351-2502; Toll Free: 1-800-387-2934
Chief Agent, D.E. Aitchison
Classes of insurance: Auto, Fire, Property, Misc
*Manitoba Mennonite Mutual Insurance Company
85 Hwy. 12 North, PO Box 3550, Steinbach MB R0A 2A0
204/326-6468; Fax: 204/326-1865
President, Delbert F. Plett, Q.C.
Classes of insurance: Property
*Manitoba Public Insurance
330 Graham Ave., 9th Fl., PO Box 6300, Winnipeg MB R3C 4A4
204/985-7000; Fax: 204/943-9851
President/General Manager, Jack W. Zacharias
Classes of insurance: Auto
The Manufacturers Life Insurance Company
(Manulife Financial)
200 Bloor St. East, Toronto ON M4W 1E5
416/926-0100; Fax: 416/926-5454; URL: http://www.manulife.com
President/CEO, Dominic D'Alessandro
Classes of insurance: Life
Marine Indemnity Insurance Company of America
#1200, 48 Yonge St., Toronto ON M5E 1G6
416/364-5485; Fax: 416/364-9068
Chief Agent, Peter T. Perkins
Classes of insurance: Property, Misc
Maritime Insurance Company Limited
60 Yonge St., Toronto ON M5E 1H5
416/362-2961; Fax: 416/362-7281
Chief Agent, A. Jervis
Classes of insurance: Property, Misc
The Maritime Life Assurance Company
Maritime Life Bldg., 2701 Dutch Village Rd., PO Box 1030, Halifax NS B3J 2X5
902/453-4300; Fax: 902/453-7041
President, Bill Black
Classes of insurance: Life
Markel Insurance Company of Canada
105 Adelaide St. West, 7th Fl., Toronto ON M5H 1P9
416/598-4500; Fax: 416/598-1252
President, Mark Ram
Classes of insurance: Auto, Accident & Sickness, Property, Misc
Massachusetts Mutual Life Insurance Company
c/o McLean & Kerr, #2800, 130 Adelaide St. West, Toronto ON M5H 3P5
416/364-5371; Fax: 416/366-8571
Chief Agent, R.B. Cumine, Q.C.
Classes of insurance: Life, Accident & Sickness
*Mennonite Mutual Fire Insurance
PO Box 190, Waldheim SK S0K 4R0
306/945-2239
*Mennonite Mutual Insurance Co. (Alberta) Ltd.
76 Skyline Cres. NE, Calgary AB T2K 5X7
403/275-6996; Fax: 403/275-3711
General Manager, Larry L. Jantzi
Classes of insurance: Auto, Property, Misc
The Mercantile & General Life Reassurance Company of Canada
Canada Trust Tower, #3000, 161 Bay St., Toronto ON M5J 2T6
416/947-3800; Fax: 416/364-2449; Toll Free: 1-800-268-9798
President/CEO, Peter B. Patterson
Classes of insurance: Life, Accident & Sickness
The Mercantile & General Reinsurance Company of Canada

Canada Trust Tower, #3000, 161 Bay St., Toronto ON M5J 2T6
416/947-3800; Fax: 416/364-2449
President/CEO, Peter B. Patterson
Classes of insurance: Auto, Accident & Sickness, Property, Misc
*Metro General Insurance Corporation Ltd.
PO Box 548, St. John's NF A1C 5K9
President & Sec.-Treas., Kevin Hutchings
Metropolitan Life Insurance Company/La Métropolitaine, Compagnie d'Assurance-Vie
99 Bank St., Ottawa ON K1P 5A3
613/560-7446; Fax: 613/560-7668
Chief Agent, William R. Prueter
Classes of insurance: Life, Accident & Sickness
Metropolitan Life Insurance Company of Canada/Compagnie d'Assurance-Vie La Métropolitan du Canada
99 Bank St., Ottawa ON K1P 5A3
613/560-7446; Fax: 613/560-7668
President/CEO, William R. Prueter
Classes of insurance: Life, Accident & Sickness
*MFQ-Vie, Corporation d'Assurance
625, rue Saint-Amable, Québec PQ G1R 2G5
418/643-3884; Fax: 418/528-0457
President/COO, Jacques Labrecque
Classes of insurance: Life, Accident & Sickness
MIC Life Insurance Corporation
#400, 8500 Leslie St., PO Box 6000, Thornhill ON L3T 4S5
905/882-3900
Chief Agent, C.W. Hastings
Classes of insurance: Life, Accident & Sickness
*Midwest Insurance Inc.
401 - 4th Ave. North, Saskatoon SK S7K 2L8
306/653-2233
The Minnesota Mutual Life Insurance Company
c/o McLean & Kerr, #2800, 130 Adelaide St. West, Toronto ON M5H 3P5
416/364-5371; Fax: 416/366-8571
Chief Agent, R.B. Cumine, Q.C.
Classes of insurance: Life
The Missisquoi Insurance Company/La Compagnie d'Assurance Missisquoi
CP 70, Frelighsburg PQ J0J 1C0
514/298-5251; Fax: 514/298-5410
President/CEO, J.P. Courtemanche
Classes of insurance: Auto, Property, Misc
Mitsui Marine & Fire Insurance Company, Ltd.
c/o D.M. Williams & Assoc. Ltd., #201, 3650 Victoria Park Ave., North York ON M2H 3P7
416/496-1148; Fax: 416/496-1089
Chief Agent, V.L. Williams
Classes of insurance: Auto, Accident & Sickness, Property, Misc
Motors Insurance Corporation
#400, 8500 Leslie St., PO Box 6000, Thornhill ON L3T 4S5
905/882-3900
Chief Agent, C.W. Hastings
Classes of insurance: Auto, Property, Misc
Munich Reinsurance Company
390 Bay St., 22nd Fl., Toronto ON M5H 2Y2
416/366-9206; Fax: 416/366-4330; Toll Free: 1-800-268-9705
Chief Agent, Life, Geoffrey R. Minns
Classes of insurance: Auto, Life, Accident & Sickness, Property, Misc
Munich Reinsurance Company of Canada
390 Bay St., 22nd Fl., Toronto ON M5H 2Y2
416/366-9206; Fax: 416/366-4330; Toll Free: 1-800-268-9705; Email: ca326flb@ibmmail.com
President, John P. Phelan
Classes of insurance: Misc
*The Municipal Insurance Association of British Columbia
#320, 5200 Hollybridge Way, Richmond BC V7C 4N3

Canadian Almanac & Directory 1997

Classes of insurance: Misc
*The Mutual Fire Insurance Company of British Columbia
#105, 10334 - 152A St., Surrey BC V3R 7P8
Classes of insurance: Auto, Fire, Property, Misc
The Mutual Life Assurance Company of Canada
227 King St. South, Waterloo ON N2J 4C5
519/888-2290; Fax: 519/888-2990
President/CEO, Robert M. Astley
Classes of insurance: Life, Accident & Sickness
Mutual of Omaha Insurance Company
500 University Ave., Toronto ON M5G 1V8
416/598-4321; Fax: 416/598-5356
Chief Agent, David R. Lafayette
Classes of insurance: Life, Accident & Sickness
*La Mutualité Société d'Assurance-Vie Inc.
2525, boul Laurier, CP 10300, Ste-Foy PQ G1V 4H5
Contact, Jacques Desbiens
La Mutuelle du Mans Assurances I.A.R.D.
c/o Mutuelles du Mans Management Ltd., #1000, 20 Queen St. West, Toronto ON M5H 3R3
416/598-1084; Fax: 416/598-1980
Chief Agent, Rui Quintal
Classes of insurance: Auto, Fire, Accident & Sickness, Property
La Mutuelle du Mans Assurances Vie
2475, boul Laurier, Sillery PQ G1T 1C4
Chief Agent, Normand Brunet
Classes of insurance: Life, Accident & Sickness
NAC Reinsurance Corporation
#200, 200 Consumers Rd., North York ON M2J 4R4
416/498-9822; Fax: 416/502-1614
Chief Agent, T.P. Flynn
Classes of insurance: Auto, Fire, Accident & Sickness, Property, Misc
National Fidelity Life Insurance Company
#1, 1375 Hopkins St., Whitby ON L1N 2C3
Chief Agent, John T. Hogan
Classes of insurance: Life, Accident & Sickness
*National Frontier Insurance Company
373 Main St. West, 2nd Fl., North Bay ON P1B 2T9
705/476-4814; Fax: 705/476-8694
Vice-President/COO, David Liddle
Classes of insurance: Auto, Fire, Property
The National Life Assurance Company of Canada
522 University Ave., Toronto ON M5G 1Y7
416/598-2122; Fax: 416/598-2195; Toll Free: 1-800-387-4326
President/COO, V.P. Tonna
Classes of insurance: Life
National Reinsurance Corporation
Canada Trust Tower, BCE Place, #2500, 161 Bay St., Toronto ON M5J 2S1
Chief Agent, Thomas J. Krause
Classes of insurance: Auto, Property, Misc
Nationwide Mutual Insurance Company
c/o John Milnes & Associates, 68 Scollard St., 2nd Fl., Toronto ON M5R 1G2
416/964-0630
Chief Agent, John R. Milnes
Classes of insurance: Auto, Accident & Sickness, Property, Misc
New Hampshire Insurance Company
145 Wellington St. West, Toronto ON M5J 1H8
Chief Agent, Gary A. McMillan
Classes of insurance: Auto, Accident & Sickness, Property, Misc
New York Life Insurance Company/Compagnie d'Assurances New York Life
#2100, Scotia Plaza, 40 King St. West, Toronto ON M5H 3C2
416/960-4500; Fax: 416/968-0901
Chief Agent, J. Brian Reeve
Classes of insurance: Life, Accident & Sickness
Niagara Fire Insurance Company
One Adelaide St. East, PO Box 219A, Toronto ON M5W 1B6
Chief Agent, Brian G. Messier

Classes of insurance: Auto, Property, Misc
Nippon Fire & Marine Insurance Company Ltd.
c/o Canadian General Insurance Company, #500, 2206 Eglinton Ave. East, Scarborough ON M1L 4S8
416/288-1800; Fax: 416/288-9756
Chief Agent, R. Lewis Dunn
Classes of insurance: Auto, Accident & Sickness, Property, Misc
NN Life Insurance Company of Canada
One Concorde Gate, North York ON M3C 3N6
416/391-2200; Fax: 416/391-1585; Email: cwalker@interlog.com; URL: http://www.ingfin.com
President/CEO, Norman A. Foran
Classes of insurance: Life, Accident & Sickness
Non-Marine Underwriters, Members of Lloyd's, London, England/Les Souscripteurs d'Assurance Non Maritime, Membres du Lloyd's de Londres (Angleterre)
#1400, 1155 rue University, Montréal PQ H3B 1S3
514/861-8361; Fax: 514/861-0470
Chief Agent, M.J. Oppenheim
Classes of insurance: Auto, Fire, Accident & Sickness, Property, Misc
*Norfolk Mutual Fire Insurance Company
37 Kent St. South, Simcoe ON N3Y 2X7
519/426-1294; Fax: 519/426-7594
Manager, Carrol E. Lambert
Classes of insurance: Auto, Fire, Property, Misc
The North America Life Assurance Co. see The Manufacturers Life Insurance Company
North American Reassurance Company
c/o Canadian Reassurance Company, 99 Yorkville Ave., Toronto ON M5R 3K5
Chief Agent, Ghislain Trepanier
Classes of insurance: Life, Accident & Sickness
The North Waterloo Farmers Mutual Insurance Company
100 Erb St. East, Waterloo ON N2J 1L9
519/886-4530; Fax: 519/746-0222
President/CEO, Robert L. Monte
Classes of insurance: Property
The North West Life Assurance Company of Canada
#800, 1040 Georgia St. West, Vancouver BC V6E 4H1
604/689-1211; Fax: 604/682-2013
Vice-President & Secretary, Arthur W. Putz
Classes of insurance: Life
Northern Indemnity Inc.
#2210, 120 Adelaide St. West, Toronto ON M5H 1T1
President, Robert Lamendola
Classes of insurance: Misc
Northwestern National Life Insurance Company
c/o D.M. Williams & Assoc. Ltd., #201, 3650 Victoria Park Ave., North York ON M2H 3P7
416/496-1148; Fax: 416/496-1089
Chief Agent, V.L. Williams
Classes of insurance: Life, Accident & Sickness
Norwich Union Fire Insurance Society Limited
60 Yonge St., Toronto ON M5E 1H5
416/362-2961; Fax: 416/362-7281
Chief Agent, A. Jervis
Classes of insurance: Fire, Accident & Sickness, Property, Misc
The Norwich Union Life Insurance Society/La Société d'Assurance-Vie Norwich Union
60 Yonge St., Toronto ON M5E 1H5
416/362-2961
Chief Agent, Guy S. Pentelow
Classes of insurance: Life
Old Republic Insurance Company of Canada/L'Ancienne Republique Compagnie d'Assurance du Canada
100 King St. West, PO Box 557, Hamilton ON L8N 3K9
905/523-5936; Fax: 905/528-4685
President/CEO, Anthony Chmiel

Classes of insurance: Auto, Property, Misc
Ontario Blue Cross see Liberty Health
*Optimum Assurance Agricole Inc./Optimum Farm Insurance Inc.
#250, 1500, rue Royale, Trois-Rivières PQ G9A 6E6
819/373-2040; Fax: 819/373-2801
President, Yvon Trépanier
Classes of insurance: Auto, Fire, Property
OTIP/RAEO Insurance Company Inc.
200 Consilium Pl., 15th Fl., Scarborough ON M1H 3E6
President/COO, Ross T. Bell
Classes of insurance: Auto, Property, Misc
*Pacific Coast Fishermen's Mutual Marine Insurance Company
#200, 4259 Canada Way, Burnaby BC V5G 1H7
Classes of insurance: Misc
*Pafco Insurance Company
#300, 1243 Islington Ave., Etobicoke ON M8X 2Y3
416/231-6983; Fax: 416/231-2806
President/CEO, Douglas E. McIntyre
Classes of insurance: Auto, Fire, Accident & Sickness, Property, Misc
*Palliser Insurance Corp.
#103, 3502 Taylor St. East, Saskatoon SK S7H 5H9
306/955-1330
The Paul Revere Life Insurance Company/Paul Revere Compagnie d'Assurance-Vie
440 Elizabeth St., PO Box 5044, Burlington ON L7R 4C1
905/681-1180, ext.201; Fax: 905/333-4598
Chief Agent, J.P. Charlebois
Classes of insurance: Life, Accident & Sickness
*Peace Hills General Insurance Company
#902, 10011 - 109 St. NW, Edmonton AB T5J 3S8
403/424-3986; Fax: 403/424-0396; Toll Free: 1-800-272-5614
President/CEO, Diane Strashok, AIIC
Classes of insurance: Auto, Fire, Property
Penncorp Life Insurance Company
#400, 90 Dundas St. West, Mississauga ON L5B 2T5
President/CEO, J. Paul Edmondson
Classes of insurance: Life, Accident & Sickness
The Personal Insurance Company of Canada
5150 Spectrum Way, Mississauga ON L4W 5G8
President/COO, Kevin McNeil
Classes of insurance: Auto, Accident & Sickness, Property, Misc
*La Personnelle-Vie Corporation d'Assurance
625, rue Saint-Amable, Québec PQ G1R 2G5
418/644-4229; Fax: 418/528-0457
Directeur général, Jacques Labrecque
Classes of insurance: Life, Accident & Sickness
Phoenix Home Life Mutual Insurance Company
Scotia Plaza, #2100, 40 King St. West, Toronto ON M5H 3C2
416/869-5300; Fax: 416/360-8877
Chief Agent, J. Brian Reeve
Classes of insurance: Life, Accident & Sickness
The Phoenix Insurance Company
Scotia Plaza, #2100, 40 King St. West, Toronto ON M5H 3C2
416/869-5300; Fax: 416/360-8877
Chief Agent, J. Brian Reeve
Classes of insurance: Auto, Fire, Property
Pictou County Farmers' Mutual Fire Insurance Company
PO Box 130, Pictou NS B0K 1H0
902/485-4542
Sec.-Treas., Heather Smith
Classes of insurance: Property, Misc
Pierce National Life Insurance Company (Canada Purple Shield Plan)
#402, 1770 - 7th Ave. West, Vancouver BC V6J 4Y8
604/736-2904; Fax: 604/737-1578
Chief Agent, Neil Lerner
Classes of insurance: Life

INSURANCE COMPANIES 7-21

*Pilot Insurance Company
90 Eglinton Ave. West, Toronto ON M4R 2E4
416/487-5141; Fax: 416/482-0220
President/CEO, Stuart Kistruck
Classes of insurance: Auto, Accident & Sickness, Property

*Pinnacle Insurance Corp.
637 Main St. North, PO Box 967, Moose Jaw SK S6H 4P6
306/694-1797

Pool Insurance Company
#1007, 220 Portage Ave., Winnipeg MB R3C 0A5
204/942-0658; Fax: 204/989-2235
President, Charles H. Swanson
Classes of insurance: Property

The Portage La Prairie Mutual Insurance Company
PO Box 340, Portage La Prairie MB R1N 3B8
204/857-3415; Fax: 204/239-6655
President, H.G. Owens
Classes of insurance: Auto, Fire, Property

*Premier Insurance Company
5905 Campus Rd., Mississauga ON L4V 1P9
905/676-1240; Fax: 905/676-9318
President, R.V. McCarron

Primerica Life Insurance Company of Canada
#301, 350 Burnhamthorpe Rd. West, PO Box 2500, Stn Malton, Mississauga ON L4T 4J4
905/848-7731; Fax: 905/270-7096
President/CEO, Michael Hagerman
Classes of insurance: Life, Accident & Sickness

*Prince Edward Island Mutual Insurance Company (PEI Mutual)
201 Water St., Summerside PE C1N 1B4
902/436-2185; Fax: 902/436-0148
General Manager, Malcolm MacFarlane
Classes of insurance: Fire, Property

Principal Mutual Life Insurance Company
c/o John Milnes & Associates, 68 Scollard St., 2nd Fl., Toronto ON M5R 1G2
Chief Agent, John R. Milnes
Classes of insurance: Life, Accident & Sickness

Progressive Casualty Insurance Company of Canada
200 Yorkland Blvd., 5th Fl., North York ON M2J 5C1
President, Andrew W. Rogacki
Classes of insurance: Auto, Property, Misc

*Promutuel Réassurance
#300, 1091, ch Saint-Louis, Sillery PQ G1S 1E2
418/683-1212; Fax: 418/683-3303
Directeur général, Jacques Douville
Classes of insurance: Auto, Property, Misc

*Promutuel Vie Inc.
134, rue St-Charles, St-Jean-Sur-Richelieu PQ J3B 2C3
514/346-5041; Fax: 514/346-0224
Directeur general, Michel Tardif
Classes of insurance: Life, Accident & Sickness

Protection Mutual Insurance Company
Ennisclare Office Centre, #810, 1275 North Service Rd. West, Oakville ON L6M 3G4
905/827-9000; Fax: 905/827-9008
Chief Agent, J. Gray
Classes of insurance: Property, Misc

Protective Insurance Company
68 Scollard St., 2nd Fl., Toronto ON M5R 1G2
Chief Agent, John R. Milnes
Classes of insurance: Auto, Property

Providence Washington Insurance Company
#1703, 155 University Ave., Toronto ON M5H 3B7
416/366-3012; Fax: 416/366-3465
Chief Agent, Jack G. Dovey
Classes of insurance: Auto, Fire, Accident & Sickness, Misc

Provident Life & Accident Insurance Company
#1000, 181 University Ave., Toronto ON M5H 3M7
Chief Agent, Thomas Langshaw
Classes of insurance: Life, Accident & Sickness

Prudential of America General Insurance Company (Canada)
200 Consilium Pl., 8th Fl., Scarborough ON M1H 3E6
416/296-0777; Fax: 416/296-3332
President, Robert McKnight
Classes of insurance: Auto, Property, Misc

Prudential of America Life Insurance Company (Canada)
#400 South, 33 Yonge St., Toronto ON M5E 1V7
President/CEO, Ronald Meredith-Jones
Classes of insurance: Life, Accident & Sickness

The Prudential Insurance Company of America/La Prudentielle d'Amérique, Compagnie d'Assurance
200 Consilium Pl., Scarborough ON M1H 3E6
416/296-0777; Fax: 416/296-3180
Chief Agent, Robert G. McKnight
Classes of insurance: Life, Accident & Sickness, Misc

The Prudential Life Assurance Company of England (Canada) see The Mutual Life Assurance Company of Canada

Prudential Reinsurance Company (of America) see Everest Reinsurance Company

Quebec Assurance Company/Compagnie d'Assurance du Québec
10 Wellington St. East, Toronto ON M5E 1L5
416/366-7511; Fax: 416/367-9869
President, R.J. Gunn
Classes of insurance: Auto, Fire, Property

*Red River Valley Mutual Insurance Company
245 Centre Ave. East, PO Box 940, Altona MB R0G 0B0
204/324-6434, 284-0684 (Winnipeg); Fax: 204/324-1316
CEO, H.G. Heinrichs
Classes of insurance: Auto, Property, Misc

The Reinsurance Corporation of New York
#4, 1101 Nicholson Rd., Newmarket ON L3Y 7V1
Chief Agent, Colleen Sexsmith
Classes of insurance: Auto, Accident & Sickness, Property, Misc

Reliable Life Insurance Company/La Reliable Compagnie d'Assurance Vie
100 King St. West, PO Box 557, Hamilton ON L8N 3K9
905/523-5587; Fax: 905/528-4685
Chair/CEO, A.T. Chmiel
Classes of insurance: Life, Accident & Sickness

Reliance Insurance Company
#1906, 200 King St. West, Toronto ON M5H 3T4
416/581-0101; Fax: 416/581-1109
Chief Agent, Daniel P. Courtemanche
Classes of insurance: Auto, Fire, Property, Misc

RGA Life Reinsurance Company of Canada
#2220, 1501, av McGill College, Montréal PQ H3A 3M8
President/CEO, André St-Amour

Royal Insurance Company of Canada/La Royale du Canada, Compagnie d'Assurance
10 Wellington St. East, Toronto ON M5E 1L5
416/366-7511; Fax: 416/367-9869
President/CEO, R.J. Gunn
Classes of insurance: Auto, Accident & Sickness, Property, Misc

Royal Life Insurance Company of Canada Ltd. (Royal Life Canada)
#300, 277 Lakeshore Rd. East, Oakville ON L6J 1H9
905/842-6200; Fax: 905/842-6294
President/CEO, Clive S. Smith
Classes of insurance: Life

Royale Belge
#1200, 425, boul de Maisonneuve ouest, Montréal PQ H3A 3G5
514/288-1900; Fax: 514/288-8099
Chief Agent, Harvey Campbell
Classes of insurance: Life

*St-Laurent, Compagnie de Réassurance
#1200, 425, boul de Maisonneuve ouest, Montréal PQ H3A 3G5
514/288-1900; Fax: 514/288-8099
President, Mario Georgiev
Classes of insurance: Life

St. Paul Fire & Marine Insurance Company/La Compagnie d'Assurance Saint Paul
#400, 55 University Ave., Toronto ON M5J 2L3
416/366-8301; Fax: 416/366-0846
Chief Agent, Charles T. Wilson
Classes of insurance: Auto, Accident & Sickness, Property, Misc

*Saskatchewan Motor Club Insurance Company Ltd.
200 Albert St. North, Regina SK S4R 5E2
306/791-4321

Saskatchewan Mutual Insurance Company
279 - 3 Ave. North, Saskatoon SK S7K 2H8
306/653-4232; Fax: 306/664-1957
President/CEO, R.W. Trost
Classes of insurance: Auto, Fire, Property

SCOR Canada Reinsurance Company
BCE Place, #5000, 161 Bay St., Toronto ON M5J 2T7
President/CEO, Laurent Thabault
Classes of insurance: Auto, Accident & Sickness, Property, Misc

SCOR Reinsurance Company
c/o SCOR Services Canada Inc., #5000, 161 Bay St., Toronto ON M5J 2S1
416/869-3670; Fax: 416/365-9393
Chief Agent, Jaya Narayan
Classes of insurance: Auto, Fire, Property

SCOR Vie
BCE Place, Canada Trust Tower, #5000, 161 Bay St., Toronto ON M5J 2S1
416/869-3670; Fax: 416/365-9393
Chief Agent, Jaya Narayan
Classes of insurance: Life, Accident & Sickness

Scotia General Insurance Company
#400, 100 Yonge St., Toronto ON M5H 1H1
President/CEO, O. Zimmerman
Classes of insurance: Accident & Sickness, Property

Scotia Life Insurance Company
Scotia Plaza, 44 King St. West, Toronto ON M5H 1H1
President/CEO, Oscar Zimmerman
Classes of insurance: Life, Accident & Sickness

*Scottish & York Insurance Co. Limited
2206 Eglinton Ave. East, Scarborough ON M1L 4S8
416/288-1800; Fax: 416/288-5888
President/CEO, R. Lewis Dunn
Classes of insurance: Auto, Accident & Sickness, Property, Misc

Seaboard Life Insurance Company
2165 West Broadway, PO Box 5900, Vancouver BC V6B 5H6
604/734-1667; Fax: 604/734-8221
President/CEO, Robert T. Smith
Classes of insurance: Life, Accident & Sickness

*La Securite, Assurances Generales Inc.
6300, boul de la Rive-Sud, Lévis PQ G6V 6P9
418/835-4771; Fax: 418/835-5599

Security Insurance Company of Hartford
c/o Wm. H. McGee & Co. of Canada Ltd., #702, 155 University Ave., Toronto ON M5H 3B7
Chief Agent, Graham A. Addington
Classes of insurance: Auto, Accident & Sickness, Property, Misc

*Security Life Insurance Company
2206 Eglinton Ave. East, Scarborough ON M1L 4S8
416/494-2497; Fax: 416/494-4616
General Manager, George Mejury

Security National Insurance Company/La Sécurité Nationale compagnie d'assurances
50, Place Crémazie, 12e étage, Montréal PQ H2P 1B6
514/382-6060; Fax: 514/385-2162

Canadian Almanac & Directory 1997

7-22 INSURANCE COMPANIES

President & COO, Alain Thibault, F.C.I.A., F.C.A.S.
Classes of insurance: Auto, Fire, Accident & Sickness, Property
Sentry Insurance - a Mutual Company
#600, 133 Richmond St. West, Toronto ON M5H 2L3
416/363-6103; Fax: 416/363-7454
Chief Agent, Donald G. Smith
Classes of insurance: Auto, Property, Misc
*SGI Canada Insurance Services
2260 - 11th Ave., Regina SK S4P 0J9
306/751-1640
Skandia Insurance Company Ltd.
c/o D.M. Williams & Associates Ltd., #201, 3650 Victoria Park Ave., North York ON M2H 3P7
Chief Agent, V. Lorraine Williams
Classes of insurance: Auto, Property, Misc
*SMDA Insurance Corporation
#330, 3303 Hillsdale St., Regina SK S4S 6W9
306/721-2920
Classes of insurance: Life, Accident & Sickness
Société Anonyme Française de Réassurances
1080, côte de Beaver Hall, 19e étage, Montréal PQ H2Z 1S8
514/878-2600; Fax: 514/866-6860
Chief Agent, R. Davis, C.A.
Classes of insurance: Auto, Fire, Life, Accident & Sickness, Property
La Société d'assurance des Caisses populaires acadiennes see Acadie Vie
*Société Nationale d'Assurance Inc./National Insurance Company
#1500, 425, boul de Maisonneuve ouest, Montréal PQ H3A 3G5
514/288-8711; Fax: 514/288-8269
Classes of insurance: Auto, Fire, Property
Société de Réassurance des Assurances Mutuelles Agricoles
#1520, 70 York St., Toronto ON M5J 1S9
416/364-3048; Fax: 416/364-1788
Chief Agent, Angus Ross
Classes of insurance: Auto, Accident & Sickness, Property
*La Solidarité Compagnie d'Assurance sur la Vie
925, ch Saint-Louis, Québec PQ G1S 1C1
418/688-8710; Fax: 418/688-1688
CEO, Andréa Latulippe
Classes of insurance: Life
*Southeastern Mutual Fire Insurance Company
115 Queen St., Moncton NB E1C 1K6
Contact, Raymond White
Classes of insurance: Property
The Sovereign General Insurance Company
#2200, 855 - 2 Ave. SW, Calgary AB T2P 4J8
403/298-4200; Fax: 403/298-4217
President, G.T. Squire
Classes of insurance: Auto, Fire, Accident & Sickness, Property
*Sphere Drake Insurance Public Limited Company
3200 Erin Mills Pkwy., PO Box 67051, Stn Millway, Mississauga ON L5L 5W9
905/828-4951; Fax: 905/828-3453
Chief Agent, Taro Asnani
*SSQ, Société d'Assurance Generales Inc.
#440, 1245, ch Ste-Foy, Québec PQ G1S 4P2
418/683-0554; Fax: 418/683-5603
President/Directeur général, Rene Hamel
Classes of insurance: Auto, Fire, Property
*SSQ, Société d'Assurance-Vie Inc.
2525, boul Laurier, CP 10500, Ste-Foy PQ G1V 4H6
418/651-7000; Fax: 418/652-2739; Email: sbussier@riq.qc.ca
Président/Directeur général, Pierre Genest
Classes of insurance: Auto, Fire, Life, Accident & Sickness, Property

The Standard Life Assurance Company/Compagnie d'Assurance Standard Life
1245, rue Sherbrooke ouest, Montréal PQ H3G 1G3
514/284-6711; Fax: 514/499-4908
President, Claude A. Garcia
Classes of insurance: Life, Accident & Sickness
The Standard Life Assurance Company of Canada/Compagnie d'Assurance Standard Life du Canada
1245, rue Sherbrooke ouest, Montréal PQ H3G 1G3
President/COO, Claude A. Garcia
Classes of insurance: Life
*Stanley Mutual Insurance Company
PO Box 70, Stanley NB E0H 1T0
Contact, James F. Pinnock
Classes of insurance: Property
State Farm Fire & Casualty Company
#102, 100 Consilium Pl., Scarborough ON M1P 3G9
416/290-4100; Fax: 416/290-4719
Chief Agent, Robert J. Cooke
Classes of insurance: Property
State Farm Life Insurance Company
#102, 100 Consilium Pl., Scarborough ON M1H 3G9
416/290-4100; Fax: 416/290-4438
Chief Agent, Robert J. Cooke
Classes of insurance: Life
State Farm Mutual Automobile Insurance Company
#102, 100 Consilium Pl., Scarborough ON M1H 3G9
416/290-4100
Chief Agent, Robert J. Cooke
Classes of insurance: Auto, Accident & Sickness
Stewart Title Guaranty Company
c/o Encon Insurance Managers Inc., #1200, 99 Metcalfe St., Ottawa ON K1P 6L7
613/238-6373; Fax: 613/238-7448
Chief Agent, Denis J. Shillington
Classes of insurance: Misc
The Sumitomo Marine & Fire Insurance Co., Ltd./Compagnie d'Assurance Maritime et Incendie Sumitomo, Ltee
One Financial Place, One Adelaide St. East, Toronto ON M5C 2V9
416/863-0550; Fax: 416/863-5010
Chief Agent, Janice M. Tomlinson
Classes of insurance: Auto, Fire, Accident & Sickness, Property
Sun Alliance & London Assurance Company (Canada) see TBD Life Insurance Co.
Sun Life Assurance Company of Canada
150 King St. West, Toronto ON M5H 1J9
416/979-9966; Fax: 416/585-9546
President/CEO, Donald A. Stewart
Classes of insurance: Life, Accident & Sickness
*La Survivance, Compagnie Mutuelle d'Assurance-Vie
1555, rue Girouard ouest, Saint-Hyacinthe PQ J2S 2Z6
514/773-6051; Fax: 514/773-6470
Directeur général, Jean Bouchard
Classes of insurance: Life, Accident & Sickness
Swiss RE Life
#1707, 1010, rue Sherbrooke ouest, Montréal PQ H3A 2R7
President, Alphonse Lepage
Classes of insurance: Life, Accident & Sickness
Swiss Reinsurance Company - Canadian Branch
99 Yorkville Ave., 3rd Fl., Toronto ON M5R 3K5
416/972-0272; Fax: 416/967-6591; Toll Free: 1-800-268-7116
Chief Agent, C. Paul Graham
Classes of insurance: Auto, Fire, Property
Swiss Reinsurance Company - Life Branch
#1707, 1010, rue Sherbrooke ouest, Montréal PQ H3A 2R7
Chief Agent, Alphonse Lepage
Classes of insurance: Life

Swiss Union General Insurance Company Limited/Union Suisse Compagnie Générale d'Assurances
#500, 1000, rue de la Gauchetière ouest, Montréal PQ H3B 4W5
Chief Agent, William J. Green
Classes of insurance: Auto, Property, Misc
TBD Life Insurance Co.
5650 Yonge St., North York ON M2M 4G4
416/362-2000; Fax: 416/362-6950
President/CEO, John G. Lynch
Classes of insurance: Life, Accident & Sickness
Terra Nova Insurance Company Limited
#740, 70 York St., Toronto ON M5J 1S9
416/864-0500; Fax: 416/864-1030
Chief Agent, J. Brian Reeve
Classes of insurance: Auto, Accident & Sickness, Property, Misc
TIG Insurance Company
c/o Canadian Insurance Consultants Inc., #600, 133 Richmond St. West, Toronto ON M5H 2L3
Chief Agent, Donald G. Smith
Classes of insurance: Auto, Accident & Sickness, Property, Misc
The Tokio Marine & Fire Insurance Company, Limited
One Adelaide St. East, Toronto ON M5C 2V9
Chief Agent, Bryan G. Messier
Classes of insurance: Auto, Property, Misc
Toronto Dominion General Insurance Company
Royal Trust Tower, 77 King St. West, 27th Fl., PO Box 307, Toronto ON M5K 1K2
President/CEO, Nick Stitt
Classes of insurance: Auto, Property
Toronto Dominion Life Insurance Company
Toronto-Dominion Tower, 34th Fl., Toronto ON M5K 1A2
President/CEO, Derek E. Thompson
Classes of insurance: Life, Accident & Sickness
Toronto Mutual Life Insurance Company
112 St. Clair Ave. West, Toronto ON M4V 2Y3
416/960-3463; Fax: 416/960-0531
President, John T. English
Classes of insurance: Life, Accident & Sickness
Trade Indemnity P.L.C.
#707, 331 Cooper St., Ottawa ON K2P 0G5
613/235-9511; Fax: 613/235-0329; Toll Free: 1-800-267-7697
Chief Agent, Tom Leonard
Classes of insurance: Misc
Traders General Insurance Company
#500, 2206 Eglinton Ave. East, Scarborough ON M1L 4S8
416/288-1800; Fax: 416/288-9756
President, R. Lewis Dunn
Classes of insurance: Auto, Accident & Sickness, Property, Misc
Trafalgar Insurance Company of Canada
#100, 425 Bloor St. East, Toronto ON M4W 3R5
416/961-5015; Fax: 416/961-8874; Toll Free: 1-800-387-5601
Vice-President, Marketing, Don Harder
Classes of insurance: Auto, Fire, Property
Transamerica Life Insurance Company of Canada
300 Consilium Pl., Scarborough ON M1H 3G2
416/486-2700; Fax: 416/486-2962
President/CEO, George A. Foegele
Classes of insurance: Life, Accident & Sickness
Transatlantic Reinsurance Company
145 Wellington St. West, Toronto ON M5J 1H8
416/596-0366; Fax: 416/971-8782
Chief Agent, Gary A. McMillan
Classes of insurance: Auto, Accident & Sickness, Property, Misc
The Travelers Indemnity Company
Scotia Plaza, #2100, 40 King St. West, Toronto ON M5H 3C2
416/869-5300; Fax: 416/360-8877
Chief Agent, J. Brian Reeve
Classes of insurance: Auto, Fire, Property

The Travelers Insurance Company
Scotia Plaza, #2100, 40 King St. West, Toronto ON M5H 3C2
416/869-5300; Fax: 416/360-8877
Chief Agent, J. Brian Reeve
Classes of insurance: Life, Accident & Sickness
Trygg-Hansa Reinsurance Company of Canada
#1402, 18 King St. East, Toronto ON M5C 1C4
416/361-0056; Fax: 416/361-0147
President, Robert W. Easton
Classes of insurance: Auto, Accident & Sickness, Property, Misc
Underwriters Insurance Company
c/o Fasken, Campbell, Godfrey, Toronto-Dominion Centre, PO Box 20, Stn Toronto-Dominion, Toronto ON M5K 1N6
416/366-8381; Fax: 416/364-7813
Chief Agent in Canada, Robert W. McDowell
Classes of insurance: Auto, Property, Misc
Unifund Assurance Company
95 Elizabeth Ave., St. John's NF A1B 1R7
709/737-1500
CEO, Paul Johnson
Classes of insurance: Auto, Accident & Sickness, Property, Misc
*Union du Canada Assurance-Vie/Union of Canada Life Insurance
325 Dalhousie St., PO Box 717, Ottawa ON K1P 5P8
613/241-3660; Fax: 613/241-4627
President/CEO, Gerard Desjardins
Classes of insurance: Life, Accident & Sickness
*L'Union Canadienne Compagnie d'Assurances
2475, boul Laurier, Sillery PQ G1T 1C4
418/651-3551; Fax: 418/651-9301
Directeur général, Paul-Henri Brochu
Classes of insurance: Auto, Life, Property
Union Fidelity Life Insurance Company
PO Box 4081, Stn A, Toronto ON M4W 1M7
416/922-1922; Fax: 416/922-1914
Chief Agent, Dan C. Evans
Classes of insurance: Life, Accident & Sickness
*L'Union-Vie, Compagnie Mutuelle d'Assurance
142, rue Hériot, Drummondville PQ J2C 1J8
819/478-1315; Fax: 819/474-1990
Directeur général, Jacques Desbiens
Classes of insurance: Life
Unione Italiana di Riassicurazione S.P.A.
#2220, 1501, av McGill College, Montréal PQ H3A 3H8
514/985-5260; Fax: 514/985-3066; Toll Free: 1-800-985-GEAM; Email: mail@rga-reinsurance.com
Chief Agent, Life, André St-Amour, 514/985-5260, Fax: 514/985-3066
Classes of insurance: Auto, Fire, Life, Accident & Sickness, Property
*L'Unique, Compagnie d'Assurances Générales
925, ch St-Louis, Québec PQ G1S 1C1
418/683-2711; Fax: 418/688-9684; Toll Free: 1-800-463-4800
Directeur géne@ral, Emilien Robichaud
Classes of insurance: Auto, Fire
United American Insurance Company
145 King St. West, Toronto ON M5H 3X6
416/366-0800
Chief Agent, Connie Vaccaro
Classes of insurance: Life, Accident & Sickness
*United General Insurance Corporation
190 Prospect St. West, Suite A, Fredericton NB E3B 2T8
Contact, Wally Jarvis
Classes of insurance: Property
UNUM Life Insurance Company of America/L'UNUM d'Amérique, Compagnie d'Assurance-Vie
Scotia Plaza, #2100, 40 King St. West, Toronto ON M5H 3C2
416/869-5300; Fax: 416/360-8877

Chief Agent, J. Brian Reeve
Classes of insurance: Life, Accident & Sickness
Utica Mutual Insurance Company
c/o Focus Group Inc., #500, 36 King St. East, Toronto ON M5C 1E5
Chief Agent, Philip H. Cook
Classes of insurance: Auto, Property, Misc
Victoria Insurance Company of Canada see Traders General Insurance Company
Virginia Surety Company, Inc.
#300, 7300 Warden Ave., Markham ON L3R 0X3
Chief Agent, Dan C. Evans
Classes of insurance: Auto, Property, Misc
Voyageur Insurance Company
#300, 44 Peel Centre Dr., Brampton ON L6T 4M8
905/791-8700; Fax: 905/791-4600
President & COO, Walter Schutte
Classes of insurance: Accident & Sickness, Misc
Waterloo Insurance Company
111 Westmount Rd. South, PO Box 2000, Waterloo ON N2J 4S4
President/CEO, Noel G. Walpole
Classes of insurance: Auto, Property, Misc
The Wawanesa Life Insurance Company
191 Broadway Ave., Winnipeg MB R3C 3P1
204/985-3811; Fax: 204/947-5192
President/CEO, G.J. Hanson
Classes of insurance: Life, Accident & Sickness
The Wawanesa Mutual Insurance Company
191 Broadway Ave., Winnipeg MB R3C 3P1
204/985-3811; Fax: 204/947-5192
President/CEO, G.J. Hanson
Classes of insurance: Auto, Property, Misc
Wellington Insurance Company
#500, 255 Queens Ave., London ON N6A 5R8
CEO, John Emory
Classes of insurance: Auto, Accident & Sickness, Property, Misc
Westbury Canadian Life Insurance Company
PO Box 2918, Hamilton ON L8N 3R5
905/528-6766; Fax: 905/523-1553
President, W. Grant Hardy
Classes of insurance: Life, Accident & Sickness
*Western Agricultural Insurance Corp.
339 Main St. North, Moose Jaw ON S6H 4N7
306/694-5959
Western Assurance Company
10 Wellington St. East, Toronto ON M5E 1L5
416/366-7511; Fax: 416/367-9869
President, R.J. Gunn
Classes of insurance: Auto, Fire, Property
Western General Mutual Insurance Company
989 Dundas St., PO Box 37, Woodstock ON N4S 7W6
519/539-9883; Fax: 519/539-0957
Sec.-Treas./General Manager, Bruce Wallis, C.G.A.
Classes of insurance: Auto, Property, Misc
Western Surety Company
PO Box 527, Regina SK S4P 2G8
306/777-0600; Fax: 306/359-0929
President & CEO, Leo C. Ell
Classes of insurance: Misc
Winterthur Life Insurance Company
1075 Bay St., Toronto ON M5S 2W5
416/928-8500; Fax: 416/928-1553
Chief Agent, William H. Gleed
Classes of insurance: Life
Winterthur Reinsurance Corporation of America
#830, 1075 Bay St., Toronto ON M5S 2W5
Chief Agent, Douglas M. Fernandes
Classes of insurance: Auto, Accident & Sickness, Property, Misc
The Yasuda Fire & Marine Insurance Company, Limited
c/o CIGNA Insurance Company of Canada, Scotia Plaza, 40 King St. West, 38th Fl., PO Box 107, Toronto ON M5H 3Y2
Chief Agent, Cynthia Santiago

Classes of insurance: Auto, Property, Misc
*York Fire & Casualty Insurance Company
#900, 130 Adelaide St. West, Toronto ON M5H 3P5
416/364-0919; Fax: 416/364-3492; Toll Free: 1-800-676-0967
President, William G. Stars
Classes of insurance: Auto, Property
Zurich Indemnity Company of Canada
400 University Ave., Toronto ON M5G 1S7
President/CEO, Stephen R. Smith
Classes of insurance: Auto, Accident & Sickness, Property, Misc
Zurich Insurance Company
400 University Ave., Toronto ON M5G 1S7
416/586-3000; Fax: 416/586-2858
Chief Agent, Stephen R. Smith
Classes of insurance: Auto, Accident & Sickness, Property, Misc
Zurich Life Insurance Company of Canada
2225 Sheppard Ave. East, North York ON M2J 5C4
416/502-3600; Fax: 416/502-3488; Toll Free: 1-800-387-4401
President/CEO, Stephen R. Smith
Classes of insurance: Life, Accident & Sickness

BOARDS OF TRADE & CHAMBERS OF COMMERCE

INTERNATIONAL CHAMBERS & BUSINESS COUNCILS

Brazil-Canada Chamber of Commerce, Carleton Tower, #720, 2 Carleton St., Toronto ON M5B 1J3 – 416/596-0992; Fax: 416/596-1257 – General Manager, Beth L. Wolff
British Canadian Chamber of Trade & Commerce, #305, 7100 Woodbine Ave., Markham ON L3R 5J2 – 905/475-3896; Fax: 905/475-0311 – Executive Director, John Archer
Canada-Arab Business Council, #1160, 55 Metcalfe St., Ottawa ON K1P 6N4 – 613/238-4000; Fax: 613/238-7643 – Chairman, J. Lambert Toupin, QC
Canada-ASEAN Business Council, Canadian Chamber of Commerce, #1160, 55 Metcalfe St., Ottawa ON K1P 6N4 – 613/238-4000; Fax: 613/238-7643
Canada China Business Council, #802, 110 Yonge St., Toronto ON M5C 1T4 – 416/954-3800; Fax: 416/954-3806 – Executive Director, David Mulroney
Canada China Business Council--Vancouver Office, SFU at Harbour Centre, #2600, 515 West Hastings St., Vancouver BC V6B 5K3 – 604/291-5190; Fax: 604/291-5039
Canada Czech Republic Chamber of Commerce, Exchange Tower, 14th Fl., 2 First Canadian Place, PO Box 198, Toronto ON M5X 1A6 – 416/367-3432; Fax: 416/367-3492 – Managing Director, Lubomir J. Novotny
Canada-Finland Chamber of Commerce, #604, 1200 Bay St., Toronto ON M5R 2A5 – 416/964-7400; Fax: 416/964-1524 – President, John Hylton
Canada-India Business Council, Canadian Chamber of Commerce, #1160, 55 Metcalfe St., Ottawa ON K1P 6N4 – 613/238-4000; Fax: 613/238-7643; Telex: 053-3360 – Executive Director, Pan Kanagaretnam
Canada-Indonesia Business Council, Box 110, 260 Adelaide St. East, Toronto ON M5A 1N1 – 416/366-8490; Fax: 416/947-1534 – Contact, Peter Dawes
Canada-Israel Chamber of Commerce, #1100, 48 St. Clair Ave. West, Toronto ON M4V 2Z2 – 416/961-7302 – President, David Goldstein
Canada-Japan Trade Council, #903, 75 Albert St., Ottawa ON K1P 5E7 – 613/233-4047; Fax: 613/233-

* BT - Board of Trade; BC - Bureau de commerce; CC - Chamber of Commerce/Chambre de commerce

Canadian Almanac & Directory 1997

2256; Email: cjtc@magi.com – President, Klaus Pringsheim
Canada-Netherlands Chamber of Commerce, #1100, 34 King St. East, Toronto ON M5C 2X8 – 416/368-0350; Fax: 416/368-7231; Email: 103123.2740@compuserve.com – Manager/International Trade Advisor, Nico Fernhout
Canada-Netherlands Chamber of Commerce--Atlantic Canada Chapter, #2100, 1801 Hollis St., Halifax NS B3J 2X6 – 902/429-4111; Fax: 902/429-8215 – Darlene Jameson
Canada-Netherlands Chamber of Commerce--Québec Chapter, #304, 300, rue St-Sacrement, Montréal PQ H2Y 1X4 – 514/847-2223; Fax: 514/288-9183 – Secretary, Virginie Sondermeyer
Canada-Netherlands Chamber of Commerce--Western Canada Chapter, #1007, 470 Granville St., Vancouver BC V6C 1V5 – 604/688-5017; Fax: 604/684-7194 – Contact, Herman Suttorp
Canada-Pakistan Business Council, 4329, av King Edward, Montréal PQ H4B 2H4 – 514/488-3979; Fax: 514/488-3979; Email: 75323.2252@compuserve.com – President, Werner R. Strub
Canada-Russia Business Council, #812, 330 Bay St., Toronto ON M5H 2S8 – 416/862-2821; Fax: 416/862-2820 – Executive Director, Susan Santiago
Canada-Sri Lanka Business Council, 30A Hazelton Ave., Toronto ON M5R 2E2 – 416/846-1214; Fax: 416/849-4823
Canada-United Kingdom Chamber of Commerce, 3 Regent St., London SW1 4N UK– (0171) 930-7711; Fax: (0171) 930-9703 – Executive Director, Geoffrey F. Bacon
Canadian Armenian Business Council Inc., #200, 12291, boul Laurentian, Montréal PQ H4K 1N5 – 514/333-7655; Fax: 514/333-7280 – President, Harry Markarian
Canadian Council for the Americas, 145 Richmond St. West, 3rd Fl., Toronto ON M5H 2L2 – 416/367-4313; Fax: 416/367-5460 – President, Halina Ostrovki
Canadian German Chamber of Industry & Commerce Inc., #1410, 480 University Ave., Toronto ON M5G 1V2 – 416/598-3355; Fax: 416/598-1840 – President & CEO, Uwe Harnack
Canadian German Chamber of Industry & Commerce Inc.--Montréal, #1604, 1010, rue Sherbrooke ouest, Montréal PQ H3A 2R7 – 514/844-3051; Fax: 514/844-1473
Canadian German Chamber of Industry & Commerce Inc.--Vancouver, #617, 1030 West Georgia St., Vancouver BC V6E 2Y3 – 604/681-4469; Fax: 604/681-4489
Canadian/Romanian Council of Trade & Commerce, #203, 2525 St. Laurent Blvd., Ottawa ON K1H 8P5 – 613/737-2922; Fax: 613/733-9501 – Chair, Robert De Valk
Chamber of Commerce for Belgium & Luxembourg in Canada, Tour de la Bourse, PO Box 528, Montréal PQ H4Z 1J8 – 514/845-4650 – President, Albert Van Herck
Chamber of Commerce of Spain in Canada, #832, 150 Bloor St. West, Toronto ON M5S 2X9 – 416/927-8787; Fax: 416/927-7888 – President, Ronald H. Rumble
Chambre de commerce Canada-Maroc, 390, rue Notre-Dame ouest, 5e étage, Montréal PQ H2Y 1T9
Chambre de commerce Canado-Tunisienne, #312, 5255, boul Henri-Bourassa ouest, St-Laurent PQ H4R 1K4 – Adel Berrais
Chambre de commerce française du Canada, 360, rue Saint-Francois-Xavier, Montréal PQ H2Y 2S8 – 514/281-1246; Fax: 514/289-9594 – Président, Pierre Lapointe
Chambre de commerce française du Canada--Ontario, #406, 347 Bay St., Toronto ON M5H 2R7 – 416/777-9658; Fax: 416/777-9659 – Président, Michel Finance
Chambre de Commerce Lao du Canada, #2, 6420, rue Victoria, Montréal PQ H3W 2S7

Chambre de Commerce Maroc-Canada, #203, Hotel Holiday Inn, Rond Point Hassan II, Casablanca Morocco – 011/212-2-29-50-31; Fax: 011/212-2-29-50-28 – Présidente, Madame Fikrai Berrada Mandri
Chambre de commerce sud-africaine à Montréal, 770, rue Sherbrooke ouest, 13e étage, Montréal PQ H3A 1G1 – Directeur, Charles Bédard
Conseil d'affaires tchèque du Québec, 8480, boul St-Laurent, Montréal PQ H2P 2M6 – Directrice exécutive, Dora Romano
Danish Canadian Chamber of Commerce, #403, 15 Wertheim Court, Richmond Hill ON L4B 3H7 – 905/882-9901; Fax: 905/882-5472 – Vice-Chairman, Secretary, Knud Westergaard
The Estonian-Canadian Chamber of Commerce, 958 Broadview Ave., Toronto ON M4K 2R6 – 416/606-3825; Fax: 416/461-0448; Email: estcancofc@neocom.ca
International Chamber of Commerce, 38, Cours Albert 1er, Paris F-7 008 France – (33 1) 49 53 28 28; Fax: (33 1) 42 25 86 63; Telex: 650770F; Email: icclib@ibnet.com – Contact, J.C. Rouher
Ireland-Canada Chamber of Commerce, #1600, 2020, rue University, Montréal PQ H3A 2A5 – 514/288-5705; Fax: 514/288-6629 – President, Helen Carrigy-McCaffrey
Italian Chamber of Commerce in Canada, #680, 550, rue Sherbrooke ouest, Montréal PQ H3A 1B9 – 514/844-4249; Fax: 514/844-4875; Toll Free: 1-800-263-4372 – President, Aldo Pier Federici
Italian Chamber of Commerce of Toronto, #306, 901 Lawrence Ave. West, Toronto ON M6A 1C3 – 416/789-7169; Fax: 416/789-7160 – Managing Director, C. Valeri
Scandinavian Canadian Chamber of Commerce, #822, 602 West Hastings St., Vancouver BC V6B 1P2 – 604/669-4428; Fax: 604/669-4420 – Executive Director, Peter Nielsen
The Swedish-Canadian Chamber of Commerce, #1504, 2 Bloor St. West, Toronto ON M4W 3E2 – 416/925-8661; Fax: 416/929-8639 – General Manager, Jeanette Kristensson
Swiss Canadian Chamber of Commerce (Montréal) Inc., 1572, av Dr. Penfield, Montréal PQ H3G 1C4 – 514/937-5822
Swiss Canadian Chamber of Commerce (Ontario) Inc., 6795 Steeles Ave. West, Etobicoke ON M9V 4R9 – 416/741-2256; Fax: 416/741-0140 – Executive Officer, A. Mettler

CANADIAN BOARDS OF TRADE & CHAMBERS OF COMMERCE
The Canadian Chamber of Commerce, #1160, 55 Metcalfe St., Ottawa ON K1P 6N4 – 613/238-4000; Fax: 613/238-7643 – National President, Timothy Reid
The Canadian Chamber of Commerce--Québec Regional Office, #1430, 1080, Côte du Beaver Hall, Montréal PQ H2Z 1T2 – 514/866-4334; Fax: 514/866-7296
The Canadian Chamber of Commerce--Toronto Office, Heritage Bldg., BCE Place, Box 818, 181 Bay St., Toronto ON M5J 2T3 – 416/868-6415; Fax: 416/868-0189
Canadian Junior Chamber, #303, 3100 Steeles Ave. East, Markham ON L3R 8T3 – 905/948-0048; Fax: 905/948-0047 – President, Colleen Neil
Chamber of Maritime Commerce, #704A, 350 Sparks St., Ottawa ON K1R 7S8 – 613/233-8779; Fax: 613/232-6211 – President, J.D. Smith
Jeune chambre de commerce de Montréal, #509, 625, av du Président-Kennedy, Montréal PQ H3A 1K2 – 514/845-4951; Fax: 514/845-0587 – Directrice générale, Annemarie Dubost
Northwestern Ontario Associated Chambers of Commerce, 857 North May St., Thunder Bay ON P7C 3S2 – 807/622-9642; Fax: 807/622-7752 – President, Dick McKenzie

PROVINCIAL & TERRITORIAL BOARDS OF TRADE & CHAMBERS OF COMMERCE
Alberta Chamber of Commerce, Edmonton Centre, #2105, TD Tower, Edmonton AB T5J 2Z1 – 403/425-4180; Fax: 403/429-1061; Toll Free: 1-800-272-8854 – Executive Director, Norman S. Leach, CAE
Atlantic Provinces Chamber of Commerce, #110, 236 George St., Moncton NB E1C 1W1 – 506/857-3980; Fax: 506/859-6131 – President & CEO, Paul J. Daigle
British Columbia Chamber of Commerce, #1607, 700 West Pender St., Vancouver BC V6C 1G8 – 604/683-0700; Fax: 604/683-0416 – Executive Director, E.A. George
Chambre de Commerce du Québec, #3030, 500, place d'Armes, Montréal PQ H2Y 2W2 – 514/844-9571; Fax: 514/844-0226; URL: http://www.ccq.ca – Président, Michel Audet
Manitoba Chamber of Commerce, #167, 167 Lombard Ave. East, Winnipeg MB R3B 0V6 – 204/942-2561; Fax: 204/942-2227 – Executive Vice-President, Lance A. Norman
Ontario Chamber of Commerce, #808, 2345 Yonge St., Toronto ON M4P 2E5 – 416/482-5222; Fax: 416/482-5879 – Executive Director, James Carnegie
Saskatchewan Chamber of Commerce, Chateau Tower, #1630, 1920 Broad St., Regina SK S4P 3V2 – 306/352-2671; Fax: 306/781-7084 – Executive Director, Mary Ann McFadyen
Yukon Chamber of Commerce, #201, 208 Main St., Whitehorse YT Y1A 2A9 – 403/667-2000; Fax: 403/667-4507; Toll Free: 1-800-661-0500 – President, Archie Graham

BY PROVINCE & TERRITORY

ALBERTA
Airdrie CC, PO Box 3661, AB T4B 2B8 – 403/948-4412; Fax: 403/948-3141 – Executive Director, Jan Peterson
Alix CC, PO Box 145, AB T0C 0B0 – 403/747-2269 – President, Connie Barritt
Athabasca & District CC, 4913B - 49 St., AB T9S 1C5 – 403/675-3999; Fax: 403/675-3038 – President, Doug Hardy, 403/698-2608
Barrhead & District CC, PO Box 4524, AB T7N 1A4 – 403/674-2338; Fax: 403/674-5648 – Executive Director, Sonny Rajoo
Bassano & District CC, PO Box 849, AB T0J 0B0 – 403/641-3512 – President, George Longmuir
Beaumont & District CC, PO Box 3026, AB T4X 1K8 – 403/929-8000; Fax: 403/929-2547 – President, Greg Bowen, 403/446-8061
Beaverlodge & District CC, PO Box 303, AB T0H 0C0 – 403/354-8785; Fax: 403/354-2101 – President, Doug Thiessen
Beiseker CC, PO Box 277, AB T0M 0G0 – 403/947-2912; Fax: 403/947-2428 – President, Derilynn Woldan
Bentley CC, PO Box 777, AB T0C 0J0 – 403/748-4411 – President, Pat Jorgensen
Berwyn & District CC, PO Box 144, AB T0H 0E0 – 403/338-3668 – President, Gail Sandboe, 403/338-3848
Blackfalds CC, PO Box 249, AB T0M 0J0 – 403/885-5886; Fax: 403/885-2655 – President, Stan Piebiak
Bluffton & District CC, PO Box 38, AB T0C 0M0 – 403/843-3583; Fax: 403/843-3392 – President, Helen Karlstrom
Bon Accord & District CC, PO Box 688, AB T0A 0K0 – Fax: 403/921-2424 – President, Marcel Hachey
Bonnyville & District CC, PO Box 6054, AB T9N 2G7 – 403/826-3252; Fax: 403/826-4525 – President, Guy Demers, 403/826-3611

BOARDS OF TRADE & CHAMBERS OF COMMERCE 7-25

Bow Island/Burdett & District CC, PO Box 569, AB T0K 0G0 – 403/545-2939; Fax: 403/545-2574 – President, Dale Wheeler, 403/545-2363

Bowden & District CC, PO Box 629, AB T0M 0K0 – 403/224-3332; Fax: 403/224-2432 – President, Ralph Beggs

Boyle & District CC, PO Box 496, AB T0A 0M0 – 403/689-2128 – President, Barry Sawka

Bragg Creek CC, PO Box 216, AB T0L 0K0 – 403/949-3220; Fax: 403/949-3254 – President, Walter Cross

Breton & District CC, PO Box 243, AB T0C 0P0 – 403/696-3557; Fax: 403/696-3797 – President, Neil Durrant

Brooks & District CC, PO Box 400, AB T1R 1B4 – 403/362-7641; Fax: 403/362-6893 – President, Norm Gerestein, 403/362-3300

Bruderheim & District CC, PO Box 512, AB T0B 0S0 – President, Carol Adamkewicz, 403/998-2121

Calgary CC, 517 Centre St. South, AB T2G 2C4 – 403/750-0400; Fax: 403/266-3413 – President, Peter Wallis

Calmar & District CC, PO Box 392, AB T0C 0V0 – 403/985-3112 – President, Phyllis McGhan, 403/985-2500

Camrose CC, 5402 - 48 Ave., AB T4V 0J7 – 403/672-4217; Fax: 403/672-1059 – Executive Director, Pat Twomey

Canmore/Kananskis CC, PO Box 1178, AB T0L 0M0 – 403/678-4094; Fax: 403/678-3455 – President, Aly Tomkinson, 403/678-3377

Cardston & District CC, PO Box 1391, AB T0K 0K0 – 403/653-2633 – President, Sharon Quinton, 403/653-4466

Caroline & District CC, PO Box 90, AB T0M 0M0 – 403/722-4066; Fax: 403/722-4066 – President, Leonard Hemphill

Cereal & District BT, PO Box 131, AB T0J 0N0 – 403/326-3817; Fax: 403/326-3817 – President, Mary Waterhouse

Coaldale CC, PO Box 1117, AB T1M 1M9 – 403/345-2358; Fax: 403/345-5888 – Executive Director, Leonard Fast

Cochrane & District CC, PO Box 1416, AB T0L 0W0 – 403/932-6810; Fax: 403/932-4569 – President, Hank Biesbroek

Cold Lake-Grand Centre CC, PO Box 454, AB T0A 1T0 – 403/594-4747; Fax: 403/594-3711 – Office Administrator, Netta Farrow

Coronation & District CC, PO Box 960, AB T0C 1C0 – 403/578-2422; Fax: 403/578-3020 – President, Barry Clampitt, 403/578-3695

Cremona Watervalley & District CC, PO Box 356, AB T0M 0R0 – 403/637-3752; Fax: 403/637-3900 – President, Evelyn Lashmar

Crowsnest Pass CC, PO Box 706, Blairmore AB T0K 0E0 – 403/562-2813; Fax: 403/562-2815 – President, Ken Sorensen

Devon & District CC, PO Box 837, AB T0C 1E0 – 403/987-5177; Fax: 403/987-2220 – President, Gary Thomson, 403/420-6850

Diamond Valley CC, PO Box 61, Turner Valley AB T0L 2A0 – 403/933-4954; Fax: 403/933-4360 – President, Dick Graham

Drayton Valley & District CC, PO Box 5318, AB T7A 1R5 – 403/542-7578; Fax: 403/542-9211 – Executive Director, Karen Kirkwood

Drumheller Regional Chamber of Development & Tourism, PO Box 999, AB T0J 0Y0 – 403/823-8100; Fax: 403/823-4469 – General Manager, Cory Campbell

Eckville & District CC, PO Box 609, AB T0M 0X0 – 403/746-2231; Fax: 403/746-2005 – President, Gordon Ebden

Edgerton & District CC, PO Box 303, AB T0B 1K0 – 403/755-3933 – President, Don Sparks, 403/755-3865

Edmonton CC, #600, 10123 - 99 St., AB T5J 3G9 – 403/426-4620; Fax: 403/424-7946; URL: http://www.tnc.com/ecc/ – Chairman, Janet Riopel

Edson & District CC, 5433 - 3 Ave., AB T7E 1L5 – 403/723-4918; Fax: 403/723-5545 – President, Fiona Fowler-Cleary

Elk Point CC, PO Box 309, AB T0A 1A0 – 403/724-3926; Fax: 403/724-4211 – President, Victor Stepa

Evansburg & Entwistle CC, PO Box 598, AB T0E 0T0 – 403/727-2757; Fax: 403/727-3526 – President, Carol Cardinal

Fairview & District CC, PO Box 1034, AB T0H 1L0 – 403/835-3483; Fax: 403/835-3483 – President, Jim Backus

Falher CC, PO Box 814, AB T0H 1M0 – 403/837-2364; Fax: 403/837-2647 – Sec./Manager, Cindy Levesque

Foremost & District CC, PO Box 272, AB T0K 0X0 – 403/867-2174 – Vice-President, P. Reyner

Fort MacLeod & District CC, PO Box 757, AB T0L 0Z0 – 403/553-4484; Fax: 403/553-3444 – President, George Gaschler

Fort McMurray CC, 200 Professional Bldg., 9908 Franklin Ave., AB T9H 2K5 – 403/743-3100; Fax: 403/790-9757; URL: http://www.tnc.com/tncn/fmcc/index.html – Executive Director, Carolyn Baikie

Fort Saskatchewan CC, 10030 - 99 Ave., PO Box 3072, AB T8L 2T1 – 403/998-4355; Fax: 403/998-1515 – Executive Director, Brygeda Renk

Fort Vermilion & Area BT, PO Box 456, AB T0H 1N0 – 403/927-4563 – President, Martin Braat

Fox Creek CC, PO Box 774, AB T0H 1P0 – 403/622-3821; Fax: 403/622-2878 – President, Vaugh Nelson, 403/622-3600

Gibbons & District CC, PO Box 38, AB T0A 1N0 – 403/923-2129; Fax: 403/923-3826 – President, Louis Jones

Girouxville CC, PO Box 57, AB T0H 1S0 – 403/323-3090; Fax: 403/323-4110 – President, Norm Doucette

Grande Cache CC, PO Box 1342, AB T0E 0Y0 – 403/827-2487; Fax: 403/827-5698 – President, Mary Stephenson

Grande Prairie & District CC, 10011 - 103 Ave., AB T8V 1B9 – 403/532-5340; Fax: 403/532-2926 – Executive Director, Trenton Parrott

Hanna CC, PO Box 2248, AB T0J 1P0 – 403/854-4659; Fax: 403/854-4917 – President, Adrian Mohl, 403/854-4659

High Level & District CC, PO Box 202, AB T0H 1Z0 – 403/926-2470; Fax: 403/926-4017 – Executive Director, Jason Sabatier

High Prairie & District CC, PO Box 519, AB T0G 1E0 – 403/523-3505; Fax: 403/523-4810 – President, Judy Shybunia, 403/523-2222

High River CC, PO Box 5244, AB T1V 1M4 – 403/652-3336; Fax: 403/652-7660 – Executive Director, Susan Cooper

Hinton & District CC, 309 Gregg Ave., AB T7V 1X3 – 403/865-2777; Fax: 403/865-1062 – Manager, Cyndy Mork

Innisfail CC, PO Box 6031, AB T4G 1S7 – 403/227-1177; Fax: 403/227-6749 – Manager, Susan Rombs

Jasper Park CC, 632 Connaught Dr., PO Box 98, AB T0B 1E0 – 403/852-3858; Fax: 403/852-4932 – General Manager, Brian Rode

Killam & District CC, PO Box 272, AB T0B 2L0 – 403/385-3949; Fax: 403/385-2129 – President, Terry Hamilton

La Crete CC, PO Box 1088, AB T0H 2H0 – 403/928-3771; Fax: 403/928-3875 – President, Jake Fehr

Lac La Biche CC, PO Box 804, AB T0A 2C0 – 403/623-2818; Fax: 403/623-3510 – Executive Director, Russ Ledger

Lacombe & District CC, 5036 - 51 St., AB T4L 1W2 – 403/782-4300; Fax: 403/782-4302 – Manager, Michelle Penhale

Leduc & District CC, 6420 - 50 St., AB T9E 7K9 – 403/986-5454; Fax: 403/986-8108; Email: commerce@tnc.com; URL: http://www.tnc.com/commerce – President, Murray Hales

Legal & District CC, PO Box 240, AB T0G 1L0 – 403/961-3820 – President, Walter Van De Walle

Lethbridge CC, #200, 529 - 6 St. South, AB T1J 2E1 – 403/327-1586; Fax: 403/327-1001 – General Manager, Jody Nilsson

Lloydminster CC, 4420 - 50 Ave., AB T9V 0W2 – 403/875-9013; Fax: 403/875-0755 – President, Elmer Nykiforuk

Mallaig CC, PO Box 144, AB T0A 2K0 – 403/635-3849; Fax: 403/635-2219 – President, Edouard Amyotte

Manning & District BT, PO Box 130, AB T0H 2M0 – 403/836-2033 – President, Beverly Kleinschroth

Mannville & District CC, PO Box 54, AB T0B 2W0 – 403/763-3800; Fax: 403/763-2110 – Executive Director, Ev Maron

Marwayne & District CC, PO Box 183, AB T0B 2X0 – President, Perry Lewis, 403/847-8190

Mayerthorpe CC, PO Box 1279, AB T0E 1N0 – 403/786-2416; Fax: 403/786-2780 – President, Doug McDermid, 403/786-2535

McLennan CC, PO Box 90, AB T0H 2L0 – 403/324-2283; Fax: 403/324-3932 – President, Darlene Bruneau

Medicine Hat & District CC, 413 - 6th Ave. SE, AB T1A 2S7 – 403/527-5214; Fax: 403/527-5182 – General Manager, Craig Couillard

Millet & District CC, PO Box 389, AB T0C 1Z0 – 403/387-4571; Fax: 403/387-5588 – President, Joe Greenwood

Morinville & District CC, PO Box 3130, AB T8R 1S1 – 403/939-2885; Fax: 403/939-4378 – President, Greg Foster, 403/939-4217

Nanton & District CC, PO Box 711, AB T0L 1R0 – 403/646-2736; Fax: 403/646-5554 – President, Marion Scott

Okotoks & District CC, PO Box 1053, AB T0L 1T0 – 403/938-2848; Fax: 403/938-5441 – President, Wes Budd, 403/938-2008

Olds & District CC, PO Box 4210, AB T4H 1P8 – 403/556-7070; Fax: 403/556-1515 – President, Allan Entwhistle, 403/556-7827

Onoway & District CC, PO Box 723, AB T0E 1V0 – 403/962-4950; Fax: 403/962-8019 – President, Janet Langman

Oyen & District CC, PO Box 420, AB T0J 2J0 – 403/664-3622; Fax: 403/664-3622 – President, Betty Lynn-Woods, 403/664-2664

Peace River BT, PO Box 6599, AB T8S 1S4 – 403/624-4166; Fax: 403/624-4663 – Manager, Tommie O'Neale

Picture Butte & District CC, PO Box 540, AB T0K 1V0 – 403/732-4623; Fax: 403/732-4703 – President, Jon Stevens

Pincher Creek & District CC, PO Box 2287, AB T0K 1W0 – 403/627-5199; Fax: 403/627-5850 – Executive Director, Alastair Maclean

Ponoka & District CC, PO Box 4188, AB T4J 1R6 – 403/783-3888; Fax: 403/783-3434 – President, Linda Steinmann

Provost & District CC, PO Box 637, AB T0B 3S0 – 403/753-6868; Fax: 403/753-3020 – President, George Meikleyohn

Rainbow Lake CC, PO Box 273, AB T0H 2Y0 – 403/956-3123; Fax: 403/956-3649 – President Elect, Dale Lederer

Red Deer CC, 3017 - 50th Ave., AB T4N 5Y6 – 403/347-4491; Fax: 403/343-6188 – Executive Director, Pat Henry

Redwater & District CC, PO Box 322, AB T0A 2W0 – President, Brian Burnstead

Rimbey CC, PO Box 87, AB T0C 2J0 – 403/843-4445 – President, Laverne Obernamer

Rocky Mountain House & District CC, PO Box 1374, AB T0M 1T0 – 403/845-5450; Fax: 403/845-7764 – Manager, Cheryl Munro

St. Albert CC, 71 St. Albert Rd., St Albert AB T8N 6L5 – 403/458-2833; Fax: 403/458-6515 – Executive Director, Natalie Zigarlick

---

* BT - Board of Trade; BC - Bureau de commerce; CC - Chamber of Commerce/Chambre de commerce

Canadian Almanac & Directory 1997

St. Paul & District CC, 4537 - 50 Ave., PO Box 887, AB T0A 3A0 – 403/645-6800; Fax: 403/645-6059 – Executive Director, Paul Pelletier

Sedgewick CC, PO Box 625, AB T0B 4C0 – 403/384-3636 – President, Chris Forster

Sexsmith CC, AB T0H 3C0 – 403/568-4031; Fax: 403/568-2833 – President, Linda Sodergren

Sherwood Park & District CC, PO Box 3103, AB T8A 2A6 – 403/464-0801; Fax: 403/449-3581 – President, Al Peterson

Slave Lake & District CC, PO Box 190, AB T0G 2A0 – 403/849-3222; Fax: 403/849-5977 – President, Ken Giblin

Spirit River & District CC, PO Box 930, AB T0H 3G0 – 403/864-3600 – Treasurer, Shenda Janis

Spruce Grove & District CC, PO Box 4210, AB T7X 3B4 – 403/962-0626; Fax: 403/962-4417; Email: sgcc@tnc.com; URL: http://www.tnc.com/sgcc – Sec./Manager, Pam Brace

Stettler & District CC, PO Box 58, AB T0C 2L0 – 403/742-3924; Fax: 403/742-3123 – President, Randall Loveseth

Stony Plain & District CC, PO Box 2300, AB T7Z 1X7 – 403/963-4545; Fax: 403/963-4542 – Manager, Sharon Dumont

Strathmore CC, PO Box 2222, AB T1P 1K2 – 403/640-3220; Fax: 403/934-3268 – President, Rick Rabb, 403/934-2528

Sundre CC, PO Box 1085, AB T0M 1X0 – 403/638-4749; Fax: 403/638-3733 – President, Dan Church

Swan Hills CC, PO Box 540, AB T0G 2C0 – 403/333-2224; Fax: 403/333-7115 – Manager, Jean McKeever

Sylvan Lake CC, PO Box 9003, AB T4S 1S6 – 403/887-5050; Fax: 403/887-4944 – President, Dave Stinson

Taber & District CC, 4702 - 50 St., AB T1G 2B6 – 403/223-2265; Fax: 403/223-2291 – President, Dennis Bryant

Thorhild CC, PO Box 384, AB T0A 3J0 – President, Wayne Lannon, 403/398-3550

Tofield CC, General Delivery, AB T0B 4J0 – 403/662-3993; Fax: 403/662-3993 – President, Rob Gillrie

Valleyview CC, PO Box 1020, AB T0H 3N0 – 403/524-3904 – President, Mina Peterson, 403/524-4552

Vegreville & District CC, 4829 - 50 St., PO Box 877, AB T9C 1R9 – 403/632-2771; Fax: 403/632-6958 – President, Bill Boyd

Vermilion & District CC, 5011 - 50 Ave., AB T9X 1A7 – 403/853-6593; Fax: 403/853-1740; Email: townvrml@agt.net; URL: http://www.agt.net/public/townvrml/index.htm – Manager, Margaret Holt

Vulcan & District CC, PO Box 1161, AB T0L 2B0 – 403/485-2996; Fax: 403/485-2878 – President, Lynda Joyce

Wainwright & District CC, PO Box 2997, AB T9W 1S9 – 403/842-4910; Fax: 403/842-2898 – President, Doug Morgan, 403/842-3145

Westlock & District CC, PO Box 2288, AB T0G 2L0 – 403/349-4444; Fax: 403/349-5551 – President, Deborah Stasiuk, 403/349-5900

Wetaskiwin CC, 4910 - 55A St., AB T9A 2R7 – 403/352-4636; Fax: 403/352-4640; Toll Free: 1-800-989-6899; Email: wcedt@ccinet.ab.ca – CEO, Bob Jeffery

Whitecourt & District CC, PO Box 1011, AB T7S 1N9 – 403/778-5363; Fax: 403/778-2351 – Executive Director, Irma Edgell

Willow Creek CC, PO Box 2211, Claresholm AB T0L 0T0 – 403/625-4427; Fax: 403/625-3229 – President, Floyd Cook, 403/625-4427

BRITISH COLUMBIA

Abbotsford CC, 2462 McCallum Rd., BC V2S 3P9 – 604/859-9651; Fax: 604/850-6880 – Manager, Leona Klingspon

Alberni Valley CC, RR#2, Site 215, C-10, BC V9Y 7L6 – 250/724-6535; Fax: 250/724-6560 – Manager, Elverna Baker

Armstrong-Spallumcheen CC, PO Box 118, BC V0E 1B0 – 250/546-8155; Fax: 250/546-8868 – Manager, Kristen Dahl

Ashcroft & District CC, PO Box 183, BC V0K 1H0 – 250/453-2642 – Secretary, Sandra Bennett

Atlin BT, PO Box 106, BC V0W 1A0 – President, George Holman

Bamfield CC, PO Box 5, BC V0R 1B0 – 250/728-3006 – President, David Payne

Barriere CC, PO Box 1190, BC V0E 1E0 – 250/672-0007; Fax: 250/672-5111 – President, Laura Christiansen

Bella Coola District BT, PO Box 371, BC V0T 1C0 – 250/799-5349; Fax: 250/799-5450 – President, Doug Pelton

Bowen Island CC, PO Box 102, BC V0N 1G0 – 604/947-2838 – President, Robert Wiltshire

Burnaby CC, #149, 9855 Austin Ave., BC V3J 1N4 – 604/421-0084; Fax: 604/421-3630; URL: http://www.bendtech.com/communities/burnaby-cofc.html – Manager, Abby Anderson

Burns Lake & District CC, PO Box 339, BC V0J 1K0 – 250/692-3773; Fax: 250/692-3493 – Manager, Susan Schienbein

Cache Creek CC, PO Box 460, BC V0K 1H0 – 250/457-9566; Fax: 250/457-9192

Campbell River & District CC, 1235 Shoppers Row, PO Box 400, BC V9W 5B6 – 250/287-4636; Fax: 250/286-6490 – Manager, Heather Pate

Castlegar & District CC, 1995 - 6 Ave., BC V1N 4B7 – 250/365-6313; Fax: 250/365-5778; Email: cacoc@knet.kootenay.net – Manager, Marlene Kruecki

Central Coast CC, PO Box 40, Bella Bella BC V0T 1C0 – 250/957-2609 – President, Tracy MacDonald

Chase & District CC, PO Box 592, BC V0E 1M0 – 250/679-8432; Fax: 250/679-3120 – Manager, Eileen McKinnon

Chemainus & District CC, PO Box 1311, BC V0R 1K0 – 250/246-3944; Fax: 250/246-3251 – Manager, Marsia Robinson

Chetwynd & District CC, 5217 North Access Rd., PO Box 1000, BC V0C 1J0 – 250/788-3345; Fax: 250/788-7843 – Manager, Valerie Simpson Bulmer

Chilliwack CC, 44150 Luckakuck Way, RR#1, BC V2R 4A7 – 604/858-8121; Fax: 604/858-0157; Toll Free: 1-800-567-9535 – Executive Director, Brenda Dehn

Christina Lake CC, Hwy. 3 & Kimura Rd., BC V0H 1E2 – 250/447-6161; Fax: 250/447-6161 – President, Valerie Sampson

Clearwater & District CC, RR#1, PO Box 1988, BC V0E 1N0 – 250/674-2646; Fax: 250/674-3693 – Manager, Marie Cornell

Clinton & District CC, PO Box 256, BC V0K 1K0 – 250/459-2661 – President, Ken Poulsen

Cloverdale BT, #106, 17564 - 56A Ave., PO Box 505, BC V3S 1G3 – 604/574-7344 – President, Anne Maguire Sharkey

Columbia Valley CC, PO Box 1019, Invermere BC V0A 1K0 – 250/342-2844; Fax: 250/342-3261; Email: columbia.valley.chamber@rockies.net – Office Manager, Bev Fraser

Comox Valley CC, 2040 Cliffe Ave., Courtenay BC V9N 2L3 – 250/334-3234; Fax: 250/334-4908; Email: chmbr@mars.ark.com; URL: http://www.ark.com/valley/chamber.html – Manager, Barry Wood

CC Serving Coquitlam, Port Coquitlam, Port Moody, #3, 1180 Pinetree Way, BC V3B 7L2 – 604/464-2716; Fax: 604/464-6796 – Manager, Elizabeth Voigt

Cranbrook CC, 2279 Cranbrook St. North, PO Box 84, BC V1C 4H6 – 250/426-5914; Fax: 250/426-3873; Email: cbkchamber@cyberlink.bc.ca; URL: http://www.cyberlink.bc.ca/chamber/cranbrook/index.html – President, Dorothy Nada

Creston CC, 1711 Canyon St., PO Box 268, BC V0B 1G0 – 250/428-4342; Fax: 250/428-9411 – Manager, Adele Miller

Cumberland CC, PO Box 74, BC V0R 1S0 – 250/336-8313; Fax: 250/336-2455 – Manager, Kathy Horsley

Dawson Creek & District CC, 10110 - 13th St., BC V1G 3W2 – 250/782-4868; Fax: 250/782-2371 – Manager, Bill Yerbury

Dease Lake & Tahltan CC, PO Box 338, BC V0C 1L0 – 250/771-3900; Fax: 250/771-3702 – Manager, Stu Pike

Delta CC, 6201 - 60 Ave., BC V4K 4E2 – 604/946-4232; Fax: 604/946-5285 – Manager, Sarah Gardner

Duncan-Cowichan CC, 381 Trans-Canada Hwy., BC V9L 3R5 – 250/746-4636; Fax: 250/746-8222 – Manager, Diane Colman

Elkford CC, 4A Front St., PO Box 220, BC V0B 1H0 – 250/865-4614; Fax: 250/865-2442 – President, Corinne Burns

Enderby & District CC, 619 Cliff Ave., PO Box 1000, BC V0E 1V0 – 250/838-6727; Fax: 250/838-0123; Email: chamber@resonet.com – Manager, Maureen Bressler

Esquimalt CC, 1153 Esquimalt Rd., PO Box 36019, Victoria BC V9A 7J5 – 250/384-3228; Fax: 250/384-5772 – President, Mark Eraut

Falkland CC, PO Box 92, BC V0E 1W0 – 250/379-2240; Fax: 250/379-2242 – President, Lynn Smart

Fernie CC, Hwy. 3 & Dicken Rd., BC V0B 1M0 – 250/423-6868; Fax: 250/423-3811 – Manager, David Keiver

Fort Fraser CC, General Delivery, BC V0J 1N0 – 250/690-7477 – President, Gilbert Sholty

Fort Langley & District CC, 9167 Glover Rd., BC V1M 2R4 – 604/888-1477; Fax: 604/888-2657 – Manager, Carollyne Haynes

Fort Nelson CC, PO Box 196, BC V0X 1R0 – 250/774-2956; Fax: 250/774-2958 – Executive Director, Mame Wevers

Fort St. John & District CC, 9323 - 100 St., BC V1J 4N4 – 250/785-6037; Fax: 250/785-7181 – Executive Director, Trudy Eklund

Fort St. James CC, PO Box 1164, Fort St James BC V0J 1P0 – 250/996-7023; Fax: 250/996-7047 – Manager, Linda Baird

Fraser Lake CC, PO Box 1059, BC V0J 1S0 – 250/699-8643 – President, Vickie Hiatt

Gabriola CC, PO Box 249, Gabriola Island BC V0R 1X0 – 250/247-9332; Fax: 250/247-9332 – Secretary, Lorraine Pickett

Gibsons & District CC, 417 Marine Dr., PO Box 1190, BC V0N 1V0 – 604/886-2325; Fax: 604/886-2379 – Manager, Emily Perry

Gold River CC, PO Box 39, BC V0P 1G0 – 250/283-2647; Fax: 250/283-2647 – Secretary, Elaine Roberts

Golden & District CC, Hwy. 95 South, PO Box 1320, BC V0A 1H0 – 250/344-7125; Fax: 250/344-6688 – Manager, Sandra Ross

Grand Forks CC, 7362 Fifth St., PO Box 1086, BC V0H 1H0 – 250/442-2833; Fax: 250/442-5688 – Manager, Sandy Elzinga

Greenwood & District BT, 278 Copper St., PO Box 430, BC V0H 1J0 – 250/445-6323; Fax: 250/445-6166 – Manager, Janet Midwinter

Harrison Hot Springs CC, PO Box 255, BC V0M 1K0 – 604/796-3425; Fax: 604/769-3188 – Manager, Laurie Ann Rolston

The Hazeltons & District CC, PO Box 1, New Hazelton BC V0J 2J0 – 250/842-6006; Fax: 250/842-6340 – President, Colin Smith

Hope & District CC, 919 Water St., PO Box 370, BC V0X 1L0 – 604/869-2021; Fax: 604/869-2160 – Manager, Inge Wilson

Houston & District CC, 3289 Hwy. 16, PO Box 396, BC V0J 1Z0 – 250/845-7640; Fax: 250/845-3682 – Manager, Diane Smith

Hudson's Hope CC, c/o District Office, PO Box 330, BC V0C 1V0 – Manager, Faye Lavallee

Juan de Fuca CC, 697 Goldstream Ave., Victoria BC V9B 2X2 – 250/478-1130; Fax: 250/478-1584 – Manager, Brady Reaume

BOARDS OF TRADE & CHAMBERS OF COMMERCE

Greater Kamloops CC, 1290 Trans Canada Hwy. West, BC V2C 6R3 – 250/372-7722; Fax: 250/828-9500 – Manager, Maureen Freeman

Kaslo CC, PO Box 329, BC V0G 1M0 – 250/353-7323; Fax: 250/353-7353 – President, Jim Embery

Kelowna CC, 544 Harvey Ave., BC V1Y 6C9 – 250/861-1515; Fax: 250/861-3624; Toll Free: 1-800-663-4345 – Manager, Bonnie Bates Gibbs

Keremeos & District CC, PO Box 490, BC V0X 1N0 – 250/499-8027; Fax: 250/499-2252 – Manager, Marcelle Lyttle

Kimberley Bavarian Society CC, 350 Ross St., BC V1A 2Z9 – 250/427-3666; Fax: 250/427-5378 – Manager, Hazel Liebscher

Kitimat CC, PO Box 214, BC V8C 2G7 – 250/632-6294; Fax: 250/632-4685 – Manager, Gail Guise

Kitsilano CC, PO Box 34369, Stn D, Vancouver BC V6J 4P3 – 604/731-4454 – President, Patricia Tracy

Kootenay Lake CC, PO Box 4, Gray Creek BC V0B 1S0 – 250/227-9267

Ladysmith CC, PO Box 598, BC V0R 2E0 – 250/245-2112; Fax: 250/245-7641 – President, Rob Johnson

Cowichan Lake District CC, PO Box 824, Lake Cowichan BC V0R 2G0 – 250/749-3244; Fax: 250/749-0187; Email: slind@islandnet.com – President, Pat Foster

Langley CC, 20420 Fraser Hwy., BC V3A 4G2 – 604/530-6656; Fax: 604/530-7066 – Manager, Lynn Whitehouse

Lillooet & District CC, 463 Russell St., PO Box 650, BC V0K 1V0 – 250/256-4364; Fax: 250/256-7262 – Manager, Helen Breault

Logan Lake CC, PO Box 1090, BC V0K 1W0 – 250/523-9525; Fax: 250/523-9670 – President, Wayne Bellwood

Lumby & District CC, PO Box 534, BC V0E 2G0 – 250/547-2300; Fax: 250/547-2300 – Manager, Lorrie Pelletier

Lytton & District CC, 400 Fraser St., PO Box 460, BC V0K 1Z0 – 250/455-2523; Fax: 250/455-6669 – Manager, Peggy Chute

Mackenzie CC, PO Box 880, MacKenzie BC V0J 2C0 – 250/997-5459; Fax: 250/997-6117 – Manager, Margaret Grant

Pender Harbour & Egmont CC, PO Box 265, Madeira Park BC V0N 2H0 – 604/883-2561; Fax: 604/883-2561 – Secretary, Michael C. Crowe

Maple Ridge CC, 22238 Lougheed Hwy., BC V2X 2T2 – 604/463-3366; Fax: 604/463-3201 – Manager, Helen Secco

Mayne Island Community CC, c/o The Oceanwood Country Inn, 630 Dinner Bay Rd., BC V0N 2J0 – 250/539-5074 – President, Jonathan Chilvers

McBride & District CC, PO Box 2, BC V0J 2E0 – 250/569-3340; Fax: 250/569-3394 – President, Robert Prentice

Merritt & District CC, PO Box 1649, BC V0K 2B0 – 250/378-5634; Fax: 250/378-6561 – Manager, Henny Stonehouse

Mission Regional CC, 34033 Lougheed Hwy., PO Box 3340, BC V2V 4J5 – 604/826-6914; Fax: 604/826-5916 – Manager, Loretta White

Nakusp & District CC, PO Box 387, BC V0G 1R0 – 250/265-4234; Fax: 250/265-3808; Toll Free: 1-800-909-8819 – Manager, Julie Gaudet

Greater Nanaimo CC, 777 Poplar St., BC V9S 2H7 – 250/753-1191; Fax: 250/754-5186 – Executive Director, Jane Hutchins

Nelson & District CC, 225 Hall St., BC V1L 5X4 – 250/352-3433; Fax: 250/352-6355 – Manager, Howard Dirks

New Westminster CC, 333 Brunette Ave., BC V3L 3E7 – 604/521-7781; Fax: 604/521-0057 – Manager, Doug Walker

North Shuswap CC, PO Box 101, Celista BC V0E 1L0 – 250/955-2534; Fax: 250/955-2534 – Manager, Gerry Kendall

Okanagan Falls CC, PO Box 246, BC V6H 1R0 – 250/497-8800; Fax: 250/497-8822 – Secretary, Marg Desmarnais

Oliver & District CC, PO Box 460, BC V0H 1T0 – 250/498-6321; Fax: 250/498-3156 – Manager, Joan Thompson

Osoyoos CC, Hwy. 3 & Hwy. 97, PO Box 277, BC V0H 1V0 – 250/495-7142; Fax: 250/495-6161 – Manager, Karey Krein

Parksville & District CC, 1275 East Island Hwy., PO Box 99, BC V9P 2G3 – 250/248-3613; Fax: 250/248-5210 – Manager, Lou Biggemann

Pemberton CC, PO Box 370, BC V0N 1L0 – 604/894-6115; Fax: 604/932-1279 – Secretary, Judy Lemke

Penticton CC, 185 Lakeshore Dr. West, BC V2A 1B7 – 250/492-4103; Fax: 250/492-6119; Toll Free: 1-800-663-5052; URL: http://www.penticton.org – Manager, James Pearmain

Pitt Meadows CC, 12492 Harris Rd., BC V3Y 2J4 – 604/465-7820; Fax: 604/465-1106 – Manager, Norah Materi

Port Hardy & District CC, 7250 Market St., PO Box 249, BC V0N 2P0 – 250/949-7622; Fax: 250/949-6653 – Manager, Heather Overy

Port McNeill & District CC, PO Box 129, BC V0N 2R0 – 250/956-4033; Fax: 250/956-4977 – Manager, Kathleen Kinley

Port Renfrew CC, 62 Parkinson St., BC V0S 1K0 – 250/647-5443 – President, Bob Corteau

Powell River CC, 6807 Wharf St., BC V8A 1T9 – 604/485-4051; Fax: 604/485-4272; URL: http://www.coc.powell-river.bc.ca/index.html – Manager, Sharon Carpenter

Prince George CC, 770 Brunswick St., BC V2L 2C2 – 250/562-2424; Fax: 250/562-6510 – Manager, Sherry Sethen

Prince Rupert & District CC, 111 - 3rd St., BC V8J 3P6 – 250/624-2296; Fax: 250/624-6105 – Manager, Lily Stewart

Princeton & District CC, PO Box 540, BC V0X 1W0 – 250/295-3103; Fax: 250/295-3255 – Manager, Christiane Gosselin

Qualicum Beach CC, 2711 West Island Hwy., BC V9K 2C4 – 250/752-9532; Fax: 250/752-2923 – Manager, Heather Macleod

Queen Charlotte Islands CC, PO Box 38, Masset BC V0T 1M0 – 250/626-3300; Fax: 250/626-3300 – Manager, Annette Fields

Quesnel & District CC, 703 Carson Ave., BC V2J 2B6 – 250/992-8716; Fax: 250/992-9606 – Manager, Marnie Burnside

Radium Hot Springs CC, PO Box 225, BC V0A 1M0 – 250/347-9331; Fax: 250/347-6459 – Secretary, Tammie Dendy

Revelstoke CC, 204 Campbell Ave., PO Box 490, BC V0E 2S0 – 250/837-5345; Fax: 250/837-4223; Email: cocrev@mindlink.bc.ca; URL: http://www.revelstokecc.bc.ca/mountns – Manager, Adelheid Bender

Richmond CC, #150, 5890 No. 3 Rd., BC V6X 3P6 – 604/278-2822; Fax: 604/278-2972; Email: richmond@jumppoint.com; URL: http://www.rpl.richmond.bc.ca/community/chamber/index.html – General Manager, Shelley Leonhardt

Rossland CC, PO Box 1385, BC V0G 1Y0 – 250/362-5666; Fax: 250/362-5399 – Manager, Maxine Mattinson

Saanich Peninsula CC, 9768 Third St., Sidney BC V8L 3A4 – 250/656-3616; Fax: 250/656-7111; Email: saanpcoc@octonet.com; URL: http://www.octonet.com/saanpcoc – Executive Director, Gary R. MacPherson

Salmo & District CC, PO Box 400, BC V0G 1Z0 – 250/357-2596 – Manager, Heather Street

Salmon Arm & District CC, 751 Marine Park Dr. NE, PO Box 999, BC V1E 4P2 – 250/832-6247; Fax: 250/832-8382 – Manager, Rosella Hillson

Salt Spring Island CC, 127 Lower Ganges Rd., PO Box 111, Ganges BC V0S 1E0 – 250/537-4223; Fax: 250/537-4276 – Manager, Jeremy Moray

Sechelt & District CC, PO Box 360, BC V0N 3A0 – 604/885-3100; Fax: 604/885-9538 – Manager, Ann Kershaw

Seton Shalath District CC, PO Box 2067, Seton Portage BC V0N 3B0 – 250/259-8318; Fax: 250/259-8218 – President, Gordon Pawloski

South Cowichan CC, RR#1, Mill Bay BC V0R 2P0 – 250/743-3566; Fax: 250/743-5332 – Manager, June Painter

Sicamous & District CC, PO Box 346, BC V0E 2V0 – 250/836-3313; Fax: 250/836-4368 – Manager, Doreen Favel

Slocan Valley CC, PO Box 488, New Denver BC V0G 1S0 – President, Gordon Brookfield

Smithers & District CC, 1425 Main St., PO Box 2379, BC V0J 2N0 – 250/847-5072; Fax: 250/847-3337 – Manager, David Ryan

Sooke-Jordan River CC, 6697 Sooke Rd., PO Box 18, BC V0S 1N0 – 250/642-6112; Fax: 250/642-6627; URL: http://www.sookenet.com/sooke/chamber/homepage.html – Manager, Gaynor Gauthier

Sorrento District CC, PO Box 7, BC V0E 2W0 – 250/675-2454 – President, John Prencipe

South Cariboo CC, PO Box 2312, 100 Mile House BC V0K 2E0 – 250/395-5353; Fax: 250/395-4085; Email: sccofc@netshop.net; URL: http://www.netshop.net/~100mile/sccofc.html – Manager, Kathy McKenzie

Sparwood & District CC, Aspen Dr., PO Box 1448, BC V0B 2G0 – 250/425-2423; Fax: 250/425-7130; Email: sparwood.chamber@rmin.net – Manager, Brian Knox

Squamish & Howe Sound CC, PO Box 1009, BC V0N 3G0 – 604/892-9244; Fax: 604/892-2034; Email: cocsqhs@mountain_inter.net – Manager, Wendy Magee

Stewart-Hyder International CC, PO Box 306, BC V0T 1W0 – 250/636-9224; Fax: 250/636-2199 – President, Ann Burton

Summerland CC, 7519 Prairie Valley Rd., PO Box 1075, BC V0H 1Z0 – 250/494-2686; Fax: 250/494-4039 – Manager, Alan Forsdick

Surrey Regional CC, 15105A - 105 Ave., BC V3R 7G9 – 604/581-7130; Fax: 604/588-7549; URL: http://www.surreycoc.com/cip/CHAMBER.HTML – Acting Manager, Red Lucas

Tahsis CC, PO Box 278, BC V0P 1X0 – 250/934-6667; Fax: 250/934-6515 – President, A.B. Ellis

Terrace & District CC, 4511 Keith Ave., BC V8G 1K1 – 250/635-2063; Fax: 250/635-2573 – Manager, Bobbie Phillips

Tofino-Long Beach CC, PO Box 476, BC V0R 2Z0 – 250/725-3414; Fax: 250/725-3296 – Manager, Nikki Lane

Trail District CC, 843 Rossland Ave., BC V1R 4S8 – 250/368-3144; Fax: 250/368-6427 – Manager, Michele Cherot

District of Tumbler Ridge CC, PO Box 606, BC V0C 2W0 – 250/242-4702; Fax: 250/242-5159 – Manager, April Moi

Ucluelet CC, PO Box 428, BC V0R 3A0 – 250/726-4641; Fax: 250/726-4611 – Manager, Kara-Lynn Bragg

Valemount CC, PO Box 298, BC V0E 2Z0 – 250/566-4464; Fax: 250/566-4333 – Secretary, Brigitta McDonald

North Vancouver CC, 131 - 2 St. East, BC V7L 1C2 – 604/987-4488; Fax: 604/987-8272 – Manager, Judi Ainsworth

Vancouver BT, #400, 999 Canada Place, BC V6C 3C1 – 604/681-2111; Fax: 604/681-0437 – Manager, Darcy Rezac

Vanderhoof District CC, 2353 Burrard Ave., PO Box 126, BC V0J 3A0 – 250/567-2124; Fax: 250/567-3316 – Manager, Glenda Olson

---

* BT - Board of Trade; BC - Bureau de commerce; CC - Chamber of Commerce/Chambre de commerce

7-28 BOARDS OF TRADE & CHAMBERS OF COMMERCE

Greater Vernon & District CC, 3700 - 33 St., BC V1T 5T6 – 250/545-0771; Fax: 250/545-3114 – Manager, Kathryn Arkell
Greater Victoria CC, 525 Fort St., BC V8W 1E8 – 250/383-7191; Fax: 250/385-3552; Email: gterrell@pinc.com; URL: http://vvv.com/Chamber – President, Bob Brown
Wells - Barkerville CC, PO Box 123, BC V0K 2R0 – 250/994-3489; Fax: 250/994-3237 – President, Madge Frigon
West Vancouver CC, 775 - 15th St., BC V7T 2S9 – 604/926-6614; Fax: 604/926-6436 – Manager, Judy Okazaki
Westbank & District CC, 2375 Pamela Rd., PO Box 26022, BC V4T 2G3 – 250/768-3378; Fax: 250/768-3465 – Manager, Trish Sol
Whistler CC, 2097 Lake Placid Rd., PO Box 181, BC V0N 1B0 – 604/932-5528; Fax: 604/932-3755; URL: http://www.whistler.net/coc/index.html – Manager, Thelma Johnstone
White Rock & South Surrey CC, 15150 Russell Ave., BC V4B 2P5 – 604/536-6844; Fax: 604/536-4994 – President, Bill Reid
Williams Lake & District CC, 1148 Broadway South, BC V2G 1A4 – 250/392-5025; Fax: 250/392-4214 – President, Brian Bramah
Zeballos BT, PO Box 208, BC V0P 2A0 – 250/761-4261; Fax: 250/761-4188 – President, Tom Weston

MANITOBA
Arborg CC, PO Box 415, MB R0C 0A0 – 204/376-5233; Fax: 204/376-5234 – President, Herman Palsson
Ashern CC, PO Box 582, MB R0C 0E0 – 204/768-2899; Fax: 204/768-2046 – Manager, Shelley Bjornson
Beausejour CC, PO Box 224, MB R0E 0C0 – 204/268-1343; Fax: 204/268-3217 – President, Rick Leclair
Birtle & District CC, PO Box 278, MB R0M 0C0 – 204/842-5250; Fax: 204/842-3349 – President, Woody Langford
Boissevain CC, PO Box 953, MB R0K 0E0 – 204/534-6400; Fax: 204/534-7188 – President, Murray Fingus
Brandon CC, 1043 Rosser Ave., MB R7A 0L5 – 204/727-5431; Fax: 204/727-2040 – General Manager, Lee Jebb
Carberry CC, PO Box 101, MB R0K 0H0 – 204/834-2353; Fax: 204/834-3073 – President, Mary-Ann Baron
Carman & Community CC, PO Box 249, MB R0G 0J0 – 204/745-3741; Fax: 204/745-6348 – Manager, Ron Funk
Churchill CC, PO Box 176, MB R0B 0E0 – 204/675-8881; Fax: 204/675-2643 – President, Bob Penwarden
Crystal City CC, PO Box 56, MB R0K 0N0 – 204/873-2499; Fax: 204/873-2450 – President, Henry Harms
Dauphin CC, 105 Main St. North, MB R7N 1C1 – 204/638-4838; Fax: 204/638-5790 – Manager, Susan Lamoureux
Deloraine CC, PO Box 748, MB R0M 0M0 – 204/747-2003; Fax: 204/747-2927 – President, Craig Adams
Elie CC, PO Box 175, MB R0H 0H0 – 204/353-2543; Fax: 204/353-2286 – President, Colin Vann
Emerson CC, Town Hall, PO Box 339, MB R0A 0L0 – 204/373-2732; Fax: 204/373-2599 – President, Menno Zacharias
Erickson CC, PO Box 188, MB R0J 0P0 – 204/636-2925; Fax: 204/636-7789 – President, Bev Turnball
Eriksdale & District CC, PO Box 434, MB R0C 0W0 – 204/739-5563; Fax: 204/739-2073 – President, Al Kelner
Falcon/West Hawk CC, Falcon Beach MB R0E 0N0 – Fax: 204/349-8450
Flin Flon CC, 84 Church St., PO Box 806, MB R8A 1N6 – 204/687-4518; Fax: 204/687-4456 – Manager, Connie Baird-Holubec
Gladstone CC, PO Box 563, MB R0J 0T0 – 204/385-3125; Fax: 204/385-2860 – President, Richard Beastall

Grunthal CC, PO Box 451, MB R0A 0R0 – 204/434-6270; Fax: 204/434-6970 – President, Jake Friesen
Hamiota CC, PO Box 430, MB R0M 0T0 – 204/764-2801; Fax: 204/764-2568 – President, Shirley Dale
Hartney & District CC, PO Box 224, MB R0M 0X0 – 204/858-2277; Fax: 204/858-2340 – President, Brenda Hicks
Headingley CC, 5434 Portage Ave., MB R4H 1G2 – 204/889-5074; Fax: 204/897-5277 – Executive Director, Jean Kuziw
Killarney CC, PO Box 809, MB R0K 1C0 – 204/523-4236; Fax: 204/523-7117 – President, Bill Janz
La Broquerie CC, PO Box 309, MB R0A 0W0 – 204/424-5551; Fax: 204/424-5552 – President, Annette Tetrault
La Salle & District CC, PO Box 603, MB R0G 1B0 – 204/736-4134; Fax: 204/736-4576 – President, Terrance Petty
Lac du Bonnet & District CC, PO Box 598, MB R0E 1A0 – 204/345-6846; Fax: 204/345-8694 – President, Rita Lansard
Leaf Rapids CC, PO Box 26, MB R0B 1W0 – 204/473-2423; Fax: 204/473-2288 – President, Barbara Bloodworth
Lorette CC, PO Box 87, MB R0A 0Y0 – 204/878-2458; Fax: 204/878-9596 – President, Robert Plett
Lynn Lake CC, PO Box 900, MB R0B 0W0 – 204/356-8444; Fax: 204/356-2940 – President, Cathie Watson
MacGregor CC, PO Box 357, MB R0H 0R0 – 204/685-2862; Fax: 204/685-2631 – Executive Director, Clare Tarr
Melita CC, PO Box 666, MB R0M 1L0 – 204/522-3215; Fax: 204/522-3176 – President, Irv Skelton
Morris CC, PO Box 98, MB R0G 1K0 – 204/746-2391; Fax: 204/746-2243 – President, Del Stevenson
Neepawa & District CC, PO Box 726, MB R0J 1H0 – 204/476-5292; Fax: 204/476-5431; URL: http://www.techplus.com/neep.htm – Manager, Janet Cochrane
Notre Dame CC, PO Box 107, Notre Dame de Lourdes MB R0G 1M0 – 204/248-2332; Fax: 204/248-2281 – President, Maurice Boisvert, Jr.
Pansy CC, General Delivery, Zhoda MB R0A 2P0 – 204/425-3434 – President, Jake Wall
Pilot Mound CC, PO Box 356, MB R0G 1P0 – 204/825-2313; Fax: 204/825-2313 – President, E.J. Collins
Portage & District CC, 11 - 2nd St. NE, Portage La Prairie MB R1N 1R8 – 204/857-7778; Fax: 204/857-4095 – President, Tony Schellenberg
Rivers & District CC, PO Box 795, MB R0K 1X0 – 204/328-7491; Fax: 204/328-7944 – President, Wally Hillier
Roblin CC, PO Box 729, MB R0L 1P0 – 204/937-2248; Fax: 204/937-8302 – President, Larry Mills
Rossburn & District CC, PO Box 579, MB R0G 1V0 – 204/859-2636; Fax: 204/859-2696 – President, Darrell Drul
Russell CC, PO Box 155, MB R0J 1W0 – 204/773-2456; Fax: 204/773-3235 – Secretary-Manager, Viola Coulter
Assiniboia CC, PO Box 42122, RPO Ferry Rd., Winnipeg MB R3J 3X7 – 204/774-4154; Fax: 204/774-4201; Email: st.chamber@accel.ca – President, Doug Sewell
Ste Rose du Lac CC, PO Box 688, MB R0L 1S0 – 204/447-2705; Fax: 204/447-2604 – President, Dave Harder
Selkirk CC, 200 Eaton, PO Box 89, MB R1A 2B1 – 204/482-7176; Fax: 204/482-5448 – President, George Hacking
Shoal Lake & District CC, PO Box 511, MB R0J 1Z0 – 204/759-2340; Fax: 204/759-2835 – President, Dan Szwaluk
Somerset CC, PO Box 187, MB R0G 1L0 – 204/744-2171; Fax: 204/744-2836
Souris & Glenwood CC, PO Box 939, MB R0K 2C0 – 204/483-2155 – President, Shelley Ross

St. Boniface CC, #2, 157 Provencher Blvd., Winnipeg MB R2H 0G2 – 204/235-1406; Fax: 204/233-8122 – President, Gabriel L. Forest
St Claude CC, PO Box 334, MB R0G 1Z0 – 204/379-2413; Fax: 204/379-2413 – President, Giles Chappelaz
St Pierre CC, 515 Jolys Ave. East, St Pierre Jolys MB R0A 1V0 – 204/433-7911; Fax: 204/433-7621 – President, Lucien Nayet
Starbuck CC, PO Box 117, MB R0G 2P0 – 204/735-2462; Fax: 204/735-2748 – President, Mark Morse
Steinbach CC, PO Box 1795, MB R0A 2A0 – 204/326-9566; Fax: 204/326-4171 – Manager, Linda Burdett
Stonewall CC, PO Box 762, MB R0C 2Z0 – 204/467-8377; Fax: 204/467-2265 – President, Shelley Stewart
Swan River CC, PO Box 1540, MB R0L 1Z0 – 204/734-3102; Fax: 204/734-4342 – President, Kevin Neely
The Pas & District CC, PO Box 996, MB R9A 1L1 – 204/623-7256; Fax: 204/623-7256 – President, Jim Scott
Thompson CC, 162 Princeton Dr., MB R8N 2A4 – 204/677-4155; Fax: 204/677-3434 – Manager, Paul Legault
Treherne CC, PO Box 344, MB R0G 2V0 – 204/723-2610; Fax: 204/723-2050 – President, Shayne Gibson
Teulon CC, PO Box 353, MB R0C 3B0 – 204/886-2084; Fax: 204/886-2315 – President, Chris Dawson
Virden CC, PO Box 899, MB R0M 2C0 – 204/747-3955; Fax: 204/748-2501 – President, Danny Pierrard
Wasagaming CC, PO Box 222, MB R0J 2H0 – 204/848-2742; Fax: 204/848-2149 – President, Bev Gowler
Waskada CC, PO Box 160, MB R0M 2E0 – 204/673-2522; Fax: 204/673-2535 – President, Gary Williams
Whitemouth CC, PO Box 189, MB R0E 2G0 – 204/348-7631; Fax: 204/348-7150 – President, Brian McDougald
Winkler CC, #335, 185 Main St., MB R6W 4B1 – 204/325-9758; Fax: 204/325-5915 – President, Robert Jones
Pinawa CC, PO Box 698, Winnipeg MB R0E 1L0 – 204/753-2674 – President, Allan Cassidy
Winnipeg CC, #500, 167 Lombard Ave., MB R3B 3E5 – 204/944-8484; Fax: 204/944-8492; Email: wcoc@escape.ca; URL: http://www.winnipegchmbr.mb.ca – President, Shelley Morris

NEW BRUNSWICK
Baie-Ste-Anne CC, RR#2, NB E0C 1A0 – 506/228-4405; Fax: 506/228-3711 – Director, Alphonse Turbide
Bath CC, PO Box 87, NB E0J 1E0 – 506/278-5213; Fax: 506/278-5963 – Director, Michael Blanchard
Bathurst CC, 275 Main St., NB E2A 1A9 – 506/548-8498; Fax: 506/548-1127 – President, Jo-Ann Ball, 506/546-2004
Beresford CC, PO Box 599, NB E0B 1H0 – 506/546-4902; Fax: 506/542-1880 – President, Gilberte Pitre, 506/542-9406
CC de Bertrand, NB E0B 1J0 – Président, Yves Thériault
Blackville CC, PO Box 208, NB E0C 1C0 – President, Leroy Stewart, 506/843-6609, Fax: 506/843-6737
Bouctouche CC, PO Box 338, Buctouche NB E0A 1G0 – 506/743-2411; Fax: 506/743-8991 – President, Benoît Michaud
Campbellton CC, PO Box 234, NB E3N 3G4 – 506/753-7856; Fax: 506/759-7557 – Executive Director, Suzanne Matte
Campobello CC, General Delivery, Wilson's Beach, NB E0G 3L0 – President, Gordon Phillips, 506/752-2233
CC de la région de Cap-Pelé, CP 699, NB E0A 1J0 – 506/577-4157; Fax: 506/577-2880 – Président, Hector Doiron
CC de Caraquet, 138, boul St-Pierre ouest, NB E1W 1B6 – 506/727-4464; Fax: 506/727-3183 – Président, Alain Foulem, 506/727-3162

Canadian Almanac & Directory 1997

Centreville CC, PO Box 147, NB E0J 1H0 – President, Randy McDougall, 506/276-4567, Fax: 506/276-4380

Greater Miramichi CC, PO Box 250, Chatham NB E1N 3A5 – 506/622-2600; Fax: 506/778-8297 – President, Dave Cadogan

CC de Cocagne & Notre-Dame, RR#1, Boite 19, Site 1, NB E0A 1K0 – 506/576-6126 – Président, Adrien Léger

Collette CC, RR#3, Boite 9, Site 18, Rogersville NB E0A 2T0 – 506/775-2898 – Président, Maurice Des-Roches

Dalhousie Region CC, PO Box 1295, NB E0K 1B0 – President, Dr. Marc Levesque, 506/684-2747

Eastern Charlotte CC, General Delivery, St. George NB E0G 2Y0 – 506/755-3376; Fax: 506/755-6688 – President, Ronnie Cousins, 506/755-3428, Fax: 506/755-6708

Eastern New Brunswick CC, PO Box 1030, Newcastle NB E1V 3V5 – 506/855-8579; Fax: 506/862-8351 – President, Claude Babineau

Edmundston CC, 74, ch Canada, NB E3V 1V5 – 506/737-1866; Fax: 506/737-1862 – Executive Director, Joanne Bérubé-Gagné

Florenceville CC, PO Box 236, NB E0J 1K0 – 506/392-5590; Fax: 506/392-6819 – President, Marg Hunter-Papineau

Fredericton CC, PO Box 275, NB E3B 4Y9 – 506/458-8006; Fax: 506/451-1119; URL: http://www.discribe.ca/chamber/ – General Manager, Krista A. Hamilton

Gagetown CC, PO Box 194, NB E0G 1V0 – President, Doug Harmon, 506/488-3161

Grand Falls & District CC, PO Box 1509, NB E3Z 1C8 – 506/473-1905; Fax: 506/475-7779 – President, Sylvie Daigle, 506/473-3276

Grand Manan CC, PO Box 110, Grand Harbour NB E0G 1X0 – 506/662-3432 – President, John Large

Grand-Digue CC, Grande-Digue NB E0A 1S0 – Secrétaire, Anne-Marie Bourque

Hampton Area CC, PO Box 329, NB E0G 1Z0 – President, David G. Carr, 506/832-7853

Inkerman CC, CP 119, NB E0B 1S9 – 506/336-8540 – Présidente, Edith Robichaud

Lameque CC, CP 113, NB E0B 1V0 – 506/344-2217; Fax: 506/344-5380 – Président, Roger Noel

CC de Maisonnette, CP 261, NB E0B 1X0 – Président, Yves Godin

McAdam CC, PO Box 411, NB E0H 1K0 – 506/784-2792; Fax: 506/784-2986 – President, Mirl Craig

Miramichi BT, Boiestown NB E0H 1A0 – 506/369-7127 – President, Cal R. Copland, 506/369-7127

Greater Moncton CC, #100, 910 Main St., NB E1C 1G6 – 506/857-2883; Fax: 506/857-9209 – President, Levi Clain, Q.C., 506/853-1970

CC de Neguac, NB E0C 1S0 – Président, Arthur Savoie

Oromocto & Area CC, PO Box 21009, NB E2V 2G5 – President, Robin L. Hanson, 506/446-6824, Fax: 506/446-6828

Perth-Andover CC, c/o Holt Flowers, NB E0J 1V0 – 506/273-2539; Fax: 506/273-4450 – President, Debbie Kinney

CC de Petite Rivière de l'Île, CP 108, Shippagan NB E0B 2P0 – 506/336-8357 – Présidente, Emilia Lanteigne

Plaster Rock Regional CC, NB E0G 1W0 – 506/356-8522 – President, Molly Ashworth

CC de Pointe-Sapin, General Delivery, NB E0A 2A0 – 506/876-3855 – President, Anne Kelly

Richibucto CC, PO Box 670, NB E0A 2M0 – 506/523-4342; Fax: 506/523-6362 – Président, Robert Robichaud

River Valley CC, PO Box 707, Grand Bay NB E0G 1W0 – 506/738-8666; Fax: 506/738-3697 – President, Diane Bormke

CC de Rivière-du-Portage, CP 127, NB E0C 1Y0 – Président, Gilles Haché, 506/395-2455

CC de Rogersville, CP 168, NB E0A 2T0 – 506/775-6738; Fax: 506/775-6002 – President, Paulette Maillet

Greater Sackville CC, 16 Lansdowne St., NB E0A 3C0 – 506/364-8911; Fax: 506/364-8082 – Executive Director, Diane Fullerton

St. Andrews CC, PO Box 89, NB E0G 2X0 – 506/529-3555; Fax: 506/529-8095 – Executive Director, Susan Corbyn

CC de Sainte-Anne-de-Madawaska, CP 390, NB E0L 1G0 – 506/445-2275; Fax: 506/445-2045 – Président, Reynald Roy

CC de Saint-Antoine, 218, rue Principale, Saint-Antoine-de-Kent NB E0A 2X0 – 506/525-2768; Fax: 506/523-9131 – President, Gilles Lemieux

CC de Saint-François, CP 378, Saint-François-de-Madawaska NB E7A 1G4 – 506/992-3362; Fax: 506/992-3930 – Président, Serge Boulet

Saint John BT, PO Box 6037, NB E2L 4R5 – 506/634-8111; Fax: 506/632-2008 – President, Bruce Dowd, 506/632-0022

CC régionale de St-Léonard, 725, rue Principale, NB E0L 1M0 – 506/423-7847 – Président, Paul Abud

CC de Saint-Louis-de-Kent, NB E0A 2Z0 – Présidente, Laurie LeBlanc

CC de Saint-Quentin Inc., CP 1116, NB E0K 1J0 – 506/235-3666; Fax: 506/235-1804 – Président, Roland Doiron

CC de St-Raphaël/Pigeon Hill, CP 117, St-Raphaël-sur-Mer NB E0B 2N0 – 506/336-2329 – Secrétaire, Humbert Savoie

CC de St-Simon, École des pêches, NB E0B 1L0 – 506/727-6531; Fax: 506/727-6265 – Président, Édard Albert

St. Stephen Area CC, PO Box 457, NB E3L 2X3 – 506/466-5416; Fax: 506/466-7001 – President, Maria Kulcher, 506/466-5519, Fax: 506/466-5558

Shediac & Area BT, c/o Frenette's Funeral Home, 248 Main St., NB E0A 3G0 – 506/532-3297 – President, Ives Frenette

CC de Shippagan, CP 201, NB E0B 2P0 – Président, Ivan Robichaud

Sussex & District CC, PO Box 1368, NB E0E 1P0 – 506/433-3429; Fax: 506/433-1886 – President, Pam Folkins

Woodstock CC, PO Box 26, NB E0J 2B0 – 506/325-9049; Fax: 506/328-4894 – President, Kelly Cummings, 506/328-3265

York North CC, PO Box 695, Nackawic NB E0H 1P0 – 506/575-9622; Fax: 506/575-2075 – President, Greg MacFarlane

NEWFOUNDLAND

Argentia Area CC, PO Box 272, Placentia NF A0B 2Y0 – 709/227-5396; Fax: 709/227-5731 – President, Gary Hynes

Baccalieu Trails CC, PO Box 29, Winterton NF A0B 3M0 – 709/749-6206; Fax: 709/583-2093 – General Manager, Peter Hiscock

Baie Verte CC, PO Box 578, NF A0K 1B0 – 709/532-4279; Fax: 709/532-4669 – President, Patrick Jim

Bay d'Espoir CC, PO Box 66, St Albans NF A0H 2E0 – 709/538-3552; Fax: 709/538-3439 – President, Tracey Perry

Bay St. George CC, PO Box 478, Stephenville NF A2N 3A3 – 709/643-5854; Fax: 709/643-3421 – President, Darren Roberts

Bell Island CC, General Delivery, NF A0A 4H0 – 709/488-2912 – Secretary, Brian Burke

Bishop's Falls CC, PO Box 940, NF A0H 1C0 – 709/258-5404; Fax: 709/258-5404 – President, Tom MacDonald

Botwood CC, PO Box 1000, NF A0H 1E0 – 709/257-3656; Fax: 709/257-2628 – President, Brian Flood

Channel-Port-aux-Basques CC, General Delivery, NF A0M 1C0 – 709/695-3402 – President, Elwyn Rose

Clarenville Area CC, PO Box 834, NF A0E 1J0 – President, Gary Decker, 709/466-2394, Fax: 709/466-2569

Conception Bay South CC, PO Box 951, Manuels NF A0A 2Y0 – President, Richard Smith, 709/834-3838, Fax: 709/834-1437

Corner Brook CC, PO Box 475, NF A2H 6E6 – 709/634-5831; Fax: 709/639-9792 – Executive Director, Mark White

Deer Lake CC, PO Box 57, NF A0K 2E0 – 709/635-2451; Fax: 709/635-5857 – President, Charles McCarthy

Exploits Regional CC, PO Box 272, Grand Falls-Windsor NF A2A 2J7 – 709/489-7512; Fax: 709/489-7532 – Executive Director, Sean Cooper

Gander & Area CC, 109 Trans Canada Hwy., NF A1V 1P6 – 709/256-7110; Fax: 709/256-4080 – General Manager, Gerald L. Gray

Harbour Breton CC, PO Box 102, NF A0H 1P0 – 709/885-2317; Fax: 709/885-2317 – President, Doreen Vallis

Harbour Grace BT, PO Box 284, NF A0A 2M0 – 709/596-5192; Fax: 709/579-4304 – President, David Weeks, 709/596-2171, Fax: 709/596-4304

Labrador West CC, PO Box 273, Labrador City NF A2V 2K5 – 709/944-3723; Fax: 709/944-5383 – President, Dr. Rehan Malik, 709/944-3131, Fax: 709/944-6835

Labrador North CC, PO Box 460, Stn B, Happy Valley-Goose Bay NF A0P 1E0 – 709/896-2421; Fax: 709/896-5028 – President, Peter Woodward

Lewisporte CC, PO Box 953, NF A0G 3A0 – 709/535-6601; Fax: 709/535-0060 – President, Don Manuals, 709/535-8492

Marystown-Burin Area CC, PO Box 728, NF A0E 2M0 – 709/279-1200; Fax: 709/279-1408 – President, Donald A. MacBeath, 709/279-2467

Mount Pearl CC, PO Box 551, NF A1N 2W4 – 709/364-8513; Fax: 709/364-8500 – President, Cheryl Rodd, 709/576-4443

St. John's BT, 159 Water St., PO Box 5127, NF A1C 5V5 – 709/726-2961; Fax: 709/726-2003 – General Manager, Bruce J. Tilley

Springdale CC, PO Box 37, NF A0J 1T0 – President, John Warr, 709/673-3925, Fax: 709/673-3920

St. Anthony CC, PO Box 191, St Anthony NF A0K 4S0 – President, Todd Hancock, 709/454-3584, Fax: 709/454-4131

NORTHWEST TERRITORIES

Yellowknife CC, #6, 4807 - 49 St., NT X1A 3T5 – 403/920-4944; Fax: 403/920-4640 – Executive Director, Cheryl Best

NOVA SCOTIA

Amherst CC, PO Box 283, NS B4H 3Z4 – 902/667-8186; Fax: 902/667-5369 – Executive Director, Betty Cochran

Annapolis Royal BT, PO Box 2, NS B0S 1A0 – 902/532-7404; Fax: 902/532-7346 – President, John Stevens

Annapolis Valley Affiliated Boards of Trade, PO Box 1149, Middleton NS B0S 1P0 – 902/825-4344; Fax: 902/825-4634 – President, Marc Blinn, 902/769-3300, Fax: 902/769-0109

Antigonish CC, PO Box 1626, NS B2G 2L8 – 902/863-6308; Fax: 902/863-6308 – President, Joeanne Mahoney, 902/863-4754, Fax: 902/863-1805

Barrington Area CC, PO Box 110, NS B0W 1E0 – 902/745-2109; Fax: 902/745-1309 – President, Bruce M. Atkinson

Bear River BT, PO Box 235, NS B0S 1B0 – 902/467-3808; Fax: 902/467-3808 – President, Brian Reynolds

Berwick & District BT, PO Box 664, NS B0P 1E0 – 902/538-9373; Fax: 902/847-3139 – President, Ken Pineo

Bridgetown BT, PO Box 467, NS B0S 1C0 – 902/665-2825 – President, Joanne Acker

* BT - Board of Trade; BC - Bureau de commerce; CC - Chamber of Commerce/Chambre de commerce

Bridgewater & Area CC, PO Box 100, NS B4V 2W8 – 902/688-2399; Fax: 902/543-0599 – President, Paul Waumback, 902/543-0515

Canso & Area BT, PO Box 235, NS B0H 1H0 – 902/533-2197; Fax: 902/533-3822 – President, Frank X. Fraser

Industrial Cape Breton BT, 140 Pitt St., PO Box 131, Sydney NS B1P 6G9 – 902/564-6453; Fax: 902/539-7487 – President, John Coleman, 902/539-5300, ext.216

Chester Municipal CC, PO Box 831, NS B0J 1J0 – 902/457-7786; Fax: 902/275-2125 – President, Ross DeMont

CC de Clare, CP 35, Church Point NS B0W 1M0 – 902/769-2040; Fax: 902/645-2861 – Présidente, Elaine Thimot

Digby & Area BT, PO Box 641, NS B0V 1A0 – 902/245-5558; Fax: 902/245-6525 – President, Geraldine Costa

East Hants CC, PO Box 76, Milford Station NS B0N 1Y0 – 902/758-4257; Fax: 902/768-5808 – President, Susan McDonell, 902/883-8403

Grand Narrows & District BT, PO Box 149, Victoria County NS B0A 1L0 – 902/725-2843 – President, Fonce Farrell

Metropolitan Halifax CC, PO Box 8990, NS B3K 5M6 – 902/468-7111; Fax: 902/468-7333 – President, Vince Marsh

Kentville & Area BT, PO Box 314, NS B4N 3X1 – 902/678-2157; Fax: 902/678-9455 – President, Alan T. Tufts

Lunenburg BT, PO Box 1300, NS B0J 2C0 – 902/634-8800; Fax: 902/634-9499 – President, Edgar Blinn

United Mosers River BT, RR#2, NS B0J 2K0 – 902/347-2527; Fax: 902/347-2498 – President, Donald Lowe

Mulgrave & Area CC, PO Box 3, Port Hawkesbury NS B0E 2G0 – 902/625-0803 – Secretary, Ray Carpenter

Musquodoboit Harbour & District BT, PO Box 64, NS B0T 1B0 – 902/889-2752; Fax: 902/889-2362 – President, Robert Stevens

Pictou County CC, East River Plaza, 980 East River Rd., New Glasgow NS B2H 3S5 – 902/755-3463; Fax: 902/755-2848 – Executive Director, Barrie MacMillan

North Queens BT, PO Box 183, Caledonia NS B0T 1B0 – 902/682-2535 – President, David Crooker

Northside CC, 84 Pleasant St., North Sydney NS B2A 1L6 – 902/736-1211 – President, Stephen MacAdam

Parrsboro & District CC, PO Box 297, NS B0M 1S0 – 902/254-3266; Fax: 902/254-2822 – President, Rick Brodie, 902/254-3881, Fax: 902/254-2588

Strait Area CC, PO Box 441, Port Hawkesbury NS B0E 6V0 – 902/625-1588; Fax: 902/625-5985 – President, Ken Anderson, 902/625-3655

Preston & Area BT, PO Box 3412, Dartmouth NS B2W 5G3 – 902/435-4464; Fax: 902/434-4615 – Executive Director, Tony Atuanya

Riverport & District BT, Deli Seafoods, NS B0J 2R0 – 902/766-4820 – President, Lynn Boone

Sheet Harbour BT, PO Box 239, NS B0J 3B0 – 902/885-3477; Fax: 902/885-3488 – President, Reg Dooks

Shelburne & Area CC, PO Box 189, NS B0T 1W0 – 902/875-1133; Fax: 902/875-4199 – President, Sharon Christie

South Queens CC, PO Box 1378, Liverpool NS B0T 1K0 – 902/354-7105; Fax: 902/354-2424 – President, Dan Swansburg

Springhill CC, PO Box 1030, NS B0M 1X0 – 902/597-2429; Fax: 902/597-2967 – President, Robert Gilroy

Northumberland CC, PO Box 279, Tatamagouche NS B0K 1V0 – 902/657-2223; Fax: 902/657-3600 – President, Marjorie Mattatall

Tiverton & District BT, PO Box 694, NS B0V 1G0 – 902/839-2687 – President, W. Outhouse

Truro & District CC, PO Box 54, NS B2N 5B6 – 902/895-6328; Fax: 902/897-6641 – Managing Director, Bob Baxter

Windsor BT, PO Box 2188, NS B0N 1T0 – 902/798-4461; Fax: 902/798-5477 – President, Kevin Saunders, 902/757-2182, Fax: 902/757-2802

Yarmouth CC, PO Box 532, NS B5A 4B4 – 902/742-3074; Fax: 902/749-1383 – President, Brian Mathews

ONTARIO

Ajax-Pickering BT, #223, 1099 Kingston Rd., ON L1V 1B5 – 905/837-6638; Fax: 905/837-1629 – Board Secretary, Lesley Whyte

Alliston & District CC, PO Box 32, ON L9R 1W5 – 705/435-7921; Fax: 705/435-1106 – General Manager, D. Gaston

Angus CC, PO Box 792, ON L0M 1B0 – 705/424-2424 – Sec.-Treas., L. Kremer

Arthur & District CC, PO Box 519, ON N0G 1A0 – 519/848-5603; Fax: 519/848-3849 – Past President, Valerie Day

Athens District CC, PO Box 543, ON K0E 1B0 – 613/924-9141; Fax: 613/924-9901 – Kathryn Hudson

Atwood & District CC, 162 Main St., PO Box 10, ON N0G 1B0 – 519/356-2216; Fax: 519/356-2832 – Manager, Neil Cockwell

Aurora CC, Aurora Shopping Centre, 14483 Yonge St., PO Box 28539, ON L4G 6S6 – 905/727-7262; Fax: 905/841-6217 – General Manager, Rosalyn Gonsalves

Baden & District CC, PO Box 130, ON N0B 1G0 – Sec.-Treas., H. Schmidt

Bancroft & District CC, PO Box 539, ON K0L 1C0 – 613/332-1513; Fax: 613/332-2119 – General Manager, Gordon MacKey

Greater Barrie CC, 89 Dunlop St. East, ON L4M 1A7 – 705/721-5000; Fax: 705/726-0973 – Executive Director, Wanda D. Collison

Beaver Valley CC, PO Box 477, Thornbury ON N0H 2P0 – 519/599-5591; Fax: 519/599-2055 – Secretary, Patricia Irish

Beaverton District CC, 412 Bay St., PO Box 699, ON L0K 1A0 – 705/426-9061; Fax: 705/426-4378 – President, J. Hudson

Belleville & District CC, 5 Moira St., PO Box 726, ON K8N 5B3 – 613/962-4597; Fax: 613/962-3911 – General Manager, R. Broadbridge

Black River-Matheson CC, 365 MacDougal Ave., PO Box 494, ON P0K 1N0 – 705/273-2475; Fax: 705/273-2340 – President, J. Barber

Blenheim & District CC, 35 Talbot St., PO Box 1353, ON N0P 1A0 – Administrative Secretary, B. Gander

Blind River CC, PO Box 9, ON P0R 1B0 – 705/356-1579

Bobcaygeon & Area CC, 34 Bolton St., PO Box 388, ON K0M 1A0 – 705/738-2202; Fax: 705/738-1534; Toll Free: 1-800-318-6173 – Office Manager, Cindy Snider

Bracebridge CC, 1-1 Manitoba St., ON P1L 1S4 – 705/645-5231; Fax: 705/645-7592; Email: bracecha@muskoka.com – General Manager, Leslie E. Talbot

Bradford & District CC, PO Box 59, ON L3Z 2A7 – 905/775-3037; Fax: 905/775-6752 – General Manager, C. Servant

The Brampton BT, #504, 8 Nelson St. West, ON L6X 4J2 – 905/451-1122; Fax: 905/450-0295 – General Manager, E. Moyer

Brantford Regional CC, 77 Charlotte St., PO Box 1294, ON N3T 5T6 – 519/753-2617; Fax: 519/753-0921 – Executive Vice-President, Anne Buchanan

Brockville & District CC, Block House Island, PO Box 1341, ON K9V 5Y6 – 613/342-6553; Fax: 613/342-6849 – Executive Director, P. Dunn

Burlington CC, 3385 Harvester Rd., ON L7N 3N2 – 905/639-0174; Fax: 905/333-3956; URL: http://wchat.on.ca/commerce/index.html – Executive Director, Scott McCammon

Caledon CC, Courtyards of Caledon, #D8, 18 King St. East, PO Box 626, Bolton ON L7E 5T5 – 905/857-7393; Fax: 905/857-7405 – General Manager, P. Green

Caledonia Regional CC, PO Box 2035, ON N3W 2G6 – 905/765-0377; Fax: 905/765-4409 – President, D. Britton

Cambridge CC, 531 King St. East, ON N3H 3N4 – 519/653-1424; Fax: 519/653-1734 – Executive Director, K.M. Thompson

Carleton Place & District CC, PO Box 301, ON K7C 3P4 – 613/257-1976; Fax: 613/257-8170 – Manager, Jackie Cowlin

Cayuga & District CC, PO Box 118, ON N0A 1E0 – 905/772-3978; Fax: 905/772-3037 – Secretary, M. Hanrath

Chatham & District CC, 235 King St. West, ON N7M 1E6 – 519/352-7540; Fax: 519/352-8741; URL: http://www.ciaccess.com/~pmartin/cdc-catog.htm – General Manager, G.A. Antaya

Cobourg & District CC, Dressler House, 212 King St. West, ON K9A 2N1 – 905/372-5831; Fax: 905/372-2411; Email: cobourg-cofc@eagle.ca; URL: http://www.eagle.ca.cobourg.chamber – Manager, Carol A. Farren

Cochrane BT, PO Box 1468, ON P0L 1C0 – 705/272-4926; Fax: 705/272-3026 – Sec.-Treas., Lynne Duquette

Collingwood CC, 155 Hurontario St., ON L9Y 2M1 – 705/445-0221; Fax: 705/445-6858 – President, P. Morrocco

Cornwall CC, 132 - 2 St. East, PO Box 338, ON K6H 5T1 – 613/933-4004; Fax: 613/933-8466; Email: strasser@glen-net; URL: http://www.busitech.com/cornwall/ – General Manager, Lezlie Strasser

Cumberland CC (Ontario) Inc., PO Box 49011, Orleans ON K1C 7E4 – 613/824-9137; Fax: 613/834-8398 – Executive Director, W. Shields

Delhi District CC, PO Box 11, ON N4B 2W8 – Fax: 582-3870 – Secretary, H. Brown

Dryden District CC, 284 Government Rd., PO Box 725, ON P8N 2Z4 – 807/223-2622; Fax: 807/223-2626; Toll Free: 1-800-667-0935; Email: chamber@moosenet.net – Manager, Barb Lyotier

Dunnville CC, 106 Main St. West, PO Box 124, ON N1A 2X1 – 905/774-3183; Fax: 905/774-9281 – Administrator, Karen Bernard

Durham & District CC, PO Box 800, ON N0G 1R0 – 519/369-5750; Fax: 519/369-5750 – Secretary, Jean Hutcheson

Dutton-Dunwich CC, PO Box 211, ON N0L 1J0 – 519/762-3128 – Sec.-Treas., Mike Gardiner

East Gwillimbury CC, PO Box 606, Sharon ON L0G 1V0 – 905/478-8142; Fax: 905/478-8074 – Secretary, Hanni Staheli

Elliot Lake & District CC, Hwy. 108 Civic Centre, ON P5A 2T1 – 705/848-3974; Fax: 705/848-2987 – Executive Assistant, R. Alger

Elmira & Woolwich CC, 5 First St. East, ON N3B 2E3 – 519/669-2605; Fax: 519/669-8251 – Executive Director, H. Greb

Elmwood & District CC, RR#2, ON N0G 1S0 – President, M. Hamel

Elora & District CC, 1 MacDonald Sq., PO Box 814, ON N0B 1S0 – 519/846-9841; Fax: 519/846-2074 – Administrator, S. Clarke

Englehart & District CC, PO Box 171, ON P0J 1H0 – 705/544-2658; Fax: 705/544-2658 – Manager, P. Woollings

Espanola & District CC, PO Box 5085, ON P5E 1S1 – R.S. Molly

Etobicoke CC, #100, 701 Evans Ave., ON M9C 1A3 – 416/622-5557; Fax: 416/622-4544 – Executive Director, Donald E. Overholt

Fenelon Falls North Kawartha District CC, PO Box 28, ON K0M 1N0 – 705/887-3409; Fax: 705/887-9259 – Office Manager, L. Matthews

Flamborough CC, #8, Hwy. 5 West, PO Box 1030, Waterdown ON L0R 2H0 – 905/689-7650; Fax: 905/689-1313 – Administrator, Jim Chambers

Flesherton & District CC, PO Box 292, ON N0C 1E0 – 519/924-3687 – President, Colleen Boer

Greater Fort Erie CC, #4, 427 Garrison Rd., ON L2A 1N1 – 905/871-3803; Fax: 905/871-1561 – Manager, C. Montana

Fort Frances CC, 474 Scott St., ON P9A 1H2 – 807/274-5773; Fax: 807/274-8706; Toll Free: 1-800-820-3678; URL: http://www.tradenet.ca/Fort_Frances – Office Manager, Heather Herbert

1,000 Islands Gananoque & District CC, 2 King St. East, ON K7G 1E6 – 613/382-3250; Fax: 613/382-1585 – Sylvia Fletcher

Georgina BT, PO Box 133, Keswick ON L4P 3E1 – 905/476-7870; Fax: 905/476-8560; Toll Free: 1-800-436-7462 – Administrative Assistant, Ron J. Brooks

Geraldton District CC, PO Box 156, ON P0T 1M0 – 807/854-1281; Fax: 807/854-1252 – President, P. Kyro

Gloucester CC, #53, 5450 Canotek Rd., ON K1J 9G3 – 613/745-3578; Fax: 613/745-8575 – Executive Director, Jim Anderson

Goderich & District CC, PO Box 414, ON N7A 4C7 – 519/524-1172; Fax: 519/524-5595 – Secretary/Business Manager, Elizabeth Kruspe

The Gogama CC, 921 Woodward Ave., Milton ON L9T 3X2 – 705/894-2788 – Chairman, John F. Rich

Grand Bend & Area CC, #1, 81 Crescent St., PO Box 248, ON N0M 1T0 – 519/238-2001; Fax: 519/238-8302 – Secretary, Pamela Reid

Gravenhurst CC/Visitors Bureau, Gravenhurst Opera House, #295, One Muskoka Rd. South, ON P1P 1J1 – 705/687-4432; Fax: 705/687-4382 – Executive Director, Ann Zangari

Grimsby & District CC, #2, 76 Main St. West, ON L3M 1R6 – 905/945-8319; Fax: 905/945-1615 – Manager, Jinny Day

Guelph CC, 485 Silvercreek Pkwy. North, PO Box 1268, ON N1H 6N6 – 519/822-8081; Fax: 519/822-8451; Email: gchamber@mgl.ca; URL: http://www.mgl.ca/~gchamber – General Manager, Gary Nadalin

Hagersville & District CC, PO Box 243, ON N0A 1H0 – 905/768-5979 – Sec.-Treas., Ted Heinrichs

Haliburton Highlands CC, PO Box 147, Minden ON K0M 2K0 – 705/286-1760; Fax: 705/286-6016; Toll Free: 1-800-461-7677 – Office Manager, B. Dean

Halton Hills CC, 170 Guelph St., Georgetown ON L7G 4A7 – 905/877-7119; Fax: 905/873-5117 – Executive Director, Anne Sidebottom

Hamilton & District CC, 555 Bay St. North, ON L8L 1H1 – 905/522-1151; Fax: 905/522-1354; URL: http://www.jmg.on.ca/chamber/home.htm – Executive Director, Lee Kirkby

Hanover CC, PO Box 20027, RPO Midtown, ON N4N 3T1 – 519/364-5777; Fax: 519/364-6456 – President, M. Robson

Harriston-Minto & District CC, PO Box 864, ON N0G 1Z0 – 519/338-3034; Fax: 519/338-3520 – Vice-President, R.A. Weiss

Hawkesbury CC, 1575 Tupper St., PO Box 798, ON K6A 3C9 – 613/632-8066; Fax: 613/632-3324 – Coordinator, Francine Fournier

Huntsville/Lake of Bays CC, #1, 8 West St. North, ON P1H 2B6 – 705/789-4771; Fax: 705/789-6191; Email: hchamber@muskoka.com – General Manager, Brenda Caskenette

Ingersoll District CC, 128 Duke St., PO Box 400, ON N5C 3V3 – 519/485-7333; Fax: 519/485-6183 – Promoter/Manager, B. Wallace

Innisfil CC, c/o Gibson & Adams, PO Box 262, Stroud ON L0L 2M0 – 705/436-1701; Fax: 705/436-1710 – President, G. MacKenzie

Iroquois Falls & District CC, 727 Synagogue Ave., PO Box 840, ON P0K 1G0 – 705/232-4656; Fax: 705/232-4656 – Office Manager, Rose-Marie Purdy-Peever

Kanata CC, #109, 275 Michael Cowpland Dr., ON K2M 2G2 – 613/592-8343; Fax: 613/592-1157 – Administrator, S. Cramm

Kapuskasing & District CC, 100 Government Rd., ON P5N 3H8 – 705/335-2332; Fax: 705/335-2359 – Secretary, D. Bliss

Kemptville & District CC, PO Box 1047, ON K0G 1J0 – 613/258-4838; Fax: 613/258-4322 – Manager, Valerie Paterson

Kenora & District CC, PO Box 471, ON P9N 3X5 – 807/467-4646; Fax: 807/468-4760 – Executive Assistant, Heather Grant

Kincardine & District CC, PO Box 115, ON N2Z 2Y6 – 519/396-9333; Fax: 519/396-5529 – Secretary, B. Eggleton

King City CC, PO Box 502, ON L0G 1K0 – 905/833-0869; Fax: 905/833-2553 – Secretary, E.L. Hinder

Greater Kingston CC, 209 Wellington St., ON K7K 2Y6 – 613/548-4453; Fax: 613/548-4743; Email: chamber@limestone.kosone.com; URL: http://www.kosone.com/chamber – General Manager, Gail Logan

Kirkland Lake & District CC, PO Box 966, ON P2N 2E6 – 705/567-5444; Fax: 705/567-1666 – Manager, Eleanor Newton

CC of Kitchener & Waterloo, 80 Queen St. North, PO Box 2367, Stn B, ON N2H 6L4 – 519/576-5000; Fax: 519/742-4760 – Executive Director, Reg Cressman

Lakefield & District CC, Water St., PO Box 537, ON K0L 2H0 – 705/652-3141; Fax: 705/652-6963 – General Manager, R. Lyons

Land O'Lakes CC, PO Box 135, Northbrook ON K0H 2G0 – 613/336-9460; Fax: 613/336-9460 – Acting Secretary, Susanne Lauper

Land-of-Nipigon CC, PO Box 760, ON P0T 2J0 – 807/887-1493 – Secretary, Gina Barnes

Leamington District CC, #303B, 33 Princess St., PO Box 321, ON N8H 3W3 – 519/326-2721; Fax: 519/326-3204 – General Manager, Chris Chopchik

Lincoln CC, 4800 South Service Rd., PO Box 1000, Beamsville ON L0R 1B0 – 905/563-5044; Fax: 905/563-6566 – Secretary/Manager, Cathy McNiven

Lindsay CC, 2 Kent St. West, ON K9V 2Y1 – 705/324-2393; Fax: 705/324-2473 – General Manager, Marje Gilligan

Listowel CC, PO Box 232, ON N4W 3H4 – 519/291-1590 – President, M. Tremblay

Manitoulin CC, PO Box 915, Little Current ON P0P 1K0 – 705/282-0713; Fax: 705/282-2989 – President, B. Barfoot

London CC, 244 Pall Mall St., PO Box 3295, ON N6A 5P6 – 519/432-7551; Fax: 519/432-8063 – President/CEO, Jack Mann

Longlac CC, PO Box 877, ON P0T 1A0 – 807/876-2273; Fax: 807/876-4337 – President, L. Tucker

Lucknow & District CC, PO Box 313, ON N0G 2H0 – 519/528-2110; Fax: 519/528-3529 – President, P. Livingston

Lyndhurst Seeleys Bay & District CC, PO Box 89, ON K0E 1N0 – 613/387-3847 – Treasurer, C. Shaw

Manitouwadge CC, PO Box 2030, ON P0T 2C0 – 807/826-3227, ext.240; Fax: 807/826-4592 – Managing Director, Terese Bullough

Marathon & District CC, PO Box 988, ON P0T 2E0 – 807/229-2112; Fax: 807/229-2112 – President, Brian Hicks

Markdale CC, PO Box 177, ON N0C 1H0 – 519/986-3677 – Sec.-Treas., Ian Drummond

Markham BT, #210, 3780 - 14th Ave., ON L3R 9Y5 – 905/474-0730; Fax: 905/474-0685 – Executive Director, Ruth Burkholder

Maryborough Township CC, PO Box 143, Moorefield ON N0G 2K0 – 519/638-3441; Fax: 519/638-5856 – President, D. Campbell

Maxville CC, PO Box 279, ON K0C 1T0 – 613/527-3131; Fax: 613/527-1119 – Secretary, J. Scott

Meaford & District CC, PO Box 4836, ON N4L 1X6 – 519/538-4020; Fax: 519/538-5295 – Executive Secretary, V. Mullin

Merrickville & District CC, PO Box 571, ON K0G 1N0 – 613/269-2229; Fax: 613/269-3713 – President, Judy Clarke

Midland CC, 208 King St., PO Box 158, ON L4R 4K8 – 705/526-7884; Fax: 705/526-1744 – General Manager/Economic Development Commissioner, Joyce A. Campbell

Milton CC, PO Box 52, ON L9T 2Y3 – 905/878-0581; Fax: 905/878-4972 – General Manager, Sandy Martin

Mississauga BT, #100, 3 Robert Speck Pkwy., ON L4Z 2G5 – 905/273-6151; Fax: 905/273-4937; URL: http://www.mbot.com – Executive Director, David A. Gordon

Morrisburg & District CC, PO Box 288, ON K0C 1X0 – 613/543-3443; Fax: 613/543-4387 – Secretary, Linda Bowers

Mount Forest District CC, 521 Main St. North, PO Box 1493, ON N0G 2L0 – 519/323-4480 – Manager, Carol Teston

Napanee & District CC, PO Box 431, ON K7R 3P5 – 613/354-2331; Fax: 613/354-5114; URL: http://chamber.napanee.on.ca – President, P. Veltheer

Nepean CC, #201, 28 Thorncliff Pl., ON K2H 6L2 – 613/828-5556; Fax: 613/828-8022 – President, Buck Arnold

New Hamburg BT, PO Box 457, ON N0B 2G0 – 519/662-3000; Fax: 519/662-2601 – Secretary, Sam Lucibello

Newmarket CC, 78 Main St. South, ON L3Y 3Y6 – 905/898-5900; Fax: 905/853-7271 – Manager, Robert T. Carter

CC of Niagara Falls, 4394 Queen St., ON L2E 2L3 – 905/374-3666; Fax: 905/374-2972 – Executive Director, Glenn Gandy

Niagara on the Lake CC, 153 King St., PO Box 1043, ON L0S 1J0 – 905/468-4263; Fax: 905/468-4930; URL: http://www.niagara.com/chamber.not1 – General Manager, N.G. Rumble

North Bay & District CC, 1375 Seymour St., PO Box 747, ON P1B 8J8 – 705/472-8480; Fax: 705/472-8027; URL: http://www.city.north-bay.on.ca/chamber.htm – Manager, G. DeVuono

North York CC, #200, 298 Sheppard Ave. West, ON M2N 1N5 – 416/226-9345; Fax: 416/590-1729 – General Manager, Tracy Blyth

Norwich Township CC, PO Box 128, ON N0J 1P0 – 519/863-2689; Fax: 519/863-2469 – President, D.M. Buck

Oakville CC, 170 Country Squire Lane, ON L6J 4Z3 – 905/845-6613; Fax: 905/845-6475 – Executive Vice-President, Brenda Kempel

Orangeville & District CC, PO Box 101, ON L9W 2Z5 – 519/941-0490; Fax: 519/941-0492 – Manager, Catherine Callum

Orillia & District CC, 150 Front St. South, ON L3V 4S7 – 705/326-4424; Fax: 705/327-7841 – Managing Director, Susan Lang

Township of Osgoode CC, PO Box 558, ON K0A 2W0 – 613/826-0661 – President, J. Bath

Oshawa/Clarington CC, 50 Richmond St. East, ON L1G 7C7 – 905/728-1683; Fax: 905/432-1259 – Executive Director, Peter Mitchell

Ottawa-Carleton BT, #1710, 350 Albert St., ON K1R 1A4 – 613/230-3631; Fax: 613/236-7498; URL: http://www.board-of-trade.org – President, W. Bagnell

Owen Sound & District CC, PO Box 1028, ON N4K 6K6 – 519/376-6261; Fax: 519/376-5647 – President, N. Osborne

Parry Sound & Area CC, 70 Church St., ON P2A 1Y9 – 705/746-4213; Fax: 705/746-6537; Toll Free: 1-800-461-4261 – Administrator/Manager, Jan Hanna

---

* BT - Board of Trade; BC - Bureau de commerce; CC - Chamber of Commerce/Chambre de commerce

7-32 BOARDS OF TRADE & CHAMBERS OF COMMERCE

Pembroke & Area CC, 2 International Dr., ON K8A 6W5 – 613/735-5381; Fax: 613/735-2738 – Treasurer, G. Gybulski

Penetanguishene-Tiny CC, Town Docks, End of Hwy. 93, PO Box 90, ON L0K 1P0 – 705/549-2232; Fax: 705/549-6640 – General Manager, Michael Ludolph

Perth CC, 80 Gore St. East, ON K7H 1H9 – 613/267-3200; Fax: 613/267-6797 – General Manager, Marion Crawford

Greater Peterborough CC, 175 George St. North, ON K9J 3G6 – 705/748-9771; Fax: 705/743-2331; URL: http://www.ptbo.igs.net/~chamber – General Manager, Don Frise

Prince Edward CC, 116 Main St., PO Box 893, Picton ON K0K 2T0 – 613/476-2421; Fax: 613/476-7461 – Secretary/Manager, Babbs Welsh

Pointe-au-Baril CC, Hwy. 69, PO Box 67, Pointe-au-Baril-Station ON P0G 1K0 – 705/366-2331; Fax: 705/366-2331 – Manager, Roxie McPhee

Port Colborne-Wainfleet CC, 76 Main St. West, ON L3K 3V2 – 905/834-9765; Fax: 905/834-1542 – Office Manager, D. Panetta

Port Dover BT, 225 Main St., PO Box 239, ON N0A 1N0 – URL: http://www.nornet.on.ca/portdover/ – President, L. Varey

Port Elgin & District CC, 515 Goderich St., ON N0H 2C4 – 519/832-2332; Fax: 519/389-3725; Toll Free: 1-800-387-3456 – General Manager, Connie Barker

Port Hope & District CC, 35 & 37 John St., ON L1A 2Z3 – 905/885-5519; Fax: 905/885-1142 – Manager, Debbie McQueen

Port Rowan-Long Point CC, Main St., PO Box 357, ON N0E 1M0 – President, P. Steiner

Port Sydney & Area CC, PO Box 1000, ON P0B 1L0 – 705/385-0162; Fax: 705/385-0163 – President, A. Lenze

Prescott & District CC, PO Box 2000, ON K0E 1T0 – 613/925-2257; Fax: 613/925-1585 – Executive Manager, Mike Boyles

Red Lake District CC, PO Box 430, ON P0V 2M0 – 807/727-3722; Fax: 807/727-3285 – Treasurer, T. Patrick

Renfrew & Area CC, PO Box 220, ON K7V 4A3 – 613/432-7015 – Manager, B. Mayhew

Richmond Hill CC, 376 Church St. South, ON L4C 9V8 – 905/884-1961; Fax: 905/884-1962 – General Manager, Barbara Scollick

Rideau Township CC, PO Box 817, Manotick ON K4M 1A7 – 613/489-0228; Fax: 613/489-2928 – President, D. Watchorn

Ridgetown & District CC, PO Box 522, ON N0P 2C0 – 519/674-0766; Fax: 519/674-0763 – President, H.J. Cole

Rodney Aldborough CC, RR#1, ON N0L 2C0 – Chairman, J. Fisher

Russell CC, PO Box 218, ON K4R 1C8 – 613/445-5308; Fax: 613/445-3140 – President, M. Ion

St Thomas & District CC, 555 Talbot St., ON N5P 1C5 – 519/631-1981; Fax: 519/631-0466; Email: chamber@ccia.st-thomas.ca; URL: http://www.mts-inc.com/chamber/ – President/CEO, Bob Hammersley

Sarnia Lambton CC, 224 North Vidal St., ON N7T 5Y3 – 519/336-2400; Fax: 519/336-2085 – General Manager, Gerry Macartney

Sauble Beach CC, General Delivery, ON N0H 2G0 – 519/422-1051 – Secretary, M. Husak

Sault Ste Marie CC, 334 Bay St., ON P6A 1X1 – 705/949-7152; Fax: 705/759-8166 – General Manager, Gene Nori

Scarborough/Metro East CC, #216, 1200 Markham Rd., ON M1H 3C3 – 416/439-4140; Fax: 416/439-4147 – Executive Director, D. Smyth

Schomberg CC, General Delivery, ON L0G 1T0 – President, B. Conzelmann

Scugog CC, 269 Queen St., PO Box 1282, Port Perry ON L9L 1B1 – 905/985-4971; Fax: 905/986-1049; URL: http://web.idirect.com/~haertel/chamber/chamber.html – 1st Vice-President, B. McIntosh

Simcoe & District CC, 76 Kent St. South, ON N3Y 2Y1 – 519/426-5867; Fax: 519/428-7718; URL: http://www.kwic.com:80/~chamber – General Manager, Yvonne Di Pietro

Sioux Lookout CC, PO Box 577, ON P8T 1A8 – 807/737-1937; Fax: 807/737-1778 – Executive Administrator, Linda Adduono

Smiths Falls & District CC, Town Hall, 77 Beckwith St. North, ON K7A 2B8 – 613/283-1334; Fax: 613/283-4764 – Manager, Victoria Ash

South River & Area CC, PO Box 600, ON P0A 1X0 – 705/386-0005 – Secretary/Manager, E. Innes

Southampton CC, Southampton Tourist Information Centre, 204 High St., PO Box 261, ON N0H 2L0 – 519/797-2215; Fax: 519/797-1222 – President, T. Thomas

St Catharines & District CC, 11 King St., PO Box 940, ON L2R 6Z4 – 905/684-2361; Fax: 905/684-2100; Email: kdrewitt@stc-chamber.com; URL: http://www.niagara.com/stc-chamber – General Manager, Kathy G. Drewitt

Stratford & District CC, #1, 121 Ontario St., 2nd Fl., ON N5A 3H1 – 519/273-5250; Fax: 519/273-2229 – General Manager, Nancy Bomasuit

Sudbury & District CC, 166 Douglas St., ON P3E 1G1 – 705/673-7133; Fax: 705/673-2944 – Executive Director, Debbi Nicholson

Tavistock CC, PO Box 670, ON N0B 2R0 – 519/655-3303; Fax: 519/655-3591 – President, J. Buffham

Thornbury & District CC, PO Box 477, ON N0H 2P0 – 519/599-3223 – President, M. Douglas

Thorold CC, 3 Front St. North, ON L2V 3Y7 – 905/680-4233; Fax: 905/680-4233 – Office Manager, Terry M. Dow

Thunder Bay CC, 857 May St. North, ON P7C 3S2 – 807/622-9642; Fax: 807/622-7752; Email: tbchamber@microage-tb.com – President, Rebecca Johnson

Tilbury & District CC, PO Box 1355, ON N0P 2L0 – 519/682-1766; Fax: 519/682-1766 – Secretary, S. Blain

Tillsonburg District CC, PO Box 113, ON N4G 4H3 – 519/842-5571; Fax: 519/842-2941; Email: matt@oxford.net – Sec.-Treas., Matthew Scholtz

Timmins CC, PO Box 985, ON P4N 7H6 – 705/360-1900; Fax: 705/360-1193 – Manager, Roberta Carey

Tobermory & District CC, PO Box 250, ON N0H 2R0 – 519/596-2452; Fax: 519/596-2536 – Coordinator, Shirley Johnstone

BT of Metropolitan Toronto, One First Canadian Place, PO Box 60, ON M5X 1C1 – 416/366-6811; Fax: 416/366-4906 – CEO, M. Elyse Allan

Trenton & District CC, 97 Front St., PO Box 536, ON K8V 5R7 – 613/392-7635; Fax: 613/394-7064 – Manager, J. Kingston

Tri-Town & District CC, #78, Hwy. 11B, PO Box 811, New Liskeard ON P0J 1P0 – 705/647-5771; Fax: 705/647-8633 – Office Manager, T. Nagy-Thisdelle

Uxbridge & District CC, PO Box 640, ON L9P 1N1 – 905/852-7683 – Secretary, Lois Bushell

Vaughan CC, #101, 8 Director Ct., Woodbridge ON L4L 3Z5 – 905/850-0024; Fax: 905/850-2441 – General Manager, Jennifer Nicholson

Walkerton & District CC, 7 Victoria St., PO Box 1344, ON N0G 2V0 – 519/881-3413; Fax: 519/881-4009 – Manager, Nicole Schnurr

Wallaceburg & District CC, PO Box 20048, ON N8A 5G1 – 519/627-1443; Fax: 519/627-9231 – General Manager, D. Keeler

Wasaga Beach CC, 35 Dunkerron St., PO Box 394, ON L0L 2P0 – 705/429-2247; Fax: 705/429-1407 – General Manager, Charlene Spooner

The Welland/Pelham CC, 32 East Main St., ON L3B 3W3 – 905/732-7515; Fax: 905/732-7175 – Executive Director, Dolores Fabiano

West Carleton District CC, PO Box 179, Carp ON K0A 1L0 – 613/839-5327; Fax: 613/839-0056 – Secretary, R. Lyall

West Lincoln CC, PO Box 555, Smithville ON L0R 2A0 – 905/957-1606; Fax: 905/957-0088 – President, M. Van Spronsen

West Muskoka CC, PO Box 536, Bala ON P0C 1A0 – 705/762-3214; Fax: 705/762-0791 – Allan Turnbull

Whitby CC, 128 Brock St. South, ON L1N 4J8 – 905/668-4506; Fax: 905/668-1894 – General Manager, Debra Cullis-Filip

Whitchurch-Stouffville CC, PO Box 1500, ON L4A 8A4 – 905/642-4227; Fax: 905/642-8966 – Office Manager, Barbara St. John

Windsor & District CC, 2575 Ouellette Place, ON N8X 1L9 – 519/966-3696; Fax: 519/966-0603 – President, Larry E. Sandre, C.A.

Wingham & Area CC, PO Box 368, ON N0G 2W0 – 519/357-1522; Fax: 519/357-1551 – Secretary, Andy Beninger

Woodstock District CC, 18 Wellington St. North, ON N4S 6P2 – 519/539-9411; Fax: 519/539-5433 – General Manager, A.A. Mowat

Belmore CC, RR#1, PO Box 21, Wroxeter ON N0G 2X0 – 519/392-8010 – Sec.-Treas., Ruth Knight

Zurich & District CC, PO Box 189, ON N0M 2T0 – 519/236-4982 – Secretary, Delores Schilbe

PRINCE EDWARD ISLAND

Greater Charlottetown CC, 127 Kent St., PO Box 67, PE C1A 7K2 – 902/628-2000; Fax: 902/368-3570 – General Manager, Harvey MacKinnon

Crapaud/Victoria CC, RR#1, PE C0A 1J0 – 902/658-2781; Fax: 902/964-3377 – President, Marion Miller

Eastern Kings Regional CC, PO Box 328, Souris PE C0A 2B0 – 902/687-2055; Fax: 902/687-3424 – President, Alice Winterhalder

Kensington & Area CC, PO Box 234, PE C0B 1M0 – 902/836-3209; Fax: 902/836-5659 – President, Austin Pendergast, 902/836-3301

Montague & District CC, PE C0A 1R0 – 902/838-2323 – President, Cameron McLean

Greater Summerside CC, #10, 263 Harbour Dr., PE C1N 5P1 – 902/436-9651; Fax: 902/436-8320 – President, David Groom

West Prince CC, Alberton PE C0B 1B0 – 902/853-2297; Fax: 902/853-3822 – President, Paul Arsenault

QUÉBEC

CC de l'Abitibi-Ouest, #100, 6 - 8e av est, La Sarre PQ J9Z 1N6

CC de la Région d'Acton, CP 1448, Acton Vale PQ J0H 1A0 – 514/546-7642

CC d'Alma, 200, av des Pins ouest, PQ G8B 6P9

CC d'Amiante, CP 572, Thetford-Mines PQ G6G 5T6 – 418/335-3441

CC d'Amos-Région, 102, av de la Gare, CP 93, PQ J9T 3A5

CC d'Amqui, CP 2317, PQ G0J 1B0

CC d'Anse-au-Griffon, CP 62, PQ G0E 1A0 – 418/892-5259

CC d'Arundel, Barkmere, Huberdeau, Montcalm, CP 183, PQ J0T 1G0

Cercle des affaires de la région d'Asbestos, CP 176, PQ J1T 3M9

CC de Baie-Comeau, 63, Place Lasalle, PQ G4Z 1J8 – 418/296-2010

CC de Barraute, CP 217, PQ J0Y 1A0

CC de Bas St-François, CP 293, Pierreville PQ J0G 1J0 – 514/568-3540

CC de Basse Côte-Nord, Secteur Est, CP 399, Lourdes-du-Blanc-Sablon PQ G0G 1W0

CC de Beauceville, 595, 9e av de Léry, CP 782, Beauceville-Est PQ G0S 1A0 – 418/774-2322; Fax: 418/774-6485 – Président, Christian Duval

CC de Beauport-Cote de Beaupré, 589, av Royale, PQ G1E 1Y5
CC de Bécancour, CP 531, St-Grégoire PQ G0X 1G0
CC de la région de Berthier, 145, ch de la Traverse, St-Ignace-de-Loyola PQ J0K 2P0
CC de Bic et St-Valérien, CP 437, PQ G0L 1B0
CC de Bois-des-Filion-Lorraine, CP 72012, PQ J6Z 4N9
CC de Bois-Francs, 122, rue Acqueduc, CP 641, Victoriaville PQ G6P 6V7
CC région Bolton, 858, route Missisquoi, Bolton Centre PQ J0E 1G0 – 514/292-4217 – Président, Richard Clinton
CC de Bonaventure, CP 848, PQ G0C 1E0
CC de Brandon, 117, rue Pacifique, CP 778, St-Gabriel-de-Brandon PQ J0K 2N0 – 514/835-2105; Fax: 514/835-2105 – Secrétaire, France Brisebois
CC de Cacouna, CP 324, PQ G0L 1G0
CC de Cap-St-Ignace, CP 115, PQ G0R 1H0
CC de Cap-de-la-Madeleine, 170, rue des Cheneaux, CP 183, PQ G8T 7W2
CC de Cap-des-Rosiers, 1127, Cap-des-Rosiers, PQ G0E 1E0
CC de Carleton, CP 209, PQ G0C 1J0
CC de Causapscal, 5, rue St-Jacques sud, PQ G0J 1J0
CC de Châteauguay, #106, 265, boul d'Anjou, PQ J6J 5J9
CC du bassin de Chambly, 1101, boul Brassard, CP 209, PQ J3L 5R4
CC de Chapais, CP 99, PQ G0W 1H0
CC de Charlesbourg-Chauveau, #295, 8500, rue Henri-Bourassa, CP 7008, PQ G1G 5E1 – 418/626-5514; Fax: 418/626-5485
CC de Charlevoix-Est, #200, 130, boul de Comporté, La Malbaie PQ G5A 1P7
CC de Charlevoix-Ouest, 11, rue St-Jean-Baptiste, CP 1900, Baie-St-Paul PQ G0A 1B0
CC de Chibougamau, 550, 3e rue, CP 600, PQ G8P 2Y8
CC de Chicoutimi, 31, rue Racine Ouest, CP 1162, PQ G7H 5G4
CC de la région de Coaticook, CP 243, PQ J1A 2T7
CC de Contrecoeur, 525, rue St-Antoine, PQ J0L 1C0 – 514/587-2353; Fax: 514/587-2353
CC de Cookshire, CP 75, PQ J0B 1M0
CC de Cowansville et région, 500, rue Sud, PQ J2K 2X8
CC de Delisle, CP 83, PQ G0W 1L0
CC Denis-Riverin, CP 422, Ste-Anne-des-Monts PQ G0E 2G0
CC des Moulins, #305, 1025, Montée Masson, Lachenaie PQ J6W 5H9
CC de Disraéli, 817, av Champlain, PQ G0N 1E0
CC de Dolbeau, CP 26, PQ G8L 2P9 – 418/276-7073; Fax: 418/276-9518
CC de Donnacona, Cap-Santé, CP 358, PQ G0A 1T0
CC de Drummond, 405, rue St-Jean, CP 188, Drummondville PQ J2B 6V7
CC de Duparquet, CP 70, PQ J0Z 1W0
CC de East-Angus, CP 490, East Angus PQ J0B 1R0
CC East Broughton, CP 209, PQ G0N 1G0 – Président, Michel Bastille
CC de Farnham et Région, #102, 477, rue de l'Hôtel de Ville, PQ J2N 2H3
CC de Ferme-Neuve, CP 715, PQ J0W 1C0 – 819/587-3882; Fax: 819/587-3861
CC de Forestville, CP 1030, PQ G0T 1E0
CC de Frampton, CP 127, PQ G0R 1M0
CC de Gaspé, CP 66, PQ G0C 1R0
CC de Gaspésie Centrale, CP 160, Grande-Vallée PQ G0E 1K0 – Présidente, Denise Mirville, 418/393-2808
CC du Coeur de la Gatineau, RR#1, Gracefield PQ J0X 1W0
CC du district de Granby - Bromont, #200, 328, rue Principale, CP 907, PQ J2G 2W4
CC et d'industrie de Grand-Mère, CP 322, PQ G9T 5L1

CC de Grande-Rivière, CP 145, PQ G0C 1V0 – 418/385-3088 – Président, Jean-Guy Boudreau, 418/385-3224
CC de Grenville et Canton, CP 219, PQ J0V 1J0
CC de Haut St-Maurice, 1525, ch de la Rivière Croche, La Tûque PQ G9X 3N7
CC Hauts-Reliefs, 1047, route 263, St-Jacques-le-Majeur PQ G0P 1G0
CC de Haut-Richelieu, 31, rue Frontenac, St-Jean-sur-Richelieu PQ J3B 2K1
CC Haute Matawinie, 721, rue Brassard, St-Michel-des-Saints PQ J0K 3B0
CC de Hemmingford, CP 295, PQ J0L 1H0 – 514/247-3310; Fax: 514/247-2389
CC d'Îles-de-la-Madeleine, CP 307, Cap-aux-Meules PQ G0B 1B0 – 418/986-4112
CC du Grand Joliette, 500, rue Dollar, PQ J6E 4M4
CC de Jonquière, 3791, rue de la Fabrique, CP 211, PQ G7X 7V9
CC de L'Assomption, CP 3027, PQ J5W 4M9 – 514/589-2405; Fax: 514/589-9213
CC de l'Érable, CP 341, Plessisville PQ G6L 2Y8
CC L'Isle-Verte, 115, rue St-Jean Baptiste, PQ G0L 1K0
CC et d'industrie de l'Outaouais, #300, 166, rue Varennes, Gatineau PQ J8T 8G4
CC et d'industrie de Ville de La Baie, 1226, 6e av, CP 1416, PQ G7B 3P5
CC de la Pocatière, CP 2080, La Pocatière PQ G0R 1Z0
CC de Labelle, 7404, boul du Curé Labelle, CP 630, PQ J0T 1H0 – 819/686-2708; Fax: 819/686-2606 – Directrice générale, Marie-Emma Rabellins
CC de Lac Brôme, CP 723, Knowlton PQ J0E 1V0
CC de Lac des Deux-Montagnes, #400, 190 - 41e av, Pointe-Calumet PQ J0N 1G2 – 819/473-2708 – Président, Rosaire Morin
CC Lac du Cerf, 141, ch du Lac Mallone, PQ J0W 1S0
CC de la région de Lac Mégantic, 3620, rue St-Adolphe, PQ G6B 1M4 – 418/583-4662; Fax: 418/583-5476
CC de Lac Robertson, La Tabatière PQ G0G 1T0 – Sec.-Trés., G. Organ
CC de Lachute, CP 517, PQ J8H 3Y1
CC et d'industrie de Laval, #200, 1555, boul Chomedey, PQ H7V 3Z1
CC de Lavaltrie, CP 691, PQ J0K 1H0
CC Le Gardeur, 333, boul Lacombe, PQ J5Z 1N2
CC Les Escoumins, CP 758, PQ G0T 1K0
CC de St-Côme-Linière, CP 827, PQ G0M 1J0
CC et d'industrie de Magog-Orford, CP 233, PQ J1X 3W8
CC de Malartic, CP 368, PQ J0Y 1Z0
CC de Maniwaki, CP 5, PQ J9E 3B3
CC de Maria, CP 1098, PQ G0C 1Y0
CC de Marieville, #2, 491, rue Ste-Marie, CP 1502, PQ J3M 1N2
CC de Mascouche, #240, 2822, ch Ste-Marie, PQ J7K 1N4 – 514/966-1536; Fax: 514/966-1531
MRC de Maskinongé, CP 35, Louiseville PQ J5V 2L6 – 819/227-2288
CC région de Matane, 968, du Phare Ouest, CP 518, PQ G4W 3P5
CC de Mirabel, 13 479, boul du Curé Labelle, PQ J7J 1H1
CC de Mistassini, CP 1330, PQ G0W 2C0
CC de la région de Mont-Joli, CP 183, PQ G5H 3K9
CC de Mont-Laurier, 177, boul A. Paquette, PQ J9L 1J2 – 819/623-3642; Fax: 819/623-5220 – Directeur général, Luc Brunet Beaudry
Mount Royal Business Centre, #110, 4480, Côte de Liesse, Mont-Royal PQ H4N 2R1 – 514/733-8600; Fax: 514/733-6343
CC de Mont-Tremblant, 140A, rue du Couvent, CP 248, PQ J0T 1Z0
CC de Montmagny, 37, rue Ste-Marie, PQ G5V 2R6
CC du Montréal métropolitain, Niveau plaza, #140, 5, Place Ville-Marie, PQ H3B 4Y2 – 514/871-4000; Fax: 514/871-1255 – Chairman, David Powell

CC du Sud-Ouest de l'Île de Montréal, 530, rue de l'Église, CP 308, Verdun PQ H4G 3E9 – Directeur général, Marc Snyder
CC de Montréal-Nord, Place Levasseur, #19, 5600, boul Henri-Bourassa est, PQ H1G 2T3 – 514/329-4453; Fax: 514/329-5373 – Directrice générale, France Huneault
CC Rive-Sud de Montréal, #100, 1000, rue de Serigny, Longueuil PQ J4H 5B1 – 514/463-2121
CC des Monts, CP 422, Ste-Anne-des-Monts PQ G0E 2G0
CC de la région de Napierville, 210, St-Nicolas, PQ J0J 1L0
CC de Nicolet, 30, rue Notre-Dame, PQ J3T 1G1 – 819/293-4537; Fax: 819/293-4537
CC du secteur de Normandin, 1048, rue St-Cyrille, CP 1080, PQ G0W 2E0 – 418/274-2004; Fax: 418/274-7171
CC de Notre-Dame-du-Lac, CP 147, PQ G0L 1X0
CC de Notre-Dame-du-Nord, CP 517, PQ J0Z 3B0
CC d'Oka, CP 310, PQ J0N 1E0
CC d'Outremont, #209, 40, rue Bates, PQ H2V 4T5
CC du Grand Paspébiac, 172, rte St-Pie-IX, PQ G0C 2K0
CC de Percé, CP 431, PQ G0C 2L0
CC de Piedmont, 100, rue de la Gare, PQ J0R 1K0
CC de Pont-Rouge, CP 744, PQ G0A 2X0
CC de Port-Cartier, CP 82, PQ G5B 2G7
CC de Princeville, CP 430, PQ G0P 1E0
CC et d'industrie du Québec métropolitain, 17, rue St-Louis, PQ G1R 3Y8 – 418/692-3853; Fax: 418/694-2286; URL: http://cciqm.megatoon.com
CC Rive-Sud de Québec, 4950, boul de la Rive-Sud, CP 312, Lévis PQ G6V 4Z6
CC de Radisson, CP 901, PQ J0Y 2X0
CC de Rawdon, 3588, rue Metcalfe, PQ J0K 1S0
CC de Repentigny, CP 140, PQ J6A 2T7
CC de la région de Richmond, CP 339, PQ J0B 2H0
CC de Rimouski, #201B, 125, boul René Lepage, CP 1296, PQ G5L 8M2
CC de Rivière St-Augustin, Pointe-à-la-Croix PQ G0C 2R0 – 418/947-2721
CC de Rivière-au-Renard, CP 54, PQ G0E 2A0
CC du Transcontinental, CP 157, Rivière-Bleue PQ G0L 2B0
CC de Rivière-des-Prairies, #200, 9708 - 4e rue, PQ H1C 1T2 – 514/494-8916 – Président, Louis Pelletier
CC de Rivière-du-Loup, 37, rue St-Louis, PQ G5R 2V3 – 418/862-5243; Fax: 418/862-5136
CC de Roberval, CP 115, Succ Bureau chef, PQ G8H 2N4
CC de Rock-Forest, Saint-Élie, Deauville, CP 6265, Rock Forest PQ J1N 3C9
CC de Rougemont, 11, ch Marieville, PQ J0L 1M0
CC et d'industrie du Rouyn-Noranda régional, CP 634, PQ J9X 5C6 – 819/797-2000; Fax: 819/762-3091 – Vice-président exécutif, Julie Bouchard
CC de Sainte-Adèle, 333, boul Sainte-Adèle, PQ J0R 1L0 – 514/229-2644
CC de St-Adolphe-d'Howard, CP 390, PQ J0T 2B0
CC du Grand de Sainte-Agathe-des-Monts, CP 323, PQ J8C 3C6 – 819/326-3731; Fax: 819/326-3936
CC de St-Anicet, 1529, rte 132, local 233, PQ J0S 1M0
CC de St-Anselme Honfleur Inc., CP 28, PQ G0R 2N0 – 418/885-4540; Fax: 418/885-9089
CC de Saint-Basile-le-Grand, CP 1064, PQ J3N 1M5
CC de St-Boniface, 1515, boul Trudel est, St-Boniface-de-Shawinigan PQ G0X 2L0
CC de Ste-Brigitte-de-Laval, CP 196, PQ G0A 3K0
CC de Saint-Bruno, 1377, rue Hillside, PQ J3V 3L3 – 514/653-2861
CC de St-Camille-de-Bellechasse, CP 288, PQ G0R 2S0
CC Jacques-Cartier, CP 53, Ste-Catherine-de-la-J. Cartier PQ G0A 3M0
CC de Saint-Césaire, 1201, av St-Paul, PQ J0L 1T0
CC de Ste-Claire, CP 728, PQ G0R 2V0
CC de Saint-Côme, 1240, rue Principale, PQ J0K 2B0

* BT - Board of Trade; BC - Bureau de commerce; CC - Chamber of Commerce/Chambre de commerce

CC de Ste-Croix, CP 488, PQ G0S 2H0
CC de St-Donat, CP 129, St-Donat-de-Montcalm PQ J0T 2C0 – 819/424-2833; Fax: 819/424-3809
CC de St-Ephrem-de-Beauce, CP 268, St-Éphrem-de-Beauce PQ G0M 1R0
CC Les Grès, CP 177, St-Étienne-des-Grès PQ G0X 2P0
CC de St-Esprit, 24, rue Principale, PQ J0K 2L0
CC de St-Eugène-de-Guigues, CP 1018, PQ J0Z 3L0
CC de la région de Saint-Eustache, 192, boul Industriel, St-Eustache PQ J7R 5C2 – 514/491-1991
CC de St-Faustin, Lac Carré, Lac Supérieur, CP 341, PQ J0T 2G0
CC de St-Félicien, CP 34, PQ G8K 2P8
Association de développement économique de Valois, CP 869, St-Félix-de-Valois PQ J0K 2M0
CC régionale de Ste-Foy, #610, 2700, boul Laurier, PQ G1V 2L8 – URL: http://www.riq.qc.ca/ccrsf
CC de St-Frédéric, 196, rue Principale, PQ G0N 1P0
CC de St-Gédéon, CP 118, PQ G0M 1T0
CC de St-Georges-de-Beauce, 12435, 1re av est, PQ G5Y 2E3 – 418/228-7879; Fax: 418/228-8074 – Directrice générale, Jeanne Bizier
CC de Ste-Germaine - Lac Etchemin, CP 128, PQ G0R 1S0
CC de St-Hubert, CP 86, St-Hubert-de-Témiscouata PQ G0L 3L0
CC du district de Saint-Hyacinthe, #260, 2685, boul Casavant ouest, PQ J2S 8B8
CC de St-Jérôme métropolitain, 324, rue Labelle, PQ J7Z 5L3
CC de St-Jean-de-Dieu, CP 392, PQ G0L 3M0
CC de St-Jean-de-Matha, 180, rue Ste-Louise, PQ J0K 2S0
CC et d'industrie de Saint-Joseph-de-Beauce, CP 507, St-Joseph-de-Beauce PQ G0S 2V0
CC de St-Jovite, CP 67, PQ J0T 2H0
CC de Ste-Julienne, CP 429, Sainte-Julienne PQ J0K 2T0 – 819/831-3551; Fax: 819/831-3551
CC de Ste-Justine, 167, Route 204, PQ G0R 1Y0
CC de St-Laurent, #105, 9900, boul Cavendish, PQ H4M 2V2 – 514/333-5222; Fax: 514/333-0937; Email: admin@chambr.saint-laurent.qc.ca; URL: http://www.cibus.ca/stlaurent – Directeur général, Alex Harper
CC de St-Léonard, #202, 4875, boul Metropolitain est, PQ H1R 3J2 – 514/325-4232; Fax: 514/325-8980 – Président, Roberto Colavecchio
CC de St-Léonard-d'Aston, CP 520, PQ J0C 1M0
CC de St-Léonard-de-Portneuf, 530, rue Lefebvre, PQ G0A 4A0 – 418/337-4469
CC de Saint-Lin, 457, rue St-Isidore, CP 250, PQ J0R 1C0
CC de St-Marc-des-Carrières, CP 579, PQ G0A 4B0
CC Ste-Marguerite du Lac Masson - Estérel, CP 480, Lac-Masson PQ J0T 1L0
CC de Sainte-Marie de Beauce, CP 684, PQ G6E 3B9
CC de Saint-Martin de Beauce, CP 31, PQ G0M 1B0
CC de Ste-Perpétue, 589, rue Principale, Ste-Perpétue-de-l'Islet PQ G0R 3Z0 – 418/359-2226
CC de Fugèreville, 490, Côte du Pont, St-Pierre PQ G0A 4E0
CC d'Île d'Orléans, 490, Côte du Pont, St-Pierre-d'Orléans PQ G0A 4E0
CC de St-Prosper, CP 519, PQ G0M 1Y0
CC de St-Raymond, CP 238, PQ G0A 4G0
CC de Saint-Rémi, CP 918, PQ J0L 2L0
CC de la Vallée de St-Sauveur, Suite M, 100, rue Guindon, PQ J0R 1R6
CC de Thérèse de Blainville, CP 465, Ste-Thérèse-de-Blainville PQ J7E 4J8
CC de la région de Salaberry-de-Valleyfield, #200, 185, rue Victoria, PQ J6T 1A7
CC de Senneterre, CP 747, PQ J0Y 2M0 – 819/737-2694; Fax: 819/737-2694 – Président, Guylaine Taillefer
CC de Sept-Îles, #204, 700, boul Laure, PQ G4R 1Y1 – 418/968-3488; Fax: 418/968-3432

CC de Shawinigan et Shawinigan-Sud, Hôtel de Ville, CP 397, PQ G9N 6V1 – 819/536-5197; Fax: 819/536-4478
CC de la région Sherbrookoise, 390, rue King ouest, CP 1356, Sherbrooke PQ J1H 5L9
CC de Sorel-Tracy métropolitain, CP 568, PQ J3P 5N9
CC de Témiscaming-Kipawa, CP 304, PQ J0Z 3R0
CC de Tring Jonction, 17, rue St-Michel, PQ G0N 1X0
CC de Trois-Pistoles, CP 876, PQ G0L 4K0
CC du district de Trois-Rivières, CP 1045, PQ G9A 5K4 – 819/375-9628; Fax: 819/375-9083 – Directeur général, Mario Côté
CC de Val-d'Or, 400, 3e av, PQ J9P 1R9
CC de Valcourt et Région, CP 900, PQ J0E 2L0
CC de Vallée de la Petite Nation, CP 590, St-André-Avellin PQ J0V 1W0
CC de Vallée du Richelieu, #304, 220, rue Brébeuf, Beloeil PQ J3G 5P3
CC et d'industrie de Varennes, CP 61, PQ J3X 1P9
CC de Vaudreuil-Dorion, #200, 417, av Roche, PQ J7V 2M9
CC Soulanges et Région, CP 122, Dorion PQ J7V 5W1 – 514/424-4190
CC de Ville Dégelis, CP 722, PQ G5T 2C9
CC de Ville-Marie, CP 308, PQ J0Z 3W0
CC de Villebois, 3070, Villebois rang 6, PQ J0Z 3V0
CC de Waterloo, CP 309, PQ J0E 2N0 – 819/539-1102
CC de la région de Weedon, CP 400, PQ J0B 3J0
CC de West-Island, #201, 1870, boul des Sources, Pointe-Claire PQ H9R 5N4 – 514/697-4228; Fax: 514/697-2562 – Directrice générale, Hélène Carrier
CC de Windsor et région, CP 115, PQ J1S 2L7

SASKATCHEWAN
Arborfield BT, c/o Arborfield Credit Union, PO Box 265, SK S0E 0A0 – 306/769-8581; Fax: 306/769-4114 – President, Alvin Alyeh, 306/769-8687
Aylsham & District BT, c/o Ken Rae Farms, PO Box 21, SK S0E 0C0 – 306/862-4849 – President, Glen Gray, 306/862-3028, Fax: 306/862-5306
Battlefords CC, Hwy. 40 & 16E, PO Box 1000, North Battleford SK S9A 3E6 – 306/445-6226; Fax: 306/445-6633 – Executive Vice-President, Henry N. Bergen
Big River CC, PO Box 473, SK S0J 0E0 – 306/469-4488 – President, Wanda Watier
Biggar & District CC, PO Box 879, SK S0K 0M0 – 306/948-5262; Fax: 306/948-5263 – President, Mike Messer
Blaine Lake & District CC, 327 - 1st Ave. East, PO Box 88, SK S0J 0J0 – 306/497-2443; Fax: 306/497-2407 – President, Barbara Woytuik, 306/497-2461
Broadview CC, 524 Main St., PO Box 40, SK S0G 0K0 – 306/696-2525; Fax: 306/696-2778 – President, Randy Heard, 306/696-2262
Candle Lake CC, c/o Brassard's Service Ltd., PO Box 68, SK S0J 3E0 – 306/929-2233; Fax: 306/929-2220 – President, Stella Brassard
Canora & District CC, PO Box 2007, SK S0A 0L0 – 306/563-5886; Fax: 306/563-6743 – President, Juliet Zbijniff
Carlyle CC, PO Box 299, SK S0C 0R0 – 306/453-2213; Fax: 306/453-2342 – President, Judy Mazurek
Carrot River & District BT, 19 Main St., PO Box 340, SK S0E 0L0 – 306/768-2533; Fax: 306/768-2532 – President, Perry C. Cavanaugh
Choiceland & District CC, c/o Grow Plan Fertilizers Ltd., 155 Railway Ave. West, PO Box 339, SK S0J 0M0 – 306/428-2300; Fax: 306/428-2424 – President, Frank H. Bond
Coronach Community CC, PO Box 57, SK S0H 0Z0 – 306/267-3251; Fax: 306/267-3234 – President, Mike Ciona, 306/267-3267
Cut Knife CC, c/o Cargill Limited, 1000 Railway Ave., PO Box 489, SK S0M 0N0 – 306/398-4914 – President, Dale Rands

Debden & District CC, PO Box 100, SK S0J 0S0 – 306/724-2233; Fax: 306/724-2129 – President, Jim Zimmerman
Eastend CC, PO Box 534, SK S0N 0T0 – 306/295-3233; Fax: 306/295-3887 – President, Scott Morvik, 306/295-4060
Eatonia & District CC, c/o Hansen's Agency Ltd., 216 Main St., PO Box 460, SK S0L 0Y0 – 306/967-2201; Fax: 306/967-2302 – President, Bruce Cooke
Edam & District BT, c/o Day's Electric, Main St., PO Box 86, SK S0M 0V0 – 306/397-2332 – President, Cameron Day
Esterhazy & District CC, PO Box 778, SK S0A 0X0 – 306/745-2667; Fax: 306/745-2446 – President, Barry Hassler, 306/745-3965
Estevan CC, 1102 - 4th St., SK S4A 0W7 – 306/634-2828; Fax: 306/634-6729 – Executive Director, Linda Mack
Eston BT, PO Box 1000, SK S0L 1A0 – 306/962-3717; Fax: 306/962-4445 – President, Audrey Tumback
Foam Lake CC, PO Box 238, SK S0A 1A0 – 306/272-3242; Fax: 306/272-4294 – President, Steve Ostapowich, 306/272-4279
Fort Qu'Appelle & District CC, PO Box 1273, SK S0G 1S0 – 306/332-5666; Fax: 306/332-5414 – President, Andy Govinchuck
Fox Valley CC, c/o Double L. Farms, PO Box 133, SK S0N 0V0 – 306/666-4447; Fax: 306/666-4448 – President, Lester Lodoen
Goodsoil & District CC, c/o Goodsoil Credit Union, PO Box 88, SK S0M 1A0 – 306/238-2033; Fax: 306/238-4441 – President, Lucille Martin, 306/238-2112, Fax: 306/238-4544
Grenfell CC, PO Box 897, SK S0G 2B0 – 306/697-2247; Fax: 306/697-3598 – President, Greg Watkins, 306/697-3510
Gull Lake & District CC, PO Box 262, SK S0N 1A0 – 306/672-4105 – President, Casey Vaskevicius
Herbert & District CC, PO Box 190, SK S0H 2A0 – 306/784-2401; Fax: 306/784-2966 – President, Jake Dyck, 306/784-2224, Fax: 306/784-2226
Hudson Bay & District CC, PO Box 130, SK S0E 0Y0 – 306/865-3808; Fax: 306/865-2251 – President, Neil Hardy
Humboldt & District CC, PO Box 480, SK S0K 2A0 – 306/682-2696; Fax: 306/682-5712 – President, Lance Unger
Ituna & District CC, PO Box 609, SK S0A 1N0 – 306/795-3188; Fax: 306/795-3636 – President, Alfred W. Moore
Kamsack & District CC, PO Box 817, SK S0A 1S0 – 306/542-3335 – President, Randy Chernoff, 306/542-2464, Fax: 306/542-3492
Kelvington & District CC, PO Box 1077, SK S0A 1W0 – 306/327-4656 – President, Carol Lowey, 306/327-5179
Kenaston & District CC, PO Box 302, SK S0G 2N0 – 306/252-2171 – President, John Boehmer
Kerrobert CC, 521 Atlantic Ave., PO Box 454, SK S0L 1R0 – 306/834-2461; Fax: 306/834-5445 – President, Robert Aellen
Kindersley CC, PO Box 1537, SK S0L 1S0 – 306/463-2320; Fax: 306/463-4607 – President, Richard Jones, 306/463-4651
Kinistino & District CC, c/o Tom's Radio & TV, 202 Dixon Ave., SK S0J 1H0 – 306/864-2244 – President, Tom Dewing
Kipling CC, PO Box 700, SK S0G 2S0 – 306/736-8211 – President, Max Krecsy, 306/736-8124
La Ronge & District CC, PO Box 286, SK S0J 1L0 – 306/425-3055; Fax: 306/425-3883
Langenburg & District CC, c/o Wardale Equipment Ltd., PO Box 190, SK S0A 2A0 – 306/743-2312; Fax: 306/743-2953 – President, Dale Kotzer
Leader BT, c/o Stueck Pharmacy, PO Box 400, SK S0N 1H0 – 306/628-3744; Fax: 306/628-4378 – President, Gordon Stueck

Canadian Almanac & Directory 1997

Lloydminster CC, c/o Lakeland College, PO Bag 6600, SK S9V 1Z3 – 403/871-5736; Fax: 403/875-5136 – President, Elmer Nykiforuk
Macklin CC, PO Box 642, SK S0L 2C0 – 306/753-2045; Fax: 306/753-2339 – President, Gary Thompson
Maidstone & District CC, PO Box 461, SK S0M 1M0 – 306/893-2273; Fax: 306/893-2909 – President, Connie McCulloch
Maple Creek CC, PO Box 1865, SK S0N 1N0 – 306/662-2811; Fax: 306/662-4131 – Co-Chair, Johanna Drury
Meadow Lake & District CC, c/o Bannerman Photos, 215 Centre St., SK S9X 1L5 – 306/236-6646; Fax: 306/236-6646 – President, Lynn Bannerman
Melfort & District CC, c/o Chamber Office, 620 Saskatchewan Ave., PO Box 2002, SK S0E 1A0 – 306/752-4636; Fax: 306/752-9505 – Manager, Sherry M. Michalyca
Melville & District CC, c/o Chamber Office, 420 Main St., PO Box 429, SK S0A 2P0 – 306/728-4177; Fax: 306/728-5911 – Manager, Dawn Melnychuk
Moose Jaw CC, 88 Sask St. East, PO Box 1359, SK S6H 4R3 – 306/692-6414; Fax: 306/692-9590 – President, Lynn Starkey, 306/692-2337
Moosomin CC, PO Box 250, SK S0G 3N0 – 306/435-2445; Fax: 306/435-3969 – President, Don Osman, 306/435-3851
Nipawin & District CC, PO Box 177, SK S0E 1E0 – 306/862-5252; Fax: 306/862-5350 – Secretary/Manager, Eileen Tebbutt
Norquay CC, PO Box 247, SK S0A 2V0 – 306/594-2005; Fax: 306/594-2300 – Secretary, Cyndi Salyniuk
Outlook & District CC, c/o Lutheran Collegiate, PO Box 459, SK S0L 2N0 – 306/867-8971; Fax: 306/867-9947 – President, Daniel Haugen
Pangman CC, PO Box 31, SK S0C 2C0 – 306/442-2122 – President, Harry Shepard, 306/442-4449
Pierceland & District CC, PO Box 555, SK S0M 2K0 – 306/839-4496; Fax: 306/839-2306 – President, Lillian Mein
Porcupine Plain & District CC, PO Box 666, SK S0E 1H0 – 306/278-3017; Fax: 306/278-3150 – Co-President, Carl Kwiatkowski
Prince Albert CC, 3700 - 2 Ave. West, SK S6W 1A2 – 306/764-6222; Fax: 306/922-4727 – General Manager, Jerry J. Paskaruk
Radville CC, PO Box 22, SK S0G 2G0 – 306/869-2729 – President, Laurie Nuspl, 306/869-2610
Regina CC, 2145 Albert St., SK S4P 2V1 – 306/757-4658; Fax: 306/757-4668 – Executive Director, Deanna Dalla-Vicenza
Rosetown & District CC, PO Box 744, SK S0L 2V0 – 306/882-2221; Fax: 306/882-2217 – President, George Leith
Rosthern CC, c/o L&L Meats Inc., 1005 - 6th St., PO Box 96, SK S0K 3R0 – 306/232-4221 – Chairman, Les Neufeld
St. Brieux & District CC, Hwy. 368, PO Box 130, SK S0K 3V0 – 306/275-2300; Fax: 306/275-2307 – President, Lorraine Perault
St Walburg CC, PO Box 303, SK S0M 2T0 – Toll Free: 1-800-665-3611 – President, Kim Rendle, 306/248-3421
Saskatoon CC, 345 - 3 Ave. South, SK S7K 1M6 – 306/244-2151; Fax: 306/244-8366 – Executive Director, Phil Mamchur
Shaunavon CC, c/o Gallery of Gold, 370 Centre St., PO Box 1450, SK S0N 2M0 – 306/297-2385; Fax: 306/297-2241 – President, Leslie Goldstein
South Shore CC, PO Box 459, Regina Beach SK S0G 4C0 – 306/729-2327; Fax: 306/729-4747 – President, Morley Alexander
Spiritwood CC, 104 Main St., PO Box 820, SK S0J 2M0 – 306/883-2058 – President, Rod Higgins
Star City BT, c/o Canada Post Corp., 112 - 4th St., PO Box 142, SK S0E 1P0 – 306/863-2509 – President, Carol Pederson
Stoughton CC, PO Box 476, SK S0G 4T0 – 306/457-3188 – President, Thomas Sangster
Swift Current CC, Route 35, Mobile Delivery, SK S9H 3V6 – 306/773-7268; Fax: 306/773-5686 – Executive Director, Marlene Arndt
Tisdale & District CC, c/o Tisdale Florists, 918 - 9 Ave., PO Box 789, SK S0E 1T0 – 306/873-2025 – President, Wayne Harrison
Unity & District CC, PO Box 117, SK S0K 4L0 – 306/228-3744; Fax: 306/228-4510 – President, Jack Fewster
Vonda CC, PO Box 190, SK S0K 4N0 – 306/258-2134; Fax: 306/258-2244 – President, Raymond Lalonde
Wadena & District CC, PO Box 962, SK S0A 4J0 – 306/338-2561; Fax: 306/338-3621 – President, Pat Casement
Waskesiu CC, PO Box 216, Waskesiu Lake SK S0J 2Y0 – 306/663-5898; Fax: 306/663-5448 – President, Myrna Nagy
Watrous & District CC, PO Box 280, SK S0K 4T0 – 306/946-3955; Fax: 306/946-3966 – President, Earl Amendt
Watson & District CC, PO Box 85, SK S0K 4V0 – 306/287-3531; Fax: 306/287-3370 – President, Leo Schmid
Weyburn CC, 411 Industrial Lane, PO Box 1300, SK S4H 3J9 – 306/842-4738; Fax: 306/842-0520 – Manager, Lois Benneweis
Wolseley & District CC, PO Box 519, SK S0G 5H0 – 306/698-2244 – President, Shirley Harris
Wynyard & District CC, PO Box 1210, SK S0A 4T0 – 306/554-2507; Fax: 306/554-2507 – President, Elizabeth Zahayko
Yorkton CC, 131 Broadway St. East, PO Box 1051, SK S3N 2X3 – 306/783-4368; Fax: 306/786-6978 – Manager, Ruth Shaw
Zenon Park BT, c/o Zenon Park Credit Union, 735 Main St., PO Box 250, SK S0E 1W0 – 306/767-2434 – President, Allen Georget

YUKON TERRITORY
Whitehorse CC, #101, 302 Steele St., YT Y1A 2C5 – 403/667-7545; Fax: 403/667-4507 – President, Anne King

CHAMBERS OF MINES
Alberta Chamber of Resources, Oxford Tower, #1410, 10235 - 101 St., Edmonton AB T5J 3G1 – 403/420-1030,1031; Fax: 403/425-4623 – Managing Director, Donald Currie
British Columbia & Yukon Chamber of Mines, 840 Hastings St. West, Vancouver BC V6C 1C8 – 604/681-5328; Fax: 604/681-2363 – Managing Director, Jack Patterson
Chamber of Mineral Resources of Nova Scotia, #1720, 1801 Hollis St., Halifax NS B3J 3N4 – 902/422-5806; Fax: 902/422-9563 – Managing Director, Dick Smyth
Chamber of Mines of Eastern British Columbia, 215 Hall St., Nelson BC V1L 5X4 – 250/352-5242; Fax: 250/352-7227 – President, George Addie
Northwest Territories Chamber of Mines, PO Box 2818, Yellowknife NT X1A 2R1 – 403/873-5281; Fax: 403/920-2145 – General Manager, Tom W. Hoefer, M.Sc., P.Geol.
Yukon Chamber of Mines, PO Box 4427, Whitehorse YT Y1A 3T5 – 403/667-2090; Fax: 403/668-7127 – Managing Director, Robert L. McIntyre

CONSULTANT LOBBYISTS

Consultant lobbyists are individuals who, for payment and on behalf of a client, communicate with a public office holder in attempts to influence government decisions. They must register when they lobby for the making, developing or amending of legislative proposals, bills or resolutions, regulations, policies or programs; and the awarding of federal grants, contributions or contracts.

The new Lobbyists Registration Act, which came into force on January 31, 1996, requires lobbyists to report their clients and employers, the parent and subsidiary companies of corporations that benefit from the lobbying, the organizational members of coalition groups that lobby, which government departments or agencies are contacted, and the specific subject matters of lobbying activities.

The Canadian Almanac listing of consultant lobbyists is based on information submitted to the Lobbyists Registration Branch. For further information, consult the Lobbyists Registry under Marketplace Services through Strategis, Industry Canada's gateway to the Internat at the following address: http://strategis.ic.gc.ca.

ALBERTA

CALGARY
Bennett Jones Verchere, Bankers Hall East, #4500, 855 - 2 St. SW, Calgary AB T2P 4K7 – 403/298-3100; Fax: 403/265-7219
C. Michael Ryer
Robert A. Brown, #1200, 205 - 5th Ave. SW, Calgary AB T2P 4B9 – 403/691-8421; Fax: 403/691-8008
Robert Brown
John R. Crawford & Associates, 6 Hawthorne Cres. NW, Calgary AB T2N 3V4 – 403/284-9733; Fax: 403/284-9733
John R. Crawford
Felesky Flynn, First Canadian Centre, #3400, 350 - 7 Ave SW, Calgary AB T2P 3N9 – 403/260-3300; Fax: 403/263-9649; Email: felesky@mail.cycor.ca
Brian A. Felesky, Q.C.
D. Blair Nixon
F. Brenton Perry
Leslie E. Skingle
Donald H. Watkins
Howard, Mackie, Canterra Tower, #1000, 400 - 3 Ave. SW, Calgary AB T2P 4H2 – 403/232-9523; Fax: 403/266-1395
Colin P. MacDonald
Macleod Dixon, Canterra Tower, #3700, 400 - 3 Ave. SW, Calgary AB T2P 4H2 – 403/267-8222; Fax: 403/264-5973; Email: md@lexcom.ab.ca
J.G. McKee
Millikin, J. Cameron Consulting Ltd., 3803 - 8A St. SW, Calgary AB T2T 3B6 – 403/243-2970; Fax: 403/287-1023
John Cameron Millikin
Milner Fenerty, Fifth Ave. Place, 30th Floor, 237 - 4th Ave. SW, Calgary AB T2P 4X7 – 403/268-7000; Fax: 403/268-3100; Email: milfen@milfen.com; URL: http://www.milfen.com
Francis M. Saville, Q.C.
Osler, Hoskin & Harcourt, #1900, 333 - 7th Ave. SW, Calgary AB T2P 2Z1 – 403/260-7044; Fax: 403/260-7024
Jack A. Silverson
Price Waterhouse, #1200, 425 - 1 Ave. SW, Calgary AB T2P 3V7 – 403/267-1277; Fax: 403/264-4745
Laurie Pare
Peter Wallis Consulting Ltd., 3617 - 7th St. SW, Calgary AB T2T 2Y2 – 403/287-3634; Fax: 403/268-3100
Peter C. Wallis
Waymar Energy Inc., #400, 550 - 5th Ave. SW, Calgary AB T2P 3Y6 – 403/281-6467; Fax: 403/281-5151
Wayne I. Bobye

EDMONTON
Government Policy Consultants (GPC), Manulife Place, #1840, 10180 - 101 St., Edmonton AB T5J 3S4 – 403/944-0696; Fax: 403/441-9849
James V. Campbell
Dwight Dibben

---
* BT - Board of Trade; BC - Bureau de commerce; CC - Chamber of Commerce/Chambre de commerce

7-36 CONSULTANT LOBBYISTS

Hill & Knowlton, Royal LePage, #990, 10130 - 103 St., Edmonton AB T5J 3N9 – 403/428-6459; Fax: 403/420-1230
Brian Wik

Lucas Bowker & White, Esso Tower, #1201, 10060 Jasper Ave., Edmonton AB T5J 4E5 – 403/426-5330; Fax: 403/428-1066; 1-800-567-7174; Email: lucas@supernet.ab.ca
Bruce D. Hirsche

BRITISH COLUMBIA

LIONS BAY
Ellen M. Gunn, PO Box 101, Lions Bay BC V0N 2E0 – 604/684-1381; Fax: 604/684-6402
Ellen M. Gunn

SIDNEY
Alexander C. Phillips, #27, 2353 Harbour Rd., Sidney BC V8L 3X8 – 250/655-1952; Fax: 250/655-1952
Alexander C. Phillips

SURREY
Prem S. Vinning, 8881 - 160 St., Surrey BC V4N 2X8 – 604/951-0500; Fax: 604/951-8899
Prem S. Vinning

VANCOUVER
Acres International Limited, 845 Cambie St., 4th Fl., Vancouver BC V6B 2P4 – 604/683-9141; Fax: 604/683-9148
Scott R. Hanna

Michael A. Bailey & Associates, Bentall Centre, Bldg Box: 49104, #1753, 595 Burrard St., Vancouver BC V7X 1G4 – 604/684-2228; Fax: 604/683-6345
Bailey Michael A.

Canadian Public Affairs Consulting Group Inc., 1028 Hamilton St., Vancouver BC V6B 2R9 – 604/688-0753; Fax: 604/688-8239
Paul Daniell
Charles Kelly

Farris, Vaughan, Wills & Murphy, Pacific Centre South, 700 West Georgia St., PO Box 10026, Vancouver BC V7Y 1B3 – 604/684-9151; Fax: 604/661-9349
A. Keith Mitchell, Q.C.

First Event, #1600, 777 Hornby St., Vancouver BC V6Z 2T3 – 604/640-4339; Fax: 604/640-4338
Warren Kinsella

GPC Pacific Public Affairs, #1515, 1188 West Georgia St., Vancouver BC V6E 4A2 – 604/688-2505; Fax: 604/688-2519
Bruce R. Drysdale
Andy Orr

Koffman Birnie & Kalef, 885 West Georgia St., 19th Fl., Vancouver BC V6C 3H4 – 604/891-3688; Fax: 604/891-3788
David A.G. Birnie

Rosenbloom & Aldridge, #1300, 355 Burrard St., Vancouver BC V6C 2G8 – 604/684-1311; Fax: 604/684-6402
James R. Aldridge
Marcus Bartley
Donald J. Rosenbloom

Stikeman, Elliott, Park Pl., #1700, 666 Burrard St., Vancouver BC V6C 2X8 – 604/631-1300; Fax: 604/681-1825
Eugene Hsiad Yu Kwan

Thomas & Davis, #1310, 1111 West Georgia St., Vancouver BC V6E 4M3 – 604/689-7522; Fax: 604/689-7525
J. Christopher Thomas

Thorsteinssons, Three Bentall Centre, 595 Burrard St., 27th Fl., PO Box 49123, Vancouver BC V7X 1J2 – 604/689-1261; Fax: 604/688-4711
Michael J. O'Keefe

MANITOBA

BRANDON
Meyers, Norris, Penny & Co., 160 - 14th St., Brandon MB R7A 7K1 – 204/727-0661; Fax: 204/726-1543
Daryl L. Ritchie

WINNIPEG
Fillmore & Riley, Winnipeg Sq., #1700, 360 Main St., Winnipeg MB R3C 3Z3 – 204/957-8321; Fax: 204/957-0516
Wayne D. Leslie

NOVA SCOTIA

BEDFORD
Angel Consulting Service, #310, 15 Dartmouth Rd., Bedford NS B4A 3X6 – 902/832-7114; Fax: 902/832-7115
John R. Angel

YARMOUTH
Pink Macdonald Harding, 379 Main St., PO Box 398, Yarmouth NS B5A 4B3 – 902/742-7861; Fax: 902/742-0425
Coline M. Campbell

ONTARIO

BRANTFORD
Neumann Consulting Services, PO Box 1505, Brantford ON N3T 5V2 – 519/759-7885; Fax: 519/759-7885
David E. Neumann

BURLINGTON
HH Environmental Inc., 4192 Inglewood Dr., Burlington ON L7L 1E2 – 905/639-2787; Fax: 905/639-4388
Hugh H. Eisler

Michael Vollmer Yacht Design Inc., 1399 Birch Ave., Burlington ON L7S 1J2 – 905/681-8778; Fax: 905/637-6712
Michael Vollmer

CRYSLER
Goodfellow Agricola Consultants Inc., RR#4, Crysler ON K0A 1R0 – 613/448-4090; Fax: 613/448-1629
Randal Goodfellow

CUMBERLAND
Murray R. Ramsbottom Enterprises Inc., 1666 Marronier Ct., Cumberland ON K4C 1C2 – 613/769-1444
R. Murray Ramsbottom

GLOUCESTER
BJV Consulting, 3207 Treetop Ct., Gloucester ON K1T 3P7 – 613/523-9579; Fax: 613/523-9195
Brian J. Veinot

MANOTIK
The Weston Group, 5638 South River Dr., Manotik ON K4M 1J4 – 613/692-4803; Fax: 613/692-3516
William Weston

MISSISSAUGA
Arthur Andersen & Co., #1200, 2 Robert Speck Pkwy., Mississauga ON L4Z 1H8 – 905/949-3900; Fax: 905/949-3911
Tony Ancimer
Craig Cowan
Derek George

Commodity Tax Services, 2373 Basswood Cres., Mississauga ON L5L 1Y2 – 905/828-1339; Fax: 905/896-1263
Barry P. Korchmar

McMillan Binch, #800, 3 Robert Speck Pkwy., Mississauga ON L4Z 2G5 – 905/566-2003; Fax: 905/566-2029
John Armstrong
David Butler

Price Waterhouse, #1100, 1 Robert Speck Pkwy., Mississauga ON L4Z 3M3 – 905/272-1200; Fax: 905/272-3937
Peter F. Kila

NEPEAN
Robert Bowen Associates Ltd., 8 Solva Dr., Nepean ON K2H 5R5 – 613/828-6219; Fax: 613/828-6684
Robert R. Bowen

Gary Brooks, 17 Cimarron Cr., Nepean ON K2G 6E1 – 613/723-2695; Fax: 613/723-3503
Gary C. Brooks

JL Consulting, 142F Valley Stream Dr., Nepean ON K2H 9C6 – 613/721-8904; Fax: 613/721-8918
Jean L.J. Lamoureux

George MacFarlane, #220, 2 Gurdwara Rd., Nepean ON K2E 1A2 – 613/226-8588; Fax: 613/226-7103
George MacFarlane

Thrust Line International, 34 Farlane Blvd., Nepean ON K2E 5H4 – 613/225-1869; Fax: 613/235-0784
A. Sean Henry

OAKVILLE
Llyod A. Hackett, 1310 Ingledene Dr., Oakville ON L6H 2J4 – 905/845-8226; Fax: 905/845-9578
Llyod A. Hackett

ORLEANS
Henault Enterprises Inc., 1204 St-Moritz Ct., Orleans ON K1C 2B3 – 613/824-2184; Fax: 613/824-2184
Philippe G. Henault

OTTAWA
Alphalink, 221 Remic Ave., Ottawa ON K1P 6L2 – 613/563-3972; Fax: 613/563-2025
J. Brian Linklater

C.D. Arthur & Associates Inc., #1004, 275 Sparks St., Ottawa ON K1R 7X9 – 613/236-5581; Fax: 613/238-0368
Douglas C. Arthur

Association House, #800, 55 Metcalfe St., Ottawa ON K1P 6L5 – 613/567-3080; Fax: 613/232-7148
James S. Deacey
Daniel Despins
John Gorman
Brian Guest
Les McIlroy
Brian P. Metcalfe
Art Silverman

Paul-Andre Baril, #311, 225 Metcalfe St., Ottawa ON K2P 1P9 – 613/238-1269; Fax: 613/238-2501
Paul-Andre Baril

BCI Regulatory Policy, #202, 2301 Carling Ave., Ottawa ON K2B 7G3 – 613/596-0257; Fax: 613/596-5040
Doug D. Blair

Berger, Gerald Consulting Inc., 384 Hamilton Ave. South, Ottawa ON K1Y 1C7 – 613/728-6177; Fax: 613/728-5827
Gerald Arthur Berger

Brogan Consulting, #202, 2301 Carling Ave., Ottawa ON K2B 7B9 – 613/596-5042; Fax: 613/596-5040
Thomas P. Brogan

P.J. Burman Consultant, 2340 Hoddington Cres., Ottawa ON K1H 8J4 – 613/733-3028; Fax: 613/733-9531
Pannalal J. Burman

Canadian Public Affairs Consulting Group Inc., #1000, 100 Sparks St., Ottawa ON K1P 5B7 – 613/238-7400; Fax: 613/563-7671
Craig Oliver

Caparim International, 37 Linden Terrace, Ottawa ON K1S 1Z1 – 613/563-3292; Fax: 613/230-3560
Richard H. Bower

Capello Consulting, 37 Claudet Cres., Ottawa ON K1G 4R4 – 613/738-7224; Fax: 613/738-7440

Canadian Almanac & Directory 1997

Gerald G. Capello
Capital Hill Group/Groupe Capital Hill, #300, 66 Queen St., Ottawa ON K1P 5C6 – 613/235-0221; Fax: 613/235-9694
David Angus
Steven Dover
David Dyer
Philippe Gervais
Herb Metcalfe
Jean-Francois Thibault
Nanci Woods
Arthur Carew & Company, 40 Signal St., Ottawa ON K2L 1B9 – 613/831-1816; Fax: 613/831-4697
Arthur V. Carew
CFN Consultants, #1502, 222 Queen St., Ottawa ON K1P 5V9 – 613/232-1576; Fax: 613/238-5519
Barry L. Code
Eldon J. Healey
William R. Oldford
George D. Simpson
Conexus Research Group Inc., #300, 55 Murray St., Ottawa ON K1N 5M3 – 613/234-7099; Fax: 613/563-7239
Paul C. Larocque
Corporation House Ltd., #1400, 60 Queen St., Ottawa ON K1P 5Y7 – 613/238-5678; Fax: 613/238-5391
Graham A.G. Hardman
Samuel F. Hughes
Robert Morton
Douglas B. Wurtele
Paul W. Couse, #1001, 275 Slater St., Ottawa ON K1P 5H9 – 613/563-2525; Fax: 613/236-3333
Paul W. Couse
Robert W. Cunningham, #406, 201 MacLeod St., Ottawa ON K2P 0Z9 – 613/567-1609; Fax: 613/567-5015
Robert W. Cunningham
De Kemp & Associates Ltd., #1127, 90 Sparks St., Ottawa ON K1P 5B4 – 613/235-7336; Fax: 613/235-5866
Philip A. De Kemp
De Valk Consulting Inc., #203, 2525 St. Laurent Blvd., Ottawa ON K1H 8P5 – 613/739-7850; Fax: 613/733-9501
Erina De Valk
Robert G. De Valk
Deacey Public Affairs Consultants Inc., #800, 55 Metcalfe St., Ottawa ON K1P 6L5 – 613/567-3080; Fax: 613/232-7148
James Deacey
Fred Doucet Consulting International Inc. (FDCI), #360, 440 Laurier Ave. West, Ottawa ON K1R 7X6 – 613/782-2336; Fax: 613/782-2428
Alfred (Fred) Doucet
Duralex Management Inc., 45 O'Connor St., 20th Fl., Ottawa ON K1P 5H9 – 613/236-3882; Fax: 613/230-6429
Leo Duguay
Earnscliffe Strategy Group Inc., #1002, 275 Sparks St., Ottawa ON K1R 7X9 – 613/563-4455; Fax: 613/236-6173
Harry J. Near
Michael W. Robinson
Evans Strategic Policy Inc., #1001, 350 Sparks St., Ottawa ON K1R 7S8 – 613/563-3205; Fax: 613/235-3111
John L. Evans
Flavell Kubrick & Lalonde, #1700, 280 Slater St., Ottawa ON K1P 1C2 – 613/230-6030; Fax: 613/230-6969
C.J. Michael Flavell
Geoffrey C. Kubrick
Paul M. Lalonde
Jason P. Flint Consulting, 236 St. Andrew, Ottawa ON K1N 5G8 – 613/241-6186; Fax: 613/563-8850
Jason P. Flint
Fraser & Beatty, #1200, 180 Elgin St., Ottawa ON K2P 2K7 – 613/783-9611; Fax: 613/238-6294

Richard J. Mahoney
Government Business Consulting Group Inc., #360, 440 Laurier Ave. West, Ottawa ON K1R 7X6 – 613/782-2336; Fax: 613/782-2428
Edmond Chiasson
Fred Doucet
Gerry Doucet
Maurice Lafontaine
Victor Little
Kenneth D. Taylor
Government Policy Consultants (GPC), #1600, 350 Albert St., PO Box 74, Ottawa ON K1R 1A4 – 613/238-2090; Fax: 613/238-9380
Gerald A. Berger
Jeremy Byatt
Pelino Colaiacovo
James Crossland
Julie E. Dickson
Alison German
John G. Harding
Stewart Lindale
Bruce Rawson
Faye Roberts
William Tretiak
Michael Von Herff
Kenneth G. Whiting
Kevin Wright
Government Policy Research Associates Inc., #514, 90 Sparks St., Ottawa ON K1P 5B4 – 613/235-5360; Fax: 613/235-5866
Gordon A. Harrison
Gowlings, #2600, 160 Elgin St., PO Box 466, Stn D, Ottawa ON K1P 1C3 – 613/233-1781; Fax: 613/563-9869; Email: marketing@gowlings.com; URL: http://www.gowlings.com
James H. Buchan
Hy Calof, Q.C.
Ronald D. Lunau
Terry D. McEwan
Sean Moore
Joel B. Taller
Grey, Clark, Shih & Associates Ltd., #1004, 275 Sparks St., Ottawa ON K1R 7X9 – 613/238-7743; Fax: 613/238-0368
Peter J. Clark
Chandra Gibbs
Chris Hines
Gordon W.R. Lafortune
Hendin, Hendin & Lyon, #726, 50 O'Connor St., Ottawa ON K1P 6L2 – 613/563-4804; Fax: 613/563-3878
Stuart E. Hendin, Q.C.
Hession, Neville & Associates, #700, 99 Bank St., Ottawa ON K1P 6B9 – 613/232-2842; Fax: 613/238-6096
Ross Christensen
Raymond V. Hession
William J. Musgrove
William H. Neville
Hill & Knowlton, #1300, 55 Metcalfe St., Ottawa ON K1P 6L5 – 613/238-4371; Fax: 613/238-8642
Carl Baltare
Gil Barrows
Donald Bell
Robert Bruchet
Glenn Chadwell
Mike McNaney
Brian L. Mersereau
David B. Miller
Peter Rutherford
Jeff Smith
E.E. Hobbs & Associates Ltd., 6 McLeod St., Ottawa ON K1R 7X9 – 613/230-6999; Fax: 613/230-2674
Ernest E. Hobbs
Hooper Lefebvre Consultants, #1400, 60 Queen St., Ottawa ON K1P 5Y7 – 613/238-5678; Fax: 613/238-5391
Ronald Charles Lefebvre

Humphreys Public Affairs Group Inc., #1620, 130 Albert St.., Ottawa ON K1P 5G4 – 613/230-3155; Fax: 613/236-2556
Jennifer A. Hartley
David L. Humphreys
James L. Lorimer
IGRG Inc. (The Industry Government Relations Group), #1110, 350 Sparks St., Ottawa ON K1R 7S8 – 613/232-1413; Fax: 613/232-9554
Robert Bolduc
Gary Leroux
David MacDonald
Robert M. Mill
Scott Proudfoot
Michael G. Teeter
Ramsey M. Withers
InterCon Consultants, #1003, 275 Slater St., Ottawa ON K1P 5H9 – 613/236-4451; Fax: 613/230-8707
Peter Cameron
Ross Campbell
Geoffrey Hugh Craven
Ernest B. Creber
Phillip R. Munro
J & IA Consulting Inc./CFN Consultants, #400, 100 Sparks St., Ottawa ON K1P 5B7 – 613/232-1194; Fax: 613/238-5519
John Allan
J.S.L. Consulting Services Ltd., #709, 99 Bank St., Ottawa ON K2P 6B9 – 613/827-2844; Fax: 613/827-5337
John S. Legate
Don Jarvis Consultants, #1127, 90 Sparks St., Ottawa ON K2C 2E8 – 613/238-7809; Fax: 613/235-5866
Donald M. Jarvis
J.R. Jenkins Consultants Inc., 1052 Cromwell Dr., Ottawa ON K1V 6K5 – 613/733-3159
John Robert Jenkins
Johnston & Buchan, #1700, 275 Slater St., Ottawa ON K1P 5H9 – 613/236-3882; Fax: 613/230-6423; Email: johnbuch@magi.com
Robert J. Buchan
Laurence J.E. Dunbar
Kelen, Michael A., #700, 99 Bank St., Ottawa ON K1P 6B9 – 613/232-6272; Fax: 613/238-6096
Michael A. Kelen
Kiedrowski & Associates, 74 Iona St., Ottawa ON K1Y 3L8 – 613/724-3857; Fax: 613/724-3891
John S. Kiedrowski
Livingston Trade Services, #1409, 130 Albert St., Ottawa ON K1P 5G4 – 613/235-7359; Fax: 613/563-1074
Kenneth H. Sorensen
Marcotte Consulting, 443 Kintyre Private, Ottawa ON K2C 3M9 – 613/727-1469; Fax: 613/727-8541
Michelle L. Marcotte
McTaggart Blais Milton, #1000, 100 Sparks St., Ottawa ON K1P 5B7 – 613/567-0762; Fax: 613/563-7671
Jean Jacques Blais
Metcalfe & Associates, #800, 55 Metcalfe St., Ottawa ON K1P 6L5 – 613/567-3080; Fax: 613/232-7148
Brian P. Metcalfe
Midpoint Consultants, #1015, 50 O'Conner St., Ottawa ON K1P 6L2 – 613/230-2727; Fax: 613/230-2934
Scott G. Walker
S.A. Murray Consulting Inc. (SAMCI), 81 Metcalfe St., 10th Fl., Ottawa ON K1P 6K7 – 613/236-3383; Fax: 613/236-4184
Kim Doran
Jim Everson
Andrew Jones
Jill Maase
Kory L. McDonald
Rick Moorcroft
Gordon Quaiattini
Lisa Stilborn
Gilles Verret
Susan Whitney

Canadian Almanac & Directory 1997

National Public Relations, #450, 55 Metcalfe St., Ottawa ON K1P 6L5 – 613/233-1699; Fax: 613/233-2431
  Gordon E. Garner
  Howard Mains
Ogilvy Renault, #1600, 45 O'Connor St., Ottawa ON K1P 1A4 – 613/780-8661; Fax: 613/230-5459
  Brenda C. Swick-Martin
Osler, Hoskin & Harcourt, #1500, 50 O'Connor St., Ottawa ON K1P 6L2 – 613/235-7234; Fax: 613/235-2867; Email: counsel@osler; URL: http://www.osler.com
  Glen A. Bloom
  Kenneth L. Boland
  Martha Healey
  J. François Lemieux
  Michael L. Phelan
  David K. Wilson
Parallax Public Affairs Inc., #800, 55 Metcalfe St., Ottawa ON K1P 6L5 – 613/230-5939; Fax: 613/238-6096
  Mark Resnick
Policy Insights Inc., #402, 222 Queen St., Ottawa ON K1P 5V9 – 613/563-8078; Fax: 613/563-4284
  Ken J.I. MacKay
Prospectus Associates in Corporate Development Inc., 346 Waverley St., Ottawa ON K2P 0W5 – 613/231-2727; Fax: 613/237-7666
  Thomas Creary
  Robert Evershed
  William J. Pristanski
Public Sector Corporation, #200, 440 Laurier Ave., Ottawa ON K1R 7X6 – 613/782-2467; Fax: 613/782-2284
  Bruce H.E. Maynard
  Peter Woods
C.G. Smallridge & Associates, #1109, 130 Albert St., Ottawa ON K1P 5G4 – 613/563-2194; Fax: 613/563-2196
  Colin G. Smallridge
Stikeman, Elliott, #914, 50 O'Connor St., Ottawa ON K1P 6L2 – 613/234-4555; Fax: 613/230-8877
  Mirko Bibic
  Randall Hofley
  Lawson A.W. Hunter, Q.C.
  T. Gregory Kane, Q.C.
  Donald A. Kubesh
  Stuart C. McCormack
Strategex Consultants Inc., #205, 541 Sussex Dr., Ottawa ON K1N 6Z6 – 613/562-3686; Fax: 613/562-3688
  Robert Landry
Stratégico Inc., 45 O'Connor St., 20th Fl., Ottawa ON K1P 6L2 – 613/235-0260; Fax: 613/235-7012
  Gordon Ritchie
Tactix Government Consulting Inc., #600, 99 Bank St., Ottawa ON K1P 6B9 – 613/566-7053; Fax: 613/233-9527
  Anthony Stikeman

ROCKCLIFFE
John A.M. Wilson, 17 Bittern Ct., Rockcliffe ON K1L 8K9 – 613/741-4605; Fax: 613/741-0007
  John A.M. Wilson

TORONTO
Sandra Anstey, #1901, 77 Bloor St. West, Toronto ON M5S 1M2 – 416/920-7950; Fax: 416/920-6409
  Sandra Anstey
Baker & McKenzie, #2100, 181 Bay St., PO Box 874, Toronto ON M5J 2T3 – 416/865-6941; Fax: 416/863-6275
  Kevin B. Coon
  Roy K. Kusano
  Brian D. Segal
Gordon R. Baker, Q.C., Exchange Tower, Bldg Box: 426, #1470, 2 First Canadian Place, Toronto ON M5X 1E3 – 416/365-7203; Fax: 416/365-7204
  Gordon R. Baker
BDO Dunwoody, PO Box 32, Stn Royal Bank, Toronto ON M5J 2J8 – 416/369-3064; Fax: 416/865-0887
  Bruce D. McLachlin
  Raymond J. Pare
Blaney, McMurtry, Stapells, Friedman, Cadillac Fairview Tower, #1400, 20 Queen St. West, Toronto ON M5H 3R3 – 416/593-1221; Fax: 416/593-5437; Email: info@blaney.com; URL: http://www.blaney.com
  Larry S. Grossman, Q.C.
Borden & Elliot, Scotia Plaza, #4400, 40 King St. West, Toronto ON M5H 3Y4 – 416/367-6000; Fax: 416/367-6749; Email: info@borden.com; URL: http://www.borden.com
  Jeffrey S. Graham
  R. Andrew G. Harrison
  John D. Hylton, Q.C.
  Eva M. Krasa
  J. Fraser Mann
  Geoffrey B. Morawetz
  Simon B. Scott, Q.C.
  Terrance A. Sweeney
  John J. Tobin
  Laura M. White
  Gordon J. Zimmerman
Bresver, Grossman, Scheininger & Davis, #2800, 390 Bay St., Toronto ON M5H 2Y2 – 416/869-0366; Fax: 416/869-0321
  Lester L. Scheininger
Burstyn Jeffery Inc., #920, 55 University Ave., Toronto ON M5J 2P8 – 416/361-1475; Fax: 416/361-1652
  Pamela Jeffery
  Catherine McKellar
C.G. Management & Communications Inc., One First Canadian Place, #780, PO Box 5100, Toronto ON M5X 1A9 – 416/362-8744; Fax: 416/362-5344
  Utilia M. Amaral
  Nancy P. Coldham
  Donald P. Gracey
Cassels Brock & Blackwell, Scotia Plaza, #2100, 40 King St. West, Toronto ON M5H 3C2 – 416/869-5300; Fax: 416/360-8877
  Stephen R. LeDrew
Coopers & Lybrand, 5160 Yonge St., Toronto ON M2N 6L3 – 416/229-3102; Fax: 416/229-3184
  Harold A. Burke
  Kevin Dancey
  Israel H. Mida
Davies, Ward & Beck, 1 First Canadian Place, 44th Fl., PO Box 63, Toronto ON M5X 1B1 – 416/863-5558; Fax: 416/863-0871
  K.A. Siobhan Monaghan
  David W. Smith, Q.C.
Deloitte & Touche, BCE Place, #1400, 181 Bay St., Toronto ON M5J 2V1 – 416/601-6270; Fax: 416/601-6151
  Mary Esteves
  James M. Vincze
G.W. Doucet Associates Ltd., #20013, 4839 Leslie St., Willowdale ON M2J 5E3 – 416/498-1994
  Gerald J. Doucet
Ernst & Young, Ernst & Young Tower, Toronto-Dominion Centre, PO Box 251, Stn Toronto Dominion, Toronto ON M5K 1J7 – 416/864-1234; Fax: 416/864-1174
  Denis Brown
Fasken Campbell Godfrey, #3600, 66 Wellington St. West, Toronto ON M5K 1N6 – 416/366-8381; Fax: 416/364-7813
  D.A. Cannon
  S.K. D'Arcy
  E.J. Johnson
  S.S. Ruby
Michael J. Finkelstein, 437 Spadina Rd., PO Box 23016, Toronto ON M5P 2W3 – 416/487-2353; Fax: 416/487-1245
  Michael J. Finkelstein
Fraser & Beatty, Madison Centre, #2300, 4950 Yonge St., North York ON M2N 6K1 – 416/733-3300; Fax: 416/221-5254
  Jules L. Lewy
  Riccardo C. Trecroce
Genest Murray DesBrisnay Lamek, #700, 130 Adelaide St. West, Toronto ON M5H 4C1 – 416/368-8600; Fax: 416/360-2625
  Bruce B. Campbell
  John C. Murray
Goodman Phillips & Vineberg, #2400, 250 Yonge St., Toronto ON M5B 2M6 – 416/979-2211; Fax: 416/979-1234
  Jon R. Johnson
  Carrie B.E. Smit
Gotlieb, Allan E., Toronto Dominion Centre, #5300, TD Bank Tower, PO Box 85, Toronto ON M5K 1E7 – 416/869-5664; Fax: 416/947-0866
  Allan E. Gotlieb
Gowlings, #4900, Commerce Court West, PO Box 438, Stn Commerce Court, Toronto ON M5L 1J3 – 416/862-4296; Fax: 416/862-7661
  Mark L. Madras
Hill & Knowlton, #800, 1 Eglinton Ave. East, Toronto ON M4P 3A1 – 416/483-5228; Fax: 416/483-4111
  Michael E. Coates
  Hon. Douglas C. Frith
  Ian Hamilton
  Cynthia Zamaria
Ken James & Associates, #906, 75 Albert St., Toronto ON K1P 5E7 – 613/236-2966; Fax: 613/236-8169
  Ken A. James
Robert P. Kaplan, Q.C., #301, 55A Avenue Rd., Toronto ON M5R 2G3 – 416/922-4444; Fax: 416/964-2584
  Hon. Robert P. Kaplan, P.C., Q.C.
Don Kerr Consulting, 110 MacPherson Ave., Toronto ON M5R 1W8 – 416/920-8114; Fax: 416/920-4905
  Donald Kerr
Koskie & Minsky, #900, 20 Queen St. West, PO Box 52, Toronto ON M5H 3R3 – 416/977-8353; Fax: 416/977-3316; URL: http://www.koskieminsky.com
  Raymond Koskie, Q.C.
Lee Associates, #506, 44 Charles St. West, Toronto ON K1P 6K7 – 416/960-8881; Fax: 416/967-0572
  Andrea L. Vincent
MacBain Public Affairs Inc., 59A Hannaford St., Toronto ON M4E 3G8 – 416/699-2337; Fax: 416/699-6613
  Robert W. MacBain
W.A. MacDonald Associates Inc., BCE Place, #3720, 161 Bay St., PO Box 621, Toronto ON M5J 2S1 – 416/865-7091; Fax: 416/865-7934
  William A. MacDonald
Macleod Dixon, BCE Place, #4520, 181 Bay St., PO Box 792, Toronto ON M5J 2T3 – 416/360-8511; Fax: 416/360-8277; Email: 75143,2536@compuserve.com
  Edward A. Heakes
McCarthy Tétrault, Toronto-Dominion Bank Tower, #4700, PO Box 48, TD Centre, Toronto ON M5K 1E6 – 416/362-1812; Fax: 416/868-0673; URL: http://www.mccarthy.ca
  Thomas B. Akin
  John W. Boscariol
  Bradley Crawford, Q.C.
  Riyaz Dattu
  C. Roderick MacKenzie
McDonald & Hayden, #1500, 1 Queen St. East, Toronto ON M5C 2Y3 – 416/364-3100; Fax: 416/601-4100; URL: http://www.mchayden.on.ca
  Clifford M. Goldlist
McIlroy & McIlroy Inc., #2725, 25 King St. West, PO Box 228, Toronto ON M5L 1E8 – 416/777-0447; Fax: 416/777-0136
  James P. McIlroy
McMillan Binch, South Tower, #3800, Royal Bank Plaza, Toronto ON M5J 2J7 – 416/865-7247; Fax: 416/865-7048

D.J. Albrecht
A.N. Campbell
P.G. Cathcart, Q.C.
R.S.G. Chester
T.J. O'Sullivan
William F. Rowley
G.W. Scott, Q.C.
D.G. Wentzell
M.M. Yaksich
Morris, Rose, Ledgett, Canada Trust Tower, BCE Pl., #2700, 161 Bay St., Toronto ON M5J 2S1 – 416/981-9400; Fax: 416/863-9500
Michael K. Eisen
Norditrade Inc., 33 Laird Dr., Toronto ON M4G 3S9 – 416/467-8438; Fax: 416/425-4858
Lars Henriksson
Osler, Hoskin & Harcourt, #6600, 1 First Canadian Pl., PO Box 501, Stn First Canadian Place, Toronto ON M5X 1B8 – 416/862-6554; Fax: 416/862-6666
S. Firoz Ahmed
David R. Allgood
Ronald G. Atkey, Q.C.
Lyndon A.J. Barnes
Monica E. Biringer
Eugene A.G. Cipparone
Peter H.G. Franklyn
Peter L. Glossop
Douglas T. Hamilton
Andrew H. Kingissepp
Norman C. Loveland
David S. McFarlane
Andrew McGuffin
David T. Tetreault
Richard G. Tremblay
R. Alan Young
Paragon Reputation Management (Canada) Inc., #1010, 6 Adelaide St. East, Toronto ON M5C 1H6 – 416/363-3111; Fax: 416/363-3944
Douglas B. Hay
Susan J. Peacock Consulting, 153 Madison Ave., Toronto ON M5R 2S8 – 416/961-1888; Fax: 416/968-1016
Susan J. Peacock
Victor Peters, TD Centre, 79 Wellington St. West, PO Box 189, Toronto ON M5K 1N2 – 416/865-7300; Fax: 416/814-3120
Victor Peters
Policy Concepts, #410, 60 Bloor St. West, Toronto ON M4W 3B8 – 416/922-6156; Fax: 416/922-4295
Peter S. Regenstreif
Price Waterhouse, #1900, 5700 Yonge St., North York ON M2M 4K7 – 416/218-1403; Fax: 416/218-1499
Bruce Harris
Public Perspectives Inc., #900, 20 Queen St. West, PO Box 52, Toronto ON M5H 3R3 – 416/971-8726; Fax: 416/581-1528; Email: ppi@koskieminsky.com
Darrell L. Brown
Raymond Koskie
Peter Landry
John O'Grady
Brock Smith
John Sweeney
Murray Wilson
Robson, Thomas Communications & Public Affairs, #400, 1235 Bay St., Toronto ON M5R 3K4 – 416/515-0535; Fax: 416/515-0950
Sandra Anstey
Tom W. Robson
Rothschild & Co. Ltd., 240 MacPherson Ave., Toronto ON M4V 1A2 – 416/801-9701; Fax: 416/533-8013
Eric W. Rothschild
Smith Lyons, Scotia Plaza, #6200, 40 King St. West, Toronto ON M5H 3Z7 – 416/369-7200; Fax: 416/369-7250; Email: rmconnelly@smithlyons.ca; URL: http://www.smithlyons.ca
H.B. Mayer, Q.C.
J.J. Shore

Stikeman, Elliott, #5300, Commerce Court West, PO Box 85, Toronto ON M5L 1B9 – 416/869-5500; Fax: 416/947-0866
Allan E. Gotlieb
Margaret E. Grottenthaler
Strategy Corp. Inc., TD Bank Tower, TD Centre, #3908, PO Box 122, Toronto ON M5K 1H1 – 416/864-7112; Fax: 416/864-7117
John R. Duffy
Tory Tory DesLauriers & Binnington, #3000, Aetna Tower, Toronto-Dominion Centre, PO Box 270, Stn Toronto Dominion, Toronto ON M5K 1N2 – 416/865-0040; Fax: 416/865-7380
James W. Welkoff
Veritas Communications Inc., #704, 161 Eglinton Ave. East, Toronto ON M4P 1J5 – 416/482-2248; Fax: 416/482-2292
David W. McLaughlin
Warren Group Inc., Bldg Box: 24, #5900, 1 First Canadian Place, Toronto ON M5X 1K2 – 416/360-7337; Fax: 416/367-3316
Robert M. Warren
Michael Wilson International Inc., #2378, 181 Bay St., PO Box 875, Toronto ON M5J 2T3 – 416/842-4000; Fax: 416/842-4001
Michael Wilson
Kathleen Winn & Associates, 911 Carlaw Ave., Toronto ON M4K 3L4 – 416/461-8874; Fax: 416/461-2525
Kathleen J. Winn
Eileen Wykes Communications, #700, 1 Eglinton Ave. East, Toronto ON M4P 3A1 – 416/921-1894; Fax: 416/921-1894
Eileen A. Wykes

WINDSOR
Belowus Easton English Holmes, 100 Ouellette Ave., 7th Fl., Windsor ON N9A 6R3 – 519/973-1900; Fax: 519/973-0225
R. Bruck Easton, Q.C.

QUÉBEC

GATINEAU
Kehoe, Blais, Major & Parent, #200, 344, boul Maloney est, Gatineau PQ J8P 7A6 – 819/663-2439; Fax: 819/663-4816
Claude Grant
Denis Tanguay, 771, boul St-Rene est, Gatineau PQ J8P 1T2 – 819/663-0961; Fax: 819/782-2428
Denis Tanguay

MONTRÉAL
Byers Casgrain, #3900, 1, Place Ville-Marie, Montréal PQ H3B 4M7 – 514/878-8811; Fax: 514/878-8197
Jean-Claude Bachand
Jean Bazin, Q.C.
William S. Grodinsky
John Hurley
CAI Corporate Affairs International, #3030, 1000, rue de la Gauchetière ouest, Montréal PQ H3B 4W5 – 514/861-9595; Fax: 514/861-9596
Steven Jast
Jean Leblond
Francoise Lyon
Howard Silverman
Canvin Consultants Inc., #110, 3300, Cote-Vertu ouest, St-Laurent PQ H4R 2B7 – 514/695-2113; Fax: 514/695-3027
Harold J. Canvin
Desjardins Ducharme Stein Monast, Tour de la Banque Nationale, #2400, 600, rue de la Gauchetière ouest, Montréal PQ H3B 4L8 – 514/878-9411; Fax: 514/878-9092; 1-800-670-0102
Guy J.H. Lord

Eckler Partners Limited, #1245, 2020, rue University, Montréal PQ H3A 2A5 – 514/848-9077; Fax: 514/848-9079
Nicholas Bauer
Forum Communications Affaires Publiques Inc., #300, 1176, rue Bishop, Montréal PQ H3G 2E3 – 514/954-1080; Fax: 514/954-1868
Marc K. Parson
Gervais Gagnon Covington & Associes Inc., #200, 606, rue Cathcart, Montréal PQ H3B 1K9 – 514/393-9500; Fax: 514/393-9324
Graham A. Covington
Richard Gervais
Goodman Phillips & Vineberg, 1, av McGill College, 26th Fl., Montréal PQ H3A 3N9 – 514/841-6400; Fax: 514/841-6499; Email: gpv@ntl.gpv.com
Alan J. Shragie
Gravenor Beck, #223, 975, boul Roméo Vachon nord, Dorval PQ H4Y 1H1 – 514/631-4494; Fax: 514/631-1226
John Thomas Keenan
Groupe Declic, #160, 1515, boul Chomedey, Laval PQ H7V 3Y7 – 514/688-1500; Fax: 514/688-9899
Paulin G.P. Grenier
Forrest C. Hume, #1100, 1200, av McGill College, Montréal PQ H3B 4G7 – 514/874-0722; Fax: 514/393-9069
Forrest Clyde Hume
Martineau, Walker, a/s Fasken Martineau, Stock Exchange Tower, #3400, 800, Place-Victoria, CP 242, Montréal PQ H4Z 1E9 – 514/397-7400; Fax: 514/397-7600; 1-800-361-6266
Hon. Francis Fox, P.C., Q.C.
Stephen S. Heller
Eric M. Maldoff
Mawussi, Epiphane, 13, ch Bord du Lac, Pointe-Claire PQ H9S 4G9 – 514/697-3712; Fax: 514/281-9887
Epiphane Ayi Mawussi
Robert D. Murray & Associates, 630, boul René-Lévesque ouest, 3e étage, CP 10, Montréal PQ H3C 2R3 – 514/397-6236; Fax: 514/397-6109
Robert Daniel Murray
Paquette Gadler Avocats, #B10, 300, Place d'Youville, Montréal PQ H2Y 2B6 – 514/849-0771; Fax: 514/849-4817
Paul Martin
Ramco Enterprises, #762, 1077, rue St-Mathieu, Montréal PQ H3H 2S4 – 514/989-9057; Fax: 514/935-3785
Richard A. Morgan
Raymond, Chabot, Martin, Pare, #1900, 600, rue de la Gauchetière ouest, Montréal PQ H3B 4L8 – 514/878-2691; Fax: 514/878-2127
Marc-Andre Morin
Stikeman, Elliott, #3900, 1155, boul René-Lévesque ouest, Montréal PQ H3B 3V2 – 514/397-3000; Fax: 514/397-3222
Marc Lalonde, P.C., O.C., Q.C.
John W. Leopold
H. Heward Stikeman, O.C., Q.C.
Towers Perrin, 1800, rue McGill College, 22e étage, Montréal PQ H3A 3J6 – 514/982-2010; Fax: 514/982-9269
Robert Blais

QUÉBEC
Aubut Chabot, #600, 900, boul René-Lévesque est, CP 910, Québec PQ G1R 4T4 – 418/524-5131; Fax: 418/524-1717; Email: aubuchab@microtec.net
Marcel Aubut, Q.C.
Boily Morency, #230, 70, rue Dalhousie, Québec PQ G1K 4B2 – 418/694-0704; Fax: 418/694-2140
Jean-Paul B. Boily
GPC Consilium, #508, 1150, rue Claire-Fontaine, Québec PQ G1R 5G4 – 418/522-4646; Fax: 418/522-2013
Claude Bechard
Remi Bujold

Canadian Almanac & Directory 1997

STE-FOY

Hill & Knowlton, 2876, de la Promenade, Ste-Foy PQ G1W 2J1 – 418/659-6887; Fax: 418/659-2798
Dennis Dawson

SASKATCHEWAN

SASKATOON

Gauley & Co., 701 Broadway Ave., PO Box 638, Saskatoon SK S7K 3L7 – 306/653-1212; Fax: 306/652-1323; Email: gauleyco@eagle.wbm.ca
J.J. Dierker, Q.C.

McKercher McKercher & Whitmore, 374 - 3rd Ave. South, Saskatoon SK S7K 1M5 – 306/653-2000; Fax: 306/244-7335; Email: mckerche@eagle.wbm.ca
D.B. Richardson

MAJOR CANADIAN COMPANIES

Listed by category; includes Crown corporations. Financial services companies (banks, trust companies, insurance companies, etc.) are excluded as they are presented elsewhere in this section.

AGRICULTURE & FISHERIES

Agrifoods International Co-Op., 6800 Lougheed Hwy., Burnaby BC V5A 1W2 – 604/420-6611; Fax: 604/420-9700 – President & CEO, David Coe

Agritek Bio Ingredients Corp., #630, 1980, rue Sherbrooke ouest, Montréal PQ H3H 1G1 – 514/935-2581; Fax: 514/935-5167 – Chairman, James D. Raymond

Alberta Wheat Pool, 505 - 2 St. SW, PO Box 2700, Calgary AB T2P 2P5 – 403/290-4910; Fax: 403/290-5550 – CEO, G.E.M. Cummings

Alta Genetics Inc., RR#2, Balzac AB T0M 0E0 – 403/226-0666; Fax: 403/226-4259 – Chairman, Eric Baker

Bunge of Canada Ltd., 300, rue Dalhousie, PO Box 2537, Québec PQ G1K 7R3 – 418/692-3761; Fax: 418/692-0182 – President, J.G. St. Onge

Canadian Dairy Commission, #300, 1525 Carling Ave., Ottawa ON K1A 0Z2 – 613/998-9490; Fax: 613/998-4492 – Chairman & CEO, Gilles Pregent

Cargill Ltd., #300, 240 Graham Ave., Winnipeg MB R3C 4C5 – 204/947-0141; Fax: 204/947-6444 – President, Kerry Hawkins

Case Canada Corp., 450 Sherman Ave. North, PO Box 2083, Hamilton ON L8N 4C4 – 905/548-3729; Fax: 905/548-3753 – General Plant Manager, Paul Meringer

Chai-Na-Ta Corp., 5965 - 205A St., Langley BC V3A 8C4 – 604/533-8883; Fax: 604/533-8891 – President & CEO, Gerry Gill

Co-Op Agricole de La Côte Sud, Route 230, La Pocatiere PQ G0R 1Z0 – 418/856-3807; Fax: 418/856-2513 – General Manager, G. Dore

Continental Grain Co. (Canada) Ltd., #2500, 200 Granville St., Vancouver BC V6C 1S4 – 604/684-7292; Fax: 604/684-8031 – President/CEO, Gerald L. McClintock

Cooperative Federée de Québec, #200, 9001, boul de L'Acadie, Montréal PQ H4N 3H7 – 514/384-6450; Fax: 514/383-7027 – President, Paul Massicotte

Fishery Products International, 70 O'Leary Ave., PO Box 550, St. John's NF A1C 5L1 – 709/570-0000; Fax: 709/570-0436 – Chairman & CEO, Victor Young

Groupe Lactil, 180, boul Begin, Ste-Claire PQ G0R 2V0 – 418/883-3301; Fax: 418/883-2134 – President, Herman Bolduc

Growmark Inc., 5600 Cancross Ct., PO Box 3020, Stn A, Mississauga ON L5A 3A4 – 905/890-8500; Fax: 905/890-4202 – Treasurer, Gay Hamilton

Humboldt Flour Mills Inc., PO Box 400, Humboldt SK S0K 2A0 – 306/682-2577; Fax: 306/682-4486 – President, John Cales

Louis Dreyfus Canada Ltd., The Commodity Exchange Tower, #1690, 360 Main St., Winnipeg MB R3C 3Z3 – 204/943-3546; Fax: 204/944-1307 – General Manager, A.P. Temple

Manitoba Pool Elevators, 220 Portage Ave., PO Box 9800, Winnipeg MB R3C 3K7 – 204/947-1171; Fax: 204/942-0570 – General Manager, Operations, D.W. Hunter

National Sea Products Ltd., PO Box 910, Lunenburg NS B0J 2C0 – 902/634-8811; Fax: 902/634-9607 – President & CEO, Henry Demone

N.M. Paterson & Sons Ltd., #609, 167 Lombard Ave., Winnipeg MB R3B 0V5 – 204/956-2090; Fax: 204/947-2386 – CEO, Andrew Patterson

Norfolk Co-Operative Co. Ltd., 645 Norfolk St., Simcoe ON N3Y 4L3 – 519/426-2740; Fax: 519/426-7203 – General Manager, Alan Hays

Nutrite Inc., #1050, 1130, rue Sherbrooke ouest, Montréal PQ H3A 2M8 – 514/849-9222; Fax: 514/849-3362 – President & CEO, Roy Parkes

Pacific Elevators Ltd., 1111 West Hastings St., 4th Fl., Vancouver BC V6E 2J5 – 604/684-5161; Fax: 604/684-7106 – General Manager, R. Butler

Saskatchewan Wheat Pool, 2625 Victoria Ave., Regina SK S4T 7T9 – 306/569-4411; Fax: 306/668-5564 – Chief Executive Officer, D.K. Loewen

Simplot Canada Limited, 1400 - 17th St. East, Brandon MB R7A 7C4 – 204/729-2900; Fax: 204/729-2886 – Plant Manager, Warren Gray

Société Québécoise d'Initiatives Agro-Alimentaires, Parc Samuel Holland, #284, 1275, ch Ste-Foy, Québec PQ G1S 4S5 – 418/643-2238; Fax: 418/643-2553 – Président, Lucien Beron

UFA Cooperative Ltd., 1016 - 68 Ave. SW, Calgary AB T2V 4J2 – 403/258-4500; Fax: 403/258-2250 – CEO, T. Semeniuk

United Farmers of Alberta Co-Operative Ltd., 1016 - 68 Ave. SW, Calgary AB T2V 4J2 – 403/258-4500; Fax: 403/258-2250 – CEO, T. Semeniuk

United Grain Growers Ltd., #2800, 201 Portage Ave., PO Box 6600, Winnipeg MB R3C 3A7 – 204/944-5411; Fax: 204/944-5454 – Chair, T.M. Allen

Western Co-Operative Fertilizers Ltd., 11111 Barlow Trail SE, PO Box 2500, Calgary AB T2P 2N1 – 403/279-1100; Fax: 403/279-1141 – President/CEO, Konrad Komitsch

W.G. Thompson & Sons Ltd., 122 George St., Blenheim ON N0P 1A0 – 519/676-5411; Fax: 519/676-8637 – President, W.D. Thompson

XL Foods Ltd., #250, 1209 - 59 Ave. SE, Calgary AB T2H 2P6 – 403/258-3233.; Fax: 403/253-5087 – President/CEO, James Pattillo

CHEMICALS, BIOTECHNOLOGY & PHARMACEUTICALS

Agrium Inc., #426, 10333 Southport Rd. SW, Calgary AB T2W 3X6 – 403/258-4600; Fax: 403/258-4692 – President & CEO, John M. Van Brunt

Allelix Biopharmaceuticals Inc., 6850 Goreway Dr., Mississauga ON L4V 1V7 – 905/677-0831; Fax: 905/677-9595 – Chairman, John R. Evans

ARC Resins International Corp., #850, 885 Dunsmuir St., Vancouver BC V6C 1N5 – 604/681-9100; Fax: 604/681-9101 – Chair, T.H. Reissner

Bayer Inc., 77 Belfield Rd., Etobicoke ON M9W 1G6 – 416/248-0771; Fax: 416/614-1058 – President, Dr. David Hillanbrand

BioChem Pharma Inc., 275, rue Armand-Frappier, Laval PQ H7V 4A7 – 514/681-1744; Fax: 514/978-7755 – President & CEO, Francesco Bellini

Biomira Inc., 2011 - 94 St., Edmonton AB T6N 1H1 – 403/450-3761; Fax: 403/463-0871 – President, Alex McPherson

Biovail Corp. International, 460 Comstock Rd., Scarborough ON M1L 4S4 – 416/285-6000; Fax: 416/285-6499 – Chairman, Eugene N. Melnyk

BOC Canada Ltd., #2, 5975 Falbourne St., Mississauga ON L5R 3W6 – 905/501-1700; Fax: 905/501-1717 – Director, Finance, Administration & Secretary, Diana Provenzano

Bristol-Myers Squibb Company, 100, boul Industrial, Condiac PQ J5R 1J1 – 514/659-9171; Fax: 514/659-9549 – General Manager, Pierre Cavalle

Cangene Corp., #3-4, 3403 American Dr., Mississauga ON L4V 1T4 – 905/673-0200; Fax: 905/673-5123 – CEO, John Langstaff

CDMV Inc., 2999, av Choquette, St-Hyacinthe PQ J2S 7C2 – 514/773-6073; Fax: 514/773-4370 – President, Paul Cusson

Celanese Canada Inc., 800, boul René-Lévesque ouest, 23e étage, Montréal PQ H3B 1Z1 – 514/871-5511; Fax: 514/871-5573 – President, Donald G. Whitcomb

Ciba-Geigy Canada Ltd., 6860 Century Ave., Mississauga ON L5N 2W5 – 905/821-4420; Fax: 905/567-2224 – President/CEO, Leon Jacobs

Connaught Laboratories Ltd., 1755 Steeles Ave. West, North York ON M2R 3T4 – 416/667-2701; Fax: 416/667-0313 – Chair/CEO, Georges Hibon

CXY Chemicals Ltd., PO Box 1500, Brandon MB R7A 6A6 – 204/728-3777; Fax: 204/726-5746 – Plant Manager, Bill Prosser

Dearborn Chemical Co. Ltd., 3451 Erindale Station Rd., Mississauga ON L5C 2S9 – 905/279-2222; Fax: 905/279-0020 – President & CEO, Ken Rosse

Degussa Canada Ltd., 4261 Mainway Dr., Burlington ON L7R 3Y8 – 905/336-3423; Fax: 905/332-6633 – President, D. Knatz

Diversey Water Technologies Ltd., 110 Second St., PO Box 2008, Cobourg ON K9A 4M2 – 905/372-3344; Fax: 905/372-2561 – President/CEO, Tony Nichols

Dow Chemical Canada Inc., PO Box 3030, Sarnia ON N7T 7M1 – 519/339-3131; Fax: 519/339-4219 – President & CEO, Dennis Lauzon

Draxis Health Inc., 6870 Goreway Dr., Mississauga ON L4V 1P1 – 905/677-5500; Fax: 905/677-5502 – President/CEO, Martin Barkin, M.D.

Drug Royalty Corp. Inc., #202, 8 King St. East, Toronto ON M5C 1B5 – 416/863-1865; Fax: 416/863-5161 – Chair & CEO, Ed Rygiel

DuPont Canada Inc., PO Box 2200, Mississauga ON L5M 2H3 – 905/821-3300; Fax: 905/821-5110 – President/CEO, A.R. Sawchuk

Eli Lilly Canada Inc., 3650 Danforth Ave., Scarborough ON M1N 2E8 – 416/694-3221; Fax: 416/699-7507 – President & CEO, Nelson Sims

General Chemical Canada Ltd., 201 City Centre Dr., 11th Fl., Mississauga ON L5B 3A3 – 905/566-3851; Fax: 905/276-6594 – President & CEO, Delyle Bloomquist

Glaxo Welcome Inc., 7333 Mississauga Rd. North, Mississauga ON L5N 6L4 – 905/819-3000; Fax: 905/819-3099 – President/CEO, P.N. Lundin

Hélène Curtis Ltée, 19501, av Clark Graham, Baie-D'Urfe PQ H9X 3T1 – 514/457-4111; Fax: 514/457-4105 – President, Jack Paque

Hemosol Inc., 115 Skyway Ave., Etobicoke ON M9W 4Z4 – 416/798-0700; Fax: 416/798-0151 – Chairman, Edward K. Rygiel

Hoechst Canada Inc., #2300, 800, boul René-Lévesque ouest, Montréal PQ H3B 1Z1 – 514/871-5511; Fax: 514/871-5573 – President, Donald G. Whitcomb

Hyal Pharmaceutical Corp., #1, 2425 Skymark Ave., Mississauga ON L4W 4Y6 – 905/625-8181; Fax: 905/625-1884 – Chairman, Donald C. Webster

Ibex Technologies Inc., 5485 Pare St., Mont-Royal PQ H4P 1P7 – 514/344-4004; Fax: 514/344-2584 – Chair, President & CEO, Dr. Robert Heft

Canadian Almanac & Directory 1997

ICI Canada Inc., 90 Sheppard Ave. East, PO Box 200, Stn A, North York ON M2N 6H2 – 416/229-7000; Fax: 416/229-8483 – President, Norm Thogersen

Interprovincial Co-op Ltd., 945 Marion St., Winnipeg MB R2J 0K7 – 204/233-3461; Fax: 204/233-8462 – President, Al Robinson

Johnson & Johnson Inc., 2155, boul Pie-IX, Montréal PQ H1V 2E4 – 514/251-5151; Fax: 514/251-5132 – President, J. Gallagher

Kronos Canada, Inc., #500, 4, Place Ville-Marie, Montréal PQ H3B 4M5 – 514/397-3501; Fax: 514/393-1186 – President, R.P. Beaulne

Liquid Carbonic Inc., 140 Allstate Pkwy., Markham ON L3R 5Y8 – 905/477-4141; Fax: 905/477-2088 – President/CEO, Abel Hauri

Methanex Corp., #1800, 200 Burrard St., Vancouver BC V6C 3M1 – 604/661-2600; Fax: 604/661-2686 – Vice-President, North America, Ron Britton

Monsanto Canada Inc., 2330 Argentia Rd., PO Box 787, Mississauga ON L5M 2G4 – 905/826-9222; Fax: 905/826-3119 – Chair, W.A. Dimma

NOVA Chemicals Ltd., PO Box 2535, Stn M, Calgary AB T2P 2N0 – 403/750-3619; Fax: 403/290-6801 – President & COO, Dan Boivan

Novopharm Ltd., 30 Nably Crt., Toronto ON M1B 2K5 – 416/291-8876; Fax: 416/754-8953 – President & CEO, Dr. Ratick Henein

Patheon Inc., Canterra Tower, #4615, 400 - 3rd Ave. SW, Calgary AB T2P 4H2 – 403/269-6795; Fax: 403/265-2887 – Chairman, President & CEO, Richard A.N. Bonnycastle

Petromont & Co. Ltd., 2931, Marie Victorin, Varennes PQ J3X 1S7 – 514/640-6400, 652-2971; Fax: 514/652-7654 – President & CEO, Marcel Emond

Potash Corp. of Saskatchewan Inc., #500, 122 - 1st Ave. South, Saskatoon SK S7K 7G3 – 306/933-8500; Fax: 306/933-8510 – President, PCS Sales, W.J. Doyle

PPG Canada Inc., 30 St. Clair Ave. West, Toronto ON M4V 3A1 – 416/923-5441; Fax: 416/924-7482 – President, Margaret H. McGrath

Praxair Canada Inc., #1200, 1 City Center Dr., Mississauga ON L5B 1M2 – 905/803-1630; Fax: 905/803-1690 – President & CEO, Joe Rivero

Prospec Chemicals, RR#3, W-4 Industrial Park, PO Box 3478, Fort Saskatchewan AB T8L 2T4 – 403/992-1522; Fax: 403/992-1302 – President/CEO, Rob McPhail

QLT Phototherapeutics Inc., #200, 520 - 6th Ave., Vancouver BC V5Z 4H5 – 604/872-7881; Fax: 604/875-0001 – President/CEO, Dr. Julia Levy

Receptagen Ltd., 3030 Beta Ave., Burnaby BC V5G 4K4 – 604/291-8846; Fax: 604/291-8863 – Chair/CEO, Albert G. Chiasson

Reckitt & Colman Canada Inc., 2 Wickman Rd., Toronto ON M8Z 5M5 – 416/255-2300; Fax: 416/255-5150 – President, Craig Chenoweth

Recochem Inc., 850, Montée de Liesse, Montréal PQ H4T 1P4 – 514/341-3550; Fax: 514/341-6553 – President/CEO, Joseph Kuchar

Rhône-Poulenc Canada Inc., Plaza Three, #400, 2000 Argentia Rd., Mississauga ON L5N 1V9 – 905/821-4450; Fax: 905/821-9339 – President/CEO, B. West

Rohm & Haas Canada Inc., 2 Manse Rd., Toronto ON M1E 3T9 – 416/284-4711; Fax: 416/284-7779 – General Manager, Bob Valgardson

Sandoz Canada Inc., 385, boul Bouchard, Dorval PQ H9S 4P5 – 514/631-6775; Fax: 514/631-1867 – Managing Director/CEO, Hans Mader

Schering Canada Inc., 3535, Rte Transcanadienne, Pointe-Claire PQ H9R 1B4 – 514/426-7300; Fax: 514/695-7641 – President, R. Mitra

Smith & Nephew Inc., 2100, 52e av, Lachine PQ H8T 2Y5 – 514/636-0772; Fax: 514/636-1684 – President & CEO, Roy Trayhern

Uniroyal Chemical Ltd., 25 Erb St., Elmira ON N3B 3A3 – 519/669-1671; Fax: 519/669-3273 – President/CEO, Walter Ruck

Witco Canada Inc., 1485 Spears Rd., Oakville ON L6L 2X5 – 905/827-1123; Fax: 905/827-0225 – Plant Manager, Adrian Roberts

FOOD & BEVERAGE

A&A Foods Ltd., 1560 Broadway St., Port Coquitlam BC V3C 6E6 – 604/942-6613; Fax: 604/942-0530 – President & CEO, Giovanni Canporese

A&W Food Services of Canada Ltd., #300, 171 West Esplanade, North Vancouver BC V7M 3K9 – 604/988-2141; Fax: 604/988-5531 – President, J.J. Mooney

Achille de la Chevrotière Ltée, 333, rue Montemurro, Rouyn-Noranda PQ J9X 5E1 – 819/797-1900; Fax: 819/797-1271 – President & CEO, Robert Cloutier

Agromex Inc., 2950, rue Ontario est, Montréal PQ H2K 1X3 – 514/527-9661; Fax: 514/527-9452 – President, Robert Desilets

Agropur, Coop Agro-Alimentaire, 510, rue Principale, CP 6000, Granby PQ J2G 7G2 – 514/375-1991; Fax: 514/375-5958 – CEO, R.C. Menard

A.L. Van Houtte Ltée, 8300, 19e av, Montréal PQ H1Z 4J8 – 514/593-7711; Fax: 514/593-8755 – President, P.A. Guillotte

Alimentation Couche-Tard Inc., #280, 1600, boul Saint-Martin est, Laval PQ H7G 4S7 – 514/662-3272; Fax: 514/662-7537 – President & CEO, Alain Bouchard

Andres Wines Ltd., PO Box 10550, Winona ON L8E 5S4 – 905/643-4131; Fax: 905/643-4944 – President & CEO, John E. Peller

Ault Foods Inc., 405 The West Mall, 10th Fl., Etobicoke ON M9C 5J1 – 416/626-1973; Fax: 416/620-3123 – President & CEO, Graham P.M. Freeman

Baxter Foods Ltd., 91 Millidge Ave., Saint John NB E2K 2M3 – 506/632-6600; Fax: 506/632-6677 – President & CEO, Malcolm R. Baxter

BC Sugar Refinery Ltd., PO Box 2150, Vancouver BC V6B 3V2 – 604/253-1131; Fax: 604/253-2517 – President/CEO, William C. Brown

BC Tree Fruits Ltd., 1473 Water St., Kelowna BC V1Y 1J6 – 250/762-2604; Fax: 250/762-5571 – President, Jamie Kidston

Beatrice Foods Inc., #600, 295 The West Mall, Etobicoke ON M9C 4Z4 – 416/626-5500; Fax: 416/626-8464 – Chair, President & CEO, Brent Ballantyne

Becker's, 671 Warden Ave., Scarborough ON M1L 3Z7 – 416/698-2591; Fax: 416/698-2907 – President, Geoffrey Pottow

Burns Foods Ltd., PO Box 2520, Stn M, Calgary AB T2P 3X4 – 403/265-8140; Fax: 403/266-2287 – President, Ronald Jackson

Cadbury Beverages Canada Inc., #500, 2700 Matheson Blvd. East, Mississauga ON L4W 4X1 – 905/629-1899; Fax: 905/629-3534 – Vice-President, Sales, Rob Granby

Campbell Soup Co. Ltd., 60 Birmingham St., Toronto ON M8V 2B8 – 416/251-1131; Fax: 416/253-8611 – Vice-President & CFO, Jeff Arnold

CAMS Inc., 219, rang St-Louis, Sherrington PQ J0L 2N0 – 514/454-4621; Fax: 514/454-6511 – President, Benoit Subtil

Canada Malting Co. Ltd., #600, 10 Four Seasons Pl., Etobicoke ON M9B 6H7 – 416/620-7575, 622-6151; Fax: 416/620-5004 – President, Jonathan Bamberger

Canada Safeway Ltd., 1020 - 64 Ave. NE, Calgary AB T2E 7V8 – 403/730-3500; Fax: 403/730-3888 – President & COO, Grant M. Hansen

Canbra Foods Ltd., 2415 - 2A Ave. North, PO Box 99, Lethbridge AB T1J 3Y4 – 403/329-5500; Fax: 403/327-3887 – President & CEO, Larry McNamara

Canola Industries Canada, #401, 1101 - 5 St., Nisku AB T9E 7N3 – 403/955-8822; Fax: 403/955-2969 – President & CEO, Tony Cabral

Cara Operations Ltd., 230 Bloor St. West, Toronto ON M5S 1T8 – 416/962-4571; Fax: 416/969-2569 – President & COO, Gabe Tsampalieros

Cascadia Brands Inc., #214, 1285 Broadway West, Vancouver BC V6H 3X8 – 604/738-9463; Fax: 604/738-0182 – President, Ian Tostenson

Clearly Canadian Beverage Corp., #1900, 999 West Hastings St., Vancouver BC V6C 2W2 – 604/683-0312; Fax: 604/683-2256 – President/CEO, Douglas L. Mason

COBI Foods Inc., PO Box 401, Hantsport NS B0P 1P0 – 902/684-1430; Fax: 902/684-1437 – Chairman, President & CEO, George E. Bishop

Coca-Cola Beverages Ltd., 42 Overlea Blvd., Toronto ON M4H 1B8 – 416/424-6000; Fax: 416/424-6079 – Executive Vice-President & COO, Shawn B. Higgins

ConPak Seafoods Inc., 31 Pippy Pl., St. John's NF A1B 3V8 – 709/726-3020; Fax: 709/726-8595 – President & CEO, Percy McDonald

Corby Distilleries Ltd., #2300, 1002, rue Sherbrooke ouest, Montréal PQ H3A 3L6 – 514/288-4181; Fax: 514/288-0749 – President & CEO, Martin Jones

Corporate Foods Ltd., 10 Four Seasons Pl., Etobicoke ON M9B 6H7 – 416/622-2040; Fax: 416/622-8954 – President/CEO, David Lees

Cott Corp., #800, 207 Queens Quay West, Toronto ON M5J 1A7 – 416/203-3898; Fax: 416/203-8168 – President, David A. Nichol

Culinar Inc., #2700, 2, Complexe Desjardins, CP 32, Montréal PQ H5B 1B2 – 514/288-3101; Fax: 514/288-3353 – President/CEO, Gaetan Lussier

Delicana Nord Ouest Inc., 680, av Chausse, Rouyn-Noranda PQ J9X 4B9 – 819/762-3555; Fax: 819/797-1039 – Executive Director, C. Fournel

Dover Industries Ltd., 4350 Harvester Rd., Burlington ON L7L 5S4 – 905/333-1515; Fax: 905/333-1584 – President/Chair, Mona Campbell

Export Packers Co. Ltd., 107 Walker Dr., Brampton ON L6T 5K5 – 905/792-9700; Fax: 905/792-7421 – Vice-President, Don Rosen

Farmers Co-operative Dairy Ltd., PO Box 8118, Halifax NS B3K 5Y6 – 902/835-3373; Fax: 902/835-1583 – President & CEO, Chris Power

Fletcher's Fine Foods Ltd., #3000, 8385 Fraser St., Vancouver BC V5X 3X8 – 604/668-5800; Fax: 604/668-5900 – President/CEO, Fred Knoedler

Foster's Brewing Group Canada Inc., #706, 175 Bloor St. East, Toronto ON M4W 3S4 – 416/921-0055; Fax: 416/921-5357 – Executive Vice-President, A.M. Hodge

Fruits Botner Ltée, #390, 615, rue Marché-Central, Montréal PQ H4W 1J8 – 514/383-1717; Fax: 514/389-7286 – President, Steve Sztern

Gainers Inc., 12425 - 66 St. NW, Edmonton AB T5J 2H8 – 403/471-0611; Fax: 403/471-0776 – Vice-President/General Manager, Brian Parteno

Gaines Pet Foods, 711 Ontario St., Cobourg ON K9A 4L3 – 905/372-0108; Fax: 905/372-1958 – President & CEO, Alex Chelico

G.E. Barbour Inc., 165 Stewart Ave., PO Box 1130, Sussex NB E0E 1P0 – 506/432-2300; Fax: 506/432-2323 – President & CEO, Grant Brenan

General Mills Canada Inc., 1330 Martin Grove Rd., PO Box 505, Etobicoke ON M9W 4X4 – 416/743-8110; Fax: 416/745-3487 – President, David Murphy

George Weston Ltd., #1901, 22 St. Clair Ave. East, Toronto ON M4T 2S7 – 416/922-2500; Fax: 416/922-8713 – Chair/President, W.G. Weston

Gilbey Canada Inc., 283 Horner Ave., Etobicoke ON M8Z 4Y4 – 416/626-2000; Fax: 416/252-4570 – President & CEO, Paul Clinton

Groupe La Cantinière Inc., 2387, rue Remembrance, Lachine PQ H8S 1X4 – 514/634-7201; Fax: 514/634-1962 – President & CEO, Eric Marceau

Hunt Wesson Canada - Conagra Ltd., #408, 1 Concorde Gate, North York ON M3C 3N6 – 416/449-4772; Fax: 416/449-6395 – President, Taketo Murata

Canadian Almanac & Directory 1997

J.M. Schneider, 321 Courtland Ave. East, PO Box 130, Kitchener ON N2G 3X8 – 519/885-8100; Fax: 519/885-8210 – President/CEO, D.W. Dodds

Kraft Canada Inc., #200, 3333, Place Cavendish, St-Laurent PQ H4M 2Y2 – 514/856-5075; Fax: 514/856-5051 – President, Irene B. Rosenfeld

Labatt Breweries of Canada, BCE Place, #200, 181 Bay St., PO Box 786, Toronto ON M5J 2T3 – 416/865-6000; Fax: 416/865-6074 – President, Hugo Powell

Lantic Sugar Ltd., 1, carré Westmount, Montréal PQ H3Z 2P9 – 514/939-3939; Fax: 514/939-1270 – President & CEO, Andre Bergeron

Lassonde Industries Inc., 170, 5e av, Rougemont PQ J0L 1M0 – 514/878-1057; Fax: 514/469-2505 – President, Jean-Paul Barre

Lilydale Co-Operative Ltd., 7727 - 127 Ave., Edmonton AB T5C 1R9 – 403/476-6261; Fax: 403/473-0020 – General Manager, Henry Van Zeggelaar

Loblaw Companies Ltd., #1500, 22 St. Clair Ave. East, Toronto ON M4T 2S8 – 416/922-8500; Fax: 416/922-7791 – President, R.J. Currie

Loeb Inc., 400 Industrial Ave., Ottawa ON K1G 3K8 – 613/737-1485; Fax: 613/737-5705 – President & CEO, Pierre Mignault

Maple Leaf Foods Inc., #1500, 30 St Clair Ave. West, Toronto ON M4V 3A2 – 416/926-2000; Fax: 416/926-2018 – President/CEO, Michael McCain

Maple Lodge Farms Ltd., RR#2, Norval ON L0P 1K0 – 905/455-8340; Fax: 905/455-8370 – CEO, Robert May

McCain Foods Ltd., Main Rd., PO Box 97, Florenceville NB E0J 1K0 – 506/392-5541; Fax: 506/392-8156 – Chairman, H. Harrison McCain

Midwest Food Products Inc., PO Box 70, Carberry MB R0K 0H0 – 204/834-2136; Fax: 204/834-3400 – Director, Operations, Joe Nicholson

Molson Companies Ltd., #3600, 40 King St. West, Toronto ON M5H 3Z5 – 416/360-1786; Fax: 416/360-5867 – President/CEO, M.A. Cohen

MRRM Inc., #100, 1600, Rte Transcanadienne, Dorval PQ H9P 1H7 – 514/683-5583; Fax: 514/683-6329 – President, Bob Blanchard

Multi-Marques Inc., #510, 1600, boul Henri-Bourassa ouest, Montréal PQ H3M 3E2 – 514/333-7246; Fax: 514/333-8782 – President, Gerald Pelletier

Nabisco Ltd., 10 Parklawn Rd., Etobicoke ON M8Y 3H8 – 416/253-3200; Fax: 416/253-3210 – Chairman, President & CEO, Bruce Wood

Nestle Canada Inc., 25 Sheppard Ave. West, Toronto ON M2N 6S8 – 416/512-9000; Fax: 416/218-2654 – Chairman/CEO & Market Head, Frank Cella

Noble China Inc., #6930, 1 First Canadian Place, PO Box 465, Toronto ON M5X 1E5 – 416/956-4906; Fax: 416/956-4907 – Chairman & President, John D. Pennal

Olymel Société en Commandité, #400, 2200, av Pratte, St-Hyacinthe PQ J2S 4B6 – 514/771-0400; Fax: 514/778-1442 – President/CEO, Jean Bienvenue

Provigo Inc., 1611, boul Crémazie est, Montréal PQ H2M 2R9 – 514/383-3000 – President & CEO, Pierre L. Mignault

The Quaker Oats Co. of Canada Ltd., Quaker Park, PO Box 4100, Peterborough ON K9J 7B2 – 705/743-6330; Fax: 705/876-4164 – President & CEO, David L. Morton

Ralston Purina Canada Inc., 2500 Royal Windsor Dr., Mississauga ON L5J 1K8 – 905/822-1611; Fax: 905/855-5712 – Vice-President, Sales, A. McCarles

Redpath Industries Ltd., 95 Queens Quay East, Toronto ON M5E 1A3 – 416/366-3561; Fax: 416/366-4177 – Chairman, M.D. McEwen

Robin Hood Multifoods Inc., 60 Columbia Way, Markham ON L3R 0C9 – 905/940-9600; Fax: 905/940-6859 – President, Consumer Foods, Don Twiner

Saputo Cheese Ltd., 6869, boul Metropolitain est, St-Leonard PQ H1P 1X8 – 514/328-6662; Fax: 514/328-3322 – Vice-President, Sales & Operations, John Saputo

Scotsburn Co-operative Services Ltd., PO Box 340, Scotsburn NS B0K 1R0 – 902/485-8023 – Chair, Donald Gunn

Scotsburn Dairy Group, PO Box 768, Truro NS B2N 5G4 – 902/485-8023; Fax: 902/485-4013 – Vice-President, Sales, Paul Works

The Seagram Company Ltd., 1430, rue Peel, Montréal PQ H3A 1S9 – 514/849-5271; Fax: 514/849-7058 – President/CEO, Edgar Bronfman

Signature Brands Ltd., 934 The East Mall, Etobicoke ON M9B 6J9 – 416/674-8554 – President/CEO, Tomas J. Asensio

Sobeys Inc., 115 King St., Stellarton NS B0K 1S0 – 902/752-8371; Fax: 902/752-2960 – President, Wholesale Operations, D.M. Rushton

Versa Services Ltd., PO Box 950, Stn U, Etobicoke ON M8Z 5Y7 – 416/255-1331; Fax: 416/255-4791 – Chair, Dixon S. Chant

Vincor International Inc., 4887 Dorchester Rd., PO Box 510, Niagara Falls ON L2E 6V4 – 905/358-7141; Fax: 905/357-2055 – President, Donald Triggs

W&H Voortman Ltd., 4455 North Service Rd., Burlington ON L7L 4X7 – 905/335-9500; Fax: 905/332-5499 – President/CEO, Harry Voortman

Westfair Foods Ltd., 3225 - 12 St. NE, Calgary AB T2E 7S9 – 403/291-7700; Fax: 403/291-7899 – President, Serge Darkazanli

Weston Foods Ltd., #501, 22 St. Clair Ave. East, Toronto ON M4T 2S3 – 416/926-1400; Fax: 416/922-7531 – President, James Fisher

ENGINEERING & CONTRACTING

ADS Associés Ltée, #200, 1220, boul Lebourgneuf, Québec PQ G2K 2G4 – 418/626-1688; Fax: 418/626-5464 – Chairman & CEO, Paul Drouin

AGRA Industries Ltd., #1900, 335 - 8 Ave. SW, Calgary AB T2P 1C9 – 403/263-9606; Fax: 403/263-9676 – President & CEO, Alex Taylor

Apex Land Corp., #1100, 500 - 4 Ave. SW, Calgary AB T2P 0L6 – 403/264-3232; Fax: 403/263-0502 – President, Frank Boyd

Armbro Enterprises Inc., #8, 25 Van Kirk Dr., Brampton ON L7A 1A6 – 905/454-3737; Fax: 905/454-5995 – Chairman & CEO, John M. Beck

Atlas Construction Inc., #200, 8200, boul Décarie, Montréal PQ H4P 2P5 – 514/739-3291; Fax: 514/341-3060 – President, Alain Boisset

Atomic Energy of Canada Ltd., 344 Slater St., 18th Fl., Ottawa ON K1A 0S4 – 613/237-3270; Fax: 613/782-2056 – President/CEO, Reid Morden

Banister Foundation Inc., 3660 Midland Ave., Scarborough ON M1V 4V3 – 416/754-8735; Fax: 416/754-8692 – President/CEO, E.R. Austin

Bennett Wright Inc., 47 Cranfield Rd., Toronto ON M4B 3H7 – 416/751-5111, ext.326; Fax: 416/751-9873 – President & CEO, David Nicholson

Bird Construction Co. Ltd., #206, 5405 Eglinton Ave. West, Etobicoke ON M9C 5K6 – 416/620-7122; Fax: 416/620-7121 – President/CEO, Paul Charette

Bracknell Corp., #1506, 150 York St., Toronto ON M5H 3S5 – 416/360-4105; Fax: 416/362-3290 – President, G.L. Ploder

Brookfield Homes, BCE Place, #4200, 181 Bay St., PO Box 746, Toronto ON M5J 2T3 – 416/369-8200; Fax: 416/369-0973 – President/CEO, W.J. Pringle

Commonwealth Construction Co., 4599 Tillicum St., Burnaby BC V5J 3J9 – 604/431-6000; Fax: 604/431-6044 – President/CEO, John Huguet

Consolidated Carma Corp., #800, 839 - 5 Ave. SW, Calgary AB T2P 3C8 – 403/231-8970; Fax: 403/231-8960 – President/CEO, Alan Norris

Delta Hudson Engineering Ltd., #400, 8500 MacLeod Trail South, Calgary AB T2H 2N1 – 403/258-6411; Fax: 403/258-6405 – President/CEO, Bernie Coady

Dumez Nord Amerique Inc., #200, 8200, boul Décarie, Montréal PQ H4P 2P5 – 514/739-3291; Fax: 514/341-5305 – President, Alain Boisset

Eastern Construction Co. Ltd., #410, 4120 Yonge St., North York ON M2P 2C8 – 416/250-7400; Fax: 416/250-7241 – President/CEO, Ed Odette

Ellis-Don Construction Ltd., 2045 Oxford St. East, London ON N5V 2Z7 – 519/455-6770; Fax: 519/455-2944 – Chair/CEO, Donald J. Smith

Fluor Constructors Canada Ltd., 10101 Southport Rd. SW, Stn F, Calgary AB T2W 3N2 – 403/259-1600; Fax: 403/259-1601 – Vice-President/CEO, John Hull

Fluor Daniel Canada Inc., 10101 Southport Rd. SW, Stn F, Calgary AB T2W 3N2 – 403/259-1110; Fax: 403/259-1222 – General Manager Operations, Bob McLeod

George Wimpey Canada Ltd., 80 North Queen St., Toronto ON M8Z 5Z6 – 416/233-5811; Fax: 416/233-2886 – Vice-President, Finance, Randy Roe

Gestion Bemacon Inc., 5181, rue Amiens, Montréal PQ H1G 6N9 – 514/324-5200; Fax: 514/329-3188 – President, J. Carola

Graham Construction & Engineering 1985, 875 - 57 St. East, Saskatoon SK S7K 5Z2 – 306/934-6644; Fax: 306/242-0605 – President/CEO, Tom Baxter

Grilli Property Group Inc., #200, 3535, boul St-Charles, Kirkland PQ H9H 5B9 – 514/694-0463; Fax: 514/694-0373 – Chair/CEO, Mario Grilli

Groupe Macyro Inc., 6140, boul Ste-Anne, L'Ange Gardien PQ G0A 2K0 – 418/822-0543; Fax: 418/822-2530 – Chairman/President, Paul Forest

Groupe Pomerleau, 521, 6e av, CP 8, St-Georges de Beauce PQ G5Y 5C4 – 418/228-6688; Fax: 418/228-3524 – Executive Vice-President, J.P. Bégin

Groupe Soprin Inc., #400, 375 boul Roland-Therrien, Longueuil PQ J4H 4A6 – 514/442-9991; Fax: 514/442-9996 – President, Real Laporte

Ledcor Industries Ltd., #1000, 1066 West Hastings St., Vancouver BC V6C 3X1 – 604/681-7500; Fax: 604/681-4385 – President, David Lede

Lessard Beaucage Lemieux Inc., 225, Montée de Liesse, St-Laurent PQ H4T 1P5 – 514/737-4533; Fax: 514/342-7772 – President/CEO, Camille Lessard

Litton Systems Canada Ltd., 25 Cityview Dr., Etobicoke ON M9W 5A7 – 416/249-1231; Fax: 416/245-0324 – President, Thomas J. McGuigan

Majestic Inc., PO Box 4947, Edmonton AB T6E 5G8 – 403/955-7167; Fax: 403/955-7160 – President, R. Marriott

M.M. Dillon Ltd., #300, 100 Sheppard Ave. East, PO Box 1850, Toronto ON M2N 6H5 – 416/229-4646; Fax: 416/229-4692 – President, Jim Balfour

Neilson Excavation Inc., 578, ch Olivier, Bernieres PQ G7A 2N6 – 418/831-2141; Fax: 418/831-8059 – President, Jean Fava

PCL Construction Group Inc., 5410 - 99 St., Edmonton AB T6E 3P4 – 403/435-9711; Fax: 403/436-2247 – President/CEO, J.A. Thompson

Reliance Construction of Canada, #300, 3400, rue Jean-Talon ouest, Montréal PQ H3R 2E8 – 514/738-7993; Fax: 514/738-2801 – President/CEO, Steve Kaplan

Richard & B.A. Ryan Ltd., 78 Logan Ave., Toronto ON M4M 2M8 – 416/461-0791; Fax: 416/461-7606 – President & CEO, V.J. Loisel

Richcraft Homes Ltd., #201, 2280 St. Laurent Blvd., Ottawa ON K1G 4K1 – 613/739-7111; Fax: 613/739-7102 – President & CEO, Chris Singhal

Robert Laframboise Mechanical, 1397 Rosemount Ave., Cornwall ON K6J 3E5 – 613/933-6664; Fax: 613/933-9910 – General Manager, Wayne Harquail

Sintra Ltd., 4984, Place de la Savane, Montréal PQ H4P 2M9 – 514/341-5331; Fax: 514/341-3915 – President/CEO, Thierry Genestar

SNC Group Inc., 2, Place Felix-Martin, Montréal PQ H2Z 1Z3 – 514/393-1000; Fax: 514/866-0795 – President/CEO, Guy Saint-Pierre

SNC-Lavalin Inc., 1100, boul René-Lévesque ouest, Montréal PQ H3B 4P3 – 514/393-1000; Fax: 514/876-9273 – President/CEO, Guy Saint-Pierre

Stuart Olson Construction Ltd., 12836 - 146 St., Edmonton AB T5L 2H7 – 403/452-4260; Fax: 403/455-4178 – President, M. MacKinnon

UMA Group Ltd., 3030 Gilmour Diversion, Burnaby BC V5G 3B4 – 604/438-5311; Fax: 604/438-5587 – BC Regional Manager, Peter Yeoman

Vibec Inc., 575, boul Industriel est, Victoriaville PQ G6P 6T2 – 819/758-7201; Fax: 819/752-5725 – President, Denis Roy

V.K. Mason Construction Ltd., #201, 2600 Skymark Ave., Mississauga ON L4W 5B2 – 905/629-8888; Fax: 905/629-8799 – President, S.M. Smith

FORESTRY & PAPER

Abitibi-Price Inc., #680, 207 Queens Quay West, Toronto ON M5J 2P5 – 416/203-5000; Fax: 416/203-5094 – President & CEO, R.Y. Oberlander

Ainsworth Lumber Co. Ltd., Exeter Rd., PO Box 67, 100 Mile House BC V0K 2E0 – 250/395-6200; Fax: 250/395-6201 – President & CEO, D. Allen Ainsworth

Alberta Newsprint Co., PO Box 9000, Whitecourt AB T7S 1P9 – 403/778-7000; Fax: 403/778-7072 – President, Fred Row

Alliance Forest Products Inc., #2820, 1000, de la Gauchetière ouest, Montréal PQ H3B 4W5 – 514/954-2100; Fax: 514/954-2145 – President/CEO, Pierre Monahan

Avenor Inc., 1250, boul René-Lévesque ouest, Montréal PQ H3B 4Y3 – 514/846-5152; Fax: 514/846-5071; URL: http://www.avenor.com – President & CEO, Paul E. Gagne

Bois Blanchet International Lumber Inc., #225, 5055, boul Hamel ouest, Québec PQ G2E 2G6 – 418/872-0810; Fax: 418/871-9755 – President, Andre Gauthier

Bowater Mersey Paper Company Ltd., PO Box 1150, Liverpool NS B0T 1K0 – 902/354-3411; Fax: 902/354-3350 – President & General Manager, Jack Dunlop

Canfor Corp., #2900, 1055 Dunsmuir St., PO Box 49420, Vancouver BC V7X 1B5 – 604/661-5241; Fax: 604/661-5464 – President/CEO, Arild Nielssen

Cascades Inc., 471, rue Marie Victorin, Kingsey Falls PQ J0A 1B0 – 819/363-5100; Fax: 819/363-5166 – President, B. Lemaire

Chemetics International Co. Ltd., 1818 Cornwall Ave., Vancouver BC V6J 1C7 – 604/734-1200; Fax: 604/737-4458 – President, Athol Trickett

CML Industries Ltd., 550 Cochrane Dr., Unionville ON L3R 8E2 – 905/513-8511; Fax: 905/513-7830 – Chair/CEO, Claude Theberge

Crestbrook Forest Industries Ltd., 220 Cranbrook St. North, Cranbrook BC V1C 3R2 – 250/426-6241; Fax: 250/426-3406 – President/COO, Jim Shepherd

Daishowa Forest Products Ltd., BCE Place, #1540, 181 Bay St., PO Box 822, Toronto ON M5J 2T3 – 416/862-5000; Fax: 416/862-7456 – President/CEO, K. Kitagawa

Doman Industries Ltd., #400, 435 Trunk Rd., Duncan BC V9L 2P9 – 250/748-3711; Fax: 250/748-6045 – Chairman, President & CEO, H.S. Doman

Domtar Inc., 395, boul De Maisonneuve ouest, Montréal PQ H3A 1L6 – 514/848-5400; Fax: 514/848-6850 – President/COO, Gilles Blondeau

Donohue Inc., 801, ch Saint-Louis, Québec PQ G1S 4W3 – 418/684-7700; Fax: 418/684-7707 – President/CEO, Michel Desbiens

Eurocan Pulp & Paper Co., PO Box 1400, Kitimat BC V8C 2H1 – 250/632-6111; Fax: 250/639-3486 – President, Dan Potts

Fletcher Challenge Canada Ltd., 700 West Georgia St., 9th Fl., PO Box 10058, Vancouver BC V7Y 1J7 – 604/654-4000; Fax: 604/654-4118 – President/CEO, Douglas Whitehead

Foresbec Inc., 1750, rue Haggerty, Drummondville PQ J2C 5P8 – 819/477-8787; Fax: 819/472-3965 – Chair, President & CEO, Guy Boisse

Green Forest Lumber Corp., #500, 194 Merton St., Toronto ON M4S 3B5 – 416/489-3336; Fax: 416/489-3312 – President, R.D. Tuckey

Groupe Forex Inc., 689 - 3e av, PO Box 296, Val d'Or PQ J9P 4P3 – 819/825-4841; Fax: 819/825-5995 – Chair, President & CEO, Jean-Jacques Cossette

Groupe Gesco-Star Ltée, #660, 2600, boul Laurier, Ste-Foy PQ G1V 4W1 – 418/657-6505; Fax: 418/657-7952 – President & CEO, M. Grondin

Husky Plywood, 15, boul Labelle, Ste-Thérèse-De-Blainville PQ J7E 4H9 – 514/435-6541; Fax: 514/435-3814 – President, W.T. Caine

International Forest Products, #3500, 1055 Dunsmuir St., Vancouver BC V7X 1H7 – 604/689-6800; Fax: 604/688-0313 – President & COO, R.M. Sitter

Kruger Inc., 3285, rue Bedford, Montréal PQ H3S 1G5 – 514/737-1131; Fax: 514/343-3124 – Chair/CEO, Joseph Kruger

Lignum Ltd., #1200, 1090 West Georgia St., Vancouver BC V6E 3V7 – 604/687-2425; Fax: 604/687-5714 – President/COO, Conrad Pinette

MacMillan Bloedel Ltd., 925 West Georgia St., 5th Fl., Vancouver BC V6C 3L2 – 604/661-8000; Fax: 604/681-8507 – President & CEO, Robert B. Findlay

Malette Inc., Hwy 101 West, PO Box 1100, Timmins ON P4N 7H9 – 705/268-1462; Fax: 705/360-1251 – President & Chief of Operations, Fred Burrows

Malette Québec Inc., 625, boul René-Lévesque ouest, Montréal PQ H3B 1R2 – 514/397-0735; Fax: 514/397-1434 – President & CEO, Gaston Malette

Materiaux Blanchet Inc., #225, 5055, boul Hamel ouest, Québec PQ G2E 2G6 – 418/871-2626; Fax: 418/871-9755 – President & CEO, Osairi Dube

Noranda Forest Inc., TD Bank Tower, TD Centre, #4414, PO Box 7, Stn Toronto Dominion, Toronto ON M5K 1A1 – 416/982-7444; Fax: 416/982-7396 – President & CEO, Linn MacDonald

Northwood Pulp & Timber Ltd., PO Box 9000, Prince George BC V2L 4W2 – 250/962-9611; Fax: 250/962-3764 – President/CEO, C.T. Hazelwood

Orenda Forest Products Ltd., #409, 545 Clyde Ave. West, Vancouver BC V7T 1C5 – 604/926-4445; Fax: 604/926-7963 – Chairman, President & CEO, Hugh Cooper

Pacific Forest Products Ltd., #1000, 1040 West Georgia St., Vancouver BC V6E 4K4 – 604/640-3400; Fax: 604/640-3480 – President & CEO, Sandy M. Fulton

Primex Forest Products Ltd., 9924 River Rd., Delta BC V4G 1B5 – 604/583-3665; Fax: 604/583-1217 – President/CEO, G.L. Malpass

Produits Forestiers Portbec, #660, 2600, boul Laurier, Québec PQ G1V 4W1 – 418/657-6505; Fax: 418/657-7952 – Président & Directeur Générale, M. Grondin

QUNO Corp., 80 King St., St Catharines ON L2R 7G1 – 905/688-5030; Fax: 905/688-6005 – President/CEO, Michael Desbiens

Repap Enterprises Inc., #3800, 1250, boul René-Lévesque ouest, Montréal PQ H3B 4W8 – 514/846-1316; Fax: 514/846-1313 – Chairman/CEO, G.S. Petty

REXFOR, 1195, av de Lavigerie, Ste-Foy PQ G1V 4N3 – 418/659-4530; Fax: 418/643-4037 – President, André L'Ecuyer

Riverside Forest Products Ltd., 820 Guy St., Kelowna BC V1Y 7R5 – 250/762-3411; Fax: 250/762-6888 – President/CEO, Gordon Steele

Rolland Inc., #1400, 2000, av McGill College, Montréal PQ H3A 3H3 – 514/282-2650; Fax: 514/285-4476 – President, Alain Lemire

Sedgwick Ltd., Toronto-Dominion Centre, PO Box 439, Toronto ON M5K 1M3 – 416/361-6742; Fax: 416/361-6764 – President/CEO, William Jarvis

Shorewood Packaging Corp. Canada, #50, 2220 Midland Ave., Scarborough ON M1P 3E6 – 416/292-3990; Fax: 416/292-0480 – Vice-President, Sales, H. Mendelson

Slocan Forest Products Ltd., #240, 10451 Shellbridge Way, Richmond BC V6X 2W8 – 604/278-7311; Fax: 604/278-7316 – President/CEO, Irving Barber

Tembec Inc., 800, boul René-Lévesque ouest, 27e étage, Montréal PQ H3B 1X9 – 514/871-0137; Fax: 514/397-0896 – President/CEO, Frank Dottori

Timberwest Forest Ltd., #2300, 1055 West Georgia St., PO Box 11101, Vancouver BC V6E 3P3 – 604/654-4600; Fax: 604/654-4662 – President/CEO, R. Keith Purchase

Toromont Industries Ltd., 1 Crothers Dr., PO Box 20011, Concord ON L4K 4T1 – 416/667-5662; Fax: 416/667-5555 – Chairman, President & CEO, R.M. Ogilvie

Weldwood of Canada Ltd., 1055 Hastings St. West, PO Box 2179, Vancouver BC V6B 3V8 – 604/687-7366; Fax: 604/662-2858 – President/CEO, George Richards

West Fraser Timber Co. Ltd., #1000, 1100 Melville St., Vancouver BC V6E 4A6 – 604/895-2700; Fax: 604/681-6061 – President/CEO, Henry Ketcham

Weyerhaeuser Canada Ltd., 11553 - 154 St., Edmonton AB T5M 3N7 – 403/452-5395; Fax: 403/452-3018 – Vice-President, Rod Dempster

GENERAL MANUFACTURING

3M Canada Inc., 1840 Oxford St. East, PO Box 5757, London ON N6A 4T1 – 519/451-2500; Fax: 519/452-6262 – President & General Manager, R.L. Harms

Algo Group Inc., 225, rue Chabanel ouest, 4e étage, Montréal PQ H2N 2C9 – 514/382-1240; Fax: 514/382-4436 – President, Joseph Schaffer

American Sensors Inc., 100 Tempo Ave., Toronto ON M2H 3S5 – 416/496-5900; Fax: 416/496-5959 – Chairman & Director, Bill Koyle

Amisco Industries Ltd., 33, 5e rue, L'Isletville PQ G0R 2C0 – 418/247-5025; Fax: 418/247-7896 – Chairman & CEO, Martin Poitras

Armstrong World Industries Canada Ltd., 6911, boul Décarie, Montréal PQ H3W 3E5 – 514/733-9981; Fax: 514/733-0661 – President, G.T. Levering

Avon Canada Inc., 5500, Rte Trans-Canada, Pointe-Claire PQ H9R 1B6 – 514/695-3371; Fax: 514/630-5440 – Vice-President, Sales Operations, B. Long

Ball Packaging Products Canada, 3060 Mainway Dr., Burlington ON L7M 1A3 – 905/336-6616; Fax: 905/332-2121 – Director, Human Resources, Bob Lauer

Bestar Inc., 4220, rue Villeneuve, Lac-Megantic PQ G6B 2C3 – 819/583-1017; Toll Free: 1-888-823-7827 – President, Paulin Tardif

Bionaire Inc., 2000, 32e av, Lachine PQ H8T 3H7 – 514/636-0790; Fax: 514/631-6069 – President/CEO, Jean-Guy Gautier

Black & Decker Canada Inc., 100 Central Ave., Brockville ON K6V 5W6 – 613/342-6641; Fax: 613/498-5812 – Site Director, Bob Larocque

Black Arrow Inc., 2889, rue Kepler, Ste-Foy PQ G1X 3V4 – 418/650-1200; Fax: 418/650-0551 – President & CEO, Serge Dompierre

Blount Canada Ltd., 505 Edinburgh Rd. North, Guelph ON N1H 6L4 – 519/822-6870; Fax: 519/822-1450 – Vice-President, Marketing, Jim Barry

Brown Shoe Co. of Canada Ltd., 1857 Rogers Rd., Perth ON K7H 3E8 – 613/267-2000; Fax: 613/267-7113 – President, K. Gilbertson

Camco Inc., 5800 Keatan Cres., Mississauga ON L2R 3K2 – 905/501-7001; Fax: 905/501-7080 – President/CEO, Nat Stoddard

Camoplast Inc., #110, 2144, rue King ouest, Sherbrooke PQ J1J 2E8 – 819/823-1777; Fax: 819/823-8772 – President, D. Choquette

Canstar Sports Inc., #600, 8000, boul Décarie, Montréal PQ H4P 2S4 – 514/738-3011; Fax: 514/738-5178 – President, P. Boibin

Canadian Almanac & Directory 1997

MAJOR CANADIAN COMPANIES

CCL Industries Inc., #800, 105 Gordon Baker Rd., North York ON M2H 3P8 – 416/756-8500; Fax: 416/756-8555 – President/CEO, Wayne McLeod

CFM International Inc., 475, Admiral Blvd., Mississauga ON L5T 2N1 – 905/670-7777; Fax: 905/670-4676 – President/CEO, Colin Adamson

Colgate-Palmolive Canada Inc., 99 Vanderhoof Ave., Toronto ON M4G 2H6 – 416/421-6000; Fax: 416/696-9539 – President, David Conn

Consolidated Enfield Corp. Ltd., BCE Place, #4501, 181 Bay St., Toronto ON M5J 2T3 – 416/359-8625; Fax: 416/865-1288 – President, Brian D. Lawson

Consolidated Mercantile Corp., 106 Avenue Rd., Toronto ON M5R 2H3 – 416/920-0500; Fax: 416/920-7851 – President, Fred A. Litwin

Consoltex Group Inc., 8555, rte Transcanadienne, St-Laurent PQ H4S 1Z6 – 514/333-8800; Fax: 514/335-7020 – President/CEO, Richard H. Willett

Coronet Carpets Inc., #106, 7420 Airport Rd., Mississauga ON L4T 4E5 – 905/678-9595; Fax: 905/678-2470 – President, Jan Lembregts

Cosmair Canada Inc., 2115, rue Crescent, Montréal PQ H3G 2C1 – 514/335-8000; Fax: 514/287-9039 – President, J. Bitton

Datamark Inc., 909 Upton, LaSalle PQ H8R 2V1 – 514/366-0652; Fax: 514/366-8254 – CEO/Chair, Frank Heller

DMO Industries, 6800 Base Line, Wallaceburg ON N8A 5E5 – 519/627-0791 – President, Norman Holesh

Dominion Textile Inc., 1950, rue Sherbrooke ouest, Montréal PQ H3H 1E7 – 514/989-6000; Fax: 514/989-6214 – President/CEO, John A. Boland

Dorel Industries Inc., 4750, boul Des Grandes-Prairies, St-Léonard PQ H1R 1A3 – 514/323-5701; Fax: 514/323-9444 – President/CEO, Martin Schwartz

Electrohome Ltd., 809 Wellington St. North, Kitchener ON N2G 4J6 – 519/744-7111; Fax: 519/749-3131 – President/COO, Dave Lowater

Estee Lauder Cosmetics Ltd., 161 Commander Blvd., Agincourt ON M1S 3K9 – 416/292-1111; Fax: 416/292-3495 – Exec. VP & Managing Director, Gary Bain

General Electric Canada Inc., 2300 Meadowvale Blvd., Mississauga ON L5N 5P9 – 905/858-5100; Fax: 905/858-5218 – Chair/CEO, Robert T.E Gillespie

Gillette Canada Inc., 16700, Transcanadienne Hwy, Kirkland PQ H9H 4Y8 – 514/426-6307; Fax: 514/426-6363 – President, Don MacDuff

Groupe Bocenor Inc., 274, rue Duchesnay, CP 1000, Ste-Marie de Beauce PQ G6E 3C2 – 418/387-7723; Fax: 418/387-3968 – Chair/CEO, Jean-Louis Bonneville

Groupe Hamelin Inc., 150, boul Industriel, Boucherville PQ J4B 2X3 – 514/641-0600; Fax: 514/641-4523 – President, Robert Hamelin

GSW Inc., #1903, 20 Eglinton Ave. West, PO Box 2047, Toronto ON M4R 1K8 – 416/489-0640; Fax: 416/489-1476 – Chair, R.M. Barford

Hubbard Holding Inc., 425, av Marien, Montréal PQ H1B 4V7 – 514/645-8833; Fax: 514/645-8838 – Chairman, Robert Lemire

ICI Paints (Canada) Inc., 8200 Keele St., Concord ON L4K 2A5 – 905/669-1020; Fax: 905/669-3497 – Vice-President, Operations, Ben Gonsko

Imperial Tobacco Ltd., 3810, rue Saint-Antoine ouest, Montréal PQ H4C 1B5 – 514/932-6161; Fax: 514/932-7033 – Chairman, President & CEO, Donald Brown

Imperial Wallcovering Canada Inc., 1051, rue Galt est, Sherbrooke PQ J1G 1Y7 – 819/566-5044; Fax: 819/563-1496 – Vice-President, Operations, Malcolm Cogan

Industries Domco Ltée, 1001, rue Yamaska est, Farnham PQ J2N 1J7 – 514/293-3173; Fax: 514/293-8385 – President/CEO, Robert VanBuren

International Wallcoverings Ltd., 151 East Dr., Brampton ON L6T 1B5 – 905/791-1547; Fax: 905/791-6655 – Chairman & CEO, Francis P. Baker

Iona Appliances Inc., 1110 Hansler Rd., PO Box 1004, Welland ON L3B 5S1 – 905/734-7476; Fax: 905/734-9955 – President/CEO, Allan Millman

Irwin Toy Ltd., 43 Hanna Ave., Toronto ON M6K 1X6 – 416/533-3521; Fax: 416/533-3257 – President/CEO, George Irwin

The John Forsyth Co. Inc., 36 Horner Ave., Toronto ON M8Z 5Y1 – 416/252-6231; Fax: 416/253-4147 – President/CEO, Oskar Rajsky

Kodak Canada, 3500 Eglinton Ave. West, Toronto ON M6M 1V3 – 416/766-8233; Fax: 416/766-5814 – President/General Manager, Ed Jurns

Lawson Packaging Inc., #700, 6733 Mississauga Rd. North, Mississauga ON L5N 6P6 – 905/821-9711; Fax: 905/821-1456 – CEO, Marcel Pilon

MAAX Inc., 600, Rte Cameron, Sainte-Marie PQ G6E 1B2 – 418/387-4155, 3646; Fax: 418/387-3507 – President/CEO, Placide Poulin

Makita Canada Inc., 1950 Forbes St., Whitby ON L1N 7B7 – 905/571-2200; Fax: 905/433-4779 – President, Harry Suzuki

Motorola Canada Ltd., 4000 Victoria Park Ave., North York ON M2H 3P4 – 416/499-1441; Fax: 416/756-5263 – Chairman, President & CEO, Eric Taylor

Mr Jax Fashions Inc., 611 Alexander St., Vancouver BC V6A 1E1 – 604/251-8600; Fax: 604/251-8602 – President, Mustata Khan

National Fibretech Inc., 25 Claireville Dr., Etobicoke ON M9W 5Z7 – 416/675-8858; Fax: 416/675-4419 – President, Ron Halton

Noma Industries Ltd., #502, 4100 Yonge St., North York ON M2P 2B5 – 416/222-6662; Fax: 416/222-9165 – Vice-President, Cathy Beck

Norwall Group Inc., 1055 Clark Blvd., Brampton ON L6T 3W4 – 905/791-2700; Fax: 905/791-5281 – Chairman, President & CEO, Jim Patton

Nu-Gro Corp., RR#4, PO Box 1148, Woodstock ON N4S 8P6 – 519/456-2021; Fax: 519/456-5002 – President/CEO, John Hill

Palliser Furniture Ltd., #55, 1155 Gateway Rd., Winnipeg MB R2G 1B9 – 204/988-5600; Fax: 204/663-1776 – President/CEO, Art DeFehr

Peerless Carpet Corp., #1700, 2, Place Alexis Nihon, Montréal PQ H3Z 3C1 – 514/989-6800; Fax: 514/989-6829 – President/CEO, David Arditi

Perkins Papers Ltd., 2345, Aut. des Laurentides, Laval PQ H7S 1Z7 – 514/688-1152; Fax: 514/682-5533 – Executive Vice-President, Suzanne Blanchet

Plastibec Ltée, 1825, boul Lionel-Bertrand, Boisbriand PQ J7H 1N8 – 514/430-9818; Fax: 514/430-9168 – Vice-President/General Manager, Mario Cadorette

Polaroid Canada Inc., 350 Carlingview Dr., Etobicoke ON M9W 5G6 – 416/675-3680; Fax: 416/675-3228 – General Manager, R. Skinner

Polygram Records, 1345 Dennison St., Markham ON L3R 5V2 – 905/415-9900; Fax: 905/415-7390 – Chair/CEO, Gerry Lacoursiere

Premdor Inc., #402, 4120 Yonge St., North York ON M2P 2B8 – 416/250-8933; Fax: 416/250-9270 – Vice-President, Sales & Marketing, C.D. Walker

Prevost Car Inc., 35, boul Gagnon, Ste-Claire PQ G0R 2V0 – 418/883-3391; Fax: 418/883-2145 – President, G. Bourelle

Procter & Gamble Inc., 4711 Yonge St., North York ON M2N 6K8 – 416/730-4711; Fax: 416/730-4415 – President, Yong H. Quek

RJR-Macdonald Inc., #600, First Canadian Place, Toronto ON M5X 1A4 – 416/601-7000 – President/CEO, Pierre Brunelle

Rothmans Inc., 1500 Don Mills Rd., North York ON M3B 3L1 – 416/449-5525; Fax: 416/442-3672 – President/CEO, J.J. Heffernan

Sanyo Canada Inc., 50 Beth Nealson Dr., Toronto ON M5H 1M6 – 416/421-8344; Fax: 416/421-8827 – President, S. Maekawa

Scott Paper Ltd., #125, 1900 Minnesota Crt., Mississauga ON L5N 3C9 – 905/812-6900; Fax: 905/812-6909 – President/CEO, Lee Griffith

Sealy Canada Ltd., 14550 - 112 Ave. NW, Edmonton AB T5M 2V1 – 403/452-3070; Fax: 403/453-7914 – Corporate Controller, Tony Fong

Shermag Inc., 2171, rue King ouest, Sherbrooke PQ J1J 2G1 – 819/566-1515; Fax: 819/566-2373 – President, CEO & Chair, Serge Racine

Shirmax Fashions Ltd., 3901, rue Jarry est, Montréal PQ H1Z 2G1 – 514/729-3333; Fax: 514/593-5758 – Chairman & President, Max Konigsberg

Sico Inc., 2505, rue De La Métropole, Longueuil PQ J4G 1E5 – 514/527-5111; Fax: 514/651-1257 – President/CEO, Pierre Dupuis

Siemens Group, 2185 Derry Rd. West, Mississauga ON L5N 7A6 – 905/819-8000; Fax: 905/819-5777 – Chair, D.S. Macdonald

Stanfield's Ltd., 1 Logan St., Truro NS B2N 5C2 – 902/895-5406; Fax: 902/893-8187 – President/CEO, F. Thomas Stanfield

Sun Ice Ltd., 1001 - 1 St. SE, Calgary AB T2G 5G3 – 403/261-4780; Fax: 403/237-8155 – President/CEO, Sylvia Rempel

Tee-Comm Electronics Inc., 775 Main St. East, Milton ON L9T 3Z3 – 905/878-8181; Fax: 905/878-2472 – President/CEO, Alvin G. Bahnman

Teledyne Canada Ltd., 15 Brydon Dr., Etobicoke ON M9W 4M8 – 416/746-2100; Fax: 416/744-7011 – Chairman, President & CEO, Gary Riley

Thomson Consumer Electronics Canada, Inc., 5925 Airport Rd., 10th Fl., Mississauga ON L4V 1W1 – 905/405-3010; Fax: 905/405-3052; Toll Free: 1-800-522-0338 – President, Mark Redmond

Unilever Canada Ltd., #1500, 160 Bloor St. East, Toronto ON M4W 3R2 – 416/964-1857; Fax: 416/964-0294 – Chair, President & CEO, R.A. Goldstein

United Canadian Shares Ltd., 1601 Church Ave., Winnipeg MB R3C 3J7 – 204/633-7042; Fax: 204/632-6779 – President, C.S. Riley

Viceroy Homes Ltd., 30 Melford Dr., Scarborough ON M1B 1Z4 – 416/298-2200; Fax: 416/298-9545 – President, Gaylord G. Lindal

Vikeda Industries, 650 King St. West, Toronto ON M5V 1M7 – 416/703-6212; Fax: 416/703-4909 – President, Vincent Wong

Warnaco of Canada Ltd., 707 St. Lawrence St. North, Prescott ON K0E 1T0 – 613/925-5981; Fax: 613/925-5983 – President, Roger Keeling

William H. Kaufman Inc., PO Box 9005, Stn C, Kitchener ON N2G 4J8 – 519/576-1500; Fax: 519/576-9794 – President, John Loucks

Workwear Corp. of Canada Ltd., #101, 6299 Airport Rd., Mississauga ON L4V 1N3 – 905/677-6161; Fax: 905/677-6289 – General Manager, Tom Moberly

Yamaha Motor Canada Ltd., 480 Gordon Baker Rd., North York ON M2H 3B4 – 416/498-1911; Fax: 416/491-3122 – Senior Vice-President, Sales & Marketing, D. McKeen

INDUSTRIAL MANUFACTURING

Albany International Canada Inc., 300, rue Westmount, Cowansville PQ J2K 1S9 – 514/263-2880; Fax: 514/263-7692 – Senior Vice-President, M.J. Bacon

Alcatel Canada Wire Inc., 250 Ferrand Dr., Don Mills ON M3C 3J4 – 416/424-5000; Fax: 416/424-1008 – CFO, Ed Edwards

Anchor Lamina Inc., 2590 Ouellette Ave., Windsor ON N8X 1L7 – 519/966-4431; Fax: 519/972-6862 – President, Clare Winterbottom

AT Plastics Inc., 134 Kennedy Rd. South, Brampton ON L6W 3G5 – 905/451-1630; Fax: 905/451-0039 – President & CEO, John G. Clarke

MAJOR CANADIAN COMPANIES

Atlas Copco Canada Inc., 745, rte Montréal-Toronto, Dorval PQ H9S 1A3 – 514/631-5571; Fax: 514/631-9217 – President/CEO, Joseph Camerata

ATS Automation Tooling Systems Inc., Preston Centre, 250 Royal Oak Rd., PO Box 32100, Cambridge ON N3H 5M2 – 519/653-6500; Fax: 519/653-6533 – President/CEO, Klaus Woerner

Babcock & Wilcox Industries, 581 Coronation Blvd., Cambridge ON N1R 5V3 – 519/621-2130; Fax: 519/622-6790 – Vice-President, P.E. Ralston

Ballard Power Systems, #107, 980 - 1 St. West, North Vancouver BC V7P 3N4 – 604/986-9367; Fax: 604/986-3262 – President/CEO, Firoz Rasul

Bay Mills Ltd., #200, 305 Church St., Oakville ON L6J 1N9 – 905/842-8808; Fax: 905/842-5966 – President & CEO, Bradford C. Mattson

Bayer Rubber Inc., 1265 Vidal St. South, PO Box 3001, Sarnia ON N7T 7M2 – 519/337-8251; Fax: 519/339-7752 – President/CEO, Richard R. White

Betz Inc., 3026 Solandt Rd., Kanata ON K2K 2A5 – 613/592-5050; Fax: 613/592-0909 – President/CEO, Don McWilliam

BICC Phillips Inc., #200, 300 Consilium Place, Scarborough ON M1H 3G2 – 416/296-0250; Fax: 416/296-0262 – President & CEO, M.J. Stagg

Blackwood Hodge (Canada) Ltd., 1220 Corporate Dr., Burlington ON L7L 5R6 – 905/332-1250; Fax: 905/332-0933 – President/CEO, J.R. Letwin

Bonar Inc., 2360 McDowell Rd., Burlington ON L7R 4A1 – 905/637-5611; Fax: 905/637-1066 – Executive Vice-President/COO, John McCabe

Brampton Brick Ltd., 225 Wanless Dr., Brampton ON L7A 1E9 – 905/840-1011; Fax: 905/840-1535 – President/CEO, Jeff Kerbel

British Steel Canada Inc., 2255, boul Cavendish, Montréal PQ H4B 2L7 – 514/481-8145; Fax: 514/481-3730 – President/CEO, Ian Taylor

Budd Canada Inc., 1011 Homer Watson Blvd., PO Box 1204, Kitchener ON N2G 4G8 – 519/895-1000; Fax: 519/895-0099 – President & General Manager, Robert Blaine

Butler Metal Products, 1574 Eagle St. North, Cambridge ON N3H 4S5 – 519/653-6286; Fax: 519/653-1352 – President, Robert Lacourciere

C-MAC Industries Inc., 3000, boul Industriel, Sherbrooke PQ J1L 1V8 – 819/821-4524; Fax: 819/563-1167 – President/CEO, Dennis Wood

Canadian Liquid Air Ltd., #1700, 1250, boul René-Lévesque ouest, Montréal PQ H3B 5E6 – 514/933-0303; Fax: 514/846-7700 – Chair/CEO, Norman Seagram

Canadian Tool & Die Ltd., 1331 Chevrier Blvd., Winnipeg MB R3T 1Y4 – 204/453-6833; Fax: 204/453-3803 – President/CEO, John W. Gatsehuffo

Canam Manac Group Inc., #500, 11535 - 1re av, St-Georges PQ G5Y 7H5 – 418/228-8031; Fax: 418/228-1750 – Chairman, President & CEO, Marcel Dutil

Cascades Paperboard International Inc., #1400, 2000, av McGill College, Montréal PQ H3A 3H3 – 514/285-4474; Fax: 514/289-1773 – Chairman, President & CEO, Laurent Lemaire

Cegelec Enterprises Ltd., #1000, 7151, rue Jean-Talon est, Anjou PQ H1M 3R4 – 514/493-4343; Fax: 514/493-4330 – President & CEO, Pierre Ranger

CFS Group Inc., 550, av Marshall, Dorval PQ H9P 1C9 – 514/631-7731; Fax: 514/631-7737 – President, M. Casey

CGC Inc., 350 Burnhamthorpe Rd. West, 5th Fl., Mississauga ON L5B 3J1 – 905/803-5600; Fax: 905/803-5688 – President/CEO, Paul J. Vanderberg

Champion Road Machinery Ltd., 160 Maitland Rd. South, PO Box 10, Goderich ON N7A 3Y6 – 519/524-2601; Fax: 519/524-3015 – President/CEO, Arthur Church

Chrysler Canada Ltd., Chrysler Centre, PO Box 1621, Windsor ON N9A 4H6 – 519/973-2000; Fax: 519/973-2895 – President/CEO, G. Yves Landry

Colortech Corp., 8027 Dixie Rd., Brampton ON L6T 3V1 – 905/792-0333; Fax: 905/792-8118 – President/CEO, Terry Breckenridge

Commonwealth Plywood Co. Ltd., CP 90, Ste-Thérèse PQ J7E 4H9 – 514/435-6541; Fax: 514/435-3814 – President, William P. Caine

Consumers Packaging Inc., #900, 401 The West Mall, Etobicoke ON M9C 5J7 – 416/232-3000; Fax: 416/232-3274 – President/CEO, John Ghaznavi

Contractors Machinery & Equipment, 1051 Heritage Rd., Burlington ON L7L 4Y1 – 905/335-3863; Fax: 905/332-6631 – President, Wally Faloney

Crane Canada Inc., 5850, ch Côte de Liesse, Montréal PQ H4T 1B2 – 514/735-3592; Fax: 514/340-9327 – Vice-President/General Manager, Plumbing Division, Maurice Marwood

Dana Inc., One St. Paul St., PO Box 3029, St Catharines ON L2R 7K9 – 905/687-4200; Fax: 905/687-4246 – President, Bill Carroll

Derlan Industries Ltd., #500, 145 King St. East, Toronto ON M5C 2Y7 – 416/364-5852; Fax: 416/362-5334 – Chair & CEO, D. Coughlan

Dofasco Inc., 1330 Burlington St. East, PO Box 2460, Hamilton ON L8N 3J5 – 905/544-3761; Fax: 905/548-4267 – President/CEO, John Mayberry

Dramex Corp., 3555 Pitfield Blvd., St-Laurent PQ H4S 1H3 – 514/745-7360; Fax: 514/745-2396 – Chair/President, Alan B. Pearson

Dresser-Rand Canada Inc., 2902 - 5 Ave. North, Lethbridge AB T1H 0P3 – 403/329-5400; Fax: 403/329-0603 – Director of Sales, W.G. McCachen

Eagle Precision Technologies Inc., 565 West St., PO Box 786, Brantford ON N3T 5R7 – 519/756-5223; Fax: 519/759-2388 – Chair/President, A. Alex Kepecs

Emco Ltd., 620 Richmond St., London ON N6A 5J9 – 519/645-3900; Fax: 519/645-2465 – President/COO, Douglas Speers

Emerson Electric Canada Ltd., 9999 Highway 48, Markham ON L3P 3J3 – 905/294-9340; Fax: 905/475-4679 – President, Lawrence C. Barrett

Enerflex Systems Ltd., 4949 - 76 Ave. SE, Calgary AB T2C 3C6 – 403/236-6800; Fax: 403/279-0367 – President/CEO, P. John Aldred

Ennisteel Corp., 200 South St., Port Robinson ON L0S 1K0 – 905/384-9794; Fax: 905/384-2120 – President, Keith Arbour

Exco Technologies Ltd., 60 Spy Ct., Markham ON L3R 5H6 – 905/477-3065; Fax: 905/477-2449 – President & CEO, Brian Robbins

Finning Ltd., 555 Great Northern Way, Vancouver BC V5T 1E2 – 604/872-4444; Fax: 604/872-2994 – President/CEO, James Shepard

Firan Corp., 353 Iroquois Shore Rd., Oakville ON L6H 1M3 – 905/844-2870; Fax: 905/844-2907 – President & CEO, Curtis Bossi

FKI Industries Canada Inc., 234 Attwell Dr., Etobicoke ON M9W 5B3 – 416/675-3820; Fax: 416/674-5129 – President/CEO, R. Miller

Fleet Aerospace Corp., #1450, 55 York St., Toronto ON M5J 1R7 – 416/365-0565; Fax: 416/365-2131 – President/CEO, D.C. Lowe

Ford Electronics Mfg. Corp., 7455 Birchmount Rd., Markham ON L3R 5C2 – 905/475-8510; Fax: 905/474-4244 – President, C. Szuluk

Ford Motor Co. of Canada Ltd., PO Box 2000, Oakville ON L6J 5E4 – 905/845-2511; Fax: 905/844-8085 – President/CEO, Mark W. Hutchins

Foremost Industries Inc., 1225 - 64 Ave. NE, Calgary AB T2E 8P9 – 403/295-5800; Fax: 403/295-5810 – President & CEO, Jack Nodwell

Galtaco Inc., #300, 174 Stanley St., Brantford ON N3S 7S3 – 519/751-1691; Fax: 519/751-1693 – Chair, President & CEO, David L. Chandler

G.E. Plastics (Canada) Ltd., Normar Rd., PO Box 10, Cobourg ON K9A 4K2 – 905/372-6801; Fax: 905/373-3909 – Plant Manager, Tom Bouchard

GEC Alsthom International Canada, 9, boul Place Du Commerce, Brossard PQ J4W 2V6 – 514/465-9795; Fax: 514/465-9596 – President, Shea O'Loughiem

General Motors of Canada Ltd., 1908 Colonel Sam Dr., Oshawa ON L1H 8P7 – 905/644-5000; Fax: 905/644-7772 – President/General Manager, Maureen Kempston Darkes

Goodfellow Inc., 225, rue Goodfellow, Delson PQ J0L 1G0 – 514/635-6511; Fax: 514/635-3730 – Marketing Manager, Andre Rashotte

Goodyear Canada Inc., 10 Four Seasons Place, Etobicoke ON M9B 6G2 – 416/626-4611; Fax: 416/695-5601 – President/CEO, Dan Patick

Great Pacific Enterprises Inc., #1600, 1055 West Hastings St., Vancouver BC V6E 2H2 – 604/688-6764; Fax: 604/687-2601 – Managing Director, Jim Pattison

Groupe Laperrière & Verreault, Parc Industriel No 2, 3100, rue Westinghouse, Trois-Rivières PQ G9A 5E1 – 819/371-8265; Fax: 819/373-4439 – Chair, President & CEO, Laurent Verreault

Groupe Permacon Inc., 8145, rue Bombardier, Anjou PQ H1J 1A5 – 514/355-4666; Fax: 514/352-9802 – President, Bertin Castonguay

Gwil Industries Inc., West Tower, #650, 555 West 12th Ave., Vancouver BC V5Z 3X7 – 604/874-4945; Fax: 604/874-4422 – President, Merv Schweitzer

H. Paulin & Co. Ltd., 55 Milne Ave., Scarborough ON M1L 4N3 – 416/694-3351; Fax: 416/694-1869 – President, Richard Paulin

Haley Industries Ltd., General Delivery, Haley Station ON K0J 1Y0 – 613/432-8841; Fax: 613/432-0743 – President/CEO, David Gorman

Hallmark Technologies Inc., 2187 Huron Church Rd., PO Box 7040, Windsor ON N9C 3Y6 – 519/966-4050; Fax: 519/966-2888 – Chair, CEO & President, R. Douglas Balint

Harris Steel Group Inc., #604, 4120 Yonge St., Toronto ON M2P 2B8 – 416/590-9549; Fax: 416/590-9560 – Chair/CEO, Milton E. Harris

Hawker Siddeley Canada Inc., #700, 3 Robert Speck Pkwy., Mississauga ON L4Z 2G5 – 905/897-7161; Fax: 905/897-1466 – President/CEO, Keith Moore

Heroux Inc., 755, rue Thurber, Longueuil PQ J4H 3N2 – 514/679-5450; Fax: 514/679-4554 – President/CEO, Gilles Labbe

Honda Canada Inc., 715 Milner Ave., Scarborough ON M1B 2K8 – 416/284-8110; Fax: 416/286-1322 – President/CEO, A. Hyogo

Honeywell Ltd., 155 Gordon Baker Rd., North York ON M2H 3N7 – 416/499-6111, 502-5200; Fax: 416/502-4059 – President & CEO, Peter Rankine

Husky Injection Molding Systems, 530 Queen St. South, Bolton ON L7E 5S5 – 905/951-5000; Fax: 905/857-7118 – President & CEO, Robert Schad

IMP Group International Ltd., #400, 2651 Dutch Village Rd., Halifax NS B3L 4T1 – 902/453-2400; Fax: 902/453-6931 – President & CEO, K.C. Rowe

Ingersoll-Rand Canada Inc., 51 Worcester Rd., Etobicoke ON M9W 4K2 – 416/213-4500; Fax: 416/213-4616 – President & CEO, S. Zalzal

Inland Cement Ltd., PO Box 3961, Edmonton AB T5L 4P8 – 403/420-2500; Fax: 403/420-2528 – President, Paul Wacko

Inter-City Products Corp., #3500, 20 Queen St. West, Toronto ON M5H 3R3 – 416/598-0101; Fax: 416/598-5261 – President/CEO, Michael Clavy

Intertape Polymer Group Inc., 110, Monteé de Liesse, Montréal PQ H4T 1N4 – 514/731-0731; Fax: 514/731-5039 – Chairman, Melbourne F. Yull

Inverpower Controls Ltd., 835 Harrington Ct., Burlington ON L7N 3P3 – 905/639-4692; Fax: 905/639-0961 – President & CEO, Shashi B. Dewan

IPL Inc., 140, rue Commerciale, St-Damien-de-Buckland PQ G0R 2Y0 – 418/789-2880; Fax: 418/789-3153 – President/CEO, Gillian Metivier

Canadian Almanac & Directory 1997

IPSCO Inc., Armour Rd., PO Box 1670, Regina SK S4P 3C7 – 306/924-7700; Fax: 306/924-9670 – President & CEO, Roger Phillips

ITT Canada Ltd., 6140 Vipond Dr., Mississauga ON L5T 2B2 – 905/670-0450; Fax: 905/670-5143 – Vice-President, Robert Eisner

ITW Canada Inc., 115 Ridgetop Rd., Scarborough ON M1P 2K3 – 416/293-2411; Fax: 416/293-9761 – President, R.F. Palach

Ivaco Inc., Place Mercantile, 770, rue Sherbrooke ouest, 20e étage, Montréal PQ H3A 1G1 – 514/288-4545; Fax: 514/284-9414 – President/CEO, Paul Ivanier

Jannock Ltd., Scotia Plaza, #5205, 40 King St. West, Toronto ON M5H 3Y2 – 416/364-8586; Fax: 416/364-9342 – President/CEO, R.J. Atkinson

John Deere Ltd., PO Box 1000, Grimsby ON L3M 4H5 – 905/945-9281; Fax: 905/945-1937 – President, G.J. Clark

Kaufel Group Ltd., 1800, boul Hymus, Dorval PQ H9P 2N6 – 514/685-2270; Fax: 514/685-0378 – President/CEO, Bruce Kaufman

Lafarge Canada Inc., #800, 606, rue Cathcart, Montréal PQ H3B 1L7 – 514/861-1411; Fax: 514/876-8900 – President/CEO, Michel Rose

Leblanc & Royle Enterprises Inc., 514 Chartwell Rd., PO Box 880, Oakville ON L6J 5C5 – 905/844-1242; Fax: 905/844-8837 – President, Keith Debelser

Linamar Corp., 301 Massey Rd., Guelph ON N1K 1B2 – 519/836-7550; Fax: 519/824-8479 – President/COO, Larry Pearson

Magna International Inc., 36 Apple Creek Blvd., Markham ON L3R 4Y4 – 905/477-7766; Fax: 905/475-0776 – President/CEO, Don Walker

Marshall Steel Ltd., 807, rue Marshall, Laval PQ H7S 1J9 – 514/668-4944; Fax: 514/663-5800 – CEO, Cecil S. Hawkins

McDonnell Douglas Canada Ltd., PO Box 6013, Mississauga ON L5P 1B7 – 905/677-4341; Fax: 905/673-4353 – President, Les Gordon

MDS Health Group Ltd., 100 International Blvd., Etobicoke ON M9W 6J6 – 416/675-7661; Fax: 416/213-4220 – President/CEO, John Rogers

Merfin Hygienic Products Ltd., 7979 Vantage Way, Delta BC V4G 1A6 – 604/946-0677; Fax: 604/946-3516 – President & CEO, Ivan B. Pivko

Meridian Technologies Inc., 2 St Clair Ave. West, 17th Fl., Toronto ON M4V 1L5 – 416/922-2050; Fax: 416/922-4282 – President & CEO, Elvio Del Sorbo

Messier-Dowty Inc., 574 Monarch Ave., Ajax ON L1S 2G8 – 905/683-3100; Fax: 905/686-2914 – President, Ken Laver

Milltronics Ltd., 730 The Kingsway, PO Box 4225, Peterborough ON K9J 7B1 – 705/745-2431; Fax: 705/741-0466 – President & CEO, David Bignell

Navistar International Corp. Canada, 120 King St. West, 9th Fl., Hamilton ON L8N 3S5 – 905/528-7700; Fax: 905/526-3057 – President, Howard Hawkins

Needler Group Ltd., 380 Hardy Rd., PO Box 1390, Brantford ON N3T 5T6 – 519/753-3408; Fax: 519/753-2912 – President, David Sterrett

Norbord Industries Inc., #500, 1 Toronto St., Toronto ON M5C 2W4 – 416/365-0710; Fax: 416/365-3292 – President, Dominic Gammiero

Norcast Castings Inc., #402, 60 Bloor St. West, Toronto ON M4W 3B8 – 416/975-8251; Fax: 416/975-8253 – President, Bruce Johnson

NQL Drilling Tools Inc., 1802 - 4 St., Nisku AB T9E 7T8 – 403/955-8828; Fax: 403/955-3309 – President, Dean Livingstone

Opron Inc., 1351, rue Newton, Boucherville PQ J4B 5H2 – 514/655-4250; Fax: 514/655-3431 – President, Conrad Gagnon

OSF Inc., 650 Barmac Dr., Etobicoke ON M9L 2X8 – 416/749-7700; Fax: 416/246-3229 – Chairman & CEO, Milton Shier

Otis Canada Inc., 710 Dorval Dr., Oakville ON L6J 5B7 – 905/842-6847; Fax: 905/845-3397 – President & CEO, E.A. Minich

Owens Corning Canada Inc., 5140 Yonge St., North York ON M2N 6T9 – 416/733-1600, 292-4000; Fax: 416/226-4159 – Plant Manager, Fred Ramquist

Paccar of Canada Ltd., 6711 Mississauga Rd. North, 3rd Fl., Mississauga ON L5N 4J8 – 905/858-7000; Fax: 905/858-3209 – Director, Sales & Marketing, Bill Currie

Peacock Inc., 8600, rue St. Patrick, Montréal PQ H8N 1V1 – 514/366-5900; Fax: 514/366-2067 – Manager, Administration & Govt. Services, Roland Bleau

Philips Electronics Ltd., 601 Milner Ave., Scarborough ON M1B 1M8 – 416/292-5161; Fax: 416/297-1019 – President, Eric Versteeg

Plasti-Fab Ltd., #207, 3015 - 5 Ave. NE, Calgary AB T2A 6T8 – 403/248-9306; Fax: 403/248-9325 – President & General Manager, Bruce Carruthers

Pratt & Whitney Canada Inc., 1000, boul Marie-Victorin, Longueuil PQ J4G 1A1 – 514/677-9411; Fax: 514/647-4016 – President/COO, Gilles Quimet

Premetalco Inc., 110 Belfield Rd., Etobicoke ON M9W 1G1 – 416/245-7386; Fax: 416/242-2839 – CEO, V.H. Sher

Premier Concrete - ESSROC Canada, 949 Wilson Ave., Toronto ON M3K 1G2 – 416/633-2180; Fax: 416/635-7651 – Sales Manager, R. Post

Procedair Industries Inc., 625, av du President Kennedy, Montréal PQ H3A 1K2 – 514/284-0341; Fax: 514/284-1326 – President & Operations Manager, S. Brunelli-Brondex

Procor Ltd., 2001 Speers Rd., Oakville ON L6J 5E1 – 905/827-4111; Fax: 905/827-0913 – President, Frank D. Lester

Prudential Steel Ltd., PO Box 1510, Calgary AB T2P 2L6 – 403/267-0300; Fax: 403/265-3426; Toll Free: 1-800-661-1050 – President & CEO, J. Donald Wilson

QIT-Fer & Titane Inc., 770, rue Sherbrooke ouest, 18e étage, Montréal PQ H3A 1G1 – 514/288-8400; Fax: 514/286-9336 – President, G.G. Charette

Reko International Group Inc., 5390 Brendan Lane, Oldcastle ON N0R 1L0 – 519/737-6974; Fax: 519/737-6975 – President & CEO, Steve Reko

Robert Mitchell Inc., 350, boul Décarie, St-Laurent PQ H4L 3K5 – 514/747-2471; Fax: 514/747-7712 – President/CEO, George H. Holland

Rockwell International of Canada Ltd., 12 Raglin Place, PO Box 843, Cambridge ON N1R 5X1 – 519/740-8656; Fax: 519/622-8350 – President, D.J. Dillon

Rolls-Royce Industries Canada Inc., 9500, Côte de Liesse, Lachine PQ H8T 1A2 – 514/631-3541; Fax: 514/636-9969 – President/CEO, Stan Todd

Royal Plastics Group Ltd., 1 Royal Gate Blvd., Woodbridge ON L4L 8Z7 – 905/264-0701; Fax: 905/264-0702 – President/CEO, Vittorio De Zen

RPM Tech Inc., 184 Route 138, Cap-Santé PQ G0A 1L0 – 418/285-1811; Fax: 418/285-4289 – President/CEO, Marshall Papillon

Russel Metals Inc., #210, 1900 Minnesota Ct., Mississauga ON L5N 3C9 – 905/819-7777; Fax: 905/819-7364 – President/CEO, John Pelton

Safety-Kleen Canada Ltd., 300 Woolwich St. South, Breslau ON N0B 1M0 – 519/648-2291; Fax: 519/648-2033 – General Manager, Gary Farrar

Samuel Manu-Tech Inc., #418, 191 The West Mall, Etobicoke ON M9C 5K8 – 416/626-2190; Fax: 416/626-5969 – President, Mark Samuel

Simard-Beaudry Inc., 4230, boul Saint-Elzear est, Laval PQ H7E 4P2 – 514/329-4747; Fax: 514/329-4608 – Directeur, Ventes, C. Brouillette

Skyjack Inc., 55 Campbell Rd., Guelph ON N1H 1B9 – 519/837-0888; Fax: 519/837-3102 – President/CEO, Wolfgang Haessler

St. Lawrence Cement Inc., 1945, boul Graham, Montréal PQ H3R 1H1 – 514/340-1881; Fax: 514/342-8154 – President/CEO, Bernard Kueng

Stackpole Ltd., #B-203, 2381 Bristol Circle, Oakville ON L6H 5S9 – 905/829-2050; Fax: 905/829-0438 – President/CEO, J. Samuel Parkhill

Strong Equipment Corp., Royal Bank Plaza, North Tower, #1525, 200 Bay St., Toronto ON M5J 2J2 – 416/364-8744; Fax: 416/364-8186 – President/CEO, J.A. Crawford

Synergistics Industries Ltd., #425, 5915 Airport Rd., Mississauga ON L4V 1T1 – 905/673-1213; Fax: 905/673-8016 – President/CEO, Kim Aagaard

Tarxien Corp., 505 Finley Ave., Ajax ON L1S 2E2 – 905/683-1681; Fax: 905/683-6969 – President, Ralph Zarboni

Tecsyn International Inc., #113, 115 Cushman Rd., PO Box 845, St Catharines ON L2R 6Z4 – 905/687-8811; Fax: 905/687-6917 – President/CEO, Zoltan Simo

Thyssen Canada Ltd., #425, 2560 Matheson Blvd. East, Mississauga ON L4W 4Y9 – 905/602-1300; Fax: 905/602-7668 – President, H. Schmidt

Timminco Ltd., 10 Bay St., 9th Fl., Toronto ON M5J 2R8 – 416/364-5171 – President/CEO, J. Thomas Timmins

Tolgeco Group Inc., 200, boul Industriel, Boucherville PQ J4B 2X4 – 514/526-2544; Fax: 514/641-4582 – President, Yvon Dion

Triam Automotive Inc., #2206, 130 Adelaide St. West, Toronto ON M5H 3P5 – 416/777-2728; Fax: 416/777-2708 – Chair/CEO, James Nicol

Tritech Precision Inc., #3400, 2 Bloor St. West, PO Box 79, Toronto ON M4W 3E2 – 416/963-8880; Fax: 416/963-8288 – President/CEO, W.B. Ferguson

Twinpak Inc., 1255, rte Transcanadienne, Dorval PQ H9P 2V4 – 514/684-7070; Fax: 514/685-5996 – President/CEO, James Allen

UAP Inc., 7025, rue Ontario est, Montréal PQ H1N 2B3 – 514/256-5031; Fax: 514/256-8469 – President/CEO, Jean Douville

Uniboard Canada Inc., #400, 3080, boul le Carresour, Laval PQ H7T 2R5 – 514/682-5240; Fax: 514/682-0550 – Vice-President, Sales, Gilles Lepine

Unicap Commercial Corp., 106 Avenue Rd., Toronto ON M5R 2H3 – 416/920-0500; Fax: 416/920-7851 – President, Mark Litwin

United Tire & Rubber Co. Ltd., 275 Belfield Rd., Etobicoke ON M9W 5C6 – 416/675-3077; Fax: 416/675-4337 – President/CEO, Charles Sherkin

Velan Inc., 2125, rue Ward, Montréal PQ H4M 1T6 – 514/748-7743; Fax: 514/748-8635 – President/CEO, A.K. Velan

Ventra Group Inc., 1 Mitten Crt, PO Box 126, Cambridge ON N1R 5S9 – 519/658-6777; Fax: 519/658-5422 – President, Rick Legate

Volvo Canada Ltd., 175 Gordon Baker Rd., North York ON M2H 2N7 – 416/493-3700; Fax: 416/493-8754 – National Marketing Manager, John Sinclair

Wajax Ltd., 8760 River Rd., Delta BC V4G 1B5 – 604/946-1171; Fax: 604/946-1319 – President/COO, John Powell

Western Star Trucks Holdings Ltd., 2076 Enterprise Way, Kelowna BC V1Y 6H8 – 250/860-3319; Fax: 250/860-1252 – President/CEO, Terrence Peabody

Winpak Ltd., 100 Saulteaux Cres., Winnipeg MB R3J 3T3 – 204/889-1015; Fax: 204/832-7781 – President/CEO, J. Robert Lavery

MINING & METALS

Aber Resources Ltd., #930, 355 Burrard St., Vancouver BC V6C 2G8 – 604/682-8555; Fax: 604/685-8359 – President, D. Grenville Thomas

Acier Francosteel Canada Inc., #300, 5890, av Monkland, Montréal PQ H4A 1G2 – 514/489-8458; Fax: 514/489-7227 – President, Bruno LeForestier

Acier Leroux Inc., 1331, rue Graham Bell, Boucherville PQ J4B 6A1 – 514/641-4360; Fax: 514/641-3671 – President, Administration, Andre Leroux

MAJOR CANADIAN COMPANIES 7-47

Adrian Resources Ltd., #900, 900 West Hastings St., Vancouver BC V6C 1E5 – 604/688-3008; Fax: 604/688-0063 – President/CEO, Chet Idziszek

Advanced Material Resources Ltd., #1740, 121 King St. West, Toronto ON M5H 3T9 – 416/367-8588; Fax: 416/367-5471 – Chairman, President & CEO, Peter V. Gundy

Agnico-Eagle Mines Ltd., #2202, 401 Bay St., Toronto ON M5H 2Y4 – 416/947-1212; Fax: 416/367-4681 – Chairman/President, Paul Penna

A.J. Perron Gold Corp., Kerr Mine/Mill Site, PO Box 390, Virginia Town ON P0K 1X0 – 705/634-2121; Fax: 705/634-2396 – President & CEO, Alexander H. Perron

Alcan Aluminum Ltd., 1188, rue Sherbrooke ouest, Montréal PQ H3A 3G2 – 514/848-8000; Fax: 514/848-1215 – President & CEO, Jacques Bougie

Algoma Steel Inc., 105 West St., Sault Ste. Marie ON P6A 5P2 – 705/945-2351; Fax: 705/945-2972 – President & CEO, W. Allan Hopkins

Ariel Resources Ltd., #1135, 1188 West Georgia St., Vancouver BC V6E 4A2 – 604/682-2201; Fax: 604/682-0318 – President, William C. Bennett

Asbestos Corporation Ltd., 840, boul Ouellet ouest, Thetford-Mines PQ G6G 7A5 – 418/338-5195; Fax: 418/338-6069 – President & CEO, M. De Rouin

Ashton Mining of Canada Inc., #123, 930 - 1 St. West, North Vancouver BC V7P 3N4 – 604/983-7750; Fax: 604/987-7107 – Chairman, David A. Robertson

Atlanta Gold Corporation, #1440, 625 Howe St., Vancouver BC V6C 2T6 – 604/669-0016; Fax: 604/683-5912 – President, Karl Rollke

Audrey Resources Inc., #850, 800, boul René-Lévesque ouest, Montréal PQ H3B 1X9 – 514/878-3166; Fax: 514/878-3324 – President & CEO, Raynald Vézina

Aur Resources Inc., #2501, 1 Adelaide St. East, Toronto ON M5C 2V9 – 416/362-2614; Fax: 416/367-0427 – President/CEO, Dr. James Gill

Aurizon Mines Inc., #1414, 700 West Georgia St., PO Box 10016, Stn Pacific Centre, Vancouver BC V7Y 1A3 – 604/687-6600; Fax: 604/687-3932 – President/CEO, David P. Hall

Barrick Gold Corp., Royal Bank Plaza, South Tower, #2700, 200 Bay St., Toronto ON M5J 2J3 – 416/861-9911; Fax: 416/861-2492 – Chairman/CEO, Peter Munk

Bema Gold Corp., #1400, 510 Burrard St., PO Box 48, Vancouver BC V6C 3A8 – 604/681-8371; Fax: 604/681-6209 – Chairman, CEO & President, Clive T. Johnson

Black Hawk Mining Inc., #2001, 44 Victoria St., Toronto ON M5C 1Y2 – 416/363-2911; Fax: 416/363-9474 – Chairman & CEO, Gordon F. Bub

Bolivar Goldfields Ltd., 172 King St. East, 2nd Fl., Toronto ON M5A 1J3 – 416/955-4554; Fax: 416/955-1206 – President, Miguel Angel De-La-Campa

Brascade Resources Inc., BCE Place, #4400, 181 Bay St., Toronto ON M5J 2T3 – 416/363-9491; Fax: 416/363-2856 – Chair & President, P.M. Marshall

Brascan Ltd., BCE Place, #4400, 181 Bay St., Toronto ON M5J 2T3 – 416/363-9491; Fax: 416/363-2856 – President/CEO, Jack Cockwell

Breakwater Resources Ltd., #2001, 44 Victoria St., Toronto ON M5C 1Y2 – 416/363-4798; Fax: 416/363-9474 – President & CEO, Gordon F. Bub

Brenda Mines Ltd., #2700, 1 Adelaide St. East, Toronto ON M5C 2Z6 – 416/982-7193; Fax: 416/982-7021 – President, David L. Bumstead

Brunswick Mining & Smelting, PO Box 3000, Bathurst NB E2A 3Z8 – 506/546-6671; Fax: 506/547-6191 – Chairman/CEO, Michael Knuckey

Caledonia Mining Corp., #16, 2150 Winston Park Dr., Oakville ON L6H 5V1 – 905/829-4848; Fax: 905/829-4238 – COO, F.C. Harvey

Cambiex Explorations Inc., #850, 800, boul René-Lévesque ouest, Montréal PQ H3B 1X9 – 514/878-3166; Fax: 514/878-3324 – President/CEO, Jean DePatie

Cambior Inc., #850, 800, boul René-Lévesque ouest, Montréal PQ H3B 1X9 – 514/878-3166; Fax: 514/878-3324 – President/CEO, Louis Gignac

Cameco Corporation, 2121 - 11 St. West, Saskatoon SK S7M 1J3 – 306/956-6200; Fax: 306/956-6201 – President/CEO, Bernard Michel

Campbell Resources Inc., #1910, 120 Adelaide St. West, Toronto ON M5H 1T1 – 416/366-5201; Fax: 416/367-3294 – President & CEO, J.O. Kachmar

Canada Tungsten Inc., #2501, 1 Adelaide St. East, Toronto ON M5C 2V9 – 416/362-2614; Fax: 416/367-0427 – President & CEO, James W. Gill

Canadian Reynolds Metals Co., #1002, 2420, rue Sherbrooke ouest, Montréal PQ H3A 3L6 – 514/842-6487; Fax: 514/842-3305 – Public Relations Manager, Guy Sarrazin

Canarc Resource Corp., #800, 850 West Hastings St., Vancouver BC V6C 1E1 – 604/685-9700; Fax: 604/685-9744 – President & CEO, Bradford Cooke

Cape Breton Development Corp., PO Box 2500, Sydney NS B1P 6K9 – 902/842-2600, 564-2848; Fax: 902/842-2589 – Vice-President, Finance, Merrill Buchanan

Caribgold Resources Inc., #1000, 36 Toronto St., Toronto ON M5C 2C5 – 416/350-2338; Fax: 416/350-3510 – Chairman, Paul Zyla

Cathedral Gold Corporation, #420, 355 Burrard St., Vancouver BC V6C 2G8 – 604/684-4659; Fax: 604/687-4030 – Chairman, N. Murray Edwards

Central Asia Goldfields Corp., #901, 1 Richmond St. West, Toronto ON M5H 3W4 – 416/867-2936; Fax: 416/867-9767 – President, John Hansuld

Chase Resource Corp., #820, 800 West Pender St., Vancouver BC V6C 2V6 – 604/685-6851; Fax: 604/685-6493 – President/CEO, Ian T. Rozier

Cheni Resources Inc., #200, 580 Hornby St., Vancouver BC V6C 3B6 – 604/688-2321; Fax: 604/684-0642 – President/CEO, Robert McMorran

Co-Steel Inc., Scotia Plaza, 40 King St. West, PO Box 130, Toronto ON M5H 3Y2 – 416/366-4500; Fax: 416/366-4616 – Chair/CEO, W.J. Shields

Cominco Ltd., #500, 200 Burrard St., Vancouver BC V6C 3L7 – 604/682-0611; Fax: 604/685-3019 – President/CEO, David A. Thompson

Consolidated Rambler Mines Ltd., 300 Union St., PO Box 937, Saint John NB E2L 4E3 – 506/632-7171; Fax: 506/632-5113 – President, W.D. Jamieson

Cornucopia Resources Ltd., Marine Bldg., #540, 355 Burrard St., Vancouver BC V6C 2G8 – 604/687-0619; Fax: 604/681-4170 – President/CEO, Andrew Milligan

CSA Management Inc., #2700, 145 King Street West, Toronto ON M5H 1J8 – 416/865-0326; Fax: 416/865-9636 – Chair, President & CEO, Robert R. McEwen

Dayton Mining Corp., #1610, 200 Burrard St., Vancouver BC V6C 3L6 – 604/662-8383; Fax: 604/684-1329 – Chair, President & CEO, Wayne D. McClay

Denison Mines Ltd., Atrium on Bay, #320, 40 Dundas St. West, Toronto ON M5G 2C2 – 416/979-1991; Fax: 416/979-5893 – President/CEO, William James

Dia Met Minerals Ltd., 1695 Powick Rd., Kelowna BC V1X 4L1 – 250/861-8660; Fax: 250/861-3649 – President, James E. Eccott

Diamond Fields Resources Inc., 200 Burrard St., 9th Fl., Vancouver BC V6C 3L6 – 604/682-2113; Fax: 604/682-2060 – President, Cliff Carson

Eden Roc Mineral Corp., #1703, 141 Adelaide St. West, Toronto ON M5H 3L5 – 416/364-9992; Fax: 416/365-0023 – Chair, Peter Crossgrove

Equity Silver Mines Ltd., PO Box 49305, Stn Bentall, Vancouver BC V7X 1L3 – 604/661-1991; Fax: 604/845-2137 – President/CEO, D.J. Fraser

Espalau Mining Corp., 1452, de la Québecoise, CP 477, Val-D'Or PQ J9P 4P5 – 819/825-1111; Fax: 819/825-9506 – President, CEO & Secretary, Normand Cliche

Euro-Nevada Mining Corp. Ltd., #1900, 20 Eglinton Ave. West, PO Box 2005, Toronto ON M4R 1K8 – 416/480-6480; Fax: 416/488-6598 – President/CEO, Pierre Lassonde

Falconbridge Ltd., #1200, 95 Wellington St. West, Toronto ON M5J 2V4 – 416/956-5700; Fax: 416/956-5757 – President & CEO, F. Pickard

First Maritime Mining Corp. Ltd., 300 Union St., PO Box 937, Saint John NB E2L 4E3 – 506/632-7171; Fax: 506/632-5113 – President, W.D. Jamieson

Fording Coal Ltd., 10th Floor, 205 - 9 Ave. SE, Calgary AB T2G 0R4 – 403/264-1063; Fax: 403/265-8794 – President/CEO, J.G. Gardiner

Franco-Nevada Mining Corp. Ltd., #1900, 20 Eglinton Ave. West, PO Box 2005, Toronto ON M4R 1K8 – 416/480-6480; Fax: 416/488-6598 – President/COO, Pierre Lassonde

Freewest Resources Canada Inc., #1525, 800 boul Rene-Levesque ouest, Montréal PQ H3B 1X9 – 514/878-3551; Fax: 514/878-4427 – President, Mackenzie I. Watson

Gerdau Courtice Steel Inc., 160 Orion Pl., PO Box 1734, Cambridge ON N1R 7G8 – 519/740-2488; Fax: 519/623-2062 – President/CEO, Paul Kelly

Gibraltar Mines Ltd., 266 Oliver St., Williams Lake BC V2G 1M1 – 250/398-6211; Fax: 250/398-8671 – President/CEO, William H. Myckatyn

Glamis Gold Ltd., Four Bentall Centre, #3324, 1055 Dunsmuir St., PO Box 49287, Vancouver BC V7X 1L3 – 604/681-3541; Fax: 604/681-9306 – President/CEO, A. Dan Rovig

Global Stone Corp., #306, 251 North Service Rd. West, Oakville ON L6M 3E7 – 905/815-1050; Fax: 905/815-1056 – President/CEO, David Singleton

Goldcorp Inc., #2700, 145 King St. West, Toronto ON M5H 1J8 – 416/865-0326; Fax: 416/865-9636 – Chair, President & CEO, Robert McEwen

Golden Knight Resources Inc., #1180, 999 West Hastings St., Vancouver BC V6C 2W2 – 604/689-3846; Fax: 604/689-3847 – President/CEO, Robert A. Quartermain

Golden Rule Resources Ltd., #1450, 125 - 9 Ave. SE, Calgary AB T2G 0P6 – 403/233-7898; Fax: 403/266-2606 – President, Glen Harper

Golden West Refining Canada Ltd., 7333 River Rd., Delta BC V4G 1B1 – 604/946-4554; Fax: 604/946-4523 – President, John Downie

Granduc Mining Corp., #2000, 95 Wellington St. West, Toronto ON M5J 2N7 – 416/363-7370; Fax: 416/362-0069 – President/CEO, Graham Clow

Greenstone Resources Ltd., #910, 26 Wellington St. East, Toronto ON M5E 1S2 – 416/862-7300; Fax: 416/862-7604 – President/CEO, Rudi Fronk

Hemlo Gold Mines Inc., #2902, 1 Adelaide St. East, Toronto ON M5C 2Z9 – 416/982-7116; Fax: 416/982-7388 – President/CEO, Ian Bayer

High River Gold Mines Ltd., #1700, 155 University Ave., Toronto ON M5H 3B7 – 416/947-1440; Fax: 416/360-0010 – President/CEO, David Mosher

Highland Valley Copper, PO Box 1500, Logan Lake BC V0K 1W0 – 250/575-2443; Fax: 250/575-3242 – President, Dave Johnston

Highwood Resources Ltd., #705, 324 - 8 Ave. SW., Calgary AB T2P 2Z2 – 403/261-3999; Fax: 403/264-2959 – President, John Smrke

Hillsborough Resources Limited, #750, 890 West Pender St., Vancouver BC V6C 1J9 – 905/684-9288; Fax: 905/684-3178 – President/CEO, George Vooro

Homestake Canada Inc., #1000, 700 West Pender St., Vancouver BC V6C 1G8 – 604/684-2345; Fax: 604/684-9831 – President & CEO, Ronald D. Parker

Hudson Bay Mining & Smelting, #1906, 201 Portage Ave., Winnipeg MB R3B 3K6 – 204/949-4261; Fax: 204/942-8177 – President/CEO, Peter C. Jones

Canadian Almanac & Directory 1997

7-48 MAJOR CANADIAN COMPANIES

Ideal Metal Inc., 3399, av Francis-Hughes, Laval PQ H7L 5A5 – 514/385-0111; Fax: 514/385-2330 – President, Henry Hildebrand

Imperial Metals Corp., #420, 355 Burrard St., Vancouver BC V6C 2G8 – 604/669-8959 – President, Pierre Lebel

Inco Ltd., #1500, 145 King St. West, Toronto ON M5H 4B7 – 416/361-7511; Fax: 416/361-7864 – President, Scott M. Hand

Inmet Mining Corp., Aetna Tower, #3400, 79 Wellington St. West, PO Box 19, Toronto ON M5K 1A1 – 416/361-6400; Fax: 416/361-3564 – President & CEO, Dr. Klaus M Zeitler

International Gold Resources Corp., 172 King St. East, 3rd Fl., Toronto ON M5A 1J3 – 416/947-9208; Fax: 416/947-1023 – President/CEO, Dan Idzal

International Mahogany Corp., 1305 - 1090 West Georgia St., Vancouver BC V6E 3V7 – 604/685-9316; Fax: 604/683-1585 – President, Nick Demare

International Minerals & Chemicals (Canada) Global Ltd., General Delivery, Esterhazy SK S0A 0X0 – 306/745-4200; Fax: 306/745-2100 – President, Eric Beaumont

Jascan Resources Inc., #2000, 95 Wellington St. West, Toronto ON M5J 2N7 – 416/362-6721; Fax: 416/362-0069 – President, John Lamacraft

Kalium Canada Ltd., PO Box 7500, Regina SK S4P 4L8 – 306/345-8400; Fax: 306/345-8200 – President, John Huber

Kap Resources Ltd., #407, 325 Howe St., Vancouver BC V6C 1Z7 – 604/669-7995; Fax: 604/684-3499 – President/CEO, Paul Deutz Jr.

Kerr Addison Mines Ltd., #2700, 1 Adelaide St. East, Toronto ON M5C 2Z6 – 416/982-7270; Fax: 416/982-7498 – President/CEO, Jeffrey Snow

Kinross Gold Corp., Scotia Plaza, 40 King St. West, 57th Fl., Toronto ON M5H 3Y2 – 416/365-5123; Fax: 416/363-6622 – President, Robert Buchan

KWG Resources Inc., #3200, 630, boul René-Lévesque ouest, Montréal PQ H3B 1S6 – 514/866-6001; Fax: 514/866-6193 – President, Norman Brewster

Laminco Resources Inc., #2380, 1055 West Hastings St., Vancouver BC V6E 2E9 – 604/684-6508; Fax: 604/682-6508 – President/COO, Edwin Morrow

Loki Gold Corp., #800, 900 West Hastings St., Vancouver BC V6C 1E5 – 604/684-8123; Fax: 604/684-5921 – President & CEO, Paul Saxton

Lytton Minerals Ltd., #501, 700 West Pender St., Vancouver BC V6C 1G8 – 604/689-7401; Fax: 604/689-7406 – President & CEO, Desmond C.B. Alexander

Manalta Coal Ltd., 700 - 9 Ave. SW, PO Box 2880, Calgary AB T2P 2M7 – 403/231-7173; Fax: 403/269-8075 – President & CEO, G.D. Chapel

Marshall Minerals Corp., 4776 Bridge St., PO Box 356, Niagara Falls ON L2E 6T8 – 905/356-9112; Fax: 905/356-0098 – Chairman, CEO & Secretary, Harry G. Quint

Mazarin Mining Corporation Inc., 116, rue St-Pierre, Québec PQ G1K 4A7 – 418/694-1123; Fax: 418/694-0331 – President/CEO, Jacques Bonneau

Mentor Exploration & Development Co. Ltd., #2302, 401 Bay St., PO Box 102, Toronto ON M5H 2Y4 – 416/947-1212; Fax: 416/367-4681 – President, Paul Penna

Minera Rayrock Inc., #500, 30 Soudan Ave., Toronto ON M4S 1V6 – 416/489-0022; Fax: 416/489-0096 – Chairman & CEO, D.R. Crombie

Minorco Canada Ltd., #720, 70 York St., Toronto ON M5J 1S9 – 416/601-9550; Fax: 416/362-3542 – Chairman & President, John Ellis

Miramar Mining Corp., 311 West First St., Vancouver BC V7M 1B5 – 604/985-2572; Fax: 604/980-0731 – President & CEO, Walter H. Berukoff

MSV Resources Inc., #3240, 630, boul René-Lévesque ouest, Montréal PQ H3B 1S6 – 514/875-9033; Fax: 514/875-9764 – President, Andre Fortier

Muscocho Explorations Ltd., 365 Bay St., 11th Fl., Toronto ON M5H 2V1 – 416/363-1124; Fax: 416/360-0728 – President, J.T. Flanagan

Nanisivik Mines Ltd., 20 Toronto St., 12th Fl., Toronto ON M5C 2B8 – 416/869-0772; Fax: 416/367-3638 – President, G. Farquharson

New Indigo Resources Inc., #501, 700 West Pender St., Vancouver BC V6C 1G8 – 604/682-0536; Fax: 604/689-7406 – Chairman & President, D.H.W. Dobson

Newhawk Gold Mines Ltd., #860, 625 Howe St., Vancouver BC V6C 2T6 – 604/687-7545; Fax: 604/689-5041 – President & CEO, Donald A. McLeod

Noble Peak Resources Ltd., #906, 50 Burnhamthorpe Rd. West, Mississauga ON L5B 3C2 – 905/897-9406; Fax: 905/897-0669 – President & CEO, Maureen Jensen

Noranda Metallurgy Inc., #2700, 1 Adelaide St. East, Toronto ON M5C 2Z6 – 416/982-7111; Fax: 416/982-7498 – President, David Goldman

Noranda Mining & Exploration Inc., #2700, 1 Adelaide St. East, Toronto ON M5C 2Z6 – 416/982-7111; Fax: 416/982-7278 – President, Michael J. Knuckey

North American Metals Corp., #1500, 700 West Pender St., Vancouver BC V6C 1G8 – 604/684-9648; Fax: 604/236-7111 – President/CEO, John Kalmet

Northgate Exploration Ltd., #2630, 1 First Canadian Place, PO Box 143, Toronto ON M5X 1C7 – 416/362-6683; Fax: 416/367-3250 – President & CEO, Terry A. Lyons

Novicourt Inc., #2700, 1 Adelaide St. East, Toronto ON M5C 2Z6 – 416/982-7111; Fax: 416/982-7278 – Vice-President, Business Development, Lance Digert

Orvana Minerals Corp., #710, 1177 West Hastings St., Vancouver BC V6E 2K3 – 604/682-4929; Fax: 604/682-3888 – Chairman & CEO, D. Neil Hillhouse

Pacific Sentinel Gold Corp., #1020, 800 West Pender St., Vancouver BC V6C 2V6 – 604/684-6365; Fax: 604/684-8092 – President, Robert Dickinson

Pan American Silver Corp., #1500, 625 Howe St., Vancouver BC V6C 2T6 – 604/684-1175 – Chairman, Ross J. Beaty

Pangea Goldfields Inc., #709, 1 Toronto St., Toronto ON M5C 2V6 – 416/350-3781; Fax: 416/350-3782 – President/CEO, Jean-Charles Potvin

Pioneer Metals Corp., #1220, 609 Granville St., Vancouver BC V7Y 1G5 – 604/669-3383; Fax: 604/669-1240 – Chairman, President & CEO, Stephen H. Sorensen

Placer Dome Inc., #1600, 1055 Dunsmuir St., PO Box 49305, Vancouver BC V7X 1P1 – 604/682-7082; Fax: 604/661-3792 – President/CEO, D.J. Fraser

Premier CDN Enterprises Ltd., 1785, 55e av, Dorval PQ H9P 2W3 – 514/631-6700; Fax: 514/631-2333 – President & CEO, Bernard Belanger

Prime Resources Group Inc., #1000, 700 West Pender, Vancouver BC V6C 1G8 – 604/684-2345; Fax: 604/684-9831 – President & CEO, Ronald Parker

Princeton Mining Corp., #2000, 1055 West Hastings St., Vancouver BC V6E 3V3 – 604/688-2511; Fax: 604/688-4772 – President, J.C. O'Rourke

QSR Ltd., 166 Pearl St., Toronto ON M5H 1L3 – 416/597-0969; Fax: 416/597-1776 – President, G. Warren Armstrong

Queenstake Resources Ltd., 900 West Hastings St., 10th Fl., Vancouver BC V6C 1E5 – 604/684-1218 – President/CEO, James Mancuso

Quest International Resources Corp., #1440, 625 Howe St., Vancouver BC V6C 2T6 – 604/682-6477; Fax: 604/683-5912 – President, Karl Rollke

Rayrock Yellowknife Resources, #500, 30 Soudan Ave., Toronto ON M4S 1V6 – 416/489-0022; Fax: 416/489-0096 – Chairman & CEO, D.R. Crombie

Rea Gold Corp., Oceanic Plaza, #1600, 1066 West Hastings St., Vancouver BC V6E 3X1 – 604/684-7527; Fax: 604/684-4428 – President & CEO, W. James Hogan

Redaurum Ltd., #600, 15 Toronto St., Toronto ON M5C 2E3 – 416/368-3553; Fax: 416/368-8957 – President, Anthony Hamilton

Redfern Resources Inc., #205, 10711 Cambie Rd., Richmond BC V6X 3G5 – 604/278-3028; Fax: 604/278-8837 – Chairman & CEO, John A. Greig

Redstone Resources Inc., #1900, 20 Eglinton Ave. West, Toronto ON M4R 1K8 – 416/480-6497; Fax: 416/488-6598 – President/CEO, David Harguail

Regional Resources Ltd., 20 Toronto St., 12th Fl., Toronto ON M5C 2B8 – 416/869-0772; Fax: 416/367-3638 – President, G. Farquharson

Repadre Capital Corp., Scotia Plaza, 40 King St. West, 57th Fl., Toronto ON M5H 3Y2 – 416/363-2410; Fax: 416/365-8065 – President/CEO, Joe Conway

Republic Goldfields Inc., #2402, 1 Dundas St. West, PO Box 13, Toronto ON M5G 1Z3 – 416/977-4653; Fax: 416/977-8335 – President, Donald Empey

RFC Resource Finance Corp., 79 Wellington St. West, Toronto ON M5K 1A1 – 416/361-6400; Fax: 416/361-3564 – President, John H. Purkis

Rhonda Mining Corp., #810, 540 - 5 Ave. SW, Calgary AB T2P 0M2 – 403/269-5369; Fax: 403/261-2866 – President, Chairman & CEO, John M. Alston

Richmont Mines Inc., 110, av Principale, Rouyn-Noranda PQ J9X 4P2 – 819/797-2465; Fax: 819/797-0166 – President/CEO, Jean-Guy Rivard

Rio Algom Ltd., 120 Adelaide St. West, 26th Fl., Toronto ON M5H 1W5 – 416/367-4000; Fax: 416/365-6810 – President/CEO, Lawrie Reinertson

Royal Canadian Mint, 320 Sussex Dr., Ottawa ON K1A 0G8 – 613/993-3500; Fax: 613/991-1741 – President, Danielle Wetherup

Slater Industries Inc., Yonge Corporate Centre, #410, 4100 Yonge St., Toronto ON M2P 2B5 – 416/733-4400; Fax: 416/733-4429 – President/CEO, B. Swirsky

Société Québécoise d'Exploration Minière, Tour Belle Cour, #2500, 2600, boul Laurier, Ste-Foy PQ G1V 4M6 – 418/658-5400; Fax: 418/658-5459 – President/CEO, Yves Harvey

Sonora Gold Corp., #1560, 141 Adelaide St. West, Toronto ON M5H 3L5 – 416/362-2090; Fax: 416/362-2295 – President/CEO, Patrick Downey

Southwestern Gold Corp., #1650, 701 West Georgia St., PO Box 10102, Vancouver BC V7Y 1C6 – 604/669-2525; Fax: 604/688-5175 – President, John Paterson

St. Andrew Goldfields Ltd., 166 Pearl St., Toronto ON M5H 1L3 – 416/597-0969; Fax: 416/597-1776 – President, Charles Gryba

St. Genevieve Resources Ltd., #3200, 630, boul René-Lévesque ouest, Montréal PQ H3B 1S6 – 514/866-6001; Fax: 514/866-6193 – President, Pierre Gauthier

Stelco Inc., Stelco Tower, 100 King St. West, PO Box 2030, Hamilton ON L8N 3T1 – 905/528-2511; Fax: 905/577-4441 – Chair/CEO, F.H. Telmer

Sydney Steel Corp., Inglis St., PO Box 1450, Sydney NS B1P 6K5 – 902/564-7900; Fax: 902/564-7905 – President, Brad Bowman

Teck Corp., #600, 200 Burrard St., Vancouver BC V6C 3L9 – 604/687-1117; Fax: 604/687-6100 – President/CEO, N.B. Keevil

Thunderwood Resources Inc., #2501, 1 Adelaide St. East, Toronto ON M5C 2V9 – 416/362-8730; Fax: 416/367-0427 – President/CEO, John Heslop

Tiomin Resources Inc., #709, 1 Toronto St., PO Box 22, Toronto ON M5C 2V6 – 416/350-3779; Fax: 416/350-3570 – President/CEO, Jean-Charles Potvin

Tombstone Explorations Co. Ltd., #1351, 409 Granville St., Vancouver BC V6C 1T2 – 604/682-1545; Fax: 604/682-1514 – President, Mario Szotlender

Trillion Resources Ltd., #800, 900 West Hastings St., Vancouver BC V6C 1E5 – 604/684-2822; Fax: 604/684-9877 – President, Jens E. Hansen

Canadian Almanac & Directory 1997

Triton Mining Corp., #1620, 1140 West Pender St., Vancouver BC V6E 4G1 – 604/689-9554; Fax: 604/688-3639 – President/CEO, Amaldo Ismay

TVX Gold Inc., #4300, 161 Bay St., Toronto ON M5J 2S1 – 416/366-8160; Fax: 416/366-8163 – Chairman/CEO, Eike Batista

United Keno Hill Mines Ltd., #1702, 150 York St., Toronto ON M5H 3S5 – 416/955-9085; Fax: 416/955-9459 – Chairman/CEO, Stephen Powell

Vengold Inc., #1788, 200 Burrard St., Vancouver BC V6C 3L6 – 604/664-7050; Fax: 604/681-9151 – President/CEO, Ian Telfer

Viceroy Resource Corp., #880, 999 West Hastings St., Vancouver BC V6C 2W2 – 604/688-9780; Fax: 604/682-3941 – President/CEO, D. Ross Fitzpatrick

Western Québec Mines Inc., 137 Church St., Toronto ON M5B 1Y5 – 416/; Fax: 416/368-0141 – Chair, Murray H. Pollitt

Westfield Minerals Ltd., #1632, 1055 West Georgia St., PO Box 11179, Stn Royal Centre, Vancouver BC V6E 3R5 – 604/669-3141; Fax: 604/687-3419 – President/CEO, Terry Lyons

Westmin Resources Ltd., The Bentall Centre, #904, 1055 Dunsmuir St., PO Box 49066, Vancouver BC V7X 1C4 – 604/681-2253; Fax: 604/681-0357 – President, Walter Segsworth

Wharf Resources Ltd., #2700, 145 King St. West, Toronto ON M5H 1J8 – 416/865-0326; Fax: 416/361-5741 – Chair, President & CEO, R.R. McEwen

Wheaton River Minerals Ltd., #515, 330 Bay St., Toronto ON M5H 2S8 – 416/860-0919; Fax: 416/367-0182 – Chair & CEO, Ian McDonald

WMC International Ltd., #3000, 181 Bay St., PO Box 815, Toronto ON M5J 2T3 – 416/869-3578; Fax: 416/869-3359 – Executive Vice-President, J.S. Parr

OIL & GAS

Akita Drilling Ltd., #1110, 505 - 3 St. SW, Calgary AB T2P 3E6 – 403/292-7979; Fax: 403/292-7990 – Chairman, Ronald D. Southern

Alberta Energy Co. Ltd., #3900, 421 - 7 Ave. SW, Calgary AB T2P 4K9 – 403/266-8111; Fax: 403/266-8154 – President & CEO, Gwyn Morgan

Alberta Natural Gas Co. Ltd., #2900, 240 - 4 Ave. SW, Calgary AB T2P 4L7 – 403/691-7777; Fax: 403/691-7893 – President & CEO, Wayne E. Lunt

Alberta Oil & Gas Ltd., #1200, 700 - 4 Ave. SW, Calgary AB T2P 3J4 – 403/269-3779; Fax: 403/266-6100 – President/CEO, Josef Hodel

Alpine Oil Services Corp., #1100, 202 - 6 Ave. SW, Calgary AB T2P 2R9 – 403/263-7800; Fax: 403/264-7260 – President & CEO, Rodney J. Hauser

Amoco Canada Petroleum Co. Ltd., 240 - 4 Ave. SW, PO Box 200, Stn M, Calgary AB T2P 2H8 – 403/233-1313; Fax: 403/233-5610 – Chairman & President, Dave Newman

Anderson Exploration Ltd., #1600, 324 - 8 Ave. SW, Calgary AB T2P 2Z5 – 403/232-7100; Fax: 403/232-7678 – President/COO, Larry Macdonald

Arakis Energy Corp., #320, 540 - 5 Ave. SW, Calgary AB T2P 0M2 – 403/263-2471; Fax: 403/263-8069 – President & CEO, John McLeod

Archer Resources Ltd., #2600, 400 - 3 Ave. SW, Calgary AB T2P 4H2 – 403/266-5522; Fax: 403/232-6008 – President & CEO, Grant A. Bartlett

Artisan Drilling, 1426 Meridian Rd. East, Calgary AB T2A 2N9 – 403/235-4000; Fax: 403/272-2923 – President/CEO, Howard Dixon

Ascentex Energy Inc., Canada Place, #3520, 150 - 6 Ave. SW, Calgary AB T2P 3Y7 – 403/265-3320; Fax: 403/262-5184 – President & CEO, Ed A. Beaman

Aztec Resources Ltd., #1000, 400 - 5 Ave. SW, Calgary AB T2P 0L6 – 403/234-8882; Fax: 403/262-8827 – CEO/President, Gregory S. Fletcher

Ballistic Energy Corporation, Bow Valley Square II, #600, 205 - 5 Ave. SW, Calgary AB T2P 2V7 – 403/290-0777; Fax: 403/290-0707 – President/CEO, John Gunn

Barrington Petroleum Ltd., Western Gas Tower, #1100, 530 - 8 Ave. SW, Calgary AB T2P 3S8 – 403/263-9464; Fax: 403/266-5794 – President & CEO, David J. Evans

BC Gas Inc., 1111 West Georgia St., Vancouver BC V6E 4M4 – 604/443-6500; Fax: 604/443-6900 – President & CEO, Steve Bellringer

Bearcat Explorations Ltd., #1700, 520 - 5 Ave. SW, Calgary AB T2P 3R7 – 403/265-6161; Fax: 403/265-0893 – President, John W. McLeod

Beau Canada Explorations Ltd., West Tower Petro Canada Centre, 150 - 6 Ave. SW, 47th Fl., Calgary AB T2P 3Y7 – 403/750-3400; Fax: 403/233-2565 – President & CEO, Thomas Bugg

Benson Petroleum Ltd., #950, 633 - 6 Ave. SW, Calgary AB T2P 2Y5 – 403/269-5158; Fax: 403/233-8304 – President/CEO, Yook Mah

Berkley Petroleum Corp., #1250, 202 - 6 Ave. SW, Calgary AB T2P 2R9 – 403/571-3600; Fax: 403/269-6510 – President/CEO, Mike Rose

Blue Range Resource Corp., #1100, 801 - 6th Ave. SW, Calgary AB T2P 3W2 – 403/264-7422; Fax: 403/262-7803 – President/CEO, Gordon Ironside

Cabre Exploration Ltd., #1400, 700 - 9 Ave. SW, Calgary AB T2P 3V4 – 403/231-8800; Fax: 403/236-4852 – Chairman/CEO, H.B. Wheeler

Camberly Energy Ltd., #700, 635 - 8 Ave. SW, Calgary AB T2P 3M3 – 403/265-5997; Fax: 403/262-6607 – President & CEO, Michael K. Duggan

Canada Southern Petroleum Ltd., One Palliser Sq., #1410, 125 - 9 Ave. SE, Calgary AB T2G 0P6 – 403/269-7741; Fax: 403/261-5667 – President, Charles J. Horne

Canadian 88 Energy Corp., Canterra Tower, #700, 400 - 3 Ave. SW, Calgary AB T2P 4H2 – 403/974-8800; Fax: 403/974-8811 – President/CEO, Greg Noval

Canadian Conquest Exploration Inc., #1100, 736 - 8 Ave. SW, Calgary AB T2P 1H4 – 403/260-6300; Fax: 403/264-2825 – President & CEO, Michael Cooke

Canadian Crude Separators Inc., #1750, 521 - 3 Ave. SW, Calgary AB T2P 3T3 – 403/233-7565; Fax: 403/261-5612 – President & CEO, David P. Werklund

Canadian Forest Oil Ltd., #600, 800 - 6 Ave. SW, Calgary AB T2P 3G3 – 403/292-8000; Fax: 403/261-7665 – President/CEO, Art Eastly

Canadian Fracmaster Ltd., #1700, 355 - 4 Ave. SW, Calgary AB T2P 0J1 – 403/262-2222; Fax: 403/266-0506 – President & CEO, Les Margetek

Canadian Hunter Exploration Ltd., #2800, 605 - 5th Ave. SW, Calgary AB T2P 3H5 – 403/260-1000; Fax: 403/260-1180 – CEO/Chairman, J.K. Gray

Canadian Jorex Ltd., Bow Valley Sq. IV, #2870, 250 - 6 Ave. SW, Calgary AB T2P 3H7 – 403/266-0930; Fax: 403/265-9033 – President & CEO, Louis J. Schneider

Canadian Natural Resources Ltd., Esso Plaza, #2000, 425 First St. SW, Calgary AB T2P 3L8 – 403/221-2100; Fax: 403/233-2182 – President/CEO, John Langille

Canadian Northstar Corp., #750, 1111 Melville St., Vancouver BC V6E 3V6 – 604/669-7624; Fax: 604/669-7693 – Chairman & President, Ian Cockwell

Canadian Occidental Petroleum, #1500, 635 - 8 Ave. SW, Calgary AB T2P 3Z1 – 403/234-6700; Fax: 403/263-8673 – President/CEO, David Hentschel

Canadian Ultramar Ltd., 2200, av McGill College, Montréal PQ H3A 3L3 – 514/499-6111; Fax: 514/499-6320 – Chairman/CEO, Jean Gaulin

Canpet Energy Group Inc., #2200, 350 - 7 Ave. SW, Calgary AB T2P 3N9 – 403/298-2100; Fax: 403/233-0399 – President/CEO, Dave Dackett

Canwest Gas Supply Inc., 1285 West Pender St., 7th Fl., Vancouver BC V6E 4B1 – 604/661-3300; Fax: 604/661-3347 – President/CEO, Hugh Gillard

Capilano International Inc., 6204 - 6A St. SE, Calgary AB T2H 2B7 – 403/258-0066; Fax: 403/258-0424 – President, M.V. Little

Carmanah Resources Ltd., #1905, 421 - 7 Ave. SW, Calgary AB T2P 4K9 – 403/266-4975; Fax: 403/266-5042 – Chairman/CEO, Richard A. Gusella

Chauvco Resources Ltd., #2900, 255 - 5 Ave. SW, Calgary AB T2P 3G6 – 403/231-3100; Fax: 403/269-9497 – President/COO, Glen Russell

Chevron Canada Ltd., #1500, 1050 West Pender St., Vancouver BC V6E 3T4 – 604/668-5300; Fax: 604/257-4030 – President/CEO, John Watson

Chevron Canada Resources Ltd., 500 - 5 Ave. SW, Calgary AB T2P 0L7 – 403/234-5000; Fax: 403/234-6206 – President, Donald Paul

Chieftain International Inc., #1201, Toronto Dominion Tower, Edmonton Centre, Edmonton AB T5J 2Z1 – 403/425-1950; Fax: 403/429-4681 – President/CEO, S.A. Milner

Cimarron Petroleum Ltd., #800, 400 - 3 Ave. SW, Calgary AB T2P 4H2 – 403/265-8900; Fax: 403/266-2780 – President/CEO, R.W. Pawliw

Cogema Resources Inc., PO Box 9204, Saskatoon SK S7K 3X5 – 306/244-2554; Fax: 306/653-1126 – Acting President, Alain Marvy

Computalog Ltd., #2000, 530 - 8 Ave. SW, Calgary AB T2P 3S8 – 403/265-6060; Fax: 403/237-8493 – President/CEO, Doug Robinson

Comstate Resources Ltd., #901, 1015 - 4 St. SW, Calgary AB T2R 1J4 – 403/237-8868; Fax: 403/265-7488 – President, G.F. Fink

Consolidated Eurocan Ventures Ltd., #1320, 885 West Georgia St., Vancouver BC V6C 3E8 – 604/689-7842; Fax: 604/689-4250 – Chair/President, Lukas H. Lundin

Consumers Co-operative Refineries Ltd., PO Box 1050, Saskatoon SK S7K 3M9 – 306/244-3311; Fax: 306/244-3403 – President, Ed Klassen

Crestar Energy Inc., #3100, 333 - 7 Ave. SW, Calgary AB T2P 4M8 – 403/231-6700; Fax: 403/231-3801 – President/CEO, S. Barry Jackson

CS Resources Ltd., #2900, 645 - 7 Ave. SW, Calgary AB T2P 4G8 – 403/260-6100; Fax: 403/260-6191 – President, D.A. Sharp

Cube Energy Corp., #800, 926 - 5 Ave. SW, Calgary AB T2P 0N7 – 403/264-4405; Fax: 403/269-3020 – President/CEO, Steven P. Dobrowolski

D.A. Stuart Inc., 43 Upton Rd., Scarborough ON M1L 2C1 – 416/757-3226; Fax: 416/757-3220 – President, Charles Santangelo

Denbury Resources Inc., #2550, 140 - 4 Ave. SW, Calgary AB T2P 3N3 – 403/266-1101; Fax: 403/263-6746 – President/CEO, Gareth Roberts

Discovery West Corp., #500, 30 Soudan Ave., Toronto ON M4S 1V6 – 416/489-0022; Fax: 416/489-0096 – President/COO, O. Michael Isaac

Dominion Explorers Inc., Bow Valley Square III, #1250, 255 - 5 Ave. SW, Calgary AB T2P 3G6 – 403/571-1100; Fax: 403/571-1101 – President/CEO, John A. Pope

Dorset Exploration Ltd., #3600, 205 - 5 Ave. SW, Calgary AB T2P 2V7 – 403/267-0700; Fax: 403/267-0777 – President/CEO, E.L. Molnar

Dreco Energy Services Ltd., Weber Centre, #1340, 5555 Calgary Trail South, Edmonton AB T6H 5P9 – 403/944-3900; Fax: 403/438-8256 – President/CEO, Robert L. Phillips

ELAN Energy Inc., #4100, 150 - 6 Ave. SW, Calgary AB T2P 3Y7 – 403/266-8500; Fax: 403/262-7337 – President/CEO, Verne G. Johnson

Encal Energy Ltd., PO Box 2310, Stn M, Calgary AB T2P 3M6 – 403/750-3300; Fax: 403/266-1072 – President, David D. Johnson

EnerMark Inc., #1300, 800 - 5 Ave. SW, Calgary AB T2P 4A4 – 403/299-2222; Fax: 403/269-2297 – President/CEO, Marcel Tremblay

MAJOR CANADIAN COMPANIES

Enertec Resource Services Inc., 3024 - 49 Ave. SE, Calgary AB T2B 2X4 – 403/569-9222; Fax: 403/569-0829 – President/CEO, Murray Olson

EnServ Corp., #1505, 505 - 3 St. SW, Calgary AB T2P 3E6 – 403/237-7660; Fax: 403/266-0885 – President/CEO, R.T. Swinton

Ensign Resource Service Group Inc., #900, 400 - 5 Ave. SW, Calgary AB T2P 0L6 – 403/262-1361; Fax: 403/266-3596 – President, Selby Porter

Foothills Pipe Lines Ltd., #3100, 707 - 8 Ave. SW, Calgary AB T2P 3W8 – 403/294-4111; Fax: 403/294-4171 – CEO/Chair, R.L. Pierce

Fortune Energy Inc., #1000, 833 - 4 Ave. SW, Calgary AB T2P 3T5 – 403/297-0230; Fax: 403/265-5268 – President/CEO, Rene Rosales

Fossil Oil & Gas Ltd., #530, 635 - 8 Ave. SW, Calgary AB T2P 3M3 – 403/290-0288; Fax: 403/262-5632 – President/CEO, Kenneth R. King

Gardiner Oil & Gas Ltd., #1600, 333 - 7 Ave. SW, Calgary AB T2P 2Z1 – 403/781-2200; Fax: 403/781-2222 – President/CEO, Wayne Thomson

Glenex Industries Inc., 185 Davenport Rd., Toronto ON M5R 1J1 – 416/962-9292 – President/CEO, Norman Glick

Grad & Walker Energy Corp., #2800, 400 - 4 Ave. SW, Calgary AB T2P 4K7 – 403/262-5622; Fax: 403/263-6920 – Chair, President & CEO, Stan Grad

Gulf Canada Resources Ltd., 401 - 9 Ave. SW, PO Box 130, Calgary AB T2P 2H7 – 403/233-4000; Fax: 403/233-5143 – President/CEO, J.P. Bryan

Gulfstream Resources Canada Ltd., #3465, 855 - 2 St. SW, Calgary AB T2P 4J8 – 403/264-8288; Fax: 403/264-8265 – Chair, J. Angus McKee

Harbour Petroleum Co. Ltd., #2700, 605 - 5 Ave. SW, Calgary AB T2P 3H5 – 403/265-5522; Fax: 403/231-1299 – Chair, Ronald A. Howard

HCO Energy Ltd., #2700, 400 - 3 Ave. SW, Calgary AB T2P 4H2 – 403/231-8400; Fax: 403/266-2850 – President & CEO, Daryl H. Connolly

Highridge Exploration Ltd., #1500, 633 - 6 Ave. SW, Calgary AB T2P 2Y5 – 403/269-2229; Fax: 403/262-4323 – President/CEO, Ross D.S. Douglas

Humboldt Capital Corp., #2100, 144 - 4 Ave. SW, Calgary AB T2P 3N4 – 403/750-4440; Fax: 403/263-2341 – Chairman, R.W. Lamond

Husky Oil Ltd., 707 - 8 Ave. SW, Calgary AB T2P 1H5 – 403/298-6111; Fax: 403/298-7464 – President, James McFarland

Imperial Oil Ltd., 111 St. Clair Ave. West, Toronto ON M4V 1N5 – 416/968-4111; Fax: 416/968-8348 – Chairman, President & CEO, R.B. Peterson

Imperial Oil Resources Limited, 237 - 4 Ave. SW, Calgary AB T2P 0H6 – 403/237-3737; Fax: 403/237-2197 – Senior Vice-President, Doug Baldwin

Intensity Resources Ltd., #2500, 425 - 1 St. SW, Calgary AB T2P 3L8 – 403/263-3440; Fax: 403/262-8508 – President/CEO, R.L. Wickwire

International Colin Energy Corp., #1000, 333 - 11 Ave. SW, Calgary AB T2R 1L9 – 403/269-6822; Fax: 403/263-1410 – President, Lloyd Mann

International Panorama Resource Corp., #600, 555 West Georgia St., Vancouver BC V6B 1Z5 – 604/687-7294; Fax: 604/682-1329 – President/CEO, L. Kenneth MacLeod

International Petroleum Corp., #1320, 885 West Georgia St., Vancouver BC V6C 3E8 – 604/689-7842; Fax: 604/689-4250 – President, Ian H. Lundin

Inuvialuit Petroleum Corp., #1100, 300 - 5 Ave. SW, Calgary AB T2P 3C4 – 403/262-6955; Fax: 403/266-4833 – President, Allan Taylor

IPL Energy Inc., #2900, 421 - 7 Ave. SW, Calgary AB T2P 4K9 – 403/231-3900; Fax: 403/231-3920 – President & CEO, Brian F. MacNeil

Jordan Petroleum Ltd., Bow Valley Sq. III, #850, 255 - 5 Ave. SW, Calgary AB T2P 3G6 – 403/266-1024; Fax: 403/266-4325 – President, Harold V. Pedersen

Lateral Vector Resources Inc., #120, 1230 Blackfoot Dr., Regina SK S4S 7G4 – 306/569-1700; Fax: 306/757-1733 – Chair/CEO, Robert B. Knight

Lynx Energy Services Corp., #500, 622 - 5 Ave. SW, Calgary AB T2P 0M6 – 403/233-0888; Fax: 403/264-6934 – Chairman & CEO, J. Verne Lyons

Maxwell Energy Corp., #3100, 350 - 7 Ave. SW, Calgary AB T2P 3N9 – 403/232-2232; Fax: 403/265-8049 – Chairman, Ted Konji

Maxx Petroleum Ltd., #1000, 112 - 4 Ave. SW, Calgary AB T2P 0H3 – 403/261-6666; Fax: 403/266-8022 – President & CEO, Burl N. Aycock

Mobil Oil Canada Ltd., 330 - 5 Ave. SW, Calgary AB T2P 2J7 – 403/260-7910; Fax: 403/260-7259 – President, Jerry Anderson

Mohawk Canada Ltd., #325, 6400 Roberts St., Burnaby BC V5G 4G2 – 604/293-4114; Fax: 604/293-4181 – President/CEO, William Duncan

Morgan Hydrocarbons Inc., #2200, 205 - 5 Ave. SW, Calgary AB T2P 2V7 – 403/298-8300; Fax: 403/298-8390 – President/CEO, William Trickett

Morrison Middlefield Resources Ltd., 1 First Canadian Place, 58th Fl., PO Box 192, Toronto ON M5X 1A6 – 416/362-0714; Fax: 416/362-7925 – Chairman & CEO, A. Gordon Stollery

Morrison Petroleums Ltd., #3000, 400 - 3 Ave. SW, Calgary AB T2P 4H2 – 403/750-3000; Fax: 403/750-3200 – President/CEO, Walt Deboni

Murphy Oil Company Ltd., #2100, 555 - 4 Ave. SW, Calgary AB T2P 3E7 – 403/294-8000; Fax: 403/294-8851 – President & CEO, Carl Thompson

New Cache Petroleums Ltd., #400, 140 - 4 Ave. SW, Calgary AB T2P 3N3 – 403/263-3447 – President, Ray Smith

Newport Petroleum Corp., Bow Valley Sq. II, #3300, 205 - 5 Ave. SW, Calgary AB T2P 2V7 – 403/531-1530; Fax: 403/531-1539 – President & CEO, Uldis Upitis

Norcen Energy Resources Ltd., 715 - 5 Ave. SW, PO Box 2595, Stn M, Calgary AB T2P 4V4 – 403/231-0111; Fax: 403/231-0187 – President/CEO, Grant Billing

Northrock Resources Ltd., #3500, 700 - 2 St. SW, Calgary AB T2P 2W2 – 403/269-3100; Fax: 403/232-4650 – President & CEO, Donald Hansen

Northstar Energy Corp., #2300, 700 - 9 Ave. SW, Calgary AB T2P 3V4 – 403/298-0500; Fax: 403/298-0579 – CEO, John Hagg

NOVA Corporation of Alberta, #2800, 801 - 7 Ave. SW, Calgary AB T2P 3P7 – 403/290-6000; Fax: 403/290-7227 – Chair/CEO, J.E. Newall

Nova Scotia Resources Ltd., PO Box 2111, Stn M, Halifax NS B3J 3B7 – 902/420-8800; Fax: 902/425-2195 – President/CEO, Don Leet

Nowsco Well Service Ltd., #2750, 801 - 6 Ave. SW, Calgary AB T2P 4L8 – 403/531-5151; Fax: 403/262-8066 – President & COO, Ron Simard

Nugas Ltd., #2100, 421 - 7 Ave. SW, Calgary AB T2P 4K9 – 403/262-7034; Fax: 403/265-8180 – Chairman/CFO, Gus A. Van Wielingen

Numac Energy Inc., 321 - 6 Ave. SW, 7th Fl., Calgary AB T2P 3H3 – 403/260-9400; Fax: 403/260-9561 – President/CEO, S.D. McGregor

Ocelot Energy Inc., Petro-Canada Centre, West Tower, 150 - 6 Ave. SW, 30th Fl., Calgary AB T2P 3Y7 – 403/299-5700; Fax: 403/299-5750 – President/COO, Glenn Gradeen

OGY Petroleums Ltd., #2270, 140 - 4 Ave. SW, Calgary AB T2P 3N3 – 403/233-0066; Fax: 403/261-6033 – President/CEO, Colin Ogilvy

Oiltec Resources Ltd., #1825, 510 - 5 St. SW, Calgary AB T2P 3S2 – 403/266-2988; Fax: 403/237-7145 – Chairman & CEO, Richard A. Schuster

Olco Petroleum Group Inc., 2561, av Georges-V, Montréal PQ H1L 6J7 – 514/645-6526; Fax: 514/645-8048 – President, Mark Kaneb

Olympia Energy Inc., #2100, 500 - 4 Ave. SW, Calgary AB T2P 2V6 – 403/265-2723; Fax: 403/265-2726 – President, Peter Salmon

Optima Petroleum Corp., #600, 595 Howe St., Vancouver BC V6C 2T5 – 604/684-6886; Fax: 604/684-6866 – President/CEO, Robert Hodgkinson

Orbit Oil & Gas Ltd., #2100, 144 - 4 Ave. SW, Calgary AB T2P 3N4 – 403/750-4440; Fax: 403/263-2341 – Chairman, Robert W. Lamond

Pacalta Resources Ltd., #1850, 633 - 6 Ave. SW, Calgary AB T2P 2Y5 – 403/266-0085; Fax: 403/266-1965 – President, Michael Chernoff

Paloma Petroleum Ltd., Guinness House, #1150, 727 - 7 Ave. SW, Calgary AB T2P 0Z7 – 403/265-9265; Fax: 403/266-3097 – President & CEO, Terry D. Brooker

Pan East Petroleum Corp., #500, 67 Richmond St. West, Toronto ON M5H 1Z5 – 416/361-0737; Fax: 416/361-0923 – President, Richard A. Walls

PanCanadian Petroleum Ltd., 150 - 9 Ave. SW, PO Box 2850, Calgary AB T2P 2S5 – 403/290-2000; Fax: 403/290-2440 – President/CEO, D.A. Tuer

Paragon Petroleum Corp., #700, 407 - 8 Ave. SW, Calgary AB T2P 1E5 – 403/266-5075; Fax: 403/266-2742 – President & CEO, Brian A. McLachlan

Paramount Resources Ltd., #4000, 350 - 7 Ave. SW, Calgary AB T2P 3W5 – 403/266-2047; Fax: 403/262-7994 – President, Clayton Riddell

Parkland Industries Ltd., #236, 4919 - 59 St., Red Deer AB T4N 6C9 – 403/343-1515; Fax: 403/346-3015 – President/CEO, Jack Donald

Pe Ben Oilfield Services Ltd., 4510 - 17 St. NW, Edmonton AB T6P 1X5 – 403/440-4425; Fax: 403/440-1134 – President & Chairman, G.R. Dawson

Penn West Petroleum Ltd., #800, 111 - 5 Ave. SW, Calgary AB T2P 3Y6 – 403/777-2500; Fax: 403/777-2699 – Chairman, Murray Edwards

Petro-Canada, PO Box 2844, Calgary AB T2P 3E3 – 403/296-8000; Fax: 403/296-3030 – President/CEO, Jim Stanford

Petromet Resources Ltd., #350, 839 - 5 Ave. SW, Calgary AB T2P 3C8 – 403/269-2627; Fax: 403/266-4150 – President & CEO, Laurie J. Smith

Petrorep Resources Ltd., #1000, 630 - 6 Ave. SW, Calgary AB T2P 0S8 – 403/750-5100; Fax: 403/233-8344 – President, Richard Elenko

Petrostar Petroleums Inc., #3750, 700 - 2 St. SW, Calgary AB T2P 2W2 – 403/265-1142; Fax: 403/265-1927 – President & CEO, Richard G. Anderson

Pinnacle Resources Ltd., #3300, 400 - 4 Ave. SW, PO Box 20067, Stn Calgary Place, Calgary AB T2P 4J2 – 403/232-9100; Fax: 403/232-9203 – President/CEO, Matthew Brister

Place Resources Corp., #1350, 140 - 4 Ave. SW, Calgary AB T2P 3N3 – 403/262-7114; Fax: 403/263-9195 – President & CEO, Keith W. Hern

Poco Petroleums Ltd., #3500, 250 - 6 Ave. SW, Calgary AB T2P 3H7 – 403/260-8000; Fax: 403/263-4098 – President/CEO, Craig Stewart

Precision Drilling Corp., #700, 112 - 4 Ave. SW, Calgary AB T2P 0H3 – 403/264-4882; Fax: 403/266-1480 – President & CEO, Hank Swartout

Profco Resources Ltd., #1500, 340 - 12 Ave. SW, Calgary AB T2R 1L5 – 403/262-5600; Fax: 403/262-8837 – Chair, President & CEO, John J. Fleming

Quaker State Inc., 1101 Blair Rd., Burlington ON L7M 1T3 – 905/335-5577; Fax: 905/332-6406; Toll Free: 1-800-463-0358 – President, John Noel

Questar Exploration Inc., #1700, 311 - 6 Ave. SW, Calgary AB T2P 3H2 – 403/265-0540; Fax: 403/234-7722 – President & CEO, Brian Skinner

Ranger Oil Limited, #1600, 321 - 6th Ave. SW, Calgary AB T2P 3H3 – 403/232-5200; Fax: 403/263-0090 – President & CEO, Fred Dyment

Remington Energy Ltd., #750, 550 - 6 Ave. SW, Calgary AB T2P 0S2 – 403/269-9309; Fax: 403/269-5592 – President/CEO, Paul Baay

Canadian Almanac & Directory 1997

Renaissance Energy Ltd., #3000, 425 - 1 St. SW, Calgary AB T2P 3L8 – 403/750-1333; Fax: 403/750-1869 – President/CEO, Clayton Woitas
Reserve Royalty Corp., #800, 205 - 5 Ave. SW, Calgary AB T2P 2V7 – 403/266-3542 – President/CEO, Fiona Read
Richland Petroleum Corp., Cadillac Fairview Tower Two, #1800, 321 - 6 Ave. SW, Calgary AB T2P 3H3 – 403/261-4080; Fax: 403/261-4083 – President/CEO, Richard Todd
Rigel Energy Corp., Bow Valley Square III, #1900, 255 - 5 Ave. SW, Calgary AB T2P 3G6 – 403/267-3000; Fax: 403/267-3006 – President/CEO, Donald T. West
Rio Alto Exploration Ltd., #1600, 111 - 5 Ave. SW, Calgary AB T2P 3Y6 – 403/264-8780; Fax: 403/261-7626 – President, Richard T. Cones
Savanna Resources Ltd., #810, 540 - 5 Ave. SW, Calgary AB T2P 0M2 – 403/269-5369; Fax: 403/261-2866 – President, John M. Alston
Shaw Industries Ltd., 25 Bethridge Rd., Rexdale ON M9W 1M7 – 416/743-7111; Fax: 416/743-8194 – President/CEO, Geoffrey F. Hyland
Shell Canada Ltd., Shell Centre, 400 - 4 Ave. SW, Calgary AB T2P 0J4 – 403/691-3111; Fax: 403/264-6487 – President/CEO, C.W. Wilson
Signal Energy Ltd., #400, 333 - 5 Ave. SW, Calgary AB T2P 3B6 – 403/262-5177; Fax: 403/265-3357 – President/CEO, Murray Berg
Société Québécoise d'Initiatives Petroliers, #180, 1175, rue de Lavigerie, Ste-Foy PQ G1V 4P1 – 418/651-9543; Fax: 418/651-2292 – Vice-President, Development, Sophie Brochu
Solid State Geophysical Inc., 7309 Flint Rd. South, Calgary AB T2H 1G3 – 403/255-9388; Fax: 403/255-4697 – President/CEO, Mitchell L. Peters
Southernera Resources Ltd., #1014, 33 Yonge St., Toronto ON M5E 1S9 – 416/359-9282; Fax: 416/359-9141 – President, Christopher Jennings
Summit Resources Ltd., #2300, 144 - 4 Ave. SW, Calgary AB T2P 3N4 – 403/269-4400; Fax: 403/269-4444 – President/CEO, Larry B. Krause
Suncor Inc., 112 - 4 Ave. SW, PO Box 38, Calgary AB T2P 2V5 – 403/269-8100; Fax: 403/269-6218 – President/CEO, R.L. George
Sunoco Inc., PO Box 307, Stn Main, Sarnia ON N7T 7J3 – 519/337-2301; Fax: 519/332-3306 – Manager, Mike Ashar
Superior Propane Inc., 75 Tiverton Crt, Markham ON L3R 9S3 – 905/940-7577; Fax: 905/940-7562 – President/CEO, Donald J. Edwards
Talisman Energy Inc., #2400, 855 - 2 St. SW, Calgary AB T2P 4J9 – 403/237-1234; Fax: 403/237-1902 – President/CEO, Dr. James Buckee
Tarragon Oil & Gas Ltd., #2500, 500 - 4 Ave. SW, Calgary AB T2P 2V6 – 403/974-7500; Fax: 403/262-5324 – President/CEO, Ed Chwyl
Texaco Canada Petroleum Inc., #3100, 150 - 6 Ave. SW, Calgary AB T2P 4M5 – 403/234-2900; Fax: 403/234-2999 – President/CEO, Alan C. Cocks
Tidal Resources Inc., #2500, 520 - 5 Ave. SW, Calgary AB T2P 3R7 – 403/231-1400; Fax: 403/231-1424 – President, R. Paul Wandlyn
Torrington Resources Ltd., #2600, 801 - 6 Ave. SW, Calgary AB T2P 3W2 – 403/263-9767; Fax: 403/237-8642 – President/CEO, Lee Anderson
Trans Mountain Pipe Line Company Ltd., #900, 1333 West Broadway, Vancouver BC V6H 4C2 – 604/739-5000; Fax: 604/739-5003 – President, T. Doyle
TransCanada Gas Services Ltd., #2400, 530 - 8 Ave. SW, Calgary AB T2P 3S8 – 403/269-5611; Fax: 403/269-4540 – President, Larry Spackman
TransCanada Pipelines Ltd., PO Box 1000, Stn M, Calgary AB T2P 4K5 – 403/267-6100; Fax: 403/267-6444 – President/CEO, George Watson
Transwest Energy Inc., #400, 255 - 5 Ave. SW, Calgary AB T2P 3G6 – 403/261-5500; Fax: 403/264-3013 – President/CEO, Joseph Ciavarra, Jr.

Tri Link Resources Ltd., 550 - 6 Ave. SW, 10th Fl., Calgary AB T2P 0S2 – 403/262-4601; Fax: 403/265-0892 – President, Gary Burns
Triumph Energy Inc., #910, 635 - 8 Ave. SW, Calgary AB T2P 3M3 – 403/266-1227; Fax: 403/262-5786 – President/CEO, William A. Friley
Truax Resources Corp., #1700, 700 - 4 Ave. SW, Calgary AB T2P 3J4 – 403/233-7122; Fax: 403/237-5403 – President/CEO, Leo G. Schnitzler
Ulster Petroleums Ltd., #1400, 144 - 4 Ave. SW, Calgary AB T2P 3N4 – 403/269-0400; Fax: 403/264-5835 – President, Donne Traxel
United Rayore Gas Ltd., #1120, 520 - 5 Ave. SW, Calgary AB T2P 3R7 – 403/262-7677; Fax: 403/262-7681 – President/CEO, Robert L. Bell
Unocal Canada Ltd., 150 - 6 Ave. SW, 48th Fl., Calgary AB T2P 3Y7 – 403/268-0176; Fax: 403/268-0507 – President, Fritz Perschon Jr.
Upton Resources Inc., 322 - 4 St., Estevan SK S4A 0T8 – 306/634-6484; Fax: 306/634-6227 – President, Scott Dutton
Wascana Energy Inc., 1777 Victoria Ave., PO Box 1550, Regina SK S4P 3C4 – 306/781-8200; Fax: 306/781-8364 – President/CEO, Frank Proto
Westcoast Energy Inc., #3400, 666 Burrard St., Vancouver BC V6C 3M8 – 604/488-8000; Fax: 604/488-8099 – President/COO, Arthur Willms
Westward Energy Ltd., Canterra Tower, #2800, 400 - 3 Ave. SW, Calgary AB T2P 4H2 – 403/262-5260; Fax: 403/261-5022 – President/CEO, Roger Hume
Zargon Oil & Gas Ltd., #2820, 250 - 6 Ave. SW, Calgary AB T2P 3H7 – 403/264-9992; Fax: 403/265-3026 – President/CEO, Craig Hansen

PRINTING & PUBLISHING
Canadian Bank Note Co. Ltd., 145 Richmond Rd., Ottawa ON K1Z 1A1 – 613/722-3421; Fax: 613/722-2548 – Chairman/CEO, Douglas R. Arends
GTC Transcontinental Group Ltd., #3315, 1, Place Ville-Marie, Montréal PQ H3B 3N2 – 514/954-4000; Fax: 514/954-4016 – Chair, President & CEO, Remi Marcoux
Hollinger Inc., 10 Toronto St., Toronto ON M5C 2B7 – 416/363-8721; Fax: 416/364-2088 – Chairman & CEO, C.M. Black
Laird Group Inc., #100, 73 Laird Dr., Toronto ON M4G 3T4 – 416/422-5151; Fax: 416/422-1363 – Chairman, President & CEO, R.M. Leith
Maclean Hunter Ltd., 777 Bay St., Toronto ON M5W 1A7 – 416/596-5000; Fax: 416/596-5195 – President/CEO, John Tory
McGraw-Hill Ryerson Ltd., 300 Water St., Whitby ON L1N 9B6 – 905/430-5000, 428-2222; Fax: 905/430-5020 – President & CEO, John Dill
PMG Financial Inc., #1300, 20 Adelaide St. East, Toronto ON M5C 2T6 – 416/366-1515; Fax: 416/366-2021 – Chairman, President & CEO, Lou Elmaleh
Québecor Inc., 612, rue St-Jacques, Montréal PQ H3C 4M8 – 514/877-9777; Fax: 514/877-9856 – President/CEO, Pierre Deledeau
Québecor Printing Inc., 612, rue St-Jacques, Montréal PQ H3C 4M8 – 514/954-0101; Fax: 514/954-9624 – Chairman & CEO, Jean Neveu
Reader's Digest Association (Canada) Ltd., 215, av Redfern, Westmount PQ H3Z 2V9 – 514/934-0751; Fax: 514/932-3637 – President/CEO, Joe Beaudin
Scholastic Canada Ltd., 123 Newkirk Rd., Richmond Hill ON L4C 3G5 – 905/883-5300; Fax: 905/883-4113 – President/CEO, Larry Muller
Southam Inc., 1450 Don Mills Rd., Toronto ON M3B 2X7 – 416/445-6641; Fax: 416/442-2077 – President/CEO, Don. Babick
St. Joseph Printing Ltd., 50 MacIntosh Blvd., Concord ON L4K 4P3 – 905/660-3111; Fax: 905/660-6820 – President/CEO, Tony Gagliano
The Thomson Corp., #2706, TD Bank Tower, TD Centre, PO Box 24, Stn Toronto-Dominion, Toronto ON M5K 1A1 – 416/360-8700; Fax: 416/360-8812 – President, W.M. Brown
Toronto Sun Publishing Corp., 333 King St. East, Toronto ON M5A 3X5 – 416/947-2222; Fax: 416/947-3119 – President/CEO, Paul Godfrey
Torstar Corp., 1 Yonge St., 6th Fl., Toronto ON M5E 1P9 – 416/869-4010; Fax: 416/869-4183 – President/CEO, David Galloway

RETAIL TRADE; DISTRIBUTION
A&P, 5559 Dundas St. West, Etobicoke ON M9B 1B9 – 416/239-7171; Fax: 416/234-6581 – Chairman/CEO, Jack Moffatt
Acklands Limited, 90 West Beaver Creek Rd., Richmond Hill ON L4B 1E7 – 905/731-5516; Fax: 905/731-9263 – President & CEO, Rai Sahi
Adventure Electronics Inc., 8155, rue Larrey, Anjou PQ H1J 2L5 – 514/352-5000 – Chairman, President & CEO, Robert Fragman
A.G. Simpson Co. Ltd., 675 Progress Ave., Scarborough ON M1H 2W9 – 416/438-6650; Fax: 416/431-8739 – President, Andries Mellema
Algonquin Mercantile Corp., #11, 668 Millway Ave., Concord ON L4K 3V2 – 905/660-7688; Fax: 905/660-1377 – President & CEO, Michael Blair
Alliance Ro-Na Home Inc., 34 Henry St., St. Jacobs ON N0B 2N0 – 519/664-2252; Fax: 519/664-3717 – General Manager, Paul Straus
Arctic Co-Operatives Ltd., 1645 Inkster Blvd., Winnipeg MB R2X 2W7 – 204/697-1625; Fax: 204/697-1880 – President, Bill Lyall
Autostock Inc., 8288, boul Pie-IX, Montréal PQ H1Z 3T6 – 514/593-8300; Fax: 514/593-6405 – President, J. Synnott
Beamscope Canada Inc., 35 Ironside Cres., Scarborough ON M1X 1G5 – 416/291-0000; Fax: 416/291-5721 – President & CEO, Morey Chaplick
Big V Pharmacies, 1005 Wilton Grove Rd., PO Box 5802, London ON N6A 5G1 – 519/686-5081; Fax: 519/686-5514 – President/CEO, Norman Puhl
Boscus Canada Inc., #504, 189, boul Hymus, Pointe-Claire PQ H9R 1E9 – 514/694-9805; Fax: 514/694-9221 – President & CEO, D. Laflame
Boutiques San Francisco Inc., 50, rue De Lauzon, Boucherville PQ J4B 1E6 – 514/449-1313; Fax: 514/449-1317 – President/CEO, Paul Roberge
Brandselite International Corp., 100 Granton Dr., Richmond Hill ON L4B 1H7 – 905/886-8300; Fax: 905/881-5932 – CEO & President, Sam Ghazouly
C Corp. Inc., 3100, Côte-Vertu, 5e étage, Saint-Laurent PQ H4R 2J8 – 514/333-5110; Fax: 514/333-8175 – Vice-President, Marie-France Gibson
Calgary Co-Operative Association Ltd., 8818 MacLeod Trail SE, Calgary AB T2H 0M5 – 403/299-4000; Fax: 403/253-5462 – CEO, Jean Syvenky
Canadian Co-Operative Wool Growers Ltd., PO Box 130, Carleton Place ON K7C 3P3 – 613/257-2714; Fax: 613/257-8896 – Executive Director, Donna Zeman
Canadian Tire Corp. Ltd., 2190 Yonge St., 6th Fl., PO Box 770, Stn K, Toronto ON M4P 2V8 – 416/480-3000; Fax: 416/480-3970 – President/CEO, Stephen E. Bachand
Canon Canada Inc., 6390 Dixie Rd., Mississauga ON L5T 1P7 – 905/795-1111; Fax: 905/795-2027 – President/CEO, Fumitaka Yamada
Cassidy's Ltd., 95 Eastside Dr., Toronto ON M8Z 5S5 – 416/231-1222; Fax: 416/231-8348 – President/CEO, A.W. Brodeur
Chapters Inc., 90 Ronson Dr., Etobicoke ON M9W 1C1 – 416/243-3132; Fax: 416/243-8964 – President/CEO, Larry Stevenson
Chirmax Fashions Ltd., 3901, rue Jarry est, Montréal PQ H1Z 2G1 – 514/729-3333; Fax: 514/593-8278 – President/CEO, Max Konigsberg

Canadian Almanac & Directory 1997

7-52 MAJOR CANADIAN COMPANIES

Co-Op Atlantic, 123 Halifax St., PO Box 750, Moncton NB E1C 8N5 – 506/858-6000; Fax: 506/858-6477 – Chair/President, Eric Meek

Comet Confectionery Ltd., 2950, rue Nelson, St-Hyacinthe PQ J2S 1Y7 – 514/774-9131; Fax: 514/774-8335 – President/CEO, Rudi Pachl

Consolidated Five Star Resources Ltd., #2, 215 Shields Court, Markham ON L3R 8V2 – 905/305-0222; Fax: 905/305-0932 – Chair/President, Edward H.K. Tan

Cotter Canada Hardware & Variety, 1530 Gamble Pl., Winnipeg MB R3T 1N6 – 204/453-9511; Fax: 204/452-6615 – President, David Grubbe

Davis Distributing Ltd., 7171 Jane St., Concord ON L4K 1A7 – 905/738-6226; Fax: 905/738-6221 – President, Bernard J. Davis

Denninghouse Inc., #201, 350 Creditstone Road, Concord ON L4K 3Z2 – 905/738-3180; Fax: 905/738-3176 – Chair, President & CEO, Dennis Klein

Drug Trading Co. Ltd., 1960 Eglinton Ave. East, Scarborough ON M1L 2M5 – 416/288-1100; Fax: 416/288-7950 – President & CEO, Willson Filion

Dylex Ltd., 637 Lakeshore Blvd. West, Toronto ON M5V 1A8 – 416/586-7000; Fax: 416/586-7277 – President/COO, Elliott Wahle

First Brands Canada Corp., #500, 100 Consilium Place, Scarborough ON M1H 3E3 – 416/290-5000; Fax: 416/290-5777 – President/COO, J.H.S. Campbell

FirstService Corp., #4000, 1140 Bay St., Toronto ON M5S 2B4 – 416/960-2724; Fax: 416/960-5333 – President/CEO, Jay S. Hennick

Forzani Group Ltd., 824 - 41 Ave. NE, Calgary AB T2E 3R3 – 403/230-8200; Fax: 403/230-8370 – Chair, President & CEO, John M. Forzani

Future Shop Ltd., 4680 Kingsway, 2nd Fl., Burnaby BC V5H 4L9 – 604/435-8223; Fax: 604/435-5349 – President/CEO, Mohammad Ziabakhsh

Gesco Industries Inc., 1965 Lawrence Ave. West, Weston ON M9N 1H5 – 416/243-0040; Fax: 416/243-1263 – Vice-President & National Sales Manager, David MacDonald

Globelle Corp., 5101 Orbitor Dr., Mississauga ON L4W 4V1 – 905/629-9990; Fax: 905/629-8510 – President, Ron Austin

Great Atlantic & Pacific Tea Co. Ltd., 5559 Dundas St. West, Etobicoke ON M9B 1B9 – 416/239-7171; Fax: 416/234-6581 – Chair/CEO, J.D. Moffatt

Groupe BMTC Inc., 8500, Place Marien, Montréal PQ H1B 5W8 – 514/648-5757; Fax: 514/648-7362 – President/CEO & Chairman, Yves des Groseillers

Groupe Ro-Na Dismat Inc., 1250, rue Nobel, Boucherville PQ J4B 5K1 – 514/599-5100; Fax: 514/599-5157 – Vice-President, Marketing, C. Bernier

Groupe Val Royal Inc., 159, rue Jean-Talon ouest, Montréal PQ H2R 2X2 – 514/270-8111; Fax: 514/270-1937 – President, Y. Archambault

Guillevin International Inc., 400, boul Montpellier, Saint-Laurent PQ H4N 2G7 – 514/747-9851; Fax: 514/747-1568 – Chair/CEO, Jeannine Guillevin Wood

GUS Canada Inc., 5375, ch Côte-De-Liesse, Montréal PQ H4P 1A2 – 514/747-6581; Fax: 514/747-9374 – President, Aaron Stuehler

Hartco Enterprises Inc., 9393, boul Louis-H-Lafontaine, Anjou PQ H1J 1Y8 – 514/354-3810; Fax: 514/354-1998 – President/CEO, Harry Hart

Hewitt Equipment Ltd., 5001, Trans Canada, Pointe-Claire PQ H9R 1B8 – 514/630-3100; Fax: 514/630-9020 – Chairman, James Hewitt

Hudson's Bay Company, 401 Bay St., Toronto ON M5H 2Y4 – 416/861-6112; Fax: 416/861-6441 – President & CEO, George J. Kosich

Hy & Zel's Inc., 7171 Yonge St., Thornhill ON L3T 2A9 – 905/886-7171; Fax: 905/886-9605 – CEO, Zelick Goldstein

Itochu Canada Ltd., #770, 999 Canada Pl., Vancouver BC V6C 3E1 – 604/683-5764; Fax: 604/688-9293 – President/CEO, I. Kanade

The Jean Coutu Group (PJC) Inc., 530, rue Beriault, Longueuil PQ J4G 1S8 – 514/646-9760; Fax: 514/646-5649 – President/COO, Jean-François Coutu

Kanematsu Canada Inc., 6430 Vipond Dr., Mississauga ON L5T 1W8 – 905/670-1977; Fax: 905/670-2510 – President, H. Kuwahata

Kimpex International Inc., 5355, rue St-Roch, Drummondville PQ J2B 6V4 – 819/472-3326; Fax: 819/472-1044 – President, Jack Ramsey

Kmart Canada Ltd./Ltée, 8925 Torbram Rd., Brampton ON L6T 4G1 – 905/792-4400; Fax: 905/792-4792 – President/CEO, Michael Lynch

Komdresco Canada Inc., 160, boul de l'Industrie, Québec PQ J5R 1J3 – 514/659-1961; Fax: 514/659-3557 – President/General Manager, J. Webster

Le Chateau Stores of Canada Ltd., 5695, rue Ferrier, Mont-Royal PQ H4P 1N1 – 514/738-7000; Fax: 514/738-3670 – Chair & President, H.H. Segal

Leon's Furniture Ltd., 88 Gordon MacKay Rd., PO Box 1100, Stn B, Weston ON M9L 2R8 – 416/243-7880; Fax: 416/243-7890 – President/CEO, Mark Leon

Les Supermarchés G P Inc., 42, av Doucet, CP 398, Mont-Joli PQ G5H 3L2 – 418/775-2214; Fax: 418/775-4173 – Directeur, Ventes, Rene Belleavance

Liquidation World Inc., 3900 - 29 St. NE, Calgary AB T1Y 6B6 – 403/250-1222; Fax: 403/291-1306 – Chairman, President & CEO, Dale Gillespie

Marchands Unis Inc., 915, rue Paradis Parc Duberger, Québec PQ G1N 4E3 – 418/687-3050; Fax: 418/687-5317 – President & CEO, Jean-Pierre Drewitt

Mark's Work Wearhouse Ltd., #30, 1035 - 64 Ave. SE, Calgary AB T2H 2J7 – 403/255-9220; Fax: 403/258-7575 – President/CEO, Garth Mitchell

Marubeni Canada Ltd., BCE Place, #2300, 161 Bay St., Toronto ON M5J 2S1 – 416/368-1171; Fax: 416/947-9004 – President, Kitaru Sato

Matco Ravary, 355, boul Sir-Wilfrid-Laurier, St-Basile-Le-Grand PQ J3N 1M9 – 514/653-7861; Fax: 514/866-6187 – President, Carmel Chaput

Matsushita Electric of Canada Ltd., 5770 Ambler Dr., Mississauga ON L4W 2T3 – 905/624-5010; Fax: 905/624-9714 – President, Syunzo Ushimaru

Mazda Canada Inc., #400, 2075 Kennedy Rd., Scarborough ON M1T 3V3 – 416/609-9909; Fax: 416/293-4535 – President/CEO, T. Sudo

MBS Bearing Service Inc., 1520, 55 av, Lachine PQ H8T 3J5 – 514/636-9336; Fax: 514/636-8936 – President/CEO, Doyle Kelly

Medis Health & Pharma Services Inc., #101, 3501, boul St-Charles, Kirkland PQ H9H 4S3 – 514/694-2100; Fax: 514/694-9341 – President & CEO, Claudio F. Bussandri

Mercedes-Benz Canada Inc., 849 Eglinton Ave. East, Toronto ON M4G 2L5 – 416/425-3550; Fax: 416/423-5027 – President, Ernst Lieb

Metro-Richelieu Inc., 11011, boul Maurice-Duplessis, Montréal PQ H1C 1V6 – 514/643-1000, 1055; Fax: 514/643-1208 – President & CEO, Pierre H. Lessard

Mitsubishi Canada Ltd., #5101, Commerce Court West, PO Box 17, Toronto ON M5L 1A5 – 416/362-6731; Fax: 416/365-1384 – President/CEO, Takesuke Miyoshi

Mitsubishi Electric Sales Canada Inc., 4299 - 14 Ave., Markham ON L3R 0J2 – 905/475-7728; Fax: 905/475-7861 – President/CEO, Emil Marx

Mitsui & Co. (Canada) Ltd., #1500, 20 Adelaide St. East, Toronto ON M5C 2T6 – 416/947-3899; Fax: 416/865-1486 – President & CEO, Shinji Teshima

MTC Electronic Technologies, #135, 13500 Maycrest Way, Richmond BC V6V 2N8 – 604/278-8788; Fax: 604/273-8889 – President, Paul Law

NBS Systems Inc., 3206 Orlando Dr., Mississauga ON L4V 1R5 – 905/672-3777; Fax: 905/672-3993 – President/CEO, Ken Kivenko

Nissan Canada Inc., 5290 Orbitor Dr., Mississauga ON L4W 4Z5 – 905/629-2888; Fax: 905/629-9742 – Vice-President & General Mgr., Richard Marcotte

The North West Co., 77 Main St., Winnipeg MB R3C 2R1 – 204/943-0881; Fax: 204/934-1555 – President/CEO, Ian Sutherland

Northwest Drug Co. Ltd., PO Box 2318, Edmonton AB T5J 2P9 – 403/484-0404; Fax: 403/489-7075 – President/CEO, Will Filion

Oshawa Group Ltd., #200, 302 The East Mall, Etobicoke ON M9B 6B8 – 416/236-1971; Fax: 416/236-2071 – Chairman/CEO, A.P. Graham

OSRAM Sylvania Ltd., 2001 Drew Rd., Mississauga ON L5S 1S4 – 905/673-6171; Fax: 905/673-1413 – President/CEO, Anthony Pucillo

Pantorama Industries Inc., 2, ch Lake, Dollard-Des-Ormeaux PQ H9B 3H9 – 514/421-1850; Fax: 514/684-3159 – President/CEO, Sidney Aptacker

Parrish & Heimbecker Ltd., #700, 360 Main St., Winnipeg MB R3C 3Z3 – 204/956-2030; Fax: 204/943-8233 – President, W.B. Parrish

Peoples Jewellers Corp., 1440 Don Mills Rd., North York ON M3B 3M1 – 416/441-1515; Fax: 416/391-7756 – President/CEO, Clare R. Copeland

Pet Valu Inc., 121 McPherson St., Markham ON L3R 3L3 – 905/946-1200; Fax: 905/946-0659 – Executive Vice-President/COO, Tony Lordanis

Price/Costco Canada Inc., 3000, av Jacques-Bureau, Laval PQ H7P 5P7 – 514/686-4444; Fax: 514/686-7455 – Vice-President, Louise Wendling

Prism Sulphur Corp., #3200, 700 - 2 St. SW, Calgary AB T2P 2W2 – 403/262-8766; Fax: 403/265-8362 – President/CEO, Walter J. Litvinchuk

The Real Canadian Superstores, PO Box 300, Stn M, Calgary AB T2P 2H9 – 403/291-7700; Fax: 403/291-7899 – President, Serge Darkazanli

Reitmans (Canada) Ltd., 250, rue Sauvé ouest, Montréal PQ H3L 1Z2 – 514/384-1140; Fax: 514/385-2634 – President/CEO, Jeremy H. Reitman

Richelieu Hardware Ltd., 1910, boul Hymus, Dorval PQ H9P 1J7 – 514/683-4144; Fax: 514/683-7256 – Chair, Jean E. Douville

The Second Cup Ltd., South Tower, #801, 175 Bloor St. East, Toronto ON M4W 3R8 – 416/975-5541; Fax: 416/975-5207 – Chairman/CEO, M. Bregman

Sharp Electronics of Canada Ltd., 335 Britannia Rd. East, Mississauga ON L4Z 1W9 – 905/890-2100; Fax: 905/890-0375 – President, Ichiro Ajshizaki

The Shopping Channel, 1400 Castlefield Ave., Toronto ON M6B 4H8 – 416/785-3500; Fax: 416/785-6534 – Warehouse Manager, Chris Brown

Sony of Canada Ltd., 675 Berry St., Winnipeg MB R3H 1A7 – 204/784-8108; Fax: 204/774-0069 – President/COO, Hirohito. Sakai

Southland Canada Inc., 3185 Willingdon Green, Burnaby BC V5G 4P3 – 604/299-0711; Fax: 604/293-5634 – President/General Manager, Frank Farr

St. Clair Paint & Wallpaper Corp., 2600 Steeles Ave. West, Concord ON L4K 3C8 – 905/738-0080; Fax: 905/738-5121 – CEO, Stan Newman

Stanley Canada Inc., 1100 Corporate Dr., Burlington ON L7L 5R6 – 905/335-0075; Fax: 905/335-5244 – President & Administrator, R. Ayers

Sulzer Canada Inc., 295, boul Hymus, Pointe-Claire PQ H9R 1G6 – 514/695-8320; Fax: 514/697-9862 – President, Jean-Claude Godel

Sumitomo Canada Ltd., PO Box 7010, Stn 1st Cdn Place, Toronto ON M5X 1C8 – 416/860-3800 – President/CEO, T. Hirano

Suzuki Canada Inc., 100 East Beaver Creek Rd., Richmond Hill ON L4B 1J6 – 905/889-2600; Fax: 905/764-1574 – President/CEO, M. Watanabe

Taiga Forest Products Ltd., 4330 Kingsway, Burnaby BC V5H 4G7 – 604/438-1471; Fax: 604/439-4242 – President/CEO, Patrick Hamill

Canadian Almanac & Directory 1997

TCG International Inc., #2800, 4710 Kingsway, Burnaby BC V5H 4M2 – 604/431-2300; Fax: 604/438-7414 – CEO, Arthur Skidmore

Tomen Canada Inc., #1770, 1500 West Georgia St., Vancouver BC V6G 2Z6 – 604/682-7436; Fax: 604/682-1209 – President, Kimio Iida

Toyota Canada Inc., 1 Toyota Pl., Scarborough ON M1H 1H9 – 416/438-6320; Fax: 416/431-1867 – President, Voshio Nakatani

TSC Shannock Corp., 4222 Manor St., Burnaby BC V5G 1B2 – 604/433-3331; Fax: 604/433-4815 – President/CEO, William G. McCartney

Uni-Select Inc., 170, boul Industriel, Boucherville PQ J4B 2X3 – 514/641-2440; Fax: 514/449-5274 – Vice-President, Sales & Marketing, M. Maheux

Univers Info Inc., 9900, Côte de Liesse, Lachine PQ H8T 1A1 – 514/828-4444; Fax: 514/828-4429 – Chair, Jean-Luc Lussier

Van Waters & Rogers Ltd., 9800 Van Horne Way, Richmond BC V6X 1W5 – 604/273-1441; Fax: 604/273-2046 – President/CEO, Larry Bullock

Volkswagen Canada Inc., 777 Bayly St. West, Ajax ON L1S 7G7 – 905/428-6700; Fax: 905/428-5898 – President/CEO, Clive Warrilow

Wal-Mart Canada Inc., 33 Adelaide St. West, Toronto ON M5H 1P5 – 416/361-2111; Fax: 416/361-3041 – President/CEO, Dave Ferguson

Westburne Inc., #400, 6333, boul Decarie, Montréal PQ H3W 3E1 – 514/342-5181; Fax: 514/342-9838 – President, Robert Chevrier

Westburne Inc., #400, 6333, boul Decarie, Montréal PQ H3W 3E1 – 514/342-5181; Fax: 514/342-9838 – President/CEO, Robert Chevrier

W.G. McMahon Canada Ltd., 1551 Church Ave., Winnipeg MB R2X 1G7 – 204/633-1020; Fax: 204/694-1649 – Executive Vice-President & COO, Bob Mason

White Rose Crafts & Nursery Sales Ltd., 4038 Hwy. 7, Unionville ON L3R 2L5 – 905/477-3330; Fax: 905/477-3902 – President/CEO, Ron MacLean

XCAN Grain Pool Ltd., #1200, 201 Portage Ave., Winnipeg MB R3B 3K6 – 204/949-1388; Fax: 204/949-1057 – President, C.H. Swanson

Yamaha Canada Music Ltd., 135 Milner Ave., Scarborough ON M1S 3R1 – 416/298-1311; Fax: 416/292-0732 – President, Motoo Azuki

Zellers Inc., 5100, boul de Maisonneuve ouest, Montréal PQ H4A 1Y6 – 514/483-7600; Fax: 514/483-8302 – President, George Kosich

SERVICE INDUSTRIES

Alert Care Corp., 145 Murray Dr., Aurora ON L4G 2C7 – 905/841-7418; Fax: 905/841-9543 – President, W. Wayne Barton

Arbor Memorial Services Inc., 2 Jane St., Toronto ON M6S 4W8 – 416/763-4531; Fax: 416/763-0381 – President & CEO, John F. Gilles

ATCO Ltd., #1600, 909 - 11 Ave. SW, Calgary AB T2R 1N6 – 403/292-7550; Fax: 403/292-7507 – President/COO, Dr. John Woods

Auberges des Gouverneurs Inc., #800, 777, rue Universisty, Montréal PQ H3C 3Z7 – 514/875-8822; Fax: 514/875-6711 – Chairman & CEO, Jacques Goupil

Bovar Inc., 4 Manning Close NE, Calgary AB T2E 7N5 – 403/235-8300; Fax: 403/248-3306 – President/CEO, Monty Davis

Caldwell Partners International Inc., 64 Prince Arthur Ave., Toronto ON M5R 1B4 – 416/920-7702; Fax: 416/922-8646 – Managing Director, Anne M. Fawcett

Canadian Commercial Corp., Metropolitan Centre, 50 O'Connor St., 11th Fl., Ottawa ON K1A 0S6 – 613/996-0034; Fax: 613/995-2121 – President, Robert G. Wright

Canadian Pacific Hotels & Resorts Inc., #1400, 1 University Ave., Toronto ON M5J 2P1 – 416/367-7111; Fax: 416/863-6097 – Chairman, President & CEO, Robert S. DeMone

Carlson Wagonlit Travel, Centre Tower, #1200, 3300 Bloor St. West, Toronto ON M8X 2Y2 – 416/236-1921; Fax: 416/236-1562 – President/Managing Director, Alan Bromfield

Cineplex Odeon Corp., 1303 Yonge St., Toronto ON M4T 2Y9 – 416/323-6600; Fax: 416/323-6677 – President/CEO, Allen Karp

Clublink Corp., 15765 Dufferin St., King City ON L7B 1K5 – 905/841-3730; Fax: 905/841-7033 – President, Bruce Simmonds

Columbia MBF, 7555 Tranmere Dr., Mississauga ON L5S 1K4 – 905/678-9191; Fax: 905/978-9323 – Vice-President, Sales, Larry Cook

Delta Hotels & Resorts, 350 Bloor St. East, Toronto ON M4W 1H4 – 416/926-7800; Fax: 416/944-7902 – Chair/CEO, Jonas J. Prince

Dynacare Inc., #1600, 20 Eglinton Ave. West, Toronto ON M4R 2H1 – 416/487-1100; Fax: 416/487-8024 – Chair/CEO, Albert Latner

Empire Maintenance Industries, 180, Montée de Liesse, Montréal PQ H4T 1N7 – 514/341-6161; Fax: 514/341-7899 – President, West Division, Fred Post

Environmental Technologies International Inc., #12, 286 Attwell Dr., Etobicoke ON M9W 5B2 – 416/674-0573; Fax: 416/674-1765 – Chair, President & CEO, Ron Williams

Extendicare Health Services Inc., #700, 3000 Steeles Ave. East, Markham ON L3R 9W2 – 905/470-4000; Fax: 905/470-4002 – President/CEO, Wes Carter

Famous Players Inc., #100, 146 Bloor St. West, Toronto ON M5S 1P3 – 416/969-7800; Fax: 416/964-6035 – President/CEO, Joseph Peixoto

FCA International Ltd., #400, 376, av Victoria, Westmount PQ H3Z 1C3 – 514/485-4525; Fax: 514/485-5178 – President, John Moynan

Federal Express Canada Ltd., 50 Burnhamthorpe Rd. West, Mississauga ON L5B 3C2 – 905/897-1803; Fax: 905/897-0605 – Vice-President, Jon Slangerup

Four Seasons Hotels Inc., 1165 Leslie St., North York ON M3C 2K8 – 416/449-1750; Fax: 416/441-4436 – President, John Sharpe

Foxboro Canada Inc., 4, ch Lake, Dollard-Des-Ormeaux PQ H9B 3H9 – 514/421-4210; Fax: 514/421-8059 – President & General Manager, John McKenna

Friesens Corp., One Printers Way, Altona MB R0G 0B0 – 204/324-6401; Fax: 204/324-1333 – President/CEO, David Friesen

The Goldfarb Corp., #1700, 4950 Yonge St., North York ON M2N 6K1 – 416/221-9200; Fax: 416/221-2214 – Chair, Martin Goldfarb

Groupe Sani Mobile Inc., #350, 6500, boul de La Rive-Sud, Levis PQ G6V 7M5 – 418/835-3750; Fax: 418/835-6679 – President/Chair, Louis Lariviere

Groupe Transat A.T. Inc., #400, 300, Léo-Pariseau, Montréal PQ H2W 2P6 – 514/987-1616; Fax: 514/982-8029 – President/CEO, Jean-Marc Eustache

H&R Block Canada Inc., #200, 340 Midpark Way SE, Calgary AB T2X 1P1 – 403/254-8689; Fax: 403/254-9949 – Senior Vice-President, General Manager, J. Bonar Irving

Halozone Technologies Inc., 4000 Nashua Dr., Mississauga ON L4V 1P8 – 905/405-8200; Fax: 905/405-8333 – President/CEO, W.H. Robert MacBean

Hudson General Aviation Services, #400, 100, boul Alexis-Nihon, Saint-Laurent PQ H4M 2N9 – 514/748-2277; Fax: 514/748-2281 – Executive Vice-President, D. Croot

Imperial Parking Ltd., #300, 601 Cordova St., Vancouver BC V6B 1G1 – 604/681-7311; Fax: 604/681-4098 – President & CEO, Paul T.C. Clough

Intermetco Ltd., 519 Parkdale Ave. North, Hamilton ON L8H 5Y6 – 905/548-9700; Fax: 905/548-9512 – President, Bernie Poplack

Ivanhoe Inc., 413, rue St. Jacques, Montréal PQ H2Y 3Z4 – 514/841-7600; Fax: 514/841-7795 – President, Rene Tremblay

Journey's End Corp., #100, 199 Front St., PO Box 6000, Belleville ON K8N 5E2 – 613/966-8020; Fax: 613/966-0867 – President, Terrance B. Ortt

Loewen Group Inc., 4126 Norland Ave., Burnaby BC V5G 3S8 – 604/299-9321; Fax: 604/473-7333 – Chairman/COO, Raymond Loewen

M-Corp. Inc., #310, 8250, boul Decarie, Montréal PQ H4P 2P5 – 514/341-5544; Fax: 514/341-5635 – President & CEO, William M. Reim

Major Drilling Group International Inc., #200, 111 St. George St., Moncton NB E1C 1T9 – 506/857-8636; Fax: 506/857-9211 – President & CEO, Ronald J. Goguen

McDonald's Restaurants of Canada, McDonald's Pl., Toronto ON M3C 3L4 – 416/443-1000; Fax: 416/446-3654 – President/CEO, Ed Garber

MDC Corp., 45 Hazelton Ave., Toronto ON M5R 2E3 – 416/960-9000; Fax: 416/960-9555 – Chair, President & CEO, Miles Nadal

Mediacom Inc., #600, 250 Bloor St. East, Toronto ON M4W 1G6 – 416/920-4311; Fax: 416/920-3042 – President/CEO, Brian McLean

Mont Saint-Sauveur International Inc., 350, rue Saint-Denis, St-Sauveur-des-Monts PQ J0R 1R3 – 514/227-4671; Fax: 514/227-4671 – Chairman, President & CEO, Jacques G. Hebert

NCR Canada Ltd., 320 Front St. West, Toronto ON M5V 3C4 – 416/599-4627; Fax: 416/351-2159 – President/CEO, Ron S. Smith

Newalta Corp., #1200, 333 - 11 Ave. SW, Calgary AB T2R 1L9 – 403/266-6556; Fax: 403/262-7348 – President/CEO, Al Cadotte

Nova Scotia Innovation Corp., PO Box 790, Dartmouth NS B2Y 3Z7 – 902/424-8670; Fax: 902/424-4679 – President & CEO, Dr. R.F. McCurdy

Pharma Plus Drugmarts Ltd., #500, 5935 Airport Rd., Mississauga ON L4V 1W5 – 905/672-0600; Fax: 905/672-5854 – President & General Manager, Rochelle Stenzler

Philip Environmental Inc., 651 Burlington St. East, Hamilton ON L8L 7W2 – 905/544-6687; Fax: 905/548-8468 – President/CEO, Alan Fracassi

Phoenix International Life Sciences Inc., 2350 Cohen St., Saint-Laurent PQ H4R 2N6 – 514/333-0033; Fax: 514/335-8349 – Chairman & President, John Hooper

Public Storage Canadian Properties, #310, 5399 Eglinton Ave. West, Etobicoke ON M9C 5K6 – 416/620-1577; Fax: 416/620-0656 – Chairman, B. Wayne Hughes

Purolator Courier Ltd., 5995 Avebury Rd., Mississauga ON L5R 3T8 – 905/712-1251; Fax: 905/712-6696 – President/CEO, Fred Manske Jr.

Sandwell Inc., 1190 Hornby St., Vancouver BC V6Z 2H6 – 604/684-9311; Fax: 604/688-5913 – Chairman, President & CEO, Alan Pyatt

Sani-Gestion Inc., 3383, boul de la Chaudière, Ste-Foy PQ G1X 4B8 – 418/872-8061; Fax: 418/871-4415 – President/General Manager, Carol Coulombe

Scott's Hospitality Inc., BCE Place, #1500, 181 Bay St., PO Box 810, Toronto ON M5J 2T3 – 416/369-9050; Fax: 416/369-2500 – President/CEO, John Lacey

Service Corp. International (Canada) Ltd., 3789 Royal Oak Ave., Burnaby BC V5G 3M1 – 604/294-9338; Fax: 604/291-9735 – CEO, W. Blair Waltrip

SHL Systemhouse Inc., #501, 50 O'Connor St., Ottawa ON K1P 6L2 – 613/236-1428; Fax: 613/238-4029 – President, Ian McLaren

Signature Vacations, #500, 111 Avenue Rd., Toronto ON M5R 3J8 – 416/967-1510; Fax: 416/967-0232 – President, Dermont Blasthead

The Spectra Group of Great Restaurants Inc., #700, 1380 Burrard St., PO Box 55, Vancouver BC V6Z 2H3 – 604/669-5333; Fax: 604/688-1854 – Vice-President, Peter Bonner

Canadian Almanac & Directory 1997

7-54 MAJOR CANADIAN COMPANIES

Sportscene Restaurants Inc., #300, 426, rue Sainte-Helene, Montréal PQ H2Y 2K7 – 514/849-9376; Fax: 514/849-8585 – President/CEO, Jean Bedard

Thomas Cook/Marlin Travel, #800, 5090 Explorer Dr., Mississauga ON L4W 4T9 – 905/238-5219; Fax: 905/206-2455 – Senior Vice-President, Gary Gaudry

Trimac Ltd., #2100, 800 - 5 Ave. SW, PO Box 3500, Calgary AB T2P 2P9 – 403/298-5100; Fax: 403/298-5258 – President/CEO, Jeffrey McCaig

Trojan Technologies, 3020 Gore Rd., London ON N5V 4T7 – 519/457-3400; Fax: 519/457-3030 – President/CEO, Henry J. Vander Laan

Veritas Energy Services Inc., #300, 615 - 3 Ave. SW, Calgary AB T2P 0G6 – 403/266-9350; Fax: 403/266-9359 – President/CEO, David B. Robson

Versacold Group, 2115 Commissioner St., Vancouver BC V5L 1A6 – 604/255-4656; Fax: 604/255-4330 – President/CEO, John Morgan

Wendy's Restaurants of Canada Inc., #301, 6715 Airport Rd., Mississauga ON L4V 1X2 – 905/677-7023; Fax: 905/677-5297 – President, Brian Grube

Westar Group Ltd., #1600, 1055 West Hastings St., Vancouver BC V6E 2H2 – 604/488-5295; Fax: 604/688-6776 – Managing Director/CEO, Kirk Henderson

William M. Mercer Ltd., BCE Place, 161 Bay St., Toronto ON M5J 2S5 – 416/868-2000; Fax: 416/868-0322 – President, Dan McCaw

Zenon Environmental Inc., 845 Harrington Ct., Burlington ON L7N 3P3 – 905/639-6320; Fax: 905/639-1812 – Chair/CEO, Andrew Benedek

TELECOMMUNICATIONS, COMMUNICATIONS, TECHNOLOGY

ABL Canada Inc., 8550, ch Côte-de-Liesse, Saint Laurent PQ H4T 1H2 – 514/344-5432; Fax: 514/344-5439 – President/CEO, William McKenzie

ACC Telenterprises Ltd., #600, 5343 Dundas St. West, Etobicoke ON M9B 6K5 – 416/236-3636; Fax: 416/236-7391 – President/CEO, Steve Dubnik

Advanced Gravis Computer Technology Ltd., #101, 3750 North Fraser Way, Burnaby BC V5J 5E9 – 604/431-5020; Fax: 604/431-5155 – President/CEO, Michael Cooper

AIT Advanced Information Technologies Corp., 9 Auriga Dr., Nepean ON K2E 7T9 – 613/226-7800; Fax: 613/226-3066 – President, Don Smith

Allied Signal Aerospace Canada, 255 Attwell Dr., Etobicoke ON M9W 6L7 – 416/675-1411; Fax: 416/675-4021 – Chairman/CEO, Basile Papaevangelo

Alphanet Telecom Inc., #260, 55 St. Clair Ave. West, Toronto ON M4V 2Y7 – 416/923-2222 – Chairman & Chief Tech. Officer, Alastair T. Gordon

Alpine Electronics of Canada, #203, 7300 Warden Ave., Markham ON L3R 9Z6 – 905/475-7280; Fax: 905/474-9146 – Vice-President, Sales, Michael Brauley

Amdahl Canada Ltd., #300, 12 Concorde Place, Toronto ON M3C 3R8 – 416/510-3111; Fax: 416/510-2296 – President, Nigel Hilliard

AmeriData Canada Ltd., #400, 1 Antares Dr., Nepean ON K2E 8C4 – 613/723-1174, 9208; Fax: 613/225-7971 – President, Jan Kaminski

Anglo Canadian Telephone Co., 4260 Still Creek Dr., Burnaby BC V5C 6C6 – 604/268-4850; Fax: 604/298-5966 – President, Alfred Giammarino

Apple Canada Inc., 7495 Birchmount Rd., Markham ON L3R 5G2 – 905/477-5800; Fax: 905/477-6305 – President, Peter Jones

Astral Communications Inc., #900, 2100, rue Sainte-Catherine, Montréal PQ H3H 2T3 – 514/939-5000; Fax: 514/939-1515 – President/CEO, Ian Greenberg

ATI Technologies Inc., 33 Commerce Valley Dr. East, Thornhill ON L3T 7N6 – 905/882-2600; Fax: 905/882-2620 – President & CEO, Kwok Yuen Ho

Atlantis Communications Inc., 65 Heward Ave., Toronto ON M4M 2T5 – 416/462-0246; Fax: 416/462-0254 – President & CEO, Seaton McLean

Avcorp Industries Inc., #200, 1001, Autoroute 440 ouest, Chomedey PQ H7L 3W3 – 514/629-5506; Fax: 514/629-5066 – President/CEO, Peter Jeffrey

Aventure Electronique Inc., 8155, rue Larrey, Anjou PQ H1J 2L5 – 514/352-5000; Fax: 514/352-1499 – President/CEO, Alain Tessous

BASF Canada Inc., 345 Carlingview Dr., Toronto ON M9W 6N9 – 416/675-3611; Fax: 416/674-2940 – President/CEO, C. Krafft

Baton Broadcasting Inc., 9 Channel Nine Ct, Scarborough ON M1S 4B5 – 416/299-2000; Fax: 416/299-2426 – President/CEO, Douglas Bassett

BC TEL, 3777 Kingsway, Burnaby BC V5H 3Z7 – 604/432-2151; Fax: 604/435-9562 – Chairman/CEO, Brian Canfield

BC Telecom Inc., 3777 Kingsway, Burnaby BC V5H 3Z7 – 604/432-2151; Fax: 604/435-9562 – Chairman & CEO, Brian A. Canfield

BCE Inc., #3700, 1000, rue de la Gauchetière ouest, Montréal PQ H3B 4Y7 – 514/397-7000; Fax: 514/397-7057 – Chairman, President & CEO, Lynton R. Wilson

BCE Mobile Communications Inc., 8501, Rte Transcanadienne, Saint-Laurent PQ H4S 1Z1 – 514/956-4800; Fax: 514/333-4616 – President/COO, Charles Laberge

Bruncor Inc., 1 Brunswick Sq., PO Box 5030, Saint John NB E2L 4L4 – 506/658-7830, 694-6330; Fax: 506/694-2168 – President/CEO, Gerald Pond

Cabletel Communications Corp., 120 Gibson Dr., Markham ON L3R 2Z3 – 905/475-0001; Fax: 905/475-9571 – President/CEO, Sheldon Rittenberg

CAE Inc., #3060, Royal Bank Plaza, PO Box 30, Toronto ON M5J 2J1 – 416/865-0070; Fax: 416/865-0337 – President/CEO, John Caldwell

Calian Technology Ltd., 300 Legget Dr., Kanata ON K2K 1Y5 – 613/599-7200; Fax: 613/592-3378 – Chairman, President & CEO, Larry O'Brien

Call-Net Enterprise Inc., 2550 Victoria Park Ave., North York ON M2J 5E6 – 416/496-1644; Fax: 416/496-0975 – President & CEO, David Parkes

Cam-Net Communications Network Inc., #795, 885 Dunsmuir St., Vancouver BC V6C 1N5 – 604/684-9016 – Chairman & CEO, Daryl Buerge

Canada Post Corp., Canada Post Place, 2701 Riverside Dr., Ottawa ON K1A 0B1 – 613/734-8440; Fax: 613/734-6084 – Chairman, The Hon. Andre Ouellet

Canadian Broadcasting Corp., 1500 Bronson Ave., PO Box 8478, Ottawa ON K1G 3J5 – 613/738-6505; Fax: 613/738-6567 – President, Perrin Beatty

Canadian Marconi Co., 600, boul Dr. Frederik Philips, Montréal PQ H4M 2S9 – 514/748-3000; Fax: 514/748-3061 – President/CEO, Lloyd Carmen

Canadian Satellite Communications Inc., #10, 50 Burnhamthorpe Rd. West, Mississauga ON L5B 3C2 – 905/272-4960; Fax: 905/272-3399; URL: http://www.cancom.ca – President/CEO, Alain Gourd

CanWest Global Comm Corp., 201 Portage Ave., 31st Fl., Winnipeg MB R3B 3L7 – 204/956-2025; Fax: 204/947-9841 – Chairman/CEO, I.H. Asper

CFCF Inc., 405, av Ogilvy, Montréal PQ H3N 1M4 – 514/273-6311; Fax: 514/276-9399 – President/CEO, A.D. Pouliot

CGI Group Inc., #700, 1130, rue Sherbrooke ouest, Montréal PQ H3A 2M8 – 514/841-3200; Fax: 514/841-3299 – Chairman, President & CEO, Serge Godin

CHUM Ltd., 1331 Yonge St., Toronto ON M4T 1Y1 – 416/925-6666; Fax: 416/926-4026 – President, Allan Waters

Cinram Ltd., 2255 Markham Rd., Scarborough ON M1B 2W3 – 416/298-8190; Fax: 416/298-0612 – President/CEO, Isadore Philosophe

Circo Craft Co. Inc., 17600, rte Transcanadienne, Kirkland PQ H9J 3A3 – 514/694-8000; Fax: 514/694-8604 – President, M. Muhlegg

Clearnet Communications Inc., #300, 1305 Pickering Pkwy., Pickering ON L1V 3P2 – 905/831-6222; Fax: 905/831-7389 – President/CEO, George Cope

Co-Operators Data Services Ltd., 1900 Albert St., Regina SK S4P 4K8 – 306/761-4000; Fax: 306/761-4329 – President/CEO, Ross Marsden

COGECO Cable Inc., #3636, 1, Place Ville-Marie, Montréal PQ H3B 3P2 – 514/874-2600; Fax: 514/874-2625 – President, Louis Audet

COGECO Inc., #3636, 1, Place Ville-Marie, Montréal PQ H3B 3P2 – 514/874-2600; Fax: 514/874-2625 – President, Louis Audet

Cognos Inc., 3755 Riverside Dr., PO Box 9707, Stn T, Ottawa ON K1G 4K9 – 613/738-1440; Fax: 613/738-0002 – President/CEO, Ron Zambonini

Comdisco Canada Ltd., 2075 Royal Bank Plaza, North Tower, Toronto ON M5J 2J3 – 416/367-4180; Fax: 416/367-5095 – President, Preston Thom

Compaq Canada Inc., 45 Vogell Rd., Richmond Hill ON L4B 3P6 – 416/707-1715; Fax: 416/229-8898 – President, Donald Woodley

Compas Electronics Inc., 1245 California Ave., Brockville ON K6V 5Y6 – 613/342-5041; Fax: 613/342-1774 – President, Robert Corson

Corel Corporation, 1600 Carling Ave., Ottawa ON K1Z 8R7 – 613/728-8200; Fax: 613/728-9790 – President/CEO, Michael Cowpland

CTV Television Network Ltd., #1800, 250 Yonge St., Toronto ON M5B 2N8 – 416/595-4100; Fax: 416/595-1203 – President/CEO, John Cassady

Delrina Corp., #500-2 Park Centre, 895 Don Mills Rd, Toronto ON M3C 1W3 – 416/441-3676; Fax: 416/441-0333 – Chairman/CEO, D. Bennie

Develcon Electronics Ltd., 856 - 51 St. East, Saskatoon SK S7K 5C7 – 306/933-3300; Fax: 306/931-1370 – President, William D. Vancoughnett

Devtek Corp., #500, 100 Allstate Pkwy., Markham ON L3R 6H3 – 905/477-6861; Fax: 905/477-0481 – Chair/CEO, Helmut Hofmann

Digital Equipment of Canada Ltd., 4110 Yonge St., North York ON M2P 2C7 – 416/730-7000; Fax: 416/730-7070 – President/CEO, Graeme Woodley

Disys Corp., Airport Square, #10, 2600 Skymark Ave., Mississauga ON L4W 5B2 – 905/625-7343; Fax: 905/625-7344 – President/CEO, James W. Leech

DMR Group Inc., #2300, 1200, av McGill College, Montréal PQ H3B 4G7 – 514/877-3301; Fax: 514/866-0423 – President/COO, Michael Poehner

Dy 4 Systems Inc., 21 Fitzgerald Rd., Nepean ON K2H 9J4 – 613/596-9911; Fax: 613/596-0574 – Chair, President & CEO, Danny B. Osadca

EDS Canada Ltd., #810, 33 Yonge St., Toronto ON M5E 1G4 – 416/814-4500; Fax: 416/814-4600 – President/CEO, Sheelagh Whittaker

Eicon Technology Corp., 9800 Cavendish Blvd., Montréal PQ H4M 2V9 – 514/745-5500; Fax: 514/745-5588 – President/CEO, Peter Brojde

EMJ Data Systems Ltd., PO Box 1012, Guelph ON N1H 6N1 – 519/837-2444; Fax: 519/836-1914 – President/CEO, James A. Estill

Epic Data International Inc., 7280 River Rd., Richmond BC V6X 1X5 – 604/273-9146; Fax: 604/273-1830 – President/CEO, Doug Bailey

Ericsson Communications Inc., 8400, boul Decarie, Montréal PQ H4P 2N2 – 514/738-8300; Fax: 514/345-6103 – President/CEO, L. Hurtubise

Fonorola Inc., #305, 500 boul Rene-Levesque ouest, Montréal PQ H2Z 1W7 – 514/954-3666; Fax: 514/954-4329 – President/CEO, Jan Peters

Fundy Cable Ltd., 199 Chesley Dr., Saint John NB E2K 4S9 – 506/634-5800; Fax: 506/634-5019 – President/CEO, C. William Stanley

Gandalf Technologies Inc., 130 Colonnade Rd. South, Nepean ON K2E 7M4 – 613/274-6500; Fax: 613/274-6501 – President/CEO, Thomas A. Vassiliades

Canadian Almanac & Directory 1997

MAJOR CANADIAN COMPANIES 7-55

Geac Computer Corporation Ltd., #300, 11 Allstate Pkwy., Markham ON L3R 9T8 – 905/475-0525; Fax: 905/475-3847 – President, S. Sadler

Gennum Corp., PO Box 489, Stn A, Burlington ON L7R 3Y3 – 905/632-2996; Fax: 905/632-2055 – President/CEO, H. Douglas Barber

Glentel Inc., #2600, 4710 Kingsway, Burnaby BC V5H 4M2 – 604/431-2300; Fax: 604/431-2259 – Chair, President & CEO, Thomas E. Skidmore

Groupe Videotron Ltée, 300, av Viger est, Montréal PQ H2X 3W4 – 514/281-1232; Fax: 514/985-8431 – Chairman/CEO, Andre Chagnon

GST Telecommunications Inc., #1030, 999 West Hastings St., Vancouver BC V6C 2W2 – 604/688-0553; Fax: 604/688-7330 – President/CEO, John Warta

Hammond Manufacturing Co. Ltd., 394 Edinburgh Rd. North, Guelph ON N1H 1E5 – 519/822-2960; Fax: 519/822-0715 – President/CEO, Robert F. Hammond

Helix Circuits Inc., 250 Finchdene Sq, Scarborough ON M1X 1A5 – 416/299-5300; Fax: 416/292-4308 – Executive Vice-President, Mark Norton

Hewlett-Packard (Canada) Ltd., 5150 Spectrum Way, Mississauga ON L4W 5G1 – 905/206-4725; Fax: 905/206-4739 – President/CEO, Dan Branda

Hitachi (HSC) Canada Inc., 6740 Campobello Rd., Mississauga ON L5N 2L8 – 905/821-4545; Fax: 905/826-6627 – President, Yutaka Matsushima

Hummingbird Communications Ltd., 1 Sparks Ave., North York ON M2H 2W1 – 416/496-2200; Fax: 416/496-2207 – Chairman, President & CEO, Fred Sorkin

IBM Canada Ltd., 3600 Steeles Ave. East, Markham ON L3R 9Z7 – 905/316-9000; Fax: 905/316-2535 – President/CEO, Khalil Barsoum

Information Technology Services, 4000 Seymour Pl., Victoria BC V8X 4S8 – 250/389-3101; Fax: 250/389-3916 – Divisional Head, Chris Bonlsbee

Intermap Technologies Ltd., #900, 645 - 7 Ave. SW, Calgary AB T2P 4G8 – 403/266-0900; Fax: 403/265-0499 – President & CEO, B.L. Bullock

International Verifact Inc., 79 Torbarrie Rd., Toronto ON M3L 1G5 – 416/245-6700; Fax: 416/245-6701 – President & COO, L. Barry Thomson

ISG Technologies Inc., 6509 Airport Rd., Mississauga ON L4V 1S7 – 905/672-2100; Fax: 905/672-2307 – President & CEO, Michael Greenberg

Island Telephone Co. Ltd., 69 Belvedere Ave., Charlottetown PE C1A 7M1 – 902/566-0195, 0131; Fax: 902/566-3265 – President & CEO, Frederick D. Morash

ISM Information Systems Management Corp., One Research Dr., Regina SK S4S 7H1 – 306/781-5151; Fax: 306/781-5382 – General Manager & Vice-President, Gerald Fiske

JVC Canada Inc., 21 Finchdene Sq., Scarborough ON M1X 1A7 – 416/293-1311; Fax: 416/293-8208 – President, Yutaka Uchiyanni

Leitch Technology Corp., 25 Dyas Rd., North York ON M3B 1V7 – 416/445-7927 – President/CEO, Stan Moote

LGS Group Inc., #1070, 1253, av McGill College, Montréal PQ H3B 2Y5 – 514/392-9193; Fax: 514/861-4114 – President, R. Lafontaine

Logistec Corp., #1500, 360, rue Saint-Jacques, Montréal PQ H2Y 1P5 – 514/844-9381; Fax: 514/843-5217 – President, Madeleine Paquin

LSI Logic Corp. of Canada Inc., #1110, 401 The West Mall, Etobicoke ON M9C 5J5 – 416/620-7400; Fax: 416/620-5005 – Vice-President/CFO, Tom Smillie

Mayne Nickless Canada Inc., #802, 50 Burnhamthorpe Rd. West, Mississauga ON L5B 3C2 – 905/272-2212; Fax: 905/272-2215 – CEO, William J. Kirk

Memotec Communications Inc., 600, rue McCaffrey, St-Laurent PQ H4T 1N1 – 514/738-4781; Fax: 514/738-4436 – President/CEO, Marco Genoni

MFP Technology Services Ltd., 2281 North Sheridan Way, Mississauga ON L5K 2S3 – 905/855-2500; Fax: 905/855-2725 – Chairman & President, Peter Wolfraim

Mirtronics Inc., 106 Avenue Rd., Toronto ON M5R 2H3 – 416/920-0500; Fax: 416/920-7851 – President, Mark Litwin

Mitel Corp., 350 Legget Dr., Kanata ON K2K 1X3 – 613/592-2122; Fax: 613/592-4784 – President/CEO, Dr. John Millard

Moffat Communications Ltd., Polo Park CKY Bldg., Winnipeg MB R3G 0L7 – 204/788-3440; Fax: 204/956-2710 – President & Chairman, R.L. Moffat

Mosaid Technologies Inc., 2171 McGee Side Rd., Carp ON K0A 1L0 – 613/836-3134; Fax: 613/831-0796 – President/CEO, George Cwynar

Newbridge Networks Corp., 600 March Rd., Kanata ON K2K 2E6 – 613/599-3660; Fax: 613/599-3615 – Vice-President, Sales & Marketing, M. Pascoe

NII Norsat International Inc., #302, 12886 - 78 Ave., Surrey BC V3W 8E7 – 604/597-6200; Fax: 604/597-6214 – President/CEO, John C. Anderson

Northern Telecom Ltd., 2920 Matheson Blvd. East, Mississauga ON L4W 4M7 – 905/238-7000; Fax: 905/238-7350 – President/CEO, Jean Monty

Okanagan Skeena Group Ltd., 4625 Lazelle Ave., Terrace BC V8G 1S4 – 250/635-6316; Fax: 250/638-6320 – President, Bryan Edwards

Park Meditech Inc., 3195, rue Louis A. Amos, Lachine PQ H8T 1C4 – 514/633-9988; Fax: 514/633-8674 – President/CEO, Dick Mullin

PC Docs Group International Inc., #800, 2005 Sheppard Ave. East, Toronto ON M2J 5B4 – 416/497-7700; Fax: 416/499-7777 – President & CEO, Rubin I. Osten

Perle Systems Ltd., 60 Renfrew Dr., Markham ON L3R 0E1 – 905/475-8885; Fax: 905/475-2377 – CEO & President, Joseph E. Perle

Petersburg Long Distance Inc., 166 Pearl St., Toronto ON M5H 1L3 – 416/593-4989; Fax: 416/979-9754 – President/CEO, James Hatt

Plaintree Systems Inc., 59 Iber Rd., Stittsville ON K2S 1E7 – 613/831-8300; Fax: 613/831-3283 – Chairman, David M. Delaney

Premier Choix : TVEC Inc., #800, 2100, rue Sainte-Catherine, Montréal PQ H3H 2T3 – 514/939-3150; Fax: 514/939-3151 – President/CEO, P. Roy

Promis Systems Corp. Ltd., #500, 175 Bloor St. East, Toronto ON M4W 3R8 – 416/960-0960; Fax: 416/960-1222 – President & CEO, Ian McKinnon

Qsound Labs Inc., 2748 - 37 Ave. NE, Calgary AB T1Y 5L3 – 403/291-2492; Fax: 403/250-1521 – President & CEO, David Gallagher

Quartex Corp., #200, 85 Scarsdale Rd., North York ON M3B 2R2 – 416/445-4823; Fax: 416/445-6228 – President, Reuben Osten

Radiomutuel Inc., 1717, boul René-Lévesque est, Montréal PQ H2L 4T9 – 514/529-3200; Fax: 514/529-3219 – President/CEO, Normand Beauchamp

Rand A Technology Corp., 5285 Solar Dr., Mississauga ON L4W 5B8 – 905/625-2000; Fax: 905/625-2012 – President, Frank Baldesarra

Raychem Canada Ltd., #101, 66303 Airport Rd., Mississauga ON L4V 1R8 – 905/671-1680; Fax: 905/671-0972 – President, Don Olechowski

Regional Cablesystems Inc., #305, 710 Dorval Dr., Oakville ON L6K 3V7 – 905/338-3133; Fax: 905/338-3137 – Chairman, Gary Kain

Rogers Cable Systems, 855 York Mills Rd., North York ON M3B 1Z1 – 416/446-6500; Fax: 416/446-6003 – President/CEO, Edward Rogers

Rogers Cantel Inc., 10 York Mills Rd., North York ON M2P 2C9 – 416/229-1400; Fax: 416/250-4010 – Chair, Edward S. Rogers

Rogers Communications Inc., Scotia Plaza, #6400, 40 King St. West, PO Box 1007, Toronto ON M5H 3Y2 – 416/864-2373; Fax: 416/864-2385 – President/CEO, Edward S. Rogers

S. Foxmeyer Sante Inc., 7900, boul Taschereau, Bldg E100, Brossard PQ J4X 2T3 – 514/877-5555; Fax: 514/877-4905 – President & CEO, Patrick Desormeau

Sand Technology Systems International, #410, 4141, rue Sherbrooke ouest, Westmount PQ H3Z 1B8 – 514/939-3477; Fax: 514/939-2042 – President/Chairman/CEO, A. Ritchie

Scintrex Ltd., 222 Snidercroft Rd., Concord ON L4K 1B5 – 905/669-2280; Fax: 905/669-5132 – President/CEO, Abe Rolnick

Semi-Tech Corporation, 131 McNabb St., Markham ON L3R 5V7 – 905/475-2670; Fax: 905/475-3652 – Chairman, President & CEO, James Ting

Shaw Communications Inc., 7605 - 50 St. NW, Edmonton AB T6B 2W9 – 403/468-1230; Fax: 403/466-4544 – Chair/President, James R. Shaw, Sr.

Sidus Systems Inc., 66 Leek Cres., Richmond Hill ON L4B 1J7 – 905/882-1600; Fax: 905/882-2429 – CEO, Alojz A. Muzar

Simmonds Capital Ltd., #1050, 5255 Yonge St., Toronto ON M2N 6P4 – 416/221-1900; Fax: 416/221-3800 – President/CEO, John G. Simmonds

Skeena Broadcasters, 4625 Lazelle Ave., Terrace BC V8G 1S4 – 250/635-6316; Fax: 250/638-6320 – President, Bryan Edwards

Spar Aerospace Ltd., #1000, 5090 Explorer Dr., Mississauga ON L4W 4X6 – 905/629-7727; Fax: 905/629-0854 – President/CEO, Colin Watson

Spectrum Signal Processing Inc., 100 Production Ct., Burnaby BC V5A 4V7 – 604/421-5422; Fax: 604/421-1764 – President/CEO, Barry Jinks

Speedware Corporation Inc., 150 John St., 10th Fl., Toronto ON M5V 3E3 – 416/408-2880; Fax: 416/408-2872 – Chairman/CEO, Ian Farquharson

SR Telecom Inc., 8150, rte Transcanadienne, Saint-Laurent PQ H4S 1M5 – 514/335-1210; Fax: 514/334-7783 – President/CEO, W. Ronald Couchman

Standard Broadcasting Corp Ltd., #1100, 2 St. Clair Ave. West, Toronto ON M4V 1L6 – 416/960-9911; Fax: 416/323-6828 – President/CEO, Allan Slaight

Sun Microsystems of Canada, 100 Renfrew Dr., Markham ON L3R 9R6 – 905/477-6745; Fax: 905/477-9423 – President, Everett Anstey

System House Ltd. Technical Services, 2000 Clark Blvd., Brampton ON L6T 4M7 – 905/793-9000 – President, Kauko Aronaho

Teleglobe Inc., 100, rue de la Gauchetiere ouest, Montréal PQ H3B 4X5 – 514/868-8124; Fax: 514/982-7580 – Chair/CEO, Charles Sirois

Telemedia Inc., #500, 1411, rue Peel, Montréal PQ H3A 1S5 – 514/845-6291; Fax: 514/845-3628 – President/CEO, R.J. McCoubrey

Telesat Canada, 1601 Telesat Crt, Gloucester ON K1B 5P4 – 613/748-0123; Fax: 613/748-8712 – President/CEO, Larry Boisvert

TELUS Corp., 10020 - 100 St., Edmonton AB T5J 0N5 – 403/498-7300; Fax: 403/498-7399 – President/CEO, George Petty

TIE/Telecommunications Canada, 7550 Birchmount Rd., Markham ON L3R 6C6 – 905/475-5577; Fax: 905/513-4714 – President, Clive Huizinga

Toshiba of Canada Ltd., 191 McNabb St., Markham ON L3R 8H2 – 905/470-5400; Fax: 905/470-3521 – President, Ichiro Tanaka

TSB International Inc., #115, 5399 Eglinton Ave. West, Etobicoke ON M9C 5K6 – 416/622-7010; Fax: 416/622-3540 – President/CEO, Jeremy Purbrick

TV Ontario, 2180 Yonge St., Toronto ON M4S 2B9 – 416/484-2600; Fax: 416/484-4234 – Chairman/CEO, Peter Herrndorf

TVA-CFTM, 1600, boul de Maisonneuve est, Montréal PQ H2L 4P2 – 514/526-9251; Fax: 514/526-6133 – Vice-President, Sales & Marketing, Robert Trempe

United Van Lines (Canada) Ltd., 7229 Pacific Cir, Mississauga ON L5T 1S9 – 905/564-6400; Fax: 905/564-0253 – Vice-President, Sales & Marketing, Anne Martin

Canadian Almanac & Directory 1997

MAJOR CANADIAN COMPANIES

Unitel Communications Holdings Company, #1601, 200 Wellington St. West, Toronto ON M5V 3C7 – 416/345-2000; Fax: 416/345-2840 – President/CEO, Bill Catucci

Wang Canada Ltd., 150 Middlefield Rd., Scarborough ON M1S 4L6 – 416/298-9400; Fax: 416/412-4800 – President/CEO, Robert Lerner

WIC Western International Communication, #1960, 505 Burrard St., Vancouver BC V7X 1M6 – 604/687-2844; Fax: 604/687-4118 – President/CEO, D.M. Holtby

TRANSPORTATION & UTILITIES

Air Canada, PO Box 14000, Saint-Laurent PQ H4Y 1H4 – 514/422-5000; Fax: 514/422-5799 – President/CEO, Lamar Durrett

Alberta Power Ltd., 10035 - 105 St., Edmonton AB T5J 2V6 – 403/420-7310; Fax: 403/420-7549 – President, J.R. Frey

Algoma Central Railway Inc., PO Box 9500, Sault Ste. Marie ON P6A 6Y1 – 705/541-2850; Fax: 705/541-2939 – Superintendent, Transportation, John Gardner

Bannister Majestic Inc., PO Box 4947, Stn South, Edmonton AB T6E 5G8 – 403/955-7167; Fax: 403/955-7160 – President, Bob Marriott

BC Gas Utility Ltd., 1111 West Georgia St., Vancouver BC V6E 4M4 – 604/443-6500; Fax: 604/443-6440 – President/CEO, Steve Bellringer

BC Hydro, 6911 Southpoint Dr., 16th Fl., Vancouver BC V3N 4X8 – 604/528-1600; Fax: 604/528-2649 – President/CEO, Michael Costello

BC Rail Ltd., 221 West Esplanade, PO Box 8770, North Vancouver BC V6B 4X6 – 604/986-2012; Fax: 604/984-5347 – President/CEO, Paul J. McElligott

BC Transit, 13401 - 108 Ave., Surrey BC V3T 5T4 – 604/540-3000; Fax: 604/540-3455 – President/CEO, Blair Trousdell

Bell Helicopter Division, Textron, 12800, rue De L'Avenir, Mirabel PQ J7J 1R4 – 514/437-3400; Fax: 514/437-6888 – President, Dell Young

Bombardier Inc., 800, boul René-Lévesque ouest, 29e étage, Montréal PQ H3B 1Y8 – 514/861-9481; Fax: 514/861-7053 – Chairman/CEO, L. Beaudoin

British Columbia Ferry Corp., 1112 Fort St., Victoria BC V8V 4V2 – 250/381-1401; Fax: 250/361-3455 – President/CEO, Frank Rhodes

Cabano Transportation Group, 6600, ch Saint-Francois, Saint-Laurent PQ H4S 1B7 – 514/332-4341; Fax: 514/332-2886 – President, J. Arthur Servant

Camvec Corp., 1190 Meyerside Dr., Mississauga ON L5T 1R7 – 905/795-3457; Fax: 905/795-3455 – Chairman & CEO, Arthur W. Walker

Canada 3000 Airlines Ltd., 27 Fasken Dr., Toronto ON M9W 1K6 – 416/674-0257, 620-2300; Fax: 416/674-2689 – President/CEO, Angus Kinnear

Canada Ports Corp., 99 Metcalfe St., 8th Fl., Ottawa ON K1A 0N6 – 613/957-6787; Fax: 613/957-6701 – Chairman, Bernie Powers

Canada Steamship Lines Inc., #60, 759 Victoria Sq, Montréal PQ H2Y 2K3 – 514/982-0231; Fax: 514/982-3846 – President/CEO, Ray. Johnston

Canadex Resources Ltd., 10 Sun Pac Blvd., Brampton ON L6S 4R5 – 905/792-2700; Fax: 905/792-8490 – President/CEO, John Riddell

Canadian Airlines Corp., #2800, 700 - 2 St. SW, Calgary AB T2P 2W2 – 403/294-2000; Fax: 403/294-2066 – President & CEO, Kevin J. Jenkins

Canadian Hydro Developers Inc., #200, 622 - 5 Ave. SW, Calgary AB T2P 0M6 – 403/269-9379; Fax: 403/262-8786 – President, John Keating

Canadian National Railway System, 935, rue de la Gauchetière ouest, Montréal PQ H3B 2M9 – 514/399-5430 – Chairman, David McLean

Canadian Utilities Ltd., 10035 - 105 St., Edmonton AB T5J 2V6 – 403/420-7757; Fax: 403/420-7010 – President & CEO, J.D. Wood

Canadian Western Natural Gas Co. Ltd., 909 - 11 Ave. SW, Calgary AB T2R 1L8 – 403/245-7110; Fax: 403/245-7400 – President, Marketing, Bill Arthur

Canutilities Holdings Ltd., Canadian Western Centre, #1600, 909 - 11 Ave. SW, Calgary AB T2R 1N6 – 403/292-7550; Fax: 403/292-7507 – Chairman, President & CEO, Ronald D. Southern

Centra Gas Inc., Park Place, #3400, 666 Burrard St., Vancouver BC V6C 3M8 – 604/488-8001; Fax: 604/488-8098 – President & CEO, Michael Phelps

Centra Gas Manitoba Inc., #540, 444 St. Mary Ave., Winnipeg MB R3C 3T7 – 204/944-9920; Fax: 204/925-0630 – President/CEO, Otto Lang

Centra Gas Ontario Inc., 200 Yorkland Blvd., North York ON M2J 5C6 – 416/491-1880; Fax: 416/496-5331; Email: cacnt193@ibmmail.com – President/CEO, John Bergsma

Charterways Transportation Ltd., #500, 248 Pall Mall St., London ON N6A 5P6 – 519/679-9150; Fax: 519/432-5819 – President/CEO, Geoff Davies

CHC Helicopters Corp., St. John's Airport, Hangar 1, PO Box 5188, St. John's NF A1C 5V5 – 709/570-0700; Fax: 709/570-0506 – President/CEO, Rudy Palladina

CN North America, 935, rue de la Gauchetière ouest, PO Box 8100, Montréal PQ H3C 3N4 – 514/399-2400; Fax: 514/399-8573 – President & CEO, P.M. Tellier

The Consumers Gas Company Ltd., PO Box 650, Scarborough ON M1K 5E3 – 416/492-6611; Fax: 416/498-2977 – President/CEO, Ronald D. Munkley

Contrans Corp., 1179 Ridgeway Rd., Woodstock ON N4S 8P6 – 519/421-4600; Fax: 519/421-3399 – Chair/President, Stan G. Dunford

CP Rail System, Windsor Stn, #401, 910, rue Peel, CP 6042, Succ Centre Ville, Montréal PQ H3C 3E4 – 514/395-5151; Fax: 514/395-7754 – President, R.J. Ritchie

Edmonton Power, #1800, 10065 Jasper Ave., Edmonton AB T5J 3B1 – 403/448-3401; Fax: 403/448-3192 – President & CEO, David Foy

Edmonton Telephones Corp., #1270, 10044 - 108 St., Edmonton AB T5J 3S7 – 403/441-2000; Fax: 403/426-2490 – President/CEO, Allan Scott

Entreposage L.A.R. Inc., 2525, Rte Transcanadienne, Pointe-Claire PQ H9R 4V6 – 514/694-6880; Fax: 514/694-5755 – President & CEO, Rene Boivin

Etobicoke Hydro, 2 Civic Centre Ct, Etobicoke ON M9C 2B4 – 416/394-3500; Fax: 416/394-3509 – President, Ron Kidd

Fednav Ltd., #3500, 1000, rue de la Gauchetière ouest, Montréal PQ H3B 4W5 – 514/878-6500; Fax: 514/878-6642 – President/CEO, Laurence G. Pathy

Gaz Metropolitain Inc., 1717, rue Du Havre, Montréal PQ H2K 2X3 – 514/598-3324; Fax: 514/521-8168 – President/CEO, Andre Caille

Gazoduc TQM, #2220, 1, Place Ville-Marie, Montréal PQ H3B 3M4 – 514/874-8800; Fax: 514/874-8888 – President & CEO, Robert Turgeon

GE Capital Fleet Services, 2300 Meadowvale Blvd., Mississauga ON L5N 5P9 – 905/858-4900; Fax: 905/567-3740 – President, Rolf Ruegg

Great Lakes Power Inc., BCE Place, #4400, 181 Bay St., Toronto ON M5J 2T3 – 416/363-9491; Fax: 416/363-2856 – President, E.C. Kress

Greyhound Lines of Canada Ltd., 877 Greyhound Way SW, Calgary AB T3C 3V8 – 403/260-0877; Fax: 403/260-0742 – President/CEO, Dick Huisman

Groupe Goyette Inc., 2825, boul Casavant ouest, St-Hyacinthe PQ J2S 7Y4 – 514/773-9615; Fax: 514/773-9832 – President & CEO, Jean-Louis Goyette

Groupe Park Avenue Inc., 5000, rue Jean-Talon est, Montréal PQ H1S 1K6 – 514/725-9811; Fax: 514/725-1414 – Chair & CEO, N.D. Hebert

Groupe Robert Inc., 20, boul Marie-Victorin, Boucherville PQ J4B 1V5 – 514/521-1011; Fax: 514/641-3476 – President, Claude Robert

Halifax Port Corp., PO Box 336, Halifax NS B3J 2P6 – 902/426-8222; Fax: 902/426-7335 – President/CEO, David Bellefontaine

Hamilton Hydro Electric Systems, 55 John St. North, Hamilton ON L8N 3E4 – 905/522-6611; Fax: 905/522-6570 – General Manager, Bill Thomas

Hughes Aircraft of Canada Ltd., 3715 - 8 St. NE, Calgary AB T2E 7H7 – 403/295-6604; Fax: 403/295-6607 – President, John Belcher

Hydro-Electric Commission of Ottawa, 3025 Albion Rd. North, Ottawa ON K1V 9V9 – 613/738-6400; Fax: 613/738-6402 – Manager, Energy Management Services, Dan Ralph

Hydro Mississauga, 3240 Mavis Rd., Mississauga ON L5C 3K1 – 905/279-9050; Fax: 905/279-3102 – General Manager, Karl Wahl

Hydro-Québec, 75, boul René-Lévesque ouest, 20e étage, Montréal PQ H2Z 1A4 – 514/289-2211; Fax: 514/289-3342 – Chairman, President & CEO, Benoit Michel

Innotech Aviation Ltd., 595, boul Stuart Graham, Dorval PQ H4Y 1E3 – 514/636-8484; Fax: 514/636-8887 – President/CEO, Stephen Plummer

Interlink Freight Systems Inc., 243 Consumers Rd., 9th Fl., Willowdale ON M2J 4W8 – 416/497-7900; Fax: 416/495-2218 – President & CEO, Bill Aziz

Kuehne & Nagel International Ltd., 5935 Airport Rd., Mississauga ON L4V 1X3 – 905/673-3981; Fax: 905/673-0006 – President, R. Lange

LEP International Inc., 401 The West Mall, 6th Fl., Etobicoke ON M9C 5J5 – 416/620-6570; Fax: 416/620-5360 – President/CEO, Peter Brown

Manitoba Hydro-Electric Board, 820 Taylor Ave., Winnipeg MB R3C 2P4 – 204/474-3311; Fax: 204/474-4974 – President/CEO, R.B. Brennan

Manitoba Telephone System, 489 Empress St., Winnipeg MB R3G 3G9 – 204/941-4111, 7314; Fax: 204/774-9015 – President/CEO, B. Fraser

Marine Atlantic Inc., 100 Cameron St., Moncton NB E1C 5Y6 – 506/851-3600; Fax: 506/851-3791 – President/CEO, Rod Morrison

Maritime Electric Co. Ltd., 180 Kent St., Charlottetown PE C1A 7N2 – 902/629-3799; Fax: 902/629-3665 – President/CEO, Philip G. Hughes

Maritime Telegraph & Telephone Co. Ltd., Maritime Centre, 1505 Barrington St., PO Box 880, Stn Central, Halifax NS B3J 2W3 – 902/487-4311; Fax: 902/425-1572 – President, Colin Latham

Montréal Port Corp., Port of Montréal Bldg., Cite du Havre, Wing No. 1, Montréal PQ H3C 3R5 – 514/283-7050; Fax: 514/283-0829 – Chairman, Raymond Lemay

Mullen Trucking Ltd., 1 Maple Leaf Rd., PO Box 87, Aldersyde AB T0L 0A0 – 403/652-8888; Fax: 403/652-2362 – President/CEO, Murray Mullen

N. Yanke Transfer Ltd., 2815 Lorne Ave., Saskatoon SK S7J 0S5 – 306/955-4221; Fax: 306/955-5663 – President & CEO, Russel Marcoux

New Brunswick Power Corp., 515 King St., 5th Fl., PO Box 2000, Fredericton NB E3B 4X1 – 506/458-4444; Fax: 506/458-4000 – President/CEO, G.L. Titus

New Brunswick Telephone Co. Ltd., 1 Brunswick Sq., 9th Fl., PO Box 1430, Saint John NB E2L 4K2 – 506/694-2340; Fax: 506/658-7163 – President, G.L. Pond

Newfoundland & Labrador Hydro, PO Box 12400, St. John's NF A1B 4K7 – 709/737-1400; Fax: 709/737-1782 – President/CEO, Bill Wells

Newfoundland Light & Power Co., 55 Kenmount Rd., St. John's NF A1B 3P6 – 709/737-5600; Fax: 709/737-2929 – President/CEO, Aidan Ryan

NewTel Communication Inc., Fort Williams Building, 10 Factory Lane, St. John's NF A1C 5H6 – 709/739-3310; Fax: 709/739-2849 – President & CEO, V.G. Withers

North York Hydro, 5800 Yonge St., North York ON M2M 3T3 – 416/226-6400; Fax: 416/229-5121 – General Manager, M.W. Butler

Northwest Territories Power, 4 Capital Dr., Hay River NT X0E 1G2 – 403/874-5200; Fax: 403/874-5251 – Vice-President, Finance & CFO, Leon Courneya

Northwestern Utilities Ltd., 10035 - 105 St., Edmonton AB T5J 2V6 – 403/420-7211; Fax: 403/420-7411 – President, Chris Sheard

Nova Scotia Power Inc., 1930 Barrington St., PO Box 910, Halifax NS B3J 2W5 – 902/428-6237, 6320; Fax: 902/428-6124 – Acting President, Thomas R. Hall

Ontario Hydro, 700 University Ave., Toronto ON M5G 1X6 – 416/592-5111; Fax: 416/592-7350 – President/CEO, Allan Kupcis

Ontario Northland Transportation Commission, 555 Oak St. East, North Bay ON P1B 8L3 – 705/472-4500; Fax: 705/476-5598 – President/CEO, John Wallace

Overland Freight Lines Ltd., 151 Spruce St., New Westminster BC V3L 5E6 – 604/520-9400; Fax: 604/520-3269 – President/CEO, Claus Jensen

Pacific Northern Gas Ltd., #1400, 1185 West Georgia St., Vancouver BC V6E 4E6 – 604/691-5680; Fax: 604/691-5863 – President/CEO, Roy Dyce

PHH Vehicle Management Services, #700, 350 Burnhamthorpe Rd. West, Mississauga ON L5B 3P9 – 905/270-8250; Fax: 905/896-6322 – Vice-President, Sales & Client Relations, M. Goddard

Port de Québec Corp., 150, Dalhousie, Québec PQ G1K 7P7 – 418/648-3640; Fax: 418/648-4160 – Chairman, Rene Paquet

Prince Rupert Port Corp., 110 - 3 Ave. West, Prince Rupert BC V8J 1K8 – 250/627-7545; Fax: 250/627-7101 – President/CEO, Don Krusel

Progas Ltd., #3300, 400 - 3 Ave. SW, Calgary AB T2P 4H2 – 403/296-0600; Fax: 403/296-0675 – President/CEO, Lorne Larson

Québec-Telephone, 6, rue Jules-A.-Brillant, Rimouski PQ G5L 7E4 – 418/723-2271; Fax: 418/722-2059 – President, Gilles Laroche

Rider Travel Group, #700, 370 King St. West, PO Box 32, Toronto ON M5V 1J9 – 416/593-8866; Fax: 416/593-7158 – Executive Vice-President, Matt Manley

Robert B. Somerville - Robert McAlpine Ltd., 13176 Dufferin St., King City ON L7B 1K5 – 905/833-3100; Fax: 905/833-3111 – President, Nick deKoning

Saint John Port Corp., 133 Prince William St., PO Box 6429, Stn A, Saint John NB E2L 4R8 – 506/636-4869; Fax: 506/636-4443 – Chair, Peter Glennie, Q.C.

Saskatchewan Telecommunications, 2121 Saskatchewan Dr., Regina SK S4P 3Y2 – 306/777-2008; Fax: 306/352-5310 – President/CEO, Don Ching

Saskatchewan Water Corp., 111 Fairford St. East, Moose Jaw SK S6H 7X9 – 306/694-3900; Fax: 306/694-3944 – Chair, Eldon Lantermilch

Socanav Inc., #600, 625, boul René-Lévesque ouest, Montréal PQ H3B 1R2 – 514/866-4881; Fax: 514/866-2878 – President/Chair, Michel Gaucher

St. John's Port Corp., PO Box 6178, St. John's NF A1C 5X8 – 709/772-4664; Fax: 709/772-4689 – Chair, Melvin Woodward

The St. Lawrence Seaway Authority, 360 Albert St., Ottawa ON K1R 7X7 – 613/598-4600; Fax: 613/598-4620 – President, Glendon Stewart

Telebec Ltée, 7151, rue Jean-Talon est, Anjou PQ H1M 3N8 – 514/493-5300; Fax: 514/493-6867 – President, Martine Corriveau-Gougeon

Toronto Hydro-Electric System, 14 Carlton St., Toronto ON M5B 1K5 – 416/599-0400; Fax: 416/591-1813 – Director, Consumer Service, C. Buckler

TransAlta Corp., 110 - 12 Ave. SW, PO Box 1900, Calgary AB T2P 2M1 – 403/267-7116; Fax: 403/267-3630 – Senior Vice-President, Sustainable Development, Jim Leslie

TransAlta Utilities Corp., 110 - 12 Ave. SW, PO Box 1900, Calgary AB T2P 0M1 – 403/267-7301; Fax: 403/267-2559 – President/COO, W. Saponja

U-Haul Co. (Canada) Ltd., 2275 Barton St. East, Hamilton ON L8E 2W8 – 905/560-0014; Fax: 905/560-0212 – President, C. Boucher

Unicorp Energy Corp., #2320, 161 Bay St., Toronto ON M5J 2S1 – 416/867-9370; Fax: 416/867-1961 – President, Ian G. Cockwell

Union Gas Ltd., 50 Keil Dr. North, Stn 2001, Chatham ON N7M 5M1 – 519/352-3100; Fax: 519/436-4621 – President/CEO, John Bergsma

Vancouver Port Corp., Granville Sq., #1900, 200 Granville St., Vancouver BC V6C 2P9 – 604/666-3226; Fax: 604/666-1207 – President/CEO, Capt. Norman Stark

Vitran Corp. Inc., 24 Mobile Dr., Toronto ON M4A 1H9 – 416/752-1411; Fax: 416/752-8510 – President & CEO, R.D. McGraw

West Kootenay Power Ltd., 1290 Esplanade, PO Box 130, Trail BC V1R 4L4 – 250/368-3321; Fax: 250/368-3211 – President/CEO, Don Bacon

Westinghouse Canada Inc., 30 Milton Ave., PO Box 2510, Stn A, Hamilton ON L8N 3K2 – 905/528-8811; Fax: 905/577-0275 – President, Gary Weimer

Winnipeg Hydro Electric System, 223 James Ave., Winnipeg MB R3B 3L1 – 204/986-2320; Fax: 204/942-7804 – Business Manager, K. Au

MISCELLANEOUS

Alberto-Culver Canada Inc., 506 Kipling Ave., Toronto ON M8Z 5E2 – 416/251-3741; Fax: 416/251-3062 – Vice-President, Operations, Dan Sulan

Alliance Communications Corp., #400, 920 Yonge St., Toronto ON M4W 3C7 – 416/967-1174; Fax: 416/960-0971 – Chairman & CEO, Robert Lantos

Arden Holdings Inc., #104, 99, rue Chabanel ouest, Montréal PQ H2N 1C2 – 514/383-4442; Fax: 514/382-5754 – President, Arden Dervishian

Canadian Film Development Corp., Tour de la Banque Nationale, 600, rue de la Gauchetière ouest, 14e étage, Montréal PQ H3B 4L8 – 514/283-6363; Fax: 514/283-8212 – President/Chairman, Robert Dinan

Canadian Pacific Enterprises Ltd., #800, Place du Canada, Montréal PQ H3C 3A4 – 514/395-6691; Fax: 514/395-6694 – Chairman, President & CEO, D.P. O'Brian

Carlson Marketing Group Ltd., 3300 Bloor St. West, 14th Fl., Toronto ON M8X 2Y2 – 416/236-1991; Fax: 416/236-1848 – President, Terry Rumsey

Cinar Films Inc., #900, 1055, boul René-Lévesque est, Montréal PQ H2L 3S8 – 514/843-7070 – Chair/CEO, Micheline Charest

Coscient Group Inc., #2400, 300, rue Leo-Pariseau, CP 1145, Montréal PQ H2W 2P4 – 514/284-2525; Fax: 514/284-0640 – President, R. Laferriere

Cree Co., #3438, 1 Place Ville-Marie, Montréal PQ H3B 3N6 – 514/861-5837; Fax: 514/861-0760 – Office Manager, Elaine Woodford

Ducks Unlimited Canada, Oak Hammock Marsh Conservation Centre, PO Box 1160, Oak Hammock Marsh MB R0C 2Z0 – 204/467-3000; Fax: 204/467-9028 – Executive Vice-President/CEO, Don Young

Federated Co-Operatives Ltd., 401 - 22 St. East, PO Box 1050, Saskatoon SK S7K 3M9 – 306/244-3311; Fax: 306/244-3403 – President, Ed Klassen

Gendis Inc., 1370 Sony Pl., PO Box 9400, Winnipeg MB R3C 3C3 – 204/474-5200; Fax: 204/474-5216 – President/COO, G.A. MacKenzie

Harrowston Inc., #3820, 181 Bay St., PO Box 758, Toronto ON M5J 2T3 – 416/777-2822; Fax: 416/956-7000 – President/CEO, Brent S. Belzberg

Hil Corporation Ltd., BCE Place, #4500, 181 Bay St., Toronto ON M5J 2T3 – 416/359-8605; Fax: 416/865-9845 – President, M.J. Walt

The Horsham Corp., BCE Place, #3900, 181 Bay St., PO Box 768, Toronto ON M5J 2T3 – 416/682-8600; Fax: 416/364-5491 – President, Gregory C. Wilkins

Imasco Ltd., 600, boul De Maisonneuve ouest, 20e étage, Montréal PQ H3A 3K7 – 514/982-9111; Fax: 514/982-0162 – President & CEO, Brian M. Levitt

Imax Corp., 45 Charles St. East, Toronto ON M4Y 1N1 – 416/960-8509; Fax: 416/960-8596 – CEO & President, Brad Wechsler

Intrawest Corp., #800, 200 Burrard St., Vancouver BC V6C 3L6 – 604/669-9777; Fax: 604/669-0605 – President & CEO, J. Houssian

James Richardson & Sons Ltd., 1 Lombard Pl., 30th Fl., Winnipeg MB R3B 0Y1 – 204/934-5811; Fax: 204/934-5811 – Managing Director, George T. Richardson

J.D. Irving Ltd., 300 Union St., PO Box 5777, Saint John NB E2L 4M3 – 506/632-7777; Fax: 506/658-0517 – President, J.K. Irving

The Jim Pattison Group, #1600, 1055 West Hastings St., Vancouver BC V6E 2H2 – 604/688-6764; Fax: 604/687-2601 – CEO/Managing Director, Jim Pattison

Laidlaw Inc., 3221 North Service Rd., PO Box 5028, Burlington ON L7R 3Y8 – 905/336-1800; Fax: 905/336-3976 – President/CEO, James R. Bullock

Landis & Gyr Ltd., 5462 Timberlee Blvd., Mississauga ON L4W 2T7 – 905/602-1320; Fax: 905/602-1910 – Manager, Finance & Admin, Greg Williamson

Lindsey Morden Group Inc., #600, 155 University Ave., Toronto ON M5H 3N5 – 416/362-6762; Fax: 416/362-8692 – President/COO, Don Cain

Livent Inc., #600, 165 Avenue Rd., Toronto ON M5R 3S4 – 416/324-5800; Fax: 416/324-5777 – President & COO, Myron I. Gottlieb

Livingston Group Inc., #480, 405 The West Mall, Etobicoke ON M9C 5K7 – 416/626-2828; Fax: 416/621-7651 – President/CEO, Jean-René Halde

Malofilm Communications Inc., #650, 3575, boul St-Laurent, Montréal PQ H2X 2T7 – 514/844-4555; Fax: 514/844-1471 – President, Jean Bureau

Maple Leaf Gardens Ltd., 60 Carlton St., Toronto ON M5B 1L1 – 416/977-1641; Fax: 416/977-3601 – Chairman/Owner & CEO, Steve Stavro

MCA Canada Ltd., #4, 2450 Victoria Park Ave., Willowdale ON M2J 4A2 – 416/491-3000; Fax: 416/491-6560 – Vice-President, Finance & Administration, Eric Pertsch

Moore Corp. Ltd., PO Box 78, Stn 1st Cdn Place, Toronto ON M5X 1G5 – 416/364-2600; Fax: 416/364-1667 – Chair, President & CEO, Reto Braun

Nelvana Ltd., 32 Atlantic Ave., Toronto ON M6K 1X8 – 416/588-5571; Fax: 416/588-5588 – President, Patrick Loubert

Nissho Iwai Canada Ltd., #1506, 150 King St. West, Toronto ON M5H 1J9 – 416/977-8182; Fax: 416/977-0241 – General Manager, Shumpei Takei

Noranda Inc., BCE Place, #4100, 181 Bay St., PO Box 755, Toronto ON M5J 2T3 – 416/982-7193, 7111; Fax: 416/982-7423 – President/CEO, D.W. Kerr

Norterra Inc., #2000, 10155 - 102 St., Edmonton AB T5J 4G8 – 403/425-6900; Fax: 403/424-1935 – President, David Burnett

Onex Corp., 161 Bay St., 49th Fl., PO Box 700, Toronto ON M5J 2S1 – 416/362-7711; Fax: 416/362-5765 – President/CEO, Gerald W. Schwartz

Ontario Store Fixtures Inc., 650 Barmac Dr., Weston ON M9L 2X8 – 416/749-7700; Fax: 416/747-5838 – President/CEO, Harry Shier

Orca Bay Sports & Entertainment, 800 Griffith Way, Vancouver BC V6B 6G1 – 604/899-4600; Fax: 604/899-7501 – President/COO, John Chapple

Oscar Poulin & Fils Ltée, 27, rue Mangin, Hull PQ J8Y 3L8 – 819/777-3893; Fax: 819/777-8712 – President & Owner, Pierre Poulin

Panval Inc., CP 340, Route 152, Sayabec PQ G0J 3K0 – 418/536-5050; Fax: 418/536-3636 – Director, A. Nerville

Paragon Entertainment Corp., #900, 119 Spadina Ave., Toronto ON M5V 2L1 – 416/977-2929; Fax: 416/977-8247 – Chairman & CEO, Jonathan Slan

Canadian Almanac & Directory 1997

7-58 MAJOR CANADIAN COMPANIES

Picker International Canada Inc., 7956 Torbram Rd., Brampton ON L6T 5A2 – 905/791-1494; Fax: 905/791-1695 – President, Bruce Ross

Pitney Bowes of Canada Ltd., #100, 2200 Yonge St., Toronto ON M4S 3E1 – 416/489-2211; Fax: 416/484-3972 – President/CEO, Ted Madden

Power Corp. of Canada, 751, Victoria Sq., Montréal PQ H2Y 2J3 – 514/286-7400; Fax: 514/286-7424 – President/CEO, Andre Desmarais

Roman Corp. Ltd., #1315, 200 King St. West, PO Box 82, Toronto ON M5H 3T4 – 416/971-3330; Fax: 416/971-9181 – Chair/CEO, Helen Roman-Barber

Sino Pac International Investments Inc., #515, 800 West Pender St., Vancouver BC V6C 2V6 – 604/682-3290; Fax: 604/682-1213 – President/CEO, R.W.C. Ng

Trionics Industries Ltd., Lake City Business Park, 8527 Eastlake Dr., Burnaby BC V5A 4T7 – 604/421-7502; Fax: 604/425-6682 – Chair/CEO, Douglas Smith

Unican Security Systems Ltd., 7301, boul Decarie, Montréal PQ H4P 2G7 – 514/735-5411; Fax: 514/735-0428 – Chairman/CEO, Aaron Fish

Viridian Inc., 10101 - 114 St., Fort Saskatchewan AB T8L 2P2 – 403/998-6911; Fax: 403/998-6568 – Chair/CEO, Ian Delaney

Xerox Canada Inc., 5650 Yonge St., 8th Fl., North York ON M2M 4G7 – 416/229-3769; Fax: 416/229-6826 – President/CEO, Diane McGarry

Canadian Almanac & Directory 1997

ns
SECTION 8

HEALTH DIRECTORY

ALBERTA	1	NEWFOUNDLAND	17	PRINCE EDWARD ISLAND	33
BRITISH COLUMBIA	8	NORTHWEST TERRITORIES	18	QUÉBEC	34
MANITOBA	11	NOVA SCOTIA	19	SASKATCHEWAN	51
NEW BRUNSWICK	15	ONTARIO	21	YUKON TERRITORY	56

See ADDENDA at the back of this book for late changes & additional information.

HOSPITALS & HEALTHCARE FACILITIES

GOVERNMENT DEPARTMENTS IN CHARGE
ALBERTA: Dept. of Health, Minister's Office, 228 Legislature Bldg., Edmonton AB T5K 2B6 – 403/427-3665; Fax: 403/429-5954
 Dept. of Health - Communications Branch, 10025 Jasper Ave., 18th Fl., Edmonton AB T5J 2N3 – 403/427-7164; Fax: 403/427-1171
BRITISH COLUMBIA: Ministry of Health, Minister's Office, Parliament Bldgs., Victoria BC V8V 1X4 – 250/387-5394; Fax: 250/387-3696
MANITOBA: Manitoba Health, Community & Mental Health Services Division, Hospital Services, 599 Empress St., PO Box 925, Winnipeg MB R3C 2T6 – 204/786-7324; Fax: 204/772-2943
NEW BRUNSWICK: Dept. of Health & Community Services - Communications, PO Box 5100, Fredericton NB E3B 5G8 – 506/453-2536; Fax: 506/444-4697
NEWFOUNDLAND: Dept. of Health, West Block, Confederation Bldg., PO Box 8700, St. John's NF A1B 4J6 – 709/729-3127; Fax: 709/729-0121
NORTHWEST TERRITORIES: Dept. of Health & Social Services, PO Box 1320, Yellowknife NT X1A 2L9 – 403/920-6173; Fax: 403/873-0266
NOVA SCOTIA: Dept. of Health, Joseph Howe Bldg., PO Box 488, Halifax NS B3J 2R8 – 902/424-5818; Fax: 902/424-0506
ONTARIO: Ministry of Health, Institutional Health Division, 5700 Yonge St., North York ON M2M 4K5 – 416/327-7126; Fax: 416/327-7763
PRINCE EDWARD ISLAND: Health & Community Services Agency, 4 Sydney St., PO Box 2000, Charlottetown PE C1A 7N8 – 902/368-6130; Fax: 902/368-6136
QUÉBEC: Ministère de la santé et des services sociaux, Service de l'infocentre, 1005, ch Ste-Foy, 4e étage, Québec PQ G1S 4N4 – 418/643-6209; Fax: 418/528-1630
SASKATCHEWAN: Saskatchewan Health - Corporate Information & Technology Branch, 3475 Albert St., Regina SK S4S 6X6 – 306/787-4636; Fax: 306/787-7095
YUKON TERRITORY: Health & Social Services, PO Box 2703, Whitehorse YT Y1A 2C6 – 403/667-3673; Fax: 403/667-3096

ALBERTA
Hosptial Districts/Health Units in Alberta provide much of the administration for individual health care facilities in their district. The Alberta listings in this section include the name of the applicable authority for each facility, where available.

HOSPITAL DISTRICTS/HEALTH UNITS
Alberta Cancer Board, 9707 - 110 St., 6th Fl., Edmonton AB T5K 2L9 – 403/482-9300; Fax: 403/488-7809 – Pres. & CEO, J.M. Turc, M.D.
Aspen Regional Health Authority #11, 10003 - 100 St., PO Box 2308, Westlock AB T0G 3E0 – 403/349-8705; Fax: 403/349-4879 – CEO, Robert Cable
Calgary Regional Health Authority, 1213 - 4 St. SW, Calgary AB T2R 0X7 – 403/541-3670; Fax: 403/541-3681 – CEO, Paul Rushforth
Capital Health Authority, 1J2 Walter C. Mackenzie Centre, 8440 - 112 St., Edmonton AB T6G 2B7 – 403/492-5000; Fax: 403/492-4257 – CEO, Brian Lemon
Chinook Health Region, 960 - 19 St. South, Lethbridge AB T1J 1W5 – 403/382-6009; Fax: 403/382-6011 – CEO, G.J. Tourigny
Crossroads Regional Health Authority, 5610 - 40 Ave., PO Box 6627, Wetaskiwin AB T9A 2G3 – 403/352-3766; Fax: 403/361-4336 – CEO, Peter Langelle
David Thompson Health Region, #602, 4920 - 51 St., PO Box 5026, Red Deer AB T4N 6A1 – 403/341-8622; Fax: 403/341-8632 – CEO, Al Martin
East Central Regional Health Authority 7, 4703 - 53 St., Camrose AB T4V 1Y8 – 403/672-8800; Fax: 403/672-5023 – CEO, Dennis Magnusson
Headwaters Health Authority, 560 - 9 Ave. West, High River AB T1V 1B3 – 403/652-0104; Fax: 403/652-0190 – CEO, Dwight Nelson
Keeweetinok Lakes Regional Health Authority #15, 5226 - 53 Ave., PO Box 874, High Prairie AB T0G 1E0 – 403/523-6641; Fax: 403/523-6642 – CEO, Brenda Langevin
Lakeland Regional Health Authority, 210 Provincial Bldg., PO Box 248, Smoky Lake AB T0A 3C0 – 403/656-2030; Fax: 403/656-2033 – CEO, Don Carley
Mistahia Regional Health Authority, Provincial Bldg., 2nd Fl., #2301, 10320 - 99 St., Grande Prairie AB T8V 6J4 – 403/538-5387; Fax: 403/538-5455 – CEO, Gerry Northam
Northern Lights Regional Health Authority, 7 Hospital St., Fort McMurray AB T9H 1P2 – 403/791-6020; Fax: 403/791-6042 – CEO, Dalton M. Russell
Northwestern Health Services Region, Regional Administration, #200, 10106 - 100 Ave., PO Box 10000, High Level AB T0H 1Z0 – 403/926-4388; Fax: 403/926-4149 – CEO, Gordon J. Voth
Palliser Health Authority, 666 - 5 St. SW, Medicine Hat AB T1A 4H6 – 403/529-8042; Fax: 403/529-8998 – Pres., Tom Seaman
Peace Regional Health Authority, 10015 - 98 St., PO Box 6178, Peace River AB T8S 1S2 – 403/624-3611; Fax: 403/624-3169 – CEO, Brian Hrab
Provincial Mental Health Advisory Board, #1360, 10025 Jasper Ave., Edmonton AB T2J 2N3 – 403/422-2233; Fax: 403/422-2472 – Exec. Dir., Nancy Reynolds, 403/422-2439
Regional Health Authority 5, 625 Riverside Dr. East, PO Box 429, Drumheller AB T0J 0Y0 – 403/823-5245; Fax: 403/823-7589 – CEO, Jim H. Ramsbottom
WestView Regional Health Authority, c/o Devon General Hospital Admin. Office, 101 Erie St. South, PO Box 438, Devon AB T0C 1E0 – 403/987-3376; Fax: 403/987-2798 – CEO, Larry Smook

GENERAL HOSPITALS
Athabasca Healthcare Centre, 3100 - 49 Ave., Athabasca AB T9S 1M9 – 403/675-6000; Fax: 403/675-

Canadian Almanac & Directory 1997

8-2 ALBERTA GENERAL HOSPITALS

7050 – 23 beds – Aspen RHA #11 – Site Suprv., Sandra Haley

Banff Mineral Springs Hospital, PO Box 1050, Banff AB T0L 0C0 – 403/762-2222; Fax: 403/762-4193 – Headwaters Health Authority – Senior Community Health Dir., West, Tom Novak

Barrhead Healthcare Centre, 4815 - 51 Ave., Barrhead AB T7N 1M1 – 403/674-2221, 424-6178; Fax: 403/674-6773, 6503 – 15 beds – Aspen RHA #11 – Site Suprv., Shelly Pusch

Bassano General Hospital, PO Box 120, Bassano AB T0J 0B0 – 403/641-3520; Fax: 403/641-2157 – 17 beds – Palliser Health Authority – Adm., Dean Roy

Beaverlodge Municipal Hospital, PO Box 480, Beaverlodge AB T0H 0C0 – 403/354-2136; Fax: 403/354-8355 – 18 beds – Site Coord., Judy White

Black Diamond: Oilfields General Hospital, PO Box 1, Black Diamond AB T0L 0H0 – 403/933-2222; Fax: 403/933-2031 – Headwaters Health Authority – Site Suprv., Emily Brookwell

Blairmore: Crowsnest Pass Health Care Centre, 2001 - 107 St., PO Box 510, Blairmore AB T0K 0E0 – 403/562-2831; Fax: 403/562-8992 – 16 acute care, 60 continuing care beds – Exec. Dir., Donna Stelmachovich

Bonnyville Health Centre & Auxiliary Centre, PO Box 1008, Bonnyville AB T9N 2J7 – 403/826-3311; Fax: 403/826-6187 – 24 acute care, 30 long term care beds – Adm., Clement Johnson

Bow Island Health Centre & Auxiliary Hospital, PO Box 3990, Bow Island AB T0K 0G0 – 403/545-2211; Fax: 403/545-2281 – 10 acute care, 20 continuing care beds – Pres., Tom Seaman

Boyle Healthcare Centre, 1004 Lakeview Rd., PO Box 330, Boyle AB T0A 0M0 – 403/689-3731; Fax: 403/689-3951 – 30 beds – Aspen RHA #11 – Site Suprv., Donna Larson

Breton Health Centre, PO Box 340, Breton AB T0C 0P0 – 403/696-4700; Fax: 403/696-4747 – 11 beds – Crossroads RHA – Site Coord., Janet Young

Brooks General & Auxiliary Hospital & Nursing Home, PO Box 300, Brooks AB T1R 1B3 – 403/362-3456; Fax: 403/362-6039 – Exec. Dir., Larry K. Smook

Calgary General Hospital - Bow Valley Centre, 841 Centre Ave. East, Calgary AB T2E 0A1 – 403/268-9111; Fax: 403/268-9222 – 439 beds – Calgary RHA – Adm., Jeanette Pick

Calgary General Hospital - Peter Lougheed Centre, 3500 - 26th Ave. NE, Calgary AB T1Y 6J4 – 403/291-8555; Fax: 403/291-8888 – 184 beds – Calgary RHA – Adm., Jeanette Pick, 403/670-1401, Fax: 403/670-1533

Calgary: Alberta Children's Hospital, 1820 Richmond Rd. SW, Calgary AB T2T 5C7 – 403/229-7211; Fax: 403/229-7221 – 115 beds – Calgary RHA – Adm., Jeanette Pick

Calgary: Foothills Provincial Hospital, 1403 - 29 St. NW, Calgary AB T2N 2T9 – 403/670-1110; Fax: 403/670-2400 – 650 beds – Calgary RHA – Adm., Jeanette Pick

Calgary: Grace Women's Health Centre, 1441 - 29 St. NW, Calgary AB T2N 4JB – 403/670-2200; Fax: 403/670-2190 – Calgary RHA – Pres., Mary Cullen

Camrose: St. Mary's Hospital, 4607 - 53 St., Camrose AB T4V 1Y5 – 403/679-6100; Fax: 403/679-6198 – 76 acute care – East Central RHA 7 – Exec. Dir., Michael Shea

Canmore Hospital, PO Box 130, Canmore AB T0L 0M0 – 403/678-5536; Fax: 403/678-9874 – Headwaters Health Authority – Site Suprv., Barb Shellian

Cardston Hospital, 144 - 2nd St. West, PO Box 1440, Cardston AB T0K 0K0 – 403/653-4411; Fax: 403/653-4399, 4115 – 25 acute care beds, 32 continuing care beds – Chinook Health Region – Exec. Dir., Roger N. Walker

Castor: Our Lady of the Rosary Hospital, PO Box 329, Castor AB T0C 0X0 – 403/882-3434; Fax: 403/882-2751 – 5 acute care, 15 continuing care beds – East Central RHA 7 – Exec. Dir., Marilyn Weber

Cereal Municipal Hospital, PO Box 130, Cereal AB T0J 0N0 – 403/326-3838; Fax: 403/326-3730 – 5 long term care beds, 11 alternate living beds – RHA 5 – Dir. of Health Servs., Stan Faupel, 403/854-3331

Claresholm General Hospital, PO Box 610, Claresholm AB T0L 0T0 – 403/625-3344; Fax: 403/625-3862 – 15 beds – Headwaters Health Authority – Site Suprv., Brian Popp

Cold Lake Regional Hospital & Auxiliary Centre, 314 - 25 St., Cold Lake AB T0A 0V1 – 403/639-3322; Fax: 403/639-2255 – Adm., Donald Carley

Consort Municipal Hospital, PO Box 310, Consort AB T0C 1B0 – 403/577-3555; Fax: 403/577-3950 – 5 acute care, 15 continuing care beds – East Central RHA 7 – Health Care Coord., Sissel Bray

Daysland Health Centre, PO Box 27, Daysland AB T0B 1A0 – 403/374-3746; Fax: 403/374-2111 – 16 acute care beds – East Central RHA 7 – Health Care Coord., Mariann Wolbeck

Devon General Hospital, 101 Erie St. South, PO Box 438, Devon AB T0C 1E0 – 403/987-3376; Fax: 403/987-4614 – 10 beds – WestView RHA – Area Team Leader, Joy Myskin

Didsbury District Health Services, PO Box 130, Didsbury AB T0M 0W0 – 403/335-9393; Fax: 403/335-4816 – 20 acute care beds, 100 continuing care beds – RHA 5 – Dir. of Health Servs., Dennis Stabbler

Drayton Valley Health Centre, 4550 Madsen Ave., Drayton Valley AB T0E 0M0 – 403/621-4841; Fax: 403/621-4966 – 100 beds – Crossroads RHA – Site Coord., Wendy Schneider

Drumheller District Health Services, PO Box 4500, Drumheller AB T0J 0Y0 – 403/823-6500; Fax: 403/823-5076 – 56 acute care beds, 110 continuing care beds – RHA 5 – Dir. of Health Servs., Heather McKee

Edmonton: Children's Health Centre of Northern Alberta, #4100, Education & Development Centre, 8308 - 114th St., Edmonton AB T6G 2V2 – 403/492-9997; Fax: 403/492-3535 – 225 beds – Pres., Brian C. Lemon

Edmonton: Grey Nuns Community Health Centre, 1100 Youville Dr. West, Edmonton AB T6L 5X8 – 403/450-7000; Fax: 403/450-7500; EMail: sfynn@caritas.ab.ca – 152 beds – Capital Health Authority – Site Adm., Beverley Rachwalski

Edmonton: Misericordia Hospital (Caritas Health Group), 16940 - 87 Ave., Edmonton AB T5R 4H5 – 403/484-8811; Fax: 403/930-5774 – 159 beds – Capital Health Authority – Site Coord., Ellen Pekeles

Edmonton: Royal Alexandra Hospital, 10240 Kingsway Ave., Edmonton AB T5H 3V9 – 403/477-4111; Fax: 403/477-4777 – 520 beds, 52 bassinets – Capital Health Authority – Senior Operating Officer, Leslee Thompson

Edmonton: Walter C. Mackenzie Health Sciences Centre, 8440 - 112 St., Edmonton AB T6G 2B7 – 403/492-8822; Fax: 403/492-4990 – 568 beds – Capital Health Authority – Dir., Human Resources, Wayne Strudwick

Edson & District Health Care Centre & Nursing Home, 4716 - 5 Ave., Edson AB T7E 1S8 – 403/723-3331; Fax: 403/723-7787 – 120 beds – WestView RHA – Area Team Leader, Laurel Becker

Elk Point General & Auxiliary Hospital & Nursing Home, PO Box 3, Elk Point AB T0A 1A0 – 403/724-3847; Fax: 403/724-3085 – Adm., C.J. Johnson

Empress Health Centre, PO Box 159, Empress AB T0J 1E0 – 403/565-3777; Fax: 403/565-3002 – 11eds – Palliser Health Authority – Area Unit Mgr., Lynne Baisley

Fairview Health Complex, PO Box 2201, Fairview AB T0H 1L0 – 403/835-6100; Fax: 403/835-5789 – 100 beds – Site Coord., Lisa Weston

Fort Macleod Health Care Centre, 744 - 26 St., PO Box 520, Fort Macleod AB T0L 0Z0 – 403/553-4487; Fax: 403/553-4567 – 12 acute care beds – Chinook Health Region – Adm., William Ayotte

Fort McMurray: Northern Lights Regional Health Centre, 7 Hospital St., Fort McMurray AB T9H 1P2 – 403/791-6161; Fax: 403/791-6042 – 105 beds – Pres., Donald M. Ford

Fort Saskatchewan General Hospital, 9430 - 95 St., Fort Saskatchewan AB T8L 1R8 – 403/998-2256; Fax: 403/992-1532 – 30 beds – Lakeland RHA – Coord., Mary Ann Iatz

Fort Vermilion: St. Theresa General Hospital, PO Box 128, Fort Vermilion AB T0H 1N0 – 403/927-3761; Fax: 403/927-4271 – 39 beds – Northwestern Health Services Region – Assistant Exec. Dir., Bill Dainard

Fox Creek Healthcare Centre, 600 - 3 St., PO Box 990, Fox Creek AB T0H 1P0 – 403/622-3545; Fax: 403/622-3474 – 4 beds – Aspen RHA #11 – Site Suprv., Carrie Howe

Glendon Municipal Hospital, PO Box 570, Glendon AB T0A 1P0 – 403/635-3861; Fax: 403/635-4213 – Adm., Donald E. Cole

Grande Cache General Hospital, PO Box 629, Grande Cache AB T0E 0Y0 – 403/827-3701; Fax: 403/827-2859 – 15 beds – Mistahia RHA – Site Coord., Julie Wakefield

Grande Prairie: Queen Elizabeth II Hospital, Auxiliary Hospital & Nursing Home, 10409 - 98 St., Grande Prairie AB T8V 2E8 – 403/538-7100; Fax: 403/538-7501 – 267 beds – Pres., Kenneth J. Fox

Grimshaw/Berwyn & District Hospital, PO Box 648, Grimshaw AB T0H 1W0 – 403/332-1155; Fax: 403/332-1177 – 15 beds – Mistahia RHA – Site Coord., Sharon Thurston

Hanna District Health Services, PO Box 730, Hanna AB T0J 1P0 – 403/854-3331; Fax: 403/854-3253 – 25 acute care beds, 65 continuing care beds – RHA 5 – Dir. of Health Servs., Stan Faupel

Hardisty Health Centre, PO Box 269, Hardisty AB T0B 1V0 – 403/888-3742; Fax: 403/888-2427 – 5 acute care, 15 continuing care beds – East Central RHA 7 – Health Care Coord., Sissel Bray

High Level General Hospital, PO Box 400, High Level AB T0H 1Z0 – 403/926-3791; Fax: 403/926-2944 – 25 beds – Northwestern Health Services Region – Adm., Bill Dainard

High Prairie Health Complex, PO Box 1, High Prairie AB T0G 1E0 – 403/523-3341; Fax: 403/523-3888 – 25 beds – Keeweetinok Lakes RHA #15 – Team Mgr. Institutional Servs., David Allen

High River Hospital & Nursing Home, 560 - 9th Ave. West, High River AB T1V 1B3 – 403/652-2222; Fax: 403/652-0199 – Headwaters Health Authority – Site Suprv., Emily Brookwell

Hinton General Hospital, 1280 Switzer Dr., Hinton AB T7V 1V2 – 403/865-3333; Fax: 403/865-1099 – 17 beds – WestView RHA – Area Team Leader, Donna Grier

Innisfail Health Care Centre, 5023 - 42nd St., Innisfail AB T4G 1A9 – 403/227-3381; Fax: 403/227-4160 – 20 acute care, 80 continuing care beds – David Thompson Health Region – Vice-Pres., South, Candace Spurrell

Jasper: Seton Hospital Jasper, 518 Robson St., PO Box 310, Jasper AB T0E 1E0 – 403/852-3344; Fax: 403/852-3413 – 33 beds – WestView RHA – Area Team Leader, Donna Grier

Lac La Biche: William J. Cadzow Hospital & Auxiliary Centre, PO Box 507, Lac La Biche AB T0A 2C0 – 403/623-4404; Fax: 403/623-4404 – Exec. Dir., Andre Remillard

Lacombe Hospital, 5430 - 47 Ave., Lacombe AB T4L 1G8 – 403/782-3336; Fax: 403/782-2818 – 95 beds – David Thompson Health Region – Vice-Pres., North, Lou Davidson

Lamont Health Care Centre - General & Extended Care, 5216 - 53 St., Lamont AB T0B 2R0 – 403/895-2279; Fax: 403/895-7305 – Exec. Dir., Harold James

Leduc Health Centre, 4210 - 48 St., Leduc AB T9E 5Z3 – 403/986-7711; Fax: 403/980-4490 – 74 beds – Crossroads RHA – Site Coord., Lynda Callioux

Lethbridge Regional Hospital, 960 - 19 St. South, Lethbridge AB T1J 1W5 – 403/382-6009; Fax: 403/382-6011 – 231 beds – Chinook Health Region

Manning General Hospital, PO Box 1250, Manning AB T0H 2M0 – 403/836-3391; Fax: 403/836-3410 – 12 beds – Peace RHA – Acting Adm., Joyce Halliday

Mannville Health Centre, PO Box 1000, Mannville AB T0B 2W0 – 403/763-3621; Fax: 403/763-3678 – 6 acute care, 20 continuing care beds – East Central RHA 7 – Health Care Coord., Jan Scott

Mayerthorpe Healthcare Centre, 4417 - 45 St., PO Box 30, Mayerthorpe AB T0E 1N0 – 403/786-2261, 2645; Fax: 403/786-2023 – 30 beds – Aspen RHA #11 – Site Suprv., Heather Thompson

McLennan Sacred Heart Community Health Centre, PO Box 2000, McLennan AB T0H 2L0 – 403/324-3730; Fax: 403/324-2267 – Peace RHA – Adm., Brian Hrab

Medicine Hat Regional Hospital, 666 - 5 St. SW, Medicine Hat AB T1A 4H6 – 403/529-8000; Fax: 403/529-8949 – Exec. Dir., T.A. Seaman

Milk River: Border Counties General Hospital, 517 Centre Ave. East, PO Box 90, Milk River AB T0K 1M0 – 403/647-3500; Fax: 403/647-2197 – 8 acute care, 21 continuing care beds – Chinook Health Region – Unit Mgr., Lorraine Dobrocane

Mundare Mary Immaculate Hospital & Auxiliary Hospital, PO Box 349, Mundare AB T0B 3H0 – 403/764-3730; Fax: 403/764-3039 – Exec. Dir., Sister Eugenia Stefaniuk

Myrnam Municipal Hospital, PO Box 220, Myrnam AB T0B 3K0 – 403/366-3870; Fax: 403/366-3919 – Adm., Ali Akbar Ali

Olds General Hospital, 3901 - 57th Ave., Olds AB T4H 1T4 – 403/556-3381; Fax: 403/556-2199 – 31 acute care, 50 continuing care beds – David Thompson Health Region – Vice-Pres., South, Candace Spurrell

Oyen Big Country Hospital & Auxiliary Hospital, PO Box 150, Oyen AB T0J 2J0 – 403/664-3526; Fax: 403/664-2074 – Adm., Pius Sauverwald

Peace River Community Health Centre, PO Box 400, Peace River AB T8S 1T6 – 403/624-7500; Fax: 403/624-9667 – Peace RHA – Acting Adm. & Dir. of Patient Care, Grace Williams

Picture Butte Municipal Hospital, 301 Cowan Ave., PO Box 430, Picture Butte AB T0K 1V0 – 403/732-4611; Fax: 403/732-5567 – 14 continuing care beds – Chinook Health Region – Institutional Coord., Bill Ayotte

Pincher Creek Municipal Hospital, 1222 Mill Ave., PO Box 968, Pincher Creek AB T0K 1W0 – 403/627-3333; Fax: 403/627-5275 – 16 acute care, 25 continuing care beds – Chinook Health Region – Adm., V. Specht

Ponoka General Hospital, 5800 - 57th Ave., Ponoka AB T4J 1P1 – 403/783-3341; Fax: 403/783-6907 – 30 acute care, 30 continuing care beds – David Thompson Health Region – Vice-Pres., North, Lou Davidson

Provost Health Centre, PO Box 270, Provost AB T0B 3S0 – 403/753-2291; Fax: 403/753-6132 – 15 acute care, 33 continuing care beds – East Central RHA 7 – Health Care Coord., Val Sorby

Raymond General Hospital, PO Box 599, Raymond AB T0K 2S0 – 403/752-4561; Fax: 403/752-3554 – 12 acute care, 35 continuing care beds – Chinook Health Region – Adm., F. Bruce Romeike

Red Deer Regional Hospital Centre, 3942 - 50A Ave., PO Box 5030, Red Deer AB T4N 4E7 – 403/343-4422; Fax: 403/343-4433 – 242 beds – David Thompson Health Region – Vice-Pres., Central, Gord Birbeck

Redwater General Hospital, PO Box 39, Redwater AB T0A 2W0 – 403/942-3932; Fax: 403/942-2373 – 109 beds – Lakeland RHA – Coord., Betty Kolewaski

Rimbey & District Health Care Centre, 5228 - 50 Ave., PO Box 440, Rimbey AB T0C 2J0 – 403/843-2271; Fax: 403/843-2506 – 15 acute care, 85 continuing care beds – David Thompson Health Region – Vice-Pres., West, Bryan Judd

Rocky Mountain House General Hospital, 5016 - 52 Ave., Rocky Mountain House AB T0M 1T3 – 403/845-3347; Fax: 403/845-7030 – 31 acute care, 30 continuing care beds – David Thompson Health Region – Vice-Pres., West, Bryan Judd

St. Albert: Sturgeon Community Health Centre, 201 Boudreau Rd., St. Albert AB T8N 6C4 – 403/460-6200; Fax: 403/460-6262 – 74 beds – Capital Health Authority – Community Health Network Adm., Wendy Hill

St. Paul: Ste. Therese Health Centre, 4713 - 48 Ave., St. Paul AB T0A 3A3 – 403/645-3331; Fax: 403/645-1809 – 70 beds – Lakeland RHA – Exec. Dir., Kevin Bestby

Slave Lake Hospital, 309 - 6 St. NE, Slave Lake AB T0G 2A2 – 403/849-3732; Fax: 403/849-5141 – 25 beds – Keeweetinok Lakes RHA #15 – Team Mgr., Institutional Services, Andrea Taylor

Smoky Lake: George McDougall Memorial Hospital, PO Box 340, Smoky Lake AB T0A 3C0 – 403/656-3034; Fax: 403/656-3010 – 48 beds – Adm., Grace Regnier

Spirit River: Central Peace General Hospital, PO Box 339, Spirit River AB T0H 3G0 – 403/864-3993; Fax: 403/864-3495 – 16 beds – Mistahia RHA – Site Coord., Karen Osborne

Stettler Health Centre, PO Box 500, Stettler AB T0C 2L0 – 403/742-7400; Fax: 403/742-1244 – 25 acute care, 90 continuing care beds – East Central RHA 7 – Health Care Coord., Marie Owen

Stony Plain Municipal Hospital, 4800 - 55 Ave., PO Box 5001, Stony Plain AB T7Z 1P9 – 403/963-2241; Fax: 403/963-7192 – 10 beds – WestView RHA – Area Team Leader, Myrene Couves

Strathmore District Health Services, 200 Brent Blvd., Strathmore AB T1P 1J9 – 403/934-4204; Fax: 403/934-3948 – 24 acute care beds, 23 continuing care beds – RHA 5 – Dir. of Health Servs., Reginald McRae

Sundre General Hospital, 709 - 1 St. NE, PO Box 3, Sundre AB T0M 1X0 – 403/638-3033; Fax: 403/638-4971 – 13 acute care, 15 continuing care beds – David Thompson Health Region – Vice-Pres., South, Candace Spurrell

Swan Hills Healthcare Centre, 29 Freeman Dr., PO Box 266, Swan Hills AB T0G 2C0 – 403/333-7000, 429-7062; Fax: 403/333-7009 – 4 beds – Aspen RHA #11 – Site Suprv., Karen Bouman

Taber & District Health Care Complex, 4326 - 50 Ave., PO Box 939, Taber AB T0K 2G0 – 403/223-4461; Fax: 403/223-1703 – 25 acute care, 70 continuing care beds – Chinook Health Region – Adm., Bob Stratychuk

Three Hills District Health Services, PO Box 340, Three Hills AB T0M 2A0 – 403/443-2444; Fax: 403/443-5565; EMail: hospadmin@kneehill.com – 19 acute care beds, 23 continuing care beds – RHA 5 – Dir. of Health Servs., Brian Sather

Tofield Health Centre, PO Box 300, Tofield AB T0B 4J0 – 403/662-3263; Fax: 403/662-3835 – 16 acute care, 50 continuing care beds – East Central RHA 7 – Health Care Coord., Betty Perras

Trochu-St. Mary's Health Care Centre, 451 DeChauney Ave., PO Box 100, Trochu AB T0M 2C0 – 403/442-3955; Fax: 403/442-3945 – 25 continuing care beds – David Thompson Health Region – Adm., Peter Verhesen

Two Hills Health Care Centre & Nursing Home, PO Box 160, Two Hills AB T0B 4K0 – 403/657-3344; Fax: 403/657-2508 – Exec. Dir., Ron Bexson

Valleyview Health Complex, PO Box 358, Valleyview AB T0H 3N0 – 403/524-3356; Fax: 403/524-4462 – 30 beds – Site Coord., Ann Polard

Vegreville: St. Joseph's General Hospital, PO Box 490, Vegreville AB T9C 1R5 – 403/632-2811; Fax: 403/632-6177 – 30 beds – Lakeland RHA – Adm., Eugene Rudyk

Vermilion Health Centre, PO Box 1050, Vermilion AB T0B 4M0 – 403/853-5305; Fax: 403/853-4786 – 25 cute care, 65 continuing care beds – East Central RHA 7 – Health Care Coord., Jan Scott

Viking Health Centre, PO Box 60, Viking AB T0B 4N0 – 403/336-4786; Fax: 403/336-4983 – 16 acute care beds – East Central RHA 7 – Health Care Coord., Kathryn Miskew

Vilna: Our Lady's Health Centre, PO Box 160, Vilna AB T0A 3L0 – 403/636-3599; Fax: 403/636-3633 – 8 beds – Lakeland RHA – Maintenance Suprv., John Romaniuk

Wabasca/Desmarais General Hospital, PO Box 450, Wabasca AB T0G 2K0 – 403/891-3007; Fax: 403/891-3784 – 10 beds – Keeweetinok Lakes RHA #15 – Team Mgr., Health Services, Linda Shea

Wainwright Health Centre, 530 - 6 Ave., Wainwright AB T9W 1R6 – 403/842-3324; Fax: 403/842-2884 – 20 acute care, 68 continuing care beds – East Central RHA 7 – Health Care Coord., Cheryl Huxley

Westlock Health Care Centre, 10220 - 93rd St., PO Box 1590, Westlock AB T0G 2L0 – 403/349-3301, 423-2238; Fax: 403/349-6973 – 22 beds – Aspen RHA #11 – Site Suprv., Joyce Nadeau

Wetaskiwin Health Centre, 6910 - 47 St., Wetaskiwin AB T9A 3N3 – 403/361-7100; Fax: 403/361-4107 – Crossroads RHA – Site Coord., Bruce Finkel

Whitecourt Healthcare Centre, 20 Sunset Blvd., Whitecourt AB T7S 1M8 – 403/778-2285, 424-7856; Fax: 403/778-5161 – 24 beds – Aspen RHA #11 – Site Suprv., Wilf Pruden

Willingdon: Mary Immaculate Hospital, PO Box 179, Willingdon AB T0B 4R0 – 403/367-2288; Fax: 403/367-2733 – Exec. Dir., Sr. Eugenia Stefaniuk

AUXILIARY HOSPITALS/HEALTH CARE CENTRES

Athabasca Healthcare Centre, *see* General Hospitals listings

Banff Mineral Springs Hospital, *see* General Hospitals listings

Barrhead Healthcare Centre, *see* General Hospitals listings

Bashaw Community Health Centre, 5308 - 53 St., PO Box 449, Bashaw AB T0B 0H0 – 403/372-3731; Fax: 403/372-4050 – 29 beds – David Thompson Health Region – Vice-Pres., North, Lou Davidson

Beaverlodge Municipal Hospital, *see* General Hospitals listings

Bentley Care Centre, 4834 - 52 Ave., PO Box 30, Bentley AB T0C 0J0 – 403/748-4115; Fax: 403/748-2727 – 16 beds – David Thompson Health Region – Vice-Pres., West, Bryan Judd

Black Diamond: Oilfields General Hospital, *see* General Hospitals listings

Blairmore: Crowsnest Pass Health Care Centre, *see* General Hospitals listings

Bonnyville Health Centre & Auxiliary Centre, *see* General Hospitals listings

Bow Island Health Centre & Auxiliary Hospital, *see* General Hospitals listings

Brooks General & Auxiliary Hospital & Nursing Home, *see* General Hospitals listings

Calgary: Bethany Care Centre, 916 - 18A St. NW, Calgary AB T3A 4N2 – 403/284-6014; Fax: 403/284-6085 – 470 beds – Calgary RHA – Adm., Paul Moore

Calgary: Carewest Cross Bow Auxiliary Hospital, 1011 Centre Ave. East, Calgary AB T2E 0A3 – 403/267-2950; Fax: 403/267-2995 – 100 beds – Calgary RHA – Site Leader, Margaret Marlin

Canadian Almanac & Directory 1997

Calgary: Carewest Dr. Vernon Fanning Extended Care Centre, 722 - 16 Ave. NE, Calgary AB T2E 6V7 – 403/276-8551; Fax: 403/230-6902 – 294 beds – Calgary RHA – Site Leader, Joan Gilmore

Calgary: Carewest Glenmore Park Auxiliary Hospital, 6909 - 14 St. SW, Calgary AB T2V 1P6 – 403/258-7650; Fax: 403/258-7676 – 170 beds – Calgary RHA – Site Leader, Iris Neuman

Calgary: Carewest Sarcee Auxiliary Hospital, 3504 - 29 St. SW, Calgary AB T3E 2L3 – 403/686-8100; Fax: 403/686-8104 – 175 beds – Calgary RHA – Site Leader, Jim Townend

Calgary: Foothills Provincial Hospital, see General Hospitals listings

Calgary: Rockyview General Hospital, 7007 - 14th St. SW, Calgary AB T2V 1P9 – 403/541-3000; Fax: 403/541-3434 – 427 beds – Calgary RHA – Adm., Jeanette Pick

Camrose: Rosehaven Care Center (The Bethany Group), 4612 - 53 St., Camrose AB T4V 1Y6 – 403/679-3000; Fax: 403/679-3001 – Exec. Dir., John Grant

Canmore Hospital, see General Hospitals listings

Carmangay: Little Bow Auxiliary Hospital, PO Box 160, Carmangay AB T0L 0N0 – 403/643-3522; Fax: 403/643-3554 – Headwaters Health Authority – Site Suprv., Brian Popp

Claresholm: Willow Creek Auxiliary Hospital & Nursing Home, 4251 - 8 St. West, PO Box 700, Claresholm AB T0L 0T0 – 403/625-3361; Fax: 403/625-3822 – Headwaters Health Authority – Site Suprv., Brian Popp

Cold Lake Regional Hospital & Auxiliary Centre, see General Hospitals listings

Coronation Health Centre, PO Box 500, Coronation AB T0C 1C0 – 403/578-3803; Fax: 403/578-3474 – 10 acute care, 23 continuing care beds – East Central RHA 7 – Health Care Coord., Carol Funnell

Didsbury District Health Services, see General Hospitals listings

Drumheller District Health Services, see General Hospitals listings

Eckville Community Health Centre, 5120 - 51 Ave. West, Eckville AB T0M 0X0 – 403/746-2201; Fax: 403/746-2185 – 20 beds – David Thompson Health Region – Adm., Kevin McEntee

Edmonton General Hospital & Continuing Care Centre (Caritas Health Group), 11111 Jasper Ave., Edmonton AB T5K 0L4 – 403/482-8111; Fax: 403/482-8035 – 484 beds – Capital Health Authority – Site Adm., Dr. Edward Papp

Elk Point General & Auxiliary Hospital & Nursing Home, see General Hospitals listings

Elnora Community Health Centre, 425 - 8th Ave., PO Box 659, Elnora AB T0M 0Y0 – 403/773-3636; Fax: 403/773-3949 – David Thompson Health Region

Elnora: Delburne Community Health Centre, 2221 - 20 St., Elnora AB T0M 0V0 – 403/749-3660; Fax: 403/749-2710 – David Thompson Health Region – Adm., Yvonne Hoppins, 403/773-3636

Fairview Health Complex, see General Hospitals listings

Fort McMurray: Northern Lights Regional Health Centre, see General Hospitals listings

Galahad Health Care Centre, PO Box 88, Galahad AB T0B 1R0 – 403/583-3788; Fax: 403/583-2105 – 15 continuing care beds – East Central RHA 7 – Health Care Coord., Sheila Fossey

Grande Prairie: Queen Elizabeth II Hospital, Auxiliary Hospital & Nursing Home, see General Hospitals listings

Hanna District Health Services, see General Hospitals listings

Hardisty Health Centre, see General Hospitals listings

High Prairie Health Complex, see General Hospitals listings

Islay Health Centre, PO Box 55, Islay AB T0B 2J0 – 403/744-3795; Fax: 403/744-3922 – 10 continuing care beds – East Central RHA 7 – Health Care Coord., Audrey Cusack

Killam Health Centre, PO Box 40, Killam AB T0B 2L0 – 403/385-3741; Fax: 403/385-3904 – 5 acute care, 40 continuing care beds – East Central RHA 7 – Exec. Dir., Alice Stafinski

Lac La Biche: William J. Cadzow Hospital & Auxiliary Centre, see General Hospitals listings

Lacombe Community Health Centre, 5010 - 51 St., Lacombe AB T4L 1W2 – 403/782-3218; Fax: 403/782-2866 – 75 continuing care beds – David Thompson Health Region – VP, Community Health Services, Denise McBain

Lamont Auxiliary Hospital, 5216 - 53 St., PO Box 10, Lamont AB T0B 2R0 – 403/895-2236; Fax: 403/895-7305 – Adm., Harold James

Lamont Health Care Centre - General & Extended Care, see General Hospitals listings

Lloydminster: Dr. Cooke Extended Care Centre, PO Box 1007, Lloydminster AB T9V 0Z7 – 403/875-2291; Fax: 403/875-3505 – Adm., Herbert Duczek

Mayerthorpe Healthcare Centre, see General Hospitals listings

McLennan Sacred Heart Community Health Centre, see General Hospitals listings

Medicine Hat Regional Hospital, see General Hospitals listings

Mundare Mary Immaculate Hospital & Auxiliary Hospital, see General Hospitals listings

Oyen Big Country Hospital & Auxiliary Hospital, see General Hospitals listings

Peace River Community Health Centre, see General Hospitals listings

Pincher Creek Municipal Hospital, see General Hospitals listings

Ponoka General Hospital, see General Hospitals listings

Provost Health Centre, see General Hospitals listings

Raymond General Hospital, see General Hospitals listings

Red Deer: Dr. Richard Parsons Auxiliary Hospital, 3929 - 52 Ave., PO Box 5030, Red Deer AB T4N 4J8 – 403/343-4422; Fax: 403/420-1605 – 100 beds – David Thompson Health Region – Pres., Gerry Vanhooren

Rimbey & District Health Care Centre, see General Hospitals listings

Rocky Mountain House Community Health Centre, 4934 - 50 St., PO Box 340, Rocky Mountain House AB T0M 1T0 – 403/845-3030; Fax: 403/845-4975 – 30 continuing care beds – David Thompson Health Region

Rocky Mountain House General Hospital, see General Hospitals listings

St. Paul: Ste. Therese Health Centre, see General Hospitals listings

Smoky Lake: George McDougall Memorial Hospital, see General Hospitals listings

Strathmore District Health Services, see General Hospitals listings

Taber & District Health Care Complex, see General Hospitals listings

Three Hills District Health Services, see General Hospitals listings

Tofield Health Centre, see General Hospitals listings

Trochu-St. Mary's Health Care Centre, see General Hospitals listings

Two Hills Health Care Centre & Nursing Home, see General Hospitals listings

Vermilion Health Centre, see General Hospitals listings

Vulcan Community Health Centre, PO Box 299, Vulcan AB T0L 2B0 – 403/485-3333; Fax: 403/485-2336 – Headwaters Health Authority – Site Suprv., Brian Popp

Wainwright Health Centre, see General Hospitals listings

Westlock Long Term Care Centre, 9732 - 100 Ave., PO Box 1100, Westlock AB T0G 2L0 – 403/349-3306; Fax: 403/429-3502 – 102 beds – Aspen RHA #11 – Site Suprv., Mona Theriault

FEDERAL HOSPITALS

Calgary: Colonel Belcher Auxiliary Hospital, 1213 - 4 St. SW, Calgary AB T2R 0X7 – 403/541-3600; Fax: 403/541-3686 – 135 beds – Calgary RHA – Site Mgr., Ruth Cox

Cardston: Blood Indian Hospital, PO Box 490, Cardston AB T0K 0K0 – 403/653-3351; Fax: 403/653-4824 – Head Adm., Dr. Charles Weasel

Medley: Canadian Forces Base Medical Squadron, Four Wing Cold Lake, General Delivery, Medley AB T0A 2M0 – 403/840-8000, ext.8749

HOME CARE OFFICES/COMMUNITY CARE SERVICES

Athabasca Health Services, 3401 - 48 Ave., Athabasca AB T9S 1M7 – 403/675-2231; Fax: 403/675-3111 – Aspen RHA #11

Banff National Park Health Unit Office, PO Box 1266, Banff AB T0L 0C0 – 403/762-2990; Fax: 403/762-5570 – Headwaters Health Authority – Pat Brooks

Barrhead Health Services, PO Box 4131, Barrhead AB T7N 1A1 – 403/674-3408; Fax: 403/674-3941 – Aspen RHA #11

Beaumont Health Unit, 5005 - 50 Ave., Beaumont AB T4X 1E7 – 403/929-4822; Fax: 403/929-4828 – Crossroads RHA

Beaverlodge/Hythe District Home Care Office, 412 - 10A St., Beaverlodge AB T0H 0C0 – 403/354-2647; Fax: 403/354-1550

Black Diamond Health Unit, 128 Centre Ave. NW, PO Box 758, Black Diamond AB T0L 0H0 – 403/933-4335; Fax: 403/933-2031 – Headwaters Health Authority – Janet Melbourne, 403/652-0139

Blairmore Community & Wellness Site, 12501 - 20 Ave., PO Box 67, Blairmore AB T0K 0E0 – 403/562-7378; Fax: 403/562-7379 – Chinook Health Region

Boyle Health Services, PO Box 201, Boyle AB T0A 0M0 – 403/689-2677; Fax: 403/689-2835 – Aspen RHA #11

Calling Lake Health Services, General Delivery, Calling Lake AB T0G 0K0 – 403/331-3760; Fax: 403/331-2200 – Aspen RHA #11

Canmore Health Unit Office, PO Box 428, Canmore AB T0L 0M0 – 403/678-5656; Fax: 403/678-5068 – Headwaters Health Authority – Elaine Spencer

Cardston Community & Wellness Site, Provincial Bldg., 576 Main St., PO Box 1590, Cardston AB T0K 0K0 – 403/653-4981; Fax: 403/653-4985 – Chinook Health Region

Claresholm Health Unit, 5221 - 2nd St. West, PO Box 1391, Claresholm AB T0L 0T0 – 403/625-4061; Fax: 403/625-4062 – Headwaters Health Authority – Janet Melbourne, 403/652-0139

Coaldale Community & Wellness Site (14th St.), 2004 - 14 St., PO Box 1000, Coaldale AB T1M 1M8 – 403/327-6507, 345-2044 (home care); Fax: 403/345-2195 – Chinook Health Region

Coaldale Community & Wellness Site (18th St.), 2018 - 18 St., PO Box 1000, Coaldale AB T1M 1M8 – 403/327-6507; Fax: 403/345-2043 – Chinook Health Region

Devon Health Unit, 101 Erie St., PO Box 567, Devon AB T0C 1E0 – 403/987-3376; Fax: 403/987-4614 – WestView RHA

Drayton Valley Health Unit, 5136 - 51 Ave., Drayton Valley AB T7A 1R4 – 403/542-4415; Fax: 403/621-4998 – Crossroads RHA

Edmonton: Home Care Administration, #402, 10216 - 124 St., Edmonton AB T5N 4A3 – 403/482-9877; Fax: 403/482-3401 – Capital Health Authority – Dir., Community Care, Jean Kipp

Edmonton: Home Care Northeast Grandin Office, 10050 - 112 St., 7th Fl., Edmonton AB T5K 2J1 – 403/496-1333; Fax: 403/482-5143 – Capital Health Authority – Client Service Mgr., Ann Semotiuk

Edmonton: Home Care Northeast Kingsway Office, #100, 11738 Kingsway Ave., Edmonton AB T5G 0X5 – 403/496-1340; Fax: 403/451-5894 – Capital Health Authority – Client Service Mgr., Carol Sims

Edmonton: Home Care Southeast Office, Grey Nuns Community Health Centre, 1100 Youville Dr. West, 5th Fl., Edmonton AB T6L 5X8 – 403/496-1330; Fax: 403/496-8446 – Capital Health Authority

Edmonton: Home Care Southwest Office, Misericordia Community Health Centre, 16940 - 87 Ave., 8th Fl., Edmonton AB T5K 2J1 – 403/496-8445; Fax: 403/944-4424 – Capital Health Authority

Edson Health Unit, 5028 - 3rd Ave., PO Box 6240, Edson AB T7E 1X4 – 403/723-4421; Fax: 403/723-6299 – WestView RHA

Edson Home Care Office, c/o Edson & District Healthcare Centre, 4716 - 5th Ave., Edson AB T7E 1S8 – 403/723-3331; Fax: 403/723-7787 – WestView RHA

Evansburg/Entwistle Health Unit, 5008 - 49 Ave., PO Box 59, Evansburg AB T0E 0T0 – 403/727-2288; Fax: 403/727-2079 – WestView RHA

Fairview District Home Care Office, 10316 - 109 St., Fairview AB T0H 1L0 – 403/835-4951; Fax: 403/835-3879

Fort Macleod Community & Wellness Site, 521 - 26 St., PO Box 727, Fort Macleod AB T0L 0Z0 – 403/553-4451; Fax: 403/553-2333 – Chinook Health Region

Fort Vermilion Community Health Services, PO Box 68, Fort Vermilion AB T0H 1N0 – 403/927-3391; Fax: 403/927-4440 – Adm., Jenny Radsma

Fox Creek Health Services, PO Box 430, Fox Creek AB T0H 1P0 – 403/622-3730; Fax: 403/622-4169 – Aspen RHA #11

Grande Cache District Home Care Office, Provincial Bldg., Grande Cache AB T0E 0Y0 – 403/827-3504; Fax: 403/827-2406

Grande Prairie: South Peace Health Unit, 10320 - 99 St., Grande Prairie AB T8V 6J4 – 403/532-4441; Fax: 403/532-1550

Gunn Health Services, c/o Lakeview Manor, General Delivery, Gunn AB T0E 1A0 – 403/967-4440; Fax: 403/967-4433 – Aspen RHA #11

High Level Community Health Services, PO Box 2000, High Level AB T0H 1Z0 – 403/926-7000; Fax: 403/926-7001 – Adm., D. Hampel

High Level: La Crete Community Health Services, PO Box 400, High Level AB T0H 1Z0 – 403/928-3242; Fax: 403/928-3080 – Adm., Jenny Radsma

High Level: Paddle Prairie Community Health Services, c/o High Level Community Health Services, PO Box 2000, High Level AB T0H 1Z0 – 403/981-2188; Fax: 403/981-2190 – Adm., Jenny Radsma

High Level: Rainbow Lake Community Health Services, PO Box 400, High Level AB T0H 1Z0 – 403/956-3646; Fax: 403/926-3338 – Adm., Jenny Radsma

High Prairie: Keeweetinok Lakes Community Health Services, PO Box 33, High Prairie AB T0G 1E0 – 403/523-4434; Fax: 403/523-5946 – Keeweetinok Lakes RHA #15 – Team Mgr. Health Servs., Valerie Beynon

High River: Foothills Health Unit, 310 MacLeod Trail, PO Box 5638, High River AB T1V 1M7 – 403/652-3297; Fax: 403/652-2537 – Headwaters Health Authority – Lori Anderson, 403/652-0142

Hinton Health Unit, 1280A Switzer Dr., Hinton AB T7V 1T5 – 403/865-2277; Fax: 403/865-3727 – WestView RHA

Innisfail Community Health Centre, 4904 - 50 St., PO Box 6094, Innisfail AB T0M 1A0 – 403/227-3636; Fax: 403/227-4170 – David Thompson Health Region – VP, Community Health Services, Denise McBain

Jasper Health Unit, PO Box 1740, Jasper AB T0E 1E0 – 403/852-4759; Fax: 403/852-4752 – WestView RHA

Kinuso Community Health Services, General Delivery, Kinuso AB T0G 1K0 – 403/775-3501; Fax: 403/775-3955 – Team Mgr., Gail Robertson

Leduc Health Unit, 5007 - 49 Ave., Leduc AB T9E 6M6 – 403/980-4644; Fax: 403/980-4666 – Crossroads RHA

Lethbridge Community & Wellness Site (2nd Ave. Office), c/o Lethbridge Train Stn. Office, 801 - 1st Ave. South, Lethbridge AB T1J 4L5 – 403/327-3827; Fax: 403/327-8494 – Chinook Health Region

Lethbridge Community & Wellness Site (Train Stn.), 801 - 1st Ave. South, Lethbridge AB T1J 4L5 – 403/327-2166; Fax: 403/328-5934 – Chinook Health Region

Magrath Community & Wellness Site, 135 West Civic Ave., PO Box 126, Magrath AB T0K 1J0 – 403/758-3331; Fax: 403/758-3332 – Chinook Health Region

Mayerthorpe Health Services, General Delivery, Mayerthorpe AB T0E 1N0 – 403/786-4198; Fax: 403/786-2383 – Aspen RHA #11

Morinville Health Services, #103, 10008 - 107 St., Morinville AB T8R 1L3 – 403/939-3699; Fax: 403/939-7126, 1216 – Aspen RHA #11

Nanton Health Unit, 2214 - 20 St., PO Box 812, Nanton AB T0L 1R0 – 403/646-2277; Fax: 403/646-3046 – Headwaters Health Authority – Lori Anderson, 403/652-0142

Okotoks Health Unit, 22 Elizabeth St., PO Box 758, Okotoks AB T0L 1T3 – 403/938-4911; Fax: 403/938-2783 – Headwaters Health Authority – Janet Melbourne, 403/652-0139

Olds Community Health Centre, 5030 - 50 St., PO Box 459, Olds AB T0M 1P0 – 403/556-8441; Fax: 403/556-6842 – David Thompson Health Region – VP, Community Health Services, Denise McBain

Picture Butte Community & Wellness Site, 301 Cowan Ave., PO Box 652, Picture Butte AB T0K 1V0 – 403/732-4762, 732-4020 (home care); Fax: 403/732-5062 – Chinook Health Region

Pincher Creek Community & Wellness Site, 782 Main St., PO Box 1685, Pincher Creek AB T0K 1W0 – 403/627-3266; Fax: 403/627-2771 – Chinook Health Region

Raymond Community & Wellness Site, 200 N. - 2nd Ave. West, PO Box 251, Raymond AB T0K 2S0 – 403/752-3303; Fax: 403/752-4655 – Chinook Health Region

Red Deer Community Health Centre, 2845 Bremner Ave., Red Deer AB T4R 1S2 – 403/341-2100; Fax: 403/341-2196 – David Thompson Health Region

Rimbey Community Health Centre, 4709 - 51 Ave., PO Box 464, Rimbey AB T0C 2J0 – 403/843-2288; Fax: 403/843-3050 – David Thompson Health Region

St. Albert: Home Care Northwest Office, Sturgeon Community Health Centre, Unit 17, 201 Boudreau Rd., St. Albert AB T8N 6C4 – 403/460-4731; Fax: 403/460-2829 – Client Service Mgr., Alice Sears

Sherwood Park: Home Care Strathcona Office, 2 Brower Dr., Sherwood Park AB T8H 1V4 – 403/467-5549; Fax: 403/449-1476 – Capital Health Authority

Slave Lake: Keeweetinok Lakes Community Health Services, 405 - 6 Ave. SW, Slave Lake AB T0G 2A4 – 403/849-3947; Fax: 403/849-3083 – Keeweetinok Lakes RHA #15 – Team Mgr., Gail Robertson

Smith Health Services, PO Box 68, Smith AB T0G 2B0 – 403/829-3758; Fax: 403/829-3830 – Aspen RHA #11

Smith: Flatbush Health Services, PO Box 68, Smith AB T0G 2B0 – 403/681-3980; Fax: 403/681-3940 – Aspen RHA #11

Spirit River District Home Care Office, PO Box 187, Spirit River AB T0H 3G0 – 403/864-3063; Fax: 403/864-4187

Spruce Grove Health Unit, 315 Jespersen Ave., PO Box 4323, Spruce Grove AB T7X 1B5 – 403/962-4072; Fax: 403/962-4994 – WestView RHA

Stony Plain Health Unit, 4905 - 47 Ave., Stony Plain AB T7Z 1S3 – 403/963-8000; Fax: 403/963-7612 – WestView RHA

Stony Plain Home Care Office, #203, 4709 - 44 Ave., Stony Plain AB T7Z 1N4 – 403/963-3366; Fax: 403/963-9267 – WestView RHA – Dir., Judy Tait

Sundre Community Health Centre, 212 - 6th Ave., PO Box 101, Sundre AB T0M 1X0 – 403/638-4063; Fax: 403/638-4460 – David Thompson Health Region

Swan Hills Health Services, PO Box 261, Swan Hills AB T0G 2C0 – 403/333-7077; Fax: 403/333-7009 – Aspen RHA #11

Sylvan Lake Community Health Centre, Lakeview Heights Mall, #4, One Sylvan Dr., Sylvan Lake AB T0M 1Z0 – 403/887-2241; Fax: 403/887-2610 – David Thompson Health Region

Taber Community & Wellness Site, 5009 - 56 St., Taber AB T1G 1M8 – 403/223-4403; Fax: 403/223-8733 – Chinook Health Region

Taber: Vauxhall Community & Wellness Site, c/o Taber Community & Wellness Site, 5009 - 56 St., Taber AB T1G 1M8 – 403/654-2232, 654-2151 (home care); Fax: 403/654-2134 – Chinook Health Region

Thorsby Health Unit, 4825 Hankin St., Thorsby AB T0C 2P0 – 403/789-4800; Fax: 403/789-4811 – Crossroads RHA

Three Hills: Trochu/Torrington Community Health Centre, PO Box 340, Three Hills AB T0M 2A0 – 403/443-5355; Fax: 403/443-2207

Valleyview District Home Care Office, 5112 - 50 Ave., PO Box 756, Valleyview AB T0H 3N0 – 403/524-3338; Fax: 403/524-3153

Vulcan Health Unit, Vulcan Community Health Centre, PO Box 214, Vulcan AB T0L 2B0 – 403/485-2285; Fax: 403/485-2639 – Headwaters Health Authority – Lori Anderson, 403/652-0142

Wabasca: Keeweetinok Lakes Community Health Services, PO Box 9, Wabasca AB T0G 2K0 – 403/891-3931; Fax: 403/891-3011 – Keeweetinok Lakes RHA #15 – Team Mgr., Linda Shea

Warner Community & Wellness Site, 300 County Rd., PO Box 8, Warner AB T0K 2L0 – 403/642-3737, 327-5578; Fax: 403/642-3944 – Chinook Health Region

Westlock Health Services, PO Box 274, Westlock AB T0G 2L0 – 403/349-3316; Fax: 403/349-5725 – Aspen RHA #11

Wetaskiwin Health Unit, 5610 - 40 Ave., Wetaskiwin AB T9A 3E4 – 403/361-4333; Fax: 403/361-4335 – Crossroads RHA

Whitecourt Health Services, 163 Provincial Bldg., Whitecourt AB T7S 1N2 – 403/778-5555, 5558; Fax: 403/778-3852 – Aspen RHA #11

Winfield Health Unit, PO Box 114, Winfield AB T0C 2X0 – 403/682-4755; Fax: 403/682-4750 – Crossroads RHA

MENTAL HEALTH HOSPITALS & COMMUNITY FACILITIES

Airdrie Mental Health Clinic, PO Box 5205, Airdrie AB T4B 2B3 – 403/948-3878 – Provincial Mental Health Advisory Board

Athabasca Mental Health Clinic, #130, 4903 - 50 St., Athabasca AB T9S 1E2 – 403/675-5404; Fax: 403/675-3994 – Provincial Mental Health Advisory Board

Barrhead Mental Health Clinic, 6203 - 49 St., Barrhead AB T0G 0E0 – 403/674-8243; Fax: 403/674-8352 – Provincial Mental Health Advisory Board

Blairmore Mental Health Clinic, PO Box 870, Blairmore AB T0K 0E0 – 403/562-8010; Fax: 403/562-2033 – Provincial Mental Health Advisory Board

Bonnyville Mental Health Clinic, PO Box 6917, Bonnyville AB T9N 2H1 – 403/826-2404; Fax: 403/

826-6114 – Provincial Mental Health Advisory Board

Brooks Mental Health Clinic, PO Box 2198, Brooks AB T1R 1C5 – 403/362-1252; Fax: 403/362-1223 – Provincial Mental Health Advisory Board

Calgary: Central Calgary Community Mental Health Clinic, #200, 1000 - 8th Ave. SW, Calgary AB T2P 3M7 – 403/297-7311; Fax: 403/297-5354 – Provincial Mental Health Advisory Board

Calgary: East Calgary Community Mental Health Clinic, #130, 920 - 36 St. NE, Calgary AB T2A 6L8 – 403/297-7196; Fax: 403/297-7160 – Provincial Mental Health Advisory Board

Calgary: Northwest Calgary Community Mental Health Clinic, #280, 1620 - 29th St. NW, Calgary AB T2N 4L7 – 403/297-7345; Fax: 403/297-4543 – Provincial Mental Health Advisory Board

Camrose Mental Health Clinic, Aspen Business Park, 4911A - 47 St., Camrose AB T4V 1J9 – 403/679-1241; Fax: 403/679-1740 – Provincial Mental Health Advisory Board

Canmore Mental Health Clinic, 800 Access Rd., PO Box 1029, Canmore AB T0L 0M0 – 403/678-4696; Fax: 403/678-1951 – Joseph Greene

Claresholm Mental Health Clinic, PO Box 2198, Claresholm AB T0L 1T0 – 403/625-1495; Fax: 403/625-4177 – 120 beds – Provincial Mental Health Advisory Board – Chief Operating Officer, Don Ehman

Claresholm/Raymond Care Centre, PO Box 490, Claresholm AB T0L 0T0 – 403/625-8585; Fax: 403/625-4318 – 18 beds – Provincial Mental Health Advisory Board – CEO, Lori Kilbank

Cochrane Mental Health Clinic, PO Box 807, Cochrane AB T0L 0W0 – 403/932-3455; Fax: 403/932-2971 – Provincial Mental Health Advisory Board

Didsbury Mental Health Clinic, c/o Victoria Square Mall, 1210 -20 Ave., Didsbury AB T0M 0W0 – 403/335-7285; Fax: 403/335-7227 – Provincial Mental Health Advisory Board

Drayton Valley Mental Health Clinic, PO Box 7276, Drayton Valley AB T0E 0M0 – 403/542-3140; Fax: 403/542-4426 – Provincial Mental Health Advisory Board

Drumheller Mental Health Clinic, PO Box 2086, Drumheller AB T0J 0Y0 – 403/823-1652; Fax: 403/823-1623 – Provincial Mental Health Advisory Board

Edmonton Mental Health Clinic, 108 St. Bldg., 5th Fl., 9942 - 108 St., Edmonton AB T5K 2J5 – 403/427-4444; Fax: 403/427-0424 – Provincial Mental Health Advisory Board

Edmonton: Alberta Hospital Edmonton, 17480 Fort Rd., PO Box 307, Edmonton AB T5J 2J7 – 403/472-5200; Fax: 403/472-5445 – 453 beds – Provincial Mental Health Advisory Board – CEO, Wayne Wright

Edson Mental Health Clinic, #100, Provincial Bldg., 111 - 54 St., Edson AB T7E 1T2 – 403/723-8294; Fax: 403/723-8297 – Provincial Mental Health Advisory Board

Fairview Mental Health Clinic, PO Box 2201, Fairview AB T0H 1L0 – 403/835-6149; Fax: 403/835-5789 – Provincial Mental Health Advisory Board

Fort McMurray Mental Health Clinic, Provincial Bldg., 9th Fl., 9915 Franklin Ave., Fort McMurray AB T9H 2K4 – 403/743-7450; Fax: 403/743-7466 – Provincial Mental Health Advisory Board

Fort Saskatchewan Mental Health Clinic, #301, 9821 - 108 St., Fort Saskatchewan AB T8L 2J2 – 403/998-5225; Fax: 403/998-7828 – Provincial Mental Health Advisory Board

Grande Cache Mental Health Clinic, 702 Pine Plaza, Grande Cache AB T0E 0X0 – 403/827-4998; Fax: 403/827-4787 – Provincial Mental Health Advisory Board

Grande Prairie Mental Health Clinic, #600, 10014 - 99 St., Grande Prairie AB T8V 3N4 – 403/538-5160; Fax: 403/538-6279 – Provincial Mental Health Advisory Board

Hanna Mental Health Clinic, Provincial Bldg., 401 McRae Dr., PO Box 1000, Hanna AB T0J 1P0 – 403/854-5585; Fax: 403/854-5597 – Provincial Mental Health Advisory Board

High River Mental Health Clinic, Andrell Bldg., 2nd Fl., 309 First St. West, High River AB T0L 1B0 – 403/652-8340; Fax: 403/652-1456 – Provincial Mental Health Advisory Board – Donavon Bentz

Hinton Mental Health Clinic, 131 Market St., PO Box 2659, Hinton AB T7V 2A2 – 403/865-8247; Fax: 403/865-8327 – Provincial Mental Health Advisory Board

Innisfail Mental Health Clinic, Provincial Bldg., 4904 - 50 St., Innisfail AB T0M 1A0 – 403/227-4601; Fax: 403/227-5683 – Provincial Mental Health Advisory Board

Lac La Biche Mental Health Clinic, 9503 Beaver Hill Rd., PO Box 3, Lac La Biche AB T0A 2C0 – 403/623-5230; Fax: 403/623-6232 – Provincial Mental Health Advisory Board

Lacombe Mental Health Clinic, Agriculture Financing Serv. Corp., Courier Bag 16, 5033 - 52 St., 2nd Fl., Lacombe AB T4L 2A6 – 403/782-3413; Fax: 403/782-3878 – Provincial Mental Health Advisory Board

Leduc Mental Health Clinic, Leduc General Hospital, NE Annex, 4210 - 48 St., Leduc AB T9E 5Z3 – 403/986-2660; Fax: 403/986-9292 – Provincial Mental Health Advisory Board

Lethbridge Mental Health Clinic, 200 - 5 Ave. South, Lethbridge AB T1J 4C7 – 403/381-5260; Fax: 403/382-4518 – Provincial Mental Health Advisory Board

Lloydminster: Mental Health Services, 4815 - 50 St., Lloydminster AB S9V 0M8 – 306/825-6410; Fax: 306/825-6159 – Provincial Mental Health Advisory Board

Olds Mental Health Clinic, Provinicial Bldg., 2nd Fl., 5025 - 50 St., Olds AB T4H 1R9 – 403/556-4204; Fax: 403/556-4265 – Provincial Mental Health Advisory Board

Peace River Mental Health Clinic, 9715 - 100 St., PO Box 900-B, Peace River AB T8S 1J7 – 403/624-6151; Fax: 403/624-6565 – Provincial Mental Health Advisory Board

Pincher Creek Mental Health Clinic, PO Box 2105, Pincher Creek AB T0K 1W0 – 403/627-1121; Fax: 403/627-3375 – Provincial Mental Health Advisory Board

Ponoka Mental Health Clinic, PO Box 4244, Ponoka AB T4J 1R6 – 403/783-7903; Fax: 403/783-7926 – Provincial Mental Health Advisory Board

Ponoka: Alberta Hospital Ponoka, PO Box 1000, Ponoka AB T4J 1R8 – 403/783-7667; Fax: 403/783-7786 – 329 beds – Provincial Mental Health Advisory Board – CEO, Rick Love

Provost Mental Health Clinic, Provincial Bldg., 5419 - 44 St., Provost AB T0B 3S0 – 403/753-2575; Fax: 403/753-2933 – Provincial Mental Health Advisory Board

Red Deer Mental Health Clinic, #209, 4920 - 51 St., Red Deer AB T4N 6K8 – 403/340-5466; Fax: 403/340-4874 – Provincial Mental Health Advisory Board

Rimbey Mental Health Clinic, Provincial Bldg., 5025 - 55 St., Rimbey AB T0C 2J0 – 403/843-2406 – Provincial Mental Health Advisory Board

Rocky Mountain House Mental Health Clinic, 4919 - 51 St., Rocky Mountain House AB T0M 1T0 – 403/845-2815; Fax: 403/845-2177 – Provincial Mental Health Advisory Board

St. Albert Mental Health Clinic, 30 St. Winston Churchill Ave., St. Albert AB T8N 3A3 – 403/459-2820; Fax: 403/460-7152 – Provincial Mental Health Advisory Board

St. Paul Mental Health Clinic, #202, Provincial Bldg., 5025 - 49 Ave., St. Paul AB T0A 3A0 – 403/645-6307; Fax: 403/645-6293 – Provincial Mental Health Advisory Board

Sherwood Park Mental Health Clinic, Strathcona Place, 340 Sioux Rd., Sherwood Park AB T8A 3X6 – 403/467-6562; Fax: 403/464-3705 – Provincial Mental Health Advisory Board

Slave Lake Mental Health Clinic, 113 - 6 Ave. NW, Slave Lake AB T0G 2A1 – 403/849-7242; Fax: 403/849-7284 – Provincial Mental Health Advisory Board

Stettler Mental Health Clinic, PO Box 600, Stettler AB T0C 2L0 – 403/742-7591; Fax: 403/742-7552 – Provincial Mental Health Advisory Board

Stony Plain Mental Health Clinic, Provincial Bldg., 4709 - 44 Ave., Stony Plain AB T7Z 1N4 – 403/963-6151; Fax: 403/963-7186 – Provincial Mental Health Advisory Board

Strathmore Mental Health Clinic, Hilton Plaza, 209 Third St., Strathmore AB T1P 1K2 – 403/934-5174; Fax: 403/934-2685 – Provincial Mental Health Advisory Board

Taber Mental Health Services Clinic, PO Box 1749, Taber AB T0K 2G0 – 403/223-7932; Fax: 403/223-7902 – Provincial Mental Health Advisory Board

Vegreville Mental Health Clinic, Provincial Bldg., Courier #7, 4809 - 50 St., Vegreville AB T9C 1R1 – 403/632-5449; Fax: 403/632-5496 – Provincial Mental Health Advisory Board

Vermilion Mental Health Clinic, PO Box 1228, Vermilion AB T0B 2M0 – 403/853-8168; Fax: 403/853-8279 – Provincial Mental Health Advisory Board

Wainwright Mental Health Clinic, Provincial Bldg., 810 - 14th Ave., PO Box 20, Wainwright AB T9W 1R2 – 403/842-7522; Fax: 403/842-7533 – Provincial Mental Health Advisory Board

Westlock Mental Health Clinic, PO Box 723, Westlock AB T0G 2L0 – 403/349-5246; Fax: 403/349-5846 – Provincial Mental Health Advisory Board

Wetaskiwin Mental Health Clinic, Dykes Bldg., 2nd Fl., 5108 - 51 Ave., Wetaskiwin AB T9A 0S6 – 403/361-1245; Fax: 403/361-1387 – Provincial Mental Health Advisory Board

Whitecourt Mental Health Clinic, Provincial Bldg., 2nd Fl., 5020 - 52 Ave., Whitecourt AB T0E 2L0 – 403/778-7147; Fax: 403/778-7212 – Provincial Mental Health Advisory Board

NURSING HOMES

Airdrie: Bethany Care Centre - Airdrie, 1736 - 1st Ave. NW, Airdrie AB T4B 2C4 – 403/948-6022; Fax: 403/948-3897 – 74 beds – Calgary RHA – Adm., Peggy Mollerup

Athabasca Extendicare, 4517 - 53 St., PO Box 119, Athabasca AB T0G 0B0 – 403/675-2291; Fax: 403/675-3833 – 50 beds – Aspen RHA #11 – Adm., Dorothy Schiller

Barrhead Healthcare Centre, *see* General Hospitals listings

Barrhead: Keir Care Centre, 5115 - 45 St., PO Box 1330, Barrhead AB T0G 0E0 – 403/674-4506; Fax: 403/674-3003 – 100 beds – Aspen RHA #11 – Site Suprv., Leslie Penny

Beaverlodge Municipal Hospital, *see* General Hospitals listings

Bentley Care Centre, *see* Auxiliary Hospitals/Health Care Centres listings

Blairmore: Crowsnest Pass Health Care Centre, *see* General Hospitals listings

Bonnyville: Extendicare Bonnyville, 4602 - 47 Ave., Bonnyville AB T9N 2E8 – 403/826-3341; Fax: 403/826-4890 – Adm., Donna Densmore

Breton Health Centre, *see* General Hospitals listings

Brooks General & Auxiliary Hospital & Nursing Home, *see* General Hospitals listings

Calgary: Bethany Care Centre, *see* Auxiliary Hospitals/Health Care Centres listings

Calgary: Bethany Care Society, Calgary, 1991 - 17th St. NW, Calgary AB T2N 2E5 – 403/284-0161; Fax: 403/284-1992 – Operates Bethany Care Centres in Airdrie, Cochrane & Calgary – Calgary RHA – Pres. & CEO, R. Greer Black

Calgary: The Beverly Centre Inc., 1729 - 90th Ave. SW, Calgary AB T2V 4S1 – 403/253-8806; Fax: 403/252-7771 – 200 beds – Calgary RHA – Adm., Sharon Cornick

Calgary: Bow-Crest Nursing Home, 5927 Bowness Rd. NW, Calgary AB T3B 0C7 – 403/288-2373; Fax: 403/247-2120 – 150 beds – Calgary RHA – Adm., Jitu Patel

Calgary: Bow View Manor, 4628 Montgomery Blvd. NW, Calgary AB T3B 0K7 – 403/288-4446; Fax: 403/288-8522 – 193 beds – Calgary RHA – Adm., Norma Jackson

Calgary: Brentwood Nursing Home, 2727 Trans Canada NW, Calgary AB T2N 3Y6 – 403/289-2576; Fax: 403/282-7027 – 120 beds – Calgary RHA – Ruth Simpson

Calgary: Carewest George Boyack Nursing Home, 1203 Centre Ave. NE, Calgary AB T2P 0A5 – 403/267-2750; Fax: 403/267-2757 – 221 beds – Calgary RHA – Site Leader, Marg Marlin

Calgary: Carewest Sarcee Auxiliary Hospital, see Auxiliary Hospitals/Health Care Centres listings

Calgary: Central Park Lodge Nursing Home, 1813 - 9th St. SW, Calgary AB T2T 3C2 – 403/244-8994; Fax: 403/244-5939 – 123 beds – Calgary RHA – Adm., Patricia Hull

Calgary: Chinook Nursing Home, 1261 Glenmore Trail SW, Calgary AB T2V 4Y8 – 403/252-0141; Fax: 403/253-0292 – 149 beds – Calgary RHA – Senior Adm., Darlene Kadonaga

Calgary: Extendicare Cedars Villa Nursing Homes, 3330 - 8th Ave. SW, Calgary AB T3C 0E7 – 403/249-8915; Fax: 403/246-7561 – 248 beds – Calgary RHA – Adm., Lori Young

Calgary: Extendicare Hillcrest Nursing Home, 1512 - 8th Ave. SW, Calgary AB T2N 1C1 – 403/289-0236; Fax: 403/289-2350 – 112 beds – Calgary RHA – Adm., Jean Jantzon

Calgary: Extendicare Scottish Nursing Home, 605 - 24 Ave. SW, Calgary AB T2S 0K7 – 403/228-5352; Fax: 403/228-2496 – 46 beds – Calgary RHA – Adm., Pierre Poirier

Calgary: Father Lacombe Nursing Home, 332 - 146 Ave. SE, Calgary AB T2X 2A3 – 403/256-4641; Fax: 403/256-1669 – 107 beds – Calgary RHA – Exec. Dir., Hilda Anderson

Calgary: Forest Grove Care Centre Ltd., 4726 - 8th Ave. SE, Calgary AB T2A 0A8 – 403/272-9831; Fax: 403/248-5788 – 225 beds – Calgary RHA – Adm., Barbara Kerr

Calgary: Glamorgan Cedars Villas Nursing Home, 105 Galbraith Dr. SW, Calgary AB T3V 4Z5 – 403/242-5911; Fax: 403/242-7613 – 55 beds – Calgary RHA – Joyce Spiers

Calgary: Mayfair Nursing Home, 8240 Collicut St. SW, Calgary AB T2V 2X1 – 403/252-4445; Fax: 403/253-6216 – 142 beds – Calgary RHA – Pres., Carl Bond

Calgary: Southwood Nursing Home, 211 Heritage Dr. SE, Calgary AB T2H 1M9 – 403/252-1194; Fax: 403/253-0393 – 120 beds – Calgary RHA – Pat Rowe

Camrose: Bethany Long Term Care Centre, 4501 - 47 St., Camrose AB T4V 1H9 – 403/679-1000; Fax: 403/679-1020 – 150 beds – East Central RHA 7 – Exec. Dir., Elvira Pain

Cardston: Grandview Nursing Home, 990 Main St., PO Box 1440, Cardston AB T0K 0K0 – 403/653-4054; Fax: 403/653-3771 – 40 beds – Chinook Health Region – Exec. Dir., Roger N. Walker

Castor: Our Lady of the Rosary Hospital, see General Hospitals listings

Cereal Municipal Hospital, see General Hospitals listings

Claresholm: Willow Creek Auxiliary Hospital & Nursing Home, see Auxiliary Hospitals/Health Care Centres listings

Cochrane: Bethany Care Centre - Cochrane, 302 Quigly Dr., Cochrane AB T0C 1C0 – 403/932-6422; Fax: 403/932-4617 – 78 beds – Calgary RHA – Adm., Jacqueline Copple

Consort Municipal Hospital, see General Hospitals listings

Coronation Health Centre, see Auxiliary Hospitals/Health Care Centres listings

Didsbury District Health Services, see General Hospitals listings

Drayton Valley Health Centre, see General Hospitals listings

Drumheller District Health Services, see General Hospitals listings

Edmonton General Hospital & Continuing Care Centre (Caritas Health Group), see Auxiliary Hospitals/Health Care Centres listings

Edmonton: Allen Gray Continuing Care Centre, 7510 - 89 St., Edmonton AB T6C 3J8 – 403/469-2371; Fax: 403/465-2073 – 52 beds – Capital Health Authority – CEO, G. Yaremko

Edmonton: Capital Care Dickinsfield, 14225 - 94 St., Edmonton AB T5E 6C6 – 403/496-3300; Fax: 403/476-4585 – 300 beds – Capital Health Authority – Vice-Pres., Operations, Susan Paul

Edmonton: Capital Care Grandview, 6215 - 124 St., Edmonton AB T6H 3V1 – 403/496-7100; Fax: 403/496-7150 – 200 beds – Capital Health Authority – Adm., Helen Lantz

Edmonton: Capital Care Lynnwood, 8740 - 165 St., Edmonton AB T5R 2R8 – 403/483-2500; Fax: 403/484-8089 – 175 beds – Capital Health Authority – VP, Operations, Robert McKim

Edmonton: Capital Care Norwood - Mount Pleasant Site, 10530 - 56 Ave., Edmonton AB T6H 0X7 – 403/496-3221; Fax: 403/496-3222 – Capital Health Authority

Edmonton: Capital Care Norwood (Angus McGugan Pavilion), 10410 - 111 Ave., Edmonton AB T5G 3A2 – 403/496-3200; Fax: 403/474-9806 – 141 beds – Capital Health Authority – Vice-Pres., Operations, Dolores Eberly

Edmonton: Central Park Lodge, 5905 - 112 St., Edmonton AB T6H 3J4 – 403/434-1451; Fax: 403/436-4300 – Capital Health Authority

Edmonton: Extendicare North, 13210 - 114 St., Edmonton AB T5E 5E2 – 403/454-8616; Fax: 403/447-5906 – Capital Health Authority

Edmonton: Extendicare South, 9510 - 80 St., Edmonton AB T6C 2T1 – 403/469-1307; Fax: 403/469-5196 – Capital Health Authority

Edmonton: Good Samaritan Auxiliary Hospital, 9649 - 71 Ave., Edmonton AB T6E 5J2 – 403/431-3600; Fax: 403/431-3699 – Capital Health Authority

Edmonton: Good Samaritan Millwoods Centre, 101 Youville Dr., Edmonton AB T6L 7A4 – 403/413-3501; Fax: 403/462-8850 – Assisted living centre – Capital Health Authority

Edmonton: Good Samaritan Mount Pleasant Care Centre, 10530 - 56 Ave., Edmonton AB T6H 0X7 – 403/431-3902; Fax: 403/431-3949 – Capital Health Authority

Edmonton: Good Samaritan Southgate Care Centre, 4225 - 107th St., Edmonton AB T6J 2P1 – 403/436-2720; Fax: 403/438-2395 – Capital Health Authority

Edmonton: Good Samaritan Wedman House, 10525 - 19 Ave., Edmonton AB T6H 5A2 – 403/438-1030; Fax: 403/435-8435 – Assisted living centre – Capital Health Authority

Edmonton: Hardisty Nursing Home Inc., 6240 - 101 Ave., Edmonton AB T6A 0H5 – 403/466-9267; Fax: 403/465-9457 – Capital Health Authority – Adm., Debbie Hoffman

Edmonton: Jasper Place Central Park Lodge, 8903 - 168th St., Edmonton AB T5R 2V6 – 403/489-4931;

Fax: 403/489-5435 – Capital Health Authority – Adm., Lynda Doll

Edmonton: Jubilee Lodge Nursing Home, 10333 -76 St., Edmonton AB T6A 3A8 – 403/469-4456; Fax: 403/466-3799 – Capital Health Authority – Adm., Blaine Turner

Edmonton: Mewburn Veterans Centre, 11440 University Ave., Edmonton AB T6G 1Z1 – 403/496-7160; Fax: 403/496-7199 – Capital Health Authority – Pres., Sheila Weatherill

Edmonton: Millwoods Shepherd's Care Centre, 6620 - 28 Ave., Edmonton AB T6K 2R1 – 403/463-9810; Fax: 403/462-1643 – Capital Health Authority – Exec. Dir., Herbert Haut

Edmonton: St. Joseph's Auxiliary Hospital, 10707 - 29 Ave., Edmonton AB T6J 6W1 – 403/430-9110; Fax: 403/430-9777 – 204 beds – Exec. Dir., R.J. Pinkoski

Edmonton: St. Michael's Extended Care Centre, 7404 - 139 Ave., Edmonton AB T5C 3H7 – 403/473-5621; Fax: 403/472-4506 – Capital Health Authority – Exec. Dir., B. Shulakewych

Edmonton: Venta Nursing Home, 13525 - 102 St., Edmonton AB T5E 4K3 – 403/476-6633; Fax: 403/476-6943 – Capital Health Authority – Adm., Ausma Birzgalis

Edson & District Health Care Centre & Nursing Home, see General Hospitals listings

Elk Point General & Auxiliary Hospital & Nursing Home, see General Hospitals listings

Fort Macleod Special Development Unit, 744 - 26 St., Fort Macleod AB T0L 0Z0 – 403/553-4482; Fax: 403/553-4567 – 31 continuing care beds – Chinook Health Region

Fort Macleod: Extendicare Ltd. - Fort Macleod, 654 - 29 St., PO Box 189, Fort Macleod AB T0L 0Z0 – 403/553-3955; Fax: 403/553-2812 – 50 beds – Chinook Health Region – Adm., Gregg Guyn

Fort McMurray: Northern Lights Regional Health Centre, see General Hospitals listings

Fort Saskatchewan: Rivercrest Lodge Nursing Home, 10104 - 101 Ave., Fort Saskatchewan AB T8L 2A5 – 403/998-2425; Fax: 403/998-5350 – Adm., Don McLeod

Galahad Health Care Centre, see Auxiliary Hospitals/Health Care Centres listings

Grande Prairie: Queen Elizabeth II Hospital, Auxiliary Hospital & Nursing Home, see General Hospitals listings

Hanna District Health Services, see General Hospitals listings

Hardisty Health Centre, see General Hospitals listings

High Prairie: J.B. Wood Nursing Home, High Prairie Health Complex, PO Box 1, High Prairie AB T0G 1E0 – 403/523-4732; Fax: 403/523-3888 – Keeweetinok Lakes RHA #15 – Coord. Regional Long Term Care, Ruth Hampton

High River Hospital & Nursing Home, see General Hospitals listings

Hythe Nursing Home, PO Box 100, Hythe AB T0H 2C0 – 403/356-3818; Fax: 403/356-3633 – 31 beds – Site Coord., Mollie Mumford

Innisfail Health Care Centre, see General Hospitals listings

Islay Health Centre, see Auxiliary Hospitals/Health Care Centres listings

Killam Health Centre, see Auxiliary Hospitals/Health Care Centres listings

Lacombe Community Health Centre, see Auxiliary Hospitals/Health Care Centres listings

Lacombe Hospital, see General Hospitals listings

Lamont Health Care Centre - General & Extended Care, see General Hospitals listings

Leduc Health Centre, see General Hospitals listings

Leduc: Extendicare Nursing Home - Leduc, 4309 - 50 St., Leduc AB T9E 6K6 – 403/986-2245; Fax: 403/986-0669 – Adm., Donna Dougan

Canadian Almanac & Directory 1997

Leduc: Salem Manor Nursing Home, 4419 - 46 St., Leduc AB T9E 6L2 – 403/986-8654; Fax: 403/986-4130 – Adm., Ed Fuellbrandt
Lethbridge: Extendicare Ltd. - Lethbridge, 1821 - 13 St. North, Lethbridge AB T1H 2V4 – 403/328-6664; Fax: 403/327-8909 – 120 beds – Adm., Joyce Adachi
Linden Nursing Home, PO Box 220, Linden AB T0M 1J0 – 403/546-3966; Fax: 403/546-4061 – Adm., Gary Barkman
Lloydminster: Dr. Cooke Extended Care Centre, see Auxiliary Hospitals/Health Care Centres listings
Magrath Hospital, 37E 2nd Ave. North, PO Box 550, Magrath AB T0K 1J0 – 403/758-3371; Fax: 403/758-3698 – 23 beds – Chinook Health Region – Coord., Bill Ayotte
Mayerthorpe Extendicare, 4706 - 54 St., PO Box 569, Mayerthorpe AB T0E 1N0 – 403/786-2211; Fax: 403/786-2274 – 50 beds – Aspen RHA #11 – Adm., Viola Oskoboiny
McLennan Sacred Heart Community Health Centre, see General Hospitals listings
McLennan: Our Lady of the Lake Nursing Home, see McLennan Sacred Heart Community Health Centre, General Hospitals listings
Medicine Hat: Central Park Lodge, 603 Prospect Dr. SW, Medicine Hat AB T1A 4C2 – 403/527-5531; Fax: 403/527-5533 – Adm., David Dennis
Medicine Hat: Sunnyside Nursing Home, 1720 Bell St. SW, Medicine Hat AB T1A 5G1 – 403/527-3838; Fax: 403/527-4690 – Adm., R.A. Weiss
Olds General Hospital, see General Hospitals listings
Peace River Community Health Centre, see General Hospitals listings
Ponoka: Northcott Care Centre, 4209 - 48 Ave., PO Box 1740, Ponoka AB T4J 1P4 – 403/783-4764; Fax: 403/783-6420 – 72 beds – Adm., Art Ulveland
Provost Health Centre, see General Hospitals listings
Red Deer Nursing Home, 4736 - 30th St., Red Deer AB T4N 5H8 – 403/343-4458; Fax: 403/341-4988 – 118 beds – David Thompson Health Region – Pres., Gerry Vanhooren
Red Deer: Valley Park Manor Nursing Home, 5505 - 60th Ave., Red Deer AB T4N 4W2 – 403/343-4722; Fax: 403/343-4433 – 100 beds – David Thompson Health Region – Pres., Gerry Vanhooren
Red Deer: West Park Nursing Home, 5715 - 41 St. Crescent, Red Deer AB T4N 1B3 – 403/343-4539; Fax: 403/341-5946 – Pres., Gerry Vanhooren
Rimbey & District Health Care Centre, see General Hospitals listings
Rocky Mountain House Community Health Centre, see Auxiliary Hospitals/Health Care Centres listings
St. Albert: Youville Home, 9 St. Vital Ave., St. Albert AB T8N 1K1 – 403/460-6900; Fax: 403/459-4139 – 162 beds – Capital Health Authority – Adm., Ken Pickard
St. Paul: Extendicare Nursing Home - St. Paul, 4614 - 47 Ave., St. Paul AB T0A 3A3 – 403/645-3375; Fax: 403/645-4290 – Adm., Steve Krim
Sherwood Park Care Centre, 2020 Brentwood Blvd., Sherwood Park AB T8A 0X1 – 403/467-2281; Fax: 403/449-1529 – Capital Health Authority – Exec. Dir., L. Dunfield
Sherwood Park: Strathcona Care Centre, 12 Brower Dr., Sherwood Park AB T8H 1V3 – 403/467-3366; Fax: 403/467-4095 – Capital Health Authority – Exec. Dir., Grace Rutledge
Smoky Lake: George McDougall Memorial Hospital, see General Hospitals listings
Stettler Health Centre, see General Hospitals listings
Stony Plain: Everglades Lodge, PO Box 360, Stony Plain AB T0E 2G0 – 403/963-6066 – 66 beds – Adm., Jae Jeung
Stony Plain: Good Samaritan Care Centre Stony Plain, 5600 - 50th St., Stony Plain AB T7Z 1P8 – 403/963-2261; Fax: 403/963-5156 – 90 beds – Pres., Phil Gaudet
Strathmore District Health Services, see General Hospitals listings
Taber & District Health Care Complex, see General Hospitals listings
Three Hills District Health Services, see General Hospitals listings
Tofield Health Centre, see General Hospitals listings
Trochu-St. Mary's Health Care Centre, see General Hospitals listings
Two Hills Health Care Centre & Nursing Home, see General Hospitals listings
Vegreville Long Term Care Centre, 5225 - 43 St., PO Box 959, Vegreville AB T9C 1S1 – 403/632-2871; Fax: 403/632-6680 – 90 beds – Area Mgr., Pearl Babiuk
Vermilion Health Centre, see General Hospitals listings
Viking: Extendicare - Viking, 5020 - 57th Ave., PO Box 430, Viking AB T0B 4N0 – 403/336-4790; Fax: 403/336-4004 – 60 beds – East Central RHA 7 – Adm., Lorie Little
Vulcan Community Health Centre, see Auxiliary Hospitals/Health Care Centres listings
Vulcan Extendicare, 715 - 2 Ave. South, PO Box 810, Vulcan AB T0L 2B0 – 403/485-2022; Fax: 403/485-2879 – Headwaters Health Authority – Adm., Dianne Harder
Wainwright Health Centre, see General Hospitals listings
Westlock Long Term Care Centre, see Auxiliary Hospitals/Health Care Centres listings
Wetaskiwin Health Centre, see General Hospitals listings

NURSING STATIONS

Chateh Hay Lakes: Hay Lakes Nursing Station, General Delivery, Chateh Hay Lakes AB T0H 1B0 – 403/495-2705 – Nurse in Charge, Louise Stacey
Fort Chipewyan Nursing Station, General Delivery, Fort Chipewyan AB T0P 1B0 – 403/697-3650; Fax: 403/697-3763 – Nurse in Charge, Lorri Frank
Fox Lake Nursing Station, General Delivery, Fox Lake AB T0H 1R0 – 403/659-3730; Fax: 403/659-3960 – Nursing Suprv., Christopher Ryan
Worsley Health Centre, General Delivery, Worsley AB T0H 3W0 – 403/685-3752; Fax: 403/685-2007

PRIVATE HOSPITALS

Canmore Pain Clinic Inc., PO Box 130, Canmore AB T0L 0M0 – 403/678-7200; Fax: 403/678-7201 – Dir., Dr. Michael Wuitchik
Coaldale Health Care Centre, 2100 - 11 St., Coaldale AB T1M 1L2 – 403/345-3075; Fax: 403/345-2681 – 47 continuing care beds – Chinook Health Region – CEO, Allan Skretting
Grande Prairie Care Centre, 10039 - 98 St., Grande Prairie AB T8V 2E7 – 403/532-3525; Fax: 403/532-6504 – Dir. of Nursing, Myrna Wendall
Lethbridge: Edith Cavell Care Centre, 1255 - 5 Ave. South, Lethbridge AB T1J 0V6 – 403/328-6631; Fax: 403/320-9061 – 100 beds – Chinook Health Region – Adm., Marian Teierle
Lethbridge: St. Michael's Health Centre - Acute Geriatrics Program, 960 - 19th St. South, Lethbridge AB T1J 1W5 – 403/382-6610; Fax: 403/382-6646 – 75 beds – Chinook Health Region – Exec. Dir., Romeo H. Paulhus, 403/382-6400, Fax: 604/382-6433
Lethbridge: St. Michael's Health Centre - Lethbridge Auxiliary, 935 - 17 St. South, Lethbridge AB T1J 3E4 – 403/382-6494; Fax: 403/320-1698 – 78 beds – Chinook Health Region
Lethbridge: St. Michael's Health Centre - Southland Nursing Home, 1511 - 15 Ave. North, Lethbridge AB T1H 1W2 – 403/382-6439; Fax: 403/320-1645 – 125 beds – Chinook Health Region

Nanton Mountainview Estates, PO Box 176, Nanton AB T0L 1R0 – 403/646-5491; Fax: 403/684-3804 – Dir./Owner, Donella Sewell

Special Treatment Centres
(Includes: Abortion Clinics, Cancer Clinics, Rehabilitation Centres, Treatment Centres)

Calgary: Alberta Cancer Board/Tom Baker Cancer Centre, 1331 - 29th St. NW, Calgary AB T2N 4N2 – 403/670-1711; Fax: 403/283-1651 – cancer treatment – Dir., Dr. Gavin Stuart
Calgary: Kensington Clinic, 2431 - 5th Ave. NW, Calgary AB T2W 0T3 – 403/283-9117; Fax: 403/283-9139 – abortion clinic
Calgary: Southern Alberta Clinic, #120, 1040 - 7 Ave. SW, Calgary AB T2P 3G9 – 403/262-4460; Fax: 403/290-0933 – breast screening clinic
Edmonton: Alberta Cancer Board/Cross Cancer Institute, 11560 University Ave. NW, Edmonton AB T6G 1Z2 – 403/432-8771; Fax: 403/432-8411 – cancer treatment – 44 beds – Dir., Dr. A.L.A. Fields
Edmonton: Glenrose Rehabilitation Hospital, 10230 - 111 Ave., Edmonton AB T5G 0B7 – 403/471-2262; Fax: 403/471-7976 – rehabilitation centre – 228 beds – Pres., Rosemary Pahl
Edmonton: Good Samaritan Wedman Village Homes, 1603/1609 Bearspaw Dr. East, Edmonton AB T6J 5E2 – 403/435-5072; Fax: 403/435-8435 – Alzheimer care centre – Capital Health Authority
Edmonton: McConnell Place North, 9113 - 144 Ave., Edmonton AB T5E 6K2 – 403/496-2575; Fax: 403/472-6699 – Alzheimer care centre – Capital Health Authority
Edmonton: Morgentaler Clinic of Edmonton, 10141 - 150th St., Edmonton AB T5P 1P2 – 403/484-1124; Fax: 403/489-3379 – abortion clinic – Exec. Dir., Susan Fox
Edmonton: Northern Alberta Clinic, 311 Kingsway Garden Mall, Edmonton AB T5G 3A6 – 403/474-4300; Fax: 403/477-8418 – breast screening clinic
Fort McMurray Cancer Clinic, c/o Fort McMurray Regional Hospital, 7 Hospital St., Fort McMurray AB T9H 1P2 – 403/791-6161 – cancer treatment
Grande Prairie Cancer Clinic, 10409 - 98th St., Grande Prairie AB T8V 2E8 – 403/538-7588; Fax: 403/532-9120 – cancer treatment – Dir., Dr. Claudia Strehlke
Lethbridge Cancer Clinic, c/o Lethbridge Regional Hospital, #2H209, 960 - 19th St. South, Lethbridge AB T1J 1W5 – 403/329-0633; Fax: 403/320-0508 – cancer treatment – Dir., Dr. Thomas Melling
Lethbridge: Children's Centre, Room A252, 2nd Fl., 200 - 5th Ave. South, Lethbridge AB T1J 4C7 – 403/381-5255; Fax: 403/381-5336 – children's assessment, rehabilitation & education centre – Chinook Health Region
Medicine Hat Cancer Clinic, 666 - 5th St. SW, Medicine Hat AB T1A 4H6 – 403/529-8817; Fax: 403/529-8007 – cancer treatment – Dir., Dr. A.R. McClelland
Peace River Cancer Clinic, c/o Peace River Auxiliary Hospital, PO Box 400, Peace River AB T0H 2X0 – 403/624-7500
Red Deer: Central Alberta Cancer Centre, 3942 - 50A Ave., PO Box 5030, Red Deer AB T4N 6R2 – 403/343-4526; Fax: 403/346-1160 – cancer treatment – Dir., Dr. Neil Graham

BRITISH COLUMBIA

HOSPITAL DISTRICTS/HEALTH UNITS
Abbotsford: Fraser Valley Regional Health Board, 34194 Marshall Rd., Abbotsford BC V2S 5E4 – 604/864-6712; Fax: 604/864-6711 – Chair, George Peary

Burnaby Regional Health Board, #113, 4940 Canada Way, Burnaby BC V5G 4K6 – 604/775-2146; Fax: 604/775-2144 – Chair, Paul McDonell

Campbell River: Upper Island/Central Coast Regional Health Board, #212, 437 - 10th Ave., Campbell River BC V9W 4E4 – 250/287-7290; Fax: 250/287-7291 – Chair, Keith Hudson

Cranbrook: East Kootenay Regional Health Board, 1212 - 2nd St. North, Cranbrook BC V1C 4T6 – 250/489-3899; Fax: 250/426-1456 – Senior Adm., Rick Robinson

Fort St. John: Peace Liard Regional Health Board, PO Box 6052, Fort St. John BC V1J 4H6 – 250/785-7812; Fax: 250/785-7813 – Chair, Sheelagh Garson

Kamloops: Thompson Regional Health Board, c/o Royal Inland Hospital, 311 Columbia St., Kamloops BC V2C 2T1 – 250/372-3284; Fax: 250/372-1464 – Chair, Sharon Frisseli

Mackenzie: Northern Interior Regional Health Board, PO Box 762, Mackenzie BC V0J 2C0 – 250/997-6510; Fax: 250/997-6880 – Chair, Stephanie Killam

Nanaimo: Central Vancouver Island Regional Health Board, #610, 495 Dunsmuir St., Nanaimo BC V9R 6B9 – 250/741-5500; Fax: 250/741-4825 – Chair, Else Strand

New Westminster: Simon Fraser Health Board, 260 Sherbrooke St., New Westminster BC V3L 3M2 – 604/520-4840; Fax: 604/520-4827 – Senior Adm., Jim Fair

North Vancouver: North Shore Health Board, #105, 200 East 23rd St., North Vancouver BC V7L 4R4 – 604/984-3841; Fax: 604/984-3840 – Senior Adm., Inge Schamborzki

Revelstoke: North Okanagan Regional Health Board, PO Box 2052, Revelstoke BC V0E 2S0 – 250/837-6803; Fax: 250/837-6803 – Chair, Mengia Nicholson

Richmond Regional Health Board, PO Box 94671, Richmond BC V6Y 4A4 – 604/244-5544; Fax: 604/244-5536 – Chair, John P. Kennedy

Sechelt: Coast Garibaldi Regional Health Board, PO Box 516, Sechelt BC V0N 3A0 – 604/885-8632; Fax: 604/885-8633 – Chair, Shawn Cardinall

Surrey: South Fraser Valley Regional Health Board, #201, 10090 - 152 St., Surrey BC V3R 8X8 – 604/951-0020; Fax: 604/951-0166 – CEO, Brian Copley

Terrace: North West Regional Health Board, 3412 Kalum St., Terrace BC V8G 4T2 – 250/638-2305; Fax: 250/638-2275 – Senior Adm., Wayne Hay

Terrace: West Kootenay-Boundary Regional Health Board, 3412 Kalum St., Terrace BC V8G 4T2 – 250/638-2305; Fax: 250/638-2275 – Senior Adm., Rick Riley

Vancouver Health Board, #601, 1285 West Broadway, Vancouver BC V6H 3X8 – 604/775-1866; Fax: 604/775-1804 – Senior Adm., John Tegenfeldt

Victoria: Capital Health Board, #207, 841 Fairfield Rd., Victoria BC V8V 3B6 – 250/389-2227; Fax: 250/389-2206 – Senior Adm., Peter McAllister

Westbank: South Okanagan/Similkameen Regional Health Board, 3115 Ridgerock Way, Westbank BC V4Y 1S7 – 250/861-7601; Fax: 250/861-7607 – Chair, Rod Barrett

Williams Lake: Cariboo Regional Health Board, 540 Borland St., Williams Lake BC V2G 1R8 – 250/398-4600; Fax: 250/398-4249 – Chair, Ivan Bonnell

GENERAL HOSPITALS

Abbotsford: Matsqui-Sumas-Abbotsford General Hospital, 2179 McCallum Rd., Abbotsford BC V2S 3P1 – 604/853-2201; Fax: 604/853-0734 – 352 beds – Pres./CEO, Larry Tokarchuk

Alert Bay: St. George's Hospital, 182 Fir St., PO Box 223, Alert Bay BC V0N 1A0 – 250/974-5585; Fax: 250/974-5422 – 14 beds – CEO, Dora Nicinski, 250/956-3655, Fax: 250/956-3653

Ashcroft & District General Hospital, PO Box 488, Ashcroft BC V0K 1A0 – 250/453-2211; Fax: 250/453-9685 – 24 beds – Adm., Sylvia Gerwien

Bella Coola General Hospital, Mackay St., PO Box 220, Bella Coola BC V0T 1C0 – 250/799-5311; Fax: 250/799-5635 – 15 beds – Adm., Mary Lynn Siwallace

Burnaby Hospital, 3935 Kincaid St., Burnaby BC V5G 2X6 – 604/434-4211; Fax: 604/431-4708 – 466 beds – CEO, Dr. John Blatherwick, 604/775-2146, Fax: 604/775-2144

Burns Lake: Lakes District Hospital & Health Centre, 741 Centre St., PO Box 479, Burns Lake BC V0J 1E0 – 250/692-3181; Fax: 250/692-3633 – 26 beds – Adm., Terry Smith

Campbell River & District General Hospital, 375 - 2 Ave., Campbell River BC V9W 3V1 – 250/287-7111; Fax: 250/287-8889 – 115 beds – CEO, Brian MacLure

Castlegar & District Hospital, 709 - 10 St., Castlegar BC V1N 2H7 – 250/365-7711; Fax: 250/365-2298 – 90 beds – Adm., Ken A. Talarico

Chemainus Health Care Centre, 9909 Esplanade St., PO Box 499, Chemainus BC V0R 1K0 – 250/246-3291; Fax: 250/246-3844 – 75 beds – Adm., Donald U. Brown

Chetwynd General Hospital, PO Box 507, Chetwynd BC V0C 1J0 – 250/788-2236; Fax: 250/788-2145 – 18 beds – Interim CEO, Meribel Miller

Chilliwack General Hospital, 45600 Menholm Rd., Chilliwack BC V2P 1P7 – 604/795-4141; Fax: 604/795-4110 – 412 beds – CEO, Etta Richmond

Clearwater: Dr. Helmcken Memorial Hospital, RR#1, Clearwater BC V0E 1N0 – 250/674-2244; Fax: 250/674-2477 – 10 beds – Adm., Linda K. Basran

Comox: St. Joseph's General Hospital, 2137 Comox Ave., Comox BC V9N 4B1 – 250/339-1402; Fax: 250/339-1432 – Exec. Dir., Michael Pontus

Cranbrook Regional Hospital, 13 - 24th Ave. North, Cranbrook BC V1C 3H9 – 250/426-5281; Fax: 250/426-5285 – Exec. Dir., Merlen W. Hokanson

Creston Valley Hospital, 312 - 15 Ave., Creston BC V0B 1G0 – 250/428-2286; Fax: 250/428-5959 – Exec. Dir., Andrew Neuner

Dawson Creek & District Hospital, 11100 - 13th St., Dawson Creek BC V1G 3W8 – 250/782-8501; Fax: 250/784-7301 – 57 beds – Interim CEO, Maureen Wood

Delta Hospital, 5800 Mountain View Blvd., Delta BC V4K 3V6 – 604/946-1121; Fax: 604/946-3086 – 158 beds – Exec. Dir., David C. Richardson

Duncan: Cowichan District Hospital, 3045 Gibbins Rd., Duncan BC V9L 1E5 – 250/746-4141; Fax: 250/746-4247 – 118 beds – CEO, Donald U. Brown

Enderby & District Memorial Hospital, 500 George St., PO Box 340, Enderby BC V0E 1V0 – 250/546-6131; Fax: 250/546-9943 – 28 beds – Transition Mgr., Brian Kines, 250/838-6441, Fax: 250/838-9530

Fernie District Hospital, 1501 - 5 Ave., PO Box 670, Fernie BC V0B 1M0 – 250/423-4453; Fax: 250/423-3732 – 50 beds – CEO, John McAulay

Fort Nelson General Hospital, PO Box 60, Fort Nelson BC V0C 1R0 – 250/774-6916; Fax: 250/774-3731 – 41 beds – Adm., Bryan Redford

Fort St. John General Hospital, 9636 - 100 Ave., PO Box 1, Fort St. John BC V1J 1Y3 – 250/785-6611; Fax: 250/785-4060 – 45 beds – CEO, Chris Wenzel

Golden & District General Hospital, 9th Ave., PO Box 1260, Golden BC V0A 1H0 – 250/344-5271; Fax: 250/344-2511 – Adm., Peter White

Grand Forks: Boundary Hospital, 7649 - 22 St., PO Box 189, Grand Forks BC V0H 1H0 – 250/442-8211; Fax: 250/442-3922 – 70 beds – Adm., Garth Burnell

Hazelton: Wrinch Memorial Hospital, Hazelton BC V0J 1Y0 – 250/842-5211; Fax: 250/842-5865 – Adm., Dr. Philip A. Muir

Hope: Fraser Canyon Hospital, 1275 - 7 Ave., RR#2, Hope BC V0X 1L0 – 604/869-5656; Fax: 604/869-7710 – 71 beds – CEO, Ray Marshall

Invermere & District Hospital, PO Box 5001, Invermere BC V0A 1K0 – 250/342-9201; Fax: 250/342-2319 – 30 beds – Adm., Milton Crawford

Kamloops: Royal Inland Hospital, 311 Columbia St., Kamloops BC V2C 2T1 – 250/374-5111; Fax: 250/314-2333 – 260 beds – Pres., Paul Chapin

Kaslo: Victorian Hospital of Kaslo, PO Box 607, Kaslo BC V0G 1M0 – 250/353-2211; Fax: 250/353-7772 – 5 beds – Interim Adm., Margaret Milner

Kelowna General Hospital, 2268 Pandosy St., Kelowna BC V1Y 1T2 – 250/862-4000; Fax: 250/862-4020 – 731 beds – CEO, Murray Ramsden

Kimberley & District Hospital, 260 - 4th Ave., Kimberley BC V1A 2R6 – 250/427-2215; Fax: 250/427-4342 – 53 beds – Adm., Joan Poweska

Kitimat General Hospital, 899 Lahakas Blvd., Kitimat BC V8C 1E7 – 250/632-2121; Fax: 250/632-3044 – 69 beds – CEO, Linda Coles

Ladysmith & District General Hospital, 1111 - 4th Ave., PO Box 10, Ladysmith BC V0R 2E0 – 250/245-2221; Fax: 250/245-3238 – 42 beds – Adm., Donald U. Brown

Langley Memorial Hospital, 22051 Fraser Hwy., Langley BC V3A 4H4 – 604/534-4121; Fax: 604/534-6411 – 451 beds – Pres., Pat Zanon

Lillooet District Hospital, 951 Murray St., PO Box 249, Lillooet BC V0K 1V0 – 250/256-4233; Fax: 250/256-4746 – 31 beds – Adm., Raelene Shea

Lytton: St. Bartholomew's Hospital, 844 Main St., PO Box 99, Lytton BC V0K 1Z0 – 250/455-2221; Fax: 250/455-6621 – 20 beds – Adm., Doug Calder

Mackenzie & District Hospital, PO Box 249, Mackenzie BC V0J 2C0 – 250/997-3263; Fax: 250/997-3940 – 12 beds – Adm., Janice Blackmore

Maple Ridge: Ridge Meadows Hospital & Health Care Centre, 11666 Laity St., PO Box 5000, Maple Ridge BC V2X 7G5 – 604/463-4111; Fax: 604/463-1888 – 250 beds – Pres., Jim Fair, 604/520-4840, Fax: 604/520-4827

McBride & District Hospital, 594 King St., PO Box 128, McBride BC V0J 2E0 – 250/569-2251; Fax: 250/569-3369 – 16 beds – Adm., Victor Chicoine

Merritt: Nicola Valley General Hospital, Hwy. 5 North, RR#1, Merritt BC V0K 2B0 – 250/378-2242; Fax: 250/378-3287 – 25 beds – Exec. Dir., Terry Frizzell

Mission Memorial Hospital, 7324 Hurd St., Mission BC V2V 3H5 – 604/826-6261; Fax: 604/826-9513 – 74 beds – Adm., Randy Wong

Nakusp: Arrow Lakes Hospital, PO Box 87, Nakusp BC V0G 1R0 – 250/265-3622; Fax: 250/265-4435 – 17 beds – Acting Adm., Barb Chwachka

Nanaimo Regional General Hospital, 1200 Dufferin Cr., Nanaimo BC V9S 2B7 – 250/754-2141; Fax: 250/755-7633 – 411 beds – Exec. Dir., E.E. (Gene) Freeborn

Nelson: Kootenay Lake District Hospital, 3 View St., Nelson BC V1L 2V1 – 250/352-3111; Fax: 250/354-2320 – 57 beds – Adm., Jack J. Miller

New Denver: Slocan Community Hospital & Health Care Centre, 401 Galena Ave., PO Box 129, New Denver BC V0G 1S0 – 250/358-7911; Fax: 250/358-7117 – 40 beds – Adm., Judy Cameron

New Westminster: Royal Columbian Hospital, 330 Columbia St. East, New Westminster BC V3L 3W7 – 604/520-4253; Fax: 604/520-3842 – 375 beds – Pres., Jim Fair, 604/520-4840, Fax: 604/520-4827

New Westminster: Saint Mary's Hospital, 220 Royal Ave., New Westminster BC V3L 1H6 – 604/521-1881; Fax: 604/527-3358 – CEO, Bernard Bilodeau

North Vancouver: Lions Gate Hospital, 231 East 15 St., North Vancouver BC V7L 2L7 – 604/988-3131; Fax: 604/984-5838 – 650 beds – CEO, Inge Schamborzki, 604/984-3840, Fax: 604/984-3841

Oliver: South Okanagan General Hospital, McKinney Rd., PO Box 760, Oliver BC V0H 1T0 – 250/498-3474; Fax: 250/498-6851 – 105 beds – Exec. Dir., Ken Doepker

100 Mile District General Hospital, 555 Cedar Ave., PO Box 399, 100 Mile House BC V0K 2E0 – 250/395-2202; Fax: 250/395-2662 – 60 beds – CEO, Bill Marshall

Penticton Regional Hospital, 550 Carmi Ave., Penticton BC V2A 3G6 – 250/492-4000; Fax: 250/492-9025 – Adm., Ken Burrows

Port Alberni: West Coast General Hospital, 3841 - 8 Ave., Port Alberni BC V9Y 4S1 – 250/723-2135; Fax: 250/723-1283 – 54 beds – Adm., Ron Mustard

Port Alice Hospital, 1090 Marine Dr., PO Box 69, Port Alice BC V0N 2N0 – 250/284-3555; Fax: 250/284-6163 – 3 beds – Site Mgr., Nancy Lee Deslauriers

Port Hardy Hospital, PO Box 790, Port Hardy BC V0N 2P0 – 250/949-6161; Fax: 250/949-7000 – 17 beds – Site Mgr., Isabel Savignac

Port McNeill & District Hospital, PO Box 790, Port McNeill BC V0N 2R0 – 250/956-4461; Fax: 250/956-4823 – CEO, Dora Nickinski, 250/956-3655, Fax: 250/956-3653

Port Moody: Eagle Ridge Hospital, 475 Guildford Way, Port Moody BC V3H 3W9 – 604/461-2022; Fax: 604/461-9972 – 175 beds – Pres., Jim Fair, 604/520-4840, Fax: 604/520-4827

Powell River General Hospital, 5000 Joyce Ave., Powell River BC V8A 5R3 – 604/485-3211; Fax: 604/485-3245 – Adm., Ed Marion

Prince George Regional Hospital, 2000 - 15 Ave., Prince George BC V2M 1S2 – 250/565-2000; Fax: 250/565-2343 – 219 beds – Interim Exec. Dir., Lucy Dobbin

Prince Rupert Regional Hospital, 1305 Summit Ave., Prince Rupert BC V8J 2A6 – 250/624-2171; Fax: 250/624-2195 – 50 beds – Interim CEO, Bernie Holden

Princeton General Hospital, 98 Ridgewood Ave., PO Box 610, Princeton BC V0X 1W0 – 250/295-3233; Fax: 250/295-3344 – 30 beds – Adm., Dorothy Cobb

Queen Charlotte Islands General Hospital, PO Box 9, Queen Charlotte City BC V0T 1S0 – 250/559-8466; Fax: 250/559-4312 – 21 beds – Adm., Elio Azzara

Quesnel: G.R. Baker Memorial Hospital, 543 Front St., Quesnel BC V2J 2K7 – 250/992-2181; Fax: 250/992-5652 – 44 beds – Adm., Kenneth T. Last

Revelstoke: Queen Victoria Hospital, PO Box 5000, Revelstoke BC V0E 2S0 – 250/837-2131; Fax: 250/837-4788 – 57 beds – Adm., James Vaillancourt

The Richmond Hospital, 7000 Westminster Hwy., Richmond BC V6X 1A2 – 604/278-9711; Fax: 604/244-5191 – 470 beds – Acting Pres., Kirk Mitchell

Rossland: Mater Misericordiae Health Care Facility, 1961 Georgia St., PO Box 1239, Rossland BC V0G 1Y0 – 250/362-7344; Fax: 250/362-7366 – 41 beds – CEO, C.F. (Rick) Riley

Saanichton: Saanich Peninsula Hospital, 2166 Mount Newton Cross Rd., Saanichton BC V8M 2B2 – 250/652-3911; Fax: 250/652-6920 – 225 beds – Adm., Robert Myers

Salmon Arm: Shuswap Lake General Hospital, PO Box 520, Salmon Arm BC V1E 4N6 – 250/833-3600; Fax: 250/833-3611 – Exec. Dir., Eugene M. Casavant

Salt Spring Island: The Lady Minto Gulf Islands Hospital, 135 Crofton Rd., Salt Spring Island BC V8K 1T1 – 250/537-5545; Fax: 250/537-1475 – 50 beds – CEO, Karen Davies

Sechelt: St. Mary's Hospital, PO Box 7777, Sechelt BC V0N 3A0 – 604/885-8614; Fax: 604/885-8628 – 83 beds – Interim CEO, Carol Brown

Smithers: Bulkley Valley District Hospital, 3950 - 8 Ave., PO Box 370, Smithers BC V0J 2N0 – 250/847-2611; Fax: 250/847-2446 – 32 beds – Public Adm., Dr. Lorne Klippert

Sparwood General Hospital, PO Box 9, Sparwood BC V0B 2G0 – 250/425-6212; Fax: 250/425-2313 – 12 beds – Adm., Lynn Noble

Squamish General Hospital, 38140 Behrner Dr., PO Box 6000, Squamish BC V0N 3G0 – 604/892-5211; Fax: 604/892-9417 – 94 beds – Adm., John R. Dillabough

Summerland General Hospital, PO Box 869, Summerland BC V0H 1Z0 – 250/494-6811; Fax: 250/494-8755 – 71 beds – Adm., Robert Heise

Surrey Memorial Hospital, 13750 - 96th Ave., Surrey BC V3V 1Z2 – 604/581-2211; Fax: 604/588-3320 – 656 beds – Pres., Bernie Blais

Terrace: Mills Memorial Hospital, 4720 Haugland Ave., Terrace BC V8G 2W7 – 250/635-2211; Fax: 250/635-7639 – 52 beds – CEO, Michael A. Leisinger

Tofino General Hospital, 261 Neill St., PO Box 190, Tofino BC V0R 2Z0 – 250/725-3212; Fax: 250/725-3324 – 21 beds – Adm., Frank Van Eynde

Trail Regional Hospital, 1200 Hospital Bench, Trail BC V1R 4M1 – 250/368-3311; Fax: 250/364-3422 – 135 beds – Acting CEO, Ron L. Parisotto

Vancouver Hospital & Health Sciences Centre, 855 - 12 Ave. West, Vancouver BC V5Z 1M9 – 604/875-4111; Fax: 604/875-4686 – 500 beds – Pres. & CEO, Murray T. Martin, 604/875-4999

Vancouver: British Columbia Children's Hospital, 4480 Oak St., Vancouver BC V6H 3V4 – 604/875-2345; Fax: 604/875-3456 – 252 beds – Interim Pres., Anne Sutherland Boal

Vancouver: Holy Family Hospital, 7801 Argyle St., Vancouver BC V5P 3L6 – 604/321-2661; Fax: 604/321-2696 – 286 beds – Pres., W.T. Frier

Vancouver: Mount Saint Joseph Hospital, 3080 Prince Edward St., Vancouver BC V5T 3N4 – 604/874-1141; Fax: 604/875-8733 – 214 beds – CEO, Rosemary Pahl

Vancouver: St. Paul's Hospital, 1081 Burrard St., Vancouver BC V6Z 1Y6 – 604/682-2344; Fax: 604/631-5135 – 448 beds – Pres. & CEO, Ron D. Mulchey

Vancouver: St. Vincent's Hospital Heather, 749 - 33rd Ave. West, Vancouver BC V5Z 2K4 – 604/876-7171; Fax: 604/876-6729 – 192 beds – CEO, Rosemary Pahl

Vancouver: Sunny Hill Health Centre for Children, 3644 Slocan St., Vancouver BC V5M 3E8 – 604/434-1331; Fax: 604/436-1743 – 28 beds – Pres., Ron Lindstrom

Vancouver: UBC Health Sciences Centre Hospital, 2211 Wesbrook Mall, Vancouver BC V6T 2B5 – 604/822-7121; Fax: 604/822-7186 – Pres. & CEO, Murray Martin, 604/875-4999

Vanderhoof: St. John Hospital, RR#2, Vanderhoof BC V0J 3A0 – 250/567-2211; Fax: 250/567-9713 – 33 beds – CEO, Ben L. Gumm

Vernon Jubilee Hospital, 2101 - 32nd St., Vernon BC V1T 5L2 – 250/545-2211; Fax: 250/545-5602 – 161 beds – Exec. Dir., Bruce Swan

Victoria General Hospital, 35 Helmcken Rd., Victoria BC V8Z 6R5 – 250/727-4212; Fax: 250/386-9119 – 464 beds – Pres., Patricia Coward, 250/370-8699

Victoria: Aberdeen Hospital, 1450 Hillside Ave., Victoria BC V8T 2B7 – 250/595-4321; Fax: 250/595-8412 – 600 beds – Adm., Peter McAllister

Victoria: The Gorge Road Hospital, 63 Gorge Rd. East, Victoria BC V9A 1L2 – 250/386-2464; Fax: 250/386-9119 – 332 beds – Pres./CEO, Patricia Coward, 250/370-8699

Victoria: Queen Alexandra Centre for Children's Health, 2400 Arbutus Rd., Victoria BC V8N 1V7 – 250/477-1826; Fax: 250/721-6837 – 50 beds – Pres., Cheryl Craver

Victoria: Royal Jubilee Hospital, 1900 Fort St., Victoria BC V8R 1J8 – 250/370-8000; Fax: 250/370-8750 – 634 beds – Pres., Patricia Coward, 250/370-8699

Waglisla: R.W. Large Memorial Hospital, Waglisla BC V0T 1Z0 – 250/957-2314; Fax: 250/957-2612 – 21 beds – Adm., Wendy MacDonald

White Rock: Peace Arch District Hospital, 15521 Russell Ave., White Rock BC V4B 2R4 – 604/531-5512; Fax: 604/531-0726 – Interim CEO, Betty Ann Busse

Williams Lake: Cariboo Memorial Hospital, 517 - 6 Ave. North, Williams Lake BC V2G 2G8 – 250/392-4411; Fax: 250/392-2157 – 76 beds – Exec. Dir., Martin Oets

AUXILIARY HOSPITALS/HEALTH CARE CENTRES

Armstrong: Pleasant Valley Health Centre, 2745 Wright Ave., PO Box 459, Armstrong BC V0E 1B0 – 250/546-6131; Fax: 250/546-9943 – Transition Mgr., Brian Kines, 250/838-6441, Fax: 250/838-9530

Barriere & District Health Centre, PO Box 659, Barriere BC V0E 1E0 – 250/672-9731; Fax: 250/672-5144 – Adm., Linda Comazzetto

Chase & District Health Centre, 825 Thompson St., PO Box 1099, Chase BC V0E 1M0 – 250/679-3312; Fax: 250/679-5329 – Adm., Gerri Rintoul

Cumberland Health Care Centre, PO Box 400, Cumberland BC V0R 1S0 – 250/336-8531; Fax: 250/336-2100 – Adm., Elaine Sparks

Dease Lake: Stikine Regional Health Centre, Hwy. 37, Box 386, Dease Lake BC V0C 1L0 – 250/771-4444; Fax: 250/771-3180 – Adm., Gerry Burland

Gold River Health Clinic, PO Box 580, Gold River BC V0P 1G0 – 250/283-2626; Fax: 250/283-7561 – Public Adm., Jennifer English

Houston Health Centre, PO Box 538, Houston BC V0J 1Z0 – 250/845-2294; Fax: 250/845-2005 – Adm., Hanne White

Logan Lake Health Centre, PO Box 1089, Logan Lake BC V0K 1W0 – 250/523-9414; Fax: 250/523-6869 – Adm., Lea Doran

New Aiyansh: Nisga's Valley Health Centre, 256 Tait Ave., PO Box 234, New Aiyansh BC V0J 1A0 – 250/633-2212; Fax: 250/633-2512 – Adm., Floyd Davis

Pemberton & District Health Centre, PO Box 310, Pemberton BC V0N 2L0 – 604/894-6633; Fax: 604/894-6918 – Adm., Richard A. Wadsworth

Qualicum Beach: Eagle Park Health Care Facility, 777 Jones St., Qualicum Beach BC V9K 2L1 – 250/752-7075; Fax: 250/752-8316 – Adm., Pat Chern

Stewart Community Health Centre, 9 St. & Brightwell St., PO Box 8, Stewart BC V0T 1W0 – 250/636-2221; Fax: 250/636-2715 – 3 beds – CEO, Linda Hyde

Tahsis Health Centre, 1085 Maquinna Dr., PO Box 399, Tahsis BC V0P 1X0 – 250/934-6322; Fax: 250/934-6404 – 3 beds – Adm., Pamela Seitz

Terrace: James Samuel Gosnell Memorial Health Centre, PO Box 724, Terrace BC V8G 4C1 – 250/633-2212; Fax: 250/633-2512 – Adm., Floyd Davis

Tumbler Ridge Health Care Centre, 220 Front St., PO Box 80, Tumbler Ridge BC V0C 2W0 – 250/242-5271; Fax: 250/242-3889 – Adm., Dennis Hickey

Valemount Health Care Centre, PO Box 697, Valemount BC V0E 2Z0 – 250/566-9138; Fax: 250/566-4319 – Adm., Roberta Roe

Victoria: Fairfield Health Centre, 841 Fairfield Rd., Victoria BC V8V 3B6 – 250/389-6300; Fax: 250/727-4221 – Pres., Ken Fyke

FEDERAL HOSPITALS

Masset: Canadian Forces Station Hospital Masset, PO Box 2000, Masset BC V0T 1M0 – 250/626-3902; Fax: 250/626-3902 – Senior Medical Officer, 250/626-3902, ext.303

NURSING HOMES

Abbotsford: Menno Hospital, 32945 Marshall Rd., Abbotsford BC V2S 1K1 – 604/859-7631; Fax: 604/859-6931 – Adm., Gerald Neufeld

Armstrong: Pleasant Valley Health Centre, see Auxiliary Hospitals/Health Care Centres listings

Burnaby: Fellburn Hospital, 6050 Hastings St. East, Burnaby BC V5B 1R6 – 604/299-7471; Fax: 604/299-

1015 – Pres. & CEO, Jim Fair, 604/520-4840, Fax: 604/520-4827
Burnaby: St. Michael's Centre Extended Care Hospital, 7451 Sussex Ave., Burnaby BC V5J 5C2 – 604/434-1323; Fax: 604/434-6469 – Exec. Dir., Gerald Herkel
Fort St. James: Stuart Lake Hospital, Stuart Dr., PO Box 1060, Fort St. James BC V0J 1P0 – 250/996-8201; Fax: 250/996-8777 – Adm., Ben. L. Gumm
Fort St. John: Peace Lutheran Extended Care Centre, 9908 - 108th Ave., Fort St. John BC V1J 2R3 – 250/785-8941; Fax: 250/785-2296 – Adm., Willy Olesen
Kamloops: Overlander Extended Care Hospital, 953 Southill St., Kamloops BC V2B 7Z9 – 250/554-2323; Fax: 250/554-3403 – Adm., Corene T. Lindsay
Nelson: Mount St. Francis Hospital, 1300 Gordon Rd., Nelson BC V1L 3M5 – 250/352-3531; Fax: 250/352-6942 – Adm., Sheila Hart
New Westminster: Queen's Park Hospital, 315 McBride Blvd., New Westminster BC V3L 5E8 – 604/525-0911; Fax: 604/525-9712 – Pres. & CEO, Jim Fair
Parksville: Trillium Lodge, 401 Moilliet St., PO Box 940, Parksville BC V9P 2G9 – 250/248-8353; Fax: 250/248-8388 – Adm., Jim Banks
Pouce Coupe Care Home, PO Box 98, Pouce Coupe BC V0C 2C0 – 250/786-5791; Fax: 250/786-5492 – Adm., Dave Gallaway
Vancouver: Louis Brier Hospital, 1055 - 41st Ave. West, Vancouver BC V6M 1W9 – 604/261-9376; Fax: 604/266-8712 – Adm., Ken Levitt
Vancouver: St. Vincent's Hospital Arbutus, 6650 Arbutus St., Vancouver BC V6P 5S5 – 604/266-4166; Fax: 604/876-6729 – CEO, Rosemary Pahl
Vancouver: St. Vincent's Hospital Langara, 255 - 62nd Ave. West, Vancouver BC V5X 2C9 – 604/325-4116; Fax: 604/877-3081 – CEO, Rosemary Pahl
Victoria: Juan de Fuca Hospitals (Aberdeen, Glengarry, Mount Tolmie, Priory), 1450 Hillside Ave., Victoria BC V8T 2B7 – 250/595-5722; Fax: 250/595-8412 – CEO, Jeanette Funke-Furber
Victoria: Mount St. Mary Hospital, 999 Burdett Ave., Victoria BC V8V 3G7 – 250/384-7158; Fax: 250/384-7631 – CEO, Colleen Black

NURSING STATIONS

Burnaby: The Canadian Red Cross Society - BC - Yukon Division, #400, 4710 Kingsway, Burnaby BC V5H 4M2 – 604/431-4200; Fax: 604/431-4275 – Responsible for Red Cross Outpost Nursing Stations in: Alexis Creek; Atlin; Bamfield; Blue River; Edgewood, & Kyuquot – Mgr., Outpost Hospitals, Elizabeth J. Chambers

PRIVATE HOSPITALS

Burnaby: Carlton Private Hospital, 4125 Canada Way, Burnaby BC V5G 1G9 – 604/438-8224 – 75 beds – Adm., Gary Bell
Burnaby: Deer Lake Private Hospital, 6907 Elwell St., Burnaby BC V5E 1K3 – 604/522-5447 – 37 beds – Admin. Coord., AnnaMae Clarke
Burnaby: Willingdon Private Hospital, 4435 Grange St., Burnaby BC V5H 1P4 – 604/433-2455 – 95 beds – Adm., A.L. Bennewith
Coquitlam: Como Lake Private Hospital, 657 Gatensbury St., Coquitlam BC V3J 5G9 – 604/939-9277 – 89 beds – Adm., Gary Bell
Coquitlam: Dufferin Care Centre, 1131 Dufferin St., Coquitlam BC V3B 7X5 – 604/552-1166
Delta: Ladner/Deltaview Private Hospital, 9321 Burns Dr., Delta BC V4K 3N3 – 604/596-8814, 8842 – 144 beds – Adm. & Supt., Salim Devji
Fort Langley: Simpson Private Hospital, 8838 Glover Rd., Fort Langley BC V0X 1J0 – 250/383-7814 – 56 beds – Adm., Richard Haliburton
Kelowna: Still Waters Private Hospital, 1450 Sutherland Ave., Kelowna BC V1Y 5Y5 – 250/860-2216 – 78 beds – Adm., Greg Kornell
Maple Ridge: Holyrood Manor, 22710 - 117th Ave., Maple Ridge BC V2X 3E6 – 604/467-8831 – 75 beds – General Mgr., Richard Haliburton
Nelson: Willowhaven Private Hospital, RR#1, Nelson BC V1L 5P4 – 250/825-4411 – 84 beds – Co-Adm., Altaf Jina
North Vancouver: North Shore Private Hospital, 1070 Lynn Valley Rd., North Vancouver BC V7J 1Z8 – 604/988-4181 – 50 beds – Adm., Medi Sherkat
Prince George: Simon Fraser Lodge, 2410 Laurier Cres., Prince George BC V2M 2B3 – 250/563-3413 – 116 beds – Adm./Supt., Kathy Giene
Vancouver: Amherst Private Hospital, 375 - West 59th Ave., Vancouver BC V5X 1X3 – 604/321-6777 – 75 beds – Adm., M. Millar
Vancouver: Braddan Private Hospital, 2450 West 2nd Ave., Vancouver BC V6X 1J6 – 604/731-2127 – 50 beds – Adm., Maureen McIntosh
Vancouver: Carlsbad Private Hospital, 2423 Cornwall Ave., Vancouver BC V6X 1B9 – 604/733-7133 – 47 beds – Adm., T. McDonald, 604/731-2273
Vancouver: Edith Cavell Private Hospital, 2855 Sophia St., Vancouver BC V5T 3L2 – 604/874-9321 – 62 beds – Adm., Kevin Svoboda
Vancouver: Glen Private Hospital, 1036 Salsbury Dr., Vancouver BC V5L 4A7 – 604/255-5727, 6426 – 65 beds – Adm., Verna Merrifield
Vancouver: Kensington Private Hospital, 750 West 41st Ave., Vancouver BC V5Z 2N3 – 604/261-8108 – 78 beds – Adm., Nujin Rana
Vancouver: Normandy Private Hospital, 4505 Valley Dr., Vancouver BC V6L 2L1 – 604/261-4292 – 180 beds – Adm., Richard Haliburton
Vancouver: Roayl Ascot Care Centre, 2455 East Broadway, Vancouver BC V5M 1Y1 – 604/254-5559, ext.28 – 75 beds – Adm., Stan Dub
Vancouver: Southpines Private Hospital, 325 West 59th Ave., Vancouver BC V5X 1X3 – 604/321-0214 – 34 beds – Adm., D. McDonald, 604/736-6460
Vancouver: Trout Lake Manor, 3490 Porter St., Vancouver BC V5N 4H2 – 604/874-2803 – 100 beds – Adm., Verna Merrifield
Victoria: Clovelly Private Hospital, 1196 Clovelly Terrace, Victoria BC V8P 1V6 – 250/383-7814 – 43 beds – Adm., Patricia Coleman
Victoria: Glenwarren Lodge, 1230 Balmoral Rd., Victoria BC V8T 1B3 – 250/383-2323 – 130 beds – Adm., Thom Murray
Victoria: Sandringham Private Hospital, 1650 Fort St., Victoria BC V8R 1H9 – 250/595-2313 – 85 beds – General Mgr., Richard Haliburton
Victoria: Wayside House, 550 Foul Bay Rd., Victoria BC V8S 4H1 – 250/598-4521 – 18 beds – Adm., P. Granham
West Vancouver Care Centre, 1675 - 27th St., West Vancouver BC V7V 4K9 – 604/925-1247 – 75 beds – Adm., Georgina Buchanan
West Vancouver: Beacon Hill Private Hospital, 525 Clyde Ave., West Vancouver BC V7T 1C4 – 604/926-6856 – 73 beds – Adm., Oriel Morrison
West Vancouver: Inglewood Private Hospital, 725 Inglewood Ave., West Vancouver BC V7T 1X5 – 604/922-9394; Fax: 604/922-2709 – 93 beds – Adm., David Ail, 604/685-8292

SPECIAL TREATMENT CENTRES

(Includes: Abortion Clinics, Cancer Clinics, Rehabilitation Centres, Treatment Centres)

Elkford & District Diagnostic & Treatment Centre, PO Box 640, Elkford BC V0B 1H0 – 250/865-2247; Fax: 250/865-2797 – Adm., Wendy Timmerman
Fraser Lake Diagnostic & Treatment Centre, PO Box 1000, Fraser Lake BC V0J 1S0 – 250/699-7742; Fax: 250/699-6987 – Adm., Ben L. Gumm
Hudson's Hope Gething Diagnostic & Treatment Centre, PO Box 599, Hudson's Hope BC V0C 1V0 – 250/783-9991; Fax: 250/783-9125 – Adm., Heather M. Wilson
Keremeos Diagnostic & Treatment Centre, PO Box 579, Keremeos BC V0X 1N0 – 250/499-5518; Fax: 250/499-2559 – Adm., Ken Doepker
Vancouver: The Arthritis Centre of B.C., 895 West 10th Ave., Vancouver BC V5Z 1L7 – 604/879-7511; Fax: 604/871-4500 – A/Exec. Dir., Mike Mahony
Vancouver: B.C. Drug & Poison Information Centre, c/o St. Paul's Hospital, 1081 Burrard St., Vancouver BC V6Z 1Y6 – 604/682-2344, ext.2126; Fax: 604/631-5262 – Managing Dir., Derek E. Daws, B.Sc.
Vancouver: British Columbia Cancer Agency, 600 - 10th Ave. West, Vancouver BC V5Z 4E6 – 604/877-6000; Fax: 604/872-4596 – cancer treatment – CEO, Dr. Donald Carlow
Vancouver: British Columbia's Women's Hospital & Health Centre, 4500 Oak St., Vancouver BC V6H 3N1 – 604/875-3060; Fax: 604/875-3136 – Pres./CEO, Lynda Cranston
Vancouver: Elizabeth Bagshaw Woman's Clinic, #40, 3195 Granville St., Vancouver BC V6H 3K1 – 604/736-7878; Fax: 604/736-8081 – abortion clinic – Adm., Bethan Everett
Vancouver: Everywoman's Health Centre, 2005 - 44th St. East, Vancouver BC V5P 1N1 – 604/322-6692 – abortion clinic
Vancouver: George Pearson Centre, 700 - 57th St. West, Vancouver BC V6P 1S1 – 604/321-3231; Fax: 604/321-7833 – treatment centre – Pres., W.G. Fraser
Vancouver: G.F. Strong Centre, 4255 Laurel St., Vancouver BC V5Z 2G9 – 604/734-1313; Fax: 604/737-6359 – treatment centre – Adm., Vacant
Victoria: British Columbia Cancer Agency - Victoria Clinic, Royal Jubilee Hospital, 1900 Fort St., Victoria BC V8R 1J8 – 250/370-8228; Fax: 250/370-8750 – cancer treatment
Whistler Diagnostic & Treatment Centre, 4380 Lorimer Rd., Whistler BC V0N 1B4 – 604/932-4911; Fax: 604/932-4992 – Acting Adm., Bill Crysler

MANITOBA

HOSPITAL DISTRICTS/HEALTH UNITS

Ashern: Lakeshore District Health System, PO Box 110, Ashern MB R0C 0E0 – 204/768-2461; Fax: 204/768-2337 – 20 beds – Adm., Wayne Lavallee
Baldur Health District, PO Box 128, Baldur MB R0K 0B0 – 204/535-2373; Fax: 204/535-2116 – 14 beds - Exec. Dir., R.J. Westwood
Beauséjour Hospital District No. 29, PO Box 1178, Beauséjour MB R0E 0C0 – 204/268-1076; Fax: 204/268-1207 – 30 beds – CEO, Arlene Gibson
Birtle Health Services District No. 10, PO Box 10, Birtle MB R0M 0C0 – 204/842-3317; Fax: 204/842-3375 – 16 beds – CEO, James Barlett
Crystal City: Rock Lake Health District, PO Box 130, Crystal City MB R0K 0N0 – 204/873-2132; Fax: 204/873-2185 – 16 beds - Exec. Dir., Terrance Hills
Deloraine: South West Health District, PO Box 447, Deloraine MB R0M 0M0 – 204/747-2745; Fax: 204/747-2160 – Acting CEO, Penny Sorensen
Emerson: Red River Valley Health District, PO Box 428, Emerson MB R0A 0L0 – 204/373-2109; Fax: 204/373-2748 – Exec. Dir., Helmut Klassen
Gimli Hospital District No.39, PO Box 250, Gimli MB R0C 1B0 – 204/642-5116; Fax: 204/642-5860 – Chair, Roger Jackson
Glenboro Health District, PO Box 310, Glenboro MB R0K 0X0 – 204/827-2438; Fax: 204/827-2199 – 14 beds – Chairman District Board, Betty Christie

Canadian Almanac & Directory 1997

Killarney: Tri-Lake Health District, PO Box 4000, Killarney MB R0K 1G0 – 204/523-4661; Fax: 204/523-8948 – 26 beds – CEO, Miriam Nichol

Lac du Bonnet: Winnipeg River Health District, PO Box 1030, Lac du Bonnet MB R0E 1A0 – 204/345-8647; Fax: 204/345-8609 – Chairman District Board, Laurie Pilon

Manitou: Pembina-Manitou Health District, PO Box 129, Manitou MB R0G 1G0 – 204/248-2092; Fax: 204/248-2499 – Chairman District Board, Dale Dobson

Minnedosa Health District, PO Box 960, Minnedosa MB R0J 1E0 – 204/867-2701; Fax: 204/867-2239 – 27 beds – Adm., Mike Kufflick

Morden Health District, 30 Stephen St., Morden MB R0M 1X8 – 204/822-4411; Fax: 204/822-4520 – 71 beds – Exec. Dir., Ray Racette

Rivers: Riverdale Health Services District, PO Box 428, Rivers MB R0K 1X0 – 204/328-7553; Fax: 204/328-7130 – 16 beds – CEO, G. Worthington

Roblin Health District, PO Box 940, Roblin MB R0L 1P0 – 204/937-2142; Fax: 204/937-8892 – 25 beds – Adm., C. Clearwater

Souris Health District, PO Box 10, Souris MB R0K 2C0 – 204/483-2121; Fax: 204/483-2310 – 30 beds – Chairman, District Board, George Torrance

Teulon-Hunter Memorial Health District, PO Box 89, Teulon MB R0C 3B0 – 204/886-2433; Fax: 204/886-2653 – 20 beds – Exec. Dir., Tannis Erickson

Treherne: Tiger Hills Health District, PO Box 130, Treherne MB R0G 2V0 – 204/723-2113; Fax: 204/723-2869 – 18 beds – Exec. Dir., R.J. Westwood

Virden: Health District No. 10, PO Box 400, Virden MB R0M 2C0 – 204/748-1230; Fax: 204/748-2053 – 24 beds – Adm., John Rakai

GENERAL HOSPITALS

Altona Community Memorial Health Centre, PO Box 660, Altona MB R0G 0B0 – 204/324-6411; Fax: 204/324-1299 – 22 beds – Exec. Dir., Peter Elias

Arborg & District Health Centre, PO Box 10, Arborg MB R0C 0A0 – 204/376-5247; Fax: 204/376-5669 – 16 beds – Exec. Dir., Tannis Erikson

Ashern: Lakeshore General Hospital, PO Box 110, Ashern MB R0C 0E0 – 204/768-2461; Fax: 204/768-2337 – 16 beds – Adm., Wayne Lavallee

Boissevain District Health Centre, PO Box 899, Boissevain MB R0K 0E0 – 204/534-2451; Fax: 204/534-6487 – 12 beds – Adm., F.J. Woodmass, 204/534-2455, Fax: 204/534-6633

Brandon General Hospital, 150 McTavish Ave. East, Brandon MB R7A 2B3 – 204/726-1122; Fax: 204/728-0528 – 319 beds – CEO, Larry E. Todd, 204/726-2119

Carberry Plains District Health Centre, PO Box 1, Carberry MB R0K 0H0 – 204/834-2144; Fax: 204/834-3333 – 27 beds – Adm., Dale Aitken

Carman Memorial Hospital, PO Box 610, Carman MB R0G 0J0 – 204/745-2021; Fax: 204/745-2756 – 30 beds – Exec. Dir., René Comte

Cartwright & District Hospital, PO Box 118, Cartwright MB R0K 0L0 – 204/529-2452; Fax: 204/529-2562 – 10 beds – CEO, Miriam Nichol

Churchill Health Centre, Churchill Town Centre, General Delivery, Churchill MB R0B 0E0 – 204/675-8881; Fax: 204/675-2643 – 31 beds – Acting Exec. Dir. & Dir. of Nursing, Joanne Kelly

Dauphin Regional Health Centre, 625 - 3 St. SW, Dauphin MB R7N 1R7 – 204/638-3010; Fax: 204/638-3183 – 103 beds – Exec. Dir., Mark Neskar

Deloraine Health Centre, PO Box 447, Deloraine MB R0M 0M0 – 204/747-2745; Fax: 204/747-2160 – 18 beds – Acting CEO, Penny Sorensen

Emerson Hospital, PO Box 428, Emerson MB R0A 0L0 – 204/373-2109; Fax: 204/373-2748 – 8 beds – Exec. Dir., Helmut Klassen

Erickson District Health Centre, PO Box 25, Erickson MB R0J 0P0 – 204/636-7777; Fax: 204/636-2471 – 12 beds – Adm., Mike Kufflick

Eriksdale: Elizabeth M. Crowe Memorial Hospital, PO Box 130, Eriksdale MB R0C 0W0 – 204/739-2611; Fax: 204/739-2065 – 17 beds – Adm., Wayne Lavallee

Fisher Branch Medical Facilities Inc., PO Box 370, Fisher Branch MB R0C 0Z0 – 204/372-6258; Fax: 204/372-6554 – Dir. of Nursing, June Caldwell

Flin Flon General Hospital, PO Box 340, Flin Flon MB R8A 1N2 – 204/687-7591; Fax: 204/687-8494 – 83 beds – Exec. Dir., Gerry Hildebrand

Gillam Hospital Inc., PO Box 2000, Gillam MB R0B 0L0 – 204/652-2600; Fax: 204/652-2536 – 10 beds – CEO, Neil McMartin

Gimli: Johnson Memorial Hospital, PO Box 250, Gimli MB R0C 1B0 – 204/642-5116; Fax: 204/642-5860 – 35 beds – Exec. Dir., Dawna Suchy

Gladstone: Seven Regions Health Centre, PO Box 1000, Gladstone MB R0J 0T0 – 204/385-2968; Fax: 204/385-2663 – 20 beds – Exec. Dir., Garry Mattin

Grandview District Hospital, PO Box 339, Grandview MB R0L 0Y0 – 204/546-2425; Fax: 204/546-3269 – 18 beds – Dir. of Nursing, Melodie Powell

Hamiota District Health Centre, 177 Birch Ave., Hamiota MB R0M 0T0 – 204/764-2412; Fax: 204/764-2049 – 22 beds – Acting Adm., Vaughn Wilson

Lynn Lake District Hospital No. 38, PO Box 2030, Lynn Lake MB R0B 0W0 – 204/356-2474; Fax: 204/356-8023 – 25 beds – Nurse Mgr., Brenda Neufeld

McCreary/Alonsa Health Centre, PO Box 250, McCreary MB R0J 1B0 – 204/835-2482; Fax: 204/835-2713 – 13 beds – Adm., Carol Everett

Melita Health Centre, PO Box 459, Melita MB R0M 1L0 – 204/522-8197; Fax: 204/522-3161 – 11 beds – Acting CEO, Penny Sorensen

Morris General Hospital, PO Box 519, Morris MB R0G 1K0 – 204/746-2301; Fax: 204/746-2197 – 27 beds – Exec. Dir., Helmut Klassen

Neepawa District Memorial Hospital, PO Box 1240, Neepawa MB R0J 1H0 – 204/476-2394, 5855 (Admin.); Fax: 204/476-5007, 3765 (Admin.) – 38 beds – Exec. Dir., Eric Gustafson

Norway House Hospital, Norway House MB R0B 1B0 – 204/359-6731; Fax: 204/359-6599 – 16 beds – Adm., Leonard T. York

Pinawa Hospital, PO Box 220, Pinawa MB R0E 1L0 – 204/753-2334; Fax: 204/753-2219 – 17 beds – Adm., Linda West

Pine Falls Health Complex, PO Box 2000, Pine Falls MB R0E 1M0 – 204/367-4441; Fax: 204/367-8981 – 27 beds – Exec. Dir., Susan Derk

Portage District General Hospital, 524 - 5 St. SE, Portage la Prairie MB R1N 3A8 – 204/239-2211; Fax: 204/239-6039 – 128 beds – Exec. Dir., Garry Mattin

Rossburn District Health Centre, PO Box 40, Rossburn MB R0J 1V0 – 204/859-2413; Fax: 204/859-2526 – 10 beds – Adm., Duane Belbeck

Russell District Hospital, Bag Service 2, Russell MB R0J 1W0 – 204/773-2125; Fax: 204/773-2142 – 38 beds – Exec. Dir./Dir. of Nursing, Marguerite Kendell

Ste Anne Hospital, 52 St. Gerard St., PO Box 10, Ste Anne MB R0A 1R0 – 204/422-8837; Fax: 204/422-9929 – 21 beds – Exec. Dir., F. Labossiere

St. Claude Hospital, PO Box 400, St. Claude MB R0G 1Z0 – 204/379-2585; Fax: 204/379-2655 – 12 beds – Exec. Dir., Ardith Rothwell

Ste Rose General Hospital, PO Box 60, Ste Rose du Lac MB R0L 1S0 – 204/447-2131; Fax: 204/447-2250 – 60 beds – Exec. Dir., John J.M. Kelly

Selkirk & District General Hospital, 100 Easton Dr., PO Box 5000, Selkirk MB R1A 2M2 – 204/482-5800; Fax: 204/785-9113 – 75 beds – Exec. Dir., Elmer Kuber

Shoal Lake - Strathclair Health Centre, PO Box 490, Shoal Lake MB R0J 1Z0 – 204/759-2336; Fax: 204/759-2480 – 19 beds – Exec. Dir., Sandra Delorme

Swan Lake: Lorne Memorial Hospital, PO Box 40, Swan Lake MB R0G 2S0 – 204/836-2132; Fax: 204/836-2044 – 21 beds – Exec. Dir., René Comte

Swan River Valley Hospital, PO Box 1450, Swan River MB R0L 1Z0 – 204/734-9451; Fax: 204/734-9081 – 77 beds – Exec. Dir., Todd Stepanuik

The Pas Health Complex Inc., PO Box 240, The Pas MB R9A 1K4 – 204/623-6431; Fax: 204/623-5372 – 60 beds – Exec. Dir., Don Solar

Thompson General Hospital, 871 Thompson Dr. South, Thompson MB R8N 0C8 – 204/677-5300; Fax: 204/778-8298 – 72 beds – Exec. Dir., Vic Wiebe

Winkler: Bethel Hospital, 133 - 6th St., PO Box 1070, Winkler MB R6W 4B1 – 204/325-4354; Fax: 204/325-5944 – 53 beds – Exec. Dir., Ray Racette

Winnipeg: Concordia Hospital, 1095 Concordia Ave., Winnipeg MB R2K 3S8 – 204/667-1560; Fax: 204/667-1049 – 196 beds – Exec. Dir., Bill Patmore, 204/661-7144

Winnipeg: Health Sciences Centre, 820 Sherbrook St., Winnipeg MB R3A 1R9 – 204/774-6511; Fax: 204/787-3912 – teaching hospital – 854 beds – Pres., A. Rodney Thorfinnson, 204/787-7346

Winnipeg: Misericordia General Hospital, 99 Cornish Ave., Winnipeg MB R3C 1A2 – 204/774-6581; Fax: 204/783-6052 – 224 beds – Pres., Ted Bartman, 204/788-8361

Winnipegosis General Hospital, PO Box 280, Winnipegosis MB R0L 2G0 – 204/656-4881; Fax: 204/656-4402 – 18 beds – Exec. Dir., Paul Quennelle

Winnipeg: Riverview Health Centre, One Morley Ave., Winnipeg MB R3L 2P4 – 204/452-3411; Fax: 204/452-3246 – 319 beds – Pres., Norman R. Kasian, 204/478-6212

Winnipeg: St. Boniface General Hospital, 409 Tache Ave., Winnipeg MB R2H 2A6 – 204/233-8563; Fax: 204/231-0640; EMail: rabnett@sbrc.umanitoba.ca – teaching hospital – 557 beds – Pres. & CEO, Kenneth Tremblay

Winnipeg: The Salvation Army Grace General Hospital, 300 Booth Dr., Winnipeg MB R3J 3M7 – 204/837-8311; Fax: 204/885-7909 – 261 beds – Pres. & CEO, Capt. John McFarlane, 204/837-0143, Fax: 204/831-0029

Winnipeg: Seven Oaks General Hospital, 2300 McPhillips St., Winnipeg MB R2V 3M3 – 204/632-7133; Fax: 204/697-2106 – 290 beds – Pres., N. Kalansky, 204/632-3327

Winnipeg: Victoria General Hospital, 2340 Pembina Hwy., Winnipeg MB R3T 2E8 – 204/269-3570; Fax: 204/261-0223 – 221 beds – Pres. & CEO, Marion Suski, 204/477-3376

AUXILIARY HOSPITALS/HEALTH CARE CENTRES

Hartney Medical Nursing Unit, PO Box 280, Hartney MB R0M 0X0 – 204/858-2078; Fax: 204/483-2310 – 9 beds – Adm., F.J. Woodmass

Lac du Bonnet District Health Centre, see Winnipeg River Health District, Hospital Districts/Health Units listings

Leaf Rapids Health Centre, PO Box 370, Leaf Rapids MB R0B 1W0 – 204/473-2441; Fax: 204/473-8273 – 8 beds – Nurse Mgr., Norma Charriere

MacGregor & District Health Centre, PO Box 250, MacGregor MB R0H 0R0 – 204/685-2850; Fax: 204/685-2529 – 6 beds – Exec. Dir., Garry Mattin

Notre Dame Medical Nursing Unit, PO Box 130, Notre Dame de Lourdes MB R0G 1M0 – 204/248-2112, 2092 (Admin.); Fax: 204/248-2499 – 10 beds – Exec. Dir., René Comte

Reston District Health Centre, PO Box 250, Reston MB R0M 1X0 – 204/877-3925; Fax: 204/877-3998 – 17 beds – Adm., John Rakai

MANITOBA NURSING HOMES

St. Pierre-Jolys: Centre Medico-Social DeSalaberry District Health Centre, PO Box 320, St. Pierre-Jolys MB R0A 1V0 – 204/433-7611; Fax: 204/433-7466 – 18 beds – Adm. & Dir. of Nursing, Suzanne Nicolas

Snow Lake Medical Nursing Unit, PO Box 453, Snow Lake MB R0B 1M0 – 204/358-2300; Fax: 204/358-7310 – 4 beds – Adm., Gerry Hildebrand

Steinbach: Bethesda Health & Social Services, PO Box 939, Steinbach MB R0A 2A0 – 204/326-6411; Fax: 204/326-6931 – 80 beds – Exec. Dir., Wilmar Chopyk

Stonewall & District Health Centre, 385 - 3rd St. West, PO Box 2000, Stonewall MB R0C 2Z0 – 204/467-5514; Fax: 204/467-9194 – 15 beds – Exec. Dir., Kevin Beresford

Vita District Health Centre Inc., 217 First Ave. West, Vita MB R0A 2K0 – 204/425-3804; Fax: 204/425-3545 – 10 beds – Adm., K.P. Aujlay

Wawanesa & District Memorial Health Centre, PO Box 309, Wawanesa MB R0K 2G0 – 204/824-2335; Fax: 204/824-2148 – 9 beds – CEO, Jim Westwood

Whitemouth District Health Centre, PO Box 160, Whitemouth MB R0E 2G0 – 204/348-7191; Fax: 204/348-7911 – 6 beds – Adm., Therese Conroy

Winkler: Eden Health Care Services, 204 Main St., PO Box 129, Winkler MB R6W 4A4 – 204/325-5355; Fax: 204/325-8742 – Exec. Dir., Ken Loewen

Winnipeg: Clinique Youville Clinic Inc., 33 Marion St., Winnipeg MB R2H 0S8 – 204/233-0262; Fax: 204/233-1520 – Exec. Dir., Marion Deegan

Winnipeg: Health Sciences Centre - Health Action Centre, 425 Elgin Ave., Winnipeg MB R3A 1P2 – 204/947-1626; Fax: 204/942-7828 – Exec. Dir., Jeanette Edwards

Winnipeg: Hope Centre Health Care Inc., 240 Powers St., Winnipeg MB R2W 5L1 – 204/589-8354; Fax: 204/586-4260 – Acting Exec. Dir., Giselle Lamy

Winnipeg: Klinic Community Health Centre, 870 Portage Ave., Winnipeg MB R3G 0P1 – 204/784-4090; Fax: 204/772-7998 – Acting Exec. Dir., Paula Lewis

Winnipeg: M.F.L. Occupation Health Centre, #102, 275 Broadway, Winnipeg MB R3C 4M6 – 204/949-0811; Fax: 204/956-0848 – Exec. Dir., Judy Cook

Winnipeg: Mount Carmel Clinic, 886 Main St., Winnipeg MB R2W 5L4 – 204/582-2311; Fax: 204/582-1341 – Exec. Dir., Thomas Kean

Winnipeg: Nor'west Health & Social Service Centre Inc., #103, 61 Tyndall Ave., Winnipeg MB R2X 2T4 – 204/633-5955; Fax: 204/632-4666 – Exec. Dir., Cheryl Susinski

Winnipeg: Village Clinic, 668 Corydon Ave., Winnipeg MB R3M 0X7 – 204/453-0045; Fax: 204/453-5214 – Exec. Dir., Patricia. Stewart

Winnipeg: Women's Health Clinic Inc., 419 Graham St., 3rd Fl., Winnipeg MB R3C 0M3 – 204/947-1517; Fax: 204/943-3844 – Exec. Dir., Barbara Wiktorowicz

FEDERAL HOSPITALS

Hodgson: Percy E. Moore Hospital, PO Box 190, Hodgson MB R0C 1N0 – 204/372-8444; Fax: 204/372-6991 – 16 beds – Adm., Elaine Kennedy

Norway House Indian Hospital, Norway House MB R0B 1B0

HOME CARE OFFICES/COMMUNITY CARE SERVICES

Beausejour: Community & Mental Health Services - Eastman Region, 20 - 1st St. South, Beausejour MB R0E 0C0 – 204/268-6114; Fax: 204/268-3890 – Acting Regional Dir., Don Gibson

Brandon: Community & Mental Health Services - Westman Region, 340 - 9th St., Brandon MB R7A 6C2 – 204/726-6294; Fax: 204/726-6536 – Regional Dir., Ray Kreitzer

Dauphin: Community & Mental Health Services - Parkland Region, 27 - 2nd Ave. SW, Dauphin MB R7N 3E5 – 204/622-2035; Fax: 204/638-3278 – Regional Dir., Yvonne Hrynkiw

Portage la Prairie: Community & Mental Health Services - Central Region, 25 Tupper St. South, Portage la Prairie MB R1N 3K1 – 204/239-3101; Fax: 204/239-3148 – Regional Dir., Sheldon Hiltz

Selkirk: Community & Mental Health Services - Interlake Region, Administration Bldg., 3rd Fl., PO Box 9600, Selkirk MB R1A 2B5 – 204/785-5160; Fax: 204/785-5210 – Regional Dir., Pat Kinrade

The Pas: Community & Mental Health Services - Norman Region, 115 - 3rd St. East, PO Box 2550, The Pas MB R9A 1M4 – 204/627-8240; Fax: 204/623-5792 – Regional Dir., John Karpan

Thompson: Community & Mental Health Services - Thompson Region, 871 Thompson Dr. South, Thompson MB R8N 0C1 – 204/677-7210; Fax: 204/677-6517 – Regional Dir., Vic Wiebe

Winnipeg: Community & Mental Health Services - Winnipeg Region, #5, 189 Evanson St., Winnipeg MB R3G 0N9 – 204/945-4505; Fax: 204/945-1735 – Regional Dir., Carol Renner

Winnipeg: Independent Living Resource Centre, #201, 294 Portage Ave., Winnipeg MB R3C 0B9 – 204/947-0194

MENTAL HEALTH HOSPITALS & COMMUNITY FACILITIES

Brandon Mental Health Centre, PO Box 420, Brandon MB R7A 5Z5 – 204/728-7110 – Adm., Clay Hutchinson

Selkirk Mental Health Centre, 825 Manitoba Ave. West, PO Box 9600, Selkirk MB R1A 2B5 – 204/482-3810; Fax: 204/785-8936 – Acting CEO, Brian Surridge

Winkler: Eden Mental Health Centre, 1500 Pembina Ave., Winkler MB R6W 1T4 – 204/325-4325; Fax: 204/325-8429 – 40 beds – Adm., Adeline Braun

NURSING HOMES

Altona & District Personal Care Home, see Altona Community Memorial Health Centre, General Hospitals listings

Altona: The Ebenezer Home for the Aged, 235 - 5th St. NE, PO Box 900, Altona MB R0G 0B0 – 204/324-6486; Fax: 204/324-8917 – 44 beds – A/Exec. Dir., Mildred Hiebert

Arborg: Pioneer Health Services Inc., PO Box 10, Arborg MB R0C 0A0 – 204/376-5226; Fax: 204/376-5669 – 40 beds – Adm., T. Erikson

Ashern Personal Care Home, see Lakeshore District Health System, Hospital Districts/Health Units listings

Baldur Manor, PO Box 128, Baldur MB R0K 0B0 – 204/535-2456; Fax: 204/535-2116 – 20 beds – Charge Nurse, Joyce Wilson

Beausejour: East-Gate Lodge Inc., 646 James Ave., PO Box 1690, Beausejour MB R0E 0C0 – 204/268-1029; Fax: 204/268-3225 – 60 – Exec. Dir., Arlene Gibson

Benito Health Centre, PO Box 490, Benito MB R0L 0C0 – 204/539-2815; Fax: 204/539-2482 – 25 beds – Exec. Dir., T. Stepanuik

Birtle Personal Care Home Inc., see Birtle Health Services District No. 10, Hospital Districts/Health Units listings

Boissevain: Evergreen Place, PO Box 899, Boissevain MB R0K 0E0 – 204/534-2451; Fax: 204/534-6487 – 20 beds – Nurse in Charge, Susan Nay

Brandon: Central Park Lodges Ltd., 3015 Victoria Ave., Brandon MB R7B 2K2 – 204/728-2030; Fax: 204/729-8351 – 89 beds – Mgr./Adm., Teresa Kindrat

Brandon: Dinsdale Personal Care Home, 510 - 6th St., Brandon MB R7A 3N9 – 204/727-3636; Fax: 204/727-2103 – 60 beds – Adm., Capt. Leslie Russell

Brandon: Fairview Home Inc., 1351 - 13th St., Brandon MB R7A 4S5 – 204/728-6696; Fax: 204/727-7616 – 248 – A/Exec. Dir., Janet Wilcox-McKay

Brandon: Hillcrest Place, 930 - 26th St., Brandon MB R7B 2B8 – 204/728-6690; Fax: 204/726-0089 – 100 beds – Adm., Kathy Sutherland

Brandon: Rideau Park Personal Care Home, 525 Victoria Ave. East, Brandon MB R7A 6S9 – 204/727-1734; Fax: 204/726-6690 – 100 beds – Adm., Larry Sage

Carberry Personal Care Home, 1st Ave., Carberry MB R0K 0H0 – 204/834-2076; Fax: 204/834-3333 – 30 beds – Adm., Dale Aitken

Carman: Boyne Lodge, PO Box 910, Carman MB R0G 0J0 – 204/745-6715; Fax: 204/745-6152 – 70 beds – Dir. of Nursing, V. Driedger

Crystal City: Rock Lake Personal Care Home, see Rock Lake Health District, Hospital Districts/Health Units listings

Dauphin Personal Care Home Inc., 625 Third St. SW, Dauphin MB R7N 1R7 – 204/638-3010; Fax: 204/638-3183 – 90 beds – Dir. of Resident Servs., Arlene Olynick

Dauphin: St. Paul's Home, 703 Jackson St., Dauphin MB R7N 2N2 – 204/638-3129; Fax: 204/638-9294 – 70 beds – Exec. Dir., Sr. Jean Zemliak

Deloraine: Delwynda Court Personal Care Home Inc., see Deloraine Health Centre, General Hospitals listings

Deloraine: Bren-Del-Win Lodge, PO Box 527, Deloraine MB R0M 0M0 – 204/747-2119; Fax: 204/747-2160 – 30 beds – CEO, Carmel Olson

Elkhorn: Elkwood Manor, PO Box 70, Elkhorn MB R0M 0N0 – 204/845-2575; Fax: 204/845-2371 – 24 beds – Adm., John Rakai

Emerson Personal Care Home (Red River Valley Lodge), PO Box 428, Emerson MB R0A 0L0 – 204/373-2208 – 20 beds – Exec. Dir., Arlene Wilgosh

Emerson: Red River Valley Lodge (Emerson), see Emerson Hospital, General Hospitals listings

Erickson Personal Care Home, see Erickson District Health Centre, General Hospitals listings

Eriksdale Personal Care Home, 1st St. NE, PO Box 130, Eriksdale MB R0C 0W0 – 204/739-2611; Fax: 204/739-2065 – 20 beds – Adm., Wayne Lavallee

Flin Flon Personal Care Corp., PO Box 340, Flin Flon MB R8A 1N2 – 204/687-9630; Fax: 204/687-8494 – 30 beds – Exec. Dir., R.J. Shaw

Flin Flon: Northern Lights Manor Inc., PO Box 340, Flin Flon MB R8A 1N2 – 204/687-7591; Fax: 204/687-8494 – 30 beds – Unit Mgr., Gail Friesen

Gilbert Plains Health District, PO Box 368, Gilbert Plains MB R0L 0X0 – 204/548-2161; Fax: 204/548-2516 – 30 beds – Adm., Jerry Mrozowich

Gimli: Betel Home Foundation, PO Box 10, Gimli MB R0C 1B0 – 204/642-5004; Fax: 204/642-7243 – 80 beds – Exec. Dir., S.L. Bruce

Gladstone: Third Crossing Manor Inc., PO Box 539, Gladstone MB R0J 0T0 – 204/385-2474; Fax: 204/385-2163 – 50 beds – Dir. of Personal Care, Donna Cymbalist

Glenboro Personal Care Home, see Glenboro Health District, Hospital Districts/Health Units listings

The Grandview Personal Care Home Inc., 308 Jackson St., PO Box 130, Grandview MB R0L 0Y0 – 204/546-2769; Fax: 204/546-2207 – 40 beds – Exec. Dir., Jerry Mrozowich

Grunthal: Menno Home for the Aged, PO Box 280, Grunthal MB R0A 0R0 – 204/434-6496; Fax: 204/434-9131 – 40 beds – Exec. Dir., Frank Klassen

Hamiota Personal Care Home, see Hamiota District Health Centre, General Hospitals listings

Killarney: Bayside Personal Care Home Inc., see Tri-Lake Health District, Hospital Districts/Health Units listings

Killarney: Lakeview Senior Citizens Home, PO Box 730, Killarney MB R0K 1G0 – 204/523-4661 – 35 beds – Head Nurse, L. Blixhavn

Canadian Almanac & Directory 1997

Lac du Bonnet Personal Care Home, PO Box 1030, Lac du Bonnet MB R0E 1A0 – 204/345-8675; Fax: 204/345-8609 – 30 beds – Dir. of Res. Servs., Judy Coleman

Lundar Personal Care Home, 1st St. South, PO Box 296, Lundar MB R0C 1Y0 – 204/762-5663, 5866; Fax: 204/762-5164 – 20 beds – Adm., W. Lavallee

MacGregor Personal Care Home, see MacGregor & District Health Centre, Auxiliary Hospitals/Health Care Centres listings

McCreary/Alonsa Personal Care Home Inc., see McCreary/Alonsa Health Centre, General Hospitals listings

Melita & Area Personal Care Home Inc., 147 Summit St., Melita MB R0M 1L0 – 204/522-3975; Fax: 204/522-3161 – 20 beds – Charge Nurse, J. Vanbeselaere

Minnedosa & District Personal Care Home, see Minnedosa Health District, Hospital Districts/Health Units listings

Morden: Tabor Home, Morden MB R0M 1Y3 – 204/822-4848; Fax: 204/822-5289 – 60 beds – Exec. Dir., L. Thiessen

Morris: Red River Valley Lodge Inc., PO Box 507, Morris MB R0G 1K0 – 204/746-2394 – 40 beds – Dir. of Care, Myrna Fitchett

Morris: The Rosenort Eventide Home Inc., RR#1, PO Box 75, Morris MB R0G 1K0 – 204/746-8455; Fax: 204/746-6288 – 26 – Exec. Dir., L. Friesen

Neepawa: East View Lodge, PO Box 1240, Neepawa MB R0J 1H0 – 204/476-2383; Fax: 204/476-3645 – 123 beds – Exec. Dir., Eric Gustafson

Norway House: Pinaow Wachi Inc., PO Box 98, Norway House MB R0B 1B0 – 204/359-6606 – 26 beds – Adm., Brian Rowden

Notre Dame de Lourdes: Foyer Notre Dame Inc., PO Box 190, Notre Dame de Lourdes MB R0G 1M0 – 204/248-2092; Fax: 204/248-2499 – 61 beds – Exec. Dir., R. Comte

Notre Dame de Lourdes: Pembina-Manitou Health Centre, PO Box 190, Notre Dame de Lourdes MB R0G 1M0 – 204/242-2744; Fax: 204/248-2499 – 8 beds – Exec. Dir., René Comte

Pilot Mound: Prairie View Lodge, PO Box 269, Pilot Mound MB R0G 1P0 – 204/825-2717 – 30 beds – Charge Nurse, C. Yake

Pilot Mound: Rock Lake Personal Care Home Inc., PO Box 269, Pilot Mound MB R0G 1P0 – 204/825-2246 – 24 beds – Charge Nurse, C. Yake

Pine Falls: Sunnywood Manor, PO Box 2000, Pine Falls MB R0E 1M0 – 204/367-8201 – 20 beds – Exec. Dir./Dir. of Nursing, Susan Derk

Portage la Prairie: Douglas Campbell Lodge, 150 - 9th St. SE, Portage la Prairie MB R1N 3T6 – 204/239-6006; Fax: 204/239-0055 – 60 beds – Personal Care Home Dir., Mary Thomas

Portage la Prairie: Lions Prairie Manor, 24 - 9th St. SE, Portage la Prairie MB R1N 3V4 – 204/857-7864; Fax: 204/857-8207 – 151 beds – Exec. Dir., M. Graham

Reston: Willowview Lodge (Reston Personal Care Home Inc.), PO Box 250, Reston MB R0M 1X0 – 204/877-3925; Fax: 204/877-3998 – 20 beds – Facility Coord., D. Obach

Rivers: Riverdale Personal Care Home Inc., 512 Québec St., PO Box 428, Rivers MB R0K 1X0 – 204/328-5321; Fax: 204/328-7130 – 20 beds – CEO, G.P. Worthington

Roblin & District Personal Care Home, see Roblin Health District, Hospital Districts/Health Units listings

Roblin: Crocus Court Personal Care Home, 15 Hospital St., PO Box 940, Roblin MB R0L 1P0 – 204/937-2149; Fax: 204/937-8892 – 60 beds – Assistant Dir. of Nursing, C. Jerome

Rossburn Personal Care Home Inc., see Rossburn District Health Centre, General Hospitals listings

Russell & District Personal Care Home Inc., PO Box 400, Russell MB R0J 1W0 – 204/773-2731; Fax: 204/773-2232 – 40 beds – Exec. Dir., E. Nernberg

St. Adolphe Nursing Home Ltd., PO Box 40, St. Adolphe MB R5A 1A1 – 204/883-2181 – 42 beds – Adm., D. Brousseau

Ste. Anne: Villa Youville Inc., 208 Central Ave., PO Box 280, Ste. Anne MB R0A 1R0 – 204/422-5624; Fax: 204/422-5842 – 66 beds – Exec. Dir., Francis LaBossiere

St. Claude: Manoir de St. Claude, see St. Claude Hospital, General Hospitals listings

St. Claude: Manoir de St. Claude inc., PO Box 400, St. Claude MB R0G 1Z0 – 204/379-2585; Fax: 204/379-2655 – 18 beds – Adm., Claude Lachance

St. Pierre-Jolys: Repos Jolys Inc., see Centre Medico-Social DeSalaberry District Health Centre, Auxiliary Hospitals/Health Care Centres listings

Ste. Rose du Lac: Dr. Gendreau Memorial Personal Care Home Inc., PO Box 420, Ste. Rose du Lac MB R0L 1S0 – 204/447-2019; Fax: 204/447-2267 – 40 beds – Exec. Dir., B.H. Kardoes

Sandy Lake Medical Nursing Home Inc., PO Box 7, Sandy Lake MB R0J 1X0 – 204/585-2107; Fax: 204/585-5352 – 36 beds – Exec. Dir., Linda Earl

Selkirk: Betel Home Foundation, 212 Manchester Ave., Selkirk MB R1A 0B6 – 204/482-7933; Fax: 204/482-4651 – 94 beds – Exec. Dir., S.L. Bruce

Selkirk: Red River Place, 133 Manchester Ave., Selkirk MB R1A 0B5 – 204/482-3036; Fax: 204/482-9499 – 104 beds – Exec. Dir., M.S. Fages

Selkirk: Tudor House Personal Care Home, 800 Manitoba Ave., Selkirk MB R1A 2C9 – 204/482-6601; Fax: 204/482-4369 – 76 beds – Adm., P.A. Martyniw

Shoal Lake: Morley House of Shoal Lake, PO Box 490, Shoal Lake MB R0J 1Z0 – 204/759-2118; Fax: 204/759-2230 – 40 beds – Exec. Dir., Garry Dunits

Souris District Personal Care Home, see Souris Health District, Hospital Districts/Health Units listings

Souris: Victoria Park Lodge, PO Box 940, Souris MB R0K 2C0 – 204/483-2487; Fax: 204/483-3805 – 20 beds – Exec. Dir., F.J. Woodmass

Steinbach: Bethesda Personal Care Home Inc., see Bethesda Health & Social Services, Auxiliary Hospitals/Health Care Centres listings

Steinbach: Rest Haven Nursing Home, 185 Woodhaven Ave., Steinbach MB R0A 2A0 – 204/326-2206; Fax: 204/326-3521 – 60 beds – Exec. Dir., L. Penner

Stonewall: Rosewood Lodge Inc., 385 - 3rd St. West, Stonewall MB R0C 2Z0 – 204/467-5514; Fax: 204/467-9194 – 30 beds – Charge Nurse, D. Shura

Swan River Valley Personal Care Home Inc., 334 - 8th Ave. South, PO Box 1390, Swan River MB R0L 1Z0 – 204/734-4521; Fax: 204/734-9081 – 60 beds – Dir. of Resident Servs., M.A. Swojanovsk

Swan Valley Lodge, see Swan River Valley Hospital, General Hospitals listings

Teulon: Goodwin Lodge Inc., PO Box 89, Teulon MB R0C 3B0 – 204/886-2108 – 20 beds – Head Nurse, Ann Heinrichs

The Pas: St. Paul's Residence, PO Box 240, The Pas MB R9A 1K4 – 204/623-9226 – 66 beds – Assistant Dir. of Nursing, M. Smith

Treherne: Tiger Hills Manor Inc., PO Box 130, Treherne MB R0G 2V0 – 204/723-2023; Fax: 204/723-2869 – 22 beds – Charge Nurse, K. Robinson

Virden: The Sherwood Lodge, PO Box 2000, Virden MB R0M 2C0 – 204/748-1546; Fax: 204/748-2822 – 50 beds – Adm., G. Danielson

Virden: West-Man Nursing Home Inc., PO Box 1630, Virden MB R0M 2C0 – 204/748-2709; Fax: 204/748-3432 – 50 beds – Exec. Dir., M. Sangster

Virden: Willowview Home, PO Box 400, Virden MB R0M 2C0 – 204/877-3921; Fax: 204/877-3998 – 20 beds – Adm., John Rakai

Vita & District Personal Care Home, see Vita District Health Centre Inc., Auxiliary Hospitals/Health Care Centres listings

Wawancsa Personal Care Home, see Wawanesa & District Memorial Health Centre, Auxiliary Hospitals/Health Care Centres listings

Whitemouth Personal Care Home Inc., see Whitemouth District Health Centre, Auxiliary Hospitals/Health Care Centres listings

Winkler: Salem Home Inc., 165 - 15 St., Winkler MB R6W 1T8 – 204/325-4316; Fax: 204/325-5442 – 125 beds – Exec. Dir., S. Janzen

Winnipeg: Beacon Hill Lodge, 190 Fort St., Winnipeg MB R3C 1C9 – 204/942-7541; Fax: 204/944-0136 – 175 beds – Adm., Phyllis Boryskiewich

Winnipeg: Bethania Mennonite Personal Care Home Inc., 1045 Concordia Ave., Winnipeg MB R2K 3S7 – 204/667-0795; Fax: 204/667-7078 – 149 beds – Exec. Dir., H. Epp

Winnipeg: Central Park Lodges of Canada Ltd. (#1), 440 Edmonton St., Winnipeg MB R3B 2M4 – 204/942-5291; Fax: 204/947-1969 – 277 beds – Mgr., Linda Norton

Winnipeg: Central Park Lodges of Canada Ltd. (#2), 70 Poseidon Bay, Winnipeg MB R3M 3E5 – 204/452-6204; Fax: 204/474-2173 – 218 beds – Mgr., Carol Johnston

Winnipeg: Concordia Hospital, 1095 Concordia Ave., Winnipeg MB R2K 3S8 – 204/661-7154; Fax: 204/667-1049 – 60 beds – Exec. Dir., Bill Patmore

Winnipeg: The Convalescent Home of Winnipeg, 276 Hugo St. North, Winnipeg MB R3M 2N6 – 204/475-1987; Fax: 204/453-7149 – 84 beds – Exec. Dir., G. Helgason

Winnipeg: Deer Lodge Centre Inc., 2109 Portage Ave., Winnipeg MB R3J 0L3 – 204/837-1301; Fax: 204/885-4983 – 253 beds – Exec. Dir., R.S. Brown

Winnipeg: Donwood Manor, 171 Donwood Dr., Winnipeg MB R2G 0V9 – 204/668-4410; Fax: 204/663-5429 – 81 beds – Exec. Dir., Herta Janzen

Winnipeg: Fort Garry Care Centre Ltd., 1776 Pembina Hwy., Winnipeg MB R3T 2G2 – 204/269-6939; Fax: 204/275-2192 – 64 beds – Exec. Dir., G. Kalef

Winnipeg: Foyer Valade Inc., 450 River Rd., Winnipeg MB R2M 5M4 – 204/254-3332; Fax: 204/254-0329 – 115 beds – Exec. Dir., R. Massicotte

Winnipeg: Fred Douglas Lodge, 1275 Burrows Ave., Winnipeg MB R2X 0B8 – 204/586-8541; Fax: 204/589-0110 – 137 beds – Exec. Dir., George Ralph

Winnipeg: Golden Door Geriatric Centre, 1679 Pembina Hwy., Winnipeg MB R3T 2G6 – 204/269-6308; Fax: 204/269-5626 – 78 beds – Adm., M.E. Lutz

Winnipeg: Golden Links Lodge, c/o PO Box 248, Stn St Vital, Winnipeg MB R2M 4A5 – 204/257-9947; Fax: 204/257-2405 – 88 beds – Exec. Dir., D.A. Buys-Holowachuk

Winnipeg: Golden West Centennial Lodge, 811 School Rd., Winnipeg MB R2Y 0S8 – 204/888-3311; Fax: 204/831-0544 – 116 beds – Exec. Dir., Maj. Wm. Loveless

Winnipeg: Heritage Lodge Personal Care Home Inc., 3555 Portage Ave., Winnipeg MB R3K 0X2 – 204/888-7940; Fax: 204/832-6544 – 86 beds – Dir. of Care, Carol Stifora

Winnipeg: Holiday Haven Nursing Home, 5501 Roblin Blvd., Winnipeg MB R3R 0G8 – 204/888-3363; Fax: 204/896-4763 – 155 beds – Adm., E.G. Robinson

Winnipeg: Holy Family Nursing Home, 165 Aberdeen Ave., Winnipeg MB R2W 1T9 – 204/589-7381; Fax: 204/589-8605 – 284 beds – Exec. Dir., J.N. Kisil

Winnipeg: Kildonan Personal Care Centre Inc., 1970 Henderson Hwy., Winnipeg MB R2G 1P2 – 204/334-4633; Fax: 204/204-334-4632 – 120 beds – Adm., Rick Kordalchuk

Winnipeg: Lions Manor, 320 Sherbrook St., Winnipeg MB R3B 2W6 – 204/784-1240; Fax: 204/784-1241 – 63 beds – Exec. Dir., A. Davies

Winnipeg: Luther Home, 1081 Andrews St., Winnipeg MB R2V 2G9 – 204/338-4641; Fax: 204/338-4643 – 80 beds – Dir., Nursing, Kathy Murdoch

Winnipeg: Manitoba Odd Fellows' Home Inc., 4025 Roblin Blvd., Winnipeg MB R3R 0E3 – 204/832-1612; Fax: 204/832-0523 – 43 beds – Exec. Dir., M. Schultz

Winnipeg: Maples Personal Care Home, 500 Mandalya Dr., Winnipeg MB R2P 1V4 – 204/632-8570; Fax: 204/697-0249 – 200 beds – Adm., Rick Kordalchuk

Winnipeg: Meadowood Manor, 577 St. Anne's Rd., Winnipeg MB R2M 5B2 – 204/257-2394; Fax: 204/254-5402 – 88 beds – Exec. Dir., G. Chernoff

Winnipeg: Metropolitan Kiwanis Courts, 2300 Ness Ave., Winnipeg MB R3J 1A2 – 204/885-7700; Fax: 204/831-1022 – 47 beds – Exec. Dir., H. Ritchie

Winnipeg: The Middlechurch Home of Winnipeg, 280 Balderstone Ave., RR#1B, Winnipeg MB R3C 2E5 – 204/339-1947; Fax: 204/338-3498 – 197 beds – Exec. Dir., L. Holgate

Winnipeg: Oakview Place, 2395 Ness Ave., Winnipeg MB R3J 1A5 – 204/888-3005; Fax: 204/831-8101 – 245 beds – Adm., Myrna King

Winnipegosis-Mossey River Personal Care Home Inc., see Winnipegosis General Hospital, General Hospitals listings

Winnipeg: Park Manor Personal Care Home Inc., 301 Redonda St., Winnipeg MB R2C 1L7 – 204/222-3251; Fax: 204/222-3237 – 100 beds – Exec. Dir., C.L. Toop

Winnipeg: River East Personal Care Home Ltd., 1375 Molson St., Winnipeg MB R2K 4K8 – 204/668-7460; Fax: 204/668-7459 – 120 beds – Adm., Len Garrett

Winnipeg: St. Joseph's Residence Inc., 1149 Leila Ave., Winnipeg MB R2P 1S6 – 204/697-8031; Fax: 204/697-8075 – 100 beds – Exec. Dir., Sr. G. Pura

Winnipeg: St. Norbert Nursing Home, 50 St. Pierre St., Winnipeg MB R3V 1J6 – 204/269-4538; Fax: 204/269-8150 – 91 beds – Adm., David Brousseau

Winnipeg: The Sharon Home Inc., 146 Magnus Ave., Winnipeg MB R2W 2B4 – 204/586-9781; Fax: 204/589-7560 – 229 beds – Exec. Vice-Pres., Daniel Ruth

Winnipeg: Tache Nursing Centre - Hospitalier Tache Inc., 185 Despins St., Winnipeg MB R2H 2B3 – 204/233-3692; Fax: 204/233-6803 – 314 beds – Exec. Dir., Renald Massicotte

Winnipeg: Tuxedo Villa, 2060 Corydon Ave., Winnipeg MB R3P 0N3 – 204/889-2650; Fax: 204/896-0258 – 213 beds – Adm., Sydney Moffitt

Winnipeg: Vista Park Lodge, 144 Novavista Dr., Winnipeg MB R2N 1P8 – 204/257-6688; Fax: 204/257-0446 – 100 beds – Adm., J. McKee

Winnipeg: West Park Manor, 3199 Grant Ave., Winnipeg MB R3R 1X2 – 204/889-3330; Fax: 204/832-9555 – 150 beds – Exec. Dir., E.A. Gallant

NURSING STATIONS
Winnipeg: Health & Welfare Canada - Medical Services Branch, 303 Main St., 5th Fl., Winnipeg MB R3C 0H4 – 204/983-4199 – Nursing stations are located at: Garden Hill (2 beds), Ste. Therese (2 beds), God's Lake Narrows (3 beds), Oxford House (3 beds), Cross Lake (4 beds), Little Grand & Rapids (2 beds), Poplar River (2 beds), Pukatawagon (2 beds), Nelson House (2 beds), Shamattawa (5 beds), Split Lake (4 beds), Brochet (3 beds), South Indian Lake (3 beds), Berens River (3 beds), Bloodvein (2 beds), Wassagamack (2 beds), Red Sucker Lake (2 beds), Lac Brochet (2 beds), God's River (1 bed), Tadoule Lake (2 beds) & York Landing (2 beds)

SPECIAL TREATMENT CENTRES
(Includes: Abortion Clinics, Cancer Clinics, Rehabilitation Centres, Treatment Centres)

Winnipeg: Community Therapy Services Inc., 35 King St., 5th Fl., Winnipeg MB R3B 1H4 – 204/949-0533; Fax: 204/942-1428 – Exec. Dir., I. Corobow

Winnipeg: Deaf Centre Manitoba Inc., 285 Pembina Hwy., Winnipeg MB R3L 2E1 – 204/284-0802; Teletype phone: 204/475-0702; Fax: 204/474-0073 – 22 beds – Exec. Dir., Doug Momotiuk

Winnipeg: Manitoba Adolescent Treatment Centre Inc., 120 Tecumseh St., Winnipeg MB R3E 2A9 – 204/477-6391; Fax: 204/783-8948 – drug rehabilitation centre – 25 beds – Exec. Dir., Paul Leveille

Winnipeg: Manitoba Cancer Treatment & Research Foundation, 100 Olivia St., Winnipeg MB R3E 0V9 – 204/787-2142, 2197; Fax: 204/787-1184, 783-6875 – cancer treatment – Pres. & CEO, Dr. Brent A. Schacter, 204/787-2241

Winnipeg: Manitoba Cardiac Institute (Refit Centre), 1390 Taylor Ave., Winnipeg MB R3M 3V8 – 204/488-8023; Fax: 204/488-4819 – rehabilitation centre – Exec. Dir., Don Fletcher

Winnipeg: Morgantalar Clinic, 883 Corydon Ave., Winnipeg MB R3M 0W7 – abortion clinic

Winnipeg: Rehabilitation Centre for Children, 633 Wellington Cres., Winnipeg MB R3M 0A8 – 204/452-4311; Fax: 204/477-5547 – rehabilitation centre – Exec. Dir., Heather Mutcheson

NEW BRUNSWICK

HOSPITAL DISTRICTS/HEALTH UNITS
Bathurst: Corporation hospitalière de la région 6, a/s Chaleur Regional Hospital, 1750 Sunset Dr., Bathurst NB E2A 4L7 – 506/548-8961; Fax: 506/547-0016 – Président, René Beaudet

Campbellton: Region 5 Hospital Corporation, c/o Campbellton Regional Hospital, PO Box 910, Campbellton NB E3N 3H3 – 506/789-5000; Fax: 506/789-5025 – CEO, Dan Arseneau

Edmundston: Corporation hospitalière de la région 4, 275, boul Hébert, PO Box 100, Edmundston NB E3V 3L2 – 506/739-2211; Fax: 506/739-2248 – Dir. gen., Gilbert St-Onge

Fredericton: Region 3 Hospital Corporation, 700 Priestman St., PO Box 9000, Fredericton NB E3B 5N5 – 506/452-5678; Fax: 506/452-5670 – CEO, John McGarry

Miramichi: Region 7 Hospital Corporation, c/o Miramichi Regional Hospital, 500 Water St., Miramichi NB E1V 3G5 – 506/623-3440; Fax: 506/623-3465 – CEO, John R. Tucker

Moncton: Corporation hospitalière de la région 1 (Beausejour), a/s Hopital Docteur Georges-L. Dumont, 330, rue Archibald, Moncton NB E1C 2Z3 – 506/862-4210; Fax: 506/858-4213 – CEO, Pierre LeBouthillier, 506/862-4210, Fax: 506/862-4213

Moncton: Region 1 Hospital Corporation (Southeast), c/o The Moncton Hospital, 135 MacBeath Ave., Moncton NB E1C 6Z8 – 506/857-5757; Fax: 506/857-5545 – CEO, Ginette Gagné-Koch

Saint John: Region 2 Hospital Corporation, c/o Saint John Regional Hospital, PO Box 2100, Saint John NB E2L 4L2 – 506/648-6000; Fax: 506/648-6364 – CEO, David Carlin

GENERAL HOSPITALS
Bath: Northern Carleton Hospital, Bath NB E0J 1E0 – 506/278-5231; Fax: 506/278-2448 – 23 beds – Facility Mgr., Dean C. Cummings

Bathurst: Chaleur Regional Hospital, 1750 Sunset Dr., Bathurst NB E2A 4L7 – 506/548-8961; Fax: 506/545-1429 – 270 beds – Président et Dir. gen., Roger Bertin

Black's Harbour: Fundy Health Centre, Black's Harbour NB E0G 1H0 – 506/456-3325; Fax: 506/456-4259 – 26 beds – Adm., C. Faith Keith

Campbellton Regional Hospital, PO Box 910, Campbellton NB E3N 3H3 – 506/789-5000; Fax: 506/789-5025 – 215 beds – Adm., Dan Arseneau

Caraquet: Centre hospitalier de l'Enfant-Jésus, 1, boul St-Pierre ouest, PO Box 900, Caraquet NB E1W 1B6 – 506/726-2166; Fax: 506/726-2188 – 50 lits – Dir. d'établissement, Fernand Rioux

Dalhousie: St. Joseph Hospital, 270 Victoria St., Dalhousie NB E0K 1B0 – 506/684-7000; Fax: 506/684-4751 – 60 beds – Facility Mgr., Diane Légère, 506/684-3391

Edmundston: Hôpital régional d'Edmundston, 275, boul Hébert, PO Box 100, Edmundston NB E3V 3K7 – 506/739-2211; Fax: 506/739-2248 – 232 beds – Exec. Dir., Jean-Claude Leclerc

Fredericton: Dr. Everett Chalmers Hospital, PO Box 9000, Fredericton NB E3B 5N5 – 506/452-5400; Fax: 506/452-5500 – 493 beds – Adm., John McGarry

Grand Falls General Hospital Inc., PO Box 1200, Grand Falls NB E3Z 1C6 – 506/473-7555; Fax: 506/473-7530 – 50 beds – Dir., Solange Bossé

Lamèque: Centre hospitalier de Lamèque, Lamèque NB E0B 1V0 – 506/344-2261; Fax: 506/344-5413 – 15 lits – Responsable de l'établissement/DSI, Roseline Hébert

McAdam: MacLean Memorial Health Centre, McAdam NB E0H 1K0 – 506/784-6300; Fax: 506/784-6306 – 4 observation beds – Adm., John Burke

Minto: Queens North Health Complex, PO Box 309, Minto NB E0E 1J0 – 506/327-3353; Fax: 506/327-4208 – 21 beds – Dir. of Operations, John Di Paola

Miramichi: Hôtel-Dieu Hospital, 53 Lobban Ave., Miramichi NB E1N 2W9 – 506/778-7000; Fax: 506/773-6519 – 110 beds – Facility Mgr., Linda Morris

Moncton Hospital, 135 MacBeath Ave., Moncton NB E1C 6Z8 – 506/857-5111; Fax: 506/857-5545 – 567 beds – Pres., Dr. Ginette Gagné-Koch

Moncton: Hôpital Dr. Georges L. Dumont, 330, rue Archibald, Moncton NB E1C 2Z3 – 506/862-4000; Fax: 506/862-4256 – 423 lits – Président et Dir. gen., Pierre J. LeBouthillier

Newcastle Hospital, 673 King George Hwy., PO Box 420, Newcastle NB E1V 3M5 – 506/627-7000; Fax: 506/627-7029 – 114 beds – Facility Mgr., Phyllis Mossman

North Head: Grand Manan Hospital Ltd., PO Box 219, North Head NB E0G 2M0 – 506/662-8411; Fax: 506/662-8819 – 14 beds – Facility Mgr., Julie Green

Oromocto Public Hospital, 103 Winnebago St., Oromocto NB E2V 1C6 – 506/357-8465; Fax: 506/357-4735 – 65 beds – Facility Mgr., John McGarry

Perth-Andover: Hôtel-Dieu de Saint-Joseph, 500 East Riverside Dr., PO Box 187, Perth-Andover NB E0J 1V0 – 506/273-2201; Fax: 506/273-7200 – 55 beds – Acting Facility Mgr., Marsha Lang

Plaster Rock: Tobique Valley Hospital Inc., Plaster Rock NB E0J 1W0 – 506/356-7361; Fax: 506/356-6618 – 15 beds – Adm., Dean P. Cummings

The Sackville Memorial Hospital, 69 Main St. West, PO Box 1170, Sackville NB E0A 3C0 – 506/364-4100; Fax: 506/536-1983 – 45 beds – Liaison Coord., Audrey Hicks

Ste-Anne-de-Kent: Hôpital Stella Maris de Kent, Ste-Anne-de-Kent NB E0A 2V0 – 506/743-2407; Fax: 506/743-8328 – 20 beds – Facility Mgr., J. Guy Hachey

Saint John Regional Hospital, PO Box 2100, Saint John NB E2L 4L2 – 506/648-6093; Fax: 506/648-6799 – 855 beds – Facility Mgr., Cherry Thorne

Saint John: Ridgewood Veterans Wing, PO Box 2100, Saint John NB E2L 4L2 – 506/635-2420; Fax: 506/635-2425 – Coord., Anne Mowatt

Saint John: St. Joseph's Hospital, 130 Bayard Dr., Saint John NB E2L 3L6 – 506/632-5555; Fax: 506/632-5551 – 140 beds – Facility Adm., Cherry Thorne

St-Quentin: Hôtel-Dieu Saint-Joseph de St-Quentin, 9, rue Canada, St-Quentin NB E0K 1J0 – 506/235-2300; Fax: 506/235-7202 – 20 beds – Adm. d'établissement, Réal Thériault

St. Stephen: The Charlotte County Hospital, Prince William St., St. Stephen NB E3L 2X2 – 506/466-

7444; Fax: 506/465-0894 – 80 beds – Adm., Arlene Haddon
Sussex Health Centre, Leonard Dr., PO Box 5006, Sussex NB E0E 1P0 – 506/432-3100; Fax: 506/432-3106 – 45 beds – Facility Mgr., Lloyd D. Secord
Tracadie-Sheila: Centre hospitalier de Tracadie, PO Box 3180, Stn Bur. chef, Tracadie-Sheila NB E1X 1G5 – 506/395-3361; Fax: 506/395-0216 – 80 lits – Dir. d'établissement, Conrad Pichette
Woodstock: The Carleton Memorial Hospital, 785 Main St., PO Box 400, Woodstock NB E0J 2B0 – 506/328-3391; Fax: 506/325-6765 – 80 beds – Adm., Dean P. Cummings

AUXILIARY HOSPITALS/HEALTH CARE CENTRES

Albert County Hospital, PO Box 28, Albert NB E0A 1A0 – 506/882-2750; Fax: 506/882-2718 – 4 beds – Facility Mgr., Ann Dowe
Baie Ste-Anne Health Centre, Baie Ste-Anne NB E0C 1A0 – 506/228-4859; Fax: 506/778-1011 – Facility Mgr., Brenda McFarlane
Blackville Health Centre, Blackville NB E0C 1C0 – 506/843-6446; Fax: 506/843-6485 – Facility Mgr., Brenda McFarlane
Campobello Health Centre, Campobello NB E0G 3H0 – 506/752-2491; Fax: 506/752-2654 – Facility Mgr., Arlene Haddon
Chipman Health Centre, Chipman NB E0E 1C0 – 506/339-6661; Fax: 506/339-6386 – Dir. of Nursing, Lisa Allard
Dalhousie: East Restigouche Community Health Care Centre, RR#1, Site 10, PO Box 1, Dalhousie NB E0K 1B0 – 506/684-8455; Fax: 506/684-4751 – Facility Mgr., Diane Légère
Deer Island Health Centre, Deer Island NB E0G 1R0 – 506/747-2394; Fax: 506/747-2417 – Adm., Arlene Haddon
Doaktown Health Centre, PO Box 10, Doaktown NB E0C 1G0 – 506/365-4637; Fax: 506/365-7128 – Facility Mgr., John Burke
Fredericton Junction Health Centre, Fredericton Junction NB E0G 1T0 – 506/368-6508; Fax: 506/368-7764 – Facility Mgr., John Burke
Harvey Station: Harvey Community Hospital Ltd., Harvey Station NB E0H 1H0 – 506/366-2812; Fax: 506/366-6403 – Adm., John Burke
Jacquet River Health Centre, Jacquet River NB E0B 1T0 – 506/237-2215; Fax: 506/684-4751 – Facility Mgr., Diane Légère
Neguac Health Centre, PO Box 34, Neguac NB E0C 1S0 – 506/776-3876; Fax: 506/778-1011 – Facility Mgr., Brenda McFarlane
Paquetville: Centre de santé-Paquetville, PO Box 130, Paquetville NB E0B 2B0 – 506/764-2424; Fax: 506/764-2425 – Adm. d'établissement, Marthe Robichaud
Petitcodiac Health Centre, PO Box 88, Petitcodiac NB E0A 2H0 – 506/756-3400; Fax: 506/756-2766 – Facility Mgr., Heather Steeves
Pointe Verte: Centre de santé Pointe Verte, PO Box 238, Pointe Verte NB E0B 2H0 – 506/783-2001; Fax: 506/545-1429 – Adm. d'établissement, Diane Sepetich
Rexton Community Health Centre, PO Box 158, Rexton NB E0A 2L0 – 506/523-4408; Fax: 506/523-9547 – Facility Mgr., Rev. Lucille Cormier
Rogersville Community Health Centre, PO Box 418, Rogersville NB E0A 2T0 – 506/775-6108; Fax: 506/775-9208 – Facility Mgr., Brenda McFarlane
Ste-Anne-de-Madawaska: Centre de santé de Ste-Anne-de-Madawaska, Ste-Anne-de-Madawaska NB E0L 1G0 – 506/445-2348; Fax: 506/735-0880 – Adm. d'établissement, Gilbert St-Onge
Shediac: Centre médical régional de Shediac, 307, rue Main, Shediac NB E0A 3G0 – 506/533-3020; Fax: 506/532-8189 – Dir. gen., J Guy Hachey

Stanley Health Centre, PO Box 130, Stanley NB E0H 1T0 – 506/367-7730; Fax: 506/367-3211 – Facility Mgr., John Burke

HOME CARE OFFICES/COMMUNITY CARE SERVICES

Caraquet: Centre de Benevolat de la Peninsule Acadienne Inc., PO Box 397, Caraquet NB E0B 1K0
Chipman Outreach, Chipman NB E0E 1C0
Fredericton: Comcare, 384 Queen St., Fredericton NB E3B 1B2 – 506/451-1303; Fax: 506/452-8565 – Mgr., Shirley Clayton
Fredericton: Olsten Kimberley Quality Care, 142 Brunswick St., Fredericton NB E3B 1G6 – 506/458-9934; Fax: 506/458-9963 – Branch Dir., Louise Billings
Fredericton: People Care, #1, Victoria Health Centre, 65 Brunswick St., Fredericton NB E3B 1G5
Fredericton: Private Care, PO Box 20116, Fredericton NB E3B 5H0 – 506/459-1888; Fax: 506/454-8707
Fredericton: Victorian Order of Nurses, 65 Brunswick St., Fredericton NB E3B 1G5 – 506/457-2171
Harvey Outreach, Harvey NB E0H 1H0
McAdam Outreach for Seniors, Wauklehegan Manor Inc., McAdam NB E0H 1K0
Minto Services to Seniors, Queens North Health Complex, Minto NB E0E 1J0
Saint John: Hospice Saint John, 116 Coburg St., Saint John NB E2K 3K1
St. Stephen: Home Support Services Inc., PO Box 293, St. Stephen NB E3L 2X2
Stanley: Paradise Lodge, Stanley NB E0H 1T0

MENTAL HEALTH HOSPITALS & COMMUNITY FACILITIES

Campbellton: Restigouche Hospital Centre Inc., PO Box 10, Campbellton NB E3N 3G2 – 506/789-7000; Fax: 506/789-7065 – 195 beds – Adm., Claudette Redstone
Saint John: Centracare of Saint John Inc., PO Box 3220, Stn B, Saint John NB E2M 4H7 – 506/635-7550; Fax: 506/635-7536 – 145 beds – Adm., Cherry Thorne

NURSING HOMES

Albert: Forest Dale Home Inc., Riverside, PO Box 4, Albert NB E0A 1A0 – 506/882-2281; Fax: 506/882-0118 – 40 beds – Adm., Eric Tracy
Baker Brook: Foyer Ste. Elizabeth Inc., 25, rue des Ormes, Baker Brook NB E7A 2J6 – 506/258-3504; Fax: 506/258-1051 – 50 beds – Dir. gen., Michel Fournier
Bath: River View Manor Inc., Bath NB E0J 1E0 – 506/278-5221; Fax: 506/278-5962 – 40 beds – Adm., Sharon Eagan
Bathurst: Le Foyer Notre-Dame de Lourdes Inc., 2055 Vallée-Lourdes, Bathurst NB E2A 4J8 – 506/548-4483; Fax: 506/548-9818 – 100 lits – Dir. gen., Claude Desrosiers
Bathurst: Villa Chaleur, DVA Unit, 795, rue Champlin, Bathurst NB E2A 4M8 – 506/548-3338; Fax: 506/548-4196 – 10 lits – Adm., Lucie Fournier
Black's Harbour: Fundy Nursing Home, Black's Harbour NB E0G 1H0 – 506/456-4213; Fax: 506/456-9200 – 20 beds – Adm., Shirley Hatt
Boiestown: Central New Brunswick Nursing Home Inc., PO Box 249, Boiestown NB E0H 1A0 – 506/369-7262; Fax: 506/369-2331 – 30 beds – Adm., Manley Black
Bouctouche: Manoir Saint-Jean Baptiste Inc., 5, rue Richard, PO Box 296, Bouctouche NB E0A 1G0 – 506/743-8917; Fax: 506/743-5270 – 50 lits – Dir. gen., Donald Daigle
Campbellton Nursing Home Inc., 101 Dover St., PO Box 850, Campbellton NB E3N 3K6 – 506/789-7800; Fax: 506/789-7808 – 100 beds – Adm., Ken Murray

Campobello Lodge Inc., Welsh Pool, Campobello NB E0G 3H0 – 506/752-2337; Fax: 506/752-2413 – 30 beds – Adm., Sherry Johnson
Caraquet: Villa Beauséjour Inc., PO Box 5608, Caraquet NB E1W 1B7 – 506/727-1144; Fax: 506/727-1145 – 62 lits – Dir. gen., Roger Landry
Chatham: Miramichi Senior Citizens Home Inc., 180 Upper Water St., Chatham NB E1N 1A4 – 506/773-5801; Fax: 506/773-7069 – 81 beds – Adm., Margaret Manderson
Dalhousie Nursing Home Inc./Le Foyer Dalhousie inc., 300 Victoria St., PO Box 1689, Dalhousie NB E0K 1B0 – 506/684-3318; Fax: 506/684-4824 – 105 beds – Adm., Gilles Richard
Edmundston: Villa Des-Jardins Inc., 50, rue Queen, Edmundston NB E3V 1A3 – 506/735-1020; Fax: 506/735-4744 – 30 lits – Dir., Cécile Paillard
Fredericton Junction: White Rapids Manor Inc., Fredericton Junction NB E0G 1T0 – 506/368-6508; Fax: 506/368-6502
Fredericton: Health Management Services, 100 Sunset Dr., Fredericton NB E3A 1A3 – 506/451-8123; Fax: 506/451-8128 – Exec. Dir., John Burke
Fredericton: Pine Grove, 521 Woodstock Rd., Fredericton NB E3B 2J2 – 506/458-9045; Fax: 506/450-1567 – 70 beds – Adm., Barbara Gregan
Fredericton: York Manor Inc., 100 Sunset Dr., Fredericton NB E3A 1A3 – 506/453-9816; Fax: 506/458-8796 – 198 beds – Adm., Kerry Wolstenholme
Gagetown Nursing Home Inc., PO Box 130, Gagetown NB E0G 1V0 – 506/488-2328; Fax: 506/488-2888 – 38 beds – Owner, Robert Corbett
Grand Falls Manor Inc./Manoir de Grand-Sault Inc., PO Box 2000, Grand Falls NB E3Z 1E2 – 506/473-6391; Fax: 506/473-9490 – 72 beds – Dir. gen., Maurice Richard
Hampton: Dr. V.A. Snow Centre Inc., RR#4, Hampton NB E0G 1Z0 – 506/832-5595; Fax: 506/832-7674 – 50 beds – Adm., Judy Paquet
Hartland: Central Carleton Nursing Home Inc., PO Box 90, Hartland NB E0J 1N0 – 506/375-4504; Fax: 506/375-4507 – 30 beds – Adm., Gwen Cullins-Jones
Harvey: Swan Haven Nursing Home Ltd., Harvey NB E0H 1H0 – 506/366-2950 – 21 beds – Owner, Frances P. Ward
Inkerman: Les Résidences Inkerman Inc., PO Box 156, Inkerman NB E0B 1S0 – 506/336-9713; Fax: 506/336-9329 – 30 lits – Dir. gen., Paul Arseneau
Lamèque: Les Résidences Lucien Saindon Inc., PO Box 480, Lamèque NB E0B 1V0 – 506/344-2201; Fax: 506/344-1033 – 54 lits – Dir. gen., Gaëtan Haché
McAdam: Waulkehegan Manor Inc., McAdam NB E0H 1K0 – 506/784-2263; Fax: 506/784-6306 – 36 beds – Adm., John Burke
Minto: W.G. Bishop Nursing Home, PO Box 309, Minto NB E0E 1J0 – 506/327-7800; Fax: 506/327-7812 – 30 beds – Adm., Lisa Allard
Miramichi: Mount Saint Joseph of Chatham N.B., 51 Lobban Ave., Miramichi NB E1N 3W4 – 506/778-6550; Fax: 506/778-0193 – 133 beds – Adm., R.B. Stewart
Moncton: Atlantic Baptist Senior (Spencer) Citizens Home Inc., 1 Atlantic Baptist Rd., PO Box 518, Moncton NB E1C 8L9 – 506/858-7870; Fax: 506/858-9674 – 200 beds – Adm., Stephen Campbell
Moncton: Villa du Repos Inc., 474 Elmwood Dr., Moncton NB E1A 2X3 – 506/857-3560; Fax: 506/859-1619 – 126 lits – Dir. gen., Paul Williams
Néguac: Le Foyer Saint-Bernard Ltée, PO Box 161, Néguac NB E0C 1S0 – 506/776-3774 – 24 lits – Propriétaire, Diane Mazerolle
North Head: Grand Manan Nursing Home Inc., North Head NB E0G 2M0 – 506/662-3522; Fax: 506/662-8898 – 30 beds – Adm., Sharon Urquhart
Paquetville: Manoir Edith B. Pinet Inc., PO Box 99, Paquetville NB E0B 2B0 – 506/764-3270; Fax: 506/764-1141 – 30 lits – Dir. gen., Marthe Robichaud

Perth: Victoria Glen Manor Inc., Perth NB E0J 1V0 – 506/273-6861; Fax: 506/273-2514 – 65 beds – Adm., Dawn Bishop

Plaster Rock: Tobique Valley Manor Inc., PO Box 99, Plaster Rock NB E0J 1W0 – 506/356-1020; Fax: 506/356-1021 – 30 beds – Adm., Eric Haddad

Port Elgin: Westford Nursing Home, PO Box 119, Port Elgin NB E0A 2K0 – 506/538-2307; Fax: 506/538-7293 – 30 beds – Adm., Judith White

Rexton Lions Nursing Home Inc., PO Box 70, Rexton NB E0A 2L0 – 506/523-4449; Fax: 506/523-1117 – 30 beds – Adm., Dianne Robichard

River Glade: Jordan Memorial Home, River Glade NB E0A 2P0 – 506/756-3355; Fax: 506/756-2081 – 100 beds – Adm., G.A. Hollingsworth

Riverview: The Salvation Army Lakeview Manor, 50 Suffolk St., Riverview NB E1B 4K6 – 506/387-2012; Fax: 506/387-7200 – 50 beds – Adm., Maj. Reginald Pell

Robertville: La Villa Sormany Inc., PO Box 250, Robertville NB E0B 2K0 – 506/783-4201; Fax: 506/783-1998 – 40 beds – Dir. gen., Raymond Bryar

Rogersville: Foyer Assomption, 22, rue Assomption, PO Box 296, Rogersville NB E0A 2T0 – 506/775-6105; Fax: 506/775-9208 – 50 lits – Dir. gen., Willie Robichaud

Sackville: Drew Nursing Home, 41 East Main St., Sackville NB E0A 3C0 – 506/536-0690; Fax: 506/536-3510 – 130 beds – Adm., Ann Johnson

St. Andrews: Passamaquoddy Lodge Inc., PO Box 370, St. Andrews NB E0G 2X0 – 506/529-1840; Fax: 506/529-1858 – 60 beds – Adm., Faith Keith

Saint Antoine: Foyer Saint-Antoine, PO Box 300, Saint Antoine NB E0A 2X0 – 506/525-2229; Fax: 506/525-1013 – 30 beds – Dir. gen., Gilles C. Ouellette

Saint-Basile: Le Foyer Saint-Joseph de Saint-Basile Inc., 475, rue Principale, Saint-Basile NB E0L 1H0 – 506/263-5561; Fax: 506/263-4101 – 126 lits – Dir. gen., Sr. Claudette Ouellet

Saint John: Carleton Kirk Lodge, 3 Carleton Kirk Pl., Saint John NB E2M 5B8 – 506/635-1444; Fax: 506/635-4097 – 70 beds – Adm., Sylvia Young

Saint John: The Church of St. John & St. Stephen Home Inc., 130 University Ave., Saint John NB E2K 4K3 – 506/634-1515; Fax: 506/634-1519 – 80 beds – Adm., Judy Heffern

Saint John: Kennebec Manor, 475 Woodward Ave., Saint John NB E2K 4N1 – 506/634-9378; Fax: 506/658-9376 – 30 beds – Adm., Jack Hiebert

Saint John: Loch Lomond Villa, 185 Loch Lomond Rd., Saint John NB E2J 3S3 – 506/633-2675; Fax: 506/648-9972 – 201 beds – Adm., Tom Jarrett

Saint John: Rocmaura Inc., 10 Park St., Saint John NB E2K 4P1 – 506/634-8940; Fax: 506/636-8229 – 150 beds – Adm., Sr. Anita Holmes

Saint John: Turnbull Home, 240 Wentworth St., Saint John NB E2L 2T6 – 506/648-1107; Fax: 506/648-9786 – 40 beds – Adm., Elizabeth Crouchman

Saint Joseph: Le Foyer St. Thomas, PO Box 120, Saint Joseph NB E0A 2Y0 – 506/758-2110; Fax: 506/758-9489 – 30 lits – Dir. gen., Pierre Landry

Saint-Léonard: Foyer Notre-Dame de Saint-Léonard Inc., PO Box 190, Saint-Léonard NB E0L 1M0 – 506/423-6457; Fax: 506/423-1914 – 37 lits – Dir. gen., Sr Ginette Bacon

Saint-Louis-de-Kent: Villa Maria Inc., Saint-Louis-de-Kent NB E0A 2Z0 – 506/876-2402; Fax: 506/876-2868 – 73 lits – Dir. gen., Laurie Vautour

Saint-Quentin: Résidences Mgr Melanson Inc., 40, rue Canada, Saint-Quentin NB E0K 1J0 – 506/235-3171; Fax: 506/235-3682 – 42 lits – Dir. gen., Louiselle Cormier

St. Stephen Nursing Home Inc., RR#4, Hwy 3, St. Stephen NB E3L 2Y2 – 506/466-1868; Fax: 506/466-6081 – 29 beds – Owner, Raymond Lee Disher

St. Stephen: Lincourt Manor Inc., 1 Chipman St., St. Stephen NB E3L 2W9 – 506/466-3007; Fax: 506/466-3845 – 60 beds – Adm., Jane Lyons

Shédiac: Villa Providence Shédiac Inc., 1215, rue Main, PO Box 340, Shédiac NB E0A 3G0 – 506/532-4484; Fax: 506/532-8189 – 204 lits – Dir. gen., Paul Williams

Shippagan: Les Résidences Mgr Chiasson Inc., PO Box 368, Shippagan NB E0B 2P0 – 506/336-2251; Fax: 506/336-3099 – 100 lits – Dir. gen., Octave Haché

Shippagan: Villa Beau Rivage Ltée, PO Box 444, Shippagan NB E0B 2P0 – 506/336-8988 – 29 lits – Propriétaire, Gisèle Duguay

Stanley: Nashwaak Villa Inc., Stanley NB E0H 1T0 – 506/367-7731; Fax: 506/367-7738 – 30 beds – Adm., Penny Higgs

Sussex: Kiwanis Nursing Home Inc., 11 Bryant St., PO Box 5002, Sussex NB E0E 1P0 – 506/432-3118; Fax: 506/432-3104 – 70 beds – Adm., Lloyd Secord

Tabusintac Nursing Home Inc., PO Box 99, Tabusintac NB E0C 2A0 – 506/779-8228; Fax: 506/779-8149 – 30 beds – Adm., Betty Blake

Tracadie-Sheila: Villa Saint-Joseph Inc., PO Box 2500, Tracadie-Sheila NB E1X 1G7 – 506/395-3384; Fax: 506/395-7542 – 64 lits – Bureau chef, Wilfred Robichaud

Woodstock: Carleton Manor Inc., PO Box 6000, Woodstock NB E0J 2B0 – 506/328-8819; Fax: 506/328-9672 – 89 beds – Adm., Patricia MacNeil

Youngs Cove Road: Mill Cove Nursing Home Inc., PO Box 518, Youngs Cove Road NB E0E 1S0 – 506/488-3033; Fax: 506/488-3037 – 75 beds – Adm., Patricia Hamilton

SPECIAL TREATMENT CENTRES

(Includes: Abortion Clinics, Cancer Clinics, Rehabilitation Centres, Treatment Centres)

Fredericton: Abortion Counselling, 88 Ferry Ave., Fredericton NB E3A 1R8

Fredericton: Stan Cassidy Centre for Rehabilitation, 180 Woodbridge St., Fredericton NB E3B 4R3 – 506/452-5225; Fax: 506/452-5190 – rehabilitation centre – 20 beds – Dir. of Specialized Rehab. Servs., Janice Eloway

Saint John West: Ridgewood Treatment & Rehabilitation Centre, PO Box 3566, Stn B, Saint John West NB E2M 4Y1 – 506/658-2525; Fax: 506/658-3774 – Exec. Dir., Bonnie Buck

St. Stephen: Valley View Manor Inc., RR#1, St. Stephen NB E3L 2Y2 – 506/466-1234 – Special care home – Owner, Wanda Higgins

NEWFOUNDLAND

HOSPITAL DISTRICTS/HEALTH UNITS

Carbonear: Avalon Health Care Institutions Board, 86 Highroad South, Carbonear NF A1Y 1A4 – 709/945-5155; Fax: 709/945-5158 – CEO, George Butt

Clarenville: Peninsulas Health Care Corporation, PO Box 2800, Clarenville NF A0E 1J0 – 709/466-5339; Fax: 709/466-1623 – CEO, W.J. (Wes) Drodge

Corner Brook: Western Health Care Corporation, PO Box 158, Corner Brook NF A2H 6C7 – 709/634-5036; Fax: 709/634-5063 – CEO, Dr. Harry Watts

Gander: Central East Health Care Institutions Board, 125 Trans Canada Hwy., Gander NF A1V 1P7 – 709/256-5530; Fax: 709/256-7800 – CEO, David Lewis

Grand Falls-Windsor: Central West Health Care Institutions Board, Union St., Grand Falls-Windsor NF A2A 2E1 – 709/292-2138; Fax: 709/292-2249 – CEO, Donald Keats

Happy Valley-Goose Bay: Health Labrador Corporation, PO Box 190, Stn A, Happy Valley-Goose Bay NF A0P 1S0 – 709/896-5351; Fax: 709/896-4032 – CEO, Keith Sansford

St Anthony: Grenfell Regional Health Services Board, St Anthony NF A0K 4S0 – 705/454-3333; Fax: 705/454-2052 – CEO, Dr. Peter Roberts

St. John's: Health Care Corporation of St. John's, South Wing, Waterford Hospital, Waterford Bridge Rd., St. John's NF A1E 4J8 – 709/758-1300; Fax: 709/758-1302 – Pres. & CEO, Elizabeth M. Davis, RSM

GENERAL HOSPITALS

Burin Peninsula Health Centre, PO Box 340, Burin NF A0E 1E0 – 709/891-1040; Fax: 709/891-3375 – 47 acute care beds – CEO, P. Coish

Carbonear General Hospital, 86 Highroad South, Carbonear NF A1Y 1A4 – 709/945-5111; Fax: 709/945-5158 – 80 acute care beds – Exec. Dir., Doris Murphy

Clarenville: Dr. G.B. Cross Memorial Hospital, PO Box 1300, Clarenville NF A0E 1J0 – 709/466-3411; Fax: 709/466-3300 – 48 acute care, 7 continuing care beds – CEO, G. Reid

Corner Brook: Western Memorial Regional Hospital, PO Box 2005, Corner Brook NF A2H 6J7 – 709/637-5000; Fax: 709/634-2649 – 207 acute care beds – CEO, L. Birmingham

Gander: James Paton Memorial Hospital, 125 TransCanada Hwy., Gander NF A1V 1P7 – 709/651-2500; Fax: 709/256-7800 – 92 acute care beds – CEO, E. Forward

Grand Falls-Windsor: Central Newfoundland Regional Health Centre, 50 Union St., Grand Falls-Windsor NF A2A 2E1 – 709/292-2500; Fax: 709/292-2249 – 142 acute care beds – CEO, H. Hynes

Happy Valley-Goose Bay: Melville Hospital, , Stn A, Happy Valley-Goose Bay NF A0P 1E0 – 709/896-2417; Fax: 709/896-8966 – 34 acute care beds – Adm., B. Rowe

Labrador City: Captain William Jackman Memorial Hospital, 410 Booth Ave., Labrador City NF A2V 2K1 – 709/944-2632; Fax: 709/944-6045 – 29 acute care, 6 continuing care beds – CEO, M. Condon

St Anthony: Charles S. Curtis Memorial Hospital, St Anthony NF A0K 4S0 – 709/454-3333; Fax: 709/454-2052 – 67 acute care beds – CEO, Dr. Peter Roberts

St. John's: The General Hospital/Health Sciences Centre, 300 Prince Philip Dr., St. John's NF A1B 3V6 – 709/758-1308; Fax: 709/737-6770 – teaching hospital – 307 acute care beds – CEO, Dr. E. Parsons

St. John's: Janeway Child Health Centre, 710 Janeway Pl., St. John's NF A1A 1R8 – 709/778-4428; Fax: 709/778-4446 – teaching hospital – 103 acute care beds – CEO, M. Pardy

St. John's: St. Clare's Mercy Hospital, 154 Lemarchant Rd., St. John's NF A1C 5B8 – 709/758-1317; Fax: 709/738-1216 – teaching hospital – 217 acute care beds – CEO, L. Jones

St. John's: Salvation Army Grace General Hospital, 241 Lemarchant Rd., St. John's NF A1E 1P9 – 709/758-1306; Fax: 709/778-6640 – teaching hospital – 204 acute care beds – CEO, G. Tilley

St. John's: Waterford Hospital, 306 Waterford Bridge Rd., St. John's NF A1E 4J8 – 709/364-0111; Fax: 709/364-0464 – 87 acute care, 159 continuing care beds – CEO, C. Simms

Stephenville: Sir Thomas Roddick Hospital, 89 Ohio Dr., Stephenville NF A2N 2V6 – 709/643-5111; Fax: 709/643-3104 – 56 acute care beds – CEO, Y. Noseworthy

AUXILIARY HOSPITALS/HEALTH CARE CENTRES

Badger's Quay: Bonavista North Health Care Complex, PO Box 209, Badger's Quay NF A0G 1B0 – 709/536-2160, 2405; Fax: 709/536-3334 – 12 acute care, 45 continuing care beds – CEO, W. Winsor

Baie Verte Peninsula Health Centre, Baie Verte NF A0K 1B0 – 709/532-4281; Fax: 709/532-4939 – 4 acute care, 19 continuing care beds – CEO, Wayne Vincent

Bell Island: Dr. Walter Templeman Community Health Centre, PO Box 580, Bell Island NF A0A 4H0 – 709/488-2821; Fax: 709/488-2600 – 6 acute care, 14 continuing care beds – CEO, T. O'Brien

Bonavista Hospital, PO Box 1, Bonavista NF A0C 1B0 – 709/468-7881; Fax: 709/468-7223 – 10 acute care, 73 continuing care beds – CEO, P. Grandy

Burgeo: Calder Health Care Centre, Burgeo NF A0M 1A0 – 709/886-3350; Fax: 709/886-3382 – 4 acute care, 18 continuing care beds – CEO, R. Staples-Payne

Fogo Island Hospital, Fogo NF A0G 2B0 – 709/266-2221; Fax: 709/266-2409 – 12 beds – Adm., R. Oake

Forteau: Labrador South Health Centre, Forteau NF A0K 2P0 – 709/931-2450; Fax: 709/931-2000

Grand Bank Community Health Centre, PO Box 310, Grand Bank NF A0E 1W0 – 709/832-2500 – CEO, J. Penney

Harbour Breton Hospital, Harbour Breton NF A0H 1P0 – 709/885-2359; Fax: 709/885-2358 – 5 acute care, 10 continuing care beds – CEO, D. Johnston

Norris Point: Bonne Bay Health Centre, Norris Point NF A0K 3V0 – 709/458-2201; Fax: 709/458-2074 – 5 acute care, 15 continuing care beds – Adm., Meta Carpenter

Old Perlican: Dr. A.A. Wilkinson Memorial Health Centre, PO Box 70, Old Perlican NF A0A 3G0 – 709/587-2200; Fax: 709/587-2275 – 6 beds – CEO, M. Oliver

Placentia & Area Health Care Complex, PO Box 480, Placentia NF A0B 2Y0 – 709/227-2013; Fax: 709/227-5476 – 6 acute care, 75 continuing care beds – CEO, A. Kennedy

Port aux Basques: Dr. Charles L. LeGrow Health Centre, PO Box 250, Port aux Basques NF A0M 1C0 – 709/695-2175; Fax: 709/695-3118 – 20 acute care, 30 continuing care beds – CEO, R. Graham

Port Saunders: Rufus Guinchard Health Care Centre, PO Box 40, Port Saunders NF A0K 4H0 – 709/861-3533; Fax: 709/861-3772 – 8 acute care, 11 continuing care beds – CEO, D. Brown

St. Lawrence: US Memorial Community Health Centre, PO Box 398, St. Lawrence NF A0E 2V0 – 709/873-2330; Fax: 709/873-2390 – 30 beds – CEO, C. Collins

Springdale: Green Bay Community Health Centre, PO Box 280, Springdale NF A0J 1T0 – 709/673-3911, 3936; Fax: 709/673-3186 – 125 continuing care beds – Adm., Wayne Vincent

Twillingate: Notre Dame Bay Memorial Health Centre, Twillingate NF A0G 4M0 – 709/884-2131; Fax: 709/884-2586 – 18 acute care, 27 continuing care beds – Exec. Dir., C. Herridge

Whitbourne: Dr. Wm. H. Newhook Community Health Centre, Whitbourne NF A0B 3K0 – 709/759-2300; Fax: 709/759-2387 – CEO, L. English

HOME CARE OFFICES/COMMUNITY CARE SERVICES

Corner Brook: Community Health - Western, PO Box 156, Corner Brook NF A2H 6C7 – 709/637-5243; Fax: 709/637-5159 – Exec. Dir., Dr. Minnie Wasmeier

Gander: Community Health - Central, 143 Bennett Dr., Gander NF A1V 2E6 – 709/256-7969; Fax: 709/651-3556 – Exec. Dir., A. Neal Ludlow

Holyrood: Community Health - Eastern, PO Box 70, Holyrood NF A0A 2R0 – 709/229-4855; Fax: 709/229-4005 – Exec. Dir., Calvin Kinden

St. John's: Community Health - St. John's Region, PO Box 13122, Stn A, St. John's NF A1B 4A4 – 709/738-4831; Fax: 709/738-4832 – Exec. Dir., Brenda Fitzgerald

NURSING HOMES

Bonavista: Golden Heights Manor, PO Box 1, Bonavista NF A0C 1B0 – 709/468-2043; Fax: 709/468-7223 – Adm., J.J. White

Botwood: Dr. Hugh Twomey Health Centre, PO Box 250, Botwood NF A0H 1E0 – 709/257-2874; Fax: 709/257-4613 – 82 beds – Adm., John W. Budgell

Buchans: A.M. Guy Memorial Health Centre, PO Box 10, Buchans NF A0H 1G0 – 709/672-3326; Fax: 709/672-3390 – 18 beds – CEO, W. Vincent

Carbonear: Harbour Lodge Nursing Home, 86 High Rd. South, Carbonear NF A1Y 1A4 – 709/596-7002; Fax: 709/596-1956 – 127 beds – CEO, D. Follett

Carbonear: Interfaith Citizens Home, 41 Water St., Carbonear NF A1Y 1B1 – 709/596-5101; Fax: 709/596-0041 – 55 beds – CEO, S, Penney

Clarke's Beach: Pentecostal Senior Citizen's Home, PO Box 130, Clarke's Beach NF A0A 1W0 – 709/786-2993; Fax: 709/786-2759 – 89 beds – Adm., Pastor W.G. Earle

Corner Brook: Dr. J.I. O'Connell Centre, PO Box 2005, Corner Brook NF A2H 6J7 – 709/637-5000; Fax: 709/634-2649 – 140 beds – CEO, M. Powell

Corner Brook: Inter Faith Home for Senior Citizens, Churchill St., Corner Brook NF A2H 5L8 – 709/639-9247; Fax: 709/639-1126 – 106 beds – CEO, A. Powell

Gander: Lakeside Homes Ltd., 95 Airport Blvd., Gander NF A1V 2L7 – 709/256-8850; Fax: 709/256-4259 – 118 beds – CEO, E. Forward

Grand Bank: Blue Crest Nursing Home, PO Box 160, Grand Bank NF A0E 1W0 – 709/832-1660; Fax: 709/832-2103 – 80 beds – CEO, J. Penney

Grand Falls-Windsor: Carmelite House Senior Citizens' Home, 21 Carmelite Rd., Grand Falls-Windsor NF A2A 1Y4 – 709/489-2274; Fax: 709/489-5778 – 94 beds – CEO, J. Budgell

Happy Valley-Goose Bay: Harry L. Paddon Memorial Home, PO Box 766, Happy Valley-Goose Bay NF A0P 1E0 – 709/896-2469; Fax: 709/896-5241 – 53 beds – CEO, J. Fry

Lewisporte: North Haven Manor Senior Citizens' Home, PO Box 880, Lewisporte NF A0G 3A0 – 709/535-6726; Fax: 709/535-8383 – 68 beds – CEO, J. Budgell

Mount Pearl: Masonic Park Senior Citizen's Home, Mount Pearl NF A1N 3K5 – 709/368-6081; Fax: 709/368-4129 – 41 beds – Adm., Marie Evans

Placentia & Area Health Care Complex, see Auxiliary Hospitals/Health Care Centres listings

St. Anthony Interfaith Home, PO Box 69, St. Anthony NF A0K 4S0 – 709/454-3506; Fax: 709/454-4134 – 49 beds – CEO, R. Patey

St. John's: Agnes Pratt Home, 239 Topsail Rd., St. John's NF A1E 2B4 – 709/579-0185; Fax: 709/739-5457 – 136 beds – Adm., Don Green

St. John's: Glenbrook Lodge, 105 Torbay Rd., St. John's NF A1A 2G9 – 709/726-1969; Fax: 709/726-0610 – 146 beds – Adm., Aux. Capt. Donald Cummings

St. John's: Hoyles-Escasoni Complex, 10 Escasoni Pl., St. John's NF A1A 3R6 – 709/570-2311; Fax: 709/753-9620 – 400 beds – Adm., Anne Morrison

St. John's: Leonard A. Miller Centre, St. John's NF A1A 1E5 – 709/737-6555; Fax: 709/737-6969 – 153 continuing care beds – CEO, L. Jones

St. John's: Saint Luke's Home, 24 Deluxe Rd., St. John's NF A1E 5C3 – 709/579-0052; Fax: 709/579-7317 – 127 beds – Adm., Margaret Boone

St. John's: St. Patrick's Mercy Home, 146 Elizabeth Ave., St. John's NF A1B 1S5 – 709/726-2687; Fax: 709/726-0722 – 214 beds – Adm., Katherine Turner

St. John's: Waterford Hospital, see General Hospitals listings

Springdale: Valley Vista Senior Citizens Home, PO Box 130, Springdale NF A0J 1T0 – 709/673-3936; Fax: 709/673-3186 – Adm., D. Vincent

Stephenville Crossing: Bay St. George Senior Citizens Home, PO Box 250, Stephenville Crossing NF A0N 2C0 – 709/646-5800; Fax: 709/646-2375 – 130 beds – Adm., C. MacDonald

NURSING STATIONS

Black Tickle Nursing Station, Black Tickle NF A0K 1N0 – 709/471-8832; Fax: 709/471-8893 – Adm., Glendene Snook

Cartwright Nursing Station, Cartwright NF A0K 1V0 – 709/938-7285; Fax: 709/938-7286 – Adm., Leela Subramanian

Charlottetown Nursing Station, Charlottetown NF A0K 5Y0 – 709/949-0259; Fax: 709/949-0259

Churchill Falls Nursing Station, PO Box 100, Churchill Falls NF A0R 1A0 – 709/925-3381; Fax: 709/925-3246 – Florence Rogers

Davis Inlet Nursing Station, Davis Inlet NF A0P 1A0 – 709/478-8842; Fax: 709/478-8817 – Adm., Delrose Gordon

Flower's Cove: Strait of Belle Isle Health Centre, Flower's Cove NF A0K 2N0 – 709/456-2401; Fax: 709/456-2562

Harbour Deep Nursing Station, Harbour Deep NF A0K 2Z0 – 709/843-3291; Fax: 709/843-4103

Hopedale Nursing Station, Hopedale NF A0P 1G0 – 709/933-3857; Fax: 709/933-3744 – Adm., Ann McElligott

Makkovik Nursing Station, Makkovik NF A0P 1J0 – 709/923-2229; Fax: 709/923-2428 – Jennifer McGrath

Mary's Harbour Nursing Station, Mary's Harbour NF A0K 3P0 – 709/921-6228; Fax: 709/921-6975

Nain Nursing Station, Nain NF A0P 1L0 – 709/922-2912; Fax: 709/922-2103 – Adm., Claudine Foster

Northwest River Nursing Station, Northwest River NF A0P 1M0 – 709/497-8351; Fax: 709/497-8521 – Adm., Joanne Montague

Port Hope Simpson Nursing Station, Port Hope Simpson NF A0K 4E0 – 709/960-0271; Fax: 709/960-0392

Postville Nursing Station, Postville NF A0P 1N0 – 709/479-9851; Fax: 709/479-9715 – Lynda Laidler

Rigolet Nursing Station, Rigolet NF A0P 1P0 – 709/947-3386; Fax: 709/947-3401 – Helen Michelin

Roddickton: White Bay Central Health Centre, Roddickton NF A0K 4P0 – 709/457-2215; Fax: 709/457-2076

St. Lewis Nursing Station, St. Lewis NF A0K 4W0 – 709/939-2230; Fax: 709/939-2342

SPECIAL TREATMENT CENTRES

(Includes: Abortion Clinics, Cancer Clinics, Rehabilitation Centres, Treatment Centres)

St. John's: Children's Rehabilitation Centre, St. John's NF A1C 5N5 – 709/754-1970; Fax: 709/754-3116 – rehabilitation centre – Adm., T. O'Brien

St. John's: Dr. H. Bliss Murphy Cancer Centre, Newfoundland Cancer Treatment & Research Foundation, 300 Prince Philip Dr., St. John's NF A1B 3V6 – 709/737-6480; Fax: 709/753-0927 – CEO, Bertha Paulse

NORTHWEST TERRITORIES

HOSPITAL DISTRICTS/HEALTH UNITS

Cambridge Bay: Kitikmeot Health Board, PO Box 200, Cambridge Bay NT X0E 0C0 – 403/983-7328; Fax:

403/983-2253; EMail: experson@assmicro.com – Exec. Dir., Alice Isnor

Inuvik Regional Health Board, PO Box 2, Inuvik NT X0E 0T0 – 403/979-2955; Fax: 403/979-2422 – CEO, Andrew Lockhart

Iqaluit: Baffin Regional Health Board, PO Box 200, Iqaluit NT X0A 0H0 – 819/979-5300; Fax: 819/979-4514 – CEO, Trevor Pollitt

Rankin Inlet: Keewatin Regional Health Board, PO Box 298, Rankin Inlet NT X0C 0G0 – 819/645-2171; Fax: 819/645-2409 – Exec. Dir., James Egan

Yellowknife: Mackenzie Regional Health Service, PO Box 520, Yellowknife NT X1A 2N4 – 403/920-6590; Fax: 403/920-4015 – Exec. Dir., Nelson McClelland

GENERAL HOSPITALS

Hay River: H.H. Williams Memorial Hospital, 3 Gaetz Dr., Hay River NT X0E 0R8 – 403/874-6512; Fax: 403/874-3449 – Exec. Dir., David Matthews

Inuvik Regional Hospital, PO Box 2, Inuvik NT X0E 0T0 – 403/979-2955; Fax: 403/979-2422 – CEO, Andrew Lockhart

Iqaluit: Baffin Regional Hospital, PO Box 200, Iqaluit NT X0A 0H0 – 819/979-5231; Fax: 819/979-4514 – CEO, Judy Watts

Yellowknife: Stanton Regional Hospital, PO Box 10, Yellowknife NT X1A 2N1 – 403/873-2254; Fax: 403/873-4382 – CEO, Dennis Cleaver

AUXILIARY HOSPITALS/HEALTH CARE CENTRES

In addition to the health centre listed below, there are 52 health centres situated in communities throughout the Northwest Territories providing primary health care.

Fort Smith Health Centre, PO Box 1080, Fort Smith NT X0E 0P0 – 403/872-2713; Fax: 403/872-2619 – Exec. Dir., Dwight Morley

NURSING HOMES

Fort Smith: Northern Lights Special Care Home, PO Box 1319, Fort Smith NT X0E 0P0 – 403/872-5403; Fax: 403/872-5404 – Adm., Cheryl Comin

Hay River: Woodland Manor, 52A Woodland Dr., Hay River NT X0E 0R8 – 403/874-2493; Fax: 403/874-3717 – Adm., Jennifer Seeley

Yellowknife: Aven Seniors' Centre, PO Box 1564, Yellowknife NT X1A 2P2 – 403/920-2443; Fax: 403/873-9915 – Adm., Wade Were

NOVA SCOTIA

HOSPITAL DISTRICTS/HEALTH UNITS

Clementsport: Western Region District Health Board, PO Box 74, Clementsport NS B0S 1E0 – 902/638-3452; Fax: 902/638-8170 – CEO, Victor Maddelena

Halifax: Central Region District Health Board, Scotia Sq., #1401, 5251 Duke St., Halifax NS B3J 1P3 – 902/420-8825; Fax: 902/420-8820 – CEO, Richard Criddle

Sydney: Eastern Region District Health Board, Ignatius Hall, 25 Churchill Dr., Sydney NS B1S 2B2 – 902/567-2620; Fax: 902/562-3764 – CEO, John Breen

Truro: Northern Region District Health Board, c/o Dept. of Health, #6, 44 Inglis Place, Truro NS B2N 4B4 – 902/897-6265; Fax: 902/893-0250 – CEO, Wayne Tucker

GENERAL HOSPITALS

Advocate Harbour: Bayview Memorial Health Centre, Advocate Harbour NS B0M 1A0 – 902/392-2859; Fax: 902/392-2625 – 10 beds – Adm., Connie Ells

Amherst: Highland View Regional Hospital, 110 East Pleasant St., Amherst NS B4H 1N6 – 902/667-3361; Fax: 902/667-6306 – Exec. Dir., David Turner

Antigonish: St. Martha's Regional Hospital, 25 Bay St., Antigonish NS B2G 2G5 – 902/863-2830; Fax: 902/863-1176 – Acting Adm., Mary Foshay

Baddeck: Victoria County Memorial Hospital, PO Box 220, Baddeck NS B0E 1B0 – 902/295-2760; Fax: 902/295-3432 – 12 beds – Adm., Peter MacKinnon

Canso: Eastern Memorial Hospital, PO Box 10, Canso NS B0H 1H0 – 902/366-2794; Fax: 902/366-2740 – 11 beds – Adm., Sheila Lawrence

Cheticamp: Sacred Heart Hospital, PO Box 129, Cheticamp NS B0E 1H0 – 902/224-4020; Fax: 902/224-2903 – Adm., Yolande LeVert

Cleveland: Strait-Richmond Hospital, RR#1, Cleveland NS B0E 1J0 – 902/625-3100; Fax: 902/625-3804 – Acting CEO, Shirley Quaade

Dartmouth General Hospital, 325 Pleasant St., Dartmouth NS B2Y 4G8 – 902/465-8300; Fax: 902/465-8537 – 126 beds – Exec. Dir., Donald Peters, 902/465-8353

Digby General Hospital, PO Box 820, Digby NS B0V 1A0 – 902/245-2501; Fax: 902/245-5517 – Adm., Linda Carter

Glace Bay Health Care Corp. (General), 300 South St., Glace Bay NS B1A 1W5 – 902/849-5511; Fax: 902/842-9775 – 144 beds – CEO, Dave Marchand

Guysborough Memorial Hospital, PO Box 170, Guysborough NS B0H 1N0 – 902/533-3702; Fax: 902/533-4066 – Acting Adm., Freda Kennedy

Halifax: IWK-Grace Health Centre for Children, Women & Families, 5980 University Ave., Halifax NS B3H 4N1 – 902/420-6600; Fax: 902/422-3009 – CEO, Richard Nurse

Halifax: Queen Elizabeth II Health Sciences Centre (Camp Hill Hospital), 1763 Robie St., Halifax NS B3H 3G2 – 902/496-4222; Fax: 902/496-2501 – CEO, Neil Roberts

Halifax: Queen Elizabeth II Health Sciences Centre (Halifax Infirmary), 1335 Queen St., Halifax NS B3J 2H6 – 902/496-4222; Fax: 902/496-2719 – CEO, Neil Roberts

Halifax: Queen Elizabeth II Health Sciences Centre (Victoria General Hospital), 1278 Tower Rd., Halifax NS B3H 2Y9 – 902/428-2240; Fax: 902/428-7052 – CEO, Neil Roberts

Inverness Consolidated Hospital, PO Box 610, Inverness NS B0E 1N0 – 902/258-2100; Fax: 902/258-3025 – Adm., Kevin MacDonald

Kentville: Valley Regional Hospital, 150 Exhibition St., Kentville NS B4N 5E3 – 902/678-7381; Fax: 902/679-1904 – Interim General Mgr., Betty Mattson

Liverpool: Queens General Hospital, PO Box 370, Liverpool NS B0T 1K0 – 902/354-3436; Fax: 902/354-2018 – Adm., Gary Slauenwhite

Lunenburg: Fishermen's Memorial Hospital, PO Box 1180, Lunenburg NS B0J 2C0 – 902/634-8801; Fax: 902/634-3668 – 53 beds – Interim Adm., Paul Haughn

Middle Musquodoboit: Musquodoboit Valley Memorial Hospital, Middle Musquodoboit NS B0N 1X0 – 902/384-2220; Fax: 902/384-3310 – Adm., Joan Murray

Middleton: Soldiers' Memorial Hospital, PO Box 730, Middleton NS B0S 1P0 – 902/825-3411; Fax: 902/825-4811 – CEO, Bruce Quigley

Musquodoboit Harbour: Twin Oaks Memorial Hospital, PO Box 309, Musquodoboit Harbour NS B0J 2L0 – 902/889-2200; Fax: 902/889-2470 – Adm., Janet Crowell

Neil's Harbour: Buchanan Memorial Hospital, Neil's Harbour NS B0C 1N0 – 902/336-2200; Fax: 902/336-2399 – 10 beds – Adm., Pauline Chubbs

New Glasgow: Aberdeen Hospital, 835 East River Rd., New Glasgow NS B2H 3S6 – 902/752-7600; Fax: 902/755-2356 – 119 beds – CEO, Patrick Flinn

New Waterford Consolidated Hospital, 716 King St., New Waterford NS B1H 3Z5 – 902/862-6411; Fax: 902/862-8277 – CEO, Sr. Marie Kelly

North Sydney: Northside Harbour View Hospital Corporation, PO Box 399, North Sydney NS B2A 3M4 – 902/794-8521; Fax: 902/794-3355 – Exec. Dir., John Higgins

Pictou: Sutherland-Harris Memorial Hospital, 20 Haliburton Rd., PO Box 1059, Pictou NS B0K 1H0 – 902/485-4324; Fax: 902/485-8835 – Adm., Norman Ferguson

Pugwash: North Cumberland Memorial Hospital, PO Box 242, Pugwash NS B0K 1L0 – 902/243-2521; Fax: 902/243-2941 – Adm., Beryl MacLean

Sheet Harbour: Eastern Shore Memorial Hospital, RR#7, Sheet Harbour NS B0J 3B0 – 902/885-2554; Fax: 902/885-3200 – 20 beds – Adm., A. Donald Batstone

Shelburne: Roseway Hospital, PO Box 610, Shelburne NS B0T 1W0 – 902/875-3011; Fax: 902/875-1580 – Exec. Dir., Jerry Fraser

Sherbrooke: St. Mary's Memorial Hospital, PO Box 279, Sherbrooke NS B0J 3C0 – 902/522-2882; Fax: 902/522-2556 – Adm., Shirley Bowen

Springhill: All Saint's Hospital, 10 Princess St., PO Box 700, Springhill NS B0M 1X0 – 902/597-3773; Fax: 902/597-3440 – 20 beds – Site Mgr., Fran McMillan

Sydney: Cape Breton Health Care Complex, 1482 George St., Sydney NS B1P 1P3 – 902/567-8000; Fax: 902/567-7878 – 311 beds – Exec. Dir., Mary MacIsaac

Tatamagouche: Lillian Fraser Memorial Hospital, PO Box 40, Tatamagouche NS B0K 1V0 – 902/657-2382; Fax: 902/657-3745 – CEO, Douglas Cunningham

Truro: Colchester Regional Hospital, 207 Willow St., Truro NS B2N 5A1 – 902/893-4321; Fax: 902/893-5559 – 133 beds – CEO, Brenda Payne

Windsor: Hants Community Hospital, PO Box 520, Windsor NS B0N 2T0 – 902/798-8351; Fax: 902/798-6002 – CEO, Donn Peters

AUXILIARY HOSPITALS/HEALTH CARE CENTRES

Annapolis Community Health Centre, PO Box 426, Annapolis Royal NS B0S 1A0 – 902/532-2381; Fax: 902/532-2113 – Adm., Abram Almeda

Arichat: St. Anne Community & Nursing Care Centre, PO Box 30, Arichat NS B0E 1A0 – 902/226-2826; Fax: 902/226-1529 – Adm., Maha St.Pierre

Berwick: Western Kings Memorial Health Centre, PO Box 490, Berwick NS B0P 1E0 – 902/538-3111; Fax: 902/538-9590 – Adm., John Dow

Halifax: Point Pleasant Lodge, 1121 South Park St., Halifax NS B3J 2W6 – 902/421-1599; Fax: 902/429-9722 – Adm., Robert Manuel

Lower Sackville: Cobequid Multi-Service Centre, 70 Memory Lane, Lower Sackville NS B4C 5A1 – 902/865-5750; Fax: 902/865-6814 – Exec. Dir., Margaret Merlin

Parrsboro: South Cumberland Community Care Centre, PO Box 489, Parrsboro NS B0M 1S0 – 902/254-2540; Fax: 902/254-2504 – Adm., Harriett McCready

Waterville: Kings Regional Health & Rehabilitation Centre, PO Box 128, Waterville NS B0P 1V0 – 902/538-3103; Fax: 902/538-7022 – Adm., Phillip Warren

MENTAL HEALTH HOSPITALS & COMMUNITY FACILITIES

Bridgewater: South Shore Regional Hospital, 90 Glen Allen Dr., Bridgewater NS B4V 3S6 – 902/543-4603; Fax: 902/543-4719 – CEO, Carolyn Johnston

Dartmouth: Nova Scotia Hospital, 300 Pleasant St., PO Box 1004, Dartmouth NS B2Y 3Z9 – 902/464-3111; Fax: 902/464-4825 – Exec. Dir., Anne McGuire

Yarmouth Regional Hospital, 60 Vancouver St., Yarmouth NS B5A 2P5 – 902/742-3541; Fax: 902/742-0369 – Exec. Dir., J.G. McEachern

NURSING HOMES

Advocate Harbour: Bayview Memorial Nursing Care Unit, *see* Bayview Memorial Health Centre, General Hospitals listings

Amherst: Gables Lodge, c/o Mr. & Mrs. S. Hussain, 260 Church St., Amherst NS B4H 3C9 – 902/667-3501; Fax: 902/667-3533 – Kathy Maltby

Annapolis Royal Nursing Home, St. George St., RR#2, Annapolis Royal NS B0S 1A0 – 902/532-2240; Fax: 902/532-7151 – Linda Bailey

Annapolis Royal: Northhills Nursing Home Ltd., PO Box 220, Annapolis Royal NS B0S 1A0 – 902/532-5555; Fax: 902/532-7449 – Adm., Frankie Sheehy

Antigonish: R.K. MacDonald Guest Home, 64 Pleasant St., Antigonish NS B2G 1W7 – 902/863-2578; Fax: 902/863-4437 – Evelyn Lindsay

Arichat: St. Anne Community & Nursing Care Centre, *see* Auxiliary Hospitals/Health Care Centres listings

Armdale: Glades Lodge, 25 Alton Dr., Armdale NS B3N 1M1 – 902/477-1777; Fax: 902/477-8174 – Adm., Jan White

Baddeck: Alderwood Home for the Aged, PO Box 218, Baddeck NS B0E 1B0 – 902/295-2644; Fax: 902/295-1698 – Adm., Marcella Roberts

Beaverbank: Scotia Nursing Homes Ltd., RR#1, Beaverbank NS B4C 2S6 – 902/865-6364; Fax: 902/865-3582 – Adm., Stephen Pace

Berwick: Grand View Manor, PO Box 309, Berwick NS B0P 1E0 – 902/538-3118; Fax: 902/538-3998 – Adm., Graham Hardy

Bridgetown: Mountain Lea Lodge, RR#1, Church St., Bridgetown NS B0S 1C0 – 902/665-4489; Fax: 902/665-2900 – Larry Marsters

Bridgewater: Hillside Pines, 77 Exhibition Ave., Bridgewater NS B4V 3K6 – 902/543-1525; Fax: 902/543-8083 – Sheila MacKinnon

Caledonia: North Queens Nursing Home, PO Box 181, Caledonia NS B0T 1B0 – 902/682-2553; Fax: 902/682-2602 – Adm., Otto Boye

Canso Seaside Manor, PO Box 70, Canso NS B0H 1H0 – 902/366-3030; Fax: 902/366-3093 – Adm., Darren Bennett

Chester: Shoreham Village, PO Box 380, Chester NS B0J 1J0 – 902/275-5631; Fax: 902/275-2586 – Adm., Brian Selig

Cheticamp: Foyer Pere Fiset, Cheticamp NS B0E 1H0 – 902/224-2087; Fax: 902/224-1188 – Adm., Lorraine Aucoin

Dartmouth: Oakwood Terrace, 10 Mount Hope Ave., Dartmouth NS B2Y 4K1 – 902/469-3702; Fax: 902/469-3824 – Adm., Glen Griffin

Digby: Tideview Terrace, PO Box 1120, Digby NS B0V 1A0 – 902/245-4718; Fax: 902/245-6674 – Gary Burlingham

Eastern Passage: Oceanview Manor, PO Box 130, Eastern Passage NS B3G 1M4 – 902/465-6020; Fax: 902/465-4929 – Adm., Keith Menzies

Glace Bay Health Care Corp., 197 Main St., Glace Bay NS B1A 4Z8 – 902/849-5531; Fax: 902/849-2287 – Adm., David Marchand

Glace Bay: Seaview Manor, 275 South St., Glace Bay NS B1A 1W6 – 902/849-7300; Fax: 902/849-7401 – Adm., Dan Munroe

Glace Bay: Victoria Haven Nursing Home, 429A Third St., Glace Bay NS B1A 4G6 – 902/849-8826 – Adm., Michael Saccary

Glenwood: Nakile Home for the Aged, RR#1, Glenwood NS B0W 1W0 – 902/643-2707; Fax: 902/643-2862 – Adm., Bertha Brannen

Guysborough: Milford Haven, PO Box 300, Guysborough NS B0H 1N0 – 902/533-2828; Fax: 902/533-4066 – Adm., Mary Jurcina-Taylor

Halifax: Armview Estates, 126 Purcell's Cove Rd., Halifax NS B3P 1B5 – 902/477-8051; Fax: 902/477-5726 – Adm., Melanie Ray

Halifax: Colonial Nursing Home, 1019 Lucknow St., Halifax NS B3H 2T2 – 902/420-0697; Fax: 902/492-3936 – Deborah Morgan-Downey

Halifax: Fairview Villa, 245 Main Ave., Halifax NS B3M 1B7 – 902/443-1971; Fax: 902/443-9037 – Carol Ann Gallant

Halifax: Melville Lodge, 50 Shoreham Lane, Halifax NS B3P 2R3 – 902/479-1030; Fax: 902/477-1663 – Adm., Dorothy Redmond

Halifax: Northwoodcare Inc., 2630 Gottingen St., Halifax NS B3K 3C6 – 902/454-8311; Fax: 902/455-6408 – Adm., Lloyd Brown

Halifax: Saint Vincent Guest Home, 2080 Windsor St., Halifax NS B3K 5B1 – 902/429-0550; Fax: 902/492-3703 – Adm., Kristin Schmitz

Inverness Memorial Nursing Care Unit, PO Box 610, Inverness NS B0E 1N0 – 902/258-2100; Fax: 902/258-3025 – Adm., Kevin MacDonald

Inverness: Inverary Manor, Maple St., PO Box 460, Inverness NS B0E 1N0 – 902/258-2581, 2842; Fax: 902/258-3865 – Joan MacLellan

Kentville: Evergreen Home for Special Care, 655 Park St., Kentville NS B4N 3V7 – 902/678-7355; Fax: 902/678-5996 – Larry D. Knowles

Liverpool: Queens Manor, PO Box 1283, Liverpool NS B0T 1K0 – 902/354-3451; Fax: 902/354-5383 – Adm., Gary Slauenwhite

Lunenburg: Harbour View Haven, Blockhouse Hill Rd., PO Box 1480, Lunenburg NS B0J 2C0 – 902/634-8836; Fax: 902/634-8792 – Adm., G.W. Crouse

Mahone Bay: Mahone Nursing Home, PO Box 320, Mahone Bay NS B0J 2E0 – 902/624-8341; Fax: 902/624-6338 – Adm., Anne Kennedy

Meteghan: Villa Acadienne, PO Box 248, Meteghan NS B0W 2K0 – 902/645-2065; Fax: 902/645-3899 – Adm., Henry Saulnier

Musquodoboit Harbour: The Birches, Musquodoboit Harbour NS B0J 2L0 – 902/889-3474; Fax: 902/889-2271 – Adm., Janet Crowell

Neil's Harbour: Highland Manor, Neil's Harbour NS B0C 1N0 – 902/336-2895 – Adm., Donna Rideout

New Germany: Rosedale Home, PO Box 8, New Germany NS B0R 1E0 – 902/644-2008; Fax: 902/644-3260 – Adm., Patricia Fraser

New Glasgow: Glen Haven Manor, 739 East River Rd., New Glasgow NS B2H 5E9 – 902/752-2588; Fax: 902/752-0053 – Adm., James Ferguson

New Waterford: Maple Hill Manor, 700 King St., New Waterford NS B1H 3Z5 – 902/862-6495; Fax: 902/862-9294 – Acting Adm., Cathy MacPhee

North Sydney: Northside Community Guest Home for the Aged, 11 Queen St., PO Box 100, North Sydney NS B2A 1A2 – 902/794-4733; Fax: 902/794-9021 – Lucy MacEachern

Pictou: Maritime Odd Fellows Home (IOOF), PO Box 850, Pictou NS B0K 1H0 – 902/485-5492; Fax: 902/485-9233 – Adm., Janet Johnston

Pictou: Shiretown Nursing Home (Edward Mortimer Place), Haliburton Rd., PO Box 250, Pictou NS B0K 1H0 – 902/485-4341; Fax: 902/485-9203 – Adm., Katherine V. Sullivan

Port Hawkesbury Nursing Home, PO Box 2105, Port Hawkesbury NS B0E 2V0 – 902/625-1460; Fax: 902/625-3232 – Adm., Fran Payne

Pugwash: East Cumberland Lodge, PO Box 250, Pugwash NS B0K 1L0 – 902/243-2504; Fax: 902/243-3375 – Adm., Donna Dill

Riverton: Valley View Villa, RR#1, Riverton NS B0K 1S0 – 902/755-5780; Fax: 902/755-3104 – Adm., David Lank

St. Peter's: Richmond Villa, PO Box 250, St. Peter's NS B0E 3B0 – 902/535-3030; Fax: 902/535-2256 – Isabelle Johnston

Sandy Point: Roseway Manor Inc., PO Box 518, Sandy Point NS B0T 1W0 – 902/875-4707; Fax: 902/875-4105 – Adm., Karl White

Sheet Harbour: Duncan MacMillan Home for the Aged, Sheet Harbour NS B0J 3B0 – 902/885-2545; Fax: 902/885-3210 – Janet Crowell

Shelburne: Surf Lodge Nursing Home, PO Box 610, Shelburne NS B0T 1W0 – 902/875-4301; Fax: 902/875-1249 – Adm., Margaret Coates

Sherbrooke: MacKaracher's Nursing Home, Sherbrooke NS B0J 3C0 – 902/522-2147; Fax: 902/522-2628 – Adm., Audrey Taylor

Springhill: Highcrest Springhill Nursing Home, 17 MacFarlane St., PO Box 2170, Springhill NS B0M 1X0 – 902/597-2797; Fax: 902/597-8339 – Mildred Carr-Shrum

Sydney Mines: Miner's Memorial Manor, 15 Lorne St., Sydney Mines NS B1V 3B9 – 902/736-1992; Fax: 902/736-0667 – Adm., Harry Blinkhorn

Sydney: Breton Bay Nursing Home, 70 St. Anthony Dr., Sydney NS B1S 2R5 – 902/539-4560; Fax: 902/567-6234 – Adm., Ellen Stoddard

Sydney: The Cove, Kings Rd., Sydney NS B1S 1B9 – 902/539-5267; Fax: 902/539-7565 – Adm., Archie MacKeigan

Sydney: MacGillivray Guest Home, 25 Xavier Dr., Sydney NS B1S 2R9 – 902/539-6110; Fax: 902/567-0437 – Adm., Jack Coffey

Tatamagouche: Willow Lodge, Blair Ave., Tatamagouche NS B0K 1V0 – 902/657-3101; Fax: 902/657-3859 – Adm., Douglas Cunningham

Truro: Glenview Lodge, RR#3, East Prince St., Truro NS B2N 5B2 – 902/895-8715; Fax: 902/897-1903 – Adm., Donna Kroonenburg

Truro: Hillcrest Manors Ltd., Manor Dr., PO Box 1210, Truro NS B2N 5H1 – 902/895-2891; Fax: 902/893-2361 – Adm., Kim Brennan

Windsor Elms, 590 King St., Windsor NS B0N 2T0 – 902/798-2251; Fax: 902/798-0914 – Rev. Ross MacDonald

Windsor: Haliburton Place, *see* Hants Community Hospital, General Hospitals listings

Windsor: Dykeland Lodge, Curry's Corner, Windsor NS B0N 2T0 – 902/798-8346; Fax: 902/798-8312 – Adm., W.R. Brooks

Wolfville Nursing Home, RR#2, 346 Main St., Wolfville NS B0P 1X0 – 902/542-2429; Fax: 902/542-2761 – Adm., Diana MacDonald

Yarmouth: Tidal View Manor, 60 Vancouver St., Yarmouth NS B5A 2P5 – 902/742-7853; Fax: 902/742-0369 – Exec. Dir., J.G. McEachern

Yarmouth: Villa St. Joseph du Lac, RR#1, Lakeside, PO Box 810, Yarmouth NS B5A 4A5 – 902/742-7128; Fax: 902/749-1342 – Adm., Sr. Estelle Arsenault

SPECIAL TREATMENT CENTRES

(Includes: Abortion Clinics, Cancer Clinics, Rehabilitation Centres, Treatment Centres)

Halifax: Camp Hill Medical Centre (Nova Scotia Breast Screening Clinic), Halifax Shopping Centre, #103, Tower 1, 7001 Mumford Rd., Halifax NS B3L 4H6 – 902/496-3956; Fax: 902/496-3959 – Mgr., Marie Peek

Halifax: Nova Scotia Cancer Centre, 5820 University Ave., Halifax NS B3H 1V7 – 902/428-4200; Fax: 902/428-4277 – cancer treatment – Clinic Mgr., Maureen MacIntyre

Halifax: Nova Scotia Hearing & Speech Clinic, Fenwick Place, 5599 Fenwick St., 32nd Fl., Halifax NS B3H 1R2 – 902/423-7354; Fax: 902/423-0981 – Dir., Dr. Brad Stach

Halifax: Queen Elizabeth II Health Sciences Centre (Cancer Treatment & Research Foundation of

Nova Scotia), #102, 1200 Tower Rd., Halifax NS B3H 4K6 – 902/425-8504; Fax: 902/425-7058 – cancer treatment – CEO, Neil Roberts

Halifax: Queen Elizabeth II Health Sciences Centre (Nova Scotia Rehabilitation Centre), 1341 Summer St., Halifax NS B3H 4K4 – 902/422-1787; Fax: 902/425-6466 – rehabilitation centre – CEO, Neil Roberts

ONTARIO

HOSPITAL DISTRICTS/HEALTH UNITS

Barrie: Simcoe County District Health Council, #216, Victoria Sq., 11 Victoria St., Barrie ON L4N 6T3 – 705/734-9960; Fax: 705/734-9987 – Exec. Dir., Floyd Dale

Belleville: Hastings & Prince Edward Counties District Health Council, #101, 375 Dundas St. West, Belleville ON K8P 1B3 – 613/962-4660; Fax: 613/962-5130 – Exec. Dir., Steve Elson

Brampton: Peel District Health Council, #220, Plaza II, 350 Rutherford Rd. South, Brampton ON L6W 4N6 – 905/455-4856; Fax: 905/455-5285 – Exec. Dir., Bob Youtz

Brantford: Brant District Health Council, #304, 233 Colborne St., Brantford ON N3T 2H4 – 519/756-1330; Fax: 519/756-6013 – Exec. Dir., Catherine Knipe

Chatham: Kent County District Health Council, 75 Thames St., Chatham ON N7L 1S4 – 519/351-1162; Fax: 519/351-6583 – Exec. Dir., Ron Shaw

Cornwall: DHC of Eastern Ontario, #301, 132 Second St., Cornwall ON K6H 1Y4 – 613/933-9585; Fax: 613/933-3977 – Exec. Dir., Jocelyne Contant

Fonthill: Niagara District Health Council, 1428 Pelham St. South, PO Box 1220, Fonthill ON L0E 1E0 – 905/892-5771; Fax: 905/892-1593 – Exec. Dir., Gary Zalot

Guelph: Wellington-Dufferin District Health Council, Woodlawn Sq., Units 217 & 218, 251 Woodlawn Rd. West, Guelph ON N1H 8J1 – 519/836-7440; Fax: 519/836-7177 – Exec. Dir., James Whaley

Hamilton-Wentworth District Health Council, #301, 10 George St., Hamilton ON L8P 1C8 – 905/570-1441; Fax: 905/570-1202 – Exec. Dir., Susan Goodman

Huntsville: East Muskoka Parry Sound District Health Council, #202, 36 Chaffey St., Huntsville ON P1H 2J4 – 705/789-4429; Fax: 705/789-6943 – Exec. Dir., Peter Deane

Keewatin: Kenora-Rainy River District Health Council, 104 Government Rd., PO Box 379, Keewatin ON P0K 1C0 – 807/547-2028; Fax: 807/547-2094 – Exec. Dir., Joe Brown

Kingston, Frontenac & Lennox & Addington District Health Council, #400, 471 Counter St., Kingston ON K7M 8S8 – 613/549-5253; Fax: 613/542-9223 – Exec. Dir., Elizabeth McIver

London: Thames Valley District Health Council, The Gordon J. Mogenson Bldg., #105, 100 Collip Circle, London ON N6G 4X8 – 519/858-5015; Fax: 519/858-5016 – Exec. Dir., Paul Huras

Mitchell: Huron-Perth District Health Council, 235 St. George St., Mitchell ON N0K 1N0 – 519/348-4498; Fax: 519/348-4300 – Exec. Dir., Fraser Bell

Newmarket: York Region District Health Council, #300, 1091 Gorham St., Newmarket ON L3Y 7V1 – 905/830-9899; Fax: 905/830-9903 – Exec. Dir., Graham Constantine

North Bay: Nipissing-Timiskaming District Health Council, 310 Algonquin Ave., North Bay ON P1B 4W2 – 705/494-9126; Fax: 705/494-9127 – Exec. Dir., Shehnaz Alidina

Oakville: Halton District Health Council, #510, 700 Dorval Dr., Oakville ON L6K 3V3 – 905/842-2120; Fax: 905/842-7131 – Exec. Dir., Linda Rothney

Ottawa-Carleton Regional Health Council, #350, 955 Green Valley Cres., Ottawa ON K2C 3V4 – 613/723-1440; Fax: 613/723-5162 – Exec. Dir., Anna Telner Wex

Owen Sound: Grey-Bruce District Health Council, 733 Ninth Ave. East, Unit 4, Owen Sound ON N4K 3E6 – 519/376-6691; Fax: 519/376-3074 – Exec. Dir., Karen Levenick

Parry Sound: West Muskoka Parry Sound District Health Council, 17 James St., 2nd Fl., Parry Sound ON P2A 1T4 – 705/746-2123; Fax: 705/746-8156 – Exec. Dir., Peter Deane

Pembroke: Renfrew County District Health Council, 12 International Dr., RR#4, Pembroke ON K8A 6W5 – 613/732-2335; Fax: 613/732-8719 – Exec. Dir., Lynn Bowering

Peterborough: Haliburton, Kawartha & Pine Ridge District Health Council, #210, 849 Alexander Ct., PO Box 544, Peterborough ON K9J 7H8 – 705/748-2992; Fax: 705/748-9600 – Exec. Dir., Marshall Elliott

Sarnia: Lambton District Health Council, #401, 265 North Front St., Sarnia ON N7T 7X1 – 519/337-5485; Fax: 519/337-9293 – Exec. Dir., Frank Chalmers

Sault Ste. Marie: Algoma District Health Council, #405, 123 March St., Sault Ste. Marie ON P6A 2Z5 – 705/942-0200; Fax: 705/942-7579 – Exec. Dir., Anthony Ubaldi

Smith Falls: Rideau Valley District Health Council, 1 Abel St., PO Box 487, Smith Falls ON K7A 4T4 – 613/283-6980; Fax: 613/283-3177 – Exec. Dir., Peter N.T. Roberts

Sudbury: Manitoulin-Sudbury District Health Council, 336 Pine St., Sudbury ON P3C 1X8 – 705/675-5654; Fax: 705/675-2870 – Acting Exec. Dir., Terry Tilleczek

Thunder Bay District Health Council, 1093 Barton St., Thunder Bay ON P7B 5N3 – 807/623-6131; Fax: 807/623-0355 – Exec. Dir., Celso Teixeira

Timmins: Cochrane District Health Council, #203, 119 Pine St. South, Timmins ON P4N 2K3 – 705/264-9539; Fax: 705/264-8620 – Exec. Dir., Anne Vincent

Toronto: Metropolitan Toronto District Health Council, #200, 4141 Yonge St., Willowdale ON M2P 2A8 – 416/222-6522; Fax: 416/222-5587 – Exec. Dir., Lorne Zon

Townsend: Haldimand-Norfolk District Health Council, 101 Nanticoke Creek Pkwy., PO Box 5081, Townsend ON N0A 1S0 – 519/587-2231; Fax: 519/587-5112 – Exec. Dir., Sally Campeau

Waterloo Region District Health Council, #218, 75 King St. South, Waterloo ON N2J 1P2 – 519/884-6390; Fax: 519/884-0445 – Exec. Dir., Gavin Grimson

Whitby: Durham Region District Health Council, #218, 1614 Dundas St. East, Whitby ON L1N 8Y8 – 905/433-4262; Fax: 905/433-2307 – Exec. Dir., Lynda Hessey

Windsor: Essex County District Health Council, 4510 Rhodes Dr., Unit 720, Windsor ON N8W 5K5 – 519/944-5888; Fax: 519/944-0619 – Exec. Dir., Hume Martin

GENERAL HOSPITALS

Ajax & Pickering General Hospital, 580 Harwood Ave. South, Ajax ON L1S 2J4 – 905/428-5200; Fax: 905/683-2618 – 116 beds – Adm., Bruce W. Cliff

Alexandria: Glengarry Memorial Hospital, Hwy. 43, Alexandria ON K0C 1A0 – 613/525-2222; Fax: 613/525-4515 – 48 beds – Chief Administrative Officer, Kurt Pristanski

Alliston: Stevenson Memorial Hospital, 200 Fletcher Cr., PO Box 4000, Alliston ON L9R 1W7 – 705/435-6281; Fax: 705/435-2327 – 43 beds – Exec. Dir., Edward Takacs

Almonte General Hospital, 75 Spring St., PO Box 940, Almonte ON K0A 1A0 – 613/256-2500; Fax: 613/256-4889 – 52 beds – Exec. Dir., Ray Timmons

Arnprior & District Memorial Hospital, 350 John St. North, Arnprior ON K7S 2P6 – 613/623-3166; Fax: 613/623-8488 – 54 beds – Chief Administrative Officer, Ron Kedrosky

Atikokan General Hospital, 120 Dorothy St., Atikokan ON P0T 1C0 – 807/597-4215; Fax: 807/597-1210 – 15 acute, 26 chronic care – Exec. Dir., Bruce Villella

Barrie: The Royal Victoria Hospital, 76 Ross St., Barrie ON L4N 1G4 – 705/728-9802; Fax: 705/728-2408 – 273 beds – Pres., E. Long

Barry's Bay: St. Francis Memorial Hospital, Siberia Rd., PO Box 129, Barry's Bay ON K0J 1B0 – 613/756-3044; Fax: 613/756-0106 – 36 beds – Adm., Keray O'Reilly

Belleville General Hospital, 265 Dundas St. East, PO Box 428, Belleville ON K8N 5A9 – 613/969-7400; Fax: 613/968-8234 – 261 beds – Pres. & CEO, Brian Steinberg

Blind River: St. Joseph's Health Centre, 525 Causley St., PO Box 970, Blind River ON P0R 1B0 – 705/356-2265; Fax: 705/356-1220 – 36 beds – CEO, Paul Davies

Bowmanville: Memorial Hospital, 47 Liberty St. South, Bowmanville ON L1C 2N4 – 905/623-3331; Fax: 905/623-0681 – 106 beds – Pres., Thomas Schonberg

Bracebridge: South Muskoka Memorial Hospital, 75 Anne St., PO Box 1570, Bracebridge ON P1L 1R6 – 705/645-4404; Fax: 705/645-4594 – 80 beds – CEO, Blaise MacNeil

Brampton: Peel Memorial Hospital, 20 Lynch St., Brampton ON L6W 2Z8 – 905/796-4066; Fax: 905/451-5552 – 418 beds – Pres. & CEO, Bruce Harber

The Brantford General Hospital, 200 Terrace Hill St., Brantford ON N3R 1G9 – 519/752-7871; Fax: 519/752-0098 – 220 beds – Pres., Richard B. Woodcock

Brantford: Lansdowne Children's Centre, 21 Preston Blvd., Brantford ON N3T 5B1 – 519/753-3153; Fax: 519/753-5927 – Adm., J. Renahan

Brantford: St. Joseph's Hospital, 63 Park Rd. North, Brantford ON N3S 6T6 – 519/753-8641; Fax: 519/753-1468 – 101 beds – Exec. Dir., Romeo Cercone

Brockville General Hospital, 75 Emma St., Brockville ON K6V 1S8 – 613/345-5645; Fax: 613/345-2529 – 149 beds – Exec. Dir., Jim Merkley

Brockville: St. Vincent de Paul Hospital, 42 Garden St., Brockville ON K6V 2C3 – 613/342-4461; Fax: 613/342-54461 – 59 beds – Exec. Dir., Tom Harrington

Burlington: Joseph Brant Memorial Hospital, 1230 North Shore Blvd., Burlington ON L7R 4C4 – 905/632-3730; Fax: 905/336-6480 – 240 beds – Pres. & CEO, Don Scott

Cambridge Memorial Hospital, 700 Coronation Blvd., Cambridge ON N1R 3G2 – 519/621-2330; Fax: 519/740-4938 – 296 beds – CEO, Helen Wright

Campbellford Memorial Hospital, 146 Oliver Rd., Campbellford ON K0L 1L0 – 705/653-1140; Fax: 705/653-4371 – 69 beds – Pres. & CEO, Richard N. Quesnel

Carleton Place & District Memorial Hospital, 211 Lake Ave. East, Carleton Place ON K7C 1J4 – 613/257-2200; Fax: 613/257-8849 – 26 beds – Exec. Dir., Robert Dahl

Chapleau General Hospital, Broomhead Rd., PO Box 757, Chapleau ON P0M 1K0 – 705/864-1520; Fax: 705/864-0449 – 30 beds – Exec. Dir., Bruce K. Peterkin

Chatham Public General Hospital, 106 Emma St., Chatham ON N7L 1A8 – 519/352-6400; Fax: 519/436-2536 – 175 beds – Exec. Dir., David Vigar

Chatham: St. Joseph's Hospital, 519 King St. West, Chatham ON N7M 1G8 – 519/352-2500; Fax: 519/352-5261 – 121 beds – Exec. Dir., Richard Kuhn

Chesley & District Memorial Hospital, 39 Second St. SE, Chesley ON N0G 1L0 – 519/881-1220; Fax: 519/881-2848 – 20 beds – Exec. Dir., Guy Kirvan

Canadian Almanac & Directory 1997

ONTARIO GENERAL HOSPITALS

Clinton Public Hospital, 98 Shipley St., Clinton ON N0M 1L0 – 519/482-3447; Fax: 519/482-5960 – 42 beds – Exec. Dir., Allan Halls

Cobourg: Northumberland Health Care Corp., 176 Chapel St., PO Box 140, Cobourg ON K9A 4K9 – 905/372-6811; Fax: 905/372-4243 – 118 beds – Exec. Dir., Roderic Potter

Cochrane: The Lady Minto Hospital at Cochrane, 241 - 8 St., PO Box 4000, Cochrane ON P0L 1C0 – 705/272-7200; Fax: 705/272-5486 – 58 beds – Exec. Dir., Daniel O'Mara

Collingwood General & Marine Hospital, 459 Hume St., Collingwood ON L9Y 1W9 – 705/445-2550; Fax: 705/444-2679 – 74 beds – CEO, Paul W. Darby

Cornwall General Hospital, 510 Second St. East, Cornwall ON K6H 1Z6 – 613/932-3300; Fax: 613/936-4605 – 100 beds – CEO, Murray Halkett

Cornwall: Hôtel-Dieu Hospital, 840 McConnell Ave., Cornwall ON K6H 5S5 – 613/938-4240; Fax: 613/938-4067 – 126 acute beds; 100 chronic care beds – Exec. Dir., John Haslehurst

Deep River & District Hospital, 1 McElligott St., Deep River ON K0J 1P0 – 613/584-3333; Fax: 613/584-4920 – 24 beds – Adm., Jennifer McDougall

Dryden District General Hospital, 58 Goodall St., PO Box 3003, Dryden ON P8N 2Z6 – 807/223-5261; Fax: 807/223-2370 – 67 beds – CEO, Andrew Skene

Dunnville: Haldimand War Memorial Hospital, 206 John St., Dunnville ON N1A 2P7 – 905/774-7431; Fax: 905/774-8672 – 65 beds – CEO, P.L. Mailloux

Durham Memorial Hospital, 320 College St., PO Box 638, Durham ON N0G 1R0 – 519/369-2340; Fax: 519/369-6180 – 32 beds – CEO, Lawrence Berge

Elliot Lake: St. Joseph's General Hospital, 70 Spine Rd., Elliot Lake ON P5A 1X2 – 705/848-7181; Fax: 705/848-1758 – 81 beds – CEO, Sarah Quackenbush

Emo Hospital, PO Box 390, Emo ON P0W 1E0 – 807/482-2881; Fax: 807/482-2493 – 23 beds – Adm., Peggy Mason

Englehart & District Hospital, 61 - 5 St., PO Box 69, Englehart ON P0J 1H0 – 705/544-2301; Fax: 705/544-8600 – 35 beds – CEO, Tim Gerkre

Espanola General Hospital, 825 McKinnon Dr., Espanola ON P5E 1R4 – 705/869-1420; Fax: 705/869-2608 – 59 beds – Exec. Dir., Paul Davies

Exeter: South Huron Hospital Association, 24 Huron St. West, Exeter ON N0M 1S2 – 519/235-2700; Fax: 519/235-3405 – 38 beds – CEO, Don Currell

Fergus: Groves Memorial Community Hospital, 235 Union St. East, Fergus ON N1M 1W3 – 519/843-2010; Fax: 519/843-7420 – 72 beds – Exec. Dir., Graham Clark

Fort Erie: Douglas Memorial Hospital, 230 Bertie St., Fort Erie ON L2A 1Z2 – 905/871-6600; Fax: 905/871-7765 – 75 beds – Adm., John Candeloro

Fort Frances: Riverside Health Care Facilities Inc., 110 Victoria Ave., Fort Frances ON P9A 2B7 – 807/274-3261; Fax: 807/274-2898 – 97 beds – Exec. Dir., Paul Brown

Georgetown & District Memorial Hospital, One Princess Anne Dr., Georgetown ON L7G 2B8 – 905/873-0111; Fax: 905/873-9653 – 80 beds – CEO, Ron Noble

Geraldton District Hospital, 500 Hogarth Ave., Geraldton ON P0T 1M0 – 807/854-1862; Fax: 807/854-1568 – 60 beds – Adm., W. Harvey Harris

Goderich: Alexandra Marine & General Hospital, 120 Napier St., Goderich ON N7A 1W5 – 519/524-8323; Fax: 519/524-5579 – 78 beds – Exec. Dir., K.T. Engelstad

Grimsby: West Lincoln Memorial Hospital, 169 Main St. East, Grimsby ON L3M 1P3 – 905/945-2253; Fax: 905/945-0504 – 78 beds – Exec. Dir., Gordon D. Gibson

Guelph General Hospital, 115 Delhi St., Guelph ON N1E 4J4 – 519/822-5350; Fax: 519/822-2170 – 142 beds – Exec. Dir., Richard Ernst

Guelph: St. Joseph's Hospital, 80 Westmount Rd., Guelph ON N1H 5H8 – 519/824-2620; Fax: 519/763-0264 – 175 beds – Pres./CEO, Sr. Margaret Myatt

Hagersville: West Haldimand General Hospital, 75 Parkview Rd., Hagersville ON N0A 1H0 – 416/768-3311; Fax: 416/768-1820 – 42 beds – Exec. Dir., Edmund Palmeroy

Haliburton Hospital, PO Box 115, Haliburton ON K0M 1S0 – 705/457-1392; Fax: 705/457-2398 – 10 beds – Unit Dir., Lynne Johnston

Hamilton Civic Hospital, 237 Barton St. East, Hamilton ON L8L 2X2 – 905/527-0271; Fax: 905/546-1861 – 704 beds – Pres. & CEO, Dr. D. McCutcheon

Hamilton: Chedoke-McMaster Hospital, 1200 Main St. West, PO Box 2000, Hamilton ON L8N 3Z5 – 905/521-2100; Fax: 905/521-5090 – 588 beds – Pres. & CEO, Dr. Jennifer Jackman

Hamilton: Hamilton Civic Hospital - Henderson Division, 711 Concession St., Hamilton ON L8V 1C3 – 905/389-4411; Fax: 905/575-2662 – Pres. & CEO, D. McCutcheon

Hamilton: St. Joseph's Hospital, 50 Charlton Ave. East, Hamilton ON L8N 4A6 – 905/522-4941; Fax: 905/521-6067 – 484 beds – Pres. & CEO, Allan J. Greve

Hamilton: St. Peter's Hospital, 88 Maplewood Ave., Hamilton ON L8M 1W9 – 905/549-6525; Fax: 905/549-2242 – 284 beds – CEO, Peter Carruthers

Hanover & District Hospital, 90 - 7 Ave., Hanover ON N4N 1N1 – 519/364-2340; Fax: 519/364-6602 – 80 beds – Exec. Dir., Peter Fabricius

Hawkesbury & District General Hospital, 1111 Ghislain St., Hawkesbury ON K6A 3G5 – 613/632-1111; Fax: 613/632-6450 – 68 beds – Pres. & CEO, Michel Lalonde

Hearst: Hôpital Nôtre-Dame Hospital, 1405 Edward St., PO Box 8000, Hearst ON P0L 1N0 – 705/362-4291; Fax: 705/372-1957 – 60 lits – CEO, R.G. Lafleur

Hornepayne Community Hospital, 278 Front St., PO Box 190, Hornepayne ON P0M 1Z0 – 807/868-2442; Fax: 807/868-2697 – 13 beds – Acting Adm., Lisa Verrino

Huntsville District Memorial Hospital, 354 Muskoka Rd. #3 North, Huntsville ON P1H 1H7 – 705/789-2311; Fax: 705/789-0557 – 75 beds – CEO, Bruce E. Laughton

Ingersoll: Alexandra Hospital, 29 Noxon St., Ingersoll ON N5C 3V6 – 519/485-1700; Fax: 519/485-7002 – 52 beds – Exec. Dir., Ross Bryant

Iroquois Falls: Anson General Hospital, 58 Anson Dr., Iroquois Falls ON P0K 1E0 – 705/258-3911; Fax: 705/258-3221 – 40 beds – CEO, Daniel O'Mara

Kapuskasing: Sensenbrenner Hospital, 101 Progress Cres., Kapuskasing ON P5N 3H5 – 705/337-6111; Fax: 705/335-6902 – 78 beds – CEO, Allan Yarush

Kemptville District Hospital, Concession Rd., PO Box 2007, Kemptville ON K0G 1J0 – 613/258-3435; Fax: 613/258-4997 – 52 beds – Exec. Dir., Lynne Budgell

Kenora: Lake of the Woods District Hospital, 21 Sylvan St. West, Kenora ON P9N 3W7 – 807/468-9861; Fax: 807/468-3939 – 109 beds – Adm., Robert Muir

Kincardine & District General Hospital, 43 Queen St., PO Box 4000, Kincardine ON N2Z 2Z2 – 519/396-3331; Fax: 519/396-3699 – 57 beds – Exec. Dir., Mike Jackson

Kingston General Hospital, 76 Stuart St., Kingston ON K7L 2V7 – 613/548-3232; Fax: 613/548-6042 – 393 beds – Pres. & CEO, Dr. Peter Glynn

Kingston: Hôtel-Dieu Hospital, 166 Brock St., Kingston ON K7L 5G2 – 613/544-3310; Fax: 613/544-7175 – 186 beds – Exec. Dir., Hugh C. Graham

Kingston: St. Mary's of the Lake Hospital, 340 Union St. West, PO Box 3600, Kingston ON K7L 5A2 – 613/544-5220; Fax: 613/544-6655 – 223 beds – Pres. & CEO, Guy Legros

Kirkland & District Hospital, 145 Government Rd. East, Kirkland Lake ON P2N 3P4 – 705/567-5251; Fax: 705/568-2102 – 62 beds – Exec. Dir., J. William C. Lewis

Kitchener: Grand River Hospital Corp. - Freeport Health Centre, 3570 King St. East, Kitchener ON N2A 2W1 – 519/893-2710; Fax: 519/893-8342 – Pres. & CEO, Al Collins

Kitchener: Grand River Hospital Corp., Kitchener-Waterloo Health Centre, 835 King St. West, Kitchener ON N2G 1G3 – 519/749-4322; Fax: 519/749-4208 – 705 beds – Pres. & CEO, Al Collins

Kitchener: St. Mary's General Hospital, 911 Queens Blvd., Kitchener ON N2M 1B2 – 519/744-3311; Fax: 519/749-6426 – 221 beds – Pres. & CEO, Bruce M. Antonello

Leamington District Memorial Hospital, 194 Talbot St. West, Leamington ON N8H 1N9 – 519/322-2501; Fax: 519/322-5584 – 88 beds – Acting Exec. Dir., Warren Chant

Lindsay: Ross Memorial Hospital, 10 Angeline St. North, Lindsay ON K9V 4M8 – 705/324-6111; Fax: 705/878-5383 – 206 beds – Exec. Dir., Anthony Vines

Lion's Head Hospital, 22 Moore St., Lion's Head ON N0H 1W0 – 519/793-3424; Fax: 519/534-1260 – 4 beds – CEO, Gwen Morris

Listowel Memorial Hospital, 255 Elizabeth St. East, Listowel ON N4W 2P5 – 519/291-3120; Fax: 519/291-5440 – 73 beds – Adm., James Van Camp

Little Current: Manitoulin Health Centre, 11 Meredith St., PO Box 640, Little Current ON P0P 1K0 – 705/368-2300; Fax: 705/368-3603 – 55 beds – Exec. Dir., Bruce Cunningham

London Health Sciences Centre - Victoria Hospital, 800 Commissioners Rd. East, PO Box 5375, London ON N6A 4G5 – 519/685-8500; Fax: 519/685-8127 – 548 beds – Pres. & CEO, Dr. Tony Dagnone

London: Parkwood Hospital, 801 Commissioners Rd. East, London ON N6C 5J1 – 519/685-4292; Fax: 519/685-4052 – 432 beds – Pres. & CEO, Michael Boucher

London: St. Joseph's Health Centre, 268 Grosvenor St., London ON N6A 4V2 – 519/646-6000; Fax: 519/646-6054 – 368 beds – Pres. & CEO, Philip C. Hassen

London: St. Mary's Hospital, 35 Grosvenor St., London ON N6A 4G5 – 519/438-6185 – 110 beds – Pres. & CEO, Philip C. Hassen

London: University Hospital, 339 Windermere Rd., London ON N6A 5A5 – 519/663-3300; Fax: 519/663-3876 – Pres. & CEO, Tony Dagnone

Manitouwadge General Hospital, Manitou Rd., Manitouwadge ON P0T 2C0 – 807/826-3251; Fax: 807/826-4216 – 18 beds – Adm., Judith C. Harris

Marathon: Wilson Memorial General Hospital, 28 Peninsula Rd., Marathon ON P0T 2E0 – 807/229-1740; Fax: 807/229-1721 – 25 beds – Exec. Dir., Eiji Tsubouchi

Markdale: Centre Grey General Hospital, 55 Isla St., PO Box 406, Markdale ON N0C 1H0 – 519/986-3040; Fax: 519/986-4562 – 38 beds – Adm., Michael Mazza

Markham-Stouffville Hospital, 381 Church St., PO Box 1800, Markham ON L3P 7P3 – 905/472-7097; Fax: 905/472-7086 – 195 beds – Pres., Marilyn J. Bruner

Matheson: Bingham Memorial Hospital, PO Box 70, Matheson ON P0K 1N0 – 705/273-2424; Fax: 705/273-2515 – 40 beds – Adm., Leo Doiron

Mattawa General Hospital, 215 Third St., PO Box 70, Mattawa ON P0H 1V0 – 705/744-5511; Fax: 705/744-0466 – 19 beds – Acting Exec. Dir., Paul Rainville

Meaford General Hospital, 229 Nelson St. West, PO Box 340, Meaford ON N0H 1Y0 – 519/538-1311; Fax: 519/538-5500 – 56 beds – Exec. Dir., Charles F. Robinson

Midland: Huronia District Hospital, 1 St. Andrews Dr., PO Box 760, Midland ON L4R 1N6 – 705/526-3751; Fax: 705/526-2007 – 106 beds – Adm., Gordon A. Key

Canadian Almanac & Directory 1997

ONTARIO GENERAL HOSPITALS

Milton District Hospital, 30 Derry Rd. East, Milton ON L9T 2X5 – 905/878-2383; Fax: 905/878-0498 – 85 beds – Exec. Dir., Brian D. Brady

Mindemoya Hospital, Mindemoya ON P0P 1S0 – 705/377-5311; Fax: 705/377-5799 – 20 beds – Patient Care Coord., Glenn Hallett

Minden: Haliburton Highlands Health Services Corp., PO Box 569, Minden ON K0M 2K0 – 705/286-4997; Fax: 705/286-4819 – 10 beds – Exec. Dir., Foster Loucks

Mississauga Hospital, 100 Queensway West, Mississauga ON L5B 1B8 – 905/848-7100; Fax: 905/848-7139 – 444 beds – Pres., Dennis Egan

Mississauga: The Credit Valley Hospital, 2200 Eglinton Ave. West, Mississauga ON L5M 2N1 – 905/813-2564; Fax: 905/813-4444 – 366 beds – Pres., Dean Sane

Moosonee: James Bay General Hospital, PO Box 370, Moosonee ON P0L 1Y0 – 705/336-2947; Fax: 705/336-2637 – 33 beds – Exec. Dir., Brent Woodford

Mount Forest: Louise Marshall Hospital, 630 Dublin St., PO Box 190, Mount Forest ON N0G 2L0 – 519/323-2210; Fax: 519/323-3741 – 37 beds – Adm., Terry Stoughton

Napanee: Lennox & Addington County General Hospital, 8 Park Dr., Napanee ON K7R 2Z4 – 613/354-3301; Fax: 613/354-7157 – 42 beds – Exec. Dir., W.A. Ronald

Nepean: Queensway-Carleton Hospital, 3045 Baseline Rd., Nepean ON K2H 8P4 – 613/721-2000; Fax: 613/721-4770 – 193 beds – Pres. & CEO, Robert Devitt

New Liskeard: Temiskaming Hospital, Shepherdson Rd., PO Box T, New Liskeard ON P0J 1P0 – 705/647-8121; Fax: 705/647-5800 – 99 beds – Exec. Dir., Wayne Coveyduck

Newbury: The Four Counties General Hospital, RR#3, Newbury ON N0L 1Z0 – 519/693-4441; Fax: 519/693-7084 – 31 beds – Exec. Dir., Janak Jass

Newmarket: York County Hospital, 596 Davis Dr., Newmarket ON L3Y 2P9 – 905/853-2209; Fax: 905/853-2220 – 246 beds – Pres., Daniel Carriere

Niagara Falls: Greater Niagara General Hospital, 5546 Portage Rd., PO Box 1018, Niagara Falls ON L2E 6X2 – 905/358-0171; Fax: 905/358-8437 – 250 beds – Pres. & CEO, J.H. Carter

Niagara-on-the-Lake Hospital, 176 Wellington St., PO Box 1270, Niagara-on-the-Lake ON L0S 1J0 – 905/468-4284; Fax: 905/468-7690 – 20 beds – Adm., Karen Tribble

Nipigon District Memorial Hospital, 125 Hogan Rd., PO Box 37, Nipigon ON P0T 2J0 – 807/887-3026; Fax: 807/887-2800 – 37 beds – CEO, Donald E. Ross

North Bay General Hospital, 750 Scollard St., North Bay ON P1B 5A4 – 705/474-8600; Fax: 705/495-7960 – 233 beds – Pres., Mark Hurst

North Bay General Hospital - McLaren Site, 720 McLaren St., North Bay ON P1B 3L9 – 705/472-6100; Fax: 705/472-2983 – Exec. Dir., L. Johnson

Oakville-Trafalgar Memorial Hospital, 327 Reynolds St., Oakville ON L6J 3L7 – 905/845-2571; Fax: 905/338-4636 – 274 beds – Pres. & CEO, John Oliver

Orangeville: Dufferin-Caledon Health Care Corporation - Dufferin Area, 32 First St., Orangeville ON L9W 2E1 – 519/941-2410; Fax: 519/942-0482 – 113 active beds; 26 chronic care beds – Exec. Dir., Nancy Ross

Orillia Soldiers' Memorial Hospital, 170 Colborne St. West, Orillia ON L3V 2Z3 – 705/325-2201; Fax: 705/325-7953 – 180 beds – Exec. Dir., Glen H. Penwarden

Oshawa General Hospital, 24 Alma St., Oshawa ON L1G 2B9 – 905/433-4400; Fax: 905/433-4338 – 619 beds – Pres., David A. Home

Ottawa Civic Hospital, 1053 Carling Ave., Ottawa ON K1Y 4E9 – 613/761-4000; Fax: 613/761-5393 – 624 beds – Pres., Ambrose Hearn, 613/761-4201

Ottawa General Hospital, 501 Smyth Rd., Ottawa ON K1H 8L6 – 613/737-7777; Fax: 613/737-8934 – 489 beds – Pres., Jacques Labelle, 613/737-8449

Ottawa: Children's Hospital of Eastern Ontario, 401 Smyth Rd., Ottawa ON K1H 8L1 – 613/737-7600; Fax: 613/738-3216 – 150 beds – Pres., Gary Cardiff

Ottawa: The Grace Hospital, 1156 Wellington St., Ottawa ON K1Y 2Z4 – 613/728-4611; Fax: 613/724-4628 – 65 beds – Pres., Capt. Malcolm D. Robinson

Ottawa: Hôpital Montfort, 713, ch Montréal, Ottawa ON K1K 0T2 – 613/746-4621; Fax: 613/748-4947 – 180 beds – Exec. Dir., Gérald Savoie

Ottawa: The Perley Hospital, 43 Aylmer Ave., Ottawa ON K1S 4R5 – 613/730-7171; Fax: 613/730-8040 – 450 beds – Exec. Dir., J.A. Lupton

Ottawa: Riverside Hospital of Ottawa, 1967 Riverside Dr., Ottawa ON K1H 7W9 – 613/738-7100; Fax: 613/738-8522 – 204 beds – Exec. Dir., D. Wayne Fyffe

Ottawa: Royal Ottawa Health Care Group - Rehabilitation Centre, 505 Smyth Rd., Ottawa ON K1H 8M2 – 613/722-6521; Fax: 613/722-4577 – 74 beds – Exec. Dir., George Langill

Ottawa: Sisters of Charity of Ottawa Health Service, 43 Bruyère St., Ottawa ON K1N 5C8 – 613/562-0050; Fax: 613/562-6367 – 689 beds – Pres. & CEO, Michel Bilodeau

Owen Sound: The Grey Bruce Regional Health Centre, 1400 - 8th St. East, PO Box 1400, Owen Sound ON N4K 6M9 – 519/376-2121; Fax: 519/376-9760 – 272 beds – Pres. & CEO, Garth Pierce

Palmerston & District Hospital, 500 White's Rd., PO Box 130, Palmerston ON N0G 2P0 – 519/343-2022; Fax: 519/343-3821 – 35 beds – Adm. & CEO, R.G. Emmerson

Paris: The Willett Hospital, 238 Grand River St. North, Paris ON N3L 2N7 – 519/442-2251; Fax: 519/442-1641 – 62 beds – Exec. Dir., Mary Sylver

Parry Sound: West Parry Sound Health Centre - Church St. Site, 88 Church St., Parry Sound ON P2A 1Z3 – 705/746-2111; Fax: 705/746-6338 – Pres., Norman Maciver

Parry Sound: West Parry Sound Health Centre, 10 James St., Parry Sound ON P2A 1T3 – 705/746-9321; Fax: 705/746-7364 – 66 acute beds; 64 chronic beds – CEO, Norman Maciver

Pembroke Civic Hospital, 425 Cecilia St., Pembroke ON K8A 1S7 – 613/735-6851; Fax: 613/735-4079 – 70 beds – Exec. Dir., William Cowan

Pembroke General Hospital, 705 MacKay St., Pembroke ON K8A 1G8 – 613/732-2811; Fax: 613/732-9986 – 104 beds – Exec. Dir., Sheila Schultz

Penetanguishene General Hospital, 25 Jeffery St., Penetanguishene ON L9M 1K6 – 705/549-7442; Fax: 705/549-4031 – 52 beds – Exec. Dir., Doris Shirriff

Peterborough Civic Hospital, 1 Hospital Dr., Peterborough ON K9J 7C6 – 705/743-2121; Fax: 705/876-5120 – 303 beds – Exec. Dir., Bill Kilpatrick

Peterborough: St. Joseph's General Hospital, 384 Rogers St., Peterborough ON K9H 7B6 – 705/743-4251; Fax: 705/740-8345 – 162 beds – Exec. Dir., Frank Lussing

Petrolia: Charlotte Eleanor Englehart Hospital, 447 Greenfield St., Petrolia ON N0N 1R0 – 519/882-1170; Fax: 519/882-3711 – 72 beds – CEO, Wayne Woods

Picton: Prince Edward County Memorial Hospital, Main Street East, PO Box 1900, Picton ON K0K 2T0 – 613/476-2181; Fax: 613/476-8600 – 46 beds – Exec. Dir., D.Monty Boultbee

Port Colborne General Hospital, 260 Sugarloaf St., Port Colborne ON L3K 2N7 – 905/834-4501; Fax: 905/834-0404 – 115 beds – Exec. Dir., Barry Lockhart

Port Hope & District Hospital, 53 Wellington St., Port Hope ON L1A 2M6 – 905/885-6371; Fax: 905/885-1948 – Exec. Dir., John Maynard

Port Perry: Community Memorial Hospital, 451 Paxton St., Port Perry ON L9L 1A8 – 905/985-7321; Fax: 905/985-0739 – 42 beds – CEO, David A. Brown

Rainy River Hospital, Rainy River ON P0W 1L0 – 807/852-3232; Fax: 807/852-3565 – 15 beds – Dir., Norma Elliott

Red Lake Margaret Cochenour Memorial Hospital, PO Box 5005, Red Lake ON P0V 2M0 – 807/727-2231; Fax: 807/727-2923 – 34 beds – CEO, Hal Fjeldsted

Renfrew Victoria Hospital, 499 Raglan St. North, Renfrew ON K7V 1P6 – 613/432-4851; Fax: 613/432-8649 – 65 beds – Exec. Dir., Randy Penney

Richards Landing: Matthews Memorial Hospital, PO Box 188, Richards Landing ON P0R 1J0 – 705/246-2570; Fax: 705/246-2569 – 9 beds – Adm., Ruth Clavet

Richmond Hill: York Central Hospital, 10 Trench St., Richmond Hill ON L4C 4Z3 – 905/883-1212; Fax: 905/883-2455 – 247 beds – Acting CEO, Bob DaCosta

St Catharines General Hospital, 142 Queenston St., St Catharines ON L2R 7C6 – 905/684-7271; Fax: 905/684-1468 – 303 beds – Pres. & CEO, T. Robert M. Lawler

St Catharines: Hôtel-Dieu Hospital, 155 Ontario St., St Catharines ON L2R 5K3 – 905/682-6411; Fax: 905/682-0663 – 124 beds – Exec. Dir., Frank Vetrano

St Catharines: The Shaver Hospital, 541 Glenridge Ave., PO Box 158, St Catharines ON L2R 6S5 – 905/685-1381; Fax: 905/687-4871 – 124 beds – Exec. Dir., K.S. Johnston

St. Mary's Memorial Hospital, 267 Queen St. West, PO Box 940, St. Mary's ON N4X 1B6 – 519/284-1332, ext.305; Fax: 519/284-4631 – 40 beds – CEO, Terry Fadelle

St. Thomas Elgin General Hospital, 189 Elm St., PO Box 2007, St. Thomas ON N5P 3W2 – 519/631-2020; Fax: 519/631-1825 – 288 beds – Pres. & CEO, Terry J. Kondrat

Sarnia General Hospital, 220 North Mitton St., Sarnia ON N7T 6H6 – 519/383-8180, ext.5520; Fax: 519/383-7152 – 166 beds – CEO, Michel Gagné

Sarnia: St. Joseph's Health Centre of Sarnia, 89 Norman St., Sarnia ON N7T 6S3 – 519/339-1389; Fax: 519/336-8780 – 260 beds – Exec. Dir., Donald McDermott

Sault Ste Marie: Plummer Memorial Public Hospital & The Sault Ste. Marie General Hospital, 969 Queen St. East, Sault Ste Marie ON P6A 2C4 – 705/759-3601; Fax: 705/759-3640 – 393 beds – Pres. & CEO, Manu Malkani

Sault Ste Marie: Rotary Children's Centre, 74 Johnson Ave., Sault Ste Marie ON P6C 2V5 – 705/759-1131; Fax: 705/759-0783 – Exec. Dir., Donna Morrison

Seaforth Community Hospital, 24 Centennial Dr., PO Box 99, Seaforth ON N0K 1W0 – 519/527-1650; Fax: 519/527-2665 – 41 beds – CEO, Bill Thibert

Shelburne: Dufferin-Caledon Health Care - Shelburne District, PO Box 190, Shelburne ON L0N 1S2 – 519/925-3340; Fax: 519/925-2130 – Exec. Dir., Nancy Ross

Simcoe: Norfolk General Hospital, 365 West St., Simcoe ON N3Y 1T7 – 519/426-0750; Fax: 519/426-8542 – 131 beds (46 chronic care beds) – Exec. Dir., Harold Shantz

Sioux Lookout General Hospital, PO Box 909, Sioux Lookout ON P8T 1B4 – 807/737-3700; Fax: 807/737-3454 – 55 beds – Exec. Dir., Mark Balcaen

Smiths Falls: The Perth & Smiths Falls District Hospital, 60 Cornellia St. West, Smiths Falls ON K7A 2H9 – 613/283-2330; Fax: 613/283-8990 – 128 beds – CEO, Caroline Manley

Smooth Rock Falls Hospital, 107 Kelly Rock, PO Box 219, Smooth Rock Falls ON P0L 2B0 – 705/338-2781; Fax: 705/338-4410 – 37 beds – Exec. Dir., Thomas H. Boyd

Canadian Almanac & Directory 1997

8-24 ONTARIO FEDERAL HOSPITALS

South Porcupine: Porcupine General Hospital, Bruce Ave., PO Box 850, South Porcupine ON P0N 1H0 – 705/235-3377; Fax: 705/235-5521 – Exec. Dir., Viola Douglas

Southampton: Saugeen Memorial Hospital, 340 High St., PO Box 310, Southampton ON N0H 2L0 – 519/797-3230; Fax: 519/797-2442 – 37 beds – Adm., Carl Crymble

Stratford General Hospital, 46 General Hospital Dr., Stratford ON N5A 2Y6 – 519/272-8202; Fax: 519/271-7173 – 169 beds – CEO, Bernard Schmidt

Strathroy Middlesex General Hospital, 395 Carrie St., Strathroy ON N7G 3C9 – 519/245-1550; Fax: 519/245-5438 – 97 beds – Exec. Dir., Thomas M. Enright

Sturgeon Falls: The West Nipissing General Hospital, 111 Coursol Rd., Sturgeon Falls ON P0H 2G0 – 705/753-3110; Fax: 705/753-0210 – 66 beds – Exec. Dir., Yves Campeau

Sudbury General Hospital, 700 Paris St., Sudbury ON P3B 3B5 – 705/674-3181; Fax: 705/675-4769 – 230 beds – Exec. Dir., Winnifred McLoughlin

Sudbury Memorial Hospital, 865 Regent St. South, Sudbury ON P3E 3Y9 – 705/671-1000; Fax: 705/671-5656 – 155 beds – Exec. Dir., Esko Vainio

Sudbury: Laurentian Hospital, 41 Ramsey Lake Rd., Sudbury ON P3E 5J1 – 705/522-2200; Fax: 705/523-7041; EMail: lhlib@vianet.on.ca – 246 beds – CEO, Janice Skot

Terrace Bay: The McCausland Hospital, 2 Cartier Dr., Terrace Bay ON P0T 2W0 – 807/825-3273; Fax: 807/825-9623 – 23 beds – CEO, C.M. Fewer

Thessalon Hospital, Thessalon ON P0R 1L0 – 705/842-2238 – Nurse in Charge, Ruth Clavet

Thunder Bay Regional Hospital - South Site (Mckellar Site), 325 South Archibald St., Thunder Bay "F" ON P7E 1G6 – 807/343-7123; Fax: 807/343-7165 – 267 beds – Pres., Gaston Levac

Thunder Bay Regional Hopsital - North Site (Port Arthur), 460 North Court St., Thunder Bay "P" ON P7A 4X6 – 807/343-6622; Fax: 807/345-9975 – 176 beds – Exec. Dir., Gaston Levac

Thunder Bay: Hogarth-Westmount Hospital, 300 North Lillie St., Thunder Bay ON P7C 4Y7 – 807/625-1110; Fax: 807/625-1155 – 198 beds – Interim CEO, Douglas Heath

Thunder Bay: St. Joseph's General Hospital, 35 North Algoma St., PO Box 3251, Thunder Bay ON P7B 5G7 – 807/343-2431; Fax: 807/345-4994 – 148 beds – Exec. Dir., Carl White

Tillsonburg District Memorial Hospital, 167 Rolph St., PO Box 3100, Tillsonburg ON N4G 4J2 – 519/842-3611; Fax: 519/842-6733 – 116 beds – Pres., James Spencer

Timmins & District Hospital, 700 Ross Ave. East, Timmins ON P4N 8P2 – 705/267-2131; Fax: 705/267-6311 – 190 beds – Exec. Dir., Irene Krys

Toronto East General & Orthopaedic Hospital, 825 Coxwell Ave., Toronto ON M4C 3E7 – 416/469-6005; Fax: 416/469-6106; EMail: teg@library.utoronto.ca – 387 beds – Pres., Gail Paech

The Toronto Hospital Corporation - Toronto General & Toronto Western Divisions, 585 University Ave., Bell Wing #658, Toronto ON M5G 2C4 – 416/340-3300; Fax: 416/340-3179 – 1,093 beds – Pres. & CEO, Alan R. Hudson

Toronto: Baycrest Centre for Geriatric Care, 3560 Bathurst St., Toronto ON M6A 2E1 – 416/785-2500; Fax: 416/785-2464 – 372 beds – Pres. & CEO, Stephen W. Herbert

Toronto: Bloorview Macmillan Centre - Bloorview Site, 25 Buchan Court, Willowdale ON M2J 4S9 – 416/494-2222; Fax: 416/494-9985 – 87 beds – CEO, Sheila Jarvis

Toronto: Centenary Health Centre, 2867 Ellesmere Rd., Scarborough ON M1E 4B9 – 416/284-8131; Fax: 416/281-7323 – 437 beds – Pres., Allan Whiting

Toronto: The Doctors' Hospital, 45 Brunswick Ave., Toronto ON M5S 2M1 – 416/923-5411; Fax: 416/923-5445 – 77 beds – Pres., R.J. Brian McFarlane

Toronto: The Etobicoke General Hospital, 101 Humber College Blvd., Etobicoke ON M9V 1R8 – 416/747-3466; Fax: 416/747-8608 – 281 beds – Acting Pres. & CEO, Donald Gordon

Toronto: Hillcrest Hospital, 47 Austin Terrace, Toronto ON M5R 1Y8 – 416/537-3421; Fax: 416/537-8628 – 85 beds – Pres. & CEO, Dr. Frank Markel

Toronto: The Hospital for Sick Children, 555 University Ave., Toronto ON M5G 1X8 – 416/813-5707; Fax: 416/813-5393 – 421 beds – Pres., Michael J. Strofolino

Toronto: Humber Memorial Hospital, 200 Church St., Weston ON M9N 1N8 – 416/243-5555; Fax: 416/243-4511 – 227 beds – Interim Pres. & CEO, Scott Dudgeon

Toronto: Lyndhurst Hospital, 520 Sutherland Dr., Toronto ON M4G 3V9 – 416/422-5551; Fax: 416/422-5216 – 79 beds – Pres. & CEO, Randy F. Swan

Toronto: Mount Sinai Hospital, 600 University Ave., Toronto ON M5G 1X5 – 416/596-4200; Fax: 416/586-8787 – 362 beds – Pres. & CEO, Theodore Freedman

Toronto: North York Branson Hospital, 555 Finch Ave. West, Willowdale ON M2R 1N5 – 416/633-2563; Fax: 416/635-2537 – 258 beds – Pres., J.A. Gallop

Toronto: North York General Hospital, 4001 Leslie St., Willowdale ON M2K 1E1 – 416/756-6000; Fax: 416/756-6384 – 345 beds – Pres., D. Murray MacKenzie

Toronto: Northwestern General Hospital, 2175 Keele St., Toronto ON M6M 3Z4 – 416/658-2028; Fax: 416/658-2192 – 186 beds – Pres., Brent Chambers

Toronto: Providence Centre Hospital, 3276 St. Clair Ave. East, Scarborough ON M1L 1W1 – 416/759-9321; Fax: 416/285-3758 – 327 beds – Pres. & CEO, Marian J. Leslie

Toronto: The Queen Elizabeth Hospital, 550 University Ave., Toronto ON M5G 2A2 – 416/597-5111; Fax: 416/597-6625 – 428 beds – Pres., Clifford A. Nordal

Toronto: Queensway General Hospital, 150 Sherway Dr., Etobicoke ON M9C 1A5 – 416/253-2935; Fax: 416/253-2505 – 200 beds – Pres., Kenneth W. White

Toronto: The Riverdale Hospital, 14 St. Matthews Rd., Toronto ON M4M 2B5 – 416/461-8251; Fax: 416/461-1670 – 646 beds – Pres. & CEO, Wayne R. Keddy

Toronto: The Runnymede Chronic Care Hospital, 274 St. Johns Rd., Toronto ON M6P 1V5 – 416/762-7316; Fax: 416/762-3836 – 114 beds – Pres., Normand A. Allaire

Toronto: St. John's Hospital, 285 Cummer Ave., North York ON M2M 2G1 – 416/226-6780; Fax: 416/226-6265 – 185 beds – Adm., Miriam Lowi

Toronto: St. Joseph's Health Centre, 30 The Queensway, Toronto ON M6R 1B5 – 416/530-6008; Fax: 416/530-6835 – 536 beds – Pres. & CEO, Leo N. Steven

Toronto: St. Michael's Hospital, 30 Bond St., Toronto ON M5B 1W8 – 416/864-5617; Fax: 416/864-5669 – 333 beds – Pres. & CEO, Jeffery Lozon

Toronto: The Salvation Army Scarborough Grace General Hospital, 3030 Birchmount Rd., Scarborough ON M1W 3W3 – 416/495-2400; Fax: 416/495-2432 – 255 beds – Pres. & CEO, Lt.-Col. Irene Stickland

Toronto: The Salvation Army Toronto Grace General Hospital, 650 Church St., Toronto ON M4Y 2G5 – 416/925-2251; Fax: 416/925-6360 – 119 beds – Pres., Lt.-Col. Wilfred Hammond

Toronto: Scarborough General Hospital, 3050 Lawrence Ave. East, Scarborough ON M1P 2V5 – 416/438-8100; Fax: 416/438-9318 – 489 beds – Pres., Ronald Bodrug

Toronto: Sunnybrook Health Sciences Centre, 2075 Bayview Ave., North York ON M4N 3M5 – 416/480-4111; Fax: 416/480-6033 – 945 beds – Pres. & CEO, Tom Closson

Toronto: The Wellesley Central Hospital - Sherbourne Site, 333 Sherbourne St., Toronto ON M5A 2S5 – 416/969-4111; Fax: 416/969-4183 – 16 beds – Exec. Dir., William Louth

Toronto: The Wellesley Central Hospital - Wellesley Site, 160 Wellesley St. East, Toronto ON M4Y 1J3 – 416/926-7002; Fax: 416/926-4908 – 299 beds – Pres. & CEO, R. Scott Rowand

Toronto: West Park Hospital, 82 Buttonwood Ave., Toronto ON M6M 2J5 – 416/243-3635; Fax: 416/243-7711 – 304 beds – Pres., Barry Monaghan

Toronto: Women's College Hospital, 76 Grenville St., Toronto ON M5S 1B2 – 416/323-7706; Fax: 416/323-7311 – 200 beds – Pres., William MacLeod

Toronto: York-Finch General Hospital, 2111 Finch Ave. West, Downsview ON M3N 1N1 – 416/747-3821; Fax: 416/747-3872 – 218 beds – Pres. & CEO, Darlene Barnes

Trenton Memorial Hospital, 242 King St., Trenton ON K8V 5S6 – 613/392-2541; Fax: 613/392-3749 – 84 beds – Pres. & CEO, Peter O'Brien

Uxbridge: The Cottage Hospital, 4 Campbell Dr., PO Box 5003, Uxbridge ON L9P 1S4 – 905/649-2223; Fax: 905/852-7844 – 36 beds – CEO, Paul Nichols

Walkerton: County of Bruce General Hospital, 21 McGivern St., Walkerton ON N0G 2V0 – 519/881-1220; Fax: 519/881-2848 – 45 beds – Exec. Dir., Guy Kirvan

Wallaceburg: Sydenham District Hospital, 325 Margaret Ave., Wallaceburg ON N8A 2A7 – 519/627-1461; Fax: 519/627-0898 – 45 beds – Exec. Dir., Lou Emery

Wawa: The Lady Dunn General Hospital, Government Rd., PO Box 179, Wawa ON P0S 1K0 – 705/856-2335; Fax: 705/856-7533 – 31 beds – CEO, Frank Buerkle

Welland County General Hospital, 65 Third St., Welland ON L3B 4W6 – 905/732-6111; Fax: 905/732-2628 – 299 beds – CEO & Pres., Timothy Wright

The Whitby General Hospital, 300 Gordon St., Whitby ON L1N 5T2 – 905/668-6831; Fax: 905/430-3421 – 81 beds – CEO, Elizabeth Woodbury

Wiarton: Bruce Peninsula Health Services, 369 Mary St., PO Box 250, Wiarton ON N0H 2T0 – 519/534-1260; Fax: 519/534-4450 – 26 beds – Exec. Dir., Gwen Morris

Winchester District Memorial Hospital, 566 Louise St., Winchester ON K0C 2K0 – 613/774-2420; Fax: 613/774-0453 – 84 beds – Pres. & CEO, Don Smith

The Windsor Regional Hospital, 1995 Lens Ave., Windsor ON N8W 1L9 – 519/254-5577; Fax: 519/254-3150 – 289 beds – Pres. & CEO, Lloyd W. Preston

Windsor Western Regional Hospital Centre, 1453 Prince Rd., Windsor ON N9C 3Z4 – 519/257-5577, ext. 6011; Fax: 519/257-5121 – Exec. Dir., Lloyd Preston

Windsor: Hôtel Dieu Grace Hospital, 1030 Ouellette Ave., Windsor ON N9A 1E1 – 519/973-4430; Fax: 519/973-0803 – 589 beds – Exec. Dir., Frank Bagatto

Wingham & District Hospital, 270 Carling Terrace, Wingham ON N0G 2W0 – 519/357-3210; Fax: 519/357-2931 – 86 beds – Exec. Dir., Lloyd Koch

Woodstock General Hospital, 270 Riddell St., Woodstock ON N4S 6N6 – 519/421-4244; Fax: 519/537-8369 – 118 beds – Pres. & CEO, W.B. Brown

FEDERAL HOSPITALS

Moose Factory General Hospital, PO Box 34, Moose Factory ON P0L 1W0 – 705/658-4544; Fax: 705/658-4452 – Adm., Meryl Huff

Ottawa: National Defence Medical Centre, 1745 Alta Vista Dr., Ottawa ON K1A 0K6 – 613/945-6600; Fax: 613/998-8093 – Commandant, Capt. R. Climie

Ottawa: Rideau Veterans Home, 363 Smyth Rd., Ottawa ON K1A 5A1 – 613/998-8198 – Adm., R. Giroux

Sioux Lookout Zone Hospital, PO Box 1500, Sioux Lookout ON P8T 1C2 – 807/737-3030 – Adm., Arlene Rein

HOME CARE OFFICES/COMMUNITY CARE SERVICES

Barrie: Simcoe County Home Care Program, 15 Sperling Dr., Barrie ON L4M 6K9 – 705/721-7330; Fax: 705/722-5237 – Dir., Lois Hill

Belleville: Hastings & Prince Edward Counties Home Care Program, c/o Belleville General Hospital, 265 Dundas St. East, PO Box 428, Belleville ON K8N 5A9 – 613/966-3530, 969-7400, ext.2206; Fax: 613/969-0996 – Dir., Elizabeth Temple

Brantford: Brant County Home Care Program, 274 Colborne St., Brantford ON N3T 2H5 – 519/759-7752; Fax: 519/759-7130 – Dir., Pat Davies, 519/759-7040, ext.223

Brockville: Leeds, Grenville & Lanark Home Care Program, c/o Leeds, Grenville & Lanark District Health Unit, 458 Laurier Blvd., Brockville ON K6V 7A3 – 613/345-0060; Fax: 613/345-3294; Tollfree: 1-800-267-4403 – Dir., Judy Killoran

Burlington: Halton Region Home Care Program, 460 Brant St., Burlington ON L7R 4B6 – 905/639-5228; Fax: 905/639-5320 – Dir., Sandra Shadwick

Chatham: Kent Chatham Home Care Program, 220 Riverview Dr., PO Box 306, Chatham ON N7M 5K4 – 519/351-9780; Fax: 519/352-1373, 351-5842 – Dir., E. Merilyn Allison

Clinton: Huron County LTC Division/Home Care Program, 80 Mary St., PO Box 458, Clinton ON N0M 1L0 – 519/482-3411; Fax: 519/482-7231 – Dir., Karen Lehnen

Cornwall: Eastern Ontario Home Care Program, 1000 Pitt St., Cornwall ON K6J 5T1 – 613/933-1375; Fax: 613/933-9916 – Dir., Jeanne Lamarche

Gloucester: Ottawa-Carleton Region Home Care Program, 1223 Michael St. North, Gloucester ON K1J 7T2 – 613/745-5525; Fax: 613/745-6984 – Dir., Catherine Danbrook

Guelph: Wellington-Dufferin-Guelph Home Care Program, #205, 2 Quebec St., Guelph ON N1H 2T3 – 519/823-2550; Fax: 519/823-8682 – Dir., Agnes Gelb

Hamilton-Wentworth Home Care Program, 414 Victoria Ave. North, Hamilton ON L8L 5G8 – 905/523-8600; Fax: 905/528-1883 – Dir., Betty Muggah

Huntsville: Muskoka-East Parry Sound Home Care Program, 354 Muskoka Rd. 3 North, PO Box 1, Huntsville ON P1H 1H7 – 705/789-6451; Fax: 705/789-1982; Tollfree: 1-800-263-2805 – Dir., Vaughn Adamson

Kenora: Northwestern Home Care Program, 21 Wolsley St., Kenora ON P9N 3W7 – 807/468-6491; Fax: 807/468-1437 – Head of Home Care, Lisa Howie

Kingston, Frontenac & Lennox & Addington Home Care Program, 471 Counter St., Kingston ON K7M 3L5 – 613/544-7090; Fax: 613/544-1494 – Dir., Nancy Sears

Kirkland Lake: Timiskaming Home Care Program, 31 Station Rd. North, PO Box 98, Kirkland Lake ON P2N 3M6 – 705/567-9355, 9350, ext.203; Fax: 705/567-5476 – Dir., Susan Donaldson

Lindsay: Haliburton, Kawartha, Pine Ridge District Home Care Program, 108 Angeline St. South, Lindsay ON K9V 3L5 – 705/324-9165; Fax: 705/324-0884; Tollfree: 1-800-347-0285 – Dir., Marg Plaunt

London: Middlesex-London Home Care Program, 50 King St., London ON N6A 5L7 – 519/663-5410; Fax: 519/432-1645 – Acting Dir., Hal Finlayson, 519/663-5332, ext.2420

Mississauga: Peel Region Home Care Program, #202, 2227 South Millway, Mississauga ON L5L 3R6 – 905/791-7800, ext.7309; Fax: 905/820-3368 – Dir., Home Care & Community Services, Linda Instance

Newmarket: York Region Home Care Program, Regional Municipality of York, 1100 Gorham St., Unit 1, Newmarket ON L3Y 7V1 – 905/895-1240, 722-4223; Fax: 905/853-6297 – Dir., Carol Dockrell

North Bay & District Home Care Program, The Thomson Bldg., 101 McIntyre St. West, PO Box 450, North Bay ON P1B 8J1 – 705/474-1400; Fax: 705/474-0080 – Dir., Yvonne Weir

Ohsweken: Six Nations Home Care Program, Ohsweken ON N0A 1M0 – 519/445-2201; Fax: 519/445-4914 – Dir. of Operations, Ken Jacobs

Owen Sound: Grey-Bruce Home Care Program, #301, 920 - 1st St., Owen Sound ON N4K 4K5 – 519/371-2112; Fax: 519/371-5612 – Dir., Judy Chalmers

Parry Sound Home Care Program, 50B Seguin St., Parry Sound ON P2A 1B4 – 705/746-9351; Fax: 705/746-4812 – Adm., Dodie Kernohan

Pembroke: Renfrew Home Care Program, Renfrew County & District Health Unit, 7 International Dr., Pembroke ON K8A 6W5 – 613/735-4133; Fax: 613/732-8752 – Acting Dir., Dr. Michael Corriveau

Peterborough Home Care Program, 10 Hospital Dr., Peterborough ON K9J 8M1 – 705/743-2212; Fax: 705/743-9559 – Dir., Ann Payne

St Catharines: Niagara Region Home Care Program, 573 Glenridge Ave., St Catharines ON L2T 4C2 – 905/684-9441; Fax: 905/684-8463, 2297 – Dir., Wanda Yarmoshuk

St. Thomas: Elgin-St. Thomas Home Care Program, 99 Edward St., St. Thomas ON N5P 1Y8 – 519/631-9907; Fax: 519/631-2236 – Dir., Carol Watson

Sarnia-Lambton Home Care Program, Bldg. #1040, 1086 Modeland Rd., PO Box 244, Stn DOW Bldg., Sarnia ON N7T 7S6 – 519/336-8112; Fax: 519/336-1419; Tollfree: 1-800-461-9196 – Adm., Peter Fitzsimmons

Sault Ste. Marie: Algoma Home Care Program, #1, 369 Queen St. East, Sault Ste. Marie ON P6A 1Z4 – 705/949-1650; Fax: 705/949-1663 – Adm., Pierrette Brown

Simcoe: Haldimand-Norfolk Home Care Program, 76 Victoria St., Simcoe ON N3Y 1L5 – 519/426-7400, 7320, ext.3301/2; Fax: 519/426-7622 – Dir., Mary Anne Baker

Stratford: Perth District Home Care Program, 653 West Gore St., Stratford ON N5A 1L4 – 519/273-2010; Fax: 519/273-2847 – Dir., Jennifer Allen

Sudbury & District Home Care Program, 1760 Regent St. South, Sudbury ON P3E 3Z8 – 705/522-3460; Fax: 705/522-3855 – Acting Dir., Diane Pacquette

Thunder Bay Home Care Program, #220, 1139 Alloy Dr., Thunder Bay ON P7B 6M8 – 807/344-0012; Fax: 807/345-3476 – Dir., Donna Opie

Timmins: Porcupine Home Care Program, 12 Elm St. North, Timmins ON P4N 6A1 – 705/267-7766; Fax: 705/267-7795; Tollfree: 1-800-890-6566 – Acting Dir., Jackie Gerrie

Toronto: Home Care Program for Metropolitan Toronto, 45 Sheppard Ave. East, Willowdale ON M2N 5W9 – 416/229-2929; Fax: 416/224-0908 – Pres., Marian Walsh, 416/229-2929, ext.5376, Fax: 416/229-1274

Waterloo Home Care Program, 99 Regina St. South, PO Box 1612, Waterloo ON N2J 4G6 – 519/883-2210; Fax: 519/883-2234 – Dir., Kevin Mercer

Whitby: Durham Region Home Care Program, 605 Brock St. North, Whitby ON L1N 4J3 – 905/430-3308; Fax: 905/430-3297 – Dir., Barbara Olsen

Windsor-Essex Home Care Program, 3000 Temple Dr., Windsor ON N8W 5J6 – 519/974-3022, ext.225; Fax: 519/974-1746 – Dir., Shirley Quick

Woodstock: Oxford County Home Care Program, 410 Buller St., Woodstock ON N4S 8A3 – 519/539-1284; Fax: 519/539-0065 – Dir., Kathy Desai

MENTAL HEALTH HOSPITALS & COMMUNITY FACILITIES

Brockville Psychiatric Hospital, Prescott Rd., PO Box 1050, Brockville ON K6V 5W7 – 613/345-1461; Fax: 613/342-6194 – 295 beds – Adm., David Hunter

Guelph: Community Mental Health Clinic, 147 Delhi St., Guelph ON N1E 4J8 – 519/821-2060 – Exec. Dir., Dr. Vernon Leditt

Guelph: Homewood Health Centre, 150 Delhi St., Guelph ON N1E 4J8 – 519/824-1010; Fax: 519/824-1827 – Exec. Dir., J.M. Dougan

Hamilton Psychiatric Hospital, 100 - 5th St. West, PO Box 585, Hamilton ON L8L 2B3 – 905/388-2511; Fax: 905/575-6038 – 245 beds – Adm., Mary Sutherland

Kingston Psychiatric Hospital, 752 King St. West, PO Box 603, Kingston ON K7L 4X3 – 613/546-1101; Fax: 613/548-5577 – 317 beds – Adm., Wayne Barnett

London Psychiatric Hospital, 850 Highbury Ave., PO Box 2532, London ON N6A 4H1 – 519/455-5110; Fax: 519/455-3712 – 346 beds – Adm., Robert Cunningham

North Bay Psychiatric Hospital, PO Box 3010, North Bay ON P1B 8L1 – 705/474-1200; Fax: 705/472-1694 – 307 beds – Adm., Dave J. Barker

Ottawa: Royal Ottawa Health Care Group, 1145 Carling Ave., Ottawa ON K1Z 7K4 – 613/722-6521; Fax: 613/722-4577 – CEO, George Langill

Penetanguishene: Mental Health Centre Penetanguishene, 500 Church St., Penetanguishene ON L9M 1G3 – 705/549-3181; Fax: 705/549-3446 – 296 beds – Adm., George Kytayko

St. Thomas Psychiatric Hospital, PO Box 2004, St. Thomas ON N5P 3V9 – 519/631-8510; Fax: 519/631-2681 – 289 beds – Adm., Robert Cunningham

Thunder Bay: Lakehead Psychiatric Hospital, 580 Algoma St. North, PO Box 2930, Thunder Bay ON P7B 5G4 – 807/343-4300; Fax: 807/343-4373 – 148 beds – Adm., Dr. Ron Saddington

Toronto: Clarke Institute of Psychiatry, 250 College St., Toronto ON M5T 1R8 – 416/979-2221; Fax: 416/599-5728 – Exec. Vice-Pres. & COO, Jean Simpson

Toronto: Queen Street Mental Health Centre, 1001 Queen St. West, Toronto ON M6J 1H4 – 416/535-8501; Fax: 416/583-4307 – 474 beds – Adm., Allison Stuart

Whitby Mental Health Centre, 700 Gordon St., PO Box 613, Whitby ON L1N 5S9 – 905/668-5881; Fax: 905/430-4032 – 287 beds – Adm., Ron Ballantyne

NURSING HOMES

Ailsa Craig: Craigholme Nursing Home, 221 Main St. East, PO Box 130, Ailsa Craig ON N0M 1A0 – 519/293-3215; Fax: 519/293-3704 – 83 beds – Acting Adm., Nancy Pratt

Ajax: Ballycliffe Lodge Nursing Home, 70 Station St., Ajax ON L1S 1R9 – 905/683-7321; Fax: 905/427-5846 – 100 beds – Adm., Carol McIlveen

Alexandria: Community Nursing Home, 92 Centre St., Alexandria ON K0C 1A0 – 613/525-2022; Fax: 613/525-2023 – 70 beds – Adm., Terry Dube

Alliston: Good Samaritan Nursing Home, 481 Victoria St. East, Alliston ON L9R 1J8 – 705/435-5722; Fax: 705/435-7982 – 55 beds – Adm., Lynda Weaver

Almonte Country Haven, 333 Country St., Almonte ON K0A 1A0 – 613/256-3095; Fax: 613/256-3096 – 82 beds – Adm., Patricia Watson

Almonte: Fairview Manor, 95 Spring St., Almonte ON K0A 1A0 – 613/256-3113; Fax: 613/256-5780 – 100 beds – Adm., G. McFarlane

Amherstburg: Richmond Terrace, 89 Rankin St., Amherstburg ON N9V 1E7 – 519/736-4295; Fax: 519/736-2995 – 115 beds – Adm., Victoria Iler

Amherstview: Helen Henderson Nursing Home, 343 Amherst Dr., Amherstview ON K7N 1X3 – 613/384-

4585; Fax: 613/384-9407 – 42 beds – Adm., Larry Gibson

Arnprior: The Grove Arnprior & District Nursing Home, 275 Ida St. North, Arnprior ON K7S 3M7 – 613/623-6547; Fax: 613/623-4844 – 60 beds – Adm., Ronald J. Kedrosky

Arthur: Caressant Care Arthur Nursing Home, 215 Eliza St., Arthur ON N0G 1A0 – 519/848-3795; Fax: 519/848-2273 – 80 beds – Adm., Gwen Good

Athens: Maple View Lodge, PO Box 100, Athens ON K0E 1B0 – 613/924-2696; Fax: 613/924-2123 – 41 beds – Adm., P. Donovan

Atikokan General Hospital, *see* General Hospitals listings

Aurora Resthaven Extended Care & Convalesance, 32 Mill St., Aurora ON L4G 2R9 – 905/727-1939; Fax: 905/727-6299 – 176 beds – Adm., Sheila Hoinkes

Aurora: The Willows Estate Nursing Home, 13837 Yonge St., Aurora ON L4G 3G8 – 905/727-0128; Fax: 905/841-0454 – 84 beds – Adm., Susan Jackson

Aylmer: Chateau Gardens Aylmer Nursing Home, 465 Talbot St. West, Aylmer ON N5H 1K8 – 519/773-3423; Fax: 519/765-2573 – 60 beds – Adm., Mary Walker

Aylmer: Terrace Lodge, 475 Talbot St. East, Aylmer ON N5H 3A5 – 519/773-9205; Fax: 519/765-2667 – 100 beds – Adm., F.J. Boyes

Bancroft: Hastings Centennial Manor, 36 Maple St., PO Box 758, Bancroft ON K0L 1C0 – 613/332-2070; Fax: 613/332-2837 – 104 beds – Adm., Rob McLaughlin

Barrie: Coleman Health Care Centre, 140 Cundles Rd. West, Barrie ON L4M 4S4 – 705/726-8691; Fax: 705/726-5085 – 112 beds – Adm., Françoise Bouchard

Barrie: Grove Park, 234 Cook St., Barrie ON L4M 4T7 – 705/726-1003; Fax: 705/726-1076 – 93 beds – Adm., D.M. Johnson

Barrie: I.O.O.F. Home, 10 Brooks St., Barrie ON L4M 3H7 – 705/728-2364; Fax: 705/728-6024 – 155 beds – Adm., R. Crawford

Barrie: Leisure World - Barrie, 130 Owen St., Barrie ON L4M 3H7 – 705/726-8621; Fax: 705/726-0821 – 57 beds – Adm., Diane Greene

Barry's Bay: Valley Manor Nursing Home, Mintha St., Lot 177, PO Box 490, Barry's Bay ON K0J 1B0 – 613/756-2643 – 70 beds – Adm., Linda Shulist

Beamsville: Albright Manor, 5035 Mountain St., Beamsville ON L0R 1B0 – 905/563-8252; Fax: 905/563-5223 – 231 beds – Adm., John Buma

Beamsville: Nipponia Home, 4505 Thirty Rd., Beamsville ON L0R 1B0 – 905/563-8312; Fax: 905/563-8312 – 35 beds – Adm., Shinichi Sawada

Beaverton: Lakeview Manor, 133 Main St., PO Box 514, Beaverton ON L0K 1A0 – 705/426-7388; Fax: 705/426-4218 – 149 beds – Adm., Elizabeth Powell

Beeton: Simcoe Manor, Main St. East, Beeton ON L0G 1A0 – 905/729-2267; Fax: 905/729-2816 – 126 beds – Adm., Brenda Urbanski

Belleville: Belcrest Nursing Home, 431 Dundas St. West, Belleville ON K8P 1B6 – 613/968-4434; Fax: 613/968-6910 – 60 beds – Adm., James A. Clegg

Belleville: Hastings Manor, 476 Dundas St. West, Belleville ON K8N 5B2 – 613/968-6467; Fax: 613/967-0128 – 251 beds – Adm., Claudette Dignard-Remillard

Belleville: Montgomery Lodge Nursing Home, 145 Farley Ave., Belleville ON K8N 4L1 – 613/968-8835; Fax: 613/968-3207 – 59 beds – Adm., James Clegg

Belleville: Westgate Lodge Nursing Home, 37 Wilkie St., Belleville ON K8P 4E4 – 613/966-1323; Fax: 613/966-5126 – 88 beds – Adm., Elizabeth McGrath

Blenheim Community Village, 10 Mary Ave., Blenheim ON N0P 1A0 – 519/676-8119; Fax: 519/676-0610 – 65 beds – Adm., Ruth A. McDougall

Blind River: Golden Birches Terrace, c/o St. Joseph's Health Centre, 525 Causley St., Blind River ON P0R 1B0 – 705/356-2265; Fax: 705/356-1220 – 20 beds – Adm., Paul Davies

Bobcaygeon: Case Manor Nursing Home, 28 Boyd St., Bobcaygeon ON K0M 1A0 – 705/738-2374; Fax: 705/738-3821 – 80 beds – Adm., Dale G. Ross

Bobcaygeon: Pinecrest Nursing Home, Lot 12, Concession 19, Bobcaygeon ON K0M 1A0 – 705/738-2366; Fax: 705/889-8127 – 58 beds – Adm., Karen White

Bolton: King Nursing Home, 49 Sterne St., Bolton ON L0P 1A0 – 905/857-4117; Fax: 905/857-5181 – 86 beds – Adm., Janice L. King

Bolton: Vera M. Davis Community Care Centre, 80 Allan Dr., Bolton ON L7E 1P7 – 905/857-0975; Fax: 905/857-7872 – 64 beds – Adm., Carolyne Clubine

Bourget Nursing Home, 2279 Laval St., Bourget ON K0A 1E0 – 613/487-2331; Fax: 613/487-3464 – 50 beds – Adm., Louise Dion

Bowanville: Strathaven Lifecare Centre, 264 King St. East, Bowanville ON L1C 1P9 – 905/623-2553; Fax: 905/623-1374 – 199 beds – Adm., Jane Noble

Bowmanville: Marnwood Lifecare Centre, 26 Elgin St., Bowmanville ON L1C 3C8 – 905/623-5731; Fax: 905/623-4497 – 60 beds – Adm., Catherine Luby

Bracebridge: The Pines, 42 Pine St., Bracebridge ON P1L 1N5 – 705/645-4488; Fax: 705/645-6857 – 105 beds – Adm., Steve O'Neil

Bradford: Beacon Hill Lodge Villa, 136 Barrie St., Bradford ON L3Z 2A9 – 905/775-8118; Fax: 905/773-0263 – 90 beds – Adm., D.K. Frosese

Brampton: Faith Manor Nursing Home, 7900 McLaughlin Rd. South, Brampton ON L6V 3N2 – 905/459-3333; Fax: 905/459-8667 – 120 beds – Adm., John Kalverda

Brampton: Peel Manor, 525 Main St. North, Brampton ON L6X 1N9 – 905/453-4140; Fax: 905/453-7802 – 177 beds – Adm., Inga Mazuryk

Brampton: Tullamore Nursing Home, 133 Kennedy Rd. South, Brampton ON L6W 3G3 – 905/459-2324; Fax: 905/459-2329 – 159 beds – Adm., Geoffrey Doff

Brantford: John Noble Home, 97 Mount Pleasant St., Brantford ON N3T 1T5 – 519/756-2920; Fax: 519/756-7942 – 361 beds – Adm., J. Mills

Brantford: Leisure World Brantford Centre, 389 West St., Brantford ON N3R 3V9 – 519/759-4666; Fax: 519/759-0200 – 90 beds – Adm., Mary Ann Owens

Brantford: Versa-Care Centre of Brantford, 425 Park Rd. North, Brantford ON N3R 7G5 – 519/759-1040; Fax: 519/759-5343 – 79 beds – Adm., Richard M. Sims

Brighton: Carewell Brighton Nursing Home, 14 Maplewood Ave., Brighton ON K0K 1H0 – 613/475-2442; Fax: 613/475-2445 – 49 beds – Adm., Mary Chester

Brockville: Fulford Home, 283 King St. East, Brockville ON K6V 1E2 – 613/342-7380; Fax: 613/342-2997 – 34 beds – Adm., Betty MacDougall

Brockville: St. Lawrence Lodge, 1803 Prescott Rd. East, PO Box 1130, Brockville ON K6V 5W2 – 613/345-0255; Fax: 613/345-1029 – 240 beds – Adm., William Luker

Brockville: Sherwood Park Manor, 1814 Highway 2 East, Brockville ON K6V 5T1 – 613/342-5531; Fax: 613/342-3767 – 75 beds – Adm., Henry Bloemen

Brunner Nursing Home, Lot 76, Concession 1W, Brunner ON N0K 1C0 – 519/595-8903; Fax: 519/595-8272 – 26 beds – Adm., Joanne Ross

Brussels: Huronlea Home for the Aged, Turnberry St. South, Brussels ON N0G 1H0 – 519/887-9267; Fax: 519/482-5263 – 61 beds – Adm., Cathy Brown

Burlington: Brantwood Lifecare Centre, 802 Hager Ave., Burlington ON L7S 1X2 – 905/637-3481; Fax: 905/637-7514 – 138 beds – Adm., Mary Scott

Burlington: Cama Woodlands Nursing Home, 159 Panin Rd., Burlington ON L7V 1A1 – 905/681-6441; Fax: 905/681-2678 – 60 beds – Adm., Andrea Pomeroy

Burlington: Maple Villa Nursing Home, 441 Maple Ave., Burlington ON L7S 1L8 – 905/639-2264; Fax: 905/639-3034 – 93 beds – Adm., Barbara Goetz

Burlington: Mount Nemo Lodge, 4486 Guelph Line, Burlington ON L9T 2X6 – 905/335-3636; Fax: 905/335-3699 – 60 beds – Adm., Allen Sybersma

Cambridge Country Manor, 3680 Speedsville Rd., Cambridge ON N3H 4R6 – 519/650-0100; Fax: 519/650-1697 – 79 beds – Adm., Lynne Lawson

Cambridge: Fairview Mennonite Home, 799 Concession Rd., Cambridge ON N3H 4L1 – 519/653-5719; Fax: 519/650-1242 – 84 beds – Adm., T. Kennel

Cambridge: Golden Years Nursing Home, 704 Eagle St. North, Cambridge ON N1R 2J2 – 519/653-5493; Fax: 519/650-1495 – 88 beds – Adm., Nancy Kauffman-Lambert

Cambridge: Hilltop Manor Nursing Home, 42 Elliott St., Cambridge ON N1R 2J2 – 519/621-3067; Fax: 519/621-3443 – 89 beds – Adm., John Heutinck

Cambridge: Riverbend Place, 650 Coronation Blvd., Cambridge ON N1R 7S6 – 519/740-3820; Fax: 519/740-0961 – 53 beds – Adm., Marg Dykeman

Cambridge: Saint Luke's Place, 1624 Franklin Blvd., Cambridge ON N3C 3P4 – 519/658-5183; Fax: 519/658-2991 – 114 beds – Adm., John Kauffman

Campbellford: Carewell Campbellford Nursing Home, 320 Burnbrae Rd. East, Campbellford ON K0L 1L0 – 705/653-4100; Fax: 705/653-2598 – 43 beds – Adm., Mary Anne Heffernan

Cannifton: E.J. McQuigge Lodge, Black Diamond Rd., Cannifton ON K0K 1K0 – 613/966-7717; Fax: 613/966-7646 – 56 beds – Adm., Anita Garland

Cannington: Bon-Air Nursing Home, 131 Laidlaw St. South, Cannington ON L0E 1E0 – 705/432-2385; Fax: 705/432-3331 – 55 beds – Adm., Lynne Disik

Carleton Place Health Care Centre/Versa-Care Centre, 256 High St., Carleton Place ON K7C 1X1 – 613/257-4355; Fax: 613/253-2190 – 60 beds – Adm., Ken Herrington

Chapleau: Cedar Grove Lodge, 101 Pine St., Chapleau ON P0M 1K0 – 705/864-1616 – 20 beds – Adm., Bruce Peterkin

Chatham: Copper Terrace LTC Facility, 91 Tecumseh Rd., Chatham ON N7M 1B3 – 519/354-5442; Fax: 519/354-2089 – 151 beds – Adm., Carolee Milliner

Chatham: Meadow Park Nursing Home, 110 Sandys St., Chatham ON N7L 4X3 – 519/351-1330; Fax: 519/351-7933 – 97 beds – Acting Adm., Debbie Lashbrook

Chatham: Thamesview Lodge, 475 Grand Ave. West, Chatham ON N7L 4R5 – 519/352-4823; Fax: 519/352-2891 – 243 beds – Adm., Shirley Clark

Chatham: Victoria Residence, 190 Stanley Ave., Chatham ON N7M 3J9 – 519/354-0610; Fax: 519/354-7741 – 90 beds – Acting Adm., Greg Keating

Chatsworth Health Care Centre/Versa-Care Centre, RR#3, Chatsworth ON N0H 1G0 – 519/794-2244; Fax: 519/794-2597 – 34 beds – Adm., Catherine Hollister

Chesley: Elgin Abbey Nursing Home, 380 First Ave. North, Chesley ON N0G 1L0 – 519/363-3195; Fax: 519/363-2747 – 27 beds – Adm., Elizabeth Elvidge

Chesley: Parkview Manor Health Care Centre, 98 - 3rd St. SE, Chesley ON N0G 1L0 – 519/363-2416; Fax: 519/363-2171 – 34 beds – Adm., Carole Wood

Clarence Creek: Centre d'accueil Roger Seguin, 435 Lemay St., PO Box 160, Clarence Creek ON K0A 1N0 – 613/488-2053; Fax: 613/488-2274 – 113 beds – Adm., Paul Mathieu

Clinton: Huronview, Lot 50, Concession 1, Tuckersmith Township, PO Box 219, Clinton ON N0M 1L0 – 519/482-3451; Fax: 519/482-5263 – 120 beds – Adm., Cathy Brown

Cobden: Lakeview Nursing Home, 49 Pembroke St., Hwy. 17, Cobden ON K0J 1K0 – 613/646-2109; Fax: 613/646-2182 – 55 beds – Adm., Vallerie Pellerin

Cobourg: Carewell Streamway Nursing Home, 19 James St. West, Cobourg ON K9A 2J8 – 416/372-0163; Fax: 416/372-0581 – 59 beds – Adm., Caroline Tompkins

Cobourg: Golden Plough Lodge, 983 Burnham St., Cobourg ON K9A 4J7 – 416/372-8759; Fax: 416/372-8525 – 161 beds – Adm., Carol Shaw
Cochenour: Owen J. Matthews, Hwy 125, Cochenour ON P0V 1L0 – 807/662-3281; Fax: 807/662-2037 – 22 beds – Adm., Kevin Queen
Cochrane: Extendicare/Cochrane, 411 - 11th Ave. North, Cochrane ON P0L 1C0 – 705/272-4144; Fax: 705/272-4155 – 62 beds – Adm., Claude Roy
Collingwood Nursing Home, 250 Campbell St., Collingwood ON L9Y 4J9 – 705/445-3991; Fax: 705/445-5060 – 60 beds – Adm., Peter Zober
Collingwood: Bay Haven Nursing Home, 499 Hume St., Collingwood ON L9Y 4H8 – 705/445-6501; Fax: 705/445-6506 – 60 beds – Adm., Karen Milligan
Collingwood: Sunset Manor, Raglan St., Collingwood ON L9Y 3Z4 – 705/445-4499; Fax: 705/445-9742 – 150 beds – Adm., Robert Morton
Corbeil: Nipissing Manor Nursing Care Centre, RR#1, Corbeil ON P0H 1K0 – 705/752-1100; Fax: 705/752-2570 – 120 beds – Adm., W.E. Graham
Cornwall: Glen-Stor-Dun Lodge, 1900 Montréal Rd., Cornwall ON K6H 5T1 – 613/933-3384; Fax: 613/933-7214 – 132 beds – Adm., F. Lafave
Cornwall: Parisien Manor Nursing Home, 439 Second St. East, Cornwall ON K6H 1Z2 – 613/933-2592; Fax: 613/933-3839 – 65 beds – Adm., Johneen Rennie
Cornwall: St. Joseph's Villa (Cornwall), 14 York St., Cornwall ON K6J 3Y6 – 613/933-6040; Fax: 613/933-9429 – 150 beds – Adm., John Haslehurst
Cornwall: Sandfield Place, 220 Emma St., Cornwall ON K6J 5V8 – 613/933-6972; Fax: 613/938-2261 – 53 beds – Adm., Joyce Kinnear
Cornwall: Tsi Ion Kwa Nonh So:Te, RR#3, Cornwall Island, Cornwall ON K6H 5R7 – 613/932-1409; Fax: 613/932-8845 – 30 beds – Adm., Bonnie Cole
Cornwall: Versa-Care Centre, Cornwall, 201 - 11th St. East, Cornwall ON K6H 2Y6 – 613/933-7420; Fax: 613/933-2759 – 118 beds – Adm., Barbara Lalonde
Courtland: Sacred Heart Villa, PO Box 279, Courtland ON N0J 1E0 – 519/688-0710; Fax: 519/688-0052 – 54 beds – Adm., Linda Hare
Creemore: Creedan Valley Nursing Home, 143 Mary St., Creemore ON L0M 1G0 – 705/466-3437; Fax: 705/466-3063 – 92 beds – Adm., Dianne Greene
Deep River: North Renfrew Long-Term Care Centre, 47 Ridge Rd., Deep River ON K0J 1P0 – 613/584-1900; Fax: 613/584-9188 – 21 beds – Adm., Ann Aikens
Delaware: Middlesex Terrace, RR#1, Delaware ON N0L 1E0 – 519/652-3483; Fax: 519/652-6915 – 105 beds – Adm., Janice McAskill
Delaware: Versa-Care Centre, Lambeth, 848 Gideon, Delaware ON N0L 1S0 – 519/472-1270; Fax: 519/472-0228 – 157 beds – Adm., Shirley Nugent
Delhi Nursing Home, 750 Gilbraltar St., Delhi ON N4B 3B3 – 519/582-3400; Fax: 519/582-0300 – 60 beds – Adm., Janet Krolouski
Dryden District General Hospital, see General Hospitals listings
Dundas: Blackadar Nursing Home, 101 Creighton Rd., Dundas ON L9H 3B7 – 905/627-5465; Fax: 905/628-2044 – 80 beds – Adm., D. Dean Blackadar
Dundas: St. Joseph's Villa (Dundas), 56 Governor's Rd., Dundas ON L9H 5G7 – 905/627-3541; Fax: 905/628-0825 – 378 beds – Adm., Paul O'Krafka
Dundas: Wentworth Lodge, 41 South St. West, Dundas ON L9H 4C4 – 905/628-6359; Fax: 905/628-3788 – 210 beds – Adm., Judith Evans
Dunnville: Grandview Lodge/Dunnville, 657 Lock St. West, Dunnville ON N1A 1V9 – 416/774-7548; Fax: 416/774-1440 – 206 beds – Adm., Arlene Lawlor
Durham: Rockwood Terrace, 575 Sadler St. East, Durham ON N0G 1R0 – 519/369-6035; Fax: 519/369-6736 – 100 beds – Adm., John Flick
Durham: St. Raphael's Nursing Home (Durham), 415 Durham Rd. East, Durham ON N0G 1R0 – 519/369-3741; Fax: 519/369-5595 – 48 beds – Adm., Tracee Givens
Dutton: Bobier Convalescent Home, 265 Shackleton St., Dutton ON N0L 1J0 – 519/762-2417; Fax: 519/762-2361 – 57 beds – Adm., Fred Boyes, 519/631-0620
Elmira: Chateau Gardens (Elmira) Nursing Home, 11 Herbert St., Elmira ON N3B 2B8 – 519/669-2921; Fax: 519/669-3027 – 48 beds – Adm., Joan Norris
Elmvale: Sara Vista Nursing Centre, 59 Simcoe St., Elmvale ON L0L 1P0 – 705/322-2182; Fax: 705/322-8326 – 60 beds – Adm., Anitta Robertson
Elora: Wellington Terrace, Wellington Dr., Elora ON N0B 1S0 – 519/846-5359; Fax: 519/846-9192 – 176 beds – Adm., Peter Barnes
Embrun: St. Jacques Nursing Home, 915 Notre Dame St., Embrun ON K0A 1W0 – 613/443-3442; Fax: 613/443-1716 – 60 beds – Adm., Louise Gaudreau
Englehart: Northview Nursing Home, 7 River Rd., Englehart ON P0J 1H0 – 705/544-8191; Fax: 705/544-8255 – 48 beds – Adm., Carol-Ann Poan
Espanola Nursing Home, 799 Queensway Ave., Espanola ON P0P 1C0 – 705/869-1420; Fax: 705/869-2068 – 30 beds – Acting Adm., Paul Davies
Essex Health Care Centre, 111 Iler Ave., Essex ON N8M 1T6 – 519/776-5243; Fax: 519/776-4450 – 142 beds – Adm., Geraldine Picken
Exeter Villa, 155 John St. East, Exeter ON N0M 1S1 – 519/235-1581; Fax: 519/235-3219 – 47 beds – Adm., Mary Jane MacDougall
Fergus: Caressant Care Fergus Nursing Home, 450 Queen St. East, Fergus ON N1M 2Y7 – 519/843-2400; Fax: 519/843-2200 – 87 beds – Adm., Marilyn Jacobi
The Fordwich Village Nursing Home, 63 Adelaide St., Fordwich ON N0G 1V0 – 519/335-3168 – 33 beds – Adm., Catherine Weber
Forest: North Lambton Rest Home, 39 Morris St., Forest ON N0N 1J0 – 519/786-2151; Fax: 519/786-2156 – 88 beds – Acting Adm., Kevin McIver
Fort Erie: Crescent Park Lodge, 4 Hagey Ave., Fort Erie ON L2A 5M5 – 905/871-8330; Fax: 905/871-9212 – 68 beds – Adm., Rosemary Turner
Fort Erie: Gilmore Lodge, 50 Gilmore Rd., Fort Erie ON L2A 2M1 – 905/871-6160; Fax: 905/871-0435 – 80 beds – Adm., Carrie Kaye
Fort Frances: Rainycrest, 550 Home St., Fort Frances ON P9A 3T2 – 807/274-9858; Fax: 807/274-7368 – 168 beds – Acting Adm., Pat Crewson
Gananoque: Carveth Care Centre, 375 James St., Gananoque ON K7G 2A1 – 613/382-4752; Fax: 613/382-8514 – 93 beds – Adm., Tim Gibson
Garson Manor Nursing Home, 219 O'Neil Dr. East, Garson ON P3L 1S5 – 705/693-2734; Fax: 705/693-5031 – 80 beds – Adm., Clifford Gavan
Geraldton District Hospital, see General Hospitals listings
Glenburnie: Fairmount Home, 2069 Battersea Rd., Glenburnie ON K0H 1S0 – 613/546-4264; Fax: 613/546-0489 – 96 beds – Adm., M.J. McCarthy
Gloucester: Extendicare/Laurier Manor, 1715 Montréal Rd., Gloucester ON K1J 6N4 – 613/741-5122; Fax: 613/741-8432 – 240 beds – Adm., William Smith
Gloucester: St. Louis Residence, 879, ch Parc Hiawatha, Gloucester ON K1C 2Z6 – 613/824-1720; Fax: 613/824-8064 – 186 beds – Adm., Sr. Diane Albert
Goderich: Versa-Care Centre, Goderich, 290 South St., Goderich ON N7A 4G6 – 519/524-7324; Fax: 519/524-8739 – 91 beds – Adm., Dana Livingstone
Gore Bay: Manitoulin Lodge, 3 Main St., Gore Bay ON P0P 1H0 – 705/282-2007; Fax: 705/282-3422 – 61 beds – Adm., Linda J. Williams
Gravenhurst: Muskoka Nursing Home, 200 Kelly Dr., Gravenhurst ON P1P 1P3 – 705/687-3444; Fax: 705/687-6319 – 71 beds – Adm., Azmina Drummond
Grimsby: Deer Park Villa, 150 Central Ave., Grimsby ON L3M 4Z3 – 905/945-4164; Fax: 905/945-7774 – 39 beds – Adm., Cornelia Tank
Grimsby: Kilean Lodge, 81-83 Main St. East, Grimsby ON L3M 1N6 – 905/945-9243; Fax: 905/945-1126 – 50 beds – Adm., Gala Casucci
Grimsby: Shalom Manor, 12 Bartlett Ave., Grimsby ON L3M 4N5 – 905/945-9631; Fax: 905/945-1211 – 132 beds – Adm., Melis Koomans
Guelph: Eden House Nursing Home, RR#2, Guelph ON N1H 6H8 – 519/856-4622; Fax: 519/856-7412 – 58 beds – Adm., John Bouwmeester
Guelph: The Elliott Home, 170 Metcalfe St., Guelph ON N1E 4Y3 – 519/822-0491; Fax: 519/822-5658 – 85 beds – Adm., David Hicks
Guelph: Lapointe-Fisher Nursing Home, 271 Metcalfe St., Guelph ON N1E 4Y8 – 519/821-9030; Fax: 519/821-6021 – 92 beds – Adm., Ann Root
Guelph: St. Joseph's Home, 325 Edinburgh Rd. North, Guelph ON N1H 1E3 – 519/824-2620; Fax: 519/767-3434 – 136 beds – Adm., Sr. Margaret Myatt
Hagersville: Norcliffe Lifecare Centre, 85 Main St. North, Hagersville ON N0A 1H0 – 416/768-1641; Fax: 416/768-1538 – 60 beds – Adm., Ben Bernardo
Haileybury: Extendicare/Tri-Town Nursing Home, 143 Bruce St., Haileybury ON P0J 1K0 – 705/672-2151; Fax: 705/672-5348 – 60 beds – Acting Adm., Françoise Denis
Haileybury: Temiskaming Lodge, 100 Bruce St., Haileybury ON P0J 1K0 – 705/672-2123; Fax: 705/672-5734 – 80 beds – Adm., Edith Schultz
Haliburton: Extendicare/Haliburton Nursing Home, Park St., PO Box 780, Haliburton ON K0M 1S0 – 705/457-1722; Fax: 705/457-3914 – 60 beds – Adm., Jane Rosenberg
Hamilton Convalescent Centre, 125 Wentworth St. South, Hamilton ON L8N 2Z1 – 905/527-1482; Fax: 905/527-0679 – 64 beds – Adm., Lorraine Preston-Orchard
Hamilton: Beacon Hill Lodge, 330 Main St. East, Hamilton ON L8N 3T9 – 905/523-7134; Fax: 905/523-7137 – 248 beds – Adm., Joan Dennison
Hamilton: Grace Villa (Hamilton) Nursing Home, 45 Lockton Cr., Hamilton ON L8V 4V5 – 905/387-4812; Fax: 905/387-4814 – 184 beds – Adm., David Baker
Hamilton: Idlewyld Manor, 449 Sanatorium Rd., Hamilton ON L9C 2A7 – 905/574-2000; Fax: 905/574-0139 – 101 beds – Adm., Beverley Preuss
Hamilton: Macassa Lodge, 701 Upper Sherman Dr., Hamilton ON L8V 3M7 – 905/546-2800; Fax: 905/546-4989 – 270 beds – Adm., Bob Malloy
Hamilton: Parkview Nursing Centre, 545 King St. West, Hamilton ON L8P 3M7 – 905/525-5903; Fax: 905/525-5907 – 126 beds – Adm., Sandra Smith
Hamilton: St. Olga's Lifecare Centre, 570 King St. West, Hamilton ON L8P 1C2 – 905/522-8572; Fax: 905/577-0644 – 90 beds – Acting Adm., Debbie Miller
Hamilton: Shalom Village Nursing Home, 60 Macklin St. North, Hamilton ON L8S 3S1 – 905/529-1613; Fax: 905/529-7542 – 60 beds – Adm., Patricia Morden
Hamilton: Townsview Lifecare Centre, 39 Mary St., Hamilton ON L8R 3L8 – 905/523-6427; Fax: 905/528-0610 – 219 beds – Adm., Robert Millar
Hamilton: Victoria Nursing Home, 176 Victoria Ave. North, Hamilton ON L8L 5G1 – 905/527-9111; Fax: 905/526-1871 – 75 beds – Adm., Rosslyn Sole
Hamilton: The Wellington Nursing Home, 1430 Upper Wellington St., Hamilton ON L9A 5H3 – 905/385-2111; Fax: 905/385-2110 – 102 beds – Adm., Mary Reid
Hanover Care Centre, 700 - 19th Ave., Hanover ON N4N 3S6 – 519/364-3700; Fax: 519/364-7194 – 41 beds – Adm., Sharon Garcia

Hanover: Versa-Care Centre of Hanover, 101 - 10th St., Hanover ON N4N 1M9 – 519/364-2620; Fax: 519/364-6953 – 70 beds – Adm., Marilyn E. Robson

Harriston: Geri-Care Nursing Home, 24 Louise St., Harriston ON N0G 1Z0 – 519/338-3700; Fax: 519/338-2744 – 89 beds – Adm., Mary T. Haid

Hawkesbury: Prescott & Russell Residence, 1020 Cartier Blvd., Hawkesbury ON K6A 1W7 – 613/632-2755; Fax: 613/632-4056 – 146 beds – Adm., Pierre Arsenault

Hearst: Extendicare/Hearst, 1317 Edward St., Hearst ON P0L 1N0 – 705/362-5825; Fax: 705/362-5519 – 61 beds – Adm., Elizabeth Howe

Hensall: Queensway Nursing Home, 100 Queen St. East, Hensall ON N0M 1X0 – 519/262-2830; Fax: 519/262-3403 – 40 beds – Adm., Edward Underwood

Hornepayne Community Hospital, see General Hospitals listings

Huntsville: Fairvern Nursing Home, 14 Mill St., Huntsville ON P0A 1K0 – 705/789-4476; Fax: 705/789-1371 – 76 beds – Adm., Bruce Laughton

Ingersoll: Oxford Regional Nursing Home, 263 Wonham St. South, Ingersoll ON N5C 3P6 – 519/485-3920; Fax: 519/485-6497 – 80 beds – Acting Adm., Gloria McKibbin

Iroquois Falls: South Centennial Manor, 240 Fyfe St., PO Box 610, Iroquois Falls ON P0K 1E0 – 705/258-3836; Fax: 705/258-3694 – 69 beds – Adm., Ken Wollan

Jasper: Carewell Easton's Manor Nursing Home, 131 Roses Bridge Rd., RR#2, Jasper ON K0G 1G0 – 613/283-5471; Fax: 613/283-9012 – 78 beds – Adm., Nelly Hobbs

Kapuskasing: Extendicare/Kapuskasing, 45 Ontario St., Kapuskasing ON P5N 2Y5 – 705/335-6633; Fax: 705/337-6051 – 60 beds – Adm., Louise Gaulin

Kapuskasing: North Centennial Manor, 2 Kimberley Dr., Kapuskasing ON P5N 1L5 – 705/335-6125; Fax: 705/337-1091 – 71 beds – Adm., Gil Dionne

Kemptville: Bayfield Manor Nursing Home, 100 Elvira St., Kemptville ON K0G 1J0 – 613/258-7484; Fax: 613/258-3838 – 66 beds – Adm., Michael J. Hall

Kenora: Birchwood Terrace Nursing Home, 237 Lakeview Dr., Kenora ON P9N 3X8 – 807/468-8625; Fax: 807/468-4060 – 96 beds – Adm., Denise Miault

Kenora: Pinecrest, 1220 Valley Dr., Kenora ON P9N 2W7 – 807/468-3165; Fax: 807/468-6346 – 161 beds – Adm., Kevin Queen

Keswick: Cedarvale Lodge, 121 Morton Dr., Keswick ON L4P 2M5 – 905/476-2656; Fax: 905/476-5689 – 60 beds – Adm., Wynanda Rosenberger

Kilworthy: Balmoral Lodge Nursing Home, RR#1, Kilworthy ON P0E 1G0 – 705/689-2029; Fax: 705/689-5844 – 42 beds – Adm., Stephen Ladanyi

Kincardine: Versa-Care Trillium Court, 550 Philip Pl., Kincardine ON N2Z 3A6 – 519/396-4400; Fax: 519/396-2199 – 40 beds – Adm., Linda Ingham

King City Lodge Nursing Home, 146 Fog Rd., King City ON L7B 1A3 – 905/833-5037; Fax: 905/833-5925 – 36 beds – Adm., Linda Albert James

Kingston: Extendicare/Kingston, 309 Queen Mary Rd., Kingston ON K7M 6P4 – 613/549-5010; Fax: 613/549-7347 – 150 beds – Adm., Marilyn C. Benn

Kingston: Providence Manor, 275 Sydenham St., Kingston ON K7K 1G7 – 613/549-4164; Fax: 613/549-7472 – 253 beds – Acting Adm., Cathy Dunne

Kingston: Rideaucrest Home, 175 Rideau St., Kingston ON K7K 3H6 – 613/547-6792; Fax: 613/531-9107 – 170 beds – Adm., J.D. Smith

Kingston: Trillium Ridge, 800 Edgar St., Kingston ON K7M 8S4 – 613/547-0040; Fax: 613/547-3734 – 90 beds – Adm., Ray Jourdain

Kirkland Lake: Extendicare/Kirkland Lake, 155 Government Rd. East, Kirkland Lake ON P2N 3P4 – 705/567-3268; Fax: 705/567-4638 – 100 beds – Adm., Margaret Orr

Kirkland Lake: Teck Pioneer Residence, 38 Churchill Dr., Kirkland Lake ON P2N 1V1 – 705/567-3257; Fax: 705/567-3737 – 74 beds – Adm., Murray Munro

Kitchener: A.R. Goudie Eventide Home (Salvation Army), 369 Frederick St., Kitchener ON N2H 2P1 – 519/744-5182; Fax: 519/744-3887 – 79 beds – Adm., Ed Hiscock

Kitchener: Central Park Lodge, 60 Westheights Dr., Kitchener ON N2N 2A8 – 519/576-3320; Fax: 519/745-3227 – 240 beds – Adm., Dianne O'Rourke

Kitchener: Sunnyside Home, 247 Franklin St. North, Kitchener ON N2A 1Y5 – 519/893-8482; Fax: 519/893-4450 – 263 beds – Adm., Gail Carlin

Kitchener: Trinity Village Care Centre (Kitchener), 2727 Kingsway Dr., Kitchener ON N2C 1A7 – 519/893-6320; Fax: 519/893-3432 – 150 beds – Adm., Arthur Schelter

Kitchener: Winston Hall Nursing Home, 695 Blockline Rd., Kitchener ON N2E 3K1 – 519/576-2430; Fax: 519/576-8990 – 95 beds – Adm., James Schlegel

Komoka: Country Terrace, 10072 Oxbow Dr., RR#3, Komoka ON N0L 1R0 – 519/657-2955; Fax: 519/657-8516 – 120 beds – Adm., Mary Raithby

Lancaster: Chateau Gardens (Lancaster) Nursing Home, 303 Military Rd., Lancaster ON K0C 1N0 – 613/347-3016; Fax: 613/347-1680 – 60 beds – Adm., Diane Morin

Leamington Mennonite Home, 22 Garrison Ave., Leamington ON N8H 2P2 – 519/326-6109; Fax: 519/326-3595 – 72 beds – Adm., Jean Marie Drummond

Leamington Nursing Home, 24 Franklin Rd., Leamington ON N8H 4B7 – 519/326-3289; Fax: 519/326-0102 – 120 beds – Adm., Roxanne Belli

Leamington: Sun Parlor Home for Senior Citizens, 175 Talbot St. East, Leamington ON N8H 1L9 – 519/326-5731; Fax: 519/326-8952 – 206 beds – Adm., Karl Samuelson

Limoges: Foyer St-Viateur Nursing Home, 1003 Limoges Rd. South, Limoges ON K0A 2M0 – 613/443-5751; Fax: 613/443-5950 – 57 beds – Adm., Richard R. Marleau

Lindsay: Caressant Care Lindsay Nursing Home, 240 Mary St. West, Lindsay ON K9V 5K5 – 705/324-1913; Fax: 705/328-3283 – 60 beds – Adm., Julia Chamberlain

Lindsay: Frost Manor, 225 Mary St. West, Lindsay ON K9V 5K3 – 705/324-8333; Fax: 705/878-5840 – 62 beds – Adm., Kay Davis

Lindsay: Victoria Manor Home for the Aged, 220 Angeline St. South, Lindsay ON K9V 4R2 – 705/324-3558; Fax: 705/324-8607 – 166 beds – Adm., Alan Cavell

Lion's Head: Golden Dawn Nursing Home, 80 Main St., Lion's Head ON N0H 1W0 – 519/793-3716; Fax: 519/793-4503 – 45 beds – Adm., Frank Walker

Listowel: Caressant Care Listowel Nursing Home, 710 Reserve Ave. South, Listowel ON N4W 2L1 – 519/291-1041; Fax: 519/291-5420 – 52 beds – Adm., Eleanor MacEwen

Little Current: Manitoulin Centennial Manor, 70 Robinson St. West, PO Box 460, Little Current ON P0P 1K0 – 705/368-2710; Fax: 705/368-2694 – 60 beds – Adm., Barbara Eadie

London: Chateau Gardens (Queens) Nursing Home, 518 Queens Ave., London ON N6B 1Y7 – 519/434-2727; Fax: 519/679-3482 – 63 beds – Adm., Darlene Fitzgerald

London: Chelsey Park (Oxford) Nursing Home, 310 Oxford St. West, London ON N6H 4N6 – 519/432-1855; Fax: 519/679-7324 – 247 beds – Adm., Jane George

London: Dearness Home for Senior Citizens, 710 Southdale Rd. East, London ON N6E 1R8 – 519/681-4400; Fax: 519/681-4491 – 396 beds – Adm., Doug Goodman

London: Extendicare/London, 860 Waterloo St., London ON N6A 3W6 – 519/433-6658; Fax: 519/642-1711 – 170 beds – Adm., Marilyn Karn

London: Kensington Village, 1340 Huron St., London ON N5V 3R3 – 519/455-3910; Fax: 519/455-1570 – 108 beds – Adm., Paulette Caldwell

London: Marian Villa, 200 College Ave., London ON N6A 1Y1 – 519/646-6000; Fax: 519/646-6148 – 247 beds – Adm., Phillip Hassen

London: The McCormick Home for the Aged, 230 Victoria St., London ON N6A 2C2 – 519/432-2648; Fax: 519/645-6982 – 150 beds – Adm., Terry Guzyk

London: Meadow Park Nursing Home, 1210 Southdale Rd. East, London ON N6E 1B4 – 519/686-0484; Fax: 519/686-9932 – 122 beds – Adm., Shirley Hodgson

London: Versa-Care Elmwood Place, 46 Elmwood Pl., London ON N6J 1J2 – 519/433-7259; Fax: 519/660-4778 – 60 beds – Adm., Mary Heppelle

Long Sault: Woodland Villa, RR#1, Long Sault ON K0C 1P0 – 613/534-2276; Fax: 613/534-8559 – 111 beds – Adm., Norm Quenneville

L'Original: Pleasant Rest Nursing Home, 428 Front Rd., L'Original ON K0B 1K0 – 613/675-4617; Fax: 613/675-1373 – 60 beds – Adm., Jean-Pierre Paquette

Lucknow: Pinecrest Manor Nursing Home, 399 Bob St., Lucknow ON N0G 2H0 – 519/528-2820; Fax: 519/528-2377 – 61 beds – Adm., Brenda Koornneef

Markdale: Grey Owen Lodge, 206 Toronto St., Markdale ON N0C 1H0 – 519/986-3010; Fax: 519/986-4644 – 41 beds – Adm., John Flick

Markham: Markhaven, 54 Parkway Ave., Markham ON L3P 2G4 – 905/294-2233; Fax: 905/294-5740 – 75 beds – Adm., A. Jennings

Markham: Versa-Care Centre, Markham, 6824 Highway 7, Markham ON L6B 1A8 – 905/294-0511; Fax: 905/471-0750 – 50 beds – Adm., Brad Lawrence

Marmora: Caressant Care Marmora, 58 Bursthall St., Marmora ON K0K 2M0 – 613/472-3130; Fax: 613/472-5388 – 84 beds – Adm., Deborah J. Warren

Maryhill Extended Care Centre, 60 Church St. North, Maryhill ON N0B 2B0 – 519/648-2117; Fax: 519/648-2570 – 31 beds – Adm., Ralph Link

Matheson: The Rosedale Centre Extended Care Unit, 507 - 8th Ave., Matheson ON P0K 1N0 – 705/273-2424; Fax: 705/273-2515 – 20 beds – Adm., Leo Doiron

Mattawa: Algonquin Nursing Home, 231 Tenth St., Mattawa ON P0H 1V0 – 705/744-2202; Fax: 705/744-2787 – 72 beds – Adm., Zena Monestime

Maxville Manor, 80 Mechanic St. West, Maxville ON K0C 1T0 – 613/527-2170; Fax: 613/527-3130 – 150 beds – Exec. Dir., Craig Munro

Meaford Nursing Home, 135 William St., Meaford ON N0H 1Y0 – 519/538-1010; Fax: 519/538-5699 – 76 beds – Adm., Doris Bilitz

Merrickville: Hilltop Manor Nursing Home, 1005 St. Lawrence St., Merrickville ON K0G 1N0 – 613/269-4707; Fax: 613/269-3534 – 60 beds – Adm., Bernard Bouchard

Metcalfe: Township of Osgoode Care Centre, 7650 Snake Island Rd., Metcalfe ON K0A 2P0 – 613/821-1034; Fax: 613/821-0070 – 70 beds – Adm., Dan Ogburn

Midland: St. Andrew's Centennial Manor, 340 Dominion Ave., Midland ON L4R 4S5 – 705/526-3781; Fax: 705/526-5656 – 70 beds – Adm., Walter Ens

Midland: The Villa Care Centre, 689 Yonge St., Midland ON L4R 2E1 – 705/526-4238; Fax: 705/526-0490 – 109 beds – Adm., Olivia Rettinger

Milton: Allendale, 185 Ontario St., Milton ON L9T 2M4 – 905/878-4141; Fax: 905/878-8797 – 300 beds – Adm., M. Strecker

Milverton: Knollcrest Lodge, 50 William St., Milverton ON N0K 1M0 – 519/595-8121; Fax: 519/595-8199 – 77 beds – Adm., Susan Rae

Minden: Hyland Crest Senior Citizen's Home, PO Box 30, Minden ON K0M 2K0 – 705/286-2140; Fax: 705/286-6384 – 62 beds – Adm., Gary McKnight

Mississauga Lifecare Centre, 55 The Queensway West, Mississauga ON L5B 1B5 – 905/270-0170; Fax: 905/270-3234 – 202 beds – Adm., Beverly McPherson

Mississauga Nursing Home, 26 Peter St. North, Mississauga ON L5H 2G7 – 905/278-2213; Fax: 905/278-1311 – 55 beds – Adm., Novak Bajin

Mississauga: Chelsey Park (Streetsville) Nursing Home, 1742 Bristol Rd. West, Mississauga ON L5M 1X9 – 905/826-3045; Fax: 905/826-9978 – 118 beds – Adm., Wendy Shelley

Mississauga: Chesley Park (Mississauga) Nursing Home, 2250 Hurontario St., Mississauga ON L5B 1M8 – 905/270-0411; Fax: 905/270-1749 – 237 beds – Adm., Lloyd Smith

Mississauga: Erin Mills Lodge Nursing Home, 2132 Dundas St. West, Mississauga ON L5K 2K7 – 905/823-6700; Fax: 905/823-2410 – 84 beds – Acting Adm., Anne Helm

Mississauga: Sheridan Villa, 2460 Truscott Dr., Mississauga ON L5J 3Z8 – 905/823-1160; Fax: 905/823-7971 – 236 beds – Adm., Verena Steger

Mississauga: Tyndall Nursing Home, 1060 Eglinton Ave. East, Mississauga ON L4W 1K3 – 905/624-1511; Fax: 905/629-9346 – 151 beds – Adm., B.D. Jolly

Mitchell Nursing Home, 184 Napier St., Mitchell ON N0K 1N0 – 519/348-8861; Fax: 519/348-4214 – 48 beds – Adm., Cathy Wight

Mitchell: Ritz Lutheran Villa, RR#5, Mitchell ON N0K 1N0 – 519/348-8612; Fax: 519/348-4420 – 83 beds – Adm., Edward Radke

Mount Forest: Saugeen Valley Nursing Centre, 465 Dublin St., Mount Forest ON N0G 2L0 – 519/323-2140; Fax: 519/323-3540 – 87 beds – Adm., Harold Lebold

Mount Pleasant: Brucefield Manor Nursing Home, 612 Mount Pleasant, Mount Pleasant ON N0E 1K0 – 519/484-2500; Fax: 519/484-2590 – 59 beds – Adm., Hazel White

Napanee: Carewell Quinte Beach Nursing Home, Hwy. 2, Napanee ON K7R 3K7 – 613/396-3438; Fax: 613/396-2729 – 78 beds – Adm., Joan Watt

Napanee: Lenadco Home for the Aged, 310 Bridge St. West, Napanee ON K7R 2G4 – 613/354-3306; Fax: 613/354-7387 – 160 beds – Adm., Richard Williams

Nepean: Carleton Lodge, 55 Lodge Rd., Nepean ON K2C 3H1 – 613/825-3763; Fax: 613/825-0245 – 160 beds – Adm., H. Lokhat

Nepean: Extendicare/Starwood, 114 Starwood Rd., Nepean ON K2G 3N5 – 613/224-3960; Fax: 613/224-9309 – 192 beds – Adm., Lynda Welch

New Hamburg: Northview Nursing Home, 200 Boulee St., New Hamburg ON N0B 2G0 – 519/662-2280; Fax: 519/662-1090 – 97 beds – Adm., Ray Schlegel

Newcastle Health Care Centre, 330 King St. West, Newcastle ON L1B 1G9 – 905/987-4702; Fax: 905/987-3621 – 88 beds – Adm., Erika Bazarin

Newmarket: Arbor Living Centres, 581 Davis Dr., Newmarket ON L3Y 2P6 – 905/895-7661; Fax: 905/895-2138 – 182 beds – Adm., Helen Lockie

Newmarket: Beacon Hill Lodge Manor, 52 George St., Newmarket ON L3Y 4V3 – 905/853-3242; Fax: 905/895-5139 – 93 beds – Adm., D.K. Forese

Newmarket: Greenacres, 194 Eagle St., Newmarket ON L3Y 1J6 – 905/895-2381; Fax: 905/895-5368 – 200 beds – Acting Adm., Shawn Turner

Newmarket: Versa-Care Centre, Newmarket, 329 Eagle St., Newmarket ON L3Y 1K3 – 905/895-5187; Fax: 905/895-2645 – 70 beds – Adm., Gwen Bate

Niagara Falls: Dorchester Manor, 6350 Dorchester Rd., Niagara Falls ON L2G 5T5 – 905/356-7430; Fax: 905/356-2199 – 98 beds – Adm., A. Whalen

Niagara Falls: Oakwood Park Lodge, 6747 Oakwood Dr., Niagara Falls ON L2E 6S5 – 905/356-8732; Fax: 905/356-2122 – 153 beds – Acting Adm., Nadia Volpatti

Niagara Falls: R.H. Lawson Eventide Home, 5050 Jepson St., Niagara Falls ON L2E 1K5 – 905/356-1221; Fax: 905/356-9609 – 100 beds – Adm., Maj. Harold Rideout

Niagara Falls: Valley Park Lodge, 6400 Valley Way, Niagara Falls ON L2E 7E3 – 905/358-3277; Fax: 905/358-3012 – 65 beds – Acting Adm., Cindy Vetrone

Niagara-on-the-Lake: Chateau Gardens (Niagara) Nursing Home, 120 Wellington St., Niagara-on-the-Lake ON L0S 1J0 – 905/468-2111; Fax: 905/468-4463 – 124 beds – Adm., Susan Norton

Niagara-on-the-Lake: Upper Canada Lodge, 272 Wellington St., Niagara-on-the-Lake ON L0S 1J0 – 905/468-4208; Fax: 905/468-0520 – 80 beds – Acting Adm., Angela Whalen

Nipigon District Memorial Hospital, see General Hospitals listings

North Bay: Cassellholme, 400 Olive St., North Bay ON P1B 6J4 – 705/474-4250; Fax: 705/474-6129 – 240 beds – Adm., Gordon Shields

North Bay: Leisure World North Bay Centre, 401 William St., North Bay ON P1A 1X5 – 705/476-2602; Fax: 705/476-1624 – 148 beds – Adm., Brenda Prieur

Northbrook: Pine Meadow Nursing Home, Lloyd St., PO Box 100, Northbrook ON K0H 2G0 – 613/336-9120; Fax: 613/336-9144 – 60 beds – Adm., Colleen M. Haley-Wicklam

Norwich: Norvilla Nursing Home, 11 Elgin St. East, Norwich ON N0J 1P0 – 519/863-2717 – 40 beds – Adm., Maureen Sinden

Norwood: Pleasant Meadow Manor, 105 Alma St., Norwood ON K0L 2V0 – 705/639-5308; Fax: 705/639-5309 – 60 beds – Adm., Jane Adams-Taylor

Oakville Lifecare Centre, 599 Lyons Lane, Oakville ON L6J 2Y2 – 905/845-9933; Fax: 905/845-9950 – 205 beds – Adm., Stephen Picott

Ohsweken: Iroquois Lodge Nursing Home, Chiefswood Rd., Ohsweken ON N0A 1M0 – 519/445-2224; Fax: 519/445-4180 – 50 beds – Adm., Belva M. Monture

Orangeville: Avalon Care Centre & Retirement Lodge, 355 Broadway Ave., Orangeville ON L9W 3Y3 – 519/941-5161; Fax: 519/941-9532 – 137 beds – Adm., David K. Holwell

Orillia: Al-Mar Nursing Home, 327 Muskoka Rd., Orillia ON L3V 4G5 – 705/326-6038; Fax: 705/327-5373 – 38 beds – Adm., Jacqueline Payne

Orillia: Hillcrest Lodge, 86 Cedar St., Orillia ON L3V 2V5 – 705/326-3181; Fax: 705/326-7867 – 48 beds – Adm., Sharon Turner

Orillia: Sunset Lodge (Salvation Army), 127 Peter St. North, Orillia ON L3V 4Z4 – 705/325-5715; Fax: 705/329-0860 – 31 beds – Adm., Maj. N. Janes

Orillia: Trillium Manor for the Aged, 12 Grace Ave., Orillia ON L3V 2K2 – 705/325-1504; Fax: 705/325-7661 – 74 beds – Adm., Sharon Turner

Orillia: Versa-Care Centre, Orillia, 291 Mississauga St. West, Orillia ON L3V 3B9 – 705/325-2289; Fax: 705/325-7178 – 94 beds – Adm., Mary Bullock

Orleans: Madonna Nursing Home, 1533 St. Joseph Blvd., Orleans ON K1C 1S9 – 613/824-2040; Fax: 613/824-5151 – 75 beds – Adm., Jacques Lemieux

Oshawa: Extendicare/Oshawa, 82 Park Rd. North, Oshawa ON L1J 4L1 – 905/579-0011; Fax: 905/579-1733 – 175 beds – Adm., Linda Grills

Oshawa: Hillsdale Manor, 600 Oshawa Blvd. North, Oshawa ON L1G 5T9 – 905/579-1777; Fax: 905/579-3911 – 446 beds – Adm., Fred Fountain

Oshawa: Versa-Care Centre, Oshawa, 186 Thornton Rd. South, Oshawa ON L1J 5Y2 – 905/576-5181; Fax: 905/576-0078 – 104 beds – Adm., Arlene Inkster

Ottawa: Beacon Hill Lodge, 2330 Carling Ave., Ottawa ON K2B 7H1 – 613/820-9328; Fax: 613/820-9774 – 326 beds – Adm., Chris Sandes

Ottawa: Extendicare/Medex, 1865 Baseline Rd., Ottawa ON K2C 3K6 – 613/225-5650; Fax: 613/225-0980 – 193 beds – Adm., Maureen Dillon

Ottawa: Extendicare/New Orchard Lodge, 99 New Orchard Ave., Ottawa ON K2B 5E6 – 613/820-2110; Fax: 613/820-6380 – 104 beds – Adm., Susan Reed

Ottawa: Extendicare/West End Villa, 2179 Elmira Dr., Ottawa ON K2C 3S1 – 613/829-3501; Fax: 613/829-3504 – 240 beds – Adm., Helen Pinel

Ottawa: Glebe Centre, 950 Bank St., Ottawa ON K1S 5G6 – 613/238-2727; Fax: 613/238-4643 – 195 beds – Adm., Susan Leconte

Ottawa: Hillel Lodge, 125 Wurtemburg St., Ottawa ON K1N 8L9 – 613/789-7132; Fax: 613/789-1371 – 48 beds – Adm., Stephen Schneiderman

Ottawa: Island Lodge, 1 Porter's Island, Ottawa ON K1N 5M2 – 613/789-5100; Fax: 613/789-3704 – 409 beds – Adm., J. Chene

Ottawa: Maycourt Convalescent Home, 114 Cameron Ave., Ottawa ON K1S 0X1 – 613/733-0760; Fax: 613/730-7903 – 50 beds – Adm., M. Wilson

Ottawa: St. Patrick's Home, 2865 Riverside Dr., Ottawa ON K1V 8N5 – 613/731-4660; Fax: 613/731-4056 – 202 beds – Adm., Sr. Mona Martin

Ottawa: Villa Marguerite, 75 Bruyere St., Ottawa ON K1N 5C8 – 613/562-6369; Fax: 613/562-6367 – 71 beds – Adm., Sr. Diane Albert

Owen Sound: Lee Manor, 875 Sixth St. East, Owen Sound ON N4K 5W5 – 519/376-4420; Fax: 519/371-5406 – 150 beds – Adm., Al Wood

Owen Sound: Lutheran Nursing Home, 1029 - 4th Ave. West, Owen Sound ON N4K 4W1 – 519/376-2522; Fax: 519/371-3304 – 29 beds – Adm., Rev. Sylvia Statham

Owen Sound: Versa-Care Georgian Heights, 1115 - 10th St. East, Owen Sound ON N4K 6B1 – 519/371-1441; Fax: 519/371-1092 – 40 beds – Adm., Catherine Hollister

Owen Sound: Versa-Care Summit Place, 850 - 4th St. East, Owen Sound ON N4K 6A3 – 519/376-3212; Fax: 519/371-0923 – 119 beds – Adm., Nan Dunbar

Palmerston: Royal Terrace, 600 Whites Rd., Palmerston ON N0G 2P0 – 519/343-2611; Fax: 519/343-2860 – 67 beds – Adm., P.K. Ramchandani

Paris: Park Lane Terrace, 295 Grand River St. North, Paris ON N3L 2N9 – 519/442-2753; Fax: 519/442-3696 – 60 beds – Adm., Beth South

Paris: Versa-Care Telfer Place, 245 Grand River St. North, Paris ON N3L 3G2 – 519/442-4411; Fax: 519/442-6724 – 45 beds – Adm., Susan Aubin

Parkhill: Chateau Gardens (Parkhill) Nursing Home, 250 Tain St., Parkhill ON N0M 2K0 – 519/294-6342; Fax: 519/294-0107 – 59 beds – Adm., Donna Letts

Parry Sound: Belvedere Heights, 21 Belvedere Ave., Parry Sound ON P2A 2A2 – 705/746-9367; Fax: 705/746-7706 – 101 beds – Adm., Jack Agema

Pembroke: Marianhill, 600 Cecelia St., Pembroke ON K8A 7Z3 – 613/735-6838; Fax: 613/732-3934 – 131 beds – Adm., Kelly Isfan

Pembroke: Miramichi Lodge, 400 Bell St., Pembroke ON K8A 2K5 – 613/735-0175; Fax: 613/735-8061 – 186 beds – Adm., Brian Burbridge

Penetanguishene: Georgian Manor, 7 Harriett St., Penetanguishene ON L0K 1P0 – 705/549-3166; Fax: 705/549-6062 – 107 beds – Adm., Robert Morton

Perth: Lanark Lodge, RR#4, Perth ON K7H 3C6 – 613/267-4225; Fax: 613/264-2668 – 164 beds – Adm., Peter Bennett

Perth: Tayview Nursing Home, 55 Sunset Blvd., Perth ON K7H 3C6 – 613/267-2506; Fax: 613/267-7060 – 93 beds – Adm., Joyce Firlotte

Peterborough: Anson House, 136 Anson St., Peterborough ON K9H 5R1 – 705/743-3172; Fax: 705/743-9028 – 42 beds – Adm., Kevin Murphy

Peterborough: Extendicare/Peterborough, 80 Alexander Ave., Peterborough ON K9J 6B4 – 705/743-7552; Fax: 705/742-9664 – 212 beds – Adm., Margaret Lazure

Peterborough: Fairhaven Home, 131 Langton St., Peterborough ON K9H 6K3 – 705/743-4265; Fax: 705/743-6292 – 253 beds – Adm., Patricia Knapp

Peterborough: Marycrest Home for the Aged, 200 St. Luke's Ave., Peterborough ON K9H 1E7 – 705/743-

Canadian Almanac & Directory 1997

4744; Fax: 705/743-7532 – 156 beds – Adm., Sr. Jacqueline Janisse

Peterborough: Riverview Manor Nursing Home, 1155 Water St., Peterborough ON K9H 3P8 – 705/748-6706; Fax: 705/742-9197 – 124 beds – Adm., Barbara Payne

Peterborough: Springdale Country Manor, 1726 Hwy. 7A, RR#5, Peterborough ON K9J 6X6 – 705/742-8811; Fax: 705/742-8812 – 65 beds – Adm., Jane Adams-Taylor

Petrolia: Fiddick's Nursing Home, 437 First Ave., Petrolia ON N0N 1R0 – 519/882-0370; Fax: 519/882-0375 – 60 beds – Adm., Michael Fiddick

Petrolia: Lambton Meadowview Villa, RR#4, Petrolia ON N0N 1R0 – 519/882-1470; Fax: 519/882-3600 – 125 beds – Adm., Doug Hutton

Pickering: Community Nursing Home, 1955 Valley Farm Rd., Pickering ON L1V 1X6 – 905/831-2522; Fax: 905/420-6030 – 169 beds – Adm., Douglas Pember

Picton: Carewell Kentwood Nursing Home, 2 Ontario St., Picton ON K0K 2T0 – 613/476-5671; Fax: 613/476-3986 – 48 beds – Adm., Norma Bongard

Picton: Carewell Picton Manor Nursing Home, 9 Hill St., Picton ON K0K 2T0 – 613/476-6140; Fax: 613/476-5240 – 78 beds – Adm., Norma Bongard

Picton: Carewell West Lake Nursing Home, West Lake Rd., Picton ON K0K 2T0 – 613/393-2055; Fax: 613/393-2057 – 47 beds – Adm., Joan Watt

Picton: McFarland (H.J.) Memorial Home, RR#2, Picton ON K0K 2T0 – 613/476-2138; Fax: 613/476-8356 – 84 beds – Adm., E. Gervais

Picton: Versa-Care Hallowell House, RR#1, Picton ON K0K 2T0 – 613/476-4444; Fax: 613/476-1566 – 101 beds – Adm., Janice Wilkes

Plantagenet: Pinecrest Nursing Home, 101 Parent St., RR#1, Plantagenet ON K0B 1L0 – 613/673-4835; Fax: 613/673-2675 – 60 beds – Adm., Lyne Simoneau

Port Colborne: Northland Manor, 485 Northland Ave., Port Colborne ON L3K 4B3 – 905/835-2463; Fax: 905/835-6518 – 87 beds – Adm., Larry Jackson

Port Dover: Versa-Care Centre, Port Dover, 501 St. George St., Port Dover ON N0A 1N0 – 519/583-1422; Fax: 519/583-3197 – 70 beds – Adm., Ellen Coffey

Port Hope: Community Nursing Home, 20 Hope St. South, Port Hope ON L1A 2M8 – 905/885-6367; Fax: 905/885-6368 – 97 beds – Adm., Douglas Palmer

Port Hope: Regency Manor Nursing Home, 66 Dorset St. East, Port Hope ON L1A 1E3 – 905/885-4558; Fax: 905/885-7386 – 50 beds – Adm., Cynthia Knight-Pocock

Port Perry: Community Nursing Home, 15941 Simcoe St. North, Port Perry ON L9L 1A6 – 905/985-3205; Fax: 905/985-3721 – 75 beds – Adm., Edna Goss

Port Stanley: Extendicare/Port Stanley, 288 East St., Port Stanley ON N5L 1J6 – 519/782-3339; Fax: 519/782-4756 – 60 beds – Adm., Charles Marczinski

Powassan: Eastholme, 200 Big Bend Ave., Powassan ON P0H 1Z0 – 705/724-2005; Fax: 705/724-5429 – 74 beds – Adm., Steven Piekarski

Prescott: Wellington House Nursing Home, 970 Edward St. North, PO Box 401, Prescott ON K0E 1T0 – 613/925-2834; Fax: 613/925-5425 – 60 beds – Adm., Bernadette Timco

Puslinch: Morriston Park Nursing Home, RR#2, Puslinch ON N0B 2J0 – 519/822-9179; Fax: 519/822-4459 – 28 beds – Adm., Alfred Urfey

Renfrew: Bonnechere Manor, 782 Raglan St. South, Renfrew ON K7V 4A5 – 613/432-4873; Fax: 613/432-7138 – 185 beds – Adm., Brian Burbridge

Renfrew: Groves Park Lodge, 470 Raglan St. North, Renfrew ON K7V 1P5 – 613/432-5823; Fax: 613/432-5287 – 75 beds – Asst. Adm., Carol Haywood

Richmond Hill: Mariann Home, 9915 Yonge St., Richmond Hill ON L4C 1V1 – 905/884-9276; Fax: 905/884-1800 – 52 beds – Adm., Sr. Mary Verhoeven

Ridgetown: Versa-Care Village, Ridgetown, 9 Myrtle St., Ridgetown ON N0P 2C0 – 519/674-5427; Fax: 519/674-2422 – 40 beds – Adm., Kathy Morningstar

Rockland: St. Joseph Nursing Home, 1615 Laurier St., Rockland ON K4K 1C8 – 613/446-5126; Fax: 613/446-1516 – 81 beds – Adm., Jacqueline Brown

St Catharines: Extendicare/St. Catharines, 283 Pelham Rd., St Catharines ON L2S 1X7 – 905/688-3311; Fax: 905/688-5774 – 152 beds – Adm., Mary Britt

St Catharines: Heidehof, 600 Lake St., St Catharines ON L2N 4J4 – 905/935-3344; Fax: 905/935-0081 – 106 beds – Adm., Gordon Midgley

St Catharines: Ina Grafton-Gage Home (Niagara), 413 Linwell Rd., St Catharines ON L2M 2P3 – 905/935-6822; Fax: 905/935-6847 – 40 beds – Adm., D. Caughey

St Catharines: Linhaven, 403 Ontario St., St Catharines ON L2N 1L5 – 905/934-3364; Fax: 905/934-6975 – 226 beds – Adm., Dan Oettinger

St Catharines: Tabor Manor, 1 Tabor Dr., St Catharines ON L2N 1V9 – 905/934-2548; Fax: 905/934-6467 – 80 beds – Adm., Rudy Siemens

St Catharines: Tufford Nursing Home, 312 Queenston Rd., St Catharines ON L2P 2X4 – 905/682-0503; Fax: 905/682-2770 – 64 beds – Adm., Cecilia Osczypko

St Catharines: Versa-Care Centre, St. Catharines, 168 Scott St., St Catharines ON L2N 1H2 – 905/934-3321; Fax: 905/934-9011 – 200 beds – Adm., Sandra Fredericks

St Catharines: West Park Health Centre, 103 Pelham Rd., St Catharines ON L2S 1S9 – 905/688-1031; Fax: 905/688-9646 – 122 beds – Adm., Michael Walter

St Jacobs: Derbecker's Heritage House, 54 Eby St., St Jacobs ON N0B 2N0 – 519/664-2921; Fax: 519/664-2380 – 72 beds – Adm., Pamela Derbecker

St Marys: Kingsway Lodge Nursing Home, 310 Queen St. East, St Marys ON N0M 2V0 – 519/284-2921; Fax: 519/284-4468 – 35 beds – Adm., Scott A. Mackay

St Marys: Wildwood Care Centre, 100 Ann St., St Marys ON N4X 1A1 – 519/284-3628; Fax: 519/284-0575 – 60 beds – Adm., Lynn Walsh

St Thomas: Caressant Care St. Thomas Nursing Home, 15 Bonnie Pl., St Thomas ON N5R 5T8 – 519/633-6493; Fax: 519/633-9329 – 116 beds – Adm., Marlene Powner

St Thomas: Elgin Manor, RR#1, St Thomas ON N5P 3S5 – 519/631-0620; Fax: 519/633-0475 – 109 beds – Adm., Fred Boyes

St Thomas: Rest Haven Nursing Home, 4 May Bucke St., St Thomas ON N5R 5J6 – 519/633-3164; Fax: 519/631-8362 – 60 beds – Adm., Ann Stansell

St Thomas: Valleyview Home for the Aged, 29 Elysian St., St Thomas ON N5P 1R5 – 519/633-1030; Fax: 519/633-7295 – 136 beds – Adm., Bob Holt

Sarnia: Marshall Gowland Manor, 1000 London Rd., Sarnia ON N7S 1N7 – 519/336-3720; Fax: 519/336-3734 – 126 beds – Acting Adm., Vicki Lucas

Sarnia: Trillium Villa Nursing Home, 1221 Michigan Ave., Sarnia ON N7S 3Y3 – 519/542-5520; Fax: 519/542-5953 – 152 beds – Adm., Jean Kimmerly

Sarnia: Versa-Care Centre, Sarnia, 1464 Blackwell Rd., Sarnia ON N7S 5M4 – 519/542-3421; Fax: 519/542-3604 – 100 beds – Acting Adm., Ann Currie

Sarnia: Vision Nursing Home, 229 Wellington St., Sarnia ON N7T 1G9 – 519/336-6551; Fax: 519/336-5878 – 60 beds – Adm., Bernard Bax

Sarsfield Nursing Home, 2861 Colonial Rd., Sarsfield ON K0A 3E0 – 613/835-2977; Fax: 613/835-2982 – 46 beds – Adm., Richard R. Marleau

Sault Ste Marie: Extendicare/Tendercare, 770 Great Northern Rd., Sault Ste Marie ON P6A 5K7 – 705/949-3611; Fax: 705/945-6303 – 119 beds – Adm., Laureanne Ryan

Sault Ste Marie: Extendicare/Van Daele, 39 Van Daele St., Sault Ste Marie ON P6B 4V3 – 705/949-7934; Fax: 705/945-0968 – 149 beds – Adm., Bill Lonergan

Sault Ste Marie: F.J. Davey Home, 860 Great Northern Rd., Sault Ste Marie ON P6A 5K7 – 705/942-2204; Fax: 705/942-2234 – 198 beds – Adm., Peter MacLean

Sault Ste Marie: Mauno Kaihla Koti, 725 North St., Sault Ste Marie ON P6B 5Z3 – 705/945-9987; Fax: 705/945-1217 – 60 beds – Exec. Dir., Lewis Massad

Seaforth Manor, 100 James St., Seaforth ON N0K 1W0 – 519/527-0030; Fax: 519/527-2862 – 63 beds – Adm., Ruth Hilderbrand

Selby: The Village Green Nursing Home, PO Box 94, Selby ON K0K 2Z0 – 613/388-2693; Fax: 613/388-2694 – 66 beds – Adm., Linda Pierce

Shelburne Residence, 200 Robert St., Shelburne ON L0N 1S0 – 519/925-3746; Fax: 519/925-1476 – 60 beds – Adm., Colin McDavid

Shelburne: Dufferin Oaks, 151 Centre St., Shelburne ON L0N 1S4 – 519/925-2140; Fax: 519/925-5067 – 165 beds – Adm., Melvin H. Lloyd

Simcoe: Cedarwood Village, 500 Queensway West, Simcoe ON N3Y 4R5 – 519/426-8305; Fax: 519/426-2511 – 90 beds – Adm., Marlene Vanham

Simcoe: The Norfolk Hospital Nursing Home, 365 West St., Simcoe ON N3Y 1T7 – 519/426-0750; Fax: 519/426-3326 – 80 beds – Adm., Harold Shantz

Simcoe: Norview Lodge, 510 Queensway West, PO Box 604, Simcoe ON N3Y 4L8 – 519/426-0902; Fax: 519/426-9867 – 186 beds – Adm., Kim Cleaver

Sioux Lookout: William A. (Bill) George Extended Care, 55 Fifth Ave., Sioux Lookout ON P0V 2T0 – 807/737-3700; Fax: 807/737-3454 – 20 beds – CEO, Mark Balcaen

Smiths Falls: Broadview Nursing Home, 210 Brockville St., Smiths Falls ON K7A 3Z4 – 613/283-1845; Fax: 613/283-7073 – 75 beds – Adm., Leonard Parsons

Smooth Rock Falls Hospital, see General Hospitals listings

Southampton Nursing Home, 140 Grey St., Southampton ON N0H 2L0 – 519/797-3220; Fax: 519/797-5487 – 84 beds – Adm., Carol Warner

Stayner Nursing Home, 244 Main St., Stayner ON L0M 1S0 – 705/428-3614; Fax: 705/428-0537 – 49 beds – Adm., Lorraine Baker

Stayner: Sweetbriar Lodge Nursing Home, RR#2, Stayner ON L0M 1S0 – 705/428-3613; Fax: 705/428-3311 – 50 beds – Adm., Nancy Archdekin

Stirling Manor Nursing Home, 218 Edward St., Stirling ON K0K 3E0 – 613/395-2596; Fax: 613/395-0930 – 75 beds – Adm., Judy Norlock

Stoney Creek Lifecare Centre, 199 Glover Rd., Stoney Creek ON L8E 5P9 – 905/643-1795; Fax: 905/643-1085 – 45 beds – Adm., Anne Fear

Stoney Creek: Clarion Nursing Home, 337 Hwy. 8, Stoney Creek ON L8G 1E7 – 905/664-2281; Fax: 905/664-2966 – 100 beds – Adm., Michael Janjic

Stoney Creek: Heritage Green Nursing Home, 353 Isaac Brock Dr., Stoney Creek ON L8J 1Y1 – 905/573-7177; Fax: 905/573-7151 – 87 beds – Adm., Kenneth D. Reimche

Stoney Creek: Pine Villa Nursing Home, 490 Hwy. 8, Stoney Creek ON L8G 1G6 – 905/662-5033; Fax: 905/662-6336 – 38 beds – Adm., Augustus Thomas

Stouffville: Green Gables Manor Nursing Home, 9th Line Rd., RR#2, Stouffville ON L4A 7X3 – 905/640-1310; Fax: 905/640-2231 – 37 beds – Adm., Kathleen Szela

Stouffville: Parkview Home, 481 Rupert Ave., Stouffville ON L4A 1T7 – 905/640-1911; Fax: 905/640-4051 – 109 beds – Adm., Wallace Kribs

Stratford: Greenwood Court, 90 Greenwood Ct., Stratford ON N5A 7W5 – 519/273-4662 – 45 beds – Adm., Victoria Stuart

Stratford: People Care Centre, 198 Mornington St., Stratford ON N5A 5G3 – 519/271-4440; Fax: 519/271-4446 – 60 beds – Adm., Pat Kelly

Stratford: Spruce Lodge, 643 West Gore St., Stratford ON N5A 1L4 – 519/271-4090; Fax: 519/271-5862 – 151 beds – Adm., Marilyn Herman

Stratford: Versa-Care Centre, Stratford, RR#5, Stratford ON N5A 6S6 – 519/393-5132; Fax: 519/393-5130 – 90 beds – Adm., Deanne Roussell

Strathroy: Sprucedale Care Centre, 150 Fraser St., Strathroy ON N7G 4C3 – 519/245-2808; Fax: 519/245-1767 – 62 beds – Adm., Darren Micallef

Strathroy: Strathmere Lodge, Albert St. West, Strathroy ON N7G 3J3 – 519/245-2520; Fax: 519/245-5711 – 220 beds – Adm., Larry Hills

Sturgeon Falls: Au Chateau, 106 Michaud St., Sturgeon Falls ON P0H 2G0 – 705/753-1550; Fax: 705/753-3135 – 50 beds – Adm., Wayne Foisy

Sudbury: Extendicare/Falconbridge, 281 Falconbridge Rd., Sudbury ON P3A 5K4 – 705/566-7980; Fax: 705/566-3300 – 234 beds – Adm., Dennis L. Boschetto

Sudbury: Extendicare/York, 333 York St., Sudbury ON P3E 5J3 – 705/674-4221; Fax: 705/674-4281 – 288 beds – Adm., Walter Squazzin

Sudbury: Pioneer Manor, 960 Notre Dame Ave., Sudbury ON P3A 2T4 – 705/566-4270; Fax: 705/524-1767 – 349 beds – Adm., Catherine Sandblom

Sutton West: River Glen Haven Nursing Home, 160 High St., Sutton West ON L0E 1R0 – 905/722-3631; Fax: 905/722-8638 – 119 beds – Adm., Susan Williams

Tavistock: Bonnie Brae Health Care Centre, 55 Woodstock St. North, Tavistock ON N0B 2R0 – 519/655-2420; Fax: 519/655-3432 – 80 beds – Adm., Joyce Penney

Tavistock: The Maples Home for Seniors, 94 William St. South, Tavistock ON N0B 2R0 – 519/655-2344; Fax: 519/655-2851 – 43 beds – Adm., Lois Riehl

Tavistock: People Care Tavistock, 28 William St. North, Tavistock ON N0B 2R0 – 519/655-2031; Fax: 519/655-3583 – 100 beds – Adm., O'Derald Gingerich

Tecumseh Health Care Centre, 1400 Banwell Rd., Tecumseh ON N8N 2M4 – 519/735-3204; Fax: 519/735-1836 – 142 beds – Adm., Patricia Pacuta

Tecumseh: Brouillette Manor Nursing Home, 11900 Brouillette Ct., Tecumseh ON N8N 1S3 – 519/735-9810; Fax: 519/735-8569 – 60 beds – Adm., Donald Hewitt

Terrace Bay: Birchwood Terrace, Hwy. 17, PO Box 250, Terrace Bay ON P0T 2W0 – 807/825-3748; Fax: 807/825-3859 – 23 beds – Adm., Michael Yakamovich

Thessalon: Algoma Manor, 1 Owen St., Thessalon ON P0R 1L0 – 705/842-2840; Fax: 705/842-2650 – 148 beds – Adm., Peter MacLean

Thornbury: Erringrung Nursing Home, 67 Bruce St., Thornbury ON N0H 2P0 – 519/599-2737; Fax: 519/599-3410 – 42 beds – Adm., Jeanne Lune

Thunder Bay: Beacon Hill Lodge, 135 South Vickers St., Thunder Bay ON P7E 1J2 – 807/623-9511; Fax: 807/623-6992 – 161 beds – Adm., Gail Henry

Thunder Bay: Bethammi Nursing Home, 63 Carrie St., Thunder Bay ON P7A 4J2 – 807/767-6263; Fax: 807/767-1672 – 109 beds – Adm., Sr. Bonnie A. MacLellan

Thunder Bay: Central Park Lodge, 315 South Syndicate Ave., Thunder Bay ON P7E 1E2 – 807/623-6919; Fax: 807/623-8499 – 107 beds – Adm., Valerie Gosse

Thunder Bay: Dawson Court, 523 North Algoma St., Thunder Bay ON P7A 5C2 – 807/625-2926; Fax: 807/345-8854 – 150 beds – Adm., Mike Kennedy

Thunder Bay: Grandview Lodge/Thunder Bay, 200 Lillie St., Thunder Bay ON P7E 2V6 – 807/625-2923; Fax: 807/623-4075 – 150 beds – Adm., Donald Holmstrom

Thunder Bay: Pinewood Court, 445 James St. South, Thunder Bay ON P7E 2V6 – 807/577-1127; Fax: 807/475-9455 – 75 beds – Adm., Michael Yakamovich

Thunder Bay: Pioneer Ridge, 750 Tungsten St., Thunder Bay ON P7B 6R1 – 807/346-3910; Fax: 807/346-3916 – 150 beds – Adm., Joyce Green

Tilbury Manor Nursing Home, 16 Fort St., Tilbury ON N0P 2L0 – 519/682-0243; Fax: 519/682-2358 – 85 beds – Adm., Gwen Waddick

Tillsonburg: Maple Manor Nursing Home, 73 Bidwell St., Tillsonburg ON N4G 3T8 – 519/842-3563; Fax: 519/842-4901 – 101 beds – Adm., George Kanuik

Timmins: Extendicare/Timmins, 15 Hollinger Lane, Timmins ON P0N 1G0 – 705/360-1913; Fax: 705/268-3975 – 119 beds – Adm., Nicole Cyr

Timmins: Golden Manor, 481 Melrose Blvd., Timmins ON P4N 5H3 – 705/264-5375; Fax: 705/267-4662 – 177 beds – Adm., Heather Bozzer

Toronto: Albion Lodge, 111 Kendleton Dr., Etobicoke ON M9V 1V2 – 416/392-2349; Fax: 416/392-4528 – 98 beds – Adm., Wayne Potty

Toronto: Altamont Nursing Home, 92 Island Rd., Scarborough ON M1C 2P5 – 416/284-4781; Fax: 416/284-3634 – 159 beds – Adm., Gladys Brett

Toronto: Barton Place Nursing Home, 914 Bathurst St., Toronto ON M5R 3G5 – 416/533-9473; Fax: 416/538-2685 – 254 beds – Adm., Derrick Hoare

Toronto: Baycrest Centre for Geriatric Care, see General Hospitals listings

Toronto: Belmont House, 55 Belmont St., Toronto ON M5R 1R1 – 416/964-9231; Fax: 416/964-1448 – 315 beds – Adm., M.J. Large

Toronto: Bendale Acres, 2920 Lawrence Ave. East, Scarborough ON M1P 2T8 – 416/397-7000; Fax: 416/397-7067 – 300 beds – Adm., Shirley Barnes

Toronto: Cana Place St. Paul's l'Amoreaux Centre, 3333 Finch Ave. East, Scarborough ON M1W 2R9 – 416/497-4770; Fax: 416/497-9069 – 50 beds – Adm., David Rudy

Toronto: Carefree Lodge, 306 Finch Ave. East, North York ON M2N 4S5 – 416/397-1500; Fax: 416/397-1501 – 127 beds – Adm., Vilma Kalu

Toronto: Casa Verde Health Centre, 3595 Keele St., North York ON M3J 1M7 – 416/633-3431; Fax: 416/633-6736 – 231 beds – Adm., Karen Kapadia

Toronto: Castleview Wychwood Towers, 351 Christie St., Toronto ON M6G 2C3 – 416/392-5700; Fax: 416/392-4157 – 437 beds – Adm., Cathy Renwick

Toronto: Central Park Lodge, 1145 Albion Rd., Etobicoke ON M9V 4J7 – 416/745-4800; Fax: 416/745-0445 – 290 beds – Adm., Tamara Christie

Toronto: Cheltenham Nursing Home, 5935 Bathurst St., North York ON M2R 1Y8 – 416/223-4050; Fax: 416/223-4159 – 170 beds – Adm., Joan O'Brien

Toronto: Chester Village, 717 Broadview Ave., Toronto ON M4K 2P5 – 416/466-2173; Fax: 416/466-6781 – 174 beds – Adm., Paul Klamer

Toronto: Chinese Community Nursing Home for Greater Toronto, 2311 McNicoll Ave., Scarborough ON M1V 5L3 – 416/321-6333; Fax: 416/321-6313 – 90 beds – Adm., Florence Wong

Toronto: Christie Gardens, 600 Melita Cres., Toronto ON M6G 3Z4 – 416/530-1330; Fax: 416/530-1686 – 88 beds – Adm., Catherine Belmore

Toronto: Copernicus Lodge, 66 Roncesvalles Ave., Toronto ON M6R 3A7 – 416/536-7122; Fax: 416/536-8242 – 108 beds – Adm., Barbara Nytko

Toronto: Craiglee Nursing Home, 102 Craiglee Dr., Scarborough ON M1N 2M7 – 416/264-2260; Fax: 416/267-8176 – 94 beds – Adm., Doris McDougall

Toronto: Cummer Lodge, 205 Cummer Ave., North York ON M2M 2E8 – 416/392-9500; Fax: 416/392-9499 – 414 beds – Adm., Leah Walters

Toronto: Dom Lipa Nursing Home, 52 Neilson Dr., Etobicoke ON M9C 1V7 – 416/621-3820; Fax: 416/621-9773 – 30 beds – Adm., Patricia King

Toronto: Drs. Paul & John Rekai Centre, 345 Sherbourne St., Toronto ON M5A 2S3 – 416/964-1599; Fax: 416/964-3907 – 126 beds – Adm., Mary Hoare

Toronto: Ehatare Nursing Home, 40 Old Kingston Rd., Scarborough ON M1E 3J5 – 416/284-0828; Fax: 416/284-4595 – 32 beds – Adm., Marika Boujoff

Toronto: Extendicare/Bayview, 550 Cummer Ave., North York ON M2K 2M2 – 416/226-1331; Fax: 416/226-2745 – 205 beds – Adm., Susan Schendel

Toronto: Extendicare/Guildwood, 60 Guildwood Pkwy., Scarborough ON M1G 1R6 – 416/266-7711; Fax: 416/269-5123 – 169 beds – Adm., Kathy Suma

Toronto: Extendicare/North York, 1925 Steeles Ave. East, North York ON M2H 2H3 – 416/493-4666; Fax: 416/493-4886 – 288 beds – Adm., Sheilagh Tasson

Toronto: Extendicare/Scarborough, 3830 Lawrence Ave. East, Scarborough ON M1G 1R6 – 416/439-1243; Fax: 416/439-4818 – 154 beds – Adm., Chris Robinson

Toronto: Fairview Nursing Home, 14 Cross St., Toronto ON M6J 1S8 – 416/534-8820; Fax: 416/538-1658 – 108 beds – Adm., Herbert Chambers

Toronto: Fudger House, 439 Sherbourne St., Toronto ON M4X 1K6 – 416/392-5252; Fax: 416/392-4174 – 250 beds – Adm., Anne Evans

Toronto: Garden Court Nursing Home, 1 Sand Beach Rd., Etobicoke ON M8V 2W2 – 416/259-6172; Fax: 416/259-7925 – 45 beds – Adm., Dean Davey

Toronto: Harold & Grace Baker Centre, 1 Northwestern Ave., Toronto ON M6M 2J7 – 416/654-2889; Fax: 416/654-0217 – 120 beds – Adm., Richard Mirabelli

Toronto: Hellenic Care for Seniors, 215 Tyrrel Ave., Toronto ON M6G 4A9 – 416/654-3904; Fax: 416/654-4988 – 78 beds – Adm., Vania Sakelaris

Toronto: The Heritage Nursing Home, 1195 Queen St. East, Toronto ON M4M 1L6 – 416/461-8185; Fax: 416/461-5472 – 201 beds – Adm., Melba Graham

Toronto: Highbourne Lifecare Centre, 420 The East Mall, Etobicoke ON M9B 3Z9 – 416/621-8000; Fax: 416/621-0671 – 257 beds – Adm., Evelyn MacDonald

Toronto: Ina Grafton-Gage Home (Toronto), 2 O'Connor Dr., Toronto ON M4K 2K1 – 416/422-4891; Fax: 416/422-1613 – 110 beds – Adm., Gordon Blowes

Toronto: Ivan Franko Home (Etobicoke), 767 Royal York Rd., Etobicoke ON M8Y 2T3 – 416/239-7364; Fax: 416/239-5102 – 85 beds – Adm., Maria Kiebalo

Toronto: Kennedy Lodge Nursing Home, 1400 Kennedy Rd., Scarborough ON M1P 2L7 – 416/752-8282; Fax: 416/752-0645 – 289 beds – Adm., Ginnette Taylor

Toronto: Kipling Acres, 2233 Kipling Ave., Etobicoke ON M9W 4L3 – 416/392-2300; Fax: 416/392-3360 – 335 beds – Adm., Brock Hall

Toronto: Lakeshore Lodge, 3197 Lakeshore Blvd. West, Etobicoke ON M8V 3X5 – 416/392-9400; Fax: 416/392-9401 – 150 beds – Adm., Lorraine Siu

Toronto: The Laughlen Centre, 110 Edward St., Toronto ON M5G 2A5 – 416/597-0373; Fax: 416/597-8234 – 215 beds – Adm., Anne Hayes

Toronto: Leisure World St. George Centre, 225 St. George St., Toronto ON M5R 2M2 – 416/967-3985; Fax: 416/967-3951 – 238 beds – Adm., Patrick Brown

Toronto: Leisure World Scarborough Centre, 130 Midland Ave., Scarborough ON M1N 4B2 – 416/264-2301; Fax: 416/264-3704 – 302 beds – Adm., Sharon Steele

Toronto: Lincoln Place Nursing Home, 429 Walmer Rd., Toronto ON M5P 2X9 – 416/967-6949; Fax: 416/928-1965 – 260 beds – Adm., Tulia Ferreira

Toronto: Maynard Nursing Home, 28 Halton St., Toronto ON M6J 1R3 – 416/533-5198; Fax: 416/533-3492 – 77 beds – Adm., Alan Bowman

Toronto: Metro Toronto Legion Village, 59 Lawson Rd., West Hill ON M1C 2J1 – 416/284-9235; Fax: 416/284-7169 – 100 beds – Adm., Catherine Hilge

Toronto: Mon Sheong Home for the Aged, 36 D'Arcy St., Toronto ON M5T 1J7 – 416/977-3762; Fax: 416/977-3231 – 65 beds – Adm., Kwong-Woon Cheng

Toronto: Nisbet Lodge, 740 Pape Ave., Toronto ON M4K 3S7 – 416/469-1105; Fax: 416/469-1107 – 103 beds – Exec. Dir., Barry Lee

Canadian Almanac & Directory 1997

Toronto: North Park Nursing Home, 450 Rustic Rd., North York ON M6L 1W9 – 416/247-0531; Fax: 416/247-6159 – 75 beds – Adm., Harry Rosenberg

Toronto: Norwood Nursing Home, 122 Tyndall Ave., Toronto ON M6K 2E2 – 416/535-3011; Fax: 416/535-6439 – 60 beds – Adm., Dr. Horst Sebald

Toronto: The O'Neill Centre, 33 Christie St., Toronto ON M6G 3B1 – 416/536-1116; Fax: 416/536-6941 – 162 beds – Adm., Anne-Marie Mohler

Toronto: Parkdale Nursing Home, 35 Elm Grove Ave., Toronto ON M6K 2J2 – 416/537-2465; Fax: 416/537-2468 – 123 beds – Adm., Tara Singh

Toronto: Providence Centre Hospital, *see* General Hospitals listings

Toronto: Rockcliffe Nursing Home, 3015 Lawrence Ave. East, Scarborough ON M1P 2V7 – 416/264-3201; Fax: 416/264-2609 – 204 beds – Adm., Phyllis Jardine

Toronto: Rotary-Laughlen Centre, 110 Edward St., Toronto ON M5G 2A5 – 416/597-0373; Fax: 416/597-8234 – Adm., Anne Hayes

Toronto: St. Clair O'Connor Community Nursing Home, 2703 St. Clair Ave. East, Toronto ON M4B 3M3 – 416/757-8757; Fax: 416/751-7315 – 25 beds – Adm., Joan Hollingshead

Toronto: Seniors' Health Centre, 2 Buchan Ct., North York ON M2J 5A3 – 416/756-1040; Fax: 416/495-9738 – 150 beds – Adm., Dianne E. Anderson

Toronto: Seven Oaks, 9 Neilson Rd., Scarborough ON M1N 5E1 – 416/392-3500; Fax: 416/392-3579 – 249 beds – Adm., Karen Wallace

Toronto: Shepherd Lodge, 3760 Sheppard Ave. East, Agincourt ON M1S 3E2 – 416/293-8241; Fax: 416/293-6229 – 150 beds – Adm., Rev. Joan Telford

Toronto: Shepherd Terrace, 3758 Sheppard Ave. East, Toronto ON M1T 3K9 – 416/609-5700; Fax: 416/293-6229 – 60 beds – Adm., Rev. Joan M. Telford

Toronto: Spencer House, 36 Spencer Rd., Toronto ON M6K 2J6 – 416/531-5737; Fax: 416/531-4722 – 120 beds – Adm., Ivor Zagroev

Toronto: Suomi-Koti Toronto Nursing Home, 795 Eglinton Ave. East, Toronto ON M4G 4E4 – 416/425-4134; Fax: 416/425-6319 – 34 beds – Adm., Tellervo Varvas

Toronto: Tendercare Living Centre, 1020 McNicoll Ave., Scarborough ON M1W 2J6 – 416/499-2020; Fax: 416/499-3379 – 254 beds – Adm., Francis Martis

Toronto: Thompson House, 1 Overland Dr., Toronto ON M3C 2C3 – 416/449-4474; Fax: 416/447-6364 – 136 beds – Adm., William Krever

Toronto: True Davidson Acres, 200 Dawes Rd., Toronto ON M4C 5M8 – 416/397-0400; Fax: 416/397-0401 – 281 beds – Adm., Sylvia Moreland

Toronto: Ukrainian Canadian Care Centre, 60 Richview Rd., Etobicoke ON M9A 5E4 – 416/243-7653; Fax: 416/243-7452 – 80 beds – Adm., Carol Jarman

Toronto: Van-Del Manor Nursing Home, 1673 Kingston Rd., Scarborough ON M1N 1S6 – 416/699-3244; Fax: 416/699-3245 – 58 beds – Adm., Stella Pinnock

Toronto: Versa-Care Centre, Etobicoke, 95 Humber College Blvd., Etobicoke ON M9V 5B6 – 416/746-7466; Fax: 416/740-5812 – 94 beds – Adm., Jane Odgen

Toronto: Versa-Care Centre, Toronto Main, 77 Main St., Toronto ON M4E 2V6 – 416/690-3001; Fax: 416/690-6866 – 150 beds – Adm., Barbara Beecroft

Toronto: Villa Colombo, 40 Playfair Ave., Toronto ON M6B 2P9 – 416/789-2113; Fax: 416/789-5986 – 268 beds – Adm., G. Glover

Toronto: The Wexford, 1860 Lawrence Ave. East, Scarborough ON M1R 5B1 – 416/752-8877; Fax: 416/752-8414 – 166 beds – Adm., Luba Funston

Toronto: White Eagle Nursing Home, 138 Dowling Ave., Toronto ON M6K 3A6 – 416/533-7935; Fax: 416/537-0309 – 56 beds – Adm., Eileen Trevors

Toronto: Yorkville Lifecare Centre, 2045 Finch Ave. West, North York ON M3N 1M9 – 416/745-0811; Fax: 416/745-0568 – 265 beds – Adm., Myrna Simms

Trenton: Crown Ridge Place, 106 Crown St., Trenton ON K8V 6R3 – 613/392-1289; Fax: 613/392-6939 – 84 beds – Adm., Fred R. Freeman

Trenton: Trent Valley Lodge Nursing Home, 195 Bay St., Trenton ON K8V 1H9 – 613/392-9235; Fax: 613/392-0688 – 70 beds – Adm., Bill Weaver Jr.

Trout Creek: Lady Isabelle Nursing Home, MacDonald St., Trout Creek ON P0H 2L0 – 705/723-5232; Fax: 705/723-5794 – 66 beds – Adm., Sadie Newman

Unionville: Bethany Lodge, 23 Second St., Unionville ON L3R 2C2 – 905/477-3838; Fax: 905/477-2888 – 101 beds – Adm., B. Stainton

Unionville: Union Villa, 4300 Hwy. 7, Unionville ON L3R 1L8 – 905/477-2822; Fax: 905/477-6080 – 162 beds – Adm., Margaret Hill

Uxbridge: Versa-Care Centre, Uxbridge, 130 Reach St., Uxbridge ON L0C 1K0 – 905/852-5191; Fax: 905/852-6467 – 100 beds – Adm., Sharon Dickinson

Vanier: Centre d'accueil Champlain, 275 Perrier St., Vanier ON K1L 5C6 – 613/746-3543; Fax: 613/746-5572 – 116 beds – Adm., G. Gagnon

Vineland: United Mennonite Home, 3311 - 2nd St., Vineland ON L0R 2C0 – 905/562-7385; Fax: 905/562-3711 – 80 beds – Adm., Art Sieb

Virgil: Heritage Place, 1743 Four Mile Creek Rd., Virgil ON L0S 1T0 – 905/468-1111; Fax: 905/468-4384 – 36 beds – Adm., Judy Gibson

Walkerton: Brucelea Haven, 41 McGivern St. West, Walkerton ON N0G 2V0 – 519/881-1570; Fax: 519/881-0231 – 144 beds – Adm., D.J. Moore

Wallaceburg: Lapointe-Fisher Nursing Home, 427 Nelson St., Wallaceburg ON N8A 4G9 – 519/627-1663 – 99 beds – Acting Adm., Tom Hudson

Wardsville: Babcock Nursing Home, 196 Wellington St., Wardsville ON N0L 2N0 – 519/693-4415; Fax: 519/693-4876 – 60 beds – Adm., Joan Enns

Warkworth: Community Nursing Home, 97 Mill St., Warkworth ON K0K 3K0 – 705/924-2311; Fax: 705/924-2329 – 60 beds – Adm., Myrna Ogden

Waterloo: Parkwood Mennonite Home Inc., 75 Cardinal Cres. South, Waterloo ON N2J 2E6 – 519/885-4810; Fax: 519/886-6720 – 58 beds – Adm., Gloria Dirks

Waterloo: Pinehaven Nursing Home, 229 Lexington Rd., Waterloo ON N2K 2E1 – 519/885-6990; Fax: 519/885-4216 – 84 beds – Adm., Connie Cox

Watford: Watford Nursing Home, 344 Victoria St., Watford ON N0M 2S0 – 519/876-2928; Fax: 519/876-2520 – 63 beds – Adm., Lynne-Anne Gallaway

Welland County General Hospital - Extended Care Unit, 65 Third St., Welland ON L3B 4W6 – 905/732-6111; Fax: 905/732-3268 – 75 beds – Adm., Susan Alexander

Welland: Foyer Richelieu Residence, 655 Tanguay St., Welland ON L3B 5W5 – 905/734-1400; Fax: 905/734-1386 – 62 beds – Adm., Dr. J. Harvey

Welland: Sunset Haven, 163 First Ave., Welland ON L3C 1Y5 – 905/735-1620; Fax: 905/735-2606 – 347 beds – Adm., Louise Doerr

Whitby: Fairview Lodge, 632 Dundas St. West, Whitby ON L1N 5S3 – 905/668-5851; Fax: 905/668-8934 – 188 beds – Adm., Sharon Swain

Whitby: Sunnycrest Nursing Home, 1635 Dundas St. East, Whitby ON L1N 2K9 – 905/686-1061; Fax: 905/686-1061 – 136 beds – Adm., Jean Forrest

Wiarton: Gateway Haven, 671 Frank St., Wiarton ON N0H 2T0 – 519/534-1113; Fax: 519/534-4733 – 96 beds – Adm., Bob Moreton

Wikwemikong Nursing Home, Wikwemikong ON P0P 2J0 – 705/859-3107; Fax: 705/859-2245 – 60 beds – Adm., Mark Manitowabi

Winchester: Dundas Manor Nursing Home, 533 Clarence St., Winchester ON K0C 2K0 – 613/774-2293; Fax: 613/774-5507 – 98 beds – Adm., Jill M. Alguire

Windsor: Beacon Hill Lodge, 350 Dougall Ave., Windsor ON N9A 4P4 – 519/256-7868; Fax: 519/256-1991 – 244 beds – Adm., Michael O'Keefe

Windsor: Chateau Park Nursing Home, 2990 Riverside Dr. West, Windsor ON N9C 1A2 – 519/254-4341; Fax: 519/254-7931 – 59 beds – Adm., Patricia Bruckman

Windsor: Huron Lodge, 1475 Huron Church Rd., Windsor ON N9C 2K9 – 519/255-6291; Fax: 519/977-8027 – 256 beds – Adm., Lucie Marcus

Windsor: Malden Park Continuing Care Centre, 1453 Prince Rd., Windsor ON N9C 3Z4 – 519/257-5111 – 225 beds – Adm., Barry Brown

Windsor: Regency Park Nursing/Retirement Centre, 567 Victoria Ave., Windsor ON N9A 4N1 – 519/254-1141; Fax: 519/254-3759 – 60 beds – Adm., Patricia Bruckman

Windsor: Riverside Health Care Centre, 6475 Wyandotte St. East, Windsor ON N8S 1N9 – 519/948-4054; Fax: 519/974-6675 – 66 beds – Acting Adm., Pat Pacuta

Windsor: Villa Maria, 2856 Riverside Dr. West, Windsor ON N9C 1A2 – 519/254-3763; Fax: 519/254-7657 – 120 beds – Acting Adm., Peggy Bauer

Wingham: Braemar Retirement Centre, RR#1, Wingham ON N0G 2W0 – 519/357-3430; Fax: 519/357-2303 – 69 beds – Adm., Murdoch C. MacGowan

Woodbridge: Kristus Darzs Latvian Home, 11290 Pine Valley Dr., Woodbridge ON L4L 1A6 – 905/832-3300; Fax: 905/832-2029 – 100 beds – Adm., Maris Inveiss

Woodbridge: Pine Grove Lodge, 8403 Islington Ave. North, Woodbridge ON L4L 1X3 – 905/850-3605; Fax: 905/850-3832 – 100 beds – Adm., Diane Cole

Woodslee: Country Village Health Care Centre, County Rd. 8, Woodslee ON N0R 1V0 – 519/839-4812; Fax: 519/839-4813 – 104 beds – Adm., Peter Burtch

Woodstock: Caressant Care Woodstock Nursing Home, 81 Fyfe Ave., Woodstock ON N4S 8A3 – 519/539-6461; Fax: 519/539-9601 – 95 beds – Adm., Annette Groulx

Woodstock: Woodingford Lodge, 423 Devonshire Ave., PO Box 308, Woodstock ON N4S 7X6 – 519/539-1245; Fax: 519/539-8937 – 258 beds – Adm., Bob Hines

Zurich: Bluewater Rest Home, PO Box 220, Zurich ON N0M 2T0 – 519/236-4373; Fax: 519/236-7685 – 65 beds – Adm., Josef Risi

NURSING STATIONS

Bearskin Lake Nursing Station, Bearskin Lake ON P0V 1E0 – Nurse in Charge, Heather Cameron

Big Trout Lake Nursing Station, Big Trout Lake ON P0V 1G0 – Nurse in Charge, Carol Rogers

Deer Lake: Oscar-Jeannette Lindokken Nursing Station, Deer Lake ON P0V 1N0 – Nurse in Charge, Catherine Mayers

Fort Albany: Kashechewan Nursing Station, Fort Albany ON P0L 1H0 – 705/275-4444; Fax: 705/275-1010 – Nurse in Charge, Mary Douhaniuk

Fort Hope: Kevin Sagutcheway Nursing Station, Fort Hope ON P0T 1L0 – Nurse in Charge, Norma Corrish

Kasabonika Nursing Station, Kasabonika Lake ON P0V 1Y0 – 807/535-1189; Fax: 807/535-1192 – Nurse in Charge, Gloria Bilyk

Lansdowne House Nursing Station, Lansdowne House ON P0T 1Z0 – 519/753-3153; Fax: 519/752-0249 – Exec. Dir., J. Renahan

New Osnaburg Nursing Station, New Osnaburg ON P0V 2H0 – 807/928-2298; Fax: 807/928-2767 – Nurse in Charge, Gabrielle Lynn

Pikangikum Nursing Station, via Red Lake GPO, Pikangikum ON P0V 2L0 – Nurse in Charge, Mary Bender

Round Lake: Sena Memorial Nursing Station, via Wegamow GPO, Round Lake ON P0V 2Y0 – Nurse in Charge, Kush Janmohammed

Sandy Lake Nursing Station, Sandy Lake ON P0V 1V0 – 807/774-3461; Fax: 807/774-1585 – Nurse in Charge, Florence Tarrant

Webequie Nursing Station, Webequie ON P0T 3A0 – Nurse in Charge, Joan Trusdale

PRIVATE HOSPITALS

Burford: Bellview Private Hospital, 54 King St. East, Burford ON N0E 1A0 – 519/449-2431; Fax: 519/449-2431 – Supt., A. Gabriel, Reg.N.

Cobourg: Sidbrook Private Hospital, 411 King St. East, Cobourg ON K9A 1M4 – 905/372-3411; Fax: 905/372-9532 – Adm., Enos Stewart

Guelph: The Homewood Sanitarium, 150 Delhi St., Guelph ON N1E 6K9 – 519/824-1010; Fax: 519/824-1827 – Exec. Dir., Dr. R.A. Pond

Kingston: Institute of Psychotherapy Limited, 113 Lower Union St., PO Box 1237, Kingston ON K7L 4Y8 – 613/546-3116; Fax: 613/546-3119 – Adm., J. Scott

Lakefield Private Hospital, 1 Grant Ave., PO Box 489, Lakefield ON K0L 2H0 – 705/652-3421 – Adm., Doreen Jolliffe

London: Grace Villa Private Hospital, 201 Riverside Dr., London ON N6H 1E5 – 519/438-7422; Fax: 519/438-9902 – Adm., Judith Abel

Ottawa: Perth Wiseman's Private Hospital, c/o Dignicare Inc., New Edinburgh Sq., 33 Beechwood Ave., Ottawa ON K1M 1M1 – 613/744-1744; Fax: 613/744-1746 – Pres., Lionel Kirby

Penetanguishene: Beechwood Private Hospital, 58 Church St., PO Box 1090, Penetanguishene ON L0K 1P0 – 705/549-7473; Fax: 705/549-4326 – 20 beds – Adm., Larry Bellisle

Thornhill: Shouldice Private Hospital, 7750 Bayview Ave., PO Box 370, Thornhill ON L3T 4A3 – 905/889-1125; Fax: 905/889-4216 – Adm., A. O'Dell

Thornhill: Vaughan Glen Hospital, 9000 Bathurst St., Thornhill ON L3T 4A1 – 905/8889-4931; Fax: 905/494-9985 – Exec. Dir., Bill Innes

Thorold: Maple Hurst Hospital, 14 St. David Rd. West, Thorold ON L2V 2K9 – 905/227-2301; Fax: 905/227-9632 – Pres., Basil Griffis

Toronto: Bellwood Health Services, 1020 McNicholl Ave., Scarborough ON M1W 2J5 – 416/495-0926; Fax: 416/495-7943 – Pres., Dr. Linda Bell

Toronto: Dewson Private Hospital, 47 Dewson St., Toronto ON M6H 1G6 – 416/536-5009; Fax: 416/536-2125 – 31 beds – Adm., L.W. Freeman

Toronto: Don Mills Surgical Unit Ltd., 20 Wynford Dr., Don Mills ON M3C 1J4 – 416/441-1947; Fax: 416/441-2144 – Adm., Dr. Dennis Evans

Toronto: Institute of Traumatic Plastic & Restorative Surgery, 215 Victoria St., Toronto ON M5B 1Z3 – 416/364-5326; Fax: 416/921-9394 – Adm., Dr. J.E. Fenn

Toronto: St. Joseph's Morrow Park Infirmary & Private Hospital, 3377 Bayview Ave., Willowdale ON M2M 2S4 – 416/222-1101; Fax: 416/250-3117 – 35 beds – Adm., Sr. Catherine McDonough

Woodbridge: Cosmetic Surgery Hospital, 4650 Hwy. 7, Woodbridge ON L4L 1S7 – 905/851-1500; Fax: 905/856-4406 – Adm., Dr. Lloyd Carlsen

Woodstock Private Hospital, 369 Huron St., Woodstock ON N4S 7A5 – 519/537-8162; Fax: 519/537-7204 – Adm., Irma C. Vander Zwaag

SPECIAL TREATMENT CENTRES

(Includes: Abortion Clinics, Cancer Clinics, Rehabilitation Centres, Treatment Centres)

Chatham: Kent County Children's Treatment Centre, 355 Lark St., Chatham ON N7L 1G9 – 519/354-0520; Fax: 519/354-7355 – Adm., Bonnie Wooten

Kitchener-Waterloo Rotary Children's Treatment Centre, 828 King St. West, Kitchener ON N2G 1E8 – 519/579-3850; Fax: 519/570-2934 – Adm., Steven Swatridge

London: Thames Valley Children's Treatment Centre, 779 Baseline Rd. East, London ON N6C 5Y6 – 519/434-7351; Fax: 519/685-8699 – Exec. Dir., Emeka. Njoku

Mississauga: Erinoak - Serving Young People with Physical Disabilities, 2277 South Millway Dr., Mississauga ON L5L 2M5 – 905/820-7111; Fax: 905/820-1333 – Exec. Dir., Diana Thomson

Oshawa: Grandview Rehabilitation & Treatment Centre of Durham Region, 600 Townline Rd. South, Oshawa ON L1H 7K6 – 905/728-1673; Fax: 905/728-2961 – Exec. Dir., Linda Watson

The Ottawa Children's Treatment Centre, 395 Smyth Rd., PO Box 8469, Ottawa ON K1G 3H9 – 613/737-0871 – Exec. Dir., J. Wallner

Peterborough: Five Counties Children's Treatment Centre, 872 Dutton Rd., Peterborough ON K9H 7G1 – 705/748-2221; Fax: 705/748-3526 – Exec. Dir., Gary Lounsbury

St Catharines: Niagara Peninsula Children's Treatment Centre, 567 Glenridge Ave., PO Box 24029, St Catharines ON L2R 7A7 – 905/688-3550; Fax: 905/688-1050 – Exec. Dir., John Tebrake

St Catharines: Niagara Peninsula Rehabilitation Centre, 547 Glenridge Ave., PO Box 924, St Catharines ON L2T 4C2 – 905/688-2980; Fax: 905/688-9905 – Exec. Dir., Candace Paris

Sarnia & District Children's Treatment Centre, 1240 Murphy Rd., Sarnia ON N7S 2Y6 – 519/542-3471; Fax: 519/542-4115 – Exec. Dir., Christine Murphy

South Porcupine: Children's Treatment Centre, PO Box 698, South Porcupine ON P0N 1H0 – 705/235-3371; Fax: 705/235-3585 – Adm., Mary MacKay

Sudbury: Laurentian Hospital Children's Treatment Centre, 1204 St. Jerome St., Sudbury ON P3A 2V9 – 705/560-8000; Fax: 705/560-4273 – Dir., Pierre Noel

Thunder Bay: George Jeffrey Children's Treatment Centre, 507 North Lillie St., Thunder Bay ON P7C 4V8 – 807/623-4381; Fax: 807/623-6626 – Exec. Dir., C. T. Kennedy

Toronto Eye Bank, c/o University of Toronto, 1 Spadina Cres., Toronto ON M5S 2J5 – 416/480-7465 – Scientific Dir., Dr. William Dixon

Toronto Rehabilitation Centre, 345 Rumsey Rd., Toronto ON M4G 1R7 – 416/425-6630; Fax: 416/425-0301 – Exec. Dir., Dr. T. Kavanagh

Toronto: Addiction Research Foundation Clinical Institute, 33 Russell St., Toronto ON M5S 2S1 – 416/595-6000; Fax: 416/979-8133 – drug rehabilitation centre – Pres., Mark Taylor

Toronto: Bloorview MacMillan Health Centre - Hugh MacMillan Site, 350 Rumsey Rd., Toronto ON M4G 1R8 – 416/425-6220; Fax: 416/425-6591 – 87 beds – COO, Sheila Jarvis

Toronto: Bob Rumball Centre for the Deaf, 2395 Bayview Ave., North York ON M2L 1A2 – 416/449-9651 – Adm., Shirley Cassell

Toronto: Cabbagetown Women's Clinic, 302 Gerrard St. East, Toronto ON M5A 2H7 – 416/323-0642; Fax: 416/323-3099 – abortion clinic – Exec. Dir., Dr. M. Burvaina

Toronto: Casey House Hospice, 9 Huntley St., Toronto ON M4Y 2K8 – 416/962-7600; Fax: 416/962-5147 – Exec. Dir., John Flannery

Toronto: Choice in Health Clinic, #207, 597 Parliament St., Toronto ON M4X 1W3 – 416/975-9300; Fax: 416/975-0314 – abortion clinic – Dir., Margaret Hancock

Toronto: The Donwood Institute, 175 Brentcliffe Rd., Toronto ON M4G 3Z1 – 416/425-3930; Fax: 416/425-7896 – 38 beds – Pres. & CEO, Dr. David Korn

Toronto: The Marvelle Koffler Breast Centre, Mount Sinai, 600 University Ave., 12th Fl., Toronto ON M5G 1X5 – 416/596-4200 – cancer treatment

Toronto: The Morgentaler Clinic, 727 Hillsdale Ave. East, Toronto ON M4S 1V4 – 416/932-0446; Fax: 416/932-0837 – abortion clinic – Dir., Dr. Henry Morgentaler

Toronto: The Ontario Cancer Treatment & Research Foundation, 620 University Ave., 15th Fl., Toronto ON M5G 2L7 – 416/971-9800; Fax: 416/971-6888 – Pres. & CEO, Dr. Charles Hollenberg

Toronto: Orthopaedic & Arthritic Hospital, 43 Wellesley St. East, Toronto ON M4Y 1H1 – 416/967-8500; Fax: 416/967-8593 – 81 beds – Pres., Roger Sharman

Toronto: The Princess Margaret Hospital, 610 University Ave., Toronto ON M5G 2M9 – 416/946-2000 – 103 beds – Pres. & CEO, Dr. Alan R. Hudson

Toronto: St. Bernard's Rehabilitation, 683 Finch Ave. West, Willowdale ON M2R 1P2 – 416/635-8422; Fax: 416/635-8507 – 59 beds – Adm., Sr. Norbert Wind

Toronto: The Scott Clinic, 157 Gerrard St. East, Toronto ON M5A 2E4 – 416/962-4108 – Medical Dir., Dr. R.H. Scott

The Windsor Regional Hospital, 1453 Prince Rd., Windsor ON N9C 3Z4 – 519/257-5232, 257-2037; Fax: 519/257-5244 – children's treatment centre – Coord., Loretta Joyce Jewer

Windsor: Children's Rehabilitation Centre of Essex County, 3945 Matchette Rd., Windsor ON N9C 4C2 – 519/252-7281; Fax: 519/252-5873 – Exec. Dir., Ross H. Byron

PRINCE EDWARD ISLAND

GENERAL HOSPITALS

Alberton: Western Hospital, PO Box 10, Alberton PE C0B 1B0 – 902/853-2330; Fax: 902/853-3240 – 20 beds – Adm., Jeannita Bernard

Charlottetown: The Hillsborough Hospital & Special Care Centre, PO Box 1929, Charlottetown PE C1A 7N5 – 902/368-5400; Fax: 902/368-5467 – Adm., Cecil Villard

Charlottetown: Queen Elizabeth Hospital, PO Box 6600, Charlottetown PE C1A 8T5 – 902/894-2111; Fax: 902/894-2146 – 282 beds – Adm., Cecil Villard

Montague: King's County Memorial Hospital, 409 McIntyre Ave., Montague PE C0A 1R0 – 902/838-3152; Fax: 902/838-3658 – 30 beds – Adm., Susan MacLeod

O'Leary Community Hospital, O'Leary PE C0B 1V0 – 902/859-3110; Fax: 902/859-2489 – 10 acute care beds – Adm., Jeannita Bernard

Souris Hospital, PO Box 339, Souris PE C0A 2B0 – 902/687-2467; Fax: 902/687-3042 – 17 beds – Regional Dir., Susan Birt

Summerside: Prince County Hospital, 259 Beattie Ave., Summerside PE C1A 2A9 – 902/436-9131; Fax: 902/436-1501 – 113 beds – Dir., Nursing, Brenda Moynard

Tyne Valley: Stewart Memorial Hospital, PO Box 10, Tyne Valley PE C0B 2C0 – 902/831-2718; Fax: 902/831-3074 – 13 beds – Adm., Kay Lewis

HOME CARE OFFICES/COMMUNITY CARE SERVICES

Charlottetown: Community & Residential Services, 3 Queen St., PO Box 2000, Charlottetown PE C1A 7N8 – 902/368-5782

Montague: Community & Residential Services, Riverview Manor, PO Box 820, Montague PE C0A 1R0 – 902/838-0772; Fax: 902/838-0770

O'Leary: Community & Residential Services, PO Box 8, O'Leary PE C0B 1V0 – 902/859-2400

Souris: Community & Residential Services, Souris Hospital, Souris PE C0A 2B0 – 902/689-3370

Summerside: Community & Residential Services, 310 Brophy Ave., Summerside PE C1N 5N4 – 902/888-8440

NURSING HOMES

Alberton: Maplewood Manor, PO Box 400, Alberton PE C0B 1B0 – 902/853-2382
Belfast: Dr. John Gillis Memorial Lodge, Eldon Belfast PO, Belfast PE C0A 1A0 – 902/659-2337 – Donald MacDonald
Charlottetown: Andrews Residence, Malpeque Rd., Charlottetown PE C1A 7J9 – 902/368-2790
Charlottetown: Beach Grove Home, PO Box 3500, Charlottetown PE C1A 7N9 – 902/368-4190
Charlottetown: Frogmore Lodge, 92 Longworth Ave., Charlottetown PE C1A 5A7 – 902/892-7607
Charlottetown: Garden Home, 310 North River Rd., Charlottetown PE C1A 3M4 – 902/892-4131
Charlottetown: Langille House, 212-214 Kent St., Charlottetown PE C1A 1P2 – 902/628-8228
Charlottetown: Lennox Nursing Home, 140 Water St., Charlottetown PE C1A 1A7 – 902/894-4968
Charlottetown: MacMillan Lodge, 230 Richmond St., Charlottetown PE C1A 1J5 – 902/894-7173
Charlottetown: McQuaid Lodge, 36 Kent St., Charlottetown PE C1A 1M8 – 902/892-0791
Charlottetown: Old Rose Lodge, 319 Queen St., Charlottetown PE C1A 4C4 – 902/368-8313
Charlottetown: Park West Lodge, 22 Richmond St., Charlottetown PE C1A 1H4 – 902/566-2260
Charlottetown: PEI Atlantic Baptist Home, 16 Centennial Dr., Charlottetown PE C1A 5C5 – 902/566-5975
Charlottetown: Prince Edward Home, 5 Brighton Rd., Charlottetown PE C1A 8T6 – 902/368-4440; Fax: 902/368-5946
Charlottetown: Sherwood, Corrigan Home, 22 Hemlock Ct., Charlottetown PE C1A 8E3 – 902/894-9686
Charlottetown: Sunset Lodge, 78 Halthen Dr., Charlottetown PE C1A 4T8 – 902/894-7217
Charlottetown: Tenderwood Lodge, 15 Hawthorne Ave., Charlottetown PE C1A 5X8 – 902/566-5174
Charlottetown: Whisperwood Villa, 160 St. Peters Rd., Charlottetown PE C1A 5P8 – 902/566-5556
Crapaud: South Shore Villa, PO Box 24, Crapaud PE C0A 1N0 – 902/658-2228
Hunter River: Rosewood Residence, Hunter River PE C0A 1N0 – 902/964-2456
Kensington: Clinton View Lodge, Clinton RR#6, Kensington PE C0B 1W0 – 902/885-2276
Lower Montague: Shady Rest, RR#2, Lower Montague PE C0A 1R0 – 902/838-4298
Miscouche Villa, Miscouche PE C0B 1T0 – 902/436-1946
Montague: Fraser Valley Inn, Main St., PO Box 233, Montague PE C0A 1R0 – 902/838-2673
Montague: MacKinnon Pines, 505 Campbellton St., Montague PE C0A 1R0 – 902/838-2656
Montague: Riverview Manor, Montague PE C0A 1R0 – 902/838-5141
New Glasgow: River View Rest Home, New Glasgow PE C0A 1N0 – 902/964-2795
O'Leary: Lady Slipper Villa, PO Box 40, O'Leary PE C0B 1V0 – 902/859-3544
Sherwood: Corrigan Lodge, 9 Valhalla Dr., Sherwood PE C1A 8N4 – 902/894-5858
Souris: Bayview Lodge, 22 Washington St., Souris PE C0A 2B0 – 902/687-3122
Souris: Colville Manor, PO Box 640, Souris PE C0A 2B0 – 902/687-2380
Summerside: MacDonald Rest Home, 197 Cambridge St., Summerside PE C1N 1N1 – 902/436-7359; Fax: 902/854-2625
Summerside: Summerset Manor, 205 Lefurgey Ave., Summerside PE C1N 2L9 – 902/888-8318
Summerside: Wedgewood Manor, 310 Brophy St., Summerside PE C1N 5N4 – 902/888-8340
Tignish: David Lodge, Tignish PE C0B 2B0 – 902/882-3721
Wellington: La Cooperative le Chez Nous Ltée, 64 Sunset Dr., Wellington PE C0B 2E0 – 902/854-3426

SPECIAL TREATMENT CENTRES
(Includes: Abortion Clinics, Cancer Clinics, Rehabilitation Centres, Treatment Centres)
Charlottetown: Special Care Unit, 65 McGill Ave., Charlottetown PE C1A 2K1 – 902/368-4720

QUÉBEC

DISTRICTS HOSPITALIERS/BUREAUX DE SANTÉ

Baie Comeau: Régie régionale de la santé et des services sociaux de la Côte-nord, 691, rue Jalbert, Baie Comeau PQ G5G 2A1 – 418/589-9845; Fax: 418/589-8574 – Dir. gen., Claude Boisjoli
Chibougamau: Regie régionale de la santé et des services sociaux du Nord-du-Québec, 51, 3e rue, Chibougamau PQ G8P 1N1 – 418/748-2676; Fax: 418/748-6391 – Dir. gen., Bernard Fortin
Chicoutimi: Régie régionale de la santé et des services sociaux du Saguenay-Lac Saint-Jean, 930, rue Jacques Cartier est, Chicoutimi PQ G7H 2A9 – 418/545-4980; Fax: 418/545-8791 – Dir. gen., Louis-Philippe Thibault
Chisasibi: Conseil cri de la santé et des services sociaux de la Baie-James, CP 420, Chisasibi PQ J0M 1E0 – 819/855-2844; Fax: 819/855-2867 – Dir. gen., James Bobbish
Gaspé: Régie régionale de la santé et des services sociaux de la Gaspésie-Îles-de-la-Madeleine, 144, boul Gaspé, CP 5002, Gaspé PQ G0G 1R0 – 418/368-2349; Fax: 418/368-4942 – Dir. gen., Denis Loiselle
Hull: Corporation d'approvisionnement du réseau de la santé et des services sociaux de l'Outaouais, 104, rue Lois, Hull PQ J8Y 3R7 – 819/770-7747; Fax: 819/771-8632 – Dir. gen., Geraldine Hutton
Hull: Régie régionale de la santé et des services sociaux de l'Outaouais, 104, rue Lois, Hull PQ J8Y 3R7 – 819/770-7747; Fax: 819/771-8632 – Planifier, organiser, mettre en oeuvre & évaluer les services sur la territoire
Joliette: Regie régionale de la santé et des services sociaux de Lanaudière, 1000, boul Ste-Anne, Joliette PQ G6E 6J2 – 514/759-1157; Fax: 514/759-0023 – Dir. gen., Raynald Bergeron
Kuujjuaq: Regie régionale de la santé et des services sociaux du Nanavik, CP 900, Kuujjuaq PQ J0M 1C0 – 819/964-2222; Fax: 819/964-2888 – Dir. gen., Lizzie Epoo York
Longueuil: Régie régionale de la santé et des services sociaux de la Montérégie, 125, boul Ste-Foy, Longueuil PQ J4J 1W7 – 514/679-6772; Fax: 514/679-6443 – Dir. gen., Hubert Gauthier
Montréal: Régie régionale de la santé et des services sociaux de Laval, #200, 4, Place Laval, Laval PQ H7N 5Y3 – 514/967-2121; Fax: 514/967-2120 – Dir. gen., Lise Denis
Montréal: Régie régionale de la santé et des services sociaux de Montréal-centre, 3725, rue St-Denis, Montréal PQ H2X 3L9 – 514/286-5500; Fax: 514/286-5669 – Dir. gen., Paul Morency, 514/286-5544
Québec: Groupe Partagec, 2255, av Vitra, Québec PQ G1J 5B3 – 418/647-1428; Fax: 418/647-3379 – Coordonateur en approvisionnement, Roger Leclerc
Québec: Regie régionale de la santé et des services sociaux de la region de Québec, 525, boul Wilfrid Hamel, Québec PQ G1M 2S8 – 418/529-5311; Fax: 418/529-4463 – Dir. gen., Monique L. Begin
Rimouski: Régie régionale de la santé et des services sociaux du Bas-Saint-Laurent, 274, rue Potvin, Rimouski PQ G5L 7P5 – 418/724-5231; Fax: 418/723-1597 – Dir. gen., Jean Miville
Rouyn-Noranda: Régie régionale de la santé et des services sociaux de l'Abitibi-Temiscamingue, 1, 9e rue, Rouyn-Noranda PQ J9X 2A9 – 819/797-3264; Fax: 819/797-1947 – Dir. gen., Marcel Lesyk
Saint-Jerome: Régie régionale de la santé et des services sociaux des Laurentides, #210, 100, rue Labelle, Saint-Jerome PQ J7Z 5N6 – 514/436-8622; Fax: 514/436-2530 – Dir. gen., Michel Leger
Ste-Marie: Régie régionale de la santé et des services sociaux de Chaudière-Appalaches, 363, rue Cameroun, Ste-Marie PQ G6E 3E2 – 418/386-3363; Fax: 418/386-3361 – Dir. gen., Lionel Chouinard
Sherbrooke: Régie régionale de la santé et des services sociaux de l'Estrie, 2424, rue King ouest, Sherbrooke PQ J1J 2E8 – 819/566-7861; Fax: 819/569-8894 – Dir. gen., Jean-Pierre Duplantis
Trois-Rivières: Régie régionale de la santé et des services sociaux de la Mauricie-Bois-Francs, 550, rue Bonaventure, 3e étage, Trois-Rivières PQ G9A 2B5 – 819/379-3771; Fax: 819/373-1627 – Dir. gen., Paulin Dumas

CENTRES HOSPITALIERS

Alma: Hôtel-Dieu d'Alma, 300, boul Champlain sud, Alma PQ G8B 5W3 – 418/662-3421; Fax: 418/668-9691 – 225 lits – Dir. gen., Gabriel Collard
Amos: Centre hospitalier Hôtel-Dieu, 622, 4e rue ouest, Amos PQ J9T 2S2 – 819/732-3341; Fax: 819/732-0425 – 145 lits – Dir. gen., Michel Michaud
Amqui: Centre hospitalier d'Amqui, 135, rue de l'Hôpital, Amqui PQ G0J 1B0 – 418/629-2211; Fax: 418/629-4498 – 111 lits – Dir. gen., Alain Paquet
Armagh: Hôpital général d'Armagh, 1, rte 281, Armagh PQ G0R 1A0 – 418/466-2115; Fax: 418/466-2245 – 20 lits – Dir. gen., Yvan Deblois
Asbestos: Centre hospitalier d'Asbestos, 475, 3e av, Asbestos PQ J1T 1X6 – 819/879-7151; Fax: 819/879-7433 – 50 lits – Dir. gen., Paul-Aime Jacques
Baie-Comeau: Centre hospitalier régional - Pavillon Boisvert, 70, av Mance, Baie-Comeau PQ G4Z 1M9 – 418/296-2281 – 62 lits – Dir. gen., Jacques A. Levesque
Baie Comeau: Centre hospitalier régional - Pavillon Le Royer, 635, boul Joliet, Baie Comeau PQ G5C 1P1 – 418/589-3701; Fax: 418/589-7101 – 155 lits – Dir. gen., Denis Boudreau
Baie-Saint-Paul: Centre hospitalier de Charlevoix, 74, rue Ambroise Fafard, CP 5000, Baie-Saint-Paul PQ G0A 1B0 – 418/435-5150; Fax: 418/435-3315 – 243 lits – Dir. gen., Robert Vallières
Beauceville: Centre hospitalier de Beauceville, 253, 108e rue, Beauceville PQ G0M 1A0 – 418/774-3304; Fax: 418/774-2304 – 257 lits – Dir. gen., Gilles Morin
Beauport: Clinique Roy Rousseau, 2579, ch de la Canardière, Beauport PQ G1J 2G2 – 418/663-5711; Fax: 418/663-5727 – 140 lits – Dir. gen., Jacques Garneau
Beauport: Hôpital de l'Enfant-Jésus (Centre St-Augustin), 2135, Terrasse Cadieux, Beauport PQ G1C 1Z2 – 418/667-3910; Fax: 418/667-4094 – 326 lits – Dir. gen., Gaston Pellan
Bernierville: Hôpital St-Julien, 220, rue Principale, Bernierville PQ G0N 1N0 – 418/428-3771; Fax: 418/428-9601 – 615 lits – Dir. gen., René Houle
Buckingham: Centre hospitalier de Buckingham, 500, rue Bélanger, Buckingham PQ J8L 2M4 – 819/986-3341; Fax: 819/986-4000 – 134 lits – Dir. gen., Jacques Prud'homme
Cap-aux-Meules: Centre hospitalier de l'Archipel, CP 730, Cap-aux-Meules PQ G0B 1B0 – 418/986-2121; Fax: 418/986-6845 – 92 lits – Dir. gen., Gaétan Doré
Cap-de-la-Madeleine: Hôpital Cloutier, 155, rue Toupin, CP 218, Cap-de-la-Madeleine PQ G8T 7W3 – 819/370-2100; Fax: 819/379-6511 – 130 lits – Dir. gen., Reynald Dessureault
Chandler: Centre hospitalier de Chandler, 451, rue Mgr Ross est, CP 3300, Chandler PQ G0C 1K0 – 418/689-2261; Fax: 418/689-5551 – 131 lits – Dir. gen., Gérald Désaulniers
Charny: Centre hospitalier Paul-Gilbert, 9330, boul du Centre-Hospitalier, Charny PQ G6X 1L6 – 418/832-

2993; Fax: 418/832-9041 – 80 lits – Dir. gen., Marcel Bernard

Châteauguay: Centre hospitalier Anna-Laberge, 200, boul Brisebois, Châteauguay PQ J6K 4W8 – 514/699-2425; Fax: 514/699-2525 – 250 lits – Dir. gen., Jacques Cotton

Chibougamau: Hôpital Chibougamau Ltée, 51, 3e rue, Chibougamau PQ G8P 1N1 – 418/748-2676; Fax: 418/748-3662 – 71 lits – Dir. gen., Régis de Roy

Chicoutimi: Complexe hospitalier de la Sagamie, 305, av Saint-Vallier, CP 5006, Chicoutimi PQ G7H 5H6 – 418/549-2195; Fax: 418/549-7081 – 628 lits – Dir. gen., Guy St-Onge

Cowansville: Hôpital Brôme-Missisquoi-Perkins, 950, rue Principale, Cowansville PQ J2K 1K3 – 514/266-4342; Fax: 514/263-8669 – 140 lits – Dir. gen., Mario Cyr

Cowansville: Hôpital St-Louis de Cowansville Inc., 133, rue Larouche, Cowansville PQ J2K 1T2 – 514/263-2220; Fax: 514/263-3401 – 28 lits – Dir. gen., Claude Codère

Des Ruisseaux: Centre Mont-Laurier, 2561, ch de Lievre sud, Des Ruisseaux PQ J9L 3G3 – 819/623-1234; Fax: 819/44-4299 – 80 lits – Dir. gen., Pierre Pagé

Dolbeau: Centre hospitalier de Dolbeau, 2000, boul Sacré-Coeur, Dolbeau PQ G8L 2R5 – 418/276-1420; Fax: 418/276-5137 – 125 lits – Dir. gen., Olivier Coté

Drummondville: Hôpital Ste-Croix, 570, rue Heriot, Drummondville PQ J2B 1C1 – 819/478-6464; Fax: 819/478-6461 – 323 lits – Dir. gen., Joaquin Bastida

Fleurimont: Centre hospitalier Universitaire de Sherbrooke, 3001, 12e av nord, Fleurimont PQ J1H 5N4 – 819/563-5555; Fax: 819/820-6417 – 388 lits – Dir. gen., Normand Simoneau

Gaspé: Centre hospitalier Mgr Ross, 150, rue Mgr Ross, CP 800, Gaspé PQ G0C 1R0 – 418/368-2291; Fax: 418/368-6730 – 241 lits – Dir. gen., Lewis Fitzpatrick

Gaspé: L'Hôtel-Dieu de Gaspé, 215, boul York, CP 120, Gaspé PQ G0C 1S0 – 418/368-3301; Fax: 418/368-6850 – 110 lits – Dir. gen., Louis-Philippe Ste-Croix

Gatineau: Centre hospitalier de Gatineau, 909, boul de la Verendrye ouest, CP 2000, Gatineau PQ J8P 7H2 – 819/561-8100; Fax: 819/561-8306 – 289 lits – Dir. gen., Jean Laporte

Granby: Centre hospitalier de Granby, 205, boul Leclerc, Granby PQ J2G 1T7 – 514/372-5491; Fax: 514/372-7197 – 227 lits – Dir. gen., Lucie Wiseman

Grand-Mère: Centre hospitalier Laflèche-Grand-Mère, 1650, 6e av, Grand-Mère PQ G9T 2K4 – 819/533-2500; Fax: 819/538-7640 – 167 lits – Dir. gen., Guy d'Anjou

Greenfield Park: Hôpital Charles Lemoyne, 121, boul Taschereau, Greenfield Park PQ J4V 2H1 – 514/466-5000; Fax: 514/466-5779 – 571 lits – Dir. gen., Jean-Pierre Montpetit

Havre-Saint-Pierre: Centre de santé Saint-Jean-Eudes, 1035, Promenade des Anciens, CP 190, Havre-Saint-Pierre PQ G0G 1P0 – 418/538-2212; Fax: 418/538-3066 – 39 lits – Dir. gen., Bill Noel

Hull: Centre hospitalier Pierre Janet, 20, rue Pharand, Hull PQ J9A 1K7 – 819/771-7761; Fax: 819/771-2908 – 93 lits – Dir. gen., Pierre Gagnon

Hull: Centre hospitalier régional de l'Outaouais, 116, boul Lionel Emond, Hull PQ J8Y 1W7 – 819/595-6000; Fax: 819/595-9007 – 369 lits – Dir. gen., Paul Moreau

Huntingdon: Centre hospitalier du Comté, 198, rue Châteauguay, CP 6000, Huntingdon PQ J0S 1H0 – 514/264-6111; Fax: 514/264-4923 – 60 lits – Dir. gen., Guy Deschenes

Jonquière: Centre hospitalier Jonquière, 2230, rue de l'Hôpital, CP 1200, Jonquière PQ G7X 7X2 – 418/695-7700; Fax: 418/695-7715 – 529 lits – Dir. gen., Jacqueline St-Cyr

Kuujjuaq: Centre de santé Tulattavik de l'Ungava, CP 149, Kuujjuaq PQ J0M 1C0 – 819/964-2905; Fax: 819/964-2653 – 25 lits – Dir. gen., Minnie Grey

La Baie: Hôpital de la Baie des Ha Ha, 100, rue Dr.-Desgagné, La Baie PQ G7B 3P9 – 418/544-3381; Fax: 418/544-0770 – 102 lits – Dir. gen., Marcel Harvey

La Malbaie: Centre hospitalier St-Joseph, 303, rue Saint-Etienne, CP 340, La Malbaie PQ G0T 1J0 – 418/665-3711; Fax: 418/665-4672 – 56 lits – Dir. gen., Jacques Tremblay

La Peche: Centre hospitalier Gatineau Memorial, CP 160, Succ Wakefield, La Peche PQ J0X 3G0 – 819/459-2342; Fax: 819/459-3947 – 31 lits – Dir. gen., Bernard Piché

La Pocatière: Hôpital de Nôtre-Dame-de-Fatima, 1201, 6e av, CP 460, La Pocatière PQ G0R 1Z0 – 418/856-3540; Fax: 418/856-4737 – 95 lits – Dir. gen., Robert Leclerc

La Sarre: Centre hospitalier La Sarre, CP 6000, La Sarre PQ J9Z 2X7 – 819/333-2311; Fax: 819/333-4316 – 82 lits – Dir. gen., Daniel Fortin

La Tûque: Centre hospitalier Saint-Joseph de La Tuque, 885, boul Ducharme, La Tûque PQ G9X 3C1 – 819/523-4581; Fax: 819/523-7992 – 160 lits – Dir. gen., Guy Lemieux

Lac-Etchemin: Le Sanatorium Begin, 331, place du Sanatorium, Lac-Etchemin PQ G0R 1S0 – 418/625-3101; Fax: 418/625-3109 – 273 lits – Dir. gen., Jean-Yves Julien

Lac-Mégantic: Centre hospitalier Lac-Mégantic, 3569, rue Laval, Lac-Mégantic PQ G6B 1A5 – 819/583-0330; Fax: 819/583-4674 – 131 lits – Dir. gen., Yves Rivard

Lachute: Hôpital d'Argenteuil, 145, boul de la Providence, Lachute PQ J8H 4C7 – 514/562-3761; Fax: 514/562-7814 – 117 lits – Dir. gen., Rene Giard

L'Annonciation: CH Laurentides et centre réadaptation Hautes-Vallees, 170, rue Principale nord, L'Annonciation PQ J0T 1T0 – 819/275-2118; Fax: 819/275-2564 – 343 lits – Dir. gen., Pierre Page

Lévis: Hôtel-Dieu de Lévis, 143, rue Wolfe, Lévis PQ G6V 3Z1 – 418/835-7121; Fax: 418/835-7143 – 492 lits – Dir. gen., Hervé Moysan

Longueuil: Centre hospitalier Pierre-Boucher, 1333, boul Jacques-Cartier est, Longueuil PQ J4M 2A5 – 514/468-8111; Fax: 514/468-8188 – 362 – Dir. gen., Gilles Dufault

Loretteville: Centre hospitalier Chauveau, 29, rue de l'Hôpital, Loretteville PQ G2A 2T7 – 418/842-3651; Fax: 418/842-8660 – 76 lits – Dir. gen., Michel Marcotte

Louiseville: Centre hospitalier Comtois, 41, boul Comtois, Louiseville PQ J5V 2H8 – 819/228-2731; Fax: 819/228-2973 – 66 lits – Dir. gen., Gerarld Desaulniers

Magog: Hôpital La Providence de Magog, 50, rue Saint-Patrice est, Magog PQ J1X 3X3 – 819/843-3381; Fax: 819/843-8262 – 81 lits – Dir. gen., Donald Langlais

Maniwaki: Centre hospitalier de Maniwaki, 309, boul Desjardins, Maniwaki PQ J9E 2E7 – 819/449-2300; Fax: 819/449-6137 – 94 lits – Dir. gen., Paul Charbonneau

Maria: Centre hospitalier Baie-des-Chaleurs, 419, boul Perron, Maria PQ G0C 1Y0 – 418/759-3443; Fax: 418/759-5063 – 183 lits – Dir. gen., Bernard Nadeau

Matane: Centre hospitalier de Matane, 333, rue Thibault, Matane PQ G4W 2W5 – 418/562-3135; Fax: 418/562-9374 – 152 lits – Dir. gen., Charles Sénéchal

Montmagny: Hôtel-Dieu de Montmagny, 350, boul Taché ouest, Montmagny PQ G5V 3R8 – 418/248-0630; Fax: 418/248-0820 – 150 lits – Dir. gen., Rodrigue Blanchette

Montréal: Centre hospitalier Catherine Booth, 4375, av Montclair, Montréal PQ H4B 2J5 – 514/481-0431; Fax: 514/481-0029 – 84 lits – Dir. gen., Joanne Davison

Montréal: Centre hospitalier Côte-des-Neiges, 4565, ch de la Reine Marie, Montréal PQ H3W 1W5 – 514/340-1424; Fax: 514/340-3500 – 397 lits – Dir. gen., Yves Jette

Montréal: Centre hospitalier de Saint-Laurent, 1275, ch Cote-Vertu, Saint-Laurent PQ H4L 4V2 – 514/747-4771; Fax: 514/747-8809 – 124 beds – Dir. gen., Jean-Pierre Massicotte

Montréal: Centre hospitalier de St. Mary, 3830, av Lacombe, Montréal PQ H3T 1M5 – 514/345-3511; Fax: 514/345-3836 – 390 lits – Dir. gen., Constant Nucci

Montréal: Centre hospitalier de Verdun, 4000, boul Lasalle, Verdun PQ H4G 2A3 – 514/765-8121; Fax: 514/765-7306 – 378 lits – Dir. gen., Georges Maillet

Montréal: Centre hospitalier Fleury, 2180, rue Fleury est, Montréal PQ H2B 1K3 – 514/381-9311; Fax: 514/383-5086 – 252 lits – Dir. gen., Lucien Hervieux

Montréal: Centre hospitalier Gouin-Rosemont, 1970, boul Rosemont, Montréal PQ H2G 1S8 – 514/273-3681; Fax: 514/273-7645 – 43 lits – Dir. gen., Juliette P. Bailly

Montréal: Centre hospitalier J. Henri Charbonneau, 3095, rue Sherbrooke est, Montréal PQ H1W 1B2 – 514/523-1173; Fax: 514/523-4196 – 213 lits – Dir. gen., Marcellin Dallaire

Montréal: Centre hospitalier Jacques Viger, 1051, rue St-Hubert, Montréal PQ H2L 3Y5 – 514/842-7181; Fax: 514/842-7689 – 347 lits – Dir. gen., Damien Dallaire

Montréal: Centre hospitalier Mont-Sinai, 5690, boul Cavendish, Côte-Saint-Luc PQ H4W 1S7 – 514/369-2222; Fax: 514/369-2225 – 107 lits – Dir. gen., Joseph Rothbart

Montréal: Centre hospitalier Nôtre-Dame de la Merci, 555, boul Gouin ouest, Montréal PQ H3L 1K5 – 514/331-3020; Fax: 514/331-5827 – 392 lits – Dir. gen., Michel Bouffard

Montréal: Centre Hospitalier Richardson, 5425, av Bessborough, Montréal PQ H4V 2S7 – 514/483-1380; Fax: 514/483-4596 – 92 lits – Dir. gen., Jean Michaud

Montréal: Cité de la santé de Laval, 1755, boul René-Laennec, CP 440, Laval PQ H7M 3L9 – 514/668-1010; Fax: 514/975-5545 – 430 lits – Dir. gen., Daniel Adam

Montréal: Hôpital Champlain de Verdun, 1325, rue Crawford, Verdun PQ H4H 2N6 – 514/766-8513; Fax: 514/766-3731 – 228 lits – Dir. gen., Ghislain Girard

Montréal: Hôpital de convalescents Julius Richardson Inc., 5425, av Bessborough, Montréal PQ H4V 2S7 – 514/483-1380; Fax: 514/483-4596 – 92 lits – Dir. gen., Jean Michaud

Montréal: Hôpital de Montréal pour enfants, 2300, rue Tupper, Montréal PQ H3H 1P3 – 514/934-4400; Fax: 514/934-4477 – 186 lits – Dir. associée, Elizabeth Riley

Montréal: Hôpital des convalescents de Montréal, 6363, ch Hudson, Montréal PQ H3S 1M9 – 514/737-3661; Fax: 514/737-0592 – 203 lits – Dir. gen., Michel A. Brunet

Montréal: Hôpital du Sacré-Coeur de Montréal, 5400, boul Gouin ouest, Montréal PQ H4J 1C5 – 514/338-2222; Fax: 514/338-2384 – 605 lits – Dir. gen., Kiem-Thien Dao

Montréal: L'Hôpital général de Lachine, 3320, rue Notre-Dame, Lachine PQ H8T 1W8 – 514/637-1161; Fax: 514/637-7851 – 147 lits – Dir. gen., Roland J. Saint-Arnaud

Montréal: Hôpital général de Montréal, 1650, av Cedar, Montréal PQ H3G 1A4 – 514/937-6011; Fax: 514/937-2455 – 672 lits – Dir. gen., Gerard Douville

Montréal: Hôpital général du Lakeshore, 160, ch Stillview, Pointe-Claire PQ H9R 2Y2 – 514/630-2225; Fax: 514/630-3302 – 257 lits – Dir. gen., Gilles Lanteigne, 514/630-2107

Canadian Almanac & Directory 1997

Montréal: Hôpital général Juif Sir Mortimer B. Davis, 3755, ch Côte Ste-Catherine, Montréal PQ H3T 1E2 – 514/340-8222; Fax: 514/340-7530 – 605 lits – Dir. gen., Henri Elbaz

Montréal: Hôpital général Lasalle, 8585, Terrasse Champlain, Lasalle PQ H8P 1C1 – 514/365-1510; Fax: 514/595-2225 – 241 lits – Dir. gen., Georges Maillet

Montréal: Hôpital Jean-Talon, 1385, rue Jean-Talon est, Montréal PQ H2E 1S6 – 514/495-6767; Fax: 514/495-6734 – 340 lits – Dir. gen., Pierre Ledoux

Montréal: Hôpital Maisonneuve-Rosemont, 5415, boul de l'Assomption, Montréal PQ H1T 2M4 – 514/252-3400; Fax: 514/252-3589 – 500 lits – Dir. gen., André Ducharme

Montréal: Hôpital Marie Enfant, 5200, rue Belanger est, Montréal PQ H1T 1C9 – 514/374-1710; Fax: 514/374-7944 – 100 lits – Dir. gen., Michel Brunet

Montréal: Hôpital neurologique de Montréal, 3801, rue Université, Montréal PQ H3A 2B4 – 514/398-1944; Fax: 514/398-8540 – 135 lits – Dir. gen., Joy Marianne Shannon

Montréal: Hôpital Nôtre-Dame, 1560, rue Sherbrooke est, Montréal PQ H2L 4M1 – 514/876-6421; Fax: 514/876-7129 – 911 lits – Dir. gen., David Levine

Montréal: Hôpital Reddy Memorial, 4039, rue Tupper, Westmount PQ H3Z 1T5 – 514/933-7511 – 241 beds – Dir. gen., Rejean Plante

Montréal: Hôpital Royal Victoria, 687, av des Pins ouest, Montréal PQ H3A 1A1 – 514/842-1231; Fax: 514/842-2271 – 610 lits – Dir. gen., Phillip P. Aspinall

Montréal: Hôpital St-Charles Borromée, 66, boul René-Lévesque est, Montréal PQ H2X 1N3 – 514/861-9331; Fax: 514/861-8385 – 275 lits – Dir. gen., Gilbert Gagnon

Montréal: Hôpital Saint-Joseph de la Providence, 11844, Bois-de-boulogne, Montréal PQ H3M 2X7 – 514/334-3120; Fax: 514/334-5881 – 140 lits – Dir. gen., Mathieu Lafrance

Montréal: L'Hôpital Saint-Luc, 1058, rue St-Denis, Montréal PQ H2X 3J4 – 514/281-2121, 3200; Fax: 514/281-4056 – 716 lits – Dir. gen., Jean Leblanc

Montréal: Hôpital Sainte-Jeanne d'Arc de Montréal, 3570, rue St-Urbain, Montréal PQ H2X 2N8 – 514/282-5000; Fax: 514/282-9206 – 318 lits – Dir. gen., François Savard

Montréal: Hôpital Sainte-Justine, 3175, ch de la Côte Ste-Catherine, Montréal PQ H3T 1C5 – 514/345-4665; Fax: 514/345-4808 – 592 lits – Dir. gen., Jean-Pierre Chicoine

Montréal: Hôpital Santa Cabrini, 5655, rue St-Zotique est, Montréal PQ H1T 1P7 – 514/252-6000; Fax: 514/252-6453 – 417 lits – Dir. gen., Irene Giannetti

Montréal: Hôtel-Dieu de Montréal, 3840, rue St-Urbain, Montréal PQ H2W 1T8 – 514/843-2611; Fax: 514/843-3065 – 570 lits – Dir. gen., Michel Lafrenière

Montréal: Institut de cardiologie de Montréal, 5000, rue Bélanger est, Montréal PQ H1T 1C8 – 514/376-3330; Fax: 514/593-2540 – 171 lits – Dir. gen., Raymond Carignan

Montréal: Institut thoracique de Montréal, 3650, rue St-Urbain, Montréal PQ H2X 2P4 – 514/849-5201; Fax: 514/849-2180 – 124 lits – Dir. gen., Phillip P. Aspinall

Montréal: Jewish Rehabilitation Hospital, 3205, Place Alton-Goldbloom, Laval PQ H7V 1R2 – 514/688-9550; Fax: 514/688-3673 – 120 lits – Dir. gen., Henry Coopersmith

Montréal: Pavillon Albert Prevost, 6555, boul Gouin ouest, Montréal PQ H4K 1B3 – 514/333-4237; Fax: 514/338-4352 – 132 lits – Dir. gen., Khien-Thien Dao

Montréal: Pavillon Chomedey, 3825, boul Lévesque ouest, Laval PQ H7V 1G6 – 514/682-3388; Fax: 514/682-6129 – 50 lits – Dir. gen., Daniel Adam

Montréal: Pavillon Rosemont, 5689, boul Rosemont, Montréal PQ H1T 2H1 – 514/252-3400 – 316 lits – Dir. gen., André Ducharme

Nicolet: Hôpital du Christ-Roi, 675, rue St-Jean-Baptiste, Nicolet PQ J3T 1S4 – 819/293-2071; Fax: 819/293-6160 – 95 lits – Dir. gen., Ginette Simard-Montplaisir

Notre-Dame-du-Lac: Hôpital Notre-Dame-du-Lac, 58, rue de l'Eglise, CP 310, Notre-Dame-du-Lac PQ G0L 1X0 – 418/899-6751; Fax: 418/899-2809 – 85 lits – Dir. gen. (interim), Michel Samson

Ormstown: Hôpital Barrie Memorial, 28, rue Gale, Ormstown PQ J0S 1K0 – 514/829-2321; Fax: 514/829-3582 – 61 lits – Dir. gen., Guy Rho

Povungnituk: Centre hospitalier de la Baie d'Hudson, Povungnituk PQ J0M 1P0 – 819/988-2802; Fax: 819/988-2796 – 15 lits – Dir. gen., Michel Garcia

Québec: Centre hospitalier universitaire de Québec - Pavillon Saint-François-d'Assise, 10, rue de l'Espinay, Québec PQ G1L 3L5 – 418/525-4303; Fax: 418/525-4426 – 632 lits – Dir. gen., Gerard Roy

Québec: Hôpital de l'Enfant-Jesus, 1401, 18e rue, Québec PQ G1J 1Z4 – 418/649-0252; Fax: 418/649-5557 – 517 lits – Dir. gen., Gaston Pellan

Québec: Hôpital général de Québec, 260, boul Langelier, Québec PQ G1K 5N1 – 418/529-0931; Fax: 418/529-0813 – 397 lits – Dir. gen., Roger Corriveau

Québec: L'Hôpital Jeffery Hale, 1250, ch Ste-Foy, Québec PQ G1S 2M6 – 418/683-4471; Fax: 418/683-8471 – 108 lits – Dir. gen., Yves Desroches

Québec: Hôtel Dieu de Québec, 11, Côte du Palais, Québec PQ G1R 2J6 – 418/525-4303; Fax: 418/691-5205 – 529 lits – Dir. gen., Gérard Roy

Québec: Hôtel Dieu du Sacre-Coeur de Jésus de Québec, 1, av du Sacre-Coeur, Québec PQ G1N 2W1 – 418/529-6851; Fax: 418/529-2971 – 120 lits – Dir. gen., Paul Robitaille

Québec: Pavillon Saint-Sacrement, 1050, ch Ste-Foy, Québec PQ G1S 4L8 – 418/682-7511; Fax: 418/682-7972 – 441 lits – Dir. gen., Gaston Pellan

Repentigny: Centre hospitalier Le Gardeur, 135, boul Claude David, Repentigny PQ J6A 1N6 – 514/654-7525; Fax: 514/585-5939 – 258 lits – Dir. gen., Gisèle Boyer

Rimouski: Centre hospitalier Régional de Rimouski, 150, av Rouleau, Rimouski PQ G5L 5T1 – 418/723-7851, 724-8442; Fax: 418/724-8615 – 344 lits – Dir. gen. (interim), Paul-André Duval

Rivière-du-Loup: Centre hospitalier régional du Grand-Portage, 75, rue St-Henri, Rivière-du-Loup PQ G5R 2A4 – 418/868-1000; Fax: 418/868-1032 – 173 lits – Dir. gen., Raymond April

Roberval: Hôtel-Dieu de Roberval, 450, rue Brassard, Roberval PQ G8H 1B9 – 418/275-0110; Fax: 418/275-6202 – 361 lits – Dir. gen., André-Guy Cloutier

Rouyn-Noranda: Centre hospitalier Rouyn-Noranda, 4, 9e rue, Rouyn-Noranda PQ J9X 2B2 – 819/764-5131; Fax: 819/764-4211 – 219 lits – Dir. gen., Gerard Marinovich

Ste-Agathe-des-Monts: Centre hospitalier Laurentien, 234, rue St-Vincent, Ste-Agathe-des-Monts PQ J8C 2B8 – 819/324-4000; Fax: 819/324-4010 – 98 lits – Dir. gen., Jacques Gaudette

Ste-Anne-de-Beaupré: Hôpital Sainte-Anne-de-Beaupré, 9974, rue Royale, Ste-Anne-de-Beaupré PQ G0A 3C0 – 418/827-3726; Fax: 418/827-6107 – 35 lits – Dir. gen., Jean-Yves Simard

Ste-Anne-des-Monts: Hôpital des Monts, 50, rue Belvedere, CP 790, Ste-Anne-des-Monts PQ G0E 2G0 – 418/763-2261; Fax: 418/763-7460 – 106 lits – Dir. gen., Robert Deschenes

Saint-Charles-Borromée: Centre hospitalier Delanaudière, 336, rue Visitation, Saint-Charles-Borromée PQ J6E 4N6 – 514/759-8222 – 10 lits – Dir. gen., Maurice Blais

St-Charles Borromée: Centre hospitalier régional DeLanaudière, 1000, rue Sainte-Anne, St-Charles Borromée PQ J6E 5B5 – 514/759-8222; Fax: 514/759-7969 – 749 lits – Dir. gen., Maurice Blais

St-Eustache: Centre hospitalier St-Eustache, 520, boul Arthur-Sauve, St-Eustache PQ J7R 5B1 – 514/473-6811; Fax: 514/473-6966 – 190 lits – Dir. gen., Jean-Guy Nadeau

Ste-Foy: Centre hospitalier de l'Université de Québec, 2705, boul Laurier, Ste-Foy PQ G1V 4G2 – 418/656-4141; Fax: 418/654-2762 – 410 lits – Dir. gen., Gérard Roy

Ste-Foy: Hôpital Laval, 2725, ch Ste-Foy, Ste-Foy PQ G1V 4G5 – 418/656-8711; Fax: 418/656-4829 – 370 lits – Dir. gen., Gilles Lagaci, 418/656-4880

St-Georges: Centre hospitalier Saint-Georges de Beauce, 1500, 18e rue ouest, St-Georges PQ G5Y 4T8 – 418/228-2031; Fax: 418/227-3825 – 155 lits – Dir. gen., Julie Doyon-Proulx

Saint-Hyacinthe: Hôtel-Dieu, 1800, rue Dessaulles, Saint-Hyacinthe PQ J2S 2T2 – 514/774-6495; Fax: 514/774-0947 – 609 lits – Dir. gen., Robert Busilacchi

St-Jean-sur-Richelieu: Hôpital du Haut-Richelieu, 920, boul du Séminaire, St-Jean-sur-Richelieu PQ J3A 1B7 – 514/359-5000; Fax: 514/359-5251 – 309 lits – Dir. gen., André Trottier

St-Jérôme: Hôtel-Dieu de St-Jérôme, 290, rue Montigny, St-Jérôme PQ J7Z 5T3 – 514/431-8200; Fax: 514/431-8280 – 444 lits – Dir. gen., Claude Guimont

St-Raymond: Centre hospitalier Portneuf, 700, rue St-Cyrille, CP 850, St-Raymond PQ G0A 4G0 – 418/337-4611; Fax: 418/337-4808 – 96 lits – Dir. gen., Fernand Morasse

Salaberry-de-Valleyfield: Centre hospitalier régional du Suroît, 150, rue St-Thomas, Salaberry-de-Valleyfield PQ J6T 6C1 – 514/371-9925; Fax: 514/371-3607; EMail: chrsbout@rocler.qc.ca – 314 lits – Dir. gen., Paul-Henri Boutin

Sept-Iles: Centre hospitalier régional de Sept-Iles, 45, rue Père Divet, Sept-Iles PQ G4R 3N7 – 418/962-9761; Fax: 418/962-2701 – 196 lits – Dir. gen., Daniel Petit

Shawinigan-Sud: Centre hospitalier régional de la Mauricie, 50, 118e rue, Shawinigan-Sud PQ G9P 4E7 – 819/536-7500; Fax: 819/536-7658 – 250 lits – Dir. gen., Pierre Lemire

Shawinigan: Centre hospitalier Sainte-Thérèse, 1705, av Georges, Shawinigan PQ G9N 2N1 – 819/537-9351; Fax: 819/537-4737 – 90 lits – Dir. gen., Jacques Veilletta

Shawville: L'Hôpital communautaire du Pontiac Inc., 200, rue Argue, Shawville PQ J0X 2Y0 – 819/647-2211; Fax: 819/647-2409 – 81 lits – Dir. gen., Gilles Lanteigne

Sherbrooke: Centre hospitalier, 375, rue Argyle, Sherbrooke PQ J1J 3H5 – 819/569-3661; Fax: 819/569-4688 – 137 lits – Dir. gen., Marie Trousdell

Sherbrooke: Hôpital de St-Vincent de Paul de Sherbrooke, 300, rue King est, Sherbrooke PQ J1G 1B1 – 819/563-2366; Fax: 819/563-5201 – 284 lits – Dir. gen., Normand Légault

Sherbrooke: Hôpital d'Youville, 1036, rue Belvedere sud, Sherbrooke PQ J1H 4C4 – 819/821-5105; Fax: 819/821-2065 – 384 lits – Dir. gen., Daniel Bergeron

Sherbrooke: Hôtel-Dieu, 580, rue Bowen sud, Sherbrooke PQ J1G 2E8 – 819/569-2551; Fax: 819/822-6766 – 322 lits – Dir. gen., Albert Painchaud

Sorel: Hôtel-Dieu de Sorel, 400, av Hôtel-Dieu, Sorel PQ J3P 1N5 – 514/746-6000; Fax: 514/746-2782 – 241 lits – Dir. gen., Pierre-Yves Desjardins

Thetford Mines: Centre hospitalier de la région de l'Amiante, 1717, rue Notre-Dame nord, Thetford Mines PQ G6G 2V4 – 418/338-7777; Fax: 418/335-7616 – 299 lits – Dir. gen., Jean-Claude Gagné

Trois-Rivières: Centre hospitalier St-Joseph, 731, rue Ste-Julie, Trois-Rivières PQ G9A 1Y1 – 819/372-3557; Fax: 819/372-3581 – 409 lits – Dir. gen., Claude Blais

Trois-Rivières: Centre hospitalier Sainte-Marie, 1991, boul du Carmel, Trois-Rivières PQ G8Z 3R9 – 819/378-9700; Fax: 819/378-9850 – 310 lits – Dir. gen., Mathieu Vaillancourt

Val-d'Or: Centre hospitalier de Val d'Or, 725, 6e rue, Val-d'Or PQ J9P 3Y1 – 819/825-6711; Fax: 819/825-4615 – 173 lits – Dir. gen., Nelson Laflamme

Vanier: Hôpital Christ-Roi, 300, boul Wilfrid-Hamel, Vanier PQ G1M 2R9 – 418/682-1711; Fax: 418/682-5784 – 178 lits – Dir. gen., Denis Carbonneau

Victoriaville: Centre d'hébergement de la MRC d'Arthabaska, 61, av de l'Ermitage, Victoriaville PQ G6P 6X4 – 819/758-7511; Fax: 819/758-4852 – 232 lits – Dir. gen., Gilles Perreault

Victoriaville: Hôtel-Dieu d'Arthabaska, 5, rue des Hospitalières, Victoriaville PQ G6P 6N2 – 819/357-2030; Fax: 819/357-4314 – 289 lits – Dir. gen., Jean Bartkowiak

Ville-Marie: Centre de santé Sainte-Famille, 22, rue Notre-Dame, CP 2 000, Ville-Marie PQ J0Z 3W0 – 819/629-2420; Fax: 819/629-3257 – 72 lits – Dir. gen., Pierre Larouche

Waterloo: Centre hospitalier de Waterloo, 5300, av Courville, CP 1230, Waterloo PQ J0E 2N0 – 514/539-5512; Fax: 514/539-1830 – 40 lits – Dir. gen., Bernard Fournelle

HÔPITAUX AUXILIAIRES/CENTRES DE SOINS DE SANTÉ

Acton Vale: CLSC la Chenaie, 1266, rue Lemay, CP 370, Acton Vale PQ J0H 1A0 – 514/546-3225; Fax: 514/546-4981 – Dir. gen., Rene Hebert

Aguanish: Dispensaire-Aguanish (CS St-Jean Eudes), Aguanish PQ G0G 1A0 – 418/533-2301 – Dir. gen., Denis R. Boudreau

Alma: CLSC Le Norois, Edifice complexe J.-Gagnon, 100, ave Saint-Joseph, Alma PQ G8B 7A6 – 418/668-4563; Fax: 418/668-5403 – Dir. gen., Jacques Levesque

Amos: CLSC de l'Elan, 1242, route 111 est, CP 729, Amos PQ J9T 3X3 – 819/732-3271; Fax: 819/732-1282 – Dir. gen., Jacques Guimond

Asbestos: CLSC le Chaumiere, 601, boul Simoneau, Asbestos PQ J1T 4G7 – 819/879-7181; Fax: 819/879-4005 – Dir. gen., Raynald Dodier

Aupaluk: Dispensaire d'Aupaluk, Aupaluk PQ J0M 1X0 – 819/491-7077 – Dir. gen., Minnie Grey

Aylmer: CLSC Grande-Rivière, 425, rue le Guerrier, Aylmer PQ J9H 6N8 – 819/684-2251; Fax: 819/684-2541 – Dir. gen., Pierre Paquin

Baie-Comeau: CLSC de l'Aquilon, 600, rue Jalbert, Baie-Comeau PQ G5C 1Z9 – 418/589-2191; Fax: 418/589-7784 – Dir. gen., Real Castonguay

Baie-James: Point de service Joutel, 100, rue Principale/Joutel, Baie-James PQ J0Y 1N0 – 819/756-2444 – Dir. gen., Louisette Pilotte

Baie-Johan-Beetz: Dispensaire-Baie-Johan-Beetz (CS St-Jean-Eudes), Baie-Johan-Beetz PQ G0C 1B0 – 418/539-0169 – Dir. gen., Denis R. Boudreau

Beloeil: CLSC le Vallée des Patriotes, 347, rue Duvernay, Beloeil PQ J3G 5S8 – 514/467-0157; Fax: 514/467-2269 – Dir. gen., Jean-Yves Leblanc

Berthierville: CLSC d'Autray, 761, rue Notre-Dame, CP 1470, Berthierville PQ J0K 1A0 – 514/836-7011; Fax: 514/836-1545 – Dir. gen., Norman Blackburn

Brossard: CLSC Samuel de Champlain, Complex Taschereau, #100, 5811, boul Taschereau, Brossard PQ J4Z 1A5 – 514/445-4452; Fax: 514/445-5535 – Dir. gen., Michel Lapointe

Buckingham: CLSC de la Vallée de la Lievre, 578, boul Cité des Jeunes, Buckingham PQ J8L 2W1 – 819/986-3359; Fax: 819/986-5671 – Dir. gen., Jacques Parenteau

Cabano: CLSC Temiscouata, 33, rue Saint-Laurent, Cabano PQ G0L 1E0 – 418/854-2572; Fax: 418/854-0660 – Dir. gen., Michel Samson

Candiac: CLSC Kateri, 90, boul Marie Victorin, Candiac PQ J5R 1C1 – 514/659-7661; Fax: 514/444-6260 – Dir. gen., André J. Coté

Cap-aux-Meules: CLSC des Iles, 420, rue Principale, CP 847, Cap-aux-Meules PQ G0B 1B0 – 418/986-5323; Fax: 418/986-4911 – Dir. gen., Germain Chevarie

Cap-de-Madeleine: CLSC du Rivage, 20, rue Notre-Dame, Cap-de-Madeleine PQ G8T 7W1 – 819/375-4849 – Dir. gen., Vital Gaudet

Causapscal: CLSC la Vallée, 558, rue Saint-Jacques nord, Causapscal PQ G0J 1J0 – 418/756-3451; Fax: 418/756-3038 – Dir. gen., Lise Chamberland

Chandler: CLSC la Saline, 633, av Daignault, CP 1090, Chandler PQ G0C 1K0 – 418/689-6695; Fax: 418/689-4707 – Dir. gen., Clement Michel

Chapais: CLSC des Grands Bois, 32, 3e av, CP 1300, Chapais PQ G0W 1H0 – 418/745-2591; Fax: 418/745-3240 – Dir. gen., René Ricard

Charlesbourg: CLSC La Source, 280, av Notre-Dame, Charlesbourg PQ G2M 1K9 – 418/849-2572; Fax: 418/849-0661 – Dir. gen., Louis Blanchette

Chateauguay: CLSC Chateauguay, 101, rue Lauzon, Chateauguay PQ J6K 1C7 – 514/691-7410; Fax: 514/691-6202 – Dir. gen., André Racine

Chertsey: CLSC de Matawinie, 8161, route 125, RR#1, Chertsey PQ J0K 3K0 – 514/882-2488; Fax: 514/882-9072 – Dir. gen., Philippe Lupien

Chicoutimi: CLSC des Coteaux, 326, rue des Sagueneens, CP 5150, Chicoutimi PQ G7H 6J6 – 418/545-1262; Fax: 418/693-0049 – Dir. gen., Helene Gobeil

Chicoutimi: CLSC Saguenay-nord, 222, rue Saint-Ephrem, Chicoutimi PQ G7G 2W5 – 418/545-1575; Fax: 418/545-7293 – Dir. gen., Carroll Malenfant

Coaticook: CLSC Albert-Samson, 228, rue Saint-Paul est, Coaticook PQ J1A 1E7 – 819/849-7041; Fax: 819/849-6430 – Dir. gen., Rosaire Provencher

Drummondville: CLSC Drummond, 350, rue Saint-Jean, Drummondville PQ J2B 5L4 – 819/474-2572; Fax: 819/474-2828 – Dir. gen., Gaetan Mercure

Fermont: Centre de santé de l'Hematite, 1, rue Aquilon, CP 550, Fermont PQ G0G 1J0 – 418/287-5461; Fax: 418/287-5281 – 5 lits – Dir. gen., Micheline Rioux

Forestville: CLSC de Forestville, 2, 7e rue, CP 790, Forestville PQ G0T 1E0 – 418/587-2212; Fax: 418/587-2865 – 15 lits – Dir. gen., Lucien Lessard

Fort-Coulonge: CLSC Pontiac, 314, route 148, CP 430, Fort-Coulonge PQ J0X 1V0 – 819/683-3000; Fax: 819/683-2008 – Dir. gen., Charlotte l'Ecuyer

Fortierville: CLSC les Bles d'Or, 216, rue Principale, Fortierville PQ G0S 1J0 – 819/287-4442

Gaspé: CLSC de la Pointe, 154, boul Renard est, CP 220, Gaspé PQ G0E 2A0 – 418/269-3391; Fax: 418/269-5294 – Dir. gen., Jdean-Claude Plourde

Gatineau: CLSC des Draveurs, 80, av Gatineau, Gatineau PQ J8T 4J3 – 819/561-2550; Fax: 819/561-3034 – Dir. gen., Gilles Gelinas

Gatineau: CLSC le Moulin, 510, boul Maloney est, Gatineau PQ J8P 1E7 – 819/663-9214; Fax: 819/663-2326 – Dir. gen., Robert Allard

Granby: CLSC de la Haute Yamaska, 294, rue Deragon, Granby PQ J2G 5J5 – 514/375-1442; Fax: 514/375-5666 – Dir. gen., Francois Blais

Grande-Vallée: CLSC l'Estran, 71, rue Saint-Francois-Xavier, CP 190, Grande-Vallée PQ G0E 1K0 – 418/393-2001; Fax: 418/393-2952 – Dir. gen., Harry Lachance

Hull: CLSC de Hull, 85, rue Saint-Redempteur, Hull PQ J8X 4E6 – 819/770-6900; Fax: 819/770-8707 – Dir. gen., Pierre Ippersiel

Huntingdon: CLSC Huntingdon, 220, rue Chateauguay, CP 820, Huntingdon PQ J0S 1H0 – 514/264-6108; Fax: 514/264-6801 – Dir. gen., Guy Deschenes

Iberville: CLSC Vallée des Forts, 874, rue Champlain, Iberville PQ J2X 3W9 – 514/358-2572; Fax: 514/347-3275 – Dir. gen., Mario Lafreniere

Joliette: CLSC de Joliette, 350, rue Beaudry nord, Joliette PQ J6E 6A6 – 514/755-2111; Fax: 514/755-4896 – Dir. gen., Pierre Boissonneault

Jonquière: CLSC de la Jonquière, 3667, boul Harvey, CP 580, Jonquière PQ G7X 7W4 – 418/695-2572; Fax: 418/695-3327 – Dir. gen., Claude Garon

Kangiqsualujjuaq: Dispensaire de Kangiqsualujjuaq, Kangiqsualujjuaq PQ J0M 1N0 – 819/337-5312 – Dir. gen., Minnie Grey

Kangiqsujuaq: Dispensaire de Kangiqsujuaq, Kangiqsujuaq PQ J0M 1K0 – 819/338-3303 – Dir. gen., Minnie Grey

Kangirsuk: Dispensaire de Kangirsuk, Kangirsuk PQ J0M 1A0 – 819/935-4225 – Dir. gen., Minnie Grey

La Baie: CLSC du Fjord, 80, rue Aime-Gravel, La Baie PQ G7B 2M4 – 418/544-7316; Fax: 418/544-0292 – Dir. gen., Armand Demers

La Guadeloupe: CLSC la Guadeloupe, 763, 14e av, La Guadeloupe PQ G0M 1G0 – 418/459-3441; Fax: 418/459-3289 – Dir. gen., Claude Lemieux

La Malbaie: CLSC Charlevoix, 600, boul de Comporte, La Malbaie PQ G5A 1S8 – 418/665-6413; Fax: 418/665-6413 – Dir. gen., Alain Ouellet

La Sarre: CLSC des Auroles Boreales, 285, 1re rue est, La Sarre PQ J9Z 3K1 – 819/333-2534; Fax: 819/333-3111 – Dir. gen., Francoise Methe

La Tuque: CLSC de Haut Saint-Maurice, 350, av Brown, La Tuque PQ G9X 2W4 – 819/523-6171; Fax: 819/523-6176 – Dir. gen., Mario Morand

Lac-Etchemin: CLSC des Etchemins, 201, rue Cluade-Bilodeau, CP 428, Lac-Etchemin PQ G0R 1S0 – 418/625-8001; Fax: 418/625-3009 – Dir. gen., Bernard Lamy

Lac-Megantic: CLSC Maria-Thibault, 3700, rue Laval, Lac-Megantic PQ G6B 1A4 – 819/583-2572; Fax: 819/583-5364 – Dir. gen., Jocelyn Ouellet

Lachute: CLSC d'Argenteuil, 551, rue Berry, Lachute PQ J8H 1S4 – 415/562-8581; Fax: 415/562-2111 – Dir. gen., Bertin Legault

Laforce: Point de service Laforce, Laforce PQ J0Z 2J0 – 819/722-2453 – Dir. gen., Pierre Larouche

L'Ancienne-Lorette: CLSC Laurentian, 1320, rue Saint-Paul, L'Ancienne-Lorette PQ G2E 1Z4 – 418/872-0881; Fax: 418/872-0463 – Dir. gen., René Laverdiere

Laurier-Station: CLSC Arthur Caux, 135, rue de la Station, CP 189, Laurier-Station PQ G0S 1N0 – 418/728-3435; Fax: 418/728-3477 – Dir. gen., Paul-Emile Coulombe

Le Gardeur: CLSC Le Meandre, 193, rue Notre-Dame, Le Gardeur PQ J5Z 3C4 – 514/654-9012; Fax: 514/654-0262 – Dir. gen., Suzanne Roy

Lebel-Sur-Quevillon: Centre de santé Lebel, 950, boul Quevillon nord, CP 5000, Lebel-Sur-Quevillon PQ J0Y 1X0 – 819/755-4881; Fax: 819/755-3581 – 14 lits – Dir. gen., O'Neil Durocher

Les Escoumins: Centre de santé de la Haute Côte-Nord, 4, rue de l'Hôpital, CP 1000, Les Escoumins PQ G0T 1K0 – 418/233-2931; Fax: 418/233-2608 – 44 lits – Dir. gen., Fernand Boutin

L'Ile-d'Anticosti: Dispensaire-Port-Meneir, Anticosti (CS St-Jean-Eudes), L'Ile-d'Anticosti PQ G0G 2Y0 – 418/535-0176 – Dir. gen., Denis R. Beaudreau

Longueuil: CLSC Longueuil-Est, 388, rue Lamarre, Longueuil PQ J4J 1T2 – 514/463-2850; Fax: 514/646-7552 – Dir. gen., Lise Latreille-Zaman

Longueuil: CLSC Longueuil-Ouest, 291, boul Curé-Poirier ouest, Longueuil PQ J4J 2G4 – 514/651-9830; Fax: 514/651-4606 – Dir. gen., Luc Genest

Lourdes-Du-Blanc-Sablon: Centre de santé de la Basse Côte Nord, CP 130, Lourdes-Du-Blanc-Sablon PQ G0G 1W0 – 418/461-2144; Fax: 418/461-2731 – 48 lits – Dir. gen., Rémy Beaudoin

Low: CLSC de la Vallée de la Gatineau, Route 105, CP 63, Low PQ J0X 2C0 – 819/422-3548; Fax: 819/422-3568 – Dir. gen., Louis-Maurice Dionne

Magog: CLSC Alfred-Desrochers, 1750, rue Sherbrooke, Magog PQ J1X 2T3 – 819/843-2572; Fax: 819/843-2940 – Dir. gen., Jean Lavigne

Maniwaki: CLSC de la Rivière Desert, 186, rue King, Maniwaki PQ J9E 3M1 – 819/449-2513; Fax: 819/449-4102 – Dir. gen., Serge Boucher

Matagami: Centre de santé Isle-Dieu, 130, boul Matagami, CP 790, Matagami PQ J0Y 2A0 – 819/739-

Canadian Almanac & Directory 1997

2515; Fax: 819/739-4777 – 15 lits – Dir. gen., Louisette Pilotte
Matane: CLSC de Matane, 349, av Saint-Jerome, Matane PQ G4W 3A8 – 418/562-5741; Fax: 418/562-9236 – Dir. gen., Lise Langevin
Matapedia: CLSC Malauze, 14, boul Perron, CP 190, Matapedia PQ G0J 1V0 – 418/865-2221; Fax: 418/865-2317 – Dir. gen., Marc Turcotte
Mistassini: CLSC des Chutes, 201, boul des Peres, Mistassini PQ G0W 2C0 – 418/276-5452; Fax: 418/276-5575 – Dir. gen., Rodrigue Gagnon
Moffet: Point de service Moffet, CP 38, Moffet PQ J0Z 2W0 – 819/747-4171 – Dir. gen., Pierre Larouche
Mont-Joli: CLSC de la Mitis, 65, av Hotel de Ville, CP 3000, Mont-Joli PQ G5H 3R3 – 418/775-2251; Fax: 418/775-7487 – Dir. gen., Gilles Tremblay
Mont-Laurier: CLSC des Hautes-Laurentides, 515, boul Albiny Paquette, Mont-Laurier PQ J9L 1K8 – 819/623-1228; Fax: 819/623-1311 – Dir. gen., Denis Bouchard
Montréal: Centre d'accueil - CLSC de Rosemont, 3245, boul Saint-Joseph est, Montréal PQ H1Y 2B6 – 514/374-8660 – Dir. gen., Michel Bourque
Montréal: CLSC Ahuntsic, 1165, boul Henri-Bourassa est, Montréal PQ H2C 3K2 – 514/381-4221; Fax: 514/389-1361 – Dir. gen., Daniel Corbeil
Montréal: CLSC Bordeaux-Cartierville, 12060, av de Bois-de-Boulogne, Montréal PQ H3M 2X9 – 514/331-2572 – Dir. gen., Mathieu Lafrance
Montréal: CLSC Centre-Sud, 1705, rue de la Visitation, Montréal PQ H2L 3C3 – 514/527-2361; Fax: 514/598-7754 – Dir. gen., Renée Spain
Montréal: CLSC Centre-Ville, 1250, rue Sanguinet, Montréal PQ H2X 3E7 – 514/847-1250; Fax: 514/847-0728 – Dir. gen., Jacques Gagné
Montréal: CLSC Cote-des-Neiges, 3600, rue Van Horne, Montréal PQ H3S 1R6 – 514/731-8531; Fax: 514/731-4012 – Dir. gen., Jacques Lorion
Montréal: CLSC des Mill-Iles, 4731, boul Levesque est, Laval PQ H7C 1M9 – 514/661-5370; Fax: 514/661-6177 – Dir. gen., Gaston Villeneuve
Montréal: CLSC du Marigot, 1351, boul des Laurentides, Laval PQ H7M 2Y2 – 514/668-1803; Fax: 514/668-4988 – Dir. gen., Henri Bradet
Montréal: CLSC du Plateau Mont-Royal, 4689, av Papineau, Montréal PQ H2H 1V4 – 514/521-7663; Fax: 514/521-1886 – Dir. gen., Marie Montpetit
Montréal: CLSC du Vieux la Chine, 1900, rue Notre-Dame, Lachine PQ H8S 2G2 – 514/639-0650; Fax: 514/639-0666 – Dir. gen., Leonard Vincent
Montréal: CLSC Hochelaga-Maisonneuve, 1620, av de Lasalle, Montréal PQ H1V 2J8 – 514/253-2181; Fax: 514/253-1239 – Dir. gen., Paul Leguerrier
Montréal: CLSC J. Octave Roussin, 13926, rue Notre-Dame est, Montréal PQ H1A 1T5 – 514/642-4050; Fax: 514/498-7507 – Dir. gen., Monique Corbeil
Montréal: CLSC Lac St-Louis, 180, av Cartier, Pointe-Claire PQ H9S 4S1 – 514/697-4110; Fax: 514/697-6341 – Dir. gen., Sandra Golding
Montréal: CLSC Lasalle, 7475, boul Newman, 2e étage, Lasalle PQ H8N 1X3 – 514/364-2572 – Dir. gen., Jean-Paul Bouchard
Montréal: CLSC Mercier-est/Anjou, 9403, rue Sherbooke est, Montréal PQ H1L 6P2 – 514/356-2572; Fax: 514/356-2571 – Dir. gen., André Lemelin
Montréal: CLSC Metro, 1801, boul de Maisonneuve ouest, Montréal PQ H3H 1J9 – 514/934-0354; Fax: 514/934-3776 – Dir. gen., Marie Beauchamp
Montréal: CLSC Montréal-nord, 11441, boul Lacordaire, Montréal PQ H1G 4J9 – 514/327-0400; Fax: 514/327-1275 – Dir. gen., Pierre Ouimet
Montréal: CLSC Norman-Bethune, 1655, rue du Couvent, Laval PQ H7W 3A8 – 514/687-5690; Fax: 514/687-5998 – Dir. gen., Richard Rivest
Montréal: CLSC Notre-Dame-de-Grace/Montréal-ouest, #110, 2525, boul Cavendish, Montréal PQ H4B 2Y4 – 514/485-1670; Fax: 514/485-6406 – Dir. gen., Terry Kaufman
Montréal: CLSC Olivier-Guimond, 5455, rue Chauveau, Montréal PQ H1N 1G8 – 514/255-2365; Fax: 514/255-1443 – Dir. gen., Renée Audy
Montréal: CLSC Parc Extension, 469, rue Jean-Talon ouest, Montréal PQ H3N 1R4 – 514/273-9591; Fax: 514/273-8954 – Dir. gen., Richard Vezina
Montréal: CLSC la Petit Patrie, 6520, rue de Saint-Vallier, Montréal PQ H2S 2P7 – 514/273-4508; Fax: 514/272-6278 – Dir. gen., Mariette Dion
Montréal: CLSC Pierrefonds, 13800, boul Gouin est, Pierrefonds PQ H8Z 3H6 – 514/626-2572; Fax: 514/626-6514 – Dir. gen., Mariette le Brun-Bohemier
Montréal: CLSC Rene-Cassin, #600, 5800, boul Cavendish, Cote-St-Luc PQ H4W 2T5 – 514/488-9163; Fax: 514/485-1612 – Dir. gen., Leon Ouaknine
Montréal: CLSC Rivière-des-Prairies, 8655, boul Perras, Montréal PQ H1E 4M7 – 514/648-4963; Fax: 514/648-8565 – Dir. gen., Jean-Pierre Deschenes
Montréal: CLSC St-Henri, 3833, rue Notre-Dame ouest, Montréal PQ H4C 1P8 – 514/933-7541; Fax: 514/933-1740 – Dir. gen., Louis-Paul Thauvette
Montréal: CLSC Saint-Leonard, 5540, rue Jarry est, Saint-Leonard PQ H1P 1T9 – 514/328-3460; Fax: 514/328-2976 – Dir. gen., Michele Vigeoz
Montréal: CLSC St-Louis du Parc, 155, boul Saint-Joseph est, Montréal PQ H2T 1H4 – 514/286-9657; Fax: 514/286-9706 – Dir. gen., Saul Panofsky
Montréal: CLSC Saint-Michel, 7950, boul Saint-Michel, Montréal PQ H1Z 3E1 – 514/374-8223; Fax: 514/374-9180 – Dir. gen., Pierre Durocher
Montréal: CLSC Ste-Rose de Laval, 280, boul Roi-du-nord, Laval PQ H7L 4L2 – 514/622-5110; Fax: 514/622-4150 – Dir. gen., Yves Matteau
Montréal: CLSC Verdun/Cote St-Paul, 1090, av de l'Eglise, Verdun PQ H4G 2N5 – 514/766-0546; Fax: 514/762-4139 – Dir. gen., Robert Capistran
Montréal: CLSC Villeray, 1425, rue Jarry est, Montréal PQ H2E 1A7 – 514/376-4141; Fax: 514/722-3758 – Dir. gen., Gyslaine Samson-Saulnier
Murdochville: Centre de santé des Hauts Bois, 600, av Dr. William May, Murdochville PQ G0E 1W0 – 418/784-2561; Fax: 418/784-3629 – 15 lits – Dir. gen., Robert Lapointe
Natashquan: Dispensaire-Natashquan (CS St-Jean-Eudes), Natashquan PQ G0G 2E0 – 418/726-3387 – Dir. gen., Denis R. Boudreau
Paspebiac: CLSC Chaleurs, 145, route 132, CP 7000, Paspebiac PQ G0C 2K0 – 418/752-6611; Fax: 418/752-6734 – Dir. gen., Jean-Marie le Brasseur
Plessisville: CLSC de l'Erable, 1331, rue Saint-Calixte, Plessisville PQ G6L 1P4 – 819/362-6301; Fax: 819/362-6300 – 40 lits – Dir. gen., Remi Moisan
Pohenegamook: CLSC des Frontières, 1922, St-Vallier, CP 70, Pohenegamook PQ G0L 2T0 – 418/859-2450; Fax: 418/859-3484 – 25 lits – Dir. gen., Marcel Lavoie
Port Cartier: Centre de santé de Port-Cartier, 103, boul des Rochelois, Port Cartier PQ G5B 1K5 – 418/766-2715; Fax: 418/766-5229 – 16 lits – Dir. gen., Jean-Marc Maloney
Port-Cartier: Centre de santé de Port-Cartier (Point de service), Edifice le Royer, 24, boul des Iles, Port-Cartier PQ G5B 2M9 – 418/766-2715 – Dir. gen., Jean-Marc Maloney
Quaqtaq: Dispensaire de Quaqtaq, Quaqtaq PQ J0M 1J0 – 819/492-9977 – Dir. gen., Minnie Grey
Québec: Centre hospitalier Courchesne/CLSC Haute-Ville, 55, ch Ste-Foy, Québec PQ G1R 1S9 – 418/641-0784 – Dir. gen., Gaetan Garon
Québec: CLSC de la Basse-Ville, 50, rue St-Joseph est, Québec PQ G1K 3A5 – 418/529-6592; Fax: 418/529-1376 – Dir. gen., André Metivier
Radisson: Centre hospitalier La Grande Rivière, CP 800, Radisson PQ J0Y 2X0 – 819/638-8240; Fax: 819/638-7496 – 11 lits – Dir. gen., Jules Pelletier
Remigny: Point de service Remigny, Remigny PQ J0Z 3H0 – 819/761-3491 – Dir. gen., Pierre Larouche
Richelieu: CLSC du Richelieu, 633, 12e av, Richelieu PQ J3L 4V5 – 514/658-7561; Fax: 514/658-7568 – Dir. gen., Julien Tremblay
Richmond: CLSC du Val Saint-Francois, 110, rue Barlow, CP 890, Richmond PQ J0B 2H0 – 819/826-3781; Fax: 819/826-3867 – Dir. gen., Gary Furlong
Rimouski: CLSC de l'Estuaire, 165, rue des Gouverneurs, Rimouski PQ G5L 7R2 – 418/724-7204; Fax: 418/724-7743 – Dir. gen., Mariette Chabot
Rivière-au-Tonnerre: Dispensaire-Rivière-au-Tonnerre (CS St-Jean-Eudes), Rivière-au-Tonnerre PQ G0G 2N0 – 418/465-2146 – Dir. gen., Denis R. Boudreau
Rivière-du-Loup: CLSC Rivières et Marées, 22, rue Saint-Laurent, Rivière-du-Loup PQ G5R 4W5 – 418/867-2642; Fax: 418/867-4713 – Dir. gen., Rejean Godbout
Rivière-Saint-Jean: Dispensaire-Rivière-St-Jean (CS St-Jean-Eudes), Rivière-Saint-Jean PQ G0G 2N0 – 418/949-2020 – Dir. gen., Denis R. Beaudreau
Roberval: Le Claire Fontaine, 835, rue Lévesque, Roberval PQ G8H 3J5 – 418/275-1360; Fax: 418/275-6211 – 19 lits – Dir. gen., Laurent Bouillon
Rouyn-Noranda: CLSC le partage des eaux, 19, rue Perreault ouest, Rouyn-Noranda PQ J9X 2T3 – 819/762-8144; Fax: 819/762-1057 – Dir. gen., Roger Dumais
Saint-Andre-Avellin: CLSC de la Petite Nation, 12, rue Saint-Andre, CP 120, Saint-Andre-Avellin PQ J0V 1W0 – 819/983-7341; Fax: 819/983-7708 – Dir. gen., Michel Audra
Saint-Esprit: CLSC Montcalm, 110, rue Saint-Isidore, Saint-Esprit PQ J0K 2L0 – 514/839-3676; Fax: 514/839-6603 – Dir. gen., Paul-Yvon Debilly
Saint-Eustache: CLSC Jean-Oliver-Chenier, 29, ch Oka, Saint-Eustache PQ J7R 1K6 – 514/491-1233; Fax: 514/491-3424 – Dir. gen., Gylaine Boucher
Saint-Fabien-de-Panet: CLSC Antoine-Rivard, 10, rue Alphonse, CP 39, Saint-Fabien-de-Panet PQ G0R 2J0 – 418/249-2572; Fax: 418/249-2507 – Dir. gen., Pierre Thibaudeau
Saint-Felicien: CLSC des Pres-Bleus, 1228, boul Sacre-Coeur, CP 10, Saint-Felicien PQ G8K 2P8 – 418/679-5270; Fax: 418/679-3510 – Dir. gen., Michel Bernard
Saint-Hubert: CLSC St-Hubert, 6800, boul Cousineau, Saint-Hubert PQ J3Y 8Z4 – 514/443-7400; Fax: 514/676-4645 – Dir. gen., Michele Laverdure
Saint-Hyacinthe: CLSC des Maskoutains, 2650, rue Morin, Saint-Hyacinthe PQ J2S 8H1 – 514/778-1144; Fax: 514/778-1899 – Dir. gen., Denis Blanchard
St-Jean-Port-Joli: CLSC des Trois-Saumons, 430, rue Jean Leclerc, St-Jean-Port-Joli PQ G0R 3G0 – 418/598-3355; Fax: 418/598-9800 – 40 lits – Dir. gen., Jean-Marc Bourgault
Saint-Jerome: CLSC Arthur-Buies, 430, rue Labelle, Saint-Jerome PQ J7Z 5L3 – 514/431-2221; Fax: 514/431-6538 – Dir. gen., Georges le Gal
Saint-Joseph-de-Beauce: CLSC Beauce-Centre, 1125, ave du Palais, CP 790, Saint-Joseph-de-Beauce PQ G0S 2V0 – 418/397-5722; Fax: 418/397-2457 – Dir. gen., Claude Jobin
Saint-Jovite: CLSC des Trois Vallées, 352, rue Leonard, Saint-Jovite PQ J0T 2H0 – 819/425-3771; Fax: 819/425-2695 – Dir. gen., Christine Lessard
Saint-Lazare: CLSC de Bellechasse, 100, rue Monseigneur Bilodeau, Saint-Lazare PQ G0R 3J0 – 418/883-2227; Fax: 418/887-6400 – Dir. gen., Michel Girard
St-Marc-des-Carrieres: CLSC de Portneuf, 1045, av Bona Dussault, CP 400, St-Marc-des-Carrieres PQ G0A 4B0 – 418/268-3571; Fax: 418/268-8533 – Dir. gen., Gilles Chartier
Saint-Maxime-du-Mont-Louis: CLSC des Berges, 19, 1re ave ouest, CP 100, Saint-Maxime-du-Mont-Louis PQ G0E 1T0 – 418/797-2744; Fax: 418/797-5122 – Dir. gen., Michelle Arcand

Saint-Omer: CLSC Malauze (Point de service), 102, boul Perron, CP 10, Saint-Omer PQ G0C 2Z0 – 418/364-7064
St-Pamphile: CLSC - Centre d'accueil des Appalaches, 103, rue du Foyer nord, CP 580, St-Pamphile PQ G0R 3X0 – 418/356-3393; Fax: 418/356-2756 – Dir. gen., Bernard Lamy
Saint-Pascal: CLSC Les Aboiteaux, 580, 25e rue, CP 850, Saint-Pascal PQ G0L 3Y0 – 418/492-1223; Fax: 418/492-5742 – Dir. gen., Gilles Michaud
Saint-Paulin: CLSC Valentine-Lupien, 2841, rue Lafleche, Saint-Paulin PQ J0K 3G0 – 819/268-2572; Fax: 819/268-2505 – Dir. gen., Henri-Paul Picotte
Saint-Remi: CLSC Jardin du Québec, 2, rue Sainte-Famille, Saint-Remi PQ J0L 2L0 – 514/454-4671; Fax: 514/454-4538 – Dir. gen., Gilles Charest
Saint-Romuald: CLSC Chutes-de-la-Chaudière-Desjardins, 2055, boul de la Rive sud, Saint-Romuald PQ G6W 2S5 – 418/839-3511; Fax: 418/839-4190 – Dir. gen., Celine L. Morin
Saint-Tite: CLSC Normandie, 750, rue du Couvent, CP 430, Saint-Tite PQ G0X 3H0 – 418/365-7555; Fax: 418/365-6009 – Dir. gen., Donat Gingras
Sainte-Adele: CLSC des Pays-d'en-Haut, 1390, boul Sainte-Adele, CP 2130, Sainte-Adele PQ J0R 1L0 – 514/229-6601; Fax: 514/229-7220 – Dir. gen., Gilles Morin
Sainte-Anne-de-Beaupre: CLSC Orleans, 9500, boul Sainte-Anne, Sainte-Anne-de-Beaupre PQ G0A 3C0 – 418/827-5241; Fax: 418/827-6107 – Dir. gen., Jean-Guy Trottier
Sainte-Genevieve-de-Batiscan: CLSC des Cheaux, 90, route Rivière-a-Veillette, RR#4, Sainte-Genevieve-de-Batiscan PQ G0X 2R0 – 418/362-2727; Fax: 418/362-3125 – Dir. gen., Gaetan Lebel
Sainte-Marie: CLSC Nouvelle Beauce, 1133, boul Vachon nord, CP 1630, Sainte-Marie PQ G6E 3C6 – 418/387-8181; Fax: 418/387-8188 – Dir. gen., Marc Tanguay
Sainte-Monique: CLSC Nicolet-Yamaska, 390, rue Principale, Sainte-Monique PQ J0G 1N0 – 819/289-2255; Fax: 819/289-2982 – Dir. gen., Marcel Nolet
Sainte-Therese: CLSC Therese-de-Blainville, 55, rue Saint-Joseph, Sainte-Therese PQ J7E 4Y5 – 514/430-4553; Fax: 514/430-0140 – Dir. gen., Luc Guenette
Salaberry-de-Valleyfield: CLSC Seigneurie de Beauharnois, 71, rue Maden, Salaberry-de-Valleyfield PQ J6S 3V4 – 514/371-0143; Fax: 514/371-7682 – Dir. gen., Christiane Brazeau-Patenaude
Schefferville: Dispensaire de Kawawachikamach, Reserve Naskapis, CP 189, Schefferville PQ G0G 2T0 – 418/585-3664
Schefferville: Dispensaire de Schefferville, 326-328, rue A.P. Low, CP 1059, Schefferville PQ G0G 2T0 – 418/585-2645
Senneterre: Centre de santé le Minordet, 961, rue de la Clinique, CP 4000, Senneterre PQ J0Y 2M0 – 819/737-2243; Fax: 819/737-8425 – Dir. gen., Sylvie Desmarais
Sept-Iles: CLSC des Sept Iles, 405, av Brochu, Sept-Iles PQ G4R 2W9 – 418/962-2572; Fax: 418/962-1858 – Dir. gen., André Tremblay
Shawinigan: CLSC du centre de la Mauricie, 1600, boul Biermans, Shawinigan PQ G9N 8L2 – 819/539-8371; Fax: 819/539-8853 – Dir. gen., Renald Turcotte
Sherbrooke: CLSC Gaston-Lessard, 1200, rue King est, Sherbrooke PQ J1G 1E4 – 819/563-0144; Fax: 819/563-9912 – Dir. gen., Denis Lalumiere
Sherbrooke: CLSC SOC, 50, rue Camirand, Sherbrooke PQ J1H 4J5 – 819/565-1330; Fax: 819/565-4411 – Dir. gen., Jaime Borja
Sorel: CLSC de Havre, 201, rue du Havre, CP 590, Sorel PQ J3P 7N7 – 514/746-4545; Fax: 514/746-7296 – Dir. gen., Claire Roussey
Tasiujaq: Dispensaire de Tasiujaq, Tasiujaq PQ J0M 1T0 – 819/633-9977 – Dir. gen., Minnie Grey
Temiscaming: Centre de santé de Témiscaming, 180, rue Anvik, CP 760, Temiscaming PQ J0Z 3R0 – 819/627-3385; Fax: 819/627-3629 – 22 lits – Dir. gen., Gilbert Ladouceur
Terrebonne: CLSC Lamater, 4625, boul des Seigneurs, Terrebonne PQ J6W 5B1 – 514/471-2881; Fax: 514/471-7134 – Dir. gen., Luc Guenette
Thetford Mines: CLSC Frontenac, 17, rue Notre-Dame sud, Thetford Mines PQ G6G 1J1 – 418/338-3511; Fax: 418/338-1668 – Dir. gen., Normand Baker
Trois-Pistoles: CLSC des Basques, 400, rue Jean Rioux, CP 39, Trois-Pistoles PQ G0L 4K0 – 418/851-1111; Fax: 418/851-4892 – Dir. gen., Raymond LeBlond
Trois-Rivieres: CLSC Les Forges, 500, rue Saint-Georges, Trois-Rivieres PQ G9A 2K8 – 819/379-7131; Fax: 819/373-7726 – Dir. gen., Laurent Pare
Val-Belair: CLSC de la Jacques-Cartier, 1465, rue de l'Etna, Val-Belair PQ G3K 1Y8 – 418/843-2572; Fax: 418/842-4662 – Dir. gen., Claude Soucy
Varennes: CLSC des Seigneuries, 2220, boul René-Gaultier, Varennes PQ J3X 1T6 – 514/652-2917; Fax: 514/652-9902 – Dir. gen., André Foisy
Vaudreuil-Dorion: CLSC le Presqu'ile, 490, boul Harwood, Vaudreuil-Dorion PQ J7V 7H4 – 514/455-6171; Fax: 514/455-9086 – Dir. gen., Doris Baril
Victoriaville-Arthabaska: CLSC Suzor-Cote, 100, rue de l'Ermitage, Victoriaville-Arthabaska PQ G6P 9N2 – 819/758-7281; Fax: 819/758-5009 – Dir. gen., Richard Desrochers
Weedon: CLSC Fleur de Lys, 460, 2e av, Weedon PQ J0B 3J0 – 819/877-3434; Fax: 819/877-3714 – Dir. gen., Guy Dufresne
Wemindji: Dispensaire de Wemindji, Wemindji PQ J0M 1L0 – 819/978-0225

HÔPITAUX PSYCHIATRIQUES ET ASSISTANCE COMMUNAUTAIRE

Alma: Villa des Lys - SAHT, 825, av Tanguay, Alma PQ G8B 5Y2 – 30 places – Dir. gen., Laurent Bouillon
Alma: Villa des Lys Inc., 400, boul Champlain sud, Alma PQ G8B 5W1 – 418/662-3447; Fax: 418/662-7860 – 37 beneficiaires – Dir. gen., Laurent Bouillon
Aylmer: Centre Mgr-Proulx, 151, rue Broad, Aylmer PQ J9H 3L7 – 819/684-1022; Fax: 819/684-8153 – 97 beneficiaires – Dir. gen., Danielle Lessard
Baie-Comeau: Pavillon de la Falaise - Le Ressac, 1250, rue Lestrat, CP 2100, Baie-Comeau PQ G5C 2S8 – 418/589-2038; Fax: 418/589-6227 – 40 places – Dir. gen., Denys Cote
Baie-Saint-Paul: SAHT St-Placide, 86, RR#4, Baie-Saint-Paul PQ G0A 1B0 – 418/435-2980 – 40 places – Dir. gen., Robert Vallieres
Beauport: Centre hospitalier Robert Giffard, 2601, rue de la Canardière, Beauport PQ G1J 2G3 – 418/663-5321; Fax: 418/666-3254 – 673 lits – Dir. gen., Réjean Cantin
Buckingham: SAHT de Buckingham, 216, rue Albert, Buckingham PQ J8L 1M6 – 819/986-3018 – 16 places – Dir. gen., Danielle Lessard
Chambly: Le SAHT de Chambly, 2135, boul Industriel, Chambly PQ J3L 4C5 – 514/658-5687 – 35 places – Dir. gen., Jean-Pierre Picard
Chicoutimi: Centre d'entrainement a la vie de Chicoutimi Inc., 766, rue du Cenacle, Chicoutimi PQ G7H 2J2 – 418/549-4003; Fax: 418/549-5281 – 56 beneficiaires – Dir. gen., Normand Dionne
Fatima: Centre de réadaptation des Iles, CP 580, Fatima PQ G0T 1G0 – 418/986-3590; Fax: 418/986-5778 – 25 places – Dir. gen., Micheline Decoste
Gatineau: Services Gatineau (Pavillon du Parc inc.), 811, boul St-René ouest, Gatineau PQ J8R 2S4 – 819/243-4443 – 40 places – Dir. gen., Danielle Lessard
Hull: Services Hull (Pavillon du Parc inc.), 178, rue Jean Proulx, Hull PQ J8Z 1V3 – 819/777-2944 – 36 places – Dir. gen., Danielle Lessard
La Malbaie: Service d'Apprentissage aux Habitudes de Travail La Malbaie, 100, rue Nairn, La Malbaie PQ G5A 1L8 – 418/665-7121 – 35 places – Dir. gen., Robert Vallieres
La Tuque: Centre de réadaptation du Lac Edouard, 1440, boul Ducharme, La Tuque PQ G9X 3N8 – 819/523-7656; Fax: 819/523-9842 – 35 places – Dir. gen., Michel Gauthier
Lac-Etchemin: SAHT Etchemins, 102, rue Giguere, Lac-Etchemin PQ G0R 1S0 – 418/625-3420 – 27 places – Dir. gen., Pierre Maheu
Lafontaine: Pavillon Ste-Marie Inc., 45, rue du Pavillon, Lafontaine PQ J7Y 3R6 – 514/438-3583; Fax: 514/438-7481 – 130 beneficiaires – Dir. gen., Francyne Jolicoeur
L'Assomption: Centre d'accueil l'Envol Inc., 391, rue Saint-Etienne, CP 29, L'Assomption PQ J0K 1G0 – 514/589-2213; Fax: 514/589-4581 – Dir. gen., Claude Ouellet
Lévis: Centre de réadaptation l'Estran, 100, rue Mgr Ignance-Bourget, Lévis PQ G6V 2Y9 – 418/833-3218; Fax: 418/833-9849 – 60 beneficiaires – Dir. gen., Michel Langlais
Longueuil: Centre d'accueil de Longueuil, 600, rue Prefontaine, Longueuil PQ J4K 3V6 – 514/670-3220 – 54 beneficiaires – Dir. gen., Jean-Pierre Picard
Magog: SAHT Memphre-Magog, 1525, rue Principale est, Magog PQ J1X 1Z8 – 819/868-6747 – 20 places – Dir. gen., Claude Lapointe
Malartic: Centre hospitalier de Malartic, 1141, rue Royale, CP 800, Malartic PQ J0Y 1Z0 – 819/757-4342; Fax: 819/757-4330 – 49 lits – Dir. gen., Christiane Glacon
Montmagny: Centre d'accueil Louis C. Dupuis, 20, av Coté, Montmagny PQ G5V 3V2 – 418/248-4970 – 79 beneficiaires – Dir. gen., Michel Langlais
Montréal: Centre d'accueil Charleroi, 6455, rue Jean Talon est, 6e étage, Saint-Leonard PQ H1S 3E8 – 514/259-2245; Fax: 514/259-5906 – 48 beneficiaires – Dir. gen., Helene Duval
Montréal: Centre d'accueil Jean-Olivier Chenier, 8000, rue Notre-Dame ouest, Saint-Pierre PQ H8R 1H2 – 514/364-2280; Fax: 514/595-5371 – 48 beneficiaires – Dir. gen., John Aung-Thwin
Montréal: Le Centre d'accueil Miriam, 4321, av Guimont, Laval PQ H7W 1E7 – 514/681-9256 – Dir. gen., Steve M. Solomon
Montréal: Centre d'accueil Senecal, 5025, boul Gouin est, Montréal-Nord PQ H1G 1A3 – 514/327-9933; Fax: 514/327-9861 – Dir. gen., Jean-Pierre Aumont
Montréal: Le Centre Garry Taylor, 231, av Elm, Beaconsfield PQ H9W 2E2 – 514/695-3914 – 60 beneficiaires – Dir. gen., François Laberge
Montréal: Le centre John Birks, 7100, boul Champlain, Verdun PQ H4H 1A8 – 514/761-5571; Fax: 514/761-7595 – 60 beneficiaires – Dir. gen., François Laberge
Montréal: Centre Louise Vachon Enr., 4390, boul Saint-Martin ouest, Laval PQ H7T 1C3 – 514/687-2970; Fax: 514/687-4184 – Dir. gen., Rolande Sabourin
Montréal: Centres Marronniers, 5695, av des Marronniers, Montréal PQ H1T 2W3 – 514/255-4025; Fax: 514/255-7620 – Dir. gen., Helene Duval
Montréal: Hôpital Douglas, 6875, boul Lasalle, Verdun PQ H4H 1R3 – 514/761-6131; Fax: 514/762-3044 – Centre hospitalier de soins psychiatriques (195 lits) & centre d'hébergement et de soins de longue durée (455 lits) – Dir. gen., Jacques Hendlisz
Montréal: Hôpital Louis-H. Lafontaine, 7401, rue Hochelaga, Montréal PQ H1N 3M5 – 514/251-4000; Fax: 514/251-0856 – 233 lits – Dir. gen., Raymond Carignan, 514/251-4028
Montréal: Hôpital Rivière-des-Prairies, 7070, boul Perras, Montréal PQ H1E 1A4 – 514/323-7260; Fax: 514/323-8622 – 350 lits – Dir. gen., Jacques Mackay
Montréal: Institut Philippe Pinel de Montréal, 10905, boul Henri-Bourassa est, Montréal PQ H1C 1H1 –

514/648-8461; Fax: 514/494-4406 – 295 lits – Dir. gen., Lionel Beliveau
Montréal: Point de service centre de jour, 4211, rue Hochelaga, Montréal PQ H1V 1B8 – 514/252-0133 – 40 places – Dir. gen., Helene Duval
Québec: Services Barbara-Rourke (Adaptation-réadaptation), 850, rue de Beaujeu, Québec PQ G1J 2R6 – 418/529-6571; Fax: 418/529-0441 – 60 beneficiaires – Dir. gen., Michel Turmel
Repentigny: La Maisonnee Laurendière, 818, rue Notre-Dame, CP 200, Repentigny PQ J5Y 1B7 – 514/582-1416; Fax: 514/582-2297 – Dir. gen., Alain Lampron
Rimouski: Atelier Tache, 292, rue Tache, Rimouski PQ G5L 1R9 – 418/724-0727 – Dir. gen., Paul-Eugene Gagnon
Roberval: Centre d'animation de Roberval, 680, boul St-Joseph, Roberval PQ G8H 2L2 – 418/275-5351 – 49 places – Dir. gen., Laurent Bouillon
Rosemere: Les centres de réadaptation du Contrefort, 140, ch Grande Côté, Rosemere PQ J7A 1H3 – 514/437-7711; Fax: 514/437-7700 – Dir. gen., Alain Gervais
Saint-Cyprien: Centre de réadaptation en déficience intellectuelle KRTB, 101, rue de l'Eglise, CP 159, Saint-Cyprien PQ G0L 2P0 – 418/963-2016; Fax: 418/963-2617 – 40 beneficiaires – Dir. gen., Gaetan Emond
Saint-Felicien: Centre d'animation de St-Felicien, 1439, boul Sacré-Coeur, Saint-Felicien PQ G8K 1B3 – 418/679-8204 – 49 places
Saint-Georges-Est: Centre Victor Cloutier, 12525, 25e av, CP 336, Saint-Georges-Est PQ G5Y 5C8 – 418/228-2051 – Dir. gen., Pierre Maheu
Saint-Jean-sur-Richelieu: Maribro Inc., 610, boul Industriel, Saint-Jean-sur-Richelieu PQ J3B 7X4 – 514/348-0947; Fax: 514/348-0949 – 55 places – Dir. gen., Gilles Bertrand
Saint-Wenceslas: Centre l'Aubier Inc., 1170, rue Sainte-Therese, CP 27, Saint-Wenceslas PQ G0Z 1J0 – 819/224-7669 – 50 beneficiaires – Dir. gen., Francine P. Lampron
Sainte-Anne-des-Monts: Le centre de réadaptation de la Gaspesie, 230, Rte du Parc, CP 370, Sainte-Anne-des-Monts PQ G0E 2G0 – 418/763-3325; Fax: 418/763-5631 – Dir. gen., Jacques Tremblay
Sainte-Marguerite-du-Lac-Masson: Residence Ste-Marguerite Inc., 88, ch Masson, Sainte-Marguerite-du-Lac-Masson PQ J0T 1L0 – 514/228-2877; Fax: 514/228-4212 – 60 beneficiaires – Dir. gen., Jean-Paul Gohier
Thetford Mines: SAHT, 17, rue Notre Dame sud, Thetford Mines PQ G6G 1J1 – 418/335-3732 – 44 places – Dir. gen., Pierre Maheu
Tois-Rivières: Carrefour Niverville, 800, rue Niverville, Tois-Rivières PQ G9A 2A8 – 819/379-6893 – Dir. gen., Mathieu Vaillancourt
Vaudreuil: Atelier de Dorion, 486, av Chicoine, Vaudreuil PQ J7V 7E4 – 514/455-6104 – 45 places – Dir. gen., Gilles Bertrand
Victoriaville-Arthabaska: Centre d'accueil Nor-Val, 26, rue Saint-Jean-Baptiste, Victoriaville-Arthabaska PQ G6P 4C7 – 819/758-6272; Fax: 819/758-4448 – Dir. gen., Michel Gauthier
Waterloo: Le Centre Butters-Savoy Inc., RR#1, Waterloo PQ J0E 2N0 – 514/539-5333 – 60 places – Dir. gen., Ronald Creary

CENTRES D'ACCUEIL ET D'HÉBERGEMENT

Acton Vale: Centre d'accueil d'Acton Vale, 1268, rue Ricard, CP 850, Acton Vale PQ J0H 1A0 – 514/546-3234; Fax: 514/546-4811 – 80 lits – Dir. gen., Maurice Coutu
Albanel: Foyer St-Joseph d'Albanel Inc., 320, rue de l'Eglise, Albanel PQ G0W 1A0 – 418/279-5205; Fax: 418/279-5202 – 24 lits – Dir. gen., Laurent Leboeuf

Alma: Domaine Lajoie Enr., 1080, rue Price ouest, Alma PQ G8B 4T7 – 418/622-9258 – 14 places – Dir. gen., Guy St-Onge
Alma: Foyer Normandie d'Alma Inc., 50, ch du Foyer nord, CP 220, Alma PQ G8B 5V6 – 418/668-8313; Fax: 418/668-2453 – 59 lits – Dir. gen., Alain Gaudreault
Amos: Foyer Harricana Inc., 632, 1e rue ouest, Amos PQ J9T 2N2 – 819/732-6521; Fax: 819/732-7526 – 92 lits – Dir. gen., Paul-Emile Doré
Amos: Pavillon Amos Inc., 121, av Gouin, Amos PQ J9T 1R9 – 819/732-6521 – 14 places – Dir. gen., Paul-Emile Doré
Asbestos: Le Centre d'hébergement et de soins de longue durée de la MRC d'Asbestos, 229, rue Chasse, Asbestos PQ J1T 2B1 – 819/879-5475; Fax: 819/879-6736 – 47 lits – Dir. gen., Jean-Yves Poisson
Asbestos: Centre hospitalier d'Asbestos, see Centres hospitaliers listings
Aylmer: Centre d'accueil Renaissance, 445, boul Wilfrid-Lavigne, Aylmer PQ J9H 6H9 – 819/684-1101; Fax: 819/684-0261 – 75 lits – Dir. gen., Aurele Dufour
Aylmer: CHSLD Aylmer, 216, ch Fraser, Aylmer PQ J9H 2H8 – 819/684-5316; Fax: 819/684-3936 – 65 lits – Dir. gen., Vincenzo Simonetta
Baie-Comeau: Centre hospitalier régional - Pavillon Boisvert, see Centres hospitaliers listings
Baie-Comeau: Pavillon Martin et Rocheleau Inc., 892, boul Joliet, Baie-Comeau PQ G5C 1P4 – 418/589-7529 – 22 places – Dir. gen., Gaetan Gauthier
Baie-Saint-Paul: Centre d'accueil Pierre-Dupre, 10, rue Boivin, CP 5500, Baie-Saint-Paul PQ G0A 1B0 – 418/435-5562 – 75 lits – Dir. gen., Robert Vallieres
Baie-Saint-Paul: Centre hospitalier de Charlevoix, see Centres hospitaliers listings
Baie-Trinite: Centre d'accueil Trinite, 3, rue Saint-Joseph, Baie-Trinite PQ G0H 1A0 – 418/939-2251 – 15 lits – Dir. gen., Gaetan Gauthier
Barraute: Pavillon Barraute, 581, 3e rue ouest, Barraute PQ J0Y 1A0 – 819/734-6606 – 16 places – Dir. gen., Paul-Emile Doré
Beauceville: Centre hospitalier de Beauceville, see Centres hospitaliers listings
Beauharnois: Centre d'accueil le Vaisseau d'Or, 55, rue Saint-Andre, Beauharnois PQ J6N 3G7 – 514/429-6403; Fax: 514/429-6602 – 91 places – Dir. gen., Lise Belanger
Beauharnois: Residence Beauharnois, 182, ch Saint-Louis, Beauharnois PQ J6N 2H9 – 514/429-2161 – 21 places – Dir. gen., Lise Belanger
Beauport: Hôpital de l'Enfant-Jesus (Centre du Fargy), 700, boul des Chutes, Beauport PQ G1E 2B7 – 418/663-9934 – 60 lits – Dir. gen., Gaston Pellan
Beauport: Hôpital de l'Enfant-Jésus (Centre St-Augustin), see Centres hospitaliers listings
Beauport: Hôpital de l'Enfant-Jesus (Centre Yvonne Sylvain), 3365, rue Guimont, Beauport PQ G1E 2H1 – 418/663-8171 – 116 lits – Dir. gen., Gaston Pellan
Beauport: Pavillon A. Thomassin Inc., 214, av Saint-Michel, Beauport PQ G1C 1G2 – 418/663-4180 – 24 places – Dir. gen., Robert Laroche
Beauport: Pavillon de l'Orme, 125, av Saint-Michel, Beauport PQ G1C 1E8 – 418/661-1425 – 16 places – Dir. gen., Rejean Cantin
Beauport: Pavillon Grenon, 827, rue Sainte-Therese, Beauport PQ G1B 1E6 – 418/663-0312 – 12 places – Dir. gen., Robert Laroche
Beaupre: L'Accueil de Notre-Dame de Beaupre, 1, rue des Erables, CP 280, Beaupre PQ G0A 1E0 – 418/827-3738 – 39 lits – Dir. gen., Jean-Yves Simard
Beaupre: Foyer Beaupre Enr., 11280, av Royale, Beaupre PQ G0A 1E0 – 418/827-5345 – 15 lits – Dir. gen., Jeanne-D'Arc Fortin
Bedford: Centre hospitalier de Bedford, 34, rue St-Joseph, CP 1140, Bedford PQ J0J 1A0 – 514/248-4304;

Fax: 514/248-4676 – 42 lits – Dir. gen., Georges Robitaille
Beloeil: Centre d'accueil Marguerite-Adam, 425, rue Hubert, Beloeil PQ J3G 2T1 – 514/467-1631 – 70 lits – Dir. gen., Ghislain Lavergne
Beloeil: Centre d'hébergement Champlain-Beloeil, 221, rue Brunelle, Beloeil PQ J3G 2M9 – 514/467-3356; Fax: 514/467-3357 – 57 lits – Dir. gen., Guy Joly
Beloeil: Villa Beausejour, 80, boul Richelieu, Beloeil PQ J3G 4N5 – 514/467-7594 – 23 places – Dir. gen., Robert Busilacchi
Bernierville: Maison du Sacre-coeur, 230, rue Principale, Bernierville PQ G0N 1N0 – 418/428-3444 – 47 lits – Dir. gen., René Houle
Bernierville: Pavillon Jean-Luc Boulet, RR#4, Bernierville PQ G0N 1N0 – 418/428-3314 – 12 places – Dir. gen., René Houle
Bernierville: Pavillon Morisset Huppe, RR#2, Bernierville PQ G0N 1N0 – 418/428-3568 – 14 places – Dir. gen., René Houle
Berthierville: Centre hospitalier le Château de Berthier Inc., 730, rue Frontenac, Berthierville PQ J0K 1A0 – 514/836-6241; Fax: 514/836-4013 – 41 lits – Dir. gen., Guy Ducharme
Berthierville: CHSLD Berthier, 400, rue Frontenac, Berthierville PQ J0K 1A0 – 514/836-3756; Fax: 514/836-1319 – 81 lits – Dir. gen., Vincenzo Simonetta
Berthierville: Foyer Sacre-coeur de Berthierville Inc., 1010, rue Montcalm, CP 30, Berthierville PQ J0K 1A0 – 514/836-3759 – 42 lits – Dir. gen., Michel Lapierre
Bishopton: La Villa du Repos, CP 124, Bishopton PQ J0B 1G0 – 819/884-5568 – 17 places – Dir. gen., Albert Kratzenberg
Black Lake: Foyer du Lac Noir Inc., 1, rue Du Foyer, CP 40, Black Lake PQ G0N 1A0 – 418/423-7508; Fax: 418/423-5250 – 26 lits – Dir. gen., André Rodrigue
Black Lake: Pavillon Ginette Lafleur, 683, boul Frontenac, CP 6, Black Lake PQ G0N 1A0 – 418/423-2265; Fax: 418/423-5250 – 15 places – Dir. gen., André Rodrigue
Black Lake: Pavillon Yves et Suzanne Boutin, 868, rue Saint-Desire, Black Lake PQ G0N 1A0 – 418/423-2945 – 13 places – Dir. gen., André Rodrigue
Boucherville: Centre d'accueil Jeanne Crevier, 151, rue de Muy, Boucherville PQ J4B 4W7 – 514/641-0590; Fax: 514/641-3082 – 59 places – Dir. gen., Robert Sabino
Boucherville: Residence de Boucherville Inc., 782, boul Marie-Victorin, Boucherville PQ J4B 1Y3 – 514/655-8045 – 18 places – Dir. gen., Robert Sabino
Bromptonville: Foyer de Bromptonville Inc., 15, rue de la Croix sud, CP 460, Bromptonville PQ J0B 1H0 – 819/846-2708; Fax: 819/846-4328 – 38 lits – Dir. gen., Real Jacques
Brossard: Centre d'accueil Champlain, 5050, Place Nogent, Brossard PQ J4Y 2K3 – 514/443-0000; Fax: 514/443-0020 – 78 lits – Dir. gen., Lucien Dansereau
Brossard: Centre d'accueil Marcelle Ferron Inc., 8600, boul Marie Victorin, Brossard PQ J4X 1A1 – 514/923-1430; Fax: 514/923-1805 – 175 lits – Dir. gen., Zeff Guiducci
Buckingham: Centre d'accueil de Buckingham, 111, rue Lucerne, Buckingham PQ J8L 3C9 – 819/986-1043; Fax: 819/986-5671 – 80 – Dir. gen., Bernard Guidon
Campbell's Bay: Manoir St-Joseph, rue Reid, CP 430, Campbell's Bay PQ J0X 1K0 – 819/648-5852; Fax: 819/648-2378 – 39 lits – Dir. gen., Michel Pigeon
Cap-aux-Meules: Villa Plaisance, 506, ch Principal, CP 970, Cap-aux-Meules PQ G0B 1B0 – 418/986-3645; Fax: 418/986-2746 – 30 places – Dir. gen., Gaetan Doré
Cap-Chat: CHSLD de Cap-Chat, 41, rue Nicholas, CP 400, Cap-Chat PQ G0J 1E0 – 418/786-5523; Fax: 418/786-5421 – 82 lits – Dir. gen., André Jalbert
Cap-de-la-Madeleine: Centre d'accueil Luc Desilets, 145, rue Toupin, Cap-de-la-Madeleine PQ G8T 3Z8

– 819/379-8441 – 32 lits – Dir. gen., Reynald Dessureault

Cap-de-la-Madeleine: Foyer Pere Frederic Inc., 80, ch du Passage, Cap-de-la-Madeleine PQ G8T 2M2 – 819/378-4163; Fax: 819/378-7980 – 121 lits – Dir. gen., Vital Gaudet

Cap-de-la-Madeleine: Pavillon Nazareth du Cap (1985) Inc., 317, boul Loranger, Cap-de-la-Madeleine PQ G8T 3V8 – 819/375-6274 – 24 places – Dir. gen., Vital Gaudet

Cap-St-Ignace: Centre d'accueil St-Ignace, 91, rue du Manoir est, Cap-St-Ignace PQ G0R 1H0 – 418/246-5644 – 43 lits – Dir. gen., Jean-Paul Lacroix

Caplan: Pavillon Manoir St-Charles de Caplan, 101, boul Perron, CP 188, Caplan PQ G0C 1H0 – 418/388-5648 – 25 places – Dir. gen., Vilmont Moreau

Chambly: Manoir Chambly, 1309, rue Barre, Chambly PQ J3L 2V3 – 514/658-1663 – 9 lits – Dir. gen., Margaret Scott

Chambly: Manoir Soleil Inc., 125, rue Daigneault, Chambly PQ J3L 1G7 – 514/658-4441; Fax: 514/658-6521 – 44 lits – Dir. gen., Suzanne Gaudet

Chambly: Residence St-Joseph de Chambly, 100, rue Martel, Chambly PQ J3L 1V3 – 514/658-6271 – 39 lits – Dir. gen., Michel Desnoyers

Chandler: Centre hospitalier de Chandler, see Centres hospitaliers listings

Chandler: Villa Pabos, 75, av des Cedres, CP 1088, Chandler PQ G0C 1K0 – 418/628-0456; Fax: 418/689-4860 – 62 lits – Dir. gen., Louisette Langlois

Charlesbourg: Centre d'accueil St-François, 600, 60e rue est, Charlesbourg PQ G1H 3A9 – 418/623-1515 – 30 lits – Dir. gen., Aline Clouthier

Charlesbourg: Centre d'hébergement St-Joseph Inc., 1430, av Notre-Dame, Charlesbourg PQ G2N 1S1 – 418/849-1891; Fax: 418/849-1892 – 30 lits – Dir. gen., Yvonette Cote-Letourneau

Charlesbourg: Centre hospitalier St-Jean-Eudes Inc., 6000, 3e av ouest, Charlesbourg PQ G1H 7J5 – 418/627-1124; Fax: 418/627-4995 – 64 lits – Dir. gen., Clemence Boucher

Charlesbourg: Le Foyer de Charlesbourg Inc., 7150, boul Cloutier, Charlesbourg PQ G1H 5V5 – 418/628-0456; Fax: 418/622-8676 – 91 lits – Dir. gen., Gratien Tardif

Charlesbourg: Pension Marie-Chantal, 8320, 1re av, Charlesbourg PQ G1G 4C2 – 418/628-7563 – 31 places – Dir. gen., Jacques Garneau

Charny: Centre hospitalier Paul-Gilbert, see Centres hospitaliers listings

Châteauguay: Centre d'hébergement Champlain-Châteauguay, 210, rue Salaberry sud, Châteauguay PQ J6K 3M9 – 514/699-1694 – 96 lits – Dir. gen., Guy Joly

Châteauguay: Le Foyer de Châteauguay Inc., 95, rue Haute-Rivière, Châteauguay PQ J6K 3P1 – 514/692-8231; Fax: 514/692-7920 – 79 lits – Dir. gen., Gaetan Roy

Chatham: Villa d'Argenteuil Inc., 21, rue Renaud (1er et 2e étage), Chatham PQ J0V 2A0 – 514/562-8738 – 22 places – Dir. gen., René Giard

Chicoutimi: Beaumanoir de Chicoutimi Inc., 904, rue Jacques-Cartier est, Chicoutimi PQ G7H 2A9 – 418/698-3900; Fax: 418/381-1091 – 92 lits – Dir. gen., Benoit Duplessis

Chicoutimi: Centre Mgr Victor Tremblay, 1236, av d'Angouleme, Chicoutimi PQ G7H 6P9 – 418/549-3941 – 50 lits – Dir. gen., Benoit Duplessis

Chicoutimi: Le Foyer Delage, 257, rue St-Armand, CP 10, Chicoutimi PQ G7G 1S4 – 418/549-3941; Fax: 418/549-5444 – 53 lits – Dir. gen., Benoit Duplessis

Chicoutimi: Foyer St-Francois Inc., 293, av Sainte-Famille, Chicoutimi PQ G7H 4J5 – 418/549-3727; Fax: 418/543-2038 – 44 lits – Dir. gen., Constant Bergeron

Chicoutimi: Institut Roland-Saucier, 150, rue Pinel, CP 2250, Chicoutimi PQ G7G 3W4 – 418/549-5474; Fax: 418/549-8143 – 10 lits – Dir. gen., Guy St-Onge

Chicoutimi: Maison Rock Boivin Enr., 2651, rue Roussel, Chicoutimi PQ G7G 1Y3 – 418/543-8819 – 20 places – Dir. gen., Guy St-Onge

Chicoutimi: Maison Saint-Antoine, 392, av St-Hilaire, Chicoutimi PQ G7J 3R1 – 418/549-3741 – 10 places – Dir. gen., Guy St-Onge

Clermont: Foyer de Clermont Inc., 6, rue du Foyer, CP 520, Clermont PQ G0T 1C0 – 418/439-4684; Fax: 418/439-4062 – 42 lits – Dir. gen., Jacques Tremblay

Cleveland: Foyer Wales, 506, rte 243, Cleveland PQ J0B 2H0 – 819/826-3266; Fax: 819/826-2549 – 222 lits – Dir. gen., Roderick MacIver

Coaticook: Centre hospitalier de Coaticook, 138, rue Jeanne-Mance, Coaticook PQ J1A 1W3 – 819/849-4876; Fax: 819/849-6735 – 67 lits – Dir. gen., Rémi Lasigne

Coaticook: Pavillon Boiscastel, 399, rue Court, Coaticook PQ J1A 1L7 – 819/849-4876 – 48 lits – Dir. gen., Remi Lavigne

Contrecoeur: Centre d'accueil Contrecoeur, 4700, rue Marie-Victorin, CP 1120, Contrecoeur PQ J0L 1C0 – 514/587-2492; Fax: 514/587-8411 – 50 lits – Dir. gen., Robert Sabino

Cookshire: Pavillon St-Camille, 140, rue Eastview, CP 490, Cookshire PQ J0B 1M0 – 819/875-3026 – 18 places – Dir. gen., Roger Couture

Côte-Nord-du-Golfe-St-Laurent: Pavillon Dr. Donald G. Hodd, Harringon Harbour, Côte-Nord-du-Golfe-St-Laurent PQ G0G 1N0 – 514/795-3353 – 14 lits – Dir. gen., Remy Beaudoin

Coteau-du-Lac: Maison de la Providence, Coteau-du-Lac, 341, ch du Fleuve, Coteau-du-Lac PQ J0P 1B0 – 514/763-5951 – 71 lits – Dir. gen., Claude-Yves de Repentigny

Coteau-du-Lac: Pavillon Denise Enr., 29, Route 338, Coteau-du-Lac PQ J0P 1B0 – 514/763-5543 – 29 lits – Dir. gen., Yvan LaFontaine

Coteau-du-Lac: Pavillon Laura Ferguson, 60, ch du Fleuve, CP 339, Coteau-du-Lac PQ J0P 1B0 – 514/267-3379 – 15 places – Dir. gen., Paul-Henri Boutin

Coteau-Landing: Hôpital Nôtre-Dame-de-Coteau-Landing ltée, 37, rue Principale, CP 180, Coteau-Landing PQ J0P 1C0 – 514/267-3581; Fax: 514/267-9263 – 44 lits – Dir. gen., Pierre Perrier

Cowansville: Centre d'accueil de Cowansville, 200, rue Principale, Cowansville PQ J2K 1J2 – 514/263-5142; Fax: 514/263-5114 – 72 lits – Dir. gen., Lucien Rioux

Cowansville: Foyer Regal, 782, rue Principale, Cowansville PQ J2K 1K1 – 514/263-1797 – 7 lits – Dir. gen., Thelma Wells

Crabtree: Pavillon Racette, 180, 8e rue, Crabtree PQ J0K 1B0 – 514/754-2804 – 14 places – Dir. gen., Maurice Blais

Danville: Centre d'hebergement de Danville, 114, rue Daniel Johnson, CP 690, Danville PQ J0A 1A0 – 819/839-2760; Fax: 819/839-3813 – 55 lits – Dir. gen., Jean-Bernard Breault

Deauville: Centre d'accueil Deauville Inc., 168, rue Dion, CP 330, Deauville PQ J1N 3H2 – 819/864-6631 – 16 lits – Dir. gen., Claudette Gregoire

Degelis: Residence Degelis Inc., 587, 6e rue, Degelis PQ G0L 1H0 – 418/853-3919 – 24 places – Dir. gen., Rejean Pelletier

Delisle: Le Domaine du Bel Age de Saint-Coeur de Marie, 4750, av Grande-Decharge, CP 157, Delisle PQ G0W 1L0 – 418/347-3394 – 35 lits – Dir. gen., Alain Gaudreault

Des Ruisseuax: Pavillon Cloutier et St-Louis Enr., 4700, ch de la Lievre nord, Des Ruisseuax PQ J9L 3G4 – 819/623-5371 – 20 places – Dir. gen., Gilles Huberdeau

Deschaillons-sur-Saint-Laurent: Foyer Deschaillons, 1045, rue Marie-Victorin, CP 219, Deschaillons-sur-Saint-Laurent PQ G0S 1G0 – 819/292-2262; Fax: 819/292-3046 – 44 lits – Dir. gen., Gisele Marquis

Deux-Montagnes: Centre d'hébergement et de soins de longue durée Deux-Montagnes Inc., 2700, ch Oka, Deux-Montagnes PQ J7R 4K1 – 514/473-5111; Fax: 514/491-4309 – 33 lits – Dir. gen., Louis-Henri Fournier

Deux-Montagnes: Le Manoir Grand Moulin Inc., 2, Croissant Grand-Moulin, Deux-Montagnes PQ J7R 6B4 – 514/473-7360; Fax: 514/473-5941 – 59 lits – Dir. gen., Denis Renaud

Disraeli: Foyer de Disraeli Inc., 260, av Champlain, CP 698, Disraeli PQ G0N 1E0 – 418/449-2020; Fax: 418/449-4006 – 47 lits – Dir. gen., André Rodrigue

Disraeli: Pavillon Saint-Rosaire, 367, av Champlain, Disraeli PQ G0N 1E0 – 418/449-2660 – 16 places – Dir. gen., André Rodrigue

Dolbeau: Pavillon Maison du Bel Age, 2020, rue Provencher, Dolbeau PQ G8L 2B4 – 418/276-1866 – 30 places – Dir. gen., Jacques Turcotte

Donnacona: Centre d'hébergement Donnacona, 250, boul Gaudreau, CP 370, Donnacona PQ G0A 1T0 – 418/285-3025 – 81 lits – Dir. gen., Fernand Morasse

Drummondville: Centre Frederick-George-Heriot, 75, rue St-Georges, Drummondville PQ J2C 4G6 – 819/477-0544; Fax: 819/477-3888 – 362 lits – Dir. gen., Nagui Habashi

Drummondville: Pavillon Marie-Reine des Coeurs, 1145, boul Mercure, Drummondville PQ J2B 3L7 – 819/477-3455 – 19 places – Dir. gen., Nagui Habashi

Drummondville: Pavillon Mona Lisa, 955, boul Jean de Breboeuf, Drummondville PQ J2B 4S9 – 819/472-2158 – 14 places – Dir. gen., Jacques Veillette

Drummondville: Villa du Boise, 100, rue Laforest, Drummondville PQ J2B 6X1 – 819/478-1292 – 34 places – Dir. gen., Nagui Habashi

East Angus: Le CHSLD de la mrc du Haunt-Saint-François, 120, rue Rosseau, CP 550, East Angus PQ J0B 1RO – 819/832-2487; Fax: 819/832-2676 – 55 lits – Dir. gen., Albert Kratzenberg

East Broughton: Foyer Sacre-coeur de Jesus d'East Broughton, 272, rue Principale, East Broughton PQ G0N 1G0 – 418/427-2068 – 33 lits – Dir. gen., André Rodrigue

Farnham: Les Foyers Farnham Inc., 800, rue Saint-Paul nord, Farnham PQ J2N 2K6 – 514/293-3168; Fax: 514/293-7878 – 62 lits – Dir. gen., Claude Codere

Fleurimont: Centre d'accueil Shermont Inc., 3220, 12e av nord, Fleurimont PQ J1H 5H2 – 819/820-8900; Fax: 819/820-8902 – 52 lits – Dir. gen., Jean Sevigny

Fort-Coulonge: Manoir Sacre-Coeur, 230, ch de la Chute, CP 610, Fort-Coulonge PQ J0X 1V0 – 819/683-2224; Fax: 819/683-3392 – 40 lits – Dir. gen., Jean Pilon

Fortierville: CHSLD les Seigneuries, 521, av du Foyer, Fortierville PQ G0S 1J0 – 819/287-4686 – 44 lits – Dir. gen., Raymond Dion

Garthby: Manoir Aylmer Inc., 9, rue Albert, Garthby PQ G0Y 1B0 – 418/458-2172; Fax: 418/458-2777 – 32 lits – Dir. gen., Real Paquette

Gaspé: Foyer Notre-Dame de Gaspé, 50, rue Bosse, CP 800, Gaspé PQ G0C 1R0 – 418/368-2125 – 29 places – Dir. gen., Lewis Fitzpatrick

Gatineau: Centre d'accueil de Gatineau, 134, rue Maple, Gatineau PQ J8P 7C3 – 819/663-2886; Fax: 819/663-2953 – 100 lits – Dir. gen., Paul-André Gervais

Gatineau: Centre d'hébergement Champlain-Gatineau, 176, rue Brian, Gatineau PQ J8P 4S1 – 819/663-9228; Fax: 819/663-9229 – 42 lits – Dir. gen., Jean-Charles Gignac

Gatineau: Centre d'hébergement Champlain-Templeton, 18, rue Hamel, Gatineau PQ J8P 1V9 – 819/663-5425 – 44 lits – Dir. gen., Guy Joly

Gatineau: Centre hospitalier Pierre Janet, 20, rue Laferriere, Gatinueau PQ J8T 3C1 – 819/771-7761; Fax: 819/771-2908 – 6 lits – Dir.-gen., Pierre Gagnon

Granby: Auberge de l'Amitie, 89, rue Drummond, Granby PQ J2G 2S8 – 514/375-6373 – 28 lits – Dir. gen., Yvan Robitaille

Granby: Centre d'accueil Marie-Berthe Couture, 230, av des Erables Ouest, Granby PQ J2G 9B1 – 514/

Canadian Almanac & Directory 1997

375-8003; Fax: 514/372-7197 – 75 lits – Dir. gen., Lucie Wiseman
Granby: Le Centre d'accueil Regina Mundi, 200, boul Robert, Granby PQ J2G 8C7 – 514/372-5125; Fax: 514/372-2828 – 24 lits – Dir. gen., Armand Gagne
Granby: Centre hospitalier de Granby, see Centres hospitaliers listings
Granby: CHSLD Horace-Boivin, 71, rue Court, Granby PQ J2G 4Y7 – 514/372-2419; Fax: 514/372-7617 – 55 lits – Dir. gen., Bernard Fournelle
Granby: L'Hôpital Notre-Dame de Granby, 363, rue Notre-Dame, Granby PQ J2G 3L4 – 514/372-7302; Fax: 514/372-5404 – 40 lits – Dir. gen., Bernard Fournelle
Grand-Mère: Centre hospitalier Laflèche-Grand-Mère, see Centres hospitaliers listings
Grand-Mère: Foyer Grand'Mère Inc., 690, 7e av, CP 400, Grand-Mère PQ G9T 2B4 – 819/538-1681; Fax: 819/538-5353 – 53 lits – Dir. gen., Raymond Guilbert
Grand-Metis: Pavillon Metis Inc., 412, Rte. 132, Grand-Metis PQ G0J 1Z0 – 418/775-7032 – 16 places – Dir. gen., Ronald Anctil
Grandes-Bergeronnes: Foyer Monseigneur Gendron Inc., 450, rue de la Mer, CP 68, Grandes-Bergeronnes PQ G0T 1G0 – 418/232-6224; Fax: 418/232-6771 – 42 lits – Dir. gen., Francis Bouchard
Ham-Nord: Foyer Saints-Anges, 493, rue Principale, CP 69, Ham-Nord PQ G0P 1A0 – 819/344-2940; Fax: 819/344-2584 – 38 lits – Dir. gen., Real Lavertu
Havre-Saint-Pierre: Foyer de Havre Saint-Pierre, 933, rue Boreale, CP 490, Havre-Saint-Pierre PQ G0G 1P0 – 418/538-2006; Fax: 418/538-3642 – 52 lits – Dir. gen., Maurice Jomphe
Herbertville: Foyer le Pionnier d'Hebertville, 640, rue Villeneuve, Herbertville PQ G0W 1S0 – 418/344-1911 – 39 lits – Dir. gen., Alain Gaudreault
Hull: Centre hospitalier Pierre Janet, 46, rue Lucien Brault, Hull PQ J8T 1H8 – 819/771-7761; Fax: 819/771-2908 – 6 lits – Dir. gen., Pierre Gagnon
Hull: Pavillon de l'Ile, 35, rue Saint-Jacques, Hull PQ J8X 2Y4 – 819/771-9176 – 23 places – Dir. gen., Jean-Pierre Allard
Hull: Pavillon du Portage, 310, rue Notre-Dame, Hull PQ J8X 3V2 – 819/776-5757 – 29 places – Dir. gen., Jean-Pierre Allard
Hull: Pavillon Siesta, 23, rue Front, Hull PQ J8Y 3M4 – 819/778-0079 – 17 places – Dir. gen., Jean-Pierre Allard
Hull: Residence foyer du Bonheur, 125, boul Lionel Emond, Hull PQ J8Y 5S8 – 819/770-1880; Fax: 819/770-8624 – 319 lits – Dir. gen., Jean-Pierre Allard
Hull: Residence la Pieta, 273, rue Laurier, Hull PQ J8X 3W8 – 819/771-1112; Fax: 819/771-3710 – 151 lits – Dir. gen., Jean-Pierre Allard
Iberville: Residence Champagnat d'Iberville Inc., 370, 5e av, CP 52, Iberville PQ J2X 1V1 – 514/347-3769; Fax: 514/347-3892 – 102 lits – Dir. gen., Jacques Gemme
Joliette: Le Centre d'accueil Saint-Eusèbe, 585, boul Manseau, Joliette PQ J6E 3E5 – 514/759-8222; Fax: 514/759-1579 – 158 lits – Dir. gen., Maurice Blais
Joliette: Le Foyer Notre-Dame, 144, rue Saint-Joseph, Joliette PQ J6E 5C4 – 514/756-8728 – 32 lits – Dir. gen., Rejeanne Marois
Jonquière: Pavillon Arvida, 1841, rue Deschênes, Jonquière PQ G7S 4K6 – 418/548-8231; Fax: 418/548-6875 – 60 lits – Dir. gen., Jacqueline St-Cyr
Jonquière: Residence des Annees d'Or, 1900, rue Fortier, Jonquière PQ G7X 4L3 – 418/547-4738 – 66 lits – Dir. gen., Jacqueline St-Cyr
Jonquière: Residence Georges Hebert, 2841, rue Faraday, CP 1490, Jonquière PQ G7S 4L1 – 418/695-7800 – 75 lits – Dir. gen., Jacqueline St-Cyr
Jonquière: Residence Ste-Marie, 2184, rue Perrier, Jonquière PQ G7X 9C9 – 418/547-4738; Fax: 418/547-1134 – 68 lits – Dir. gen., Jacqueline St-Cyr
Kingsey Falls: Foyer de Kingsey Falls Inc., 2, rue Saint-Aime, CP 60, Kingsey Falls PQ J0A 1B0 – 819/363-2243; Fax: 819/363-2345 – 57 lits – Dir. gen., Gilles Perreault
Kuujjuaq: Centre de santé Tulattavik de l'Ungava, see Centres hospitaliers listings
La Baie: Foyer de Bagotville, 300, rue Victoria, La Baie PQ G7B 3M6 – 418/544-2853; Fax: 418/544-6012 – 51 lits – Dir. gen., Marcel Harvey
La Baie: Foyer St-Joseph de la Baie Inc., 2002, rue Alexis-Simard, La Baie PQ G7B 2K9 – 418/544-2865; Fax: 418/544-8936 – 55 lits – Dir. gen., Marcel Harvey
La Guadeloupe: Le Pavillon Notre-Dame Inc., 437 - 15e rue ouest, CP 490, La Guadeloupe PQ G0M 1G0 – 418/459-3476; Fax: 418/459-6428 – 49 lits – Dir. gen., Richard Busque
La Malbaie: Accueil Bellerive (1970) Inc., 367, rue Saint-Etienne, CP 490, La Malbaie PQ G5A 1M3 – 418/665-3724; Fax: 418/665-2249 – 57 lits – Dir. gen., Jacques Tremblay
La Pêche: Centre d'accueil de la Basse-Gatineau, 9, ch Passe-Partout, CP 59, La Pêche PQ J0X 2W0 – 819/456-3863 – 32 lits – Dir. gen., Louis-Philippe Mayrand
La Peche: Le Foyer d'accueil de Gracefield, CP 59, La Peche PQ J0X 2W0 – 819/456-3863; Fax: 819/456-4531 – 31 lits – Dir. gen., Louis-Philippe Mayrand
La Pocatière: Centre d'accueil Sainte-Anne-de-la-Pocatière, 402, 1e rue, CP 460, La Pocatière PQ G0R 1Z0 – 418/856-3118 – 42 lits – Dir. gen., Robert Leclerc
La Prairie: Centre d'accueil la Prairie, 500, boul Balmoral, La Prairie PQ J5R 4N5 – 514/659-9148; Fax: 514/659-9989 – 134 lits – Dir. gen., Gaetan Roy
La Prairie: Foyer Notre-Dame de Laprairie Inc., 444, rue Leon Bloy, La Prairie PQ J5R 3G6 – 514/659-5828; Fax: 514/659-0753 – 28 lits – Dir. gen., Robert Legault
La Sarre: Le Foyer de l'age d'Or Inc., 22, 1e av est, La Sarre PQ J9Z 1C4 – 819/333-5525; Fax: 819/333-4903 – 39 lits – Dir. gen., Camil Dion
Labelle: Centre d'accueil de Labelle, 50, rue de l'Eglise, CP 38, Labelle PQ J0T 1H0 – 819/686-2372 – 48 lits – Dir. gen., Yvan Lachaine
Labelle: Pavillon Gagnon, 36, rue de l'Eglise, Labelle PQ J0T 1H0 – 819/686-2493 – 15 places – Dir. gen., Pierre Page
Labelle: Pavillon LeTourneau, 13411, rue Cure Labelle, Labelle PQ J0T 1H0 – 819/686-3484 – 15 places – Dir. gen., Pierre Page
Lac-au-Saumon: Residence Marie-Anne Ouellet, 6, rue Turbide, Lac-au-Saumon PQ G0J 1M0 – 418/778-5816 – 96 lits – Dir. gen., Alain Paquet
Lac-Bouchette: Le Foyer de Lac Bouchette Inc., 99, rte de l'Ermitage, Lac-Bouchette PQ G0W 1V0 – 418/348-6313; Fax: 418/348-6342 – 38 lits – Dir. gen., Claude J.Y. Theberge
Lac-Etchemin: Foyer Lac-Etchemin, 227, 1e av, CP 369, Lac-Etchemin PQ G0R 1S0 – 418/625-6661; Fax: 418/625-6661 – 78 lits – Dir. gen., Jean-Yves Julien
Lac-Etchemin: Le Sanatorium Begin, see Centres hospitaliers listings
Lac-Kenogami: Pavillon St-Dominique Enr., 3528, rue Fortin, Lac-Kenogami PQ G7X 1B7 – 418/547-5289 – 19 places – Dir. gen., Guy St-Onge
Lac-Megantic: La Maison Paternelle, 3675, rue du Foyer, Lac-Megantic PQ G6B 2K2 – 819/583-4222; Fax: 819/583-0900 – 48 lits – Dir. gen., Raymonde Lapointe-Lagueux
Lac-Nominingue: Pavillon Lachaine & Lajeunesse Enr., 237, rue Martineau, CP 452, Lac-Nominingue PQ J0W 1R0 – 819/278-4529 – 15 places – Dir. gen., Pierre Page
Lac-Nominingue: Pavillon Monique et Noel Thibault, 2234, rue Sacre-Coeur, CP 152, Lac-Nominingue PQ J0W 1R0 – 819/278-3242 – 10 places – Dir. gen., Pierre Page
Lac-Nominingue: Pavillon St-Louis Enr., 2188, ch Tour du Lac, Lac-Nominingue PQ J0W 1R0 – 819/278-3774 – 18 places – Dir. gen., Pierre Page
Lac-Norminingue: Pavillon Thibault Enr., 330, rue des Merles, CP 164, Lac-Norminingue PQ J0W 1R0 – 819/278-4257 – 14 places – Dir. gen., Pierre Page
Lachute: Pavillon d'Argenteuil, 150, rue du Pavillon, Lachute PQ J8H 4E7 – 514/562-3761 – 82 lits – Dir. gen., René Giard
Lachute: La Residence de Lachute, 377, rue Principale, Lachute PQ J8H 1Y1 – 514/562-5203; Fax: 514/562-4156 – 52 lits – Dir. gen., Jane Thomson
Lachute: Residence Robitaille Enr., 350, rue Bethany, CP 458, Lachute PQ J8H 3X9 – 514/562-2862 – 39 lits – Dir. gen., René Giard
Lacolle: Pavillon d'accueil Lacolle, 71, rue de l'Eglise nord, Lacolle PQ J0J 1J0 – 514/246-2602 – 26 lits – Dir. gen., Fernand Tremblay
Ladore: Centre d'accueil de la Dore, 4921, rue des Peupliers, Ladore PQ G0W 2J0 – 418/256-3851; Fax: 418/256-3852 – 21 lits – Dir. gen., Claude J.Y. Theberge
Lambton: Le Castel des Aieux, 310, rue Principale, CP 490, Lambton PQ G0M 1H0 – 418/486-7417 – 41 lits – Dir. gen., Raymonde Lapointe-Lagueux
L'Annonciation: Accueil Come Cartier, 101, rue Labelle sud, CP 698, L'Annonciation PQ J0T 1T0 – 819/275-3430; Fax: 819/275-1988 – 43 lits – Dir. gen., Gilles Huberdeau
L'Annonciation: CH Laurentides et centre réadaptation Hautes-Vallees, see Centres hospitaliers listings
Lanoraie-d'Autray: Centre Alphonse Rondeau, 419, rue Faust, Lanoraie-d'Autray PQ J0K 1E0 – 514/887-2343 – 75 lits – Dir. gen., Yvon Poirier
L'Assomption: Centre de l'Assomption, 410, boul l'Ange Gardien, CP 890, L'Assomption PQ J0K 1G0 – 514/589-2101 – 103 lits – Dir. gen., Yvon Poirier
L'Assomption: Residence l'Assomption Enr., 1980, ch Bas L'Assomption, L'Assomption PQ J0K 1G0 – 514/585-9944 – 40 lits – Dir. gen., Roger Fortin
Laurentides: Centre d'accueil St-Antoine de Padoue, 521, rue Saint-Joseph, CP 219, Laurentides PQ J0R 1C0 – 514/439-3217 – 110 lits – Dir. gen., Jacques Beaupre
Laurentides: Residence S.M., 169, 12e av, Laurentides PQ J0R 1C0 – 514/439-2385 – 14 places – Dir. gen., Maurice Blais
Laurierville: Villa Provencher, 501, rue Provencher, Laurierville PQ G0S 1P0 – 819/365-4558 – 21 lits – Dir. gen., Jean Gauthier
Le Gardeur: Centre Alexandre Archambeault, 37, Notre-Dame, Le Gardeur PQ J5Z 1R3 – 514/582-8704 – 46 lits – Dir. gen., Yvon Poirier
Lennoxville: Foyer Grace Christian, 1501, rue Campbell, RR#2, Lennoxville PQ J1M 2A3 – 819/842-2164 – 49 lits – Dir. gen., John Degrace
Lévis: Centre d'accueil Saint-Joseph de Lévis Inc., 107, rue Saint-Louis, CP 1188, Lévis PQ G6V 6R9 – 418/833-3414; Fax: 418/833-3417 – 125 lits – Dir. gen., Monique Leveille
Lévis: Pavillon Bellevue Inc., 543, rue Saint-Joseph est, Lévis PQ G6V 1G9 – 418/833-3490; Fax: 418/833-6874 – 50 lits – Dir. gen., Claude Talbot
Lévis: Pavillon de Lauzon, 82, boul des Erables, Lévis PQ G6V 2G4 – 418/833-4469 – 17 places – Dir. gen., Benoit Guillemette
Lévis: Pavillon St-Antoine Enr., 28, rue Fraser, Lévis PQ G6V 3R7 – 418/833-8797 – 15 places – Dir. gen., Yvan Deblois
Lévis: Villa Mon Domaine Inc., 109, av Mont-Marie, Lévis PQ G6V 8B4 – 57 lits – Dir. gen., Jean-Noel Begin
L'Ile-aux-Coudres: Pavillon Restons Chez-Nous, 1, rue Royale est, L'Ile-aux-Coudres PQ G0A 1X0 – 418/438-2757 – 12 places – Dir. gen., Robert Vallieres
L'Ile-Perrot: Centre d'accueil Laurent-Bergevin, 200, boul Perrot, L'Ile-Perrot PQ J7V 7M7 – 514/453-

5860; Fax: 514/453-8939 – 82 lits – Dir. gen., Lise Belanger

L'Islet-sur-Mer: Foyer Bon-Secours Inc., 125, Rte. des Pionniers ouest, L'Islet-sur-Mer PQ G0R 2B0 – 418/247-5149 – 33 lits – Dir. gen., Pierrette D. Guimond

Longueuil: Centre d'accueil Chevalier de Lévis, 40, rue Lévis, Longueuil PQ J4H 1S5 – 514/670-5110 – 105 lits – Dir. gen., France Larin

Longueuil: Centre d'accueil le Manoir Trinite, 15, rue Pratt est, Longueuil PQ J4H 3S9 – 514/674-4948 – 115 lits – Dir. gen., France Larin

Longueuil: Centre d'accueil Mgr-Coderre, 2761, rue Beauvais, Longueuil PQ J4M 2A1 – 514/468-1516 – 100 lits – Dir. gen., France Larin

Longueuil: Centre d'accueil René-Lévesque, 1901, rue Claude, Longueuil PQ J4G 1Y5 – 514/651-2210 – 224 lits – Dir. gen., France Larin

Longueuil: Centre d'accueil St-Laurent Inc., 675, boul Quinn, Longueuil PQ J4H 2N6 – 514/670-5480; Fax: 514/670-9874 – 22 lits – Dir. gen., Marc-André Domingue

Longueuil: CHSLD St-Felix de Longueuil Inc., 650, ch Chambly, Longueuil PQ J4H 3L8 – 514/677-5253; Fax: 514/677-5384 – 54 lits – Dir. gen., Vincenzo Simonetta

Longueuil: Pavillon le Baron, 1500, boul Marie-Victorin est, Longueuil PQ J4G 1A4 – 514/647-1985 – 24 places – Dir. gen., France Larin

Longueuil: Pavillon Renaissance, 2381, av Dieppe, Longueuil PQ J4L 2K3 – 514/679-5826 – 16 places – Dir. gen., France Larin

Longueuil: Pavillon St-Patrick, 90, boul Guimond, Longueuil PQ J4G 1L5 – 514/677-8414 – 25 places – Dir. gen., Robert Sabino

Lorraine: Pavillon Lorraine Enr., 153, rue Fraser, Lorraine PQ J6Z 3B2 – 514/621-1151 – 15 places – Dir. gen., Yvon Poirier

Lorretteville: Foyer de Lorretteville inc., 165, rue Lessard, Lorretteville PQ G2B 2V9 – 418/842-9191; Fax: 418/842-4472 – 76 lits – Dir. gen., Michel Marcotte

Lotbinière: Le Foyer de Lotbinière, 7472, rue Marie-Victorin, CP 87, Lotbinière PQ G0S 1S0 – 418/796-2015 – 38 lits – Dir. gen., André Paquet

Louiseville: Centre hospitalier Comtois, see Centres hospitaliers listings

Louisville: Centre d'accueil de Louisville Inc., 181, av Choisy, Louisville PQ J5V 1V3 – 819/228-2706; Fax: 819/228-9944 – 129 lits – Dir. gen., Micheline Bonner Lesage

Louisville: Pavillon Dupuis, 820, rue Notre-Dame sud, Louisville PQ J5V 1Y9 – 819/228-3586 – 14 places – Dir. gen., Jacques Veillette

Louisville: Pavillon Lefrançois Inc., 741, rang Village des Gravel, Louisville PQ J5V 2L4 – 819/228-5060 – 15 places – Dir. gen., Jacques Veillette

Luceville: Pavillon de Luceville Inc., 48, boul Saint-Pierre, Luceville PQ G0K 1E0 – 418/739-4905 – 24 places – Dir. gen., Ronald Anctil

Luceville: Pavillon Dionne Inc., 56, rue Saint-Louis, Luceville PQ G0K 1E0 – 418/739-3708 – 14 places – Dir. gen., Ronald Anctil

Luceville: Pavillon Therese Lepage, 52, rue Saint-Antoine, Luceville PQ G0K 1E0 – 418/739-3901 – 18 places – Dir. gen., Ronald Anctil

Lyster: Foyer de Lyster, 2180, rue Becancour, Lyster PQ G0S 1V0 – 819/389-5923; Fax: 819/389-5969 – 35 lits – Dir. gen., Michel Lauzon

Macamic: Centre hospitalier St-Jean, 169, 7e av est, Macamic PQ J0Z 2S0 – 819/782-4661; Fax: 819/782-2400 – 222 lits – Dir. gen., Camil Dion

Macamic: Pavillon Royal Roussillon Inc., 171, 7e av, Macamic PQ J0Z 2S0 – 819/782-2522 – 12 places – Dir. gen., Camil Dion

Magog: Foyer du Sacre-Coeur, 50, rue Saint-Patrice est, Magog PQ J1X 1T4 – 819/843-3381; Fax: 819/843-8262 – 108 lits – Dir. gen., Donald Langlais

Magog: Pavillon Place Victoria, 147, rue Victoria, Magog PQ J1X 2J7 – 819/843-7333 – 18 places – Dir. gen., Donald Langlais

Magog: Residence Ste-Marguerite Marie, 64, rue St-Pierre, Magog PQ J1X 3A2 – 819/843-0202 – 27 lits – Dir. gen., Serge Lacourse

Malartic: Villa St-Martin Inc., 701, rue de la Paix, CP 639, Malartic PQ J0Y 1Z0 – 819/757-3663; Fax: 819/757-3309 – 52 lits – Dir. gen., Jean-Pierre Cote

Maniwaki: Foyer Pere Guinard, 177, rue des Oblats, Maniwaki PQ J9E 1G5 – 819/449-4900; Fax: 819/449-2079 – 77 lits – Dir. gen., Louis-Philippe Mayrand

Manseau: Pavillon Charles-Aime Vachon, 970, Rte. 218, Manseau PQ G0X 1V0 – 819/356-2203 – 12 places – Dir. gen., Raymond Dion

Manseau: Pavillon Robert Morin, 305, Moose Park, CP 122, Manseau PQ G0X 1V0 – 418/356-2455 – 15 places – Dir. gen., Raymond Dion

Maria: Centre hospitalier Baie-des-Chaleurs, see Centres hospitaliers listings

Maria: Residence Saint-Joseph, 491, Rte. 132, CP 10, Maria PQ G0C 1Y0 – 418/759-3458; Fax: 418/759-5103 – 125 lits – Dir. gen., Bernard Nadeau

Marieville: Centre Rouville (Residence Sainte-Croix), 300, rue du Docteur Poulin, Marieville PQ J3M 1L7 – 514/460-4475; Fax: 514/460-4104 – 180 lits – Dir. gen., Michel Desnoyers

Martinville: Pavillon St-Gabriel Enr., 213, ch de l'Eglise, Martinville PQ J0B 2A0 – 819/835-5355 – 15 places – Dir. gen., Real Jacques

Mascouche: Pavillon des Pins, 1151, ch Pincourt, Mascouche PQ J7L 2X8 – 514/474-4772 – 16 places – Dir. gen., Joyce Boillat

Mashteuiatsh: Centre Tshishemishk, 410, rue Amish, Mashteuiatsh PQ G0W 2H0 – 418/275-5535 – 20 lits – Dir. gen., Edouard Robertson

Massueville: Foyer Familial St-Aime (1986) Inc., 201, rue Cartier, Massueville PQ J0G 1K0 – 514/788-2223; Fax: 514/788-2223 – 65 lits – Dir. gen., Serge Cournoyer

Matane: Foyer d'accueil de Matane, 150, av Saint-Jerome, Matane PQ G4W 3A2 – 418/562-4154; Fax: 418/562-9281 – 106 lits – Dir. gen., Clement Gauthier

McMasterville: Pavillon McMasterville, 329, ch du Richelieu, McMasterville PQ J3G 1T8 – 514/464-8827 – 14 places – Dir. gen., Raymond Carignan

Metabetchouan: Le CHSLD de Lac-Saint-Jean-Est, 40, rue de l'Hôpital, Metabetchouan PQ G0W 2A0 – 418/349-2861; Fax: 418/349-2288 – 200 lits – Dir. gen., Alain Gaudreault

Metabetchouan: Pavillon Diane Enr., 27, rue Saint-Pierre, Metabetchouan PQ G0W 2A0 – 418/349-2364 – 14 places – Dir. gen., Laurent Bouillon

Mirabel: Centre d'accueil de St-Benoit, 9100, rue Dumouchel, Mirabel PQ J0N 1K0 – 514/258-2481; Fax: 514/258-4980 – 75 lits – Dir. gen., André C. Desuatels

Mistassini: CHSLD Maria-Chapdelaine, 116, av des Chutes, Mistassini PQ G0W 2C0 – 418/276-1153; Fax: 418/276-4355 – 64 lits – Dir. gen., Jacques Turcotte

Mont-Joli: Foyer Ste-Bernadette Inc., 1039, boul Jacques-Cartier, CP 292, Mont-Joli PQ G5H 3L1 – 418/775-2241 – 24 lits – Dir. gen., Lucette Berube-Goyette

Mont-Joli: Hôpital de Mont-Joli Inc., 800, ch du Sanatorium, Mont-Joli PQ G5H 3L6 – 418/775-7261; Fax: 418/775-8607 – 303 lits – Dir. gen., Ronald Anctil

Mont-Joli: Pavillon Jacques-Cartier Enr., 1147, boul Jacques-Cartier nord, Mont-Joli PQ G5H 2S5 – 418/775-5984 – 16 places – Dir. gen., Ronald Anctil

Mont-Joli: Pavillon Lamarre-Pinel Enr., 1049, boul Jacques-Cartier, Mont-Joli PQ G5H 2S4 – 418/775-2727 – 17 places – Dir. gen., Ronald Anctil

Mont-Joli: Pavillon St-Joseph, 31, rue du Lac, Mont-Joli PQ G5H 3P1 – 418/775-3041 – 20 places – Dir. gen., Roanld Anctil

Mont-Joli: La Residence de Mont-Joli Inc., 75, av des Retraites, Mont-Joli PQ G5H 1E7 – 418/775-4351; Fax: 418/775-6284 – 47 lits – Dir. gen., Ronald Anctil

Mont-Laurier: Centre d'accueil Sainte-Anne de Mont-Laurier, 411, rue de la Madone, Mont-Laurier PQ J9L 1S1 – 819/623-5940; Fax: 819/623-7347 – 61 lits – Dir. gen., Gilles Huberdeau

Mont-Laurier: Pavillon Alain Campeau, 244, rue Chapleau, Mont-Laurier PQ J9L 2N5 – 819/623-2199 – 12 places – Dir. gen., Gilles Huberdeau

Mont-Laurier: Pavillon Therrien Inc., 278, rue de la Madone, Mont-Laurier PQ J9L 1R5 – 819/623-6315 – 24 places – Dir. gen., Gilles Huberdeau

Montmagny: Foyer d'Youville, 168, rue Saint-Joseph, Montmagny PQ G5V 1H8 – 418/248-0182; Fax: 418/248-4464 – 111 lits – Dir. gen., Jean-Paul Lacroix

Montmagny: Pavillon Goulet & Labrecque Inc., 44, rue Saint-Thomas, Montmagny PQ G5V 1L3 – 418/248-7268 – 18 places – Dir. gen., Jean-Paul Lacroix

Montmagny: Pavillon Labrie, 155, Place des Meuniers, Montmagny PQ G5V 1M6 – 418/248-5577 – 15 places – Dir. gen., Jean-Paul Lacroix

Montréal: L'Accueil Demers Enr., 1016, 51e av, Montréal PQ H1A 2A4 – 514/642-3544 – 13 places – Dir. gen., Raymond Carignan

Montréal: Assn Montréalaise pour les Aveugles - Res. Gilman, 7000, rue Sherbrooke ouest, Montréal PQ H4B 1R3 – 514/489-8201; Fax: 514/489-3477 – 59 lits – Dir. gen., John A. Simms

Montréal: C.A. Armand Lavergne, 3500, rue Chapleau, Montréal PQ H2K 4N3 – 514/527-8921 – 188 lits – Dir. gen., Rolande Laurin-Dorval

Montréal: Les Cedres-Centre d'accueil pour personnes agée, 95, boul Gouin est, Montréal PQ H3L 1A6 – 514/389-1023; Fax: 514/389-0581 – 22 lits – Dir. gen., Diane Chaunt

Montréal: Centre Biermans, 7905, rue Sherbrooke est, Montréal PQ H1L 1A4 – 514/351-9891; Fax: 514/351-1556 – 242 lits – Dir. gen., Jacques Hould

Montréal: Centre Le Cardinal Inc., 12900, rue Notre-Dame est, Montréal PQ H1A 1R9 – 514/645-2766; Fax: 514/640-6267 – 174 lits – Dir. gen., André Groulx

Montréal: Centre d'accueil Alfred Desrochers, 5325, av Victoria, Montréal PQ H3W 2P2 – 514/731-3891 – 125 lits – Dir. gen., Yves Jette

Montréal: Centre d'accueil Chevalier de Lorimer, 4625, av Delorimer, Montréal PQ H2H 2B4 – 514/526-2894; Fax: 514/526-9942 – 75 lits – Dir. gen., Jean-Louis Vaillancourt

Montréal: Centre d'accueil Chomedey, 4115, 9e rue, Laval PQ H7W 1Y2 – 514/688-4393 – 23 lits – Dir. gen., Michel de Luca

Montréal: Centre d'accueil Dante, 6887, rue Chatelain, Montréal PQ H1T 3X7 – 514/252-1535 – 100 lits – Dir. gen., Irene Giannetti

Montréal: Centre d'accueil de Lachine, 650, Place d'Accueil, Lachine PQ H8S 3Z5 – 514/634-7161; Fax: 514/634-8751 – 211 lits – Dir. gen., Jean-Guy Poirier

Montréal: Centre d'accueil Denis-Benjamin Viger, 3292, boul Cherrier est, Saint-Raphael-de-l'Ile-Bizard PQ H9C 2C2 – 514/620-6310; Fax: 514/620-6553 – 125 lits – Dir. gen., André Cote

Montréal: Centre d'accueil Dorchester, 1800, rue Saint-Jacques ouest, Montréal PQ H3J 2R5 – 514/935-4681; Fax: 514/935-6189 – 192 lits – Dir. gen., André Paquette

Montréal: Centre d'accueil Edmond Laurendeau, 1725, boul Gouin est, Montréal PQ H2C 3H6 – 514/384-2020; Fax: 514/384-4245 – 300 lits – Dir. gen., André Soucy

Montréal: Centre d'accueil Eloria Lepage, 3090, av de la Pepinière, Montréal PQ H1N 3N4 – 514/252-1710 – 160 lits – Dir. gen., Gisele Besner

Montréal: Centre d'accueil Ernest Routhier, 2110, rue Wolfe, Montréal PQ H2L 4V4 – 514/525-2546 – 96 lits – Dir. gen., Damien Dallaire

Canadian Almanac & Directory 1997

Montréal: Centre d'accueil Father Dowd, 6565, ch Hudson, Montréal PQ H3S 2T7 – 514/731-9601; Fax: 514/731-7253 – 135 lits – Dir. gen., John R. Walker

Montréal: Centre d'accueil Fernand Larocque, 5436, boul Lévesque est, Laval PQ H7C 1N7 – 514/661-5440; Fax: 514/661-6554 – 100 lits – Dir. gen., Michel Briere

Montréal: Centre d'accueil Francois Seguenot, 13950, rue Notre-Dame est, Montréal PQ H1A 1T5 – 514/642-7741 – 77 lits – Dir. gen., Monique Corbeil

Montréal: Centre d'accueil Gouin-Rosemont, 5900, rue de Saint-Vallier, Montréal PQ H2S 2P3 – 514/273-3681 – 105 lits – Dir. gen., Juliette P. Bailly

Montréal: Centre d'accueil Henri Bradet, 6465, av Chester, Montréal PQ H4V 2Z8 – 514/483-1380 – 125 lits – Dir. gen., Jean Michaud

Montréal: Centre d'accueil Heritage Inc., 5716, ch de la Cote-Saint-Antoine, Montréal PQ H4A 1R9 – 514/484-2645 – 15 lits – Dir. gen., Michael Pomilo

Montréal: Centre d'accueil Idola St-Jean, 250, boul Cartier ouest, Laval PQ H7N 5S5 – 514/668-6750 – 100 lits – Dir. gen., Michel Briere

Montréal: Centre d'accueil Jean XXIII, 6900, 15e av, Montréal PQ H1X 2V9 – 514/725-2190 – 24 lits – Dir. gen., Marie-Claire Lamontagne

Montréal: Centre d'accueil Jeannine Gingras, 6770, boul Pie IX, Montréal PQ H1X 2C8 – 514/725-7757 – 20 lits – Dir. gen., Rita Bloutier

Montréal: Centre d'accueil Judith Jasmin, 8850, rue Bisaillon, Montréal PQ H1K 4N2 – 514/354-5990 – 75 lits – Dir. gen., Claude Desjardins

Montréal: Centre d'accueil Juif, 5750, rue Lavoie, Montréal PQ H3W 3H5 – 514/735-9999; Fax: 514/735-9094 – 160 lits – Dir. gen., Isaac Katofsky

Montréal: Centre d'accueil Louis Riel, 2120, rue Augustin-Gantin, Montréal PQ H3K 3G3 – 514/931-2263; Fax: 514/931-2299 – 100 lits – Dir. gen., Germain Harvey

Montréal: Centre d'accueil Marie-Rollet, 5003, rue Saint-Zotique est, Montréal PQ H1T 1N6 – 514/729-5281 – 125 lits – Dir. gen., Michel Brunet

Montréal: Centre d'accueil Nazaire Piche, 150, 15e av, Lachine PQ H8S 3L9 – 514/637-2326; Fax: 514/637-1224 – 100 lits – Dir. gen., Leonard Vincent

Montréal: Centre d'accueil Ovila Legare, 1615, av Emile Journault, Montréal PQ H2M 2G3 – 514/384-5490 – 105 lits – Dir. gen., André Soucy

Montréal: Centre d'accueil la Piniere, 4895, rue Saint-Joseph, Laval PQ H7C 1H6 – 514/661-3305 – 100 lits – Dir. gen., Michel Briere

Montréal: Centre d'accueil Providence Auclair, 6910, rue Boyer, Montréal PQ H3W 2M4 – 514/844-3463 – 160 lits – Dir. gen., André Paquette

Montréal: Centre d'accueil Real Morel, 3500, rue Wellington, Verdun PQ H4G 1T3 – 514/761-5874; Fax: 514/761-7264 – 152 lits – Dir. gen., Germain Harvey

Montréal: Centre d'accueil Robert Cliche, 3730, rue de Bellechasse, Montréal PQ H1X 3E5 – 514/374-8660 – 100 lits – Dir. gen., Michel Bourque

Montréal: Centre d'accueil St-Margaret, 50, av Hillside, Westmount PQ H3Z 1V9 – 514/845-2141; Fax: 514/932-4379 – 96 lits – Dir. gen., John R. Walker

Montréal: Centre d'accueil Ste-Marie Inc., 4045, rue Prieur est, Montréal PQ H1H 2M9 – 514/322-0650; Fax: 514/322-5176 – 30 lits – Dir. gen., Micheline Gauthier

Montréal: Centre d'accueil la Salle, 8686, rue Centrale, LaSalle PQ H8P 3N4 – 514/364-6700; Fax: 514/364-0484 – 202 lits – Dir. gen., Jean-Paul Bouchard

Montréal: Centre de gerontologie Manoir Dorval inc., 2400, ch Herron, Dorval PQ H9S 5W3 – 514/631-7288 – 60 lits – Dir. gen., Howard Modlin

Montréal: Le Centre de soins prolonges de Montréal, 5155, rue Ste-Catherine est, Montréal PQ H1V 2A5 – 514/255-2833; Fax: 514/255-6275 – 280 lits – Dir. gen., Caroline Barbir

Montréal: Centre d'hébergement Champlain - Marie-Victorin, 7150, rue Marie-Victorin, Montréal PQ H1G 2J5 – 514/324-2044; Fax: 514/324-4096 – 310 lits – Dir. gen., Guy Joly

Montréal: Centre d'hébergement Champlain-Villeray, 1640, rue Tillemont, Montréal PQ H2E 1C2 – 514/725-9881; Fax: 514/725-9883 – 28 lits – Dir. gen., Guy Joly

Montréal: Centre d'hébergement Emilie Gamelin, Armand-Lavergne, 1440, rue Dufresne, Montréal PQ H2K 3J3 – 514/527-8921 – 194 lits – Dir. gen., Rolande Laurin-Dorval

Montréal: Centre d'hébergement et de soins de longue durée Bourget inc., 11570, rue Notre-Dame est, Montréal PQ H1B 2Z4 – 514/645-1673; Fax: 514/645-1673 – 112 lits – Dir. gen., Yvon Girard

Montréal: Centre d'hébergement et de soins de longue durée Bussey (Québec) inc., 2069, boul Saint-Joseph, Lachine PQ H8S 4B7 – 514/637-1127 – 42 lits – Dir. gen., Marie-Helene Girard

Montréal: Centre d'hébergement et de soins de longue durée Gouin inc., 4445, boul Henri-Bourassa est, Montréal PQ H1H 5M4 – 514/327-6209; Fax: 514/327-9912 – 93 lits – Dir. gen., Francesco Ieraci

Montréal: Centre d'hébergement le Royer, 7351, rue Jean Desprez, Anjou PQ H1K 5A6 – 514/493-9397; Fax: 514/493-9103 – 96 lits – Dir. gen., Jean-Bernard Breault, 514/849-1357

Montréal: Centre d'hébergement St-Albert-le-Grand Inc., 4357, av Charlemagne, Montréal PQ H1X 2H2 – 514/259-6905; Fax: 514/259-8984 – 18 lits – Dir. gen., Simonne Chabot

Montréal: Centre d'hébergement St-Francois inc., 4105, Montée Masson, Laval PQ H0A 1G0 – 514/666-6541; Fax: 514/666-1601 – 53 lits – Dir. gen., Marie-Christine Moulin

Montréal: Centre d'hébergement St-Georges Inc., 1205, rue Labelle, Montréal PQ H2L 4C1 – 514/849-1357; Fax: 514/849-8465 – 280 lits – Dir. gen., Jean-Bernard Breault

Montréal: Centre d'Hébergement St-Vincent-Marie Inc., 1175, ch Cote Vertu, St-Laurent PQ H4L 5J1 – 514/744-1175; Fax: 514/744-0557 – 66 lits – Dir. gen., Mary Maley

Montréal: Centre Geriatrique le Bel Age de Fabre, 5200, 80e av, Laval PQ H7R 1J9 – 514/627-7990; Fax: 514/627-7993 – 64 lits – Dir. gen., Kenneth Courville

Montréal: Centre hospitalier Côte-des-Neiges, see Centres hospitaliers listings

Montréal: Centre hospitalier de Lachine, 637, 13e av, Lachine PQ H8S 3K3 – 514/637-2351; Fax: 514/637-2285 – 128 lits – Dir. gen., Camille Lefebvre

Montréal: Centre hospitalier du Trés-Saint-Rédempteur Inc., 3591, rue Ste-Catherine est, Montréal PQ H1W 2E6 – 514/522-2257; Fax: 514/522-3504 – 16 lits – Dir. gen., Denise Savoie

Montréal: Centre hospitalier gériatrique Maimonides, 5795, av Caldwell, Cote-Saint-Luc PQ H4W 1W3 – 514/483-2121; Fax: 514/483-1561 – 387 lits – Dir. gen., Vacant

Montréal: Centre hospitalier Jacques Viger, see Centres hospitaliers listings

Montréal: Centre hospitalier Juif de l'Espérance, 5725, av Victoria, Montréal PQ H3W 3H6 – 514/738-4500; Fax: 514/738-2611 – 160 lits – Dir. gen., Isaac Katofsky

Montréal: Centre Triest, 4900, boul Lapointe, Montréal PQ H1K 4W9 – 514/353-1227 – 275 lits – Dir. gen., Jacques Hould

Montréal: Chateau sur le Lac, 16289, boul Gouin ouest, Sainte-Geneviève PQ H9H 1E2 – 514/620-9794 – 50 lits – Dir. gen., B.S. Kachra

Montréal: Chateau Westmount, 250, av Victoria, Westmount PQ H3Z 2M7 – 514/369-3000; Fax: 514/369-0014 – 29 lits – Dir. gen., Ginette Villeneuve

Montréal: CHSLD Bois-Menu, 2710, boul Gouin est, Montréal PQ H2B 1Y6 – 514/387-5876; Fax: 514/387-1218 – 13 lits – Dir. gen., Vincenzo Simonetta

Montréal: CHSLD Dollard-des-Ormeaux, 197, rue Thornhill, Dollard-des-Ormeaux PQ H9B 3H8 – 514/684-0173; Fax: 514/684-0179 – 160 lits – Dir. gen., Vincenzo Simonetta

Montréal: CHSLD Jeanne-Leber, 7445, Hochelaga, Montréal PQ H1N 3V2 – 514/251-6000 – 400 lits – Dir. gen., Juliette P. Bailly

Montréal: CHSLD Mont Royal, 275, av Brittany, Mont-Royal PQ H3P 3C2 – 514/739-5593 – 260 lits – Dir. gen., Vincenzo Simonetta

Montréal: CHSLD Pierrefonds, 14775, boul Pierrefonds, Pierrefonds PQ H9H 4Y1 – 514/620-1220; Fax: 514/620-0024 – 64 lits – Dir. gen., Vincenzo Simonetta

Montréal: CHSLD Ste-Germaine Cousin, 14241, av Victoria, Montréal PQ H1A 1P2 – 514/642-5341; Fax: 514/642-5343 – 46 lits – Dir. gen., Vincenzo Simonetta

Montréal: CHSLD Ste-Rita, 11720, av Desy, Montréal PQ H1G 4C3 – 514/323-5210; Fax: 514/323-2136 – 50 lits – Dir. gen., Vincenzo Simonetta

Montréal: CHSLD Ville-Emard, 6935, rue Hamilton, Montréal PQ H4E 3C8 – 514/769-3812; Fax: 514/769-7581 – 53 lits – Dir. gen., Vincenzo Simonetta

Montréal: Les Entreprises Simone Letourneau Inc., 15156, rue Notre-Dame est, Montréal PQ H1A 1W6 – 514/642-7825 – 23 places – Dir. gen., Raymond Carignan

Montréal: Foyer Bon Accueil Enr., 16201, rue Bureau, Montréal PQ H1A 1Z2 – 514/642-9686 – 17 places – Dir. gen., Raymond Carignan

Montréal: Foyer Dorval, 225, av de la Presentation, Dorval PQ H9S 3L7 – 514/631-9094; Fax: 514/631-4420 – 84 lits – Dir. gen., Leonard Vincent

Montréal: Foyer du Sourire Inc., 12140, boul René-Lévesque, Montréal PQ H1B 2C7 – 514/645-8861 – 19 places – Dir. gen., Raymond Carignan

Montréal: Foyer Lachapelle, 752, 14e av, Montréal PQ H1B 3T1 – 514/645-7851 – 23 places – Dir. gen., Monique Corbeil

Montréal: Foyer Lefebvre, 16056, boul Gouin ouest, Sainte-Geneviève PQ H9H 1C8 – 514/620-6140 – 27 lits – Dir. gen., Leonard Vincent

Montréal: Foyer Notre-Dame, 223, boul Je-me-Souviens, Laval PQ H7L 1W2 – 514/622-8539 – 29 places – Dir. gen., Michel Brière

Montréal: Foyer pour personnes agées Saint-Laurent Inc., #18, 1055, ch Cote-Vertu, Saint-Laurent PQ H4L 1Y8 – 514/744-4981 – 144 lits – Dir. gen., Mariette Lebrun-Bohemier

Montréal: Foyer Rejeane Martineau Inc., 11780, rue Notre-Dame est, Montréal PQ H1B 2X5 – 514/645-8912 – 19 places – Dir. gen., Raymond Carignan

Montréal: Foyer Rousselot, 5655, rue Sherbrooke est, Montréal PQ H1N 1A4 – 514/254-9421; Fax: 514/254-3967 – 157 lits – Dir. gen., Robert Boucher

Montréal: Foyer St-Andre Enr., 779, 17e av, Montréal PQ H1B 3K4 – 514/645-4956 – 14 places – Dir. gen., Raymond Carignan

Montréal: Foyer Ste-Dorothee, 690 rue Mandel, Laval PQ H7X 1L4 – 514/689-5844 – 12 lits – Dir. gen., Therese Moise

Montréal: Foyer St-Marc, 3300, boul Cremazie est, Montréal PQ H2A 1A3 – 514/374-2420; Fax: 514/288-7076 – 64 lits – Dir. gen., Michel Duchesne

Montréal: Foyer Senneville, 55, ch Senneville, Senneville PQ H9X 1C1 – 514/457-2440 – 220 lits – Dir. gen., Richard Watkins

Montréal: Foyer Villa Gamelin Enr., 21, 58e av, Montréal PQ H1A 2P4 – 514/642-1832 – 13 places – Dir. gen., Raymond Carignan

Montréal: Les Foyers Presbyteriens de St-Andrew Inc., 3350, boul Cavendish, Montréal PQ H4B 2M7 – 514/489-8190; Fax: 514/489-7253 – 70 lits – Dir. gen., John R. Walker

Montréal: Gestion Groupe 5 Ltée (Pavillon St-Laurent), 8, 60e av, Montréal PQ H1A 2N5 – 514/642-3019 – 39 places – Dir. gen., Claude Desjardins

Montréal: Gestion J. Jacques Inc., 1058, 51e av, Montréal PQ H1A 2W4 – 514/642-7012 – 18 places – Dir. gen., Raymond Carignan

Montréal: Griffith McConnell Residence, 5790, av Parkhaven, Côte-Saint-Luc PQ H4W 1Y1 – 514/482-0590; Fax: 514/482-2643 – 348 lits – Dir. gen., Davis F. Walls

Montréal: L'Hôpital Chinois de Montréal, 7500, rue St-Denis, Montréal PQ H2R 2E6 – 514/273-9154; Fax: 514/273-2446 – 108 lits – Dir. gen., Pierre Lalonde

Montréal: Hôpital général Juif Sir Mortimer B. Davis, *see* Centres hospitaliers listings

Montréal: Hôpital Grace Dart, 6085, rue Sherbrooke est, Montréal PQ H1N 1C2 – 514/256-9021; Fax: 514/251-2391 – 101 lits – Dir. gen., Caroline Barbir

Montréal: Hôpital Jean-Talon, *see* Centres hospitaliers listings

Montréal: Hôpital Louis-H. Lafontaine, 7401, rue Hochelaga, Montréal PQ H1N 3M5 – 514/251-4000; Fax: 514/251-0856 – 837 lits – Dir. gen., Raymond Carignan

Montréal: Hôpital Mont-Sinai, 5690, boul Cavendish, Cote-Saint-Luc PQ H4W 1S7 – 514/369-2222; Fax: 514/369-2225 – 107 lits – Dir. gen., John R. Walker

Montréal: Hôpital St-Denis, 2870, boul Rosemont, Montréal PQ H1Y 1L7 – 514/727-8173; Fax: 514/465-7017 – 19 lits – Dir. gen., Gisèle Désilets

Montréal: Hôpital Sainte-Anne, 305, rue Saint-Pierre, Sainte-Anne-de-Bellevueuw PQ H9X 1Y9 – 514/457-3440; Fax: 514/457-5741 – 910 lits – Dir. gen., Richard Watkins

Montréal: Hôpital La Visitation, 161, boul Henri-Bourassa ouest, Montréal PQ H3L 1N2 – 514/331-2220; Fax: 514/331-8572 – 70 lits – Dir. gen., Michel Bouffard

Montréal: Iakhihsohtha Lodge, CP 40, Akwesasne PQ H0M 1A0 – 613/575-2507 – 30 lits – Dir. gen., Michael Mitchell

Montréal: Institut Canadien-Polonais du Bien-Etre Inc., 5655, rue Belanger est, Montréal PQ H1T 1G2 – 514/259-2551; Fax: 514/259-9948 – 126 lits – Dir. gen., Anna Brychcy

Montréal: Ma Maison St-Joseph, 5605, rue Beaubien est, Montréal PQ H1T 1X4 – 514/254-4991; Fax: 514/257-1742 – 93 lits – Dir. gen., Sr. Bernice Marie

Montréal: Maison Bellerive, 9493, rue Bellerive, Montréal PQ H1L 3S8 – 514/493-7628 – 13 places – Dir. gen., Raymond Carignan

Montréal: Maison Brabant Inc., 10881, av Laurentides, Montréal PQ H1H 4W1 – 514/325-2083 – 23 lits – Dir. gen., Antoine Dodard

Montréal: Maison de santé Woodlawn Enr., 1391, rue du College, Saint-Laurent PQ H4L 2L4 – 514/747-1433 – 13 lits – Dir. gen., Fernand Tremblay

Montréal: Manoir l'Age-d'Or, 3430, rue Jeanne-Mance, Montréal PQ H2X 2J9 – 514/842-1147; Fax: 514/842-1146 – 212 lits – Dir. gen., Gilbert Gagnon

Montréal: Manoir Beaconsfield, 34, av Woodland, Beaconsfield PQ H9W 4V9 – 514/694-2000 – 23 lits – Dir. gen., Annie Maffre

Montréal: Manoir Cartierville, 12235, rue Grenet, Montréal PQ H4J 2N9 – 514/337-7300; Fax: 514/337-4188 – 284 lits – Dir. gen., Francois Lamarre

Montréal: Manoir des Roseraies, 1050, av Gordon, Verdun PQ H4G 2S2 – 514/768-6605 – 50 lits – Dir. gen., Jean-Claude Goyer

Montréal: Manoir Fleury Enr., 2145, rue Fleury est, Montréal PQ H2B 1J8 – 514/388-1553 – 25 lits – Dir. gen., Mariana Lavoie

Montréal: Manoir Ile de l'ouest, 17725, boul Pierrefonds, Pierrefonds PQ H9J 3L1 – 514/620-9850 – 63 lits – Dir. gen., John Karakas

Montréal: Manoir Pierrefonds Inc., 18465, boul Gouin ouest, Pierrefonds PQ H9K 1A6 – 514/626-6651 – 100 lits – Dir. gen., Ginette Villeneuve

Montréal: Manoir Saint-Germain inc., 3420, rue Germain, Montréal PQ H1W 2V5 – 514/598-7792 – 14 places – Dir. gen., Jean Leblanc

Montréal: Manoir St-Patrice Inc., 3615, boul Perron, Laval PQ H7V 1P4 – 514/681-5854; Fax: 514/681-6120 – 132 lits – Dir. gen., Elmer Carey

Montréal: Manoir Verdun, 5500, boul Lasalle, Verdun PQ H4N 1N9 – 514/769-8801 – 215 lits – Dir. gen., Alain Gaudreault

Montréal: Pavillon Bruchesi, 225, rue Rachel est, Montréal PQ H2H 1R4 – 514/528-1603 – 83 lits – Dir. gen., Jean Leblanc

Montréal: Pavillon de l'Espoir, 6546, rue Azilda, Anjou PQ H1K 2Z9 – 514/355-3268 – 11 places – Dir. gen., Raymond Carignan

Montréal: Pavillon Duguay Enr., 3934, ch du Souvenir, Laval PQ H7W 1A8 – 514/688-9053 – 21 places – Dir. gen., Michel Brière

Montréal: Pavillon Evelyne Robert Inc., 1041, 53e av, Montréal PQ H1A 2T8 – 514/642-4624 – 15 places – Dir. gen., Raymond Carignan

Montréal: Pavillon Fabre, 943, 40e av, Laval PQ H7R 4X4 – 514/627-4612 – 29 places – Dir. gen., Pierre Marson

Montréal: Pavillon Hubert, 13192, rue Notre-Dame est, Montréal PQ H1A 1S6 – 514/692-5527 – 17 places – Dir. gen., Raymond Carignan

Montréal: Pavillon Laurendeau Enr., 19, av Laurendeau, Montréal PQ H1B 4X9 – 514/645-3782 – 19 places – Dir. gen., Raymond Carignan

Montréal: Pavillon Louis Riel Inc., 201, av Broadway, Montréal PQ H1B 5A4 – 514/645-6802 – 29 places – Dir. gen., Raymond Carignan

Montréal: Pavillon Louise inc., 6995, rue Lafontaine, Montréal PQ H1N 2C2 – 514/252-9122 – 16 places – Dir. gen., Jean Leblanc

Montréal: Pavillon Louvain Inc., 9600, rue Saint-Denis, Montréal PQ H2M 1P2 – 514/381-7256 – 155 lits – Dir. gen., André Soucy

Montréal: Le Pavillon M. & D. des Chenes inc., 522, av Hector, Montréal PQ H1L 3W9 – 514/354-4255 – 18 places – Dir. gen., Jean Leblanc

Montréal: Pavillon Mess, 13902, rue de Montigny, Montréal PQ H1A 1J4 – 514/642-5712 – 15 places – Dir. gen. Pavillon Morand Inc., Claude Desjardins

Montréal: Pavillon Morand inc., 12412, rue Notre-Dame est, Montréal PQ H1B 2Z1 – 514/640-5353 – 29 places – Dir. gen., Jean Leblanc

Montréal: Pavillon Omer Inc., 1505, rue de Beaurivage, Montréal PQ H1L 5V3 – 514/353-5467 – 20 places – Dir. gen., Raymond Carignan

Montréal: Pavillon Pilote, 644, rue Bourgeoys, Montréal PQ H3K 2M6 – 514/933-8241 – 14 places – Dir. gen., Joyce Boillat

Montréal: Pavillon Rejean Longpre enr., 13952, rue de Montigny, Montréal PQ H1A 1J6 – 514/642-1841 – 20 places – Dir. gen., Raymond Carignan

Montréal: Pavillon Robert Enr., 1385, 12e av, Montréal PQ H1B 3Y6 – 514/645-0594 – 18 places – Dir. gen., Raymond Carignan

Montréal: Pavillon Rosemont, *see* Centres hospitaliers listings

Montréal: Pavillon Saint-Clement, 549, rue Theodore, Montréal PQ H1V 3B1 – 514/433-2421 – 27 places – Dir. gen., Jean Leblanc

Montréal: Pavillon St-Henri, 5205, rue Notre-Dame ouest, Montréal PQ H4C 3L2 – 514/931-0851; Fax: 514/931-2993 – 237 lits – Dir. gen., André Paquette

Montréal: Pavillon St-Hubert, Sherbrooke est, 2047-2049, rue Saint-Hubert, Montréal PQ H2L 3Z6 – 514/526-7941 – 21 places – Dir. gen., Jean Leblanc

Montréal: Pavillon St-Marc (2618-4341 Québec Inc.), #1844, 1854 - 17e av, Montréal PQ H1B 3L9 – 514/645-7715 – 18 places – Dir. gen., Claude Desjardins

Montréal: Pavillon Suzanne Blanchard Inc., 1919, 9e av, Montréal PQ H1B 4E7 – 514/645-3204 – 29 places – Dir. gen., Raymond Carignan

Montréal: Pavillon Villa Ste-Maria, 16170, Terrasse Sainte-Maria-Goretti, Montréal PQ H1A 1X9 – 514/642-1099 – 16 places – Dir. gen., Claude Desjardins

Montréal: Pavillon Yolande et Gilles Inc., 3655, rue Sherbrooke est, Montréal PQ H1W 1E3 – 514/529-7897 – 239 places – Dir. gen., Claude Desjardins

Montréal: Residence Angelica Inc., 3435, boul Gouin est, Montréal PQ H1H 1B1 – 514/324-6110; Fax: 514/324-9332 – 400 lits – Dir. gen., Sr. Anne-Marie Marolo

Montréal: Residence Berthiaume-duTremblay, 1635, boul Gouin est, Montréal PQ H2C 1C2 – 514/381-1841; Fax: 514/381-1090 – 248 lits – Dir. gen., Gaston Bouchard

Montréal: Residence a la Bonne Étoile Inc., 7401, av Churchill, Verdun PQ H4H 2L5 – 514/767-4739 – 29 places – Dir. gen., Joyce Boillat

Montréal: Residence Claude & Claire, 12650, 41e av, Montréal PQ H1E 2E7 – 514/494-0935 – 20 places – Dir. gen., Jacques Mackay

Montréal: Residence Dandurand, 3841, rue Dandurand, Montréal PQ H1X 1P3 – 514/729-5902; Fax: 514/729-5902 – 18 lits – Dir. gen., Guy Gauthier

Montréal: Residence Dorion, 1360, rue Jean-Talon est, Montréal PQ H2E 1S2 – 514/270-9271; Fax: 514/270-6779 – 147 lits – Dir. gen., Gilles Saint-Pierre

Montréal: Residence du Bonheur Enr., 5855, rue Boulard, Laval PQ H0A 1G0 – 514/666-1567 – 30 lits – Dir. gen., Linda Sirois

Montréal: Residence Fleur de Lys, 15304, rue Notre-Dame est, Montréal PQ H1A 1S6 – 514/642-3317 – 29 places – Dir. gen., Raymond Carignan

Montréal: La Residence Fulford, 1221, rue Guy, Montréal PQ H3H 2K8 – 514/933-7975 – 40 lits – Dir. gen., Ingrid Leuzy

Montréal: Residence Jean de la Lande, 4255, av Papineau, Montréal PQ H2H 2P6 – 514/526-4981; Fax: 514/526-0645 – 312 lits – Dir. gen., Jean-Louis Vaillancourt

Montréal: Residence Maisonneuve, 2300, rue Nicolet, Montréal PQ H1W 3L4 – 514/527-2161 – 228 lits – Dir. gen., Gisele Besner

Montréal: Residence Marie-Christine Inc., 1487, boul des Laurentides, Laval PQ H7M 2Y3 – 514/663-3901; Fax: 514/663-7916 – 38 lits – Dir. gen., Marie-Christine Moulin

Montréal: Residence Notre-Dame, 13540, rue Notre-Dame est, Montréal PQ H1A 1T2 – 514/642-2165 – 15 places – Dir. gen., Monique Corbeil

Montréal: Residence Paul Lizotte, 6850, boul Gouin est, Montréal PQ H1G 6L7 – 514/326-7140 – 129 lits – Dir. gen., Pierre Ouimet

Montréal: Residence Rive Soleil, 15150, rue Notre-Dame est, Montréal PQ H1A 1W6 – 514/642-5509; Fax: 514/642-4120 – 43 lits – Dir. gen., Roger-G. Bergeron

Montréal: Residence Riviera Inc., 3860, boul Lévesque ouest, Laval PQ H7V 1G7 – 514/682-0111; Fax: 514/682-0154 – 84 lits – Dir. gen., Marilyn Nadon

Montréal: Residence Ste-Jeanne-d'Arc, 7300, boul des Laurentides, Laval PQ H7H 1V8 – 514/963-3208 – 14 places – Dir. gen., Pierre Marson

Montréal: Residence St-Maxime Inc., 3717, boul Lévesque ouest, Laval PQ H7V 1G4 – 514/682-0414 – 46 lits – Dir. gen., Madeleine Bourbeau

Montréal: Residence Sainte-Claire Inc., 8950, rue Sainte-Claire est, Montréal PQ H1L 1Z1 – 514/351-3877 – 38 lits – Dir. gen., Marcel Daniel

Montréal: Residence Sainte-Dorothée, 350, boul Samson, Laval PQ H7X 1J4 – 514/689-0933; Fax: 514/689-3147 – 280 lits – Dir. gen., Lise Groleau

Montréal: Residence Villeray, 6767, rue Cartier, Montréal PQ H2G 3G2 – 514/270-9271 – 100 lits – Dir. gen., Gilles Saint-Pierre

Montréal: Residence Yvon-Brunet, 6250, av Newman, Montréal PQ H4E 4K4 – 514/765-8000; Fax: 514/765-8064 – 191 lits – Dir. gen., Germain Harvey

Montréal: Residences Marois Ltée, 14, boul Daniel-Johnson, Laval PQ H7V 2C2 – 514/681-2100; Fax: 514/681-7494 – 39 lits – Dir. gen., Normand Goyette

Canadian Almanac & Directory 1997

Montréal: Villa Belle Rive Inc., 5320, boul Gouin est, Montréal PQ H1G 1B4 – 514/321-1367 – 27 lits – Dir. gen., Francoise Chapleau

Montréal: Villa Ste-Genevieve (1986) Inc., 5002, boul Saint-Charles, Pierrefonds PQ H9H 3G1 – 514/620-8780 – 42 lits – Dir. gen., Dr. Lambros Chaniotis

New Carlisle: Centre d'accueil de la Baie, 108, rue Principale, CP 577, New Carlisle PQ G0C 1Z0 – 418/752-3386; Fax: 418/752-6483 – 75 lits – Dir. gen., Vilmont Moreau

Newport: La Maison de l'Anse Inc., CP 58, Newport PQ G0C 2A0 – 418/777-2008 – 12 places – Dir. gen., Louisette Langlois

Nicolet: Foyer de Nicolet, 175, rue Marguerite d'Youville, Nicolet PQ J3T 1T3 – 819/293-2142; Fax: 819/293-8510 – 215 lits – Dir. gen., Sr. Rejeanne Letendre

Nicolet: Hôpital du Christ-Roi, see Centres hospitaliers listings

Normandin: Foyer St-Cyrille de Normandin Inc., 1153, av des Ecoles, CP 490, Normandin PQ G0W 2E0 – 418/274-3416; Fax: 418/274-5679 – 23 lits – Dir. gen., Jacques Turcotte

Normandin: Pavillon Ghislain Genest, 1162, av des Ecoles, CP 132, Normandin PQ G0Q 2E0 – 418/274-2993 – 18 places – Dir. gen., Jacques Turcotte

North Hatley: Foyer Connaught, CP 178, North Hatley PQ J0B 2C0 – 819/842-2164 – 49 lits – Dir. gen., John Degrace

North Hatley: La Maison Blanche de North Hatley Inc., 977, rue Massawippi, CP 298, North Hatley PQ J0B 2C0 – 819/842-2478; Fax: 819/842-2470 – 60 lits – Dir. gen., Gisele Croteau

Notre-Dame-du-Bon-Conseil: L'Accueil de Notre-Dame-du-Bon-Conseil Inc., 91, rue Saint-Thomas, CP 90, Notre-Dame-du-Bon-Conseil PQ J0C 1A0 – 819/336-2122; Fax: 819/336-2453 – 57 lits – Dir. gen., Nagui Habashi

Notre-Dame-du-Mont-Carmel: Pavillon Valmont Inc., Lac Doucet, 260, 3e rue, Notre-Dame-du-Mont-Carmel PQ G0X 3J0 – 819/375-8744 – 18 places – Dir. gen., Vital Gaudet

Notre-Dame-du-Nord: Pavillon Tete du Lac Inc., 15, rue Ontario, CP 550, Notre-Dame-du-Nord PQ J0Z 3B0 – 418/723-2787 – 21 places – Dir. gen., Nicole Landry

Oka: Manoir Oka Inc., 2083, ch Oka, CP 567, Oka PQ J0N 1E0 – 514/479-6447; Fax: 514/479-6447 – 34 lits – Dir. gen., Robert Fournier

Ormstown: Le Centre d'accueil Ormstown-Huntingdon, 65, rue Hector, Ormstown PQ J0S 1K0 – 514/829-2346 – 75 lits – Dir. gen., Claude-Yves de Repentigny

Palmarolle: Le Foyer Mgr Halde, 136, rue Principale est, CP 70, Palmarolle PQ J0Z 3C0 – 819/787-2612; Fax: 819/787-3293 – 33 lits – Dir. gen., Fabiola Pelletier

Pierreville: Foyer Lucien Shooner Inc., 50, rue Paul-Comtois, CP 220, Pierreville PQ J0G 1J0 – 514/568-2712; Fax: 514/568-3658 – 59 lits – Dir. gen., Pierre Levasseur

Plessisville: Foyer des Bois Francs Inc., 1450, av Trudelle, Plessisville PQ G6L 1T9 – 819/362-3558; Fax: 819/362-9266 – 40 lits – Dir. gen., Michel Lauzon

Plessisville: Pavillon Foyer Plessis, 3351, 8e rang est, Plessisville PQ G6L 2Y2 – 819/362-7454 – 34 places – Dir. gen., Jacques Veillette

Plessisville: Pavillon LS.-PH. Cote, 1801, av Michaud, Plessisville PQ G6L 1C5 – 819/362-2984 – 15 places – Dir. gen., Jean Gauthier

Pointe-a-la-Croix: Pavillon Ste-Helene, 41, rue Sarto, CP 69, Pointe-a-la-Croix PQ G0C 1L0 – 418/788-5654 – 20 places – Dir. gen., Martin Savoie

Pointe-au-Pic: Villa des Erables, 54, rue Principale, Pointe-au-Pic PQ G0T 1M0 – 418/665-2542 – 13 places – Dir. gen., Jacques Tremblay

Pontbriand: Pavillon Gaetane Grondin Enr., 214, 3e rang, Pontbriand PQ G0N 1K0 – 418/338-3310 – 14 places – Dir. gen., André Rodrigue

Povungnituk: Centre hospitalier de la Baie d'Hudson, see Centres hospitaliers listings

Price: Pavillon de Price, 4, rue du Centre, Price PQ G0J 1Z0 – 418/775-2882 – 22 places – Dir. gen., Ronald Anctil

Price: Pavillon Lavoie Chouinard Enr., 26, rue de la Gare, Price PQ G0J 1Z0 – 418/775-3544 – 19 places – Dir. gen., Ronald Anctil

Princeville: Foyer St-Eusebe Inc., 435, rue Saint-Jacques est, CP 610, Princeville PQ G0P 1E0 – 819/364-2355; Fax: 819/362-9266 – 27 lits – Dir. gen., Michel Lauzon

Québec: Centre d'accueil le Faubourg, 925, av Turnbull, Québec PQ G1R 2X6 – 418/524-2463 – 96 lits – Dir. gen., Gerard Roy

Québec: Le Centre d'accueil Nazareth Inc., 715, rue des Glacis, Québec PQ G1R 3P8 – 418/694-0492; Fax: 418/694-9452 – 75 lits – Dir. gen., Louise Gaudreault

Québec: Centre d'accueil St-Antoine, 1451, boul Pere-Lelievre, Québec PQ G1M 1N8 – 418/683-2516 – 283 lits – Dir. gen., Gerard Roy

Québec: Centre d'accueil Sainte-Marie-des-Anges, 2390, boul Masson, Québec PQ G1P 1J4 – 418/871-1186 – 17 lits – Dir. gen., Gisele Boivin

Québec: Centre de services Notre-Dame-de-Lourdes, 105, rue Hermine, Québec PQ G1K 1Y5 – 418/529-2501; Fax: 418/529-1693 – 226 lits – Dir. gen., Robert Laroche

Québec: Centre d'hébergement Champlain-Limoilou, 220, rue de la Sapinière Dorion est, Québec PQ G1L 1P5 – 418/623-1824; Fax: 418/623-1824 – 32 lits – Dir. gen., Guy , oly

Québec: Centre hospitalier St-François Inc., 1604, 1re av, Québec PQ G1L 3L6 – 418/524-6033; Fax: 418/524-9542 – 29 lits – Dir. des soins, Josée Gosselin

Québec: Centre Louis-Hebert, 1550, rue de la Pointe-aux-Lievres nord, Québec PQ G1L 4M8 – 418/524-2496; Fax: 418/529-3450 – 55 lits – Dir. gen. par interim, Richard Rousseau

Québec: La Champenoise, 990, rue Gerard Moriseet, Québec PQ G1S 1X6 – 418/681-4637 – 20 lits – Dir. gen., André la Roche

Québec: Habitation Grande Allee, 1175, rue Turnbull, Québec PQ G1R 5L5 – 418/522-3979 – 78 lits – Dir. gen., Michel Baumont

Québec: Hôpital de l'Enfant-Jésus (Centre Maizerets), 2480, ch de la Canardière, Québec PQ G1J 2G1 – 418/663-3518; Fax: 418/663-8501 – 54 lits – Dir. gen., Gaston Pellan

Québec: Hôtel Dieu du Sacre-Coeur de Jésus de Québec, see Centres hospitaliers listings

Québec: Pavillon Demers, 325, 18e rue, Québec PQ G1L 2E3 – 418/522-8696 – 12 places – Dir. gen., Robert Laroche

Québec: Pavillon la Residence Langelier, 350, boul Langelier, Québec PQ G1K 5N3 – 418/524-1477 – 26 places – Dir. gen., Robert Laroche

Québec: Pavillon Saint-Sacrement, see Centres hospitaliers listings

Québec: Pavillon Ste-Therese inc., 1990, av Bardy, Québec PQ G1J 4S1 – 418/663-3379 – 12 places – Dir. gen., Jacques Garneau

Québec: La Residence Grande-Allee, 1175, rue Turnbull, Québec PQ G1R 5L5 – 418/522-3979 – 29 places – Dir. gen., Robert Laroche

Québec: Les Residences Kirouac, 765, rue Kirouac, Québec PQ G1N 2J5 – 418/527-1616 – 29 places – Dir. gen., Robert Laroche

Rawdon: Centre d'accueil Heather II, 3468, 3e av, Rawdon PQ J0K 1S0 – 514/834-2512; Fax: 514/834-5805 – 40 lits – Dir. gen., Paul Arbec

Rawdon: Foyer Beaudoin, 3472, rue Melcalfe, Rawdon PQ J0K 1S0 – 514/834-6747 – 14 places – Dir. gen., Jacques Hendlisz

Rawdon: Foyer Bouleaux Argentes, 3567, rue Church, Rawdon PQ J0K 1S0 – 514/834-2794 – 16 lits – Dir. gen., Remy Landry

Rawdon: Pavillon André Etheir Inc., 3380, rue Cedar, Rawdon PQ J0K 1S0 – 514/834-6715 – 14 places – Dir. gen., Maurice Blais

Rawdon: Pavillon Longpre, 3832, rue Queen, Rawdon PQ J0K 1S0 – 514/834-3463 – 14 places – Dir. gen., Maurice Blais

Repentigny: Centre le Gardeur, 60, boul Aubert, Repentigny PQ J6A 4N8 – 514/585-5933 – 80 lits – Dir. gen., Yvon Poirier

Repentigny: Pavillon Bellefeuille, 699, rue Notre-Dame, Repentigny PQ J6A 2X1 – 514/581-4951 – 13 places – Dir. gen., Yvon Poirier

Repentigny: Pavillon LeBlanc - Longpre Enr., 14, rue Leonie, Repentigny PQ J6A 3A8 – 514/585-4206 – 24 places – Dir. gen., Yvon Poirier

Repentigny: Pavillon-Ste-Therese Enrg., 697, rue Notre-Dame, Repentigny PQ J6A 2W9 – 514/581-6143 – 21 places – Dir. gen., Claude Desjardins

Richmond: Foyer Richmond Inc., 980, rue McGauran, CP 860, Richmond PQ J0B 2H0 – 819/826-3711; Fax: 819/826-5724 – 64 lits – Dir. gen., Nicole Corbin

Rigaud: Foyer de Rigaud Inc., 7, rue d'Armour, CP 370, Rigaud PQ J0P 1P0 – 514/451-5328; Fax: 514/451-6370 – 58 lits – Dir. gen., Lise Belanger

Rimouski: Le Foyer de Rimouski Inc., 645, boul Saint-Germain, Rimouski PQ G5L 3S2 – 418/724-4111; Fax: 418/724-0604 – 242 lits – Dir. gen., Gilles Gauvreau

Rimouski: Manoir de Caroline Inc., 280, rue Belzile, Rimouski PQ G5L 8K7 – 418/723-0611; Fax: 418/723-0615 – 85 lits – Dir. gen., André Bisaillon

Ripon: Centre d'accueil de Ripon, 46, rue Principale, CP 70, Ripon PQ J0V 1V0 – 819/983-6173; Fax: 819/983-1494 – 42 lits – Dir. gen., Denise Bergevin

Rivière-Beaudette: Pavillon Ste-Anne Enr., 990, ch Sainte-Claire, Rivière-Beaudette PQ J0P 1R0 – 514/269-2167 – 22 places – Dir. gen., Paul-Henri Boutin

Rivière-Bleue: CHSLD du Temiscouata, 45, rue du Foyer, CP 98, Rivière-Bleue PQ G0L 2B0 – 418/893-5511; Fax: 418/893-7151 – 41 lits – Dir. gen., Rejean Pelletier

Rivière-du-Loup: Hôpital Saint-Joseph, 28, rue Joly, Rivière-du-Loup PQ G5R 3H2 – 418/862-6385; Fax: 418/862-1986 – 142 lits – Dir. gen., Raymond April

Rivière-du-Loup: Villa Fraserville Inc., 70, rue Saint-Henri, Rivière-du-Loup PQ G5R 2A1 – 418/862-7251; Fax: 418/862-2902 – 39 lits – Dir. gen., Raymond April

Rivière-Ouelle: Centre d'accueil Therese Martin, 100, ch de la Petite Anse, Rivière-Ouelle PQ G0L 2C0 – 418/856-4433; Fax: 418/856-4381 – 126 lits – Dir. gen., Jean-Claude Rousseau

Robertsonville: Pavillon Jacinthe Vachon, 95, rue Notre-Dame nord, Robertsonville PQ G0N 1L0 – 418/338-8818 – 13 places – Dir. gen., André Rodrigue

Roberval: Le Claire Fontaine, see Hôpitaux auxiliaires/Centres de soins de santé listings

Roberval: Le Domaine du Bon Temps, 400, av Bergeron, Roberval PQ G8H 1K8 – 418/275-3623 – 65 lits – Dir. gen., Claude J.-Y. Theberge

Roberval: Pavillon Colombe Gagnon, 507, rue Notre-Dame, Roberval PQ G8H 2M5 – 418/275-2884 – 12 places – Dir. gen., Laurent Bouillon

Roberval: Pavillon Ferland, 992, boul Saint-Joseph, Roberval PQ G8H 2L9 – 418/275-4376 – 23 places – Dir. gen., Laurent Bouillon

Rouyn-Noranda: Centre d'accueil Youville, 3, 9e rue, Rouyn-Noranda PQ J9X 2A9 – 819/764-3281 – 75 lits – Dir. gen., Gerard Marinovich

Rouyn-Noranda: Maison Pie XII, 512, av Richard, Rouyn-Noranda PQ J9X 4M1 – 819/762-0908; Fax: 819/764-5036 – 82 places – Dir. gen., Daniel Bergeron

Rouyn-Noranda: Pavillon Claude Larouche, 30, rue Monseigneur Tessier est, Rouyn-Noranda PQ J9X 3B9 – 819/764-4706 – 29 places – Dir. gen., Daniel Bergeron

Sacre-Coeur-de-Marie-Partie-Sud: Pavillon Alidor et Cecile Jacques Inc., 1310, 8e rang, Sacre-Coeur-de-Marie-Partie-Sud PQ G0N 1W0 – 418/338-1308 – 16 places – André Rodrigue

Ste-Agathe-de-Lotbinière: Pavillon Chantal et Noel Tardif Inc., 144, rue Saint-Georges, Ste-Agathe-de-Lotbinière PQ G0S 2A0 – 418/599-2975 – 12 places – Dir. gen., André Paquet

Ste-Agathe-des-Monts: Centre hospitalier Laurentien - Foyer Ste-Agathe, 21, rue Godon ouest, Ste-Agathe-des-Monts PQ J8C 1E5 – 819/326-1141 – 55 lits – Dir. gen., Jacques Gaudette

Ste-Agathe-des-Monts: Centre hospitalier Laurentien - Pavillon Grignon, 2, rue Préfontaine ouest, Ste-Agathe-des-Monts PQ J8C 1C3 – 514/326-3551; Fax: 514/324-4010 – 32 lits – Dir. gen., Jacques Gaudette

Ste-Agathe-des-Monts: Centre hospitalier Laurentien - Pavillon Sinai, 100, ch Mont Sinai, Ste-Agathe-des-Monts PQ J8C 3A4 – 819/326-2303 – 67 lits – Dir. gen., Jacques Guadetie

Saint-Alexandre: Foyer Villa Maria Inc., 404, av du Foyer, Saint-Alexandre PQ G0L 2G0 – 418/495-2914; Fax: 418/495-2829 – 78 lits – Dir. gen., Jean-Claude Rousseau

Saint-Alexis-de-Matapedia: Pavillon le Gite de Saint-Alexis Inc., 187, rue Principale, Saint-Alexis-de-Matapedia PQ G0J 2E0 – 418/299-2723 – 15 places – Dir. gen., Marc Turcotte

Saint-Amable: Pavillon St-Amable, 125, rue Saint-Thomas, Saint-Amable PQ J0L 1N0 – 514/649-0458 – 10 places – Dir. gen., Robert Sabino

Saint-André-Avellin: Centre d'accueil la Petite Nation, 76, rue Saint-André, CP 230, Saint-André-Avellin PQ J0V 1W0 – 819/983-2731; Fax: 819/983-7812 – 72 lits – Dir. gen., André Dupuis

Ste-Anne-de-la-Pérade: Foyer de la Pérade Inc., 60, rue de la Fabrique, CP 217, Ste-Anne-de-la-Pérade PQ G0X 2J0 – 418/325-2313; Fax: 418/325-2313 – 47 lits – Dir. gen., Gilles Cossette

Saint-Anselme: Pavillon André Breton, 357, rue Principale, Saint-Anselme PQ G0R 2N0 – 418/885-4212 – 12 places – Dir. gen., Herve-Emile Allen

Saint-Anselme: Pavillon de l'Age d'Or St-Anselme Inc., 40, rue Saint-Marc, Saint-Anselme PQ G0R 2N0 – 418/885-4482 – 48 lits – Dir. gen., Yvan de Blois

Saint-Antoine-sur-Richelieu: Accueil du Rivage Inc., 1008, rue du Rivage, CP 60, Saint-Antoine-sur-Richelieu PQ J0L 1R0 – 514/787-3163; Fax: 514/787-1156 – 36 lits – Dir. gen., J. André Bergeron

Saint-Antoine: Le Medaillon d'Or enr., 905, boul des Laurentides, Saint-Antoine PQ J7Z 6W7 – 514/431-7555 – 12 places – Dir. gen., Germain Beausejour

Saint-Antonin: Le Foyer de St-Antonin Inc., 286, rue Principale, Saint-Antonin PQ G0L 2J0 – 418/862-7993; Fax: 418/862-5278 – 41 lits – Dir. gen., Raymond April

Saint-Apollinaire: La Lignée Lotbinière, 32, rue Industrielle, Saint-Apollinaire PQ G0S 2E0 – 418/881-3982; Fax: 418/881-3482 – 40 lits – Dir. gen., André Paquet

St-Augustin-De-Desmaures: CHSLD St-Augustin, 4954, rue Marie Le Franc, St-Augustin-De-Desmaures PQ G3A 1V5 – 418/871-1232; Fax: 418/871-0744 – 87 lits – Dir. gen., Vincenzo Simonetta

St-Augustin-de-Desmaures: Jardins du Haut Saint-Laurent (1992) Inc., 4770, rue Saint-Felix, St-Augustin-de-Desmaures PQ G3A 1B1 – 418/999-9999; Fax: 418/872-4245 – 110 lits – Dir. gen., Jeannine Dulude

St-Barthélémy: Pavillon André Desroches, 1021, rang York, St-Barthélémy PQ J0K 1X0 – 514/885-3012 – 14 places – Dir. gen., Maurice Blais

Saint-Basile: Pavillon Saint-Basile, 329, rue de l'Eglise, Saint-Basile PQ G0A 3G0 – 418/329-2066 – 21 places – Dir. gen., Fernand Morasse

Ste-Béatrix: Pavillon Michelle Gravel et Roland Mondor, 1011, rue Principale, Ste-Béatrix PQ J0K 1Y0 – 514/883-5616 – 14 places – Dir. gen., Maurice Blais

Ste-Béatrix: Pavillon Ste-Béatrix Enr., #1100-1102, rang Sainte-Cecile, Ste-Béatrix PQ J0K 1Y0 – 514/883-8405 – 14 places – Dir. gen., Maurice Blais

St-Benoît-Labre: Pavillon Baillargeon Inc., 357, Rte 271, St-Benoît-Labre PQ G0M 1P0 – 418/228-9141 – 28 places – Dir. gen., Richard Busque

Saint-Bernard-de-Lacolle: Residence Florence Groulx Inc., 7, rang Saint-Louis, Saint-Bernard-de-Lacolle PQ J0J 1V0 – 514/246-2232; Fax: 514/246-4111 – 50 lits – Dir. gen., André Gaudette

St-Boniface-de-Shawinigan: Pavillon St-Boniface Inc., 50, rue Principale, St-Boniface-de-Shawinigan PQ G0X 2L0 – 819/535-3223 – 16 places – Dir. gen., Jacques Veillette

St-Bruno: Centre d'accueil de Montarville, 265, boul Seigneuriale ouest, St-Bruno PQ J3V 2H4 – 514/461-2650 – 150 lits – Dir. gen., Ghislain Lavergne

St-Casimir: Centre d'hébergement St-Casimir, 605, rue Fleury, CP 10, St-Casimir PQ G0A 3L0 – 418/339-2861 – 63 lits – Dir. gen., Fernand Morasse

Ste-Cecile: Pavillon Ste-Cecile, 4581, rue Principale, Ste-Cecile PQ G0Y 1J0 – 819/583-0400 – 15 places – Dir. gen., Raymonda Lapointe-Lagueux

St-Célestin: Foyer de St-Célestin, 475, rue Houde, CP 90, St-Célestin PQ J0C 1G0 – 819/229-3617; Fax: 819/229-1165 – 52 lits – Dir. gen., Rita Leclerc

St-Césaire: Residence Val-Joli, 1425, rue Notre-Dame, St-Césaire PQ J0L 1T0 – 514/469-3194 – 55 lits – Dir. gen., Michel Desnoyers

St-Charles Borromée: Centre hospitalier régional DeLanaudière, see Centres hospitaliers listings

Ste-Claire: Villa Prevost Inc., 84, boul Begin sud, Ste-Claire PQ G0R 2V0 – 418/883-3357; Fax: 418/883-4204 – 51 lits – Dir. gen., Yvan Deblois

St-Cléophas: Pavillon A & N Deschenes Enr., 560, rue Principale, St-Cléophas PQ J0K 2A0 – 514/889-2725 – 14 places – Dir. gen., Maurice Blais

St-Côme: Pavillon Gaston Larochelle, 1531, rue Principale, St-Côme PQ J0K 2B0 – 514/883-5537 – 14 places – Dir. gen., Maurice Blais

St-Cóme: Pavillon Gerald Baillargeon Inc., 51, 50e av, St-Cóme PQ J0K 2B0 – 514/883-6619 – 14 places – Dir. gen., Maurice Blais

St-Cóme: Pavillon St-Cóme Inc., 1051, rue Principale, St-Cóme PQ J0K 2B0 – 514/883-6693 – 14 places – Dir. gen., Maurice Blais

Ste-Croix: Centre d'accueil de Ste-Croix, 6245, rue Principale, Ste-Croix PQ G0S 2H0 – 418/926-3247 – 48 lits – Dir. gen. Villa Suite-Anne de St-Cuthbert Inc., André Paquet

St-Cyprien: Foyer St-Cyprien Inc., 175, rue Principale, CP 118, St-Cyprien PQ G0L 2P0 – 418/963-2018; Fax: 418/963-2499 – 46 lits – Dir. gen., Robert Gagnon

St-Damien-de-Buckland: Pavillon Rosaire Deblois, 164, rue Commerciale, St-Damien-de-Buckland PQ G0R 2Y0 – 418/789-2262 – 16 places – Dir. gen., Yvan Deblois

St-David: Centre d'accueil St-David Inc., 10, rue Rivière, St-David PQ J0G 1L0 – 514/789-2033; Fax: 514/789-2994 – 45 lits – Dir. gen., Mohammed Settouche

St-Denis-sur-Richelieu: Foyer St-Joseph St-Denis sur Richelieu Inc., 577, ch des Patriotes, CP 245, St-Denis-sur-Richelieu PQ J0H 1K0 – 514/787-2040 – 35 lits – Dir. gen., Jean-Guy Lavoie

St-Donat: Foyer de St-Donat Inc., 430, rue Bellevue, CP 250, St-Donat PQ J0T 2C0 – 819/424-2503; Fax: 819/424-5639 – 41 lits – Dir. gen., Rejean Gaudet

St-Donat: Pavillon Poudrier Enr., 225, av du Lac, St-Donat PQ J0T 2C0 – 819/424-2200 – 11 places – Dir. gen., Pierre Poudrier

St-Édouard-de-Frampton: Les CHSLD Nouvelle-Beauce-Frampton, 148, rue Principale, St-Édouard-de-Frampton PQ G0R 1M0 – 418/479-2970 – 33 lits – Dir. gen., Benoit Guillemette

Ste-Élisabeth: Centre d'accueil Ste-Élisabeth, 2410, rue Principale, Ste-Élisabeth PQ J0K 2J0 – 514/759-8355; Fax: 514/759-9750 – 108 lits – Dir. gen., Paul-Yves Laviolette

Ste-Élisabeth: Pavillon France Lefebvre, 110, rue Pelland, Ste-Élisabeth PQ J0K 2J0 – 514/759-0588 – 14 places – Dir. gen., Maurice Blais

Ste-Élisabeth: Residence Ste-Élisabeth Enr., 250, rue Principale, Ste-Élisabeth PQ J0A 1M0 – 819/358-2771 – 17 places – Dir. gen., Gilles Perreault

St-Éphrem-de-Beauce: Foyer Ste-Famille Inc., 1, rue Plante, CP 310, St-Éphrem-de-Beauce PQ G0M 1R0 – 418/484-2121; Fax: 418/484-2144 – 36 lits – Dir. gen., Real Roy

St-Eugene: Centre d'accueil de St-Eugene de l'Islet Inc., 24, rue Commerciale, St-Eugene PQ G0R 1X0 – 418/247-3927; Fax: 418/247-3928 – 36 lits – Dir. gen., Pierrette D. Guimond

St-Eustache: Manoir St-Eustache, 55, rue Chenier, St-Eustache PQ J7R 4Y8 – 514/472-0013; Fax: 514/472-0016 – 79 lits – Dir. gen., Denis Renaud

St-Eustache: Pavillon St-Louis Inc., 154, rue St-Louis, St-Eustache PQ J7R 1Y2 – 514/472-9002 – 23 places – Dir. gen., Denis Renaud

St-Eustache: Société en commandite centre d'accueil l'Ermitage, 112, 25e av, St-Eustache PQ J7P 2V2 – 514/473-5961; Fax: 514/491-1847 – 70 lits – Dir. gen., Kevin Shemie

Saint-Fabien-de-Panet: Centre d'accueil de Saint-Fabien-de-Panet, 19, rue Principale, Saint-Fabien-de-Panet PQ G0R 2J0 – 418/249-4051; Fax: 418/249-2371 – 45 lits – Dir. gen., Jean-Paul Lacroix

St-Fabien: Foyer St-Fabien, 142, 1re rue, CP 367, St-Fabien PQ G0L 2Z0 – 418/869-2709 – 27 places – Dir. gen., Gilles Gauvreau

St-Félicien: Le Foyer de la Paix Inc., 1229, boul Sacre-Coeur, CP 400, St-Félicien PQ G8K 1A5 – 418/679-1585; Fax: 418/679-2376 – 46 lits – Dir. gen., Claude J.Y. Theberge

St-Félicien: Pavillon Daniel Girard, 1567, boul Sacre-Coeur, St-Félicien PQ G8K 1B4 – 418/679-3768 – 14 places – Dir. gen., Laurent Bouillon

St-Félicien: Pavillon de l'Amitie, 996, 1e rue, St-Félicien PQ G8K 1Y4 – 418/679-1777 – 20 places – Dir. gen., Claude J.Y. Theberge

St-Félicien: Pavillon Florent Perron, 1414, rue Bellevue, St-Félicien PQ G8K 1J2 – 418/679-0713 – 11 places – Dir. gen., Laurent Bouillon

Saint-Félicien: Pavillon Gilaine, 1163, boul Lefebvre, Saint-Félicien PQ G8K 1Y5 – 418/679-0474 – 10 places – Dir. gen., Laurent Bouillon

St-Félicien: Pavillon Therese, 1139, rue Notre-Dame, St-Félicien PQ G8K 1Z7 – 418/679-0732 – 10 places – Dir. gen., Laurent Bouillon

Ste-Félicité: Pavillon Marie-Anna, 170, boul Perron, CP 188, Ste-Félicité PQ G0J 2K0 – 418/733-4851 – 16 places – Dir. gen., Clement Gauthier

Saint-Félix-de-Valois: Residence de Lanaduière (1989) Inc., 1450, ch Barrette, Saint-Félix-de-Valois PQ J0K 2M0 – 514/889-4707 – Dir. gen., Roger Guertin

St-Flavien: Le Foyer de St-Flavien, 82, rue Principale, St-Flavien PQ G0S 2M0 – 418/728-2727 – 41 lits – Dir. gen., André Paquet

St-Flavien: Pavillon Real et Michelle Demers Enr., 36, rue Bernatchez, St-Flavien PQ G0S 2M0 – 418/728-2727 – 12 places – Dir. gen., André Paquet

Ste-Foy: Foyer Notre-Dame de Foy Inc., 2580, ch Sainte-Foy, Ste-Foy PQ G1V 1T9 – 418/653-3626; Fax: 418/654-9307 – 18 lits – Dir. gen., Jean-René Desmarais

Ste-Foy: Maison Legault, 3035, ch St-Louis, Ste-Foy PQ G1W 1R5 – 418/682-0667 – 9 lits – Dir. gen., Francoise Legault

Canadian Almanac & Directory 1997

Ste-Foy: Pavillon Hélène-de-Champlain, 809, rue du Chanoine Scott, Ste-Foy PQ G1V 3N5 – 418/656-6957 – 23 places – Dir. gen., Jacques Garneau

Ste-Foy: Residence Paul Triquet, 789, rue de Belmont, Ste-Foy PQ G1V 4V2 – 418/657-6890 – 64 lits – Dir. gen., Gérard Roy

Ste-Foy: Residence Paul Triquet, 789, rue de Belmont, Ste-Foy PQ G1V 4V2 – 418/675-6890 – 64 lits – Dir. gen., Michel Tremblay

Saint-François de Sales: Pavillon St-François de Sales, 306, rue du Foyer, CP 28, Saint-François de Sales PQ G0W 1M0 – 418/348-6798 – 20 places – Dir. gen., Claude J.-Y. Theberge

St-Gabriel-de-Brandon: Au Second Bonheur Enr., 63, rue Provost, CP 1777, St-Gabriel-de-Brandon PQ J0K 2N0 – 514/835-4994 – 21 lits – Dir. gen., Ginette Simard-L'Abbee

St-Gabriel-de-Brandon: Centre d'accueil Desy Inc., 90, rue Maskinonge, CP 840, St-Gabriel-de-Brandon PQ J0K 2N0 – 514/835-4712; Fax: 514/835-7606 – 54 lits – Dir. gen., Real Naud

St-Gabriel-de-Brandon: Pavillon Laurette Boucher, 200, rue Saint-Gabriel, St-Gabriel-de-Brandon PQ J0K 2N0 – 514/835-5083 – 13 places – Dir. gen., Real Naud

St-Gabriel-de-Brandon: Pavillon Lucille S. Desalliers Enr., 76, rue Grenier, St-Gabriel-de-Brandon PQ J0K 2N0 – 514/835-5683 – 14 places – Dir. gen., Maurice Blais

St-Gabriel-de-Brandon: Pavillon Ma-Mi Enr., 156, rue Dequoy, St-Gabriel-de-Brandon PQ J0K 2N0 – 514/835-4969 – 15 places – Dir. gen., Real Naud

St-Gabriel-de-Brandon: Pavillon St-Gabriel Enr., 179, rue Maskinonge, St-Gabriel-de-Brandon PQ J0K 2N0 – 514/835-5309 – 14 places – Dir. gen., Maurice Blais

St-Gabriel-de-Brandon: Residence Chez Maman Enr., 1780, rang 6, St-Gabriel-de-Brandon PQ J0K 2N0 – 514/835-5123 – 20 lits – Dir. gen., Guylaine Comtois-Lavoie

St-Gabriel-de-Rimouski: Pavillon Fortin Enr., 309, rue Principale, CP 130, St-Gabriel-de-Rimouski PQ G0K 1M0 – 418/798-8888 – 25 places – Dir. gen., Ronald Anctil

St-Gédéon-de-Beauce: Foyer Saint-Gedeon, 131, 1e av sud, St-Gédéon-de-Beauce PQ G0M 1T0 – 418/582-3322; Fax: 418/582-3068 – 36 lits – Dir. gen., Richard Busque

Saint-Georges Est: L'Accueil de Ville Saint-Georges Inc., 11515, 8e av, Saint-Georges Est PQ G5Y 1J5 – 418/228-2021 – 50 lits – Dir. gen., Richard Busque

St-Georges: Centre d'accueil St-Louis Inc., 16705, 1re av, St-Georges PQ G5Y 2G6 – 418/228-2041; Fax: 418/228-9365 – 45 lits – Dir. gen., Gerard Gendreau

St-Georges: Foyer du Repos Enr., 3135, 120e rue est, St-Georges PQ G5Y 5B9 – 418/228-4550 – 14 lits – Dir. gen., Patrice Gilbert

St-Georges: Le Foyer Saint-Georges de Beauce Inc., 405, 18e rue, St-Georges PQ G5Y 4T2 – 418/228-2081 – 55 lits – Dir. gen., Richard Busque

St-Georges: Residence du Bon Pasteur, 300, 18e rue, St-Georges PQ G5Y 4S9 – 418/228-9015 – 29 places – Dir. gen., Richard Busque

St-Gérard: Pavillon St-Gérard, 339, rue Roy nord, St-Gérard PQ G0Y 1K0 – 819/877-2032 – 17 places – Dir. gen., Albert Kratsenberg

St-Gervais: Foyer St-Gervais Inc., 70, rue Saint-Etienne, St-Gervais PQ G0R 3C0 – 418/887-3387; Fax: 418/887-3388 – 37 lits – Dir. gen., Yvan Deblois

Ste-Hénédine: Le Foyer Paroissial de Ste-Hénédine, 104, Rte Langevin, CP 40, Ste-Hénédine PQ G0S 2R0 – 418/935-3658 – 47 lits – Dir. gen., Benoit Guillemette

Ste-Hénédine: Pavillon Gaetan Labbe, 103, rue Langevin, Ste-Hénédine PQ G0S 2R0 – 418/935-3756 – 15 places – Dir. gen., Estelle Cliche

St-Honoré-de-Beauce: Centre d'accueil St-Honoré, 452, rue Principale, CP 160, St-Honoré-de-Beauce PQ G0M 1V0 – 418/485-6357; Fax: 418/485-6232 – 33 lits – Dir. gen., Richard Busque

St-Hubert: Centre d'accueil Henriette Cere, 6435, ch Chambly, St-Hubert PQ J3Y 3R6 – 514/678-3291 – 79 lits – Dir. gen., Lucien Dansereau

St-Hubert: CHSLD Montérégie, 2042, boul Marie, St-Hubert PQ J4T 2B4 – 514/671-5596; Fax: 514/671-5079 – 90 lits – Dir. gen., Vincenzo Simonetta

St-Hubert: Pavillon Residence St-Hubert, 5160, montee St-Hubert, St-Hubert PQ J3Y 1V7 – 514/676-8411 – 38 places – Dir. gen., Jean-Pierre Montpetit

St-Hubert: Pavillon St-Hubert Enr., 3823, rue Grand boulevard, St-Hubert PQ J4T 2M3 – 514/445-3598 – 13 lits – Dir. gen., Lucien Dansereau

St-Hyacinthe: Pavillon Girouard, 2320, rue Girouard, St-Hyacinthe PQ J2S 3B1 – 514/774-9022 – 30 places – Dir. gen., Ghislaine Lavergne

St-Hyacinthe: Residence Gaucher-Heroux Inc., 2935, rue St-Pierre ouest, St-Hyacinthe PQ J2T 1R7 – 514/774-1927 – 29 lits – Dir. gen., Yvon St-Laurent

St-Hyacinthe: Villa des Frenes Inc., 2755, av Raymond, St-Hyacinthe PQ J2S 5W8 – 514/773-4688; Fax: 514/467-4210 – 77 lits – Dir. gen., Ghislaine Lavergne

St-Isidore-de-Dorchester: Les CHSLD Nouvelle-Beauce-St-Isidore, 102, rue Saint-Albert, St-Isidore-de-Dorchester PQ G0S 2S0 – 418/882-5601 – 45 lits – Dir. gen., Benoit Guillemette

St-Isidore-de-Dorchester: Pavillon Parent Enr., 134, rue Sainte-Jean, St-Isidore-de-Dorchester PQ G0S 2S0 – 418/882-6236 – 12 places – Dir. gen., Benoit Guillemette

St-Isidore-de-Laprairie: Pavillon d'accueil St-Isidore, 675, rue Saint-Regis, St-Isidore-de-Laprairie PQ J0L 2A0 – 514/454-3121; Fax: 514/699-2425 – 16 places – Dir. gen., Jacques Cotton

St-Jacques: Foyer St-Jacques, 30, rue Sainte-Anne, St-Jacques PQ J0K 2R0 – 514/839-2695 – 55 lits – Dir. gen., Jacques Beaupre

Saint-Jean-de-Boischatel: Pavillon des Chutes, 5500, boul Sainte-Anne, Saint-Jean-de-Boischatel PQ G0A 1H0 – 418/822-2578 – 29 places – Dir. gen., Robert Laroche

Saint-Jean-de-Dieu: Le Pavillon Rochapel Inc., 22, rue Principale nord, Saint-Jean-de-Dieu PQ G0L 3M0 – 418/963-2124 – 27 places – Dir. gen., Raymond April

St-Jean-de-Dieu: Villa Dube Inc., 20, rue de la Villa, CP 10, St-Jean-de-Dieu PQ G0L 3M0 – 418/963-2713; Fax: 418/963-2493 – 42 lits – Dir. gen., Donald Gagnon

St-Jean-d'Orléans: Gestion Lafrance - Chandonnet Inc., 1473, ch Royal, St-Jean-d'Orléans PQ G0A 3W0 – 418/829-3987 – 16 places – Dir. gen., Rejean Cantin

St-Jean-sur-Richelieu: Centre Georges Phaneuf, 230, rue Jacques-Cartier nord, St-Jean-sur-Richelieu PQ J3B 6T4 – 514/346-1133; Fax: 514/346-2199 – 135 lits – Dir. gen., André Trottier

St-Jean-sur-Richelieu: Centre Gertrude Lafrance, 150, boul St-Luc, St-Jean-sur-Richelieu PQ J3A 1G2 – 514/348-4941; Fax: 514/348-7693 – 211 lits – Dir. gen., André Trottier

St-Jérôme: L'Auberge (St-Jérôme) Inc., 66, rue Danis, St-Jérôme PQ J7Y 2R3 – 514/436-3131; Fax: 514/436-4139 – 81 lits – Dir. gen., Germain Beauséjour

St-Jérôme: Centre d'Youville, 531, rue Laviolette, Saint-Jérôme PQ J7Y 2T8 – 514/436-3061; Fax: 514/436-8328 – 128 lits – Dir. gen., Germain Beauséjour

St-Jérôme: Foyer Soleil Inc., 225, ch du Lac Bertrand, RR#2, St-Jérôme PQ J7Z 5T5 – 514/438-1704; Fax: 514/438-6594 – 53 lits – Dir. gen., Richard Parisien

St-Joseph-de-Beauce: Foyer Mgr O. Roy, 755, rue Sainte-Christine, St-Joseph-de-Beauce PQ G0S 2V0 – 418/397-6817; Fax: 418/397-6642 – 78 lits – Dir. gen., Richard Busque

St-Joseph-de-Coleraine: Pavillon Coulombe, 212, av Proulx, St-Joseph-de-Coleraine PQ G0N 1B0 – 418/423-4527 – 20 places – Dir. gen., André Rodrigue

St-Jovite: CHSLD des Valles du Nord, 925, rue Ouimet, CP 910, St-Jovite PQ J0T 2H0 – 819/425-2793 – 57 lits – Dir. gen., Yvan Lachaine

Ste-Justine: Foyer Ste-Justine, 100, rue du Foyer, CP 129, Succ Langevin, Ste-Justine PQ G0R 1Y0 – 418/383-3413 – 28 lits – Dir. gen., Jean-Yves Julien

Saint-Lambert: L'Hôpital Saint-Lambert, 831, av Notre-Dame, Saint-Lambert PQ J4R 1S1 – 514/672-3320; Fax: 514/672-3370 – 120 lits – Dir. gen., Jean-Denis Godbout

St-Lazare-de-Bellechasse: Pavillon Leblond & Fontaine, 412, 41e rang ouest, St-Lazare-de-Bellechasse PQ G0R 3J0 – 418/883-3622 – 11 places – Dir. gen., Yvan Deblois

St-Lazare-de-Bellechasse: Pavillon V. Audet, 121, rue Principale, St-Lazare-de-Bellechasse PQ G0R 3J0 – 418/883-2384 – 14 places – Dir. gen., Yvan Deblois

Saint-Leon-de-Standon: Pavillon Lucien Labrecque Enr., 99, rue Saint-Pierre, Saint-Leon-de-Standon PQ G0R 4L0 – 418/642-2125 – 11 places – Dir. gen., Yvan Deblois

St-Liguori: Foyer St-Liguori, 771, rue Principale, St-Liguori PQ J0K 2X0 – 514/753-7062 – 44 lits – Dir. gen., Jacques Beaupre

St-Louis-du-Ha-Ha: Foyer Beausejour Inc., 25, rue Saint-Philippe, St-Louis-du-Ha-Ha PQ G0L 3S0 – 418/854-2631; Fax: 418/854-0430 – 54 lits – Dir. gen., Rejean Pelletier

Ste-Luce: Pavillon Ste-Luce, 51, rte du Fleuve ouest, CP 166, Ste-Luce PQ G0K 1P0 – 418/739-3555 – 16 places – Dir. gen., Ronald Anctil

Saint-Luc: Pavillon Brouillet Inc., 359, rue de Bretagne, Saint-Luc PQ J0J 2A0 – 514/348-8518 – 18 places – Dir. gen., Michel Tremblay

St-Ludger: Pavillon St-Ludger Inc., 210, rue de la Salle, CP 99, St-Ludger PQ G0M 1W0 – 819/548-5551; Fax: 819/548-5553 – 39 lits – Dir. gen., Raymonde Lapointe-Lagueux

St-Magloire: Foyer St-Magloire Inc., 15, rue de la Caisse Populaire, CP 39, St-Magloire PQ G0R 3M0 – 418/257-2881; Fax: 418/257-2187 – 33 lits – Dir. gen., Jean-Yves Julien

St-Magloire: Pavillon Lefrance Enr., 104, rue Principale, St-Magloire PQ G0R 3M0 – 418/257-2951 – 14 places – Dir. gen., Jean-Yves Julien

St-Marc-des-Carrières: Centre d'hébergement St-Marc-des-Carrières, 444, rue Beauchamps, CP 220, St-Marc-des-Carrières PQ G0A 4B0 – 418/268-3511 – 53 lits – Dir. gen., Fernand Morasse

Saint-Maxime-du-Mont-Louis: Centre d'accueil du Littoral Inc., 12, 5e rue est, Saint-Maxime-du-Mont-Louis PQ G0E 1T0 – 418/797-2960; Fax: 418/797-2038 – 35 lits – Dir. gen., Alain Berube

Ste-Mélanie: Les Entreprises G. Blouin Inc., 141, rue Principale, Ste-Mélanie PQ J0K 3A0 – 514/889-5221 – 19 places – Dir. gen., Raymond Carignan

Saint-Methode-de-Frontenac: Foyer Valin Inc., 28, rue des Erables, CP 160, Saint-Methode-de-Frontenac PQ G0N 1S0 – 418/422-2362; Fax: 418/422-2448 – 72 lits – Dir. gen., André Rodrigue

Saint-Methode-de-Frontenac: Pavillon Gaetane Tardif, 75, rue Principale, Saint-Methode-de-Frontenac PQ G0N 1S0 – 418/422-2027 – 10 places – Dir. gen., André Rodrigue

St-Michel-de-Bellechasse: CHSLD Notre-Dame de Lourdes, 80, rue Principale, CP 10, St-Michel-de-Bellechasse PQ G0R 3S0 – 418/884-2811; Fax: 418/884-3714 – 80 lits – Dir. gen., Giovanni Simonetta

St-Michel-des-Saints: Centre d'accueil Brassard Inc., 390, rue Brassard, CP 309, St-Michel-des-Saints PQ J0K 3B0 – 514/833-6331; Fax: 514/833-6093 – 35 lits – Dir. gen. par intérim, Jean-Jacques Lamarche

Saint-Michel-du-Squatec: Hôpital Saint-Michel-du-Squatec, 10, rue Saint-Andre, Saint-Michel-du-Squatec PQ G0L 4H0 – 418/855-2442; Fax: 418/855-2357 – 15 lits – Dir. gen., Réjean Pelletier

St-Narcisse: Centre d'accueil de St-Narcisse Inc., 361, rue du College, St-Narcisse PQ G0X 2Y0 – 418/328-

3351; Fax: 418/328-4140 – 37 lits – Dir. gen., Gilles Cossette

St-Norbert Berthier: Foyer St-Norbert Enr., 2200, rang Sainte-Anne, St-Norbert Berthier PQ J0K 3C0 – 514/836-3297 – 14 places – Dir. gen., Maurice Blais

St-Odilon: Villa St-Odilon, 377, rue Langevin, CP 160, St-Odilon PQ G0S 3A0 – 418/464-4731; Fax: 418/464-4732 – 28 lits – Dir. gen., Richard Busque

Saint-Pacôme: CHSLD Regroupement Kamouraska, Centre Anjou, 127, rue Galarneau, Saint-Pacôme PQ G0L 3X0 – 418/852-2281; Fax: 418/852-3230 – 72 lits – Dir. gen., Jean-Claude Rousseau

Saint-Pamphile: Residence Bellevue, 88, rue du Foyer, Saint-Pamphile PQ G0R 3X0 – 418/356-3843 – 33 lits – Dir. gen., Bernard Lamy

Saint-Pascal: Villa Saint-Pascal Inc., 575, av Martin, Saint-Pascal PQ G0R 3X0 – 418/492-2342; Fax: 418/492-1793 – 82 lits – Dir. gen., Jean-Claude Rousseau

St-Patrice-de-Beaurivage: Pavillon St-Patrice, 445, rue Principale, St-Patrice-de-Beaurivage PQ G0S 1B0 – 418/596-2402 – 11 places – Dir. gen., Germain Leblond

St-Paul-d'Industrie: Pavillon Claude Bouchard, 465, rue Brassard, St-Paul-d'Industrie PQ J0K 3E0 – 514/754-2995 – 14 places – Dir. gen., Maurice Blais

St-Paul-d'Industrie: Pavillon Matte, 392, rue Brassard, St-Paul-d'Industrie PQ J0K 3E0 – 514/754-2079 – 14 places – Dir. gen., Maurice Blais

St-Paulin: Pavillon St-Paulin Inc., 2680, rang Saint-Louis, St-Paulin PQ J0K 3G0 – 819/268-5202 – 30 places – Dir. gen., Jacques Veillette

Ste-Perpétue-de-L'Islet: Residence du Bonheur, 8, av du Foyer, Ste-Perpétue-de-L'Islet PQ G0R 3Z0 – 418/359-2247 – 40 lits – Dir. gen., Bernard Lamy

St-Philémon: Pavillon Diane Pouliot, 1405, rue Principale, St-Philémon PQ G0R 4A0 – 418/469-3393 – 10 places – Dir. gen., Yvan Deblois

St-Pierre-D'Orléans: Hôpital de l'Enfant-Jesus (Villa Alphonse Bonenfant), 1199, ch Royal, St-Pierre-D'Orléans PQ G0A 4E0 – 418/828-9114 – 50 lits – Dir. gen., Gaston Pellan

St-Pierre-les-Becquets: Foyer Romain Becquet Inc., 255, Rte. Marie-Victorin, St-Pierre-les-Becquets PQ G0X 2Z0 – 819/263-2245; Fax: 819/263-2636 – 40 lits – Dir. gen., Raymond Dion

St-Prime: Pavillon Julien, 598, rue Principale, St-Prime PQ G0W 2W0 – 418/251-3145 – 11 places – Dir. gen., Laurent Bouillon

St-Prosper-de-Dorchester: Pavillon de l'hospitalité, 2770, 20e av, St-Prosper-de-Dorchester PQ G0M 1Y0 – 418/594-8174 – 46 lits – Dir. gen., Jean-Yves Julien

St-Raphaël-de-Bellechasse: Foyer St-Raphael Inc., 84, rue du Foyer, St-Raphaël-de-Bellechasse PQ G0R 4C0 – 418/243-2855; Fax: 418/243-2990 – 61 lits – Dir. gen., Yvan Deblois

Saint-Raymond: Centre d'hébergement St-Raymond, 324. rue Saint-Joseph, CP 490, Saint-Raymond PQ G0A 4G0 – 418/337-4661 – 64 lits – Dir. gen., Fernand Morasse

St-Raymond: Centre hospitalier Portneuf, see Centres hospitaliers listings

St-Rémi: Centre d'accueil Pierre-Remi-Narbonne, 110, rue du College, St-Rémi PQ J0L 2L0 – 514/454-4694; Fax: 514/454-3614 – 52 lits – Dir. gen., Gaetan Roy

St-Romuald: Le Foyer Chanoine Audet Inc., 2155, ch du Sault, St-Romuald PQ G6W 2K7 – 418/839-8845; Fax: 418/839-2800 – 55 lits – Dir. gen., Marcel Bernard

St-Romuald: Villa Beausejour, 2230, boul Rive sud, St-Romuald PQ G6W 2S4 – 418/839-7801 – 38 places – Dir. gen., Marcel Bernard

St-Sauveur-des-Monts: Villa du Vieux Sapin Inc., 55, rue Hochard, St-Sauveur-des-Monts PQ J0R 1R0 – 514/227-2241; Fax: 514/227-6186 – 34 lits – Dir. gen., Colette Desjardins

St-Siméon: Foyer de Notre-Dame du Sacre-Coeur de St-Simeon, 371, rue Saint-Laurent, CP 7, St-Siméon PQ G0T 1X0 – 418/638-2414; Fax: 418/638-2470 – 38 lits – Dir. gen., Benoit Guerin

Ste-Sophie: Centre d'hébergement Jaclo Inc., 2319, rue Sainte-Marie, Ste-Sophie PQ J0R 1S0 – 514/436-5627; Fax: 514/436-6663 – 31 lits – Dir. gen., Claude Briere

St-Stanislas-de-Champlain: Centre d'accueil St-Stanislas Inc., 255, rue Principale, CP 99, St-Stanislas-de-Champlain PQ G0X 3E0 – 418/328-3142; Fax: 418/328-4172 – 43 lits – Dir. gen., Paul Sills

St-Sulpice: Pavillon St-Sulpice, 1625, rue Notre-Dame, St-Sulpice PQ J0K 3J0 – 514/581-7141 – 14 places – Dir. gen., Yvon Poirier

St-Sylvestre: Le Foyer de St-Sylvestre Inc., 828, rue Principale, St-Sylvestre PQ G0S 3C0 – 418/596-2217; Fax: 418/596-2218 – 31 lits – Dir. gen., Germain Leblond

St-Sylvestre: Pavillon Michel Blais Inc., 53, rang Sainte-Catherine, St-Sylvestre PQ G0S 3C0 – 418/596-2764 – 14 places – Dir. gen., Germain Leblond

St-Thecle: Foyer de Sainte-Thecle Inc., 651, rue Saint-Jacques, CP 246, St-Thecle PQ G0X 3G0 – 418/289-2114; Fax: 418/289-3538 – 47 lits – Dir. gen., Gilles Cossette

Ste-Thérèse: Centres Drapeau et Deschambault, 100, rue Chanoine Lionel Groulx, Ste-Thérèse PQ J7E 5E1 – 514/437-4267; Fax: 514/437-0788 – 237 lits – Dir. gen., André Poirier

Ste-Thérèse: Pavillon Marie-Therese Inc., 44, rue Dagenais, Ste-Thérèse PQ J7E 3C8 – 514/435-0451 – 12 places – Dir. gen., André Poirier

Ste-Thérèse: Villa Labelle Inc., 440, boul Labelle, Ste-Thérèse PQ J7E 2Y1 – 514/430-4440 – 8 places – Dir. gen., André Poirier

St-Thomas-de-Joliette: Centre d'accueil St-Thomas - Siege Social, 791, rue Principale, St-Thomas-de-Joliette PQ J0K 3L0 – 514/759-1513 – 36 lits – Dir. gen., Paul-Yves Laviolette

St-Timothée: La Maison des Aine(e)s, 1, rue des Aines, St-Timothée PQ J0S 1X0 – 514/377-3925; Fax: 514/377-3490 – 38 lits – Dir. gen., Denis Charland

St-Tite-des-Caps: Centre d'accueil St-Tite-des-Caps, 97, av de la Montagne, St-Tite-des-Caps PQ G0A 4J0 – 418/823-2440 – 86 lits – Dir. gen., Jean-Yves Simard

St-Tite: Foyer Mgr Paquin Inc., 580, rue du Couvent, CP 400, St-Tite PQ G0X 3H0 – 418/365-5107; Fax: 418/365-7914 – 63 lits – Dir. gen., Gilles Cossette

St-Tite: Pavillon Beauregard enr., 771, rue Marchand, St-Tite PQ G0X 3H0 – 418/365-3172 – 14 places – Dir. gen., Gilles Cossette

St-Urbain-de-Charlevoix: Pavillon le Gite, 1070, rue Saint-Edouard, St-Urbain-de-Charlevoix PQ G0A 4K0 – 418/439-3362 – 20 places – Dir. gen., Robert Vallieres

Ste-Véronique: Pavillon Filion Enr., 1772, Rte. 117, Ste-Véronique PQ J0W 1X0 – 819/275-2845 – 15 places – Dir. gen., Pierre Page

Ste-Véronique: Pavillon Michel et Liliane Heafey, 1808, Rte. 117, CP 323, Ste-Véronique PQ J0W 1X0 – 819/275-3116 – 16 places – Dir. gen., Pierre Page

St-Zacharie: Pavillon Garant, 668, 12e av, St-Zacharie PQ G0M 2C0 – 418/593-3267 – 26 places – Dir. gen., Jean-Yves Julien

Sainte-Agathe-des-Monts: Foyer Sainte-Agathe, 21, rue Godon ouest, Sainte-Agathe-des-Monts PQ J8C 1E5 – 819/326-1141 – 55 lits – Dir. gen., Jacques Gaudette

Sainte-Angele-de-Premont: Pavillon Bergeron, 2000, rang Paul Lemay, Sainte-Angele-de-Premont PQ J0K 1R0 – 819/268-5747 – 10 places – Dir. gen., Jacques Veillette

Sainte-Anne-de-Beaupré: Pavillon Sainte-Anne, 10632, boul Sainte-Anne, Sainte-Anne-de-Beaupré PQ G0A 3C0 – 418/827-5093 – 16 places – Dir. gen., Rejean Cantin

Sainte-Marguerite-du-Lac-Masson: Manoir de la Pointe Blueue (1978), 428, av Baron Empain, RR#1, Sainte-Marguerite-du-Lac-Masson PQ J0T 1L0 – 514/228-2503; Fax: 514/228-2503 – 91 lits – Dir. gen., Jacqueline Gagnon

Sainte-Marie: Les CHSLD Nouvelle-Beauce-Sainte-Marie, 40, boul Vachon, CP 99, Sainte-Marie PQ G6E 3B4 – 418/387-5228; Fax: 418/387-3782 – 65 lits – Dir. gen., Benoit Guillemette

Sainte-Marie: Pavillon Familial Carrier, 299, rue Sainte-Anne, Sainte-Marie PQ G6E 2B9 – 418/387-2911 – 12 places – Dir. gen., Gertrude Beaulieu

Sainte-Marthe-du-Cap: Pavillon des Aines, 2460, rue Notre-Dame, Sainte-Marthe-du-Cap PQ G8T 8B3 – 819/374-6551 – 31 places – Dir. gen., Vital Guadet

Sainte-Sophie: Centre d'hébergement Jaclo Inc., 2319, rue Sainte-Marie, CP 129, Sainte-Sophie PQ J0R 1S0 – 514/436-5627 – Dir. gen., Claude Briere

Salaberry-de-Valleyfield: Le Centre d'accueil du Haut St-Laurent, 18, rue de la Fabrique, Salaberry-de-Valleyfield PQ J6T 4G8 – 514/373-4013; Fax: 514/373-0325 – 133 lits – Dir. gen., Claude-Yves de Repentigny

Sayabec: Foyer Sainte-Marie de Sayabec, 1, rue Saindon, CP 130, Sayabec PQ G0J 3K0 – 418/536-5456 – 31 lits – Dir. gen., Alain Paquet

Senneterre: Ilot d'Or Inc., 951, rue de la Clinique, Senneterre PQ J0Y 2M0 – 819/737-8341 – 14 places – Dir. gen., Jean-Pierre Cote

Sept-Îles: Pavillon des Iles, 540, av Franquelin, Sept-Îles PQ G4R 2M1 – 418/962-9801; Fax: 418/962-6420 – 60 lits – Dir. gen., Charlotte Audet

Shawinigan-Sud: Centre d'accueil de Shawinigan-Sud Inc., 80, 118e rue, CP 1160, Shawinigan-Sud PQ G9P 4E8 – 819/537-0111; Fax: 819/537-1895 – 41 lits – Dir. gen., Raymond Guilbert

Shawinigan-Sud: Residence Linteau, 95, 118e rue, Shawinigan-Sud PQ G9P 3E5 – 819/537-5636 – 18 places – Dir. gen., Raymond Guilbert

Shawinigan: Centre d'accueil les Chutes Inc., 5000, av Albert-Tessier, Shawinigan PQ G9N 6T6 – 819/533-5751; Fax: 819/539-5400 – 64 lits – Dir. gen., Jacques Moreau

Shawinigan: Centre d'accueil Dr. Joseph Garceau, 243, 1e rue, CP 4017, Shawinigan PQ G9N 7Y5 – 819/537-5173 – 90 lits – Dir. gen., Raymond Guilbert

Shawinigan: Centre hospitalier Sainte-Thérèse, see Centres hospitaliers listings

Shawinigan: Foyer Dehauffe, 750, boul Saint-Maurice, Shawinigan PQ G9N 1L6 – 819/536-5601; Fax: 819/536-4994 – 107 lits – Dir. gen., Raymond Guilbert

Shawinigan: La Residence les Chutes Inc., 2353, 49e rue, Shawinigan PQ G9N 6T6 – 819/539-6152 – 29 places – Dir. gen., Jacques Veillette

Shawville: Centre d'accueil Pontiac, rue Marion, CP 2001, Shawville PQ J0X 2Y0 – 819/647-5755; Fax: 819/647-2453 – 50 lits – Dir. gen., Michel Pigeon

Shawville: L'Hôpital communautaire du Pontiac Inc., see Centres hospitaliers listings

Sherbrooke: Le Foyer St-Joseph de Sherbrooke, 611, boul Queen nord, Sherbrooke PQ J1H 3R6 – 819/564-6655; Fax: 819/564-6504 – 252 lits – Dir. gen., Real Jacques

Sherbrooke: Hôpital d'Youville, see Centres hospitaliers listings

Sherbrooke: Hôtel-Dieu, see Centres hospitaliers listings

Sherbrooke: Maison Reine Marie Inc., 1630, rue Galt ouest, Sherbrooke PQ J1H 2B5 – 819/566-1414; Fax: 819/346-5081 – 48 lits – Dir. gen., Yoland Gregoire

Sherbrooke: Mont St-Dominique, 361, rue Moore, Sherbrooke PQ J1H 1C1 – 819/346-5512; Fax: 819/563-5023 – 50 lits – Dir. gen., Matija Bojanic

Sherbrooke: Le Pavillon Catherine, 165, rue Moore, Sherbrooke PQ J1H 1B8 – 819/567-7519 – 35 places – Dir. gen., Real Jacques

Sherbrooke: Pavillon l'Eden enr., 223, rue Murray, Sherbrooke PQ J1G 2K2 – 819/821-4458 – 20 places – Dir. gen., Real Jacques

Sherbrooke: Pavillon Fontaine Enr., 215, 41e rue, Sherbrooke PQ J1G 2L2 – 819/563-2307 – 15 places – Dir. gen., Real Jacques

Sherbrooke: Pavillon St-Marc Enr., 511, rue Prospect, Sherbrooke PQ J1H 1A9 – 819/567-0459 – 14 places – Dir. gen., Real Jacques

Sherbrooke: Pavillon Simon Cote Inc., 44, rue Kennedy sud, Sherbrooke PQ J1G 2H6 – 819/563-2242 – 25 places

Sherbrooke: La Residence de l'Estrie de Sherbrooke Inc., 500, rue Murray, Sherbrooke PQ J1G 2K6 – 819/569-5131; Fax: 819/822-4102 – 175 lits – Dir. gen., Real Jacques

Sillery: Pavillon Saint-Dominique, 1045, boul Saint-Cyrille ouest, Sillery PQ G1S 1V3 – 418/681-3561; Fax: 418/687-9196 – 142 lits – Dir. gen., Jeanne Laliberte

Sillery: Saint Brigid's Home Inc., 1645, ch Saint-Louis, Sillery PQ G1S 4M3 – 418/681-4689; Fax: 418/527-6882 – 162 lits – Dir. gen., Henry-J. Hannon

Sorel: Foyer Richelieu Inc., 40, rue de Ramesay, Sorel PQ J3P 3Y7 – 514/742-5936 – 71 lits – Dir. gen., Yvan Rheault

Sorel: L'Hôpital général de Sorel, 151, rue George, Sorel PQ J3P 1C8 – 514/746-5555; Fax: 514/746-4897 – 175 lits – Dir. gen., Jacques Blais

Sorel: Hôpital Richelieu Inc., 30, rue Ferland, Sorel PQ J3P 3C7 – 514/743-5569; Fax: 514/743-1803 – 26 lits – Dir. gen., Jacques Blais

Sutton: Foyer Sutton, 50, rue Western, CP 719, Sutton PQ J0E 2K0 – 514/538-3332; Fax: 514/538-0514 – 75 lits – Dir. gen., Claude Codere

Temiscaming: Pavillon de Temiscaming, 48, 5e rue, Temiscaming PQ J0Z 3R0 – 819/627-3543 – 14 places – Dir. gen., Nicole Landry

Terrebonne: Centre d'accueil Lorrain inc., 834, rue Dupre, Terrebonne PQ J6W 3K7 – 514/471-3303; Fax: 514/471-3498 – 24 lits – Dir. gen., Jacques Lorrain

Terrebonne: Centre d'hébergement des Moulins inc., 934, rue St-Sacrement, Terrebonne PQ J6W 3G2 – 514/471-4885; Fax: 514/471-5095 – 55 lits – Dir. gen., Gerald Asselin

Terrebonne: Pavillon Longpre - Gravel, 575, rue Saint-Louis, Terrebonne PQ J6W 1J3 – 514/471-8557 – 18 places – Dir. gen., Yvon Poirier

Thetford-Mines: Pavillon Jacques Boutin Enr., 736, boul Ouellet ouest, Thetford-Mines PQ G6G 4X5 – 418/335-7681 – 26 places – Dir. gen., André Rodrigue

Thetford-Mines: Residence Denis Marcotte, 56, 9e rue est, Thetford-Mines PQ G6G 5H5 – 418/338-4556; Fax: 418/338-6242 – 70 lits – Dir. gen., André Rodrigue

Tracy: Le Centre d'hébergement de Tracy, 4205, rue Frontenac, Tracy PQ J3R 4G8 – 514/743-4924; Fax: 514/743-4374 – 36 lits – Dir. gen., Jacques Blais

Tracy: Residence Sorel-Tracy Inc., 4025, rue Frontenac, Tracy PQ J3R 4G8 – 514/742-9427 – 64 lits – Dir. gen., Wilner Bien-Aime

Trois-Pistoles: Centre hospitalier de Trois-Pistoles, 550, rue Nôtre-Dame est, Trois-Pistoles PQ G0L 4K0 – 418/851-3301; Fax: 418/851-2934 – 125 lits – Dir. gen., Donald Gagnon

Trois-Rivières: Centre d'accueil Louis Dennoncourt, 435, rue Saint-Roch, Trois-Rivières PQ G9A 2L9 – 819/376-2566 – 75 lits – Dir. gen., Gervais Morissette

Trois-Rivières: Centre hospitalier Cooke, 3450, rue Ste-Marguerite, Trois-Rivières PQ G8Z 1X3 – 819/375-7713; Fax: 819/375-5659 – 149 lits – Dir. gen., Gervais Morissette

Trois-Rivières: Foyer Joseph-Denys Inc., 1274, rue Laviolette, Trois-Rivières PQ G9A 1W4 – 819/378-4838; Fax: 819/374-6697 – 122 lits – Dir. gen., Gervais Morissette

Trois-Rivières: Pavillon la Cathedrale, 645, rue Bonaventure, Trois-Rivières PQ G9A 2B8 – 819/373-9887 – 18 places – Dir. gen., Gervais Morissette

Upton: Domaine du Bel Age Enr., 906, rue Lanoi, Upton PQ J0H 2E0 – 514/549-4405 – 9 lits – Dir. gen., Jacqueline Gosslin

Val-Brillant: Villa Mon Repos, 31, rue Saint-Pierre ouest, Val-Brillant PQ G0J 3L0 – 418/742-3230 – 29 places – Dir. gen., Alain Paquet

Val-d'Or: Foyer de Val-d'Or Inc., 1212, av Brebeuf, Val-d'Or PQ J9P 2C9 – 819/825-3093; Fax: 819/824-8745 – 98 lits – Dir. gen., Jean-Pierre Coté

Val-d'Or: L'Oasis du Repos, 1543, 7e rue, Val-d'Or PQ J9P 4Z9 – 819/824-4093 – 15 places – Dir. gen., Jean-Pierre Coté

Valcourt: Foyer de Valcourt Inc., 1150, rue Champlain, CP 459, Valcourt PQ J0E 2L0 – 514/532-3190; Fax: 514/532-3233 – 41 lits – Dir. gen., Nicole Corbin

Vallée-Jonction: Les CHSLD Nouvelle-Beauce-Vallée, 228, rue du Foyer, Vallée-Jonction PQ G0S 3J0 – 418/253-5469 – 49 lits – Dir. gen., Benoit Guillemette

Varennes: Foyer Lajemmerais, 60, rue d'Youville, CP 450, Varennes PQ J3X 1T6 – 514/652-2995; Fax: 514/652-2998 – 83 lits – Dir. gen., Robert Sabino

Vaudreuil: Centre d'accueil Vaudreuil, 408, boul Roche, Vaudreuil PQ J7V 7M9 – 514/455-6176 – 100 lits – Dir. gen., Lise Belanger

Vaudreuil: Manoir Harwood Enr., 170, rue Boileau, Vaudreuil PQ J7V 8A3 – 514/424-6458 – 51 lits – Dir. gen., Denis Charland

Victoriaville: Centre d'accueil l'Ermitage, 45, av de l'Ermitage, Victoriaville PQ G6P 6X4 – 819/758-7511 – 133 lits – Dir. gen., Gilles Perreault

Victoriaville: Centre hospitalier des Bois-Francs, 61, av de l'Ermitage, Victoriaville PQ G6P 6X4 – 819/758-7511; Fax: 819/758-4852 – 100 lits – Dir. gen., Gilles Perreault

Victoriaville: Pavillon Bujold-Lefebvre enr., 60, rue Olivier, Victoriaville PQ G6P 5G7 – 819/752-4411 – 28 places – Dir. gen., Gilles Perreault

Victoriaville: Pavillon Familial des Bois-Francs Inc., 21, rue Marchand, Victoriaville PQ G6P 4J5 – 819/752-9920 – 36 places – Dir. gen., Gilles Perreault

Ville-Marie: Centre d'accueil Duhamel, 37, rue Saint-Jean Bapiste sud, CP 3500, Ville-Marie PQ J0Z 3W0 – 819/629-3027; Fax: 819/629-2805 – 61 lits – Dir. gen., Nicole Landry

Warwick: Foyer Étoiles d'Or Inc., 10, rue l'Heureux, CP 610, Warwick PQ J0A 1M0 – 819/358-6833; Fax: 819/358-6150 – 55 lits – Dir. gen., Gilles Perreualt

Waterville: Foyer de Waterville, 265, rue Compton est, CP 210, Waterville PQ J0B 3H0 – 819/877-2500; Fax: 819/837-2916 – 20 lits – Dir. gen., Jeannette Delage

Weedon: Foyer de Weedon Inc., 245, rue Saint-Janvier, CP 250, Weedon PQ J0B 3J0 – 819/877-2500; Fax: 819/877-3089 – 52 lits – Dir. gen., Albert Kratzenberg

Wendake: Centre d'hébergement Marie-Dolores, 20, boul Maurice Bastien, Wendake PQ G0A 4V0 – 418/843-8004 – 9 lits – Dir. gen., Richard Picard

Windsor: Hôpital St-Louis de Windsor inc., 23, rue Ambroise-Dearden, CP 2000, Windsor PQ J1S 1G8 – 819/845-2751; Fax: 819/845-5834 – 36 lits – Dir. gen., Nicole Corbin

Wotton: Le Centre d'accueil de Wotton, 666, rue Saint-Jean, Wotton PQ J0A 1N0 – 819/828-2251 – 32 lits – Dir. gen., Jean-Yves Poisson

Yamachiche: Foyer Ernest Jacob Inc., 610, rue Sainte-Anne, Yamachiche PQ G0X 3L0 – 819/296-3787; Fax: 819/296-2170 – 57 lits – Dir. gen., Micheline Bonner Lesage

HÔPITAUX PRIVÉS

Greenfield Park: Centre hospitalier Rive-Sud Inc., 860, ch Victoria, Greenfield Park PQ J4V 1M8 – 514/465-7017; Fax: 514/465-7017 – 30 lits – Dir. gen., Benoit Desilets

Kahnawake: Centre hospitalier Kateri Memorial, CP 10, Kahnawake PQ J0L 1B0 – 514/638-3930; Fax: 514/638-4634 – 43 lits – Dir. General, Irene Tschernmor

Montréal: Centre d'hébergement et de soins de longue durée St-Jude, 4410, boul Saint-Martin ouest, Chomedey PQ H7T 1C3 – 514/687-7714; Fax: 514/682-0330 – 204 lits – Dir. gen., Louis-Marie Leclair

Montréal: Centre hospitalier Bayview Inc., 27, ch Lakeshore, Pointe-Claire PQ H9S 4H1 – 514/695-9384; Fax: 514/695-5723 – 128 lits – Dir. gen., George Guillon

Montréal: Centre hospitalier Guy Laporte, 30, boul St-Joseph est, Montréal PQ H2T 1G9 – 514/845-4241; Fax: 514/845-4428 – 31 lits – Dir. gen., Jules Robert

Centre métropolitain de Chirurgie Plastique Inc., 999, rue de Salaberry, Montréal PQ H3L 1L2 – 514/332-7091; Fax: 514/382-5784 – 17 lits – Dir. gen., Marcel-A. Dion

Montréal: Clinique communautaire de Pointe St-Charles, 500, av Ash, Montréal PQ H3K 2R4 – 514/937-9251; Fax: 514/937-3492 – Dir. gen., Jocelyne Bernier

Montréal: Hôpital Marie Claret, 3530, boul Gouin est, Montréal PQ H1H 1B7 – 514/322-8800; Fax: 514/326-8811 – 204 lits – Dir. gen., Louise Beaulac

Montréal: Hôpital Notre-Dame-de-Lourdes, 1870, boul Pie-IX, Montréal PQ H1V 2C6 – 514/527-4595; Fax: 514/527-4475 – 162 lits – Dir. gen., Robert St-Pierre

Montréal: Hôpital Ste-Thérèse inc., 9307, boul La Salle, La Salle PQ H8R 2M7 – 514/366-3556 – 47 lits – Dir. gen., Réjeanne Lemieux-Labbé

Montréal: Hôpital Shriners pour l'enfant infirme (Québec) inc., 1529, av Cedar, Montréal PQ H3G 1A6 – 514/842-4464; Fax: 514/842-7553 – 40 lits – Dir. gen., Allen Hicks

Montréal: Hôpital Ville-Marie Inc., 7015, boul Gouin est, Montréal PQ H1E 5N2 – 514/955-8242; Fax: 514/955-4733 – 70 lits – Dir. gen., Louis Gariépy

Montréal: Villa Medica Inc., 225, rue Sherbrooke est, Montréal PQ H2X 1C9 – 514/288-8201; Fax: 514/288-7076 – 207 lits – Dir. gen. (interim), Michel Duchesne

Québec: Centre hospitalier Nôtre-Dame du Chemin Inc., 510, ch Ste-Foy, Québec PQ G1S 2J5 – 418/681-7882; Fax: 418/681-5387 – 50 lits – Dir. gen., Antoine Pichette

Québec: Centre hospitalier St-Sacrement Ltée, 1165, ch Ste-Foy, Québec PQ G1S 2M8 – 418/527-4836; Fax: 418/527-1743 – 63 lits – Dir. gen., Jacques Pichette

Québec: Hôpital Ste-Monique (1988) Inc., 4805, boul Wilfrid Hamel, Québec PQ G1P 2J7 – 418/871-8701; Fax: 418/871-0105 – 58 lits – Dir. gen., Andrée Begin

Rawdon: Centre hospitalier Heather Inc., 3931 Lakeshore Dr., Rawdon PQ J0K 1S0 – 514/834-2512; Fax: 514/834-5805 – 76 lits – Dir. gen., Paul Arbec

Saint-Georges: Centre hospitalier de l'Assomption Inc., 16750, boul Lacroix, Saint-Georges PQ G5Y 2G4 – 418/228-2041; Fax: 418/228-9366 – 117 lits – Dir. gen., Gerard Gendreau

Sillery: La Maison Michel Sarrazin, 2101, ch St-Louis, Sillery PQ G1T 2P5 – 418/688-0878; Fax: 418/681-8636 – 15 lits – Dir. gen., Louis Dionne

Waterloo: Centre gériatrique Courville Inc., 5305, av Courville, CP 580, Waterloo PQ J0E 2N0 – 514/539-1821; Fax: 514/539-1937 – 32 lits – Dir. gen., Georges W. Courville

CENTRES DE TRAITEMENTS SPÉCIALISÉS

(comprend: cliniques d'avortement, cliniques de soins aux cancéreux, centres de réadaptation professionnelle, centres de traitement)

Amos: Centre d'accueil Normand, 621, rue Harricana, Amos PQ J9T 2P9 – 819/732-8241; Fax: 819/727-2210 – centre de réadaptation des drogues – Dir. gen., Jacques-A. Noel

Baie-Comeau: Centre N.-A.-Labrie, 659, boul Blance, Baie-Comeau PQ G5C 2B2 – 418/589-5704; Fax: 418/589-6371 – centre de réadaptation des drogues – 63 lits – Dir. gen., Gaetan Gauthier

Charlesbourg: Institut des Sourds de Charlesbourg Inc., 775, rue Saint-Viateur, Charlesbourg PQ G2L 2S2 – 418/623-9801; Fax: 418/626-3914 – centre de réadaptation (déficience auditive) – Dir. gen., Claudette Gauvreau

Chicoutimi: Maison d'accueil Doris Pineault, 2888, rue Roussel, Chicoutimi PQ G7G 1Y9 – 418/549-5474 – 27 lits de néonatalogie – Dir. gen., Guy St-Onge

Drummondville: Module de services externes de Drummondville, 420, rue St-Georges, Drummondville PQ J2C 4H4 – 819/477-9010 – Centre de réadaptation (déficience motrice) – Dir. gen., Raymond Beaudry

East Angus: Atelier du Haut St-François, 197, rue Saint-Hilaire, East Angus PQ J0B 1R0 – 819/832-2222 – centre de réadaptation (déficience motrice) – 10 places – Dir. gen., Gilles Servant

Hull: Centre de réadaptation la ressource, 325, rue Laramee, Hull PQ J8Y 3A4 – 819/777-6261; Fax: 819/777-0073 – centre de réadaptation (déficience auditive, visuelle, & motrice) – Dir. gen., Jean-Pierre Blais

Hull: Pavillon Jellinek, 25, rue Saint-François, Hull PQ J9A 1B1 – 819/776-5584; Fax: 819/776-0255 – centre de réadaptation des drogues – 26 beneficiaires – Dir. gen., Guy Charpentier

Joilette: Centre d'accueil de réadaptation le Bouclier, 260, rue Lavaltrie sud, Joilette PQ J6E 5X7 – 514/755-2741; Fax: 514/755-4895 – centre de réadaptation (déficience motrice) – Dir. gen., Lise Bolduc

Lac-Megantic: Atelier le Sept de Trefle, 6435, rue Notre-Dame, Lac-Megantic PQ G6B 2M9 – 819/583-0407 – centre de réadaptation (déficience motrice) – 25 places – Dir. gen., Gilles Servant

Lemoyne: Clinique externe Foster, #200, 2475, rue St-Georges, Lemoyne PQ J4R 2T4 – 514/466-7981 – centre de réadaptation des drogues – Dir. gen., Jean-Guy Poirier

Longueuil: Atelier Protege/Bibliotheque Braille, 1255, rue Beauregard, Longueuil PQ J4K 2M3 – 514/463-1710 – centre de réadaptation (déficience visuelle)

Longueuil: Institut Nazareth et Louis-Braille, 1111, rue Saint-Charles ouest, Longueuil PQ J4K 5G4 – 514/463-1710; Fax: 514/463-0243 – centre de réadaptation (déficience visuelle) – Dir. gen. par interim, Julien Tremblay

Montréal: Assn Montréalaise pour les Aveugles - Maison Penfield, 7000, rue Sherbrooke ouest, Montréal PQ H4B 1R3 – 514/489-8201; Fax: 514/489-3477 – centre de réadaptation (déficience visuelle) – Dir. gen., John A. Sims

Montréal: Centre d'accueil Prefontaine, 3100, rue Rachel est, Montréal PQ H1W 1A1 – 514/521-1280; Fax: 514/521-7854 – centre de réadaptation des drogues – 30 beneficiaires – Dir. gen., Pierre Lamarche

Montréal: Centre d'accueil Prefontaine II, 4055, av Papineau, Montréal PQ H2K 4K2 – 514/521-8054 – centre de réadaptation des drogues – 18 beneficiaires – Dir. gen., Pierre Lamarche

Montréal: Centre de réadaptation alternatives, 10555, boul St-Laurent, Montréal PQ H3L 2P5 – 514/385-6444; Fax: 514/385-5186 – centre de réadaptation des drogues – Dir. gen., Pierre Lamarche

Montréal: Centre de réadaptation Constance-Lethbridge, 7005, boul de Maisonneuve ouest, Montréal PQ H4B 1T3 – 514/487-1770; Fax: 514/487-5494 – centre de réadaptation (déficience motrice) – Dir. gen., Howard G. Martin

Montréal: Centre de réadaptation Lucie-Bruneau, 2222, av Laurier est, Montréal PQ H2H 1C4 – 514/527-4521 – centre de réadaptation (déficience motrice) – 60 beneficiaires – Dir. gen., Leon Lafleur

Montréal: Centre Mackay, 3500, boul Decarie, Montréal PQ H4A 3J5 – 514/482-0500; Fax: 514/482-4536 – centre de réadaptation (déficience motrice) – 35 beneficiaires – Dir. gen., John Spencer

Montréal: Domremy-Montréal, 15693, boul Gouin ouest, Sainte-Geneviève PQ H9H 1C3 – 514/626-0220 – centre de réadaptation des drogues – Dir. gen., Pierre Lamarche

Montréal: Domremy-Montréal (point de service Laval), 1, place Laval, Laval PQ H7N 1A1 – 514/967-5054 – centre de réadaptation des drogues – Dir. gen., Pierre Lamarche

Montréal: Domremy-Montréal secteur externe, 10140, rue Lajeunesse, Montréal PQ H3L 2E2 – 514/385-0046 – centre de réadaptation des drogues – Dir. gen., Pierre Lamarche

Montréal: L'Institut de réadaptation de Montréal, 6300, av Darlington, Montréal PQ H3S 2J4 – 514/340-2085; Fax: 514/340-2149 – 104 lits – Dir. gen., Jacques R. Nolet

Montréal: Institut Raymond-Dewar, 3600, rue Berri, Montréal PQ H2L 4G9 – 514/284-2581; Fax: 514/284-0699 – centre de réadaptation (déficience motrice) – Dir. gen., Pierre-Paul Lachapelle

Pointe-du-Lac: Domremy, 2931, rue Notre-Dame, CP 70, Pointe-du-Lac PQ G0X 1Z0 – 819/377-2441; Fax: 819/377-2560 – centre de réadaptation des drogues – 24 beneficiaires – Dir. gen., Gratien Thibeault

Prevost: Centre d'accueil le Portage, 1790, ch du Lac Echo, RR#1, Prevost PQ J0R 1T0 – 514/224-2944 – centre de réadaptation des drogues – 110 beneficiaires – Dir. gen., Peter Vamos

Québec: Centre François-Charon, 525, boul Wilfrid Hamel, Québec PQ G1M 2S8 – 418/529-9141; Fax: 418/529-7318 – centre de réadaptation (déficience motrice) – 153 beneficiaires – Dir. gen., Louis Champoux

Rouyn-Noranda: La Maison (Rouyn-Noranda) Inc., 100, ch Docteur Lemay, CP 1055, Rouyn-Noranda PQ J9X 5C8 – 819/762-6592; Fax: 819/797-9313 – centre de réadaptation (déficience motrice) – Dir. gen., Jean-Claude Beauchemin

Rouyn-Noranda: SAHT de Rouyn-Noranda - Deficience Physique, 1, 9e rue, Rouyn-Noranda PQ J9X 2A9 – 819/762-6592 – centre de réadaptation (déficience motrice) – 18 places – Dir. gen., Jean-Claude Beauchemin

Ste-Anne-des-Monts: Centre réadaptation pour personnes toxicomanes l'Escale, 145, 7e rue ouest, Ste-Anne-des-Monts PQ G0E 2G0 – 418/763-2261; Fax: 418/763-7460 – centre de réadaptation des drogues – Dir. gen., Robert Deschenes

Ste-Foy: Centre Cardinal-Villeneuve, 2975, ch Saint-Louis, Ste-Foy PQ G1W 1P9 – 418/653-8766 – centre de réadaptation (déficience motrice) – 34 beneficiaires – Dir. gen., Bernard Tremblay

Ste-Foy: Ilot de Ste-Foy, 3620, av des Compagnons, Ste-Foy PQ G1X 3Z5 – 418/651-1332 – centre de réadaptation (déficience motrice) – 10 beneficiaires – Dir. gen., Louis Champoux

Saint-Hubert: Centre de réadaptation Montergie, 5110, boul Cousineau, Saint-Hubert PQ J3Y 7G5 – 514/443-2100; Fax: 514/443-4196 – centre de réadaptation des drogues – Dir. gen., Pierre Menard

Saint-Jerome: Pavillon André Boudreau, 910, rue Labelle, Saint-Jerome PQ J7Z 5M5 – 514/432-1395 – centre de réadaptation des drogues – 10 beneficiaires – Dir. gen., Denis Paquin

Saint-Philippe: Pavillon Foster, 6, rue Foucreault, CP 119, Saint-Philippe PQ J0L 2K0 – 514/659-8911 – centre de réadaptation des drogues – Dir. gen., Jean-Guy Poirier

Shawinigan: Domremy-Shawinigan (Centre de services externes), 1600, boul Biermans, Shawinigan PQ G9N 8L2 – 819/539-8714 – centre de réadaptation des drogues – Dir. gen., Gratien Thibeault

Sherbrooke: Atelier Federal, 932, rue Federal, Sherbrooke PQ J1H 5A7 – 819/346-8411 – centre de réadaptation (déficience motrice) – 40 places – Dir. gen., Gilles Servant

Sherbrooke: Atelier King Ouest, 1930, rue King ouest, Sherbrooke PQ J1J 2E2 – 819/346-8411; Fax: 819/564-7670 – centre de réadaptation (déficience motrice) – 36 places – Dir. gen., Gilles Servant

Sherbrooke: Foyer Jean-Patrice Chiasson, 1270, rue Galt ouest, Sherbrooke PQ J1H 2A7 – centre de réadaptation des drogues – 9 places; 4 beneficiaires – Dir. gen., Yves d'Ambroise

Sherbrooke: La Maison St-Georges (Sherbrooke) Inc., 433, rue Marquette, Sherbrooke PQ J1H 1M5 – 819/562-1533 – centre de réadaptation des drogues – Dir. gen., Claude Dussault

Trois-Rivières: Clinique de réadaptation de Trois-Rivières inc., 4100, rue Jacques de Labadie, CP 1960, Trois-Rivières PQ G9A 5M6 – 819/378-4083; Fax: 819/378-1354 – centre de réadaptation (déficience motrice) – Dir. gen., Raymond Beaudry

Trois-Rivières: Domremy-Trois-Rivières (Centre de services externes), 1420, Royale, Trois-Rivières PQ G9A 4J7 – 819/374-4744 – centre de réadaptation des drogues – Dir. gen., Gratien Thibeault

Victoriaville-Arthabaska: Domremy-Victoriaville (Centre de services externes), 100, rue de l'Ermitage, Victoriaville-Arthabaska PQ G6P 9N2 – 819/752-5668 – centre de réadaptation des drogues – Dir. gen., Gratien Thibeault

Victoriaville-Arthabaska: Module de services externes de Victoriaville, 80, rue St-Paul, Victoriaville-Arthabaska PQ G6P 9C8 – 819/378-4083 – centre de réadaptation (déficience motrice) – Dir. gen., Raymond Beaudry

SASKATCHEWAN

HOSPITAL DISTRICTS/HEALTH UNITS

Assiniboia: South Country Health District, PO Box 1120, Assiniboia SK S0H 0B0 – 306/642-5733; Fax: 306/642-5433 – CEO, Dale Schmeichel

Estevan: Southeast Health District, 721 Henry St., Estevan SK S4A 2B7 – 306/634-7626; Fax: 306/634-7824 – CEO, Dan Florizone

Fort Qu'Appelle: Touchwood Qu'Appelle Health District, PO Box 850, Fort Qu'Appelle SK S0G 1S0 – 306/332-6431; Fax: 306/332-1824 – CEO, James (Jim) Cawsey

Grenfell: Pipestone Health District, PO Box 970, Grenfell SK S0G 2B0 – 306/697-3577; Fax: 306/697-2686 – CEO, Alvin Gallinger

Humboldt: Central Plains Health District, PO Box 690, Humboldt SK S0K 2A0 – 306/682-5526; Fax: 306/682-3596 – CEO, Gren Smith-Windsor

Kamsack: Assiniboine Valley Health District, PO Box 368, Kamsack SK S0A 1S0 – 306/542-3007; Fax: 306/542-2995 – CEO, Sandra Delorme

Kindersley: Prairie West Health District, 1003 - 1st St. West, Kindersley SK S0L 1S2 – 306/463-2611; Fax: 306/463-3362 – CEO, Patrick Dumelie

Lanigan: Living Sky Health District, PO Box 1060, Lanigan SK S0K 2M0 – 306/365-2522; Fax: 306/365-2099 – Acting CEO, Andy Cebryk

Lloydminster Region Health District, 3820 - 43rd Ave., Lloydminster SK S9V 1Y5 – 306/825-9090; Fax: 306/825-9880 – Exec. Dir., Brian Heidt

Maidstone: Twin Rivers Health District Inc., PO Box 629, Maidstone SK S0M 1M0 – 306/893-4850; Fax: 306/893-4480 – CEO, Vern McCelland

Meadow Lake: Northwest Health District, PO Box 820, Meadow Lake SK S0M 1V0 – 306/236-5777; Fax: 306/236-5801 – CEO, Irene Denis

Canadian Almanac & Directory 1997

SASKATCHEWAN GENERAL HOSPITALS

Melfort: North Central Health District, PO Box 1990, Melfort SK S0E 1A0 – 306/752-9600; Fax: 306/752-2276 – CEO, David Fan

Melville: North Valley Health District, 256 - 2nd Ave. West, PO Box 1090, Melville SK S0A 2P0 – 306/728-4762; Fax: 306/728-4925 – CEO, Barb Hunter

Moose Jaw-Thunder Creek Health District, 455 Fairford St. East, Moose Jaw SK S6H 1H3 – 306/694-0295; Fax: 306/692-5596 – CEO, John Borody

Nipawin: North-East Health District, PO Box 389, Nipawin SK S0E 1E0 – 306/862-5900; Fax: 306/862-9310 – CEO, Rayann Ulvick

North Battleford: Battlefords Health District, 1092 - 197 St., 4th Fl., North Battleford SK S9A 1Z1 – 306/446-6606; Fax: 306/446-4114 – CEO, George Gillies

Outlook: Midwest Health District, PO Box 1100, Outlook SK S0L 2N0 – 306/867-9700; Fax: 306/867-1877 – CEO, Doug Ball

Prince Albert Health District, 2345 - 10th Ave. West, PO Box 5700, Prince Albert SK S6V 7V6 – 306/953-0500; Fax: 306/763-1501 – CEO, Stan Rice

Regina Health District, 2180 - 23 Ave., Regina SK S4S 0A5 – 306/359-5287; Fax: 306/359-5222 – CEO, Dr. Glenn S. Bartlett

Rosthern: Gabriel Springs Health District, PO Box 309, Rosthern SK S0K 3R0 – 306/232-4305; Fax: 306/232-5218 – CEO, Alex Horner

Saskatoon Health District, Royal University Hospital, 6th Fl., 103 Hospital Dr., Saskatoon SK S7N 0W8 – 306/966-1576; Fax: 306/966-1037 – Acting CEO, Jim Ferguson

Shaunavon: Southwest Health District, PO Box 339, Shaunavon SK S0N 2M0 – 306/297-2523; Fax: 306/297-3881 – CEO, Alan Ruetz

Spiritwood: Parkland Health District, 511 - 4 St. East, PO Box 427, Spiritwood SK S0J 2M0 – 306/883-3300; Fax: 306/883-3700 – CEO, C. Jean Morrison

Swift Current Health District, 429 - 4th Ave. SE, Swift Current SK S9H 2J9 – 306/778-5100; Fax: 306/773-9513 – CEO, Gordon A. Allsen

Swift Current: Rolling Hills Health District, 429 - 4th Ave. NE, PO Box 1527, Swift Current SK S9H 4G5 – 306/773-2224; Fax: 306/773-0033 – CEO, Marlene Weston

Tisdale: Pasquia Health District, PO Box 1780, Tisdale SK S0E 1T0 – 306/873-3100; Fax: 306/873-5994 – CEO, Gordon Denton

Unity: Greenhead Health District, PO Box 1538, Unity SK S0K 4L0 – 403/228-4499; Fax: 403/228-3860 – CEO, Michael Kukurudza

Wawota: Moose Mountain Health District, PO Box 61, Wawota SK S0G 5A0 – 306/739-2593; Fax: 306/739-2668 – CEO, Warren Wallin

Weyburn: South Central Health District, PO Box 218, Weyburn SK S4H 2J9 – 306/842-7211; Fax: 306/842-7237 – CEO, Lee Spencer

Yorkton: East Central Health District, 270 Bradbrooke Dr., Yorkton SK S3N 2K6 – 306/786-3155; Fax: 306/786-3151 – CEO, Dr. James Millar

GENERAL HOSPITALS

Arcola Health Centre, Arcola SK S0C 0G0 – 306/455-2771; Fax: 306/455-2397 – 18 beds – Mgr., Health Services, Joanne Hollingshead

Assiniboia Union Hospital, Assiniboia SK S0H 0B0 – 306/642-3351; Fax: 306/642-3804 – 12 beds – Dir., Nursing, Betty Peterson

Balcarres Union Hospital, Balcarres SK S0G 0C0 – 306/334-2636; Fax: 306/334-2674 – 16 beds – Adm., Ann Barnsley

Big River Hospital, PO Box 100, Big River SK S0J 0E0 – 306/469-2220; Fax: 306/469-2237 – CEO, Jean Morrison

Biggar Union Hospital, Biggar SK S0K 0M0 – 306/948-3323; Fax: 306/948-2011 – 16 beds – Dir., Health Services, Ed Krizanowski

Broadview Union Hospital, Broadview SK S0G 0K0 – 306/696-2441; Fax: 306/696-2611 – 16 beds – Facility Mgr., Lynda Beutler

Canora Hospital, Canora SK S0A 0L0 – 306/563-5621; Fax: 306/563-5571 – 33 beds – Nurse Adm., Mavis Bouey

Carrot River Hospital, Carrot River SK S0E 0L0 – 306/768-2722; Fax: 306/768-2734 – 18 beds – Community Coord., Lynda Blum

Central Butte Union Hospital, Central Butte SK S0H 0T0 – 306/796-2190; Fax: 306/796-4610 – 30 beds – Adm.-Coord., Myrna Peterson

Cudworth: St. Michael's Hospital, PO Box 220, Cudworth SK S0K 1B0 – 306/256-3443; Fax: 306/256-3311 – 10 acute care, 4 continuing care beds – Adm., Joseph P. Habetler

Davidson Union Hospital, Davidson SK S0G 1A0 – 306/567-2801; Fax: 306/567-4380 – 13 beds – Adm., Suanne Laurent

Esterhazy: St. Anthony's Hospital, PO Box 280, Esterhazy SK S0A 0X0 – 306/745-3973; Fax: 306/745-3388 – 18 beds – Adm., Gordon Karpinka

Estevan: St. Joseph's Hospital, 1176 Nicholson Rd., Estevan SK S4A 0H3 – 306/634-0400; Fax: 306/634-8785 – Exec. Dir., Harvey Fox

Foam Lake Union Hospital, PO Box 190, Foam Lake SK S0A 1A0 – 306/272-3737 – Adm., Ray King

Fort Qu'Appelle: Indian Hospital, PO Box 220, Fort Qu'Appelle SK S0G 1S0 – 306/332-5611; Fax: 306/332-4352 – Adm., Nick Hassack

Gravelbourg: St. Joseph's Hospital, 216 Bettez St., Gravelbourg SK S0H 1X0 – 306/648-3185; Fax: 306/648-3440 – 9 acute care, 50 continuing care beds – Adm., Raymond Mulaire

Hafford Hospital & Special Care Centre, PO Box 130, Hafford SK S0J 1A0 – 306/549-2108; Fax: 306/549-4660 – 26 beds – Dir., Care, Linda Findelet

Herbert-Morse Union Hospital, PO Box 220, Herbert SK S0H 2A0 – 306/784-2533; Fax: 306/784-3452 – 17 beds – Hospital Coord., Monique Sedgwick

Hudson Bay Union Hospital, Hudson Bay SK S0E 0Y0 – 306/865-2219; Fax: 306/865-2429 – 18 beds – Community Mgr., Irene Fenson

Humboldt: St. Elizabeth's Hospital, PO Box 10, Humboldt SK S0K 2A0 – 306/682-2603; Fax: 306/682-4046 – Adm., Jim Ramsay

Ile a la Crosse: St. Joseph's Hospital, PO Bag 500, Ile a la Crosse SK S0M 1C0 – 306/833-2081; Fax: 306/833-2556 – 42 beds – Adm., Judy Rutko

Indian Head Union Hospital, PO Box 340, Indian Head SK S0G 2K0 – 306/695-3878; Fax: 306/695-2525 – Adm., Kathy Grad

Kamsack Hospital, Kamsack SK S0A 1S0 – 306/542-2636; Fax: 306/542-4360 – Adm., P. Ratushny

Kelvington Union Hospital, PO Box 70, Kelvington SK S0A 1W0 – 306/327-4711; Fax: 306/327-5115 – Adm., Lawrence Wytrykusz

Kerrobert Union Hospital, PO Box 320, Kerrobert SK S0L 1R0 – 306/834-2646; Fax: 306/834-1007 – Adm., Todd Stepanuik

Kindersley Hospital, Kindersley SK S0L 1S0 – 306/463-2611; Fax: 306/463-4550 – Adm., Todd Stepanuik

Kinistino Union Hospital, PO Box 460, Kinistino SK S0J 1H0 – 306/864-2292; Fax: 306/864-2440 – Adm., Carol Pryznyk

Kipling Memorial Union Hospital, PO Box 420, Kipling SK S0G 2S0 – 306/736-2553; Fax: 306/736-8407

La Ronge: La Ronge Hospital, PO Box 6900, La Ronge SK S0L 1L0 – 306/425-2422

LaLoche: St. Martin's Hospital, LaLoche SK S0M 1G0 – 306/822-2011; Fax: 306/822-2112 – 12 beds – Adm., Violet Lemaigre

Lanigan Hospital, Lanigan SK S0K 2M0 – 306/365-2022; Fax: 306/365-2099 – Adm., T. Andy Cebryk

LaRonge Hospital, LaRonge SK S0J 1L0 – 306/425-2422; Fax: 306/425-3298 – Sec.-Treas., Mark Belanger

Leader Union Hospital, Leader SK S0N 1H0 – 306/628-3343; Fax: 306/628-4413 – Adm., Helen Thorburn

Lestock: St. Joseph's Union Hospital, PO Box 280, Lestock SK S0A 2G0 – 306/274-2215; Fax: 306/274-2045 – Exec. Dir., Pamela Heinrichs

Lloydminster Hospital, 3820 - 43 Ave., Lloydminster SK S9V 1Y5 – 306/825-2211; Fax: 306/825-9880 – CEO, Brian Heidt

Loon Lake Union Hospital & Special Care Home, PO Box 68, Loon Lake SK S0M 1L0 – 306/837-2114; Fax: 306/837-2268 – 12 beds – Sec.-Treas., Marlene Chapellaz

Maidstone Union Hospital, PO Box 160, Maidstone SK S0M 1M0 – 306/893-2622; Fax: 306/893-2922 – Adm., Greg Trotter

Maple Creek Union Hospital, Maple Creek SK S0N 1N0 – 306/662-2611; Fax: 306/662-3210 – Exec. Dir., Sheila Mulatz

Meadow Lake Union Hospital, PO Box 600, Meadow Lake SK S0M 1V0 – 306/236-3661; Fax: 306/236-3244 – Adm., Irene Denis

Melfort Union Hospital, PO Box 1480, Melfort SK S0E 1A0 – 306/752-2811; Fax: 306/742-5578 – Adm., Wilfred Veller

Melville: St. Peter's Hospital, PO Box 1810, Melville SK S0A 2P0 – 306/728-5407; Fax: 306/728-4870 – 50 beds – CEO, Terri Hodges

Moose Jaw Union Hospital, 455 Fairford St. East, Moose Jaw SK S6H 1H3 – 306/694-1515; Fax: 306/692-5596 – Pres. & CEO, John Borody

Moosomin Union Hospital, PO Box 400, Moosomin SK S0G 3N0 – 306/435-3303; Fax: 306/435-3211 – Adm., Skuli Bjornson

Nipawin Union Hospital, PO Box 2104, Nipawin SK S0E 1E0 – 306/862-4643; Fax: 306/862-9310 – Adm., Rayaun Ulrich

North Battleford: Battlefords Union Hospital, 1092 - 107 St., North Battleford SK S9A 1Z1 – 306/446-7350; Fax: 306/446-7301 – Adm., Bob Miller

Outlook Union Hospital, Outlook SK S0L 2N0 – 306/867-8676; Fax: 306/867-9449 – Sec.-Treas., Mervin Dewing

Paradise Hill Hospital, Paradise Hill SK S0M 2G0 – 306/344-2255; Fax: 306/344-2277 – Adm., Brenda Rutherford

Porcupine-Carragana Union Hospital, PO Box 70, Porcupine Plain SK S0E 1H0 – 306/278-2233; Fax: 306/278-3088 – Sec./Mgr., Leslie R. Merriman

Preeceville Hospital, PO Box 469, Preeceville SK S0A 3B0 – 306/547-2102; Fax: 306/547-2223 – Adm., Thom Carnahon

Prince Albert: Holy Family Hospital, 675 - 15 St. West, Prince Albert SK S6V 3R8 – 306/922-2605, 953-1217 (admin.); Fax: 306/763-1882 – 90 beds – Exec. Dir., Sr. Rose Ketchum

Prince Albert: Victoria Union Hospital, 1200 - 24th St. West, Prince Albert SK S6V 5T4 – 306/764-1551; Fax: 306/763-2871 – Exec. Dir., David Fan

Redvers Health Centre, PO Box 30, Redvers SK S0C 2H0 – 306/452-3553; Fax: 306/452-3556 – Mgr., Health Services, Vacant

Regina General Hospital, 1440 - 14 Ave., Regina SK S4P 0W5 – 306/766-4444; Fax: 306/766-4723 – 350 beds – Pres. & CEO, Dr. Glenn Barlett

Regina: Pasqua Hospital, 4101 Dewdney Ave., Regina SK S4T 1A5 – 306/766-2222; Fax: 306/359-2497 – 268 beds – Pres. & CEO, Dr. Glenn Barlett

Rosetown & District Health Centre, PO Box 850, Rosetown SK S0L 2V0 – 306/882-2672; Fax: 306/882-3335 – Adm., Robert Legoffe

Rosthern Union Hospital, Rosthern SK S0K 3R0 – 306/232-4811; Fax: 306/232-4887 – Adm., Nestor Yaganiski

Saskatoon City Hospital, 701 Queen St., Saskatoon SK S7K 0M7 – 306/655-8000; Fax: 306/655-8269 – Pres., John Malcolm

Canadian Almanac & Directory 1997

Saskatoon: Royal University Hospital, 103 Hospital Dr., Saskatoon SK S7N 0W8 – 306/656-1018; Fax: 306/655-1037 – 429 beds – Pres., John Malcom
Saskatoon: St. Paul's Hospital, 1702 - 20 St. West, Saskatoon SK S7M 0Z9 – 306/655-5000; Fax: 306/655-5716 – Pres., Walter Podiluk
Shaunavon Union Hospital, PO Box 789, Shaunavon SK S0N 2M0 – 306/297-2644; Fax: 306/297-2502 – 15 beds – Program Coord., Gloria Illerbrun
Shellbrook Hospital, Shellbrook SK S0J 2E0 – 306/747-2603; Fax: 306/747-3004 – Adm., Clifford E. Skange
Spalding Community Health Centre, Spalding SK S0K 4C0 – 306/872-2022; Fax: 306/872-2186 – Sec.-Treas., Maria Leonard
Spiritwood Hospital, PO Box 69, Spiritwood SK S0J 2M0 – 306/883-2133; Fax: 306/883-2136 – Adm., David W. McLachlan
Swift Current Union Hospital, 499 - 4th Ave. NE, Swift Current SK S9H 2K1 – 306/778-9400; Fax: 306/778-0189 – Exec. Dir., Gordon A. Allsen
Tisdale Union Hospital, Tisdale SK S0E 1T0 – 306/873-2621; Fax: 306/873-5994 – Adm., Gordon Denton
Turtleford: Riverside Memorial Union Hospital, PO Box 10, Turtleford SK S0M 2Y0 – 306/845-2195; Fax: 306/845-2772 – Adm., Lionel Chabot
Unity Union Hospital, PO Box 741, Unity SK S0K 4L0 – 306/228-2666; Fax: 306/228-2292 – Adm., Merv Dewing
Uranium City Hospital, Uranium City SK S0J 2W0 – 306/498-2412; Fax: 306/498-2577 – 28 beds – Adm., Ian Berg
Wadena Union Hospital, PO Box 10, Wadena SK S0A 4J0 – 306/338-2515; Fax: 306/338-2720 – Adm., Eugene Kalenchuk
Wakaw Union Hospital, PO Box 309, Wakaw SK S0K 4P0 – 306/233-4611; Fax: 306/233-5990 – Acting Adm., Pat Taciuk
Watrous Hospital, Watrous SK S0K 4T0 – 306/946-3341; Fax: 306/946-2880 – Adm., Annita Romich
Wawota Health Centre, Wawota SK S0G 5A0 – 306/739-2244; Fax: 306/739-2802 – Sec./Mgr., Bruce Norsworthy
Weyburn General Hospital, 201 - 1st Ave. NE, Weyburn SK S4H 0N1 – 306/842-8400; Fax: 306/842-0737 – Adm., V.B. Wilde
Wilkie Union Hospital, Wilkie SK S0K 4W0 – 306/843-2644; Fax: 306/843-3222 – Adm., Miles Sookocheff
Wolseley Memorial Union Hospital, PO Box 458, Wolseley SK S0G 5H0 – 306/698-2377; Fax: 306/698-2988
Wynyard Hospital, Wynyard SK S0A 4T0 – 306/554-2586; Fax: 306/554-2247 – Adm., L. Haraasen
Yorkton Regional Health Centre, 270 Bradbrooke Dr., Yorkton SK S3N 2K6 – 306/782-2401; Fax: 306/782-3359 – Acting Pres., Glen Kozak

AUXILIARY HOSPITALS/HEALTH CARE CENTRES
Arborfield Health Centre & Arborfield Special Care Lodge, PO Box 160, Arborfield SK S0E 0A0 – 306/769-8722; Fax: 306/769-8640 – Sec.-Treas., A. Lindsay
Beechy Health Centre, 306/859-2118; Fax: 306/859-2206 see Midwest Health District, Hospital Districts/Health Units listings
Bengough Health Centre/Twilight Home Inc., Bengough SK S0C 0K0 – 306/268-2944; Fax: 306/268-4339 – Sec.-Treas., Jodi Bartlett
Birch Hills Memorial Health Centre, PO Box 578, Birch Hills SK S0J 0G0 – 306/749-3331; Fax: 306/749-2440 – CEO, Karl Humeniuk
Borden Community Health Centre, Borden SK S0K 0N0 – 306/997-2110; Fax: 306/997-2114 – Adm., Monica Kohlhammer
Cabri: Prairie Health Care Centre, PO Box 79, Cabri SK S0N 0J0 – 306/587-2623; Fax: 306/587-2751 – 18 beds – Acting CEO, E. Jackson

Canora: Norquay Health Centre/Gateway Lodge Inc., c/o Canora, PO Box 1387, Canora SK S0A 0L0 – 306/594-2133; Fax: 306/594-2488 – Adm., Daniel Florizone
Climax: Border Community Health Centre, Climax SK S0N 0N0 – 306/293-2222; Fax: 306/293-2860 – Sec.-Treas., Michelle Balfour
Coronach & District Health Centre, Coronach SK S0H 0Z0 – 306/267-2233; Fax: 306/267-2324 – 13 beds – Adm., Ann Benoit
Craik & District Health Centre, PO Box 208, Craik SK S0G 0V0 – 306/734-2288; Fax: 306/734-2248 – 15 beds – CEO, Elaine M. Spencer
Cupar Health Centre, Cupar SK S0G 0Y0 – 306/723-4300; Fax: 306/723-4416 – Adm., Betty Smith
Cut Knife Health Complex, PO Box 220, Cut Knife SK S0M 0N0 – 306/398-4718; Fax: 306/398-2206 – Sec.-Treas., Sonja Pellerin
Delisle Community Health & Social Centre, Delisle SK S0L 0P0 – 306/493-2323
Dinsmore Health Care Centre, PO Box 219, Dinsmore SK S0L 0T0 – 306/846-2222; Fax: 306/846-2225 – 20 beds – Adm., Anne Rankin
Dodsland Health Centre, Dodsland SK S0L 0V0 – 306/356-2172; Fax: 306/356-2042
Eastend Wolf Willow Health Centre, PO Box 220, Eastend SK S0N 0T0 – 306/295-3534; Fax: 306/295-3223 – 24 beds – Adm., Barry Grant
Eatonia Health Care Centre, PO Box 400, Eatonia SK S0L 0Y0 – 306/967-2591; Fax: 306/967-2373 – 13 beds – Adm., C. Cooke
Edam: Lady Minto Health Care Centre, PO Box 178, Edam SK S0M 0V0 – 306/397-2222; Fax: 306/397-2225 – 17 beds – Adm., Brenda Kirtzinger
Elrose Health Centre, PO Box 100, Elrose SK S0L 0Z0 – 306/378-2882; Fax: 306/378-2812 – 36 beds – Adm., Suanne Laurent
Eston Health Centre, Eston SK S0L 1A0 – 306/962-3667; Fax: 306/962-3242 – Team Mgr., Care, Margaret Bogel
Fillmore Union Health Centre/Fillmore Special-Care Home Inc., PO Box 246, Fillmore SK S0G 1N0 – 306/722-3315; Fax: 306/722-3877 – 20 beds – Adm., Heather Haupstein
Gainsborough & Area Health Centre, Gainsborough SK S0C 0Z0 – 306/685-2277; Fax: 306/685-4636 – 14 beds – Adm., Laurie Cole
Goodsoil: L. Gervais Memorial Health Centre, PO Box 100, Goodsoil SK S0M 1A0 – 306/238-2100; Fax: 306/238-4449 – 14 beds – Sec.-Treas., Fred Puffer
Grenfell Health Centre, Grenfell SK S0G 2B0 – 306/697-2853; Fax: 306/697-3459 – Adm., Peter Rousay
Gull Lake Health Centre, Gull Lake SK S0N 1A0 – 306/672-4147; Fax: 306/672-4475 – Sec.-Treas., Theresa Moritz
Hodgeville Community Health & Social Centre, Hodgeville SK S0H 2B0 – 306/677-2292; Fax: 306/677-2466
Imperial: Long Lake Valley Integrated Facility, PO Box 180, Imperial SK S0G 2J0 – 306/963-2210; Fax: 306/963-2480 – 13 beds – Adm., Wanda Gustafson
Invermay Health Centre/Gateway Lodge Inc., Invermay SK S0A 0L0 – 306/593-2133; Fax: 306/593-4566
Ituna Health Centre, Ituna SK S0A 1N0 – 306/795-2622; Fax: 306/795-3592 – Adm., Sharon Henchert
Kincaid Health Centre, PO Box 179, Kincaid SK S0H 2J0 – 306/264-3233; Fax: 306/264-3878 – Sec.-Treas., Pat Williamson
Kyle & District Health Centre, PO Box 70, Kyle SK S0L 1T0 – 306/375-2251; Fax: 306/375-2422 – 19 beds – Sec.-Treas., Evelyn Mazzel
LaFleche & District Health Centre, LaFleche SK S0H 2K0 – 306/472-5230; Fax: 306/472-5405 – 13 beds – Sec.-Treas., Pauline Dumont
Lampman Community Health Centre, PO Box 238, Lampman SK S0C 1N0 – 306/487-2561; Fax: 306/487-3103 – 21 beds – Sec.-Treas., Linda Grimes

Langenburg Health Centre, PO Box 9, Langenburg SK S0A 2A0 – 306/743-2661; Fax: 306/743-2844 – Adm., Darwyn MacKenzie
Leoville: Evergreen Health Centre, PO Box 160, Leoville SK S0J 1N0 – 306/984-2136; Fax: 306/984-2046 – 16 beds – CEO, Adrian Sakundiak
Leroy Community Health & Social Centre, Leroy SK S0K 2P0 – 306/286-3347
Lucky Lake Health Centre, PO Box 250, Lucky Lake SK S0L 1Z0 – 306/858-2133; Fax: 306/858-2312 – 19 beds – Sec.-Treas., Peggy M. Erickson
Macklin: St. Joseph's Health Centre, Macklin SK S0L 2C0 – 306/ 753-2115; Fax: 306/753-2181 – Adm., Deborah King
Mankota: Prairie View Health Centre, Mankota SK S0H 2W0 – 306/478-2200; Fax: 306/478-2462 – Adm., Sheila Gebhart
Maryfield Community Health & Social Centre, Maryfield SK S0G 3K0 – 306/646-2133
Midale: Mainprize Manor & Health Care Corporation, PO Box 239, Midale SK S0C 1S0 – 306/458-2446 – 16 beds – Adm., Arlice Adderley
Milden Health Centre, Milden SK S0L 2L0 – 306/935-2142; Fax: 306/935-2200 – Sec.-Treas., Doug Ball
Montmartre Health Centre, PO Box 206, Montmartre SK S0G 3M0 – 306/424-2222; Fax: 306/424-2227 – 14 beds – Adm., Peter Rousay
Moosomin: Whitewood Health Centre, PO Box 400, Moosomin SK S0G 3N0 – 306/735-2688; Fax: 306/ 435-2512 – Adm., Skuli Bjornson
Mossbank Community Health & Social Centre, Mossbank SK S0H 3G0 – 306/354-2300
Neilburg: Manitou Health Centre, PO Box 190, Neilburg SK S0M 2C0 – 306/823-4262; Fax: 306/823-4590 – Sec.-Treas., Carolyn Watsch
Neudorf Community Health & Social Centre, Neudorf SK S0A 2T0 – 306/748-2566
Nokomis Health Centre/Pufer Special Care Home Corp., PO Box 98, Nokomis SK S0G 3R0 – 306/528-2114; Fax: 306/528-4655 – 16 beds – Sec.-Treas., T. Andy Cebryk
Oxbow: Galloway Health Centre, PO Box 268, Oxbow SK S0C 2B0 – 306/483-2956; Fax: 306/483-5178 – 14 beds – Adm., Mary Ackerman
Pangman Hospital, Pangman SK S0C 2C0 – 306/442-2044; Fax: 306/442-4416 – Sec.-Treas., Kathy Jacques
Ponteix Health Centre, Ponteix SK S0N 1Z0 – 306/625-3366; Fax: 306/625-3764 – Sec.-Treas., Sr. G. Bonneville
Quill Lake Community Health & Social Centre, Quill Lake SK S0A 3E0 – 306/383-2266
Rabbit Lake Integrated Facility, PO Box 156, Rabbit Lake SK S0M 2L0 – 306/824-2020; Fax: 306/824-2011 – Sec.-Treas., Gwen Moore
Radville: Marian Health Centre, Radville SK S0C 2G0 – 306/869-2224; Fax: 306/869-2653 – Adm., Sheila Jubenville
Raymore Community Health & Social Centre, Raymore SK S0A 3J0 – 306/746-2231
Regina: Plains Health Centre, 4500 Wascana Pkwy., Regina SK S4S 5W9 – 306/766-6211; Fax: 306/766-6769; EMail: phc@max.cc.ur – Associate Vice-Pres., Patient Care Services, R. Mireau
Rockglen: Grasslands Health Centre, PO Box 19, Rockglen SK S0H 3R0 – 306/476-2030; Fax: 306/476-2534 – 13 beds – Sec.-Treas., Louise Todd
Rose Valley & District Integrated Care Facility, PO Box 310, Rose Valley SK S0E 1M0 – 306/322-2115 – 12 beds – Adm., Ian Begg
St. Walburg Helath Centre, St. Walburg SK S0M 2T0 – 306/248-3355; Fax: 306/248-3413 – Sec.-Treas., Linda English
Smeaton & District Health Centre, PO Box 59, Smeaton SK S0J 2J0 – 306/426-2051; Fax: 306/426-2229 – Sec.-Treas., Roni Jean Grunerud
Strasbourg & District Health Centre, Strasbourg SK S0G 4V0 – 306/725-3220

Canadian Almanac & Directory 1997

Theodore Health Centre, Theodore SK S0A 4C0 – 306/647-2115; Fax: 306/647-2238 – Adm., Gerald Hoffman

Vanguard Health Centre, Vanguard SK S0N 2V0 – 306/582-2044; Fax: 306/582-4833 – Sec.-Treas., R.W. Kehoe

Watson Community Health Centre & Quill Plains Lodge, PO Box 220, Watson SK S0K 4V0 – 306/287-3791; Fax: 306/287-3909 – Adm., Edna Favreau

Willow Bunch Community Health & Social Centre, Willow Bunch SK S0H 4K0 – 306/473-2310

Zenon Park Community Health & Social Centre, Zenon Park SK S0E 1W0 – 306/767-2221

FEDERAL HOSPITALS
Fort Qu'appelle Indian Hospital, PO Box 220, Fort Qu'appelle SK S0G 1S0 – 306/332-5611

MENTAL HEALTH HOSPITALS & COMMUNITY FACILITIES
North Battleford: Saskatchewan Hospital North Battleford, PO Box 39, North Battleford SK S9A 2X8 – 306/446-7860 – Adm., L. Spencer

NURSING HOMES
Arborfield Health Centre & Arborfield Special Care Lodge, see Auxiliary Hospitals/Health Care Centres listings

Assiniboia Pioneer Lodge Inc., PO Box 1388, Assiniboia SK S0H 0B0 – 306/642-3311 – 62 beds – Adm., James Larson

Assiniboia Pioneer Lodge Inc. (Ross Payant Nursing Home), PO Box 1388, Assiniboia SK S0H 0B0 – 306/642-3304 – 63 beds

Balcarres: Parkland Lodge Corporation, PO Box 488, Balcarres SK S0G 0C0 – 306/334-2677 – 35 beds – Adm., Elizabeth Jarocki

The Battlefords Regional Care Centre, PO Box 69, Battleford SK S0M 0E0 – 306/937-2628 – 156 beds – Adm., Ted King

Bengough: Twilight Centennial Home Inc., PO Box 399, Bengough SK S0C 0K0 – 306/268-2058 – 28 beds – Adm., Linda Hagen

Big River: Lake-Wood Lodge Inc., PO Box 760, Big River SK S0J 0E0 – 306/469-2333 – 30 beds – Adm., Jack De Vlaming

Biggar: Diamond Lodge Co. Ltd., PO Box 340, Biggar SK S0K 0M0 – 306/948-3385 – 60 beds – Adm., Eugene Motruk

Birch Hills Memorial Health Centre, see Auxiliary Hospitals/Health Care Centres listings

Broadview & District Centennial Lodge Inc., PO Box 670, Broadview SK S0G 0K0 – 306/696-2459 – 36 beds – Adm., Gordon Wyatt

Cabri: Prairie Health Care Centre, see Auxiliary Hospitals/Health Care Centres listings

Canora: Gateway Lodge Inc., PO Box 1387, Canora SK S0A 0L0 – 306/563-5685 – 78 beds – Adm., J. Matsalla

Canora: Norquay Health Centre/Gateway Lodge Inc., see Auxiliary Hospitals/Health Care Centres listings

Canwood: Whispering Pine Place Inc., PO Box 418, Canwood SK S0J 0K0 – 306/468-2900 – 30 beds – Adm., Brenda Person

Carlye: Moose Mountain Lodge Company Inc., PO Box 729, Carlye SK S0C 0R0 – 306/453-2434 – 36 beds – Adm., Terry Steininger

Carnduff: The Border-Line Housing Co. (1975) Inc. (Sunset Haven), PO Box 250, Carnduff SK S0C 0S0 – 306/462-3424 – 68 beds – Adm., Clara Irwin

Carrot River: Pasquia Special Care Home, PO Box 250, Carrot River SK S0E 0L0 – 306/768-2725 – 38 beds – Adm., Wanda Kiteley

Central Butte & District Regency Manor Inc., PO Box 430, Central Butte SK S0H 0T0 – 306/796-4338 – 30 beds – Adm., Laurie Stephens

Coronach & District Health Centre, see Auxiliary Hospitals/Health Care Centres listings

Craik & District Health Centre, see Auxiliary Hospitals/Health Care Centres listings

Cudworth Nursing Home, PO Box 190, Cudworth SK S0K 1B0 – 306/256-3423 – 29 beds – Adm., Betty Lewandoski

Cupar & District Nursing Home Inc. (Shalom), PO Box 310, Cupar SK S0G 0Y0 – 306/723-4666 – 48 beds – Adm., Richard Jensen

Cut Knife Health Complex, see Auxiliary Hospitals/Health Care Centres listings

Dalmeny: Spruce Manor Special Care Home, PO Box 190, Dalmeny SK S0K 1E0 – 306/254-2162 – 36 beds – Adm., Jacob Frosse

Davidson: Arm River Housing Corporation (Prairie View Lodge), PO Box 756, Davidson SK S0G 1A0 – 306/567-3111 – 37 beds – Adm., Dianne Birch

Dinsmore Health Care Centre, see Auxiliary Hospitals/Health Care Centres listings

Duck Lake & District Nursing Home Inc., PO Box 370, Duck Lake SK S0K 1J0 – 306/467-4440 – 30 beds – Adm., Eric Goretzky

Eastend Wolf Willow Health Centre, see Auxiliary Hospitals/Health Care Centres listings

Eatonia Health Care Centre, see Auxiliary Hospitals/Health Care Centres listings

Edam: Lady Minto Health Care Centre, see Auxiliary Hospitals/Health Care Centres listings

Elrose Health Centre, see Auxiliary Hospitals/Health Care Centres listings

Esterhazy: Centennial Special Care Home, PO Box 310, Esterhazy SK S0A 0X0 – 306/745-2323 – 60 beds – Adm., Sherrell Fox

Estevan Regional Nursing Home, 1921 Wallock Rd., Estevan SK S4A 2B5 – 306/634-2689 – 80 beds – Adm., Brenda Rabman

Estevan: Souris Valley Housing Company, 1028 Hillcrest Dr., Estevan SK S4A 1Y7 – 306/634-4154 – 27 beds – Adm., Norman Vall

Eston: Jubilee Lodge Inc., PO Box 667, Eston SK S0L 1A0 – 306/962-3215 – 35 beds – Adm., Garry Johnson

Fillmore Union Health Centre/Fillmore Special-Care Home Inc., see Auxiliary Hospitals/Health Care Centres listings

Foam Lake Jubilee Home, PO Box 460, Foam Lake SK S0A 1A0 – 306/272-4141 – 54 beds – Adm., Mervin Prystupa

Fort Qu'Appelle: Qu'Appelle Valley Housing Corp. (Echo Lodge), Fort Qu'Appelle SK S0G 1S0 – 306/332-4300 – 51 beds – Adm., Norm Zimmer

Gainsborough & Area Health Centre, see Auxiliary Hospitals/Health Care Centres listings

Goodsoil: L. Gervais Memorial Health Centre, see Auxiliary Hospitals/Health Care Centres listing

Gravelbourg: Foyer d'Youville, 216 Bettez St., Gravelbourg SK S0H 1X0 – 306/648-3185 – 50 beds – Adm., Raymond Mulaire

Grenfell & District Pioneer Home, PO Box 760, Grenfell SK S0G 2B0 – 306/697-2842 – 39 beds – Adm., Ernest C. Schmidt

Gull Lake & District Special Care Home Ltd., PO Box 539, Gull Lake SK S0N 1A0 – 306/672-3366 – 36 beds – Adm., Terry Hardy

Hafford & District Nursing Home, PO Box 130, Hafford SK S0J 1A0 – 306/549-2126 – 15 beds – Adm., John Sawyshyn

Herbert Nursing Home Inc., PO Box 520, Herbert SK S0H 2A0 – 306/784-2661 – 55 beds – Adm., Kenneth J. Isaak

Herbert Senior Citizens Home, PO Box 10, Herbert SK S0H 2A0 – 306/784-3167 – 32 beds – Adm., Brian D. Penner

Hudson Bay Pioneer Lodge, PO Box 940, Hudson Bay SK S0E 0Y0 – 306/865-2566 – 23 beds – Adm., Kathy Zimmer

Humboldt & District Housing Corp. (St. Mary's Villa), PO Box 1360, Humboldt SK S0K 2A0 – 306/682-3962 – 101 beds – Adm., Tom Ferguson

Imperial: Long Lake Valley Integrated Facility, see Auxiliary Hospitals/Health Care Centres listings

Indian Head: Golden Prairie Home Ltd., PO Box 250, Indian Head SK S0G 2K0 – 306/695-3636 – 47 beds – Adm., Dona M. Jones

Invermay Health Centre/Gateway Lodge Inc., see Auxiliary Hospitals/Health Care Centres listings

Ituna & District Pioneer Lodge, PO Box 430, Ituna SK S0A 1N0 – 306/795-2683 – 36 beds – Adm., Murray McIntosh

Kamsack & District Nursing Home, PO Box 99, Kamsack SK S0A 1S0 – 306/542-3666 – 62 beds – Adm., Roger Zelinski

Kamsack Senior Housing Ltd. (Eaglestone Lodge), PO Box 1330, Kamsack SK S0A 1S0 – 306/542-2620 – 25 beds – Adm., Anita Dixon

Kelvington: Kelvindell Lodge Company, PO Box 280, Kelvington SK S0A 1W0 – 306/327-5151 – 46 beds – Adm., L. Wytrykusz

Kerrobert: Buena Vista Lodge, PO Box 440, Kerrobert SK S0L 1R0 – 306/834-2463 – 28 beds – Adm., Edward L. Kryzanowski

Kerrobert: Pioneer Haven Co. Ltd., PO Box 650, Kerrobert SK S0L 1R0 – 306/834-5255 – 30 beds – Adm., B. Ernie Tendler

Kindersley Senior Care Inc. (Heritage Manor), 901 - 1st St. West, Kindersley SK S0L 1S1 – 306/463-6401 – 80 beds – Adm., Brian Martin

Kinistino & District Housing Corporation (Jubilee Lodge), PO Box 370, Kinistino SK S0J 1H0 – 306/864-2851 – 36 beds – Adm., Carol Pryznyk

Kipling: Willowdale Lodge Care Home, PO Box 537, Kipling SK S0G 2S0 – 306/736-2218 – 26 beds – Adm., Murray Goeres

Kyle & District Health Centre, see Auxiliary Hospitals/Health Care Centres listings

La Ronge: La Ronge Hospital, see General Hospitals listings

LaFleche & District Health Centre, see Auxiliary Hospitals/Health Care Centres listings

Lampman Community Health Centre, see Auxiliary Hospitals/Health Care Centres listings

Langenburg: Centennial Special Care Home, PO Box 9, Langenburg SK S0A 2A0 – 306/734-2232 – 46 beds – Adm., Janice Veal

Langham Senior Citizens Home, PO Box 287, Langham SK S0K 2L0 – 306/283-4210 – 28 beds – Adm., Margaret Balzer

Lanigan: Central Parkland Lodge, PO Box 459, Lanigan SK S0K 2M0 – 306/365-3015 – 35 beds – Adm., Kathy Cole

Leader: Western Senior Citizens Home, PO Box 69, Leader SK S0N 1H0 – 306/628-3565 – 36 beds – Adm., Fenton Yeo

Leask: Wheatland Lodge Inc., PO Box 130, Leask SK S0J 1M0 – 306/466-4949; Fax: 306/466-2205 – 30 beds – Adm., Gail Cote

Leoville: Evergreen Health Centre, see Auxiliary Hospitals/Health Care Centres listings

Leroy: LeRose Lodge, PO Box 280, Leroy SK S0K 2P0 – 306/286-3331 – 26 beds – Adm., David Moore

Lloydminster & District Senior Citizens Lodge (Jubilee Home), 3902 - 45th Ave., Lloydminster SK S9V 1Z2 – 403/825-2132 – 50 beds – Adm., Linda Graham

Loon Lake Union Hospital & Special Care Home, see General Hospitals listings

Lucky Lake Health Centre, see Auxiliary Hospitals/Health Care Centres listings

Lumsden & District Heritage Home Inc., PO Box 479, Lumsden SK S0G 3C0 – 306/731-2247 – 30 beds – Adm., Matthew A. Kalp

Macklin: Golden Twilight Lodge Incorporated, Macklin SK S0L 2C0 – 306/753-2217 – 25 beds – Adm., Mervin Dewing

Maidstone: Pine Island Lodge Ltd., PO Box 40, Maidstone SK S0M 1M0 – 306/893-2223 – 27 beds – Adm., Varn McClelland

Mankota: Prairie View Health Centre, see Auxiliary Hospitals/Health Care Centres listings

Maple Creek: Cypress Lodge Corp., PO Box 878, Maple Creek SK S0N 1N0 – 306/662-2671 – 61 beds – Adm., Bryce Wirachowsky

Meadow Lake: Northland Pioneers Lodge Inc., PO Box 40, Meadow Lake SK S0M 1V0 – 306/236-5812 – Adm., Floyd Gibb

Melfort & District Pioneer Lodge (Nirvana), PO Box 5000, Melfort SK S0E 1A0 – 306/752-2130 – 60 beds – Adm., Joe Rybinski

Melfort: Parkland Regional Care Centre, 302 Bemister Ave. East, PO Box 2260, Melfort SK S0E 1A0 – 306/752-2767 – 92 beds – Adm., Robert J. Duns

Melville: St. Paul Lutheran Home, PO Box 1390, Melville SK S0A 2P0 – 306/728-4591 – 154 beds – Adm., Don Whittmire

Midale: Mainprize Manor & Health Care Corporation, see Auxiliary Hospitals/Health Care Centres listings

Middle Lake: Bethany Pioneer Village Inc., PO Box 8, Middle Lake SK S0K 2X0 – 306/367-2033 – 36 beds – Adm., Glenn McDougall

Montmartre Health Centre, see Auxiliary Hospitals/Health Care Centres listings

Moose Jaw: Extendicare Ltd., 1151 Coteau St. West, Moose Jaw SK S6H 5G5 – 306/693-5191 – 127 beds – Adm., Tarry Vanbocquestal

Moose Jaw: Ina Grafton Gage Home, 200 Iriquois St. East, Moose Jaw SK S6H 4T3 – 306/692-4882 – 39 beds – Adm., Dolores Willfong

Moose Jaw: Pioneer Housing Association of Moose Jaw, 1000 Albert St., Moose Jaw SK S6H 2Y2 – 306/692-6711 – 103 beds – Adm., Donald Campbell

Moosomin: Eastern Saskatchewan Pioneer Lodge Nursing Home, 405 Windover Ave., PO Box 858, Moosomin SK S0G 3N0 – 306/435-2100 Nursing Home, 435-2326 Lodge – 46 beds – Adm., Larry Signarowski

Nipawin District Nursing Home Inc. (Pineview Lodge), PO Box 2105, Nipawin SK S0E 1E0 – 306/862-9828 – 106 beds – Adm., Michael Kukurudza

Nokomis Health Centre/Pufer Special Care Home Corp., see Auxiliary Hospitals/Health Care Centres listings

North Battleford: The Battlefords River Heights Lodge Corporation, 2001 - 99th St., PO Box 657, North Battleford SK S9A 0S3 – 306/445-2497 – 142 beds – Adm., William H. Smith

North Battleford: Societe Joseph Breton Inc. (Villa Pascal), 1301 - 113th St., North Battleford SK S9A 3K1 – 306/445-8465 – 40 beds – Adm., Normand Poirier

Outlook & District Pioneer Home Inc., PO Box 396, Outlook SK S0L 2N0 – 306/867-8321 – 52 beds – Adm., Judy Jeska

Oxbow: Galloway Health Centre, see Auxiliary Hospitals/Health Care Centres listings

Ponteix Housing Company Ltd., PO Box 148, Ponteix SK S0N 1Z0 – 306/625-3511 – 18 beds – Adm., Jackie Shaddock

Ponteix: Foyer St. Joseph Nursing Home, PO Box 450, Ponteix SK S0N 1Z0 – 306/625-3810 – 30 beds – Adm., Sr. Marie P. Beliveau

Porcupine Plain: Red Deer Nursing Home, PO Box 70, Porcupine Plain SK S0E 1H0 – 306/278-2469 – 50 beds – Adm., L. Merriman

Preeceville Lions Housing Corporation Ltd. (Lyons Lodge), PO Box 348, Preeceville SK S0A 3B0 – 306/547-3112 – 30 beds – Adm., Marlene Shapherd

Prince Albert: Mont St. Joseph Home Inc., 125 - 25th St. East, Prince Albert SK S6V 1S6 – 306/764-2856 – 81 beds – Adm., Marianne Sherwood

Prince Albert: Northern Housing Development Inc. (Herb Bassett Home), 1220 - 25th St. West, Prince Albert SK S6V 7P7 – 306/764-7777 – 144 beds

Prince Albert: Northern Housing Development Inc. (Pineview Terrace), 701 - 13th St. West, Prince Albert SK S6V 3E9 – 306/764-7777 – 53 beds

Rabbit Lake Integrated Facility, see Auxiliary Hospitals/Health Care Centres listings

Radville: Marian Home, PO Box 310, Radville SK S0M 2L0 – 306/869-2254 – 49 beds – Adm., Sheila Jubenville

Raymore: Silver Heights Special Care Home, PO Box 549, Raymore SK S0A 3J0 – 306/746-5744 – 30 beds – Adm., Loralee Bailey

Redvers Centennial Haven, PO Box 399, Redvers SK S0C 2H0 – 306/452-3331 – 24 beds – Adm., Lori Hinz

Regina Lutheran Home, 1925 - 5th Ave. North, Regina SK S4R 8P6 – 306/543-4055 – 91 beds – Adm., Allan Hoffman

Regina Pioneer Village Ltd., 430 Pioneer Dr., Regina SK S4T 6L8 – 306/757-5646 – 405 beds – Adm., Ron Reavley

Regina: Extendicare Elmwood, 4125 Rae St., Regina SK S4S 3A5 – 306/586-1787 – 65 beds – Adm., Marion Ogrodnick

Regina: Extendicare Parkside, 4540 Rae St., Regina SK S4S 3B4 – 306/586-0220 – 228 beds – Adm., Shirley Van Moorleham

Regina: Extendicare Sunset, 260 Sunset Dr., Regina SK S4S 2S3 – 306/586-3355 – 152 beds – Adm., Doreen Werry

Regina: Martin Luther Nursing Home Inc., 5161 Sherwood Dr., Regina SK S4C 4C1 – 306/543-0288 – 22 beds – Adm., Lorne Wettstein

Regina: The Qu'Appelle Diocesan Housing Company, 1425 College Ave., Regina SK S4P 1B4 – 306/522-0335 – 34 beds – Adm., Lucille Meaney

Regina: The Salvation Army William Booth Special Care Home, 50 Angus Rd., Regina SK S4R 6P6 – 306/543-0655 – 83 beds – Adm., Maj. John Foley

Regina: Santa Maria Senior Citizens Home, 4215 Regina Ave., Regina SK S4S 0J5 – 306/584-5566 – 162 beds – Adm., Beverly Olineck

Rockglen: Grasslands Health Centre, see Auxiliary Hospitals/Health Care Centres listings

Rosetown & District Health Centre, see General Hospitals listings

Rosetown: Wheatbelt Centennial Lodge Inc., PO Box 250, Rosetown SK S0L 2V0 – 306/882-3567 – 28 beds – Adm., Robert LeGoffe

Rosthern: Mennonite Nursing Home Inc., PO Box 370, Rosthern SK S0K 3R0 – 306/232-4861 – 86 beds – Adm., David Ratzlaff

St Brieux: Chateau Providence Inc., PO Box 340, St Brieux SK S0K 3V0 – 306/275-2227 – 30 beds – Adm., Wendy Smith

St Walburg: Lakeland Lodge Inc., PO Box 70, St Walburg SK S0M 2T0 – 306/248-3677 – 28 beds – Adm., Maryanne Hill

Saltcoats: Lakeside Manor Care Home Inc., PO Box 340, Saltcoats SK S0A 3R0 – 306/744-2353 – 30 beds – Adm., Dorothy Dawson

Saskatoon Convalescent Home, 101 - 31st St. West, Saskatoon SK S7L 0P6 – 306/244-7155 – 60 beds – Adm., Nathaniel Swaan

Saskatoon: Central Haven Special Care Home Inc., 1020 Avenue I North, Saskatoon SK S7L 2H7 – 306/665-6180 – 60 beds – Adm., Clarence Sawatzky

Saskatoon: Circle Drive Special Care Home Inc., 3055 Preston Ave. South, PO Box 60020, Saskatoon SK S7K 7L2 – 306/955-4800 – 50 beds – Adm., Leonard Enns

Saskatoon: Convent of Sion, 333 Acadia Dr., Saskatoon SK S7H 3V5 – 306/374-9566 – 16 beds – Adm., Sr. Beth Linthicum

Saskatoon: Del Haven Lodge, 316 - 4th Ave. North, Saskatoon SK S7K 2L7 – 306/653-2867 – 52 beds – Adm., Jean Neudorf, R.P.N.

Saskatoon: Elmwood Residences Inc. (Kinsmen Elmwood Lodge), 2012 Arlington Ave., Saskatoon SK S7J 2H5 – 306/374-5151 – 50 beds – Adm., Richard Baxter

Saskatoon: Extendicare Preston, 2225 Preston Ave., Saskatoon SK S7J 2E7 – 306/374-2242 – 82 beds – Adm., Pat Amos

Saskatoon: Jubilee Residences Inc. (Porteous), 833 Ave. P North, Saskatoon SK S7L 2W5 – 306/382-2626 – 117 beds – Adm., Ivan Kresak

Saskatoon: Jubilee Residences Inc. (Stensrud), 2202 McEown Ave., Saskatoon SK S7L 3L6 – 306/373-5580 – 100 beds – Adm., Heather Anderson

Saskatoon: Lutheran Sunset Home, 1212 Osler St., Saskatoon SK S7N 0T9 – 306/652-8566 – 129 beds – Adm., Harold Hesje

Saskatoon: Oliver Lodge, 1405 Faulkner Cres., Saskatoon SK S7L 3R5 – 306/382-4111 – 121 beds – Adm., M. Mitchell

Saskatoon: Parkridge Lodge, 110 Gropper Cres., Saskatoon SK S7M 5N9 – 306/978-2333 – 238 beds – Adm., Dave Gibson

Saskatoon: St. Ann's Senior Citizens Village Corporation, 2910 Louise St., Saskatoon SK S7J 3L8 – 306/374-8900 – 80 beds – Adm., L.J. Moxness

Saskatoon: St. Joseph's Home for the Aged, 33 Valans Dr., Saskatoon SK S7L 3S2 – 306/382-6306 – 85 beds – Adm., Sr. Theodosia

Saskatoon: The Salvation Army Eventide Home, 2221 Adelaide St. East, Saskatoon SK S7J 0J6 – 306/374-5737 – 60 beds – Adm., Maj. Travis S. Wagner

Saskatoon: Sherbrooke Community Centre, 301 Acadia Dr., Saskatoon SK S7H 2E7 – 306/374-7955 – 286 beds – Adm., E. Marleau

Saskatoon: Sunnyside Nursing Home, 2200 St. Henry Ave., Saskatoon SK S7M 0P5 – 306/653-1267 – 106 beds – Adm., Desmond Dobroskay

Saskatoon: Ursuline Sisters of St. Angela's Convent, 1212 College Dr., Saskatoon SK S7N 0W4 – 306/653-2134 – 5 beds

Shaunavon Special Care Inc., 632 - 2nd St. East, Shaunavon SK S0N 2M0 – 306/297-2245 Lodge, 297-2353 Nursing Home – 23 beds – Adm., Shannon Pomeroy

Shellbrook: Parkland Housing Company, Parkland Terrace, PO Box 670, Shellbrook SK S0J 2E0 – 306/747-2639 – 36 beds – Adm., Faith Mazurek

Spiritwood: Idylwild Senior Citizens Lodge, PO Box 159, Spiritwood SK S0J 2M0 – 306/883-2267 – 36 beds – Adm., Ted Boddy

Stoughton: Newhope Pioneer Lodge Incorporated, PO Box 38, Stoughton SK S0G 4T0 – 306/457-2552 – 30 beds – Adm., Edith Raiwet

Strasbourg: Last Mountain Pioneer Home, PO Box 549, Strasbourg SK S0G 4V0 – 306/725-3342 – 43 beds – Adm., Maxine Flotre

Swift Current: Chantelle Management Ltd., Swift Current Centre, 700 Aberdeen St. SE, Swift Current SK S9H 3E3 – 306/773-9371 – 70 beds – Adm., Vera Hyde

Swift Current: Palliser Regional Care Centre, PO Box 1420, Swift Current SK S9H 3G6 – 306/773-8307 – 105 beds – Adm., Keith Dalby

Swift Current: Prairie Pioneers Lodge, 300 Central Ave. South, Swift Current SK S9H 3G3 – 306/773-7524 – 58 beds – Adm., Esther Wall

Theodore Health Centre, see Auxiliary Hospitals/Health Care Centres listings

Tisdale & District Housing Company (Newmarket Manor), PO Box 2620, Tisdale SK S0E 1T0 – 306/873-5828 – 40 beds – Adm., Gordon Denton

Tisdale & District Housing Company (Sasko Park Lodge), PO Box 1330, Tisdale SK S0E 1T0 – 306/873-2404 – 35 beds – Adm., Gordon Denton

Turtleford: Turtle River Nursing Home, PO Box 10, Turtleford SK S0M 2Y0 – 306/845-2195 – 15 beds – Adm., Vern McClelland

Canadian Almanac & Directory 1997

Unity: Unimac Pioneers Lodge, PO Box 970, Unity SK S0K 4L0 – 306/228-2744 – 43 beds – Adm., Mervin Dewing

Wadena: Pleasant View Care Home, Wadena SK S0A 4J0 – 306/338-3275 – 46 beds – Adm., Mike Koval

Wakaw: Lakeview Pioneer Lodge Housing Company, PO Box 544, Wakaw SK S0K 4P0 – 306/233-4621 – 50 beds – Adm., Claudia Vachon, R.N.

Waldheim: Menno Home of Saskatchewan, PO Box 130, Waldheim SK S0K 4S0 – 306/965-2070 – 43 beds – Adm., Marlin Roth

Warman Mennonite Special Care Home, Warman SK S0K 4S0 – 306/933-2011 – 31 beds – Adm., Norman Wiens

Watrous: Manitou Lodge, PO Box 10, Watrous SK S0K 4T0 – 306/946-3718 – 36 beds – Adm., John Knoch

Watson Community Health Centre & Quill Plains Lodge, see Auxiliary Hospitals/Health Care Centres listings

Wawota & District Special Care Home Inc., PO Box 99, Wawota SK S0G 5A0 – 306/739-2400 – 30 beds – Adm., Aaron Fornwald

Weyburn & District Special Care Homes Corporation, 704 - 5th St. NE, Weyburn SK S4H 1A3 – 306/842-4455 – 110 beds – Adm., Alex Horner

Weyburn: Souris Valley Regional Care Centre, PO Box 2001, Weyburn SK S4H 2L7 – 306/842-7481 – 241 beds – Adm., Warren Wallin

Whitewood & District Nursing Home Inc., PO Box 699, Whitewood SK S0G 5C0 – 306/735-2634 – 30 beds – Adm., Dan Shiplack

Wilkie & District Centennial Nursing Home, PO Box 459, Wilkie SK S0K 4W0 – 306/843-2668 – 30 beds – Adm., Bryce Martin

Wolseley: Lakeside Home, PO Box 10, Wolseley SK S0G 5H0 – 306/698-2573 – 80 beds – Adm., Arthur Colclough

Wynyard & District Housing Corporation (Golden Acres), PO Box 190, Wynyard SK S0A 4T0 – 306/554-3312 – 51 beds – Adm., Gary Hilderman

Yorkton & District Nursing Home Corporation, 200 Bradbrooke Dr., Yorkton SK S3N 2K5 – 306/782-2117 – 160 beds – Adm., Glen Kozak

Yorkton: Anderson Lodge, 150 Independent St., Yorkton SK S3N 0S7 – 306/783-4911 – 61 beds – Adm., Kerry Bodnarchuk

SPECIAL TREATMENT CENTRES

(Includes: Abortion Clinics, Cancer Clinics, Rehabilitation Centres, Treatment Centres)

Moose Jaw: Providence Place for Holistic Health, 100 Second Ave. NE, Moose Jaw SK S6H 1B8 – 306/694-8081; Fax: 306/694-8804 – 188 beds – Exec. Dir., Bill Bell

Regina: Wascana Rehabilitation Centre, 2180 - 23 Ave., Regina SK S4S 0A5 – 306/766-6211; Fax: 306/359-5339 – rehabilitation centre – Adm., Donna Bjore

YUKON TERRITORY

GENERAL HOSPITALS

Watson Lake Hospital, PO Box 500, Watson Lake YT Y0A 1C0 – 403/536-4444; Fax: 403/536-7302 – 10 beds – Nurse in Charge, Sue Rudd

Whitehorse General Hospital, 5 Hospital Rd., Whitehorse YT Y1A 3H7 – 403/667-8700; Fax: 403/667-2451 – CEO, Marny Willis

AUXILIARY HOSPITALS/HEALTH CARE CENTRES

Beaver Creek Health Centre, General Delivery, Beaver Creek YT Y0B 1A0 – 403/862-4444; Fax: 403/862-7909

Carcross Health Centre, PO Box 27, Carcross YT Y0A 1B0 – 403/821-4444; Fax: 403/821-3909

Carmacks Health Centre, General Delivery, Carmacks YT Y0B 1C0 – 403/863-4444; Fax: 403/863-6612

Destruction Bay Health Centre, General Delivery, Destruction Bay YT Y0B 1H0 – 403/841-4444; Fax: 403/841-5274

Haines Junction Health Centre, General Delivery, Haines Junction YT Y0B 1L0 – 403/634-4444; Fax: 403/634-2733

Pelly Crossing Health Centre, General Delivery, Pelly YT Y0B 1P0 – 403/537-4444; Fax: 403/537-3611

Ross River Health Centre, General Delivery, Ross River YT Y0B 1S0 – 403/969-4444; Fax: 403/969-2014

Teslin Health Centre, General Delivery, Teslin YT Y0A 1B0 – 403/390-4444; Fax: 403/390-2217

Watson Lake Health Centre, see Watson Lake Hospital, General Hospitals listings

Whitehorse Health Centre, #300, 211 Main St., Whitehorse YT Y1A 2B3 – 403/667-6371; Fax: 403/667-2707

Whitehorse: Mt. McIntyre Native Health Centre, PO Box 1217, Whitehorse YT Y1A 5A5 – 403/668-7289; Fax: 403/633-6095

MENTAL HEALTH HOSPITALS & COMMUNITY FACILITIES

Whitehorse: Mental Health Services, 2 Hospital Rd., Whitehorse YT Y1A 3H8 – 403/667-8346; Fax: 403/667-8372

NURSING STATIONS

Dawson City Nursing Station, PO Box 10, Dawson YT Y0B 1G0 – 403/993-4444; Fax: 403/993-5811

Faro Nursing Station, PO Box 99, Faro YT Y0B 1K0 – 403/994-4444; Fax: 403/994-3457

Mayo Nursing Station, PO Box 98, Mayo YT Y0B 1M0 – 403/996-4444; Fax: 403/996-2018

Old Crow Nursing Station, General Delivery, Old Crow YT Y0B 1N0 – 403/996-4444; Fax: 403/966-3614

SECTION 9

EDUCATION DIRECTORY

ALBERTA	1
BRITISH COLUMBIA	6
MANITOBA	13
NEW BRUNSWICK	17
NEWFOUNDLAND	19
NORTHWEST TERRITORIES	21
NOVA SCOTIA	21
ONTARIO	23
PRINCE EDWARD ISLAND	41
QUÉBEC	41
SASKATCHEWAN	51
YUKON TERRITORY	55
INDEX TO SELECTED FACULTIES/SCHOOLS	56

See ADDENDA at the back of this book for late changes & additional information.

ALBERTA

Alberta Advanced Education & Career Development
10155 - 102 St., 7th Fl., Edmonton AB T5J 4L5
403/422-4488; Fax: 403/422-5126

Alberta Education
Communications Branch, Devonian Bldg., 11160 Jasper Ave., Edmonton AB T5K 0L2
403/427-2285; Fax: 403/427-0591

CURRICULUM INFORMATION
Acting Director, Curriculum Branch, Wayne Keith, 403/427-2984; Fax: 422-3745

ALBERTA DISTANCE LEARNING CENTRE
Box 4000, Barrhead AB T7N 1P4
403/674-5333; Fax: 403/674-6561
Director, Garry Popowich

For detailed departmental listings, see Index: "Education, Depts."

PUBLIC SCHOOL BOARDS & DIVISIONS
Includes counties, francophone educational regions, public school districts, Roman Catholic public school districts, regional divisions, regional school districts & school divisions.

Boards with an enrollment of more than 12,000 are in bold print.

Aspen View Regional Division #19
  3602 - 48 Ave., Athabasca AB T9S 1M8
  403/675-2273; Fax: 403/675-5512 – Supt., John Ord; Asst. Sec.-Treas., Maurice Gushta
Battle River Regional Division #31
  5402 - 48A Ave., Camrose AB T4V 0L3
  403/672-6131; Fax: 403/672-6137 – Supt., Merle A. Stover; Sec.-Treas., Bill Schulte
Black Gold Regional Division #18
  Nisku Centre, 1101 - 5 St., Nisku AB T9E 7N3
  403/955-6025; Fax: 403/955-6050 – Supt., Lowell Throndson; Sec.-Treas., Gordon Handke
Buffalo Trail Regional Division #28
  #2, 1041 - 10A St., Wainwright AB T9W 2R4
  403/842-6144; Fax: 403/842-3255 – Supt., Terry Pearson; Sec.-Treas., Vince Rodgers
Calgary School District #19
  Education Centre Bldg., 515 Macleod Trail SE, Calgary AB T2G 2L9
  403/294-8100; Fax: 403/294-8336
  Chief Supt., Donna Michaels
  Supt. & Treas., Finance, Ursula Mergny
Canadian Rockies Regional Division #12
  PO Box 748, Banff AB T0L 0C0
  403/762-5581; Fax: 403/762-8271 – Supt., Brian Callaghan; Sec.-Treas., David Mackenzie
Chinook's Edge Regional Division #5
  4904 - 50 St., PO Box 6080, Innisfail AB T4G 1W4
  403/227-4272; Fax: 403/227-3652 – Supt., Altha Neilson; Treas., Susan Roy
Clearview Regional Division #24
  PO Box 1420, Stettler AB T0C 2L0
  403/742-3331; Fax: 403/742-1388 – Supt., Gillian Bushrod; Sec.-Treas., Robert Dick
East Central Francophone Education Region #3
  PO Box 249, St. Paul AB T0A 3A0
  403/645-3888; Fax: 403/645-2045 – Supt., Donald Michaud; Sec.-Treas., Yvan Beaubien
Edmonton School District #7
  Centre for Education, One Kingsway, Edmonton AB T5H 4G9
  403/429-8080; Fax: 403/429-8318
  Acting Supt., Emery Dosdall
  Treas., Dean Power
Elk Island Public School Regional Division #14
  2001 Sherwood Dr., Sherwood Park AB T8A 3W7
  403/464-3477; Fax: 403/464-8056
  Supt., Terry Gunderson
  Treas., Brian J. Smith
Foothills School Division #38
  PO Box 5700, High River AB T1V 1M7
  403/652-3001; Fax: 403/652-4204 – Supt., David Lynn; Sec.-Treas., Clair O. Belsher
Fort McMurray School District #2833
  9401 Franklin Ave., Fort McMurray AB T9H 3Z7
  403/799-7900; Fax: 403/791-3027 – Supt., John Waddell; Sec.-Treas., Randy Hoffman
Fort Vermilion School Division #52
  PO Box 1, Fort Vermilion AB T0H 1N0
  403/927-3766; Fax: 403/927-4625 – Supt., Michael Davenport; Sec.-Treas., Grant Mann
Golden Hills Regional Division #15
  435A Hwy. #1, Strathmore AB T1P 1J4
  403/934-5121; Fax: 403/934-5124 – Supt., Dr. G. McKinnon; Sec.-Treas., Wayne Bralin
Grande Prairie School District #2357
  10213 - 99 St., Grande Prairie AB T8V 2H3
  403/532-4491; Fax: 403/539-4265 – Supt., Derek Taylor; Sec.-Treas., Bob Leech
Grande Yellowhead Regional Division #35
  3656 - 1 Ave., Edson AB T7E 1S8
  403/723-4471; Fax: 403/723-2414 – Supt., Klaus Puhlmann; Sec.-Treas., Earl Trathen
Grasslands Regional Division #6
  408 First St. West, Brooks AB T1R 0V8
  403/362-2555; Fax: 403/362-8225 – Supt., Duncan Gillespie; Sec.-Treas., Leeann Woods
High Prairie School Division #48
  PO Box 870, High Prairie AB T0G 1E0
  403/523-3337; Fax: 403/523-4639 – Supt., Verne Evans; Sec.-Treas., Laurie Marston
Horizon School Division #67
  6304 - 52 St., Taber AB T1G 1J7
  403/223-3547; Fax: 403/223-2999 – Supt., Dr. Eric Johnson; Sec.-Treas., Viola Powell
Lethbridge School District #51
  433 - 15 St. South, Lethbridge AB T1J 2Z5
  403/380-5301; Fax: 403/327-4387 – Supt., Gary Kiernan; Sec.-Treas., Don Lussier
Livingstone Range School Division #68
  PO Box 1959, Claresholm AB T0L 0T0
  403/625-3356; Fax: 403/325-2424 – Supt., Lloyd Cavers; Treas., Don Olsen
Lloydminster Public School Division #1753
  5017 - 46 St., Lloydminster AB T9V 1R4
  403/875-5541; Fax: 403/875-7829 – Supt., Don Duncan; Treas., Beverley Henry
Medicine Hat School District #76

Canadian Almanac & Directory 1997

601 - 1 Ave. SW, Medicine Hat AB T1A 4Y7
403/528-6730; Fax: 403/529-5339 – Supt., Harold T. Storlien; Sec.-Treas., Doug Pudwell
North Central Francophone Education Region #4
8815D - 92 St., Edmonton AB T6C 3P9
403/468-6440; Fax: 403/440-1631 – Supt., Gerard Bissonnette; Sec.-Treas., Paulette Briand
Northern Gateway Regional Division #10
4104 Kepler St., Whitecourt AB T7S 1M8
403/778-2800; Fax: 403/778-6719 – Supt., L. Larson; Treas., Cody McClintock
Northern Lights School District #69
6005 - 50 Ave., Bonnyville AB T9N 2L4
403/826-3145; Fax: 403/826-4600 – Supt., Ed Wittchen; Sec.-Treas., Gary Krawchuk
Northland School Division #61
PO Bag 1400, Peace River AB T8S 1V2
403/624-2060; Fax: 403/624-5914 – Supt., Colin Kelly; Sec.-Treas., Fred deKleine
Northwest Francophone Education Region #1
PO Box 1220, St. Isidore AB T0H 3B0
403/624-8855; Fax: 403/624-8554 – Supt., Denise Bourassa; Sec.-Treas., Anita Belzile
Palliser Regional Division #26
#101, 905 - 4 Ave. South, Lethbridge AB T1J 0P4
403/328-4111; Fax: 403/380-6890 – Supt., John Bolton; Sec.-Treas., John J. Gleason
Parkland School Division #70
4603 - 48 St., Stony Plain AB T7Z 2A8
403/963-4010; Fax: 403/963-4169 – Supt., Dr. David Young; Sec.-Treas., Thomas Olson
Peace River School Division #10
PO Box 6960, Peace River AB T8S 1S7
403/624-3601; Fax: 403/624-5941 – Supt., David Van Tamelan; Sec.-Treas., Bruce Moltzan
Peace Wapiti Regional Division #33
8611A - 108 St., Grande Prairie AB T8V 4C5
403/532-8133; Fax: 403/532-4234 – Supt., R. Gerald Mazer; Sec.-Treas., Murray Donaghy
Pembina Hills Regional Division #7
5310 - 49 St., Barrhead AB T7N 1P3
403/674-8500; Fax: 403/674-3262 – Supt., Sig Schmold; Treas., Tracy Meunier
Prairie Land Regional Division #25
PO Box 1400, Hanna AB T0J 1P0
403/854-4881; Fax: 403/854-2803 – Supt., Robert Tredger; Sec.-Treas., Dennis Moss
Prairie Rose Regional Division #8
918 - 2 Ave., PO Box 204, Dunmore AB T0J 1A0
403/527-5516; Fax: 403/528-2264 – Supt., Keith Jones; Sec.-Treas., Patricia Cocks
Red Deer School District #104
4747 - 53 St., Red Deer AB T4N 2E6
403/342-3710; Fax: 403/347-8190 – Supt., David Blacker; Asst. Supt., Business Service, Ray Congdon
Rocky View School Division #41
2616 - 18 St. NE, Calgary AB T2E 7R1
403/291-6313; Fax: 403/250-3281 – Supt., Colleen Brownlee; Sec.-Treas., Darrell Couture
St. Paul Education Regional Division #1
4901 - 47 St., St. Paul AB T0A 3A3
403/645-3323; Fax: 403/645-5789 – Supt., Ted Cabaj; Sec.-Treas., Jean Champagne
Sturgeon School Division #24
9820 - 104 St., Morinville AB T8R 1L8
403/939-4341; Fax: 403/939-5520 – Supt., John Hogarth; Sec.-Treas., Murray R. Lloyd
Westwind Regional Division #9
PO Box 10, Cardston AB T0K 0K0
403/653-4991; Fax: 403/653-4641 – Supt., Dr. Mel Cottle; Sec.-Treas., Drew Chipman
Wetaskiwin County Board of Education #11
4710 - 55 St., Wetaskiwin AB T9A 3B7
403/352-6018; Fax: 403/352-7886 – Supt., Hal Kluczny; Sec.-Treas., Donna Mogg
Wild Rose School Division #66
PO Box 8000, Rocky Mountain House AB T0M 1T0

403/845-3376; Fax: 403/845-3850 – Supt., Jim McLellan; Sec.-Treas., Alex Weber
Wolf Creek Regional Division #32
6000 Hwy. 2A, Pononka AB T4J 1P6
403/783-3473; Fax: 403/783-3483 – Supt., Lyle Lorenz; Sec.-Treas., Joe Henderson

PROTESTANT SEPARATE SCHOOL DISTRICTS
St. Albert Protestant Separate School District #6
60 Sir Winston Churchill Ave., St. Albert AB T8N 0G4
403/460-3712; Fax: 403/460-7686 – Supt., Ruth Leblanc; Sec.-Treas., Mel Poole

ROMAN CATHOLIC SEPARATE SCHOOL DISTRICTS
Calgary Roman Catholic Separate School District #1
1000 - 5th Ave. SW, Calgary AB T2P 4T9
403/298-1383; Fax: 403/237-9694
Chief Supt., Bill Dever
Sec.-Treas., Deborah Achen
Christ Redeemer Catholic Separate Regional Division #3
PO Box 3, Okotoks AB T0L 1T0
403/938-2659; Fax: 403/938-4575 – Supt., Ronald Wallace; Treas., Dennis Schneider
East Central Alberta Catholic Separate School Regional Division #16
223 - 10 St., Wainwright AB T9W 1N7
403/842-3992; Fax: 403/842-5322 – Supt., George Bunz; Treas., Marilyn Bachmann
Edmonton Roman Catholic Separate School District #7
9807 - 106 St., Edmonton AB T5K 1C2
403/441-6001; Fax: 403/425-8759
Supt., Terry Fortin
Sec.-Treas., R. G. Bennett
Evergreen Catholic Separate Regional Division #2
PO Box 4265, Spruce Grove AB T7X 3B4
403/962-5627; Fax: 403/962-4664 – Supt., Jim Collins; Sec.-Treas., Gary Innes
Fort McMurray Roman Catholic Separate School District #32
9809 Main St., Fort McMurray AB T9H 1T7
403/799-5700; Fax: 403/799-5706 – Acting Supt., Dan McIsaac; Sec.-Treas., Vacant
Fort Saskatchewan Roman Catholic Separate School District #104
#124, 8818 - 111 St., Fort Saskatchewan AB T8L 3T4
403/998-4622; Fax: 403/998-1100 – Supt., James Sheasgreen; Sec.-Treas., Andrew Isbister
Good Shepherd Roman Catholic Regional Division #13
4921 - 43 St., Drayton Valley AB T7A 1P5
403/542-5267; Fax: 403/542-6060 – Supt., Bryce Knudson; Sec.-Treas., Joyce Murray
Grande Prairie Roman Catholic Separate School District #28
9902 - 101 St., Grande Prairie AB T8V 2P5
403/532-3013; Fax: 403/532-3430 – Supt., Lorne Radbourne; Sec.-Treas., Grant Burge
Greater St. Albert Catholic Regional Division #29
6 St. Vital Ave., St. Albert AB T8N 1K2
403/459-7711; Fax: 403/458-3213 – Supt., Lee Lucente; Sec.-Treas., Al Summers
Holy Family Catholic Separate Regional Division #17
PO Box 789, High Prairie AB T0G 1E0
403/523-3771; Fax: 403/523-4603 – Supt., Marcel Michaud; Sec.-Treas., Diana Hildebrand
Holy Spirit Roman Catholic Separate Regional Division #4
534 - 18 St. South, Lethbridge AB T1J 3E7
403/327-9555; Fax: 403/327-9595 – Supt., Frank Letain; Sec.-Treas., Karel Meulenbroek
Holy Trinity Catholic Regional Division #21
3804B - 47 St., Whitecourt AB T7S 1M8
403/778-5666; Fax: 403/778-2727 – Supt., Bryan Kulmatycki; Sec.-Treas., Frank Booth

Lakeland Roman Catholic Separate School District #150
4810 - 46 St., Bonnyville AB T9N 1B5
403/826-3235; Fax: 403/826-7576 – Supt., Henri Lemire; Sec.-Treas., Adele Coates
Medicine Hat Catholic Separate School Regional Division #20
1251 - 1 Ave. SW, Medicine Hat AB T1A 8B4
403/527-2292; Fax: 403/529-0917 – Supt., Patrick Glashan; Sec.-Treas., Tony Giesinger
North Peace Roman Catholic Separate School District #43
10307 - 99 St., Peace River AB T8S 1R5
403/624-3956; Fax: 403/624-1154 – Supt., Wayne Doll; Sec.-Treas., Huguette Ropchan
Red Deer Roman Catholic Separate School District #17
3827 - 39 St., Red Deer AB T4N 0Y6
403/343-1055; Fax: 403/347-6410 – Supt., Lloyd Baumgarten; Sec.-Treas., Richard M. Dornstauder
St. Thomas Aquinas Regional Division #22
5108A - 47 St., Leduc AB T9E 6Y9
403/986-2500; Fax: 403/986-8620 – Supt., Eugene Miller; Sec.-Treas., Ron Beakhouse
Sherwood Park Catholic Separate School District #105
2017 Brentwood Blvd., Sherwood Park AB T8A 0X2
403/467-8896; Fax: 403/467-5469 – Supt., Patrick Maguire; Sec.-Treas., Alberta M. Hutchings
Slave Lake Roman Catholic Separate School District #364
109 - 6 Ave. SE, Slave Lake AB T0G 2A3
403/849-3020; Fax: 403/849-5900 – Supt., Michel Beaudoin; Sec.-Treas., Noel Moriyama
Sundance Catholic Separate Regional Division #10
PO Box 6210, Hinton AB T7V 1X5
403/865-3811; Fax: 403/856-5633 – Supt., Joffre Plaquin; Sec.-Treas., Cheryl Freeman
Vegreville Catholic Separate School District #16
5121 - 52 Ave., Vegreville AB T9C 1M2
403/632-6821; Fax: 403/632-3448 – Supt., Bernard McCracken; Sec.-Treas., Daniel Dubuc

CHARTER SCHOOLS
Action for Bright Children – Gr. 1-9
717 Ranchview Circle NW, Calgary AB T3G 1A9
403/239-1285 – Supt., Vacant; Sec.-Treas., Stan Doherty
Boyle Street Service Society – Gr. 1-12
9331 - 105 Ave., Edmonton AB T5H 0J7
403/425-4903 – Supt., Emery Dosball; Sec.-Treas., Deanna Bright
Centre for Academic & Personal Excellence – Gr. 1-9
51 - 6 St. SE, Medicine Hat AB T1A 1G5
403/528-3979 – Supt., Teresa Bimimmo; Sec.-Treas., Judy Herring
Education for the Gifted Society – Gr. Pre.-9
#205, 1604 Sherwood Dr., Sherwood Park AB T8A 0Z2
403/467-6409 – Supt., Vacant; Treas., Greg Paton
Society for Talent Education – Gr. Pre.-9
7211 - 96A Ave., Edmonton AB T6B 1B5
403/468-2598 – Administrator, Loretta Isaac

NATIVE SCHOOLS
(Jurisdiction of Indian & Northern Affairs Canada.)

BANDS, BOARDS OF EDUCATION
Alexander Band, PO Box 1440, Morinville AB T0G 1P0 – 403/939-3868 – Adm., E. Arcand
Alexis Band, PO Box 27, Glenevis AB T0E 0X0 – 403/967-5919 – Adm., Roderick Alexis
Beaver Lake Tribe #131, PO Box 960, Lac La Biche AB T0A 2C0 – 403/623-4548 – Adm., D. Kirby
Cree Band #461, c/o Sturgeon Lake Band School, PO Box 5, Valleyview AB T0H 3N0 – 403/524-4590 – Adm., Nareen Narayan

Dene Tha Band, PO Box 118, Chateh AB T0H 0S0 – 403/321-3842 – Supt., Education, Russell Lahti
Driftpile Band, General Delivery, Driftpile AB T0G 0V0 – 403/355-3615 – Dir. of Ed., Steven Kulmatycki
Ermineskin Band, General Delivery, Hobbema AB T0C 1N0 – 403/585-2118 – Adm., Don Sinclaire
Ermineskin Smallboy Band, General Delivery, Robb AB T0E 1X0 – 403/794-3784 – Adm., Melvin Nadeau
Federally Administered Schools, c/o Indian & Inuit Affairs, #630, 9700 Jasper Ave., Edmonton AB T5J 4G2
Frog Lake Band, General Delivery, Frog Lake AB T0A 1M0 – 403/943-3918 – Dir., Clarence Faithfull
Heart Lake Band, PO Box 936, Lac La Biche AB T0A 2C0 – 403/623-2600 – Adm., Sidney Rodnunsky
Horse Lake First Nation, PO Box 303, Hythe AB T0H 2C0 – 403/356-2248; Fax: 403/356-3666
Kainaiwa Board of Education, PO Box 240, Standoff AB T0L 1Y0 – 403/737-3966; Fax: 403/737-2361
Kehewin Band, PO Box 6218, Bonnyville AB T8N 2G8 – 403/826-3333 – Adm., Victor John
Kiseputinow Education Dept., PO Box 130, Hobbema AB T0C 1N0 – 403/585-3978; Fax: 403/585-3799
Kitaskinaw Education Authority, RR#1, Site 2, PO Box 25, Winterburn AB T0E 2N0
Little Red River Board of Education, PO Box 1830, High Level AB T0H 1Z0 – 403/759-3810 – Supt., Marvin Fyten
Montana Community School, PO Box 129, Hobbema AB T0C 1N0 – 403/585-2000
O'chiese Education Authority, PO Box 337, Rocky Mountain House AB T0M 1T0 – 403/989-2000; Fax: 403/989-2122
Paul Band Education Authority, PO Box 89, Duffield AB T0E 0N0 – 403/892-2691
Peigan Band, PO Box 130, Brochet AB T0K 0H0 – 403/965-3910; Fax: 403/965-3713 – Dir., Ben Kawaguchi
Saddle Lake Education Authority, PO Box 70, Saddle Lake AB T0A 3T0 – 403/726-3730 – Dir., Charles Wood
Samson Band, PO Box 658, Hobbema AB T0C 1N0 – 403/585-2211; Fax: 403/585-3857 – Adm., Grace Buffalo
Sarcee Band, 3700 Anderson Rd. SW, PO Box 131, Calgary AB T2W 3C4
Siksika Board of Education, PO Box 249, Gleichen AB T0J 1N0 – 403/734-5220 – Dir., Robert Breaker
Stoney Band, PO Box 40, Morley AB T0L 1N0 – 403/881-3966
Sunchild First Nation Band, PO Box 747, Rocky Mountain House AB T0M 1T0 – 403/989-3787
Swan River First Nation, PO Box 270, Kinuso AB T0G 1K0 – 403/775-3536; Fax: 403/775-3796
Tallcree Band, PO Box 310, Fort Vermilion AB T0H 1N0 – 403/927-4381 – Adm., Michael J. Campbell
Whitefish Lake Educational Authority, PO Box 274, Goodfish AB T0A 1R0 – 403/428-9501
Yellowhead Tribal Council, 17304 - 105 Ave., 3rd Fl., Edmonton AB T5S 1G4 – 403/962-0303; Fax: 403/481-7275 – Dir. of Ed., Jim Brule

UNIVERSITIES

Athabasca University
PO Box 10000, Athabasca AB T9S 2B6
403/675-6111; Fax: 403/675-6450; URL: http://www.athabascau.ca
Registrar, Alex Reed
President, Dominique Abrioux, Ph.D.
Vice-President, Academic, Alan Davis, Ph.D.
Vice-President, University Development, A. Bleiken
Vice-President, Finance, Art Nutt, C.A.
Head, Tutorial Services, C. Nelson, B.A., B.Ed.
University Librarian, L. Aitken
Executive Director, Student Services, Judith Hughes, Ph.D.

FACULTIES WITH DEANS
Acting Dean, Administration Studies, Harvey Pasis
Arts, David Gregory, Ph.D.
Sciences, K. Mailer, Ph.D.

SCHOOLS WITH DIRECTORS
Centre for Distance Education, R. Spencer, Ph.D.
Computing Services, W. Gray, B.Sc.
Marketing & Communications, M. Jean-Louis, B.A.
Media Services, P.A. Nedza, M.Ed.

Augustana University College
4901 - 46 Ave., Camrose AB T4V 2R3
403/679-1100; Fax: 403/679-1129; URL: gopher://gopher/augustana.ab.ca:70/1
President, Rev. Richard Husfloen
Chair, Board of Regents, Sandra Anderson
Dean & Vice-President, Academic Affairs, Janet Wright
Vice-President, Student Services, Erhard Pinno
Vice-President, Finance & Administration, Raymond Smith
Registrar, Raymond Blacklock
Librarian, Nancy Goebel
Director, Alumni & Public Relations, Kenneth Fredrick
Manager, Bookstore, Elaine Duchscherer
Vice-President, Development & Institutional Relations, James Rasmussen

University of Alberta
26 University Campus NW, Edmonton AB T6G 2E8
403/492-3111, 2325; Fax: 403/492-2997; URL: http://web.cs.ualberta.ca/UAlberta.html
Chancellor, L. Hyndman, O.C., LL.B.
President, R. Fraser, Ph.D.
Chair, Board of Governors, J. Ferguson, B.Comm.
Vice-President, Academic, D. Owram, Ph.D.
Vice-President, Finance & Administration, G. Harris, M.A.Sc.
Vice-President, Research & External Affairs, M. Piper, Ph.D.
Executive Director, External Relations, T.R. Flannigan, Ph.D.
Comptroller & Assoc. Vice-President, L. Jamernik, B.B.M.
Registrar & Assoc. Vice-President, B.J. Silzer, M.Ed.
Director, Public Affairs, J.A. Myers, LL.B.
Director, Materials Management, R.A. Bennett, M.B.A.
Manager, Bookstore, J. Malone, B. Com.
Director, School of Library & Information Studies, S. Bertram, Ph.D.
Director, School of Native Studies, J. Dempsey, M.A.
Dean, Students, J. Newton, Ph.D.

FACULTIES WITH DEANS
Agriculture, Forestry & Home Economics, I.N. Morrison, Ph.D.
Arts, P. Clements, D.Phil.
Business, R. Schneck, Ph.D.
Education, L. Beauchamp, Ph.D.
Engineering, D. Lynch, Ph.D.
Extension, R. Garrison, Ph.D.
Faculté Saint-Jean, Claudette Tardif, Ph.D.
Graduate Studies & Research, M. Gray, Ph.D.
Law, T. Christian, LL.B.
Medicine & Oral Health Sciences, D.L. Tyrrell, Ph.D.
Nursing, M. Wood, Ph.D.
Pharmacy & Pharmaceutical Sciences, R.E. Moskalyk, Ph.D.
Physical Education & Recreation, A. Quinney, Ph.D.
Rehabilitation Medicine, A. Cook, Ph.D.
Science, R.E. Peter, Ph.D.

AFFILIATED COLLEGES
Canadian Union College, PO Box 430, College Heights AB T0C 0Z0 – 403/782-3381; Fax: 403/782-3170; Toll Free: 1-800-661-8129 – President, Victor Fitch
Concordia College, 7128 Ada Blvd., Edmonton AB T5B 4E4 – 403/479-8481; Fax: 403/474-1933
King's College, 10766 - 97 St., Edmonton AB T5H 2M1 – 403/465-3500; Fax: 403/425-8166; URL: http://www.kingsu.ab.ca – Chair, Board of Governors, William Wildeboer
North America Baptist College, 11525 - 23rd Ave., Edmonton AB T6J 4T3 – 403/437-1960
St. Joseph's College, c/o University of Alberta, Edmonton AB T6G 2J5 – 403/492-7681 – President, Rev. R.J. Barringer, C.S.B., D.Phil.
St. Stephen's College, c/o University of Alberta, Edmonton AB T6G 2J5 – 403/439-7311 – Principal, Dr. G.I. Mundle, D.Min.

The University of Calgary
2500 University Dr. NW, Calgary AB T2N 1N4
403/220-5110; Fax: 403/282-7298; Telex: 03-821545; URL: http://www.ucalgary.ca/
Chancellor, M.A. McCaig, B.Ed.
Chair, Board of Governors, J.E. Newall, B.Comm.
President & Vice-Chancellor, T. White, B.Sc., M.A., Ph.D.
Registrar, G.J.P. Krivy, B.Ed., M.Ed., Ph.D.
Vice-President, Academic, J.D. Calkin, B.Sc.N., M.Sc.N., Ph.D.
Vice-President, Finance & Services, G.K. Winter, B.Sc., M.Sc., Ph.D.
Vice-President, Research, C.H. Langford, A.B., Ph.D.
Director, Information Services, A.H. MacDonald, B.A., B.L.S., A.L.I.A.A.
Director, Libraries, T.M. Eadie, B.A., M.A., M.L.S.
Director, University Secretariat, R. Williams, B.A. (Hons.)
Executive Director, External Relations, S. Reid, B.Sc.

FACULTIES WITH DEANS
Continuing Education, T.P. Keenan, M.S., Ed.M.
Education, I. Winchester, D.Phil.
Engineering, S.C. Wirasinghe, Ph.D., P.Eng.
Environmental Design, R.J.D. Page, B.A., M.A., D.Phil.
Fine Arts, Maurice Yacowar, Ph.D.
General Studies, M.J. McMordie, B.Arch., Ph.D.
Graduate Studies, D.J. Bercuson, B.A., M.A., Ph.D., F.R.S.C.
Humanities, R.B. Bond, B.A., M.A., Ph.D., A.R.C.T., A.R.C.C.O.
Kinesiology, W.L. Veale, B.Sc., M.Sc., Ph.D., F.R.S.C.
Law, M. Wylie, B.A., LL.B., B.C.L.(Oxon)
Management, P.M. Maher, B.E., M.B.A., Ph.D., P.Eng.
Medicine, E.R. Smith, M.D., FRCP(C) (F.R.C.P.C)
Acting Dean, Nursing, Carol Rogers, R.N., M.H.Sc.
Science, E.J.M. Kendall, B.Sc., M.Sc., Ph.D.
Social Sciences, S.J. Randall, B.A., M.A., Ph.D.
Social Work, R.J. Thomlison, B.Sc., B.S.W., M.S.W., Ph.D.

University of Lethbridge
4401 University Dr., Lethbridge AB T1K 3M4
403/320-5700; Fax: 403/329-5159; URL: http://www.uleth.ca
President, H.E. Tennant
Director, Development, Charlotte Caton
Vice-President, Academic, Seamus O'Shea
Assoc. Vice-President, Academic, L. Stebbins
Director, Research Services, R. McHugh
Dean, Student Affairs, Vacant
Manager, Materials Management, Barry Kimery
Manager, Bookstore, Donna Kampen

FACULTIES WITH DEANS
Arts & Science, Bhagwan Dua

Education, L. Walker
Management, George Lermer

SCHOOLS WITH DIRECTORS
Dean, Fine Arts, Vondis Miller
Dean, Nursing, Una Ridley

INSTITUTES OF TECHNOLOGY

THE NORTHERN ALBERTA INSTITUTE OF TECHNOLOGY
11762 - 106 St., Edmonton AB T5G 2R1
403/471-7400; Fax: 403/471-8583; URL: http://www.schoolfinder.com/profiles/colleges/nait.htm
President, Stan G. Souch

THE SOUTHERN ALBERTA INSTITUTE OF TECHNOLOGY
1301 - 16 Ave. NW, Calgary AB T2M 0L4
403/284-8581; Fax: 403/281-8940; Telex: 03-821989; URL: http://www.sait.ab.ca/
President, Dale Landry, Email: dale.landry@sait.ab.ca

PUBLIC COLLEGES

FAIRVIEW COLLEGE
PO Box 3000, Fairview AB T0H 1L0
403/835-6600; Fax: 403/835-6670; Email: sroy@fairviewc.ab.ca
President, Fred Trotter

GRANDE PRAIRIE REGIONAL COLLEGE
10726 - 106 Ave., Grande Prairie AB T8V 4C4
403/539-2024; Fax: 403/539-2749
President, Gordon Gilgan

GRANT MACEWAN COMMUNITY COLLEGE
c/o Administration Office, City Centre Campus, 10700 - 104 Ave., Edmonton AB T5J 4S2
403/497-5401; Fax: 403/497-5405; URL: http://www.gmcc.ab.ca/
President, Dr. Gerald Kelly, Email: Kellyg@admin.gmcc.ab.ca
City Centre Campus, 10700 - 104 Ave., Edmonton AB T5J 4S2 – 403/497-5040; Fax: 403/497-5045
Jasper Place Campus, 10045 - 156 St., Edmonton AB T5P 2P7 – 403/497-4340; Fax: 403/497-4300
Mill Woods Campus, 7319 - 29 Ave., Edmonton AB T6K 2P1 – 403/497-4040; Fax: 403/497-4045

KEYANO COLLEGE
8115 Franklin Ave., Fort McMurray AB T9H 2H7
403/791-4800; Fax: 403/791-1555
President, Dr. Douglas MacRae

LAKELAND COLLEGE
c/o Corporate Offices, Bag 5100, Vermilion AB T0B 4M0
403/853-8400; Fax: 403/853-7355
President, Dr. Steve Pawluk
Lloydminster Campus, Bag 6600, Lloydminster SK S9V 1Z3 – 403/871-5700; Fax: 403/875-5136

LETHBRIDGE COMMUNITY COLLEGE
3000 College Dr. South, Lethbridge AB T1K 1L6
403/320-3200; Fax: 403/329-0530; Email: pr@lethbridgec.ab.ca; URL: http://www.lethbridgec.ab.ca
President, Donna Allan

MEDICINE HAT COLLEGE
299 College Dr. SE, Medicine Hat AB T1A 3Y6
403/529-3803; Fax: 403/526-7750
President, D. Ralph Weeks, Ph.D., Email: rweeks@acd.mhc.ab.ca

MOUNT ROYAL COLLEGE
4825 Richard Rd. SW, Calgary AB T3E 6K6
403/240-6111; Fax: 403/240-5938; Email: dkoop@mtroyal.ab.ca; URL: http://www.mtroyal.ab.ca/
President, Thomas L. Wood

OLDS COLLEGE
4500 - 50th St., Olds AB T4H 1R6
403/556-8281; Fax: 403/556-4698
President, Robert Turner

PRAIRIE BIBLE COLLEGE & GRADUATE SCHOOL
PO Box 4000, Three Hills AB T0M 2N0
403/443-5511; Fax: 403/443-5540; Toll Free: 1-800-661-2425
President, Paul W. Ferris
Chancellor, Ted S. Rendall

RED DEER COLLEGE
56 Ave. & 32 St., PO Box 5005, Red Deer AB T4N 5H5
403/342-3300; Fax: 403/340-8940
President, Dan Cornish

POST-SECONDARY & SPECIALIZED INSTITUTIONS

ALBERTA COLLEGE OF ART & DESIGN
1407 - 14 Ave. NW, Calgary AB T2N 4R3
403/284-7600; Fax: 403/289-6682
President, Arthur Greenblatt

BANFF CENTRE FOR THE ARTS & CENTRE FOR MANAGEMENT & CENTRE FOR CONFERENCES
PO Box 1020, Stn 1, Banff AB T0L 0C0
403/762-6100; Fax: 403/762-6444; Telex: Artsbanff 03-826657; URL: http://www-nmr.banffcentre.ab.ca
Director, Communications & Development, Jon Bjorgum
President/CEO, Dr. Graeme D. McDonald

NATIONAL SCREEN INSTITUTE
10022 - 103 St., 3rd Fl., Edmonton AB T5J 0X2
403/421-4084; Fax: 403/425-8098

PETROLEUM INDUSTRY TRAINING SERVICE
#13, 2115 - 27 Ave. NE, Calgary AB T2E 7E4
403/250-9606; Fax: 403/291-9408; Telex: 03-822806
Executive Director, Paul Schoenuhals

VOCATIONAL CENTRES

ALBERTA VOCATIONAL COLLEGE
Downtown Campus, 10215 - 108 St., Edmonton AB T5J 1L6
427/427-2823; Fax: 427/427-5465; Email: info@edma.avc.calgary.ab.ca
President, Irene Lewis, Email: ILewis@EDMA.AVC.Calgary.ab.ca
Lynn Lauren Campus, 5606 - 47 St., Wetaskiwin AB T9A 2A2 – 403/352-6009; Fax: 403/352-7092
South Campus, 10330 - 71 Ave., Edmonton AB T6E 0W8 – 403/427-8750; Fax: 403/427-5486
Winnifred Stewart Campus, 11140 - 131 St., Edmonton AB T5M 1C1 – 403/422-9061

ALBERTA VOCATIONAL COLLEGE (CALGARY)
332 - 6 Ave. SE, Calgary AB T2G 4S6
403/297-3930; Fax: 403/297-4081; Email: info@avc.calgary.ab.ca
President, Nancy Lynch

ALBERTA VOCATIONAL COLLEGE (LAC LA BICHE)
PO Box 417, Lac La Biche AB T0A 2C0
403/623-5551; Fax: 403/623-5639
Director, William Lieshoff

ALBERTA VOCATIONAL COLLEGE (LESSER SLAVE LAKE)
1201 Main St. SE, Slave Lake AB T0G 2A3
403/849-8611; Fax: 403/849-2570; Email: neidig@grda.avc.calgary.ab.ca
President, Dan Vandermeulen
Acting Vice-President, Rick Neidig

INDEPENDENT & PRIVATE SCHOOLS

Schools with five teachers or more, listed alphabetically by city.

Airdrie Koinonia Christian School, Big Hill Springs Rd., RR#1, Airdrie AB T4B 2A3 – 403/948-5100; Fax: 403/948-5563 – Gr. Pre.-10
Banff International College, PO Box 1020, Stn 3, Banff AB T0L 0C0 – 403/762-6430; Fax: 403/762-8423 – Gr. 9-12
Banff Mountain Academy, PO Box 1020, Banff AB T0L 0C0 – 403/762-5287; Fax: 403/762-8585 - Gr. 10-12
Bow Island: Cherry Coulee Christian Academy, PO Box 1037, Bow Island AB T0K 0G0 – 403/542-2107; Fax: 403/542-2107 – Gr. Pre.-12; Special Ed.
Calgary: Akiva Academy, 140 Haddon Rd. SW, Calgary AB T2V 2Y3 – 403/258-1312; Fax: 403/258-3812 – Gr. Pre.-6
Calgary: Banbury Crossroads Private School, #101, 1410 - 1st St. SW, Calgary AB T2R 0V8 – 403/269-5261 – Gr. Pre.-12; Special Ed.
Calgary Academy, Site 2, SS #3, PO Box 103, Calgary AB T3C 3N9 – 403/686-6444; Fax: 403/240-3427 – Gr. 1-12; Special Ed.; Evening Credit
Calgary Christian High School, 5029-26 Ave. SW, Calgary AB T3E 0R5 – 403/242-2896; Fax: 403/686-1281 – Gr. 7-12; Special Ed.
Calgary Christian School, 5029 - 49 Ave. SW, Calgary AB T3E 3X9 – 403/242-2896; Fax: 403/242-6682 – Gr. Pre.-6; Special Ed.
Calgary: The Calgary French School, 6304 Larkspur Way SW, Calgary AB T3E 5P7 – 403/240-1500; Fax: 403/249-5899 – Gr. Pre.-6
Calgary International College, #1100, 833 - 4 Ave. SW, Calgary AB T2P 3T5 – 403/233-2982; Fax: 403/269-7568 – Gr. 7-12
Calgary Jewish Academy, 6700 Kootenay St. SW, Calgary AB T2V 1P7 – 403/253-3992; Fax: 403/255-0842 – Gr. Pre.-12
Calgary Montessori School, c/o Clem Gardner Elementary School, 5915 Lewis Dr. SW, Calgary AB T3E 5Z4 – 403/246-2275 – Gr. Pre.-12
Calgary Waldorf School, 1915 - 36 Ave. SW, Calgary AB T2T 2G6 – 403/287-1868; Fax: 403/287-3414 – Gr. Pre.-9
Calgary: Chinook Winds Adventist Academy, Site 12, S.S.#1, PO Box 23, Calgary AB T2M 4N3 – 403/286-5686; Fax: 403/247-1623 – Gr. 1-12
Calgary: Christopher Robin School, 1011 Beverley Blvd. SW, Calgary AB T2V 2C4 – 403/252-6063 – Gr. Pre.-3
Calgary: Columbia College, 805 Manning Rd. NE, Calgary AB T2E 7N8 – 403/235-9309; Fax: 403/272-3805 – Gr. 1-12; Special Ed.
Calgary: Delta West Academy, #307, 1111 - 11 Ave. SW, Calgary AB T2R 0G5 – 403/228-4746; Fax: 403/228-4748 – Gr. 1-12; Special Ed.
Calgary: Equilibrium Inter-Educational Institute, #360, 703 - 6 Ave. SW, Calgary AB T2P 0T9 – 403/237-7239; Fax: 403/237-7239 – Gr. 10-12; Evening Credit
Calgary: Foothills Academy, 745 - 37 St. NW, Calgary AB T2N 4T1 – 403/270-9400; Fax: 403/270-9438 – Gr. 1-12; Special Ed.
Calgary: German Language School of Calgary, #201, 3112 - 11 St. NE, Calgary AB T2E 7J1 – 403/291-3515; Fax: 403/931-2628 – Gr. 10-12; Evening Credit
Calgary: Glenmore Christian Academy, 16520 - 24 St., Calgary AB T2J 5G5 – 403/254-9050; Fax: 403/256-9695 – Gr. Pre.-9; Special Ed.
Calgary: Heritage Christian School, 155 Falconridge Cres. NE, Calgary AB T3J 1Z9 – 403/280-4800; Fax: 403/280-4817 – Gr. Pre.-12
Central Campus, 2020 - 6 St. NW, Calgary AB T2M 3G3 – 403/289-8213; Fax: 403/282-5878
Northwest Campus, 5300 - 53 Ave. NW, Calgary AB T3A 2G8 – 403/247-1314; Fax: 403/286-9933

Calgary: Italian School of Calgary, 24 Beddington Way NE, Calgary AB T3K 1N9 – 403/246-2399; Fax: 403/246-2399 – Gr. 1-12; Evening Credit
Calgary: Lycée Louis Pasteur, 4416 - 16 St. SW, Calgary AB T2T 4H9 – 403/243-5420; Fax: 403/287-2245 – Gr. Pre.-9
Calgary: Menno Simons School, 307 - 55 Ave. SW, Calgary AB T2H 0A1 – 403/531-0745 – Gr. Pre.-9
Calgary: North Calgary Christian Academy, 719 - 44 Ave. NW, Calgary AB T2K 0J5 – 403/282-3405; Fax: 403/220-0326 – Gr. Pre.-12
Calgary: Prince of Peace Lutheran School, RR#7, Box 10, Site 17, Calgary AB T1X 1E1 – 403/285-2288; Fax: 403/285-2855 – Gr. Pre.-9
Calgary: Renfrew Educational Services, PO Box 52013, Edmonton Trail RPO, Calgary AB T2K 8K9 – 403/276-2211; Fax: 403/286-9875 – Gr. Pre.-2
Calgary: Rundle Academy, 414 - 11A St. NE, Calgary AB T2E 4P3 – 403/262-2411; Fax: 403/263-3782 – Gr. 4-6
  Rundle College, 2612 - 37 Ave. NE, Calgary AB T1Y 5L2 – 403/250-7180; Fax: 403/250-7184
Calgary: Trinity Christian School, 11024B Oakfield Dr. SW, Calgary AB T2W 5G6 – 403/251-2884; Fax: 403/251-2884 – Gr. Pre.-10
Calgary: West Island College, 7410 Blackfoot Trail SE, Calgary AB T2H 1M5 – 403/255-5300; Fax: 403/252-1434 – Gr. 7-12
Coaldale Christian School, 2008 - 8 St., Coaldale AB T1M 1L1 – 403/345-4055; Fax: 403/345-6436 – Gr. Pre.-9; Special Ed.
College Heights Adventist Junior Academy, 185 College Ave., College Heights AB T4L 1Z6 – 403/782-6212; Fax: 403/782-7507 – Gr. Pre.-9
College Heights: Parkview Adventist Academy, 251 College Ave., College Heights AB T4L 2E7 – 403/782-3381; Fax: 403/782-7308 – Principal, J. Janes – Gr. 10-12
Devon Christian School, PO Box 960, Devon AB T0C 1E0 – 403/987-4157; Fax: 403/987-3331 – Gr. Pre.-9
Edmonton: Alberta College, 10050 MacDonald Dr., Edmonton AB T5J 2B7 – 403/428-1851; Fax: 403/424-6371 – Gr. 10-12; Evening Credit
Edmonton: The Bilingual Montessori Learning Centre, 7200 - 156 St., Edmonton AB T5R 1X3 – 403/484-4796; Fax: 403/489-7548 – Gr. 1-8
Edmonton: Centennial Montessori School, 6755 - 88 St., Edmonton AB T6E 4Y4 – 403/465-5752; Fax: 403/437-4817 – Gr. Pre.-12
Edmonton: Concordia College, 7128 Ada Blvd., Edmonton AB T5B 4E4 – 403/479-8481; Fax: 403/474-1933 – Gr. 10-12; Lutheran
Edmonton: Concordia College of Continuing Education, 9359 - 67A St., Edmonton AB T6B 1R7 – 403/466-6633; Fax: 403/466-9394 – Gr. 10-12; Evening Credit
Edmonton: Coralwood Adventist Academy, 13510 - 122 Ave., Edmonton AB T5L 2V8 – 403/454-2173; Fax: 403/455-6946 – Gr. Pre.-10
Edmonton: Dante Alighieri Italian School, c/o St. Alphonsus School, 11624 - 81 St., Edmonton AB T5B 2S2 – 403/453-6182 – Gr. 1-4, 10-12
Edmonton Academy, 10231 - 120 St., Edmonton AB T5K 2A4 – 403/482-5449; Fax: 403/482-0902 – Gr. 5-12; Spec. Ed.
Edmonton Christian High School, 14304 - 109 Ave., Edmonton AB T5N 1H6 – 403/454-0791; Fax: 403/454-0793 – Gr. 10-12
Edmonton Islamic School, 13070 - 113 St., Edmonton AB T5E 5A8 – 403/454-3498; Fax: 403/452-1243 – Gr. Pre.-6; Special Ed.
Edmonton Menorah Academy, 10735 - 144 St., Edmonton AB T5N 3L1 – 403/451-1848; Fax: 403/451-2254 – Gr. Pre.-11
Edmonton: Elves Memorial Child Development Centre, 10825 - 142 St., Stn E, Edmonton AB T5N 3Y7 – 403/454-5310; Fax: 403/454-5889 – Special Ed.

Edmonton: Faith Lutheran School, 9359 - 67A St., Edmonton AB T6B 1R7 – 403/496-9302; Fax: 403/496-9394 – Gr. Pre.-9
Edmonton: German Saturday School, Trinity Lutheran Church, 10014 - 81 Ave., Edmonton AB T6E 1W8 – 403/433-1604; Fax: 403/433-6623 – Gr. 1-5; 10-12
Edmonton: Heritage School, 8540 - 69 Ave., Edmonton AB T6E 0R6 – 403/469-6689; Fax: 403/465-7181 – Gr. P-12; Special Ed.
Edmonton: Manning Adult Learning Centre, 21611 Meridian St., PO Box 2290, Edmonton AB T5J 3H7 – 403/472-6052; Fax: 403/495-6036 – Gr. 1-12
Edmonton: Meadowlark Christian School, 9825 - 158 St., Edmonton AB T5P 2X4 – 403/483-6476; Fax: 403/487-8992 – Gr. Pre.-9
Edmonton: Millwoods Christian School, 8704 Millwoods Rd., Edmonton AB T6K 3J3 – 403/462-2627; Fax: 403/462-9322 – Gr. Pre.-12; Special Ed.
Edmonton: North Edmonton Christian School, 13470 Fort Rd., Edmonton AB T5A 1C5 – 403/475-2818; Fax: 403/478-1728 – Gr. Pre.-9
Edmonton: Opportunity Avenues Program, #301, 10526 Jasper Ave., Edmonton AB T5J 1Z7 – 403/428-7590; Fax: 403/425-1549 – Gr. 7-12
Edmonton: Parkland Immanuel Christian School, 21304 - 35 Ave. NW, Edmonton AB T5P 4B7 – 403/444-6443; Fax: 403/444-6448 – Gr. Pre.-12
Edmonton: Progressive Academy, 12245 - 131 St., Edmonton AB T5L 1M8 – 403/455-8344; Fax: 403/455-8344 – Gr. Pre-12; Special Ed.
Edmonton: St. Luke's College, 10419 - 159 St., Edmonton AB T5P 3A6 – 403/486-7422; Fax: 403/486-7423 – Gr. 9-12
Edmonton: Tempo School, 5603 - 148 St., Edmonton AB T6H 4T7 – 403/434-1190; Fax: 403/430-6209 – Gr. 1-12; Special Ed.
Edmonton: West Edmonton Christian School, 14345 McQueen Rd., Edmonton AB T5N 3L5 – 403/455-8515; Fax: 403/452-5669 – Gr. Pre.-9
Fort Saskatchewan Christian School, 9935 - 93 Ave., Fort Saskatchewan AB T8L 1N5 – 403/998-7044; Fax: 403/998-7388 – Gr. Pre.-9; Special Ed.
Grande Prairie Christian School, 10404 - 102 St., Grande Prairie AB T8V 2W3 – 403/539-4566; Fax: 403/539-4748 – Gr. Pre.-12
Grande Prairie: Hillcrest Christian School, 10306 - 102 St., Grande Prairie AB T8V 2W3 – 403/539-9161; Fax: 403/532-3244 – Gr. Pre.-9
Hobbema: Maskwachees Cultural School, PO Box 360, Hobbema AB T0C 1N0 – 403/585-3925; Fax: 403/585-2080 – Gr. 10-12
Innisfail: Buffalo Creek Learning Centre, PO Box 6000, Innisfail AB T4G 1V1 – 403/227-3391; Fax: 403/227-6022 – Gr. 1-12
Kingman: Cornerstone Christian Academy, PO Box 99, Kingman AB T0B 2M0 – 403/672-7197; Fax: 403/672-7197 – Gr. Pre.-12; Special Ed.
Lacombe: Central Alberta Christian High School, 22 Eagle Rd., Lacombe AB T4L 1G7 – 403/782-4535; Fax: 403/782-2542 – Gr. 10-12
Lacombe Christian School, 5206 - 58 St., Lacombe AB T4L 1G9 – 403/782-6531; Fax: 403/782-5760 – Gr. Pre.-9
Leduc: Covenant Christian School, PO Box 3827, Leduc AB T9E 6M7 – 403/986-8353; Fax: 403/986-8360 – Gr. Pre.-9; Special Ed.
Lethbridge: Edu-Cater Skills Centre, PO Box 1446, Lethbridge AB T1J 4K2 – 403/381-7768 – Gr. 1-12; Special Ed.
Lethbridge: Immanuel Christian School, 802 - 6 Ave. North, Lethbridge AB T1H 0S1 – 403/328-4783; Fax: 403/328-4082 – Gr. Pre.-12; Special Ed.
Lethbridge Christian School, 2010 - 5 Ave. North, Lethbridge AB T1H 0N5 – 403/320-0677; Fax: 403/320-0828 – Gr. Pre.-12
Lethbridge: Taber Christian School, 802 - 6 Ave. North, Lethbridge AB T1H 0S1 – 403/223-4550; Fax: 403/223-4693 – Gr. Pre.-9; Special Ed.

Medicine Hat Christian School, 68 Rice Dr. SE, Medicine Hat AB T1B 3X2 – 403/526-3246; Fax: 403/528-9048 – Gr. Pre.-9
Monarch: Calvin Christian School, PO Box 40, Monarch AB T0L 1M0 – 403/381-3030; Fax: 403/381-4241 – Gr. Pre.-12; Special Ed.
Neerlandia: Covenant Canadian Reformed School, PO Box 67, Neerlandia AB T0G 1R0 – 403/674-4774; Fax: 403/674-4774 – Gr. 1-11; Special Ed.
Okotoks: Strathcona-Tweedsmuir School, RR#2, Okotoks AB T0L 1T0 – 403/938-4431; Fax: 403/938-4492 – Gr. 1-12
Olds Koinonia Christian School, PO Box 4039, Olds AB T4H 1P7 – 403/556-4038; Fax: 403/556-4038 – Gr. Pre.-12
Ponoka: Mamawi Atosketan Native School, RR#4, Ponoka AB T4J 1R4 – 403/783-4362 – Gr. Pre.-9
Ponoka Christian School, 6300 - 50 St., Ponoka AB T4J 1E6 – 403/783-6563; Fax: 403/783-6687 – Gr. Pre.-9
Red Deer: Koinonia Christian School of Red Deer, 6014 - 57 Ave., Red Deer AB T4N 4S9 – 403/346-1818; Fax: 403/347-3013 – Gr. Pre.-12
Red Deer Christian School, 14 McVicar St., Red Deer AB T4N 0M1 – 403/346-5795; Fax: 403/347-3003 – Gr. Pre.-9
Red Deer: Word of Life School Society, RR#4, Site 4, PO Box 30, Red Deer AB T4N 5E4 – 403/343-6510; Fax: 403/343-8480 – Gr. Pre.-12
Rimbey Christian School, PO Box 90, Rimbey AB T0C 2J0 – 403/843-3904; Fax: 403/843-3904 – Gr. Pre.-10; Special Ed.
Rocky Christian School, 5204 - 54 Ave., Rocky Mountain House AB T0M 1T3 – 403/845-3516; Fax: 403/845-4370 – Principal, William Slofstra – Gr. Pre.-9; Spec. Ed.
Sherwood Park: Alberta Boscoe Homes, PO Box 4100, Sherwood Park AB T8A 2A7 – 403/922-4790; Fax: 403/449-3344 – Gr. 1-11; Special Ed.
Sherwood Park: German School Edelweiss-MacDonald, #253, 51308 RR#224, Sherwood Park AB T8C 1H3 – 403/922-3665; Fax: 403/922-3665 – Gr. 1-12
Sherwood Park: Strathcona Christian Academy, 1011 Cloverbar Rd., Sherwood Park AB T8A 4V7 – 403/464-7127; Fax: 403/467-1454 – Gr. Pre.-9
Siksika: Old Sun Community College, PO Box 1250, Siksika AB T0J 3W0 – 403/264-9658; Fax: 403/734-5110 – Gr. 10-12; Evening Credit
Spruce Grove: Living Waters Christian Academy, 5 Grove Dr. West, Spruce Grove AB T7X 3X8 – 403/962-3331; Fax: 403/962-3958 – Gr. Pre.-9
Stony Plain: St. John's School of Alberta, RR#5, Stony Plain AB T7Z 1X5 – 403/429-4140; Fax: 403/848-2395 – Gr. 7-12
Stony Plain: St. Matthew Lutheran School, 5014 - 53 Ave., Stony Plain AB T7Z 1R8 – 403/963-2715; Fax: 403/963-7324 – Gr. Pre.-9
Three Hills: Prairie Elementary School, c/o Prairie Bible Institute, PO Box 4000, Three Hills AB T0M 2N0 – 403/443-5511; Fax: 403/443-5540 – Gr. Pre.-6; Special Ed.
Three Hills: Prairie High School, c/o Prairie Bible Institute, PO Box 4000, Three Hills AB T0M 2N0 – 403/443-5536; Fax: 403/443-7005 – Gr. 10-12
Three Hills: Prairie Junior High, c/o Prairie Bible Institute, PO Box 4000, Three Hills AB T0M 2N0 – 403/443-5511; Fax: 403/443-5125 – Gr. 7-9
Vegreville: Ivan Franko Ukrainian School, 5234 - 45B Ave., Vegreville AB T9C 1L3 – 403/632-4907 – Gr. 8-12

BRITISH COLUMBIA

Ministry of Education
Parliament Bldgs., Victoria BC V8V 2M4
250/356-2500; Fax: 250/356-5945
Minister, Hon. Moe Sihota

CURRICULUM INFORMATION
Technology, Distance Learning & Continuing Education Branch, Dr. B. Carbol, 604/326-2326
Acting Director, Curriculum Development Branch, David Williams, 604/356-2317

For detailed departmental listings, see Index: "Education, Depts."

SCHOOL DISTRICTS

The British Columbia Ministry of Education has set up 75 School Districts in the province, each managed by a Superintendent. Elections for school trustees are held in November throughout the Province. Enrollment figures shown below are from the 1995/96 academic year. Included in the school district figures are students at containment centres (institutions operating under the Ministry of the Attorney General); students in provincial resource programs (provide services to students with special needs); alternate programs offered at facilities such as rehabilitation centres; correspondence regional schools.

Districts with an enrollment of more than 10,000 are in bold print.

Abbotsford School District #34
  2790 Tims St., Clearbook BC V2T 4M7
  604/859-4891; Fax: 604/852-8587
  *17,520
  Supt., Dr. Robin Arden
  Sec.-Treas., Hugh Finlayson
Agassiz-Harrison School District #76 – *988
  PO Box 69, Agassiz BC V0M 1A0
  604/796-2225; Fax: 604/796-2767 – Supt., Jim Latham; Sec.-Treas., Ken Mackie
Alberni School District #70 – *6,354
  4690 Roger St., Port Alberni BC V9Y 3Z4
  250/723-3565; Fax: 250/723-0318 – Supt., Gary Murton; Sec.-Treas., Robert Kanngiesser
Armstrong-Spallumcheen School District #21 – *2,054
  PO Box 430, Armstrong BC V0E 1B0
  250/546-3031; Fax: 250/546-3161 – Supt., Ron Samborski; Sec.-Treas., John Reid
Arrow Lakes School District #10 – *929
  PO Box 340, Nakusp BC V0G 1R0
  250/265-3638; Fax: 250/265-3701 – Supt., Dan Russell; Sec.-Treas., Vic Pirie
Bulkley Valley School District #54 – *3,132
  PO Box 758, Smithers BC V0J 2N0
  250/847-3261; Fax: 250/847-4276 – Supt., A.W. Cooper; Sec.-Treas., Jim Floris
Burnaby School District #41
  5325 Kincaid St., Burnaby BC V5G 1W2
  604/664-8441; Fax: 604/664-8382
  *23,282
  Supt., Dr. Elmer Froese
  Sec.-Treas., Robert Ingram
Burns Lake School District #55 – *1,636
  PO Box 2000, Burns Lake BC V0J 1E0
  250/692-7141; Fax: 250/692-7145 – Supt. & Sec.-Treas., Jerry Smit
Campbell River School District #72 – *7,874
  425 Pinecrest Rd., Campbell River BC V9W 3P2
  250/286-0651; Fax: 250/287-2616 – Supt., Brendan Croskery; Sec.-Treas., Murray Ruehlen
Cariboo-Chilcotin School District #27 – *9,411
  350 - 2 Ave. North, Williams Lake BC V2G 1Z9
  250/398-3800; Fax: 250/392-3600 – Supt., Brian Butcher; Sec.-Treas., Andrew. Sullivan
Castlegar School District #9 – *2,522
  865 Columbia Ave., Castlegar BC V1N 1H3
  250/365-7731; Fax: 250/365-3817 – Supt., Everette Surgenor; Sec.-Treas., Bill Babakaiff
Central Coast School District #49 – *422
  PO Box 130, Hagensborg BC V0T 1H0
  250/982-2691; Fax: 250/982-2319 – Supt., Walter Robinson; Sec.-Treas., Duncan Morgan
Central Okanagan School District #23
  1940 Haynes Rd., Kelowna BC V1X 5X7
  250/860-8888; Fax: 250/860-9799
  *21,762
  Supt. of Schools, Ron. Rubadeau
  Sec.-Treas., Harvey Peatman
Chilliwack School District #33
  46361 Yale Rd. East, Chilliwack BC V2P 2P9
  604/792-1321; Fax: 604/792-9665
  *10,994
  Supt., Phil Halladay
  Sec.-Treas., Don Murray
Comox Valley School District #71
  607 Cumberland Rd., Courtenay BC V9N 7G5
  250/334-5500; Fax: 250/334-4472
  *10,189
  Supt., Bruce Thompson
  Sec.-Treas., William A. Burns
Coquitlam School District #43
  550 Poirier St., Coquitlam BC V3J 6A7
  604/939-9201; Fax: 604/939-6400
  *30,566
  Supt., Tom Harris
  Sec.-Treas., Peter Boyle
Cowichan School District #65 – *9,372
  2557 Beverly St., Duncan BC V9L 2X3
  250/748-0321; Fax: 250/748-6591 – Supt., Geoff Johnson; Sec.-Treas., William Brown
Cranbrook School District #2 – *4,694
  940 Industrial Rd. No. 1, Cranbrook BC V1C 4C6
  250/426-4201; Fax: 250/489-5460 – Supt., George Watson; Sec.-Treas., Robert Norum
Creston-Kaslo School District #86 – *2,635
  PO Box 250, Creston BC V0B 1G0
  250/428-2217; Fax: 250/428-4990 – Supt., D. MacKinlay; Sec.-Treas., Dave Douglas
Delta School District #37
  4629 - 51 St., Delta BC V4K 2V9
  604/946-4101; Fax: 604/946-3910
  *18,231
  Supt., Dr. Rod A. Wickstrom
  Sec.-Treas., Steven Pillar
Distance Education District #101 – *8,498
  Ministry of Education, Victoria BC V8V 4W6
  250/387-4311; Fax: 250/387-1452
Fernie School District #1 – *3,332
  PO Box 160, Fernie BC V0B 1M0
  250/423-4631; Fax: 250/423-7277 – Supt., Roy McLean; Sec.-Treas., Elaine Sabo
Fort Nelson School District #81 – *1,305
  PO Box 87, Fort Nelson BC V0C 1R0
  250/774-2591; Fax: 250/774-2598 – Supt. & Sec.-Treas., Anne Cooper
Golden School District #18 – *1,587
  PO Box 1110, Golden BC V0A 1H0
  250/344-5241; Fax: 250/344-6052 – Supt., Anita Ure; Sec.-Treas., Terry Kirkham
Grand Forks School District #12 – *1,703
  PO Box 640, Grand Forks BC V0H 1H0
  250/442-8258; Fax: 250/442-8800 – Supt., Denny Kemprud; Sec.-Treas., Woody Kehler
Greater Victoria School District #61
  PO Box 700, Victoria BC V8W 2R1
  250/475-3212; Fax: 250/475-4110
  *23,999
  Sec.-Treas., Robert Whitmore
Gulf Islands School District #64 – *1,834
  112 Rainbow Road, Salt Spring Island BC V8K 2K3
  250/537-5548; Fax: 250/537-4200 – Supt., Dr. Michael Marshall; Sec.-Treas., Ken Starling
Haida Gwaii - Queen Charlotte School District #50 – *1,150
  PO Box 69, Queen Charlotte City BC V0T 1S0
  250/559-8471; Fax: 250/559-8849 – Supt. & Sec.-Treas., William Roper
Hope School District #32 – *1,634
  PO Bag 3200, Hope BC V0X 1L0
  604/869-2411; Fax: 604/869-7400 – Supt., Keith Lanphear; Sec.-Treas., Ken Campbell
Howe Sound School District #48 – *4,351
  PO Box 250, Squamish BC V0N 3G0
  604/892-5228; Fax: 604/892-1038 – Supt., Douglas Courtice; Sec.-Treas., Nancy Edwards
Kamloops School District #24
  1383 - 9 Ave., Kamloops BC V2C 3X7
  250/374-0679; Fax: 250/372-2731
  *17,057
  Supt., T.D. Grieve
  Sec.-Treas., Jim Sheldon
Keremeos School District #16 – *701
  PO Box 10, Keremeos BC V0X 1N0
  250/499-5825; Fax: 250/499-5866 – Supt., Dan Cairnie; Sec.-Treas., Gina Nixon
Kettle Valley School District #13 – *653
  PO Box 640, Midway BC V0H 1M0
  250/449-2300; Fax: 250/449-2277 – Supt., Brian Fichter; Sec.-Treas., Beverly Smith
Kimberley School District #3 – *1,766
  PO Box 70, Kimberley BC V1A 2Y5
  250/427-2245; Fax: 250/427-2044 – Supt., Gary Doi; Sec.-Treas., Russell Horswill
Kitimat School District #80 – *2,439
  1515 Kingfisher Ave. North, Kitimat BC V8C 1S5
  250/639-9161; Fax: 250/632-4363 – Supt., Sharon Beedle; Sec.-Treas., Ron Bernt
Lake Cowichan School District #66 – *1,239
  21 Oak Lane, PO Box 10, Lake Cowichan BC V0R 2G0
  250/749-6636; Fax: 250/749-3543 – Supt. & Sec.-Treas., Brian Hoole
Langley School District #35
  4875 - 222 St., Langley BC V3A 3Z7
  604/534-7891; Fax: 604/533-1115
  *20,122
  Supt., Susan Everett
  Sec.-Treas., Don Dunaway
Lillooet School District #29 – *1,117
  PO Box 820, Lillooet BC V0K 1V0
  250/256-4282; Fax: 250/256-7848 – Supt., William Sturn; Sec.-Treas., Joan Norton
Maple Ridge School District #42
  22225 Brown Ave., Maple Ridge BC V2X 8N6
  604/463-4200; Fax: 604/463-4181
  *13,916
  Supt., D. Therrien
  Sec.-Treas., Adam Andruschak
Merritt School District #31 – *2,288
  Bag 4100, Merritt BC V0K 2B0
  250/378-2022; Fax: 250/378-6263 – Supt., Mike Henderson; Sec.-Treas., H. Bruce Tisdale
Mission School District #75 – *7,162
  33046 - 4 Ave., Mission BC V2V 1S5
  604/826-6286; Fax: 604/826-4517 – Supt., Keith Cameron; Sec.-Treas., Guy Bonnefoy
Nanaimo School District #68
  395 Wakesiah Ave., Nanaimo BC V9R 3K6
  250/754-5521; Fax: 250/741-5309
  *17,048
  Supt., Jim Dyck
  Sec.-Treas., Dean Cooper
Nechako School District #56 – *3,975
  PO Drawer 129, Vanderhoof BC V0J 3A0
  250/567-2284; Fax: 250/567-4639 – Supt. & Sec.-Treas., Louise Burgart
Nelson School District #7 – *4,272
  308 Anderson St., Nelson BC V1L 3Y2
  250/352-6681; Fax: 250/352-6686 – Supt., Don Truscott; Sec.-Treas., Ben Martin

Canadian Almanac & Directory 1997

BRITISH COLUMBIA — UNIVERSITIES

New Westminster School District #40 – *5,930
821 - 8th St., New Westminster BC V3M 3S9
604/527-8240; Fax: 604/522-6653 – Supt., Tom Rothney; Sec.-Treas., Charles T. Condon
Nisga'a School District #92 – *550
2500 Tait Ave., New Aiyansh BC V0J 1A0
250/633-2228; Fax: 250/633-2425 – Supt., Alvin McKay; Sec.-Treas., Alvin Azak
North Thompson School District #26 – *1,199
PO Box 1314, Clearwater BC V0E 1N0
250/674-3313; Fax: 250/674-2508 – Supt., Nancy Wells Nelson; Sec.-Treas., Sterling Olson

North Vancouver School District #44
721 Chesterfield Ave., North Vancouver BC V7M 2M5
604/987-8141; Fax: 604/987-7154
*18,365
Supt., Dr. Robin Brayne
Sec.-Treas., Leonard Berg

Peace River North School District #60 – *5,615
9803 - 102 St., Fort St. John BC V1J 4B3
250/785-6785; Fax: 250/787-0461 – Supt., Wayne Cheesman; Sec.-Treas., Edna Barber
Peace River South School District #59 – *6,025
929 - 106 Ave., Dawson Creek BC V1G 2N9
250/782-8571; Fax: 250/782-3204 – Supt., C.G. Parslow; Sec.-Treas., Cathy Esselink
Penticton School District #15 – *6,067
425 Jermyn Ave., Penticton BC V2A 1Z4
250/492-2721; Fax: 250/492-2295 – Supt., Stewart R. Ladymar; Sec.-Treas., Frank Regehr
Powell River School District #47 – *3,459
4351 Ontario Ave., Powell River BC V8A 1V3
604/485-6271; Fax: 604/485-6435 – Supt., Mike Heron; Sec.-Treas., E.A. Byng

Prince George School District #57
1894 - 9 Ave., Prince George BC V2M 1L7
250/561-6800; Fax: 250/561-6801
*20,435
Supt., Phil Redmond
Sec.-Treas., Bryan Mix

Prince Rupert School District #52 – *4,016
634 - 6 Ave. East, Prince Rupert BC V8J 1X1
250/624-6717; Fax: 250/624-6517 – Supt., Bob David; Sec.-Treas., Walt Dallamore
Princeton School District #17 – *879
PO Box 460, Princeton BC V0X 1W0
250/295-6914; Fax: 250/295-7727 – Supt., Victor Dikaitis; Sec.-Treas., Marcel Georges
Qualicum School District #69 – *4,193
499 West Island Hwy., PO Box 430, Parksville BC V9P 2G5
250/248-4241; Fax: 250/248-5767 – Supt., John C. Moss; Sec.-Treas., Daniel Whiting
Quesnel School District #28 – *5,573
401 North Star Rd., Quesnel BC V2J 5K2
250/992-8802; Fax: 250/992-7652 – Supt., Ed Napier; Sec.-Treas., Tim Klotz
Revelstoke School District #19 – *1,865
PO Bag 5800, Revelstoke BC V0E 2S0
250/837-2101; Fax: 250/837-9335 – Supt., Tom Williams; Sec.-Treas., Bruce Buchannon

Richmond School District #38
7811 Granville Ave., Richmond BC V6Y 3E3
604/668-6000; Fax: 604/668-6006
*23,931
Supt., Chris Kelly
Sec.-Treas., K.L. Morris

Saanich School District #63 – *8,689
2125 Keating Cross Rd., Saanichton BC V8M 2A5
250/652-7300; Fax: 250/652-6421 – Supt., Hank Stefaniak; Sec.-Treas., Bruce Hunt
Shuswap School District #89 – *6,800
PO Box 129, Salmon Arm BC V1E 4N2
250/832-2157; Fax: 250/832-9428 – Supt., Doug Pearson; Sec.-Treas., Bernard Dogterom
Sooke School District #62 – *9,363
3143 Jacklin Rd., Victoria BC V9B 5R1

* indicates enrollment figure.

250/474-9800; Fax: 250/474-9825 – Supt., Leo J. Chaland; Sec.-Treas., David Lockyer
South Cariboo School District #30 – *1,388
PO Box 250, Ashcroft BC V0K 1A0
250/453-9101; Fax: 250/453-2425 – Supt., John Wiens; Sec.-Treas., Alan Franks
Southern Okanagan School District #14 – *2,638
Bag 5000, Oliver BC V0H 1T0
250/498-3481; Fax: 250/498-4070 – Supt., Hart Doerksen; Sec.-Treas., Terry P. Killough
Stikine School District #87 – *434
PO Box 190, Dease Lake BC V0C 1L0
250/771-4440; Fax: 250/771-4441 – Supt. & Sec.-Treas., Garry Roth
Summerland School District #77 – *2,044
PO Box 339, Summerland BC V0H 1Z0
250/494-7511; Fax: 250/494-3766 – Supt., Larry Thomas; Sec.-Treas., Kelly Grittner
Sunshine Coast School District #46 – *4,072
PO Box 220, Gibsons BC V0N 1V0
604/886-8811; Fax: 604/886-4652 – Supt., Clifford Smith; Sec.-Treas., Tim Anderson

Surrey School District #36
14225 - 56 Ave., Surrey BC V3X 3A3
604/596-7733; Fax: 604/597-0191
*53,380
Supt., Dr. Fred Renihan
Sec.-Treas., J. Leigh Anderson

Terrace School District #88 – *5,608
3211 Kenney St., Terrace BC V8G 3E9
250/635-4931; Fax: 250/635-4287 – Supt., F.M. Hamilton; Sec.-Treas., Barry Piersdorff
Trail School District #11 – *3,713
2079 Columbia Ave., Trail BC V1R 1K7
250/368-6434; Fax: 250/364-2470 – Supt., Pat Dooley; Sec.-Treas., G. Ivan Bell
Vancouver Island North School District #85 – *3,032
PO Box 90, Port Hardy BC V0N 2P0
250/949-6618; Fax: 250/949-8792 – Supt., Larry Naidoo; Sec.-Treas., John R. Martin
Vancouver Island West School District #84 – *939
PO Box 100, Gold River BC V0P 1G0
250/283-2241; Fax: 250/283-7352 – Supt., Andris Freimanis; Sec.-Treas., Kevin Cormack

Vancouver School District #39
1595 - 10 Ave. West, Vancouver BC V6J 1Z8
604/731-1131; Fax: 604/736-8564
*61,569
Supt., Allan Mcleod
Sec.-Treas., Dave Yuen

Vernon School District #22
1401 - 15 St., Vernon BC V1T 8S8
250/542-3331; Fax: 250/549-9200
*10,308
Supt., Michael McAvoy
Sec.-Treas., David Greenan

West Vancouver School District #45 – *6,573
1075 - 21 St., West Vancouver BC V7V 4A9
604/981-1000; Fax: 604/981-1001 – Supt., Doug Player; Sec.-Treas., Len Archer
Windermere School District #4 – *1,575
PO Box 430, Invermere BC V0A 1K0
250/342-6313; Fax: 250/342-6966 – Supt., Dick Chambers; Sec.-Treas., Cameron Dow

CORRESPONDENCE SCHOOLS

Central Interior Distance Education, 1788 Diefenbaker Ave., PO Box 7400, Prince George BC V2N 4V7 – 250/563-1818; Fax: 250/563-1150 – Principal, Harry Hufty – *459
Greater Vancouver Distance Education, 530 - 41st Ave. East, Vancouver BC V5W 1P3 – 604/660-7947; Fax: 604/660-5042 – Principal, Judy Dallas – *2,009
Kootenay Distance Education, 570 Johnstone Rd., RR#1, Nelson BC V1L 5P4 – 250/354-4311; Fax: 250/354-6629 – Principal, Bob McLure – *691
North Coast Distance Education, 3211 Kenney St., PO Box 5000, Terrace BC V8G 5K2 – 250/635-7944;

Fax: 250/638-3649 – Principal, Joe Vander Kwaak – *338
North Island Distance Education, 2080 Wallace Ave., Comox BC V9N 1W9 – 250/339-6119; Fax: 250/339-5555 – Principal, John Anderson – *842
Northern BC Distance Education, 10704 - 97th Ave., Fort St. John BC V1L 6L7 – 250/785-1333; Fax: 250/785-1188 – Principal, Chuck Froese – *445
Okanagan Distance Education, 2475 Merritt Ave., PO Box 4700, Merritt BC V0K 2B0 – 250/378-1440; Fax: 250/378-1447 – Principal, Paul Montgomery – *1,573
South Island Distance Education, 4575 Wilkinson Rd., Victoria BC V8Z 7E8 – 250/479-6839; Fax: 250/479-9870 – Principal, Gregory Bunyan – *1,198

SCHOOL FOR THE HEARING IMPAIRED
Provincial School for the Deaf
c/o Burnaby South Secondary School, 5455 Rumble St., Burnaby BC V5J 2B7 – 604/664-8560; Fax: 604/664-8561 – Principal, Provincial Program for the Deaf, John Anderson

UNIVERSITIES

Royal Roads University
2005 Sooke Rd., Victoria BC V9B 5Y2
250/391-2511; Fax: 250/391-2500; Toll Free: 1-800-788-8028; URL: http://www.royalroads.ca
President, Gerald Kelly
Exec. Asst. to President/Board Secretary, Lyla Smith
Vice-President, Administration, Nick Rubidge

Simon Fraser University
Burnaby BC V5A 1S6
604/291-4641; Fax: 604/291-4860; URL: http://www.sfu.ca/
Chancellor, Joseph Segal, LL.D.
President & Vice-Chancellor, John O. Stubbs, B.A., M.Sc., D.Phil.
Vice-President, Academic & Provost, David P. Gagan, B.A., M.A., Ph.D.
Vice-President, Finance & Administration, Roger Ward, B.Sc., M.Sc., Ph.D.
Vice-President, Research, Bruce P. Clayman, B.Sc., M.Sc., Ph.D.
Vice-President, Harbour Centre & Continuing Studies, Jack P. Blaney, B.Ed., M.Ed., Ed.D.
Assoc. Vice-President, Academic, Judith Osborne, LL.B., M.A., LL.M.
Executive Director, External Relations, Gregg Macdonald, B.A., M.A.
Executive Director, University Development, Meg Clarke, B.A., M.A.
Registrar & Dean, Student Services, W. Ronald Heath, B.S.A.
University Librarian, Theodore (Ted) C. Dobb, B.A., B.L.S.
Manager, Purchasing Services, R. Szczotko
Director, Bookstore, Biff Savoie, B.A.

FACULTIES WITH DEANS
Applied Sciences, Ronald Marteniuk, B.P.E., M.A., Ph.D.
Arts, Evan Alderson, B.A., M.A., Ph.D.
Business Administration, Stanley J. Shapiro, A.B., M.B.A., Ph.D.
Education, Robin Barrow, B.A., Cert.Ed., Ph.D.
Graduate Studies, Bruce P. Clayman, B.Sc., Ph.D.
Science, Colin H.W. Jones, B.Sc., Ph.D.

Trinity Western University
7600 Glover Rd., Langley BC V3A 6H4
604/888-7511; Fax: 604/888-5336; URL: http://www.twu.ca
Director, Admissions, Cam Lee
Director, Finance, Harvey Ouellette

Canadian Almanac & Directory 1997

Director, Libraries, David A. Twiest, B.A., M.A., M.R.E.
President, R. Neil Snider, B.A., B.Ed., M.Ed., Ph.D.
Registrar, R. Orville Lyttle, B.A., M.A., M.A. (Ed.)
Vice-President & Dean, Academic Affairs, Donald Page, B.A., M.A., Ph.D.
Assoc. Academic Dean, Deane E.D. Downey, B.A., M.A., Ph.D.
Vice-President, Development, Ron Kuehl, B.A.
Vice-President, Student Affairs, Thomas F. Bulick, Th.B., M.A., Ph.M.
Vice-President, University Advancement, Guy S. Saffold, B.Sc., M.Div., Ed.D.
Executive Assistant & University Secretary, Glen C. Forrester, B.Sc., M.Sc.
Vice-President, University Enterprises, Lou Sawchenko, B.R.E., M.A., Ph.D.

FACULTIES WITH DEANS
Arts & Religious Studies, Philip Wiebe, B.A., M.A., Ph.D.
Business & Economics, John Sutherland, B.Comm., M.B.A., M.A.
Graduate Studies, Donald Page, B.A., M.A., Ph.D
Natural & Applied Sciences, John D. Van Dyke, B.Sc., Ph.D.
Social Sciences & Education, Harro Van Brummelen, B.Sc., M.Ed., Ed.D.

AFFILIATED COLLEGES
The Associated Canadian Theological Colleges of Trinity Western University, 7600 Glover Rd., Langley BC V3A 6H4 – 604/888-7511; Fax: 604/888-5729 – Coordinator, Guy Saffold, B.Sc., M.Div., Ed.D.
Canadian Baptist Seminary, 7600 Glover Rd., Langley BC V3A 6H4 – 604/888-1265; Fax: 604/888-5729 – President, Barrie Palfreyman, B.Ed., M.Ed., M.Min., Ed.D.
Northwest Baptist Theologic College & Seminary, PO Box 790, Langley BC V3A 8B8 – 604/888-3310 – Acting President, Donald Launstein, B.A., Th.M., Th.D.
Trinity Western Seminary, 7600 Glover Rd., Langley BC V3A 6H4 – 604/888-6158; Fax: 604/888-5729 – President, R.N. Snider, B.A., B.Ed., M.Ed., Ph.D

University of British Columbia
Vancouver BC V6T 1Z2
604/822-2211; Telex: 04-51233; URL: http://view.ubc.ca:80/
Visitor, The Hon. David C. Lam, Lt. Governor of British Columbia
Chancellor, William L. Sauder, B.Comm., LL.D.
President, David W. Strangway, M.A., Ph.D., P.Eng., F.R.A.S., F.R.S.C., D.Litt.S.
Vice-President, Academic & Provost, Daniel Birch, B.A., M.A., Ph.D.
Vice-President, Administration & Finance, Terry E. Sumner, C.A.
Vice-President, External Affairs, Peter W. Ufford
Vice-President, Research, B.H. Bressler, B.Sc., M.Sc., Ph.D.
Vice-President, Student & Academic Services, M.M. Klawe, B.Sc., Ph.D.

FACULTIES WITH DEANS
Agricultural Sciences, J.F. Richards, B.Sc., M.Sc., Ph.D., P.Ag.
Applied Science, Axel Meisen, B.Sc., M.Sc., Ph.D., A.C.G.C., F.C.I.C., P.Eng.
Arts, Shirley Neuman, B.A., M.A., Ph.D.
Commerce & Business Administration, M.A. Goldberg, B.A., M.A., Ph.D.
Dentistry, Edwin H.K. Yen, D.D.S., Dip.Ortho., Ph.D.
Education, Nancy Sheehan, B.A., B.Ed., M.Ed., Ph.D.
Forestry, C.S Binkley, A.B., M.S., Ph.D.
Graduate Studies, Frieda Granot, B.Sc., M.Sc., Ph.D.
Law, C. Lynn Smith, B.A., LL.B.
Medicine, John A. Cairns, M.D., F.R.C.P.C.
Pharmaceutical Sciences, Frank S. Abbott, B.S.P., M.S., Ph.D.
Science, B.C. McBride, M.Sc., Ph.D.

DIRECTORS & OTHER OFFICERS
Registrar, R.A. Spencer, B.E., Ph.D., P.Eng.
Athletics & Sport Services, Robert Philip, B.Ed., M.A.
Bookstore, Debbie Harvey
Centre for Continuing Education, Walter Uegama, Ph.D.
Ceremonies & Community Relations, Charles E. Slonecker, D.D.S., Ph.D.
Counselling & Resource Centre, Mary Stott
Extra-sessional Studies, Kenneth Slade, M.Ed., Ph.D.
Financial Services, Jacqueline Rice
Purchasing, K. Bowler
University Computing Services, J. Leigh, M.Sc., C.D.P.

SCHOOLS WITH DIRECTORS
Architecture, Sanford Hirshen, A.B., B.Arch., M.Arch., F.A.I.A.
Audiology & Speech Sciences, Judith R. Johnston, B.A., M.A., Ph.D.
Community & Regional Planning, William E. Rees, B.Sc., Ph.D.
Family & Nutritional Sciences, Margaret Arcus, B.Sc., M.Ed., Ph.D.
Principal, Green College, Richard Ericson
Library, Archival & Information Studies, Kenneth Haycock, B.A., M.Ed., A.M.L.S., Ed.D.
Music, Jesse Read, B.Mus., M.Mus.
Nursing, Kathryn May, B.S.N., M.S., D.NSc.
Physical Education & Recreation, Robert W. Schutz, B.P.E., M.Sc., Ph.D.
Rehabilitation Sciences, Angelo Belcastro, B.A., B.Sc., M.Sc., Ph.D.
Social Work, Elaine Stolar, B.A., M.S.W., M.A.

AFFILIATED COLLEGES
Regent College, 5800 University Blvd., Vancouver BC V6T 2ET – 604/224-3245 – Walter C. Wright, Jr., B.A., M.Div., Ph.D.
St. Mark's College (Roman Catholic), 5935 Iona Dr., Vancouver BC V6T 1J7 – 604/822-4463 – Rev. Paul C. Burns, C.S.B., B.A., S.T.B., M.A., B.Litt., Ph.D.

University of Northern British Columbia
3333 University Way, PO Box 1950, Prince George BC V2N 4Z9
250/960-5555; Fax: 250/960-5794; URL: http://www.unbc.edu
President, Geoffrey Weller
Vice-President, Academic, Ken Coates
Secretary to the Board of Governors, Wendy Fletcher
Director, Communications, Clive Keen
Director, University Development, Michael Hamer
University Librarian, Pat Appavoo

FACULTIES WITH DEANS
Arts & Sciences, Dr. Robin Fisher
Health & Human Sciences, Dr. David Fish
Management & Administration, Dr. Doug Nord
Natural Resources & Environmental Studies, Dr. Fred Gilbert
Research & Graduate Studies, Dr. Bill Morrison

University of Victoria
PO Box 1700, Victoria BC V8W 2Y2
250/721-7211; Fax: 250/721-6223; URL: http://www.uvic.ca
Chancellor, Robert G. Rogers, O.C., K.St.J., C.D., O.B.C.
President & Vice-Chancellor, David F. Strong, B.Sc., M.Sc., Ph.D., F.R.S.C.
Vice-President, Academic & Provost, Penelope W. Codding, B.S., Ph.D.
Vice-President, Finance & Operations, J. Donald Rowlatt, B.Comm., Ph.D., Bursar
University Secretary, Sheila Sheldon Collyer, B.A.
Administrative Registrar, D. Cledwyn Thomas, B.A.
Director, Public Relations & Information Services, Bruce Kilpatrick, B.A.

FACULTIES WITH DEANS
Arts & Science, John A. Schofield, B.A., M.B.A., Ph.D.
Business, Roger N. Wolff, B.Sc., M.B.A., D.B.A.
Education, Bruce L. Howe, Dip.Ed., B.S., M.S., Ph.D.
Engineering, James W. Provan, B.Sc., M.Sc., Ph.D., O.I.Q.
Fine Arts, Anthony Welch, B.A., M.A., Ph.D.
Graduate Studies, Gordana Lazarevich, Artist & Licentiate Dip., B.Sc., M.Sc., Ph.D.
Human & Social Development, Anita E. Molzahn, B.Sc., M.N., Ph.D.
Humanities, G.R. Ian MacPherson, B.A., M.A., Ph.D.
Law, David S. Cohen, B.Sc., LL.B., LL.M.
Acting Dean, Science, Terence E. Gough, B.Sc., Ph.D., F.C.I.C.
Social Sciences, John A.. Schofield, B.A., M.B.A., M.A., Ph.D.

COMMUNITY COLLEGES

CAMOSUN COLLEGE
Lansdowne Campus, 3100 Foul Bay Rd., Victoria BC V8P 5J2
250/370-3000; Fax: 250/370-3660; URL: http://www.camosun.bc.ca
President, Dr. Elizabeth Ashton
Interurban Campus, 4461 Interurban Rd., RR#3, Victoria BC V8X 3X1 – Fax: 604/370-3750

CAPILANO COLLEGE
2055 Purcell Way, North Vancouver BC V7J 3H5
604/986-1911; Fax: 604/984-4985; Email: glee@capcollege.bc.ca; URL: http://www.capcollege.bc.ca/
President, Greg Lee, Ph.D.

COLLEGE OF NEW CALEDONIA
3330 - 22 Ave., Prince George BC V2N 1P8
250/562-2131; Fax: 250/561-5816
President, Dr. Terence Weninger
Lakes District Campus, Hwy. 16 West, PO Box 5000, Burns Lake BC V0J 1E0 – 250/692-3175; Fax: 250/692-3809
Mackenzie Campus, Evergreen Mall, PO Box 2110, Mackenzie BC V0J 2C0 – 250/997-4333; Fax: 250/997-3779
Nechako Campus, RR#2, Vanderhoof BC V0J 3A0 – 250/567-9291; Fax: 250/567-9584
Quesnel Campus, 488 McLean St., Quesnel BC V2J 2P2 – 250/992-3906; Fax: 250/992-7876

COLLEGE OF THE ROCKIES
PO Box 8500, Cranbrook BC V1C 5L7
250/489-2751; Fax: 250/489-1790
President, William Berry Calder
Manager, Communications Services, Joan Vickers
Creston Campus, PO Box 1978, Creston BC V0B 1G0
Fernie Campus, PO Box 1770, Fernie BC V0B 1M0
Golden Campus, PO Box 376, Golden BC V0A 1H0
Invermere Campus, PO Box 960, Invermere BC V0A 1K0

DOUGLAS COLLEGE
PO Box 2503, New Westminster BC V3L 5B2
604/520-5400; Fax: 604/527-5095; URL: http://www.douglas.bc.ca/
President, Dr. Susan Hunter-Harvey

KWANTLEN UNIVERSITY COLLEGE
PO Box 9030, Surrey BC V3W 2M8
604/599-2100; Fax: 604/599-2068; URL: http://www.kwantlen.bc.ca/

President, Dr. G.B. Kilcup
Langley Campus, 20901 Langley Bypass, Langley BC V3A 8G9 – 250/599-2100; Fax: 250/599-3277
Newton Campus, 13479 - 77 Ave., Surrey BC V3W 6Y1 – 250/599-2100; Fax: 250/599-2975
Richmond Campus, 8771 Lansdowne Rd., Richmond BC V6X 3V8 – 250/599-2100; Fax: 250/599-2716
Surrey Campus, 12666 - 72 Ave., Surrey BC V3T 5H8 – 250/599-2100; Fax: 250/599-2068

MALASPINA UNIVERSITY COLLEGE
900 Fifth St., Nanaimo BC V9R 5S5
250/753-3245; Fax: 250/755-8725; URL: http://www.mala.bc.ca
President, Richard Johnston
Cowichan Campus, 222 Cowichan Way, RR#6, Duncan BC V9L 4T8 – 250/748-2591; Fax: 250/746-3529
Nanaimo Campus, 900 Fifth St., Nanaimo BC V9R 5S5 – 250/753-3245; Fax: 250/755-8725
Parksville-Qualicum Office, Box 42, 223 Mills St., Parksville BC V9P 2G3 – 250/248-9792
Powell River Campus, 3960 Selkirk, Powell River BC V8A 3C6 – 604/485-2878; Fax: 604/485-2868

NORTH ISLAND COLLEGE
2300 Ryan Rd., Courtenay BC V9N 8N6
250/334-5271; Fax: 250/334-5274; Email: nicad3.nic.bc.ca; URL: http://www.nic.bc.ca
President, Dr. M. Neil Murphy
Director, Communications & Community Liaison, Susan Toresdahl
Campbell River Regional Campus, 1480 Elm St., Campbell River BC V9W 3A6 – 250/286-8911; Fax: 250/286-8900
Comox Valley Regional Campus, 2300 Ryan Rd., Courtenay BC V9N 8N6 – 250/334-5000; Fax: 250/334-5018
Port Alberni Regional Campus, 3699 Roger St., Port Alberni BC V9Y 8E3 – 250/724-8711; Fax: 250/724-8700
Port Hardy Regional Campus, PO Box 901, Port Hardy BC V0N 2P0 – 250/949-7912; Fax: 250/949-2617

NORTHERN LIGHTS COLLEGE
11401 - 8 St., Dawson Creek BC V1G 4G2
250/782-5251; Fax: 250/782-5233; URL: http://www.nlc.bc.ca
President, J.B. Kassen, Email: jkassen@nlc.bc.ca
Director, Community Relations, C. Lorincz, 604/784-7513; Email: clorincz@nlc.bc.ca
Chetwynd Campus, PO Box 1180, Chetwynd BC V0C 1J0 – 250/788-2248; Fax: 250/788-9706 – Principal, Merlin Nichols
Dawson Creek Campus, 11401 - 8 St., Dawson Creek BC V1G 4G2 – 250/782-5251; Fax: 250/782-6069 – Principal, Carolyn Rochon
Fort Nelson Campus, PO Box 860, Fort Nelson BC V0C 1R0 – 250/774-2741; Fax: 250/774-2750 – Principal, John Boraas
Fort St. John Campus, 9820 - 120 St., PO Box 1000, Fort St. John BC V1J 6K1 – 250/785-6981; Fax: 250/785-1294 – Principal, Finola Finlay

NORTHWEST COMMUNITY COLLEGE
College Services, 5331 McConnell Ave., PO Box 726, Terrace BC V8G 4X2
250/635-6511; Fax: 250/635-3511
President, Michael Hill
Hazelton Campus, Omenica St., PO Box 338, Hazelton BC V0J 2N0 – 250/842-5291; Fax: 250/842-5813
Houston Campus, 3221 - 14 St., PO Box 1277, Houston BC V0J 1Z0 – 250/845-7266; Fax: 250/845-3521
Kitimat Campus, 606 Mountainview Sq., Kitimat BC V8C 2N2 – 250/632-4766; Fax: 250/632-5069
Masset Campus, PO Box 289, Masset BC V0T 1M0 – 250/626-3627; Fax: 250/626-3699
Nass Campus, c/o Nisga'a Tribal Council, General Delivery, New Aiyansh BC V0J 1A0 – 250/633-2292; Fax: 250/633-2463
Prince Rupert Campus, 130 - 1 Ave. West, Prince Rupert BC V8J 1A8 – 250/624-6054; Fax: 250/624-4920
Queen Charlotte Islands Campus, PO Box 67, Queen Charlotte City BC V0T 1S0 – 250/559-8222; Fax: 250/559-8219
Smithers Campus, 3966 - 2 Ave., PO Box 3606, Smithers BC V0J 2N0 – 250/847-4461; Fax: 250/847-4568
Stewart Campus, c/o Stewart Secondary School, PO Box 919, Stewart BC V0T 1W0 – 250/636-9184; Fax: 250/636-2770
Terrace Campus, 5331 McConnell Ave., Terrace BC V8G 4X2 – 250/635-6511; Fax: 250/638-5432

OKANAGAN UNIVERSITY COLLEGE
3333 College Way, Kelowna BC V1V 1V7
250/762-5445; Fax: 250/470-6004; URL: http://www.okanagan.bc.ca/
President, W.D. Bowering, 604/470-6026
Information Officer, Garry Gaudet, 604/862-5662; Fax: 604/862-5476
Penticton Campus, 583 Hastings Ave., Penticton BC V2A 8E1 – 250/492-4305; Fax: 250/492-5355 – Centre Director, Allan Markin
Salmon Arm Campus, PO Box 189, Salmon Arm BC V1E 4N3 – 250/832-2126; Fax: 250/832-4368 – Centre Director, Clyde Tucker
Vernon Campus, 7000 College Way, Vernon BC V1B 2N5 – 250/545-7291; Fax: 250/545-3277 – Centre Director, Whitney Buggey

SELKIRK COLLEGE
301 Frank Beinder Way, PO Box 1200, Castlegar BC V1N 3J1
250/365-7292; Fax: 250/365-3929; URL: http://www.selkirk.bc.ca/
President, Leo Perra, Email: perra@selkirk.bc.ca
Nelson Campus, 2001 Silver King Rd., Nelson BC V1L 1C8 – 250/352-6601; Fax: 250/352-3180
Trail Campus, 900 Helena St., Trail BC V1R 4S6 – 250/368-5236; Fax: 250/368-4983

UNIVERSITY COLLEGE OF THE CARIBOO
PO Box 3010, Kamloops BC V2C 5N3
250/828-5000; Fax: 250/828-5086; URL: http://www.cariboo.bc.ca/
President, A.J. Wright
100 Mile House Campus, Provincial Bldg., 572 South Birch Ave., PO Box 2109, 100 Mile House BC V0K 2E0 – 250/395-3115; Fax: 250/395-2894
Merritt Campus, 1600 Voght St., PO Box 4400, Merritt BC V0K 2B0 – 250/378-2967; Fax: 250/378-8231
Williams Lake Campus, 351 Hodgson Rd., Williams Lake BC V2G 3P7 – 250/392-8000; Fax: 250/392-4984

UNIVERSITY COLLEGE OF THE FRASER VALLEY
33844 King Rd., RR#2, Abbotsford BC V2S 4N2
604/853-7441; Fax: 604/853-7558; URL: gopher://gopher.ucfv.bc.ca/
President, Dr. Peter Jones

VANCOUVER COMMUNITY COLLEGE
1155 East Broadway, Vancouver BC V5N 5T9
604/871-7171; Fax: 604/871-7200
President, J. Cruickshank
Vice-President, Education, D. Dorn
Vice-President, Educational Support Services, L. Martin
City Centre Campus, 250 West Pender St., Vancouver BC V6B 1S9 – 604/443-8300; Fax: 604/443-8588
King Edward Campus, 1155 East Broadway, Vancouver BC V5T 4N3 – 604/871-7000; Fax: 604/871-7100

TECHNICAL & VOCATIONAL INSTITUTES

BC INSTITUTE OF TECHNOLOGY
3700 Willingdon Ave., Burnaby BC V5G 3H2
604/434-3304; Fax: 604/434-6243; URL: http://www.bcit.bc.ca
Vice-President, Education, Brian Gillespie
Vice-President, Finance & Administration, Clayton E. McKinley
Vice-President, Student Services & Educational Support, Gerry Moss
President, John Watson
Burnaby Campus, 3700 Willingdon Ave., Burnaby BC V5G 3H2 – 604/434-5734
Downtown Education Centre, Vancouver BC – 250/687-4666
Pacific Marine Training Campus, 265 West Esplanade, North Vancouver BC V7M 1A5 – 604/985-0622; Fax: 604/985-2862 – Associate Dean, Capt. Roman Piechocki
Vancouver Int'l. Airport Campus, 5301 Airport Rd. South, Richmond BC V7B 1B5 – 604/278-4831

EMILY CARR INSTITUTE OF ART & DESIGN
1399 Johnston St., Vancouver BC V6H 3R9
604/844-3800; Fax: 604/844-3801; URL: http://www.eciad.bc.ca/
Acting President, Brad Campbell

JUSTICE INSTITUTE OF B.C.
715 McBride Blvd., New Westminster BC V3L 5T4
604/525-5422; Fax: 604/528-5518
President, Larry Goble

OPEN LEARNING AGENCY
4355 Mathissi Pl., Burnaby BC V5G 4S8
604/431-3000; Fax: 604/431-3333
President, Dr. Glen Farrell

POST-SECONDARY & SPECIALIZED INSTITUTIONS

ANNA WYMAN SCHOOL OF DANCE ART
1457 Marine Dr., West Vancouver BC V7T 1B8
604/926-6535

COLUMBIA ACADEMY OF RADIO, TELEVISION & RECORDING ARTS
1295 West Broadway, Vancouver BC V6H 3X8
604/736-3316; Fax: 604/731-5458
M. Hasselbach

INSTITUTE OF INDIGENOUS GOVERNMENT
342 Water St., 3rd Fl., Vancouver BC V6B 1B6
250/684-0231; Fax: 250/684-5726

LANGARA COLLEGE
100 West 49th Ave., Vancouver BC V5Y 2Z6
604/323-5511; Fax: 604/323-5555; URL: http://www.langara.bc.ca
President, Linda Holmes

LESTER B. PEARSON COLLEGE OF THE PACIFIC
RR#1, Victoria BC V9B 5T7
250/391-2411; Fax: 250/391-2412
President, Peter D. Bavinton

OUTWARD BOUND WESTERN CANADA
109, 1367 West Broadway, Vancouver BC V6H 4A9
604/737-3093; Fax: 604/737-3109; Email: ob@uniserve.com
Executive Director, Andrew Orr

TREBAS INSTITUTE
#305, 112 East 3rd Ave., Vancouver BC V5T 1C8
604/872-2666
President, David P. Leonard

VANCOUVER ART THERAPY INSTITUTE
#350, 1425 Marine Dr., West Vancouver BC V7T 1B9
604/926-9381; Fax: 604/926-5728

VANCOUVER SCHOOL OF THEOLOGY
6000 Iona Dr., Vancouver BC V6T 1L4
604/228-9031; Fax: 604/228-0189
Director, Degree Programs, The Rev. Dr. James A. McCullum
Principal, The Rev. Dr. W.J. Phillips

WESTERN PENTECOSTAL BIBLE COLLEGE
PO Box 1700, Abbotsford BC V2S 7E7
604/853-7491; Fax: 604/853-8951
President, James G. Richards

INDEDENDENT & PRIVATE SCHOOLS

Schools with enrollment of 50 or more, listed alphabetically by city.

100 Mile House: Bethel Christian Academy, PO Box 670, 100 Mile House BC V0K 2E0 – 250/395-4637 – Principal, Judith Liske – *50 – Gr. K-9

100 Mile House: Cariboo Christian School, PO Box 670, 100 Mile House BC V0K 2E0 – 250/395-4637; Fax: 250/395-4648 – Principal, Paul Brown – *67 – Gr. K.-10

Abbotsford Christian School, 35011 Old Clayburn Rd., Abbotsford BC V2S 7L7 – 604/850-5342; Fax: 604/859-2240 – Principal, Dwight L. Moodie – *1,253 – Gr. K.-12

Abbotsford: Cornerstone Christian School, 3970 Gladwin Rd., PO Box 520, Abbotsford BC V2S 5Z5 – 604/859-7867; Fax: 604/855-9367 – Principal, Ward McGowan – *442 – Gr. K.-12

Abbotsford: Dasmesh Punjabi School, 33094 South Fraser Way, Abbotsford BC V2S 2A9 – 604/852-8986; Fax: 604/852-8924 – Principal, Dalip Singh Gill – *197 – Gr. K.-8; Gen. & Sikh Studies

Abbotsford: St. Ann's School, 2767 Townline Rd., RR#8, Abbotsford BC V2S 6A9 – 604/852-1788 – Principal, Catherine Kraemer – *215 – Gr. K.-7/Learning Assistance

Abbotsford: St. James School, 2767 Townline Rd., Abbotsford BC V2S 6A9 – 604/852-1788; Fax: 604/850-5376 – Principal, Catherine Kraemer – *228 – Gr. K.-7

Abbotsford: St. John Brebeuf, 2747 Townline Rd., Abbotsford BC V2S 5E1 – 604/855-0571; Fax: 604/855-0572 – Principal, Wendell MacCormack – *214 – Gr. 8-11

Abbotsford: Valley Christian School, 1681 McCallum Rd., Abbotsford BC V2S 3M4 – 604/859-4847; Fax: 604/859-7973 – Principal, I. Cann – *61 – Gr. K.-4

Agassiz Christian School, 7571 Morrow Rd., PO Box 3230, Agassiz BC V0M 1A0 – 604/796-9310; Fax: 604/796-9519 – Principal, Henry Tuininga – *101 – Gr. K.-7

Agassiz: Seabird Island Community School, 5 Chowat Rd., PO Box 930, Agassiz BC V0M 1A0 – 604/796-3061; Fax: 604/796-3068 – Principal, Barbara Rose – *152 – Gr. 1-10

Ahousat: Maaqtusiis School, General Delivery, Ahousat BC V0R 1A0 – 250/670-9589; Fax: 250/670-9543 – Principal, Gregory Louie – *191 – Gr. 1-12

Aldergrove: Fraser Valley Adventist Academy, 26026 - 48 Ave., PO Box 249, Aldergrove BC V4W 2T8 – 604/856-7852; Fax: 604/856-1002 – Principal, Marjorie Fortney – *217 – Gr. 1-12

Alert Bay: T'Lisalagi'Lakw School, Front St., PO Box 50, Alert Bay BC V0N 1A0 – 250/974-5591; Fax: 250/974-5900 – Principal, Evangeline Kuzio – *91 – Gr. K.-7

Armstrong: North Okanagan Junior Academy, RR#3, C9 Evan Site, Armstrong BC V0E 1B0 – 250/546-8330; Fax: 250/546-8330 – Principal, Karen Wallace – *64 – Gr. K.-10

Burnaby: Columbia College, 6037 Marlborough Ave., Burnaby BC V5H 3L6 – 604/430-6422; Fax: 604/439-0548 – Principal, Michael Weiss – *182 – Sec.

Burnaby: Deer Lake SDA School, 5550 Gilpin St., Burnaby BC V5G 2H6 – 604/434-5844; Fax: 604/434-5845 – Principal, Murray Cooper – *197 – Gr. K.-10

Burnaby: Holy Cross School, 1450 Delta Ave., Burnaby BC V5B 3G2 – 604/299-3530; Fax: 604/299-3534 – Principal, Jennifer Gallivan – *228 – Gr. K.-7

Burnaby: John Knox Christian School, 8260 - 13 Ave., Burnaby BC V3N 2G5 – 604/522-1410; Fax: 604/522-4606 – Principal, Peter Valkenier – *220 – Gr. K.-7; Special Ed.

Burnaby: Kenneth Gordon School, 7855 Meadow Ave., Burnaby BC V3N 2V8 – 604/524-5224; Fax: 604/524-8297 – Principal, Ellen Baglot – *56 – Elem.

Burnaby: Our Lady of Mercy School, 7481 - 10 Ave., Burnaby BC V3N 2S1 – 604/526-7121; Fax: 604/520-3194 – Principal, Colleen Burrell – *237 – Gr. K.-7

Burnaby: St. Francis de Sales School, 6656 Balmoral St., Burnaby BC V5E 1J1 – 604/435-5311; Fax: 604/434-4798 – Principal, Cecilia McLaren – *211 – Gr. K.-7

Burnaby: St. Helen's School, 3894 Triumph St., Burnaby BC V5C 1Y7 – 604/299-2234; Fax: 604/299-3565 – Principal, Waldemar Sambor – *248 – Gr. K.-7

Burnaby: St. Michael's School, 9387 Holmes St., Burnaby BC V3N 4C3 – 604/526-9768 – Principal, Ethel Jackson – *237 – Gr. K.-7

Burnaby: St. Thomas More Collegiate, 7450 - 12 Ave., Burnaby BC V3N 2K1 – 604/521-1801; Fax: 604/520-0725 – Principal, Hugh O'Neill – *599 – Gr. 8-12; Boys

Burns Lake Christian School, Hwy. 35, Gerow Island, Burns Lake BC V0J 1E0 – 250/692-3532 – Principal, Donald Cram – *74 – Gr. 1-8

Campbell River Christian School, 250 South Dogwood St., Campbell River BC V9W 6Y7 – 250/287-4266; Fax: 250/287-3130 – Principal, Gordon Wickens – *569 – Gr. K.-12

Chemainus: St. Joseph's School, 9735 Elm St., PO Box 900, Chemainus BC V0R 1K0 – 250/246-3191; Fax: 250/246-2921 – Principal, Eleanor Greveling – *204 – Gr. K.-7

Chilliwack Christian School, 9750 McNaught, PO Box 161, Chilliwack BC V2P 6G2 – 604/792-4171; Fax: 604/792-0640 – Principal, Doyle Smiens – *217 – Gr. K.-7

Chilliwack: Highroad Academy, 46641 Chilliwack Central Rd., Chilliwack BC V2P 1K3 – 604/792-4680; Fax: 604/792-2465 – Principal, Berne J. Watters – *276 – Gr. K.-12

Chilliwack: John Calvin School, 4268 Stewart Rd., Chilliwack BC V2R 5G3 – 604/823-6814; Fax: 604/823-6791 – Principal, Pieter H. Torenvliet – *274 – Gr. 1-7

Chilliwack: Mount Cheam Christian School, 48988 Yale Rd. East, Chilliwack BC V2P 6H4 – 604/794-3072; Fax: 604/794-3078 – Principal, Adrian Stoutjesdyk – *308 – Gr. K.-12

Chilliwack: St. Mary's School, 8909 Mary St., Chilliwack BC V2P 4J4 – 604/792-7715; Fax: 604/792-3013 – Principal, Shelley MacDonell – *243 – Gr. K.-7

Chilliwack: Timothy Christian School, 50420 Castleman Rd., Chilliwack BC V2P 6H4 – 604/794-7114; Fax: 604/794-3520 – Principal, James Beeke – *396 – Gr. K.-12

Chilliwack: Valley Christian School, 8700 Young Rd., Chilliwack BC V2P 4P4 – 604/793-7997; Fax: 604/793-7991 – Principal, Philip Hills – *103 – Gr. K.-7

Clearbrook: Mennonite Educational Institute, 4081 Clearbrook Rd., PO Box 2240, Clearbrook BC V2T 3X8 – 604/859-8813, 9762; Fax: 604/859-9206 – Principal, Leo Regehr – *918 – Gr. K.-1, 8-12

Cobble Hill: Evergreen Independent School, 3805 Cobble Hill Rd., PO Box 166, Cobble Hill BC V0R 1L0 – 250/743-2433 – Principal, Penny Pope – *57 – Gr. K.-7

Coquitlam: British Columbia Christian Academy, 2665 Runnel Dr., Coquitlam BC V3B 7M6 – 604/941-8426; Fax: 604/945-6455 – Principal, John MacPhail – *120 – Gr. K.-12

Coquitlam College, 516 Brookmere Ave., Coquitlam BC V3J 1W9 – 604/939-6633; Fax: 604/939-0336 – Principal, Roger Kopf – *183 – Elem.

Coquitlam: Our Lady of Fatima School, 315 Walker St., Coquitlam BC V3K 4C7 – 604/936-4228; Fax: 604/936-4403 – Principal, Robertson Wood – *236 – Gr. K.-7/French Immersion

Cranbrook: St. Mary's Catholic Public School, 1701 - 5 St. South, PO Box 250, Cranbrook BC V1C 1K1 – 250/426-5017; Fax: 250/426-5076 – Principal, Douglas F. Mitchell – *307 – Gr. K.-7, Learning Assistance, French A.S.L.

Dawson Creek: Mountain Christian School, 11501 - 17th St., PO Box 2308, Dawson Creek BC V1G 4P2 – 250/782-9528 – Principal, Abram Born – *73 – Gr. K.-12

Dawson Creek: Notre Dame School, 925 - 104 Ave., Dawson Creek BC V1G 2H8 – 250/782-4923; Fax: 250/782-4388 – Principal, Eileen Materi – *179 – Gr. K.-7; Learning Assistance, Enrichment

Dawson Creek: Ron Pettigrew Christian School, PO Box 688, Dawson Creek BC V1G 4H7 – 250/782-4580; Fax: 250/782-9805 – Principal, Debbie Maddigan – *105 – Gr. K.-12

Delta Christian School, 4789 - 53 St., Delta BC V4K 2Y9 – 604/946-2514; Fax: 604/946-2589 – Principal, Jacob Lieuwen – *219 – Gr. K.-7

Delta: Immaculate Conception School, 8840 - 119 St., Delta BC V4C 6M4 – 604/596-6116; Fax: 604/596-4338 – Principal, Sr. Alexis Taphorn – *443 – Gr. K.-7

Delta: Sacred Heart School, 3900 Arthur Dr., PO Box 10, Delta BC V4K 3N5 – 604/946-2611; Fax: 604/604-4533 – Principal, Mary-Joyce Derouin – *228 – Gr. K.-7

Delta: Traditional Learning Academy, 10680 - 84th Ave., Delta BC V4C 2L2 – 604/582-7898; Fax: 604/582-7898 – Principal, Tom McRae – *87 – Gr. K.-7

Duncan Christian School, 5781 Chesterfield St., Duncan BC V9L 3M1 – 250/746-5341; Fax: 250/746-3615 – Principal, Jacoba M. Spyksma – *352 – Gr. K.-12; Special Ed.

Duncan: Queen of Angels School, RR#5, Duncan BC V9L 4T6 – 250/746-5919; Fax: 250/746-8689 – Principal, Ellen McMillan – *446 – Gr. K.-9

Duncan: Queen Margaret's School, 660 Brownsey Ave., Duncan BC V9L 1C2 – 250/746-4185; Fax: 250/746-4187 – Principal, M. Rees Davies – *242 – Gr. K.-12

Duncan: Sunrise Waldorf School, RR#7, 4344 Peters Rd., Duncan BC V9L 4W4 – 250/743-7253 – Principal, Peter Morris – *136 – Gr. K.-8

Enderby Christian School, 104 Meadow Cres., PO Box 339, Enderby BC V0E 1V0 – 250/838-6035; Fax: 250/838-6085 – Principal, Michael Wilson – *440 – Gr. K.-7

Fort James: St. Maria Goretti School, PO Box 1390, Fort James BC V0J 1P0 – 250/996-8441; Fax: 250/996-2229 – Principal, Simon Waltham-Smith – *84 – Gr. K.-6

Fort St. John: Christian Life School, 8923 - 112th Ave., Fort St. John BC V1J 5H8 – 250/785-1437; Fax: 250/785-4852 – Principal, Richard Flake – *205 – Gr. K.-11

Fort St. John: Church at Blueberry School, PO Box 6227, Fort St. John BC V1J 4H6 – 250/774-1013; Fax: 250/774-1013 – Principal, Charity Titas – *55 – Gr. K.-12

Fort St. John: Immaculata Catholic School, 10011 - 96 St., Fort St. John BC V1J 1L2 – 250/785-3524; Fax: 250/785-0049 – Principal, Gary Boechler – *204 – Gr. K.-7; Special Ed.

Hazelton: Kispiox Elementary, 1279 Lax Seel St., PO Box 418, Hazelton BC V0J 1Y0 – 250/842-6148; Fax: 250/842-5720 – Principal, Brian Pritchard – *101 – Gr. 1-8

Houston Christian School, Hillside Dr., PO Box 237, Houston BC V0J 1Z0 – 250/845-7736 – Principal, Jack Vanden Born – *161 – Gr. K.-11

Iskut: Klappan Independent Day School, PO Box 30, Iskut BC V0J 1K0 – 250/234-3331; Fax: 250/234-3200 – Principal, I. Wightman – *107 – Gr. K.-9

Kamloops Christian School, 685 Tranquille Rd., Kamloops BC V2B 3H7 – 250/376-6900; Fax: 250/376-6904 – Principal, Bob Adams – *580 – Gr. K.-12

Kamloops: Our Lady of Perpetual Help School, 235 Poplar St., Kamloops BC V2B 4B9 – 250/376-2343; Fax: 250/376-2361 – Principal, Sr. Mary Macdonald – *244 – Gr. K.-7

Kamloops: St. Ann's Academy, 205 Columbia St., Kamloops BC V2C 2S7 – 250/372-5452; Fax: 250/372-5257 – Principal, Bth. Peter O'Loughlin – *608 – Gr. K.-12

Kelowna: Heritage Christian School, 295 Gerstmar Rd., Kelowna BC V1X 4A6 – 250/862-2377; Fax: 250/862-4943 – Principal, Don Irwin – *362 – Gr. K.-12

Kelowna: Immaculata High School, 1493 KLO Rd., Kelowna BC V1W 3N8 – 250/762-2730; Fax: 250/861-3028 – Principal, John Campbell – *189 – Gr. 8-12

Kelowna Christian School, 3285 Gordon Dr., Kelowna BC V1W 3N4 – 250/861-3238; Fax: 250/861-4844 – Principal, Dr. Kenneth Penner – *555 – Gr. K.-12

Kelowna: Okanagan Adventist Academy, 1035 Hollywood Rd., Kelowna BC V1X 4N3 – 250/860-5305; Fax: 250/868-9703 – Principal, Robert Crux – *205 – Gr. K.-12

Kelowna: St. Joseph Elementary School, 839 Sutherland Ave., Kelowna BC V1Y 5X4 – 250/763-3371; Fax: 250/763-2740 – Principal, Beverly Pulyk – *337 – Gr. K.-7; Learning Assistance

Kemano: Lord Alexander School, General Delivery, Kemano BC V0T 1K0 – 250/634-5577; Fax: 250/634-5441 – Principal, Ken Allison – *50 – Gr. K.-8

Kitimat: St. Anthony's School, 1750 Nalabila Blvd., Kitimat BC V8C 1E6 – 250/632-6313; Fax: 250/632-6313 – Principal, Ann M. Herz – *214 – Gr. K.-7

Kitwanga: Gitanyow Independent School, PO Box 369, Kitwanga BC V0J 2A0 – 250/849-5528 – Principal, Laura Derrick – *78 – Gr. 1-9

Ladner: Boundary Bay Montessori House School, 5008 - 47th Ave., Ladner BC V4K 1T9 – 604/940-9844; Fax: 604/943-7827 – Principal, Heather Main – *58 – Gr. 1-7

Langley: Credo Christian Elementary School, 21919 - 52 Ave., Langley BC V3A 4R1 – 604/530-1131; Fax: 604/530-4268 – Principal, J.A. Roukema – *213 – Gr. K.-7/Spec. Ed.

Langley: Credo Christian High School, 21846 - 52 Ave., PO Box 3457, Langley BC V3A 4R8 – 604/530-5396; Fax: 604/530-8965 – Principal, Ed Vanderboom – *322 – Gr. 8-12

Langley: The King's School, 21783 - 76B Ave., Langley BC V0X 1T0 – 604/888-0969; Fax: 604/888-0977 – Principal, Robert Beck – *199 – Gr. K.-11

Langley Christian School, 21789 - 50 Ave., Langley BC V3A 3T2 – 604/533-2222; Fax: 604/533-7276 – Principal, Leo Smit – *528 – Gr. K.-9

Langley: St. Catherine's School, 20244 - 32 Ave., Langley BC V2Z 2C9 – 604/534-6564; Fax: 604/534-4871 – Principal, Patricia F. Delany – *225 – Gr. K.-7; Learning Assistance

Lister: Bountiful Elementary/Secondary School, 4702 Lyons Rd., PO Box 226, Lister BC V0B 1Y0 – 604/428-4679; Fax: 604/428-4789 – Principal, Merrill R. Palmer – *142 – Gr. K.-10

Lytton: Mestanta Technological Institute, PO Box 300, Lytton BC V0K 1Z0 – 250/455-2522; Fax: 250/455-2512 – Principal, Dr. Glenn Sinclair – *375 – Gr. K.-12

Mansons Landing: Linnaea School, PO Box 98, Mansons Landing BC V0P 1K0 – 250/935-6747 – Principal, Donna Bracewell – *62 – Gr. K.-8

Maple Ridge: Haney-Pitt Meadows Christian School, 12140 - 203 St., Maple Ridge BC V2X 4V5 – 604/465-4442; Fax: 604/465-1685 – Principal, Rodney Berg – *337 – Gr. K.-8

Maple Ridge: Meadowridge School, 12224 - 240th St., Maple Ridge BC V4R 1N1 – 604/467-4444; Fax: 604/467-4989 – Principal, Otto Hookey – *386 – Gr. K.-12; University Prep.

Maple Ridge: St. Patrick's School, 22589 - 121 Ave., Maple Ridge BC V2X 3T5 – 604/467-1571; Fax: 604/467-2686 – Principal, Anne Kully – *226 – Gr. K.-7

Matsqui: Valley Christian School, 5930 Riverside St., PO Box 220, Matsqui BC V4X 3R2 – 604/826-1388; Fax: 604/826-2744 – Principal, Dorothy Peters – *682 – Gr. K.-11

Merritt: Maranatha Christian School, 2150 Burgess St., PO Box 849, Merritt BC V0K 2B0 – 250/378-2626; Fax: 250/378-2408 – Principal, Dale Johnson – *116 – Gr. K.-12

Merville: Comox Valley Christian School, 1050 Larkin Rd., PO Box 425, Merville BC V0R 2M0 – 250/337-5335; Fax: 250/337-5632 – Principal, Ron Gamache – *148 – Gr. K.-9

Mill Bay: Brentwood College School, PO Box 1000, Mill Bay BC V0R 2P0 – 250/743-5521; Fax: 250/743-2911 – Principal, William Ross – *405 – Gr. 8-12

Moricetown Elementary School, Site 15, RR#1, Beaver Rd., PO Box 25, Moricetown BC V0J 2N0 – 250/847-3166; Fax: 250/847-3813 – Principal, Victor Jim – *67 – Gr. 1-5

Nanaimo Christian School, 198 Holland Rd., Nanaimo BC V9R 5K3 – 250/754-4512; Fax: 250/754-4271 – Principal, John Reems – *235 – Gr. K.-10; Special Ed.

Nanaimo Montessori School, 945 Waddington Rd., Nanaimo BC V9S 4V1 – 250/753-0649 – Principal, James Nelson – *56 – Gr. K.-7

Nanoose Bay: Parksville Christian School, Morello Rd., PO Box 53, Nanoose Bay BC V0R 2R0 – 250/468-9433; Fax: 250/468-7748 – Principal, Arend Bakker – *121 – Gr. K.-8

Nelson Waldorf School, PO Box 165, Nelson BC V1L 5P9 – 250/352-6919 – Principal, D. Oese-Lloyd – *175 – Gr. K.-8; Learning Assistance, French & German A.S.L.

Nelson: St. Joseph's School, 523 Mill St., Nelson BC V1L 4S2 – 250/352-3041; Fax: 250/352-9188 – Principal, Mary Gris – *188 – Gr. K.-6; Special. Ed.

New Westminster: Tavistock Academy, 811 Royal Ave., New Westminster BC V3M 1K1 – 604/522-3312; Fax: 604/522-3316 – Principal, Shirley Russell Cox – *74 – Gr. K.-12

North Vancouver: Holy Trinity Elementary School, 128 West 27 St., North Vancouver BC V7N 2H1 – 604/987-4454; Fax: 604/987-0360 – Principal, Chris Sumner – *241 – Gr. K.-7

North Vancouver: Mulgrave School, 1325 East Keith Rd., North Vancouver BC V7J 1J3 – 604/984-9034; Fax: 604/984-9034 – Principal, Linda Hamer – *66 – Gr. K.-4

North Vancouver: St. Edmund's School, 535 Mahon Ave., North Vancouver BC V7M 2R7 – 604/988-7364; Fax: 604/988-7350 – Principal, Pat Hamilton – *195 – Gr. K.-7

North Vancouver: St. Thomas Aquinas School, 541 West Keith Rd., North Vancouver BC V7M 1M5 – 604/987-4431; Fax: 604/987-7816 – Principal, Marilyn Williams – *424 – Gr. 8-12

North Vancouver: Vancouver Waldorf School, 2725 St. Christopher's Rd., North Vancouver BC V7K 2B6 – 604/985-7435; Fax: 604/985-4948 – Principal, Colin Dutson – *272 – Gr. K.-12

Okanagan Mission: Kelowna Waldorf School, 429 Collet Rd., PO Box 93, Okanagan Mission BC V0H 1S0 – 250/764-4130; Fax: 250/764-4130 – Principal, Lynn Wallace – *99 – Gr. K.-8

Oliver: Sen Pok Chin, RR#3, Site 25, Comp 13, Oliver BC V0H 1T0 – 250/498-2019; Fax: 250/498-6577 – Principal, Brent Kaulback – *55 – Gr. K-11

Penticton: Holy Cross Elementary School, 1299 Manitoba St., Penticton BC V2A 5Z9 – 250/492-4480; Fax: 250/493-0773 – Principal, Bernard Hopley – *888 – Gr. K.-7

Penticton Community Christian School, #102, 148 Roy Ave., PO Box 910, Penticton BC V2A 7G1 – 250/493-5233; Fax: 250/493-0733 – Principal, Alistair Jackson – *94 – Gr. K.-8

Port Alberni: Ha-Ho-Payuk, 5000 Mission Rd., PO Box 1279, Port Alberni BC V9Y 7M1 – 250/724-5542; Fax: 250/724-7335 – Principal, Mary Chambers – *87 – Gr. K.-6

Port Coquitlam: Archbishop Carney Secondary School, 1335 Dominion St., Port Coquitlam BC V3B 7M6 – 604/942-7465; Fax: 604/942-5289 – Principal, Peter Dawe – *186 – Gr. 8-9

Port Coquitlam: Our Lady of the Assumption School, 2255 Fraser Ave., Port Coquitlam BC V3B 6G8 – 604/942-5522; Fax: 604/942-8313 – Principal, John Van Der Pauw – *240 – Gr. 1-Sec.

Port Hardy: Avalon Adventist Church School, 4640 Byng Rd., PO Box 974, Port Hardy BC V0N 2P0 – 250/949-8243; Fax: 250/949-6770 – Principal, Anthony Oucharek – *106 – Gr. K.-10

Port Hardy: Gwa'Sala-'Nakwaxda'Xw Band School, PO Box 1799, Port Hardy BC V0N 2P0 – 250/949-7743; Fax: 250/949-7422 – Principal, Robert Regier – *113 – Elem.

Powell River: Assumption School, 7091 Glacier St., Powell River BC V8A 1R8 – 604/485-9894; Fax: 604/485-7984 – Principal, Mimi Richardson – *234 – Gr. K.-7

Prince George: Cedars Christian School, 701 North Nechako Rd., Prince George BC V2K 1A2 – 250/564-0707; Fax: 250/564-0729 – Principal, Vic Wiens – *271 – Gr. K.-10

Prince George: Immaculate Conception School, Cathedral Ave., PO Box 1487, Prince George BC V2L 4V5 – 250/964-4362; Fax: 250/964-9465 – Principal, Lucie Redmond – *183 – Gr. K.-7, Spec. Ed.

Prince George: O'Grady Catholic High School, O'Grady Rd., PO Box 8000, Prince George BC V2N 3Z2 – 250/964-4455; Fax: 250/964-4456 – Principal, H.L. Bucher – *341 – Gr. 8-12

Prince George Academy, 1919 - 17 Ave., Prince George BC V2L 5R2 – 250/563-3167; Fax: 250/564-6800 – Principal, Susan Steeves – *132 – Gr. K.-12

Prince George: Sacred Heart School, 785 Patricia Blvd., Prince George BC V2L 3V5 – 250/563-5201; Fax: 250/563-5283 – Principal, Terry Wilson – *199 – Gr. K.-7, Spec. Ed.

Prince George: St. Mary's School, 1088 Gillett St., Prince George BC V2M 2V3 – 250/563-7502; Fax: 250/563-7818 – Principal, Sr. Margaret Quinn – *227 – Gr. K.-7

Prince George: Westside Academy, SS#2, Site 10, Comp. 13, Prince George BC V2N 2K6 – 250/964-9600; Fax: 250/964-9604 – Principal, Marlo Johnson – *140 – Gr. K.-Sec.

Prince Rupert: Annunciation School, 627 - 5 Ave. West, Prince Rupert BC V8J 1V1 – 250/624-5873; Fax: 250/627-4486 – Principal, Flora D'Angelo – *251 – Gr. K.-7

Prince Rupert Christian School, 1220 Portage Rd., Prince Rupert BC V8J 4H9 – 250/627-7515 – Principal, Edward Bieber – *69 – Gr. K.-11

Quesnel: St. Ann's School, 150 Sutherland Ave., Quesnel BC V2J 2J5 – 250/992-6237 – Principal, Donald Murphy – *103 – Gr. K.-7

Richmond: Choice Learning Centre, 20451 Westminster Hwy., Richmond BC V6V 1B3 – 604/273-2418;

* indicates enrollment figure.

Fax: 604/273-2419 – Principal, Lorraine. Ford – *109 – Gr. 1-Elem.
Richmond: Muslim School, 12300 Blundell Rd., PO Box 94415, Richmond BC V6W 1B3 – 604/270-2511; Fax: 604/270-2511 – Principal, Manzoor Cokar – *307 – Gr. 1-10
Richmond Christian School, 5240 Woodwards Rd., Richmond BC V7E 1H1 – 604/272-5720; Fax: 604/272-7370 – Principal, Ian Codling – *569 – Gr. K.-12
Richmond International High School & College, 8671 Odlin Cres., Richmond BC V6X 1G1 – 604/244-0100; Fax: 604/244-0102 – Principal, Jindra Repa – *88 – Gr. 10-12
Richmond Jewish Day School, 9711 Geal Rd., Richmond BC V7E 1R4 – 604/275-3393; Fax: 604/275-9322 – Principal, Eleanor Braude – *129 – Gr. K.-6
Richmond: St. Joseph the Worker School, 4451 Williams Rd., Richmond BC V7E 1J7 – 604/277-1115; Fax: 604/272-5214 – Principal, Lesya Balsevich – *217 – Gr. K.-7
Richmond: St. Paul's School, 8251 St. Alban's Rd., Richmond BC V6Y 2L2 – 604/277-4487; Fax: 604/277-1810 – Principal, Frank Dragojevich – *215 – Gr. K.-7
Salmon Arm: Shuswap Christian, 51 Hudson St., PO Box 789, Salmon Arm BC V1E 4N9 – 250/832-7994 – Principal, D. Kendig – *53 – Gr. K.-7
Saltspring Centre School, 355b Blackburn Rd., Saltspring Island BC V8K 2B8 – 250/537-9130 – Principal, Frances Rautenbach – *63 – Gr. K.-Sec.
Sechelt: New Life Christian Academy, PO Box 2163, Sechelt BC V0N 3A0 – 604/886-7450 – Principal, David Cliff – *53 – Gr. K.-12
Shawnigan Lake: Maxwell International Baha'i School, PO Box 1000, Shawnigan Lake BC V0R 2W0 – 250/743-7144; Fax: 250/743-3522 – Principal (Interim), Dr. K.y Hein – *214 – Gr. 7-12
Shawnigan Lake School, RR#1, 1975 Renfrew Rd., Shawnigan Lake BC V0R 2W0 – 250/743-5516; Fax: 250/743-6200 – Principal, Simon Bruce-Lockhart – *340 – Gr. 8-12
Smithers: Bulkley Valley Christian School, PO Box 3635, Smithers BC V0J 2N0 – 250/847-4238; Fax: 250/847-3564 – Principal, Evert A. Vroon – *367 – Gr. K.-7
Smithers: Ebenezer Canadian Reformed School, PO Box 3635, Smithers BC V0J 2N0 – 250/847-4238; Fax: 250/847-3564 – Principal, Henk Vanbeelen – *143 – Gr. K.-12
Smithers: St. Joseph's School, 4054 Broadway Ave., PO Box 454, Smithers BC V0J 2N0 – 250/847-9414; Fax: 250/847-3221 – Principal, Rosemary McKenzie – *179 – Gr. K.-7
Summerland: The Glenfir School, 9533 Main St., PO Box 1800, Summerland BC V0H 1Z0 – 250/494-0004; Fax: 250/494-0058 – Principal, Thomas Meredith – *101 – Gr. 1-7
Surrey: Bible Fellowship Academy, 15100 - 66A Ave., Surrey BC V3S 2A6 – 604/599-8171; Fax: 604/597-9090 – Principal, Rev. Darrell Steeves – *197 – Gr. K.-Sec.
Surrey: Cloverdale Catholic School, 17511 - 59 Ave., Surrey BC V3S 1P3 – 604/574-5151; Fax: 604/574-5160 – Principal, Trudy Desjardine – *230 – Gr. K.-7/Learning Assistance
Surrey: Cornerstone Kindergarten, 14724 - 84 Ave., Surrey BC V3S 2M5 – 604/599-9918 – Principal, Dale Gausman – *66 – Gr. K.
Surrey: Diamond Elementary, 18620 - 56th Ave., Surrey BC V3S 1G1 – 604/576-1146; Fax: 604/574-9831 – Principal, Robert Sarginson – *136 – Gr. K.-7
Surrey: Fraser Valley Christian High School, 15353 - 92 Ave., Surrey BC V3R 1C3 – 604/581-1033; Fax: 604/581-1712 – Principal, Al Boerema – *420 – Gr. 8-12; Special Ed.
Surrey: Heritage Christian School, 3487 King George Hwy., Surrey BC V4P 1B7 – 604/536-5967; Fax: 604/536-5967 – Principal, Clayton Mills – *182 – Gr. K.-8

Surrey: Holy Cross Regional High School, 16193 - 88 Ave., Surrey BC V4N 1G3 – 604/581-3023; Fax: 604/583-4795 – Principal, Robert Dejulius – *801 – Gr. 8-12
Surrey: Khalsa School Surrey, 6933 - 124th St., Surrey BC V3W 3W6 – 604/591-2248; Fax: 604/591-3396 – Principal, Harchand Gill – *747 – Gr. 1-10
Surrey: Our Lady of Good Counsel School, 10504 - 139 St., Surrey BC V3T 4L5 – 604/581-3154 – Principal, Corina Meisl – *242 – Gr. K.-7
Surrey: Pacific Academy, 10238 - 168 St., Surrey BC V4N 1Z4 – 604/581-5353; Fax: 604/581-0087 – Principal, Raymond C. Sutton – *884 – Gr. K.-12
Surrey: Regent Christian Academy, 15100 - 66A Ave., Surrey BC V3S 2A6 – 604/599-8171; Fax: 604/597-9090 – Principal, Paul Johnson – *189 – Gr. K.-12
Surrey: Relevant High, 18620 - 56 Ave., Surrey BC V3S 1G1 – 604/574-4736; Fax: 604/574-9831 – Principal, Robert Sarginson – *102 – Gr. 8-12
Surrey: Roots & Wings Montessori, 6962 - 124th St., Surrey BC V3W 3W7 – 604/590-2717; Fax: 604/590-2724 – Principal, Kristin Cassie – *73 – Gr. K.-Elem.
Surrey: St. Bernadette School, 13130 - 65B Ave., Surrey BC V3W 9M1 – 604/596-1101; Fax: 604/597-9534 – Principal, Doreen Junk – *220 – Gr. K.-7
Surrey: South Ridge School, 2656 - 160 St., Surrey BC V4P 2M7 – 604/535-5056; Fax: 604/535-3676 – Principal, Alan Brown – *180 – Gr. K.-9
Surrey: Star of the Sea School, 15024 - 24 Ave., Surrey BC V4A 2H8 – 604/531-6316; Fax: 604/531-0171 – Principal, Rita Smith – *260 – Gr. K.-7
Surrey Christian School, 9115 - 160 St., Surrey BC V4N 2X7 – 604/581-2474; Fax: 604/581-5211 – Principal, Anthonie Jansen – *465 – Gr. K.-7
Surrey: White Rock Christian Academy, 2265 - 152 St., Surrey BC V4A 4P1 – 604/531-9186; Fax: 604/531-1727 – Principal, Susan Penner – *276 – Gr. K.-12
Surrey: William of Orange Christian School, 5790 - 175 St., PO Box 34090, Surrey BC V3S 8C4 – 604/576-2144 – Principal, Apko Nap – *127 – Gr. 1-7
Surrey: Zion Lutheran School, 5950 - 179 St., Surrey BC V3S 4J9 – 604/576-6313; Fax: 604/576-1399 – Principal, James Murray – *147 – Gr. K.-7/Learning Assistance
Terrace: Centennial Christian School, 3608 Sparks St., Terrace BC V8G 2V6 – 250/635-6173; Fax: 250/635-9385 – Principal, Frank Voogd – *275 – Gr. K.-10
Terrace: Veritas Catholic School, 4836 Straume Ave., Terrace BC V8G 4G3 – 250/635-3035; Fax: 250/635-7588 – Principal, Frances P. Nuyten – *210 – Gr. K.-7
Trail: St. Michael's Elementary School, 1329 - 4 Ave., Trail BC V1R 1S3 – 250/368-6151; Fax: 250/368-9962 – Principal, Maureen Johnson – *226 – Gr. K.-7
Vancouver: Blessed Sacrament School, 3020 Heather St., Vancouver BC V5Z 3K3 – 604/876-7211; Fax: 604/876-7280 – Principal, Pauline Teglasi – *209 – Gr. K.-7; French Immersion
Vancouver: Bodwell College, 2026 - West 12th Ave., Vancouver BC V6J 2G2 – 604/737-8221; Fax: 604/737-8213 – Principal, Dr. Lawrence Fast – *221 – Gr. 8-12
Vancouver: Corpus Christi School, 6344 Nanaimo St., Vancouver BC V5P 4K7 – 604/321-1117; Fax: 604/327-1410 – Principal, Marian McDermott – *223 – Gr. K.-7; Learning Assistance
Vancouver: Crofton House School, 3200 West 41 Ave., Vancouver BC V6N 3E1 – 604/263-3255; Fax: 604/263-4941 – Principal, Barbara Walker – *652 – Gr. 1-12; University Prep.
Vancouver: Dorset College, 200 City Square, 555 - 12th Ave. West, Vancouver BC V5Z 3X7 – 604/879-8686; Fax: 604/874-8686 – Principal, Margaret Misfeldt – *198 – Sec.
Vancouver: Effective Education School, 8610 Ash St., Vancouver BC V6P 3M2 – 604/322-8666; Fax: 604/322-8666 – Principal, Jennifer Jaehriling – *55 – Gr. K-Sec.

Vancouver: Fraser Academy, 2294 West 10 Ave., Vancouver BC V6K 2H8 – 604/736-5575; Fax: 604/736-5578 – Principal, Scott Armstrong – *126 – Gr. 1-12
Vancouver: Immaculate Conception School, 3745 West 28 Ave., Vancouver BC V6S 1S6 – 604/224-5012; Fax: 604/224-3721 – Principal, Mary Paetsch – *210 – Gr. K.-7
Vancouver: Khalsa School Vancouver, 5987 Prince Albert St., Vancouver BC V5W 3E2 – 604/321-1226 – Principal, Amar Dhaliwal – *99 – Gr. 1-6; Gen. & Sikh Studies
Vancouver: Life Song School, 4196 - 4th Ave. West, Vancouver BC V6J 4M1 – 604/222-1900 – Principal, Susan Brown – *463 – Gr. K.-8
Vancouver: Little Flower Academy, 4195 Alexandra St., Vancouver BC V6J 4C6 – 604/738-9016; Fax: 604/738-5749 – Principal, Sr. Eileen Kelly – *430 – Gr. 8-12; Girls
Vancouver: Maimonides School, 5465 Baillie St., Vancouver BC V5Z 3M6 – 604/263-9700; Fax: 604/263-4848 – Principal, Edward Collins – *62 – Gr. 8-12
Vancouver: Notre Dame Regional Secondary School, 2855 Parker St., Vancouver BC V5K 2T8 – 604/255-5454; Fax: 604/255-2115 – Principal, Michael Cooke – *636 – Gr. 8-12
Vancouver: Our Lady of Perpetual Help School, 2550 Camosun St., Vancouver BC V6R 3W6 – 604/228-8811; Fax: 604/224-6822 – Principal, Maria Fasan – *321 – Gr. K.-7
Vancouver: Our Lady of Sorrows School, 575 Slocan St., Vancouver BC V5K 3X5 – 604/253-2434 – Principal, Anne Coulombe – *228 – Gr. K.-7
Vancouver: St. Andrew's School, 450 - 47 Ave. East, Vancouver BC V5W 2B4 – 604/325-6317; Fax: 604/325-0920 – Principal, Ruth Cash – *229 – Gr. K.-7
Vancouver: St. Augustine's School, 2145 West 8 Ave., Vancouver BC V6K 2A5 – 604/731-8024; Fax: 604/739-1712 – Principal, Catherine Oberndorf – *226 – Gr. K.-7/Learning Assistance
Vancouver: St. Francis of Assisi School, 870 Victoria Dr., Vancouver BC V5L 4E7 – 604/253-7311; Fax: 604/253-7375 – Principal, Laila Maravillas – *209 – Gr. K.-7/Learning Assistance
Vancouver: St. Francis Xavier School, 884 East Pender St., Vancouver BC V6A 1W1 – 604/254-2714; Fax: 604/254-2514 – Principal, Therese Leung – *337 – Gr. 1-7
Vancouver: St. George's School, 4175 West 29 Ave., Vancouver BC V6S 1V6 – 604/224-1304; Fax: 604/224-7066 – Principal, Gordon Atkinson – *893 – Gr. 1-12; Boys
Vancouver: St. John's International, 1088 Homer St., Vancouver BC V6B 2W9 – 604/683-4572; Fax: 604/683-4679 – Principal, David Sage – *103 – Gr. 7-12
Vancouver: St. John's School, 1811 - 16 Ave. West, Vancouver BC V6J 2M3 – 604/732-4434; Fax: 604/732-1074 – Principal, Christopher McGill – *131 – Gr. 1-12
Vancouver: St. Joseph's School, 3261 Fleming St., Vancouver BC V5N 3V6 – 604/872-5715; Fax: 604/872-5700 – Principal, Michael Boreham – *212 – Gr. K.-7/Spec. Ed.
Vancouver: St. Jude's School, 2953 East 15 Ave., Vancouver BC V5M 2K7 – 604/434-1633; Fax: 604/434-8677 – Principal, Maria Anzulovich – *222 – Gr. K.-7
Vancouver: St. Mary's School, 5239 Joyce St., Vancouver BC V5R 4G8 – 604/437-1312; Fax: 604/437-1193 – Principal, Sandra Marshall – *223 – Gr. K.-7
Vancouver: St. Patrick's Elementary School, 2850 Quebec St., Vancouver BC V5T 3A9 – 604/879-4411; Fax: 604/879-3737 – Principal, Sheila Roberts – *264 – Gr. 1-7
Vancouver: St. Patrick's Regional Secondary School, 115 East 11 Ave., Vancouver BC V5T 2C1 – 604/874-6422; Fax: 604/874-5176 – Principal, Eugene Luttrell – *476 – Gr. 8-12
Vancouver: Traditional Learning Academy, 1370 West 73rd Ave., Vancouver BC V6P 3E8 – 604/264-4655;

Fax: 604/264-4655 – Principal, Martin Dale – *1,144 – Gr. K.-12

Vancouver Christian School, 3496 Mons Dr., Vancouver BC V5M 3E6 – 604/435-3113; Fax: 604/430-1591 – Principal, Ronald Donkersloot – *371 – Gr. K.-10; Learning Assistance

Vancouver College, 5400 Cartier St., Vancouver BC V6M 3A5 – 604/261-4285; Fax: 604/261-2284 – Principal, Br. Kieran Murphy – *1,000 – Gr. K.-12; Learning Assistance

Vancouver Hebrew Academy, 5750 Oak St., Vancouver BC V6M 2V9 – 604/266-1245; Fax: 604/264-0648 – Principal, Shayndel Feuerstein – *116 – Gr. K.-7

Vancouver Montessori School, 8650 Bernard St., Vancouver BC V6P 5G5 – 604/261-0315 – Principal, Prasannata Runkel – *135 – Gr. K.-Elem.

Vancouver Talmud Torah, 998 West 26 Ave., Vancouver BC V5Z 2G1 – 604/736-7307; Fax: 604/736-9754 – Principal, Hugh Burke – *395 – Gr. K.-7

Vancouver: Wondertree Learning Centre, 4196 - 4th Ave. West, Vancouver BC V6R 4J5 – 604/224-3663; Fax: 604/739-6903 – Principal, Rebecca Irwin – *265 – Elem.

Vancouver: York House School, 4176 Alexandra St., Vancouver BC V6J 2V6 – 604/736-6551; Fax: 604/736-6530 – Principal, G. Ruddy – *603 – Gr. K.-12; University Prep, French Program

Vanderhoof: Northside Christian School, RR#2, PO Box 1, Vanderhoof BC V0J 3A0 – 250/567-9335; Fax: 250/567-9332 – Principal, W. Shenk – *181 – Gr. 1-12

Vanderhoof: Rainbow Christian School, 448 Connaught, PO Box 1339, Vanderhoof BC V0J 3A0 – 250/567-3107; Fax: 250/567-3177 – Principal, Wilfred Loewen – *105 – Gr. K.-7

Vanderhoof: St. Joseph's School, PO Box 1429, Vanderhoof BC V0J 3A0 – 250/567-2794; Fax: 250/567-4564 – Principal, Claire Petrucci – *124 – Gr. K.-7; Learning Assistance

Vernon: Pleasant Valley Academy, 1802 - 45th Ave., Vernon BC V1T 3M7 – 250/545-7852; Fax: 250/545-7852 – Principal, Daniel Self – *61 – Gr. K.-9

Vernon: St. James School, 2700 - 28 Ave., Vernon BC V1T 1V7 – 250/542-4081; Fax: 250/542-5696 – Principal, Mary Manton – *275 – Gr. K.-9; Learning Assistance, Enrichment

Vernon Christian School, RR#3, S-19A, C-4, Vernon BC V1T 6L6 – 250/545-7345; Fax: 250/545-0254 – Principal, Elco Vandergrift – *208 – Gr. K.-8

Victoria: Cathedral School, 912 Vancouver St., Victoria BC V8V 3V7 – 250/383-5125; Fax: 250/386-4013 – Principal, Laura Heintzman – *56 – Gr. K.-Elem.

Victoria: Crossroads Christian School, 3460 Shelbourne St., Victoria BC V8P 4G5 – 250/592-1335 – Principal, Colleen Brewer – *73 – Gr. K.-7

Victoria: Glenlyon-Norfolk School, 801 Bank St., Victoria BC V8S 4A6 – 250/598-2621, 2522; Fax: 250/598-4505, 3439 – Principal, David Brooks – *774 – Gr. 1-7, Jr. Boys & Jr. Girls; 8-12 Senior

Victoria: Island Pacific Adventist School, 729 Cordova Bay Rd., Victoria BC V8Y 1P7 – 250/658-5082; Fax: 250/658-5072 – Principal, Malcolm Pedlar – *50 – Gr. 1-10

Victoria: Lighthouse Christian Academy, 1289 Parkdale Dr., Victoria BC V9B 4G9 – 250/474-5311; Fax: 250/474-5021 – Principal, Dorothy Spencelayh – *111 – Gr. K.-10

Victoria: Maria Montessori Academy, 4052 Wilkinson Rd., Victoria BC V8Z 5A5 – 250/479-4746; Fax: 250/479-4746 – Principal, Ann Stevens – *95 – Gr. K.-6

Victoria: Montessori Centre of Victoria, 1530 Lionel St., Victoria BC V8R 2X8 – 250/592-3414; Fax: 250/592-3446 – Principal, Karen L. Colussi – *116 – Gr. K.-Elem.

Victoria: Pacific Christian School, 654 Agnes St., Victoria BC V8Z 2E6 – 250/479-4832; Fax: 250/479-3511 – Principal, John Messelink – *702 – Gr. K.-12

Victoria: St. Andrew's Regional High School, 880 MacKenzie Ave., Victoria BC V8X 3G5 – 250/479-1414; Fax: 250/479-5356 – Principal, Arthur Therrien – *296 – Gr. 8-12

Victoria: St. Andrew's School, 1002 Pandora Ave., Victoria BC V8V 3P5 – 250/382-3815; Fax: 250/385-3830 – Principal, James O'Reilly – *329 – Gr. K.-7; Learning Assistance, Enrichment

Victoria: St. Joseph's Catholic School, 757 West Burnside Rd., Victoria BC V8Z 1M9 – 250/479-1232; Fax: 250/479-1907 – Principal, Ken Leason – *201 – Gr. K.-7

Victoria: St. Margaret's School, 1080 Lucas Ave., Victoria BC V8X 3P7 – 250/479-7171; Fax: 250/479-8976 – Principal, Stephen Clayton – *368 – Gr. K.-12

Victoria: St. Michael's University School (Junior), #1906, 820 Victoria Ave., Victoria BC V8S 4N3 – 250/598-3922; Fax: 250/592-0783 – Principal, H. Gray Stone – *159 – Gr. 1-5

Victoria: St. Michael's University School (Middle), 3400 Richmond Rd., Victoria BC V8P 4P5 – 250/592-3549; Fax: 250/592-3942 – Principal, Clifford. Yorath – *183 – Gr. 6-8

Victoria: St. Michael's University School (Senior), Admin. Office, #1906, 3400 Richmond Rd., Victoria BC V8P 4P5 – 250/592-2411; Fax: 250/592-2812 – Principal, Peter Tongue – *485 – Gr. 9-12

Victoria: St. Patrick's School, 2368 Trent St., Victoria BC V8R 4Z3 – 250/592-6713; Fax: 250/592-6717 – Principal, Joseph Colistro – *398 – Gr. K.-7

Victoria: Trinity Christian School, 98 Cadillac Ave., Victoria BC V8Z 4T1 – 250/475-2977; Fax: 250/475-2988 – Principal, Mark Langley – *170 – Gr. K.-Sec.

Victoria: West-Mont School, 1016 Marwood Rd., Victoria BC V9C 3C4 – 250/474-2626 – Principal, Lois Harvey – *79 – Gr. K.-6

West Vancouver: Collingwood School, 70 Morven Dr., West Vancouver BC V7S 1B2 – 604/925-3331; Fax: 604/925-3373 – Principal, Graham M. Baldwin – *720 – Gr. K.-12

West Vancouver: Horseshoe Bay Christian School, 6355 Bruce St., West Vancouver BC V7W 2G5 – 604/921-9978; Fax: 604/983-8768 – Principal, Jeanne Wegner – *56 – Gr. K-9

West Vancouver: St. Anthony's School, 595 Keith Rd., West Vancouver BC V7T 1L8 – 604/922-0011; Fax: 604/922-3196 – Principal, Geraldine Jang – *197 – Gr. K.-7/Learning Assistance

Westbank: Our Lady of Lourdes Elementary School, 2547 Hebert Rd., Westbank BC V4T 2J6 – 250/768-9008; Fax: 250/768-0168 – Principal, Roman Mahnic – *55 – Gr. K.-7

Williams Lake: Cariboo Adventist Academy, 1405 South Lakeside Dr., Williams Lake BC V2G 3A7 – 250/392-4741; Fax: 250/392-6583 – Principal, Larry Murrin – *172 – Gr. K.-12

Williams Lake: Maranatha Christian School, 1100 - 11th Ave., Williams Lake BC V2G 3T9 – 250/392-7410 – Principal, Kathy Shetler – *58 – Elem./Sec.

Williams Lake: Sacred Heart Catholic School, 455 Pigeon Ave., Williams Lake BC V2G 4R5 – 250/398-7770; Fax: 250/398-7725 – Principal, Marlene Kosolofski – *69 – Gr. K.-4

OVERSEAS STUDENT SELECTION OFFICES

Hong Kong: British Columbia Student Selection Office, International Education & Student Services Centre Ltd., #901, Hutchinson House, 10 Harcourt Rd., Hong Kong Hong Kong – 852-845-1155; Fax: 852-845-4114 – BC Education Officer, Mei Mei Yiu

Japan: British Columbia Student Selection Office, BC Trade Office, Place Canada 3F, 3-37, Akasaka 7-chome, Minato-ku, Tokyo 107 Japan – 813-3-408-6171; Fax: 813-3-408-6340 – BC Education Officer, Jean Maeda

Taiwan R.O.C.: British Columbia Student Selection Office, Kamsun Development Ltd., Room 2202, 22/F, #333, Keelung Rd., Sec. 1, Taipei Taiwan R.O.C. – 886-2-722-08; Fax: 886-2-757-6593 – BC Education Officer, Sherry Yuan

MANITOBA

Manitoba Education & Training
#162, 450 Broadway, Winnipeg MB R3C 0V8
204/945-3752; Fax: 204/945-8330

EDUCATION ADMINISTRATION SERVICES BRANCH
#507, 1181 Portage Ave., Winnipeg MB R3G 0T3
204/945-6899; Fax: 204/948-2154

PLANNING & POLICY DEVELOPMENT BRANCH
#409, 1181 Portage Ave., Winnipeg MB R3G 0T3
204/945-6177; Fax: 204/945-0194

PROFESSIONAL CERTIFICATION & STUDENT RECORDS
402 Main St. North, PO Box 700, Russell MB R0J 1W0
204/773-2998; Fax: 204/773-2411; Toll Free: 1-800-667-2378

PROGRAM DEVELOPMENT BRANCH
#W120, 1970 Ness Ave., Winnipeg MB R3J 0Y9
204/945-8806; Fax: 204/945-5060

PROGRAM IMPLEMENTATION BRANCH
#W130 - 1970 Ness Ave., Winnipeg MB R3J 0Y9
204/945-7967; Fax: 204/945-5060

For detailed departmental listings, see Index: "Education, Depts."

SCHOOL DIVISIONS & DISTRICTS

The Province of Manitoba is divided into 57 educational units: 48 School Divisions; 6 Remote School Districts; 3 Special Revenue School Districts. The 6 Remote School Districts, one Special Revenue District, & the 48 School Divisions are controlled by elected school boards. Elections are held in accordance with the Local Authorities Election Act.

Fifty-six educational units are responsible for the provision of elementary & secondary education; one for secondary technical education only.

Boards with an enrollment of more than 10,000 are in bold print.

Agassiz School Division #13 – *2,877
PO Box 1206, Beausejour MB R0E 0C0
204/268-2465; Fax: 204/268-4149 – Supt., Waldo Klassen

Antler River School Division #43 – *938
PO Box 370, Melita MB R0M 1L0
204/522-3292; Fax: 204/522-3776 – Supt., Bob Bell

Assiniboine South School Division #3 – *6,738
3401 Roblin Blvd., Winnipeg MB R3R 0C6
204/889-5523; Fax: 204/896-0409 – Supt., Steve Dvorak

Beautiful Plains School Division #31 – *1,733
PO Box 700, Neepawa MB R0J 1H0
204/476-2388; Fax: 204/476-3606 – Supt., Dennis Wrightson

Birdtail River School Division #38 – *1,376
General Delivery, Crandall MB R0M 0H0
204/562-3677; Fax: 204/562-3634 – Supt., Ron Van Den Bussche

Boundary School Division #16 – *759
PO Box 1001, Dominion City MB R0A 0H0
204/427-2091; Fax: 204/427-2531 – Supt., Keith Bricknell

Brandon School Division #40 – *8,345
1031 - 6 St., Brandon MB R7A 4K5

* indicates enrollment figure.

204/729-3100; Fax: 204/727-2217 – Supt., Bob Swayze
Dauphin-Ochre School (Area #1) Division #33 – *2,168
　505 Main St. South, Dauphin MB R7N 1L3
　204/638-3001; Fax: 204/638-7250 – Supt., James Dalton
Duck Mountain School Division #34 – *860
　PO Box 400, Winnipegosis MB R0L 2G0
　204/656-4885; Fax: 204/656-4980 – Supt., Syl Didur
Evergreen School Division #22 – *1,801
　PO Box 1200, Gimli MB R0C 1B0
　204/642-5186; Fax: 204/642-7273 – Supt., James Daltow
Flin Flon School Division #46 – *1,715
　PO Box 578, Flin Flon MB R8A 1N4
　204/687-3413; Fax: 204/687-3517 – Supt., Dan Reagan
Fort la Bosse School Division #41 – *1,835
　PO Box 1420, Virden MB R0M 2C0
　204/748-2692; Fax: 204/748-2436 – Supt., Bonnie Thiessen
Fort Garry School Division #5 – *7,025
　181 Henlow Bay, Winnipeg MB R3Y 1M7
　204/488-1757; Fax: 204/488-2095 – Supt., Henry Izatt
Franco-Manitobaine Division Scolaire #49 – *4,267
　#204, 131 Provencher Boul., Winnipeg MB R2H 0G2
　204/982-8950; Fax: 204/982-8955 – Acting Supt., Georges Druwè
Frontier School Division #48 – *5,521
　1402 Notre Dame Ave., Winnipeg MB R3E 3G5
　204/775-9741; Fax: 204/775-9940 – Supt., Keven Van Camp
Garden Valley School Division #26 – *2,757
　PO Box 3000, Winkler MB R6W 4C8
　204/325-8335; Fax: 204/325-4132 – Supt., John A. Janzen
Hanover School Division #15 – *5,687
　PO Box 2170, Steinbach MB R0A 2A0
　204/326-6471; Fax: 204/326-9901 – Supt., Gilbert Unger
Interlake School Division #21 – *3,700
　PO Box 4000, Stonewall MB R0C 2Z0
　204/467-8485; Fax: 204/467-8334 – Acting Supt., Wendell Sparkes
Intermountain School Division #36 – *1,272
　PO Box 160, Grandview MB R0L 0Y0
　204/546-2068; Fax: 204/546-2770 – Supt., Howard Smith
Kelsey School Division #45 – *1,944
　PO Box 4700, The Pas MB R9A 1R4
　204/623-6421; Fax: 204/623-7704 – Supt., Al Yaskiw
Lakeshore School Division #23 – *1,534
　PO Box 100, Eriksdale MB R0C 0W0
　204/739-2101; Fax: 204/739-2145 – Supt., Ronald Weston
Lord Selkirk School Division #11 – *4,682
　205 Mercy St., Selkirk MB R1A 2C8
　204/482-5942; Fax: 204/482-3000 – Supt., Gail Bagnall
Midland School Division #25 – *1,658
　182 Main St. South, Carman MB R0G 0J0
　204/745-2003; Fax: 204/745-3699 – Supt., Eugene Wiebe
Morris-MacDonald School Division #19 – *1,655
　PO Box 400, Morris MB R0G 1K0
　204/746-2317; Fax: 204/746-2785 – Supt., Larry McCrady
Mountain School Division #28 – *903
　PO Box 160, Notre-Dame-de-Lourde MB R0G 1M0
　204/248-2228; Fax: 204/248-2482 – Supt., Henri Bouvier
Norwood School Division #8 – *1,075
　200 St. Mary's Rd., Winnipeg MB R2H 1H9
　204/237-0212; Fax: 204/231-1912 – Supt., Alex Boyes
Pelly Trail School Division #37 – *1,122
　PO Box 640, Russell MB R0J 1W0
　204/773-3107; Fax: 204/773-3909 – Supt., Marshall Draper
Pembina Valley School Division #27 – *889
　PO Box 459, Manitou MB R0G 1G0
　204/242-2797; Fax: 204/242-3275 – Supt., Lorne Miller
Pine Creek School Division #30 – *1,439
　PO Box 420, Gladstone MB R0J 0T0
　204/385-2216; Fax: 204/385-2825 – Supt., Ed Sklar
Portage la Prairie School Division #24 – *3,728
　535 - 3 St. NW, Portage la Prairie MB R1N 2C4
　204/857-8756; Fax: 204/239-5998 – Supt., Gary Little
Red River School Division #17 – *654
　PO Box 219, St. Pierre-Jolys MB R0A 1V0
　204/433-7815; Fax: 204/433-7102 – Supt., Ron Perron
Rhineland School Division #18 – *1,410
　PO Box 390, Altona MB R0G 0B0
　204/324-6491; Fax: 204/324-1664 – Supt., Don Wiebe
River East School Division #9
　589 Roch St., Winnipeg MB R2K 2P7
　204/667-7130; Fax: 204/661-5618
　*13,264
　Supt., George Wall
　Asst. Supt., Dr. Bob Cross
　Asst. Supt., Henry Kojima
Rolling River School Division #39 – *2,299
　PO Box 1170, Minnedosa MB R0J 1E0
　204/867-2754; Fax: 204/867-2037 – Supt., Neil Whitley
St. Boniface School Division #4 – *4,924
　50 Monterey Rd., Winnipeg MB R2J 1X1
　204/253-2681; Fax: 204/257-4805 – Supt., Jean-Yves Rochon
St. James-Assiniboia School Division #2 – *9,741
　2574 Portage Ave., Winnipeg MB R3J 0H8
　204/888-7951; Fax: 204/831-0859 – Sec.-Treas. & Dir., Education, George Buchholz
St. Vital School Division #6 – *9,856
　900 St. Mary's Rd., Winnipeg MB R2M 3R3
　204/257-7827; Fax: 204/256-8553 – Supt., Norbert Philippe
Seine River School Division #14 – *3,983
　PO Box 1146, Ste. Anne MB R0A 1R0
　204/422-8807; Fax: 204/422-8141 – Supt., Roy Seidler
Seven Oaks School Division #10 – *9,209
　830 Powers St., Winnipeg MB R2V 4E7
　204/586-8061; Fax: 204/589-2504 – Supt., John Wiens
Souris Valley School Division #42 – *1,188
　PO Box 820, Souris MB R0K 2C0
　204/483-2128; Fax: 204/483-2296 – Supt., Lloyd Paulson
Swan Valley School Division #35 – *1,995
　PO Box 995, Swan River MB R0L 1Z0
　204/734-4531; Fax: 204/734-2273 – Supt., William Schaffer
Tiger Hills School Division #29 – *1,248
　PO Box 130, Glenboro MB R0K 0X0
　204/827-2881; Fax: 204/827-2050 – Supt., Ray Le Neal
Transcona-Springfield School Division #12 – *8,246
　760 Kildare Ave. East, Winnipeg MB R2C 3Z4
　204/958-6565; Fax: 204/224-2783 – Supt., Dr. Gerry Saleski
Turtle Mountain School Division #44 – *1,325
　PO Box 280, Killarney MB R0K 1G0
　204/523-7531; Fax: 204/523-7269 – Supt., Gary Maxwell
Turtle River School Division #32 – *1,150
　PO Box 309, McCreary MB R0J 1B0
　204/835-2067; Fax: 204/835-2426 – Supt., Joe Mudry
Western School Division #47 – *1,390
　215 - 12th St., Morden MB R6M 1X4
　204/822-4448; Fax: 204/822-4262 – Supt., Colin Jamieson
White Horse Plain School Division #20 – *1,042
　PO Box 160, Elie MB R0H 0H0
　204/353-2828; Fax: 204/353-2480 – Supt., Norbert Delaquis
Winnipeg School Division #1
　1577 Wall St. East, Winnipeg MB R3E 2S5
　204/775-0231; Fax: 204/783-0118
　*34,325
　Chief Supt., Jack Smyth
　Supt., Schools, Pauline Clarke
　Supt., Schools, Al Krahn
　Supt., Schools, Jan Schubert

SPECIAL REVENUE SCHOOL DISTRICTS
Pine Falls School District #2155 – *138
　PO Box 190, Pine Falls MB R0E 1M0
　204/367-2254; Fax: 204/367-8809
Whiteshell School District #2408 – *379
　PO Box 130, Pinawa MB R0E 1L0
　204/753-8366; Fax: 204/753-2237

REMOTE SCHOOL DISTRICTS
Churchill School District #2264 – *232
　PO Box 338, Churchill MB R0B 0E0
　204/675-2218; Fax: 204/675-2648
Leaf Rapids School District #2460 – *393
　PO Box 697, Leaf Rapids MB R0B 1W0
　204/473-2423; Fax: 204/473-2288
Lynn Lake School District #2312 – *264
　PO Box 730, Lynn Lake MB R0B 0W0
　204/356-8444; Fax: 204/356-2940
Mystery Lake School District #2355 – *3,636
　408 Thompson Dr. North, Thompson MB R8N 0C5
　204/677-6150; Fax: 204/677-9528
Snow Lake School District #2309 – *252
　PO Box 220, Snow Lake MB R0B 1M0
　204/358-7708; Fax: 204/358-2451
South Winnipeg Technical Centre School Division #3000 – *1,006
　130 Henlow Bay, Winnipeg MB R3Y 1G5
　204/989-6500; Fax: 204/488-4159
Sprague School District #2439 – *149
　PO Box 69, Sprague MB R0A 1Z0
　204/437-2175; Fax: 204/437-2893

NATIVE SCHOOLS

FEDERAL SCHOOLS
Lac Brochet School, Lac Brochet MB R0B 2E0 – 204/337-2270 – Gr. Pre.-9
Tadoule Lake School, Tadoule Lake MB R0B 2C0 – 204/684-2279 – Gr. K.-7

BAND OPERATED SCHOOLS
Southeast Tribal School District #7400, Division for Schools Inc., #205, 511 Ellice Ave., Winnipeg MB R3B 1Y8 – 204/477-6050; Fax: 204/772-1226

INDIVIDUAL BAND OPERATED SCHOOLS
Abraham Beardy School, General Delivery, Shamattawa MB R0B 1K0 – 204/565-2022 – Gr. Pre.-10
Amos Okemow Memorial School, God's River MB R0B 0N0 – 204/366-2070 – Gr. Pre.-10
Anicinabe School, PO Box 219, Pine Falls MB R0E 1M0 – 204/367-2285 – Gr. Pre.-9
Birdtail Sioux N & K School, Beulah MB R0M 0B0 – 204/586-4634 – Gr. Pre.-K.
Charles Sinclair School, PO Box 1, Koostatak MB R0C 1S0 – 204/645-2206 – Gr. Pre.-12
Chemawawin School, Easterville MB R0C 0V0 – 204/329-2115 – Gr. Pre.-10
Chief Clifford Lynxleg Anishinabe School, Valley River Reserve, Shortdale MB R0L 1W0 – 204/546-2641 – Gr. Pre.-9
Chief Sam Cook Mahmuwee Education Centre, Split Lake MB R0B 1P0 – 204/342-2134 – Gr. Pre.-12
Dakota Plains School, PO Box 110, Portage la Prairie MB R1N 3B2 – 204/252-2895 – Gr. Pre.-5
Dakota Tipi School, PO Box 1569, Portage la Prairie MB R1N 3P1 – 204/857-4772 – Gr. K.-6

Dauphin River School, PO Box 140, Gypsumville MB R0C 1J0 – 204/659-5268 – Gr. 1-9
Donald Ahmo School, General Delivery, Crane MB R0L 0M0 – 204/732-2548 – Gr. Pre.-8
Fox Lake Native Spiritual School, PO Box 279, Gillam MB R0B 0L0 – 204/486-2307 – Gr. K.-8
Garden Hill First Nations High School, Island Lake MB R0B 0T0 – 204/456-2886 – Gr. 7-12
Garden Hill School, Island Lake MB R0B 0T0 – 204/456-2391 – Gr. Pre.-10
George Knott School, Waasagamach Bay MB R0B 1Z0 – 204/457-2493 – Gr. Pre.-10
George Saunders Memorial School, York Landing MB R0B 2B0 – 204/341-2118 – Gr. Pre.-9
Ginew School, PO Box 10, Ginew MB R0A 2R0 – 204/427-2490 – Gr. Pre.-9
God's Lake Narrows First Nation School, God's Narrows MB R0B 0M0 – 204/335-2003 – Gr. Pre.-9
Indian Springs School (Swan Lake Band), PO Box 1, Mariapolis MB R0K 1K0 – 204/836-2332 – Gr. Pre.-8
Jackhead School, Dallas MB R0C 0S0 – 204/394-2378 – Gr. Pre.-9
Joe A. Ross School, Opasquiak Education Authority, PO Box 1078, The Pas MB R9A 1L1 – 204/623-4286 – Gr. Pre.-12
Keeseekoowenin School, PO Box 100, Elphinstone MB R0J 0N0 – 204/625-2062 – Gr. Pre.-8
Lake Manitoba School, General Delivery, Vogar MB R0C 3C0 – 204/768-2728 – Gr. Pre.-12
Lake St. Martin School, PO Box 2020, Gypsumville MB R0C 1J0 – 204/659-5774 – Gr. Pre.-9
Little Saskatchewan School, Gypsumville MB R0C 1J0 – 204/659-2672 – Gr. Pre.-8
Long Plain School, Long Plain Education Authority, Long Plain Reserve, Edwin MB R0H 0G0 – 204/252-2326 – Gr. Pre.-9
Mikisew Middle School, Cross Lake MB R0B 0J0 – 204/676-3030 – Gr. 5-8
Miskooseepi School, Bloodvein MB R0C 0J0 – 204/395-2012 – Gr. Pre.-9
Otetiskewin Kiskinwamahtowekamik, Nelson House MB R0B 1A0 – 204/484-2242 – Gr. Pre.-12
Otter Nelson River, Cross Lake Education Authority, Cross Lake MB R0B 0J0 – 204/676-2050 – Gr. Pre.-12
Oxford House School, Oxford House MB R0B 1C0 – 204/538-2318 – Gr. Pre.-12
Peguis Central School, PO Box 220, Hodgson MB R0C 1N0 – 204/645-2164 – Gr. Pre.-12
Pinaymootang School, Fairford Reserve, Fairford MB R0C 0X0 – 204/659-2045 – Gr. Pre.-12
Pine Creek School, PO Box 160, Camperville MB R0L 0J0 – 204/524-2354 – Gr. Pre.-9
Pukatawagan School, Pukatawagan MB R0B 1G0 – 204/553-2163 – Gr. K.-10
Red Sucker Lake School, Red Sucker Lake MB R0B 1H0 – 204/469-5039 – Gr. Pre.-11
Sagkeeng Anicinabe High School, PO Box 1610, Pine Falls MB R0E 1M0 – 204/367-2244 – Gr. 9-12
Sagkeeng School, PO Box 610, Pine Falls MB R0E 1M0 – 204/367-2588 – Gr. Pre.-8
St. Theresa Point School, St. Theresa Point MB R0B 1J0 – 204/462-2600 – Gr. Pre.-10
Sandy Bay School, Marius MB R0H 0T0 – 204/843-2407 – Gr. Pre.-12
Sergeant Tommy Prince School, Scanterbury MB R0E 1W0 – 204/766-2636 – Gr. Pre.-6
Sioux Valley School, Sioux Valley Reserve, PO Box 99, Griswold MB R0M 0S0 – 204/855-2536 – Gr. Pre.-9
Waywayseecappo Community School, Wayayseecappo Reserve, PO Box 40, Rossburn MB R0J 1S0 – 204/859-2811 – Gr. Pre.-8
Wuskwisipihk School, PO Box 307, Birch River MB R0L 0E0 – 204/236-4201 – Gr. Pre.-8
Yellowquill College, Crescent Rd. West, PO Box 1599, Portage la Prairie MB R1N 3P1 – 204/239-1570 – Gr. 10-12

* indicates enrollment figure.

INSTITUTIONAL SCHOOLS
Agassiz Youth Centre, 2 River Rd., PO Box 1342, Portage la Prairie MB R1N 3A9 – 204/239-3028 – Gr. 1-12
Manitoba Development Centre, Portage la Prairie MB R1N 3C6 – 204/239-6435 – Gr. K.-12
Manitoba School for the Deaf, 500 Shaftesbury Blvd., Winnipeg MB R3P 0M1 – 204/945-8934 – Gr. K.-12
Manitoba Youth Centre, 170 Doncaster St., Winnipeg MB R3N 1X9 – 204/475-2010 – Gr. K.-12
Marymound School, 442 Scotia St., Winnipeg MB R2V 1X4 – 204/338-7971 – Gr. 6-10
Pine Ridge School, PO Box 420, Brandon MB R7A 5Z5 – 204/726-2631 – Gr. 6-12

UNIVERSITIES

Brandon University
#270 - 18th St., Brandon MB R7A 6A9
204/728-9520; Fax: 204/726-4573; URL: http://www.brandonu.ca; gopher://gopher.brandonu.ca
Chancellor, Ron Bell, Q.C.
Purchasing Agent, Robert Pearson
President & Vice-Chancellor, C. Dennis Anderson
Acting Vice-President, Academic & Research, Patrick Carrabré
Acting Vice-President, Administration & Finance, Scott Lamont
Executive Assistant to the President, Lee Clark
Manager, Book Store, Elaine Rust
Registrar, Tom Mitchell
Executive Director, Development & External Relations, Shari Decter Hirst

FACULTIES WITH DEANS
Arts, R. Florida
Acting Dean, Education, G. Richards
Science, R. Smith

SCHOOLS WITH DIRECTORS
Dean, Music, R. Goddard

University of Manitoba
#202, Admin. Building, Winnipeg MB R3T 2N2
204/474-8880; URL: http://www.umanitoba.ca; gopher://gopher.cc.umanitoba.ca
Chancellor, Arthur V. Mauro, O.C., LL.D.
President & Vice-Chancellor, Emoke Szathmary, B.A., Ph.D.
Executive Assistant to the President, W.F.W. Neville, B.A.(Hons), M.A.
Vice-President, Administration, Terry Falconer, C.A.
Vice-President, Academic & Provost, J. Gardner, B.Sc.(Hons), M.Sc., Ph.D.
Vice-President, Research & External Programs, T.P. Hogan, B.A., M.A., Ph.D.
Assoc. Vice-President, B.A. Fijal
Assoc. Vice-President, D. McCallum, B.Sc.
Assoc. Vice-President, Research, J. Kesselman, B.A., M.A., Ph.D.
Vice-Provost, Student Affairs, D.R. Morphy, B.A., M.A., Ph.D.
Vice-Provost, Staff Development, K. Ogden, A.B., M.A.T.
Vice-Provost, Programs, R.A. Johnson, B.Sc. (E.E.)
Admissions, D. Halstead
Director, Human Resources, C. Farr, B.A.
Director, Libraries, C. Presser, A.B., M.L.S.

FACULTIES WITH DEANS
Agricultural & Food Sciences, J. Elliot
Architecture, M.G. Cox
Arts, R. Currie
Acting Dean, Continuing Education, A. Percival
Dentistry, J. Wright
Education, R. Magsino
Engineering, D. Sheilds
Graduate Studies, K.R. Hughes
Human Ecology, R. Berry
Law, A. Braid
Interim Dean, Management, Jerry Gray
Medicine, N. Anthonisen
Nursing, J. Beaton
Pharmacy, W. Hindmarsh
Physical Education & Recreation Studies, H. Janzen
Science, J. Jamieson
Social Work, D. Fuchs

SCHOOLS WITH DIRECTORS
Art, D. Amundson
Dental Hygiene, E. Brownstone
Div. of Occupational Therapy, Ann D. Booth
Div. of Physical Therapy, B. Loveridge
Medical Rehabilitation, F. Stein
Music, R.B. Wedgewood

AFFILIATED COLLEGES
Collège universitaire de Saint-Boniface, 200, av de la Cathédrale, Winnipeg MB R2H 0H7 – 204/233-0210 – Rector, P. Ruest, B.A.Lat.(Phil.), B.Ed., M.Ed., Ph.D.
St. Andrew's College, 475 Dysart Rd., Winnipeg MB R3T 2M7 – 204/474-8895 – Principal, R. Yereniuk, B.A., M.A., Ph.D.
St. John's College, 400 Dysart Rd., Winnipeg MB R3T 2M5 – 204/474-8531 – Warden, M. McLean, B.A., L.Th., M.A., D.Phil.
St. Paul's College, 430 Dysart Rd., Winnipeg MB R3T 2M6 – 204/474-8575 – Rector, J. Stapleton, B.S., M.T.S., M.A., Ph.D.
University College, 500 Dysart Rd., Winnipeg MB R3T 2M8 – 204/474-9388 – Provost, C.C. Bigelow, B.A.Sc., M.Sc., Ph.D.

APPROVED TEACHING CENTRES
Canadian Mennonite Bible College, 600 Shaftesbury Blvd., Winnipeg MB R3P 0M4 – 204/888-6781 – President, Rev. J. Neufeld
Canadian Nazarene College, 1301 Lee Blvd., Winnipeg MB R3T 2P7 – 204/269-2120 – President, Dr. R. Coulter
Catherine Booth Bible College, 447 Webb Pl., Winnipeg MB R3B 2P2 – 204/947-6701, 6702, 6950 – President, Major Earl Robinson
Prairie Theatre Exchange, Unit Y, 300-393 Portage Ave., Winnipeg MB R3B 2H6 – 204/942-7291 – Artistic Director, M. Springate

University of Winnipeg
515 Portage Ave., Winnipeg MB R3B 2E9
204/786-7811; Fax: 204/786-8983; Email: http://www.uwinnipeg.ca
Chancellor, Carol Shields
Chair, Board of Regents, R. Purves
President, M. Hanen
Vice-President, Administration, G. Lane
Vice-President, Academic, George Tomlinson
Controller, H. McMullin
University Secretary, R. Kingsley
Executive Director, University Relations, J. Anderson
Purchasing Agent, B. Bater
Manager, Bookstore, Vacant
President, Menno Simons College, G. Richert

SCHOOLS WITH DIRECTORS
Dean, Arts & Science, J. Hofley
Dean, Collegiate, D. Price
Dean, Continuing Education, C. Nordman
Dean, Theology, H. King

ASSOCIATED INSTITUTION
Concord College, 169 Riverton Ave., Winnipeg MB R2L 2ES – 204/669-6583

COMMUNITY COLLEGES

ASSINIBOINE COMMUNITY COLLEGE
1430 Victoria Ave. East, Brandon MB R7A 2A9
204/726-6600; Fax: 204/726-6753; Email: info@adminet.assiniboinec.mb.ca; URL: http://www.assiniboinec.mb.ca
President, B. Cooke
Parkland Campus, 520 Whitmore Ave. East, PO Box 4000, Dauphin MB R7N 2V5 – 204/622-2023; Fax: 204/638-3941

ÉCOLE TECHNIQUE ET PROFESSIONNELLE
c/o Collège Universitaire de Saint-Boniface, 200, av de la Cathédrale, Saint-Boniface MB R2H 0H7
204/233-0210; Fax: 204/237-3240
Director, Raymonde Gagné, B.A., Cert.Ed., M.B.A.

KEEWATIN COMMUNITY COLLEGE
436 - 7 St. East, PO Box 3000, The Pas MB R9A 1M7
204/627-8500; Fax: 204/623-7316; Toll Free: 1-800-238-8508; URL: http://www.keewatincc.mb.ca
President, W.A. Sam Shaw, Email: sshaw@keewatincc.mb.ca

RED RIVER COMMUNITY COLLEGE
2055 Notre Dame Ave., Winnipeg MB R3H 0J9
204/632-2311; Fax: 204/632-9661
President, Dr. Tony Knowles, Email: tknowles@rrcc.mb.ca

PRIVATE VOCATIONAL SCHOOLS

ACADEMY OF LEARNING - NORTH
1109 Henderson Hwy., Winnipeg MB R2G 1L4
204/334-2121; Fax: 204/334-2129; Email: rolan bisson@mbnet.mb.ca

ACADEMY OF LEARNING - SOUTH
106B Scurfied Blvd., Winnipeg MB R3Y 1G4
204/489-7684

CAMBRIAN COLLEGE
909 - 24th St., Brandon MB R7B 1Y5
204/725-3492

CANADIAN COLLEGE OF TAXIDERMY
419 - 1st Ave., McCreary MB R0J 1B0
204/835-2639; Fax: 204/835-2764

CANADIAN SCHOOL OF FLORAL ART
569 St. Mary's Rd., Winnipeg MB R2M 3M6
204/233-2426

CAREER DEVELOPMENT INSTITUTE
#400, 393 Portage Ave., Winnipeg MB R3B 2H6
204/942-1773

COMPUTER MULTIMEDIA TECHNOLOGY CENTRE
491 Portage Ave., Winnipeg MB R3B 2E4
204/772-4411

HERZING CAREER COLLEGE
723 Portage Ave., Winnipeg MB R3G 0M8
204/775-8175

THE JACKS INSTITUTE
2 Alpine Ave., PO Box 52028, Winnipeg MB R3M 5P9
204/255-1550

MID-OCEAN RECORDING STUDIO
1578 Erin St., Winnipeg MB R3E 2T1
204/774-3715

NATIONAL INSTITUTE OF BROADCASTING
831 Portage Ave., 4th Fl., Winnipeg MB R3G 0N6
204/772-6720

NATIONAL TRAINING INSTITUTE
831 Portage Ave., 2nd Fl., Winnipeg MB R2G 0N6
204/775-8751; Fax: 204/772-6720

ROBERTSON COLLEGE INC.
696 Portage Ave., Winnipeg MB R3G 0M6
204/774-9444; Fax: 204/774-9345

SCHOOL OF RECORDING ARTS OF MANITOBA
275 Selkirk Ave., Winnipeg MB R2W 2L6
204/586-8057

SUCCESS/ANGUS BUSINESS COLLEGE
#215, 267 Edmonton St., Winnipeg MB R3C 1S2
204/942-6495

INDEPENDENT & PRIVATE SCHOOLS

Schools with enrollment of 50 or more, listed alphabetically by city.

Arborg: Interlake Mennonite Fellowship School, PO Box 388, Arborg MB R0C 0A0 – 204/364-2328 – Gr. 1-10
Arborg: Lake Centre Mennonite Fellowship School, PO Box 417, Arborg MB R0C 0A0 – 204/364-2201 – Gr. 1-9
Arborg: Morweena Christian School, PO Box 1030, Arborg MB R0C 0A0 – 204/364-2466 – Gr. 1-12
Austin Christian School, PO Box 226, Austin MB R0H 0C0 – 204/637-2303 – Gr. 1-12
Austin Mennonite School, PO Box 267, Austin MB R0H 0C0 – 204/637-2008 – Gr. 1-10
Austin: Pine Creek School, Pine Creek Colony, PO Box 299, Austin MB R0H 0C0 – 204/466-2822 – Gr. 1-8
Beausejour: Willow Grove School, PO Box 783, Beausejour MB R0E 0C0 – 204/268-3207 – Gr. 3-9
Birnie: Shady Oak Christian Academy, General Delivery, Birnie MB R0J 0J0 – 204/966-3477 – Gr. 1-9
Brandon: Christian Heritage School, PO Box 1242, Brandon MB R7A 6K4 – 204/725-3209 – *87 – Gr. K.-9
Brandon: Early Years Development Centre, 911 - 26th St., Brandon MB R7B 2B7 – 204/728-3275 – Gr. Pre.-K.
Carman: Dufferin Christian School, Box 1450, Carman MB R0G 0J0 – 204/745-2278 – *156 – Gr. K.-12
Cartwright Community Independent School, General Delivery, Cartwright MB R0K 0L0 – 204/529-2357 – Gr. 10-12
Cartwright: Rock Lake School, PO Box 69, Cartwright MB R0K 0L0 – 204/529-2349 – Gr. 1-9
Dauphin: Western Christian College, PO Box 5000, Dauphin MB R7N 2V5 – 204/638-8801 – *83 – Gr. 7-12
Edwin: Grace Christian Academy, General Delivery, Edwin MB R0H 0G0 – 204/252-2217 – Gr. 1-12
Elma: Riverside School, PO Box 136, Elma MB R0E 0Z0 – 204/348-2686 – Gr. 1-9
Fort Whyte: McGillivray Montessori School, PO Box 99, Fort Whyte MB R0G 0G0 – 204/488-5046 – *88 – Gr. Pre.-6
Grandview: Poplar Grove School, PO Box 70, Grandview MB R0L 0Y0 – 204/546-2691 – Gr. 1-9
Gretna: Mennonite Collegiate Institute, PO Box 250, Gretna MB R0G 0V0 – 204/327-5891 – *161 – Gr. 9-12
Horndean Christian Day School, PO Box 79, Horndean MB R0G 0Z0 – 204/829-3865 – Gr. 2-9
Île-des-Chênes: Blackmore Private School, Rainbow Colony, PO Box 310, Île-des-Chênes MB R0A 0T0 – 204/878-2428 – Gr. 4-12
Kenville: Emmanuel Fellowship Christian School, PO Box 9, Kenville MB R0L 0B0 – 204/734-2651 – Gr. 1-12
Kenville: Riverdale School, RR#1, Kenville MB R0L 0Z0 – 204/734-2660 – Gr. 1-9

Killarney Christian Academy, PO Box 1150, Killarney MB R0K 1G0 – 204/523-7318 – Gr. 1-12
Killarney: Lakeside Christian School, PO Box 894, Killarney MB R0K 1G0 – 204/523-8240 – Gr. K.-7
Kleefeld: New Hope Christian School, PO Box 120, Kleefeld MB R0A 0V0 – 204/377-4204 – Gr. 1-12
Kleefeld: Wild Rose School, PO Box 167, Kleefeld MB R0A 0V0 – 204/377-4778 – Gr. 1-8
Lorette: New Life Academy, PO Box 468, Lorette MB R0A 0Y0 – 204/878-2521 – Gr. 3-12
Morden College, 514 Stephen St., Morden MB R6M 1T7 – 204/822-6156 – Gr. 10-12
Morris: Albright Private School, PO Box 819, Morris MB R0G 1K0 – 204/746-8933 – Gr. K.-8
Morris Christian Day School, PO Box 447, Morris MB R0G 1K0 – 204/746-8130 – Gr. 1-10
Neepawa: Living Hope School, PO Box 2158, Neepawa MB R0J 1H0 – 204/966-3274 – Gr. 1-10
Pine Falls: Christian Faith Academy, PO Box 459, Pine Falls MB R0E 1M0 – 204/367-2056 – Gr. 1-12
Plum Coulee: Prairie Mennonite School, PO Box 53, Plum Coulee MB R0G 1R0 – 204/829-3336 – Gr. 1-9
Portage Christian Academy, PO Box 1300, Portage la Prairie MB R1N 3L5 – 204/857-3780 – Gr. 2-12
Portage La Prairie: Westpark School, PO Box 91, Portage La Prairie MB R1N 3B2 – 204/857-3726 – *138 – Gr. K.-12
Rapid City: Potter's Wheel Christian School, PO Box 315, Rapid City MB R0K 1W0 – 204/826-2607 – Gr. 2-9
Riverton: Mennville Christian School, Box 448, Riverton MB R0C 2R0 – 204/378-5576 – *51 – Gr. K.-10
Roblin: Parkland Christian School, PO Box 480, Roblin MB R0L 1P0 – 204/937-2870 – Gr. 1-9
Roblin: St. Vladimir's College, PO Box 789, Roblin MB R0L 1P0 – 204/937-2173 – Gr. 10-12
Rosenort: Prairie View School, PO Box 117, Rosenort MB R0G 1W0 – 204/746-8837
Ste. Anne: Greenland School, RR#1, Ste. Anne MB R0A 1R0 – 204/355-4922 – Gr. 1-9
Sinclair: Stony Creek School, PO Box 64, Sinclair MB R0M 2A0 – 204/662-4431 – Gr. 1-9
Steinbach: Country View School, PO Box 3910, Steinbach MB R0A 2A0 – 204/326-1481 – Gr. 1-9
Steinbach: Mennonite Christian Academy, PO Box 20749, Steinbach MB R0A 2T2 – 204/434-9315 – Gr. 1-10
Steinbach Christian Academy, PO Box 20629, Steinbach MB R0A 2T2 – 204/326-5553 – Gr. K.-10
Steinbach Christian High School, PO Box 1420, Steinbach MB R0A 2A0 – 204/326-3537 – *69 – Gr. 10-12
Swan River: Community Bible Fellowship Christian School, PO Box 1630, Swan River MB R0L 1Z0 – 204/734-2174 – Gr. K.-9
Tolstoi: Border View Christian Day School, PO Box 83, Tolstoi MB R0A 2E0 – 204/427-2932 – Gr. K-9
Winkler: Valley Mennonite Academy, Grp. 7, RR#1, PO Box 139, Winkler MB R6W 4A1 – 204/325-8172 – Gr. 1-12
Winnipeg: Balmoral Hall, 630 Westminster Ave., Winnipeg MB R3C 3S1 – 204/784-1600; Fax: 204/774-5534 – Head, Diane Bieber – *437 – Gr. K.-12
Winnipeg: Calvin Christian School, 245 Sutton Ave., Winnipeg MB R2G 0T1 – 204/338-7981 – *307 – Gr. K.-9
Winnipeg: Children's House, 150 Pacific Ave., Winnipeg MB R3B 3K8 – 204/956-1622 – Gr. Pre.-K
Winnipeg: Christ the King School, 8 Lennox Ave., Winnipeg MB R2M 1A6 – 204/257-0027 – *164 – Gr. Pre.-6
Winnipeg: Faith Academy, 600 Jefferson Ave., Winnipeg MB R2V 0P2 – 204/338-6150 – *183 – Gr. K.-12
Winnipeg: Holy Cross School, 300 Dubuc St., Winnipeg MB R2H 1E4 – 204/237-4936 – *258 – Gr. K.-8
Winnipeg: Holy Ghost School, 333 Selkirk Ave., Winnipeg MB R2W 2L8 – 204/582-1053 – *225 – Gr. K.-8

Winnipeg: Immaculate Heart of Mary School, 650 Flora Ave., Winnipeg MB R2W 2S5 – 204/582-5698 – *188 – Gr. K.-8
Winnipeg: Immanuel Christian School, 215 Rougeau Ave., Winnipeg MB R2C 3Z9 – 204/661-8937 – *131 – Gr. K.-12
Winnipeg: Indian Metis & Holiness School, Mr. Mark Becker, 388 Elgin Ave., Winnipeg MB R3A 0K4 – 204/949-0870 – Gr. 1-11
Winnipeg: Joseph Wolinsky Collegiate, 437 Matheson Ave., Winnipeg MB R2W 0E1 – 204/589-5345 – *256 – Gr. 7-12
Winnipeg: Keystone Christian School, 1770 King Edward St., Winnipeg MB R2R 0M5 – 204/987-8811 – Gr. K-12
Winnipeg: The King's School, 851 Panet Rd., Winnipeg MB R2K 4C9 – 204/989-6581 – *109 – Gr. K.-10
Winnipeg: The Laureate Academy, 367 Hampton St., Winnipeg MB R3J 1P7 – 204/831-7107 – Gr. 1-11
Winnipeg: Linden Christian School, 877 Wilkes Ave., Winnipeg MB R3P 1B8 – 204/989-6730 – *114 – Gr. K.-9
Winnipeg: Mennonite Brethren Collegiate Institute, 180 Riverton Ave., Winnipeg MB R2L 2E8 – 204/667-8210 – *508 – Gr. 7-12
Winnipeg: The Montessori Learning Centre, 170 Ashland Ave., Winnipeg MB R3L 1L1 – 204/475-1039 – Gr. Pre.-K.
Winnipeg: Msgr. James K. MacIsaac School, 249 Arnold Ave., Winnipeg MB R3L 0W5 – 204/452-7632 – *122 – Gr. K.-8
Winnipeg: Oholei Torah School, 2095 Sinclair St., Winnipeg MB R2V 3K2 – 204/334-8222 – Gr. Pre.-7
Winnipeg: Ramah Hebrew School, 705 Lanark St., Winnipeg MB R3N 1M4 – 204/488-4493 – *338 – Gr. Pre.-6
Winnipeg: Red River Valley Junior Academy, 56 Grey St., Winnipeg MB R2L 1V3 – 204/667-2383 – *76 – Gr. K.-10
Winnipeg: St. Alphonsus School, 343 Munroe Ave., Winnipeg MB R2K 1H2 – 204/667-6271 – *231 – Gr. K.-8
Winnipeg: St. Boniface Diocesan High School, 282 Dubuc St., Winnipeg MB R2H 1E4 – 204/233-7385 – *213 – Gr. 9-12
Winnipeg: St. Charles Academy, 331 St. Charles St., Winnipeg MB R3K 1T6 – 204/837-1520 – *185 – Gr. K.-8
Winnipeg: St. Edward's School, 836 Arlington St., Winnipeg MB R3E 2E4 – 204/774-8773 – *188 – Gr. K.-6
Winnipeg: St. Emile School, 552 St. Anne's Rd., Winnipeg MB R2M 3G4 – 204/253-9331 – *220 – Gr. K.-8
Winnipeg: St. Gerard's School, 40 Foster St., Winnipeg MB R2L 1V7 – 204/667-4862 – *104 – Gr. K.-6
Winnipeg: St. Ignatius School, 239 Harrow St., Winnipeg MB R3M 2Y3 – 204/475-1386 – *263 – Gr. Pre.-8
Winnipeg: St. John Brebeuf School, 605 Renfrew St., Winnipeg MB R3N 1J8 – 204/489-2115 – *244 – Gr. K.-8
Winnipeg: St. John's-Ravenscourt School, 400 South Dr., Winnipeg MB R3T 3K5 – 204/477-2402 – *683 – Gr. 1-12
Winnipeg: St. Joseph the Worker School, 505 Brewster St., Winnipeg MB R2C 2W6 – 204/222-1832 – *129 – Gr. K.-6
Winnipeg: St. Mary's Academy, 550 Wellington Cres., Winnipeg MB R3M 0C1 – 204/477-0244 – *520 – Gr. 7-12
Winnipeg: St. Maurice School, 1639 Pembina Hwy., Winnipeg MB R3T 2G6 – 204/452-2873 – *303 – Gr. K.-12
Winnipeg: St. Michael's School, 174 Maple St., Winnipeg MB R2W 3L4 – 204/582-4664 – Gr. 1-10
Winnipeg: St. Paul's High School, 2200 Grant Ave., Winnipeg MB R3P 0P8 – 204/888-1605 – *504 – Gr. 9-12

Winnipeg: St. Raphael's Academy, 480 McKenzie St., Winnipeg MB R2W 5B9 – 204/589-0759 – Gr. K.-7
Winnipeg: Springs Christian Academy, 261 Youville St., Winnipeg MB R2H 2S7 – 204/235-0863 – *88 – Gr. K.-9
Winnipeg: Talmud Torah, I.L. Peretz School, 427 Matheson Ave., Winnipeg MB R2V 0E1 – 204/586-8366 – *166 – Gr. Pre.-6
Winnipeg: University of Winnipeg Collegiate, #2W04, 515 Portage Ave., Winnipeg MB R3B 2E9 – 204/786-9221 – *458 – Gr. 11-12
Winnipeg: Victorious Faith Centre, 50 Scurfield Rd., Winnipeg MB R3Y 1G4 – 204/488-2487 – Gr. Pre.-12
Winnipeg Mennonite Elementary School, 250 Bedson St., Winnipeg MB R3K 1R7 – 204/885-1032 – *297 – Gr. K.-6
Winnipeg Montessori Schools Inc., 1525 Willson Pl., Winnipeg MB R3T 4H1 – 204/452-3315 – Gr. Pre.-K
Winnipeg: Zion Christian Academy, 305 Machray Ave., Winnipeg MB R2W 1A3 – 204/582-6541 – Gr. K.-9

NEW BRUNSWICK

Department of Advanced Education & Labour
416 York St., PO Box 6000, Fredericton NB E3B 5H1
506/453-2597; Fax: 506/453-7913
Director, Curriculum & Evaluation, Peter Kilburn, 506/453-8226

Department of Education
PO Box 6000, Fredericton NB E3B 5H1
506/453-3678; Fax: 506/453-3325

CURRICULUM INFORMATION
Curriculum Development, Barry Lydon, 506/453-2155; Fax: 506/453-3325
Direction des services pédagogiques, Donata Thériault, 506/453-2743; Fax: 506/453-3325

CORRESPONDENCE EDUCATION SERVICE
NBCC/CCNB, 1234 Mountain Rd., PO Box 2100, Stn A, Moncton NB E1C 8H9
506/856-2237; Fax: 506/856-2665

For detailed departmental listings, see Index: "Education, Depts."

SCHOOL DISTRICTS
New Brunswick is divided into 18 school districts under the direction of eight superintendents of schools. Each school district has a director of education. Instruction is offered in both official languages. The administration of public school education in each school district is the responsibility of a locally elected Board of School Trustees.

Boards with an enrollment of more than 10,000 are in bold print.
District Scolaire #1 – *9,869
  533, rue Main, PO Box 398, Shédiac NB E0A 3G0
  506/533-3300 – Dir. gén., Lucille Collette; Dir. de l'éducation, Annette Roy
District Scolaire #11 – *5,524
  18B, boul Cartier, CP 40, Richibouctou NB E0A 2M0
  506/523-7655 – Dir. gén., Lucille Collette; Dir. de l'éducation, Ronald LeVasseur
District Scolaire #3 – *8,555
  532, ch Madawaska, Grand-Sault NB E3Y 1A3
  506/473-7360 – Dir. de l'éducation, Leo-Paul Charest; Dir. gén., Jocelyne Mallet-Parent
District Scolaire #5 – *4,773
  21, rue King, Campbellton NB E3N 1C5
  506/789-2255 – Dir. gén., Jocelyne Mallet-Parent; Dir. de l'éducation, Jean-Guy Levesque

District Scolaire #7 – *4,786
  970, rue Principale, CP 1000, Beresford NB E0B 1H0
  506/547-2771 – Dir. gén., Keith Coughlan; Dir. de l'éducation, Yolande McLaughlin
District Scolaire #9
  3376, Place du Quai, rue Principale, CP 3668, Tracadie-Sheila NB E1X 1G5
  506/394-3400
  *10,849
  Dir. gén., Keith Coughlan
  Dir. de l'éducation, Fernande McLaughlin
School District #10 – *4,712
  11 School St., St. Stephen NB E0J 2B0
  506/466-7300 – Supt., Vernon Goodfellow; Dir. of Education, Paul Sweeney
School District #12 – *4,838
  138 Chapel St., PO Box 40, Woodstock NB E0J 2B0
  506/325-4432 – Supt., Vernon Goodfellow; Dir. of Education, Frank Hayes
School District #13 – *4,872
  566 East Riverside Dr., PO Box 160, Perth-Andover NB E0J 1V0
  506/273-4777 – Supt., Vernon Goodfellow; Dir. of Education, Colleen Sprague
School District #14 – *2,740
  464 Montgomery St., PO Box 400, Dalhousie NB E0K 1B0
  506/684-7555 – Supt., Robin Roe; Dir. of Education, Donald Thompson
School District #15 – *2,710
  270 Douglas Ave., PO Box 1058, Bathurst NB E2A 4H8
  506/547-2777 – Supt., Robin Roe; Dir. of Education, Gene Bishop
School District #16 – *7,431
  78 Henderson St., Chatham NB E1N 2R7
  506/778-6075 – Supt., Robin Roe; Dir. of Education, Kathy Grebenc
School District #17 – *5,965
  2 Civic Ct., PO Box 190, Chipman NB E0E 1C0
  506/339-7000 – Supt., Victor Martin; Dir. of Education, Marilyn Ball
School District #18
  #301, 565 Priestman St., PO Box 10, Fredericton NB E3B 4Y4
  506/453-5454
  *13,267
  Supt., Victor Martin
  Dir. of Education, Pam Campbell
School District #2
  1077 St. George Blvd., Moncton NB E1E 4C9
  506/856-3222
  *14,356
  Supt., Marilyn Adams-Smith
  Dir. of Education, William Strugnell
School District #4 – *6,073
  1022 Main St., PO Box 1079, Sussex NB E0E 1P0
  506/432-2016 – Supt., Marilyn Adams-Smith; Dir. of Education, Greg West
School District #6 – *8,409
  70 Hampton Rd., PO Box 820, Rothesay NB E2E 5A8
  506/847-6262 – Supt., Dennis Cochrane; Dir. of Education., James Stevenson
School District #8
  384 Lancaster Ave., Saint John NB E2M 2L5
  506/658-5300
  *15,325
  Supt., Dennis Cochrane
  Dir. of Education, Brian McCarthy

NATIVE SCHOOLS
Big Cove School – *351
  RR#1, Site 11, PO Box 6, Rexton NB E0A 2L0
  506/523-6880 – Principal, K. Francis
Burnt Church School – *221
  RR#2, Lagaceville NB E0C 1K0

* indicates enrollment figure.

506/776-3776 – Principal, Sharon Millar
Eel Ground Federal School – *65
PO Box 265, Newcastle NB E1V 3M3
506/622-4979 – Principal, Peter MacDonald
Eel River Kindergarten – *14
PO Box 1444, Dalhousie NB E0K 1B0
506/684-4533 – Principal, Doreen Gagne
Kingsclear School – *36
RR#6, Fredericton NB E3B 4X7
506/363-3019 – Principal, Sherry Graham
Red Bank Federal School – *59
PO Box 30, Red Bank NB E0C 1W0
506/836-7500 – Principal, Gail McKibbon
St. Mary's Kindergarten – *23
c/o St. Mary's Band Hall, 25 Dedham St., Fredericton NB E3A 2V3
506/472-5768 – Principal, V. Brooks
Tobique Mah-Sos School – *121
PO Box 840, Perth-Andover NB E0J 1V0
506/273-6815 – Principal, Tim Nicholas
Woodstock Indian Community Kindergarten – *12
c/o Woodstock Bank, Box 8, Site 1, RR#1, Woodstock NB E0J 2B0
506/328-3303 – Principal, June Tomah

UNIVERSITIES

Mount Allison University
Sackville NB E0A 3C0
506/364-2275; URL: http://www.mta.ca/
Chancellor, Harold Purdy Crawford, Q.C., B.A., LL.M., LL.D.
President & Vice-Chancellor, I.D.C. Newbould, B.A., M.A., Ph.D., F.R.H.S.
Chair, Board of Regents, J. James Keith, B.A., M.A.
Vice-President, Academic, W.R. Driedzic, B.Sc., M.Sc., Ph.D.
Vice-President, Administration & Finance, Sharon MacFarlane, B.B.A., C.A.
Asst. Vice-President, Student Service, J. Hollett, B.A., B.Ed.
Dean, B.J. Ellard, B.Mus., M.A., Ph.D.
Dean, P.M. Ennals, B.A., M.A., Ph.D.
Dean, J.A. Stanton, B.A., M.A., Ph.D.
Dean, J.M. Stewart, B.Sc., M.Sc.
Registrar, L.A. Owen, B.A., M.A.

Université de Moncton
Moncton NB E1A 3E9
506/858-4000; Fax: 506/858-4379; URL: gopher://gopher.umoncton.ca
Chancelier, Antonine Maillet
Recteur, Jean-Bernard Robichaud, Email: recteur@umoncton.ca
Secrétaire générale, Simone Leblanc-Rainville, Email: secgen@umoncton.ca
Vice-recteur, Administration et ressources humaines, Fernand Landry, Email: landryf@umoncton.ca
Vice-recteur, Enseignement et recherche, Léandre Desjardins, Email: desjarl@umoncton.ca
Directeur, Développement universitaire, Rhéal Bérubé
Directrice, Education permanente, Colette Landry Martin, Email: martine@umoncton.ca
Directeur, Service des finances, Donald Cormier, Email: cormied@umoncton.ca
Directeur, Services administratifs,
Directeur, Services aux étudiants, Gilles Nadeau
Bibliothécaire en chef, Gilles Chiasson
Directeur, Services techniques, Eustache Haché
Directeur, Service du personnel, Rhéal Belliveau
Directeur, Service des communications, Paul-Emile Benoit, Email: benoitpe@umoncton.ca
Directeur, Service des anciens et amis, William Boucher

FACULTÉS AVEC DOYENS
Administration, George Wybouw
Arts, Zenon Chiasson
Droit, Michel Doucet
Études supérieures et de la recherche, Truong Vo-Van
Sciences, Victorin Mallet
Sciences de l'éducation, Rodrigué Landry
Sciences sociales, Renaud LeBlanc

ÉCOLES AVEC DIRECTEURS
Education physique et loisir, Hermel Couturier
Génie, Nassir El-Jabi
Nutrition et d'études familiales, Lita Villalon
Sciences forestières, Edgar Robichaud
Sciences infirmières, Michèle Trudeau

CENTRES UNIVERSITAIRES
Vice-recteur, Saint-Louis-Maillet, Normand Carrier
Vice-recteur, Shippigan, Armand Caron

University of New Brunswick
PO Box 4400, Stn A, Fredericton NB E3B 5A3
506/453-4666; Fax: 506/453-4599; URL: http://degaulle.hil.unb.ca
Saint John Campus, PO Box 5050, Saint John NB E2L 4L5 – 506/648-5500; Fax: 506/648-5528 – Vice-President, F.C. Miner
Chancellor, F.S. Eaton, O.C., B.A., LL.D.
President, Elizabeth Parr-Johnston, B.A., M.A., Ph.D., Email: epj@unb.ca
Vice-President, Academic, L. Visentin, B.Sc., M.S., Ph.D., Email: visentin@UNB.CA
Vice-President, Finance & Administration, J. F. O'Sullivan, B.B.A., LL.D., Email: jos@UNB.CA
Vice-President, Research & International Cooperation, F.R. Wilson, B.Sc.E., M.Sc.E., Ph.D., F.C.S.C.E., Email: frw@UNB.CA
Comptroller, D.V. Murray, B.Comm., C.A.
University Secretary, S. Strople, B.A., M.A., Email: sstrople@UNB.CA
Registrar, Deanne Dennison, B.A., Email: denn@UNB.CA
Personnel, J.D. Horn, B.Sc., Email: jdhorn@unb.ca
Dean, Students, T.A. Austin, B.A., B.Ed., M.Sc.(C.S.), Email: austin@unb.ca
Purchasing Agent, L.M. Spencer, Email: lspencer@unb.ca
Manager, Bookstore, D.G. McConnell, Email: mcconnel@unb.ca

FACULTIES WITH DEANS
Administration,
Arts, P.C. Kent, B.A., B.Ed., M.Sc.Econ., Ph.D.
Computer Science, W.D. Wasson, B.Sc.E., S.M., Ph.D.
Acting Dean, Education, H. Cowan, B.Comm., M.Ed.
Engineering, W. Faig, Dip.Ing., M.Sc.E., Dr.Ing.
Forestry & Environmental Management, I.R. Methven, B.Sc.F., Ph.D.
Kinesiology, T. Haggerty, B.A., B.P.H.E., M.A., Ph.D.
Law, Anne LeForest, B.A., LL.B., LL.M.
Nursing, Penelope K. Ericson, B.S.N., M.S.N.
Science, I. Unger, B.Sc., M.Sc., Ph.D.

SCHOOLS WITH DIRECTORS
Dean, Graduate Studies, M.A. Edwards, B.Sc., M.Sc., Ph.D.

AFFILIATED COLLEGES
Maritime Forest Ranger School, RR#10, Fredericton NB E3B 6H6 – 506/458-0199 – Director, Stephen Hoyt, B.Sc.F., M.Sc., M.Sc.F.

ASSOCIATED INSTITUTION
St. Thomas University, PO Box 4569, Fredericton NB E3B 5G3 – 506/452-7700; Fax: 506/450-9615; URL: http://www.stthomasu.ca – Chancellor, Most Rev. J. Edward Troy, B.A., B.Ph., Lic.in Phil., Ph.D., LL.D.

COMMUNITY COLLEGES

NEW BRUNSWICK COMMUNITY COLLEGE (BATHURST)/ COLLÈGE COMMUNAUTAIRE DU NOUVEAU-BRUNSWICK(BATHURST)
PO Box 266, Bathurst NB E2A 3Z2
506/547-2145; Fax: 506/547-2741
Principal, Maurice Roy, Email: roymauri@nbnet.nb.ca

NEW BRUNSWICK COMMUNITY COLLEGE (CAMPBELLTON)/ COLLÈGE COMMUNAUTAIRE DU NOUVEAU-BRUNSWICK (CAMPBELLTON)
PO Box 309, Campbellton NB E3N 3G7

NEW BRUNSWICK COMMUNITY COLLEGE (DIEPPE)/COLLÈGE COMMUNAUTAIRE DU NOUVEAU-BRUNSWICK (DIEPPE)
PO Box 4519, Dieppe NB E1A 6G1
506/856-2200
Principal, M. Richard

NEW BRUNSWICK COMMUNITY COLLEGE (EDMUNDSTON)/ COLLÈGE COMMUNAUTAIRE DU NOUVEAU-BRUNSWICK (EDMUNSTON)
PO Box 70, Edmundston NB E3V 3K7
506/735-2504; Fax: 506/735-1108
Principal, Michel Laroche, Email: mlaroche@gov.nb.ca

NEW BRUNSWICK COMMUNITY COLLEGE (MIRAMICHI)/ COLLÈGE COMMUNAUTAIRE DU NOUVEAU-BRUNSWICK (MIRAMICHI)
PO Box 1053, Chatham NB E1N 3W4
506/773-9451
Principal, A. Heckel

NEW BRUNSWICK COMMUNITY COLLEGE (MONCTON)/ COLLÈGE COMMUNAUTAIRE DU NOUVEAU BRUNSWICK (MONCTON)
1234 Mountain Rd., Moncton NB E1C 8H9
506/856-2230; Fax: 506/856-3382
Principal, John Lean, Email: JohnLean@gov.nb.ca

NEW BRUNSWICK COMMUNITY COLLEGE (SAINT JOHN)/ COLLÈGE COMMUNAUTAIRE DU NOUVEAU-BRUNSWICK (SAINT JOHN)
PO Box 2270, Saint John NB E2L 3V1
506/658-6600; Fax: 506/658-6792
Principal, Cheryl M.G. Robertson

NEW BRUNSWICK COMMUNITY COLLEGE (ST. ANDREWS)/ COLLÈGE COMMUNAUTAIRE DU NOUVEAU-BRUNSWICK (ST. ANDREWS)
PO Box 427, St. Andrews NB EOG 2XO
Principal, Gerald Ingersoll
Registrar, Peter Acheson, 506/529-5025; Fax: 506/529-5078; Email: pa5025@gov.nb.ca

POST-SECONDARY & SPECIALIZED INSTITUTIONS

NEW BRUNSWICK COLLEGE OF CRAFT & DESIGN
15 Carleton St., PO Box 6000, Fredericton NB E3B 5H1
506/453-2305; Fax: 506/457-7352
Director, Janice Gillies

INDEPENDENT & PRIVATE SCHOOLS

Schools with enrollment of 50 or more, listed alphabetically by city.
Fredericton: Devon Park Christian School, 145 Clark St., PO Box 3510, Stn B, Fredericton NB E3A 5J8 – 506/458-9377 – Principal, Bev Amos – *168 – Gr. K.-12
Moncton Wesleyan Academy, 945 St. George Blvd., Moncton NB E1E 2C9 – 506/857-2293 – Principal, Willie Brownlee – *114 – Gr. K.-12
Plaster Rock: Apostolic Christian School, PO Box 28, Plaster Rock NB E0J 1W0 – 506/356-8690 – Principal, Sanford Goodine – *96 – Gr. K.-12

Rothesay: RCS-Netherwood School, College Hill, Rothesay NB E0G 2W0 – 506/847-8224 – Principal, Paul Kitchen – *142 – Gr. 7-12

Rothesay Baptist Christian School, PO Box 788, Rothesay NB E2E 5A8 – 506/847-7897 – Principal, Dexter Stults – *52 – Gr. K-12

NEWFOUNDLAND

Department of Education
PO Box 8700, St. John's NF A1B 4J6
709/729-5097; Fax: 709/729-5896

ADVANCED STUDIES BRANCH
Director, Institutional and Industrial Training, Barry Roberts, 709/729-2350

PRIMARY, ELEMENTARY & SECONDARY BRANCH
Manager, Curriculum Learning Resources, Wilbert Boone, 709/729-2739
Director, Program Development, Dr. Glen Loveless, 709/729-3004

For detailed departmental listings, see Index: "Education, Depts."

SCHOOL BOARDS
There are presently 16 Integrated School Boards (Anglican, United Church & Salvation Army), 9 Roman Catholic School Boards, one Pentecostal Assemblies School Board, one Seventh Day Adventist School Board, for a total of 27 School Boards.

School boards are undergoing fundamental reorganization. The current 27 denominational school boards will be replaced by ten regional boards. At time of going to press, details were incomplete. Below is a list of the new school boards, with Chair and Treasurer.

Labrador
  Chair, Lt. Marshall Dean
  Treas., Pastor Everett Flight
Northern Peninsula/Labrador South
  Chair, Robert Mesher
  Treas., Don Brown
Corner Brook/Deer Lake/St. Barbe South
  Chair, John Edgar
  Treas., Owen Whalen
Stephenville/Port aux Basques
  Chair, James Mercer
  Treas., Michael Finn
Baie Verte/Central/Connaigre
  Chair, George Woodman
  Treas., Grace Hedges
Lewisporte/Gander
  Chair, Everett Saunders
  Treas., Scott Pritchett
Burin
  Chair, Bill Hodder
  Treas., Jim Farrell
Clarenville/Bonavista
  Chair, Ross Wiseman
  Treas., Joe Stringer
Avalon West
  Chair, Lorraine Brown
  Treas., Frank Antle
Avalon East
  Chair, Kevin Breen
  Treas., Robert Haliday

Boards with an enrollment of more than 10,000 are in bold print.

INTEGRATED SCHOOL BOARDS
Avalon Consolidated Integrated #111
  PO Box 1980, St. John's NF A1C 5R5
  709/754-0710; Fax: 709/754-0122
  *11,074

* indicates enrollment figure.

  Business Manager, A.R. Johnston, C.A.
  Supt., W.C. Lee
  Asst. Supt., Thelma Whalen
Avalon North Integrated #110 – *7,577
  PO Box 500, Bay Roberts NF A0A 1G0
  709/786-7182; Fax: 709/786-4451 – Supt., Dr. Max Trask
Bay-d'Espoir-Hermitage-Fortune Bay Integrated #113 – *1,456
  English Harbour West, PO Box 1100, Fortune Bay NF A0H 1M0
  709/888-3391; Fax: 709/888-6371 – Supt., Max Taylor
Bonavista-Trinity-Placentia Integrated #109 – *6,198
  PO Box 2001, Clarenville NF A0E 1J0
  709/466-3401; Fax: 709/466-3987 – Supt., Wade Sheppard
Burin Peninsula Integrated #112 – *2,803
  PO Box 1172, Marystown NF A0E 2M0
  709/891-2150; Fax: 709/891-2736 – Supt., Ron Brown
Conception Bay South Integrated #129 – *3,490
  Manuels, PO Box 220, Conception Bay NF A1W 1M8
  709/834-5511; Fax: 709/834-4735 – Supt., Randell A. Dawe
Deer Lake-St. Barbe South Integrated #103 – *3,611
  PO Box 2001, Deer Lake NF A0K 2E0
  709/635-2155; Fax: 709/635-5852 – Supt., Graham Blundon
Exploit's Valley Integrated #105 – *3,519
  PO Box 70, Grand Falls NF A2A 2J3
  709/489-2168; Fax: 709/489-6585 – Supt., Stanley Cole
Green Bay Integrated #104 – *2,388
  PO Box 550, Springdale NF A0J 1T0
  709/673-3855; Fax: 709/673-4224 – Supt., Dr. G.L. Moss
Labrador East Integrated #117 – *2,259
  PO Box 3021, Stn B, Happy Valley NF A0P 1E0
  709/896-2431; Fax: 709/896-9638 – Supt., Cal Patey
Labrador West Integrated #118 – *1,538
  669 Tamarack Dr., Labrador City NF A2V 2V2
  709/944-7628; Fax: 709/944-3480 – Supt., Barry Ledrew
Notre Dame Integrated #106 – *2,436
  PO Box 70, Lewisporte NF A0G 3A0
  709/535-6919; Fax: 709/535-3522 – Supt., John Hunt
Nova Consolidated School District #107 – *6,983
  203 Elizabeth Dr., Gander NF A1V 1H6
  709/256-2547; Fax: 709/651-3044 – Supt., Jack Waye
Port aux Basques Integrated #114 – *1,983
  PO Box 970, Port aux Basques NF A0M 1C0
  709/695-3422; Fax: 709/695-7097 – Supt., Joseph Roberts
Vinland-Strait of Belle Isle Integrated #101 – *3,191
  PO Box 89, Flower's Cove NF A0K 2N0
  709/456-2232; Fax: 709/456-2809 – Supt., Dr. Keith Ludlow
Western Integrated #115 – *5,480
  PO Box 190, Corner Brook NF A2H 6C7
  709/639-9823; Fax: 709/639-1733 – Supt., Tony Genge

ROMAN CATHOLIC SCHOOL DISTRICTS
Appalachia RC #512 – *4,826
  PO Box 5200, Stephenville NF A2N 3M5
  709/643-9525; Fax: 709/643-9235 – Supt., Andrew D. Butt
Burin Peninsula RC #502 – *3,701
  PO Box 69, Marystown NF A0E 2M0
  709/279-2870; Fax: 709/279-2177 – Supt., Mike Siscoe
Exploit's-White Bay RC #506 – *2,253
  PO Box 278, Grand Falls-Windsor NF A2A 2J7
  709/489-5796; Fax: 709/489-1233 – Supt., Dennis Fewer
Ferryland RC #507 – *1,866
  PO Box 90, Mobile NF A0A 3A0
  709/334-2606 – Supt., Francis Galgay

Gander-Bonavista-Connaigre RC #508 – *2,166
  PO Box 386, Gander NF A1V 1W8
  709/256-3319; Fax: 709/256-5045 – Supt., Frank Smith
Humber-St. Barbe Roman Catholic #509 – *3,500
  PO Box 368, Corner Brook NF A2H 6G9
  709/634-5052; Fax: 709/634-1828 – Supt., David Quick
Labrador RC #510 – *2,494
  PO Box 1300, Wabush NF A0R 1B0
  709/282-6838; Fax: 709/282-5307 – Supt., Patrick Furlong
St. John's Roman Catholic #514
  Belvedere, 67 Bonaventure Ave., St. John's NF A1C 3Z4
  709/753-8530; Fax: 709/753-8407
  *18,899
  Supt., Brian Shortall., B.A., B.Ph., M.Ed.
  Asst. Supt., Maureen Dunne
  Asst. Supt., David Locke
Western Avalon RC #504 – *6,789
  Conception Bay Centre Division, PO Box 70, Avondale NF A0A 1B0
  709/229-3931; Fax: 709/229-4322 – Supt., Joyce Fewer

PENTECOSTAL ASSEMBLIES SCHOOL BOARDS
Pentecostal Assemblies School Board #401 – *5,345
  34 Bond St, Grand Falls-Windsor NF A2B 1J4
  709/489-5751; Fax: 709/489-7129 – Supt., Domino Wilkins

SEVENTH DAY ADVENTIST SCHOOL BOARDS
Seventh Day Adventist School Board #701 – *271
  PO Box 2520, Mt. Pearl NF A1N 4M7
  709/745-4051; Fax: 709/745-1600 – Chair, E. Gerald Mews

NATIVE SCHOOL BOARDS
St. Anneway Kegnamogwon All-Grade School – *179 – Gr. K.-12
  Conne River NF A0H 1J0
  709/882-2747; Fax: 709/882-2528 – Director, Craig Benoit

UNIVERSITIES

Memorial University of Newfoundland
PO Box 4200, St. John's NF A1C 5S7
709/737-8000; Fax: 709/737-4569; URL: http://www.mun.ca; gopher://gopher.mun.ca
University Librarian, R.H. Ellis, B.A., M.L.S.
Official Visitor, The Hon. Frederick W. Russell, Lt. Governor of Newfoundland
Chancellor, J.C. Crosbie, B.A., LL.B., LL.D.
President & Vice-Chancellor, A.W. May, B.Sc.(Hons), M.Sc., Ph.D., D.U., D.Sc.
Vice-President, Academic & Pro Vice-Chancellor, J. Tuinman, B.Ed., M.A., M.O.A., Ph.D., Email: jtuinman@morgan.ucs.mun.ca
Vice-President, Admin. & Finance & Legal Counsel, W.W. Thistle, B.Sc., B.Ed., M.A., LL.B., Email: wthistle@morgan.ucs.mun.ca
Vice-President, Research, K.M.W. Keough, B.Sc., M.Sc., Ph.D., Email: kkeough@kean.ucs.mun.ca
Registrar, G.W. Collins, B.Sc., B.Ed., M.Sc., Email: gcollins@kean.ucs.mun.ca
Comptroller, T. Pound-Curtis, B.Com, C.A., Email: tcurtis@morgan.ucs.mun.ca

FACULTIES WITH DEANS
Arts, T. Murphy, B.A., M.A., Ph.D.
Business Administration, W. Blake, B.A.(Com.), M.B.A., Ph.D.
Continuing Education, Vacant
Education, T. Piper, B.A., M.A., Ph.D.
Engineering & Applied Science, R. Seshadri, B.E.(Hons.), M.Tech., M.Sc., Ph.D., FCSME

Acting Dean, Graduate Studies, C. Sharpe, B.A., M.A., Ph.D.
Medicine, H.I. Bowmer, B.Sc., M.D., C.M., F.R.C.P.C.
Science, A. Law, B.A., M.A., Ph.D.
Student Affairs & Services, W.E. Ludlow, B.Sc., B.Ed., M.Ed., Ed.D.

OTHER DIRECTORS & OFFICERS
Alumni Affairs & Development, K. Smith, B.A., B.A.(Ed.), M.Ed.
Animal Care Services, L. Husa, M.V.Dr.
Chair, Archaeology Unit, J.A. Tuck, A.B., Ph.D., F.R.S.C.
Art Gallery, P. Grattan, B.A.(Hons.), B.F.A.
Botanical Garden, P. Scott, B.Sc., Ph.D.
Budget & Audits, H. Squires, F.C.G.A.
Pres./CEO, C-CORE, J. Clark, B.Sc., B.Eng., M.Sc., Ph.D., P.Eng.
Cartographic Laboratory, C.H. Wood, B.S., M.S.
Acting Dir., Centre for Earth Resources Research, G. Quinlan, B.Sc., Ph.D.
Centre for International Business Studies, B. Winsor, B.A., LL.B., M.B.A.
Centre for Management Development, G. Rowe, B.Comm., M.B.A., Ph.D.
Centre for Offshore & Remote Medicine, H. Manson, M.B., Ch.B., F.F.A.R.C.S., F.R.C.P.C.
Computing & Communications, W. Bussey, B.A.
Continuing Studies, D. Whalen, Dip. A.A., B.Voc.Ed., M.B.A.
Counselling Centre, G. Hurley, B.A., M.S., Ph.D.
Educational Technology, Vacant
Facilities Management, G. Bradshaw, B.Eng., M.B.A., P.Eng.
Faculty Relations, J. Strawbridge, B.A., M.A., Ph.D.
Folklore & Language Archive, M.J. Lovelace, B.A., M.A., Ph.D.
General Student Services, W.C. Leonard, B.Sc., B.Ed., M.Ed.
Human Resources, G.A. Hickman, B.A.(Ed.), M.Ed., Ed.D.
Institute of Social & Economic Research, J.A. Tuck, A.B., Ph.D., F.R.S.C.
Labrador Institute of Northern Studies, C. Brice-Bennett, B.A., M.A.
Archivist, Maritime History Archive, H. Wareham, B.A.
Maritime Studies Research Unit, D. Vickers, B.A., Ph.D.
Ocean Engineering Research Centre, N. Bose, B.Sc., Ph.D., C.Eng., P.Eng.
Ocean Sciences Centre, L. Crim, B.A., M.Sc., Ph.D.
Office of Research, B. Cox, B.A.
P.J. Gardiner Institute for Small Business Studies, W.F. King, B.Com., C.A., M.B.A.
School of Music, M. Volk, B.Mus., M.Mus., D.M.
School of Nursing, M. Lamb, B.Sc., N.Ed., M.N.
School of Pharmacy, G.R. Duncan, B.Sc.Phm., M.Sc.Phm, D.Phil.
School of Physical Education & Athletics, W. Redden, B.P.E., M.S.(P.E.), M.Ed. (G.P.S.), Ph.D.
School of Social Work, J.. Pennell, A.B., M.S.W., Ph.D..
Pres. & CEO, Seabright Corporation Ltd., D. King, B.Comm., M.B.A., C.A.
Staff Relations, C. Horlick, B.Comm.
Student Development, D. Hardy Cox, B.S.W., M.S.W., Ed.D., R.S.W.
Student Health Service, R. Harpur, M.B., B.Ch., C.C.F.P.
Student Housing & Food Services, B. Johnston, B.A., B.Ed., M.Ed., Ed.D.
Technical Services, Vacant
Telemedicine Centre, M. House, MD, CM, FRCPC
University Relations, V. Collins, B.A.

AFFILIATED INSTITUTIONS
Fisheries & Marine Institute of Memorial University, PO Box 4920, St. John's NF A1C 5R3 – 709/778-0200; Fax: 709/778-0346 – Executive Director, Les O'Reilly, B.A.(Ed.), Dip.Ed., M.Admin.
Queen's College, Prince Philip Dr., St. John's NF A1B 3R6 – 709/753-0116 – Provost, Rev. B. Morgan, B.A., M.Div., M.A.
Sir Wilfred Grenfell College, Memorial University of Newfoundland, University Dr., Corner Brook NF A2H 6P9 – 709/637-6200; Fax: 709/639-8125; Email: kbindon@morgan.ucs.mun.ca – Principal, Dr. Kathryn Bindon

COMMUNITY COLLEGES

CABOT COLLEGE OF APPLIED ARTS, TECHNOLOGY & CONTINUING EDUCATION
PO Box 1693, St. John's NF A1C 5P7
709/778-2400; Fax: 709/738-2182
President, Dr. Edna Turpin-Downey, Email: edowney@admin.cabotnf.ca
Engineering Technology Centre, PO Box 1150, St. John's NF A1C 6L8 – 709/758-7007; Fax: 709/758-7126 – Campus Director, Daniel Wong
Seal Cove Campus, PO Box 10, Seal Cove NF A0A 3T0 – 709/744-2047; Fax: 709/744-3929 – Campus Manager, Dennis Power
Topsail Road Campus, PO Box 1693, St. John's NF A1C 5P7 – 709/758-7624; Fax: 709/758-7634 – Campus Director, Dr. Donna B. Henderson

CENTRAL NEWFOUNDLAND COLLEGE OF APPLIED ARTS, TECHNOLOGY & CONTINUING EDUCATION
PO Box 745, Grand Falls-Windsor NF A2A 2M4
709/489-2807; Fax: 709/489-4358
President, James Forward, Email: jforward@calvin.stemnet.nf.ca
Registrar, Joseph Hudon, 709/489-8500; Fax: 709/489-8504; Email: jhudon@calvin.stemnet.nf.ca
Baie Verte Campus, Baie Verte NF A0K 1B0 – 709/532-8066; Fax: 709/532-4624 – Principal, Colin Forward
Gander Campus, PO Box 395, Gander NF A1V 1W8 – 709/256-4481; Fax: 709/651-3376 – Principal, Mac Moss
Grand Falls-Windsor Campus, PO Box 413, Grand Falls-Windsor NF A2A 2J8 – 709/489-4317; Fax: 709/489-4180 – Principal, Pauline Power

EASTERN COLLEGE OF APPLIED ARTS, TECHNOLOGY & CONTINUING EDUCATION
PO Box 3600, Clarenville NF A0E 1J0
709/466-1991; Fax: 709/466-2777
President, Fred R. Green, Email: fred@pinky.east-coll.nf.ca
Bonavista Campus, PO Box 670, Bonavista NF A0C 1B0 – 709/468-2610; Fax: 709/468-2004 – Campus & Area Director, Marilyn Coles-Hayley
Burin Campus, PO Box 369, Burin NF A0E 1E0 – 709/891-1253; Fax: 709/891-2256 – Campus & Area Director, Ray Kavanagh
Carbonear Campus, PO Box 60, Carbonear NF A1Y 1B5 – 709/596-6139; Fax: 709/596-2688 – Campus & Area Director, Graham Sheppard
Clarenville Campus, PO Box 308, Clarenville NF A0E 1J0 – 709/466-2250; Fax: 709/466-2771 – Campus & Area Director, Steve Quinton
Placentia Campus, PO Box 190, Placentia NF A0B 2Y0 – 709/227-2037; Fax: 709/227-7185 – Campus & Area Director, Gerald O'Reilly

LABRADOR COLLEGE OF APPLIED ARTS, TECHNOLOGY & CONTINUING EDUCATION
Labrador Headquarters, PO Box 3013, Happy Valley NF A0P 1E0
709/896-3876; Fax: 709/896-9533
President, Ronald Sparkes
Division of Extension Services, PO Box 248, North West River NF A0P 1M0 – 709/497-8595; Fax: 709/497-8796 – Director, F. Pye
Happy Valley Campus, PO Box 3013, Happy Valley NF A0P 1E0 – 709/896-3307; Fax: 709/896-9533 – Principal, Larry McPherson
Labrador West Campus, Campbell Dr., Labrador City NF A2V 2Y1 – 709/944-7210; Fax: 709/944-6581 – Principal, Shirley Alport

WESTVIKING COLLEGE OF APPLIED ARTS, TECHNOLOGY & CONTINUING EDUCATION
PO Box 5400, Stephenville NF A2N 2Z6
709/643-7701; Fax: 709/643-5407
President, Douglas Fowlow
Registrar, Linda Dunne, 709/643-7730
Bay St. George Campus, PO Box 5400, Stephenville NF A2N 2Z6 – 709/643-7736; Fax: 709/643-5407 – Area Director, Patrick J. Power
Corner Brook Campus, PO Box 822, Corner Brook NF A2H 6H6 – 709/637-8519; Fax: 709/634-2126 – Area Director, William Barker
Port-aux-Basques Campus, PO Box 760, Port-aux-Basques NF A0M 1C0 – 709/695-3528, 3343; Fax: 709/695-2963 – Area Director, George Anderson
St. Anthony Campus, PO Box 550, St. Anthony NF A0K 4S0 – 709/454-3559, 3835; Fax: 709/454-8808 – Area Director, Bill Carpenter

POST-SECONDARY & SPECIALIZED INSTITUTIONS

ACADEMY CANADA
#167, 169 Kenmount Rd., PO Box 8747, St. John's NF A1B 3T2
709/739-6767; Fax: 709/739-6797

ACADEMY OF LEARNING
332 Water St., PO Box 204, St. John's NF A1C 2J5
709/579-7771; Fax: 709/579-7774

ADULT CAREER CENTRES INC.
25 Anderson Ave., St. John's NF A1B 3E4
709/579-8080

AQUATIC RESOURCES INC.
PO Box 36, St. Alban's NF A0H 2E0
709/538-3359; Fax: 709/538-3439

ATLANTIC CONSTRUCTION TRAINING
PO Box 1872, St. John's NF A1C 5R4
709/726-6264; Fax: 709/726-6255

AVIATION CAREER ACADEMY
PO Box 9460, St. John's NF A1A 2Y4
709/576-1891; Fax: 709/576-1802

CANADIAN DIVER TRAINING CENTRE INC.
1 Crosbie Place, St. John's NF A1B 3Y8
709/738-8800; Fax: 709/738-8810

CAREER ACADEMY
189 Higgin's Line, St. John's NF A1B 4N4
709/753-1123; Fax: 709/753-1142

CAREERS PLUS
PO Box 1059, Bay Roberts NF A0A 1G0
709/786-3030; Fax: 709/786-9507

CENTRAC COLLEGE OF BUSINESS, TRADES & TECHNOLOGY
PO Box 473, Gander NF A1V 1W8
709/256-2670; Fax: 709/256-3697
Vice-Principal, Jason Saunders
Creston, PO Box 160, Creston NF A0E 1K0 – 709/279-1999; Fax: 709/279-2004; Toll Free: 1-800-563-1910 – Principal, Darlene Pike
St. John's, 25 Pippy Place, St. John's NF A1B 3V8 – 709/722-9151; Fax: 709/722-9152; Toll Free: 1-800-563-5296 – Principal, Beverley Whalen

CENTRAL TECHNICAL COLLEGE
Comfort Cove, Newstead NF A0G 3K0
709/244-4400

CENTRAL TRAINING ACADEMY
15 Main St., Badger NF A0H 1A0
709/539-5150

COASTAL COMPUTER ACADEMY
42 Elizabeth Ave., St. John's NF A1A 1W4
709/754-7773; Fax: 709/754-7773

COMPUCOLLEGE SCHOOL OF BUSINESS
275 Duckworth St., PO Box 6325, St. John's NF A1C 6J9
709/722-8580; Fax: 709/722-8318

CORONA TRAINING INSTITUTE
PO Box 819, Grand Falls-Windsor NF A2A 2P7
709/489-7825; Fax: 709/489-5001
Principal, Marilyn Bennett
Manager, Operations, Jacqueline Butler

INDUSTRY & ARTS ACADEMY
General Delivery, Great Harbour Deep NF A0K 2Z0
709/843-3291; Fax: 709/843-4103

KEYIN TECHNICAL COLLEGE
7 Austin St., PO Box 13609, Stn A, St. John's NF A1B 4G1
709/579-1061; Fax: 709/579-6002

LAWRENCE COLLEGE INC.
35 Blackmarsh Rd., St. John's NF A1E 1S4
709/738-1053; Fax: 709/738-3350

NEWFOUNDLAND MUSIC ACADEMY
General Delivery, Baie Verte NF A0K 1B0
709/329-3161; Fax: 709/329-3161

OPERATING ENGINEERS, EDUCATION & DEVELOPMENT INC.
62 Commonwealth Ave., Mount Pearl NF A1N 1W8
709/747-9040

PROVINCIAL LEARNING CENTRES
310 LeMarchant Rd., St. John's NF A1E 1R3
709/722-5537; Fax: 709/364-5047

PROVINCIAL TECHNICAL INSTITUTE
137 Crosbie Rd., PO Box 74, St. John's NF A1E 4N1
709/738-8890; Fax: 709/738-8890

INDEPENDENT & PRIVATE SCHOOLS

Schools with enrollment of 50 or more, listed alphabetically by city.

Churchill Falls: Eric G. Lambert All-Grade School, PO Box 40, Churchill Falls NF A0R 1A0 – 709/925-3371; Fax: 709/925-8306 – Principal, Adrian Clarke – *187 – Gr. K.-12

St. John's: Lakecrest Independent School, 74 The Boulevard, St. John's NF A1A 1K2 – 709/738-1212 – Principal, Francine Frisson-Tuinman – *105 – Gr. K.-8

Whitbourne: Newfoundland-Labrador Youth Centre, PO Box 40, Whitbourne NF A0B 3K0 – 709/729-0944; Fax: 709/759-2611 – Principal, Bill Tucker – *69 – Gr. 7-12

NORTHWEST TERRITORIES

Department of Education, Culture & Employment
PO Box 1320, Yellowknife NT X1A 2L9
403/873-7110; Fax: 403/873-0155, 0200, 0109;
URL: http://siksik.learnnet.nt.ca

* indicates enrollment figure.

CULTURE & CAREERS BRANCH
Assistant Deputy Minister, Mark Cleveland

EDUCATIONAL DEVELOPMENT BRANCH
Assistant Deputy Minister, Eric Colbourne

INCOME SUPPORT REFORM
Assistant Deputy Minister, Conrad Pilon

For detailed departmental listings, see Index: "Education, Depts."

EDUCATION DISTRICTS
Yellowknife Education District No. 1
  PO Box 788, Yellowknife NT X1A 2N6
  403/873-5050; Fax: 403/873-5051 – Supt., Dr. Kenneth Woodley
Yellowknife Education District No. 2
  PO Box 1830, Yellowknife NT X1A 2P4
  403/873-2200; Fax: 403/873-2701 – Supt., Dr. Loretta Foley

BOARDS OF EDUCATION
Baffin Divisional Board of Education
  PO Box 1330, Iqaluit NT X0A 0H0
  819/979-5236; Fax: 819/979-4868 – Director, C. McGregor
Beaufort/Delta Divisional Board of Education
  c/o Bag Service No. 12, Inuvik NT X0E 0T0
  403/979-7130; Fax: 403/979-2469 – Director, Pauline Gordon
Dehcho Divisional Board of Education
  PO Box 376, Fort Simpson NT X0E 0N0
  403/695-7260; Fax: 403/695-2035 – Director, Nolan Swartzentreber
Dogrib Divisional Board of Education
  Bag Service #1, Rae Edzo NT X0E 0Y0
  403/371-3026; Fax: 403/371-3053 – Director, J. Martin
Keewatin Divisional Board of Education
  PO Box 90, Baker Lake NT X0C 0A0
  819/793-2740; Fax: 819/793-2996 – Director, Curtis Brown
Kitikmeot Divisional Board of Education
  Coppermine NT X0E 0E0
  403/982-7220; Fax: 403/982-3054 – Director, T. Stewart
Sahtu Divisional Board of Education
  PO Box 64, Norman Wells NT X0E 0V0
  403/587-2367; Fax: 403/587-2462 – Director, Michael Campbell
South Slave Divisional Board of Education
  Fort Smith NT X0E 0P0
  403/872-7215; Fax: 403/872-2150 – Director, Dr. Walter Curtis

POST-SECONDARY EDUCATION

AURORA COLLEGE
PO Box 1290, Fort Smith NT X0E 0P0
403/872-7009; Fax: 403/872-4730
President, C. Parker
Aurora Campus, PO Box 1008, Inuvik NT X0E 0T0 – 403/979-7878; Fax: 403/979-2850 – Campus Director, Miki O'Kane
Thebacha Campus, PO Box 600, Fort Smith NT X0E 0P0 – 403/872-7520; Fax: 403/872-4511 – Campus Director, R. Holtorf
Yellowknife Campus, #500, 5022 - 49 St., Yellowknife NT X1A 3R7 – 403/920-3030; Fax: 403/873-0333 – Campus Director, Dan Daniels

NUNAVUT ARCTIC COLLEGE
PO Box 160, Iqaluit NT X0A 0H0
819/979-4114; Fax: 819/979-4118
President, Greg Welch

Keewatin Campus, PO Bag 002, Rankin Inlet NT X0C 0G0 – 819/645-2529; Fax: 819/645-2387 – Director, M. Shouldice
Kitimeot Campus, PO Bag 200, Cambridge Bay NT X0E 0C0 – 403/983-7234; Fax: 403/983-2404 – Director, C. Isnor
Nunatta Campus, PO Box 600, Iqaluit NT X0A 0H0 – 819/979-7217; Fax: 819/979-4579 – Director, D. Wilman

NOVA SCOTIA

Department of Education
Trade Mart, PO Box 578, Halifax NS B3J 2S9
902/424-5168; Fax: 902/424-0519

CURRICULUM INFORMATION
Director, French Program Services, Margelaine Holding, 902/424-6646; Fax: 902/424-0613
Director, English Program Services, Bob Leblanc, 902/424-5991; Fax: 902/424-0613

CORRESPONDENCE STUDIES
PO Box 1650, Halifax NS B3J 2Z2
902/424-4054

For detailed departmental listings, see Index: "Education, Depts."

SCHOOL BOARDS

The 22 district school boards in Nova Scotia were amalgamated in 1996. The following is a breakdown of the amalgamated boards, and the district school boards they replaced:

Cape Breton-Victoria
  Cape Breton
  Northside-Victoria
Strait
  Antigonish
  Guysborough
  Inverness; Richmond
Chignecto-Central
  Colchester-East Hants
  Cumberland
  Pictou
Halifax
  Dartmouth
  Halifax
  Halifax County-Bedford
Annapolis Valley
  Annapolis
  Hants West
  Kings
Southwest
  Clare-Argyle
  Digby
  Lunenburg
  Queens
  Shelburne
  Yarmouth
Acadien provincial
  Antigonish
  Cape Breton
  Clare-Argyle
  Grand Havre;
  Inverness
  Kings
  Richmond

Boards with an enrollment of more than 15,000 are in bold print.

Annapolis Valley Regional School Board
PO Box 220, Kentville NS B4N 3W8
902/678-2161; Fax: 902/679-3023
*18,455
Supt., Dr. James Gunn

Director., Finance & Operations, Stuart Jamieson
Cape Breton-Victoria Regional School Board
275 George St., Sydney NS B1P 1J7
902/564-8293; Fax: 902/564-0123
*24,318
Supt., Dr. Hayes MacNeil
Director., Finance, Doug Peach
Chignecto-Central Regional School Board
#303, 14 Court St., Truro NS B2N 3H7
902/893-6317; Fax: 902/893-6104
*28,186
Supt., Elmer MacDonald
Finance Officer, Robert Renouf
Conseil scolaire acadien provincial – *4,123
PO Box 360, Meteghan NS B0W 2J0
Fax: 902/645-3032; Email: 1-888-533-2727 – Supt., Réjean. Sirois; Director, Finance & Operations, Janine Saulnier
Halifax Regional School Board
PO Box 1000, Lower Sackville NS B4C 3Z5
902/864-1928; Fax: 902/864-2760
*57,786
Supt., Dr. Don Trider
Director, Finance, David Gray
Southwest Regional School Board
46 Parade St., Yarmouth NS B5A 3A9
902/742-9266; Fax: 902/742-1149
*19,494
Supt., Ann Jones
Director, Finance & Operations, David Eyre
Strait Regional School Board – *11,658
PO Box 5100, Port Hawkesbury NS B0E 2V0
902/625-2191; Fax: 902/625-2281 – Supt., Jack Sullivan; Director, Finance & Operations, John Cameron

FEDERAL & BAND-OPERATED SCHOOLS

Eskasoni Elementary & Junior High School, Eskasoni NS B0A 1J0 – 902/379-2825; Fax: 902/379-2273 – Principal, Philomena Moore
Mi'kmawey School, RR#1 St. Peter's, Richmond County NS B0E 3B0 – 902/535-2307; Fax: 902/535-3004 – Principal, Charles Boudreau
Muin Seboo Mi'kmaq Elementary School, PO Box 210, Bear River NS B0S 1B0 – 902/467-4193; Fax: 902/467-4143
Wagcobah Federal School, PO Box 209, Whycocomagh NS B0E 3M0 – 902/756-9000; Fax: 902/756-2171 – Principal, Dave Maston
Wagmatcook School, PO Box 525, Baddeck NS B0E 1B0 – 902/295-3491; Fax: 902/295-1331 – Principal, Josephine Peck

SCHOOLS FOR THE VISUALLY/HEARING IMPAIRED

Atlantic Provinces Special Education Authority, 5940 South St., Halifax NS B3H 1S6 – 902/424-7765; Fax: 902/424-5819 – Acting Supt., Deborah Pottie

UNIVERSITIES

Acadia University
15 University Dr., Wolfville NS B0P 1X0
902/542-2201; Fax: 902/542-7224 (Info.); Email: all Acadia email addresses are in the format first-name.lastname@acadiau.ca; URL: http://www.acadiau.ca; gopher://gopher.acadiau.ca
President's Office Fax: 902/542-1516; Library Fax: 902/542 4727
President, K.K. Ogilvie, B.Sc., Ph.D., D.Sc.
Acting Vice-President, Academic, S. Maurice Tugwell, B.Sc., M.Sc., Ph.D.
Vice-President, Finance, Harold D. Austin, B.A., R.I.A
Director, Human Resources, Garry Alexa, B.A., C.H.R.P.
Equity Officer, Kathy Meade, B.P.E., M.A.

Associate Comptroller & Director, Budgets, Gary Draper, B.B.A., C.A.
Director, Development, Harvey Gilmour, B.A., LL.B.
Director, Student Affairs, Dima Utgoff, B.A., M.S.Ed.
Director, Personnel, Robert T. Flecknell, B.Sc.
Registrar, Jane Cayford, B.A., B.Ed.
Director, Support Services, W.K. Horton, B.Sc.
Director, Office of Public Affairs, Bruce E. Choon, B. Comm., B.Ed.
Executive Director, Associated Alumni, Steve M. Pound, B.Sc., B.Ed., M.Sc., Ph.D.
Manager, Bookstore, Doug Mosher

FACULTIES WITH DEANS/
Arts, Thomas G. Regan, B.A., M.A., Ph.D.
Acting Dean, Management & Education, William McLeod, B.Sc., M.Sc., D.P.E.
Pure & Applied Science, Michael P. Leiter, B.A., M.A., Ph.D.
Theology, A.D. MacRae, M.A., B.D., D.D.

SCHOOLS WITH DIRECTORS
Acting Director, Business Administration, Steven Enman, B.B.A., LL.B., LL.M.L.
Computer Science, Leslie Oliver, B.Sc., M.Sc., Ph.D.
Education, James H. Fasano, B.Sc., B.Ed., M.Ed., Ph.D.
Acting Director, Engineering, Douglas Seamone, C.A.S., B.Eng., M.Sc., P.Eng.
Acting Director, Music, Gordon J. Callon, B.Mus., M.M.A., D.M.A.
Nutrition & Food Science, E.M. Johnston, B.Sc., M.S., Ph.D.
Recreation & Physical Education, Alex Wright, D.P.E., B.Sc., M.Sc., Ed.D.

AFFILIATED COLLEGES
Acadia Divinity College, 31 Horton Ave., Wolfville NS B0P 1X0 – 902/542-2285 – Principal, Andrew D. MacRae, M.A., B.D., D.D.

Dalhousie University
1236 Henry St., Halifax NS B3H 3J5
902/494-2211; Fax: 902/494-2319; Email: http://www.dal.ca; gopher://ac.dal.ca; URL: http://www.da.ca; gopher://ac.dal.ca
Chancellor, Sir Graham Day
Vice-Chancellor & President, Dr. Tom Traves
Chair, Board of Governors, Allan C. Shaw
Vice-President, Academic & Research, Deborah Hobson
Vice-President, Administration & Finance, Bryan Mason
Vice-President, External, Vacant
Vice-President, Student Services, Eric McKee
Registrar, Gudrun Curri

FACULTIES WITH DEANS
Arts & Social Sciences, Graham D. Taylor
Dentistry, William MacInnis
Graduate Studies, Peter Ricketts
Health Professions, Lynn MacIntyre
Henson College of Public Affairs & Continuing Education, Mary Morrisey
Law, Dawn Russell
Management, Philip J. Rosson
Medicine, John Ruedy
Science, Warwick Kimmins

SCHOOLS WITH DIRECTORS
Business Administration, Leonard C. MacLean
College of Pharmacy, Frank Chandler
Dental Hygiene, Joanne Clovis
Health Services Administration, Ingrid Sketris
Human Communications Disorders, Walter Green
Library & Information Studies, Dr. Louis Vagianos
Maritime School of Social Work, Joan Gilroy
Nursing, Joyce Black

Occupational Therapy, Barbara J. O'Shea
Physiotherapy, Lydia Makrides
Public Administration, Dale Poel
Recreation, & Physical & Health Education, Larry Maloney
Resource & Environmental Studies, Dr. Ray Côté

AFFILIATED COLLEGES
Atlantic School of Theology, 640 Francklyn St., Halifax NS B3H 3B5 – 902/423-6939 – Registrar, Mary Schaefer
Technical University of Nova Scotia, PO Box 1000, Halifax NS B3J 2X4 – 902/420-7500 – President & Vice-Chancellor, Dr. Edward Rhodes
University of King's College, Halifax NS B3H 2A1 – 902/422-1271; URL: http://www.ukings.ns.ca – President, Colin J. Starnes

Mount Saint Vincent University
166 Bedford Hwy., Halifax NS B3M 2J6
902/457-6788; Fax: 902/445-3960; URL: http://www.msvu.ca/
President & Vice-Chancellor, Sheila A. Brown, Ph.D.
Chair, Board of Governors, Carole Taylor

St. Francis Xavier University
PO Box 5000, Antigonish NS B2G 2W5
902/863-3300; Fax: 902/867-5153; URL: http://www.stfx.ca/
President, Sean E. Riley, Ph.D., Email: sriley@stfx.ca
Vice-President, Academic, Hugh Gillis, Ph.D., Email: hgillis@stfx.ca
Vice-President, Administration, J.T. Langley, M.S., C.G.A., Email: tlangley@stfx.ca
Comptroller, J.C. Hagar, B.Comm., C.G.A.
Director, Student Services & Registrar, Carson Duncan, Ph.D., Email: cduncan@stfx.ca
Associate Registrar, Janet Stark, Email: jstark@stfx.ca
Public Relations Officer, Kimberly Dickson, B.Ed., Email: kdickson@stfx.ca
Manager, Procurement Services, Lorris Keizer
Manager, Bookstore, Dave Renny

FACULTIES WITH DEANS
Arts, Ken den Heyer, Ph.D.
Science, Ed McAlduff, Ph.D.

SCHOOLS WITH DIRECTORS
Interim Director, Coady International Institute, Eric Amit, B.A., M.A.
Extension Dept., Tom Webb, B.A., M.A.

AFFILIATED COLLEGE
Mount Saint Bernard College, 10 Hillcrest St., Antigonish NS B2G 2N5 – 902/867-3859; Fax: 902/867-3866; URL: http://www.stfx.ca/msbresid/ – Principal, Sr. Margaret McDonell, Ph.D.

Saint Mary's University
923 Robie St., Halifax NS B3H 3C3
902/420-5400; Fax: 902/420-5566; URL: http://www.st-marys.ca
Chancellor, Most Rev. Austin E. Burke, B.A., M.T.L., D.D., D.Lit.
President, Kenneth L. Ozmon, B.A., M.A., Ph.D.
Vice-President, Academic & Research, J.Colin Dodds, B.Sc., M.A., Ph.D.
Vice-President, Administration, G. Noël, B.Eng., P.Eng.
Director, University Advancement, D.P. Keleher, Dip. Eng., B.E.
Director, Continuing Education, J.F. Sharpe, B.Sc., M.A.
Comptroller, R.L. Cochrane, B.Comm., C.G.A.
Registrar, Elizabeth A. Chard, B.A., B.Ed., M.A.
Director, Public Affairs, C.R. Bridges, M.B.A.

FACULTIES WITH DEANS
Arts, M.J. Larsen, B.A., M.A., Ph.D.
Acting Dean, Commerce, Paul Dixon, Ph.D.
Education, M.J. Larsen, B.A., M.A., Ph.D.
Science, D.H.S. Richardson, B.Sc., M.Sc., M.A., Ph.D.

Technical University of Nova Scotia
1360 Barrington St., PO Box 1000, Halifax NS B3J 2X4
902/420-7500; Fax: 902/420-7551; URL: http://www.tuns.ca/index.html
Chancellor Emeritus, Ruth M. Goldbloom, C.M., D.Hum.L., LL.D.
President, Edward Rhodes, B.Sc.Tech., M.Sc.Tech., Ph.D., P.Eng.
Vice-President, Administration, J.R. Dexter Kaulbach, B.Eng., P.Eng.
Registrar, LaMont Pelletier, B.Sc., B.Ed.
Dean, Students, Ronald C. Gilkie, Ph.D., P.Eng., F.C.S.C.E.
Treasurer, Rick Lowery, C.A.
Librarian, Donna Richardson, B.A., M.L.S.
Director, Community Relations, Barbara Watt, B.A.

FACULTIES WITH DEANS
Architecture, Frank Palermo, B.Arch., M.Arch.U.D., MRAIC, MCIP
Engineering, Adam Bell, B.Eng., S.M., M.E., Sc.D., P.Eng.

SCHOOLS WITH DIRECTORS
Continuing Education & Conference Centre, Carol Connor
School of Computer Science, Jonathan Barzilai, B.Sc., M.Sc., D.Sc.

OTHER DIRECTORS & OFFICERS
Physical Plant, Carl Day, B.Sc., B.Eng., P.Eng.

Université Sainte Anne
Pointe-de-l'Église NS B0W 1M0
902/769-2114; Fax: 902/769-3120; URL: http://www.isisnet.com/ustanne
President, Harley d'Entremont
Vice-President, Academic, Ian Richmond
Secretary General, Gérald Boudreau
Registrar, Murielle Comeau
Information Officer, Richard Landry
Manager, Bookstore, Claire Dol
Comptroller, Eric Tufts

University College of Cape Breton
PO Box 5300, Stn A, Sydney NS B1P 6L2
902/539-5300; Fax: 902/562-6949; URL: http://www.uccb.ns.ca
President, Jacquelyn Thayer Scott, Ph.D.
Executive Director, Research & Development, Robert Morgan, Ph.D.
Acting Director, Dept. of Institutional Advancement, Germaine LeMoine, B.A.
Alumni Officer, Deborah MacAuley
Registrar, Denis Cassivi, M.A.
Executive Director, Human Resources & Dean of Student Services, David White
University Librarian, Penelope Marshall, M.L.S.
Director, Human Resources Buildings & Grounds, Gordon MacLean
Manager, Builings & Grounds, Don MacIsaac, P.Eng.
Director, Centre for International Studies, Brian Tennyson, Ph.D.
Curator, Art Gallery, Barry Gabriel, B.F.A., B.A.

FACULTIES WITH DEANS
Arts & Letters, Thomas Rendall, Ph.D.
Business, Steve Kavanagh, M.B.A.
Community Studies, Silver Donald Cameron, Ph.D.

* indicates enrollment figure.

Dean (Acting), Extension & Community Affairs, Keith Brown, B.A., M.B.A.
Science & Technology, Stephen Manley, B.S., M.S., Ph.D.

COMMUNITY COLLEGES

NOVA SCOTIA COMMUNITY COLLEGE
Central Office, 5685 Leeds St., Halifax NS B3J 3C4
902/424-4055; Fax: 902/424-4225
President, Jack Buckley
Vice-President, Extension Services, John Keating
Vice-President, Program Services, Bill Cruden
Vice-President, Administrative Services, Robert Shedden
Director, Curriculum Development, Kelly McKnight
Communications Officer, Wilma Butts
Coordinator, Customized Training, Anne Rodger
Manager, Human Resources, David McKillop
Manager, Information Technology, Lindsay Estabrooks
Annapolis Campus, 295 Commercial St., Middleton NS B0S 1P0 – 902/825-3491; Fax: 902/825-2285 – Principal, Paul LaFleche
Burridge Campus, 372 Pleasant St., Yarmouth NS B5A 2L2 – 902/742-3501; Fax: 902/742-0519 – Principal, Marcel Cottreau
College of Geographic Sciences, RR#1, Lawrencetown, Annapolis County NS B0S 1M0 – 902/584-2226; Fax: 902/584-7211 – Principal, Paul LaFleche
Cumberland Campus, 1 Main St., PO Box 550, Springhill NS B0M 1X0 – 902/597-3737; Fax: 902/597-8548 – Principal, George R. Laird
Halifax Campus, 1825 Bell Rd., Halifax NS B3H 2Z4 – 902/424-7529; Fax: 902/424-0534 – Principal, Allister Thorne
I.W. Akerley Campus, 21 Woodlawn Rd., Dartmouth NS B2W 2R7 – 902/434-2020; Fax: 902/462-4320 – Principal, Gerry Mahar
Institute of Technology Campus, 5685 Leeds St., PO Box 2210, Halifax NS B3J 3C4 – 902/424-7529; Fax: 902/424-0534 – Principal, Allister Thorne
Kingstec Campus, Belcher St., PO Box 487, Kentville NS B4N 3X3 – 902/678-7341; Fax: 902/679-1141 – Principal, Janet Kirk
Lunenburg Campus, 75 High St., Bridgewater NS B4V 1V8 – 902/543-4608; Fax: 902/543-0190 – Principal, Sandra Forsythe
Marconi Campus, Glace Bay Highway, PO Box 1042, Sydney NS B1P 6J7 – 902/563-2450; Fax: 902/563-0511
Pictou Campus, Acadia St., PO Box 820, Stellarton NS B0K 1S0 – 902/752-2002; Fax: 902/752-5446 – Principal, Carol Forbes
Shelburne Campus, 1575 Lake Rd., PO Box 760, Shelburne NS B0T 1W0 – 902/875-8640; Fax: 902/875-3797 – Principal, Gordon Patton
Strait Area Campus, Reeves St., PO Box 1225, Port Hawkesbury NS B0E 2V0 – 902/625-2380; Fax: 902/625-0193
Truro Campus, 36 Arthur St., Truro NS B2N 1X5 – 902/893-5385; Fax: 902/893-5390

POST-SECONDARY & SPECIALIZED INSTITUTIONS

ATLANTIC BROADCASTING INSTITUTE
#500, 6009 Quinpool Rd., Halifax NS B3K 5J7
902/423-2001; Fax: 902/429-6692
A. Walling

ATLANTIC HOME BUILDERS TRAINING
53 Leary's Cove Rd., East Dover NS B0J 3L0
902/852-2151; Fax: 902/852-3193

GAELIC COLLEGE OF CELTIC ARTS & CRAFTS
PO Box 9, Baddeck NS B0E 1B0

902/295-3411; Fax: 902/295-2912
Executive Director, Sam MacPhee

THE INSTITUTE FOR EARLY CHILDHOOD EDUCATION & DEVELOPMENTAL SERVICES
480 Beech Hill Rd., Princeport RR#1, Truro NS B2N 5A9
902/893-3342; Fax: 902/895-4487
Executive Director, Jane M. Norman, Ph.D

MARITIME CONSERVATORY OF MUSIC
6199 Chebucto Rd., Halifax NS B3L 1K7
902/423-6995; Fax: 902/423-6029
Director, Jack Brownell

NOVA SCOTIA AGRICULTURAL COLLEGE
PO Box 550, Truro NS B2N 5E3
902/893-6600; Fax: 902/897-9399; URL: gopher://gopher.nsac.ns.ca
Interim Principal, B.M. MacDonald

NOVA SCOTIA TEACHERS COLLEGE
PO Box 810, Truro NS B2N 5G5
902/895-5300; Fax: 902/893-5610; URL: http://fox.nstn.ca:89/~ptiwana/nstc.html
Principal, David White

INDEPENDENT & PRIVATE SCHOOLS

Schools with enrollment of 50 or more, listed alphabetically by city.
Cambridge Station: Kings County Christian School, 6185 Hwy. #1, Cambridge Station NS B0P 1G0 – 902/679-6641 – Principal, Barbara C. Billings – *66 – Gr. Pre.-9
Halifax: Armbrae Academy, 1400 Oxford St., Halifax NS B3H 3Y8 – 902/423-7920 – Principal, Eric T. MacKnight – *207 – Gr. Pre.-12
Halifax Grammar School, 5750 Atlantic St., Halifax NS B3H 1G9 – 902/422-6497 – Principal, John A. Messenger – *313 – Gr. Pre.-12
Halifax: Sacred Heart School of Halifax, 5820 Spring Garden Rd., Halifax NS B3H 1X8 – 902/423-1358 – Principal, Joan Dormington – *410 – Gr. Pre.-12
Sydney Mines: Northside Christian Academy, 302 Main St., Sydney Mines NS B1V 2M6 – 902/736-6465 – Principal, Pastor Blair Bridle – *82 – Gr. Pre.-12
Timberlea: Halifax Christian Academy, 2020 St. Margaret's Bay Rd., Timberlea NS B3T 1C3 – 902/876-8497 – Principal, Joan Dennis – *248 – Gr. Pre.-12
Truro: Colchester Christian Academy, 15 Elm St., PO Box 393, Truro NS B2N 5C5 – 902/895-6520 – Principal, Colin Murphy – *145 – Gr. Pre.-12
Tusket: Living Waters Christian Academy, PO Box 175, Tusket NS B0W 3M0 – 902/648-2676 – Principal, Kevin Cribby – *79 – Gr. Pre.-9
Windsor: Kings-Edgehill School, 254 College Rd., Windsor NS B0N 2T0 – 902/798-2278 – Principal, David R. Penaluna – *259 – Gr. 6-12
Wolfville: Landmark East School, 476 Main St., PO Box 1270, Wolfville NS B0P 1X0 – 902/542-2237 – Principal, G. Fred Atkinson – *60 – Remedial, Learning disabled, Residential

ONTARIO

Ministry of Education & Training
15th Fl., Mowat Block, Queen's Park, Toronto ON M7A 1L2
416/325-2929; TDD: 1-800-263-2892; Toll Free: 1-800-387-5514
Minister, Hon. John Snobelen, 416/325-2600; Fax: 416/325-2608
Deputy Minister, Richard Dicerni, 416/325-2180

CENTRE D'ÉTUDES INDÉPENDANTES
2141, boul Lasalle, Sudbury ON P3A 2A3
705/688-3045; Toll Free: 1-800-461-6257

INDEPENDENT LEARNING CENTRE
#400, 20 Bay St., Toronto ON M5J 2W1
416/325-4388; Toll Free: 1-800-387-5512

MINISTRY OF EDUCATION & TRAINING REGIONAL OFFICES:
Central Ontario Region : Heron's Hill Bldg., #3201, 2025 Sheppard Ave. East, North York ON M2J 1W4 – 416/491-0330; Fax: 416/491-9962 – Director, R. DiCecco
Eastern Ontario Region: 1580 Merivale Rd., 4th Fl., Nepean ON K2G 4B5 – 613/225-9210; Fax: 613/225-2881 – Director, Maurice Poirier
Midnorthern Ontario Region : 199 Larch St., 7th Fl., Sudbury ON P3E 5P9 – 705/675-4401; Fax: 705/675-4186 – Director, Michel Robineau
Northeastern Ontario Region : 447 McKeown Ave., PO Box 3020, North Bay ON P1B 8K7 – 705/474-7210; Fax: 705/494-4075 – Acting Director, Lise Presseault
Northwestern Ontario Region : #111, 435 James St. South, Thunder Bay ON P7C 5G6 – 807/475-1581; Fax: 807/475-1550 – Director, Jacqueline Dojack
Western Ontario Region : 759 Hyde Park Rd., London ON N6H 3S6 – 519/472-1440; Fax: 519/472-6178 – Acting Director, Terry Boucher

For detailed departmental listings, see Index: "Education, Depts."

PUBLIC SCHOOL BOARDS

Boards with an enrollment of more than 20,000 are in bold print.

Atikokan Board of Education – *702
    110 Clark St., Atikokan ON P0T 1C0
    807/597-6941; Fax: 807/597-6935 – Chair, Judy Eluik; Dir., Wayne McAndrew
Beardmore, Geraldton, Longlac & Area Board of Education – *558
    PO Box 909, Geraldton ON P0T 1M0
    807/854-1470; Fax: 807/854-1148 – Chair, Stephanie Drajanoff; Dir., Joe Virdiramo
Brant County Board of Education – *17,562
    349 Erie Ave., Brantford ON N3T 5V3
    519/756-6301; Fax: 519/756-9181 – Chair, Dorleen Allen; Dir., Peter Moffatt
Bruce County Board of Education – *11,207
    PO Box 190, Chesley ON N0G 1L0
    519/366-2014; Fax: 519/363-3448 – Chair, Donald Stobo; Dir., Paul Martindale
Carleton Board of Education
    133 Greenbank Rd., Nepean ON K2H 6L3
    613/721-1820; Fax: 613/820-6968
    *47,634
    Chair, Carol Parker
    Dir., E. Kyle Murray
Central Algoma Board of Education – *2,257
    PO Box 10, Richards Landing ON P0R 1J0
    705/246-2441; Fax: 705/246-2151 – Chair, Lorraine Aelick; Dir., Melvin L. Baird
Chapleau Board of Education – *445
    31 Birch St. East, PO Box 220, Chapleau ON P0M 1K0
    705/864-1750; Fax: 705/864-0518 – Chair, Earle Freeborn
Cochrane/Iroquois Falls/Black River Matheson Board of Education – *2,194
    457 Zealand Ave., PO Box 820, Iroquois Falls ON P0K 1G0
    705/232-4015; Fax: 705/232-5450 – Chair, Jamie Kydd; Dir., Craig Shelswell
Dryden Board of Education – *4,248
    Lower Level, 79 Casimir Ave., Dryden ON P8N 2Z6 807/223-5311; Fax: 807/223-4703 – Chair, David Penney; Dir., John Borst
Dufferin County Board of Education – *8,331
    40 Amelia St., Orangeville ON L9W 3T8
    519/941-6191; Fax: 519/942-2450 – Chair, Laura Ryan; Dir., David C. Baldwin
Durham Board of Education
    400 Taunton Rd. East, RR#2, Whitby ON L1N 5R5
    905/666-5500; Fax: 905/576-1457
    *59,704
    Chair, Patricia Bowman
    Dir., P. Laing
East Parry Sound Board of Education – *4,055
    24-26 Marie St., PO Box 40, South River ON P0A 1X0
    705/386-2387; Fax: 705/386-0670 – Chair, But Whitmell; Dir., Norman J. Mason
East York, Board of Education for the Borough of – *14,995
    840 Coxwell Ave., Toronto ON M4C 2V3
    416/396-2000; Fax: 416/461-7356 – Chair, Constance Culbertson; Dir., Eric B. Lewis
Elgin County Board of Education – *13,835
    400 Sunset Dr., St. Thomas ON N5R 3C8
    519/633-2700; Fax: 519/633-1622 – Chair, Malcolm B. Wood; Dir., Demra L. Walker
Espanola Board of Education – *1,772
    210 Mead Blvd., PO Box 429, Espanola ON P0P 1C0
    705/869-3103; Fax: 705/869-5304 – Chair, Louis Bourcier; Dir., John Cottenden
Essex County Board of Education – *17,726
    Essex County Civic & Education Centre, 360 Fairview Ave. West, Essex ON N8M 1Y4
    519/776-6421; Fax: 519/776-4457 – Chair, Joan Flood; Dir., Paul de Sadeleer
Etobicoke, Board of Education for the City of
    1 Civic Centre Court, Etobicoke ON M9C 2B3
    416/394-7000; Fax: 416/394-7397
    *37,094
    Chair, Lorraine Nowina
    Dir., Bill McIntosh
Fort Frances-Rainy River Board of Education – *3,489
    522 Second St. East, Fort Frances ON P9A 1N4
    807/274-9855; Fax: 807/274-5078 – Chair, Peggy Johnson; Dir., John McLeod
Frontenac County Board of Education
    220 Portsmouth Ave., PO Box 610, Kingston ON K7L 4X4
    613/544-6920; Fax: 613/544-6804
    *20,201
    Chair, Ross Drummond
    Dir., J.H. Bates
Grey County Board of Education – *14,915
    55 Victoria St., PO Box 100, Markdale ON N0C 1H0
    519/986-3410; Fax: 519/986-3691 – Chair, Wally Reif; Dir., Berry B. Dobie
Haldimand Board of Education – *8,301
    #72, Hwy. 54, PO Box 2000, Cayuga ON N0A 1E0
    905/772-3391; Fax: 905/772-3878 – Chair, Kevin Young; Dir., Frank J. Kelly
Haliburton County Board of Education – *2,451
    PO Box 507, Haliburton ON K0M 1S0
    705/457-1980; Fax: 705/457-3040 – Chair, Wally Bunn; Dir., Alexander Saunders
Halton Board of Education
    2050 Guelph Line, PO Box 5005, Burlington ON L7R 3Z2
    905/335-3663; Fax: 905/335-9802
    *43,805
    Chair, David Coons
    Dir., Bob Williams
Hamilton, Board of Education for the City of
    100 Main St. West, PO Box 2558, Hamilton ON L8N 3L1
    905/527-5092; Fax: 905/521-2539
    *40,804
    Chair, Bert Allen
    Dir., Donald W. Goodridge

Hastings County Board of Education
    Education Centre, 156 Ann St., Belleville ON K8N 1N9
    613/966-1170; Fax: 613/966-0939
    *20,413
    Chair, D.E. Maracle
    Dir., Ronald Denyes
Hearst Board of Education – *353
    923 Edward St., PO Box 7000, Hearst ON P0L 1N0
    705/372-1459; Fax: 705/362-8093 – Chair, Ruby Brunet
Hornepayne Board of Education – *264
    PO Box 69, Hornepayne ON P0M 1Z0
    807/868-2253; Fax: 807/868-2352 – Sec., Carol Ann Latoski
Huron County Board of Education – *10,448
    103 Albert St., Clinton ON N0M 1L0
    519/482-3496; Fax: 519/482-7358 – Chair, Roxanne Brown; Dir., Paul Carroll
Kapuskasing-Smooth Rock Falls & District Board of Education – *880
    62 Devonshire Ave., Kapuskasing ON P5N 1C3
    705/335-6025; Fax: 705/335-5066 – Chair, Dorothy Enright; Dir., David B. Duchesne
Kenora Board of Education – *3,294
    100 First Ave. West, Kenora ON P9N 3Z7
    807/468-5571; Fax: 807/468-3857 – Chair, Marion Helash; Dir., Richard W. Coburn
Kent County Board of Education – *15,912
    476 McNaughton Ave. East, PO Box 1000, Chatham ON N7M 5L7
    519/354-3770; Fax: 519/354-0662 – Chair, Richard L. Whittington; Dir., Douglas W. Houston
Kirkland Lake Board of Education – *2,131
    35 Second St., PO Box 2610, Kirkland Lake ON P2N 3P4
    705/567-3271; Fax: 705/568-8503 – Chair, Eileen Miko
Lake Superior Board of Education – *2,718
    12 Helmo Dr., PO Bag A, Marathon ON P0T 2E0
    807/229-0436; Fax: 807/229-1471 – Chair, Guy Champagne; Dir., Ted Lake
Lakehead Board of Education – *17,244
    2135 Sills St., Thunder Bay ON P7E 5T2
    807/625-5100; Fax: 807/623-5833 – Chair, Linda Rydholm; Dir., Jim McCuaig
Lambton County Board of Education – *19,159
    200 Wellington St., PO Box 2019, Sarnia ON N7T 7L2
    519/336-1500; Fax: 519/336-0992 – Chair, Steve Morris; Dir., Grant Yeo
Lanark County Board of Education – *10,118
    15 Victoria St., Perth ON K7H 2H7
    613/267-4210; Fax: 613/267-3860 – Chair, Janet Duncan; Dir., William John Laughlin
Leeds & Grenville County Board of Education – *14,337
    25 Central Ave. West, Brockville ON K6V 5X1
    613/342-0371; Fax: 613/342-7444 – Chair, David Paul; Dir., Frank Kinsella
Lennox & Addington County Board of Education – *7,117
    264 Camden Rd., PO Box 70, Napanee ON K7R 3M1
    613/354-3391; Fax: 613/354-4732 – Chair, John Ibey; Dir., Willis F. Boston
Lincoln County Board of Education
    191 Carleton St., St. Catharines ON L2R 7P4
    905/641-1550; Fax: 905/685-8511
    *26,300
    Chair, Lora E. Campbell
    Dir., Willian McLean
London, Board of Education for the City of
    1250 Dundas St., PO Box 5888, London ON N6A 5L1
    519/452-2000; Fax: 519/455-7648; URL: http://www.lbe.edu.on.ca
    *49,569

Chair, John Townshend
Dir., Darrel D. Skidmore
Manitoulin Board of Education – *1,950
PO Box 489, Little Current ON P0P 1K0
705/368-2860; Fax: 705/368-3811 – Chair, Rob Scott; Dir., Doug M. Hall
Metropolitan Toronto School Board – *621
45 York Mills Rd., North York ON M2P 1B6
416/397-2500; Fax: 416/397-2640 – Chair, Ann Vanstone; Dir., Donald J. McVicar
Michipicoten Board of Education – *909
Winston Rd., PO Box 560, Wawa ON P0S 1K0
705/856-2309; Fax: 705/856-4332 – Chair, Robert Moore
Middlesex County Board of Education – *10,890
1120 Hyde Park Rd., Hyde Park ON N0M 1Z0
519/471-3510; Fax: 519/471-1913 – Chair, Donna McImoyle; Dir., Ted D. Anderson
Muskoka Board of Education – *8,575
14 Pine St., Bracebridge ON P1L 1N4
705/645-8704; Fax: 705/645-8452 – Chair, Doris Monahan; Dir., Dusty L.G. Papke
Niagara South Board of Education
250 Thorold Rd. West, Welland ON L3C 3W3
905/735-3840; Fax: 905/735-5285
*26,780
Chair, Mickey Mayne
Dir., William T. Millar
Nipigon-Red Rock Board of Education – *803
Frost St., PO Box 448, Red Rock ON P0T 2P0
807/886-2243; Fax: 807/886-2316 – Chair, Betty P. Chambers; Dir., J.S. Virdiramo
Nipissing Board of Education – *10,917
200 McIntyre St. East, PO Box 3110, North Bay ON P1B 8H1
705/472-8170; Fax: 705/472-9927 – Chair, Kathy Hewitt; Dir., Robert Kennedy
Norfolk Board of Education – *10,083
PO Box 486, Simcoe ON N3Y 4L7
519/428-1880; Fax: 519/428-2484 – Chair, Howard Clark; Dir., J.G. Townsend
North Shore Board of Education – *4,125
160 Spruce Ave., Elliot Lake ON P5A 2C5
705/848-3661; Fax: 705/848-9225 – Chair, Robert Whitehead; Dir., Michael J. Lewis
North York, Board of Education for the City of
5050 Yonge St., North York ON M2N 5N8
416/395-4661; Fax: 416/225-0297
*64,173
Chair, Elsa Chandler
Dir., Veronica Lacey
Northumberland/Clarington Board of Education
834 D'Arcy St., PO Box 470, Cobourg ON K9A 4L2
905/372-6871; Fax: 905/372-1133
*24,814
Chair, Judi Armstrong
Dir., Richard T. Malowney
Ottawa Board of Education
330 Gilmour St., Ottawa ON K2P 0P9
613/239-2211; Fax: 613/230-6408
*33,303
Chair, Bill G. Gowling
Dir., Robert C. Gillett
Oxford County Board of Education – *16,454
94 Grahman St., PO Box 636, Woodstock ON N4S 7Z8
519/539-4821; Fax: 519/539-1905 – Chair, Patricia Smith; Dir., Michael J. Weeks
Peel Board of Education
5650 Hurontario St., Mississauga ON L5R 1C6
905/890-1099; Fax: 905/890-1277
*96,318
Chair, Beryl Ford
Dir., Harold M. Brathwaite
Perth County Board of Education – *11,985
210 Water St., Stratford ON N5A 3C5
519/271-0930; Fax: 519/271-2324 – Chair, Peter Stulp; Dir., A. Paul R. Sherratt

Peterborough County Board of Education – *18,549
150 O'Carroll Ave., PO Box 719, Peterborough ON K9J 7A1
705/743-7431; Fax: 705/743-0341 – Chair, Barbara Jinkerson; Dir., Len Budden
Prescott & Russell County Board of Education – *4,457
411 Stanley St., Hawkesbury ON K6A 3E8
613/632-0144; Fax: 613/632-0147 – Chair, Allan Anderson; Dir., D.A. Farrow
Prince Edward County Board of Education – *3,478
5 Stanley St. East, PO Box 220, Bloomfield ON K0K 1G0
613/393-3153; Fax: 613/393-2990 – Chair, Ruth Hart; Dir., Larry L. Langdon
Red Lake Board of Education – *1,411
20 Young St., Red Lake ON P0V 2M0
807/727-2676; Fax: 807/727-3335 – Chair, G. Williamson; Dir., David C. McLeod
Renfrew County Board of Education – *13,953
1270 Pembroke St. West, Pembroke ON K8A 4G4
613/735-0151; Fax: 613/735-6315 – Chair, Ted Barron; Dir., Peter W. Hiscott
Sault Ste. Marie Board of Education – *11,770
644 Albert St. East, Sault Ste. Marie ON P6A 2K7
705/945-7111; Fax: 705/942-2540 – Chair, Donald T. Edwards; Dir., R.C. Rosario
Scarborough, Board of Education for the City of
Civic Centre, 140 Borough Dr., Scarborough ON M1P 4N6
416/396-7100; Fax: 416/396-4215
*79,824
Chair, David F. Horrox
Dir., Earl Campbell
Simcoe County Board of Education
Hwy. 26, Midhurst ON L0L 1X0
705/728-7570; Fax: 705/728-2265
*50,938
Chair, Ken Snelgrove
Dir., Terry Lynch
Stormont, Dundas & Glengarry County Board of Education – *13,566
902 Second St. West, Cornwall ON K6H 5S6
613/933-6990; Fax: 613/933-4089 – Chair, Art Buckland; Dir., J.W. Dilamarter
Sudbury Board of Education – *19,560
Civic Square, West Tower, 5th Fl., 200 Brady St., Sudbury ON P3E 5K3
705/674-3171; Fax: 705/647-3167 – Chair, Dr. Ernie Checkeris; Dir., J.D. Smith
Timiskaming Board of Education – *3,708
213 Whitewood Ave., PO Box 40, New Liskeard ON P0J 1P0
705/647-7394; Fax: 705/647-9212 – Chair, Juergen Leukert; Dir., Thomas McGrory
Timmins Board of Education – *4,886
153 Third Ave., PO Box 1020, Timmins ON P4N 7H7
705/360-1151; Fax: 705/268-7100 – Chair, Heather Bozzer; Dir., John Huggins
Toronto, Board of Education for the City of
155 College St., Toronto ON M5T 1P6
416/598-4931; Fax: 416/393-9969
*77,570
Chair, David Moll
Dir., John Davies
Victoria County Board of Education – *11,811
Verulam Rd. South, PO Box 420, Lindsay ON K9V 4S3
705/324-6776; Fax: 705/328-2036 – Chair, Alex Istchenko; Dir., Dianne E. Dalton, Ed.D.
Waterloo County Board of Education
51 Ardelt Ave., PO Box 68, Kitchener ON N2G 3X5
519/570-0300; Fax: 519/742-1364
*55,672
Chair, Elaine Gross
Dir., Patti Gross
Wellington County Board of Education
500 Victoria Rd. North, Guelph ON N1E 6K2

519/822-4420; Fax: 519/822-4487
*24,486
Chair, Donald Ross
Dir., Dr. Martha C. Rogers
Wentworth County Board of Education – *17,959
Memorial Bldg., 357 Wilson St. East, Ancaster ON L9G 4B7
905/523-8621; Fax: 905/648-5583 – Chair, Jack Duncan; Dir., Allan A. Greenleaf
West Parry Sound Board of Education – *3,190
70 Isabella St., Parry Sound ON P2A 1M6
705/746-9372; Fax: 705/746-7367 – Chair, Sue Woodhouse; Dir., Bradley Burt
Windsor, Board of Education for the City of – *19,989
451 Park St. West, PO Box 210, Windsor ON N9A 6K1
519/255-3200; Fax: 519/255-7053 – Chair, Beth Cooper; Dir., S.C. Payne
York, Board of Education for the City of – *18,199
2 Trethewey Dr., Toronto ON M6M 4A8
416/394-2270; Fax: 416/394-3137 – Chair, Karen Hen; Dir., Norman Ahmet
York Region Board of Education
60 Wellington St. West, PO Box 40, Aurora ON L4G 3H2
905/969-8131; Fax: 905/727-3984
*74,601
Chair, Bill Crothers
Dir., Bill Hogarth

COUNTY & DISTRICT COMBINED ROMAN CATHOLIC SEPARATE SCHOOL BOARDS

Boards with an enrollment of more than 20,000 are in bold print.
Brant County Roman Catholic Separate School Board – *6,100
322 Fairview Dr., PO Box 217, Brantford ON N3T 5M8
519/756-6369; Fax: 519/756-9913 – Chair, Dan Dignard; Dir., Carol Cigagna
Bruce-Grey County Roman Catholic Separate School Board – *4,527
799 - 16 Ave., Hanover ON N4N 3A1
519/364-5820; Fax: 519/364-5882 – Chair, Thomas O'Dwyer; Dir., Rosemary Kennedy
Carleton Roman Catholic Separate School Board
1695 Merivale Rd., Nepean ON K2G 3R4
613/224-2222; Fax: 613/224-5063
*23,227
Chair, June Flynn-Turner
Acting Dir., R.P. Larkin
Chapleau District Roman Catholic Separate School Board – *404
31 Birch St. East, PO Box 788, Chapleau ON P0M 1K0
705/864-1100; Fax: 705/864-0518 – Chair, Jean P. Brais
Cochrane/Iroquois Falls/Black River Matheson Roman Catholic Separate School Board – *1,649
540, Ste. Hélène St., PO Box 858, Iroquois Falls ON P0K 1G0
705/232-4061; Fax: 705/232-6748 – Chair, Florian Chartier; Dir., Rheal M. Bazinet
Conseil des écoles catholiques de Timmins/Timmins Roman Catholic School Board – *5,951
36 Birch St. South, Timmins ON P4N 2A5
705/267-1421; Fax: 705/267-7247 – Chair, Maureen Beaulne-Harvey; Dir., Michael Serre
Dryden District Roman Catholic Separate School Board – *742
105 King St., PO Box 781, Dryden ON P8N 2Z4
807/223-4663; Fax: 807/223-4014 – Chair, Frank Bastone; Dir., Garry F. Bates
Dufferin-Peel Roman Catholic Separate School Board
40 Matheson Blvd. West, Mississauga ON L5R 1C5
905/890-1221; Fax: 905/890-7610
*73,065

* indicates enrollment figure.

Chair, John J. Doran
Dir., Michael Bates

Durham Region Roman Catholic Separate School Board
650 Rossland Rd. West, Oshawa ON L1J 7C4
905/576-6150; Fax: 905/576-0953
*24,084
Chair, Tom Oldman
Dir., Grant A. Andrews

Elgin County Roman Catholic Separate School Board – *2,149
21 Parish St., St. Thomas ON N5R 4W7
519/631-8300; Fax: 519/631-1619 – Chair, William Hall; Dir., J.K. Couchman

Essex County Roman Catholic Separate School Board – *15,343
360 Fairview Ave. West, Essex ON N8M 1Y5
519/776-6431; Fax: 519/776-6663 – Chair, Donald Petrozzi; Dir., Ronald J. Reddam

Fort Frances-Rainy River District Roman Catholic Separate School Board – *721
555 Flinders Ave., Fort Frances ON P9A 3L2
807/274-2931 – Chair, Orielle DeGagne; Dir., Garry F. Bates

Frontenac, Lennox & Addington County Roman Catholic Separate School Board – *7,804
84 Stephen St., PO Box 1058, Kingston ON K7L 4Y5
613/544-4927; Fax: 613/544-9616 – Chair, Thomas Foley; Dir., G.T. Cosgrove

Geraldton District Roman Catholic Separate School Board – *558
308 - 4 St. North, PO Box 370, Geraldton ON P0T 1M0
807/854-1421; Fax: 807/854-0446 – Chair, Jack Duhaime

Haldimand-Norfolk Roman Catholic Separate School Board – *2,966
55 Park Rd., PO Box 278, Simcoe ON N3Y 4L1
519/426-8370; Fax: 519/426-5333 – Chair, Paul Serruys; Dir., Denis I. Tschirhart

Halton Roman Catholic Separate School Board – *19,838
802 Drury Lane, PO Box 5308, Burlington ON L7R 3Y2
905/632-6300; Fax: 905/333-4661 – Chair, Irene McCauley; Dir., Fred Sweeny

Hamilton-Wentworth Roman Catholic Separate School Board
90 Mulberry St., PO Box 2012, Hamilton ON L8N 3R9
905/525-2930; Fax: 905/525-1724
*27,134
Chair, Patrick Daly
Dir., James Daly

Hastings-Prince Edward County Roman Catholic Separate School Board – *5,538
3 Applewood Dr., Belleville ON K8P 4E3
613/966-9210; Fax: 613/966-0204 – Chair, Leona Dombrowsky; Dir., Barbara A. Lynn

Hearst District Roman Catholic Separate School Board – *1,744
923 Edward St., PO Box 1660, Hearst ON P0L 1N0
705/362-4337; Fax: 705/362-8093 – Chair, Rémi Lessard; Dir., L. Papineau

Huron-Perth County Roman Catholic Separate School Board – *4,517
87 Mill St., PO Box 70, Dublin ON N0K 1E0
519/345-2440; Fax: 519/345-2449 – Chair, Louise Martin; Dir., James S. Brown

Kapuskasing District Roman Catholic Separate School Board – *2,781
75 Queen St., Kapuskasing ON P5N 1H5
705/335-6091; Fax: 705/335-8258 – Chair, Louis Veilleux; Dir., André Bordeleau

Kenora District Roman Catholic Separate School Board – *1,349
200 First St. North, Kenora ON P9N 2K4
807/468-9851 – Chair, David McCann; Dir., Patrick M. Gillen

Kent County Roman Catholic Separate School Board – *7,546
535 Baldoon Rd. North, PO Box 2003, Chatham ON N7M 5L9
519/354-5170; Fax: 519/354-4173 – Chair, Gerard Couture; Dir., Sandy J. Easton

Kirkland Lake-Timiskaming District Roman Catholic Separate School Board – *3,221
21 Armstrong St., PO Bag R, New Liskeard ON P0J 1P0
705/647-7304; Fax: 705/647-8410 – Chair, Marcel A. Joliat; Dir., Paul St-Cyr

Lakehead District Roman Catholic Separate School Board – *8,943
212 Miles St. East, Thunder Bay ON P7C 4Y5
807/625-1555; Fax: 807/623-0431 – Chair, Joleene Kemp; Dir., J.W. Tennier

Lambton County Roman Catholic Separate School Board – *7,941
430 Christina St. South, Sarnia ON N7T 2N8
519/336-6139; Fax: 519/336-5160 – Chair, Mary Cowley; Dir., John F. Ross

Lanark, Leeds & Grenville County Roman Catholic Separate School Board – *5,709
PO Box 427, Smiths Falls ON K7A 4T4
613/283-5007; Fax: 613/283-2782 – Chair, Thomas Barr; Dir., Frank B. Musca

Lincoln County Roman Catholic Separate School Board – *9,859
80 Grantham Ave., St Catharines ON L2P 3H1
905/682-8354; Fax: 905/682-0012 – Chair, Susan Venditti; Dir., Vincent C. Monaghan

London & Middlesex Roman Catholic Separate School Board – *17,084
165 Elmwood Ave. East, PO Box 5474, London ON N6A 4X5
519/663-2088; Fax: 519/663-9250 – Chair, Joe Kraemer; Dir., Patrick J. Dunne

Metropolitan Separate School Board
80 Sheppard Ave. East, Toronto ON M2N 6E8
416/222-8282; Fax: 416/229-5345
*104,370
Chair, Elvira Demonte
Dir., Anthony J. Barone

Michipicoten District Roman Catholic Separate School Board – *550
PO Box 560, Wawa ON P0S 1K0
705/856-2309 – Chair, Gerald Beerkens

Nipissing District Roman Catholic Separate School Board – *9,054
1140 Front St., North Bay ON P1B 6P2
705/472-1520; Fax: 705/472-9398 – Chair, Robert Lucenti; Dir., Brian D. Giroux

North Shore District Roman Catholic Separate School Board – *1,990
8 Woodward Ave., PO Box 460, Blind River ON P0R 1B0
705/356-2223; Fax: 705/356-2563 – Chair, Robert Gallagher; Dir., David R. Hubbert

North of Superior District Roman Catholic Separate School Board – *1,054
13 Simcoe Plaza, PO Box 610, Terrace Bay ON P0T 2W0
807/825-3209; Fax: 807/825-3885 – Chair, Paul Paradis; Dir., Maureen McGoey

Ottawa Roman Catholic Separate School Board – *10,736
140 Cumberland St., Ottawa ON K1N 7G9
613/746-3025; Fax: 613/746-3081 – Chair, Jim Kennelly; Dir., W. Dennis Nolan

Oxford County Roman Catholic Separate School Board – *2,832
912 Dundas St., PO Box 97, Woodstock ON N4S 7W5
519/539-4877; Fax: 519/539-1732 – Chair, Cliff Roach; Dir., Robert Gutcher

Peterborough-Victoria-Northumberland & Clarington Roman Catholic Separate School Board – *12,093
459 Reid St., Peterborough ON K9H 4G7
705/748-4861; Fax: 705/748-9734 – Chair, James Lynch; Dir., Donald Folz

Prescott & Russell County Roman Catholic Separate School Board (English Language) – *1,163
999 Promenade Heritage, Rockland ON K4K 1R2
613/446-7979; Fax: 613/446-5899 – Chair, Karen Leonard; Dir., William Crossan

Renfrew County Roman Catholic Separate School Board – *6,252
499 Pembroke St. West, Pembroke ON K8A 5P1
613/735-1031; Fax: 613/735-2649 – Chair, Robert Schreader; Dir., J.E. Stunt

Sault Ste. Marie District Roman Catholic Separate School Board – *7,103
90 Ontario Ave., Sault Ste. Marie ON P6B 6G7
705/949-5400; Fax: 705/949-4503 – Chair, Karen Fata; Dir., William Struk

Simcoe County Roman Catholic Separate School Board – *17,138
46 Alliance Blvd., Barrie ON L4M 5K3
705/722-3555; Fax: 705/722-6534 – Chair, Ernest Vaillancourt; Dir., M.J. Obee

Stormont, Dundas & Glengarry County Roman Catholic Separate School Board – *10,564
835 Campbell St., PO Box 130, Cornwall ON K6H 5S8
613/933-1720; Fax: 613/933-5127 – Chair, Alphonse Lafrance; Dir., Roger Davidson

Sudbury District Roman Catholic Separate School Board – *17,940
201 Jogues St., Sudbury ON P3C 5L7
705/673-5621; Fax: 705/673-9160 – Chair, Louie De Longhi; Dir., Léo Lefebvre

Waterloo County Roman Catholic Separate School Board
91 Moore Ave., PO Box 1116, Kitchener ON N2G 4G2
519/578-3660; Fax: 519/578-5291; URL: http://www.watrc.edu.on.ca
*23,342
Chair, Stephen P. Haller
Dir., Dr. William A. Brown

Welland County Roman Catholic Separate School Board – *14,881
427 Rice Rd., Welland ON L3C 7C1
905/735-0240; Fax: 905/735-8807 – Chair, Donald J. Lefebvre; Dir., Angelo Di Ianni

Wellington County Roman Catholic Separate School Board – *6,776
75 Woolwich St., Guelph ON N1H 6N6
519/821-4600; Fax: 519/824-3088 – Chair, John Lambertus; Dir., John A. Wheatley

Windsor Roman Catholic Separate School Board – *16,434
1485 Janette Ave., Windsor ON N8X 1Z2
519/253-2481; Fax: 519/253-8397 – Chair, Catherine Curran; Dir., James Molnar

York Region Roman Catholic Separate School Board
320 Bloomington Rd. West, Aurora ON L4G 3G8
905/713-2711; Fax: 905/713-1261
*42,787
Chair, Terrance G. Ryan
Dir., F.S. Bobesich

ROMAN CATHOLIC SEPARATE SCHOOL BOARDS

Atikokan Roman Catholic Separate School Board – *261
120 Marks St., Atikokan ON P0T 1C0
807/597-6748; Fax: 807/597-1209 – Chair, E.A. Morrissette

Cardiff-Bicroft Combined Roman Catholic Separate School Board
c/o Hastings-Prince Edward County R.C.S.S. Board, 3 Applewood Dr., Belleville ON K8P 4E3

613/966-9210; Fax: 613/966-0204 – Chair, Kelly Krick
Dubreuilville Roman Catholic Separate School Board – *160
 1, av du Parc, PO Box 69, Dubreauilville ON P0S 1B0
 705/884-2309 – Chair, Pauline Tremblay Guylaine
Foleyet Roman Catholic Separate School Board – *40
 52 Theodore Pl., Timmins ON P4N 7P6
 705/267-3521 – Chair, Suzanne Roch
Gogama Roman Catholic Separate School Board – *55
 PO Box 70, Gogama ON P0M 1W0
 705/894-2775; Fax: 705/894-2866 – Chair, Roger Carriere
Hornepayne Roman Catholic Separate School Board – *91
 5 High St., PO Box 430, Hornepayne ON P0M 1Z0
 807/868-2010; Fax: 807/868-3026 – Chair, C. MacEachern
Ignace Roman Catholic Separate School Board – *44
 Hwy. 17, PO Box 930, Ignace ON P0T 1T0
 807/934-6426; Fax: 807/934-6282 – Chair, Diane Thibault
Moosonee Roman Catholic Separate School Board – *149
 PO Box 340, Moosonee ON P0L 1Y0
 705/336-2605 – Chair, Gerard Heaney
Parry Sound Roman Catholic Separate School Board – *118
 70 Isabella St., Parry Sound ON P2A 1M6
 705/746-6231; Fax: 705/746-7568 – Chair, Roger Kolbuc
Red Lake Area Combined Roman Catholic Separate School Board – *162
 48 Discovery Rd., PO Box 888, Red Lake ON P0V 2M0
 807/727-3470; Fax: 807/727-3211 – Chair, Teresa Van Dusen

SECONDARY SCHOOL BOARDS
James Bay Lowlands Secondary School Board – *294
 Keewatin Dr., PO Box 157, Moosonee ON P0L 1Y0
 705/336-2903; Fax: 705/336-2170 – Chair, Ernie Sutherland

DISTRICT SCHOOL AREA BOARDS (PUBLIC SCHOOLS)
Airy & Sabine District School Area Board – *29
 PO Box 190, Whitney ON K0J 2M0
 613/637-2019; Fax: 613/637-2019 – Chair, Jane Dumas; Dir., Dave pace
Asquith-Garvey District School Area Board – *23
 General Delivery, Shining Tree ON P0M 2X0
 705/263-2847; Fax: 705/263-2009 – Chair, Heather Winslow; Dir., Eichard Dominico
Caramat District School Area Board – *29
 PO Box 5, Caramat ON P0T 1J0
 807/872-2645; Fax: 807/872-2683 – Chair, Raymond Lelievre
Collins District School Area Board – *14
 General Delivery, Collins ON P0V 1M0
 807/583-2593; Fax: 807/475-6945 – Chair, Mike Yellowhead
Connell & Ponsford District School Area Board – *112
 8 Dickenson Dr., PO Box 280, Pickle Lake ON P0V 3A0
 807/928-2952; Fax: 807/928-2144 – Chair, Gordon Williams
Foleyet District School Area Board – *33
 PO Box 100, Foleyet ON P0M 1T0
 705/899-2942; Fax: 705/899-2950 – Chair, G. Bromley
Gogama District School Area Board – *16
 PO Box 11, Gogama ON P0M 1W0
 705/894-2445 – Chair, A. Carrière
Kashabowie District School Area Board
 Kashabowie ON P0T 1Y0
 807/926-2471 – Chair, I. Mayo

Kilkenny District School Area Board – *36
 411 Morse St., Thunder Bay ON P7A 1G7
 807/683-3949 – Chair, A. Adams
Mine Centre District School Area Board – *88
 PO Box 128, Mine Centre ON P0W 1H0
 807/599-2836; Fax: 807/599-2815 – Chair, Donald A. Hyatt
Missaranda District School Area Board – *10
 PO Box 62, Missanabie ON P0M 2H0
 705/234-2820 – Chair, M.C. Anglehart
Moose Factory Island District School Area Board – *526
 PO Box 160, Moose Factory ON P0L 1W0
 705/658-4571; Fax: 705/658-4768 – Chair, Patrick S. Chilton
Moosonee District School Area Board – *326
 PO Box 398, Moosonee ON P0L 1Y0
 705/336-2300; Fax: 705/336-2170 – Chair, Jackie Spindloe
Murchison & Lyell District School Area Board – *17
 PO Box 39, Madawaska ON K0J 2C0
 613/637-5592; Fax: 613/637-2052 – Chair, Jill Bresnahan
Nakina District School Area Board – *91
 59 Algoma St., PO Box 330, Nakina ON P0T 2H0
 807/329-5257; Fax: 807/329-5207 – Chair, T. Swanson
Northern District School Area Board – *174
 PO Box 98, Armstrong ON P0T 1A0
 807/583-2010; Fax: 807/583-2614 – Chair, Bette Hughes
Slate Falls District School Area Board – *42
 405 Isabella St. West, Thunder Bay ON P7E 5E5
 807/475-6989; Fax: 807/475-6945 – Chair, Elsie Sakakeesic
Sturgeon Lake District School Area Board
 PO Box 660, Ignace ON P0T 1T0
 807/934-6932; Fax: 807/475-6945 – Chair, Carol Groves
Summer Beaver District School Area Board – *88
 Summer Beaver ON P0T 3B0
 807/593-2110 – Chair, C. Oskineegish
Umfreville District School Area Board
 405 Isabella St. West, Thunder Bay ON P7E 5E5
 807/475-6989; Fax: 807/475-6945 – Chair, Art Gouriluk
Upsala District School Area Board – *35
 General Delivery, Upsala ON P0T 2Y0
 807/986-2207; Fax: 807/986-2206 – Chair, B. Johnson

PROTESTANT SEPARATE SCHOOL BOARDS
Penetanguishene Protestant Separate School Board – *202
 39 Burke St., PO Box 550, Penetanguishene ON L0K 1P0
 705/549-6422; Fax: 705/549-2768 – Chair, Kathyrn Contois

HOSPITALS & TREATMENT CENTRE SCHOOL BOARDS
Campbell Children's School Board of Education, 600 Townline Rd. South, Oshawa ON L1H 7K6 – 905/576-8403 – Chair, K.V. Peacock – *19
Essex County Children's Rehabilitation Centre Board of Education, 3945 Matchette Rd., Windsor ON N9C 4C2 – 519/252-7281; Fax: 519/252-5873 – Chair, John Zangari – *36
Hugh MacMillan Centre Board of Education, 350 Rumsey Rd., Toronto ON M4G 1R8 – 416/424-3831; Fax: 416/425-6591 – Chair, G. Wilson – *91
Niagara Peninsula Children's Centre Board of Education, 567 Glenridge Ave., PO Box 1454, Fonthill ON L0S 1E0 – 905/688-3550; Fax: 905/688-1055 – Chair, Anne Finley – *66
Ottawa Children's Treatment Centre Board of Education, 395 Smyth Rd., Ottawa ON K1H 8L2 – 613/737-0871 – Dir., Ruth Koch-Schulte – *25

Waterloo North Children's Centre Board of Education, 500 Hallmark Dr., Waterloo ON N2K 3P5 – 519/886-8886; Fax: 519/570-2934 – Chair, Linda Hendry – *56

FRENCH LANGUAGE SCHOOL BOARDS
Conseil des Écoles Catholiques de Langue Française de la Region d'Ottawa-Carleton/Ottawa-Carleton French Catholic School Board – *14,999
 4000 Labelle St., Gloucester ON K1J 1A1
 613/241-5660; Fax: 613/241-2597 – Prés., Pierre Marcil; Chair, Albert Potvin
Conseil des écoles françaises de la communauté urbaine de Toronto – *1,627
 #207, 1 Concorde Gate, North York ON M3C 3N6
 416/391-1264; Fax: 416/391-3892 – Chair, Anne-Marie Couffin; Dir., Alice Ducharme
Conseil des Écoles Publiques d'Ottawa-Carleton/Ottawa-Carleton Public School Board (French) – *6,417
 140 Genest St., Vanier ON K1L 7Y9
 613/742-8960; Fax: 613/747-3810 – Prés., Denis Chartrand; Dir., Robert J.C. Pilon
Conseil des écoles séparées catholiques de langue française de Prescott-Russell – *11,758
 875, rte 17, PO Box 570, L'Orignal ON K0B 1K0
 613/675-4691; Fax: 613/675-2921 – Prés., Ronald Lalonde; Dir., Denis Vaillancourt

CANADIAN FORCES BASE SCHOOL BOARDS
CFB Borden Board of Education, Building E-105, CFB Borden, Borden ON L0M 1C0 – 705/423-2172; Fax: 705/423-2367 – Dir., Martin F. Des Roches – *1,443
CFB Trenton Board of Education, CFB Trenton, Astra ON K0K 1B0 – 613/392-9500; Fax: 613/965-7091 – Chair, L.Col. P.A. Tinsley – *690

SCHOOLS FOR HEARING OR VISUALLY IMPAIRED STUDENTS
The Ernest C. Drury School – *262
 255 Ontario St. South, Milton ON L9T 2M5
 905/878-2851 – Sec., R. Dodds; Elem., J. Vanderzand
The Robarts School – *115
 1090 Highbury Ave., London ON N5Y 4V9
 519/453-4400 – C. Barry
The Sir James Whitney School – *92
 350 Dundas St. West, Belleville ON K8P 1B2
 613/967-2823 – C. Barnes
The W. Ross Macdonald School – *215
 350 Brant Ave., Brantford ON N3T 3J9
 519/759-0730 – Sec., D.F. Bethune; Elem., C. Hudson

DEMONSTRATION SCHOOLS FOR CHALLENGED STUDENTS
The Amethyst School, 1090 Highbury Ave., PO Box 7300, London ON N5Y 4V9 – 519/453-4400 – P. Rouble – *41
Centre Jules-Léger, 1495 Heron Rd, Ottawa ON K1V 6A6 – 613/521-4000 – Roger Frappier – *45
Sagonaska School, 350 Dundas St. West, Belleville ON K8P 1B2 – 613/967-2830 – P.G. Healey – *39
Trillium School, 347 Ontario St. South, Milton ON L9T 3X9 – 905/878-8428 – C. Hodder – *40

FIRST NATION EDUCATION AUTHORITIES
Ahkwesasne Mohawk Board of Education, PO Box 819, Cornwall ON K6H 5T7 – 613/575-2934; Fax: 613/575-2289 – Chair, Angela Barnes – *581 – Elem.
Attawapiskat First Nation Education Authority, General Delivery, Attawapiskat ON P0L 1A0 – 705/997-2114, 2232; Fax: 705/997-2357 – Acting Chair, Steve Hookimaw – *532 – Elem./Sec.
Beausoleil First Nation Education Authority, Cedar Point PO, Christian Island ON L0K 1C0 – 705/247-

* indicates enrollment figure.

2051; Fax: 705/247-2239 – Chair, Henry Jackson – *113 – Elem.
Big Grassy River Education Authority, General Delivery, Morson ON P0W 1J0 – 807/488-5916; Fax: 807/488-5345 – Dir., Roger Kangas – *60 – Elem.
Chippewas of Nawash First Nations Board of Education, RR#5, Wiarton ON N0H 2T0 – 519/534-0882; Fax: 519/534-5138 – Education Adm., Verlyn Akiwenzie – *124 – Elem.
Chippewas of Sarnia Education Committee, 978 Tashmoo Ave., Sarnia ON N7T 7H5 – 519/336-8410; Fax: 519/336-0382 – Chair, Patricia Adams – *14 – Elem.
Chippewas of the Thames First Nation Education Board, RR#1, Muncey ON N0L 1Y0 – 519/289-5555; Fax: 519/289-2351 – Chair, Dwayne Kechego – *180 – Elem.
Constance Lake Education Authority, General Delivery, Calstock Via Hearst ON P0L 1B0 – 705/463-4101; Fax: 705/463-4124 – Dir., Stella Etherington – *125 – Elem.
Deer Lake Education Authority, General Delivery, Deer Lake ON P0V 1N0 – 807/775-2367; Fax: 807/775-2398 – Chair, Barbara Rae – *200 – Elem.
Eabametoong First Nation Education Authority, General Delivery, Fort Hope ON P0T 1L0 – 807/242-1305; Fax: 807/242-1313 – Chair, Ron Missewache – *305 – Elem.
Hishkoonikun Education Authority, 430 Riverside Rd., Kashechewan ON P0L 1S0 – 705/275-4538; Fax: 705/275-4515 – Dir., John Hughie – *400 – Elem.
Kingfisher Lake Education Authority, General Delivery, Kingfisher ON P0V 1Z0 – 807/532-2057; Fax: 807/532-2153 – Chair, James Mamakwa – *90 – Elem.
Marten Falls Education Authority, Ogoki Post via Nakina ON P0T 2L0 – 807/349-2509; Fax: 807/349-2511 – Chair, Mel Baxter – *45 – Elem.
Michikan Education Authority, PO Box 78, Bearskin Lake ON P0V 1E0 – 807/363-1011; Fax: 807/363-2519 – Chair, Greta Mosquito – *113 – Elem.
Mishkeegogamang Education Authority, General Delivery, Mishkeegogamang ON P0V 2H0 – 807/928-2284; Fax: 807/928-2382 – Education Coordinator, Isabelle Skunk – *217
Mundo Peetabeck Education Authority, PO Box 31, Fort Albany ON P0L 1H0 – 705/278-3390; Fax: 705/278-1049 – Chair, Peter Sutherland – *185 – Elem.
Muskrat Dam Education Authority, General Delivery, Muskrat Dam ON P0V 3B0 – 807/471-2650; Fax: 807/471-2649 – Dir., Roy Morris – *64 – Elem./Sec.
Neskantaga Education Authority, PO Box 103, Lansdowne House ON P0T 1Z0 – 807/479-2570; Fax: 807/479-1138 – Chair, Lillian Moonais – *70 – Elem.
North Caribou Lake First Nation Education Office, PO Box 155, Weagamow Lake ON P0V 2Y0 – 807/469-1222, 1254; Fax: 807/469-1351 – Chair, Chief Caleb Sakchekapo – *145 – Elem.
Obishikokaang Education Authority, General Delivery, Lac Seul ON P0V 2A0 – 807/582-3420; Fax: 807/582-3430 – Dir., Raymond Ningewance – *107
Onyota'a:ka Kalthuny Nihtsla Tehatilihutakwas (OKT) Education Authority, RR#2, Southwold ON N0L 2G0 – 519/652-1580, 1582; Fax: 519/652-3219 – Chair, Arnold Antone – *208
Pic River First Nation Education Authority, General Delivery, Heron Bay ON P0T 1R0 – 807/229-1749; Fax: 807/229-1944 – Chair, Clyde Cooke – *95 – Elem.
Pikangikum Education Authority, General Delivery, Pikangikum ON P0V 2L0 – 807/773-1093; Fax: 807/773-1014 – Chair, Charlie Pascal – *520 – Elem./Sec.
Sachigo Lake Education Authority, General Delivery, Sachigo Lake ON P0V 2P0 – 807/595-2577; Fax: 807/595-1134 – Education Coordinator, James Chapman – *112 – Elem./Sec.
Sandy Lake Education Authority, PO Box 2, Sandy Lake ON P0V 1V0 – 807/774-1135; Fax: 807/774-1166 – Dir., Peter Goodman – *550 – Elem./Sec.
Shoal Lake Chief & Council: Education Authority, General Delivery, Kejick ON P0X 1E0 – 807/733-2315; Fax: 807/733-3115 – Band Councillor, Education Portfolio, Vernon Redsky – *46 – Elem.
Sineonokway Education Authority, PO Box 73, Kasabonika ON P0V 1Y0 – 807/535-2547; Fax: 807/535-1152 – Chair, Ida Morris – *207
Six Nations of the Grand River, Indian & Northern Affairs, 188 Mohawk St., PO Box 1960, Brantford ON N3T 5W5 – 519/758-2405; Fax: 519/754-0639 – Program Services Dir., Allan Raslack – *1,128 – Elem.
Tyendinaga Territory, Indian & Northern Affairs Canada, 188 Mohawk St., PO Box 1960, Brantford ON N3T 5W5 – 519/758-2405; Fax: 519/754-0639 – Program Services Dir., Allan Rasluck – *300 – Elem.
Wabigoon Lake Chief & Council: Education Authority, Site 112, PO Box 24, Dinorwic ON P0V 1P0 – 807/938-6684; Fax: 807/938-1166 – Chair, Chief Ruben Cantin – *25 – Elem.
Walpole Island First Nation Board of Education, RR#3, Wallaceburg ON N8A 4K9 – 519/627-0708; Fax: 519/627-8596 – Dir., Jim Cassin – *374 – Elem.
Wasaho Education Authority, General Delivery, Fort Severn ON P0V 1W0 – 807/478-2571; Fax: 807/478-1103 – Chair, Moses Kakekaspan – *102 – Elem.
Weenusk First Nation Education Services, PO Box 2, Peawanuck ON P0L 2H0 – 705/473-2527; Fax: 705/473-2528 – Chair, Abraham Hunter – *50 – Elem.
West Bay Board of Education, PO Box 297, West Bay ON P0P 1G0 – 705/377-4988; Fax: 705/377-5080 – Education Coord., Melvina Corbiere – *170 – Elem.
Whitefish Bay: Northwest Angle Education Authority, General Delivery, Pawitik ON P0X 1L0 – 807/226-5710; Fax: 807/226-1066 – Dir., William Bird – *300 – Elem./Sec.
Wikwemikong Board of Education, PO Box 112, Wikwemikong ON P0P 2J0 – 705/859-3122; Fax: 705/859-3851 – Dir., Grace Fox – *458 – Elem.
Wunnumin Lake Education Authority, General Delivery, Wunnumin Lake ON P0V 2Z0 – 807/442-2559; Fax: 807/442-2627 – Dir., Matthew Angees – *120 – Elem.

UNIVERSITIES

Brock University
500 Glenridge Ave., St. Catharines ON L2S 3A1
905/688-5550; Fax: 905/688-2789; URL: http://www.brocku.ca
Chancellor, Robert S.K. Welch
Acting President & Vice-Chancellor, Susan M. Clark
Acting Vice-President, Academic, William H. Cade
Vice-President, Administration, Terrence B. Varcoe
Registrar, Lou Ariano
Secretary to the University, Evelyn Janke
Executive Director, Office of External Relations, Grant Dobson
Development Manager, Scott Hayter
Alumni Manager, Michael Somerville

FACULTIES WITH DEANS
Business, Ronald McTavish
Education, Terrance Boak
Humanities, John Sivell
Acting Dean, Mathematics & Sciences, Richard Cheel
Physical Education, Robert Kerr
Social Sciences, William G. Webster
Acting Dean, Student Affairs, David Siegel

Carleton University
1125 Colonel By Dr., Ottawa ON K1S 5B6
613/520-7400; URL: http://www.carleton.ca; gopher://gopher.carleton.ca
Chancellor, Arthur Kroeger, B.A., M.A.
President & Vice-Chancellor, Richard J. Van Loon, B.Sc., M.A., Ph.D.
Vice-President, Student & Academic Services, Susan Gottheil, B.A., M.A.
Vice-President, Finance & Administration, J.S. Riordon, M.Eng., D.I.C., Ph.D., P.Eng.
Assoc. Vice-President, Finance & Administration, Duncan Watt, M.B.A., P.Eng.
Asst. Vice-President, International, D.R.F. Taylor, M.A., P.G.C.E., Ph.D.
Vice-President, Academic & University Registrar, John W. ApSimon, B.Sc., Ph.D.
Clerk of Senate, Chong Hon Chan, B.Sc., M.A.Sc., Ph.D.
Secretary, Board of Governors, Donald C. McEown, B.A., Dip. Bus. Admin.
Director, University Services, Katherine Main
Director, Finance, Vacant
Controller, Katherine Downs, C.A.
Director, Carleton International, D.R.F. Taylor, M.A., P.G.C.E., Ph.D.
Director, Public Relations & Information, Patrick O'Brien, B.A., D.P.A.
Director, Development & Alumni Relations, Kim McCuaig, B.A., B.P.H.E.
Bookstore Manager, Joe Gosset, B.A.
Purchasing Manager, Ed Kane
Director, Admissions & Academic Records, Victor J. Chapman, B.A., DPA, M.A.
Director, Physical Plant, Vacant

FACULTIES WITH DEANS
Arts, G. Stuart Adam, B.J., M.A., Ph.D.
Engineering, Malcolm J. Bibby, Ph.D., P.Eng.
Graduate Studies & Research, Roger C. Blockley, B.A., M.A., Ph.D.
Science, D.R. Gardiner, B.Sc., Ph.D.
Social Sciences, Tom Wilkinson, B.Sc., Ph.D.

SCHOOLS WITH DIRECTORS
Architecture, Benjamin Gianni, B.A., M.Arch.
Biochemistry, Peter Buist, B.Sc., Ph.D., M.C.M.
Business, Vinod Kumar, B.Sc., B.Eng., M.Eng., Ph.D., P.Eng.
Canadian Studies, Pat Armstrong, B.A., M.A., Ph.D.
Central/East European & Russian-Area Studies, Carl H. McMillan, M.A., Ph.D.
Computer Science, Evangelos Kranakis, B.Sc., Ph.D.
Continuing Education, Bernadette Landry, B.A.
Industrial Design, Martien Leevw, B.Sc., B.I.D., M.B.A.
Journalism & Communications, Peter Johansen, B.A., M.A.
Public Administration, Frances D. Abele, B.A., M.A., Ph.D.
Social Work, Allan Moscovitch, B.A., M.A.
The Norman Paterson School of International Affairs, M.A. Molot, B.A., M.A., Ph.D.

Lakehead University
955 Oliver Rd., Thunder Bay ON P7B 5E1
807/343-8110; Fax: 807/343-8023; URL: http://www.lakeheadu.ca; gopher://flash.lakeheadu.ca
Chancellor, L.B. Wilson
President, R.G. Rosehart, 807/343-8200; Email: Bob.Rosehart@Lakeheadu.ca
Vice-President, Academic, J. Whitfield
Registrar, P.A. Paularinne, 807/343-8269; Email: Pentti.Paularinne@Lakeheadu.ca
Chief Librarian,, 807/343-8205
Director, Services, E.G. Walsh
Director, Finance, L. A. Miller
Director, Continuing Education, D. Pakulak
Director, Campus Development, J. Podd
Director, Student Services & Community Relations, J. Himmelman, 807/343-8899; Email: Joy.Himmelman@Lakeheadu.ca

Director, Human Resources, F.W. Bragnalo, 807/343-8757; Email: Bill.Bragnalo@Lakeheadu.ca

FACULTIES WITH DEANS
Arts & Sciences, J. Gellert
Business Administration, B. Dadgostar
Education, J.D. Bates
Engineering, G. Locker
Forestry, D. Evler
Research & Graduate Studies, C. Nelson

Laurentian University of Sudbury/Université Laurentienne de Sudbury
Ramsey Lake Rd., Sudbury ON P3E 2C6
705/675-1151; Fax: 705/675-4812; Email: admissions@nickel.laurentian.ca; URL: http://www.laurentian.ca/
Teaching is in French & English. Certain faculties offer parallel programs in both languages.
President, Ross H. Paul, B.A., M.A., Ph.D.
Vice-President, Academic, Vacant
Asst. Vice-President, French Programs & Service, Gratien Allaire, B.A., M.A., L.ès.L., Ph.D.
Director, Services, R. Bertoli
Director, Centre for Continuing Education, D. Mayer, M.Sc.
Executive Director, University Advancement, M.E. Croft, B.Sc., M.Sc.
Registrar, J. Porter, B.B.A., M.Ed.
Director, Division of Physical Education, B. Tihanyi, B.P.E., M.P.E., Ph.D.
Director, Library, Joyce C. Garnette, B.Sc., M.L.S.
Co-ordinator, Université canadienne en France programme, Denis Lauzon
Director, Financial Services, Gerry Labelle, B.Comm., CA

FACULTIES WITH DEANS
Humanities, Paul Collili, B.A., M.A., Ph.D.
Professional Schools, J. Mount, B.A., B.L.S., M.B.A., Ph.D.
Science & Engineering, Reid R. Keays, B.Sc., Ph.D.
Social Sciences, Geoffrey Tesson, B.Sc., M.A., Ph.D.

SCHOOLS WITH DIRECTORS
Commerce, Louis Zanibbi, B.Sc., M.B.A., Ph.D., C.M.A., C.D.P.
Education, Elvive Gignac-Pharand, B.Ed., B.A., M.A., Ph.D.
Graduate Studies, Dieter K. Buse, B.A., M.A., Ph.D.
Human Movement, S. Knox, B.A., M.S., Ph.D.
Nursing, W. Gerhard, B.Sc.N., M.Sc.N., R.N.
Social Work, M. Reitsma-Street, B.A., B.S.W., M.S.W., Ph.D.
Sports Administration, G. Zorbas, B.P.H.E., M.A.
Translators & Interpreters, Denise Merkle, B.A., M.A., B.Ed.

AFFILIATED COLLEGES
Algoma University College, Sault Ste. Marie ON P6A 2G4 – President, J. Douglas Lawson, B.A.Sc., M.Sc., Ph.D.
Collège Universitaire de Hearst, Hearst ON P0L 1N0 – Recteur, Raymond Tremblay, B.A., B.Sc., M.A.

FEDERATED UNIVERSITIES
Huntington University, Ramsey Lake Rd., Sudbury ON P3E 2C6 – 705/673-4126 – Principal, K.G. MacQueen, B.A., B.D., M.A., Ph.D.
Thorneloe University, Ramsey Lake Rd, Sudbury ON P3E 2C6 – Provost & Vice-Chancellor, Donald Thompson, B.A., M.T.S., Ph.D.
University of Sudbury, Ramsey Lake Rd, Sudbury ON P3E 2C6 – 705/673-5661 – President, Jacques Monet, s.j., B.A., Ph.L., M.A., Ph.D., Th.L.

McMaster University
1280 Main Street West, Hamilton ON L8S 4L8

* indicates enrollment figure.

905/525-9140; Fax: 905/527-0100; URL: http://www.mcmaster.ca; gopher://gopher.mcmaster.ca
Chair, Board of Governors, G.M. Luxton
Chancellor, J.H. Taylor
President & Vice-Chancellor & Chair of Senate, Peter George
Vice-President, Administration, A.L. Darling
Provost & Vice-President, Academic, H. Weingarten
Vice-President, Health Sciences, J. Bienenstock
Vice-President, Research, Vacant
Assoc. Vice-President, Academic, M.M. Atkinson
Executive Director, University Advancement, R. Trull
Secretary, Board of Governors, W.B. Frank
Registrar, G. Granger
Asst. Provost, Student Affairs, M.E. Keyes
Secretary of Senate, J.E. Morris
Manager, Bookstore, R.C. Crawford

FACULTIES WITH DEANS
Business, D. Conrath
Engineering, M. Shoukri
Health Sciences, J. Bienenstock
Humanities, D.P.J.E. Simpson
Science, P. Sutherland
Social Sciences, J.A. Johnson

SCHOOLS WITH DIRECTORS
Dean, Arts & Science Program, B.M. Ferrier
Continuing Education, Dale Schenk
Dean, Graduate Studies, J.C. Weaver
Dean, Social Work, J.M. Macintyre

AFFILIATED COLLEGE
McMaster Divinity College, Hamilton ON L8S 4L8 – 905/525-9140, ext.24401 – Principal, W.H. Brackney

Nipissing University
100 College Dr., North Bay ON P1B 8L7
705/474-3450; Fax: 705/474-1947
Chair, Board of Governors, David Liddle, Email: davel@admin.unipissing.ca
President, David Marshall, Email: davem@admin.unipissing.ca
Vice-President, Murray Green, Email: murrayg@admin.unipissing.ca
Executive Director, University Relations, Al Carfagnini, Email: alc@admin.unipissing.ca
Registrar, Denis Lawrence, Email: denisl@admin.unipissing.ca
Executive Director, Library Services, Brian Nettleford, Email: briann@admin.unipissing.ca
Dean, Arts & Science, Ted Chase, Email: tedc@admin.unipissing.ca
Dean, Education, Lavern Smith, Email: lavernes@admin.unipissing.ca

Queen's University
99 University Ave., Kingston ON K7L 3N6
613/545-2000; Fax: 613/545-6300; URL: http://info.queensu.ca/
Chancellor, Agnes M. Benidickson, O.C., B.A., LL.D.
Vice-Chancellor & Principal, William C. Leggett, B.A., M.Sc., Ph.D., D.Sc., LL.D., F.R.S.C.
Rector, Peter Gallant, B.Sc.(Hons.), M.Sc.
Vice-Principal, Academic, David H. Turpin, B.Sc., Ph.D.
Vice-Principal, Advancement, Florence M. Campbell, B.A.
Vice-Principal, Health Sciences, Duncan G. Sinclair, D.V.M., V.S., M.S.A., Ph.D.
Vice-Principal, Operations & Finance, John Cowan, B.Sc., M.Sc., Ph.D.
Registrar, Vacant
Secretary of the Senate, University & Board, Alison Morgan, B.Com., M.A.
Director, University Communications, Anji Husain, B.A., M.A.

Secretary of the University Council, Catherine Perkins, B.A.
Dean of Women, Pamela Dickey Young, B.A., M.Div., Ph.D.
Director, Purchasing Services, Mike Stefano
Bookstore Manager, James Patterson

FACULTIES WITH DEANS
Applied Science, Carl Hamacker, B.Sc., M.Sc., Ph.D., P.Eng.
Arts & Science, Leslie Monkman, B.A., M.A., Ph.D.
Education, Rena Upitis, B.A., LL.B., M.Ed., Ed.D.
Law, Donald Carter, B.A., LL.B., B.C.L.
Medicine, Duncan G. Sinclair, D.V.M., V.S., M.S.A., Ph.D.

SCHOOLS WITH DIRECTORS
Business, Dr. Margaret Northey, B.A., M.A., Ph.D.
Centre for Canada/Asian Studies, Lorna L. Wright, B.A., M.A., P.G.C.E., M.I.M., Ph.D.
Centre for International Relations, Neil MacFarlane
Centre for Resource Studies, Vacant
Graduate Studies, Ronald J. Anderson, B.Sc., Ph.D., P.Eng.
Industrial Relations Centre, Bryan Downie, B.A., M.B.A., Ph.D.
Institute of Intergovernmental Relations, Doug Brown, B.A., M.A.
Nursing, Alice Baumgart, R.N., B.Sn., M.Sc., Ph.D.
Physical & Health Education, J. Gavin Reid, T.D., D.P.E., M.A., Ph.D.
Policy Studies, Keith G. Banting, B.A.(Hons.), Ph.D.
Rehabilitation Therapy, Malcom Peat, B.P.T., M.Sc., Ph.D.
Sudbury Nutrino Observatory, Arthur B. MacDonald, B.Sc., M.Sc., Ph.D.
Principal, Theological College, Hallett E. Llewellyn, B.A., B.D., TH.M., Ph.D.
Urban & Regional Planning, Mohammad A. Qadeer, B.Sc., M.A., M.S., M.C.P., Ph.D., M.C.I.P., A.I.C.

Royal Military College of Canada
Kingston ON K7K 5L0
613/541-6000; URL: http://www.rmc.ca/
Commandant, B.Gen. J.C.A. Emond, C.D.
Principal & Director of Studies, B.J. Plant, O.M.M., C.D.
Director of Cadets, L.Col. J.J.C. Michaud, C.D.
Director of Administration, L.Col. D.J. Southen, C.D.
Registrar, Dr. M.A. Labbe
Protocol & Information Officer, Lt. A.M. Martin

FACULTIES WITH DEANS
Academic Services, D.W. Kirk
Arts, R.G. Haycock
Engineering, A.Y. Chikhari
Graduate Studies, W.F. Furter
Science, A.J. Barrett

Ryerson Polytechnic University
350 Victoria St., Toronto ON M5B 2K3
416/979-5000; Fax: 416/979-5341; Email: inquire@acs.ryerson.ca; URL: http://www.ryerson.ca/
Chair, Board of Governors, John Sharpe
Chancellor, David Crombie
President & Vice-Chancellor, Claude Lajeunesse
Vice-President, Academic, Dennis Mock
Vice-President, Faculty & Staff Affairs, Michael Dewson
Vice-President, Administration, Linda Grayson
Registrar, Keith Alnwick
Executive Director, University Development, Bob Crow
Asst. Director, Community Relations, Ian Marlatt
Manager, Purchasing Dept., Doug Perks
Manager, Bookstore, Peter Brunner
Secretary of the Board of Governors, Ed Valin

FACULTIES WITH DEANS
Applied Arts, Ira Levine
Arts, Errol Asperig
Business, Stanley Heath
Community Services, Judith Sandys
Continuing Education, Marilynn Booth
Engineering & Applied Science, William White

Trent University
PO Box 4800, Peterborough ON K9J 7B8
705/748-1011; Fax: 705/748-1246; URL: http://www.trentu.ca
Chair, Jalynn Bennett, B.A.
Chancellor, Mary May Simon, C.M., LL.D.
President & Vice-Chancellor, Leonard W. Conolly, B.A., M.A., Ph.D.
Vice-President, Administration & University Services, W. Fraser Wilson, B.A., M.A., Ph.D.
Dean, Arts & Science, Robert Campbell, B.A., M.A., Ph.D.
Vice-President, Advancement, Susan Mackle, B.A.
Registrar, Paul Thomson, B.A.
Secretary of the Senate, Dianne Choate, B.A.
Master, Peter Robinson College, Vacant
Principal, Catharine Parr Traill College, Heather Avery, M.A.
Master, Champlain College, Stephen Brown, M.A., Ph.D., F.S.A.
Principal, Lady Eaton College, Ken Field, B.Mus.Ed., M.L.S.
Master, Otonabee College, Robert Annett, B.Sc., Ph.D.
Associate Dean & Director, Julian Blackburn College, John Syrett, B.A., M.A., Ph.D.
Director, Financial Services, A.A. van Hoeckel
Manager, Purchasing/Accounts Payable, Lorraine Hayes, B.Sc.
Acting Director, Communications, Kathleen Bain, B.A., B.J.
Director, Athletics, P.S.B. Wilson, B.A.
Bookstore Manager, Ralph Colley, B.A.

University of Guelph
#158, 50 Stone Rd. East, Guelph ON N1G 2W1
519/824-4120; Fax: 519/824-7962; URL: http://www.uoguelph.ca/
Chancellor, The Honourable Lincoln Alexander
President & Vice-Chancellor, M. Rozanski
Provost & Vice-President, Academic, J.L. Campbell
Assoc. Vice-President & Registrar, Academic, C. Rooke
Vice-President, Development & Public Affairs, J.D. Mabley
Assoc. Vice-President, Student Affairs, B. Sullivan
Vice-President, Research, L.P. Milligan
Vice-President, Finance & Administration, N. Sullivan
Chair, D. Dodds
Director, Development & Alumni Affairs, P. Samson
Acting Director, Communication & Public Affairs, S. Webster
Asst. Vice-President, Finance, J.M. Miles
Director, Office of Open Learning, V. Gray

FACULTIES WITH DEANS/DIRECTORS
Arts, C. Stewart
Biological Science, R. Sheath
Family & Consumer Studies, M. Nightingale
Graduate Studies, Vacant
Ontario Agricultural College, R.J. McLaughlin
Ontario Veterinary College, A.H. Meek
Acting Dean, Physical Science, R. McCrindle
Social Science, D. Knight

SCHOOLS WITH DIRECTORS
Engineering, L. Otten
Hotel & Food Administration, K.M. Haywood
Landscape Architecture, J. Taylor
Rural Planning & Development, J. FitzGibbon

University of Ottawa/Université d'Ottawa
PO Box 450, Stn A, Ottawa ON K1N 6N5
613/562-5800; Fax: 613/562-5103; URL: http://www.uottawa.ca; gopher://gopher.uottawa.ca
Chancellor, Huguette Labelle, O.C., B.Sc.N.Ed., B.Ed., M.Ed., Ph.D., D.U., LL.D., D.Sc., D.Hum.L.
Rector & Vice-Chancellor, Marcel Hamelin, B.A., L.ès L., D.ès L., M.S.R.C.
Vice-Rector, Academic, Bernard Philogène, B.Sc., M.Sc., Ph.D.
Asst. Vice-Rector, Research, Howard Alper, B.Sc., Ph.D., F.R.S.C.
Asst. Vice-Rector, Teaching, Denis Carrier, M.Sc.Com., Dipl.E.S. (sc.pol.), D.U.
Vice-Rector, Resources, Carole Workman, B.Comm., C.A.
Vice-Rector, University Relations & Development, J.M. Beillard, M.A., Ph.D.
Asst. Vice-Rector, Institutional Research & Planning, Joseph Lloyd-Jones, B.A., M.A., M.B.A., Ph.D.
Secretary, Pierre-Yves Boucher, B.A., LL.B., Dipl.E.S.D.
Asst. Vice-Rector, Alumni & Development, Bonnie Morris
Registrar, Henri Wong, B.Sc., M.Sc., Ph.D.
Chief Librarian, Richard Greene, B.A., B.Bibl., M.L.S.
Director General, Student Affairs, Michel Leduc, B.Adm.
Director, Public Relations & Information Services, Vacant
Legal Counsel, Darryl A. Grandbois, B.A., LL.B.

FACULTIES WITH DEANS
Administration, Jean-Louis Malouin, B.Comm., M.Sc., Ph.D.
Acting Dean, Arts, David Staines, B.A., M.A., Ph D.
Education, Pierre Calvé, B.Péd., M.S., Ph.D.
Engineering, Gilles Patry, B.A.Sc., M.A.Sc., Ph.D.
Graduate Studies & Research, Joseph-M. De Koninck, B.A., B.A. (Psy.), M.A. (Psy.), Ph.D.
Health Sciences, Hon. Monique Bégin, B.A., M.A., LL.D.
Law, Civil Law Section, Louis Perret, LL.L., Dipl.E.S.D.
Law, Common Law Section, Sanda Rodgers, B.A., LL.B., B.C.L., LL.M.
Medicine, Peter Walker, M.D., F.R.C.P.C.
Science, Hugh French, B.A., Ph.D.
Social Sciences, Henry P. Edwards, B.A., M.A., Ph.D.

AFFILIATED UNIVERSITY
Saint Paul University, 223 Main St., Ottawa ON K1S 1C4 – 613/236-1393 – Rector, Dale Schlitt, O.M.I., S.T.B., S.T.L., M.A., Ph.D.

University of Toronto
Saint George St., Toronto ON M5S 1A1
416/978-2011; URL: http://www.utoronto.ca/
Chancellor, Rose Wolfe
Chair of the Governing Council, Anthony Comper
President, J. Robert S. Prichard
Vice-President & Provost, Adel S. Sedra
Deputy Provost, Carolyn J. Tuohy
Vice-Provost, Paul W. Gooch
Vice-Provost, Derek McCammond
Vice-Provost, Arnold Aberman
Vice-President, Research & International Relations, Heather Munroe-Blum
Vice-President, Administration & Human Resources, Michael G. Finlayson
Vice-President & Chief Development Officer, Jon S. Dellandrea
Assistant Vice-President, Planning & Budget, Daniel W. Lang
Chief Financial Officer, Robert G. White
Comptroller, Anthony Pieterse
University Ombudsman, Elizabeth Hoffman
Associate University Registrar, Admissions & Awards, Karel Swift, 416/978-2190; Fax: 416/978-6089; Email: ask@adm.utoronto.ca
Director, Alumni & Development, Rivi Frankle
Director, Public Affairs, Susan Bloch-Nevitte, 416/978-5947; Fax: 416/978-1632

FACULTIES WITH DEANS
Applied Science & Engineering, Michael E. Charles
Architecture & Landscape Architecture, Anthony Eardley
Arts & Science, Marsha A. Chandler
Vice-Dean, Arts & Science, Donald N. Dewees
Assoc. Dean, Arts & Science (Development), Robert Vipond
Assoc. Dean, Arts & Science (Humanities), Janet Paterson
Assoc. Dean, Arts & Science (Science), Ian Orchard
Assoc. Dean, Arts & Science (Social Sciences), Michael W. Donnelly
Dentistry, Barry J. Sessle
Assoc. Dean, Div. 1, Heather J. Jackson
Assoc. Dean, Div. 2, Donald E. Moggridge
Assoc. Dean, Div. 3, Don Cormack
Assoc. Dean, Div. 4, G. Harvey Aderson
Education, Michael G. Fullan
Forestry, Rorke Bryan
Graduate Studies, Jon S. Cohen
Vice-Dean, Graduate Studies, John N.H. Britton
Information Studies, Lynne Howarth
Law, Ronald J. Daniels
Management, Hugh J. Arnold
Medicine, Arnold Aberman
Assoc. Dean, Medicine (Continuing Education), Dave Davis
Assoc. Dean, Medicine (Postgraduate Medical Education), Murray B. Urowitz
Assoc. Dean, Medicine (Research), Cecil Yip
Assoc. Dean, Medicine (Student Affairs), Miriam Rossi
Assoc. Dean, Medicine (Undergraduate Medical Education), Richard Frecker
Vice-Dean, Medicine (Education), Andrew Baines
Music, David Beach
Nursing, Dorothy Pringle
Pharmacy, Donald G. Perrier
Social Work, Wesley Shera

SCHOOLS WITH DIRECTORS
Aerospace Studies, A.A. Haasz
Canadian Institute for Theoretical Astrophysics, J. Richard Bond
Centre for Biomaterials, Robert Pilliar
Centre for Comparative Literature, Peter Nesselroth
Centre for Computer Integrated Engineering, J.D. Gorrie
Centre for Industrial Relations, Morley Gunderson
Centre for International Studies, Leonard Waverman
Centre for Medieval Studies, R. Frank
Centre for Reformation & Renaissance Studies, Konrad Eisenbichler
Centre for Research in Information Studies, Barbara Craig
Centre for Russian & East European Studies, Robert E. Johnson
Centre for South Asian Studies, N.K. Wagle
Centre for Technology & Social Development, W.H. Vanderburg
Acting Director, Centre for Urban & Community Studies, Richard Stren
Centre of Criminology, Clifford D. Shearing
Cinema Studies Program, Cameron Tolton
Computer Systems Research Institute, Ken Sevick
Continuing Studies, Mary Barrie
David Dunlap Observatory, E.R. Seaquist
Encyclopedia of Ukraine, Danylo H. Struk
Graduate Centre for the Study of Drama, Colin Visser
Institute for Environmental Studies, Rodney R. White

Institute for History & Philosophy of Science & Technology, Trevor H. Levere
Institute for Policy Analysis, James E. Pesando
Institute of Biomedical Engineering, Hans Kunov
Institute of Medical Science, Mel Silverman
Institute on Human Development, Life Course & Aging, Victor W. Marshall
Interim Director, Joint Centre for Asia Pacific Studies, Bernie Frolic
Joint Program in Transportation, G.N. Steuart
McLuhan Program in Culture & Technology, Derrick de Kerckhove
Museum Studies Program, T. Cuyler Young, Jr.
Peace & Conflict Studies Program, Thomas Homer-Dixon
Pontifical Institute for Medieval Studies, James K. McKonica
School of Physical & Health Education, Bruce Kidd
Toronto School of Theology, Jean-Marc Laporte
Transitional Year Program, Jack Wayne

AFFILIATED COLLEGES
Emmanuel College, 75 Queen's Park Cres. East, Toronto ON M5S 1K6 – 416/585-4539; Fax: 416/585-4516 (Registrar) – Principal, Robert C. Hutchinson
Knox College, 59 Saint George St., Toronto ON M5S 1A1 – 416/978-4503; Fax: 416/971-2133 – Principal, Rev. Arthur Van Seters
Wycliffe College, Hoskin Ave., Toronto ON M5S 1J6 – 416/979-2870; Fax: 416/979-0471 – Principal Archdeacon, Rev. Michael Pountney

FEDERATED COLLEGES
St. Michael's College, 50 Saint Joseph St., Toronto ON M4Y 1J4 – 416/926-1300; Fax: 416/926-7266 (Registrar) – President, Richard M.H. Alway
Trinity College, Hoskin Ave., Toronto ON M5S 1J6 – 416/978-2522; Fax: 416/978-2831 (Registrar) – Provost, Robert Painter
Victoria College, 73 Queen's Park Cres. East, Toronto ON M5S 1K7 – 416/585-4524; Fax: 416/585-4459 (Registrar) – President, Roseann Runte

UNIVERSITY COLLEGES
Erindale College, 3359 Mississauga Rd., Mississauga ON L5L 1C6 – 905/828-5399; Fax: 905/569-4301 (Registrar); URL: http://www.erin.utoronto.ca/ – Principal, Robert H. McNutt
Innis College, 2 Sussex Ave., Toronto ON M5S 1J6 – 416/978-2513; Fax: 416/978-5503 – Principal, John W. Browne
Massey College, 4 Devonshire Pl., Toronto ON M5S 2E1 – 416/978-2895; Fax: 416/978-1759 – Master, John Fraser
New College, 300 Huron, Toronto ON M5S 1A1 – 416/978-2460; Fax: 416/978-0554 – Principal, Vacant
Scarborough College, 1265 Military Trail, Scarborough ON M1C 1A4 – 905/287-7080; Fax: 905/287-7525 (Registrar); URL: http://www.scar.utoronto.ca/ – Principal, R. Paul Thompson
University College, 15 King's College Circle, Toronto ON M5S 2V9 – 416/978-3170; Fax: 416/978-6019 (Registrar) – Principal, Lynd W. Forguson
Woodsworth College, 119 Saint George St., Toronto ON M5S 1A1 – 416/978-4444; Fax: 416/978-4088 (Registrar) – Principal, Noah M. Meltz

University of Waterloo
200 University Ave. West, Waterloo ON N2L 3G1
519/885-1211; Fax: 519/884-8009; URL: http://www.uwaterloo.ca/
Chancellor, S. Ostry, C.C., B.A., M.A., Ph.D., LL.D, F.R.S.C.
Chair, Board of Governors, P.H. Sims, Q.C., LL.B., B.Comm.
President & Vice-Chancellor, J. Downey, B.A., B.Ed., M.A., Ph.D., D.H.L., D.Litt., LL.D.
Vice-President, Academic & Provost, J.G. Kalbfleisch, B.Sc., M.A., Ph.D.
Vice-President, University Relations, Vacant
Vice-President, University Research, C.M. Hansson, B.Sc., A.R.S.M., Ph.D., D.I.C., P.Eng.
Associate Provost, Academic & Student Affairs, T.G. Waller, B.S., M.S., Ph.D.
Associate Provost, Human Resources & Student Services, A.C. Scott, B.A.
Associate Provost, General Services & Finance, D. Huber, B.B.A., C.M.A.
University Secretary, L.H.P. Claxton, B.A., B.L.S., M.L.S.
Registrar, Vacant

FACULTIES WITH DEANS
Applied Health Sciences, R.W. Norman, B.A., B.P.E., M.Sc., Ph.D.
Arts, B.P. Hendley, B.A., M.A., Ph.D.
Engineering, D.J. Burns, B.Sc., Ph.D., P.Eng., C.Eng.
Environmental Studies, J. Kay, B.A., M.S., Ph.D.
Graduate Studies, P.M. Rowe, B.A., M.A., Ph.D.
Mathematics, J.D. Kalbfleisch, B.Sc., M.Math., Ph.D., F.R.S.C.
Science, J.E. Thompson, B.S.A., Ph.D., F.R.S.C.

AFFILIATED COLLEGES
Conrad Grebel College, Waterloo ON N2L 3G6 – President, J.E. Toews, B.A., M.A., Ph.D.
Renison College, Waterloo ON N2L 3G4 – Principal, G. Cuthbert Brandt, B.A., M.A., Ph.D.
St. Paul's United College, Waterloo ON N2L 3G5 – Principal, H. Mills, B.A., M.A., Ph.D.
University of St. Jerome's College, Waterloo ON N2L 3G3 – President, D.R. Letson, B.A., M.A., Ph.D.

University of Western Ontario
1151 Richmond St. North, London ON N6A 5B8
519/679-2111; URL: http://www.uwo.ca/
President & Vice-Chancellor, Paul Davenport
Chair, Board of Governors, Libby Fowler
Chancellor, Peter Godsoe
Vice-President, Academic & Provost, Greg Moran
Vice-President, Administration, Peter Mercer
Vice-President, External, Ted Garrard
Vice-President, Research, Bill Bridger
Vice-Provost & Registrar, Roma Harris
Secretary, Board of Governors & Senate, J.K. Van Fleet

FACULTIES WITH DEANS
Applied Health Sciences, J.D. Cooke
Arts, J.M. Good
Dentistry, R.I. Brooke
Education, Allen Pearson
Engineering Science, R.M. Mathur
Acting Dean, Graduate School of Journalism, D. Spencer
Acting Dean, Graduate School of Library & Information Science, B. Frohmann
Graduate Studies, Alan Werdon
Kinesiology, A.W. Taylor
Law, Eileen Gillese
Medicine, R. McMurtry
Music, J. Stokes
Nursing, L. Bramwell
Part Time & Continuing Education, C. Farber
Richard Ivey School of Business, Larry Tapp
Science, Y. Kang
Social Science, Peter Neary
*Note: The Faculties of Journalism, Part Time & Continuing Education, & the Graduate School of Library & Information Sciences are merging to form the Faculty of Communication & Open Learning; Acting Dean is Catherine Ross.

SCHOOLS WITH DIRECTORS
Applied Electrostatics Research Centre, I. Inculet
Boundary Layer Wind Tunnel Laboratory, A.G. Davenport
Centre for Activity & Aging, Nancy Ecclestone
Centre for Cognitive Science, Z.W. Pylyshyn
Centre for Health & Well-Being, W. Avison
Centre for Human Nutrition, K.K. Carroll
Centre for Interdisciplinary Studies in Chemical Physics, M. Stillman
Centre for Mass Media Studies, A.M. Osler
Centre for Olympic Studies, B. Barney
Centre for Research & Teaching of Canadian Native Languages, R. Darnell
Centre for Studies in Construction, A.G. Davenport
Centre for Studies in Family Medicine, M. Bass
Centre for Textual Scholarship, R.J. Shroyer
Centre for Women's Studies & Feminist Research, M. Fleming
Centre for the Study of International Economic Relations, J. Whalley
Centre for the Study of Theory & Criticism, T. Rajan
Chemical Reactor Engineering Centre, I. DeLasa
Geotechnical Research Centre, K. Lo
John P. Robarts Research Institute, M. Poznansky
Museum of London Archaeology, W.D. Finlayson
National Centre for Management Research, K. Hardy
National Tax Centre, B.J. Arnold
Population Studies Centre, R. Fernando
Research Centre in Tribology, W.K. Wan
Surface Science Western, N.S. McIntyre
Westminster Institute for Ethics & Human Values, C.B. Hoffmaster

OTHER DIRECTORS & OFFICERS
Ombudsman, F. Bauer
Public Affairs Officer, J. Noordermeer
Industrial Liaison Officer, Tim Walzak
Alumni Relations, H. Luckman
Assoc. Dir., Communications, A.B. Johnston
Assoc. Director, Development, M. Rodney
Financial Aid Office, D. Whitehead
Senior Director, Financial Services, W.R. Dickie
Executive Director, Foundation Western, Jim Bristow
Senior Director, Housing & Food Services, S. Grindrod
Senior Director, Human Resources, B. Trimble
Senior Director, Information Technology Services, M. Bauer
Institutional Planning & Budgeting, R. Chelladurai
Libraries, C. Quinlan
Occupational Health & Safety, D.G. Barratt
Office of the Registrar, R.J. Tiffin
Part-Time Studies, J.H. Stevenson
Physical Plant, D.V.B. Riddell
Purchasing, R. Moore
Research Services, Susan Hodoinott
Student Development Centre, G.E. Hutchinson
Student Health Services, T. Macfarlane
University Police, N. Coutu

AFFILIATED COLLEGES
Brescia College, 1285 Western Rd., London ON N6G 1H2 – Principal & Dean, Sr. Dolores Kuntz
Huron College, 1349 Western Rd., London ON N6G 1H3 – Principal, D. Bevan
King's College, 266 Epworth Ave., London ON N6A 2M3 – Principal, P. Mueller

University of Windsor
401 Sunset Ave., Windsor ON N9B 3P4
519/253-4232; Fax: 519/973-7050; URL: http://www.cs.uwindsor.ca/index.html; gopher://access/cs.uwindsor.ca70/1
Chairman of the Board, Peter Cathcart, B.Comm., LL.B.
Chancellor, Vacant
Vice-Chancellor & President, Ronald W. Ianni, B.A., B.Comm., C.U.E.C.E., I.H.E.I., LL.B., Ph.D.
Vice-President, Academic, William E. Jones, B.Sc., M.Sc., Ph.D., F.C.I.C.

Senior Vice-President, Development & Alumni Affairs, Paul V. Cassano, B.A., M.A., Ph.D.
Vice-President, Administration & Finance, Eric Harbottle, B.A., M.B.A.
Registrar, F.L. Smith, B.A., M.Ed.
Secretary & General Counsel, D. Charles James, B.A., LL.B.
Director, Human Resources, Jim Butler, B.A., M.A.
Director, Community Relations & Publications, Joan Carter, B.A.
Director, Alumni Affairs, Susan Lester
Director, Physical Plant, Gary A. McMann, B.A.Sc.

FACULTIES WITH DEANS
Arts, Sue Martin, B.A., M.A., Ph.D.
Interim Dean, Business Administration, Norman Solomon, B.S., M.A., Ph.D.
Education, Michael Awender, B.A., M.A., M.Ed., Ph.D.
Engineering, Hoda ElMaraghy, B.Eng., M.Eng., Ph.D., P.Eng.
Graduate Studies, Sheila Cameron, R.S.C.N., B.A., M.A. Nurse. Educ., Ed.D., F.A.A.M.R.
Human Kinetics, Michael Salter, B.P.E., M.A., Ph.D.
Law, Juanita Westmoreland-Traoré, B.A., Ll.l.D.es., Doctorate of State, Bar of Québec
Science, Brian Fryer, B.Sc., Ph.D.
Social Science, Kathleen McCrone, B.A., M.A., Ph.D.

SCHOOLS WITH DIRECTORS
Computer Science, Richard A. Frost, B.Sc., M.S.E., Ph.D.
Dramatic Art, Diana Mady Kelly, B.A., M.A.
Music, E. Gregory Butler, A.R.C.T., B.M., M.M., D.M.A.
Nursing, Martha E. Horsburgh, Reg.N., Ph.D.
Social Work, James Chacko, B.A, B.S.W., M.S.W., Ph.D
Acting Director, Visual Arts, Iain Baxter, B.Sc., M.Ed., M.F.A., R.C.A.

FEDERATED & AFFILIATED INSTITUTIONS
Assumption University, 400 Huron Church Rd., Windsor ON N9B 3P4 – 519/973-7033; Fax: 519/973-7089 – President, Rev. Ulysse Paré, C.S.B., B.A., S.T.L., S.S.L., D.D.
Canterbury College, 172 Patricia Rd., Windsor ON N9B 3B9 – 519/256-6442 – Principal, David T.A. Symons, B.A.Sc., M.A., Ph.D., P.Eng.
Iona College, 208 Sunset Ave., Windsor ON N9B 3A7 – 519/973-7039 – Acting Principal, Dietmar Lage, B.A., M.A., Ph.D.

Wilfrid Laurier University
75 University Ave. West, Waterloo ON N2L 3C5
519/884-1970; Fax: 519/886-9351
Chair of the Board, Betty Sims
President, L.R. Marsden, Email: lmarsden@mach2.wlu.ca
Vice-President, Academic, Rowland J. Smith, Email: rsmith@mach2.wlu.ca
Vice-President, Finance & Administration, A. Berczi, Email: aberczi@mach2.wlu.ca
Acting Registrar, Doug Witmer, Email: dwitmer@mach2.wlu.ca
Acting Vice-President, University Advancement, Arthur Stephen, Email: astephen@mach1.wlu.ca
Acting Bookstore Manager, Shelley Worden, Email: sworden@mach2.wlu.ca
Librarian, Virginia Gillham, Email: vgillham@mach2.wlu.ca

FACULTIES WITH DEANS
Dean, Arts & Science, L.A.A. Read
Dean, Graduate Studies, Barry D. McPherson
Dean, Music, Anne Hall
Dean, School of Business & Economics, J.A. Murray
Dean, Social Work, Jannah Hurn Mather
Dean, Waterloo Lutheran Seminary, Richard Crossman

York University
4700 Keele St., North York ON M3J 1P3
416/736-2100; Fax: 416/736-5700; URL: http://www.yorku.ca
Chair of the Board, W.A. Dimma, B.A.Sc., M.B.A., D.B.A., P.Eng.
Chancellor, A.R. Haynes, O.C., B.Comm., Hon.D.C.L., Hon.LL.D.
President, S. Mann, B.A., M.A., Ph.D., Hon.LL.D., F.R.S.C.
Vice-President, Academic Affairs, H.M. Stevenson, B.A., M.A., Ph.D.
Vice-President, External Relations, I.H. Lithgow, B.A.
Vice-President, Institutional Affairs, S. Levy, B.Sc., M.A.
Assoc. Vice-President, Research & Faculties, M.B. Fenton, B.Sc., M.Sc., Ph.D.
Assoc. Vice-President, Registrar & Technological Services, G. Denzel, B.Sc., M.S., Ph.D.
University Counsel, H.I. Lewis, B.A., M.A., LL.B.
Secretary of the University, M.W. Ransom, B.A.
Asst. Vice-President, Academic Resource Planning, B. Abner, B.A., M.A.
Asst. Vice-President, Campus Relations & Student Affairs, C.M. Dusk, B.A., B.Mus., M.Ed.
Asst. Vice-President, Finance & Human Resources, P. Clark, B.A., M.A., Ph.D.
Asst. Vice-President, Management Information, D. Smith, B.Sc., M.B.A.
Asst. Vice-President, Facilities & Business Operations, P. Struk, B.Mec.Eng., M.A.Sc.
University Librarian, E. Hoffman, B.A., M.A. in L.S.
Chair, Counselling & Development, M. Wilchesky, B.A., M.A., Ph.D.
Director, Hospitality, Food & Beverage Services, N.D. Crandles
Executive Director, Safety & Security, Parking Services, P.A. MacDonald, B.A.
Master Planner, Facilities and Business Operations, M.L. Reimer, MLandArch.
President, York University Development Corporation, R. Hunt, B.Com.

FACULTIES WITH DEANS
Arts, G.B. Fallis, B.A., Ph.D.
Education, S.M. Shapson, B.Sc., M.A., Ph.D.
Environmental Studies, D.V.J. Bell, B.A., A.M., Ph.D.
Fine Arts, S. Feldman, B.A., Ph.D.
Glendon College, Principal, D. Adam, B.A., B.Ps., M.A., Ph.D.
Graduate Studies, D.R. Leyton-Brown, B.A., M.A., Ph.D.
Joseph E. Atkinson College, H.A. Bassford, B.A., M.A., Ph.D.
Osgoode Hall Law School, M.L. Pilkington, B.A., LL.B.
Schulich School of Business, D. Horvath, B.A., M.B.A., Ph.D.
Science, R.H. Prince, B.A.Sc., M.Sc., Ph.D.

SCHOOLS WITH DIRECTORS
Atmospheric Chemistry, G.W. Harris, B.Sc., Ph.D.
Centre for Feminist Research, N. Mandell, B.A., B.Ed., M.A., Ph.D.
Centre for Health Studies, G.D. Feldberg, B.A., M.A., Ph.D.
Centre for International & Strategic Studies, D.B. Dewitt, B.A., M.A., Ph.D.
Centre for Jewish Studies, M.G. Brown, A.B., A.M., M.H.L., Ph.D.
Centre for Practical Ethics, C.D. MacNiven, B.A., M.A., Ph.D.
Centre for Public Law & Public Policy, P.J. Monaghan, B.A., M.A., LL.B., LL.M.
Centre for Refugee Studies, A.F. Bayefsky, B.A., M.A., LL.B., M.Litt.
Centre for Research in Earth & Space Science, G.G. Shepherd, B.Sc., M.Sc., Ph.D., F.R.S.C.
Centre for Research on Latin America & the Caribbean, R. Grinspun, B.A., M.A., Ph.D.
Centre for Research on Work & Society, C. Lipsig-Mummé, B.A., M.A.,Ph.D.
Centre for Vision Research, I.P. Howard, B.Sc., Ph.D.
Centre for the Study of Computers in Education, R.D. Owston, B.Sc., B.Ed., M.Ed., Ph.D.
Institute for Social Research, J.P. Grayson, B.A., M.A., Ph.D.
Joint Centre for Asia Pacific Studies, P.M. Evans, B.A., M.A., Ph.D.
La Marsh Centre for Research on Violence & Conflict Resolution, D.J. Pepler, B.A., B.Ed., M.Sc., Ph.D.
Robarts Centre for Canadian Studies, D. Drache, B.A., M.A.

OTHER DIRECTORS & OFFICERS
Academic Staff Relations, P.H. O'Reilly, B.A., LL.B.
Admissions, T.A.T. Meininger, B.A., M.A., Ph.D.
Director/Curator, Art Gallery of York University, L. Yarlow, B.A., M.Ed.
Academic Director, Centre for Support of Teaching, P.B.R. Doob, B.A., M.A., Ph.D.
Communications, J.M. Rowntree, B.A.
Computer Operations & Telecommunications, Admin. Computing, P. Busby
Computing & Communications Services, S. Spence
Assoc. Campaign Director, Corporations & Foundations, B. Petruck
English Language Institute, M. McNerney, B.A., M.A.
Facilities Development, T. Mohammed, B.Sc., M.Sc., P.Eng.
Facilities Management, K. Irani, B.E., P.Eng.
Facilities Planning, K.M. Brunelle, B.A.
Financial Aid, E.S. Rudyk, B.A.
Assoc. Campaign Director, Individuals, D. Peck
Innovation York, M.B. Fenton, B.Sc., M.Sc., Ph.D.
Instructional Technology Centre, P. Pow, B.A., M.Ed.
Internal Audit, B. Blackstock, B.A., C.M.A.
Library Computing Services, R. Thompson, B.A.
Management Information Systems, I. Marley, B.E.S., M.B.A.
Occupational Health & Safety, Vacant
Research Administration, N. Swatman, B.A.
Sport & Recreation, Vacant
Student Affairs, D.L. Glass, B.A., B.Ed., M.E.D.
Student Information System Architecture, R.A. Cobb, B.A., Ph.D.
York International, M.L. Cioni, M.A., Ph.D.
Glendon Campus, 2275 Bayview Ave., Toronto ON M4N 3M6 – 416/487-6710

COLLEGES OF APPLIED ARTS & TECHNOLOGY

ALGONQUIN COLLEGE
1385 Woodroffe Ave., Nepean ON K2G 1V8
613/727-4723; Fax: 613/727-7743; Email: gilletr@algonquinc.on.ca; URL: http://algonquinc.on.ca/
President, Robert Gillett

CAMBRIAN COLLEGE/COLLÈGE CAMBRIAN
1400 Barrydowne Rd., Sudbury ON P3A 3V8
705/566-8101; Fax: 705/524-7329; URL: http://www.cambrianc.on.ca/
President, Glenn N. Crombie
Regent Street Campus, 885 Regent St. South, Sudbury ON P3E 4T2

CANADORE COLLEGE/COLLÈGE CANADORE
100 College Dr., PO Box 5001, North Bay ON P1B 8K9
705/474-7600; Fax: 705/474-2384; URL: http://canadorec.on.ca/
President, Dr. Patricia Groves

CENTENNIAL COLLEGE
PO Box 631, Stn A, Scarborough ON M1K 5E9
416/289-5000; Fax: 416/439-7358; Telex: 06-963824; URL: gopher://cenvmc.cencol.on.ca
President, Catherine Henderson

LA CITÉ COLLÉGIALE
801, promenade de l'Aviation, Ottawa ON K1K 5H8
613/742-2483; Fax: 613/742-2481; Toll Free: 1-800-267-2483; URL: http://www.lacitec.on.ca

COLLÈGE BORÉAL
261, av Notre-Dame, Sudbury ON P3C 5K4
705/675-6673; Fax: 705/675-2370; Toll Free: 1-800-361-6673; URL: http://www.borealc.on.ca

COLLÈGE DES GRANDS LACS
76, rue Division, 5e étage, Welland ON L3B 3Z7
905/735-2130; Fax: 905/735-2438; Toll Free: 1-800-590-5227

CONESTOGA COLLEGE
299 Doon Valley Dr., Kitchener ON N2G 4M4
519/748-5220; Fax: 519/748-3505; URL: http://www.conestogac.on.ca/
President, Dr. John W. Tibbits, Email: jtibbits@cs7.conestogac.on.ca

CONFEDERATION COLLEGE
1415 Nakina Dr., PO Box 398, Stn F, Thunder Bay ON P7C 4W1
807/475-6110; Fax: 807/623-4512; URL: http://spiderweb.confederationc.on.ca/
President, Roy Murray

DURHAM COLLEGE
2000 Simcoe St. North, PO Box 385, Oshawa ON L1H 7L7
905/721-2000; Fax: 905/721-3115; URL: http://durham.durhamc.on.ca/index.html
President, Gary Polonsky

FANSHAWE COLLEGE
1460 Oxford St. East, London ON N5V 1W2
519/452-4100; Fax: 519/452-3570; URL: http://www.fanshawec.on.ca/
President, Dr. Howard W. Rundle

GEORGE BROWN COLLEGE
PO Box 1015, Stn B, Toronto ON M5T 2T9
416/867-2000; Fax: 416/867-2272; Toll Free: 1-800-263-8995; URL: http://www.gbrownc.on.ca/
President, John J. Rankin

GEORGIAN COLLEGE
One Georgian Dr., Barrie ON L4M 3X9
705/728-1988; Fax: 705/722-5123; Email: GOPHER@gel.georcoll.on.ca; URL: http://www.georcoll.on.ca
President, Bruce W. Hill
Collingwood Office, 49 Huron St., Collingwood ON L9Y 1L5 – 705/445-2961
Kempenfelt Conference Centre, RR#4, Barrie ON L4M 4S6 – 705/722-8080
Midland Office, 478 Bay St., Midland ON L4R 1K9 – 705/526-3666
Orangeville Office, 5 Armstrong St., Orangeville ON L9W 3H6 – 519/940-0666
Orillia Campus, 825 Memorial Ave., PO Box 2316, Orillia ON L3V 6S2 – 705/325-2740
Owen Sound Campus, PO Box 700, Owen Sound ON N4K 5R4 – 519/376-0840
Parry Sound Office, 26 James St.,Upper Level, Parry Sound ON P2A 1T5 – 705/746-9222
The Georgian Source, 301 Byrne Dr., Barrie ON L4M 6E7 – 705/722-5150
Walkerton Office, #10, 106 Colborne St. North, PO Box 940, Walkerton ON N0G 2V0 – 519/881-2795

HUMBER COLLEGE
North Campus/Etobicoke, PO Box 1900, Etobicoke ON M9W 5L7
416/675-6622; Fax: 416/675-2427; Toll Free: 1-800-268-4867; URL: http://www.humberc.on.ca/
President, Robert Gordon
Humber College Sailing Centre, Humber Bay Park West, Lakeshore Blvd., Toronto ON M8V 3A7 – 416/251-7005
Humber Tower, 6700 Finch Ave. West, Etobicoke ON M9W 5P5
Keelesdale Campus, 88 Industry St., Toronto ON M6M 4L8 – 416/763-5141
Lakeshore Campus, 3199 Lakeshore Blvd. West, Toronto ON M8V 1K8 – 416/252-5571
Theatre Humber, 829 The Queensway, Toronto ON M8Z 1N6
Woodbine Centre Campus, 500 Rexdale Blvd., Etobicoke ON M9W 6V3
York Eglinton Centre, 1669 Eglinton Ave. West, Toronto ON M6E 2H4 – 416/763-5141

LAMBTON COLLEGE
Main Campus, PO Box 969, Sarnia ON N7T 7K4
519/542-7751; Fax: 519/542-6667; URL: http://www.lambton.on.ca/
President, Dr. A.T. Easley
Centre for Advanced Process Technology, PO Box 969, Sarnia ON N7T 7K4 – 542/542-5033; Fax: 542/542-1017
Riverside Campus, PO Box 969, Sarnia ON N7T 7K4 – 519/542-7751; Fax: 519/332-6583

LOYALIST COLLEGE
PO Box 4200, Belleville ON K8N 5B9
613/969-1913, ext.200; Fax: 613/967-5804
President, Douglas A.L. Auld

MOHAWK COLLEGE
PO Box 2034, Hamilton ON L8N 3T2
905/575-1212; Fax: 905/575-2378; URL: http://www.mohawkc.on.ca/
President, K.L. McIntyre
Brantford Campus, 411 Elgin St., Brantford ON N3T 5V2 – 519/ 759-7200
Brantford General Campus, 235 St. Paul Ave., Brantford ON N3R 5Z3 – 519/759-2770
Chedoke Campus, Health Sciences Education Centre, Sanatorium Rd., Hamilton ON L8N 3T2 – 905/575-1515; Fax: 905/575-2378
Fennell Campus, Fennell Ave. & West 5th, Hamilton ON L8N 3T2 – 905/575-1212; Fax: 905/575-2378
Industrial Training Centre, 350 Dosco Dr., Stoney Creek ON L8E 2N5 – 905/662-3700
Stoney Creek Campus, 481 Barton St. East, PO Box 9901, Stoney Creek ON L8G 3Y4 – 905/662-3700
Wentworth Campus, 196 Wentworth St. North, Hamilton ON L8L 5V7 – 905/575-2310

NIAGARA COLLEGE
300 Woodlawn Rd., PO Box 1005, Welland ON L3B 5S2
905/735-2211; Fax: 905/735-5671; Email: webmaster@niagarac.on.ca; URL: http://www.niagarac.on.ca/
President, Dan Patterson
Horticultural Centre, Ivan D. Buchanan Hall, 360 Niagara St., St Catharines ON L2M 4W1 – 905/684-4315; Fax: 905/684-3167
Mack Nursing Education Centre, 178 Queenston St., St. Catharines ON L2R 2Z7 – 905/688-5310
Maid of the Mist Centre for Hospitality & Tourism, 5881 Dunn St., Niagara Falls ON L2G 2N9 – 905/374-7454; Fax: 905/374-1116
St Catharines Campus, 59 Welland Vale Rd., St Catharines ON L2R 6V6 – 905/684-4315; Fax: 905/684-3167
Ventures Centre, PO Box 20162, Stn Grantham, St Catharines ON L2M 7W7 – 905/641-2252; Fax: 905/641-2611

NORTHERN COLLEGE
Hwy. 101 East, South Porcupine, PO Box 3211, Timmins ON P4N 8R6
705/235-3211; Fax: 705/235-7279; Email: gervairj@kirk.northernc.on.ca; URL: http://www.northernc.on.ca/
President, R. Gervais, Fax: 705/235-7277
Haileybury School of Mines Campus, 640 Latchford, Haileybury ON P0J 1K0 – 705/672-3376; Fax: 705/672-2014
James Bay Education Centre Campus, First St., Moosonee ON P0L 1Y0 – 705/336-2913; Fax: 705/336-2393
Kapuskasing Campus, 3 Aurora Ave., Kapuskasing ON P5N 1J6 – 705/335-8504; Fax: 705/335-8343
Kirkland Lake Campus, 140 Government Rd. East, Kirkland Lake ON P2N 3L8 – 705/567-9291; Fax: 705/568-8186

ST. CLAIR COLLEGE
2000 Talbot Rd. West, Windsor ON N9A 6S4
519/966-1656; Fax: 519/966-2737; TDD: 966-0053; URL: http://www.stclairc.on.ca/
President, J.E. McGee
Thames Campus, 1001 Grand Ave. West, Chatham ON N7M 5W4 – 519/354-9100 – Principal, Patricia McFarlane

ST. LAWRENCE COLLEGE
King & Portsmouth, Kingston ON K7L 5A6
613/544-5400; Fax: 613/345-2231; Toll Free: 1-800-463-0752; URL: http://www.stlawrencec.on.ca/
President, Dan Corbett
Brockville Campus, 2288 Parkedale Ave., Brockville ON K6V 5X3 – 613/345-0660; Fax: 613/345-4721 – Principal, J.M. Butt
Cornwall Campus, Windmill Point, Cornwall ON K6H 4Z1 – 613/933-6080; Fax: 613/937-1523 – Principal, A.L. Martin
Kingston Campus, King & Portsmouth, Kingston ON K7L 5A6 – 613/544-5400; Fax: 613/545-3920 – Principal, G. Welch

THE SAULT COLLEGE
443, Northern Ave., PO Box 60, Sault Ste. Marie ON P6A 5L3
705/759-6774; Fax: 705/759-1319; Toll Free: 1-800-461-2260; URL: http://www.saultc.on.ca/
President, Gerry McGuire
Chapleau Campus, 34 Birch St., PO Box 787, Chapleau ON P0M 1K0
Elliot Lake Campus, 1 College Place, Elliot Lake ON P5A 3G9
North Algoma Campus, 3 Maple St., PO Box 1490, Wawa ON P0S 1K0
North Shore Campus, PO Box 1238, Blind River ON P0R 1B0

SENECA COLLEGE
c/o Newnham Campus, 1750 Finch Ave. East, North York ON M2J 2X5
416/491-5050; Fax: 416/491-3081; Telex: 06-966659; URL: http://www.senecac.on.ca/
President, Stephen E. Quinlan
Don Mills Campus, 1380 Don Mills Rd., North York ON M3B 2X2 – 416/491-5050
Dufferin Campus, 1000 Finch Ave. West, North York ON M3J 2V5 – 416/491-5050
Glen Park Campus, 100 Dalemount Ave., North York ON M6B 3C9 – 416/491-5050
Jane Campus, 21 Beverley Hills Dr., North York ON M3L 1A2 – 416/491-5050
King Campus, RR#3, King City ON L0G 1K0 – 905/833-3333

Leslie Campus, 1255 Sheppard Ave. East, North York ON M2K 1E2 – 416/491-5050

Management Development Centre, RR#3, King City ON L0G 1K0 – 905/833-4500

Newmarket Campus, 11775 Yonge St. South, Newmarket ON L3Y 8J4 – 905/898-6199

Richmond Hill Campus, #222, 10720 Yonge St., Richmond Hill ON L4C 3E1 – 905/770-5211

School of Communication Arts, 1124 Finch Ave. West, North York ON M3J 2E2 – 416/491-5050

Sheppard Campus, 43 Sheppard Ave. East, North York ON M2N 2Z8 – 416/491-5050

Vaughan Campus, 3901 Hwy. 7 West, Vaughan ON L4L 6B1 – 905/856-0404

Yorkdale Campus, 2999 Dufferin St., North York ON M6B 3T4 – 416/491-5050

SHERIDAN COLLEGE

Trafalgar Road Campus, 1430 Trafalgar Rd., Oakville ON L6H 2L1

905/845-9430; Fax: 905/815-4043; Email: infoSheridan@sheridanc.on.ca; URL: http://www.sheridanc.on.ca

President, Mary E. Hofstetter

Davis Campus, McLaughlin Rd., PO Box 7500, Brampton ON L6V 1G6 – 905/459-7533; Fax: 905/874-4345

Dixie Campus, #5-8, 100 Wilkinson Rd., Brampton ON L6T 4Y9 – 905/457-6112; Fax: 905/874-4570

Skills Training Centre, 407 Iroquois Shore Rd., Oakville ON L6H 1M3 – 905/845-9430; Fax: 905/815-4105

SIR SANDFORD FLEMING COLLEGE

Sutherland Campus, Peterborough ON K9J 7B1

705/749-5530; Fax: 705/749-5540; Email: ggallaghers@flemingc.on.ca; URL: http://www.flemingc.on.ca/

President, Brian L. Desbiens

Lakeshore Campus, 1005 William St., Cobourg ON K9A 5J4 – 905/372-6865; Fax: 905/372-8570 – Principal, Vacant

School of Fine Arts, Haliburton Campus, PO Box 339, Haliburton ON K0M 1S0 – 705/457-1680; Fax: 705/457-2255 – Principal, Barbara Bolin

School of Natural Resources, Frost Campus, PO Box 8000, Lindsay ON K9V 5E6 – 705/324-9144; Fax: 705/324-9716 – Academic Team Leader, Jim Madder

POST-SECONDARY & SPECIALIZED INSTITUTIONS

Accountancy Programs

THE CERTIFIED GENERAL ACCOUNTANTS ASSOCIATION OF ONTARIO

The Director of Student Services, 240 Eglinton Ave. East, Toronto ON M4P 1K8

416/322-6520; Toll Free: 1-800-668-1454

THE INSTITUTE OF CHARTERED ACCOUNTANTS OF ONTARIO

69 Bloor St. East, Toronto ON M4W 1B3

416/962-1841; Fax: 416/962-8900; Email: exof@icao.on.ca; Toll Free: 1-800-387-0735; URL: http://www.icao.on.ca

Chief Executive Officer, David A. Wilson, M.B.A., F.C.A.

THE SOCIETY OF MANAGEMENT ACCOUNTANTS OF ONTARIO

The Assistant Executive Director, Member Programs & Services, #300, 70 University Ave., Toronto ON M5J 2M4

416/977-7741; Fax: 416/977-6079; Toll Free: 1-800-387-2991

Agricultural Colleges

ALFRED COLLEGE OF AGRICULTURE & FOOD TECHNOLOGY

PO Box 580, Alfred ON K0B 1A0

613/679-2218; Fax: 613/679-2550

Principal, M. Paulhus

KEMPTVILLE COLLEGE OF AGRICULTURAL TECHNOLOGY

PO Bag 2003, Kemptville ON K0G 1J0

613/258-8336; Fax: 613/258-8384

Director, David Beattie

Registrar, K. Cavanagh

NEW LISKEARD COLLEGE OF AGRICULTURAL TECHNOLOGY

New Liskeard ON P0J 1P0

705/647-6738; Fax: 705/647-7008

Director, D. Beattie

Administrative Officer, A. Labonte

ONTARIO AGRICULTURAL COLLEGE

c/o University of Guelph, Guelph ON N1G 2W1

519/824-4120, ext.2284; Fax: 519/767-1692; Telex: 069-56645

Dean, F.L. McEwen, B.Sc., M.Sc., Ph.D.

ONTARIO AGRICULTURAL TRAINING INSTITUTE

#405, 491 Eglinton Ave. West, Toronto ON M5N 1A8

416/485-3677; Fax: 416/485-5661; Email: infooati@oati.com; Toll Free: 1-800-668-6284

RIDGETOWN COLLEGE OF AGRICULTURAL TECHNOLOGY

Ridgetown ON N0P 2C0

519/674-1500; Fax: 519/674-1515

Director, M. Kathryn Biondi, B.A., M.A., P.Ag.

Administrative Officer, J.M. Brooks

Art Schools

DUNDAS VALLEY SCHOOL OF ART

21 Ogilvie St., Dundas ON L9H 2S1

905/628-6357; Fax: 905/628-1087

Director, T. Hodgson

ONTARIO COLLEGE OF ART & DESIGN

100 McCaul St., Toronto ON M5T 1W1

416/977-6000; Fax: 416/977-0235; Email: ocad.on.ca

President, Alan Barkley

Vice-President, Administration & Finance, Peter Caldwell

Acting Vice-President, Academic, Alan Barkley

Dean, Academic & Student Services, Arthur Wood

Manager, Student Services, Josephine Polera

Dean, Faculty of Art, Katherine Knight

Asst. Dean, Curriculum Planning & Student Advising, Greg Murphy

Asst. Dean, Studio Management, Peter Sramek

Dean, Faculty of Design, Lenore Richards

Asst. Dean, Curriculum Planning & Studetn Advising, Steve Quinlan

Asst. Dean, Studio Management, Heather Whitton

Dean, Foundation Studies, Katherine Wild

Director, Library & Audio Visual Services, Jill Patrick

Project Director, Information Services, Lise Patton

Manager, Academic Computer Centre, Asa Weinstein

OCA Gallery & Exhibitions Coordinator, Christine Swiderski

Executive Director, Development & Communication Services, Katharine Rajczak

Manager, Fundraising & Foundations, Cindy Ball

Manager, Marketing & Promotions, Margaret McWhinnie

Manager, Public Relations & Special Events, Jack Kado

Manager, Recruitment & Admissions, Jan Sage

Director, Finance, Peter Fraser

Director, Human Resources, Nicky Davis

Director, Plant Services, Peter Lashko

Manager, Health, Safety & Security, Ted Rickard

OTTAWA SCHOOL OF ART

35 George St., Ottawa ON K1N 8W5

613/241-7471; Fax: 613/241-4391; Email: osa@magi.com; URL: http://infoweb.magi.com/~osa/

Executive Director, Jeff Stellick

Church-Affiliated Schools

CANADIAN CHURCHES' FORUM FOR GLOBAL MINISTRIES

11 Madison Ave., Toronto ON M5R 2S2

416/924-9351; Fax: 416/924-5356; Email: ccforum@web.apc.org

Coordinator, Outreach & Communication, Robert Faris

ONTARIO BIBLE COLLEGE & THEOLOGICAL SEMINARY

25 Ballyconnor Ct., North York ON M2M 4B3

416/226-6380

Chair, Dr. J. Gordon Freeland

President, Dr. Bruce E. Gordon

REDEEMER COLLEGE

777 Hwy. 53 East, Ancaster ON L9K 1J4

905/648-2131; Fax: 905/648-2134; Email: dekorte@redeemer.on.ca

President, Justin Cooper, Ph.D.

Chair, Board of Governors, Rev. John Zantingh

Vice-President, Academic, M. Elaine Botha, Ph.D.

Vice-President, Advancement, William Smouter, F.I.C.B.

Vice-President, Administration & Finance, William can Staalduinen, M.A.

Associate Dean, Jacob Ellens, Ph.D.

Registrar, Marian Ryks-Szelekovszky, M.Ed.

Community Relations Director, Henry Dekorte, M.Div.

TORONTO BAPTIST SEMINARY & BIBLE COLLEGE

130 Gerrard St. East, Toronto ON M5A 3T4

416/925-3263; Fax: 416/925-8305; Email: tbsedu@io.org; URL: http://www.io.org/~tbsedu/

Principal, A.M. Fountain, B.Sc., M.Div., Ph.D.

Financial Education

CANADIAN INSTITUTE OF FINANCIAL PLANNING

151 Yonge St., 5th Fl., Toronto ON M5C 2W7

416/865-1237; Fax: 416/366-1527

Executive Director, John Kaszel

CANADIAN INVESTMENT FUNDS COURSE

c/o Education Division of The Investment Funds Institute of Canada, 151 Yonge St., 5th Fl., Toronto ON M5C 2W7

416/363-2158; Fax: 416/861-9937

Québec Branch, 407, boul St-Laurent, 1er étage, Montréal PQ H2Y 2Y3 – 514/874-3729; Fax: 514/866-5580

CANADIAN SECURITIES INSTITUTE

#1550, 121 King St. West, PO Box 113, Toronto ON M5H 3T9

416/364-9130; Fax: 416/359-0486

CREDIT INSTITUTE OF CANADA

#501, 5090 Explorer Dr., Mississauga ON L4W 3T4

905/629-9805; Fax: 905/629-9809

Health-Related Education

THE CANADIAN COLLEGE OF NATUROPATHIC MEDICINE

60 Berl Ave., Etobicoke ON M8Y 3C7

416/251-5261; Fax: 416/251-5883

Director, Communications, Audrey Adams-White

CANADIAN MEMORIAL CHIROPRACTIC COLLEGE

1900 Bayview Ave., Toronto ON M4G 3E6

416/482-2340; Fax: 416/482-9745; URL: http://www.cmcc.ca
Chair, Board of Governors, V. Sinclair, D.C.
President, J.A. Moss, D.C., M.B.A., Email: president@cmcc.ca
Clinic Director, H. Morrison, D.C.
Registrar, J. Morrison

INTERNATIONAL ACADEMY OF NATURAL HEALTH SCIENCES (CANADA)
380 Forest St., Ottawa ON K2B 8E6
613/820-0318; Fax: 613/828-7107; Toll Free: 1-800-267-8732
Executive Director, Dorothy Marshall, Ph.D., N.D., C.H.H.P., N.H.C.

MEDICAL LABORATORY TECHNOLOGY
The Canadian Society of Laboratory Technologists, PO Box 2830, Stn LCD1, Hamilton ON L8N 3N8
905/528-8642; Fax: 905/528-4968
Executive Director, E. Valerie Booth

MEDICAL RADIATION TECHNOLOGY
c/o Ontario Association of Medical Radiation Technologists, PO Box 1054, Brantford ON N3T 5S7
519/753-6037; Fax: 519/753-6408; Toll Free: 1-800-387-4674

SHIATSU SCHOOL OF CANADA INC.
547 College St., Toronto ON M6G 1A9
416/323-1818; Fax: 416/323-1681; Toll Free: 1-800-263-1703
Director, Kaz Kamiya

TORONTO INSTITUTE OF PHARMACEUTICAL TECHNOLOGY
55 Town Centre Ct., Scarborough ON M1P 4X4
416/296-8860; Fax: 416/296-7077; URL: http://www.tipt.on.ca/tipt.html

COLLEGE OF PHYSIOTHERAPISTS
230 Richmond St. West, 10th Fl., Toronto ON M5V 1V6
416/591-3828; Fax: 416/591-3834; Email: collegpt@worldchat.com
President, Karen Lee
Registrar, Dianne Milette

Language Education

E.L.L. ENGLISH AS A LIVING LANGUAGE PRIVATE SCHOOL
288 Dupont St., Toronto ON M5R 1V9
416/975-4901
Principal, Miriam Speers

THE LANGUAGE WORKSHOP
#202, 180 Bloor St. West, Toronto ON M5S 2V6
416/968-1405; Fax: 416/968-6667
Director, Marylou Heenan

LSC LANGUAGE STUDIES CANADA/METRO TORONTO LANGUAGE SCHOOL
#300, 20 Eglinton Ave. East, Toronto ON M4P 1A9
416/488-2200; Fax: 416/488-2225
Principal, David S. Diplock

OMNICOM PROFESSIONAL LANGUAGE SERVICES LTD.
#1002, 2 Sheppard Ave. East, Willowdale ON M2N 5Y7
416/224-0750; Fax: 416/224-0813

Music Schools

THE ROYAL CONSERVATORY OF MUSIC
273 Bloor St. West, Toronto ON M5S 1W2
416/408-2824; Fax: 416/408-3096
President, Dr. Peter. C. Simon
General Manager, RCM Schools, Nancy Bell

Roman Catholic Theological Seminaries & Pre-Theological Schools

DOMINICAN COLLEGE OF PHILOSOPHY & THEOLOGY
96 Empress Ave., Ottawa ON K1R 7G3
613/233-5696; Fax: 613/233-6064
Chancellor, Rev. Thomas R. Potvin, O.P.
President, Rev. Michel Gourgues, O.P.
Master of Studies/Registrar, Rev. M.-Thérèse Nadeau, C.N.D.
Dean, Faculty of Philosophy, Gabor Csepregi
Dean, Faculty of Theology, Rev. Yvon-D. Gélinas, O.P.
Director, Institute of Pastoral Theology, Rev. J.-Louis Larochelle, O.P.
Sec.-Treas., Jean-Jacques Robillard, O.P.

IGNATIUS COLLEGE
PO Box 1238, Guelph ON N1H 6N6
519/824-1250
Rector, Rev. John English, S.J.
Director of Novices, Rev. George Leach, S.J.
Administrator, Rev. Lorne Trainor, S.J.
Treasurer, Barry Leidl

ST. AUGUSTINE'S SEMINARY OF TORONTO
2661 Kingston Rd., Scarborough ON M1M 1M3
416/261-7207; Fax: 416/261-2529
Rector, Rev. John A. Boissoneau, B.A., S.T.B., S.T.L., Th.D.
Dean, Bishop Attila Mikloshazy, S.J., L.Ph., M.A., S.T.D.

ST. BASIL'S COLLEGE
95 St. Joseph St., Toronto ON M5S 2R9
416/925-4368
Rector, J. Leo Walsh, CBS, S.T.L., S.T.D.

ST. PETER'S SEMINARY
1040 Waterloo St. North, London ON N6A 3Y1
519/432-1824
Rector, Very Rev. T.C. Collins, B.A., B.TH., M.A., S.S.L., S.T.D.
Vice Rector & Dean, Philosophy, Rev. M. Smith, Ph.D.
Dean, Theology, W.T. McGrettan, B.G.Sc., M.Div., S.T.L.
Registrar, Rev. J.J. O'Flaherty, B.A., Dip. Catechetics
Spiritual Director, Rev. T.F. O'Connor, M.A., M.T.S., M.Th.
Business Administrator, Frank A. Vita, B.A., B.Comm., M.B.A.
Librarian, Lois Côte, B.A., B.L.S., M.L.S., M.Div.

Other Colleges, Institutions, Specialized Schools

ADVANCED LEARNING INSTITUTE
#7, 873 Avenue Rd., Toronto ON M5P 2K5
416/485-5149
Director of Programs, Ruta Lovett

CANADIAN CENTRE FOR CREATIVE TECHNOLOGY
8 Young St. East, Waterloo ON N2J 2L3
519/884-8844; Fax: 519/884-8191
President, Jack Pal
Vice-President, Ron Champion

CANADIAN EMERGENCY PREPAREDNESS COLLEGE
PO Box 40, Arnprior ON K7S 3H2
613/623-7931; Fax: 613/563-9095
Acting Director, T.A. George

CANADIAN INSTITUTE FOR ADVANCED RESEARCH
#701, 179 John St., Toronto ON M5T 1X4
416/971-4255
President, Dr. J. Fraser Mustard

CANADIAN JEWELLERS INSTITUTE
#1108, 20 Eglinton Ave. West, PO Box 2021, Toronto ON M4R 1K8
416/480-1424; Fax: 416/480-2342
Assoc. General Manager, Karen Bassels

CANADIAN POLICE COLLEGE/COLLÈGE CANADIEN DE POLICE
PO Box 8900, Ottawa ON K1G 3J2
613/998-0785; Fax: 613/990-9738
Management Training Unit, Sgt. John J. Gaudet, B.A.

COMPUTER COMMUNICATIONS INSTITUTE
98 Peckham Ave., Willowdale ON M2R 2V5
416/222-3145
Director, Carlos Laredo

CONSTELLATION COLLEGE OF HOSPITALITY
900 Dixon Rd., Etobicoke ON M9W 1J7
416/675-2175; Fax: 416/675-6477
Director, Sharon Turner-Brown

FRONTIER COLLEGE
35 Jackes Ave., Toronto ON M4T 1E2
416/923-3591; Fax: 416/323-3522
The Governor General of Canada, Patron
Chair of the Board, Campbell Mackie
President, John Daniel O'Leary

GRAND RIVER POLYTECHNICAL INSTITUTE
Grand River Territory, Six Nations, PO Box 728, Hagersville ON N0A 1H0
905/768-0448; Fax: 905/768-0424

INSTITUTE FOR ADVANCED TECHNOLOGY
#202, 110 Bloor St. West, Toronto ON M5S 2W7
416/964-8664; Fax: 416/920-6856
Director, Dr. N. Beylerian
Registrar, Lori Trenton
Registrar, Joy Baldwin

THE INSTITUTE FOR COMPUTER STUDIES
#402, 155 Gordon Baker Rd., North York ON M2H 3N5
416/499-9522; Fax: 416/499-9386

INTERNATIONAL ACADEMY OF MERCHANDISING & DESIGN LTD.
31 Wellesley St. East, Toronto ON M4Y 1G7
416/922-3666; Fax: 416/922-7504; Email: iaod.com; Toll Free: 1-800-361-6664; URL: http://www.iaod.com
President, Stephen Bartolini
Vice-President, Larry Gross
Chancellor, Barbara Ann Scott King
Québec Académie at Mart, Place Bonaventure, D-36 Dawson, CP 55, Montréal PQ H5A 1A3 – 514/875-9777; Fax: 514/875-9297

NDE INSTITUTE OF CANADA
135 Fennell Ave. West, Hamilton ON L8N 3T2
905/387-1655; Fax: 905/574-6080; Email: karunaa@operatns.mohawkc.on.ca
Acting Managing Director, Douglas Marshall

NIAGARA PARKS BOTANICAL GARDENS & SCHOOL OF HORTICULTURE
PO Box 150, Niagara Falls ON L2E 6T2
905/356-8554; Fax: 905/356-5488; URL: http://www.niagara.com/~;shoup/botanic_gardens.html
Director, Deborah Whitehouse

ONTARIO INSTITUTE FOR STUDIES IN EDUCATION
252 Bloor St. West, Toronto ON M5S 1V6
416/923-6641; Fax: 416/926-4725; TLX: 06-217720
Director, Angela Hildyard, Ph.D., Email: ahildyard@oise.on.ca
Assistant Director, Academic, Malcolm Levin, Ed.D.
Chair, Board of Governors, V. Jane Knox, Ph.D.

Canadian Almanac & Directory 1997

TORONTO ART THERAPY INSTITUTE
216 St. Clair Ave. West, Toronto ON M4V 1R2
416/924-6221; Fax: 416/924-0156
Executive Director, Dr. J. Baker
Director, Academic Program & Internships, Gilda Grossman

TORONTO MONTESSORI INSTITUTE
8569 Bayview Ave., Richmond Hill ON L4B 3M7
905/889-9201; Fax: 905/886-6516
Co-Director, Charles Terranova
Co-Director, Jaime Torres

TREBAS INSTITUTE
410 Dundas St. East, Toronto ON M5A 2A8
416/966-3066; Fax: 416/966-0030
Executive Director, David P. Leonard

INDEPENDENT & PRIVATE SCHOOLS

Schools with enrollment of 50 or more, listed alphabetically by city.

Ajax: Faithway Baptist Church School, 1964 Salem Rd., Ajax ON L1S 4S7 – 905/686-0951 – L. Allen Homan – *54 – Gr. K./Elem./Sec.

Ajax: Pickering Christian School, 1030 Ravenscroft Rd., Ajax ON L1S 4S7 – 905/427-4120 – Paul Douglas Ogborne – *177 – Elem.

Alliston Community Christian School, PO Box 1122, Alliston ON L0M 1A0 – 705/435-4611 – Gerty Baarda – *82 – Gr. K./Elem.

Ancaster: Hamilton District Christian Private School, 92 Gloucester Rd., RR#1, Ancaster ON L9G 3K9 – 905/648-6655 – Jim Vanderkooy – *434 – Sec.

Athens Christian School, PO Box 264, Athens ON K0E 1B0 – 613/924-9500 – Jannie Feenstra – *53 – Elem.

Aurora Montessori School, RR#2, Aurora ON L4G 3G8 – 905/841-0065 – Sharon Kashani – *103 – Elem.

Aurora: St. Andrew's College, 15800 Yonge St. North, Aurora ON L4G 3H7 – 905/727-3178 – Robert P. Bedard – *457 – Sec.

Aylmer: Amish-Mennonite School, RR#4, Aylmer ON N5H 2R3 – 519/773-9225 – D. Eicher – *87 – Gr. K./Elem.

Aylmer: Carlton Christian School, RR#6, Aylmer ON N5H 2R5 – 519/765-1721 – Steven Martin – Elem./Sec. (Amish)

Aylmer: Immanuel Christian School Society, 75 Caverly Rd., Aylmer ON N5H 2P6 – 519/773-8476 – Andrew Vanderploeg – *181 – Gr. K./Elem.

Aylmer: Old Colony Christian School, PO Box 127, Aylmer ON N5H 2R8 – 519/765-1138 – Ben Bergen – *160 – Elem./Sec.

Bancroft Christian Academy, PO Box 657, Bancroft ON K0L 1C0 – 613/332-3670 – Mike West – *55 – Elem.

Barrie: Heritage Christian Academy, 79 Ardagh Rd., Barrie ON L4M 4S7 – 705/733-0097 – David Bartz – *71 – Gr. K./Elem./Sec.

Barrie: St. Paul's Evangelical Christian School, 50 Anne St. North, Barrie ON L4N 2B6 – 705/728-9026 – Mark Kennedy – Elem.

Barrie: Timothy Christian School, 49 Ferris Lane, Barrie ON L4M 2Y1 – 705/726-6621 – Jane Tjeerdsma – *177 – Gr. K./Elem.

Barwick: Pineview Mennonite School, PO Box 34, Barwick ON P0W 1A0 – 807/487-2443 – Robert Heatwoler – *56 – Elem.

Beamsville: Great Lakes Christian College, 4875 King St., Beamsville ON L0R 1B0 – 905/563-5374 – Brian F. Boden – *100 – Sec.

Beamsville: Heritage Christian School, PO Box 363, Beamsville ON L0R 1B0 – 905/563-3212 – Joanne Bakker – *468 – Elem./Sec.

Belleville: Albert College, 160 Dundas St. West, Belleville ON K8P 1A6 – 613/968-5726; Fax: 613/968-9651; Toll Free: 1-800-952-5237; URL: http:// www.telos.ca/quinta/albertc – E. John Rose – *198 – Elem./Sec.

Belleville District Christian School, RR#5, Belleville ON K8N 4Z5 – 613/962-7849 – Martin Vandyk – *109 – Gr. K./Elem.

Belleville: Quinte Christian Private School, 289 Pinnacle St., PO Box 158, Belleville ON K8N 5A2 – 613/968-7870 – Leo Vanarragon – *126 – Elem./Sec.

Bethany: The Bethany Hills School, PO Box 10, Bethany ON L0A 1A0 – 705/277-2866; Fax: 705/277-1279 – Janis J. Smith – *76 – Elem./Sec.

Big Trout Lake: Aglace Chapman Education Centre, Big Trout Lake ON P0V 1G0 – 807/537-2264 – Thomas Shura – *251 – Gr. K./Elem./Sec.

Bowmanville: Durham Christian High School, RR#1, Bowmanville ON L1C 3K2 – 905/623-5940 – Fred Spoelstra – *113 – Sec.

Bowmanville: Knox Christian School, RR#1, Bowmanville ON L1C 3K2 – 905/623-5871 – W. Helmus – *247 – Gr. K./Elem.

Bracebridge: Cedarbrook Christian School, RR#3, District Rd. 37, Bracebridge ON P1L 1X1 – 705/645-4769 – Wayne Potts – *50 – Elem.

Brampton Montessori School, PO Box 553, Brampton ON L6V 2L6 – 905/457-2496 – Alan Shine – *149 – Gr. K./Elem.

Brampton: John Knox Christian School, 82 McLaughlin Rd. South, Brampton ON L6Y 2C7 – 905/451-3236 – Hilda Roukema – *308 – Gr. K./Elem.

Brampton: KRT Christian School, RR#2, Brampton ON L6V 1A1 – 905/846-3771 – Robert J. Boshart – *426 – Gr. K./Elem./Sec.

Brampton: Rowntree Montessori School, 93 Autumn Blvd., Brampton ON L6T 2W1 – 905/793-2196 – Dr. Y.H. Alonso – *137 – Gr. K./Elem.

Brampton: Tall Pines School, 8525 Torbram Rd., Brampton ON L6T 5K4 – 905/458-6770 – Elaine Flett – *183 – Elem.

Brantford Christian School, 7 Calvin St., Brantford ON N3S 3E4 – 519/752-0433 – Chris Vanderveen – *139 – Gr. K./Elem.

Brantford: Central Baptist Academy, 300 Fairview Dr., Brantford ON N3R 2X6 – 519/448-1445 – Nevel Bevington – *215 – Gr. K./Elem.

Brantford: Montessori House of Children, 85 Charlotte St., Brantford ON N3L 3E2 – 519/759-7290 – Perin Alarakhia – *495 – Gr. K./Elem.

Breslau: St. John's-Kilmarnock School, PO Box 179, Breslau ON N0B 1M0 – 519/648-2183 – W.K. Langford – *255 – Elem./Sec.

Breslau: Woodland Christian Private School, RR#1, Breslau ON N0B 1M0 – 519/648-2114 – Gary VanArragon – *162 – Sec.

Brockville Seventh Day Adventist Private School, 100 Perth St., PO Box 794, Brockville ON K6V 5W1 – 613/342-0590 – Sigrid Arnie Robinson – Gr. K./Elem.

Brockville: Grenville Christian College, RR#2, PO Box 610, Brockville ON K6V 5V8 – 613/345-5521 – Rev. Charles Farnsworth – *209 – Gr. K./Elem./Sec.

Burlington: John Calvin Christian School, 607 Dynes Rd., Burlington ON L7N 2V4 – 905/634-8015 – F.C. Ludwig – *330 – Gr. K./Elem.

Burlington: Niagara Montessori Schools, 3132 South Dr., Burlington ON L7N 1H7 – 905/632-2374 – Shirley Gray – *100 – Elem.

Burlington: Park Academy, 1500 Kerns Rd., Burlington ON L4P 3A7 – 905/336-0447 – Bob Euesden – *242 – Gr. K./Elem.

Burlington: Trinity Christian School, 650 Walker's Line, Burlington ON L7N 2E7 – 905/634-3052 – G. Hoytema – *173 – Gr. K./Elem.

Caledonia: Johnsfield Baptist School, PO Box 362, Caledonia ON N0A 1A0 – 519/445-2872 – Duane Wilson – Elem.

Cambridge Christian School, 229 Myers Rd., Cambridge ON N1R 7H3 – 519/623-2261 – Peter Van Dyken – *198 – Gr. K./Elem.

Cambridge: Temple Baptist Christian Academy, 400 Holiday Inn Dr., Cambridge ON N3T 3C1 – 519/658-9001 – Stephen Limmer – *247 – Gr. K./Elem./Sec.

Campbellville: The Halton Waldorf School, 83 Campbell Rd., PO Box 184, Campbellville ON L0P 1B0 – 905/854-0191 – Janet Myers – *136 – Elem.

Campbellville: Hitherfield Preparatory School, 2439 - 10th Sideroad, Campbellville ON L0P 1B0 – 905/854-0890 – Ann J. Scott – *65 – Elem./Sec.

Carp: Venta Preparatory School, 2013 Old Carp Rd., Carp ON K0A 1L0 – 613/839-2175 – Marilyn C. Mansfield – *52 – Elem./Sec.

Cayuga: Grand River Academy of Christian Education, RR#1, Cayuga ON N0A 1E0 – 905/772-5808 – John Elgersma – *133 – Elem./Sec.

Chatham Christian School, 72 Tissiman Ave., Chatham ON N7M 4G5 – 519/352-4980 – Fredric Klooster – *218 – Gr. K./Elem.

Chatham District Christian Secondary School, 90 Park Ave. East, Chatham ON N7M 4G5 – 519/352-4041 – Bruce Mitchell – *82 – Elem./Sec.

Chatham: Eben-Ezer School, 485 McNaughton Ave. East, Chatham ON N7L 2H2 – 519/354-1142 – B. Hart – *92 – Elem.

Claremont: Stouffville Christian School, RR#3, Claremont ON L0H 1E0 – 905/640-3297 – Margaret L. Mack – *129 – Gr. K./Elem./Sec.

Clinton & District Christian School, PO Box 658, Clinton ON N0M 1L0 – 519/482-7851 – Ralph Schuurman – *227 – Gr. K./Elem.

Cobourg: Northumberland Christian School, RR#5, Cobourg ON K9A 4J8 – 905/372-8766 – Henry Lise – *73 – Gr. K./Elem.

Copetown: Rehoboth Christian School, 198 Inksetter Rd., PO Box 70, Copetown ON L0R 1J0 – 905/627-5977 – Jack Weterink – *288 – Gr. K./Elem./Sec.

Cornwall: Islamic Institute Al-Rasheed, RR#1, Cornwall ON K6H 5R5 – 613/931-2895 – M.M. Alam – *60 – Elem./Sec.

Cottam: Emmanuel Christian Academy, PO Box 220, Cottam ON N0R 1B0 – 519/839-4874 – Velma McCombe – *64 – Gr. K./Elem.

Deep River: The Deep River Science Academy, Mackenzie High School, PO Box 600, Deep River ON K0J 1P0 – 613/584-4541 – John M. Gray – Sec.

Don Mills: Northmount School for Boys, 156 Duncan Mills Rd., Don Mills ON M3B 3N2 – 416/250-9442 – Robert Hartley – *65 – Elem./Sec.

Downsview: Bnei Akiva Schools, 159 Almore Ave., Downsview ON M3H 2H9 – 416/630-6772 – Dr. N. Smith – *201 – Sec.

Drayton: Calvin Christian School, High St., PO Box 141, Drayton ON N0G 1P0 – 519/638-2935 – A.J. Vanderstoel – *227 – Gr. K./Elem.

Dresden Private Mennonite School, RR#3, Dresden ON N0P 1M0 – 519/683-6610 – Elizabeth Friesen – *61 – Elem.

Dundas: Calvin Christian School, 542 Ofield Rd. North, RR#2, Dundas ON L9H 5E2 – 905/627-1411 – Jack Zondag – *210 – Gr. K./Elem.

Dunnville Christian School, RR#1, Dunnville ON N1A 2W1 – 905/774-5142 – Richard VanEgmond – *185 – Gr. K./Elem.

Etobicoke: Centennial Montessori School, 2 Remington Dr., Etobicoke ON M9A 2J1 – 416/239-2929 – Susan C. Morand – *167 – Gr. K./Elem.

Etobicoke: International Language Centre Ltd., #300, 5233 Dundas St. West, Etobicoke ON M9B 1A6 – 416/233-3991 – G.M. Banuelos – *1,132 – Sec.

Etobicoke: Kingsley Primary School, 516 The Kingsway, Etobicoke ON M9A 3W6 – 416/233-0150 – U. Morton – *58 – Gr. K./Elem.

Etobicoke: Kingsway College School, 4600 Dundas St. West, Etobicoke ON M9A 1A5 – 416/234-5073 – Harold C. Hannaford – *148 – Elem.

Etobicoke: Leonardo Da Vinci Academy of Arts & Sciences, 100 Allanhurst Dr., Etobicoke ON M9A 4K4 – 416/247-6137 – Salavatore Ritacca – *53 – Gr. K./Elem.

Etobicoke: Mississauga Private School, 30 Barrhead Cres., Etobicoke ON M9W 3Z7 – 416/745-1328 – Diane Proctor – *340 – Gr. K./Elem.

Etobicoke: Timothy Christian School, 28 Elmhurst Dr., Etobicoke ON M9W 2J5 – 416/741-5770 – Coby Jonker – *498 – Elem.

Fergus: Emmanuel Christian High School, RR#3, Fergus ON N1M 2W4 – 519/843-3029 – Peter Witten – *91 – Elem./Sec.

Fergus: Maranatha Christian School, RR#3, Fergus ON N1M 2W4 – 519/843-3029 – Allard Gunnin – *155 – Elem.

Fort Erie: Niagara Christian College, 2619 Niagara Blvd., Fort Erie ON L2A 5M4 – 905/871-6980 – Clare D. Lebold – *139 – Elem./Sec.

Fort Frances: Emmanuel Christian Academy, 308 Butler Ave., Fort Frances ON P9A 2N9 – 807/274-3963 – Fay Edwards – *81 – Elem.

Fort Frances: Lac La Croix High School, PO Box 640, Fort Frances ON P9A 3M9 – 807/485-2446 – Betty Ann LaRocque – *85 – Elem./Sec.

Fort Frances: Rainy Lake First Nation School, PO Box 297, Fort Frances ON P9A 3M6 – 807/274-2796 – David Lovisa – *128 – Sec.

Fort Hope via Pickle Lake: John C. Yesno School, Fort Hope via Pickle Lake ON P0T 1L0 – 807/242-8421 – Derek Smith – Gr. K./Elem./Sec.

Fort Severn: Wasaho First Nation School, Fort Severn ON P0V 1W0 – 807/478-2590 – Anne Marie Levi – *90 – Sec.

Fruitland: John Knox Memorial Christian School, Hwy. 8, PO Box 795, Fruitland ON L0R 1L0 – 905/643-2460 – Julius DeJager – *309 – Gr. K./Elem.

Georgetown District Christian School, Trafalgar Rd., RR#1, Georgetown ON L7G 4S4 – 905/877-4221 – Treena Sybersma – *176 – Gr. K./Elem.

Gloucester: Life Christian Academy, 2214 Innes Rd., Gloucester ON K1B 3K5 – 613/834-6585 – Karen Middleton – *73 – Elem./Sec.

Guelph: Crestwicke Christian Academy, 400 Victoria Rd. North, Guelph ON N1E 5J7 – 519/836-2132 – Neil Paton – *208 – Gr. K./Elem.

Guelph: Elora Road Christian School, Elora Rd., RR#5, Guelph ON N1H 6J2 – 519/824-1890 – James Gordon – *51 – Gr. K./Elem.

Hamilton: Calvin Christian School, 547 West 5 St., Hamilton ON L9C 3P7 – 905/388-2645 – A. Ben Harsevoort – *329 – Gr. K./Elem.

Hamilton: Columbia International College, 1033 Main St. West, Hamilton ON L8S 1B7 – 905/572-7883 – Anna Shkolnik – *240 – Sec.

Hamilton: Guido de Bres Private School, PO Box 20098, RPO Upper James, Hamilton ON L9C 7M5 – 905/383-6744 – J.G. Vandooren – *3059 – Sec.

Hamilton Hebrew Academy Zichron Meir School, 60 Dow Ave., Hamilton ON L8S 2T9 – 905/528-0330 – Rabbi W. Eisenstein – *258 – Elem.

Hamilton: Hillfield - Strathallan College, 299 Fennell Ave. West, Hamilton ON L9C 1G3 – 905/389-1367 – M.B. Wansbrough – *989 – Gr. K./Elem./Sec.

Hamilton: Southern Ontario College, 35 Brant St., Hamilton ON L8L 4C6 – 905/546-1500 – Martin Harvey – *69 – Sec.

Hamilton: Timothy Canadian Reformed School, PO Box 20007, RPO Upper James, Hamilton ON L9C 7M5 – 905/385-3953 – H.J. Nobel – *171 – Gr. K./Elem.

Hamilton: Yeshiva of Hamilton - Yitzchak, 235 Bowman St., Hamilton ON L8S 2T9 – 905/528-5451 – Rabbi W. Eisenstein – *77 – Sec.

Hastings: Columbine School for Exceptional Children, RR#2, Hastings ON K0L 1Y0 – 705/696-3295 – Margaret Santon – *50 – Elem./Sec.

Hastings: The Learning Centre, PO Box 312, Hastings ON K8P 5A5 – 613/966-5603 – Michael Maloney – *72 – Elem./Sec.

Hawkesville: Countryside Christian School, PO Box 65, Hawkesville ON N0B 1X0 – 519/699-5793 – Orval D. Zehr – *103 – Gr. K./Elem./Sec.

Hyde Park: Christian Academy of Western Ontario, General Delivery, Hyde Park ON N0M 1Z0 – 519/473-3332 – Philip J. Conley – *245 – Gr. K./Elem./Sec.

Jarvis District Christian School, PO Box 520, Jarvis ON N0A 1J0 – 519/587-4444 – Garry Glashergen – *262 – Gr. K./Elem.

Jordan Station: Netherlands Reformed Christian School, 15 St. South, PO Box 69, Jordan Station ON L0R 1S0 – 905/562-4023 – Foppe Vander Zwaag – *93 – Gr. K./Elem.

King City: The Country Day School, RR#3, King City ON L0G 1K0 – 905/833-5366 – Paul C. Duckett – *473 – Gr. K./Elem./Sec.

Kingston Christian School, 1212 Woodbine Rd., RR#3, Kingston ON K7L 4V2 – 613/384-9572 – Hugo Marcus – *156 – Gr. K./Elem.

Kingston Learning Centre, 740-742 Arlington Pl., Kingston ON K7M 8H9 – 613/384-6194 – A.S. Stayer – Gr. K./Elem./Sec.

Kingston Montessori School, PO Box 1416, Kingston ON K7L 5C6 – 613/542-7193 – Linda Karshmar – Gr. K./Elem.

Kingsville: Old Colony Christian Academy, 1521 County Rd. 4 West, RR#2, Kingsville ON N9Y 2E5 – 519/733-2891 – Frank Martens – *170 – Elem./Sec.

Kitchener: Christ Lutheran School, 146 Trafalgar Ave., Kitchener ON N2A 1Z7 – 519/896-0615 – Richard Orlowski – *181 – Elem.

Kitchener: Laurentian Hills Christian School, 11 Laurentian Dr., Kitchener ON N2E 1C1 – 519/576-6700 – Luke Janssen – *146 – Gr. K./Elem.

Kitchener: Rockway Mennonite Collegiate, 110 Doon Rd., Kitchener ON N2G 3C8 – 519/743-5209 – Albert J. Lobe – *300 – Elem./Sec.

Kitchener: Sunshine Montessori School, 527 Bridgeport St., Kitchener ON N2K 1N6 – 519/744-1423 – Roshima Shamji – *143 – Elem.

Lakefield College School, Lakefield ON K0L 2H0 – 705/652-3324 – David J. Hadden – *281 – Elem./Sec.

Lambeth: Faith Community Christian School, 7 Howard Ave, Lambeth ON N0L 1S2 – 519/668-0015 – Jennifer Charlton – *112 – Gr. K./Elem.

Laurel: Dufferin Area Christian School, Laurel ON L0N 1L0 – 519/941-4368 – N. Mans – *99 – Elem.

Leamington: United Mennonite Educational Institute, RR#5, Leamington ON N8H 3V8 – 519/326-7448 – Paul Warkentin – *92 – Sec.

Lindsay: Heritage Christian School, 159 Colborne St. West, Lindsay ON K9V 5Z8 – 705/324-8363 – R.W. Moore – *176 – Gr. K./Elem.

Listowel: Brookside Christian School, RR#4, Listowel ON N4W 3G9 – 519/595-8459 – Clarice Plett – *56 – Gr. K./Elem.

Listowel Christian School, PO Box 151, Listowel ON N4W 3H2 – 519/291-3086 – Mary Gibbon – *115 – Gr. K./Elem.

Listowel: West Hesson Parochial School, RR#4, Listowel ON N4W 3G9 – 519/595-8644 – Josiah Weber – *56 – Elem.

London: Askin Montessori School, 115 Askin St., London ON N6C 1E7 – 519/433-2671 – Madalaine Milli – *56 – K./Elem.

London: Central Christian School, 602 Queens Ave., London ON N6B 1Y8 – 519/439-0144 – Susan R. Fountain – *72 – Gr. K./Elem.

London Community Hebrew Day School, 247 Epworth Ave., London ON N6A 2M2 – 519/439-8419 – Janet Nish Lapidus – *58 – Gr. K./Elem.

London District Christian School, 24 Braesyde Ave., London ON N5W 1V3 – 519/455-4360 – Henry Kooy – *268 – Sec.

London Parental Christian School, 202 Clarke Rd., London ON N5W 5E4 – 519/455-0360 – Herb Goodhoofd – *212 – Gr. K./Elem.

London Waldorf School, 1697 Trafalgar St., London ON N5W 1X2 – 519/451-7971 – Merwin Lewis – *118 – Gr. K./Elem.

London: Matthews Hall Private School, 1370 Oxford St. West, London ON N6H 1W2 – 519/471-1506 – F.P. Marchese – *248 – Gr. K./Elem./Sec.

London: Montessori House of Children, 711 Waterloo St., London ON N6A 3W1 – 519/433-9121 – Sharon Keenan – *495 – Gr. K./Elem.

Lucknow & District Christian School, RR#1, PO Box 550, Lucknow ON N0G 2H0 – 519/528-2016 – Lawrence Uyl – *68 – Gr. K./Elem.

Maple: North York Montessori Learning Centre, 9600 Bathurst St., Maple ON L6A 1R9 – 905/633-2636 – Florence Miller – *133 – Gr. K./Elem.

Markham: Somerset Academy, 7700 Brimley Rd., Markham ON L3R 0E5 – 905/940-8990 – M. Vanloon – *105 – Elem.

Markham: Town Centre Montessori School, Main Office, #201, 7077 Kennedy Rd., Markham ON L3R 0N8 – 905/470-1200 – Marie Vanderlugt – *277 – Gr. K./Elem.

Markham: Wishing Well Montessori School, #30, 455 Cochrane Dr., Markham ON L3R 9R4 – 905/498-0331 – Connie Xuereb – *313 – Gr. K./Elem.

Metcalfe: Community Christian School-Metcalfe, PO Box 540, Metcalfe ON K0A 2P0 – 613/821-3669 – M.B. Ripmeester – *53 – Elem.

Millgrove: Covenant Christian School, PO Box 2, Millgrove ON L0R 1V0 – 905/689-3191 – G. Hofsink – *194 – Elem.

Mississauga: Aristotle Greek School, 2146 Waycross Cres., Mississauga ON L5K 1H9 – 905/855-0774 – Chrissanthi Pachiadakisi – *90 – Gr. K./Elem./Sec.

Mississauga: Cedar Grove School, 1884 Lakeshore Rd., Mississauga ON L5J 1J9 – 905/271-6006 – Susan Kendall – *60 – Elem.

Mississauga: The Froebel Kindergarten & School, 1576 Dundas St. West, Mississauga ON L5C 1E5 – 905/277-9371 – Barbara E. Corbett – Elem.

Mississauga: Isna Islamic School, 1525 Sherway Dr., Mississauga ON L4X 1C5 – 905/272-4303 – A.I. Ali – *326 – Gr. K./Elem.

Mississauga: Mentor College, 40 Forest Ave., Mississauga ON L5G 1L1 – 905/271-3393 – Arthur Steinberg – *883 – Gr. K./Elem./Sec.

Mississauga Christian Academy, 2720 Gananoque Dr., Mississauga ON L5N 2R2 – 905/826-4114 – Joy Elliot – *255 – Gr. K./Elem.

Mississauga: Queensway Cathedral Christian School, 1542 Rometown Dr., Mississauga ON L5E 2T9 – 905/255-0141 – D. Broomer – Gr. K./Elem./Sec.

Mississauga: Rotherglen Private School, 3553 South Common Ct., Mississauga ON L5L 2B3 – 905/820-9445 – Marie Lanigan – *376 – Elem.

Mississauga: Sherwood Heights School, 3065 Glen Erin Dr., Mississauga ON L5L 1J3 – 905/569-8999 – Edward Mutlak – *100 – Elem.

Mississauga: Springfield Manor Mississauga, 1444 Dundas Cres., Mississauga ON L5C 1E9 – 905/277-1085 – Winefride Johnson – *123 – Elem.

Mississauga: The Toronto Ability School, 1146 Clarkson Rd. North, Mississauga ON L5T 2W2 – 905/855-3800 – Magvite Wilhans – *52 – Gr. K./Elem.

Mississauga: Tutorial & Educational Assistance in Mississauga (T.E.A.M.), 275 Rudar Rd., Mississauga ON L5A 1S2 – 905/279-7200 – Kenneth B. Philbrook – *184 – Gr. K./Elem./Sec./Spec. Ed.

Mobert: Netamisakomik Centre for Education, General Delivery, Mobert ON P0M 2J0 – 807/822-2011 – Chris Courage – *71 – Elem./Sec.

Mount Forest: Farewell Parochial, RR#5, Mount Forest ON N0G 2L0 – Noreen Horst – *53 – Elem.

* indicates enrollment figure.

Mount Hope: Grandview Seventh-Day Adventist Academy, 3975 Hwy. #6, Mount Hope ON L0R 1W0 – 905/679-4492 – Garry Proctor – *55 – Elem./Sec.

Nepean: Canadian Montessori Academy, 2 Peter St., Nepean ON K2G 1K2 – 613/727-9427 – Sherie DeMel – *70 – Elem.

Nepean: École Maimonides School, 23 Esquimault Ave., Nepean ON K2H 6Z5 – 613/820-9484 – Rabbi Mordecai Berger – *156 – Gr. K./Elem./Spec. Ed.

Nestleton: Lighthouse Academy, RR#3, Nestleton ON L0B 1L0 – 905/986-5569 – Erika Kiezerbrink – Gr. K./Elem.

Nestor Falls: O-Ne-Ga-Ming School, PO Box 339, Nestor Falls ON P0X 1K0 – 807/484-2510 – Sylvan Chadee – *96 – Gr. K./Elem./Sec.

Newmarket: Elizabeth Simcoe Private School, 95 Carlson Dr., Newmarket ON L3Y 3G9 – 905/898-6208 – Gail E. Cheetham – *64 – Elem./Sec.

Newmarket: Holland Marsh District Christian School, RR#2, Newmarket ON L3Y 4V9 – 905/775-3701 – Henry Lise – *322 – Gr. K./Elem.

Newmarket & District Christian Academy, 221 Carlson Dr., PO Box 297, Newmarket ON L3Y 4X1 – 905/895-1119 – David Balik – *207 – Gr. K./Elem.

Newmarket Montessori School, #110, 1100 Stellar Dr., Newmarket ON L3Y 7B7 – 905/895-1921 – S. Soni – Gr. K./Elem.

Newmarket: Pickering College, 16945 Bayview Ave., Newmarket ON L3Y 4X2 – 905/895-1700 – Peter C. Sturrup – *257 – Elem./Sec.

Niagara Falls: Bible Baptist Academy, 9674 Upper's Lane, Niagara Falls ON L2E 6S4 – 905/356-7717 – J. Cunningham – *64 – Elem./Sec.

Niagara Community Church School, 9527 McLeod St., RR#2, Niagara Falls ON L2E 6S5 – 905/357-9519 – Chris Halls – *69 – Gr. K./Elem.

Nobleton: Montessori Country School, PO Box 455, Nobleton ON L0G 1N0 – 905/859-4739 – Marianne Perks – *82 – Gr. K./Elem.

North Gower Christian Academy, c/o Pilgrim Holiness Church, PO Box 605, North Gower ON K0A 2T0 – 613/489-2501 – Rev. Lloyd Wolenfeld – Gr. K./Elem./Sec.

North Gower: Viewmount Christian Academy, 2659 Roger Stevens Dr., North Gower ON K0A 2T0 – 613/489-2175 – Ellen Hackett – *81 – Elem.

North York: ARS Armenian Private School, 45 Hallcrown Pl., North York ON M2J 4Y4 – 416/491-2675 – Markar Saraphanian – *365 – Gr. K./Elem.

North York: Associated Hebrew Schools of Toronto, 252 Finch Ave. West, North York ON M2R 1M9 – 416/223-4845 – S. Rabinowitz – *2,394 – Gr. K./Elem.

North York: Bayview Glen Junior School, 275 Duncan Mill Rd., North York ON M3B 2Y1 – 416/443-1030 – J.T.M. Guest – *419 – Gr. K./Elem./Sec.

North York: Community Hebrew Academy, 200 Wilmington Ave., North York ON M3H 5J8 – 416/636-5984 – Shelden Friedman – *605 – Sec.

North York: Crawford Adventist Academy, 531 Finch Ave. West, North York ON M2R 3X2 – 416/633-0090 – Vernon Langdon – *470 – Gr. K./Elem./Sec.

North York: The Crescent School, 2365 Bayview Ave., North York ON M2L 1A2 – 416/449-2556 – J. Tansey – *529 – Elem./Sec.; Boys

North York: Crestview Junior Private School, 350 Seneca Hills Dr., PO Box 101, North York ON M2J 4S7 – 416/491-1949 – Leila Esper – *66 – Gr. K./Elem.

North York: Crestwood School, 411 Lawrence Ave. East, North York ON M3C 1N9 – 416/444-5858 – Dalia Eisen – *310 – Elem.

North York: Eitz Chaim Day Schools, 475 Patricia Ave., North York ON M2R 2N1 – 416/225-1187 – Rabbi Jakabovitz – *1,063 – Gr. K./Elem./Sec.

North York: Ellesmere Montessori Private School, 5350 Yonge St., North York ON M2N 5R5 – 416/447-1059 – Jill Weinberger – *110 – Gr. K./Elem.

North York: Hawthorn School for Girls, 230 The Donway West, North York ON M3B 2V8 – 416/444-3054 – Dr. Teresa Tomory – *90 – Elem./Sec.

North York: Holy Cross Armenian School, 61 Curlew Dr., North York ON M3A 2P8 – 416/441-2152 – Diana Hanimyam – *92 – Gr. K./Elem.

North Toronto Christian School, 50 Page Ave., North York ON M2K 2B4 – 416/226-3366 – Stuart W. Cooke – *619 – Gr. K./Elem./Sec.

North York Christian School, 43 Drewry Ave., North York ON M2M 1C9 – 416/222-1675 – Gregory J. Spencer – *58 – Gr. K./Elem./Sec.

North York: Or Haemet Sefaradic School, 37 Southborne Ave., North York ON M3H 1A4 – 416/635-9881 – Rabbi E. Rokach – *189 – Gr. K./Elem.

North York: The Oswald J. Smith Elementary School, 374 Sheppard Ave. East, North York ON M2N 3B6 – 416/222-3341 – Donald J. McNiven – *135 – Gr. K./Elem.

North York: The Paul B. Smith Academy, 374 Sheppard Ave. East, North York ON M2N 3B6 – 416/222-3341 – Donald F. McNiven – *180 – Sec.

North York: She'Arim Hebrew Day School, 100 Elder St., North York ON M3H 5G7 – 416/633-8247 – Elaine Runbinoff – *50 – Elem./Spec. Ed.

North York: Sidney Ledson School Ltd., #107, 220 Duncan Mill Rd., North York ON M3B 3J5 – 416/447-5355 – Vee Ledson – *89 – Gr. K./Elem.

North York: Willow Wood School, 157 Willowdale Ave., North York ON M2N 4Y7 – 416/222-0631 – Joy Kurtz – *136 – Elem./Sec./Spec. Ed.

North York: Willowdale Christian School, 60 Hilda Ave., North York ON M2M 1V5 – 416/222-1711 – Rick Nonnekes – *170 – Gr. K./Elem.

Norwich: Rehoboth Reformed Private School, PO Box 220, Norwich ON N0J 1P0 – 519/863-2403 – M.C. Vanderspek – *413 – Gr. K./Elem./Sec.

Oakville: Appleby College, 540 Lakeshore Rd. West, Oakville ON L6K 3P1 – 905/845-4681 – Guy S. McLean – *535 – Elem./Sec.

Oakville: Bronte College of Canada, 320 Bronte Rd., Oakville ON L6L 3C8 – 905/825-9871 – James Forrester – *84 – Sec.

Oakville: Chisholm Educational Centre, 440 Inglehart St., Oakville ON L6J 3J6 – 905/844-3240 – Dr. Howard A. Bernstein – *111 – Elem./Sec.

Oakville: Dearcroft Montessori School, 1167 Lakeshore Rd. East, Oakville ON L6J 1L3 – 905/844-2114 – Barbara Phippen – *163 – Gr. K./Elem.

Oakville: Fern Hill School, 3300 Ninth Line, RR#1, Oakville ON L6J 4Z2 – 905/257-0022 – Wendy Dennick – *367 – Gr. K./Elem./Sec.

Oakville: Glenburnie School, 2035 Upper Middle Rd., Oakville ON L6J 4Z2 – 905/338-6236 – Linda Sweet – *158 – Gr. K./Elem.

Oakville: John Knox Christian School, 2232 Sheridan Garden Dr., Oakville ON L6J 7T1 – 905/822-8131 – Lorna Keith – *228 – Gr. K./Elem.

Oakville: MacLachlan College, 337 Trafalgar Rd., Oakville ON L6J 3Y2 – 905/844-0372 – Audrey Hadfield – *234 – Elem./Sec.

Oakville: The Oakville Christian School, 112 Third Line, Oakville ON L6L 3Z7 – 905/825-1247 – Wesley L. Mack – *211 – Gr. K./Elem.

Oakville: St. Mildred's - Lightbourn School, 1080 Linbrook Rd., Oakville ON L6J 2L1 – 905/845-2386 – Lynda Duckworth – *599 – Gr. K./Elem./Sec; Girls

Orangeville: Hillcrest School, #74A, 90 Lawrence Ave., Orangeville ON L9W 3S4 – 519/942-3251 – Gail P. Hooper – *124 – Gr. K./Elem.

Orangeville Christian School, RR#5, PO Box 176, Orangeville ON L9W 2Z6 – 519/941-3381 – George Hoytema – *55 – Gr. K./Elem.

Orillia: Bethel Christian Academy, 300 Coldwater Rd. West, Orillia ON L3V 6X5 – 705/326-4561 – Ross W. Draper – *59 – Gr. K./Elem./Sec.

Orillia: Canadian Christian Academy, PO Box 937, Orillia ON L3V 6K8 – 705/327-8975 – Rev. C.K. Fear – *336 – Elem./Sec.

Orillia Christian School, PO Box 862, Orillia ON L3V 6K8 – 705/326-0532 – George Kamphuis – *120 – Gr. K./Elem.

Oshawa: College Park School, 1300 King St. East, PO Box 31054, Stn Kingsway, Oshawa ON L1H 8N9 – 905/723-0163 – Ruth Satelmajer – *168 – Gr. K./Elem.

Oshawa: Durham Christian Academy, 900 King St. East, Oshawa ON L1H 1H2 – 905/436-6354 – Michael Broomer – *128 – Gr. K./Elem.

Oshawa: Immanuel Christian School, 849 Rossland Rd. West, Oshawa ON L1H 7K4 – 905/728-9071 – Stan Baker – *133 – Gr. K./Elem.

Oshawa: Kingsway College, 1200 Leland Rd, Oshawa ON L1K 2H4 – 905/433-1144 – Ralph Janes – *206 – Sec.

Ottawa: Ashbury College, 362 Mariposa Ave., Ottawa ON K1M 0T3 – 613/749-5954 – Robert P. Napier – *559 – Elem./Sec.

Ottawa: Bishop Hamilton School, 2199 Regency Terrace, Ottawa ON K2C 1H2 – 613/596-4971 – Elaine Hopkins – *151 – Gr. K./Elem.

Ottawa: École Parsifal, 630 Island Park, Ottawa ON K1Y 0B7 – 613/729-7545 – Michéle Auger – *96 – Gr. K./Elem.

Ottawa: Elmwood School, 261 Buena Vista Rd., Ottawa ON K1M 0V9 – 613/749-6761 – Morag S. Gundy – *355 – Gr. K./Elem./Sec.

Ottawa: Hillel Academy, 881 Broadview Ave., Ottawa ON K2A 2M6 – 613/722-0020 – Mark Weinberg – *452 – Gr. K./Elem./Sec.

Ottawa: Joan of Arc Academy, 130 Keyworth Ave., Ottawa ON K1V 0E6 – 613/728-6364 – Nancy Reid – *71 – Gr. K./Elem.; Girls

Ottawa: Lycée Claudel, 1635 Promenade Riverside, Ottawa ON K1G 0E5 – 613/733-8522 – Irene Fesdjian – *856 – Gr. K./Elem./Sec.

Ottawa Christian School, 2191 Benjamin Ave., Ottawa ON K2A 1P6 – 613/722-5836 – William A. VanDyke – *198 – Gr. K./Elem.

Ottawa Iranian School, 100 Dufferin St., Ottawa ON K1M 2A6 – 613/236-2714 – Shokoh Najmi – *339 – Elem./Sec.

Ottawa Islamic School, 10 Coral St., Ottawa ON K2E 5Z6 – 613/727-5066 – Ali A. Hersi – *227 – Elem.

Ottawa Languages Institute Ltd., 1990 Leslie St., Ottawa ON K1H 5M3 – 613/521-3331 – Tin S. Yap – Sec.

Ottawa Montessori Schools, 335 Lindsay St., Ottawa ON K1G 0L6 – 613/521-5185 – Patricia McLaughlin – *339 – Gr. K./Elem.

Ottawa: Parsifal School, 630 Island Park Dr., Ottawa ON K1Y 0B7 – 613/729-7545 – Michèle Auger – *68 – Elem.

Ottawa: Redeemer Christian High School, 2199 Regency Terrace, Ottawa ON K2C 1H1 – 613/721-8233 – Derek R.S. Maggs – *97 – Sec.

Ottawa: Turnbull Learning Centre, #2, 111 Sherwood Dr., Ottawa ON K1Y 3V1 – 613/729-9940 – Mary Ann S. Turnbull – *97 – Elem./Sec.

Owen Sound Montessori School, 1701 - 3 Ave. East, Owen Sound ON N4K 2M3 – 519/376-9710 – Pamela Uair – *86 – Gr. K./Elem.

Owen Sound: Timothy Christian School, 199 - 4 Ave. West, Owen Sound ON N4K 4V1 – 519/371-9151 – Garth Bierma – *115 – Gr. K./Elem.

Oxford: Springford School with the Bible, PO Box 8, Oxford ON N0G 1X0 – 519/879-6898 – Pastor Lieuwe Schaafsma – *67 – Elem./Sec.

Pawitik: Baibombeh Anishinabe School, Pawitik ON P0X 1L0 – 807/226-5698 – Michael Leahy – *304 – Gr. K./Elem./Sec.

Peterborough: Grace Christian Academy, PO Box 2217, Peterborough ON K9J 7Y4 – 705/745-4400 – Gerry Libby – *100 – Gr. K./Elem.

Peterborough: Rhema Christian School, 3195 Parkhill Rd. East, Peterborough ON K9L 1B8 – 705/743-1400 – Ray Hendriks – *196 – Gr. K./Elem.

Pickering: Montessori Learning Centre of Pickering, 401 Kingston Rd., Pickering ON L1V 1A3 – 905/509-1722 – N. Phillips – *157 – Gr. K./Elem.

Picton: Sonrise Christian Academy, 48 Johnson St., Picton ON K0K 2T0 – 613/476-7883 – Matthew J. Bittel – *52 – Elem.

Pikangikum: Eenchokay Birchstick School, General Delivery, Pikangikum ON P0V 2L0 – 807/773-5561 – Lynda Worrod – *84 – Gr. K./Elem./Sec.

Poole: Fair Haven Christian Day School, RR#1, Poole ON N0K 1S0 – 519/595-4568 – Howard Bean – *84 – Gr. K./Elem.

Port Hope: Trinity College School, 190 Ward St., Port Hope ON L1A 3W2 – 905/885-9690 – Roger C. Wright – *405 – Elem./Sec.

Prince Albert: Scugog Christian School, PO Box 3308, Prince Albert ON L9L 1C3 – 905/985-3741 – John Lunshof – *58 – Elem.

Richmond Hill: Academy for Gifted Children, 12 Bond Cres., Richmond Hill ON L4E 3K2 – 905/773-0997 – Barbara Rosenberg – *73 – Elem./Sec.

Richmond Hill: Holy Trinity School, 11300 Bayview Ave., Richmond Hill ON L4C 4X7 – 905/737-1114 – George Rutherford – *555 – Elem./Sec.

Richmond Hill: Lifetime Learning Day School, 9206 Yonge St., Richmond Hill ON L4C 7A2 – 905/764-2579 – Lynn Howarth – *66 – Elem.

Richmond Hill Montessori & Elementary School, 85 - 16th Ave., Richmond Hill ON L4C 7A6 – 905/882-6000 – Eveline Kopachkov – *199 – Gr. K./Elem.

Richmond Hill: Toronto Montessori Schools, 8569 Bayview Ave., RR#2, Richmond Hill ON L4C 7B5 – 905/789-7828 – P. Glasgow – *689 – Gr. K./Elem.

Rosseau Lake College, PO Box 1967, Rosseau ON P0C 1J0 – 705/732-4351 – William J. McCracken – *99 – Elem./Sec.

Sachigo Lake: Martin McKay Memorial School, General Delivery, Sachigo Lake ON P0V 2P0 – 807/595-2526 – Anna Delaney – *101 – Sec.

St Catharines: Beacon Christian High School, 2 O'Malley Dr., St Catharines ON L2N 6N7 – 905/937-7411 – Ted Harris – *77 – Sec.

St Catharines: Calvary Christian School, 89 Scott St., St Catharines ON L2N 1G8 – 905/935-3854 – Walter Litowski – *131 – Gr. K./Elem.

St Catharines: Calvin Memorial Christian School, 300 Scott St., St Catharines ON L2N 1J3 – 905/937-6302 – Karen Gerritsma – *255 – Gr. K./Elem.

St Catharines: Garden City Christian Academy, 265 Linwell Rd., St Catharines ON L2N 1S4 – 905/937-6440 – Douglas Osborn – *65 – Gr. K./Elem./Sec.; Boys

St Catharines: Grey Gables Day School, One Dexter St., St Catharines ON L2S 2L4 – 905/685-4577 – Kathleen Marion – *87 – Gr. K./Elem./Sec.

St Catharines: Ridley College, PO Box 3013, St Catharines ON L2R 7C3 – 905/684-8193 – Rupert D. Lane – *576 – Elem./Sec.

St Catharines Montessori Day School, PO Box 1673, St Catharines ON L2R 7K1 – 905/684-6110 – Ellen Smith – *53 – Gr. K./Elem.

St Catharines: The Wheatley School of Montessori Education, 154 Martindale Rd., St Catharines ON L2S 2X9 – 905/641-3012 – Eda Varalli – *105 – Elem.

St. Mary's: Brookside Parochial School, RR#4, St. Mary's ON N0M 2V0 – Henry Troyer – Elem.

St. Thomas: Ebenezer Christian School, 77 Fairview Ave., St. Thomas ON N5R 4X7 – 519/633-0690 – Anthony Dekoter – *160 – Elem.

St. Thomas: Faith Christian Academy, 109 Chestnut St., St. Thomas ON N5R 2B1 – 519/633-0943 – Thomas Lancaster – *110 – Gr. K./Elem.

Sandy Lake: Thomas Fiddler Memorial School, Via Favorable Lake Post Office, Sandy Lake ON P0V 1V0 – 807/774-4491 – Sarah Sawanas – Elem./Sec.

Sarnia: Lambton Christian High School, 295 Essex St., Sarnia ON N7T 4S3 – 519/337-9122 – Wayne Drost – *94 – Sec.

Sarnia: New Life School, 867 London Rd., Sarnia ON N7T 4S3 – 519/336-6082 – Elizabeth DeGroot – *53 – Elem.

Sarnia Christian School, 1273 Exmouth St., Sarnia ON N7S 1W9 – 519/344-4562 – P. Weening – *233 – Gr. K./Elem.

Sarnia: Temple Christian Academy, 1410 Quinn Dr., Sarnia ON N7T 7H4 – 519/542-1427 – James D. Loosemore – *74 – Elem.

Scarborough: Agbu Zaroukian School, 30 Progress Crt., Scarborough ON M1G 3T5 – 416/431-2428 – Hriar Kafessian – *114 – Gr. K./Elem.

Scarborough: Blaisdale Montessori School, 885 Scarborough Golf Club Rd., Scarborough ON M1G 1J6 – 416/289-2273 – Eleanor Wilson – *342 – Gr. K./Elem.

Scarborough: Ellington Montessori School, 2102 Lawrence Ave. East, Scarborough ON M1R 2Z9 – 416/759-8363 – Deborah Renwick – *56 – Elem.

Scarborough: The Hart Academy, #101, 3090 Kingston Rd., Scarborough ON M1M 1P2 – 416/261-0510 – Annette M.P. Dunleavy – Elem.; Special Ed.

Scarborough: Our Lady of Victory Academy, 24 Rowatson Rd., Scarborough ON M1E 1K1 – 416/659-1421 – Penelope Anne Costin – Elem./Sec.

Scarborough Christian Private School, 614 Brimley Rd., Scarborough ON M1J 1B8 – 416/477-4433 – Keith Davies – *489 – Gr. K./Elem./Sec.

Scarborough: Whitefield Christian Jr. Academy, 5810 Finch Ave. East, Scarborough ON M1B 4Y6 – 416/297-1212 – Ruth E. Slade – *175 – Elem.

Sebringville: Stratford District Christian School, 130 Huron Rd., Sebringville ON N0K 1X0 – 519/595-8644 – Peter C. Van Manen – *116 – Gr. K./Elem.

Sharon: The East Gwillimbury Country Day School, RR#1, Sharon ON L0G 1V0 – 905/853-3301 – Mary Pape – Elem.

Simcoe: Bethel Baptist Academy, PO Box 752, Simcoe ON N3Y 2T2 – 519/426-8421 – Rev. G. Kevin Schular – *67 – Gr. K./Elem./Sec.

Sioux Lookout: Pelican Falls First Nation High School, PO Box 4127, Sioux Lookout ON P8T 1J9 – 807/737-1110 – Wayne McElhone – *141 – Sec.

Sioux Lookout: Washa Distance Education Centre, PO Box 1118, Sioux Lookout ON P8T 1B7 – 807/737-1488 – Norma Kejick – *465 – Sec.

Smithville: John Calvin School of Smithville, Station St., PO Box 280, Smithville ON L0R 2A0 – 905/957-3161 – Judy Kingma – *333 – Gr. K./Elem.

Smithville Covenant Christian School, Townline Rd., RR#1, Smithville ON L0R 2A0 – 905/957-7796 – M. Elzinga – *156 – Elem.

Smithville District Christian High School, 6488 Smithville Rd., Smithville ON L0R 2A0 – 905/957-3255 – M.B. Stroobosscher – *189 – Sec.

Stittsville: Ottawa Waldorf School, 1 Goulbourn Ave., Stittsville ON K2S 1N9 – 613/836-1547 – Elizabeth MacMillan – *50 – Gr. K./Elem.

Strathroy: John Calvin Christian School, 48 York St., Strathroy ON N7G 2E5 – 519/245-1924 – Henry Wiersema – *178 – Gr. K./Elem.

Strathroy Community Christian School, 48 York St., Strathroy ON N7G 2E5 – 519/245-1924 – Henry Wiersema – *182 – Gr. K./Elem.

Sudbury Christian Day School, PO Box 1291, Stn B, Sudbury ON P3E 4S7 – 705/523-5550 – L. Mohns – *50 – Gr. K./Elem.

Tecumseh: Our Lady of Mercy School, 2078 St. Anne St., Tecumseh ON N8N 1V7 – 519/735-0746 – Donna Hayes – Elem.

Thornhill: Cheder Chabad, 770 Chabad Gate, Thornhill ON L4J 3V9 – 905/764-8721 – Rabbi Chanowitz – *92 – Elem.

Thornhill: The Leo Baeck Day School, 36 Atkinson Ave., Thornhill ON L4J 8C9 – 905/709-3636 – Zita J. Gardner – *501 – Gr. K./Elem.

Thornhill: Ner Israel Yeshiva College, 8950 Bathurst St., Thornhill ON L4J 8A7 – 905/731-1224 – T. Widrich – *145 – Sec.

Thornhill: Netivot Hatorah Day School, 18 Atkinson Ave., Thornhill ON L4J 8C8 – 905/771-1234 – Avrom Schochet – *470 – Gr. K./Elem.

Thornhill: Toronto Waldorf School, 9100 Bathurst St., PO Box 220, Thornhill ON L3T 3N3 – 905/881-1611 – Les Black – *396 – Gr. K./Elem.

Thornton: Thor Secondary Prep School, RR#3, Thornton ON L0L 2P0 – 705/458-9705 – W.H. Madden – *108 – Elem.

Thunder Bay Christian School, RR#2, Stn F, Thunder Bay ON P7C 4V1 – 807/939-1209 – Richard Poortinga – *272 – Gr. K./Elem./Sec.

Timmins: Faith Christian Academy, PO Box 1434, Timmins ON P4N 7N2 – 705/267-5463 – Pastor Gerald Vaillancourt – Elem./Sec.

Timmins Trinity Christian School, PO Box 734, Timmins ON P4N 7G2 – 705/268-4498 – Sally Bidwell – *50 – Elem.

Toronto: Alan Howard Waldorf School, 250 Madison Ave., Toronto ON M4V 2W6 – 416/962-6447 – Alan Hughes – *129 – Elem.

Toronto: Associated Hebrew Schools of Toronto Junior High Division, 3630 Bathurst St., Toronto ON M6A 2E3 – 416/789-7471 – J.H. Rosenfield – Elem./Sec.

  Associated Hebrew Schools of Toronto Junior High Division, 6100 Leslie St., North York ON M2H 3J1

Toronto: Bais Yaakov Elementary School, 85 Stormont Ave., Toronto ON M5N 2C3 – 416/783-6181 – M. Drebin – *462 – Gr. K./Elem.; Girls

Toronto: Beth Jacob Private School, 410 Lawrence Ave. West, Toronto ON M5M 1C2 – 416/787-4949 – Rabbi A. Stefansky – *302 – Sec.; Girls

Toronto: Bialik Hebrew Day School, 12 Viewmount Ave., Toronto ON M6B 1T3 – 416/783-3346 – Dr. Uri Korin – *793 – Gr. K./Elem./Sec.

Toronto: Bishop Strachan School, 298 Lonsdale Rd., Toronto ON M4V 1X2 – 416/483-4325 – Rev. Ann E. Tottenham – *782 – Gr. K./Elem./Sec.

Toronto: Branksome Hall, 10 Elm Ave., Toronto ON M4W 1N4 – 416/920-9741 – Rachel Belash – *814 – Gr. K./Elem./Sec.

Toronto: Cambridge International College of Canada, 35 Ourland Ave., Toronto ON M8Z 4E1 – 416/252-9195 – Irwin Diamond – *145 – Sec.

Toronto: Canadian Heritage School, 110 Eglinton Ave. West, 3rd Fl., Toronto ON M4P 1R3 – 416/322-6010 – Merle Langbord Levine – Elem./Sec.

Toronto: Canadian Outward Bound Wilderness School, #302, 150 Laird Dr., Toronto ON M4G 3Y7 – 416/421-8111 – Philip Blackford – *200 – Sec.

Toronto: Cathedral Christian Academy, 1901 Jane St., PO Box 410, Stn W, Toronto ON M6M 5C1 – 416/241-1100 – Dr. P.D. Melnichuk – *61 – Gr. K./Elem./Sec.

Toronto: Dominion College, 111 Gerrard St. East, Toronto ON M5B 1G8 – 416/348-8708 – Barbara Wehrmann – *63 – Sec.

Toronto: The Great Lakes College of Toronto, 323 Keele St., Toronto ON M6P 2K6 – 416/763-4121 – Murray R. Gaziuk – *148 – Sec.

Toronto: Havergal College, 1451 Avenue Rd., Toronto ON M5N 2H9 – 416/483-3519 – Priscilla Winn Barlow – *839 – Gr. K./Elem./Sec.

Toronto: High Park Montessori School, 35 High Park Gdns., Toronto ON M6R 1S8 – 416/763-6097 – Karen L. Fagan – *111 – Gr. K./Elem.

Toronto: Higher Marks Educational Institute, Main Campus, 941 Bathurst St., Toronto ON M5R 3G4 – 416/532-5563 – Ronald E. Blake – *214 – Elem./Sec.; Spec. Ed.

* indicates enrollment figure.

Toronto: Humberside Montessori School, 411 Clendenan Ave, Toronto ON M6P 2X7 – 416/763-8888 – Felix Bednarski – *81 – Elem./Ungraded

Toronto: Imperial College of Toronto, 20 Queen Elizabeth Blvd., Toronto ON M8Z 1L8 – 416/251-4970 – Vojin Stefancic – *369 – Sec.

Toronto: Institute of Child Study, 45 Walmer Rd., Toronto ON M5R 2X2 – 416/978-3454 – Elizabeth Morley – *193 – Elem.

Toronto: Islamic Foundation School, 441 Nugget Ave., Toronto ON M1S 5E1 – 416/321-3776 – Salma Khokhar – *90 – Elem.

Toronto: Lena Brown Seventh Day Adventist School, c/o Knobhill Public School, #201, Seminole Ave., Toronto ON M1J 1M8 – 416/439-2029 – Randolph F. Dixon – Elem.

Toronto: The Mabin School, 50 Poplar Plains Rd., Toronto ON M4V 2M8 – 416/964-9594 – Geraldine Mabin – *151 – Gr. K./Elem.

Toronto: Maria Montessori School, 125 Brentcliffe Rd., Toronto ON M4G 3Y7 – 416/423-9123 – James Brand – *123 – Elem.

Toronto: Metro Toronto Language School, 20 Eglinton Ave. East, Toronto ON M4P 1A9 – 416/488-2200 – D.S. Diplock – *289 – Sec./Ungraded

Toronto: Metropolitan Preparatory Academy, 49 Mobile Dr., Toronto ON M4A 1H5 – 416/285-0870 – Wayne McKelvey – *311 – Elem./Sec.

Toronto: Montcrest School, 4 Montcrest Blvd., Toronto ON M4K 1J7 – 416/469-2008 – Elaine Danson – *165 – Gr. K./Elem.

Toronto: Montessori Learning Centre (Ajax), 22 Delavan Ave., Toronto ON M5P 1T3 – 905/428-3122 – Dorothy Graziani – *73 – Gr. K./Elem.

Toronto: National Ballet School, 105 Maitland St., Toronto ON M4Y 1E4 – 416/964-3780 – Mora I. Oxley – *144 – Elem./Sec.

Toronto: Pathways College, #1801, 1 Yonge St., Toronto ON M5E 1W7 – 416/367-3940 – F. Manson – *66 – Sec.

Toronto: Royal St. George's College, 120 Howland Ave., Toronto ON M5R 3B5 – 416/533-9481 – John R. Latimer – *400 – Elem./Sec.; Boys

Toronto: St. Clement's School, 21 St. Clement's Ave., Toronto ON M4R 1G8 – 416/483-4835 – Janette Doupe – *439 – Gr. K./Elem./Sec.; Girls

Toronto: St. Louis Delia Secondary School, 111 Bond St., Toronto ON M5B 1Y2 – 416/979-0301 – Anthony Ho – *73 – Sec.

Toronto: St. Michael's College School, 1515 Bathurst St., Toronto ON M5P 3H4 – 416/653-3180 – *914 – Sec.; Boys

Toronto: De La Salle College, 131 Farnham Ave., Toronto ON M4V 1H7 – 416/969-8771; Fax: 416/969-9175 – Br. D. Viggiani – Elem./Sec.

Toronto: School of Liberal Arts, #200, 44 Eglinton Ave. West, Toronto ON M4R 1A1 – 416/489-7652 – David L. Ferguson – *85 – Sec.

Toronto: The Sterling Hall School of Toronto, 99 Cartwright Ave., Toronto ON M6A 1V4 – 416/449-3410 – Darlene Ferris – *171 – Elem.; Boys

Toronto: Sunnybrook School, 469 Merton St., Toronto ON M4S 1B4 – 416/487-5308 – Irene Davy – *136 – Gr. K./Elem.

Toronto: Thornton Hall Senior Private School, 241 Poplar Plains Rd., Toronto ON M4V 2N8 – 416/923-3291 – Stuart E. Mackey – *50 – Sec.

Toronto: The Toronto French School, Main Campus, 306 Lawrence Ave. East, Toronto ON M4N 1T7 – 416/484-6533; Fax: 416/488-3090 – Headmaster, Jean Brugniau – *1,144 – Gr. K./Elem./Sec.

Toronto: United Synagogue Day School, 1700 Bathurst St., Toronto ON M5P 3K3 – 416/781-5658 – Aaron M. Nussbaum – *1,388 – Gr. K./Elem./Sec.; Boys

Toronto: University of Toronto Schools, 371 Bloor St. West, Toronto ON M5S 2R8 – 416/978-3209 – Stan Pearl – *455 – Elem./Sec.

Toronto: Upper Canada College, 200 Lonsdale Rd., Toronto ON M4V 1W6 – 416/488-1125 – J. Douglas Blakey – *1,050 – Elem./Sec.

Toronto: Weston Montessori School, 40 South Station St., Toronto ON M9N 2B3 – 416/242-3725 – Mark W. Berger – *63 – Elem.

Toronto: Yeshiva Bnei Tzion of Bobov, 44 Champlain Blvd., Toronto ON M3H 2Z1 – 416/633-6332 – David Kessler – *157 – Gr. K./Elem.; Boys

Toronto: Yeshiva Yesadei Hatorah, 77 Glen Rush Blvd., Toronto ON M2N 2T8 – 416/787-1101 – A. Bornstein – *390 – Gr. K./Elem.; Boys

Toronto: Yeshivas Nachalas Zvi, 475 Lawrence Ave. West, Toronto ON M5M 1C6 – 416/782-8912 – J. Rosenfield – *58 – Elem./Sec.

Toronto: York Montessori School, 65 Sheldrake Blvd., Toronto ON M4P 2B1 – 416/483-0541 – Barbara Zeibots – *208 – Gr. K./Elem

Toronto: The York School, 65 Sheldrake Boulevard, Toronto ON M4P 2B1 – 416/483-0541

Toronto Island Montessori School, 18 Wyandot Ave., Toronto Island ON M5J 2M9 – 416/368-1919 – Susan Roy – Gr. K./Elem.

Trenton Christian School, 20 - 4 Ave., Trenton ON K8V 5N3 – 613/392-3600 – J. Van Duyvendyk – *208 – Gr. K./Elem.

Unionville: Some Place Special Christian Academy, 100 Lee Ave., Unionville ON M1V 2W6 – 905/754-7314 – Marjorie Serio – *60 – Elem.

Unionville: Trillium Montessori School, 7781 Kennedy Rd., Unionville ON L3R 2C8 – 416/946-1181 – Lily Moon – Elem.

Utterson: Muskoka Christian School, PO Box 150, Utterson ON P0B 1M0 – 705/385-2847 – William Fitch – *91 – Gr. K./Elem.

Vanier: L'Etincelle, 268 Durocher St., Vanier ON K1L 7S6 – 613/733-6919 – Claudette Giguere – Gr. K./Elem.

Vaughan: Children's College Private Elementary School, 7909 Kipling Ave., Vaughan ON L4L 1Z7 – 905/742-0434 – Lynne Taylor – *80 – Gr. K./Elem.

Vaughan: Toronto District Christian High School, 377 Woodbridge Ave., Vaughan ON L4L 2S8 – 905/851-1772 – W. Barneveld – *294 – Sec.

Wallaceburg Christian School, 693 Albert St., Wallaceburg ON N8A 1Y8 – 519/627-6013 – Trevor J. Tristram – *94 – Gr. K./Elem.

Wasaga Beach: Silvercrest Christian School, 380 Zoo Park Rd., Wasaga Beach ON L0L 2P0 – 705/429-4303 – Grey Ayrheart – *84 – Gr. K./Elem.

Waterloo: Fellowship Christian School, 306 Erb St. West, Waterloo ON N2L 1W3 – 519/886-6530 – Marilyn Lambert – *55 – Elem.

Waterloo: Kitchener Waterloo Bilingual School, 600 Erb St. West, Waterloo ON N2J 3Z4 – 519/886-6510 – Michel Poinot – *163 – Gr. K./Elem.

Waterloo: Kitchener-Waterloo Montessori School, 194 Allen St. East, Waterloo ON N2J 1K1 – 519/742-1051 – Elizabeth Black – Gr. K./Elem.

Waterloo: St. Judes School, 419 Phillip St., Waterloo ON N2L 3X2 – 519/888-6620 – Frederick Gore – *55 – Elem./Sec./Spec. Ed.

Wellandport: Robert Land Academy, RR#3, Wellandport ON L0R 2J0 – 905/386-6203 – G. Scott Bowman – *86 – Elem./Sec.

Wellandport Christian School, RR#1, Wellandport ON L0R 2J0 – 905/386-6272 – William J. Thies – *283 – Elem.

Wheatley: Old Colony Christian Academy, RR#2, Wheatley ON N0P 2P0 – 519/825-4400 – Milton Friesen – *106 – Elem.

Whitby: Trafalgar Castle School, 401 Reynolds St., Whitby ON L1N 3W9 – 905/668-3358 – C.T.C. Kamcke – *144 – Elem./Sec.

Whitby Montessori School, 301 Byron St. South, Whitby ON L1N 4P9 – 905/430-8201 – Kathleen Natsuhara – *134 – Elem.

White Dog: Wabeseenmoong School, White Dog ON P0X 1P0 – 807/927-2286 – Valerie Henry – *251 – Gr. K./Elem./Sec.

Williamsburg: Timothy Christian School, Williamsburg ON K0C 2H0 – 613/535-2687 – Gary Postma – *145 – Gr. K./Elem.

Willowdale: People's Christian Academy, 374 Sheppard Ave. East, Willowdale ON M2N 3B6 – 416/222-3341 – Donald F. McNiven – *502 – Elem./Sec.

Windsor: Academie Ste-Cecile Private School, 925 Cousineau Rd., Windsor ON N9G 1V8 – 519/961-1291 – Therese H. Gadoury – *86 – Elem./Sec.

Windsor: Marantha Christian Academy, 939 Northwood St., Windsor ON N9E 2B4 – 519/966-7424 – Peter Baljeu – *90 – Gr. K./Elem.

Windsor: Temple Christian Academy of Windsor, 3005 Temple Dr., Windsor ON N8W 5E5 – 519/945-7077 – Agnita Solomon – *72 – Gr. K./Elem.

Windsor Christian Fellowship Academy, 4490 - 7th Concession, RR#1, Windsor ON N9A 6J3 – 519/972-5977 – Thomas Collins – *124 – Elem.

Woodbridge: Calvary Christian School, c/o Calvary Baptist Church, 26 Bruce St., Woodbridge ON L4L 1J4 – 905/851-2273 – Mark Kennedy – *72 – Gr. K./Elem.

Woodbridge: Credo Christian School, 8260 Huntington Rd., Woodbridge ON L4L 1A5 – 905/851-1620 – L.P. Maat – *97 – Gr. K./Elem.

Woodbridge: Maple Leaf Montessori School Inc., 8066 Kipling Ave., Woodbridge ON L4L 2A1 – 905/856-3359 – Johanna Madeley – *174 – Elem.

Woodstock: John Knox Christian School, 800 Juliana Dr., PO Box 243, Woodstock ON N4S 7W8 – 519/539-1492 – A. Bouma – *249 – Gr. K./Elem.

Woodstock: Kettle Creek Private School, PO Box 167, Woodstock ON N4S 7W8 – 519/539-3473 – Dora Force – *56 – Elem./Sec.

Wunnummin Lake: Lydia Lois Beardy Memorial School, General Delivery, Wunnummin Lake ON P0V 2Z0 – 807/442-2402 – Georgina Nahwegahbo – *126 – Elem./Sec.

Wyoming: John Knox Christian School of Wyoming, PO Box 81, Wyoming ON N0N 1T0 – 519/845-3112 – William Hordyk – *158 – Gr. K./Elem.

OVERSEAS SCHOOLS

France: Lycée canadien en France, Place du Centenaire, 06230 St.-Jean-Cap-Ferrat France – 011-33-9301-4884; Fax: 011-33-9376-1402 – Principal, Gary O'Meara – *85 – OSSD

Offering the final year or OAC year of high school. Instruction in English. Students are housed locally with French families. Co-educational. Diploma.

Hong Kong: Delia School of Canada, Tai Fung Road, Tai Koo Shing, Quarry Bay Hong Kong – 011-852-884-41654166; Fax: 011-852-886-0813 – Principal, William McGarvie – *852

Hong Kong: S.E.A. Canadian Overseas Sec. School, 166-166A Boundary St., Kowloon Hong Kong – 011-852-336-1116; Fax: 011-852-336-4782 – Principal, Morley Mason – *271

Japan: Columbia International College, #709, Harada Bldg., 2-14-2 Takadanobaga, Shinjuku-ku, Tokyo 169 Japan – 011-81-3-04 2423-3711; Fax: 011-813-03-3204-7404 – Principal, Don McCallum

Malaysia: Sunway College, No. 5 Jalan Kolej, Sengalor Darul Ehsan, 46150 Petaling Jaya Malaysia – 011-603-735-8622; Fax: 011-603-735-8633 – Principal, Rex Sharman – *315

Malaysia: Taylor's College, No. 1, Jalan SS15/8, Subang Jaya New Town Centre, 47500 Petaling Jaya Malaysia – 011-03-734-5211; Fax: 011-03-734-5209 – Principal, Bert Naylor – *503

Romania: A.A.C. Cernavoda School, Centrala Nucleara Cernavoda, Constanta Romania – 011-40-01-239340; Fax: 011-40-1-312-0519

Singapore: Canadian International School, 5 Toh Tuck Rd., Singapore 21659 Singapore – 011-65-467-1732;

Fax: 011-65-467-1729 – Principal, Wayne MacInnis – *432

Switzerland: Neuchatel Jr. College, Cret-Taconnet, 4, 2000 Neuchatel Switzerland – 011-41-38-252700; Fax: 011-41-252-38-244259 – Principal, Jim McMurtry – *107

PRINCE EDWARD ISLAND

Department of Education
PO Box 2000, Charlottetown PE C1A 7N8
902/368-4600; Fax: 902/368-4663; Telex: 014-44154

CURRICULUM INFORMATION
Director, French Programs & Services, Tilmon Gallant, 902/368-4680; Fax: 902/368-4622
Director, English Programs & Services, Eldon Rogerson, 902/368-4670; Fax: 902/368-4622

Office of Higher Education, Training and Adult Learning
PO Box 2000, Charlottetown PE C1A 7N8
902/368-5988; Fax: 902/368-6144; Telex: 014-44154
Director, Policy & Programs, Calvin Caiger

For detailed departmental listings, see Index: "Education, Depts."

REGIONAL ADMINISTRATIVE SCHOOL UNITS
There are three regional administrative school boards. The two English boards consist of fifteen elected members; the French school board has nine elected members.

Eastern School District
 PO Box 8600, Charlottetown PE C1A 8V7
 902/368-6990; Fax: 902/368-6960 – Supt., David McCabe
French Language School Board
 Abram's Village, RR#3, Wellington PE C0B 2E0
 902/854-2975; Fax: 902/854-2981 – Supt., Gabriel Arsenault
Western School Board
 PO Box 312, Slemon Park PE C0B 2A0
 902/888-8400; Fax: 902/888-8449 – Supt., Sonia Pritchard; Asst. Supt., Alan Kennedy; Asst. Supt., Jim MacNeill

BAND-OPERATED INDIAN SCHOOLS
John J. Sark Memorial School, PO Box 124, Lennox Island PE C0B 1P0 – 902/831-2777 – Principal, Sr. Bernice Smith

UNIVERSITIES

University of Prince Edward Island
550 University Ave., Charlottetown PE C1A 4P3
902/566-0300; Fax: 902/566-0420; URL: http://www.upei.ca
President & Vice-Chancellor, Elizabeth Epperly, B.A., M.A., Ph.D.
Chancellor, Norman Webster, B.A., M.A.
Chair of the Board, John A. O'Keefe, B.B.A., LL.B.
Registrar, John DeGrace, B.Sc.(Eng.), M.Sc.
Vice-President, Academic Support, John Crossley, B.A., M.A., Ph.D.
Director, Alumni, Development & Public Relations, Sonya Banks, B.A., M.B.A.
Public Afairs Officer, S.L. Copan, B.P.R.
Business Manager, M.S. Stevenson
Purchasing Agent, R.A. Cooke
Manager, Bookstore, E.R. Gallant

FACULTIES WITH DEANS
Arts, Philip Smith, B.A., M.A., Ph.D.
Business Administration, J. Ronald Collins, B.Sc., M.B.A., Ph.D.
Education, Vianne Timmons, B.A., B.Ed., M.Ed., Ph.D.
School of Nursing, Margaret F. Munro, R.N., Ph.D.
Science, Winston Pineau, B.Sc., M.Sc.
Veterinary Medicine, Lawrence E. Heider, D.V.M.

POST-SECONDARY SCHOOLS

HOLLAND COLLEGE OF APPLIED ARTS AND TECHNOLOGY
Administrative Services, 140 Weymouth St., Charlottetown PE C1A 4Z1
902/566-9510; Fax: 902/566-9509; Email: doiron@reggys.cc.hollandc.pe.ca
President, Alex MacAulay
Atlantic Police Academy, PO Box 156, Slemon Park PE C0A 2A0 – 902/888-6700; Fax: 902/888-6725
Culinary Institute of Canada, 140 Weymouth St., Charlottetown PE C1A 4Z1 – 902/566-9550
Harbourside Centre, 298 Water St., Summerside PE C1N 1B8 – 902/888-6450; Fax: 902/888-6401
Marine Centre, 100 Water St., Summerside PE C1N 1A9 – 902/888-6485; Fax: 902/888-6404
Royalty Centre, 40 Enman Cres., Charlottetown PE C1E 1E6 – 902/566-9330; Fax: 902/566-1955
School of Justice, PO Box 156, Slemon Park PE C0B 2A0 – 902/888-6700; Fax: 902/888-6725
Souris Centre, 120 Main St., Souris PE C0A 2B0 – 902/687-3341; Fax: 902/687-4360
Summerside Centre, 425 Granville St., Summerside PE C1N 3C4 – 902/888-6420; Fax: 902/888-6402
West Prince Centre, PO Box 37, Elmsdale PE C0B 1K0 – 902/853-2200; Fax: 902/853-3586

INDEPENDENT & PRIVATE SCHOOLS
Charlottetown: Fair Isle Adventist School, 20 Lapthorne Ave., Charlottetown PE C1A 2M3 – 902/894-9301 – Sheila Bergey – Gr. 1-9; Seventh-day Adventist
Charlottetown: Grace Christian School, 50 Kirkdale Rd., Charlottetown PE C1E 1N6 – 902/368-2218 – Principal, Carol Johnston – *132 – Gr. K.-12; Baptist
Charlottetown: Immanuel Christian School, 65 Kirkwood Dr., Charlottetown PE C1A 8C3 – 902/628-6465 – Principal, Allen Bron – *48 – Gr. 1-6

QUÉBEC

Ministère de l'Éducation
Direction des communications, 1035, rue De La Chevrotière, 11e étage, Québec PQ G1R 5A5
418/643-7095; Fax: 418/646-6561
Minister, Pauline Marois, 418/644-0664; Fax: 418/646-7551
Deputy Minister, Pierre Lucier, 418/643-3810; Fax: 418/644-4591

DIRECTIONS RÉGIONALES
Direction Régionale 1: Bas St-Laurent/Gaspésie-Îles-de-La-Madeleine: 376, av de la Cathédrale, Rimouski PQ G5L 5K9 – 418/727-3600; Fax: 418/727-3557 – Directeur régionale, Michel Doré
Direction Régionale 2: Saguenay-Lac-Saint-Jean: 3950, boul Harvey, 2e étage, Jonquière PQ G7X 0L5 – 418/695-2633; Fax: 418/695-7990 – Directeur régional, Claude Pagé
Direction Régionale 3: Québec-Chaudière-Appalaches: 1020, rte de l'Église, 3e étage, Ste-Foy PQ G1V 3V9 – 418/643-7934; Fax: 418/643-0972 – Directeur régional, Jeannot Bordeleau
Direction Régionale 4: La Mauricie-Bois- Francs: 100, rue Laviolette, 2e étage, Trois-Rivières PQ G9A 5S9 – 819/371-6711; Fax: 819/371-6075 – Directeur régional, Jean-Paul Bournival
Direction Régionale 5: L'Estrie: #3.05, 200, rue Belvédère nord, Sherbrooke PQ J1H 4A9 – 820/820-3382; Fax: 820/820-3947 – Directeur général, Marcel Veillette
Direction Régionale 6.1: Laval-Laurentides-Lanaudière: 300, rue Sicard, 2e étage, Ste-Thérèse-de-Blainville PQ J7E 3X5 – 514/430-3611; Fax: 514/430-4005 – Directeur régional, Michel Monfet
Direction Régionale 6.2: La Montérégie: 201, Place Charles-Lemoyne, 6e étage, Longueuil PQ J4K 2T5 – 514/928-7438; Fax: 514/928-7451 – Directeur régional, Claude Fortier
Direction Régionale 6.3: Montréal: 600, rue Fullum, 6e étage, Montréal PQ H2K 4L1 – 514/873-4630; Fax: 514/873-0620 – Directeur régionale, Michel de Celles
Direction Régionale 7: L'Outaouais: 170, rue Hôtel-de-Ville, 4e étage, Hull PQ J8X 4C2 – 819/772-3382; Fax: 819/772-3955 – Directeur régional, Denis Dugal
Direction Régionale 8: L'Abitibi-Témiscamingue: #2.02, 180, boul Rideau, Rouyn-Noranda PQ J9X 1N9 – 819/797-1766; Fax: 819/797-5074 – Directeur régional, Oliva Carrier
Direction Régionale 9: Côte-Nord: #1.812 625, boul Laflèche, Baie-Comeau PQ G5C 1C5 – 418/589-5748; Fax: 418/589-4467 – Directrice régional, Margaret Rioux-Dolan

For detailed departmental listings, see Index: "Education, Depts."

COMMISSIONS SCOLAIRES
The Québec school board networks are denominational. The elementary course usually lasts six years & the secondary course five years. The secondary education is polyvalent in that the students may choose professional options at the same time as general options. In the listings below, (Prot.) indicates Protestant; (RC) indicates Roman Catholic.

Boards with an enrollment of more than 15,000 are in bold print.

Commission des écoles catholiques de Montréal
 3737, rue Sherbrooke est, Montréal PQ H1X 3B3
 514/596-6021; Fax: 514/596-7570
 (RC)
 Dir. gén., Yves Archambault
 Prés., Michel Pallascio
Commission des écoles catholiques de Québec – (RC)
 1460, ch Ste-Foy, Québec PQ G1S 2N9
 418/682-2041; Fax: 418/682-6058 – Dir. gén., Lise Doyon-Forques; Prés., Lucien Flamand
Commission des écoles catholiques de Verdun – (RC)
 1100, 5e av, Verdun PQ H4G 2Z7
 514/765-7555; Fax: 514/765-7599 – Dir. gén., Guy Dupuis; Prés., Daniel O'Reilly
Commission des écoles protestantes du Grand-Montréal
 6000, av Fielding, Montréal PQ H3X 1T4
 514/483-7202; Fax: 514/483-7324
 (Prot.)
 Dir. gén., Michael D. George
 Prés., Allan Butler
Commission scolaire Abitibi – (RC)
 500, rue Principale, LaSarre PQ J9Z 2A2
 819/333-5411; Fax: 819/333-3044 – Dir. gén., Robert Caron; Prés.e, Marguerite Houle
Commission scolaire de l'Argile Bleue – (RC)
 480, boul Laurier, Mont-St-Hilaire PQ J3H 4R9
 514/467-9323; Fax: 514/467-9375 – Dir. gén., Ginette Jacques; Prés.e, Denise Asselin
Commission scolaire de l'Asbesterie – (RC)
 309, rue Chassé, Asbestos PQ J1T 2B4
 819/879-6907; Fax: 819/879-4350 – Dir. gén., Yvon Raymond; Prés., Camille Côté
Commission scolaire d'Aylmer – (RC)
 115, rue Principale, 2e étage, Aylmer PQ J9H 3M2
 819/684-3056; Fax: 819/684-7709 – Dir. gén., Guy Benoit; Prés.e, Nicole Desjardins
Commission scolaire de Baie-des-Chaleurs – (RC)

*indicates enrollment figure.

151 - 7e rue A, CP 8000, Paspébiac PQ G0C 2K0
418/752-3328; Fax: 418/752-5716 – Dir. gén., Bertrand Poirier; Prés., Pierre Arsenault
Commission scolaire Baie-des-Ha Ha – (RC)
3111, rue Monseigneur-Dufour, La Baie PQ G7B 4H5
418/544-3307; Fax: 418/544-0257 – Dir. gén., Réjean Simard; Prés.e, Liz Gagné
Commission scolaire Baldwin-Cartier
10, boul des Sources, Pointe-Claire PQ H9S 5K8
514/697-6320; Fax: 514/697-5908
(RC)
Dir. gén., France Goulet
Prés., Jacques Mongeau
Commission scolaire de Barraute-Senneterre – (RC)
391, 4e rue ouest, CP 250, Senneterre PQ J0Y 2M0
819/737-2382; Fax: 819/237-2039 – Dir. gén., Suzanne Néron; Prés., Paul Veilleux
Commission scolaire Des Basques – (RC)
9, rue Notre-Dame est, CP 1660, Trois-Pistoles PQ G0L 4K0
418/851-3341; Fax: 418/851-4968 – Dir. gén., Denis Leclerc; Prés.e, Cécile N. Lamarre
Commission scolaire de la Beauce-Abénaquis – RC
#A, 700, Notre-Dame nord, Ste-Marie PQ G6E 2K9
418/387-5960; Fax: 418/387-6885 – Dir. gén., Jacques Ouellet; Prés., Daniel Fecteau
Commission scolaire Beauport – (RC)
643, av du Cénacle, Beauport PQ G1E 1B3
418/666-6015; Fax: 418/666-9783 – Dir. gén., Diane Provencher; Prés.e, Lise C. Harvey
Commission scolaire des Belle-Rivières – (RC)
1900, Place Côté, Québec PQ G1N 3Y5
418/688-7818; Fax: 418/688-4071 – Dir. gén., Chantal Dolbec; Prés., Jean Roy
Commission scolaire de Bersimis – (RC)
#16, 5e av, CP 190, Forestville PQ G0T 1E0
418/587-2235; Fax: 418/587-6104 – Dir. gén., Guy Lemieux; Prés., Donald Perron
Commission scolaire Berthier-Nord-Joli – (RC)
4671, rue Prinicpale, St-Felix-de-Valois PQ J0K 2M0
514/889-5531; Fax: 514/889-8604 – Dir. gén., Jacques Laperrière; Prés., Bernard Lacasse
Commission scolaire Black Lake-Disraëli – (RC)
304, rue Saint-Désiré, Black Lake PQ G6H 1L7
418/423-4281; Fax: 418/423-7300 – Dir. gén., Uriel Rouleau; Prés., Raymond Lemieux
Commission scolaire de Brossard – (RC)
5885, av Auteuil, Brossard PQ J4Z 3P6
514/656-1450; Fax: 514/656-2411 – Dir. gén., Jean-Jacques Maurin; Prés., Réal Hébert
Commission scolaire des Cantons – (RC)
55, rue Court, CP 9000, Granby PQ J2G 9H7
514/372-0221; Fax: 514/372-3150 – Dir. gén., Michel Bilodeau; Prés.e, Viviane Schofield
Commission scolaire Des Cascades-l'Achigan – (RC)
3461, rue Queen, CP 850, Rawdon PQ J0K 1S0
514/834-2591; Fax: 514/834-5495 – Dir. gén., Johanne Paradis; Prés.e, Diane Bernard-Riberdy
Commission scolaire catholique de Sherbrooke
2955, boul de l'Université, Sherbrooke PQ J1K 2Y3
819/822-5534; Fax: 819/822-5631
(RC)
Dir. gén. intérimaire, Jean De Francesco
Prés., Noel Richard
Commission scolaire du Centre de la Mauricie – (RC)
2072, rue Gignac, CP 580, Shawinigan PQ G9N 6V7
819/539-6971; Fax: 819/539-7797 – Dir. gén., Robert Rivard; Prés., Normand Lajoie
Commission scolaire de Chapais-Chibougamau – (RC)
596, 4e rue, Chibougamau PQ G8P 1S3
418/748-7621; Fax: 418/748-2440 – Dir. gén., Léo-Paul Larouche; Prés.e, Clémence Tremblay
Commission scolaire de Charlesbourg – (RC)
7260, boul Cloutier, Charlesbourg PQ G1H 3E8
418/622-7800; Fax: 418/622-7809 – Dir. gén., Cécile Mélançon; Prés.e, Marguerite Dorion

Commission scolaire de Châteauguay – (RC)
184, boul Salaberry nord, Châteauguay PQ J6J 4K9
514/691-5028; Fax: 514/691-9201 – Dir. gén., Maurice Brossard; Prés.e, Marie-Louise Kerneis
Commission scolaire de la Chaudière-Etchemin – (RC)
1925, 118e rue, Saint-Georges-de-Beauce PQ G5Y 7R7
418/226-2503; Fax: 418/228-5549 – Dir. gén., Gilles Lapierre; Prés., Marc-Yvon Poulin
Commission scolaire de Chavigny – (RC)
7175, boul Marion, CP 1804, Trois-Rivières-Ouest PQ G9A 5M4
819/379-2843; Fax: 819/379-5634 – Dir. gén., Richard Théoret; Prés.e, Gaétane Martin
Commission scolaire des Chênes
211, rue St-Édouard, CP 846, Drummondville PQ J2B 6X1
819/478-6700; Fax: 819/478-9166
(RC)
Dir. gén., Monique Bertrand Deslauriers
Prés., Gaétan Mercure
Commission scolaire de Chicoutimi – (RC)
36, rue Jacques-Cartier est, Chicoutimi PQ G7H 1W2
418/698-5068; Fax: 418/698-5262 – Dir. gén., Pierre Tchernof; Prés., Jean-Marie Beaulieu
Commission scolaire Chomedey de Laval
125, boul des Prairies, Laval PQ H7N 2T6
514/662-5601; Fax: 514/662-7040
(RC)
Dir. gén., Luc Mauger
Prés., André Ferron
Commission scolaire des Chutes-de-la-Chaudière – (RC)
1860, 1re rue, St-Romuald PQ G6W 5M6
418/839-0505; Fax: 418/839-0536 – Dir. gén., Bertrand Laroche; Prés., Anicet A. Gagné
Commission scolaire des Chutes-Montmorency – (RC)
2233, av Royale, Beauport PQ G1C 1P3
418/664-1717; Fax: 418/664-1203 – Dir. gén., Roger Boudreau; Prés.e, Jeanne d'Arc Marcoux
Commission scolaire de Coaticook – (RC)
249, rue St-Jean-Baptiste, Coaticook PQ J1A 2J4
819/849-7051; Fax: 819/849-9495 – Dir. gén., Gérard Ruest; Prés., André Lafaille
Commission scolaire de la Côte-du-Sud – (RC)
157, rue Saint-Louis, Montmagny PQ G5V 4N3
418/248-2016; Fax: 418/248-9797 – Dir. gén., Gaston Caron; Prés., Richard Couillard
Commission scolaire Crie
282, rue Principale, Mistissini, CP 1210, Baie-du-Poste PQ G0W 1C0
819/923-2764; Fax: 819/923-2072 – Dir. gén., Gordon Blackned; Prés., Luke MacLeod
Commission scolaire Davignon – (RC)
112, rue John, Cowansville PQ J2K 1X2
514/263-3087; Fax: 514/263-9583 – Dir. gén. intérimaire, Donald Proteau; Prés.e, Ghislaine Delisle
Commission scolaire des Découvreurs – (RC)
945, rue Wolfe, CP 244, Ste-Foy PQ G1V 4E2
418/652-2120; Fax: 418/652-2146 – Dir. gén., Sylvain Blanchette; Prés., Claude Gélinas
Commission Scolaire Deux-Montagnes – (RC)
95, ch Principale, St-Joseph-du-Lac PQ J0N 1M0
514/473-2010; Fax: 514/473-9585 – Dir. gén., Pierre Alary; Prés., Mario Desormiers
Commission scolaire dissidente catholique de Greenfield-Park – (RC)
#280, 899, boul Taschereau, Greenfield-Park PQ J4V 2J2
514/672-7505; Fax: 514/672-4958 – Dir. gén., Denise Benoît-Lussier; Prés., Gilbert Dionne
Commission scolaire dissidente catholique de Portage-du-Fort – (RC)
CP 10, Portage-du-Fort PQ J0X 2T0
819/648-2353; Fax: 819/647-2046 – Dir. gén., Gordon Brennan; Prés., Benedict Tanquay

Commission scolaire dissidente protestante de Baie-Comeau – (Prot.)
39, av Marquette, Baie-Comeau PQ G4Z 1K4
418/296-2832; Fax: 418/296-4883 – Dir. gén., Raymond Haché; Prés., Jaan Kull
Commission scolaire dissidente protestante de Laurentienne – (Prot.)
26, rue Napoléon, Ste-Agathe-des-Monts PQ J8C 1Z3
819/326-2563; Fax: 819/327-7563 – Dir. gén., Augustino Santini; Prés., William S. Pollock
Commission scolaire dissidente protestante de Rouyn – Prot.
218, av Portage, CP 266, Rouyn-Noranda PQ J9X 5C3
819/762-2196 – Prés., Walter Charchuk
Commission scolaire District of Bedford – (Prot.)
CP 20, Cowansville PQ J2K 3H2
514/266-0944; Fax: 514/266-0954 – Dir. gén., James R. Bissel; Prés., Peter Quilliams
Commission scolaire de Dolbeau – (RC)
1950, boul Sacré-Coeur, Dolbeau PQ G8L 2R3
418/276-2032; Fax: 418/276-8819 – Dir. gén., André Perron; Prés.e, Jeannine Caouette
Commission scolaire des Draveurs
225, rue Notre-Dame, Gatineau PQ J8P 1K3
819/663-9221; Fax: 819/663-6176
(RC)
Dir. gén., Jean-Guy Binet
Prés.e, Christine Émond-Lapointe
Commission scolaire Eastern Townships – (Prot.)
257, rue Queen, CP 5004, Lennoxville PQ J1M 2A5
819/821-9570; Fax: 819/821-9586 – Dir. gén., Walter Duszara; Prés., Margaret Paulette
Commission scolaire de l'Eau-Vive – RC
790, boul Quinn, Longueuil PQ J4H 2N5
514/463-2230; Fax: 514/463-2241 – Dir. gén., André Barrette; Prés., Gabriel Ducharme
Commission scolaire Les Écores – (RC)
#210, 3100, boul de la Concorde est, Laval PQ H7E 2B9
514/664-1300; Fax: 514/664-2835 – Dir. gén., Denis Roy; Prés.e, Diane Latour-Gadbois
Commission scolaire des Falaises – (RC)
102, rue Jacques-Cartier, CP 2003, Gaspé PQ G0C 1R0
418/368-3499; Fax: 418/368-6531 – Dir. gén., Carol Paré; Prés., François Tardif
Commission scolaire Fermont – (RC)
130, rue Le Carrefour, CP 190, Fermont PQ G0G 1J0
418/287-5491; Fax: 418/287-3576 – Dir. gén., Diane Fortin; Prés., Jocelyn Caron
Commission scolaire Des Frontières – (RC)
474, rue des Étudiants, CP 99, Pohénégamook PQ G0L 4J0
418/893-5555; Fax: 418/893-2822 – Dir. gén., Serge Pelletier; Prés., Roger Bélanger
Commission scolaire de Le Gardeur
80, rue Jean-Baptiste-Meilleur, Repentigny PQ J6A 6C5
514/581-6411; Fax: 514/581-8199
(RC)
Dir. gén., Thomas Duzyk
Prés., Claude Giguère
Commission scolaire Gaspésie-Les Îles – (Prot.)
40, rue Mont-Sorel, CP 500, New Carlisle PQ G0C 1Z0
418/752-2247; Fax: 418/752-6447 – Dir. gén., Wade Gifford; Prés.e, Audrey Acteson
Commission scolaire du Goéland – (RC)
50, boul Taschereau, La Prairie PQ J5R 4V3
514/444-4484; Fax: 514/659-7131 – Dir. gén., Normand Lapointe; Prés., Jacques Perreault
Commission scolaire du Gouffre – (RC)
50, rue Racine, CP 70, Baie-St-Paul PQ G0A 1B0
418/435-2003; Fax: 418/435-2223 – Dir. gén., Gilles E. Bouchard; Prés., Benoit Simard

Commission scolaire de Grandpré – (RC)
100, rue St-Jacques, Louiseville PQ J5V 1C2
819/228-2771; Fax: 819/228-8570 – Dir. gén., Denis Chrétien; Prés., Michael Marcotte
Commission scolaire de Greater Québec – (Prot.)
2046, ch Saint-Louis, Sillery PQ G1T 1P4
418/688-8621; Fax: 418/682-5891 – Dir. gén., William Pennefather; Prés., Martin Hicks
Commission scolaire Harricana – (RC)
341, rue Principale nord, Amos PQ J9T 2L8
819/732-6561; Fax: 819/732-1623 – Dir. gén., Jean-Marc Matthieu; Prés., Clément Roy
Commission scolaire du Haut St-Maurice – (RC)
445, rue Lacroix, CP 490, La Tuque PQ G9X 3P4
819/523-7582; Fax: 819/523-8554 – Dir. gén., René Piché; Prés.e, Lise Lapointe
Commission scolaire de la Haute Gatineau – (RC)
331, rue du Couvent, Maniwaki PQ J9E 1H5
819/449-7866; Fax: 819/449-6083 – Dir. gén., Louis Pelletier; Prés., Daniel Moreau
Commission scolaire de Huntingdon – (RC)
64, rue Châteauguay, CP 1090, Huntingdon PQ J0S 1H0
514/264-6191; Fax: 514/264-4536 – Dir. gén., Jean Beauchamp; Prés., Normand Demeule
Commission scolaire d'Iberville – (RC)
600, 4e rue, Iberville PQ J2X 3N2
514/347-8556; Fax: 514/347-8388 – Dir. gén., Jean-Pierre Fontaine; Prés., Luc Mercier
Commission scolaire des Îles – (RC)
CP 610, Cap-aux-Meules PQ G0B 1B0
418/986-5511; Fax: 418/986-3552 – Dir. gén., Rosaire Arseneau; Prés.e, Lise Thériault-Duguay
Commission scolaire Des Îlets – (RC)
80, rue de l'Église, Charlesbourg PQ G2N 1C5
418/849-1299; Fax: 418/849-1200 – Dir. gén., Paul-Eugène Roger; Prés., André Caron
Commission scolaire de l'Industrie – (RC)
333, rue Sir-Mathias-Tellier, Joliette PQ J6E 6E6
514/755-7000; Fax: 514/755-7290 – Dir. gén., Michel Ratelle; Prés., Christian Perron
Commission scolaire L'Islet-Sud – (RC)
25, rue Principale, St-Pamphile PQ G0R 3X0
418/356-3361; Fax: 418/356-2811 – Dir. gén., Thérèse Lachance; Prés., Jacques-Yvan Pelletier
Commission scolaire Jacques-Cartier – (RC)
13, rue Saint-Laurent est, 1er étage, Longueuil PQ J4H 4B7
514/670-0730; Fax: 514/670-0250 – Dir. gén., Claude Capistran; Prés., Michel Poulin
Commission scolaire Jean-Chapais – (RC)
325, av Chapleau, CP 1000, St-Pascal PQ G0L 3Y0
418/492-9970; Fax: 418/492-9792 – Dir. gén., Arthur Bouchard; Prés., Claude Langlois
Commission scolaire de Jean-Rivard – (RC)
1783, av Saint-Édouard, Plessisville PQ G6L 2K8
819/362-4400; Fax: 819/362-9157 – Dir. gén., Réal Ouellet; Prés., Michel Bernier
Commission scolaire Jérôme-Le Royer
550, 53e av, Montréal PQ H1A 2T7
514/642-9520; Fax: 514/642-1590
(RC)
Dir. gén., Micheline Sabourin
Prés., Vincenzo Arciresi
Commission scolaire de La Jeune-Lorette – (RC)
184, rue Racine, Loretteville PQ G2B 1E3
418/847-8110; Fax: 418/847-8163 – Dir. gén., Jean-Marie Pépin; Prés.e, Lili Paillé
Commission scolaire de la Jonquière – (RC)
3644, rue St-Jules, CP 1600, Jonquière PQ G7X 7X4
418/542-7551; Fax: 418/542-2407 – Dir. gén., André Garon; Prés.e, Monique Villeneuve
Commission scolaire Kativik
305, av Mimosa, Dorval PQ H9S 3K5
514/636-8120; Fax: 514/636-1261 – Dir. gén., Gilbert Legault; Prés., George Peters
Commission scolaire de La Pocatière – (RC)
1011, 6e av, CP 940, La Pocatière PQ G0R 1Z0

418/856-3690; Fax: 418/856-3232 – Dir. gén., Richard Bernier; Prés., Gaétan Grondin
Commission scolaire du Lac-Mégantic – (RC)
4730, rue Dollard, Lac-Mégantic PQ G6B 1G6
819/583-2351; Fax: 819/583-0624 – Directrice général, Colette Roy Laroche; Prés.e, Suzanne Durivage
Commission scolaire du Lac Saint-Jean – (RC)
350, boul Champlain sud, Alma PQ G8B 5W2
418/669-6000; Fax: 418/669-6016 – Dir. gén., Jean-Claude Lindsay; Prés., Michel Hudon
Commission scolaire Lac-Témiscamingue – (RC)
2, rue Maisonneuve, CP 700, Ville-Marie PQ J0Z 3W0
819/629-2472; Fax: 819/629-2791 – Dir. gén., Rémi Barrette; Prés.e, Doris Roberge
Commission scolaire de Lakeshore – (Prot.)
257, boul Beaconsfield, Beaconsfield PQ H9W 4A5
514/697-2480; Fax: 514/697-5919 – Dir. gén., John Killingbeck; Prés., Marcus Tabachnick
Commission scolaire Laure-Conan – (RC)
350, boul de Comporté, CP 5000, La Malbaie PQ G5A 1T5
418/665-3905; Fax: 418/665-6805 – Dir. gén., Gilbert Dumont; Prés., Pierre Asselin
Commission scolaire Laurentian – (Prot.)
171, rue Mary, Lachute PQ J8H 2C1
514/562-3721; Fax: 514/562-1541 – Dir. gén., Dominic Martini; Prés., Peter Haldimand
Commission scolaire des Laurentides – (RC)
13, rue Saint-Antoine, Ste-Agathe-des-Monts PQ J8C 2C3
819/326-0333; Fax: 819/326-2121 – Dir. gén., Gaétan St-Pierre; Prés., Michel Vallières
Commission scolaire Laurenval – (Prot.)
1105, rue Victor-Morin, Laval PQ H7G 4B8
514/668-4380; Fax: 514/668-3555 – Dir. gén., Scott Conrod; Prés., Ronald G. Edwards
Commission scolaire de Lévis – (RC)
30, Champagnat ouest, Lévis PQ G6V 6P5
418/838-8338; Fax: 418/838-8393 – Dir. gén., Richard Gagnon; Prés., Serge Bouchard
Commission scolaire du Littoral
652, rue Dequer, Sept-Îles PQ G4R 2R5
418/962-5558; Fax: 418/968-2942 – Adm., Mederic O'Brien
Commission scolaire du Long Sault – (RC)
189, rue Mary, Lachute PQ J8H 2C3
514/562-8841; Fax: 514/562-1905 – Dir. gén., Ghislain Levert; Prés., Jacques Sabourin
Commission scolaire de Lotbinière – (RC)
1159, rue Principale, CP 430, St-Agapit PQ G0S 1Z0
418/888-3947; Fax: 418/888-3627 – Dir. gén., Guy Godin; Prés., Alain Lavoie
Commission scolaire de Malartic – (RC)
340, rue La Sarre, CP 4077, Malartic PQ J0Y 1Z0
819/757-3695; Fax: 819/757-6614 – Dir. gén., Robert Paquin; Prés.e, Ginette McFadden
Commission scolaire de Manicouagan – (RC)
771, boul Joliet, Baie-Comeau PQ G5C 1P3
418/589-0813; Fax: 418/589-2711 – Dir. gén., Gilles-Maurice Bouchard; Prés.e, Ginette Côté-Fortin
Commission scolaire des Manoirs – (RC)
775, rue St-Louis, Terrebonne PQ J6W 1J7
514/492-3555; Fax: 514/492-3563 – Dir. gén., Jean-Claude Brisson; Prés.e, Francine Dyon
Commission scolaire de Marieville – (RC)
500, rue Docteur-Poulin, Marieville PQ J3M 1R7
514/460-2181; Fax: 514/460-4683 – Dir. gén., Gilles Roy; Prés.e, Cécile Dubé Marier
Commission scolaire de Matane – (RC)
530, av Saint-Jérôme, Matane PQ G4W 3B5
418/566-2502; Fax: 514/562-4805 – Dir. gén., René Ouellet; Prés.e, Liane Lebrun-Imbeault
Commission scolaire de Memphrémagog – RC
449, rue Percy, Magog PQ J1X 1B5
819/897-1500; Fax: 819/847-3632 – Dir. gén., Lucien Carrier; Prés., Nellie Vandal

Commission scolaire Miguasha – (RC)
24, rue du Centre Civique, CP 330, Carleton PQ G0C 1J0
418/364-3371; Fax: 418/364-7598 – Dir. gén., Gérard Thériault; Prés.e, Roseline Arsenault
Commission scolaire des Mille-Îles
2275, rue Honoré-Mercier, Laval PQ H7L 2T1
514/625-6951; Fax: 514/625-2042
(RC)
Dir. gén., Jocelyne Darveau
Prés.e, Lyne Deschamps
Commission scolaire de La Mitis – (RC)
1624, rue Aubin, Mont-Joli PQ G5H 2R8
418/775-6000; Fax: 418/775-9192 – Dir. gén., Jean-Marie Thibeault; Prés., Bernard Côté
Commission scolaire des Moissons – (RC)
660, rue Ellice, Beauharnois PQ J6N 1Y1
514/429-4671; Fax: 514/429-5046 – Dir. gén., Denis Girard; Prés.e, Francine Daigle
Commission scolaire Mont-Fort – (RC)
1740, rue Roberval, St-Bruno-de-Montarville PQ J3V 3R3
514/441-2919; Fax: 514/441-0838 – Dir. gén., Serge Dubé; Prés., Richard Schiller
Commission scolaire Des Montagnes – (RC)
381, av Principale, Dégelis PQ G5T 1L3
418/853-2226; Fax: 418/853-3778 – Dir. gén., Claude Lavoie; Prés., Guilmont Pelletier
Commission scolaire Morilac – (RC)
65, 1re av, Windsor PQ J1S 2A4
819/845-2761; Fax: 819/845-2571 – Dir. gén., Susan Tremblay; Prés.e, Manon Beaudry-Roberge
Commission scolaire de la Moyenne-Côte-Nord – (RC)
1235, rue de la Digue, CP 940, Havre-St-Pierre PQ G0G 1P0
418/538-3044; Fax: 418/538-3268 – Dir. gén., Yves Thériault; Prés.e, Édith Jomphe
Commission scolaire La Neigette – (RC)
435, av Rouleau, Rimouski PQ G5L 8V4
418/723-5927; Fax: 418/722-1978 – Dir. gén., Jeanne-Paule Berger; Prés., Raymond Tudeau
Commission scolaire de Normandie – (RC)
581, rue Saint-Paul, CP 10, St-Tite PQ G0X 3H0
418/365-5938; Fax: 418/365-3132 – Dir. gén., Jean Lavoie; Prés.e, Martine Duchemin
Commission scolaire de Normandin – (RC)
1013, rue du Centre Sportif, Normandin PQ G8M 4L7
418/274-0000; Fax: 418/274-7183 – Dir. gén., Gaston Plourde; Prés.e, Marlène Tremblay-Potvin
Commission scolaire du Nouveau-Québec – (RC)
7, rue Petite Allée, CP 190, Matagami PQ J0Y 2A0
819/739-4361; Fax: 819/739-4524 – Dir. gén., Bernard Le Régent; Prés.e, Liliane Pronovost Gingras
Commission scolaire de Outaouais-Hull – (RC)
225, rue Saint-Rédempteur, Hull PQ J8X 2T3
819/771-4548; Fax: 819/771-6964 – Dir. gén., René Nadeau; Prés.e, Denise Laferrière
Commission scolaire des Patriotes – (RC)
430, boul Arthur-Sauvé, St. Eustache PQ J7R 6V6
514/974-7000; Fax: 514/974-7718 – Dir. gén., Pierre Leduc; Prés., Claude St-Jacques
Commission scolaire Pierre-Neveu – (RC)
525, De la Madone, Mont-Laurier PQ J9L 1S4
819/623-4310; Fax: 819/623-7979 – Dir. gén., Roger Lapointe; Prés., Gilles Létourneau
Commission scolaire de Pontiac – (RC)
185, rue Principale, CP 520, Fort-Coulonge PQ J0X 1V0
819/683-3483; Fax: 819/683-3808 – Dir. gén., Jean-Louis Brizard; Prés., Roland Vallières
Commission scolaire de Port-Cartier – (RC)
12A, rue Boisvert, Port-Cartier PQ G5B 1W7
418/766-2912; Fax: 418/766-6034 – Dir. gén., Richard Banville; Prés.e, Fatmi Asri
Commission scolaire de Portneuf – (RC)
310, rue de l'Église, Donnacona PQ G0A 1T0

Canadian Almanac & Directory 1997

418/285-2600; Fax: 418/285-2738 – Dir. gén., Russel Gilbert; Prés., Alfred Gauthier
Commission scolaire Prince-Daveluy – (RC)
50, rue Saint-Charles, CP 790, Princeville PQ G0P 1E0
819/364-2074; Fax: 819/364-3508 – Dir. gén., Diane Grandmaitre; Prés.e, Paulette Rancourt
Commission scolaire protestante de Châteauguay Valley – (Prot.)
214, rue McLeod, Châteauguay PQ J6J 2H4
514/691-1440; Fax: 514/691-0643 – Dir. gén., Keith Fitzpatrick; Prés.e, Doreen Newell
Commission scolaire protestante de Greater Seven Islands – (Prot.)
530, av Brochu, Sept-Îles PQ G4R 2X3
418/968-9804; Fax: 418/962-9601 – Dir. gén., J. Kenneth Robertson; Prés., Dave Johnson
Commission scolaire protestante St-Maurice – Prot.
1241, rue Nicolas-Perrot, Trois-Rivières PQ G9A 1C2
418/688-8730; Fax: 418/682-5891 – Dir. gén., William Pennefather; Prés., Raymond MacDonald
Commission scolaire Provençal – (RC)
1730, av du Frère-André, St-Césaire PQ J0L 1T0
514/469-3112; Fax: 514/469-5239 – Dir. gén., Denise Renaud; Prés., Robert Chicoine
Commission scolaire de Quévillon – (RC)
223, Place Quévillon, CP 70, Lebel-sur-Quévillon PQ J0Y 1X0
819/755-4833; Fax: 819/755-4763 – Dir. gén., Laurent Therrien; Prés., Robert Picard
Commission scolaire régionale Eastern Québec – (Prot.)
2046, ch Saint-Louis, Sillery PQ G1T 1P4
418/688-0602; Fax: 418/682-5891 – Dir. gén., William Pennefather; Prés., Peter Marshall
Commission scolaire La Riveraine – RC
1580, boul Port-Royal, Bécancour PQ G0X 2T0
819/233-2757; Fax: 819/233-3300 – Dir. gén., Pâquerette Gagnon; Prés., Robert Boucher
Commission scolaire de Rivière-du-Loup – (RC)
464, rue Lafontaine, CP 910, Rivière-du-Loup PQ G5R 3Z5
418/862-8201; Fax: 418/862-0964 – Dir. gén., Marcien Proulx; Prés., André Thériault
Commission scolaire Des Rivières – (RC)
707, rue Saint-Paul nord, Farnham PQ J2N 2K4
514/293-5358; Fax: 514/293-2731 – Dir. gén., Jean Rivard; Prés.e, Jacqueline Lafrance-Tougas
Commission scolaire Roberval – (RC)
828, boul Saint-Joseph, Roberval PQ G8H 2L5
418/275-4136; Fax: 418/275-6217 – Dir. gén., Julien Guillemette; Prés.e, Pierrette Fortin
Commission scolaire de Rocher-Percé – (RC)
348, La Grande Allée est, CP 400, Grande-Rivière PQ G0C 1V0
418/385-2231; Fax: 418/385-4446 – Dir. gén. intérimaire, Alain Desmeules; Prés., Jean-Pierre Johnson
Commission scolaire Rouyn-Noranda – (RC)
70, rue des Oblats est, CP 908, Rouyn-Noranda PQ J9X 5C9
819/762-8161; Fax: 819/797-5125 – Dir. gén., Yves Charlebois; Prés., Denis Bureau
Commission scolaire de Saguenay – (Prot.)
1770, rue Joule, Jonquière PQ G7S 3B1
418/548-0853; Fax: 418/548-9498 – Dir. gén., William Pennefather; Prés.e, Judy Francis-Fay
Commission scolaire Ste-Croix – (RC)
1100, ch Côte-Vertu, Saint-Laurent PQ H4L 4V1
514/748-6991; Fax: 514/748-7529 – Dir. gén., Pierre Grou; Prés.e, Thérèse LeBrock-Lalonde
Commission scolaire St-Hyacinthe-Val-Monts – RC
2255, av Sainte-Anne, St-Hyacinthe PQ J2S 5H7
514/773-8401; Fax: 514/773-6876 – Dir. gén., Jacques Dupré; Prés.e, Lise Desmarais-Grimard
Commission scolaire St-Jean-sur-Richelieu – (RC)
210, rue Notre-Dame, St-Jean-sur-Richelieu PQ J3B 6N3
514/359-6411; Fax: 514/359-4623 – Dir. gén., Jacques Bédard; Prés.e, June Galipeau
Commission scolaire St-Jérôme – (RC)
995, rue Labelle, St-Jérôme PQ J7Z 5N7
514/436-5040; Fax: 514/436-5277 – Dir. gén., Yves Gaugeon; Prés., Guy Michaud
Commission scolaire de Ste-Thérèse – (RC)
6, rue Tassé, CP 390, Ste-Thérèse PQ J7E 4J6
514/433-4601; Fax: 514/433-4626 – Dir. gén., Jean Poitras; Prés.e, Jeanne d'Arc Duval Paquette
Commission scolaire Samuel-De Champlain – (RC)
41, rue Bellerive, CP 190, Cap-de-la-Madeleine PQ G8T 7W2
819/378-6146; Fax: 819/378-5120 – Dir. gén., André Pelletier; Prés., Yvon Lemire
Commission scolaire La Sapinière – (RC)
308, av Palmer, CP 418, East Angus PQ J0B 1R0
819/832-4953; Fax: 819/832-4863 – Dir. gén., Roger DesBiens; Prés., Yvon Turcotte
Commission scolaire du Sault-Saint-Louis – (RC)
8700, boul Champlain, LaSalle PQ H8P 3H7
514/365-4600; Fax: 514/595-2083 – Dir. gén., Pierre Beauchamp; Prés., Patrick K. Carroll
Commission scolaire Seigneurie – (RC)
378A, rue Papineau, Papineauville PQ J0V 1R0
819/427-6258; Fax: 819/427-8350 – Dir. gén., Marc Anctil; Prés., Jacques Montreuil
Commission scolaire de Sept-Îles – (RC)
30, rue Comeau, Sept-Îles PQ G4R 4N2
418/968-9901; Fax: 418/962-7760 – Dir. gén., Richard Roy; Prés., Gaétan Lavoie
Commission scolaire de Sorel – (RC)
41, av de l'Hôtel-Dieu, Sorel PQ J3P 1L1
514/746-3990; Fax: 514/746-4474 – Dir. gén., Michel Faust; Prés., Denis Rajotte
Commission scolaire South Shore – (Prot.)
6e étage, 6, boul Désaulniers, St-Lambert PQ J4P 1L6
514/672-4010; Fax: 514/465-8809 – Dir. gén., David C. D'Aoust; Prés., E.N. Gould
Commission scolaire de Tadoussac – (RC)
184, rue de l'Église, CP 130, Tadoussac PQ G0T 2A0
418/235-4489; Fax: 418/235-4674 – Dir. gén., Thomas Maher; Prés.e, Luciana Hovington
Commission scolaire Taillon – (RC)
1890, boul Marie, St-Hubert PQ J4T 3R6
514/465-0280; Fax: 514/465-0859 – Dir. gén., Jacquelin Bergeron; Prés.e, Fernande Leblanc-Sénéchal
Commission scolaire de Témiscouata – (RC)
14, rue Vieux-Chemin, Cabano PQ G0L 1E0
418/854-2370; Fax: 418/854-2715 – Dir. gén. intérimaire, Gaston Caron; Prés., Michel Samson
Commission scolaire de Thetford-Mines – (RC)
650, rue Lapierre, Thetford-Mines PQ G6G 7P1
418/338-7801; Fax: 418/338-7845 – Dir. gén., Réal Boucher; Prés., Denis Langlois
Commission scolaire de La Tourelle – (RC)
27, ch du Parc, CP 488, Ste-Anne-des-Monts PQ G0E 2G0
418/763-2206; Fax: 418/763-5533 – Dir. gén., Yvan Landry; Prés., Michel Thibault
Commission scolaire Tracy – (RC)
1015, rue Saint-Pierre, St-Joseph-de-Sorel PQ J3R 1B3
514/743-7991; Fax: 514/743-6907 – Dir. gén., Robert Blanchette; Prés., Jean Cournoyer
Commission scolaire des Trois-Lacs – RC
400, av St-Charles, Vaudreuil PQ J7V 6B1
514/455-9311; Fax: 514/455-0259 – Dir. gén., Jean-Paul Régis; Prés.e, Gaëtane Trempe-Koszegi
Commission scolaire de Trois-Rivières – (RC)
1025, Marguerite-Bourgeois, CP 100, Trois-Rivières PQ G9A 5E7
819/379-6565; Fax: 819/379-3450 – Dir. gén., Jean Sauvageon; Prés., Pierre Tremblay
Commission scolaire Val-Mauricie – (RC)
800, 6e av, Shawinigan-Sud PQ G9P 4E6
819/536-5606; Fax: 819/536-3057 – Dir. gén., Jean-Pierre Hogue; Prés., Jean-Yves Laforest
Commission scolaire de Val d'Or – (RC)
799, boul Forest, Val d'Or PQ J9P 2L4
819/825-4220; Fax: 819/825-5305 – Dir. gén., Adrien Boucher; Prés., Gaétan Gilbert
Commission scolaire Vallée-de-la-Lièvre – (RC)
582, boul Cité des Jeunes, Buckingham PQ J8L 2W2
819/986-8511; Fax: 819/986-9283 – Dir. gén., Réjean Chalifoux; Prés.e, Marthe Bergeron
Commission scolaire Vallée de la Matapédia – (RC)
93, av du Parc, CP 2000, Amqui PQ G0J 1B0
418/629-6223; Fax: 418/629-6280 – Dir. gén., Laval Morin; Prés., Laurent Boudreau
Commission scolaire Vallée-de-Mistassini – (RC)
68, rue Savard, Mistassini PQ G8M 3B9
418/276-5444; Fax: 418/276-8841 – Dir. gén., Claude Dauphinais; Prés., Rémi Rousseau
Commission scolaire de Valleyfield – (RC)
29, rue Fabre, CP 2000, Salaberry-de-Valleyfield PQ J6S 5G3
514/371-1401; Fax: 514/371-4757 – Dir. gén., Michel St-Jacques; Prés., Jacques Derepentigny
Commission scolaire La Vallière – (RC)
1322, boul Sacré-Coeur, CP 7900, St-Félicien PQ G8K 2R4
418/679-3620; Fax: 418/679-3887 – Dir. gén., Roger Guillemette; Prés.e, Ghislaine Dallaire
Commission scolaire de Victoriaville – (RC)
40, boul Bois-Francs nord, CP 40, Victoriaville PQ G6P 6S5
819/758-6453; Fax: 819/758-4925 – Dir. gén., Roger Richard; Prés., Henri-Paul Roux
Commission scolaire de Warwick – (RC)
14, rue Hôtel-de-Ville, Warwick PQ J0A 1M0
819/358-6801; Fax: 819/358-5668 – Dir. gén., André Moreau; Prés.e, Estelle Luneau
Commission scolaire Western Québec – (Prot.)
170, rue Principale, Aylmer PQ J9H 6K1
819/684-2336; Fax: 819/684-9061 – Dir. gén., H.A. Macdonald; Prés., Jerry Barber
Conseil scolaire de l'Île de Montréal
500, boul Crémazie est, Montréal PQ H2P 1E7
514/384-1830; Fax: 514/384-2139 – Dir. gén., Nicole Ranger; Prés., Jacques Mongeau

NATIVE SCHOOLS (FEDERAL)

Schools with enrollment of 50 or more.

École fédérale Notre-Dame-du-Nord, CP 428, Notre-Dame-du-Nord PQ J0Z 3B0 – 819/723-2533 – *88 – Gr. K./Elem.
École indienne de Lorette, 20, rue de l'Ours, Wendake PQ G0A 4V0 – 418/842-3740 – *126 – Gr. K./Elem.
École indienne de Manawan, 150, rue Wapoc, St-Michel-des-Saints PQ J0K 1M0 – 819/971-8817 – *452 – Sec.
École indienne de Natashquan, Natashquan PQ G0G 2E0 – 418/726-3671 – *219 – Gr. K./Elem./Sec.
École Jimmy Sandy Memorial, Secteur Schefferville, 2046, ch Saint-Louis, Sillery PQ G1T 1P4 – 418/688-8730 – *146 – Gr. K./Elem./Sec.
École Johnny-Pilot, 460, rue Évangéline, Sept-Îles PQ G4R 2N5 – 418/968-8225 – *175 – Gr. K./Elem.
École Manikanetish, CP 430, Moisie PQ G0G 2B0 – 418/927-2250 – *87 – Sec.
École Mikwan, RR#4, Amos PQ J9T 3A3 – 819/732-5213
École Olamen, CP 222, La Romaine PQ G0G 1M0 – 418/229-2450 – *216 – Gr. K-12
École Pakuaushipu, CP 68, Saint Augustin PQ G0G 2R0 – 418/947-2729 – *61 – Gr. K-8
École primaire Nussiem et Kapotakam, 4, rue Pulis, CP 70, Betsiamites PQ G0H 1B0 – 418/567-2215 – *317 – Gr. K./Elem.

École primaire de Pointe-Bleue, 403, rue Amishk, Pointe-Bleue PQ G0W 2H0 – 418/275-1243 – *226 – Elem.
École secondaire de Pointe-Bleue, 400, rue Amishk, Pointe-Bleue PQ G0W 2H0 – 418/275-2473 – *61 – Sec.
École secondaire Uashkaikan, 63, rue Messek, Betsiamites PQ G0H 1B0 – 418/567-2271 – *223 – Sec.
École Teuaikan, CP 159, Mingan PQ G0G 1V0 – 418/949-2113
École Tshishteshinu, CP 430, Moisie PQ G0G 2B0 – 418/927-2956 – *152 – Elem.
École Wejgwapniag, CP 1280, Gesgapegiag PQ G0C 1Y0 – 418/759-3422
École de Weymontachie, CP 39, Weymontachie PQ G0X 3R0 – 819/666-2226 – *196 – Gr. K./Elem.
Kahnawake Survival School, Nation Mohawk, CP 1978, Kahnawake PQ J0L 1B0 – 514/682-8831
Kanatamat Tsitipenitamunu, 224, rue Lorraine, CP 1000, Schefferville PQ G0G 2T0 – 418/585-2842 – *170 – Gr. K./Elem./Sec.
Kanesatake Indian School, 681A, Ste-Philomène, RR#1, Oka PQ J0N 1E0 – 514/479-8827
Karonhianonhnha School, CP 100, Kahnawake PQ J0L 1B0 – 514/632-6854
Kateri School, CP 100, Kahnawake PQ J0L 1B0 – 514/632-3350
Kitigan Zibi School, CP 10, Maniwaki PQ J9E 3B3 – 819/449-2848
Rapid Lake School, Parc de la Vérendrye, Lac-Rapide PQ J0W 2C0 – 819/794-1711

CANADIAN FORCES BASE SCHOOLS
École Alexander-Wolff, 17, rue Roy, Courcelette PQ G0A 1R0 – 418/844-5669 – *415
École Alouette, BFC Bagotville, Édifice 116, La Baie PQ G0V 1A0 – 418/693-2352 – *256
École Dollard-des-Ormeaux, 18, rue Ladas, Courcelette PQ G0A 1R0 – 418/844-5633 – *282
St. Michael's School, BFC Montréal, Immeuble 101, St-Hubert PQ J3Y 5T4 – 514/462-7596 – *196

SCHOOLS OPERATED BY THE MINISTÈRE DE LA SANTÉ ET DES SERVICES SOCIAUX (Health & Social Services)
Centre d'accueil La Clairière, 950, rue de Louvain est, Montréal PQ H2M 2E8 – 514/382-6160
Centre d'accueil l'Escale, 4515, rue de la Colline, Cap-Rouge PQ G1Y 3A1 – 418/653-5241 – *50
Centre Marie-Vincent, 840, ch Côte-Vertu, St-Laurent PQ H4L 1Y4 – 514/748-7901 – *22
Centre de Rééducation Boscoville, 10950, boul Perras est, Montréal PQ H1C 1B3 – 514/648-7426 – *46
Centre Rose-Virginie-Pelletier, 9469, boul Gouin ouest, Pierrefonds PQ H8Y 1T2 – 514/685-3200 – *52

SCHOOLS FOR HEARING IMPAIRED STUDENTS
École Orale de Montréal pour les Sourds – Gr. K./Elem.
5851, Upper Lachine Rd., Montréal PQ H4A 2B7
514/488-4946; Fax: 514/488-0802 – Directrice, Agnes H. Phillips

COLLÈGES D'ENSEIGNEMENT GÉNÉRAL ET PROFESSIONNEL (CÉGEP)

With Directeur général.
Cégep de l'Abitibi-Témiscamingue
  425, boul du Collège, CP 1500, Rouyn-Noranda PQ J9X 5E5
  819/762-0931; Fax: 819/762-3815
Cégep Ahuntsic
  9155, rue St-Hubert, Montréal PQ H2M 1Y8
  514/389-5921; Fax: 514/389-5276 – Paul Inchauspé
Cégep d'Alma
  675, boul Auger ouest, Alma PQ G8B 2B7
  418/668-2387; Fax: 418/668-3808 – Louisette Perreault
Cégep André-Laurendeau
  1111, rue Lapierre, LaSalle PQ H8N 2J4
  514/364-3320; Fax: 514/364-7130 – Jean-Yves Bourque
Cégep de Baie-Comeau
  537, boul Blanche, Baie-Comeau PQ G5C 2B2
  418/589-5707; Fax: 418/589-9842 – Jean-Marc Cliche
Cégep Beauce-Appalaches
  #1055, 116e rue, St-Georges PQ G5Y 3G1
  418/228-8896; Fax: 418/228-0562 – Jocelyn Benoît
Cégep de Bois-de-Boulogne
  10555, av de Bois-de-Boulogne, Montréal PQ H4N 1L4
  514/332-3000; Fax: 514/332-5857 – Bernard Lachance
Cégep de Chicoutimi
  534, rue Jacques-Cartier est, Chicoutimi PQ G7H 1Z6
  418/549-9520; Fax: 418/549-1315 – Alex G. Potter
Cégep de Drummondville
  960, rue St-Georges, Drummondville PQ J2C 6A2
  819/478-4671; Fax: 819/474-6859 – Paul G. Lemire
Cégep Édouard-Montpetit
  945, ch de Chambly, Longueuil PQ J4H 3M6
  514/679-2630; Fax: 514/679-5570 – Yves Sanssouci
Cégep François-Xavier-Garneau
  1660, boul de l'Entente, Québec PQ G1S 4S3
  418/688-8310; Fax: 418/681-9384 – Jean Asselin
Cégep de la Gaspésie et des Îles
  96, rue Jacques-Cartier, CP 590, Gaspé PQ G0C 1R0
  418/368-2201; Fax: 418/368-7003 – Jules Bourque
Cégep de Granby-Haute-Yamaska
  50, rue St-Joseph, Granby PQ J2G 9H7
  514/372-6614; Fax: 514/372-6565 – Yvan Vaillancourt
Cégep Joliette-De Lanaudière
  20, rue St-Charles sud, Joliette PQ J6E 4T1
  514/759-1661 – Donald Fortin
Cégep de Jonquière
  2505, rue St-Hubert, Jonquière PQ G7X 7W2
  418/547-2191; Fax: 418/547-3359 – Jacques Vézina
Cégep de La Pocatière
  140, 4e av, La Pocatière PQ G0R 1Z0
  418/856-1525; Fax: 418/856-4913 – Michel Toussaint
Cégep de Lévis-Lauzon
  205, rue Mgr-Ignace-Bourget, Lévis PQ G6V 6Z9
  418/833-5110; Fax: 418/833-3428 – Gaétan Poirier
Cégep de Limoilou
  1300, 8e av, CP 1400, Québec PQ G1K 7H3
  418/647-6600; Fax: 418/647-6798 – Yvon Beaulieu
Cégep Lionel-Groulx
  100, rue Duquet, Ste-Thérèse PQ J7E 3G6
  514/430-3120; Fax: 514/971-7883 – Marie-Hélène Desrosiers
Cégep de Maisonneuve
  3800, rue Sherbrooke est, Montréal PQ H1X 2A2
  514/254-7131; Fax: 514/254-5496 – Pierre Leduc
Cégep Marie-Victorin
  7000, rue Marie-Victorin, Montréal PQ H1G 2J6
  514/325-0150 – Gilles Lépine
Cégep de Matane
  616, av St-Rédempteur, Matane PQ G4W 1L1
  418/562-1240; Fax: 418/566-2115 – Jean-Pierre Clermont
Cégep Montmorency
  475, boul de l'Avenir, Laval PQ H7N 5H9
  514/975-6100 – Michel Brisson
Cégep de l'Outaouais
  333, boul Cité-des-Jeunes, CP 5220, Succ A, Hull PQ J8Y 6M5
  819/770-4012; Fax: 819/770-8167 – Émile Demers
Cégep de la Région de l'Amiante
  671, boul Smith sud, Thetford-Mines PQ G6G 1N1
  418/338-8591; Fax: 418/338-3498 – Vincent Guay
Cégep de Rimouski
  60, rue de l'Évêché ouest, Rimouski PQ G5L 4H6
  418/723-1880; Fax: 418/724-4961 – Alcide Daigneault
Cégep de Rivière-du-Loup
  80, rue Frontenac, Rivière-du-Loup PQ G5R 1R1
  418/862-6903; Fax: 418/862-4959 – Gilles Bacon
Cégep de Rosemont
  6400, 16e av, Montréal PQ H1X 2S9
  514/376-1620; Fax: 514/376-1440 – Réginald Lavertu
Cégep de St-Félicien
  1105, boul Hamel, CP 7300, St-Félicien PQ G8K 2R8
  418/679-5412; Fax: 418/679-8357 – Ghislain Parent
Cégep de Ste-Foy
  2410, ch Ste-Foy, Ste-Foy PQ G1V 1T3
  418/659-6600; Fax: 418/657-3529 – Denys Larose
Cégep de St-Hyacinthe
  3000, rue Boullé, St-Hyacinthe PQ J2S 1H9
  514/773-6800; Fax: 514/773-9971 – Serge Larivière
Cégep St-Jean-sur-Richelieu
  30, boul du Séminaire, CP 1018, St-Jean-sur-Richelieu PQ J3B 7B1
  514/347-5301; Fax: 514/358-9350 – Gilles Perreault
Cégep de St-Jérôme
  455, rue Fournier, St-Jérôme PQ J7Z 4V2
  514/436-1580; Fax: 514/436-1756 – Jean-Denis Asselin
Cégep de Saint-Laurent
  625, av Ste-Croix, Saint-Laurent PQ H4L 3X7
  514/747-6521; Fax: 514/748-1250 – Claude Boily
Cégep de Sept-Îles
  175, rue De La Vérendrye, Sept-Îles PQ G4R 5B7
  418/962-9848 – Octove Deraps
Cégep de Shawinigan
  2263, boul du Collège, CP 610, Shawinigan PQ G9N 6V8
  819/539-6401; Fax: 819/539-8819 – Francine Bonicalzi
Cégep de Sherbrooke
  475, rue Parc, Sherbrooke PQ J1H 5M7
  819/564-6350 – Jocelyn Vallée
Cégep de Sorel-Tracy
  3000, boul de la Mairie, Tracy PQ J3R 5B9
  514/742-6651; Fax: 514/742-0014 – Roland Gaudreau
Cégep de Trois-Rivières
  3500, rue De Courval, CP 97, Trois-Rivières PQ G9A 5E6
  819/376-1721; Fax: 819/376-1026 – Guy Forgues
Cégep de Valleyfield
  169, rue Champlain, Valleyfield PQ J6T 1X6
  514/373-9441; Fax: 514/373-7719 – Jacques Turgeon
Cégep de Victoriaville
  475, rue Notre-Dame est, Victoriaville PQ G6P 4B3
  819/758-6401; Fax: 819/758-0333 – Réjean Fortin
Cégep du Vieux-Montréal
  255, rue Ontario est, Montréal PQ H2X 1X6
  514/982-3437, ext.2162; Fax: 514/982-3400 – Alain Lallier
Champlain Regional College
  1301, boul Portland, CP 5000, Sherbrooke PQ J1H 5N1
  819/564-3637; Fax: 819/564-3639 – Gerald R. Cutting
Dawson College
  3040, rue Sherbrooke ouest, Montréal PQ H3Z 1A4
  514/931-8731; Fax: 514/931-3567 – Patrick Woodsworth
Heritage College
  205, rue Laurier, CP 1757, Hull PQ J8X 4J3
  819/778-2270; Fax: 819/778-7364 – Lawrence Kolesar
John Abbott College
  21275, ch Bord-du-Lac, CP 2000, Ste-Anne-de-Bellevue PQ H9X 3L9
  514/457-6610; Fax: 514/457-4730 – Gerald J. Brown

* indicates enrollment figure.

Vanier College
821, av Ste-Croix, Saint-Laurent PQ H4L 3X9
514/744-7500; Fax: 514/744-7916 – Michael Macchiagodena

UNIVERSITIES

Bishop's University
PO Box 5000, Lennoxville PQ J1M 1Z7
819/822-9600; Fax: 819/822-9661; Email: sboard@admin.ubishops.ca; Telex: 05-836168; Toll Free: 1-800-567-2792; URL: http://www.ubishops.ca
Chancellor, Alex K. Paterson, O.C., O.Q., Q.C.
President of Corporation, Ronald E. Lawless
Vice-President of Corporation, J. Ferrabee, B.A.
Registrar, A. Montgomery, B.A.
Chair, Executive Committee, N. Webster, B.A., O.C.L.
Principal, J.M. Hodder, B.A., M.A.
Vice-Principal, Administration, J.-L. Grégoire, C.M.A.
Director, Athletics, T. Allen, B.A.
Director, Graduate School of Education, W.D. Van Balkom, B.A., Ph.D.
Director, Liaison, D. McBride, B.A.
Director, Admissions, J. Wilson, B.A.
Director, Continuing Education, M. Bandrauk, B.A., M.A.
Director, Development, P. McPhail, B.A., M.A.
Director, Alumni & Public Relations, E.B. Stevenson, B.A.
Manager, Bookstore, D. Mimnaugh

FACULTIES WITH DEANS
Business Administration, W.J. Robson, B.Com., M.B.A.
Humanities, R.W.E. Forrest, B.A., M.A., Ph.D.
Natural Sciences, R.D. Cook, B.Sc., Ph.D.
Social Sciences, F.A. Siddiqui, B.Sc., M.Sc.
Student Affairs, T. Nowers, B.Sc., M.Ed.

Concordia University
1455, boul de Maisonneuve ouest, Montréal PQ H3G 1M8
514/848-2424; Fax: 514/848-3494; URL: http://www.concordia.ca; gopher://gopher.concordia.ca
Loyola Campus, 7141, rue Sherbrooke ouest, Montréal PQ H4B 1R6
Sir George Williams Campus, 1455, boul de Maisonneuve ouest, Montréal PQ H3G 1M8
Chancellor, Eric H. Molson
Chair, Board of Governors, Reginald K. Groome, Q.C.
Rector & Vice-Chancellor, Frederick Lowy
Vice-Rector, Services, Charles Bertrand
Vice-Rector, Academic, Jack Lightstone
Vice-Rector, Institutional Relations, Marcel Danis
University Registrar, Lynne Prendergast
Treasurer, Larry Lauly
Director, Libraries, Roy Bonin
Interim Director, Public Relations, Laurie Zack, Email: laurie@domingo.concordia.ca

FACULTIES WITH DEANS
Arts & Science, Gail Valaskakis
Commerce & Administration, Mohsen Anvari
Engineering & Computer Science, Don Taddeo
Fine Arts, Christopher Jackson
Graduate Studies & Research, Martin Kusy

McGill University
845, rue Sherbrooke ouest, Montréal PQ H3A 2T5
514/398-4455; Fax: 514/514/398-4455; URL: http://www.mcgill.ca
Chancellor, Gretta Chambers, O.Q., B.A.
Chair of Board, Richard Pound, O.C., O.Q., Q.C.
Principal & Vice-Chancellor, Bernard J. Shapiro, B.A., M.A.T., Ed.D.
Vice-Principal, Academic, Tak-Hang Chan, B.Sc., M.A., Ph.D., FCIC, FRSC
Vice-Principal, Administration & Finance, Phyllis Heaphy, C.A.
Vice-Principal, Planning & Computer Services, François Tavenas, Dr.Eng.
Vice-Principal, Research, Pierre R. Bélanger, Ph.D., E.E., S.M., B.Eng.
Secretary General, Victoria Catherine Lees, A.B., M.Phil., Ph.D.
Registrar, J.P. Schuller, B.A.
Director, Admissions, Mariela Johansen
Director, University Relations Office, Kate Williams, B.A., M.A.

FACULTIES WITH DEANS
Agricultural & Environmental Sciences, Buszard Deborah, B.Sc., Ph.D.
Arts, Carman Miller, Ph.D., M.A., B.Ed., B.A.
Director, Centre for Continuing Education, Morty Yalovsky, B.Sc., M.Sc., Ph.D.
Dentistry, James Percy Lund, B.D.S., Ph.D.
Education, A. Edward Wall, B.Ed., M.A., Ph.D.
Engineering, John M. Dealy, B.S., Ch.E., M.F.E., Ph.D.
Graduate Studies & Research, Pierre R. Belanger, Ph.D., E.E., S.M., B.Eng.
Law, Stephen J. Toope, A.B., B.C.L., LL.B., Ph.D.
Management, W.B. Crowston, B.A.Sc., S.M., M.S.C., Ph.D.
Medicine, Abraham Fuks, B.Sc., M.D., C.M.
Music, Richard Lawton, B.Mus., M.Mus.
Religious Studies, D. Runnalls, B.A., B.D., Ph.D.
Science, Alan G. Shaver, B.Sc., Ph.D.

SCHOOLS WITH DIRECTORS
Architecture, Derek Drummond, B.Arch., F.R.A.I.C., O.A.Q., O.A.A.
Communication Sciences & Disorders, Tanya M. Gallagher, B.Sc., M.A., Ph.D.
Computer Science, Luc Devroye
Dietetics & Human Nutrition, Peter Jones, B.Sc., M.Sc., Ph.D.
International Executive Institute, Alistair Duff
Library & Information Studies, J. Andrew Large, B.Sc.A., Ph.D.
Nursing, Laurie Gotlieb, R.N., B.N., M.Sc.(a), Ph.D.
Physical & Occupational Therapy, Sharon Wood-Dauphinée, B.Sc., Dip. Ed., M.S.
Social Work, William Rowe, B.A., M.S.W., D.S.W.
Urban Planning, Jeanne M. Wolfe, B.Sc., M.Sc., M.A.

AFFILIATED THEOLOGICAL COLLEGES
The Montréal Diocesan Theological College, 3473, rue University, Montréal PQ H3A 2A8 – 514/849-3004, 5997 – Principal, A.C. Capon, M.A., B.D.
The Presbyterian College of Montréal, 3495, rue University, Montréal PQ H3A 2A8 – 514/288-5256 – Principal, W.J. Klempa, B.A., M.A., B.D., Ph.D.
The United Theological College of Montréal, 3521, rue University, Montréal PQ H3A 2A9 – 514/849-2042 – Principal, Pierre Goldberger, B.A., B.Sc., L.h., D.E.A.

INCORPORATED COLLEGES
Macdonald College, 21, 111, ch Bord-du-Lac, Ste-Anne-de-Bellevue PQ H9X 1C0 – 514/398-4455 – Vice-Principal, Buszard Deborah, B.Sc., Ph.D.
Royal Victoria College, 3425, rue University, Montréal PQ H3A 2A8 – 514/398-6378

Université Laval
Cité Universitaire, Québec PQ G1K 7P4
418/656-2131; Fax: 418/656-2809; URL: http://www.ulaval.ca/index.html
Recteur, Michel Gervais, 418/656-2695; Fax: 418/656-7917; Email: rec@rec.ulaval.ca
Vice-recteur exécutif, Jacques Racine, Email: vrex@vrex.ulaval.ca
Vice-recteur, services, Benoît Dumais, Email: vrs@vrs.ulaval.ca
Vice-recteur, ressources humaines, Alain Vinet
Vice-recteur, recherche, Denis Gagnon
Vice-recteur, études, Louise Milot
Secrétaire général, Jacques Genest, Email: sg@sg.ulaval.ca
Dir. gén., Premier cycle, Gilles Kirouac
Registraire par intérim, Jacques Loiselle, Email: reg@reg.ulaval.ca
Directeur, Service des communications, Michel Héroux, 418/656-2571; Fax: 418/656-2809; Email: scom@scom.ulaval.ca

FACULTÉS AVEC DOYENS
Architecture, Takashi Nakajima
Arts, François Demers
Droit, André C. Côté
Études supérieures, Dinh N. Nguyen
Foresterie et géomatique, Claude Godbout
Lettres, Jacques Desautels
Médecine, Louis Larochelle
Médecine dentaire, Diane Lachapelle
Philosophie, Jean-Marc Narbonne
Sciences de l'administration, Bernard Garnier
Sciences de l'agriculture et de l'alimentation, André Gosselin
Sciences de l'éducation, Jean-Claude Gagnon
Sciences et de génie, André Cardinal
Sciences sociales, Lise Darveau-Fournier
Théologie, René-Michel Roberge

ÉCOLES AVEC DIRECTEURS
Actuariat, André Prémont
Architecture, Alexis Ligougne
Arts visuels, André Theberge
Directeur par intérim, Langues vivantes, Jean-Louis Tremblay
Musique, Raymond Ringuette
Pharmacie, Gilles Barbeau
Psychologie, Robert Rousseau
Sciences infirmières, Edith Côté
Service social, Lise Tessier

Université de Montréal
CP 6128, Succ Centre-Ville, Montréal PQ H3C 3J7
514/343-6111; Fax: 514/343-2098; Email: bisaillo@ere.umontreal.ca; URL: http://www.umontreal.ca
Recteur, René Simard
Vice-recteur, administration, Patrick A. Molinari
Vice-rectrice, enseignement, Irène Cinq-Mars
Vice-rectrice, affaires publiques, Claire McNicoll
Vice-recteur, recherche & planification, Maurice St-Jacques
Vice-recteur, ressources humaines, Michel Trahan
Secrétaire général, Michel Lespérance
Directeur, finances, André Racette
Registraire, Fernand Boucher

FACULTÉS AVEC DOYENS
Aménagement, Michel Gariépy
Arts et des sciences, Mireille Mathieu
Directeur, Département d'éducation physique, Claude Alain
Droit, Claude Fabien
Directeur, École d'optométrie, Pierre Simonet
Éducation permanente, Jacques Boucher
Études supérieures, Louis Maheu
Médecine, Patrick Vinay
Médecine dentaire, Jean Turgeon
Médecine vétérinaire, Serge Larivière
Musique, Robert Leroux
Pharmacie, Robert Goyer
Sciences de l'éducation, Gisèle Painchaud
Sciences infirmières, Suzanne Kérouac
Théologie, Laval Létourneau

AFFILIATED COLLEGES
École des Hautes Études Commerciales, 5255 av Decelles, Montréal PQ H3T 1V6 – 514/340-6151 – Directeur, Jean-Marie Toulouse
École Polytechnique, CP 6079, Succ Centre-Ville, Montréal PQ H3C 3A7 – 514/340-4724; URL: http://www.polymtl.ca – Directeur, André Bazergui

Université du Québec
2875, boul Laurier, Ste-Foy, Québec PQ G1V 2M3
418/657-3551; Fax: 418/657-2132; URL: http://www.uquebec.ca
Prés., Claude Hamel
Vice-président, administration, Michel Leclerc
Vice-présidente, enseignement et recherche, Paule Leduc
Secrétaire général, Michel Quimper
Directeur, affaires publiques, Guy Reeves

INSTITUTS ET ÉCOLES AFFILIÉS
École Nationale d'Administration publique, 945, av Wolfe, Ste-Foy PQ G1V 3J9 – 418/657-2485 – Dir. gén., Pierre De Celles
École de Technologie Supérieure, 4750, av Henri-Julien, Montréal PQ H2T 2C8 – 514/289-8800 – Dir. gén., Robert-L. Papineau
Institut Armand-Frappier, 531, boul des Prairies, Laval PQ H7V 1B7 – 514/687-5010 – Directeur General, Claude Pichette
Institut National de la Recherche Scientifique (INRS), 2600, boul Laurier, 6e étage, CP 7500, Ste-Foy PQ G1V 4C7 – 418/654-2500; URL: http://www.inrds-urb.uquebec.ca – Directeur, Alain Soucy
Télé-Université, 2600, boul Laurier, 7e étage, CP 10700, Ste-Foy PQ G1V 4V9 – 418/657-2262; Fax: 418/657-2094; URL: http://www.teluq.uquebec.ca/ – Dir. gén., Anne Marrec
Télé-Université (Montréal), 1001, rue Sherbrooke est, 4e étage, Montréal PQ H2X 3M4 – ; Toll Free: 1-800-463-4728

UNIVERSITÉS AFFILIÉS
Université du Québec à Chicoutimi, 555, boul de l'Université, Chicoutimi PQ G7H 2B1 – 418/545-5011; URL: http://www.uqac.uquebec.ca – Recteur, Bernard Angers
Université du Québec à Hull, 170, rue de L'Hôtel-de-Ville, CP 1250, Succ B, Hull PQ J8X 3X7 – 819/595-3900; Toll Free: 1-800-567-1283; URL: http://www.uqah.uquebec.ca/ – Recteur, Francis R. Whyte
Université du Québec à Montréal, CP 8888, Succ Centre-ville, Montréal PQ H3C 3P8 – 514/987-3000; URL: http://www.uqam.ca – Rectrice, Paule Leduc
Université du Québec à Rimouski, 300, Allée des Ursulines, Rimouski PQ G5L 3A1 – 418/723-1986; URL: http://www.uqar.uquebec.ca – Recteur, Pieere Couture
Université du Québec à Trois-Rivières, 3351, boul Des Forges, CP 500, Trois-Rivières PQ G9A 5H7 – 819/376-5011 – Recteur, Jacques Plamondon
Université du Québec en Abitibi-Témiscamingue, 42, Mgr Rhéaume est, Rouyn-Noranda PQ J9X 5E4 – 819/762-0971; URL: http://www.uqat.uquebec.ca/ – Recteur, Jules Arsenault

Université de Sherbrooke
2500, boul de l'Université, Sherbrooke PQ J1K 2R1
819/821-7000
Recteur, Pierre Reid
Vice-recteur, Enseignement, Jean-Pierre Kesteman
Vice-recteur, Administration, Daniel Hade
Vice-recteur, Personnel et Étudiants, Trefflé Michaud
Vice-recteur, Recherche, Alain Caillé
Vice-recteur, Relations Extérieures, Jean Comtois
Secrétaire général, Michel Poirier

FACULTÉS AVEC DOYENS
Administration, John Ingham
Droit, Jean-Guy Bergeron
École de musique, Normand Wener
Éducation, Mario Laforest
Éducation physique et sportive, Johanne Sarrassin
Lettres et sciences humaines, Normand Wener
Médecine, Michel Bureau
Sciences, Pierre-Yves Leduc
Sciences appliquées, Yves Van Hoenacker
Théologie, Éthique et Philosophie, Jean-François Malherbe

SERVICES ET BUREAUX
Registraire intérimaire, Jean-Pierre Bertrand
Directeur intérimaire, Approvisionnement, Denis Viens
Directeur, Appui aux programmes, Denis Marceau
Directeur, Archives, Guy Cloutier
Responsable, Audiovisuel, Benoit Hallée
Directeur intérimaire, Bibliothèques, Michele Beaudoin
Directeur, Centre culturel, Jacques Labrecque
Directeur, Centre sportif, Jean Poirier
Directeur, Communications et soutien institutionnel, Michel Turgeon
Directeur, Coordination, Renald Mercier
Directeur, Équipement, Julien Beaudette
Directrice, Finances, Carole Langlois
Directeur, Informatique, André Croteau
Directeur, Liaison entreprises-Université, Sylvain Desjardins
Directeur, Montérégie, Jean-Louis Martel
Directeur, Personnels, Pierre Lemieux
Directeur, Recherche, Jacques Oliva Bélair
Directeur intérimaire, Services aux étudiants, Jean-Pierre Bertrand
Directeur, Services auxiliaires, Jean-Louis Lareau
Directeur, Système intégré d'information de gestion, Jean-Guy Léveillé

POST-SECONDARY & SPECIALIZED INSTITUTIONS

ACADÉMIE DE L'ENTREPRENEURSHIP QUÉBÉCOIS
#325, 5245, boul Cousineau, St-Hubert PQ J3Y 6G8
514/676-5826

ACADÉMIE INTERNATIONALE DU DESIGN
Mart D-36, Dawson, Place Bonaventure, CP 55, Montréal PQ H5A 1A3
514/875-9777; Fax: 514/875-9297
Managing Director, Larry Gross
President, Doris O'Keefe
Chancellor, Barbara Ann Scott King

ATELIERS DE DANSE MODERNE DE MONTRÉAL
#234, 372, rue Ste-Catherine ouest, Montréal PQ H3B 1A2
514/866-9814

COLLÈGE D'INFORMATIQUE MARSAN
#3200, 1600, rue Berri, Montréal PQ H2L 4E4
514/842-7776

COLLÈGE DE MODE CHÂTELAINE
1705, ch de Canardière, Ste-Foy PQ G1J 2E2
418/660-5242; Fax: 418/660-6268

COLLÈGE DE PHOTOGRAPHIE MARSAN
#3200, 1600, rue Berri, Montréal PQ H2L 4E4
514/842-7776

COLLÈGE TECHNIQUE DE MONTRÉAL
1863, boul René Lévesque ouest, Montréal PQ H3H 1R4
514//932-6444
Director, E. Kefalidis

CONSERVATOIRES DE MUSIQUE
Conservatoire de musique de Chicoutimi, 202, rue Jacques-Cartier est, Chicoutimi PQ G7H 6R8 – 418/549-9560 – Directeur, Jacques Clément
Conservatoire de musique de Hull, 430, boul Alexandre-Taché, Hull PQ J9A 1M7 – 819/772-3283; Fax: 819/772-3346 – Directeur, Yvon Pépin
Conservatoire de musique de Montréal, 100, rue Notre-Dame est, Montréal PQ H2Y 1C1 – 514/873-4031; Fax: 514/873-4601 – Directeur, Albert Grenier
Conservatoire de musique de Québec, 270, rue St-Amable, Québec PQ G1R 5G1 – 418/643-2190; Fax: 418/644-9658 – Directeur, Wilfrand Guillemette
Conservatoire de musique de Rimouski, 22, rue Ste-Marie, CP 1210, Rimouski PQ G5L 8M2 – 418/722-3706; Fax: 418/722-3818 – Directrice, Josée Blackburn
Conservatoire de musique de Trois-Rivières, 587, rue Radisson, CP 1146, Trois-Rivières PQ G9A 5K8 – 819/371-6748; Fax: 819/371-6955 – Directeur, Pierre Normandin
Conservatoire de musique de Val-d'Or, 88, rue Allard, Val-d'Or PQ J9P 2Y1 – 819/825-3585; Fax: 819/825-3297 – Directeur, Gilles Simard

ÉCOLE NATIONALE D'AÉROTECHNIQUE
5555, Place de la Savane, St-Hubert PQ J3Y 5K2
514/678-3560; Fax: 514/678-3240

ÉCOLE NATIONALE DE CIRQUE
417, rue Berri, Montréal PQ H2Y 3E1
514/982-0859; Toll Free: 1-800-267-0859

ÉCOLE NATIONALE DE L'HUMOUR
#310, 3575, boul Saint-Laurent, Montréal PQ H2X 2T7
514/849-7876; Fax: 514/849-3307

ÉCOLE DE RADIO ET D'ÉLOCUTION PROMÉDIA
#700, 1118, rue Ste-Catherine ouest, Montréal PQ H3B 1H5
514/861-8951
P. Dufault

ÉCOLE SUPÉRIEURE DE MUSIQUE
251, rue St-Jean-Baptiste, Nicolet PQ J0G 1E0
819/293-2011
Directeur, Alyne Martin

ÉCOLE VINCENT D'INDY
628, ch de la Côte Ste-Catherine, Outremont PQ H2V 2C5
514/735-5261; Fax: 514/735-5266
Directrice des études musicales, Jocelyne Desjardins-Melanson

IAT
#1400, 2021, rue Union, Montréal PQ H3A 2S9
514/285-4520; Fax: 514/285-1254
Registrar, I. Garand

INSTITUT CARRIÈRE ET DÉVELOPPEMENT
#10, 3, Place Laval, Laval PQ H7G 3S2
514/662-9090
ICD Longueuil, #101, 1111, rue St-Charles ouest, CP 7, Longueuil PQ J4K 5G4 – 514/677-9191
ICD Montréal, #500, 300, Léo-Pariseau, CP 335, Stn Place du Parc, Montréal PQ H2W 2N8
IDC Québec, #200, 900, Place d'Youville, Québec PQ G1R 3P7 – 418/694-0211

INSTITUT DE CRÉATION ARTISTIQUE ET DE RECHERCHE EN INFOGRAPHIE ICARI
#402, 2070, rue Clark, Montréal PQ H2X 2R7
514/982-0922; Email: icari@cam.org

INSTITUT DE FORMATION AUTOCHTONE DE QUÉBEC
225, ch du Chef-Michel-Laveau, Village-des-Hurons PQ G0A 4V0
418/843-6857

INSTITUT D'INFORMATIQUE DE QUÉBEC
#385, 1275, ch Ste-Foy, Québec PQ G1S 4S5
418/687-5801

INSTITUT DE TECHNOLOGIE AGRO-ALIMENTAIRE DE LA POCATIÈRE
401, rue Poirée, La Pocatière PQ G0R 1Z0
418/856-1110; Fax: 418/856-1719

INSTITUT DE TECHNOLOGIE AGRO-ALIMENTAIRE DE ST-HYACINTHE
3230, rue Sicotte, PO Box 70, St-Hyacinthe PQ J2S 7B3
514/778-6504; Fax: 514/778-6536

THE INTERNATIONAL COLLEGE OF SPIRITUAL & PSYCHIC SCIENCES
1974, boul de Maisonneuve ouest, CP 1445, Succ H, Montréal PQ H3G 2N3
514/937-8359; Fax: 514/937-5380
Dean, Dr. Marilyn Zwaig Rossner, Ph.D.

NATIONAL THEATRE SCHOOL OF CANADA/ÉCOLE NATIONALE DE THÉÂTRE DU CANADA
5030, rue St-Denis, Montréal PQ H2J 2L8
514/842-7954; Fax: 514/842-5661
Director General, Monique Mercure, C.C.
Administrative Director, Simon Brault, c.g.a.
Director, Communications & Development, Rachel Martinez
Director, Design Section, Michael Eagan
Director, English Acting & Playwriting Section, Perry Schneiderman
Director, English Technical Section, Norberts Muncs
Director, French Acting & Playwriting Section, André Brassard
Director, French Technical Section, Pierre Phaneuf

TREBAS INSTITUTE
451, rue St-Jean, Montréal PQ H2Y 2R5
514/845-4141
President, David P. Leonard

INDEPENDENT & PRIVATE SCHOOLS

Private schools delivering the official educational program must, according to the Private Education Act, either be declared public interest institutions & recognized for grant purposes or hold a teaching permit. An institution that is recognized for grant purposes is an institution which has not been declared of public interest but which must meet the criteria as defined in the relevant regulations. Public interest institutions & degree granting institutions receive grants as determined annually by the Ministry of Education. The institutions which operate under the Private Schools Act & its regulations receive a teaching permit but are not eligible for grants from the Ministry of Education.

Schools with enrollment of 50 or more, listed alphabetically by city.
Note: "Sec." in Québec is Gr. 7-11
Arthabaska: Collège d'Arthabaska, 905, boul Bois-Francs sud, Arthabaska PQ G6P 5W1 – 819/357-8215; Fax: 819/357-8218 – Directeur, Claude Cloutier – Sec.; Boys
Ayer's Cliff: Collège Notre-Dame des Servites, 580, Route 141, Ayer's Cliff PQ J0B 1C0 – 819/838-4221; Fax: 819/838-4222 – Directeur, Jean-Jacques Marchand – Sec.; Boys
Aylmer: École Montessori de l'Outaouais Inc., 114, rue Principale, Aylmer PQ J9H 3M1 – 819/682-3299 – Directrice, Anne McConnel – Gr. K./Elem.
Baie-Comeau: École secondaire Jean-Paul II, 20, av Ramesay, Baie-Comeau PQ G4Z 1B2 – 418/296-6212; Fax: 418/296-3654 – Directrice, Suzanne Fortin – Sec.
Baie-d'Urfé: Ecole allemande Alexander Von Humbold inc., 216, ch Victoria, Baie-d'Urfé PQ H9X 2H9 – 514/457-2886; Fax: 514/457-2885 – Horst Studte – Gr. K./Elem./Sec.; German
Beauceville: École Jesus-Marie de Beauceville, 670, 9e av de Léry, Beauceville PQ G0S 1A0 – 418/774-3709; Fax: 418/774-3775 – Directrice, Paula Bourque – Sec.
Beauport: École Secondaire François-Bourrin, 50, av des Cascades, Beauport PQ G1E 6B3 – 418/661-6978; Fax: 418/661-4778 – Directrice, Mireille Alexandre – Sec.
Beauport: Pensionnat Saint-Coeur-de-Marie, 30, av des Cascades, Beauport PQ G1E 2J8 – 418/663-0605 – Directrice, Jocelyne Thériault – Elem.
Boucherville: École Les Trois Saisons inc., 80, rue du Puits, Boucherville PQ J4B 4V7 – 514/641-2000; Fax: 514/641-0927 – Directrice, Monique Mathieu – Elem.
Bromptonville: École Secondaire de Bromptonville, 125, rue du Frère-Theode, Bromptonville PQ J0B 1H0 – 819/846-2738; Fax: 819/846-4808 – Directeur, André Choquette – Sec.; Boys
Brossard: Académie Marie-Laurier, 1555, Stravinski, Brossard PQ J4X 2H5 – 514/923-2787; Fax: 514/923-2291 – Directrice, Monique Bergeron – Gr. K./Elem.; Eng./Fr.
Cap-de-la-Madeleine: Val Marie, 88, ch du Passage, Cap-de-la-Madeleine PQ G8T 2M3 – 819/379-8040 – Directrice, Sr Madeleine Lacombe – Gr. K./Elem.
Charlesbourg: Externat St-Jean-Eudes, 650, av du Bourg Royal, Charlesbourg PQ G2L 1M8 – 418/627-1550; Fax: 418/627-0770 – Directeur, Carol Pelletier – Sec.
Châteauguay: Collège Héritage de Châteauguay, 270, boul Youville, Châteauguay PQ J6J 4R6 – 514/692-5578; Fax: 514/692-5579 – Directeur, Richard Lépine – Elem./Sec.
Chicoutimi: École apostolique de Chicoutimi, 913, rue Jacques-Cartier est, Chicoutimi PQ G7H 2A3 – 418/549-3302; Fax: 418/693-8609 – Directrice, Denise Villeneuve – Elem.
Chicoutimi: Lycée du Saguenay Inc., 658, rue Racine est, Chicoutimi PQ G7H 1V1 – 418/543-4448; Fax: 418/543-1716 – Directrice, Irenée Beaulieu – Sec.; Girls
Chicoutimi: Séminaire de Chicoutimi, 679, rue Chabanel, Chicoutimi PQ G7H 1Z7 – 418/549-0190; Fax: 418/549-1524 – Directeur, Marcel Bergeron – Sec.
Chomedey-Laval: École Démosthène, 3730, boul Lévesque ouest, Chomedey-Laval PQ H7V 1E8 – 514/686-8000; Fax: 514/686-2757 – Directeur, Theodore Maniakas – Gr. K./Elem.
Coaticook: College Rivier, 343, rue St-Jacques, Coaticook PQ J1A 2R2 – 819/849-4833; Fax: 819/849-3621 – Directeur, Mario Asselin – Sec.; Girls
Compton: Pensionnat de Compton Inc., 250, route 147 nord, Compton PQ J0B 1L0 – 819/835-9503; Fax: 819/835-9506 – Directeur, Serge Goyette – Elem.
Côte-St-Luc: Académie Hébraïque Inc., 5700, av Kellert, Côte-St-Luc PQ H4W 1T7 – 514/489-5321; Fax: 514/489-8607 – Directrice, Linda Lehrer – Gr. K./Elem./Sec.; Eng./Fr.
Côte-St-Luc: École Yechivat or Torah, #7, 7005, rue Kildare, Côte-St-Luc PQ H4W 1C1 – 514/488-4449; Fax: 514/738-2972 – Directeur, Benot Hanna – Gr. K./Elem.
Dolbeau: Juvénat Saint-Jean (F.I.C.), 200, boul Walberg, Dolbeau PQ G8L 2R2 – 418/276-3340; Fax: 418/276-1757 – Jean-Claude Hould – Sec.
Dollard-des-Ormeaux: Collège de l'Ouest de l'Île Inc., 851, rue Tecumseh, Dollard-des-Ormeaux PQ H9B 2L2 – 514/683-4660; Fax: 514/683-1702 – Directeur, Terry D. Davies – Sec.; Eng./Fr.
Dollard-des-Ormeaux: École Chrétienne Emmanuel, 4698, boul Saint-Jean, Dollard-des-Ormeaux PQ H9H 4S5 – 514/696-6430; Fax: 514/696-3687 – Directeur, Roderick S. Cornell – Gr. K./Elem./Sec.; Eng.
Dollard-des-Ormeaux: École de formation hébraique de la Congrégation Beth Tikvah, 2, prom Hope, Dollard-des-Ormeaux PQ H9A 2V5 – 514/684-6270 – Directeur, Rabbin Zev Lanton – Gr. K./Elem.; Eng./Fr.
Dorval: Queen of Angels Academy, 100, boul Bouchard, Dorval PQ H9S 1A7 – 514/636-0900; Fax: 514/633-8969 – Directrice, Elizabeth Terrien Scanlan – Sec.; Girls; Eng.
Drummondville: Collège St-Bernard, 25, av des Frères, Drummondville PQ J2B 6A2 – 819/478-3330; Fax: 819/478-2582 – Directeur, Rolland Dumais – Sec.
Drummondville: Pensionnat de Drummondville, 235, rue Moisan, Drummondville PQ J2C 1W9 – 819/472-4389; Fax: 819/472-3486 – Directrice, Marielle Cliche – Sec.; Girls
Gatineau: Collège St-Alexandre, 850, rue Principale, Gatineau PQ J8V 1E7 – 819/561-3812; Fax: 819/561-5205 – Directeur, René Martineau – Sec.
Granby: Collège Mont Sacré-Coeur, 210, rue Denison est, Granby PQ J2G 8E3 – 514/372-6882; Fax: 514/372-9219 – Directeur, Frère René Goyette, S.C. – Sec.
Granby: École Présentation de Marie, 232, rue Principale, Granby PQ J2G 2V8 – 514/372-2925; Fax: 514/372-9642 – Directeur, Raynald Jean – Sec.; Girls
Granby: École Secondaire du Verbe Divin, 1021, rue Cowie, Granby PQ J2G 8W8 – 514/378-3469; Fax: 514/378-4566 – Directeur, Pierre Labbé – Sec.
Hull: École Secondaire St-Joseph, 174, rue Notre-Dame, Hull PQ J8X 3T4 – 819/776-3123; Fax: 819/776-0992 – Directrice, Alice Labrie – Sec.; Girls
Iberville: École Secondaire Marcellin-Champagnat, 14, rue Bord-de-l'Eau, Iberville PQ J2X 4J3 – 514/347-5343; Fax: 514/347-2423 – Directeur, Jacques Bélisle – Sec.
Joliette: Académie Antoine Manseau, 20, St-Charles-Borromée sud, Joliette PQ J6E 3Z9 – 514/753-4271; Fax: 514/753-3661 – Directeur, Gilles Émond – Sec.
Joliette: École les Mélèzes, 393, rue de Lanaudière, Joliette PQ J6E 3L9 – 514/752-4433; Fax: 514/752-4337 – Directrice, Sr Thérèse Thibodeau – Gr. K./Elem.; Girls
Kirkland: Académie Kuper, 2, rue Aesop, Kirkland PQ H9H 4K7 – 514/426-3426 – Directrice, Janet H. Perdue – Gr. K./Elem.; Eng.
La Pocatière: Collège de Ste-Anne de la Pocatière, 100, 4e av, La Pocatière PQ G0R 1Z0 – 418/856-3012; Fax: 418/856-5611 – Directeur, Adrien Vaillancourt – Sec.
La Prairie: Collège Jean-de-la-Mennais, 870, ch de St-Jean, La Prairie PQ J5R 2L5 – 514/659-7657; Fax: 514/659-3717 – Directeur, Hervé Lacroix – Sec.
Lachine: Collège Ste-Anne de Lachine, 1250, boul St-Joseph, Lachine PQ H8S 2M8 – 514/637-3571; Fax: 514/637-8906 – Directrice, Jeannine Serres, S.S.A. – Sec.
Lafontaine: Académie Lafontaine Inc., 2171, boul Maurice, Lafontaine PQ J7Z 5V3 – 514/431-3733; Fax: 514/431-7390 – Directeur, Yvon Robert – Gr. K./Elem./Sec.
L'Assomption: Collège de l'Assomption, 270, boul l'Ange-Gardien, L'Assomption PQ J5W 1R7 – 514/589-5621; Fax: 514/589-2910 – Directeur, Normand Therrien – Sec.
Lauzon: École Sainte-Famille (Fraternite St-Pie X) Inc., 10425, boul de la Rive-Sud, Lauzon PQ G6V 7M5 – 418/837-3028; Fax: 418/837-7070 – Directeur, Jacques Emily – Elem./Sec.
Laval: Collège Laval, 275, rue Laval, Laval PQ H7C 1W8 – 514/661-7714; Fax: 514/661-7146 – Directeur, Richard Roy – Sec.; Boys

Laval: École Notre-Dame de Nareg Inc., 2450, rue Rosemère, Laval PQ H7E 2J8 – 514/688-4990; Fax: 514/688-4991 – Directeur, Abbé Paul Kazandjian – Gr. K./Elem.
Lennoxville: Bishop's College School, PO Box 5001, Lennoxville PQ J1M 1Z8 – 819/566-0227; Fax: 819/822-8917 – Director, Nancy J. Layton – Sec.; Eng.
Léry: École alternative la clé des champs de Léry, 200, boul Rene'-Lévesque, Léry PQ J6N 3N6 – 514/699-6802; Fax: 514/699-6802 – Patrick Chaput – Gr. K./Elem./Sec.
Lévis: Collège de Lévis, 9, rue Mgr-Gosselin, Lévis PQ G6V 5K1 – 418/833-1249; Fax: 418/833-1974 – Directeur, Denis Delamarre – Sec.
Lévis: Couvent Notre-Dame-de-Toutes-Grâces, 51, rue Déziel, Lévis PQ G6V 3T7 – 418/833-7691; Fax: 418/833-1843 – Directrice, Jacqueline Bureau – Sec.; Girls
Longueuil: École Secondaire Notre-Dame de Lourdes, 845, ch Tiffin, Longueuil PQ J4P 3G5 – 514/670-4700; Fax: 514/670-2800 – Directrice, Thérèse Messier – Sec.; Girls
Métabetchouan: Services educatifs du Séminaire Marie-Reine-du-Clergé, 110, rang Caron, Métabetchouan PQ G0W 2A0 – 418/349-2816; Fax: 418/349-8055 – Directeur, Serge Tremblay – Sec.
Mont-St-Hilaire: Collège St-Hilaire Inc., 800, rue Rouillard, Mont-St-Hilaire PQ J3G 4S6 – 514/467-7001; Fax: 514/467-9040 – Directeur, André Dufault – Sec.
Montebello: Sedbergh School Association/Association de l'École Sedbergh, Côte Azélie, Montebello PQ J0V 1L0 – 819/423-5523; Fax: 819/423-5769 – Directeur, Duncan Hossack – Elem./Sec.; Eng.
Montréal: Académie Beth Rivkah pour filles, 5001, rue Vézina, Montréal PQ H3W 1C2 – 514/731-3681; Fax: 514/342-4956 – Leib Kramer – Gr. K./Elem./Sec.; Girls
Montréal: L'Académie Centennale, 3641, av Prud'homme, Montréal PQ H4A 3H6 – 514/486-5533; Fax: 514/486-1401 – Directeur, Barry S. Stevens – Sec.; Eng.
Montréal: Académie Kells, 6865, boul Maisonneuve ouest, Montréal PQ H4B 1T1 – 514/485-8565; Fax: 514/485-8505 – Directrice, Irene Woods – Elem./Sec.; Eng./Fr.; Spec. Ed.
Montréal: Académie Michèle-Provost Inc., 1517, av des Pins ouest, Montréal PQ H3G 1B3 – 514/934-0596; Fax: 514/934-2390 – Directrice, Michele Provost – Elem./Sec.
Montréal: Académie Saint-Louis de France, 4430, rue Bélanger est, Montréal PQ H1T 3D1 – 514/725-0340 – Directeur, François Labbé – Gr. K./Elem.
Montréal: Académie Solomon Schechter, 5555, Côte Saint-Luc, Montréal PQ H3X 2C9 – 514/485-0866; Fax: 514/485-2267 – Directrice, Rosa Finestone – Gr. K./Elem.; Eng./Fr.
Montréal: Adventist School of Montreal/École adventiste de Montréal, 2330, West Hill Ave., Montréal PQ H4B 2S3 – 514/486-5092 – Directeur, James Duberry – Elem./Sec.
Montréal: Centre académique Fournier, 1039, av Parc-Georges, Montréal PQ H1H 4Y4 – 514/321-2642; Fax: 514/321-0278 – Marie-Claire Fournier – Elem./Sec./Spec. Ed.
Montréal: Centre de l'enseignement vivant, 4975, rue Amos, Montréal PQ H1G 2X2 – 514/325-8500; Fax: 514/325-2797 – Danielle Sormany – Elem./Spec. Ed.
Montréal: Centre François-Michelle, 10095, rue Meunier, Montréal PQ H3L 2Z1 – 514/381-4418; Fax: 514/381-2895 – Nicole Rheault
Montréal: Centre d'intégration scolaire inc., 2651, boul Crémazie est, Montréal PQ H1Z 2H6 – 514/374-8490; Fax: 514/374-3978 – Jean-Marc Rousseau – Elem./Sec.
Montréal: Clinique pédagogique de Montréal, 11015, rue Tolhurst, Montréal PQ H3L 3A8 – 514/334-2189; Fax: 514/334-4402 – Jean-Claude Giroux – Elem./Sec./Spec. Ed.
Montréal: Collège Ahuntsic, 9155, rue Saint-Hubert, Montréal PQ H2M 1Y8 – 514/389-5921; Fax: 514/389-4554
Montréal: Collège Français (1965) Inc., 185, av Fairmount ouest, Montréal PQ H2T 2M6 – 514/495-2581; Fax: 514/279-5131 – Directeur, Louis Portal – Gr. K./Elem./Sec
Montréal: Collège Jean-de-Brebeuf Inc., 3200, ch Côte Ste-Catherine, Montréal PQ H3T 1C1 – 514/342-9342; Fax: 514/342-0693 – Directeur, Benoit Lauzière – Sec.
Montréal: Collège Jean-Eudes, 3535, boul Rosemont, Montréal PQ H1X 1K7 – 514/376-5740; Fax: 514/376-4325 – Origéne Voisine
Montréal: Collège Mont-Royal, 2165, rue Baldwin, Montréal PQ H1L 5A7 – 514/351-7851; Fax: 514/351-3124 – Directeur, Guy Brulé – Sec.
Montréal: Collège Mont St-Louis, 1700, boul Henri-Bourassa est, Montréal PQ H2C 1J3 – 514/382-1560; Fax: 514/382-5886 – Directeur, Ralph Smith – Sec.
Montréal: Collège de Montréal, 1931, rue Sherbrooke ouest, Montréal PQ H3H 1E3 – 514/933-7397; Fax: 514/933-3225 – Directeur, Jean-Guy Perras – Sec.; Boys
Montréal: Collège Notre-Dame-du-Sacré-Coeur, 3791, ch Reine Marie, Montréal PQ H3V 1A8 – 514/739-3371; Fax: 514/739-4833 – Directeur, Charles Edouard Smith – Sec.
Montréal: Collège Prep International, 7475, rue Sherbrooke ouest, Montréal PQ H4B 1S4 – 514/489-7287; Fax: 514/489-7280 – Ursulene-Mora Farmer – Elem./Sec.; Eng.
Montréal: Collège rabbinique du Canada, 6405, av Westbury, Montréal PQ H3W 2X5 – 514/735-2201 – Directeur, Rabbin Leib Kramer – Gr. K./Elem.
Montréal: Collège Rachel, 310, rue Rachel est, Montréal PQ H2W 1E7 – 514/287-1944; Fax: 514/287-7523 – Directrice, Marie Lachapelle – Sec.
Montréal: Collège Regina Assumpta, 1750, rue Sauriol est, Montréal PQ H2C 1X4 – 514/382-4121; Fax: 514/387-7825 – Directrice, Annette Bellavance – Sec.; Girls
Montréal: Collège St-Jean-Vianney, 12630, boul Gouin est, Montréal PQ H1C 1B9 – 514/648-3821; Fax: 514/648-8401 – Directeur, Roger Bergeron – Sec.
Montréal: Collège Ste-Marcelline, 9155, boul Gouin ouest, Montréal PQ H4K 1C3 – 514/334-9651; Fax: 514/334-0210 – Directrice, Sr Orietta Roda – Gr. K./Elem./Sec.
Montréal: Collège Ville-Marie, 2850, rue Sherbrooke est, Montréal PQ H2K 1H3 – 514/525-2516; Fax: 514/525-7675 – Directeur, Yves Robillard – Sec.
Montréal: École Ali Ibn Abi Talib, 1800, boul René-Lévesque ouest, Montréal PQ H3H 2H2 – 514/251-8753 – Bilai Jundi – Gr. K./Elem.
Montréal: École arménienne Sourp Hagop, 3400, rue Nadon, Montréal PQ H4J 1P5 – 514/332-1373; Fax: 514/332-8303 – Directeur, Hagop Boulgarian – Gr. K./Elem./Sec.
Montréal: École Augustin Roscelli Inc., 11960, boul de l'Acadie, Montréal PQ H3M 2T7 – 514/334-0057; Fax: 514/334-4060 – Directrice, Sr Germaine Castonguay – Gr. K./Elem.
Montréal: École ECS Inc./ECS School Inc., 525, av Mount Pleasant, Montréal PQ H3Y 3H6 – 514/935-6357; Fax: 514/935-1099 – Directrice, Michèle Gorry – Elem./Sec.; Girls; Eng.
Montréal: École au Jardin Bleu Inc., 1690, rue Sauvé est, Montréal PQ H2C 2A8 – 514/388-4949 – Directrice, Nicole Normand – Gr. K./Elem.
Montréal: École Marie-Clarac, 3530, boul Gouin est, Montréal PQ H1H 1B7 – 514/322-1161; Fax: 514/322-4364 – Directrice, Sr Pierre-Anne Mandato – Gr. K./Elem.
Montréal: École Montessori Ville-Marie Inc., 6520, boul Gouin ouest, Montréal PQ H4K 1B2 – 514/747-2232 – Directrice, Claudette Debbane – Gr. K./Elem.
Montréal: École Pasteur, 12345, rue de la Miséricorde, Montréal PQ H4J 2E8 – 514/331-0850; Fax: 514/331-2312 – Directeur, Roger Évrard – Gr. K./Elem./Sec.
Montréal: École Première Mesifta du Canada, 2325, av Ekers, Montréal PQ H3S 1C6 – 514/342-0977; Fax: 514/738-9963 – Directeur, Rabbin Leon Mund – Gr. K./Elem.
Montréal: École primaire de l'Institut Garvey/The Garvey Institute Day School, 2515, rue Delisle, Montréal PQ H3C 2T1 – 514/933-9013 – Director, June A. Bertley – Gr. K./Elem.; Eng.
Montréal: École primaire Socrates, 5757, av Wilderton, Montréal PQ H3S 2K8 – 514/738-2421 – Directrice, Nicole St-Germain – Gr. K./Elem.
Montréal: École Rudolf Steiner de Montréal, 8205, ch Mackle, Montréal PQ H4W 1B1 – 514/481-5686; Fax: 514/481-6935 – Directeur, Serge Langlois – Gr. K./Elem./Sec.
Montréal: École Sacré-Coeur de Montréal, 3635, av Atwater, Montréal PQ H3H 1Y4 – 514/937-2845; Fax: 514/937-8214 – Directrice, Mary Burns – Sec.; Girls; Eng.
Montréal: École St-Georges de Montréal Inc., 3100, The Boulevard, Montréal PQ H3Y 1R9 – 514/937-9289; Fax: 514/933-3621 – Gr. K./Elem./Sec.; Eng.
Montréal: École Saint-Joseph 1985 Inc., 4080, De Lorimier, Montréal PQ H2K 3X7 – 514/526-8288 – Directrice, Lucille Castonguay – Elem.
Montréal: École Secondaire Duval Enr., 9900, av d'Auteuil, Montréal PQ H3L 2K1 – 514/382-6070; Fax: 514/382-7207 – Directeur, Jacques Duval – Sec.
Montréal: Ecole secondaire Jeanne-Normandin, 690, boul Crémazie est, Montréal PQ H2P 1E9 – 514/381-3945; Fax: 514/381-1695 – Laurent Méthot – Sec.
Montréal: École Secondaire Letendre Inc., 9615, rue Papineau, Montréal PQ H2B 1Z6 – 514/389-3513; Fax: 514/385-5545 – Directeur, Renald Larrivée – Sec.
Montréal: École Weston Inc., 5460, rue Connaught, Montréal PQ H4V 1X7 – 514/488-9191; Fax: 514/488-9192 – Directeur, James Heywood – Elem./Sec.; Eng.
Montréal: Les Écoles juives populaires et les Écoles Peretz Inc., 5170, Van Horne, Montréal PQ H3W 1J6 – 514/731-6456; Fax: 514/731-0343 – Gr. K./Elem./Sec.; Eng./Fr.
Montréal: Écoles musulmanes de Montréal, 7445, av Chester, Montréal PQ H4V 1M4 – 514/484-8845; Fax: 514/484-3802 – Directeur, Dr Mohammed Amin – Gr. K./Elem./Sec.
Montréal: Greaves Academy, 2330, av West Hill, Montréal PQ H4B 2S3 – 514/486-5092; Fax: 514/486-0515 – James Duberry – Gr. K./Elem./Sec.; Eng.
Montréal: Institut Reine-Marie, 9300, boul St-Michel, Montréal PQ H1Z 3H1 – 514/382-0484; Fax: 514/858-1401 – Directrice, Johanne Kenyon – Sec.; Girls
Montréal: Lower Canada College, 4090, av Royale, Montréal PQ H4A 2M5 – 514/482-9916; Fax: 514/482-0195 – Directeur, Edmond G. Staunton – Elem./Sec.; Eng./Fr.
Montréal: Loyola High School, 7272, rue Sherbrooke ouest, Montréal PQ H4B 1R6 – 514/486-1101; Fax: 514/486-7266 – Directeur, Leonard G. Altiliaitsch – Sec.; Boys; Eng.
Montréal: Pensionnat Notre-Dame-des-Anges, 5690, boul Rosemont, Montréal PQ H1T 2H2 – 514/254-6447; Fax: 514/254-6261 – Directrice, Sr Réjeanne Paquette – Elem.
Montréal: Priory School Inc., 3120, The Boulevard, Montréal PQ H3Y 1R9 – 514/935-5966 – Directrice, Teresa McConnon – Gr. K./Elem.; Eng.
Montréal: The Study, 3233, The Boulevard, Montréal PQ H3Y 1S4 – 514/935-9352; Fax: 514/935-1721 – Director, Eve Marshall – Gr. K./Elem./Sec.; Eng.

Canadian Almanac & Directory 1997

QUÉBEC — INDEPENDENT & PRIVATE SCHOOLS

Montréal: Talmud Torahs Unis de Montréal Inc., 4840, av Saint-Kevin, Montréal PQ H3W 1P2 – 514/739-2291; Fax: 514/739-3579 – Directrice, Elaine Cohen – Gr. K./Elem./Sec.; Eng./Fr.

Montréal: Trafalgar School for Girls, 3495, rue Simpson, Montréal PQ H3G 2J7 – 514/935-2644; Fax: 514/935-2359 – Director, Geoffrey Dowd – Sec.; Girls; Eng.

Montréal: Villa Maria, 4245, boul Décarie, Montréal PQ H4A 3K4 – 514/484-4950; Fax: 514/484-4492 – Directeur, Sr Arlita Matte – Sec.; Girls; Eng./Fr.

Montréal: Yeshivah Gedola Merkaz Hatorah, 6155, ch Deacon, Montréal PQ H3S 2P4 – 514/735-6611 – Directeur, Rabbin Moshe Glustein – Gr. K./Elem./Sec.; Eng./Fr.

Montréal-Nord: Académie Louis-Pasteur, 11280, rue Jules-Dorion, Montréal-Nord PQ H1G 4W8 – 514/322-6123; Fax: 514/322-6787 – Directeur, Noel Lauzon – Gr. K./Elem.

Montréal-Nord: École élémentaire Marie-Soleil, 12550, boul Lacordaire, Montréal-Nord PQ H1G 4L8 – 514/321-7198 – Directrice, Lise Hade – Gr. K./Elem.

Montréal-Nord: École Michelet Inc., 10550, av Pelletier, Montréal-Nord PQ H1H 3R5 – 514/321-9551; Fax: 514/321-9111 – Directrice, Arlette Spandonide – Elem.

Montréal-Nord: École Secondaire Marie-Victorin, 10748, boul St-Vital, Montréal-Nord PQ H1H 4T3 – 514/322-8111; Fax: 514/322-8112 – Directeur, Gilles Léger – Sec.

Nicolet: Collège Notre-Dame de l'Assomption, 251, rue St-Jean-Baptiste, Nicolet PQ J3T 1X9 – 819/293-2011; Fax: 819/293-2099 – Directrice, Aline Vadnais – Sec.; Girls

Outremont: Centre François-Michelle, 5210, rue Durocher, Outremont PQ H2V 3Y1 – 514/948-6434; Fax: 514/948-6436 – Nicole Rheault – Gr. K./Elem./Sec./Spec. Ed.

Outremont: École Beth Jacob, 1750, av Glendale, Outremont PQ H2V 1B3 – 514/739-3614; Fax: 514/739-0172 – Directeur, Rabbin S. Aisenstark – Gr. Pre./Elem./Sec.; Eng./Fr.

Outremont: École Buissonnière, centre de formation artistique inc., 215, av de l'Épée, Outremont PQ H2V 3T3 – 514/272-4739 – Jacqueline Tremblay – Gr. K./Elem.

Outremont: Ecole communautaire Belz, 1495, av Ducharme, Outremont PQ H2V 1E8 – 514/271-0611; Fax: 514/271-9329 – Ernest Kisner

Outremont: École communautaire Hassidique, 1495, av Ducharme, Outremont PQ H2V 1E2 – 514/271-0611; Fax: 514/271-9329 – Directeur, Ernest Kiszner – Gr. K./Elem/.Elem./Sec.; Eng./Fr.

Outremont: Écoles communautaires Skver, 1235, av Ducharme, Outremont PQ H2V 1E2 – 514/274-8241; Fax: 514/279-3948 – Directeur, Fred Gestetner – Gr. K./Elem./Sec.; Eng./Fr.

Outremont: Externat Mont-Jésus-Marie, 1360, boul Mont-Royal, Outremont PQ H2V 4P3 – 514/272-1035; Fax: 514/272-5908 – Directrice, Lise Bluteau – Gr. K./Elem.

Outremont: Pensionnat du St-Nom-de-Marie, 628, ch Ste-Catherine, Outremont PQ H2V 2C5 – 514/735-5261; Fax: 514/735-5266 – Directrice, Sr Rolande Coderre – Sec.; Girls

Philipsburg: Pensionnat Saint-Jean-Baptiste, 15, route 133, Philipsburg PQ J0J 1N0 – 514/248-7301; Fax: 514/248-7787 – Directrice, Rita Morissette – Elem.; Boys

Pierrefonds: Collège Beaubois, 9509, boul Gouin ouest, Pierrefonds PQ H8Y 1T7 – 514/684-7642; Fax: 514/684-3011 – Directeur, Louis Dion – Gr. K./Elem./Sec.

Pierrefonds: Collège Charlemagne Inc., 5000, rue Pilon, Pierrefonds PQ H9K 1G4 – 514/626-7060; Fax: 514/626-1806 – Directeur, Bernard Laudy – Gr. K./Elem./Sec.

Pierrefonds: École Charles Perrault, 11950, boul Gouin, Pierrefonds PQ H8Z 1V6 – 514/684-5043; Fax: 514/975-2248 – Directeur, Denis Faber – Gr. K./Elem./Sec.

Pointe-aux-Chênes: Séminaire du Sacré-Coeur, 1042, rte 148, Pointe-aux-Chênes PQ J0V 1T0 – 819/242-0957; Fax: 819/242-4089 – Directeur, Richard Dupuis – Sec.; Boys

Québec: Académie St-Louis (Québec), 1500, rue De La Rive-Boisée, Québec PQ G2C 2B3 – 418/845-5121; Fax: 418/845-5244 – Directeur, Jocelyn Lee – Sec.

Québec: Collège Marie-Moisan, 640, 8e av, Québec PQ G1J 3L7 – 418/529-7522; Fax: 418/529-0332 – Directrice, Denise Sauvageau – Sec.; Girls

Québec: Collège Notre-Dame de Bellevue, 1605, ch Ste-Foy, Québec PQ G1S 2P2 – 418/681-7781; Fax: 418/681-1244 – Directrice, Sr Lucille Bedard – Sec.; Girls

Québec: Collège St-Charles-Garnier, 1150, boul René-Lévesque ouest, Québec PQ G1S 1V7 – 418/681-0107; Fax: 418/681-9631 – Directeur, Henri Marineau – Sec.

Québec: École Saint-Joseph, 1090, boul René-Lévesque ouest, Québec PQ G1S 1V5 – 418/527-1072; Fax: 418/526-9346 – Directrice, Sr Claudette Hamel – Gr. K./Elem.

Québec: École des Ursulines de Québec, 4, rue du Parloir, Québec PQ G1R 4S7 – 418/692-2612; Fax: 418/692-1240 – Directeur, Remi Boudreau – Elem./Sec.; Girls

Québec: Externat Saint-Jean-Berchmans, 1160, ch Ste-Foy, Québec PQ G1S 2M4 – 418/687-5871 – Directrice, Sr Colette Gagnon – Elem.

Québec: Institut Saint-Joseph Inc., 550, ch Ste-Foy, Québec PQ G1S 2J5 – 418/688-0736 – Directrice, Sr Jeannine Roy – Gr. K./Elem.

Québec: Pensionnat Saint-Louis-de-Gonzague, 980, rue Richelieu, Québec PQ G1R 1L5 – 418/692-1072 – Directrice, Pierrette Desrochers – Elem.; Boys

Québec: Le Petit Séminaire de Québec, 6, rue de l'Université, Québec PQ G1R 5K2 – 418/694-1020; Fax: 418/694-0803 – Directeur, Louis Bouchard – Sec.

Rawdon: Collège Champagneur, 3713, rue Queen, Rawdon PQ J0K 1S0 – 514/834-5401; Fax: 514/834-6500 – Directeur, Raymond Gravel – Sec.; Boys

Rawdon: École Marie-Anne, 3766, rue Queen, Rawdon PQ J0K 1S0 – 514/834-4668 – Directrice, Carole Lalancette – Gr. K./Elem.

Repentigny: Académie François-Labelle, 1227, rue Notre-Dame, Repentigny PQ J5Y 3H2 – 514/582-2020; Fax: 514/582-9732 – Raymond Girard – Gr. K./Elem.

Repentigny: Centre académique Lanaudière, 930, boul L'Assomption, Repentigny PQ J6A 5H5 – 514/654-5026 – Directrice, Denise Normandin – Gr. K./Elem.

Repentigny: Centre pédagogique Nicolas et Stéphanie inc., 50, rue Thouin, Repentigny PQ J6A 4J4 – 514/585-3001; Fax: 514/585-5050 – Diane Harvey Monette – Gr. K./Elem./Sec./Spec. Ed.

Rigaud: Collège Bourget, 65, rue St-Pierre, Rigaud PQ J0P 1P0 – 514/451-0815; Fax: 514/451-4171 – Directeur, Jean-Marc Saint-Jacques – Elem./Sec.

Rimouski: École Claire-L'Heureux-Dubé, 77, 2e rue ouest, Rimouski PQ G5L 4X3 – 418/724-2511; Fax: 418/724-2524 – Directeur, Marcel Samson – Sec.

Rivière-du-Loup: École Secondaire Notre-Dame, 56, rue St-Henri, Rivière-du-Loup PQ G5R 3Z5 – 418/862-8257; Fax: 418/862-8495 – Directeur, Fernand Chouinard – Sec.

Rock Forest: Collège du Mont-Ste-Anne, 2100, ch Ste-Catherine, Rock Forest PQ J1N 3V5 – 819/823-3003; Fax: 819/569-9636 – Directeur, Andre Bessette – Sec.; Boys

Rosemère: Externat Sacré-Coeur Rosemère, 535, rue Lefrançois, RR#1, Rosemère PQ J7E 4H4 – 514/621-6720; Fax: 514/621-1525 – Directeur, Jacques Lafontaine – Sec.

Rosemont: École Sainte-Anne, 6500, 39e av, Rosemont PQ H1T 2W8 – 514/725-4179; Fax: 514/725-9962 – Directrice, Monique Cloutier – Gr. K./Elem.

Ste-Angèle-de-Laval: École Secondaire Mont-Bénilde, 1325, av des Pensées, Ste-Angèle-de-Laval PQ G0X 2H0 – 819/222-5601; Fax: 819/222-5825 – Directeur, Frère Louis-Paul Lavallée – Sec.

Ste-Anne-de-Beaupré: Séminaire St-Alphonse, 10026, av Royale, Ste-Anne-de-Beaupré PQ G0A 3C0 – 418/827-3744; Fax: 418/827-3745 – Directrice, Nicole Marcotte – Sec.

St-Augustin: Collège St-Augustin, 4950, rue Lionel-Groulx, St-Augustin PQ G3A 1V2 – 418/872-0954; Fax: 418/872-8249 – Directeur, Charles Fournier – Sec.

St-Augustin: Séminaire St-François, 4900, rue St-Félix, St-Augustin PQ G3A 1X3 – 418/872-0611; Fax: 418/872-5845 – Directeur, Père Jean-Marc Boule – Sec.

St-Bruno-de-Montarville: Pensionnat des Sacrés-Coeurs, 1575, ch des Vingt, St-Bruno-de-Montarville PQ J3V 4P6 – 514/653-3681; Fax: 514/653-0816 – Directrice, Louisette Reid – Gr. K./Elem.

St-Bruno-de-Montarville: Séminaire de la Trés Ste-Trinité, 1475, ch des Vingt, St-Bruno-de-Montarville PQ J3V 4P6 – 514/653-2409; Fax: 514/441-4786 – Directeur, Roland Martin – Sec.

Ste-Catherine: Collège Charles-Lemoyne Inc., 3507, boul Marie-Victorin, Ste-Catherine PQ J0L 1E0 – 514/638-1282; Fax: 514/638-5975 – Directeur, Jean-Yves Ferland – Sec.

St-Césaire: Collège de St-Césaire, 1390, rue Notre-Dame, St-Césaire PQ J0L 1T0 – 514/469-3143; Fax: 514/469-5455 – Directrice, Joscelyne Charbonneau – Elem./Sec.

Ste-Foy: Centre psycho-pédagogique de Québec inc., 1000, av Joli-Bois, Ste-Foy PQ G1V 3Z6 – 418/650-1171; Fax: 418/650-1145 – Jean Marieguay – Elem./Sec./Spec. Ed.

Ste-Foy: Collège de Champigny, 1400, rte de l'Aéroport, Ste-Foy PQ G2G 1G6 – 418/872-0508; Fax: 418/872-6266 – Directeur, Henri Piolain – Sec.

Ste-Foy: Collège Marguerite-d'Youville, 2700, ch des Quatres-Bourgeois, Ste-Foy PQ G1V 1X5 – 418/656-9313; Fax: 418/656-9885 – Directrice, Sr Anita Lepage – Sec.; Girls

St-Gabriel-de-Valcartier: École Secondaire Mont St-Sacrement, 200, boul St-Sacrement, St-Gabriel-de-Valcartier PQ G0A 4S0 – 418/844-3771; Fax: 418/844-2517 – Directeur, Jean-Claude Grondin – Sec.

St-Guillaume: Juvénat Saint-Louis-Marie, 96, rue Saint-Jean-Baptiste, St-Guillaume PQ J0C 1L0 – 819/396-2076; Fax: 819/396-3331 – Jean-Pierre Vallée – Sec.

St-Hyacinthe: Collège Antoine-Girouard, 700, rue Girouard est, St-Hyacinthe PQ J2S 2Y2 – 514/773-4334; Fax: 514/773-8011 – Directeur, Roger Gauvin – Sec.

St-Hyacinthe: Collège St-Maurice, 630, rue Girouard ouest, St-Hyacinthe PQ J2S 2Y3 – 514/773-7478; Fax: 514/773-1413 – Directrice, Huguette Seguin – Sec.; Girls

St-Hyacinthe: Ecole secondaire Saint-Joseph de Saint-Hyacinthe, 2875, av Bourdages nord, St-Hyacinthe PQ J2S 5S3 – 514/774-7087; Fax: 514/773-6340 – Michel Lanctot

St-Hyacinthe: La Petite Académie du Boisé Inc., 1090, rue Pratte, St-Hyacinthe PQ J2S 2B6 – 514/771-0644; Fax: 514/773-8011 – Directrice, Sr Estelle Moreau – Gr. K./Elem.

St-Jacques: Institut Esther Blondin, 101, rue Ste-Anne, St-Jacques PQ J0K 2R0 – 514/839-3672; Fax: 514/839-3951 – Directrice, Claudette Forget – Sec.; Girls

St-Lambert: Collège Durocher St-Lambert, 857, prom Riverside, St-Lambert PQ J4P 1C2 – 514/465-7213; Fax: 514/465-0860 – Directrice, Sr. Jocelyne Latreille – Sec.

Canadian Almanac & Directory 1997

St-Laurent: Collège Hillel, 2190, rue Ward, St-Laurent PQ H4M 1T7 – 514/744-9707; Fax: 514/744-9747 – Ruth Bensimhon – Gr. K./Elem./Sec.

Saint-Laurent: École Armen-Québec de l'UGAB, 755, Manoogian, Saint-Laurent PQ H4N 1Z5 – 514/744-5636; Fax: 514/744-2785 – Directeur, Dr Archavin Gundjian – Gr. Pre./Elem./Sec.

Saint-Laurent: École Maimonide, Campus Saint-Laurent, 1900, rue Bourdon, Saint-Laurent PQ H4M 1V1 – 514/744-5300; Fax: 514/331-6311 – Directrice, Lucienne Azoulay – Gr. K./Elem./Sec.

Saint-Laurent: École Peter Hall, 1455, rue Rochon, Saint-Laurent PQ H4L 1W1 – 514/748-6727; Fax: 514/748-5122 – Directeur, Victor P. Elbert – Gr. Pre./Elem./Sec.; Eng./Fr.; Spec. Ed.

St-Laurent: Ecole le Sommet, 1750, rue Deguire, St-Laurent PQ H4L 1M7 – 514/744-2867; Fax: 514/744-6410 – Gloria Cherney – Gr. K./Elem./Sec./Spec. Ed.; Eng.

Saint-Laurent: École Vanguard Québec Ltée, 1150, rue Deguire, Saint-Laurent PQ H4L 1M2 – 514/747-5500; Fax: 514/747-2831 – Directeur, Paul-Émile Cuerrier – Elem./Sec.; Eng./Fr.; Spec. Ed.

St-Léonard: École adventiste de Montréal est, 8885, boul Lacordaire, St-Léonard PQ H1K 2B4 – 514/328-2617; Fax: 514/486-0515 – Robert O.A. Samms – Gr. K./Elem.

St-Michel: Collège Dina Bélanger, 1, rue St-Georges, St-Michel PQ G0R 3S0 – 418/884-2360 – Directrice, Suzanne Dubois – Sec.

St-Romuald: Juvénat Notre-Dame du Saint-Laurent, 30, rue du Juvénal, St-Romuald PQ G6V 6P5 – 418/839-9592; Fax: 418/839-3523 – Omer Tessier – Sec.

Ste-Thérèse: Académie Sainte-Thérèse, 425, Blainville est, Ste-Thérèse PQ J7E 1N7 – 514/434-1130; Fax: 514/434-0010 – Directeur, Jacques About – Elem./Sec.

Sept-Îles: Institut d'Enseignement de Sept-Îles Inc., 737, rue Gamache, Sept-Îles PQ G4R 2J8 – 418/968-9104; Fax: 418/962-8561 – Directeur, Jean-Claude Ruest – Sec.

Shawinigan: Séminaire Ste-Marie, 5655, boul des Hètres, Shawinigan PQ G9N 4V9 – 819/539-5493; Fax: 819/539-1749 – Directeur, Jean Gignac – Sec.

Shawinigan-Sud: Institution Secondaire Montfort, 1805, rang St-Mathieu est, Shawinigan-Sud PQ G9N 6T5 – 819/536-2544; Fax: 819/536-3609 – Directeur, André Roberge – Sec.

Sherbrooke: Collège Mont Notre-Dame de Sherbrooke inc., 114, rue de la Cathédrale, Sherbrooke PQ J1H 4M1 – 819/563-4104; Fax: 819/563-8689 – Directrice, Michelle Drolet – Sec.; Girls

Sherbrooke: Collège du Sacré-Coeur, 155, rue Belvédère nord, Sherbrooke PQ J1H 4A7 – 819/569-9457; Fax: 819/820-0636 – Directeur, Onil Boilard – Sec.; Girls

Sherbrooke: École Plein-Soleil (Association coopérative), 300, rue Montréal, Sherbrooke PQ J1H 1E5 – 819/569-8359 – Directrice, Huguette Larose – Gr. K./Elem.

Sherbrooke: Séminaire Salesien, 135, rue Don Bosco nord, Sherbrooke PQ J1L 1E5 – 819/566-2222; Fax: 819/566-6969 – Directeur, Pierre Duclos – Sec.; Boys

Sherbrooke: Séminaire de Sherbrooke, 195, rue Marquette, CP 790, Sherbrooke PQ J1H 1L6 – 819/563-2050; Fax: 819/562-8261 – Directeur, André Nuyt – Sec.; Boys

Sillery: Collège Jésus-Marie de Sillery, 2047, ch St-Louis, Sillery PQ G1T 1P3 – 418/687-9250; Fax: 418/687-9847 – Directrice, Sr Odile Fortin – Elem./Sec./Girls

Sillery: École Montessori de Québec, 1265, av Du Buisson, Sillery PQ G1T 2C4 – 418/688-7646 – Directeur, Benoit Dubuc – Gr. K./Elem.

Sillery: Séminaire des Pères Maristes, 2315, ch St-Louis, Sillery PQ G1T 1R5 – 418/651-4944; Fax: 418/651-6841 – Directeur, Jean-Claude Trotter – Sec.

* indicates enrollment figure.

Stanstead: Pensionnat des Ursulines de Stanstead, 26, rue Dufferin, Stanstead PQ J0B 3E0 – 819/876-2795; Fax: 819/876-2797 – Directeur, Benoît Larue – Sec.; Girls

Stanstead College, 4, rue Dufferin, Stanstead PQ J0B 3E0 – 819/876-2702; Fax: 819/876-5891 – Directeur, Barry Gallant – Sec.; Eng.

Terrebonne: École Secondaire St-Sacrement, 901, rue St-Louis, Terrebonne PQ J6W 1K1 – 514/471-6615; Fax: 514/471-5904 – Directeur, Yves Lemire – Sec.

Trois-Rivières: Collège Marie-de-l'Incarnation, 725, rue Hart, Trois-Rivières PQ G9A 5S3 – 819/379-3223; Fax: 819/379-3226 – Directeur, Pierre Papillon – Elem./Sec.; Girls

Trois-Rivières: Institut secondaire Keranna, 6205, boul des Chenaux, Trois-Rivières PQ G9A 5S3 – 819/378-4833; Fax: 819/378-2417 – Directrice, Solange Guimond – Sec.; Girls

Trois-Rivières: Séminaire St-Joseph de Trois-Rivières, 858, boul Laviolette, Trois-Rivières PQ G9A 5S3 – 819/376-4459; Fax: 819/378-0607 – Directeur, Pierre Leclerc – Sec.; Boys

Val-Morin: Académie Laurentienne (1986) Inc., 1200, 14e av, Val-Morin PQ J0T 2R0 – 819/322-2913; Fax: 819/322-3466 – Directeur, Laurier Labonté – Elem./Sec.

Varennes: Centre éducatif Chante Plume, 104, Montée Ste-Julie, Varennes PQ J3X 1Z5 – 514/652-6869 – Colette Cardin – Gr. K./Elem.

Varennes: École Secondaire St-Paul de Varennes, 235, rue Ste-Anne, Varennes PQ J3X 1P9 – 514/652-2941; Fax: 514/652-4461 – Directeur, Richard Doyle – Sec.

Victoriaville: Collège Clarétain, 663, boul Gamache, Victoriaville PQ G6P 6R8 – 819/752-4571; Fax: 819/752-4572 – Directeur, Jean-Roch Angé – Sec.; Boys

Waterville: Collège François Delaplace, 365, Compton est, Waterville PQ J0B 3H0 – 819/837-2882; Fax: 819/837-2916 – Directrice, Sr Jocelyne Boulanger – Sec.; Girls

Westmount: École Akiva, 450, rue Kensington, Westmount PQ H3Y 3A2 – 514/939-2430; Fax: 514/939-2432 – Directrice, Frances Levy – Gr. K./Elem.; Eng./Fr.

Westmount: Institut canadien pour le développement neuro-intégratif, 11, av Hillside, Westmount PQ H3Z 1V8 – 514/935-1911; Fax: 514/935-9768 – Darlene Berringer

Westmount: Selwyn House Association, 95, ch Côte-St-Antoine, Westmount PQ H3Y 2H8 – 514/931-9481; Fax: 514/931-6118 – Directeur, William Mitchell – Elem./Sec.; Eng.

Westmount: Villa Ste-Marcelline, 815, av Upper Belmont, Westmount PQ H3Y 1K5 – 514/488-2528; Fax: 514/488-5384 – Directrice, Sr Mathilde Fantone – Gr. K./Elem./Sec.

SCHOOLS OFFERING FRENCH BACCALAURÉAT PROGRAMS

Collège de Marie-France, 4635, ch Queen Mary, Montréal PQ H3W 1W3 – 514/737-1177; Fax: 514/737-0789 – Directeur, Jean-Claude Guidicelli – Gr. K./Elem./Sec.

Collège Stanislas, 780, boul Dollard, Outremont PQ H2V 3G5 – 514/273-9521; Fax: 514/273-3409 – Directeur, Jacques Bourdon – Gr. K./Elem./Sec.

SASKATCHEWAN

Saskatchewan Education
2220 College Ave., Regina SK S4P 3V7
306/787-2280; Fax: 306/787-7392; Email: ENVOY: SK.EDUC

REGIONAL OFFICES IN SASKATCHEWAN

Region One: J. Auburn Bldg., 110 Souris Ave., PO Box 2003, Weyburn SK S4H 2Z9 – 306/848-2431; Fax: 306/848-2455 – Regional Director, Art Scherr

Region Two: 350 Cheadle St. West, Swift Current SK S9H 4G3 – 306/778-8247; Fax: 306/778-8583 – Regional Director, Gary Luke

Region Three: #312, 3085 Albert St., Regina SK S4P 3V7 – 306/787-6075; Fax: 306/787-6139 – Regional Director, Gil Dumelie

Region Four: 122 - 3 Ave. North, 8th Fl., Saskatoon SK S7K 2H6 – 306/933-5028; Fax: 306/933-7469 – Regional Director, Don Sangster

Region Five: 107 Crawford Ave. East, PO Box 6500, Melfort SK S0E 1A0 – 306/752-6166; Fax: 306/752-6168 – Regional Director, Darlene Thompson

Region Six: 1146 - 102 St., North Battleford SK S9A 1E9 – 306/446-7434; Fax: 306/446-7586 – Regional Director, Glenn Wouters

Northern Region: PO Box 5000, La Ronge SK S0J 1L0 – 306/425-4382; Fax: 306/425-4383 – Regional Director, Glenn McKenzie

For detailed departmental listings, see Index: "Education, Depts."

PUBLIC SCHOOL DIVISIONS

Saskatchewan schools are organized as follows: Public School Divisions, Roman Catholic Separate School Divisions, High School Divisions, Comprehensive School Boards.

Under the Education Act, proclaimed 1979, school units & independent school districts became school divisions. All high school districts, with one exception, & all school districts in school units ceased to exist.

The members of school divisions are elected under the Local Government Elections Act for a term of three years on the fourth Wednesday in October. For divisions situated wholly or in part within a town or city, elections are conducted by the town or city clerk. Elections in the other divisions are conducted by a returning officer who is the secretary-treasurer.

The members of comprehensive school boards are not elected, but are appointed from other school boards.

Divisions with an enrollment of more than 10,000 are in bold print.

Arcola School Division #72 – *1,591
PO Box 327, Arcola SK S0C 0G0
306/455-2377; Fax: 306/455-2767 – Dir., Thomas E. Chell; Sec.-Treas., Huguette P. Lutz

Battle River School Division #60 – *1,540
5017 - 46th St., PO Box 827, Lloydminster SK S9V 1C2
403/825-2828; Fax: 403/875-7829 – Supt. of Adm., Walter Hardy; Dir., K. Stuart Keys

Battleford School Division #58 – *1,203
122 - 23 St., PO Box 460, Battleford SK S0M 0E0
306/937-7702; Fax: 306/937-7721 – Supt. of Adm., Kenneth R. Tebb; Dir., Barry Werth

Biggar School Division #50 – *974
119 Main St., PO Box 310, Biggar SK S0K 0M0
306/948-3348; Fax: 306/948-2005 – Dir., R.B. Arnold; Sec.-Treas., Don R. Cleaveley

Blaine Lake School Division #57 – *602
207 - 2 Ave. West, PO Box 400, Blaine Lake SK S0J 0J0
306/497-2626; Fax: 306/497-3151 – Dir., Glen Penner; Sec.-Treas., Phil J. Weimer

Borderland School Division #68 – *1,087
205 Railway Ave., PO Box 89, Rockglen SK S0H 3R0
306/476-2101; Fax: 306/476-2414 – Dir., Ed. I. Stelmaschuk; Sec.-Treas., Wilfred Hotsko

Broadview School Division #18 – *1,142
PO Box 130, Broadview SK S0G 0K0

Canadian Almanac & Directory 1997

9-52 SASKATCHEWAN — PUBLIC SCHOOL DIVISIONS

306/696-2566; Fax: 306/696-3267 – Supt. of Adm., Maurice J. Lemieux; Dir., Dexter D. Samida
Buffalo Plains School Division #21 – *3,020
3080 Albert St. North, PO Box 1937, Regina SK S4P 3E1
306/949-3366; Fax: 306/543-1771 – Dir., Jim Hopson; Sec.-Treas., Bruce W. Lipinski
Canora School Division #37 – *766
140 - 1 Ave. West, PO Box 869, Canora SK S0A 0L0
306/563-5562; Fax: 306/563-5295 – Dir., Gerry Joynt; Sec.-Treas., Janice Chicilo
Centennial Park School Board – *25
#161, 1791 - 110 St., North Battleford SK S9A 3E7
306/445-3827; Fax: 306/445-4332 – Supt. of Adm., Jim Gondziola; Dir., Merv F. Grosse
Conseils Scolaires Fransaskois
216, 514 Victoria Ave. East, Regina SK S4N 0N7
306/757-7541; Fax: 306/757-2040 – Dir., Florent Bilodeau; Sec. Treas., Gilbert Hautcoeur
Conseils Scolaires Fransaskois
2213 East Hanselman Court, Saskatoon SK S7L 6A8
306/653-8490; Fax: 306/653-8495 – Dir., André Moquin; Sec.-Treas, Lise Garneau
Creighton School Division #111 – *440
325 Main St., PO Box 158, Creighton SK S0P 0A0
306/688-5825; Fax: 306/688-3131 – Dir., Don Smith; Sec.-Treas., Virginia R. Hamm
Cupar School Division #28 – *1,207
708 Qu'Appelle Ave., PO Box 250, Cupar SK S0G 0Y0
306/723-4404; Fax: 306/723-4354 – Dir., Wayne Dahlgren; Sec.-Treas., Gary P. Kreklewich
Davidson School Division #31 – *942
PO Box 696, Davidson SK S0G 1A0
306/567-2811, 2812; Fax: 306/567-2878 – Dir., Christine Boyczuk; Sec.-Treas., Jeff D. Alexander
Deer Park School Division #26 – *381
633 Main St., PO Box 1930, Melville SK S0A 2P0
306/728-4426; Fax: 306/728-2351 – Dir., A.A. (Tony) Wihlidal; Sec.-Treas., Gordon Majeran
Eastend School Division #8 – *636
427 Redcoat Dr., PO Box 550, Eastend SK S0N 0T0
306/295-3771; Fax: 306/295-3703 – Dir. (Interim), Lynne Hepfner; Sec.-Treas., Louise Wanlin
Estevan Comprehensive High School Board – *863
130 King St., Estevan SK S4A 2T5
306/634-4777; Fax: 306/634-6768 – Dir., Larry E. Steeves; Sec.-Treas., Glen G. Bell
Estevan Rural School Division #62 – *1,107
130 King St., PO Box 1600, Estevan SK S4A 2L7
306/634-4741; Fax: 306/634-6768 – Dir., J. Ellery Peters; Sec.-Treas., Glen G. Bell
Estevan School Division #95 – *1,097
130 King St., Estevan SK S4A 2T5
306/634-4777; Fax: 306/634-6768 – Dir., Larry E. Steeves; Sec.-Treas., Glen G. Bell
Eston-Elrose School Division #33 – *1,012
220 - 4th Ave. East, PO Box 430, Elrose SK S0L 0Z0
306/378-2522; Fax: 306/378-4133 – Dir., James D. Gunningham; Sec.-Treas., Rhonda Saathoff
Glenn McGuire School Board – *11
874 Prospect, PO Box 509, Oxbow SK S0C 2B0
306/483-2964; Fax: 306/483-5230 – Dir., Thomas E. Chell; Sec.-Treas., Huguette Lutz
Grand Coulee School Division #110 – *97
RR#2, Site #200, PO Box 65, Regina SK S4P 2Z2
306/757-2051; Fax: 306/757-1944 – Dir., Helen Horsman; Sec., Judith Vallance; Treas., Les Barrett
Gravelbourg School Division #109 – *395
Elementary School Bldg., PO Box 748, Gravelbourg SK S0H 1X0
306/648-3229; Fax: 306/684-2269 – Dir., Marion Piche; Sec.-Treas., Ray Perzan
Gray School Division #101 – *11
PO Box 38, Gray SK S0G 2A0
306/569-1234 – Dir., Helen Horsman; Sec.-Treas., Ried Mossing
Gull Lake School Division #76 – *636

PO Box 30, Gull Lake SK S0N 1A0
306/672-3515; Fax: 306/672-3267 – Supt. of Adm., Robert V. Francis; Dir., Cliff Chutskoff
Herbert School Division #79 – *955
501 Herbert Ave., PO Box 100, Herbert SK S0H 2A0
306/784-2433; Fax: 306/784-3565 – Dir., J. Timothy Peake; Sec.-Treas., Joanne P. Dales
Hudson Bay School Division #52 – *1,252
210 Main St., PO Box 579, Hudson Bay SK S0E 0Y0
306/865-2444, 3163; Fax: 306/865-2128 – Dir., Glen Holmwood; Sec.-Treas., Dora J. Thack
Humboldt High School Division – *356
14th Ave., PO Box 780, Humboldt SK S0K 2A0
306/682-5659; Fax: 306/682-3239 – Dir., Gene Pulak; Sec.-Treas., Fred W. Saliken
Humboldt Rural School Division #47 – *1,363
Hwy. 5 East, PO Box 40, Humboldt SK S0K 2A0
306/682-2558; Fax: 306/682-5154 – Dir., Murray Huck; Sec.-Treas., Mona Johns
Humboldt School Division #104 – *219
14th Ave., PO Box 780, Humboldt SK S0K 2A0
306/682-5659; Fax: 306/682-3239 – Dir., Gene Pulak; Sec.-Treas., Fred W. Saliken
Ile a la Crosse School Division #112 – *472
PO Box 89, Ile a la Crosse SK S0M 1C0
306/833-2141; Fax: 306/833-2104 – Dir., William J. Duffee, 306/752-2390; Sec.-Treas., Wanda Chaboyer
Indian Head School Division #19 – *1,731
708 Otterloo St., PO Box 639, Indian Head SK S0G 2K0
306/695-2208; Fax: 306/695-2541 – Dir., Michael R. Fulton; Sec.-Treas., Gerald Meyer
Kamsack School Division #35 – *843
431 - 3 St., PO Box 339, Kamsack SK S0A 1S0
306/542-2511; Fax: 306/542-2832 – Dir., Wes Prosser; Sec.-Treas., Janet Patterson
Kerrobert School Division #44 – *1,290
433 Manitoba Ave., PO Box 470, Kerrobert SK S0L 1R0
306/834-2624; Fax: 306/834-2210 – Dir., Harvey Morissette; Sec.-Treas., Gloria Bahm
Kindersley School Division #34 – *1,886
112 - 5 Ave., PO Box 1209, Kindersley SK S0L 1S0
306/463-4657; Fax: 306/463-3077 – Dir., Ken Moore; Sec.-Treas., Dianne Gordon
Kinistino School Division #55 – *829
PO Box 549, Kinistino SK S0J 1H0
306/864-2404; Fax: 306/864-2889 – Dir., Ken Passler; Sec.-Treas., Dennis A. Moniuk
Lanigan School Division #40 – *1,014
110 Main St., PO Box 100, Lanigan SK S0K 2M0
306/365-2015; Fax: 306/365-2808 – Dir., Lance M. Macsymic; Sec.-Treas., Joan Adams
Last Mountain School Division #29 – *1,416
PO Box 10, Govan SK S0G 1Z0
306/484-2060; Fax: 306/484-2000 – Dir. (Interim), Ernie Dawson; Sec.-Treas., Marrion Wolff
Leader School Division #24 – *752
106 - 3rd St. West, PO Box 420, Leader SK S0N 1H0
306/628-3881; Fax: 306/628-4403 – Dir., Ernest Sweeney; Sec.-Treas., Darlene Fitterer
Lloydminster School Division – *1,420
5017 - 46 St., Lloydminster SK T9V 1R4
403/875-5541; Fax: 403/875-7829 – Dir., Dr. Donald B. Duncan; Treas., Beverley Henry
Long Lake School Division #30 – *1,158
116 Main St., PO Box 520, Watrous SK S0K 4T0
306/946-3332; Fax: 306/946-3442 – Dir., Ralph Eliasson; Sec.-Treas., Phil J. Benson
Maple Creek School Division #17 – *1,0467
217 Marsh St., PO Box 400, Maple Creek SK S0N 1N0
306/662-2424, 2892; Fax: 306/662-3173 – Dir., Ed Bath; Sec.-Treas., Beverley A. Drader
Meadow Lake School Division #66 – *2,675
606 - 5th Ave. West, Meadow Lake SK S9X 1A9

306/236-5614; Fax: 306/236-3922 – Dir., Larry Zemlak; Sec.-Treas., Marilyn Y. Wiklund
Melfort School Division #100 – *1,176
113 Burrows West, PO Box 6000, Melfort SK S0E 1A0
306/752-5741; Fax: 306/752-4347 – Dir., Bob Kroeker; Sec.-Treas., Raymond Kopera
Melville Compehensive School Board – *495
633 Main St., PO Box 1930, Melville SK S0A 2P0
306/728-4426; Fax: 306/728-2351 – Dir., A.A. (Tony) Wihlidal; Sec.-Treas., Gordon Majeran
Melville School Division #108 – *399
633 Main St., PO Box 1930, Melville SK S0A 2P0
306/728-4426; Fax: 306/728-2351 – Dir., A.A. (Tony) Wihlidal; Sec.-Treas., Gordon Majeran
Moose Jaw School Division #1 – *5,016
1075 - 9 Ave. NW, Moose Jaw SK S6H 4J6
306/693-4631; Fax: 306/694-4686 – Dir., Larry T. Booth; Sec.-Treas., James N. Trites
Moosomin School Division #9 – *1,298
1103 Broadway Ave. East, PO Box 700, Moosomin SK S0G 3N0
306/435-3389; Fax: 306/435-2331 – Dir., David B Steele; Sec.-Treas., Laurel St. Onge
Nipawin School Division #61 – *2,155
214 - 1 St. West, PO Box 2044, Nipawin SK S0E 1E0
306/862-4616; Fax: 306/862-9733 – Dir., Gary L. Broker; Sec.-Treas., Len J. Skulmoski
North Battleford School Division #103 – *2,131
#161, 1791 - 110 St., North Battleford SK S9A 3E7
306/445-3827; Fax: 306/445-4332 – Dir., Merv F. Grosse; Sec.-Treas., Jim Gondziola
Northern Lakes School Division #64 – *1,171
116 - First St. East, PO Box 669, Spiritwood SK S0J 2M0
306/883-2424; Fax: 306/883-2415 – Dir., Dennis Tetu; Sec.-Treas., Carol Boechler
Northern Lights School Division #113 – *4,489
Bag Services #6500, La Ronge SK S0J 1L0
306/425-3302; Fax: 306/425-3377 – Dir., Dennis Lokinger; Sec.-Treas., Linda Chapman
Outlook School Division #32 – *1,289
305 Saskatchewan Ave. West, PO Box 280, Outlook SK S0L 2N0
306/867-8622; Fax: 306/867-9999 – Dir., Ivan Yackel; Sec.-Treas., Darrel Guy
Oxbow School Division #51 – *1,101
874 Prospect, PO Box 509, Oxbow SK S0C 2B0
306/483-2964; Fax: 306/483-5230 – Dir., Thomas E. Chell; Sec.-Treas., Huguette Lutz
Parkland School Division #63 – *1,670
PO Box 100, Shellbrook SK S0J 2E0
306/747-2611; Fax: 306/747-2618 – Dir., David Thomson; Sec.-Treas., Robert L. Dows
Paynton School Division #102 – *51
123 Railway Ave., PO Box 100, Paynton SK S0M 2J0
306/895-2045; Fax: 306/895-2046 – Dir., Eugene Thera; Sec.-Treas., Garth Merryweather
Pense School Division #98 – *137
PO Box 122, Pense SK S0G 3W0
306/345-2261 – Dir., Helen Horsman; Sec.-Treas., Carol Seaberly
Potashville School Division #80 – *1,796
PO Box 700, Esterhazy SK S0A 0X0
306/745-6641; Fax: 306/745-6549 – Supt. of Adm., Ed M. Boyechko; Dir., Lawrence Chomos
Prairie View School Division #74 – *914
232 Main St., PO Box 60, Milestone SK S0G 3L0
306/436-2160; Fax: 306/436-2128 – Dir., Merv S. Renz; Sec.-Treas., Raymond P. Trew
Prairie West School Division #75 – *973
110 - 11 Ave. NW, Swift Current SK S9H 1B8
306/773-9358; Fax: 306/778-2668 – Dir., Kenneth Ladouceur; Sec.-Treas., Vince Gaudet
Prince Albert Comprehensive High School Board – *1,570
545 - 11 St. East, Prince Albert SK S6V 1B1

Canadian Almanac & Directory 1997

306/764-1571; Fax: 306/763-4460 – Dir., Shirley Gange; Sec.-Treas., Dennis A. Moniuk
Prince Albert Rural School Division #56 – *1,822
1308 - 5 Ave. East, Prince Albert SK S6V 2H7
306/764-1511; Fax: 306/763-4072 – Dir., Gordon Rutten; Sec.-Treas., Wayne Kabatoff
Prince Albert School Division #3 – *4,042
545 - 11 St. East, Prince Albert SK S6V 1B1
306/764-1571; Fax: 306/763-4460 – Dir., Shirley Gange; Sec.-Treas., Dennis A. Moniuk
Radville School Division #67 – *507
420 Floren St., PO Box 189, Radville SK S0C 2G0
306/869-2525, 2282; Fax: 306/869-2733 – Dir., Bob Demencuik; Sec.-Treas., Marlene Pilsner
Red Coat Trail School Division #69 – *1,154
500 - 1 Ave. East, PO Box 1330, Assiniboia SK S0H 0B0
306/642-3341; Fax: 306/642-3455 – Dir., Edward H. Maksymiw; Sec.-Treas., Arthur J. Warnecke
Regina (East) School Division #77 – *1,134
424 Railway Ave., PO Box 128, Odessa SK S0G 3S0
306/957-2172; Fax: 306/957-2073 – Supt. of Adm., Don L. Pearson; Dir., R.V. Mokelky
Regina School Division #4
1600 - 4 Ave., Regina SK S4R 8C8
306/791-8200; Fax: 306/352-2898
*24,226
Dir., Larry Huber
Sec.-Treas., Debra Burnett
Rosetown School Division #43 – *1,417
501 First St. West, PO Box 700, Rosetown SK S0L 2V0
306/882-2677; Fax: 306/882-3366 – Dir., John Ulsifer; Sec.-Treas., Maureen Sample
Saskatchewan Valley School Division #49 – *4,225
121 Klassen St. East, PO Box 809, Warman SK S0K 4S0
306/933-4414; Fax: 306/934-8221 – Dir., Michael James McLeod; Sec.-Treas., Keith R. Kraft
Saskatoon (East) School Division #41 – *1,965
620 Heritage Lane, Saskatoon SK S7H 5P5
306/374-2433; Fax: 306/955-0806 – Dir., Norman Dray; Sec.-Treas., James R. Shields
Saskatoon (West) School Division #42 – *2,605
1359 Fletcher Rd., Saskatoon SK S7M 5H5
306/664-0010; Fax: 306/664-0020 – Dir., Brian Keegan; Sec.-Treas., Ronald W. Walter
Saskatoon School Division #13
405 - 3 Ave. South, Saskatoon SK S7K 1M7
306/683-8200; Fax: 306/683-8207
*22,604
Dir., Pat Dickson
Sec.-Treas., Ralph Paquin
Scenic Valley School Division #117 – *1,191
PO Box 100, Neudorf SK S0A 2T0
306/748-2523; Fax: 306/748-2753 – Dir., Lynne Saas; Sec.-Treas., Sharon Bender
Shamrock School Division #38 – *1,276
340 Cameron St., PO Box 130, Foam Lake SK S0A 1A0
306/272-3377; Fax: 306/272-3239 – Dir., Siegrid Schergel; Sec.-Treas., William P. Saban
Shaunavon School Division #71 – *897
499 Centre St., PO Box 10, Shaunavon SK S0N 2M0
306/297-2627; Fax: 306/297-2439 – Dir., Ray J. Dickie; Sec.-Treas., Herb H. Conrad
Swift Current Comprehensive High School Board – *1,135
600 Chaplin St. East, Swift Current SK S9H 1J3
306/778-4600; Fax: 306/773-8011 – Supt. of Adm., Clifford D. Belter; Dir., Bryan Tallon
Swift Current School Division #94 – *1,580
600 Chaplin St. East, Swift Current SK S9H 1J3
306/778-4600; Fax: 306/773-8011 – Supt. of Adm., Clifford D. Belter; Dir., Bryan Tallon
Thunder Creek School Division #78 – *1,226
15 Thatcher Dr. East, PO Box 730, Moose Jaw SK S6H 4P4

306/694-2121; Fax: 306/694-4955 – Dir., Wayne Kiel; Sec.-Treas., Dale S. Clark
Tiger Lily School Division #54 – *1,023
150 McLeod Ave. East, PO Box 550, Melfort SK S0E 1A0
306/752-9391; Fax: 306/752-1933 – Dir., Lynell Pylatiuk; Sec.-Treas., James W. Martin
Timberline School Division #45 – *950
209 - 1 Ave. SE, PO Box 220, Sturgis SK S0A 4A0
306/548-2024; Fax: 306/548-2020 – Dir., Gerry Joynt; Sec.-Treas., Shirley Olson
Tisdale School Division #53 – *1,557
1010 - 102 Ave., PO Box 400, Tisdale SK S0E 1T0
306/873-2674; Fax: 306/873-5222 – Dir., Dwayne Brownridge; Sec.-Treas., Valerie Hvidston
Turtleford School Division #65 – *1,259
318 Railway Ave., PO Box 280, Turtleford SK S0M 2Y0
306/845-2150; Fax: 306/845-3392 – Dir., Robert Lockwood; Sec.-Treas., Gregory C. Gerwing
Wadena School Division #46 – *1,773
245 Main St., PO Box 160, Wadena SK S0A 4J0
306/338-2325, 2167; Fax: 306/338-3527 – Dir., Harvey Bowers; Sec.-Treas., Glen Lazeski
Wakaw School Division #48 – *1,032
200 - 2 St. South, PO Box 280, Wakaw SK S0K 4P0
306/233-4623; Fax: 306/233-4649 – Dir., Harold Mueller; Sec.-Treas., Sandy Gessner
Weyburn Central School Division #73 – *606
21 - 5 St. NE, Weyburn SK S4H 0Y9
306/842-2674; Fax: 306/842-1261 – Dir., Crandall Hrynkiw; Sec.-Treas., Patricia Jones
Weyburn Comprehensive School Board – *575
617 King St. NW, Weyburn SK S4H 2S5
306/842-2811, 2068; Fax: 306/842-2335 – Dir., Ed E. Kolybaba; Sec.-Treas., Gord Young
Weyburn School Division #97 – *1,591
617 King St. NW, Weyburn SK S4H 2S5
306/842-2811, 2068; Fax: 306/842-2335 – Dir., Edward E. Kolybaba; Sec.-Treas., Gord Young
Wilcox School Division #105 – *54
PO Box 280, Wilcox SK S0G 5E0
306/732-4522 – Dir., Leigh Calnek; Sec.-Treas., Pat Maguire
Wilkie School Division #59 – *1,289
206 - 2 St. West, PO Box 360, Wilkie SK S0K 4W0
306/843-2665; Fax: 306/843-2422 – Dir., Ray Johnson; Sec.-Treas., Guy Denton
Wood River School Division #70 – *663
38 - 2 Ave. North, PO Box 280, Lafleche SK S0H 2K0
306/472-5242; Fax: 306/472-3277 – Dir., Sharon Compton; Sec.-Treas., Ray Perzan
Yorkdale School Division #36 – *1,242
91 Broadway East, Yorkton SK S3N 0L1
306/783-8526; Fax: 306/783-0355 – Dir., Michael J. Clarke; Sec.-Treas., Sandra Wilson
Yorkton Regional High School Board – *1,167
33 Darlington St. West, Yorkton SK S3N 0E4
306/786-5500; Fax: 306/782-3223 – Dir., Leonard Bode; Sec.-Treas., Florence Halldorson
Yorkton School Division #93 – *2,034
33 Darlington St. West, Yorkton SK S3N 0E4
306/786-5500; Fax: 306/782-3223 – Dir., Leonard Bode; Sec.-Treas., Florence Halldorson

ROMAN CATHOLIC SEPARATE SCHOOL DIVISIONS

Christ the King Roman Catholic Separate School Division #83 – *122
PO Box 1084, Shaunavon SK S0N 2M0
306/297-4119; Fax: 306/297-2321 – Dir., Ray Dickie; Sec.-Treas., Carol Ann Hansen
Estevan Roman Catholic Separate School Division #27 – *556
1329 Third St., Estevan SK S4A 0S1
306/634-6711; Fax: 306/634-7023 – Dir., Austin Gerein; Sec.-Treas., Holley Odgers

Humboldt Roman Catholic Separate School Division #15 – *590
809 -10th St., PO Box 2830, Humboldt SK S0K 2A0
306/682-2287; Fax: 306/682-2055 – Dir., Stan Digout; Sec.-Treas., Janet Mueller
Lloydminster Roman Catholic Separate School District #89
5411 - 50 Ave., Lloydminster SK S9V 0R1
306/825-8911; Fax: 306/825-9855 – Dir., James McLoughlin; Sec.-Treas., Tom Schinold
Lloydminster Roman Catholic Separate School Division – *691 (Sask. only)
5411 - 50 Ave., Lloydminster SK S9V 0R1
306/825-8911; Fax: 306/825-9855 – Dir., Dr. Jim McLoughlin; Sec.-Treas., Tom Schinold
Mankota Our Lady of Fatima Roman Catholic Separate School Division #90 – *36
PO Box 280, Lafleche SK S0H 2K0
306/472-5242; Fax: 306/472-3277 – Dir., Sharon Compton; Sec.-Treas., Ray Perzan
Moose Jaw Roman Catholic Separate School Division #22 – *1,711
502 - 6 Ave. NE, PO Box 1087, Moose Jaw SK S6H 4P8
306/694-5333; Fax: 306/692-2238 – Dir., Jerry Zimmer; Sec.-Treas., Gerry Gieni
North Battleford Roman Catholic Separate School Division #16 – *1,617
9301 - 19 Ave., North Battleford SK S9A 3N5
306/445-6158; Fax: 306/445-3993 – Supt. of Adm., G. Paul Baskey; Dir., Ken J. Loehndorf
Prince Albert Roman Catholic Separate School Division #6 – *2,548
717 MacArthur Dr., Prince Albert SK S6V 5X6
306/953-7500; Fax: 306/763-1723 – Dir., Dr. Garry Andrews; Sec.-Treas., Don Orr
Regina Roman Catholic Separate School Division #81
2160 Cameron St., Regina SK S4T 2V6
306/791-7200; Fax: 306/347-7699
*11,113
Dir., Gwen Keith
Sec.-Treas., Curt Van Parys
St. Alphonse Roman Catholic Separate School Division #2 – *27
PO Box 71, Viscount SK S0K 4M0
306/944-4446; Fax: 306/944-4446 – Dir., Joe Kammermayer; Sec.-Treas., Mary B. Comeault
St. Gabriel's Roman Catholic Separate School Division #23 – *271
234 - 3 Ave. West, PO Box 1177, Biggar SK S0K 0M0
306/948-3889; Fax: 306/948-5254 – Dir., Ron Arnold; Sec.-Treas., Jean Silvernagle
St. Henry's Roman Catholic Separate School Division #5 – *381
633 Main St., PO Box 1029, Melville SK S0A 2P0
306/728-4426; Fax: 306/728-2351 – Dir., A.A. (Tony) Wihlidal; Sec.-Treas., Gordon Majeran
St. Olivier Roman Catholic Separate School Division, #12 – *143
325 Beckwell Ave., PO Box 579, Radville SK S0C 2G0
306/869-3259 – Dir., Robert Demencuik; Sec.-Treas., Louise Tuchscherer
St. Paul's Roman Catholic Separate School Division #20
420 - 22 St. East, Saskatoon SK S7K 1X3
306/668-7000; Fax: 306/668-7085
*14,210
Dir., Ken McDonough
Sec.-Treas., Donald Lloyd
Spiritwood Roman Catholic Separate School Division #82 – *89
PO Box 353, Spiritwood SK S0J 2M0
306/883-2328 – Dir., Denis Tetu; Sec.-Treas., Gail Ferster
Swift Current Roman Catholic Separate School Division #11 – *365
247 - 2 Ave. SE, Swift Current SK S9H 3J3

* indicates enrollment figure.

306/778-4666; Fax: 306/773-8331 – Dir., Bryan Tallon; Sec.-Treas., Deborah L. DeMars
Unity Roman Catholic Separate School Division #88 – *224
PO Box 598, Unity SK S0K 4L0
306/228-3118; Fax: 306/228-3598 – Dir., Eugene Thera; Sec.-Treas., Dianna Wildeman
Weyburn Roman Catholic Separate School Division #84 – *425
433 - 4 St. NE, Weyburn SK S4H 0Y8
306/842-5256; Fax: 306/842-4544 – Dir., Crandall Hrynkiw; Sec.-Treas., Colleen Court
Wilkie St. George Roman Catholic Separate School Division #85 – *183
PO Box 744, Wilkie SK S0K 4W0
306/843-2665; Fax: 306/843-2422 – Dir., Eugene Thera; Sec.-Treas., Guy Denton
Yorkton Roman Catholic Separate School Division #86 – *1,246
259 Circlebrooke Dr., Yorkton SK S3N 2S8
306/783-8787; Fax: 306/783-4992 – Dir., Brian Boechler; Sec.-Treas., Wilfred R. Maier

NATIVE SCHOOLS
Joe Duquette High School, 919 Broadway Ave., Saskatoon SK S7N 1B8 – 306/668-7490 – *170

SCHOOLS FOR CHILDREN WITH SOCIAL, EMOTIONAL, BEHAVIOURAL CHALLENGES
Cornwall Alternative School
40 Dixon Cres., Regina SK S4N 1V4
306/522-0044; Fax: 306/359-0720
Radius Community Centre for Education & Employment
#200, 245 - 3rd Ave. South, Saskatoon SK S7K 1M4
306/665-0362
Schaller School
PO Box 570, Pilot Butte SK S0G 3Z0
306/352-1694

UNIVERSITIES

The University of Regina
#100, 3737 Wascana Pkwy., Regina SK S4S 0A2
306/585-4402; Fax: 306/585-4997; Email: http://www.uregina.ca
Visitor, Lt. Gov. J.E.N. Wiebe
Chairman, Board of Governors, Arleen Hynd
Chancellor, Verda Lucille Petry, B.A., B.Ed., M.Ed.
President & Vice-Chancellor, Donald O. Wells, B.Sc., M.Sc., Ph.D.
Vice-President, Academic, Dianne L. Common, Ph.D., M.Ed., B.Ed., B.A.
Vice-President, Administration, David Barnard, B.Sc., M.Sc., Ph.D.
Assoc. Vice-President, Academic, Robert G. McCulloch, Ph.D., M.Sc., B.S.P.E.
Assoc. Vice-President & Dean, Research & Graduate Studies, Nicholas J. Cercone, B.S., M.S., Ph.D.
Executive Director, University Development, M. Hutchings, B.A., M.B.A.
Registrar & Director, Student Affairs, G. Meehan, B.A., M.Ed.
University Secretary, R. Reid Robinson, B.A., D.Phil.

FACULTIES WITH DEANS
Administration, Garnet Garven, B.A., M.B.A., Ph.D. (a.b.d.)
Arts, K. Murray Knuttila, B.A., M.A., Ph.D.
Education, Michael Tymchak, B.A.Hons., Ph.D.
Engineering, Amit Chakma, M.A.Sc., Ph.D..
Fine Arts, Michael J. Rushton, B.A., M.A., Ph.D.
Physical Activity Studies, Ralph Nilson, B.A., M.Sc., Ph.D.
Science, Keith Denford, B.Sc.Hons., Ph.D.
Social Work, Sharon McKay, B.A., M.S.W.
University Extension, Morris Maduro, A.A., B.A., M.A., Ph.D.

SCHOOLS WITH DIRECTORS
Canadian Plains Research Centre, David A. Gauthier, B.A., M.A., Ph.D.
Centre for Advanced Systems, Michael Wong, B.Sc., M.A., Ph.D.
Communications, Frank Flegel
Conservatory of Music & Dance, John Griffiths, B.Mus.Ed., M.Mus.
Counselling Services, Brian Sveinson, B.A., M.A., Ph.D.
Energy Research Institute, Brian D. Kybett, B.Sc., Ph.D.
Institute for Health Studies, R.G. Haennel, Ph.D.
Institute for Northeast Asian Studies, Vacant
Language Institute, A.N. Lalonde, B.A., M.A., Ph.D.
Mackenzie Art Gallery, Andrew J. Oko, M.A., B.A.
Prairie Justice Research, R. Schriml, B.A., M.S.W.
Saskatchewan Instructional Development & Research Unit, C. Krentz, B.A., M.Ed., Ph.D.
Social Administration Research Unit, D. Durst, B.A., M.S.W., Ph.D.
The Development Institute of Saskatchewan, G. Parsons
Water Research Institute, Donald R. Cullimore, B.Sc., Ph.D.

AFFILIATED COLLEGES
Canadian Theological Seminary, 4400 - 4th Ave., Regina SK S4T 0H8 – 306/545-1515 – Acting President, Melvin Syvestre
Gabriel Dumont Institute of Native Studies & Applied Research, 121 Broadway Ave. East, Regina SK S4N 0Z6 – 306/347-4100 – Director, Robert Devrome

FEDERATED COLLEGES
Campion College, c/o University of Regina, Regina SK S4S 0A2 – 306/586-4242; URL: http://www.uregina.ca/calendar/fedcoll/html#camp – President, Joseph G. Schner, S.J., A.B., M.A., M.Div., Ph.D.
Luther College, c/o University of Regina, Regina SK S4S 0A2 – 306/585-5333, 5025 – President, Richard Hordern, B.A., M.Div., S.T.M., M.Phil., Ph.D.
Saskatchewan Indian Federated College, 118 College St. West, Regina SK S4S 0A2 – 306/ 584-8333, 8334; URL: http://www.uregina.ca/calendar/fedcoll.html#sifc – President, Eber Hampton, B.A., Ed.D.

University of Saskatchewan
105 Admin. Place, Saskatoon SK S7N 5A2
306/966-4343; Fax: 306/966-8670; URL: http://www.usask.ca/
Visitor, The Hon. J.E.N. Wiebe, Lt. Governor of Saskatchewan
Chancellor, Margaret L. McKercher, C.M., B.A.
Chair, Board of Governors, H.E. Wyatt, B.Comm.
President, J.W.G. Ivany, B.Sc., Dip.Ed., M.A., Ph.D.
Vice-President (Acting), Academic, Sylvia Wallace, B.S.P., Ph.D.
Vice-President, Finance & Administration, A.J. Whitworth, B.Sc., Ph.D., M.B.A., M.Ed., C.Chem., C.M.A.
University Secretary, R.I. MacLean, B.A.
Registrar, K.M. Smith, A.B., M.S., Ph.D.
Controller, L. Kennedy, B. Comm., C.A.
Assoc. Vice-President, Research, D. Johnson, B.S.P., M.Sc., Ph.D.
Assoc. Vice-President, Information Technology Services, R.N. Kavanagh, B.E., M.Sc., Ph.D.

FACULTIES WITH DEANS
Agriculture, J.W.B. Stewart
Arts & Science, D. Atkinson
Commerce, V.L. Pearson
Dentistry, R. McDermott
Education, K. Jacknicke
Engineering, F. Berruti
Extension, G. Thompson
Graduate Studies & Research, G. Kachonoski
Law, R.P. MacKinnon
Medicine, D. Popkin
Nursing, Y.M.R. Brown
Pharmacy, J.L. Blackburn
Physical Education, R. Faulkner
Veterinary Medicine, A. Livingston

SCHOOLS WITH DIRECTORS
Physical Therapy, E. Harrison, B.P.T., M.Sc., M.C.P.A.

AFFILIATED COLLEGES
Central Pentecostal College, 1303 Jackson Ave., Saskatoon SK S7H 2M9 – 306/374-6655 – President, Rev. R. Kadyschuk
College of Emmanuel & St. Chad, 1337 College Dr, Saskatoon SK S7N 0W6 – 306/975-3753 – Principal, Rev. W.N. Christensen
Lutheran Theological Seminary, 114 Seminary Cres., Saskatoon SK S7N 0X3 – 306/975-7004; Fax: 306/975-0084 – President, Rev. F. Rohrbough
St. Andrew's College, Saskatoon SK S7N 0W3 – Co-President, Rev. Charlotte Caron
St. Peter's College, PO Box 10, Muenster SK S0K 2Y0 – 306/682-1755 – Co-President, B. Popowich

FEDERATED COLLEGES
St. Thomas More College, 1437 College Dr., Saskatoon SK S7N 0W6 – 306/966-8900 – President, J.R. Thompson

TECHNICAL INSTITUTIONS

SASKATCHEWAN INDIAN INSTITUTE OF TECHNOLOGIES
c/o Asimakaniseekan Askiy Reserve, #100, 103A Packham Ave., Saskatoon SK S7N 4K4
306/244-4444; Fax: 306/244-1391
President, Joan Greyeyes
Information Officer, Joyce Sasbrink Harkema

SASKATCHEWAN INSTITUTE OF APPLIED SCIENCE & TECHNOLOGY
c/o Secretariat, #1401, 606 Spadina Cres. East, Saskatoon SK S7K 2H6
306/933-7331
Communications Officer, Colleen Gallant, Email: gallant@siast.sk.ca
President, Art Knight
Kelsey Institute, PO Box 1520, Saskatoon SK S7K 3R5 – 306/933-6350; Toll Free: 1-800-567-3263
Palliser Institute, PO Box 1420, Moose Jaw SK S6H 4R4 – 306/694-3200; Toll Free: 1-800-667-0055
Wascana Institute, 221 Winnipeg St. North, PO Box 556, Regina SK S4P 3A3 – 306/787-4356; Toll Free: 1-800-667-7730
Woodland Institute, Main Bldg., 1100 - 15 St. East, PO Box 3003, Prince Albert SK S6V 6G1 – 306/953-7000; Toll Free: 1-800-667-9664

REGIONAL COLLEGES

CARLTON TRAIL REGIONAL COLLEGE
623 - 7 St., PO Box 720, Humboldt SK S0K 2A0
306/682-2623; Fax: 306/682-3101
Principal, Dave Kraft

CUMBERLAND REGIONAL COLLEGE
201 - 1 Ave. West, PO Box 2225, Nipawin SK S0E 1E0
306/862-9833; Fax: 306/862-4940
CEO, Steve Rudy

CYPRESS HILLS REGIONAL COLLEGE
129 - 2 Ave. NE, Swift Current SK S9H 2C6
306/773-1531; Fax: 306/773-2384; Email: emilr@sasknet.sk.ca
Acting Principal, Emily Rempel

Gravelbourg Learning Centre, 7 Athabasca St., PO Box 652, Gravelbourg SK S0H 1X0 – 306/648-3244; Fax: 306/648-2983

Maple Creek Learning Centre, 110 Jasper St., PO Box 1738, Maple Creek SK S0N 1N0 – 306/662-3829; Fax: 306/662-3849

Shaunavon Learning Centre, #307 - 7 Ave. West, PO Box 1478, Shaunavon SK S0N 2M0 – 306/297-3462; Fax: 306/297-3420

NORTH WEST REGIONAL COLLEGE

1381 - 101 St., North Battleford SK S9A 0Z9
306/937-5100; Fax: 306/445-1575
President, Brian Campbell

Meadow Lake Campus, 607 Centre St., Meadow Lake SK S9X 1E1 – 306/236-5659; Fax: 306/236-6379

Shellbrook Adult Education Centre, PO Box 1026, Shellbrook SK S0J 2E0 – 306/747-3038; Fax: 306/747-2276

Spiritwood Adult Education Centre, PO Box 567, Spiritwood SK S0J 2M0 – 306/883-2341; Fax: 306/883-3002

St. Walburg Adult Education Centre, PO Box 4, St. Walburg SK S0M 2T0 – 306/248-3288; Fax: 306/248-3203

Unity Adult Education Centre, PO Box 1438, Unity SK S0K 4L0 – 306/228-4191; Fax: 306/228-2383

NORTHLANDS COLLEGE

PO Box 1000, Air Ronge SK S0J 3G0
306/425-4480; Fax: 306/425-3002
CEO, Bill McLaughlin

Central Region Office, PO Box 509, La Ronge SK S0J 1L0 – 306/425-4353; Fax: 306/425-2696

Eastern Region Office, PO Box 400, Creighton SK S0P 0A0 – 306/688-3474; Fax: 306/688-7710

Western Region Office, PO Box 190, Buffalo Narrows SK S0M 0J0 – 306/235-1765; Fax: 306/235-4346

PARKLAND REGIONAL COLLEGE

290 Prince William Dr., PO Box 790, Melville SK S0A 2P0
306/728-4471; Fax: 306/728-2576
Principal, W.J. Rieger

PRAIRIE WEST REGIONAL COLLEGE

PO Box 700, Biggar SK S0K 0M0
306/948-3363; Fax: 306/948-2094
Principal, Richard Krahn

Kindersley Office, PO Box 488, Kindersley SK S0L 1S0 – 306/463-6431; Fax: 306/463-1161

Outlook Office, PO Box 1237, Outlook SK S0L 2N0 – 306/867-8857; Fax: 306/867-8722

Rosetown Office, PO Box 610, Rosetown SK S0L 2V0 – 306/882-4236; Fax: 306/882-2262

Warman Office, PO Box 1001, Warman SK S0K 4S0 – 306/242-5377; Fax: 306/242-8662

SOUTHEAST REGIONAL COLLEGE

Box 880, Weyburn SK S4H 2L1
306/848-2500; Fax: 306/848-2517
Principal, Arthur Whetstone

POST-SECONDARY & SPECIALIZED INSTITUTIONS

BSD TRAINING & RESOURCES LTD.

609 - 25 St. East, Saskatoon SK S4P 0L7
306/244-7504; Fax: 306/978-2230
Skills training for employment.

CAREER DEVELOPMENT INSTITUTES LTD.

315 - 25 St. East, Saskatoon SK S7K 0L4
306/244-8585; Fax: 306/244-0788
Computer maintenance; automated office administration.

SASKATOON ACADEMY OF LEARNING

226 - 20th St. East, Saskatoon SK S7K 0A6
306/665-5577; Fax: 306/653-1808
Secretarial; microcomputer business applications.

WESTERN ACADEMY BROADCASTING COLLEGE LTD.

321 Ave. F South, PO Box 6082, Saskatoon SK S7K 4E5
306/665-1771; Fax: 306/668-1219

WESTERN CANADIAN MANAGEMENT INSTITUTE

3300 Second Ave. West, PO Box 2975, Prince Albert SK S6V 7M4
306/922-4287; Fax: 306/953-0910
Hotel/restaurant; small business.

WESTERN TRADE TRAINING INSTITUTE

2206 Speers Ave., Saskatoon SK S7L 5X7
306/665-7709; Fax: 306/665-7795
Crane & hoist upgrading.

INDEPENDENT & PRIVATE SCHOOLS

Schools with enrollment of 50 or more, listed alphabetically by city.

All day & residential, & co-educational, except as noted

Caronport High School, PO Box 73, Caronport SK S0H 0S0 – 306/756-3303 – Principal, A. Robert Adam – *274 (Non-Denom.) – Gr. 9-12

Gravelbourg: Collège Mathieu, PO Bag 20, Gravelbourg SK S0H 1X0 – 306/648-3105 – Principal, Bernard Roy – *150 (RC) – Gr. 8-12; French

Outlook: Lutheran Collegiate Bible Institute, Outlook SK S0K 2N0 – 306/867-8971 – Principal, Tony Peter – *150 (Lutheran) – Gr. 10-12; Residential only

Prelate: St. Angela's Academy, PO Box 220, Prelate SK S0N 2B0 – 306/673-2200 – Principal, Sr. Dianne Sehn – *73 (RC) – Gr. 10-12; Residential; Girls

Prince Albert: Rivier Academy, 1405 - 5 Ave. West, Prince Albert SK S6V 5J1 – 306/764-6289 – Principal, Sr. Rose Marie Sanche – *232 (RC) – Gr. 7-12; Girls

Regina: Harvest City Christian Academy, 40 Sheppard St., Regina SK S4R 3M6 – 306/569-1935 – Principal, Todd Harrison – *105 – Gr. K.-12 (Non-Denom.); Day only

Regina: Luther College High School, 1500 Royal St., Regina SK S4T 5A5 – 306/791-9150 – Principal, Bert McNair – *396 (Lutheran) – Gr. 9-12

Rosthern Junior College, Rosthern SK S0K 3R0 – 306/232-4222 – Principal, Erwin Tiesson – *135 (General Conference Mennonite) – Gr. 10-12

Saskatoon: Christian Centre Academy, 102 Pinehouse Dr., Saskatoon SK S7K 5H7 – 306/242-7141 – Principal, Lou Brunelle – *164; (Non-Denom.) – Gr. K.-12; Day only

Saskatoon: Faith Alive Christian Academy, 637 University Dr., Saskatoon SK S7N 0H8 – 306/652-2230 – Principal, Leslie Semchuk – *66 – Gr. K.-12; (Non-Denom.); Day only

Saskatoon Christian School, 2410 Haultain Ave., Saskatoon SK S7J 1R3 – 306/343-1494 – Principal, Wes Vanstone – *92 (Non-Denom.) – Gr. K.-8; Day only

Wilcox: Athol Murray College of Notre Dame, PO Box 174, Wilcox SK S0G 5E0 – 306/732-2080 – Principal, Gerry Scheibel – *421 (RC) – Gr. 9-12

YUKON TERRITORY

Department of Education

PO Box 2703, Whitehorse YT Y1A 2C6
403/667-5141; Fax: 403/393-6254

ADVANCED EDUCATION BRANCH

Director, Training Services, Ken Smith
Manager, Student Financial Assistance, Carole Theriault
Acting Assistant Deputy Minister, Roland McCaffrey

PUBLIC SCHOOLS BRANCH

Supt. of Schools, Accreditation, Carol McCauley
Supt. of Schools, Special Programs, Wally Seipp
Supt. of Schools, Program Support, Fred Smith
Supt. of Schools, Curriculum & French Programs, Mavis Fisher
Manager, School Services (Facilities & Transportation), Gordon deBruyn
Director, Communications, Policy & Legislative Support, Sheila Rose
Director, Libraries & Archives, Linda Johnson
Assistant Deputy Minister, Roland McCaffrey

For detailed departmental listings, see Index: "Education, Depts."

The Yukon has 29 public schools (15 in Whitehorse, 14 in other communities) & three private schools. The public schools are administered directly by the Department of Education, although elected officials are gradually assuming more powers under the 1990 Education Act, & may evolve into school boards in the near future.

Curriculum is largely based on that of British Columbia, with flexibility for locally developed courses, particularly from a First Nations perspective (one quarter of the Yukon's 5,800 students are of native ancestry). Seven different native languages are taught in various Yukon schools, as well as French immersion & a French first language school in Whitehorse.

POST-SECONDARY EDUCATION

YUKON COLLEGE

PO Box 2799, Whitehorse YT Y1A 5K4
403/668-8704; Fax: 403/668-8896
Chair, Board of Governors, Jim Holt
Manager, Marketing & College Development, Karen King
President, Sally Ross

* indicates enrollment figure.

INDEX TO SELECTED FACULTIES/SCHOOLS

The following is compiled from universty listings found in Section 9; please contact the Editor in the case of omissions.

ADMINISTRATION/MANAGEMENT
Athabasca University
Dalhousie University
McGill University
Université Laval
Université de Montréal
Université de Sherbrooke
The University of Calgary
University of Lethbridge
University of Manitoba
Université de Moncton
University of New Brunswick
University of Northern British Columbia
University of Ottawa/Université d'Ottawa
University of Toronto
The University of Regina

AGRICULTURE
McGill University
Université Laval
University of Alberta
University of British Columbia
University of Guelph
University of Manitoba
University of Saskatchewan

ARCHITECTURE
Carleton University
McGill University
Technical University of Nova Scotia
Université Laval
University of British Columbia
University of Manitoba
University of Toronto
University of Waterloo

BUSINESS/COMMERCE
Acadia University
Bishop's University
Brock University
Carleton University
Concordia University
Dalhousie University
École des Hautes Études Commerciales (Université de Montréal)
Lakehead University
Laurentian University of Sudbury/Université Laurentienne de Sudbury
McMaster University
Memorial University of Newfoundland
Queen's University
Ryerson Polytechnic University
Saint Mary's University
Simon Fraser University
Trinity Western University
Wilfrid Laurier University
University of Alberta
University of British Columbia
University of Prince Edward Island
University of Saskatchewan
University of Victoria
University College of Cape Breton
University of Western Ontario
University of Windsor
York University

COMPUTER SCIENCE/INFORMATION TECHNOLOGY
Acadia University
Athabasca University
Carleton University
Concordia University
McGill University
Memorial University of Newfoundland
Technical University of Nova Scotia
University of New Brunswick
University of Toronto
University of Waterloo
University of Western Ontario
University of Windsor

DENTISTRY
Dalhousie University
McGill University
Université Laval
Université de Montréal
University of Alberta
University of British Columbia
University of Manitoba
University of Saskatchewan
University of Toronto
University of Western Ontario

EDUCATION
Acadia University
Brandon University
Brock University
Lakehead University
Laurentian University of Sudbury/Université Laurentienne de Sudbury
McGill University
Memorial University of Newfoundland
Nipissing University
Nova Scotia Teachers College
Queen's University
Saint Mary's University
Simon Fraser University
Trent University
Trinity Western University
Université Laval
Université de Moncton
Université de Montréal
Université de Sherbrooke
University of Alberta
University of British Columbia
The University of Calgary
University of Lethbridge
University of Manitoba
University of New Brunswick
University of Ottawa/Université d'Ottawa
University of Prince Edward Island
The University of Regina
University of Saskatchewan
University of Toronto
University of Western Ontario
University of Windsor
University of Victoria
York University

ENGINEERING
Acadia University
Carleton University
Concordia University
Lakehead University
Laurentian University of Sudbury/Université Laurentienne de Sudbury
McGill University
McMaster University
Memorial University of Newfoundland
Royal Military College of Canada
Ryerson Polytechnic University
Simon Fraser University
Technical University of Nova Scotia
Université Laval
Université de Moncton
Université de Sherbrooke
University of Alberta
University of British Columbia
The University of Calgary
University of Guelph
University of Manitoba
University of New Brunswick
University of Ottawa/Université d'Ottawa
The University of Regina
University of Saskatchewan
University of Toronto
University of Victoria
University of Waterloo
University of Western Ontario
University of Windsor

FINE ARTS/VISUAL ARTS
Concordia University
Université Laval
The University of Calgary
University of Lethbridge
The University of Regina
University of Victoria
University of Waterloo
University of Windsor
York University

FORESTRY
Lakehead University
Université Laval
Université de Moncton
University of Alberta
University of British Columbia
University of New Brunswick
University of Toronto

LAW
Carleton University
Dalhousie University
McGill University
Queen's University
Université Laval
Université de Moncton
Université de Montréal
Université du Québec
Université de Sherbrooke
University of Alberta
University of British Columbia
The University of Calgary
University of Manitoba
University of New Brunswick
University of Ottawa/Université d'Ottawa
University of Saskatchewan
University of Toronto
University of Victoria
University of Western Ontario
University of Windsor
York University

LIBRARY/INFORMATION SCIENCE
Dalhousie University
McGill University
Université de Montréal
University of Alberta
University of British Columbia
University of Toronto
University of Western Ontario

MEDICINE
Dalhousie University
McGill University
McMaster University
Memorial University of Newfoundland

Queen's University
Université Laval
Université de Montréal
Université de Sherbrooke
University of Alberta
University of British Columbia
The University of Calgary
University of Manitoba
University of Ottawa/Université d'Ottawa
University of Saskatchewan
University of Toronto
University of Western Ontario

MUSIC
Acadia University
Brandon University
McGill University
Memorial University of Newfoundland
Mount Allison University
Université Laval
Université de Montréal
Université de Sherbrooke
University of British Columbia
University of Manitoba
University of Toronto
University of Western Ontario
University of Windsor
Wilfrid Laurier University

NURSING
Dalhousie University
Lakehead University
Laurentian University of Sudbury/Université Laurentienne de Sudbury
McGill University
McMaster University
Memorial University of Newfoundland
Queen's University
Ryerson Polytechnic University
St. Francis Xavier University
Université Laval
Université de Moncton
Université de Montréal
University of Alberta
University of British Columbia
The University of Calgary
University of Lethbridge
University of Manitoba
University of New Brunswick
University of Ottawa/Université d'Ottawa
University of Prince Edward Island
University of Saskatchewan
University of Toronto
University of Western Ontario
University of Windsor
York University

PHARMACY
Dalhousie University
Memorial University of Newfoundland
Université Laval
Université de Montréal
University of Alberta
University of British Columbia
University of Manitoba
University of Saskatchewan
University of Toronto

SOCIAL WORK
Carleton University
Dalhousie University
Laurentian University of Sudbury/Université Laurentienne de Sudbury
McGill University
McMaster University
Memorial University of Newfoundland
University of British Columbia
The University of Calgary
University of Manitoba
The University of Regina
University of Toronto
University of Windsor
Wilfrid Laurier University

VETERINARY MEDICINE
Université de Montréal
University of Guelph
University of Prince Edward Island
University of Saskatchewan

SECTION 10

LEGAL DIRECTORY

COURTS & JUDGES	1	MANITOBA	43	ONTARIO	49
OFFICIAL RECEIVERS	21	NEW BRUNSWICK	45	PRINCE EDWARD ISLAND	93
DIRECTORY OF LAW FIRMS	22	NEWFOUNDLAND	47	QUÉBEC	93
ALBERTA	22	NORTHWEST TERRITORIES	47	SASKATCHEWAN	100
BRITISH COLUMBIA	33	NOVA SCOTIA	47	YUKON TERRITORY	103

See ADDENDA at the back of this book for late changes & additional information.

COURTS & JUDGES

FEDERAL

SUPREME COURT OF CANADA

Supreme Court Bldg., Wellington St., Ottawa ON K1A 0J1

613/995-4330; Fax: 613/996-3063

The Supreme Court of Canada, first established in 1875 by the Supreme Court & Exchequer Act, is now governed by the Supreme Court Act.

The Supreme Court sits at Ottawa & exercises general appellate jurisdiction throughout Canada in civil & criminal cases. The judgement of the Court is final & conclusive. The Court is also required to advise on questions referred to it by the Governor in Council. Under section 53 of the Supreme Court Act, the constitutionality or interpretation of any federal or provincial law, the powers of Parliament or of the provincial legislatures or of both levels of government, among other matters, may be referred by the Government to the Supreme Court for consideration.

In civil cases, appeals may be brought from any final judgement of the highest court of last resort in a province or territory by obtaining leave to do so from that court or from the Supreme Court itself. The Supreme Court will grant permission to appeal if it is of the opinion that a question of public importance is involved, one that transcends the immediate concerns of the parties to the litigation.

In criminal cases, the Court will hear appeals as of right concerning indictable offenses where an acquittal has been set aside or where there has been a dissenting judgement on a point of law in a provincial court of appeal. The Supreme Court may, in addition, hear appeals on questions of law concerning both summary convictions & indictable offenses if permission to appeal is first granted by the Court.

There are three sessions of the Court each year, beginning normally on the fourth Tuesday in January, the fourth Tuesday in April & the first Tuesday in October.

The Court consists of a Chief Justice, who is called the Chief Justice of Canada, & eight puisne judges. They are appointed by the Governor in Council & hold office during good behaviour but are removable by the Governor-General on address of the Senate & the House of Commons. They cease to hold office on attaining the age of 75 years.

The Court is responsible for its own administration and budgeting. Its estimates are submitted to Parliament by the Minister of Justice. The Registrar has the rank of Deputy Head and, subject to the direction of the Chief Justice, is responsible for the Registry, the Library, the Supreme Court Reports as well as the general administration of the Court.

Chief Justice of Canada, The Rt. Hon. Mr. Justice A. Lamer

Puisne Judges (The Hon. Mr./Madam Justice):
Peter Cory; Charles Gonthier; Frank Iacobucci; Claire L'Heureux-Dubé; Gérard La Forest; John C. Major; Beverley McLachlin; John Sopinka

Registrar, Anne Roland
Executive Legal Officer, Robin Elliot
Deputy Registrar, Louise Meagher
Legal Services, B. Kincaid
Manager, Process Registry, Danielle Beaulieu
Head, Registry & Court Record Services, M.K. Larmour
Director, Reports, Odile Calder
Law Editors, Sally Griffin, Claude Marquis, Archie McDonald
Revisors, L. Baribeau, R.D. Berberi
Director, Administrative Services, Irene O'Connor
Director, Library & Research Services, Diane Teeple
Director, Informatics, Terry Hamm
Director, Corporate Services, Anneliese Villeneuve

FEDERAL COURT OF CANADA

Supreme Court of Canada Bldg., Kent & Wellington Sts., Ottawa ON K1A 0H9

613/996-6795; Fax: 613/995-5442

The Federal Court of Canada consists of a Chief Justice, an Associate Chief Justice & not more than 29 other Judges, & has two divisions: the Federal Court of Appeal & the Federal Court (Trial Division).

The Federal Court of Appeal has jurisdiction on appeals from a judgement of the Federal Court (Trial Division) & Tax Court of Canada, a determination on a reference made by federal tribunals, boards or commissions or the Attorney General of Canada & on judicial review in respect of decisions of federal boards, commissions or tribunals listed in section 28 of the Federal Court Act.

The Federal Court (Trial Division) has jurisdiction in claims generally by & against the Crown, miscellaneous cases involving the Crown, claims against or concerning Crown officers, agents & servants, relief, including judicial review, against Federal boards, commissions and tribunals, intergovernmental disputes, conflicts with respect to industrial property, including patent, copyright & trade-mark, maritime law, citizenship appeals, aeronautics, inter-provincial works & undertakings, residuary jurisdiction for relief if there is no other Canadian court that has such jurisdiction, & jurisdiction in specific matters conferred by Federal Statutes.

The Court has a Senior Prothonotary, Associate Senior Prothonotary & Prothonotary (Sec. 12 of the Act). Prothonotaries sittings are held in open Court to hear motions at the direction of the Associate Chief Justice (Federal Court Rule 318). A prothonotary has the power to dispose of any interlocutory application, or any action not exceeding a $5,000 claim, assigned to him by direction of the Chief Justice or the Associate Chief Justice (Federal Court Rule 336).

Chief Justice, The Hon. Mr. Justice Julius A. Isaac
Assoc. Chief Justice, The Hon. Mr. Justice James A. Jerome, P.C.
Justices (The Hon. Mr./Madam Justice):
Appeal Division: Robert Décary; Alice Desjardins; James K. Hugessen; Gilles Létourneau; Allen M. Linden; Mark R. MacGuigan; Louis Marceau; F. Joseph McDonald; Louis Pratte; Joseph T. Robertson; Arthur J. Stone; Barry L. Strayer
Trial Division: Douglas R. Campbell; Bud Cullen; Pierre Denault; Jean-Eudes Dubé, P.C.; Frederick E. Gibson; L. Marcel Joyal; Allan Lutfy; W. Andrew

Canadian Almanac & Directory 1997

MacKay; Donna C. McGillis; William P. McKeown; Francis C. Muldoon; Marc Nadon; Marc Noël; Yvon Pinard; Barbara J. Reed; John D. Richard; Marshall E. Rothstein; Paul U.C. Rouleau; Sandra J. Simpson; Max M. Teitelbaum; Danièle Tremblay-Lamer; Howard I. Wetston

Administrator of the Court, Robert Bijan
Judicial Administrator, Trial Division, Monique Major
Senior Prothonotary, Jacques Lefebvre
Assoc. Senior Prothonotary, Peter A.K. Giles
Prothonotaries, John A. Hargrave, Richard Morneau

LOCAL OFFICES
(with Regional Director or District Administrator)

Calgary Office: 635 - 8 Ave. SW, 3rd Fl., Calgary AB T2P 3M3 – 403/292-5920 – Dan Buell
Charlottetown Office: Sir Louis Henry Davies Court House, 42 Water St., PO Box 2200, Charlottetown PE C1A 8B9 – 902/892-9900 – E. Dorothy Kitson
Edmonton Office: Tower 1, 10060 Jasper Ave., 5th Fl., Edmonton AB T5J 3R8 – 403/495-4561 – R. Orrin J. Splane
Fredericton Office: Westmorland Pl., 82 Westmorland St., Fredericton NB E3B 3L3 – 506/452-3016 – Gerald Parlee
Halifax Office: #1720, 1801 Hollis St., Halifax NS B3J 3N4 – 902/426-3282 – F. Pilon
Montréal Office: 30, rue McGill, Montréal PQ H2Y 3Z7 – 514/283-4820 – Monique Giroux
Québec Office: Palais du Justice, #500, 300, boul Jean Lesage, Québec PQ G1K 8K6 – 418/648-4920 – Mireille Bonin
Regina Office: Court House, 2425 Victoria Ave., Regina SK S4P 3V7 – 306/780-5268 – Jan Kernaghan
Saint John Office: Provincial Bldg., #427, 110 Charlotte St., PO Box 5001, Saint John NB E2L 4Y9 – 506/636-4990 – George S. Thériault
St. John's Office: Court House, 301 Duckworth St., PO Box 937, St. John's NF A1C 5M3 – 709/772-2884 – Vacant
Saskatoon Office: Court House, 520 Spadina Cr. East, Saskatoon SK S7K 3G7 – 306/975-4509 – D. Berezowski
Toronto Office: Canada Life Bldg., 250 University Ave., 3rd Fl., Toronto ON M5G 1R7 – 416/973-3356 – Peter Pace
Vancouver Office: The Pacific Centre, 700 West Georgia St., PO Box 10065, Vancouver BC V7Y 1B6 – 604/666-3232 – C. Stinson
Whitehorse Office: Andrew A. Phillipsen Law Centre, 2134 - 2 Ave., Whitehorse YT Y1A 5H6 – 403/667-5441; Fax: 403/667-4116 – Linda Adam
Winnipeg Office: 363 Broadway St., 4th Fl., Winnipeg MB R3C 3N9 – 204/983-2509 – Terry Johnston
Yellowknife Office: Court House, 4905 - 49th St., Yellowknife NT X1A 2N4 – 403/873-2044 – Lysette Deyelle

REGISTRY OF THE COURT
Principal Office, Supreme Court of Canada Building, Kent & Wellington Sts., Ottawa ON K1A 0H9
613/996-6795
Deputy Administrators:
 Facilities & Management, Pierre R. Gaudet
 Appeal Division, W. Wendt
 Trial Division, Paul F. Scott
 Human Resources & Security, M.E. Doherty
 Judicial Information Services, W. Wendt
 Resource Management, Gerald Parlee
Asst. Administrator, Management Services, Robert Misener

COURT MARTIAL APPEAL COURT OF CANADA
Supreme Court of Canada Bldg., Kent & Wellington Sts., Ottawa ON K1A 0H9
613/996-6795; Fax: 613/952-7226
Chief Justice, The Hon. Mr. Justice Barry L. Strayer, 613/995-7886

Puisne Judges (The Hon. Mr./Madam Justice):
Alphonse Barbeau; André G. Biron; John Watson Brooke; Douglas R. Campbell; J.S.G. Bud Cullen, P.C.; Robert Décary; Pierre Denault; Alice Desjardins; J.S. Armand Desroches; Jean-Eudes Dubé, P.C.; Roland Durand; Eugene G. Ewaschuk; Frederick E. Gibson; Walter R.E. Goodfellow; N.H.A. Goodridge; Gordon L.S. Hart; Bonnie M. Helper; Benjamin Hewak; James K. Hugessen; Julius A. Isaac; James A. Jerome, P.C.; L. Marcel Joyal; Louis-Philippe Landry; Gilles Létourneau; Hugh P. Legg; Allen M. Linden; Kenneth M. Lysyk; Mark R. MacGuigan, P.C.; W. Andrew MacKay; Edward C. Malone; Louis Marceau; William Roy Matheson; F. Joseph McDonald; Elizabeth C. McFadyen; Donna C. McGillis; William P. McKeown; Perry Meyer; Francis C. Muldoon; Marc Nadon; Marc Noël; Yvon Pinard, P.C.; Lawrence A. Poitras; Joseph H. Potts; Louis Pratte; Barbara J. Reed; John D. Richard; Guy A. Richard; Joseph T. Robertson; Marshall E. Rothstein; Paul Rouleau; Melvin E. Shannon; Sandra J. Simpson; Allyre Louis Sirois; Arthur J. Stone; Barry L. Strayer; Max M. Teitelbaum; William J. Trainor; Danièlle Tremblay-Lamer; Jacques Vaillancourt; Joanne B. Veit; Karen M. Weiler; Howard I. Wetston; Mark M. de Weerdt

Administrator of the Court, Robert Bijan, 613/995-6719
Deputy Assistant, Registry of the Court, W. Wendt
Coordinator, Registry of the Court, Greg Smith

REGISTRY OF THE COURT
Asst. Administrator, William Wendt
Coordinator, Gregory Smith

TAX COURT OF CANADA
200 Kent St., Ottawa ON K1A 0M1
613/992-0901; Fax: 613/957-9034

Established by the Tax Court of Canada Act, S.C. 1980-81-82-83, c. 158, the Tax Court of Canada was proclaimed in force on July 18, 1983. It replaced the Tax Review Board, the members of which became Judges. On September 22, 1988, an Act to amend the Tax Court of Canada Act & other Acts in consequence thereof (S.C. 1988, c. 61) received Royal Assent.

The Tax Court of Canada has exclusive original jurisdiction to hear & determine references & appeals on matters arising under the Income Tax Act, the Canada Pension Plan, the Old Age Security Act, the Petroleum & Gas Revenue Tax Act, Part III of the Unemployment Insurance Act, & Part IX of the Excise Tax Act for the Goods & Services Tax where references or appeals to the Court are provided in those Acts. The Court also has exclusive original jurisdiction to hear & determine appeals on matters arising under the War Veterans Allowance Act & the Merchant Navy & Civilian War-related Benefits Act as referred to in section 17 of the Veterans Appeal Board Act.

Appeals from assessments or reassessments under the Income Tax Act follow two procedures: an informal & expeditious procedure where the amount in issue is small & a general procedure in other cases. Under the informal procedure, paperwork is kept to a minimum &, generally speaking, the rules of evidence are not stringently applied. In cases involving larger amounts, the general procedure is analogous to that in the Federal Court of Canada - Trial Division & the rules of evidence are applied in the ordinary way. The practice & procedures in appeals, other than those under the Income Tax Act, are governed by other rules, for example, Tax Court of Canada Rules Procedure (Unemployment Insurance Act).

The Court, with its principal office in Ottawa, consists of a Chief Judge, an Associate Judge and 24 other Judges. To ensure the expeditious hearing of appeals, the Chief Judge may, with the approval of the Governor in Council, appoint Deputy Judges. There are currently 11 Deputy Judges.

Chief Judge, The Hon. Mr. Justice J.-C. Couture
Assoc. Chief Judge, The Hon. Mr. Justice D.H. Christie
Judges (His/Her Hon.):
P. Archambault; D.W. Beaubier; R.D. Bell; M.J. Bonner; E.A. Bowie; D.G.H. Bowman; J.A. Brulé (Supernumerary); P.R. Dussault; A. Garon; D. Hamlyn; Louise Lamarre; L. Lamarre Proulx; T.E. Margeson; C. McArthur; M.A. Mogan; T. O'Connor; G.J. Rip; A.A. Sarchuk; R.E. Sobier; Roland St-Onge (Supernumerary); A. Tardif; D.E. Taylor (Supernumerary); G. Teskey; G. Tremblay (Supernumerary)
Registrar of the Court, R.P. Guenette

LOCAL OFFICES
(with Regional Director or District Administrator)

Montréal Office: #1800, 500, Place d'Armes, 18e étage, Montréal PQ H2Y 2W2 – 514/283-9912; Fax: 514/496-1996 – Regional Director, Denis Lussier
Toronto Office: Sun Life Centre, #902, 200 King St. West, Toronto ON M5H 3T4 – 416/973-9181; Fax: 416-973-5944 – Regional Director, Dorothée McKinlay
Vancouver Office: Pacific Centre, 700 West Georgia St., 17th Fl., Vancouver BC V7Y 1A1 – 604/666-7987; Fax: 604/666-7967 – Regional Director, Denis Reeve

PENSION APPEALS BOARD
#327, 381 Kent St., PO Box 8567, Ottawa ON K1G 3H9
613/995-0612; Fax: 613/995-6834
Chair, The Hon. Mr. Justice Armand Dureault
Vice-Chair, The Hon. Mr. Justice D.J.A. Rutherford
Registrar, Mina McNamee
Deputy Registrar, René Ducharme

OFFICE OF THE COMMISSIONER FOR FEDERAL JUDICIAL AFFAIRS
110 O'Connor St., Ottawa ON K1A 1E3
613/992-9175; Fax: 613/995-5615

The Office administers Part I of the Judges Act, which provides for the payment of salaries, allowances and annuities to the judges of the Federal Court of Canada, the Tax Court of Canada and all other federally appointed judges of the superior courts of the provinces. It also provides administrative services to the Canadian Judicial Council and is responsible for the preparation of budgetary submissions of the Federal Court of Canada, the Tax Court of Canada and the Canadian Judicial Council. Also included in the services provided by the Office are language training for federally appointed judges, the publication of the Federal Court Reports and the administration of the fifteen Advisory Committees on Judicial Appointments.

Commissioner, Guy Y. Goulard, Q.C.
Deputy Commissioner, Denis Guay
Judges Administration Officer, Ginette Beauparlant
Executive Editor, Federal Court Reports, W.J. Rankin
Executive Secretary, Judicial Appointments Secretariat, Andre S. Millar

ALBERTA

ALBERTA COURT OF APPEAL
Law Courts Bldg., 1A Sir Winston Churchill Sq., 5th Fl. South, Edmonton AB T5J 0R2
403/422-2416; Fax: 403/427-5507

The Court of Appeal has appellate jurisdiction in all civil & criminal matters.
Chief Justice, The Hon. Catherine A. Fraser
Justices of Appeal (The Hon. Mr./Madam Justice):
Roger H. Belzil (Supernumerary); Jean E. Coté; Rene P. Foisy; Howard L. Irving; Samuel S. Lieberman (Supernumerary); John W. McClung; Ellen I. Picard; Anne H. Russell

Registrar, Lynn E. Varty, 403/422-2415; Fax: 403/422-4127
- Calgary: Court of Appeal, Court of Appeal Bldg., 530 - 7 Ave. SW, Calgary AB T2P 0Y3 – 403/297-7447; Fax: 403/297-5294
    Justices of Appeal (The Hon. Mr./Madam Justice): John D. Bracco (Supernumerary); Carole M. Conrad; Asa Milton Harradence (Supernumerary); Mary M.M. Hetherington; Constance D. Hunt; Roger P. Kerans; Elizabeth A. McFadyen; Willis O'Leary
    Deputy Registrar, Ileen Moore, 403/297-2206; Fax: 403/297-5294

ALBERTA COURT OF QUEEN'S BENCH
Court House, 611 - 4 St. SW, Calgary AB T2P 1T5
403/297-7211; Fax: 403/297-8617

The Court of Queen's Bench has original jurisdiction in all civil & criminal matters arising in Alberta, unless otherwise indicated by statute.

Surrogate Court has jurisdiction in respect of testamentary matters & all matters arising out of the issue of revocation of grants of probate & administration of estates.

Chief Justice, The Hon. Mr. William K. Moore
Justices (The Hon. Mr./Madam Justice):
Suzanne M. Bensler; Robert M. Cairns; Paul S. Chrumka; Roy V. Deyell; Russell A. Dixon (Supernumerary); William G.N. Egbert; Gregory R. Forsythe (Supernumerary); Robert P. Fraser; Adelle Fruman; Dennis Hart; Ernest A. Hutchinson; Colleen Lynn Kenny; M. Earl Lomas; Sal Joseph Lovecchio; Arthur M. Lutz; Donald I. MacLeod; Peter Macdonnell Clark; D. Blair Mason; Ross T.G. McBain; Peter J. McIntyre; Terrence F. McMahon; Donald H. Medhurst (Supernumerary); Robert A.F. Montgomery; John S. Moore; Virgil P. Moshansky (Supernumerary); C.S. Phillips; Peter C.G. Power (Supernumerary); Hubert S. Prowse (Supernumerary); Bonnie L. Rawlins; John D. Rooke; Melvin E. Shannon; Allen B. Sulatycky; William P. Sullivan; Charles G. Virtue; Jack H. Waite (Supernumerary); Lloyd David Wilkins
Masters in Chambers:
    Keith Roy Laycock
    Robert B. Waller, Q.C.
    L. Alberstat, 403/297-7385
    J.P. Floyd, Q.C., 403/297-7385
- Edmonton: Court of Queen's Bench, Law Courts Bldg., 1A Sir Winston Churchill Sq., Edmonton AB T5J 0R2 – 403/422-2200; Fax: 403/422-9742
    Assoc. Chief Justice, The Hon. Mr. Allan H.J. Wachowich
    Justices (The Hon. Mr./Madam Justice):
    John A. Agrios; Alexander Andrekson (Supernumerary); R. Paul Belzil; Ronald L. Berger; Myra B. Bielby; Mel Binder; Robert Allan Cawsey (Supernumerary); C. Philip Clarke; Alan T. Cooke; Peter T. Costigan; John B. Dea; Joseph Bernard Feehan (Supernumerary); Tellex W. Gallant; William J. Girguilis; Cecilia Johnstone; Lionel L. Jones; C. Adele Kent; Donald Lee; Erik Lefsrud; James L. Lewis; Edward P. MacCallum; Richard P. Marceau; Ernest A. Marshall; Tevie H. Miller (Supernumerary); M.T. Moreau; Alex T. Murray; Eileen M. Nash; Michael B. O'Byrne (Supernumerary); Delmar W. Perras; Keith G. Ritter; Vernor W.M. Smith (Supernumerary); Marguerite J. Trussler; Joanne B. Veit; William E. Wilson
    Masters in Chambers:
    M.B. Funduk, 403/422-2328
    W.J. Quinn, 403/422-2328
    W. Breitkreuz, 403/422-2328
- Lethbridge: Court of Queen's Bench, Court House, 320 - 4 St. South, Lethbridge AB T1J 1Z8 – 403/329-5196; Fax: 403/381-5762
    Justices (The Hon. Mr./Madam Justice):
    W. Vaughan Hembroff; James H. Langston; Lawrence D. MacLean (Supernumerary); Clarence G. Yanosik (Supernumerary)
- Red Deer: Court of Queen's Bench, Court House, 4909 - 48 Ave., Red Deer AB T4N 3T5 – 403/340-5533; Fax: 403/340-7984
    Justices (The Hon. Mr./Madam Justice):
    James L. Foster; Jack K. Holmes (Supernumerary); John H. MacKenzie

ADMINISTRATORS/MANAGERS
Red Deer: Court House, 4909 – 403/340-5220; Fax: 403/340-7984 – Joe Doyle
Calgary: Court House, 611 - 4 St. SW, Calgary AB T2P 1T5 – 403/297-2395; Fax: 403/297-8617 – Manager, Kevin Hoschka
Drumheller: Court House, 511 - 3 Ave. West, PO Box 759, Drumheller AB T0J 0Y0 – 403/823-1700; Fax: 403/823-6073 – Maureen Gendron
Edmonton: Law Courts Bldg., 1A Sir Winston Churchill Sq., Main Fl. South, Edmonton AB T5J 0R2 – 403/422-2492; Fax: 403/422-9742 – Manager, Wayne Samis
Fort McMurray: Court House, 9700 Franklin Ave., Fort McMurray AB T9H 4W3 – 403/743-7136; Fax: 403/743-7395 – Bev Patterson
Grande Prairie: Court House, 10260 - 99 St., Grande Prairie AB T8V 6J4 – 403/538-5340; Fax: 403/538-5454 – Wendy Smith
Lethbridge: Court House, 320 - 4 St. South, Lethbridge AB T1J 1Z8 – 403/381-5196; Fax: 403/381-5128 – Acting Administrator, Gwen Luchia
Medicine Hat: Law Courts Bldg., 460 - 1 St. SE, Medicine Hat AB T1A 0A8 – 403/529-8710; Fax: 403/529-8607 – Joe Hay
Peace River: Court House, 9905 - 97 Ave., PO Box 900-34, Peace River AB T8S 1T4 – 403/624-6256; Fax: 403/624-6563 – Iris Caillioux
Wetaskiwin: Law Courts, 4605 - 51 St., Wetaskiwin AB T9A 1K7 – 403/361-1258; Fax: 403/361-1319 – Bob Mahaffey

ALBERTA PROVINCIAL COURT
Law Courts Bldg., 1A Sir Winston Churchill Sq., 6th Fl. North, Edmonton AB T5J 0R2
403/427-6330

The Provincial Court has jurisdiction in small claims, family & select criminal matters & is a youth court.

Chief Provincial Court Judge, The Hon. Mr. Edward R. Wachowich
- Calgary: Provincial Court (Civil Division), 603 - 6 Ave. SW, Calgary AB T2P 0T3
    Judges (The Hon.):
    Sandra Hunt McDonald, 403/297-7361; William C. Kerr (Supernumerary), 403/297-7749; Ronald H. O'Neil, 403/297-7309; Brian E. Scott (Asst. Chief Judge), 403/297-7233; Douglas J. Tompkins, 403/297-5273
    Administrator, Penny Shortridge, 403/297-7217; Fax: 403/297-7374
    Sheriff's Office: Court House Annex, 603 - 6 Ave. SW, PO Box 1830, Stn M, Calgary AB T2P 2L8 – 403/297-4477; Fax: 403/297-7374 – Asst. Sheriff, Gordon Fofonoff
- Calgary: Provincial Court (Criminal Division), Provincial Courts Bldg., 323 - 6 Ave. SE, 5th Fl., Calgary AB T2G 4V1 – 403/297-3156
    Judges (The Hon.):
    Garry G. Cioni; Cheryl L. Daniel; Robert H. Davie; Manfred Delong; Anthony P. Demong; Robert S. Dinkel; Allan A. Fradsham; William N. Gilbert; William N. Gilbert; Sandra A. Hamilton; Kathleen E. Helmer (Supernumerary); John D. James; Heather A. Lamoureux; Bernard N. Laven (Supernumerary); Francis L. Maloney; Douglas M. McDonald; Thomas B. McMeekin; William R. Pepler; Michael H. Porter; Brian C. Stevenson (Asst. Chief Judge); William Arthur Troughton (Supernumerary); Sharon L. Van De Veen
    Manager, Criminal & Traffic, David L. Paul, 403/297-3122; Fax: 403/297-3179
- Calgary: Provincial Court (Family & Youth Division), J.J. Bowlen Bldg., 620 - 7 Ave. SW, Calgary AB T2P 0Y8 – 403/297-3474, 3478
    Judges (The Hon.):
    Herbert A. Allard (Senior Judge); John S. Brownlee; Edward R.R. Carruthers; Lynn T.L. Cook; Nancy A. Flatters; Karen J. Jordan; Hugh F. Landerkin; N. Peter Leveque; Sharron Prowse-O'Ferrall
    Manager, Lorette Olson, 403/297-3470; Fax: 403/297-3461
- Camrose: Provincial Court, Court House, 5210 - 49 Ave., Camrose AB T4V 3Y2 – 403/679-1240
    Judges (The Hon.):
    Harry D. Gaede
    Administrator, Debbie Ekholm, 403/679-1240; Fax: 403/679-1253
- Canmore: Provincial Court, Provincial Bldg., 800 Access Rd., Canmore AB T0L 0M0 – 403/678-2355
    Judges (The Hon.):
    John D. Reilly
    Administrator, Cheryl Dubuc, 403/378-2355; Fax: 403/678-4936
- Drumheller: Provincial Court, Court House, 511 - 3 Ave. West, PO Box 759, Drumheller AB T0J 0Y0 – 403/823-5740
    Judges (The Hon.):
    Gordon W. Clozza
    Administrator, Maureen Gendron, 403/823-1700; Fax: 403/823-6073
- Edmonton: Provincial Court (Civil Division), Law Courts Bldg., 1A Sir Winston Churchill Sq., 6th Fl. North, Edmonton AB T5J 0R2 – 403/427-0106
    Judges (The Hon.):
    Jack Allford, 403/422-4015; Margaret M. Donnelly, 403/422-4012; Ken D. Hope, 403/422-4019; James L. Skitsko, 403/422-4003; Harry F. Wilson (Supernumerary), 403/422-4021
    Administrator, Donna Farley, 403/422-2510; Fax: 403/427-4348
    Sheriff's Office: Law Courts Bldg., 1A Sir Winston Churchill Sq., Main Fl. North, Edmonton AB T5J 0R2 – 403/422-2481; Fax: 403/422-3011 – Sheriff, Dwayne Weatherall
- Edmonton: Provincial Court (Criminal Division), Law Courts Bldg., 1A Sir Winston Churchill Sq., 5th Fl. North, Edmonton AB T5J 0R2 – 403/427-7817
    Judges (The Hon.):
    Daniel C. Abbott; Paul L. Adilman; P.R. Broda (Supernumerary); Peter M. Caffaro (Asst. Chief Judge); H. Ralph Chisholm; Albert G. Chrumka; Pierre-Michael Dubé; Russell L. Dzenick; Sam A. Friedman (Supernumerary); Philip G.C. Ketchum; David J. MacNab; Percy C.C. Marshall; William M. Mustard; Ken J. Plomp; Edward R. Saddy; Dean Saks (Supernumerary); Edward D. Stack (Supernumerary); Michael Stevens-Guille; David J. Tilley; Leo Wenden; Darlene R. Wong
    Manager, Criminal, Ron Babyn, 403/427-7868; Fax: 403/422-9736
    Manager, Traffic, Erwin Stoik, 4103/427-4724; Fax: 403/427-5791
- Edmonton: Provincial Court (Family & Youth Division), Law Courts Bldg., 1A Sir Winston Churchill Sq., 6th Fl. North, Edmonton AB T5J 0R2 – 403/427-7805
    Judges (The Hon.):
    Jonetta G. Bradburn; Donald J. Buchanan; Jack G. Easton; Richard S. Fowler; J. Peter Jorgensen; Walder G.W. White (Asst. Chief Judge); Lawrence S. Witten; Sidney E.W. Wood

- Edmonton: Provincial Court (Rural Division), Law Courts Bldg., 1A Sir Winston Churchill Sq., 6th Fl. North, Edmonton AB T5J 0R2 – 403/427-0110
  Judges (The Hon.):
  Raymond W. Bradley; Kenneth A. Cush; Norman A.F. Mackie; Lawrence E. Nemirsky; Ernest J.M. Walter (Asst. Chief Judge)
- Fort MacLeod: Provincial Court, Court House, 244 Chief Red Crow Blvd., PO Box 1360, Fort MacLeod AB T0L 0Z0 – 403/553-5010; Fax: 403/553-5045
  Administrator, Cecilia Baker
- Fort McMurray: Provincial Court, Court House, 9700 Franklin Ave., Fort McMurray AB T9H 4W3 – 403/743-7195
  Judges (The Hon.):
  Michael Horrocks
  Administrator, Bev Patterson, 403/743-7195; Fax: 403/743-7395
- Fort Saskatchewan: Provincial Court, Court House, 10504 - 100 Ave., Fort Saskatchewan AB T8L 3S9 – 403/998-1200
  Judges (The Hon.):
  Raymond W. Bradley
  Administrator, Wendy Komarnisky, 403/998-1200; Fax: 403/998-7222
- Grande Prairie: Provincial Court, Court House, 10260 - 99 St., Grande Prairie AB T8V 6J4 – 403/538-5364; Fax: 403/538-5454
  Judges (The Hon.):
  J.N. Gary Mitchell; Donald E. Patterson (Asst. Chief Judge)
  Administrator, Wendy Smith, 403/538-5360; Fax: 403/538-5454
- High Level: Provincial Court, 10106 - 100 Ave., PO Box 1560, High Level AB T0H 1Z0 – 403/926-3715; Fax: 403/926-4068
- High Prairie: Provincial Court, 4911 - 53 Ave., PO Box 1470, High Prairie AB T0G 1E0 – 403/523-6600
  Judges (The Hon.):
  Thomas R. Goodson; Roger P. Smith
  Administrator, Mae Fjeld, 403/523-6600; Fax: 403/523-6643
- Hinton: Provincial Court, Court House, 237 Jasper St., PO Box 6450, Hinton AB T7V 1X7 – 403/865-8280
  Judges (The Hon.):
  Donald C. Norheim
  Administrator, Karen Hanington, 403/865-8280; Fax: 403/865-8253
- Leduc: Provincial Court, Court House, 4612 - 50 St., Leduc AB T9E 6L1 – 403/986-6911
  Judges (The Hon.):
  Michael G. Tomyn
  Administrator, Ursula Owre, 403/986-6911; Fax: 403/986-0345
- Lethbridge: Provincial Court, Court House, 320 - 4th St. South, Lethbridge AB T1J 1Z8 – 403/381-5275
  Judges (The Hon.):
  Fred W. Coward; Gerald R. DeBow; Timothy G. Hironaka; Lloyd B. Hogan; Ron A. Jacobson; Jerry N. LeGrandeur; Laurie B. Levine (Supernumerary); Eric W. Peterson; James Arthur Wood (Asst. Chief Judge)
  Administrator, Gerdy Krogman, 403/381-5223; Fax: 403/381-5763
- Medicine Hat: Provincial Court, Law Courts Bldg., 460 - 1 St. SE, Medicine Hat AB T1A 0A8 – 403/529-8675; Fax: 403/592-2566
  Judges (The Hon.):
  Dietrich Brand; James P. Wambolt
  Administrator, Miles C. Weatherall, 403/529-8644; Fax: 403/529-8606
- Peace River: Provincial Court, Court House, 9905 - 97 Ave., PO Box 900-34, Peace River AB T8S 1T4 – 403/524-6260
  Judges (The Hon.):
  James R. McIntosh; E. Darrell Riemer
  Administrator, Iris Callioux, 403/624-6256; Fax: 403/624-6563

- Red Deer: Provincial Court, Court House, 4909 - 48 Ave., Red Deer AB T4N 3T5 – 403/340-5546
  Judges (The Hon.):
  Doug L. Crowe (Asst. Chief Judge); N. Patrick Lawrence; David P. MacNaughton; David J. Plosz; Thomas G. Scholie
  Acting Administrator, Sandra Mitchell, 403/340-5250; Fax: 403/340-7985
- St. Albert: Provincial Court, Court House, 3 St. Anne St., St. Albert AB T8N 2E8 – 403/458-7300
  Judges (The Hon.):
  Norman A.F. Mackie; Robert B. Spevakow
  Administrator, Sharon Boisvert, 403/458-7300; Fax: 403/460-2963
- St. Paul: Provincial Court, Court House, 4704 - 50 St., PO Box 1900, St. Paul AB T0A 3A0 – 403/645-6324
  Judges (The Hon.):
  Donald D. Demetrick; Brian H. Fraser; Marshall W. Hopkins (Supernumerary); Lawrence E. Nemirsky
  Administrator, Patricia Laramee, 403/645-6324; Fax: 403/645-6273
- Sherwood Park: Provincial Court, Court House, 190 Chippewa Rd., Sherwood Park AB T8A 4H5 – 403/464-0114
  Judges (The Hon.):
  John Maher
  Administrator, Wendy Komarnisky, 403/464-0114; Fax: 403/449-1490
- Stony Plain: Provincial Court, Court House, 4711 - 44 Ave., Stony Plain AB T0E 2G0 – 403/963-6205
  Judges (The Hon.):
  Peter P. Ayotte; M. Jeanne Burch; James E. Enright; Michael Stevens-Guille
  Administrator, Maureen McCulloch, 403/963-6205; Fax: 403/963-6402
- Vegreville: Provincial Court, Provincial Bldg., 4701 - 50 St., PO Box 1812, Vegreville AB T0B 4L0 – 403/632-5428
  Judges (The Hon.):
  Kenneth A. Cush
- Vermilion: Provincial Court, Provincial Bldg., 4701 - 52nd St., PO Box 149, Vermilion AB T0B 4M0 – 403/853-8111
  Judges (The Hon.):
  Ronald L. Tibbitt
  Administrator, Craena Coyne, 403/853-8130; Fax: 403/853-8200
- Wetaskiwin: Provincial Court, Law Courts, 4605 - 51 St., Wetaskiwin AB T9A 1K7 – 403/361-1204
  Judges (The Hon.):
  Norman A. Rolf
  Administrator, Susan O'Connor, 403/361-1204; Fax: 403/361-1338

ALBERTA COURT OPERATIONS

Calgary: Court House, 611 - 4 St. SW, 1st Fl., Calgary AB T2P 1T5 – 403/297-2210; Fax: 403/297-7152 – Director, James McLaughlin

Edmonton: Law Courts Bldg., 1A Sir Winston Churchill Sq., Mezz. Fl., Edmonton AB T5J 0R2 – 403/422-2426, 2428, 2429; Fax: 403/422-9585 – Director, John Bachinski

North (Rural): Court House, 4612 - 50 St., Leduc AB T9E 6L1 – 403/986-6903, 6904; Fax: 403/986-2429 – Director, Ed Towers

Lethbridge, Fort MacLeod, Medicine Hat, Drumheller: Court House, #115, 320 - 4 St. South, Lethbridge AB T1J 1Z8 – 403/381-5450; Fax: 403/381-5762 – District Manager, Clara Finan

South (Rural): Court House, 4909 - 48 Ave., Red Deer AB T4N 3T5 – 403/340-5220; Fax: 403/340-7984 – Director, Owen Lowe

BRITISH COLUMBIA

BRITISH COLUMBIA COURT OF APPEAL

Law Courts, 800 Smithe St., Vancouver BC V6Z 2E1
Law Courts, 850 Burdett Ave., Victoria BC V8W 1B4
604/660-2800

An appeal lies to the Court of Appeal from an order of the Supreme Court or an order of a judge of that court & in any matter where jurisdiction is given to it by statute.

Chief Justice, The Hon. Mr. Allan McEachern
Justices of Appeal (The Hon. Mr./Madam Justice):
A.B.B. Carrothers; G.S. Cumming; I.T. Donald; William A. Esson; L.S.G. Finch; R.J. Gibbs; D.M.M. Goldie; D.B. Hinds; E.E. Hinkson; H.A. Hollinrake; C.M. Huddart; J.D. Lambert; A.B. Macfarlane (Victoria); H.P. Legg; Carol Mahood Huddart; M.V.M. Newbury; P.M. Proudfoot; J.E. Prowse; M.A. Rowles; C.A. Ryan; Mary F. Southin; B. Williams
Registrar, Jennifer Jordan

BRITISH COLUMBIA SUPREME COURT

Law Courts, 800 Smithe St., Vancouver BC V6Z 2E1
604/660-2800

The Supreme Court is a court of original jurisdiction having jurisdiction in all civil & criminal matters arising in B.C., save & except matters expressly excluded by statute.

Chief Justice, The Hon. Mr. Bryan Williams
Assoc. Chief Justice, The Hon. Mr. P.D. Dohm
Justices (The Hon. Mr./Madam Justice):
M.J. Allan; W.G. Baker; R.J. Bauman; M.E. Boyd; T.R. Braidwood; D.I. Brenner; H.A. Callaghan; D.H. Campbell; M.I. Catliff; D.L. Clancy; B.I. Cohen; Francis W. Cole; F.W. Cole; Ross Collver; G.R.B. Coultas; V.R. Curtis; J.R. Dillon; I.L. Drost; E.R.A. Edwards; J.L.T. Edwards; G.P. Fraser; K.M. Gill; J.E. Hall; S.J. Hardinge; R.B. Harvey; A.G. Henderson; R.R. Holmes; S.W. Hood; M.A. Humphries; P.A. Kirkpatrick; M.M. Koenigsberg; R.E. Levine; R.T.A. Low; P.D. Lowry; K.M. Lysyk; A.W. MacKenzie; B.D. Macdonald; K.C. Mackenzie; Frank Maczko; K.E. Meredith; W.T. Oppal; R.M.P. Paris; S.R. Romilly; M.E. Saunders; W.B. Scarth; D.W. Shaw; J.S. Sigurdson; J.A. Sinclair Prowse; H.L. Skipp; K.J. Smith; J.E. Spencer; A.M. Stewart; J.D. Taylor; A.D. Thackray; D.F. Tysoe; D.H. Vickers; T.P. Warren; L.P. Williamson; R.S.K. Wong; Mark M. de Weerdt
District Registrar in Bankruptcy, K. Wellburn
Registrars in Bankruptcy & Masters of the Supreme Court:
Kenneth Doolan, 604/660-0255; Fax: 604/660-2420
Alan Patterson, 604/660-0255; Fax: 604/660-2420
Alan Donaldson, 604/660-2879; Fax: 604/660-2420
Neil Bolton, 604/660-0255; Fax: 604/660-2420
Susan Brandeth-Gibbs, 604/660-2879; Fax: 604/660-2420
Ronald Barber, 604/660-2879; Fax: 604-660-2420
Dennis Tokarek, 604/660-2879; Fax: 604/660-2420

OTHER SUPREME COURT LOCATIONS
(with Registry/County, District Registrars, Registrars in Bankruptcy)

- Chilliwack: Supreme Court, Court House, 9391 College St., Chilliwack BC V2P 4L7
  Registry (County): Westminster
  Justices (His/Her Hon.):
  W.H. Davies; W.G.E. Grist
  Manager, Court Services, Sheilah Chequer
- Cranbrook: Supreme Court, Court House, 102 - 11 Ave. South, Cranbrook BC V1C 2P3
  Registry (County): Kootenay
  Justices (His/Her Hon.):
  T.J. Melnick
  Deputy District Registrar, Beth Glassford
- Dawson Creek: Supreme Court, Court House, 1201 - 103 Ave., Dawson Creek BC V1G 4J2

Registry (County): Cariboo
Justices (His/Her Hon.):
R.D. Wilson
District Registrar, G.W. Schmidt
• Kamloops: Supreme Court, Court House, 455 Columbia St., Kamloops BC V2C 6K4
Registry (County): Yale
Justices (His/Her Hon.):
R.M.L. Blair; R.B. Hunter; G.W. Lamperson; Robert Robinson
Deputy District Registrar, Cindy Friesen
District Registrar, Registrar in Bankruptcy & Master of Supreme Court, Robert Powers, 250/828-4343; Fax: 250/828-4332
• Kelowna: Supreme Court, Court House, 1355 Water St., Kelowna BC V1Y 9R3 – 250/470-6900
Registry (County): Yale
Justices (His/Her Hon.):
N.A. Drossos; H.J. Hamilton; C.W. Wilkinson
Registrar in Bankruptcy & Master of the Supreme Court, Michael Bishop, 250/470-6896; Fax: 250/470-6884
District Registrar, Gene C. Watt
• Nanaimo: Supreme Court, Court House, 35 Front St., Nanaimo BC V9R 5J1
Registry (County): Vancouver Island
Justices (His/Her Hon.):
K.K. Downs; R.M.J. Hutchinson; S.J. Shabbits
Registrar in Bankruptcy & Master of the Supreme Court, John W. Horn, 250/741-3846; Fax: 250/741-3845
Deputy District Registrar, B. Murphy
• Nelson: Supreme Court, Court House, 320 Ward St., Nelson BC V1L 1S6
Registry (County): Kootenay
District Registrar, District Registrar in Bankruptcy, Elaine Beaulac
• New Westminster: Supreme Court, Court House, Begbie Sq., New Westminster BC V3M 1C9
Justices (His/Her Hon.):
H.D. Boyle; T.K. Fisher; D.A. Hogarth; I.B. Josephson; C.R. Lander; S.M. Leggatt; R.A. McKinnon; B.M. Preston; J.F. Rowan; D.A.S. Satanove; T.M. Singh; S.S. Stromberg-Stein; M.M. de Weerdt
Registrar in Bankruptcy & Master of the Supreme Court, Brian Joyce, 604/660-8615; Fax: 604/660-2072
• Prince George: Supreme Court, Court House, 1600 - 3rd Ave., Prince George BC V2L 3G6
Registry (County): Cariboo
Justices (His/Her Hon.):
I.C. Meiklem; W.G. Parrett; A.F. Wilson
Registrar in Bankruptcy & Master of the Supreme Court, Eric Chamberlist, 250/565-7051; Fax: 250/565-6127
Deputy District Registrar, Joan Foisy
• Prince Rupert: Supreme Court, Court House, 100 Market Pl., Prince Rupert BC V8J 1B8
Registry (County): Prince Rupert
Justices (His/Her Hon.):
R.T. Errico
District Registrar, District Registrar in Bankruptcy, J. Jones
• Vernon: Supreme Court, Court House, 3001 - 27th St., Vernon BC V1T 4W5
Registry (County): Yale
Justices (His/Her Hon.):
K.F. Arkell; B.M. Davies
District Registrar, District Registrar in Bankruptcy, Stan R. Smith
• Victoria: Supreme Court, Court House, 850 Burdett Ave., Victoria BC V8W 1B4
Registry (County): Vancouver Island
Justices (His/Her Hon.):
J.C. Bouck; J.C. Cowan; J.L. Dorgan; M.L. Drake; R.B. McD. Hutchison; F.A. Melvin; P.J. Mill-

ward; K.C. Murphy; D.D. Owen-Flood; G.M. Quijano
Registrar in Bankruptcy & Master of the Supreme Court, William McCallum, 250/387-0095; Fax: 250/356-6806
Registrar in Bankruptcy & Master of the Supreme Court, Elizabeth Dunn, 250/387-0095; Fax: 250/356-6806
District Registrars, Linda Kieran, Pat Hoshal
Operations Manager, Wayne Phalen

DISTRICT REGISTRARS
(with Registry/County, District Registrars; for District Registrars attached to Supreme Court locations, see above)

Ashcroft: PO Box 639, Ashcroft BC V0K 1A0 – 250/453-9174; Fax: 250/453-9049
Registry (County): Cariboo
District Registrar, D.S. McCoy
Campbell River: 500 - 13 Ave., Campbell River BC V9W 6P1 – 250/286-7510; Fax: 250/286-7512
Registry (County): Vancouver Island
District Registrar, Michael Hammell
Courtenay: Court House, #100, 420 Cumberland Rd., Courtenay BC V9N 2C4 – 250/334-1115; Fax: 250/334-1191
Registry (County): Vancouver Island
District Registrar, R. Krayenhoff
Creston: Court House, 224 - 10 Ave. North, PO Box 1790, Creston BC V0B 1G0 – 250/428-3200; Fax: 250/428-3243
Registry (County): Kootenay
District Registrar, Brian J. Gatto
Duncan: Court House, 238 Government St., Duncan BC V9L 1A5 – 250/746-1227; Fax: 250/746-1244
Registry (County): Vancouver Island
District Registrar, Derek D'Altroy
Fernie: Court House, 401 - 4 Ave., PO Box 1000, Fernie BC V0B 1M0 – 250/423-4601; Fax: 250/423-6973
Registry (County): Kootenay
District Registrar, Marva Black
Fort Nelson: PO Box 1000, Fort Nelson BC V0C 1R0 – 250/774-6990; Fax: 250/774-6904
Registry (County): Cariboo
District Registrar, Shawn Checkley
Fort St. John: Court House, 10600 - 100 St., Fort St. John BC V1J 4L6 – 250/787-3231; Fax: 250/787-3518
Registry (County): Cariboo
District Registrar, Gloria Morton
Golden: 837 Park Dr., PO Box 1500, Golden BC V0A 1H0 – 250/344-7581; Fax: 250/344-7715
Registry (County): Kootenay
District Registrar, Bonnie Carter
Grand Forks: 524 Central Ave., PO Box 1059, Grand Forks BC V0H 1H0 – 250/442-5464; Fax: 250/442-8606
Registry (County): Kootenay
District Registrar, Dave Henly
Kitimat: 603 City Centre, Kitimat BC V8C 2N1 – 250/632-4781; Fax: 250/632-4946
Registry (County): Prince Rupert
District Registrar, Norman Lee
Lillooet: 615 Main St., PO Box 700, Lillooet BC V0K 1V0 – 250/256-7445; Fax: 250/256-7458
Registry (County): Cariboo
District Registrar, Cindy Frederick
Merritt: PO Box 4400, Merritt BC V0K 2B0 – 250/378-9350; Fax: 250/378-1431
Registry (County): Yale
District Registrar, Elaine Ohata
100 Mile House: 160 Cedar Ave. South, PO Box 1060, 100 Mile House BC V0K 2E0 – 250/395-5562; Fax: 250/395-5519
Registry (County): Cariboo
District Registrar, Maureen Menzies
Penticton: Court House, #116, 100 Main St., Penticton BC V2A 5A5 – 250/492-1220; Fax: 250/492-1378
Registry (County): Yale
District Registrar, Maureen Corrado

Port Alberni: 2999 - 4 Ave., Port Alberni BC V9Y 8A5 – 250/720-2424; Fax: 250/720-2426
Registry (County): Vancouver Island
District Registrar, Diane Heidner
Powell River: #103, 6953 Alberni St., Powell River BC V8A 2B8 – 604/485-3630; Fax: 604/485-3637
Registry (County): Vancouver Island
District Registrar, Lowell S. Boran, Jr.
Princeton: Court House, 151 Vermilion Ave., PO Box 1210, Princeton BC V0X 1W0 – 250/295-3113; Fax: 250/295-7928
Registry (County): Yale
District Registrar, Vivian Hedrich
Quesnel: Court House, 350 Barlow Ave., Quesnel BC V2J 2C1 – 250/992-4256; Fax: 250/992-4171
Registry (County): Cariboo
District Registrar, Wayne Hakanson
Richmond: Unified Family Court, 6931 Granville Ave., Richmond BC V7C 4M9 – 604/660-4693; Fax: 604/660-1797
Registry (County): Vancouver
District Registrar, E.D. Kae
Rossland: Court House, 2288 Columbia Ave., PO Box 639, Rossland BC V0G 1Y0 – 250/362-7368; Fax: 250/362-9632
Registry (County): Kootenay
District Registrar, Howard Bondaroff
Salmon Arm: Court House, 20 Hudson St. NE, PO Box 100, Salmon Arm BC V1E 4S4 – 250/832-1610; Fax: 250/832-1607
Registry (County): Yale
District Registrar, Gordon Redding
Smithers: #40, PO Box 5000, Smithers BC V0J 2N0 – 250/847-7376; Fax: 250/847-7710
Registry (County): Prince Rupert
District Registrar, L. MacGillivray
Terrace: Court House, 3408 Kalum St., Terrace BC V8G 2N6 – 250/638-2111; Fax: 250/638-3637
Registry (County): Prince Rupert
District Registrar, Irene Blackstone
Vanderhoof: PO Box 1220, Vanderhoof BC V9A 3A0 – 250/567-6330; Fax: 250/567-6460
Registry (County): Cariboo
District Registrar, Gloria Edwards
Williams Lake: Court House, 540 Borland St., Williams Lake BC V2G 1R8 – 250/398-4301; Fax: 250/398-4459
Registry (County): Cariboo
District Registrar, Robert Girvin

BRITISH COLUMBIA PROVINCIAL COURT
Pacific Centre, #501, 700 West Georgia St., PO Box 10287, Vancouver BC V7Y 1E8
604/660-2864; Fax: 604/660-1108
The Provincial Court has jurisdiction in small claims, family & select criminal matters & is a youth court.
Chief Judge, The Hon. Mr. R.W. Metzger
Assoc. Chief Judge, His/Her Hon. E.D. Schmidt
Judges (The Hon.):
C.E. Bakony; P. Collings; M. Friesen; R.C.S. Graham; F.S. Green; I.G. Hanley; J.K. Shaw
• Abbotsford: Provincial Court, 32203 South Fraser Way, Abbotsford BC V2T 1W6 – 604/855-3200
Judges (The Hon.):
Harvey Field; M.I. MacAlpine; C.B. MacArthur; C.G. Maltby
• Burnaby: Provincial Court, 6263 Deer Lake Ave., Burnaby BC V5G 3Z8 – 604/660-7147
Judges (The Hon.):
W.J. Diebolt; T.J. Gove; D.R. Holmes; K.D. Page; D.M.B. Steinberg; J. Watchuk
• Campbell River: Provincial Court, 500 - 13 Ave., Campbell River BC V9W 6P1 – 250/286-7510
Judges (The Hon.):
P.M. Doherty; B. Saunderson
• Castlegar: Provincial Court, 555 Columbia Ave., Castlegar BC V1N 1G8 – 250/365-8511

Judges (The Hon.):
D.L. Sperry
- Chilliwack: Provincial Court, 9391 College St., Chilliwack BC V2P 4L7 – 604/795-8340; Fax: 604/795-8345
Judges (The Hon.):
B.G. Hoy; D.M. Vamplew
- Courtney: Provincial Court, #211, 420 Cumberland Rd., Courtney BC V9N 5M6 – 250/334-1115
Judges (The Hon.):
C. Lazar
- Cranbrook: Provincial Court, 102 - 11 Ave. South, Cranbrook BC V1C 2P3 – 250/426-1232; Fax: 250/426-1352
Judges (The Hon.):
D.C. Carlgren (Admin. Judge); D.M. Waurynchuk
- Dawson Creek: Provincial Court, 1201 - 103 Ave., Dawson Creek BC V1G 4J2 – 250/784-2278; Fax: 250/784-2339
Judges (The Hon.):
D.M. Levis
- Delta: Provincial Court, 5540 Clarence Taylor Cr., Delta BC V4K 3W3 – 604/940-4350; Fax: 604/940-4364
Judges (The Hon.):
A.E. Rounthwaite
- Duncan: Provincial Court, 238 Government St., Duncan BC V9L 1A5 – 250/746-1234; Fax: 250/746-1244
Judges (The Hon.):
R.A. Higinbotham
- Fort St. John: Provincial Court, 10600 - 100 St., Fort St. John BC V1J 4L6 – 250/787-3231; Fax: 250/787-3518
Judges (The Hon.):
C.D. Cleaveley
- Kamloops: Provincial Court, 455 Columbia St., Kamloops BC V2C 6K4 – 250/828-4081; Fax: 250/828-4368
Judges (The Hon.):
W.A. Blair (Admin. Judge); J.P. Gordon; H. Rohrmoser; T.W. Shupe; B. Sundhu
- Kelowna: Provincial Court, 1355 Water St., Kelowna BC V1Y 8M3 – 250/470-6811
Judges (The Hon.):
J.P. Cartwright; B.J. Grannary; W.W. Klinger (Adm. Judge); H.A. Stansfield; B.C. Weddell
- Langley: Provincial Court, 20389 Fraser Hwy., Langley BC V3A 7N2 – 604/530-1164; Fax: 604/533-4853
- Maple Ridge: Provincial Court, 11960 Haney Pl., Maple Ridge BC V2X 6G1 – 604/467-1515; Fax: 604/467-9906
Judges (The Hon.):
S.C. Antifaev
- Nanaimo: Provincial Court, Court House, 35 Front St., Nanaimo BC V9R 5J1 – 250/741-3851; Fax: 250/741-3809
Judges (The Hon.):
S.G. Clark; D.J. Cowling; R.A. Gould; E.L. Iverson (Admin. Judge); J.I.D. Joe
- Nelson: Provincial Court, 320 Ward St., Nelson BC V1L 1S6 – 250/354-6165; Fax: 250/354-6539
Judges (The Hon.):
S.W. Enderton
- New Westminster: Provincial Court, Law Courts, Begbie Sq., New Westminster BC V3M 1C9 – 604/660-8565; Fax: 604/660-8977
Judges (The Hon.):
L.P. Clare; K.J. Husband; D. Stone
- North Vancouver: Provincial Court, 200 East 23 St., North Vancouver BC V7L 4R4 – 604/983-4059; Fax: 604/983-4034
Judges (The Hon.):
D.E. Moss; J.B. Paradis (Adm. Judge); W.J. Rodgers
- Penticton: Provincial Court, 100 Main St., Penticton BC V2A 5A5 – 250/492-1378
Judges (The Hon.):
G.G. Sinclair
- Port Alberni: Provincial Court, 2999 - 4 Ave., Port Alberni BC V9Y 8A5 – 250/724-5741
Judges (The Hon.):
B.R. Klaver
- Port Coquitlam: Provincial Court, 2620 Mary Hill Rd., Unit J, Port Coquitlam BC V3C 3B2 – 604/927-2166; Fax: 604/927-2233
Judges (The Hon.):
M.R. Buller; L.A.T. Nimsick; A.J. Spence (Admin. Judge); J. Threlfall
- Powell River: Provincial Court, 6953 Alberni St., Powell River BC V8A 2B8 – 604/485-2861; Fax: 604/485-7938
Judges (The Hon.):
S.E. Giroday
- Prince George: Provincial Court, 1033 - 4 Ave., Prince George BC V2L 5H9 – 250/565-6692; Fax: 250/565-6927
Judges (The Hon.):
B.L. Dollis (Admin. Judge); P.V. Hogan; R.B. Macfarlane; D.W. Ramsay
- Prince Rupert: Provincial Court, 100 Market Pl., Prince Rupert BC V8J 1B7 – 250/624-7548; Fax: 250/627-0538
Judges (The Hon.):
A.K. Krantz
- Quesnel: Provincial Court, 350 Barlow Ave., Quesnel BC V2J 2C1 – 250/992-4256; Fax: 250/992-4171
Judges (The Hon.):
J.S. de Villiers
- Richmond: Provincial Court (Criminal Division), 6900 Minoru Blvd., Richmond BC V6Y 1Y1 – 604/660-6900; Fax: 604/660-1797
Judges (The Hon.):
R.D. Fratkin; J.R. Groberman
- Richmond: Provincial Court (Family & Small Claims Division), 6931 Granville Ave., Richmond BC V7C 4M9 – 604/448-2550; Fax: 604/660-1525
Judges (The Hon.):
B.K. Davis
- Rossland: Provincial Court, Court House, PO Box 639, Rossland BC V0G 1Y0 – 250/362-7368; Fax: 250/362-9632
Judges (The Hon.):
R.G. Fabbro
- Salmon Arm: Provincial Court, Court House, PO Box 100, Salmon Arm BC V1E 4S4 – 250/832-1610; Fax: 250/832-1749
Judges (The Hon.):
E.R. Brecknell
- Smithers: Provincial Court, PO Box 5000, Smithers BC V0J 2N0 – 250/847-7379; Fax: 250/847-7710
Judges (The Hon.):
Raymond R. Low; C.J. Trueman
- Squamish: Provincial Court, PO Box 1580, Squamish BC V0N 3G0 – 604/892-5911; Fax: 604/892-2272
Judges (The Hon.):
C.I. Walker
- Surrey: Provincial Court, 14340 - 57th Ave., Surrey BC V3X 1B2 – 604/572-2200; Fax: 604/572-2301
Judges (The Hon.):
T. Alexander; G.J.F. Baker; Norman Collingwood; T.D. Devitt; G. Gill; T.J. Gove; F.E. Howard; P.A. Hyde; R. Lemiski; J.R. Lytwyn; W.G. MacDonald (Admin. Judge); R.D.M. Miller; R. Raven; Jill Rounthwaite; E.D. Scarlett; W.F. Stewart; M.H. Thomas
- Terrace: Provincial Court, #200, 3408 Kalum St., Terrace BC V8G 2N6 – 250/638-3242; Fax: 250/638-2116
Judges (The Hon.):
P.R. Lawrence; E.F. deWalle (Admin. Judge)
- Vancouver: Provincial Court (Criminal Division), 222 Main St., Vancouver BC V6A 1E8 – 604/660-4200, 4300; Fax: 604/660-4322
Judges (The Hon.):
E.A. Arnold; C.L. Bagnall; C.C. Baird-Ellan (Admin. Judge); B.E. Bastin; E.H. Bendrodt; W.G. Craig; E.J. Cronin; W.J. Kitchen; K.J. Libby; P.L. Maughan; J.L. McCarthy; T.D. McGee; H.J. McGivern; J.K. Scherling; K.A.P.D. Smith; D.I. Smith; H. Weitzel
- Vancouver: Provincial Court (Family & Small Claims Division), 800 Hornby St., PO Box 33, Vancouver BC V6Z 2C5 – 604/660-8989; Fax: 604/660-8405
Judges (The Hon.):
Family Division: Jane Auxier (Adm. Judge); M. Borowicz; G.D. Gillis; M.E. Rae
Small Claims Division: E.M. Burdett; R.M. Gallagher; D.J. Martinson; M.R. Mondin; M.S. Puhach; E.D. Schmidt (Assoc. Chief Judge); R. Tweedale (Adm. Judge); J.F. Werier; H.A. White
- Vernon: Provincial Court, 3001 - 27 St., Vernon BC V1T 4W5 – 250/549-5422; Fax: 250/549-5415
Judges (The Hon.):
D.B. Overend
- Victoria: Provincial Court, Western Communities Court House, 1756 Island Hwy., Victoria BC V9B 1H8 – 250/474-9700; Fax: 250/474-9704
Judges (The Hon.):
A.J. Palmer
- Victoria: Provincial Court (Criminal & Small Claims Division), 850 Burdett Ave., Victoria BC V8W 1B4 – 250/356-1478; Fax: 250/356-6779
Judges (The Hon.):
J.K. Bracken; A.I. Ehrcke; A.E. Filmer; L.J.M. Harvey; J.M. Hubbard; J.N. Kay; B.D. MacKenzie; B.M. Neal; L.W. Smith (Admin. Judge)
- Victoria: Provincial Court (Family Division), 1119 Pembroke St., Victoria BC V8V 1X4 – 250/387-1925; Fax: 250/387-8881
Judges (The Hon.):
L.F.E. Chaperon
- West Vancouver: Provincial Court, 1310 Marine Dr., West Vancouver BC V7T 1B5 – 604/660-1232; Fax: 604/775-0311
Judges (The Hon.):
R.D. Grandison
- Williams Lake: Provincial Court, 540 Borland St., Williams Lake BC V2G 1R8 – 250/398-4301; Fax: 250/398-4459
Judges (The Hon.):
C.C. Barnet (Admin. Judge); T.C. Smith

MANITOBA

MANITOBA COURT OF APPEAL
Law Courts Bldg., 408 York Ave., Winnipeg MB R3C 0P9

The Court of Appeal has appellate jurisdiction in all civil & criminal cases adjudicated by the Court of Queen's Bench & indictable offences adjudicated by the Provincial Court.
Chief Justice, The Hon. Mr. R.J. Scott
Justices of Appeal (The Hon. Mr./Madam Justice):
B.M. Helper; C.R. Huband; G.J. Kroft; S.R. Lyon, P.C.; M. Monnin; A.R. Philip (Supernumerary); A.K. Twaddle
Registrar, B.T. Cadger, 204/945-2647

MANITOBA COURT OF QUEEN'S BENCH
Law Courts Bldg., 408 York Ave., Winnipeg MB R3C 0P9

The Court of Queen's Bench is a court of original jurisdiction & has jurisdiction in all civil & criminal cases arising in Manitoba, except matters expressly excluded by statute.
Chief Justice, The Hon. Mr. B. Hewak
Assoc. Chief Justice, The Hon. Mr. J.J. Oliphant
Assoc. Chief Justice, The Hon. Mr. G.W.J. Mercier
Judges (The Hon. Mr./Madam Justice): G.J. Barkman (Supernumerary); H.C. Beard; A.R. Clearwater;

W.M. Darichuk; W.R. DeGraves; A. Dureault (Supernumerary); L.A. Duval; T.M. Glowacki; B.M. Hamilton; K.R. Hanssen; A.A. Hirschfield (Supernumerary); G.O. Jewers; D.P. Kennedy; B. Keyser; R. Krindle; A. MacInnis; P.S. Morse (Supernumerary); N. Nurgitz; P. Schulman; S.I. Schwartz; J.A. Scollin; V. Simonsen; J.G. Smith; F. Steel; W.S. Wright (Supernumerary)
Family Division: C.M. Bowman; R. Carr; C.M. Davidson; R.M. Diamond; G.R. Goodman; S. Guertin-Riley; JOhn A. Menzies; J.A. Mullally; K.F. Stefanson
Administrator, St. Boniface, P. Beaulieu
Masters of Court of Registrars & Court of Bankruptcy: F. Lee
Anne Bolton, Q.C.
•Brandon: Court of Queen's Bench, 1104 Princess Ave., PO Box 68, Brandon MB R7A 5Y6
Judges (The Hon. Mr./Madam Justice): R. Mykle
Family Division: J.A. Duncan
Master of Court of Registrars in Bankruptcy, Errick G. Harrison
•Dauphin: Court of Queen's Bench, 114 River Ave. West, Dauphin MB R7N 0J7
Judges (The Hon. Mr./Madam Justice): K. Galanchuk
•The Pas: Court of Queen's Bench, 300, East 3 St., PO Box 1259, The Pas MB R9A 1L2
•Portage la Prairie: Court of Queen's Bench, 3 St. SE, Portage la Prairie MB R1N 1M9
•Thompson: Court of Queen's Bench, 59 Elizabeth Dr., Thompson MB R8N 1X9

MANITOBA PROVINCIAL COURT
Law Courts Bldg., 408 York Ave., Winnipeg MB R3C 0P9
The Provincial Court has jurisdiction in family, youth & select criminal matters.
Chief Judge, The Hon. J.M. Webster
Assoc. Chief Judge, The Hon. B.D. Giesbrecht
Assoc. Chief Judge, The Hon. C.M. Sinclair
Assoc. Chief Judge, The Hon. B. Miller
Judges (His/Her Hon.):
F. Acquila; F. Allen; P.L. Ashdown; R.J. Chartier; H. Collerman; A.J. Conner; B.M. Corrin; R.J.B. Cramer; S.V. Devine; I.V. Dubienski (Supernumerary); J.J. Enns (Supernumerary); M. Garfinkel; L.M. Giesbrecht; J.P. Guy; H.F. Gyles (Supernumerary); R.H. Harris; M.W. Howell; R.A. Johnston; E.C. Kimelman (Supernumerary); L. Kopstein; T.J. Lismer; G.B. McTavish (Supernumerary); R.J. Meyers; S. Minuk; L.R. Mitchell (Supernumerary); R.J. Morlock (Supernumerary); C.K. Newcombe; W.E. Norton; H.R. Pullen; C.N. Rubin; W.H. Swail
•Brandon: Provincial Court, 1104 Princess Ave., Brandon MB R7A 0P9
Judges (His/Her Hon.):
D.D.S. Coppleman; A. James (Supernumerary); K. Tarwid
Sheriff, M. Drosdoski, 204/726-6552
•Dauphin: Provincial Court, 114 River Ave. West, Dauphin MB R7N 0J7
Judges (His/Her Hon.):
K.P. Peters; R.W. Thompson
Sheriff, D. Bertnick, 204/622-2088
•The Pas: Provincial Court, 300 - 3 St. East, The Pas MB R9A 1L2
Judges (His/Her Hon.):
Roger Grégoire; W.R. Martin (Supernumerary)
Sheriff, G. Wilson, 204/627-8431
•Portage la Prairie: Provincial Court, 25 Tupper St., Portage la Prairie MB R1N 3K1
Judges (His/Her Hon.):
R.G. Cummings
Sheriff, R. Sim, 204/239-3379
•Thompson: Provincial Court, 59 Elizabeth Dr., Thompson MB R8N 1X4
Judges (His/Her Hon.):
B.G. Colli; J.P. Drapack; R.A. Johnson (Supernumerary)
Sheriff, R. Meneer, 204/677-6764

NEW BRUNSWICK

NEW BRUNSWICK COURT OF APPEAL
PO Box 6000, Fredericton NB E3B 5H1
The Court of Appeal has appellate jurisdiction in civil & criminal matters.
Chief Justice, The Hon. Mr. W.L. Hoyt
Justices of Appeal (The Hon. Mr./Madam Justice):
L.C. Ayles; Michel Bastarache; R.C. Rice; P.A.A. Ryan; W.S. Turnbull
Registrar, A.M. DiGiacinto, Q.C., 506/453-2452
Deputy Registrar, Line Pinet

NEW BRUNSWICK COURT OF QUEEN'S BENCH
PO Box 6000, Fredericton NB E3B 5H1
The Court of Queen's Bench is a court of original jurisdiction, having jurisdiction in all civil and criminal matters arising in New Brunswick, except those expressly excluded by statute. The Court is comprised of two divisions: Trial and Family
Chief Justice, The Hon. Joseph Z. Daigle
Registrar, Bankruptcy/Divorce & Matrimonial Causes, A.M. DiGiacinto, Q.C., 506/453-2452
Deputy Registrar, Bankruptcy, Line Pinet, 506/453-2452
•Bathurst: Court of Queen's Bench, Court House, 254 St. Patrick St., PO Box 5001, Bathurst NB E2A 3Z9
Judicial District: Gloucester County
Judges (His/Her Hon.):
Family Division: G.W. Boisvert
Trial Division: A. Deschenes; J.R. McIntyre
Regional Manager, R.G. Boudreau
Clerk (Trial Division) & Administrator (Family Division), Donald Arseneau
Sheriff/Coroner, Edgar Aubé
•Campbellton: Court of Queen's Bench, Court House, 157 Water St., PO Box 5001, Campbellton NB E3N 3H5
Judicial District: Restigouche, Parishes of Saint Quentin & Grimmer Counties
Judges (His/Her Hon.):
Trial Division: Gladys J. Young
Clerk (Trial Division) & Administrator (Family Division), Lucien Leblanc
Sheriff/Coroner, Walter Thompson
•Edmundston: Court of Queen's Bench, 121 Church St., PO Box 5001, Edmundston NB E3V 3L3
Judicial District: Madawaska County, Parishes of Drummond & Town of Grand Falls of Victoria County
Judges (His/Her Hon.):
Family Division: J.A. Sirois
Trial Division: J.E. Angers; J.Z. Daigle
Clerk, Administrator (Family Division) & Regional Manager, Richard J. Keeley
Sheriff/Coroner, Jérôme Ouellette
•Fredericton: Court of Queen's Bench, Court House, 423 Queen St., PO Box 6000, Fredericton NB E3B 5H1
Judicial District: York, Sunbury & Queens Counties
Judges (His/Her Hon.):
Family Division: Myrna Athey
Trial Division: W.L.M. Creaghan; M.E.L. Larlee; D.H. Russell
Regional Manager, Beth Nicholas
Sheriff/Coroner, Vaughn Fraser
Clerk (Trial Division) & Administrator (Family Division), A. Mehta
•Moncton: Court of Queen's Bench, 770 Main St., PO Box 5001, Moncton NB E1C 8R3
Judicial District: Westmorland, Kent & Albert Counties
Judges (His/Her Hon.):
Family Division: Paul J.-M. Godin; Roger Savoie; David D. Smith
Trial Division: P.S. Creaghan; J. Alfred Landry; C.I.L. Leger; R.L. Miller; Guy R. Richard
Regional Manager, David Leger
Clerk (Trial Division) & Administrator (Family Division), Michael Bray
Sheriff/Coroner, Rhéal LeBlanc
•Newcastle: Court of Queen's Bench, Court House, 599 King George Hwy., Newcastle NB E1V 1N6
Judicial District: Northumberland County
Judges (His/Her Hon.):
Trial Division: Thomas Riordon
Deputy Clerk (Trial Division) & Deputy Administrator (Family Division), Matthew Cripps
Sheriff/Coroner, James Muck
•Saint John: Court of Queen's Bench, Court House, 110 Charlotte St., PO Box 5001, Saint John NB E2L 2J4
Judicial District: Saint John, Kings & Charlotte Counties
Judges (His/Her Hon.):
Family Division: Weldon Graser; R.J. Guerette; R.E. Logan
Trial Division: R.J. Higgins; H.H. McLellan; J.W. Turnbull
Regional Manager, Donna Beaton
Clerk (Trial Division) & Administrator (Family Division), George S. Thériault
Sheriff/Coroner, Joan Collins
•Woodstock: Court of Queen's Bench, Court House, 689 Main St., PO Box 5001, Woodstock NB E0J 2B0
Judicial District: Victoria & Carleton Counties
Judges (His/Her Hon.):
Trial Division: Judy L. Clendening
Deputy Clerk (Trial Division) & Deputy Administrator (Family Division), Jean Sewell
Sheriff/Coroner, Gerald Girerson

NEW BRUNSWICK PROVINCIAL COURT
PO Box 6000, Fredericton NB E3B 5H1
506/453-2935
The provincial Court has jurisdiction in select criminal matters as well as youth matters.
Chief Judge, His Hon. H. Hazen-Strange
•Carleton County: Provincial Court, PO Box 1329, Woodstock NB E0J 2B0
Judges (His/Her Hon.):
Graydon Nicholas
•Charlotte County: Provincial Court, 41 King St., St. Stephen NB E3L 2C1
Judges (His/Her Hon.):
D.E. Rice
•Gloucester County (Bathurst): Provincial Court, PO Box 5001, Bathurst NB E2A 3Z9
Judges (His/Her Hon.):
Frederic Arsenault; Camille Dumas
•Gloucester County (Tracadie): Provincial Court, PO Box 806, Tracadie NB E0C 2B0
Judges (His/Her Hon.):
Jocelyne Moreau-Bérubé
•Kent County: Provincial Court, PO Box 5001, Richibucto NB E0A 2M0
Judges (His/Her Hon.):
Joseph C. Michaud
•Kings County: Provincial Court, PO Box 137, Hampton NB E0J 1Z0
Judges (His/Her Hon.):
M.F. Cain
•Madawaska County: Provincial Court, Carrefour Assomption, #235, 121 Church St., PO Box 5001, Edmunston NB E3V 3L3 – 506/739-9803
Judges (His/Her Hon.):
George S. Perusse
•Northumberland County: Provincial Court, 599 King George Hwy., Newcastle NB E1V 1N6

Judges (His/Her Hon.):
Dennis Lordon; Andrew Stymiest
- Restigouche County: Provincial Court, PO Box 5001, Campbellton NB E3N 3H5
  Judges (His/Her Hon.):
  Pierre Arsenault; Steve Hutchinson
- Saint John County: Provincial Court, 15 Market Sq., 3rd Fl., Saint John NB E2L 1E8
  Judges (His/Her Hon.):
  Alfred H. Brien; Gerald T. Casey; William J. McCarroll; James G. McNamee
- Sunbury-Queens Counties: Provincial Court, PO Box 94, Oromocto NB E2V 2G4
  Judges (His/Her Hon.):
  G.W.N. Cockburn
- Victoria County: Provincial Court, PO Box 5001, Grand Falls NB E0J 1M0
  Judges (His/Her Hon.):
  Jacques Desjardins
- Westmorland County: Provincial Court, PO Box 5001, Moncton NB E1C 8R3
  Judges (His/Her Hon.):
  Irwin Lampert; Ian P. Mackin; Michael McKee; Sylvio Savoie; Camille Vautour
- York County: Provincial Court, Justice Bldg., PO Box 6000, Fredericton NB E3B 5H1
  Judges (His/Her Hon.):
  Patricia Cumming; J.D. Harper

NEW BRUNSWICK: PROBATE COURT
PO Box 6000, Fredericton NB E3B 5H1
506/453-2805
The Probate Court has jurisdiction in estate matters.
Clerk, Ashwin Mehta

NEWFOUNDLAND & LABRADOR

NEWFOUNDLAND SUPREME COURT: COURT OF APPEAL
Court House, 355 Duckworth St., St. John's NF A1C 1H6
709/729-5147
The Court of Appeal has appellate jurisdiction in criminal and civil matters from decisions of the lower courts and designated administrative boards and tribunals.
Chief Justice, The Hon. Mr. James R. Gushue
Justices of Appeal (The Hon. Mr./Madam Justice):
James P. Adams; J.W. Mahoney; William W. Marshall; Arthur S. Mifflin (Supernumerary); H.B. Morgan; John J. O'Neill; G.L. Steele

NEWFOUNDLAND SUPREME COURT: TRIAL DIVISION
Court House, 355 Duckworth St., St. John's NF A1C 1H6
709/729-1059
The Trial Division is a court of original jurisdiction having jurisdiction in all civil and criminal matters arising in Newfoundland, except those excluded by statute. With the exception of the judicial area of St. John's, the Trial Division's original jurisdiction extends to particular family matters.
Chief Justice, The Hon. Mr. T.A. Hickman
Judges (His/Her Hon.):
James P. Adams; William G. Adams; F. Aylward; H.H. Cummings (Supernumerary); Raymond J. Halley; G. Lang; Nathaniel S. Noel (Supernumerary); J. James Puddester; David G. Riche; David L. Russell; Robert Wells
Supreme Court Registrar, Barry R. Sparkes, Q.C.
Senior Deputy Registrar, Vacant
Sheriff, L.R. Thoms

NEWFOUNDLAND SUPREME COURT: JUDICIAL CENTRES
Court House, 355 Duckworth St., St. John's NF A1C 1H6
709/729-5147
The Supreme Court has jurisdiction in Bankruptcy.
Registrar in Bankruptcy, Vacant
Asst. Deputy Registrar, Bankruptcy, Louise King
Asst. Deputy Registrar, Bankruptcy, Elaine Burke
- Brigus: Supreme Court, PO Box 100, Brigus NF A0A 1K0
  Judges (His/Her Hon.):
  Rupert W. Bartlett
- Corner Brook: Supreme Court, PO Box 2006, Corner Brook NF A2H 6J8
  Judges (His/Her Hon.):
  Denis Roberts (Supernumerary); Frederick R. Woolridge
  Deputy Registrar, Bankruptcy, Camille Pennell
- Gander: Supreme Court, PO Box 40, Gander NF A1V 2E1
  Judges (His/Her Hon.):
  Kevin Barry
- Grand Bank: Supreme Court, PO Box 910, Grand Bank NF A0E 1W0
  Judges (His/Her Hon.):
  G. Easton
- Grand Falls: Supreme Court, Provincial Bldg., Grand Falls NF A2A 1W9
  Judges (His/Her Hon.):
  Abraham Schwartz
- Happy Valley/Goose Bay: Supreme Court, PO Box 423, Stn B, Happy Valley/Goose Bay NF A0P 1C0
  Judges (His/Her Hon.):
  Seamus O'Regan

NEWFOUNDLAND SUPREME COURT: UNIFIED FAMILY COURT
21 Kingsbridge Rd., St. John's NF A1C 3K4
709/753-5873
The Unified Family Court has exclusive jurisdiction for all family matters within the judicial area of metropolitan St. John's.
Judge, Her Hon. Mary E. Noonan
Administrator, Berkley Reynolds

NEWFOUNDLAND PROVINCIAL COURT
Atlantic Pl., PO Box 5144, St. John's NF A1C 5V5
709/726-7181; Fax: 709/729-2161
The Provincial Court has jurisdiction in select criminal and family (outside the judicial area of St. John's) matters as well as small claims and youth matters.
Chief Judge, His Hon. Donald S. Luther
Judges (His/Her Hon.): W.J. Baker; Gregory Brown; O.M. Kennedy; J. LeClair; M.R. Reid; John F. Rorke; Robert T. Smith; J. Woodrow
Traffic Court: Vacant
Youth Court: Robert B. Hyslop
- Bell Island: Provincial Court, Bell Island NF A0A 4H0
- Bonne Bay: Provincial Court, Woody Point NF A0K 1P0
- Channel-Port-aux-Basques: Provincial Court, Channel-Port-aux-Basques NF A0M 1C0
- Clarenville: Provincial Court, Clarenville NF A0E 1J0
  Judges (His/Her Hon.):
  R.J. Whiffen
- Corner Brook: Provincial Court, Corner Brook NF A2H 6J4
  Judges (His/Her Hon.):
  James Igloliorte; Richard D. LeBlance; Michael W. Roche
- Gander: Provincial Court, Gander NF A1V 1W7
  Judges (His/Her Hon.):
  Kymil Howe; D. Peddle
- Goose Bay: Provincial Court, Goose Bay NF A0P 1C0
  Judges (His/Her Hon.):
  David E. Power
- Grand Bank: Provincial Court, Grand Bank NF A0E 1W0
  Judges (His/Her Hon.):
  G. Handrigan
- Grand Falls: Provincial Court, Grand Falls NF A2A 1W9
  Judges (His/Her Hon.):
  R. Fowler; K. Goulding
- Harbour Grace: Provincial Court, Harbour Grace NF A0A 2M0
  Judges (His/Her Hon.):
  J. Kean
- Placentia: Provincial Court, Placentia NF A0B 2Y0
  Judges (His/Her Hon.):
  G. Barnable
- Springdale: Provincial Court, Springdale NF A0J 1T0
- Stephenville: Provincial Court, Stephenville NF A2N 3K9
  Judges (His/Her Hon.):
  B. LeGrow
- Wabush: Provincial Court, Wabush NF A0R 1B0

NORTHWEST TERRITORIES

NORTHWEST TERRITORIES COURT OF APPEAL
Court House, PO Box 1320, Yellowknife NT X1A 2L9
403/920-8759
The Court of Appeal has appellate jurisdiction in criminal and civil matters from the Supreme Court and Territorial Court.
Chief Justice, The Hon. Mr./Madam C.A. Fraser
Justices of Appeal (The Hon. Mr./Madam Justice):
R.E. Hudson; C. Hunt; W. O'Leary; E. Picard; J.E. Richard; A.H. Russell; J.Z. Vertes; M.M. de Weerdt
Calgary: John D. Bracco; C.M. Conrad; A.M. Harradence; M.M. Hetherington; R.P. Kerans
Edmonton: R.H. Belzil; J.E. Coté; R.P. Foisy; H.L. Irving; S.S. Lieberman; J.W. McClung; E.A. McFadyen; J.J. Stratton
Regina: C.F. Tallis
Whitehorse: H.C.B. Maddison
Registrar, Lysette A. Deyelle

NORTHWEST TERRITORIES SUPREME COURT
Court House, PO Box 1320, Yellowknife NT X1A 2L9
The Supreme Court is a court of original jurisdiction and has jurisdiction in all civil and criminal matters arising in the Northwest Territories, except those expressly excluded by statute.
Judges (The Hon. Mr./Madam Justice):
J. Edward Richard; J.Z. Vertes; M.M. de Weerdt
Ex-Officio Judges (The Hon. Mr./Madam Justice):
R.E. Hudson; H.C.B. Maddison
Deputy Judges (The Hon. Mr./Madam Justice): B. Hewak
Brigus: R.W. Bartlett
Calgary: John D. Bracco; Paul Chrumka; Carole M. Conrad; Mary M. Hetherington; M. Earl Lomas; Arthur M. Lutz; Peter Power; Charles Virtue
Chilliwack: William H. Davies
Edmonton: Alan T. Cooke; Tellex W. Grant; Howard L. Irving; S.S. Lieberman; E.P. MacCallum; Ernest A. Marshall; Elizabeth McFadyen; T.H. Miller; Ellen I. Picard; Joanne B. Veit; A.H. Wachowich
Halifax: W.J. Grant
Montréal: Jean-Guy Boilard; R.F. Paul; M.L. Rothman
Ottawa: W. Dan Chilcott; J.K. Hugesson
Picton: J.D. O'Flynn
Québec: Paul Trudeau
Regina: C.F. Tallis
Simcoe: J. Pringle
St. John's: Mary E. Noonan
Toronto: D.H. Carruthers; W.D. Griffiths; J.H. Potts; F.K. Roberts

Vancouver: Howard A. Callaghan; Kenneth M. Lysyk; Wallace Oppal; Patricia M. Proudfoot; Randall S.K. Wong
Whitehorse: R.E. Hudson; H.C.B. Madison
Winnipeg: W.R. Degraves; Daniel P. Kennedy
Clerk, Administrator & Registrar, Bankruptcy, Lysette A. Deyelle
Sheriff, Colin McCluskie
Chief Court Reporter, L.A. Young

NORTHWEST TERRITORIAL COURT
PO Box 550, Yellowknife NT X1A 2M4
403/873-7643
The Territorial Court has jurisdiction in small claims, youth, family and select criminal matters.
Chief Judge, The Hon. R.W. Halifax
Judges (His/Her Hon.): R.M. Bourássa; T. Davis
Inuvik: B. Bruser
Iqaluit: B. Browne
Acting Clerk, R.A. Mould

NORTHWEST TERRITORIES: JUSTICE OF THE PEACE COURT
PO Box 1320, Yellowknife NT X1A 2L9
The Justice of the Peace has jurisdiction in summary conviction matters arising out of territorial statutes and municipal by-laws.

NORTHWEST TERRITORIES: SMALL CLAIMS COURT
PO Box 1320, Yellowknife NT X1A 2L9
The Small Claims Court has jurisdiction in civil matters not exceeding the amount prescribed by statute.

NOVA SCOTIA

NOVA SCOTIA COURT OF APPEAL
The Law Courts Bldg., 1815 Upper Water St., Halifax NS B3J 1S7
The Nova Scotia Court of Appeal has appellate jurisdiction in civil and criminal matters.
Chief Justice, The Hon. Mr. Lorne O. Clarke
Justices of Appeal (The Hon. Justice):
Nancy J. Bateman; David R. Chipman; E.J. Flinn; Gerald B. Freeman; J. Doane Hallett; Gordon L.S. Hart (Supernumerary); Malachi C. Jones (Supernumerary); Kenneth M. Matthews (Supernumerary); Ronald N. Pugsley; Elizabeth Roscoe
Registrar, Court of Appeal, Gretchen Pohlkamp, 902/424-9968

NOVA SCOTIA SUPREME COURT
The Law Courts Bldg., 1815 Upper Water St., Halifax NS B3J 1S7
902/424-4900
The Supreme Court is a court of original jurisdiction having jurisdiction in all civil and criminal matters arising in Nova Scotia, except those matters expressly excluded by statute. The Supreme Court's civil jurisdiction also extends to select family matters.
Chief Justice, The Hon. Constance R. Glube
Assoc. Chief Justice, The Hon. Ian M. Palmeter
Judges (The Hon. Justice):
N. Robert Anderson; Allan P. Boudreau; Felix A. Cacchione; Hiram J. Carver; John M. Davison; Walter Goodfellow; David W. Gruchy; Charles E. Haliburton; Donald M. Hall; M. Jill Hamilton; Suzanne M. Hood; F.B. William Kelly; A. David MacAdam; Simon J. MacDonald; J. Michael MacDonald; Hugh MacDonnell; Douglas L. MacLellan; Hilroy S. Nathanson; D. Merlin Nunn; K. Peter Richard; Jamie W.S. Saunders; Ted Scanlan; Margaret J. Stewart; Gordon Tidman
Prothonotary, Clerk of the Crown & Registrar in Bankruptcy, Gretchen G. Pohlkamp, 902/424-6905

NOVA SCOTIA PROVINCIAL COURT
5250 Spring Garden Rd., Halifax NS B3J 1E7
902/424-8718
The Provincial Court has jurisdiction in select criminal matters and acts as a Youth Court for cases involving youths aged 12 to 15 years.
Chief Judge, The Hon. Joseph Kennedy
Judges (The Hon.):
Barbara J. Beach; Patrick H. Curran; Sandra E. Oxner; Hughes Randall; Michael B. Sherar; Castor H.F. Williams; Brian D. Williston
- Amherst: Provincial Court, PO Box 326, Amherst NS B4H 3Z5 – 902/667-2256
  Judges (The Hon.):
  Ross Archibald; David Cole
- Annapolis Royal: Provincial Court, PO Box 425, Annapolis Royal NS B0S 1A0 – 902/532-5137
  Judges (The Hon.):
  Jean-Louis Batiot
- Antigonish: Provincial Court, PO Box 1506, Antigonish NS B2G 2L8 – 902/863-3676
  Judges (The Hon.):
  John D. Embree
- Bridgewater: Provincial Court, 84 Pleasant St., Bridgewater NS B4V 1N1 – 902/543-7143
  Assoc. Chief Judge, Joseph P. Kennedy
  Judges (The Hon.):
  Anne Crawford
- Dartmouth: Provincial Court, #200, 277 Pleasant St., Dartmouth NS B2Y 3S2 – 902/424-2390
  Judges (The Hon.):
  R. Brian Gibson; R.B. Kimball; F.K. Potts
- Digby: Provincial Court, PO Box 1089, Digby NS B0V 1A0 – 902/245-4567
  Judges (The Hon.):
  John R. Nichols
- Kentville: Provincial Court, PO Box 457, Kentville NS B4N 3X3 – 902/679-6070
  Judges (The Hon.):
  Claudine MacDonald; J.A. MacLellan
- New Glasgow: Provincial Court, Bridgeview Sq., 115 MacLean St., New Glasgow NS B2H 4M5 – 902/755-5106
  Judges (The Hon.):
  Clyde Macdonald; Robert Stroud
- Port Hawkesbury: Provincial Court, PO Box 404, Port Hawkesbury NS B0E 2V0 – 902/625-2605
  Judges (The Hon.):
  John D. Embree
- Sydney: Provincial Court, Harbour Place, 136 Charlotte St., 2nd Fl., Sydney NS B1P 1C3 – 902/563-3502
  Judges (The Hon.):
  S.D. Campbell; D.L. Matheson; A.P. Ross
- Truro: Provincial Court, 540 Prince St., Truro NS B2N 1G1 – 902/893-5840
  Judges (The Hon.):
  J.G. MacDougall
- Yarmouth: Provincial Court, 403 Main St., Yarmouth NS B5A 1G3 – 902/742-0500
  Judges (The Hon.):
  Robert M.J. Prince

NOVA SCOTIA: PROBATE COURT
5151 Terminal Rd., PO Box 7, Halifax NS B3J 2L6
902/424-7129
The Probate Court has jurisdiction in respect of estate matters.
Director of Probate, Shauna Wilson
- Amherst: Probate Court, PO Box 581, Amherst NS B4H 4B8 – 902/667-8062
  Registrar, Wm. Fairbanks
- Annapolis Royal: Probate Court, PO Box 129, Annapolis Royal NS B0S 1A0 – 902/532-5462
  Registrar, Lynn Durkee
- Arichat: Probate Court, PO Box 119, Arichat NS B0E 1A0 – 902/226-2818
  Registrar, A.A. Bowen
- Guysborough: Probate Court, PO Box 123, Guysborough NS B0H 1N0 – 902/533-4001
  Registrar, Lorna M. Chisholm
- Halifax: Probate Court, #910, 1660 Hollis St., Halifax NS B3J 1V7 – 902/424-7422
  Registrar, Sharron Grant
- Kentville: Probate Court, 87 Cornwallis St., Kentville NS B4N 2E5 – 902/679-5339
  Registrar, Susan Campbell-Baltzer
- Lunenburg: Probate Court, PO Box 760, Lunenburg NS B0J 2C0 – 902/634-8885
  Registrar, Armenia Corkum
- Pictou: Probate Court, PO Box 1199, Pictou NS B0K 1H0 – 902/485-4351
  Registrar, Laura Lannon
- Port Hawkesbury: Probate Court, PO Box 909, Port Hawkesbury NS B0E 2V0 – 902/625-4215
  Registrar, Arthur Bowen
- Sydney: Probate Court, PO Box 157, Sydney NS B1P 6H1 – 902/563-3545
  Registrar, Shauna Wilson
- Truro: Probate Court, Church St., Truro NS B2N 3Z5 – 902/893-5870
  Registrar, Kenneth Starratt
- Yarmouth: Probate Court, Court House, Yarmouth NS B5A 1G3 – 902/742-5469
  Registrar, Aileen Smith

NOVA SCOTIA: FAMILY COURT
5151 Terminal Rd., PO Box 7, Halifax NS B3J 2L6
902/424-4632
The Family Court has jurisdiction in family matters and also functions as a Youth Court for cases involving youths aged 12 to 15 years.
Chief Judge, His. Hon. Robert Ferguson, 902/424-6824; Fax: 902/424-0395
Director, Family Court Services, Jock Mackinnon, Fax: 902/424-4556
- Amherst: Family Court, PO Box 1148, Amherst NS B4H 4L1 – 902/667-3598; Fax: 902/667-1108
  (His Hon.):
  David Milner (Judge)
- Annapolis: Family Court, Provincial Bldg., 136 Exhibition St., Kentville NS B4N 4E5 – 902/679-6079; Fax: 902/679-6081
  Judges (His Hon.):
  Robert Levy
- Bridgewater: Family Court, #102, 84 Pleasant St., Bridgewater NS B4V 1N1 – 902/543-4222; Fax: 902/543-0524
  Judges (His Hon.):
  Robert C. Hebb
- Dartmouth: Family Court, 45 Alderney Dr., PO Box 1253, Dartmouth NS B2Y 4B9 – 902/424-4600; Fax: 902/424-0567
  Judges (His/Her Hon.):
  Moira Legere; Paul S. Niedermayer; Robert J. Williams
- Halifax: Family Court, 3380 Devonshire Ave., PO Box 8988, Stn A, Halifax NS B3K 5M6 – 902/424-3990; Fax: 902/424-0562
  Judges (His/Her Hon.):
  T.T. Daley; William Dyer; Deborah Gass; Corrine E. Sparks
- Kentville: Family Court, 136 Exhibition St., Kentville NS B4N 4E5 – 902/679-6079; Fax: 902/679-6081
  Judges (His Hon.):
  Robert Levy
- New Glasgow: Family Court, PO Box 518, New Glasgow NS B2H 5E7 – 902/755-6520; Fax: 902/755-7176
  Judges (His Hon.):
  Robert J.L. White; James C. Wilson
- Sydney: Family Court, #11, 360 Prince St., Sydney NS B1P 5L1 – 902/563-2200; Fax: 902/563-3666
  Judges (His/Her Hon.):
  J.V. MacDonald; Clare MacLellan; Daryl W. Wilson

- Truro: Family Court, PO Box 1680, Truro NS B2N 5Z5 – 902/893-5930; Fax: 902/893-6100
  Judges (His Hon.):
  David R. Hubley
- West Hants: Family Court, 136 Exhibition St., Kentville NS B4N 4E5 – 902/679-6079; Fax: 902/679-6081
  Judges (His Hon.):
  Robert Levy
- Yarmouth: Family Court, PO Box 460, Yarmouth NS B5A 4B4 – 902/742-0550; Fax: 902/742-0582
  Assoc. Chief Judge, His Hon. John Comeau

NOVA SCOTIA: SMALL CLAIMS COURT

5151 Terminal Rd., PO Box 7, Halifax NS B3J 2L6
902/424-7525

The Small Claims Court has jurisdiction in civil claims not exceeding the amount prescribed by statute.
Administrator, Alden Rennie

NOVA SCOTIA JUDICIAL CENTRES,

Amherst: c/o Sheriff's Office, 16 Church St., PO Box 326, Amherst NS B4H 3Z5 – 902/667-8750; Fax: 902/667-1108 – District Court Administrator, David Burke

Antigonish: c/o Provincial Court, Kirk Place, 219 Main St., PO Box 1506, Antigonish NS B2G 2L8 – 902/863-7300; Fax: 902/863-7451 – District Court Administrator, Terry MacDonald

Bridgewater: c/o Provincial Court, 80 Pleasant St., PO Box 369, Bridgewater NS B4V 2W9 – 902/543-0588; Fax: 902/543-0639 – District Court Administrator, Margaret Mesiner

Kentville: c/o Probate Office, 87 Cornwallis St., PO Box 457, Kentville NS B4N 3X3 – 902/679-4358; Fax: 902/679-6178 – District Court Administrator, Bernie Conrad

New Glasgow: c/o Family Court, 196 Riverside Pkwy., PO Box 518, New Glasgow NS B2H 5E7 – 902/755-6520; Fax: 755-7176 – District Court Administrator, Jim Hahnen

Sydney: c/o Provincial Court, Harbour Place, 136 Charlotte St., 2nd Fl., Sydney NS B1P 1C3 – 902/563-3515; Fax: 902/563-3421 – District Court Administrator, David Muise

Truro: c/o Provincial Court, 540 Prince St., Truro NS B2N 1G1 – 902/893-5840; Fax: 902/893-6119 – District Court Administrator, Carmel Standen

Yarmouth: c/o Provincial Court, 403 Main St., Yarmouth NS B5A 1G3 – 902/742-0500; Fax: 902/742-0678 – District Court Administrator, Lynn Strang

ONTARIO

ONTARIO COURT OF APPEAL

Osgoode Hall, 130 Queen St. West, Toronto ON M5H 2N5
416/327-5020; Fax: 416/327-5032

The Court of Appeal is the final court of appeal for Ontario. Appeals from the Court of Appeal may be pursued in the Supreme Court of Canada.
Chief Justice, The Hon. Mr. Roy McMurtry
Assoc. Chief Justice, The Hon. Mr. John Wilson Morden
Justices of Appeal (The Hon. Mr./Madam Justice):
Rosalie S. Abella; Louise Arbour; A.M. Austin; John Watson Brooke; James J. Carthy; Marvin Adrian Catzman; Louise Charron; David H. Doherty; George Duncan Finlayson; Lloyd William Houlden; Horace Krever; Jean-Marc Labrosse; John I. Laskin; Hilda M. McKinlay; Coulter Arthur Anthony Osborne; Sydney Lewis Robins; M. Rosenberg; Karen M. Weiler
Court of Appeal Office, John Kromkamp, 416/327-5208

ONTARIO COURT OF JUSTICE,

All Ontario courts (except the Court of Appeal & the Unified Family Court) form part of the Ontario Court of Justice, which consists of two divisions, the General Division & the Provincial Division. For judicial purposes, Ontario is divided into eight regions.

GENERAL DIVISION

Osgoode Hall, 130 Queen St. West, Toronto ON M5H 2N5
Fax: 416/326-2224

In addition to its regular trial court functions, the General Division has two branches: the Divisional Court which generally hears appeals from a final order of a Judge of the General Division involving disputes of up to $25,000, & the Small Claims Court which generally hears cases involving claims up to $6,000. The Governor General appoints the Judges to all but the Ontario Court (Provincial Division).
Chief Justice, The Hon. Mr. P.J. Lesage
Assoc. Chief Justice, The Hon. Madam H.J. Smith
Registrar in Bankruptcy, J.M. Ferron
Deputy Registrars in Bankruptcy:
G.C. Saunders, H. Garfield, D.H. Sandler, S.D. Cork, H.F.H. Sedgwick, W.R. Donkin, B. Sischy, D.A. Peppiatt, R. Linton, R.B. Peterson, B.T. Clark
- Central East Region, 50 Eagle St. West, 4th Fl., Newmarket ON L3Y 6B1 – 905/853-4810
  Justices (The Hon. Mr./Madam Justice):
  Barrie: M.P. Eberhard; P.G.M. Hermiston; H.D. Logan; C. Marchand; C. Perkins; P.B. Tobias; T.M. Wood
  Bracebridge: S.B. Hogg (Supernumerary); R.N. Weekes
  Cobourg: H.R. McLean
  Lindsay: B.G. MacDougall
  Newmarket: R. Boyko; J.A. Goodearle; P.H. Howden; G.R. Klowak; J.R. MacKinnon; D.J. Taliano
  Peterborough: S.H. Murphy
  Whitby: D.S. Ferguson; J. Jenkins; H.S. Laforme; W.B. Lane; J.R. McIsaac; J.E. Sheppard; A.J. Stong
- Central South Region, 50 Main St. East, Hamilton ON L8N 1E9 – 905/308-7200
  Justices (The Hon. Mr./Madam Justice):
  Brantford: E.O. Fanjoy (Supernumerary); J.C. Kent
  Cayuga: T.D. Marshall
  Hamilton: T.A. Beckett (Supernumerary); N. Borkovich; J.J. Cavarzan; David S. Crane; G. Czutrin; E. Fedak; C.S. Glithero; T. Lofchik; Randolph Mazza; D. Mendes Da Costa; P.W. Perras (Supernumerary); P.J. Philp; J.C. Scime; W. Stayshyn; D. Steinberg; J.E. Van Duzer (Supernumerary); P.H. Wallace; G. Yates
  Kitchener: D.F. Mossop (Supernumerary); R.D. Reilly; R.E. Salhany; R.C. Sills; E.F. West (Supernumerary)
  Simcoe: J.A. Pringle (Supernumerary); G.I. Thomson
  St Catharines: G.W. Dandie; R.T.P. Gravely (Supernumerary); F.J. Kovacs (Supernumerary); J.W. Quinn
  Welland: J.J. Fleury; M.P. Forestell; E. MacDonald; G.G. Nicholls (Supernumerary)
- Central West Region, 7755 Hurontario St., PO Box 8000, Brampton ON L6V 2M7 – 905/452-6623
  Justices (The Hon. Mr./Madam Justice):
  Brampton: John R. Belleghem; M.L. Caswell; T.M. Dunn; S.C. Hill; Emile Kruzick; K.A. Langdon; A. Donald K. MacKenzie; J.M. Simmons; R.G. Thomas; L.M. Walters; J.B. Webber
  Guelph: C. Herold; G.B. Smith
  Milton: J.D. Carnwath; J.H. Clarke; W.J. Morrison; C.M. Speyer; R.E. Zelinski
  Owen Sound: T.P. O'Connor; R.M. Thompson
  Walkerton: J.I. McKay (Supernumerary)

- East Region, 161 Elgin St., Ottawa ON K2P 2K1 – 613/239-1400
  Justices (The Hon. Mr./Madam Justice):
  Belleville: R.G. Byers; B.W. Hurley (Supernumerary)
  Brockville: P.J. Cosgrove
  Cornwall: A.J. Roy
  Kingston: M. Dunbar; T.J. Lally; H.K. MacLeod; C. Robertson; L.A. Woods (Supernumerary)
  L'Orignal: R.J.A. Cusson
  Ottawa: J.M. Bell; K.C. Binks; J.B. Chadwick; W.D. Chilcott; J.D. Cunningham; Robert C. Desmarais; C.F. Doyle (Supernumerary); J.A. Forget; Roydon Kealey; Colin McKinnon; D.L. McWilliam; P. Mercier; M. Metivier; F.H. Poulin (Supernumerary); D.J.A. Rutherford; G.G. Sedgwick; J.G. Sirois; J.P.E.H. Soubliere
  Pembroke: E.R. Millette
  Perth: G.R. Morin
  Picton: J.D. O'Flynn (Supernumerary)
- Northeast Region, 155 Elm St. West, Sudbury ON P3C 1V1 – 705/671-5968
  Justices (The Hon. Mr./Madam Justice):
  Cochrane: R.P. Boissonneault; N.M.J. Karam
  Gore Bay: R.G. Trainor (Supernumerary)
  Haileybury: J.D. Bernstein
  North Bay: M.G. Bolan; G.T. Valin
  Parry Sound: E. Loukidelis
  Sault Ste. Marie: F.R Caputo; C. Bruce Noble; G.I. Pardu; R. Stortini (Supernumerary); W. Larry Whalen
  Sudbury: M.C. DiSalle; I.M. Gordon; R.J. Huneault; Spyros D. Loukidelis; M.R. Meehan; C.T. Murphy (Supernumerary); J.S. Poupore
- Northwest Region, 277 Camelot St., Thunder Bay ON P7A 4B3 – 807/343-2712
  Justices (The Hon. Mr./Madam Justice):
  Kenora: G.F. Kinsman (Supernumerary); E.W. Stach
  Thunder Bay: L.C. Kozak; S.R. Kurisko (Supernumerary); A. William Maloney; John McCartney; T.A. Platana; J. deP. Wright
- Southwest Region, 80 Dundas St. East, 15th Fl., London ON N6A 2P3 – 519/660-3027; Fax: 519/660-2294
  Justices (The Hon. Mr./Madam Justice):
  Chatham: E. Browne; J.G. Kerr
  Goderich: J.M. Donnelly
  London: David Aston; Grant Campbell; R.J. Flinn (Supernumerary); B. Thomas Granger; R.J. Haines; Peter B. Hockin; W.A. Jenkins; J.C. Kennedy; G.P. Killeen; Lynne Leitch; M. Marshman; J.F. McCart (Supernumerary); D.R. McDermid; H. Vogelsang
  Sarnia: John Desotti; W.F. Higgins (Supernumerary); K.F. Ross
  St. Thomas: J.F. McGarry
  Stratford: J.A. Mullen (Supernumerary)
  Windsor: R. Abbey; J.H. Brockenshire; A.E. Cusinato; R.M.P. Daudlin; J.P. McMahon (Supernumerary); L.R. Morin; K.G. Ouellette; C. Zalev (Supernumerary); T.G. Zuber (Supernumerary)
  Woodstock: C.C. Misener (Supernumerary)
- Metropolitan Toronto, 361 University Ave., Toronto ON M5G 1T3 – 416/327-5752
  Justices (The Hon. Mr./Madam Justice):
  G.W. Adams; L.A. Beaulieu; Mary Lou Benotto; R.A. Blair; J.L. Boland (Supernumerary); S. Borins; W.J.L. Brennan; D.R. Cameron; Archie G. Campbell; D.H. Carruthers (Supernumerary); S. Chapnik; N.D. Coo (Supernumerary); M. Corbett; J. Crossland; P.A. Cumming; M.R. Dambrot; G.F. Day; A.P. Dilks; T. Dunnet; N.D. Dyson; G.J. Epstein; E.G. Ewaschuk; J.M. Farley; K.N. Feldman; G.S.P. Ferguson (Supernumerary); L.K. Ferrier; W. Festeryga; S.N. Filer; N.E. Garton; P. German (Supernumerary); K.M. Gibson (Supernumerary); L. Gotlib; S.E. Greer;

P.A. Grossi; J.D. Ground; D.J. Haley; J.F. Hamilton; E.P. Hartt (Supernumerary); B.C. Hawkins; K.A. Hoilett; D.G. Humphrey (Supernumerary); P.G. Jarvis; J.R.R. Jennings; J.C. Kane (Supernumerary); H.J. Keenan; F.P. Kiteley; G.D. Lane; S.E. Lang; Joan Lax; S.N. Lederman; C.H. Lissaman; H.R. Locke (Supernumerary); W.D. Lyon (Supernumerary); J.L. MacFarland; E. Macdonald; J.A.B. Macdonald; J.C. Macpherson; A. Mandel (Supernumerary); P.T. Matlow; J.D. McCombs; E.G. McNeely (Supernumerary); N.D. McRae; A.M. Molloy; J.W. O'Brien; H.M. O'Connell; J.G.J. O'Driscoll; D.F. O'Leary (Supernumerary); V. Paisley; R.R.M. Pitt; J.H. Potts; F.K. Roberts; A.B. Rosenberg (Supernumerary); R.C. Rutherford (Supernumerary); E. Saunders (Supernumerary); R.J. Sharpe; J.D. Sheard (Supernumerary); W.P. Somers; J.B.S. Southey (Supernumerary); G. Speigel; J.M. Spence; D.R. Steele (Supernumerary); R.A.F. Sutherland; E. Then; W.B. Trafford; G.T. Walsh; J.D. Watt; S.P. Webb (Supernumerary); B.J. Wein; A.C. Whealy (Supernumerary); J.G.M. White; J.C. Wilkins; J. Wilson; W.K. Winkler; W.F. Wren (Supernumerary); B. Wright

PROVINCIAL DIVISION

#2600, 1 Queen St. East, PO Box 91, Toronto ON M5C 2W5

The Provincial Division generally performs functions assigned to it by Acts such as the Provincial Offences Act, the Family Law Act, the Children's Law Reform Act & the Child & Family Services Act & is a youth court for the purposes of the Young offenders Act. The Lieutenant Governor in Council, on the recommendation of the Attorney General, appoints Provincial Division Judges.

Chief Justice, Provincial Division, The Hon. Sidney B. Linden, 416/327-5660

Assoc. Chief Judge, The Hon. Brian W. Lennox, 416/327-6826

Assoc. Chief Judge, The Hon. Marietta L.D. Roberts, 416/327-5653

- Central East Region, 440 Kent St. West, PO Box 4000, Lindsay ON K9V 5P2 – 705/324-1610

  Regional Senior Judge, The Hon. John D.D. Evans, 705/324-1410

  Judges (The Hon.):

  Barrie: T.P. Cleary, 705/739-6518; James C. Crawford, 705/739-6518; J.M. Gammell, 705/739-6518; Roland C. Harris, 705/739-6517; Donald R. Inch, 705/739-6517; Robert P. Main, 705/739-6517; Norman J. Nadeau, 705/739-6517; Gary V. Palmer, 705/739-6517; Bruce E. Payne, 705/739-6517; James T. Robson, 705/739-6517

  Bracebridge: Douglas G. Bice, 705/645-2269

  Cobourg: John D. Bark, 905/372-0193; John Rhys Morgan, 705/372-3751

  Lindsay: George F.W. Inrig, 705/324-1414; Karen E. Johnston, 705/324-1414; T.C. Whetung, 705/324-1414

  Newmarket: Roy E. Bogusky, 905/853-4812; W.W. Bradley, 905/853-4812; M.H. Caney, 905/853-4812; Elizabeth Earle-Renton, 905/853-4812; Stephen E. Foster, 905/853-4802; V.A.R. Lampkin, 905/853-4802; R.A. Minard, 905/853-4802; Terence O'Hara, 905/853-4802; Charles E. Purvis, 905/853-4802; John Sherrill M. Rogers, 905/853-4812; David G. Scott, 905/853-4802; Hugh E. Zimmerman, 905/853-4802

  Orillia: Leonard T. Montgomery, 705/326-2671

  Oshawa: Hubert J. Campbell, 905/723-9680; Donald B. Dodds, 905/723-9680; R.H. Donald (Senior Judge), 905/728-1623; Norman H. Edmondson, 905/723-9680; Donald J. Halikowski, 905/723-9680; P.Z. Magda, 905/728-1623; R.J. Richards, 905/723-9680; M.A. Scott, 905/728-1623; David M. Stone, 905/723-9680; Raymond P.V. Taillon, 905/723-9680; D. Timms, 905/728-1623

  Peterborough: Richard B. Batten, 705/876-3846; L.T.G. Collins, 705/876-3846; A.P. Ingram, 705/876-3846

- Central South Region, 50 Main St. East, 1st Fl., Hamilton ON L8N 1E9 – 905/508-7207

  Regional Senior Judge, The Hon. Anton Zuraw, 905/308-7207

  Judges (The Hon.):

  Brantford: P.H. Marjoh Agro, 519/758-3470; Kenneth G. Lenz, 519/758-3470

  Cambridge: Paddy A. Hardman, 519/621-9220

  Hamilton: Norman Bennett, 905/577-8410; D.S. Cooper, 905/577-8410; Peter R. Mitchell, 905/577-8410; Morris J. Perozak, 905/577-8410; D. Terry Vyse, 905/577-8410; Robert T. Weseloh, 905/577-8318; Bernd E. Zabel, 905/577-8410

  Kitchener: J.E. Allen, 519/741-3366; T.A. Culver, 519/741-3366; Donald C. Downie, 519/741-3366; Heather L. Katarynych, 519/741-3366; Donald J. MacMillan, 519/741-3366; Gordon H. McConnell (Senior Judge), 519/741-3366; Colin R. Westman, 519/741-3366; Margaret F. Woolcott, 519/741-3366

  Simcoe: W. Brian Stead, 519/426-1408

  St. Catharines: Harry W. Edmondstone, 905/988-6200; Kathleen Ellin McGowan, 905/988-6200; Wayne D. Morrison, 905/988-6200; J.W. Scott, 905/988-6200; Donald J. Wallace, 905/988-6200

  Welland: R.L. Budgell (Senior Judge), 905/734-4164; Marc J. Girard, 905/734-4164; Douglas H. Gowan, 905/734-4164

- Central West Region, #404, 201 County Court Blvd., Brampton ON L6W 4L2 – 905/874-4006

  Regional Senior Judge, The Hon. W. Gonet, 905/874-4006

  Chief Judge (Family), The Hon. H. Tedford G. Andrews, 905/878-4161

  Judges (The Hon.):

  Brampton: H.K. Atwood, 905/450-4733; W.B. Blacklock, 905/450-4733; L.M. Budzinski, 905/450-4733; N.S. Douglas, 905/450-4733; P.W. Dunn, 905/452-6611; Roderick J. Flaherty, 905/450-4733; Peter A.J. Harris, 905/450-4733; Kathryn L. Hawke, 905/450-4733; J.D. Karswick, 905/452-6611; Jane Kerrigan Brownridge, 905/452-6610; Elinore Ready, 905/450-4733; V.T. Rosemay, 905/450-4733; John D. Smith, 905/450-4733; R.E. Stauth, 905/452-6611; J. David Wake, 905/450-4733; G.W. Waldman, 905/450-4733; Brian Weagant, 905/450-4733; Theo Wolder, 905/452-6611

  Milton: F. Stewart Fisher, 905/637-4125; A. James Fuller, 905/878-4161; Douglas V. Latimer, 905/878-4161; John E.C. Robinson, 905/637-4125; William S. Sharpe, 905/878-4161; John D. Takach, 905/842-8380

  Orangeville: J.B. Allen, 519/941-5802; William G. Richards, 519/941-5802

  Owen Sound: James F. Laing, 519/376-0185

  Walkerton: R.S. MacKenzie, 519/881-0211; Francis W. Olmstead, 519/881-2333

- East Region, 161 Elgin St., Ottawa ON K2P 2K1 – 613/239-1343

  Regional Senior Judge, The Hon. P.R. Belanger, 613/239-1339

  Judges (The Hon.):

  Belleville: S.J. Hunter, 613/962-3468; D.K. Kirkland, 613/968-8583; W.J. Pickett, 613/968-8583

  Brockville: Charles D. Anderson, 613/342-5003, ext.46; Rommel G. Masse, 613/342-5003

  Cornwall: Johanne Lafrance-Cardinal, 613/933-7500; Gilles Renaud, 613/933-7500

  Kingston: E.D. Baker (Senior Judge), 613/548-6215, ext.6710; Ross H. Fair, 613/548-6790, ext.322; Paul H. Meggison, 613/548-6215, ext.6711; K.E. Pedlar, 613/548-6790

  L'Orignal: J.R. Reginald Levesque, 613/675-4625

  Napanee: J. Peter Coulson, 613/354-5450

  Ottawa: Jennifer A. Blishen, 613/239-1339; Jean M. Bordeleau, 613/239-1339; J.A. Cousineau, 613/239-1339; David W. Dempsey, 613/239-1339; James A. Fontana, 613/239-1339; H.L. Fraser, 613/239-1339; Maria T. Linhares de Sousa, 613/239-1339; Bruce Edward MacPhee, 613/239-1339; J.P. Michel, 613/239-1339; John D. Nadelle, 613/239-1339; Dianne M. Nicholas, 613/239-1339; Lynn D. Ratushny, 613/239-1339; Bernard T. Ryan, 613/239-1339; A.D. Sheffield, 613/239-1339; Patrick D. White, 613/239-1339; J.P. Wright, 613/239-1339

  Pembroke: L.P. Foran, 613/735-6886; C. Russell Merredew, 613/735-6886

  Perth: Inger Hansen, 613/283-1932

- Northeast Region, #146, 1 Elm St., Sudbury ON P3C 1T7 – 705/671-5944

  Regional Senior Judge, The Hon. Louise L. Gauthier, 705/671-5944

  Judges (The Hon.):

  Cochrane: Gerard E. Cloutier, 705/272-4358

  Elliot Lake: George Normand Glaude, 705/848-2500

  Haileybury: Robert N. Fournier, 705/672-3395

  North Bay: L. Duchesneau-McLachlan, 705/495-8308; Jean-Gilles Lebel, 705/495-8315

  Parry Sound: Lewis S. Geiger, 705/746-4237

  Sault Ste. Marie: Wayne W. Cohen, 705/759-9400; James D. Greco, 705/759-9400; John Kukurin, 705/759-9400

  Sudbury: William F. Fitzgerald, 705/671-5929; Andre L. Guay, 705/670-7250, ext.45; W. Guy Mahaffy, 705/671-5929; Gilles R. Matte, 705/671-5929; Gerald Edward Michel (Senior Judge), 705/671-5945; R.T. Runciman, 705/671-5986

  Timmins: W.E. Carr, 705/267-7799; Richard Lajoie, 705/267-7799

- Northwest Region, 1805 East Arthur St., 2nd Fl., Thunder Bay ON P7E 5N7 – 807/625-1625

  Regional Senior Judge, The Hon. Raymond J. Walneck, 807/625-1625

  Judges (The Hon.):

  Dryden: Peter T. Bishop, 807/223-2348

  Kenora: Donald Fraser, 807/468-2882; Judythe Little, 807/468-2884

  Thunder Bay: Dianne P. Baig, 807/625-1610; Roderick D. Clarke, 807/625-1610; P.S. Glowacki, 807/625-1600; G.R. Kunnas, 807/625-1600; R.B. Lester, 807/625-1610; Frank A. Sargent, 807/625-1610

- Southwest Region, 80 Dundas St. East, 15th Fl., London ON N6A 2P3 – 519/660-2292; Fax: 519/660-2294

  Regional Senior Judge, The Hon. Donald A. Ebbs, 519/660-2292

  Judges (The Hon.):

  Chatham: L.G. DeKoning, 519/352-9070

  Goderich: R.G.E. Hunter, 519/524-2447

  London: Alan J. Baker (Senior Judge), 519/660-3014; Walter E. Bell, 519/660-3014; Deborah Kristin Livingstone, 519/660-3014; John L. Menzies, 519/660-3014; Eleanor Schnall, 519/660-3045; John M. Seneshen, 519/660-3014; J. Douglas R. Walker, 519/660-3014; A.R. Webster, 519/660-3014

  Sarnia: Deborah J. Austin, 519/336-8830; A.L. Eddy, 519/336-8830; D.F. Kent, 519/337-3474

  St. Thomas: George A. Phillips, 519/633-1230

  Stratford: Peter R.W. Isaacs, 519/271-2640; G.A. Pockele, 519/271-9252

  Windsor: Guy F. DeMarco, 519/254-3741; Harry Momotiuk, 519/254-3741; Saul Nosanchuk, 519/254-3741; Douglas W. Phillips, 519/254-6670; Micheline Rawlins, 519/254-3741; S.G. Zaltz, 519/973-6670

  Woodstock: Alexander M. Graham, 519/539-6187

Canadian Almanac & Directory 1997

- Metropolitan Toronto, Old City Hall, 60 Queen St. West, Toronto ON M5H 2M4

    Regional Senior Judge, The Hon. Bernard M. Kelly, 416/327-5659

    Judges (The Hon.):

    Downsview: William P. Bassel, 416/314-4218; C.J. Cannon, 416/314-4218; George E. Carter, 416/314-4218; Faith M. Finnestad, 416/314-4218; Eric S. Lindsay, 416/314-4218; S.E. Marin, 416/314-4218; Lauren E. Marshall, 416/314-4218; Arthur K. Meen, 416/314-4218; Harold A. Rice (Assoc. Chief Judge), 416/314-4218; C.H. Vaillancourt, 416/314-4218

    Etobicoke: Jack J. Belobradic, 416/314-3975; Harvey P.. Brownstone, 416/327-6300, ext.216; M.L. Cohen, 416/327-6300, ext.215; Ayres Couto, 416/314-3975; Derek T. Hogg, 416/314-3975; M.F. Khoorshed, 416/314-3975; Stanley W. Long, 416/314-3975; Salvatore Merenda, 416/314-3975; M.G. Morten, 416/314-3975; William P. Ross, 416/314-3975

    North York: James P. Felstiner, 416/326-3539, ext.221

    Scarborough: C.R. Ball, 416/325-0978, ext.365; D.P. Cole, 416/325-0861; Donna G. Hackett, 416/325-0861; John P. Kerr, 416/325-0861; Marion E. Lane, 416/325-0861; Petra E. Newton, 416/325-0861; R.J. Otter, 416/325-0861; Sheila Ray, 416/325-0861; P.A. Sheppard, 416/325-0861; Marvin A. Zuker, 416/325-0978, ext.365

    Toronto: W. Donald August (Senior Judge), 416/327-5907; William J.C. Babe, 416/327-5907; D.A. Bean, 416/327-6891; P. Bentley, 416/327-5907; June T. Bernhard, 416/327-5907; R.G. Bigelow, 416/327-5907; Annemarie Erika Bonkalo, 416/314-4218; Joseph William Bovard, 416/327-5907; Milton A. Cadsby, 416/325-8972; J.F. Casey, 416/327-5907; B. Cavion, 416/327-5907; Samuel E. Darragh, 416/327-5907; David Fairgrieve, 416/327-5907; E. Gordon Hachborn, 416/325-8972; Monte H. Harris, 416/327-5907; Mary Jane Hatton, 416/327-6891; M.L. Hogan, 416/327-5907; Walter P. Hryciuk, 416/327-5907; Peter Hryn, 416/327-5907; J.C.M. James, 416/327-6891; Penny Jones, 416/327-6891; R. Khawly, 416/372-5907; Lynn King, 416/327-6891; Brent Knazan, 416/327-5907; Ian A. MacDonnell, 416/327-5907; D.R. Main, 416/327-6891; Michael E. Martin, 416/327-5907; Thomas Mercer, 416/325-8972; James Murphy, 416/325-8972; J.P. Nevins, 416/327-6891; Maryka Omatsu, 416/325-8972; Edward Francis Ormston, 416/327-5907; Claude H. Paris, 416/327-5907; Paul B. Pickett, 416/325-8972; Hugh D. Porter, 416/325-8972; Paul Henry Reinhardt, 416/327-5907; Harvey M. Salem, 416/327-5907; Charles Scullion (Senior Judge), 416/325-8972; S. Rebecca Shamai, 416/327-5907; Hugh W. Silverman, 416/327-5907; Geraldine Sparrow, 416/327-5907; Robert J.K. Walmsley (Assoc. Chief Judge), 416/327-6891; Bruce J. Young, 416/327-5907

    Willowdale: W.E. MacLatchy, 416/326-3539, ext.221; N. Weisman, 416/326-3539, ext.221; H.D. Wilkins, 416/326-3539, ext.221

COURTS ADMINISTRATION

720 Bay St., Toronto ON M5G 2K1

Asst. Deputy Attorney General, Courts Administration, Heather Cooper, 416/326-2609

Director, Program Development Branch, Janet Faas, 416/326-4264

Director, Facilities & Special Court Services Branch, Matt Veskimets, 416/326-4033

Asst. Director, Family Support Plan, Vacant, 416/326-4710

REGIONAL COURT: CENTRAL EAST

Areas served: Durham, Muskoka, Northumberland, Peterborough, Simcoe, Victoria-Haliburton, York Region

Regional Municipality of Durham, Court House, 605 Rossland Rd. East, PO Box 640, Whitby ON L1N 9G7

   Manager, Court Services, Terry Cyr, 905/430-5810

   Enforcement & Process Serving, Barbara Munro, 905/430-5808

   General Division/Small Claims Court, Alfred Ruttan, 905/430-5800

   Provincial Division (Criminal): 242 King St. East, Oshawa ON L1H 3Z8 – 905/723-5251 – Val McGraw

   Small Claims Court/Provincial Division (Family): 44 Bond St. West, 2nd Fl., Oshawa ON L1G 6R2 – 905/728-1623 – Linda Kurelo

District Municipality of Muskoka, Court House, 3 Dominion St. North, PO Box 1080, Bracebridge ON P1L 2E6

   Local Registrar, Provincial Division, Cathy Larsen, 705/645-8793

   Small Claims Court, Owen McQuillen, 705/645-8793

Northumberland County, Court House, 860 William St., PO Box 910, Cobourg ON K9A 3A9 – 905/372-3751

   Provincial Division/Enforcement & Process Serving, Jean Wilson, 905/372-3751

   Court Services: 440 Kent St. West, PO Box 4000, Lindsay ON K9V 5P2 – 705/324-7110 – Asst. Manager, Terry Cyr

Peterborough County, Court House, 470 Water St., Peterborough ON K9H 3M3

   Manager, Court Services, Dianne Wylie, 705/876-3817

   Small Claims/Enforcement & Process Serving, Helen Boyd, 705/876-3809

   Provincial Division: 70 Simcoe St., Peterborough ON K9H 7G9 – 705/876-3822 – Helen Boyd

Simcoe County, Court House, 114 Worsley St., Barrie ON L4M 1M1

   Manager, Court Services, Lynn Wagner, 705/739-6577

   Enforcement & Process Serving, John Wilson, 705/739-6100

   Local Registrar, Small Claims Court, Sue Whalen, 705/739-6144, 6116, 6136

   Counter Services for Criminal Matters: Court House, 30 Poyntz St., PO Box 284, Barrie ON L4M 5L4 – 705/739-6500 – Inez Diamond-Gleeson

   Small Claims Court/Provincial Division: PO Box 218, Orillia ON L3V 6J3 – 705/326-5652 – Joan Scott

Victoria-Haliburton Counties, Court House, 440 Kent St. West, PO Box 4000, Lindsay ON K9V 5P2 – 705/324-1400

   Provincial Division/Enforcement & Process Serving, Nora McIsaac

   Counter Services for Civil Matters: 10 New Castle St., PO Box 270, Minden ON K0M 2K0 – 705/286-6417 – Nancy Russell

Regional Municipality of York, Court House, 50 Eagle St. West, Newmarket ON L3Y 6B1

   Manager, Court Services, Mary Louise Porcelli, 905/853-4822

   Provincial Division/Enforcement & Process Serving, Mike Terzievski, 905/853-4809

   Provincial Division, Evelyn Thompson, 905/853-4801

   Small Claims Court: 855 Major MacKenzie Dr., Richmond Hill ON L4C 4X7 – 905/737-4416 – Nicole Cole

REGIONAL COURT: CENTRAL SOUTH

Areas served: Brant, Haldimand-Norfolk, Hamilton-Wentworth, Niagara (St. Catharines), Niagara (Welland), Waterloo

Brant County, Court House, 70 Wellington St., Brantford ON N3T 2L9

   Manager, Court Services, Cathy Hiuser, 519/752-9069

   Enforcement & Process Serving/Counter for Civil Matters, Ken Hamilton, 519/752-7828

   Provincial Division: 44 Queen St., Brantford ON N3T 3B2 – 519/758-3460 – Ken Hamilton

Regional Municipality of Haldimand-Norfolk (Cayuga), Court House, 55 Munsee St. North, PO Box 70, Cayuga ON N0A 1E0 – 905/772-3335

   Provincial Division/Enforcement & Processing Serving, Sharon Warring

Regional Municipality of Haldimand-Norfolk (Simcoe), 530 Queensway West, PO Box 308, Simcoe ON N3Y 4L2 – 519/426-1408

   Provincial & General Divisions/Enforcement & Process Serving, Susan Bridge

Regional Municipality of Hamilton-Wentworth, Court House, 55 Main St. West, Hamilton ON L8P 1H4

   Manager, Court Services, Joanne Spriet, 905/577-8326

   Provincial Division (Family), Bernadette Flis, 905/525-1550

   Provincial Division (Criminal): 125 Main St. East, Hamilton ON L8N 3Z3 – 905/525-1840 – Mary Hudacin

   Small Claims Court: 140 Hunter St., Hamilton ON L8N 4H1 – 905/522-9063 – Robert Stone

Hamilton, 50 Main St. East, Hamilton ON L8N 1E9

   Enforcement & Process Serving, Reno Violin, 905/308-7221

   Local Registrar, Relph Beam-Parker, 905/308-7218

Regional Municipality of Niagara North (St. Catharines), Court House, 59 Church St., St. Catharines ON L2R 7N8 – 905/988-6200

   Manager, Court Services, Patricia Clark

   Enforcement & Process Serving/Provincial Division, Ralph Beam-Parker

   Counter Services for Civil Matters, Mary Ellen Hilko

Regional Municipality of Niagara South (Welland), 3 Cross St., Welland ON L3B 5X6

   Provincial Division (Family), Connie Novosel, 905/734-7451

   Provincial Division (Criminal)/Sheriff's Office, Pam Stringer, 905/732-2493

   Counter Services for Civil Matters: 102 Main St. East, Welland ON L3B 5R4 – 905/735-0010 – R. Morin

Niagara Falls, 4635 Queen St., Niagara Falls ON L2E 2L7

   Provincial Division (Criminal), Odette Briggs, 905/354-2789

   Bailiff/Small Claims Court, Jan Huntington, 905/354-3360

Regional Municipality of Waterloo, Court House, 20 Weber St. East, Kitchener ON N2H 1C3

   Manager, Court Services, Michel Gauvreau, 519/741-3234

   Local Registrar, Enforcement & Process Serving, Larry Ketchmark, 519/741-3203

   Provincial Division: #1000, 200 Frederick St., Kitchener ON N2H 6P1 – 519/741-3396 – Carol Gogos

   Small Claims Court: #520, 50 Queen St. North, Kitchener ON N2H 6P4 – 519/745-5842 – Elizabeth Belyea

REGIONAL COURT: CENTRAL WEST

Areas served: Bruce, Dufferin, Grey, Halton, Peel, Wellington

Bruce County, Court House, 215 Cayley St., Walkerton ON N0G 2V0

Manager, Court Services, Sheriff & Bailiff, Glenna McComb, 519/881-1772
Small Claims Court, David Ellis, 519/881-1772
Local Registrar, Gerald Johnson, 519/881-0211
Provincial Division, Nancy Coleman, 519/881-0211
Dufferin County, Court House, 10 Louisa St., Orangeville ON L9W 3P9
Local Registrar, Sheriff, Bailiff, Small Claims Court, Thom Collyer, 519/941-9701, 4744
Provincial Division, Diane Golden, 905/941-5802
Grey County, Court House, 595 - 9 Ave. East, Owen Sound ON N4K 3E3
Local Registrar, Small Claims Court, Pat Kay, 519/376-3812
Bailiff & Sheriff, Muriel Parkes, 519/376-7535
Owen Sound, 1133 - 2 Ave. East, Owen Sound ON N4K 2J1
Manager, Court Services, Sharon Vickers, 519/371-2226
Regional Municipality of Halton, Court House, 491 Steeles Ave. East, Milton ON L9T 1Y7 – 905/878-2672
Manager, Court Services, Local Registrar, Provincial/General Divs., Marion Maslach
Small Claims Court, Fiona MacPherson, 905/878-7281
Small Claims Court: 2021 Plains Rd. East, Burlington ON L7R 4M3 – 905/637-4125 – Gloria Owen
Small Claims Court: 1225 Trafalgar Rd., PO Box 84020, Oakville ON L6H 3P1 – 905/842-8380 – Clare Patterson
Regional Municipality of Peel, Court House, 7765 Huronontario St., PO Box 548, Brampton ON L6V 2L1
Manager, Court Services & Provincial Division (Criminal), Bob Gleason, 905/452-6601
Bailiff/Sheriff, Barbara Turner, 905/452-6600
Local Registrar/Small Claims Court: 7755 Huronontario St., PO Box 8000, Brampton ON L6V 2M7 – 905/452-6617 – Joyce Lazic
Provincial Division (Family): 7765 Huronontario St., 2nd Fl., PO Box 220, Brampton ON L6V 2L1 – 905/452-6608 – Shan Georgsen
Small Claims Court: 2301 Haines Rd., Mississauga ON L4Y 1Y5 – 905/275-3083 – Joan Zammit
Wellington County, Court House, 74 Woolwich St., Guelph ON N1H 3T9
Manager, Court Services, Bill Hansford, 519/824-4100
Provincial Division(Family)/Counter Servs. for Civil Matters, Norma McDonald, 519/824-4100
Small Claims Court, Bonnie Epoch, 519/824-4169
Guelph, 36 Wyndham St. South, Guelph ON N1G 3T9 – 519/836-2501
Enforcement & Process Serving, Kathleen Cross, 519/824-4430
Provincial Division (Criminal), Joanne Riddell, 519/836-2501

REGIONAL COURT: EAST
Areas served: Frontenac, Hastings, Lanark, Leeds-Grenville, Lennox-Addington, Ottawa-Carleton, Prescott-Russell, Prince Edward, Renfrew, Stormont-Dundas-Glengarry
Frontenac County, Court House, 279 Wellington St., Kingston ON K7L 6E1
Manager, Court Services, Dianne Aziz, 613/548-6202
Provincial Division (Criminal), Arlene Stoness, 613/548-6200
Provincial Division (Family): 469 Montreal St., Kingston ON K7K 3H9 – 613/548-6789 – Vivianne Carpenter
Small Claims Court: General Delivery, Sharbot Lake ON K0H 2P0 – 613/279-2537 – Bailiff, Donna Ladouceur
Kingston, Court House, 5 Court St., Kingston ON K7L 2N4 – 613/548-6816
Small Claims Court, Dianne Aziz
Local Registrar, Jackie Gumienny
Hastings County, Court House, 235 Pinnacle St., Belleville ON K8N 3A9
Manager, Court Services, Local Registrar, Sheriff & Bailiff, Robert C. Coveney, 613/962-9106, 9694
Small Claims Court, Cyndi Hunt, 613/962-2300
Small Claims Court: 5 Fairway Blvd., Bancroft ON K0L 1C0 – 613/332-4613 – Yvonne Trollope
Provincial Division (Criminal): 15 Victoria Ave., Belleville ON K8N 1Z5 – 613/962-3468 – Bonnie Gryce
Provincial Division (Family): #402, Century Pl., PO Box 906, Belleville ON K8N 5B6 – 613/968-6759 – Bonnie Gryce
Small Claims Court: 80 Division St., Trenton ON K8V 5S5 – 613/392-1655 – Kaye Coling
Lanark County, Court House, 43 Drummond St. East, Perth ON K7H 1G1 – 613/267-2021
Manager, Court Services, Valerie Neville
Leeds & Grenville County, District Court House, PO Box 8, Brockville ON K6V 5T7
Small Claims Court, Jean Jensen, 613/342-2833
Local Registrar & Sheriff, Andrew Gransden, 613/342-2288
Provincial Division: 75 Water St. West, PO Box 1300, Brockville ON K6V 5Y6 – 613/342-5003 – Andrew Gransden
Lennox & Addington County, 41 Dundas St. West, PO Box 266, Napanee ON K7R 1Z5 – 613/354-3845
Provincial Division/Enforcement & Process Serving/Civil Matters, Pamela Crockett
Small Claims Court: Hwy. 7, PO Box 88, Kaladar ON K0H 1Z0 – 613/336-2050 – Bailiff, Frances Boomhour
Regional Municipality of Ottawa-Carleton, Court House, 161 Elgin St., Ottawa ON K2P 2K1
Bailiff, Sheriff, Provincial Division (Criminal), Jackie Henderson, 613/239-1098
Manager, Court Services, Carol O'Brien, 613/239-1490
Local Registrar, Small Claims Court, Joanne Williams, 613/239-1105
Provincial Division (Family), Lynda Emerson, 613/239-1034
Prescott & Russell County, Court House, 59 Court St., L'Orignal ON K0B 1K0 – 613/675-4695
Manager, Court Services, Small Claims Court/Provincial Division, Liette Giroux
Rockland: 1783 St. Laurent Blvd., PO Box 2, Rockland ON K1K 1C2 – 613/446-5698 – Bailiff, Dennis Houle
Prince Edward County, Court House, 44 Union St., Picton ON K0K 2T0
Local Registrar & Sheriff, James Bervie, 613/476-6236
Bailiff, Small Claims Court, Donna Stever, 613/476-6236
Provincial Division, Gloria Stone, 613/476-2606
Renfrew County, Court House, 297 Pembroke St. East, Pembroke ON K8A 3G2
Local Registrar, Sheriff, Provincial Division (Family), Monique Rousseau, 613/732-8581
Small Claims Court, C. Harkins, 613/732-2541
Bailiff, Harry Blackley, 613/732-8581
Court Services: #415, 417 Pembroke St., Pembroke ON K8A 6X3 – 613/735-6886 – Manager, Helen Mick
Small Claims Court: 315 Raglan St. South, PO Box 386, Renfrew ON K7V 4A6 – 613/432-3193 – Joanne O'Gorman
Pembroke, 415-417 Pembroke St. West, PO Box 218, Pembroke ON K8A 6X3 – 613/732-8581
Manager, Court Services, Helen Mick
Provincial Division (Criminal), A.M. Hamilton
Stormont, Dundas & Glengarry County, Court House, 340 Pitt St., 4th Fl., PO Box 56, Cornwall ON K6H 5R9 – 613/933-7500
Manager, Court Services, Diane Brunet-Mongeon
Small Claims Court, M. McMartin
Provincial Division (Criminal), Lyse Pichie
Provincial Division (Family), Diane Plamondon
Local Registrar, Beverly Roy
Enforcement & Process Serving, Anne Senecal
Small Claims Court/Provincial Division (Criminal): Shopping Mall, Hwys. 2 & 31, Morrisburg ON K0C 1X0 – 613/543-2193 – Monique LeFebvre
Alexandria, 110 Main St. North, PO Box 699, Alexandria ON K0C 1A0
Provincial Division (Criminal), Gabrielle Blais, 613/525-4330
Small Claims Court, J. Wensink, 613/525-1057

REGIONAL COURT: NORTHEAST REGION
Areas served: Algoma, Cochrane, Manitoulin, Nipissing, Parry Sound, Sudbury, Timiskaming
Algoma District, Court House, 426 Queen St. East, Sault Ste. Marie ON P6A 1Z7
Manager, Court Services, Small Claims Court, Lesley Benderavage, 705/759-9450
Provincial Division (Criminal), Anna Callon, 705759-9466
Local Registrar, Provincial Division (Family), Lonnie Ostroski, 705/759-9418
Small Claims Court, Provincial Division: 200 Ontario St., Elliott Lake ON P5A 1Y4 – 705/848-2500 – Bailiff, Louise Greco
Cochrane District, Court House, 149 - 4 Ave., PO Box 2069, Cochrane ON P0L 1C0 – 705/272-4256
Manager, Court Services, Paul Langlois
Provincial Division, Lise Koslosksi
Enforcement & Process Serving/Counter for Civil Matters, Chris Robin
Sheriff, Rene Lamarche
Enforcement & Process Serving; Counter for Civil Matters, Chris Robin
Small Claims Court: 885 Centennial St., PO Box 874, Iroquois Falls ON P0K 1G0 – 705/232-7744 – Bailiff, Adrien Cyr
Small Claims Court: #35, 25 Brunetville, Kapuskasing ON P5N 2E9 – 705/337-1477 – Lorese Lauzon
Timmins: #127, 38 Pine St., Timmins ON P4N 6K6 – 705/267-7799
Bailiff, Edward Colbert
Provincial Division, Theresa Miller
Manitoulin District, Court House, 27 Phipps St., PO Box 265, Gore Bay ON P0P 1H0
Local Registrar, Sheriff & Bailiff, Small Claims Court, Ron Lane, 705/282-2461
Provincial Division, Sharon Sloss, 705/282-2531
Small Claims Court: 15 Robinson St., PO Box 358, Little Current ON P0P 1K0 – 705/368-2205 – Mary McHarg
Nipissing District, Court House, 360 Plouffe St., North Bay ON P1B 9L5 – 705/495-8309
Manager, Court Services, Small Claims Court, Nestor Prisco
Bailiff, Bob Raycraft
Small Claims Court: 229 Main St., PO Box 416, Sturgeon Falls ON P0H 2G0 – 705/753-1090 – Bailiff, Marlene Bertrand
Parry Sound District, Court House, 89 James St., Parry Sound ON P2A 1T7
Manager, Court Services, Nestor Prisco, 705/746-1414
Provincial Division, Marilyn Helmkay, 705/746-4237
Bailiff, Local Registrar & Sheriff, Small Claims Court, Michael Ryman, 705/746-4251
Small Claims Court: PO Box 119, Burks Falls ON P0A 1C0 – 705/382-2571 – Bailiff,
Sudbury District, Court House, 155 Elm St. West, Sudbury ON P3C 1T9
Manager, Court Services, David Lafreniere, 705/671-5923
Local Registrar, Doug Seaton, 705/671-5958

Small Claims Court, Provincial Division: #3, 100 Tudhope St., Espanola ON P5E 1S6 – 705/869-4334 – Linda Fuller
Sudbury: 38 Larch St., Sudbury ON P3E 5M7 – 705/675-4164 – Bailiff,
Sudbury, 159 Cedar St., 2nd Fl., Sudbury ON P3E 6A5
Small Claims Court, Ruth-Anne Ingram, 705/670-7251
Provincial Division, 705/670-7250
Timiskaming District, Court House, 393 Main St., PO Box 609, Haileybury ON P0J 1K0
Local Registrar, Susan Rennie, 705/672-3321
Enforcement & Process Serving/Civil Matters, Carmen MacKewn
Provincial Division, Nancy Young, 705/672-3395
Small Claims Court: 50 Third St., PO Box 147, Englehart ON P0J 1H0 – 705/544-8177 – Patricia Ann Proctor
Kirkland Lake, 4 Kirkland St. West, Kirkland Lake ON P2N 2G2
Provincial Division, Lina Chartrand-Carriere
Small Claims Court, Wendy Lee Rogoza, 705/567-9381

REGIONAL COURT: NORTHWEST REGION
Areas served: Kenora, Rainy River, Thunder Bay
Kenora District, Court House, 216 Water St., Kenora ON P9N 1S4 – 807/468-2842
Manager, Court Services, Margaret Mathieson
Local Registrar/Sheriff/Bailiff, Small Claims Court, Peter Hall
Provincial Division, Susan Newton
Dryden, #127, 479 Government St., PO Box 636, Dryden ON P8N 3B3
Provincial Division, Adrianne Ridgeway, 807/223-2348
Bailiff, Small Claims Court, Florence Smith, 807/223-2613
Red Lake, PO Box 1070, Red Lake ON P0V 2M0
Provincial Division, Norma Ewen, 807/727-2376
Bailiff, Small Claims Court, Judy Jeffrey, 807/727-3310
Rainy River District, Court House, 333 Church St., Fort Frances ON P9A 1C9 – 807/274-5961
Local Registrar/Sheriff/Bailiff, Small Claims Court/Provincial Division, John E. Bradley
Thunder Bay District, Court House, 277 Camelot St., Thunder Bay ON P7A 4B3
Regional Manager, Court Services, Bob Gordon, 807/343-2747
Local Registrar/Sheriff/Bailiff, Small Claims Court, Alvin Franks, 807/343-2728, 2725
Provincial Division, Bruce McLean, 807/625-1600, 1610
Small Claims Court: 624 Main St., PO Box 39, Geraldton ON P0T 1M0 – 807/854-1488 – Bailiff, Laurette Payeur
Small Claims Court: 10 Front St., Nipigon ON P0T 2J0 – 807/887-3829 – Bailiff, Edna Aubut
Bailiff: 223 Walker Lake Dr., PO Box 248, Schreiber ON P0T 2S0 – 807/824-2543 – Keith Scott

REGIONAL COURT: SOUTHWEST
Areas served: Elgin, Essex, Huron, Kent, Lambton, Middlesex, Oxford, Perth
Elgin County, Justice Bldg., 145 Curtis St., St. Thomas ON N5P 3Z7
Sheriff & Manager, Court Services, Small Claims Court, Gordon Button, 519/631-3530
Local Registrar, Provincial Division (Family), Karen Moule, 519/633-1720
Provincial Division (Criminal), Anne Patton, 519/633-1230
Essex County, Court House, 245 Windsor Ave., Windsor ON N9A 1J2
Manager, Court Services, Brian Lemire, 519/973-6604
Local Registrar, Donna Downes, 519/973-6620

Small Claims Court, Marie-Anne Kelly-Lalonde, 519/973-6665
Small Claims Court: #303C, 33 Princess St., Leamington ON N8H 5C5 – 519/326-9854 – Pat Mailing
Provincial Division (Criminal): Provincial Court, City Hall Sq., PO Box 607, Windsor ON N9A 6N4 – 519/254-2591 – Mara Conrad
Windsor, Ontario Govt. Bldg., 250 Windsor Ave., 4th Fl., Windsor ON N9A 6V9
Bailiff/Sheriff, Judy Harris, 519/973-6603
Provincial Division (Family), Linda Peltier, 519/973-6669
Huron County, Court House, 1 Court House Sq., PO Box 400, Goderich ON N7A 1M2
Manager, Court Services, Bailiff/Sheriff, Small Claims Court, Gord Button, 519/524-7322, 2519
Provincial Division, Linda McIvor, 519/524-9342
Kent County, Court House, 21 - 7th St., PO Box 2021, Chatham ON N7M 5L9 – 519/352-9070
Local Registrar/Bailiff/Sheriff, Small Claims Court/Provincial Division, Joy Shaun
Lambton County, Court House, 700 North Christina St., PO Box 2587, Sarnia ON N7V 3C2
Manager, Court Services, Rosemarie Gandz, 519/337-5314
Local Registrar, Pat Wemple, 519/337-5314
Provincial Division (Criminal), Marie Burns, 519/336-8830
Provincial Division (Family), Carol McKerracher, 519/337-2346
Bailiff, Jim Lowry, 519/337-7964
Sheriff, Kim Policelli, 519/337-8940
Middlesex County, Court House, 80 Dundas St., London ON N6A 6A3
Manager, Court Services, Ron Marks, 519/660-3049
Local Registrar, Provincial Division/Counter Servs. for Civil Matters, Connie Holmes, 519/660-3054
Enforcement & Process Serving, Pam Johnson, 519/660-3004
Small Claims Court, Fran Martellotti, 519/660-3000
Small Claims Court: 52 Frank St., Strathroy ON N7G 2R4 – 519/245-1477 – Bailiff, Dean Dolbear
Oxford County, Court House, 415 Hunter Rd., PO Box 70, Woodstock ON N4S 7W5 – 519/539-6187
Manager, Court Services, Gord Button
Local Registrar/Sheriff/Bailiff, Small Claims Court/Provincial Division, Virginia Taylor
Perth County, Administration of Justice Bldg., 100 St. Patrick St., PO Box 1010, Stratford ON N5A 6W4 – 519/271-9252
Manager, Court Services, Gord Button
Provincial Division, Shirley Creek
Small Claims Court: Court House, PO Box 726, Stratford ON N5A 6V6 – 519/271-1850 – Local Registrar/Sheriff/Bailiff, Don Misener

REGIONAL COURT: METROPOLITAN TORONTO
Areas served: Toronto, Metro North (North York), Metro East (Scarborough), Metro West (Etobicoke)
Downsview, 1000 Finch Ave. West, North York ON M3J 2V5 – 416/314-4208
Provincial Division (Criminal), Rosa Martelli
Etobicoke, 80 The East Mall, Etobicoke ON M8Z 5X6 – 416/314-3967
Provincial Division, Kapeel Karandat
Court Services: 2265 Keele St., 2nd Fl., Toronto ON M6M 3Z7 – 416/326-6731 – Manager, Lynn Norris
Small Claims Court: #209, 2265 Keele St., Toronto ON M6M 5B8 – 416/326-6707 – Nora Gauer
North York, 47 Sheppard Ave. East, 3rd Fl., North York ON M2N 5N1
Small Claims Court, Graham Beeby, 416/326-3554
Provincial Division (Family), Carmen Carnovale, 416/326-3568
Provincial Division (Family), Gemma Castellino, 416/326-3592

Scarborough, 1911 Eglinton Ave. East, Scarborough ON M1L 4P4
Manager, Court Services, Sylvia Orgias, 416/325-0357
Provincial Division, Neville Clement, 416/325-0975
Provincial Division, Micheline Seguin, 416/325-0974
Small Claims Court: #300, 2130 Lawrence Ave. East, Scarborough ON M1R 5B9 – 416/327-1155 – Carol Gottschalk
Toronto, Court House, 361 University Ave., Toronto ON M5G 1T3
Manager, Court Services, Huguette Malyon, 416/327-5545
Sheriff, Graham Hall, 416/327-6326
Toronto, Court House, 60 Queen St. West, Toronto ON M5H 2M4
Manager, Court Services, Marie Cardno, 416/327-5896
Provincial Division (Criminal), Donna Johnstone, 416/327-5831
Criminal Court: 444 Yonge St., 2nd Fl., Toronto ON M5B 1H4 – Manager, Graham Borton
Family Court: 311 Jarvis St., Toronto ON M5B 2C4 – 416/963-0677 – Manager, Hazel Davis
Family Court: 311 Jarvis St., Toronto ON M5B 2C4 – 416/963-0677 – Manager, Val Fillippilli
Small Claims Court: 444 Yonge St., 2nd Fl., Toronto ON M5B 2M4 – 416/324-7367 – Manager, June Caldwell
Toronto, 444 Yonge St., 2nd Fl., Toronto ON M5B 2H4 – 416/325-8925
Small Claims Court/Provincial Division (Criminal), Graham Borton
Toronto, #174, 130 Queen St. West, Toronto ON M5H 2N5 – 416/327-5036
Local Registrar, General Division, Mary Dayton
Toronto, 311 Jarvis St., Toronto ON M5B 2C4 – 416/327-6853
Provincial Division (Family), Dorothy Marcil
Toronto, 439 University Ave., 3rd Fl., Toronto ON M5H 1Y8 – 416/326-2940
Estates, Joel Persaud
Toronto, #127, 145 Queen St. West, Toronto ON M5H 2N9 – 416/327-6935
Local Registrar, Marie Singh

PRINCE EDWARD ISLAND

PRINCE EDWARD ISLAND SUPREME COURT
Sir Louis Henry Davies Law Courts Bldg., 42 Water St., PO Box 2000, Charlottetown PE C1A 7N8
Chief Justice, The Hon. Norman H. Carruthers

SUPREME COURT: COURT OF APPEAL
Sir Louis Henry Davies Law Courts Bldg., 42 Water St., PO Box 2000, Charlottetown PE C1A 7N8
The Court of Appeal has appellate jurisdiction in criminal and civil matters.
Chief Justice, The Hon. Mr. Norman H. Carruthers
Judges (The Hon. Mr./Madam Justice): John McQuaid; Gerard E. Mitchell
Deputy Registrar, Appeal Division, Gloria Panting

SUPREME COURT: TRIAL DIVISION
Sir Louis Davies Law Courts Bldg., 42 Water St., PO Box 2000, Charlottetown PE C1A 7N8
The Supreme Court is a Court of original jurisdiction and has jurisdiction in all civil (including family, estate and small claims) and criminal matters arising in Prince Edward Island.
Chief Justice, The Hon. Mr. Kenneth R. MacDonald
Justices (The Hon. Mr./Madam Justice):
J. Armand Desroches; Joseph A. Ghiz; David Jenkins; Jacquiline Matheson
Registrar, Bankruptcy, George E. MacMillan, 902/368-6025

Deputy Registrar, Estates Section, Gloria Panting
Deputy Registrar, General Section, Marjorie MacDonald
Deputy Registrar, Small Claims Section, Elva Costello
Deputy Registrar, Family Section, Anne Clough

PRINCE EDWARD ISLAND PROVINCIAL COURT,
The Provincial Court has jurisdiction in select criminal matters as well as youth matters.
- Prince County: Provincial Court, Law Courts Bldg., PO Box 2020, Summerside PE C1N 4M1
  Chief Judge, The Hon. Ralph C. Thompson
- Queens & Kings Counties: Provincial Court, Law Courts Bldg., PO Box 2290, Charlottetown PE C1A 8C1
  Judges (The Hon.):
  G.L. Fitzgerald; Nancy K. Orr

JUDICIAL OFFICERS,
Kings County: Judicial Officers, Court House, Georgetown PE C0A 1L0
  Sheriff, Howard Kerwin, 902/652-2215
  Deputy Registrar, Aurell Johnston, 902/652-2308
  Registrar of Deeds, Charlottetown, Kathy Toole, 902/368-4591
Prince County: Judicial Officers, Court House, PO Box 2020, Summerside PE C1N 4M1
  Sheriff, Ed Dornan, 902/888-8191
  Deputy Registrar, Wayne Lilly, 902/888-8190
  Registrar of Deeds, Eileen Gaudet
Queens County: Judicial Officers, Law Courts, PO Box 2000, Charlottetown PE C1A 7N8
  Chief Sheriff, Frank Driscoll, 902/368-6055
  Prothonotary, G.E. MacMillan
  Registrar of Deeds, Kathy Toole, 902/368-4591
  Registrar of Supreme Court & Chief Provincial Court Clerk, Dorothy Kitson, 902/368-6005

QUÉBEC

QUÉBEC: COUR D'APPEL,
The Court of Appeal has appellate jurisdiction in all civil and criminal matters.
Montréal: Cour d'Appel, 1, rue Notre-Dame est, Montréal PQ H2Y 1B6
Juge en chef, L'Honorable Pierre Michaud
Juges (Les Honorables):
Jean Louis Baudouin; Marc Beauregard; André Brossard; Jacques Chamberland; Marie Deschamps; Morris J. Fish; André Forget; Louise Mailhot; Joseph R. Nuss; Michel Proulx; Michel J. Robert; Melvin L. Rothman (surnum.); Claude Vallerand
- Québec: Cour d'Appel, 300, boul Jean-Lesage, Québec PQ G1K 8K6
  Juges (Les Honorables):
  Roger Chouinard (surnum.); Jacques Deslile; René Dussault; Paul-Arthur Gendreau; Louis Le Bel; Louise Otis; Thérèse Rousseau-Houle; Christine Tourigny

QUÉBEC: COUR SUPÉRIEURE
300, boul Jean-Lesage, Québec PQ G1K 8K6
418/649-3501
The Superior Court has original jurisdiction in all civil and criminal matters arising in Québec, unless otherwise indicated by statute. Judges of the Superior Court have jurisdiction in Bankruptcy.
Juge en chef, L'Honorable Lyse Lemieux
Juge en Chef associé, L'Honorable René W. Dionne
Juges (Les Honorables):
Yves Alain; Jules Allard; Frank Barakett; Jean-Claude Beaulieu; Camille L. Bergeron (surnum.); Bruno Bernard; Jean Bienvenue (surnum.); Jacques Blanchard; Danielle Blondin-Gingras (surnum.); Gérald Boisvert; Armand Carrier; Pierre Côté (surnum.); Louis De Blois; Gaston Desjardins; André Desmeules; Jacques Dufour (surnum.); André Gervais; Ross Goodwinn; Jean-Roch Landry; Henri Larue; Gérard Lebel; Robert Lesage; René Letarte; Édouard Martin; Benoît Morin; Gaétan Pelletier; Jacques Philippon; Paul Reeves (surnum.); Jean Richard; Claude Rioux (surnum.); Louis Rochette; France Thibault; François Tremblay; André Trottier (surnum.); Hubert Walters
Registraire de Faillite, Rm. #1.32, 418/649-3505
- Abitibi: Registraires de Faillite, 900, 7e rue, Val-d'Or PQ J9P 3P8 – 819/825-6462
- Alma: Cour Supérieure, 725, boul Harvey ouest, Alma PQ G8B 1P5
  Juges (Les Honorables):
  Gratien Duchesne
  Registraire de Faillite, #31, 418/668-3334
- Amos: Cour Supérieure, 891, rue 3e ouest, Amos PQ J9T 2T4
- Arthabaska: Registraire de Faillite, 800, boul Bois-Francs sud, Arthabaska PQ G6P 5W5 – 819/357-2054
  Registraires, Denis Noël, Nicole Simoneau
- Baie-Comeau: Cour Supérieure, Palais de Justice, 71, av Mance, Baie Comeau PQ G4C 1N2
  Juges (Les Honorables):
  Baie Comeau/Mingan: Paul A. Corriveau
  Registraire de Faillite, 418/296-5534
- Beauce: Registraire de Faillite, 795, av du Palais, CP 820, St-Joseph-de-Beauce PQ G0S 2V0 – 418/397-4188
- Beauharnois: Registraire de Faillite, 180, rue Salaberry, Valleyfield PQ J6T 2J2 – 514/370-4006
- Bedford: Registraire de Faillite, 920 rue Principale, Cowansville PQ J2K 1K2
  77, rue Principale, Granby PQ J2G 9B3 – 514/263-3520
- Bonaventure: Registraire de Faillite, 87, rue Principale, CP 517, New Carlisle PQ G0C 1Z0 – 418/752-3376
- Chicoutimi: Cour Supérieure, 227, rue Racine est, Chicoutimi PQ G7H 1S2
  Juges (Les Honorables):
  Jacques Babin; J. Roger Bandford; Pierre Bergeron; Claude Larouche
  Registraire de Faillite, 418/696-9927; Fax: 418/696-9944
- Drummondville: Registraire de Faillite, 1680, boul St-Joseph, Drummondville PQ J2C 2G3 – 819/478-2513
- Frontenac: Registraire de Faillite, 693, rue St-Alphonse ouest, CP 579, Thetford Mines PQ G6G 3X3 – 418/338-2118
- Gaspé: Registraire de Faillite, Palais de Justice, 124, rte 132, CP 188, Percé PQ G0C 2L0 – 418/782-2055
- Hull: Cour Supérieure, 17, rue Laurier, Hull PQ J8X 4C1
  Juges (Les Honorables): Charles B. Major (surnum.); Jean-Pierre Plouffe
  Hull, Labelle & Pontiac: Jean R. Dagenais; Orville Frenette (surnum.); Louis-Philippe Landry; Johanne Trudel
  Registraire de Faillite, #0.210, 819/776-8100, poste 8323
- Iberville: Registraire de Faillite, 109, rue St-Charles, Saint-Jean-sur-Richelieu PQ J3B 2C2 – 514/347-3715
- Joliette: Registraire de Faillite, 200, rue St-Marc, Joliette PQ J6E 8C2 – 514/753-4819
- Kamouraska: Registraire de Faillite, 33, rue de la Cour, Rivière-du-Loup PQ G5R 1J1 – 418/862-3579
- Laval: Cour Supérieure, 2800, boul Saint-Martin ouest, Laval PQ H7T 2S9
  Juges (Les Honorables):
  Jean Filiatreault; Yvan A. Macerola; Paul Trudeau
- Mingan: Registraire de Faillite, 425, boul Laure, Sept-Îles PQ G4R 1X6 – 418/962-2154
- Montréal: Cour Supérieure, 1, rue Notre-Dame est, Montréal PQ H2Y 1B6 – 514/873-3227
  Juges (Les Honorables): Jean Archambault; Guy Arsenault; Georges Audet; Roger Baker; Alphonse Barbeau (surnum.); François Bélanger; Pierre Béliveau; Nicole Bénard; Marc Beaudoin; Jules Beauregard (surnum.); Marcel Belleville (surnum.); Claude Benoit (surnum.); Anthime Bergeron (surnum.); Rodolphe Bilodeau; André G. Biron; Yvan Bisaillon (surnum.); John Bishop; Jules Blanchet; Jean-Guy Boilard; Sylvianne Borenstein; Pierre Boudreault; Jean-Marie Brassard (surnum.); Paul P. Carrière; Jean-Jude Chabot; Paul Chaput; Vital Cliche; Lise Côté; Michel Coté; Jean Crépeau; J.F. Louis Crête; Jean-Jacques Crôteau; Pierre J. Dalphond; Wilbrod Décarie; André Denis; André Deslongchamps (Juge en chef adjoint); Kevin Downs; Jacques Dugas (surnum.); Roland Durand; Denis Durocher; Nicole Duval-Hesler; Robert T. Flahiff; Bernard Flynn; Jean Frappier; John H. Gomery; Benjamin J. Greenberg; Danielle Grenier; Claude Guérin; Jean Guibault; Derek A. Guthrie; Irving J. Halperin; Gilles Hébert; René Hurtubise; Pierre Jasmin; Paul Jolin; Claire Barrette Joncas; Pierre Journet; Carole Julien; James T. Kennedy; Maurice E. Lagacé; Claude Larouche; Jean Louis Léger; Denis Lévesque; Hélène Lebel; Jean Legault; Louise Lemelin; Anatole Lesyk (surnum.); Diane Marcelin-Laurin; Jean Marquis (surnum.); Fraser J. Martin; Herbert Marx; Israël S. Mass; Yves Mayrand; Victor Melançon; Gilles Mercure; Maurice Mercure (surnum.); Perry Meyer (surnum.); Nicole Morneau; Jean-Claude Nolin (surnum.); Jean-L. Normand; Luc Parent; Réjean F. Paul; Ginette Piché; Pierre Pinard; Jean Provost (surnum.); Pierrette Rayle; Danielle Richer; André Rochon; François Rolland; Gontran Rouleau; Jeannine M. Rousseau; Gérald-J. Ryan (surnum.); Jean-Piere Sénécal; Pierrette Sévigny-McConomy; Lou S. Tannenbaum; Claude Tellier; Pierre Tessier; Daniel H. Tingley; Anne-Marie Trahan; Roland Tremblay; Clement Trudel; Gérard Turmel (surnum.); Jacques Vaillancourt; Jocelyn Verrier; Pierre Viau; Dionysia Zerbisias; Jack J. Zigman
  Longueuil: Bernard Gratton
  Registraire de Faillite, #1.195, 514/393-2058
- Richelieu: Registraire de Faillite, 46, rue Charlotte, Sorel PQ J3P 6N5 – 514/742-2786
- Rimouski: Cour Supérieure, 183, av de la Cathédrale, CP 800, Rimouski PQ G5L 7C9
  Juges (Les Honorables):
  Gilles Blanchet; Robert Pidgeon
  Registraire de Faillite, 418/722-3852
- Roberval: Registraire de Faillite, 750, boul Saint-Joseph, Roberval PQ G8H 2L5 – 418/275-5073
- Rouyn: Cour Supérieure, 2, av du Palais, Rouyn PQ J9X 2N9
  Juges (Les Honorables):
  Abitibi: Ivan St-Julien
  Abitibi & Rouyn: Jacques Viens
  Abitibi, Rouyn-Noranda & Témiscamingue: Laurent Guertin
  Registraire de Faillite, Rouyn-Noranda & Témiscamingue, 819/764-6709
- St-François: Registraire de Faillite, 375, rue King ouest, Sherbrooke PQ J1H 6B9 – 819/822-6902
- St-Hyacinthe: Registraire de Faillite, 1550, rue Dessaules, St-Hyacinthe PQ J2S 2S8 – 514/773-8471
- St-Maurice: Registraire de Faillite, 212, rue 6e, Shawinigan PQ G9N 8B6 – 819/536-2571
- Shawinigan: Cour Supérieure, 212, rue 6e, Shawinigan PQ G1K 8B6
  Juges (Les Honorables):
  St-Maurice: Gilles Gauthier
- Sherbrooke: Cour Supérieure, 375, rue King ouest, Sherbrooke PQ J1H 6B9
  Juges (Les Honorables):

Mégantic & St-François: Leo Daigle; Pierre C. Fournier

St-François: Raynald Frechette; Paul M. Gervais (surnum.); Jean-Louis Péloquin (surnum.); Georges Savoie (surnum.); Thomas Toth (surnum.)

St-François & Bedford: Paul-Marcel Bellavance; Pierre Boily; Louis-Philipe Galipeau

St-François, Bedford & Sherbrooke: Suzanne Mireault

- Terrebonne: Registraire de Faillite, 400, rue Laviolette, St-Jerôme PQ J7Y 2T6 – 514/431-4407
- Trois-Rivières: Cour Supérieure, 250, rue Laviolette, Trois-Rivières PQ G9A 1T9
  Juges (Les Honorables):
  Guy Lebrun; Robert Legris; Jacques J. Levesque
  Registraire de Faillite, 819/372-4150
- Val-d'Or: Cour Supérieure, 900, rue 7e, Val-d'Or PQ J9P 4P8

QUÉBEC: COUR DU QUÉBEC
300, boul Jean Lesage, Québec PQ G1R 8K6
39, rue St-Louis, Québec PQ G1R 3Z2

The Québec Court has jurisdiction in select civil, criminal and penal matters as well as youth, expropriation, small claims and provincial tax matters.

Juge en chef, L'Honorable Louis Morin
Juge en chef associé, L'Honorable Yvon Mercier
Juges (Les Honorables):

Chambre Civile: Richard Beaulieu; Gilles Bergeron; Lina Bond; Gérald Bossé; Raymond Boucher; André C. Cartier; Pierre Choquette; André Cloutier; Gill Fortier (Juge en chef adjoint); Louis-Charles Fournier; Bertrand Gagnon; Denis Gobeil; G. André Gobeil; François Godbout (Juge en chef adjoint); Anne Laberge; Guy Lambert; Daniel Lavoie; André Marceau; Guy Pinsonneault; Gilles Plante; Michael Sheehan; Michel Simard; Michel St-Hilaire; Jean-Marc Tremblay; Louis Vézina; Pierre Verdon

Chambre Criminelle et Pénale: Michel Babin; Gilles Bergeron; André Bilodeau; Rémi Bouchard (Juge en chef adjoint); Louis Carrier; Marc Choquette; René De La Sablonnière; Jean-François Dionne; Jean Drouin; Laurent Dubé; Marc Dufour; Jean Dutil; Gilles Garneau; Gilles La Haye; Guy Lambert; Denis R. Lanctôt; Roch Lefrançois; Alain Morand; André Plante; Narcisse Proulx; Pierre-L. Rousseau

Chambre de la Jeunesse: Jean Alarie (Juge en chef adjoint); Andreé Bergeron; Claude C. Boulanger; Louise Galipeault-Moisan; Paule Gaumont; Daniel Lavoie; Lucie Rondeau; André Sirois; Alain Turgeon

- Alma: Cour du Québec, 725, rue Harvey ouest, Alma PQ G8B 1P5
  Juges (Les Honorables):
  Chambre Civile: Maurice Abud
- Amos: Cour du Québec, 891, av 3e ouest, Amos PQ J9T 2T4
  Juges (Les Honorables):
  Chambre Civile, Chambre Criminelle et Pénale: Normand Bonin; Guy Gagnon
- Arthabaska: Cour du Québec, 800, boul Bois-Francs sud, Arthabaska PQ G6P 5W5
  Juges (Les Honorables):
  Chambre Civile: Claude Pinard
- Baie Comeau: Cour du Québec, 71, av Mance, Baie Comeau PQ G4Z 1N2
  Juges (Les Honorables):
  Chambre Civile: Sarto Cloutier
  Chambre de la Jeunesse: Claude Tremblay
- Chicoutimi: Cour du Québec, 227, rue Racine, Chicoutimi PQ G7H 1S2
  Juges (Les Honorables):
  Chambre Civile: Jean-Paul Aubin; Claude Gagnon; Micheline Paradis; Jean Simard; Guy Tremblay; Lucien Tremblay; Jean-Yves Tremblay

Chambre de la Jeunesse: Paul Casgrain; Bernard Gagnon; Micheline Paradis

- Drummondville: Cour du Québec, 1680, boul St-Joseph, Drummondville PQ J2C 2G3
  Juges (Les Honorables):
  Chambre Civile: Gilles Gagnon
- Granby: Cour du Québec, 77, rue Principale, Granby PQ J2G 9B3
  Juges (Les Honorables):
  Chambre Civile; Chambre Criminelle et Pénale: Donald Bissonnette
  Chambre Criminelle et Pénale: Pierre Bachand
  Chambre de la Jeunesse: Gilles Therriault
- Hull: Cour du Québec, 17, rue Laurier, Hull PQ J8X 4C1
  Juges (Les Honorables):
  Chambre Civile: Jules Barrière; Bernard Dagenais; Jean-François Gosselin; Raymond Séguin
  Chambre Civile; Chambre Criminelle et Pénale: Nicole Gibeault
  Chambre Civile; Chambre de la Jeunesse: Réal Lapointe
  Chambre Criminelle et Pénale: Pierre Chevalier; Jean-François Gosselin; Réal R. Lapointe; Raymond Séguin; Louise Turpin
  Chambre de la Jeunesse: Jean-François Gosselin; Michel Séguin; Raymond Séguin; Louise Turpin
- Joliette: Cour du Québec, 200, rue St-Marc, Joliette PQ J6E 8C2
  Juges (Les Honorables):
  Chambre Civile: Monique Sylvestre; Louis Vaillancourt
  Chambre Criminelle et Pénale: L. Michel Hétu; François Landry; Maurice Parent; Céline Pelletier; Marc Vanasse
  Chambre de la Jeunesse: Lise Gaboury; Paul Grégoire
- Laval: Cour du Québec, #1.03, 2800, boul Saint-Martin ouest, Laval PQ H7T 2S9
  Juges (Les Honorables):
  Chambre Civile: Micheline Sasseville
  Chambre Criminelle et Pénale: Michel Duceppe; Micheline Dufour; Claude Melançon
  Chambre de la Jeunesse: Normand Lafond; Jacques Lamarche; Claude Melançon
- Longueuil: Cour du Québec, 1111, boul Jacques-Cartier est, Longueuil PQ J4M 2J6
  Juges (Les Honorables):
  Chambre Civile: Jean-Pierre Bourduas; Claude H. Chicoine; Micheline Laliberté; Michel Lassonde
  Chambre Criminelle et Pénale: Denis Bouchard; Robert Lafontaine; Yves Lagacé; Ellen Paré; Claude Provost; Gérard Rouleau; Lucien Roy
  Chambre de la Jeunesse: Mireille Allaire; Claude Crete; Pierre-G. Dorion; Jean-Pierre Saintonge
- Matane: Cour du Québec, 382, av St-Jérôme, Matane PQ G4W 3B3
  Juges (Les Honorables):
  Chambre Civile: Marc Gagnon
- Montmagny: Cour du Québec, 25, rue du Palais, Montmagny PQ G5V 1P6
- Montréal: Cour du Québec, 1, rue Notre-Dame est, Montréal PQ H2Y 1B6
  Chambre de la Jeunesse: 410, rue Bellechasse est, Montréal PQ H2S 1X3
  Juge en chef, L'Honorable Albert Gobeil
  Juge en chef associé, L'Honorable Paul Mailloux
  Juge en chef associé, L'Honorable Huguette St-Louis
  Juge en chef associé, L'Honorable Louis Vaillancourt
  Juges (Les Honorables):
  Chambre Civile: Armando Aznar; Raol Barbe; René Beaulac; Jacques Biron; Guy Boissonneault; Serge Boisvert; Simon Brossard; Denis Charette; Brigitte Charron; Charles Cimon; Lucien Dansereau; Antonio De Michèle; Michel Desmarais; Jacques Desormeau; Jean Dionne; Michel Duchesne; Claude-René Dumais; Pierre Durand; François Michel Gagnon; Brigitte Gouin; Luc Grammond; Gaston Labrèche; Gilson Lachance; Jacques Lachapelle; Paule Lafontaine; Jean-Louis Lamoureux; Bernard Lesage (Juge en chef adjoint); Jean-Pierre Lortie; Eliana Marengo; Huguette Marleau; Yvan Mayrand; Yves Morier; Léon Nichols; Michèle Pauzé; Gilles Poirier; Claude Pothier; André Quesnel; Louis Rémillard; André Renaud; Michèle Rivet; René Roy; Bernard Tellier; Gilles Trudel; Claude Vaillancourt; Pierre M. Verdy; Clermont Vermette
  Chambre Criminelle et Pénale: John D'Arcy Asselin; Bernard Bilodeau; Jean-Pierre Boniin; Jean-Pierre Bonin (Juge en chef adjoint); Pierre Brassard; Gilles Cadieux; Micheline Corbeil-Laramée; Suzanne Coupal; Rosaire Desbiens; François Doyon; Monique P. Dubreuil; Michel Duchesne; André Duranleau; Jean B. Falardeau; Gérard Girouard; Bernard Grenier; Joël L. Guberman; Maurice Johnson; Claude Joncas; Céline Lacerte-Lamontagne; Lorraine Laporte-Landry; Louis-A. Legault; Jean Longtin; Rolande Matte; Claude Millette; Gilbert Moirier; Yves Morier; Albert Ouellette; Claude Parent; Maximilien Polak; Claude Provost; ouise Provost; Lucien Roy; Robert Sansfaçon; Jean Sirois; J. Roch St-Germain; Joseph Tarasofsky; Luc Trudel; Roger Vincent
  Chambre de la Jeunesse: Gérard Beaudry; Nicole Bernier; Omer Boudreau; Jean-Paul Braun; Barrie H. Brown; Henri Choinière; Oscar D'Amours; Élaine Demers-Nadeau; Ginette Durand-Brault; Françoise Garneau-Fournier; François Godbout; Lucie Godin; Michel Jasmin (Juge en chef adjoint); Isabelle Lafontaine; Guy Lévesque; Gilles L. Ouellet; Jacques R. Roy; Robert Sacchitelle; André Saint-Cyr; Gaetan Zonato
- Montréal: Cour du Québec (Chambre Civile), 255, boul Crémazie est, Montréal PQ H2M 1L5
  Juges (Les Honorables): Marc Brière
  Chambre Civile: Robert Burns; Lise Langlois; Louise Ménard; Bernard Prudhomme; Claude Saint-Arnaud
- New Carlisle: Cour du Québec, CP 84, New Carlisle PQ G0C 1Z0
  Chambre Criminelle et Pénale, Chambre de la Jeunesse: 87, rue Principale, CP 517, New Carlisle PQ G0C 1Z0
  Juges (Les Honorables):
  Chambre Civile: Jean Bécu
  Chambre Criminelle et Pénale; Chambre de la Jeunesse: Robert Lévesque
- Percé: Cour du Québec, 124, rte 132, CP 188, Percé PQ G0C 2L0
  Juges (Les Honorables):
  Chambre Civile; Chambre Criminelle et Pénale; Jeunesse: Embert Whittom
- Rimouski: Cour du Québec, 183, rue de la Cathédrale, Rimouski PQ G5L 5J1
  Chambre Criminelle et Pénale: CP 800, Rimouski PQ G5L 7C9
  Juges (Les Honorables):
  Chambre Civile: Marc Gagnon; Raoul Poirier
  Chambre Civile; Chambre Criminelle et Pénale: Jean-Paul Decoste
  Chambre Criminelle et Pénale: Richard Côté
- Rivière-du-Loup: Cour du Québec, 33, rue de la Cour, Rivière-du-Loup PQ G5R 1J1
  Juges (Les Honorables):
  Chambre Civile; Chambre Criminelle et Pénale: Gérald Laforest; Guy Ringuet
  Chambre de la Jeunesse: Bertrand Laforest
- Roberval: Cour du Québec, 750, boul St-Joseph, Roberval PQ G8H 2L5
  Juges (Les Honorables):

Chambre Civile; Chambre Criminelle et Pénale: Rosaire Larouche
- Rouyn-Noranda: Cou du Québec, 2, rue du Palais, Rouyn-Noranda PQ J9X 2N9
  Juges (Les Honorables):
  Chambre Civile: Paul J. Bélanger; Jean-Charles Coutu
  Chambre de la Jeunesse: Gilles Gendron
- Ste-Foy: Cour du Québec, 2050, boul St-Cyrille ouest, Ste-Foy PQ G1V 2K8
  2875, boul Laurier, Ste-Foy PQ G1V 2M2
- St-Hyacinthe: Cour du Québec, 1550, rue Dessaules, St-Hyacinthe PQ J2S 2S8
  Chambre de la Jeunesse: 1150, rue Ste-Anne, St-Hyacinthe PQ J2S 5G9
  Juges (Les Honorables):
  Chambre Civile: Denis Robert
  Chambre Criminelle et Pénale: Guy Fortier
  Chambre de la Jeunesse: Constant Cordeau
- St-Jean-sur-Richelieu: Cour du Québec, 109, rue St-Charles, St-Jean-sur Richelieu PQ J3B 2C2
  Juges (Les Honorables):
  Chambre Civile: Jacques Rancourt
- St-Jérôme: Cour du Québec, 400, rue Laviolette, St-Jérôme PQ J7Y 2T6
  Juges (Les Honorables):
  Chambre Civile: Denis Charette; Diane Girard; Jean-Claude Paquin; André Soumis
  Chambre Criminelle et Pénale: Valmont Beaulieu; Carole Richer
  Chambre de la Jeunesse: Jean-Claude Gagnon; Jean La Rue; Marie Lapointe-Prevost; Andrée Ruffo
- St-Joseph-de-Beauce: Cour du Québec, 795, rue du Palais, St-Joseph-de-Beauce PQ G0S 2V0
  Juges (Les Honorables):
  Chambre Civile: Marcel Blais
  Chambre Criminelle et Pénale: Hubert Couture
- Sept-Îles: Cour du Québec, 425, boul Laure, Sept-Îles PQ G4R 1X6
  Juges (Les Honorables):
  Chambre Civile: Bernard Lemieux
  Chambre Criminelle et Pénale: Gabriel de Pokomandy
- Shawinigan: Cour du Québec, 212, rue 6e, Shawinigan PQ G9N 8B6
  Juges (Les Honorables):
  Chambre Civile; Chambre Criminelle et Pénale: Raymond Pronovost
- Sherbrooke: Cour du Québec, 375, rue King ouest, Sherbrooke PQ J1H 6B9
  Juges (Les Honorables):
  Chambre Civile: Louis-Denis Bouchard; Danielle Côté; Jacques Pagé; Yvon Roberge
  Chambre Criminelle et Pénale: Michel Beauchemin; Michel Côté; Danielle Côté; Gérald-E. Desmarais; Gabriel Lassonde
  Chambre de la Jeunesse: Lise Dubé; Michel Dubois; Michel Durand
- Sorel: Cour du Québec, 46, rue Charlotte, Sorel PQ J3P 6N5
  Juges (Les Honorables):
  Chambre Criminelle et Pénale: Ronald Dudamaine
- Terrebonne: Cour du Québec,
  Juges (Les Honorables):
  Chambre Criminelle et Pénale: François Beaudoin; Jean R. Beaulieu; Paul Chevallier; Jean La Rue; Hughes St-Germain; Michel Toupin
- Thetford-Mines: Cour du Québec, 693, St-Alphonse ouest, Thetford-Mines PQ G6G 3X3
  Juges (Les Honorables):
  Chambre Civile, W. James Johnson
- Trois-Rivières: Cour du Québec, 250, rue Laviolette, Trois-Rivières PQ G9A 1T9
  878, rue de Tonnancourt, #1.10, Trois-Rivières PQ G9A 4P8
  Juges (Les Honorables):
  Chambre Civile: Serge Gagnon; Nicole Maillette

Chambre Criminelle et Pénale: René Crochetière; Jacques Trudel
Chambre de la Jeunesse: Pierre Houde
Val-d'Or: Cour du Québec, 900, rue 7e, Val-d'Or PQ J9P 3P8
  Juges (Les Honorables):
  Chambre Civile: Denis Lavergne; Miville Saint-Pierre
  Chambre de la Jeunesse: Normand Bonin; Denyse LeDuc
- Valleyfield: Cour du Québec, 180, rue Salaberry ouest, Valleyfield PQ J6T 2J2
  Juges (Les Honorables):
  Chambre Civile: Raymond Boyer; Pierre Laberge; Odette Perron
  Chambre Civile; Chambre Criminelle et Pénale: Michel Mercier; Marie-Andrée Villeneuve
  Chambre Criminelle et Pénale: Odette Perron
  Chambre de la Jeunesse: Jean Gravel

COURS MUNICIPALES
The Municipal Courts have jurisdiction in select civil, penal and criminal matters.
Juge en Chef, Pierre Lalande
- Acton Vale: Cour municipale, 1025, rue Boulay, Acton Vale PQ J0H 1A0
  Chefs de la cour: Louise-B Grignon
- Alma: Cour municipale, 140, av St-Joseph sud, Alma PQ G8B 3R1
  Chefs de la cour: Jacques Turcotte, Jean-M. Morency
- Anjou: Cour municipale, 7701, boul Louis-H-Lafontaine, Anjou PQ H1K 4B9
  Chefs de la cour: Richard Chassé, Claude Simard
- Asbestos: Cour municipale, 300, boul St-Luc, Asbestos PQ J1T 2W2
  Chefs de la cour: Roland Lamoureax, Gilles J. Geoffroy
- L'Assomption: Cour municipale, 399, rue Dorval, L'Assomption PQ J0K 1G0
  Chefs de la cour: Louis Laporte, Gilles Thouin
- D'Autray: Cour municipale, 588, rue Montcalm, D'Autray PQ J0K 1A0
  Chefs de la cour: Marguerite M. Brochu, Louis Laporte
- Aylmer: Cour municipale, 120, rue Principale, Aylmer PQ J9H 3M3
  Chefs de la cour: Raymond Séguin, Jacques Sauvé
- Baie-Comeau: Cour municipale
  Chefs de la cour: Jean Blouin, Micheline Fournier
- La-Baie: Cour municipale, 200, rue Victoria, La-Baie PQ G7B 3M4
  Chefs de la cour: Robert Côté, René Lambert
- Barkmère: Cour municipale, RR#1, CP 11, Argenteuil PQ J0T 1A0
  Chefs de la cour: Gavin Wyllie
- Beaconsfield: Cour municipale, 303, boul Beaconsfield, Beaconsfield PQ H9W 4A7
  Chefs de la cour: Pierre G. Bouchard, Bernard Lefebvre
- Beauharnois: Cour municipale, 103, rue St-Laurent, Beauharnois PQ J6N 1V8
  Chefs de la cour: Paul-Émile L'Écuyer, Jean F. Cordeau
- Beaupré: Cour municipale, 216, rue Prévost, Beaupré PQ G0A 1E0
  Chefs de la cour: Michael E. Hickson
- Bedford: Cour municipale, 14, rue Corriveau, Bedford PQ J0J 1A0
  Chefs de la cour: Claude Hamann, Alain Boisvert
- Bellechasse: Cour municipale, 100, rue Mgr Bilodeau, St-Lazare PQ J0R 3J0
  Chefs de la cour: Claude Fortin
- Beloeil: Cour municipale, 777, boul Laurier, Beloeil PQ J3G 4S9
  Chefs de la cour: Pierre J. Raiche, Luc Alarie
- Blainville: Cour municipale, 1000, rue de la Mairie, Blainville PQ J7C 3B5

Chefs de la cour: Robert Diamond, Guy Saulnier
- Boisbriand: Cour municipale, 940, boul Grande-Allée, Boisbriand PQ J7G 2J7
  Chefs de la cour: Guy Saulnier, André Hotte
- Boucherville: Cour municipale, 500, rue de la Rivière-aux-Pins, Boucherville PQ J4B 2Z7
  Chefs de la cour: Claude Simard, Michel Jetté
- Bromptonville: Cour municipale, 133, rue Laval, Bromptonville PQ J0B 1H0
  Chefs de la cour: Roland Lamoureux, Gerald Lafrance
- Brossard: Cour municipale, 3200, boul Lapinière, Brossard PQ J4Z 2B4
  Chefs de la cour: Philippe Clément, Jacques P. Dansereau
- Candiac: Cour municipale, #430, 9, boul Montcalm nord, Candiac PQ J5R 3L5
  Chefs de la cour: Georges E. Laurin, Jean-Pierre Dépelteau
- Cap-de-la-Madeleine: Cour municipale, 10, rue de l'Hôtel-de-Ville, CP 220, Cap-de-la-Madeleine PQ G8T 7W4
  Chefs de la cour: Joselyn Crête, Claude Trudel
- Chambly: Cour municipale, 1, Place de la Mairie, Chambly PQ J3L 4X1
  Chefs de la cour: Pierre J. Raiche, Denis Favreau
- Charlesbourg: Cour municipale, 160, rue 76e est, Charlesbourg PQ G1H 7H5
  Chefs de la cour: Jean-Pierre Gignac
- Charny: Cour municipale, 5333, rue de la Symphonie, Charny PQ G6X 3B6
  Chefs de la cour: Raymond Lavoie
- Château-Richer: Cour municipale, 8006, av Royale, Château-Richer PQ G0A 1N0
  Chefs de la cour: Michel-N. Dugal
- Châteauguay: Cour municipale, 55, boul Maple, Châteauguay PQ J6J 3P9
  Chefs de la cour: Jean-F. Cordeau, Paul-Émile L'Écuyer
- Chibougamau: Cour municipale, 650, rue 3e, Chibougamau PQ G8P 1P1
  Chefs de la cour: Michel Lapointe, Robert Côté
- Chicoutimi: Cour municipale, 201, rue Racine est, Chicoutimi PQ G7H 1S3
  Chefs de la cour: Robert Côté, René Lambert
- Coaticook: Cour municipale, 150, rue Child, CP 85, Coaticook PQ J1A 2B3
  Chefs de la cour: Pierre A. Cloutier, Roland Lamoureux
- Côte St-Luc: Cour municipale, 5801, boul Cavendish, Côte St-Luc PQ H4W 3C3
  Chefs de la cour: Donald W. Seal, Alfred N. Segall
- Cowansville: Cour municipale, 220, Place Municipale, Cowansville PQ J2K 1T4
  Chefs de la cour: Claude Hamann, Pierre Raiche
- Delson: Cour municipale, 50, Ste-Thérèse, Delson PQ J0L 1G0
  Chefs de la cour: Jacques Laurier
- Deux-Montagnes: Cour municipale, 803, ch Oka, Deux-Montagnes PQ J7R 4K1
  Chefs de la cour: Robert Diamond, Jacques Lamontagne
- Dolbeau: Cour municipale, 1100, boul Walberg, Dolbeau PQ G8L 1G7
  Chefs de la cour: Jacquelin Légaré, Robert Côté
- Dollard-des-Ormeaux: Cour municipale, 12001, boul de Salaberry ouest, Dollard-des-Ormeaux PQ H9B 2A7
  Chefs de la cour: Pierre Mondor, Donald W. Seal
- Donnaconna: Cour municipale, 138, av Pleau, Donnaconna PQ G0A 1T0
  Chefs de la cour: Jean-R. Côté, Claude Fournier
- Dorion: Cour municipale, 190, St-Charles, CP 70, Dorion PQ J7V 5V8
  Chefs de la cour: Manon Bourbonnais
- Dorval: Cour municipale, 530, boul Bouchard, Dorval PQ H9S 1B2

Canadian Almanac & Directory 1997

Chefs de la cour: Jean-Pierre Dépelteau, Georges É. Laurin
- Drummondville: Cour municipale, 413, rue Lindsay, Drummondville PQ J2B 1G8
 Chefs de la cour: Jacques Guertin, Michel Houle
- East Angus: Cour municipale, 146, rue Angus, East Angus PQ J0B 1R0
 Chefs de la cour: Léonard Bergeron, Gilles J. Geoffroy, Roland Lamoureux
- Farnham: Cour municipale, 477, rue de l'Hôtel de Ville, Farnham PQ J2N 2H3
 Chefs de la cour: Alain Boisvert, Claude Hamann
- Gatineau: Cour municipale, 280, boul Maloney est, Gatineau PQ J8P 1C6
 Chefs de la cour: François Gravel, Jacques Sauvé
- Granby: Cour municipale, 125, rue Simonds sud, Granby PQ J2J 1P7
 Chefs de la cour: Hélène Poulin, Pierre Raiche
- Grand'Mère: Cour municipale, 333, av 5e, Grand'Mère PQ G9T 2M2
 Chefs de la cour: Jean-Marc Champagne, Jean-Louis Sanschagrin
- Greenfield Park: Cour municipale, 158, boul Churchill, Greenfield Park PQ J4V 2M3
 Chefs de la cour: Denis Boudrias, Jean-Guy Clément
- Hampstead: Cour municipale, 5569 Queen Mary Rd., Hampstead PQ H3X 1W5
 Chefs de la cour: Donald W. Seal, Alfred N. Segall
- Haut-Saint Laurent: Cour municipale
 Chefs de la cour: Manon Bourbonnais, Paul-Émile L'Écuyer
- Hudson: Cour municipale, rue Principale, Hudson PQ J0P 1H0
 Chefs de la cour: Robert La Haye
- Hull: Cour municipale, 25, rue Laurier, CP 1970, Hull PQ J8X 3Y9
 Chefs de la Cour, François Gravel
- Iberville: Cour municipale, 855, rue 1er, Iberville PQ J2X 3C7
 Chefs de la cour: Pierre-Armand Tremblay
- Île-Perrot: Cour municipale, 110, boul Perrot, Île-Perrot PQ J7V 3G1
 Chefs de la cour: Jacques Laverdure
- Joliette: Cour municipale, 733, rue Richard, Joliette PQ J6E 2T8
 Chefs de la cour: Marguerite M. Brochu, Louis Laporte
- Jonquière: Cour municipale, 2201, rue De Montfort, CP 278, Jonquière PQ G7X 4P6
 Chefs de la cour: Jean M. Morency, Jean-Jacques Turcotte
- La Pocatière: Cour municipale, 412, rue 9e, La Pocatière PQ G0R 1Z0
 Chefs de la cour: Jean Blouin, Louis-Marie Vachon
- Lac Mégantic: Cour municipale, #200, 5527, rue Frontenac, Lac Mégantic PQ G6B 1H6
 Chefs de la cour: Gabriel Garneau, Jean-Pierre Gignac
- Lachine: Cour municipale, 1800, boul St-Joseph, Lachine PQ H8S 2N4
 Chefs de la cour: Yves Fournier, Jacques Laurier
- Lachute: Cour municipale, 380, rue Principale, Lachute PQ J8H 1Y2
 Chefs de la cour: André Hotte, Guy Saulnier
- Lasalle: Cour municipale, 55, av Dupras, Lasalle PQ H8R 4A8
 Chefs de la cour: Philippe Clément, Denis Laberge
- Laval: Cour municipale, 55, boul des Laurentides, Pont-Viau PQ H7G 2T1
 Chefs de la cour: Bernard Caron, Jean-H. Charbonneau
- Lennoxville: Cour municipale
 Chefs de la cour: Roland Lamoureux
- Lévis: Cour municipale, 225, côte du Passage, Lévis PQ G6V 5T4
 Chefs de la cour: Gilles Charest, Raymond Lavoie
- Longueuil: Cour municipale, #290, Place Charles-Lemoyne, Longueuil PQ J4K 2T4
 Chefs de la cour: Richard Alary, Jacques Lamontagne
- Loretteville: Cour municipale, 305, rue Racine, Loretteville PQ G2B 1E7
 Chefs de la cour: Gilles Charest, Claude Fournier
- Louiseville: Cour municipale, 105, av St-Laurent ouest, Louiseville PQ J5V 2L6
 Chefs de la cour: Jocelyn Crête, Claude Trudel
- Magog: Cour municipale, 7, rue Principale est, Magog PQ J1X 1Y4
 Chefs de la cour: Leonard Bergeron, Roland Lamoureux
- Marieville: Cour municipale, 682, rue St-Charles, Marieville PQ J0L 1J0
 Chefs de la cour: Louis-B. Grignon
- Mascouche: Cour municipale,
 Chefs de la cour: Claude Lemire
- Matawinie: Cour municipale,
 Chefs de la cour: Michel Lalande
- Mirabel: Cour municipale, 1411, rue St-Jean, Ste-Monique-deux-Montagnes PQ J0N 1R0
 Chefs de la cour: André Hotte, Michel Paquin
- Mistassini: Cour municipale, 173, St-Michel, CP 219, Mistassini PQ G0W 2C0
 Chefs de la cour: Michel J. Lapointe, Jacquelin Légaré
- Mont-Royal: Cour municipale, 90, av Roosevelt, Mont-Royal PQ H3R 1Z4
 Chefs de la cour: Pierre G. Bouchard, Jérôme C. Smyth
- Mont-St-Hilaire: Cour municipale, 100, rue du Centre-Civique, Mont-St-Hilaire PQ J3H 3M8
 Chefs de la cour: Luc Alarie, Pierre J. Raiche
- Montcalm: Cour municipale,
 Chefs de la cour: Marguerite M. Brochu, Louis Laporte
- Montmagny: Cour municipale, 134, rue St-Jean-Baptiste est, Montmagny PQ G5V 1K6
 Chefs de la cour: Jean Blouin, Louis-Marie Vachon
- Montréal-Est: Cour municipale, 11370, rue Notre-Dame est, Montréal PQ H1B 2W6
 Chefs de la cour: Florent Bisson, Jean Hébert
- Montréal-Nord: Cour municipale, 4240, rue Amos, Montréal-Nord PQ H1H 1P3
 Chefs de la cour: Richard Alary, Jacques Lamontagne
- Montréal-Ouest: Cour municipale, 50, av Westminster sud, Montréal PQ H4X 1Y7
 Chefs de la cour: Frank Schlesinger, Alfred N. Segall
- Montréal: Cour municipale, 775, rue Gosford, Montréal PQ H2Y 3B9
 Juge en chef adjoint, Jean-Pierre Bessette
 Juge en chef, Raymonde Verreault
 Chefs de la Cour: Louise Baribeau, Denis Boisvert, Louise Bourdeau, René Déry, Pierre D. Denault, Antonio Discepola, Gérard Duguay, Pierre Fontaine, Pierre Gaston, Dennis Laliberté, Louis-Jacques Léger, Évasio Massagnini, André Massé, Jean Massé, Morton S. Minc
- Nicolet: Cour municipale, 180, rue Panet, CP 670, Nicolet PQ J0G 1E0
 Chefs de la cour: Jacques Desaulniers
- Outremont: Cour municipale, 510, av Davaar, Outremont PQ H2V 2B9
 Chefs de la cour: Georges E. Laurin, Adrien R. Paquette
- Pierrefonds: Cour municipale, 13665, boul Pierrefonds, Pierrefonds PQ H9H 4N2
 Chefs de la cour: Philippe Clément, Pierre Mondor
- Pincourt: Cour municipale, 919, ch Duhamel, Pincourt PQ J7V 4G8
 Chefs de la cour: Robert La Haye
- Plessisville: Cour municipale, 1700, rue St-Calixte, Plessisville PQ G6L 1R3
 Chefs de la cour: Jules Bellavance, Jean-Louis Provencher
- Pointe-Claire: Cour municipale, 401, St-Jean, Pointe-Claire PQ H9R 3J2
 Chefs de la cour: Philippe Clément, Pierre Mondor
- La Prairie: Cour municipale, 600, Ste-Elizabeth, La Prairie PQ J5R 1V1
 Chefs de la cour: Claude Céré, Jean Hébert
- Princeville: Cour municipale, 50, av St-Jacques ouest, CP 370, Princeville PQ G0P 1E0
 Chefs de la cour: Jules Bellavance, Claude Caron
- Québec: Cour municipale, Centrale de Police, 275, rue Gignac, Québec PQ G1K 2L3
 Juge en chef, Laurent Cossette
 Chefs de la cour: J.-Charles Brochu
- Repentigny: Cour municipale, 435, boul d'Iberville, Repentigny PQ J6A 2B6
 Chefs de la cour: Claude Lemire, Gilles Thouin
- Rimouski: Cour municipale, 205, av de la Cathédrale, CP 710, Rimouski PQ G5L 7C7
 Chefs de la cour: Jean Blouin, Raymond Lavoie
- Roberval: Cour municipale, 851, boul St-Joseph, Roberval PQ G8H 2L6
 Chefs de la cour: Michel J. Lapointe, Jacquelin Légaré
- Rosemère: Cour municipale, 100, rue Charbonneau, Rosemère PQ J7A 3W1
 Chefs de la cour: Michel J. Lapointe, Guy Saulnier, Robert Diamond
- Roxboro: Cour municipale, 13 Centre Commercial, Roxboro PQ H8Y 2N9
 Chefs de la cour: Philippe Clément, Ronald J. Montcalm
- Ste-Adele: Cour municipale, 1381, boul Sainte-Adele, Sainte-Adele PQ J0R 1L0
 Chefs de la cour: J.-H. Denis Gagnon, Michel Lalande
- Ste-Agathe-des-Monts: Cour municipale, 50, St-Joseph, Sainte-Agathe-des-Monts PQ J8C 1M9
 Chefs de la cour: J.H. Denis Gagnon, Michel Lalande
- Ste-Anne-de-Bellevue: Cour municipale, 109, Ste-Anne, CP 40, Sainte-Anne-de-Bellevue PQ H9X 1M2
 Chefs de la cour: Jacques Chanimé, Pascal Pillarella
- St-Antoine: Cour municipale, 854, boul St-Antoine, St-Antoine PQ J7Z 3C5
- St-Bruno-de-Montarville: Cour municipale, 1585, boul Montarville, St-Bruno-de-Montarville PQ J3V 3T8
 Chefs de la cour: Marc Gravel, Guy Houle
- St-Césaire: Cour municipale, 1111, St-Paul, Saint-Césaire PQ J0L 1T0
 Chefs de la cour: Louis B. Grignon
- St-Constant: Cour municipale, 147, rue St-Pierre, Saint-Constant PQ J5A 2G2
 Chefs de la cour: Yves Fournier, Jacques Laurier
- St-Eustache: Cour municipale, 168, rue Dorion, St-Eustache PQ J7R 5S4
 Chefs de la cour: Réne Boismenu, Robert Diamond
- St-Félicien: Cour municipale, 1058, boul Sacré-Coeur, CP 7000, St-Félicien PQ G8K 2R5
 Chefs de la cour: Robert Côté, Michel J. Lapointe
- Ste-Foy: Cour municipale, 1000, rte de l'Eglise, CP 218, Ste-Foy PQ G1V 4E1
 Chefs de la cour: Marc Jessop, René Paquet
- St-Georges: Cour municipale, 11700, boul Lacroix est, St-Georges PQ G5Y 1L3
 Chefs de la cour: Gabriel Garneau, Jean-Pierre Gignac
- St-Hilaire: Cour municipale, 100, du centre-civique, St-Hilaire PQ J3H 3M8
 Chefs de la cour: Pierre J. Raiche
- St-Hubert: Cour municipale, 5900, boul Cousineau, St-Hubert PQ J3Y 7K8
 Chefs de la cour: Jean-Pierre Gignac, Jean Herbert
- St-Hyacinthe: Cour municipale, 700, av de l'Hôtel de Ville, St-Hyacinthe PQ J2S 5B2
 Chefs de la cour: Gérald Locas

- St-Jean-Chrysostome: Cour municipale, 959, rue de l'Hôtel de Ville, St-Jean-Chrysostome PQ G6Z 2N8
  Chefs de la cour: Claude Fortin, Jean-Pierre Gignac
- St-Jean-sur-Richelieu: Cour municipale, 188, rue Jacques Cartier nord, St-Jean-sur-Richelieu PQ J3B 7B2
  Chefs de la cour: Louis B. Grignon, Pierre-Armand Tremblay
- St-Jérôme: Cour municipale, 280, boul Labelle, St-Jérôme PQ J7Z 5L1
  Chefs de la cour: René Boismenu, Robert Diamond
- St-Lambert: Cour municipale, 55, Argyle, Saint-Lambert PQ J4P 2H3
  Chefs de la cour: Marc Gravel, Guy Houle
- St-Laurent: Cour municipale, 777, Laurentien, Saint-Laurent PQ H4M 2M7
  Chefs de la Cour, Jérôme C. Smyth
- St-Léonard-de-Port-maurice: Cour municipale, 8400, boul Lacordaire, St-Léonard PQ H1R 3B1
  Chefs de la cour: Richard Chassé, Claude Simard
- St-Luc: Cour municipale, 347, boul St-Luc, Saint-Luc PQ J0J 2A0
  Chefs de la cour: Denis Boudrias, Pascal Pillarella
- Ste-Marie-de-Beauce-Nord: Cour municipale, 270, rue Marguerite Bourgeois, CP 1750, Ste-Marie-de-Beauce-Nord PQ G6E 3C7
  Chefs de la cour: Jean-Pierre Gignac, Paul Routhier
- St-Nicolas, St-Rédempteur, Bernières, St-Étienne-de-Lauzon: Cour municipale, 85, rue 19e, St-Rédempteur PQ G6K 1C3
  Chefs de la cour: Claude Fournier, Jacques Ouellet
- St-Pierre: Cour municipale, 69, av 5e, St-Pierre PQ H8R 1P1
  Chefs de la cour: Pierre G. Bouchard, Yves Fournier
- St-Raymond: Cour municipale, 375, St-Joseph, St-Raymond PQ G0A 4G0
  Chefs de la cour: Jean R. Côté, Claude Fournier
- St-Rémi-de-Napierville: Cour municipale, 105, Perras, St-Rémi-de-Napierville PQ J0L 2L0
  Chefs de la cour: Robert La Haye, Pascal Pillarella
- Ste-Thérèse: Cour municipale, 6, rue de l'Église, CP 100, Ste-Thérèse PQ J7E 4H7
  Chefs de la cour: André Hotte, Michel Paquin
- St-Tite: Cour municipale, 540, rue Notre-Dame, St-Tite PQ G0X 3H0
  Chefs de la cour: Jean-Marc Champagne, Jean L. Sanschagrain
- Salaberry-de-Valleyfield: Cour municipale, 61, rue Ste-Cécile, Salaberry-de-Valleyfield PQ J6T 1L8
  Chefs de la cour: Michel Lalande, Paul Lemieux
- Senneville: Cour municipale, 35, rue Senneville, Senneville PQ H9X 1B8
  Chefs de la cour: Philippe Clément, Pierre Mondor
- Sept-Îles: Cour municipale, 546, rue Dequen, Sept-Îles PQ G4R 2R4
  Chefs de la cour: Jean Blouin, Guy Pettigrew
- Shawinigan-Sud: Cour municipale, 1550, rue 118e, Shawinigan PQ G9P 3G8
  Chefs de la cour: Jocelyn Crête, Claude Trudel
- Shawinigan: Cour municipale, 550, av Hôtel de Ville, CP 400, Shawinigan PQ G9N 6V3
  Chefs de la cour: Jocelyn Crête, Claude Trudel
- Sherbrooke: Cour municipale, 191, rue Palais, Sherbrooke PQ J1H 4R1
  Chefs de la cour: Pierre A. Cloutier, Roland Lamoureux
- Sillery: Cour municipale, 1445, av Maguire, Sillery PQ G1T 1Z2
  Chefs de la cour: Marc Jessop, René Paquet
- Sorel: Cour municipale, 71, rue Charlotte, CP 368, Sorel PQ J3P 7K1
  Chefs de la cour: Jacques Guertin, Michel Houle
- Terrebonne: Cour municipale, 775, rue St-Jean Baptiste, Terrebonne PQ J6W 1B5
  Chefs de la cour: Claude Lemire, Michel Paquin
- Thetford-Mines: Cour municipale, 144, rue Notre-Dame sud, CP 489, Thetford-Mines PQ G6G 5T3

  Chefs de la cour: Gilles Ouellet, Jean-Louis Provencher
- Tracy: Cour municipale, 3025, boul de la Mairie, Tracy PQ J3R 1C2
  Michel Houle
- Trois-Rivières-Ouest: Cour municipale, 500, côte du Richelieu, Trois-Rivières PQ G9A 2Z1
  Chefs de la cour: Jocelyn Crête, Claude Trudel
- Trois-Rivières: Cour municipale, 1193, rue Laviolette, CP 969, Trois-Rivières PQ G9A 5K2
  Chefs de la cour: Jocelyn Crête, Claude Trudel
- La Tuque: Cour municipale, 558, rue Commerciale, La Tuque PQ G9X 3A9
  Chefs de la cour: Jocelyn Crête, Claude Trudel
- Val-Bélair: Cour municipale, 1105, av de l'Église nord, Val-Bélair PQ G3K 1X5
  Chefs de la cour: Claude Fortin, Jean-Pierre Gignac
- Val-d'Or: Cour municipale, 855, av 2e, Val-d'Or PQ J9P 4P4
  Chefs de la cour: Jacques Barbès
- Val-St-François: Cour municipale,
  Chefs de la cour: J.-Gilles Geoffroy
- Vaudreuil-Soulanges: Cour municipale,
  Chefs de la cour: Manon Bourbonnais
- Verdun: Cour municipale, #104, 4555, av Verdun, Verdun PQ H4G 1M4
  Chefs de la cour: Denis Boudrias, Jacques Ghanimé
- Victoriaville: Cour municipale, 1, rue Notre-Dame ouest, CP 370, Victoriaville PQ G6P 6T2
  Chefs de la cour: Jean-Louis Provencher, Gilles ouellet
- Waterloo: Cour municipale, 417, rue de la Cour, Waterloo PQ J0E 2N0
  Chefs de la cour: Michel Brun
- Westmount: Cour municipale, 21, rue Stanton, Westmount PQ H3Y 3B1
  Chefs de la cour: Keith A. Ham, Alfred N. Segall

REGISTRATEURS

Abitibi: 552, av 1er ouest, CP 160, Amos PQ J9T 3A6
Argenteuil: 505, rue Bethanie, CP 337, Lachute PQ J8H 3X5
Arthabaska: 800, boul des Bois Francs sud, Arthabaska PQ G6P 5W5
L'Assomption: 300, rue Dorval, L'Assomption PQ J0K 1G0
Beauce: 111, rue 107e, Beaceville-est PQ G0S 1A0
Beauharnois: Registraeurs, 39, rue Richardson, Beauharnois PQ J6N 2T4
Bellechasse: 23, av Chanoine-Audet, St-Raphael PQ G0R 4C0
Berthier: 180, rue Champlain, CP 299, Berthierville PQ J0K 1A0
Bonaventure, Division No. 1: Palais de Justice, CP 250, New Carlisle PQ G0C 1Z0
Bonaventure, Division No. 2: 17, rue Lacroix, Carleton PQ G0C 1J0
Brôme: Registratreurs, 550, ch Knowlton, Lac Brôme PQ J0E 1V0
Chambly: 2555, boul Roland Therrien, R.C. 05, Longueuil PQ J4M 2J4
Champlain: 211, rue de l'Église, Ste-Geneviève-de-Batiscan PQ G0X 2R0
Charlevoix, Division No. 1: #250, 237, rue St-Etienne, CP 310, La Malbaie PQ G5A 1T8
Charlevoix, Division No. 2: #102, 4, Place de l'Église, Baie-St-Paul PQ G0A 1B0
Châteauguay: 164, rue St-Joseph, Ste-Martine PQ J0S 1V0
Chicoutimi: 227, rue Racine est, Chicoutimi PQ G7H 5C5
Coaticook: Hôtel de ville, #04, 150, rue Child, Coaticook PQ J1A 2B3
Compton: 89, rue du Parc, CP 459, Cookshire PQ J0B 1M0
Deux-Montagnes: #204, 140, rue St-Eustache, St-Eustache PQ J7R 2K9

Dorchester: 115, rue Langevin, Ste-Hénédine PQ G0S 2R0
Drummond: Palais de Justice, 1680, rue St-Joseph, 2e étage, Drummondville PQ J2C 2G3
Frontenac: #219, 5527, rue Frontenac, CP 157, Lac Mégantic PQ G6B 2S6
Gaspé: Palais de Justice, CP 128, Percé PQ G0C 2L0
Gatineau: #307, 266, rue Notre-Dame, Maniwaki PQ J9E 2J8
Hull: #3.120, 170, rue de l'Hôtel de Ville, Hull PQ J8X 4C2
Huntington: 25, rue King, Huntington PQ J0S 1H0
Îles-de-la-Madeleine: Palais de Justice, CP 97, Hâvre-Aubert PQ G0B 1J0
L'Islet: 34, rue Fortin, CP 578, St-Jean-Port-Joli PQ G0R 3G0
Joliette: #1.04, 450, rue St-Louis, Joliette PQ J6E 2Y9
Kamouraska: 395, rue Chapleau, St-Pascal PQ G0L 3Y0
Labelle: 440, boul Albiny-Paquette, Mont-Laurier PQ J9L 1K6
Lac St-Jean Est: Palais de Justice, 725, boul Harvey ouest, Alma PQ G8B 1P5
Lac St-Jean Ouest: Palais de Justice, 1221, boul St-Dominique, Roberval PQ G8H 3B8
Laval: #1.03, 2800, boul St-Martin ouest, Laval PQ H2T 2S9
Lévis: 45B, rue Desjardins, Lévis PQ G6V 4Z3
Lotbinière: 6375, rue Garneau, Ste-Croix PQ G0S 2H0
Maskinongé: 121, rue Petite-Rivière, Louiseville PQ J5V 2H3
Matane: 750, rue du Phare ouest, Matane PQ G4W 3W8
Matapédia: 27, boul St-Benoît, CP 1508, Amqui PQ G0J 1B0
Missisquoi: 4, rue Adhémar Cusson, CP 300, Bedford PQ J0J 1A0
Montcalm: 2450, rue Victoria, CP 190, Ste-Julienne PQ J0K 2T0
Montmagny: #101, 25, boul Taché ouest, Montmagny PQ G5V 2Z9
Montmorency: 7007, av Royal, Château-Richer PQ G0A 1N0
Montréal: Palais de Justice, #2.175, 1, rue Notre-Dame est, Montréal PQ H2Y 1B6
Nicolet: Palais de Justice, 395, Mgr Couchesne, Nicolet PQ J3T 1X6
Papineau: 266, rue Viger, Papineauville PQ J0V 1R0
Pontiac: Palais de Justice, CP 310, Campbell's Bay PQ J0X 1K0
Portneuf: 185, rte 138, Cap-Santé PQ G0A 1L0
La Prairie: 214, rue St-Ignace, La Prairie PQ J5R 1E5
Québec: 300, boul Jean-Lesage, R.C. 32, Québec PQ G1K 8K6
Richelieu: Maison du Québec, 46, rue Charlotte, Sorel PQ J3P 6N5
Richmond: Hôtel de Ville, 745, rue Gouin, Richmond PQ J0B 2H0
Rimouski: #04, 337 rue Moreault, Rimouski PQ G5L 1P4
Rouville: 500, rue Desjardins, Marieville PQ J3M 1E1
Rouyn-Noranda: 2, av du Palais, Rouyn-Noranda PQ J9X 2N9
Saguenay: Palais de Justice, 71, av Mance, Baie-Comeau PQ G4Z 1N2
Ste-Anne-des-Monts: Palais de Justice, 10, boul Ste-Anne, CP 517, Ste-Anne-des-Monts PQ G0E 2G0
St-Hyacinthe: #200, 1150, av Ste-Anne, St-Hyacinthe PQ J2S 5G9
St-Jean: 109, rue Saint-Charles, local 1.01, St-Jean PQ J3B 2C2
Sept-Îles: 425, boul Laure, Sept-Îles PQ G4R 1X6
Shawinigan: Centre Administratif, 212, rue 6e, CP 608, Shawinigan PQ G9N 6V6
Shefford: 77, rue Principale, Granby PQ J2G 9B3
Sherbrooke: 375, rue King ouest, Sherbrooke PQ J1H 6B9

Canadian Almanac & Directory 1997

10-20 COURTS & JUDGES – SASKATCHEWAN

Stanstead: 100, ch Dufferin, CP 240, Stanstead Plain PQ J0B 3E0

Témiscamingue: 8, rue St-Gabriel nord, CP 757, Ville-Marie PQ J0Z 3W0

Témiscouata: 310, rue Ste-Pierre, Rivière-du-Loup PQ G5R 3V3

Terrebonne: #4.3, 85, rue De Martigny ouest, St-Jérôme PQ J7Y 3R8

Thetford: 865, av l'abbé, Thetford-Mines PQ G6G 2A6

Trois-Rivières: Palais de Justice, 878, de Tonnancourt, Trois-Rivières PQ G9A 4P8

La Tuque: 290, rue St-Joseph, 2e étage, La Tuque PQ G9X 3Z8

Vaudreuil: #101, 420, boul Roche, Vaudreuil PQ J7V 2N1

Verchères: #92, 461, boul St-Joseph, Ste-Julie PQ J3E 1W8

PROTONOTAIRES ET SHERIFS

Abitibi: 891, 3e rue ouest, Amos PQ J9T 2T4 – 819/732-6577

Alma: #RC31, 725, rue Harvey ouest, Alma PQ G8B 1P5 – 418/668-3334

Arthabaska: 800, boul Bois-Franc sud, Arthabaska PQ G6P 5W5 – 819/357-2054

Baie Comeau: 71, av Mance, Baie-Comeau PQ G4Z 1N2 – 418/296-5534

Beauce: 795, av du Palais, St-Joseph-de-Beauce PQ G0S 2V0 – 418/397-4188

Beauharnois: 180, rue Salaberry, Valleyfield PQ J6T 2J2 – 514/370-4006

Bedford: 920, rue Principale, Cowansville PQ J2K 1K2 77, rue Principale, Granby PQ J2G 9B3 – 514/263-3520

Bonaventure: 87, rue Principale, CP 517, New Carlisle PQ G0C 1Z0 – 418/752-3376

Charlevoix: 30, ch de la Vallée, La Malbaie PQ G5A 1T8 – 418/665-3991

Chicoutimi: 227, rue Racine est, CP 370, Chicoutimi PQ G7H 5C5 – 418/696-9927

Drummond: 1680, boul St-Joseph, Drummondville PQ J2C 2G3 – 819/478-2513

Frontenac: #1.23, 693, rue St-Alphonse ouest, CP 579, Thetford-Mines PQ G6G 3X3 – 418/338-2118

Gaspé: 124, rte 132, CP 188, Percé PQ G0C 2L0 – 418/782-2055

Hull: #0.210, 17, rue Laurier, Hull PQ J8X 4C1 – 819/776-8100

Iberville: 109, rue St-Charles, St-Jean-sur-Richelieu PQ J3B 2C2 – 514/347-3715

Joliette: 200, rue St-Marc, Joliette PQ J6E 8C2

Kamouraska: 33, rue de la Cour, Rivière-du-Loup PQ G5R 1J1 – 418/862-3579

Labelle: 645, rue de la Madone, Mont-Laurier PQ J9L 1T1 – 819/623-9666

Lac Mégantic: #316, 5527, rue Frontenac, Lac Mégantic PQ G6B 1H6 – 819/583-1268

Longueuil: 1111, boul Jacques-Cartier est, Longueuil PQ J4M 2J6 – 514/646-4011

Mingan: 425, boul Laure, Sept-Îles PQ G4R 1X6 – 418/962-2154

Montmagny: 25, rue du Palais, Montmagny PQ G5V 1P6 – 418/248-0909

Montréal: 1, rue Notre-Dame est, Montréal PQ H2Y 1B6

Pontiac: 27, rue John, CP 159, Campbell's Bay PQ J0X 1K0 – 819/648-5222

Québec: 300, boul Jean-Lesage, Québec PQ G1K 8K6 – 418/649-3501

Richelieu: 46, rue Charlotte, Sorel PQ J3P 6N5 – 514/742-2786

Rimouski: 183, rue de la Cathédrale, CP 800, Rimouski PQ G5L 7C9 – 418/727-3852

Roberval: 750, boul St-Joseph, Roberval PQ G8H 2L5 – 418/275-5073

Rouyn-Noranda: 2, av du Palais, Rouyn-Noranda PQ J9X 2N9 – 819/764-3058

St-François: 375, rue King ouest, Sherbrooke PQ J1H 6B9 – 819/822-6901

St-Hyacinthe: 1550, rue Dessaulles, St-Hyacinthe PQ J2S 2S8 – 514/773-8471

St-Maurice: 212 - 6e rue, Shawinigan PQ G9N 8B6 – 819/536-2571

Témiscamingue: 8, rue St-Gabriel nord, CP 550, Ville-Marie PQ J0Z 3W0 – 819/629-2773

Terrebonne: 400, rue Laviolette, St-Jérôme PQ J7Y 2T6 – 514/431-4407

Trois-Rivières: 250, rue Laviolette, Trois-Rivières PQ G9A 1T9 – 819/372-4150

SASKATCHEWAN

SASKATCHEWAN: COURT OF APPEAL
Court House, 2425 Victoria Ave., Regina SK S4P 3V7

The Court of Appeal has appellate jurisdiction with respect to any judgement, order or decree made by the Court of Queen's Bench and any matter granted to it by statute.

Chief Justice of Saskatchewan, The Hon. Mr./Madam E.D. Bayda

Justices of Appeal (The Hon. Mr./Madam Justice):
S.J. Cameron; M.A. Gerwing; G.R. Jackson; J.G. Lane; N.W. Sherstobitoff; C.F. Tallis; W.J. Vancise; T.C. Wakeling (Supernumerary)

Registrar, M. Herauf

SASKATCHEWAN: FAMILY LAW DIVISION
224 - 4 Ave. South, Saskatoon SK S7K 2H6

Judges (The Hon. Mr./Madam Justice):
M.Y. Carter (Supernumerary); F.G. Dickson

Coordinator, D. Scott

SASKATCHEWAN COURT OF QUEEN'S BENCH
2425 Victoria Ave., Regina SK S4P 3V7

The Court of Queen's Bench is a court of original jurisdiction having jurisdiction in civil & criminal matters arising in Saskatchewan, except those matters expressly excluded by statute.

Chief Justice, The Hon. Mr. D.K. MacPherson

Justices (The Hon. Mr./Madam Justice):
G.H.M. Armstrong; R.L. Barclay; C.L. Dawson; E.J. Gunn; D.C. Hunter; L.A. Kyle; K.R. MacLeod (Supernumerary); E.C. Malone; W.R. Matheson; G.A. Maurice; D.E. McIntyre; E.A. Scheibel; C.R. Wimmer

Registrar of the Court of Queen's Bench & Provincial Court, J. Kernaghan

Local Registrar, G. Ullman

Acting Sheriff, J. Rhinelander

- Assiniboia: Court of Queen's Bench, Assiniboia SK S0H 0B0
  Deputy Sheriff/Local Registrar & Court Clerk, D. Green
- Battleford: Court of Queen's Bench, Battleford SK S0M 0E0
  Justices (The Hon. Mr./Madam Justice):
  D.K. Kreuger
  Sheriff, Court Clerk & Local Registrar, D.I. Dament
- Estevan: Court of Queen's Bench, Estevan SK S4A 0W5
  Justices (The Hon. Mr./Madam Justice):
  G.N. Allbright
  Deputy Sheriff/Local Registrar & Court Clerk, P. Boxrud
- Humboldt: Court of Queen's Bench, Humboldt SK S0K 2A0
  Justices (The Hon. Mr./Madam Justice):
  P.J. Dielschneider (Supernumerary)
  Deputy Sheriff/Local Registrar & Court Clerk, Elaine Lange
- Melfort: Court of Queen's Bench, Melfort SK S0E 1A0
  Deputy Sheriff/Local Registrar & Court Clerk, J. Gabrysh
- Moose Jaw: Court of Queen's Bench, Moose Jaw SK S6H 4P1
  Justices (The Hon. Mr./Madam Justice):
  R.A. MacLean
  Deputy Sheriff/Local Registrar & Court Clerk, J.R.D. Paquin
- Prince Albert: Court of Queen's Bench, Prince Albert SK S6V 4W7
  Justices (The Hon. Mr./Madam Justice):
  J.D. Milliken; A. Rothery
  Sheriff, Court Clerk & Registrar, David Sinclair
- Saskatoon: Court of Queen's Bench, 520 Spadina Cr. East, Saskatoon SK S7K 2H6
  Justices (The Hon. Mr./Madam Justice):
  G.W. Baynton; P. Blacklock Linn; T.L. Geatros (Supernumerary); W.F. Gerein; I. Goldenberg; I. Grotsky (Supernumerary); P. Hrabinsky; J. Klebuc; R.D. Laing; G.E. Noble (Supernumerary); A.L. Sirois (Supernumerary); Marian Wedge; D.H. Wright
  Local Registrar, D. Berezowsky
  Sheriff, G. Laing
- Swift Current: Court of Queen's Bench, Swift Current SK S9H 0J4
  Justices (The Hon. Mr./Madam Justice):
  I.D. McLellan
  Sheriff, Court Clerk & Local Registrar, R. Peterson
- Weyburn: Court of Queen's Bench, Weyburn SK S4H 0L4
  Sheriff, Court Clerk & Local Registrar, W. Dammann
- Wynyard: Court of Queen's Bench, Wynyard SK S0A 4T0
  Deputy Sheriff/Local Registrar & Court Clerk, G. Fewster
- Yorkton: Court of Queen's Bench, Yorkton SK S3N 0C2
  Justices (The Hon. Mr./Madam Justice):
  J. Pritchard
  Sheriff, Court Clerk & Local Registrar, S. Urbanoski

SASKATCHEWAN PROVINCIAL COURT
1815 Smith St., Regina SK S4P 3V7

The Provincial Court has jurisdiction in both civil (including small claims and family) and select criminal (including young offender) matters.

Chief Judge, The Hon. Brosi Nutting

- Estevan: Provincial Court, Court House, 1016 - 4th St., Estevan SK S4A 0W5 – 306/634-0771
  Judges (The Hon.):
  R.E. Lee
- Lloyminster: Provincial Court, 4815 - 50 St., Lloydminster SK S9V 0M8
  Judges (The Hon.):
  K.J. Young
- Meadow Lake: Provincial Court, PO Box 849, Meadow Lake SK S0M 1V0
  Judges (The Hon.):
  J. Nightingale; T.W. White
- Melfort: Provincial Court, PO Box 6500, Melfort SK S0E 1A0
  Judges (The Hon.):
  E.C. Diehl; E.R. Gosselin
- Moose Jaw: Provincial Court, 110 Ominica St. West, Moose Jaw SK S6H 6V2 – 306/694-3612
  Judges (The Hon.):
  G.C. King; D. Orr
- North Battleford: Provincial Court, 1002 - 103 St., North Battleford SK S9A 1K4
  Judges (The Hon.):
  L.P. Deshaye; D. Kaiser; V.H. Meekma
- Prince Albert: Provincial Court, PO Box 3003, Prince Albert SK S6V 6G1
  Judges (The Hon.):

T.B. Bekolay; Stephen Carter; Stephen Carter; T.W. Ferris; W.V. Goliath
- Regina: Provincial Court, 1815 Smith St., Regina SK S4P 3V7
  Judges (The Hon.):
  R.H. Allan; K.E. Bellerose; D.E. Fenwick; L. Halliday; B.D. Henning; E.A. Lewchuk; J.E. McMurtry; D. Morris; G.R. Moxley; L.J. Smith
- La Ronge: Provincial Court, PO Box 500, La Ronge SK S0J 1L0
  Judges (The Hon.):
  C. Fafard; W.K. Tucker
- Saskatoon: Provincial Court, 230 - 20 St. East, Saskatoon SK S7K 2H6
  Judges (The Hon.):
  R.G. Bell; B.P. Carey; R. Finley; B. Goldstein; B.L. Huculak; D.A. Lavoie; J.B.J. Nutting; E. Schmeise; G.T. Seniuk; S.P. Whelan
- Swift Current: Provincial Court, Court House, 121 Lorne St. West, Swift Current SK S9H 0J4 – 306/778-8390
  Judges (The Hon.):
  L.A. Matsulla; G.B. Shaner
- Weyburn: Provincial Court, Court House, 301 Prairie Ave., Weyburn SK S4H 0L4 – 306/848-2357
  Judges (The Hon.):
  W.V. Goliath
- Wynyard: Provincial Court, Court House, PO Box 1449, Wynyard SK S0A 4T0 – 306/554-2155
  Judges (The Hon.):
  D. Ebert
- Yorkton: Provincial Court, Court House, 120 Smith St. East, Yorkton SK S3N 3V3
  Judges (The Hon.):
  K.A. Andrychuck; E.S. Bobowski; R. Rathgeber

YUKON TERRITORY

YUKON TERRITORY: COURT OF APPEAL
PO Box 4010, Whitehorse YT Y1A 3S9
403/667-3524; Fax: 403/667-3079

The Court of Appeal has appellate jurisdiction in all civil and criminal matters from decisions by the Territorial Court and Supreme Court.
Justices of Appeal (The Hon. Mr./Madam Justice):
Vancouver: A.B.B. Carrothers; G.S. Cumming; I.T. Donald; William A. Esson; L.S.G. Finch; R. Gibbs; D.B. Gibbs; D.M.M. Goldie; E.E. Hinkson; H.A. Hollinrake; H. Hutcheon; J.D. Lambert; H. Legg; A.B. Macfarlane; A. McEachern; P. Proudfoot; J. Prowse; M.A. Rowles; C.A. Ryan; M.F. Southin; M.R. Taylor; J. Wood
Whitehorse: R.E. Hudson; H.C.B. Maddison
Yellowknife: E. Richard; John C. Vertes
Registrar, Edna Delisle Jackson

YUKON TERRITORY: SUPREME COURT
PO Box 4010, Whitehorse YT Y1A 3S9
403/667-3524; Fax: 403/667-3079

The Supreme Court is a superior court of record having original jurisdiction in all civil and criminal matters arising in the Yukon, unless excluded by statute.
Judges (The Hon. Mr./Madam Justice):
Whitehorse: Ralph E. Hudson; Harry C.B. Maddison
Ex-Officio Judges (The Hon. Mr./Madam Justice):
Yellowknife: J. Ted Richard; Virginia A. Schuler; John Z. Vertes
Deputy Judges (The Hon. Mr./Madam Justice):
Calgary: Paul S. Chrumka; Carole M. Conrad; Mary M. Hetherington; Roger P. Kerans; Earl Lomas; Arthur M. Lutz; Peter McIntyre; Peter C.G. Power
Edmonton: William J. Girgulis; Edward P. MacCallum; Ernest A. Marshall; Mary Moreau; Allan H. Wachowich
Lethbridge: Clarence G. Yanosik
London: R.J. Haines
Montréal: Perry Meyer; J.E. Marcel Nichols
Nanaimo: Ralph Hutchinson
Québec: Ross Goodwin
Regina: Edward D. Bayda; Calvin F. Tallis
Thunder Bay: Anthony William Maloney
Toronto: Lucien A. Beaulieu; Stephen Borins; Douglas Carruthers; W. David Griffiths; Stanley R. Kuristo
Vancouver: Marion Jean Allan; John C. Bouck; George Peter Fraser; Kenneth M. Lysyk; A. Gordon MacKinnon; Kenneth E. Meredith; Wallace T. Oppal; I. Lee Skipp; David Vickers
Winnipeg: A. Aubrey Hirschfield; Guy J. Kroft
Registrar, Bankruptcy, Edna Delisle-Jackson
Sheriff, Paul Cowan
Deputy Sheriff, R. Taylor
Deputy Sheriff, Gavin Shaw
Deputy Sheriff, J. Tiedman

YUKON TERRITORY: TERRITORIAL COURT
PO Box 2703, Whitehorse YT Y1A 2C6
403/667-5438; Fax: 403/667-3079

The Territorial Court has jurisdiction in family, youth and select criminal matters.
Chief Judge, The Hon. John E. Faulkner
Puisne Judges (The Hon.):
Heino Lilles; Barry D. Stuart
Senior Court Clerk, Sharon Kerr
Territorial Court Clerks:
Linda Balcaen, Sue Cleaver, Norma Davignon, Edwige Graham, Norm Hamilton, Stella Hearty (Watson Lake), Dorothy Irwin (Dawson City), Sharon Kerr, S.J. McCullough, Sharman Morrison, Arlene Ogden, Iris Warde

OFFICIAL RECEIVERS

(UNDER THE BANKRUPTCY & INSOLVENCY ACT)

Superintendent of Bankruptcy, G. Redling, Industry Canada, 365 Laurier Ave. West, 8th Fl., Ottawa, ON K1A 0C8 613/941-1000; Fax: 613/941-2862

Alberta
Industry Canada, Bankruptcy, 10225 - 100 Ave., Edmonton AB T5J 0A1; 403/495-2476, Fax: 403/495-2466
  Division No. 1: Edmonton; Red Deer; Wetaskiwin; Camrose (sub-district); Stettler; Peace River; Grande Prairie (sub-district)
Industry Canada, Bankruptcy, Standard Life Tower Bldg., #400, 639 - 5 Ave. SW, Calgary AB T2P ; 403/292-567, Fax: 403/292-5188
  Division No. 2: Calgary; Medicine Hat; Lethbridge; Taber (sub-district); Bassano (sub-district); Hanna; MacLeod

British Columbia
Industry Canada, Bankruptcy, #1900, 300 West Georgia St., Vancouver BC V6B 6E1, 604/666-5007, Fax: 604/666-4610
  Division No. 1: Prince Rupert
  Division No. 2: Victoria; Nanaimo
  Division No. 3: Vancouver ; New Westminster
  Division No. 4: Yale; Cariboo
  Division No. 5: West Kootenay; East Kootenay
  Division No. 6: Parts of Yale and Cariboo; north of 52nd parallel

Manitoba
Industry Canada, Bankruptcy, 400 St..Mary Ave., 4th Fl., Winnipeg MB 204/983-3229, Fax: 204/983-8904

New Brunswick
Same as Nova Scotia
  Division No. 1: Saint John; Queens; Kings; Charlotte
  Division No. 2: York; Sunbury; Carleton; Victoria; Madawaska
  Division No. 3: Gloucester; Northumberland; Restigouche
  Division No. 4: Westmorland; Kent; Albert

Newfoundland
Same as Nova Scotia

Northwest Territories
Same as Alta. Div. 1 (Edmonton)

Nova Scotia
Industry Canada, Bankruptcy Branch, Halifax Insurance Bldg., #900, 5670 Spring Garden Rd., Halifax NS B3J 1H6; 902/426-2900; Fax: 902/426-7275
  Division No. 1: Halifax; Hants; Lunenburg; Queens; Annapolis; Kings
  Division No. 2: Pictou; Guysborough; Cumberland; Colchester; Antigonish
  Division No. 3: Cape Breton; Inverness; Richmond; Victoria
  Division No. 4: Digby; Yarmouth; Shelburne

Ontario
Industry Canada, Bankruptcy, 330 Portage Ave., PO Box 981, Winnipeg MB R3C 0M6; 204/983-3229, Fax: 204/983-8904
  Division No. 1: Thunder Bay; Rainy River
Industry Canada, Bankruptcy, 25 St. Clair Ave. East, 7th Fl., Toronto ON M4T 1M2; 416/973-6486, Fax: 416/973-7440
  Division No. 2: Sudbury; Algoma
  Division No. 3: Manitoulin; Simcoe; Muskoka
  Division No. 9: Peel; York
  Division No. 10: Peterborough; Northumberland & Durham; Victoria & Haliburton
  Division No. 13: Nipissing
  Division No. 14: Parry Sound
  Division No. 15: Temiskaming
  Division No. 16: Cochrane
Industry Canada, Bankruptcy, The Federal Bldg., #303, 451 Talbot St., London ON N6A 5C9; 519/645-4034, Fax: 519/645-5139
  Division No. 4: Dufferin; Grey; Bruce
  Division No. 5: Middlesex; Huron; Perth; Oxford; Elgin
  Division No. 6: Essex; Lambton; Kent
  Division No.8: Waterloo; Wellington
Industry Canada, Bankruptcy, 69 John St. South, 4th Fl., Hamilton ON L8N 2B9; 905/572-2847; Fax: 905/572-4066
  Division No. 7: Wentworth ; Norfolk; Haldimand; Welland; Brant; Lincoln; Halton
  Division No. 9: Peel; York
Industry Canada, Bankruptcy, 255 Argyle Ave., Ottawa ON K2P 1B8; 613/995-2994, Fax: 613/996-0949
  Division No. 11: Frontenac; Lennox & Addington; Hastings; Prince Edward
  Division No. 12: Carleton; Renfrew; Lanark; Russell & Prescott; Stormont, Dundas & Glengarry; Leeds & Grenville

Prince Edward Island
Same as Nova Scotia

Québec
Industrie Canada, Direction des Faillites, #800, 5, Place Ville-Marie, Montréal PQ H3B 2G2; 514/283-6192, Fax: 514/283-9795
  Division No. 1: Montréal; Richelieu; St. Hyacinthe; Beauharnois
  Division No. 8: Joliette

Division No. 18: Terrebonne; Labelle
Division No. 19: Iberville
Industrie Canada, Direction des Faillites, 1040, av Belvedère, 2e étage, Sillery PQ G1S 3G3; 418/648-4280, Fax: 418/648-4120
Division No. 2: Québec; Montmagny (Anticosti)
Division No. 3: Rimouski
Division No. 5: Trois-Rivières; St. Maurice
Division No. 7: Chicoutimi; Saguenay
Division No. 9: Roberval
Division No. 10: Kamouraska
Division No. 11: Gaspé; Bonaventure
Division No. 13: Beauce
Division No. 14: Îles-de-la-Madeleine

Division No. 15: Arthabaska
Division No. 17: Megantic
Division No. 22: Hauterive; Mingan
Industrie Canada, Direction des Faillites, #600, 2665, rue King ouest, Sherbrooke PQ J1J 2B8 ; 819/564-5742, Fax: 819/564-5743
Division No. 4: St. François
Division No. 20: Bedford
Division No. 21: Drummond
Same as Ontario Division No. 11 (Ottawa)
Division No. 6: Hull; Pontiac
Division No. 12: Abitibi
Division No. 16: Rouyn-Noranda-Temiscamingue

Saskatchewan
Industry Canada, Bankruptcy, #1020, 2002 Victoria Ave., Regina SK S4P 0R7; 306/780-5391, Fax: 780-6947
Division No. 1: Regina
Division No. 3: Moose Jaw
Industry Canada, Bankruptcy, 123 - 2nd Ave. South, 7th Fl., Saskatoon SK S7K 7E6; 306/975-4298, Fax: 306/975-5317
Division No. 2: Saskatoon

Yukon Territory
Same as B.C. Div.1 (Vancouver)

DIRECTORY OF LAW FIRMS

ALBERTA

AIRDRIE .... Calgary
R.J. Hashizume, Airdrie Professional Centre, 142 - 1 Ave. NW, PO Box 3700, T4B 2B8 – 403/948-3335 – *1
M. John Wilson, 121E Centre Ave. West, PO Box 3444, T4B 2B7 – 403/948-7302, Fax: 403/948-4347 – *1

ATHABASCA .... Edmonton
Kozina & Gregory, Athabasca Centre Bldg., #4907, 4907 - 51 St., PO Box 1287, T0G 0B0 – 403/675-3443, Fax: 403/675-3282 – *2

BANFF .... Calgary
Karras, Rathbone, 205 Bear St., PO Box 899, T0L 0C0 – 403/762-2770, Fax: 403/762-5961 – *3
Robert M. Nesbitt, Q.C., PO Box 2129, T0L 0C0 – 403/762-3438, Fax: 403/762-9458 – *2
Dennis R. Shuler, 217 Bear St., PO Box 1600, T0L 0C0 – 403/762-3888, Fax: 403/762-5229 – *1

BARRHEAD .... Edmonton
Andrew, Donahoe & Oake, PO Box 470, T0G 0E0 – 403/426-4570
Driessen & Roy, 5006 - 50 Ave., PO Box 4220, T7N 1A2 – 403/674-2276, Fax: 403/674-4592 – *2
Marvin L. Perry, 5104 - 49A St., PO Box 158, T0G 0E0 – 403/674-2002, Fax: 403/674-4438 – *1

BASSANO .... Medicine Hat
Ben R. Plumer, PO Box 329, T0J 0B0 – 403/641-4131, Fax: 403/641-4133 – *1

BEAUMONT .... Wetaskiwin
Jackie & Handerek, 5002 - 50 St., T0C 0H0 – 403/929-8608

BEAVER LODGE .... Grande Prairie
Roger Jewitt, PO Box 780, T0H 0C0 – 403/354-2271 – *1

BLAIRMORE .... Macleod
King & Young, 12305 - 20 Ave., PO Box 450, T0K 0E0 – 403/562-2804 – *2
North & Company, 13013 - 20th Ave., T0K 0E0 – 403/562-2055
Paterson North, 1303 - 20 Ave., T0K 0E0 – 403/562-2131, Fax: 403/320-8958 – *2

BONNYVILLE .... Edmonton
Allan Wayne Fraser, Muller Plaza, 4816 - 50 Ave., PO Box 6710, T9N 2H2 – 403/826-3355, Fax: 403/826-6132 – *1
Michel D. Meunier, 5022 - 50 Ave., PO Box 7670, T9N 2H9 – 403/826-3384 – *1
Dale L. Wilson, PO Box 7238, T9N 2H6 – 403/826-6150 – *1

Wood & Wiebe, #101, 5001 - 49 Ave., PO Box 8060, T9N 2J3 – 403/826-5767, Fax: 403/826-4654 – *2

BROOKS .... Medicine Hat
Kay, Kay & Riggins, #B, 212 - 3 Ave, PO Box 1227, T0J 0J0 – 403/362-5733 – *3
Lutes, Shantz & Bell, 103 - 2 Ave West, PO Box 670, T1R 1B6 – 403/362-3447, Fax: 403/362-4379 – *3

CALGARY .... Calgary
Diane Ablonczy, 112 Edgedale Dr. NW, T3A 2R5 – 403/269-2525, Fax: 403/241-2268 – *1
Adel A. Abougoush, 1409 - 18A St. NE, T2E 4W7 – 403/276-8415
Adamson Willoughby & D'Souza, #217, 495 - 36 St. NE, T2A 6K3 – 403/531-9520, Fax: 403/272-6586 – *4
W. Adamson, Lancaster Bldg., #412, 304 - 8 Ave. SW, T2P 1C2 – 403/262-3946 – *1
Ady, Blumell & Rasmusen, #208, 2004 - 14 St. NW, T2M 3N3 – 403/282-4544, Fax: 403/284-4503 – *3
Ahlsten & Company, #320, 521 - 3 Ave. SW, T2P 3T3 – 403/233-7600, Fax: 403/263-2713 – *3
John W. Aikenhead, 124 Westview Dr. SW, T3C 2R9 – 403/242-6699
Anderson Law Firm, #610, 7015 Macleod Tr. South, T2H 2K6 – 403/253-4597, Fax: 403/253-4599 – *2
D.G. Anderson, #800, 640 - 8 Ave. SW, T2P 1G7 – 403/265-9100
Arkell & Charnock, #600, 777 - 8 Ave. SW, T2P 3R5 – 403/265-5665
G.R. Auck, #706, 6455 Macleod Tr. South, T2H 0K9 – 403/258-3330 – *1
T.J. Bachynski, 112 - 4 Ave. SW, 28th Fl., PO Box 38, T2P 2V5 – 403/269-8690, Fax: 403/269-6213 – *1
Balbi & Company, 1501 MacLeod Tr. SE, T2G 2N6 – 403/269-7300, Fax: 403/265-9790
Verna G. Baldwin, 15 Hillary Cres. SW, T2V 3J3 – 403/255-8739
Ballem McDill MacInnes Eden, Petro Canada Centre, West Tower, 150 - 6 Ave. SW, 40th Fl., T2P 3Y7 – 403/292-9800, Fax: 403/233-8979 – *28
Barron & Barron, Southland Court Building, #231, 10601 Southport Rd. SW, T2W 3M6 – 403/278-3730, Fax: 403/271-8016 – *2
Walter C. Barron, Q.C., First Alberta Pl., 777 - 8 Ave. SW, T2P 3R5 – 403/269-2277, Fax: 403/263-3256 – *1
Robert J. Batting, #500, 736 - 6 Ave. SW, T2P 3T7 – 403/263-4949
A.V.M. Beattie, Q.C., 3108 Carleton St. SW, T2T 5Y6 – 403/245-5255, Fax: 403/228-0254 – *1
Beaumont Church, AGT Tower, #2200, 411 - 1 St. SE, T2G 5E7 – 403/264-0000, Fax: 403/264-0478 – *13
R.E. Beninger, 503 - 6 St. SW, T2P 1X4 – 403/237-0983 – *1
Bennett Jones Verchere, Bankers Hall East, #4500, 855 - 2 St. SW, T2P 4K7 – 403/298-3100, Fax: 403/265-7219 – *134
Gary E. Bilyk, #202, 703 - 6 Ave. SW, T2P 0T9 – 403/266-2810, Fax: 403/237-0327 – *1
R. Michael Birnbaum, B.A., LL.B., Rocky Mountain Plaza, #670, 615 Macleod Tr. SE, T2G 4T8 – 403/

265-9050, Fax: 403/262-1379; Email: birnbaum@nucleus.com
Bishop & McKenzie, #2230, 700 - 9th Ave. SW, T2P 3V4 – 403/237-5550, Fax: 403/263-3423; Email: bishmc@agt.net – *5
Barry C. Bishop, 2460 - 23 St. NW, T2M 3Y2 – 403/289-0204
Christopher D. Bixby, #300, 840 - 6 Ave. SW, T2P 3E5 – 403/229-0772
S.L. Blaine, PO Box 1164, T2P 2K9 – 403/246-1733 – *1
Blake, Cassels & Graydon, Bankers Hall East, #3500, 855 - 2nd St. SW, T2P 4J8 – 403/260-9600, Fax: 403/263-9895 – *41
Vivian J. Blochert, 8948 Bayridge Dr. SW, T2V 3M8 – 403/251-3947
Nevine S. Booth, 8 Edgeland Cres. NW, T3A 4C3 – 403/547-0991
Richard W. Bourassa, #504, 706 - 7th Ave. SW, T2P 0Z1 – 403/276-1167
Laurence E. Bowes, #509, 5920 - 1A St. SW, T2H 0G3 – 403/255-8521 – *1
Robert M. Boyer, #1100, 800 - 5 Ave. SW, T2P 3T6 – 403/269-9266
James A. Bradford, 2712 - 10 St. SW, T2T 3H2 – 403/245-2694
Bridges, Dick & Jamison, 3527 - 18 St. SW, T2T 4T9 – 403/243-8360 – *3
Britton & Jones, #406, 501 - 18 Ave. SW, T2S 0C7 – 403/229-9333
Beverly A.B. Broadhurst, #830, 615 Macleod Trail SE, T2G 4T8 – 403/234-9477 – *1
Brown & Curran, #316, 6707 Elbow Dr. SW, T2V 0E5 – 403/252-8876 – *1
Brunnen, Sturgeon, #400, 1167 Kensington Cres. NW, T2N 1X7 – 403/270-3572 – *5
Bryan & Co., First Canadian Place, #3520, 350 - 7th Ave., T2P 3N9 – 403/269-7220, Fax: 403/269-9304 – *4
Debra Bulmer, PO Box 2211, Stn M, T2P 2M4 – 403/541-8944, Fax: 403/873-0110 – *1
David R. Burge, Brentwood Village Mall, #232C, 3630 Morley Trail NW, T2L 1K8 – 403/282-2888 – *1
Burnet, Duckworth & Palmer, First Canadian Centre, #1400, 350 - 7 Ave. SW, T2P 3N9 – 403/260-0100, Fax: 403/260-0332; Email: central@mhs.bdplaw.compuserve.com – *69
Gordon J. Burrell, #401, 1110 Centre St. North, T2E 2R2 – 403/277-3133
Burstall Ward, #1800, 800 - 5 Ave. SW, T2P 3T6 – 403/264-1915 – *14
D.W. Busheikin, 8240 Elbow Dr. SW, T2V 1K4 – 403/255-8643 – *1
Butlin, Biggs & Coultry, #405, 1509 Centre St. South, T2G 2E6 – 403/290-0047 – *3
Tari Y.P. Carey, #500, 333 - 11 Ave. NW, T2R 1L9 – 403/266-7110
Carscallen Lockwood & Cormie, #1500, 407 - 2 St. SW, T2P 2Y3 – 403/262-3775, Fax: 403/262-2952 – *5
C. Yvonne Chenier Professional Corporation, #303, 1204 Kensington Rd. NW, T2N 3P5 – 403/270-8700 – *1

Malcom P.Y. Chow, #328, 1015 Centre St. North, T2E 2P8 – 403/277-1688, Fax: 403/277-1699

T. Catherine Christopher, #840, 407 - 2 St. SW, T2P 2Y3 – 403/237-8084, Fax: 403/263-6413

S.M. Chumir, #280, 521 - 3 Ave. SW, T2P 3T3 – 403/269-1949 – *1

Clark Dymond Crump, Calgary House, #1400, 550 - 6 Ave. SW, T2P 0S2 – 403/265-7070, Fax: 403/232-6750 – *4

B.N. Clark, #209, 2411 - 4 St. NW, T2M 2Z8 – 403/284-4651, Fax: 403/282-0790 – *1

Clarke Bonnycastle, #220, 1100 - 8 Ave. SW, T2P 3T9 – 403/237-6300 – *3

Rosemary J. Clarke, 6347 Lynch Cres. SW, T3E 5V1 – 403/240-0008

Code Hunter Wittmann, #1200, 700 - 2 St. SW, T2P 4V5 – 403/298-1000, Fax: 403/263-9193; Email: chw@cad-vision.com – *62

John C. Cohen, #210, 2323 - 32 Ave. NE, T2E 6Z3 – 403/250-1582 – *1

Maggie F. Collins, #900, 840 - 7 Ave. SW, T2P 3G2 – 403/269-4222

Donald J. Colton, #220, 240 Midpark Way SE, T2X 1N4 – 403/256-9644 – *1

Cook Duke Cox, #2700, 645 - 7 Ave. SW, T2P 4G8 – 403/298-2400, Fax: 403/262-0007; Email: cdc@ccinet.ab.ca – *19

R.G. Couch, 611 - 25 Ave. NE, T2E 1Y6 – 403/276-7126 – *1

Richard L. Cragg, #204, 495 - 36 St. NE, T2A 6K3 – 403/273-7686, Fax: 403/272-2511 – *1

Brian J. Crawford, Sunlife Plaza South, #2500, 144 - 4 Ave. SW, T2P 3N4 – 403/264-9999 – *1

L.H.A. Creighton, #400, 4600 Crowchild Trail NW, T3B 2C6 – 403/247-1643 – *1

Cummings Verstraten Kugelmass, Deerfoot Ct., Bldg Box: 106, 1144 - 29 Ave. NE, T2E 7P1 – 403/250-3570, Fax: 403/291-0389 – *3

Charles R. Darwent, 414 - 8 St. SW, T2P 1Z9 – 403/261-9048 – *1

T.M. Dawe, #200, 1409 Edmonton Tr. NE, T2E 3K8 – 403/276-8802

Deborah Dalton, City of Calgary, Law Department, PO Box 2100, Stn M, T2P 2M5 – 403/244-2517

H.R. Densmore, #800, 603 - 7 Ave. SW, T2P 2T5 – 403/263-0950 – *1

J.S. Dhanda, #5, 15 Millrise Blvd. SW, T1Y 2X1 – 403/254-1777, Fax: 403/254-1779

Arline F. Diamond, #745, 610 - 8 Ave. SW, T2P 1G5 – 403/237-9592

Leslie M. Diamond, Bow Valley Sq. II, #3000, 205 - 5 Ave. SW, T2P 2V7 – 403/263-4360, Fax: 403/265-6429 – *1

Divorce By Mediation, 3222 - 3 St. SW, T2S 1V3 – 403/243-4899 – *1

Donahue Rondeau, Bow Valley Sq. II, #1800, 205 - 5 Ave SW, T2P 2V7 – 403/262-7250 – *6

M.M. Donlevy-Konkin, 27 Cornwallis Dr. NW, T2K 1T6 – 403/284-0639

Doucette & Phipps, #209, 6036 - 3 St. SW, T2H 0H9 – 403/531-0181, 0182, Fax: 403/531-0180

Margaret-Ann R. Douglas, #4, 3820 Bow Trail SW, T3C 2E7 – 403/249-1176

Drummond Phillips & Sevalrud, #900, 521 - 3 Ave. SW, T2P 3T3 – 403/221-8700, Fax: 403/264-6654 – *7

Dudelzak & Landry, #325, 4400 Macleod Tr. South, T2G 4Y7 – 403/287-3330, Fax: 403/243-6743 – *3

Dukeshire Law Office, Provident Professional Bldg., #201, 4161 Valiant Dr. NW, T3A 0X9 – 403/286-7008, Fax: 403/286-7644 – *1

Dunkley & Company, 5219 - 4 St. NE, T2K 6J5 – 403/275-9292 – *1

Dunphy Calvert, #2100, 777 - 8 Ave. SW, T2P 3R5 – 403/265-7777, Fax: 403/269-8911 – *10

Dworkin & Dworkin, Elveden House, #340, 717 - 7th Ave. SW, T2P 0Z3 – 403/261-3050, Fax: 403/266-5847 – *2

G.M. Eamon, #630, 11012 Macleod Tr. South, T2J 6A5 – 403/271-3221, Fax: 403/271-5909 – *1

Ebbert & Company, 2020 - 10 St. NW, T2M 3M2 – 403/284-1131, Fax: 403/282-1621 – *3

Peter M.B. Eberhard, #606, 734 - 7 Ave. SW, T2P 3T8 – 403/266-3715

B.A.F. Edy, #17, 6624 Centre St. South, T2H 0C6 – 403/253-1228 – *1

Engel & Company, #1000, 808 - 4 Ave. SW, T2P 3E8 – 403/269-9808, Fax: 403/269-3285 – *1

P. Robert Enns, Westmount Pl., #222, 1100 - 8 Ave. SW, T2P 3T9 – 403/262-6588, Fax: 403/262-6590

Evans Bascom, #510, 604 - 1 St. SW, T2P 1M7 – 403/233-0443 – *3

Faber Gurevitch Bickman, #350, 603 - 7 Ave SW, T2P 2T5 – 403/263-1540, Fax: 403/269-2653 – *9

A.W. Facey, 1213 - 17 St. SW, T3C 1G9 – 403/269-7209 – *1

Felesky Flynn, First Canadian Centre, #3400, 350 - 7 Ave SW, T2P 3N9 – 403/260-3300, Fax: 403/263-9649; Email: felesky@mail.cycor.ca – *14

W.A. Ferguson, #210A, 5403 Crowchild Tr. NW, T3B 4Z1 – 403/288-7601, Fax: 403/228-3689 – *1

D.W. Fetherston, 5311 Bannerman Dr. NW, T2L 1W1 – 403/289-6556 – *1

Field Atkinson Perraton, First Canadian Centre, #1900, 350 - 7 Ave. SW, T2P 4H2 – 403/290-0990, Fax: 403/266-4466 – *33

P.L. Fiess, #825, 603 - 7 Ave. SW, T2P 2T5 – 403/266-0033, Fax: 403/261-4958 – *1

N.A. Flatters, 1307 Klondike Ave. SW, T2V 2L9

Fleming Kambeitz, #1500, 738 - 6 Ave. SW, T2P 3T7 – 403/266-5550, Fax: 403/265-5910 – *8

G. Lyle Ford, 30 Eagle Ridge Dr. SW, T2V 2V4 – 403/255-5555, Fax: 403/255-5555 – *1

Forsyth & Associates, #100, 1300 - 8 St. SW, T2R 1B2 – 403/244-3829, Fax: 403/229-4063

Fox Chittick Munn, #314, 1167 Kensington Cres. NW, T2N 1X7 – 403/221-9800 – *3

Fric & Lowenstein, Sunridge Professional Centre, #406, 2675 - 36 St. NE, T1Y 6H6 – 403/291-2594, Fax: 403/291-2668 – *3

Karen Gainer, #316, 1167 Kensington Cres. NW, T2N 1X7 – 403/270-0660 – *1

Richard D. Galbraith, 163 Midvalley Pl. SE, T2X 1K3 – 403/254-0779

Robert W. Gee, 1725 - 10 Ave. SW, 2nd Fl., T3C 0K1 – 403/245-0640, Fax: 403/244-7955 – *1

German Fong Albus Lam, #610, 715 - 5 Ave. SW, T2P 2X6 – 403/263-7880, Fax: 403/237-7075 – *5

H. Carl Gerwing, #610, 11012 Macleod Tr. South, T2J 6A5 – 403/278-4400 – *1

Gillis, Dartnell, #530, 11012 Macleod Tr. South, T2J 6A5 – 403/278-7140 – *3

Jim Gladstone, 3700 Anderson Rd. SW, PO Box 1470, T2W 3C4 – 403/251-7272, Fax: 403/251-5871 – *1

G.J. Godlovitch, #412, 10325 Bonaventure Dr. SE, T2J 5R8 – 403/225-1584 – *1

Irvin Goldman, #204, 1015 - 4 St. SW, T2R 1J4 – 403/234-7100

W.D. Goodfellow, Q.C., #1660, 540 - 5 Ave. SW, T2P 0M2 – 403/262-4610, Fax: 403/262-4625

Goodman & Company, #602, 805 - 8 Ave. SW, T2P 1H7 – 403/269-7171 – *2

Gorman, Gorman & Burns, #300, 1333 - 8 St. SW, T2R 1M6 – 403/244-5515, Fax: 403/244-5605 – *2

Mark Avrom Gottlieb, #200, 222 - 16 Ave. NE, T2E 1J8 – 403/282-2516, 230-0712 – *1

George R.D. Goulet, 350 - 7 Ave. SW, 18th Fl., T2P 3N9 – 403/262-1677 – *1

Laura Lee Grant, #250, 525 - 28 St. SE, T2A 6W9 – 403/235-2111 – *1

Green & McIlhargey, #210, 999 - 8 St. SW, T2R 1J5 – 403/228-4425 – *2

Marvin A. Greenblatt, #300, 1717 - 10 St. NW, T2M 4S2 – 403/289-9999, Fax: 403/289-3114 – *1

Gregg & Company, Kipling Sq., #300, 611 - 10 Ave. SW, T2R 0B2 – 403/263-3086, Fax: 403/262-6677 – *2

E. Noel Grey, #305, 8181 Flint Rd. SE, T2H 2B8 – 403/253-0332, Fax: 403/278-2965 – *1

Grier, Allen & Company, #400, 4600 Crowchild Tr. NW, T3A 2L6 – 403/247-2761, Fax: 403/233-2798 – *5

Gruman, Brown & Crossfield, #201, 1717 - 10 St. NW, T2M 4S2 – 403/284-4614 – *2

Harrison Guild, #502, 5920 - 1A St., T2H 0G3 – 403/259-5256

Rita J. Guthrie, 3026 Linden Dr., T3E 6C5 – 403/242-9704 – *1

Bryan F. Hagel, 2026 - 33 Ave. SW, T2T 1Z4 – 403/249-5505, Fax: 403/240-0632 – *1

McGuire Hagel, #300, 4515 Bow Trail SW, T3C 2G3 – 403/249-1176, Fax: 403/242-9455 – *1

Bruce J. Halliday, #1200, 840 - 7 Ave. SW, T2P 3G2 – 403/266-3321, Fax: 403/266-3463 – *1

E.B. Hammelburg, 55 Dalcastle Way NW, T3A 2N4 – 403/286-6239

K.M. Hansen, 3810 - 6 St. SW, T2S 2M8 – 403/243-3625 – *1

Hanson & Associates, 3515 - 17 Ave. SE, 2nd Fl., T2A 0R5 – 403/235-5556 – *1

Hanson & Company, #1000, 815 - 8 Ave SW, T2P 3P2 – 403/261-6890, Fax: 403/263-1632 – *2

Harben, Aaron & Rynd, #501, 665 - 8 St. SW, T2P 3K7 – 403/233-7616

B.D. Harris, #605, 5940 Macleod Tr. South, T2H 2G4 – 403/255-0799 – *1

Gregory R. Harris, #500, 630 - 4 Ave. SW, T2P 0J9 – 403/266-5035, Fax: 403/265-6368

O.W. Harris, #3, 610 - 8 Ave. SW, T2P 1G5 – 403/266-2261 – *1

Harrison & Company, #300, 1201 - 5 St SW, T2R 0Y6 – 403/531-9500 – *2

Doucet Harrison, #2050, 300 - 5 Ave. SW, T1P 3C4 – 403/237-7970 – *2

M.P. Hartney, #209, 2411 - 4 St. NW, T2M 2Z8 – 403/284-4651, Fax: 403/282-0790 – *1

Hawley, W.D., #595, 700 - 4 Ave. SW, T2P 3J4 – 403/234-8185 – *1

L.S. Heald, #300, 840 - 6 Ave. SW, T2P 3E5 – 403/269-2336

Thomas T.E. Helgeson, 1770 - 7 Ave. SW, T2N 0Z4

Henders & Company, #2, 1225A Kensington Rd. NW, T2N 3P8 – 403/270-7746 – *1

G.W. Henderson, #900, 441 - 5 Ave. SW, T2P 2V1 – 403/290-1282

Dale Hensley, #230, 1210 - 8 St. SW, T2R 1L3 – 403/229-2938, Fax: 403/229-2977

Hess DeVries, #300, 1717 - 10 St. NW, T2M 4S2 – 403/289-9999 – *2

Higgs & Hooker, #120, 1330 - 15 Ave. SW, T3C 3N7 – 403/245-3493 – *2

C.R. High Wo, #515, 1110 Centre St. NE, T2E 2R2 – 403/276-9877 – *1

K.L. Hill, #10, 1032 - 1 Ave. NW, T2N 0A7 – 403/270-0887

Ho MacNeil Jenuth, #500, 100 - 4 Ave SW, T2G 3N2 – 403/233-2812, Fax: 403/237-8312 – *3

Timothy S. Hoar, North Tower, SunLife Plaza, #700, 140 - 4 Ave. SW, T2P 3N3 – 403/262-4866

Hoffman Dorchik, #500, 222 - 58 Ave. SW, T2H 2S3 – 403/258-0800, Fax: 403/253-0738 – *4

Howard Bernhardt Stevenson, #1400, 400 - 3 Ave. SW, T2P 4H2 – 403/266-5222 – *3

Howard, Mackie, Canterra Tower, #1000, 400 - 3 Ave. SW, T2P 4H2 – 403/232-9523, Fax: 403/266-1395 – *68

James Hubbell, #6, 2439 - 54 Ave. SW, T3E 1M4 – 403/287-2922

Sharon A. Huckell, Home Oil Tower, Home Oil Company Limited, Bldg Box: 1600, 324 - 8 Ave. SW, T2P 2Z5

M. Ann Hughes, 940 Coachside Cres. SW, T3H 1A5 – 403/560-4579

Ivo Hula, #438, 1421 - 7 Ave. NW, T2M 0Z3 – 403/283-9329

---

* indicates number of lawyers in law firm.

L.D. Hurd, #521, 206 - 7 Ave. SW, T2P 0W7 – 403/262-8280 – *1

H.J. Hurov, #535, 540 - 5 Ave. SW, T2P 0M2 – 403/263-8220 – *1

M.A. Hutchings, #310, 9737 Macleod Tr. South, T2J 0P6 – 403/531-0200

J.E. Hutchison, 14004 Park Estates Dr. SE, T2J 3W2 – 403/278-1719

James & Company, #3250, 700-2nd St. SW, T2P 2W2 – 403/298-2000, Fax: 403/298-2024 – *3

James & Company, #204, 1015 - 4 St. SW, T2R 1J4 – 403/262-7141 – *3

B.D. Janusz, #700, 805 - 8 Ave. SW, T2P 1H7 – 403/269-9595 – *1

Jarvis & Company, 135 Whitefield Dr. NE, T1Y 5X1 – 403/293-2191 – *2

D.E. Jermyn, #1060, 340 - 12 Ave. SW, T2R 1L5 – 403/264-5810 – *1

Harold M. Joffe, #301, 604 - 1 St. SW, T2P 1M7 – 403/292-0700

Johnson & Shibley, #116, 8220 Centre St. North, T3K 1J7 – 403/275-3230 – *2

R.S. Johnson, #228, 3715 - 51 St., T3E 6V2 – 403/249-4426

Kenneth C. Johnston, #600, 510 - 5 St., T2P 3S2 – 403/262-3122

Marcia L. Johnston, #480, 708 - 11 Ave. SW, T2R 0E3 – 403/261-7600

Ali S. Jomaa, #500, 333 - 11 Ave. SW, T2R 1L9 – 403/269-5177

Joshi & Company, #301, 1000 - 8 Ave. SW, T2P 3M7 – 403/262-8200 – *3

G.M. Jumaga, #201, 2411 - 4 St. NW, T2M 2Z8 – 403/284-4587 – *1

Kelly & Kelly, #1640, 700 - 4 Ave. SW, T2P 3J4 – 403/266-6296, Fax: 403/264-2954 – *4

Kennedy & Company, #400, 805 - 8 Ave. SW, T2P 1H7 – 403/234-7721 – *2

P. Donald Kennedy, Q.C., 59 Cherovan Dr. SW, T2V 2P3 – 403/255-6331, Fax: 403/264-2993

Kenney & Company, #550, 1121 Centre St. North, T2E 7K6 – 403/230-3751, Fax: 403/276-8139 – *3

Jack A. King, Q.C., 10 Forest Grove Pl. SE, T2A 7G6 – 403/235-4600 – *1

G.R. Klatt, #606, 734 - 7 Ave. SW, T2P 3P8 – 403/266-3693

Knibbe McClintock Piercey, #900, 441 - 5 Ave. SW, T2P 2V1 – 403/290-1282, Fax: 403/261-5772 – *3

S. Kushwaha, #203, 4908 - 17 Ave. SE, T2A 0V4 – 403/569-9129

Kutz Hotzel, #316, 1167 Kensington Cres. NW, T2N 1X7 – 403/270-4098, Fax: 403/270-0660 – *3

Guy L. Lacoiurciére, #200, 839 - 5 Ave. SW, T1P 2T5 – 403/262-2421, Fax: 403/262-2423 – *1

Clément E. Lagassé, #514, 206 - 7 Ave. SW, T2P 0W7 – 403/269-7188 – *1

Laird Armstrong, #770, 340 - 12 Ave. SW, T2R 1L5 – 403/233-0050, Fax: 403/266-1238 – *3

Lang Michener Lawrence & Shaw, #200, 630 - 4 Ave. SW, T2P 0J9 – 403/237-5858, Fax: 403/266-5272 – *5

Langlois Legal Centre, 3333 - 23 St. NE, T2E 6V8 – 403/531-9300 – *1

Linda S. Laratta, 3938 Edenstone Rd. NW, T3A 3Z6 – 403/239-7052, Fax: 403/241-2455

Leach & Davison, Texaco Building, #1010, 505 - 5 St. SW, T2P 3J2 – 403/262-7745 – *2

Lee & Company, #610, 140 - 4 Ave. SW, T2P 3N3 – 403/233-9432, Fax: 403/237-9614 – *2

K.W. Leech, #230, 3715 - 51 St., T3E 6V2 – 403/246-3411 – *1

Lefebvre Bergman, 3144 - 35 Ave SW, T3E 0Z7 – 403/249-4444 – *2

Lenhardt & Company, #1180, 840 - 7 Ave. SW, T2P 3G2 – 403/237-6970 – *1

Dennis A. Lerner, #204, 1632 - 14 Ave. NW, T2N 1M7 – 403/282-9156

L.G. Lien, #301, 1204 Kensington Rd. NW, T2N 3P5 – 403/270-7787

Lilburn Ellert, #400, 603 - 7 Ave. SW, T2P 2T5 – 403/269-3315, Fax: 403/269-3329 – *4

Lirenman Peterson, #300, 255 - 17 Ave. SW, T2S 2T8 – 403/245-0111, Fax: 403/245-0115 – *6

Litwiniuk & Company, #205, 4020 - 17 Ave. SE, T2A 0S7 – 403/273-8580, Fax: 403/273-9045 – *2

Sheryl Malca Livergant, #400, 7015 Macleod Tr. SE, T2H 2K6 – 403/259-2377 – *1

W.E. Logan, #301, 609 - 14 St. NW, T2N 2A1 – 403/283-0999

J.G. Lomow, #304, 1609 - 14 St. NW, T3E 1E3 – 403/245-5777 – *1

Lord Russell, #600, 706 - 7 Ave. SW, T2P 0Z1 – 403/262-7722, Fax: 403/262-5991 – *6

Low & Company, #210, 7260 - 12 St. SE, T2H 2S5 – 403/259-5255 – *5

Low, Dalton & Heming, #17, 6624 Centre St. South, T2H 0C6 – 403/253-1228 – *5

Low, Glenn & Card, 3475 - 26 Ave. NE, T1Y 6L4 – 403/291-2532, Fax: 403/291-2534; Email: lgc-law@supernet.ab.ca; URL: http://www.canfind.com/index.html – *4

James A. MacDonald, #710, 304 - 8 Ave. SW, T2P 1C2 – 403/221-9444

Ronald C. MacDonald, 54 Granlea Pl. SW, T3E 4K2 – 403/249-0658

Machida Mack Shewchuk, #304, 1204 Kensington Rd. NW, T2N 3P5 – 403/221-8333, Fax: 403/221-8339 – *3

MacKenzie Welbourn, Mount Royal Pl., #640, 1414 - 8 St. SW, T2R 1J6 – 403/229-9093, Fax: 403/229-1553 – *2

MacKimmie Matthews, Gulf Canada Sq., #700, 401 - 9 Ave. SW, PO Box 2010, T2P 2M2 – 403/232-0611, Fax: 403/232-0888 – *47

Macleod Dixon, Canterra Tower, #3700, 400 - 3 Ave. SW, T2P 4H2 – 403/267-8222, Fax: 403/264-5973; Email: md@lexcom.ab.ca – *96

S.C.R. Mah Toy, #1530, 255 - 5 Ave. SW, T2P 3G6

Brian E. Mahoney, 1740 - 10 St. SW, T2T 3E8 – 403/228-0040 – *1

Mahony & Dawson, #500, 1040 - 7 Ave. SW, T2P 3G9 – 403/263-0880 – *2

Major, Caron, #1600, 400 - 3 Ave. SW, T2P 4H2 – 403/262-3000, Fax: 403/237-0111; Email: major.caron@cadvision.com; URL: majorcaron.com – *8

Patricia H. Major, 2812 - 26 St. SW, T3E 2B2 – 403/249-3383 – *1

Marshall Bondar, Bankers Hall, #2100, 855 - 2 St., T2P 4J9 – 403/237-4860, Fax: 403/237-4809

Martin C. Matheron, #204, 5403 Crowchild Trail NW, T3B 4Z1 – 403/247-2359, Fax: 403/286-4517 – *1

Lionel S. Matthews, #500, 736 - 6 Ave. SW, T2P 3T7 – 403/262-7566

O.J. Mayrl, #500A, 805 - 8 Ave. SW, T2P 1H7 – 403/266-6831

N.E. McArdle, #600, 11012 Macleod Tr. South, T2J 6A5 – 403/278-8238

David G. McBean, 7815 - 5 St. SW, T2V 1C2 – 403/252-1221 – *1

Karen Leigh McBean, 44 Hawksbrow Rd. NW, T3G 2S7 – 403/239-9704 – *1

McCaffery Goss, #1800, 350 - 7 Ave. SW, T2P 3N9 – 403/263-7570 – *14

McCarthy Tétrault, #3200, 421 - 7 Ave. SW, T2P 4K9 – 403/260-3500, Fax: 403/260-3501; Email: calgary@mccarthy.ca; URL: http://www.mccarthy.ca/ – *37

McConnell MacInnes, #534, 11012 Macleod Tr. South, T2J 6A5 – 403/278-7001 – *4

McCormick Van Harten, #302, 805 - 8 Ave. SW, T2P 1H7 – 403/269-3655 – *3

McDonald & Hayden, #650, 603 - 7 Ave. SW, T2P 2T5 – 403/265-5862, Fax: 403/269-2004 – *1

M.J. McDonald, 1111 - 11 Ave. SW, PO Box 1680, Stn M, T2P 2L7 – 403/253-0000; 245-2024, Fax: 403/228-1749 – *1

McDonald, Plotkins, Anderson & Company, Western Union Bldg., 640 - 8 Ave. SW, 8th Fl., T2P 1G7 – 403/265-9100, Fax: 403/265-7438 – *2

McGown & Johnson, #245, 1209 - 59 Ave. SE, T2H 2P6 – 403/255-5114, Fax: 403/258-3840 – *3

Neil R. McKay, 5331 LaSalle Cres. NW, PO Box 1284, Stn M, T2P 2L2 – 403/240-1082

Kerry W. McLelland, Crowchild Square, #204, 5403 Crowchild Trail NW, T3B 4Z1 – 403/247-2359, Fax: 403/286-4517 – *1

McLeod & Company, #800, 11012 Macleod Tr. South, T2J 6A5 – 403/278-9411, Fax: 403/271-1769 – *17

McLeod Ferner & Bruni, 600 - 6 Ave. SW, T2P 0S5 – 403/266-5664, Fax: 403/262-6343 – *4

McManus Anderson Miles, Bow Valley Sq. IV, #2200, 250 - 6 Ave. SW, T2P 3H7 – 403/263-2190, Fax: 403/263-6840 – *22

McNiven Kelly, #1400, 530 - 8 Ave. SW, T2P 3S8 – 403/263-8230, Fax: 403/263-8950 – *15

Anne E. McTavish, 4620 Manilla Rd. SE, T2G 4B7 – 403/255-4400, Fax: 403/252-1581 – *1

Megaffin Higgerty Anderson, #360, 525 - 28 St. SE, T2A 6W9 – 403/273-8086, Fax: 403/569-0741 – *7

Merchant Law Group, #200, 1221A - 11th Ave. SW, T3C 0M5 – 403/250-9777

Mary J. Metz, #253, 1632 - 14 Ave. NW, T2N 1M7 – 403/289-3399 – *1

Meurin Johns Wilson & Smith, #605, 520 - 5 Ave. SW, T2P 3R7 – 403/269-8989, Fax: 403/237-0327 – *7

Meurin Johns Wilson & Smith, #605, 520 - 5 Ave. SW, T1P 3R7 – 403/269-8989, Fax: 403/237-0327 – *1

Meyers Clark, #3000, 205 - 5 Ave. SW, T2P 2N7 – 403/264-7288 – *2

Ronald A. Miles, #214, 5720 Macleod Tr. South, T2H 0J6 – 403/255-6033, Fax: 403/252-7304 – *1

Millar & Associates, 1124 Kensington Rd. NW, T2N 3P3 – 403/283-1925, Fax: 403/270-8033 – *2

Millard, Johnson & Maxwell, 812A - 16 Ave. SW, T2R 0S9 – 403/228-4317, Fax: 403/228-3391 – *2

Milne & Company, #708, 5920 Macleod Tr. South, T2H 0K2 – 403/252-3357 – *1

Milne & Papp, #550, 10281 Southport Rd. SW, T2W 4X9 – 403/258-1930, Fax: 403/255-5794 – *2

Milne, Davis, #850, 933 - 17 Ave. SW, T2T 5R6 – 403/229-3000, Fax: 403/229-3282 – *2

Milner Fenerty, Fifth Ave. Place, 30th Floor, 237 - 4th Ave. SW, T2P 4X7 – 403/268-7000, Fax: 403/268-3100; Email: milfen@milfen.com; URL: http://www.milfen.com – *100

Mootoo & Lambert, #219, 222 - 16 Ave. NE, T2E 1J8 – 403/230-2800 – *1

Moreau, Ogle & Hursh, #402, 1015 - 4 St. SW, T2R 1J4 – 403/269-5352, Fax: 403/266-5823 – *3

Scott D. Morgan, #205, 4500 - 16 Ave. NW, T3B 0M6 – 403/286-5056

Jonathan H.B. Moss, #240, 999 - 8 St. SW, T2R 1J5 – 403/229-0514

Robert C. Muir, 622 - 5 Ave. SW, 2nd Fl., T2P 0M6 – 403/262-8410

G. Mungan, 1039 Durham Ave. SW, T2T 0P8 – 403/229-4002, Fax: 403/299-7728

J.B. Munholland, #280, 251 Midpark Blvd. SE, T2X 1S3 – 403/254-9266 – *1

K.P. Murphy, #130, 2116 - 27 Ave. NE, T2E 7A6 – 403/250-1110 – *1

Kevin F. Murphy, #204, 1632 - 14 Ave. NW, T2N 1M7 – 403/282-9156

V.M. Naimish, #1200, 640 - 8 Ave. SW, T2P 1G7 – 403/262-7088 – *1

B.F. Nattrass, 925 Riverdale Ave. SW, T2S 0X7 – 403/234-6529, Fax: 403/272-6278 – *1

Jean-Anne Naysmith, 3409 - 6 St. SW, T2S 2M5 – 403/243-4996

Nelson & Nelson, #311, 1716 - 16 Ave. NW, T2M 0L7 – 403/289-9216 – *2

A.J. Nesbitt, Site 24, RR#12, PO Box 24, T3E 6W3 – 403/246-5778 – *1

Stephen G. Ney, #505, 1110 Centre St. North, T2E 2R2 – 403/230-3931, Fax: 403/276-9770 – *1

E.M. Nicholson, #1701, 520 - 5 Ave. SW, T2P 3R7 – 403/237-6336, Fax: 403/237-6338 – *1

D.M. Nielsen, 207 - 14 St. NW, T2N 1Z6 – 403/283-1244 – *1

Nikitiuk Blain Roszler, #712, 2710 - 17 Ave. SE, T2A 0P6 – 403/235-3838

O'Brien Devlin Markey Macleod, #3110, 421 - 7th Ave. SW, T2P 4K9 – 403/265-5616, Fax: 403/264-8146 – *6

Karen M. O'Brien, 1947 - 12 St. SW, T2T 3N3 – 403/245-4745

O'Neil Dunn, 306 - 10 St. NW, T2N 1V8 – 403/270-0800 – *2

Ogilvie & Company, Canada Pl., #1600, 407 - 2 St. SW, T2P 2Y3 – 403/237-9050, Fax: 403/262-7896 – *17

Brett E. Olsen, #205, 5940 Macleod Tr. SE, T2G 2R7 – 403/252-8111, Fax: 403/252-8455

Oughton & Company, #101, 635 - 6 Ave. SW, T2P 0T5 – 403/262-0504 – *1

Owens & Sattin, #2000, 801 - 6 Ave. SW, T2P 3W2 – 403/269-5131, Fax: 403/264-0194 – *2

Park Sullivan, #1330, 734 - 7 Ave. SW, T2P 3P8 – 403/262-6292 – *2

Judith E.R. Park, #101, 1122 - 4 St. SW, T2R 1M1 – 403/262-5636

Parken & Company, #1200, 407 - 2 St. SW, T2P 2Y3 – , Fax: 403/237-5816 – *2

Parlee McLaws, Western Canadian Pl., #3400, 707 - 8th Ave. SW, T2P 1H5 – 403/294-7000, Fax: 403/265-8263 – *32

Brian A. Paterson, 1111 - 8 St. SW, T2R 1L4 – 403/229-2938

M.H. Patterson, #222, 20 Coachway Rd. SW, T3H 1E6 – 403/240-2573

Kathy I. Pawluk, 115 Forest Cres. SE, T2A 5B1 – 403/272-5642 – *1

Pearce & Smyth, 1850 - 14 St. SW, T2T 3S9 – 403/245-8835 – *3

M.E. Peters, #700, 933 - 17 Ave. SW, T2T 5R6 – 403/245-3176

Peterson, Shields, Galbraith & Hutchinson, #204, 755 Lake Bonavista Dr. South, T2J 0N3 – 403/271-9710, Fax: 403/271-3942 – *4

M.A. Pettem, 306 - 10 St. NW, T2N 1V8 – 403/230-3777

Pickton & Company, #830, 615 Macleod Tr. SE, T2G 4T8 – 403/234-9477 – *3

Jeffrey B. Pike, 3907 - 45 St. SW, T3E 6P2 – 403/240-2435

Pipella, Warren, #600, 404 - 6 Ave. SW, T2P 0R9 – 403/265-8733, Fax: 403/263-3153 – *7

Pittman MacIsaac & Roy, Western Canadian Pl., Bldg Box: 2200, 700 - 9 Ave. SW, T2P 3V4 – 403/263-1970, Fax: 403/263-8145 – *3

Leonard S. Polsky, #850, 639 - 5 Ave. SW, T2P 0M9 – 403/266-4500, Fax: 403/265-3824 – *3

Pomerance & Company, #700, 10655 Southport Rd. SW, T2W 4Y1 – 403/278-5840, Fax: 403/271-6929 – *4

Poole Laycraft & McMahon, #212, 908 - 17 Ave., T2T 0A3 – 403/244-4454 – *3

Lawrence S. Portigal, 6638 Bow Cres. NW, T3B 2B9 – 403/286-6380, Fax: 403/286-1888 – *1

Graham Price, #210, 1010 - 8 Ave. SW, T2P 1J2 – 403/262-8616 – *1

Prodanchuk Dickson, #250, 999 - 8 St. SW, T2R 1J5 – 403/245-4616, Fax: 403/245-4621 – *3

Pulak & Fulton, #1100, 840 - 7 Ave. SW, T2P 3G2 – 403/265-0575, Fax: 403/265-0575 – *3

Purdy & Purdy, 1603 - 10 Ave. SW, T3C 0J7 – 403/244-1811, Fax: 403/228-0918 – *2

D. Allan Radke, #201, 8820A Macleod Trail SE, T2H 0M4 – 403/252-4466 – *1

Ranson Law Office, #1700, 633 - 6 Ave. SW, T2P 2Y5 – 403/269-5400, Fax: 403/262-8118

R. Brickard Ratcliffe, #220, 3016 - 19 St. NE, T2E 6Y9 – 403/250-5444, Fax: 403/291-0410 – *1

Raymaker, Forrest, #825, 521 - 3 Ave. SW, T2P 3T3 – 403/262-7200, Fax: 403/233-9250 – *2

Reesor Martin, #1200, 700 - 9 Ave. SW, T2P 3V4 – 403/237-5400 – *2

Reich Law Office, #212, 4935 - 40 Ave., T3A 2N1 – 403/288-6500 – *1

G.B.E. Reiman, 1700 Varsity Estates Dr. NW, T3B 2W9 – 403/286-7711 – *1

Reynolds, Mirth, Richards & Farmer, Sunlife Plaza, North Tower, #1790, 140 - 4 Ave. SW, T2P 3N3 – 403/234-9192, Fax: 403/234-9194

Katherine Richmond, #690, 1414 - 8 St. SW, T2R 1J6 – 403/228-0503

Robert A. Rivard, #605, 5940 Macleod Tr. South, T2H 2G4 – 403/255-0799 – *2

Robb & Evenson, #550, 333 - 11 Ave. SW, T2R 1L9 – 403/265-6862 – *2

Robertson & Associates, #812, 700 - 4 Ave. SW, T2P 3J4 – 403/237-5488 – *1

T.W. Robinson, #930, 300 - 5 Ave. SW, T2P 3C4 – 403/261-7600, Fax: 403/269-5866; Email: 104400.2363@compuserve.com

Rogers & Company, #400, 1010 - 8 Ave. SW, T2P 1J2 – 403/263-6805, Fax: 403/263-6800 – *6

K.J. Rogers, #1, 4404 - 14 St. NW, T2K 1J5 – 403/284-3371 – *1

W.W. Rollins, #201, 333 - 17 Ave. SW, T2S 0A7 – 403/228-2590 – *1

Ross Hepner Baker & Ross, Monenco Pl., #1850, 801 - 6 Ave. SW, T2P 3W2 – 403/269-2600, Fax: 403/265-2455 – *4

Ross, Lerner & Murphy, #204, 1632 - 14 Ave. NW, T2N 1M7 – 403/282-9156 – *3

A. Charles Ruff, #202, 1409 Edmonton Tr. NE, T2E 3K8 – 403/276-2880, Fax: 403/230-3835 – *1

J.P. St. Pierre, 1221A - 11 Ave. SW, T3C 0M5 – 403/229-1129

Salmon & Company, #1180, 840 - 7 Ave. SW, T2P 3G2 – 403/266-6066 – *1

K.A. Sarjeant, 48 Woodhaven Rd. SW, T2W 5P9 – 403/238-1290

Schultz & Company, Glenmore Landing, #A211, 1600 - 90 Ave. SW, T2V 5A8 – 403/252-3200 – *1

T. Schwartzberg, #235, 1935 - 32 Ave. NE, T2E 7C8 – 403/291-3391, Fax: 403/291-9831 – *1

Scott & Company, #635, 10201 Southport Rd. SW, T2W 4X9 – 403/253-5656 – *3

Scott, Vinci, Phillips, #403, 628 - 12 Ave. SW, T2P 3W2 – 403/265-4323 – *3

Sefcik Hudson, #206, 5940 Macleod Tr. South, T2H 2G4 – 403/258-1124 – *2

Semenuk McCrimmon Hill McKay, McFarlane Twr., #600, 700 - 4 Ave. SW, T2P 3J4 – 403/269-8282, Fax: 403/269-8295 – *3

W.J. Shachnowich, 1700 Varsity Estates Dr., NW, T3B 2W9 – 403/269-1313, Fax: 403/247-3127 – *1

Carole A. Shaw, #302, 1550 - 8 St. SW, T2R 1K1 – 403/245-8200 – *1

John R. Shaw, #610, 615 Macleod Tr. SE, T2G 4T8 – 403/294-1414

Shellnutt McKenna Bryant, #405, 603 - 7 Ave. SW, T2P 2T5 – 403/234-8811, Fax: 403/234-7911 – *3

W.J.E. Shepherdson, #900, 840 - 7 Ave. SW, T2P 3G2 – 403/262-6185

S.M. Shuler, 3040 Glencoe Rd. SW, T2S 2L8 – 403/287-2087

Shymka & Company, #401, 239 - 8 Ave. SW, T2P 1B9 – 403/263-0000 – *2

Silver Gelmon, First Alberta Pl., #1500, 777 - 8 Ave. SW, T2P 3R5 – 403/234-8874, Fax: 403/266-5813 – *2

D.J. Simpson, 348 - 14 St. NW, T2N 1Z7 – 403/283-8018

Singleton Urquhart Scott, Calgary Pl., Bldg Box: 3, #1900, 355 - 4 Ave. SW, T2P 0J1 – 403/261-9043 – *11

L.F. Sjoman, 2239 - 2 Ave. NW, T2N 0H1 – 403/283-5799

Smith & Smith, #206, 7 Glenbrook Place SW, T3E 6W4 – 403/242-9711 – *2

Smith Lamarsh, Mount Royal Pl., #550, 1414 - 8 St. SW, T2R 1B8 – 403/228-3476, Fax: 403/244-2479 – *3

Smith Law Office, 348 - 14 St. NW, T2N 1Z7 – 403/283-8018, Fax: 403/270-3065 – *1

Smith, Creet, #1600, 520 - 5 Ave. SW, T2P 3R7 – 403/234-9400, Fax: 403/266-1996 – *3

Smith, Smith, Premji & Adler, #503, 1300 - 8 St. SW, T2R 1B2 – 403/229-1727 – *3

W. Murray Smith, #333, 1015 Centre St. North, T2E 2P8 – 403/277-1688, Fax: 403/277-1699

W.S. Soboren, 2444 Palisade Dr. SW, T2V 3V3 – 403/281-3741 – *1

Soby, Boyden, Lenz, #440, 1010 - 8 Ave. SW, T2P 1J2 – 403/237-0553 – *3

Soltysiak & Sparks, #205, 2411 - 4 St. NW, T2M 2Z8 – 403/282-9215, Fax: 403/289-3729 – *2

Hugh D. Sommerville, Rocky Mountain Plaza, #830, 615 Macleod Tr. SE, T2G 4T8 – 403/234-9477

Spackman & Matt, #475, 1550 - 5 St. SW, T2R 1K3 – 403/229-2429, Fax: 403/228-6415 – *2

Craig A. Sparrow, #10, 628 - 12 Ave. SW, T2R 0H6 – 403/234-0722

Spier Harben, #1000, 665 - 8th St. SW, T2P 3K7 – 403/263-5130, Fax: 403/264-9600 – *8

Patricia E. Stark, #600, 706 - 7 Ave. SW, T2P 0Z1 – 403/262-7722, Fax: 403/262-5991 – *1

Kenneth E. Staroszik, #400, 1010 - 8 Ave. SW, T1P 1J2 – *1

Starr Cairns, #205, 212 - 7 Ave. SW, T2P 0W6 – 403/237-7550 – *2

Donald V. Steele, 2020 - 10 St. NW, T2M 3M2 – 403/284-2940

Stemp & Company, #505, 100 - 4 Ave. SW, T2P 3N2 – 403/237-9135 – *1

Stengl Everard, #406, 1212 - 31 Ave. NE, T2E 7S8 – 403/250-7105, Fax: 403/291-5473 – *3

Stephens & Holman, #200, 1040 - 3 Ave. SW, T2P 3G9 – 403/265-6400 – *1

Stewart & McCullough, 1138 Kensington Rd. NW, T2N 3P3 – 403/270-2641 – *5

Stewart & Stewart, #700, 603 - 7 Ave. SW, T2P 2T5 – 403/265-5440, Fax: 403/262-1367 – *3

Stikeman, Elliott, Bankers Hall, #1500, 855 - 2nd St. SW, T2P 4J7 – 403/266-9000, Fax: 403/266-9034 – *11

R.M. Stirling, 1221A - 11 Ave. SW, T3C 0M5 – 403/229-1129, Fax: 403/245-9660 – *1

Tracey D. Stock, #602, 523 - 15 Ave. SW, T2R 0R3 – 403/245-3386

J.N.M. Strilchuk, One Palliser Sq., #255, 125 - 9 Ave. SE, T2G 0P6 – 403/269-1981 – *1

Haruji Suga, 414 - 8 St. SW, T2P 1Z9 – 403/264-3004

Sugimoto & Company, #204, 2635 - 37 Ave. NE, T1Y 5Z6 – 403/291-4650, Fax: 403/291-4099 – *8

T.G.D. Sullivan, #605, 5940 Macleod Tr. South, T2H 2G4 – 403/255-0799, Fax: 403/253-3274 – *1

John A. Sutherland, 2619 - 14 St. SW, PO Box 32053, T2T 5X6 – 403/270-0727, Fax: 403/270-0325 – *1

Arthur A.M. Szabo, 1221A - 11 Ave. SW, T3C 0M5 – 403/229-1129, Fax: 403/245-9660

L.J. Szmolyan, #601, 2303 - 4 St. SW, T2S 2S7 – 403/263-5591; 228-4679 – *1

Michael J. Tadman, #10, 628 - 12 Ave. SW, T2R 0H6 – 403/234-9722, Fax: 403/237-8748 – *1

George A. Tapp, 2026 - 33 Ave. SW, T2T 1Z5 – 403/249-5505

Taylor & Company, #200, 9919 Fairmount Dr. SE, T2J 0S3 – 403/271-6223 – *2

C.L. Taylor, Site 11, SS#3, PO Box 16, T3C 3N9 – 403/249-7798

T.N. Taylor, #610, 615 Macleod Tr. SE, T2G 4T8 – 403/269-7561, Fax: 403/232-6535

Donald E. Teed, #338, 8500 Macleod Tr. SE, T2H 2N1 – 403/259-8485 – *1

Tharp Sinclair Watson Quigley Taylor, #800, 933 - 17 Ave. SW, T2T 5R6 – 403/245-3666, Fax: 403/245-3777 – *5

Joan C. Thomas, #205, 259 Midpark Way SE, T2X 1M2 – 403/256-2249

* indicates number of lawyers in law firm.

Thompson, Ball & Anderson, #200, 5824 - 2 St. SW, T2H 0H2 – 403/259-4434, Fax: 403/259-4660 – *3

Thornborough, Smeltz & Company, #630, 11012 Macleod Trail South, T2P 6A5 – 403/271-6684, Fax: 403/271-3221 – *5

Wayne M. Tinker, #760, 999 - 8 St. SW, T2R 1J5

K.R. Tobler, 68 Signal Hill Circle SW, T3H 2G6 – 403/249-4195

Bruno J. Todesco, #1111, 10 Coachway Rd. NW, T3H 1E5 – 403/242-7757

Townsend & Christensen, #508, 5920 - 1A St. SW, T2H 0G3 – 403/258-2700 – *1

Richard T. Tumanon, Petro Chemical Bldg., #500A, 805 - 8 Ave. SW, T2P 1H7 – 403/262-3841

Turnbull Barristers & Solicitors, #1410, 1122 - 4 St. SW, T2R 1M1 – 403/237-0669

D.M. Underdahl, 12 Lenton Pl. SW, T3E 5C8 – 403/287-2292 – *1

Uniacke & Yanko, #610, 2710 - 17 Ave. SE, T2A 0P6 – 403/272-8787 – *4

Vallance & Company, #1400, 550 - 6 Ave. SW, T2P 0S2 – 403/264-3244, Fax: 403/232-6750 – *2

Joseph P.P. Vautour, 594 Strathcona Dr. SW, T3H 1K4 – 403/249-1129

Viccars & Associates, #1000, 1122 - 4 St. SW, T2R 1M1 – 403/265-9697 – *3

Harold R. Vickers, Bankers Hall, Bldg Box: 2025, 855 - 2 St. SW, T2O 4J8 – 403/269-9400 – *1

E. Vomberg, PO Box 8053, Stn F, T2J 5R8 – 403/278-3505, Fax: 403/271-4936 – *1

Lawrence A. Wagar, #1001, 505 - 3 Ave. SW, T2P 3E6 – 403/266-5414, Fax: 403/266-5439

Wakerich & Company, #504, 4600 Crowchild Trail NW, T3A 2L6 – 403/247-2111 – *2

Walsh Wilkins, #2800, 801 - 6 Ave. SW, T2P 4A3 – 403/267-8400, Fax: 403/264-9400; Toll Free: 1-800-304-3574 – *18

Samuel D.C. Wan Professional Corporation, #600, 805 - 5 Ave. SW, T2P 1H7 – 403/269-7630

P.M. Ward, #202, 229 - 11 Ave. SE, T2G 0Y1 – 403/263-1158 – *1

Warren Tettensor, 1413 - 2 St. SW, T2R 0W7 – 403/228-7007, Fax: 403/244-1948 – *8

Charles G. Watkins, 914 Royal Ave. SW, T2T 0L5 – 403/244-5142

S.R. Watkins, 3631 - 12 St. SW, T2T 3P1 – 403/287-2051 – *1

K. Grant Watson, #304, 707 - 10 Ave. SW, T2R 0B3 – 403/269-5377 – *1

Watts Gottlieb, #8, 5602 - 4 St. NW, T2K 1B2 – 403/275-4881 – *1

John S. Webb, #312, 902 - 11 Ave. SW, T2R 0E7 – 403/228-3332

William G. Webb, Rocky Mountain Plaza, #610, 615 Macleod Tr. South, T2G 4T8 – 403/294-1414, Fax: 403/263-4784

Brett O. Webber, 2832 - 12 Ave. NW, T2N 1K8 – 403/284-4624

Wedekind Demiantschuck Larsen & Singer, #1400, 700 - 4 Ave. SW, T2P 3J4 – 403/262-8888, Fax: 403/262-3292 – *4

White & Company, #204, 3716 - 61 Ave. SE, T2C 1Z4 – 403/236-2110 – *2

Harold W. White, #812, 603 - 7 Ave. SW, T2P 2T5 – 403/265-5400 – *1

Whitt & Company, #1500, 112 - 4 Ave. SW, T2P 0H3 – 403/265-3232 – *4

Widdowson MacPhail Webber Harding, #300, 1121 Centre St. North, T2E 7K6 – 403/230-4617, Fax: 403/277-8930 – *5

Witwicki Perovich, #200, 1134 - 8 Ave. SW, T2P 1J5 – 403/265-3833 – *2

Stephen R. Wojcik, #302, 805 - 8 Ave. SW, T2P 1H7 – 403/269-3655

Wolfman & Company, #300, 116 - 8 Ave. SW, 3rd Fl., T2P 1B3 – 403/263-6710, Fax: 403/266-1896 – *2

Wolfman Ryder, #212A, 805 - 1 St. SW, T2P 7N2 – 403/266-4433 – *2

Judy K. Wong, #825, 101 - 6 Ave. SW, T2P 3P4 – 403/262-8308

Madeline J. Wood, #301, 540 - 12 Ave. SW, T2R 0H4 – 403/266-6766, Fax: 403/233-8429

Woolliams, Korman, Moore, Wittman, #2700, 801 - 6 Ave. SW, T2P 3W2 – 403/269-2111, Fax: 403/263-5600 – *6

Derek R. Worden, #1008, 505 - 5 St. SW, T2P 3J2 – 403/269-9344

Paul G. Wozniak, #300, 840 - 6 Ave. SW, T2P 3E5 – 403/266-2123

William Wuttunee, 4924 Valiant Dr. NW, T3A 0Y4 – 403/286-0857

Zenith Hookenson Vogel, #1050, 10201 Southport Rd. SW, T2W 4X9 – 403/255-2636, Fax: 403/253-8036 – *5

Zinner & Company, #1530, 255 - 5 Ave. SW, T2P 3G6 – 403/269-2425 – *3

CAMROSE .... Wetaskiwin

Andreassen Olson, #200, 4870 - 51 St., T4V 1S1 – 403/672-3181, Fax: 403/672-0682 – *6

Wilf K. Backhaus, #102, 4909A - 48 St., T4V 1L7 – 403/672-1121, Fax: 403/679-2242 – *1

Farnham Schaffter & Ziebart, 5016 - 52 St., T4V 1V7 – 403/679-0444, Fax: 403/679-0958 – *3

Fielding, Syed & Smith, #201, 5015 - 50 Ave., T4V 3P7 – 403/672-8851, Fax: 403/672-4707 – *4

Knaut Johnson Sawle, 4925 - 51 St., PO Box 1630, T4V 1X6 – 403/672-5561, Fax: 403/672-5565 – *3

CANMORE .... Calgary

Carmen H. Colborne, PO Box 2922, T0L 0M0 – 403/678-2927

Robert Elliott, PO Box 2310, T0L 0M0 – 403/678-6078, Fax: 403/678-5173 – *1

Rencz & McAvity, #208, 705 - 8 St., PO Box 1860, T0L 0M0 – 403/678-5823, Fax: 403/678-4890 – *2

Soper & Parker, #202, 820 - 8 St., PO Box 2879, T0L 0M0 – *2

CARDSTON .... Lethbridge

T.M. Matkin, 87 - 2 Ave. West, PO Box 1209, T0K 0K0 – 403/653-3391, Fax: 403/653-2786 – *1

Stringam Denecky, PO Box 182, T0K 0K0 – 403/653-3282, Fax: 403/327-1141

CARSTAIRS .... Calgary

Stephen Stiles, 315 - 10 Ave. South, PO Box 790, T0M 0N0 – 403/337-3358 – *2

James B. Wilde, 417 - 10th Ave., T0M 0N0 – 403/337-3105

CHESTERMERE .... Calgary

Karl H.H. Trobst, 368 West Chestermere Dr., T1X 1B3 – 403/272-1056, Fax: 403/569-2968 – *1

CLARESHOLM ....

North & Company, 208 - 50 Ave. West, T0L 0T0 – 403/625-4404, Fax: 403/625-4186

Townsend & Malcolm, PO Box 2226, T0L 0T0 – 403/625-3777

Welbourn, Maloney, 208 - 50 Ave. West, PO Box 1300, T0L 0T0 – 403/625-4404; 553-3833, Fax: 403/625-4186 – *2

COALDALE .... Lethbridge

Leonard D. Fast, 1709 - 20 Ave., PO Box 1360, T1M 1N2 – 403/345-4415, Fax: 403/345-2719

Vincent A. Lammi, 1910 - 18 St., PO Box 1329, T0K 0L0 – 403/345-3922 – *1

COCHRANE .... Calgary

M.J. Rothecker, 123 - 4 Ave. West, PO Box 279, T0L 0W0 – 403/932-3843, Fax: 403/932-3108

CORONATION .... Red Deer

E. Roger Spady, Coronation Mall, PO Box 328, T0C 1C0 – 403/578-3131 – *1

DEVON .... Wetaskiwin

Jackie & Handerek, 14B Athabasca Ave., T0C 1E0 – 403/987-4219

DIDSBURY .... Calgary

J.S. Fisher, PO Box 1027, T0M 0W0 – 403/335-3347 – *2

Brian M.M. Forestell, Victoria Sq. Mall, #207, PO Box 625, T0M 0W0 – 403/335-8491; 262-7335, Fax: 403/335-8581

DRAYTON VALLEY .... Yellowhead

Barr, Wensel, Nesbitt, Reeson, 5203 Industrial Rd., T0E 0M0 – 403/542-4567

Prentice, Chow, 5202 - 52 Ave., PO Box 6777, T7A 1S2 – 403/542-4447, Fax: 403/542-3392; Email: michow@ccinet.ab.ca – *2

DRUMHELLER .... Drumheller

Ross, Todd & Company, 98 - 3 Ave. West, PO Box 970, T0J 0Y0 – 403/823-5186, Fax: 403/823-6407 – *5

Schumacher, Gough & Pedersen, 180 Riverside Dr. East, PO Box 2800, T0J 0Y0 – 403/823-2424, Fax: 403/823-6984 – *3

J.L. Sparling, 150 - 3 Ave. West, Lower Level, PO Box 2859, T0J 1Y0 – 403/823-5500, Fax: 403/823-6472

ECKVILLE .... Red Deer

R.S. Paston, PO Box 517, T0M 0X0 – 403/746-2160 – *1

EDMONTON .... Edmonton

Abbey Davies Greaves Hunter, MacDonald Place, #200, 9939 Jasper Ave., T5J 2W8 – 403/421-8585, Fax: 403/425-0472 – *5

David R. Abbey, #412, 9707 - 110 St., T5K 2L9 – 403/488-8945, Fax: 403/488-5017; Email: drabbey@oanet.com – *1

Raj Kumar Abbi, #230, 4144A - 97 St. NW, T6E 5Y6 – 403/450-6141

Ackroyd, Piasta, Roth & Day, 10665 Jasper Ave., 15th Fl., T5J 3S9 – 403/423-8905, Fax: 403/423-8946 – *17

G.W. Acorn, Q.C., #313, 11523 - 100 Ave., T5K 0J8 – 403/482-2379 – *1

Agard & Company, Royal Trust Tower, #750, Edmonton Centre, T5J 2Z2 – 403/423-3518, Fax: 403/426-6444 – *3

Jack N. Agrios, Q.C., Scotia Place, #1900, 10060 Jasper Ave., T5J 3V4 – 403/424-2861 – *1

Neena Ahluwalia, #777, 10024 Jasper Ave., T5J 1R9 – 403/422-6162

Charles R. Allard, 13723 Summit Point, T5N 3S6 – 403/438-2626

Wes D. Alton, 5818 - 181 St., T6M 1V7 – 403/444-5910 – *1

Amerongen Spencer, #2170, 10123 - 99 St., T5J 3H1 – 403/423-2481

Anderson Carter & Callaghan, #460, 4445 Calgary Trail Southbound NW, T6H 5R7 – 403/438-1787, Fax: 403/437-3089 – *3

Anderson, Dawson, Knisely & Stevens, #300, 9924 - 100 St., T5K 1C4 – 403/424-9058, Fax: 403/425-0172; Toll Free: 1-800-661-3176 – *5

Andrew, Donahoe & Oake, #314, 10310 - 102 Ave., T5J 2X6 – 403/429-3391, Fax: 403/424-8483 – *9

Ares Kvill Rattan, LeMarchand Tower, 11507 - 100 Ave., T5K 2R2 – 403/488-1951, Fax: 403/482-6048 – *3

Askin Sciur, #700, 10020 - 101A Ave., T5J 3G2 – 403/429-7070 – *2

D.C. Averback, #3, 11536 Jasper Ave., T5K 0M8 – 403/482-2638 – *1

Baker & Purdon, 10263 - 178 St., T5S 1M3 – 403/489-5566 – *3

Laurine E. Balson, Children's Advocate, #201, 10109 - 106 St., T5J 3L7 – 403/422-6056

Donald S. Barber, PO Box 26, T5J 2G9 – 403/453-2386
Barr, Wensel, Nesbitt, Reeson, #1200, 10303 Jasper Ave., T5J 3N6 – 403/421-9900, Fax: 403/421-4151 – *21
Barry M.W. Basaraba, 9706 - 153 Ave., T5X 5V2 – 403/473-8910
Bassie & Zilinski, Wentworth Bldg., #200, 10209 - 97 St., T5J 0L6 – 403/423-2161, Fax: 403/426-1720 – *4
Dennis E. Bayrak, #800, 10310 Jasper Ave., T5J 2W4 – 403/426-4884
Therese M.A. Beaudoin, 10263 - 178 St., T5S 1M3 – 403/489-5566, Fax: 403/486-7735 – *1
Becker & McKay, #520, 4445 Calgary Trail Southbound NW, T6H 5R7 – 403/435-4726 – *3
David A. Beckwith, #360, 10123 - 99 St., T5J 3H1 – 403/426-6820 – *1
Beller Carreau & Associates Inc., 4634 - 90 Ave., T6B 2P9
Bennett Jones Verchere, Canadian Utilities Centre, #1000, 10035 - 105 St. NW, T5J 3T2 – 403/421-8133, Fax: 403/421-7951 – *10
Beresh DePoe Cunningham, MacLean Block, Bldg Box: 300, #300, 10110 - 107 St., T5J 1J4 – 403/421-4766, Fax: 403/429-0346 – *8
Barry R. Berman, #202, 9644 - 54 Ave. NW, T6E 5V1 – 403/438-4972, Fax: 403/436-7771
Helmut Berndt, 8617 - 104 St., T6E 4G6 – 403/439-6643 – *1
Marc Berzins, 10426 - 81 Ave., T6E 1X5 – 403/433-4717, Fax: 403/433-6718 – *1
Biamonte Cairo & Shortreed, Midland Walwyn Tower, #1600, 10205 - 101 St., T5J 2Z2 – 403/425-5800, Fax: 403/426-1600 – *13
Bishop & McKenzie, #2500, 10104 - 103 Ave., T5J 1V3 – 403/426-5550, Fax: 403/426-1305; Email: bishmc@mail.planet.eon.net – *26
Eleanor K. Boddy, Royal LePage Building, #1120, 10130 - 103 St., T5E 0C1 – 403/429-4520, Fax: 403/429-4591
Patricia A. Bokenfohr, #206, 17872 - 106 Ave., T5S 1V4 – 403/484-0665
Margaret E. Bonar, #2300, 10123 - 99 St., T5J 3H1 – 403/488-0899
Bosecke & Knol, #1, 9301 - 50 St., T6B 2L5 – 403/469-0494 – *2
Peter C. Bowal, #1980, 10123 - 99 St., T5J 3H1 – 403/425-6741
Angus M. Boyd, #405, 10408 - 124 St., T5N 1R5 – 403/488-7477, Fax: 403/488-0965
E.L. Boyd, #205, 11523 - 100 Ave., T5K 0J8 – 403/488-0971 – *1
Braithwaite Boyle, 11816 - 124 St., T5L 0M3 – 403/451-9191, Fax: 403/451-9198; Toll Free: 1-800-661-4902; Email: bba@ccinet.ab.ca; URL: http://www.edmonton.com/web/injurylaw/ – *12
Braul Gaffney, Sun Life Place, #2170, 10123 - 99 St., T5J 3H1 – 403/423-2481, Fax: 403/423-2474 – *8
M.S. Brett, #2501, 10004 - 104 Ave., T5J 0K1 – 403/429-2737 – *1
Brimacombe, Sanderman, Stroppel & Finlayson, Canada Trust Tower, #747, 10104 - 103 Ave., T5J 0H8 – 403/424-5156, Fax: 403/425-5883 – *5
Broda & Company, #103, 15333 Castle Downs Rd., T5X 3Y7 – 403/456-9330, Fax: 403/456-9339 – *2
Brooks Woollard, #208, 12406 - 112 Ave., T5M 2S9 – 403/454-3100
Brosseau & Associates, Century Pl., #1900, 9803 - 102A Ave., T5J 3A3 – 403/426-4000 – *3
Brownlee Fryett, Commerce Place, #2200, 10155 - 102 St., T5J 4G8 – 403/497-4800 – *30
Brumlik Lees, Oxford Tower, Edmonton Centre, #2100, 10235 - 101 St., T5J 3G1 – 403/423-4445, Fax: 403/424-6688 – *3
Bryan & Co., Bldg Box: 2600, 10180 - 101 St., T5J 3Y2 – 403/423-5730, Fax: 403/428-6324 – *34
Bubel, Boll & Sorenson, Royal Bank Bldg., #610, 10117 Jasper Ave., T5J 3G2 – 403/421-4040, Fax: 403/421-4146 – *3

Ronald J.L. Butler, #2698, 10060 Jasper Ave., T5J 3R8 – 403/429-3105
J.T. Byrne, 8003 - 101 St., T6E 5E2 – 403/425-4187 – *1
Scott W. Caine, #2, 6328A - 104 St., T6H 2K9 – 403/438-4111
Myron W. Calof, #900, 9707 - 110 St., T5K 2L9 – 403/488-8191 – *1
Campbell & Company, 318 Saddleback Rd., T6J 4R7 – 403/434-6565 – *3
Campbell Thurston Van Doesburg, Westgrove Professional Bldg., #300, 10230 - 142 St., T5N 3Y6 – 403/451-2661 – *3
A.F. Campbell, #777, 10024 Jasper Ave., T5J 1R9 – 403/428-8882 – *1
J.K.J. Campbell, #208, 4245 - 97 St. NW, T6E 5Y7 – 403/434-8777, Fax: 403/436-6357
Joseph A. Caruk, #1209, 10104 - 103 Ave., T5J 0H8 – 403/424-7145, Fax: 403/426-2980
Jack L. Chapman, #4833, 9027 Saskatchewan Dr., T5J 3V4 – 403/439-2639
K.J. Chapman Professional Corporation, Esso Tower, Scotia Pl., #901, 10060 Jasper Ave., T5J 3R8 – 403/420-0501, Fax: 403/420-1256 – *1
Chatwin Belzil, Scotia Pl., #800, 10060 Jasper Ave., T5J 3R8 – 403/421-7667, Fax: 403/424-7231 – *5
Chivers Greckol, #301, 10328 - 81 Ave., T6E 1X2 – 403/439-3611 – *3
Chomicki Baril, Esso Tower, #2101, 10060 Jasper Ave., T5J 4K1 – 403/423-3441, Fax: 403/420-1763 – *15
Chopra & Chopra, Sun Life Pl., #565, 10123 - 99 St., T5J 3H1 – 403/429-4961 – *2
R.P. Christensen, 11450 - 124 St., T5M 0K3 – 403/454-0387, Fax: 403/454-0389 – *2
Michael H. Clancy, 9844 - 106 St., T5K 1B8 – 403/424-9014, Fax: 403/424-9023 – *1
Cleall Pahl, Commerce Place, #2500, 10155 - 102 St., T5J 4G8 – 403/425-2500, Fax: 403/425-1222 – *10
Coley, Ewasiuk & Young, #100, 4936 - 87 St. NW, T6E 5W3 – 403/468-2551, Fax: 403/466-8006 – *2
A.R. Collins, #520, 10303 Jasper Ave., T5J 3N6 – 403/423-1815 – *1
Combe & Kent, #800, 10310 Jasper Ave., T5J 1Y8 – 403/428-0792 – *2
Colleen M. Connolly, 9902 - 111 St., T5K 1K2 – 403/482-0802, Fax: 403/482-7148
Cook Duke Cox, Commerce Place, #2700, 10155 - 102 St., T5J 4G8 – 403/429-1751, Fax: 403/424-5866; Email: cdc@ccinet.ab.ca – *43
Gary K. Cooper, Q.C., #200, 10020 - 101A Ave., T5J 3G2 – 403/420-6745, Fax: 403/424-8584
Coulter, Kerby & Power, Metropolitain Pl., #2200, 10303 Jasper Ave., T5J 3N6 – 403/423-3331, Fax: 403/420-0049 – *6
C.D. Cousineau, Centre 111, #202, 11830 - 111 Ave., T5G 0E1 – 403/455-0485 – *1
Jean K. Coutts, First Edmonton Pl., 10665 Jasper Ave., 15th Fl., T5J 3S9 – 403/423-4357, Fax: 403/423-8946 – *1
Covey & Behm, #850, 10665 Jasper Ave., T5J 3S9 – 403/423-1962 – *2
Richard W. Covlin, 11211 - 76 Ave., T6G 0K2
Cox Trofimuk Campbell - Sulyma Stewart, Manulife Pl., Bldg Box: 2750, 10180 - 101 St., T5J 3S4 – 403/422-6242, Fax: 403/426-1137 – *6
E.M. Crane, 12125 Jasper Ave., T5N 3X9 – 403/488-8101 – *1
Cruickshank Karvellas, Manulife Pl., #3400, 10180 - 101 St., T5J 4W9 – 403/424-3800, Fax: 403/424-1311 – *23
Cruikshank Karvellas Law Office, Manulife Place, #3400, 10180 - 101 St., T5J 4W9 – 403/424-3800, Fax: 403/424-1311
M.D. Cullen, #403, 10310 - 102 Ave., T5J 2X6 – 403/424-9354 – *1
Cummings Andrews & Mackay, #500, 10150 - 100 St., T5J 0P6 – 403/428-8222, Fax: 403/426-2670 – *8
Robert H. Davidson, 10138 - 121 St., T5N 1K4 – 403/482-5496 – *1

Davies & Co., TD Tower, Edmonton Centre, #1103, 10060 Jasper Ave., T5J 2Z1 – 403/423-3661, Fax: 403/426-1293 – *2
Roger Davies, #442, 10113 - 104 St., T5J 1A1 – 403/421-4040 – *1
C.B. Davison, 10039 - 117 St., T5K 1W7 – 403/488-5078
Paul K. Dawson, #830, 10020 - 101A Ave., T5J 3G2 – 403/424-9058, Fax: 403/424-0172; Toll Free: 1-800-661-3176 – *6
Robert C. Day, Phipps McKinnon Bldg., #950, 10020 - 101A Ave., T5J 3G2 – 403/423-2107
de Villars Jones, Noble Bldg., #300, 8540 - 109 St., T6G 1E6 – 403/433-9000 – *2
A.D. Demco, #600, 10089 Jasper Ave., T5J 1V2 – 403/423-2159 – *1
R.W. Derrah, #201, 9562 Whyte Ave., T6C 0Z8 – 403/439-3400, Fax: 403/439-6284 – *1
Dlin & Harker, #202, 9644 - 54 Ave. NW, T6E 5V1 – 403/438-4972 – *2
Joseph Doz, #2830, 10180 - 101 St., T5J 3S4 – 403/422-6228 – *1
Duncan & Craig, Scotia Pl., #2800, 10060 Jasper Ave., T5J 3V9 – 403/428-6036, Fax: 403/428-9683 – *51
D.F. Dunwoodie, #320, 10055 - 106 St., T5J 2Y2 – 403/424-3200
Durocher Simpson, Scotia Place, #801, 10060 Jasper Ave., T5J 3R8 – 403/420-6850, Fax: 403/425-9185; Email: durocher@oanet.com; URL: http://www.tgx.com/durocher – *11
E.L. Eccleston, 235 North Town Mall, T5E 6C1 – 403/478-6635, Fax: 403/476-8587 – *1
Dennis Edney, #420, 10123 - 99 St., T5J 3H1 – 403/424-6425; 426-6651, Fax: 403/424-6477
E.A.O. Elford, 50 Westridge Rd., T5T 1B4 – 403/487-3579
David C. Elliott, #313, 11523 - 100 Ave., T5K 0J8 – 403/482-2379
Embury & McFayden, #401, 10508 - 82 Ave., T6E 2A4 – 403/439-7302 – *1
Emery Jamieson, Oxford Tower, #1700, 10235 - 101 St., T5J 3G1 – 403/426-5220, Fax: 403/420-6277; Email: emery@freenet.edmonton.ab.ca – *29
Environmental Law Centre, #201, 10350 - 124 St., T5N 3V9 – 403/482-4891, Fax: 403/488-6779; Toll Free: 1-800-661-4238; Email: elc@web.apc.org – *4
Sol Estrin Law Offices, #400, 11456 Jasper Ave., T5K 0M1 – 403/488-2222, Fax: 403/488-0599 – *3
Evans & Co., Weber Centre, #1535, 5555 Calgary Trail South, T6H 5P9 – 403/438-4493, Fax: 403/436-1019 – *4
Felesky Flynn, Canada Trust Tower, #2600, 10104 - 103 Ave., T5J 0H8 – 403/428-8310, Fax: 403/421-8820; Email: felesky@planet.eon.net – *7
David A. Fennell, Royal Trust Tower, #2302, Edmonton Centre, T5J 2Z2 – 403/423-1619 – *2
Field Atkinson Perraton, Oxford Tower, #2000, 10235 - 101 St., T5J 3G1 – 403/423-3003, Fax: 403/428-9329, 424-7116 – *46
L.R. Fleming, #205, 11523 - 100 Ave., T5K 0J8 – 403/482-4142
L.R. Flynn, 4731 - 147A St., T6H 5N3
G.J. Fontaine, #508, 10235 - 101 St., T5J 3E8 – 403/428-0707 – *1
Fuller St. Arnaud & McAllister, #800, 10150 - 100 St., T5J 0P6 – 403/423-2663, Fax: 403/424-4873 – *3
Galbraith Law Offices, 654 Kingsway Garden Mall, T5G 3E6 – 403/455-6111, Fax: 403/471-6211 – *2
Galbraith, Larocque & Empson, #1800, 10123 - 99 St., T5J 3H1 – 403/424-9558 – *3
R.G. Gariepy, #411, 11523 - 100 Ave., T5K 0J8 – 403/482-7370 – *2
William G. Geddes, #200, 10123 - 99 St., T5J 3H1 – 403/423-1546
B.M. Geiger, #202, 9644 - 54 Ave. NW, T6E 5V1 – 403/438-4972
Klaus Gessert, #610, 10506 Jasper Ave., T5J 2W9 – 403/421-4325 – *1

* indicates number of lawyers in law firm.

DIRECTORY OF LAW FIRMS – ALBERTA

R.D. Gillespie, #300, 10209 - 97 St., T5J 0L6 – 403/424-3255

H.S. Gillett, #304, 10209 - 97 St., T5J 0L6 – 403/426-1361, Fax: 403/429-2828

Gledhill Reid, #1950, 10205 - 101 St., T5J 2Z2 – 403/425-3511, Fax: 403/426-5919 – *7

R.M. Gold, #502, 10109 - 106 St., T5J 3L7 – 403/429-9933 – *1

D.C. Goldie, #1103, 10104 - 103 St., T5J 0H8

Grace Parrotta-King Professional Corporation, #795, 10020 - 101A Ave., T5J 3G2 – 403/424-2333, Fax: 403/424-3777

Ingolf F. Grape, Campus Tower, #209, 8625 - 112 St., T6G 1K8 – 403/436-8421, Fax: 403/436-8420; Email: grapelaw@oanet.com – *1

Graziano & Associates, 11428 - 100 Ave., T5K 0J4 – 403/482-5846, Fax: 403/482-2191 – *3

Grotski & Hochachka, #800, One Thornton Court NW, T5J 2E7 – 403/426-0566 – *3

Gunn & Company, #220, 9707 - 110 St., T5K 2L9 – 403/488-4460, Fax: 403/488-4783 – *2

Renuka Gupta, 10516 - 31 Ave., T6J 2Y3 – 403/437-1069

Wittold L. Gutter, 6030 - 88 St., T6E 6G4 – 403/448-9100

Hagen, Feehan & Gilchrist, 8623 - 149 St., T5R 1B2 – 403/486-0207, Fax: 403/483-0848 – *4

P. Haljan, Empire Bldg., Bldg Box: 908, 10080 Jasper Ave., T5J 1V9 – 403/428-0055 – *1

Hall & Burchak, 12026 - 102 Ave., T5K 0R9 – 403/482-5732 – *2

Ivan A. Hall, 10807 - 124 St., T5M 0H4 – 403/452-1651 – *1

Hanington, Cavanaugh & Wheelwright, #570, 10123 - 99 St., T5J 3H1 – 403/426-1452, Fax: 403/428-1827 – *3

D.L. Hansen, 828 Lee Ridge Rd., T6K 0P8 – 403/426-0734 – *1

Hansma & Associates, 13907 - 127 St., T6V 1A8 – 403/456-3661, Fax: 403/457-9381 – *3

Harwardt, MacPherson & Hodgson, 10035 Saskatchewan Dr., T6E 4R4 – 403/433-9431 – *3

Wayne D. Hatt, #1209, 10104 -103 Ave., T5J 0H8 – 403/423-3391, Fax: 403/426-2980

Hattersley & Company, #2240, 10123 - 99 St., T5J 3H1 – 403/423-4081, Fax: 403/423-3221 – *2

Hauptman, Hart, Cherkawsky, #201, 4990 - 92 Ave., T6B 2V4 – 403/465-9191, Fax: 403/469-8889 – *4

D.R. Hayward, 4628 - 151 St., T6H 5N8

M.A. Heaton, 4420 - 97 St. NW, T6E 5R9 – 403/438-3848

Henderson & Meiklejohn, 4416 - 97 St. NW, T6E 5R9 – 403/436-6400

H.J.D. Henderson, #205, 10715 - 124 St., T5M 0H2 – 403/451-2769, Fax: 403/455-2769

Henderson, MacEachern & Burgener, #442, 10113 - 104 St., T5J 1A1 – 403/428-1079 – *3

Patricia Henderson, 4416 - 97 St. NW, T6E 5R9 – 403/436-6400 – *1

Hendrickson Gower & Massing, Phipps McKinnon Bldg., #680, 10020 - 101A Ave., T5J 3G2 – 403/421-8816, Fax: 403/424-5864 – *5

Jana Hennessy, 9254 Strathearn Dr., T6C 4E2 – 403/465-2231 – *1

B.J. Herring, 10402 - 155 St., T5P 2M3 – 403/453-6068 – *1

Adlynn Miskew Hewitt, Q.C., 7013 - 101 Ave., T6A 0M6 – 403/466-0906 – *1

John D. Hill, Q.C., Phipps McKinnon Bldg., #1600, 10020 - 101A Ave., T5J 3G2 – 403/429-3889, Fax: 403/426-1146 – *1

Leroy N. Hiller, #1209, 10104 -103 Ave., T5J 0H8 – 403/424-6660, Fax: 403/426-2980 – *2

Harold Hinz, #202, 9644 - 54 Ave. NW, T6E 5V1 – 403/438-4972

Hladun & Company, #100, 10187 - 104 St., T5J 0Z9 – 403/423-1888, Fax: 403/424-0934 – *5

A.C. Hoff, 2512 - 132 Ave., T5A 3Z6 – 403/476-9738 – *1

G.D. Honey, #210, 8930 Jasper Ave., T5H 4E9 – 403/428-4531 – *1

H. Horbay, 10912 - 97 St., T5H 2M5 – 403/422-6433 – *1

William K. Horwitz, #105, 10423 - 178 St., T5S 1R5 – 403/486-3100, Fax: 403/489-0671 – *1

Richard A. Hunt, Centre 104, #612, 5241 Calgary Trail Southbound NW, T6H 5G8 – 403/437-6050, Fax: 403/437-5481 – *1

T.S.A. Hunt, #201, 8709 - 156 St., T5R 1Y5 – 403/481-2323, Fax: 403/483-2140 – *1

George E. Illsley, #202, 15241 Stony Plain Rd., T5P 3Y4 – 403/484-7765 – *1

Ingersoll & Ingersoll, Phipps McKinnon Bldg., #460, 10020 - 101A Ave., T5J 3G2 – 403/422-6207, Fax: 403/424-9955 – *1

M.A. Irving, 8356 - 120 St., T6G 1X2

Jackson, Arlette, MacIver, #700, 10020 - 101A Ave., T5J 3G2 – 403/424-5146, Fax: 403/426-6566 – *6

Bodil Jelhof Jensen, 10703 - 54 St., T6A 2H7 – 403/469-4241 – *1

Barclay W. Johnson, #150, 12225 - 105 Ave., T5N 0Y3 – 403/488-8181 – *1

James E.B. Johnston, #205, 11523 - 100 Ave., T5K 0J8 – 403/488-0971 – *1

Jones, Bolton, Royal Trust Tower, #1528, Edmonton Centre, T5J 2Z2 – 403/424-3165 – *2

James W. Joosse, #420, 10123 - 99 St., T5J 3H1 – 403/426-6651, Fax: 403/426-6656 – *1

J.T. Joyce, #2220, 10123 - 99 St., T5J 3H1 – 403/424-3175, Fax: 403/425-5157 – *1

Kalil Haymour, #900, 10665 Jasper Ave., T5J 3S9 – 403/425-5700, Fax: 403/421-8400 – *1

R.E. Kampitsch, #2210, 10060 Jasper Ave., T5J 3R8 – 403/428-1390 – *1

Edward W.S. Kane, #205, 11523 - 100 Ave., T5K 0J8 – 403/488-0971

T.H. Kantor, #740, 10150 - 100 St., T5J 0P6 – 403/423-7786, Fax: 403/426-0101

Karoles Mintz Majeski, The Dorchester, #400, 10357 - 109 St., T5J 1N3 – 403/425-2041, Fax: 403/425-2195 – *7

Saul Katz, #900, 9707 - 110 St., T5K 2L9 – 403/482-7800, Fax: 403/482-7803 – *1

Robert M. Kelcher, Blue Quill Centre, 292 Saddleback Rd., T6J 4R7 – 403/436-0011, Fax: 403/436-7000

Kennedy & Edlund, #115, 17220 Stony Plain Rd., T5S 1K6 – 403/486-3000 – *3

Robert J. Kennedy, 10311 - 174 St., T5S 1H1 – 403/484-5723

Kirwin Kobewka, 14820 Stony Plain Rd., T5N 3S5 – 403/451-1441 – *2

Kiss & Davidson, #202, 15241 Stony Plain Rd., T5P 3Y4 – 403/484-7704 – *2

G.M. Kitt, #300, 10036 Jasper Ave., T5J 2W2 – 403/422-6009 – *1

Knight & Company, 11408 - 103 Ave., T5K 0S4 – 403/488-3333, Fax: 403/482-6200 – *1

Koch & Company, #1404, 10024 Jasper Ave., T5J 1R9 – 403/424-0246 – *3

Kolthammer, Zazula & Fedorak, #208, 11062 - 156 St., T5P 4M8 – 403/489-5003, Fax: 403/486-2107 – *4

Glenn R. Kosak, 9726 - 145 St., T5N 2W9 – 403/429-2942 – *1

Koshman & Johnson, #700, 10117 Jasper Ave., T5J 1W8 – 403/428-0636 – *2

Methodius Koziak, #204, 7104 - 109 St., T6G 1B8 – 403/438-3090, Fax: 403/437-1905 – *1

I.S. Kravinchuk, #800, 10310 Jasper Ave., T5J 1Y8 – 403/426-4834 – *1

Oskar H. Kruger & Company, #304, 10209 - 97 St., T5J 0L6 – 403/423-3511, Fax: 403/423-3514 – *3

H.W. Kuckertz, #202, 8003 - 102 St., T6E 4A2 – 403/432-9308, Fax: 403/439-9950 – *1

P.M.W. Kuehn, #102, 7603 - 104 St., T6E 4C3 – 403/433-2603 – *1

Kuzmicz & Associates, #810, 10089 Jasper Ave., T6J 1V1 – 403/426-6352 – *1

Lavallee Buchanan, #705, 10240 - 124 St., T5N 3W6 – 403/488-4801 – *4

Gregory C. Lazin Professional Corporation, #203, 10171 Saskatchewan Dr., T6E 4R5 – 403/433-6600, Fax: 403/439-6696

Donald Lee, #408, 10506 Jasper Ave., T5J 2W9 – 403/448-0340

Lennie & Company, #1250, 10180 - 101 St., T5J 3L8 – 403/425-2110, Fax: 403/426-6977 – *3

Keith M. Leslie, 3657 - 73 St., T6K 0L8 – 403/463-4019, Fax: 403/463-2360 – *1

M.L. Leung, Royal Trust Tower, #404, Edmonton Centre, T5J 2Z2 – 403/424-7684 – *1

C.W. Leviston, 14615 - 91 Ave., T5R 4Y7 – 403/484-7540 – *1

K.S.V. Linton, 10415 - 80 Ave., T6E 1V1 – 403/439-8357

M.R. Lippe, #2210, 10060 Jasper Ave., T5J 3R8 – 403/428-1390 – *1

Lister & Associates, #777, 10024 Jasper Ave., T5J 1R9 – 403/422-6114 – *3

R.V. Lloyd, #1400, 10303 Jasper Ave., T5J 3N6 – 403/421-1818, Fax: 403/429-4453 – *1

Linda L. Long, 10835 - 124 St., 2nd Fl., T5M 0H4 – 403/455-7373, Fax: 403/454-3167 – *1

Peter T.K. Loong, #320, 10055 - 106 St., T5J 2Y2 – 403/424-3200

Lucas Bowker & White, Esso Tower, #1201, 10060 Jasper Ave., T5J 4E5 – 403/426-5330, Fax: 403/428-1066; Toll Free: 1-800-567-7174; Email: lucas@supernet.ab.ca – *31

G.R. Ludwig, #201, 9111 - 39 Ave. NW, T6E 5Y2 – 403/461-5681

Philip Lupul, #803, 8220 Jasper Ave., T5H 4B6 – 403/424-4024

L.R. Lyman, #2440, 10180 - 101 St., T5J 3S4 – 403/429-2700 – *1

Lyons Albert & Cook, Weber Centre, #905, 5555 Calgary Tr. Southbound, T6H 5P9 – 403/437-0743, Fax: 403/438-6695; Email: alalbert@compusmart.ab.ca – *3

Macdonald & Freund, #750, 10665 Jasper Ave., T5J 3S9 – 403/424-7201, Fax: 403/428-7667; Email: gfreund@accessweb.com; bmacdonald@accessweb.com – *2

Reginald S. Macdonald, #306, 10328 - 81 Ave., T6E 1X2 – 403/439-7000

D.C. MacPherson, #300, 10209 - 97 St., T5J 0L6 – 403/424-9086

Majaesic, Dueck & Baird, Toronto Dominion Tower, #2701, Edmonton Centre, T5J 2Z1 – 403/424-4200, Fax: 403/425-1407 – *4

Majeski, Johnson, #1040, 10405 Jasper Ave., T5J 3N4 – 403/428-9628 – *4

Malhotra & Company, #315, 10909 Jasper Ave., T5J 3L9 – 403/423-5792 – *2

James W. Mandick, #1900, 10123 - 99 St., T5J 3H1 – 403/423-3311

A.A. Marchesich, #401, 10036 Jasper Ave., T5J 2W2 – 403/425-5201 – *1

M.B. Marcovitch, #304, 10209 - 97 St., T5J 0L6 – 403/425-1816 – *1

Matheson & Company, Matheson Bldg., 10410 - 81 Ave., T6E 1X5 – 403/433-5881, Fax: 403/432-9453 – *13

Cheryl J. Matheson, #202, 11714 - 95 St., T5G 1L9 – 403/474-1455, Fax: 403/474-2559 – *1

E. Mazzolini, #2210, 10060 Jasper Ave., T5J 3R8 – 403/428-1390 – *1

McBean Becker Cochard Gordon Zwaenepoel & Martin, Park Plaza, #104, 10611 - 98th Ave., T5K 2P7 – 403/425-9777, Fax: 403/425-9779 – *6

McCuaig Desrochers, Bank of Montreal Bldg., #500, 10199 - 101 St., T5J 3Y4 – 403/426-4660, Fax: 403/426-0982 – *16

Canadian Almanac & Directory 1997

Timothy Douglas McFetridge, Manulife Pl., #2740, 10180 - 101 St., T5J 3S4 – 403/421-1071, Fax: 403/421-7533 – *1

Dennis W. McGechie, #205, 11523 - 100 Ave., T5K 0J8 – 403/488-1974, Fax: 403/482-7417 – *1

McGee Richard, Weber Centre, #1301, 5555 Calgary Trail South, T6H 5P9 – 403/437-2240, Fax: 403/438-5788 – *3

W.N. McKay, #205, 11523 - 100 Ave., T5K 0J8 – 403/488-0971, Fax: 403/482-7417 – *1

T.L. McKee, #213, 14065 Victoria Tr., T5Y 2B6 – 403/473-7244 – *1

McLennan Ross, West Chambers, #600, 12220 Stony Plain Rd., PO Box 12040, T5J 3L2 – 403/482-9200, Fax: 403/482-9100; Toll Free: 1-800-567-9200; Email: mross@supernet.ab.ca – *40

R. McPhail, #150, 12225 - 105 Ave., T5N 0Y3 – 403/482-5947 – *1

Ingrid E. Meier, Bomira, 9411 - 20 Ave., T6N 1E5 – 403/450-3761

Ian L. Meikle, #304, Kingsway Garden Mall, T5G 3A6 – 403/474-8047 – *1

Melnyk & Co., 11054 - 86 Ave., T6G 0W9 – 403/432-7464, Fax: 403/431-1039 – *2

D.M. Memela, #101, 10621 - 80 Ave., T6E 1V6 – 403/439-7604

Joseph J. Michaels, #500, One Thornton Ct., T5J 2E7 – 403/424-0354 – *1

Marla S. Miller, 11835 - 102 Ave., T5K 0R6 – 403/482-2888, Fax: 403/482-4600 – *1

Milner Fenerty, Manulife Pl., #2900, 10180 - 101 St., T5J 3V5 – 403/423-7100, Fax: 403/423-7276 – *62

Minsos & Edwards, #220, 8723 - 82 Ave., T6C 0Y9 – 403/466-1175 – *2

W. Robert Mitchell, #405, 10408 - 124 St., T5N 1R5 – 403/482-5791, Fax: 403/488-0965 – *1

A.S. Mlonzi, #803, 9725 - 106 St., T5K 1B5 – 403/425-5269

Wendy M. Molnar, #2501, 10004 - 104 Ave., T5J 0K1 – 403/429-1891, Fax: 403/420-6345 – *1

Molstad Gilbert, #700, 10104 - 103 Ave., T5J 0H8 – 403/426-4535 – *13

Nick Mosychuk, #500, One Thornton Ct., T5J 2E7 – 403/424-9364 – *1

Murray, Chilibeck & Horne, #208, 10464 Mayfield Rd., T5P 4P4 – 403/484-2323, Fax: 403/486-4289 – *3

A.M. Myers, 12936 - 116 St., T5E 5H4 – 403/455-7551

Ness & Hum, #105, 8704 - 51 Ave., T6E 5E8 – 403/465-1818 – *2

Neuman Thompson, 11507 - 100 Ave., T5K 2R2 – 403/482-7645 – *3

Nicholl & Akers, #200, 10187 - 104 St., T5J 0Z9 – 403/429-2771, Fax: 403/425-1665 – *8

Neil W. Nichols, PO Box 4668, T6E 5G5 – 403/465-0100, Fax: 403/465-1981 – *1

Ian A. Nicholson, #203, 12303 - Jasper Ave., T5N 3K7 – 403/482-1019 – *1

Nickerson, Roberts & Hilborn, #300, 10004 Jasper Ave., T5J 1R3 – 403/428-0041 – *7

Peter G. Northcott, 9902 - 111 St., T5K 1K2 – 403/448-0300, Fax: 403/482-7148 – *2

Odishaw & Odishaw, Sun Life Pl., #2200, 10123 - 99 St., T5J 3H1 – 403/429-1600 – *3

B.V. Odsen, #300, 10209 - 97 St., T5J 0L6 – 403/429-2615, Fax: 403/424-9123

Ogilvie & Company, Metropolitan Pl., #1400, 10303 Jasper Ave., T5J 3N6 – 403/421-1818, Fax: 403/429-4453; Email: ogilvie@compusmart.ab.ca – *25

Miyako R. Okubo, 7750 Jasper Ave., T5H 3R8 – 403/429-2381 – *1

Olekshy & Company, 10418 - 80 Ave. NW, T6E 5T7 – 403/433-1448, Fax: 403/433-3888 – *2

Oliver & Grant, #2140, 10123 - 99 St., T5J 3H1 – 403/424-6948, Fax: 403/424-6972 – *2

Osborne & Company, #204, 15205 Stony Plain Rd., T5P 3Y4 – 403/484-5347 – *2

Oshry & Company, Canada Trust Tower, Bldg Box: 1004, 10104 - 103 Ave., T5J 0H8 – 403/428-1731 – *2

T.R. Owen, #2350, 10060 Jasper Ave., T5J 3R8 – 403/425-6530

Hermo Toribio Pagtakhan, #1840, 10123 - 99 St., T5J 3H1 – 403/425-6611, Fax: 403/429-4695 – *1

Michael M. Park, 8534 - 109 St., T6G 1E5 – 403/432-1694, Fax: 403/433-7757

M. George Parker, #1290, 10130 - 103 St., T5J 3N9 – 403/421-1277, Fax: 403/426-6478 – *1

Parlee McLaws, Manulife Pl., #1500, 10180 - 101 St., T5J 4K1 – 403/423-8500, Fax: 403/423-2870 – *94

Richard E. Parr, 10345 Glenora Cres., T5N 3J5 – 403/451-2170

Paton Croll, #1300, 10665 Jasper Ave., T5J 3S9 – 403/424-4042, Fax: 403/428-6936 – *4

Patrick & Patrick, #800, 10310 Jasper Ave., T5J 2W4 – 403/426-4884 – *2

David N. Paull, #304, 10209 - 97 St., T5J 0L6 – 403/426-2307

Pawlowski & Associates, #107, 11831 - 123 St., T5L 0G7 – 403/451-0027 – *2

K.A. Pazder, #300, 10230 - 142 St., T5N 3Y6 – 403/453-6161 – *1

K.W. Penonzek, #420, 10123 - 99 St., T5J 3H1 – 403/424-7700

Lynn K. Penrod, 9626 - 85 Ave., T6C 1H4 – 403/433-2205

G. Perdicaris, #835, 10310 Jasper Ave., T5J 2W4 – 403/423-1097

Peterson Hustwick Wetsch & Moffat, Capital Pl., #200, 9707 - 110 St., T5K 2L9 – 403/482-6555, Fax: 403/482-6613

Peterson Ross, Capital Pl., #200, 9707 - 110 St., T5K 2L9 – 403/482-6555, Fax: 403/482-6613 – *1

Patrick J. Phelan, Sun Life Pl., #1990, 10123 - 99 St., T5J 3H1 – 403/424-7730, Fax: 403/423-3350 – *1

R.A. Philion, #1910, 10180 - 101 St., T5J 3S4 – 403/423-2977 – *2

Philp & Collins, 10374 - 172nd St., T5S 1G9 – 403/484-8708, Fax: 403/484-8894 – *2

William R. Picton, 10722 - 113 St., T5H 3H8 – 403/425-8936, Fax: 403/425-8936

Pierzchalski & Company, 11914 - 129 Ave., T5E 0N3 – 403/455-6678, Fax: 403/453-1093 – *2

Ronald W. Poitras, #300, 10209 - 97 St., T5J 0L6 – 403/422-6251 – *1

Polack, Meindersma, Smith & Liddell, Denton Centre, #300, 14925 - 111 Ave., T5M 2P6 – 403/486-0926, Fax: 403/444-1393 – *4

M.L. Pollock, #701, 10240 - 124 St., T5N 3W6 – 403/488-7027

R.G. Powelson, 9685 - 85 Ave., T6E 2J1 – 403/439-8424, Fax: 403/439-7786

Glen Power, #1110, 10117 Jasper Ave., T5J 1W8 – 403/426-2838, Fax: 403/426-2838 – *1

Alexander Pozniak, #3, 9430 - 118 Ave., T5G 0N6 – 403/474-6314, Fax: 403/479-3732

Pringle, Renouf & Associates, #200, 10237 - 104 St., T5J 4A1 – 403/424-8866, Fax: 403/426-1470 – *5

Proulx & Associates, #201, 9111 - 39 Ave. NW, T6E 5Y2 – 403/462-3663 – *1

Prowse & Chowne, Strathcona Professional Centre, #100, 10328 - 81 Ave., T6E 1X2 – 403/439-7171, Fax: 403/439-0475; Email: prowse@planet.eom.net – *21

Pundit Chotalia, Oxford Tower, #808, 10235 - 101 St., T5J 3G1 – 403/421-0861 – *2

Rand Moreau, Liberty Bldg., #1101, 10506 Jasper Ave., T5J 2W9 – 403/423-1984 – *3

M. Naeem Rauf, First Edmonton Pl., #900, 10665 Jasper Ave., T5J 3S9 – 403/424-4591, Fax: 403/421-8400

P.E. Recto, #600, 10089 Jasper Ave., T5J 1V2 – 403/423-1283, Fax: 403/426-2233 – *1

Michele J. Reeves, #320, 10055 - 106 St., T5J 2Y2 – 403/424-3200

H.M. Reich, Sun Life Pl., #1990, 10123 - 99 St., T5J 3H1 – 403/424-7732 – *1

Rennick & DiPinto, Metropolitan Pl., #502, 10303 Jasper Ave., T5J 3N6 – 403/426-5510 – *2

Jerome Reyda, Q.C., 240 Riverside Cres., T5N 3M5 – 403/452-7702 – *1

Reynolds, Mirth, Richards & Farmer, Manulife Pl., #3200, 10180 - 101 St, T5J 3W8 – 403/425-9510, Fax: 403/429-3044; Toll Free: 1-800-661-7673; Email: reynolds@law.ualberta.ca; URL: http://www.ualberta.ca/~law/firms/reynolds/ – *27

Aubrey C. Rice, #570, 10123 - 99 St., T5J 3H1 – 403/426-1452

G.W. Robertson, #205, 11523 - 100 Ave., T5K 0J8 – 403/488-0971, Fax: 403/482-7417 – *1

Roddick & Peck, #2, 4716 - 91 Ave., T6B 2L1 – 403/469-0451, Fax: 403/468-4389 – *4

David W. Ross, #900, 10024 Jasper Ave., T5J 1S2 – 403/425-1965 – *1

Rowand, Lopatka & Savich, 12304 - 107 Ave., T5M 1Z1 – 403/451-3152 – *3

Royal, McCrum, Duckett & Glancy, Palomar Bldg., #215, 8204 - 104 St., T6E 4E6 – 403/432-0919, Fax: 403/439-6562 – *4

Kenneth J. Rusnak, #2240, 10123 - 99 St., T5J 3H1 – 403/424-1112 – *1

Russell & Company, #500, 10104 - 103 Ave., T5J 0H8 – 403/420-1004, Fax: 403/426-2582 – *4

W. Byron Rutley, #102, 7603 - 104 St., T6E 4C3 – 403/433-2392 – *1

St. Pierre, Spelliscy & Van Vliet, Callingwood Professional Centre, #213, 6650 - 177 St., T5T 4J5 – 403/444-4041, Fax: 403/481-5018 – *4

Samy F. Salloum, #1090, 10020 - 101A Ave., T5J 3G2 – 403/426-7777 – *1

Savaryn & Savaryn, Bank of Montreal Bldg., #403, 10089 Jasper Ave., T5J 1V2 – 403/422-7548 – *2

R.H. Sawchuk, #403, 10089 Jasper Ave., T5J 0H8 – 403/428-8848

Saxton & Company, Sun Life Pl., #1920, 10123 - 99 St., T5J 3H1 – 403/428-6060 – *2

J.F. Sayers, 2756 - 105 St., T6J 4J3 – 403/437-1141

B.M. Schloss, #101, 17505 - 107 Ave., T5S 1E5 – 403/448-9300

Schwab, Rowe & Parsons, 9908 - 106 St., T5K 1C4 – 403/426-6715 – *3

D.L. Schwartz, #430, 10036 Jasper Ave., T5J 2W2 – 403/424-0259 – *1

Scott & Murray, TD Tower, #750, 10205 - 101 St., T5J 2Z2 – 403/423-3271, Fax: 403/428-1963 – *3

Donna V.T. Sekida, 7609 - 152 St., T5R 1K6 – 403/444-0736

R.A. Semenchuk, #200, 10923 - 101 St., T5H 2S7 – 403/424-4161 – *1

A.J.W. Semotiuk, #332, 10113 - 104 St., T5J 1A1 – 403/428-8241, Fax: 403/425-0539

Shaw & Tamke, #203, 8657 - 51 Ave. NW, T6E 6A8 – 403/465-9001, Fax: 403/468-2532 – *2

Sheckter & Company, #408, 9707 - 110 St., T5K 2L9 – 403/454-2060

G.P. Shewchuk, Tower One, Scotia Pl., Bldg Box: 2110, 10060 Jasper Ave., T5J 3R8 – 403/421-1641, Fax: 403/446-3580

W.K.F. Shim, #2, 10627A - 101 St., T5H 2S2

Shoctor Ferguson, #2800, 10060 Jasper Ave., T5J 3V9 – 403/423-2461, Fax: 403/424-5244 – *3

Shtabsky & Tussman, #400, 10235 - 101 St., T5J 3G1 – 403/429-4671, Fax: 403/424-3580; Email: stlaw@oanet.com; URL: http://www.stlaw.com – *12

W.J. Shymko, #200, 10105 - 108 Ave., T5H 1A7 – 403/425-6414 – *1

Silverman & Shafir, #1104, 10117 Jasper Ave., T5J 1W8 – 403/428-0731, Fax: 403/428-0733 – *2

Sim, Reid & Birenbaum, Toronto Dominion Tower, #1607, Edmonton Centre, T5J 2Z1 – 403/422-7126 – *3

Simons & Company, #618, 10216 - 124 St., T5N 4A3 – 403/482-1536 – *3

Larry A. Sitko, 9531 - 144 Ave., T5E 2H8 – 403/476-7686 – *1

John G. Skinner, 318 Saddleback Rd., T6J 4R7 – 403/434-6565, 1692, Fax: 403/454-2424 – *1

* indicates number of lawyers in law firm.

Smith Bresee, #205, 11714 - 95 St., T5G 1L9 – 403/474-8284, Fax: 403/477-8659 – *5
Smith Gawlinski Parkatti, #1780, 10123 - 99 St., T5J 3H1 – 403/428-6645, Fax: 403/428-6639 – *4
F.P. Smith, #206, 14925 - 111 Ave., T5M 2P6 – 403/489-2503 – *1
L.M. Snaychuk, #903, 10060 Jasper Ave., T5J 2R8 – 403/422-2115 – *1
P.R. Solotki, Wentworth Bldg., #304, 10209 - 97 St., T5J 0L6 – 403/424-8110 – *1
Spitz & Carr, #1870, 10303 Jasper Ave., T5J 3N6 – 403/428-0792 – *3
John Stadnyk, Terra Losa Centre, 9760 - 170 St., T5T 5L4 – 403/483-8383
Laura K. Stevens, #830, 10020 - 101A Ave., T5J 3G2 – 403/425-4671
Stewart & Karoles, #200, 10446 - 122 St., T5N 1M3 – 403/482-5743 – *4
I.M. Stillman, #101, 18067 - 107 Ave., T5S 1K3 – 403/484-4445
M.P. Stone, #616-21, 10405 Jasper Ave., T5J 3S2 – 403/486-5146 Fax: 403/483-7791 – *1
Stuffco Olsen, #404, 10216 - 124 St., T5N 4A3 – 403/482-3405, Fax: 403/488-3738 – *7
Sulyma Stewart, Manulife Pl., #2750, 10180 - 101 St., T5J 3S4
Gerald S. Swersky, #1104, 10117 Jasper Ave., T5J 1W8 – 403/424-0864
Swist & Company, #2300, 10123 - 99 St., T5J 3H1 – 403/426-6780 – *3
Tarrabain & Company, Tower One, Scotia Place, #2150, 10060 Jasper Ave., T5J 3R8 – 403/429-1010, Fax: 403/429-0101 – *7
W.J. Tatarchuk, #411, 11523 - 100 Ave., T5K 0J8 – 403/482-7370
C. Taylor, #1810, 10130 - 103 St., T5H 3N9 – 403/424-1055 – *1
James P. Taylor, #201, 12910 - 50 St., T5A 4L2 – 403/475-3692
M.E.G. Taylor, 14412 - 63 St., T5A 2B6 – 403/475-9303 – *1
Jan A. Terhart, 10020 - 95 St., T5H 2A4 – 403/424-9014 – *1
M.A.T. Terrell, #200, 9707 - 110 St., T5K 2L9 – 403/488-5500
Leonard Thom, Greystone VI Bldg., #106, 4246 - 97 St., T6E 5Z9 – 403/434-5870, Fax: 403/436-8420
Janet L. Thompson, #2240, 10123 - 99 St., T5J 3H1 – 403/423-3091
J.A. Thygesen, 9807 - 149 St., T5P 1K5 – 403/451-1316
Tkachuk & Patterson, Energy Sq., Bldg Box: 305, 10109 - 106 St., T5J 3L7 – 403/428-1593, Fax: 403/426-6679 – *2
B.R. Touchings, #410, 10310 - 102 Ave., T5J 2X6 – 403/424-6487, Fax: 403/424-7516 – *2
George E. Trott, #2440, 10180 - 101 St., T5J 3S4 – 403/429-2700
Helen S. Tymoczko, 12125 Jasper Ave., T5N 3X9 – 403/488-8103 – *1
Lee A.I. Tyrrell, 121 Laurier Dr., T5R 5P6
V.P. Hardman Professional Corporation, #201, 10335 - 178 St., T5S 1R5 – 403/484-2041, Fax: 403/484-8950 – *1
Venkatraman & Associates, Terrace Tower Office Plaza, #440, 4445 Calgary Trail South, T6H 5R7 – 403/436-7060, Fax: 403/436-7060 – *4
R. Douglas Vigen, 9677 - 45 Ave. NW, T6E 5Z8 – 403/438-2151, Fax: 403/438-2197
James A. Wachowich, 12431 Grandview Dr., T6H 4K3 – 403/427-4901
Walker, Butler & O'Laughlin, #300, 10209 - 97 St., T5J 0L6 – 403/426-6651
J.M. Walker, Sun Life Place, #575, 10123 - 99 St., T5J 3H1 – 403/426-6651, Fax: 403/441-9835 – *1
Wallace & Spitz, 18121 - 107 Ave., T5S 1K4 – 403/483-9223 – *2

David C. Ward Professional Corp., Centre 104, #506, 5241 Calgary Trail Southbound NW, T6H 5G8 – 403/434-8751 – *1
Weeks Doherty Schuldhaus & Spencer, Millwoods Office, Bldg Box: 1810, 4227 - 23 Ave., T6L 5Z3 – 403/450-0945, Fax: 403/461-8612
Weeks Doherty Schuldhaus & Spencer, 1120 One Thornton Ct., T5J 2E7 – 403/426-1382, Fax: 403/426-2094 – *8
Weir Bowen, #1600, 10104 - 103 Ave., T5J 0H8 – 403/424-2030 – *2
Welsh & Company, #888, 4445 Calgary Trail Southbound NW, T6H 5R7 – 403/438-3500, Fax: 403/438-3129 – *1
Uwe Welz, 7904 - 103 St., T6E 6C3 – 403/432-7711, Fax: 403/439-1177 – *1
John F. Werbicki, #201, 12910 - 50 St., T5A 4L2 – 403/473-1216 – *1
Wheatley Sadownik, #2000, 10123 - 99 St., T5J 3H1 – 403/423-6671, Fax: 403/420-6327; Email: makuch@compusmart.ab.ca – *5
John G. Wheelwright, #420, 10123 - 99 St., T5J 3H1 – 403/424-6425
Whiting, Sachs & Company, #445, 10020 - 101A Ave., T5J 3G2 – 403/424-5577 – *2
William A. Wiese, Noble Bldg., #303, 8540 - 109 St, T6G 1E6 – 403/432-1144 – *1
Louis A.T. Williams, #206, 4615 - 106A St., T6H 5H2 – 403/435-5441 – *2
H.D. Williamson, 8715 Saskatchewan Dr., T6G 2A9 – 403/439-2898 – *1
David R. Willson, 10316 - 121 St., T5N 1K8 – 403/482-6670, Fax: 403/482-2518 – *1
Richard A. Winter, Toronto-Dominion Tower, #2735, Edmonton Centre, T5J 2Z1 – 403/421-8777
Witten Binder, #2500, 10303 Jasper Ave., T5J 3N6 – 403/428-0501 – *27
Wolff Leia, Tower One, Scotia Place, #500, 10060 Jasper Ave., T5J 3R8 – 403/421-0222, Fax: 403/429-0503 – *2
Collin Wong, 10811 - 148 St., T5N 3H4 – 403/454-4433
Woo & Fok, #200, 10708 - 97 St., T5H 2L8 – 403/424-9050 – *2
Craig W. Wood, 10811 - 148 St., T5N 3H4 – 403/454-4433
Worton & Hunter, #1270, 5555 Calgary Trail Southbound NW, T6H 5P9 – 403/436-8554 – *2
Wright & McMenemy, #305, 10328 - 81 Ave., T6E 1X2 – 403/439-3991 – *3
B.K. Yiu, #635, 10180 - 102 St., T5J 0W5 – 403/428-1540 – *1
Ronald J. Young, #780, 10020 - 101A Ave., T5J 3G2 – 403/424-3311 – *1
A.R. Zariwny, 9211 - 96 St., T6C 3Y5 – 403/469-6791, Fax: 403/439-6456
A.A. Zwikstra, #530, 10020 - 101A Ave., T5J 3G2 – 403/424-5121

EDSON .... Edmonton
Robert W. Anderson, PO Box 6748, T7E 1V1 – 403/723-4829, Fax: 403/723-5443 – *1
Dennis C. Calvert, 107 - 50 St., PO Box 6658, T0E 0P0 – 403/723-6047, Fax: 403/723-3602 – *1
Duane H. Catterall, 5008 - 3 Ave., PO Box 6568, T7E 1T9 – 403/723-5111, 5112, Fax: 403/723-6179 – *1

ENOCH .... Edmonton
Mandamin & Associates, PO Box 300, T7X 3Y3 – 403/470-5777, Fax: 403/470-3909 – *3

EVANSBURG .... Edmonton
William R. Picton, 4900 - 50 Ave., T0E 0T0 – 403/727-2427

FAIRVIEW .... Peace River
H.A. Byers, PO Box 2200, T0H 1L0 – 403/835-4100, Fax: 403/835-4171 – *1

FORT MACLEOD .... MacLeod
J.C. Davis, PO Box 660, T0L 0Z0 – 403/553-3277 – *1
Gaschler & Vallance, 249 - 24 St., PO Box 757, T0L 0Z0 – 403/553-4484 – *2
North & Company, 324 - 24 St., T0L 0Z0 – 403/553-4998
Welbourn, Maloney, Professional Building, T0L 0Z0 – 403/553-4998

FORT MCMURRAY .... Fort McMurray
Campbell & Cooper, #212, 9714 Main St., T9H 1T6 – 403/743-5370, Fax: 403/791-0750 – *2
Adam W. Germain (1993) Professional Corp., #212, 9714 Main St., T9H 1T6 – 403/743-0045, Fax: 403/791-0750 – *1
Gorsalitz Law Office, 9912 Manning Ave., T9H 2B9 – 403/791-4115, Fax: 403/743-0040 – *1
Gregory L. Marullo, 243 Berens Place, T9K 2C6 – 403/791-3602
Samuel N. Mason, #104, 10012 Franklin Ave., T9H 2K6 – 403/743-5002 – *1
Weeks Doherty Schuldhaus & Spencer, #102, 9908 Franklin Ave., T9H 2K5 – 403/791-5505, Fax: 403/743-2428
Wolff Taitinger, #201, 10010 Franklin Ave., T9H 2K6 – 403/791-1403 – *2

FORT SASKATCHEWAN .... Edmonton
Jenkins & Jenkins, #200, 9835 - 104 St., T8L 2E5 – 403/998-4200, Fax: 403/998-4370 – *3
Valens, Fotty & Torok-Both, 10509 - 100 Ave., T8L 1Z5 – 403/998-4841, Fax: 403/998-4821 – *4
W.H. Wiebe, #4, 10307 - 100 Ave., T8L 1Y9 – 403/998-3331 – *1

GIBBONS .... Edmonton
T.M. Walter, PO Box 1200, T0A 1N0 – 403/923-3500

GRAND CENTRE .... Edmonton
Kowalski & Thomas, PO Box 480, T0A 1T0 – 403/594-7531 – *2
Todd & Drake, 4807 - 51 St., PO Box 908, T0A 1T0 – 403/594-7151 – *2

GRANDE CACHE .... Edmonton
Harry Arnesen, PO Box 385, T0E 0Y0 – 403/827-2458, Fax: 403/827-3734 – *1

GRANDE PRAIRIE .... Grande Prairie
Burgess & Gurevitch, 9931 - 106 Ave., T8V 1J4 – 403/539-3710, Fax: 403/532-2788 – *3
Carter, Lock & Repka, Whitby House, #200, 9803 - 101 Ave., T8V 0X6 – 403/532-8350 – *7
Dobko Innes & Hougestol, #201, 9914 - 109 Ave., T8V 1R6 – 403/539-6200, Fax: 403/532-9052
Angela L. Howey, 9927B Richmond Ave., T8V 0V1 – *1
Kay, Shipley, McVey & Smith, Windsor Ct., #600, 9835 - 101 Ave., T8V 5V4 – 403/532-7771, Fax: 403/532-1158 – *8
Lewis Clackson Mochan & Chrenek, Richmond Sq., #300, 9804 - 100 Ave., T8V 0T8 – 403/539-6800, Fax: 403/539-7975 – *4
Logan Watson & Company, #202, 10027 - 101 Ave., T8V 0X9 – 403/532-0315 – *4
MacDonell & McNaught, #202, 9934 Richmond Ave., T8V 0T9 – 403/539-3666 – *2
Robert S. Pollick, #200, 10009 - 101 Ave., T8V 0X9 – 403/532-4458, Fax: 403/538-4515 – *1
Wadey & Scragg, 9734B Richmond Ave., T8V 0T6 – 403/538-3731 – *2

GRIMSHAW .... Peace River
G.W.J. Paul, 4905 - 55 Railway Ave., PO Box 829, T0H 1W0 – 403/332-4647, Fax: 403/332-4614 – *1

HANNA .... Hanna
Kush & Daughter, PO Box 369, T0J 1P0 – 403/854-3361, Fax: 403/854-3985 – *2

DIRECTORY OF LAW FIRMS – ALBERTA

HIGH PRAIRIE .... Calgary
Susan Grattan, Drake Building, PO Box 1680, T0G 1E0 – 403/523-3432 – *1
Harry J. Jong, PO Box 1379, T0G 1E0 – 403/523-4554, Fax: 403/523-5550 – *1
Susan M. Lamothe, 5119 - 48 St., PO Box 1507, T0G 1E0 – 403/523-4944, Fax: 403/523-5055

HIGH RIVER .... Calgary
W.J. Andresen, PO Box 2080, T0L 1B0 – 403/652-3702 – *1
Arnold & Arnold, PO Box 250, T0L 1B0 – 403/652-2242 – *1
A. George Dearing, #103, 14 - 2 Ave. SE, T1V 1G4 – 403/652-2771, Fax: 403/652-2699 – *1

HINTON .... Edmonton
Johnson & McClelland, 213 Pembina Ave., PO Box 6060, T7V 2B3 – 403/865-2222, Fax: 403/865-8857 – *3
R. Rooneem, 121 Jasper St., PO Box 6539, T7V 1V7 – 403/865-2185, Fax: 403/865-7882 – *1
Woods & Robson, 110 Brewster Dr., T7V 1B4 – 403/865-3086, Fax: 403/865-7149 – *3

HOBBEMA .... Wetaskiwin
T.R. Goodson, Ermineskin Indian Reserve, PO Box 900, T0C 1N0 – 403/585-4100 – *1
J.W. Littlechild, PO Box 370, T0C 1N0 – 403/585-3038 – *1
Judith Sayers, PO Box 900, T0C 1N0 – 403/585-3037, Fax: 403/585-2025
Rodney Soonias, #70, c/o Montana Band, T0C 1N0 – 403/585-3998, Fax: 403/585-3264

INNISFAIL .... Red Deer
Miller, Lehane & Wild, 5035 - 49 St., PO Box 699, T0M 1A0 – 403/227-3361, Fax: 403/227-2929 – *3
Gary J. Shudra, #201, 4733 - 50 St., PO Box 1625, T0M 1A0 – 403/227-1950
Tulloch & Stretch, 5030 - 50 St., PO Box 6099, T4G 1S7 – 403/227-5591, Fax: 403/227-1230 – *2

JASPER .... Edmonton
Archibald & Edwards, 100A Connaught St., PO Box 1558, T0E 1E0 – 403/852-4501 – *1
Rodger & Ireland, PO Box 130, T0E 1E0 – 403/852-4905,4501, Fax: 403/852-4440 – *2
Smith Gawlinski Parkatti, #204, 416 Connaught Dr., T0E 1E0 – 403/852-2399, Fax: 403/428-6645

KILLAM .... Vegreville
Gaede, Fielding, Syed & Smith, 5011 - 50 St., T0B 2L0 – 403/385-3555

LAC LA BICHE .... Edmonton
Kozina & Gregory, PO Box 1439, T0A 2C0 – 403/623-4818, Fax: 403/623-2933 – *2
Thomas R. Maccagno, 10120 - 101 Ave., PO Box 1270, T0A 2C0 – 403/623-4177, Fax: 403/623-2266
D.L. McCallum, T0A 2C0 – 403/623-2514
Tarrabain & Company, PO Box 1710, T0A 2C0

LACOMBE .... Red Deer
Advani, Rose, Cruickshank & Adair, 5025 - 51 St., PO Box 129, T0C 1S0 – 403/782-3391 – *4
J.A.T. Fredeen, PO Box 1240, T0C 1S0 – 403/782-5210 – *1
Roger C. Holteen, 5015 - 50 Ave., PO Box 639, T0C 1S0 – 403/782-6661 – *1

LEDUC .... Wetaskiwin
Elgert & Neufeld, 5206 - 50 St., PO Box 5290, T9E 6L6 – 403/986-3487 – *2
Jackie & Handerek, 4710 - 50 St., T9E 6W2 – 403/986-5081, Fax: 403/986-8807 – *4
E. Kahlke, PO Box 5236, T9E 6L6 – 403/986-8427, Fax: 403/986-3108 – *1

Karoles Mintz Majeski, Nortec Bldg., #205B, 5904 - 50 St., T9E 6J3 – 403/986-5335
Zalapski & Pahl, 5304 - 50 St., PO Box 3715, T9E 6M4 – 403/986-8428, Fax: 403/986-2552; Email: zap@tnc.com; URL: http://www.tnc.com/zap/ – *4

LETHBRIDGE .... Lethbridge
Robert F. Babki, #250, 220 - 4 Ave. South, T1J 4J7 – 403/320-5300 – *1
Fred D. Burton, 190 Oxford Rd. West, T1K 4V6 – 403/381-6968
A.E. Dahl, #4, 1122 - 3 Ave. South, T1J 0J6 – 403/329-8188
Davidson & Williams, 220 - 3 Ave South, 5th Fl., PO Box 518, T1J 3Z4 – 403/328-1766 – *7
de Walle & McDonald, 323 - 7 St. South., T1J 2G4 – 403/328-8800 – *2
D.B. Hepburn, 118A - 8 St. South, T1J 2J3 – 403/320-5350
Huckvale & Company, 612 - 3 Ave. South, PO Box 1028, T1J 4A2 – 403/328-8856 – *5
Terrence J. Huzil, #9, 402 - 5th Ave. South, T1J 0T5 – 403/320-0222, Fax: 403/327-5630 – *1
Ives & Carleton, Lacidem Bldg., #200, 542 - 7 St. South, PO Box 728, T1J 3Z6 – 403/327-3116 – *1
Jervis & Oishi, 418 Stafford Dr. South, T1J 2L2 – 403/320-1000 – *1
Peter J. Keebler, #407, 740 - 4 Ave. South, T1J 0N9 – 403/329-1444, Fax: 403/320-1844 – *1
Kubara & Ruston, 118 - 8 St. South, T1J 2J3 – 403/320-1180 – *2
R.F. Llewellyn, #103, 1410 Mayor Magrath Dr. South, T1K 2R3 – 403/329-0222
MacLachlan McNab Hembroff, 1003 - 4th Ave. South, T1J 0P7 – 403/329-4966, Fax: 403/327-0927 – *6
Maxwell, Larson & Co., PO Box 1058, T1J 4A2 – 403/329-1411 – *6
Millar, Thiessen & Keith, #302 - 10 St. South, 2nd Fl., PO Box 937, T1J 3Z8 – 403/327-5716, Fax: 403/329-4063 – *4
Milne McCallum & Pritchard, #907, 400 - 4 Ave. South, T1J 4E1 – 403/329-1133, Fax: 403/329-0395 – *3
D.M. Moffatt, #404, 740 - 4 Ave. South, T1J 0N9 – 403/328-7723
Harold N. Moodie, 212 - 5 St. South, 2nd Fl., PO Box 9, T1J 3Y3 – 403/328-5926 – *2
North & Company, Chancery Ct., #600, 220 - 4 St. South., PO Box 219, Stn Main, T1J 3Y5 – 403/328-7781, Fax: 403/320-8958; Toll Free: 1-800-552-8022 – *13
Ludvik L. Pahulje, #217, 740 - 4 Ave. South, T1J 0N9 – 403/327-6747
Peterson & Purvis, 537 - 7th St. South, PO Box 1165, T1J 4A4 – 403/328-9666, Fax: 403/320-1393 – *6
Pocock & Quan, 449 Mayor Magrath Dr., T1J 3L8 – 403/320-6645, Fax: 403/328-6308 – *2
Pollock & Company, PO Box 1386, T1J 4K1 – 403/653-4606 – *2
Pritchard & Stokes, Professional Bldg., #202, 740 - 4 Ave. South, PO Box 127, T1J 3Y3 – 403/328-7728, Fax: 403/328-5589 – *2
Roman Scholdra, PO Box 236, T1J 3Y5 – 403/328-3944 – *1
Shapiro & Company, #200, 427 - 5 St. South., T1J 2B6 – 403/328-9300, Fax: 403/328-9307 – *2
Stringam Denecky, Lethbridge Centre Tower, #900, PO Box 757, T1J 3Z6 – 403/328-5576, Fax: 403/327-1141; Email: lethlaw@agt.net; URL: http://www.agt.net/public.lethlaw/sd.htm – *7
Blaine A. Thacker, #206, 268 - 7 Ave. South, T1J 1N4 – 403/328-9877
Townsend & Malcolm, #202, 714 - 5 Ave. South, T1J 0V1 – 403/329-0001, Fax: 403/329-0868 – *2

LLOYDMINSTER .... Battleford
Bodnar Law Office, 4820 - 47 St., PO Box 2399, T9V 0E8 – 403/825-2101

Kirzinger, Hall & Revering, 4620 - 50 Ave., PO Box 1277, T2V 0W3 – 403/875-4949 – *4
J.A. Macrae, #505, 5116 - 50 St., PO Box 1440, T9V 0M3 – 403/875-5488 – *1
Politeski Milen & Ballegooyen, 5009 - 47 St., PO Box 20, S9V 0X9 – 403/875-2288, Fax: 403/875-3479 – *12

MEDICINE HAT .... Medicine Hat
Biddell, Fisher & Link, 666 - 4 St SE, PO Box 758, T1A 0H4 – 403/527-7735 – *2
Henry Binder, #2, 643 - 2 St. SE, T1A 0C8 – 403/526-1811
G.R. Côté, #209, 1899 Dunmore Rd. SE, T1A 1Z8 – 403/529-1888
Gordon, Smith & Company, 378 - 1 St. SE, PO Box 490, T1A 7G2 – 403/527-5506, Fax: 403/527-0577 – *5
R.W. Jensen, 29 - 8 St. NW, T1A 6N9 – 403/529-5353 – *1
Kolody, Leis & Weise, 675 - 3 St. SE, T1A 0H4 – 403/527-7766 – *3
MacLean, MacDonald, Wiedermann & Pitcher, 525 - 2 St. SE, PO Box 1240, T1A 7G5 – 403/527-3343 – *5
Niblock & Company, 420 Macleod Tr. SE, PO Box 609, T1A 7G5 – 403/526-2806 – *6
Francis A. O'Connell, 546 - 2 St. SE, T1A 0C6 – 403/526-0504
Pritchard, Lerner & Co., Professional Bldg., Bldg Box: 100, #204, 430 - 6th Ave. SE, T1A 7E8 – 403/527-4411, Fax: 403/527-9806 – *9
Rombough & Yarshenko, #202, 132 - 4 Ave. SE, T1A 8B5 – 403/527-3030 – *2
D.G. Schindel, #1, 3295 Dunmore Rd. SE, T1B 3R2 – 403/529-5548, Fax: 403/529-2694 – *1
Sihvon, Carter, Fisher & Berger, 499 - 1st St. SE, T1A 1Z8 – 403/526-2600, Fax: 403/526-3217 – *6
Wahl & Co., #104, 533 - 2 St. SE, PO Box 1446, T1A 7N4 – 403/526-7222 – *2

MILK RIVER ....
North & Company, 125 Main St. NW, T0K 1M0 – 403/647-3662

MORINVILLE .... Edmonton
Allan W. Damer, 10201 - 100 Ave., PO Box 1165, T0G 1P0 – 403/939-2936 – *1
Goldsman & Ritzen, 10018 - 100 Ave., T0G 1P0 – 403/939-5233

NANTON .... Lethbridge/MacLeod
Roddie & McLellan, 2113 - 20 St., PO Box 100, T0L 1R0 – 403/646-2211, Fax: 403/646-3159 – *2

OKOTOKS .... Calgary
Charles A. Dixon, 126 Elizabeth St., PO Box 1169, T0L 1T0 – 403/938-8131 – *1
E.D. Simper, PO Box 1117, T0L 1T0 – 403/938-2101, Fax: 403/938-6020 – *1

OLDS .... Calgary
Ronald B. Carlyle, 5001 - 50 Ave., PO Box 2387, T0M 1P0 – 403/556-7762
Alvin F. Ganser, 4834 - 50 St., PO Box 3207, T0M 1P0 – 403/556-8481, Fax: 403/556-3830
James L. MacInnis, 5037 - 50 St., PO Box 2340, T0M 1P0 – 403/556-8412 – *1
Douglas S. Martinson, 5126 - 46 St., PO Box 1800, T0M 1P0 – 403/556-8955
James B. Wilde, 5126 - 46 St., T0M 1P0 – 403/337-3105

PEACE RIVER .... Peace River
Donald W. Freeland, #255, 9913 - 100 Ave., PO Box 6239, T8S 1S2 – 403/624-2944, Fax: 403/624-4225 – *1
Mann & Ambrose, 9902 - 97 Ave., PO Box 2880, T0H 2X0 – 403/624-4860
Mathieu, Hryniuk, Shynkar & Erickson, 10012 - 101 St., PO Box 6210, T8S 1S2 – 403/624-2565, Fax: 403/624-5766 – *6

* indicates number of lawyers in law firm.

Simpson, Thietke & Associates, 9910 - 97 Ave., PO Box 6778, T8S 1S5 – 403/624-1122,5040, Fax: 403/624-4443 – *2

PICTURE BUTTE .... **Lethbridge/MacLeod**
North & Company, 316 Jamieson Ave., T0K 1W0 – 403/732-4436

PINCHER CREEK .... **MacLeod**
Douglas J. Evans, PO Box 2457, T0K 1W0
G.L. Jasman, 752 Schofield St., PO Box 335, T0K 1W0 – 403/627-2877, Fax: 403/627-4495 – *1
W.M.K. McGurk, 345 Canyon Drive, PO Box 1598, T0K 1W0 – 403/627-3862 – *1
North & Company, 765 Main St., T0K 1W0 – 403/627-4688

PONOKA .... **Wetaskiwin**
Lowden & Bradley, 5034 - 50 Ave., PO Box 1048, T0C 2H0 – 403/783-5571, Fax: 403/783-2130 – *2
Noble & Kidd, 5024 - 51 Ave., PO Box 4278, T4J 1R7 – 403/783-3325, Fax: 403/783-5080 – *2
Richard D. Wyrozub, PO Box 698, T0C 2H0 – 403/783-5521 – *1

PROVOST .... **Vegreville**
Ackroyd, Piasta, Roth & Day, 5101 - 50 St., T0B 3S0

RED DEER .... **Red Deer**
Altvater Law Office, #1, 5000 - 51 Ave., T4N 4H8 – 403/342-1336, Fax: 403/341-4688 – *1
A.B. Armstrong, #302, 4820 Gaetz Ave., T4N 4A4 – 403/347-7701 – *1
G.M. Boris, #202, 4921 - 49 St., T4N 1V2 – 403/340-2222 – *1
Glen D. Capeling, #307, 4822 - 50 St., T4N 1X4
Norman J. Cavanagh, #308, 4808 Ross St., T4N 1X5 – 403/341-5404
Chapman Riebeek, Professional Bldg., #208, 4808 Ross St., T4N 1X5 – 403/346-6603, Fax: 403/340-1280 – *8
Duhamel Manning Feehan Warrender Glass, 5233 - 49 Ave., 2nd Fl., T4N 6G5 – 403/343-0812, Fax: 403/340-3545 – *8
Fielding & Dixon, 4811 - 48 St., 2nd Fl., T4N 1S6 – 403/343-1160 – *2
Flanagan, Sully & Surkan, Park Pl., #200, 4825 - 47 St., T4N 1R3 – 403/342-7711 – *4
C.E. Forgues, 4604 - 49 St., PO Box 1214, T4N 6S6 – 403/342-7044
Gerig Hamilton Neeland Handel, #501, 4901 - 48 St., T4N 6M4 – 403/343-2444, Fax: 403/343-6522 – *5
Brian E. Grice, #150, 4919 - 59 St., T4N 6C9 – 403/342-2544, Fax: 403/347-9895
Don A. Gross, #274, 4919 - 59 St., T4N 6C9 – 403/343-3715 – *1
J.N. Hawthorne, #306, 4805 - 48 St., T4N 1S6 – 403/343-2121, Fax: 403/342-2550 – *1
M.R. Hetherington, #300, 4808 Ross St., T4N 1S8 – 403/346-4199
Johnston, Ming, Manning, Royal Bank Bldg., 4943 - 50 St., 3rd & 4th Fl., T4N 1Y1 – 403/346-5591, Fax: 403/346-5599 – *10
Beverly Keeshing, 111 Piper Dr., T4P 1L5 – 403/343-0842, Fax: 403/341-3612
Lee & Short, Parkland Sq., #402, 4901 - 48 St., T4N 6M4 – 403/343-1212 – *4
N.W. Lockerby, #202, 4921 - 49 St., T4N 1V2 – 403/343-8660 – *1
Harold Loney, #507, 4808 Ross St., T4N 1X5 – 403/343-0122, Fax: 403/343-2623 – *2
Brian S. MacNairn, Woodward Place, #201, 5008 Ross St., T4N 1Y3 – 403/347-2700
Pamela S. MacNaughton, 4811 - 48 Ave., PO Box 279, T4N 5E8 – 403/340-1600
P.E.B. MacSween, 4824 - 51 St., T4N 2A5 – 403/342-5595, Fax: 403/341-3130 – *1
McIntosh & Schollie, #206, 4808 Ross St., T4N 1X5 – 403/340-8877, Fax: 403/347-3833 – *2

E.F. Murphy, Q.C., 5008 - 50 St., 2nd Fl., T4N 1Y4 – 403/343-8824
Robert M. Oxman, #3, 4909 - 48 St., 2nd Fl., T4N 1S8 – 403/346-5500 – *1
Roxanne V. Prior, #201, 4909 - 50 Ave., T4N 4A7 – 403/340-0400
Klaus G. Ruschin, #274, 4919 - 59 St., T4N 6C9 – 403/340-3737 – *1
Schnell, MacSween & Hardy, #601, 4808 Ross St., T4N 1X5 – 403/342-7400 – *5
Siewert Bothwell, Central Block, #204, 5000 - 50 Ave., T4N 6C2 – 403/346-1123, Fax: 403/346-1198 – *2
Sisson Warren Sinclair, First Red Deer Pl., #600, 4911 - 51 St., T4N 6V4 – 403/343-3320, Fax: 403/343-6069; Email: sws@ccinet.ab.ca – *11
Vanden Brink & Elgersma, #500, 4808 Ross St., T4N 1X5 – 403/343-6664, Fax: 403/346-9292; Email: benbrink@agt.net – *2

REDWATER .... **Edmonton**
D.L. McCallum, PO Box 892, T0A 2W0 – 403/942-3040, Fax: 403/942-2003 – *1
Smith Gawlinski Parkatti, 4918 - 49 St., T0A 2W0 – 403/942-3331, Fax: 403/428-6645

RIMBEY .... **Wetaskiwin**
Flanagan, Sully & Surkan, 5059 - 50 Ave., T0C 2J0 – 403/843-2676
David R. Pfau, PO Box 1009, T0C 2J0 – 403/843-2296 – *1

ROCKY MOUNTAIN HOUSE .... **Red Deer**
Dunsford & Scott, 4920 - 51 Ave., PO Box 370, T0M 1T0 – 403/845-7112, Fax: 403/845-4670 – *3
P.A. Jenson, Westco Bldg., 5039 - 45 St., PO Box 1108, T0M 1T0 – 403/845-2828, Fax: 403/845-4630 – *1
Woollard Hopkins & Company, 5133 - 49 St., PO Box 700, T0M 1T0 – 403/845-2545, Fax: 403/845-2285 – *2

SHERWOOD PARK .... **Edmonton**
W.D. Abercrombie, Lower Concourse, #17, 2016 Sherwood Dr., T8A 3X3 – 403/467-5579, Fax: 403/467-8155 – *1
Ahlstrom Wright, #200, 80 Chippewa Rd., T8A 3Y1 – 403/464-7477 – *4
V.M. Anthonysamy, 1 Newport Dr., PO Box 3141, T8A 5H1 – 403/464-5805 – *1
Ashton & Company, #201, 2 Athabascan Ave., T8A 4E3 – 403/467-5534 – *2
Peter L. Court, #8, 140 Athabascan Ave., T8A 4E3 – 403/464-3756, Fax: 403/467-0927
Alexander Hogan, 7 Yew Ct., T8A 1H8
Stanley H. King, 957 Ordze Rd., T8A 4L7 – 403/449-1404 – *1
Wayne Ledrew, #10, 140 Athabascan Ave., T8A 4E3 – 403/467-3014, Fax: 403/467-0927 – *1
Nigro, McPike, #201, 912 Ash St., T8A 2G1 – 403/464-4666, Fax: 403/467-0720 – *2
Spratlin Tonnellier, 363 Sioux Rd., T8A 4H2 – 403/464-5404 – *2
Maureen L. Towns, 78 Highland Way, T8A 2A7 – 403/467-7947

SLAVE LAKE .... **Peace River**
Wayne D. Hatt, #301, 101 Main St. South, T0G 2A0
Holtby, Anderson, Dawson & Knisely, 301 Lakeland Centre, P5J 3G2 – 403/849-2443
Philip Lokken, 401 - 3 Ave. NE, T0G 2A2 – 403/849-5540, Fax: 403/849-5499 – *1
Larry W. Schimpf, PO Box 818, T0G 2A0 – 403/849-3547 – *1
Catherine M. Twinn, Sawridge Admin. Bldg., 2nd Fl., Caribou Trail, PO Box 1460, T0G 2A0 – 403/849-4319 – *1

SPRUCE GROVE .... **Edmonton**
Heil & Robinson, Cumbria Centre, #201, 93 McLeod Ave., T7X 2Z9 – 403/962-3505, Fax: 403/962-9329 – *2

ST. ALBERT .... **Edmonton**
Campbell & Company, #118, 7 St. Anne St., T8N 2X4 – 403/459-2220 – *3
Goldsman & Ritzen, Grandin Park Tower, #609, 22 Sir Winston Churchill Ave., T8N 1B4 – 403/458-0500, Fax: 403/459-2472 – *4
M.C. Good, #201, 7 Perron St., T8N 1E3 – 403/459-1284
David A. Haas, Grandin Park Tower, Bldg Box: 505, 22 Sir Winston Churchill Sq., T8N 1B4 – 403/459-6914, Fax: 403/459-0875 – *1
Alexander S. Romanchuk, #322, 7 St. Anne St., T8N 2X4 – 403/459-8420 – *1
Weary & Company, 1500 Tudor Glen Market, T8N 3V4 – 403/459-5596 – *3

ST. PAUL .... **Edmonton**
L.E. Langager Q.C., 4705 - 50 Ave., PO Box 2350, T0A 3A0 – 403/645-3366, Fax: 403/645-5185; Email: lelpc@cgt.net – *1
Ouellette & Hajduk, 4713 - 50 St., PO Box 2228, T0A 3A0 – 403/645-5202, Fax: 403/645-6507 – *4

STANDOFF .... **Calgary**
E.J. Creighton, PO Box 270, T0L 1Y0 – 403/737-3763
Walsh Wilkins, PO Box 270, T0L 1Y0 – 403/737-8050, Fax: 403/264-9400

STETTLER .... **Red Deer**
D.C. Ellis, #1, 5002 - 51 Ave., T0C 2L0 – 403/742-4440
Grant, Hunter & Reesor, 4910 - 51 St., PO Box 430, T0C 2L0 – 403/742-4436, Fax: 403/742-1455 – *3
J.M. Grindley, PO Box 1785, T0C 2L0 – 403/742-4401, Fax: 403/742-1270 – *1
Sloan Landman & Anderson, 4819 - 51 St., PO Box 1630, T0C 2L0 – 403/742-3411, Fax: 403/742-1246 – *3

STONY PLAIN .... **Edmonton**
Birdsell Grant Gardner, #102, 5300 - 50 St., T7Z 1T8 – 403/963-8181, Fax: 403/963-9618 – *4
Braul Gaffney, PO Box 1624, T0E 2G0 – 403/963-2360 – *1
Joly & McAllister, Park House, Bldg Box: 203, #203, 50318 - 48 St., PO Box 927, T0E 2G0 – 403/963-2245, Fax: 403/963-2145 – *3

STRATHMORE .... **Calgary**
Getz & Associates, 225D Wheatland Trail, PO Box 2370, T1P 1K3 – 403/934-2500, Fax: 403/934-2794 – *2
R.E.J. Jarvis, PO Box 1479, T0J 3H0 – 403/934-5000

SYLVAN LAKE .... **Red Deer**
Burchak & Flanagan, 5043 - 50A St., PO Box 396, T0M 1Z0 – 403/887-5441 – *3
Chapman Riebeek, 5020 - 50A St., T0M 1Z0 – 403/887-2024, Fax: 403/887-2036
Shaun C. Langin, #4, 5004 - 46 St., PO Box 29, T4S 1C2 – 403/887-2233, Fax: 403/887-4646

TABER .... **Lethbridge**
Baldry Sugden, 5401 - 50 Ave., T1G 1V2 – 403/223-3585, Fax: 403/223-1732 – *2
E.R. Hirch, 5302 - 48 Ave., PO Box 2107, T0K 2G0 – 403/223-1970, Fax: 403/223-4881
North & Company, 4822 - 53 St., T0K 2G0 – 403/223-4015
Stringam Denecky, 5216 - 48 Ave., PO Box 757, T1J 3Z6 – 403/223-2550, Fax: 403/327-1141

THREE HILLS .... Drumheller
Tainsh Howard, 205 Main St., PO Box 1234, T0M 2A0 – 403/443-2200, Fax: 403/443-2025; Email: tainhow@kneehill.com – *2

TOFIELD .... Vegreville
Braul Gaffney, PO Box 299, T0B 4J0 – 403/662-3143, Fax: 403/662-3423
Nancy A. Buchko, PO Box 549, T0B 4J0 – 403/662-3293, Fax: 403/662-4902

TROCHU .... Calgary
F.N. Vanderkley, 314 St. John St., PO Box 640, T0M 2C0 – 403/442-2395

TURNER VALLEY .... Calgary
D.L. McKillop, PO Box 570, T0L 2A0 – 403/933-4378 – *1
Mootoo & Lambert, #2, 118 Main St., PO Box 501, T0L 2A0 – 403/933-3255, Fax: 403/230-2820 – *1

VALLEYVIEW .... Grande Prairie
Dobko Innes & Hougestol, 5007 - 50 Ave., PO Box 1588, T0H 3N0 – 403/524-5535, Fax: 403/524-3955 – *3

VEGREVILLE .... Vegreville
Duncan & Craig, 4925 - 50 St., PO Box 700, T9C 1R7 – 403/632-2877, Fax: 403/632-2898
D.D. Himsl, PO Box 1838, T0B 4L0 – 403/632-6301 – *1
M.W. Kawulych, PO Box 989, T0B 4L0 – 403/632-2944 – *1
Kuzyk & Bombak, Bldg Box: 929, #301, 5038 - 50 Ave., T0B 4L0 – 403/632-4522 – *2
R.M. Semeniuk, 5341 - 50 Ave., PO Box 1796, T0B 4L0 – 403/632-4300
L.M. Starko, PO Box 1178, T9C 1S3 – 403/632-3551 – *1
D.C. Weetman, 5004 - 50 Ave., PO Box 445, T0B 4L0 – 403/632-6899 – *1

VERMILION .... Vegreville
Reynolds & Flemke, #11, 5125 - 50 Ave., T9X 1A8 – 403/853-5339, Fax: 403/853-4200 – *2
Wheat Law Office, 5042 - 49 Ave., T9X 1B7 – 403/853-4707, Fax: 403/853-4499 – *2

VIKING .... Vegreville
J.D. Hunter, PO Box 110, T0B 4N0 – 403/336-3143 – *1

VULCAN .... Calgary
Roy W. Elander, 115 - 2 Ave. North, PO Box 479, T0L 2B0 – 403/485-2039, Fax: 403/485-6043 – *1
North & Company, 104 Center St. East, T0L 2B0 – 403/485-2070

WAINWRIGHT .... Vegreville
Rodnunsky & Marchant, 1032 - 1 Ave., PO Box 1560, T0B 4P0 – 403/842-3396, Fax: 403/842-6104 – *2
P. Van Winssen, PO Box 1325, T0B 4P0 – 403/842-5140 – *1

WARNER .... Lethbridge/MacLeod
North & Company, 304 - 2nd St., T0K 2L0 – 403/642-3644

WESTLOCK .... Edmonton
Gerlach Barlow, 10030 - 106 St., PO Box 326, T0G 2L0 – 403/349-3321 – *2
Logan & Lennon, 9936 - 107 St., PO Box 220, T0G 2L0 – 403/349-4426 – *2
W.V. Stilwell, 10030 - 106 St., PO Box 100, T0G 2L0 – 403/349-4448 – *1
Tims & Company, 9531 - 107 St., PO Box 490, T0G 2L0 – 403/349-5366, Fax: 403/349-6510 – *2

WETASKIWIN .... Wetaskiwin
Lorne P. Kroetch, 100 Northwood Cres., T9A 3L4

* indicates number of lawyers in law firm.

MacDonald Street Law Office, 4408 - 51 St., T9A 1K5 – 403/352-0369 – *1
Dennis W. Pike, PO Box 7050, T9A 2Y9 – 403/352-3305
Sirrs Deckert Allen Cymbaluk, 5201 - 51 Ave., PO Box 6060, T9A 2E8 – 403/352-3301, Fax: 403/352-5976; Email: sirrsdec@ccinet.ab.ca – *4
Sockett & Associates, #100, 5108 - 50 Ave., T9A 0S6 – 403/352-6691 – *2
Vickerson & Hankinson, 5111 - 50 Ave., PO Box 6600, T9A 0S6 – 403/352-3393 – *2
George G. Watson, 5008B - 51 Ave., PO Box 6716, T9A 2G4 – 403/352-1771, Fax: 403/352-8546 – *1

WHITECOURT .... Edmonton
Durocher Simpson, 4907 - 52 Ave., PO Box 685, T7S 1N7 – 403/778-3699, Fax: 403/778-6666
Kenney & Pinchbeck, 5011 - 51 Ave., PO Box 2039, T7S 1P7 – 403/778-6644, Fax: 403/778-4199
Roderick W. Koski, 5032 - 51 Ave., PO Box 960, T7S 1N9 – 403/778-2243, Fax: 403/778-3591 – *1
McConnell & Company, 5115 Highway St., PO Box 1795, T0E 2L0 – 403/778-4945 – *2

WINTERBURN .... Edmonton
Eileen Powless, PO Box 100, RR#1, Site 2, T0E 2N0 – 403/470-3535, Fax: 403/470-5751
Sharon Venne, Site 2, RR#1, PO Box 100, T0E 2N0 – 403/470-3535, Fax: 403/470-3380

BRITISH COLUMBIA

100 MILE HOUSE .... Cariboo
Johann Erickson, PO Box 1690, V0K 2E0 – 250/395-3831, Fax: 250/395-3940 – *1
Messner & Foster, PO Box 819, V0K 2E0 – 250/395-3881, Fax: 250/345-2644 – *2

ABBOTSFORD .... Westminster
Baker, Newby & Company, #200, 2955 Gladwin Rd., V2S 6W8 – 604/852-3646, Fax: 604/852-5194; Toll Free: 1-800-533-0990
Gordon J. Dykstra, #204, 2306 McCallum Rd., V2S 3P4 – 604/853-4793 – *1
Eric J. Janzen, #2, 32056 South Fraser Way, V2T 1V7 – 604/853-6424, Fax: 604/853-9601 – *1
MacAdams Law Firm, #205, 2955 Gladwin Rd., V2S 6W8 – 604/850-1675, Fax: 604/850-1937 – *2
Matsqui-Abbotsford Community Legal Services, #100, 2955 Gladwin Rd., V2S 6W8 – 604/859-2755, Fax: 604/853-3059
McLachlan Brown Anderson Holmes, #300A, 32555 Simon Ave., V2T 4Y5 – 604/857-1693, Fax: 604/859-8838
Robertson, Downe & Mullally, #301, 33695 South Fraser Way, V2S 2C1 – 604/853-0774; 856-3627 (Vancouver), Fax: 604/852-3829 – *12
Lloyd H. Wilson, 2644 Montrose Ave., V2S 3T6 – 604/853-3355, Fax: 604/853-2644 – *2

ASHCROFT .... Yale
Morelli, Chertkow, 401 Railway Ave., V0K 1A0 – 250/453-2320, Fax: 250/453-2622; Email: mclawyer@mail.netshop.net

BARRIERE .... Cariboo
Mair Jensen Blair, #3, 621 Barriere Town Rd., PO Box 298, V0E 1E0 – 604/272-5654

BRENTWOOD BAY .... Vancouver Island
Stevenson Rachue Jenko, 7103 West Saanich Rd., PO Box 177, V0S 1A0 – 250/652-5151, Fax: 250/652-9687

BURNABY .... Westminster
Becker, Mathers, Rogers Dantel Tower, Eaton Centre, #2148, 4710 Kingsway, V5H 4M2 – 604/438-8234, Fax: 604/438-1497 – *8
C.H. Bergen, #200, 5000 Kingsway, V5H 2E4 – 604/430-4244, Fax: 604/430-4210 – *1
W.E. Bergmann, 4550 East Hastings St., V5C 2K4 – 604/298-8211, Fax: 604/298-8216 – *1
Carlos A. Brito, #303, 4501 North Rd., V3N 4R7 – 604/444-4747, Fax: 604/444-4757 – *1
Cobbett & Cotton, 4259 East Hastings St., V5C 2J5 – 604/299-6251, Fax: 604/299-6627 – *2
Doig, Baily, McLean, Greenbank & Murdoch, 7297 Kingsway, V5E 1G6 – 604/521-6611 – *10
Annabelle Donovan, 4853 East Hastings St., V5C 2L1 – 604/291-8211, Fax: 604/291-2676 – *1
Dorman Baird Bernardino Baker & Baker, #2030, 4710 Kingsway, V5H 4M2 – 604/430-3421, Fax: 604/430-0636 – *6
DuMoulin & Boskovich, Metro-Pointe Bldg., #205, 4603 Kingsway, V5H 4M4 – 604/435-0877, Fax: 604/435-5480 – *2
Edwards, Edwards, Edwards & Maskall, #510, 5021 Kingsway, V5H 4A5 – 604/433-2445, Fax: 604/433-8209 – *5
Robin Fischer, #180, 4664 Lougheed Hwy., V5C 5T5 – *1
James K. Fraser Law Corporation, #200, 5000 Kingsway, V5H 2E4 – 604/433-0010, Fax: 604/435-0269 – *1
Harris, Threlfall, O'Neill, 4729 East Hastings St., V5C 2K8 – 604/294-8311, Fax: 604/294-5278 – *4
Hawthorne, Piggott, Emerson & Petronio, #208, 1899 Willingdon Ave., V5C 5T1 – 604/299-8371, Fax: 604/299-1523 – *4
Hean Wylie Peach DeStefanis, #1501, 4330 Kingsway, V5H 4H9 – 604/434-5784, Fax: 604/434-7707 – *11
Sue M. Kelly, #124A, 4664 Lougheed Hwy., V5C 5T5 – 604/293-4110, Fax: 604/293-1372 – *1
Kerfoot, Cameron & Company, #314, 9600 Cameron St., V3J 7N3 – 604/421-7144, Fax: 604/421-2912 – *7
Philip T. Lau, #402, 3701 East Hastings St., V5C 2H6 – 604/293-1231, Fax: 604/293-1232 – *1
Martin, MacLeod, #1830, 4720 Kingsway, V5H 4N2 – 604/430-8444, Fax: 604/430-1164 – *2
F.T.D. McGovern, #6, 4857 Kingsway, V5H 2C8 – 604/433-0939, Fax: 604/433-9374 – *1
John W. Motiuk, #201, 6125 Sussex Ave., V5H 4G1 – 604/437-8684, Fax: 604/437-9874 – *1
Ogilvie Law Offices, #201, 3975 North Rd., V3J 1S2 – 604/421-1622, Fax: 604/421-8197 – *1
Pihl & Company, #205, 5481 Kingsway, V5H 2G1 – 604/437-3529, Fax: 604/437-8837 – *2
B.C.E. Russell, 220 - 4411 Hastings East, V5C 2K1 – 604/298-1038, Fax: 604/298-1037 – *1
Saucier & Company, 4750 Kingsway, V5H 2C2 – 604/434-7200, Fax: 604/432-9803 – *2
Smith & Company, #148, 4664 Lougheed Hwy., V5C 5T5 – 604/473-9330, Fax: 604/473-9334 – *3
Starr & Company, #315, 5000 Kingsway, V5H 2E4 – 604/435-5588, Fax: 604/430-2912 – *3
L.P. Stewart, #206, 5050 Kingsway, V5H 4H2 – 604/435-0010, Fax: 604/435-0758 – *1
Joseph W. Tarnowski, #8, 9500 Erickson St., V3J 1M8 – 604/444-4949 – *1
Donald M. Tenant, #515, 4710 Kingsway, V5H 4M2 – 604/434-2512, Fax: 604/432-9556 – *1
Audrey H. Vandervelden, #4, 6344 Kingsway, V5E 1C5 – 604/433-8706, Fax: 604/435-5915 – *1
Maureen J. Wesley, 4270 McGill St., V5C 1M9 – 604/298-6555, Fax: 604/298-6555 – *1
Wood, Wong, Wexler & Maerov, #210, 4603 Kingsway, V5H 4M4 – 604/436-3315, Fax: 604/436-3302 – *1

CACHE CREEK .... Yale
Mair Jensen Blair, #6, 1054 South Trans Canada Hwy., V0K 1H0 – 250/457-9641

Canadian Almanac & Directory 1997

DIRECTORY OF LAW FIRMS – BRITISH COLUMBIA

CAMPBELL RIVER .... **Vancouver Island**
John F. Grant & Associates, 964 Island Highway, V9W 2C5 – 250/287-8855, Fax: 250/286-6227 – *1
McVea, Shook, Wickham & Bishop, 906 Island Hwy., V9W 2C3 – 250/287-8355, Fax: 250/287-8112 – *8
B. Ettie O'Connell, 2200 Shetland Rd., V9W 3Y5 – 250/287-3844 – *1
Sinnott, Stamp & Associates, 480 - 10 Ave., V9W 4E3 – 250/287-7185 – *2
Tees Lloyd Clare & Kiddle, Royal Court Bldg., #200, 1260 Island Highway, V9W 2C8 – 250/287-7755, Fax: 250/287-3999 – *7

CASTLEGAR .... **West Kootenay**
Moran & Company, 1233 - 3rd St., V1N 1Z6 – 250/365-7741, Fax: 250/365-2620 – *4
Polonicoff, Jones & Perehudoff, 1115 - 3 St., V1N 2A1 – 250/365-3343, Fax: 250/365-6307 – *3
Spilker, Bridgeman, 210 Columbia Ave., V1N 1G7 – 250/365-2183, Fax: 250/365-8111 – *2
Wyllie & Okros, #100, 1444 Columbia Avve., V1N 3K3 – 250/365-8451

CHASE .... **Yale**
Mair Jensen Blair, 560 Shuswap., V0E 1M0 – 250/679-3121, Fax: 250/374-6992 – *1

CHILLIWACK .... **Westminster**
Baker, Newby & Company, 9259 Main St., PO Box 390, V2P 6K2 – 604/792-1376, Fax: 604/792-8711; Toll Free: 1-800-881-3646; Email: info@bakernewby.com; URL: http://www.bakernewby.com – *21
Patten, MacDonald & Crabtree, PO Box 379, V1P 6J4 – 604/795-9188, Fax: 604/795-6340 – *4
Point & Shirley, #3, 9360 Mill St., V2P 4N2 – 604/792-3640, Fax: 604/792-0663 – *2
Rempel, Kaye, Toews & Grist, 9202 Young St., PO Box 372, V2P 6J4 – 604/792-1977, Fax: 604/792-7077 – *4
Thome, Jespersen, Hansford, #201, 45820 Wellington Ave., V2P 2C9 – 604/792-9100, Fax: 604/792-1331 – *5

CLAYBURN .... **Westminster**
Bryan J. Haber, 34810 Clayburn Rd, V0X 1E0 – 604/852-8177, Fax: 604/852-1464

CLEARBROOK .... **Westminster**
Cope Martyn, #210, 32112 South Fraser Way, V2T 1W4 – 604/859-1388 – *4
Fast & Welwood, #203, 31943 South Fraser Way, V2T 1V5 – 604/850-6640, 6616, Fax: 604/850-6616 – *4
Brian Juriloff, 2642B Cedar Park Pl., V2T 3S5 – 604/853-9268, Fax: 604/853-2226 – *1
Kuzminski & Haraldsen, 2890 Garden St., V2T 4W7 – 604/853-5401 – *3
Linley, Duignan & Company, 2548 Clearbrook Rd, PO Box 2040, V1T 3T8 – 604/859-7134 – *7
Viba Panchmatia, 32086 South Fraser Way, V2T 1V7 – 604/853-8199, Fax: 604/853-3233 – *1

CLEARWATER .... **Cariboo**
Mair Jensen Blair, 74 Young, V0E 1N0 – 250/674-2255

COBBLE HILL .... **Vancouver Island**
George E. Asp, 896 Chapman, RR#2, V0R 1L0 – 250/748-6315, Fax: 250/748-2812

COQUITLAM .... **Westminster**
Antifaev & Associates, #221, 3030 Lincoln Ave., V3B 6B4 – 604/464-6822, Fax: 604/464-7335 – *4
Burke Tomchenko, #258, 3020 Lincoln Ave., V3B 6B4 – 604/942-1166 – *5
Feller, Drysdale, #211, 1015 Austin Ave., V3K 3N9 – 604/939-7584, Fax: 604/939-8321 – *9
Goddard & Company, #302, 566 Lougheed Hwy., V3K 3S3 – 604/937-7791, Fax: 604/937-3340 – *1

R. Larry Nixon, #260, 1140 Austin Ave., V3K 3P5 – 604/931-4555, Fax: 604/931-7465 – *1
Spraggs & Company, #202, 1030 Westwood St., V3C 4L4 – 604/464-3333, Fax: 604/464-4335 – *1
Taylor Bardal & Dorchester, #2, 1111 Austin Ave., V3K 3P4 – 604/931-3477, Fax: 604/931-1277 – *4
Dave R. Way, #302, 566 Lougheed Hwy., V3K 3S3 – 604/937-7791, Fax: 604/937-3340 – *1
Zipp & Company, 820 Henderson Ave., V3K 1P2 – 604/936-7743 – *2

COURTENAY .... **Vancouver Island**
Gibson & Kelly, 505 - 5 St., V9N 1K2 – 250/334-2416, Fax: 250/334-3198 – *4
H. Huibers, 917 Fitzgerald Ave., V9N 2R6 – 250/334-3108, Fax: 250/334-0621 – *1
C.H.L. Morris, 949 Fitzgerald Ave., V9N 2R6 – 250/338-5311, Fax: 250/338-1818 – *1
Muir, Sinclare, #200, 575 - 10 St., V9N 1P9 – 250/338-6744, Fax: 250/334-3325 – *2
Olstead & Holekamp, 512 - 4th St., V9N 1H2 – 250/338-6747, Fax: 250/338-1833 – *4
Swift Datoo & Company, #201, 467 Cumberland Rd., V9N 2C5 – 250/334-4461, Fax: 250/334-2335 – *7

CRANBROOK .... **East Kootenay**
R.G. Buddenhagen, #205, 14A - 13 Ave. South, V1C 2V3 – 250/426-3377, Fax: 250/426-3357 – *1
Graham Apps & Company, 122 - 11 Ave. South, V1C 2P2 – 250/426-2277, Fax: 250/426-1903 – *3
Hislop & Company, 915B Baker St., PO Box 160, V1C 4H7 – 250/426-6211, Fax: 250/426-3338 – *2
Robert Mayne & Company, 30 - 11 Ave. South, V1C 2P1 – 250/489-2585
Rella Docking & Paolini, #6, 10 Ave. South, 2nd Fl., V1C 2M8 – 250/426-8981, Fax: 250/426-8987 – *3
Robertson & Company, #100, 125 - 10 Ave. South, V1C 2N1 – 250/489-4346, Fax: 250/489-1899 – *1
Steidl Kambeitz & Donald, 828D Baker St., V1C 1A2 – 250/426-7211, Fax: 250/426-6100 – *3

CRESTON .... **West Kootenay**
Miller, Dan & Associates, PO Box 1429, V0B 1G0 – 250/428-2208, Fax: 250/428-2200 – *1

DAWSON CREEK .... **Cariboo**
Gibb & Syal, #201, 10312 - 12 St., PO Box 510, V1G 4H5 – 250/782-8556, Fax: 250/782-5239 – *3
Mitchell, Schuller & Dellow, #2, 933 - 103 Ave., V1G 2G4 – 250/782-8155, Fax: 250/782-4525 – *4
Plenert Higson, #201, 1136 - 103 Ave., V1G 2G7 – 250/782-9134, Fax: 250/782-9135 – *2
Valair & Company, 10206 - 10 St., V1G 3T4 – 250/782-3347 – *2

DELTA .... **Vancouver**
James Broad, 9349 Scott Rd., V4C 6R8 – 604/585-3422, Fax: 604/585-3613 – *1
Buckley & Buckley, 9453 - 120 St., V4C 6S2 – 604/588-0431 – *4
Harris, Stuart & Tomyn, 7929 - 120 St., V3W 3N6 – 604/591-1166, Fax: 604/591-8722 – *6
Kaminsky & Company, #202, 8435 - 120 St., V4C 6R2 – 604/591-7877, Fax: 604/591-1978 – *5
Kane, Shannon & Weiler, #301, 6935 - 120 St., V4E 2A8 – 604/591-7321, Fax: 604/591-7149 – *12
Terry D. Millichamp, #2, 1323 - 56 St., V4L 2A6 – 604/943-7401, Fax: 604/943-7402 – *1
Ulf K. Ottho, 4873 Delta St., V4K 2T9 – 604/946-1175, Fax: 604/946-8818 – *4
R.E. Piters, #110, 4977 Trennant St., V4K 2K5 – 604/946-0466, Fax: 604/946-0467 – *2
Simpson & Company, 7329 - 120 St., V4C 6P5 – 604/591-8885, Fax: 604/591-9972 – *1
P.A. Smith, 151 - 67 St., V4L 1M2 – 604/943-0205, Fax: 604/943-6089 – *1
Souch Severide, #210, 4882 Delta St., V4K 2T8 – 604/946-1249 – *2

G.G. Walters, #405, 11861 - 88 Ave., V4C 3C6 – 604/596-3300, Fax: 604/596-9111 – *1

DENMAN ISLAND .... **Vancouver Island**
Sally Campbell, 1536 Northwest Rd., PO Box 52, V0R 1T0 – 250/335-2505, Fax: 250/335-2221; Email: salal@comox.island.net – *1

DUNCAN .... **Vancouver Island**
Coleman LaCroix Fraser & Whittome, #201, 58 Station St., V9L 1M4 – 250/748-1013, Fax: 250/748-2733 – *5
Jean E. Hamilton, #209, 225 Canada Ave., V9L 1T6 – 250/748-5858, Fax: 250/748-6060 – *1
MacCarthy Ridgway, 170 Craig St., V9L 1W1 – 250/746-7121, Fax: 250/746-4070 – *6
MacIsaac & Company, Top Floor, 190 Ingram St., V9L 1P1 – 250/746-4422, Fax: 250/746-1811 – *1
Sandra McEwan, 5784 Alderlea St., PO Box 482, V9L 3X8 – 250/748-4433
Peter M. Moir, PO Box 951, V9L 3Y2 – 250/746-7114, Fax: 250/746-7115 – *1
Molnar, Desjardins & Associates, Financial Centre, #206, 435 Trunk Rd., V9L 2P5 – 250/746-5253, Fax: 250/746-1511; Email: gmolnar@island.net.ca – *3
Robert Morales, PO Box 356, V9L 3X5 – 250/748-5233
Richard J.P. Nesbitt, #2, 271 Ingram St., V9L 1P3 – 250/748-1464, Fax: 250/748-4819 – *1
Whittome & Whittome, #201, 58 Station St., V9L 1M4 – 250/748-3151 – *2

ENDERBY .... **Okanagan**
Andrew Kern, 604 Cliff St., V0E 0V0 – 250/838-9666 – *1

FERNIE .... **East Kootenay**
R.W. Bentley, PO Box 2038, V0B 1M0 – 250/423-9241, Fax: 250/423-9241 – *1
Majic, Leffler & Purdy, PO Box 369, V0B 1M0 – 250/423-4497 – *3

FORT ST. JAMES .... **Cariboo**
Hope Heinrich, 122 Stuart St., V0J 1P0 – *1

FORT ST. JOHN .... **Cariboo**
Callison & Company, 10419 - 100 St., V1J 3Z3 – 250/785-8033, Fax: 250/785-4346 – *2
Lewis Daley Strandberg, 10740 - 100 St., V1J 3Z6 – 250/785-6961, Fax: 250/785-6967 – *4
Pomeroy & Harrison, 9947 - 100 Ave., V1J 1Y4 – 250/785-6688, Fax: 250/785-6465 – *2
Walsh Cleaveley Fus, 9940 - 104 Ave., V1J 2K3 – 250/785-4477, Fax: 250/785-1467 – *3

GANGES .... **Vancouver Island**
I.H. Clement, PO Box 248, V0S 1E0 – 250/537-5505, Fax: 250/655-3512 – *1
P.B. Joyce, PO Box 780, V0S 1E0 – 604/669-3644, Fax: 604/669-3634 – *1
McKimm & Lott, Ganges Centre, PO Box 70, V0S 1E0 – 250/537-9951, Fax: 250/537-4341

GOLD RIVER .... **Comox**
Lloyd G. Roberts, PO Box 154, V0P 1G0 – 250/283-7431 – *1

GOLDEN .... **East Kootenay**
C. Davis & Company, 510 - 9 Ave. North, PO Box 989, V0A 1H0 – 250/344-2241, Fax: 250/344-6118 – *2
Ewan & McKenzie, PO Box 429, V0A 1H0 – 250/344-5258, Fax: 250/344-7374 – *2

GRAND FORKS .... **West Kootenay**
Ronald C.E. Mellett, PO Box 1870, V0H 1H0 – 250/442-5599, Fax: 250/442-8466 – *1
Somerville & Company, 135 Market Ave., PO Box 1016, V0H 1H0 – 250/442-2105, Fax: 250/442-5262 – *1

Canadian Almanac & Directory 1997

INVERMERE — East Kootenay

W.J. MacDonald, PO Box 2400, V0A 1K0 – 250/342-6921, Fax: 250/342-3237 – *1
Randall K. McRoberts, 613 - 12 St., PO Box 1049, V0A 1K0 – 250/342-6975, Fax: 250/342-6299 – *1

KAMLOOPS — Yale

Peter Allik-Petersenn, #205, 141 Victoria St., V2C 1Z5 – 250/828-9545, Fax: 250/828-1297 – *1
P.R. Bianco, 1023 Schubert Dr., V2B 2G6 – 250/376-9911, Fax: 250/372-1514 – *1
Coutlee & Company, 101 - 310 Nicola St., V2C 2P5 – 250/372-9922, Fax: 250/372-1114 – *3
Elaine Dixon, #204, 655 Victoria St., V2C 2B3 – 250/828-6662, Fax: 250/828-1156 – *1
Fulton & Company, 248 - 2nd Ave., V2C 2C9 – 250/372-5542, Fax: 250/851-2300; Email: fultonco@netshop.net – *17
J.G. Gnitt, #2, 703 St. Paul St., V2C 2K3 – 250/374-3156 – *1
D.J. Goar, #440, 175 - 2 Ave., V2C 5W1 – 250/374-4627, Fax: 250/374-0035 – *1
Horne Marr Zak, #600, 175 - 2 Ave., V2C 5W1 – 250/372-1221, Fax: 250/372-8339 – *5
Jensen, Mitchell & Co., Old Firehall #1, #300, 125 - 4 Ave. SW, V2C 3N3 – 250/372-8811, Fax: 250/828-6697 – *5
Vincent M. Kong, 408 Victoria St., V2C 2A7 – 250/828-0081, Fax: 250/828-1038 – *1
J. Kurta, #400, 235 First Ave., V2C 3J4 – 250/372-8248, Fax: 250/372-1274 – *1
Bruce I. Macallum, #204, 300 Columbia St., V2C 6L1 – 250/372-1282, Fax: 250/374-1295 – *1
Mair Jensen Blair, #700, 275 Lansdowne St., V2C 6H6 – 250/374-3161, Fax: 250/374-6992 – *21
McKechnie Watt, 790 Seymour St., V2C 2H3 – 250/374-4123, Fax: 250/374-2226 – *2
Morelli, Chertkow, #300, 180 Seymour St., V2C 2E3 – 250/374-3344, Fax: 250/374-1144; Toll Free: 1-888-374-3350; Email: mclawyer@mail.netshop.net – *13
B.I. Murphy, 703 St. Paul St., V2C 2K3 – 250/372-1515, Fax: 250/372-1514 – *1
Nixon & Nixon, #8, 345 Victoria St., V2C 2A3 – 250/374-1555, Fax: 250/374-9992 – *2
Roger R. Plested, 441 Tranquille Rd., V2B 3G9 – 250/376-1211, Fax: 250/376-1207 – *1
Rogers & Hyslop, 533 Nicola St., V2C 2P9 – 250/374-7179, Fax: 250/374-3818 – *2
Schaefer, Cundari, Woitas & McMillan, #810, 175 - 2 Ave., V2C 5W1 – 250/372-3368, Fax: 250/372-5554 – *4
Taylor Epp & Dolder, #300, 153 Seymour St., V2C 2C8 – 250/374-3456 – *3
Stefan Wasserberger, #440, 175 - 2 Ave., V2C 5W1 – 250/828-6221 – *1

KELOWNA — Yale

Beairsto & Company, #100, 1449 St. Paul St., V1Y 2E5 – 250/762-6111, Fax: 250/762-6480 – *3
Alison J. Beames, #200, 537 Leon Ave., V1Y 2A9
Berge & Company, #101, 346 Lawrence Ave., V1Y 6L4 – 250/762-4222, Fax: 250/762-8616 – *8
Lyndon A. Best, #202, 1636 Pandosy St., V1Y 1P7 – 250/762-2345, Fax: 250/862-5133 – *1
Heather J. Dunlop, 1974 McDougall St., V1Y 1A3 – 250/862-9292
Kimmit & Company, #202, 1433 St. Paul St., V1Y 2E4 – 250/763-6441, Fax: 250/763-1633
Larson Baron, #200, 215 Lawrence Ave., V1Y 6L2 – 250/763-0307, Fax: 250/763-6878 – *4
Levin, Kendall & Company, 147 Park Rd., PO Box 2130, Stn R, V1X 4K5 – 250/765-9733, Fax: 250/765-7773 – *5
Robert Louie, 515 Hwy. 97 South, V1Z 3J2 – 250/769-5666
McAfee, Harder Hattori & Shaw, #207, 1433 St. Paul St., V1Y 2E4 – 250/762-2252, Fax: 250/762-2246 – *4
Pattie & Company, #203, 1980 Cooper Rd., V1Y 9G8 – 250/762-0333, Fax: 250/868-2161 – *4
R.G. Phelps, #10, 1638 Pandosy St., V1Y 1P8 – 250/762-2345, Fax: 250/862-5133 – *1
Pihl & Associates, #301, 678 Bernard Ave., V1Y 6P3 – 250/762-5434, Fax: 250/762-5450 – *3
Porter Ramsay, #200, 1465 Ellis St., V1Y 2A3 – *6
Pushor, Mitchell, Davies, Montgomery & Company, #301, 1665 Ellis St., V1Y 2B3 – 250/762-2108, Fax: 250/762-9115; Toll Free: 1-800-558-1155; Email: pmdm@pmdm.com – *19
Salloum Doak, Chancery Place, #200, 537 Leon Ave., V1Y 2A9 – 250/763-4323, Fax: 250/763-4780; Toll Free: 1-800-661-4959; Email: salloum.doak@awinc.com – *14
Schlosser, Gunnlaugson & Schlosser, 3032 Pandosy St., V1Y 1W2 – 250/763-1393, Fax: 250/862-3779 – *2
Thomas, MacDonald, Van Blarcom & Butler, #207, 1664 Richter St., V1Y 8N3 – 250/763-0200, Fax: 250/762-8848 – *5
Tinker, Kueng & Company, 1573 Ellis St., PO Box 309, V1Y 7N8 – 250/763-7333, Fax: 250/763-5507 – *3
Wageman Bailey, 1674 Bertram St., 2nd Fl., V1Y 9G4 – 250/763-3343, Fax: 250/763-9524 – *8
Weddell, Horn & Company, #1, 1737 Pandosy St., V1Y 1R2 – 250/762-2011, Fax: 250/861-3980 – *4

KIMBERLEY — East Kootenay

Robert C. Apps, 230 Spokane St., V1A 2E4 – 250/427-2235, Fax: 250/426-5168
Robert Mayne & Company, 104 Deer Park Ave., V1A 2J4 – 250/427-4844, Fax: 250/427-4891 – *2
Smaill, Van Steinburg, #200, 144 Deer Park Ave., V1A 2J4 – 250/427-2231, Fax: 250/427-5353 – *2

KITIMAT — Prince Rupert

K.P. Douglas, #104, 369 City Centre, V8C 1T6 – 250/632-4727, Fax: 250/632-4885 – *1
Wozney & Donaldson, 366 City Centre, V8C 1T6 – 250/632-7151, Fax: 250/632-7100 – *2

LAC LA HACHE — Yale

Brian I. Murphy, Comp. 16, Forbes Rd., RR#1, V0K 1T0 – 250/396-4284, Fax: 250/396-4285

LADYSMITH — Vancouver Island

MacIsaac & Company, 19 Gatacre St., PO Box 1589, V0R 2E0 – 250/245-7670, Fax: 250/245-7614 – *1

LAKE COWICHAN — Vancouver Island

Molnar, Desjardins & Associates, 76 Cowichan Lake Rd., PO Box 964, V0R 2G0 – 250/749-6442, Fax: 250/749-4155

LANGLEY — Westminister

William J. Alexander, 206 - 20641 Logan Ave., V3A 7R3 – 604/533-3886, Fax: 604/731-7839 – *1
Bell, Meugens & Van Duffelen, #107, 20644 Eastleigh Cres., V3A 4C4 – 604/533-1451, Fax: 604/533-0476 – *2
Bryenton, Rosberg & Company, #300, 20689 Fraser Hwy., V3A 4G4 – 604/530-7155, Fax: 604/530-8081 – *2
Campbell, Burton & McMullan, #202, 22242 - 48th Ave., V3A 3N5 – 604/533-3821, Fax: 604/533-5521 – *6
K.A. Christofferson, 20580 - 102B Ave., RR#5, V3A 4P8 – 604/888-7641, Fax: 604/888-7217 – *1
Fleming, Olson & Taneda, 4038 - 200B St., V3A 1N9 – 604/533-3411, Fax: 604/533-8749 – *3
Gaynor Smith & Scott, 5525 - 208 St., V3A 2K4 – 604/533-4110, 3029, Fax: 604/533-8338 – *1
Lindsay Kenney, #110, 5769 - 201A St., V3A 8H9 – 604/534-5114, Fax: 604/534-5927
MacCallum McIntyre, 6345 - 197 St., V2Y 1K8 – 604/530-4161, Fax: 604/530-5716 – *6
MacDonald, Boyle & Jeffery, 20450 Fraser Hwy., V3A 4G2 – 604/530-9571, Fax: 604/530-9573 – *3
Alan G. Major, 20491 Fraser Highway, V3A 4G3 – 604/530-0422, Fax: 604/530-4935 – *1
Meighen & Sissons, #201C, 20651 - 56 Ave., V3A 3Y9 – 604/534-6061, Fax: 604/534-1640 – *3
Milne Selkirk, Bldg. #5, 21183 - 88th Ave., V1M 2G5 – 604/882-5015, Fax: 604/882-5025
Minten Critchley, #221, 20316 - 56 Ave., V3A 3Y7 – 604/530-7187, Fax: 604/530-0237 – *3
Nundal, Cherrington, Easingwood & Kearl, 20570 - 56 Ave., V3A 3Z1 – 604/530-2191, Fax: 604/530-6282 – *4
Joseph M. Prodor, PO Box 3189, Stn A, V3A 4R5 – 604/534-7907, Fax: 604/535-8981 – *1
Severide, Staplin McCallum & Company, 20432 Douglas Cres., PO Box 3400, V3A 4R7 – 604/534-8551, Fax: 604/534-1021 – *5
Marvyn A. Shore, #212, 20316 - 56 Ave., V3A 3Y7 – 604/533-3694 – *1

LILLOOET — Cariboo

Mair Jensen Blair, 682 Main St., PO Box 280, V0K 1V0 – 250/256-7822

LIONS BAY — Vancouver

M.A. Roell, 150 Sunset Dr., PO Box 502, V0N 2E0 – 604/921-6972 – *1

MACKENZIE — Cariboo

Hope Heinrich, PO Box 209, V0J 2C0 – *1

MAPLE RIDGE — Westminster

Becker & Company, #304, 11965 Fraser St., V1X 8H7 – 604/463-5121 – *1
Meighen & Sissons, 11910A - 207 St., V2X 1X7 – 604/467-5122, Fax: 604/467-1439 – *2
Norquist, Davies, 22299 Dewdney Trunk Rd., V2X 3J1 – 604/467-3477, Fax: 604/467-0018 – *3
Shantz & Associates, 22326 McIntosh Ave., V2X 3C1 – 604/463-8890, Fax: 604/463-6760 – *2
Vernon & Thompson, 22311 - 119 Ave., V2X 2Z2 – 604/463-6281, Fax: 604/463-7497 – *6

MERRITT — Yale

Mair Jensen Blair, 2038 Nicola, V0K 2B0 – 250/378-6686
Merritt Legal Services, 1964 Quilchena Ave., PO Box 4400, V0K 2B0 – 250/378-6112, Fax: 250/378-4550 – *1
Nixon & Nixon, 2051 Quilchena Ave., V0K 2B0 – 250/378-4966

MILL BAY — Vancouver Island

Gibson & Hicks, PO Box 83, V0R 2P0 – 250/743-3245 – *2
Molnar, Desjardins & Associates, 109 Mill Bay Centre, PO Box 178, V0R 2P0 – 250/743-1030, Fax: 250/743-1029

MISSION — Westminster

W. Gordy, 33056 - 1 Ave, V1V 1G3 – 604/826-6633 – *1
Walker, Lacusta & Ross, 33137 North Railway Ave., PO Box 3250, V2V 4J4 – 604/826-7104, Fax: 604/826-3229 – *2

NANAIMO — Vancouver Island

Allin, Anderson, Mullen & MacNeil, #505, 495 Dunsmuir St., PO Box 10, V9R 5K4 – 250/753-6435, Fax: 250/753-5285 – *6
Bergen & Company, 503 Comox Rd, 1st Fl., PO Box 455, Stn A, V9R 3J2 – 250/754-1295, Fax: 250/753-7977 – *6
Clark & Company, 30 Front St., PO Box 189, V9R 5K9 – 250/754-2361, Fax: 250/754-8080 – *13
John D. Ewert, #506, 495 Dunsmuir St., V9R 6B9 – 605/753-6444, Fax: 605/753-9750 – *1
Heath, Giovando, Downs & Hansen, #1, 345 Campbell St., PO Box 490, V9R 5L5 – 250/753-2202, Fax: 250/753-3949 – *4

* indicates number of lawyers in law firm.

Hobbs Harvey Hargrave, 301 Franklyn St., V9R 2X5 – 250/753-3477, Fax: 250/753-7927 – *3

S.M. Hogan, 515 Campbell St., V9R 3G9 – 250/754-1222 – *1

Patricia E. Lebedovich, 151 Skinner St., V9R 5E8 – 250/753-4108, Fax: 250/754-4439 – *1

MacIsaac & Company, 503 Comox Rd., PO Box 455, Stn A, V9R 5L5 – 250/754-1295, Fax: 250/753-7977 – *8

A. Ronald McAfee, 486C Franklyn St., PO Box 1106, V9R 6E7 – 250/754-2337, Fax: 250/754-1352 – *1

John B. Morgan, 55 Front St., V9R 5H9 – 250/754-6122 – *1

D.J. Mulligan, 149 Wallace St., V9R 5B2 – 250/754-4612 – *1

Plazzer & Geselbracht, #3, 4488 Wellington Rd., V9T 2H3 – 250/758-2825, Fax: 250/758-7412

Ramsay Thompson Lampman, #5, 1611 Bowen Rd., PO Box 667, V9R 5L9 – 250/754-3321, Fax: 250/754-1148 – *15

Saunders, Fabris & Murphy, 40 Cavan St., PO Box 778, V9R 5M2 – 250/753-6661, Fax: 250/753-6648 – *9

NELSON .... West Kootenay

Hamilton & Company, #105, 465 Ward St., V1L 1S7 – 250/352-3171 – *3

D.W. Skogstad, PO Box 140, V1L 5P7 – 250/352-7228, Fax: 250/352-5299 – *1

Stacey, Wallach, #1, 405 Baker St., V1L 4H7 – 250/352-3135, Fax: 250/352-3460 – *2

Suffredine Burch, 466 Josephine St., V1L 1W3 – 250/352-6631, Fax: 250/352-6634 – *3

Eric E. Watson, 525 Vernon St., V1L 4E9 – 250/354-4416, Fax: 250/352-7398 – *1

Wyllie & Okros, #2, 385 Baker St., V1L 4H6 – 250/354-4844, Fax: 250/354-4882 – *2

NEW HAZELTON .... Kitimat-Stikine

Terrance P. Brown, Willowdale Plaza, 3517 Churchill St., PO Box 250, V0J 2J0

NEW WESTMINSTER .... Westminster

Baumgartal & Gould, #370, 550 - 6 St., V3L 3B7 – 604/526-1805, Fax: 604/526-8056 – *2

Gordon J. Bondoreff, #202, 713 Columbia St., V3M 1B2 – 604/526-4491, Fax: 604/526-5979 – *1

Cassady, Insley, Lauener & Burgess, #330, 522 - 7 St., V3M 5T5 – 604/525-3431, Fax: 604/525-5721 – *6

E.M. Doricic, #609, 534 - 6th St., V3L 5K7 – 604/525-8636, Fax: 604/521-1747

Goodwin & Mark, #217, 713 Columbia St., V3M 1B2 – 604/522-9884, Fax: 604/526-8044 – *5

Edel Hass, #202, 713 Columbia St., V3M 1B2 – 604/526-4491, Fax: 604/526-5979 – *1

Howard Smith, & Company, 628 Carnavon St., V3M 1E5 – 604/525-7688, Fax: 604/525-7698 – *6

M.J. Hughes, 815 Massey St., V3L 4S8

McDonald & Co., 725 Carnarvon St., V3M 1E6 – 604/521-8885, Fax: 604/521-3611 – *2

D.D. McLellan, #609, 534 - 6th St., V3L 5K7 – 604/521-1080, Fax: 604/521-1447 – *1

McQuarrie Hunter, #400, 713 Columbia St., V3M 1B2 – 604/526-1821, Fax: 604/526-4656 – *23

Milne Selkirk, #400, 555 - 6 St., V3L 4Y4 – 604/522-2785, Fax: 604/522-4971 – *9

Nordman & Company, 443 - 6 St., V3L 3B1 – 604/526-4404, Fax: 604/526-0860 – *3

Nyack & Persad, #270, 550 - 6 St., V3L 3B7 – 604/521-8808, Fax: 604/521-6166 – *2

Oliver, Hughes & Drabik, 725 Carnarvon St., 2nd Fl., V3M 1E6 – 604/526-4875, Fax: 604/526-1936 – *5

Rhodes, McShane, Percival, #220, 26 Lorne St., V3M 3L7 – 604/525-4681 – *3

Gary L.F. Somers, #107, 765 - 6 St., V3M 3C6 – 604/525-2451, Fax: 604/525-2932 – *3

Thompson, MacDonald, #250, 550 Sixth St., V3L 3B2 – 604/522-9744, Fax: 604/522-7929 – *2

Richard Turner, #609, 534 - 6th St., V3L 5K7 – 604/521-1080 – *1

NORTH VANCOUVER .... Vancouver

Barrie R. Adams, #405, 145 Chadwick Ct., PO Box 20, V7M 3K1 – 604/987-1213, Fax: 604/987-1297 – *1

Ardagh Hunter Turner, #300, 1401 Lonsdale Ave., V7M 2H9 – 604/986-4366, Fax: 604/986-9286 – *3

Baldwin & Company, #40, 1199 Lynn Valley Rd., V7J 3H2 – 604/985-8000, Fax: 604/985-5999 – *1

J. Howard Bayntun, International Plaza, Bldg Box: 100, 1999 Marine Dr., V7P 3J3 – 604/986-9156, Fax: 604/985-6632 – *1

Begin & Company, 117 - 1st St. West, V7M 1B1 – 604/987-5297, Fax: 604/987-6044 – *2

Trevors Bjurman, #22, 1501 Lonsdale Ave., V7M 2J2 – 604/983-3728, Fax: 604/983-0148 – *1

Bradbrooke, Crawford & Green, #600, 171 West Esplanade, V7M 3J9 – 604/980-8571; 254-8555, Fax: 604/980-4019 – *7

P.S. Faminow, 743 Roslyn Blvd., V7G 1P4 – 604/929-5141 – *1

Forrest, Gray, Lewis & Gillett, #201, 145 East 15th St., V7L 2P7 – 604/988-5244, Fax: 604/988-0093 – *2

M. Hollander, #320, 145 West 17 St., V7M 1V5 – 604/986-4354, Fax: 604/986-9183 – *1

Jabour, Sudeyko, Stewart, #300, 233 West 1 St., V7M 1B3 – 604/986-8600, Fax: 604/986-4872 – *5

R.F. Jackson, #200, 132 East 14 St., V7L 2N3 – 604/988-4155, Fax: 604/980-7426 – *1

Robert W. Johnson, #200, 2609 Westview Dr., V7N 3W9 – 604/984-0305, Fax: 604/984-0304 – *1

E.B. Kroon, #100, 132 East 14 St., V7L 2N3 – 604/980-7021, Fax: 604/980-7428 – *1

Lakes, Straith & Bilinsky, #301, 145 - 15th St. West, V7M 1R9 – 604/984-3646, Fax: 604/984-8573 – *3

R.W. Perrick, #480, 145 West 17 St., V7M 1V5 – 604/984-9521, Fax: 604/984-9104 – *1

Poyner & Baxter, #408, 145 Chadwick Ct., V7M 3K1 – 604/988-6321, Fax: 604/988-3632 – *3

Ratcliff & Company, #103, 133 - 15 St. West, V7M 1R8 – 604/988-5201, Fax: 604/988-1452 – *13

Reid & Walsoff, #233, 1433 Lonsdale Ave., V7M 2H9 – 604/984-4357, Fax: 604/984-4326 – *2

D.A. Roper, 334 - 15th St. West, V7M 1B5 – 604/986-0488, Fax: 604/984-3463 – *1

L. Thomas Symons & Company, #200, 2609 Westview Dr., V7N 3W9 – 604/984-0305, Fax: 604/984-0304 – *1

Kenneth N. Taschuk, #5, 3046 Edgemont Blvd., V7R 2N4 – 604/986-3338, Fax: 604/986-1129 – *1

W.D. Yager Personal Law Corporation, 4017 Capilano Park Rd., V7R 4L2 – 604/985-4733, Fax: 604/985-9851 – *1

OLIVER .... Yale

Pugh & Frank, PO Box 1800, V0H 1T0 – 250/498-4941, Fax: 250/498-4100 – *1

PARKSVILLE .... Vancouver Island

Davis & Avis, #201, 156 Morison Ave., PO Box 1600, V9P 2H5 – 250/248-5731, Fax: 250/248-5730 – *2

J.A. Hossack, 163 Memorial Ave., V0R 2S0 – 250/248-9241, Fax: 250/248-8375 – *1

PEMBERTON .... Vancouver

Race & Company, #201, 7432 Prospect Ave., V0N 2L0 – 604/894-5153

PENTICTON .... Yale

Anderson & Company, 60 Nanaimo Ave. West, V2A 1N1 – 250/493-2414, Fax: 250/493-3964 – *2

Boyle & Company, #201, 100 Front St., V2A 1H1 – 250/492-6100, Fax: 250/492-4877; Toll Free: 1-800-665-8244 – *11

Wm. Randall Fowle, 173 West Westminster Ave., V2A 1J7 – 250/493-6786

Gilchrist & Company, #201, 575 Main St., V2A 5C6 – 250/492-3033, Fax: 250/492-6162 – *2

Halbauer & Company, 496 Main St., V2A 5C5 – 250/492-7225 – *4

Kinsman & Company, #100, 166 Main St., PO Box 40, V2A 6J9 – 250/492-2624, Fax: 250/492-5525 – *8

PITT MEADOWS .... Westminster

E. John Becker, #202, 12165 Harris Rd., V3Y 2E9 – 604/465-9993, Fax: 604/465-0066 – *1

Thomas Eaton Sprague, #202, 12165 Harris Rd., V3Y 2E9 – 604/465-9993, Fax: 604/465-0066 – *1

PORT ALBERNI .... Vancouver Island

Badovinac, Scoffield & Mosley, 3290 - 3 Ave., V9Y 4E1 – 250/724-1275, Fax: 250/724-7200 – *3

Beckingham, William & Co., 5029 Argyle St., V9Y 1V5 – 250/724-0111 – *3

Mary T. Margetis, Site 312, C-44, V9Y 7L7 – 250/724-4907 – *1

Stofer, Smith & Company, 5169 Argyle St., V9Y 1V3 – 250/724-3253, Fax: 250/724-5169 – *3

PORT COQUITLAM .... Westminster

Bell Marsden Spagnuolo, #440, 2755 Lougheed Hwy., V3B 5Y9 – 604/464-2024, Fax: 604/464-8976 – *4

Garton & Harris, 1542 Prairie Ave., V3B 1T4 – 604/941-9661, Fax: 604/941-5198 – *5

Eugene Lesyk, #1, 2628 Shaughnessy St., V3C 3V1 – 604/941-4055, Fax: 604/941-4002 – *1

Macleod Thorson Darychuk, #310, 2755 Lougheed Hwy., V3B 5Y9 – 604/464-2644, Fax: 604/464-2533 – *5

PORT HARDY .... Vancouver Island

Jeffrey Jones & Company, 8755 Granville St., PO Box 1949, V0N 2P0 – 250/949-8533, Fax: 250/949-9255 – *1

Donald L. Mancell, PO Box 1770, V0N 2P0 – 250/949-6777, Fax: 250/949-9091 – *1

PORT MCNEILL .... Vancouver Island

Dick & Jones, 1488 Beach Dr., PO Box 70, V0N 2R0 – 250/956-3358, Fax: 250/956-4093 – *2

Elaine Evans, 1705 Campbell Way, PO Box 190, V0N 2R0 – 250/956-4451 – *1

PORT MOODY .... Westminster

Roderick A. Brown, #6, 86 Moody St., V3H 2P6 – 604/461-2434, Fax: 604/461-9662 – *1

POWELL RIVER .... Vancouver

Giroday & Company, 4571 Marine Ave., V8A 2K5 – 604/485-2771, Fax: 604/485-2197 – *2

PRINCE GEORGE .... Cariboo

Harold J. Bogle, Q.C., Scotiabank Bldg., #515, 1488 - 4 Ave., PO Box 699, Stn A, V2L 4T2 – 250/562-4324, Fax: 250/561-0969

J.H. Cluff, #303, 1575 - 5 Ave., V2L 3L9 – 250/563-5339, Fax: 250/563-1567 – *1

John A. Davis, Bank of BC Bldg., #1, 1515 - 2 Ave., V2L 3B8 – 250/564-5544, Fax: 250/562-9427 – *1

Dungate & Company, 1209 - 4 Ave., PO Box 130, V1L 4R9 – 250/563-7747 – *3

William Firman, #309, 1705 - 3 Ave., V1L 3G7 – 250/564-1917 – *1

Fletcher Repstock, #608, 1488 - 4 Ave., V2L 4Y2 – 250/564-1313, Fax: 250/564-4362 – *2

Gibbs & Company, #205, 715 Victoria St., V2L 2K5 – 250/564-6460, Fax: 250/562-0671 – *2

Heather Sadler Jenkins, #700, 550 Victoria St., PO Box 4, V2L 2K1 – 250/564-5144 – *12

Hope Heinrich, 1598 - 6 Ave., V2L 5G7 – 250/563-0681, Fax: 250/562-3761; Toll Free: 1-800-663-8230; Email: mail@hh.bc.ca – *16

F.A. Howard-Gibbon, #302, 1370 Seventh Ave., V2L 3P1 – 250/562-7261 – *1

E. John, 435 Québec St., V2L 1W5 – 250/562-1726, Fax: 250/562-1704 – *1
Leverman & Company, #200, 444 Victoria St., V2L 2J7 – 250/564-1212, Fax: 250/563-1879 – *3
Charles I.M. Lugosi, #201, 411 Quebec St., V2L 1W5 – 250/564-1000, Fax: 250/564-9000 – *1
R.W. Madill, #901, 299 Victoria St., V2L 5B8 – 250/562-5000, Fax: 250/562-9444 – *1
Ramsay Nosè Traxler, Scotia Bank Bldg., #614, 1488 - 4 Ave., V2L 4Y2 – 250/563-7741, Fax: 250/563-2953 – *8
Wilbur & Company, #200, 1110 Sixth Ave., V1L 3M6 – 250/564-1444 – *2
Wilson, King & Company, #1000, 299 Victoria St., V2L 5B8 – 250/960-3200, Fax: 250/562-7777 – *14

PRINCE RUPERT .... Prince Rupert
McLean & Kan, #1, 741 Second Ave. West, V8J 1H4 – 250/624-6060, Fax: 250/624-6451 – *2
Punnett & Johnston, #7, 222 - 3 Ave. West, PO Box 456, V8J 3R2 – 250/624-2106 – *4
David J. Sestak, #2, 330 - 3 Ave. West, PO Box 756, V8J 3S1 – 250/627-1726 – *1
Silversides, Wilson & Seidemann, 330 Second Ave. West, PO Box 188, V8J 3P7 – 250/624-2116, Fax: 250/627-7786 – *7
C.J. Trueman, #1, 521 - 2 Ave. West, V8J 1G9 – 250/627-7771 – *1

PRINCETON .... Yale
Stanley G. Turner, PO Box 568, V0X 1W0 – 250/295-6722, 6972, Fax: 250/295-6722 – *1

QUALICUM BEACH .... Vancouver Island
Clark & Company, 710 Memorial Ave., PO Box 879, V9K 1T2 – 250/752-5615, Fax: 250/752-2055 – *1
Walker & Wilson, 707 Primrose St., PO Box 2100, V9K 1T6 – 250/752-6951, Fax: 250/752-6022 – *2

QUESNEL .... Cariboo
Chudiak, Schmit & Co., 531 Reid St., V2J 2M8 – 250/992-8341, Fax: 250/992-7349 – *2
Coffey & Bernath, #3, 375 Reid St., V2J 2M5 – 250/992-8317, Fax: 250/992-3224 – *2

REVELSTOKE .... Yale
S.G. Bernacki, 109 - 2 St. East, PO Box 2699, V0E 2S0 – 250/837-4971 – *1
Christopher H. Johnston, #201, 101 First St. East, PO Box 2639, V0E 2S0 – 250/837-6171, Fax: 250/837-7194 – *1
Bernard Lavallee, PO Box 244, V0E 2S0 – 250/837-5168 – *1
R.A. Lundberg, PO Box 2490, V0E 2S0 – 250/837-5196, Fax: 250/837-4746 – *1

RICHMOND .... Vancouver
Altman Kahn Zack, #270, 10711 Cambie Rd., V6X 3C9 – 604/270-9571, Fax: 604/270-8282; Email: altman_kahn_zack@akz.com – *14
Brodie & Morrice, #250, 5611 Cooney Rd., V6X 3J6 – 604/270-9411, Fax: 604/270-7704 – *3
Campbell Froh May & Rice, #200, 5611 Cooney Rd., V6X 3J6 – 604/273-8481, Fax: 604/273-4729 – *9
V.N. Carvalho, 13811 Gilbert Rd., V7E 2H8 – 604/274-5636, Fax: 604/274-5694 – *1
S.R. Chamberlain, Q.C., #1, 7100 River Rd., V6X 1X5 – 604/244-0646, Fax: 604/244-0617 – *1
Cobb Michaels, #550, 5900 - 3rd St., V6X 3P7 – 604/273-2748, Fax: 604/273-2703 – *3
Cohen, Buchan, Edwards, #208, 4940 - 3 Rd., V6X 3A5 – 604/273-6411, Fax: 604/273-4512 – *3
A. Ted Ewachniuk & Associates, 8331 River Rd., V6X 1Y1 – 604/273-1844, Fax: 604/273-5625 – *4
Fitzsimmons & Scammells, #550, 5900 - 3rd St., V6X 3P7 – 604/276-8982, Fax: 604/273-2703 – *2
Michael J. Frank, #152, 10551 Shellbridge Way, V6X 2W9 – 604/270-6878, Fax: 604/276-0566 – *1
Friesen & Epp, #220, 8120 Granville Ave., V6Y 1P3 – 604/273-2941, Fax: 604/273-1381 – *4
D.B. Graves, #317, 8055 Anderson Rd., V6Y 1S2 – 604/276-0069 – *1
Bernard Hoodekoff, North Tower, #206, 5811 Cooney Rd., V6X 3M1 – 604/278-8451, Fax: 604/278-8453 – *1
W.G. Hughes, #335, 8120 Granville Ave., V6Y 1P3 – 604/273-5164, Fax: 604/273-5454 – *1
Humphry Paterson, #205, 8171 Park Rd., V6Y 1S9 – 604/278-3031, Fax: 604/278-3021 – *2
Sharen Janeson, 3711 Moncton St., 2nd Fl., V7E 3A5 – 604/272-5171, Fax: 604/275-5578 – *1
Phillips Paul, #215, 4800 - 3 Rd., V6X 3A6 – 604/273-5297, Fax: 604/273-1643 – *4
Pryke Lambert Leathley Russell, North Tower, #500, 5811 Cooney Rd., V6X 3M1 – 604/276-2765, Fax: 604/276-8045 – *17
Scardina & Co., #140, 8351 Alexandra Rd., V6X 3P3 – 604/273-5558, Fax: 604/273-5550 – *1
Arne Silverman, #120, 11181 Vayager Way, V6X 3N9 – 604/270-1430, Fax: 604/270-4588 – *1
Simpson & Company, #1405, 4380 No. 3 Rd., V6X 3V7 – 604/270-0880, Fax: 604/270-7308 – *1
John Skapski, 3711 Moncton St., 2nd Fl., V7E 3A5 – 604/274-2526, Fax: 604/275-5578 – *1
David Sky, #270, 10711 Tanbie Rd., V6X 3C9 – 604/273-4315, Fax: 604/270-8282 – *1
Stark Christian Henderson, 12011 - 3 Ave., V7E 3K1 – 604/241-2855, Fax: 604/241-2866 – *7
Wong & Tsang, #310, 8120 Granville Ave., V6Y 1P3 – 604/279-9023, Fax: 604/279-9025 – *2

ROSSLAND .... West Kootenay
A.R. Dahlstrom, PO Box 699, V0G 1Y0 – 250/362-5786, Fax: 250/362-7250 – *1

SALMON ARM .... Yale
H.R. Bartlett, 401 Okanagan Ave., PO Box 910, V1E 4P1 – 250/832-7061, Fax: 250/832-5493 – *1
Brooke, McManus, Jackson, #303, 370 Lakeshore Dr. NE, PO Box 67, V1E 4N2 – 250/832-9311, Fax: 250/832-4787 – *3
Sivertz, Kiehlbauch & Zachernuk, 316 Hudson Ave. NE, PO Box 190, V1E 4N3 – 250/832-8031, Fax: 250/832-6177 – *3
Garrett N. Wynne, #102, 310 Hudson Ave., PO Box 3009, V1E 4R8 – 250/837-9611, Fax: 250/832-9788 – *1

SECHELT .... Vancouver
Eastwood & Company, #102, 5630 Dolphin St., PO Box 1280, V0N 3A0 – 604/885-5831, Fax: 604/885-5441 – *2

SICAMOUS .... Yale
Brooke, McManus, Jackson, PO Box 422, V0E 2V0 – 250/836-2874

SIDNEY .... Vancouver Island
Alice Finall, #304, 9775 - 4th St., V8L 2Z8 – 250/656-6668, Fax: 250/656-9366 – *1
Henley & Walden, #201, 2377 Bevan Ave., V8L 4M9 – 250/656-7231, Fax: 250/656-0937 – *4
Lloyd A. Johnson, 9751 - 5 St., V8L 2X1 – 403/656-0934, Fax: 403/656-9334 – *1
McKimm & Lott, 9830 - 4 St., V8L 2Z3 – 250/656-3961, Fax: 250/655-3329 – *7

SMITHERS .... Prince Rupert
G.E. Greene, 3895 Alfred St., PO Box 940, V0J 2N0 – 250/847-4777, Fax: 250/847-4029 – *1
Perry & Company, PO Box 790, V0J 2N0 – 250/847-4341, Fax: 250/847-5634 – *4
Mark G. Takahashi, 3868 Broadway Ave., PO Box 2501, V0J 2N0 – 250/847-4222, Fax: 250/846-4282 – *1

SOOKE .... Vancouver Island
Dinning Hunter & Company, #1, 6631 Sooke Rd., PO Box 91, V0S 1N0 – 250/642-2553, Fax: 250/642-7859
Hallgren & Company, 6595 Sooke Rd., PO Box 939, V0S 1N0 – 250/642-5271, Fax: 250/642-6006 – *1

SQUAMISH .... Vancouver
Race & Company, #201, 7432 Pemberton Ave., PO Box 1850, V0N 3G0 – 604/892-5254, Fax: 604/892-5461 – *6
Sanguinetti & Company, 201 - 1364 Pemberton Ave., V0N 3G0 – 604/892-9311 – *2
V. Donald R. Wilson, #201, 38133 Cleveland Ave., PO Box 1910, V0N 3G0 – 604/892-5284, Fax: 604/892-9725 – *1

SUMMERLAND .... Yale
Johnston, Bell & Company, 9921 Main St., PO Box 520, V0H 1Z0 – 250/494-6621, Fax: 250/494-8055 – *3

SURREY .... Westminster
Becker, Mathers, #111, 15225 - 104 Ave., V3R 6Y8 – 604/583-2200, Fax: 604/583-3469 – *4
Gordon Bowen, #402, 15127 - 100th Ave., V3R 0N9 – 604/588-4434, Fax: 604/588-4487 – *1
S.A. Bowers, 8893 - 160 St., V3R 4N1 – 604/951-9224, Fax: 604/951-9224 – *1
Brawn & Randall, #301, 15117 - 101 Ave., V3R 8P7 – 604/588-5344, Fax: 604/588-2331 – *3
Bull, Housser & Tupper, #201, 9468 - 128 St., V3T 2X9 – 604/581-4677, Fax: 604/581-5947 – *1
R.R. Coumont, #402, 15127 - 100th Ave., V3R 0N9 – 604/588-4434, Fax: 604/588-4487 – *1
James L. Davidson & Company, #403, 16033 - 108 Ave., PO Box 271, V4N 1P2 – 604/951-2990, Fax: 604/951-9368 – *2
Kane, Shannon & Weiler, #104, 2055 - 152nd St., V4A 4N7 – 604/535-8770, Fax: 604/535-8771
J. Kelso, 8950 - 152 St., V3R 4E4 – 604/589-1414, Fax: 604/589-2044 – *1
MacMillan, Tucker, Krieger & Mackay, #5690, 176A St., V3S 4H1 – 604/574-7431, Fax: 604/574-3021 – *5
Maier & Co., #310, 10524 King George Hwy., V3S 2X2 – 604/582-5951, Fax: 604/588-0779 – *1
A.L. McAndrew, #240, 13711 - 72 Ave., V3W 2P2 – 604/591-2288, Fax: 604/591-7366 – *1
McCarthy Tétrault, Station Tower, Gateway, #1300, 13401 - 108th Ave., V3T 5T3 – 604/583-9100, Fax: 604/583-9150; Email: adj@mccarthy.ca; URL: http://www.mccarthy.ca – *2
McNeney & McNeney, Sunwest Pl., 14888 - 104 Ave., V3R 1M4 – 604/588-7858, Fax: 604/581-7084 – *2
McQuarrie Hunter, #200, 13889 - 104th Ave., V3T 1W8 – 604/581-0461, Fax: 604/581-7110
Mosher & Treleaven, 13762 - 72 Ave., V3W 2P4 – 604/591-8211, Fax: 604/596-9907 – *2
Norquist Davies, #200, 10330 - 152 St., V3R 4G8 – 604/585-1196, Fax: 604/585-3293 – *4
Nyack & Persad, #201, 9380 - 120 St., V3V 4B9 – 604/588-9933, Fax: 604/588-2731 – *4
Peterson Stark, #300, 10366 - 136A St., V3T 5R3 – 604/588-9321, Fax: 604/589-5391
Richards & Richards, 10325 - 150 St., V3R 4B1 – 604/588-6844, Fax: 604/588-8800 – *2
E.H. Skands, 10246B - 152 St., V3R 6N7 – 604/581-1621, Fax: 604/588-9365 – *1
Marvin N. Stern, #402, 15127 - 100th Ave., V3R 0N9 – 604/588-4434, Fax: 604/588-4487 – *1
Stilling Blackmore Raven Hoem, #220, 7525 King George Hwy., V3W 5A8 – 604/591-2241, Fax: 604/597-0389 – *5
E.R. Swedahl, #11, 15243 - 91 Ave., V3R 8P8 – 604/581-3232, Fax: 604/589-3741 – *1
Thompson & McConnell, #300, 1676 Martin Dr., V4A 6E7 – 604/531-1421, Fax: 604/531-8402; Toll Free: 1-800-667-1421 – *9
Watchorn & McLellan, 10334 - 152A St., V3R 7P8 – 604/585-4321, Fax: 604/585-8195 – *8

* indicates number of lawyers in law firm.

Worthington, Simm & David, 10430 - 144 St., V3T 4V5 – 604/588-9721, Fax: 604/585-6020 – *5

TERRACE .... Prince Rupert

Crampton, Brown & Arndt, #3, 4623 Park Ave., V8G 1V5 – 250/635-6330, Fax: 250/635-4795 – *3

Halfyard, O'Byrne & Wright, 4730 Lazelle Ave., V8G 1T2 – 250/638-0354 – *3

Cecil C. Pratt, 4509 Lakelse Ave., PO Box 459, V8G 4B5 – 250/638-1161, Fax: 250/638-1162 – *1

Leslie Ann Strike, c/o Deputy Regional Crown Court, #110, 3408 Kalum St., V8G 2N6 – 250/387-3840, Fax: 250/638-3298 – *1

Talstra & Company, #203, 4650 Lazelle Ave., V8G 1S6 – 250/638-1137, Fax: 250/638-1306 – *2

Warner Bandstra, #200, 4630 Lazelle Ave., V8G 1S6 – 250/635-2622, Fax: 250/635-4998 – *2

TRAIL .... West Kootenay

Adair & Company, 1402 Bay Ave., V1R 4B1 – 250/368-9171, Fax: 250/368-3369 – *1

J. Ghilarducci, 1309 Bay Ave., V1R 4A7 – 250/368-6455, Fax: 250/368-6107 – *3

McEwan, Harrison & Co., 1432 Bay Ave., V1R 4B1 – 250/368-8211 – *4

Moran & Company, 1309 Bay Ave., V1R 4A7 – 250/368-6455, Fax: 250/368-6107

VALEMOUNT .... Cariboo

Mair Jensen Blair, 1275 - 5 Ave., V0E 2Z0 – 250/566-4364 – *1

VANCOUVER .... Vancouver

Aaron, MacGregor, Gordon & Daykin, #506, 815 Hornby St., V6Z 2E6 – 604/689-7571, Fax: 604/685-8563 – *4

A.S. Alafriz, #401, 1385 West 8 Ave., V6H 3V9 – 604/732-3345, Fax: 604/736-5522 – *1

Alexander, Holburn, Beaudin & Lang, #2700, 700 West Georgia St., PO Box 10057, V7Y 1B8 – 604/688-1351, Fax: 604/669-7642; Email: ahbluser@ahbl.bc.ca – *58

Allan & Lougheed, 1628 - 7 Ave. West, V6J 1S5 – 604/733-2411, Fax: 604/736-6225 – *2

Allard & Company, #600, 815 Hornby St., V6Z 2E6 – 604/689-3885, Fax: 604/687-0814 – *4

Tony D. Allen, #1400, 1166 Alberni St., V6E 3Z3 – 604/682-7794, Fax: 604/669-0869 – *2

Stafford D.R. Alliston, 12 Gaoler's Mews, V6B 4K7 – 604/681-9371, Fax: 604/682-3687 – *1

Alperstein Law Corp., #707, 1281 West Georgia, V6E 3J7 – 604/688-8390, Fax: 604/688-8063 – *1

M.M. Altman, #270, 5655 Cambie St., V5Z 3A4 – 604/263-0808, Fax: 604/263-3093 – *1

Bruce D. Ames, #1400, 1166 Alberni St., V6E 3Z3 – 604/662-7550, Fax: 604/669-0860 – *1

Andersen Paul, #306, 1530 West 8 Ave., V6J 4R8 – 604/734-8411, Fax: 604/734-8511 – *3

Anderson & Galati, #607, 808 Nelson St., Box 12152, V6Z 2H2 – 604/669-2445, Fax: 604/669-4395 – *4

Brian Anderson, #411, 470 Granville St., V6C 1V5 – 604/684-5367 – *1

A. Stewart Andree, Esq., #1130, 1040 West Georgia St., V6E 4H1 – 604/685-8121, Fax: 604/685-8120 – *1

George P. Angelomatis, #601, 134 Abbott St., V6B 2K4 – 604/689-8788, Fax: 604/689-3327 – *1

G.J. Arbour, #202, 2100 West 3 Ave., V6K 1L1 – 604/736-0287 – *1

Ardagh Hunter Turner, #300, 1401 Lonsdale Ave. North, V7M 2H9 – 604/986-4366, Fax: 604/986-9286 – *3

Armstrong & Company, Scotia Tower, #480, 650 West Georgia St., PO Box 11622, V6B 4N9 – 604/683-7361, Fax: 604/662-3231 – *3

K.T. Au, #201, 124 East Pender St., V6A 1T3 – 604/681-0933 – *1

Aydin & Co., North Office Tower, #530, 650 West 41 Ave., V5Z 2M9 – 604/266-5828, Fax: 604/266-3929 – *1

Richard D. Ballentyne, #1400, 100 West Pender St., 14th Fl., V6B 1R8 – 604/669-8899, Fax: 604/689-8278 – *1

Sandra I. Banister, #880, 1090 West Georgia St., V6E 3V7 – 604/662-7276, Fax: 604/662-8782 – *2

Barbeau & Company, #1450, 700 West Georgia St., PO Box 10019, V7Y 1A1 – 604/688-4900, Fax: 604/688-0649 – *3

Baria & Company, #300, 6330 Fraser St., V5W 3A4 – 604/321-8300, Fax: 604/321-9163 – *2

Gail Barnes, #105, 12 Water St., V6B 1A5 – 604/684-1124, Fax: 604/684-1122 – *1

Barrigar & Moss, #480, 601 West Cordova St., V6B 1G1 – 604/669-3432, Fax: 604/681-4081 – *8

David G. Batist, 575 Richard St., 4th Fl., V6B 2Z7 – 604/682-6122, Fax: 604/682-2919 – *1

Lawrence W. Beadle, PO Box 35279, V6M 4G5 – 604/266-8008 – *1

Dorothy Beck, #328, 470 Granville St., V6C 1V5 – 604/687-8711, Fax: 604/687-8711 – *1

Beck, Robinson & Company, #700, 686 West Broadway, V5Z 1G1 – 604/874-0204, Fax: 604/874-0820 – *5

W.D.O. Bees, #104, 1128 Hornby St., V6Z 2L4 – 604/669-6990, Fax: 604/669-6944 – *1

Robert W. Bellows, #401, 1385 West 8 Ave., V6H 3V9 – 604/736-5500, Fax: 604/736-5522 – *1

Bennett, Parkes, #400, 2609 Granville St., V6H 3H3 – 604/734-6838, Fax: 604/738-6789 – *3

Berger & Nelson, #300, 171 Water St., V6B 1A7 – 604/684-1311, Fax: 604/684-6402 – *4

Peter P. Bieg, #606, 1155 Robson St., V6E 1B5 – 604/688-5471, Fax: 604/688-6176 – *1

Bisaro & Company, Vancouver Centre, #2020, 650 West Georgia St., PO Box 11547, V6B 4N7 – 604/683-9621, Fax: 604/683-5084 – *4

Bitney & Co., #405, 675 West Hastings St., V6B 1N2 – 604/682-8504, Fax: 604/682-5124 – *1

Blake, Cassels & Graydon, #1700, 1030 West Georgia St., V6E 2Y3 – 604/631-3300, Fax: 604/631-3309 – *36

Barbara R. Bluman, 3906 Quesnel Dr., V6L 2X2 – 604/732-6028, Fax: 604/732-5801 – *2

Bolton & Muldoon, #400, 1045 Howe St., V6Z 2A9 – 604/687-7078, Fax: 604/687-3022 – *7

Bose, Deborah, #102, 873 Beatty St., V6B 2M6 – 604/682-9535, Fax: 604/682-7365 – *2

Boughton Peterson Yang Anderson, Four Bentall Centre, #2500, 1055 Dunsmuir St., PO Box 49290, V7X 1S8 – 604/687-6789, Fax: 604/683-5317 – *32

Joyce W. Bradley, #202, 3195 Granville St., V6H 3K2 – 604/732-3886, Fax: 604/736-7387 – *1

J.F.C. Bridal, 12 Gaolers Mews, V6B 4K7 – 604/687-4551, Fax: 604/682-3687 – *1

Brown Benson, #1450, 701 West Georgia St., PO Box 10137, V7Y 1C6 – 604/684-7274, Fax: 604/669-9120 – *5

H.K. Brown, #1504, 100 West Pender St., 15th Fl., V6B 1R8 – 604/684-1021, Fax: 604/688-6243 – *1

Brown, McCue, #1650, 999 West Hastings St., V6C 2W2 – 604/684-8411, Fax: 604/687-7430 – *2

P.W. Brown, 2081 - 37 Ave. West, V6M 1N7 – 604/261-0300, Fax: 604/261-0312 – *1

J.G. Buchanan, #707, 777 West Broadway, V5Z 4J7 – 604/876-0343, Fax: 604/876-9035 – *1

Bull, Housser & Tupper, Royal Centre, #3000, 1055 West Georgia St., PO Box 11130, V6E 3R3 – 604/687-6575, Fax: 604/641-4949; Email: general@bht.com – *104

Donald R. Burton, King Edward Mall, 928 West King Edward Ave., V5Z 2E2 – 604/733-7201 – *1

M.L. Cacchioni, 820 Millbank, V5Z 4A1 – 604/872-0607 – *1

Bradley M. Caldwell, #480, 650 West Georgia, PO Box 11622, V6B 4N9 – 604/689-8894, Fax: 604/662-3231 – *1

E.A. Cameron, #205, 1510 Nelson St., V6G 1M1 – 604/689-2414, Fax: 604/684-7190 – *1

Camp Church & Associates, Randall Bldg., 555 West Georgia St., 7th Fl., B6B 1Z5 – 604/689-7555, Fax: 604/689-7554 – *4

T.J. Campbell, Q.C., #611, 543 Granville St., V6C 1X8 – 604/681-3401 – *1

Campney & Murphy, #2100, 1111 West Georgia St., PO Box 48800, V7X 1K9 – 604/688-8022, Fax: 604/688-0829; Email: cmlaw@campneymurphy.com – *55

J.A. Carr, #1510, 777 Hornby St., V6Z 1S4 – 604/681-4158, Fax: 604/688-9981 – *1

Carr-Harris & Company, CN Bldg., #210, 900 Howe St., V6Z 2M4 – 604/669-4922, Fax: 604/669-4969 – *2

Douglas R. Chalke, #1800, 70 West Georgia St., V7Y 1C6 – 604/683-5096, Fax: 604/980-6469 – *1

Chan Yue & Lee, #212, 475 Main St., V6A 2T7 – 604/687-4576, Fax: 604/683-3258 – *7

Chapman & Company Law Corporation, #204, 5511 West Blvd., V6M 4H3 – 604/266-6294, Fax: 604/266-2352 – *2

Bruce H. Chapman, #1300, 666 Burard St., V6C 3J8 – 604/731-3344, Fax: 604/688-2419 – *1

George G. Chapman, 2475 West 37 Ave., V6M 1P4 – 604/266-3122, Fax: 604/263-7408 – *1

Bernard Charles, 206 - 111 Water St., V6B 1A7 – 604/689-9545, Fax: 604/688-1425

Charlton & Buxton, #880, 999 West Broadway, V5Z 1K5 – 604/736-6781, Fax: 604/736-1463 – *2

Chen & Leung, North Tower, Oakridge Centre, #728, 650 - 41st Ave. West, V5Z 2M9 – 604/264-8331, Fax: 604/264-8387 – *10

Clark, Wilson, Hongkong Bank of Canada Bldg., #800, 885 West Georgia St., V6C 3H1 – 604/687-5700, Fax: 604/687-6314 – *52

A.T. Clarke, #960, 777 Hornby St., V6Z 1S4 – 604/683-4493, Fax: 604/683-4416 – *1

Robert C. Claus, 1002 - 777 West Broadway, V5Z 4J7 – 604/873-9098, Fax: 604/361-9600

M.E. Cofman, #2020, 650 West Georgia St., V6B 4N7 – 604/683-9621, Fax: 604/683-5084 – *1

D.E. Comparelli, #704, 510 West Hastings St., V6B 1L8 – 604/683-6888, Fax: 604/688-4497 – *1

Connell Lightbody, Royal Centre, #1900, 1055 West Georgia St., PO Box 11161, V6E 4J2 – 604/684-1181, Fax: 604/641-3916 – *25

J. Cove, 923 Denman St., V6G 2L9 – 604/683-6505, Fax: 604/683-2176 – *1

Hartley E. Cramer, #300, 896 Cambie St., V6B 2P6 – 604/684-6301, Fax: 604/684-6303 – *1

F.D. Crane, #780, 999 West Broadway, V5Z 1K5 – 604/730-0375, Fax: 604/730-0376

F.S. Crestani, #204, 1651 Commercial Drive, V5L 3Y3 – 604/251-1168, Fax: 604/253-7726 – *1

H. Crosby, #201, 5316 Victoria Dr., V5P 3V7 – 604/321-6922, Fax: 604/327-8873 – *2

Dallas, Kinney & Company, 852 Seymour St., V6B 3L6 – 604/681-6171, Fax: 604/683-1000 – *3

A. Kenneth Dangerfield, #2500, 1055 Dunsmere St., PO Box 49290, V7X 1S8 – 604/687-6789, Fax: 604/683-5317 – *1

Gail Y. Davidson, #102, 1648 West 7 Ave., V6J 1S4 – 604/736-1175, Fax: 604/736-7402 – *1

Davies & Co., #780, 1333 West Broadway, V6H 4C1 – 604/736-8338, Fax: 604/736-3391 – *2

Davis & Company, Park Pl., #2800, 666 Burrard St., V6C 2Z7 – 604/687-9444, Fax: 604/687-1612 – *118

Brian Day, #1102, 2050 Nelson St., V6G 1N6 – 604/681-0744, Fax: 604/669-0222 – *1

A.J. DeMeulemeester, 1976 - 4th Ave. West, V6J 1M5 – 604/731-1388 – *1

Derpak & White, 1933 West Broadway, V6J 1Z3 – 604/736-9791, Fax: 604/736-7197 – *3

Diana M. Davidson & Company, #303, 2695 Granville St., V6H 3H4 – 604/736-3638, Fax: 604/736-8308 – *4

J.W. Dobbin, #704, 510 West Hastings St., V6B 1L8 – 604/683-6888, Fax: 604/683-4497 – *1
Hans J.R. Doehring, #100, 1215 Beach Ave., V6E 1V5 – 604/669-3414
Dohn & Jaffer, #268, 3316 Kingsway, V5R 5K7 – 604/438-3369, Fax: 604/438-5578 – *1
M. Dong, 4347 James St., V5V 3H8 – 604/876-5094 – *1
Frank Dorchester, #1800, 999 West Hastings St., V6C 2W2 – 604/683-2784, Fax: 604/683-1375 – *1
Dosanjh & Company, #202, 5887 Victoria Dr., V5P 3W5 – 604/327-6381, Fax: 604/327-2923 – *3
Douglas, Symes & Brissenden, One Bentall Centre, Bldg Box: 2100, #2100, 505 Burrard St., V7X 1R4 – 604/683-6911, Fax: 604/669-1337; Email: lawyer@ds_b.com – *48
DuMoulin & Boskovich, Oceanic Plaza, #1440, 1066 West Hastings St., PO Box 12539, V6E 3X1 – 604/669-5500, Fax: 604/688-8491 – *11
Eastwood & Company, #610, 1112 West Pender St., V6C 2R9 – 604/689-1636, Fax: 604/683-0890 – *4
Kenneth C. Eberhardt, #203, 2609 Westview Dr., V7N 4M2 – 604/983-2818, Fax: 604/980-2624 – *1
Edwards, Kenny & Bray, 1040 West Georgia St., 19th Fl., V6E 4H3 – 604/689-1811, Fax: 604/689-5177 – *26
Norman Einarsson, #306, 1530 West 8 Ave., V6J 4R8 – 604/734-8411, Fax: 604/734-8511 – *1
Ellis, Nauss & Jones, #600, 1665 West Broadway, V6J 1X1 – 604/731-9276, Fax: 604/734-0206 – *3
Ellis, Roadburg, #200, 853 Richards St., V6B 3B4 – 604/669-7131, Fax: 604/669-7684 – *2
Epstein Wood Logie Wexler & Maerov, #650, 1500 West Georgia St., V6G 3A9 – 604/685-4321, Fax: 604/685-7901 – *9
Evans, Goldstein & Eadie, #1400, 700 West Georgia St., PO Box 10014, V7Y 1A1 – 604/685-5235, Fax: 604/685-9104 – *5
R.J. Falconer, Q.C., #320, 666 Burrard St., V6C 2X8 – 604/683-5674, Fax: 604/682-2534 – *1
Fan & Co., #601, 609 Gore Ave., V6A 2Z8 – 604/683-0471, Fax: 604/638-8748 – *2
Farris, Vaughan, Wills & Murphy, Pacific Centre South, 700 West Georgia St., PO Box 10026, V7Y 1B3 – 604/684-9151, Fax: 604/661-9349 – *45
Fayers & Company, #380, 5740 Cambie St., V5Z 3A6 – 604/325-1246, Fax: 604/325-1261 – *3
J.J. Fedyk, 930 - 57th Ave. West, V6P 1S3 – 604/263-6290, Fax: 604/263-9410 – *1
Feller Drysdale, Bldg Box: 58, #1550, 400 Burrard St., V6C 3A6 – 604/689-2626, Fax: 604/681-5354 – *9
Ferguson Gifford, Park Place, #500, 666 Burrard St., V6C 3H3 – 604/687-3216, Fax: 604/683-2780; Email: 102107.1705@compuserve.com; URL: http://www.fergif.com – *22
K.L.D. Findlay, #1900, 1055 West Georgia, V6E 4J2 – 604/684-1181, Fax: 604/641-3916 – *1
Flader & Phelps, #500, 999 West Broadway, V5Z 1K5 – 604/736-3722 – *2
Flanagan & Assoc., #1400, 1166 Alberni St., V6E 3Z3 – 604/669-0886, Fax: 604/669-0860 – *2
C.C. Fogal, #401, 207 West Hastings St., V6B 1H7 – 604/687-0588, Fax: 604/688-0550 – *1
Robert A. Foran, Oceanic Plaza, #1700, 1066 West Hastings St., PO Box 12546, V6E 3X2 – 604/689-3431, Fax: 604/685-1035 – *1
Thomas Dean Fox, #1050, 1188 West Georgia St., V6E 4A2 – 604/682-6121, Fax: 604/682-4428 – *2
Fraser & Beatty, Grosvenor Bldg., 1040 West Georgia St., 15th Fl., V6E 4H8 – 604/687-4460, Fax: 604/683-5214; URL: http://www.fraserbeatty.ca – *30
Fraser & Company, #900, 777 Hornby St., V6Z 1S4 – 604/669-5244, Fax: 604/669-5791 – *9
Friesen & Epp, #1, 3103 Kingsway, V5R 5J9 – 604/437-4777, Fax: 604/437-1575 – *2
H.G.N. Frith, #614, 198 West Hastings St., V6B 1H2 – 604/681-3811 – *1
George T.H. Fuller, 5261 Dunbar St., V6N 1W1 – 604/261-3199, 3417, Fax: 604/261-3199 – *1

Ganapathi, Ashcroft, Cruickshank & Levine, 225 Smithe St., V6B 4X7 – 604/669-9000, Fax: 604/684-9277 – *6
Gayle D. Gavin, #920, 777 Hornby St., V6Z 1S4 – 604/685-6235, Fax: 604/681-6375 – *1
G.C. Geraghty, 301 - 701 West Georgia St., V7Y 1C6 – 604/684-8247 – *1
R.P. Gibbons, #2080, 777 Hornby St., V6Z 1S4 – 604/689-7124 – *1
Giusti Barrett Ellan, #2080, 777 Hornby St., V6Z 1S4 – 604/669-7723 – *3
Giusti, Barrett & Ellan, #500, 190 Alexander St., V6A 1B5 – 604/669-2238, Fax: 604/669-4679 – *3
Glasner & Schwartz, #707, 1281 Georgia St., V6E 3J7 – 604/683-4181, Fax: 604/683-0226 – *1
Goldman Mathisen, #1788, 1111 West Georgia, V6E 4M3 – 604/682-6181, Fax: 604/683-5723 – *1
Goldsmith & Hartshorne, Vancouver Centre, #1601, 650 West Georgia St., 16th Fl., PO Box 11505, V6B 4N7 – 604/687-6641, Fax: 604/687-6966 – *8
W.C. Gorham, #268, 2025 West 42 Ave., V6M 2B5 – 604/263-1878, Fax: 604/261-8515 – *1
P.C. Gorick, #1140, 1311 Chestnut St., V6J 3K1 – 604/736-3337 – *1
P.D. Gornall, #960, 355 Burrard St., V6C 2G8 – 604/681-7932, Fax: 604/687-7935 – *1
Gowlings, #2414, 1055 Dunsmuir St., PO Box 49122, V7X 1J1 – 604/683-6498, Fax: 604/683-3558 – *10
A.G. Graham, 1316 West 57 Ave., V6P 1S8 – 604/684-8171 – *1
Murray H. Grant, #2020, 650 West Georgia St., PO Box 11547, V6B 4N7 – 604/683-9621, Fax: 604/683-5084 – *1
Greenall & Company, #200, 2443 Kingsway, V5R 5G8 – 604/430-5637, Fax: 604/430-5642 – *1
Harry Greenberg, 3450 West 10 Ave., V6R 2E8 – 604/733-4281 – *1
Greyell & MacPhail, #1811, 808 Nelson St., V6Z 2H2 – 604/687-4232, Fax: 604/687-4234 – *4
Grossman & Stanley, #800, 1090 West Georgia St., PO Box 55, V6E 3V7 – 604/683-7454, Fax: 604/683-8602 – *3
Guild, Yule, Sullivan, Yule, Truscott & Slivinski, Three Bentall Centre, #2000, 595 Burrard St., PO Box 49170, V7X 1R7 – 604/688-1221, Fax: 604/688-1315 – *27
W.F. Guinn, 671G Market Hill, V5Z 4B5 – 604/872-6658, Fax: 604/876-3304 – *1
Gutkin, Siddal & Cashman, #500, 650 - 41st Ave. West, V5Z 2M9 – 604/266-1130, Fax: 604/266-9046 – *5
Guy & Company, #510, 190 Alexander St., V6A 1B5 – 604/681-6164, Fax: 604/681-9420 – *2
Hara & Company, #301, 460 Nanaimo St., V5L 4W3 – 604/255-4800, Fax: 604/255-8111 – *3
Garry A. Harmel, #270, 5655 Cambie St., V5Z 3A4 – 604/266-3266, Fax: 604/266-5066 – *1
Harper Grey Easton, 3100 Vancouver Centre, 650 West Georgia St., PO Box 11504, V6B 4P7 – 604/687-0411, Fax: 604/669-9385 – *3
Harris & Company, #2200, 1111 West Georgia St., V6E 4M3 – 604/684-6633, Fax: 604/684-6632 – *1
Harris Atkinson Brun, #600, 1155 West Georgia St., V6E 3H4 – 604/683-2466, Fax: 604/683-4541 – *5
Harrop, Phillips, Powell & Gibbons, 2 Gaolers Mews, V6B 4K7 – 604/688-8211 – *8
P.A. Hart, #975, 200 Burrard St., V6C 3L6 – 604/688-6232, Fax: 604/687-7089 – *1
Heenan Blaikie, #600, 1199 West Hastings St., V6E 3T5 – 604/669-0011, Fax: 604/669-5101 – *13
A.G. Helgason, #1510, 777 Hornby St., V6Z 1S4 – 604/681-3448, Fax: 604/688-9981 – *1
John E. Helsing, #204, 1651 Commercial Dr., V5L 3Y3 – 604/253-7731, Fax: 604/253-7726 – *1
Hemsworth, Schmidt, #430, 580 Hornby St., V6C 3B6 – 604/687-4456, Fax: 604/687-0586 – *2
M.B. Hicks, #307, 815 Hornby St., V6Z 2E6 – 604/660-4100, Fax: 604/660-4198 – *1

Hogan & Company, 195 Alexander St., 5th Fl., V6A 1B8 – 604/687-8806 – *4
Holmes, Greenslade, 401 West Georgia St., 17th Fl., V6B 5A1 – 604/688-7861, Fax: 604/688-0426 – *4
Hordo & Ross, Nelson Sq., #1801, 808 Nelson St., PO Box 12146, V6Z 2H2 – 604/682-5250, Fax: 604/682-7872 – *6
B.D. Hoy & Associate, #209, 539 Main St., V6A 2V1 – 604/682-0596, Fax: 604/682-6709 – *1
S. Huberman, 796 Granville St., V6Z 1K1 – 604/654-2262, Fax: 604/682-8879 – *1
Peter J. Hull, 869 West 20 Ave., V5Z 1Y3 – 604/874-1242 – *1
Hungerford Simon, #1725, 555 Burrard St., V7X 1J8 – 604/682-7800, Fax: 604/682-8565 – *6
Hutchinson, Cristall, 796 Granville St., 5th Fl., V6Z 1K1 – 604/682-2821, Fax: 604/682-8879 – *2
L. Hyman, #800, 1200 Burrard St., V6Z 2C7 – 604/685-9277, Fax: 604/681-1576 – *4
Brian Jackson, #1502, 100 West Pender St., V6B 1R8 – 604/681-7766, Fax: 604/688-6243 – *2
Roy B. Jacobsen, #1500, 777 Hornby St., V6Z 1S4 – 604/681-5256 – *1
Jarvis & Company, 1080 Hornby St., 3rd Fl., V6Z 1V6 – 604/682-3771 – *5
Jarvis & Goulet, #600, 1125 Howe St., V6Z 2K8 – 604/682-0587 – *2
Jeffery & Calder, #601, 815 Hornby St., V6Z 2E6 – 604/669-5534, Fax: 604/669-7563 – *7
A. Jeletzky, 100 West Pender St., V6B 1R8 – 604/687-1037 – *1
J.L. Jessiman, 5550 Maple St., V6M 3T7 – 604/984-4975, Fax: 604/263-5670 – *1
Jones McCloy Peterson, 3 Bentall Centre, #1700, 595 Burrard St., 17th Fl., PO Box 49117, V7X 1G4 – 604/682-1851, Fax: 604/682-7329 – *9
D. Jung, 416 Columbia St., V6A 2R8 – 604/682-7151, Fax: 604/669-8042 – *1
R.N. Jussa, 4680 Main St., V5V 3R7 – 604/872-4745, 8191, Fax: 604/872-8217 – *1
E.W. Kagna, #612, 825 Granville St., V6Z 1K9 – 604/683-8722, Fax: 604/683-8722 – *1
Kane, Shannon & Weiler, #348, 1275 West 6th Ave., V6H 1A6 – 604/732-4070, Fax: 604/738-7134 – *1
Kaplan & Waddell, #102, 2590 Granville St., V6H 3H1 – 604/736-8021, Fax: 604/736-3845 – *4
Katz & Company, Nelson Square, #1018, 808 Nelson St., PO Box 12135, V6Z 2H2 – 604/669-6226, Fax: 604/669-6752 – *1
M.K. Keating, 2658 West 34 Ave., V6N 2J2 – 604/266-5169, Fax: 604/266-5169 – *1
Stephen Kelleher, #650, 475 West Georgia St., V6B 4M9 – 604/683-0122, Fax: 604/683-3846 – *1
C. Robert Kennedy, #206, 190 Alexander St., V6A 1B5 – 604/684-3927, Fax: 604/684-3228 – *1
J. Ross Ker, 2021 West 41 Ave., V6M 1Y7 – 604/266-7151, Fax: 604/266-8781 – *1
Kerfoot, Cameron & Company, #300, 5687 Yew St., V6M 3Y2 – 604/263-2565, Fax: 604/263-2737 – *12
Killam, Whitelaw & Twining, #100, 200 Granville St., PO Box 25, V6C 1S4 – 604/682-5466, Fax: 604/682-5217 – *17
L.A. King, #1510, 777 Hornby St., V6Z 1S4 – 604/688-9921, Fax: 604/688-9981 – *1
William N. King, United Kingdom Bldg., #400, 409 Granville St., V6C 1T2 – 604/682-1245, Fax: 604/682-8417 – *1
Norman C. Kliman, 465 West 26 Ave., V5Y 2K1 – 604/876-3544, Fax: 604/683-1620 – *1
James R. Klopping, #215, 402 West Pender St., V6B 1T6 – 604/682-8288 – *1
Koffman Birnie & Kalef, 885 West Georgia St., 19th Fl., V6C 3H4 – 604/891-3688, Fax: 604/891-3788 – *4
Kontou & Routhwarte, #301, 134 Abbott St., V6B 2K4 – 604/662-7244, Fax: 604/687-3097 – *2
Koo, McKee & Sharpe, Four Bentall Centre, #3354, 1055 Dunsmuir St., PO Box 49304, V7X 1L3 – 604/682-9555, Fax: 604/682-6425 – *4

* indicates number of lawyers in law firm.

Kornfeld & Company, #301, 796 Granville St., V6Z 1J8 – 604/689-3838, Fax: 604/689-0526 – *2

E.L. Kornfeld, #1116, 736 Granville St., V6Z 1H7 – 604/688-8241 – *1

Kowarsky & Company, #1050, 1185 West Georgia St., V6E 4E6 – 604/683-6875, Fax: 604/683-2737 – *8

G.R. Kroll, #400, 409 Granville St., V6C 1T2 – 604/682-4704, Fax: 604/682-8417 – *1

Theodore Kuchta, #1500, 777 Hornby St., V6Z 1S4 – 604/681-5256, Fax: 604/681-5103 – *1

Donna L. Kydd, 970 West - 22 Ave., V5Z 2A1 – 604/732-5031, Fax: 604/732-5046 – *1

Denis T. LaCharité, #208, 131 Water St., V6B 4M3 – 604/684-2315 – *1

Ladner Downs, Waterfront Centre, #1200, 200 Burrard St., PO Box 48600, V7X 1T2 – 604/687-5744, Fax: 604/687-1415; Email: ldmaster@ladner.com; URL: http://www.ladner.com/ladner – *106

Benedict S.K. Lam, 88 East Pender St., V6A 1T1 – 604/683-7282, Fax: 604/688-6388 – *1

Lando & Company, Four Bentall Centre, #1774, 1055 Dunsmuir St., PO Box 49345, V7X 1L4 – 604/682-6821, Fax: 604/662-8293 – *7

Lang Michener Lawrence & Shaw, Three Bentall Centre, #2500, 595 Burrard St., PO Box 49200, V7X 1L1 – 604/689-9111, Fax: 604/685-7084 – *47

Langdon, LaCroix & Toews, #1300, 1100 Melville St., V6E 4A6 – 604/681-1188, Fax: 604/681-3019 – *3

Lauk & La Liberte, #225, 701 West Georgia St., PO Box 10106, V7Y 1C6 – 604/669-8808, Fax: 604/669-2719 – *2

R.E. Lawrence, 1500 West Georgia St., 15th Fl., V6Z 1S4 – 604/681-4171, Fax: 604/681-5103 – *1

Lawson, Lundell, Lawson & McIntosh, Cathedral Place, #1600, 925 West Georgia St., V5C 3L2 – 604/685-3456, Fax: 604/669-1620; Email: genmail@lawsonlundell.com – *79

Laxton & Company, 1285 West Pender St., 10th Fl., V6E 4B1 – 604/682-3871, Fax: 604/682-3704 – *3

G.C. Layne, #402, 2366 Wall St., V5L 4Y1 – 604/253-1320 – *1

Leask, Daniells & Bahen, #201, 111 Water St., V6B 1A7 – 604/683-3206, Fax: 604/662-7511 – *5

LeBlanc & Company, 1826 West Broadway, V6J 1Y9 – 604/731-4628, Fax: 604/731-4620 – *2

Lecovin & Company, #300, 896 Cambie St., V6B 2P6 – 604/687-1721, Fax: 604/684-6303 – *2

Lee & Company, #388, 1190 Hornby St., V6Z 2K5 – 604/687-1212, Fax: 604/669-6868 – *2

Jack L. Lee, 127 East Pender St., 3rd Fl., V6A 1T6 – 604/683-7241 – *1

Legge & Company, #605, 815 Hornby St., V6Z 2E6 – 604/688-8211 – *1

Lew & Lee, #108, 329 Main St., V6A 2S9 – 604/685-8331, Fax: 604/685-6334 – *3

Chuck Lew, #1010, 207 West Hastings St., V6B 1H7 – 604/688-3601, Fax: 604/688-7866 – *1

H.H. Lew, 210 West Broadway., V5Y 3W2 – 604/879-3151, Fax: 604/879-3707 – *1

Libby, Moss & Beirne, 157 Alexander St., 3rd Fl., V6A 1B8 – 604/683-4311, Fax: 604/683-4317 – *2

Liddle, Burns, Beechinor & Fitzpatrick, #1210, 400 Burrard St., V6C 3A6 – 604/685-0121, Fax: 604/685-2104 – *9

Lidstone, Young, Anderson, Nelson Sq., #1616, 808 Nelson St., PO Box 12147, V6Z 2H2 – 604/689-7400, Fax: 604/689-3444; Toll Free: 1-800-665-3540 – *13

Lindsay Kenney, 700 West Pender St., 17th Fl., V6C 1G8 – 604/687-1323, Fax: 604/687-2347 – *25

A.L. Lipetz, #201, 2902 West Broadway, V6K 2G8 – 604/733-5611, Fax: 604/738-5611 – *1

P. Litsky, 6330 Fremlin St., V5Z 3X5 – 604/266-7806 – *1

Keith A. Lo, #338, 237 Keefer St., V6A 1X6 – 604/687-4315, Fax: 604/681-2289 – *2

Blair E. Lockhart, #400, 1045 Howe St., V6Z 2A9 – 604/688-5625 – *1

A.D. Long, 375 Southborough Dr., V7S 1M3 – 604/922-8228 – *1

Long, Miller & Co., #400, 409 Granville St., V6C 1T2 – 604/682-1311, Fax: 604/682-8417 – *1

R.H. Long & Co., #102, 4088 Cambie St., V5Z 2Y8 – 604/876-7797, Fax: 604/876-1105 – *1

Lorimer O'Dyer Adelman, #341, 5021 Kingsway, V5H 4A5 – 604/438-7443, Fax: 604/438-7642 – *2

Macaulay McColl, #600, 840 Howe St., V6Z 2L2 – 604/687-9811, Fax: 604/683-8716 – *11

Macdonald, Lewis, Pacific Centre, #1625, 609 Granville St., PO Box 10078, V7Y 1B6 – 604/669-6824, Fax: 604/681-8028 – *2

MacKenzie Fujisawa Brewer Stevenson Koenig, #1800, 400 Burrard St., V6C 3A6 – 604/689-3281, Fax: 604/685-6494 – *15

MacKenzie Murdy & McAllister, Four Bentall Centre, 1055 Dunsmuir St., 31st Fl., PO Box 49059, V7X 1C4 – 604/689-5263, Fax: 604/689-9029 – *4

R.H. MacKenzie, #2020, 650 West Georgia St., PO Box 11547, V6B 4N7 – 604/683-9621, Fax: 604/683-5084 – *1

MacKinlay Woodson Diebel, #1170, 1040 West Georgia St., V6E 4H1 – 604/669-1511, Fax: 604/669-1566 – *3

MacLean, Nicol & Wong, #200, 900 Howe St., V6Z 1M4 – 604/682-6466 – *4

J. Raymond MacLeod, #1240, 701 West Georgia St., V7Y 1A1 – 604/685-2361, Fax: 604/669-3477 – *1

MacQuarrie Hobkirk, #2020, 777 Hornby St., V6Z 1T7 – 604/684-6255, Fax: 604/684-7575 – *5

Mair Jensen Blair, #1110, 777 Dunsuir St., V7Y 1K4 – 604/684-9511

Maitland & Company, Standard Life Bldg., #700, 625 Howe St., V6C 2T6 – 604/681-7474, Fax: 604/681-3896 – *9

Mandell, Pinder, #300, 111 Water St., V6B 1A7 – 604/681-4146, Fax: 604/681-0959 – *9

Leonard F. Maracle, #206, 111 Water St., V6B 1A7 – 604/689-9545

Margach, Carr-Harris, Griffiths, #210, 900 Howe St., V6Z 2M4 – 604/669-4922 – *3

Marinakis & Company, #114, 900 Beach Ave., V6Z 2N9 – 604/684-1237, Fax: 604/688-0034 – *1

Alan Marsden, #303, 1431 Howe St., V6Z 1R9 – 604/669-3238, Fax: 604/669-7173 – *1

Gerald K. Martin, #308, 650 - 41st Ave. West, V5Z 2M9 – 604/266-1988, Fax: 604/263-0880 – *1

S.E. Martin, #201, 110 Cambie St., V6B 2M8 – 604/687-0134, Fax: 604/687-5176 – *1

M.V. Mass, #302, 2695 Granville St., V6H 3H4 – 604/736-8741, Fax: 604/736-3241 – *1

Maxwell, Schuman & Company, 900 Helmcken St., V6Z 1B3 – 604/669-4912, Fax: 604/662-3975 – *7

McAlpine & Associates, The Landing, #250, 375 Water St., V6B 5C6 – 604/685-6272, Fax: 604/685-8434

McCandless & Company, #900, 885 Dunsmuir St., V6C 1N5 – 604/662-3771, Fax: 604/669-9828 – *4

McCarthy Tétrault, Pacific Centre, #1300, 777 Dunsmuir St., PO Box 10424, V7Y 1K2 – 604/643-7100, Fax: 604/643-7900; Email: twb@mccarthy.ca; URL: http://www.mccarthy.ca – *79

Joanne S. McClusky, #300, 744 West Hastings, V6C 1A5 – 604/689-4010, Fax: 604/684-2349 – *1

McCrea & Associates, #102, 1012 Beach Ave., V6E 1T7 – 604/662-8200, Fax: 604/662-8225 – *3

McEwen Schmitt & Company, #1615, 1055 West Georgia St., 11174, V6E 3R5 – 604/683-1223, Fax: 604/683-2359 – *4

F.G. McGinley, #303, 555 Howe St., V6C 2C2 – 604/687-6916, Fax: 604/687-2933 – *1

McGrady, Askew & Fiorillo, #500, 2695 Granville St., V6H 3H4 – 604/734-4777, Fax: 604/734-1109 – *4

J.E. McInnes, 808 Nelson St., 17th Fl., PO Box 12148, V6Z 2H2 – 604/891-0214, Fax: 604/685-8992 – *1

McKenzie & Company, #920, 938 Howe St., V6Z 1N9 – 604/687-7811, Fax: 604/685-4358 – *2

D.J. McKinlay, #2500, 595 Burrard St., V7X 1L1 – 604/691-7477, Fax: 604/689-9111 – *1

R.M. McKitrick, #302, 2695 Granville St., V6H 3H4 – 604/736-6717, Fax: 604/736-3241 – *1

McLachlan Brown Anderson, #1001, 601 West Broadway, V5Z 4C2 – 604/873-4351 – *11

Harry P. McLaughlin, #1001, 750 West Pender St., V6C 2T8 – 604/682-2771, Fax: 604/682-1183 – *1

E.M. McMahon, #215, 1075 West Georgia St., V6E 3C9 – 604/683-6828, Fax: 604/683-8456 – *1

McNeney & McNeney, 970 Richard St., V6G 3C1 – 604/687-1766, Fax: 604/687-0181 – *4

McTaggart, Ellis & Company, #1400, 1030 West Georgia St., V6E 2Y3 – 604/682-3131, Fax: 604/682-3353 – *9

Brian E. Mickelson, 100 West Pender St., 2nd Fl., V6B 1R8 – 604/688-8588, Fax: 604/681-0652 – *1

J.L. Mickleson, #302, 1110 Hamilton St., V6B 2S2 – 604/684-0040, Fax: 604/684-0048 – *1

Micner & Company, #720, 943 West Broadway, V5Z 1K3 – 604/732-1800, Fax: 604/732-7500 – *2

Milan Uzelac, Law Offices, Personal Law Corporation, #200, 1737 West 3 Ave., V6J 1K7 – 604/734-2444, Fax: 604/734-3243 – *2

Moir Associates, #1107, 808 Nelson St., PO Box 12150, V6Z 2H2 – 604/685-7996, Fax: 604/685-7466 – *3

Montaine, Black & Company, #217, 900 West Georgia St., V6C 2W6 – 604/685-5361, Fax: 604/685-1564 – *1

Mortimer & Rose, 1243 Hornby St., V6Z 1W4 – 604/669-0440, Fax: 604/669-0228 – *2

Morton & Company, #1750, 750 West Pender Blvd., V6C 2T8 – 604/681-1194, Fax: 604/681-9652 – *4

Munro & Crawford, 5670 Yew St., V6M 3Y3 – 604/266-7174, Fax: 604/266-7998 – *4

Murphy, Battista, Vancouver Centre, #2020, 650 West Georgia St., PO Box 11547, V6B 4N7 – 604/683-9621, Fax: 604/683-5084 – *4

Murray, Remedios & Stewart, Burrard Bldg., Bldg Box: 507, #1010, 1030 West Georgia St., V6E 2Y3 – 604/688-9337, Fax: 604/688-5590 – *7

Myers Johnson & Co., 195 Alexander St., 5th Fl., V6A 1B8 – 604/688-8331, Fax: 604/688-8350 – *4

Myers, Johnson & Company, 195 Alexander St., 5th Fl., V6A 1B8 – 604/688-8331, Fax: 604/688-8350 – *4

Roderick Naknakim, #101, 1292 West Georgia St., V6E 3J3 – 604/684-1937, Fax: 604/685-4271

B.J. Nelson, #103, 1012 Beach Ave., V6E 1T7 – 604/685-7317, Fax: 604/682-3965 – *1

Kimball R. Nichols, #1050, 1188 West Georgia, V6E 4A2 – 604/682-0541, Fax: 604/682-4428 – *1

Allan S. Nicol, #1800, 999 West Hastings, V6C 2W2 – 604/683-4478, Fax: 604/683-1375 – *1

K.F. Nordlinger, Q.C., #109, 1008 Beach Ave., V6E 1T7 – 604/689-5134, Fax: 604/689-5323 – *3

Norton Stewart, #1200, 1055 West Georgia St., PO Box 11104, V6E 3P3 – 604/687-0555, Fax: 604/689-1248 – *7

O'Neill & Company, 1190 Hornby St., 12th Fl., V6Z 2L3 – 604/687-5792, Fax: 604/687-6650 – *6

N.R. Oddy, #1402, 1166 Alberni St., V6E 3Z3 – 604/687-6339, Fax: 604/687-3256 – *1

A. Barry Oland, Vancouver Centre, Bldg Box: 2020, 650 West Georgia St., PO Box 11547, V6B 4N7 – 604/683-9621, Fax: 604/689-4556 – *2

Oliver & Company, #1920, 777 Hornby St., V6Z 2L1 – 604/681-5232, Fax: 604/681-1331 – *5

Oreck, Chernoff, Tick, Farber & Folk, #1800, 701 West Georgia St., PO Box 10142, V7Y 1E9 – 604/689-8741, Fax: 604/682-7643 – *8

Osten & Osten, #114, 990 Beach Ave., V6Z 2N9 – 604/683-9104, Fax: 604/688-0034 – *2

Owen, Bird, Three Bentall Centre, #2900, 595 Burrard St., PO Box 49130, V7X 1J5 – 604/688-0401, Fax: 604/688-2827; Email: owenbird.com – *48

Paine Edmonds, #1100, 510 Burrard St., V6C 3A8 – 604/683-1211, Fax: 604/681-5084; Toll Free: 1-800-669-8599 – *17

Canadian Almanac & Directory 1997

R. Pandya, #720, 475 Howe St., V6C 2B3 – 604/685-0507, Fax: 604/685-7249 – *1

Pape & Salter, #400, 220 Cambie St., V6B 2M9 – 604/681-3002, Fax: 604/681-3050 – *3

Al Paquette, #103, 8584 Granville St., V6P 4Z7 – 604/261-3211, Fax: 604/266-1120 – *1

J.C. Paterson & Associates, #340, 1090 Homer St., V6B 2W9 – 604/669-7311, Fax: 604/669-2340 – *2

Patterson & Price, #1500, 736 Granville St., V6Z 1G3 – 604/684-5951, Fax: 604/684-2449 – *2

Peterson Stark, #500, 1195 West Broadway, V6H 3X5 – 604/736-9811, Fax: 604/736-2859; Toll Free: 1-800-663-1667 – *15

S.L. Polinsky, 671D Market Hill, V5Z 4B5 – 604/876-9995, Fax: 604/879-4934 – *1

S.L. Polsky Shamash, #200, 1700 - 75th Ave. West, V6P 6G2 – 604/664-7800, Fax: 604/664-7898 – *1

John E. Potter, 1370 West King Edward, V6H 1Z9 – 604/736-6831, Fax: 604/873-3989 – *1

Poulsen & Co., #1800, 999 West Hastings St., V6C 2W2 – 604/681-0123, Fax: 604/683-1375 – *3

Price Shimizu, #718, 808 Nelson St., PO Box 12159, V6Z 2H2 – 604/685-6426, Fax: 604/685-6412 – *2

William C. Prowse, 2215 Commissioner St., V5L 1B5 – 604/254-5751, Fax: 604/254-0957 – *1

Raibmon & Goulet, #880, 1090 West Georgia St., V6E 3V7 – 604/688-8551, Fax: 604/662-8782 – *2

B.H. Ralston, #1300, 100 West Pender, V6B 1R8 – 604/669-9488, Fax: 604/669-0459 – *1

Ramsay Thompson Lampman, #730, 580 Hornby St., V6C 3B6 – 604/685-7590 – *12

Rand, Edgar & Sedun, #2200, 885 West Georgia St., V6C 3E8 – 604/687-9931, Fax: 604/681-7116 – *4

W.A. Randall, #102, 535 West Georgia St., V6B 1Z6 – 604/685-9411 – *1

Rankin & Company, 195 Alexander St., 4th Fl., V6A 1N8 – 604/682-2781, Fax: 604/682-8649 – *5

Rankin, Bond, 157 Alexander St., V6A 1V8 – 604/682-3621, Fax: 604/682-3919 – *2

Raphanel Cantillon, #102, 853 Richards St., V6B 3B4 – 604/681-5383, Fax: 604/681-6021 – *2

Richards Buell Sutton, #300, 1111 Melville St., V6E 4H7 – 604/682-3664, Fax: 604/688-3830; Email: rbs2@rbs.com – *29

Riecken & Sherman, 1035 Cambie St., V6B 5L7 – 604/682-0494 – *3

Ritchie & Company, #1002, 777 West Broadway, V52 4J7 – 604/877-0778, Fax: 604/879-2852 – *2

Roberts & Griffin, #901, 840 Howe St., V6Z 2L2 – 604/682-9766, Fax: 604/682-6746 – *5

Roberts & Stahl, #500, 220 Cambie St., V6B 2M9 – 604/684-6377, Fax: 604/684-6387 – *2

Daniel J. Rogers, #101, 925 West 8 Ave., V5Z 1E4 – 604/736-7754, Fax: 604/736-9023 – *1

Paul E.A. Romeril, #107, 2298 McBain Ave., V6L 3B1 – 604/732-4845 – *1

V. Romilly, 3536 Point Grey Rd., V6R 1A8 – 604/736-7040, Fax: 604/738-5143 – *1

Jeffrey A. Rose, 1243 Hornby St., V6Z 1W4 – 604/688-3288

Rosenberg & Rosenberg, 671D Market Hill, V5Z 4B5 – 604/879-4505, Fax: 604/879-4934 – *3

Rosenbloom & Aldridge, #1300, 355 Burrard St., V6C 2G8 – 604/684-1311, Fax: 604/684-6402 – *4

J.H. Rosner, #770, 475 West Georgia St., V6B 4M9 – 604/687-6638, Fax: 604/682-2481 – *1

R.D. Ross, 4741 West 2 Ave., V6T 1C1 – 604/228-9701, Fax: 604/228-9055 – *1

K. Roth, #501, 595 Howe St., V6C 2T5 – 604/681-7161, Fax: 604/683-7043 – *1

Ronald D. Roth, #1440, 1066 West Hastings, V6E 3X1 – 604/669-2336

Sunny Rothschild, 2081 - 37 Ave. West, V6M 1N7 – 604/261-0300, Fax: 604/261-0312; Email: sunny@cyberstore.ca – *1

Rubin & Maisonville, 100 West Pender St., 9th Fl., V6B 1R8 – *2

J.M. Ruckwood, #403, 1720 Balsam St., V6K 3M2 – 604/732-6637 – *1

Rush, Crane, Guenther & Adams, #300, 111 Water St., V6B 1A7 – 604/687-5611, Fax: 604/681-0912 – *6

Russell & DuMoulin, #2100, 1075 West Georgia St., V6E 3G2 – 604/631-3131, Fax: 604/631-3232; Email: rdcounsel@rdcounsel.com; URL: http://rd-counsel.com/rd - *107

Sabatino Moscovich & Aikenhead, #316, 2800 East 1 Ave., V5M 4P3 – 604/253-4525, Fax: 604/253-1080 – *5

E.A. Safarik, 2215 Commissioner St., V5L 1A8 – 604/254-5751, Fax: 604/254-0957 – *1

C.A. Sandberg, #108, 2786 West 16 Ave., V6K 4M1 – 604/734-7768, Fax: 604/733-1229 – *1

J.P. Sanders, #222, 470 Granville St., V6C 1V5 – 604/685-6238 – *1

Dale Sands, #300, 3665 Kingsway, V5R 5W2 – 604/431-8452, Fax: 604/462-0407 – *1

Iqbal Sara, #1, 2535 SW Marine Dr., V6P 6C3 – 604/327-1911 – *1

Henry K. Sarava, 2222 Spruce St., V6H 2P3 – 604/737-1226, Fax: 604/737-1230 – *1

Alison Sawyer, #3, 1163 Commercial Dr., V5L 3X3 – 604/255-1979, Fax: 604/255-6589 – *1

P.N. Scarisbrick, 234 Abbott St., V6B 2K8 – 604/688-0495, Fax: 604/688-0201 – *3

Bernard Schachter, #401, 796 Granville St., V6Z 1J6 – 604/688-1474, Fax: 604/688-5191 – *1

Schiffer & Company, #1470, 1188 Georgia St. West, V6E 4A2 – 604/681-1171, Fax: 604/681-1329 – *3

Schroeder Pidgeion & Company, #1119, 808 Nelson St., PO Box 12168, V6Z 2H2 – 604/888-6737, Fax: 604/888-0271 – *9

D.A. Schwartz, #304, 700 West Pender St., V6C 1G8 – 604/687-0811, Fax: 604/688-9611 – *1

Stanley A. Schwartz, #1800, 701 West Georgia St., PO Box 10142, V7Y 1E9 – 604/681-1077, Fax: 604/682-7643 – *1

Seaton Promislow, Pender Pl., Bldg Box: 1202, 700 West Pender St., V6C 1G8 – 604/688-1466, Fax: 604/688-4157 – *1

A.P. Serka, #707, 777 West Broadway, V5Z 4J7 – 604/876-8761, Fax: 604/876-9035 – *1

Murray H. Shapiro, #702, 686 West Broadway, V5Z 1G1 – 604/879-6777, Fax: 604/874-0820 – *1

S.S. Shelton, 2245 Commercial Dr., V5N 4B6 – 604/251-2144, Fax: 604/251-2781 – *1

Merril Shepard, #2100, 1075 West Georgia St., V6E 3G2 – 604/631-4929, Fax: 604/631-3232

Shortt & Company, #400, 789 West Pender, V6C 1H2 – 604/669-4447, Fax: 604/669-4737 – *4

Shrimpton & Company, 1325 Kingsway, V5V 3E3 – 604/879-2458, Fax: 604/879-4643 – *3

Sierra Legal Defence Fund, #214, 131 Water St., V6B 4M3 – 604/685-5618, Fax: 604/685-7813; Email: sldf@wimsey.com – *6

Sikula Werbes Sasges, #708, 1111 West Hastings St., V6E 2J3 – 604/669-3233, Fax: 604/689-4626 – *3

Silbernagel & Company, #700, 595 Howe St., V6C 2T5 – 604/687-9621, Fax: 604/687-5960 – *2

Simon, Wener & Adler, #401, 1385 West 8 Ave., V6H 3V9 – 604/736-5500, Fax: 604/736-5522 – *5

Simpson & Company, #750, 999 West Broadway, V5Z 1K5 – 604/734-2272, Fax: 604/734-4570 – *4

Simpson & Company, #600, 1001 West Broadway, V6H 4B1 – 604/734-1234, Fax: 604/734-8327 – *4

Singleton Urquhart Scott, #1200, 1125 Howe St., V6Z 2K8 – 604/682-7474, Fax: 604/682-1283 – *19

Sisett & Co., #603, 601 West Broadway, V5Z 4C2 – 604/879-8811, Fax: 604/879-7346 – *1

Smart & Biggar, Vancouver Centre, #2200, 650 West Georgia St., PO Box 11560, V6B 4N8 – 604/682-7295, Fax: 604/682-0274 – *3

Smith & Hughes, #321, 1525 Robson St., V6G 1C3 – 604/683-4176, Fax: 604/683-2621 – *4

Smith Lyons, World Trade Centre, #550, 999 Canada Pl., V6C 3C8 – 604/662-8082, Fax: 604/891-2700 – *17

Smith, Hutchison, #410, 355 Burrard St., V6C 2G8 – 604/683-6858

Snarch & Allen, #907, 1030 Georgia St. West, V6E 2Y3 – 604/684-8000, Fax: 604/684-8003 – *3

Sobolewski Anfield, Stock Exchange Twr., Pacific Centre, #1600, 609 Granville St., PO Box 10068, V7Y 1C3 – 604/669-1322, Fax: 604/669-3877 – *5

Soronow & Soronow, 1628 West 7 Ave., V6J 1S5 – 604/733-2411, Fax: 604/736-6225 – *1

Michael P.S. Spearing, #880, 1500 West Georgia St., V6G 2Z6 – 604/681-0699, Fax: 604/682-0713 – *1

Spring Brammall & Gemmill, 2774 Granville St., V6H 3J3 – 604/732-3881, Fax: 604/723-3883 – *2

Vina A. Starr, #608, 1033 Davie St., V6E 1M7 – 604/683-7383, Fax: 604/683-0272 – *2

Steinberg & Company, #390, 2600 Granville St., V6H 3V3 – 604/733-6130, Fax: 604/733-6160 – *1

D.M.B. Steinberg, #601, 134 Abbott St., V6B 2K4 – 604/689-0051, Fax: 604/689-3327 – *1

Stephens & Holman, #320, 1600 West 6 Ave., V6J 1R3 – 604/736-0431 – *7

Stewart & Company, Chancery Pl., #903, 865 Hornby St., V6Z 2G3 – 604/688-0033, Fax: 604/685-5238 – *5

Stewart Aulinger & Company, #1200, 805 West Broadway, V5Z 1K1 – 604/879-0291 – *6

Stikeman, Elliott, Park Pl., #1700, 666 Burrard St., V6C 2X8 – 604/631-1300, Fax: 604/681-1825 – *21

Street Morrison Hall, #1701, 1166 Alberni St., V6E 3Z3 – 604/688-7211, Fax: 604/688-4481 – *3

J.M. Sumpton, 10 Gaolers Mews, V6B 4K7 – 604/688-7252 – *1

Swinton & Company, Robson Ct., #1000, 840 Howe St., V6Z 2M1 – 604/687-2242, Fax: 604/643-1200; Toll Free: 1-800-794-6866; Email: svd@swinton.ca – *37

Ruth Lea Taylor, #3, 1163 Commercial Dr., V5L 3X3 – 604/255-1979, Fax: 604/255-6589 – *1

G.J. Te Hennepe, #203, 4545 West 10 Ave., V6R 4N2 – 604/228-1433, Fax: 604/228-9822 – *1

P.G. Theocharis, #1510, 777 Hornby St., V6Z 1S4 – 604/669-7726, Fax: 604/688-9981 – *1

J.G. Thomson, #419, 1033 Davie St., V6E 1M7 – 604/683-3371 – *1

Bonnie L. Thorpe, 6909 Cambie St., V6P 3H1 – 604/685-9721 – *1

Thorsteinssons, Three Bentall Centre, 595 Burrard St., 27th Fl., PO Box 49123, V7X 1J2 – 604/689-1261, Fax: 604/688-4711 – *27

Torrie & Associates, 1221 Bidwell St., V6G 2K7 – 604/683-8111, Fax: 604/685-0194 – *2

Trower & Company, #1180, 666 Burrard St., V6C 2X8 – 604/683-5781, Fax: 604/683-5826 – *2

Tupper, Jonsson & Yeadon, #1710, 1177 West Hastings St., V6E 2L3 – 604/683-9262, Fax: 604/683-9635 – *9

C.J. Van Twest, #404, 1160 Burrard St., V6Z 2E8 – 604/683-8874, Fax: 604/683-8874 – *1

Varty & Company, Bldg Box: 12155, #1300, 808 Nelson St., V6Z 2H2 – 604/684-5356, Fax: 604/685-8972 – *6

Vertlieb Anderson, 835 Granville St., 2nd Fl., V6Z 1K7 – 604/688-7761, Fax: 604/688-7291 – *4

Vick, McPhee & Liu, #1275, 1185 West Georgia St., V6E 4E6 – 604/682-0926, Fax: 604/688-8615 – *5

Victory Square Law, #200, 198 West Hastings, V6B 1H2 – 604/684-8421 – *1

Von Dehn & Company, #700, 595 Howe St., V6C 2T5 – 604/688-4541, Fax: 604/687-5960 – *2

T. Wing Wai, #205, 475 Main St., V6A 2T7 – 604/688-2291, Fax: 604/688-8983 – *2

Walden & Company, #327, 736 Granville St., V6Z 1G3 – 604/683-5943 – *2

Walker & Company, 1500 - 1030 West Georgia St., V6E 2Y3 – 604/682-8521, Fax: 604/682-8753 – *8

G.B. Walker, #750, 609 West Hastings St., PO Box 14, V6B 4W4 – 604/681-9577 – *1

Warren Aaron MacGregor & Gordon, #1101, 808 Nelson St., V6Z 2H2 – 604/689-7571 – *4

---

* indicates number of lawyers in law firm.

C.E. Warren, #506, 815 Hornby St., V6Z 2E6 – 604/689-7571, Fax: 604/685-8563 – *1
Derril T. Warren, Q.C., Intl. Commercial Arbn. Centre, #670, 999 Canada Place, V6C 2E2 – 604/684-2821 – *1
Warren, Eder, #201, 110 Cambie St., V6B 2M8 – 604/687-0134, Fax: 604/687-5176 – *3
G.A. Wasko, #D, 1306 Bidwell St., V6C 2L1 – 604/662-3032 – *1
Wasson & Wasson, #222, 470 Granville St., V6C 1V5 – 604/681-2147, Fax: 604/681-5355 – *1
Watson Goepel Maledy, Three Bentall Centre, #3023, 595 Burrard St., PO Box 49096, V7X 1G4 – 604/688-1301, Fax: 604/688-8193 – *16
Watts, Nabata, #570, 999 West Broadway, V5Z 1K5 – 604/734-2766, Fax: 604/731-5274 – *2
R.H. Watts, #740, 475 West Georgia St., V6B 4M9 – 604/682-2671, Fax: 604/682-2348 – *1
K.S. Westlake, #975, 200 Burrard St., V6C 3L6 – 604/687-9831, Fax: 604/687-7089 – *1
White, John M. & Associates, #312, 1281 West Georgia St., V6E 3J7 – 604/683-4161 – *3
Williamson, Walker & Company, #1500, 1030 West Georgia St., V6E 2Y3 – 604/682-8521, Fax: 604/682-8753 – *1
Wilson, Danderfer, Banno & Mitchell, #1450, 1075 West Georgia St., V6E 3C9 – 604/682-0701, Fax: 604/682-7359 – *7
P.J. Wilson, 195 Alexander St., 3rd Fl., V6A 1B8 – 604/684-4751, Fax: 604/684-8319 – *1
Wirick & Klassen, 6625 Fraser St., 2nd Fl., V5X 3T6 – 604/324-5115, Fax: 604/324-6996 – *2
Lorne Wise, #202, 2628 Granville St., V6H 4B4 – 604/731-0248 – *1
Wittchen, Macintosh & Larson, 1035 Cambie St., V6B 5L7 – 604/682-0494, Fax: 604/682-4258 – *3
Wizinsky, Dadson & Longpre, #930, 800 West Pender St., V6C 2V6 – 604/688-3800, Fax: 604/688-3818 – *4
P.L. Wong, #407, 1541 West Broadway, V6J 1W7 – 604/731-5301, Fax: 604/731-1266 – *1
W.G. Wong, 145 Keefer St., 2nd Fl., V6A 1X3 – 604/685-9361, Fax: 604/684-1299 – *1
A.K. Wooster, 1176 West Georgia St., PO Box 18, V6E 4A2 – 604/684-1204, Fax: 604/682-4428 – *1
Worrall, Scott & Page, #100, 200 Granville St., Box 25, V6C 1S4 – 604/683-5731 – *12
Patricia Yaremovich, #610, 207 West Hastings St., V6B 1H7 – 604/688-3469, Fax: 604/681-1533 – *1
D.W.H. Yerxa, #1200, 805 West Broadway, V5Z 1K1 – 604/873-5225, Fax: 604/874-5551 – *1
David L. Youngson, #204, 5701 Granville St., V6M 4J7 – 604/266-6588, Fax: 604/266-6393 – *1

VANDERHOOF .... Cariboo
Hope Heinrich, 2416 Burrard St., V0J 3A0 – *1
Steven F. Peleshok, 2608 Burrard Ave., PO Box 1128, V0J 3A0 – 250/567-9277, Fax: 250/567-2657 – *1

VERNON .... Yale
R.V. Blakely, #102, 2802 - 30 St., V1T 8G7 – 250/549-1544, Fax: 250/549-4233 – *1
Alan M. Gaudette, 13004 Kinlock Dr., V1B 1C2 – 250/545-3132, Fax: 250/545-1617
Kenny Diebert Gaudette, 3009 - 28 St., V1T 4Z7 – 250/545-3132, Fax: 250/545-1617 – *3
Andrew, Kern, #1, 2906 - 32 St., V1T 5M1 – 250/549-2184, Fax: 250/549-2207
Howard Lawrence, 2903 - 28 St., V1T 4Z5 – 250/549-1555 – *1
Nixon, Wenger & Co., 3201 - 30 Ave., 4th Fl., V1T 2C6 – 250/542-5353, Fax: 250/542-7273 – *10
Yvonne D. Orr, #201, 3131 - 29 St., V1T 5A8 – 250/549-3101 – *1
Pattie & Company, 2805 - 30 Ave., V1T 5C7 – 250/542-1266, Fax: 250/549-1214 – *4
Sigalet, Maguire & Cole, 2904 - 29th Ave., V1T 1V7 – 250/545-6054, Fax: 250/545-7227; Email: djsiglet@nocdc.bc.ca – *4
Steiner & Company, 3107A - 31 Ave., V1T 2G9 – 250/545-1371, Fax: 250/542-5630 – *1

VICTORIA .... Vancouver Island
Acheson Shaw, #400, 535 Yates St., V8W 2Z6 – 250/384-6262, Fax: 250/384-5353 – *3
Achtem Alexander, Bank of Commerce Bldg., Bldg Box: 667, #808, 1175 Douglas St., V8W 2E1 – 250/388-4444, Fax: 250/388-4777 – *4
J. Trevor Alexander, #520, 645 Fort St., V8W 1G2 – 250/360-1777, Fax: 250/360-1778 – *1
Amicus Law Centre, 207 Menzies St., V8V 2G6 – 250/383-5012, Fax: 250/385-1174 – *1
Anniko & Hunter, #201, 300 Gorge Rd. West, V9A 1M8 – 250/385-1233, Fax: 250/385-4078 – *3
Cardinal, Edgar, Emberton & Macaulay, #101, 2945 Jacklin Rd., V9B 5E3 – 250/474-2274 – *8
R.W. Chard, #421, 645 Fort St., V8W 1G2 – 250/384-9932, Fax: 250/384-9932 – *1
Pinder K. Cheema, #312, 645 Fort St., V8W 1C4 – 250/383-6332 – *1
D.H. Christie, 810 Courtney St., V8W 1C4 – 250/385-1022 – *1
Clapp & Company, 1005 Cook St., V8V 3Z6 – 250/388-5266, Fax: 250/388-5663 – *2
Robert C. Claus, 1161 Fort St., V8V 3K9 – 250/361-9600, Fax: 250/361-9181 – *1
Clay & Company, 837 Burdett Ave., PO Box 961, V8W 2S4 – 250/386-2261, Fax: 250/389-1336 – *6
Considine & Lawler, International House, #700, 880 Douglas St., V8W 2B7 – 250/381-7788, Fax: 250/381-1042 – *6
Cook Roberts, 777 Fort St., 4th Fl., V8W 1G9 – 250/385-1411, Fax: 250/381-0300; Email: lawmark@cookroberts.bc.ca – *12
Robert S. Cosburn, #316, 10 Paul Kane Pl., V9A 7J8 – 250/360-1777
Cox, Taylor, Burnes House, 26 Bastion Sq., 3rd Fl., V8W 1H9 – 250/388-4457, Fax: 250/382-4236 – *11
Crease, Harman & Company, #800, 1070 Douglas St., PO Box 997, V8W 2S8 – 250/388-5421, Fax: 250/388-4294 – *24
G.J. Davies, #207, 895 Fort St., V8W 1H7 – 250/380-9978 – *1
H.H. Decter, 138 Linden Ave., V8V 4E1
Dinning Hunter & Company, #201, 895 Fort St., V8W 1H7 – 250/381-2151, Fax: 250/386-2123 – *9
Dinning Hunter & Company, 813 Goldstream Ave., V9B 2X8 – 250/478-1731, Fax: 250/478-9500
D.G. Fetterley, #312, 645 Fort St., V8W 1G2 – 250/382-6952 – *1
Vincent R. Giles, #203A, 947 Fort St., V8V 3K3 – 250/386-6181 – *1
Gordon & Velletta, #203, 919 Fort St., V8V 3K3 – 250/383-9104, Fax: 250/383-1922 – *3
Green Higinbotham & Claus, 1161 Fort St., V8V 3K9 – 250/361-9600, Fax: 250/361-9181 – *4
Lenore B. Harlton, #209, 703 Broughton St., V8W 1E2 – 250/382-5161, Fax: 250/383-0611 – *1
Hatter, Thompson & Shumka, #201, 919 Fort St., V8V 3K3 – 250/388-4931, Fax: 250/386-8088 – *4
Heath, Irving & Walton, 3371 Oak St., V8X 1R2 – 250/386-1336, Fax: 250/386-3363 – *3
John A. Hills, #202, 3 Fan Tan Alley, V8W 3G9 – 250/381-6171, Fax: 250/381-3460 – *1
Holmes & Isherwood, 1190 Fort St., V8V 3K8 – 250/383-7157, Fax: 250/383-1535 – *2
Horne, Coupar, Royal Trust Bldg., 612 View St., 3rd Fl., V8W 1J5 – 250/388-6631, Fax: 250/388-5974 – *11
Jawl & Bundon, 1007 Fort St., 4th Fl., V8V 3K5 – 250/385-5787, Fax: 250/385-4364 – *6
Johns, Southward, Glazier & Walton, PO Box 847, V8W 2R9 – 250/381-7321, Fax: 250/381-1181 – *5
Jones Emery, #1212, 1175 Douglas St., V8W 2E9 – 250/382-7222, Fax: 250/382-5436 – *9
R.E.M. Jones, 910 Government St., 3rd Fl., V8V 1X4 – 250/387-4481 – *1
Kardish Ashurst, 409 - 3960 Quadra St., V8X 4A3 – 250/479-9336, Fax: 250/479-6845 – *7
Kjellander Pope & Company, #200, 764 Yates St., V8W 1L4 – 250/382-2632, Fax: 250/382-4542 – *2
Latham, Dennis A., & Associate, #210, 612 View St., V8W 1J5 – 250/388-7575, Fax: 250/388-9642 – *2
Lidstone, Young, Anderson, 501 - 1803 Douglas St., V8T 5C3 – 250/383-2063, Fax: 250/689-3444
Linge Carr & Davies, #110, 1315 Esquimalt Rd., V9A 3P5 – 250/384-7877, Fax: 250/388-7327 – *1
S.P. MacCarthy, 1879 Forrester St., V8R 3G7 – 250/387-0483, Fax: 250/387-0527 – *1
MacIsaac & Company, #320, 560 Johnson St., PO Box 933, V8W 2R9 – 250/381-5353, Fax: 250/380-7272 – *9
MacIsaac & Company, 2227 Sooke Rd., V9B 1W8 – 250/474-1940 – *2
D.A. Main, #209, 703 Broughton St., V8W 1E2 – 250/383-4541, Fax: 250/383-0611 – *1
McConnan, Bion, O'Connor & Peterson, #420, 880 Douglas St., V8W 2B7 – 250/385-1383, Fax: 250/385-2841 – *13
McKimm & Lott, 800 Fort St., V8W 1H4 – 250/389-0809, Fax: 250/386-6244
McMicken, Shaver, Alexander and Bennett, 990 Fort St., 3rd Fl., V8V 3K2 – 250/385-9555, Fax: 250/385-9841 – *4
Meyer & Company, #401, 645 Fort St., V8W 1G2 – 250/384-1951, Fax: 250/381-1954 – *2
Robert Moore-Stewart, #616, 620 View St., V8W 1J6 – 250/380-1887, Fax: 250/380-9134 – *1
Morahan & Aujla, #203, 821 Burdett Ave., V8W 1B3 – 250/383-3542, Fax: 250/385-8748 – *2
Mullin Demeo Dalsin, #102, 3930 Shelbourne St., V8P 5P6 – 250/477-3327, Fax: 250/477-0980 – *3
O'Grady Associates, #906, 1175 Douglas St., V8W 2E1 – 250/384-7119 – *2
Parsons & Company, 714A Goldstream Ave., V8B 2X3 – 250/474-3144, Fax: 250/474-5571 – *1
Pearlman & Lindholm, 736 Broughton St., PO Box 1327, V8W 1E1 – 250/388-4433, Fax: 250/388-5856 – *14
Clark R. Purves, 620 View St., 7th Fl., V8W 1J6 – 250/386-2225, 688-9801, Fax: 250/386-6609 – *1
Randall & Company, 103 - 1006 Fort St., V8V 3K4 – 250/382-9282, Fax: 250/382-0366 – *7
Heather Raven, 215 Begbie Bldg., Faculty of Law, University of Victoria, PO Box 2400, V8W 3H7 – 250/721-8185, Fax: 250/721-8149
R. Keith Reed, 535 - 645 Fort St., V8W 1G2 – 250/383-3838, Fax: 250/385-4324 – *1
Victor W. Simeoni, 4051 Ebony Place, V8N 3Z1 – 250/477-3331 – *1
Sidney B. Simons, 620 View St., 7th Fl., V8W 1J6 – 604/688-9801, 386-2225, Fax: 604/386-6609 – *1
Skillings & Company, 880 Douglas St., V8W 2B7 – 250/388-5136, Fax: 250/388-5195 – *2
Smith, Hutchison, 823 Broughton St., V8W 1E5 – 250/388-6666, Fax: 250/389-0400 – *7
Stevenson, Doell & Company, 999 Fort St., V8V 3K3 – 250/388-7881, Fax: 250/388-7324 – *7
Straith & Company, 1070 Douglas St., PO Box 1052, V8W 2C4 – 250/386-1434, Fax: 250/386-1421 – *5
Christine A. Stretton, #300, 506 Fort St., V8W 1E6 – 250/388-5333, Fax: 250/382-8644 – *1
E.G.L. Tomlinson, #209, 703 Broughton St., V8W 1E2 – 250/383-6432, Fax: 250/383-0611 – *1
Turnham Woodland, 1002 Wharf St., V8W 1T4 – 250/385-1122, Fax: 250/385-6522 – *6
Wilson Marshall, #200, 911 Yates St., V8V 4X3 – 250/385-8741, Fax: 250/385-0433 – *3
Wood & McMillan, #500, 645 Fort St., V8W 1G2 – , Fax: 604/380-7299 – *2
Woods Adair, #201, 4500 West Saanich Rd., V8Z 3G2 – 250/479-9367, Fax: 250/727-3356 – *4
Jack Woodward Barristers & Solicitors, Penthouse, 3 Fan Tan Alley, V8W 1N7 – 250/383-2356, Fax: 250/380-6560

WEST VANCOUVER .... Vancouver

Donald E. Brister, #216, 2438 Marine Dr., V7V 1L2 – 604/922-6158 – *1

K.A. Davis, 475 Keith Rd., V7T 1L6 – 604/926-7887 – *1

Daniel B. Geller, 5349 Monteverdi Place, V7W 2W8 – 604/921-5948 – *1

George Davis & Company, #205, 1455 Bellevue Ave., V7T 1C3 – 604/922-2151, Fax: 604/925-0457 – *1

Goluboff, Mazzei, #201, 585 - 16th St., PO Box 91700, V7V 3R8 – 604/925-1156, Fax: 604/926-7817 – *4

Gourlay Spencer Slade & Winch, #205, 1455 Bellevue Ave., V7T 1C3 – 604/922-3386, Fax: 604/925-1304 – *5

Christopher H. Hebb, #30, 2231 Folkestone Way, V7S 2Y6 – 604/922-9766 – *1

McCrea & Company, #101, 2221 Folkestone Way, V7S 2Y6 – 604/926-4524, Fax: 604/926-0222 – *1

T.E. Rafael, 475 Keith Rd., V7T 1L6 – 604/926-7887 – *1

A.M. Sweeney, 1590 Bellevue Ave., V7V 1A7 – 604/922-0131, Fax: 604/922-0171 – *1

Dianne M. Tingey, #201, 585 - 16th St., PO Box 91700, V7V 3P3 – 604/925-1156, Fax: 604/926-7817 – *1

Lorne W. Topham, #21, 285 - 17 St., V7V 3S6 – 604/922-9364, Fax: 604/922-9370 – *1

Williams & Ross, 1010 Esquimalt Ave., V7T 1J8 – 604/922-9140, Fax: 604/922-9175 – *2

WESTBANK .... Yale

Bassett & Company, 2524 Main St., PO Box 938, V4T 2E3 – 250/768-5152, Fax: 250/768-3003 – *2

Gerhard E. Schauble, c/o Bassett, Gordon & Company, 2524 Hwy. 97 South, PO Box 938, V0H 2A0 – 250/768-5152, Fax: 250/768-3003

WHISTLER .... Vancouver

Race & Company, #332, 4370 Lorimer Rd., V0N 1B4 – 604/932-3211; 682-3117(Vancouver), Fax: 604/932-2515 – *6

WHITE ROCK .... Westminster

Auerbach, Green & Bradford, 15261 Russell Ave., 3rd Fl., PO Box 75300, V4B 5C6 – 604/531-1041, Fax: 604/538-5356 – *3

J.H. Bateman, #101, 15261 Russell Ave., V4B 2P7 – 604/531-6421, Fax: 604/536-9001 – *1

Alan J. Benson, #203, 1959 - 152 St., V4A 9E3 – 604/538-4911 – *1

Ginther & Cleveland, #204, 15225 Thrift Ave., V4B 2K9 – 604/531-9121, Fax: 604/531-8100 – *2

Kruse, Adams, #305, 1656 Martin Dr., V4A 6E7 – 604/531-5501, Fax: 604/531-6256 – *2

A.D. McRae, #309, 1656 Martin Dr., V6Z 2A9 – 604/538-1511 – *1

Medland & Company, 14582 - 18th Ave., V4A 5V5 – 604/230-8476, Fax: 604/835-4145 – *1

WILLIAMS LAKE .... Cariboo

Michael M. Barbour, #B, 315 Yorston St., V2G 1H1 – 250/398-7045, Fax: 250/398-7710 – *1

Kenneth Grant, #301, 35 - 2nd Ave. South, V1G 3W3 – 250/392-2383, Fax: 250/392-7458 – *1

Oliver, Smith & Co., #106, 235 Oliver St., V1G 1M2 – 250/392-2395 – *2

Thomas A. Rhodes, Q.C., PO Box 4734, V2G 2V7 – 250/392-6856 – *1

Vanderburgh, Scott, Halpin & O'Brian, 5 - 123 Barland St., V2G 1R1

MANITOBA

ARBORG .... Winnipeg

Frank Lawrence, General Delivery, R0C 0A0 – 204/376-2333 – *1

ASHERN .... Winnipeg

D.E., Geisler, PO Box 200, R0C 0E0 – 204/768-2848 – *1

BEAUSEJOUR .... Beausejour

Bellan Wasylin Thompson, 527 Park Ave., R0E 0C0 – 204/268-2000, Fax: 204/268-3519 – *3

Middleton, Hawranik, PO Box 1150, R0E 0C0 – 204/268-1405 – *2

BIRTLE .... Russell

M.D. Butcher & Associates, Main St. & 7th Ave., PO Box 190, R0M 0C0 – 204/842-3355, Fax: 204/842-3446 – *2

Brian A. Langford, PO Box 131, R0M 0C0 – 204/842-3355 – *1

Sims & Company, PO Box 190, R0M 0C0 – 204/842-3355, Fax: 204/842-3446

BOISSEVAIN .... Killarney

Michael Waldron, PO Box 235, R0K 0E0 – 204/534-6266, Fax: 204/534-2388 – *1

BRANDON .... Brandon

David Campbell, Q.C., Scotia Towers, #201, 1011 Rosser Ave., R7A 0L5 – 204/727-0170 – *1

Terri E. Deller Law Office, 801 Princess Ave., R7A 0P5 – 204/726-0128 – *1

Hunt, Miller & Combs, 148 - 8 St., PO Box 875, R7A 5Z9 – 204/727-8491, Fax: 204/727-4350 – *8

Gladys F. Lowes, 2044 Currie Blvd., R7A 5Y1 – 204/728-0412, Fax: 204/727-4906 – *1

Paula Mallea, 136 - 11 St., R7A 4J4 – 204/725-1452 – *1

Meighen, Haddad & Company, 110 - 11 St., R7A 4T4 – 204/727-8461, Fax: 204/726-1948 – *11

Paterson Bass Ross, Carriage House, 1 - 1040 Princess Ave., PO Box 1034, R7A 6A3 – 204/727-2424, Fax: 204/728-4670 – *3

Roy Johnston & Company, 363 - 10 St., R7A 5Z7 – 204/727-0761, Fax: 204/726-1339 – *8

Smith Legal, Scotia Towers, #603, 1011 Rosser Ave., R7A 0L5 – 204/725-1502, Fax: 204/727-8686 – *2

CARMAN .... Morden

Lee & Lee, 5 Centre Ave. West, R0G 0J0 – 204/745-6751, Fax: 204/745-3481 – *2

McKenzie, Mooney & Brown, 71 Main St., R0G 0J0 – 204/745-2028, Fax: 204/745-3513 – *3

CRYSTAL CITY .... Morden

Treble & Company, PO Box 10, R0K 0N0 – 204/873-2427, Fax: 204/873-2656 – *1

DAUPHIN .... Dauphin

Hawkins & Sanderson, PO Box 552, R7N 2V4 – 204/638-4121 – *2

DUGALD .... Winnipeg

A.H. Mackling, Q.C., RR#1, R0E 0K0 – *1

ELIE .... Portage La Prairie

Miller Miller Pressey, PO Box 36, R0H 0H0 – 204/353-2317

ERICKSON .... Minnedosa

St. John & St. John, PO Box 428, R0J 1E0 – 204/867-2231

FISHER BRANCH .... Winnipeg

Nathan Golas, PO Box 305, R0C 0Z0 – 204/372-6552, Fax: 204/372-8479 – *1

FLIN FLON .... Flin Flon

Ginnell, Bauman & Associates, 47 Main St., PO Box 697, R8A 1N5 – 204/687-3431, 8208, Fax: 204/687-5219, 8051 – *3

FORT ALEXANDER .... Eastern

Roy A. Yerex, Fort Alexander Medical Centre, R0E 0P0 – 204/367-2208

GIMLI .... Winnipeg

Tupper & Adams, Lighthouse Mall, R0C 0B0 – 204/642-8192

HAMIOTA .... Minnedosa

McNeill, Poole & Company, PO Box 41, R0M 0T0 – 204/764-2885, Fax: 204/264-2063 – *3

HEADINGLEY .... Winnipeg

Patricia Grace Ritchie, Q.C., #2, 126 Bridge Rd., PO Box 142, R0H 0J0 – 204/889-1142, Fax: 204/832-5090 – *1

HOLMFIELD .... Killarney

Harrison & Harrison, PO Box 26, R0K 1A0 – 204/523-7357 – *1

KILLARNEY .... Killarney

Heming & Arraf, 541 Broadway Ave., PO Box 1300, R0K 1G0 – 204/523-4671, Fax: 204/523-8885 – *2

Roy Johnston & Company, PO Box 99, R0K 1G0 – 204/523-4464, Fax: 204/726-1339 – *1

LAC DU BONNET .... Beausejour

W.D. Besel, Hwy. 313, PO Box 566, R0E 1A0 – 204/345-8145 – *1

MANITOU .... Morden

Selby & Jones, PO Box 279, R0G 1G0 – 204/242-2801, Fax: 204/242-2723 – *2

MELITA .... Killarney

Holmes R.A., Main & Souris Sts., PO Box 397, R0M 1L0 – 204/522-3225

MINNEDOSA .... Minnedosa

Sims & Company, 76 Main St. South, PO Box 460, R0J 1E0 – 204/867-2717, Fax: 204/867-2434; Email: ajackson@mail.techplus.com – *4

MORDEN .... Morden

Hoeschen & Stewart, 326 Stephen St., PO Box 70, R0G 1J0 – 204/822-4463 – *2

Wiens Gilmour & Co., 278 Stephen St., PO Box 20, R0G 1J0 – 204/822-5466, Fax: 204/822-6984 – *2

MORRIS .... Winnipeg

G.B. Schmidt, 125 Main St., PO Box 580, R0G 1K0 – 204/746-2193 – *1

NEEPAWA .... Minnedosa

Paterson Ross, 390 Mountain Ave., PO Box 310, R0J 1H0 – 204/476-3311, Fax: 204/476-5430 – *4

Taylor Law Office, PO Box 309, R0J 1H0 – 204/476-2336, Fax: 204/476-5783 – *1

PORTAGE LA PRAIRIE .... Portage La Prairie

Miller Pressey Selinger, 103 Saskatchewan Ave. East, PO Box 368, R1N 3B7 – 204/857-3436, Fax: 204/857-9238 – *2

Sing & Sing, 21 Royal Rd. North, PO Box 548, R1N 3B9 – 204/857-4121 – *1

RIVERS .... Brandon

Cram & Juce, 505 - 2 Ave., R0K 1X0 – 204/328-7563

ROBLIN .... Dauphin

M.J.J.R. Gregoire, 204 Main St., R0L 1P0 – 204/937-2117 – *1

RUSSELL .... Russell

M.D. Butcher & Associates, PO Box 70, R0J 1W0 – 204/773-2172, Fax: 204/773-3950

* indicates number of lawyers in law firm.

SELKIRK — Selkirk

Kohaykewych, Weipert & Associates, 413 Main St., R1A 1V2 – 204/482-7925 – *2

D.F. Williams, Q.C., 407 Main St., R1A 2B2 – 204/482-3921 – *3

SHOAL LAKE — Minnedosa

Sims & Company, #1, 515 - 4th Ave., PO Box 430, R0J 1Z0 – 204/759-2733, Fax: 204/759-2411

SOMERSET — Morden

Teffaine Labossière, General Delivery, R0G 2L0 – 204/744-2415 – *2

SOURIS — Brandon

Forrest & Forrest, 4 Crescent Ave., PO Box 276, R0K 2C0 – 204/483-2171, Fax: 204/483-3389 – *2

M.J. Murray, PO Box 276, R0K 2C0 – 204/483-2171, Fax: 204/483-3389 – *1

ST. BONIFACE — St. Boniface

Teffaine Labossière, #201, 185, boul Provencher, CP 36, R2H 3B4 – 204/233-4359, Fax: 204/233-5770 – *3

STEINBACH — Minnedosa

Ruth McNeill, PO Box 21330, R0A 2T3 – 204/204-6424 – *1

Plett Goossen Harasym, PO Box 1960, R0A 2A0 – 204/326-6454 – *2

Smith, Neufeld, Jodoin, PO Box 1267, R0A 2A0 – 204/326-3442 – *4

Wohlgemuth & Loewen, #101, 344 Main St., PO Box 3820, R0A 2A0 – 204/326-4486, Fax: 204/326-5562 – *2

STONEWALL — Winnipeg

Goodman & Grantham, Westdale Plaza, #15, 353 Main St., PO Box 1400, R0C 2Z0 – 204/467-5527, Fax: 204/942-0473 – *2

SWAN RIVER — Swan River

Burnside & Company, 509 Main St. East, PO Box 340, R0L 1Z0 – 204/734-3485, Fax: 204/734-2872 – *3

Palsson Law Office, PO Box 1238, R0L 1Z0 – 204/734-4528, Fax: 204/734-5085 – *1

THE PAS — The Pas

Lionel Chartrand, 236 Edwards Ave., R9A 0J2 – 204/623-7864, Fax: 204/623-3595

D.R. Knight & Associates, 237 Fischer St., PO Box 1769, R9A 0K3 – 204/623-5432, Fax: 204/623-2258 – *6

D.N. MacIver & Associates, 236 Edwards Ave., R9A 1M1 – 204/623-7864, Fax: 204/623-7925

THOMPSON — Thompson

Bancroft, Whidden, Mayer & Beard, 7 Selkirk Ave., R8N 0M4 – 204/677-2393, Fax: 204/778-8125 – *3

Morrison, McDonald, Thompson, #309, 83 Churchill Dr., R8N 0L6 – 204/677-2366, Fax: 204/677-3249 – *3

VIRDEN — Virden

McNeill Poole, Buckingham Bldg., 243 Raglan St. West, PO Box 520, R0M 2C0 – 204/748-1220 – *3

WINKLER — Morden

Hoeschen & Stewart, 583 Main St., R6W 4A2 – 204/325-4233, Fax: 204/822-6416

Wiens Gilmour & Co., 564 Mountain Ave., PO Box 1150, R6W 4B2 – 204/325-8807, Fax: 204/325-8352 – *3

WINNIPEG — Eastern

Abrams & Tweed, #2, 549 Regent Ave. West, R2C 1R9 – 204/949-3080, Fax: 204/949-3089 – *3

Aikins, MacAulay & Thorvaldson, Commodity Exchange Tower, 360 Main St., 30th Fl., R3C 4G1 – 204/957-0050, Fax: 204/957-0840; Email: amt@aikins.com – *79

Stephen D. Alsip, 137 Scott St., R3L 0K9 – 204/475-9420, Fax: 204/453-8522 – *1

F.R. Avanthay, #25, 185, boul Provencher, R2H 0G4 – 204/233-5029 – *1

Baker & Company, Winnipeg Sq., Bldg Box: 300, #300, 360 Main St., R3C 3Z3 – 204/957-1700, Fax: 204/942-2325; 947-5995 – *5

Allan P. Baker, #603, 294 Portage Ave., R3C 0B9 – 204/947-0057 – *1

W.L. Barker, #500, 125 Garry St., R3C 3P2 – 204/943-3247 – *1

Bernstein & Hirsch, #508, 283 Portage Ave., R3B 2B5 – 204/942-0706, Fax: 204/957-1345 – *2

Booth, Dennehy, Ernst & Kelsch, 387 Broadway Ave., R3C 0V5 – 204/957-1717, Fax: 204/943-6199 – *13

D.E. Bowman, Q.C., 241 Harvard Ave., R3M 0K1 – 204/477-0484 – *1

Marshall Braunstein, #600, 294 Portage Ave., R3C 0B9 – 204/942-2961 – *1

Brotman & Cramer, #100H, 1485 Portage Ave., R3G 0W4 – 204/942-3168 – *1

Buchwald Asper Gallagher Henteleff, Commodity Exchange Tower, #2500, 360 Main St., R3C 4H6 – 204/956-0560, Fax: 204/957-0227; Email: bagh@escape.ca – *37

Campbell Marr, 10 Donald St., R3C 1L5 – 204/942-3311, Fax: 204/943-7997 – *10

John E. Carstairs, #1, 525 Wellington Cres., R3M 0A1

Chapman Goddard Kagan Tallin & Kristjansson, 1864 Portage Ave., R3J 0H2 – 204/888-7973, Fax: 204/943-9810 – *5

T.L. Charne, Q.C., #1600, 155 Carlton St., R3C 3H8 – 204/944-8393 – *1

Cherniack Allen, #200, 100 Osborne St., R3L 1Y5 – 204/989-5600 – *5

L. Cholakis, #300, 275 Portage Ave., R3B 2B3 – 204/947-0531, Fax: 204/942-3631 – *1

S. Cohan, #508, 386 Broadway, R3C 3R6 – 204/944-1413, Fax: 204/943-9563 – *1

D'Arcy & Deacon, Royal Trust Bldg., 330 St. Mary Ave., 12th Fl., R3C 4E1 – 204/942-2271, Fax: 204/943-4242 – *29

De Lucia & De Lucia, Lindsay Bldg., #900, 228 Notre Dame Ave., R3B 1N7 – 204/942-2316, 1482, Fax: 204/943-6579

Deniset & Boily, 202, boul Provencher, 2nd Fl., R2H 0G3 – 204/235-1378, Fax: 204/233-9762 – *4

Derksen & Co., #200, 1135 Henderson Hwy., R2G 1L4 – 204/339-1671, Fax: 204/339-5078 – *2

Diamond & Adleman, 1300 Plessis Rd., R2C 2Y6 – 204/224-2221 – *3

Dowhan & Dowhan, Newport Centre, Bldg Box: 1810, 330 Portage Ave., R3C 0C4 – 204/942-4235, Fax: 204/956-4560 – *3

S.J. Drache, Q.C., Bancolare House, 128 Montrose St., R3M 3M6 – 204/488-0665, Fax: 204/956-5262

Edmond & Associates, #204, 1120 Grant Ave., R3M 2A6 – 204/452-5314, Fax: 204/452-5989 – *6

Barry C. Effler, A1150 Waverley St., R3T 0P4 – 204/284-2988, Fax: 204/474-1867 – *1

Neil Enns, #605, 386 Broadway, R3C 3R6 – 204/956-2428, Fax: 204/947-1013 – *1

Fillmore & Riley, Winnipeg Sq., #1700, 360 Main St., R3C 3Z3 – 204/957-8321, Fax: 204/957-0516 – *47

Fishman & Associates, #1118, 363 Broadway, R3C 3N9 – 204/944-1897 – *2

Flatt Law Office, 242 Dunkirk Dr., R2M 3W9 – 204/253-2253 – *1

Antoine Fréchette, 155, boul Provencher, R2H 0G2 – 204/231-1333

Zachary I. Garber, #508, 386 Broadway, R3C 3R6 – 204/943-7454, Fax: 204/943-9563 – *1

Gindin, Smith, Pearlman, #950, 363 Broadway Ave., R3C 3N9 – 204/943-6292, Fax: 204/943-4120 – *8

Glowacki & Libitka, Lindsay Bldg., #1001, 228 Notre Dame Ave., R3B 1N7 – 204/942-3385, Fax: 204/943-6354 – *2

Stanley Goldberg, #1212, 363 Broadway Ave., R3C 3N9 – 306/942-4160, Fax: 306/942-4301 – *1

Gould Goszer, 175 Carlton St., 2nd Fl., R3C 3H9 – 204/943-0571, Fax: 204/943-4498 – *3

Grafton & Rosenberg, #304, 213 Notre Dame Ave., R3B 1N3 – 204/942-5401 – *2

Renald Guay, 300 Provencher Blvd., R2H 0G7 – 204/233-6659, Fax: 204/231-1950 – *1

Ronald M. Habing & Associates, 2643 Portage Ave., R3J 0P9 – 204/832-8322, Fax: 204/832-3906 – *2

M.L. Halkewycz, #204, 952 Main St., R2W 3P4 – 204/589-6301, Fax: 204/589-2743 – *1

Halprin & Halprin, #1110, 213 Notre Dame Ave., R3B 1N3 – 204/943-6691, Fax: 204/947-1861 – *1

A.D. Hoffer, #700, 444 St. Mary Ave., R3C 3T1 – 204/947-6801, Fax: 204/947-6800 – *1

A.A. Hoffman, #1212, 363 Broadway Ave., R3C 3N9 – *1

Hogue, Kushnier, 194 Provencher Blvd., R2H 0G3 – 204/237-1231, Fax: 204/233-2689 – *2

Hook & Smith, #201, 3111 Portage Ave., R3K 0W4 – 204/885-4520, Fax: 204/837-9846 – *3

H.A. Huppe, Q.C., 51 St. Anne's Rd., R2M 2Y4 – 204/237-1647 – *1

Inkster, Christie, Hughes, Mackay, #700, 444 St. Mary Ave., R3C 3T1 – 204/947-6801, Fax: 204/947-6800 – *14

Iwanchuk, Nickel, #17A, 2136 McPhillips St., R2V 3C8 – 204/694-5588, Fax: 204/697-3813 – *2

Juravsky, Jury & Associates, #2701, 83 Garry St., R3C 4J9 – 204/943-8544 – *3

Kaufman Cassidy, #300, 360 Main St., R3C 3Z3 – 204/943-7454, Fax: 204/943-9563 – *7

J. Scott Kennedy & Associates, #303, 175 Hargrave St., R3C 3R8 – 204/949-0298, Fax: 204/942-0336 – *2

W.D. Koshowski, #101, 1311 Portage Ave., R3G 0V3 – 204/942-7764 – *1

F. Lawrence, #202, 1382 Henderson Hwy., R2G 1M8 – 204/338-9705 – *1

Victoria E. Lehman, 412 Wardlaw Ave., R3L 0L7 – 204/453-6416 – *1

Loewen, Martens & Rempel, 1101 Henderson Hwy., R2G 1L4 – 204/338-9364, Fax: 204/338-8379 – *3

Allan Ludkiewicz, #204, 150 Henry Ave., PO Box 7000, R3C 4E9 – 204/946-3341, Fax: 204/946-3305 – *1

MacInnes, Burbidge, #500, 177 Lombard Ave., R3B 0W5 – 204/942-5256, Fax: 204/942-5259 – *2

D.N. MacIver & Associates, #1530, 155 Carlton St., R3C 3H8 – 204/943-6222, Fax: 204/957-5874 – *1

A.J. MacKenzie, 123 St. Vital Rd., R2M 2A1 – 204/254-8416 – *1

Martens & Associates, 137 Scott St., R3L 0K9 – 204/475-9420, Fax: 204/453-8522 – *1

David Matas, 205 Edmonton St., 2nd Fl., R3C 1R4 – 204/944-1831 – *1

Marilyn McConigal, 500 - 125 Garry St., R3C 3P2 – 204/943-6011

McCreedy, Knight & Associates, 931 Nairn Ave., R2L 0X9 – 204/668-7320, Fax: 204/667-5104 – *3

Marilyn McGonigal, #500, 125 Garry St., R3C 3P2 – 204/943-3247 – *1

McJannet Rich, Newport Centre, #1420, 330 Portage Ave., R3C 0C4 – 204/985-8100, Fax: 204/956-0098 – *4

John P. McKinnon, 41 Cambridge St., R3M 3E6 – 204/488-0399 – *1

D. Neil McTavish, 1002 Pembina Hwy., R3T 1Z5 – 204/284-3221 – *1

Meltzer Essers Duboff Schachter, 175 Carlton St., 2nd Fl., R3C 3H9 – 204/942-3361, Fax: 204/943-4498 – *7

Michaels & Potash, 800 - 310 Broadway Ave., R3C 0S6 – 204/989-5500, Fax: 204/947-5845 – *3

Minuk & Company, #508, 386 Broadway, R3C 3R6 – 204/942-7294, Fax: 204/943-9563 – *1

Monk, Goodwin, #800, 444 St. Mary Ave., R3C 3T1 – 204/956-1060, Fax: 204/957-0423 – *16
James A. Muller, 179 Spence St. NW, 2nd Fl., R3C 1Y5 – *1
Myers Weinberg Kussin Weinstein Bryk, Cargill Bldg., #724, 240 Graham Ave., R3C 0J7 – 204/942-0501, Fax: 204/956-0625 – *18
Nemy, Brown & Roy, #200, 2727 Portage Ave., R3J 0R2 – 204/888-8890 – *3
Nozick, Sinder & Associates, #903, 386 Broadway, R3C 0V6 – 204/944-8227 – *7
R.L. Olesky, #200, 62 Hargrave St., R3C 1N1 – 204/956-0903, Fax: 204/956-4200 – *1
Oliver, Derksen, Arkin, #800, 310 Broadway, R3C 0S6 – 204/947-2007 – *4
Parashin Law Office, 404 McGregor St., R2W 4X5 – 204/582-3558 – *1
Parker, Sarbit, 175 Carlton St., 2nd Fl., R3C 3H9 – 204/944-9682, Fax: 204/943-4498 – *3
Perlov Stewart Lincoln, #1400, One Lombard Place, R3B 3G5 – 204/944-9295, Fax: 204/956-4270 – *7
Pitblado & Hoskin, Commodity Exchange Tower, #1900, 360 Main St., R3C 3Z3 – 204/942-0391, Fax: 204/957-1790; Email: lawyers@pitblado.mb.ca; URL: http://www.mts.net/~lawyers/text/pitblado.html – *53
A.P. Pittarelli, #803, 213 Notre Dame Ave., R3B 1N3 – 204/942-8886 – *1
G.S. Posner, #200, 938 Corydon Ave., R3M 0Y5 – 204/453-9221 – *1
Pullan Guld Kammerloch, #600, 330 Portage Ave., R3C 0C4 – 204/956-0490, Fax: 204/947-3747 – *5
Robertson & Bond, #807, 294 Portage Ave., R3C 0B9 – 204/943-8439 – *1
Robertson Shypit, 202 - 1555 St. Mary's Rd., R2M 3W2 – 204/257-6061, Fax: 204/254-7183 – *6
James F.C. Rose, Grain Exchange Bldg., Bldg Box: 709, 167 Lombard Ave., R3B 0V3 – 204/943-1995, Fax: 204/949-9232 – *1
Albert Rosen, #709, 167 Lombard Ave., R3B 0V3 – *1
Sheldon Rosenstock, 647 Borebank St., R3N 1G1 – 204/488-4121, Fax: 204/488-1869 – *1
Ross & Associates, 641 St. Mary's Rd., R2M 3M2 – 204/257-0675, Fax: 204/254-7074 – *2
Rutledge & Dyker, #310, 3025 Portage Ave., R3K 2E2 – 204/987-7575, Fax: 204/837-3638 – *2
Schulman & Schulman, #808, 444 St. Mary Ave., R3C 3T1 – 204/943-5428, Fax: 204/944-8019 – *1
M.H. Schwartzwald, #912, 363 Broadway Ave., R3C 3N9 – 204/943-2477, Fax: 204/943-2573 – *1
Simpson Law Office, #310, 2265 Pembina Hwy., R3T 5J3 – *1
Slusky & Slusky, #1212, 363 Broadway, R3C 3N9 – 204/943-5455, Fax: 204/942-4301 – *1
Smith & Moss, #204, 584 Pembina Hwy., R3M 3X7 – 204/284-7090, Fax: 204/477-5179 – *2
Remi Smith, #302, 131 Provencher Blvd., R2H 0G2 – 204/958-6851, Fax: 204/958-6855 – *1
Smordin, Soronow & Ludwig, #805, 386 Broadway, R3C 3T5 – 204/944-0603, Fax: 204/943-5102 – *16
Alice Steinbart, #400, 55 Donald St., R3C 1L8 – 204/947-1475 – *1
Swystun Karsevich Windsor, #102, 5 Donald St. South, R3L 2T4 – 204/477-0285, Fax: 204/453-8876 – *6
Tacium, Vincent, Orlikow, 246A St. Anne's Rd., R2M 3A4 – 204/989-4220, Fax: 204/254-7744 – *4
Taylor McCaffrey, 400 St. Mary Ave., 9th Fl., R3C 4K5 – 204/949-1312, Fax: 204/957-0945; Email: taylorm@mbnet.mb.ca – *50
Léo V. Teillet, #302, 131 Provencher Blvd., R2H 0G2 – 204/958-6850, Fax: 204/958-6855 – *1
Thompson Dorfman Sweatman, Toronto-Dominion Centre, 2200 - 201 Portage Ave., R3B 3L3 – 204/957-1930, Fax: 204/943-6445 – *72
M.T. Tracey, 137 Scott St., R3L 0K9 – 204/477-1040, Fax: 204/453-8522 – *1
Tupper & Adams, 200 Portage Ave., 4th Fl., R3C 3X2 – 204/942-0161, Fax: 204/942-2385 – *17

W.R. Van Walleghem, #206, 1120 Grant Ave., R3M 2A6 – 204/477-0210, Fax: 204/452-9746 – *2
Walsh, Micay & Company, Richardson Bldg., One Lombard Pl., 10th Fl., R3B 3H1 – 204/942-0081, Fax: 204/957-1261 – *24
Warkentin & Calver, N3025 Ness Ave., R2Y 2J2 – 204/885-4452, Fax: 204/837-9021 – *3
E. Waskiw, 441 Perth Ave., R2V 0T9 – 204/334-7372 – *1
R.D. Watson, One Lakeview Sq., #1510, 155 Carleton St., R3C 3H8 – 204/944-1960 – *1
Wilder Wilder & Langtry, Richardson Bldg., #1500, 1 Lombard Place, R3B 0X3 – 204/947-1456, Fax: 204/957-1368; Email: wilder@mb.sympatico.ca – *15
D.F. Williams, Q.C., 740 Queenston Ave., PO Box 26, Stn A, R3K 1Z9 – 204/475-8633, Fax: 204/488-2540
Wolch, Pinx, Tapper, Scurfield, #1000, 330 St. Mary Ave., R3C 3Z5 – 204/949-1700, Fax: 204/947-2593; Email: wolchpts@mts.net – *31
Wolchock & Company, #804, 310 Broadway, R3C 0S6 – 204/925-3500, Fax: 204/925-3509 – *3
Yanofsky, Kelsch & Associates, #709, 167 Lombard Ave., R3B 0V3 – 204/942-6387, Fax: 204/949-9232 – *5
Roy A. Yerex, #500, 125 Garry St., R3C 3P2 – 204/947-0438; 947-0455, Fax: 204/943-3247 – *1
Ken B. Young, #590, 125 Garry St., R3C 3P2 – 204/944-0133, Fax: 204/943-7094
Zimmerman & Zimmerman, #101, 207 Donald St., R3C 1M5 – 204/942-6329, Fax: 204/944-8383

NEW BRUNSWICK

BATHURST .... Bathurst
John Douglas Hazen, 240 King Ave., PO Box 690, E2A 3Z6 – 506/546-9988, Fax: 506/546-3344 – *1
Robichaud, Godin, Williamson, Theriault & Johnstone, Keystone Place, 270 Douglas Ave., PO Box 747, E2A 4A5 – 506/548-8821, Fax: 506/548-5297 – *9
Siscoe & Savoie, #8, 195 Main St., E2A 1A7 – 506/546-4488 – *2

CAMPBELLTON .... Restigouche
Dubé & Dubé, 72 Roseberry St., PO Box 126, E3N 3G1 – 506/753-7641, Fax: 506/753-5428 – *2
John D. Larlee, #703, 157 Water St., PO Box 914, E3N 3H3 – 506/753-5008, Fax: 506/759-7275 – *1
Richard J. Tingley, Q.C., #5, 78 Roseberry St., PO Box 546, E3N 3G9 – 506/753-7743, Fax: 506/759-7535

CAP PELE .... Westmorland
Jean A. Cormier, PO Box 339, E0A 1J0 – 506/577-4321 – *1
MacIntyre Finn Richard, PO Box 235, E0A 1J0 – 506/577-4358, Fax: 506/577-2768 – *1

CHIPMAN .... Fredericton
Sharon R. Lockwood, 122 Northside Dr., PO Box 58, E0E 1C0 – 506/339-6632, Fax: 506/339-5130 – *1

DALHOUSIE .... Restigouche
D. Paul Hayes, 391 Adelaide St., PO Box 190, E0K 1B0 – 506/684-5571, Fax: 506/684-4717 – *1
McIntyre & Kierstead, PO Box 248, E0K 1B0 – 506/684-3304 – *2

DIEPPE .... Westmorland
J.E. Michel Bastarache, 341, rue Lavoie, E1A 6P8 – 506/388-2865, Fax: 506/853-5421

DOAKTOWN .... Northumberland
R. Alex Mills, Old River Lodge, RR#2, E0C 1G0 – 506/365-2253, Fax: 506/365-7134 – *1

EDMUNDSTON .... Madawaska
Cyr & Ouellette, 77, rue Rice, E3V 1S8 – 506/735-4791, Fax: 506/735-3942 – *2
McLaughlin Durette McNeil, Edifice du Centre, 176, rue Church, E3V 1K2 – 506/735-8845, Fax: 506/739-5506 – *4

FLORENCEVILLE .... Woodstock
Crocco, Hunter, Purvis, PO Drawer 240, E0J 1K0 – 506/392-6258, Fax: 506/392-8315 – *6

FREDERICTON .... York
Ashfield, DeWitt, LeBlanc & Yerxa, 181 Brunswick St., PO Box 1150, E3B 5C2 – 506/458-9600, Fax: 506/450-0758 – *5
Athey, Gregory & Hughes, Rookwood Centre, #200, 206 Rookwood Ave., E3B 2M2 – 506/458-8060, Fax: 506/459-8288 – *4
Atkinson & Atkinson, 108 Queen St., PO Box 700, E3B 5B4 – 506/451-7777, Fax: 506/451-1029 – *6
Buchanan Bell, Frederick Sq., #340, 77 Westmorland St., PO Box 1418, Stn A, E3B 5E3 – 506/453-0900 – *5
Richard B. Cochrane, Q.C., 98 Prospect St. West, E3B 2T8 – 506/452-2844, Fax: 506/452-8225 – *1
Guy Daigle, Services Juridiques, Ministère de la Justice, CP 6000, E3B 5H0 – 506/453-2514, Fax: 506/453-3275 – *1
Eddy, Young, Hoyt & Downs, Barker House, #600, 570 Queen St., PO Box 610, E3B 5A6 – 506/458-8572, Fax: 506/458-9903; Email: eddyb@nbnet.nb.ca – *9
Leslye Lynne Fraser, PO Box 1384, E3B 1G8 – 506/458-9010, Fax: 506/450-9390 – *1
Freeze, Walker, Lourensse, Janssens, #208, 212 Queen St., PO Box 397, E3B 4Z9 – 506/458-8555 – *6
Hanson, Hashey, Phoenix Sq., #400, PO Box 310, E3B 4Y9 – 506/453-7771, Fax: 506/453-9600 – *23
John D. Harper, PO Box 155, E3B 4Y9 – 506/458-8290, Fax: 506/450-9391 – *1
J.R. Howie, Q.C., 678 Churchill Row, E3B 1P6 – 506/458-9987 – *1
M. Mck. Hoyt, Q.C., 120 Edinburgh St., E3B 2C9 – 506/454-3136 – *1
Hughes, Cooper & Campbell, 551 Charlotte St., PO Box 295, E3B 4Y9 – 506/458-8140 – *3
Jane Keenan, 15A Currie Cres., E3E 1A1 – 506/458-5287, Fax: 506/459-4146; Email: devlinpm@mi.net – *1
Kenny, Jackson & Murray, 228 Brunswick St., PO Box 1572, E3B 5G2 – 506/458-1108, Fax: 506/458-2645; Email: kenny@nbnet.nb.ca – *7
Matthews Oliver Theriault, 255 Main St., E3A 1E1 – 506/458-5959, Fax: 506/450-3834 – *3
Barbara E. McQueen, Site 9, RR#6, PO Box 22, E3B 4X7 – 506/363-5583 – *1
Mockler, Allen & Dixon, 836 Churchill Row, PO Box 1388, E3B 5E3 – 506/459-5515 – *14
George A. Noble, 560 Queen St., PO Box 1387, E3B 5E3 – 506/458-9887 – *1
E. Joanne Oley, 6 Hermitage Ct., E3B 2P2 – 506/455-6599, Fax: 506/455-7009 – *1
Claude J. Pardons, 895 Mitchell, E3B 6E8 – 506/457-0663 – *1
Mark C. Paul-Elias, 352 George St., PO Box 1302, E3B 5C8 – 506/458-1880, Fax: 506/458-9868 – *1
Gerald R. Pugh, 48 Hillcourt Dr., E3A 1S1 – 506/450-2666, Fax: 506/453-1793 – *1
Ruben & Kingston, 259 Brunswick St., PO Box 1142, E3B 5C2 – 506/458-0000, Fax: 506/451-8766; Email: dflood@nbnet.nb.ca – *4
Smith & Irvine, #103, 212 Queen St., PO Box 487, E3B 4Z9 – 506/453-9919, Fax: 506/453-1882 – *3
Smith, Townsend, Myatt, Toronto-Dominion Tower, #430, 77 Westmorland St., PO Box 38, E3B 4Y2 – 506/452-9900, Fax: 506/452-6726 – *7
Stevenson & Stevenson, 127 George St., PO Box 245, E3B 4Y9 – 506/458-9884, Fax: 506/450-2844 – *2

* indicates number of lawyers in law firm.

J.E. Warner, Q.C., PO Box 1522, E3B 5G2 – 506/455-7392 – *1

A.E. Wilby, Q.C., 526 Queen St., E3B 1B9 – 506/454-4286, Fax: 506/457-1651 – *2

GRAND FALLS....................................**Edmundston**

Duffie, Friel & Deschènes, 346 Chapel St., PO Box 747, E3Z 1C2 – 506/473-2221, Fax: 506/473-3253; Email: friel@sympatico.nb.ca – *3

Terrance A. McCarthy, PO Box 900, E3Z 1C4 – 506/473-2750, Fax: 506/473-2759 – *1

Pichette, Toner & Murchison, 257 Broadway, PO Box 2050, E3Z 1E3 – 506/473-4776, Fax: 506/473-6493 – *3

Peter Seheult, PO Box 2440, E0J 1M0 – 506/473-2164, Fax: 506/473-5543 – *1

HAMPTON..**Kings**

Lutz, Longstaff & Richards, PO Box 500, E0G 1Z0 – 506/832-1500, Fax: 506/832-3848 – *5

HARTLAND..**Albert**

G. Peter Hyslop, PO Box 337, E0J 1N0 – *1

KINGSHURST.....................................**Saint John**

John B.M. Baxter, Q.C., 143 Green Rd., E2H 1T2 – *1

LAMEQUE..**Gloucester**

R.A. Noel, PO Box 330, E0B 1V0 – 506/344-2217 – *1

MIRAMICHI...**Miramichi**

Maynes, Mahoney & Tremblay, 1723 Water St., PO Box 518, E1N 3A8 – 506/778-8336, Fax: 506/778-2103 – *4

MONCTON..**Westmorland**

Doris Alfonso-Desjardins, #307, 1111, rue Main, E1C 1H3 – 506/858-1830, Fax: 506/856-6092 – *1

Anderson, McWilliam, LeBlanc & MacDonald, 633 Main St., PO Box 20010, E1C 9M1 – 506/857-2171, Fax: 506/858-0284 – *4

Michel C. Arsenault, #5, 207 Robinson St., E1C 5C5 – 506/857-8008, Fax: 506/857-1702 – *2

H. Reuben Cohen, Q.C., #205, 1111 Main St., E1C 1H3 – 506/857-9510, Fax: 506/858-5462 – *1

Drapeau Robichaud & McNally, 86 Botsford, PO Box 665, E1C 8M7 – 506/857-0360, Fax: 506/859-6038 – *4

Forbes Roth Basque, Heritage Ct., #201, 95 Foundry St., PO Box 480, E1C 8L9 – 506/857-4880, Fax: 506/857-0151 – *7

Fowler & Fowler, #11, 885 Main St., PO Box 721, E1C 8M9 – 506/857-8811, Fax: 506/857-9297 – *4

Goodwin & Ellsworth, PO Box 626, E1C 8M7 – 506/857-8228, Fax: 506/859-4219 – *5

John D. Hughes, 225 Lutz St., PO Box 29072, E1C 9N5 – 506/853-3333

Innes, Bossé & Eddie, 9 Dominion St., E1C 6G4 – 506/857-8273, Fax: 506/859-9096 – *3

Jones, Beardsworth & Maclean, 63 Church St., E1C 9G1 – 506/853-1131, Fax: 506/853-1139 – *2

Mary Anne Kimball, PO Box 5001, E1C 8R3 – 506/856-2270, Fax: 506/856-2076 – *2

LeBlanc Boucher Rodger & Bourque, 740 Main St., E1C 1E6 – 506/858-0110, Fax: 506/858-9497 – *6

Donald MacLean, PO Box 191, E1C 8K9 – 506/858-9990 – *1

Gregg McAllister & Assoc., 155 Cornhill St., E1C 6L3 – 506/853-3040 – *2

McGrath Tuck Sutherland, PO Box 831, E1C 8N6 – 506/850-0838, Fax: 506/857-9965 – *3

McIntyre & Finn, Pl. de l'Assomption, 770 Main St., E1C 1E7 – 506/857-1820, Fax: 506/857-1830 – *4

Murphy Collette Murphy, PO Box 869, E1C 8N6 – 506/856-8560, Fax: 506/856-8579; URL: http://www.discribe.ca/marco – *8

Murphy, Murphy & Mollins, 89 Church St., E1C 4Z4 – 506/855-2120, Fax: 506/857-9129 – *3

Patterson Palmer Hunt Murphy, Blue Cross Centre, PO Box 20100, E1C 9M1 – 506/856-9800, Fax: 506/856-8150 – *7

Roy, Yeoman, Savoie, LeBlanc, 86 Church St., E1C 4Z5 – 506/858-9000, Fax: 506/859-0829 – *8

Samuelsen Rideout & Doucet, Blue Cross Postal Outlet, 644 Main St., PO Box 20111, E1C 9M1 – 506/858-9830, Fax: 506/857-0917

Alan D. Schelew, #100, 803 Main St., PO Box 182, E1C 8K9 – 506/857-2272, Fax: 506/857-2276 – *1

Scobie & Marriner, 190 Cameron St., E1C 5Z2 – 506/857-2056, Fax: 506/857-1711 – *2

Stewart & Cooper, 325 Baig Blvd., PO Box 889, E1C 8N8 – 506/857-2110 – *7

Stewart McKelvey Stirling Scales, Blue Cross Centre, #601, 644 Main St., PO Box 20070, E1C 9M1 – 506/853-1970, Fax: 506/858-8454; Email: smss@email.smss.com – *7

Tedford Delehanty Rinzler, 272 George St., PO Box 1083, E1C 8P6 – 506/857-3030 – *3

Joseph E. Weir, #205, 111 Main St., E1C 1H3 – 506/857-9510, 857-2162, Fax: 506/858-5462, 857-0450 – *1

NEWCASTLE....................................**Northumberland**

Maynes, Mahoney & Tremblay, 170 Thomas St., PO Box 629, E1V 3T7 – 506/622-8353, Fax: 506/622-5350 – *4

John L. McAllister, 499 King George Hwy., PO Box 442, E1V 3M6 – 506/622-4822, Fax: 506/622-1946 – *1

D.W. Morris, 55 Pleasant St., E1V 3M2 – 506/622-0067, Fax: 506/622-6178

Smith & Smith, 155 Pleasant St., PO Box 100, E1V 3M2 – 506/622-0722, Fax: 506/622-7499 – *3

OROMOCTO...**Sunbury**

Roach & Morris, #24, 101 Hersey St., PO Box 232, E2V 2G5 – 506/357-3385, Fax: 506/357-5868 – *2

PERTH-ANDOVER................................**Woodstock**

Johnson & Hyslop, PO Box 698, E0J 1V0 – 506/273-6818, Fax: 506/273-6590 – *2

PETIT-ROCHER...................................**Gloucester**

Robert M. Boudreau & Assoc., CP 520, E0B 2E0 – 506/783-4246 – *2

PETITCODIAC....................................**Westmorland**

Jones, Beardsworth & Maclean, 2 Kay St., E0A 2H0 – 506/756-3374

QUISPAMSIS..**Kings**

Clark, Drummie & Company, Lakefield Plaza, 186 Old Hampton Rd., E2E 4L8 – 506/849-3800

RICHIBUCTO..**Kent**

Michaud, LeBlanc & Co., 103 Main St., PO Box 28, E0A 2M0 – 506/523-4442, Fax: 506/523-4819 – *4

SACKVILLE......................................**Westmorland**

Forbes Roth Basque, 84 West Main St., E0A 3C0 – 506/536-4880

Meldrum & Meldrum, 5 Bridge St., PO Box 1720, E0A 3C0 – 506/536-3870, Fax: 506/536-2131; Email: meldrumk@nbnet.nb.ca – *3

Ove B. Samuelsen, PO Box 90, E0A 3C0 – 506/536-0511, Fax: 506/536-1169 – *1

SAINT JOHN.......................................**Saint John**

Barry & O'Neil, Royal Bank Bldg., 85 Charlotte St., PO Box 6010, Stn A, E2L 4R5 – 506/633-4226, Fax: 506/633-4206 – *23

Clark, Drummie & Company, 40 Wellington Row, PO Box 6850, Stn A, E2L 4S3 – 506/633-3800, Fax: 506/633-3811 – *21

Harry G. Colwell, #302, 102 Prince William St., PO Box 7027, Stn A, E2L 4G4 – 506/634-7035, Fax: 506/634-6194 – *1

Bruce A. Drost, 300 Union St., 12th Fl., PO Box 5777, E2L 4M3 – 506/632-5110, Fax: 506/658-0517 – *1

Gilbert, McGloan, Gillis, Mercantile Centre, 55 Union St., PO Box 7174, Stn A, E2L 4S6 – 506/634-3600, Fax: 506/634-3612; Email: gmg@nb.sympatico.co – *17

Gorman Nason Ljungstrom, PO Box 7286, Stn A, E1L 4S6 – 506/634-8600, Fax: 506/634-8685 – *10

Hanson, Hashey, #1212, 1 Brunswick Sq., E2L 4V1

John M. Henderson, Bank of Canada Bldg., #417, 75 Prince William St., E2L 2B2 – 506/635-5471, Fax: 506/634-1795 – *1

M.L. McCluskey, 56 Canterbury St., E2L 2C5 – 506/634-0400 – *1

Mosher Chedore, 57 King St., E2L 1G5 – 506/634-1600, Fax: 506/634-0740 – *7

Neill, Tonning, Horgan, PO Box 102, Stn A, E2L 4S2 – 506/658-1700, Fax: 506/658-0951 – *3

Northrup, Bamford & Company, #311, 75 Prince William St., E2L 2B2 – 506/634-8130, Fax: 506/633-0389 – *2

Riley, John G., Bank of Canada Bldg., #417, 75 Prince William St., E2L 2B2 – 506/634-1188, Fax: 506/634-1795 – *1

Ritchie, Cannell, 120 Prince William St., PO Box 7143, Stn A, E2L 4S5 – 506/632-0006, Fax: 506/632-9015 – *2

Ralph J. Stephen, 135 Douglas Ave., E2K 1E5 – 506/634-7970, Fax: 506/634-7979 – *1

Stewart McKelvey Stirling Scales, Brunswick House, 44 Chipman Hill, 10th Fl., PO Box 7289, Stn A, E2L 4S6 – 506/632-1970, Fax: 506/652-1989; Email: saint-john@email.smss.com; URL: http://www.nstn.ca/smss – *29

Teed & Teed, 127 Prince William St., PO Box 6639, Stn A, E2L 4S1 – 506/634-7320, Fax: 506/634-7423 – *2

Whelly & Whelly, 122 Carleton St., E2L 2Z7 – 506/634-1193, Fax: 506/693-9040 – *5

David Zed, PO Box 518, E2L 3Z8 – 506/633-1973 – *1

Thomas J. Zed, 15 Market Square, E2L 1E7 – 506/634-0800 – *1

SHEDIAC...**Westmorland**

Michel C. Leger, CP 1900, E0A 3G0 – 506/533-3820, Fax: 506/532-6332 – *1

Jamie M. Storey, 324 Main St., PO Box 1658, E0A 3G0 – 506/532-6572, Fax: 506/532-6599 – *2

SHIPPAGAN......................................**Gloucester**

Godin, Lizotte, Robichaud, CP 590, E0B 2P0 – 506/336-2336, Fax: 506/336-9013 – *3

ST. ANDREWS....................................**Saint John**

Bartlett & Smart, 159 Water St., E0G 2X0 – 506/529-4000, Fax: 506/529-4777; Email: barsmart@nbnet.nb.ca – *2

Nicholson, Turner, Walker & White, 177 Water St., PO Box 569, E0G 2X0 – 506/529-8831, Fax: 506/529-3066 – *4

ST. GEORGE.......................................**Charlotte**

D'Arcy Leycester, Q.C., Main St., PO Box 367, E0G 2Y0 – 506/755-2810

ST. QUENTIN.....................................**Restigouche**

Louise B. Somers, PO Box 789, E0K 1J0 – 506/235-2056, Fax: 506/235-3323 – *1

ST. STEPHEN......................................**Charlotte**

G.W.A. Cockburn, #101, 123 Milltown Blvd., PO Box 206, E3L 2X1 – 506/466-6292, Fax: 506/466-3577 – *1

Hansen, MacDonald, Ames & Wilson, 184 King St., PO Box 188, E3L 2X1 – 506/466-2400, Fax: 506/466-6234 – *1

Dana W. McConkey, 196 King St., E3L 2E2 – 506/466-3626 – *1

Nicholson, Turner, Walker & White, 46 Milltown Blvd., PO Box 218, E3L 2X1 – 506/466-2338, Fax: 506/466-0160 – *4

Ronald W. Sutherland, 71 King St., PO Box 427, E3L 2X3 – 506/466-5330, Fax: 506/466-3692 – *1

SUSSEX .... Kings

Emily Palmer Law Office, 17 Queen St., PO Box 1020, E0E 1P0 – 506/433-2168, Fax: 506/433-4740 – *3

TRACADIE .... Gloucester

Doiron, Lavoie & Lebouthillier, 3376, rue Principale, CP 1120, E0C 2B0 – 506/395-3387, Fax: 506/395-6866 – *4

Guy Paulin, CP 1608, E0C 2B0 – 506/395-2256 – *1

A. Poirier, CP 1000, E0C 2B0 – 506/395-2227 – *1

WOODSTOCK .... Carleton

Crocco, Hunter, Purvis & Depow, 105 Connell St., PO Box 280, E0J 2B0 – 506/325-3331, Fax: 506/325-3355 – *6

McCue & Associates, 179 Broadway St., PO Box 848, E0J 2B0 – 506/325-2835, Fax: 506/328-6248 – *2

NEWFOUNDLAND

CHANNEL-PORT-AUX-BASQUES .... Burin-St. Georges

Stagg, Marks & Mills, PO Box 640, A0M 1C0 – 709/695-7341, Fax: 709/695-3944 – *3

CORNER BROOK .... Humber

Martin, Avis & King, 20 Central St., A2H 2M6 – 709/639-7184 – *3

Monaghan, Seaborn, Marshall, Matthews & Allen-Westby, Bldg Box: 815, 17 West St., A2H 6H9 – 709/634-3231, Fax: 709/634-8889 – *7

E.R. Ozon, PO Box 1166, A2H 6T2 – 709/639-7126 – *1

Poole, Althouse, Clarke, Thompson & Thomas, #49, 51 Park St., PO Box 812, A2H 6H7 – 709/634-3136, Fax: 709/634-8247 – *9

Graham C. Watton & Company, 1 Riverside Dr., PO Box 188, A2H 6C7 – 709/634-3132, Fax: 709/634-7229 – *3

GANDER .... Gander-Gr. Falls

Easton, Facey & Hillier, Polaris Bldg., 61 Elizabeth Dr., PO Box 408, A1V 1W8 – 709/256-4006, Fax: 709/651-2850 – *5

GRAND FALLS-WINDSOR .... Gander

Blackmore/Inder, 2 Mill Rd., PO Box 731, A2A 2K2 – 709/489-2226, Fax: 709/489-7004 – *2

Brenda P. Boyd, 1 Junction Rd., A2A 1K2 – 709/489-5671, Fax: 709/489-9233 – *3

Michael J. Griffin, PO Box 400, A1A 2J8 – 709/489-7700, Fax: 709/489-2760 – *1

KELLIGREWS .... St. John's

Chalker, Pink, Kelligrews Professional Bldg., PO Box 237, A0A 2T0 – 709/834-2071, Fax: 709/834-3717 – *2

LABRADOR CITY .... Labrador

Miller & Hearn, 450 Avalon Dr., PO Box 129, A1V 2K3 – 709/944-3666, Fax: 709/944-5494 – *2

MARYSTOWN .... St. George's

MacBeath, Colbourne, Wiscombe Bldg., PO Box 218, A0E 2M0 – 709/279-2467, 2468, 2469, Fax: 709/279-3863 – *4

MOUNT PEARL .... St. John's

Heywood, Kennedy, Belbin, 184 Park Avenue, PO Box 250, A1N 2C3 – 709/747-9613, Fax: 709/747-9723 – *4

* indicates number of lawyers in law firm.

ST. JOHN'S .... St. John's

Barry, Smyth, Walsh, 365 Duckworth St., PO Box 5818, A1C 5X3 – 709/754-1666, Fax: 709/754-0106 – *4

Chalker, Green & Rowe, Baine Johnson Centre, 10 Fort William Place, PO Box 5939, A1C 5X4 – 709/722-8735, Fax: 709/722-1763 – *18

Chalker, Pink, Avalon Mall, PO Box 28010, A1B 4J8 – 709/754-3600, Fax: 709/754-4002

Curtis, Dawe, Royal Trust Bldg., 139 Water St., 11th Fl., PO Box 337, A1C 5J9 – 709/722-5181, Fax: 709/722-7521 – *13

E. Gerard Doucette, PO Box 220, A1C 5J2 – *1

A.M. Ted Goodridge, 21 Military Rd., A1C 2C3 – 709/754-2292 – *1

Greene & Fraize, PO Box 5217, A1C 5W1 – 709/726-7978, Fax: 709/726-8201 – *2

Patrick J.B. Kennedy, 5 Church Hill, PO Box 5186, A1C 5V5 – 709/753-9500, Fax: 709/753-6400 – *1

Learmonth, Dunne, Clarke & Simmonds, Fortis Bldg., 139 Water St., PO Box 700, A1C 5L4 – 709/739-8585, Fax: 709/739-8151 – *5

Lewis, Day, Dawe & Burke, Toronto-Dominion Pl., #600, 140 Water St., A1C 6H6 – 709/753-2545, Fax: 709/722-2266 – *7

Martin, Whalen, Hennebury & Stamp, 15 Church Hill, PO Box 5910, A1C 5X4 – 709/754-1400, Fax: 709/754-0915 – *12

McGrath, Rose, 18 Argyle St., A1A 1V3 – 709/726-5250, Fax: 709/738-0614 – *2

McInnes Cooper & Robertson, Scotia Centre, #602, 235 Water St., PO Box 547, A1C 5K8 – 709/726-9500, Fax: 709/726-9550 – *3

Morris & Pittman, 139 Water St., PO Box 2355, A1C 6E7 – 709/754-8474, Fax: 709/754-8036 – *2

Noonan, Oakley, PO Box 5303, A1C 5W1 – 709/726-9598, Fax: 709/726-9614; Email: oakley@new-comm.net – *2

James E. Nurse, Q.C., 70 Portugal Cove Rd., A1B 2M3 – 709/726-7664 – *1

O'Dea, Earle, 323 Duckworth St., PO Box 5955, A1C 5X4 – 709/726-3524, Fax: 709/726-9600 – *10

O'Dea, Greene, 263 Duckworth St., PO Box 686, A1C 5L4 – 709/726-3740, Fax: 709/726-6014 – *1

O'Reilly, Noseworthy, Scotia Centre, #401, 235 Water St., A1C 1B6 – 709/726-3321, Fax: 709/726-2992 – *17

Patterson, Palmer, Hunt, Murphy, Scotia Centre, 235 Water St., PO Box 610, A1C 5L3 – 709/726-6124, Fax: 709/722-0483 – *22

Pike Law Offices, 272 Duckworth St., A1C 1H3 – 709/726-5600 – *1

Claude A.J. Sheppard, Jr., Cabot Pl., #300, 100 New Gower St., A1C 6K3 – 709/753-5655, Fax: 709/753-7431 – *1

Barry R. Sparkes, 29 Carpasian Rd., A1B 2P9 – 709/739-9423, Fax: 709/739-9423 – *1

Stack & Associates, 325 Duckworth St., PO Box 637, A1C 5K8 – 709/753-6066, Fax: 709/753-3608 – *2

Stewart McKelvey Stirling Scales, Cabot Place, 100 New Gower St., PO Box 5038, A1C 5V3 – 709/722-4270, Fax: 709/722-4565 – *23

White, Ottenheimer & Baker, Baine Johnson Centre, 10 Fort Williams Pl., PO Box 5457, A1C 5W4 – 709/722-7584, Fax: 709/722-9210 – *14

Williams, Roebothan, McKay & Marshall, 209 Duckworth St., PO Box 5236, A1C 5W1 – 709/753-5805, Fax: 709/753-5221; Toll Free: 1-800-563-5563 – *14

STEPHENVILLE .... Stephenville

William J. Gallant, 87 Gallant St., PO Box 447, A2N 3A3 – 709/643-5688, Fax: 709/643-2906 – *1

NORTHWEST TERRITORIES

FORT SMITH .... Western Arctic

Louis Sebert, PO Box 780, X0E 0P0 – 403/872-2199 – *1

INUVIK .... Western Arctic

Joyce Lillegran, PO Box 1966, X0E 0T0 – 403/979-3366

YELLOWKNIFE .... Western Arctic

Lucy Austin, PO Box 1282, X1A 2N9 – 403/920-4982, Fax: 403/873-3787

Bayly Williams, Scotia Centre, #203, 5102 - 50 Ave., PO Box 2882, X1A 2R2 – 403/920-4542, Fax: 403/873-4790 – *4

Boyd, Denroche, PO Box 2910, X1A 2R2 – 403/920-4151, Fax: 403/920-4252 – *6

Thomas H. Boyd, PO Box 2788, X1A 2N8 – 403/873-8808

Cooper, Peach & Gullberg, 4908 - 49 St., PO Box 818, X1A 2N6 – 403/669-5500, Fax: 403/920-2206 – *8

Davis & Company, Northwest Tower, #802, 5201 - 50th Ave., X1A 3S9 – 403/873-6455, Fax: 403/873-6456

Valdis Foldats, 56 Morrison Dr., X1A 1Z2 – 403/873-2000

Peter C. Fuglsang & Associates, 5016 - 48 St., PO Box 2459, X1A 2P8 – 403/920-4344, Fax: 403/873-3386 – *3

Rick Hardy, #180, 4908 Franklin Ave., X1A 2N6 – 403/873-2451

Elaine Keenan Bengts, PO Box 262, X1A 2N2 – 403/873-8631

Lawson, Lundell, Lawson & McIntosh, #204, 4817 - 49th St., X1A 3S7 – 403/669-9990, Fax: 403/669-9991

Austin F. Marshall, PO Box 1236, X1A 2N9 – 403/873-4969

Thomas McCauley, PO Box 386, X1A 2N3 – 403/873-5364

Jill A. Murray, PO Box 415, X1A 2N3 – 403/920-4144, Fax: 403/920-7985

Patrick A. Penny, PO Box 2438, X1A 2P8 – 403/873-8576 – *1

Peterson, Hudson, Stang & Malakoe, 4902 - 49 St., PO Box 939, X1A 2N7 – 403/873-4456, 6321, Fax: 403/873-6543 – *11

Phillips & Wright, PO Box 1855, X1A 2P4 – 403/873-3335 – *5

R. Clark Rehn, 5406 - 46 St., X1A 2N1 – 403/873-3634, Fax: 403/920-4406 – *1

Richard Spaulding, PO Box 2517, X1A 2P8 – 403/873-6300, Fax: 403/873-3787 – *1

NOVA SCOTIA

AMHERST .... Cumberland

Archibald, Morley, PO Box 548, B4H 4A1 – 902/667-3856, Fax: 902/667-0104 – *4

Creighton & Shatford, 14 Electric St., PO Box 398, B4H 3Z5 – 902/667-8490, Fax: 902/667-6081 – *4

Fairbanks Law Office, PO Box 103, B4H 3Y6 – 902/667-7579, Fax: 902/667-0644 – *1

Hicks, LeMoine, 23 La Planche St., PO Box 279, B4H 3G2 – 902/667-7214, Fax: 902/667-5886 – *8

Larry A. McKim, Q.C., 39 Victoria St., B4H 3Z2 – 902/667-2013 – *1

ANNAPOLIS ROYAL .... Annapolis

MacArthur & Associates, PO Box 366, B0S 1A0 – 902/532-2129, Fax: 902/532-5424 – *2

ANTIGONISH .... Antigonish

LeBlanc, MacDonald & Pickup, 133 Church St., B2G 2E3 – 902/863-2120, Fax: 902/863-0030

James C. MacIntosh, 16 Bay St., B2G 2G8 – 902/863-4805, Fax: 902/863-8086 – *1

MacPherson MacNeil Macdonald, 42 West St., B2G 2H5 – 902/863-2925 – *3

Susan E. Woolway, #201, 219 Main St., B2G 2C1 – 902/863-6231, Fax: 902/863-6729 – *1

BARRINGTON — Shelburne
G. David Eldridge, PO Box 157, B0W 1E0 – 902/637-2878, Fax: 902/637-2025 – *1

BARRINGTON PASSAGE — Shelburne
Pink Macdonald Harding, PO Box 580, B0W 1G0 – 902/637-2266, Fax: 902/637-3283

BEDFORD — Halifax
Blackburn English, Bedford House, Sunnyside Mall, #231, 1595 Bedford Hwy., B4A 3Y4 – 902/835-8544, Fax: 902/835-4310
Rhindress, Rusk & Kent, 1394 Bedford Hwy., B4A 1E2 – 902/835-7444 – *3

BERWICK — Kings
Stewart & Turner, 196 Cottage St., B0P 1E0 – 902/538-3123, Fax: 902/538-7933 – *2
Waterbury, Newton & Johnson, 188 Commercial St., PO Box 475, B0P 1E0 – 902/538-3168, Fax: 902/538-8680

BRIDGETOWN — Annapolis
D.H. Hatherly, Q.C., PO Box 269, B0S 1C0 – 902/665-4544 – *1
Orlando & Hicks, 3 Queen St., B0S 1C0 – 902/665-4471, Fax: 902/665-4039 – *2

BRIDGEWATER — Lunenburg
Conrad & Feindel, 70 Dufferin St., B4V 2G3 – 902/543-4655, Fax: 902/543-6853 – *2
Coughlan & Coughlan, 48 Pleasant St., PO Box 169, B4V 2W8 – 902/543-7888, Fax: 902/543-0225 – *3
Gordon M. Davidson, 764 King St., B4V 1B4 – 902/453-4556, Fax: 902/453-5293 – *1
Ferrier, Fownes, 137 Queen St., PO Box 69, B4V 2W6 – 902/543-1421, Fax: 902/543-1359
Milner Morris Naugler & Reid, 344 King St., PO Box 250, B4V 1A9 – 902/543-6661, Fax: 902/543-6639 – *4
Theakston, Allen & Peers, 455 King St., B4V 1B2 – 902/543-2437, Fax: 902/543-0243 – *4

CHESTER — Lunenburg
David S. Fraser, Q.C., PO Box 4, B0J 1J0 – 902/275-4654, Fax: 902/275-4798 – *1
Hennigar, Wells, Lamey & Baker, 24 Pleasant St., B0J 1J0 – 902/275-3544 – *3

CHESTER BASIN — Lunenburg
B.J. Preeper, Q.C., PO Box 99, B0J 1K0 – 902/275-2155, Fax: 902/275-3088 – *1

DARTMOUTH — Halifax
Ramey Ayres, 14A Josephine Ct., L2W 5Z9 – *1
Boyne Clarke, PO Box 876, Stn Halifax, B2Y 3Z5 – 902/469-9500, Fax: 902/463-7500; Email: admin@boyneclarke.ns.ca – *29
John D. Filliter, Q.C., 56 Lorne Avenue, B2Y 3E7 – 902/466-8424, Fax: 902/463-4168 – *1
David A. Grant, 63 Tacoma Drive, B2W 3E7 – 902/463-6300, Fax: 902/435-7910 – *1
Horne Langille Sealy, CIBC Bldg., #200, 56 Portland St., PO Box 767, B2Y 3Z3 – 902/463-5200, Fax: 902/465-5200 – *9
Huestis - Holm, Royal Bank Bldg., 44 Portland St., PO Box 913, B2Y 3Z6 – 902/469-3080, Fax: 902/465-3751 – *8
Landry, McGillivray, 33 Ochterloney St., PO Box 1200, B1Y 4B8 – 902/463-8800, Fax: 902/463-0590 – *8
Livingstone & Company, 12 Queen St., PO Box 664, B2Y 3Y9 – 902/461-5111, Fax: 902/461-4911 – *4
Pettipas & Richey, PO Box 723, B2Y 3Z3 – 902/465-4481, Fax: 902/463-4319 – *2
Tippett, Leary, #302, 177 Main St., B2X 1S1 – 902/434-1512, Fax: 902/434-1513
Weldon, Beeler & Mont, 19 Portland St., PO Box 465, B1Y 3Y8 – 902/469-2421, Fax: 902/463-4452 – *4

Wolfson, Schelew, Green & Zatzman, Bank of Commerce Bldg., #500, 73 Tacoma Dr., PO Box 2308, B2W 3Y4 – 902/435-7000, Fax: 902/435-4085 – *3

ENFIELD — Hants
Blackburn English, 287 Old Truro Hwy., PO Box 277, B0N 1N0 – 902/883-2264, Fax: 902/883-8744 – *4

GLACE BAY — Cape Breton
Crosby, Burke & Macrury, PO Box 86, B1A 5V2 – 902/849-3971, Fax: 902/849-7009 – *3

GREENWOOD — Kings
Durland, Gillis & Parker, Greenwood Shopping Mall, PO Box 629, B0P 1N0 – 902/765-4992, Fax: 902/765-4120
William J. Dyer, PO Box 1940, B0P 1N0 – 902/765-3301, Fax: 902/765-6493 – *1

GUYSBOROUGH — Guysborough
LeBlanc, MacDonald & Pickup, PO Box 200, B0H 1N0 – 902/533-2644

HALIFAX — Halifax
Armsworthy Lynch, 5443 Cogswell St., B3J 1R1 – 902/425-8740, Fax: 902/423-6891 – *4
Blois, Nickerson & Bryson, 1568 Hollis St., PO Box 2147, B3J 3B7 – 902/425-6000, Fax: 902/429-7347; Email: blois@fox.nstn.ca – *16
Buchan, Derrick & Ring, #100, 5525 Artillery Pl., B3J 1J2 – 902/422-7411, Fax: 902/423-3544
Burchell, MacAdam & Hayman, 1801 Hollis St., PO Box 36, B3J 2L4 – 902/423-6361, Fax: 902/420-9326 – *15
Burchell, MacDougall & Gruchy, One Sackville Pl., #400, 5121 Sackville St., B3J 1K1 – 902/421-1536, Fax: 902/425-0085 – *4
R.D. Campbell, #2003, 1470 Summer St., B3H 3A3 – 902/429-5454, Fax: 902/429-5457 – *1
Chandler Moore, 3476 Dutch Village Rd., B3N 2R9 – 902/445-2500, Fax: 902/445-5187 – *7
Coady Filliter, #208, 880 Spring Garden Rd., B3H 1Y1 – 902/429-6264, Fax: 902/423-3044 – *5
Cox Downie, Purdy's Wharf Tower, Bldg Box: 1100, 1959 Upper Water St., PO Box 2380, Stn Central RPO, B3J 3E5 – 902/421-6262, Fax: 902/421-3130; Email: admin@coxdownie.ns.ca – *43
Crowe Dillon Robinson, #2000, 7075 Bayers Rd., B3L 2C1 – 902/453-1732, Fax: 902/454-9948 – *8
Daley, Black & Moreira, PO Box 355, B3J 2N7 – 902/423-7211, Fax: 902/420-1744 – *23
Flinn Merrick, PO Box 1054, B3J 2X6 – 902/429-4111, Fax: 902/429-8215; Email: fmhfx@fox.nstn.ca – *16
Simon L. Gaum, Q.C., Tower One, Halifax Shopping Centre, #200, 7001 Mumford Rd., B3L 4N9 – 902/423-6391, Fax: 902/455-0974 – *1
Goldberg Thompson, PO Box 306, B3J 2N7 – 902/421-1161, Fax: 902/425-0266 – *8
Green Parish, PO Box 1134, B3J 2X1 – 902/422-3100, Fax: 902/425-2504 – *6
Mary B. Helleiner, PO Box 325, B3J 2N7 – 902/422-8335, Fax: 902/492-0424 – *1
Huestis - Holm, Bank of Commerce Bldg., #708, 1809 Barrington St., B3J 3K8 – 902/429-3400, Fax: 902/422-4713 – *15
Lambert & Duncan, #903, 1649 Hollis St., B3J 2R7 – 902/423-9143, Fax: 902/422-7837 – *2
MacInnis, Kenneth A. Associates, #340, 1801 Hollis St., B3J 3N4 – 902/421-1817, Fax: 902/423-8504 – *3
McInnes Cooper & Robertson, Summit Place, 1601 Lower Water St., PO Box 730, B3J 2V1 – 902/425-6500, Fax: 902/425-6350; Email: mcrhfx@mcrlaw.com; URL: http://fox.nstn.ca/~mcrhfx/ – *50
Medjuck & Medjuck, PO Box 1074, B3J 2X1 – 902/429-4061 – *2
Metcalf, Hayashi, 1459 Hollis St., B3J 1V1 – 902/420-1990, Fax: 902/429-1171 – *3

Moore & Associates, 1554 Hollis St., PO Box 3068, B3J 3G6 – 902/420-1066, Fax: 902/420-1938 – *5
Murrant Brown, Tower II, Purdy's Wharf, #1800, 1969 Upper Water St., PO Box 2067, B3J 2Z1 – 902/421-2121, Fax: 902/421-2125 – *1
Robert W. Newman & Associates, #207, 7071 Bayers Rd., B3L 2C2 – 902/454-9827 – *1
Paton & Paton, 1529 Granville St., B3J 1W7 – 902/429-4343, Fax: 902/423-9293 – *1
Patterson Palmer Hunt Murphy, #1600, 5151 George St., PO Box 247, B3J 2N9 – 902/492-2000, Fax: 902/429-5215 – *55
Clyde A. Paul & Associates, 349 Herring Cove Rd., B3R 1V9 – 902/477-2518 – *2
Jack P. Rafuse, Q.C., #200, 6265 Quinpool Rd., B3L 1A4 – 902/422-9621 – *1
Reierson & Associates, Bldg Box: 300, 1869 Upper Water St., B3J 1S9 – 902/420-9181, Fax: 902/429-6232 – *1
Ross Wood & Scott, PO Box 502, B3J 2R7 – 902/422-6512 – *1
Scaravelli & Garson, 1869 Upper Water St., B3J 1S9 – 902/429-4104, Fax: 902/423-4009 – *4
Stewart McKelvey Stirling Scales, Purdy's Wharf Tower One, #900, 1959 Upper Water St., PO Box 997, B3J 2X2 – 902/420-3200, Fax: 902/420-1417; Email: halifax@email.smss.com; URL: http://www.nstn.ca/smss/ – *56
Walker, Dunlop, PO Box 3366, Stn South, B3J 3J1 – 902/423-8121, Fax: 902/429-0621 – *6
H.A.J. Wedderburn, #3007, 7001 Mumford Rd., B3L 4R3 – 902/453-1281 – *1

KENTVILLE — Kings
Donald C. Fraser, PO Box 668, B4N 3X9 – 902/678-4006, Fax: 902/678-2999 – *1
Gary J. Steele, 12 Cornwallis St., PO Box 730, B4N 3X9 – 902/678-8969, Fax: 902/678-5349 – *1
D.E. Thompson-Sheppard, Q.C., Drawer 578, B4N 3X7 – 902/681-6169, Fax: 902/681-1099
Thorpe Buntain Muttart Forse, PO Box 515, B4N 3X3 – 902/678-2157, Fax: 902/678-9455 – *8
Waterbury, Newton & Johnson, 469 Main St., PO Box 98, B4N 3V9 – 902/678-3257, Fax: 902/678-7727 – *15

LIVERPOOL — Queens
Conrad & Feindel, 267 Main St., PO Box 1600, B0T 1K0 – 902/354-5723, Fax: 902/543-4308
Ferrier, Fownes, 333 Main St., PO Box 1739, B0T 1K0 – 902/354-2744, Fax: 902/354-2746 – *3

LOWER SACKVILLE — Halifax
Robert W. Newman & Associates, 453 Sackville Dr., B4C 2S1 – 902/864-2722, Fax: 902/864-3164 – *1

LUNENBURG — Lunenburg
D.W.T. Brattston, PO Box 1599, B0J 2C0 – 902/634-8474 – *1
Burke & Macdonald, PO Box 549, B0J 2C0 – 902/634-8354, Fax: 902/634-4226 – *2
Walton W.M. Cook, 118 Montague St., PO Box 457, B0J 2C0 – 902/634-8713, Fax: 902/634-8943 – *1

MAHONE BAY — Lunenburg
Haysom & Kinley, PO Box 279, B0J 2E0 – 902/624-8337, Fax: 902/624-9401 – *3

MIDDLETON — Annapolis
Durland, Gillis & Parker, 76 Commercial St., B0S 1P0 – 902/825-3415, Fax: 902/825-2522 – *3

NEW GLASGOW — Pictou
Goodman MacDonald & Patterson, Goodman Pl., PO Box 697, B2H 5G2 – 902/752-5090, Fax: 902/755-3545 – *3
John G. Langley, Q.C., Squire Fraser's Pl., 130 George St., B2H 2K6 – 902/752-1131, Fax: 902/752-7737 – *1

Canadian Almanac & Directory 1997

MacIntosh, MacDonnell & MacDonald, 159 George St., PO Box 368, B2H 5E5 – 902/752-8441, Fax: 902/752-7810 – *8
Ian A. MacKay, Q.C., 559 East River Rd., PO Box 926, B2H 5K7 – 902/752-6803 – *1
H. Elizabeth MacKay O'Farrell, 465 Westville Rd., PO Box 1422, B0K 1S0 – 902/752-4227, Fax: 902/755-6218 – *1
J.G. Proudfoot, 260 Westville Rd., B1H 2J5 – 902/752-6220, Fax: 902/755-1763 – *1

NEW MINAS .... **Kings**
Waterbury, Newton & Johnson, 1095 Commercial St., B4N 3E3 – 902/678-3257, 1466, Fax: 902/679-1315

NEW WATERFORD .... **Cape Breton**
Charles Broderick, 3316 Plummer Ave., PO Box 151, B1H 4K4 – 902/862-6471, Fax: 902/862-9513 – *1

NORTH SYDNEY .... **Cape Breton**
Alfred J. Dinaut, PO Box 272, B1A 3M3 – 902/794-7729, Fax: 902/794-7692 – *1
M. Mora B. MacLennan, 33 Archibald Ave., B2A 2W6 – 902/794-2060, Fax: 902/794-3558
Ryan & Ryan, 208 Commercial St., PO Box 278, B2A 3M3 – 902/794-4784, Fax: 902/794-3042 – *4

PARRSBORO .... **Cumberland**
Hicks, LeMoine, 4B Spring St., PO Box 267, B0M 1S0 – 902/254-2477, Fax: 902/254-3311

PICTOU .... **Pictou**
MacLean & MacDonald, 90 Coleraine St., PO Box 730, B0K 1H0 – 902/485-4347, Fax: 902/485-8887 – *3
K.E.W. Roddam, Q.C., 94 Church St., PO Box 280, B0K 1H0 – 902/485-4385 – *1

PORT HAWKESBURY .... **Inverness**
Evans, MacIsaac, MacMillan, PO Box 69, B0E 2V0 – 902/625-0580, Fax: 902/625-2811 – *7
LeBlanc MacDonald & Pickup, 301 Pitt St., PO Box 700, B0E 2V0 – 902/625-2120 – *10

SHELBURNE .... **Shelburne**
Pink Macdonald Harding, 30 John St., PO Box 549, B0T 1W0 – 902/875-3611, Fax: 902/875-3414 – *2
W.S. Rideout, PO Box 508, B0T 1W0 – 902/875-3236 – *1

SHERBROOKE .... **Shelburne**
Robin W. Archibald, PO Box 176, B0J 3C0 – 902/522-2067; 833-2713, Fax: 902/522-2299 – *1

SPRINGHILL .... **Cumberland**
Hicks, LeMoine, 49 Main St., PO Box 899, B0M 1X0 – 902/597-3725, Fax: 902/597-5880 – *2

STELLARTON .... **Pictou**
Paul Graham, 276 Foord St., B0K 1S0 – 902/755-4522 – *1
Skoke & Company, 286 Foord St., PO Box 850, B0K 1S0 – 902/755-5711, Fax: 902/752-6561 – *3

SYDNEY .... **Cape Breton**
Nash Terrance Brogan, 290 George St., B1P 1J6 – 902/539-1390, Fax: 902/564-6722 – *1
Elizabeth Cusack Walsh, 205 Charlotte St., PO Box 5, B1P 1C4 – 902/564-8396, Fax: 902/564-0030 – *2
Elman, Kuna, 327 Charlotte St., B1P 6G9 – 902/562-5577, Fax: 902/564-4495 – *3
Dominic P. Goduto, 161 Townsend St., B1P 5E3 – 902/564-9503, Fax: 902/562-0365 – *1
Khattar & Khattar, 378 Charlotte St., PO Box 387, B1P 6H2 – 902/539-9696, Fax: 902/562-7147 – *5
MacDonald & MacLennan, 295 George St., PO Box 1148, B1P 6J7 – 902/564-4429, Fax: 902/539-2303 – *2
R.G. MacLellan, Q.C., PO Box 854, B1P 6J1 – 902/564-4463, Fax: 902/564-3845 – *1

* indicates number of lawyers in law firm.

McIntyre MacLellan, 245 Charlotte St., PO Box 788, B1P 6J1 – 902/562-4224, Fax: 902/562-0606 – *4
Murrant Brown, c/o E.C. Walsh, 205 Charlotte St., PO Box 595, B1P 6H4 – 902/564-8396, Fax: 902/564-0030
Parsons, D.L. & Associate, 240 Kings Rd., B1P 1A6 – 902/539-2777 – *2
Sampson McDougall, 642 King's Rd., B1S 1B9 – 902/539-2425, Fax: 902/564-0954 – *7
Stewart McKelvey Stirling Scales, 50 Dorchester St., PO Box 820, B1P 6J1 – 902/539-5135, Fax: 902/539-8256 – *1

TANTALLON .... **Halifax**
Smith-Camp, Reierson, Site 1, RR#2, PO Box 11, B0J 3J0 – 902/826-2193, Fax: 902/826-2347 – *2

TATAMAGOUCHE .... **Colchester**
W.R. Kennedy, PO Box 186, B0K 1V0

TRURO .... **Colchester**
Burchell MacDougall & Gruchy, 710 Prince St., PO Box 1128, B2N 5H1 – 902/895-1561, Fax: 902/895-7709 – *20
Curtis & Associates, 559 Prince St., PO Box 458, B2N 1G2 – 902/895-0528, Fax: 902/893-1158 – *2
Grant, MacNeill, 35 Inglis St., PO Box 188, B3N 5C1 – 902/893-7217 – *4
W.R. Kennedy, 56 Elm St., B1N 3H6 – *1
Patterson Palmer Hunt Murphy, 10 Church St., PO Box 1068, B2N 5B9 – 902/897-2000, Fax: 902/893-3071 – *1
Patterson Palmer Hunt Murphy, 26 Union St., B4A 2B5 – 902/835-7111, Fax: 902/835-3847

WAVERLEY .... **Halifax**
Conrad & Kelly, PO Box 310, B0N 2S0 – 902/861-1088, Fax: 902/861-4555 – *2

WINDSOR .... **Hants**
Adams & Company, 87 Gerrish St., B0N 2T0 – 902/798-8384, Fax: 902/798-0432 – *2
William R. Lawrence, Q.C., PO Box 788, B0N 2T0 – 902/798-8395 – *1
McGrath Alexander & MacKenzie, 99 Water St., PO Box 280, B0N 2T0 – 902/798-5734, Fax: 902/798-5739 – *4
Nelson & Associates, 258 King St., PO Box 2018, B0N 2T0 – 902/798-5797, Fax: 902/798-2332 – *2

WOLFVILLE .... **Kings**
Eric G. DeMont, Q.C., 180 Main St., PO Box 1449, B0P 1X0 – 902/542-5701, Fax: 902/542-7230 – *2
Kimball & Associates, 232 Main St., PO Box 670, B0P 1X0 – 902/542-5757, Fax: 902/542-5759 – *2

YARMOUTH .... **Yarmouth**
Chipman, Fraser, Pink & Nickerson, 390 Main St., PO Box 580, B5A 4B4 – 902/742-9224, Fax: 902/742-9383 – *6
Pink Macdonald Harding, 379 Main St., PO Box 398, B5A 4B3 – 902/742-7861, Fax: 902/742-0425 – *9

ONTARIO

AJAX .... **Durham**
Daniel J. Balena, 110 Hunt St., L1S 1P5 – 905/683-9601, Fax: 905/683-4610 – *1
L.A. Berg, Q.C., 36 Harwood Ave. South, PO Box 228, L1S 3C3 – 905/683-6171, Fax: 905/428-3473 – *1
Walker D. Clark, 20 Church St. North, L1T 2W5 – 905/683-2741, Fax: 905/683-2752 – *1
William E. Foden, 60 Randall Dr., Unit 2, L1S 6L3 – 905/428-8200, Fax: 905/428-8666 – *1
R.J. Fromstein, 15 Harwood Ave. South, L1S 2B9 – 905/683-8900, Fax: 905/683-8534 – *1

Greening & Associate, 50 Commercial Ave., L1S 2H5 – 905/683-7037, Fax: 905/683-7627 – *1
Todd J. Hoffman, 15 Harwood Ave. South, L1S 2B9 – 905/619-2535, Fax: 905/619-6780 – *1
J.E. Ort, #1, 30 Hunt St., L1S 3M2 – 905/427-9919, Fax: 905/427-9910 – *1
Polak, McKay & Hawkshaw, 467 Westney South, L1S 6V8 – 905/683-6880, Fax: 905/428-2063 – *4
P.G. Singh, Q.C., 158 Harwood Ave. South, L1S 2H6 – 905/683-1042, Fax: 905/683-7794 – *1
George D. Wright, PO Box 123, L1S 3L2 – 905/427-7200

ALEXANDRIA .... **Glengarry**
Jean-Marc Lefebvre, Q.C., 32 Main St. North, PO Box 519, K0C 1A0 – 613/525-1358, Fax: 613/525-3411 – *2
Macdonald & Aubry, 40 Main St. North, PO Box 1000, K0C 1A0 – 613/525-1055, Fax: 613/525-5080 – *2

ALLISTON .... **Simcoe**
John W. Clarke, PO Box 408, L9R 1V6 – 705/435-4301, Fax: 705/435-4307 – *1
Darling, Smith, McLean, 22 Church St. South, PO Box 1330, L0M 1A0 – 705/435-4324, Fax: 705/435-2628 – *4
Feehely, Gastaldi & Hayes, 18 Victoria St. East, PO Box 339, L9R 1T4 – 705/435-4386, Fax: 705/435-9256 – *3
Greenfield, Gilmore, 458 Victoria St. East, PO Box 250, L9R 1V5 – 705/435-4339, Fax: 705/435-6520 – *2
James W. Smith, PO Box 730, L9R 1V9 – 705/435-0160, Fax: 705/435-5049 – *1

ALMONTE .... **Lanark**
L.G. William Chapman, 77 Little Bridge St., PO Box 362, K0A 1A0 – 613/256-3072, Fax: 613/256-5164 – *1
Galligan & Mavis, 78 Mill St., PO Box 1150, K0A 1A0 – 613/256-2840, Fax: 613/256-4669 – *2
Patrick Galway, 359 Ottawa St., K0A 1A0 – 613/256-3480, Fax: 613/256-5895 – *1
Wheeler/Mackey, 38 Mill St., PO Box 1540, K0A 1A0 – 613/256-4148, Fax: 613/256-4708 – *2

AMHERSTBURG .... **Essex**
Barat Farlam Millson, 145 Sandwich St. South, PO Box 9, N9V 2Z2 – 519/736-5425, Fax: 519/736-8505 – *7
Bondy, Belowus, 41 Sandwich St. South, N9V 1Z5 – 519/736-2154, Fax: 519/736-2466 – *7
DiPierdomenico Law Firm, 285 Sandwich St. South, N9V 2A7 – 519/736-2126 – *1

AMHERSTVIEW .... **Lennox**
W.E.M. Vince, 3 Manitou Cres. West, K7N 1S3 – 613/389-6727 – *1

ANGUS .... **Simcoe**
Greenfield, Gilmore, 189 Mill St., PO Box 600, L0M 1B0 – 705/424-1331, Fax: 705/424-6441 – *1

ARNPRIOR .... **Renfrew**
McLean & Moore, 141 John St. North, PO Box 8, K7S 3H2 – 613/623-3177, Fax: 613/623-9166 – *2
Mulvihill & Murray, 84 John St. North, PO Box 187, K7S 3H4 – 613/623-4246, Fax: 613/623-8547 – *1

ARTHUR .... **Wellington**
Smith Janzen & Alaimo, 197 George St., PO Box 220, N0G 1A0 – 519/848-3916, Fax: 519/848-2395 – *3

ATHENS .... **Leeds**
Quigley, Ross & Cliffen, 10 Main St. East, PO Box 604, K0E 1B0 – 613/924-2673

AURORA .... **York Region**
W.H.C. Bailey, 33 Victoria St., PO Box 186, L4G 3H3 – 905/727-9473, Fax: 905/841-8492 – *1

Canadian Almanac & Directory 1997

Timothy P. Boland, 14996 Yonge St., L4G 1M6 – 905/841-5717 – *1
Roland J. Deschamps, 15032 Yonge St., L4G 1M4 – 905/841-2085 – *1
Mark W. Kushner, 330 Kennedy St. West, L4G 6L7 – 905/841-1086, Fax: 905/841-7184 – *1
Laurion Jack Law Office, 15105 Yonge St., L4G 1M3 – 905/841-2222
Lonny W. Mark, 15032 Yonge St., L4G 1M4 – 705/727-4285, Fax: 705/727-5569 – *1
McPherson, Shugart, Vrancic & Sorley, 15220 Yonge St., PO Box 338, L4G 3H4 – 905/727-3151, Fax: 905/841-2164 – *4
Murray, Kenneth D., 50 Wellington St. East, L4G 1H5 – 905/841-1850, Fax: 905/841-3659 – *1
Peddle, Boland, 138 Yonge St., L4G 1M6 – *2
Kent F. Pollard, 13 Church St., L4G 1G5 – 905/727-8354, Fax: 905/841-1749 – *1
Shortill & Young, #18, 2 Orchard Heights Blvd., L4G 3W3 – 905/727-1335 – *2
Smith & Thompson Associates, PO Box 100, L4G 1L9 – 905/727-3127, Fax: 905/727-7096 – *2
Steinberg Still & Bruce, 15139 Yonge St., L4G 1M3 – 905/713-1080, Fax: 905/713-1083 – *3
Barry W. Switzer, PO Box 246, L4G 1L8 – 905/727-9488, Fax: 905/841-8647 – *1
Michael L. Young, #160, 34 Berczy St., L4G 1W9 – 905/727-1335 – *1

AYLMER .... **Elgin**
Fordham, Watterworth & Marshall, 34 Talbot St. West, N5H 1J7 – 519/773-3130 – *4
Gloin, Hall & Shields, 139 Talbot St. East, PO Box 8, N5H 2R8 – 519/773-9221, Fax: 519/765-1885 – *6
M.L. Riddell, 200 Talbot St. East, N5H 1H7 – 519/773-5230

BANCROFT .... **Hastings**
O. Gregory Anderson, Q.C., 129 Hastings St., PO Box 700, K0L 1C0 – 613/332-3773, Fax: 613/332-5079 – *1
L.C. Plater, 61 Hastings St. North, K0L 1C0 – 613/332-1605, Fax: 613/332-2619 – *1

BARRIE .... **Simcoe**
R. Bruce Algie, 84 Worsley St., PO Box 804, L4M 4Y5 – 705/722-3634, Fax: 705/734-1435 – *1
Allison, Nancy Lee, 103 Collier St., PO Box 308, L4M 4T2 – 705/737-5702, Fax: 705/737-1614
Armstrong Meakings, 111 Toronto St., L4N 1V1 – 705/739-9111, Fax: 705/739-8111 – *2
Bell, Temple, 58 Collier St., PO Box 907, L4M 4Y6 – 705/726-4511, Fax: 705/726-0613 – *2
Brian Bond, 25 Poyntz St., L4M 3N8 – 705/734-1550, Fax: 705/734-0306
James Bowden, 85 Bayfield St., L4M 3A7 – 705/739-7310, Fax: 705/739-7091
Thomas Bryson, 11 Sophia St. West, L4N 1H9 – 705/728-2232, Fax: 705/728-7525 – *1
Burgar, Rowe, 90 Mulcaster St., PO Box 758, L4M 4Y5 – 705/721-3377, 726-6511, Fax: 705/721-4025 – *10
Francis Edward Burns, #101, 89 Dunlop St. East, L4M 5E2 – 705/722-7700, Fax: 705/722-0218 – *1
Stephen R. Canning, 91 Toronto St., L4N 1V1 – 705/739-1264, Fax: 705/739-1265
Carroll, Heyd, 77 Mary St., PO Box 548, L4M 4T7 – 705/722-4400, Fax: 705/722-0704 – *3
Cockburn & Smith, 89 Collier St., PO Box 955, L4M 4Y6 – 705/726-7351, Fax: 705/721-9445 – *2
Cowan & Carter, 107 Collier St., PO Box 722, L4M 4Y5 – 705/728-4521, Fax: 705/728-8744 – *1
Cugelman & Eisen, #201, 28 Owen St., L4M 3G7 – 705/721-1888, Fax: 705/721-7755 – *2
Paul J. Daffern & Associates, LWR 111 Toronto St., L4N 1V1 – 705/725-9670, Fax: 705/725-8764 – *1
Sam Delmar, 99 Burke St., L4N 7H9 – 705/739-1043, Fax: 705/728-0455
Alfred W.J. Dick, 80 Worsley St., L4M 1L8 – 705/728-9006, Fax: 705/728-9876 – *1

Julianne Ecclestone, 302-89 Dunlop St. East, L4M 1A7 – 705/725-8050, Fax: 705/722-0189 – *1
Graham, Wilson & Green, 190 Cundles Rd. East, PO Box 987, L4M 5E1 – 705/737-1811, Fax: 705/737-5390 – *4
Hogben Mayhew Hill, 39 Owen St., PO Box 501, L4M 4T7 – 705/726-3712, Fax: 705/726-3895 – *3
Klaus N. Jacoby, 34 Clapperton St., PO Box 350, L4M 4T5 – 705/726-0238, Fax: 705/726-9197 – *1
Carolyn L. Jones, 34A Clapperton St., L4M 3G8 – 705/737-0111, Fax: 705/734-0046 – *1
Mark A. Kelly, 17 Poyntz St., L4M 3N6 – 705/739-6955, Fax: 705/739-8816
Kenneth P. Kinnear, 23 Owen St., PO Box 646, L4M 4V1 – 705/726-6497, Fax: 705/722-4749 – *2
Peter Lamprey, 78 Worsley St., L4M 1L8 – 705/722-1114 – *1
Legal Aid, #104, 150 Dunlop St. East, L4M 6H1 – 705/737-3400, Fax: 705/739-0002
K. Joy Levison, 34A Clapperton St., L4M 3E7 – 705/737-5410, Fax: 705/737-5418 – *1
Livingston, Myers & Levison, 89 Collier St., PO Box 698, L4M 4Y5 – 705/726-6407, Fax: 705/726-3732 – *3
Norman E. Long, #206, 150 Dunlop St. East, L4M 6H1 – 705/737-3960, Fax: 705/722-6734
Gary W. Luhowy, 178 Bayfield St., PO Box 1063, L4M 5E1 – 705/737-5115, Fax: 705/721-0263 – *1
Gavin J. May, 88 Mulcaster St., L4M 3M5 – 705/739-9913, Fax: 705/722-6920 – *1
Peter McPhie, 78 Worsley St., L4M 1L8 – 705/722-1115, Fax: 705/722-5484 – *1
J. Marvin Menzies, #101, 89 Dunlop St. East, PO Box 1175, L4M 5E2 – 705/722-5432, Fax: 705/722-0218 – *1
Miller Pickard, 119 Collier St., L4M 1H5 – 705/734-1181, Fax: 705/722-6387 – *2
Albert Miller, 119 Collier St., PO Box 774, L4M 4Y5 – 705/737-2042, Fax: 705/737-2042 – *1
Wendy Miller, 80 Worsley St., PO Box 1117, L4M 5E2 – 705/737-5192, Fax: 705/734-0276 – *1
Mills Alexander, #230, 400 Bayfield St., L4M 5A1 – 705/739-7472, Fax: 705/739-5060
R.J. Mitchell, 40 Clapperton St., PO Box 1, L4M 4S9 – 705/725-8855, Fax: 705/721-0782 – *1
Christine Murray, 1296 Dunlop St. East, L4M 1A6 – 705/737-3229, Fax: 705/737-5380
Gerald E. Norman, 99 Bayfield St., PO Box 732, L4M 3A9 – 705/726-2772, Fax: 705/734-1942 – *1
Oatley, Purser, 151 Ferris Lane, L4M 4Y5 – 705/726-9021, Fax: 705/726-2132 – *7
J.S. Otton, Q.C., 15 Owen St., L4M 3G8 – 705/728-5822 – *1
Owen, Dickey, 26 Owen St., PO Box 848, L4M 4Y6 – 705/726-1181, Fax: 705/726-1463 – *3
G.W. Paisley, 30 Owen St., L4M 3G7 – 705/737-0688 – *1
K. Danielle Park, 18 Collier St., L4M 1H4 – 705/739-0929, Fax: 705/725-7977 – *2
Catherine Rogers, 115 Collier St., L4M 1H2 – 705/734-2800, Fax: 705/734-2807
Robert C. Rowe, 20 Bowman Ave., L4M 1V3 – 705/737-3119
Charles F. Ruttan, 23 Owen St., PO Box 7, L4M 4Y5 – 705/737-0688 – *1
Service Nichols Macleod, 78 Mary St., PO Box 40, L4M 4S9 – 705/737-2123, Fax: 705/737-2194 – *3
Simcoe Legal Services Clinic, 80 Bradford St., Unit 20, L4M 1A5 – 705/722-3421
Smith, McLean, 118 Collier St., PO Box 515, L4M 4T8 – 705/728-5907, Fax: 705/728-1897 – *3
Helena Song, 58 Mary St., L4N 1T1 – 705/728-0751, Fax: 705/737-5380 – *1
Stewart, Esten, 100 Collier St., L4M 4V3 – 705/728-5591, Fax: 705/728-3566 – *8
Dennis Tascona, 218 Bradford St., L4N 3B6 – 705/734-1801, Fax: 705/734-2324

Joseph Neil Tascona, 84 Worsley St., L4M 5E1 – 705/725-1769, Fax: 705/725-1772 – *1
Eric C. Taves, 86 Worsley, PO Box 295, L4M 4T2 – 705/728-4770, Fax: 705/728-7642 – *1
George Taylor, Q.C., 119 Collier St., L4M 1H5 – 705/722-0221, Fax: 705/722-6387 – *1
W. Michael Temple, Q.C., c/o Ontario Provincial Police Association, 119 Ferris Lane, L4M 2Y1 – 705/728-6161
Judith Turner-MacBeth, 86 Worsley St., PO Box 295, L4M 4T2 – 705/721-5907, Fax: 705/728-7642 – *1
Robin Vogl, #203, 28 Owen St., L4M 3G7 – 705/739-1770
Deborah L. Wall-Armstrong, 631 Yonge St., L4N 4E7 – 705/722-7272, Fax: 705/722-3568 – *1
Webb Graham, #206, 150 Dunlop St., L4M 6H1 – 705/722-8580, Fax: 705/722-6734
David S. White, Q.C., 89 Dunlop St. East, L4M 1A7 – 705/734-0100, Fax: 705/734-1303 – *1
David Wilcox, #206, 150 Dunlop St. East, L4M 6H1 – 705/721-6642, Fax: 705/722-6734 – *1
E.C. Wildman, 11 Sophia St. West, PO Box 1, L4M 4S9 – 705/739-7493, Fax: 705/739-1145 – *1
R.A. Wildman, 80 Worsly St., L4M 1L8 – 705/739-7495, Fax: 705/739-7442 – *1
Charles L. Wilson, Q.C., 25 Berczy St., PO Box 601, L4M 4V1 – 705/726-6581, Fax: 705/739-1420 – *1
Zwicker, Evans & Lewis, 201-48 Alliance Blvd., L4M 5K3 – 705/722-6221, Fax: 705/722-4072 – *4

BARRY'S BAY .... **Renfrew**
Robert B. Howe, PO Box 790, K0J 1B0 – 613/756-2087, Fax: 613/756-5818 – *1

BEAMSVILLE .... **Niagara North**
Arthur D. Fleming, 5041 King St., PO Box 694, L0R 1B0 – 905/563-7000, Fax: 905/563-7740
M.G. Vandeyar, Kingsway Plaza, Bldg Box: 5041, #7, 5041 King St., L0R 1B0 – 905/563-8818, Fax: 905/563-7750 – *1

BEAVERTON .... **Durham**
C.C. Calder, PO Box 221, L0K 1A0 – 705/426-7354, Fax: 705/426-9043 – *1
Ivan G. Tomlinson, 402 Simcoe St., PO Box 512, L0K 1A0 – 705/426-7317, Fax: 705/426-5740 – *1

BELLE RIVER .... **Essex**
Mousseau, DeLuca, 419 Notre Dame St., N0R 1A0

BELLEVILLE .... **Hastings**
B. Bates, General Delivery, Belleville Plaza, K8N 1G1 – 613/969-1222, Fax: 613/969-1132 – *1
M.A. Black, 210 Church St., PO Box 652, K8N 5B3 – 613/969-8346, Fax: 613/968-8985 – *1
Boyle & Keilty, 49 Campbell St., K8N 1S8 – 613/966-2515, Fax: 613/966-2601 – *2
R.W. Cass, Q.C., 17 Campbell St., PO Box 1, K8N 5A2 – 613/962-1451 – *1
J.B. Corbett, 308 North Front St., K8P 3C4 – 613/966-6662 – *1
Follwell & Follwell, 24 Catharine St., K8P 4Z9 – 613/968-3471, Fax: 613/968-9441 – *1
Raymond Kaufmann, 187B Front St. North, K8P 3C1 – 613/966-7771, Fax: 613/966-6415 – *1
R.R. Ketcheson, 212 1/2 Front St., K8N 2Z2 – 613/966-1123 – *1
Peter B. McCabe, PO Box 1508, K8N 5J2 – 613/966-0924 – *1
O'Brien & Wright, 280 Pinnacle St., K8N 3B1 – 613/962-5337, Fax: 613/962-6833 – *3
Reynolds O'Brien Kline Selick, 183 Front St., PO Box 1327, K8N 5J1 – 613/966-3031, Fax: 613/966-2390 – *7
C. Roderick Rolston, #202, 175 Front St., K8N 2Z1 – 613/962-9154
J. David M. Ross, PO Box 501, K8N 5B2 – 613/966-5355, Fax: 613/966-6915 – *1

Paul Russell, 221 Coleman St., K8N 3H8 – 613/962-3433 – *1
Scott & Richardson, 400 Century Place, PO Box 1029, K8N 5B6 – 613/966-4554, Fax: 613/966-5830 – *2
Templeman, Menninga, Kort, Sullivan & Fairbrother, #200, 205 Dundas St. East, PO Box 234, K8N 5A2 – 613/966-2620, Fax: 613/966-2866; Email: tmksf_jm@loyalistcon.ca – *12
Van Huizen, Scholten, 210 Church St., PO Box 1372, K8N 5J1 – 613/962-8645, Fax: 613/962-7689 – *2

BLENHEIM .... Kent
Thomas G. Chalmers, 116 Talbot St. West, N0P 1A0 – 519/676-4044 – *1
Lucy C. Glenn, 23 Marlborough St. South, PO Box 1870, N0P 1A0 – 519/676-5451, Fax: 519/676-4911 – *1
Kerr & Wood, 15 George St., PO Box 1150, N0P 1A0 – 519/676-5465,5466, Fax: 519/676-3918 – *2
T.R. Warwick, Q.C., 4 Talbot St. West, N0P 1A0 – 519/676-3266, Fax: 519/676-0001 – *1

BLIND RIVER .... Algoma
Peterson & Peterson, 12 Lawton Ave., PO Box 1607, P0R 1B0 – 705/356-9877, Fax: 705/356-7498

BOBCAYGEON .... Victoria
Warner, Cork & Siegel, 116 Main St., PO Box 999, K0M 1A0 – 705/738-5126, Fax: 705/738-5129 – *1

BOLTON .... Peel
Jean P. Carberry, 210 Bolton Professional Bldg., 30 Martha St., L7E 5V1 – 905/857-2332 – *1
Marilyn Conway Jones, UPR-284 Queen St. South, L7E 4Z5 – 905/951-0504, Fax: 905/951-0074 – *1
Sandra Morra, PO Box 75006, L7E 1H6 – 905/951-2886, Fax: 905/951-2893 – *1
Allan L. Naiman, 69 King St. West, PO Box 822, L7E 5T2 – 905/857-0861, Fax: 905/857-0866
Neiman, Bissett, 12 King St. West, PO Box 550, L7E 5T4 – 905/857-2373 – *3
Palmateer & Muise, 58 King St. West, PO Box 665, L7E 5T5 – 905/857-0847, Fax: 905/857-4410 – *2
Mark E. Penfold, 49 Queen St. North, PO Box 225, L7E 5T2 – 905/857-2835, Fax: 905/857-0091 – *1
Carol E. Struthers, 30 Martha St., L7E 5V1 – 905/951-0503, Fax: 905/951-2929 – *1

BOURGET .... Russell
Houle Assaly Morissette, 3792 Champlain St., PO Box 536, K0A 1E0 – 613/487-3229

BOWMANVILLE .... Durham
Douglas J. Barber, PO Box 339, L1C 3L1 – 905/623-2525, Fax: 905/623-7666 – *1
William Brown, 68 King St. East, L1C 3X2 – 905/623-3305, Fax: 905/623-3287 – *1
Stephen A. Cooper, 36B King St. East, L1C 1N2 – 905/623-5554, Fax: 905/623-3961 – *2
Craig Fromstein, 181 Church St., L1C 1T8 – 905/623-7181, Fax: 905/623-8192 – *1
Hamilton & Mutton, 1 Division St., PO Box 39, L1C 3K8 – 905/623-7744, Fax: 905/623-7759 – *2
Mervyn B. Kelly, 38A King St. East, PO Box 159, L1C 3K9 – 905/623-4444, Fax: 905/623-4712; Email: bkel@istar.ca – *1
Strike, Salmers & Furlong, 38 King St. West, PO Box 7, L1C 3K8 – 905/623-5791, Fax: 905/623-8336 – *3

BRACEBRIDGE .... Muskoka
A.R. Black, 50 Ball's Dr., PO Box 1197, P1L 1V3 – 705/645-5251, Fax: 705/645-9193 – *1
Jacques & Huycke, 46 Kimberley Ave., P1L 1R8 – 705/645-8743, Fax: 705/645-8895 – *2
Lee, Roche & Kelly, 6 Dominion St., PO Box 990, P1L 1R6 – 705/645-2286, Fax: 705/645-5541 – *3
D.R. Lisso, Attorney General Office, PO Box 487, P1L 1R6 – 705/545-2411 – *1

Judith L. Stephenson, 58 Ontario St., P1L 2A6 – 705/645-5251, Fax: 705/645-9193 – *1
Sugg & Fitton, 5 Chancery Lane, PO Box 1109, P1L 1S6 – 705/645-5211, Fax: 705/645-8021 – *3
Bruce McLeod Thompson, PO Box 99, P1L 1T5 – 705/646-1000, Fax: 705/645-9193; Email: 1-800-661-8080
R.A. Tweedie, 62 Kimberley Ave., P1L 1R8 – 705/645-2221, Fax: 705/645-3943 – *1
Wyjad & Grimmett, 39 Dominion St., P1L 1R6 – 705/645-8787, Fax: 705/645-3390 – *1

BRADFORD .... Simcoe
Evans & Evans, 21 Holland St. West, PO Box 190, L3Z 2A8 – 905/775-3381, Fax: 905/775-8835 – *2
Zygmunt J. Fenik, 22 Barrie St., PO Box 100, L3Z 2A7 – 905/775-5313, Fax: 905/775-5462 – *1
W. Roy Gordon, 57 John St. West, PO Box 1660, L3Z 2B9 – 905/775-5301, Fax: 905/775-8152 – *1
Diana S. Riffert, 84 Barrie St., PO Box 1555, L3Z 2B8 – 905/775-5383, Fax: 905/775-6580 – *1
E. Pauline Taylor, 107 Holland St. East, L3Z 2B6 – 905/775-9606, Fax: 905/775-0692 – *1

BRAMPTON .... Peel
Acri, MacPherson, Fader & Baldock, #101, 134 Queen St. East, L6V 1B2 – 905/459-6160 – *4
Agree Dispute Resolution, #410, 7700 Hurontario St., L6Y 4M3 – 905/455-9900, Fax: 905/455-3066 – *2
Linda B. Alexander, #300, 197 County Court Blvd., L6W 4P6 – 905/450-7757, Fax: 905/455-9190 – *1
Richard A. Allman, 1 Cornwall Rd., L6W 1M8 – 905/454-0397, Fax: 905/454-5072 – *1
Andre Irving, #20, 1 Bartley Bull Pkwy., L6W 3T7 – 905/459-1399, Fax: 905/459-5534
Stephen I. Beck, 400 Queen St. W., L6X 1B3 – 905/451-9898, Fax: 905/451-9427 – *1
Louise Berman, 14 Nelson St. West., L6X 1B7 – 905/459-8383 – *1
Bowyer, Greenslade & Hall, 6 George St. South, L6Y 1P3 – 416/451-1300, Fax: 416/451-4451 – *5
Brampton Community Legal Services, 37 George St. North, L6X 1R5 – 905/455-0160, Fax: 905/455-0832 – *2
Edmond O'Donoghue Brown, #100, 205 County Court Blvd., L6W 4R6 – 905/454-4141, Fax: 905/454-4463 – *1
Alan M. Buchanan, #1804, 83 Kennedy Rd. S., L6W 3G1 – 905/459-6331, Fax: 905/459-2674 – *1
Shawn K. Campbell, #200, 5 Conestoga Dr., L6Z 4N5 – 905/846-4991 – *1
Bonnie Caplan-Stroeder, 480 Main St. North, L6V 1P8 – 905/455-7096, Fax: 905/455-5848 – *1
Coffin & Bhattacharya, 83 Kennedy Rd. S, L6W 3P3 – 905/457-5027, Fax: 905/457-3991 – *4
David Cohen, #116, 44 Peel Centre Dr., L6T 4B5 – 905/792-7000, Fax: 905/792-2036 – *1
Jane A. Connan, 165 Main St. North, L6X 1N1 – 905/454-3070, Fax: 905/454-2964 – *1
Elliott Dale, 480 Main St. North, L6V 1P8 – 905/455-7300, Fax: 905/455-5848 – *1
Dalzell, Inglis, Waite, 1 Bartley Bull Pkwy., L6W 3T7 – 905/454-2288, Fax: 905/454-2297 – *3
Davis, Webb & Schulze, Brampton Executive Centre, #600, 8 Nelson St. West, L6X 4J2 – 905/451-6714, Fax: 905/454-1876 – *3
DeFaria & DeFaria, 8 Strathearn Ave., L6T 4L9 – 905/458-4440, Fax: 905/458-4441 – *2
Douma, John D., 103 Queen St. West, L6Y 1M3 – 905/451-7234, Fax: 905/455-7356 – *1
Douglas G. Edward, #707, 24 Queen St. East, L6V 1A3 – 905/456-3600, Fax: 905/456-3622 – *1
Furlong Collins, 182 Queen St. West, L6W 4P6 – 905/450-9050 – *2
James A. Garvie, 350 Rutherford Rd. South, Unit 3, L6W 3M2 – 905/451-4050, Fax: 905/451-5517 – *1
Peter A. Girouard, 35 Cox Cres., L6X 3G8 – 905/451-2138, Fax: 905/451-5655 – *1

Donald R. Good, #204, 60 Queen St., L6V 2L3 – , Fax: 905/453-1176; Toll Free: 1-800-661-8837
Linda S. Gudz, #301, 197 County Court Blvd., L6W 4P6 – 905/455-2255, Fax: 905/459-2826
Henderson Law Office, #407, 7700 Hurontario St., L6Y 4M3 – 905/451-7700, Fax: 905/451-6620 – *1
Hendy & Hendy, 280 Main St. North, L6V 1P6 – 905/457-8230, Fax: 905/457-3075 – *2
Hillier & Hillier, 165 Main St. North, L6X 1N1 – 905/453-8636, Fax: 905/453-6267 – *2
Stephen A. Holmes, #201, 60 Queen St. E., L6V 1A9 – 905/796-3030, Fax: 905/796-2157 – *1
Irving, Joseph W., 121 Braidwood Lake Rd., L6Z 4L4 – 905/840-5858, Fax: 905/840-7353 – *1
J. Stephen Braganca, #503, 201 County Court Blvd., L6W 4L2 – 905/450-9111, Fax: 905/450-9640 – *5
J.D. Barnett Law Offices, #222, 284 Queen St. E., L6V 1C2 – 905/796-6000, Fax: 905/796-9994 – *6
James & Associates, 1 Conestoga Dr., Unit 3, L6Z 4N6 – 905/846-0000, Fax: 905/846-0001
Ken James & Associates, #210, 1C Conestoga Dr., L6Z 4N5 – 905/846-0000, Fax: 905/846-0001
Paul W. Jeffries, #412, 7700 Hurontario St., L6Y 4M3 – 905/451-1991, Fax: 905/451-7619 – *1
Eric M. Kelday, #200, 197 County Court Blvd., L6W 4P6 – 905/459-8281, Fax: 905/459-8284 – *1
Larry Konrad, #200, 2 County Court Blvd., L6W 3W8 – 905/453-9944, Fax: 905/453-1313 – *1
Meyer Korman, 2 Fisherman Dr., Unit 7, L7A 1B5 – 905/840-7108
Lawrence, Lawrence, Stevenson, 43 Queen St. West, L6Y 1L9 – 905/451-3040, Fax: 905/451-5058 – *16
D.R. Lent, 38 Queen St. West, L6X 1A1 – 905/457-4215 – *1
Robert S. Leschied, #201, 60 Queen St. East, L6V 1A9 – 905/455-7111, Fax: 905/454-4234 – *1
A. Randall Longfield, 303 Main St. North, L6X 1N5 – 905/452-8622, Fax: 905/452-9761 – *1
C.G. MacPherson, 134 Queen St. East, L6V 1B2 – 905/459-6160, Fax: 905/459-4606 – *1
Narin N. Malik, 7700 Hurontario St., Unit 311A, L6Y 4M3 – 905/450-9473, Fax: 905/450-9479 – *1
Peter Maloney, 499 Main St. South, L6Z 1N7 – 905/450-0941, Fax: 905/450-1124 – *1
Marcos Associates, 5 Church St. East, L6V 1E8 – 905/451-0002, Fax: 905/451-0003 – *1
John W. May, 58 Elizabeth St. N., L6X 1S4 – 905/452-7004, Fax: 905/452-7006 – *1
McCabe Kelly & Filkin, #300, 195 County Court Blvd., L6W 4P7 – 905/452-7400, Fax: 905/452-6444
W.J. McCulligh, #301, 197 County Court Blvd., L6W 4P6 – 905/459-1545, Fax: 905/459-2826 – *1
Robert D. Mcintyre, Q.C., 44 Peel Centre Drive, L6T 4B5 – 905/791-6262, Fax: 905/791-6446 – *1
Sarah E. Mott-Trille, 268 Main St. N., L6V 1P5 – 905/459-6000, Fax: 905/459-6108 – *1
John P. Mullen, 412-7700 Hurontario St., L6Y 4M3 – 905/453-7600, Fax: 905/451-7619 – *1
O'Grady, Stephenson, 5A Conestoga Dr., L6Z 4N5 – 905/840-0011, Fax: 905/840-1909 – *2
Offman & Raby, #207, 7956 Torbram Rd., L6T 5A2 – 905/791-3320, Fax: 905/791-3324 – *2
Pandy & Company, Bldg 1E, 1 Conestoga Dr., 3rd Fl., L6Z 4N5 – 905/840-9955, Fax: 905/840-9280 – *2
Peel Law Association, 7755 Hurontario St., L6V 2L7 – 905/451-2924
Peel Legal Aid, 200-205 County Court Blvd., L6W 4R6 – 905/453-1723, Fax: 905/453-1743
Susan S. Powell, 400 Queen St. W., L6X 1B3 – 905/455-6677, Fax: 905/455-6724 – *1
Thomas W.G. Pratt, #600, 24 Queen St. East, L6V 1A3 – 905/456-3900 – *1
Prouse, Dash & Crouch, 50 Queen St. West, L6X 4H3 – 905/451-6610, Fax: 905/451-1549 – *7
Frank Racioppo, #18, 1 Bartley Bull Pkwy., L6W 3T7 – 905/848-6100, Fax: 905/896-1111
H. Ram, #703, 24 Queen St. East, L6V 1A3 – 905/453-9966 – *1

* indicates number of lawyers in law firm.

Carol L. Reid, 400 Queen St. W., L6X 1B3 – 905/451-9539, Fax: 905/455-6724 – *1

Richardson, Schnall & Sanderson, 13 Queen St. East, L6W 2A7 – 905/451-1593 – *1

Peter L.T. Rickards, 341 Main St. North, L6X 1N5 – 905/450-5858, Fax: 905/450-9772 – *1

Kenneth D. Robb, Q.C., #200, 197 County Court Blvd., L6W 4P6 – 905/451-1460, Fax: 905/457-0598 – *1

Samuel, L.F., 21 John St., L6W 1Z1 – 905/453-3500 – *1

Santos Associates, #203, 195 County Court Blvd., L6W 4P7 – 905/452-8622, Fax: 905/452-9761 – *2

Donald M. Seeback, 134 Queen St. E., L6V 1B2 – 905/459-4389, Fax: 905/459-5274 – *1

Segal, Coffin, Bhattacharya, #20, 83 Kennedy Rd. South, L6W 3P3 – 905/457-5027, Fax: 905/457-3991 – *3

Simmons, Da Silva & Sinton, #200, 201 County Court Blvd., L6W 4L2 – 905/457-1660, Fax: 905/457-5641 – *11

Mark E. Skursky, #101, 380 Bovaird Dr., L6Z 2S8 – 905/840-0001 – *1

George Paul Smith, 280 Main St. North, L6V 1P6 – 905/457-9791, Fax: 905/457-9798 – *1

George T. Snowdon, #200, 197 County Court Blvd., L6W 4P6 – 905/457-2340, Fax: 905/457-0598 – *1

Speigel Nichols Fox, 44 Peel Centre Dr., L6T 4B5 – 905/791-6262 – *7

Brian Starkman, 50 Kennedy Rd. S., L6W 3E7 – 905/456-1053, Fax: 905/456-1206 – *1

Andrea Steiner, 480 Main St. North, L6V 1P8 – 905/455-5441, Fax: 905/455-5848 – *1

Craig A. Stephenson, #11, 1 Bartley Bull Pkwy., L6W 3T7 – 905/457-3644, Fax: 905/457-2531 – *1

R.C. Stockey, #312, 25 Peel Centre Dr., L6T 3R5 – 905/793-3026, Fax: 905/793-2446 – *1

George Struk, #405, 37 George St. North, L6X 1R5 – 905/453-9591, Fax: 905/453-9722 – *1

Marvin Talsky, 45 Bramalea Rd., L6T 2W4 – 905/791-7171, Fax: 905/678-6626 – *1

Tannahill, Lockhart & Clark, #200, 2 County Court Blvd., L6W 3W8 – 905/453-5770, Fax: 905/453-1313 – *4

Cynthia K. Waite, 2 County Court Blvd., L6W 3W8 – 905/450-3800, Fax: 905/450-8376 – *1

Madanjit S. Walia, 860 North Park Dr., L6S 4N5 – 905/459-5117, Fax: 905/459-8418 – *1

Walker Fox & Schwarz, 20 Wilkinson Rd., L6T 5B2 – 905/457-5503 – *3

Michael J. Walsh, 280 Main St. North, L6V 1P6 – 905/453-4105, Fax: 905/457-3075 – *1

Wanda L. Warren, 400 Queen St. West, L6X 1B3 – 905/840-7034, Fax: 905/840-6395 – *1

J.T. Wiley, #100, 205 County Court Blvd., L6W 4P3 – 905/454-5600, Fax: 905/454-4463 – *1

Wise, Zeldin, 480 Main St. North, L6V 1P8 – 905/796-9220

Alan M. Zuker, #201, 118 Queen St. West, L6X 1A5 – 905/451-5665, Fax: 905/451-2105 – *1

BRANTFORD .... **Brant**

Boddy, Ryerson, 42 Wellington St., PO Box 1265, N3T 5T3 – 519/753-8417, Fax: 519/753-7421 – *6

Donald C. Calder, #201, 70 Market St., PO Box 1882, N3T 5W4 – 519/759-1910, Fax: 519/759-2881 – *1

Gethin Edward, #1417, 82 Charlotte St., N3T 5T7 – 519/756-5217

J.M. Hart, Q.C., 25 West St., PO Box 784, N3T 5R7 – 519/759-1181, Fax: 519/759-6963 – *1

Hospodar, Davies & Goold, 120 Market St., N3T 5N3 – 519/759-0082, Fax: 519/759-8490 – *3

Jaskula, Sherk, Flaherty, Weston & Brock, #201, 222 Fairview Dr., N3R 2W9 – 519/751-3325, Fax: 519/577-7775

Lawrence, Giles, 63 Charlotte St., PO Box 216, N3T 5M8 – 519/756-8700, Fax: 519/756-5454 – *1

Lefebvre & Lefebvre, 75 Chatham St., PO Box 488, N3T 5N9 – 519/756-3350, Fax: 519/756-4727 – *5

Miller & Miller, 41 George St., N3T 5T3 – 519/753-4118 – *1

Ernest W. Painter, 58 Brant Ave., N3T 3G7 – 519/756-8330

Brian T. Pennell, 65 King St., PO Box 1857, N3T 5W4 – 519/752-2555, Fax: 519/752-1648 – *1

Staats, Edward, 188 Mohawk St., PO Box 1417, N3T 5T7 – 519/756-5217, Fax: 519/756-4783 – *2

Trepanier, Hagey, Kneale & Wiacek, 63 Charlotte St., PO Box 144, N3T 5M3 – 519/756-5227, Fax: 519/756-5454 – *4

Vandervet, Karkkainen, 107 Wellington St., PO Box 1495, N3T 5V6 – 519/759-4240, Fax: 519/759-4863 – *2

Verity Daboll Gregory & Jones, Holstein Place, 171 Colborne St., PO Box 278, N3T 5M8 – 519/759-4426, Fax: 519/759-1770 – *6

D. Warner, 25 Wellington St., N3T 2L5 – 519/759-4100 – *1

Waterous, Holden, Amey, Hitchon, 20 Wellington St., PO Box 1510, N3T 5V6 – 519/759-6220, Fax: 519/759-8360 – *15

F.B. Wray, RR#8, N3T 5M1 – 519/753-1333 – *1

Wyatt, Purcell, Will, Stillman & Scott, 103 Darling St., N3T 2K8 – 519/756-5800 – *6

BRECHIN .... **Simcoe**

Joseph J. McDonald, GD PO, L0K 1B0 – 705/484-0308, Fax: 705/484-0804 – *1

BRIDGENORTH .... **Peterborough**

H. Girvin Devitt, Causeway Plaza, Ward St., PO Box 269, K0L 1H0 – 705/292-9235

BRIGDEN .... **Lambton**

W.E. Tennyson, 1579 Main St., N0N 1B0 – 519/864-1189, Fax: 519/864-1966 – *1

BRIGHTON .... **Northumberland**

Joseph T. Banbury, 24 Prince Edward St., PO Box 868, K0K 1H0 – 613/475-2421, Fax: 613/475-4087 – *1

Philip S. Staddon, 17 Prince Edward St., PO Box 1360, K0K 1H0 – 613/475-3522, Fax: 613/475-3651 – *1

BROCKVILLE .... **Leeds**

Beale, Macintosh, Lewis, O'Shaughnessy & Johnston, 2 Court House Ave., PO Box 338, K6V 5V5 – 905/345-5653, Fax: 905/345-6022 – *4

R.W. Flood, 13 Hartley St., PO Box 682, K6V 5V8 – 613/345-0087 – *1

Fraser, Best, 9 Pine St., PO Box 206, K6V 5V2 – 613/245-1435, Fax: 613/345-2007 – *2

David A. Hain, 84 King St. West, K6V 5W1 – 613/342-5577, Fax: 613/342-1773. – *1

Henderson, Johnston, Fournier & Hammond, 61 King St. East, PO Box 217, K6V 5V4 – 613/345-5613, Fax: 613/345-6473 – *4

Jacqueline Regina, #109, 133 King St. West, K6V 3R4 – 613/342-5888, Fax: 613/342-1831 – *1

D.W. Wyatt, 10 Broad St., K6V 4T7 – 613/342-7205, Fax: 613/342-0995 – *1

BRUCE MINES .... **Algoma**

Peterson & Peterson, 76 Taylor St., PO Box 100, P0R 1C0 – 705/785-3491, Fax: 705/785-3768

Wishart & Partners, 2 Taylor St., P0R 1C0 – 705/785-3465

BRUSSELS .... **Huron**

Crawford, Mill & Davies, 570 Turnberry St., PO Box 104, N0G 1H0 – 519/887-9491, Fax: 519/887-9148 – *3

BURK'S FALLS .... **Parry Sound**

Linda Heyder, 139 Ontario St., PO Box 546, P0A 1C0 – 705/382-3031, Fax: 705/382-2886 – *1

Powell, Cunningham, Kennedy & Grandy, 178 Ontario St., PO Box 460, P0A 1C0

R. Vander Wijst, PO Box 541, P0A 1C0 – 705/382-2746 – *1

BURLINGTON .... **Halton**

Patricia E. Anderson, 496 Brant St., L7R 2G4 – 905/333-0903 – *1

Noel R. Bates, 1422A Ontario St., L7S 1G4 – 905/681-1196, Fax: 905/637-0042 – *1

Brechin & Huffman, 3365 Harvester Rd., L7N 3N2 – 905/681-2476, Fax: 905/333-4298 – *2

Bridle & Bridle, 3310 South Service Rd., L7N 3M6 – 905/637-5213 – *2

Brooks Alexandre, 2019 Caroline St., L7R 1L1 – 905/333-6619, Fax: 905/634-5585

Cass & Bishop, 3455 Harvester Rd., Unit 31, L7N 3P2 – 905/632-7744, Fax: 905/632-9076 – *2

Cleaver, Crawford, Hunt, O'Driscoll & Fraser, 2019 Caroline St., L7R 1L1 – 905/634-5581, Fax: 905/634-1563 – *5

Forbes Conant, #2, 3455 Harvester Rd., L7N 3P2 – 905/333-1622, Fax: 905/333-1624 – *1

Michael J. Darling, 3419 Mainway Dr., L7M 1A9 – 905/332-6696, Fax: 905/332-0021 – *1

Dingle, Charlebois & Swybrous, 2079 Gore St., L7R 1E2 – 905/634-5541; 825-0502, Fax: 905/333-4499 – *2

Dunlop & Associates, 3556 Commerce Ct., L7N 3L7 – 905/681-3311, Fax: 905/681-3635

R.B. Easterbrook, #200, 1013 St. Matthew's Ave., L7T 2J3 – 905/333-1633 – *1

Adam A. Gall, 7A-355 Plains Rd. E., L7T 4H7 – 905/639-4113, Fax: 905/639-4148 – *1

David Godard, 3540 Commerce Crt, L7N 3L7 – 905/632-2600, Fax: 905/632-2722 – *1

Green Germann, 411 Guelph Line, PO Box 400, L7R 3Y3 – 905/639-1222, Fax: 905/632-6977 – *7

Haber, Haber & Associates, 3370 South Service Rd., L7N 3M6 – 905/639-8894; 825-1953, Fax: 905/639-0459 – *3

Hastings, Charlebois, Feltmate, Fur & Delibato, #100, 3410 South Service Rd., L7N 3T2 – 905/632-0366 – *6

John Hicks, #7, 541 Brant St., L7R 2G6 – 905/681-3131, Fax: 905/333-6688 – *1

Hofbauer Associates, 1455 Lakeshore Rd., L7S 2J1 – 905/634-0040, Fax: 905/634-9119; Email: ideas@cap-atents.com – *2

Kerr & Hawken, 442 Brant St., L7R 2G4 – 905/632-2822, Fax: 905/333-9594 – *2

Paul A. Lafleur, 518 Brant St., L7R 2G7 – 905/632-3842, Fax: 905/632-6821 – *1

Lakeshore Law Chambers, 2122 Lakeshore Rd., L7R 1A3 – 905/637-5641, Fax: 905/637-5404 – *1

Law Line, 1422A Ontario St., L7S 1G4 – , Fax: 905/637-0042

Lithgow Penelope, 216-2349 Fairview St., L7R 2E3 – 905/634-6060

MacIsaac & MacIsaac, 7-107 Plains Rd. W., L7T 1E8 – 905/333-1246, Fax: 905/333-1248 – *3

Mitchell T. MacLeod, 2122 Lakeshore Rd., L7R 1A3 – 905/637-5641 – *1

Martin Hillyer Bryant, 2122 Lakeshore Rd., L7R 1A3 – 905/637-5641, 847-5277 (Toronto), Fax: 905/637-5404 – *8

McEniry & McEniry, 3310 South Service Rd., L7R 3Y7 – 905/529-1151, Fax: 905/634-9180 – *1

Nancy A. Millar, 2079 Gore St., L7R 1E2 – 905/639-2580, Fax: 905/333-4499 – *1

Patrick M. Mlot, #204 South, 1455 Lakeshore Rd., L7S 2J1 – 905/634-3677, Fax: 905/681-6510 – *1

Moores & Reynolds, 2-2021 Plains Rd. E., L7R 4M3 – 905/333-0100, Fax: 905/333-9675 – *3

Michael D. Morgan, 4380 South Service Rd., Unit 26, L7L 5Y6 – 905/681-8747, Fax: 905/681-8769 – *1

Douglas W. Muir, Q.C., 468 Elizabeth St., L7R 2M2 – 905/639-8030, Fax: 905/333-4613 – *2

Gloria Nardi-Bell, #218, 2349 Fairview St., L7R 2E3 – 905/639-4113, Fax: 905/639-4148 – *1

Pichelli & Turingia, 3390 South Service Rd., L7N 3J5 – 905/639-0731, Fax: 905/333-4290 – *2
Rayner, White, Mills, Grant, #210, 3600 Billings Court, L7N 3N6 – 905/632-8123, Fax: 905/632-4520 – *4
J. Douglas Redfearn, 442 Brant St., L7R 2G4 – 905/333-5322, Fax: 905/333-9835 – *1
J.C. Savchuk, 1100 Burloak Dr., L7L 6B2 – 905/336-9111 – *1
Simpson & Rich, #12, 460 Brant St., L7R 4B6 – 905/681-1521, 825-0522, Fax: 905/333-5075 – *2
Simpson, Wigle, Sims Square Building #1, #501, 390 Brant St., L7R 4J4 – 905/639-1052, Fax: 905/333-3960 – *6
D. Bruce Smith, 2349 Fairview St., L7R 2E3 – 905/333-9702 – *1
Sandra J. Stephenson, 3168 Trailwood Dr., L7M 2Z8 – 905/332-6788, Fax: 905/332-6788 – *1
T.R. Sutherland Q.C., #201, 3190 Harvester Rd., L7N 3T1 – 905/634-5521, Fax: 905/634-5153 – *1
Harold Kim Taylor, 204 South-1455 Lakeshore Rd, L7S 2J1 – 905/681-6400, Fax: 905/681-6510 – *1
Thatcher, Wands & Culver, 501 John St., L7R 2L1 – 905/681-0444, Fax: 905/681-2937 – *3
E.A. Urban, 496 Brant St., L7R 2G4 – 905/333-6640 – *1
Clayton J. Wallace, 2122 Lakeshore Rd., L7R 1A3 – 905/637-5641 – *1
J.B. Watters, 482 Elizabeth St., L7R 2M2 – 905/639-3775 – *1

CALEDON .... Peel
Richard A. Allman, RR#1, L0N 1C0 – 519/940-0415

CALEDON EAST .... Peel
George W. Jenney, 9 Airport Rd. South, L0N 1E0 – 905/584-9300 – *1

CALEDONIA .... Haldimand
Arrell, Brown, Osier & Murray, 41 Caithness St. West, N0A 1A0 – 905/765-5414, Fax: 905/765-5144 – *4
Benedict & Ferguson, 322 Argyle St. South, N3W 1K8 – 905/765-4004, Fax: 905/765-3001 – *2
L.S. Humenik, 35 Caithness St. East, PO Box 2112, N3W 2G6 – 905/765-3162, Fax: 905/765-4313 – *1

CAMBRIDGE .... Waterloo
D. St.C. Bond, 57 Ainslie St. North, PO Box 22104, N1R 8E3 – 519/623-2311, Fax: 519/623-6957 – *1
Copp, Cosman, Pavey, Law & Wannop, 19 Cambridge St., PO Box 1707, N1R 7G8 – 519/621-7260, Fax: 519/621-1304 – *6
Dufresne & Dufresne, 30 George St. North, PO Box 783, N1R 5W6 – 519/621-7910, Fax: 519/621-1940 – *1
Gary Flaxbard, #140, 1315 Bishop St., PO Box 1578, N1R 6Z2
Goad & Goad, 53 Cambridge St., PO Box 907, N1R 5X9 – 519/623-7660, Fax: 519/623-2594 – *3
Gowlings, 19 Thorne St., N1R 5W1 – 519/621-6910, Fax: 519/621-5028 – *7
Grant & Sheilds, 2 Water St. North, N1R 3B1 – 519/623-7530, 622-2150, Fax: 519/623-0997 – *2
P.A. Hardman, 1270 King St. East, N3H 3P8 – 519/653-1214, Fax: 519/650-2282 – *1
Gary E.J. Hauser, 1666 King St. East, N3H 3R7 – 519/653-1521, Fax: 519/650-1466 – *1
Hilborn & Konduros, 39 Queen St. West, N3C 1G2 – 519/658-6341, Fax: 519/654-9127 – *2
Claude Isaacksz, 1434 King St. East, N3H 3R4 – 519/653-0341, Fax: 519/653-9521 – *1
Calvin G. Johnson, PO Box 876, N1R 5X9 – 519/623-9160, Fax: 519/740-6023 – *1
Paul M. Mann, 679 Coronation Blvd., N1R 3G5 – 519/623-0700, Fax: 519/622-4091 – *1
Matlow, Miller, Harris, Thrasher, 39 Dickson St., PO Box 607, N1R 5W1 – 519/621-2430 – *4

Onorato & Zboril & McKnight, 708 Duke St., PO Box 32184, N3H 5M2 – 519/653-3217, Fax: 519/653-3702 – *3
Pearson, Flynn, Preston Towne Centre, 553 King St. East, PO Box 32088, N3H 4M2 – 519/653-5747; 621-2540, Fax: 519/650-1477 – *4
Pettitt, Schwarz, #403, 73 Water St. North, N1R 7L6 – 519/621-2450, Fax: 519/621-5750 – *2
David M. Tugender, PO Box 3455, N3H 5C6 – 519/653-1032, Fax: 519/653-0492 – *1
J. Craig Wilson, 2 Water St. North, PO Box 1297, N1R 7G6 – 519/622-0192 – *1
W.C. Wraight, 15 Main St., N1R 7G9 – 519/623-3330 – *1

CAMPBELLFORD .... Northumberland
Wallace J. Brown, 17 Front St. South, PO Box 1269, K0L 1L0 – 705/653-2041, Fax: 705/653-4063 – *1
J. Wayne C. Buck, 6 Queen St., PO Box 1630, K0L 1L0 – 705/653-4022, Fax: 705/653-2365 – *1
N.R.H. Burgess, 64 Front St., K0L 1L0 – 705/653-3400
Paul M.G. Smith, Q.C., 32 Pellissier St., PO Box 1057, K0L 1L0 – 705/653-1860, Fax: 705/653-4903 – *1

CANNINGTON .... Durham
Brandon Miller McGrath, 17 Cameron St. West, L0E 1E0 – 705/432-2361, Fax: 705/432-2680 – *1

CARDINAL .... Leeds
Gorrell, Grenkie, Leroy & Rémillard, PO Box 580, K0E 1E0 – 613/657-3184

CARLETON PLACE .... Lanark
Bruun & Bennett, 74 Bridge St., PO Box 190, K7C 3P4 – 613/257-1655, Fax: 613/257-8837 – *2
P.D. Courtice, 164 Bridge St., PO Box 29, K7C 3P3 – 613/257-5001, Fax: 613/257-8797 – *1
McNabb, Brooke, 38 Mill St., PO Box 152, K7C 3P4 – 613/257-7620, Fax: 613/257-8830 – *2

CASSELMAN .... Prescott/Russell
Baribault, Campbell, Martel, LaViolette, 759 St. Jean St., PO Box 179, K0A 1M0 – 613/443-5683, Fax: 613/443-3285 – *1

CAYUGA .... Haldimand
Slimon & Gallagher, 45 Munsee St. North, PO Box 250, N0A 1E0 – 905/772-3369, Fax: 905/772-5113 – *2
Larry P. Thibideau, PO Box 508, N0A 1E0 – 905/772-3513, Fax: 905/772-5918 – *1

CHAPLEAU .... Sudbury
Weaver, Simmons, Pine St., PO Box 329, P0M 1K0 – 705/864-1505

CHATHAM .... Kent
Archibald & Creed, 237 Wellington St. West, N7M 1J9 – 519/354-2383, Fax: 519/354-3250 – *1
Benoit, Van Raay, Spisani & Fuerth, 124 Thames St., PO Box 1087, N7L 2Y8 – 519/352-8580 – *4
Carscallen, Reinhart, Mathany, 111 1/2 St. Clair St., PO Box 1444, N7M 5W8 – 519/351-2261, Fax: 519/351-2860 – *1
J. Bernard Comiskey, 84 Dover St., PO Box 525, N7M 5K6 – 519/352-1360, Fax: 519/352-7300 – *1
Bernard J. Goodal, 5 - 6 St., N7M 4V1 – 519/352-9963 – *1
K.E. Hansen, Q.C., 186 Wellington St., PO Box 579, N7M 5K6 – 519/352-2040, Fax: 519/352-9522 – *1
Juba, Elliott, 84 Dover St., PO Box 848, N7M 5L1 – 519/354-9911, Fax: 519/351-7300 – *2
Kee & Robertson, 334 King St. West, PO Box 189, N7M 5K3 – 519/354-1490 – *1
R.A. Kirby, PO Box 607, N7M 5K8 – 519/351-6849 – *1
W.P. Magee, 36 - 4 St., N7M 5K5 – 519/352-7950, Fax: 519/352-2699 – *1
McNevin, Gee & O'Connor, 43 William St. North, N7M 5K1 – 519/352-5450, Fax: 519/352-5452 – *1

William M. Myers Q.C., 186 Wellington St. West, PO Box 579, N7M 5K6 – 519/352-2040, Fax: 519/352-9522 – *1
Paroian, Raphael, Courey, Cohen & Houston, 214 Queen St., PO Box 548, N7M 5K6 – 519/352-0190, Fax: 519/352-0565 – *37
Patricia L. Poole, 65 Adelaide St. South, N7M 4R1 – 519/351-3500 – *1
Robert K. Rankin, Q.C., #402, 48 - 5 St., PO Box 341, N7M 5K4 – 519/354-8550, Fax: 519/354-2255 – *1
Rhodes Law Firm, PO Box 1358, N7M 5W8 – 519/352-4700, Fax: 519/352-5616 – *2

CHELMSFORD .... Sudbury
Gerard E. Guimond, 164 Errington St., PO Box 2225, P0M 1L0 – 705/855-4511, Fax: 705/855-5631
Mailloux & Gray, 128 Errington St., 1347, P0M 1L0 – 705/855-9091, Fax: 705/855-4038

CHESLEY .... Bruce-Grey
Loucks & Loucks, 84 First Ave. South, PO Box 430, N0G 1L0 – 519/363-3223, Fax: 519/363-2133 – *2
Ross C. McLean, PO Box 118, N0G 1L0 – 519/363-3190, Fax: 519/363-2213 – *1

CHESTERVILLE .... Dundas
David J. Barnhart, PO Box 730, K0C 1H0 – 613/448-3057, Fax: 613/774-5731
Cass, Grenkie, 13 Ralph St., PO Box 700, K0C 1H0 – 613/448-2735, Fax: 613/448-1395 – *4

CLINTON .... Huron
Hiltz D. Gerald, 52 Huron St., PO Box 1087, N0M 1L0 – 519/482-3414
E. Beecher Menzies, Q.C., 49 Albert St., PO Box 68, N0M 1L0 – 519/482-3475, Fax: 519/482-3779 – *1

COBOCONK .... Durham
Tyler P. Higgins, PO Box 219, K0M 1K0 – 705/454-2665

COBOURG .... Northumberland
Karl G. Bernhardt, #102, 1005 William St., K9A 5J4 – 905/372-8789, Fax: 905/373-0376 – *1
Rodger F. Cooper, PO Box 188, K9A 4K5 – 905/372-8727 – *1
J.B. Halls, 203 Durham St., PO Box 664, K9A 4R5 – 905/372-8791, Fax: 905/372-4819 – *1
Irvine & Irvine, 72 King St. West, PO Box 427, K9A 4L1 – 905/372-5449, Fax: 905/372-1707 – *4
William C. Lifeso, PO Box 248, K9A 4K8 – 905/372-0119, Fax: 905/372-4819 – *1
Stewart, Mitchell & Macklin, #205, 1005 William St., K9A 5J4 – 905/372-3395, Fax: 905/372-1695 – *4
D.E. Stokes, 3A King St. West, K9A 2L8 – 905/372-2791 – *1
V.W. Targon & Associates, 287 Division St., PO Box 475, K9A 4L1 – 905/372-5424, Fax: 905/372-4285 – *1
John Van Duzer, 35 King St. East, PO Box 667, K9A 4R5 – *1

COCHRANE .... Cochrane
Evans, Bragagnolo & Sullivan, 138 Third St., P0L 1C0 – 705/272-5197, Fax: 705/272-7424 – *1
David L. Lanthier, 153 - 3 St., PO Box 2020, P0L 1C0 – 705/272-4205, Fax: 705/272-3467 – *1

COLBORNE .... Northumberland
J.A. Carter, PO Box 699, K0K 1S0 – 905/355-3322, Fax: 905/355-3104 – *1

COLDWATER .... Simcoe
Raymond J. Morhan, RR#4, L0K 1E0 – 705/835-5752, Fax: 705/835-5742 – *1
Stewart, Esten, GD PO, L0K 1E0 – 705/835-3231 – *3

* indicates number of lawyers in law firm.

COLLINGWOOD .... Simcoe
Bellamy, Besse, Augaitis & Merrifield, 100 Pretty River Parkway, PO Box 129, L9Y 3Z4 – 705/445-4722, Fax: 705/445-9295 – *6
J.D. Bulmer, Q.C., 137 Hurontario St., PO Box 23, L9Y 3Z4 – 705/445-9244, Fax: 705/444-5741 – *1
Christie Cummings, 115 Hurontario St., PO Box 187, L9Y 3Z4 – 705/444-3650, Fax: 705/444-0024 – *2
Corcoran, Thompson, Baulke & Wright, 150 Hurontario St., PO Box 100, L9Y 3Z4 – 705/445-4930, Fax: 705/445-1871 – *3
Brian Greasley, 33 Ste. Marie St., PO Box 490, L9Y 4B2 – 705/445-9300, Fax: 705/445-2996 – *1
Robert Jacks, Q.C., 31 Simcoe St., L9Y 1H5 – 705/445-0381 – *1
L.E. Lant, 60 Hume St., PO Box 248, L9Y 3Z5 – 705/445-2886, Fax: 705/444-5837 – *3
Paul Lee & Associates, 207 Hurontario St., L9Y 2M1 – 705/444-0077, Fax: 705/444-9241 – *2
Neathery & Mumford, #4, 450 Hume St., L9Y 1W6 – 705/445-6051, Fax: 705/444-0969 – *2
Shaw, McLellan & Ironside, 10 Schoolhouse Lane, PO Box 280, L9Y 3Z5 – 705/445-1382, Fax: 705/445-7042 – *3
Simcoe Legal Services Clinic, 159 First St., L9Y 1A6 – 705/444-1177, Fax: 705/445-1516
Victor L. Vandergust, 11 Hurontario St., PO Box 39, L9Y 3Z4 – 705/445-4544, Fax: 705/445-4160 – *1
Kechin Wang, Q.C., 536 The Oxbow, Cranberry Village, PO Box 4088, L9Y 4T9 – 705/444-2407 – *1

CONCORD .... York
Joseph Bagliari, #312, 1600 Steeles Ave. West, L4K 4M2 – 905/660-1800, Fax: 905/660-7828 – *1
Chehab Talal, #300, 3100 Steeles Ave. West, L4K 3R1 – 905/738-2463, Fax: 905/738-4901
Ralph Ciccia, #300, 3100 Steeles Ave. West, L4K 3R1 – 905/748-4900, Fax: 905/738-4901 – *1
Danson, Recht & Freedman, #15, 3000 Langstaff Rd., L4K 4R7 – 905/660-0818, Fax: 905/660-0891
DiMonte Law Offices, #208, 3100 Steeles Ave. West, L4K 3R1 – 905/738-2101, Fax: 905/738-1168 – *1
Mark W. Kushner, #231, 1600 Steeles Ave. West, L4K 4M2 – 905/669-7079, Fax: 905/669-7080
Enzo Salvatori, #203, 2100 Steeles Ave. West, L4K 2V1 – 905/738-1777, Fax: 905/738-2065 – *1
Savage, Bourque & Raffaghello, #310, 3300 Hwy. 7, L4K 4M3 – 905/660-4633, Fax: 905/660-0384 – *3
Sherwin H. Shapiro, #309, 3100 Steeles Ave. West, L4K 3R1 – 905/660-4404, Fax: 905/660-4711 – *1

CORNWALL .... Stormont
Adams, Sherwood, Swabey & Follon, 305 Second St. East, K6H 1Y8 – 613/938-3330, Fax: 613/938-7885 – *7
Bergeron, Filion & McClelland, 103 Sydney St., K6H 5V3 – 613/932-2911, Fax: 613/932-2356 – *3
Barry A. Desrosiers, 11 - 4 St. West, K6J 2R5 – 613/938-0430 – *1
Fennell, Rudden, Stevenson & Levesque, 35 - 2 St. East, K6H 5S7 – 613/932-7654, Fax: 613/932-1692 – *5
Guindon, MacLean, McDonald & Castle, 50 - 2 St. East, K6H 1Y3 – 613/933-3931, Fax: 613/933-6123 – *4
Lamoureux, Gauthier, McDerby & Associates, 402 - 132 St. East, PO Box 1205, K6H 5V3 – 613/932-1220, Fax: 613/936-1624 – *4
Leduc, Giovanniello, Bellefeuille, 340 - 2nd St. East, K6H 1Y9 – 613/938-0294, Fax: 613/932-2374 – *3
Duncan J. MacDonald, 126 Sydney St., K6H 3H2 – 613/932-3640, Fax: 613/932-3643 – *1
Parisien, Willis, 229 Augustus St., PO Box 127, K6H 5S7 – 613/937-3333, Fax: 613/933-2200 – *2
Stephen A. Renner, 122 Sydney St., K6H 3H2 – 613/933-6540 – *1
Ross & Duncan, 120 Sydney St., K6H 3H2 – 613/932-2044, Fax: 613/937-0993 – *2

Michael R. Salhany, 504 Pitt St., PO Box 912, K6H 5V1 – 613/932-4140 – *1
Barrie M. Wilson, 132 - 2nd St. West, K6J 1G5 – 613/938-2224, Fax: 613/938-8005 – *1
Wise & Brunet, 1302 - 2 St. West, K6J 1J3 – 613/938-1826 – *2

CORUNNA .... Lambton
Allan Brock, 447 Lyndock St., N0N 1G0 – 519/862-2211 – *1

CREEMORE .... Simcoe
Brian Greasley, PO Box 27, L0M 1G0 – 705/466-3336 – *1

DEEP RIVER .... Renfrew
Roche & Dakin, 11 Champlain St., PO Box 1240, K0J 1P0 – 613/584-3392, Fax: 613/854-4922 – *2

DELHI .... Norfolk
John R. Hanselman, 138 Eagle St., N4B 1S5 – 519/582-0770, Fax: 519/582-1876 – *1
Harrison & Harrison, PO Box 98, N4B 2W8 – 519/582-1900 – *1
Kapusta, Sayeau & Gouthro, 237 Main St., N4B 2M4 – 519/582-1552, Fax: 519/582-1941 – *2

DESERONTO .... Hastings
Elton Brant, RR#1, K0X 1X0 – 613/966-9414

DRESDEN .... Kent
Timothy D. Mathany, 347 St. George St. South, PO Box 568, N0P 1M0 – 519/683-6219 – *1

DRYDEN .... Kenora
McAuley & Partners, 4 Whyte Ave., PO Box 159, P8N 2Y8 – 807/223-2254, Fax: 807/223-3794 – *4
Vermeer & Van Walleghem, PO Box 938, P8N 2Z5 – 807/223-3311, Fax: 807/223-4133 – *3

DUNDALK .... Grey
Harris, Willis, McGarry & Ferris, PO Box 520, N0C 1B0 – 519/923-2212, Fax: 519/923-3493
Shepherd & Osyany, PO Box 10, N0C 1B0 – 519/923-3201

DUNDAS .... Hamilton-Wentworth
Hines & Stevens, 161 King St. West, PO Box 8, L9H 1V3 – 905/627-3531, Fax: 905/628-0038 – *2
Johnson, Ramsbottom & Castle, PO Box 8180, L9H 5G1 – 905/628-2214; 627-5487, Fax: 905/627-5639 – *3
Lee & Lee, PO Box 8587, L9H 5G1 – 905/628-6321, Fax: 905/628-2767; Email: wilklaw@netaccess.on.ca – *1

DUNNVILLE .... Haldimand
G.D. Chambers, 106 Lock St. East, N1A 1J7 – 905/744-7485, Fax: 905/774-7486 – *1
Hedley & McQuatty, PO Box 217, N1A 2X5 – 905/774-7688, Fax: 905/774-6637 – *2
J.F. Jacob, 129 Queen St., N1A 1H6 – *1

DURHAM .... Grey
Fallis, Fallis & McMillan, 195 Lambton St. East, N0G 1R0 – 519/369-2515 – *3
I.C. Johnson, 157 Garafraxa St. North, N0G 1R0 – 519/369-6931, Fax: 519/369-2423 – *1
Allen Wilford, RR#1, N0G 1R0 – 519/369-6466, Fax: 519/369-5701 – *1

EARLTON .... Temiskaming
Ramsay, Ramsay, Kemp, Andrew & Maille, P0J 1E0 – 705/563-8368

EGANVILLE .... Renfrew
H.S. Lavigueur, PO Box 9, K0J 1T0 – 613/628-2153, Fax: 613/628-2915 – *1

ELGIN .... Leeds
J.T. Monaghan, PO Box 190, K0G 1E0 – 613/359-5108, Fax: 613/359-6105 – *1

ELLIOT LAKE .... Algoma
Aubé, Fabris Associates, PO Box 310, P5A 2J8 – 705/848-6993, Fax: 705/848-8621 – *2
André L.J. Berthelot, 13 Elizabeth Walk, P5A 1Z2 – 705/848-2208, Fax: 705/848-2200 – *1

ELMIRA .... Waterloo
Haney & Weir, 11A Arthur St. South, N3B 2M4 – 519/669-1644, Fax: 519/669-3592 – *2
Waters & Hastings-Zinck, 21 Arthur St. South, N3B 2M4 – 519/669-1641, Fax: 519/669-1944 – *2
Woods & Clemens, 9 King St., PO Box 216, N3B 2Z6 – 519/669-5101, Fax: 519/669-5618 – *2
Zinszer & Associates, 30 Church St. West, N3B 1M5 – 519/669-1539, Fax: 519/669-1530 – *4

ELMVALE .... Simcoe
John H. Heacock, 12 Queen St. West, L0L 1P0 – 705/322-2101, Fax: 705/322-0822 – *2

ELORA .... Wellington
J.E. Morris, PO Box 338, N0B 1S0 – 519/846-5366, Fax: 519/846-8170 – *1

EMBRUN .... Prescott & Russel
Baribault, Campbell, Martel, LaViolette, #1, 165 Bay St., K0A 1W1 – 613/443-5683, Fax: 613/443-3285 – *4
Beaudet Davidson, 945 Notre Dame, PO Box 220, K0A 1W0 – 613/443-3372 – *1

ENGLEHART .... Temiskaming
Ramsay, Ramsay, Kemp, Andrew & Maille, P0J 1H0 – 705/544-2223

ERIN .... Peel
Kenneth Torrens, 194 Main St., PO Box 325, N0B 1T0 – 519/833-9081, Fax: 519/833-0259 – *1

ESSEX .... Essex
Bondy, Belowus, #100, 72 Talbot St. North, N8M 1A2 – 519/776-4244, Fax: 519/776-7277 – *8
Hickey & Brown, 14 Centre St., N8M 1N9 – 519/776-7349, Fax: 519/776-8161 – *2
W.K. Kendrick, 114 Talbot St. South, N8M 1B2 – 519/253-4431 – *1
Outerbridge, Miller, Sefton, Willms & Shier, 115 Talbot St., N8M 2C5 – 519/776-9020, Fax: 519/776-9027 – *2

EXETER .... Huron
Robert J. Deane, Q.C., 417 Main St., N0M 1S6 – 519/235-0440 – *1
Little & Grant, 71 Main St. North, N0M 1S3 – 519/235-0670, Fax: 519/235-1603 – *2
Raymond & McLean, 387 Main St., PO Box 100, N0M 1S6 – 519/235-2234, Fax: 519/235-2671 – *2

FENELON FALLS .... Victoria
David J. Gowanlock, PO Box 607, K0M 1N0 – 705/887-2582, Fax: 705/887-1871 – *1
McQuarrie, Hill, Walden, Chester, McLeod, 68 Colborne St., K0M 1N0 – 705/887-2941

FERGUS .... Wellington
Wilson, Jack & Grant, PO Box 128, N1M 2W7 – 519/843-1960, Fax: 519/843-6888 – *4

FINCH .... Stormont
C.A. Martin-Hrycak, PO Box 170, K0C 1K0 – 613/984-2759, Fax: 613/984-2533 – *1

FLESHERTON .... Grey
Harris, Willis, McGarry & Ferris, PO Box 100, N0C 1E0 – 519/924-2031, Fax: 519/924-3198

DIRECTORY OF LAW FIRMS – ONTARIO   10-55

FONTHILL .... **Niagara South**
Jill Anthony, 1450 Pelham St., PO Box 743, L0S 1E0 – 905/892-2621, Fax: 905/892-1022 – *1
Blackadder Lacavera, 10 Hwy. 20 East, L0S 1E0 – 905/892-2423

FORT ERIE .... **Niagara South**
G.M. Berman, 25A Jarvis St., PO Box 545, L2A 5M6 – 905/871-6699, Fax: 905/871-0442 – *1
David A. Hurren, 1264 Garrison Rd., PO Box 1190, L2A 5Y2 – 905/871-2424, 6868, Fax: 905/871-4848 – *1
D.J. Jacobi, 1321 Garrison Rd., PO Box 1028, L2A 5N8 – 905/871-4244, Fax: 905/871-8693 – *1
G.A. Marchand, PO Box 68, L2A 5M6 – 905/871-4440, Fax: 905/871-7344 – *1
R.B. Miller, 1222 Garrison Rd., L2A 1P1 – 905/871-4556, Fax: 905/871-5215 – *1
J.T. Teal, PO Box 247, L2A 5M9 – 905/871-5796, Fax: 905/871-9151 – *1
Louis Ziff, Q.C., 660 Garrison Rd., L2A 6E2 – 905/871-3300, Fax: 905/871-9955 – *1

FORT FRANCES .... **Rainy River**
Eustace, Morgan & Derksen, 510 Portage Ave., P9A 2A3 – 807/274-3247, Fax: 807/274-6447 – *3
Ian J. McLennan, 356 Church St., PO Box 254, P9A 3M6 – 807/274-5343, Fax: 807/274-8489 – *1
Watt & Brunetta, 420 Victoria Ave., PO Box 636, P9A 3M9 – 807/274-9800, Fax: 807/274-8760 – *2

FRANKFORD .... **Hastings**
D.J. Parsons, 17 Mill St., PO Box 180, K0K 2C0 – 613/398-6162 – *1

GANANOQUE .... **Leeds**
Clarke & Wright, 280 King St. East, K7G 2T8 – 613/382-2112 – *2
Henry J. Knotek, 82 King St. East, K7G 1G1 – 613/382-4567, Fax: 613/382-8586 – *1
Steacy & Delaney, PO Box 70, K7G 2T6 – 613/382-2137 – *2

GARSON .... **Sudbury**
Duane D. Drager, 3493 Falconbridge Hwy., PO Box 1090, P0M 1V0 – 705/693-2743, Fax: 705/693-3914 – *1

GEORGETOWN .... **Halton**
Arnold & Banbury, #2, 211 Guelph St., L7G 4A8 – 905/877-5251, Fax: 905/877-4100 – *3
Jeffrey L. Eason, 116 Guelph St., PO Box 159, L7G 4Y5 – 905/877-6961; 846-1557, Fax: 905/877-9725 – *1
Helson, Kogon, Ashbee, Schaljo, 132 Mill St., L7G 2C6 – 905/877-5206, 454-2889 (Toronto), Fax: 905/877-3948 – *5
W. Glen How & Associates, PO Box 4100, L7G 4Y4 – 905/873-4100, Fax: 905/873-4522 – *3
Julian W. Lipkowski, #306, 16 Mountainview Rd. South, L7G 4K1 – 905/873-1648 – *1
William H. Manderson, 2 Guelph St., L7G 3Y9 – 905/873-0121, Fax: 905/873-4114 – *1
O'Connor MacLeod, 134 Main St. South, L7G 3E6 – 905/873-8000, Fax: 905/873-7865
Daniel G. Pole, PO Box 208, L6S 5Y9 – 905/874-0100, Fax: 905/874-0229
Sopinka & Kort, 145 Mill St., L7G 2C2 – 905/846-2515, Fax: 905/877-0604 – *2

GLENCOE .... **Middlesex**
Gary R. Merritt, 213 Main St., PO Box 309, N0L 1M0 – 519/287-3432, Fax: 519/287-2498 – *1
Brian K. Morris, PO Box 428, N0L 1M0 – 519/287-2456, Fax: 519/287-3608 – *1

GLOUCESTER .... **Ottawa-Carleton**
Anderson Law Office, 2663 Innes Rd., K1B 3J7 – 613/830-1112, Fax: 613/830-7998 – *2

Bunning & Farnand, 2580 Innes Rd., K1B 4N7 – 613/824-0000, Fax: 613/824-9164 – *2
Bruce A. Freeborn, 21 Ryeburn Dr., K1G 3N3 – 613/822-0774, Fax: 613/822-7079 – *1

GODERICH .... **Huron**
Carey & Ottewell, 50 North St., N7A 2T4 – 519/524-2634, Fax: 519/524-5538 – *2
Donnelly & Murphy, 18 The Square, PO Box 38, N7A 3Y7 – 519/524-2154, Fax: 519/524-8550 – *4
Norman B. Pickell, PO Box 430, N7A 4C7 – 519/524-8335, Fax: 519/524-1530 – *1
Troyan & Fincher, 44 North St., PO Box 97, N7A 3Y5 – 519/524-2115, Fax: 519/524-4481 – *2

GORE BAY .... **Manitoulin**
James E. Weppler, 65 Meredith St., P0P 1H0 – 705/282-3354, Fax: 705/282-3211 – *1

GORRIE .... **Huron**
Crawford, Mill & Davies, General Delivery, N0G 1X0 – 403/335-3528

GRAVENHURST .... **Muskoka**
J.C. Malvern, 190 Hotchkiss, P0C 1G0 – 705/687-2241 – *1
Stuart, Cruickshank & Beatty, PO Box 1270, P1P 1V4 – 705/687-3441, Fax: 705/687-5405 – *4
Sullivan & Weekes, 225 Muskoka Rd. South, P1P 1H6 – 705/687-2219, Fax: 705/687-7951 – *1

GRIMSBY .... **Niagara North**
Morris Cree, 15 Main St. East, PO Box 69, L3M 4G1 – 905/945-2077, Fax: 905/945-2078 – *1
John C. Lovett, Q.C., PO Box 100, L3M 4G1 – 905/945-2269, 2581; 563-4845 – *2
Paul A. MacLeod, #204, 155 Main St. East, L3M 1P2 – 905/945-9659, Fax: 905/945-0838 – *1
Nicholls & Greenhow, 18 Ontario St., PO Box 187, L3M 4G3 – 905/945-5431, Fax: 905/945-5286 – *2
Sinclair, Murakami & Loney, 55 Main St. West, L3M 1R3 – 905/945-9271, Fax: 905/945-3066 – *3
J.L. Wolfe, 63 Main St. East, L3M 1M7 – 905/945-9231, Fax: 905/945-9166 – *1

GUELPH .... **Wellington**
Abraham Acker, Q.C., 18 Douglas St., PO Box 846, N1H 2S9 – 519/822-5660, Fax: 519/822-0411 – *1
Braida & Henry, 28 Paisley St., PO Box 1082, N1H 8N6 – 519/824-2242 – *2
Izaak de Rijcke, 258 Woolwich St., N1H 3W1 – 519/837-2551, Fax: 519/837-0958
Dunbar Goetz Cameron, 32 Douglas St., PO Box 366, N1H 6K5 – 519/822-4260, Fax: 519/822-3370 – *1
T. Flaherty, 29 Cork St. West, N1H 2W9 – 519/836-5730, Fax: 519/836-8654 – *1
Flesher & Mann, 376 Woolwich St., PO Box 1788, N1H 7A1 – 519/821-6406 – *2
Flynn & Sorbara, 336 Speedvale Ave. West, N1H 7M7 – 519/836-1510, Fax: 519/836-9215 – *1
Hastings, Hogg & Pellizzari, 166 Woolwich St., PO Box 964, N1H 3V3 – 519/822-8511 – *3
Hungerford, Guthrie & Berry, 59 Woolwich St., PO Box 187, N1H 6J9 – 519/824-2020, Fax: 519/824-2023 – *3
Kearns, McKinnon, 512 Woolwich St., PO Box 930, N1H 6M8 – 519/822-4680, Fax: 519/822-1583 – *11
Maiocco & DiGravio, 230 Speedvale Ave. West, N1H 1C4 – 519/836-2710, Fax: 519/836-7312 – *2
McElderry & Morris, 84 Woolwich St., PO Box 875, N1H 3T9 – 519/822-8150, Fax: 519/822-1921 – *4
Moon, Heath, 164 Norfolk St., PO Box 180, N1H 6K1 – 519/824-2540, Fax: 519/763-6785 – *7
Richard R. Morrow, 185 Woolwich St., N1H 3V4 – 519/836-4020
Moyer, Malak, Jackman & Rowles, 17 Cork St. West, Box 37, N1H 6J6 – 519/824-4883, Fax: 519/821-2910 – *3

Nelson, Watson, 183 Norfolk St., N1H 4K1 – 519/821-9610, Fax: 519/821-8550 – *3
Nicholson & Doney, 137 Norfolk St., PO Box 1505, N1H 6N9 – 519/837-3000 – *3
W. Gerald Punnett, 150 Norfolk St., N1H 4J1 – 519/821-5840, Fax: 519/821-7247 – *1
J.A. Runions, Q.C., Canada Trust Bldg., #300, 55 Cork St., PO Box 1117, N1H 6N3 – 519/821-3300, Fax: 519/821-7431 – *1
Judith P. Ryan, RR#2, N1H 6H8 – 519/856-2223, Fax: 519/856-2223
Smith, Smith, Gazzola, Sansom & Holub, 285 Woolwich St., PO Box 1025, N1H 6N1 – 519/821-0010, Fax: 519/821-6821 – *8
Turkstra Garrod Hodgson, 221 Woolwich St., N1H 3V4 – 519/837-0500, Fax: 519/763-2204 – *4
Valeriote & Valeriote, 373 Woolwich St., N1H 7A1 – 519/837-0300, Fax: 519/837-1617 – *3
Vorvis, Anderson, Gray, Armstrong & Vorvis, 5 Douglas St., N1H 6J9 – 519/824-7400, Fax: 519/824-7521 – *5

HAGERSVILLE .... **Haldimand**
James R. Baxter, 39 King St. East, N0A 1H0 – 905/768-3363, Fax: 905/768-1550 – *1
McCarthy & Fowler, 17 Main St. South, N0A 1H0 – 905/768-3553

HAILEYBURY .... **Temiskaming**
Robbie D. Gordon, 488 Ferguson Ave., PO Box 490, P0J 1K0 – 705/672-3338, Fax: 705/672-2451 – *2
Smith, Byck & Grant, 514 Ferguson St. West, PO Box 1240, P0J 1K0 – 705/672-2102, Fax: 705/647-8575 – *2

HALIBURTON .... **Haliburton**
Bishop & Rogers, PO Box 472, K0M 1S0 – 705/457-1440 – *1
R.G. Selbie, PO Box 186, K0M 1S0 – 705/457-2435, Fax: 705/457-3074 – *1

HAMILTON .... **Hamilton-Wentworth**
Agro, Zaffiro, Parente, Orzel & Baker, 1 James St. South, 4th Fl., PO Box 2069, Stn LCD 1, L8N 3G6 – 905/527-6877, Fax: 905/527-6843 – *21
R. Bartkiw, 57 John St., South, L8N 2B9 – 905/528-8800 – *1
T.N. Basciano, 115 Hughson St. North, L8R 1G7 – 905/525-4396 – *1
Alec Z. Beasley, #808, 20 Hughson St. South, L8N 2A1 – 905/527-8348, Fax: 905/527-3863 – *1
Bennett & Bennett, #701, 20 Hughson St. South, L8N 2A1 – 905/527-1784 – *1
Jerome Bergart, 77 Hunter St. East, L8N 1M4 – 905/524-1060 – *1
Borkovich & Ingrassia, 1 Main St. East, L8N 1E7 – 905/522-7442, Fax: 905/522-7191 – *3
Braden & Braden, 123 Ottawa St. North, L8H 3Y9 – 905/547-1987 – *1
Burns, Vasan, Christmas, McLeod, Cimba, PO Box 987, L8N 4B7 – 905/522-1381 – *8
Cain, Gzik & Gardner, 340 Main St. East, L8N 1J1 – 905/528-7933, Fax: 905/528-1326 – *3
Peter J. Cassidy, 360A Queenston Rd., L8K 1H9 – 905/545-0442 – *1
Philip Castrodale, #1008, 20 Hughson St. South, L8N 2A1 – 905/523-7903 – *1
Channan & Associates, 947 Main St. East, L8M 1M9 – 905/544-9441, Fax: 905/544-6155 – *2
Gary Chertkoff, Q.C., #502, 20 Jackson St. West, L8P 1L2 – 905/522-2439, Fax: 905/522-9198 – *1
L.J. Cohen, Q.C., #407, 20 Hughson St. South, L8N 2A1 – 905/525-0400, Fax: 905/572-1190 – *1
Cooper & Cooper, Union Gas Bldg., #702, 20 Hughson St. South, L8N 2A1 – 905/527-1611 – *1
R.J. Cornale, Norwich Union Bldg., 4 Hughson St. South, 2nd Fl., L8N 3Z1 – 905/521-9989, Fax: 905/572-6509

* indicates number of lawyers in law firm.

Canadian Almanac & Directory 1997

F.J. Corner, #1002, 143 James St. South, L8P 3A1 – 905/529-6544 – *1
David S. Crane, Q.C., #2225, 25 Main St. West, 22nd Fl., L8P 1H1 – 905/525-4489, Fax: 905/525-4465
K.W. Dechert, 636 Upper James St., L9C 2Z2 – 905/387-2711 – *1
John DiPietro, 72 James St. North, L8R 2K5 – 905/526-0736 – *1
Joseph Dubeck, 172 Main St. East, L8N 3R1 – 905/522-1321 – *1
Dudzic, Barristers & Solicitors, #1014, 105 Main St. East, PO Box 988, Stn A, L8N 3R1 – 905/528-4251, Fax: 905/528-5325 – *2
M.D. Dyck, #1008, 105 Main St. East, L8N 1G6 – 905/526-7395, Fax: 905/522-6677 – *1
Eddy & Montcalm, 329 Ottawa St. North, L8H 3Z8 – 905/549-2451
Paul H. Ennis, Q.C, #502, 105 Main St. East, L8N 1G6 – 905/525-9335, Fax: 905/525-9988 – *1
Evans, Husband, #901, 20 Hughson St. South, L8N 2A1 – 905/528-0084, Fax: 905/528-7692 – *7
Evans, Philp, PO Box 930, Stn A, L8N 3P9 – 905/525-1200, Fax: 905/525-7897 – *13
Raymond L. Fazakas, 942 King St. West, L8S 1K8 – 905/528-8666 – *1
Fedak Law Offices, 1252 Barton St. East, L8H 2V9 – 905/547-6232, Fax: 905/547-8305 – *1
L.A. Ferro, #903, 1 King St. West, L8P 1A4 – 905/522-8702, Fax: 905/522-0841 – *1
Findlay & McCarthy, #1100, 21 King St. West, L8P 4W7 – 905/526-8943 – *2
Genesee & Clarke, 143 Main St. East, L8N 1G4 – 905/522-7066, Fax: 905/522-7085 – *4
Colin David Gibson, Q.C., 550 Concession St., L8V 1A9 – 905/522-1163, Fax: 905/574-3299 – *1
Gowlings, #600, 120 King St. West, L8P 4V2 – 905/540-8208, Fax: 905/528-5833 – *5
John Grant, #201, 224 King St. West, L8P 1A9 – 905/521-8901, Fax: 905/527-9564 – *1
Guyatt & Gaasenbeek, #201, 131 John St. South, L8N 2C3 – 905/528-8369, Fax: 905/528-9187 – *1
Halford, Findley, 336 Sanatorium Rd., L9C 2A4 – 905/388-0973, Fax: 905/388-2797 – *1
Sidney M. Halpern, 1164 Barton St. East, L8H 2V6 – 905/544-2812 – *1
J.W. Hammond, Q.C., 152 James St. South, L8P 3A2 – 905/527-3865 – *1
R. John Harper, #1215, 25 Main St. West, L8P 1H1 – 905/522-3517, Fax: 905/522-3555 – *1
Harrington & Harrington, 550 Concession St., L8V 1A9 – 905/383-3331 – *3
Harris & Henderson, 92 King St. East, L8N 1A8 – 905/528-4242, Fax: 905/528-8808 – *6
D.E. Horlacher, 75 Young St., PO Box 867, L8N 1V4 – 905/528-5105, Fax: 905/523-5867 – *1
Hovius, John, #425, 135 James St. South, L8P 2Z6 – 905/526-0780, Fax: 905/526-0783 – *1
Howell & Howell, 105 Main St. East, L8N 1G6 – 905/528-1141, Fax: 905/528-9669 – *2
Hughes, Amys, #1401, One King St. West, L8P 1A4 – 905/577-4050, Fax: 905/577-6301
Douglas L.L. Inch, Q.C., 1164 Barton St. East, L8H 2V6 – 905/544-2812, Fax: 905/544-2815 – *1
Inch, Easterbrook & Shaker, 1 King St. West, 15th Fl., L8P 4X8 – 905/525-4481, Fax: 905/525-0031 – *9
Jaskula, Sherk, Flaherty, Weston & Brock, 135 James St. South, 3rd Fl., L8P 2Z6 – 905/577-1040, Fax: 905/577-7775 – *5
W. Jazvac, 124 Young St., L8N 1V6 – 905/523-0872, Fax: 905/529-5112 – *1
Richard E. Jennis, 75 Hunter St. East, L8N 4B8 – 905/528-7922 – *1
Johnston & Peart, #403, 20 Hughson St. South, L8N 2A1 – 905/527-4521, Fax: 905/527-0447 – *2
H.E. Katz, 2 Ray St. South, L8P 3V2 – 905/522-0040, Fax: 905/522-2981 – *1
Katz, Harvey & Associates, 14 Hess St. South, L8P 3M8 – 905/523-1442, Fax: 905/525-3817 – *5

M.J. Kemeny, 126 MacNab St. South, L8P 3C3 – 905/528-8711 – *1
William E. Kosar, #3800, 100 Main St. East, L8N 3W6 – 905/524-0011, Fax: 905/524-1879 – *1
Landeg & Stonkus, #1004, 20 Hughson St. South, L8N 2A1 – 905/529-7462, Fax: 905/528-6787 – *2
Lazier Hickey Langs O'Neal, 25 Main St. West, 17th Fl., L8P 1H1 – 905/525-3652, Fax: 905/525-6278 – *9
Lees & Lees, #2225, 25 Main St. West, L8P 1H1 – 905/523-7830, Fax: 905/523-4677 – *3
Leggat, Keesmaat & Dixon, LCD 1, #201, 20 Hughson St. South, PO Box 916, L8N 3P6 – 905/527-0202, 529-8403, Fax: 905/527-4948 – *5
Patrick D. Lennon, #101, 100 Main St. East, L8N 3W7 – 905/529-4357, Fax: 905/529-4752
Lewis, Brown, Scarfone, Hawkins, 120 King St. West, L8N 3P9 – 905/523-1333, Fax: 905/523-5878 – *11
Gary R. Livesey, 75 Young St., L8N 1V4 – 905/523-5850, Fax: 905/523-5867 – *1
C.E. Logan, 1394 Main St. East, L8K 1C1 – 905/545-0680 – *1
Luchak, Lofchik, Sullivan, #101, 46 Jackson St. East, PO Box 91066, Stn Effort Sq., L8N 4G3 – 905/529-1939, Fax: 905/527-3497 – *6
Michael Lypka, #711, 20 Hughson St. South, L8N 2A1 – 905/527-0255 – *1
Mackesy, Smye, Turnbull, Grilli, Jones, Winward & Mahler, 117 Hughson St. South, L8N 1G7 – 905/525-2341, Fax: 905/525-6300 – *7
E.R. Madronich, 1 Charlton Ave. West, L8P 2B8 – 905/523-4191 – *1
W.J.I. Malcolm, 20 Hughson St. South, L8N 2A1 – 905/528-4291, Fax: 905/528-4292 – *1
Marck & Marck, 42 James St. North, L8R 2K2 – 905/522-1811 – *1
Martin & Martin, 4 Hughson St. South, L8N 3Z1 – 905/528-5936, Fax: 905/523-4144 – *8
Anthony E. McCusker, #1001, 105 Main St. East, L8N 1G6 – 905/523-0593 – *1
McHugh, Mowat, Whitmore, 337 Queenston Rd., L8K 1H7 – 905/549-4676 – *4
McLaren & McLaren, 1278 Barton St. East, L8H 2W1 – 905/544-5761 – *2
McLelland & Dean, #700, 1 King St. West, L8P 1A4 – 905/522-9261 – *1
Milligan, Gresko, Charuk & Rogers, #330, 110 King St. West, PO Box 57099, L8P 4W9 – 905/522-7700, Fax: 905/522-1502 – *4
Mitchnick & Mitchnick, 1 King St. West, PO Box 907, L8N 3P6 – 905/528-1409, Fax: 905/526-0732 – *2
F. Mohideen, 360 Queenston Rd., L8K 1H9 – 905/545-0442, Fax: 905/545-2645 – *1
B.W. Morison, Q.C., 25 Main St. West, L8P 1H1 – 905/528-8311 – *1
Morris, Waxman, Carpenter-Gunn, 151 John St. South, L8N 2C3 – 905/526-8080, Fax: 905/521-1927 – *4
John W. Nicholson, 117 Hunter St. East, L8N 1M5 – 905/529-9982 – *1
Nolan, Nolan, McLean & Associates, #700, 1 King St. West, L8P 1A4 – 905/522-9261 – *8
J.Z. Olenski, #203, 1039 Upper James St., L9C 3A6 – 905/387-3922, Fax: 905/387-0291; Email: john.olenski@freenet.hamilton.ca – *1
Leonard H.P. Panek, Effort Sq., #504, 105 Main St. East, L8N 1G6 – 905/527-1119 – *1
George J. Parker, 14 Bold St., L8P 1T2 – 905/523-5636, Fax: 905/523-4910 – *1
Pelech, Otto & Powell, 149 Main St. East, PO Box 91206, L8N 4G4 – 905/522-4696, Fax: 905/528-6608 – *4
Albert K. Perl, #1420, 25 Main St., L8P 1H1 – 905/527-5316, Fax: 905/527-0114 – *1
Petrini, Rubenstein & Waxman, 242 James St. South, L8P 3B3 – 905/529-9632, Fax: 905/521-0690 – *3
Leon Price, #610, 135 James St. South, L8P 2Z6 – 905/529-8146 – *1
Geoffrey M. Read, 172 Main St. East, L8N 1G9 – 905/529-2028, Fax: 905/522-6677 – *1

Robinson, McCallum, McKerracher, Graham, #720, 110 King St. West, L8P 4S6 – 905/528-1435, Fax: 905/529-1570 – *2
Rocchi & Rocchi, 120 Hughson St. South, PO Box 868, L8N 3N9 – 905/527-1518, Fax: 905/527-7022 – *2
C.J. Rosart, 57 John St. South, PO Box 867, L8N 2B9 – 905/528-8800 – *1
Ross & McBride, 1 King St. West, 10th Fl., PO Box 907, L8N 3P6 – 905/526-9800, Fax: 905/526-0732 – *19
Ross & Ross, #414, 20 Jackson St. West, L8P 1L2 – 905/522-4657, Fax: 905/527-8550 – *2
Schreiber & Smurlick, 288 Ottawa St. North, L8H 3Z9 – 905/545-1107 – *1
Schreiber, Bordonaro, 126 Jackson St. East, L8N 1L3 – 905/527-4477 – *1
Sharpe, Inglis, Litwiller, #2225, 25 Main St. West, L8P 1H1 – 905/528-5918, Fax: 905/529-5855 – *2
B.B. Shekter, Q.C., 103 John St. South, L8N 2C2 – 905/527-1133 – *1
S. Simpson, #407, 20 Hughson St. South, L8N 2A1 – 905/523-7400, Fax: 905/527-1190 – *1
Simpson, Watson & Vujnovic, 950 King St. West, L8S 1K8 – 905/527-1174, Fax: 905/577-0661 – *3
Simpson, Wigle, King St. West, PO Box 990, L8N 3R1 – 905/528-8411, Fax: 905/528-9008 – *21
Spears, Smith & Associates, 44 Hughson St. South, L8N 2A7 – 905/526-0626, Fax: 905/521-1976 – *3
State & Garman, 1036 Upper James St., L9C 3A8 – 905/388-8022, Fax: 905/574-1991 – *4
J.J. Steadman, 126 MacNab St. South, L8P 3C3 – 905/528-7981 – *1
Sullivan, Festeryga, Lawlor & Arrell, 39 James St. South, 3rd Fl., L8P 4X6 – 905/528-7963 – *10
Swaye, Gerald A., Q.C., 155 James St. South, L8P 3A4 – 905/524-2861, Fax: 905/524-2313 – *4
Szpiech, Ellis, Skibinski, Shipton, 414 Main St. East, L8N 1J9 – 905/524-2454, 522-8660, Fax: 905/523-1733 – *4
Thoman, Soule, Gage, 46 Jackson St. East, PO Box 187, L8N 3C5 – 905/529-8195, Fax: 905/529-7906 – *9
William J. Tidball, 172 Main St. East, L8N 1G9 – 905/521-8922, Fax: 905/522-6677 – *2
Tkach & Tokiwa, 520 Upper Sherman, L8V 3L8 – 905/383-3545, Fax: 905/574-3020 – *1
Turkstra Garrod Hodgson, 15 Bold St., L8P 1T3 – 905/529-3476, Fax: 905/529-3663 – *3
Turkstra, Mazza, Shinehoft, Mihailovich, Associates, 15 Bold St., L8P 1T3 – 905/529-3476, Fax: 905/529-3663 – *17
Vance & Vance, Royal Bank Bldg., #212, 32 James St. South, L8P 2Y1 – 905/528-6346, Fax: 905/528-8200 – *1
R.F. Vero, #300, 143 James St. South, L8P 3A1 – 905/523-6363, Fax: 905/523-5130 – *1
Waller & Homer, 241 King St. West, L8P 1A7 – 905/525-6120, Fax: 905/525-6127 – *2
Weisz, Rocchi & Scholes, Effort Trust Bldg., #200, 242 Main St. East, L8N 1H5 – 905/523-1842, Fax: 905/528-9254 – *5
Wellenreiter, A., Q.C., 46 Forest Ave., L8N 1X1 – 905/525-4520 – *2
Terence A. Whelan, Q.C., #403, 393 Rymal Road West, L9B 1V2 – 905/383-6381 – *1
William J. Wilkins, #610, 1 Young St., L8N 1T8 – 905/528-6151, Fax: 905/528-6168 – *1
Williams and Johnson, 1 James St. South, 16th Fl., L8P 4R5 – 905/522-9287; 572-0885, Fax: 905/522-9296 – *3
Terry L. Winchie, Q.C., 112 Hughson St. South, L8N 2B2 – 905/525-8911, Fax: 905/529-6688
Yachetti, Lanza & Restivo, #800, 105 Main St. East, PO Box 950, L8N 3P9 – 905/528-7534, Fax: 905/528-5275 – *7
Zimmerman & Associates, #4201, 100 Main St. East, L8N 3W6 – 905/524-0231, Fax: 905/524-2023 – *9

DIRECTORY OF LAW FIRMS – ONTARIO 10-57

HANMER..Sudbury
Stanley J. Thomas, Hanmer Valley Shopping Centre, PO Box 3003, P0M 1Y0 – 705/969-4448, Fax: 705/969-7770

HANOVER..Grey
Barker & Halpin, 570 - 10 St., N4N 1R7 – 519/364-4720, Fax: 519/364-2407 – *2
Crockford & Duffy, 282 - 10 St., N4N 1P2 – 519/364-1440, Fax: 519/364-6023 – *2
Robert W. Garcia, PO Box 37, N4N 3C3 – 519/364-3643, Fax: 519/364-6594 – *1
Donald R. Neilson, 320 - 10 St., N4N 1P3 – 519/364-3100 – *1

HARROW..Essex
Karl G. Melinz, 41A Centre St. West, PO Box 880, N0R 1G0 – 519/738-2232, Fax: 519/738-2233 – *1

HAVELOCK.......................................Northumberland
Wallace J. Brown, 11 George St. West, K0L 1Z0 – 705/778-3381, Fax: 705/778-7722

HAWKESBURY..Prescott
Charbonneau, Smith, 482 Main St. East, K6A 1A9 – 613/632-7083, Fax: 613/632-2800 – *7
Houle Assaly Morissette, 444 McGill St., PO Box 306, K6A 2R9 – 613/632-7032, Fax: 613/632-5472 – *4
Robert G. Julien, 132 Race St., K6A 1V2 – 613/632-0148, Fax: 613/632-1810 – *2
Langlois Wilkins Berthiaume Perrier, #500, 1 Main St., K6A 1A1 – 613/632-8541, Fax: 613/632-5274 – *5
Woods Parisien, #200, 115 Main St. East, PO Box 249, K6A 2R9 – 613/632-7015, 8557, Fax: 613/632-3524 – *5

HEARST..Cochrane
G. Boivin, 826, rue George, PO Box 850, P0L 1N0 – 705/362-4268, Fax: 705/362-5614 – *1
Bourgeault, Nadeau, Brunelle, 914 Prince St., P0L 1N0 – 705/362-5922 – *3

HILLSBURGH..Wellington
Robert P. Harper, 89 Main St., PO Box 10, N0B 1Z0 – 519/855-4961, Fax: 519/855-4029 – *2

HUNTSVILLE..Muskoka
James S. Anderson, The East Mall Court, 110 Main St. East, PO Box 1447, P0A 1K0 – 705/789-8823, Fax: 705/789-1272
A.B. Cochran, 110 Main St. East, PO Box 2220, P0A 1K0 – 705/789-5538, Fax: 705/789-1272 – *1
J. Chris Ireland, PO Box 1628, P0A 1K0 – 705/789-4495 – *1
G.A. Smith, #1, 3 Fairy Ave., P1H 1G7 – 705/789-8829 – *1

INGERSOLL..Oxford
McBride, McIntyre & McIntyre, 167 Thames St. South, PO Box 125, N5C 3K1 – 519/485-2160 – *2
Nesbitt Coulter Carr, 183 Thames St. South, PO Box 55, N5C 3K1 – 519/485-5651, Fax: 519/485-6582 – *8
Parker, Ross & Blain, 36 King St. East, PO Box 160, N5C 3K5 – 519/485-0300, Fax: 519/485-6588 – *4

IROQUOIS..Dundas
Gorrell, Grenkie, Leroy & Rémillard, PO Box 469, K0E 1K0 – 613/652-4839

IROQUOIS FALLS....................................Cochrane
Alexander, Barber, 328 Main St., PO Box 290, Stn A, P0K 1G0 – 705/232-4309, 6311, Fax: 705/232-5274 – *3
Susan T. McGrath, PO Box 700, P0K 1G0 – 705/232-4055, Fax: 705/232-6301

KALADAR..................................Lennox & Addington
Hogle & Doreleyers, PO Box 51, K0H 1Z0 – 613/336-8230, Fax: 613/336-8087

KANATA......................................Ottawa-Carleton
Adam & Miller, #400, 300 March Rd., K2K 2E2 – 613/592-6290 – *2
Niebergall Bowles & Shelston, 150 Katimavik Rd., K2L 2N2 – 613/592-5748, Fax: 613/592-8230
Perley-Robertson, Panet, Hill & McDougall, 600 Terry Fox Dr., K2L 4B6 – 613/592-5561, Fax: 613/592-0526 – *4

KAPUSKASING..Cochrane
Bourgeault, Nadeau, Brunelle, Dumais, 7 Cain Ave., PO Box 446, P5N 1S8 – 705/335-6121, Fax: 705/335-8127 – *4
Bill Matwichuk, Q.C., 4A Drury St., PO Box 220, P5N 1K8 – 705/335-2375, Fax: 705/335-6575 – *1

KEMPTVILLE...Grenville
Quist & Humphreys, RR#5, Hwy. 43, K0G 1J0 – 613/258-5711 – *2
R.G. Shaw, 202 Prescott St., PO Box 100, K0G 1J0 – 613/258-5191, Fax: 613/258-5191 – *1
Warren and Jansen, 215 Van Buren St., PO Box 820, K0G 1J0 – 613/258-7462, Fax: 613/258-7761 – *2

KENORA..Kenora
Compton, Shewchuk, MacDonell, Ormiston, Richardt & Fregeau, 214 Main St. South, PO Box 1970, P9N 1T2 – 807/468-9828, Fax: 807/468-5504 – *6
David James Elliott, Stone House, 225 Main St. South, P9N 1T3 – 807/468-3355, Fax: 807/468-7858 – *2
Bruce H. Findlay, PO Box 129, P9N 3X1 – 807/468-9849 – *1
Gibson & Wexler, 111 Main St. South, PO Box 2450, P9N 3X8 – 807/468-3061, Fax: 807/468-7940 – *3
Hook, Seller & Zrum, Bannister Centre, #204, 301 - 1 Ave. South, P9N 3X8 – 807/468-9831, Fax: 807/468-8384,6505 – *5
T.A. O'Flaherty, Q.C., 213B Main St. South, P9N 3X6 – 807/468-9888, Fax: 807/468-3272 – *1

KESWICK..York
Robert Wm. Bailey, 4 The Queensway South, L4P 1Y7 – 905/476-4391, Fax: 905/476-6597 – *1
Joseph O. Dales, Q.C., 314 The Queensway South, L4P 2B7 – 905/476-5135, Fax: 905/476-5415 – *1
Clare C. Green, PO Box 37, L4P 3E1 – 905/476-4271, Fax: 905/476-8977 – *1
R.E. Pollock, 183 The Queensway South, L8P 3T6 – 905/476-0021 – *1

KINCARDINE..Bruce
Diane S. Barker, 329 Durham Market, PO Box 14, N2Z 2Y6 – 519/396-9542, Fax: 519/396-3599 – *1
Graham E. Mahood, PO Box 388, N2Z 2Y8 – 519/396-8144, Fax: 519/396-9446 – *1
William S. Mathers, 863B Queen St., N2Z 2Y2 – 519/396-8918, Fax: 519/396-3395 – *1

KING CITY..York
John A. Geisler, Q.C., RR#1, L0G 1K0 – 905/727-6326 – *1

KINGSTON..Frontenac
D.J. Atkinson, #201, 105 Wellington St., PO Box 1941, K7L 5J7 – 613/544-4497, Fax: 613/544-3200 – *1
Wm. J.F. Bishop, 338 Montreal St., PO Box 1403, K7L 5C6 – 613/544-0644, Fax: 613/544-2197 – *3
Black & Black, 225 Bagot St., PO Box 607, K7L 4X1 – 613/549-2222, Fax: 613/549-8882 – *1
Black & Lloyd, 249 Brock St., PO Box 247, K7L 4V8 – 613/546-3286, 549-3262, Fax: 613/549-1193 – *3
Caldwell & Moore, 260 Barrie St., K7L 3K7 – 613/545-1860, Fax: 613/545-1862 – *3

Cartwright & Cartwright, 89 Clarence St., PO Box 758, K7L 4X6 – 613/544-6212 – *1
Jack W. Chong, 273 King St. East, PO Box 1382, K7L 5C6 – 613/549-1225, Fax: 613/549-3882 – *2
Cunningham, Swan, Carty, Little & Bonham, Empire Life Bldg., #500, 259 King St. East, PO Box 460, K7L 4W6 – 613/544-0211, Fax: 613/542-9814 – *16
James F. Donnelly, Q.C., 221 King St. East, K7L 3A7 – 613/548-7761 – *1
Ecclestone O'Connor-Kaiser, 730 Arlington Park Pl., K7M 8H9 – 613/384-0735, Fax: 613/384-0731 – *1
John R. Gale, 18 Market St., K7L 1W8 – 613/546-4283, Fax: 613/546-9861 – *1
Gerretsen & Conacher, 195 Sydenham St., PO Box 636, K7L 4X1 – 613/544-5660, Fax: 613/546-5369 – *2
Good & Elliott, 153 Brock St., K7L 1S2 – 613/544-1330, Fax: 613/547-4538 – *3
Headrick & Lord, 770 Bath Rd., K7M 4Y2 – 613/384-4403, Fax: 613/384-7056 – *2
B.R.A. Heder & Associates, 255 Bagot St., K7L 4V6 – 613/544-1022 – *2
Hickey & Hickey, 93 Clarence St., PO Box 110, K7L 4V6 – 613/548-3191, Fax: 613/548-8195 – *2
Mary Ann Higges, 231 Brock St., 2nd Fl., PO Box 700, K7L 4X1 – 613/548-7399, Fax: 613/548-1862 – *1
N.C. Jackson, City Hall, 216 Ontario St., K7L 2Z3 – 613/546-4291
Jacob Macpherson Hogan, 237 Queen St., PO Box 668, K7L 4X1 – 613/544-4780, Fax: 613/544-4286 – *4
Johnston & MacNaughton, 231 Brock St., PO Box 670, K7L 4X1 – 613/547-6790, Fax: 613/547-6815 – *1
Kamin & Letourneau, #304, 863 Princess St., K7L 5N4 – 613/542-7334, Fax: 613/542-7386 – *2
A.L. Mandell, 355 Frontenac St., K7L 3T1 – 613/549-4668 – *1
M.A. McCue, 104 Queen, K7K 1A6 – 613/544-5117, Fax: 613/544-7346 – *1
G.Y. McDiarmid, PO Box 1010, K7L 4X8 – 613/546-3274, Fax: 613/546-1493 – *1
Judith A. Millard, 3 Rideau St., PO Box 1010, K7L 4X8 – 613/546-3274, Fax: 613/546-1493 – *1
A. Laurel Montrose, Macdonald-Cartier Bldg., 49 Place d'Armes, 2nd Fl., K7L 5J3 – 613/548-6305, Fax: 613/548-6650 – *1
O'Connor & Napier, PO Box 1959, K7L 5J7 – 613/546-5581, Fax: 613/546-5540 – *2
Philip D. Quintin, PO Box 310, K7P 1R7 – 613/549-3000, 384-0830, Fax: 613/384-0831 – *1
Peter J. Radley, Q.C., #208, 303 Bagot St., K7K 5W7 – 613/544-5612, Fax: 613/544-5614 – *1
David G. Rayner, 464 Princess St., K7L 1C2 – 613/549-3400, Fax: 613/549-3142 – *1
Harvey M. Rosen, #203, 863 Princess St., PO Box 1055, K7L 5N4 – 613/544-1816, Fax: 613/542-6793 – *1
Douglas M. Slack, #1, 817 Blackburn Mews, K7P 2N6 – 613/384-7260, Fax: 613/384-7262 – *1
A.B. Smith, Q.C., 80 Johnson St., K7L 1X7 – 613/544-6673 – *1
Soloway, Wright, Victor, #210, 366 King St. East, K7K 6Y3 – 613/544-7334, Fax: 613/544-4689; Toll Free: 1-800-263-4257 – *1
George N. Speal, Q.C., 74 Brock St., PO Box 81, K7L 4V6 – 613/544-0001, Fax: 613/545-9865 – *1
L.M. Steele, 104 Queen St., K7K 1A6 – 613/544-5117, 5116, Fax: 613/544-7346 – *1
Terence J. Tait, Q.C., 544 Armstrong Rd., K7M 7N8 – 613/544-4770, Fax: 613/544-6266 – *1
Y. Tarnowecky, #5, 633 Norris Ct., K7P 2R9 – 613/384-2354, Fax: 613/384-8904 – *1
Geraldine R. Tepper, 461 Princess St., K7L 1C4 – 613/546-1169, Fax: 613/546-6992 – *1
L.H. Tepper, Q.C., 461 Princess St., K7L 1C4 – 613/546-1168, Fax: 613/546-4162 – *1
Thomson, A.G., 232 Brock St., 2nd Fl., K7L 1S4 – 613/549-5111, Fax: 613/549-4074
I.G. Thorne, PO Box 370, K7L 4W2 – 613/544-1833 – *1
Thomas W. Troughton, 164 Queen St., PO Box 487, K7L 4W5 – 613/546-3277, Fax: 613/546-6825 – *1

* indicates number of lawyers in law firm.

Canadian Almanac & Directory 1997

Trousdale & Trousdale, #200, 184 Wellington St., K7L 3E4 – 613/546-2231, Fax: 613/546-9001 – *2

Bogart W. Trumpour, Q.C., 89 Clarence St., K7L 1X2 – 613/548-7728, Fax: 613/548-3548 – *1

Willoughby MacLeod Scheulderman, 299 Concession St., K7L 4X8 – 613/546-5523, Fax: 613/546-6018 – *3

J.C.A. Wilson, 1412 Princess St., K7M 3E5 – 613/549-4404, Fax: 613/549-8376 – *1

Stephen L. Zap, #203, 863 Princess St., K7L 5N4 – 613/542-3688, Fax: 613/542-6793 – *1

KINGSVILLE .... **Essex**

Clark, McGregor Sims & O'Neil, 58 Main St. East, N9Y 1A2 – 519/733-8441, Fax: 519/733-6874 – *4

Dunnion & Beneteau, 59 Main St. East, N9Y 1A1 – 519/733-6573 – *2

Karry & Laba, 25 Main St. East, PO Box 9, N9Y 2E8 – 519/733-2372, Fax: 519/733-3110 – *2

Karl G. Melinz, 59 Main St. East, N9Y 1A1 – 519/733-6575 – *1

KIRKLAND LAKE .... **Temiskaming**

G. Shorrock, PO Box 490, P2N 3J5 – 705/567-5213, Fax: 705/567-3987 – *1

KITCHENER .... **Waterloo**

G.C. Amos, 276 Frederick St., N2H 2N4 – 519/576-8480, Fax: 519/579-3042 – *1

Artindale & Partners, #510, 101 Frederick St., PO Box 996, N2G 4E6 – 519/744-3331, Fax: 519/744-5062 – *9

John S. Askin, Q.C., 35 Roy St., N2H 4B4 – 519/744-4178, Fax: 519/579-1944 – *1

A.D. Barron, #209B, 385 Frederick St., N2H 2P2 – 519/579-5340 – *1

Sidney S. Bergstein, Q.C., 39 Weber St. East, N2H 1C4 – 519/744-3531, Fax: 519/744-2194 – *1

Brock & Brock, PO Box 933, N2G 4E3 – 519/578-8290, Fax: 519/741-0071 – *1

Steven O. Casey & Associates, PO Box 515, Stn C, N2G 4A2 – 519/576-4320, Fax: 519/576-3604 – *3

Chris & Richard, 194 Weber St. East, N2H 1E4 – 519/570-4400, Fax: 519/570-4242 – *3

J.D. Coleman, 115 Victoria St. North, N2H 5C3 – 519/743-9432 – *1

N.A. Crawford, 1444 King St. East, N2G 2N7 – 519/743-3615, Fax: 519/743-2218 – *1

Fehrenbach Schmidt, Market Sq. Tower, Bldg Box: 1112, 22 Frederick St., N2H 6M6 – 519/578-4525, Fax: 519/745-0914 – *3

Lee Fitzpatrick, 276 Frederick St., N2H 2N4 – 519/579-3150 – *1

Flynn & Sorbara, 300 Victoria St. North, N2H 6R9 – 519/576-0460, Fax: 519/576-3234 – *9

Giesbrecht, Griffin, 60 College St., N2H 5A1 – 519/579-4300, Fax: 519/579-8745 – *4

Giffen, Lee, Wagner, Morley & Garbutt, Commerce House, #500, 50 Queen St. North, PO Box 2396, Stn B, N2H 6M3 – 519/578-4150, Fax: 519/578-8740 – *9

J.C.M. Gothard, Q.C., 30 Duke St. West, N2H 3W5 – 519/578-3250, Fax: 519/742-7126 – *1

Gowlings, #1100, 50 Queen St. North, N2H 6M2 – 519/576-6910, Fax: 519/576-6030 – *21

R.S. Grant, #55, 503 King St. West, N2G 4W1 – 519/744-3397 – *1

J.R. Guy, 245 Frederick St., N2H 2M7 – 519/744-4466, Fax: 519/744-4468 – *1

Haalboom & Schafer, #914, 22 Frederick St., N2H 6M6 – 519/579-2920, Fax: 519/576-0471 – *2

Peter B. Hambly, The Prudential Centre Frederick Tower, #911, 101 Frederick St., N2H 6R2 – 519/579-2924, Fax: 519/744-8008 – *2

John A. Harder, PO Box 2368, Stn B, N2H 6R2 – 519/570-1010, Fax: 519/570-2436 – *1

R.J. Hare, 741 King St. West, N2G 1E3 – 519/576-6710, Fax: 519/576-7040 – *1

J. Joseph Kelly & Associates, Corporation Sq., #500, 30 Duke St. West, PO Box 2277, N2H 6M2 – 519/579-3360, Fax: 519/579-2256 – *4

Sheldon Kosky, 71 Weber St. East, N2H 1C6 – 519/578-1480, Fax: 519/578-2537 – *1

James M. Krakovsky, 51 Francis St. North, N2H 5B4 – 519/570-3700, Fax: 519/570-3399 – *1

Eric M. Kraushaar, 675 Riverbend Dr., N2K 3S3 – 519/743-3911, Fax: 519/742-1841 – *1

Lang, Lang & Lang, #101, 678 Belmont Ave. West, N2M 1N6 – 519/578-3330, Fax: 519/578-3337 – *3

Diane J. Larocque, #15, 842 Victoria St. North, N2B 3C1 – 519/579-1920, Fax: 519/741-9956 – *1

R.G.R. Lawrence, Q.C., 194 Weber St. East, N2H 1E4 – 519/742-4443, Fax: 519/570-4242 – *1

Madorin, Snyder, Carere, Lackenbauer & Hertzberger, 235 King St. East, PO Box 1234, N2G 4G9 – 519/744-4491, Fax: 519/741-8060 – *12

J.J. Marentette, #810, 50 Queen St. North, N2H 6P4 – 519/743-7530 – *1

Harald A. Mattson, Commerce House, #810, 50 Queen Street North, N2H 6P4 – 519/743-7530

McIntyre, McMurray, 51 Scott St., N2H 2P9 – 519/576-7360, Fax: 519/576-7400 – *2

Morscher & Morscher, #905, 101 Frederick St., N2H 6R2 – 519/749-8100, Fax: 519/749-8141 – *3

Neeb, J.W.W., Q.C., #201, 7 Duke St. West, N2H 6M2 – 519/578-4400, Fax: 519/578-3450 – *3

Paquette & Travers, #911, 101 Frederick St., N2H 6R2 – 519/744-2281, Fax: 519/744-8008 – *4

Judith E. Phipps, 314 Frederick St., N2H 2N7 – 519/578-9660, Fax: 519/578-9668 – *3

R.C. Potwarka, 18 Irvin St., N2H 1K8 – 519/578-4200 – *1

Roetsch & Schaffer, 284 Frederick St., N2H 2N4 – 519/576-5310, Fax: 519/576-2797 – *2

Daryl W. Schnurr, PO Box 2607, Stn B, N2H 6N2 – 519/578-5650, Fax: 519/576-2030; Toll Free: 1-800-265-2220; Email: schnurr@ibm.net – *1

J.D.E. Shannon, 30 Spetz St., N2H 1K1 – 519/743-3654, Fax: 519/578-9521 – *1

Shuh Cline & Grossman, 17 Weber St. West, N2H 3Y9 – 519/578-9010, 961-4078 (Toronto) – *6

Sims Clement Eastman, Market Sq. Tower, #700, 22 Frederick St., PO Box 578, N2G 4A2 – 519/579-3660, Fax: 519/743-2540 – *2

Margaret Skowronska-Binek, #911, 101 Frederick St., N2H 6R2 – 519/744-3570, Fax: 519/744-8008 – *1

Smyth, Hobson, Corporation Sq., #902, 30 Duke St. West, N2H 3W5 – 519/578-9400, Fax: 519/578-7482 – *2

Somer, Nanson, PO Box 725, Stn C, N2G 4B6 – 519/579-5700, Fax: 519/741-8259 – *2

Sutherland, Hagarty, Mark & Somerville, 22 Water St. South, N2G 4K4 – 519/745-6801 – *8

Tait, McDonald, 9 Ahrens St. West, N2H 4B6 – 519/576-6500, Fax: 519/744-7811 – *2

C.D. Trotter, 27 Roy St., N2H 4B4 – 519/743-4324 – *1

R.M. Van Buskirk, 31 Roy St., PO Box 1786, N2G 4R3 – 519/745-5570 – *1

Villemaire, Levato, 82 Weber St. East, N2H 1C7 – 519/745-5676, Fax: 519/745-9573 – *2

Voll, Elstner & Santos, 30 Spetz St., N2H 1K1 – 519/578-3400, Fax: 519/578-9521 – *3

Vujic, Dragan, Lawyers, 372 Queen St. South, N2G 1W7 – 519/743-2670 – *1

Walters Sagel Gubler, 151 Frederick St., N2H 2M2 – 519/578-8010, Fax: 519/578-9395 – *4

Bernd G. Wolf, 82 Weber St. East, N2H 1C7 – 519/742-6599, Fax: 519/571-9023 – *1

Orlin C. Wood, 155 Frederick St., N2H 2M6 – 519/576-7630, Fax: 519/570-4022 – *1

Jim Ziegler, 3171 King St. East, N2A 1B1 – 519/893-3171 – *1

Zinszer & Associates, 1183 King St. East, N2G 2N3 – 519/744-8181, Fax: 519/744-8606 – *4

Zinszer & Associates, 1183 King St. East, PO Box 2563, Stn B, N2H 6N2 – 519/744-8181

LAKEFIELD .... **Peterborough**

G.A. Booth, 74 Bridge St., K0L 2H0 – 705/652-3378, Fax: 705/652-6823 – *1

T.E. Cole, 6 Bridge St., K0L 2H0 – 705/652-8161, Fax: 705/652-7088 – *1

Alex Ramsay, PO Box 1088, K0L 2H0 – 705/652-6000, Fax: 705/652-6966 – *1

LAMBETH .... **Middlesex**

Bitz, Szemenyei & Ferguson, 30 Main St., PO Box 482, N0L 1S0 – 519/652-1616, Fax: 519/652-1622

LASALLE .... **Essex**

Ute Wigley-Mueller, 1620 Front Rd., N9J 2B6 – 519/734-1303 – *1

LEAMINGTON .... **Essex**

Pearsall & Marshall, 22 Queens Ave., N8H 3G8 – 519/326-4415, Fax: 519/326-1844 – *3

Reid, Reynolds, Collins & Ricci, 60 Talbot St. West, N8H 1M4 – 519/326-3237 – *4

Sawatzky & Balzer, 5 Russell St., N8H 1T7 – 519/322-2341, Fax: 519/322-2668 – *3

Scaddan & Jakob, 16 Wellington St., N8H 2X4 – 519/326-8638 – *2

Spettigue Spettigue & Cartlidge, 21 Talbot St. East, PO Box 327, N8H 3W3 – 519/326-2687, Fax: 519/326-1344 – *3

LINDSAY .... **Victoria**

Dianne J. Ballam, 18 Cambridge St. North, PO Box 277, K9V 4S1 – 705/324-9811, Fax: 705/324-7720 – *1

R. Dan Cornell, 272 Kent St. West, PO Box 536, K9V 4S5 – 705/324-4312, Fax: 705/324-7525 – *1

J.W. Evans, 219 Kent St., PO Box 427, K9V 4S5 – 705/324-3207, Fax: 705/328-1128 – *1

Flett, Douglas M., Kent Pl., #218, 189 Kent St. West, PO Box 535, K9V 4S5 – 705/324-1161, Fax: 705/324-3726 – *1

Glass, Farn & Reynolds, 6 Albert St. North, PO Box 58, K9V 4R8 – 705/324-3577, Fax: 705/324-0060 – *3

Timothy W. Johnston, 40 Lindsay St. South, K9V 2L8 – 705/328-2393, Fax: 705/878-1765 – *1

I.T. McEachern, 18 Cambridge St. North, PO Box 277, K9V 4S1 – *1

McQuarrie, Hill, Walden, Chester, McLeod, 64 Lindsay St. South, PO Box 457, K9V 4S5 – 705/324-6711, Fax: 705/324-5723 – *4

Mortlock & Sillberg, #210, 189 Kent St. West, K9V 5G6 – 705/324-8511 – *2

Wallace A.W. Scott, Q.C., #219, 189 Kent St. West, PO Box 660, K9V 4S5 – 705/324-5181, Fax: 705/324-8077 – *1

Staples, Swain & Gunsolus, 10 William St. South, PO Box 455, K9V 4S5 – 705/324-6222, Fax: 705/324-4168 – *3

Warner, Cork & La Mantia, 22 Peel St., PO Box 208, K9V 4S1 – 705/324-6196, Fax: 705/324-7440 – *3

LISTOWEL .... **Perth**

Benson, Giller, Tarbush & Carter, 140 Barber Ave. South, N4W 3H2 – 519/291-2710, Fax: 519/291-5231 – *3

Robert S. Johns, 218 Main St. West, PO Box 248, N4W 3H4 – 519/291-3420 – *1

Pratt & Pratt, 280 Inkerman St. West, PO Box 10, N4W 3H2 – 519/291-3612, Fax: 519/291-3613 – *1

LITTLE CURRENT .... **Manitoulin**

Stephen B. Marshall, PO Box 607, P0P 1K0 – 705/368-2424, Fax: 705/368-2967; Email: 1-800-881-1108 – *1

LONDON .... **Middlesex**

Norman M. Aitken, #207, 795 Wonderland Rd., N6K 3C2 – 519/472-8463, Fax: 519/472-1814 – *1

Karl Arvai, Talbot Centre, #1508, 140 Fullarton St., N6A 5P2 – 519/672-0911, Fax: 519/642-1272 – *1

Aston, Berg, Kennedy, & Morrissey, Talbot Centre, #1900, 140 Fullarton St., N6A 5P2 – 519/679-8000, Fax: 519/679-8042 – *13
Baccarea Camman & Steele, 535 Talbot St., N6A 2S5 – 519/432-3468, Fax: 519/679-2150 – *5
Barnes, S.C., 305 Oxford St. East, N6A 1V3 – 519/439-0558, Fax: 519/439-8938 – *3
Beechie, Madison, Sawchuk & Seabrook, 439 Waterloo St., N6B 2P1 – 519/673-1070, Fax: 519/439-4363 – *4
Behr & Rady, 64 Fullarton St., N6A 1K1 – 519/438-4530, Fax: 519/679-6576 – *2
G.P. Belch, #1014, 300 Dufferin Ave., PO Box 5035, N6A 4L9 – 519/661-4940, Fax: 519/661-5530
Bitz, Szemenyei & Ferguson, 341 Talbot St., N6A 2R5 – 519/433-8155, Fax: 519/660-4857 – *7
Bitz, Szemenyei & Ferguson, 538 Adelaide St. North, N6B 3J4 – 519/654-7255, Fax: 519/660-4857
Brown, Beattie, O'Donovan, City Centre Tower, 380 Wellington St., 16th Fl., N6A 5B5 – 519/679-0400, Fax: 519/679-6350 – *13
J.M. Brown, 64 Fullarton St., N6A 1K1 – *1
Burgard, Robinson, 585 Talbot St. North, N6A 2T2 – 519/679-9900, Fax: 519/679-8546 – *2
Carrier, Robert, 585 Springbank Dr., N6J 1H3 – 519/673-3370, Fax: 519/641-2114 – *2
Chambers & Mueller, 141 Wortley Rd., N6C 3P4 – 519/673-1300, Fax: 519/673-1728 – *4
Rano Channan, 68 Tamarack Cres., N6K 3J7
Chapman & Fowler, 540 Queens Ave., N6B 1Y8 – 519/673-1113, Fax: 519/673-5060 – *2
Chinneck Thomson Mahoney Elliott Delorey, 145 Wharncliffe Rd., N6J 2K4 – 519/673-1151, Fax: 519/673-3632 – *7
Chizmar Law Firm, 478 Waterloo St., N6B 2P6 – 519/672-8440, Fax: 519/679-1994 – *2
Cockburn, Foster, Townsend, Graham & Associates, 551 Waterloo St., N6B 2R1 – 519/672-5272, Fax: 519/672-9313 – *10
Cohen Highley Vogel & Dawson, 1 London Pl., 255 Queens Ave., 11th Fl., N6A 5R8 – 519/672-9330, Fax: 519/672-5960; Email: chvd@icis.on.ca; URL: http://www.icis.on.ca/chvd – *20
J.A. Tory Colvin, 466 Ridout St. North, N6A 2P7 – 519/433-0500, Fax: 519/434-9279 – *1
J.W. Cooper, 1555 Glenora Dr., N5X 1V7 – 519/672-8342, Fax: 519/672-5322 – *1
Cousins Trudell, 782 Richmond St., N6A 3H5 – 519/438-5185, Fax: 519/438-4687 – *3
Cram & Associates, #514, 200 Queens Ave., N6A 1J3 – 519/673-1670, Fax: 519/439-5011 – *3
Crawford, Squire & Hampson, #801, 150 Dufferin Ave., N6A 5N6 – 519/673-1233, Fax: 519/661-0594 – *4
Downs, M.P., 489 Talbot St., N6A 2S4 – 519/679-0063 – *2
Kenneth Duggan, #203, 111 Waterloo St., N6B 2M4 – 519/672-5360, Fax: 519/433-6975 – *1
Dunlop Steacy Phillips, 320 Princess Ave., N6B 2A6 – 519/433-6111, Fax: 519/438-9933 – *3
Dyer, Brown, 495 Richmond St., PO Box 818, Stn B, N6A 4Z3 – 519/673-1100, Fax: 519/679-6108 – *15
Eberhard & Morden, 1029 Hyde Park Rd., N0M 1Z0 – 519/473-2100, Fax: 519/472-0768 – *5
R.D. Farrington, #201, 255 Dufferin Ave., N6A 5K6 – 519/434-6821 – *1
Filion, Wakely & Thorup, One London Place, #1610, 255 Queens Ave., N6A 5R8 – 519/433-7270, Fax: 519/433-4453; Email: london@filion.on.ca; URL: http://www.filion.on.ca
G.E. Fitzgerald, 308 Wortley Rd., N6C 3R5 – 519/673-0942 – *1
Fulton Rivett Shanfeld, 625 Wellington St., N6A 3R8 – 519/432-6755 – *3
P.C. Gillespie, 1240 Commissioners Rd. West, N6K 1C7 – 519/473-4440, Fax: 519/473-4443 – *1
J.H. Groom, 47 Grand Ave., N6C 1L4 – 519/433-9201 – *1

William B. Hagarty, 517 Dufferin Ave., N6B 2A3 – 519/434-6064 – *1
D.J. Hamilton, RR#5, N6A 4B9 – 519/432-6653, Fax: 519/660-8060 – *1
Hanes, Buchner & Uren, 783 Richmond St., N6A 3H4 – 519/434-7371, Fax: 519/672-5012 – *3
J.G. Harding, 635 Wellington St., N6A 3R8 – 519/439-0641, Fax: 519/439-0643 – *1
Harrison, Elwood, 450 Talbot St., PO Box 3237, N6A 4K3 – 519/679-9660, Fax: 519/667-3362, 663-9341 – *38
Haskett, Menear Associates, 100 Fullarton St., N6A 1K1 – 519/672-7370, Fax: 519/663-1165 – *6
Henry L. Hennick, #908, 383 Richmond St., N6A 3C4 – *1
E.P. Heyninck, 34 Willingdon Ave., N6A 2Y6 – 519/432-4405 – *1
Hicks Morley Hamilton Stewart Storie, #1608, 148 Fullarton St., N6A 5P3 – 519/433-7515, Fax: 519/433-8827
Godfrey Jefferson, 505 Talbot St., N6A 2S6 – 519/438-1727 – *1
Jeffery Associates, 174 King St., PO Box 2095, N6A 4E1 – 519/434-6881, Fax: 519/673-5376 – *9
R.D.W. Keating, Q.C., #908, 383 Richmond St., N6A 3C4 – 519/432-4553 – *1
Donald Leahy, #6, 575 Wharncliffe Rd. South, N6J 2N6 – *1
Lerner & Associates, 80 Dufferin Ave., PO Box 2335, N6A 4G4 – 519/672-4131, 4510, Fax: 519/672-2044 – *68
V. Libis, #201, 255 Dufferin Ave., N6A 5K6 – 519/434-6821 – *1
Lipson, Frauts, 784 Richmond St., N6A 3H5 – 519/679-3115, Fax: 519/661-0725 – *2
John R. Lisowski, 607 Queens Ave., N6B 1Y9 – 519/679-5000, Fax: 519/673-1717 – *1
J.M. Litterick, 693 Hale St., N5W 1J1 – 519/451-2790 – *1
Little & Jarrett, 412 King St., PO Box 2757, N6A 4H4 – 519/672-8121, Fax: 519/432-0784 – *6
Little, Parker & Ingus, 300 Dundas St., N6B 1T6 – 519/672-5415, Fax: 519/672-3906 – *3
Little, Reeves, Mahoney & Jarrett, 412 King St., N6B 1S6 – 519/672-8121, Fax: 519/438-9818 – *8
Littlejohn & Dupré, City Centre, #902, 275 Dundas St., N6B 3L1 – 519/434-4523, Fax: 519/667-4867 – *2
Charles L. Mackenzie, Q.C., #4, 175 Dundas St., N6A 1G4 – 519/672-1772, Fax: 519/672-1880
MacKewn, Winder, Kirwin, 383 Richmond St., PO Box 96, N6A 4V3 – 519/672-2040 – *5
Alfred A. Mamo & Associates, #201, 380 Queens Ave., N6B 1X6 – 519/672-5952, Fax: 519/672-8736 – *3
Marcus, Tobin, #601, 137 Dundas St., N6A 1E9 – 519/663-0792 – *3
McCarthy Tétrault, One London Place, #2000, 255 Queens Ave., N6A 5R8 – 519/660-3587, Fax: 519/660-3599; URL: http://www.mccarthy.ca – *18
McGrath, Braiden, 4 Covent Market Pl., N6A 1E2 – 519/672-7410, Fax: 519/645-8516 – *2
McKenzie Nash Bryant, 300 Dundas St., PO Box 3120, Stn B, N6A 4J4 – 519/672-5666, Fax: 519/672-2674 – *9
McKenzie R.J. McMillan, 607 Queens Ave., PO Box 516, Stn B, N6A 4W8 – 519/672-2116, Fax: 519/679-2020 – *1
L.D. Miller, 1333 Brydges St., N5W 2C5 – 519/659-3261 – *1
Mitches & Mitches, 88 York St., Box 98, N6A 1A7 – 519/663-5300, Fax: 519/663-2199 – *1
H.D. Morgan, PO Box 143, Stn B, N6A 4V6 – 519/673-1270, Fax: 519/434-4380 – *1
Murphy & Brown, 311 Dufferin Ave., PO Box 443, N6B 1Z3 – 519/679-8800, Fax: 519/433-7267 – *3
Murphy, Durdin, McNamara & Pizzale, #38, 267 Dundas St., N6A 1H2 – 519/434-2174, Fax: 519/642-7654 – *3

J.M. Neilson, Q.C., 479 Talbot St., N6A 2S4 – 519/672-8470 – *1
Nelligan & Nelligan, #48, 267 Dundas St., N6A 1H2 – 519/438-1709, Fax: 519/672-7455 – *1
Nicholson, Seabrook, Epstein & Ste. Marie, #101, 450 Talbot St., N6A 5J6 – 519/679-9250 – *5
James R. O'Donnell, #16, 440 Wellington St., N6A 3P2 – 519/673-0600 – *1
Wendy Oliver, 369 Hamilton Rd., N5Z 1R6 – 519/672-7582 – *1
Norman Peel, Q.C., 466 Ridout St. North, N6A 2P7 – 519/433-2111 – *1
Pensa & Associates, Dufferin Corporate Centre, #1000, 130 Dufferin Ave., PO Box 816, Stn B, N6A 4Z3 – 519/667-4010, Fax: 519/434-9656 – *19
Jeffrey M. Phillips, 11 York St., N6A 1A3 – 519/673-4214, Fax: 519/672-8721 – *1
R. Rohrer, 204 Central Ave., N6A 1M7 – 519/679-8004 – *1
Ross, Bennett & Lake, 400 Queens Ave., N6B 1X9 – 519/672-3630, Fax: 519/672-8795 – *12
Eleanor M. Schnall, 370 Princess Ave., N6B 2A8 – 519/672-7300 – *1
H. Peter Sengbusch, #509, 220 Dundas St., N6A 1H3 – 519/433-0693 – *1
Robert C. Sheppard, 4 Covent Market Pl., N6A 1E2 – 519/432-3575, Fax: 519/645-8516 – *1
Siskind, Cromarty, Ivey & Dowler, 680 Waterloo St., PO Box 2520, N6A 3V8 – 519/672-2121, Fax: 519/672-6065; Email: lawyers@siskind.com – *43
Joseph Sommerfreund, 400 Ridout St. North, N6A 2P4 – 519/438-2708 – *1
David E. Storry, #226, 1255 Commissioners Rd. West, N6K 3N5 – 519/472-2200 – *1
F.E. Troller, 511 Talbot St., N6A 2S5 – 519/672-8335, Fax: 519/672-8972 – *1
Underhill & Joles, 379 Dufferin Ave., N6B 1Z5 – 519/438-1413, 432-4644, Fax: 519/438-3936 – *2
Walker & Wood, 399 Ridout St. North, 3rd Fl., N6A 2P1 – 519/672-3500, Fax: 519/672-2420 – *2
E.M. Walsh, #104, 396 Queens Ave., N6B 1X7 – 519/438-2484, Fax: 519/439-3229 – *1

LUCKNOW .... Bruce
George J. Brophy, 567 Campbell St., PO Box 610, N0G 2H0 – 519/528-2818, Fax: 519/528-2848 – *1

MANOTICK .... Ottawa-Carleton
Carolyn R. Green, 5478 West River Dr., K4M 1G7 – 613/692-0748, Fax: 613/692-0871 – *1
Donald P. Hamilton, Q.C., PO Box 510, K4M 1A5 – 613/692-3511, Fax: 613/692-0724 – *1
Wilson, Prockiw, 5542 Main St., PO Box 429, K4M 1A4 – 613/692-3547, Fax: 613/692-0826 – *2

MAPLE .... York Region
M.D. Newman, 62 Lancer Dr., L6A 1C9 – 905/832-5602 – *1

MARATHON .... Thunder Bay
Filipovic, Brothers & Conway, #4, 65 Peninsula Rd., P0T 2E0 – 807/229-2566, Fax: 807/229-1200 – *1

MARKDALE .... Grey
Harris, Willis, McGarry & Ferris, 45 Main St. West, PO Box 466, N0C 1H0 – 519/986-2740, Fax: 519/986-4205 – *5

MARKHAM .... York
Michael Barmherzig, #550, 11 Allstate Pkwy., L3R 9T8 – 905/477-8855, Fax: 905/477-2488 – *1
Martin Barratt, 201 Whitehall Dr., L3R 9Y3 – 905/475-9738 – *1
Berlin & Azoulay, 101, 16 Esna Park Dr., L3R 5X1 – 905/470-9444, Fax: 905/470-9449
Jay I. Bernholtz, Pilsbury Tower, #505, 675 Cochrane Dr., L3R 0R8 – 905/946-9689, Fax: 416/969-8167

* indicates number of lawyers in law firm.

Bongard & Associate, 10 Washington St., PO Box 509, L3P 2R2 – 905/294-7555, Fax: 905/294-8360 – *1
Stephen D. Brown, 60 Columbia Way, L3R 0C9 – 905/513-9765, Fax: 905/513-6914 – *1
Burstein, Greenglass & Hochman, #200, 7481 Woodbine Ave., L3R 2W1 – 905/475-1266, Fax: 905/475-7851 – *4
Steven J. Carr, #550, 11 Allstate Pkwy., L3R 9T8 – 905/470-9455, Fax: 905/477-2488 – *1
Cattanach Hindson Sutton Van Veldhuizen, 52 Main St. North, L3P 1X5 – 905/294-0666, Fax: 905/294-5688 – *4
Anna Chung, #209, 80 Acadia Ave., L3R 9V1 – 905/940-6800, Fax: 905/970-6804 – *1
Bryan Dale, 123-7225 Woodbine Ave., L3R 1A3 – 905/513-1959, Fax: 905/513-6417 – *1
Stephen R. Dyment, #500, 7030 Woodbine Ave., L3R 6G2 – 905/474-1718, Fax: 905/474-9309 – *1
M. Fagan, 60 Esna Park Dr., L3R 1E1 – 905/475-1933, Fax: 905/475-1578 – *1
D. Gregory Flude, 180 Renfrew Dr., L3R 8B7 – 905/513-1550 – *1
Irving Gleiberman, #208, 50 McIntosh Dr., L3R 9T3 – 905/940-5525, Fax: 905/940-5528
Lawrence S. Gold, 555 Denison St., L3R 1B8 – 905/475-4230, Fax: 905/475-3021 – *1
Fritz Greenblatt, #550, 11 Allstate Pkwy., L3R 9T8 – 905/477-0166, Fax: 905/477-2488 – *1
Gordon H. Hall, #550, 11 Allstate Pkwy, L3R 9T8 – 905/940-1581
Sheri Hirschberg, 2800-14th Ave., L3R 0E4 – 905/946-8282 – *1
Robert F. Hopkins, 15 Ambleside Cres., L3R 7T1 – 905/940-1050, Fax: 905/940-1950 – *1
Alexander Jozefacki, 4961 Hwy.#7 East, L3R 1N1 – 905/940-3141 – *1
Kennedy, Dymond, #404, 140 Allstate Pkwy., L3R 5Y8 – 905/470-2077, Fax: 905/470-2075
Patrick Kirby, 65 Ferrier St., 2nd Fl., L3R 3K6 – 905/479-1615, Fax: 905/479-2277 – *1
Gary M. Kuchar, #S550, 11 Allstate Pkwy., L3R 9T8 – 905/513-8822, Fax: 905/477-2488 – *1
Paul Kupferstein, #550, 11 Allstate Pkwy., L3R 9T8 – 905/477-5520, Fax: 905/477-2466 – *1
H.P. Albert Liang, 80 Acadia Ave., L3R 9V1 – 905/513-9022, Fax: 905/513-8657 – *1
Henry Lue, 808-3100 Steeles Ave., L3R 8T3 – 905/513-6528, Fax: 905/513-6526 – *1
Alan J. Luftspring, #219, 7100 Woodbine Ave., L3R 5J2 – 905/479-1200, Fax: 905/479-9769 – *1
Irene L. Matthews, #104, 7225 Woodbine Ave., L3R 1A3 – 905/475-9716, Fax: 905/475-9716 – *1
S.A. McClyment, #220, 60 Columbia Way, L3R 0C9 – 905/513-7560, Fax: 905/513-7563 – *1
W.J. Melko, 180 Renfrew Dr., L3R 8B7 – 905/881-0430 – *1
Metcalfe, Blainey & Burns, #202, 18 Crown Steel Dr., L3R 9X8 – 905/492-8310, Fax: 905/475-6226 – *5
Midanik, Saul Associates, #550, 11 Allstate Pkwy., L3R 9T8 – 905/477-1721, Fax: 905/477-2488 – *2
Miller Thomson, #800, 625 Cochrane Dr., L3R 9R9 – 905/475-8060, Fax: 905/475-8104; Email: env.group@miltom.com – *11
Mingay & Vereshchak, 81 Main St. North, L3P 1X7 – 905/294-0550, Fax: 905/294-9141 – *5
G. Arthur Moad, #206, 5762 Hwy. 7, L3P 1A8 – 905/294-6446, Fax: 905/294-4436 – *1
Parker & Zener, #705, 7030 Woodbine Ave., L3R 6G2 – 905/470-6226, Fax: 905/475-4082 – *2
Ian Ross Pelman, #100, 100 Allstate Pkwy., L3R 6H3 – 905/946-8161, Fax: 905/477-7601 – *1
William Popovski, 7725 Birchmount Rd., L3R 9X3 – 905/513-7144, Fax: 905/513-7147 – *1
E.M.D. Read, #110, 1 West Pearce St., L4B 3K3 – 905/882-8666, Fax: 905/882-1082 – *1
Theodore Rotenberg Barristers, #205, 80 Tiverton Crt., L3R 0G4 – 905/479-3331, Fax: 905/479-5017 – *2

Michael A. Siegel, #500, 7030 Woodbine Ave., L3R 6G2 – 905/474-1717, Fax: 905/474-9309 – *1
Sigal & Cairns, #404, 8300 Woodbine Ave., L3R 9Y7 – 905/940-1945, Fax: 905/940-2193 – *2
Paul F. Smith, #202, 5762 Hwy. 7, L3P 1A8 – 905/294-9955, Fax: 905/294-4004 – *1
Solomon & Balinsky, 7507 Kennedy Rd., L3R 0L8 – 905/479-1900, Fax: 905/479-9793 – *3
D.M. Starzynski, Q.C., The 16th Ave. Shopping Centre, 9275 Hwy. 48 North, L6E 1A3 – 905/294-3891, Fax: 905/471-2550 – *1
Still Thompson McGee, 20 Main St. North, L3P 1X2 – 905/472-1072, Fax: 905/472-1077 – *6
Tan & Associates, #603, 160 Bullock Dr., L3P 1W2 – 905/471-9000, Fax: 905/471-9090 – *2
Tsubouchi & Nichols, 71 Main St. North, L3P 1X7 – 905/294-7780, Fax: 905/294-9883 – *4
Stanley Udell, #102, 7030 Woodbine Ave., L3R 1A2 – 905/474-1770, Fax: 905/474-1692 – *1
Deborah L. Wilkins, 107-7225 Woodbine Ave., L3R 1A3 – 905/475-0242, Fax: 905/475-0852 – *1
Wilson, Vukelich, #710, 60 Columbia Way, L3R 0C9 – 905/940-8700 – *7
Judith M. Wolf, #550, 11 Allstate Pkwy., L3R 9T8 – 905/477-0043, Fax: 905/477-2488 – *1
Patrick A. Wymes, #550, 11 Allstate Pkwy., L3R 9T8 – 905/470-7089 – *1
Jack Zwicker, #306, 7100 Woodbine Ave., L3R 5J7 – 905/470-2544 – *1

MEAFORD .... **Grey**
Norman Kopperud, 76 Sykes St. North, N0H 1Y0 – 519/538-2044, Fax: 519/538-5323 – *1
Scheifele, Erskine & Renken, 39 Nelson St. West, PO Box 3395, N4L 1A5 – 519/538-2510, Fax: 519/538-1843 – *5

MIDLAND .... **Simcoe**
Berthin & Associates, 237 Second St., L4R 3P7 – 705/526-0525
Joseph Blake, 366 First St., L4R 3P2 – 705/526-7894 – *1
Chin & Orr, 382 King St., L4R 3M9 – 705/526-5529, Fax: 705/526-3071 – *3
Deacon Taws Friend, 476 Elizabeth St., PO Box 247, L4R 4K8 – 705/526-3791, Fax: 705/526-2688 – *3
Ferguson & Boeckle, 531 King St., PO Box 306, L4R 4L1 – 705/526-1471, Fax: 705/526-1067; Toll Free: 1-800-563-6348 – *4
Hacker Gignac Rice, 518 Yonge St., L4R 2C5 – 705/526-2231, Fax: 705/526-0313 – *6
Heacock & DiTomaso, 361 King St., PO Box 640, L4R 3M7 – 705/526-7886, Fax: 705/526-6872 – *2
James Lunnie, 509 Dominion Ave., PO Box 567, L4R 4L3 – 705/526-6735 – *1
Prost & Associates, 323 Midland Avenue, PO Box 96, L4R 4K6 – 705/526-9328, Fax: 705/526-1209 – *2
Symons & Grisé, 266 King St., PO Box 187, L4R 4K8 – 705/526-2251, Fax: 705/526-2601 – *5
John Winter & Mark Kowalsky, 362 Midland Ave., L4R 3K7 – 705/526-4560, Fax: 705/528-8499 – *2

MILTON .... **Halton**
Flannagan & Greenwood, #105, 13 Charles St., L9T 2G5 – 905/878-2804, Fax: 905/878-5610 – *2
Furlong Collins, 64 Ontario St. North, L9T 2T1 – 905/878-8123, Fax: 905/878-2555 – *2
Hedley Grieves, 24 Martin St., L9T 2P9 – 905/878-8843, Fax: 905/876-4891 – *2
Nigel A. Gunding, #203, 15 Martin St., L9T 2R1 – 905/875-4678, Fax: 905/878-3723
Ingrid Hibbard, 623 Laurier Ave., L9T 4G9 – 905/875-3828, Fax: 905/875-3829 – *1
P.K. McWilliams, Q.C., #203, 15 Martin St., L9T 2R1 – 905/878-4681, Fax: 905/878-3723 – *2
Nichols & Servos, 207 Mary St., L9T 1M1 – 905/878-4149, Fax: 905/878-4984 – *2

D.J. Pressé, #301, 205 Main St. East, L9T 1N7 – 905/876-4721, Fax: 905/878-4282 – *1
Leonard A. Walker, 205 Main St. East, L9T 1N7 – 905/875-0732, Fax: 905/875-2366 – *1

MILVERTON .... **Perth**
Byers, Kenny, Parlee & Thorn, 11 Main St. North, N0K 1M0 – 519/595-8171

MINDEN .... **Haliburton**
Donald J. Finn, 13 NewCastle St., PO Box 158, K0M 2K0 – 705/286-2611, Fax: 705/286-4460 – *1

MISSISSAUGA .... **York**
Calvin V. Agard, #111, 93 Dundas St. East, L5A 1W7 – 905/276-6920
David A. Aiken, #330, 1420 Burnhamthorpe Rd. East, L4X 2Z9 – 905/602-5230, Fax: 905/602-0722 – *1
Carol Allen, 6050 Bidwell Trail, L5V 1V6 – 905/826-6799, Fax: 905/826-6799 – *1
David A. Allport, 1646 Dundas St. West, L5C 1E6 – 905/270-2008, Fax: 905/270-2148 – *1
Jeffrey A. Alter, #6, 2145 Dunwin Dr., L5L 4L9 – 905/828-1195, Fax: 905/828-4602 – *1
Mark E. Alter, 7330 Goreway Dr., L4T 4J2 – 905/672-0770 – *1
Anderson, Sinclair, 2170 Torquay Mews, L5N 2M6 – 905/821-8522 – *13
David Arthur & Associates, #6, 2145 Dunwin Dr., L5L 4L9 – 905/828-2300, Fax: 905/828-4602 – *1
Mary E. Atkinson, #227, 92 Lakeshore Rd. East, L5G 4S2 – 905/278-4910, Fax: 905/271-6065 – *1
Robert A. Ault, #6, 25 Watline Ave., L4Z 2Z1 – 905/712-2726, Fax: 905/712-2727 – *1
John R.E. Bacon, Barrister & Solicitor, #15, 1100 Central Pkwy. West, L5C 4E5 – 905/949-4300 – *1
H. Ross R. Bain, Emerald Business Centre, #600, 10 Kingsbridge Garden Circle, L5R 3K6 – 905/568-0000, Fax: 905/568-0080 – *1
Paul Bannon, #360, 33 City Centre Dr., L5B 2N5 – 905/272-3412, Fax: 905/272-1065 – *2
Barie Benaich, 30 Village Centre Pl., L4Z 1V9 – 905/275-7731, Fax: 905/275-3315
Barlow & Hancock, #708, 1 City Centre Dr., L5B 1M2 – 905/273-7380, Fax: 905/273-7386 – *2
Barrigar & Moss, #1250, 2 Robert Speck Pkwy., L4Z 1H8 – 905/276-2300, Fax: 905/276-7687 – *7
N. Bartels, #102, 2600 Edenhurst Dr., L5A 3Z8 – 905/276-8286 – *1
Bateman & Bowen, #606, 6711 Mississauga Rd. North, L5N 2W3 – 905/567-4440, Fax: 905/821-1572 – *2
Richard T. Bennett, 82 Queen St. South., L5M 1K6 – 905/826-1453, Fax: 905/826-7185 – *2
R.M. Bindoo, ##200, 4265 Sherwoodtowne Blvd., L4Z 1Y5 – 905/803-8255, Fax: 905/803-0843 – *1
Binsky Howard & Associates, #6, 2145 Dunwin Dr., L5L 4L9 – 905/828-2247, Fax: 905/828-4607
S.R. Biss, #102, 2600 Edenhurst Dr., L5A 3Z8 – 905/273-3322 – *1
Susan Margaret Black, 42 Peter St. North, L5H 2G8 – 905/274-4738, Fax: 905/274-4948 – *1
Bobesich, Gordon, Zlatko, #301, 918 Dundas St. East, L4Y 2B8 – 905/566-1779, Fax: 905/566-1951
Broadhurst Main, 4257 Sherwoodtowne Blvd., L4Z 1Y5 – 905/275-3511, Fax: 905/275-6330 – *5
Lori K. Brown, 168 Queen St. South, L5M 1K8 – 905/567-5352 – *1
D.E. Buckman, 50 Burnhamthorpe Rd. West, L5B 3C2 – 905/276-7497, Fax: 905/276-7590 – *1
Michael J. Bukovac, 1325 Burnhamthorpe Rd. East, L4Y 3V8 – 905/238-1411, Fax: 905/629-9277 – *1
J. Paul Burk, Q.C., #206, 1310 Dundas St. East, L4Y 2L6 – 905/848-1653, Fax: 905/848-5989 – *1
Byrnes, Chan & Associates, #42, 145 Traders Blvd. East, L4Z 3L3 – 905/712-2888, Fax: 905/712-3838
Carey, Froud & McCallum, #100C, 131 Brunel Rd., L4Z 1X3 – 905/568-1900, Fax: 905/568-3854 – *3

J.C. Chapman, 2572 Stanfield Rd., L4Y 1S2 – 905/270-7034, Fax: 905/270-1001 – *1
Chojnacki, Fuller & O'Neail, #301, 6733 Mississauga Rd. North, L5N 6J5 – 905/821-3644, Fax: 905/821-8355 – *3
P.G.B. Cooke, 2600 Edenhurst Dr., L5A 3Z8 – 905/276-7560 – *1
Winfield Corcoran, #130, 2155 Leanne Blvd., L5K 2K8 – 905/822-2121, Fax: 905/822-2172 – *3
R.J. Cornale, 2070 Hadwen Ave., L8K 2C9 – 905/403-1433, Fax: 905/403-1400 – *1
Cousins & Nadler, 30 Village Centre Place, Upper Level, L4Z 1V9 – 905/275-6042, Fax: 905/275-3315 – *3
Albert Cunningham, 130 Dundas St. East, L5A 3V8 – 905/272-0616, Fax: 905/272-0067 – *2
Douglas M. Davidson, 15 Dundas St. West, L5B 1H2 – 905/279-3330, Fax: 905/279-2735 – *1
Michael J. Day, 93 Queen St. South, L5M 1K7 – 905/826-5670, Fax: 905/826-5673; Email: daylaw@idirect.com – *1
M.G. DeCosimo, 7 Helene St. South, L5G 3A8 – 905/278-7248, Fax: 905/278-7718 – *1
Carmen A. Defacendis, #202, 120 Traders Blvd. East, L4Z 2H7 – 905/712-2655, Fax: 905/712-2654 – *1
Greg Dimitriou, #102, 160 Traders Blvd., L4Z 3K7 – 905/568-9800, Fax: 905/568-9802 – *1
P.E. Dubas, #500, 3025 Hurontario St., L5A 2H2 – 905/848-8484, Fax: 905/848-8489 – *1
L. Murray Eades, 7229 Pacific Circle, L5T 1S9 – 905/795-4040, Fax: 905/564-2315
Peter Everett, #577, 33 City Centre Dr., L5B 2N5 – 905/896-3121, Fax: 905/896-3123 – *1
Richard Alan Fellman, #100, 46 Village Centre Pl., L4Z 1V9 – 905/275-2231, Fax: 905/275-8323 – *1
Harold Fink, #200, 19 Dundas St. West, L5B 1H2 – 905/276-1024, Fax: 905/276-4646 – *1
Kim Fullerton, 1347 Crestdale Rd., L5H 1X9 – 905/274-6708 – *1
Hugh H. Galbraith, 2863 Derry Rd. East, L4T 1A6 – 905/671-2462, Fax: 905/671-0859 – *1
Gardner, Cutler, 30 Village Centre Pl., L4Z 1V9 – 905/275-6132, Fax: 905/276-2193
Garvey & Garvey, 972 Clarkson Rd. South, L5J 2V7 – 905/823-4400, Fax: 905/823-5153 – *2
Stanley Gelman, Q.C., #602, 50 Burnhamthorpe Rd. West, L5B 3C2 – 905/270-5110, Fax: 905/220-3002 – *4
Stephen Joel Goldman, #104, 1454 Dundas St. East, L4X 1L4 – 905/281-0119, Fax: 905/281-1013 – *1
William D. Gray & Associates, #6-12, 2145 Dunwin Dr., L5L 1X2 – 905/828-2300 – *1
D.F. Hardacre, #830, 2 Robert Speck Pkwy., L4Z 1H8 – 905/276-5646 – *1
K.R. Harris, 1370 Hurontario St., L5G 3H4 – 905/271-4277, Fax: 905/271-8027 – *1
Jack Harrison, Q.C., 80-4 Robert Speck Pkwy., L4Z 1S1 – 905/275-4673, Fax: 905/275-4680 – *1
Holmes & Stewart, #6, 2624 Dunwin Dr., L5L 3T5 – 905/607-8879, Fax: 905/607-1074 – *2
R. Allan Horwood, #300, 57 Village Centre Pl., L4Z 1V9 – 905/848-0287, Fax: 905/848-8584 – *1
James Hoyt, #114, 1801 Lakeshore Rd. West, L5J 1J6 – 905/823-4567, Fax: 905/823-5025
George K. Hutcheson, #105, 3034 Palstan Rd., L4Y 2Z6 – 905/848-3600, Fax: 905/272-1682 – *1
D. Grant Isaac, Emerald Business Centre, #803, 10 Kingsbridge Garden Circle, L5R 3K6 – 905/507-0303, 791-0619, Fax: 905/507-4618 – *1
M. Janjua, #14, 7050 Bramalea Rd., L5S 1T1 – 905/672-2220, Fax: 905/672-2190 – *1
Wm. G. Jeffery, #301, 8 Stavebank Rd. North, L5G 2T4 – 905/278-7271, Fax: 905/278-7514 – *1
Jerry S. Korman & Associates, 46 Village Centre Pl., L4Z 1V9 – 905/270-6660, Fax: 905/270-2665 – *2
Kain & Ball, #240, 1900 Dundas St. West, L5K 1P9 – 905/855-4888, Fax: 905/855-3760; Email: 73617.3151@compuserve.com – *2

Kaiser Reide, #708, 1 City Centre Dr., L5B 1M2 – 905/272-6930, Fax: 905/273-7386
Keller Treloar & Sehmi, #301, 25 Watline Ave., L4Z 2Z1 – 905/890-2211, Fax: 905/890-2246 – *3
Kemp Boswell Berger, 200-4303 Village Centre Crt., L4Z 1S2 – 905/275-7171, Fax: 905/275-7062 – *3
Kennedy & Associates, 20 Hurontario St., L5G 3G7 – 905/271-1010, Fax: 905/271-8104 – *2
Thomas D. Kerr, 3102 O'Hagan Dr., L5C 2C6 – 905/279-9004, Fax: 905/279-9004 – *1
Keyser Mason Ball, #701, 201 City Centre Dr., L5B 2T4 – 905/276-9111, Fax: 905/276-2298; Email: kmb@kmblaw.com; URL: http://www.kmblaw.com – *25
Killaby, Peter C., 93 Queen St., L1M 1K3 – 905/542-3151 – *3
Korman McNulty, 46 Village Centre Pl., L4Z 1V9 – 905/270-6660, Fax: 905/270-2665 – *2
Michael Krepakevich, 2572 Stanfield Rd., L4Y 1S2 – 905/273-3811, Fax: 905/273-5648 – *1
Frank Laconte, 4311 Village Crater Court, L4Z 1S2 – 905/897-1982, Fax: 905/897-9287 – *1
D. Lafferty, Q.C., 1743 Lakeshore Rd. West, L5J 1J4 – 905/822-3111, Fax: 905/822-8885 – *1
T.K. Lalla, 19 Dundas St. West, L5B 1H2 – 905/566-0532, Fax: 905/532-4942 – *1
Letman, Forth & Associates, 34 Lakeshore Rd. East, L5G 1C8 – 905/271-0102, Fax: 905/274-0169 – *2
Frank Loconte, #100, 4311 Village Centre Ct., L4Z 1S2 – 905/789-3436, Fax: 905/897-9287 – *1
C.P. Lum, #200, 4265 Sherwoodtowne Blvd., L4Z 1Y5 – 905/949-0799, Fax: 905/949-1749 – *1
Arthur MacColl, #16, 6645 Kitimat Rd., L5N 6J3 – 905/821-3213, Fax: 905/821-2582 – *1
W.E. MacDonald, Q.C., 1370 Hurontario St., L5G 3H4 – 905/271-6223 – *1
MacKay & MacKay, #202, 776A Dundas St. East, L4Y 2B6 – 905/848-3446 – *2
Carol E. MacPherson, 6711 Mississauga Rd. North, L5N 2W3 – 905/5567-9740, Fax: 905/821-1572 – *1
B.R. Madigan, #101, 20 Stavebank Rd., L5G 2T4 – 905/278-7766, Fax: 905/278-4233 – *1
Malicki & Malicki, 3020 Kirwin Ave., L5A 2K6 – 905/279-6250, Fax: 905/279-3878 – *1
Mangat Manjit Singh, #16, 7033 Delford Way, L5S 1V4 – 905/677-4124, Fax: 905/677-7134
Markowitz & Associates, #401, 10 Kingsbridge Garden Circle, L5R 3K6 – 905/890-1800, Fax: 905/890-8400 – *2
William E. Mathers, #200, 2386 Haines Rd., L4Y 1Y6 – 905/270-8811, Fax: 905/270-2977 – *1
Mazzucco & Boguski, 1090 Dundas St. East, L4Y 2B8 – 905/272-0303 – *3
McClintock, Ingle & O'Connor, 4263 Sherwoodtowne Blvd., L4Y 1Y5 – 905/896-4370, Fax: 905/896-4926 – *3
Cindy McGoldrick, #121, 1454 Dundas St. East, L4X 1L4 – 905/279-0872, Fax: 905/279-1349 – *1
Hugh G. McLean, 1599 Hurontario St., L5G 3H7 – 905/271-1010, Fax: 905/271-1012 – *1
McMillan Binch, #800, 3 Robert Speck Pkwy., L4Z 2G5 – 905/566-2003, Fax: 905/566-2029 – *4
Donald McPherson, 34 Village Centre Pl., L4Z 1V9 – 905/848-7737
David S.H. Mimms, #708, 1 City Centre Dr., L5B 1M2 – 905/276-4211, Fax: 905/273-7386 – *1
Mississauga Community Legal Services, #501A, 130 Dundas St. East, L5A 3V8 – 905/896-2050, Fax: 905/273-4255
David A. Morrison, 67 Lakeshore Rd. East, L5G 1C9 – 905/274-5370, Fax: 905/274-5387 – *6
Ronald F. Mossman, #300, 34 Village Centre Place, L4Z 1V9 – 905/848-4020, Fax: 905/848-4026 – *1
Mussani Law Office, 3701 Price Ct., L5L 4S6 – 905/828-6623, Fax: 905/828-6623
John O'Donnell, #7, 1015 Matheson Blvd. East, L4W 3A4 – 905/625-2522, Fax: 905/625-0614
O.J. Osmak, #2A, 702 Burnhamthorpe Rd. East, L4Y 2X3 – 905/277-0229, Fax: 905/277-4966 – *1

Toomas Ounapuu, 3070A Hurontario St., L5B 1N7 – 416/972-1999, Fax: 416/276-1063 – *1
Ovenden & Ovenden, 1 City Centre Dr., L5B 1M2 – 905/270-8544, Fax: 905/273-7386 – *2
Pallett Valo, #1600, 90 Burnhamthorpe Rd. West, L5B 3C3 – 905/273-3300, Fax: 905/273-6920 – *22
Roland Paskar, 1450 Hurontario St., L5G 3H4 – 905/271-3343, Fax: 905/271-3352 – *2
Wesley M. Philip, #203, 7420 Airport Rd., L4T 4E5 – 905/673-8088, Fax: 905/673-8098
Larry R. Plener, 2564 Confederation Pkwy., L5B 1S2 – 905/897-8611, Fax: 905/897-8807 – *1
Annalisa Pressaco, #606, 6711 Mississauga Rd. North, L5N 2W3 – 905/821-9055, Fax: 905/821-1572 – *1
Pretam K. Prewal, #210A, 7071 Airport Rd., L4T 4J3 – 905/678-0084, Fax: 905/678-1493
David G. Price, 1370 Hurontario St., L5G 3H4 – 905/271-0191 – *1
Purdon & Ronka, 1348 Hurontario St., L4Z 3G1 – 905/271-3636, Fax: 905/271-7779 – *2
Peter Quirt, #102, 6850 Mill Creek Dr., L5N 4J9 – 905/858-1366, Fax: 905/858-3622 – *1
Racioppo Zuber Dionne, Corporate Centre III, #200, 1290 Central Pkwy. West, L5C 4R3 – *1
Bonnie Racz, #318, 1 City Centre Dr., L5B 1M2 – 905/949-9555 – *1
Reddington & White, #100, 53 Village Centre Pl., L4Z 1V9 – 905/896-7533, Fax: 905/896-7573 – *2
George Rethy Law Office, 4261 Sherwoodtowne Blvd., L4Z 1Y5 – 905/270-9585
Sheri Richardson, 30 Village Centre Pl., L5A 3R6 – 905/270-4264, Fax: 905/275-3315 – *1
Terry D. Richardson, 18 Mississauga Rd. North, L5H 2H4 – 905/891-0011, Fax: 905/891-1410 – *1
G. Martin Rosen, #101, 160 Traders Blvd., L4Z 3K7 – 905/507-4771, Fax: 905/507-0467 – *1
Peter M. Rowland, 872 Whittier Cres., L5H 2X3 – 905/274-4841 – *1
T.D. Salomaas, 2572 Stanfield Rd., L4Y 1S2 – 905/270-7034, Fax: 905/270-1001 – *1
J. Saltzman, #15, 7205 Goreway Dr., L4T 2T9 – 905/671-1178, Fax: 905/671-8030 – *1
Sargeant & Sargeant, #202, 120 Traders Blvd. East, L4Z 2H7 – 905/568-1200, Fax: 905/568-1206 – *2
Susan J. Schell, #59, 6535 Mill Creek Dr., L5N 2M2 – 904/567-7037 – *1
Edgar Schink, 6549B Mississauga Rd., L5N 1A6 – 905/826-8448, Fax: 905/826-2652 – *1
Martin C. Schulz, 2564 Confederation Pkwy., L5B 1S2 – 905/897-2200, Fax: 905/897-8807 – *1
J.H. Selley, 1719 Lakeshore Rd. West, L5J 1J4 – 905/855-2908 – *1
Shadlock, Barycky, Roche, #2300, 4 Robert Speck Pkwy., L4Z 2J1 – 905/270-1900, Fax: 905/270-5750 – *3
Donald N. Shaw, Q.C., 2294 Camilla Road, L5A 2K3 – 905/279-9831 – *1
Jeremy Sheppard, 4303 Village Centre Ct., L4Z 1S2 – 905/949-5364, Fax: 905/949-5201 – *1
Shivarattan Sudeesh, #4, 7305 Bramalea Rd., L5S 1C5 – 905/677-3114, Fax: 905/667-3665
Allan Shulman, 2225 Erin Mills Pky., L5K 1T9 – 905/822-3563, Fax: 905/822-6342 – *1
Thomas Simpson, 1721 Lakeshore Rd. West, L5J 1J4 – 905/855-8200, Fax: 905/855-8858 – *1
Barry Smith, #117, 377 Burnhamthorpe Rd. East, L5A 3Y1 – 905/276-9701, Fax: 905/276-1973 – *1
Speciale & Assoc., #11, 150 Brittania Rd. East, L4Z 2A4 – 905/890-1666, Fax: 905/890-8322 – *2
Sproule & Girouard, 6509 Mississauga Rd., L5N 1A6 – 905/826-5800 – *1
W.F. Summers, #230, 2155 Leanne Blvd., L5K 2K8 – 905/823-9893, Fax: 905/823-6135 – *1
Suter Law, 100 City Centre Dr., L5B 2G6 – 905/273-6640, Fax: 905/270-7518 – *2
Thompson, MacColl & Stacy, #5, 1020 Matheson Blvd. East, L4W 4J9 – 905/625-5591, Fax: 905/238-3313 – *5

* indicates number of lawyers in law firm.

10-62 DIRECTORY OF LAW FIRMS – ONTARIO

Thompson, MacColl & Stacy, #5, 1020 Matheson Blvd. East, L4W 4J9 – 905/625-5591, Fax: 905/238-3313 – *7
Helen M. Thomson, #101, 295 Matheson Blvd. East, L4Z 1X8 – 905/507-3616, Fax: 905/507-3617 – *1
Lynda J. Townsend, 1556 Dundas St. West, L5C 1E4 – 905/275-4111 – *1
Barry Trembetzky, 2564 Confederation Pkwy., L5B 1S2 – 905/279-8561 – *1
Turk, Jonah Law Office, #208, 1325 Eglinton Ave. East, L4W 4L9 – 905/625-5883, Fax: 905/625-5885 – *2
Turkstra, Mazza, Reininger Associates, #1250, 2 Robert Speck Pkwy., L4Z 1H8 – 905/276-9000, Fax: 905/276-9822 – *1
Marina Ushycky, #316, 6855 Meadowvale Town Circle, L5N 2Y1 – 905/826-6324, Fax: 905/826-3279 – *1
Verbeek & Verbeek, #12, 1020 Matheson Blvd East, L4W 4J9 – 905/602-6000, Fax: 905/602-5000 – *2
Donald P. Warren, #760, 2 Robert Speck Pkwy., L4Z 1H8 – 905/848-2770, Fax: 905/848-2773 – *1
Brian M. Watson, #105, 3034 Palston Rd., L4Y 2Z6 – 905/272-0942, Fax: 905/272-1682 – *1
Weir & Foulds, #902, 50 Burnhamthorpe Rd. West, L5B 3C2 – 905/896-1100, Fax: 905/896-0803
Weir Associates, #710, 1290 Central Pkwy. West, L5C 4R3 – 905/279-7930, Fax: 905/279-3421 – *5
Wheeler & Associates, 10 Front St. North, L5H 2C9 – 905/274-7881, Fax: 905/274-7883 – *2
Willis & Torry, #355, 35 Queen St. South, L5M 1K2 – 905/819-8377 – *2
Annette Wilson, #201, 1515 Matheson Blvd. East, L4W 2P5 – 905/602-1989, Fax: 905/602-6513 – *1
Michael Woods, #209, 5805 Whittle Rd., L4Z 2J1 – 905/568-3810, Fax: 905/568-5816 – *1
Yeoman, Ament Associates, #B, 6549 Mississauga Rd. North, L5N 1A6 – 905/826-6660, Fax: 905/826-2652 – *2

MITCHELL .... **Perth**
William E. Wilson, 89 Ontario Rd., N0K 1N0 – 519/348-8488, Fax: 519/348-4226 – *1

MOOSONEE .... **Cochrane**
Keewaytinok Native Legal Services, 40 Revillon Rd. North, PO Box 218, P0L 1Y0 – 705/336-2981, 2982, Fax: 705/336-2577 – *2

MORRISBURG .... **Dundas**
Gorrell, Grenkie, Leroy & Rémillard, PO Box 820, K0C 1X0 – 613/543-2922, Fax: 613/543-4228 – *4
McInnis & MacEwen & Ault, PO Box 733, K0C 1X0 – 613/543-2946, Fax: 613/543-3867 – *4

MOUNT ALBERT .... **York Region**
Urquhart, Urquhart, Aiken & Medcof, #707, 330 University Ave., PO Box 40, L0G 1M0 – 905/595-1111, Fax: 905/595-7312 – *1
Wilson, Martin, 19139 Centre St., L0G 1M0 – 905/852-3353 – *3

MOUNT BRYDGES .... **Middlesex**
Sylvia A. Loyens, 22 Adelaide St. North, N0L 1W0 – 519/264-9440, Fax: 519/264-2921 – *1

MOUNT FOREST .... **Wellington**
Fallis, Fallis & McMillan, 150 Main St. South, N0G 2L0 – 519/323-2800, Fax: 519/323-4115 – *3
Grant Deverell Lemaich & Barclay, 166 Main St. South, N0G 2L0 – 519/323-1600, Fax: 519/323-3877 – *5

NAPANEE .... **Lennox**
G. Graeme G. Dempster, 21 Market Sq., PO Box 310, K7R 3M4 – 613/354-2141, Fax: 613/354-3171 – *1
W.A. & J.M. Grange, PO Box 26, K7R 3L4 – 613/354-3359, Fax: 613/354-6786 – *2
Hogle & Doreleyers, 35 Dundas St. East, PO Box 398, K7R 3P5 – 613/354-3375, Fax: 613/354-5641 – *3

Frank T. Horn, 22 Meadow Lane, K7R 3R8 – 613/354-6954
Madden, Sirman & Cowle, 3 Bridge St., K7R 3L8 – 613/354-2161, Fax: 613/354-5027 – *3
J.K. Pearce, Q.C., PO Box 308, K7R 3M4 – 613/354-2101, Fax: 613/354-7694 – *1
Smart & Griffin, 130 Centre St. North, PO Box 206, K7R 3M3 – 613/354-9716, Fax: 613/354-3120 – *2

NEPEAN .... **Ottawa-Carleton**
Doraty & Ferris, 28 Northside Rd., K2H 5Z3 – 613/829-7171, Fax: 613/829-0244 – *3
Donald R. Good, Merivale Depot, PO Box 5118, K2C 3H4 – 613/739-8872, Fax: 613/736-7809; Toll Free: 1-800-661-8837 – *1
Ronald J. Houlahan, Q.C., #214, 3730 Richmond Rd., K2H 5B4 – 613/828-2236, Fax: 613/828-0210 – *1
McLeod, D.G., 1447 Woodroffe Ave., K2G 1W1 – 613/225-0037 – *2
Mirsky Pascoe Lithwick, #300, 39 Robertson Rd., K2H 8R2 – 613/828-2120 – *4
Charles Schwartzman, 15 Saddlebrook St., K2G 5N7 – *1
Danyl Stotland, #C, 273 Craig Henry Dr., K2G 4C7 – 613/723-7179, Fax: 613/727-0573 – *1
E.W. Tennant, #105, 3740 Richmond Rd., K2H 5B9 – 613/829-5121 – *1
R.A. Vanier, #202, 1370 Clyde Ave., K2G 3H8 – 613/226-3336, Fax: 613/226-8767
Jo-Anne E. Ward, 12 Harrogate Pl., K2H 5L7 – 613/829-2317 – *1
John Wyatt, 17 Fitzgerald Rd., K2H 9G1 – 613/820-1886 – *1

NEW HAMBURG .... **Waterloo**
N.A. Thomas, PO Box 1000, N0B 2G0 – 519/662-1760 – *1

NEW LISKEARD .... **Temiskaming**
Ramsay, Ramsay, Kemp, Andrew & Maille, 22 Armstrong St., PO Box 1540, P0J 1P0 – 705/647-7353, Fax: 705/647-1540 – *4
D. Cragg Ross, Q.C., 18 Paget St. North, PO Box 9, P0J 1P0 – 705/647-6819, Fax: 705/647-9525 – *1
Smith, Byck & Grant, 22 Paget St., PO Box 1210, P0J 1P0 – 705/647-7307, Fax: 705/647-7511 – *3

NEWBURGH .... **Lennox**
Thomas Grant Smyth, PO Box 163, K2K 2S0 – 613/378-6429, Fax: 613/378-6429 – *1

NEWCASTLE .... **York**
Sam L. Cureatz, Q.C., 104 James St., L1B 1C6 – 905/987-3500, Fax: 905/987-3503; Email: dn00123@mail.durham.net – *1
Pollitt, Walters, Dizenbach, 29 King St. East, PO Box 2, L1B 1H3 – 905/987-4735, Fax: 905/987-1061 – *3

NEWMARKET .... **York**
Boyd Cumming Eady, 130 Main St. S., L3Y 3Y7 – 905/898-6471, Fax: 905/898-5941 – *3
Penelope Bryan, 130 Mulock Dr., Unit 1, L3Y 7C5 – 905/853-4577, Fax: 905/830-1451 – *1
Chisvin Murphy & Lewis, #300, 30 Prospect St., L3Y 3S9 – 905/836-1027, Fax: 905/836-6691 – *3
Christopher & Fysh, 474 Bathford St., L3Y 1T3 – 905/898-7331, Fax: 905/853-9382 – *3
Iain Stewart Cunningham, 227 Eagle St. East, L3Y 1J8 – 905/836-4151, Fax: 905/836-1059 – *1
Joan Cushon, 17705B Leslie St., L3Y 3E3 – 905/898-1673, Fax: 905/898-2477 – *1
Di Cecco, Jones, #200, 496 Davis Dr., L3Y 2P3 – 905/898-1911, Fax: 905/853-9893 – *2
C.E. Dresner, 39 Parkside Dr., L3Y 4R7 – 905/898-6800, Fax: 905/853-7073 – *1
Dunsmuir & Dunsmuir, 330 Yonge St. South, PO Box 2003, L3Y 6W4 – 905/895-7741, Fax: 905/853-5851 – *2

S. Eisen, #8, 1111 Davis Dr., L3Y 7V1 – *1
J. David Hobson, Q.C., 34 Eagle St. East, L3Y 1J1 – 905/895-6528, Fax: 905/853-1108 – *1
Hunter, Corbett & Losell, 68 Prospect St., L3Y 3T2 – 905/898-1541, Fax: 905/898-5596 – *3
Karnis & Bourgeois, 3-22 Main St. N, L3Y 3Z7 – 905/836-4977, Fax: 905/836-2851 – *1
Neal J. Kearney, 17035 Yonge St., L3Y 5Y1 – 905/898-3012, Fax: 905/853-9894 – *1
Legal Aid, 50 Eagle St., L3Y 6B1 – 905/888-1575, Fax: 905/898-4932
McChesney, Rogers, Hill & Callaghan, 69 Main St. South, PO Box 234, L3Y 4X7 – 905/895-1007, Fax: 905/895-4064 – *4
D.J. McKee, #213, 16610 Bayview Ave., L3X 1X3 – 905/898-4116, Fax: 905/898-3838 – *1
Monteith Baker & Howe, 227 Eagle St. East, PO Box 281, L3Y 4X1 – 905/895-8600, 773-8910, Fax: 905/895-8269 – *5
Paul Montgomery, 890 Wildrush Pl., L3X 1L7 – 905/898-1533 – *1
Peter S. Oliver, #36, 17665 Leslie St., L3Y 3E3 – 905/836-4946, Fax: 905/836-0364 – *1
Elizabeth Ann Patrick, 130 Davis Dr., Unit 203, L3Y 2N1 – 905/853-7031, Fax: 905/853-2274 – *1
Anne L. Roberts, 712 Davis Dr., L3Y 8C3 – 905/895-1090, Fax: 905/895-1090 – *1
Rubin Wintraub, 207 Main St. S., L3Y 3Y9 – 905/898-4440; Toronto Line: 773-6526, Fax: 905/898-3291 – *2
Heather M. Saunders, 17665 Leslie St., L3Y 3E3 – 905/836-5040, Fax: 905/836-0364 – *1
A. Schneider, 291 Davis Dr., L3Y 2N6 – 905/898-1342 – *1
Ainslie Smith, #203, 130 Davis Dr., L3Y 2N1 – 905/853-2671, Fax: 905/853-2274 – *1
Kimberley Smith, #202, 1091 Gorham St., L3Y 7V1 – 905/853-1746, Fax: 905/853-7603 – *2
Stevens & Stevens, Empire Centre, #15, 350 Harry Walker Pkwy. North, L3Y 8L3 – 905/887-5807, Fax: 905/853-7214 – *2
Stiver Vale, 195 Main St., L3Y 4X4 – 905/895-4571, 773-6323, Fax: 905/853-2958 – *9
William D. Turville, Q.C., 34 Eagle St. East, L3Y 1J1 – 905/887-5023, Fax: 905/895-8618 – *1
Wrock & Assoc., 17837 Yonge St., RR#1, L3Y 4V8 – 905/898-5161, Fax: 905/898-1821 – *2

NIAGARA FALLS .... **Niagara South**
Broderick, Marinelli, Amadio, Sullivan & Rose, 4625 Ontario Ave., PO Box 897, L2E 3P8 – 905/356-2621, Fax: 905/356-6904 – *8
J.D. Conte, 4624 Ontario Ave., PO Box 928, L2E 6V8 – 905/357-1144, Fax: 905/357-5560 – *1
David P. Czifra, 5146 Victoria Ave., L2E 4E3 – 905/357-6633, Fax: 905/357-6659
Charles A. Galloway, 5146 Victoria Ave., L2E 4E3 – 905/356-2512, Fax: 905/357-6659 – *1
Douglas Goslin, 4780 Portage Rd., L2E 6A8 – 905/357-0500, Fax: 905/357-0501 – *1
Geoffrey G. Hadfield, 4552A Victoria Ave., PO Box 2173, L2E 6Z3 – 905/357-3500, Fax: 905/356-5850 – *1
Kenneth B. Harris, 4444 Drummond Rd., PO Box 206, L2E 6T3 – 905/374-2121, Fax: 905/374-8546 – *1
Hopkins & Kirkham, 4683 Queen St., PO Box 687, L2E 6V5 – 905/357-5820, Fax: 905/357-9686 – *2
Margaret A. Hoy, 4786 Queen St., PO Box 868, L2E 6V6 – 905/357-3500, Fax: 905/356-3635 – *1
Jaluvka & Sauer, 4231 Portage Rd., L2E 6A2 – 905/356-6484 – *2
R.O. Kallio, City Solicitor, City Hall, L2E 6X5 – 905/356-7521, Fax: 905/356-2354
S. James Knight, Q.C., 4683 Queen St., L2E 2L9 – 905/356-1524, Fax: 905/357-9686 – *1
Philip C. Lococo, 5079 Victoria Ave., PO Box 958, L2E 6V8 – 905/356-7661, Fax: 905/356-6330 – *1

Canadian Almanac & Directory 1997

Joseph A. LoConte, 5146 Victoria Ave., L2E 4E3 – 905/357-5554, Fax: 905/357-6659 – *1
Patricia Lucas, 6268 Colbourne St., L2J 1E6 – 905/357-4510, Fax: 905/357-9757 – *1
Martin, Sheppard, Fraser, 4607 Huron St., PO Box 900, L2E 6V7 – 905/354-1611, Fax: 905/354-5540 – *8
McBurney, Durdan, Henderson & Corbett, 4759 Queen St., PO Box 2148, L2E 6Z2 – 905/356-4511, Fax: 905/356-8938 – *3
D.J. McDonald, 4683 Queen St., L2E 2Z9 – 905/356-1524, Fax: 905/357-9686 – *1
McKay, Heath, Marshall & Gajer, 4673 Ontario Ave., PO Box 23001, Stn Downtown E, L2E 7J4 – 905/357-0660, Fax: 905/357-5680 – *5
G.F. McNab, Q.C., 6268 Colbourne St., L2J 1E6 – 905/357-4510, Fax: 905/357-9757 – *1
N. Minov, 3879 Portage Rd., L2J 2L2 – 905/356-4420, Fax: 905/356-0333 – *1
Michael J. Moberg, 5089 Victoria Ave., L2E 4E2 – 905/374-0036, Fax: 905/374-6684 – *1
Nicoletti & DiPaul, 5001 Victoria Ave., PO Box 2238, L2E 6Z3 – 905/356-5053, Fax: 905/356-9487 – *2
Stephen Paine, 4786 Queen St., PO Box 868, L2E 6V6 – 905/357-3500, Fax: 905/356-3635 – *1
George Radojcic, 4672 Queen St., L2E 2L8 – 905/374-7727, Fax: 905/227-4031 – *1
Andrew Rasuse, 4786 Queen St., PO Box 868, L2E 6V6 – 905/357-3500, Fax: 905/356-3635 – *1
James Rocca, 4056 Dorchester Rd., L2E 6M9 – 905/357-3730, Fax: 905/356-6185 – *1
Ryall, Walker, 4190 Bridge St., PO Box 816, L2E 6V6 – 905/374-3000, Fax: 905/374-6456 – *3
Sharpe, Beresh & Gnys, 4700 St. Clair Ave., L2E 3S8 – 905/357-5555, Fax: 905/357-5760 – *3
Sinclair Crowe, 6617 Drummond Rd., PO Box 58, L2E 6S8 – 905/356-7755, Fax: 905/356-7772 – *2
Slovak, Stockton, Henderson & Hoy, 4786 Queen St., PO Box 868, L2E 6V6 – 905/357-3500, Fax: 905/356-3635 – *2
Guy Ungaro, #201, 6225 Huggins St., L2J 1H2 – 905/357-5310, Fax: 905/357-9677; Email: gung@vaxxine.com – *1
George F. Walker, Q.C., 4786 Queen St., PO Box 868, L2E 6V6 – 905/357-3500, Fax: 905/356-3635 – *1
Brian C. Wilcox, 3964 Portage Rd., L2J 2K9 – 905/358-0782, Fax: 905/358-0783; Email: bcwlaw@niagara.com – *1

NIAGARA-ON-THE-LAKE
Richard J.W. Andrews, 431 Mississauga St., PO Box 900, L0S 1J0 – 905/468-3272, Fax: 905/468-5441 – *1
A.C. Dekany, RR#1, L0S 1J0 – 905/262-5521
Heelis, Williams & Little, 126 Queen St., L0S 1J0 – 905/687-8200 – *1
W.R. King, 431 Mississauga St., PO Box 900, L0S 1J0 – 905/468-3272, Fax: 905/468-5441 – *1
Larry H. Kroeker, 431 Mississauga St., PO Box 1570, L0S 1J0 – 905/646-4447, Fax: 905/468-3898
Lampard, Ellis & Walsh, 355 Mary St., L0S 1J0 – 905/468-3222 – *1

NIPIGON .... **Thunder Bay**
Peter G.F. Young, 64 Front St., P0T 2J0 – 807/887-3204, Fax: 807/345-9886 – *1

NOBLETON .... **York Region**
Joseph Vroom, PO Box 1037, L0G 1N0 – 905/859-0014, Fax: 905/859-5113 – *1
Zimmerman & Zimmerman, 25 Hwy. 27 North, L0G 1N0 – 905/859-1117, Fax: 905/859-1732 – *2

NOELVILLE .... **Sudbury**
Desmarais, Keenan, 9, rue Notre Dame, P0M 2N0 – 705/898-2245

NORTH BAY .... **Nipissing**
Donnelly, Birnie, 116 McIntyre St. West, PO Box 100, P1B 8G8 – 705/497-1900, Fax: 705/497-1700 – *7

Lucenti, Rivard & Orlando, 108 Main St. East, PO Box 358, P1B 8H5 – 705/472-9500, Fax: 705/472-4814 – *4
McLachlan Wilcox & DuCharme, 705 Cassells St., P1B 4A3 – 705/476-6333, Fax: 705/476-4397 – *3
Olah & Olah, 457 Main St. West, PO Box 985, P1B 8K3 – 705/476-1323 – *2
Tafel, Trussler & Eggert, 477 Sherbrooke St., P1B 2C2 – 705/472-4890, Fax: 705/472-9612 – *3
Valin Partners, 140 Main St. West, PO Box 97, P1B 2T5 – 705/474-1220, Fax: 705/474-5630 – *3
Wallace & Carr, 225 McIntyre St. West, PO Box 37, P1B 8G8 – 705/474-2920, Fax: 705/474-1758 – *4
Douglas D. Woltz, 325 Main St. West, P1B 2T9 – 705/476-1710, Fax: 705/476-8277 – *1
Donald W. Wood, 355 Main St. West, P1B 8H5 – 705/476-1710, Fax: 705/476-8277 – *1

NORWICH .... **Oxford**
White, Coad, Patience, Bennett & Oliver, 6 Stover St. North, N0J 1P0 – 519/863-2710, 2091, Fax: 519/863-2469

OAKVILLE .... **Halton**
Baggs, Henderson & Brown, 228 Lakeshore Rd., PO Box 249, L6J 5A2 – 905/844-3218, Fax: 905/844-3699 – *1
George A. Benak, 418 North Service Rd. East, L6H 5R2 – 905/845-4004, Fax: 905/845-6917 – *1
David Bereskin, 418 North Service Rd. East, L6H 5R2 – 905/845-6914, Fax: 905/845-6917 – *1
H.D. Brown, #705, 700 Dorval Dr., L6K 3V3 – 905/842-8710 – *1
Roger B. Campbell, #200, 200 Lakeshore Rd. East, L6J 1H6 – 905/849-7000, Fax: 905/849-7145 – *1
Carson Law Office, 2902 South Sheridan Way, 3rd Fl., L6J 7L6 – 950/844-6404, Fax: 950/844-6426 – *1
CAW Legal Services Plan, #406, 700 Dorval Dr., L6K 3V3 – 905/842-3101, Fax: 905/842-1389; Toll Free: 1-800-465-9701
Stephen B. Collinson, #11, 250 Wyecroft Rd., L6K 3T7 – 905/842-1600, Fax: 905/842-2775 – *1
Coutts, Crane, Ingram, #300, 627 Lyons Lane, L6J 2Y2 – 905/338-0802, Fax: 905/338-3168 – *1
Diane Daly, #509, 345 Lakeshore Rd. East, L6J 1J5 – 905/844-5883, Fax: 905/844-9765 – *1
Diab DeCosimo, #A101, 2381 Bristol Cir., L6H 5S9 – 905/829-2900, Fax: 905/829-2903 – *2
J.I.A. Docherty, 1170 Willowbrook Dr., L6L 2J8 – 905/825-2245, Fax: 905/847-9379 – *1
Gordon M. Edwards, #308, 251 North Service Rd. West, L6M 3E7 – 905/844-1604, Fax: 905/844-9592 – *1
William Elias, 301 Church St., L6J 1N9 – 905/842-2070, Fax: 905/842-5334 – *1
J.B. Gardner, 228 Lakeshore Rd. East, PO Box 249, L6J 5A2 – 905/844-3218, Fax: 905/844-3699 – *1
M. Edward Graham, 420 North Service Rd. East, L6H 5R2 – 905/842-3211, Fax: 905/842-3765 – *1
J.H. Ham, Q.C., 228 Lakeshore Rd. East, PO Box 249, L6J 5A2 – 905/844-3218 – *1
Steven Harrington, 2441 Lakeshore Rd. West, L6L 1H6 – 905/827-8738 – *1
D.K. Haxell, 467 Speers Rd., 2nd Fl., L6K 3S4 – 905/845-0767, Fax: 905/845-7674 – *1
Darrel N. Hotz, #11, 1155 North Service Rd. West, L6M 3E3 – 905/847-7199, Fax: 905/847-8840 – *1
E.N. Hretzay, 1432 Grand Blvd., L6H 3E6 – 905/849-4187 – *1
L.S. Jackson, 107 Maurice Dr., L6K 2W6 – 905/842-3072, Fax: 905/842-1982; URL: http://web.idirect.com/~kid – *1
William B. Kerr, 233 Robinson St., L6J 1G5 – 905/842-8600, Fax: 905/842-4774 – *1
Brian W. King, Q.C., Hopedale Mall, #23, 1515 Rebecca St., L6L 5G8 – 905/827-0808, Fax: 905/827-8380 – *1
LeDressay Van Melle, #101, 700 Kerr St., L6K 3W5 – 905/842-4977, Fax: 905/842-4977 – *2

Matthew J. Leslie, 164 Trafalgar Rd., L6J 3G6 – 905/844-2550, Fax: 905/842-6166 – *1
Lush, Bowker Aird, 261 Lakeshore Rd. East, PO Box 734, L6J 1H9 – 905/844-0381 – *5
Marler & Kyle, 86 Chisholm St., L6K 3H7 – 905/338-2300 – *2
Thomas H. Marshall, Q.C., 296 Randall St., PO Box 955, L6J 5E8 – 905/844-0464, Fax: 905/844-3983 – *1
W. McCrea, #302, 88 Dunn St., L6J 3C7 – 905/844-8881, Fax: 905/844-9970 – *1
David L. McKenzie, #23, 323 Church St., PO Box 906, L6J 5E8 – 905/842-3421, Fax: 905/842-3422 – *1
McLeod, Horner & Axon, #314, 345 Lakeshore Rd. East, L6J 1J5 – 905/338-2555, Fax: 905/338-2961 – *2
Patricia McNamara, 2227 Wyandotte Dr., L6L 2T4 – 905/847-0356 – *1
Kathryn S. Naumetz, 263 Church St., L6J 1N7 – 905/845-2241, Fax: 905/845-0193 – *1
O'Connor MacLeod, 700 Kerr St., L6K 3W5 – 905/842-8030, Fax: 905/842-2460 – *14
J.G. O'Reilly, 187A Lakeshore Rd. East, L6J 1H5 – 905/845-4111, Fax: 905/845-0011 – *1
John Paladino, #200B, 447 Speers Rd., L6K 3S7 – 905/842-3311, Fax: 905/842-7433 – *1
P. William Perras, Jr., #610, 1275 North Service Rd. West, L6M 3G4 – 905/827-2700, Fax: 905/827-2766 – *1
David J. Pilo, #301, 88 Dunn St., L6J 3C7 – 905/338-2002, Fax: 905/338-3810 – *1
J. Jeffrey Richey, #301, 88 Dunn St., L6J 3C7 – 905/845-5880, Fax: 905/338-3810 – *1
R.M. Rose, 2163 - 6 Line, L6H 3N7 – 905/338-9555 – *1
Ruth A.M. Ross, 226 Randall St., L6J 1P7 – 905/849-8377, Fax: 905/849-8344 – *1
Ryrie, Ford, Kerr, 233 Robinson St., PO Box 100, L6J 4Z5 – 905/842-8600 – *7
Angelo A. Serafini, #202, 447 Speers Rd., L6K 3S7 – 905/842-0300, Fax: 905/842-7433 – *1
Shepherd Grenville-Wood, 1391 Fieldcrest Lane, L6M 2W3 – 905/847-0589
Skrow & Indovina, #208, 243 North Service Rd. West, L6M 3E5 – 905/842-6625, Fax: 905/842-6197 – *1
David B. Smith, #2, 760 Pacific Rd., L6L 6M5 – 905/827-3113 – *1
Randolph I. Smith, 710 Dorval Dr., PO Box 517, L6K 3V7 – 905/849-6700, Fax: 905/849-7145 – *1
Karen A. Thompson, #4, 132 Allan St., L6J 3N5 – 905/338-7941, Fax: 905/844-9765 – *1
Trafalgar Village Law Office, 125 Cross Ave., L6J 2W8 – 905/842-8786
Anthony A. Vale, 420 North Service Rd. East, L6H 5R2 – 905/842-0300, Fax: 905/842-3765 – *1

OHSWEKEN .... **Norfolk**
Lonny Bomberry, Iroquois Village Centre, N0A 1M0 – 519/445-2984

ORANGEVILLE .... **Dufferin**
Wayne D. Ball, 279 Broadway Ave., L9W 1L2 – 519/942-4492, Fax: 519/942-1530 – *1
Bourque, White, 30 Mill St., L9W 2M3 – 519/941-9440, Fax: 519/941-3803 – *2
William Church, Q.C., 31 First St., L9W 2C8 – 519/941-3782, Fax: 519/941-3837 – *1
Evans, Adams & Adams, 107 Broadway St., L9W 1K2 – 519/941-0810, Fax: 519/941-3333 – *2
Shirley Griffin, 47 First St., L9W 2E3 – 519/942-0190 – *1
Richard J. Harbour, 162 Broadway Ave., L9W 1K3 – 519/942-8555, Fax: 519/942-8583 – *1
Margot L. Hornseth, 12 First Ave., L9W 1H8 – 519/941-2620, Fax: 519/941-6888 – *1
Deborah L. MacLeod, 267 Broadway Ave., L9W 1K8 – 519/940-4500, Fax: 519/940-4502 – *1
McAlpine & Vroom, #201, 70 First St., L9W 2E5 – 519/941-0218, Fax: 519/941-8057 – *2
Lorna Paradis, 28 Mill St., L9W 2M3 – 519/942-1042 – *1

* indicates number of lawyers in law firm.

Canadian Almanac & Directory 1997

DIRECTORY OF LAW FIRMS – ONTARIO

Gillian Shute, #18, 28 Mill St., L9W 2M3 – 519/940-0333, Fax: 519/940-0234 – *1

William W. Stutz, 269 Broadway Ave., L9W 1K8 – 519/941-7500, Fax: 519/941-8381 – *1

Tilson & Birchall, 5 Mill St., L9W 2M2 – 519/941-6671, Fax: 519/941-2354 – *2

Wardlaw, Mullin, Carter & Thwaites, 235 Broadway Ave., PO Box 67, L9W 2Z5 – 519/941-1760, Fax: 519/941-3688 – *6

L. Anne Welwood, 14 Zina St., L9W 1E1 – 519/941-9710, Fax: 519/941-9244 – *1

L'ORIGNAL .... Prescott

Tolhurst & Miller, 28 Court St., K0B 1K0 – 613/675-4512, Fax: 613/675-1103

ORILLIA .... Simcoe

Douglas S. Anderson, #B, 190 Memorial Ave., L3V 5X6 – 705/327-1841, Fax: 705/327-3188 – *1

Bourne, Jenkins & Mulligan, 27 Peter St. North, PO Box 368, L3V 6J8 – 705/326-3565, Fax: 705/326-8360 – *3

George Clegg, 31 Peter St. North, PO Box 277, L3V 6J6 – 705/325-6137, Fax: 705/325-4699 – *1

Crawford, Worling, McKenzie & Donnelly, 40 Coldwater St. East, PO Box 520, L3V 6K4 – 705/325-2753, Fax: 705/325-4913 – *6

Richard Crothers, 674 Atherley Rd., PO Box 205, L3V 6J3 – 705/326-2525 – *1

Michael Drury, 4 Cowan St., L3V 4G2 – 705/326-6256 – *1

Margaret P. Eberhard, PO Box 2306, L3V 6V7 – 705/326-8013 – *1

Aubrey J.F. Ford & Associate, 110 Neywash St., PO Box 788, L3V 6K7 – 705/325-7462, Fax: 705/325-8527 – *2

R.C. Allan French, 241 West St. North, PO Box 338, L3V 6J6 – 705/327-6671 – *1

R.M. Haidle, 13 Mississauga St. West, PO Box 2389, L3V 6V7 – 705/325-9524, Fax: 705/325-7079 – *1

W.H. Hamilton, 354 Laclie St., PO Box 2326, L3V 6V7 – 705/325-4556, Fax: 705/325-3108 – *1

W.M. Holdsworth, 63 Coldwater Rd. West, L3V 3L3 – 705/325-4411, Fax: 705/327-3442 – *1

Lowell C. Hunking, 62 Colborne St. East, PO Box 430, L3V 6J8 – 705/329-2615, Fax: 705/788-0222 – *1

Lisa James, 27 Peter St. North, PO Box 368, L3V 6J8 – 705/325-2762, Fax: 705/326-8360 – *1

Linda D. Lewis, 41 Peter St. North, L3V 4Y9 – 705/329-1957, Fax: 705/329-1574 – *1

Scott Lindsey, 273 Coldwater Rd. West, L3V 3M1 – 705/325-3638, Fax: 705/325-8193 – *1

Winsor MacDonnell, 31 Peter St. North, PO Box 277, L3V 6J6 – 705/326-3431, Fax: 705/325-4699 – *1

John H. Madden, Q.C., 62 Colborne St. East, PO Box 430, L3V 6J8 – 705/326-1166, Fax: 705/326-2972 – *1

Nils Peterson, 66 Matchedash St. South, L3V 4W5 – 705/325-5659, Fax: 705/325-0721 – *1

Russell, Christie, Miller, Koughan, 76 Coldwater St. East, PO Box 158, L3V 6J3 – 705/325-1326, Fax: 705/327-1811 – *6

Ronald W. Sillick, 31 Mississauga St. West, PO Box 428, L3V 6J8 – 705/327-5121, Fax: 705/327-5122 – *1

Simcoe Legal Services Clinic, 71 Colborne St. East, PO Box 275, L3V 6J6 – 705/326-6444, Fax: 705/326-9757

R.G. Sparks, 32 Matchedash St. North, PO Box 2357, L3V 6V7 – 705/325-0082, Fax: 705/327-7537 – *1

Stong, Blackburn, Machon, Bohm & Pond, RR#7, L3V 6H7 – 705/329-2983 – *1

Wilford L.S. Trivett, Q.C., 27 Front St. North, PO Box 157, L3V 6J3 – 705/326-3579, Fax: 705/326-3570 – *1

Brian M. Turnbull, #111, 200 Memorial Ave., L3V 5X6 – 705/327-2110, Fax: 705/327-1952 – *1

Bernard J. Varcoe, PO Box 2195, L3V 6S1 – 705/325-2668 – *1

R. Bruce Waite, 241 West St. North, PO Box 338, L3V 6J6 – 705/327-6655, Fax: 705/325-2081 – *2

Zwicker, Evans & Lewis, 93 Coldwater St. East, PO Box 310, L3V 6J7 – 705/325-6146, Fax: 705/325-0044

ORLEANS .... Ottawa-Carleton

Beament, Green, Dust, 2589 St. Joseph Blvd., K1C 1E9 – 613/837-1010, Fax: 613/837-9670 – *4

ORONO .... Durham

W.K. Lycett, Q.C., 5301 Main St., PO Box 87, L0B 1M0 – 905/983-5007, Fax: 905/983-9022 – *1

OSHAWA .... Durham

Affleck & Payne, 197 Bond St. East, L1G 1B4 – 905/436-8400, Fax: 905/436-9959 – *2

James Aitchison, Office Galeria, #185, Oshawa Shopping Centre, PO Box 30608, Stn Centre, L1J 8L8 – 905/433-1174, Fax: 905/433-1645 – *1

Alan Berk, #209, 650 King St. East, L1H 1G5 – 905/579-2888, Fax: 905/579-7586 – *1

Aleksandr Bolotenko, 221 Simcoe St. North, L1G 4T1 – 905/433-1176, Fax: 905/433-0283 – *1

Boychyn & Boychyn, 36 1/2 King St. East, L1H 1B3 – 905/576-2670 – *3

Kay M. Carlson, 106 Stevenson Rd. South, L1J 5M1 – 905/433-0622, Fax: 905/571-7706 – *1

D.H. Creighton, 90 Simcoe St. North, PO Box 2188, L1H 7V4 – 905/579-6561 – *1

Creighton, Victor, Alexander, Hayward & Morison, 235 King St. East, PO Box 26010, Stn 206, L1H 8R4 – 905/723-3446, Fax: 905/432-2323 – *4

Diamond & Fischman, 206 King St. East, PO Box 26008, L1H 8R4 – 905/723-5243, Fax: 905/436-6041 – *3

G.K. Drynan, Q.C., #1001, 44 Bond St. West, L1G 1A4 – 905/576-9304, Fax: 905/432-2380 – *1

Dutka & Associates, 142 Simcoe St. North, L1G 4S7 – 905/571-1411, Fax: 905/436-6098 – *2

Elliott, Hughes & Green, 106 Stevenson Rd. South, L1J 5M1 – 905/571-1774, Fax: 905/571-7706 – *3

Barry L. Evans, 419 King St. West, L1J 2K5 – 905/433-1200, Fax: 905/433-2555 – *1

Farquharson, Adamson, 74 Simcoe St. South, L1H 4G6 – 905/404-1947, Fax: 905/404-9050 – *2

Pasquale Gelsomino, 304 Stevenson Rd. North, L1J 5M9 – 905/571-1916, Fax: 905/571-4254 – *1

Greer, Seiler & Zochodne, 88 Centre St. North, PO Box 917, L1H 7N1 – 905/576-5153, Fax: 905/571-4376 – *3

Harris, Fletcher, Tesluk Associates, 70 Albert St., L1H 4P9 – 905/434-8766, Fax: 905/362-4181 – *2

Higgins, Clark, Cornwall-Taylor, 32 Elgin St. East, L1G 1T1 – 905/434-6411, Fax: 905/571-6114 – *3

Stacy Howell, 1913 Dundas St. East, L1N 2L5 – 905/432-7772, Fax: 905/725-4211

John D. Humphreys, Q.C., 36 1/2 King St. East, L1H 1B3 – 905/571-2555, Fax: 905/725-7299 – *1

Shan K. Jain, Q.C., 215 Simcoe St. North, L1G 4T1 – 905/432-7787, Fax: 905/432-2343 – *1

Kelly, Zuly, Greenway, Bruce, 114 King St. East, PO Box 886, L1H 7N1 – 905/723-2278; 686-5156, Fax: 905/432-2663 – *4

Kitchen, Kitchen, Simeson & McFarlane, 86 Simcoe St. South, PO Box 428, L1H 7L5 – 905/579-5302, Fax: 905/479-6073 – *5

Koziar, Reczulski, 72 Centre St. North, L1G 4B6 – 905/571-3214, Fax: 905/571-3832 – *2

Myrna L. Lack, 174 Athol St. East, PO Box 1098, Stn B, L1J 5Y9 – 905/579-8866, Fax: 905/579-8913 – *1

K.L. Lancaster, 52 Division St., L1G 5L9 – 905/571-3901, Fax: 905/571-4241 – *1

A.E. Laskowsky, 73 Centre St. South, L1H 4A1 – 905/579-0777, Fax: 905/576-9918 – *1

Legal Aid, 500 King St. West, L1J 2K9 – 905/576-2124, Fax: 905/721-1859

Mack, Kisbee & Nicholson, 146 Simcoe St. North, L1G 4S7 – 905/571-1400, Fax: 905/571-0735 – *3

Mackey, Bailey & Korb, #400, 22 King St. West, PO Box 518, L1H 7L9 – 905/436-7600, Fax: 905/576-9427 – *3

MacVicar, MacLean, 850 King St. West, L1J 2L5 – 905/404-2233, Fax: 905/404-2234 – *4

Marks & Marks, 16 Lloyd St., L1H 1X3 – 905/728-5151, Fax: 905/433-4018 – *2

Mazar & Associates, 419 King St. West, L1J 2K5 – 905/571-2558, Fax: 905/571-3548 – *2

McGibbon, Bastedo, Armstrong & Armstrong, National Trust Bldg., 32 Simcoe St. South, PO Box 2396, L1H 7V6 – 905/686-5251, Fax: 905/432-2348 – *3

John N. McKay, 146 Simcoe St. North, L1G 4S7 – 905/571-1400, Fax: 905/571-0735 – *1

McNeely & Kelly, 146 Simcoe St. North, PO Box 735, L1H 7M9 – 905/579-1121, Fax: 905/579-0214 – *2

Kenneth R. McPherson, 85 Bond St. West, L1G 1A6 – 905/434-6555 – *1

Michaels & Michaels, 50 Colborne St. East, PO Box 2395, L1G 1L9 – 905/579-5522 – *3

Frank Minich, 86 Colborne St. West, L1G 1L7 – 905/728-7597, Fax: 905/728-4181 – *1

Joseph Neal, 142 Simcoe St. North, L1G 4S7 – 905/436-9015, Fax: 905/436-6098 – *1

Josef Neubauer, 106 Stevenson Rd. South, L1J 5M1 – 905/433-1991, Fax: 905/433-7038 – *1

O'Brien, Balka & Frayne, 219 King St. East, L1H 1C5 – 905/427-2908, Fax: 905/576-3913 – *3

Palter, McCarthy, 219 King St. East, L1H 1C5 – 905/576-7501, Fax: 905/576-2909 – *2

Margot Poepjes, 231 King St. East, 2nd Fl., L1H 8R4 – 905/433-4020 – *1

Pollitt, Walters, Dizenbach, Bldg Box: 832, 218 Centre St. North, L1G 4C5 – 905/579-1066, Fax: 905/579-6811 – *4

Gregory G. Price, 455 Bond St. East, L1G 1B9 – 905/576-4944, Fax: 905/576-4898 – *1

Reid, Brown & Bell, #202, 200 Bond St. West, L1J 2L7 – 905/571-1301, Fax: 905/576-5022 – *3

Risen, Espey, Scott, Kimball & Olver, Lord Simcoe Place, #1C, 57 Simcoe St. South, PO Box 278, L1H 7L3 – 905/571-3942, Fax: 905/683-4699 – *5

Salmers, Strike & Furlong, 55 William St. East, PO Box 2096, L1H 7V4 – 905/723-1101, Fax: 905/723-1157 – *4

James A. Scott, 1050 Simcoe St. North, L1G 4W5 – 905/571-2001, Fax: 905/571-2002 – *1

Seetner & Associate, 1913 Dundas St. East, L1N 2L5 – 905/725-3350, Fax: 905/725-4211

Stephen F. Shine, 231 King St. East, L1H 8R4 – 905/571-2559, Fax: 905/579-2846 – *1

Sims Brady Thomson & Babbs, #715, 2 Simcoe St. South, PO Box 395, L1H 7L5 – 905/571-2558, Fax: 905/571-3548 – *3

Frank H.M. Stolwyk, 25 Brock St. West, PO Box 235, L1G 1R2 – 905/576-8100, Fax: 905/579-6762 – *1

E.L. Stone, #8B, 50 Richmond St. East, L1G 7C7 – 905/432-3827, Fax: 905/432-3182 – *1

Ronald L. Swartz, 231 Simcoe St. North, L1G 4T1 – 905/576-3392 – *1

Debra J. Sweetman, 111 Simcoe St. North, L1G 4S4 – 905/404-0386, Fax: 905/404-1202

David B. Thomas, 90 Simcoe St. North, L1G 4S2 – 905/576-5666, Fax: 905/576-5289 – *1

George R. Vella, 231 King St. East, L1H 1C5 – 905/576-0520, Fax: 905/576-0326 – *1

J.T. Wilbur, 218 Centre St. North, PO Box 2307, L1H 7V5 – 905/436-0165, Fax: 905/436-0167 – *1

R. Worboy, 153 Simcoe St. North, PO Box 21, L1G 7K8 – 905/723-2288, Fax: 905/576-1355 – *2

OTTAWA .... Ottawa-Carleton

Douglas R. Adams, #400, 100 Sparks St., K1P 5B7 – 613/238-8076, Fax: 613/238-5519 – *1

R.D. Allard, #2, 213 Kent St., K1P 1Z8 – 613/238-2245 – *1

F. James Altimas, PO Box 1168, K1P 5R2 – 613/731-7918, Fax: 613/830-9201 – *1

Janis Apse, #100, 1785 Alta Vista Dr., K1G 3Y6 – 613/738-1713, Fax: 613/738-5056 – *1

Jacqueline Asselin, #110, 261 Cooper St., K2P 0G3 – 613/232-3574 – *1

William T. Badcock, Q.C., 130 Albert St., K1A 0H8 – 613/941-0387, Fax: 613/957-4697 – *1

Gary R. Barnes, #402, 200 Elgin St., K1P 1L5 – 613/238-8111, Fax: 613/238-5551 – *2

Barnes, Sammon, #400, 200 Elgin St., K2P 1L5 – 613/594-8000, Fax: 613/235-7578 – *13

Barrigar & Moss, 81 Metcalfe St., 7th Fl., K1P 6K7 – 613/238-6404, Fax: 613/230-8755 – *4

Bayne, Sellar, Boxall, #500, 200 Elgin St., K2P 1L5 – 613/236-0535, Fax: 613/236-6958 – *6

Beaudet Davidson, #1110, 141 Laurier West, K1P 5J3 – 613/234-8497, Fax: 613/236-0989

Bell, Baker, #500, 116 Lisgar St., K2P 0C2 – 613/237-3444, Fax: 613/237-1413 – *12

Bennett Jones Verchere, #1800, 350 Albert St., PO Box 25, K1R 1A4 – 613/230-4935, Fax: 613/230-3836 – *1

Adèle Berthiaume, #200, 440 Laurier Ave. West, K1R 7X6 – 613/782-2248, Fax: 613/521-8561 – *1

Binks, Simpson, 180 Waller St., K1N 9B9 – 613/233-4063, Fax: 613/233-0450 – *4

Peggy J. Blair, 400 Piccadilly Ave., K1Y 0H4 – 403/722-0947 – *1

Blake, Cassels & Graydon, World Exchange Plaza, 45 O'Connor St., 20th Fl., K1P 1A4 – 613/788-2200, Fax: 613/788-2247; Email: ottawa@blakes.ca – *9

John E. Bogue, #802, 200 Elgin St., K2P 1L5 – 613/234-4901, Fax: 613/236-8906 – *1

Bosada & Associates, 280 Metcalfe St., 2nd Fl., K2P 1R7 – 613/563-1001, Fax: 613/563-1031 – *2

Boyle & Associates, #203, 130 Albert St., K1P 5G4 – 613/238-3434 – *2

Robert N. Boyle, Q.C., 208 - 130 Albert St., K1P 5G4 – 613/238-1304 – *1

Brennan & Hedges, 292 Somerset St. West, K2P 0J6 – 613/238-7733, Fax: 613/234-0954 – *2

Brennan, Tunney & Emond, #300, 200 Elgin St., K1P 1L5 – 613/232-9441, Fax: 613/232-0448

Bulger, Young, #500, 120 Holland Ave., K1Y 0X6 – 613/728-5881, Fax: 613/728-6158 – *4

Burke-Robertson, 70 Gloucester St., K2P 0A2 – 613/233-4195, Fax: 613/235-4430, 233-4195 – *27

Charles, Merovitz & Potechin, #301, 200 Catherine St., K1P 2K9 – 613/563-7544 – *5

Charron, Hollander, Mattar, #440, 325 Dalhousie, K1N 7G2 – 613/236-9951, Fax: 613/232-1166 – *4

Chiarelli, Cramer, Witteveen & Ritchie, 1700 Woodward Dr., K1B 6R1 – 613/723-9100, Fax: 613/723-9105 – *4

Paul-Emile Chiasson, #800, 180 Elgin St., K2P 2K6 – 613/230-8800, Fax: 613/233-6643 – *1

Cogan & Cogan, Bank St. Chambers, 102 Bank St., K1P 5N4 – 613/237-4000, Fax: 613/237-4906 – *4

Conlin & McAlpin, 1678 Bank St., K1V 7Y6 – 613/737-4140, Fax: 613/737-7903 – *3

Counsellor Law Offices, #4000, 210 Gladstone Ave., K1P 0Y6 – 613/237-0505 – *5

Curran Associates, 1125 Baxter Rd., K2C 3R4 – 613/596-2804, Fax: 613/596-2316 – *2

Daigneault & Caron, #201, 200 Elgin St., K1P 1L5 – 613/238-4411, Fax: 613/238-4413 – *1

Davis & Company, World Exchange Plaza, #810, 45 O'Connor St., K1P 1A4 – 613/235-9444, Fax: 613/232-7525

Dent & Francis, #300, 309 Cooper St., K2P 0G5 – 613/232-9611 – *1

Dixon McCulloch & More, #314, 2249 Carling Ave., K1B 7E9 – 613/726-1136, Fax: 613/726-0097 – *3

Dunlap, Dunlap & McInenly, 1350 Wellington St., K1Y 3C1 – 613/729-0572 – *3

Farber, Segal & Robillard, Westboro Manor, 330 Churchill Ave., K1Z 5B9 – 613/722-9418, Fax: 613/722-5981 – *3

Michael J. Farrell, 34 Hawthorne Ave., K1S 0B1 – 613/238-8006, Fax: 613/230-8855 – *1

Finlayson & Singlehurst, 70 Gloucester St., 4th Fl., K2P 0A2 – 613/232-0227, Fax: 613/232-0542 – *3

Ann L. Flint, #203, 190 Somerset St. West, K2P 0J4 – 613/594-5461 – *1

Forbes, Singer & Smith, 302 Waverley St., K2P 0W3 – 613/238-1424, Fax: 613/238-6741 – *4

Fortey, Scott & McGuire, #420, 1335 Carling Ave., K1Z 8N8 – 613/725-3723, Fax: 613/729-8613 – *3

Fraser & Beatty, #1200, 180 Elgin St., K2P 2K7 – 613/783-9611, Fax: 613/238-6294 – *6

Gibson & Augustine, #1520, 360 Albert St., K1R 7X7 – 613/238-8865, Fax: 613/238-7930 – *4

Goldberg, Shinder, Gardner & Kronick, 280 Slater St., 18th Fl., K1P 1C2 – 613/237-4922, Fax: 613/237-2920; Email: gsgklaw@ottawa.net – *11

Goss, Chan, 211 Pretoria Ave., K1S 1X1 – 613/563-0105 – *3

Gowlings, #2600, 160 Elgin St., PO Box 466, Stn D, K1P 1C3 – 613/233-1781, Fax: 613/563-9869; Email: marketing@gowlings.com; URL: http://www.gowlings.com – *103

Shirley E. Greenberg, #330, 440 Laurier Ave. West, K1R 7X6 – 613/235-7774, Fax: 613/230-7356 – *1

Ronald G. Guertin, #601, 200 Elgin St., K2P 1L5 – 613/238-5448, Fax: 613/238-4824 – *1

Hale & May, #500, 77 Metcalfe St., K1P 5L6 – 613/230-6524, Fax: 613/237-1156 – *2

Hall, Ray & Button, #508, 359 Kent St., K2P 0R6 – 613/232-4848, Fax: 613/232-3662 – *2

Hamilton Appotive Callan, 150 Metcalfe St., 11th Fl., K2P 1P1 – 613/238-8400, Fax: 613/238-4085 – *8

James D. Harbic, #700, 200 Elgin St., K2P 1L5 – 613/235-4365, Fax: 613/237-9450 – *1

Hendin, Hendin & Lyon, #726, 50 O'Connor St., K1P 6L2 – 613/563-4804, Fax: 613/563-3878 – *7

Hewitt, Hewitt, Nesbitt, Reid, Fuller Bldg., #604, 75 Albert St., K1P 5E7 – 613/563-0202, Fax: 613/563-0445 – *12

Honey, MacMillan, Gilhooly & Baldwin, 146 Richmond Rd., K1Z 6W2 – 613/722-2493, Fax: 613/722-2773 – *4

Hughes & Hughes, #604, 225 Metcalfe St., K2P 1P9 – 613/563-1131, Fax: 613/230-8297 – *4

Hughes, Laishley, Touhey & Sigouin, 116 Lisgar St., K1P 0C2 – 613/236-7333, Fax: 613/236-7075 – *7

Ken James & Associates, #906, 75 Albert St., K1P 5E7 – 613/236-2966, Fax: 613/236-8169 – *6

Johnston & Buchan, #1700, 275 Slater St., K1P 5H9 – 613/236-3882, Fax: 613/230-6423; Email: johnbuch@magi.com – *13

Eric A. Johnston, 111 Percy St., K1R 6C5 – 613/560-6025, ext.1215, Fax: 613/560-1383 – *1

Karr & Associates, #700, 222 Somerset St. West, K2P 2G3 – 613/236-9001, Fax: 613/236-9059 – *2

Kealey & Batts, #401, 2249 Carling Ave., K2B 7E9 – 613/828-7710 – *2

Kealey & Kealey, 451 Metcalfe St., K2P 1T1 – 613/238-4611, Fax: 613/238-8672 – *2

Kelly, Howard, Santini, #320, 2249 Carling Ave., K2B 7E9 – 613/238-6321, Fax: 613/596-5695 – *1

J.K. Kerr, Q.C., 71 Bank St., K1P 5N2 – 613/232-7902 – *1

Kershman & Warren, 283 McLeod St., K2P 1A1 – 613/238-1924, Fax: 613/238-4490; Email: info@bankruptlaw.com; URL: http://www.bankruptlaw.com – *1

Morris Kertzer, #902, 200 Elgin St., K2P 1L5 – 613/236-0743 – *1

L. Kos-Rabcewicz-Zubkowski, 214 Roger Road, K1H 5C6 – 613/737-3116; 232-1476, Fax: 613/564-9800 – *1

Lafleur & Aubin, 45 Rideau St., K1P 0Y1 – 613/235-5159 – *1

Lalonde, Chartrand, Colonnier & O'Connor, 214, ch Montreal Rd, K1L 8E3 – 613/745-9446 – *4

Lang Michener, #300, 50 O'Connor St., K1P 6L2 – 613/232-7171, Fax: 613/231-3191 – *25

Lavery, de Billy, 48 O'Connor St., K1P 1A4 – 613/594-4936, Fax: 613/594-8783

Lavery, O'Brien, #1600, 50 O'Connor St., K1P 6L2 – 613/238-2229 – *1

Lette, Whittaker, #1000, 100 Sparks St., PO Box 2486, Stn D, K1P 5W6 – 613/232-8389, 237-6430, Fax: 613/563-7671 – *7

Robert A. Lewis & Associates, #301, 1889 Baseline Rd., K2C 0C7 – 613/226-8815, Fax: 613/226-4930 – *1

Low, Murchison, #1200, 220 Laurier Ave. West, K1P 5Z9 – 613/236-9442, Fax: 613/236-7942 – *12

Macera & Jarzyna, 81 Metcalfe St., 12th Fl., PO Box 2088, Stn D, K1P 5W3 – 613/238-8173, Fax: 613/235-2508; Email: macjar@ibm.net – *8

J. William MacKinnon, Q.C., 46 Dunvelan Rd., K1K 3L3 – 613/746-6038, Fax: 613/746-6038 – *1

Maclaren, Corlett, #450, 45 O'Connor St., K1P 1A4 – 613/233-1146, Fax: 613/233-7190 – *9

Kay V. Marshall, 1875 Highland Terrace, K1H 5A5 – 613/526-3908, Fax: 613/233-3154 – *1

Mayo, Curley, Siu, #16, 99 - 5 Ave., K1S 5K4 – 613/232-1178, Fax: 613/232-2672 – *3

McCann & Giamberardino Law Office, #300, 222 Somerset St. West, K2P 2G3 – 613/236-1410, Fax: 613/563-1367 – *3

McCarthy Tétrault, #1000, 275 Sparks St., K1R 7X9 – 613/238-2000, Fax: 613/563-9386 – *9

McGuire, Mills & Harrington, #1408, 1 Nicholas St., K1N 7B7 – 613/236-0695, Fax: 613/236-0914 – *4

Ronald McGurk, 1130 Agincourt Rd., K2C 2H7 – 613/224-4443, Fax: 613/224-0828 – *1

McHugh Devine, 182 Isabella St., K1S 1V8 – 613/237-5610, Fax: 613/235-7996 – *4

McKechnie, Tallim, #702, 325 Dalhousie St., K1N 7G2 – 613/232-1976 – *2

R. Warden McKimm, #1201, 180 Elgin St., K1P 2K7 – 613/238-6294 – *1

William R. Meredith, Q.C., 141 Laurier Ave. West, K1P 5J3 – 613/238-2001, Fax: 613/238-8727 – *1

T.P. Metrick, Q.C., #1508, 1 Nicholas St., K1N 7B7 – 613/232-1735 – *1

Marthe Montreuil, #110, 261 Cooper St., K2P 0G3 – 613/232-3574 – *1

J.C. Moore, #201, 117 Murray St., K1N 5M5 – 613/233-9334 – *1

J.B. More, #200, 1320 Carling Ave., K1Z 7K8 – 613/725-2002, Fax: 613/725-0675 – *1

Donald A. Morgan, #505, 200 Elgin St., K2P 1L5 – 613/234-9571 – *1

Anne L. Moxley, #204, 185 Somerset St. West, K2P 0J2 – 613/832-4378, Fax: 613/832-0745 – *1

Nahwegahbow Jones, 1338 Wellington St., K1Y 3B7 – 613/729-9491, Fax: 613/729-6903 – *3

Nelligan Power, #1900, 66 Slater St., K1P 5H1 – 613/238-8080, Fax: 613/238-2098; Email: cchoquet@nplaw.com – *41

Neville & Selkirk, 222 Somerset St. West, 3rd Fl., K2P 2G3 – 613/237-7092, Fax: 613/237-1156 – *2

Nicholls & Jennings, #1000, 100 Sparks St., K1P 5B7 – 613/238-8300, Fax: 613/563-7671 – *2

Nicol & Lazier, #400, 331 Cooper St., K1P 0G5 – 613/232-4241 – *3

Niebergall Bowles & Shelston, #300, 200 Elgin St., K1P 1L5 – 613/232-8508, Fax: 613/232-0448 – *5

Noble & Gadient, Toronto-Dominion Bank Bldg., #203, 245 Stafford Rd., K1H 9E8 – 613/726-9500, Fax: 613/596-9958 – *2

O'Connor, Lavigne & Engel King, #504, 1 Nicholas St., K1N 7B7 – 613/235-4366, Fax: 613/235-0971 – *2

O'Dea, Earle, 151 Slater St., K1P 5H3 – 613/238-2327 – *1

Ogilvy Renault, #1600, 45 O'Connor St., K1P 1A4 – 613/780-8661, Fax: 613/230-5459 – *13

Osler, Hoskin & Harcourt, #1500, 50 O'Connor St., K1P 6L2 – 613/235-7234, Fax: 613/235-2867;

* indicates number of lawyers in law firm.

Canadian Almanac & Directory 1997

Email: counsel@osler.com; URL: http://www.osler.com – *32
Paradis Jones Pollon Horowitz, #401, 200 Elgin St., K1P 1L5 – 613/238-5074 – *4
Perley-Robertson, Panet, Hill & McDougall, #830, 99 Bank St., K1P 6C1 – 613/238-2022, Fax: 613/238-8775 – *41
Perley-Robertson, Panet, Hill & McDougall, 99 Bank St., K1P 6C1 – 613/238-2022, Fax: 613/238-8775
Piazza, Polowin, Brooks & Siddons, 66 Lisgar St., K1P 0C1 – 613/238-2244 – *4
Potvin Law Office, Gillin Bldg., #1000, 141 Laurier Ave. West, K1P 5J3 – 613/236-6628, Fax: 613/234-7529 – *2
W.F. Prachter, #1212, 130 Albert St., K1P 5G4 – 613/232-2683 – *1
Helene Bruce Puccini, #800, 180 Elgin St., K2P 2K3 – 613/230-6295, Fax: 613/594-8729 – *1
Peter A. Pyper, #300, 100 Sparks St., K1P 5B7 – 613/230-5443, Fax: 613/230-2238 – *1
Quain, Dioguardi, #700, 200 Elgin St., K2P 1L5 – 613/237-2222 – *4
Natu P. Radia, #314, 2249 Carling Ave., K1B 7E9 – 613/726-1136
Radnoff, Pearl, Slover, Swedko, Dwoskin, 100 Gloucester St., K2P 0A4 – 613/594-8844, Fax: 613/594-9092 – *9
Raven, Jewitt & Allen, 1600 - 220 Laurier Ave. West, K1P 5Z9 – 613/567-2901 – *8
Shirley Ramey Rayes, #415, 396 Cooper St., K2P 2H7 – 613/563-3098 – *1
Richer & Richer, #702, 325 Dalhousie St., K1N 7G2 – 613/238-1401 – *2
Rock, Talarico, Wong, 355 Waverley St., K2P 0W4 – 613/232-1161, Fax: 613/594-8630 – *5
Larry A. Roine, #203, 1419 Carling Ave., K1Z 7L6 – 613/729-1171, Fax: 613/729-3781 – *1
Scott & Aylen, 60 Queen St., K1P 5Y7 – 613/237-5160, Fax: 613/230-8842 – *42
M.S. Shaikh, #505, 200 Elgin St., K2P 1L5 – 613/234-9571 – *1
Shanbaum & Semanyk, #700, 81 Metcalfe St., 7th Fl., K1P 6K7 – 613/238-6969, Fax: 613/238-8724 – *2
Shapiro, Cohen, Andrews, Finlayson, 112 Kent St., PO Box 3440, Stn D, K1P 6P1 – 613/232-5300 – *6
Shepherd Grenville-Wood, 43 Florence St., K2P 0W6 – 613/232-2688, Fax: 613/232-2680 – *3
Glenn R. Sheppy, PO Box 500, Stn A, K1N 8T7
Sim & Morrison, #1400, 130 Albert St., K1P 5G4 – 613/237-2355, Fax: 613/237-0042 – *3
Smart & Biggar, #900, 55 Metcalfe St., PO Box 2999, Stn D, K1P 5Y6 – 613/232-2486, Fax: 613/232-8440 – *18
Smith Lyons, #1700, 45 O'Connor St., K1P 1A4 – 613/230-3988, Fax: 613/230-7085 – *5
Soloway, Wright, Victor, 427 Laurier Ave. West, 9th Fl., K1R 7Y2 – 613/236-0111, Fax: 613/238-8507 – *17
R. Ben Sorensen, Q.C., 1315 Richmond Rd., K1B 8J7 – 613/596-1792, Fax: 613/569-6289 – *1
Sterling & Young, 1510 Merivale Rd., K2G 3J6 – 613/224-7799, Fax: 613/224-9150 – *1
Stikeman, Elliott, #914, 50 O'Connor St., K1P 6L2 – 613/234-4555, Fax: 613/230-8877 – *11
Thom, Malcolm & Associates, #701, 150 The Driveway, K2P 1E7 – 613/594-3469, Fax: 613/594-8985 – *1
Thomas & Winship, #303, 251 Bank St., K2P 1X3 – 613/235-6721 – *2
Eileen Mitchell Thomas, Q.C., #500, 77 Metcalfe St., K1P 5L6 – 613/230-6316, Fax: 613/232-1156 – *1
Tierney, Tierney, Tierney, Stauffer, 175 Holland Ave., 2nd Fl., K1Y 0Y2 – 613/728-8057, Fax: 613/728-9866 – *7
Gilad Vered, 1801 Woodward Dr., K2C 0R3 – 613/226-2000, Fax: 613/225-0391 – *1
Vice & Hunter, 344 Frank St., K2P 0Y1 – 613/232-5773, Fax: 613/232-3509 – *4

Vincent Dagenais Gour Roy, #600, 325 Dalhousie St., K1N 7G2 – 613/238-2701, Fax: 613/235-2599 – *11
Robert Wakefield, 169 Lisgar St., K2P 0C3 – 613/238-1895 – *1
G.D. Warren, #700, 200 Elgin St., K2P 1L5 – 613/236-0852 – *1
Wentzell & Wentzell, #204, 190 Somerset St. West, K2P 0J4 – 613/235-6756 – *2
Wilson, Monaghan, #707, 141 Laurier Ave. West, K1P 5J3 – 613/238-1515, Fax: 613/238-1323 – *8

OWEN SOUND .... **Grey**
Herbert E. Boyce, Canada Trust Bldg., #201, 983 - 2 Ave. East, PO Box 968, N4K 6H6 – 519/371-4160, Fax: 519/371-1604 – *1
P.S. Dykstra, 151 - 8 St. East, PO Box 906, N4K 6H6 – 519/376-4500, Fax: 519/376-7273 – *1
Greenfield & Barrie, 142 - 10 St. West, PO Box 665, N4K 5R4 – *2
Edward P. Horton, Q.C., 1390 - 2 Ave. West, PO Box 787, N4K 5W9 – 519/376-8650, Fax: 519/371-3512 – *2
Catherine A. Laing, 935 - 2 Ave. West, PO Box 664, N4K 5R4 – 519/371-2202, Fax: 519/376-4683 – *1
McKerroll & McKerroll, 854 - 1 Ave. West, PO Box 607, N4K 5R4 – 519/376-2050, Fax: 519/371-1256 – *3
Middlebro & Stevens, 1030 - 2 Ave. East, PO Box 100, N4K 5P1 – 519/376-8730, Fax: 519/376-7135 – *4
Julia A. Morneau, 935 - 2 Ave. West, PO Box 664, N4K 5R4 – 519/371-0148, Fax: 519/376-4683 – *1
Murray, Thomson, 912 - 2 Ave. West, PO Box 1060, N4K 6K6 – 519/376-6350, Fax: 519/376-0835 – *3
Van Wyck, Kirby, 930 -1 Ave. West, PO Box 730, N4K 5W9 – 519/376-7450, Fax: 519/376-8288 – *5

PAISLEY .... **Bruce**
Patrick L.J. Kelly, PO Box 190, N0G 2N0 – 519/353-5697 – *1

PALMERSTON .... **Wellington**
Fallis, Fallis & McMillan, 233 Main St., N0G 2P0 – 519/343-3527, Fax: 519/343-3528 – *3
Nesbitt Coulter Carr, PO Box 309, N0G 2P0 – 519/343-3796, Fax: 519/539-6832 – *1

PARIS .... **Brant**
Thomas H. Buck, 139 Grand River St. North, N3L 2M4 – 519/442-2218, Fax: 519/442-6810 – *1
Theresa A. McClenaghan, 7 William St. North, N3L 1K7 – 519/442-5571, 5572, Fax: 519/442-5567; Email: tmcclena@web – *1

PARKHILL .... **Middlesex**
Robert G. Waters, 197 Main St., N0M 2K0 – 519/294-6884 – *1

PARRY SOUND .... **Parry Sound**
Larry W. Douglas, #201, 1 Church St., PO Box 520, P2A 2X5 – 705/746-9471, Fax: 705/746-9606 – *2
David A. Holmes, #10, 16 Seguin St., P2A 1B1 – 705/746-4223, Fax: 705/746-6368 – *1
A. Wayne Piddington, #1, 43A James St., P2A 1T6 – 705/746-9365, Fax: 705/746-7159 – *1
Powell & Powell, 34 Mary St., P2A 1E4 – 705/746-8756, Fax: 705/746-2336 – *2
Powell, Cunningham, Kennedy & Grandy, 88 James St., P2A 1T9 – 705/746-4207, Fax: 705/746-2945 – *6
D. Andrew Thomson, 7 William St., P2A 1V2 – 705/746-5938, Fax: 705/746-4351 – *1
Joseph B. Wilson, 97 James St., P2A 1T7 – 705/746-4215, Fax: 705/746-5357 – *1
Wyjad & Associates, 43A James St., P2A 1T7 – 705/746-7760, Fax: 705/746-7551

PEMBROKE .... **Renfrew**
Kenneth J. Conroy, 358 Pembroke St. East, PO Box 1266, K8A 6Y6 – 613/735-0645, Fax: 613/732-2603 – *1
B. Lynne Felhaber, 258 Nelson St., K8A 6X9 – 613/735-0666, Fax: 613/732-8825 – *1
Huckabone, Shaw, O'Brien, Radley-Walters & Reimer, 284 Pembroke St. East, PO Box 487, K8A 6X7 – 613/735-2341, Fax: 613/735-0920 – *9
Johnson, Fraser, 259 Pembroke St. East, K8A 3J9 – 613/735-0624, Fax: 613/735-0625 – *1
Bruce Leach, 256 Nelson St., PO Box 546, K8A 6X7 – 613/735-1013, Fax: 613/732-8825 – *1
McCann & Sheppard, 290 Pembroke St. East, PO Box 817, K8A 7M5 – 613/732-3621, Fax: 613/732-3594 – *3
Rod L. Sauriol, 238 Pembroke St. West, K8A 6X1 – 613/735-0654 – *1
H. Graham Walsh, Q.C., 220 Pembroke St. East, K8A 6X3 – 613/732-3625, Fax: 613/732-8040 – *2

PENETANGUISHENE .... **Simcoe**
Deacon Taws Friend, 90 Main St., PO Box 869, L0K 1P0 – 705/549-3131, Fax: 705/549-4682 – *3
Kathleen D. Flint, 4 Robert West, L0K 1P0 – 705/549-4367, Fax: 705/549-4349 – *1
Hacker Gignac Rice, 142 Main St., PO Box 599, L0K 1P0 – 705/549-3114, Fax: 705/549-4415
A.W. Rubens, 67A Robert St. West, L0K 1P0 – 705/549-7487, Fax: 705/549-7487 – *1

PERTH .... **Lanark**
Barker, Willson, Butterworth, James & Scott, 31 Foster St., PO Box 308, K7H 3E4 – 613/267-2800, Fax: 613/267-4852 – *6
O'Donnell, Dulmage, Bond, March & Anderson, 10 Market Square, K7H 1V7 – 613/267-1212, Fax: 613/267-7059 – *4
Michael P. Reid, 83 Gore St. East, PO Box 63, K7H 3E2 – 613/267-7280, Fax: 613/267-7285 – *1
Rubino & Chaplin, 10A Gore St. West, PO Box 338, K7H 3E4 – 613/267-5227, Fax: 613/267-3951 – *1
K.W. Smith, 27 Foster St., PO Box 157, K7H 3E3 – 613/267-5910, Fax: 613/264-0789 – *1

PETAWAWA .... **Renfrew**
Huckabone, Shaw, O'Brien, Radley-Walters & Reimer, 7 Hilda St., PO Box 148, K8H 2X2 – 613/687-8128 – *10
Roche & Dakin, 17 Hwy. 31, PO Box 38, K8H 2X1 – 613/687-2223, Fax: 613/584-4922

PETERBOROUGH .... **Peterborough**
Richard Aitken, 308 Park St. North, PO Box 1237, K9J 3W5 – 705/742-0440 – *1
R.W. Beninger, 310 Rubidge St., PO Box 310, K9J 7X6 – 705/743-0065, Fax: 705/742-8718 – *1
William M. Carruthers, 404 Water St., PO Box 1117, K9J 7H4 – 705/743-6471, Fax: 705/743-9306 – *1
Roger Clark, 220 Simcoe St., PO Box 1328, K9J 7H5 – 705/743-9070, Fax: 705/743-7484 – *1
Corkery & Corkery, 164 Hunter St. West, PO Box 331, K9J 6Z3 – 705/742-3869, Fax: 705/742-7311 – *2
G.W. Coros, 394A George St. North, K9H 3R3 – 705/748-4311, Fax: 705/748-3332 – *1
Crook & Collins, 257 George St. North, PO Box 1539, K9J 7H7 – 705/742-5415
H. Girvin Devitt, 858 Chemong Rd., K9H 5Z8 – 705/742-5471 – *1
M.J. Dwyer, 359 Aylmer St. North, PO Box 327, K9J 7A5 – 705/743-4221, Fax: 705/743-2187 – *1
Farquharson Daly, 161 Hunter St. West, PO Box 1087, K9J 7H4 – 705/742-9241, Fax: 705/741-1601 – *3
J.E. Fitzpatrick, Q.C., 331 Reid St., PO Box 1155, K9J 7H5 – 705/743-9334, Fax: 705/743-7253 – *1
Galvin, Murphy & Bosch, 176 McDonnel St., PO Box 1118, K9J 7H4 – 705/743-7500 – *3

Gowland, Boriss, 371 Reid St., K9H 4G4 – 705/743-7252, Fax: 705/743-1850 – *3
Grant, Whetung & Willcox, 457 Water St., PO Box 29, K9J 6Y5 – 705/743-6470, Fax: 705/743-3128 – *3
Howell, Fleming, 415 Water St., PO Box 148, K9J 6Y5 – 705/745-1361, Fax: 705/745-6220 – *9
Rod E. Johnston, 244 Aylmer St. North, PO Box 1718, K9J 7X6 – 705/748-2241, Fax: 705/748-9125 – *2
E.J. Jordan, 359 Aylmer St. North, PO Box 327, K9J 7A5 – 705/743-4221, Fax: 705/743-2187 – *1
Lech, Lightbody & O'Brien, 116 Hunter St. West, PO Box 809, K9J 7A2 – 705/742-3844, Fax: 705/742-0121 – *3
MacDougall & McGarrity, 438 Sheridan St., PO Box 775, K9J 7A2 – 705/743-1822, Fax: 705/743-4870 – *2
McMichael, Davidson, 172 Hunter St. West, K9H 2L2 – 705/745-0571, Fax: 705/745-0411 – *2
Millard, Johnston, McGillen, 244 Aylmer St. North, PO Box 1718, K9J 7X6 – 705/748-2241, Fax: 705/748-9125 – *3
Moldaver, McFadden & Moorcroft, 121 George St. North, K9J 7H6 – 705/743-1801, Fax: 705/743-0397 – *3
M.B. Moser, 184 Charlotte St., PO Box 717, K9J 6Z8 – 705/748-5661 – *1
Harry W. Robertson, 191 Hunter St. West, K9H 2L1 – 705/741-3337 – *1
John S. Robertson, Q.C., 191 Hunter St. West, K9H 2L1 – 705/741-2220 – *1
G.H. Usher, 359 Aylmer St. North, PO Box 327, K9J 6Z3 – 705/743-4221, Fax: 705/743-8692 – *1
Douglas F. Walker, 308 Park St. North, PO Box 1237, K9J 7H5 – 705/748-3012, Fax: 705/748-2746 – *1
J. Ross Whittington, 359 Aylmer St. North, PO Box 327, K9J 6Z3 – 705/743-4221, Fax: 705/743-8692 – *1
J.C. Edgar Wood, PO Box 565, K9J 6Z6 – 705/743-9320 – *1

PETROLIA .... **Lambton**
F. Jordan Edward, PO Box 125, N0N 1R0 – 519/882-0510 – *1

PICKERING .... **Durham**
Daniel A. Barna, 1848 Liverpool Rd., L1V 1W3 – 905/831-8000, Fax: 905/831-1493 – *1
Stephen A. Cooper, #703, 1305 Pickering Pkwy., L1V 3P2 – 905/686-6406, Fax: 905/837-7762 – *1
G.W. Edmiston, 1281 Commerce St., L1W 1C7 – 905/839-8270 – *1
John G. Howes, #702, 1305 Pickering Pkwy., L1V 3P2 – 905/420-8628, Fax: 905/420-8634; Email: 1-800-373-6641 – *1
Scott Magder, 1 Evelyn Ave., L1V 1N3 – 905/509-3720, Fax: 905/509-5270 – *1
Ronald A. Rubinoff, 1020 Brock Rd., L1W 3H2 – 905/839-1195, Fax: 905/839-1345 – *1
Henry Silver, 345 Kingston Rd., L1V 1A1 – 905/509-2556, Fax: 905/509-5441 – *1
Harvey Storm, 1128 Kingston Rd., L1V 1B4 – 905/839-5121, Fax: 905/420-4062 – *1
Murray Stroud, 356 Kingston Rd., L1V 1A2 – 905/509-1353, Fax: 905/509-2370 – *2
Cameron J.H. Suggitt, #209, 1550 Kingston Rd., L1V 1C3 – 905/420-4020, Fax: 905/420-4508 – *1
G.P. Vanular, 1460 Bayly St., L1W 1L8 – 905/837-0340, Fax: 905/837-0994 – *1
Timothy Vanular, #13, 1450 Kingston Rd., L1V 1C1 – 905/427-4886, Fax: 905/420-0808 – *1
Walker, Head, Corporate Centre, #506, 1305 Pickering Pkwy., L1V 3P2 – 905/839-4484, Fax: 905/420-1073 – *6

PICTON .... **Prince Edward**
Campbell & Mathers, 194 Main St., PO Box 1260, K0K 2T0 – 613/476-2366, 2733, Fax: 613/476-6064 – *1
Hurley & Williams, 199 Main St., PO Box 1200, K0K 2T0 – 613/476-3241, Fax: 613/476-5985 – *2

Walmsley & Walmsley, 340 Main St., PO Box 1500, K0K 2T0 – 613/476-5516 – *1
Jack H. Ward, 51 Mary St., PO Box 530, K0K 2T0 – 613/476-3640, Fax: 613/476-3435 – *1

POINT EDWARD .... **Lambton**
Dawson, Carpento & Gallaway, #202, 805 North Christina St., N7V 1X6 – 519/337-2321, Fax: 519/332-6588 – *3
Elliott, Porter, McFadyen & McFadyen, 137 Kendall St., N7V 4G6 – 519/336-4600, Fax: 519/336-0400 – *4

PORT CARLING .... **Muskoka**
Grimmett & Fraser, 2 Bailey St., PO Box 365, P0B 1J0 – 705/765-3191, Fax: 705/765-6740 – *2

PORT COLBORNE .... **Niagara South**
Brendon J. Bulger, 333 Wellington St., L3K 2K4 – 905/835-1445, Fax: 905/834-9085 – *1
Davies, Ebert & Wilson, 190 Elm St., PO Box 99, L3K 5V7 – 905/835-1163, Fax: 905/835-2171 – *3
F.N. Gibbs, 262 Catherine St., L3K 4K9 – 905/835-5650, Fax: 905/732-1015 – *1
Macdonald, Tuck & Associates, 196 West St., PO Box 334, L3K 5W1 – 905/834-4525, Fax: 905/834-3254 – *3
Maloney & Maloney, 178 Clarence St., L3K 5V8 – 905/835-5633, Fax: 905/835-8801 – *2
Reilly, Railton & Lambie, PO Box 127, L3K 5V8 – 905/835-1141, Fax: 905/835-2185 – *3

PORT DOVER .... **Norfolk**
A.M. Lee Gaunt, 110 St. Andrew St., PO Box 580, N0A 1N0 – 519/583-1411, Fax: 519/583-1110 – *1
Oswald W. Stahl, 725 Main St., PO Box 610, N0A 1N0 – 519/583-2460, Fax: 519/583-1772 – *1

PORT ELGIN .... **Bruce**
George D. Gruetzner, 667 Goderich St., PO Box 10, N0H 2C0 – 519/832-2482 – *1
Ryder & Planz, 669 Gustavus St., PO Box 209, N0H 2C0 – 519/832-6941, Fax: 519/832-2537 – *2

PORT HOPE .... **Northumberland**
Brooks, Harrison, Mann & McCracken, 114 Walton St., L1A 1N5 – 905/885-2451, 7291, Fax: 905/885-7474 – *4
Bruce H. Coleman, 50 Walton St., L1A 1N1 – 905/885-8149, Fax: 905/885-7471 – *1
Wilfred A. Day, 45 Mill St. South, PO Box 65, L1A 3V9 – 905/885-8118, Fax: 905/885-7470 – *1
A. Ronald Good, 11 Mill St. North, PO Box 208, L1A 3W3 – 905/885-2428, Fax: 905/885-6060 – *1
James Thomas Hunt, 4 Diane Pl., L1A 3Y6 – 905/885-2874
Gordon C. Kelly, Q.C., 160 Walton St., L1A 1N6 – 905/885-8127, Fax: 905/885-8129 – *1

PORT PERRY .... **Durham**
Fowler, Davies, 175 North St., L9L 1B7 – 905/985-8411, Fax: 905/985-0029 – *4
Harris, Fletcher, Tesluk Associates, 171 Shanly St., L9L 1J4 – 905/985-8488 – *2
Siksay & Fraser Law Offices, 204 Casimir St., L9L 1B7 – 905/985-4141, Fax: 905/985-4595
George L. Smith, 226 Queen St., PO Box 5243, L9L 1B9 – 905/985-8465, Fax: 905/985-3758 – *1

POWASSAN .... **Parry Sound**
R.J. van der Wijst, PO Box 428, P0H 1Z0 – 705/724-3520 – *1

PRESCOTT .... **Grenville**
Peter R. Adams, 111 King St. West, K0E 1T0 – 613/925-2825, Fax: 613/925-2826 – *1
Beaumont & Laushway, 214 King St. West, PO Box 190, K0E 1T0 – *1

R.M. Tobin, 257 King St. West, PO Box 760, K0E 1T0 – 613/925-2853, Fax: 613/925-5741 – *1

RED LAKE .... **Kenora**
Glenda R. Bishop, PO Box 323, P0V 2M0 – 807/727-3256, Fax: 807/727-3948 – *1
Russel S. Smart, #201, Discovery Rd. Centre, PO Box 307, P0V 2M0 – 807/727-3200, Fax: 807/727-1126 – *1

RENFREW .... **Renfrew**
Chown & Crosby, 297 Raglan St. South, PO Box 188, K7V 4A3 – 613/432-3669, Fax: 613/432-2874 – *2
Dawe & Edmondstone, PO Box 332, K7V 4A4 – 613/432-4513, Fax: 613/432-5011 – *2
Lawrence E. Gallagher, 33 Renfrew Ave. East, PO Box 481, K7V 4B1 – 613/432-8537, Fax: 613/432-8538 – *1
McNab, Stewart & Prince, 117 Raglan St. South, PO Box 338, K7V 4A4 – 613/432-5844, Fax: 613/432-7832 – *4
N. Jane Wilson, 29 Raglan St. South, PO Box 520, K7V 4B1 – 613/432-4806, Fax: 613/432-2453 – *1

RICHARDS LANDING .... **Algoma**
Bradley J. Allison, PO Box 234, P0R 1J0 – 705/246-2901, Fax: 705/246-1058 – *1

RICHMOND HILL .... **York**
Ken Anders, 176 Stouffville Rd., L4E 3P4 – 905/773-1290, Fax: 905/773-1659 – *1
Joseph G. Argier, 70 Leek Cres., L4B 1H1 – 905/882-8666, Fax: 905/882-1082 – *1
D.E. Buckman, 34 Tomlin Cres., L4C 7T1 – 905/737-4721 – *1
R. Laurent Carrier, 69 Red Oak Dr., L4B 1W2 – 905/731-4951, Fax: 905/731-4951 – *1
Christie, Saccucci, Matthews, Caskie & Chilco, #202, 9050 Yonge St., L4C 9S6 – 905/882-2211, Fax: 905/882-5585 – *1
Stephen Codas, 9555 Yonge St., L4C 9M5 – 905/883-8212, Fax: 905/737-7691 – *1
Counter & Mitchell, PO Box 2959, Stn B, L4E 3C5 – 905/773-4301, Fax: 905/773-7439 – *2
Stanley C. Ehrlich, 330 Hwy 7 East, L4B 3P8 – 905/881-7209 – *1
Jack Elie, #700, 225 East Beaver Creek, L4B 3P4 – 905/731-2189, Fax: 905/731-5534
S.P. Fienberg, 116 Church St. South, L4C 1W3 – 905/883-5557, Fax: 905/883-4619 – *1
Filipovich, Nielsen, #314, 9050 Yonge St., L4C 9S6 – 905/764-2505, Fax: 905/764-2507 – *2
Roger A. Gosbee, #310, 350 Hwy 7 East, L4B 3N2 – 905/882-2559, Fax: 905/882-9573 – *1
P.C. Hengen, 10330 Yonge St., L4C 5N1 – 905/884-9257, Fax: 905/884-9470 – *1
Martin M. Herman, #202, 9350 Yonge St., L4C 5G2 – 905/884-0222, Fax: 905/884-0442 – *1
Richard M Ittleman, #206, 10350 Yonge St., L4C 5K9 – 905/737-8284, Fax: 905/737-8289 – *1
Jordan Kolman, #700, 225 East Beaver Creek Rd., L4B 3P4 – 905/731-2189, Fax: 905/731-5534
Lawlor & LeClaire, #408, 9555 Yonge St., L4C 9M5 – 905/884-9133, Fax: 905/884-9507 – *2
G.E. Levine, #205, 10620 Yonge St., L4C 3C8 – 905/883-4855 – *1
S. Lawrence Liquornik, #421, 9555 Yonge St., L4C 9M5 – 905/883-8193, Fax: 905/737-7691 – *1
Malach & Fidler, #6, 30 Wertheim Court, L4B 1B9 – 905/889-1667, Fax: 905/889-1139 – *8
Peter L. May, 14 Church St. South, L4C 1W2 – 905/884-1167, Fax: 905/884-5446 – *1
Stuart P. Parker, Q.C., #1, 174 West Beavercreek Rd., L4B 1B4 – 905/889-7246, Fax: 905/881-8150 – *1
Plaxton & Mann, 10350 Yonge St., L4C 3B8 – 905/884-1115, Fax: 905/884-6722 – *3
Michael Polisuk, 9555 Yonge St., L4C 9M5 – 905/508-8203, Fax: 905/737-7691 – *1

* indicates number of lawyers in law firm.

Canadian Almanac & Directory 1997

Sidney Poon, Golden Plaza, 212-330 Hwy. 7 East, L4B 3P8 – 905/881-8229, Fax: 905/881-9833

I. Prydatok, #200, 650 Hwy #7 East, L4B 2N7 – 905/886-4666 – *2

Reycraft & Saunders, #102, 10211 Yonge St., L4C 3B3 – 905/884-6806, Fax: 905/884-6806 – *1

Corinne M. Rivers, #104, 13311 Yonge St., L4E 3L6 – 905/773-9911, Fax: 905/773-9927 – *1

Robins, Appleby & Taub, #201, 95 Mural St., L4B 3G2 – 905/731-6622, Fax: 905/731-6986 – *3

Rosenberg, Chadwick, Shankman & Wall, #700, 225 East Beaver Creek Rd., L4B 3P4 – 905/731-7100, Fax: 905/731-5534 – *4

Rumack & Bines, 174 West Beaver Creek Rd., L4B 1B4 – 905/881-5111, Fax: 905/881-8150 – *2

David Seed, #503, 330 Hwy. 7 East, L4B 3P8 – 905/886-2984, Fax: 905/881-8856 – *1

Brian Sherman, #203, 14 Oxford St., L4C 4L5 – 905/508-0248, Fax: 905/508-0248

Dennis R. Steinberg, #200, 9350 Yonge St., L4C 5G2 – 905/884-6353, Fax: 905/884-2655 – *1

Stong, Blackburn, Machon, Bohm & Pond, 10350 Yonge St., 4th Fl., L4C 5K9 – 905/884-9242; 773-5921, Fax: 905/884-5445 – *5

Gary Sugar, #700, 225 East Beaver Creek Rd., L4B 3P4 – 905/731-2189, Fax: 905/731-5534

Verskin, Milton, #700B, 225 East Beaver Creek Rd., L4B 3P4 – 905/731-2189, Fax: 905/731-5584

Joseph Virgilio, 70 Leek Cres., L4B 1H1 – 905/882-1082, Fax: 905/882-1082 – *1

Gordon E. Watkin, #200, 9350 Yonge St., L4C 5G2 – 905/884-3778, Fax: 905/884-2655 – *1

Winemaker, Kilgour & Todd, 10023 Yonge St., L4C 1T7 – 905/884-9235, Fax: 905/884-0438 – *2

Irene S.L. Yee, 42 Trinity Crescent, L4B 3L7 – 905/886-4277 – *1

T. Raciunas Zenon, 10330 Yonge St., L4C 5N1 – 905/883-8592 – *1

RIDGETOWN .... **Kent**

Shaw, Nicol, & Little, 64 Main St. East, PO Box 7, N0P 2C0 – 519/674-3372, Fax: 519/674-3352 – *2

Stirling, Faussett, McGuire, McFarlane & Thomas, 43 Main St. West, N0P 2C0 – 519/674-5401, Fax: 519/674-3579 – *4

Watson & Walker, PO Box 549, N0P 2C0 – 519/674-5407, Fax: 519/674-5568 – *1

RIDGEWAY .... **Niagara South**

Thom W. Arthur, 241 Ridge Rd. North, L0S 1N0 – 905/894-3884, Fax: 905/894-4818 – *1

Peter R. BonEnfant, PO Box 340, Stn GD PO, L0S 1N0 – 905/894-3410 – *1

Community Legal Services of Niagara South Inc., PO Box 430, Stn GD PO, L0S 1N0 – 905/894-4775, Fax: 905/894-6101

Jones, Jamieson & Redekop, 288 Ridge Rd. North, PO Box 340, L0S 1N0 – 905/894-0220; 382-2061, Fax: 905/894-5356 – *3

RIPLEY .... **Bruce**

Crawford, Mill & Davies, 38 Queen St., PO Box 100, N0G 2R0 – 519/395-2633, Fax: 519/395-4947 – *3

ROCKLAND .... **Russell**

Houle Assaly Morissette, 2784 Laurier St., PO Box 880, K4K 1L5 – 613/446-6411, Fax: 613/446-4513 – *5

RUSSELL .... **Russell**

Dianne Custance, 97 Mill St., PO Box 520, K4R 1E1 – 613/445-3183, Fax: 613/445-3424 – *1

SARNIA .... **Lambton**

Beaudet & De Sena, 251 Exmouth St., PO Box 2162, N7T 7L7 – 519/337-1LAW, 1529 – *1

Roderick Brown, Q.C., 442 Christina St. North, PO Box 909, N7T 5W2 – 519/336-7880, Fax: 519/336-5848 – *1

Dally, Elliott & Ruffilli, 500 Exmouth St., N7T 5P4 – 519/336-2253, Fax: 519/336-5870 – *3

Joseph M. Donohue, 521 Christina St. North, PO Box 1058, N7T 7K2 – 519/344-7425 – *1

J.A. Farina, 425 Christina St. North, N7T 5V8 – 519/337-5468, Fax: 519/337-8939 – *1

Fleck & Daigneault, PO Box 2072, N7T 7L1 – 519/337-5288, Fax: 519/336-9550 – *2

Foreman, Dawson, 1350 L'Héritage Dr., N7S 6H8 – 519/542-7711, 1240, Fax: 519/542-5577 – *7

George, Murray & Shipley, 2 Ferry Dock Hill, PO Box 2196, N7T 7L8 – 519/336-8770, Fax: 519/336-1811 – *10

Gray, Bruce, Kowalyshyn, Cimetta, 1166 London Rd., PO Box 2259, N7T 7L7 – 519/336-9700, Fax: 519/336-3289 – *4

Habel, Jacques, 2121 Huron Shores, N7T 7H6 – 519/869-6324 – *1

Jules J. Kovac, 219 Lochiel St., PO Box 485, N7T 7J4 – 519/336-3261 – *1

Peter Westfall, 1778 Churchill Rd., N7T 7H3 – 519/344-1155 – *1

Wyrzykowski, Higgins, Austin & Robb, 722 Lite St., PO Box 2200, N7T 7L7 – 519/336-6118, Fax: 519/336-9550 – *4

SAUBLE BEACH .... **Grey**

Ross C. McLean, 202 Main St., PO Box 1-15, N0H 1P0 – 519/422-2888, Fax: 519/422-3309

SAULT STE. MARIE .... **Algoma**

Bisceglia & Associates, #201, 405 Queen St. East, P6A 1Z5 – 705/942-5856, Fax: 705/942-6493 – *3

Aldona V. Bondar, 482 MacDonald Ave., P6B 1H9 – 705/759-6861 – *1

Bortolussi & Palombi, 470 Albert St. East, P6A 2J8 – 705/942-1333, Fax: 705/949-7684 – *2

Caputo Sarlo O'Neill, 116 Spring St., P6A 3A1 – 705/949-6901, Fax: 705/949-0618 – *5

R. Jack Falkins, 176 Wellington St. East, P6A 2L5 – 705/942-2022, Fax: 705/942-2027 – *2

Gaetz, N. Douglas, Q.C., 446 Albert St. East, P6A 2J8 – 705/949-6600

Hamilton, Nixon & Marchand, 67 Elgin St., PO Box 249, P6A 5L8 – 705/759-8498, Fax: 705/759-8781 – *3

Harry & Renaud, 138 Brock St., P6A 3B5 – 705/942-7900, Fax: 705/942-7902 – *2

E.R. Hornstein, 527 Queen St. East, P6A 2A2 – 705/942-8024, Fax: 705/942-9060 – *1

I.D. Hugill, #505, 421 Bay St., PO Box 457, P6A 1X3 – 705/949-4504, Fax: 705/949-3904 – *1

Kelleher, Laidlaw, Paciocco, 421 Bay St., 6th Fl., PO Box 819, P6A 5N3 – 705/949-7790, Fax: 705/949-5816 – *3

Henry M. Lang, Q.C., 157 East St., P6A 3C8 – 705/949-3300, Fax: 705/949-3312 – *1

Gerald P. Maich, 434 Albert St. East, P6A 2J8 – 705/254-6821 – *1

F.N. Mantello, Q.C., 183 Albert St. East, P6A 2J2 – 705/945-9900, Fax: 705/945-8044 – *1

R.C. Peres, Q.C., #201, 212 Queen St. East, P6A 5X8 – 705/949-9411, Fax: 705/949-3759 – *2

Peterson & Peterson, 626 Wellington St. East, PO Box 1169, P6A 2M5 – 705/942-1011, Fax: 705/942-9543 – *2

Pritchard, Benjamin F., 642 Queen St. East, P6A 2A4 – 705/759-1991, Fax: 705/759-2571 – *1

Provenzano, Provenzano & McMillan, 422 Albert St. East, PO Box 519, P6A 5M6 – 705/949-5411 – *3

Lorna Rudolph, 182 March St., P6A 2Z7 – 705/949-5131 – *1

William R. Scott, #1, 224 Queen St. East, P6A 1Y8 – 705/949-4333, Fax: 705/945-0958 – *1

Roderick W.A. Sonley, #1, 121 Brock St., P6A 3B6 – 705/759-8692 – *1

Walker, Thompson, 421 Bay St., PO Box 428, P6A 5M4 – 705/949-7806, Fax: 705/759-0457 – *2

Wishart & Partners, 390 Bay St., P6A 1X2 – 705/949-6700, Fax: 705/949-2465 – *9

Roy Youngson, 9 Texas St., PO Box 141, P6A 5L2 – 705/949-7931 – *1

SCHOMBERG .... **York**

M.J. Black, 233 Main St., L0G 1T0 – 905/939-8515, Fax: 905/939-8279 – *2

Clarke Smith, 250 Main St., L0G 1T0 – 905/939-2344, Fax: 905/727-7096 – *1

SEAFORTH .... **Huron**

McConnell, Stewart & Devereaux, 77 Main St. South, PO Box 220, N0K 1W0 – 519/527-0850 – *1

SHELBURNE .... **Dufferin**

Robert A. Donaldson, GD PO, L0N 1S0 – 519/925-1211

Ford-Arnold Beverly, 119 Owen Sound St., L0N 1S0 – 519/925-3737

Shepherd & Osyany, PO Box 760, L0N 1S0 – 519/925-5331, Fax: 519/925-3202 – *2

Timmerman & Haskell, 305 Owen Sound St., PO Box 216, L0N 1S0 – 519/925-2608,2260, Fax: 519/925-2268 – *2

SIMCOE .... **Norfolk**

Brimage, Tyrrell, Van Severen & Homeniuk, 21 Norfolk St. North, N3Y 4L1 – 519/426-5840, Fax: 519/426-7515 – *7

Cline, Backus & Nightingale, 28 Colborne St. North, N3Y 3T9 – 519/426-6763 – *4

Cobb & Jones, 2 Talbot St. North, N3Y 4N5 – 519/428-0170, Fax: 519/428-3105 – *6

B.J. Hogan, 81 Norfolk St. South, PO Box 544, N3Y 4N5 – 519/426-8911, Fax: 519/426-8912 – *1

Sheppard, MacIntosh, Lados & Herter, 58 Peel St., PO Box 677, N3Y 4T2 – 519/426-1382, Fax: 519/426-1392 – *4

Smelko Law Office, 25 Norfolk St. North, N3Y 3N6 – 519/426-1711, Fax: 519/426-7863 – *2

Tisdale & Reid, 49 Robinson St., PO Box 69, N3Y 4K8 – 519/426-0503, Fax: 519/426-4364 – *2

SIOUX LOOKOUT .... **Kenora**

Catherine M. Beamish, 65 King St., PO Box 1437, P0V 2T0 – 807/737-2809, Fax: 807/737-1211 – *1

Young & Young, #101, 73 King St., PO Box 38, P0V 2T0 – 807/737-2562, Fax: 807/737-2571 – *2

SMITHS FALLS .... **Lanark**

Dixon & Dixon, 40 Main St. West, K7A 4T2 – 613/283-4735 – *3

G.W. Fournier, 35 Daniel St., PO Box 752, K7A 4W6 – 613/283-8818, Fax: 613/283-8951 – *1

Howard & Ryan, 2 Main St. East, PO Box 548, K7A 4T6 – 613/283-6772, Fax: 613/283-8840 – *2

Kirkland, Murphy & Ain, 15 Russell St. East, PO Box 220, K7A 4T1 – 613/283-0515, Fax: 613/283-8557 – *3

Quigley, Ross & Cliffen, 30 Russell St. East, PO Box 804, K7A 4W6 – 613/283-7331, Fax: 613/283-6792 – *4

Rubino & Chaplin, 10 Church St. West, K7A 4T2 – 613/283-6501 – *1

SMITHVILLE .... **York**

John W. Shipton, 176 Griffin St. South, L0R 2A0 – 905/957-7898, Fax: 905/957-1085 – *1

Van Der Woerd, Faber & Olij, Village Square Mall, Hwy. 20, L0R 2A0 – 905/957-7240, Fax: 905/957-2599 – *2

SMOOTH ROCK FALLS .... **Cochrane**

David L. Lanthier, 142 - 1 Ave., P0L 2B0 – 705/338-2717, Fax: 705/272-2584

SOUTH PORCUPINE .... **Cochrane**
Albert Ristimaki, 69 Harold Ave., PO Box 1060, P0N 1H0 – 705/235-2211, Fax: 705/235-3084 – *1

SOUTHAMPTON ...., **Bruce**
Robert E. Forsyth, Q.C., 243 High St., PO Box 779, N0H 2L0 – 519/797-3223, Fax: 519/797-3192 – *1

ST. CATHARINES .... **Niagara North**
Leslie R. Allen, 8 Church St., PO Box 96, L2R 6R4 – 905/685-1701, Fax: 905/685-7651 – *2
O.D. Babij, 110 Church St., L2R 3C8 – 905/684-1159, Fax: 905/684-1150 – *1
Bakker, Atamanuk, Taylor & Wenglowski, 60 James St., L2R 7E7 – 905/688-1520, Fax: 905/688-6002 – *4
Barr, Giannotti & Leach, 1 Church St., L2R 3B1 – 905/688-6161, Fax: 905/688-6144 – *3
G.L. Black, 55 King St., L2R 6Z1 – 905/641-1551, Fax: 905/641-1830 – *1
W.J. Garry Bracken, 50 Dunvegan Rd., L2P 1H6 – 905/988-9389
Wayne Norris Brooks, Barrister & Solicitor, 20 Lake St., PO Box 1501, L2R 6S4 – 905/685-0010, Fax: 905/685-7301 – *1
CAW Legal Services Plan, #206, 55 King St., L2R 3H5 – 905/641-1313, Fax: 905/641-0967; Toll Free: 1-800-318-0782
J. Ronald Charlebois, 172 James St., PO Box 1626, L2R 7K1 – 905/988-5000, Fax: 905/688-0034 – *1
Chown, Cairns, 80 King St., PO Box 760, L2R 6Y8 – 905/688-4500, Fax: 905/688-0015; Email: lawyers@chown-cairns.com; URL: http://www.chown-cairns.com/northland/cc – *20
Tracy J. Middleton Collini, 234 Vine St., L2M 4T1 – 905/937-9229, Fax: 905/937-9228
Covello, Dennis, 23 Centre St., PO Box 638, L2R 3A8 – 905/688-0066, Fax: 905/688-0477 – *1
Coy, Barch, 46 Ontario St., L2R 5J4 – 905/641-1146, Fax: 905/641-1151 – *4
Crossingham, Brady, Miller, Stewart & Morningstar, #200, 63 Church St., PO Box 307, L2R 6V2 – 905/641-1622, Fax: 905/685-1461 – *8
Daniel, Wilson, Dominion Bldg., 39 Queen St., PO Box 24022, L1R 6V7 – 905/688-9411, Fax: 905/688-5747 – *18
Daniel, Wilson, #10, 201 Martindale Rd., L2W 1A2 – 905/687-9922
Mark F. Dedinsky, 154 James St., L2R 5C5 – 905/688-6275, Fax: 905/682-0264
Michael M. DelGobbo, #304, 110 James St., L2R 7E8 – 905/988-1400, Fax: 905/988-1414
B.W. Doliszny, Q.C., 69 Queen St., L1R 6W8 – 905/682-8321 – *1
Terence J. Donohue, 603, 110 James St., L2R 7E8 – 905/684-8533 – *1
Michael J. Dube, #Lwr., 19 Wellington St., L2R 5P5 – 905/684-8171 – *1
Forster, Lewandowski & Cords, #2, 82 Lake St., PO Box 1180, L2R 7A7 – 905/688-9110, Fax: 905/688-0901 – *3
Freeman, Frayne & Hummell, 9 Raymond St., PO Box 253, L1R 6S4 – 905/684-1147, Fax: 905/684-7147 – *2
Fullerton & Fullerton, 30 Duke St., L2R 5W5 – 905/688-2080, Fax: 905/641-1006 – *2
R.A. Gordon, Q.C., 31 Church St., PO Box 1296, L2R 7A7 – 905/685-8435, Fax: 905/685-9126 – *1
Graves & Associates, #702, 55 King St., L2R 7K1 – 905/641-2020, Fax: 905/641-0484 – *5
Erik Grinbergs, 205 King St., L2R 3J5 – 905/688-9800, Fax: 905/685-8836
B. John Hanna, #604, 55 King St., PO Box 24044, L2R 7P7 – 905/687-9347, Fax: 905/687-3939 – *1
Bernard H. Hawkins, 8 Church St., PO Box 1661, L2R 6R4 – 905/687-9900, Fax: 905/685-7651
Heelis, Williams & Little, 14 Church St., PO Box 1056, L2R 7A3 – 905/687-8200, Fax: 905/684-4844 – *5

Donald M. Henderson, Q.C., #601, 110 James St., PO Box 1268, L2R 7A7 – 905/984-4366, Fax: 905/687-6553
Ricky J. Hesp, 5 Race St., L2R 3M1 – 905/687-1766
Hetherington & Allen, 8 Church St., PO Box 96, L2R 6R4 – 905/685-1701, Fax: 905/685-7651 – *2
D. Ceri Hugill, #18, 235 Martindale, L2R 6P9 – 905/687-4000, Fax: 905/687-6842 – *1
William A. Huska, Q.C., #3, 8 Church St., L2R 6R4 – 905/684-1163, Fax: 905/685-7651 – *1
Jason, Robert, 5 Race St., L2R 3M1 – 905/682-2021, Fax: 905/687-8816; Toll Free: 1-888-862-2444; Email: resolve@vaxxine.com
Edward F. Kravcik, 281 Saint Paul St., PO Box 216, L2R 6S4 – 905/984-5822, Fax: 905/685-9102
Charles M. Kray, #206B, 15 King St., PO Box 1473, L2R 7J9 – 905/688-0377, Fax: 905/688-0373 – *1
Larry H. Kroeker, 215 Scott St., L2N 1H5 – 905/646-4447 – *1
Lampard, Ellis & Walsh, 51 Queen St., PO Box 338, L2R 6V5 – 905/682-8663, Fax: 905/684-1000 – *2
Lancaster, Mix & Welch, 55 King St., PO Box 790, L2R 6Z1 – 905/641-1551, Fax: 905/641-1830; Email: lmw@lmw.com; URL: http://www.lmw.com – *15
Legal Aid, 110 James St., L2R 7E8 – 905/685-1012, Fax: 905/685-7202
MacNaughton & Boyko, #401, 55 King St., PO Box 1082, L2R 7A3 – 905/685-1364, Fax: 905/685-9487 – *2
Frank M. Marotta, 21 Duke St., L2R 5W1 – 905/688-5401, Fax: 905/688-6204 – *1
Martens, Lingard, Walters & Maddalena, #601, 110 James St., PO Box 1286, L2R 7A7 – 905/687-6551, Fax: 905/687-6553 – *5
A.J. Mascarin, #303, 15 King St., PO Box 398, L1R 6V9 – 905/684-6567, Fax: 905/684-9669 – *1
Alan McGarvie, 6 Clark St., L2R 5G2 – 905/688-5115 – *1
McKenzie, Lefurgey & Hunt, 205 King St., L2R 3J5 – 905/685-4321, Fax: 905/685-8836 – *3
Paula McPherson, 5 Race St., L2R 3M1 – 905/687-9455, Fax: 905/687-8816; Toll Free: 1-888-862-2444; Email: resolve@vaxxine.com
Morgan, Dilts & Toppari, 281 St. Paul St., PO Box 216, L2R 6S4 – 905/685-7391, Fax: 905/685-9102 – *3
Niagara North Community Legal Assistance, 8 Church St., PO Box 1266, L2R 7A7 – 905/682-6635 – *4
O'Neill & Radford, 154 James St., PO Box 1163, L2R 7A3 – 905/685-1377, Fax: 905/682-0264 – *2
Peter Partington, Q.C., 70 James St., L2R 5C1 – 905/685-6755, Fax: 905/685-4774
Ian G. Pearson, 30 Duke St., L2R 5W5 – 905/688-2080, Fax: 905/641-1006 – *1
Pedwell & Pedwell, 2 Church St., L2R 3B2 – 905/688-0710, Fax: 905/688-4100 – *2
Reid, McNaughton, 63 Ontario St., PO Box 577, L2R 6W8 – 905/685-5435, Fax: 905/685-3143; Email: lawyers@reidlaw.com; URL: http://reidlaw.com/lawyers – *7
Repei, Richard, 284 Geneva St., L2N 2E8 – 905/646-4437, Fax: 905/646-4173 – *2
Brenda V. Sandulak, 172 James St., L2R 7K1 – 905/988-5000, Fax: 905/688-0034
D.S. Shantz, #303, 110 James St., L2R 7A7 – 905/688-4650, Fax: 905/984-6314 – *1
M.J. Shea, 101 King St., PO Box 1360, L2R 3H6 – 905/688-6561 – *1
S.E. Sherk, 63 Front St. South, PO Box 412, L2V 4J6 – 905/227-7581, Fax: 905/227-5352 – *1
David N. Sider, 6 Clark St., L2R 5G2 – 905/688-1180, Fax: 905/688-8026
Brian C. Smith, 5 St. Paul Cres., L2R 3P6 – 905/688-9550, Fax: 905/688-9953 – *1
Sullivan, Mahoney, 40 Queen St., PO Box 1360, L2R 6Z2 – 905/688-6655, Fax: 905/688-5814 – *23
A.E. Tessmer, 15 Church St., PO Box 1688, L2R 7K1 – 905/688-9552, Fax: 905/935-8772 – *1

A. Tolonen, 166 James St., L2R 6Z4 – 905/688-4636, Fax: 905/688-4637 – *1
George F. Walker, Q.C., 1 Church St., L2R 3B1 – 905/685-3500, Fax: 905/688-6144 – *1
Wilson & Wilson, #604, 110 James St., L2R 7E8 – 905/688-1272, Fax: 905/388-0198 – *2
Daniel Wilson, 39 Queen St., PO Box 24022, L2R 7P7 – 905/688-9411, Fax: 905/688-5747
Paul J. Wintemute, 20 Lake St., PO Box 638, L2R 6W8 – 905/687-7044, Fax: 905/687-7085
Donald L. Wolfe, 17 Beecher St., L2R 5S4 – 905/688-4566

ST. THOMAS .... **Elgin**
James R. Carrie, 555 Talbot St., PO Box 617, N5P 4B1 – 519/631-8200, Fax: 519/633-9635 – *2
Fordham, Watterworth & Marshall, 4 Elgin St., N5R 3L6 – 519/631-9090, Fax: 519/633-1371 – *4
Gloin, Hall & Associates, 12 Pearl St., PO Box 66, N5P 2N9 – 519/633-3100, Fax: 519/633-9362 – *5
J.A. Gundry, 16 Pearl St., PO Box 518, N5P 3V6 – 519/631-9060, Fax: 519/631-7304 – *1
Gunn & Associates, 108 Centre St., PO Box 459, N5P 3V5 – 519/631-0700, Fax: 519/631-1468 – *5
Hennessey, Bowsher & Associates, 108 Centre St., PO Box 548, N5P 3V6 – 519/633-3310 – *4
W.O. Herold, Q.C., 130 Centre St., N5R 2Z9 – 403/631-3250, Fax: 403/631-0557 – *1
William W. Johnson, 651 Talbot St., N5P 1C9 – 519/633-3200 – *1
Brian W. Kempster, 48 Stanley St., N5R 3E9 – 519/633-2580, Fax: 519/633-0832 – *1
E.W. Popovich, 24 Curtis St., PO Box 580, N5P 3V6 – 519/631-5600, Fax: 519/631-9789 – *1
T.A. Por, 79 Stanley, PO Box 190, N5P 3T7 – 519/631-7100, Fax: 519/768-1270 – *1
M.L. Riddell, 360 Talbot St. East, PO Box 88, N5P 3T5 – 519/631-3211, Fax: 519/631-8586 – *1
Sanders, Cline, 14 Southwick St., PO Box 70, N5P 3T5 – 519/633-0800, Fax: 519/633-9259 – *3
Brian D. Scott Associates, #200, 408 Talbot St., N5R 1B8 – 519/633-3230, Fax: 519/633-9232 – *1
Larry D.N. Smith, Q.C., 142 Centre St., PO Box 129, N5P 3T7 – 519/663-2052, Fax: 519/633-2104 – *1
Robert J. Upsdell, 59 Metcalfe St., PO Box 486, N5P 3V2 – 519/633-7100, Fax: 519/633-6762 – *1
Arnold B. Walker, 651 Talbot St., PO Box 20022, Stn Centre, N5P 4H4 – 519/633-3273, 3200, Fax: 519/633-9558 – *1

STAYNER .... **Simcoe**
Bumstead & Demery, 233 Main St., PO Box 820, L0M 1S0 – 705/428-6000, Fax: 705/428-6427 – *2

STIRLING .... **Hastings**
S. Ward, 45 Front St., K0K 3E0 – 613/395-2131, Fax: 613/395-5089 – *1
Alex Winkler, Q.C., 33 Mill St., K0K 3E0 – 613/395-3397, Fax: 613/359-3398 – *1

STITTSVILLE .... **Ottawa-Carleton**
Watson/Boivin & Associates, Highway 7, Savage Dr., PO Box 199, K0A 3G0 – 613/836-6335 – *2

STONEY CREEK .... **Hamilton-Wentworth**
R.T. James, 99 Hwy. 8, PO Box 9309, Stn 4, L9H 4V5 – 905/664-6683, Fax: 905/664-2382 – *1
S.W. Peglar, 286 Barton St. East, L8E 2K6 – 905/662-5404, Fax: 905/664-1977 – *1
Richard P. Startek & Associates, 141 Hwy. 8, L8G 5C1 – 905/662-7727

STOUFFVILLE .... **York**
Button, Armstrong & Ness, 6361 Main St., PO Box 220, L4A 7Z5 – 905/640-3530, Fax: 905/640-7027 – *3
Donald J. Kimura, 6140 Main St., L4A 1A5 – 905/640-5454, Fax: 905/640-8090 – *3

* indicates number of lawyers in law firm.

André E. Kozak, 6290 Main St., PO Box 940, L4A 8A1 – 905/640-2211, Fax: 905/640-8161 – *1
H.J. MacLean, 4920 Bethesda Rd., L4A 7X5 – 905/640-0901, Fax: 905/640-9278 – *1

STRATFORD .... **Perth**

W.W. Aitchison, 42 Albert St., PO Box 411, N5A 6T3 – 519/273-4822 – *1
Byers, Kenny, Parlee & Thorn, 25 William St., PO Box 722, N5A 6V6 – 519/271-6700, Fax: 519/271-7419 – *3
A.G. Goodwin, 4 Ontario St., N5A 3G8 – 519/271-4522 – *1
Gregory & Buechler, 30 Waterloo St. South, N5A 4A6 – 519/271-3520, Fax: 519/271-1490 – *2
Hastings & Fair, 92 Ontario St., PO Box 844, N5A 6W3 – 519/271-2066 – *2
Mountain, Mitchell, Hill, Monteith & Ritsma, PO Box 846, N5A 6W3 – 519/271-6770, Fax: 519/271-9261 – *6
Neilson, Bell, Skinner, Rogerson & Dunphy, 1 Ontario St., N5A 6T7 – 519/271-7330, Fax: 519/271-1762 – *5
John H. Stratton, Q.C., 313 St. David St., N5A 1E1 – 519/271-7360 – *1
W.E. Sylvester, 15 Downie St., PO Box 130, N5A 6S8 – 519/273-1550, Fax: 519/273-6170 – *1

STRATHROY .... **Middlesex**

Robert J. Dack, 16 Front St. East, N7G 1Y4 – 519/245-0370, Fax: 519/245-0523 – *1
Jones, Gibbons & Reis, 39 Front St. West, N7G 1X5 – 519/245-1110, Fax: 519/245-5859 – *3
Quinlan & Somerville, PO Box 28, N7G 3J1 – 519/245-0342, Fax: 519/245-0108 – *2
George E. Sinker, 53 - 55 Front St. West, PO Box 250, N7G 3J2 – 519/245-1144, Fax: 519/245-6090 – *2

STREETSVILLE .... **Peel**

M.C. Foster & Assoc., 151 Queen St. South, L5M 1L1 – 905/826-1177, Fax: 905/826-4926 – *3

STROUD .... **Simcoe**

Gibson & Adams, PO Box 100, L0L 2M0 – 705/436-1701, Fax: 705/436-1710 – *3
Myles F. McLellan, 1000 Innisfil Beach Rd., PO Box 6500, L0L 2M0 – 705/436-6957, Fax: 705/436-7601

STURGEON FALLS .... **Nipissing**

Conrad Proulx, 65 Queen St., P0H 2G0 – 705/753-2780, Fax: 705/753-4753 – *1

SUDBURY .... **Sudbury**

William G. Beach, 224 Applegrove St., P3C 1N3 – 705/675-5685, Fax: 705/675-5685 – *1
Walter Chmara, #4, 54 Elgin St. South, P3E 3N2 – 705/673-2090 – *1
Conroy, Trebb, Scott, Hurtubise, 164 Elm St. West, P3C 1T7 – 705/674-6441, Fax: 705/673-9567 – *7
Desmarais, Keenan, Mackey Bldg., Bldg Box: 100, 30 Durham St., P3C 5E5 – 705/675-7521, Fax: 705/675-7390 – *10
Edmonstone Barnett Associates, 264 Elm St., P3C 1B4 – 705/674-3210, Fax: 705/674-1265 – *3
Gatien Law Firm, 111 Larch St., P3E 4T5 – 705/675-5414, Fax: 705/675-8252 – *3
Gerard E. Guimond, #300, 96 Larch St., P3E 1C1 – 705/674-5551, Fax: 705/675-2051 – *1
Richard Guy, 143 Applegrove St., P3C 1N2 – 705/673-1101, Fax: 705/673-1134 – *2
Horeck, Beckett & Babij, 135 Applegrove St., P3C 1N3 – 706/673-9551, Fax: 706/673-0476 – *3
B.N. Howe, 235 Elm St. West, P3C 1T8 – 705/674-8317 – *1
Lacroix, Forest & Del Frate, Place Balmoral, 36 Elgin St., P3C 5B4 – 705/674-1976, Fax: 705/674-6978 – *6
Mailloux & Gray, 142 Paris St., P3E 3E1 – 705/674-5267, Fax: 705/674-2109 – *2

Mensour & Mensour, #101, 238 Elm St., P3C 1V3 – 705/673-6787, Fax: 705/673-1418 – *3
Miller, Maki, 176 Elm St., P3C 1T7 – 705/675-7503 – *9
Orendorff Vrbanac, #1, 17 Frood Rd., P3C 4Y9 – 705/673-1200, Fax: 705/673-3050 – *2
Paquette, Lalande & Keast, #200, 1188 St. Jerome St., P3A 2V9 – 705/560-2121, Fax: 705/560-8072 – *4
Parisé, Hennessy & Gervais, PO Box 1, P3E 4N3 – 705/674-4040, Fax: 705/674-4242 – *4
Pharand, Kuyek, 229 Elm St. West, P3C 1T8 – 705/675-1227, Fax: 705/675-5350 – *2
Robert C. Torr, Banngton, 149 Pine St., P3C 1X3 – 705/674-0500 – *3
Steinberg, Renzini & Fabbro, 54 Elgin St., P3E 3N2 – 705/675-1336, Fax: 705/675-5445 – *3
Norman G. Stoner, 88 Larch St., P3E 1B9 – 705/675-8307, Fax: 705/675-7245 – *1
Sullivan & Horton, 158 Elm St. West, P3C 1T7 – 705/674-7567 – *2
Stanley J. Thomas, #200, 174 Larch St., P3E 1C6 – 705/674-8306, Fax: 705/674-6789
Law Office of Serge F. Treherne, 158 Elm St. West, 2nd Fl., PO Box 1269, P3C 1T7 – 705/670-9689, Fax: 705/670-9141 – *1
Valin, Innes & Treherne, 96 Larch St., P3E 1C1 – 705/673-3655, Fax: 705/673-8758 – *2
Vere, Gray & Bland, 54 Elgin St., P3E 3N2 – 705/675-2454, Fax: 705/675-2820 – *3
Weaver, Simmons, PO Box 158, P3E 4N5 – 705/674-6421, Fax: 705/674-9948 – *20
Zito Associates, 85 Durham St., P3E 3M5 – 705/674-2134, Fax: 705/674-6085 – *3

SUNDRIDGE .... **Parry Sound**

Smith & Hardy, PO Box 234, P0A 1Z0 – 705/384-5388, Fax: 705/384-7713 – *2

SUTTON .... **York**

Fahey & Reeder, 100 High St., L0E 1R0 – 905/722-3771, Fax: 905/722-9852 – *3
McChesney, Rogers, Hill & Callaghan, #101, 152 High St., L0E 1R0

TAVISTOCK .... **Oxford**

Shuh Cline & Grossman, 14 Hope St. West, N0B 2R0 – 519/578-9010, Fax: 519/578-1590

TEMAGAMI .... **Nipissing**

Smith, Byck & Grant, PO Box 516, P0H 2H0 – 705/672-2102 (Haileybury), Fax: 705/647-8575 – *2

THAMESFORD .... **Oxford**

Godfrey Jefferson, 136 Dundas St., N0M 2M0 – 519/285-2531

THORNDALE .... **Middlesex**

P.S. McBirnie, RR#3, N0M 2P0 – 519/462-1300 – *1

THORNHILL .... **York**

M. Adelson, #216, 2900 Steeles Ave. East, L3T 4X1 – 905/881-8800, Fax: 905/881-7391 – *1
Thomas A. Adler, #207, 1600 Steeles Ave. West, L4K 4M2 – 905/660-3637, Fax: 905/660-3863 – *1
Agueci & Calabretta, #312, 1600 Steeles Ave. West, L4K 4M2 – 416/638-8400, Fax: 416/660-7828 – *5
A.M. Arrigo, Q.C., 48 Guardsman Rd., L3T 6L4 – 905/889-6131 – *1
William G. Atwell, 11874 Keele St., L4K 2S3 – 905/669-1300 – *1
Auciello Franschman, #580, 8500 Leslie St., L3T 7M8 – 905/882-8080, Fax: 905/882-5483 – *2
Baker & Associates, #404, 100 York Blvd., L4B 1J8 – 905/882-6507, Fax: 905/886-7701
Beglaubter, Greenberg, Sinukoff & Ernst, 7626A Yonge St., L4J 1V9 – 905/886-9535, Fax: 905/886-9540 – *4
Warren W. Biback, 175 Commerce Valley Dr. West, L3T 7P6 – 905/882-2020, Fax: 905/764-0308

Edward L. Burlew, #510, 8500 Leslie St., L3T 7M8 – 905/882-2422, Fax: 905/882-2431
Chauhan & Associates, #309, 330 Hwy. 7 East, L4B 3P8 – 905/771-1235, Fax: 905/771-1237 – *2
Anthony D'Avella, #200, 300 West Beaver Creek, L4B 3B1 – 905/882-1504, Fax: 905/882-4065
Damiani & Associates, #300, 3300 Hwy. 7 West, L4K 4M3 – 905/660-3333, Fax: 905/660-0990 – *5
De Lucia & Associates, #208, 1600 Steeles Ave., L4K 4M2 – 905/660-4500, Fax: 905/660-5580 – *1
Deverett Law Offices, Bldg Box: 10, 324 Hwy 7 East, L4B 1A6 – 905/882-9308, Fax: 905/882-8609 – *1
Direnfeld, A.D., #205, 7089 Yonge St., L3T 2A7 – 905/881-2345, Fax: 905/881-8949 – *1
A. Christopher Dymond, 30 Wertheim Crt., L4B 1B9 – 905/882-9400, Fax: 905/882-6266 – *1
Hercules E. Faga, 137 Langstaff Rd. East, L3T 3M6 – 905/881-2624, Fax: 905/881-0593 – *1
Edward L. Fingold, 77 Hetherington Cres., L4J 2M9 – 905/882-9666, Fax: 905/881-6427
Fish & Associates, 7951 Yonge St., PO Box 956, L3T 2C4 – 905/881-1500 – *4
A.I. Goldstein, #43, 165 Beaver Creek Rd., L4B 2N2 – 905/882-2275, Fax: 905/882-6999 – *1
C. Rodney Green, Q.C., #700, 225 East Beaver Creek, L4B 3P4 – 905/771-9373, Fax: 905/731-5534 – *9
Herman Murray Law Office, 1 Promenade Cir., L4J 4P8 – 905/889-2502
Gerri C. Holder, 75 Dundurn Cres., L4J 6Z3 – 905/764-9732 – *1
Hughes, Etigson, #200, 175 Commerce Valley Dr. West, L3T 7P6 – 905/771-6414, Fax: 905/771-6420 – *2
Hui, Ling, Wong & Assoc., #301, 350 Hwy. 7 East, L4B 3N2 – 905/881-7387, Fax: 905/881-0106 – *6
J.D. Barnett Law Offices, 8500 Leslie St., L3T 7M8 – 905/709-1888
A.L. Jackson, PO Box 81, L3T 3N1 – 905/881-5945, Fax: 905/884-3532 – *1
Barry Klady, #300, 8199 Yonge St., L3T 2C6 – 905/731-6071, Fax: 905/731-4058 – *1
Thomas Ko, 512-330 Hwy 7 East, L4B 3P8 – 905/881-4842, Fax: 905/881-1119
Kotick & Associates, 60 Commerce Valley Dr. East, L3T 7P9 – 905/882-1200, Fax: 905/882-0086 – *2
Jerry Lapowich, Q.C., #305, 202-404 Steeles Ave. West, L4J 6X3 – 905/771-9904, Fax: 905/771-1507 – *1
Lecker Gorodensky Assoc., #222, 1600 Steeles Ave. West, L4K 4M2 – 905/669-7400, Fax: 905/669-9403 – *4
Leslie Brown, #400, 300 John St., L3T 5W4 – 905/731-5083
Janet MacDougall, #202, 8108 Yonge St., L4J 1W4 – 905/886-4907, Fax: 905/886-8070 – *1
Mandel, Hirsch, #218, 180 Steeles Ave. West, L4J 2L1 – 905/881-3666 – *3
Martino, Rossi, #203, 8108 Yonge St., L4J 1W4 – 905/882-9504, Fax: 905/882-2417 – *2
Derrick McNamara, 665 Millway, L4K 3T8 – 905/660-4849, Fax: 905/660-4852
R.G. Merritt, 7061 Yonge St., L3T 2A6 – 905/889-3430, Fax: 905/889-7290 – *1
Dan Moshinsky, 54 Chabad Gate, L4J 2R3 – 905/889-7985
W.S. Novak, #310, 1 Promenade Cir., L4J 4P8 – 905/882-1818, Fax: 905/882-8775 – *1
Rocco Palmieri, #212, 2180 Steeles Ave. West, L4K 2Z5 – 905/669-6232
Tania Perlin, 218-180 Steeles Ave. West, L4J 2L1 – 905/881-3456, Fax: 905/881-9859
Frank Pizzimenti, #300, 8400 Jane St., L4K 4L8 – 905/660-5253, Fax: 905/738-0528 – *1
D.J. Reeve, 278 Badessa Circle, L4J 6C5 – 905/738-9826, Fax: 905/669-2577 – *1
Riesz, Thomas, #218, 180 Steeles Ave. West, L4J 2L1 – 905/881-5609, Fax: 905/881-9859
Ronald S. Minken & Assoc., 310-330 Hwy 7 East, L4B 3P8 – 905/771-0025, Fax: 905/771-0805 – *2

Sol Rosenfeld, #11, 30 Wertheim Crt., L4B 1B9 – 905/709-0090, Fax: 905/882-6266
Lloyd Rubinoff, 300 John St., L3T 5W4 – 905/886-3110, Fax: 905/886-0989 – *1
Sheldon Rudolph, 613 York Hill Blvd., L4J 5L3 – 905/886-7988, Fax: 905/886-9388 – *1
Marc E. Schiffer, 83 Breckonwood Cres., L3T 5G8 – 905/881-0056 – *1
A.S. Schorr, 210-175 Commerce Valley Dr. West, L3T 7P6 – 905/764-0282, Fax: 905/764-0308 – *1
Seymour Iseman & Associate, #216, 2900 Steeles Ave. East, L3T 4X1 – 905/881-8800, Fax: 905/881-7391 – *1
Alan G. Silverstein, #30, 180 Steeles Ave. West, L4J 2L1 – 905/882-8811, Fax: 905/882-8927 – *1
Stewart Floyd Sklar, 175 Newport Sq., L4J 7N6 – 905/505-5556, Fax: 905/886-4482 – *1
Stern & Morganstein, 402-8199 Yonge St., L3T 2C6 – 905/881-8288, Fax: 905/881-8665 – *2
L. Stulberg, #402, 300 John St., L3T 5W4 – 905/764-1422 – *1
Suter Law, The Promenade Mall, 1 Promenade Circle, L4J 4P8 – 905/886-0529
Warga, Katz, #10A, 1 Applewood Cr., L4K 1K1 – 905/669-1979, Fax: 905/669-6699 – *2
O.C. Wong, #503, 330 Hwy 7 East, L4B 3P8 – 905/881-2992

THOROLD .... Niagara North
Dennis Gross, 9 Pine St. North, L2V 3Z9 – 905/227-8111
Peter J. Jurmain, 21 1/2 Front St. South, PO Box 235, L2V 3Y9 – 905/227-2731, Fax: 905/227-9206
James V. McManamy, 21 1/2 Front St. South, PO Box 235, L2V 3Y9 – 905/227-2731, Fax: 905/227-9206 – *1
John J. Simon, 7 Front St. North, PO Box 505, L2V 4M5 – 905/227-9191, Fax: 905/227-7234 – *1
Young, McNamara, 18 Albert St., PO Box 68, L1V 3Y7 – 905/227-3777, Fax: 905/227-5988 – *3

THUNDER BAY .... Thunder Bay
Atwood, Shaw, Labine, 501 East Donald St., P7E 6N6 – 807/623-4342, Fax: 807/623-2098 – *4
David J. Auger, 195 Park Ave., P7B 1B9 – 807/345-7466, Fax: 807/345-8450
B. Lee Baig, Q.C., 384 Fort William Rd., P7B 2Z3 – *1
Buset & Partners, 1121 Barton St., P7B 5N3 – 807/623-2500, Fax: 807/622-7808 – *9
Carrel & Partners, West Arthur Place, 1265 East Arthur St., 6th Fl., PO Box 638, P7C 4W6 – 807/623-4000, Fax: 807/623-7309 – *12
Cheadle Johnson Shanks MacIvor, #2000, 715 Hewitson St., PO Box 429, P7C 4V9 – 807/622-6821, Fax: 807/623-3892 – *7
Christie & Potestio, 263 Park Ave., PO Box 3047, P7B 5G5 – 807/344-6651, Fax: 807/345-1105 – *3
Edwards & Carfagnini, 69 North Court St., PO Box 2237, Stn P, P7B 5E8 – 807/345-0711, Fax: 807/345-3571 – *2
Erickson Larson, 291 South Court St., PO Box 1240, P7C 4X9 – 807/345-1213, Fax: 807/345-2526 – *8
Filipovic, Brothers & Conway, Tomlinson Block, #20, 8A North Cumberland St., P7A 4L1 – 807/343-9090, Fax: 807/345-1397 – *3
Terry Gilbert, 217 Van Norman St., P7A 4B6 – 807/345-6538 – *1
Kajander, Blanchard, Conway, Heerema & Paivalainen, 76 North Algoma St., P7A 4Z4 – *5
G.W. Kostyshyn, 123 Brodie St. South, P7E 1B8 – 807/623-5400 – *1
Kovanchak Ferris Ross, 79 North Court St., PO Box 3197, P7B 5G6 – 807/344-5771, Fax: 807/345-1642 – *3
R.E. Lauder, 217 Van Norman St., P7A 4B6 – 807/345-6538, Fax: 807/345-0337 – *1
Donald J. Lees, 1820 Victoria Ave. East, P7C 1E2 – 807/623-5892, Fax: 807/623-1580 – *1

Lukinuk & McKenzie, #403, 135 Syndicate Ave. North, PO Box 26, P7C 3V6 – 807/622-6413 – *2
Macgillivray-Poirier & Mullen, 384 Fort William Rd., PO Box 3445, P7B 5J9 – 807/344-5847, Fax: 807/345-3036 – *4
Martin & Scrimshaw, 43 North Ct., PO Box 3260, P7B 5G6 – 807/345-3600, Fax: 807/344-8152 – *3
McCartney, Judge, Murray, 1151 Barton St., P7C 1B7 – 807/623-5595 – *5
McKitrick, Jones, Kislock, 17A Cumberland St. South, P7B 5G1 – 807/345-1251 – *5
Thomas C. Mitton, Chapple Bldg., Bldg Box: 305, 101 North Syndicate Ave., PO Box 173, P7C 4V8 – 807/623-4320, Fax: 807/622-8038 – *1
Petrone Hornak Garofalo Mauro, 76 Algoma St. North, PO Box 3446, P7B 5J9 – 807/344-9191, Fax: 807/345-8391; Toll Free: 1-800-465-3988 – *5
Celina M. Reitberger, 215 Camelot St., P7A 4B2 – 807/345-0563 – *1
Shaffer, Jobbitt, Stead, Halabisky, Karlstedt, Fillmore & Barker, 1020 Victoria Ave. East, PO Box 125, P7C 4V5 – 807/623-4442, Fax: 807/623-8140 – *8
Kenneth R. Tilson, #17, 4 Court St. South, P7B 2W4 – 807/345-1451 – *1
Weiler, Maloney, Nelson, Chapple Bldg., 101 Syndicate Ave. North, 2nd Fl., PO Box 10, P7C 3V5 – 807/623-1111, Fax: 807/623-4947; Email: weiler@air.on.ca – *12
W.C. Wieckowski, 293 Park Ave., P7B 1C4 – 807/345-6566, Fax: 807/345-9982 – *1
Peter G.F. Young, 244 Camelot St., P7A 4B1 – 807/344-0881, Fax: 807/345-9886 – *1

TILBURY .... Kent
Thomas C. Odette Jr., Q.C., 13 Queen St. North, N0P 2L0 – 519/682-1644 – *1

TILLSONBURG .... Oxford
Gibson, Linton, Toth & Campbell, 36 Broadway, N4G 3P1 – 519/842-3658 – *4
Groom & Szorenyi, 25 Harvey St., N4G 3J7 – 519/842-4205 – *1
Mandryk & Heeney, 65 Bidwell St., N4G 3T8 – 519/842-4228, Fax: 519/842-7659 – *2
Morris, Jenkins & Kee, 19 Ridout St. East, N4G 4H8 – 519/842-9017, Fax: 519/842-3394 – *2
Odorjan, Battin & Slivocka, 35 Bidwell St., PO Box 397, N4G 4H8 – 519/842-9079, Fax: 519/842-6091 – *3

TIMMINS .... Cochrane
Alexander, Barber, #1, 192 - 3 Ave., P4N 1C8 – 705/264-5221, Fax: 705/267-1336 – *3
Suzanne Desrosiers, #3, 24 Pine St. South, P4N 2J8 – 705/268-6492, Fax: 705/264-1940 – *1
Ellery, Cox, #202, 85 Pine St. South, PO Box 1540, P4W 7W7 – 705/264-9591, Fax: 705/264-1393 – *2
Evans, Bragagnolo & Sullivan, The 101 Mall, #131, 38 Pine St. North, P4N 6K6 – 705/264-1285, Fax: 705/264-7424 – *6
John Kukurin, 30 Spruce St. North, PO Box 1125, P4N 7H9 – 705/267-8441, Fax: 705/267-6811 – *1
Racicot, Bonney, Aubé, Gauthier, 15 Balsam St. South, P4N 2C7 – 705/264-2385, Fax: 705/268-3949 – *3
Robert A. Riopelle, #202, 85 Pine St. South, PO Box 1540, P4N 7W7 – 705/264-9591, 1396, Fax: 705/264-1393 – *1

TORONTO .... York
A.S.C. Wilson, North York Hydro, 5800 Yonge St., M2M 3T3 – 416/221-5501 – *1
Aaron & Aaron, #1400, 10 King St. East, M5C 1C3 – 416/364-5895, Fax: 416/364-3818 – *2
C.J. Abbass, #1200, 595 Bay St., M5G 2C2 – 416/593-5599 – *1
Abesamis Law Office, 2-2 Lombard St., M5C 1M1 – 416/861-8336, Fax: 416/861-8337 – *1
G.J. Abols, #101A, 1000 Finch Ave. West, M3J 2V5 – 416/661-1166, Fax: 416/661-7048 – *2

Abraham Duggan, 17 Dundonald St., M4Y 1K3 – 416/921-1700, Fax: 416/921-8936 – *9
Peter Abrahams, #504, 2 Sheppard Ave. East, M2N 5Y7 – 416/250-1313, Fax: 416/250-1303 – *1
G. Chalmers Adams, #100, 1255 Yonge St., M4T 1W6 – 416/929-7232, Fax: 416/929-7225 – *1
Richard W. Addinall, #1202, 180 Bloor St. West, M5S 2V6 – 416/925-4822, Fax: 416/967-5468 – *1
Addy & Addy, #210, 1560 Bayview Ave., M4G 3B8 – 416/322-5973 – *1
Bessie Adelman, 98 Roberta Dr., M6A 2J7 – 416/785-6660 – *1
Leo Adler, #3204, 20 Queen St. West, PO Box 40, M5H 3R3 – 416/598-1745, Fax: 416/340-7025 – *1
Advocacy Centre for the Elderly, #902, 120 Eglinton Ave. East, M4P 1E2 – 416/487-7157, Fax: 416/487-1342
Advocacy Resource Centre for the Handicapped, 255-40 Orchard View Blvd., M4R 1B9 – 416/482-8255, Fax: 416/482-2981 – *5
Advocacy Resource Centre For the Hearing Impaired, 40 Orchard View Blvd., M4R 1B9 – 416/482-1254 (Hearing Impaired)
Joseph Agostino, 321 Bloor St. East, M4W 1H1 – 416/413-3707, Fax: 416/413-3696 – *1
Agozzino Baker Gray, #200, 3875 Keele St., M3J 1N6 – 416/398-1200, Fax: 416/398-8585 – *4
Ahee, McMahon & Meikle, #550, 135 Queen's Plate Dr., M9W 6V1 – 416/745-2433, Fax: 416/745-6017 – *3
Aiken Associates, Richmond-Adelaide Centre, #410, 120 Adelaide St. West, M5H 1T1 – 416/947-0199, Fax: 416/947-0370 – *1
Melvyn H. Aiken, 878 Wilson Ave., M3K 1E7 – 416/635-7243, Fax: 416/635-7681 – *1
Aird & Berlis, #1800, 181 Bay St., M5J 2T9 – 416/364-1241 – *61
Irwin Aisen, 1921 Eglinton Ave. East, M1L 2L6 – 416/285-9988, Fax: 416/285-6801 – *1
Michael V. Akai, #204, 3459 Sheppard Ave. East, M1T 3K5 – 416/292-2565, Fax: 416/292-0473 – *1
Jerome T. Albert, #444, 100 Richmond St. West, M5H 2M9 – 416/368-8480, Fax: 416/368-0950
G.W. Alexandrowicz, 618A Queen St. West, M6J 1E4 – 416/368-5441, Fax: 416/368-5441 – *1
George Alexiou, #203, 785 Carlaw Ave., M4K 3L1 – 416/465-5515, Fax: 416/465-5554 – *1
Demo Aliferis, #200, 717 Pape Ave., M4K 3S9 – 416/778-4498, Fax: 416/463-1216 – *1
Allan & Associate, #2707, 401 Bay St., M5K 2Y4 – 416/363-5431, Fax: 416/363-2506 – *4
Allen and Phelan, #300, 100 Front St. East, M5A 1E1 – 416/865-0295, Fax: 416/865-1241 – *3
Carol Allen, #200, 166 Pearl, M5H 1L3 – 416/351-8600, Fax: 416/351-8331
K. Patricia Alletson, Commerce Court West, #5500, PO Box 85, Stn Commerce Court, M5L 1B9 – 416/869-5600, Fax: 416/947-0866 – *1
Alpert & Associates, #900, 1 St. Clair Ave. East, M4T 2V7 – 416/923-0809, Fax: 416/923-1549 – *2
Harriet Altman, 68 Gamier Court, M2M 4C9 – 416/224-5240, Fax: 416/224-0360 – *1
Sheldon L. Altman & Associates, 9 Gloucester St., M4Y 1L8 – 416/929-1313, Fax: 416/972-6885 – *1
Altwerger, Baker, Weinberg, #1701, 5650 Yonge St., M2M 4G3 – 416/733-2906, Fax: 416/733-3023 – *5
Joseph Amorim, 1310 Dundas St. West, M6J 1Y1 – 416/537-4121, Fax: 416/537-4123 – *4
Amsterdam & Peroff, #1902, 150 York St., M5N 3S5 – 416/367-0076, Fax: 416/367-1334 – *2
Anand, Bragança, Levy & Jebb, #1800, 4950 Yonge St., M2N 6K1
Anderson & Wylde, #2112, 401 Bay St., M5H 2Y4 – 416/363-0338, Fax: 416/868-0332 – *3
Anderson, Burgess, #403, 2333 Dundas St. West, M6R 3A6 – 416/535-1131, Fax: 416/536-3651
Dwight Anderson, #200, 2200 Bloor St. West, M6S 1N4 – 416/769-3522, Fax: 416/763-2522 – *1

indicates number of lawyers in law firm.

Anderson, Sinclair, #209, 3416 Dundas St. West, M6S 2S1 – 416/767-2127 – *1

Edmond Andrade & Associates, 32 Applemore Rd., M1B 1R6 – 416/609-8040, Fax: 416/609-1582 – *1

R. Andreansky, #305, 2161 Yonge St., M4S 3A6 – 416/485-1400, Fax: 416/489-7528 – *1

William Andrews, Q.C., #305, 27 Queen St. East, M5C 2M6 – 416/366-0740, Fax: 416/366-2861 – *1

Andriessen & Associate, #901, 701 Evans Avenue, M9C 1A3 – 416/620-7020, Fax: 416/622-8952; URL: http://ourworld.compuserve.com/homepages/andriessen_and_associates – *2

Raymond Ang, #850, 439 University Ave., M5G 1Y8 – 416/596-7077, Fax: 416/596-7629 – *1

M.J. Angevine, c/o The Law Society of Upper Canada, 130 Queen St. West, M5H 2N6 – 416/947-3301

V. Charles Anipare, 4002 Sheppard Ave. East, M1S 4R5 – 416/609-0540 – *1

R.A. Anisio, #5900, 1 First Canadian Place, PO Box 24, M5X 1K2 – 416/863-0820, Fax: 416/367-3316 – *1

Philip Anisman, #1905, 80 Richmond St. West, M5H 2A4 – 416/363-4200, Fax: 416/363-6200 – *1

Larry Anklewicz, #203, 5000 Dufferin St., M3H 5T5 – 416/961-6119 – *1

Mel Antflyck, 1501 Ellesmere Rd., M1P 4T6 – 416/431-1500, Fax: 416/431-1912 – *1

S.J. Antonette, #213, 455 Spadina Ave., M5S 2G8 – 416/979-2363, Fax: 416/979-0456 – *1

Sandra Antoniani, #780, 439 University Ave., M5G 1Y8 – 416/410-0608, Fax: 416/593-0225 – *1

Sam J. Apelbaum, #202, 4599 Kingston Rd., M1E 2P3 – 416/282-5779 – *1

Dennis Apostolides, 463 Danforth Ave., M4K 1P1 – 416/463-1147, Fax: 416/463-1762 – *1

M.G. Appel, Q.C., #3102, 130 Adelaide St. West, M5H 3P5 – 416/832-1111 – *1

Cheryl L. Appell, #306, 10 Alcorn Ave., M4V 1E4 – 416/927-0891, Fax: 416/927-0385

Jerry Applebaum, 36 Covington Rd., M6A 1G1 – 416/785-1140 – *1

M.I. Applebaum, Q.C., 4800 Dufferin St., M3H 5S9 – 416/661-9290, Fax: 416/661-6971 – *1

Frank A. Aprile, 2494 Danforth Ave., M4C 1K9 – 416/694-3117 – *1

C.E. Archibald, Q.C., #301, 817 Bloor St. West, M6G 1M1 – 416/534-6369 – *1

Kenneth Arenson, #1901, 8 King St. East, M5C 1B5 – 416/368-1500, Fax: 416/368-1516 – *1

Argiris & Associates, 693 Pape Ave., M4K 3S6 – 416/466-2184, Fax: 416/466-8707 – *3

Armel, Cohen, Stieber, #800, 55 University Ave., M5J 2K4 – 416/368-1400, Fax: 416/368-0016 – *19

Brian J. Armstrong, 5100 Dundas St. West, M9A 1C2 – 416/232-1358, Fax: 416/234-0259 – *1

Armstrong, Schiralli, Dunne & Singer, #1400, 141 Adelaide St. West, M5H 3L5 – 416/868-0180, Fax: 416/863-1814 – *10

D.W. Arn, 380 Bathurst St., M5T 2S6 – 416/364-3658, Fax: 416/368-0379 – *1

Arnold, Falzone & Fyshe, #2210, 439 University Ave., M5G 1Y8 – 416/977-1521, Fax: 416/977-4927 – *4

M.S. Aronoff, 166 Sheppard Ave. East, M2N 3A4 – 416/224-5806, Fax: 416/224-5087 – *1

Aronovitch, Robinson, #1200, 595 Bay St., M5G 2C2 – 416/593-1608, Fax: 416/593-4326

Judith Arrillaga, #200, 111 Eglinton Ave. East, M4P 1H4 – 416/488-3138, Fax: 416/482-4165 – *1

Harvey Ash, #900, 5799 Yonge St., M2M 3V3 – 416/250-0080, Fax: 416/225-1124; Email: justice@hookup.net – *1

Ashbourne & Caskey, 2077 Lawrence Ave. West, PO Box 403, M9N 1H7 – 416/247-6677, Fax: 416/247-3519 – *1

Christopher Ashby, #1200, 8 King St. East, M5C 1B5 – 416/368-4422, Fax: 416/364-1282

John Au, #830, 210 Dundas St. West, M5G 2E8 – 416/979-2663, Fax: 416/979-8681 – *1

Frank Austin, Q.C., 3092 Danforth Ave., M1L 1B1 – 416/691-5557 – *1

S.J. AvRuskin, 101 Charles St. East., M4Y 1V2 – 416/922-4147, Fax: 416/920-1554 – *1

Aylesworth, Thompson, Phelan, O'Brien, #3000, South Tower, Royal Bank Plaza, PO Box 15, Stn Royal Bank, M5J 2J1 – 416/865-0101, Fax: 416/865-1398 – *21

Kenneth Back & Associates, 3420 Finch Ave. East, M1W 2R6 – 416/499-2144 – *6

J.W. Baerg, #1610, 8 King St. East, M5C 1B5 – 416/366-3705, Fax: 416/366-0157 – *1

Sarah Bagnall, #2000, 390 Bay St., M5H 2Y2 – 416/862-9945, Fax: 416/860-0580 – *1

John H. Bailey, #901, 701 Evans Ave., M9C 1A3 – 416/622-7970, 2725, Fax: 416/622-8952 – *1

Karen Bailey, 56 Temperence St., 8th Fl., M5H 3V5 – 416/214-4646, Fax: 416/214-4699 – *1

Bain, Coleman, #400, 225 Richmond St. West, M5V 1W2 – 416/593-4813, Fax: 416/593-6157

W.N. Bain, #212, 120 Carlton St., M5A 4K2 – 416/924-7647 – *1

Baker & Company, #3300, 130 Adelaide St. West, M4W 1B9 – 416/366-8833, Fax: 416/366-3992 – *3

Baker & Janssen, #822, 207 Queen's Quay West, M5J 1A7 – 416/368-0881, Fax: 416/368-3312 – *5

Baker & McKenzie, #2100, 181 Bay St., PO Box 874, M5J 2T3 – 416/865-6941, Fax: 416/863-6275 – *42

Gordon R. Baker, Q.C., Exchange Tower, Bldg Box: 426, #1470, 2 First Canadian Place, M5X 1E3 – 416/365-7203, Fax: 416/365-7204 – *1

Morris A. Baker, 794 Bathurst St., M5R 3G1 – 416/534-7986, 7987 – *1

Baker, Ranieri, #403, 164 Eglinton Ave. East, M4P 1G4 – 416/932-1313, Fax: 416/932-1903 – *2

Baker, Schneider, Swartz, #1000, 120 Adelaide St. West, M5H 3V1 – 416/363-2211, Fax: 416/363-0645 – *3

W.G. Baker, 5179 Yonge St., M2N 5P5 – 416/221-1106 – *1

Baksh & Associates, #1204, 347 Bay St., M5H 2R7 – 416/867-1111, Fax: 416/867-2939 – *2

I. Vernon Balaban, Bldg Box: 1900, #2200, 181 University Ave., M5K 1B7 – 416/601-6760, Fax: 416/601-1322 – *1

Philip E. Band, Q.C., 668 Briar Hill, M6B 1L3 – 416/782-9808 – *1

Banks & Starkman, #303, 222 Dixon Rd., M9P 3S5 – 416/243-3394, Fax: 416/243-9692 – *4

D. Stuart Barber, #301, 250 Dundas St. West, M5T 2Z5 – 416/596-6636

T. Gary Bard, 415 Yonge St., 3rd Fl., M5B 2E7 – 416/975-7742, Fax: 416/975-3453 – *1

David A. Barker, #210, 45 Sheppard Ave. East, M2N 5W9 – 416/512-6010, Fax: 416/512-6846 – *1

Anne Barrett, 213 Armour Blvd., M3H 1M6 – 416/638-2990 – *1

Barrigar & Moss, #1108, 120 Adelaide St. West, M5H 1T1 – 416/364-4733 – *12

Harvey Barron, #202, 2986 Danforth Avenue, M4C 1M6 – 416/691-2666 – *1

J.R. Barrs, #2412, 401 Bay St., M5H 2Y4 – 416/366-6466, Fax: 416/364-2308 – *1

Basman Smith Rose, #1400, 111 Richmond St. West, M5H 2G4 – 416/365-0300, Fax: 416/365-9276 – *13

Bassel & Bassel, 39 Hayden St., M4Y 2P2 – 416/968-1266 – *1

Bassel Sullivan, #2100, 20 Queen St. West, PO Box 61, M5H 3R3 – 416/813-0600, Fax: 416/813-0470 – *5

James P. Bassel, 486 Briar Hill Ave., M5N 1M7 – 416/487-2315 – *1

Robert J. Bassermann, #212, 120 Carlton, M5A 4K2 – 416/323-3741, Fax: 416/922-3939 – *1

Bastedo, Sheldon, McGivney & Peck, #1800, 180 Dundas St. West, M5G 1Z8 – 416/595-5151, Fax: 416/596-7538

Batcher, Wasserman & Associates, #500, 718 Wilson Ave., M3K 1E2 – 416/635-6300, Fax: 416/635-6376 – *4

G. Richard Batty, 36 Adelaide St. East, PO Box 728, M5C 2J8 – 416/979-1772 – *1

Beach, Hepburn, #1000, 36 Toronto St., M5C 2C5 – 416/350-3500, Fax: 416/350-3510; Email: lawyer@beachlaw.com – *7

Alexander Beadie, 810 Queen St. East, M4M 1H7 – 416/463-8008, Fax: 416/469-9662 – *1

Beard, Winter, #900, 150 King St. West, M5H 2K4 – 416/593-5555, Fax: 416/593-7760 – *27

J.E.C. Beatty, Q.C., 138 Hanna Rd., M4G 3N7 – 416/488-8429 – *1

Beaudoin & Pepper, #800, 439 University Ave., M5G 1Y8 – 416/598-4775 – *3

Sandra Bebris, #3, 900 Don Mills Rd., M3C 1V8 – 416/510-1324, Fax: 416/441-6898 – *1

Allan J. Belisle, #1801, 1 Yonge St., M5E 1W7 – 416/777-9055, Fax: 416/365-0515 – *1

D. Casson Bell, Q.C., #811, 44 Victoria St., M5C 1Z2 – 416/363-9011, Fax: 416/363-9012 – *1

Bell, Temple, #1501, 393 University Ave., M5G 1E6 – 416/596-0969, Fax: 416/596-0952 – *15

Steven Bellissimo, #700, 357 Bay St., M5H 2T7 – 416/362-6437 – *1

Bellmore & Moore, #1600, 393 University Ave., M5G 1E6 – 416/581-1818, Fax: 416/581-1279 – *2

Bennett & Company, #2125, 130 King St. West, M5X 1A6 – 416/363-8688, Fax: 416/363-8083 – *2

Bennett Best Burn, #1700, 150 York St., M5H 3S5 – 416/362-3400, Fax: 416/362-2211; Email: bbbsuper@bbburn.com – *10

Bennett Jones Verchere, 1 First Canadian Place, #3400, PO Box 130, M5X 1A4 – 416/863-1200, Fax: 416/863-1716 – *24

Benson Percival Brown, #800, 250 Dundas St. West, M5T 2Z6 – 416/977-9777, Fax: 416/977-1241 – *12

Jeff Benson, 2901 Bayview Ave., M2K 1E6 – 416/730-8005 – *1

Sheldon Berg, 1595 Bloor St. West, M6P 1A6 – 416/533-9445, Fax: 416/537-8500 – *1

Percy Bergart, 120 Eglinton Ave. East, 5th Fl., M4P 1E2 – 416/482-1311, Fax: 416/483-8017 – *1

Bergstein & Kelly, 113 Davenport Rd., M5R 1H8 – 416/961-3100 – *2

Bradley F. Berns, #2307, 2025 Sheppard Ave. East, M2J 1V7 – 416/490-6456, Fax: 416/490-6439 – *1

Colin M. Berry, 74 - 38 St., M8W 3M3 – 416/251-4698 – *1

David C. Besant, #404, 3601 Victoria Park Ave., M1W 3Y3 – 416/756-4566, Fax: 416/756-3663 – *1

Michael Betcherman, 142 Robert St., M5S 2K3 – 416/924-2143 – *1

Myer Betel, #932, 20 Dundas St. West, Box 77, M5G 2C2 – 416/977-7114, Fax: 416/977-4069 – *1

Bhatia, Minipreet, #405, 3601 Victoria Park Ave., M1W 3Y3 – 416/493-1727, Fax: 416/756-3663

Bigelow, Hendy, #200, 789 Don Mills Rd., M3C 1T5 – 416/429-3110, Fax: 416/429-3057 – *4

R.G. Bigelow, 45 St. Nicholas St., M4Y 1W6 – 416/964-7497, Fax: 416/925-8122 – *1

Mary L. Biggar, #1000, 33 Bloor St. East, M4W 3H1 – 416/961-4100, Fax: 416/961-2531 – *1

Biles & Wratten, #1200, 10 King St. East, M5C 1C3 – 416/368-6178, Fax: 416/368-6170 – *2

Birchall Northey, #400, 144 Front St. West, M5J 2L7 – 416/599-0992, Fax: 416/599-4800 – *2

Birenbaum & Bernstein, #101, 3042 Keele St., M3M 2H5 – 416/633-3720, Fax: 416/633-4546 – *2

Birenbaum, Koffman, Steinberg, #1000, 33 Bloor St. East, M4W 3H1 – 416/961-4100, Fax: 416/961-2531 – *6

Birks, Langdon & Elliott, #2114, 85 Richmond St. West, M5H 1T1 – 416/363-3431, Fax: 416/363-0098 – *2

Irving I. Birnbaum, 108 Combe Ave., M3H 4J9 – 416/633-1870 – *1

Donald H. Bitter, Q.C., 308-100 Richmond St. West, M5H 3K6 – 416/360-4357 – *1

Black & Cook, #2109, 2 Bloor St. West, M4W 1A1 – 416/924-3311, Fax: 416/925-1711 – *2

Christopher C. Black, 1650 Yonge St., 2nd Fl., M47 2A2 – 416/487-1333, Fax: 416/482-2779

Donald D. Black, #101, 5859 Yonge St., M2M 3V6 – 416/225-8806 – *1

Black, Sutherland & Crabbe, #2700, 401 Bay St., PO Box 101, M5H 2Y4 – 416/361-1500, Fax: 416/361-1674 – *9

Harry Blaier, #1800, 4950 Yonge St., M2N 6K1 – 416/224-0200, Fax: 416/224-0758 – *1

Blake, Cassels & Graydon, Commerce Court West, 46th Fl., PO Box 25, M5L 1A9 – 416/863-2400, Fax: 416/863-2653, 4250; Email: toronto@blakes.ca – *208

Edith M. Blake, #130, 130 Don Mills Rd., M3B 2W6 – 416/445-0310, Fax: 416/445-0316

Blaney, McMurtry, Stapells, Friedman, Cadillac Fairview Tower, #1400, 20 Queen St. West, M5H 3R3 – 416/593-1221, Fax: 416/593-5437; Email: info@blaney.com; URL: http://www.blaney.com – *74

M.E. Blankstein, #100, 133 Berkeley St., M5A 2X1 – 416/363-9024, Fax: 416/363-9291 – *1

Jeffrey A. Blayways, 129 John St., M5V 2E2 – 416/598-3401, Fax: 416/977-3660 – *1

Bliss & Associates, #402, 133 Richmond St. West, M5H 2L3 – 416/361-0801 – *4

Bloom & Lanys, #100, 250 Roehampton Ave., M4P 1R9 – 416/486-9913, Fax: 416/485-6054 – *1

Deborah M. Bloomberg, 75 Lowther Ave., M5R 1C9 – 416/960-1822, Fax: 416/961-9905 – *1

Joseph L. Bloomenfeld, #2110, 120 Adelaide St. West, M5H 1T1 – 416/363-7315, Fax: 416/363-7697 – *1

Bloor Information & Legal Services, 1072 Dovercourt Rd., M6H 2X8 – 416/531-7376, Fax: 416/531-7580

Harold Bocknek, 460 College St., M6G 1A1 – 416/961-8280, 8229, Fax: 416/961-3628 – *1

Bodnaruk & Capone, 720 Spadina Ave., M5S 2T9 – 416/923-7000 – *4

Bogart, Robertson & Chu, #1608, 141 Adelaide St. West, M5H 3L5 – 416/601-1991, Fax: 416/601-0006 – *4

John M. Bolton, 97 Munro Blvd., M2P 1C5 – 416/225-1091 – *1

Robert E. Bombier, 1366 Dundas St. West, M6J 1Y2 – 416/532-1926, Fax: 416/534-2870 – *1

G.H. Bomza, #2303, 180 Dundas St. West, M5G 1Z8 – 416/598-2244 – *1

Bondzi-Simpson Company, 1650 Yonge St., 2nd Fl., M4T 2A2 – 416/482-2601, Fax: 416/482-2779 – *2

Richard Borchiver, #900, 119 Spadina Ave., M5V 2L1 – 416/977-2929, Fax: 416/977-0489 – *1

Borden & Elliot, Scotia Plaza, #4400, 40 King St. West, M5H 3Y4 – 416/367-6000, Fax: 416/367-6749; Email: info@borden.com; URL: http://www.borden.com – *221

Borden, Wearing, #507, 330 University Ave., M5G 1R7 – 416/351-1213, Fax: 416/351-1434 – *2

Harry J. Borenstein, #304, 3335 Yonge St., M4N 2M1 – 416/482-0990, Fax: 416/482-6511 – *1

Howard Borenstein, 9 Gloucester St., M4Y 1L8 – 416/925-1601, Fax: 416/972-6885 – *1

Alex Borman, #601, 130 Bloor St. West, M5S 1N5 – 416/960-5090, Fax: 416/923-1391 – *1

N.H.R. Borski, Q.C., #201, 2256B Bloor St. West, M6S 1N6 – 416/766-2441 – *1

Y.R. Botiuk, Q.C., #212, 2323 Bloor St. West, M6S 4W1 – 416/763-4333 – *1

Botnick & Botnick, #53, 2300 Finch Ave. West, M9M 2Y3 – 416/741-3584, Fax: 416/741-3529 – *4

N. Boutet, 350 Bay St., 9th Fl., M5H 2S6 – 416/363-0650, Fax: 416/367-4098 – *1

Bowlby & Bowlby, 330 Bay St., M5H 2S8 – 416/363-4147 – *2

Bowman, Farber & Ceresney, #110, 2100 Ellesmere Rd., M1H 3B7 – 416/438-9450, Fax: 416/438-9236 – *3

Jerry Boyaner, 100 Adelaide St. West, M5H 1S3 – 416/360-5765, Fax: 416/360-6551 – *1

Mary Boyce, 69 Elm St., M5G 1H2 – 416/591-7588, Fax: 416/971-9092 – *1

Neil L. Boyko, 878 Wilson Ave., M3K 1E7 – 416/635-1411, Fax: 416/635-7681 – *1

R. Bradburn, #304, 2 Dunbloor Rd., M9A 2E4 – 416/239-8119, Fax: 416/239-6922 – *1

P.G. Bradley, 1051 Tapscott Rd., M1X 1A1 – 416/298-0066, Fax: 416/299-8008 – *1

L.A. Braithwaite, Q.C., 250 Wincott Dr., M9R 2R5 – 416/249-2288, Fax: 416/249-2280 – *1

Carl A. Brand, #2, 2034 Queen St. East, M4L 1J4 – 416/698-1799, Fax: 416/691-9760 – *1

David Brannan, 845 Wilson Ave., M3K 1E6 – 416/636-9770 – *1

Brans, Lehun, Baldwin & Champagne, #1700, 120 Adelaide St. West, M5H 1T1 – 416/601-1040, Fax: 416/601-0655

George F. Brant, #212, 120 Carlton St., M5A 4K2 – 416/922-4820, Fax: 416/924-7166 – *2

Bratty & Partners, Madison Centre, 4950 Yonge St., 20th Fl., M2N 6K1 – 416/226-0660, Fax: 416/226-6395; Email: mourisin@bratty.com; URL: http://www.bratty.com – *17

G.K.C. Braund, Q.C., #204, 3333 Bayview Ave., M2K 1G4 – 416/223-0862 – *1

W. Braverman, 771 St. Clair Ave. West, M6C 1B4 – 416/654-8160 – *1

Chaim P. Bredin, #214, 2175 Sheppard Ave. East, M2J 1W8 – 416/496-0045, Fax: 416/496-0542 – *1

Brennen Partners, #530, 21 Four Seasons Place, M9B 6J8 – 416/620-9500, Fax: 416/620-1837 – *3

Brent & Paul, #100, 99 Scarsdale Rd., M3B 2R2 – 416/441-2830, Fax: 416/441-4011 – *1

Bresver, Grossman, Scheininger & Davis, #2800, 390 Bay St., M5H 2Y2 – 416/869-0366, Fax: 416/869-0321 – *11

Stephen W. Brett, #1200, 595 Bay St., M5G 2C2 – 416/595-9603 – *1

Domenic C. Brigante, #23, 1170 Sheppard Ave. West, M3K 2A3 – 416/636-6969, Fax: 416/636-6740 – *1

Brigden, George W., Q.C., #602, 425 University Ave., M5G 1T6 – 416/977-3775, Fax: 416/595-0825

Royden Brigham, #800, 75 The Donway West, M3C 2E9 – 416/444-1193, Fax: 416/444-1194 – *1

Barry Brissenden, #205, 2095 Weston Rd., M9N 1X7 – 416/244-5555, Fax: 416/241-2711 – *1

Broadhurst Main, #2812, 20 Queen St. West, M5H 3R3 – 416/408-4088, Fax: 416/408-4188 – *9

Peter E. Brodey, Q.C., 298 Avenue Rd., Main Fl., M4V 2H1 – 416/923-1175 – *1

Brodkin, Comba, #1200, 595 Bay St., M5G 2C2 – 416/340-0404, Fax: 416/340-7229 – *3

Michael Brodzky, 69 Elm St., M5G 1H2 – 416/581-8898, Fax: 416/971-9092 – *1

Natalie Bronstein, #1200, 595 Bay St., M5G 2C2 – 416/408-0444, Fax: 416/593-1352 – *1

Brown & Forbes, #2700, 390 Bay St., M5H 2Y2 – 416/366-7927, Fax: 416/363-9602 – *12

Brown & Jones Associates, #104, 5803 Yonge St., M2M 3V5 – 416/223-9126, Fax: 416/223-9343 – *3

Arthur C. Brown, 183 Queen St. East, M5A 1S2 – 416/362-9590 – *1

Constance M. Brown, Q.C., #1530, 439 University Ave., M5G 1Y8 – 416/598-3388, 3389, Fax: 416/598-2145 – *1

G.P. Brown, 1154 Morningside Ave., M1B 3A4 – 416/283-1200 – *1

Brown, Joseph, #1803, 2 Sheppard Ave. East, M2N 5Y7 – 416/222-3295, Fax: 416/733-8090

Kenneth J. Brown, 45 Mogul Dr., M2H 2M8 – 416/499-8005, Fax: 416/499-8048 – *1

M.H. Brown, 38 Berwick Ave., M5P 1H1 – 416/487-5122, Fax: 416/487-5168 – *1

Peter Brown, 3048 Bloor St. West, M8X 1C4 – 416/234-8682 – *1

Phillip A. Brown, 317 Grace St., M6G 3A7 – 416/538-8328, Fax: 416/533-5174 – *1

Milton J. Brown Q.C. & Associates, Thomson Bldg., 65 Queen St. West, M5H 2M5 – 416/361-1313 – *2

Colin A. Browne, #700, 4 King St. West, M1S 5B3 – 416/864-0246, Fax: 416/864-0912 – *1

Jack Brudner, #203, 2753 Eglinton Ave. East, M1J 2C7 – 416/267-1148, Fax: 416/267-4741 – *1

Arnold Bruner, 167 Danforth Ave., M4K 1N2 – 416/461-0983 – *1

G.J. Bruner, 167 Danforth Ave., M4K 1N2 – 416/461-0983, Fax: 416/462-3347 – *1

Brunner & Lundy, #1800, 401 Bay St., M5H 2Z1 – 416/777-9375, Fax: 416/777-9381 – *2

A.G. Bryant, 370 Bloor St. East, M4W 3M6 – 416/927-7441 – *1

David G. Bryce, #108, 100 Lombard St., M5C 1M3 – 416/364-9916, Fax: 416/364-7505 – *1

Buckland Werbowyj, #401, 302 The East Mall, M9B 6C7 – 416/233-9461

Frederic Buckland, #401, 302 The East Mall, M9B 6C7 – 416/236-0906, Fax: 416/233-1524 – *1

Lowell Budd, #1700, 150 King St. West, M5H 1J9 – 416/598-2332 – *1

Elizabeth Slava Budi, 94 Walmer Rd., M5R 2X7 – 416/922-2151, Fax: 416/960-8630 – *1

Victor Bulger, #610, 4211 Yonge St., M2P 2A9 – 416/590-7744, Fax: 416/590-9998

N. Bullard, #412, 120 Carlton St., M5A 4K2 – 416/515-1742 – *1

Bunn & Ehrlich, #112, 5803 Yonge St. M2M, M2M 3V5 – 416/226-4486 – *2

J.J. Burke, #302, 2405 Lakeshore Blvd. West, M8V 1C6 – 416/252-9101, Fax: 416/503-0627 – *1

R.H. Burke, Q.C., #612, 330 Bay St., M5H 2S8 – 416/214-1162, Fax: 416/214-0870 – *1

Burkman & Twiss, One First Canadian Pl., #1410, PO Box 129 Stn First Canadian Place, M5X 1A4 – 416/364-3831, Fax: 416/364-3832 – *2

Burnett & Jacobson, 48 St. Clair Ave. W., M4T 2Z2 – 416/922-8710, Fax: 416/964-5840 – *2

Terry Burrell, 317 Grace St., M6G 3A7 – 416/538-0842, Fax: 416/533-5174 – *1

Burt, Burt, Wolfe & Bowman, #202, 2 Adelaide St. West, M5H 1L6 – 416/366-5431, Fax: 416/369-1135 – *2

Bernard Burton, #410, 120 Carlton St., M5A 4K2 – 416/922-1263, Fax: 416/922-1963 – *1

Michael P. Bury, #1001, 65 Queen St. West, M5H 2M5 – 416/363-9966 – *1

Burych, Raimonde, 2200 Lakeshore Blvd. West, M8V 1A4 – 416/252-6550, Fax: 416/252-1843 – *2

Bussin & Bussin, #1822, 181 University Ave., M5H 3M7 – 416/364-4925, Fax: 416/868-1818 – *3

Fernandez Buternowsky, 605-10 Saint Mary St., M4Y 1P9 – 416/323-6783, Fax: 416/323-0867 – *1

G.C. Butterill, 92 Hanna Rd., M4G 3N3 – 416/488-5352 – *1

B. Clive Bynoe, Q.C., 480 University Ave., 7th Fl., M5G 1V2 – 416/977-0853, Fax: 416/977-5331 – *1

Byrne, Crosby, #1600, 8 King St. East, M5C 1B5 – 416/364-1616, Fax: 416/363-6455; Email: ccrosby@byrnecrosby.com – *4

Byrne, Johnson & Calzavara, #106, 81 The East Mall, M8Z 5W3 – 416/253-0253, Fax: 416/253-1243 – *3

Thomas J. Byron, #208, 5353 Dundas St. West, M9B 6H8 – 416/234-9171 – *1

C A W Legal Services Plans, #830, 102 Bloor St. West, M5S 1M8 – 416/960-2410, Fax: 416/960-8047

Frank Calandra, 392 Dundas St. East, M5A 2A5 – 416/944-8544, Fax: 416/944-8085 – *1

Paul Calarco, #1000, 65 Queen St. West, M5H 2M5 – 416/366-9202, Fax: 416/367-3949 – *1

Paul Calarco, #780, 439 University Ave., M5G 1Y8 – 416/598-1948 – *1

* indicates number of lawyers in law firm.

Ruth L. Cameron, 720 Spadina Ave., M5S 2T9 – 416/929-9562 – *1
Alistair Campbell, #201, 181 Eglinton Ave. East, M4P 1J9 – 416/482-6500, Fax: 416/488-2477 – *1
H.B. Campbell & Associates, #6000, 40 King St. West, M5H 3Z7 – 416/365-1986 – *1
Campbell, Jarvis, McKenzie & Fulton, 372 Bay St., M5H 2W9 – 416/363-6279 – *1
John R. Campbell, Q.C., #107, 8 King St. East, M5C 1B5 – 416/363-5086, Fax: 416/961-0510 – *1
Campbell, Waisberg, 2373 Bloor St. West, M6S 1P6 – 416/760-8868, Fax: 416/760-8493
Campione & Vaturi, #400, 1110 Finch Ave. West, M3J 2T2 – 416/665-8133, Fax: 416/665-5752 – *2
Canada Loan Litigation Inc., #1606, 401 Bay St., PO Box 62, M5H 2Y4 – 416/864-7424, Fax: 416/366-9505
G.H. Cancilla, #1606, 401 Bay St., M5H 2Y4 – 416/366-9504, Fax: 416/366-9505 – *1
Cannings, John, #400, 145 Adelaide St. West, M5H 3H4 – 416/366-1985, Fax: 416/366-2482 – *4
Ruth Canton, 2489A Bloor St. West, M6S 1R6 – 416/769-5759, Fax: 416/769-3132 – *1
Rochelle F. Cantor, #204, 100 Lombard St., M5C 1M3 – 416/861-1625, Fax: 416/861-1466 – *1
Capp, Shupak, #1703, 2 St. Clair Ave. West, M4V 1L5 – 416/323-1116, Fax: 416/323-0697 – *2
Stephen L. Cappe, #1704, 55 University Ave., M5J 2H7 – 416/366-7305, Fax: 416/366-3513
Ernest J. Cappellacci, #1400, 65 Queen St. West, M5H 2M5 – 416/203-2988 – *2
Carbonaro, Dakin, Flude & Mikulinski, 2910-390 Bay St., M5H 2V6 – 416/368-2500, Fax: 416/368-0909 – *4
L.C. Caroe, #1800, 4950 Yonge St., M2N 6K1 – 416/224-0200, Fax: 416/224-0758 – *1
Michael W. Caroline, #5012, 40 King St. West, M5H 3Y2 – 416/366-4300, Fax: 416/366-7076 – *1
Juan F. Carranza, #317, 1315 Finch Ave. West, M3J 2G6 – 416/633-1065, Fax: 416/633-9782 – *1
John S.H. Carriere, #1810, 65 Queen St. West, PO Box 81, M5H 2M5 – 416/363-5594, Fax: 416/363-8492 – *1
F.L. Carruthers, #250, 70 University Ave., M5J 2M4 – 416/597-1777, Fax: 416/977-2895 – *1
Carson, Gross & McPherson, #1400, 401 Bay St., M5H 2Y4 – 416/361-0900, Fax: 416/361-3459 – *8
Carter & Wong, #401, 302 Spadina Ave., M5T 2E7 – 416/593-8820, Fax: 416/593-9611 – *2
George Carter, 180 Dundas St. West, M5G 1Z8 – 416/599-2877 – *1
John R. Casey, Q.C., 119 Underhill Dr., M5G 1V2 – 416/441-1279 – *1
Joy Casey, #1402, 151 Yonge St., M5C 2W7 – 416/368-3847, Fax: 416/366-9808
Caspar Sinnige, 470 King St. East, M5A 1L7 – 416/362-5700, Fax: 416/362-0847 – *1
Cass & Cass, #700, 55 University Ave., M5J 2H7 – 416/943-4711, Fax: 416/368-0016 – *2
G.M. Cass, #206, 2040 Yonge St., M4S 1Z9 – 416/488-9718, Fax: 416/488-9116 – *1
Marilynne Cass, #210, 335 Bay St., M5H 2R3 – 416/863-9744, Fax: 416/863-9541 – *1
Cass, Miller & Associates, #100, 272 Lawrence Ave. West, M5M 4M1 – 416/787-0641, Fax: 416/787-0645 – *2
Cassels Brock & Blackwell, Scotia Plaza, #2100, 40 King St. West, M5H 3C2 – 416/869-5300, Fax: 416/360-8877 – *126
Cassels, Mitchell, 497 Eglinton Ave. West, M5N 1A7 – 416/485-9435 – *1
Donald J. Catalano, O.C., 84 Avenue Rd., M5R 2H2 – 416/928-2803, Fax: 416/925-1536 – *1
Licio E. Cengarle, 1151 Martin Grove Rd., M9W 4W8 – 416/248-5505, Fax: 416/248-2100 – *1
Oren H. Chaimovitch, #300, 230 Sheppard Ave. West, M2N 1N1 – 416/223-1840
Chaiton & Chaiton, 185 Sheppard Ave. West, M2N 1M9 – 416/222-8888, Fax: 416/222-8402 – *20
Chan & Li, #202, 3640 Victoria Park Ave., M2H 3B2 – 416/498-3333, Fax: 416/498-3340 – *2

Chapin & Chapin, #300, 8 King St. East, M5C 1B5 – 416/867-1799, Fax: 416/366-4892 – *2
Chapnick & Associates, 228 Carlton St., M5A 2L1 – 416/968-2160, Fax: 416/975-9338 – *4
Chappell, Bushell, Stewart, #3310, 20 Queen St. West, M5H 3R3 – 416/351-0005, Fax: 416/351-0002
Gerald J. Charney, Q.C., #200, 70 Bond St., M5B 1X3 – 416/360-8820, Fax: 416/365-7702 – *1
Chatarpaul & Associates, #402, 2065 Finch Ave. West, M3N 2V7 – 416/742-3150, Fax: 416/742-3163 – *2
Max P. Cheng, #1020, 180 Dundas St. West, M5G 1Z8 – 416/598-2998, Fax: 416/598-4374 – *2
Jackson L Chercover, Q.C., #805, 111 Avenue Rd., M5R 3J8 – 416/920-7411, Fax: 416/925-6811 – *2
Chernin & Kirsh, #204, 1497 Yonge St., M4T 1Z2 – 416/925-2444, Fax: 416/925-2446 – *1
Chernos, Conway, #2600, 130 Adelaide St. West, M5H 3P5 – 416/363-2443, Fax: 416/363-2448
M. Chernovsky, 61 Saint Nicholas St., M4Y 1W6 – 416/927-7048, Fax: 416/925-0162 – *1
Sydney B. Chertkoff, Q.C., #1701, 5650 Yonge St., M2M 4G3 – 416/733-2906, Fax: 416/733-3023 – *1
Adam Ching, #212, 885 Progress Ave., M1H 3G3 – 416/431-4311, Fax: 416/431-5445 – *1
Ronald W. Chisholm, Q.C., #707, 330 University Ave., M5G 1R7 – 416/586-0777, Fax: 416/586-0267 – *2
David Chong, #207, 1370 Don Mills Rd., M3B 3N7 – 416/510-2233, Fax: 416/510-2234 – *1
Christopher E. Chop, #300, 8 King St. East, M5C 1B5 – 416/867-1799; 922-7099, Fax: 416/366-4892 – *1
Raymond Chow, 2 Lansing Sq., M2J 4P8 – 416/502-2200 – *1
Shirley Chow, #3, 3030 Midland Ave., M1S 5C9 – 416/298-0203, Fax: 416/298-1339 – *1
Chowbay Valmiki, #407, 1315 Finch Ave. West, M3J 2G6 – 416/638-9273, Fax: 416/638-7721
Robert C. Christie, #1000, 65 Queen St. West, M5H 2M5 – 416/866-8436, Fax: 416/367-3949 – *1
Christie, Saccucci, Matthews, Caskie & Chilco, Confederation Sq., #301, 20 Richmond St. East, M5C 2R9 – 416/367-0680, Fax: 416/367-0429 – *7
B.N. Christoff, 4 Ranleigh Ave., M4N 1W9 – 416/489-5604 – *1
Paul Chumak, 75 Lowther Ave., M5R 1C9 – 416/927-1977, Fax: 416/961-9905 – *1
Andrea Chun, One Corporate Plaza, #700, 2075 Kennedy Rd., M1T 3V3 – 416/754-3060, Fax: 416/754-3321 – *1
Arthur K. Chung, 63 Elm St., M5G 1H2 – 416/977-2700, Fax: 416/977-4359 – *1
Chusid, Friedman, #900, 30 St. Clair Ave West, M4V 3A1 – 416/963-4990 – *19
G.J. Ciglen, #5, 1474 Bathurst St., M5P 3G9 – 416/656-8400, Fax: 416/656-9823 – *1
Cimetta & Cimetta, #207, 834 Yonge St., M4W 2H1 – 416/921-7470 – *2
Wayne Paul Cipollone, #2330, 130 Adelaide St. West, M5H 3P5 – 416/368-5366, Fax: 416/368-5361 – *3
D.J. Cirone, #206, 2494 Danforth Ave., M4C 1K9 – 416/691-1000, Fax: 416/694-5369 – *1
Arthur H. Clairman, #C, 1966 Yonge St., M4S 1Z4 – 416/481-8658, Fax: 416/481-6055
Clapp & Gibson, 18 Erskine Ave., M4P 1Y2 – 416/484-4827, Fax: 416/484-0821 – *2
J.S. Clarfield, #1106, 45 Bunfield Ave., M4S 2H4 – 416/638-6768 – *1
Deta J. Clark, #201, 5075 Yonge St., M2N 6C6 – 416/733-3135 – *1
S.R. Clark, #1901, 65 Queen St. West, M5H 2M5 – 416/601-1518, Fax: 416/369-0085 – *1
Clarke, Freeman, Miller & Ryan, 1863 Danforth Ave., M4C 1J3 – 416/698-9323, Fax: 416/698-9110 – *3
M.J. Clarke, 251 Wellesley St. East, M4X 1G8 – 416/961-9801, Fax: 416/961-9880 – *1
Bernard Clayman, #1500, 2 St. Clair Ave. East, M4T 2T5 – 416/922-4777, Fax: 416/927-0305 – *1
J.T. Clement, Q.C., #2800, 390 Bay St., M5H 2Y2 – 416/362-1685, Fax: 416/869-0321 – *1

Eric Cliche, #204, 3875 Keele St., M3J 1N6 – 416/398-2290, Fax: 416/398-8358
Peter Clyne, 155 Harbord St., M5S 1H1 – 416/922-0864, Fax: 416/922-6856 – *1
Robert G. Coates, #307, 120 Carlton St., M5A 4K3 – 416/925-6490, Fax: 416/925-4492 – *1
Coatsworth, Richardson & Hart, #406, 347 Bay St., M5H 2R7 – 416/363-0113 – *1
Codina & Pukitis, #1708, 390 Bay St., M5H 2Y2 – 416/361-1404, Fax: 416/361-1390 – *8
Susan Coen, 45 Saint Nicholas St., M4Y 1W6 – 416/925-0004, Fax: 416/925-8122 – *1
Cohen & Associates, #801, 1 St. Clair Ave. East, M4T 2V7 – 416/323-0907, Fax: 416/324-8053 – *1
B.C. Cohen, #201, 1001 Sandhurst Circle, M1V 1Z6 – 416/293-6000, Fax: 416/293-4027 – *1
Cohen, Goodman, #1500, 439 University Ave., M5G 1Y8 – 416/595-5555, Fax: 416/595-7020 – *2
Harold B. Cohen, Q.C., 10 Foxbar Rd., M4V 2G6 – 416/961-7255 – *1
Howard Cohen, #2412, 401 Bay St., M5H 2Y4 – 416/364-7436, Fax: 416/364-2308 – *1
Kenneth J. Cohen, #200, 65 Queen St. West, M5H 2M5 – 416/363-3351, Fax: 416/363-0252 – *1
M.V. Cohen, #1905, 400 Walmer Rd., M5P 2X7 – 416/927-7891 – *1
Neil Cohen, #115, 2 College St., M5G 1K3 – 416/921-0617, Fax: 416/921-9542 – *1
David Cohn, 401 Bay St., M5H 2Y4 – *1
Victoria Colby, #212, 120 Carlton, M5A 4K2 – 416/323-9660, Fax: 416/924-7166 – *1
V.K. Colebourn, Q.C., #210, 335 Bay St., M5H 2R3 – 416/863-9744, Fax: 416/863-9541 – *1
Allen R. Collins, #1704, 55 University Ave., M5J 2H7 – 416/362-1566, Fax: 416/366-3513 – *1
John Collins, #Penthouse, 121 Richmond St. West, M5H 2K1 – 416/364-9006, Fax: 416/861-0554 – *1
David J. Colman, 344 Bloor St. West, M5S 3A7 – 416/944-8046, Fax: 416/944-8756 – *1
Colman, Greenwood & Posen, 4580 Dufferin St., M3H 5Z1 – 416/665-9111
David I. Conn, #1202, 330 Bay St., M5H 2S8 – 416/363-1868, Fax: 416/364-7885 – *1
John R. Connolly, #1202, 390 Bay St., M5H 2Y2 – 416/865-1558, Fax: 416/363-8451 – *1
Nils R. Connor, 69 Elm St., M5G 1H2 – 416/591-2203, Fax: 416/971-9092 – *1
David R. Conway, #601, 130 Bloor St. West, M5S 1N5 – 416/923-4720, Fax: 416/923-1391 – *1
E.A. Conway, #1402, 151 Yonge St., M5C 2W7 – 416/368-2124, Fax: 416/366-9808 – *1
R.H.W. Cook, #2880, Royal Bank Plaza, M5J 2J3 – 416/368-1041, Fax: 416/865-0896 – *1
Roger P.P. Cooney, 3080 Yonge St., M4N 3N1 – 416/481-5604
Cooper & Cooper, #700, 357 Bay St., M5H 2T7 – 416/362-6459, Fax: 416/363-4130 – *2
Cooper & Stein, #303, 1035 McNicoll Ave., M1W 3W6 – 416/490-9299, Fax: 416/490-1018 – *2
Gregory W. Cooper, #1501, 1 Queen St. East., M5C 2W5 – 416/867-1400, Fax: 416/867-1873 – *2
Harry S. Cooper, #510, 45 Sheppard Ave. East, M1N 5W9 – 416/225-7321, Fax: 416/225-8751 – *1
Kirk J. Cooper, 348 Danforth Ave., M4K 1N8 – 416/778-1200, Fax: 416/778-1291 – *1
Morris Cooper, 99 Yorkville Ave., M5R 3K5 – 416/961-2626, Fax: 416/961-4000 – *1
Cooper, Sandler, West & Skurka, #1900, 439 University Ave., M5G 1Y8 – 416/585-9191, Fax: 416/408-2372 – *3
Stephen E. Cooper, 671 St. Clair Ave. West, M6C 1A8 – 416/651-2641, Fax: 416/651-1295 – *1
Copeland, Campbell, 31 Prince Arthur Ave., M5R 1B2 – 416/964-8126, Fax: 416/960-5456 – *3
Copeland, McKenna, 3638 Lakeshore Blvd. West, M8W 1P1 – 416/252-3351, Fax: 416/252-7519 – *4
J. Copelovici, #707, 40 Sheppard Ave. West, M2N 6K9 – 416/512-2181, Fax: 416/250-6546 – *1

Canadian Almanac & Directory 1997

Cornish Advocates, #500, 210 Dundas St. West, M5G 2E8 – 416/971-5011, Fax: 416/971-6108 – *7

Lori A. Cornwall, #1000, 65 Queen St. West, M5H 2M5 – 416/361-0909, Fax: 416/367-3949 – *1

Willa J. Corse, 78 Shields Ave., M5N 2K4 – 416/488-0257 – *1

Cosman & Associates, #200, 5109 Steeles Ave. West, M9L 2Y8 – 416/746-2213 – *2

F.D. Costa, 1389 Dundas St. West, M6J 1Y4 – 416/534-6357 – *1

Angela M. Costigan, #410, 120 Carlton St., M5A 4K2 – 416/922-8611, Fax: 416/922-1963

Donald Cosway, #208, 4218 Lawrence Ave. East, M1E 4X9 – 416/281-2502, Fax: 416/281-8957 – *1

D.B. Cousins, #300, 111 Elizabeth St., M5G 1P7 – 416/977-8871 – *1

Coutts, Crane, Ingram, #700, 480 University Ave., M5G 1V2 – 416/977-0956, Fax: 416/977-5331 – *8

Ronald Cowitz, #3, 794 Bathurst St., M5R 3G1 – 416/588-6614, Fax: 416/588-6146 – *1

Cox, Armstrong & Smith, #907, 8 King St. East., M5C 1B5 – 416/861-8695, Fax: 416/861-9074 – *2

Christopher G. Cox, #3, 900 Don Mills Rd., M3C 1V8 – 416/447-4274, Fax: 416/447-3823 – *1

Peter B. Cozzi, #300, 111 Eglinton Ave. East, M4P 1H4 – 416/440-0046, Fax: 416/440-1682

Crabtree & Ringer, #1600, 8 King St. East, M5C 1B5 – 416/364-4491, Fax: 416/364-0364 – *2

Gordon Crann & Associates, 535 Adelaide St. East, M5A 1N8 – 416/214-2722, Fax: 416/214-4787 – *1

Crawford & Scott, 198 Delaware Ave., M6H 2T3 – 416/531-4229 – *1

T.D. Crawford, #302, 2280A Bloor St. West, M6S 1N9 – 416/760-8118, Fax: 416/760-8175 – *1

F.H. Cremer, #201, 1593 Wilson Ave., M3L 1A5 – 416/244-5575, Fax: 416/247-3844 – *1

Crewe & Marks, #1100, 111 Elizabeth St., M5G 1P7 – 416/506-0423, Fax: 416/506-9173 – *4

Robert C. Cronish, Q.C., #2828, 2 Bloor St. East, M4W 1A8 – 416/961-1088 – *3

Howard Crosner, 1961A Queen St. East, M4L 1H8 – 416/690-8664, Fax: 416/690-8107 – *1

L.A. Crosse, #1002, 365 Bloor St. East, M4W 3L4 – 416/962-3740, Fax: 416/962-3902 – *1

Crossley, Mann, #706, 1 First Canadian Place, PO Box 405, M5X 1E3 – 416/860-1663, Fax: 416/868-2368

Paul J. Crowe, #3, 4901A Yonge St., M2N 5N4 – 416/733-0255, Fax: 416/221-9965 – *1

Crum-Ewing & Poliacik, 56 Sheppard Ave. West, M1N 1M2 – 416/733-9292, Fax: 416/733-9654 – *2

Sheila Crummey, #300, 100 Front St. East, M5A 1E1 – 416/363-3363, Fax: 416/865-1241 – *1

L.J. Cuddy, #209, 3550 Victoria Park Ave., M2H 2N5 – 416/498-0865, Fax: 416/498-0667 – *1

Patricia A. Cullen, #1704, 55 University Ave., M5J 2H7 – 416/366-7802, Fax: 416/366-3513

G.A.J. Cundari, 1684 Dufferin St., M6H 3M1 – 416/654-9000, Fax: 416/658-7653 – *1

Curtis, Carole, 288 Jarvis St., M5B 2C5 – 416/340-1850 – *3

J. Cusmariu, #2, 1272 Dundas St. West, M6J 1X7 – 416/533-1173 – *1

Harry K. Cuttler, #3, 794 Bathurst St., M5R 3G1 – 416/588-6614 – *1

Timothy P. Czajkowski, Plaza 100, #112, 100 Wellesley St. East, M4Y 1H5 – 416/925-9551 – *1

Czuma, Ritter, #502, 481 University Ave., M5G 2E9 – 416/599-5799 – *2

E.L. D'Alimonte, #203, 1111 Albion Rd., M9V 1A9 – 416/741-5373, Fax: 416/740-1154 – *1

Dale & Lessman, Commercial Union Tower, #2000, Toronto-Dominion Centre, PO Box 73, M5K 1E7 – 416/863-1010, Fax: 416/863-1009

H.A. Dale, #412, 120 Carlton St., M5A 4K2 – 416/922-8787, Fax: 416/922-3939 – *1

Daley, Byers, #700, 4 King St. West, M5C 1B6 – 416/864-0246, Fax: 416/864-0192 – *6

Damery & Mamak, 101 Roncesvalles Ave., M6R 2K9 – 416/532-3349 – *2

Timothy Dang, #910, 65 Queen St. West, M5H 2M5 – 416/368-2851, Fax: 416/360-1056

Daniels & Associates, #601, 4711 Yonge St., M2N 6K8 – 416/226-6602, Fax: 416/226-6388 – *1

Leah Daniels, 1035 McNicoll Ave., M1W 3W6 – 416/502-0144, Fax: 416/497-1992 – *2

Danielson & Fox, #3B, 1911 Eglinton Ave. East, M1L 2L6 – 416/755-3735, Fax: 416/755-3595 – *2

D.A. Danielson, 9 Gloucester St., M4Y 1L8 – 416/972-6966, Fax: 416/972-6885 – *1

Danson, Recht & Freedman, 30 College St., 2nd Fl., M5G 1K2 – 416/929-2200, Fax: 416/929-2192 – *7

Danson, Zucker & Connelly, #500, 70 Bond St., M5B 1X3 – 416/863-9955 – *6

W.G. Danyliw, Q.C., #200, 319 King St. West, M5V 1J5 – 416/591-1588, Fax: 416/977-1282 – *1

Jeffrey Danziger, 969 Gerrard St. East, M4M 1Z4 – 416/778-7062, Fax: 416/778-5442 – *1

David & Co., #1020, 130 Adelaide St. West, M5H 3P5 – 416/366-5900, Fax: 416/366-1799 – *5

David & David, #E224, 2255 Sheppard Ave. East, M2J 4Y1 – 416/499-4444, Fax: 416/499-8247 – *3

A.E. Davidson, #2408, 180 Dundas St. West, M5G 1Z8 – 416/596-1852 – *1

Davies & Tackaberry Associates, 1920 Ellesmere Rd., M1H 2V6 – 416/289-1777 – *3

David Davies, 2010A Queen St. East, M4L 1J3 – 416/699-5098 – *1

Davies, Ward & Beck, 1 First Canadian Place, 44th Fl., PO Box 63, M5X 1B1 – 416/863-5558, Fax: 416/863-0871 – *104

Davis Sullivan, 31 Prince Arthur Ave., M5R 1B2 – 416/921-2500 – *2

Abraham Davis, #804, 55 Eglinton Ave. East, M4P 1G8 – 416/482-1506, Fax: 416/486-8789 – *1

Marie Davison, #102, 327 Eglinton Ave. East, M4P 1L7 – 416/486-9701, Fax: 416/483-1397 – *1

J. David Day, 500 Danforth Ave., M4K 1P6 – 416/461-4888, Fax: 416/461-4296

Day, McDonald, #203, 1941 Weston Rd., M9N 1W8 – 416/247-5327, Fax: 416/247-5328 – *1

Zahava Day, 4901A Yonge St., M2N 5N4 – 416/224-8010, Fax: 416/665-7186 – *1

Wayne V.C. De Landro, 1474 Bathurst St., M5P 3G9 – 416/658-6324, Fax: 416/652-2709 – *1

M.B. de Munik, #601, 2161 Yonge St., M4S 3A5 – 416/483-5354, Fax: 416/483-5360 – *1

J.N. De Sommer, #1510, 5140 Yonge St., M2N 6L7 – 416/223-1020, Fax: 416/250-7008

Deacon, Benevides & Thomson, #307, 347 Bay St., M5H 2R7 – 416/364-3477, Fax: 416/364-2571 – *2

Alp Debreli, 80 Richmond St. West, M5H 2A4 – 416/366-2084

F. Timothy Deeth, #200, 25 Lesmill Rd., M3B 2T3 – 416/443-0080, Fax: 416/443-0279 – *1

Deeth, Williams, Wall, #400, 150 York St., M5H 3S5 – 416/941-9440, Fax: 416/941-9443 – *9

Defensa, Hispana, #204, 2365 Finch Ave. West, M9M 2W8 – 416/742-3351, Fax: 416/742-1693

Christopher DeGeer, #1515, 390 Bay St., M5H 2Y2 – 416/860-7175, Fax: 416/860-1474 – *1

James S. Deitch, 120 Carlton St., M5A 4K2 – 416/922-5529, Fax: 416/924-7166 – *1

Robert P. Della Libera, 25 Lesmill Rd., M3B 2T3 – 416/449-4565, Fax: 416/449-2060 – *1

DelZotto, Zorzi, #D, 4810 Dufferin St., M3H 5S8 – 416/665-5555, Fax: 416/665-9653 – *14

Anthony DeMarco, 2950 Keele St., M3M 2H2 – 416/638-0680, Fax: 416/638-9760 – *1

A.M. Dempsey, Q.C., 533 Queen St. East, M5A 1V1 – 416/364-6755 – *1

David L. Dennis, Q.C., Plaza Tower, Park Plaza Hotel, #300, 4 Avenue Rd., M5R 2E8 – 416/920-8121, Fax: 416/920-5672 – *1

Muneshwar Deopaul, #202, 16 Humber College Blvd., M9V 4E4 – 416/746-7300, Fax: 416/746-3300 – *1

Bonnie E.T. Derby, #604, 130 Bloor St. West, M5S 1N5 – 416/515-7500, Fax: 416/924-2371 – *1

P.G. Derry, #816, 181 University Ave., M5H 2X7 – 416/868-6483, Fax: 416/364-1697 – *1

Richard G.J. Desrocher, #203, 3425 Dundas St. West, M6S 2S4 – 416/769-5855, Fax: 416/769-9173 – *1

Deverett Law Offices, 250 Sheppard Ave. East, M2N 6M9 – 416/222-5867, Fax: 416/222-7605

Jane H. Devlin, #1017, 111 Richmond St. West, M5H 2G4 – 416/366-3091, Fax: 416/366-0879 – *1

Devry, Smith & Frank, #100, 95 Barber Greene Rd., M3C 3E9 – 416/449-1400, Fax: 416/449-7071; Email: enquiries@derrylaw.on.ca – *8

Dewar & Graham, 4889 Dundas St. West, M9A 1B2 – 416/231-2211, Fax: 416/234-8553 – *2

Iqbal Ismail Dewji, #810, 225 Duncan Mill Rd., M3B 3H9 – 416/449-9600, Fax: 416/449-9348 – *1

Diamond & Diamond, #350, 700 Lawrence Ave. West, M6A 3B4 – 416/256-9490, Fax: 416/256-0100 – *1

Diamond & Tevel, #200, 111 Eglinton Ave. East, M4P 1H4 – 416/482-2666, Fax: 416/482-4165 – *2

Diamond, Fairbairn, #2000, 393 University Ave., M5G 1E6 – 416/971-7000, Fax: 416/971-7885 – *15

DiCecco & Associates, #213, 250 Eglinton Ave. West, M4R 1A7 – 416/484-7470, Fax: 416/484-7471 – *1

DiCenzo & Associates, #200, 212 King St. West, M5H 1K5 – 416/598-2958, Fax: 416/598-3458 – *1

Ernest Dicker, Q.C., #605, 111 Peter St., M5V 2H1 – 416/593-8941, Fax: 416/598-2815 – *1

Irvine P. Dickler, Q.C., #1603, 80 Richmond St. West, M5H 2C2 – 416/364-1656 – *1

Dickson, Sachs, Appell & Beaman, #306, 10 Alcorn Ave., M4V 3A9 – 416/927-0891, Fax: 416/927-0385 – *10

DiGregorio & Associates, 723 Lawrence Ave. West, M6A 1B4 – 416/785-8135, Fax: 416/785-6088 – *2

Dingwall, McLauchlin, #2100, Commercial Union Tower, Toronto-Dominion Centre, PO Box 69, Stn Toronto Dominion, M5K 1E7 – 416/863-1000, Fax: 416/863-1007 – *14

M. DiPaolo, #400, 7050 Weston Rd., L4L 8G7 – 905/850-7575, Fax: 905/850-7050 – *1

Direnfeld & Nurgitz, #336, 200 Finch Ave. West, M2R 3W4 – 416/226-6060, Fax: 416/226-6900 – *2

Dispute Services, #200, 70 Bond St., M5B 1X3 – 416/366-8009, Fax: 416/365-7702 – *1

H.J. Doan, 18 Wild Briarway, M2J 2L2 – 416/491-2700, Fax: 416/502-9373 – *1

J.J. Doane, 39 Hayden St., 2nd Fl., M4Y 2P2 – 416/968-3454, Fax: 416/968-1211 – *1

Paul L. Dodds, 180 Dundas St. West, M5G 1Z8 – 416/593-6611, Fax: 416/593-1323 – *1

T.R. Doidge, Q.C., #404, 170 The Donway West, M3C 2G3 – 416/444-6603, Fax: 416/444-9038 – *1

William B. Donaldson, Q.C., 228 Braymore Blvd., M1B 2G8 – 416/281-2006 – *1

Donnelly & Daigneault, 101 Charles St. East, M4Y 1V2 – 416/920-1553, Fax: 416/920-1554 – *2

Donnelly & Powell, #1509, 180 Dundas St. West, M5G 1Z8 – 416/597-2191 – *2

B.J. Donnelly, #201, 1165A St. Clair Ave. West, M6E 1B2 – 416/653-0311, Fax: 416/653-6653 – *1

John J. Donohue, 75 Lowther Ave., M5R 1C9 – 416/920-0405, Fax: 416/961-9905 – *1

C.H. Dove, #324, 255 Morningside Ave., M1E 3E6 – 416/284-8707, Fax: 416/284-9150 – *1

Downsview Community Legal Services, 520 Wilson Heights Blvd., M3H 2V6 – 416/635-8388, Fax: 416/635-8786

Downtown Legal Services, 84 Queens Park Cres., M5S 1A1 – 416/978-6497, Fax: 416/978-0819; Email: law.dls@utoronto.ca – *1

E.E. Doyle, #1000, 65 Queen St. West, M5H 2M5 – 416/362-4650, Fax: 416/367-3949 – *1

Michael M. Doyle, 4-329 Saint George St., M4W 3R1 – 416/920-6180 – *1

Doyle, Speirs, 345 Kingston Rd., M4L 1T8 – 905/509-4882 – *2

*indicates number of lawyers in law firm.

Draimin, Fine Barristers, #300, 30 St. Clair Ave. West, M4V 3A1 – 416/922-6768, Fax: 416/960-0698 – *2

Linda S. Dranoff, #314, 1033 Bay St., M5S 3A5 – 416/925-4500 – *2

Sheldon L. Drebin, Q.C., #1401, 111 Richmond St. West, M5H 2G4 – 416/364-6777, Fax: 416/365-9276 – *1

William Mark Dresser, 1018 - 31 Alexander St., M4Y 1B2 – 416/323-0166 – *1

V.L. Drevnig, Q.C., #1402, 30 St. Clair Ave. West, M4V 3A1 – 416/922-8760, Fax: 416/964-5954 – *1

Drexler & Budd, 1033 Pape Ave., M4K 3W1 – 416/425-7101, Fax: 416/425-7103 – *2

J. Blair Drummie, 39 Hayden St., M4Y 2P2 – 416/921-0915, Fax: 416/925-6181 – *1

D.A. Drynan, #502, 15 Erskine Ave., M4P 1Y5 – 416/485-1262 – *1

Du Vernet, Stewart, Fenn, #1100, 170 Bloor St. West, M5S 1T9 – 416/921-4770, Fax: 416/921-6440 – *3

Todd Ducharme, #2714, 130 Adelaide St. West, M5H 3P5 – 416/868-1825, Fax: 416/868-1990 – *1

Julian O. Dudley, #1000, 65 Queen St. West, M5H 2M5 – 416/867-1442, Fax: 416/367-3949 – *1

P.S. Duffy, Q.C., #305, 180 Dundas St. West, M5G 1Z8 – 416/599-0848 – *1

Mangesh Duggal, #1604, 372 Bay St., M5H 2W9 – 416/363-9421, Fax: 416/363-6950 – *1

Duncan, Fava, Schermbrucker, 56 Temperance St., 8th Fl., M5H 3V5 – 416/861-0313, Fax: 416/214-4699 – *3

John D. Duncan, 160 John St., 4th Fl., M5V 2E5 – 416/593-2513, Fax: 416/593-2514 – *1

T.S. Dungey, 46 Fairview Blvd., M4K 1L9 – 416/469-3088 – *1

Hamish Dunlop, 103 Charles St. East, M4Y 1V2 – 416/925-8880 – *1

Brian R. Dunn, 1510-5140 Yonge St., M2N 6L7 – 416/250-5366, Fax: 416/250-0182 – *1

Edwin Z. Durbin, #2407, 401 Bay St., M5H 2Y4 – 416/214-0487

N.L. Durbin, 2530 Jane St., M3L 1S1 – 416/743-2345, Fax: 416/743-0645 – *1

Durno Shea & McMurter, #3, 505 Ellesmere Rd., M1R 4E5 – 416/752-0720, Fax: 416/752-1439 – *3

Reginald J. Dutrizac, #A, 1977 Avenue Rd., M5M 4A3 – 416/483-7409, Fax: 416/483-6957 – *1

Dutton, Brock, MacIntyre & Collier, #1700, 438 University Ave., M5G 2L9 – 416/593-4411, Fax: 416/593-5922 – *16

H.S. Dyment, #910, 390 Bay St., M5H 2Y2 – 416/861-0087 – *1

D.C. Dzwiekowski, 260 Willard Ave., M6S 3R2 – 416/762-7251, Fax: 416/762-7252 – *1

T. Allen Eagleson, 37 Maitland, M4Y 1C8 – 416/924-4116, Fax: 416/924-3005 – *1

East Toronto Community Legal Services, 1320 Gerrard St. East, M4L 3X1 – 416/461-8102, Fax: 416/461-7497 – *4

Bernard L. Eastman, Q.C., 2547 Eglinton Ave. West, M6M 1T2 – 416/656-1420, Fax: 416/766-5957 – *1

G.W. Ecclestone, Q.C., 20 Gypsy Rose Way, M2N 5Y9 – 416/229-0231

M. Edelstein, 625 Sheppard Ave. West, M3H 2S3 – 416/638-3911, Fax: 416/638-3148 – *1

Edgar, MacMahon, 2901 Bloor St. West, M8X 1B3 – 416/231-3261 – *2

George Edmonds, Q.C., #2500, 145 King St. West, M5H 3T6 – 416/955-0947, Fax: 416/863-3997 – *1

David V. Eisenkrein, #405, 3601 Victoria Park Ave., M1W 3Y3 – 416/494-4110, Fax: 416/756-3663 – *1

Elgie & Walsh, #502, 145 Adelaide St. West, M5H 3H4 – 416/364-5418, Fax: 416/364-9357 – *1

James Elia, #802, 55 Queen St. East, M5C 1R6 – 416/364-5211 – *1

Elkind, Lipton & Jacobs, #1900, 1 Queen St. East, M5C 2W6 – 416/367-0871, Fax: 416/367-9388; Email: eljtoronto@aol.com – *8

Elliott, Rodrigues & Daffern, #1050, 181 University Ave., M5H 3M7 – 416/362-1989 – *3

Ellis Clinton, #1005, 5160 Yonge St., M2N 6L9 – 416/250-1300, Fax: 416/250-5097

R.D. Ellwood, 2857 Lakeshore Blvd. West, M6V 1H8 – 416/252-1128, Fax: 416/259-1992 – *1

Anne Empke, Colonia Tower, #1500, 2 St. Clair Ave. East, 15th Fl., M4T 2T5 – 416/923-8748, Fax: 416/927-0305 – *1

Enfield, Hemmerick, Adair & Wood, #810, 1 Queen St. East, M5C 2W5 – 416/863-1230, Fax: 416/863-1241 – *10

Samuel Eng, #205, 3320 Midland Ave., M1V 5E6 – 416/299-8855, Fax: 416/299-0969

Michael Ephraim, #718, 1000 Finch Ave. West, M3J 2V5 – 416/661-9900, Fax: 416/661-0643 – *1

Arnold Epstein, #1, 16 Four Season Pl., M9B 6E5 – 416/621-7070, Fax: 416/620-6535 – *1

Epstein, Cole, #3200, 401 Bay St., PO Box 52, M5H 2Y4 – 416/862-9888, Fax: 416/862-2142 – *11

Norman Epstein, #417, 45 Sheppard Ave. East, M2N 5W9 – 416/225-5577, Fax: 416/225-2504 – *1

Harry Erlich, #475, 700 Lawrence Ave. West, M6A 3B4 – 416/256-1555, Fax: 416/256-0918 – *1

Thora H. Espinet, 3459 Sheppard Ave. East, M1T 3K5 – 416/321-2631, Fax: 416/292-4508 – *1

Etobicoke North Community Information Centre, #205, 1530 Albion Rd., M9V 1B4 – 416/741-1553, Fax: 416/741-1547

John Paul Evans, 926 The East Mall, M9B 6K1 – 416/620-7300, Fax: 416/620-1679 – *1

John A. Eversley, #1610, 11 King St. West, M5H 1A3 – 416/360-4038, Fax: 416/360-5211 – *1

George C. Eyre, #206, 730 Yonge St., M4Y 2B7 – 416/924-3108 – *1

Sydney Ezrin, 135 Torresdale Ave., M2R 3K2 – 416/739-6568, Fax: 416/739-6584 – *1

John F. Fagan, 6000 Yonge St., M2M 3W1 – 416/222-3186

Charles F. Fair, #210, 45 Sheppard Ave. East, M2N 5W9 – 416/512-6012, Fax: 416/512-6846 – *1

Faivish, Jerry, #203, 120 Carlton St., M5A 4K2 – 416/924-1090, Fax: 416/924-5310

Farano, Green, #1100, 22 St. Clair Ave. East, M4T 2Z6 – 416/961-2344, Fax: 416/961-0585; Email: fargreen@fargreen.com; URL: http://www.inforamp.net/~goldfarb/ – *13

Farb, Warren, Bergman, 2313A Bloor St. West, M6S 1P1 – 416/763-4183, Fax: 416/763-1310; Email: farb.warren@sympatico.ca – *3

V. Fargnoli, 1 First Canadian Place, #5900, PO Box 24 Stn First Canadian Place, M5X 1K2 – 416/363-3658, Fax: 416/367-3316 – *1

Joseph S. Farkas, 3089 Bathurst St., M6A 2A4 – 416/784-9550, Fax: 416/784-9552 – *1

Fasken Campbell Godfrey, #3600, 66 Wellington St. West, M5K 1N6 – 416/366-8381, Fax: 416/364-7813 – *204

Klemens Fass, #308, 2401 Eglinton Ave. East, M1K 2M5 – 416/750-4824, Fax: 416/750-4827 – *1

Francis X. Fay, Q.C., #301, 215 Victoria St., M5B 1T9 – 416/366-6510 – *1

Ricardo G. Federico, Carlton on the Park, #412, 120 Carlton St., M5A 4K2 – 416/928-1458, Fax: 416/922-3939; Toll Free: 1-800-928-1668 – *1

W.B. Fedunchak, #5, 885 Progress Ave., M1H 3G3 – 416/431-1122, Fax: 416/431-1133 – *1

Fefergrad, Dizgun, #2407, 401 Bay St., PO Box 35, M5H 2Y4 – 416/366-7686, Fax: 416/366-0134 – *5

Steven M. Fehrle, 350 Bay St., 9th Fl., M5H 2S6 – 416/777-2077, Fax: 416/367-4098 – *1

R. Eric Feige, #3300, 130 Adelaide St. West, M5H 3P5 – 416/366-6833, Fax: 416/366-3992 – *3

Leonard Feigman, #200, 70 Bond St., M5B 1X3 – 416/363-2233 – *1

Fejer & Associates, #2355, 2 First Canadian Place, M5X 1B1 – 416/364-7710, Fax: 416/364-1828 – *1

Feldman & Weisbrot, #1700, 2300 Yonge St., PO Box 2443, M4P 1E4 – 416/484-6363, Fax: 416/484-6840; Email: sabsav@io.org – *3

Howard J. Feldman, #1100, 372 Bay St., M5H 2W9 – 416/863-9333, Fax: 416/863-6080 – *2

Jodi L. Feldman, #303, 21 St. Clair Ave. East, M4T 1L9 – 416/922-3233, Fax: 416/922-3234

Lawrence T. Feldman, #103, 1000 Finch Ave. West, M3J 2V5 – 416/667-9796, Fax: 416/667-8048 – *1

Stephen Feldman, #415, 4580 Dufferin St., M3H 5Y2 – 416/667-0980, Fax: 416/667-0765 – *1

Avrum Fenson, Legislative Library c/o Legislative Research Service, 3rd Fl., North Wing, Legislative Bldg., Queen's Park, M7A 1A9 – 416/325-3689, Fax: 416/325-3696 – *4

Alan Fenster, 258 Wilson Ave., M3H 1S6 – 416/631-6601, Fax: 416/631-6828 – *1

John Peter Ferreira, 802 St. Clair Ave. West, M6C 1B6 – 416/656-9524, Fax: 416/636-7368 – *1

Field, Turner, #1000, 439 University Ave., M5G 1Y8 – 416/595-1111, Fax: 416/595-7312 – *3

Gerald Fields, #1705, 95 Wellington St. West, M5J 2N7 – 416/862-8000, Fax: 416/862-8001 – *1

Wm. Fienberg, Q.C., 175 Keewatin Ave., M4P 2A3 – 416/486-5211, Fax: 416/486-0074 – *1

Filion, Wakely & Thorup, #2601, 150 King St. West, M5H 4B6 – 416/408-3221, Fax: 416/408-4814 – *21

Fine & Deo, #220, 124 Eglinton Ave. West, M4R 2G8 – 416/489-6600, Fax: 416/489-0036 – *1

Andrew Fine, 2768 Dufferin St., M6B 3R7 – 416/785-9499 – *1

Daniel M. Fine, #506, 4950 Yonge St., M2N 6K1 – 416/733-8815, Fax: 416/733-3758 – *1

Richard Fink, 466 Dupont St., M5R 1W6 – 416/537-0108, Fax: 416/537-1604; Email: macneill@interlog.com – *2

A.C. Finkelstein, #1709, 2 Carlton St., M5B 1J3 – 416/977-1162 – *1

Finkelstein, Harvey, Q.C., #3, 4901A Yonge St., M2N 5N4 – 416/221-8890, Fax: 416/221-9965 – *1

Fireman & Regan, 181 University Ave., M5H 3M7 – 416/601-1000, Fax: 416/601-9255; Email: mailbox@firemanregan.on.ca – *19

J.Y. Fisch, 394 College St., 2nd Fl., M5T 1S7 – 416/920-6312, Fax: 416/920-1780 – *1

Steven M. Fishbayn, #415, 4580 Dufferin St., M3H 5Y2 – 416/677-0980, Fax: 416/667-0765 – *1

Barry B. Fisher, #1200, 595 Bay St., M5G 2C2 – 416/585-2330, Fax: 416/585-2105 – *1

R.A. Fisher, #300, 95 Barber Greene Rd., M3C 3E9 – 416/449-6890, Fax: 416/449-6482 – *1

Issie Fishman, 5987 Bathurst St., M2R 1Z3 – 416/222-6526, Fax: 416/222-6663 – *1

Donald R. Fiske & Associates, West Tower, Mutual Group Centre, #760, 3300 Bloor St. West, M8X 2X2 – 416/234-2177, Fax: 416/234-9039 – *1

Jean A. Fitzgerald, #3, 123 John St., M5V 2E2 – 416/597-9707, Fax: 416/597-9750 – *1

John Fitzmaurice. 317 Grace St., M6G 3A7 – 416/533-5053, Fax: 416/533-5174 – *1

Fitzsimmons, MacFarlane, Slocum & Harpur, #2500, 180 Dundas St. West, M5G 1Z8 – 416/977-5545, Fax: 416/977-8426 – *10

Flaccavento and Kreger, 2181 Danforth Ave., M4C 1K4 – 416/698-8000, Fax: 416/698-8015 – *2

Flaherty Dow Elliott, #1901, 120 Adelaide St. West, M5H 1T1 – 416/368-0231, Fax: 416/368-9229

Fleischer Kochberg & Laimon, 4 Finch Ave. West, M1N 6L1 – 416/223-8102, Fax: 416/225-5992 – *3

Fleming, White, Burgess, Brown, #605, 160 Bloor St. East, M4W 1B9 – 416/961-2868, Fax: 416/961-2964 – *6

Flemingdon Community Legal Services, #350, 10 Gateway Blvd., M3C 3A1 – 416/424-1965, Fax: 416/424-4204

Fleury, Comery, #104, 215 Morrish Rd., M1C 1E9 – 416/282-5754, Fax: 416/282-9906 – *5

A.M. Flisfeder, 785 Carlaw Ave., M4K 3L1 – 416/469-0375, Fax: 416/469-0375 – *1

Ronald Flom, #712, 2345 Yonge St., M4P 2E5 – 416/482-2777, Fax: 416/482-2599 – *1

Floras & Murray, #801, 55 Queen St. West, M5C 1R6 – 416/869-3151, Fax: 416/869-1762 – *3
Fogelman Herschel, #303, 21 St. Clair Ave. East, M4T 1L9 – 416/929-7739, Fax: 416/922-3234
Fogler, Rubinoff, #4400, 77 King St. West, PO Box 95, M5K 1G8 – 416/864-9700, Fax: 416/941-8852 – *46
Peter Folkins, 10 Foxbar Rd., M4V 2G6 – 416/944-0997, Fax: 416/924-9541 – *1
William J. Fong, #305, 155 Marlee Ave., M6B 4B5 – 416/783-3534 – *1
Jamie A. Ford, 372 Bay St., M5H 2W9 – 416/360-1770 – *1
Michael Forrester & Associates, 171 Ravel Rd., M2H 1T1 – 416/495-1411, Fax: 416/495-9128 – *1
Jeffrey M. Fortinsky, #358, 1111 Finch Ave. West, M3J 2E5 – 416/665-5688, Fax: 416/741-1765 – *1
R. Brian Foster Q.C., #218, 111 Richmond St. West, M5H 2G4 – 416/368-3363, Fax: 416/368-4532
Barry Fox, 9 Gloucester St., M4Y 1L8 – 416/972-6966, Fax: 416/972-6885 – *1
Walter Fox, #312, 100 Richmond St. West, M5H 3K6 – 416/363-9238, Fax: 416/363-9230 – *1
David A. Fram, #901, 701 Evans Ave., M9C 1A3 – 416/622-2665, Fax: 416/622-8952 – *2
David Franklin, #700, 21 Dundas Sq., M5B 1B8 – 416/365-1971, Fax: 416/365-1824 – *1
Fraser & Beatty, #100, One First Canadian Place, PO Box 100, Stn First Canadian Place, M5X 1B2 – 416/863-4748, Fax: 416/863-4592 – *204
Fraser & Beatty, Madison Centre, #2300, 4950 Yonge St., M2N 6K1 – 416/733-3300, Fax: 416/221-5254 – *2
Fraser, Simms and Reid, 1944 Weston Rd., M9N 1W2 – 416/241-0111 – *1
Anne E. Freed, 10 King St. East, 14th Fl., M5C 1C3 – 416/368-7800, Fax: 416/364-3818 – *1
Harvey Freedman, #100, 79 Shuter St., M5B 1B3 – 416/363-1737, Fax: 416/861-9919 – *3
J.P. Freedman, #313, 1415 Lawrence Ave. West, M6L 1A9 – 416/248-6231, Fax: 416/241-0080 – *1
L.S. Freedman, 1577 Bloor St. West, M6P 1A6 – 416/536-1159, Fax: 416/536-3618 – *1
N.J. Freedman, Q.C., #1906, 20 Queen St. West, M5H 3R3 – 416/979-7767, Fax: 416/979-7772
Freeman & Associates, #1803, 2 Sheppard Ave. East, M2N 5Y7 – 416/733-3600, Fax: 416/733-8090 – *1
Freeman & Reim, #2310, 4950 Yonge St., M2N 6K1 – 416/733-3400, Fax: 416/733-9810 – *2
C.H. Freeman, 392 Dundas St. East, M5A 2A5 – 416/944-8544, Fax: 416/944-8083 – *1
D.V. Freeman, #902, 5799 Yonge St., M2M 3V3 – 416/224-5600 – *1
S.V. Freeman, 111 Bermondsey Rd., M4A 2T7 – 416/288-1919 – *1
Boris G. Freesman, Q.C., 4 Rollscourt Dr., M2L 1X5 – 416/512-8965, Fax: 416/512-8964 – *1
Andrew Frei, 181 University Ave., M5H 3M7 – 416/601-6838, Fax: 416/601-9107 – *1
Allan Friedland, #212, 3555 Don Mills Rd., M2H 3N3 – 416/498-1323, Fax: 416/498-8562 – *1
J. Friedman, Q.C., 1 First Canadian Place, #7060, PO Box 169, Stn First Canadian Place, M5X 1C7 – 416/364-5451, Fax: 416/364-9764 – *1
David G. Friend, Q.C., #202, 3459 Sheppard Ave. East, M1T 3K5 – 416/754-0333, Fax: 416/292-0473 – *1
Frolick & Frolick, #200, 131 Davenport Rd., M5R 1H8 – 416/924-1015, Fax: 416/924-8532 – *1
Mark Fromkin, 700-5160 Yonge St., M2N 6L9 – 416/250-0818, Fax: 416/250-0818 – *1
C. Sydney Jr. Frost, Q.C., 50 Bayview Wood, M4N 1R7 – 416/489-5844 – *1
Damien R. Frost, 81 Wellesley St. East, M4Y 1H6 – 416/923-1900, Fax: 416/960-1498 – *1
Harry Frymer, #320, 100 Richmond St. West, M5H 3K6 – 416/869-1073, Fax: 416/869-1840 – *4
Fuerst Fay, 406 King St. East, M5A 1L4 – 416/366-5444, Fax: 416/466-5688
Derrick Fulton, 390 Bay St., M5H 2Y2 – 416/594-3338, Fax: 416/860-1474 – *1

Greta M. Fung, #2320, 2025 Sheppard Ave. East, M2J 1V6 – 416/494-8383 – *1
A.L. Furguiele, #202, 1013 Wilson Ave., M3K 1G1 – 416/630-7900, Fax: 416/630-8671 – *1
Furqan Ahmed Legal Services, 100 McLevin Ave., M1B 2V5 – 416/754-0443, Fax: 416/754-1142
Futerman & Futerman, #1500, 2 St. Clair Ave. East, M4T 2R1 – 416/925-4100, Fax: 416/323-9132 – *5
F.A. Gabriel, #300, 111 Elizabeth St., M5G 1P7 – 416/593-6621 – *1
Gaertner & Math, #400, 144 Front St. West, M5J 2L7 – 416/599-7761, Fax: 416/977-8587 – *4
G.J. Gaglione, #104, 2300 Sheppard Ave. West, M9M 3A4 – 416/747-7010, Fax: 416/747-7011 – *1
J. Mark Gahan, #303, 489 College St., M6G 1A5 – 416/927-7253, Fax: 416/972-1992 – *1
Rocco Galati, 372 Bay St., M5H 2W9 – 416/864-1382 – *1
Gary M. Gampel, #203, 345 Wilson Ave., M3H 5W1 – 416/398-0104, Fax: 416/398-0106
F.H. Ganz, Q.C., #305, 27 Queen St. East, M5C 2M6 – 416/364-9212, Fax: 416/364-4813 – *1
Gardiner, Blumberg, #1202, 390 Bay St., M5H 2Y2 – 416/361-1982, Fax: 416/363-8451 – *11
Gardiner, Roberts, #3100, 40 King St. West, PO Box 105, M5H 3Y2 – 416/865-6600, Fax: 416/865-6636; Email: colbert@gardiner-roberts.on.ca – *44
John H. Gardner, Q.C., #801, 67 Yonge St., M5E 1J8 – 416/366-7791, Fax: 416/366-7110 – *1
Karan Singh Garewa, 747 Don Mills Rd., M3C 1T2 – 416/410-2696, Fax: 416/467-1240 – *1
Susan W. Garfin, #1200, 595 Bay St., M5G 2C2 – 416/599-9933, Fax: 416/599-5497
Garfin, Zeidenberg, CenterPoint Mall, Entrance #1, 6400 Yonge St., M2M 3X4 – 416/512-8000, Fax: 416/512-9992 – *4
Garfinkle, Biderman, One Financial Place, #1401, 1 Adelaide St. East, M5C 2V9 – 416/869-1234, Fax: 416/869-0547 – *11
Jacqueline Garrity, 45 Saint Nicholas St., M4Y 1W6 – 416/925-6443, Fax: 416/925-8122 – *1
Garvey, Ferriss, South Tower, Bldg Box: 3100, Royal Bank Plaza, PO Box 56, M5J 2J2 – 416/865-0222, Fax: 416/865-0410 – *10
Gass & Associates, #PH, 121 Richmond St. West, M5H 2K1 – 416/365-9878 – *2
Cheryl Gaster, #600, 20 Richmond St. East, M5C 2R9 – 416/360-0463 – *1
Gauthier & Associates, Canada Trust Tower, BCE Place, #4800, 161 Bay St., PO Box 528, M5J 2S1 – 416/868-4848, Fax: 416/868-4840 – *5
Leon Gavendo, Law Chambers, University Centre, #2000, 393 Bay St., M5G 1E6 – 416/366-9591, Fax: 416/366-2107 – *1
L.B. Geffen, #205, 2907 Kennedy Rd., M1V 1S8 – 416/292-6688, Fax: 416/292-6649 – *1
Geller & Minster, 2 Keewatin Ave., M4P 1Z8 – 416/480-2200, Fax: 416/480-2693 – *2
J.W. Gemmell, Q.C., #1605, 8 King St. East, M5C 1B5 – 416/364-4129 – *1
Genest Murray DesBrisnay Lamek, #700, 130 Adelaide St. West, M5H 4C1 – 416/368-8600, Fax: 416/360-2625 – *40
Basil L. Georgieff, 3543 St. Clair Ave. East, M1K 1L6 – 416/267-1452 – *1
Seymour E. German, #104, 49 St. Clair Ave. West, M4V 1K6 – 416/920-7800, Fax: 416/920-4580 – *1
Stanley Gershman, 556 Atlas Ave., M6C 3R6 – 416/781-2931 – *1
Lorne Gershuny, 1577 Bloor St. West, M6P 1A6 – 416/539-0989, Fax: 416/536-3618 – *1
A.C. Gerstl, #612, 330 Bay St., M5H 2S8 – 416/214-1165, Fax: 416/214-0870 – *1
Gertler & Associates, #300, 120 Eglinton Ave. East, M4P 1E2 – 416/485-9585, Fax: 416/485-3313 – *1
J.M.P. Ghalioungui, 1033 Bay St., M5S 3A5 – 416/347-7475 – *1

Stuart Ghan, 1035 McNicoll Ave., M1W 3W6 – 416/502-8845, Fax: 416/497-1999 – *1
Ghose, Kotak, #708, 1243 Islington Ave., M8X 1Y9 – 416/234-5610, Fax: 416/234-2881 – *2
Lorne Giacomelli, #201, 40 Eglinton Ave. East, M4P 3A2 – 416/484-9115, Fax: 416/484-0161 – *1
Giacomini, Davis, Turk, 1002-347 Bay St., M5H 2R7 – 416/363-1077, Fax: 416/363-4188 – *3
Gilbert & Yallen, 204 Saint George St., 3rd Fl., M5R 2N5 – 416/927-0001, Fax: 416/927-0930 – *2
Jack A. Gilbert, Q.C., #703, 123 Edward St., M5G 1E2 – 416/593-4093, Fax: 416/593-0656 – *1
Gilbert, Wright & Kirby, #1800, 155 University Ave., M5H 3B7 – 416/363-3100, Fax: 416/363-1379 – *6
Gilbertson, Davis, Herceg, Emerson, McCaskill, #1002, 111 Richmond St. West, M5H 2G4 – 416/366-8404, Fax: 416/366-6419 – *8
John D. Gilfillan, Q.C., #1200, 8 King St. East, M5C 1B5 – 416/861-1881, Fax: 416/364-1282 – *1
Leslie M. Giroday, 190 Sixth St., M8V 3A5 – 416/255-1063, Fax: 416/251-8699 – *1
Robert M. Girvan, #1000, 65 Queen St. West, M5H 2M5 – 416/368-4960, Fax: 416/367-3949
Roseanne M Giulietti, 212 King St. West, M5H 1K5 – 416/593-6100, Fax: 416/971-9391 – *1
Glaholt & Tamblyn, #806, 141 Adelaide St. West, M5H 3L5 – 416/368-8281, Fax: 416/368-3467
Glass & Friedland, #2108, 2 Bloor St. West, M4W 3E2 – 416/968-3995, Fax: 416/968-6899 – *3
Alan A. Glass, #415, 4580 Dufferin St., M3H 5Y2 – 416/667-0980, Fax: 416/667-0765 – *1
Donna M. Glassman, #505, 4100 Bathurst St., M3H 3P2 – 416/398-8738, Fax: 416/532-5089 – *1
Jeffrey D. Glatt, 506 Russell Hill Rd., M5P 2S9 – 416/484-7498, Fax: 416/484-8169 – *1
Louis Glatt, 2354 Danforth Ave., M4C 1K7 – 416/422-2107, Fax: 416/422-2606 – *1
Saul I. Glober, #2600, 250 Yonge St., M5B 2M6 – 416/979-2211, Fax: 416/979-1234 – *1
Andrew G.E. Goddard, #PH, 121 Richmond St. West, M5H 2K1 – 416/368-1211
Godfrey & Associates, #702, 5160 Yonge St., M2N 6L9 – 416/250-5061, Fax: 416/250-5925 – *1
Godfrey & Corcoran, #702, 55 Queen St. East, M5C 1R6 – 416/363-0484, Fax: 416/363-0485 – *1
Sheldon J. Godfrey, 49 Front St. East, 3rd Fl., M5E 1B3 – 416/362-7788 – *1
Alan D. Gold, 29 Tanbark Cr., M3V 1N7 – 416/445-1328 – *1
Peter M. Gold, 39A Hazelton Ave., M5R 2E3 – 416/925-3101, Fax: 416/925-8118 – *1
Stanley Goldberg, #1402, 151 Yonge St., M5C 2W7 – 416/363-2299, Fax: 416/366-9808 – *1
Golden, Green & Chercover, #200, 101 Yorkville Ave., M5R 1C1 – 416/968-3333, Fax: 416/968-0325 – *8
Sydney L. Goldenberg, #2600, 250 Yonge St., M5B 2M6 – 416/591-6610, Fax: 416/979-1234 – *1
Henry Goldentuler, #220, 1018 Finch Ave. West, M3J 2E1 – 416/663-9309, Fax: 416/650-1782 – *1
H.A. Goldgut, #700, 2 St. Clair Ave. East, M4T 2T5 – 416/968-6400, Fax: 416/968-6985 – *1
Goldhar & Nemoy, #212, 120 Carlton St., M5A 2K1 – 416/928-1488, Fax: 416/924-7166 – *2
H.A. Goldkind, #320, 100 Richmond St. West, M5H 3K6 – 416/366-5280 – *1
Goldman Sloan Nash & Haber, #2100, 181 University Ave., M5H 3M7 – 416/862-8200, Fax: 416/862-9953 – *1
Gordon Goldman, #320, 100 Richmond St. West, M5H 3K6 – 416/367-2388, Fax: 416/869-1840
Jeffrey W. Goldman, #600, 3101 Bathurst St., M6A 2A6 – 416/787-1818, Fax: 416/787-1810 – *1
R.M. Goldman, #2412, 401 Bay St., M5H 2Y4 – 416/860-9900, Fax: 416/364-2308; Email: rmg@counsel2.com – *1
Goldman, Spring, Schwartz & Kichler, #700, 40 Sheppard Ave. West, M2N 6K9 – 416/225-9400, Fax: 416/225-4805 – *7

* indicates number of lawyers in law firm.

Cheryl S. Goldsmith, #1314, 181 University Ave., M5H 3M7 – 416/368-5626, Fax: 416/861-0706

Goldstein & Grubner, #212, 3459 Sheppard Ave. East, M1T 3K5 – 416/292-0414, Fax: 416/292-4508 – *2

Goldstein & Rosen, 1648 Victoria Park Ave., M1R 1P7 – 416/757-4156 – *2

H.S. Goldstein, #202, 4889 Yonge St., M1N 5N4 – 416/221-3494, Fax: 416/221-7155 – *1

L.C. Goldstein, #410, 212 King St. West, M5H 1K5 – 416/599-3000, Fax: 416/599-5582 – *1

Thomas Goldstein, #601, 2161 Yonge St., M4S 3A6 – 416/488-2100, Fax: 416/488-2794 – *1

Harry Golish, #403, 2828 Bathurst St., M6B 3A7 – 416/789-2438 – *1

Paul Gollom, #804, 55 Eglinton Ave. East, M4P 1G8 – 416/932-9300, Fax: 416/483-2737; Email: gollom@servtech.com – *1

Goodman & Carr, #2300, 200 King St. West, M5H 3W5 – 416/595-2300, Fax: 416/595-0567; Email: mail@goodmancarr.com; URL: http://www.goodman-carr.com – *78

Goodman Phillips & Vineberg, #2400, 250 Yonge St., M5B 2M6 – 416/979-2211, Fax: 416/979-1234 – *118

Henry G. Goodman, #510, 25 Imperial St., M5P 1B9 – 416/488-3303, Fax: 416/488-7085 – *1

I. Goodman, #605, 111 Peter St., M5V 2H1 – 416/598-0246, Fax: 416/598-2815 – *1

Louis Goodman, 29 Pleasant Blvd., M4T 1K2 – 416/923-2512, Fax: 416/923-6013 – *1

Nancy Goodman, #1130, 20 Dundas St. West, Stn 180, M5G 2G8 – 416/977-8045, Fax: 416/591-7333 – *1

Stanley Goodman, Q.C., #1800, 4950 Yonge St., M1N 6K1 – 416/224-0200, Fax: 416/224-0758 – *1

John L.Z. Gora, Penthouse, 481 University Ave., M5G 2E9 – 416/977-6439 – *1

Barbara J. Gordon, #210, 12 Birch Ave., M4V 1C8 – 416/928-0856, Fax: 416/928-0577 – *1

Gordon, Traub, #2600, 21 King St. West, M5H 3T9 – 416/214-6500, Fax: 416/214-7275 – *10

S.L. Gore, 10 Silver Birch Ave., M4E 3K9 – 416/690-2160 – *1

William A. Gorewich, 49 Saint Nicholas St., M4Y 1W6 – 416/927-1109, Fax: 416/924-5443 – *1

Mark Gorlick, 699 Coxwell Ave., M4C 3C1 – 416/778-7788, Fax: 416/778-1876 – *1

J.D. Gorrell, Q.C., 533 Queen St. East, M5A 1V1 – 416/361-1411 – *1

T.G. Gorrie, Q.C., #1100, 27 Queen St. East, M5C 2M6 – 416/368-2928, Fax: 416/368-2955 – *1

Nathan Gotlieb, Madison Centre, #1800, 4950 Yonge St., M2N 6K1 – 416/224-0200, Fax: 416/224-0758 – *1

Gottlieb & Pearson, #1800, 4950 Yonge St., M2N 6K1 – 416/250-1550, Fax: 416/250-7889 – *3

Gottlieb, Connie, #200, 70 Bond St., M5B 1X3 – 416/214-0650, Fax: 416/365-7765

G.L. Gottlieb, Q.C., #309, 600 Bay St., M5G 1M6 – 416/977-3835 – *1

Gottlieb, Hoffman & Kumer, 1214 Lawrence Ave. West, M6A 1E3 – 416/789-0584 – *3

Max A. Gould, #200, 101 Yorkville Ave., M5R 1C1 – 416/964-0290, Fax: 416/964-7102 – *1

Michael J. Gould, #308, 801 York Mills Rd., M3B 1X7 – 416/510-3030, Fax: 416/510-3034 – *1

Gowlings, #4900, Commerce Court West, PO Box 438, Stn Commerce Court, M5L 1J3 – 416/862-4296, Fax: 416/862-7661 – *140

Graci & Associates, 350 Bay St., 9th Fl., M5H 2S6 – 416/360-1991, Fax: 416/367-4098 – *1

D.J. Grant, #205, 250 Sheppard Ave. East, M2N 6M9 – 416/225-1161, Fax: 416/225-1243 – *1

Grant, Grant & Fraser, 39 Hayden St., M4Y 2P2 – 416/968-1266, Fax: 416/925-6181 – *1

Grasset, Fleisher, Toronto-Dominion Bank Tower, #5104, Toronto-Dominion Centre, PO Box 317, Stn TD Centre, M5K 1K2 – 416/214-5651, Fax: 416/214-5655; Email: gflaw@netcom.ca – *3

Jeffrey Gray, #200, 4211 Yonge St., M2P 2A9 – 416/512-1694, Fax: 416/221-8372 – *1

William D. Gray & Associates, Toronto Colony Hotel, #100, 89 Chestnut St., M5G 1R1 – 416/977-1300 – *2

B. Michael Grayson, Q.C., #Penthouse, 121 Richmond St. West, M5H 2K1 – 416/363-1022 – *1

Green & Spiegel, #2200, 121 King St. West, PO Box 114, M5H 3T9 – 416/862-7880, Fax: 416/862-1698 – *8

D.J. Green, 399 Spadina Ave., M5T 2G6 – 416/979-2333, Fax: 416/597-8966 – *1

Elliott Green, Q.C., #1404, 2 Carlton St., M5B 1J3 – 416/977-5575, Fax: 416/977-5576 – *1

Michael S. Green, 1415 Bathurst St., M5R 3H8 – 416/538-2737 – *1

Norman Green, Q.C., 302 Richview Ave., M5P 3G5 – 416/487-7191 – *1

Paul J. Green, #1600, 8 King St. East, M5C 1B5 – 416/860-1723 – *1

Pauline Green, 978 Kingston Rd., M4E 1S9 – 416/699-3826 – *1

Weldon F. Green, Q.C., #1601, 65 Queen St. West, M5H 2M5 – 416/364-4465, Fax: 416/364-3657 – *1

Donald M. Greenbaum, Q.C., 258 Wilson Ave., M3H 1S6 – 416/631-7504, Fax: 416/631-9895 – *1

Greenberg, Jack, #201, 40 Holly St., M4S 3C3 – 416/485-8833, Fax: 416/485-3246 – *3

Morton Greenglass Q.C., Royal Trust Tower, #4400, 77 King St. West, M5K 1G8 – 416/214-1000, Fax: 416/941-8852

Greening & Associate, 1436 Danforth Ave., M4J 1N4 – 416/462-9010, Fax: 416/462-3858 – *2

David B. Greenspan, Q.C., 1201, 131 Bloor St. West, M5S 1S3

Greenspan, Humphrey, #2714, 130 Adelaide St. West, M5H 3P5 – 416/868-1755, Fax: 416/868-1990 – *4

Greenspan, Rosenberg & Buhr, Simpson Tower, #3200, 401 Bay St., M5H 1T7 – 416/366-3961, Fax: 416/366-7994 – *3

Rose Greenstein, #101, 861 College St., M6H 1A1 – 416/533-6044, Fax: 416/532-9845 – *1

E.J. Gresik, 101 Scollard St., M5R 1G4 – 416/924-0781, Fax: 416/960-9650 – *1

John W. Grice, 350 Bay St., 9th Fl., M5H 2S6 – 416/360-4160, Fax: 416/367-4098 – *1

Allan H. Griesdorf, #406, 43 Eglinton Ave. East, M4P 1A2 – 416/482-2602, Fax: 416/482-1075 – *1

Griffiths & Powell, #523, 524, 1315 Lawrence Ave. East, M3A 3R3 – 416/441-1253, Fax: 416/441-9757 – *3

Saul Grillo, 1463 Wilson Ave., M3M 1J5 – 416/614-6000, Fax: 416/614-6082 – *1

C. Grimanis, 904 Logan Ave., M4K 3E4 – 416/469-1176, Fax: 416/469-4252 – *1

Sheldon, Grimson, #803, 525 University Ave., M5G 2L3 – 416/596-7517 – *1

Gerald Gringorten, #424, 100 Richmond St. West, M5H 3K6 – 416/365-7376, Fax: 416/365-1474

Groll & Groll, 112 St. Clair Ave. West, M4V 2Y3 – 416/968-1177, Fax: 416/968-1178 – *2

James J. Grosberg, #415, 4580 Dufferin St., M3H 5Y2 – 416/667-0980, Fax: 416/667-0765 – *1

Grosman, Grosman & Gale, #1410, 1 Queen St. East, M5C 2W5 – 416/364-9599, Fax: 416/364-2490 – *6

A.H. Gross, #101, 861 College St., M6H 1A1 – 416/533-6044, Fax: 416/532-9845 – *1

J.M. Grossman, 335 Bay St., M5H 2R3 – 416/864-9550 – *1

Grubner, Krauss, #1540, 5140 Yonge St., M2N 6L7 – 416/222-4446, Fax: 416/222-9788 – *4

Grudeff, Berg, 1595 Bloor St. West, M6P 1A6 – 416/533-5909, Fax: 416/537-8500

Gerald Grupp, #302, 120 Carlton St., M5A 4K2 – 416/972-6063 – *1

Isak Grushka, #7, 1267A St. Clair Ave. West, M6E 1B8 – 416/656-2631, Fax: 416/656-8328 – *1

Guberman, Garson, #1920, 130 Adelaide St. West, M5H 3P5 – 416/363-1234, Fax: 416/363-8760; Email: guberman@passport.ca; URL: http://www.gubermangarson.com – *4

Anand Gucharan, #901, 2 Carlton St., M5B 1J3 – 416/593-5252, Fax: 416/593-4511

Guiste, Haynes, #313, 120 Carlton St., M5A 4K2 – 416/944-1222, Fax: 416/961-0779 – *2

Gulycz, Galati, #112, 82 Lombard St., M5C 2S8 – 416/363-7979, Fax: 416/363-7974

J.M. Guoba, 1 St. Clair Ave. East, M4T 2V7 – 416/923-7002, Fax: 416/923-7590 – *1

Albert Gurland, #212, 1210 Sheppard Ave. East, PO Box 41, M2K 1E3 – 416/490-0414, Fax: 416/492-1926 – *1

Gutstein Mandel, #2015, 120 Adelaide St. West, M5H 1T1 – 416/364-7717, Fax: 416/364-4813 – *2

Peter F. Haber, #410, 120 Carlton St., M5A 4K2 – 416/961-0265, Fax: 416/922-1963 – *1

L. Hadbavny, #404, 1415 Lawrence Ave. West, M6L 1A9 – 416/247-5357, Fax: 416/247-4307 – *1

Michael P. Haddad, 208 Carlton St., M5A 2L1 – 416/926-8151, Fax: 416/927-9005 – *1

Haffey, Sherwood, Hunt, #2330, 120 Adelaide St. West, M5H 3P5 – 416/366-7976, Fax: 416/366-0580 – *3

Sidney S. Hagler, 3702 Kingston Rd., M1J 3H3 – 416/269-4999, Fax: 416/269-4998 – *1

K.A. Hahn, #13, 5230 Dundas St. West, M9B 1A8 – 416/231-3353 – *1

Miles M. Halberstadt, Q.C., #412, 120 Carlton St., M5A 4K2 – 416/944-0441, Fax: 416/922-3939 – *1

Sheila K. Halladay, 2126 1/2 Queen St. East, M4E 1E3 – 416/694-5609, Fax: 416/694-4908 – *1

Halman & Halman, #300, 365 Bay St., M5H 2V1 – 416/363-8481, Fax: 416/363-8536 – *2

F. Halpern, 94 Overbrook Pl., M3H 4P6 – 416/630-4828 – *1

Hamalengwa Munyonzwe, #708, 2 Sheppard Ave. East, M2N 5Y7 – 416/222-8111, Fax: 416/733-1625

V.W. Hamara, 20 Madison Ave., M5R 2S1 – 416/961-5010, Fax: 416/963-8387 – *1

Hamilton & Associates, 360 Bay St., 10th Fl., M5H 2V6 – 416/869-7150 – *2

Patricia A. Hamilton, #201, 1969 Weston Rd., PO Box 300, Stn A, M9N 3M7 – 416/235-0105, Fax: 416/235-0750 – *1

Hamilton, Wilkie, #1400, 20 Queen St. West, M5H 2V3 – 416/598-3441, Fax: 416/398-3902 – *2

Hans & Hans, 10 Foxbar Rd., M4V 2G6 – 416/960-5445 – *2

Haque & Associates, #507, 80 Richmond St. West, M5H 2A4 – 416/366-2337, Fax: 416/366-0936 – *1

Zakaul Haque, #205, 1058A Albion Rd., M9V 1A7 – 416/743-6302, Fax: 416/743-4783 – *1

George M. Harasymowycz, 2311A Bloor St. West, M6S 1P1 – 416/766-2472, Fax: 416/766-3297 – *1

Aaron B. Harnett, 75 Lowther Ave., M5R 1C9 – 416/960-3676, Fax: 416/961-9905 – *1

M.G. Harnum, 1887A Lawrence Ave. East, M1R 2Y3 – 416/752-4994, Fax: 416/752-5640 – *1

Murray P. Harrington, #215, 3447 Kennedy Rd., M1V 3S1 – 416/321-8621, Fax: 416/321-8622 – *1

Harris & Henderson, #Penthouse, 121 Richmond St. West, M5H 2K1 – 416/862-1661 – *1

Harris & Partners, #1040, 151 Yonge St., M5C 2W7 – 416/865-0504, Fax: 416/865-9567 – *1

Harris Sheaffer, #310, 4100 Yonge St., M2P 2B5 – 416/250-5800, Fax: 416/250-5300

David E. Harris, 439 University Ave., M5G 1Y8 – 416/585-9329, Fax: 416/408-2372 – *1

Harris, Direnfeld & Christie, 190 Attwell Dr., M9W 6H8 – 416/798-2722, Fax: 416/798-2715 – *7

Gerald Harris, 4122 Bathurst St., M3H 3P2 – 416/638-7277 – *1

W.A. Harrison, #1102, 2 Sheppard Avenue East, M2N 5Y7 – 416/222-7668, Fax: 416/222-9253 – *1

Al Hart, 45 Saint Nicholas St., M4Y 1W6 – 416/925-6443, Fax: 416/925-8122 – *1

Robert S. Hart, Q.C., #313, 120 Carlton St., M5A 2K1 – 416/961-9861 – *1

Paul E. Harte, 119 John St., M5V 2E2 – 416/595-1391, Fax: 416/595-0717; Toll Free: 1-800-966-0339;

Email: pharte@litigate.com; URL: http://www.hartelaw.com – *1

S.E. Hartley, 1180 Weston Rd., M6M 4P4 – 416/243-0444 – *1

Ruth Hartman, c/o Workers Compensation Appeals Tribunal, 505 University Ave., M5G 1X4 – 416/531-9714 – *1

Klaus Anton Hartmann, 391 Willowdale Ave., M2N 5A8 – 416/395-0311, Fax: 416/590-0312 – *1

Hartrick & Associates, 116-118 Parliament St., M5A 2Y9 – 416/366-8755, Fax: 416/366-5158 – *5

Jane Harvey Associates, #187, 300 Borough Dr., M1P 4P5 – 416/296-1607, Fax: 416/296-1757 – *2

W.K. Hastings, 60 Sheldrake Blvd., M4P 2B3 – 416/483-5973 – *1

Gabrielle Hauser, 937 Broadview Ave., M4K 2R3 – 416/696-8808, Fax: 416/696-8579 – *1

Frederick Simon Hawa, #1900, 1 Queen St. East, M5C 2W6 – 416/362-2317, Fax: 416/367-9388 – *1

John J. Hazel, #G-9, 4195 Dundas St. West, M8X 1Y4 – 416/234-1500, Fax: 416/234-9357 – *1

Hazzard & Hore, #1002, 141 Adelaide St. West, M5H 3L5 – 416/868-0074, Fax: 416/868-1468 – *2

Alfred C. Heakes, Q.C., 1920 Weston Rd., M9N 1W4 – 416/249-2237, Fax: 416/249-1200 – *1

David P.V. Healey, 1577 Bloor St. West, M6P 1A6 – 416/532-3036, Fax: 416/536-3618 – *1

Rod Heather, Q.C., #305, 180 Dundas St. West, M5G 1Z8 – 416/979-7416, Fax: 416/599-0847 – *1

Marian D. Hebb, 52A St. Patrick St., 2nd Fl., M5T 1V1 – 416/971-6618, Fax: 416/971-4144 – *1

William S. Hechter, #PH, 121 Richmond St. West, M5H 2K1 – 416/364-9517, Fax: 416/364-9391 – *1

Heenan Blaikie, South Tower, Royal Bank Plaza, #3350, PO Box 185, Stn Royal Bank, M5J 2J4 – 416/360-6336, Fax: 416/360-8425 – *4

E.S. Heiber, #200, 70 Bond St., M5B 1X3 – 416/362-2768, Fax: 416/365-7702 – *1

Heifetz, Crozier, #704, 55 University Ave., M5J 2H7 – 416/863-1717, Fax: 416/368-3133 – *3

Heller, Feldman., #902, 130 Adelaide St. West, M5H 3P5 – 416/364-2404, Fax: 416/364-0793 – *4

Heller, Rubel, #208, 111 Richmond St. West, M5H 2G4 – 416/863-9311, Fax: 416/863-9465 – *4

A. Henderson, #1812, 2 Carlton St., M5B 1J3 – 416/977-7700, Fax: 416/977-8570 – *1

Ian S. Hennessey, #108, 100 Lombard St., M5C 1M3 – 416/364-4211, Fax: 416/364-7505 – *1

Harry Herberman, 648 Danforth Ave., M4K 1R3 – 416/461-3171 – *1

Alfred H. Herman & Associates, 1948 Weston Rd., M9N 1W2 – 416/245-2400 – *3

Lawrence L. Herman, #2200, 40 King St. West, M5H 3C2 – 416/488-2696, Fax: 416/488-5752 – *1

W.B. Herman, Q.C., #810, 1 Toronto St., M5C 2V7 – 416/868-0773, Fax: 416/868-6700 – *1

Louis Hermant, Q.C., #206, 74 Victoria St., M5C 2A5 – 416/364-9766 – *1

John S. Herron, #3102, 130 Adelaide St. West, M5H 3P5 – 416/363-6067, Fax: 416/862-2124 – *1

William Hershorn, #103, 964 Albion Rd., M9V 1A7 – 416/741-9494, Fax: 416/741-9479 – *1

Joel Hertz, #200, 111 Eglinton Ave. East, M4P 1H4 – 416/482-8242, Fax: 416/482-4165 – *1

Hicks Morley Hamilton Stewart Storie, TD Bank Tower, 30th Fl., Box 371, TD Centre, M5K 1K8 – 416/362-1011, Fax: 416/362-9680 – *44

J.R. Higgins, #201, 161 St. George St., M5R 2M3 – 416/921-6093 – *1

Enid G. Hildebrand, 39A Hazelton Ave., M5R 2E3 – 416/925-2711, Fax: 416/925-8118 – *1

Hills & Associate, 1168 Warden Ave., M1R 2R1 – 416/752-7078, Fax: 416/752-8769 – *2

D'Arcy Hiltz, #408, 94 Cumberland St., M5R 1A3 – 416/968-6575, Fax: 416/968-3424 – *1

M. Hlinka, 1486 Dundas St. West, M6K 1T5 – 416/763-3553 – *1

Howard P.C. Ho, #405, 120 Carlton St., M5A 4K2 – 416/928-1300, Fax: 416/928-5079 – *1

Rufus Ho, #306, 45 Sheppard Ave. East, M2N 5W9 – 416/590-7737, Fax: 416/590-7738 – *1

J. Gardner Hodder, #2200, 181 University Ave., M5H 3M7 – 416/601-6809, Fax: 416/947-0909 – *1

A. John Hodgins, 603 Evans Ave., M8W 2W3 – 416/251-9390, Fax: 416/251-0449 – *1

Hodgson, Parker, 2346 Danforth Ave., M4C 1K7 – 416/422-2110, Fax: 416/422-0814 – *2

Norman Hoffman, Q.C., #200, 1810 Avenue Rd., M5M 3Z2 – 416/787-1161, Fax: 416/787-3894 – *1

Hoffman, Sillery, Buckstein & Chuback, #200, 1810 Avenue Rd., M5M 3Z2 – 416/787-1161, Fax: 416/787-3894 – *3

Robert Hogan, 21 Lanewood Cres., M1W 1W9 – 416/499-6553, Fax: 416/499-6728 – *1

Holden Day Wilson, Toronto-Dominion Bank Tower, Toronto-Dominion Centre, #2400, PO Box 52, M5K 1E7 – 416/361-1444, Fax: 416/361-1258 – *63

R.L. Holden, #304, 375 University Ave., M5G 2G1 – 416/979-1446, Fax: 416/979-8669 – *1

P. Virginia Holmes, #1, 35 Lesmill Rd., M3B 2T3 – 416/444-7342, Fax: 416/444-2507

Holmestead & Sutton, #1001, 4 King St. West, M5H 1B6 – 416/364-9317, Fax: 416/364-9118

Holmsted & Sutton, 4 King St. West, M5H 1B3 – 416/364-9317, Fax: 416/364-9118 – *6

Christopher Holoboff, #500, 27 Queen St. East, M5C 2M6 – 416/868-0878, Fax: 416/362-5013 – *1

Shireen E. Hooshangi, 379 Broadview Ave., M4K 2M7 – 416/463-5248, Fax: 416/463-0420 – *1

Hope Jack, #500, 3500 Dufferin St., M3K 1N2 – 416/398-5222, Fax: 416/398-7847

Laron Paul Hopkins, #1900, 180 Dundas St. West, M5G 1Z8 – 416/598-1300 – *1

Hoppe, Carter, #100, 196 Adelaide St. West, M5H 1W7 – 416/599-8500, Fax: 416/599-7318

P.G. Hopperton, #5064, 3080 Yonge St., M4N 3N3 – 416/482-6233 – *1

William B. Horkins, #1900, 439 University Ave., M5G 1Y8 – 416/591-1218, Fax: 416/408-2372; Email: horkins@interlog.com; URL: http://www.interlog.com/~horkins – *1

Horlick Kleinman Associates, #1402, 151 Yonge St., M5C 2W7 – 416/366-6000, Fax: 416/366-9808 – *1

Brian J. Hornsby, #4068, 3080 Yonge St., M4N 3N1 – 416/482-5853, Fax: 416/322-7097 – *1

Horwitz, Finder, 30 St. Clair Ave. West, M4V 3A1 – 416/961-1177, Fax: 416/961-1251 – *2

Houlihan & McCrie, Belfield Pl., 15 Belfield Rd., M9W 1E8 – 416/243-9501, Fax: 416/243-2990 – *2

Houser, Henry & Syron, #2000, 145 King St. West, M5H 2B6 – 416/362-3411, Fax: 416/362-3757 – *13

Howard & Cook, #200, 70 Bond St., M5B 1X3 – 416/366-9411, Fax: 416/366-9416 – *2

Janet Howard, 406 King St. East, M5A 1L4 – 416/362-5700, Fax: 416/362-0847 – *1

Richard S. Howard, 305-3768 Bathurst St., M3H 3M6 – 416/398-9895, Fax: 416/633-3303 – *1

John A. Howlett, #1200, 100 Adelaide St. West, M5H 1S3 – 416/941-9444, Fax: 416/363-1019 – *1

Peter Hryn, Old City Hall, 60 Queen St. West, M5H 2M4 – 416/926-0798 – *1

Hubbard, Favaro, 142 King St. East, M5C 1G7 – 416/366-9558 – *2

Hughes, Amys, Bldg Box: 401, #5050, 1 First Canadian Place, M5X 1E3 – 416/367-1608, Fax: 416/367-8821; Email: mail@h-amys.mhs.compuserve.com; URL: http://www.hughes-amys.on.ca/h-amys – *27

Hughes, Archer, Dorsch, #1405, 372 Bay St., M5H 2X8 – 416/868-1300, Fax: 416/861-1147 – *4

Frank T.L. Hughes, 69 Elm St., M5G 1H2 – 416/599-5311, Fax: 416/971-9092 – *1

R.A. Hummel, Q.C., #208, 4218 Lawrence Ave. East, M1E 4X9 – 416/281-2502, Fax: 416/281-8957 – *1

Edward F. Hung, #319, 1033 Bay St., M5S 3A5 – 416/926-8777, Fax: 416/926-1799 – *1

David J. Hunt, #110, 1468 Victoria Park Ave., M4A 2M2 – 416/751-2064, Fax: 416/750-3794 – *1

Gary Patrick Huskins, #301, 500 Danforth Ave., M4K 1P6 – 416/778-8885 – *1

David V. Hutchinson, 701 Evans Ave., M9C 1A3 – 416/620-0553, Fax: 416/622-8952 – *1

Ken Hutchinson, #300, 48 Kennebec Cres., M9W 2R7 – 416/742-4858 – *1

David L. Hynes, The Mutual Group Centre, West Tower, #550, 3300 Bloor St. West, M8X 2X2 – 416/742-6900, Fax: 416/742-8744 – *1

Iacono Brown, 130 Adelaide St. West, 31st Fl., M5H 3P5 – 416/869-0123, Fax: 416/869-0271 – *15

Marvin Igelman, #220, 1018 Finch Ave. West, M3J 2E1 – 416/650-1601, Fax: 416/650-1782 – *1

Iler, Campbell, 160 John St., 2nd Fl., M5V 2E5 – 416/598-0103, Fax: 416/598-3484 – *8

Industrial Accident Victims Group of Ontario, #203, 489 College St., M6G 1A5 – 416/924-6477, Fax: 416/924-2472 – *1

Injured Workers Consultants, #307, 815 Danforth Ave., M4J 1L2 – 416/461-2411, Fax: 416/461-7138 – *1

Di Iorio, 821 The Queensway, M8Z 1N6 – 416/253-1223, Fax: 416/253-0186

Sheridan Ippolito, #506, 2 Jane St., M6S 4W3 – 416/763-3399, Fax: 416/763-3443 – *1

Ira E. Book & Associates, 1400 Kingston Rd., M1N 1R3 – 416/698-1157, Fax: 416/698-7680 – *1

Ireland, Nicoll, #1505, 330 Bay St., M5H 2S8 – 416/362-1354, Fax: 416/362-1465 – *2

Alan Irwin, 26 Woburn Ave., M5M 1K6 – 416/322-3142 – *1

Joan M. Irwin, #11, 2300 Lawrence Ave. East, M1P 2R2 – 416/288-9200, Fax: 416/288-1093 – *1

Claude Isaacksz, #602, 18 Wynford Dr., M3C 3S2 – 416/444-6006, Fax: 416/449-6969

Philip D. Isbister, #2200, 181 University Ave., M5H 3M7 – 416/601-6797, Fax: 416/363-7875 – *1

A. Isenberg, #804, 5075 Yonge St., M2N 6C6 – 416/225-5136, Fax: 416/225-6877 – *1

Miriam Isenberg, Q.C., 11 Bentworth Ave., M6A 1P1 – 416/785-8787, Fax: 416/785-6266 – *1

Irwin Z. Isenstein, 1202-390 Bay St., M5H 2Y2 – 416/368-2181, Fax: 416/363-8451

Sonny Itzkovitch, #207, 2175 Sheppard Ave. East, M2J 1W8 – 416/498-1311, Fax: 416/498-1397 – *1

Iwasykiw, J.A., 2115 Bloor St. West, M6S 1M5 – 416/762-5605, Fax: 416/236-1434 – *1

J.D. Barnett Law Offices, 1278 St. Clair Ave. West, M6E 1B9 – 416/656-8888, Fax: 416/232-0232

J.D. Barnett Law Offices, 5233 Dundas St. West, M9B 1A6

Jackman & Associates, #200, 196 Adelaide St. West, M5H 1W7 – 416/599-7070, Fax: 416/599-2861; Email: kevinmac@inforamp.net – *13

Carol E. Jackson, #300, 8 King St. East, M5C 1B5 – 416/363-3292, Fax: 416/366-4892 – *1

M.H. Jacobs, #612, 330 Bay St., M5H 2S8 – 416/214-1151, Fax: 416/214-0870 – *1

Wm. F. Jacobs, #511, 45 Sheppard Ave. East, M2N 5W9 – 416/229-4496, Fax: 416/229-4497 – *1

Harvey Jacobson, #222, 3089 Bathurst St., M6A 2A4 – 416/787-0611, Fax: 416/787-4873 – *1

Brandon Jaffe, #424, 100 Richmond St. West, M5H 3K6 – 416/368-2809, Fax: 416/365-1474

Sadrudin B. Jaffer, 1053 McNicoll Ave., M1W 3W6 – 416/495-9935, Fax: 416/497-1992 – *1

James Jagtoo, #110, 1468 Victoria Park Ave., M4A 2M2 – 416/750-3791, Fax: 416/750-3794 – *1

James & Boyden, #905, 555 Richmond St. West, M5V 3B1 – 416/361-6111, Fax: 416/504-6177 – *2

James & Davies, #1100, 55 Queen St. East, M5C 1R6 – 416/860-0166, Fax: 416/860-0041 – *3

Michael W. Jameson, Q.C., 101 Chaplin Cres., M5P 1A4 – 416/481-7529, Fax: 416/481-7626 – *1

D.M. Jamieson, #912, 390 Bay St., M5H 2Y2 – 416/366-8742, Fax: 416/366-5182 – *1

* indicates number of lawyers in law firm.

Katharina Janczaruk, #312, 720 Spadina Ave., M5S 2T9 – 416/944-8151, Fax: 416/929-2474 – *1

Jane Finch Community Legal Services, #409, 1315 Finch Ave. West, M3J 2G6 – 416/398-0677, Fax: 416/398-7172 – *3

Mary Jarrell, #106, 81 The East Mall, M8Z 5W3 – 416/253-1840, Fax: 416/253-1243 – *1

Johannes Jarvalt, #102, 958 Broadview Ave., M4K 2R6 – 416/463-2737

M.I. Jeffery, Q.C., 40 Plymbridge Cres., M2P 1P5 – 416/487-2307, Fax: 416/487-2307 – *1

Jeffery, Robertson, Watson & Pendrith, #1812, 2 Carlton St., M5B 1J3 – 416/977-7700, Fax: 416/977-8570 – *2

M.M. Jemmott, Q.C., 470 Dupont St., M5R 1W6 – 416/588-2440 – *1

Robert L. Jenkins, #1200, 20 Toronto St., M5C 2B8 – 416/368-5248, Fax: 416/363-1457

Jesin & Watson, #204, 4580 Dufferin St., M3H 5Y3 – 416/736-7331, Fax: 416/736-7426 – *2

Jewell, Michael & Obradovich, #700, 390 Bay St., M5H 2Y2 – 416/862-7020, Fax: 416/862-2135 – *5

Larry B. Joffe, 700-55 Town Centre Crt., M1P 4X4 – 416/290-6138, Fax: 416/296-1259 – *1

Stanley Joffe, #312, 2 St. Clair Ave. East, M4T 2T5 – 416/968-6477, Fax: 416/968-6743 – *2

Johnston & Douglas, 2974A Lakeshore Blvd. West, M8V 3B7 – 416/259-4267 – *1

Daphne Johnston, #1130, 20 Dundas St. West, M5G 2G8 – 416/599-9635, Fax: 416/591-7333 – *1

Douglas Senn Johnston, 2974A Lakeshore Blvd. West, M8V 1J9 – 416/259-4267 – *1

Gary Johnston, 340 Eglinton Ave. East, M4P 1L8 – 416/481-8663

Kerry W. Johnston, #1110, 36 Toronto St., M5C 2C5 – 416/360-1834, Fax: 416/360-1845 – *1

Johnston, Malcolm & Associates, #505, 133 Richmond St. West, M5H 2L3 – 416/365-0316, Fax: 416/365-0384 – *2

Richard T. Johnston, #1401, 67 Yonge St., M5E 1J8 – 416/364-8508 – *1

G.P. Johnstone, #1601, 65 Queen St. West., M5H 2M5 – 416/364-3200, Fax: 416/364-3657 – *1

William R. Johnstone, #1515, 390 Bay St., M5H 2Y2 – 416/860-7150, Fax: 416/860-1474 – *1

Gerald F. Jonas, #1607, 80 Richmond St. West, M5H 2C2 – 416/366-3838, Fax: 416/366-8041 – *1

S. Jonas, #304, 559 College St., M6G 1A9 – 416/961-3474, Fax: 416/961-8094 – *1

Brian D. Jones, #320, 100 Richmond St. West, M5H 3K6 – 416/364-0707, Fax: 416/869-1840 – *2

Gregory Jones, #300, 111 Elizabeth St., M5G 1P7 – 416/977-3796, Fax: 416/599-8075 – *1

Kevin Jones, 284 Sherbourne St., M5A 2S1 – 416/923-1685 – *1

Jones, Rogers, #1600, 155 University Ave., M5H 3B7 – 416/361-0626, Fax: 416/361-6303; Email: jr_law@istar.ca – *7

Joseph & O'Donoghue, #1301, 2200 Yonge St., M4S 2B8 – 416/932-0545, Fax: 416/932-0541 – *7

Mary K.E. Joseph, #1050, 181 University Ave., M5H 3M7 – 416/363-8048, Fax: 416/363-8554 – *1

Vesna Josifovski, #604, 130 Bloor St. West, M5S 1N5 – 416/960-0143, Fax: 416/924-2371 – *1

Ron Jourard, 802 St. Clair Ave. West, M6C 1B6 – 416/656-9667, Fax: 416/656-7368 – *1

E.A. Jupp, Q.C., #1712, 130 Adelaide St. West, M5H 3P5 – 416/868-0626, Fax: 416/868-0352 – *1

Juriansz & Li, #1709, 5650 Yonge St., M2M 4G3 – 416/226-2342, Fax: 416/222-6874; Email: justice@io.org – *3

M. Jurjans, #201, 785 Carlaw Ave., M4K 3L1 – 416/466-1101, Fax: 416/466-6335 – *1

Justice for Children & Youth, #405, 720 Spadina Ave., M5S 2T9 – 416/920-1633, Fax: 416/920-5855 – *4

Larry Kagan, #101, 2171 Avenue Rd., M5M 4B4 – 416/485-1193 – *1

Marsha Kagan, #101, 2171 Avenue Rd., M5M 4B4 – 416/485-1195 – *1

R.B. Kallmeyer, #305, 2968 Dundas St. West, M6P 1Y8 – 416/763-2297, Fax: 416/763-2298 – *1

Bernard J. Kamin, #401, 111 Eglinton Ave. East, M4P 1H4 – 416/932-1236, Fax: 416/932-1747 – *1

A. Victor Kanbergs, #101, 5859 Yonge St., M2M 3V6 – 416/225-8806 – *1

Speros Kanellos, 61 Hayden St., M4Y 2P2 – 416/968-1717, Fax: 416/968-7559

C.Y. Kang, #210, 280 Sheppard Ave. East, M2N 3B1 – 416/228-1417, Fax: 416/221-1732 – *1

N.S. Kanji, 61 Alness St., M3J 2H2 – 416/650-0901, Fax: 416/650-0900 – *1

Kaplan & Associates, #210, 69 Bloor St. East, M4W 1A9 – 416/961-2600, Fax: 416/961-2534 – *1

Jacob Kaplan, Q.C., 185 Old Yonge St, M2P 1R2 – 416/226-3262 – *1

William Kaplan, #200, 70 Bond St., M5B 1X3 – 416/360-4429, Fax: 416/365-7702 – *1

Anil K. Kapoor, #2714, 130 Adelaide St. West, M5H 3P5 – 416/363-2700, Fax: 416/868-1990 – *1

Joseph H. Kappy, 392 Parliament St., M5A 2Z7 – 416/922-0202, Fax: 416/922-0404 – *1

N.H. Karal, Q.C., 17 Joyce Pkwy., M6P 2S7 – 416/787-6101, Fax 416/787-6102 – *1

Karas & Associates, #410, 212 King St. West, M5H 1K5 – 416/506-1800, Fax: 416/599-5582; Email: karas@karas.ca; URL: http://www.karas.ca – *1

C.N. Karbaliotis, #201, 101 Richmond St. East, M5C 1N9 – 416/364-0388, Fax: 416/364-3756; Email: kartis@techne.com; URL: http://www.techne.com – *1

H.B. Kasman, 500 Danforth Ave., M4K 1P6 – 416/465-7593 – *1

Sheldon L. Kasman & Associates, #201, 1622 Eglinton Ave. West, M6E 2G8 – 416/789-1888, Fax: 416/789-5928 – *2

B.M. Kassirer, Q.C., #1200, 595 Bay St., M5G 2C2 – 416/591-7607 – *1

Kates & Goldkind, #206, 3850 Sheppard Ave. East, M1T 3L4 – 416/291-5587 – *2

Barry M. Kaufman, #201, 2050 Sheppard Ave. East, M2J 5B3 – 416/498-7297, Fax: 416/498-0792 – *1

S.D. Kaufman, 381 Broadview Ave., M4K 2M7 – 416/424-4388 – *1

C.M. Kavanagh, 121 Wineva Ave., M4E 2T1 – 416/410-0486 – *1

J.M. Kavanagh, Q.C., 706 Kennedy Rd., M1K 2B5 – 416/265-3560, Fax: 416/265-1944 – *1

Kavinoky & Cook, #455, 207 Queen's Quay West, M5J 1A7 – 416/203-0631, Fax: 416/203-0639 – *3

Bernard L. Kay, 2901 Bayview Ave., PO Box 91035, M2K 2Y6 – 416/922-9395 – *1

Robert C. Kay, 31 Adelaide St. East, PO Box 961, Stn Adelaide, M5C 2K3 – 416/362-9999, Fax: 416/362-9999 – *1

D.H. Kayfetz, 55 York St., M4W 1R7 – 416/364-8131 – *1

Kazman & Associates, #210, 3701 Chesswood Dr., M3J 2P6 – 416/630-9950, Fax: 416/630-9159 – *2

Keel Cottrelle, #920, 36 Toronto St., M5C 2C5 – 416/367-2900, Fax: 416/367-2791

Jennifer E. Keenan, #1708, 372 Bay St., M5H 2W9 – 416/368-2811, Fax: 416/368-3425

Keith & Kramer, #404, 1200 Bay St., M5R 2A5 – 416/922-4417, Fax: 416/922-9328 – *2

J. Robert Kellermann, #303, 489 College St., M6G 1A5 – 416/926-8034, Fax: 416/972-1992 – *1

Kelly Affleck Greene, #840, One First Canadian Place, Bldg Box: 489, PO Box 489, M5X 1E5 – 416/360-2800, Fax: 416/360-5960 – *12

Miriam A. Kelly, #1500, 2 St. Clair Ave. East, M4T 2R1 – 416/926-1602, Fax: 416/926-7532 – *1

Timothy C. Kelly, #405, 11 Church St., M5E 1W1 – 416/941-8952, Fax: 416/366-1799 – *1

F.S. Kelman, #303, 4120 Yonge St., M2P 2B8 – 416/250-6400, Fax: 416/250-6411 – *1

Saul B. Kelner, #230, 165 The Queensway, M8Y 1H8 – 416/366-7988, Fax: 416/259-9177 – *1

Evan Kenley, #307, 111 Eglinton Ave. East, M4P 1H4 – 416/932-1148, Fax: 416/932-1108 – *1

Kennedy Dymond, #2500, 55 Avenue Rd., M5R 3L2 – 416/968-2939

Kennedy Dymond, #200, 4211 Yonge St., M2P 2A9 – 416/733-2807

Mary Ann Kennedy, 202-2323 Yonge St., M4P 2C9 – 416/486-1339

William I. Kennedy, #500, 370 King St. West, M5V 1J9 – 416/599-1930, Fax: 416/599-1377

Kensington-Bellwoods, #205, 489 College St., M6G 1A5 – 416/924-4244, Fax: 416/924-5904 – *3

Kerbel & Associates, #2700, 181 University Ave., M5H 3M7 – 416/777-2160, Fax: 416/601-0805 – *1

M. Kerbel, Q.C., #2412, 401 Bay St., M5H 2Y4 – 416/366-7621, Fax: 416/364-2308 – *1

M.L. Kerbel, #1001, 65 Queen St. West, M5H 2M5 – 416/364-9532 – *2

Carrolyne Kerr, #305, 1033 Bay St., M5S 3A5 – 416/921-4554, Fax: 416/925-2860 – *1

Catherine Kerr, #1720, 180 Dundas St. West, M5G 1Z8 – 416/977-3657, Fax: 416/977-9516 – *1

Kerr, Oster & Wolfman, 133 Berkeley St., M5A 2X1 – 416/365-7163 – *3

Helen M. Kersley, 308-100 Richmond St. West, M5H 3K6 – 416/947-1124, Fax: 416/947-1236 – *1

Kerzner Papazian MacDermid, #500, 121 King St. West, M5H 3T9 – 416/367-4900, Fax: 416/367-8197

Louis I. Kesten, Q.C., 887 Queen St. East, M4M 1J2 – 416/461-0865, Fax: 416/461-1869 – *3

Kestenberg Siegal Lipkus, 65 Granby St., M5B 1H8 – 416/597-0000, Fax: 416/597-6567 – *7

Kettner, Philp, Gold, Frydman & Rumack, #300, 500 University Ave., M5G 1V7 – 416/598-3277, Fax: 416/340-0884 – *4

Khaki El-Farouk, 81 Pembroke St., M5A 2N9 – 416/925-7227, Fax: 416/925-2450; Email: elfin925@aol.com

Abdul A. Khalifa, #5, 1 Willingdon Blvd., M8X 2H1 – 416/234-0640, Fax: 416/234-9064 – *1

Kidd, J. Kenneth, Q.C., #406, 347 Bay St., M5H 2R7 – 416/363-6097 – *2

Theodore J. Kielb, Scotia Plaza, 40 King St. West, 41st Fl., M5H 3Y4 – 416/367-1643 – *1

C.W. Kilian, #308, 2401 Eglinton Ave. East, M1K 2M5 – 416/750-4824, Fax: 416/750-4827 – *1

Kimberley, Vaillancourt & Henry, 1937 Gerrard St. East, M4L 2C2 – 416/690-1708, Fax: 416/690-4976 – *1

R.S. Kimel, 444 Adelaide St. West, M5V 1S7 – 416/361-1877, Fax: 416/861-9216 – *1

King & King, #810, 390 Bay St., M5H 2W9 – 416/368-4678, Fax: 416/947-0482 – *1

James H. King, 2-692 Eglinton Ave. East, M4G 2K5 – 416/425-0276

W.A. King, 120 Eglinton Ave. East, 5th Fl., M4P 1E2 – 416/483-8877, Fax: 416/483-8017 – *1

J. Kingstons, #100, 185 Glencairn Ave., M4R 1N3 – 416/322-0612, Fax: 416/322-6488 – *1

Kirby, Lyon, Gatward & Clark, #2405, 1 Dundas St. West, M5G 1Z3 – 416/351-1010, Fax: 416/351-1130 – *4

Terry L. Kirichenko, 1316-181 University Ave., M5H 3M7 – 416/861-0123 – *1

Fern Kirsch, 5160 Yonge St., PO Box 85, M2N 6L9 – 416/590-7090 – *1

Pamela L. Kirsch, 1661B Eglinton Ave. East, M6E 2H1 – 416/787-5420, Fax: 416/787-2926 – *1

Ernest J. Kirsh, #200, 2901 Bayview Ave., M2K 1E6 – 416/226-4198 – *1

Sheila Kirsh, #816, 181 University Ave., M5H 2X7 – 416/367-1765, Fax: 416/364-1697 – *1

Sheldon E. Kirsh, #306, 27 Queen St. East, M5C 2M6 – 416/360-6411, Fax: 416/360-5738 – *1

Howard Joshua Kirshenbaum, 70 Bond St., M5B 1X3 – 416/777-9237 – *1

Kissoon Pachai, #207, 5353 Dundas St. West, M9B 1Y4 – 416/234-1446, Fax: 416/234-1446
Klaiman, Edmonds, #1020, 121 King St. West, PO Box 27, M5H 3T9 – 416/867-9600, Fax: 416/867-9783 – *2
Klein Law Office, 307 Danforth Ave., M4K 1N7 – 416/469-2540, Fax: 416/469-5216 – *1
Murray Klein, 12 Highgate Road, M8X 2B2 – 416/231-5476 – *1
A. Klemencic, 332 Brown's Line, M8W 3T6 – 416/251-5281, Fax: 416/251-0029 – *1
Klotz Associates, 700-347 Bay St., M5H 2R7 – 416/360-4500 – *2
A.W. Klymko, #430, 100 Richmond St. West, M5H 3K6 – 416/366-4583 – *1
Frances A. Knoll, #307, 42 Glen Elm Ave., M4T 1T7 – 416/487-7688 – *1
Kohm Seto & MacLean, #602, 1 St. Clair Ave. East, M4T 2V7 – 416/921-6256, Fax: 416/416-921-6398 – *3
Linda H. Kolyn, #503, 2 Jane St., M6S 4W3 – 416/604-7677, Fax: 416/762-8494; URL: http://www.pathcom.com/~dadey/homepage.htm – *1
Marc Kopowitz, #700, 55 University Ave., M5J 2K4 – 416/368-1100, Fax: 416/368-0016
Mark B. Koreen, 2424 Bloor St. West, M6S 1P9 – 416/766-2416, Fax: 416/769-5365 – *1
Rinas Korn, #201, 344 Dupont St., M5R 1V9 – 416/515-1500, Fax: 416/515-1295 – *1
Koroloff & Huckins, #304, 1110 Sheppard Ave. East, M2K 2W2 – 416/229-6226, Fax: 416/229-6517 – *2
E.C. Korzen, 1392 Eglinton Ave. West, M6E 2E4 – 416/789-7183, Fax: 416/785-7192 – *1
Koskie & Minsky, #900, 20 Queen St. West, PO Box 52, M5H 3R3 – 416/977-8353, Fax: 416/977-3316; URL: http://www.koskieminsky.com – *28
A.I. Kostman, 392 Parliament St., M5A 2Z7 – 416/962-8800, Fax: 416/922-0404 – *1
R.M. Kostuk, Q.C., 2195 Bloor St. West, M6S 1N2 – 416/766-7666 – *1
Kostyniuk & Associates, 2481A Bloor St. West, M6S 1P8 – 416/762-8238 – *5
Robert Kostyniuk, Q.C., #612, 390 Bay St., M5H 2Y2 – 416/364-4025, Fax: 416/364-4631 – *3
Bernard Kott, Q.C., #1115, 330 Bay St., M5H 2S8 – 416/365-7866 – *1
I. Koziebrocki, #2600, 250 Yonge St., M5B 2M6 – 416/598-2167, Fax: 416/598-3167 – *1
Jeffrey W. Kramer, #1904, 120 Adelaide St. West, M5H 1T1 – 416/601-6820, Fax: 416/601-0712 – *1
S.B. Kravetz, #202, 69 Elm St., M5G 1H2 – 416/971-8704, Fax: 416/971-9092 – *1
E.A. Kremer, 845 St. Clair Ave. West, M6C 1C3 – 416/654-4111, Fax: 416/653-3891 – *1
Stephen Krepakevich, Q.C., 58 Edenvale Cres., M9A 4A6 – 416/241-1717 – *1
Timothy J. Kreutzer, #1506, 141 Adelaide St. West, M5H 3L5 – 416/364-7292, Fax: 416/864-0175 – *1
J.H. Krieger, 4 Finch Ave. West, M2N 6L1 – 416/223-9577, Fax: 416/225-5992 – *1
Kathleen Kroeger, 2249 Queen St. East, M4E 1G1 – 416/699-8494, Fax: 416/699-8494 – *1
Krol & Krol, #201, 14A Hazelton Ave., M5R 2E2 – 416/964-0138 – *2
Kronis, Rotsztain, Margles, Cappel, #700, 25 Sheppard Ave. West, M2N 6S6 – 416/225-8750, Fax: 416/225-3910 – *10
Steven Kruck, #211, 2498 Yonge St., M4P 2H8 – 416/484-1607
Ronald A. Krueger, #1000, 65 Queen St. West, M5H 2M5 – 416/867-1440, Fax: 416/367-3949 – *1
Diane Kruger, #600, 20 Richmond St. East, M5C 2R9 – 416/360-8338 – *1
George J. Kubes, 360 Bloor St. West, M5S 1X1 – 416/926-9298 – *1
E.M. Kudrac, #108, 1415 Lawrence Ave. West, M6L 1A9 – 416/248-0181, Fax: 416/240-1219 – *1
Ernie Kung, #1708, 372 Bay St., M5H 2W9 – 416/777-1722, Fax: 416/777-1624 – *1

Howard Kutner & Associates, 2347 Kennedy Rd., M1T 3T8 – 416/297-4949 – *2
Enn Allan Kuuskne, #1510, 5140 Yonge St., M2N 6L7 – 416/224-2267, Fax: 416/250-7008 – *1
Kuzmochka & Kotylo, 89 Elizabeth St., 2nd Fl., M5G 1P4 – 416/597-1747, Fax: 416/597-2242 – *2
Aaron B. Kwinter, #100, 76 Densley Ave., M6M 2R3 – 416/245-5040, Fax: 416/249-9573 – *1
Wolfgang H. Kyser, #303, 101 Yorkville Ave., M5R 1C1 – 416/928-5999, Fax: 416/928-5987 – *1
Ted Laan, #1508, 330 Bay St., M5H 2S8 – 416/861-1071, Fax: 416/861-1968 – *1
John F. LaBerge, #800, 1243 Islington Ave., M8X 1Y9 – 416/233-4631, Fax: 416/234-0258 – *1
Stephen M. Labow, #700, 357 Bay St., M5H 2T7 – 416/947-1172, Fax: 416/363-4130 – *1
Tony Lacaria, #612, 330 Bay St., M5H 2S8 – 416/214-1390, Fax: 416/214-0870
B.F. Lackie, #201, 16 Isabella St., M4Y 2A1 – 416/922-0770, Fax: 416/922-5069 – *1
K.D.L. Lackner, 692 Coxwell Ave., M4C 3B6 – 416/461-8106, Fax: 416/461-8011 – *1
Lafleur Brown, #920, 1 First Canadian Place, PO Box 359, M5X 1E1 – 416/869-0994, Fax: 416/362-5818 – *12
Laforme, Harry, #1702, 100 Yonge St., M5C 1T4 – 416/954-2760, Fax: 416/954-2765 – *1
Laird & Laird, #521, 1315 Lawrence Ave. East, M3A 3R3 – 416/449-0993, Fax: 416/449-9396 – *2
W.W. Laird, Q.C., #1707, 57 Widdicombe Hill Blvd., M9R 1Y4 – 416/245-3114 – *1
Benjamin Laker, Q.C., 121 Westgate Blvd., M3H 1P5 – 416/636-9600, Fax: 416/636-9601 – *1
Laks & Rabinovici, #502, 133 Richmond St. West, M5H 2L3 – 416/863-9887, Fax: 416/863-9905 – *2
W.N. Lalka, #208, 5399 Eglinton Ave. West, M9C 5K6 – 416/620-9999, Fax: 416/620-7433 – *1
Christine Lall, #268, 5 Fairview Mall Dr., M2J 2Z1 – 416/498-4688, Fax: 416/498-6201 – *1
Lalonde & Eisen, #200, 70 Bond St., M5B 1X3 – 416/367-0136, Fax: 416/365-7702 – *2
Lambert Tweyman & Assoc., #800, 789 Don Mills Rd., M3C 1T5 – 416/467-5555, Fax: 416/467-9906 – *2
Jack S. Lambert, 203-5075 Yonge St., M2N 6C6 – 416/226-6333, Fax: 416/226-6344
W.W. Lamberton, Q.C., #101, 1262 Don Mills Rd., M3B 2W7 – 416/445-6800, Fax: 416/445-5468 – *1
Lawrence Lamey, #201, 84 Avenue Rd., M5R 2H2 – 416/925-6762, Fax: 416/925-1536 – *1
Lamont & Lamont, #810, 1 Queen St. East, M5C 2W5 – 416/363-0173, Fax: 416/363-0176 – *2
Garry Lamourie, #1509, 180 Dundas St. West, M5G 1Z8 – 416/533-1153, Fax: 416/536-3529 – *1
Landlord Self-Help Centre, 110 Atlantic Ave., M6K 1X9 – 416/532-4467 – *1
Sharon S. Landsman, #2000, 80 Richmond St. West, M5H 2A4 – 416/363-5478, Fax: 416/364-9707 – *1
Landy Marr & Associates, #1000, 2 Sheppard Ave. East, M2N 5Y7 – 416/221-9343, Fax: 416/221-8928
Landy, Marr & Associates, #1000, 2 Sheppard Ave. East, M2N 5Y7 – 416/221-9343, Fax: 416/221-8928 – *3
Lane, Allen, Standard Life Centre, #2330, 121 King St. West, PO Box 34, M5H 3T9 – 416/863-9686, Fax: 416/863-1811 – *3
Lang Michener, BCE Pl., #2500, 181 Bay St., PO Box 747, M5J 2T7 – 416/360-8600, Fax: 416/365-1719; Email: nwatson@toronto.langmichener.ca – *98
Aaron Lang, #200, 710 Wilson Ave., M3K 1E2 – 416/398-2210, Fax: 416/398-3317 – *1
C. Robert Langdon, Q.C., 140 Dinnide Cres., M4N 1L8 – 416/483-6272 – *1
George Lantos, 519A Bloor St. West, M5S 1Y4 – 416/535-4111 – *1
Simonetta A. Lanzi, #700, 357 Bay St., M5H 2T7 – 416/861-8142, Fax: 416/363-4130 – *1
G. Jonathan Lapid, #2200, 4950 Yonge St., M2N 6K1 – 416/222-4324, Fax: 416/222-6223

P.K. Large, #610, 372 Bay St., M5H 2W9 – 416/867-8669, Fax: 416/867-3079 – *1
Sam Laufer, #1200, 595 Bay St., M5G 2C2 – 416/598-7766, Fax: 416/598-0510 – *1
Stephen J. Lautens, #210, 335 Bay St., M5H 2R3 – 416/863-9744, Fax: 416/863-9541; Email: sjl@interlog.com; URL: http://beachnet.org/sjl – *1
Rosemary LaValley, #430, 100 Richmond St. West, M5H 3K6 – 416/863-6870 – *1
Law Offices, #780, 439 University Ave., M5G 1Y8 – 416/593-9300, Fax: 416/593-0225 – *6
Law Society of Upper Canada, 1-130 Queen St. West, M5H 2N5 – 416/947-3300, Fax: 416/947-5967
John V. Lawer, Q.C., #306, 40 St. Clair Ave. East, M4T 1M9 – 416/922-0737, Fax: 416/922-1896 – *1
Daniel Lawson, #1515, 390 Bay St., M5H 2Y2 – 416/594-1234, Fax: 416/860-1474 – *1
Lawson, McGrenere, Wesley, Rose & Clemenhagen, #700, 120 Adelaide St. West, M5H 1T1 – 416/862-8294, Fax: 416/862-2232 – *14
Lax, Smith & Assoc., 348A Queen St. West, 3rd Fl., M5V 2A2 – 416/408-3553, Fax: 416/408-3811 – *2
Laxton, Glass & Swartz, #1000, 80 Richmond St. West, M5H 2B1 – 416/363-2353, Fax: 416/363-7112
Paul Layefsky, #308, 100 Richmond St. West, M5H 3K6 – 416/947-1234, Fax: 416/947-1236 – *1
M.J. Leach, 4 Synnybrae Cres., M6M 4W5 – 416/248-5559, Fax: 416/240-9684 – *1
Timothy Leach, #1300, 100 Adelaide St. West, M5H 1S3 – 416/868-0265, Fax: 416/868-0478 – *1
Timothy E. Leahy, #408, 5075 Yonge St., M2N 6C6 – 416/226-9889, Fax: 416/226-2882; Email: teleahy@istar.ca
R.N. Lebi, 1331 St. Clair Ave. West, M6E 1C3 – 416/656-6157 – *1
H.W. Lebo, #302, 75 Eglinton Ave. East, M4P 2Z9 – 416/487-4504, Fax: 416/487-4073 – *1
Randy H. Lebow, #100, 480 Lawrence Ave., M5M 1C4 – 416/787-1681, Fax: 416/787-5814 – *1
Lee & Associates, #1402, 30 St. Clair Ave. West, M4V 3A1 – 416/922-9220, Fax: 416/964-5845
Lee Julia Yuen-Nam, #302, 607 Gerrard St. East, M4M 1Y2 – 416/466-6888
Edward Lee, #1003, 100 Yonge St., M5C 2W1 – 416/363-8220, Fax: 416/868-0478 – *1
John Y.C. Lee, #418, 4002 Sheppard Ave. East, M1S 1S6 – 416/299-8900, Fax: 416/299-8242 – *1
M.Y. Lee, 42 Fulham St., M1S 2A5 – 416/298-4476, Fax: 416/321-1717 – *1
Paul Lee & Associates, 20 Maitland St., M4Y 1C5 – 416/961-2707, Fax: 416/961-5575; Email: pauleee@inforamp.net – *8
Sunda Lee, #301, 302 Spadina Ave., M5T 2E7 – 416/596-8960, Fax: 416/596-1490 – *1
Legal Aid - Environmental Law, #401, 517 College St., M6G 1A8 – 416/960-2284, Fax: 416/960-9392 – *4
Legge & Legge, 60 St. Clair Ave. East, M4T 1N5 – 416/923-1776 – *5
Anita Leggett, #1300, 100 Adelaide St. West, M5H 1S3 – 416/360-1759, Fax: 416/360-6551 – *1
J.L. Leibel, Q.C., 104 Waterloo Ave., M3H 3Y5 – 416/635-8653 – *1
Jay Leider, #800, 75 Donway West, M3C 2E9 – 416/444-2465, Fax: 416/391-0650
Janet A. Leiper, #1900, 439 University Ave., M5G 1Y8 – 416/593-5805
J.C. Lemire, #500, 70 Bond St., M5B 1X3 – 416/363-1097, Fax: 416/863-4896 – *1
Lenczner, Slaght, Royce, Smith & Griffin, #2300, 130 Adelaide St, West, M5H 3P5 – 416/360-0023, Fax: 416/360-1054
Lende & Associates, #1900, 180 Dundas St. West, M5G 1Z8 – 416/598-7876, Fax: 416/979-0430
Lende & Associates, #1900, 180 Dundas St. West, M5G 1Z8 – 416/598-7876, Fax: 416/979-0434 – *1
Dennis K. Lenzin, 1724-390 Bay St., M5H 2Y2 – 416/869-3422 – *1

* indicates number of lawyers in law firm.

A. Lerek, #902, 1200 Bay St., M5R 2A5 – 416/927-9222, Fax: 416/927-8772 – *1

Lerner & Associates, Continental Bank of Canada Bldg., #2400, 130 Adelaide St. West, M5H 3P5 – 416/867-3076, Fax: 416/867-9192

Thomas J. Leroy, 45 Saint Nicholas St., M4Y 1W6 – 416/925-3968, Fax: 416/925-8122 – *1

Lette, Whittaker, #2800, 20 Queen St. West, CP 33, M5H 3R3 – 416/971-4849, Fax: 416/971-4849 – *2

B.J.B. Letterio, Q.C., #201, 1295A St. Clair Ave. West, M6E 1C2 – 416/652-0780, Fax: 416/652-2723 – *2

Leve & Zeller, #1306, 200 King St. West, M5H 3T4 – 416/368-8717 – *2

Levesque & Taylor, #5030, 3080 Yonge St., M4N 3N1 – 416/322-1458, Fax: 416/322-7493 – *1

Gérard Lévesque, 184 Lake Promenade, M8W 1A8 – 416/253-0129, Fax: 416/253-4737 – *1

Hugh A. Levin, #902, 5799 Yonge St., M2M 3V3 – 416/221-2800 – *1

Levine Associates, #1400, 10 King St. East, M5C 1C3 – 416/364-2345, Fax: 416/364-3818; Email: levlaw@interlog.com; URL: http://www.interlog.com/~levlaw/ – *3

Lorne Levine, #512, 90 Eglinton Ave. East, M4P 2T3 – 416/483-1251, Fax: 416/483-2903 – *1

Myer S. Levine, #1250, 180 Dundas St. West, M5G 1Z8 – 416/348-0114, Fax: 416/977-0714 – *1

R.A. Levine, #801, 1110 Finch Ave. West, M3J 2T2 – 416/736-4173 – *1

R.M. Levine, 627 Bloor St. West, M6G 1K8 – 416/533-8539 – *1

Levine, Sherkin, Boussidan & Linden, #200, 70 Bond St., M5B 1X3 – 416/360-6511, Fax: 416/360-1524 – *4

Yehudah H.J. Levinson, #410, 212 King St. West, M5H 1K5 – 416/591-8484, Fax: 416/599-5582; Email: levinson@pssnet.com – *1

Levinter & Levinter, #2520, 130 Adelaide St. West, M5H 3P5 – 416/863-1930, Fax: 416/361-6168 – *3

Jerry Levitan, #200, 70 Bond St., M5B 1X3 – 416/368-4600, Fax: 416/368-1166

Sherr Levitan, 10 Alcorn Ave., M4V 1E4 – 416/924-5664, Fax: 416/924-5664 – *1

Shirley E. Levitan, #303, 489 College St., M6G 1A5 – 416/927-7263, Fax: 416/972-1992 – *1

Howard Levitt & Associates, #7500, 401 Bay St., M5H 2Y4 – 416/594-3900, Fax: 416/594-2323 – *1

Levitt, Levitt & Lightman, #1, 16 Four Seasons Place, M9B 6E5 – 416/620-0362, Fax: 416/620-5158 – *3

Levitt, Levitt & Lightman, 21 Isabella St., M4Y 1M7 – 416/323-1377, Fax: 416/323-9355; Email: shlevitt@netcom.ca – *1

E.J. Levy, Q.C., #2600, 250 Yonge St., M5B 2M6 – 416/598-2167, Fax: 416/598-3167 – *1

Paul S. Lewin, #405, 3601 Victoria Park Ave., M1W 3Y3 – 416/499-7945, Fax: 416/756-3663

Lewis & Collyer, #401, 160 John St., M5V 2E5 – 416/598-4357, Fax: 416/598-1067 – *2

Eric Lewis & Assoc., 116 Parliament St., M5A 2Y8 – 416/367-1918, Fax: 416/362-1918

Jacqueline Lewis, 175 Harbord St., M5S 1H3 – 416/533-4100, Fax: 416/533-4120 – *3

Joseph E. Lewis, 327 Eglinton Ave. East, 2nd Fl., M4P 1L7 – 416/486-0084, Fax: 416/486-7363 – *1

R.K. Lewis, #2001, 372 Bay St., M5H 2W9 – 416/362-6966 – *1

Peter K. Libman, #405, 372 Bay St., M5H 2W9 – 416/368-1861

Lorne Lichtenstein, 1604-55 University Ave., M5J 2H7 – 416/947-0550, Fax: 416/866-7946 – *1

Ronald M. Lieberman, 42 Thelma Ave., M4V 1X9 – 416/488-9080

S.J. Lieberman, #236, 2900 Warden Ave., M1W 2S8 – 416/497-4300 – *1

Lilly, Anderson, Morgan, #900, 330 Bay St., M5H 2S8 – 416/365-6300, Fax: 416/365-7965 – *4

Angela Y. Lin, #412, 90 Eglinton Ave. East, M4P 2Y3 – 416/483-1328, Fax: 416/481-6171 – *1

C.O. Lindberg, #207, 191 Eglinton Ave. East, M4P 1K1 – 416/489-3325 – *1

Lindenberg & Lindenberg, 287 Eglinton Ave. East, M4P 1L3 – 416/484-8177, Fax: 416/322-0807 – *2

C. Lindhout, 16 Northcliffe Blvd., M6H 3H1 – 416/653-3073 – *1

Linett & Karoly, 101 Richmond St. East, M5C 1N9 – 416/366-5100 – *3

Lipman, Zener & Waxman, 1200 Bay St. West, M6C 2E3 – 416/789-0652 – *7

Murray M. Lipton, #1108, 8 King St. East, M5C 1B5 – 416/364-8283 – *1

Richard Litkowski, #1001, 65 Queen St. West, M5H 2M5 – 416/504-0996 – *1

Charles Litman, 26 Densley Ave., M6M 2R1 – 416/248-2002, Fax: 416/248-2024 – *1

G.E. Litowitz, #5, 2020 Bathurst St., M5P 3L1 – 416/789-7221 – *1

C.E. Litwack, 802 St. Clair Ave. West, M6C 1B6 – 416/656-7007, Fax: 416/656-7368 – *1

Nadia Liva, #700, 480 University Ave., M5G 1V2 – 416/598-0106, Fax: 416/977-5331 – *1

Lloyd, Speigel, #810, 111 Richmond St. West, M5H 2H5 – 416/362-2255, Fax: 416/362-7910 – *2

Shirley K.T. Lo, #206, 4002 Sheppard Ave. East, M1S 1S6 – 416/754-8454, Fax: 416/754-7737 – *1

David H. Locke, #1901, 65 Queen St. West, M5H 2M5 – 416/601-1525, Fax: 416/369-0085 – *1

Lockwood & Associates, #2100, 439 University Ave., M5G 1Y8 – 416/598-2323, Fax: 416/598-5581 – *6

Lofranco Longley & Vickar, #201, 622 College St., M6G 1B4 – 416/516-3715, Fax: 416/516-3719

Lofranco, Daly, #1300, 5255 Yonge St., M2N 6P4 – 416/223-8333, Fax: 416/223-3404 – *8

Michael Lomer, 81 Wellesley St. East, M4Y 1H6 – 416/960-0049, Fax: 416/960-1498 – *1

Lon Hall Attorneys, #808, 121 Bloor St. East, M4W 3M5 – 416/920-3849, Fax: 416/920-8373; Email: 103202.3406@compuserve.com; URL: http:/ourworld.compuserve.com/homepages/lha_ent_law – *2

Longley & Vickar, #900, 970 Lawrence Ave. West, M6A 3B6 – 416/256-2020, Fax: 416/256-2811 – *1

Loopstra, Nixon & McLeish, Woodbine Place, #600, 135 Queens Plate Dr., M9W 6V7 – 416/746-4710, Fax: 416/746-8319 – *16

Benedict J. Lopes, #111, 215 Morrish Rd., M1C 1E9 – 416/284-2119, Fax: 416/284-4837 – *1

Thomas Lorenz, #307, 500 Danforth Ave., M4K 1P6 – 416/461-1101, Fax: 416/465-9560

Lorenzetti Wolfe, #201, 133 Richmond St. West, M5H 2L5 – 416/366-3064, Fax: 416/366-0208 – *3

Frank Loreto, #7, 2007 Lawrence Ave. West, M9N 3V1 – 416/244-0700, Fax: 416/244-0389 – *1

S.I. Lovas, #2000, 390 Bay St., M5H 2Y2 – 416/977-7500, Fax: 416/860-0580 – *1

M. Lubek, #200, 65 Queen St. West, M5H 2M5 – 416/363-6651, Fax: 416/363-0252 – *1

Patricia Lucas, #1515, 123 Edward St., M5G 1E2 – 416/597-1061, Fax: 416/598-2943 – *1

Olga Luftig, 201-100 Sheppard Ave. W., M2N 1M6 – 416/224-2244, Fax: 416/225-0832 – *1

Patricia M. Lukasewich, 3386 Lakeshore Blvd. West, M8W 1M9 – 416/259-3747, Fax: 416/259-5177 – *1

R.E. Lund, 549 The Kingsway, M9A 3W9 – 416/232-1551 – *1

Arthur Lundy, #210, 3701 Chesswood Dr., M3J 2P6 – 416/630-9818, Fax: 416/630-9159 – *1

Karen D. Lundy, #2150, 1 Queen St. East, M5H 2W9 – 416/866-8152, Fax: 416/866-8197 – *1

Earl L. Lutes, #15B, 777 Danforth Ave., M4J 1L2 – 416/463-4411 – *1

Helen Luzius, #1610, 372 Bay St., M5H 2W9 – 416/368-3264, Fax: 416/866-8197

Michael M. Lynch, Q.C., 99 Charles St. East, M4Y 1V2 – 416/972-9828, Fax: 416/964-0823 – *1

P.M. Lynch, #707, 330 University Ave., M5G 1R7 – 416/596-0609 – *1

Gordon A. Macartney Q.C., #700, 390 Bay St., M5H 2Y2 – 416/366-7854, Fax: 416/862-2135

MacBeth & Johnson, #301, 133 Richmond St. West, M5H 2L7 – 416/368-8311, Fax: 416/368-1645 – *6

Janette M.F. MacDonald, 76 Harper Ave., M4T 2L3 – 416/488-9126, Fax: 416/488-9126 – *1

Norman MacDonald, 200-70 Bond St., M5B 1X3 – 416/865-2950, Fax: 416/365-7702 – *1

Peter MacDonald, #500, 70 Bond St., M5B 1X3 – 416/864-1130, Fax: 416/863-4896 – *1

MacKay & Associates, 939 Lawrence Ave. East, M3C 1P8 – 416/443-9494, Fax: 416/510-1935 – *1

Alison R. Mackay, 2519 Mainroyal St., L5L 1E1 – 905/820-3866, Fax: 905/820-3866 – *1

Donald J. MacKay, #5044, 3080 Yonge St., M4N 3N3 – 416/482-6233 – *1

Mackenzie, Magill, #1000, 65 Queen St. West, M5H 2M5 – 416/367-9100, Fax: 416/367-3949; Email: mmlaw@idirect.com – *2

Judy D. MacLachlan, 70 Bude St., M6C 1X8

Lennox A. MacLean, Q.C., 46 Kingland Cr., M2J 2B7 – 416/496-8985, Fax: 416/496-2445 – *1

D.J. MacLennan, Q.C., 497 Eglinton Ave. West, M5N 1A7 – 416/482-9209 – *1

T.J. MacLennan, 25 Isabella St., M4Y 1M7 – 416/925-6400, Fax: 416/969-8678 – *1

Macleod Dixon, BCE Place, #4520, 181 Bay St., PO Box 792, M5J 2T3 – 416/360-8511, Fax: 416/360-8277; Email: 75143,2536@compuserve.com – *1

Doug MacLeod, #701, 123 Edward St., M5G 1E2 – 416/591-1735, Fax: 416/591-9200 – *1

Terence Macli, #1100, 372 Bay St., M5H 2W9 – 416/863-6655, Fax: 416/863-6080

MacMaster, Poolman & DeVries, #1140, 121 King St. West, PO Box 17, M5H 3T9 – 416/365-0258, Fax: 416/365-1355 – *2

MacMillan, Rooke & Boeckle, #702, 401 Bay St., PO Box 96, M5H 2Y4 – 416/360-1194, Fax: 416/360-8469; Toll Free: 1-800-661-7606 – *8

S.G.R. MacMillan, #2110, 120 Adelaide St. West, M5H 1T1 – 416/363-0100, Fax: 416/363-7697 – *1

MacTavish, de Lint, Hamersfeld, #200, 196 Adelaide St. West, M5H 1W7 – 416/599-7070, Fax: 416/599-2861; Email: mdlh@inforamp.net; URL: http://www.inforamp.net/~mdlh – *3

Magder & Associates, #420, 90 Eglinton Ave. East, M4P 2Y3 – 416/480-1940, Fax: 416/480-2176 – *3

Magerman & Page, #203, 2141 Jane St., M3M 1A2 – 416/241-8681 – *5

Maksymiw, Tokar, Hrycyna & Vieira-Hanna, #200, 1081 Bloor St. West, M6H 1M5 – 416/532-3373, Fax: 416/531-4189 – *4

Malach & Fidler, #1700, 439 University Ave., M5G 1Y8 – 416/598-1667, Fax: 416/598-5222 – *8

Dan Malamet, 95 St. Clair Ave. West, M4V 1N7 – 416/324-7984, Fax: 416/926-2888 – *1

D.I. Malcolm, 274A Avenue Rd., M4V 2G7 – 416/927-8375, Fax: 416/924-7120 – *1

T.R. Anthony Malcolm, #850, 36 Toronto St., M5A 1J3 – 416/864-1608, Fax: 416/864-1549 – *1

G.A. Maldoff, 55 Medulla Ave., M8Z 5L6 – 416/232-1733, Fax: 416/232-2194 – *1

Anna Mallin, 78 Bideford Ave., M3H 1K4 – 416/638-8897 – *1

Paul E. Mallon, #700, 2 Bloor St. West, M4W 3E2 – 416/944-1442 – *1

Jean MacKinnon Mallory, #700, 2 Bloor St. West, M4W 3R1 – 416/923-3514, Fax: 416/923-2071 – *1

Malo & Pilley, 1067 Bloor St. West, M6H 1M5 – 416/534-7543, Fax: 416/534-7625 – *2

Murray N. Maltz, #203, 3875 Keele St., M3J 1N6 – 416/398-6900, Fax: 416/398-6845

M.A. Manchee, 31 Clarendon Ave., M4V 1J2 – 416/972-0057, Fax: 416/323-9460 – *1

Mancia & Mancia, #701, 390 Bay St., M5H 2Y2 – 416/363-7422, Fax: 416/363-4975 – *2

Mang, Steinberg & Skultety, 707 College St., M6G 1C2 – 416/531-3516, Fax: 416/538-4412 – *3

Manning & Simone, 174 Avenue Rd., M5R 2J1 – 416/944-8460, Fax: 416/944-8461 – *2
Hubert E. Mantha, #216, 215 College St., M5T 1R1 – 416/591-7345, Fax: 416/591-8814 – *1
The Marchant Practice, #1801, One Yonge St., M5E 1W7 – 416/365-1544, Fax: 416/369-0515 – *1
A.M. Marchetti, 12 Karen Ann Cres., M1G 1M3 – 416/289-7184 – *1
Denise Marchildon, #506, 4576 Yonge St., M2N 6N4 – 416/229-2133, Fax: 416/229-9256 – *1
Pierre F. Marchildon, Dundas-Lambton Centre, #308, 4195 Dundas St. West, M8X 1Y4 – 416/236-0686, Fax: 416/236-0650 – *1
Harvey Margel, #202, 2365 Finch Ave. West, M9M 2W8 – 416/745-9933, Fax: 416/745-9290 – *1
Markle, May, Phibbs, Bldg Box: 114, 438 University Ave., 21st Fl., M5G 2K8 – 416/593-4385, Fax: 416/593-4478 – *9
Marko, Rose, #Lower, 70 Bond St., M5B 1X3 – 416/867-6196, Fax: 416/867-6199 – *4
Michael A. Markoff, 4950 Yonge St., M2N 6K1 – 416/224-0200 – *1
H. David Marks, Q.C., #300, 133 Berkeley St., M5A 2X1 – 416/863-1550, Fax: 416/863-9670 – *1
G.A. Marron, Q.C., 99 Charles St. East, M4Y 1V2 – 416/920-1504, Fax: 416/964-0823 – *1
Larry M. Marshall, #710, 25 Sheppard Ave. W., M2N 6S6 – 416/512-6171, Fax: 416/229-0278 – *1
Ben Martin, 469 Queen St. East, M5A 1T9 – 416/366-9901, Fax: 416/363-4603
Calvin Martin, Q.C., 600 Church St., M4Y 2E7 – 416/922-5854, Fax: 416/922-5854; Email: duc14@fox.nstn.ca; URL: http://fox.nstn.ca/~duc14/law.html – *1
David Martin, #402, 20 Adelaide St. East, M5C 2T6 – 416/362-7673, Fax: 416/362-0550 – *1
E.J.S. Martin, Q.C., #215, 555 Burnhamthorpe Rd., M9C 2X3 – 416/622-2224 – *1
J. David Martin, #2200, 181 University Ave., M5H 3M7 – 416/601-0555, Fax: 416/363-7875 – *1
Malcolm Martin, 577 Jarvis St., M4Y 2J3 – 416/961-0501, Fax: 416/961-2749 – *1
R.W. Martin, #1000, 65 Queen St. West, M5H 2M5 – 416/362-3887, Fax: 416/367-3949 – *1
Thomas Martin, #203, 1114A Wilson Ave., M3M 1G7 – 416/636-0056, Fax: 416/636-5908 – *1
W.D. Martin, 1152 Yonge St., M4W 2L9 – 416/968-0322, Fax: 416/968-3725 – *1
Waldo W. Martin, #305, 2401 Eglinton Ave. East, M1K 2M5 – 416/750-0795, Fax: 416/750-0090 – *1
Martinello & Associates, United Centre, #208, 255 Duncan Mill Rd., M3B 3H9 – 416/510-8866, Fax: 416/449-9977 – *4
Dawn C. Maruno, 54 Broadleaf Rd., M3B 1C4 – 416/444-9334 – *1
Ray M. Maruschak, 63 Beaver Bend Cres., M9B 5R2 – 416/626-2877, Fax: 416/626-2700 – *1
Dan Marc Mascioli, 467 Roehampton Ave., M4P 1S3 – 416/488-3257 – *1
W.J. Massey, #225, 85 Ellesmere Rd., M1R 4B9 – 416/444-5223, Fax: 416/444-6806 – *1
Masters & Masters, #440, 65 Queen St. West, M5H 2M5 – 416/361-1399, Fax: 416/361-6181 – *2
Gary J. Matalon, 403 Saint Clements Ave., M5N 1M2 – 416/481-8596
Mathews, Dinsdale & Clark, #2500, 1 Queen St. East, M5C 2Z1 – 416/862-8280, Fax: 416/862-8247 – *25
David Maubach & Assoc., 810 Queen St. East, M4M 1H7 – 416/469-1115, Fax: 416/469-9662 – *3
Frank D. Mauro, #203, 1029 McNicoll Ave., M1W 3W6 – 416/502-9232, Fax: 416/502-3061 – *1
William R. Maxwell, Q.C., Penthouse, 121 Richmond St. West, M5H 2K1 – 416/364-7771, Fax: 416/364-9842 – *1
J.W. May, #304, 250 Dundas St. West, M5T 2Z5 – 416/593-4385, Fax: 416/593-4478 – *1
D.C. Mayne, 577 Jarvis St., M4Y 2J3 – 416/961-0470, Fax: 416/961-2749 – *1

Harry Mayzel, #2718, 401 Bay St., M5H 2Y4 – 416/366-1969, Fax: 416/366-0116 – *1
Karen M. McArthur, 37 Prince Arthur Ave., M5R 1B2 – 416/972-1900 – *2
Joseph M. McBride, 5150 Dundas St. West, M9A 1C3 – 416/231-6555, Fax: 416/231-6630 – *1
McBride, Wallace & Laurent, 150 Dundas St. West, M9A 1C3 – 416/231-6555, Fax: 416/231-6630 – *4
McCarthy Tétrault, Toronto-Dominion Bank Tower, #4700, PO Box 48, TD Centre, M5K 1E6 – 416/362-1812, Fax: 416/868-0673; URL: http://www.mccarthy.ca – *184
D.V. McCarthy, #303, 100 Consilium Pl., M1H 3E3 – 416/296-1611 – *1
David R. McCaskill, #412, 120 Carlton St., M5A 4K2 – 416/929-9352, Fax: 416/922-3939 – *1
Robert L. McClelland, #313, 2498 Yonge St., M4P 2H8 – 416/481-7360, Fax: 416/481-7360
Susan McClennan, #200, 2200 Bloor St. West, M6S 1N4 – 416/767-5320, Fax: 416/763-2522 – *1
McComb & Associates, Toronto-Dominion Bank Tower, Toronto-Dominion Centre, PO Box 17, M5K 1A1 – 416/366-5558, Fax: 416/366-0608 – *2
Patrick T. McCool, #110, 964 Albion Rd., M9V 1A7 – 416/740-3684, Fax: 416/740-8495 – *1
K. Wayne McCracken, 90 Sandringham Dr., M3H 1C9 – 416/398-9483 – *1
Lisa McCullough, #2550, 55 King West, M4W 1E7 – 416/921-5011, Fax: 416/927-7318 – *1
McDonald & Hayden, #1500, 1 Queen St. East, M5C 2Y3 – 416/364-3100, Fax: 416/601-4100; URL: http://www.mchayden.on.ca – *15
Peter McGaw & Associates, #1007, 3266 Yonge St., M4N 2P6 – 416/864-1464, Fax: 416/322-4852 – *1
J.G. McGee, 332 Sheppard Ave. East, M2N 3B4 – 416/223-2604, Fax: 416/223-9819 – *1
Robert B. McGee, Q.C., 99 Charles St. East, M4Y 1V2 – 416/925-2232, Fax: 416/964-0823 – *1
David McGhee, #902, 360 Bay St., M5H 2V6 – 416/362-9736, Fax: 416/362-9736 – *1
Edward McGill, 112 Sheppard Ave. West, M1N 1M5 – 416/223-6800, Fax: 416/226-9730 – *1
D.R. McGregor, #706, 161 Eglinton Ave. East, M4P 1J5 – 416/485-1123, Fax: 416/485-1124 – *1
Bruce McGuire, 2643 Eglinton Ave. West, M6M 1T6 – 416/653-1891 – *1
McIver & McIver, #900, 372 Bay St., M5H 2W9 – 416/864-9000, Fax: 416/864-9190 – *3
McKechnie, Jurgeit & MacKenzie, 655 Dixon Rd., M9W 1J4 – 416/245-5454 – *4
D.L. McKelvey, 533 Queen St. East, M5A 1V1 – 416/365-0550 – *1
Lois McKenzie, 75 Lowther Ave., M5R 1C9 – 416/961-8540 – *1
McKeon, Poss, Halfnight & Corey, #3100, 130 Adelaide St. West, M5H 3P5 – 416/361-3200, Fax: 416/361-1405 – *3
Donald J. McKillop, Q.C., #700, 30 St. Clair Ave. West, M4V 3A1 – 416/483-6969, Fax: 416/975-9766 – *1
McLachlan, Winter, #1500, 123 Edward St., M5G 1E2 – 416/596-7077, Fax: 416/596-7629 – *2
Mary R. Mclaughlin, #1000, 120 Eglinton Ave. East, M4P 1E2 – 416/486-4939, Fax: 416/326-6371 – *1
McLean & Kerr, #2800, 130 Adelaide St. West, M5H 3P5 – 416/364-5371, Fax: 416/366-8571 – *23
Gordon W. McLean, #404, 600 Eglinton Ave. East, M4P 1P3 – 416/488-4712, Fax: 416/482-4043 – *1
Reginald M. McLean, #1601, 2 Sheppard Ave. E., M2N 5Y7 – 416/512-1200, Fax: 416/512-1217 – *1
Donald I. McLennan Q.C., #2700, 390 Bay St., M5H 2Y2 – 416/366-7837
McMahon, Raine, #307, 145 Sheppard Ave. West, M1N 3A7 – 416/222-2529, Fax: 416/222-8177 – *2
McMaster, McIntyre & Smyth, 2777 Dundas St. West, M6P 1Y4 – 416/769-4188, Fax: 416/769-4147 – *4
William McMaster, #2408, 180 Dundas St. West, M5G 1Z8 – 416/598-4810 – *1

McMillan Binch, South Tower, #3800, Royal Bank Plaza, M5J 2J7 – 416/865-7247, Fax: 416/865-7048 – *128
McNally & Dawson, 4953 Dundas St. West, M9A 1B6 – 416/236-7500, Fax: 416/236-7501 – *2
Neil D. McNish, #506, 2221 Yonge St., M4S 2B4 – 416/485-0717 – *1
I.D.C. McPhail, 207 Queen St. East, M5A 1S2 – 416/869-3400, Fax: 416/869-0094 – *1
Kenneth McQuaid, 2171 Danforth Ave., M4C 1K3 – 416/690-6939, Fax: 416/690-6941 – *1
McTague Law Firm, #300, 95 Barber Greene Rd., M5C 3E9 – 416/283-2449, Fax: 416/449-6482 – *1
Faye Mcwatt, 74 Lowther Ave., M5R 1C9 – 416/927-7430, Fax: 416/961-9905 – *1
Peter Meier, #303, 100 Consilium Pl., M1H 3E3 – 416/296-1510, Fax: 416/296-0836 – *1
Meighen Demers, Merrill Lynch Canada Tower, Bldg Box: 11, #1100, 200 King St. West, M5H 3T4 – 416/977-8400, Fax: 416/977-5239 – *32
Meisels & Associates, #200, 79 Shuter St., M5B 1B3 – 416/363-7700, Fax: 416/861-9919 – *1
Menzies, von Bogen, 1071B Bloor St. West, M6H 1M5 – 416/532-2833, Fax: 416/532-6553 – *2
Paul Mergler, #401, 302 The East Mall, M9B 6C7 – 416/232-9589, Fax: 416/232-9201 – *1
E.H. Merifield, #202, 4889 Yonge St., M2N 5N4 – 416/221-3494, Fax: 416/221-4169 – *1
Edwin Norman Merkur, #4052, 3080 Yonge St., M4N 3N1 – 416/487-3445, Fax: 416/487-9674 – *1
Ephry N. Merkur, Q.C., #Penthouse, 175 Keewatin Ave., M4P 2A3 – 416/486-5211, Fax: 416/486-2254
A.B. Mervin, 99 Charles St. East, M4Y 1V2 – 416/962-3780, Fax: 416/964-0823 – *1
Ruth E. Mesbur, #210, 335 Bay St., M5H 2R3 – 416/863-9744, Fax: 416/863-9541 – *1
Meyer, Wassenaar & Banach, 4856 Yonge St., M1N 5N2 – 416/223-9191, Fax: 416/222-9405 – *4
Michela & Gord, #1200, 595 Bay St., M5G 2C2 – 416/972-1137, Fax: 416/966-5053 – *1
David M. Midanik, 470 King St. East, M5A 1L7 – 416/364-1780, Fax: 416/362-0847 – *1
J.S. Midanik, Q.C., 296 Russell Hill Rd, M4V 2T6 – 416/924-1575 – *1
Yaroslav Mikitchook, #210, 204 Richmond St. West, M5V 1V6 – 416/599-2811, Fax: 416/599-2971 – *1
Janet G. Miliaris, #11, 2300 Lawrence Ave. East, M1P 2R2 – 416/288-0887, Fax: 416/288-1093 – *1
J.A. Millard, #109, 964 Albion Rd., M9V 1A7 – 416/742-1233, Fax: 416/742-1237 – *1
Miller & Miller, 1577 Bloor St. West, M6P 1A6 – 416/536-1159, Fax: 416/536-3618 – *2
Miller Thomson, Bldg Box: 27, #2700, 20 Queen St. West, M5H 3S1 – 416/595-8500, Fax: 416/595-8695; Email: env.group@miltom.com – *78
Dan Miller, #2200, 121 King St. West, M5H 3T9 – 416/862-2473, Fax: 416/862-1698 – *1
Duncan R. Miller, #1110, 36 Toronto St., M5C 2C5 – 416/362-0234, Fax: 416/860-1845 – *1
G.R. Miller, #402, 43 Eglinton Ave. East, M4P 1A3 – 416/486-7917, Fax: 416/487-4444 – *1
Glen M.A. Miller, 3850 Finch Ave. East, M1T 3T4 – 416/299-6785 – *1
H.L. Miller, Q.C., #204, 825 Eglinton Ave. West, M5N 1E7 – 416/783-1171, Fax: 416/783-7822 – *1
Jeffrey L. Miller, #704, 55 University Ave., M5J 2H7 – 416/363-6029, Fax: 416/363-3445 – *1
Jonathan Miller, #600, 1120 Finch Ave. West, M3J 3H7 – 416/665-6016, Fax: 416/667-0048 – *1
Mills & Mills, #2500, 145 King St. West, M5H 3T6 – 416/863-0125, Fax: 416/863-3997 – *16
Douglas J. Millstone, #309, 2100 Ellesmere Rd., M1H 3B7 – 416/289-7996, Fax: 416/289-7998 – *1
Milrad & Agnew, 215 Carlton St., M5A 2K9 – 416/964-0021, Fax: 416/964-0744 – *2
Minden, Gross, Grafstein & Greenstein, #600, 111 Richmond St. West, M5H 2H5 – 416/362-3711, Fax: 416/864-9223 – *46

* indicates number of lawyers in law firm.

DIRECTORY OF LAW FIRMS – ONTARIO

Richard R. Minster, #428, 105 Gordon Baker Rd., M2H 3P8 – 416/499-9829, Fax: 416/499-1620 – *1

Allan Mintz, Penthouse, 121 Richmond St. West, M5H 2K1 – 416/864-0330 – *1

Paul Minz, #1, 3520 Pharmacy Ave., M1W 2T8 – 416/499-9350, Fax: 416/499-1463 – *1

Nick Mircheff, #2B, 3030 Midland Ave., M1S 5C9 – 416/321-2885, Fax: 416/321-3345 – *1

Vishnu Misir & Associates, #212, 2357 Finch Ave. West, M9M 2W8 – 416/744-2796, Fax: 416/744-7772 – *5

Mitchell, Bardyn & Zalucky, #200, 3029 Bloor St. West, M8X 1C5 – 416/234-9111, Fax: 416/234-9114 – *10

Heather Mitchell, #306, 10 Alcorn Ave., M4V 1E4 – 416/972-6565, Fax: 416/973-3999 – *1

M.J. Mitchell, Q.C., #1704, 55 University Ave., M5J 2H7 – 416/362-0901, Fax: 416/366-3513 – *1

L.R. Mitz, 185 King St. East, M5A 1J4 – 416/365-7979, Fax: 416/361-0229 – *1

J.W.P. Mo, #207, 834 Yonge St., M4W 2H1 – 416/923-3292, Fax: 416/923-3292 – *1

M.S. Mogil, #610, 4211 Yonge St., M2P 2A9 – 416/590-7999, Fax: 416/590-9998 – *1

Mohan & Mohan, #225, 3300 McNicoll Ave., M1V 5J6 – 416/609-8200, Fax: 416/609-8202 – *2

Alawi K. Mohideen, #207, 2131 Lawrence Ave. East, M1R 5G4 – 416/752-9814, Fax: 416/752-6356 – *2

B. Monaco, #103, 1205 St. Clair Ave. West, M6E 1B5 – 416/651-2299, Fax: 416/651-1954 – *1

Bernard J. Monaghan, 3080 Yonge St., M4N 3N1 – 416/486-9919, Fax: 416/486-1885 – *1

Moore & Costello, #365, 5 Fairview Mall Dr., M1J 2Z1 – 416/493-4148, Fax: 416/493-3979 – *2

John C. Moore, 533 Queen St. East, M5A 1V1 – 416/364-6755 – *1

Pasquale Morabito, #222, 61 Alness St., M3J 2H2 – 416/665-9944 – *1

Robin Morch, #601, 130 Bloor St. West, M5S 1N5 – 416/926-1219, Fax: 416/923-1391

Morlock & Associates, #500, 1 Richmond St. West, M5H 3W4 – 416/862-0500, Fax: 416/862-9063 – *6

Morris & Morris, #920, 390 Bay St., M5H 2Y2 – 416/366-2277, Fax: 416/366-5988 – *6

Morris Silver Lewis, 1 Yorkdale Rd., M6A 3A1 – 416/781-5222, Fax: 416/781-3110 – *3

D.S. Morris, 129 John St., M5V 2E2 – 416/977-4799, Fax: 416/977-4472 – *1

L.J. Morris, 101 Scollard St., M5R 1G4 – 416/924-0711, Fax: 416/960-9650 – *1

Morris, Rose, Ledgett, Canada Trust Tower, BCE Pl., #2700, 161 Bay St., M5J 2S1 – 416/981-9400, Fax: 416/863-9500 – *59

Steven A. Morris, #306, 500 Danforth Ave., M4K 1P6 – 416/778-9795 – *1

Warren J. Morris, #2200, 181 University Ave., M5H 3M7 – 416/601-6795, Fax: 416/363-7875 – *1

D.A. Morrison, 2773 Lakeshore Blvd. West, M8V 1H4 – 416/251-3364, Fax: 416/251-9331

Stephen Morrison, 112 Adelaide St. East, M5C 1K9 – 416/363-0453, Fax: 416/363-1877 – *1

Michael Morse, #412, 120 Carlton St., M5A 4K2 – 416/922-3253, Fax: 416/922-3939 – *1

Mortimer, Clark, Grey & Martin, 153 Glencairn Ave., M4R 1N1 – 416/486-0816, Fax: 416/486-1755

Moses & Associates, #410, 212 King St. West, M5H 1K5 – 416/599-8812, Fax: 416/599-5582 – *1

S.S. Moskowitz, 740 Spadina Ave., M5S 2J2 – 416/961-8864, Fax: 416/961-7654 – *1

Clifford Moss, #336, 200 Finch Ave. West, M2R 3W4 – 416/226-6060, Fax: 416/226-6900 – *1

Mostyn, Mostyn & Naiman, 845 St. Clair Ave. West, 4th Fl., M6C 1C3 – 416/653-3819, Fax: 416/653-3891 – *5

Anthony Moustacalis, #902, 372 Bay St., M5H 2W9 – 416/363-2656 – *1

Movat, Eccleston., #803, 130 Spadina Ave., M5V 2L4 – 416/504-2722, Fax: 416/504-2686 – *1

Matthew Moyal, 8 Finch Ave. West, M2N 6L1 – 416/733-0330, Fax: 416/250-1818; Email: moyal@idirect.com – *1

Steven Mucha, #300, 50 Richmond St. East, M5C 1N7 – 416/366-5114, Fax: 416/366-1722 – *1

Richard Muir, 420 Nugget Ave., M1S 4A4 – 416/291-1459 – *1

Murrant Brown, 130 Yorkville Ave., M5R 1C2 – 416/975-0821, Fax: 416/975-1531

Murray & Gregory, 160 John St., M5V 2E5 – 416/598-1643, Fax: 416/598-9520 – *2

Muyal, Moses, #307, 55 Eglinton Ave. East, M4P 1G8 – 416/932-0786, Fax: 416/932-1198 – *1

Naftolin & Associates, #500, 180 Attwell Dr., M9W 6A9 – 416/675-3521, Fax: 416/675-3541 – *4

F.G. Nasello, 2737 Danforth Ave., M4C 1L8 – 416/698-2501, Fax: 416/698-0289 – *1

Ken H. Nathens, #3, 4901A Yonge St., M2N 5N4 – 416/222-6980, Fax: 416/221-9965 – *1

J. Naumovich, #101, 813 Broadview Ave., M4K 2P8 – 416/466-2119, Fax: 416/466-2581

Neal & Smith, #300, 3443 Finch Ave. East, M1W 2S1 – 416/494-4545 – *3

Neighbourhood Legal Services, 333 Queen St. East, M5A 1S9 – 416/861-0677, Fax: 416/861-1777

Neinstein & Singer, #402, 1183 Finch Ave. West, M3J 2G2 – 416/665-8411, Fax: 416/665-4291 – *2

C. Ann Nelson, #400, 2490 Bloor St. West, M6S 1R4 – 416/760-7076, Fax: 416/760-7338 – *1

Nelson, McNamee, 238 Jane St., M6S 3Z1 – 416/762-7477, Fax: 416/762-0182 – *2

Theodore Nemetz, #801, 1 St. Clair Ave. East, M4T 2V7 – 416/961-6560, Fax: 416/964-2494; Email: nemetz@inforamp.net – *1

Richard Nemis, #1210, 111 Richmond St. West, M5H 2G4 – 416/864-1456, Fax: 416/947-0807 – *1

A.R.D. Nesbitt, #1806, 2 Bloor St. West, M4W 3E2

Neuman & Grant, 508 Bathurst St., M5S 2P9 – 416/961-7400, Fax: 416/921-2949 – *2

R. Geoffrey Newbury, The Exchange Tower, #2125, 130 King St. West, M5X 1A6 – 416/362-4048, Fax: 416/362-4049; Email: newbury@io.org – *1

Newman Weinstock, #906, 43 Eglinton Ave. East, M4P 2W1 – 416/484-7766, Fax: 416/484-8264 – *1

D.H. Newman, Q.C., 70 Dundas St. East, M5B 1C7 – 416/598-4922 – *1

James L. Newman, #300, 133 Richmond St. West, M5H 2L3 – 416/863-0440, Fax: 416/863-5241 – *1

S.H. Newman, #1201, 44 Charles St. West, M4Y 1R7 – 416/925-8165, Fax: 416/925-8122 – *1

Steve Newman, #305, 343 Wilson Ave., M3H 1T1 – 416/630-8910, Fax: 416/630-8489 – *1

Alexandra Ngan, #306, 1033 Bay St., M5S 3A5 – 416/925-3333, Fax: 416/925-3339 – *1

Peter Ngan, 1911 Kennedy Rd., M1P 2L9 – 416/298-1828, Fax: 416/298-2186 – *1

Cindy Nicholas, 2891 Kingston Rd., M1M 1N3 – 416/266-3080, Fax: 416/264-2330 – *1

E.B. Nicholson, 307 Davenport Rd., M5R 1K5 – 416/921-8287 – *1

A.R. Nicol, 111 Elizabeth St., 3rd Fl., M5G 1P7 – 416/340-9909, Fax: 416/599-8075 – *1

Niebler, Liebeck, Singer & Associates, 595 Bay St., M5G 2C2 – 416/597-6689, Fax: 416/597-8683 – *3

Howard Nightingale, #411, 1111 Finch Ave. West, M3J 2E5 – 416/663-4423, Fax: 416/663-4424 – *1

Nobbs, Woods & Clark, #250, 70 University Ave., M5J 2M4 – 416/977-1000, Fax: 416/977-2895 – *5

Cinnie Noble, #1505, 330 Bay St., M5H 2S8 – 416/363-8680, Fax: 416/362-1465 – *1

Noik & Associates, #400, 3410 Sheppard Ave. East, M1T 3K4 – 416/754-1020, Fax: 416/754-1784; Email: bern@inforamp.net – *3

James G. Norton, #5210, 40 King St. West, M5H 3Y2 – 416/362-2600, Fax: 416/362-9185 – *1

C. Randall Nowlan, #1200, 595 Bay St., M5G 2C2 – 416/595-0106, Fax: 416/593-1352 – *1

R. Otto Nupponen, #806, 43 Eglinton Ave. East, M4P 1A2 – 416/488-7113 – *1

Nuttall, Rekai, #3204, 20 Queen St. West, M5H 3R3 – 416/598-2311 – *2

O'Connor & Gold, 198 Davenport Road, M5R 1J2 – 416/962-8200, Fax: 416/964-7498 – *3

David F. O'Connor, 75 Lowther Ave., M5R 1C9 – 416/960-1951, Fax: 416/961-9905 – *1

J.F. O'Donnell, #906, 95 Wellington St. West, PO Box 40, M5J 2N7 – 416/862-7330, Fax: 416/368-0549 – *1

R. Allan O'Donnell, #2200, 181 University Ave., M5H 3M7 – 416/366-0323, Fax: 416/366-3205

O'Donnell, Robertson & Sanfilippo, #2100, 1 Queen St. East, PO Box 100, M5C 2W5 – 416/214-0606, Fax: 416/214-0605 – *2

O'Donohue & O'Donohue, #1600, 390 Bay St., M5H 2Y2 – 416/361-3231, Fax: 416/361-3472 – *4

Kevin J. O'Hara, #424, 100 Richmond St. West, M5H 3K6 – 416/868-1555, Fax: 416/365-1474 – *1

O'Neill, Browning, Pineau, #200, 372 Bay St., M5H 2W9 – 416/868-0544, Fax: 416/868-0724 – *2

O'Reilly, Moll, 300 Main St., M4C 4X5 – 416/690-3324, Fax: 416/690-3330 – *1

Patrick O'Rourke, 75 Lowther Ave., M5R 1C9 – 416/927-7041, Fax: 416/961-9905 – *1

Ogilvie, Ishbel S., 469 Queen St. East, M5A 1T9 – 416/956-4848 – *1

Ogilvy Renault, Royal Trust Tower, TD Centre, #2100, 77 King St. West, PO Box 141, M5K 1H1 – 416/216-4000, Fax: 416/216-3930 – *6

Okell & Weisman, 352 Bedford Park Ave., M5M 1J8 – 416/787-1105, Fax: 416/787-2130 – *2

Maurice K. Olanick, Q.C., #212, 2323 Bloor St. West, M6S 4W1 – 416/766-1930 – *1

Olch, Torgov, Cohen, #1014, 111 Richmond St. West, M5H 2J5 – 416/363-8366, Fax: 416/367-4043 – *2

Oleskiw, Anweiler, #701, 123 Edward St., M5G 1E2 – 416/591-1746, Fax: 416/591-9200; Email: anweiler@inforamp.net – *2

Diane Oleskiw, #701, 123 Edward St., M5G 1E2 – 416/591-1261, Fax: 416/591-9200 – *1

Laura A. Onischuk, 350 Bay St., 9th Fl., M5H 2S6 – 416/869-0751, Fax: 416/367-4098 – *1

Thomas T. Onizuka, Q.C., #201, 425 University Ave., M5G 1T6 – 416/598-2002, Fax: 416/598-8183 – *1

Joanna Opalinski, 131 Silverhill Dr., M9B 3W6 – 416/234-1740, Fax: 416/234-1740 – *1

Delia Opekokew, #2, 2034 Queen St. East, M4L 1J4 – 416/698-1832, Fax: 416/691-9760 – *1

Chris Opoka-Okumu, 206 - 530 Wilson Ave., M3H 5Y9 – 416/630-2016, Fax: 416/630-3229 – *1

Karen Or, #200, 69 Elm St., M5G 1H2 – 416/595-9665, Fax: 416/971-9092 – *1

Orbach, Katzman & Herschorn, 417 Parliament St., M5A 3A1 – 416/967-6777, Fax: 416/967-1506 – *3

J.N. Ormston, 739 Bloor St. West, M6G 1L6 – 416/535-3888 – *1

Orr & Darrah, #700, 4 King St. West, M5H 1B6 – 416/860-0141, Fax: 416/860-0140 – *2

Morris C. Orzech, 4121 Lawrence Ave. East, M1E 2S2 – 416/282-1121, Fax: 416/283-6117 – *1

Osak, Osak & Osak, #904, 1000 Finch Ave. West, M3J 2V5 – 416/736-1736, Fax: 416/736-1546 – *3

M.A. Osborne, #201, 100 Sheppard Ave. West, M2N 1M6 – 416/225-1145, Fax: 416/225-0832 – *1

Osler, Hoskin & Harcourt, #6600, 1 First Canadian Pl., PO Box 501, Stn First Canadian Place, M5X 1B8 – 416/862-6554, Fax: 416/862-6666 – *224

J.A. Ostrowski, #900, 5075 Yonge St., M2N 6C6 – 416/364-3835, Fax: 416/730-1227 – *1

Samy Ouanounou, #500, 3500 Dufferin St., M3K 1N2 – 416/635-5002, Fax: 416/630-3930 – *1

Outerbridge, Miller, Sefton, Willms & Shier, #900, 4 King St. West, M5H 1B3 – 416/863-0711, Fax: 416/863-1938 – *12

Owens, Wright, 14 Birch Ave., M4V 1C8 – 416/926-9800 – *11

Canadian Almanac & Directory 1997

Anthony Paas, 81 Wellesley St. East, M5A 2Z7 – 416/960-0049, Fax: 416/960-1498 – *1
Page, Hill, #2200, 439 University Ave., M5G 1Y8 – 416/595-9935, Fax: 416/595-1731 – *6
Pallett Valo, #1401, 67 Yonge St., M5E 1J8 – 416/368-3890, Fax: 416/368-6366 – *2
Pallo Holdings, #252, 250 Eglinton Ave. West, M4R 1A7 – 416/487-8220, Fax: 416/487-4503 – *1
Susanne I. Palmer, 4 Hillholm Rd., M5P 1M2 – 416/482-2492 – *1
Demetrius Pantazis, 870 Danforth Ave., M4J 1L7 – 416/469-5355, Fax: 416/469-8136 – *1
Papernick & Papernick, #206, 4580 Dufferin St., M3H 5Y2 – 416/665-5660, Fax: 416/665-5662 – *1
Allan Papernick, Q.C., #204, 1711 McCowan Rd., M1S 2Y3 – 416/291-2965, Fax: 416/291-0161 – *1
Lawrence J. Papoff, #315, 1315 Finch Ave. West, M3J 2G6 – 416/398-9336, Fax: 416/398-9179
Ado Park Q.C., #401, 365 Bay St., M5H 2V1 – 416/363-4451, Fax: 416/363-9256 – *1
John Y.S. Park, #203, 53 Spring Garden Ave., M2N 3G1 – 416/512-8755, Fax: 416/512-0074 – *1
Mary Park, #200, 60 St. Clair Ave. East, M4T 1N5 – 416/323-0331, Fax: 416/323-0162 – *1
Parkdale Community Legal Services, 165 Dufferin St., M6K 1Y9 – 416/531-2411 – *1
Mary Lou Parker, #1200, 595 Bay St., M5G 2C2 – 416/593-7595 – *1
William J. Parker, Q.C., Penthouse, 121 Richmond St. West, M5H 2K1 – 416/862-8210, Fax: 416/364-9842 – *1
John R. Parkinson, #200, 2401 Eglinton Ave. East, M1K 2M5 – 416/757-8855 – *1
Paroian, Raphael, Courey, Cohen & Houston, #1812, 181 University Ave., M5H 3M7 – 416/594-1812, Fax: 416/594-0868 – *37
Carolyn Parpasniak, 271 Queen St. East, M4E 1G5 – 416/691-9355
Pascale, Zentil, 3800 Steeles Ave. West, L4L 4G9 – 416/746-7420, Fax: 416/746-2100 – *3
Stanley Pasternak, #401, 111 Avenue Rd., M5R 3J8 – 416/961-8144, Fax: 416/961-8730 – *1
Paterson, MacDougall, #2100, 1 Queen St. East, PO Box 100, M5C 2W5 – 416/366-9607 – *19
A. Bonwyn Patterson, #204, 345 Wilson Ave., M3H 5W1 – 416/630-2266, Fax: 416/630-6696 – *4
Philip Patterson, #305, 1033 Bay St., M5S 3A5 – 416/968-9188 – *1
Paul & Paul, 39 Hayden St., M4Y 2P2 – 416/968-1777, Fax: 416/968-1211 – *2
J.G. Paul, #5, 1778 Bloor St. West, PO Box 465, M6P 3K4 – 416/767-9919, Fax: 416/767-6272 – *1
Jeffrey Paul, #10, 1278 St. Clair Ave. West, M6E 1B9 – 416/653-3131, Fax: 416/653-6343 – *1
Robert J. Paul, #5, 74 Upper Canada Pl., M2P 2A3 – 416/226-3967 – *1
Pay Equity Legal Clinic, #804, 40 Eglinton Ave. East, M4P 3A2 – 416/482-1338, Fax: 416/482-1650; Toll Free: 1-800-565-6059 – *4
David A. Payne, #1503, 372 Bay St., M5H 2W9 – 416/863-3901 – *1
Murray E. Payne, 3329 Bloor St. West, M8X 1E7 – 416/232-1242, Fax: 416/231-1280 – *1
Wolfgang J. Pazulla, 16 Four Seasons Pl., M9B 6E5 – 416/622-6669, Fax: 416/622-1440 – *1
Peace, Burns, Halkiw & Manning, Harbord House, 546 Euclid Ave., M6G 2T2 – 416/533-1025, Fax: 416/588-6936 – *3
Roselyn Pecus, #407, 1280 Finch Ave. West, M3J 3K6 – 416/665-6449, Fax: 416/665-7488 – *1
Peikes & Halpert, 35 Howard St., M4X 1J6 – 416/968-7733, Fax: 416/968-7192 – *3
Paul S. Pellman, #2200, 181 University Ave., M5H 3M7 – 416/601-6808, Fax: 416/601-1702 – *1
Penman & Penman, 1938 Weston Rd., M9N 1W2 – 416/244-1149 – *2
Craig J. Penney, #15, 123 Edward St., M5G 1E2 – 416/863-6517, Fax: 416/863-9463 – *1

Glenn B. Peppiatt, #401, 11 Yorkville Ave., M4W 1L3 – 416/323-3232 – *1
Perks & Hanson, #901, 130 Adelaide St. West, M5H 3P5 – 416/362-3366, Fax: 416/362-3174 – *3
Peters & Kestelman, 245 Coxwell Ave., M4L 3B4 – 416/465-3561, Fax: 416/468-3563 – *1
Peterson, D'Andrea, 2547 Eglinton Ave. West, M6M 1T2 – 416/656-6500, Fax: 416/656-1420 – *7
Mendo Petrovski, 2336 Danforth Ave., M4C 1K7 – 416/423-8455, Fax: 416/423-1581 – *1
V. Walter Petryshyn, 1247 Dundas St. West, M6J 1X6 – 416/534-8431, Fax: 416/531-2455 – *1
Phillips & Phillips, #2200, 181 University Ave., M5H 3M7 – 416/601-6802, Fax: 416/601-9590 – *1
Douglas N. Phillips, 13 Reno Dr., M1K 2V5 – 416/757-3445 – *1
Picov & Kleinberg, #601, 2161 Yonge St., M4S 3A6 – 416/488-2100, Fax: 416/488-2794 – *2
Pikkov, Mart, #108, 100 Lombard St., M5C 1M3 – 416/601-0368
L.A. Piller, #700, 390 Bay St., M5H 2Y2 – 416/862-7020, Fax: 416/862-2135 – *1
G.F. Pinos, Q.C., 174 Avenue Rd., M5R 2J1 – 416/944-8623, Fax: 416/944-8461 – *1
Piscelli & Faieta, #100, 866 The Queensway, M8Z 1N7 – 416/255-7392, Fax: 416/255-7394 – *2
R.W.M. Pitt, #1002, 365 Bloor St. East, M4W 3L4 – 416/962-7220, Fax: 416/962-3902 – *1
Jillian M. Pivnick, #410, 350 Lonsdale Rd., M5P 1R6 – 416/484-6306 – *1
Frank Pizzimenti, 370 Bloor St. East, M4W 3M6 – 416/927-9000, Fax: 416/927-9069
Fred A. Platt, #1600, 151 Yonge St., M5C 2W7 – 416/777-1818, Fax: 416/777-1819 – *1
Pledge & Associates, #1, 951 Wilson Ave., M3K 1G1 – 416/630-8702, Fax: 416/630-8714 – *1
Poch Environmental Lawyer, 236 Old Forest Hill Rd., M6C 2H4 – 416/789-9787, Fax: 416/789-9209 – *1
Pocock & Rogers, #5044, 3080 Yonge St., M4N 3N3 – 416/482-6155 – *2
F. Polla, 1684 Dufferin St., M6H 3M1 – 416/651-2888, Fax: 416/658-7653 – *1
A.S. Pollack, 648 Bedford Park Ave., M5M 1K3 – 416/787-1791 – *1
J.B. Pollock, #304, 3200 Dufferin St., PO Box 8, M6A 2T3 – 416/787-4223, Fax: 416/787-5530 – *1
Eric P. Polten, Guardian of Canada Tower, #2200, 181 University Ave., M5H 3M7 – 416/601-6766, Fax: 416/947-0909; Email: ph@interlog.com; URL: http://www.poltenhodder.com/~ph – *1
H.M. Pomerantz, 1035 McNicoll Ave., M1W 3W6 – 416/497-2210, Fax: 416/497-1992 – *1
William Pomerantz, 1035 McNicoll Ave., M1W 3W6 – 416/502-0770
Stephen P. Ponesse, #1600, 111 Richmond St. West, M5H 2G4 – 416/361-3582, Fax: 416/368-7217 – *1
Poole Milligan, #330, 4100 Yonge St., M2P 2B5 – 416/221-4100, Fax: 416/221-6340; Email: avainfo@poolemilligan.ca; URL: http://www.poolemilligan.ca – *6
Poole, A.F.N., Q.C., 133 Avenue Rd., M5R 2H7 – 416/967-5711, Fax: 416/967-4428; Email: afnpoole@interlog.com; URL: http://web.idirect.com/~poole/ – *3
Porter Posluns & Harris, #1201, 100 Yonge St., M5C 2W1 – 416/367-0148, Fax: 416/367-4279
Don Poscente, 115 Pembroke St., M5A 2N9 – 416/924-9912, Fax: 416/924-9912 – *1
E.G. Posen, #900, 1 St. Clair Ave. East, M4T 2V7 – 416/962-4180, Fax: 416/923-1549 – *1
Gary Posesorski, #202, 2323 Yonge St., M4P 2C9 – 416/488-5323, Fax: 416/488-3716 – *1
W.G. Posthumus, #1900, 900 Bay St., M5G 1Z6 – 416/598-0747, Fax: 416/971-7656 – *1
S.J. Potter, #1, 640 Bloor St. West, M6G 1K9 – 416/533-2328, Fax: 416/536-3529 – *1
Potts, Weisberg & Musil, #202, 586 Eglinton Ave. East, M4P 1P2 – 416/485-7366, Fax: 416/485-7368 – *3

Powell, Michael L., #523, 1315 Lawrence Ave. East, M3A 3R3 – 416/441-6840, Fax: 416/441-0330; Email: powlaw@interlog.com – *1
Powers & Associates, 112 Adelaide St. East, M5C 1K9 – 416/214-2900, Fax: 416/307-0014; Email: powerlaw@inforamp.net – *1
Mark Prager, Barr & Solctr, 2 Sheppard Ave. East, M2N 5Y7 – 416/223-2108, Fax: 416/221-8928
C.G. Preobrazenski, 99 Charles St. East, M4Y 1V2 – 416/964-1717, Fax: 416/964-0823 – *1
Robert Presler, #1230, 65 Queen St. West, M5H 2M5 – 416/364-2000, Fax: 416/364-7027 – *1
Jack J. Press, 394 Old Orchard Grove, M5M 2E9 – 416/783-4256, Fax: 416/783-6528 – *1
Price Grenville, C., Q.C., 1624 Bayview Ave., 2nd Fl., M4G 3B7 – 416/481-6488, Fax: 416/481-5275
Robert G. Price Q.C., #402, 372 Bay St., M5H 3W1 – 416/365-7756, Fax: 416/863-0324
Stephen Price & Associates, #3204, 20 Queen St. West, M5H 3R3 – 416/598-1522, Fax: 416/340-7025 – *1
D.R. Proctor, Q.C., 1921 Eglinton Ave. East, Unit 8A, M1L 2L6 – 416/751-0467, Fax: 416/751-3770 – *1
Prousky & Biback, 2 Toronto St., M5C 2B6 – 416/863-1300, Fax: 416/863-4942 – *3
F.T.M. Pujolas, 2773 Lakeshore Blvd. West, M8V 1H4 – 416/251-3364, Fax: 416/251-9331 – *1
V.E. Purcell, Q.C., 893 O'Connor Dr., M4B 2S7 – 416/757-2801, Fax: 416/757-1130 – *1
Purdon & Ronka, #200, 5415 Dundas St. West, M9B 1B5 – 416/239-4369 – *2
R.G. Pyne, 3329 Bloor St. West, M8X 1E7 – 416/231-3339 – *1
Quirk, McGillicuddy & Sutton, 1661 Dufferin St., M6H 3L9 – 416/652-3543, Fax: 416/652-2730 – *1
Rachlin & Wolfson, #1500, 390 Bay St., M5H 2Y2 – 416/367-0202, Fax: 416/367-1820 – *9
Danuta H. Radomski, #164, 66 Princess St., M5A 2T1 – 416/366-3875, Fax: 416/368-0620 – *1
Louis Radomsky, 10 Otter Cres., M5N 2W2 – 416/364-7764, Fax: 416/787-5059 – *1
John Ragonetti, 120 Carlton St., M5A 4K2 – 416/920-7499 – *1
Martin N. Rain, #407, 1183 Finch Ave. West, M3J 2G2 – 416/661-4518, Fax: 416/661-2688 – *1
Harvey Ram, #200, 1969 Weston Rd., M9N 1W8 – 416/245-2222, Fax: 416/245-5615 – *1
Adi M. Raman, 1944 Eglinton Ave. West, M6E 2J8 – 416/783-3421, Fax: 416/783-9131 – *1
R. Sam Ramlall, #902, 5799 Yonge St., M2M 3V3 – 416/512-6465, Fax: 416/224-1511 – *1
Brigitte L. Raney, 7 Ansley St., M4R 1X5 – 416/484-6418, Fax: 416/484-6418 – *1
R.P. Rawana, #209, 8130 Sheppard Ave. East, M1B 3W3 – 416/281-8505, Fax: 416/286-4353 – *1
Raymond & Honsberger, Thomson Building, 65 Queen St. West, 17th Fl., M5H 2M5 – 416/366-3726, Fax: 416/367-2502 – *14
Rayson, Kohn Evelyn, #302, 3845 Bathurst St., M3H 3N2 – 416/630-5600, Fax: 416/630-5906
Raza Arif, #207, 2131 Lawrence Ave. East, M1R 5G4 – 416/752-9810, Fax: 416/752-6356
Reble, Ritchie, Green & Ketcheson, #100, 1 Eva Rd., M9C 4Z5 – 416/622-6601, Fax: 416/622-4713 – *6
Redway & Butler, 3080 Yonge St., M4N 3N1 – 416/481-5604 – *2
F. Vincent Regan, Q.C., #1507, 65 Queen St. West, M5H 2M5 – 416/864-9010, Fax: 416/864-9013 – *1
T.S. Reiber, #601, 135 Bay St., M5R 3K4 – 416/927-9841, Fax: 416/975-1531 – *1
William V. Reid, #201, 1114A Wilson Ave., M3M 1G7 – 416/398-5200, Fax: 416/398-9930 – *1
Reid, Wilmer H., Q.C., 2938 Danforth Ave., M4C 1M5 – 416/699-1131, Fax: 416/699-1958 – *1
Dorothy J. Reilly, 701 Coxwell Ave., M4C 3C1 – 416/461-7553, Fax: 416/461-2679 – *1
Michael P. Reilly, #201, 1919 Lawrence Ave. East, M1R 2Y6 – 416/757-7773, Fax: 416/757-0771 – *3

* indicates number of lawyers in law firm.

Canadian Almanac & Directory 1997

Anthony S. Rein, #8, 145 Sheppard Ave E., M2N 5N4 – 416/226-2020, Fax: 416/226-2044 – *1
Peter Reiner, #307, 55 Eglinton Avenue East, M4P 1G8 – 416/932-9959, Fax: 416/932-1108 – *1
Jack Reingold, Q.C., #2050, 3080 Yonge St., M4N 3N1 – 416/483-3364 – *1
A.C.J. Reisler, #1500, 1 Queen St. East, M5C 2Y3 – 416/362-4263, Fax: 416/601-4100 – *1
Stanley Reisman, 740 Spadina Ave., M5S 2J2 – 416/961-8864, Fax: 416/961-7654 – *1
Moishe Reiter, Q.C., #2030, 130 Adelaide St. West, M5H 3P5 – 416/369-1717, Fax: 416/369-1723 – *1
Rekai & Johnson, #604, 130 Bloor St. West, M5S 1N5 – 416/960-8876 – *4
Rendeiro, Ducas Associates, #400, 489 King St. West, M5V 1L3 – 416/595-5595, Fax: 416/595-5524
R.J. Renton, #400, 2 Billingham Rd., M9B 6E1 – 416/237-0294, Fax: 416/232-9291 – *1
Rexdale Community Legal Clinic, #215, 1530 Albion Rd., M9V 1B4 – 416/741-5201, Fax: 416/741-5281
Reznick, Parsons, #2314, 120 Adelaide St. West, M5H 1T1 – 416/863-6026, Fax: 416/863-9334 – *3
Lewis J. Richardson, #1200, 595 Bay St., M5G 2C2 – 416/599-1226, Fax: 416/599-8415 – *1
Riches, McKenzie & Herbert, #2900, 2 Bloor St. East, M4W 3J5 – 416/961-5000 – *6
Richman & Richman, #405, 255 Duncan Mill Rd., M3B 3H9 – 416/510-1575, Fax: 416/510-1580 – *1
D.S. Rickerd, Q.C., #3516, 79 Wellington St. West, PO Box 105, M5K 1G8 – 416/601-4770, Fax: 416/601-1630; Email: drickerd@yorku.ca – *1
Ricketts, Harris, Guardian of Canada Tower, #816, 181 University Ave., M5H 2X7 – 416/364-6211, Fax: 416/364-1697 – *11
Ridout & Maybee, #2400, 1 Queen St. East, M5C 3B1 – 416/868-1482, Fax: 416/362-0823 – *24
Gerald Rifkin, #415, 4580 Dufferin St., M3H 5Y2 – 416/667-0980, Fax: 416/667-0765 – *1
Riley & Associates, #906, 151 Yonge St., M5C 2W7 – 416/364-7611, Fax: 416/364-1636 – *2
J.T. Riley, #901, 55 University Ave., M5J 2H7 – 416/862-0077 – *1
Henry Ritchie, #100, 20 York Mills Rd., M2P 2C2 – 416/733-3590, Fax: 416/733-3591 – *1
Roach, Schwartz & Associates, 688 St. Clair Ave. West, M6C 1B1 – 416/657-1465, Fax: 416/657-1511; Email: charoa@globalserve.net – *6
Robert Adourion, 900 Don Mills Rd., M3C 1W3 – 416/441-4141, Fax: 416/441-6898 – *2
William H. Roberts, #1, 6 Ripley Ave., M6S 3N9 – 416/769-3162 – *1
Robertson & Keith, 2481 Kingston Rd., M1N 1V4 – 416/261-1220, Fax: 416/261-1716 – *1
Paul Robertson, 533 Queen St. East, M5A 1V1 – 416/361-9555, Fax: 416/364-7049 – *1
Robertson, Perrett, #2408, 180 Dundas St. West, M5G 1Z8 – 416/598-4819, Fax: 416/598-0974 – *2
Robins, Appleby & Taub, #2500, 130 Adelaide St. West, PO Box 102, M5H 2M2 – 416/868-1080, Fax: 416/868-0306 – *14
S.M. Robins, #400, 330 Bay St., M5H 2S8 – 416/361-0404, Fax: 416/868-1818 – *1
Robinson Hinkson, #904, 4950 Yonge St., M2N 6K1 – 416/223-7787, Fax: 416/223-7679; Toll Free: 1-800-387-7260 – *3
Mary Grace Robinson, #700, 390 Bay St., M5H 2Y2 – 416/368-7122, Fax: 416/862-2135
Lawlor Rochester, #806, 141 Adelaide St. West, M5H 3L5 – 416/366-2267, Fax: 416/368-3467 – *1
R.A. Rodney, Q.C., 85 Scollard St., M5R 1G4 – 416/924-0905 – *1
Roebuck & Roebuck, #801, 40 Pleasant Blvd., M4T 1J9 – 416/925-8003, 7328, Fax: 416/925-9278 – *1
Roebuck, Garbig, #3200, 401 Bay St., M5H 2Y4 – 416/862-7822, Fax: 416/862-2568 – *4
Rogers & Rowland, #2600, 121 King St. West, PO Box 120, M5H 3T9 – 416/364-2333, Fax: 416/864-0271 – *2

Rogers, Bereskin & Parr, Bldg Box: 401, 40 King St. West, M5H 3Y2 – 416/364-7311, Fax: 416/361-1398 – *30
Rogers, Campbell, Mickleborough, #1600, 111 Richmond St. West, M5H 2G4 – 416/366-3999, Fax: 416/862-0049 – *4
E.S. Rogers, Commercial Union Tower, #2600, POBox 249, Stn Toronto Dominion, M5K 1J5 – 416/864-2101, Fax: 416/864-2333 – *1
Rogers, Smith, Dick & Thomson, #2606, 2 Bloor St. West, M4W 3E2 – 416/968-7270, Fax: 416/968-6299 – *3
Rohmer & Fenn, #1E, 20 Prince Arthur Ave., PO Box 408, M5R 1B1 – 416/921-2299, Fax: 416/921-2999 – *2
Roland Nelson, #704, 130 Spadina Ave., M5V 2L4 – 416/368-2538, Fax: 416/360-6764
William L. Roland, 2900, 390 Bay St., M5H 2Y2
George A. Rolston, #703, 55 Eglinton Ave. East, M4P 1G8 – 416/489-2277, Fax: 416/489-2289 – *1
M.B. Romanick, Q.C., #1607, 80 Richmond St. West, M5H 2C2 – 416/362-2585 – *1
Paul F. Rooney, 5075 Yonge St., M1N 6C6 – 416/222-4446 – *1
Patrick S. Roopchand, #303, 745 Danforth Ave., M4J 1L4 – 416/469-5367, Fax: 416/469-9809 – *1
Rosati, Di Zio, 968 Wilson Ave., 3rd Fl., M3K 1E7 – 416/630-6993, Fax: 416/630-1289 – *2
Rose & Rose, #300, 230 Sheppard Ave. West, M2N 1N1 – 416/590-9990, Fax: 416/590-9991 – *3
Rose, Persiko, Rakowsky, #700, 55 University Ave., M5J 2K4 – 416/868-1908, Fax: 416/868-1708 – *2
V.T. Rosemay, Q.C., 3339A Bloor St. West, M8X 1E9 – 416/236-1681, Fax: 416/236-1682 – *1
A.C. Rosen, #904, 27 Queen St. East, M5C 2M6 – 416/363-1601, Fax: 416/363-5620 – *1
Rosen, Fleming, 370 Bloor St. East, M4W 3M6 – 416/927-9000, Fax: 416/927-9069 – *7
Paul Rosen, #102, 20 Queen St. West, M5H 3R3 – 416/599-1221, Fax: 416/599-2123 – *1
S.L. Rosen, 2933 Dufferin St., M6B 3S7 – 416/789-7133 – *1
Rosenbaum Dickison McKay & Grant, 257 Danforth Ave., M4K 1N2 – 416/466-6264, Fax: 416/466-8465 – *4
Brian Rosenbaum, #102, 1245 Caledonia Rd., M6A 2X6 – 416/785-1157, Fax: 416/787-9709 – *1
Martin Z. Rosenbaum, #1202, 330 Bay St., M5H 2S8 – 416/364-1919, Fax: 416/364-7885 – *1
Rosenberg & Robinson, #1606, 150 York St., M5H 3S5 – 416/361-5875, Fax: 416/361-3440 – *2
Rosenberg & Smith, #1800, 120 Adelaide St. West, M5H 1S8 – 416/863-1900, Fax: 416/863-1966 – *3
Rosenberg Irving, #203, 345 Wilson Ave., M3H 5W1 – 416/398-0102, Fax: 416/398-0106
Elliot F. Rosenberg, #201, 4949 Bathurst St., M2R 1Y1 – 416/512-7373, Fax: 416/512-7374 – *1
Hy Rosenberg, 61 Saint Nicholas St., M4Y 1W6 – 416/592-7034, Fax: 416/925-0162 – *1
Rosenblatt Associates, 335 Bay St., 10th Fl., M5H 2R3 – 416/861-9429, Fax: 416/861-1215 – *1
Stanley Rosenfarb, #512, 4002 Sheppard Ave. East, M1S 4R5 – 416/298-8828, Fax: 416/298-7142 – *1
Jonathan M. Rosenthal, #500, 70 Bond St., M5B 1X3 – 416/360-7768, Fax: 416/863-4896 – *1
Stewart Rosenthall, #1402, 151 Yonge St., M5C 2W7 – 416/359-0000, Fax: 416/368-9808 – *1
Ross & Ross, 111 Elizabeth St., M5G 1R9 – 416/977-1007 – *1
Michael Ross, 197 Sheppard Ave. West, 1st Fl., M2N 1M9 – 416/730-9399, Fax: 416/730-9476 – *1
R.M. Ross, #700, 390 Bay St., M5H 272 – 416/363-1186, Fax: 416/862-2135 – *1
Ted Ross, 272 Roncesvalles Ave., M6R 2M2 – 416/533-7878 – *1
A.M. Sinclair, #200, 2901 Bayview Ave., M2K 1E6 – 416/226-6508 – *1

Cecil L. Rotenberg, Q.C., United Centre, #808, 255 Duncan Mill Rd., M3B 3H9 – 416/449-8866, Fax: 416/510-9090 – *3
J.S. Rotenberg, 17 Isabella Ave., M4X 1M7 – 416/925-4940, Fax: 416/925-4571 – *1
Robert Rotenberg, 75 Lowther Ave., M5R 1C9 – 416/515-1753, Fax: 416/515-1754 – *1
Rotfleisch & Samulovitch, 350 Bay St., 9th Fl., M5H 2S6 – 416/367-4222, Fax: 416/367-4098 – *2
Frank L. Roth, #500, 70 Bond St., M5B 1X3 – 416/963-8776 – *1
Neal H. Roth, #100, 191 Church St., M5B 1Y7 – 416/366-6666, Fax: 416/366-7684 – *1
Rothman & Rothman, #403, 133 Richmond St. West, M5H 2L3 – 416/367-9901, Fax: 416/367-9979 – *2
Nancy-Gay Rotstein, #200, 808 Mount Pleasant Rd., M4P 2L2 – 416/488-3322, Fax: 416/488-8350 – *1
Allan Rouben, #200, 70 Bond St., M5B 1X3 – 416/360-5444, Fax: 416/365-7765 – *1
Frederick Rowell, Q.C., 99 Charles St. East, M4Y 1V2 – 416/920-9251, Fax: 416/964-0823 – *1
S.J. Ruben, #200, 45 St. Clair Ave. West, M4V 1K6 – 416/922-0511, Fax: 416/967-3945 – *1
D.A. Rubenstein, #201, 3292 Bayview Ave., M2M 3R7 – 416/730-0303, Fax: 416/730-0645 – *1
Benjamin Rubin & Associates, 229 Russell Hill Rd., M4V 2T3 – 416/929-2919 – *1
Janice Rubin, #1200, 595 Bay St., M5G 2C2 – 416/593-4463, Fax: 416/593-4109 – *1
Barry Rubinoff, #1200, 595 Bay St., M5G 2C2 – 416/596-7423, Fax: 416/596-1117 – *1
Ruby & Edwardh, 11 Prince Arthur Ave., M5R 1B2 – 416/964-9664, Fax: 416/964-8305 – *7
Victor E. Rudinskas, 27 John St., 2nd Fl., M9N 1J4 – 416/240-0594 – *1
George A. Rudnik, #202, 720 Spadina Ave., M5S 2T9 – 416/927-7788 – *1
Martin K.I. Rumack, #202, 2 St. Clair Ave. East, M4T 2T5 – 416/961-3441, Fax: 416/961-1045 – *1
Brian A. Rumanek, #15, 200 Evans Ave., M8Z 1J7 – 416/252-9115, Fax: 416/253-0494 – *1
Henry Rusak, 8 Beamish Dr., M9B 3P3 – 416/233-6224, Fax: 416/236-2066 – *1
R.E. Rusek, 1623 Bloor St. West, 2nd Fl., M6P 1A6 – 416/533-8563, Fax: 416/533-8564 – *1
Rush, G.C., #400, 2970 Lake Shore Blvd. West, M8V 1J7 – 416/251-2291, Fax: 416/251-2292 – *1
M.H. Rusonik, 4515 Chesswood Dr., Unit B, M3J 2V6 – 416/638-4111, Fax: 416/638-2257 – *1
Russell & Russell, 663 Greenwood Ave., M4J 4B4 – 416/461-0788 – *1
Russell Juriansz, 1501-65 Queen St. West, M5H 2M5 – 416/867-7590, Fax: 416/867-7594
C.H. Rutherford, #220, 4580 Dufferin St., M3H 5Y2 – 416/667-1338 – *1
Rebecca Rutherford, #300, 111 Elizabeth St., M5G 1P7 – 416/598-3928, Fax: 416/599-8075 – *1
Judith P. Ryan, #207, 12 Birch Ave., M4V 1C8 – 416/928-1154, Fax: 416/925-6684 – *1
Ryder, Whitaker, Wright, #1812, 438 University Ave., M5G 2K8 – 416/340-9070, Fax: 416/340-9250 – *3
Rye & Partners, #1200, 65 Queen St. West, M5H 2M5 – 416/362-4901, Fax: 416/362-8291 – *5
Lorne Sabsay, 317 Grace St., M6G 3A7 – 416/537-1204, Fax: 416/533-5174 – *1
R.L. Sachter, Q.C., #402, 801 Eglinton Ave. West, M5N 1E3 – 416/787-1165, Fax: 416/787-6532 – *1
Sack Goldblatt Mitchell, #1130, 20 Dundas St. West, PO Box 180, M5G 2G8 – 416/977-6070, Fax: 416/591-7333 – *20
M. Sack, Q.C., #2412, 401 Bay St., M5H 2Y4 – 416/364-7197 – *1
Geraldine Sadoway, #303, 489 College St., M6G 1A5 – 416/926-1447, Fax: 416/972-1992 – *1
H.A. Saffrey, #1704, 55 University Ave., M5J 2H7 – 416/593-8794, Fax: 416/366-3513 – *1
H. Saginur, #200, 4211 Yonge St., M2P 2A9 – 416/512-1912 – *1

R. Sahadeo, #208, 2357 Finch Ave. West, M9M 2W8 – 416/744-4395 – *1

Sam Sahoy, #208, 738 Sheppard Ave. East, M2K 1C4 – 416/224-0550, Fax: 416/224-5169 – *1

F.G. Salehmohamed, #105, 747 Don Mills Rd., M3C 1T2 – 416/421-7000 – *1

Salter, Apple, Cousland & Kerbel, #1000, 67 Yonge St., M5E 1J8 – 416/363-3366, Fax: 416/363-0561 – *5

M. Saltman Arbitrations Ltd., #1017, 111 Richmond St. West, M5H 2G4 – 416/366-3091, Fax: 416/366-0879 – *1

Samis, Blouin, Dunn, #1100, 123 Front St. West, PO Box 11, M5J 2M2 – 416/365-0000, Fax: 416/365-9993 – *12

William Samis, 258 Wilson Ave., M3H 1S6 – 416/601-6832, Fax: 416/631-9895 – *1

Sanderson & Cochrane, #1707, 8 King St. East, M5C 1B5 – 416/366-8068 – *1

Paul Sanderson Barrister & Solicitor, 52 St. Patrick St., 2nd Fl., M5T 1V2 – 416/971-6616, Fax: 416/971-4144 – *1

Sandler, Gordon, Saperia & Walman, #702, 1240 Bay St., M5R 2A7 – 416/961-0001, Fax: 416/961-9461 – *4

D.A. Sands, 663 Greenwood Ave., M4J 4B4 – 416/463-5982 – *1

S.K. Sanwalka, Q.C., #602, 18 Wynford Dr., M3C 3S2 – 416/449-7755, Fax: 416/449-6969 – *1

Umberto Sapone, 1859A Eglinton Ave., West, M6E 2J3 – 416/789-2689 – *1

Sawers, Liswood, Hickman, #2901, 1 Adelaide St. East, M5C 2Z7 – 416/861-0330, Fax: 416/861-9886 – *9

Sax, Isaacs, #802, 111 Richmond St. West, M5H 2G4 – 416/869-0400, Fax: 416/869-3405 – *3

Michael M. Sax, #1700, 22 St. Clair Ave. East, M4T 2S3 – 416/921-5669, Fax: 416/925-5753

Dianne Saxe, 66 Russell Hill Rd., M4V 2T2 – 416/962-5882, Fax: 416/962-8817; Email: dsaxe@envirolaw.com; URL: http://www.magic.ca/saxe/ – *1

Scandiffio & Gariepy, 89 Dupont St., M5R 1V4 – 416/928-2066, Fax: 416/925-5528 – *2

P.M. Scandiffio, Q.C., #308, 344 Bloor St. West, M5S 3A7 – 416/515-1660, Fax: 416/515-1526 – *1

Scarborough Community Legal Services, #9, 695 Markham Rd., M1H 2A5 – 416/438-7182, Fax: 416/438-9869

Arthur Scauzillo, 824 Wilson Ave., M3K 1E5 – 416/635-0050, Fax: 416/636-4385 – *1

L.H. Schipper, Q.C., #1010, 22 St. Clair Ave. East, M4T 2S3 – 416/961-5355, Fax: 416/961-7011 – *1

Schmidt Preben, 900-350 Bay St., M5H 2S6 – 416/368-8869, Fax: 416/367-4098

Richard D. Schneider, 49 Saint Nicholas St., M4Y 1W6 – 416/922-6147 – *1

M.M. Schnier, #1500, 2 St. Clair Ave. East, M4T 2T5 – 416/927-0300, Fax: 416/927-0305 – *1

Edmund L. Schofield, #1314, 181 University Ave., M5H 3M7 – 416/868-0824, Fax: 416/861-0706 – *1

P.J. Schrieder, Q.C., 1123 Albion Rd., M9V 1A9 – 416/749-6000, Fax: 416/749-6004 – *1

Jeffrey R. Schroeder, 103 Charles St. East, M4Y 1V2 – 416/944-9465, Fax: 416/925-8882 – *1

Schwartz & Schwartz, #432, 700 Lawrence Ave. West, M6A 1B6 – 416/787-1863, Fax: 416/787-0793 – *2

Cecil Schwartz, #200, 2901 Bayview Ave., M2K 1E6 – 416/250-0083, Fax: 416/226-1162 – *1

Schwartz, De Pasquale, #403, 225 Richmond St. West, M5V 1W2 – 416/596-0477, Fax: 416/596-8784 – *2

Arnold B. Schwisberg, #101, 515 Consumers Rd., M2J 4Z2 – 416/502-3360, Fax: 416/502-3957 – *1

Sclodnick & Kavassalis, 145 Berkeley St., M5A 2X1 – 416/361-0707, Fax: 416/361-1242 – *4

Scott & Aylen, Royal Trust Tower, Toronto Dominion Centre, 34th Fl., #1903, PO Box 194, Stn Toronto Dominion, M5K 1H6 – 416/368-2400, Fax: 416/363-7246; Email: sscaylen@inforamp.net – *6

N.D. Scott, #803, 525 University Ave., M5G 2L3 – 416/585-2593, Fax: 416/585-2577 – *1

B.M. Scully, 31 Prince Arthur Ave., M5R 1B2 – 416/968-2456, Fax: 416/960-5456 – *1

Peter B. Scully, 31 Prince Arthur Ave., M5R 1B2 – 416/968-2456, Fax: 416/960-5456 – *1

V.M. Seabrook, Q.C., #2200, 181 University Ave., M5H 3M7 – 416/601-6826, Fax: 416/363-7875 – *1

E.M. Searles, Q.C., #221, 501 Yonge St., M4Y 1Y4 – 416/922-6618 – *1

Gary L. Segal, #402, 111 Avenue Rd., M5R 3J8 – 416/967-5400, Fax: 416/967-7877; Email: segalimm@istar.ca – *1

Seligman, Robin, #100, 33 Bloor St. East, M4W 3H1 – 416/967-7878, Fax: 416/967-9069

Barry Seltzer, #101, 2642 Eglinton Ave. East, M1K 2S3 – 416/265-1500, Fax: 416/265-0720 – *5

Erwin S. Seltzer, #101, 2642 Eglinton Ave. East, M1K 2S3 – 416/265-0192, Fax: 416/265-0720 – *1

Semple, Jones, #205, 505 Consumers Rd., M2J 4V8 – 416/494-7669 – *2

Seon, Gutstadt, Lash & First, #1800, 4950 Yonge St., M2N 6K1 – 416/224-0224, Fax: 416/224-0758 – *8

Sera, Harrison & Daniels, #1102, 2 Sheppard Ave. East, M2N 5Y7 – 416/222-7668, Fax: 416/222-9253 – *3

Sereda & Sereda, #500, 365 Evans Ave., M8Z 1K2 – 416/251-8600, Fax: 416/251-5680 – *2

Frederick J. Shanahan, The Thomson Building, #1508, 65 Queen St. West, PO Box 67, M5H 2M5 – 416/362-6449 – *1

Martin A. Shanahan, #1508, 65 Queen St. West, PO Box 67, M5H 2M5 – 416/366-7781, Fax: 416/362-3210 – *1

Shapiro & Shapiro, #200, 55 St. Clair Ave. West, M4V 2Y7 – 416/960-5853, Fax: 416/960-8265 – *2

Lawrence N. Shapiro, #208, 2040 Sheppard Ave. East, M2J 5B3 – 416/494-4899, Fax: 416/499-6416 – *1

P.H. Shapiro, #405, 40 St. Clair Ave. West, M4V 1M2 – 416/323-9744, Fax: 416/323-9744 – *2

David Share Associates, Malvern Town Centre, #31, 31 Tapscott Rd., M1B 4Y7 – 416/754-8822, Fax: 416/754-8915

Chet Sharma, #7, 1658 Victoria Park Ave., M1R 1P7 – 416/285-1550, Fax: 416/285-1698 – *1

Roop N. Sharma, 942 Gerrard St. East, M4M 1Z2 – 416/461-0467, Fax: 416/461-5817 – *1

A.J. Shaul, Q.C., 305 Milner Ave., M1B 3V4 – 416/299-6688, Fax: 416/299-6774 – *1

Joel E. Shaw, #1702, 2200 Yonge St., M4S 2C6 – 416/486-3400 – *1

Victor Shaw, 3416 Dundas St. West, M6S 2S1 – 416/766-3700 – *1

Shearman & Sterling, 199 Bay St., PO Box 247, M5L 1E8 – 416/360-8484, Fax: 416/360-2958

G. James M. Shearn, #4300, 40 King St. West, M5H 3Y4 – 416/367-1325, Fax: 416/367-6749

Brian Shell, 615 Lonsdale Rd., M5P 1R8 – 416/656-6003, Fax: 416/654-8469

Shepherd Grenville-Wood, #502, 2200 Yonge St., M4S 2C6 – 416/322-1556, Fax: 416/322-1562 – *3

Harold Shepherd, #311, 500 Danforth Ave., M4K 1P6 – 416/465-8580, Fax: 416/465-9560

T.M. Sheppard, #1200, 595 Bay St., M5G 2C2 – 416/596-6885, Fax: 416/593-1352 – *1

Irvin H. Sherman, Q.C., #604, 130 Bloor St. West, M5S 1N5 – 416/960-8876, Fax: 416/924-2371; Email: irv.sherman@westonia.com; URL: http://www.teraport.net/sherman/shermanl.html – *1

S.L. Sherman, 2645 Eglinton Ave. East, M1K 2S2 – 416/261-7161, Fax: 416/261-7163 – *1

Sherwin & Associates, #1010, 2 Sheppard Ave. East, M2N 5Y7 – 416/221-8181, Fax: 416/221-8149 – *3

Sherwin & Associates, #1010, 2 Sheppard Ave. East, M2N 5Y7 – 416/221-8181, Fax: 416/221-8199 – *2

Michelle Sherwood, 317 Grace St., M6G 3A7 – 416/533-3191, Fax: 416/533-5174 – *1

Shi Chi Kun, #1801, One Yonge St., M5E 1E5 – 416/214-1260, Fax: 416/369-0515

Shibley Righton, The Simpson Tower, #1800, 401 Bay St., PO Box 32, M5H 2Z1 – 416/363-9381, Fax: 416/214-5438 – *24

A. Shields, #1300, 5255 Yonge St., M2N 6P4 – 416/223-8333, Fax: 416/223-3404 – *1

B.S. Shier, 219 Carlton St., M5A 2L2 – 416/923-8997, Fax: 416/923-8380 – *1

Stanley I. Shier, Q.C., #1700, 390 Bay St., M5H 2Y2 – 416/366-9591, Fax: 416/366-2107 – *1

Ralph Shiff, #605, 1120 Finch Ave. West, M3J 3H7 – 416/665-3003, Fax: 416/665-3004 – *1

Gary Shiffman, #504, 505 Eglinton Ave. West, M5N 1B2 – 416/482-4555 – *1

Charles Shifman, #900, 5799 Yonge St., M2M 3V3 – 416/225-1123, Fax: 416/225-1124 – *1

Albert Shifrin, Q.C., Sterling Tower, #603, 372 Bay St., M5H 2W9 – 416/363-1473 – *1

O.B. Shime, Q.C., #200, 70 Bond St., M5B 1X3 – 416/366-8009 – *1

Shamim Shivji, #305, 489 College St., M6G 1A5 – 416/927-7224, Fax: 416/927-8129 – *1

E.I. Shoihet, #408, 100 Adelaide St. West, M5H 1S3 – 416/863-9594 – *1

Thomas J. Shoniker, 719 Yonge St., M4Y 2B5 – 416/921-4444, Fax: 416/499-9870 – *1

M.H. Shore, 61 St. Nicholas St., M4Y 1W6 – 416/925-6416, Fax: 416/925-0162 – *1

Geary B. Shorser, #1130, 20 Dundas St. West, PO Box 180, M5G 2G8 – 416/977-7749 – *1

Gary E. Shortliffe, #832, 150 Bloor St. West, M5S 2X9 – 416/927-7088, Fax: 416/927-7888 – *1

Shostack & Dorsey, #600, 5075 Yonge St., M2N 6C6 – 416/222-4550, Fax: 416/730-0603 – *2

Ian C. Shoub, #415, 4580 Dufferin St., M3H 5Y2 – 416/667-0980, Fax: 416/667-0765 – *1

R.A.L. Shour, #1200, 595 Bay St., M5G 2C2 – 416/977-4492 – *1

J.D. Shulman, #212, 120 Carlton St., M5A 4K2 – 416/961-2934, Fax: 416/924-7166 – *1

A.B. Shusterman, #207, 3320 Midland Ave., M1V 5E6 – 416/291-6176, Fax: 416/291-6047 – *1

Obaid R. Siddiqui, #212, 85 Ellesmere Rd., M1R 4B7 – 416/444-5597, Fax: 416/445-9487 – *1

F. Scott Sievert, 15 Belfield Rd., M9W 1E8 – 416/243-8756, Fax: 416/243-2990 – *1

Louis D. Silver, Q.C., #2600, 250 Yonge St., M5B 2M6 – *1

Silverberg & Weisberg, 4240 Sheppard Ave. East, M1S 1T5 – 416/291-7701, Fax: 416/291-1766 – *3

Murray D. Silverberg, 1100-5799 Yonge St., M2M 3V3 – 416/226-6006, Fax: 416/225-9846

Silverman & Freed, 700 Bay St., 19th Fl., M5G 1Z6 – 416/979-2335, Fax: 416/597-3828 – *2

Anne M. Silverman, #301, 5075 Yonge St., M2N 6C6 – 416/250-0045, Fax: 416/250-1984 – *1

P.A. Silverman, Q.C., 76 St. Clair Ave. West, 4th Fl., M4V 1N2 – 416/967-5868, Fax: 416/967-1441 – *1

Sheldon N. Silverman, #638, 121 Richmond St. West, M5H 2K1 – 416/363-6295, Fax: 416/363-3047 – *1

Silverstein & Gelfand, #208, 212 King St. West, M5H 1K5 – 416/595-0655, Fax: 416/595-0799 – *2

Sim, Hughes, Ashton & McKay, #701, 330 University Ave., M5G 1R7 – 416/595-1155, Fax: 416/595-1163 – *9

Lionel Simbrow, 66 Charles St. East, M4Y 2R3 – 416/964-9292, Fax: 416/928-9484 – *1

Monty M. Simmonds, Q.C., #1000, 2 St. Clair Ave. West, M4V 1L5 – 416/967-6706, Fax: 416/967-9483 – *1

Morris Simon, 2788 Bathurst St., M6B 3A3 – 416/782-3004 – *1

P.C. Simonelis, 1579 Bloor St. West, M6P 1A6 – 416/532-3443 – *1

Michael B. Simrod, #415, 4580 Dufferin St., M3H 5Y2 – 416/667-0980, Fax: 416/667-0765 – *1

Angus G. Sinclair, 271 Wolverleigh Blvd., M4C 1S3 – 416/947-9553 – *1

* indicates number of lawyers in law firm.

Canadian Almanac & Directory 1997

Irwin Singer, #906, 101 Richmond St. West, M5H 1T1 – 416/364-9126, Fax: 416/364-2527 – *1
Isaac Singer, 2424 Bloor St. West, M6S 1P9 – 416/766-1135, Fax: 416/769-5365 – *1
Singer, Kwinter, Polo Centre, #214, 1033 Bay St., M5S 3A5 – 416/961-2882, Fax: 416/961-6760 – *4
Michael S. Singer, 35A Hazelton Ave., M5R 2E3 – 416/926-1934, Fax: 416/922-2636 – *1
Mimi Singh, 378 Berkeley St., M5A 2X7 – 416/968-6649, Fax: 416/921-1398 – *1
J.R.N. Sintzel, Q.C., 33 Harbour Sq., M5J 2G2 – 416/361-1994, Fax: 416/361-1994 – *1
Joel Skapinker, #1100, 372 Bay St., M5H 2W9 – 416/214-1500, Fax: 416/214-0658; Email: jskapinker@usa.net
J.T. Skells, Q.C., #2000, 372 Bay St., M5H 2W9 – 416/363-2371, Fax: 416/363-8032 – *1
S.H. Skolnik, #512, 4002 Sheppard Ave. East, M1S 4R5 – 416/297-7300, Fax: 416/298-7142 – *1
Slansky & Pringle, 601-260 Richmond St. West, M5V 1W5 – 416/596-8192, Fax: 416/596-8449 – *2
Slater & Spiller, 450 Rathburn Rd., M9C 3S6 – 416/622-3233, Fax: 416/622-3302 – *2
Slater, Huston, Wells Associates, 644 Evans Ave., M8W 2W6 – 416/259-4293, Fax: 416/259-1286 – *3
Sloan Barristers & Solicitors, #1020, 121 King St. West, PO Box 27, M5H 3T9 – 416/867-9600, Fax: 416/867-9783 – *2
Barry S. Small, #601, 1235 Bay St., M5R 3K4 – 416/929-4783 – *1
Smart & Biggar, #2300, 439 University Ave., PO Box 39, Stn P, M5S 2S6 – 416/593-5514, Fax: 416/591-1690 – *11
Andrea Smart, #301, 2490 Bloor St. West, M6S 1R4 – 416/766-9989, Fax: 416/763-6876 – *1
Smith & Hukowich, #400, 2405 Lakeshore Blvd. West, M8V 1C6 – 416/259-7638, Fax: 416/259-7424 – *2
Smith & Jacobs, #600, 123 Edward St., M5G 1E2 – 416/593-6601, Fax: 416/597-1581 – *2
Smith & Smith, #15, 695 Markham Rd., M1H 2A5 – 416/439-3010, Fax: 416/439-3014 – *2
Smith & Zoldhelyi, 2424 Bloor St. West, M6S 1P9 – 416/968-7037 – *2
Smith Lyons, Scotia Plaza, #6200, 40 King St. West, M5H 3Z7 – 416/369-7200, Fax: 416/369-7250; Email: rmconnelly@smithlyons.ca; URL: http://www.smithlyons.ca – *135
B.A. Smith, #601, 2161 Yonge St., M4S 3A6 – 416/483-1331 – *1
Chester Smith, 216-4195 Dundas St. West, M8X 1Y4 – 416/234-8248, Fax: 416/234-8252 – *1
Smith, Chester, Q.C., #216, 4195 Dundas St. West, M8X 1Y4 – 416/234-8248, Fax: 416/234-8252 – *1
Cindy L. Smith, #1509, 180 Dundas St. West, M5G 1Z8 – 416/408-0008, Fax: 416/597-9808
Gary Smith, 101 Scollard St., M5R 1G4 – 416/961-1339, Fax: 416/960-9650 – *1
K.D. Smith, #500, 70 Bond St., M5B 1X3 – 416/361-0232 – *1
Les Smith, #2500, 1 First Canadian Place, PO Box 199, M5X 1A6 – 416/777-0594 – *2
Stanley Smither, #B1, 309 Mt. Pleasant Rd., M4T 2C2 – 416/485-7511 – *1
Smookler & Smookler, #1604, 55 University Ave., M5J 2H7 – 416/360-1712, Fax: 416/866-7946 – *2
Sneath, Samac & Darling, #811, 44 Victoria St., M5C 1Z5 – 416/363-5195, Fax: 416/363-7485 – *4
D.B. Snider, 978 Kingston Rd., M4E 1S9 – 416/699-0424, Fax: 416/699-0285 – *1
Kenneth E. Snider, #309, 2100 Ellesmere Rd., M1H 3B7 – 416/438-4515, Fax: 416/289-7998 – *1
Irving Snitman, 554 Annette St., M6S 2C2 – 416/767-0805, Fax: 416/767-4619 – *1
Samual Sochaczewski, 692 Euclid Ave., M6G 2T9 – 416/533-9099 – *1
Louis Sokolov, 31 Prince Arthur Ave., M5R 1B2 – 416/921-7626, Fax: 416/960-5456 – *1

A. Melvin Sokolsky, #605, 505 Consumers Rd., M1J 4V8 – 416/493-3993, Fax: 416/493-2653 – *1
Solish, Fellen, #200, 277 Victoria St., M5B 1W2 – 416/977-7345, Fax: 416/977-8177 – *3
Solmon, Rothbart, Goodman, #1600, 18 King St. East, M5C 1C4 – 416/947-1093, Fax: 416/947-0079 – *8
Victor Solnicki, 53 Hilholm Rd., M5P 1M4 – 416/486-5498, Fax: 416/486-6433 – *1
Sidney Solnik, 2991 Dundas St. West, M6P 1Z4 – 416/767-7506, Fax: 416/767-4738 – *1
Solomon & Solomon, Penthouse, 481 University Ave., 10th Fl., M5G 2E9 – 416/977-7786, Fax: 416/340-0064 – *2
Solomon, Grosberg, #1704, 55 University Ave., M5J 2H7 – 416/366-7828 – *6
Andreas H. Solomos, 1182 Danforth Ave., 2nd Fl., M4J 1M3 – 416/465-9955, Fax: 416/465-8114
A. David Soloway, #12B, 500 Rexdale Blvd., M9W 6K5 – 416/674-5820, Fax: 416/674-8825 – *1
Morrey Solway, #1250, 180 Dundas St. West, M5G 1Z8 – 416/599-3960, Fax: 416/977-0717 – *1
Somer & Associates, #300, 365 Bay St., M5H 2V1 – 416/362-1997, Fax: 416/363-8536 – *2
J.J. Somjen, #906, 94 Cumberland St., M5R 1A3 – 416/922-8083, Fax: 416/922-4234 – *1
Sommers & Roth, 268 Avenue Rd., M4V 2G7 – 416/961-1212, Fax: 416/961-2827 – *2
L.S. Sonenberg, 1123 Albion Rd., M9V 1A9 – 416/749-6000, Fax: 416/749-6004 – *1
Sookram & Levine, #710, 43 Eglinton Ave. East, M4P 1A2 – 416/480-9920, Fax: 416/480-9923
Frank Soppelsa, 75 Cuffley Cres. North, M3K 1Y1 – 416/636-9043, Fax: 416/213-5678 – *1
L.B. Sosna, 2627 Eglinton Ave. East, M1K 2S2 – 416/266-2133 – *1
Sosnowski & Mikolajko, #408, 2333 Dundas St. West, M6R 3A6 – 416/538-8493
Sotos, Karvanis, #1250, 180 Dundas St. West, M5G 1Z8 – 416/977-0007, Fax: 416/977-0717 – *9
Souraya, Abdu, #307, 5400 Yonge St., M2N 5R5 – 416/222-0243, Fax: 416/222-9304
R.J. Spence, #1200, 595 Bay St., M5G 2C2 – 416/977-4492, Fax: 416/977-4971 – *1
Spencer Romberg Associates, #700, 21 Dundas Square, M5B 1B8 – 416/869-1571, Fax: 416/869-1735 – *3
Steve Speropoulos, 802 St. Clair Ave. West, M6C 1B6 – 416/656-6150, Fax: 416/656-7360 – *1
Solomon Spiro, 11 King St. West, M5H 1A3 – 416/361-0717 – *1
Larry Spodek, #220, 1018 Finch Ave. W., M3J 2E1 – 416/667-0987, Fax: 416/667-1022 – *1
Harvey Spring, #488, 22 College St., M5G 1K2 – 416/967-0800 – *1
Spurr, Forsythe, #514, 90 Eglinton Ave. East, M4P 2Y3 – 416/483-1242, Fax: 416/483-2903 – *2
C.A. Stafford, 1036 Coxwell Ave., M4C 3G5 – 416/421-3211 – *1
Barry C. Stagg, #8, 1033 Pape Ave., M4K 3W1 – 416/425-7101, Fax: 416/425-0644 – *1
Stainton & Murray, 1624 Bayview Ave., M4G 3B7 – 416/481-1146 – *1
Barb Stalbecker-Pountney, #100, 577 Annette St., M6S 2C3 – 416/763-4606 – *1
R.J. Stanbrook, #200, 2901 Bayview Ave., M2K 1E6 – 416/490-1611, Fax: 416/490-1751 – *1
Stancer, Sidenberg, #2000, 332 Dupont St., M5R 1V9 – 416/925-6768, Fax: 416/925-9072 – *2
Jerome Stanleigh, #212, 120 Carlton St., M5A 4K2 – 416/924-0151, Fax: 416/924-2887 – *1
Richard Stanwick, #300, 3443 Finch Ave. East, M1W 2S1 – 416/502-1841, Fax: 416/494-4660 – *1
Brian F. Stark, 198 Davenport Rd., M5R 1J2 – 416/923-8000, Fax: 416/964-7498 – *1
N.D. Starkman, #308, 801 York Mills Rd., M5B 1X7 – 416/510-3030, Fax: 416/510-3034 – *1
Fred Stasiuk, 250 The East Mall, M9B 3Y8 – 416/236-1487, Fax: 416/236-1518 – *1

R.B. Statton, 52 Hayden St., M4Y 1V8 – 416/922-3200, Fax: 416/922-7377 – *1
James Stefoff, #1505, 80 Richmond St. West, M5H 2A4 – 416/366-7984 – *1
M.M. Steidman, Q.C., #505, 335 Bay St., M5H 2R3 – 416/366-7661, Fax: 416/360-6868 – *1
D.A. Stein, #800, 5075 Yonge St., M2N 5P3 – 416/225-5007 – *1
F.P. Stein, 66 Charles St. East, M4Y 2R3 – 416/928-9390, Fax: 416/928-9484 – *1
Larry C. Stein, #711, 1000 Finch Ave. West, M3J 2V5 – 416/665-3440, Fax: 416/663-5491 – *1
J.M. Steinberg, #203, 2304 Islington Ave., M9W 3W9 – 416/741-5261, Fax: 416/741-6650 – *1
Steinberg, Olyan, #408, 1200 Sheppard Ave. East, M2K 2S5 – 416/497-2777, Fax: 416/497-0221 – *9
R.B. Steinberg, #1001, 65 Queen St. West, M5H 2M5 – 416/368-8223 – *1
J. Stephens, Q.C., #407, 1280 Finch Ave. West, M3J 3K6 – 416/665-1499, Fax: 416/665-7488 – *1
Peter D. Stephens, 802 St. Clair Ave. West, M6C 1B6 – 416/656-6152 – *2
Stephenson & Stephenson, #313, 1033 Bay St., M5S 3A5 – 416/925-2200, Fax: 416/925-0858 – *2
J.A. Stephenson, Q.C., Bldg Box: 91, #5820, First Canadian Place, M5X 1B1 – 416/362-3909, Fax: 416/362-4136 – *1
H.P. Steponaitis, 1613 Bloor St. West, M6P 1A6 – 416/532-4413, Fax: 416/538-3205 – *1
Michael Sterlin, 55 Town Centre Court, M1P 4X4 – 416/296-7383, Fax: 416/296-1259 – *1
Sterling & Devlin, 2488A Kingston Rd., M1N 1V3 – 416/267-8274, Fax: 416/267-8430 – *1
Stern & Lenzin, #1724, 390 Bay St., M5H 2Y2 – 416/869-3422 – *3
W.G. Stevenson, 44 St. Clair Ave. East, M4T 1M9 – 416/425-6385, Fax: 416/962-7926 – *1
Stewart Roper & Assoc, #906, 95 Wellington St. West, M5J 2N7 – 416/368-7881, Fax: 416/368-0549 – *5
Deborah L. Stewart, #201, 5075 Yonge St., M2N 6C6 – 416/226-9340, Fax: 416/226-5341 – *1
John K.H. Stiff, 257 Coxwell Ave., M4L 3B5 – 416/469-5119, Fax: 416/469-0328
Stikeman, Elliott, #5300, Commerce Court West, PO Box 85, M5L 1B9 – 416/869-5500, Fax: 416/947-0866 – *119
Stikeman, Graham & Keeley, Bldg Box: 45, #1001, 95 Wellington St. West, M5J 2N7 – 416/367-1930, Fax: 416/365-1813 – *4
Frederick C. Stinson, Q.C., #610, 372 Bay St., M5H 2W9 – 416/867-8669, Fax: 416/867-3079 – *2
Stockwood, Spies, Craigen & LeVay, #2512, 150 King St. West, M5H 1J9 – 416/593-7200, Fax: 416/593-9345
Stone & Osborne, #201, 100 Sheppard Ave. West, M2N 1M6 – 416/225-1145, Fax: 416/225-0832 – *2
Stone & Yack, #608, 1120 Finch Ave. West, M3J 3H7 – 416/663-5656 – *1
Stortini Lee-Whiting, #1907, 80 Richmond St. West, M5H 2C6 – 416/368-1091, Fax: 416/368-7234 – *3
Stortini, Derubeis Galluzzo, #305, 1033 Bay St., M5S 3A5 – 416/925-4000, Fax: 416/925-2860 – *3
Allan Strader, 49 Saint Nicholas St., M4Y 1W6 – 416/924-4488, Fax: 416/924-5443 – *1
David S. Strashin, #702, 55 Eglinton Ave. East, M4P 1G8 – 416/482-8171 – *1
Michael Strathman, 219 Carlton St., M5A 2L2 – 416/923-8997, Fax: 416/923-8380 – *1
James B. Stratton, 60 Glengowan Rd., M4N 1G4 – 416/489-9167, Fax: 416/482-1822 – *1
Earle H. Straus, 15 Purdon Dr., M3H 4W9 – 416/596-3642 – *1
Strauss, Cooper, 1802-11 King St. West, M5H 1A3 – 416/869-1950, Fax: 416/869-0305 – *5
Marcel Strigberger, 69 Elm St., M5G 1H2 – 416/971-7272, Fax: 416/971-9092 – *2
Stringer, Brisbin, Humphrey, #1100, 110 Yonge St., M5C 1T4 – 416/862-1616, Fax: 416/363-7358 – *12

J.F. Stroz, Q.C., 2275 Dundas St. West, M6R 1X6 – 416/536-2131, Fax: 416/536-5451 – *1
J.A.F. Struyk, 1144 Queen St. East, M4M 1L1 – 416/463-1188, Fax: 416/463-9020 – *1
Alan Sugarman, #500, 4002 Sheppard Ave. East, M1S 4R5 – 416/297-7200, Fax: 416/297-7307 – *1
Paul J. Sullivan & Associates, 116 Hazelton Ave., M5R 2E4 – 416/967-1311 – *1
Summers & Nogueira, #205, 622 College St., M6G 1B4 – 416/531-3030, Fax: 416/531-3069 – *2
Summerville & Riley, #1, 2084 Danforth Ave., M4C 1J9 – 416/423-4412 – *2
Jimmy Sun, #207, 4190 Finch Ave. East, M1S 4T7 – 416/299-8909, Fax: 416/299-3189 – *1
Leonard Susman, 6420A Yonge, M2M 3X4 – 416/222-6000
Suter Law, 102 Annette St., M6P 1N6 – 416/760-0529
Ian Sutherland, 568 Annette St., M6S 2C2 – 416/763-0787, Fax: 416/763-0675 – *1
Ralph A. Sutton, #1800, 4950 Yonge St., M1N 6K1 – 416/224-0200, Fax: 416/224-0758 – *1
Nigel Svami, #204, 550 St. Clair Ave. West, M6C 1A5 – 416/656-4500, Fax: 416/656-5595 – *1
Swadron Associates, #1100, 30 St. Patrick St., M5T 3A3 – 416/598-3000, Fax: 416/598-3685 – *3
Kenneth P. Swan, #200, 70 Bond St., M5B 1X3 – 416/368-5279, Fax: 416/365-7702
Swanick, Shnier, D'Oliveira, #101, 225 Duncan Mill Rd., M3B 3K9 – 416/510-1888, Fax: 416/510-1945 – *6
Ernie Tadman, 185 Strachan Ave., M6J 2T1 – 416/362-9864, Fax: 416/362-7622 – *1
M.E. Taharally, #23, 1270 Finch Ave. West, M3J 3J7 – 416/661-4301, Fax: 416/661-5447 – *1
J.G. Tait, Q.C., #405, 121 Richmond St. West, M5H 2K1 – 416/364-3117, Fax: 416/364-2178 – *1
Mimi Tang, #229, 40 Dundas St. West, M5G 2C2 – 416/597-8583, Fax: 416/597-3846 – *1
Robert G. Tanner, #1300, 55 Queen St. East, M5C 1R6 – 416/862-7745, Fax: 416/862-7874 – *1
Sandra Tanner, #700, 2 Bloor St. West, M4W 3R1 – 416/969-9887, Fax: 416/969-9554 – *1
Tanzola & Sorbara, 2950 Keele St., M3M 2H2 – 416/638-0680, Fax: 416/638-9760 – *8
G.E. Tapper, 17 Lynwood Ave., M4V 1K3 – 416/927-7320 – *1
Brian I. Taran, 838 Mount Pleasant Rd., M4P 2L3 – 416/483-7834, Fax: 416/484-1089 – *1
Tatham, Pearson, 5524 Lawrence Ave. East, M1C 3B2 – 416/284-4749, Fax: 416/284-3086 – *2
William Tatsiou, #200, 121 Richmond St. West, M5H 2K1 – 416/362-4318, Fax: 416/362-6003 – *1
Stanley Taube, #1005, 21 St. Clair Ave. East, M4T 1L9 – 416/922-4545 – *1
Brahm M. Taveroff, #1000, 2 Sheppard Ave. East, M2N 5Y7 – 416/221-9343, Fax: 416/221-8928 – *2
Fred Tayar & Associates, #1600, 151 Yonge St., M5C 2W7 – 416/363-1800, Fax: 416/363-3356 – *3
R.R. Taylor, 340 Eglinton Ave. East, M4P 1L8 – 416/489-3030, Fax: 416/322-0524 – *1
Techman & Associates, 8 Finch Ave. West, M2N 6L1 – 416/250-9090 – *1
Teichman S. Blake, 42 Strathearn Blvd., M5P 1T1 – 416/488-0964
Moshe Teller, #208, 4455 Sheppard Ave. East, M1S 3G9 – 416/297-9400, Fax: 416/297-9402 – *1
Kelly J. Martin, 45 Sheppard Ave. East, M2N 5W9 – 416/733-1771 – *1
Tamara Tenebaum, #3313, 77 King St. West, M5K 1H6 – 416/601-4811, Fax: 416/504-0276 – *1
Teplitsky, Colson, #200, 70 Bond St., M5B 1X3 – 416/365-9320, Fax: 416/365-7702 – *21
B. Tepper, Q.C., 460 College St., M6G 1A1 – 416/961-8228, Fax: 416/961-3628 – *1
Kenneth Tepper, #301, 801 York Mills Rd., M3B 1X7 – 416/445-4502, Fax: 416/445-9060 – *1
Helen L. Terry, 3216 Yonge St., M4N 2L2 – 416/481-9992, Fax: 416/481-0314 – *1

Rod B. Thibodeau, #200, 225 Duncan Mills Rd., M3B 3K9 – 416/444-2244, Fax: 416/444-3222 – *2
Stephen Thom, #500, 70 Bond St., M5B 1X3 – 416/364-3371, Fax: 416/364-3376 – *1
Shaun Thompson, 4945A Dundas St. West, M9A 1B6 – 416/233-0399, Fax: 416/233-0399 – *1
Thompson, Tooze, McLean & Scott, 2938 Danforth Ave., M4C 1M5 – 416/591-1131, Fax: 416/699-1958 – *8
W.A.D. Thompson, #102, 175 Shaughnessy Blvd., M2J 1K1 – 416/609-2044 – *1
William H. Thompson, #2825, Commerce Ct. North, PO Box 124, M5L 1E2 – 416/368-0721, Fax: 416/368-0721 – *1
Thomson, Rogers, #3100, 390 Bay St., M5H 1W2 – 416/868-3100, Fax: 416/868-3134 – *37
W.J. Thorne, #9, 290 The West Mall, M9C 1C6 – 416/621-9644, Fax: 416/621-9668 – *1
Ian Thornhill, 902-5255 Yonge St., M2N 6P4 – 416/224-2004, Fax: 416/224-2101 – *1
Thorsteinssons, BCE Place, 161 Bay St., 36th Fl., PO Box 611, M5J 2S1 – 416/864-0829, Fax: 416/864-1106 – *8
Barbara J. Thurston, 201-5075 Yonge St., M2N 6C6 – 416/590-9161, Fax: 416/590-9941 – *1
R.W. Thurston, Q.C., 1425 Bloor St. West, M6P 3L6 – 416/536-4588 – *2
Carmine Tiano, #704, 130 Spadina Ave., M5V 2L4 – 416/360-1985, Fax: 416/360-6764 – *1
Ann Tierney, 470 King St. East, M5A 1L7 – 416/362-5700, Fax: 416/362-0847 – *1
Tikal & Associates, 178 St. George St., M5R 2N2 – 416/968-7070, Fax: 416/968-1876 – *4
Yunus Timol, 815 College St., 1st Fl., M6G 1C9 – 416/531-4388, Fax: 416/940-0074 – *1
Philip Tinianov, #1000, 65 Queen St. West, M5H 2M5 – 416/363-0866, Fax: 416/367-3949 – *1
Tinkler, Morris, #1050, 181 University Ave., M5H 3M7 – 416/362-2900, Fax: 416/362-6204
M.K. Titherington, 46 Northcliffe Blvd., M6H 3H2 – 416/656-6465 – *1
J. Tobias, #3516, 79 Wellington St. West, M5K 1G8 – 416/360-4600, Fax: 416/601-1630 – *1
Warren W. Tobias, #700, 357 Bay St., M5H 2T7 – 416/947-0911, Fax: 416/363-4130 – *1
Norman W. Tomas, 954A Royal York Rd., M8X 2E5 – 416/233-5567, Fax: 416/233-5567 – *1
Paul V. Tomlinson, 305-180 Dundas St. West, M5G 1Z8 – 416/597-0477, Fax: 416/599-0847 – *1
Toome Holmberg Laar, #1510, 5140 Yonge St., PO Box 10, M2N 6L7 – 416/250-7000, Fax: 416/250-7008 – *4
Dennis M. Topp, #103, 1750 Brimley Rd., M1P 4X7 – 416/291-9161 – *1
Tordoff Thomas, #1708, 390 Bay St., M5H 2Y2 – 416/368-3460, Fax: 416/361-1390
Torkin, Manes, Cohen & Arbus, #1500, 151 Yonge St., M5C 2W7 – 416/863-1188, Fax: 416/863-0305 – *34
Toronto Legal Aid Office, #204, 375 University Ave., M5G 2G1 – 416/598-0200, Fax: 416/598-0558
Tory Tory DesLauriers & Binnington, #3000, Aetna Tower, Toronto-Dominion Centre, PO Box 270, Stn Toronto Dominion, M5K 1N2 – 416/865-0040, Fax: 416/865-7380 – *203
Wayne Trainer, 388A Browns Line, M8W 3T8 – 416/251-3331 – *1
Philip J. Traversy, #100, 272 Lawrence Ave. West, M5M 4M1 – 416/787-0641, Fax: 416/787-4245 – *1
Treloar, Mergler, #401, 302 The East Mall, M9B 6C7 – 416/232-2919, Fax: 416/232-9201 – *3
Paul R. Trethewey, #2150, 1 Queen St. East, M5C 2W5 – 416/364-3800, Fax: 416/364-3866; Email: trethewy@terraport.net – *1
Quoc Toan Trinh, 1577 Bloor St. West, M6P 1A6 – 416/533-8987, Fax: 416/536-3618 – *1
Paul W. Trollope, 400 Dundas St. East, M5A 2A5 – 416/967-5259 – *1
K.F. Trotter, 106 Southvale Dr., M4G 1G7 – 416/467-1763

William M. Trudell, #700, 480 University Ave., M5G 1V2 – 416/598-2019, Fax: 416/977-5331 – *1
Alexander Tsang, 228-40 Dundas St. West, M5G 2C2 – 416/581-0226, Fax: 416/581-0229 – *1
C. Tsantis, 69 Elm St., M5G 1H2 – 416/599-6689, Fax: 416/971-9092 – *1
Tsapralis & Stanoulis, #303, 717 Pape Ave., M4K 3S9 – 416/466-1900, Fax: 416/466-1919 – *4
Tse Kee Sheung, #403, 2347 Kennedy Rd., M1T 3T8 – 416/298-1232, Fax: 416/298-5722
Mary Helen Tso, #1540, 439 University Ave., M5G 1Y8 – 416/598-5545, Fax: 416/598-9834 – *1
M.L. Tucker, 43 Madawaska Ave., M2M 2R1 – 416/221-5122, Fax: 416/226-9737 – *1
Tufman & Associates, 350 Bay St., 9th Fl., M5H 2S6 – 416/360-1689, Fax: 416/367-4098
Arthur Tugwood, 3458 Danforth Ave., M1L 1E1 – 416/694-3263, Fax: 416/694-3266 – *1
Tuovi & Yen, #705, 390 Bay St., M5H 2Y2 – 416/956-7755, Fax: 416/956-7754 – *2
Noel W. Turk, 38 Elderwood Dr., M5P 1W7 – 416/968-7848 – *1
Turkstra Garrod Hodgson, #200, 212 King St. West, M5H 1K5 – 416/593-1465, Fax: 416/971-9391 – *2
Turkstra, Mazza, Shinehoft, Mihailovich, Associates, #200, 212 King St. West, M5H 1K5 – 416/340-8407, Fax: 416/593-9559 – *3
Tytler & Sproule, #1618, 44 Victoria St., M5C 1Y2 – 416/364-3283 – *1
Ulrich & Sherr, #202, 2978 Islington Ave., M9L 2K6 – 416/745-7720, Fax: 416/745-5692 – *2
Richard D. Ulster, 41 Elliotwood Ct., M2L 2P8 – 416/446-1151 – *1
Howard Ungerman, 37 Maitland St., M4Y 1C8 – *1
United States Immigration Law Office, #404, 11 Church St., M5E 1W1 – 416/283-2515, Fax: 416/854-0294; Toll Free: 1-800-854-7330
H.S. Urman, 2857 Lawrence Ave. East, M1P 2S9 – 416/266-7784, Fax: 416/266-7785 – *1
I. Usprech, 21 Dundas Sq., M5B 1B7 – 416/363-0185 – *1
Gordon C. Vadum, Q.C., 463 Danforth Ave., M4K 1P1 – 416/778-9272, Fax: 416/778-0685 – *1
Robert Valentine, #300, 111 Elizabeth St., M5G 1P7 – 416/596-0722 – *1
Simon P. Valleau, #305, 180 Dundas St. West, M5G 1Z8 – 416/593-5511, Fax: 416/599-0847 – *1
Sheldon C. Vanek & Associate, #1610, 8 King St. East, M5C 1B5 – 416/366-1109, Fax: 416/366-0157
George Vano, 528 St. Clair Ave. West, 2nd Floor, M6C 1A2 – 416/653-1148, Fax: 416/653-1148 – *1
Anil Varma, 53 Chicora Ave., M5R 1T7 – 416/921-8880, Fax: 416/921-0440 – *1
Leslie Vasilaros, #1500, 2 St. Clair Ave. East, M4T 2T5 – 416/927-0300, Fax: 416/927-0305 – *1
K.C. Vaughan, #3, 900 Don Mills Rd., M3C 1V8 – 416/441-6313, Fax: 416/441-6898 – *1
Velanoff & Velanoff, 344 Sheppard Ave. East, 2nd Fl., M1N 3B4 – 416/225-3425, Fax: 416/733-3776 – *1
Elana Velensky, #415, 4580 Dufferin St., M3H 5Y2 – 416/789-5373, Fax: 416/667-0763 – *1
Vella & Pratt, #600, 200 Ronson Dr., M9W 5Z9 – 416/244-7706, Fax: 416/244-2288
Peter A. Vesa, Q.C., 1028 Danforth Ave., M4J 1M2 – 416/463-3392 – *1
Vine, Van Houten, #1604, 80 Richmond St. West, M5H 2A4 – 416/863-9341, Fax: 416/863-9342 – *2
Carl Vipavec, 770 Brown's Line, M8W 3W2 – 416/255-7500, Fax: 416/255-6667 – *1
Julia M. Viva, #305, 1256 Yonge St., M4T 1W5 – 416/922-0221, Fax: 416/922-1264 – *1
James D. Vlasis, 99 Charles St. East, M4Y 1V2 – 416/920-3447, Fax: 416/964-0823 – *1
Norfi Volpe, 112 Sheppard Ave. West, M1N 1M5 – 416/223-6800, Fax: 416/226-9730 – *1
H.J. von Monteton, #8F, 20 Prince Arthur Ave., M5R 1B1 – 416/925-0167 – *1

*indicates number of lawyers in law firm.

M.G. Wade, #202, 181 Eglinton Ave. East, M4P 1J9 – 416/487-7181, Fax: 416/487-4199 – *1

Michael T. Wadsworth, #209, 1252 Lawrence Ave. East, M3A 1C3 – 416/447-6479 – *1

Shale Wagman, #200, 145 Berkeley St., M5A 2X1 – 416/361-0807, Fax: 416/361-1242 – *1

Wagman, Sherkin, #200, 756A Queen St. East, M4M 1H4 – 416/465-1102, Fax: 416/465-3941 – *2

Mark Wainberg, 81 Wellesley St. East, M4Y 1H6 – 416/960-0049, Fax: 416/960-1498 – *1

G.R. Wakefield, 1 Evelyn Cres., M6P 3C8 – 905/509-5267, Fax: 905/509-5270 – *2

Waldin, de Kenedy, #2150, One Queen St. East, M5C 2W5 – 416/364-6761, Fax: 416/364-3866; Email: waldin@waldin.on.ca – *4

Lorne Waldman, 281 Eglinton Ave. East, M4P 1L3 – 416/482-6501, Fax: 416/489-9618 – *1

David Walfish, Q.C., 156 Danforth Ave., M4K 1N1 – 416/461-3583, Fax: 416/461-7466 – *1

Henry Walfish, 156 Danforth Ave., M4K 1N1 – 416/461-3583 – *1

Bruce E. Walker, 65 Wellesley St. East, M4Y 1G7 – 416/961-7451 – *1

Walker, Ellis & Pezzack, Yonge-Richmond Centre, #1302, 151 Yonge St., M5C 2W7 – 416/363-2144, Fax: 416/363-1541 – *3

Trevor Walker, #612, 330 Bay St., M5H 2S8 – 416/214-1162, Fax: 416/214-0870

J.H.G. Wallace, 551 Gerrard St. East, M4M 1X7 – 416/463-6666, Fax: 416/463-8259 – *1

John Walsh, #502, 145 Adelaide St. West, M5H 3H4 – 416/239-1161, Fax: 416/869-5630 – *1

Walsh, McLuskie, Lennox, #935, 525 University Ave., M5G 2L3 – 416/598-8177, Fax: 416/598-5466 – *4

Walton & Kelly, 893 O'Connor Dr., M4B 2S7 – 416/757-2801, Fax: 416/757-1130 – *1

Wanigasekera Gamini, #600, 75 Donway West, M3C 2E9 – 416/449-4294, Fax: 416/449-4369

Wappel & Associates, #303, 500 University Ave., M5G 1V7 – 416/598-1333, Fax: 416/598-5024 – *2

J.P. Warner, #1600, 372 Bay St., M5H 2W9 – 416/322-3015 – *1

C.B. Warren, #300, 124 Eglinton Ave. West, M4R 2G8 – 416/482-1011, Fax: 416/487-4724 – *1

Howard E. Warren, 167 Danforth Ave., M4K 1N2 – 416/461-0983, Fax: 416/462-3347 – *1

Robert D. Warren, #210, 20 Adelaide St. East, M5C 2T6 – 416/368-5393, Fax: 416/368-6811

Cynthia D. Watson, #705, 130 Spadina Ave., M5V 2L4 – 416/360-1967, Fax: 416/360-6764 – *1

M.O. Watson, 129 John St., M5V 2E2 – 416/977-3879, Fax: 416/977-3660 – *1

Richard Watson, #1402, 151 Yonge St., M5C 2W7 – 416/365-3358, Fax: 416/366-9808 – *1

Michael J. Waud, 968 Wilson Ave., 3rd Fl., M3K 1E7 – 416/633-4301, Fax: 416/630-1289 – *1

Weatherhead, Weatherhead, #500, 27 Queen St. East, M5C 2M6 – 416/362-1369, Fax: 416/362-5013 – *2

Ian D.A. Webb, 2 First Canadian Place, #2345, PO Box 75, Stn First Canadian Place, M5X 1B1 – 416/777-9583 – *1

Matt Webber, 317 Grace St., M6G 3A7 – 416/533-4086, Fax: 416/533-5174 – *1

John David Webster, Q.C., 290 Lytton Blvd., M5N 1R6 – 416/489-6255, Fax: 416/488-7582 – *1

Michael Edward Webster, #910, 65 Queen St. West, M5H 2M5 – 416/364-6000, Fax: 416/360-1056 – *1

R.L. & J.H. Webster, 2600 Danforth Ave., M4C 1L3 – 416/699-9644, Fax: 416/699-8905 – *2

C.J. Weiler, 207 McCaul St., M5T 1W6 – 416/598-3434, Fax: 416/598-3437 – *1

Robert D. Weiler, Q.C., 2300-439 University Ave., M5G 1Y8 – 416/598-0453 – *1

Allen W. Weinberg, #1002, 347 Bay St., M5H 2R7 – 416/360-8489, Fax: 416/366-3712 – *1

John Weingust, Q.C., #3300, 130 Adelaide St. West, M5H 3P5 – 416/868-1150, Fax: 416/366-3992 – *1

F. Sheldon Weinles, 1275 Dundas St. West, M6J 1X8 – 416/535-0915 – *1

Marcie I. Weinman, #305, 5400 Yonge St., M2M 5R5 – 416/229-9242, Fax: 416/229-0278 – *1

Arthur Weinreb, 44 Woodrow Ave., M4C 5S2 – 416/690-9220 – *1

Ben Weinstein, 340 Rimrock Rd., M3J 3A6 – 416/633-2120, Fax: 416/633-4113 – *1

Gilbert Weinstock, #401, 1850 Victoria Park Ave., M1R 1T1 – 416/759-1354, Fax: 416/759-3256 – *1

Weir & Foulds, 2 First Canadian Place, Exchange Tower, #1600, Box 480, M5X 1J5 – 416/365-1110, Fax: 416/365-1876; Email: firm@weirfoulds.com; URL: http://www.weirfoulds.com – *65

John Weisdorf, Q.C., 810-65 Queen St. West, M5H 2M5 – 416/861-1000, Fax: 416/363-7558 – *1

M.S. Weisleder, 516 Glencairn Ave., M6B 1Z1 – 416/787-2424 – *1

Stanley J. Weisman, Q.C., 3802 Bloor St. West, M9B 6C2 – 416/236-1141, Fax: 416/237-0458 – *1

Steven Weiss, #1701, 5650 Yonge St., M2M 4G3 – 416/733-2906, Fax: 416/733-3023 – *1

William W.B. Weissglass, #303, 100 Consilium Pl., M1H 3E3 – 416/296-9800, Fax: 416/296-0836 – *1

Weldon, Sproule, 8 King St. East, M5C 1B5 – 416/364-4235, Fax: 416/364-4689 – *4

A.P. Welman, 1034A Bloor St. West, M6H 1M3 – 416/532-2871, Fax: 416/532-5089 – *1

Weltman, Breatross, #127, 5050 Dufferin St., M3H 5T5 – 416/665-5222, Fax: 416/665-4483 – *2

Wengle Associates, #501, 133 Richmond St. West, M5H 2L3 – 416/364-7201, Fax: 416/364-7203 – *2

Irwin Wenus, 27 Acton Ave., M3H 4G6 – 416/633-5830 – *1

West Scarborough Community Legal Services, 6-565 Kennedy Rd., M1K 2B2 – 416/264-4384, Fax: 416/264-2491

R.L. Westell, #200, 303 Eglinton Ave. East, M4P 1L3 – 416/481-3331

Wetstein & Shulman, #204, 3845 Bathurst St., M3H 3N2 – 416/398-1444, Fax: 416/398-1447 – *2

M.J. Wheldrake, Q.C., 2 Alvarado Pl., M3A 3E9 – 416/444-2746

Henry L.E. White, #203, 239 Sheppard Ave. East, M2N 3A8 – 416/224-1757 – *1

J. Edward R. White, #339A, 200 Finch Ave. West, M2R 3W4 – 416/730-0713, Fax: 416/730-0975 – *1

White, Kelly & Wong, #405, 11 Church St., M5E 1W1 – 416/366-5900, Fax: 416/366-1799 – *3

Lionel B. White, Q.C., #2314, 120 Adelaide St. West, M5H 1T1 – 416/364-1127, Fax: 416/364-6903 – *1

J.A. William Whiteacre, Q.C., #605, 160 Bloor St. East, M4W 1B9 – 416/961-9318, Fax: 416/961-9478 – *1

A.B. Whitelaw, Q.C., 100 Adelaide St. West, M5H 1S3 – 416/366-5514 – *1

A.H. Whittaker, #1250, 180 Dundas St. West, M5G 1Z8 – 416/971-9068, Fax: 416/977-0717 – *1

S. Whitzman, #412, 120 Carlton St., M5A 4K2 – 416/960-0059, Fax: 416/922-3939 – *1

Barry B. Widman, #1515, 123 Edward St., M5G 1E2 – 416/597-0702, Fax: 416/597-1581 – *1

J. Wildgoose, 645 Carlaw Ave., M4K 3K6 – 416/469-4390, Fax: 416/469-0682

Willard & Devitt, 155 Roncesvalles Ave., M6R 2L3 – 416/531-1136, Fax: 416/531-4096 – *1

Sian E. Williams, #1610, 372 Bay St., M5H 2W9 – 416/866-8152, Fax: 416/866-8197 – *1

Paul T. Willis, 600 Church St., M4Y 2E7 – 416/926-9806, Fax: 416/926-9737 – *1

Norman A. Wills, #1707, 8 King St. East, M5C 1B5 – 416/366-8060 – *1

Catherine E. Willson, #346, 67 Mowat Ave., M6K 3E3 – 416/534-9504, Fax: 416/534-9503 – *2

Julie Wilmot, 7 Westlake Crescent, M4C 2X3 – 416/696-7222 – *1

Wilson & Bartlett, #904, 27 Queen St. East, M5C 2M6 – 416/363-1601 – *1

Wilson, Christen, #401, 47 Colborne St., M5E 1P8 – 416/360-6336, Fax: 416/360-7912

David S. Wilson, #810, 111 Richmond St. West, M5H 2H5 – 416/943-1223, Fax: 416/943-1049 – *1

David S. Wilson, 180 Dundas St. West, M5G 1Z8 – 416/979-1223, Fax: 416/972-0717 – *1

Robert Wilson, #221, 2928 Yonge St., M4N 2K1 – 416/489-2576 – *1

T.H. Wilson, #404, 372 Bay St., M5H 2W9 – 416/363-0249 – *1

S.L. Winberg, #400, 44 Eglinton Ave. West, M4R 1A1 – 416/483-3400, Fax: 416/483-3409 – *1

Winch, Gasee & Cohen, #200, 65 Queen St. West, M5H 2M5 – 416/363-3351, Fax: 416/363-0252 – *4

C.F. Winer, Q.C., #201, 270 The Kings Way, M9A 3T7 – 416/233-5524, Fax: 416/233-5526 – *1

Norman Winter, #801, 1 St. Clair Ave. East, M4T 2V7 – 416/964-0325, Fax: 416/964-2494; Email: saresh@inforamp.net – *1

J.K. Winters, Q.C., 118 Holcolm Rd., M2N 2C9 – 416/223-8637 – *1

Wise & Partner, 7 Frost St., M9W 1Y5 – 416/747-1229, Fax: 416/740-2549 – *1

G.R. Wise, 3329 Bloor St. West, M8X 1E7 – 416/231-7399, Fax: 416/231-1280 – *1

Garry J. Wise, #200, 70 Bond St., M5B 1X3 – 416/362-1800, Fax: 416/362-0809 – *1

Roy Wise, #1604, 55 University Ave., PO Box 12, M5J 2H7 – 416/866-4144, Fax: 416/866-7946 – *2

Gary L. Wiseman, #7703, 2 St. Clair Ave. West, M4V 1L5 – 416/324-8777, Fax: 416/323-0697 – *1

Juanita Wislesky, 11 Grand Marshall Dr., M1B 5N6 – 416/724-6780, Fax: 416/724-9166

Peter J. Woebbolt, 1554A Bloor St. West, M6P 1A4 – 416/516-4621, Fax: 416/516-1679 – *1

Harold B. Wolfe, #1906, 80 Richmond St. West, M5H 4A7 – 416/863-0333, Fax: 416/863-4968 – *1

N.S. Wolicki, #200, 2200 Bloor St. West, M6S 1N4 – 416/763-3553, Fax: 416/763-2522 – *1

Wilfred Wolman, Q.C., 240 Heath St. West, M5P 3L5 – 416/482-4996 – *1

Lawrence Wong, 49 Placentia Blvd., M1S 4C6 – 416/321-3233 – *1

Mavin Wong, 810 Queen St. East, M4M 1H7 – 416/778-6861, Fax: 416/969-9662 – *1

O.C. Wong, #1900, 180 Dundas St. West, M5G 1Z8 – 416/593-9776, Fax: 416/593-1329 – *1

Wing H. Wong, #202, 4433 Sheppard Ave. East, M1S 1V3 – 416/298-6767, Fax: 416/298-3844 – *1

H.F. Wood, #202, 1900 Eglinton Ave. East, M1L 2L9 – 416/751-4600, Fax: 416/751-3095 – *1

Mary Jane Woods, #3, 1923 Weston Rd., M9N 1W7 – 416/242-5896, Fax: 416/242-9014 – *1

R.L.H. Woolf, 1474 Bathurst St., M5P 3G9 – 416/658-1234, Fax: 416/652-2709 – *1

Woolfson & Woolfson, 3429 Bathurst St., M6A 2C3 – 416/783-1801, Fax: 416/783-2421 – *2

Woolgar, VanWiechen, #506, 56 The Esplanade, M5E 1A7 – 416/867-1331, 1881, Fax: 416/867-1434; Email: woolvan@inforamp.net – *3

Robert L. Woolner, 782 Broadview Ave., M4K 2P7 – 416/465-7895, Fax: 416/465-3857

Wootten, George A., Q.C., #901, 701 Evans Ave., M9C 1A3 – 416/622-7970, Fax: 416/622-8952 – *2

Nestor Woychyshyn, #301, 2259 Bloor St. West, M6S 1N8 – 416/604-2091 – *1

K.E. Wright, #1601, 65 Queen St. West, M5H 2M5 – 416/364-1157 – *1

Sara Wunch, #3204, 20 Queen St. West, PO Box 40, M5H 3R3 – 416/595-7001, Fax: 416/340-7025 – *1

S.L. Yale, 42 Strathearn Blvd., M5P 1T1 – 416/488-1297, Fax: 416/488-0622 – *1

Amy Yao, 209-210 Midland Ave., M1V 4W7 – 416/292-3232, Fax: 416/292-2139 – *1

John Yaremko, Q.C., 1 Connable Dr., M5R 1Z7 – 416/921-7158 – *1

Gerald B. Yasskin, #415, 4580 Dufferin St., M3H 5Y2 – 416/667-0980, Fax: 416/667-0765 – *1

Brenda L. Yeates, #1506, 141 Adelaide St. West, M5H 3L5 – 416/777-1114, Fax: 416/864-0174 – *1

K. Dock Yip, 236 Torrens Ave., M4J 2P5 – 416/425-6485 – *1

Yoannou & Petropoulos, #802, 55 Eglinton Ave. East, M4P 1G8 – 416/484-9640, Fax: 416/487-3274 – *2

York Community Services, 1651 Keele St., M6M 3W2 – 416/653-5400, Fax: 416/653-1696

Albert Young, #112, 1801 Eglinton Ave. West, M6E 2H8 – 416/789-4183, Fax: 416/789-4184 – *1

Joseph R. Young, #1808, One Queen St. East, PO Box 88, M5C 2W5 – 416/866-8888, Fax: 416/866-8889 – *1

Judith Young, #600, 344 Bloor St. West, M5S 3A7 – 416/929-3811, Fax: 416/944-8756 – *1

Younger & Associates, #3400, Toronto Dominion Centre, PO Box 21, Stn T-D, M5K 1A1 – 416/868-7535 – *3

G.R. Youngs, Q.C., #1203, 45 Livingston Rd., M1E 1K8 – 416/265-6901 – *1

Simon Yiu L. Yu, #850, 439 University Ave., M5G 1Y8 – 416/340-8388, Fax: 416/340-8080 – *1

D.R. Zadorozny, #307, 4195 Dundas St. West, M8X 1Y4 – 416/239-2333, Fax: 416/239-1752 – *1

Zaldin & Fine, #1012, 111 Richmond St. West, M5H 2G4 – 416/868-1431, Fax: 416/868-6381 – *4

Ronald V. Zaldin, #1405, 5650 Yonge St., M2M 4G3 – 416/225-3396, Fax: 416/225-3852 – *2

Zammit, Dash & Semple, #601, 130 Bloor St. West, M5S 1N5 – 416/923-2601, Fax: 416/923-1391 – *3

Marisa Zanini, #205, 3875 Keele St., M3J 1N6 – 416/398-9292, Fax: 416/398-8358

C. Zapf, 2424 Bloor St. West, 2nd Fl., M6S 1P9 – 416/766-4208, Fax: 416/769-5365 – *1

E.J. Zaraska, 119 Dunvegan Rd., M4V 2R2 – 416/482-4500, Fax: 416/482-8075 – *1

Daniel Zaretsky, #302, 240 Richmond St. West, M5V 1V6 – 416/599-5254, Fax: 416/599-5330 – *1

Martin R. Zaretsky, #360, 100 Cowdray Crt., M1S 5C8 – 416/754-4404, Fax: 416/754-7280

B.B. Zarowsky, Q.C., #101, 2150 Bloor St. West, M6S 1M8 – 416/763-4671 – *1

M. David Zbarsky, 533 Queen St. East, M5A 1V1 – 416/361-0354, Fax: 416/364-7049 – *1

Sidney I. Zelewicz, 1034A Bloor St. West, M6H 1M3 – 416/532-2871, Fax: 416/532-5089 – *1

Carl S. Zeliger, #300, 303 Eglinton Ave. East, M4P 1L3 – 416/489-7207 – *1

Mannie L. Zeller, #205, 505 Consumers Rd., M1J 4V8 – 416/492-8510 – *1

Zender & Klotz, 1175 Weston Rd., M6M 4P5 – 416/243-2222 – *2

Vincent Zenobio, #415, 4580 Dufferin St., M3H 5Y2 – 416/667-0980, Fax: 416/667-0765 – *1

Zeppieri & Associates, 851 Wilson Ave., M3K 1E6 – 416/631-7800, Fax: 416/631-6170 – *2

David L. Zifkin, 92 Isabella St., M4Y 1N4 – 416/927-7720, Fax: 416/964-9348 – *1

Ryan Zigler, #404, 3420 Finch Ave. East, M1W 1W9 – 416/499-6553, Fax: 416/499-6728 – *1

Stephen M. Zikman, #802, 130 Spadina Ave., M5V 2L4 – 416/504-2300, Fax: 416/504-2299 – *1

Zimmerman, Kirshenblat, #16, 1170 Sheppard Ave. West, M3K 2A3 – 416/638-9511 – *2

Bram M. Zinman, #1800, 4950 Yonge St., M2N 6K1 – 416/224-0200, Fax: 416/224-0758 – *1

R. Zisman, #307, 120 Carlton St., M5A 4K3 – 416/925-6490, Fax: 416/925-4492 – *1

Morrie Zucker, 637 Lake Shore Blvd. West, M5V 1A8 – 416/591-9300 – *1

Stanley R. Zupan, Q.C., #214, 47 Sheppard Ave. East, M2N 5X5 – 416/223-4014 – *1

Arthur Zutis, #1401, 80 Richmond St. West, M5H 2A4 – 416/366-5946 – *1

Howard G. Zweig, #1601, 2 Sheppard Ave. E., M2N 5Y7 – 416/512-1201, Fax: 416/512-1212 – *1

B.E. Zyla, #200, 3029 Bloor St. West, M8X 1C5 – 416/234-9111, Fax: 416/234-9114 – *1

* indicates number of lawyers in law firm.

TOTTENHAM .... **Simcoe**

Feehely, Gastaldi & Hayes, 5 Mill St. East, PO Box 370, L0G 1W0 – 905/936-4262; 859-0065 (Toronto), Fax: 905/936-5102 – *4

Catherine Rogers, 17 Queen St. South, PO Box 399, L0G 1W0 – 705/936-3793, Fax: 705/936-3793 – *3

TRENTON .... **Hastings**

G.W. Bonn, 80 Division St., K8V 5S5 – 613/392-9207, Fax: 613/392-6367 – *3

Davis & Tuckey, 469 Dundas St. West, K8V 3S4 – 613/392-1221 – *1

C. Vincent Graham, 2 King St., PO Box 601, K8V 5R7 – 613/965-6666, Fax: 613/392-0681 – *1

Grant, Donald L., Q.C., 41 Heber St., K8V 1M7 – 613/965-1280, Fax: 613/965-1282; Toll Free: 1-800-387-1280 – *1

Raymond Kaufmann, 257 Dundas St. East, K8V 1M1 – 613/394-3315, Fax: 613/394-6752 – *1

J.S. Robertson, 188 Dundas St. East, K8V 1L6 – 613/392-3659, Fax: 613/392-3521 – *1

Philip S. Staddon, 469 Dundas St. West, K8V 3S4 – 613/394-2228, Fax: 613/475-3651

J.S. Wonnacott, 80 Division St., K8V 5P7 – 613/392-9207, Fax: 613/392-6367 – *1

UNIONVILLE .... **York**

Susan Ambrose, 178 Main St., L3R 2G9 – 905/477-0624, Fax: 905/477-5846 – *1

Peter J. Lewarne, 4701 Hwy. 7, L3R 1M7 – 905/477-4381, Fax: 905/477-7668

R. Parnes, 4480 Hwy. 7., L3R 1M3 – 905/477-5151, Fax: 905/477-6778 – *1

W.B. Thomas, Q.C., 4701 Hwy. 7., L3R 1M7 – 905/477-2233, Fax: 905/477-7668 – *1

UXBRIDGE .... **Durham**

Bailey & Sedore, PO Box 1030, L4P 1N3 – 905/852-3363, Fax: 905/852-3480 – *2

E.E.P. Iglar, 92 Brock St. West, L9P 1P4 – 905/852-3367, Fax: 905/852-9254 – *1

John M. McKay, 10 Brock St. East, PO Box 519, L9P 1P1 – 905/852-3379; 571-1400, Fax: 905/852-3370 – *1

P.D. Turner, Q.C., #103, 29 Toronto St. South, L9P 1V9 – 905/362-1951, Fax: 905/852-6197; Email: dturner@hookup.net – *1

R.J. Wigdor, 23 Franklin St., PO Box 850, L9P 1K3 – 905/852-6402, Fax: 905/852-6496; Email: rwigdor@netcom.ca – *1

Wilson & Martin, 22 Brock St. East, PO Box 1420, L9P 1P1 – 905/852-3353 – *3

VANIER .... **Ottawa-Carleton**

Jean Paul Guertin, Chateau Vanier Mall, 158 McArthur Ave., K1L 7E7 – 613/741-7565, Fax: 613/741-7566 – *1

VANKLEEK HILL .... **Prescott**

Tolhurst & Miller, 115 Main St., PO Box 730, K0B 1R0 – 613/678-3345, Fax: 613/678-3251 – *3

VAUGHAN .... **York**

Bianchi, Presta, #300, 8400 Jane St., L4K 4L8 – 905/738-1078, Fax: 905/738-0528 – *6

Gambin Associates, 3300 Hwy 7 West, 9th Fl., L4K 4M3 – 905/660-6600, Fax: 905/669-5770 – *9

Gardiner, Roberts, #300, 3300 Hwy. 7, L4K 4M3 – 905/660-3333, Fax: 905/660-0990

Piersanti & Company, Royal Centre, #800, 3300 Hwy #7, L4K 4M3 – 905/738-2176, Fax: 905/738-5182; Toll Free: 1-800-531-0708 – *6

WALKERTON .... **Bruce**

Brian R. Linley, 240 Durham St., PO Box 1448, N0G 2V0 – 519/881-2502, Fax: 519/881-1981 – *1

D.O. McCray, 240 Durham St. East, N0G 2V0 – 519/881-0950, Fax: 519/881-1981 – *1

Reichenbach, Gilbert, 3 Colborne St., PO Box 1448, N0G 2V0 – 519/881-2441, Fax: 519/881-1981 – *2

Waechter, Magwood, Van De Vyvere & Thompson, 215 Durham St., N0G 2V0 – 519/881-3230, Fax: 519/881-3595 – *4

WALLACEBURG .... **Kent**

Burgess & Burgess, 218 Duncan St., N8A 4E3 – *2

Carscallen, Reinhart, Mathany, 619 James St., N8A 4L5 – 519/627-2261, Fax: 519/627-1030 – *2

Hyde, Hyde & McGregor, 233 Creek St., N8A 4L6 – 519/627-2081, Fax: 519/627-1615 – *2

WASAGA BEACH .... **Simcoe**

Maurice Loton, 984 Mosley St., PO Box 500, L0L 2P0 – 705/429-4332 – *1

Carl Mandrish, 310 River Rd. East, L0L 2P0 – 905/847-1780, Fax: 905/847-5054 – *1

Donald F. McKay, #311, RR#3, PO Box 61, L0L 2P0 – 705/429-3280 – *1

WATERLOO .... **Waterloo**

Amy, Appleby & Brennan, 372 Erb St. West, N2L 1W6 – 519/884-7330, Fax: 519/884-7390 – *3

Biggs, Sloan & Strype, 92 Erb St. East, PO Box 547, N2J 4B8 – 519/886-1590, Fax: 519/886-8545 – *4

Chris & Volpini, 375 University Ave. East, N2K 3M7 – 519/888-0999, Fax: 519/888-0995 – *3

W. Marlene Fitzpatrick, 421 King St. North, N1J 4E4 – 519/725-9500, Fax: 519/725-2379 – *1

Gehl, Gehl, 421 King St. North, N2J 4E4 – 519/886-8120, Fax: 519/886-8223 – *2

Haney, Haney & Kendall, 41 Erb St. East, PO Box 185, N2J 3Z9 – 519/747-1010, Fax: 519/747-9323 – *6

Heimbecker, Richardson & Petker, 354 King St. North, PO Box 546, N2J 4B8 – 519/886-1750, Fax: 519/886-8754 – *4

Hicks Morley Hamilton Stewart Storie, #290, 100 Regina St. South, N2J 4P9 – 519/746-0411, Fax: 519/747-4829

Hobson, Wellhauser, Taylor & Oldfield, 172 King St. South, PO Box 16580, N2G 4X4 – 519/576-7200, Fax: 519/576-0131 – *7

Anthony T. Keller, #205, 151 Frobisher Dr., N2V 2C9 – 519/725-2518, Fax: 519/725-2519 – *1

Kominek, Gladstone, Ross, 601 Waterloo Sq., N2J 1P2 – 519/886-1050, Fax: 519/747-9565 – *3

McDowell, Welch, Waterloo City Centre, #290, 100 Regina St. South, N2J 4P9 – 519/747-4504, Fax: 519/747-4829 – *3

McGibbon & Woodworth, #215, 50 Westmount Rd. North, N2L 2R5 – 519/886-5050, Fax: 519/886-1791 – *3

P.M. Miller, 15 Westmount Rd. South, N2L 2K2 – 519/884-1332, Fax: 519/884-1161 – *1

James E. Pitcher, 421 King St. North, N2J 4E4 – 519/725-9444, Fax: 519/725-2379 – *1

Shepherd Grenville-Wood, #550, 180 King St. South, N2J 1P8 – 519/571-8331

Shortt, Hanbidge & Snider, 7 Union St. East, PO Box 550, N2J 4B8 – 519/579-5600, Fax: 519/579-2725 – *4

Snyder, Dueck & Sauer, #3, 465 Phillip St., N3L 6C7 – 519/884-2620, Fax: 519/884-0254

J.R. Weber, 192 King St. South, N2J 1P9 – 519/742-1004 – *1

White, Jenkins, Duncan & Ostner, 45 Erb St. East, PO Box 457, N2J 4B5 – 519/886-3340 – *12

WAWA .... **Algoma**

Michael Allemano, PO Box 10, P0S 1K0 – 705/856-4970, Fax: 705/856-2713 – *1

Wishart & Partners, 71 Broadway Ave., P0S 1K0 – 705/856-7260

WELLAND .... **Niagara South**

G.C.M. Banks, 191 Division St., L3B 5P2 – 905/735-1770, Fax: 905/735-7031 – *1

Canadian Almanac & Directory 1997

Blackadder Lacavera, 136 East Main St., PO Box 580, L3B 5R3 – 905/735-3620, Fax: 905/735-1577 – *6

Brooks, Macfarlane & Bielby, 247 East Main St., PO Box 67, L3B 5N9 – 905/735-5684; 384-9788, Fax: 905/735-3340 – *4

Community Legal Services of Niagara South Inc., 80 King St., L3B 3J2 – 905/735-1559, Fax: 905/732-6133

Flett, Beccario, 190 Division St., PO Box 340, L8B 5P9 – 905/732-4481, Fax: 905/732-2020 – *5

William V. Frith, #301, 76 Division St., PO Box 757, L3B 5R5 – 905/735-7582, Fax: 905/735-0093 – *1

F.N. Gibbs, Q.C., 59 Empire St., PO Box 414, L3B 5P7 – 905/732-6145, Fax: 905/732-1015 – *1

Gordon & Adams, 800 Niagara St. North, PO Box 820, L3B 5Y5 – 905/735-0181 – *3

Houghton & Sloniowski, 170 Division St., L3B 5R2 – 905/734-4577, Fax: 905/732-3765 – *4

D.G. Humphries, Q.C., 136 Main St. East, PO Box 39, L3B 5N9 – 905/735-8334, Fax: 905/735-4710 – *1

Johnston & Marotta, 189 Main St. East, PO Box 306, L3B 5P7 – 905/734-4517, Fax: 905/734-3987 – *2

Rodney J. Kajan, #102, 60 King St., PO Box 130, L3B 5P2 – 905/732-1352, Fax: 905/732-0531 – *1

Kormos & Evans, 663 King St., L3B 3L5 – *2

LaRose, Taylor & Fazari, 149 Main St. West, PO Box 366, L3B 5P7 – 905/735-2921, Fax: 905/735-4519 – *3

Anthony W. Pylypuk, 80 King St., PO Box 605, L3B 5R4 – 905/735-2300, Fax: 905/735-9230 – *2

Donald A. Riou, #301, 76 Division St., PO Box 757, L3B 5R5 – 905/735-7582, Fax: 905/735-0093 – *1

Talmage, Stratton, Latinovich & DiFiore, 221 Division St., PO Box 97, L3B 5P2 – 905/732-4477 – *3

WESTPORT . . . . Leeds
Barker, Wilson, Butterworth, James & Scott, Church St., PO Box 159, K0G 1X0 – 613/273-3166, Fax: 613/273-3676 – *6

WHEATLEY . . . . Kent
Scaddan & Jakob, 37 Erie St. North, N0P 2P0 – 519/825-7745

WHITBY . . . . Durham
Louis S. Allore, #206, 701 Rossland Dr. East, L1N 8Y9 – 905/666-5111, Fax: 905/666-5181 – *1

Brooks, Whittington, 326 Dundas St. East, L1N 2J1 – 905/430-1755 – *2

Terence Clarke, 101 Dundas St. West, L1N 2M2 – 905/430-8446, Fax: 905/430-3695 – *1

Coath, Livingstone, 128 Byron St. North, PO Box 327, L1N 4M9 – 905/668-3375, Fax: 905/668-7037 – *2

Dixon & Spong, 124 Byron St. North, L1N 4M9 – 905/668-8571, Fax: 905/668-7936 – *3

Flaherty Dow Elliott, 132 Dundas St. West, L1N 2L9 – 905/666-0231, Fax: 905/686-6447 – *2

David J. Franklin, 326 Dundas St. East, L1N 2J1 – 905/668-8651, Fax: 905/668-8373 – *1

D.G. Goodaire, 126 Byron St. North, PO Box 123, L1N 5R7 – 905/668-1842, Fax: 905/668-8576 – *1

Jenkins & Newman, 126 Byron St. North, L1N 4M9 – 905/666-8588, Fax: 905/666-4873 – *2

Johnston, Morton, Burch & Boland, 201 Byron St. South, L1N 4P7 – 905/666-2252, 686-0306 (Toronto), Fax: 905/430-0878 – *4

M.F. Madill, 610 John St. West, L1N 2V8 – 905/666-8499 – *1

Martial & Martial, 103 Dundas St. West, L1N 2M1 – 905/427-7474, Fax: 905/668-3761 – *1

Murray Miskin, 501 Brock St. South, L1N 4K8 – 905/428-8000, Fax: 905/430-0772 – *1

Edward P. Schein, 107 Kent St., L1N 4Y1 – 905/666-1266, Fax: 905/668-2023 – *1

Schilling, Evans, 330 Bryon St. South, PO Box 267, L1N 5S1 – 905/668-3392, Fax: 905/668-0407 – *2

Schneider, Howard, 107 Kent St., L1N 4Y1 – 905/668-1677, Fax: 905/668-2023 – *1

Robin D. Scott, 306 Dundas St. West, L1N 2M5 – 905/666-2011, Fax: 905/666-2022 – *1

Shewan, Rapoport, #206, 701 Rossland Rd. East, L1N 8Y9 – 905/668-1712, Fax: 905/430-0772 – *1

Siksay & Fraser Law Offices, 618 Athol St., L1N 3Z8 – 905/666-4772, Fax: 905/666-3233 – *2

Sims Brady Thomson & Babbs, 117 King St., PO Box 358, L1N 5S4 – 905/668-7704, Fax: 905/668-1268 – *3

Sosna & Shaughnessy, 214 Colborne St. West, L1N 1X2 – 905/686-1286, Fax: 905/668-6999 – *2

B.P. Stelmach, #5, 11 Stanely Ct., L1N 8P9 – 905/430-6611, Fax: 905/430-6828 – *1

Debra J. Sweetman, 340 Byron St. South, L1N 4P8 – 905/428-6944, Fax: 905/666-8163 – *1

WIARTON . . . . Bruce
H.R. Hendry, 343 William St., N0H 2T0 – 519/534-2610, Fax: 519/534-1372 – *1

Peter Pegg, 847 Berford St., PO Box 569, N0H 2T0 – 519/534-2011, 2012, Fax: 519/534-4494 – *1

WILLIAMSFORD . . . . Grey
Harry Landra, Q.C., RR#1, N0H 2V0 – 519/794-3066 – *1

WINCHESTER . . . . Dundas
David J. Barnhart, 489 Main St., PO Box 730, K0C 2K0 – 613/774-2808, Fax: 613/774-5731 – *1

Cass, Grenkie, 489 Main St., PO Box 820, K0C 2K0 – 613/774-2004, Fax: 613/448-1395

Robert Lamb, PO Box 850, K0C 2K0 – 613/774-3706 – *1

McInnis, MacEwen & Ault, 522 St. Lawrence St., K0C 2K0 – 613/774-2670, Fax: 613/774-2266 – *2

WINDSOR . . . . Essex
Roland J. Baldassi, 380 Ouellette Ave., N9A 6X5 – 519/258-4992 – *1

Barat, Farlam, Millson, 510 Westcourt Pl., N9A 6V2 – 519/258-2424, Fax: 519/258-2451 – *6

Bartlet & Richardes, Canada Bldg., #1000, 374 Ouellette Ave., N9A 1A9 – 519/253-7461, Fax: 519/253-2321 – *19

Anita M. Berecz, #300, 33 University Ave. West, N9A 5N8 – 519/258-8306, Fax: 519/258-4184

Bondy, Belowus, #1004, 100 Ouellette Ave., 7th Fl., N9A 6T3 – 519/973-1900, Fax: 519/973-0225 – *8

Bondy, Kuzak, Riggs & Hurst, #400, 1500 Ouellette Ave., N8X 1K7 – 519/258-9494, Fax: 519/258-9985 – *7

Bondy, Riley, Koski, Stewart, Canada Trust Bldg., #310, 176 University Ave. West, N9A 5P1 – 519/258-1641, Fax: 519/258-1725 – *5

Ellen C. Brudner, 3072 Dougall Ave., N9E 1S4 – 519/966-6661, Fax: 519/966-7098 – *1

Helen M. Carefoot, 397 Moy Ave., N9A 2N1 – 519/252-2761 – *1

Cowan, McWilliams & Salvador, 100 Ouellette Ave., PO Box 1449, N9A 6R5 – 519/258-1100, Fax: 519/258-7384 – *3

Croll & Croll, 185 City Hall Sq. South, N9A 6W5 – 519/256-1829 – *1

K.I. Dodick, Q.C., Canada Trust Bldg., #711, 176 University Ave. West, N9A 5P1 – 519/252-3432, Fax: 519/252-9789 – *1

Donaldson, Donaldson, Greenaway, Canada Bldg., #904, 374 Ouellette, N9A 1B1 – 519/255-7333, Fax: 519/255-7173 – *8

Fazio Law Firm, 333 Wyandotte St. East, N9A 3H7 – 519/258-5030, Fax: 519/971-9051 – *4

Julie Fodor, #3, 1922 Wyandotte St. East, N8Y 1E4 – 519/256-8239, Fax: 519/258-5780 – *1

Furlong Chodola Reynolds, #1010, 100 Ouellette Ave., N9A 6T3 – 519/254-6433, Fax: 519/254-7990 – *4

Gatti, Iannetta & Associates, #400, 267 Pelissier St., N9A 4K4 – 519/258-1010, Fax: 519/258-0163 – *5

Gignac, Sutts, Westcourt Place, #600, 251 Goyeau St., N9A 6V2 – 519/258-9333, Fax: 519/258-9527 – *21

Kamin, Fisher, Burnett & Ziriada, 42 Pitt St. West, N9A 5L4 – 519/252-1123 – *6

Kirwin Partners, 423 Pelissier St., PO Box 1703, N9A 4L2 – 519/255-9840, Fax: 519/255-1413 – *8

Leonard Lyons, 139 University West, N9A 5P4 – 519/258-3492 – *1

MacMillan & Stipic, #508, 251 Goyeau St., N9A 6V2 – 519/258-3201, Fax: 519/258-2665 – *3

MacPhee Law Firm, #1000, 176 University Ave. West, N9A 5P1 – 519/258-8240 – *2

A.R. Mariotti, #500, 267 Pelissier St., N9A 4K4 – 519/258-1931, Fax: 519/973-7575 – *1

McPherson, Prince & Geddes, Canada Bldg., #200, 374 Ouellette Ave., N9A 6S5 – 519/258-6600, Fax: 519/258-9669 – *6

McTague, Clark, 455 Pelissier St., N9A 6Z9 – 519/255-4300, Fax: 519/255-4360 – *19

Norando Meconi, Q.C., 447 Wyandotte St. East, N9A 3H8 – 519/254-4958 – *1

Samuel A. Mossman, #400, 1500 Ouellette Ave., N8X 1K7 – 519/258-0903, Fax: 519/977-0282 – *1

Mousseau, DeLuca, Canada Trust Bldg., 176 University Ave. West, N9A 5P3 – 519/258-0615, Fax: 519/258-6833 – *7

Louis Mullins, #1, 2825 Lauzon Pkwy., N8T 3H5 – 519/944-7705, Fax: 519/944-6512 – *2

Paul L. Mullins, 691 Ouellette Ave., N9A 4J4 – 519/255-7707, Fax: 519/255-7114 – *1

Ohler, Mingay, 134 University Ave. West, N9A 5N9 – 519/256-5496 – *2

Paroian, Raphael, Courey, Cohen & Houston, 875 Ouellette Ave., PO Box 970, Stn A, N9A 6S7 – 519/258-1166, Fax: 519/258-8361

D.R. Revait, Royal Windsor Terrace, #209, 380 Pelissier, N9A 6W8 – 519/258-7030, Fax: 519/258-2629 – *1

Rivait & Stevens, 185 City Hall Square South, N9A 6W5 – 519/255-1250 – *2

Barrie Rubin, 635 Tecumseh Rd. West, N8X 1H4 – 519/258-0650 – *1

Schwartz, Udell, Shanfield & Hawrish, 670 Goyeau St., N9A 1H4 – 519/258-3333, Fax: 519/258-1663 – *4

Brian Sherwell, 827 Pillette Rd., N8Y 3B4 – 519/945-1109, Fax: 519/948-0003 – *1

Cynthia A. Thrasher, Canada Trust Bldg., #909, 176 University Ave. West, N9A 5P1 – 519/253-8882 – *1

G.S. Tuck, 691 Ouellette Ave., N9A 4J4 – 519/253-3509 – *1

Wilson, Walker, Hochberg, Slopen, #300, 443 Ouellette Ave., PO Box 1390, N9A 6R4 – 519/977-1555, Fax: 519/977-1566 – *17

Yuffy, Roberts, Goldstein & Benmanzocco, Canada Trust Bldg., #900, 176 University Ave. West, N9A 5P1 – 519/253-5242, Fax: 519/253-0218 – *3

Floyd Zalev, 2776 Whelpton St., N8Y 1V9 – 519/258-1238 – *1

WINGHAM . . . . Huron
Crawford, Mill & Davies, 217 Josephine St., PO Box 1028, N0G 2W0 – 519/357-3630 – *2

WOODBRIDGE . . . . York
F. Borgatti, 7135 Islington Ave., 2nd Fl., L4L 1V9 – 905/851-2883, Fax: 905/851-2887 – *1

Borlak & Associates, #300, 140 Woodbridge Ave., L4L 4K9 – 416/324-2610 – *1

Capo, Sgro, Dilena, Hemsworth, Mendicino, #400, 7050 Weston Rd., L4G 8G7 – 905/850-7000, Fax: 905/850-7050 – *8

Lynda L. Ciaschini, #301, 7050 Weston Rd., L4L 8G7 – 905/850-6080, Fax: 905/850-6082 – *1

Mancini Associates, #505, 7050 Weston Rd., L4L 8G7 – 905/851-7717 – *3

Anthony Maniaci, 4000 Steeles Ave., L4L 4V9 – 905/851-3400, Fax: 905/851-5108 – *1

Joseph Paradiso, #502, 216 Chrislea Rd., L4L 7W3 – 905/781-6171, Fax: 905/850-5616 – *1

Piccin, Bottos, #201, 4370 Steeles Ave. West, L4L 4Y4 – 905/850-0155, Fax: 905/850-0498 – *5

Jan Poot & Maria Pede, 268 Woodbridge Ave., L4L 2T2 – 905/851-1540,1125, Fax: 905/851-1908 – *2

Felix Rocca, #103, 2 Director Ct., L4L 3Z5 – 905/851-7747, Fax: 905/851-7834 – *1

Stabile & Associates, #109, 4 Director Ct., L4L 3Z5 – 905/851-6711, Fax: 905/851-5773 – *3

S. Suppa, #103E, 3800 Steeles Ave. West, L4K 4G9 – 905/739-5050, Fax: 905/856-1633 – *1

Turner, Brooks & Diamond, #102, 7000 Pine Valley Dr., L4L 4Y8 – 905/677-3445; 851-7110, Fax: 905/851-4229 – *3

P.M. Valenti, West Bldg., #300, 3800 Steeles Ave., L4L 4G9 – 905/635-9998, Fax: 905/850-9998 – *1

WOODLAWN .... Ottawa-Carleton
Bruce R. Coates, 935 Bayview Dr., RR#1, PO Box 59, K0A 3M0 – 613/832-1945 – *1

WOODSTOCK .... Oxford
Beatty & Associates, 487 Princess St., PO Box 336, N4S 7X6 – 519/537-6629, Fax: 519/539-2459 – *3

George A. Calder, Q.C., 77 Light St., N4S 6G9 – 519/539-9861, Fax: 519/539-0516 – *1

J.F. Hutchinson, 395 Dundas St., N4S 1B6 – 519/539-2345 – *1

Kratzmann, Peter H., 48 Vansittart Ave., PO Box 550, N4S 7Y5 – 519/537-6248, Fax: 519/537-5150 – *1

Nesbitt Coulter Carr, 432 Simcoe St., PO Box 125, N4S 7W8 – 519/539-1234, Fax: 519/539-6832 – *8

Odorjan, Battin & Slivocka, 35 Wellington St. North, N4S 6P4 – 519/421-2323, Fax: 519/421-3878

J.R. Park, 45 Light St., N4S 6G7 – 519/539-5686, Fax: 519/539-8259 – *1

Searle & Lemon, 13 Light St., PO Box 515, N4S 6G7 – 519/537-5554, Fax: 519/537-7532 – *2

D.J.B. Stock, Q.C., 530 Adelaide St., PO Box 337, N4S 7X6 – 519/537-5578, Fax: 519/537-7202 – *1

White, Coad, Patience, Bennett & Oliver, 5 Wellington St. North, PO Box 1059, N4S 8A4 – 519/421-1500, Fax: 519/539-6926 – *7

WYOMING .... Lambton
W.M. Dawson, Q.C., 595 Broadway, N0N 1T0 – 519/845-3224

Elliott, Porter, McFadyen & McFadyen, 630 Broadway St., N0N 1T0 – 519/845-0051

PRINCE EDWARD ISLAND

ALBERTON .... Prince
Diane Campbell, 472 Church St., C0B 1B0 – 902/853-2894

CHARLOTTETOWN .... Queens
Campbell, Lea, Michael, McConnell & Pigot, 15 Queen St., PO Box 429, C1A 7K7 – 902/566-3400, Fax: 902/566-9266 – *7

Campbell, Stewart, #201, 137 Queen St., PO Box 485, C1A 7L1 – 902/894-5573, Fax: 902/566-9101 – *4

Carr, Stevenson & MacKay, Peake House, 50 Water St., PO Box 522, C1A 7L1 – 902/892-4156, Fax: 902/566-1377 – *5

Horace B. Carver, Q.C., 104 Kent St., PO Box 2698, C1A 8C3 – 902/892-1224, Fax: 902/368-3311 – *1

Farmer MacLeod MacMillan Fortier, PO Box 2500, C1A 8C2 – 902/368-3003, Fax: 902/566-4265 – *6

John J. Holmes, 138 Richmond St., C1A 1H9 – 902/892-6145 – *1

Donald P. Large, Q.C., PO Box 1265, C1A 7M8 – 902/566-3773, Fax: 902/368-3039 – *1

Hugh D. MacIntosh, 209 Queen St., PO Box 2257, C1A 8B9 – 902/566-5580 – *1

MacLeod, MacDougall, Crane & Parkman, 82 Fitzroy St., PO Box 1056, C1A 7M4 – 902/892-3544, Fax: 902/894-7686 – *5

Macnutt & Dumont, 57 Water St., PO Box 965, C1A 7M4 – 902/894-5003, Fax: 902/368-3782 – *3

Matheson & Murray, 106 Kent St., PO Box 875, C1A 7L9 – 902/894-7051, Fax: 902/368-3762 – *3

Philip Mullally, PO Box 2560, C1A 8C2 – 902/892-5452, Fax: 902/892-7013 – *2

Patterson, Palmer, Huni, Murphy, Landing Place, 20 Great George St., PO Box 486, C1A 7L1 – 902/628-1033, Fax: 902/566-2639; Email: pphmpei@peinet.pe.ca – *14

Theodore & Elizabeth Reagh, 17 West St., C1A 3S3 – 902/892-7667

Stewart McKelvey Stirling Scales, 65 Grafton St., PO Box 2140, C1A 8B9 – 902/892-2485, Fax: 902/566-5283 – *18

MONTAGUE .... Kings
Patterson, Palmer, Huni, Murphy, 35 Main St. North, C0A 1R0 – 902/838-2644, Fax: 902/838-3440

MOUNT STEWART .... Cardigan
M.R. Clark, PO Box 63, C0A 1T0 – 902/676-2954

SUMMERSIDE .... Prince
Diane Campbell, 740 Water St., PO Box 1300, C1N 4K2 – 902/436-2232, Fax: 902/436-0318 – *1

George A. Lyle, PO Box 300, C1N 4Y8 – 902/436-4296, Fax: 902/436-4072 – *1

McCabe, Bernard & Associates, 268 Water St., C1N 1B6 – 902/436-6510 – *2

Ramsay, Campbell & Riley, 307 Water St., PO Box 96, C1N 4P6 – 902/436-4891 – *2

Taylor, McLellan, 37 Central St., C1N 4P6 – 902/436-9211, Fax: 902/436-1514 – *5

Walker & Alyward, PO Box 1326, C1N 4K2 – 902/436-2535 – *2

QUÉBEC

ALMA .... Alma
Morency, Duchesne & Associé, 521, rue Sacré-Coeur ouest, G8B 1M4 – 418/668-3011, Fax: 418/668-0209 – *7

AMOS .... Abitibi
St-Julien, Bigué, 91, av 1er ouest, CP 66, J9T 1T7 – 819/732-6448, Fax: 819/732-1470 – *3

AYLMER .... Hull
A.P. Foster, Q.C., 15, rue Port Royal, J9C 1C7 – 819/777-0892

BAIE-COMEAU .... Hauterive
Carrier, Blouin, Dostie & Associés, #101, 67, Place Lasalle, J4Z 1K2 – 418/296-2251, Fax: 418/296-8454 – *4

Lavoie, Langlois, Forest et Associés, 790, rue Bossé, G5C 1L6 – 418/589-5647, Fax: 418/589-9957 – *3

Savard, Nadeau, Francoeur & Associés, 250, boul La-Salle, G4Z 1S7 – 418/296-4921

BEAUPORT .... Québec
J.C. Lord, 637, av du Cenacle, G1E 1B3 – 418/661-7715, Fax: 418/488-7716 – *1

BEDFORD .... Bedford
Michel Cambrini, 7, Place d'Estrie, J0J 1A0 – *1

François-Lévesque, 14, rue Rivière, CP 540, J0J 1A0 – 514/248-3353 – *1

Paradis, Poulin, 1, rue Rivière, CP 690, J0J 1A0 – 514/248-3355, Fax: 514/248-2491 – *4

BELOEIL .... St. Hyacinthe
Bastien, Morand et Tourigny, #200, 201, boul Laurier, J3G 4G8 – 514/467-5849, Fax: 514/467-3152 – *5

BERNIERES .... Québec
Beland & Tremblay, 581, route Lagueux, G7A 1A7 – 418/831-6011, Fax: 418/831-3433 – *4

BOUCHERVILLE .... Longueuil
Rocheleau, St-Germain, Labranche, Beaudoin, #201, 650, rue de Montbrun, J4B 5E4 – 514/449-7922, Fax: 514/449-3978 – *2

BROSSARD .... Longueuil
Lussier, Jean-Pierre, #202, 4, Place du Commerce, J4W 3B3 – 514/671-1925, Fax: 514/671-1915 – *2

CHANDLER .... Gaspé
Gilles Gaul, 484, Place Hotel de Ville, CP 757, G0C 1K0 – 418/689-6500, Fax: 418/689-2136 – *1

Roy & Arseneau, CP 489, G0C 1K0 – 418/689-2211, Fax: 418/689-5542 – *2

CHATEAUGUAY .... Beauharnois
Serge Allen, 5, boul Youville, J6J 2P8 – 514/692-6701, Fax: 514/692-7359 – *1

Chevrefils & Montpetit, 264, boul d'Anjou, J6K 1C5 – 514/691-2133, Fax: 514/691-8006 – *2

CHICOUTIMI .... Chicoutimi
Aubin, Fillion & Associates, 98, rue Racine est, G7H 1R1 – 418/543-0786 – *7

Carol Girard, #202, 200, rue Racine est, G7H 1S1 – 418/543-0725, Fax: 418/543-1765 – *1

COWANSVILLE .... Bedford
Andre Bachand, 145, rue Principale, J2K 1J3 – 514/263-3226, Fax: 514/263-9719 – *1

Boisvert, Champoux, Complexe Goyer, #205, 505, rue Sud, J2K 2X9 – 514/263-0656, Fax: 514/263-8582 – *2

DRUMMONDVILLE .... Drummond
Paul Biron, #202, 150, rue Marchand, J2C 4N1 – 819/477-8741, Fax: 819/477-7166 – *1

Blais & Associés, 215, rue Lindsay, J2C 1N8 – 819/477-2235, Fax: 819/477-8674 – *2

Jutras et Associés, 449, rue Hériot, J2B 1B4 – 819/477-6321, Fax: 819/474-5691 – *8

FARNHAM .... Bedford
Remi Pageau, 54, boul Normandie Nord, J2N 1W3 – 514/293-6678 – *1

Paradis, & Associés, CP 150, J1N 2R4 – 514/293-5367 – *3

GASPE .... Gaspé
Luc Houle, 107, rue de la Reine, CP 2255, G0C 1R0 – 418/368-1723, Fax: 418/368-6474 – *1

Joncas & Desbois, CP 1160, G0C 1R0 – 418/368-3358, Fax: 418/368-3432 – *2

Michaud & Coté, 147, rue de la Reine, CP 208, G0C 1R0 – 418/368-2633 – *3

GATINEAU .... Hull
Beaudry, Bertrand, Carrefour des Affaires, #203, 160, boul de l'Hôpital, J8T 8J1 – 819/246-2323, Fax: 819/246-1217

Kehoe, Blais, Major & Parent, #200, 344, boul Maloney est, J8P 7A6 – 819/663-2439, Fax: 819/663-4816 – *5

Lapointe et Lapointe, #200, 370, boul Gréber, J8T 5R6 – 819/568-0663, Fax: 819/568-0226 – *5

Laporte, Angès, #104, 365, boul Gréber, J8T 5R3 – 819/568-2011 – *1

Legault, Roy, Mantha & Associés, Édifice l'Atrium, #260, 85, rue Bellehumeur, J8T 6K5 – 819/561-1042 – *10

Letellier & Associates, #127, 139, boul de l'Hôpital, J8T 8A3 – 819/243-7293, Fax: 819/243-5913

GRANBY .... Bedford
Choinière & Hill, 26, rue Court, J2G 4Y5 – 514/372-7332, Fax: 514/372-1222 – *2

* indicates number of lawyers in law firm.

Normandin Brisebois Faucher, 35, rue Dufferin, J1G 4W5 – 514/372-3545, Fax: 514/372-5854 – *3

GRAND-MERE .... St. Maurice
Goulet & Cote, 570, av 6e, G9T 2H5 – 819/538-1791, Fax: 819/538-3616 – *2

GRANDE-RIVIERE .... Gaspé
Guy Gendron, CP 488, G0C 1V0 – 418/385-2333, Fax: 418/385-4418 – *1

HULL .... Hull
Beaudry, Bertrand, Maison du Citoyen, #400, 25, rue Laurier, J8X 4C8 – 819/770-4880, Fax: 819/595-4979, 770-9190 – *15
Robert Bélanger, #100, 305, boul St-Joseph, J8Y 3Y6 – 819/771-6679 – *1
Bergeron, Gaudreau & Pinet, 167, rue Notre-Dame, J8X 3T3 – 819/770-7928, Fax: 819/770-1424 – *3
Serge Côté, 44, boul Montclair, J8Y 2E6 – 819/776-3101, Fax: 819/776-3954 – *1
Desjardins & Associates, 241, rue Papineau, J8X 1W7 – 819/778-6105, Fax: 819/778-1580 – *1
Desjardins & Gauthier, 132, rue St-Raymond, J8Y 1T2 – 819/771-7415, Fax: 819/771-2658 – *3
Pierre Fontaine, 25, rue Bernier, J8Z 1E7 – 514/771-6578 – *1
M.R. Paul Frechette, 188, rue Archambault, J8Y 5E2 – 819/771-6896, Fax: 819/771-7010 – *2
Roger Gosselin, 44, boul Montclair, J8Y 2E6 – 819/776-3101, Fax: 819/776-3954 – *1
Hamon, Dufour & Isabelle, #301, 200, rue Montcalm, J8Y 3B5 – 819/778-1870 – *8
Leduc, Bouthillette, 12, rue Ste-Marie, J8Y 2A3 – 819/771-6257, Fax: 819/771-3973 – *4
Letellier & Associates, #500, 15, ch Gamelin, J8Y 1V4 – 819/778-7293, Fax: 819/778-1145 – *13
E. Wayne Lora, 175, rue Champlain, J8X 3R3 – 819/778-6522 – *2
Noël Berthiaume, Aubry, 111, rue Champlain, J8X 3R1 – 819/771-7393, Fax: 819/771-5397 – *11
Ste-Marie, McLean, 175, rue Champlain, J8X 3R3 – 819/777-3864, Fax: 819/777-8378 – *1
Sarrazin, Charlebois, Édifice Themis, 162, rue Wellington, J8X 2J4 – 819/770-4888, Fax: 819/770-0712 – *3
Taché, Pharand, Bédard, Bélanger, 166, rue Wellington, CP 1456, Succ B, J8X 2J4 – 819/771-7781, Fax: 819/771-0608 – *6
Arnaud Voyer, 6, rue Villeneuve, J8Y 1L2 – 819/771-3712 – *1

JOLIETTE .... Joliette
Ferland & Bélair, 70, Place Bourget sud, J6E 5E8 – 514/759-7412, Fax: 514/759-5366 – *3
Roy, Laporte & Sylvestre, 386, boul Manseau, J6E 3E1 – 514/759-7788, 514/589-2266 (Montreal), Fax: 514/759-8501 – *4

JONQUIERE .... Québec
Cain, Lamarre, Wells, #201, 3750, boul du Royaume, G7S 0A4 – 418/695-4580, Fax: 418/547-9590 – *29
Gauthier, Simard, Ouellet, Mazurette & Tremblay, 3687, boul Harvey, G7X 7V9 – 418/542-3545 – *10
Tremblay & Marceau, 1939, rue Davis, CP 1217, G7S 4K8 – 418/548-8283 – *2
Turcotte Fortin Guay & Cantin, 2332, rue St-Dominique, CP 2040, G7X 7X6 – 418/547-2108, Fax: 418/547-9519 – *4

KAHNAWAKA .... Bedford
Bishop & McKenzie, Mohawk Counsel, PO Box 720, J0L 1B0 – 514/638-3011 – *1

LA TUQUE .... St-Maurice
Hénaire, Roy, 290, rue St-Joseph, 2e étage, G9X 3Z8 – 819/676-8002, Fax: 819/379-1227

LAC MEGANTIC .... Mégantic
Pierre Greffard, 5284, rue Frontenac, G6B 1H3 – 819/583-2776 – *1
Monty, Coulombe, 5109, rue Frontenac, G6B 1H2 – 819/583-3833, Fax: 819/583-5673 – *3
André Turgeon, 5175, rue Frontenac, G6B 1H2 – 819/583-1477 – *1

LACHUTE .... Terrebonne
Michel J.J. Chartrand, 415, rue Principale, J8H 1Y1 – 514/562-2742 – *1

LEVIS .... Québec
Gosselin & Associés, #6500, 310, boul de la Rive-Sud, G6V 7M5 – , Fax: 418/833-6130 – *4

LONGUEUIL .... Longueuil
Raymond Allard, 1150, boul Marie-Victorin, J4G 2M4 – 514/442-8600, Fax: 514/463-1043 – *1
Bernard, Cimoné, Poupart, Despatis, Cormier, Proulx, #200, 101, boul Roland Therrien, J4H 4B9 – 514/670-7900, Fax: 514/670-0673 – *8
Brassard, Roy & Gagnon, #200, 785, ch Chambly, J4H 3M2 – 514/679-8880 – *3
Brissette, St-Jacques, Trépanier, Lamarre, #200, 370, ch Chambly, J4H 3Z6 – 514/677-9144, Fax: 514/677-3241 – *8
R.E. Fusey, 1115, boul Desaulniers, J4K 1K5 – 514/442-3222, Fax: 514/442-3222 – *1
Lamoureux, Morin & Lamoureux, 1909, ch Chambly, J4J 3Y1 – 514/670-3663 – *3
Montgrain, McClure, Marois, Chandonnet, Gibeau, #300, 550, ch Chambly, J4H 3L8 – 514/679-0720 – *9
Periard, Ledoux, 175, ch Chambly, G4H 3L3 – 514/646-2116, Fax: 514/646-3828 – *2

MANIWAKI .... Pontiac
Desjardins & Gauthier, 185, boul Desjardins, J9E 2C9 – 819/449-6075, Fax: 819/449-5679 – *2

MATAGAMI .... Abitibi
Bigué, Dufresne, Ferron, St-Julien, 195, boul Matagami, J0Y 2A0 – 819/739-2277 – *1

MATANE .... Rimouski
Chamberland Fillion Avocats, #311, 159, rue St-Pierre, G4W 3M9 – 418/562-1806, Fax: 418/562-7248 – *2
Deschenes, Doiron et Houde, 352, av St-Jérôrme, G4W 3B1 – 418/562-2097, Fax: 418/562-2926 – *3

MONT-LAURIER .... Labelle
Jean-Marc Roy, 634, rue de la Madone, J9L 1S9 – 819/623-3355 – *1

MONTMAGNY .... Montmagny
Réal Garant, 77, av de la Gare, G5V 2T1 – 418/248-0194, Fax: 418/248-0195 – *1
Morin, Lemieux & Associés, #205, 25, boul Taché ouest, G5V 2Z9 – 418/248-3114 – *4
Pelletier, Lavoie, #201, 5, boul Taché est, G5V 1B6 – 418/248-7474, Fax: 418/248-8294 – *3

MONTRÉAL .... Montréal
Jacob Aaron, #303, 200, ch Bates, H3S 1A3 – 514/731-7714, Fax: 514/341-1771 – *1
Abbey, Pass, #840, 1310, av Greene, H3Z 2B2 – 514/931-3881, Fax: 514/932-1451 – *2
Abrams & Associates, #1005, 2001, rue University, H3A 2A6 – 514/849-9794, Fax: 514/843-7967 – *1
Allan Adel, #305, 276, rue St-Jacques, H2Y 1N3 – 514/845-4151, Fax: 514/845-0306 – *1
Ahern, Lalonde, Nuss, Drymer, #3333, 1, Place Ville Marie, H3B 3N2 – 514/866-9757 – *7
Alarie, Legault, Beauchemin, Paquin, Nadon, Jobin & Brisson, 1259, rue Berri, 10e étage, H2L 4C7 – 514/844-6216, Fax: 514/844-8129 – *13
Alepin Gauthier, #601, 3080, boul Le Carrefour, H7T 2K9 – 514/681-3080, 338-3037 (Montréal), Fax: 514/681-1476 – *9
Joseph Allen & Associés, #200, 7170, boul St-Laurent, H2S 3E2 – 514/274-9393, Fax: 514/274-5614 – *2
Jak Almaleh, #101, 5725, Côte St. Luc, H3X 2E6 – 514/488-1096 – *1
Amaron, Stead & Viberg, #200, 280, av Dorval, H9S 3H4 – 514/636-4992, Fax: 514/636-8122 – *4
Jean Arsenault, #800, 407, boul St-Laurent, H2Y 2Y5 – 514/866-3045, Fax: 514/866-8230 – *7
Aster & Aster, #410, 345, av Victoria, H3Z 2N2 – 514/483-2444, Fax: 514/483-2477 – *2
Aster & Aster, #410, 345, av Victoria, H3Z 2N2 – 514/483-2444, Fax: 514/483-2477 – *2
Axelrod, Price, Brossard, #2314, 1155, boul René-Lévesque ouest, H3B 2K2 – 514/878-9951, Fax: 514/878-3883 – *3
Raymond G. Ayoup, #805, 1255, Carré Phillips, H3B 3G1 – 514/861-9955, Fax: 514/866-4101 – *1
Baker, Nudleman & Lamontagne, La Tour CIBC, #2720, 1155, boul René-Lévesque ouest, H3B 2K8 – 514/866-6674, Fax: 514/866-9822 – *7
Barkowitz, Strauber, Goldman & Tiger, #300, 4141, rue Sherbrooke ouest, H3Z 1B8 – 514/931-1788, Fax: 514/931-3061 – *4
Baron & Abrams, #450, 5180, ch Queen-Mary, H3W 3E7 – 514/487-7783, Fax: 514/483-2280 – *4
Barza & Lagana, #700, 2015, rue Peel, H3A 1T8 – 514/288-9322, Fax: 514/288-2562 – *5
Basile Angelopoulos, Phillips, Vineberg, 5, Place Ville Marie, 17e étage, H3B 2G2 – 514/866-8541, Fax: 514/875-0344 – *1
Beauchamp, Pomerleau & Huot, #201, 84, rue Notre-Dame ouest, H2Y 1S6 – 514/845-8227, Fax: 514/845-7910 – *3
Robert Beaudet, 5331, rue Bannantyne, H4H 1E8 – 514/769-8527, Fax: 514/769-7466 – *3
Beaudry, Marion, #100, 443, rue St-Vincent, H2Y 3A6 – 514/866-4167, Fax: 514/866-0230 – *2
Beaulieu, Semeniuk & Gagnon, #218, 1405, rue Bishop, H3G 2E4 – 514/844-2811, Fax: 514/499-8536 – *3
Beaupré, Trudeau, #1600, 2000, av McGill College, H3A 3H3 – 514/281-1533, Fax: 514/281-1527 – *16
Bélanger & Bélanger, 8136, rue St-Denis, H2P 2G6 – 514/381-7626, Fax: 514/381-0339 – *2
Bélanger, Sauvé, #1700, 1, Place Ville Marie, H3B 2C1 – 514/878-3081, Fax: 514/878-3053 – *54
Bell Rudick Edelstein, #3404, 1155, boul René-Lévesque ouest, H3B 3T3 – 514/866-1977, Fax: 514/866-1639 – *5
J.M. Bellaiche, #2280, 800, boul René-Lévesque ouest, H3B 1X9 – 514/954-8888, Fax: 514/954-5077 – *1
Edouard J. Belliardo, #603, 10, rue St-Jacques, H1Y 1L3 – 514/845-6253, Fax: 514/845-8056 – *1
Bennett Jones Verchere, #3900, 1000, rue de La Gauchetière, H3B 4W5 – 514/871-1200, Fax: 514/871-8115 – *9
Robert Benoit, 5325, rue Jean-Talon est, H1S 1L4 – 514/725-9577, Fax: 514/725-8763 – *1
Berger & Winston, #400, 615, boul René-Lévesque ouest, H3B 1P5 – 514/288-4177, Fax: 514/876-1090 – *2
Bergman, Michael N., #1515, 1, Carré Westmount, H3Z 2P9 – 514/866-8686, Fax: 514/937-7953 – *3
Berkowitz Strauber Goldman Tiger, #300, 4141, rue Sherbrooke ouest, H3Z 1B8 – 514/931-1788, Fax: 514/931-3061 – *5
Bernstein & Feifer, #713, 1411, rue Forth, H3H 2N7 – 514/270-3192, Fax: 514/939-3318 – *4
Jean Berthiaume, 1800, rue Sherbrooke est, H2K 1B3 – 514/521-2144, Fax: 514/525-0182 – *1
Bertrand, Guerard, 134, av Laurentides, H7G 2T3 – 514/663-0851 – *2
Michael Besner, #500, 1210, rue Sherbrooke ouest, H3A 1H6 – 514/288-5252, Fax: 514/288-7479 – *1
Alexander Biega, Q.C., #705, 276, rue St-Jacques, H2Y 1N3 – 514/842-1126, Fax: 514/842-1290 – *1

Bissonnet, Mercadente & Associés, #202, 5450, rue Jarry est, H1P 1T9 – 514/326-3300 – *7

Elaine Bissonnette, #102, 4139, rue Amiens – 514/323-8770, Fax: 514/323-8700 – *1

Harry Blank, #1416, 1255, rue University, H3B 3X1 – 514/866-1125, Fax: 514/866-6898 – *2

Danielle Blier, #402, 266, rue Notre-Dame ouest, H2Y 1T6 – 514/844-8693, Fax: 514/842-6808 – *1

Monique Blondin, #401, 10, rue St-Jacques, H1Y 1L3 – 514/844-2535 – *1

Bloomfield Bellemare, #1720, 1080, Côte du Beaver Hall, H2Z 1S8 – 514/871-9571, Fax: 514/397-0816 – *3

Jack Bobrove, Q.C., #1530, 1080, Côte du Beaver Hall, H2Z 1S8 – 514/875-4350, Fax: 514/875-9552 – *1

Boivin, Manon, #208, 1101, rue Jeanne-Mance, H2Z 1W8 – 514/288-0770 – *1

Michele Bolduc, #1608, 1050, Côte du Beaver Hall, H2Z 1S4 – 514/870-8891 – *1

Bouchard & Associés, #1010, 10, rue St-Jacques, H2Y 1L3 – 514/842-2913, Fax: 514/842-5353 – *7

Boucher, Champoux, 1816, rue Sherbrooke est, H2K 1B3 – 514/524-3591 – *2

Jean-Pierre Boucher, 1816, rue Sherbrooke est, H2K 1B3 – 514/524-3632 – *1

Boule Lamontagne, #500, 266, rue Notre-Dame ouest, H2Y 1T6 – 514/284-9681, Fax: 514/284-6606 – *2

Maurice J. Boxer, 1276, boul Cure-Labelle, H7V 2W1 – *1

Boyer, Gariépy, Duplessis, #200, 417, rue St-Nicholas, H2Y 2P4 – 514/287-9585, Fax: 514/844-5243 – *5

Alain Brabant, 8263, Place Montrichard, H1K 1H9 – 514/354-3121, Fax: 514/351-2160 – *1

Jean-Yves Brière, #2158, 5199, rue Sherbrooke est, H1T 3X1 – 514/252-0277, Fax: 514/252-4338 – *3

Sarto Brisebois, 710, rue St-Jacques, H2Y 1L3 – 514/849-9444, Fax: 514/849-0119 – *2

Julius Briskin, #200, 1255, rue University, H3B 3B2 – 514/737-3564, Fax: 514/874-7693 – *1

Brisset des Nos, Gravel, Lévesque, Normand, Rioux, #300, 777, rue de la Commune ouest, H3C 1Y1 – 514/875-7975, Fax: 514/875-9433 – *7

Brodeur, Matteau, #300, 204, rue Notre-Dame ouest, 3e étage, H2Y 1T4 – 514/281-0033, Fax: 514/284-9328 – *3

Donald R. Brown, 149, Ashley Rd., H9W 1K7

Brunelle, Sirois, Arseneault & Ledoux, #703, 465, rue St-Jean, H1Y 2R6 – 514/844-2802 – *4

Jacques Brunet, 3714, rue Ontario est, H1W 1R9 – 514/524-6638 – *1

Byers Casgrain, #3900, 1, Place Ville-Marie, H3B 4M7 – 514/878-8811, Fax: 514/878-8197 – *70

Daniel Caisse, #508, 10, rue St-Jacques, H2Y 1L3 – 514/288-2250, Fax: 514/288-2402 – *1

Campbell, Cohen, Seidman, #1802, 2, Place Alexis-Nihon, H3Z 3C1 – 514/937-9445 – *3

J.B. Carisse, #300, 19, rue Le Royer ouest, H2Y 1W4 – 514/843-4569, Fax: 514/843-6612

Carriére, Londéi, Dame, 2356, rue Jean-Talon est, H1E 1V9 – 514/593-1977, Fax: 514/593-4762 – *1

Raymond A. Cartwright, #600, 615, boul René-Lévesque ouest, H3B 1P6 – 514/861-7454, Fax: 514/861-6180 – *1

Jean Caumartin, 6688, av Christophe-Colomb, H2S 2G8 – 514/274-1126 – *1

Cayer Lapointe, #200, 11903, boul Ste-Gertrude, H1G 5R1 – 514/327-1201, Fax: 514/322-5624 – *3

Cayer, Lapointe, #200, 11903, boul Ste-Gertrude, H1G 5R1 – 514/327-1201, Fax: 514/322-5624 – *3

Cerundolo & Maiorino, 1807, rue Jean-Talon est, H1E 1T4 – 514/376-0335, Fax: 514/376-6334 – *3

Chaikelson & Spector, #1600, 2000, rue Mansfield, H3A 3A4 – 514/288-2500, Fax: 514/288-7128 – *8

Chait Amyot, #1900, 1, Place Ville Marie, H3B 2C3 – 514/879-1353, Fax: 514/879-1460 – *25

Champagne & Kouri, #104, 6494, rue Beaubien est, H1M 1A9 – 514/255-1223, Fax: 514/255-0635 – *3

Claude Champagne, 4237, rue St-Hubert, H1J 2W6 – 514/526-0817, Fax: 514/526-0397 – *1

François Chapados, #204, 1010, rue Sherbrooke ouest, H3A 2R7 – 514/844-2234, Fax: 514/844-9330 – *1

Charbonneau & Archambault, 2300, rue Sherbrooke est, H2K 1E5 – 514/527-4561, Fax: 514/522-3364 – *2

Michel, Charbonneau, #201, 4403, rue Beaubien est, H1T 1T2 – 514/725-4773, Fax: 514/725-4828 – *2

Pierre Charbonneau, #1000, 550, rue Sherbrooke ouest, H3A 1B9 – 514/288-9150, Fax: 514/288-9307 – *1

Charness, Charness & Charness, #1100, 440, boul René-Lévesque ouest, H2Z 1V7 – 514/878-1808, Fax: 514/871-1149 – *3

Jean-Yves Chartrand, 376, boul St-Joseph est, H2T 1J6 – 514/287-9796, Fax: 514/843-7471 – *2

Chassé & Therien, #400, 4001, boul Crémazie est, H1Z 2L2 – 514/374-6211, Fax: 514/376-2717 – *2

Claude Chauret, #300, 3535, rue St-Charles, H9H 3C4 – 514/697-1421, Fax: 514/426-8677 – *1

Fred Cheftechi, 800, boul René-Lévesque ouest, H3B 1X9 – 514/397-8700, Fax: 514/397-8608 – *2

Marc Chenard, #205, 5174, Côté des Neiges, H3T 1X8 – 514/733-3669, Fax: 514/733-2006 – *1

Maurice Chevalier, #1407, 3555, rue Berri, H1L 4G4 – 514/845-5551 – *1

Choquette Bernstein Rheaume, #200, 5316, av du Parc, H2V 4G7 – 514/270-3192, Fax: 514/270-8876 – *4

Ciampini & Ciampini, #203, 7655, boul Newman, H8N 1X7 – 514/364-4750, Fax: 514/264-2730 – *2

Clark & LaTraverse, #4200, 1250, boul René-Lévesque ouest, H3B 4W8 – 514/938-1313, Fax: 514/938-3691 – *9

Coblentz & Coblentz, #1500, 555, boul René-Lévesque ouest, H2Z 1B1 – 514/866-8901, Fax: 514/866-8901 – *2

Paul B. Cohen, #809, 4000, boul de Maisonneuve ouest, H3Z 1J9 – 514/931-3691 – *1

Ralph A. Cohen, #514, 1117, rue Ste-Catharine est, H3B 1H9 – *1

Colby, Monet, Demers, Delage, Crevier, #2900, 1561, av McGill College, H3A 3M8 – 514/284-3663, Fax: 514/284-1961 – *14

Colby, Rioux & Demers #3301, 1155, boul René-Lévesque ouest, H3B 3T1 – 514/866-4301, Fax: 514/879-0626 – *12

A.B. Coleman, #440, 4141, rue Sherbrooke ouest, H3Z 1B8 – 514/935-5030, Fax: 514/935-3559 – *1

Mortimer J. Constantine, #1600, 2000, rue Mansfield, H3A 3A4 – 514/849-8111, Fax: 514/849-8113 – *1

S. Cooperstein, #1051, 400, boul de Maisonneuve ouest, H3A 1L4 – 514/845-1094 – *1

Normand Corbeil, #1021, 50, Place Crémazie ouest, H2P 2T7 – 514/381-1851, Fax: 514/389-1924 – *1

Cordeau & Associés, #300, 8535, rue Sherbrooke est, H1L 1B4 – 514/352-5200, Fax: 514/352-4040 – *1

Côté & Associates, #2050, 1501, av McGill College, H3A 3M8 – 514/843-4499, Fax: 514/843-4864 – *1

Diane L. Côté, 6977, St. Denis, H2S 2S5 – 514/274-0988, Fax: 514/274-8622 – *1

Hyman J. Crystal, #826, 276, rue St-Jacques, H2Y 1N3 – 514/284-1125, Fax: 514/284-2413 – *1

Jacques Cyr, #204, 13000, rue Sherbrooke est, H1A 3W2 – 514/642-2676, Fax: 514/642-1663 – *1

Giles Daoust, #304, 4, rue Notre-Dame est, H2Y 1B7 – 514/861-0753, Fax: 514/861-5600 – *1

David & Touchette, #3600, 1155, boul René-Lévesque ouest, H3B 3T9 – 514/871-8174, Fax: 514/871-8052 – *2

De Grandpré, Godin, #2900, 1000, rue de la Gauchetière ouest, H3B 4W5 – 514/878-4311, Fax: 514/878-4333 – *44

Claude de la Madeleine, 3600, boul Henri-Bourassa, H1H 1J4 – 514/323-2112, Fax: 514/323-2112 – *1

De Latremoille & Chaussegros de Lery, 847, rue Cherrier, H2L 1H6 – 514/596-0299 – *1

Décary Francescucci & Monty, 3467, rue St-Hubert, H1L 3Z8 – 514/525-2589, Fax: 514/525-2580 – *2

Delvecchio & Bouliane, 5898, av 3e, H1Y 2X1 – 514/376-7569 – *3

Demarais & Hargreaves, #201, 410, boul Henri-Bourassa est, H3L 1C4 – 514/382-8122 – *3

Derome & Rouillier, 935, boul St-Joseph est, H2J 1K7 – 514/272-2930, Fax: 514/272-3869 – *2

Claude Des Marais, 1206, boul St. Joseph, H2J 1L6 – 514/521-0047 – *1

Desjardins Ducharme Stein Monast, Tour de la Banque Nationale, #2400, 600, rue de la Gauchetière ouest, H3B 4L8 – 514/878-9411, Fax: 514/878-9092; Ligne sans frais: 1-800-670-0102 – *76

Bruno Desjardins, #1502, 2045, rue Stanley, H3A 2V4 – 514/849-3113, Fax: 514/849-2061 – *1

Desjardins, Lapointe, Delage, Mousseau, Bélanger, #2185, 600, rue de la Gauchetière ouest, H3B 4L8 – 514/875-5404, Fax: 514/875-5647 – *13

Robert Desjardins, 4515, rue Notre-Dame ouest, H4C 1S3 – 514/766-6285, Fax: 514/932-0412 – *1

Desmarais Picard Garceau Pasquin, 204, Place d'Youville, H2Y 2B4 – 514/845-5171, Fax: 514/845-5578 – *15

Jean Desrosiers, 4192, av Girouard, H4A 3C9 – 514/482-7428 – *1

Desrosiers, Turcotte, Marchant, Latulippe, Groulx, 303, rue St-Sulpice, 5e étage, H2Y 3W2 – 514/287-9284, Fax: 514/287-9792 – *6

Deveau, Lavoie & Associates, #400, 3131, rue de la Concorde est, H7E 4W4 – 514/664-1515, Fax: 514/664-1438 – *3

Joseph Di Clementi, #224, 759, Victoria Sq., H2Y 2J7 – 514/288-1891, Fax: 514/288-3833 – *1

Donato Di Tullio, 7647, boul Gouin est, H1E 1A7 – 514/648-1048, Fax: 514/648-3288 – *1

Lawrence Diner, #400, 1310, av Greene, H3Z 2B2 – 514/931-3883, Fax: 514/939-1469 – *1

Hrair Djihanian, #300, 320, rue Notre-Dame est, H2Y 1C7 – 514/395-0543, Fax: 514/395-2476 – *1

Donald, Duggan, #365, 1253, av McGill College, H3B 2Y5 – 514/871-2844, Fax: 514/866-1901 – *4

André R. Dorais Avocats, #1810, 1, Carré Westmount, H3Z 2P9 – 514/938-0808, Fax: 514/938-8888 – *2

Dostie, Robert & Associés, #1800, 507, Place d'Armes, H2Y 2W8 – 514/282-0722, Fax: 514/282-9770

Doyon, Nivoix & Goulet, #501, 6455, rue Jean-Talon est, H1S 3E8 – 514/253-3338, Fax: 514/251-0560 – *3

Daniel Drouin, #1802, 666, rue Sherbrooke ouest, H3A 1E7 – 514/287-9050, Fax: 514/897-1592 – *1

Druker & Marcovitch, #605, 1255, Carré Phillips, H3B 3G5 – 514/871-1300 – *4

Du Mesnil & Lavigne, #1605, 555, boul René-Lévesque ouest, H2Z 1B1 – 514/866-1529, Fax: 514/866-7725 – *2

Serge Dubé, #2707, 1, Place Ville-Marie, H3B 4G4 – 514/871-9796, Fax: 514/954-1774 – *1

Dubuc, Marcaix, Trudeau, #2610, 300, rue Léo-Pariseau, CP 963, H1L 1K3 – 514/843-5444 – *3

Duceppe, Jolicoeur & Associés, 1595, rue St-Hubert, H2L 3Z2 – 514/526-6621, Fax: 514/524-4341 – *5

Laurier Dugas, 4545, av Pierre-de-Coubertin, H1V 3N7 – 514/252-3137, Fax: 514/251-8038 – *1

Duguay, Salois, Dionne, Morneau, Massicotte & Tellier, 425, ch St-Sulpice, H2Y 2V7 – 514/842-9631, Fax: 514/842-1255 – *7

Francine Dumont, 404, rue Saint-Dizier, H2Y 3T3 – 514/288-6050, Fax: 514/288-0630 – *1

Dunton, Rainville, Toupin, Perrault, 800, Place Victoria, Boite: 800, #4300, CP 303, H4Z 1H1 – 514/866-6743, Fax: 514/866-8854 – *12

Thuc D.D. Duong, 1252, rue Saint-Matthew, 1e étage, H3H 2H8 – 514/939-5851 – *1

Gilles Dupont, #400, 1594, rue St-Hubert, H2L 3Z2 – 514/526-6621, Fax: 514/524-4341 – *1

Robert Dupuis, 509, rue Lartigue, H7N 3T6 – 514/663-5280, Fax: 514/663-5281 – *1

Elsassy & Rose, #600, 10, rue Notre-Dame est, H2Y 1B7 – 514/861-9092, Fax: 514/861-8113 – *7

* indicates number of lawyers in law firm.

Jean-Guy Farley, 2544, boul Rosemont, H1Y 1K4 – 514/254-9519 – *1

Emile J. Fattal, #705, 1134, rue Ste-Catherine ouest, H3B 1H4 – 514/861-4545, Fax: 514/874-1639 – *1

Barry Feinstein, #300, 1384, av Greene, H3Z 2B1 – 514/846-4045, Fax: 514/846-4027 – *1

Feldman & Spina, #908, 10, rue St-Jacques, H2Y 1L3 – 514/842-8378, Fax: 514/849-4457 – *1

Maurice Ferron, Tour Chomedy, #310, 1600, boul Cure-Labelle, H7V 2W2 – 514/687-4200 – *1

Filion & Bisson, 3422, rue St-Hubert, H2L 3Z7 – 514/282-2022, Fax: 514/282-0281 – *4

W.H. Finkelberg, #400, 1155, rue Sherbrooke ouest – 514/284-1186, Fax: 514/849-0527 – *1

Fiske, Emery & Associés, #1102, 1425, boul René-Lévesque ouest, H3G 1T7 – 514/866-3601, Fax: 514/866-3604 – *2

C.A. Fitzwilliam, 93, av Easton, H4X 1L3 – 514/484-8722, Fax: 514/485-5719 – *1

I. David Fleming, #523, 1440, Ste. Catherine ouest, H3G 1R8 – 514/866-9988, Fax: 514/861-4116 – *1

Flynn, Rivard & Associés, #444, 2020, rue University, H3A 2A5 – 514/288-7156, Fax: 514/288-2534

Maggie Fortin, 3967, av Verdun, H4G 1L1 – 514/769-4731 – *1

Marie Fournelle, 4216, rue St-Hubert, H1J 2W7 – *1

Fournier, Frenette, #1108, 2500, boul Daniel-Johnson, H7T 2P6 – 514/682-7011, Fax: 514/682-0303 – *3

Yves Fournier & Associés, #301, 8190, boul Newman, H8N 1X9 – 514/364-1912, Fax: 514/364-4270 – *1

Frankel & Frankel, #908, 10, rue St-Jacques, H2Y 1L3 – 514/849-3544, Fax: 514/849-4457 – *2

Franklin & Franklin, Westmount Life Bldg, Boite: 545, #545, 4141, rue Sherbrooke ouest, H3Z 1B8 – 514/935-3576, Fax: 514/935-6862 – *3

Frumkin, Feldman & Glazman, #2270, 1010, de la Gauchetière ouest, H3B 2N2 – 514/861-2812, Fax: 514/861-6062 – *1

Jean-Pierre Gagné, 4797, av Victoria, H3W 2M9 – 514/341-7677, Fax: 514/486-9682 – *1

Gagnon & Haines, 545A, ch Lakeshore, H9S 2B1 – 514/631-6429, Fax: 514/631-5606 – *2

Hervé Gagnon, #310, 1030, rue Cherrier, H1L 1H9 – 514/525-0086 – *1

Richard Gareau, #220, 4400, ch Côte-de-Liesse, H4N 2P7 – 514/344-5614, Fax: 514/344-5613 – *1

Gasco, Lelange, #2100, 1080, Côte du Beaver Hall, H2Z 1S8 – 514/397-0066, Fax: 514/397-0393 – *9

Gauthier, Gregory & Robitaille, #1100, 615, boul René-Lévesque ouest, H3B 1P5 – 514/879-9294, Fax: 514/879-1456 – *6

Ulrich Gautier, #912, 10, rue St-Jacques, H2Y 1L3 – 514/842-1006, Fax: 514/842-1811 – *1

Stanley Gelfand, #306, 189, boul Hymus, H9R 1E9 – 514/695-4542, Fax: 514/695-7975 – *1

Philippe Gélinas, Q.C., 232, rue Fleury est, H3L 1E8 – 514/383-1983 – *1

Généreux & Associates, #905, 276, rue St-Jacques, H2Y 1N3 – 514/286-9100, Fax: 514/286-9453 – *4

Geoffrion Bernier Barbeau Perreault, 8088, rue St-Denis, H2R 2G1 – 514/388-0555, Fax: 514/388-1421 – *9

Geoffrion, Jetté, #1680, 550, rue Sherbrooke ouest, H3A 3G8 – 514/288-7422 – *11

Geoffroy Ferron, #503, 1030, rue Cherrier, H2L 1H9 – 514/522-5445, Fax: 514/522-4386 – *2

Gervais & Robert, #1500, 507, Place d'Armes, H2Y 2W8 – 514/288-4241, Fax: 514/843-8104 – *3

Ghanime et Cordeau, 5777, av Verdun, H4H 1L7 – 514/769-9639, Fax: 514/769-5899 – *2

Mario Girard, #200, 10, rue Notre-Dame est, H2Y 1B7 – 514/861-6794 – *1

Larry Gitman, #2440, 2020, rue University, H3A 2A5 – 514/849-4511, Fax: 514/849-1584 – *1

Larry H. Gitman, #2440, 2020, rue University, H3A 2L4 – 514/849-4511, Fax: 514/849-1854 – *1

Glasz, Miedzigorski, 772, rue Sherbrooke ouest, 3e étage, H3A 1G1 – 514/284-9551, Fax: 514/284-3419 – *3

Gliserman, Ackman, Cutler & Bernfeld, 1200, av McGill College, H3B 4J8 – 514/849-9141 – *6

Allan J. Gold, #605, 388, rue St-Jacques ouest, H2Y 1S1 – 514/849-1621, Fax: 514/849-1624 – *1

Gold, Fridhandler, Goldberg, Place du Parc, #2000, 300, rue Leo-Parizeau, CP 994, H1W 2N1 – 514/288-7929, Fax: 514/844-7290 – *4

A. Goldman & Associates, #400, 1310, av Greene, H3Z 2B2 – 514/931-3883, Fax: 514/939-1469 – *1

Goldstein & Associates, #4100, 1250, boul René-Lévesque ouest, H3B 4W8 – 514/932-4100 – *1

Goldwater & Dubé, #2330, 630, boul René-Lévesque ouest, H3B 1S6 – 514/861-4367, Fax: 514/861-7601 – *2

Goloff & Boucher, #904, 5, Place Ville-Marie, H3B 2G2 – 514/398-9549, Fax: 514/398-9792 – *4

Albert Gomberg, 5740, av Blossom, H4W 2T3 – 514/488-9778 – *1

Gonzales, Sloan, #306, 10, rue Ontario ouest, H2X 1Y6 – 514/289-9877, Fax: 514/289-9612 – *3

Goodman Phillips & Vineberg, 1, av McGill College, 26th Fl., H3A 3N9 – 514/841-6400, Fax: 514/841-6499; Email: gpv@ntl.gpv.com – *1

R.A. Gordy, #1600, 2000, rue Mansfield, H3A 3A4 – 514/849-8111, Fax: 514/849-8113 – *1

Harold Gossack, #2440, 2020, rue University, H3A 2L4 – 514/849-4511, Fax: 514/849-1854 – *1

Gottlieb & Pearson, #1600, 2020, rue University, H3A 2A5 – 514/288-1744, Fax: 514/288-6629 – *10

R. Goulet, 505, Place St-Henri, 2e étage, H4C 2S1 – 514/933-4211, Fax: 514/933-3394 – *1

Philip Goulston, 1631, rue de Ville-Marie, H1V 3K2 – 514/259-5066, Fax: 514/259-5066 – *1

Gourd & Monette, #5055, 2000, rue Peel, H3A 2R4 – 514/849-0639, Fax: 514/849-2875 – *2

Grana, Djihanian & Pouliot, #100, 245, rue St-Jacques, H1Y 1M6 – 514/849-5631, Fax: 514/282-1890 – *1

Gravel & Bolduc, 5, Place Ville-Marie, H3B 2X3 – 514/871-1850, Fax: 514/871-1997 – *1

Gravenor Beck, #223, 975, boul Roméo Vachon nord, H4Y 1H1 – 514/631-4494, Fax: 514/631-1226 – *5

Ura Greenbaum, Boite: 2, 2222, rue René-Lévesque ouest, H3H 1R6 – 514/931-7291, Fax: 514/931-7882 – *3

Jean-Marc Grenier, #103, 1666, rue Thierry, H8N 2K4 – 514/368-0454 – *2

Grondin, Poudrier, Bernier, #710, 425, boul de Maisonneuve ouest, H3A 3G5 – 514/982-0701, Fax: 514/499-9725 – *2

Gross, Pinsky, 2, Place Alexis Nihon, #1000, 3500, boul de Maisonneuve ouest, H3Z 3C1 – 514/934-1333, Fax: 514/933-0810 – *11

Isabelle Grou, #520, 50, Place Crémazie ouest, H2P 2T2 – 514/382-9670, Fax: 514/382-9676 – *3

Gurman, Aumais, #520, 125, rue Chabanel ouest, H2N 1E4 – 514/858-1118, Fax: 514/858-1121 – *4

Guy & Gilbert, #2300, 770, rue Sherbrooke ouest, H3A 1G1 – 514/281-1766, Fax: 514/281-1059, 9948, 5799 – *78

Blanka Gyulai, Q.C., 2, av McCulloch, H2V 3L4 – 514/271-6569, Fax: 514/271-6168 – *1

Hadjis & Feng, #707, 1117, rue Ste-Catherine ouest, H3B 1H9 – 514/849-3526, Fax: 514/849-1595 – *3

Hallée, Hamel, #300, 5835, av Léger, H1G 6E1 – 514/323-9000, Fax: 514/328-8748 – *2

Handelman, Handelman & Schiller, #1610, 1255, rue Université, H3B 3X3 – 514/866-5071, Fax: 514/866-4210 – *3

Hanna, Glace & Sher, 772, rue Sherbrooke ouest, 3e étage, H3A 1G1 – 514/284-9551, Fax: 514/284-3419 – *3

Harkins, Laramee, 2544, boul Rosemont, H1Y 1K4 – 514/271-2879, Fax: 514/271-5914 – *6

G.I. Harris, Q.C., 3410, rue Peel, H3A 1W8 – 514/844-3314 – *1

Hart, Saint-Pierre, #2125, 1, Place Ville Marie, H3B 2C6 – 514/866-6883, Fax: 514/866-8323 – *9

Hébert & Bourque, #2405, 500, Place d'Armes, H1Y 2W2 – 514/284-2351, Fax: 514/284-2354 – *3

Hébert Denault, 359, Place Royale, H2Y 2V3 – 514/288-4424, Fax: 514/288-7859 – *20

Heenan Blaikie, #2500, 1250, boul René-Lévesque ouest, H3B 4Y1 – 514/846-1212, Fax: 514/846-3427 – *95

Heller Clarke Blond, 1210, rue Sherbrooke ouest, H3A 1H6 – 514/288-5252, Fax: 514/288-7479 – *13

Jack Hendler, #703, 10, rue St-Jacques, H1Y 1L3 – 514/844-1373 – *1

Hudon, Gendron, Harris, Thomas & Cie, 630, boul René-Lévesque ouest, H3B 1S6 – 514/871-1398, Fax: 514/871-9987; Email: hght@hght.com – *41

Huot, Laflamme, 470, rue du Champ-de-Mars, H1Y 1B4 – 514/288-0937, Fax: 514/844-9786 – *9

Hussey, Frégeau, 1590, av des Pins ouest, H3G 1B4 – 514/932-1119, Fax: 514/932-5908 – *2

Hutchins, Soroka & Dionne, #400, 245, rue St-Jacques, H2Y 1M6 – 514/849-2403, Fax: 514/849-4907 – *6

Michel A. Iacono, #2000, 300, av Leo-Pariseau, CP 1141, H2W 2P4 – 514/288-1414, Fax: 514/844-7290 – *1

Iadeluca Morabito & Venneri, #350, 5167, rue Jean-Talon est, H2A 2A9 – 514/727-0332, Fax: 514/727-9315 – *3

Ionata & Lazaris, 615, boul René Lévesque ouest, H3B 1P5 – 514/397-1515, Fax: 514/397-6823 – *2

Izzi & L'Heureux, #307, 700, boul Crémazie ouest, H3N 1A1 – 514/495-1840, Fax: 514/495-2580 – *2

Jallbert, Séguin, Verdon, Caron, Mahoney, 500, Place d'Armes, 21e étage, H2Y 3W9 – 514/872-2993, Fax: 514/872-2828 – *23

Ahmed Jazouli, #22, 5336, ch Queen-Mary, H3X 1T8 – 514/485-6577, Fax: 514/485-6577 – *1

Kalman Samuels, Q.C. & Assoc., 1200, rue du Fort, H3H 2B3 – 514/939-1200, Fax: 514/939-1201 – *4

Harvey S. Kalnitsky, #315, 360, rue St-Jacques, H2Y 1P5 – 514/288-6066, Fax: 514/288-6550 – *2

I.H. Kaufman, #711, 1117, rue Ste-Catherine ouest, H3B 1H1 – 514/282-7401, Fax: 514/282-9209 – *1

Kelada Tremblay Avocats, #5, 8687, rue St-Denis, H2P 2H4 – 514/384-8732, Fax: 514/384-5001 – *2

Kessner, N.S., #1632, 2020, rue University, H3A 2A5 – 514/866-7266, Fax: 514/288-1381 – *2

Kierans & Guay, #440, 606, rue Cathcart, H3B 1K9 – 514/866-3394, Fax: 514/866-3398 – *3

Kirshenblatt Crestohl & Bogante, #1200, 1, Carré Westmount, H3Z 2P4 – 514/932-7392, Fax: 514/932-0990 – *5

Duncan Kisilenko, Q.C., #615, 6600, rte Trans-Canada, H9R 4S2 – 514/695-0750, Fax: 514/698-7428 – *1

Kliger & Kliger, #808, 1255, Carré Phillips, H3B 3G1 – 514/281-1720, Fax: 514/281-0678 – *2

Lillian Kliger, #550, 4999, rue Ste-Catherine ouest, H3Z 1T3 – 514/481-2180, Fax: 514/481-6707 – *1

Kochenburger Rochefort, #800, 625, boul René Lévesque ouest, H3B 1R2 – 514/874-0491, Fax: 514/874-0489 – *3

H. Kooiman, #705, 276, rue St-Jacques, H2Y 1N3 – 514/288-4900, Fax: 514/842-1290 – *4

Jon Kosorwich, #1006, 7800, boul Gouin ouest, H4K 2K2 – 514/334-3229 – *1

Daniel Kouri, #104, 6494, rue Beaubien est, H1M 1A9 – 514/255-1223 – *1

Kravitz & Kravitz, 750, boul Marcel-Laurin, H4M 2M4 – 514/748-2889, Fax: 514/748-5191 – *4

Kugler & Kandestin, #211, 1, Place Ville Marie, H3B 2C6 – 514/878-2861 – *10

Kushnir & Waters, #260, 4950, ch Queen-Mary, H3W 1X3 – 514/340-1807, Fax: 514/340-9945 – *2

J.E. Labelle, 800, Carré Victoria, 17e étage, CP 246, H4Z 1G3 – 514/873-5326, Fax: 514/873-3090 – *1

Lucien Lachapelle, 5971, rue St-Hubert, H1S 2L8 – 514/277-2164, Fax: 514/277-1120 – *1

Lackstone & Turner, 256, rue Devon, H3R 1B9 – 514/731-3544, Fax: 514/737-3770 – *2

Lacoste Langévin, #1400, 2000, rue Mansfield, H3A 3A2 – 514/284-0426, Fax: 514/284-2319 – *4

Laflamme Rousseau, #1100, 801, rue Sherbrooke est, H2L 1K7 – 514/527-3691, Fax: 514/527-3911 – *5

Lafleur Brown, 1, Place Ville Marie, H3B 3P4 – 514/878-9641, Fax: 514/878-1450 – *50

Gaston Lafleur, #1000, 550, rue Sherbrooke ouest, H3A 1B9 – 514/288-9150, Fax: 514/288-9307 – *1

Gaetan Lagarde, #201, 1554, boul Mont-Royal est, H2J 1Z2 – 514/521-2442, Fax: 514/525-5561 – *1

LaHaye, Moisan, Boucher, Gaudreau, Doray, Richard, Paquette, #202, 28, rue Notre-Dame est, H2Y 1B9 – 514/878-1316, Fax: 514/878-1318 – *7

Lamarche, Pierre, 237A, boul des Prairies, H7N 2T8 – 514/667-9802 – *1

Lamarre, Charbonneau, #2905, 500, Place d'Armes, H1Y 2W2 – 514/842-0754 – *4

Lamy, Turbide, Lefebvre, #301, 1030, rue Beaubien est, H2S 1T4 – 514/271-1336 – *3

Raymond Landry, #700, 2015, rue Peel – 514/288-9322, Fax: 514/288-2562 – *1

Langlois Robert, #2600, 1002, rue Sherbrooke ouest, H3A 3L6 – 514/842-9512, Fax: 514/845-6573; Email: langloir@odyssee.net – *27

John P. Lanthier, #127, 1015, Côte du Beaver Hall, H2Z 1S1 – 514/393-8751 – *1

Lapin, Polisuk, Mauer, 1155, boul René-Lévesque ouest, H3B 4S5 – 514/861-8546, Fax: 514/861-1298 – *7

Lapointe Rosenstein, Place Sherbrooke, #1100, 1010, rue Sherbrooke ouest, H3A 2R7 – 514/844-6392, Fax: 514/288-7390 – *45

Lapointe, Schachter, Champagne & Talbot, #100, 511, Place d'Armes, H2Y 2W7 – 514/288-8200, Fax: 514/288-6962 – *8

Daniel Latour, #1000, 550, rue Sherbrooke ouest, H3A 1B9 – 514/288-9150, Fax: 514/288-9307 – *1

Laurier, Cêré, 356, av 90, H8R 2Z7 – 514/363-0220, Fax: 514/363-9495 – *4

Francine Lauzé, #610, 8000, boul Lange Lier, H1P 3K2 – 514/329-3560, Fax: 514/852-4505 – *3

Lavery, de Billy, #4000, 1, Place Ville-Marie, H3B 4M4 – 514/871-1522, Fax: 514/285-6355 – *138

Leo D. Lavut, 400, boul de Maisonneuve ouest, H3A 1L4 – 514/844-4462 – *1

Lazare & Altschuler, #2812, 1800, av McGill College, H3A 3J6 – 514/288-3341, Fax: 514/288-7634 – *2

Lazarus, Charbonneau, #505, 606, rue Cathcart, H3B 1K9 – 514/875-6446, Fax: 514/875-9757 – *4

Leo Leblanc, 4058, av de Vendôme, H4A 3N1 – 514/842-2002 – *1

Leo R. Leblanc, Q.C., 10, rue St-Jacques, H2Y 1L3 – 514/842-2002 – *1

Lebovics, Cytrynbaum, Marchessault & Peizler, 4098, rue Ste-Catherine ouest, 2e étage, H3Z 1P2 – 514/866-2995, Fax: 514/861-4359 – *9

Lebrun Papineau, #310, 495, boul St-Martin ouest, H7M 1Y9 – 514/668-4550, Fax: 514/387-5602 – *3

Micheline Lebrun-Sylvestre, #305, 10500, boul de l'Acadie, H4N 2V4 – 514/331-0177 – *1

Lechter & Segal, #1110, 2, Place Alexis-Nihon, H3Z 3C1 – 514/937-2222, Fax: 514/937-8729 – *3

John E. Lechter, #202, 2015, rue Drummond St., H3G 1W7 – 514/845-4287, Fax: 514/845-1803 – *1

Leduc Lambert, #400, 2550, boul Daniel-Johnson, 7e étage, H7T 2L1 – 514/686-4000, Fax: 514/686-6000 – *13

Marcel Lefebvre, #210, 1010, rue Ste-Catherine est, H2L 2G3 – 514/842-3466, Fax: 514/842-1044 – *1

Legault Longtin Laurin Haloin, #1800, 630, boul René-Lévesque ouest, H3B 1S6 – 514/879-1124, Fax: 514/397-0370 – *10

Legault, Joly, #315, 390, rue Notre-Dame ouest, H1Y 1T9 – 514/842-8891, Fax: 514/842-6202 – *12

Léger, Robic & Richard, 1514, rue Penfield, H3G 1X5 – 514/934-0785 – *20

Lemoine & Major, 11553, av Brunet, H1G 5G2 – 514/327-4777 – *2

Mario Létourneau, #102, 480, av Gilford, H1J 1N3 – 514/589-7827, Fax: 514/598-9811 – *1

Levasseur, Fréchette, #202, 2600, boul Saint-Joseph est, H1Y 2A4 – 514/526-0101, Fax: 514/526-5067

Fernand Levesque, #504, 4, rue Notre-Dame est, H2Y 1B8 – 514/861-4719, Fax: 514/861-8467 – *1

Levine, Frishman, #904, 5, place Ville-Marie, H3B 2G2 – 514/398-9549, Fax: 514/398-9792 – *4

Liberman Segall Finkelberg, #650, 4150, rue Ste-Catherine ouest, H3Z 2Y5 – 514/937-3976, Fax: 514/397-3415 – *3

Liebman & Associates, #1800, 1, Carré Westmount, H3Z 2P9 – 514/846-0666, Fax: 514/935-2380 – *1

Judith Lifshitz, #2500, 1250, boul René-Lévesque ouest, H3B 4Y1 – 514/846-2229, Fax: 514/846-3427 – *1

Lightstone, Riback, #900, 615, boul René-Lévesque ouest, H3B 1P5 – 514/861-6373, Fax: 514/861-5218 – *2

Linetsky, Hartman, #200, 1255, Carré Phillips, H3B 3G1 – 514/871-8971, Fax: 514/871-8974 – *3

N. Lord, #210, 1010, rue Ste-Catherine est, H2L 2G3 – 514/842-3466, Fax: 514/842-1044 – *1

Robert Loulou, 7924, rue St-Denis, H2R 2G1 – 514/388-3511, Fax: 514/388-3211 – *1

Luterman, Stotland, Davis, #1800, 1, Carré Westmount, H3Z 2P9 – 514/935-7433, Fax: 514/935-2380 – *5

Kelvin J. MacDougall, Q.C., #1163, 1155, rue Metcalfe St., H3B 2V6 – 514/875-8024, Fax: 514/875-8025 – *1

Mackenzie Gervais, #1300, 770, rue Sherbrooke ouest, H3A 1G1 – 514/842-9831, Fax: 514/288-7389; Email: @macger.qc.ca – *45

T.R. Anthony Malcolm, #2, 3468, rue Drummond, H3G 1Y4 – 514/849-4134, Fax: 514/849-4137 – *1

Maliniak & Ironside, #3, 388, rue St-Jacques, H1Y 1S1 – 514/844-2507 – *2

Malo, Dansereau, Cyr & Larue, #1500, 507, Place d'Armes, H1Y 2W8 – 514/288-4241 – *7

Mao Chambers, Tour de la Cité, #1909, 300, rue Leo-Parizeau, CP 982, H1W 2N1 – 514/849-7381, Fax: 514/849-7382

Léo René Maranda, 31, rue St-Jacques, H2Y 1K9 – 514/842-6871, Fax: 514/845-3372 – *1

Marchand & Associés, #2000, 300, av Leo-Pariseau, CP 989, H2W 2N1 – 514/844-8631, Fax: 514/844-6691 – *5

Marchand & Kosorwich, #600, 1118, rue Ste-Catherine ouest, H3B 1H5 – 514/866-5061, Fax: 514/866-8741 – *2

Marchand, Magnan, Melançon, Forget, #1640, 600, de la Gauchetière ouest, H3B 4L8 – 514/393-1155, Fax: 514/861-0727 – *19

André Martin, 276, rue St-Jacques, H1Y 1N3 – 514/845-3101 – *1

Martineau, Walker, a/s Fasken Martineau, Stock Exchange Tower, #3400, 800, Place-Victoria, CP 242, H4Z 1E9 – 514/397-7400, Fax: 514/397-7600; Ligne sans frais: 1-800-361-6266 – *117

André Matteau, 450, rue St-Pierre, H2Y 2M9 – 514/388-3754, Fax: 514/843-9946 – *1

Maynard & Zaor, #1101, 507, Place d'Armes, H2Y 2W8 – 514/288-1101, Fax: 514/499-8548 – *3

McCarthy Tétrault, 1170, rue Peel, H3B 4S8 – 514/397-4100, Fax: 514/875-6246 – *70

McDougall, Caron, #2600, 1000, rue de la Gauchetière ouest, H3B 4W5 – 514/399-1000, Fax: 514/399-1026 – *19

Robert E. McFetridge, #365, 1253, av McGill College, H3B 2Y5 – 514/395-8662, Fax: 514/866-1901 – *1

McGilton & Johnston, 1130, rue Sherbrooke ouest, H3A 2M8 – 514/842-1714, Fax: 514/842-1718 – *5

McMaster Meighen, #900, 1000, rue de la Gauchetière ouest, H3B 4W5 – 514/879-1212, Fax: 514/878-0605 – *58

Melançon, Marceau, Grenier et Sciortino, #300, 1717, boul René-Lévesque est, H2L 4T3 – 514/525-3414, Fax: 514/525-2803 – *12

Ménard & Hurtubise, #500, 266, rue Notre-Dame ouest, H2Y 1T6 – 514/284-0600, Fax: 514/284-6606 – *2

Ménard, Boucher, 3530, rue Jean-Talon ouest, H3R 2G3 – 514/341-3124, Fax: 514/341-4287 – *5

Jean-Pierre Ménard, 5969, rue Hochelaga, H1N 1X3 – 514/253-8044, Fax: 514/253-9404 – *5

Michel A. Ménard, #414, 50, Place Crémazie ouest, H2P 2T1 – 514/384-4800, Fax: 514/384-4807 – *1

Yves Ménard, #301, 10, rue Notre-Dame sud, H2Y 1B7 – 514/861-0469, Fax: 514/861-0460 – *1

Mendelsohn Rosentzveig Shacter, 1000, rue Sherbrooke ouest, 27e étage, H3A 3G4 – 514/987-5000, Fax: 514/987-1213 – *44

Mercier Leduc Boulay, #450, 750, boul Marcel-Laurin, H4M 2M4 – 514/747-3549, Fax: 514/747-4206 – *6

Jean Mercier, Q.C., #200, 4059, rue Hochelaga, H1W 1K4 – 514/723-0908 – *1

Meyerovitch, Goldstein, Flanz & Fishman, #1800, 300, av Leo-Pariseau, CP 959, H2W 2P9 – 514/288-4070, Fax: 514/288-4078 – *9

Michon, Ferland, #900, 84, rue Notre-Dame ouest, H2Y 1S6 – 514/288-3901, Fax: 514/844-4491 – *5

Jean Mignault, 1730, rue Cunard, H7S 2B2 – 514/332-4110, Fax: 514/334-6043 – *1

Miller & Khazzam, #2200, 800, boul René-Lévesque ouest, H3B 1X9 – 514/875-8040, Fax: 514/875-8044 – *3

Miller, Adel & Associés, #805, 276, rue St-Jacques, H2Y 1N3 – 514/845-4151, Fax: 514/845-0306 – *3

Suzanne Moisan-Gerard, ##202, 28, rue Notre-Dame est, H2Y 1B9 – 514/878-1316, Fax: 514/878-1318 – *1

Michele Monast, #1700, 1, Place Ville-Marie, H3B 2C1 – 514/878-3081, Fax: 514/878-3053 – *1

Mondor, Fournier, #2140, 1, Place Ville-Marie, H3B 2C6 – 514/878-1900, Fax: 514/878-3679 – *8

Morin & Associates, #1935, 500, Place d'Armes, H2Y 2W2 – 514/281-1010, Fax: 514/288-3144 – *5

Morin, Chamberland, #100, 1030, rue Beaubien est, H2S 1H5 – 514/272-1764, Fax: 514/278-1664 – *2

Morris & Morris, #1500, 1, Carré Westmount, H3Z 2P9 – 514/935-6226, Fax: 514/935-2314

Daniel Morris, Q.C., #1600, 2000, rue Mansfield, H3A 3A4 – 514/288-2500, Fax: 514/288-7128 – *4

Morris, Morris & Morris, #1500, 1, Carré Westmount, H3Z 2P9 – 514/935-6226, Fax: 514/935-2314 – *2

I. Myszka, 4781, av Van Horne, H3W 1J1 – 514/737-4069 – *1

Nadeau, Desroches, Seers, 3689, rue St-Hubert, H1L 3Z9 – 514/522-5549, Fax: 514/522-6487 – *6

Nanci, Tommaso, 4755, rue Jarry est, H1R 1X7 – 514/722-3788 – *1

Narvey, Green & Lack, #2270, 800, boul René-Lévesque ouest, H3B 1X9 – 514/871-4992, Fax: 514/871-4995 – *3

O'Reilly & Associates, #1007, 1155, rue University, H3B 3A7 – 514/871-8117, Fax: 514/871-9177 – *4

O'Reilly & Grodinsky, CP 1270, Succ B, H3B 3K9 – 514/878-3711 – *1

Ogilvy Renault, #1100, 1981, McGill College Ave., H3A 3C1 – 514/847-4747, Fax: 514/286-5474; Email: info@ogilvyrenault.ca – *144

Oligny & Jacques, #1100, 800, boul René-Lévesque ouest, H3B 1X9 – 514/871-2240, Fax: 514/871-8772 – *2

Overland Rosenzveig, #2875, 630, boul René-Lévesque ouest, H3B 1S9 – 514/875-6200, Fax: 514/875-9708 – *3

J. René Paiement, 3150, rue Linton, H3S 1S7 – 514/737-6199 – *1

B. Papachristou, 10, rue St-Jacques, H2Y 1L3 – 514/288-8700 – *1

Papillon HeSert Guilbault, #201, 315, boul René-Lévesque est, H2X 3P3 – 514/844-8804, Fax: 514/844-5927 – *3

* indicates number of lawyers in law firm.

Paquette, Perreault, Trudeau & Associés, #900, 200, rue St-Jacques, H2Y 1M1 – 514/842-1864, Fax: 514/842-1868 – *5

Paquin Danis, 55, rue St-James ouest, 6e étage, H2Y 3X2 – 514/842-1884, Fax: 514/842-0605 – *1

Parenteau Archambault, 240, rue St-Jacques, H2Y 1L9 – 514/849-6644, Fax: 514/849-5233 – *5

Parizeau, Richer, #2020, 500, Place d'Armes, H2Y 2W2 – 514/849-6325, Fax: 514/849-9438 – *5

Pateras & Iezzoni, #2314, 500, Place d'Armes, H1Y 2W2 – 514/284-0860, Fax: 514/843-7990 – *6

Denis R. Paul, 4145A, rue St-Denis, H2W 2M7 – 514/287-1884 – *1

Pearl & Associates, 1170 Place du Frère André, 4e étage, H3B 3C6 – 514/861-1170, Fax: 514/861-0850 – *3

Denis Peloquin, #600, 407, boul St-Laurent, H2Y 2Y5 – 514/842-9185 – *1

Pepin, Létourneau, #2200, 500, Place D'Armes, H2Y 3S3 – 514/284-3553, Fax: 514/284-2173 – *20

John J. Pepper, Q.C & Associates, #955, 1253, av McGill College, H3B 2Y5 – 514/875-5311, Fax: 514/875-8381 – *6

John J. Pepper, Q.C & Associates, #2500, 1155, boul René-Lévesque ouest, H3B 2K4 – 514/875-5454, Fax: 514/875-8967 – *1

Gregore Perron & Assoc., 84, rue Notre-Dame ouest, H2Y 1S6 – 514/285-6441, Fax: 514/285-8589 – *4

Serge Petit, #3821, 1, Place Ville-Marie, H3B 4M6 – 514/395-0208, Fax: 514/395-0207 – *1

Phillips & Vineberg, 5, Place Ville-Marie, 17 étage, H3B 2G2 – 514/866-8541, Fax: 514/875-0344 – *48

Frederick R. Phillips, 6039, av Verdun, H4H 1M8 – 514/762-0112, Fax: 514/762-0114 – *1

Phillips, Friedman, Kotler, Place du Canada, #900, 1010, rue de la Gauchetière ouest, H3B 2P8 – 514/878-3371, Fax: 514/878-3691, 4676 – *22

André Piché, #101, 6664, rue St-Denis, H2S 2R9 – 514/277-4141, Fax: 514/277-1614 – *2

Pascal Pillarella, #202, 7925, boul Newman, H8N 2N9 – 514/364-3100, Fax: 514/364-1604 – *1

Roger Pilon, 89, av Giroux, H7N 3H3 – *1

Pinker & Associates, #2440, 2020, rue Université, H2A 2L4 – 514/849-4511, Fax: 514/849-1854 – *5

Marcel Plante, 6984, rue St-Denis, H1S 2S4 – 514/272-8217, Fax: 514/272-3823 – *5

Pollack Group, #600, 1210, rue Sherbrooke ouest, H3A 1H6 – 514/284-0864, Fax: 514/284-2968 – *1

Pollack, Machlovitch, Kravitz & Teitelbaum, #2640, 800, boul René-Lévesque ouest, H3B 1Y2 – 514/871-0205, Fax: 514/871-2809 – *6

Pouliot, Caron, Prévost, Bélisle, Galarneau, 300, av Leo-Pariseau, H2W 2N1 – 514/849-3787, Fax: 514/849-8085 – *6

Pouliot, Mercure, 1155, boul René-Lévesque ouest, 31e étage, H3B 3S6 – 514/875-5210, Fax: 514/875-4308 – *40

Poupart & Cournoyer, 3431, rue St-Hubert, H2L 3Z8 – 514/526-0861, Fax: 514/526-9646 – *5

Armand Poupart & Associés, 261, rue St-Jacques, H2Y 1M6 – 514/845-6126, Fax: 514/845-0320 – *2

Claude F. Proulx, #23, 460, rue St-Gabriel, H2Y 2Z9 – 514/395-9521, Fax: 514/392-1566 – *1

Racine, Perrault & Lussier, #407, 7575, rte Transcanadienne, H4T 1V6 – 514/331-8511, Fax: 514/321-0027 – *3

J.L. Ranger, Place Chaumont, 8676, av Chaumont, H1K 1N6 – 514/353-7529 – *1

Jacques Ranger, 5694, av Laurendeau, H4E 3W4 – 514/766-0756, Fax: 514/766-0756 – *1

Sylvain Rheault, #202, 4004, rue Wellington, H4G 1V3 – 514/765-0691 – *1

Alain Richard, #508, 10, rue St-Jacques, H1Y 1L3 – 514/288-2250 – *1

Simon Richter, 455, rue St-Antoine ouest, H1Z 1H9 – 514/866-2981, Fax: 514/866-2983 – *1

Pierre Riopel, 2418, rue Jolicoeur, H4E 1Y2 – 514/765-0014, Fax: 514/765-0831 – *7

Robert & Champagne, #810, 306, Place d'Youville, H1Y 2B6 – 514/845-0274, Fax: 514/845-9630 – *5

Pierre Robert, 2907, boul Pierre-Bernard, H1L 4R2 – 514/355-1214, Fax: 514/355-8657 – *1

Robinson Sheppard Shapiro, Tour Stock Exchange, #4700, 800, Place Victoria, CP 322, H4Z 1H6 – 514/878-2631, Fax: 514/878-1865 – *33

Rousseau, Gaudry, Labelle, #2736, 1, Place Ville-Marie, H3B 4G4 – 514/875-8243, Fax: 514/875-8801 – *3

Roy, Dagenais, Allen & Associés, #110, 1515, boul Chomedey, H7V 3Y7 – 514/686-0500, Fax: 514/337-2733 – *12

Marie Claude Roy, 935, boul St-Joseph est, H2J 1K7 – 514/272-2930, Fax: 514/272-3869 – *1

Isabelle Roy-Egan, 3285, rue Viel, H3M 1H8 – 514/334-4328, Fax: 514/956-9471 – *1

Leonard I. Sabloff & Associates, 6600, rte Trans-Canada, H9R 4S2 – 514/683-1502 – *2

Louise Saint-Amour, #3, 1375, rue Notre-Dame, H8S 2C9 – 514/634-8243, Fax: 514/634-1741 – *1

Normand Saint-Amour, 368, boul Henri-Bourassa est, H3L 1C3 – 514/382-0373, Fax: 514/383-7730 – *3

J.J.J. St. Michael, #660, 4141, rue Sherbrooke ouest, H3Z 1B8 – 514/935-5030, Fax: 514/935-3559 – *1

Johanne St. Pierre, #60, 1395, rue Fleury est, H2C 1R7 – 514/388-8922, Fax: 514/388-3672 – *1

Leo St. Pierre, 7110, av Somerled, H4V 1W1 – 514/488-4191 – *1

Sand & Associates, #1810, 1, Carré Westmount, H3Z 2P9 – 514/938-1056, Fax: 514/935-6098 – *1

Jean Saulnier, 7190, rue St-Denis, H2R 2E2 – 514/273-1525 – *1

Sauvé, Hébert, 1130, boul Cure-Labelle, H7V 3T7 – 514/687-2030 – *2

David I. Schatie, #200, 1255, av Greene, H3Z 2A4 – 514/935-7470, Fax: 514/937-6245 – *1

Schlesinger & Schlesinger, 1, Carré Westmount, 15e étage, H3Z 2P9 – 514/935-6226, Fax: 514/935-2314 – *3

Schnaiberg & Associates, 245, rue St-Jacques, 4e étage, H2Y 1M6 – 514/288-8717, Fax: 514/288-6646 – *2

Irwin Schnaiberg, #812, 1117, rue Ste-Catherine ouest, H3B 1H9 – 514/845-2143, Fax: 514/845-1057 – *1

Bernard K. Schneider, #3, 5365, av Victoria, H2J 2J5 – 514/736-1694, Fax: 514/736-1693 – *1

Howard Schnitzer, 2017, rue St-Hubert, H2L 3Z6 – 514/289-9549 – *1

Schratz, Wong & Melancon, 3614, av du Musée, H3G 2C9 – 514/289-9362 – *3

Norman Schwartz, #805, 1255, Carré Phillips, H3B 3G1 – 514/866-5507, Fax: 514/866-4101 – *1

Sciascia, Fargnoli, Corbeil, Poletto & Associates, #300, 7012, boul St-Laurent, H2S 3E2 – 514/272-0709 – *4

Sciascia, Iadeluca, Coulanges & Corbeil, #7206, 2125, rue Jean-Talon est, H2E 1V4 – 514/721-1474 – *5

Abraham Segal, #1110, 3500, boul de Maisonneuve ouest, H3Z 3C1 – 514/937-2222, Fax: 514/937-8729 – *1

Séguin & Prévost, 2316, rue Sherbrooke est, H2K 1E5 – 514/526-0821, Fax: 514/521-5397 – *4

Shaffer & Shaffer, #1200, 2075, rue University, H3A 2L1 – 514/842-5074, Fax: 514/842-3479 – *4

William P. Shaw, #311, 477, rue St-François-Xavier, H2Y 2T2 – 514/849-4525 – *1

Brian Sher, 772, rue Sherbrooke ouest, H3A 1G1 – 514/284-9551, Fax: 514/284-3419 – *1

Shriar, Polak, Cooperstone, #1500, 1, Carré Westmount, H3Z 2P9 – 514/935-6226, Fax: 514/935-2314 – *3

Silver, Braun et Avocats, #400, 510, boul St. Laurent, H1Y 2Y9 – 514/282-9112, Fax: 514/282-0600 – *8

Roger Simard, #1300, 777, rue Sherbrooke ouest, H3A 1G1 – 514/847-3557, Fax: 514/288-7389 – *1

Henri Simon, #500, 400, rue St-Jacques, H2Y 1S1 – 514/985-0995, Fax: 514/985-0944 – *2

Laizer Sirota, #504, 10, rue St-Jacques, H1Y 1L3 – 514/844-1123, Fax: 514/844-4071 – *1

Smart & Biggar, #3400, 1000, rue de la Gauchetière ouest, H3B 4W5 – 514/954-1500, Fax: 514/954-1396 – *4

Solomon & Solomon, 300, rue Leo-Pariseau, H1W 2N1 – 514/845-5239 – *2

Spector Seymour, #4, 1236, rue St-Mark, H3H 2E5 – 514/932-6941, Fax: 514/933-4236

Roland H. Sperlich, #200, 1980, rue Sherbrooke ouest, H3H 1E8 – 514/939-3273, Fax: 514/939-6394 – *1

Spiegel Sohmer, #1203, 5, Place Ville-Marie, H3B 2G2 – 514/875-2100, Fax: 514/875-8237 – *21

Sproule, Castonguay, Pollack, #2330, 1, Place Ville Marie, H3B 3M5 – 514/879-1737, Fax: 514/879-1733 – *13

A.H. Steckler, 5115, av de Gaspé, H1T 3B7 – 514/273-8891, Fax: 514/273-1576 – *1

Stern & Blumer, 300, av Leo-Pariseau, CP 983, H2W 2N1 – 514/842-1133, Fax: 514/842-3105 – *2

Sternthal Katznelson Montigny, Place du Canada, #1020, 1010, rue de la Gauchetière ouest, H3B 2N2 – 514/878-1011, Fax: 514/878-9195 – *12

Stikeman, Elliott, #3900, 1155, boul René-Lévesque ouest, H3B 3V2 – 514/397-3000, Fax: 514/397-3222 – *114

William Sullivan, #557, 555, boul René-Lévesque ouest, H2Z 1B1 – 514/397-1504, Fax: 514/397-1505 – *1

Hayk Sumbulian, #1610, 1350, rue Sherbrooke ouest, H3G 1J1 – 514/281-1955, Fax: 514/281-1956 – *1

Sweibel, Richter, Usher & Vineberg, 2, Place Alexis-Nihon, H3Z 3C2 – 514/934-3434, Fax: 514/934-3408 – *3

Rosalie Szewczuk, 4420, rue Ste-Catherine ouest, H3Z 1R2 – 514/933-4453, Fax: 514/934-3134 – *1

Taillefer, Sheitoyan, #737, 1801, av McGill College, H3A 2N4 – 514/288-3366 – *8

Charles Takefman, #402, 266, rue Notre-Dame ouest, H2Y 1T6 – 514/842-9662, Fax: 514/842-6808 – *1

Talbot & Clément-Talbot, 4519, rue St-Denis, H2J 2L4 – 514/849-2930, Fax: 514/982-0716 – *2

Talbot, Drapeau, #600, 2525, boul Daniel-Johnson, H7T 1S9 – 514/687-9660; 337-4540 – *5

Tannenbaum & Associates, #100, 203, Place d'Youville, H2Y 2B3 – 514/849-1221, Fax: 514/849-7992 – *6

Tanny & Fine, #110, 1253, av McGill College, H3B 2Y5 – 514/395-5800, Fax: 514/395-8847 – *2

Joanne Tasse, 935, rue St-Joseph est, H2J 1K7 – 514/272-2930, Fax: 514/272-3869 – *1

Tassé, Themens, 2421, rue Allard, H4E 2L3 – 514/769-9654, Fax: 514/769-7363 – *3

Tessier, Poupart & Coursol, 400, boul Curé Labelle, H7P 2P3 – 514/687-5883 – *4

Therrien, Plante, Vanasse, Trovencher, 4220, boul St-Martin ouest, H7T 1C1 – 514/687-7660, 331-1197, Fax: 514/687-7609 – *4

Pierre Thomas, #100, 245, rue St-Jacques, H2Y 1M6 – 514/849-5631, Fax: 514/282-1890 – *1

Toulch & Assoc., #406, 1117, rue St. Catherine ouest, H3B 1T9 – 514/849-1289, Fax: 514/849-3101 – *3

Toupin & Barrette, 1344, rue Jean-Talon est, H2E 1S1 – 514/278-5400, Fax: 514/278-7584 – *3

Pierre Tremblay, 7044, boul Pie IX, H1A 2G4 – 514/725-2411, Fax: 514/728-7783 – *1

Claude Trinque, #1202, 3030, boul Le Carrefour, H2W 2N1 – 514/688-7964, Fax: 514/688-7998 – *1

Trudeau, Provençal, Saint-Pierre & Côte, 7390, rue St-Denis, H2R 2E4 – 514/277-3138, Fax: 514/277-3318 – *4

Trudel, Nadeau, Lesage, Larivière & associés, CP 993, Succ Place du Parc, #2500, 300, av Leo-Pariseau, H2W 2N1 – 514/849-5754, Fax: 514/499-0312 – *28

Tsimberis, Philpot, Marion, CP 986, Succ Place du Parc, #2201, 300, av Leo-Pariseau, H2W 2N1 – 514/982-0144, Fax: 514/982-0149 – *4

Sergio Tucci, 201, rue St-Zotique est, H2S 1L2 – 514/271-0650, Fax: 514/270-2164 – *1

Turcotte, Nolet, Perras, #300, 1515, boul Chomedey, H7V 3Y7 – 514/681-1400, Fax: 514/681-2099 – *4
Unterberg, Labelle, Lebeau & Associés, #700, 1980, rue Sherbrooke ouest, H3H 1E8 – 514/934-0841, Fax: 514/937-6547 – *7
Yves Vaillancourt, #912, 10, rue St-Jacques, H2Y 1L3 – 514/842-1006, Fax: 514/842-1811 – *1
Angelo Velentzas, 1255, rue University, H3B 4A3 – 514/861-3742 – *1
Sergio Venneri, #200, 3556, rue Belair, H2A 2A9 – 514/727-0332, Fax: 514/727-9315 – *3
Villeneuve, Pigeon, Clément, Laurendeau & Herbert, #501, 235, boul René-Lévesque est, H2X 1N8 – 514/866-8674, Fax: 514/866-0092 – *6
Warren Baer, #1530, 1080, Côte du Beaver Hall, H2Z 1S8 – 514/875-4350, Fax: 514/875-9552 – *3
Mark Wener, #2440, 2020, rue University, H3A 2L4 – 514/849-4511, Fax: 514/849-1854 – *1
Wingender, Laplante, #925, 1200, boul Chomedey, H7Y 3L3 – 514/682-8000, Fax: 514/682-6099 – *1
Wiseman, Hamerman, #2720, 1155, boul René-Lévesque ouest, H3B 2K8 – 514/879-1208, Fax: 514/861-1632 – *2
Judah Lyon Wolofsky, #100, 388, rue St-Jacques, H2Y 1S1 – 514/849-1621, Fax: 514/849-1624 – *1
J.H. Woloshen, 1980, rue Sherbrooke ouest, 11e étage, H3H 1E8 – 514/939-4633, Fax: 514/939-2786 – *1
Yarosky, Daviault, La Haye, Stober & Isaacs, #2536, 800, boul René-Lévesque ouest, H3B 1X9 – 514/878-3505, Fax: 514/861-3065 – *7
Joyce Yedid, 2017, rue St-Hubert, H2L 3Z6 – 514/522-6515, Fax: 514/522-9952 – *2
Allan Zilbert, #805, 1255, Carré Phillips, H3B 3G1 – 514/866-5507, Fax: 514/866-4101 – *1
Zimmerman & Blitt, #410, 345, av Victoria, H3Z 2N2 – 514/483-2444, Fax: 514/483-2477 – *2

QUEBEC .... Québec
Aubut Chabot, #600, 900, boul René-Lévesque est, CP 910, G1R 4T4 – 418/524-5131, Fax: 418/524-1717; Email: aubuchab@microtec.net – *14
Henri Beaudry, C.R., #300, 105, Côte de la Montagne, G1K 7A1 – 418/692-0160 – *3
Bernatchez, Robitaille & Associés, #310, 400, boul Jean-Lesage, G1K 8W1 – 418/648-0456, Fax: 418/648-9587 – *5
Boutin, Roy, & Associés, #444, 2, rue des Jardins, G1R 4S9 – 418/691-6360, Fax: 418/691-7622 – *9
DeBlois, Gauthier, Samson, #315, 2, Place Québec, G1R 2B5 – 418/529-1784, Fax: 418/529-6077 – *9
Des Rivieres & Vermette, #701, 71, rue St-Pierre, CP 245, Succ B, G1K 7A9 – 418/692-0616, Fax: 418/692-0689 – *10
Desjardins Ducharme Stein Monast, #300, 1150, rue de Claire-Fontaine, G1R 5G4 – 418/529-6531, Fax: 418/523-5391 – *30
Desjardins Ducharme Stein Monast, #300, 1150, rue de Claire-Fontaine, G1R 5G4
Gagné, Letarte, Sirois, Beaudet, #400, 79, boul René-Lévesque est, G1R 5N5 – 418/522-7900, Fax: 418/523-7900 – *18
Grondin, Poudrier, Bernier, #200, 801, ch St-Louis, G1S 1C1 – 418/683-3000, Fax: 418/683-8784 – *41
La société d'avocats Garneau, Turgeon, Verdon, 67, rue Ste-Ursule, G1R 4E7 – 418/692-3010, Fax: 418/692-1742 – *6
Labrie & Bellemare, 1247, rue St-Joseph-Vezina, G1T 2L1 – 418/688-4367 – *2
Langlois Robert, Édifice Mérici, #160, 801, ch St-Louis, G1S 1C1 – 418/682-1212, Fax: 418/682-2272 – *19
Lavery, de Billy, #800, 925, ch St-Louis, G9S 1C1 – 418/688-8000, Fax: 418/688-3458
Levasseur, Fréchette, #200, 1150, rue de Claire-Fontaine, G1R 5G4 – 418/647-1713, Fax: 418/647-3006 – *7
Mailhot, Drapeau, #7, 250, Grande Allée ouest, G1R 2H4 – 418/647-2121 – *2
Marquis, Huot Société d'Avocats, #102, 500, Grande Allée est, G1R 2J7 – 418/522-2701, Fax: 418/649-0097 – *9
Martineau, Walker, a/s Fasken Martineau, Immeuble le Saint-Patrick, #800, 140, Grande Allée est, G1R 5M8 – 418/640-2000, Fax: 418/647-2455; Ligne sans frais: 1-800-463-2827 – *13
McCarthy Tétrault, Le Complexe St-Amable, #700, 1150, rue de Claire-Fontaine, G1R 5G4 – 418/521-3000, Fax: 418/521-3099 – *10
Pierre Montreuil, #13, 860, av Marguerite Bourgeois, G1S 3W9 – 418/683-9966 – *1
Néron, Trudel & Associés, #204, 771, boul St-Joseph est, G1K 3C7 – 418/647-4260, Fax: 418/647-1425 – *5
Gilbert-M. Noreau, 689, Grande Allée est, G1R 2K4 – 418/524-5251, Fax: 418/524-0272 – *1
O'Brien, #420, 500, Grande Allée est, G1R 2J7 – 418/648-1511, Fax: 418/648-9335 – *5
Ogilvy Renault, #520, 500, Grande Allée est, G1R 2J7 – 418/640-5000, Fax: 418/640-1500 – *16
Savard, Nadeau, Kallis & Associates, 838, St-Joachim, G1R 1X1 – 418/648-9771, Fax: 418/648-2778 – *7
Trudel, Nadeau, Lesage, Larivière & associés, #300, 5000, boul des Gradins, G2J 1N3 – 418/623-0610, Fax: 418/622-7000 – *8
Vaillancourt, St-Pierre, #410, 3075, ch des Quatre-Bourgeois, G1W 4Y9 – 418/657-6789, Fax: 418/658-7454 – *4

RIMOUSKI .... Rimouski
Biron, Dolbec & Lacroix, 9, rue Jules-A. Brillant, G5L 1W7 – 418/722-5587, Fax: 418/722-5949 – *3
Casgrain, Blanchet, Gagnon & Desrosiers, Edifice Trust General, #400, 2, boul St-Germain est, CP 580, G5L 7C6 – 418/723-3302 – *6
Marc, Doucet, 205, rue de la Cathédrale, G5L 5G1 – 418/724-3125, Fax: 418/724-3180 – *1
Norman Dumais, 165, av Belzile, CP 998, G5L 7E1 – 418/723-3179, Fax: 418/723-3195 – *1
Gendreau & Beaulieu, 41, rue de l'Évèché ouest, CP 8, G5L 7C9 – 418/724-4416 – *5
J.H. Roy, #200, 162, av de la Cathédrale, CP 416, G5L 7C3 – 418/723-0434, Fax: 418/723-9432 – *1

RIVIERE-DU-LOUP .... Kamouraska
Rioux Bosse Masse & Associés, 12, rue de la Cour, CP 487, G5R 3Z1 – 418/862-3565 – *6

SEPT-ILES .... Mingan
Caron, Coté, Paradis, Bibeau, Desmarais, #72, 690, boul Laure, G4R 4N8 – 418/968-1140 – *7
de Pokomandy, Besnier & Parvu, Dion, 865, boul Laure, G4R 1Y6 – 418/962-9775 – *5
Desrosiers & Ricard, 512, av Brochu, G4R 2X3 – 418/962-7392, Fax: 418/962-6100 – *2
Gauthier, Nepveu, Leblanc & Brouillette, 1, Place Mingan, G4R 4L8 – *6
Landry, Savard & Lynch, #210, 390, av Brochu, G4R 2W6 – 418/962-7575 – *3

SHERBROOKE .... St-François
Pierre Belhumeur, #101, 380, rue King ouest, J1H 1R4 – 819/566-1676, Fax: 819/563-7734 – *1
Gerard G. Boudreau, 92, rue Wellington nord, J1H 5B8 – 819/562-0848 – *1
Delorme, Bessette, #201, 225, rue King ouest, J1H 1P8 – 819/566-6222, Fax: 819/566-4331 – *14
Demers Bureau Borduas, #400, 455, rue King ouest, J1H 6E9 – 819/569-9056, Fax: 819/569-1259 – *9
Gervais Dube, 144, rue Wellington nord, J1H 5B7 – 819/563-0333, Fax: 819/563-0155 – *1
Grenier, Martel & Company, #110, 337, rue Dufferin, J1H 4M6 – 819/563-0334, Fax: 819/563-5434 – *3
Hackett, Campbell, Bouchard, 80, rue Peel, J1H 4K1 – 819/565-7885, Fax: 819/566-0888 – *6
Huard, Théroux & Associés, 191, rue Palais, CP 610, J1H 4R1 – 819/821-5700, Fax: 819/822-6064 – *5
Lamoureux, Roland, 520, rue Bowen, J1G 2E1 – 819/563-0500 – *2
Monty, Coulombe, #200, 234, rue Dufferin, J1H 4M2 – 819/566-4466, Fax: 819/565-2891 – *24

SILLERY .... Québec
Boivin, Hamel, #200, 1330, av Maguire, G1T 1Z3 – 418/681-0693, Fax: 418/681-5121 – *2
Dumas, Gagne, Mercier & Associés, 1965, rue St-Michel, G1S 1J7 – 418/527-9516, Fax: 418/527-3246 – *4
Fortin Dignard Reny Fiset, #200, 1091, ch St-Louis, CP 3425, G1S 1E2 – 418/683-1177, Fax: 418/683-1224 – *4
Hickson, Martin & Blanchard, 1170, ch St-Louis, G1S 1E5 – 418/681-9671, Fax: 418/527-6938; Email: hmb@rtq.qc.ca – *20

SOREL .... Richelieu
Jacques Guertin & Associés, #1, 50, rue du Roie, J3P 4M7 – 514/743-9719, Fax: 514/743-4074 – *2

ST-EUSTACHE .... Terrebonne
Saulnier, Leroux & associés, #5070, 430, boul Arthur Sauvé, J7R 6V6 – 514/472-0031, Fax: 514/472-7910 – *4

ST-GEORGES .... Beauce
Flynn, Rivard Avocats, #410, 11505, av 1re ouest, G5Y 7X3 – 418/228-2074, Fax: 418/228-6016 – *2

ST-HILAIRE .... St-Hyacinthe
Edith Des Lauriers, 721, rue P.E. Borduas, J3H 4W7 – 514/446-7055, Fax: 514/446-2497 – *1

ST-HYACINTHE .... St-Hyacinthe
Brodeur & Boileau, 1700, rue Girouard ouest, J2S 3A1 – 514/773-8566, Fax: 514/778-3749 – *3
Gerald Locas, 975, boul du Palais, J2S 5C6 – 514/773-2514 – *1
Diane Poirier, 1600, rue Girouard ouest, 3e étage, J2S 2Z8 – 514/773-5176, Fax: 514/773-6788 – *1
Sylvestre & Associés, #236, 1600, rue Girouard ouest, J2S 2Z8 – 514/773-8445, Fax: 514/773-2112 – *5

ST-JEAN-SUR-RICHELIEU .... Iberville
Bédard, Lord, 188, rue Longueuil, J3B 6P1 – 514/347-8220, Fax: 514/347-3693 – *2
Jacques Cartier, 215, rue Jacques-Cartier nord, J3B 6T3 – 514/346-6817 – *1
Gregoire, Lanthier Avocats, 123, rue St-Jacques, J3B 2K2 – 514/347-5511, Fax: 514/346-3483 – *2
Paradis, Paradis, #302, 200, rue Macdonald, J3B 8J6 – 514/359-8100, Fax: 514/359-8027 – *5
Roland Tremblay, Q.C., 220, rue Longueuil, J3B 6P4 – 514/347-5531; 658-4511, Fax: 514/358-9915 – *1

ST-JEROME .... Terrebonne
Boismenu & Racicot, #200, 395, rue Laviolette, J7Y 2P2 – 514/432-4331, Fax: 514/432-4331 – *3
Filfe, Paquin, Filion, Laure & Laferriere, 316, rue St-Georges, J7Z 5A5 – *5
Levac & Cotte-Levac, 474, rue Laviolette, J7Y 2T7 – 514/432-3274 – *2
Lord, Lalonde, Gendron & Riendeau, 450, rue Laviolette, J7Y 2T7 – *4
Morin, Perras et La Rue, #200, 30A, rue Legault, J7Z 2B8 – 514/436-8166, Fax: 514/436-6321 – *3
Prévost, Auclair, Fortin & D'Aoust, #400, 55, rue Castonguay, J7Y 2H9 – 514/436-8244, Fax: 514/436-9735 – *17
Ross & Geraghty, #102, 480, rue St-Georges, J7Z 5B4 – 514/436-8022 – *5

ST-LAMBERT .... Longueuil
Paul Joffe, 360, av Putney, J4P 3B6 – 514/465-3654, Fax: 514/465-5730 – *1

* indicates number of lawyers in law firm.

Edmond D. Pinsonnault, 130, av de Normandie, J4S 1K1 – 514/671-0916 – *1
Luc Racicot, 439, rue Notre-Dame, J4P 2K5 – 514/466-6633, Fax: 514/466-7315 – *1

ST-ROMUALD... Québec
Huguette Gagnon, 1779, ch du Fleuve, G6W 1Z6 – 418/839-2045, Fax: 418/839-2061 – *1

STE-AGATHE-DES-MONTS....................... Terrebonne
Paul Gelinas, Q.C., 45, rue St-Antoine, J8C 2C4 – 819/326-4221, Fax: 819/326-6272 – *1

STE-FOY.. Québec
Brisset des Nos, Gravel, Lévesque, Normand, Rioux, #107, 3350, rue de la Pérade, G1X 2L7 – 418/656-1313, Fax: 418/652-1844 – *5
Brochet, Dussault & Associés, #450, 2795, boul Laurier, G1V 4M7 – 418/657-2424, Fax: 418/657-1793 – *8
Dergerom, Saindon & Trembley, 2750, ch Ste-Foy, G1V 1V6 – 418/651-5901, Fax: 418/651-7467 – *2
Jolin, Fournier, Morisset, Place Iberville Trois, #500, 2960, boul Laurier, G1V 4S1 – 418/651-1900, Fax: 418/651-7410 – *25
Pothier Delisle, #400, 3075, ch des Quatre-Bourgeois, G1W 4X5 – 418/651-9900, Fax: 418/651-5184 – *29
Tremblay, Bois, Mignault & Lemay, Iberville Un, #200, 1195, av Lavigerie, G1V 4N3 – 418/658-9966, Fax: 418/658-6100; Email: avocats@riq.qc.ca – *27
Vézina, Pouliot, Tour des Laurentides, 2525, boul Laurier, 10e étage, G1V 2L2 – 418/658-1080, Fax: 418/658-1414 – *23

STE-MARIE.. Beauce
Sylvain, Parent, Gobeil, 225, rue du College, CP 40, G6E 3B4 – 418/387-2727, Fax: 418/387-7070 – *4

STE-THERESE-DE-BLAINVILLE .... Terrebonne
Brazeau, Grégoire, 72, rue Blainville ouest, J7E 1X3 – 514/430-1530, Fax: 514/430-3607 – *3

THETFORD MINES................................... Frontenac
Gosselin, Ouellette, Grondin, Houle, 163, rue Pie XI, CP 667, G6G 5V1 – 418/335-9151, Fax: 418/338-4874 – *4
Warren & Ouellet, 108, rue Notre-Dame sud, CP 714, G6G 5V1 – 418/338-3191, Fax: 418/338-5267 – *3

TROIS-RIVIERES.................................. Trois Riviéres
Ayotte, Mallette, Gamache, St-Hilaire & Roy, #603, 1350, rue Royale, G9A 5H5 – 819/379-3766 – *1
Beaumier, Richard, 90, rue des Casernes, CP 365, G9A 5G9 – 819/379-1221, Fax: 819/371-1214 – *6
Biron & Spain, 154, rue Radisson, G9A 2C3 – 819/375-4187, Fax: 819/375-7395 – *3
Jacques Desaulniers, 543, boul Laviolette, 2e étage, G9A 1V4 – 819/378-3717, Fax: 819/375-2462 – *1
Godin & Saint-Amant, 190, rue Bonaventure, CP 1474, G9A 5L6 – 819/379-5225, Fax: 819/379-4545 – *3
Heenan Blaikie, #360, 1500, boul Royal, CP 1900, G9A 6E6 – 819/373-7000, Fax: 819/373-0943
Louis Henaire, 983, rue Hart, CP 1745, G9A 5M4 – 819/379-3355, Fax: 819/379-1227 – *2
Lajoie, Roy, Lambert & Associés, 1350, boul Royal, G9A 5N6 – 819/376-9213 – *8
Pierre Marchand, 1637, rue des Forges, G8Z 1T7 – 819/378-3535 – *1
Pierre Soucy, #212, 3550, rue Cherbourg, G8Y 6S6 – 819/379-0307, Fax: 819/378-9586 – *1

VAL-D'OR... Abitibi
Cliche & Cliche, 1121, rue 6e, CP 460, J9P 4P5 – 819/825-3010, Fax: 819/825-7375 – *10
St-Julien, Bigué, #202, 855, av 3e, CP 520, J9P 4P5 – 819/825-4153, Fax: 819/825-9769 – *4
Denis Tousignant, 1218, rue 6e, CP 969, J9P 4P8 – *1

VALLEYFIELD.. Beauharnois
Blanchard, Plante, Bourbonnais & Gaulin, 70, rue Nicholson, J6T 4N2 – 514/373-1414, Fax: 514/373-6833 – *8
Brassard & Gaulin, 50, rue Jacques-Cartier, J6T 4R3 – 514/371-4320 – *1
Lecompte, Drouin & Assoociés, 151, rue Salaberry St., G6T 2H8 – 514/371-6066, Fax: 514/371-5139 – *4
Massé, Gingras, Robert & Toulouse, 145, rue Salaberry, J6T 2H8 – 905/371-4266 – *4
Rancourt, Legault, Boucher & Godbout, 175, rue Salaberry, J6T 2J1 – 514/371-2221, Fax: 514/371-2094 – *4
Vachon & Martin, 72, rue de Montcalm, J6T 2C9 – 514/371-7771 – *2

VARENNES... Richelieu
Desjardins, Lessard, 1950, boul René Gaultier, J0L 2P0 – 514/652-2957, Fax: 514/652-3484 – *2

VAUDREUIL... Beauharnois
René Boucher, 382, boul Roche, J7V 2M6 – 514/455-3943 – *1

VICTORIAVILLE...................................... Arthabaska
Caron, Dubois & Associes, 268, boul Bois Francs nord, G6P 1G5 – 819/758-8251, Fax: 819/752-4520 – *4
Provencher, Coté & Garneau, 42, boul Carignan, G6P 4Z6 – 819/758-0529 – *3

VILLE DE LA BAIE.................................. Saguenay
Aubin, Bédard et Associés, 1262, 6e av, G7B 1R4 – 418/544-6845

SASKATCHEWAN

ALAMEDA.. Estevan
McLellan, Cundall, Bridges & Baumgartner, 115 Fifth St., S0C 0A0 – 306/489-2216, Fax: 306/489-4602

ASSINIBOIA.. Assiniboia
Lewans & Associates, 228 Centre St., PO Box 759, S0H 0B0 – 306/642-4520, Fax: 306/642-5777 – *2
Marlin Law Office, 105 - 2 Ave. East, PO Box 1088, S0H 0B0 – 306/642-3933, Fax: 306/642-3933 – *1
Mountain & Mountain, 101 - 4 Ave. West, PO Box 459, S0H 0B0 – 306/642-3866, Fax: 306/642-5848; Email: lee.mountain@sk.sympatico.ca – *2

BENGOUGH.. Assiniboia
Mountain & Mountain, PO Box 40, S0C 0K0 – 306/268-2825, 642-3866 – *2

BIGGAR... Battleford
Stuart A. Busse Q.C., Credit Union Bldg., 302 Main St., PO Box 669, S0K 0M0 – 306/948-3346, Fax: 306/948-3366 – *2

BIRCH HILLS..................................... Prince Albert
Mills & Zuk, PO Box 790, S0J 0G0 – 306/922-4700

BROADVIEW.. Melville
Gary G. Moore, PO Box 610, S0G 0K0 – 306/696-2454 – *1

BROWNLEE... Moose Jaw
Frederick R.C. Rawlings, PO Box 70, S0H 0M0 – 306/759-2621 – *1

CANORA.. Yorkton
Peet Law Firm, 106 First Ave. East, PO Box 1298, S0A 0L0 – 306/563-5200, Fax: 306/547-5590

CARLYLE...
McLellan, Cundall, Bridges & Baumgartner, Falco Place Bldg., 205 Main St., S0C 0R0 – 306/453-2252, Fax: 306/634-9995

CARNDUFF..
McLellan, Cundall, Bridges & Baumgartner, 1 Street West, S0C 0S0 – 306/482-3282, Fax: 306/482-3669

CARROT RIVER..................................... Melfort
Irwin B. Carson, PO Box 98, S0E 0L0 – 306/768-3411 – *1

CUPAR.. Regina
Pedersen, Norman, McLeod & Todd, 210 Stanley, S0G 0Y0 – 306/723-4213, Fax: 306/723-4201

EASTEND... Shaunavon
Benison Law Office, 302 Redcoat Dr., S0N 0T0 – 306/295-3250

ESTERHAZY.. Melville
MacKenzie & MacKenzie, 500 Maple St., S0A 0X0 – 306/745-3952 – *2

ESTEVAN.. Estevan
Chicoine, Billesberger & Grimsrud, 403 - 9th Ave., S4A 2L7 – 306/634-5644, Fax: 306/634-8610 – *3
Ignatiuk Law Offices, PO Box 460, S4A 2A4 – 306/634-6477 – *2
Kohaly & Elash, Drawer 580, S4A 2A5 – 306/634-3631, Fax: 306/634-6901 – *4
Komarnicki & Orlowski, #305, 1133 - 4 St., PO Box 725, S4A 2A6 – 306/634-2616, Fax: 306/634-9881 – *2
McLellan, Cundall, Bridges & Baumgartner, 1138 Third St., PO Box 609, S4A 2A5 – 306/634-2673, Fax: 306/634-9995 – *7
Merchant Law Group, Estevan-Weyburn, 305 Main St., S0G 4T0 – 306/634-9777

ESTON... Kerrobert
Hughes Law Office, PO Box 729, S0L 1A0 – 306/962-4111, Fax: 306/962-3302 – *1

FOAM LAKE.. Wynyard
Owen Klebeck, 412 Main St., PO Box 779, S0A 1A0 – 306/272-4330, Fax: 306/272-4330

FORT QU'APPELLE................................. Melville
Niel Halford, PO Box 817, S0G 1S0 – 306/332-5661 – *1
Pedersen, Norman, McLeod & Todd, 140 Braodway, S0G 1S0 – 306/332-5269

GOVAN.. Regina
Pedersen, Norman, McLeod & Todd, 124 Elgin, S0G 1Z0 – 306/484-2177, Fax: 306/484-4333

GRAVELBOURG.................................... Gravelbourg
Guy J. Dauphinais, PO Box 480, S0H 1X0 – 306/648-3325 – *1
Louis E. Stringer, PO Box 927, S0H 1X0 – 306/648-2582 – *1

HUDSON BAY...................................... Melfort
S.J. Nesdoly, PO Box 968, S0E 0Y0 – 306/865-2775 – *1

HUMBOLDT.. Humboldt
Holt, Munkler & Halderman, 607 - 9 St., PO Box 1510, S0K 2A0 – 306/682-2516, Fax: 306/682-5053 – *3
Sutherland, Behiel & Wil, 602 - 9 St., PO Box 878, S0K 2A0 – 306/682-2642, Fax: 306/682-5165; Email: sbw@sk.sympatico.ca – *2

INDIAN HEAD.................................... Regina
Kraus McKay Pederson, General Delivery, S0G 2K0 – 306/761-6226, Fax: 306/761-6222 – *2

KAMSACK . . . . Yorkton
Rosowsky & Campbell, 445 - 2 St., S0A 1S0 – 306/542-2646, Fax: 306/542-2510 – *2

KELVINGTON . . . . Wynyard
Bertram, Scrivens & Prior, PO Box 220, S0A 1W0 – 306/327-5111, Fax: 306/327-4765 – *3
Peet Law Firm, #5, 201 Main St., S0A 1W0 – 306/327-4343, Fax: 306/547-5590

KINDERSLEY . . . . Kerrobert
Anderson, Nimegeers, Walter, Gibbings, Ryan, Froslee & Keene, S0L 1S0
Roberts & Company, 115 - 1 Ave. East., PO Box 1510, S0L 1S0 – 306/463-4647, Fax: 306/463-6133 – *3
Monte J. Sheppard, Bldg Box: 1567, 207 Main St., PO Box 1567, S0L 1S0 – 306/463-2035, Fax: 306/463-6270 – *1

LAMPMAN . . . . Estevan
Chicoine & Billesberger, PO Box 40, S0C 1N0 – 306/487-2880, Fax: 306/634-8610

LLOYDMINSTER . . . . Battleford
Clements & Wells, #203, 5101 - 48 St., PO Box 440, S9V 0Y4 – 403/875-7999 – *2
Johnston, Bennett, 5105 - 49 St., S9V 0Y6 – 403/875-9105, Fax: 403/875-6748 – *3
S.L. Lonsdale, 5009 - 48 St., PO Box 1248, S9V 1G1 – 403/875-5185, Fax: 403/875-6547 – *1

MAPLE CREEK . . . . Swift Current
McLaughlin, Forrester, Heinrichs, 42 Pacific Ave., S0N 1N0 – 306/662-2744
W.R. Orr, PO Box 608, S0N 1N0 – 306/662-2282, Fax: 306/662-2111 – *1

MEADOW LAKE . . . . Battleford
Cariou, Partyka & Francis, 306 Centre St., PO Box 939, S0M 1V0 – 306/236-5648, Fax: 306/236-3660 – *3

MELFORT . . . . Melfort
Annand Law Office, 208 Main St., PO Box 69, S0E 1A0 – 306/752-2707, Fax: 306/752-4484 – *1
Carson & Co., Bldg Box: 1600, 803 Main St., S0E 1A0 – 306/752-5781, Fax: 306/752-4797 – *3
Eisner Mahon Burningham, 101 McLeod West, PO Box 2680, S0E 1A0 – 306/752-2832, Fax: 306/752-4399 – *4
Kapoor Selnes Klimm & Brown, PO Box 2200, S0E 1A0 – 306/752-5777, Fax: 306/752-2712 – *4
Ronald Price-Jones, #3 Highway East, PO Box 129, S0E 1A0 – 306/752-5701, Fax: 306/752-2444 – *1

MELVILLE . . . . Melville
Ozirny, Fisher, Bell & Matthews, Triton Pl., 147 - 3 Ave. East, S0A 2P0 – 306/728-5468, Fax: 306/728-4444 – *5

MIDALE . . . . Estevan
Chicoine & Billesberger, S0C 1S0 – 306/458-2277

MOOSE JAW . . . . Moose Jaw
Murray D. Acton, 330 Main St. North, S6H 3J9 – 306/694-0052, Fax: 306/691-0445 – *1
Chow & MacLowich, 113 High St. West, PO Box 160, S6H 4N8 – 306/693-7536, Fax: 306/693-6444 – *3
Dickinson, Ansell & Zimmer, Hammond Bldg, #414, 310 Main St. North, S6H 3K1 – 306/692-4124, Fax: 306/692-7718 – *2
Grayson & Company, 350 Langdon Cres., PO Box 908, S6H 4P6 – 306/693-6176, Fax: 306/693-1515 – *7
Merchant Law Group, 53 Stadacona West, S6H 1Z2 – 306/693-7777
Terrance Ocrane Law Office, #106, 12 High St. East, S6H 0B9 – 306/694-4922, Fax: 306/692-6386; Email: terrance.ocrane@sk.sympatico.ca – *1

Whittaker, Craik, Chow & MacLowich, 109 Ominica St. West, PO Box 1178, S6H 4P9 – 306/694-4677, Fax: 306/694-5747 – *4

MOOSOMIN . . . . Souris/Moose Mtn.
Olive, Waller, Zinkhan & Waller, 714 Main St., 2nd Fl., S0G 3N0 – 306/435-2131
Osman, Gardner, Gordon, Bldg Box: 280, 626 Carleton St., PO Box 280, S0G 3N0 – 306/435-3851, Fax: 306/435-3962 – *3

NIPAWIN . . . . Melfort
Carson Law Office, 116 - 1 Ave. East, PO Box 1983, S0E 1E0 – 306/862-9807 – *2

NORTH BATTLEFORD . . . . Battleford
Cawood-Walker, #201, 1291 - 102 St., PO Box 905, S9A 2Z3 – 306/445-6177, Fax: 306/445-7076 – *5
David Conroy, #101, 1351 - 101 St., S9A 0Z9 – 306/445-3613, Fax: 306/445-9088 – *1
Lojek, Jones & Hudec, 10211 - 12 Ave., PO Box 1179, S9A 3K2 – 306/446-2211, Fax: 306/446-3022 – *4
Maher, Lindgren, Blais & Frank, 1301 - 101 St., PO Box 940, S9A 2Z3 – 306/445-2422, Fax: 306/445-2313 – *6
Wilhelm Migneault Gibbons Greenwood, PO Box 520, S9A 2Y8 – 306/445-4436, 8151, Fax: 306/445-6444 – *5

OUTLOOK . . . . Saskatoon
Clark Law Office, 109 Saskatchewan Ave., PO Box 1040, S0L 2N0 – 306/867-8655 – *1

OXBOW . . . . Estevan
Chicoine & Billesberger, S0C 2B0 – 306/483-2721
McLellan, Cundall, Bridges & Baumgartner, 408 Main St., S0C 2B0 – 306/483-2250, Fax: 306/483-2302

PORCUPINE PLAIN . . . . Melfort
Kapoor, Selnes, Klimm, Schnell & Brown, McAlister Ave., S0E 1H0 – 306/278-2230

PREECEVILLE . . . . Yorkton
Peet Law Firm, 17 First Ave. NW, PO Box 1210, S0A 3B0 – 306/547-3322, Fax: 306/547-5590 – *1

PRINCE ALBERT . . . . Prince Albert
Balicki, Popescul, Forsyth & Neudorf, #200, 110 - 11 St. East, S6V 1A1 – 306/764-2222, Fax: 306/764-2221 – *4
Balon Krishan Law Firm, 1335B - 2nd Ave. West, S6V 5B2 – 306/922-5151, Fax: 306/763-1755 – *2
Balon, Krishan, 1335B - 2 Ave. West, S6V 5B2 – 306/922-5151, Fax: 306/763-1755 – *3
Cherkewich, Yost & Heffernan, 1005 Central Ave., S6V 4V4 – 306/764-1537, Fax: 306/763-0505 – *4
Delbert M. Dynna, 100A - 10 St. East, S6V 0Y7 – 306/764-6856 – *1
Eggum, Abrametz & Stewart, 88 - 13 St. East, S6V 1C6 – 306/763-7441, Fax: 306/764-2882 – *4
Harradence, Longworth, Logue & Harradence, 1102 - 1 Ave. West, PO Box 2080, S6V 6V4 – 306/764-4244, Fax: 306/764-4949; Toll Free: 1-800-661-6690 – *4
Loewen & Bell, #21, 969 - 1 Ave. East, PO Box 520, S6V 5R8 – 306/922-0212, Fax: 306/922-2422 – *2
Mills, Wilcox, Zuk , 20 - 12 St. West, S6V 3B3 – 306/922-4700, Fax: 306/922-0633 – *3
Pandila Morin, 15 - 15 St. West, S6V 3P4 – 306/764-2720, Fax: 306/763-8096 – *3
Pandila Morin, Opawikoscikan Reserve #201, PO Box 2890, S6V 7M4 – 306/764-2715, Fax: 306/763-8095
Leo Pinel, 1100 - 1 Ave. East, S6V 2A7 – 306/763-1300 – *1
Philip E. West, Q.C., 1109 Central Ave., S6V 4V7 – 306/763-7467, Fax: 306/763-7469 – *2
Wilcox, MacLean, 706 - 15 Ave. East, S6V 7A4 – 306/922-4277, Fax: 306/763-4479 – *2
Zatlyn, Holash, 25 - 11 St. East, S6V 0Z8 – 306/922-1444, Fax: 306/922-5848 – *3

QUINTON . . . . Mackenzie
Don Worme, Kawacatoose Reserve, PO Box 127, S0G 3G0

REDVERS . . . . Moosomin
Osman, Gardner, Gordon, 38 Railways Ave., S0C 2H0 – 306/452-3445

REGINA . . . . Regina
Andrews, Butler & Associates, #201, 1771 Rose St., S4P 1Z4 – 306/525-8136, Fax: 306/525-3318 – *2
Balfour Moss, #700, 2103 - 11th Ave., S4P 4G1 – 306/347-8300, Fax: 306/347-8350; Email: balfourmoss.regina@eagle.wbm.ca; URL: http://saskweb.com/~balfourmoss – *20
Robert M. Barr, #116, 1765 Hamilton St., S4P 2B4 – 306/352-4565 – *2
Bertram, Scrivens, Prior & Stradecki, #1730, 2002 Victoria Ave., S4P 0R7 – 306/525-2737, Fax: 306/565-3244 – *5
Cuelenaere, Hunter, Miller, #600, 2500 Victoria Ave., S4R 1A6 – 306/525-6103, Fax: 306/565-8806 – *4
Dahlem, Findlay & von Ledebur, 2100 Smith St., S4P 2P2 – 306/522-3631, Fax: 306/565-2616 – *3
Gates & Company, 3132 Avonhurst Dr., S4R 3J7 – 306/949-5544, Fax: 306/775-2995 – *7
Gauley & Co., #400, 2201 - 11 Ave., S4P 0J8 – 306/352-1643, Fax: 306/525-8499 – *3
Gerrand Mulatz, Toronto Dominion Bank Bldg., #701, 1914 Hamilton St., S4P 3N6 – 306/525-3561, Fax: 306/781-8150 – *7
Gritzfeld & Associates, #801, 1867 Hamilton St., S4P 2C2 – 306/757-1601, Fax: 306/757-8017 – *2
John L. Harms, 2550 Reynolds St., S4N 3N9 – 306/352-0865 – *1
Hleck Kanuka Thuringer, North Canadian Oils Bldg., #1400, 2500 Victoria Ave., S4P 3X2 – 306/525-7200, Fax: 306/359-0590 – *23
Elaine Husk, 2269 Hamilton St., S4P 2E7 – 306/525-8311, Fax: 306/565-2766 – *1
Kraus McKay Pederson, #400, 1900 Albert St., S4P 4K8 – 306/761-6200, Fax: 306/761-6222 – *10
M.A. Kuziak, 1872 Angus St., S4T 1Z5 – 306/757-0154 – *1
Leier Law Office, 230 Doiron Rd., S4Y 1G4 – 306/543-7000, Fax: 306/543-9022 – *1
Leslie, Shirkey, Laurin, 2731 - 13 Ave., PO Box 4, S4P 3Y3 – 306/525-8176, Fax: 306/525-3337 – *3
MacKay & McLean, #124, 2001 Cornwall St., S4P 2K6 – 306/569-1301, Fax: 306/569-8560 – *2
MacLean Keith, Nicol Ct., 2398 Scarth St., S4P 2J7 – 306/757-1611, Fax: 306/757-0712
MacPherson Leslie & Tyerman, #1500, 1874 Scarth St., S4P 4E9 – 306/347-8000 – *30
McDougall, Ready, Royal Bank Bldg., #700, 2010 - 11 Ave., S4P 0J3 – 306/757-1641, Fax: 306/359-0785 – *28
McKercher McKercher & Whitmore, #1000, 1783 Hamilton St., S4P 2B6 – 306/352-7661, Fax: 306/781-7113 – *7
Merchant Law Group, Saskatchewan Drive Plaza, #100, 2401 Saskatchewan Dr., S4P 4H8 – 306/359-7777, Fax: 306/522-3299 – *28
Morgan, Khaladkar & Skinner, 2510 - 13 Ave., S4P 0W2 – 306/525-9191, Fax: 306/525-0006 – *4
Murphy & Murphy, #401, 1900 Albert St., S4P 4K8 – 306/757-1656, Fax: 306/347-7931 – *4
Olive, Waller, Zinkhan & Waller, 2255 - 13 Ave., S4P 0V6 – 306/359-1888, Fax: 306/352-0771 – *15
Pedersen, Norman, McLeod & Todd, Bank of Canada Building, #500, 2220 - 12 Ave., PO Box 1037, S4P 3B2 – 306/565-4100, Fax: 306/757-4858 – *14
Phillips & Milen, 2343 Broad St., S4P 1Y9 – 306/569-0811, Fax: 306/565-3434 – *3
Randall, McCannell & Wellsch, #300, 2445 - 13 Ave., S4P 0W1 – 306/569-1530, Fax: 306/569-0121 – *3
Rath Johnson Hart, #1101, 1867 Hamilton St., S4P 2C2 – 306/757-8571, Fax: 306/757-8017 – *7

* indicates number of lawyers in law firm.

Rendek McCrank, #208, 2208 Scarth St., S4P 2J6 – 306/525-2191, Fax: 306/757-8138 – *7
Robertson Stromberg, #100, 1777 Victoria Ave., S4P 4K5 – 306/569-9000, Fax: 306/757-6443; Email: rs.regina@robertsonstromberg.com; URL: http://www.robertsonstromberg.com – *8
Edwin C. Robinson, 2164 Smith St., S4P 2P2 – 306/569-3322 – *1
S.G. Segal, #1530, 1855 Victoria Ave., S4P 3T2 – 306/757-5651 – *1
Sheppard, Braun & Muma, #204, 3988 Albert St., PO Box 4228, S4S 3R1 – 306/586-6020, Fax: 306/586-8525 – *4
Shumiatcher Alberts, 2100 Scarth St., S4P 2H6 – 306/352-2651, Fax: 306/781-8171 – *4
Smith Law Offices, #105, 2505 - 11 Ave., S4P 0K6 – 306/352-1515, Fax: 306/522-3877 – *2
Tkach, Duchin, Bayda & Kroczynski, 2500 - 13 Ave., S4P 0W2 – 306/359-3131, Fax: 306/359-3372 – *4
Tulloch & Tulloch, 310 Gardiner Park Ct., S4V 1R9 – 306/789-0666, Fax: 306/789-1405 – *4
Tyerman & Egan, #412, 2120 Scarth St., S4P 2H9 – 306/525-8101, Fax: 306/525-9973 – *2
Willows Howe Goudie Linka, #300, 533 Victoria Ave., S4N 0P6 – 306/525-6113, Fax: 306/352-1393 – *6
Woloshyn Mattison, Saskatchewan Pl., #200, 1870 Albert St., S4P 4B7 – 306/352-9676, Fax: 306/569-8411 – *5

ROCANVILLE .... Moosomin
Osman, Gardner, Gordon, General Delivery, S0A 3L0 – 306/645-2825

ROSETOWN .... Kerrobert
Aseltine & Turner, 106 Main St., PO Box 158, S0L 2V0 – 306/882-2121, Fax: 306/882-3177 – *2
Skelton & Spencer, Drawer 1120, S0L 2V0 – 306/882-4244, Fax: 306/822-3969 – *2

ROSTHERN .... Saskatoon
Balicki, Popescul, Forsyth & Neudorf, 716 Railway Ave., PO Box 779, S0K 3R0 – 306/232-4482, Fax: 306/232-5595 – *1
R.M. Simpson, Q.C., 601 - 1 Ave., S0K 3R0 – 306/232-4331 – *1

SASKATOON .... Saskatoon
Agnew & Company, 279 - 3 Ave. North, S7K 2H8 – 306/244-7966, Fax: 306/244-8010; Email: dagnew@eagle.wbm.ca – *4
Balfour Moss, #600, 123 - 2nd Ave. South, S7K 7E6 – 306/665-7844, Fax: 306/662-1586; Email: balfourmoss.saskatoon@eagle.wbm.ca; URL: http://saskweb.com/~balfourmoss – *6
Beerling Hjelte Tangjerd Ritchie, #710, 119 - 4 Ave. South, S7K 5X2 – 306/934-3803, Fax: 306/665-1764 – *3
Benesh Bitz & Company, #19, 1738 Quebec Ave., S7K 1V9 – 306/664-0033, Fax: 306/664-8633; Email: benesh@link.com – *4
Bennett Jones Verchere, #600, 410 - 22 St. East, S7K 5T6 – 306/664-6755, Fax: 306/242-3611 – *2
Bodnar & Wanhella, 812 Spadina Cres. East, S7K 3H4 – 306/664-3314 – *3
Rose Boyko, #220, 212 - 10 St. East, S7N 2T6 – 306/665-6816
Brayford - Shapiro, 311- 21 St. East., S7K 0C2 – 306/244-5656, Fax: 306/244-5644 – *2
Brent & Greenhorn, #216, 3501 - 8 St. East, S7H 5K5 – 306/955-9544, Fax: 306/955-2656; Email: bandg@eagle.wbm.ca; URL: http://broadwaynet.com/~bandglaw – *3
Burlingham Cuelenaere, 1043 - 8 St. East, S7H 0S2 – 306/343-9581, Fax: 306/343-1947 – *4
Cuelenaere, Kendall, Katzman & Richards, #510, 128 - 4 Ave. South, S7K 1M8 – 306/653-5000, Fax: 306/652-4171; Email: cuelenaere@getthe.net – *16

Donlevy and Company, #500, 402 - 21 St. East, S7K 0C3 – 306/244-8494, Fax: 306/665-7042 – *3
Leila M. Ewing, 1222 Elliott St., S7N 0V6 – 306/652-9610, Fax: 306/652-2187 – *1
Gauley & Co., 701 Broadway Ave., PO Box 638, S7K 3L7 – 306/653-1212, Fax: 306/652-1323; Email: gauleyco@eagle.wbm.ca – *24
Goldstein Jackson Gibbings, #700, 201 - 21 St. East, S7K 0B8 – 306/653-2838, Fax: 306/652-4747 – *4
Halyk Dovell Stooshinoff Wright, 321 - 6 Ave. North, S7K 2S3 – 306/665-3434, Fax: 306/652-1915 – *5
Haubrich, Borden, Trach, Carlson & Clark, Canada Bldg., #400, 105 - 21 St. East, S7K 0B3 – 306/244-6561, Fax: 306/652-2514; Email: haubrich@sk.sympatico.ca – *5
Henderson Campbell, #202, 135 - 21 St. East, S7K 0B4 – 306/652-1234, Fax: 306/244-6640 – *4
Holgate & Kowalchuk, 9 - 315 Ave. South, S7M 2K5 – 306/978-2222, Fax: 306/384-2820 – *2
Linda Jaine, 247 Sylvian Way, S7H 5G1 – 306/374-4952
Jamieson Bains, #801, 119 - 4 Ave. South, S7K 5X2 – 306/653-5410, Fax: 306/652-3031; Email: info@jblawyers.com; URL: http://www.jblawyers.com – *8
Khan, Hanna & Company, #100, 219 Robin Cres., S7L 6M8 – 306/665-9995 – *3
Kloppenburg & Kloppenburg, Spadina Towers, #333, 728 Spadina Cres. East, S7K 4H7 – 306/665-7600, Fax: 306/665-7800 – *2
Knott Jackson, #413, 220 - 3 Ave. South, S7K 1M1 – 306/664-6900 – *2
Koskie & Company, #4, 2175 Airport Dr., S7L 7E1 – 306/242-8478, Fax: 306/653-2120; Email: tkoskie@eagle.wbm.ca; URL: http://www.wbm.ca/koskie/ – *2
Kraus McKay Pederson, #300, 333 - 3 Ave. North, S7K 2H9 – 306/652-8833, 653-5700, Fax: 306/652-3333 – *7
R.J. Leibel, 303 - 21 St. East, S7K 0C1 – 306/665-7700, Fax: 306/664-4135 – *1
MacDermid Lamarsh, #905, 201 - 21 St. East, S7K 0B8 – 306/652-9422, Fax: 306/653-4884, 242-1554 – *19
MacLean Keith, #1210, 410 - 22 St. East, S7K 5T6 – 306/664-9200, Fax: 306/664-1960
MacPherson Leslie & Tyerman, #1500, 410 - 22nd St. East, S7K 5T6 – 306/975-7100, Fax: 306/975-7145 – *16
Louis E. Martel, 830 - 4 St., S7H 1K4 – 306/652-6830 – *1
Mathiason & Valkenburg, #208, 165 - 3 Ave. South, PO Box 609, S7K 3L6 – 306/242-1202 – *2
McDougall, Ready, #300, 110 - 21 St. East, S7K 0B6 – 306/653-1641, Fax: 306/665-8511 – *4
McKercher McKercher & Whitmore, 374 - 3rd Ave. South, S7K 1M5 – 306/653-2000, Fax: 306/244-7335; Email: mckerche@eagle.wbm.ca – *32
Merchant Law Group, Canterbury Towers, #501, 224 Fourth Ave. South, S7K 5M5 – 306/653-7777, Fax: 306/975-1983 – *5
William Nykyforuk, Q.C., #208, 165 - 3 Ave. South, S7K 1L8 – 306/242-1202, Fax: 306/244-4423 – *1
Reg Parker, Bessborough Hotel, Bldg Box: 702, 601 Spadina Cr. East, S7K 3G8 – 306/652-7433 – *1
E.C. Partridge, #604, 224 - 4 Ave. South, S7K 5M5 – 306/955-5535, Fax: 306/652-1110 – *1
Ron Peigan, Saskatoon Sq., #850, 410 - 22 St. East, S7K 5T6 – 306/665-7844
Michael A. Power, #804, 230 - 22 St. East, S7K 0E9 – 306/242-0072, Fax: 306/242-0071 – *1
Priel, Stevenson, Hood & Thornton, 902 Spadina Cres. East, S7K 3H5 – 306/244-0132, Fax: 306/653-1118 – *10
Quon, Ferguson MacKinnon & Walters, #704, 224 - 4 Ave. South, S7K 5M5 – 306/665-8828, Fax: 306/665-5519 – *4
Robertson Stromberg, #600, 105 Twenty First St. East, S7K 0B3 – 306/652-7575, Fax: 306/652-2445;

Email: rs.stoon@robertsonstromberg.com; URL: http://www.robertsonstromberg.com – *22
Roe, Beckie & Olson, #313, 220 - 3rd Ave. South, S7K 1M1 – 306/244-9865, Fax: 306/934-6827 – *2
Sandstrom & Scott, #701, 224 - 4 Ave. South, S7K 5M5 – 306/244-0002, Fax: 306/652-2424 – *4
Schulman, Serne, Boryski & Gall, #604, 224 - 4 Ave. South, S7K 5M5 – 306/933-2233, Fax: 306/652-1110 – *4
Skarsgard Law Office, 1515 Shannon Cres., S7H 2T6 – 306/373-2688, Fax: 306/373-2688 – *1
Sonnenschein Law Office, Lincoln's Inn, 313 - 20th St. East, S7K 0A9 – 306/652-4730, Fax: 306/653-5760 – *1
Leslie G. Tallis, 2410 Irvine Ave., S7J 2A8 – *1
Thomson & Company, #303, 416 - 21 St. East, S7K 0C2 – 306/652-1620, Fax: 306/664-6732 – *1
Walker, Plaxton & Co., #200, 402 - 21 St. East, S7K 0C3 – 306/653-1500, Fax: 306/664-6659 – *4
Colleen L. Wilson, #1120, 606 Spadina Cres. East, S7K 3H1 – 306/665-6335, Fax: 306/244-0004 – *1
Woloshyn Mattison, Scotiabank Bldg., Bldg Box: 200, #200, 111 - 2nd Ave. South, S7M 4P7 – 306/244-2242 – *19
Woloshyn Mattison, Scotiabank Bldg., #200, 111 - 2 Ave. South, S7K 1K6 – 306/244-2242, Fax: 306/652-0332 – *9

SHAUNAVON .... Shaunavon
Benison Law Office, 407 Centre St., S0N 2M0 – 306/297-2633, Fax: 306/297-2808 – *1

SOUTHEY .... Regina
Pedersen, Norman, McLeod & Todd, 234 Railway, S0G 4P0 – 306/726-2040

STRASBOURG .... Regina
Pedersen, Norman, McLeod & Todd, 204 Mountain, S0G 4V0 – 306/725-3247

SWIFT CURRENT .... Swift Current
Anderson Nimegeers, 40 Cheadle St. West, PO Box 610, S9H 3W4 – 306/773-2891, Fax: 306/778-3364 – *8
Douglas J. Heinricks, 327 Central Ave. North, PO Box 1327, S9H 3X4 – 306/773-7226, Fax: 306/773-5696 – *1
MacBean Tessem, Bldg Box: 550, 151 First Ave. NE, PO Box 550, S9H 3W4 – 306/773-9343, Fax: 306/773-3828 – *1
McLaughlin, Forrester, Heinrichs, #9, 244 - 1 Ave. NE, PO Box 100, S9H 3V5 – 306/773-7205, Fax: 306/773-9715 – *4
M.S. Nakonechny, #6, 244 - 1 Ave. NE, S9H 2B4 – 306/778-3239, Fax: 306/773-7062 – *1

TISDALE .... Melfort
Annand Nystuen, 1105 Main St., S0E 1T0 – 306/873-2145
Kapoor, Selnes, Klimm, Schnell & Brown, PO Box 760, S0E 1T0 – 306/873-4535 – *4

UNITY .... Kerrobert
Hepting & Piché, 257 - 2 Ave. West, PO Box 600, S0K 4L0 – 306/228-2631, Fax: 306/228-4449 – *2
L. Kenneth Neil, 100 - 1 Ave. West, PO Box 128, S0K 4L0 – 306/228-2693, Fax: 306/228-4465 – *1

WATROUS .... Humboldt
B.H. Lannan, 106 - 2 Ave. East, PO Box 580, S0K 4T0 – 306/946-3512 – *2

WEYBURN .... Weyburn
Hardy & Thorson, 102 Coteau Ave. NE, S4H 2Z5 – 306/842-2772, Fax: 306/848-3539 – *2
MacDonald, Dawson, Fabian, Bldg Box: 97, 5 First Ave. NE, S4H 2J8 – 306/842-7419 – *5

Nimegeers, Schuck, Wormsbecker & Bobbitt, 319 Souris Ave. NE, PO Box 8, S4H 2J8 – 306/842-4654 – *4

Stinson & Company, Bldg Box: 1060, 8 - 4 St. NE, S4H 0X7 – 306/842-2657, Fax: 306/842-1999 – *3

WHITEWOOD..Moosomin

J.R. Ashfield, 940 Lalonde St., PO Box 880, S0G 5C0 – 306/735-2321 – *1

Osman, Gardner, Gordon, 717 Lalonte St., S0G 5C0 – 306/735-4503

WILKIE...Battleford

Lojek, Jones & Hudec, 106 - 2 Ave. East, PO Box 4, S0K 4W0 – 306/843-2661, Fax: 306/446-3022

WYNYARD..Wynyard

Owen Klebeck, Bldg Box: 1120, 115 Ave. East, S0A 4T0 – 306/554-2523,2278, Fax: 306/554-2099 – *2

YORKTON...Yorkton

Kyba, Yaholnitsky & Taylor, 41 Betts Ave., S3N 2W8 – 306/782-2283, Fax: 306/782-2284 – *4

Stamatinos, Leland, Koskie & Wellsch, Bldg Box: 188, 36 - 4 Ave. North, S3N 2V7 – 306/783-8541, Fax: 306/786-7484 – *4

Wrubell & Company, 18 - 1 Ave. North, S3N 1J4 – 306/783-9440, Fax: 306/786-1838 – *2

YUKON TERRITORY

PELLY CROSSING...Tatchun

James Harper, General Delivery, Y0B 1P0 – 403/537-3503

WHITEHORSE..Whitehorse

Anton, Campion, Macdonald, Phillips, Oyler & Buchan, #200, 204 Lambert St., Y1A 3T2 – 403/667-7885, Fax: 403/667-7600 – *9

Barbara Buffy Blakely, 107 Jarvis St., Y1A 2G7 – 403/668-4402

James Francis Burchill, #13, 501 Alexander St., Y1A 2L9

Robin Roy Dalziel, 6 Lewes Blvd., Y1A 3J2 – 403/668-2888

Davis & Company, #101, 307 Jarvis St., Y1A 2H3 – 403/668-6444, Fax: 403/667-2669

Barry Ernewein, #105, 107 Main St., Y1A 2A7 – 403/667-4000 – *1

David Joe, #101, 307 Jarvis St., Y1A 2H3 – 403/668-6681

Brian L. Morris, Horwoods Mall, #202, 100 Main St., Y1A 2A8 – 403/668-3390, Fax: 403/668-6213

O'Brien & Horembala, #3, 3089 - 3 Ave., Y1A 5B3 – 403/668-7272 – *3

Willard L. Phelps, Government of Yukon, Legislative Assembly Office, PO Box 2703, Y1A 2C6 – 403/667-5639

Pitzel & Coffin, #205, 205A Main St., Y1A 2B2 – 403/668-2700, Fax: 403/667-6308 – *2

Preston, Willis & Lackowicz, 2093 - 2 Ave., Y1A 1B5 – 403/668-5252, Fax: 403/668-5251; Email: yukonlaw@yknet.yk.ca – *10

Eloise P. Spitzer, 67 Walnut Cr., Y1A 5C7

Veale, Kilpatrick, Austring & Farkvam, 3081 - 3 Ave., Y1A 4Z7 – 403/668-4405, Fax: 403/668-3710 – *6

Stephen J. Walsh, #101, 307 Jarvis St., Y1A 2H3 – 403/668-7353, Fax: 403/667-6303 – *1

F. Edith Walters, 107 Jarvis St., Y1A 2G7 – 403/667-7024

Eric J. Woodhouse, Yukon Development Corporation, 410 Jarvis St., PO Box 2703, Y1A 2C6 – 403/667-5028

---

* indicates number of lawyers in law firm.

COPP CLARK PROFESSIONAL

INFORMATION FORM

PHOTOCOPY THIS FORM FOR CONVENIENCE

CHANGE TO LISTING:

You may find it most convenient to photocopy your existing listing indicating any changes. Fax or mail the form.

PAGE NUMBER:_____

NAME OF FIRM/ORGANIZATION/GOVERNMENT BODY:_____

PLEASE CHANGE OUR LISTING TO REFLECT THE FOLLOWING:

_____
_____
_____
_____
_____
_____
_____

NEW LISTING:

WE ARE NOT REPRESENTED IN THE DIRECTORY. HERE IS THE INFORMATION ON OUR FIRM/ORGANIZATION/GOVERNMENT BODY:

(Please examine the guidelines in the front of the directory and the entries of similar organizations for an indication of how best to present your data).

_____
_____
_____
_____
_____
_____
_____
_____

WE WOULD LIKE TO SEE MORE INFORMATION ON:

_____
_____

MAIL INFORMATION TO:	EMAIL TO:	FAX INFORMATION TO:
COPP CLARK PROFESSIONAL	info@mail.canadainfo.com	THE EDITOR
200 ADELAIDE STREET WEST		CANADIAN ALMANAC & DIRECTORY
3RD FLOOR		(416) 597-1617
TORONTO, ONTARIO M5H 1W7		

INDEX

EDITOR'S NOTE:
Wherever possible the listings in this index are arranged alphabetically according to the main word in each entry. Thus the Canadian Bankers Association is listed under "Bankers Assn., Cdn.", and the National Energy Board is listed under "Energy Bd., Ntl.". Government Departments are listed under the name of the Department, and not under the names of provinces. Thus if you are looking for the Ontario Transportation Department, look under "Transportation, Depts.," not under "Ontario".

Listings (such as the International Boundary Commission) are sometimes duplicated, when it was difficult to determine which word a user might consider the main one, or where it was felt that a user would look for an entry under a title that is well-known (such as the National Arts Centre).
See Index Page 74 for commonly used abbreviations.
Page numbers in bold refer to illustrations found in the colour section followig page 1-46.

See ADDENDA at the back of this book for late changes & additional information.

A
A.B.A.A.P.A.S., 2-17
AA, 2-10
AADAC, 3-96
Abbotsford
   City Govt., 4-153
   Sch. District (B.C.), 9-6
Abbreviations
   Academic, 1-35
   Astronomical, 1-15
   Business, 1-39
   Ecclesiastical, 1-35
   Forms of address, 1-33
   of Honours & Decorations, 1-32
   Measurement, 1-60
   Prov. Postal Code, 1-46
   Shipping, 1-39
ABC Canada, 2-111
ABCDEF-Canada, 2-117
Abilities
   Council, Sask., 2-43
   Fdn. of N.S., 2-42
Abitibi-Témscamingue, Univ. du Qué. en, 9-47
Aboriginal (*see also* Native)
   Affairs
      Brs./Divs. (Govt.): Alta., 3-99; Nfld., 3-141
      Depts. (Govt.)(*see also* Indian & Northern Affairs): Quick Ref., 3-1; B.C., 3-108; N.B., 3-137; N.W.T., 3-152
   AIDS Prevention Soc., Feather of Hope, 2-18
   Assn., Ont. Metis &, 2-133
   Business
      Canada (Fed.), 3-75
      Cdn. Council for, 2-132
   Capital Corp., 3-75
   Councils, 2-133
   Educ. Br. (B.C.), 3-111
   Forestry Assn., Ntl., 2-75
   Friendship Ctrs., 2-134
   Issues Project (B.C. Transp.), 3-119
   Justice (Fed.), 3-77
   Mgmt. Bd., Ntl., 3-73
   Magazines, 5-191
   Nurses Assn., 2-132

Aboriginal (cont.)
   Orgs., 2-132
   People(s)
      Business Assn., 2-132
      Congress of, 2-133; Alta., 2-133
      Council, N.B., 2-133
   Policing (Fed.), 3-89
   Programs Br., Universities & (B.C.), 3-111
   Science & Engrg. Assn., Cdn., 2-132
   Tourism Assn., Cdn. Ntl., 2-185
   Trappers Fedn., 2-77
   Urban Alliance of Ont., 2-132
   Women's Assns., 2-134
Abortion
   Clinics (*see also* Special Treatment Ctrs.)
      Ont. Coalition for, 2-154
   Rights Action League, Cdn., 2-154
AboutFace, 2-41
Abstracting Soc. of Canada, Indexing &, 2-119
Academic
   Abbrevs., 1-35
   Accounting Assn., Cdn., 2-8
   Degrees, 1-35
   Exchanges, Canada-Israel Fdn. for, 2-129
   Journals, 5-195
   Medicine, Cdn. Inst. of, 2-86
Academy Canada (Nfld.), 9-20
Acadia
   Divinity College (N.S.), 9-22
   Univ. (N.S.), 9-22
Acadian
   Affairs Dir. (N.S.), 3-155
   Language Servs. (N.S.), 3-158
Acadie, Soc. ntle de l', 2-39
Acadien(ne)(s)
   Congrès mondial, 2-38
   Fédn des communautés francophones et, 2-39
   Le Musée (N.-B.), 6-11
   du N.-B., Soc. des, 2-39
   de la N.-E., Fédn, 2-39
Access
   to Info. & Privacy: Alta., 3-102
   Nova Scotia, 3-157

Accessories, Assn. of Canada, Luggage, Leathergoods, Handbags &, 2-68
Accident(s)
   industriels majeurs, Conseil cdn des, 2-160
   et de maladies du travail, L'Alliance cdnne des victimes d', 2-110
   Prevention Assns., 2-158
   du travail, Assn des commissions des, 2-110
Accouchement vaginal après césarienne, 2-36
Accountancy Educ. (Ont.), 9-34
Accounting
   Assn(s)., 2-8
   Shows/Conferences, 1-72
Accommodation Motel Ont. Assn., 2-183
Accueil
   et d'hébergement du Qué., Ctrs d', 8-40
   intl pour l'enfance, 2-108
   privés, Assn des centres d' (Qué.), 2-100
ACEL, 3-54
Acier
   d'Armature
      du Canada, 2-181
      du Qué., Inst. d', 2-181
   Assn cdnne des producteurs d', 2-181
   Conseil cdn de la construction en, 2-181
   Inst cdn de la construction en, 2-181
ACOA, 3-54
Acoustic Neuroma Assn., 2-81
Acoustical Assn., Cdn., 2-57
Act for Disarmament Coalition, 2-107
Action
   Canada Network, 2-187
   on Waste Div. (Alta.), 3-99
Actionnaires, Assn cdnne des services aux, 2-69
Active Living Alliance for Cdns. with a Disability, 2-172
Actors'
   Equity Assn., Cdn., 2-198
   Fund, 6-35
ACTRA, 2-196
Actuaries, Cdn. Inst. of, 2-105
Acupuncteurs du Qué., Corp. profle des, 2-91
Acupuncture
   Assn., Chinese Medicine &, 2-91
   Fdn. of Canada, 2-81

Canadian Almanac & Directory 1997

Acute Care Servs. (*see also* Long Term Care) Dir.: B.C., 3-116
Addiction(s) (*see also* Drugs; Alcohol)
  Assns., 2-10
  Fdn. of Man., 2-10
  Research Fdn., Ont., 2-10
Address, Official Forms of, 1-33
Adjusters Assn., Cdn. Indep., 2-105
Administrateurs(trices)
  agréés
    au Canada, Inst des secrétaires et, 2-122
    du Qué., Ordre des, 2-122
  des corporations, l'Inst des, 2-122
  de la législation ouvrière, 2-110
  de recherche universitaire, Assn cdnne d', 2-47
  scolaires, Assn cdnne des, 2-121
  de services sociaux en milieu de santé, Assn cdnne des, 2-100
  en transport motorisé, Conseil cdn des, 2-188
Administratif
  cdn aux orgs, Service, 2-121
  Universitaire, Assn cdnne de pérsonnel, 2-46
Administration (*see also* Public Administration)
  Assns., 2-120
  Faculties/Schs., Index to, 9-56
  publique du Canada, Inst d', 2-80
  publique, École ntle d' (Qué.), 9-47
Administrative
  Assistants, Assn. of, 2-120
  Housekeepers Assn., 2-100
  Mgrs., Insts. of Certified, 2-121
  Sciences Assn. of Canada, 2-120
Administrators
  Assn. of
    Cdn. Court, 2-113
    Records Mgrs. &, 2-120
  Cdn. Assn. of
    Nurse, 2-135
    School, 2-121
    University Research, 2-47
  in Health Facilities, Cdn. Assn. of Social Work, 2-100
  Inst. of Chartered Secretaries &, 2-122
  of Labour Legislation, Cdn. Assn. of, 2-110
  of Large Urban Public Libraries, Council of, 2-119
  of Medium Public Libraries of Ont., 2-116
  Municipal (Cities & Towns), 4-1
Adoption(s)
  Appeal Bd., (Nfld.), 3-149
  Branch (Ont.), 3-173
  Govt. Quick Ref., (*see* Child Welfare), 3-7
  Reunion Register, Cdn., 2-168
  Triad Soc. for Truth in, 2-169
Adult
  Career Ctrs. (Nfld.), 9-20
  Children of Alcoholics, 2-10
  Corrections, *see* Correctional Services; Corrections
  Education
    Advisor (P.E.I.), 3-191
    Cdn. Assn. for, 2-47
    Intl. Council for, 2-52
    Min. of State (N.B.), 3-191
    Learning (P.E.I.), Office of Higher Educ., Training &, 3-191
Adultes
  Conseil intl d'éduc des, 2-52
  Inst cdn d'éduc. des, 2-52
Advanced
  Education (*see also* Skills Development; Post Secondary)
    Brs./Divs. (Govt.): Man., 3-124; Yukon, 3-222
    & Career Devel., Dept., Alta., 3-94, 9-1
    Depts. (Govt.): Alta., 3-94; N.B., 3-132
  Learning Inst. (Ont.), 9-35
  Manufacturing Tech., Institute for (NRC), 3-81
  Research, Cdn. Inst. for (Ont.),199, 9-35
  Study, Intl. Fedn. of Insts. for, 2-52

Advanced (cont.)
  Technology
    Assn., Cdn., 2-57
    Inst. for (Ont.), 9-35
Advent, 1-24
Advertisers, Assn. of Cdn., 2-11
Advertising
  Agencies, Soc. of Ont., 2-12
  Agency
    Assn(s)., 2-10
    Network, Trans-Canada, 2-12
    Print Production Assn., 2-10
  Assn(s)., 2-10
    Outdoor, 2-12
  Awards, 1-92
  Benevolent Soc., Ntl., 2-11
  Conventions, 1-72
  & Design Club, 2-11
  Fdn., Cdn., 2-13
  Inst. of Cdn., 2-14
  Magazines, 5-159
  & Mktg. Assns., 2-10
  Research Fdn., Cdn., 2-11
  Standards Councils, 2-11
  Trade Shows, 1-72
Advocacy
  Centre, Public Interest, 2-115
  Resource Ctr. for the Handicapped, 2-43
Advocates Soc., 2-113
AECB, 3-54
AECL, 3-54
Aerial Photographs, Govt. Quick Ref., 3-26
Aérien, Assn du transport, 2-27
Aériennes intles, Assn cdnne des passagers de lignes, 2-28
Aeronautical Preservation Assn., Cdn., 2-27
Aeronautics
  Assn., Model, 2-152
  & Space Inst., Cdn., 2-28
Aéronautique et spatial du Canada, l'Inst, 2-28
Aéronefs,
  Assn du groupe des opérations d', 2-196
  Conseil cdn de l'entretien des, 2-28
Aerophilatelic Soc., Cdn., 2-149
Aéroports du Canada, Conseil des, 2-28
Aerospace (*see also* Aviation)
  & Agricl. Implement Wkrs. Union, Intl. Automobile, 2-203
  Assns., 2-27
  Defense Command (NORAD), 3-247
  Industries
    Assn., 2-27
    Devel. (Man.), 3-127
  Magazines, 5-160, 5-178
  Medicine, Cdn. Soc. of, 2-89
  Research, Inst. for (NRC), 3-81
  Studies, Inst. for, 2-28
  Transportation & General Workers Union (CAW), 2-203
  Wkrs., Intl. Assn. of Machinists &, 2-202
Aérospatiale(s)
  Assn
    des industries, 2-27
    intle des machinistes et des travailleurs de l', 2-202
    du transport et des autres travailleurs et travailleuses, Synd. ntl de l'automobile, de l', 2-203
Aérotechnique, École ntle d' (Qué.), 9-47
AESS, 2-256
Aesthetics, Cdn. Soc. for, 2-155
Affaires
  culturelles, Inst cdn des, 2-108
  indiennes et du Nord Canada (Fed.), 3-73
  internationales, Inst cdn des, 2-108
  publiques du Canada, Assn des, 2-80
  sociales, Fédn des, 2-200
Affichage extérieur, L'Assn cdnne de, 2-12

AFL-CIO, 2-195
Africa Inland Mission, 2-6
African(s)
  Medical & Research Fdn., 2-81
  Missions Fdn., Cdn., 2-6
  in Partnership Against AIDS, 2-16
  Studies, Cdn. Assn. of, 2-47
AFS Interculture Canada, 2-107
Against Drunk Driving, 2-10
  Mothers, 2-10
Agape House, 2-167
AGCare, 2-12
Age d'or, Fédn de l', 2-164
Aged, Help the, 2-164
Agency Owners Roundtable, 2-11
Aggregate Prodrs. Assn. of Ont., 2-30
Aging
  Ctr. for Activity & (U.W.O.), 9-31
  Councils on: Alta, 2-163 ; Man., 3-126
  Inst. on Human Devel., Life Course &, (U. of T.), 9-31
  Ntl. Adv. Council on, 3-78
Agneaux et moutons, Fédn des producteurs d' (Qué.), 3-198
Agoraphoric Fdn. of Canada, 2-125
Agricole(s)
  Assurances, Régie des (Qué.), 3-198
  du Canada, Inst, 2-12
  Canada, Soc. du crédit, 3-66
  Commn de protection du territoire (Qué.), 3-198
  Conseil ntl des produits, 3-80
  Fédn de la relève (Qué.), 3-198
  Fédn des synds. de gestion (Qué.), 3-198
  et forestiers, Fonds d'assurance-prêts (Qué.), 3-198
  Groupe géstion & économie (Qué.), 3-198
  de langue française, Assn des rédacteurs, 2-193
  Régies (Qué.), 3-198
  Soc. de financement (Qué.), 3-198
  Temple cdn de la renommée, 2-13
  Tribunal d'appel en matière de protection du territoire (Qué.), 3-198
  Union des producteurs (Qué.), 2-16, 3-198
Agricorp (Ont.), 3-169
Agriculteurs chrétien de l'Ontario, Fédn des, 2-14
Agricultrices, Fédn des (Qué.), 2-15, 3-198
Agricultural
  Assn(s)., 2-12
  Awards, 1-92
  Bds. & Commns.: Ont. 3-169
  Colleges in: Alta., 3-95; B.C., 3-108; Man., 3-122; N.B., 3-134; Nfld., 3-144; N.S., 9-23; Ont., 9-34
  Credit Corps.: Man., 3-122; Sask., 3-212
  Devel. (Govt.): Man., 3-122; N.B., 3-134; N.S., 3-156; P.E.I., 3-189
  Economics & Farm Mgmt. Soc., Cdn., 2-44
  Engrg., Cdn. Soc. of, 2-14
  Exhibitions, 1-79, 1-80
  Extension Ctr. (Man.), 3-122
  Fairs, 1-80
  Financing (Qué.), 3-198
  Groups Concerned about Resources & the Environment, 2-12
  Hall of Fame, Cdn., 2-13
  Implement Wkrs. Union, Intl. Union, 2-203
  Implements Bd., Sask., 3-217
  Industry Servs. Dir. (Fed.), 3-53
  Inst. of Canada, 2-12
  Insurance Bd., Qué., 3-198
  Land(s)
    Commn., B.C., 3-108
    Preservation (Qué.), 3-198
    Soc., Preservation of., 2-15
  Licensing & Reg'n Review Bd. (Ont.), 3-170
  Loans Bd. of Ont., 3-169
  Machinery Inst., Prairie, 3-212
  Magazines, *see* Farm Publications
  Mktg. Bds., *see* Marketing; *see* names of individual crops & animals

Agricultural (cont.)
  Museum, Ont., 3-169
    Adv. Bd., Ont., 3-170
  Orgs., 2-12
  Producers, Keystone, 2-13
  Production Canada, Resource Efficient, 2-64
  Products Mktg.
    Bd., (Nfld.), 3-144
    Councils: Alta., 3-95; Qué., 3-198
  Rehab. & Devel. Dir. (Ont.), 3-170
  Research
    Division (Fed.), 3-54
    Insts. (Govt.): Alta., 3-96; Ont., 3-169
    Jubilee Ctr. for, 2-15
  Shows, 1-80
  Socs.
    Adv. Bd., Man., 3-122
    Alta. Assn. of, 2-12
    & Exhibitions, Sask. Assn of, 2-15
  Stabilization Program, Ntl. Tripartite (Man), 3-122
  Tech., Colleges of (Ont.), 9-34
  Trade, *see* Trade
  Training Inst., Ont., 9-34
  Winter Fair Assn., Royal, 2-67
Agriculture
  & Agri-Food Canada, 3-52
  Assn(s), 2-12
    Sustainable, 2-16
  Awards, 1-92
  biologique du Qué., Fédn de l', 2-15
  Br. (Yukon), 3-224
  Cdn. Fedn. of, 2-13
  in Christian Perspective, Food &, 2-14
  Companies, Cdn., 7-40
  Depts. (Govt.): Quick Ref., 3-1; Alta., 3-95; B.C., 3-108; Fed., 3-52; Man., 3-121; N.B., 3-133; Nfld., 4-144; N.S., 3-156; Ont., 3-168; P.E.I., 3-188; Qué., 3-197; Sask., 3-212
  Exhibitions, Shows & Events, 1-80
  Faculties/Schs., Index to, 9-56
  Fedns. of, 2-13
  Financial Serv. Corp. (Alta.), 3-95
  Fisheries
    & Food, Min. (B.C.), 3-108; Qué., 3-197
    & Forestry, Dept. (P.E.I.), 3-188
  Food & Rural
    Affairs, Dept. (Ont.), 3-168
    Devel., Dept. (Alta.), 3-95
  & Food
    Laboratory Servs. (Ont.), 3-169
    Marketing Bd., Qué., 3-198
    Tech., Alfred College of, 9-34
  & Forest Insurance Fund (Qué.), 3-198
  Govt. Quick Ref., 3-1
  & Mktg., Dept. (N.S.), 3-156
  Net Income Stabilization Admin. (Fed.), 3-53
  Orgs., 2-12
  Publications, *see* Farm Publications
  & Rural Devel. Dept. (N.B.), 3-133
  Statistics, 1-56
  & Veterinary Medicine, Conf. of Cdn. Faculties of, 2-47
Agri-Food(s)
  Agriculture &, Dept. (Fed.), 3-52
  Council, Sask., 3-212
  Forest Resources & (Nfld.), 3-144
  Industries Devel. (Man.), 3-127
Agrifoods Intl. Coop., 2-14
Agri-Retailers, Cdn. Assn. of, 2-35
Agro-alimentaire(s)
  Assn des technologistes, 2-13
  Canada, Agriculture et (Fed.), 3-52
  Club export (Qué.), 2-188
  Insts de technologie (Qué.), 9-48
  Soc. qué. d'initiatives, 3-198
Agrologists
  Assn., Cdn. Consulting, 2-13
  Insts. of, 2-12

Agrologists (cont.)
  of Que., Order of, 2-15
Agronomes
  -conseils, L'Assn cdnne des, 2-13
  du Qué., Ordre des, 2-15
Agronomy, Cdn. Soc. of, 2-14
Ahmadiyya Movement in Islam, 2-2
Aid & Relief, Cdn. Physicians for, 2-108
AIDS
  Adv. Commn. (Govt.), N.S., 3-160
  Assns., 2-16
  Care, Cdn. Assn. of Nurses in, 2-136
  Committees, 2-16
  Fdn., 2-16
  Govt. Quick Ref., 3-2
  Hotline (B.C.), 3-116
  Policy Coord. (Fed.), 3-71
  Research, Cdn. Fdn. for, 2-19
  Soc., Cdn., 2-16
AIM Canada, 2-6
Aîné(e)s
  Aide aux, 2-164
  Assn intl francophone des, 2-163
  Conseil des (Qué.), 3-207
  Francophones du Canada, L'Assemblée des, 2-163
  de l'Ont., Assn des centres pour, 2-164
  Séjours culturels des, 2-164
  La Voix - Le Réseau cdn des, 2-164
Air
  Cadet League of Canada, 2-126
  Command (Natl. Defence), 3-79
  Conditioning
    Assns., 2-94
    Contractors Assn., Cdn. Refrigeration &, 2-95; Ont., 2-95
    Sheet Metal &, 2-182
    Engrs., Amer. Soc. of Heating, Refrigerating &, 2-94
    Exhibitions, Shows & Events, 1-84
    Inst., Heating, Refrigeration &, 2-95
    Magazines, 5-168
  Cushion Tech. Soc., 2-57
  Force
    Assn., 2-126
    Benevolent Fund, Royal Cdn., 2-127
    Telecom Assn., 2-183
    Veterans, Army, Navy &, 2-126
  & Gas Machinery Mfrs. Assn., Compressed, 2-66
  Handling Group, Ont., 2-182
  Line (*see also* Airline)
    Dispatchers' Assn., 2-198
    Pilots Assn., Cdn., 2-198
  Pollution, *see* Environment
  Quality Brs./Divs. (Govt.): N.B., 3-135; N.S., 3-159; N.W.T., 3-153; P.E.I., 3-190
  Resources, Govt. Quick Ref., 3-2
  Search & Rescue Assn., 2-55
  Shows, 1-72
  Traffic Control Assn., Cdn., 2-198
  Transport Assns.
    of Canada, 2-27
    Intl., 2-28
    Northern, 2-28
  & Waste Mgmt. Assn., 2-59
Aircraft
  Assns.
    Cdn. Business, 2-188
    Recreational, 2-28
  Engrs. Assn., (Atlantic), 2-27
  Magazines, *see* Aviation
  Maintenance Engrs. Assn. of Ont., 2-28
  Operations Group Assn., 2-196
Airline
  Companies, 1-67
  Inflight Magazines, 5-177
  Passengers Assn., Intl., 2-28
  Safety (Fed.), 3-91

Airport(s)
  Council, Cdn., 2-28
  Govt. Quick Ref., 3-2
  Group (Fed. Transp.), 3-90
  Mgmt. Conf. of Ont., 2-27
Ajax Town of, Govt., 4-153
Al-Anon Family Groups, 2-10
Alarm & Security Assn., Cdn., 2-159
Alberta
  Archives in, 5-112
  Art Galleries in, 6-29
  Bds. of Trade in, 7-24
  Botanical Gardens in, 6-45
  Chambers of
    Commerce in, 7-24
    Resources, 7-35
  Cities & Towns in, 4-1
  Colleges in, 9-4
  Courts & Judges in, 10-2
  Educ. in, 9-1
  Flag & Coat of Arms, **9**
  FreeNets, 5-232
  Government in, 3-92
  Hospitals in, 8-1
  Law Firms in, 10-22
  Libraries in, 5-2
  Lobbyists in, 7-35
  Meeting, Conference, Exhibit & Event Planners in, 1-68
  Municipal Govt. in, 4-1
  Museums in, 6-2
  Native Schs. in, 9-2
  Newspapers in, 5-130
  Nursing Homes in, 8-6
  Online Service Providers, 5-230 (& *see* Addenda)
  Post Secondary & Specialized Insts. in, 9-4
  Private Schs. in, 9-4
  Prov. Museum of, 6-2
  Public Colleges in, 9-4
  Stock Exchange, 7-9
  Technical Institutions, 9-4
  Treasury Brs., 7-3
  Univs. in, 9-3
  Vocational Colleges, 9-4
  Zoos in, 6-44
Alcohol & Drug (*see also* Drug Dependency Services; Substance Abuse)
  Agencies (Govt.): Quick Ref., 3-13; Alta., 3-96
  Concerns, 2-10
  Information (B.C.), 3-116
Alcoholics
  Adult Children of, 2-10
  Anonymous, 2-10
  Cdn. Assn. for Children of, 2-10
Alcoholism
  Council of Man., Native, 2-134
  Govt. Quick Ref., *see* Drugs & Alcohol, 3-13; Liquor Control, 3-25
Alcool, Régie des (Qué.), 3-208
Alcoolisme et les toxicomanies, Centre cdn de lutte contre, 2-10, 3-57
Alcools
  des courses et des jeux, Régie des (Qué.), 3-208
  du Qué., Synd.
    des employées de magasins et de bureaux de la Soc. des, 2-206
    du personnel technique et profl de la Soc. des, 2-206
  Soc. des (Govt.): N.B., 3-138; Qué., 3-203
Alcuin Soc., 2-143
ALÉNA Secretariat (Fed.), 3-84
Alfred College of Agric. (Ont.), 9-34
Algoma Univ. College (Ont.), 9-29
Algonquin
  College, AA & T (Ont.), 9-32
  Forestry Auth., 3-184

Alimentaires
  Assn
    cdnne des banques, 2-166
    des distributeurs aux services, 2-72
    des manufacturiers de produits, 2-72
  Conseil cdn de la distribution, 2-72
  Fabricants cdns de produits, 2-73
  Inst cdn de science et tech., 2-162
  Régie des marchés (Qué.), 3-198
Alimentation
  Agriculture, des pêcheries &, Min. de l' (Qué.), 3-197
  animale, Assn cdnne des industries de l', 2-14
  Assn
    cdnne des courtiers en, 2-72
    des détaillants en, 2-158
Aliments
  pour animaux familiers, Assn des fabricants, 2-74
  fins, L'Assn cdnne des, 2-72
  Inst des, 2-73
  Qualité des, Dir. gén. (Qué.), 3-198
  de santé, Assn cdnne des, 2-72
All-Terrain Vehicles
  Distrs. Council, 2-26
  Govt. Quick Ref., (*see* Leisure Craft) & Vehicle Regulations, 3-25
Allergy
  Asthma Info. Assn., 2-81
  & Clinical Immunology, Cdn. Soc. of, 2-89
  Fdn. of Canada, 2-81
Alliance(s)
  Church, 2-3
  Québec, 2-38
Almanacs, 5-181
Allstate Fdn. of Canada, 2-208
Alphabétisation
  en français, Fédn cdnne pour l', 2-112
  Laubach, 2-112
  mondiale Canada, 2-112
  Rassemblement cdn pour l', 2-112
Alpine Club of Canada, 2-172
Alternative
  Energy (*see* Energy, Alternative)
  Newspapers Assn., 2-144
ALS Soc. of Canada, 2-81
Alsek Renewable Resources Council (Yukon), 3-225
Aluminium
  Assn de l'industrie de l', 2-181
  Fédn des synds du secteur de l', 2-201
Aluminum Brick & Glass Wkrs. Intl. Union, 2-197
Alzheimer
  Fdn., Interior, 2-92
  Member Assns. & Socs., 2-81
  Soc. of Canada, 2-81
AM Radio Stations, 5-199
AMA Intl., Cdn. Mgmt. Ctr. of, 2-121
  Sport Dir. (P.E.I.), 3-190
Ambassadors
  (to Canada), 3-248
  (Cdn.), Abroad, 3-259
  Forms of Address, 1-36
Ambulance
  du Qué., Corp. des services d', 2-55
  St. John, 2-55
  Services (Govt.): B.C., 3-116; Man., 3-126; N.B., 3-136; N.S., 3-160; Que., 3-207
Ambulancier, Service (Qué.), 3-207
Aménagement
  régl, Soc. d' (N.-B.), 3-139
  rural Dept, Agriculture et de l' (N.B.), 3-133
Aménagistes municipaux du Qué., Assn des urbanistes et des, 2-79
American
  Govt.
    Depts./Agencies, 3-244
    Equivalency Table, 3-227
    States, Org. of, 3-247
  Studies, Cdn. Assn. for, 2-47

Americas, Cdn. Fdn. for the, 2-107
Amérique française, Musée de l', 6-24
Amiante
  Assn des Mines d' (Qué.), 2-127
  Conseil Ntl Cdn de, 2-35
  Inst de l', 2-127
  Soc. ntle de l' (Qué.), 3-205
Amish Church, Old Order, 2-5
Amitié, Assn ntle des centres d', 2-134
Ammunition Assn., Cdn. Sporting Arms &, 2-178
Amnesty Intl. (English), 2-102
Amnistie Intle (Francophone), 2-102
Among Equals, 2-109
Amputations of Canada, War, 2-172
Amputee Sports Assn., Cdn., 2-173
Amusement(s)
  Machine Operators of Canada, 2-149
  Reg. Bd., (N.S.), 3-161
Amyotrophic Lateral Sclerosis Soc. of Canada, 2-81
Anaesthetists' Soc., Cdn., 2-83
Anatomy, Neurobiology & Cell Biology, Cdn. Assn. for, 2-162
Ancestral Languages, Man. Assn. for Promotion of, 2-112
Anciens Combattants
  de l'armée, de la marine et des forces aériennes, 2-126
  Assn liaison des, 2-127
  Canada (Féd.), 3-92
Andrology Soc., Cdn. Fertility &, 2-154
Anemie falciforme, La soc. de l', 2-89
Anesthésistes, Soc. cdnne des, 2-83
Anglais (langue seconde), Soc. pour la promotion de l'enseignement de l', 2-54
Anglers & Hunters, Ont. Fedn. of, 2-152
Anglican(s)
  Church, 2-2; Forms of Address, 1-34
  Fdn., 2-208
  Magazines, *see* Religious Magazines
Anglophone(s)
  Communauté, Sous-ministre adjoint (Qué. Éduc.), 3-200
  Servs. (Qué. Educ.), 3-200
Angus Assn., Cdn., 2-19
Animal(s)
  Alliance of Canada, 2-21
  Assn. for the Protection of Fur-Bearing, 2-77
  Breeders, Assn(s)., 2-19
    Cdn., Assn. of, 2-19
  Cdns. for Ethical Treatment of Food, 2-22
  Care, Cdn. Council on, 2-21
  Council, Ont. Farm, 2-21
  Defence League of Canada, 2-21
  Health
    Brs./Div. (Govt.): Nfld., 3-144; Qué., 3-198
    Inst., Cdn., 2-21
    Technologists & Technicians, Cdn. Assn. of, 2-21
    Trust of Canada, 2-19
  Industry Brs./Divs. (Govt.): Alta., 3-95; Man., 3-122; N.S., 3-156
  Magazines, 5-177
  & Plant Health Dir. (Fed.), 3-53
  Products Council (Qué.), 3-198
  Rights
    Cdn. Vegans for, 2-22
    Network, Cdn., 2-21
  Science
    Cdn.
      Assn. for Laboratory, 2-21
      Soc. of, 2-22
    Orgs., 2-21
  Socs. for Prevention of Cruelty to, 2-27
  Welfare Fdn., 2-208
  World Soc. for Protection of, 2-23
Animale(s)
  La Fdn cdnne de la santé, 2-19
  Qualité des aliments et Santé, (Qué.), 3-198
  du Qué., Conseil des productions, 3-198

Animation Prodrs. Assn., Cdn., 2-68
Animaux
  Conseil cdn de protection des, 2-21
  Fédn des socs cdnnes d'assistance aux, 2-21
  de Qué., Soc. protectrice des, 2-22
  Société
    cdnne d'enregistrement des, 2-20
    mondiale pour la protection des, 2-23
  Socs pour la défense des, 2-21
Anishinabek, 2-134
Anna Wyman Sch. of Dance Art (B.C.), 9-9
Annapolis Valley Regl. Sch. Bd. (N.S.), 9-21
Anniversaries, Fixed & Movable Festivals &, 1-24
Annonceurs, Assn cdnne des, 2-11
Annuités, Assn des courtiers, 2-104
Anthem, Ntl., 1-25
Anthropologie appliquée, Soc. d', 2-157
Anthropology
  Assn., Cdn. Sociology &, 2-155
  Museum of (B.C.), 6-4
  Soc. of Applied, 2-157
Anti-
  Poverty Orgs.: Ntl., 2-168; Man., 2-167
  Racism Secretariat, Ont., 3-172
Antiochan Orthodox Christian Archdiocese, 2-2
Antiquarian Booksellers Assn., 2-23
Antique(s)
  Assn(s)., 2-23; Man., 2-23
  Automobile Club of Amer., 2-23
  & Classic
    Boat Soc., 2-23
    Car Club of Canada, 2-23
  Dealers Assn., Cdn., 2-23
  Magazines, 5-160, 5-177
  Shows, 1-72
Antiquities, Soc. for the Study of Egyptian, 2-157
ANZA Club, 2-128
APICS Region VIII, 2-123
Aplastic Anemia Assn. of Canada, 2-81
Apostolic Church, 2-2
  Armenian Holy, 2-2
  New, 2-4
  of Pentecost, 2-2
Appaloosa Horse Club of Canada, 2-19
Apparel (*see also* Fashion)
  Fedn., Cdn., 2-67
  Manufacturers
    Assn.
      Children's, 2-67
      of Ont., 2-67
    Guild, Qué. Fashion, 2-68
    Inst. of Qué., 2-68
  Markets, 2-67
Appareils domestique, Org. cdnne de service d', 2-54
Appeal(s)
  Commn., Island Regulatory & (P.E.I.), 3-191
  Court, Court Martial, 10-2
  Courts: Alta., 10-2; B.C., 10-4; Fed. (Supreme), 10-1; Man., 10-6; N.B., 10-7; Nfld., 10-8; N.W.T., 10-8; N.S., 10-9; Ont., 10-10; P.E.I., 10-14; Qué., 10-15; Sask., 10-20; Yukon, 10-21
Appel, Cour d' (Qué.), 10-15
Apple Mktg. Agencies: N.B., 3-134; Ont., 3-170; Qué., 3-198
Appliance
  Manufacturers Assn., Cdn., 2-123
  Serv. Assn., Cdn. Electronic &, 2-54
Applied
  Arts & Tech.
    Colleges, *see* Community Colleges
    of Ont., Assn. of Colleges of, 2-45
  Economists, Atlantic Assn. of, 2-44
  Mineralogy, Intl. Council for, 2-128
  Negotiation, Cdn. Intl. Inst. of, 2-34
Appraisal
  Assns., 2-146
  Inst. of Canada, 2-146
Appraisers, Intl. Inst. of Public, 2-147

Apprenticeship (*see also* Industrial Training; Occupational; Training)
   Bds. (Govt.), Alta., 3-95; B.C., 3-117; N.B., 3-133; N.S., 3-158
   Brs./Divs. (Govt.): Alta., 3-95; B.C., 3-117; N.S., 3-158; Ont., 3-177; P.E.I., 3-191
   Programs, Govt. Quick Ref., 3-2
   Qué., *see* Formation profl de la main-d'oeuvre
   & Trade Certification Bd. (N.W.T.), 3-151
Appropriate Devel., The Pembina Inst. for, 2-64
Approvisionnements (Govt.): Qué., 3-209
APRO - The Canadian Tech. Network, 2-154
Aquaculture
   Assn. Ont., 2-72
   Brs./Divs. (Govt.): Quick Ref. *see* Fisheries, 3-17; B.C., 3-108; Nfld., 3-143; N.S., 3-160; P.E.I., 3-188
   Dept. (Govt.) N.B., 3-136; Nfld., 3-144
   Exhibitions, Shows & Events, 1-82
   Govt. Quick Ref., *see* Fisheries, 3-17
   Industry Alliance, Cdn., 2-71
   Publications, *see* Fisheries Magazines
Aquaria, 6-45
Aquarium(s) (*see also* Aquaria)
   Cdn. Assn. of Zoological Parks &, 2-21
   & Marine Ctr., N.B., 3-136
Aquatic Fedn. of Canada, 2-172
   Resources Inc. (Nfld.), 9-20
Aquiculture/pêches
   commerciales, Dir. gén. (Qué.), 3-197
   Dept. (N.B.), 3-136
Arab Fedn., Cdn., 2-129
Arabian Horse Registry, Cdn., 2-19
Arabic Magazines, 5-191
Arbitrage
   commercial
      Fédn intle des insts d', 2-111
      Ntl & intl du Qué., Centre d', 2-110
   Insts d', 2-110
Arbitration (*see also* Labour)
   Bd., Mediation & (B.C.), 3-112
   Commission, Inter-American Commercial, 2-111
   Institutions, Intl. Fedn. of Commercial, 2-111
   & Mediation Insts., 2-110
Arboretum, *see* Botanical Gardens
Archaeological
   Assn., Cdn., 2-23
   Soc. of B.C., Underwater, 2-24
Archaeologists, Nfld. & Lab. Assn. of Amateur, 2-23
Archaeology
   Assns., 2-23
   Brs./Divs. (Govt.): B.C., 3-118; N.B., 3-138
   & History, Pointe-à-Callière, Museum of (Qué.), 6-24
   Ont. Soc. of Industrial, 2-23
Archbishop, Forms of Address, 1-34
Archdeacon, Forms of Address, 1-34
Archéologie cdnne, Assn, 2-23
Archéologues du Qué., Assn des, 2-23
Archers, Fedn. of Cdn., 2-179
Architectes
   paysagistes, Assn des (Qué.), 2-98; du Canada, 2-99
   en pratique privée du Qué., Assn des, 2-24
   du Qué., Ordre des, 2-24
Architects' Assns., 2-24
Architectural
   Assns., 2-24
   Awards, 1-96
   Conservancy of Ont., 2-24
   Heritage Soc., Sask., 2-98
   Inst.
      of B.C., 2-24
      of Canada, Royal, 2-24
   Magazines, 5-160
   Metal Assn., 2-30
   Orgs., 2-24
   Soc., NWT, 2-24
   Technologists of Ont., Assn. of, 2-24
   Woodwork Mfrs. Assn., 2-30

Architecture
   Assns., 2-24
   Awards, 1-96
   in Canada, Soc. for Study of, 2-24
   Cdn. Ctr. for, 6-24
   Faculties/Schs., Index to, 9-56
   Magazines, 5-160
Archival Appraisal Bd., Ntl., 2-119
Archives, 5-112
   Assn(s)., 2-116
      of Cdn. Map Libraries &, 2-116
      of Ont., 2-116
   of Canada, Ntl., 3-78, 5-112
   Cdn.
      Council of, 2-117
      Lesbian & Gay, 2-98
   Councils, 2-117/118
   Govt.: Quick Ref. (History/), 3-20; Alta., 3-96; B.C., 3-114; Fed. (Ntl.), 3-78; Man., 3-123; N.B., 3-140; Nfld., 3-149; Ont., 3-173; P.E.I., 3-189; Qué., 3-199; Sask., 3-213; Yukon, 3-222
   In: Alta., 5-112; B.C., 5-113; Man., 5-113; N.B., 5-113; Nfld., 5-113; N.S., 5-113; Ont., 5-113; P.E.I., 5-114; Qué., 5-114; Sask., 5-115
   nationales du Canada, 3-78, 5-112
Archivistes
   Bureau cdn des, 2-117
   du Qué., Assn des, 2-116
Archivists
   Assns., 2-116
   Bureau of Cdn., 2-117
   Govt., *see* Archives
Arctic
   College (N.W.T.), 9-21
   Environmental Strategy Info. (Fed.), 3-73
   Govt. Quick Ref., 3-3
   Inst. of N. Amer., 2-161
   Winter Games Intl. Com., 2-172
Area
   of Canada, 1-63
   Codes for Canada, 1-46
   of Major Cities, 4-153
   Measurements, 1-62
   Pressure, Force per, 1-63
   of Provinces: Alta., 3-92; B.C., 3-105; Man., 3-120; N.B., 3-131; Nfld., 3-140; N.S., 3-154; Ont., 3-164; P.E.I., 3-187; Qué., 3-193; Sask., 3-210
   of Terrs.: N.W.T., 3-150; Yukon, 3-221
ARF, 2-10
ARK II, 2-21
ARMA Intl., 2-120
Armand-Frappier Inst. (Qué.), 9-47
Armateurs cdns, Assn des, 2-188
Armed Forces Badge, Cdn., **8**
Armenian
   Evangelical Church, 2-2
   Holy Apostolic Church, 2-2
   Magazines, 5-191
   National
      Com. of Canada, 2-128
      Fedn., 2-128
Armoires de cuisine, Assn cdnne de fabricants d', 2-123
Arms & Ammunition Assn., Cdn. Sporting, 2-178
Army
   Benevolent Fund (Fed.), 3-92
   Cadet League of Canada, 2-126
   Navy & Air Force Veterans, 2-126
Arpenteurs-géomètres
   Conseil cdn des, 2-182
   du N.-B., Assn des, 2-182
   du Qué., Ordre des, 2-182
Art (*see also* Arts)
   Assn(s)., 2-24
      Western Canada, 2-191
      Women's, 2-193
   Awards, *see* Culture, Visual Arts
   Cdn. Soc. for Educ. through, 2-50
   Collectors Assn., Corp., 2-190

Art (cont.)
   Colleges: Alta, 9-4; B.C., 9-9; Ont., 9-34
   Conseil des métiers d' (Qué.), 2-190
   contemporain de Montréal, Musée d', 6-34
   Critics, Intl. Assn of, 2-191
   Dealers Assn., Profl., 2-191
   & Design
      Alta. College of, 9-4
      Emily Carr Inst. of (B.C.), 9-9
   dramatique du Qué., Conservatoires, 3-199
   Exhibitions, Shows & Events, 1-73
   Fdns.: Cdn., 2-190; Inuit, 2-133
   Galleries, 6-29; Assns., 2-77
      Ont. Assn. of, 2-78
   Gallery Assn., Atlantic Provs., 2-77
   Industry & Science, Cdn. Soc. for Color in, 2-59
   Libraries Soc. of N. Amer., 2-116
   Magazines, 5-160, 5-177
   Museum Dirs. Org., Cdn., 2-77
   National
      Assn. for Photographic, 2-140
      du Canada, Fond. d', 2-191
   Ontario
      College of, 9-34
      Soc. for Educ. through, 2-191
   Resource Ctr., Women's, 2-193
   Schs., Ont., 9-34
   Shows, 1-73
   Soc., SIAS Intl., 2-191
   Therapy
      Assn., Cdn., 2-190
      Insts., (Toronto), 9-36; (Vancouver), 9-10
Arthritis Soc., 2-81
Arthur Ellis Awards, 1-105
Artisans, Council of Man., 2-191
Artiste(s)
   cdns: Le Front des, 2-24; Soc. des, 2-191
   des centres alternatifs, Regroupement des, 2-24
   Commn de reconnaissance des assns d', 3-199
   -producteurs, Tribunal cdn des relations professionnelles, 3-56
   Union des, 2-207
Artistic Assn., Cdn. Literary &, 2-111
Artist(s)
   Awards & Prizes, *see* Culture
   Ctrs., Assn. of Ntl. Non-Profit, 2-24
   Fedn. of Cdn., 2-25
   Managers, Cdn. Assn. of, 2-24
   & Producers Profl. Relations Tribunal, Cdn. 3-56
   Representation, Cdn., 2-24
   Soc. of Cdn., 2-191
   in Stained Glass, 2-190
Arts (*see also* Art)
   Alta. Fdn. for the, 2-24
   Alliance, Sask., 2-25
   Assn(s)., 2-24
      Cdn. Celtic, 2-24
   Awards, 1-96 (*see also* Broadcasting & Film; Literary Arts; Performing Arts)
   Banff Ctr. for the, 9-4
   Bd., Sask., 3-219
   Brs./Divs. (Govt.): Quick Ref., 3-3; Alta., 3-96; Fed., 3-58; Man., 3-123; N.B., 3-138; Ont., 3-172; Sask., 3-219; Yukon, 3-225
   Canada Council, 3-55
   Cdn. Conf. of the, 2-25
   Cdn. Soc. of Decorative, 2-190
   Centre, Ntl., 3-79
   Conseil des, 3-55
   Council(s)
      Assembly of B.C., 2-24
      for Business & the, 2-25
      Canada, 3-55
      Prov: B.C., 3-119; Man., 2-25, 3-123; N.B., 2-25; Nfld. & Lab., 2-25; N.W.T., 2-25, 3-151; Ont., 2-32, 3-173; P.E.I., 2-25; Sask., 2-25; Yukon, 2-25

Canadian Almanac & Directory 1997

Arts (cont.)
   & Culture
      Directory, 6-1
      Govt. Quick Ref., 3-3
   Décoratifs
      Cercle cdn des, 2-190
      Musée des, 6-24
   Directory, 6-1
   Exhibitions, Shows & Events, 1-73
   Faculties/Schs., Index to, 9-56
   Festivals, 1-73
      Associated Man., 2-66
      Assn., Intl. Native, 2-133
   Foundation
      Cdn. Native, 2-133
      Governor General's Performing, 2-25
      of Greater Toronto, 2-24
   Govt. Quick Ref., 3-3
   Graphic, see Graphic Arts
   Graphiques du Qué., Assn des, 2-143
   Guild, Metal, 2-191
   et des lettres, Conseil des (Qué.), 2-25; 3-199
   Magazines, 5-177
   Montréal Museum of Fine, 6-34
   Musée des beaux-, 6-34
   Orgs., 2-24
   Place des, de Montréal, 3-200
   Policy Br. (Fed.), 3-58
   Populaires, Conseil cdn des, 2-190
   Presenting Assn., Cdn., 2-24
   Publicists Assns., Performing, 2-25
   Royal
      Cdn. Academy of, 2-191
      Soc. for the Encouragement of, 2-157
   Soc., B.C. Festival of the, 3-119
   textiles du Qué., Conseil des, 2-190
   Websites, 5-233
   for Young Audiences, Cdn. Inst. of the, 2-25
Asbestos
   Council, Cdn. Ntl., 2-35
   Inst., 2-127
   Mining Assn., Qué., 2-127
   Natl. Soc. (Qué.), 3-205
   Wkrs., Intl. Assn. of, 2-202
Ash Wednesday, 1-24
Asia Pacific
   Fdn., 2-187, 3-112
   Studies, Joint Ctr. for Research on: U. of T., 9-31; York Univ., 9-32
Asian
   AIDS Project, Gay, 2-18
   Studies
      Assn., Cdn., 2-47
      Ctr. for
         Canada/(Queen's Univ.), 9-29
         Northeast (U. of Regina), 9-54
         South (U. of T.), 9-30
ASM Intl., 2-103
Asparagus Growers' Mktg. Bd., Ont., 3-170
Asphalt Assn., Cdn. Technical, 2-59
Assainissement
   des eaux, Soc. qué. d', 2-65; 3-202
   de l'énergie, Soc. planétaire pour l', 2-57
Assemblée ntle (Qué.), 3-194
Assessment
   Appeal
      Bds.: B.C., 3-118; Yukon, 3-222
      Tribunal of N.W.T., 3-152
   Authority, B.C., 3-118
   Mgmt. Agency, Sask., 3-213
   Review Bds.: N.B. (Regional), 3-138, (Ont. Att. Gen.), 3-172
Assessors
   N.S. Inst of, 2-102
   of Ont., Inst. of Mun., 2-102
Assinibone
   Community College (Man.), 9-16
   River Mgmt. Auth. (Man.), 3-130

Assistance, Victims, see Crimes Compensation; Justice Depts.
Association
   Executives, Cdn. Soc. of, 2-121
   Research & Education, Fdn. for, 2-121
Associations
   Incorporation of, Govt. Quick Ref., 3-22
   du Québec, Centre pour l'avancement des, 2-121
   & Socs., 2-8
Assumption Univ. (Windsor), 9-32
Assurance
   automobile, Soc. de l' (Qué.), 2-27; 3-208
   du barreau cdn, Assn d', 2-113
   du Canada, Bureau, 2-105
   Dépôts (Govt.): Fed., 3-55; Qué., 3-203
   de Dommages du Qué., L'Inst d', 2-106
   Institutes, 2-106
   -maladie, Régie de l' (Qué.), 3-207
   de personnes du Qué., Assn des intermédiaires, 2-104
   Regroupement des cabinets de courtage d', 2-105
   -vie
      Assn cdnne des directeurs médicaux en, 2-105
      Institut d', 2-106
Assurances
   agricoles, Régie des (Qué.), 3-198
   Assns des courtiers d', 2-105
   Commn. admin. des régimes de retraite et (Qué.), 3-120
   de dommages, Conseil des, 2-105
   de personnes, Assn cdnne des companies d', 2-105
   Surintendant (Qué.), 3-203
Assureurs
   automobiles, Groupement des, 2-105
   en bris des machines, 2-104
   Cdns, Assn des, 2-104
   Laboratoires des, 2-106
   Service anti-crime des, 2-105
   -vie, L'Assn des, 2-106
ASTED, 2-117
Asthma
   Info. Assn., Allergy, 2-81
   Soc. of Canada, 2-82
Astronauts Program, Cdn., 3-62
Astronomical
   Calculations, 1-1
   Soc.
      Cdn., 2-161
      Royal, 2-163
   Symbols, 1-15
   Tables, 1-8
Astronomy
   Awards, see Science Awards
   in Canada, 1-1
   Govt. Quick Ref., 3-36
   Reading Suggestions, 1-22
   Websites, 1-22
Astrophysics
   Cdn. Inst. of Theoretical (U. of T.), 9-30
   Herzberg Inst. of (NRC), 3-81
Asylum (Fed.), 3-63
Ataxie de Friedreich, Assn cdnne de l', 2-81
Athabasca Univ. (Alta.), 9-3
Athlete Fedn., Cdn. Master, 2-176
Athletic
   Assn(s)., 2-172
      Alta. Schools, 2-172
      Cdn. Colleges, 2-174
      Man. High Schs., 2-179
      Ont. Fedn. of School, 2-179
   Awards, see Sport(s)
   Commr., Ont., 3-174
   Fedn.: Nfld. & Lab. High School, 2-179; N.S. School, 2-179; P.E.I. School, 2-180
   Therapists Assn., Cdn., 2-84
   Union, Cdn. Interuniv., 2-47
Athletics Canada, 2-172
Atkinson College, (York Univ.), 9-32

Atlantic
   Broadcasting Inst. (N.S.), 9-23
   Canada
      Assn. of Free Will Baptists, 2-2
      Opportunities Agency, 3-54
      Plus Assn., 2-121
   Communication & Technical Wkrs.' Union, 2-198
   Construction Training (Nfld.), 9-20
   Council of Canada, 2-107
   Dairy Council, 2-13
   Ecumenical Council of Churches, 2-6
   Farmers Council, 2-13
   Filmmakers' Coop., 2-68
   First Nations AIDS Task Force, 2-17
   Fisheries
      Museum of the (N.S.), 6-13
      Orgs., 3-278
   Fishery, Task Force on Incomes & Adjustment in the, 3-68
   Home Builders Training (N.S.), 9-23
   Lottery Corp. (N.B.), 3-136
   Marine Trades Assn., 2-124
   Maritime Museum of the (N.S.), 6-13
   Oil Wkrs., 2-198
   Pilotage Auth., 3-54
   Police Academy (P.E.I.), 9-41
   Provinces
      Art Gallery Assn., 2-77
      Council on the Sciences, 2-161
      Economic Council, 2-44, 3-131
      Education Fdn., 2-47, 3-131
      Hatchery Fedn., 2-142
      Library Assn., 2-117
      Pharmacy Council, 2-139
      Special Educ. Authority, 9-22
      Transp. Commn., 2-188
   Salmon Fedn., 2-71
   School of
      Chartered Accountancy, 2-8
      Theology (N.S.), 9-22
   Tunas, Intl. Commn. for the Conservation of, 3-248
   Univs., Assn. of, 2-46
Atlantique
   Administration de pilotage de l', 3-54
   Agence de promotion économique du Canada, 3-54
Atmospheric
   Chemistry, Cdn. Inst. for Research in, 2-162
   Environment Service (Fed.), 3-65
Atomic Energy
   Agency, Intl. (in Canada), 3-247
   of Canada Ltd., 3-54
   Control Bd., 3-54
   Govt. Quick Ref., (see Nuclear Energy), 3-28
Atomique
   du Canada ltée, Énergie, 3-54
   Commn de contrôle de l'Énergie, 3-54
Attorney(s) (see also Crown Attorneys)
   Assns., Crown: Man., 2-115; Ont., 2-115
   General (see also Justice)
      Depts.: Alta. (Justice), 3-101; B.C., 3-109; Fed. (Justice), 3-77; Man. (Justice), 3-77; N.B. (Justice), 3-128; Nfld., 3-146; Ont., 3-170; P.E.I., 3-191; Sask., 3-217
Audio Engrg. Soc., 2-28
Audiologistes, Ordre des orthophonistes et, (Qué.), 2-94
Audiologists, Cdn. Assn. of Speech-Lang. Pathologists &, 2-84
Audit
   Bd., Cdn. Circulations, 2-144
   Bur. of Circulations, 2-11
   Canada, 3-85
Auditifs, Assn du Qué. pour enfants avec problèmes, 2-41
Auditing Fdn., Cdn. Comprehensive, 2-8

Auditor(s)
　Certification Bd., B.C., 3-115
　Generals (Govt.): Quick Ref., 3-3; Alta., 3-96; B.C., 3-110; Fed., 3-54; Man., 3-122; N.B., 3-134; Nfld., 3-142; N.S., 3-156; Ont., 3-172; P.E.I., 3-189; Qué., 3-210; Sask., 3-213
　Inst. of Internal, 2-9
Augustana Univ. College (Alta.), 9-3
AUPELF-UREF, 2-45
Aurora Research Inst. (N.W.T.), 3-151
Australia-New Zealand Assn., 2-128
Auteurs
　et Compositeurs
　　cdns, Assn des, 2-194
　　dramatiques, Ctr. des, 6-35
　　et éditeurs de musique, Soc. cdnne des, 2-139
　Recherchistes, documentalistes et compositeurs, Soc. des, 2-206
Authors
　Assn., Cdn., 2-194
　Awards see Literary Awards
　Cdn. Soc. of Children's, 2-194
　& Music Publishers, Soc. of Composers, 2-139
Autism
　Assns., 2-82/83
　Soc. of Canada, 2-82
　Treatment Services, 2-83
Auto (see also Automobile; Automotive)
　Insurance (Qué.), 3-208
　League, Ntl., 2-27
Auto-Distribution, L'Assn Cdnne d', 2-11
Auto Immune Deficiency Syndrome see AIDS
Autobus
　Assn cdnne de l', 2-188
　du Qué., Assn des propriétaires, 2-25
Autochtone(s)
　Affaires (Govt.): N.B., 3-137; Qué., 3-196
　Assn des infirmières et infirmiers, 2-132
　Centres d'Amitié, 2-134
　Commn d'appel pour les (Qué. Santé), 3-207
　Orgs, 2-132
　du Qué., Alliance, 2-133
　　Femmes, 2-134
　de Québec, Inst. de formation, 9-48
　pour le tourisme, Assn cdnne ntle des, 2-185
Automated Bldgs. Assn., Cdn., 2-58
Automatic
　Merchandising Assn., Cdn., 2-11
　Sprinkler Assn., Cdn., 2-159
Automatisation des bâtiments, Assn cdnne pour l', 2-58
Automobile(s) (see also Auto; Automotive)
　Aerospace
　　& Agricl. Implement Wkrs. of Amer., Intl. Union, 2-203
　　Transportation & General Wkrs. Union, Ntl. (CAW), 2-203
　Assn(s)., 2-26; Cdn., 2-26
　Club of Amer., Antique, 2-23
　Corp. des concessionnaires d' (Qué.), 2-26
　Dealers'
　　Assns. (see also Motor): Nfld., 2-25; N.B., 2-27; N.S., 2-27; Ont., 2-27; P.E.I., 2-27; Sask., 2-27
　　Cdn. Assn. of Japanese, 2-26
　　in Ont., Org. of Reg'rd, 2-27
　　Registrars, see Motor Vehicles
　Groupement des assureurs, 2-105
　Injury Compensation Appeal Commn. (Man.), 3-123
　Insurance
　　Bd., Alta., 3-105
　　Govt. Quick Ref., 3-4
　Journalists Assn. of Canada, 2-25
　Magazines, 5-178
　Manufacturers
　　Assn., Japan, 2-26
　　of Canada, Assn. of Intl., 2-187
　Orgs., 2-25
　Parking Soc. (Qué.), 3-210

Automobile(s) (cont.)
　Protection Assn., 2-25
　Racing Assn. of Canada, Vintage, 2-23
　Reg. (Fed.), 3-91
　Shows, 1-71
　Sports Clubs, Cdn., 2-26
Automotive
　Aftermarket Retailers of Ont., 2-25
　Assns., 2-25
　Equipment Assn., Ntl., 2-27
　Exhibition, Shows & Events, 1-73
　Industries Assn. of Canada, 2-25
　Magazines, 5-160
　Parts Mfrs. Assn. of Canada, 2-25
　Repair & Service Inst., Cdn., 2-26; Council, 2-26
　Retailers Assn. of B.C., 2-26
　Trades Assns.: Man., 2-26
Autoplan, B.C., 3-117
Autumn begins, 1-3
Auxiliaires bénévolés des établissements de santé, Assns 2-100
Auxiliary Hosps. in Canada, List of, 8-1
Avalanche Assn., Cdn., 2-55
Avalon Consolidated Integrated Sch. Bd. (Nfld.), 9-19
Aveugles
　Assn cdnne des sports pour, 2-174
　Conseil cdn des, 2-42
　Inst ntl cdn pour les, 2-42
　du Qué., Assn sportive des, 2-174
　Soc. John Milton pour les, Canada, 2-43
Aviation
　Assns., 2-27
　Career Academy (Nfld.), 9-20
　civile intle, Org. de l', 2-28
　Councils: Alta., 2-27; B.C., 2-27
　Flood & Fire Mgmt., Dir. (Ont.), 3-184
　Govt. Quick Ref., 3-2
　Hist'l Soc., Cdn., 2-28
　Magazines, 5-160, 5-178
　Maintenance Council, Cdn., 2-28
　Musée ntl de l', 6-1
　Museum, Ntl., 6-1
　Org., Intl. Civil, 2-28, 3-247
　Regulation (Fed.), 3-91
　Shows see Air Shows
　Transp. Canada, 3-91
Avicultural Adv. Council of Canada, 2-134
Aviron, Rowing Canada, 2-180
Avortement, Assn cdnne pour le droit à, 2-154
Awards, Major Cdn., 1-92
Ayrshire Breeders Assn. of Canada, 2-19
Azimuths of Sun, 1-7

B

Babies & Mothers Magazines, 5-178
Bach-Elgar Choral Soc., 6-39
Backpackers Intl. Assn., 2-149
Bacterial Diseases Network, Cdn., 2-154
Badminton Assns., 2-172
Baha'i
　Calendar, 1-2
　Faith, 2-2
　Studies, Assn. for, 2-45
Baie-Comeau-Hauterive, Soc. du port ferroviaire, 3-208
Bakery
　Confectionery & Tobacco Wkrs. Intl. Union, 2-198
　Council of Canada, 2-72; Qué., 2-73
Baking & Bakers' Magazines, 5-161
Balais, Assn cdnne des fabricants de, 2-123
BALANCE, 2-41
Baldwin-Cartier, Commn Scolaire (Qué.), 9-42
Ball Hockey Assn., Cdn., 2-174
Ballet(s)
　Assns. & Companies, 6-41
　Awards, see Performing Arts
　of Canada, National, 6-43

Ballet(s) (cont.)
　Royal Winnipeg, 6-44
Balloon Owners & Pilots Assn., Fantasy, 2-151
Baltic Fedn. in Canada, 2-128
Band
　Assns., 6-39
　Operated Schs., see Native Schs.
Banff Centre, 9-4
Bangladesh Awami League of Canada, 2-129
Bank(s), 7-1, (see also Trust Cos.; Loan Cos.; Credit Unions)
　Business Devel. (Fed.), 3-55
　of Canada, 3-55
　　Currency Museum of the, 6-1
　Chartered, 7-1
　Domestic, 7-1
　Foreign, Subsidiaries, 7-2
　Savings, 7-3
　Schedule I, 7-1; Schedule II, 7-2
　Statistics, 1-57
Bankers
　Assn., Cdn., 2-69
　Inst. of Cdn., 2-70
Banking
　Govt. Quick Ref., 3-4
　Ombudsman, Cdn., 7-1
Bankruptcy
　Govt. Quick Ref., 3-4
　Official Receivers, 10-21
　Registrars: B.C., 10-4; Man., 10-7; N.B., 10-7; Nfld., 10-8; N.W.T., 10-9; N.S., 10-9; Ont., 10-10; P.E.I., 10-14; Qué., 10-15; Yukon, 10-21
　Supt. of, (Fed.), 3-76
Banque(s), 7-1
　du Canada, 3-55
　de Devéloppement du Canada, 3-55
　laurentienne du Canada, 7-2
　ntle du Canada, 7-1
　d'yeux du Qué., 2-92
Banquiers Cdns
　Assn des, 2-69
　Inst des, 2-70
Banting Research Fdn., 2-208
Baptist(s)
　Atlantic Canada Assn. of Free Will, 2-2
　Cdn. Conv. of Southern, 2-2
　Churches
　　Assn. of Regular, 2-6
　　Fellowship of Evangelical, 2-4
　　Union of French, 2-2
　College, N. Amer. (Alta.), 9-3
　Conf., N. Amer., 2-4
　Convention
　　of Atlantic Provs., United, 2-3
　　of Ont. & Qué., 2-2
　General Conf. of Canada, 2-2
　Intl. Ministries, Cdn., 2-3
　Ministries, Cdn., 2-2
　Seminary: Cdn., 9-8; Northwest, 9-8; Toronto, 9-34
　Theologic College (B.C.), 9-8
　Union of Western Canada, 2-2
Baptiste(s)
　françaises, Union d'églises, 2-2
　des provinces de l'Atlantique, La Convention, 2-2
Bar
　Assn(s)., 2-113
　　Cdn., 2-113
　　Québec, 2-113
　Fdn., Cdn., 2-113
　Insurance Assn., Cdn., 2-113
　of Montréal, 2-113
Barbers
　Assn. of B.C., 2-67
　Magazines, 5-161
Barber Shop Quartet Singing, Soc. for Preservation of, 6-41
Barils, Assn cdnne de saut de, 2-149

Barley
    Growers Assn., Western, 2-16
    Research Inst., Brewing & Malting, 2-72
Baronets, Cdn., 1-30
Barons, Cdn., 1-30
Barreau
    Cdn
        Assn du, 2-113
        Fdn du, 2-113
    de Montréal, 2-113
    du Québec, 2-113
        Fdn du, 2-114
Barrel Jumping Assn., Cdn., 2-149
Barrie City Govt., 4-153
Barristers Soc., N.S., 2-144
Baseball
    Assns., 2-172
    Players' Assn., Major League, 2-203
Basketball
    Assns., 2-173; Cdn. Wheelchair, 2-178
    Fdn., Dr. James Naismith, 2-179
Bataille ntl, Commn des champs de, 3-79
Bâtiment, Régie du, 3-209
Bâtiments, Assn cdnne pour l'automatisation des, 2-58
Baton Twirling Fedn., Cdn., 2-149
Battery Assn., Cdn., 2-123
Battle of Normandy Fdn., Cdn., 2-126
Battlefields Commn., Ntl., 3-79
Bayfield Inst. for Marine Science & Surveys, 3-68
Bayhurst Gas Ltd. (Sask.), 3-220
BBM, Bur. of Measurement, 2-28
BBYO Canada, 2-36
B.C. (*see also* British Columbia)
    Rail, 1-68, 3-112
    Social Credit Party, 2-141
    Stats, 3-114
Bean Mktg. Bds.: N.S., 3-156; Ont., 3-170
Beauport, Ville de, Govt., 4-153
Beauticians Magazines, 5-161
Beauty Assn., Allied, 2-67
Beaux arts, Musée des: du Canada, 6-29; de Montréal, 6-34
Beaver, Operation, 2-167
Beaverbrook Cdn. Fdn., 2-208
Bedford Inst. of Oceanography, 3-68
Beef (*see also* Cattle)
    Commn., N.S., 3-156
    Export Fedn., Cdn., 2-187
    Info. Ctr., 2-13
Beekeepers Assns. (*see also* Honey): N.S., 2-15; Ont., 2-15; Sask., 2-15
Belarusian Cdn. Alliance, 2-129
Belgian
    Govt.
        Depts./Agencies, 3-230
        Equivalency Table, 3-226
    Horse Assn., Cdn., 2-19
Belgium, Govt., 3-226, 3-230
Belgo-Cdn. Assn., 2-129
Benefits Conf., Cdn. Pension &, 2-70
Benevolent & Protective Order of Elks, 2-75
Bénévole
    de l'Ont., Assn des centres' d'action: Ont., 2-168; Qué., 2-167
Bénévoles, Regroupement des orgs ntles, 2-166
Bereaved Families of Ont., 2-165
Bétail, Assn cdnne des éleveurs de, 2-19
Béton
    Assn cdnne des
        fabricants de Tuyaux de, 2-30
        manufacturiers de maçonnerie en, 2-30
    Canada, 2-32
    précontraint, Inst cdn du, 2-31
    Québec, Assn, 2-30
Better
    Basic Educ., Intl. Assn. for, 2-52
    Business Bureaus, Cdn. Council of, 2-33

Beverage
    Companies, Cdn., 7-41
    Exhibitions, Shows & Events, 1-83
    Industry Assns., 2-72
    Magazines, Food &, 5-182
Beverly & Qamanirjuag Cariboo Mgmt. Board, 3-74
Biathlon Canada, 2-173
Bible
    Colleges in: Alta., 9-4; B.C., 9-10; Man., 9-15; Ont., 9-34
    Assn. of Cdn., 2-45
    Holiness Movement, 2-6
    Hour, Canada's Ntl., 2-6
    League of Canada, 2-6
    Soc. cdnne pour la dist. de la, 2-6
    Society, Cdn., 2-6
    & Tract Soc. of Canada, Watch Tower, 2-6
Biblical
    Assn. of Canada, Catholic, 2-7
    Studies, Cdn. Soc. of, 2-50
Bibliographic Services, Govt. Quick Ref., 3-4
Bibliographical Soc. of Canada, 2-117
Bibliothécaires
    Awards, *see* Literary Awards
    parlementaires, Assn des, 2-116
    profls du
        N.-B., Assn des, 2-116
        Qué., Corp des, 2-119
    du Qué., Assn des, 2-119
Bibliotechniciens de l'Ont., Assn des, 2-119
Bibliothéconomie, Conseil cdn des écoles de, 2-118
Bibliothèque(s), 5-1
    archives et centres de doc. musicaux, Assn cdnne des, 2-117
    Centres de documentation universitaires et recherche d'expression française, Assn des responsables, 2-117
    de droit
        Assn cdnne des, 2-117
        de Montréal, Assn des, 2-116
    du gouvernement fédéral, Conseil des, 2-119
    ntle du Canada, 5-1
    du Parlement, 3-78
    publiques (Qué.), 5-85
        de l'Abitibi-Témiscamingue, 2-120
        du Bas-Saint-Laurent, 2-117
        de la Côte-Nord, 2-120
        de l'Estrie, Assn des, 2-116
        du Lac-Saint-Jean et Saguenay, 2-120
        Montérégie, 2-117
    de recherche, Assn des, 2-117
    de la région
        Mauricie-Bois-Francs, 2-116
        du Nord de Montréal, 2-119
        des régions de Québec et Chaudière-Appalaches, 2-117
    de la santé, Assns des, 2-118
Biblio-santé de la région de Qué., Groupe, 2-119
Biblique cdnne, Soc., 2-6
Bien-être, Conseil de la santé et du (Qué.), 3-207
Big
    Brothers
        of B.C. & Affiliated Big Sisters, 2-164
        & Big Sisters of Canada, 2-164
    Sisters Assn. of Ont., 2-164
Bijoutiers du Qué., La Corp. des, 2-78
Bilingual Educ., Manitoba Assn. for, 2-52
Bilingualism
    Govt. Quick Ref., 3-5
    Translation Servs. (Fed.), 3-87
Billings, World Org. Ovulation Method, 2-154
Biochemistry & Molecular Biology, Cdn. Soc. of, 2-162
Biochemists, Cdn. Assn. of Medical, 2-83
Biodiagnostics, Inst. for (NRC), 3-81
Biodiversity Dir. (Fed.), 3-65
Biodynamie du Qué., Assn de, 2-161
Bio-Industries du Qué., Conseil des, 2-62

Biological
    Engrg. Soc., Cdn. Medical &, 2-162
    Sciences, Inst. for (NRC), 3-81
    Socs., Cdn. Fedn. of, 2-161
Biologie végétale, Inst de recherche en, 2-63
Biologique du Qué., Fédn de l'agriculture, 2-15
Biologistes du Qué., Assn des, 2-161
Biologists
    Alta. Soc. of Profl., 2-161
    of B.C., Assn. of Profl., 2-161
    Cdn. Soc. of Environmental, 2-61
Biology Chairs, Cdn. Council of Univ., 2-47
Biomass & Biotechnology Promotion (Qué.), 3-200
Biomasses, Centre qué. de valorisation de la, 3-200
Biomaterials, Ctr. for (U. of T.), 9-30
Biomedical Engineering, Inst. (U. of T.), 9-31
Biophysical Soc. of Canada, 2-161
Biotechnologies, Ctr. qué. de valorisation des, 3-200
Biotechnology
    Assn., Industrial, 2-163
    Cdn. Inst. of, 2-162
    Companies, Cdn., 7-40
    Govt. Quick Ref., 3-5
    Research Ctr. (NRC), 3-81
Bird(s) (*see also* Wildlife)
    Fdn. Jack Miner, Migratory, 2-135
    Provincial, **9**
    Sanctuary, Reifel, 2-135
Birks Family Fdn., 2-208
Birmanie, Les Amis Cdns de la, 2-108
Birth
    Assns., 2-36
    Certificates (Govt.): Govt. Quick Ref., 3-39; Alta., 3-103; B.C., 3-116; Man., 3-122; N.B., 3-136; Nfld., 3-145; N.W.T., 3-154; N.S., 3-157; Ont., 3-174; P.E.I., 3-191; Qué., 3-204; Sask., 3-215; Yukon, 3-223
    & Death Statistics, 1-48 (*see also* Vital Statistics)
Birthparent & Relative Group Soc., 2-165
Birthright, 2-154
Biscuit Mfrs., Assn. of Cdn., 2-72
Bishops
    Conf. of Catholic: Cdn., 2-5; Ont., 2-5
    Forms of Address, 1-34
    Univ. (Qué.), 9-46
Bison Assn., Cdn., 2-19
Black
    Coalition for AIDS Prevention, 2-17
    Community Magazines, 5-191
    Cultural Ctr. for N.S., 2-129
    History Soc., Ont., 2-97
    Secretariat, The, 2-129
    Women of Canada, Congress of, 2-192
Blé, Commn cdnne du, 3-62
Blessures de la route, Fdn de recherches sur, 2-157
Blind (*see also* Visually Impaired)
    Cdn. Council of the, 2-42
    Cdn.
        Guide Dogs for the, 2-42
        Ntl. Inst. for the, 2-42
    John Milton Soc. for the, 2-43
    Ntl. Camps for the, 2-42
    Sports Assns., 2-174
Blindness, E.A. Baker Fdn. for Prev. of, 2-209
Bloc Québécois, 2-141; Office of the Leader (Fed. Opposition), 3-46
Block Parents Programs: B.C., 2-165; Canada, 2-165; Ont., 2-168; P.E.I., 2-168; Sask., 2-169; Yukon, 2-172
Blonde d'Aquitaine Assn., Cdn., 2-19
Blood Transfusion Service Employees Assn. (Cdn. Red Cross), 2-199
Blue Cross
    Employees Assn., 2-204
    Plans, Cdn. Council of, 2-104
Bluegrass, *see* Music
B'nai B'rith
    Canada, 2-128
    League for Human Rights of, 2-102
    Youth Org., 2-36

Boards
    of Educ. (*see also* Education)
        in: Alta., 9-1; B.C., 9-6; Man., 9-13; N.B., 9-17;
            Nfld., 9-19; N.W.T., 9-21; N.S., 9-21; Ont., 9-24;
            P.E.I., 9-41; Qué., 9-41; Sask., 9-51
    of Examiners, *see* Examiners
    Parole (*see* Parole Boards)
    of Review (Govt.): Quick Ref., 3-5; Alta., 3-102;
        B.C., 3-110; Man., 3-164
    of Trade in: Alta., 7-24; B.C., 7-26; Cdn., 7-23; Intl.,
        7-23; Man., 7-28; N.B., 7-28; Nfld., 7-29; N.W.T., 7-
        29; N.S., 7-29; Ont., 7-30; P.E.I., 7-32; Prov.,
        Territorial, 7-24; Qué., 7-32; Sask., 7-34; Yukon, 7-
        35
Boat(s)
    Govt. Quick Ref., (*see* Leisure Craft), 3-25
    Shows, *see* Boating
    Soc., Antique & Classic, 2-23
Boating
    Assn., Maritime, 2-152
    Exhibitions, Shows & Events, 1-74
    Fedn., Cdn., 2-149
    Magazines, 5-161, 5-178
    Regs., Govt. Agencies, *see* Leisure Craft Regs., 3-25
Bob Rumball Ctr. for the Deaf, 2-41
Bobsleigh Canada, 2-173
Body
    Building, Cdn. Fedn. of, 2-149
    Guards of the Govt. of Qué., Profl. Assn., 2-198
Boiler
    Insp., *see* Boilers
    & Machinery Underwriters' Assn., Cdn., 2-104
    Soc., Cdn., 2-123
Boilermakers, Intl. Broth. of, 2-202
Bois
    Assn cdnne de l'industrie du, 2-74
    Bureau cdn de la préservation du, 2-75
    Conseil cdn du, 2-75
    dur, Assn cdnne du contreplaqué de, 2-74
    Fédn des producteurs de (Qué.), 2-75; 3-198
    de sciage des Maritimes, 2-75; Ont., 2-75; Qué., 2-74
    traités, Inst cdn des, 2-74
Boissons gazeuses, Assn
    cdnne de l'industrie des, 2-73
    des embouteilleurs des (Qué.), 2-73
Boîtes en cartons, Assn cdnne des fabricants de, 2-138
BOMA Canada, 2-147
Bombardier, Fdn. J. Armand, 2-210
Book(s)
    Artists Guild, 2-144
    Assn. for Export of Cdn., 2-144
    Award(s), 1-104
        in Canada First Novel Award, 1-104
    Centre, Cdn. Children's, 2-144
    Exchange Ctr., Cdn., 5-1
    Exhibitions, Shows & Events, 1-74
    Magazines, 5-161, 5-185
    Manufacturers Assn., Cdn., 2-144
    & Periodical Council, 2-144
    Promoters' Assn., 2-144
    Publishers, 5-115
        Assns., 2-144
    Publishing Industry Devel. Program (Fed.), 3-58
    Rare (National Library), 5-1
    for Young People, Intl. Bd. on, 2-145
Bookbinders & Book Artists Guild, Cdn., 2-144
Booksellers
    Assn.
        Antiquarian, 2-23
        Cdn., 2-144
        Christian, 2-145
Border Servs., Customs (Fed.), 3-86
Boréal, Collège (Ont.), 9-33
Borstal Assn., B.C., 2-145
Botanical
    Assn., Cdn., 2-161
    Garden, Friends of the Montréal, 2-98
    Gardens, 6-45; Royal, 2-99

Bottled Water Fedn., Cdn., 2-72
Boulangerie, Conseil cdn de la, 2-72; du Qué., 2-73
Boulingrin Canada, 2-152
Boundaries Commns.
    B.C.
        -Alberta, 3-113
        -Yukon-N.W.T., 3-113
    Intl., 3-76
Boundary
    Arbitration, Canada-France Maritime (Cdn.
        Agent), 3-69
    Commn., Intl., 3-76
    Layer Wind Tunnel Laboratory (U.W.O.), 9-31
Bourse de Montréal, 7-10
Bovins
    Cdns, Soc. des éleveurs de, 2-19
    Fédn des producteurs (Qué.), 2-21; 3-198
Bowlers' Assn., Cdn. 5 Pin, 2-173
Bowling
    Council, Ntl. Youth, 2-179
    Fedn., Canada, 2-173
    Proprietors' Assns., 2-173
Box Mfrs. Assn., Cdn. Paper, 2-138
Boxe amateur, Assn cdnne de, 2-173
Boxing
    Assn., Cdn. Amateur, 2-173
    Fedn., Cdn. Profl., 2-176
Boy Scouts of Canada, 2-37
Boys & Girls' Clubs of Canada, 2-36
B.P.O. Elks of Canada, 2-75
Brain
    Injury Coalition, Cdn., 2-42
    Tissue Bank, Cdn., 2-84
Brampton City Govt., 4-154
Brandon
    City Govt., 4-154
    Univ., 9-15
Brantford City Govt., 4-154
Brass Devel. Assn., Cdn., 2-127
Brasseurs, Assns.: Canada, 2-72; Qué., 2-72
Bravery
    Awards, 1-95
    Decorations, Cdn., **16**, 1-28
        Cross of Valour, **16**, 1-28
        Medal of Bravery, **16**, 1-28
        Star of Courage, **16**, 1-28
Bravoure, Décorations cdnne pour actes, **16**, 1-28
Breakfast Cereals Mfrs. of Canada, 2-72
Breast Cancer
    Action, 2-191
    Soc. of Canada, 2-83
Breeders Assns., 2-19
Brescia College (Ont.), 9-31
Brethren
    in Christ, 2-2
    Church, United, 2-6
    Plymouth, 2-3
Brevets & marques, Inst cdn des, 2-138
Brewers Assn.
    of the Americas, Master, 2-73
    of Canada, 2-72; Qué., 2-72; Sask., 2-74
Brewery
    & Gen. Wkrs., Cdn. Union of, 2-204
    General & Profl. Wkrs. Union, 2-204
Brewing & Malting Barley Research Inst., 2-72
Brick & Glass Wkrs. Intl. Union, Aluminum, 2-197
Bricklayers
    & Allied Craftsmen, Intl. Union of, 2-196
    Masons Indep. Union of Canada, 2-198
Bridal
    Magazines, 5-179
    Shows, 1-75
Bridge
    Fedn., Cdn., 2-149
    Structural & Ornamental Iron Wkrs. Intl. Assn. of,
        2-202
Bridgehead Inc., 2-107

Bright Children (*see also* Gifted)
    Assns. for: Alta., 2-36; Man., 2-37; Ont., 2-36
Brique d'arquile cuite, Assn cdnne de, 2-32
Britain, *see* United Kingdom
British Columbia
    Aquaria in, 6-45
    Archives in, 5-113
    Art Galleries in, 6-30
    Boards of Trade in, 7-26
    Botanical Gardens in, 6-46
    Boundary Commns., 3-113
    Chamber(s) of
        Commerce, 7-26
        Mines of Eastern, 7-35
    Cities & Towns in, 4-12
    Community Colleges in, 9-8
    Correspondence Schs. in, 9-7
    Courts & Judges in, 10-4 (& *see* Addenda)
    Educ. in, 9-6
    Flag & Coat of Arms, **9**
    FreeNets, 5-232
    Government in, 3-105
    Hospitals in, 8-8
    House, Ottawa, 3-106
    Indep. Schs. in, 9-10
    Inst. of Techn., 9-9
    Law Firms in, 10-33
    Libraries in, 5-12
    Lobbyists in, 7-36
    Meeting, Conference, Exhibit & Event Planners in,
        1-69
    Municipal Govt. in, 4-12
    Museum, Royal, 6-4
    Museums in, 6-4
    Newspapers in, 5-132
    Nursing Homes in, 8-10
    Online Service Providers, 5-230
    Overseas Educ., 9-13
    Post-Sec. & Specialized Insts. in, 9-9
    Private Schs. in, 9-10
    Regl. Mun. in, 4-171
    Sch. Districts, 9-6
    Technical & Vocational Insts. in, 9-9
    Univs. in, 9-7
    & Yukon Chamber of Mines, 7-35
    Zoos in, 6-44
British
    Commonwealth, 3-246
    & Commonwealth Honours, 1-29
    Consuls in Canada, 3-258
    Govt.
        Depts./Agencies, 3-242
        Equivalency Table, 3-227
    High Commn. in Canada, 3-258
    Methodist Episcopal Church, 2-2
Broadcast
    Consultants, Cdn. Assn. of, 2-29
    Educators Assn. of Canada, 2-28
    Employees Union, Cdn., 2-200
    Engineers, Western Assn. of, 2-30
    Execs.' Soc., 2-29
    Research Council of Canada, 2-29
Broadcasters
    Assns., 2-28
    Awards, 1-93 (*see also* Performing Arts)
    Cdn. Assn. of, 2-29
    Magazines, 5-161
Broadcasting
    Assns., 2-28
    Awards, 1-93 (*see also* Performing Arts)
    CBC, 3-56
    College, Western Academy (Sask.), 9-55
    Corporate Head Offices, 5-198
    Corp., Cdn., 3-56
    CRTC, 3-61
    Friends of Cdn., 2-29
    Govt. Quick Ref., 3-5
    Inst., Atlantic (N.S.), 9-23

Canadian Almanac & Directory 1997

Broadcasting (cont.)
    Magazines, 5-161
    National Inst. of (Man.), 9-16
    Networks, 5-198
    Stations
        AM Radio, 5-199
        Cable, 5-223
        FM Radio, 5-206
        Television, 5-198
Brock Univ. (Ont.), 9-28
Broiler (*see also* Chicken; Egg)
    Hatching Egg
        Agencies: B.C., 3-108; Cdn., 3-80; Man., 3-122; Ont., 3-170; Sask., 3-212
        Mktg. Agency, Cdn., 2-142
        Prodrs. Assn., B.C., 2-142
Brokers, Insurance, Assns., 2-105
Bronfman (Samuel & Saidye) Family Fdn., 2-213
Bronte Soc., 2-111
Broom Mfrs. Assn., Cdn., 2-123
Brossard, Ville de, Govt., 4-154
Brosses, Assn cdnne des fabricants de, 2-123
Brown Swiss Assn., Cdn., 2-19
Bruce Trail Assn., 2-149
Brush Mfrs. Assn., Cdn., 2-123
BSD Training & Resources Ltd. (Sask.), 9-55
Buccale, l'academie cdnne
    de pathologie, 2-39
    de radiologie, 2-39
Buddhist
    Assn. of Canada, 2-6
    Churches of Canada, 2-2
        Union of Vietnamese, 2-6
Budget Offices (Govt.): Alta., 3-104; N.B., 3-135; Ont., 3-178
Builders'
    Assns., 2-30
    Hardware Mfrs. Assn. of Canada, 2-30
    Publications, *see* Building Magazines
Building (*see also* Construction)
    Assns., 2-30
    Contractors Assns., 2-30
    Envelope Council, Ntl., 2-33
    Inspectors Assn. of N.S., 2-146
    Magazines, 5-161
    Maintenance Contractors Assn., 2-30
    Officials Assns.: Man., 2-147; N.B., 2-147; Ont., 2-147; Sask., 2-148
    Owners & Mgrs. Assn., 2-147
    Products Trade Shows, 1-77
    Standards Dir. (Govt.), B.C., 3-118
    Supply
        Council, Cdn. Retail, 2-32
        Dealers' Assns., 2-32
    Trades Council, Prov. (Ont.), 2-111
Buildings
    Assn., Cdn. Automated, 2-58
    Corps. (Govt.): B.C., 3-112; Qué., 3-210
Bureaux
    de commerce, 7-23
    d'éthique commerciale, 2-33/34
Burlington City Govt., 4-154
Burma, Cdn. Friends of, 2-108
Burn Nurses, Cdn. Assn. of, 2-135
Burnaby
    Govt., 4-155
    School District, 9-6
Bursaries, Student, *see* Student Aid
Bus
    Assn., Cdn., 2-188
    History Assn., 2-95
    Magazines, 5-177
    Owners Assn., Qué., 2-25
Business (*see also* Companies)
    Abbreviations, 1-39
    Affairs Br. (Ont.), 3-174
    Aircraft Assn., Cdn., 2-188
    & the Arts, Council for, 2-25

Business (cont.)
    Assistance, Govt. Quick Ref., (*see* Industry) 3-22
    Assn(s)., 2-33
        Aboriginal Peoples, 2-132
        Latin American Cdn., 2-188
    Awards, 1-94
    Bureaus, Cdn. Council for Better, 2-33
    Cdn.
        Council for
            Aboriginal, 2-132
            Intl., 2-34
        Fedn. of Indep., 2-34
        Org. of Small, 2-34
    College, Success/Angus (Man.), 9-16
    Communicators, Intl. Assn. of, 2-35
    in the Community, Cdn. Ctr. for, 2-33
    Compucollege Sch. of (Nfld.), 9-21
    Conferences, 1-75
    & Consumer Servs. (N.S.), 3-156
    Council(s) (*see also* Boards of Trade)
        of B.C., 2-33
        on the Environment, N.S., 2-64
        Intl., 7-23
        on Ntl. Issues, 2-33
    Credit Corp., N.W.T., 3-153
    Development (*see also* Small Business; Economic Development; Development; Trade; Industry; Industrial Development)
        Adv. Bd., Yukon, 3-222
        Bank (Fed.), 3-55
        Br., Intl. (Fed. For. Affairs), 3-69
        Govt. Quick Fed., 3-6
        N.S., 3-158
    Economics, Cdn. Assn. for, 2-44
    Education Teachers, Cdn. Assn. of, 2-47
    Equity Br., (B.C.), 3-118
    Excellence, Canada Awards for, 1-95
    Exhibitions, Shows & Events, 1-75
    Faculties/Schs., Index to, 9-56
    & Finance, 5-179
    Forms, Assn., Cdn., 2-143
    Forms of Address, 1-35
    Govt. Quick Ref., 3-6
    Immigration Brs. (Govt.): B.C., 3-110; Fed., 3-63
    Inst. of Canada, Native, 2-134
    Loans Admin., Small (Fed.), 3-75
    Magazines, 5-159, 5-162, 5-164, 5-179
    Officers, Cdn. Assn. of Univ., 2-46
    Officials, Man. Assn. of Sch., 2-53; Ont., 2-53
    Orgs., 2-33
    & Profl. Women's Clubs, Cdn. Fedn. of, 2-192
    Publications, 5-159, 5-162, 5-164
    Regs., Govt. Quick Ref., 3-6
    Schs., Index to, 9-56
    School Deans, Cdn. Fedn. of, 2-48
    Service(s)
        Ctrs.: Cdn. (Fed.), 3-76; N.B., 3-134; N.S., 3-157
        Govt. Quick Ref. (*see* Industry), 3-22
    Statistics (Fed.), 3-89
    Teacher Educators, Assn. of, 2-45
    Telecomm. Alliance, Cdn., 2-183
    Trade
        Awards, 6-45
        Shows, 1-75
    Travel Assns.: Cdn., 2-184; Montréal, 2-184
    Valuators, Cdn. Inst. of Chartered, 2-34
    The Voice of, 2-34
    Websites, 5-236
Businessmen's Assn., Ont. Korean, 2-131
Businesswomen's Assn., Western, 2-193
Buyers Assn., Ont. Public, 2-35
Byzantinists, Cdn. Com. of, 2-155

C

CAA Assns., (Automobiles), 2-26
Cabinet, Mgmt. Bd. of (Ont.), 3-181

Cabinets (Govt.): Alta., 3-92; B.C., 3-106; Fed., 3-46; Man., 3-120; N.B., 3-131; Nfld., 3-141; N.W.T., 3-150; N.S., 3-154; Ont., 3-165; P.E.I., 3-187; Qué., 3-194; Sask., 3-210; Yukon, 3-221
    Committees, *see* Standing Cabinet
    Forms of Address, 1-33
Cable
    Telecomm. Assn., Ont., 2-183
    Television
        Assn., Cdn., 2-29
        Networks, 5-223
        Standards Fdn., 2-181
Cablodistrs du Qué., Assn des, 2-183
Cabot College of Applied Arts & Tech. (Nfld.), 9-20
Cadets: Air, 2-126; Army, 2-126
Cadres
    Confédn ntle des (Qué.), 2-121
    financiers mun., Assn des, 2-69
    de la fonction publique, L'Assn profle des, 2-120
    d'institutions culturelles, Assn des, 2-120
    scolaires du Qué., Assn des, 2-45
Caesarian, Vaginal Birth After, 2-36
Café, Assn du, 2-73
Caisse(s)
    de dépôt et placement du Qué., 3-202
    d'économie Desjardins, Fédn des, 2-70
Caisses populaires
    et d'économie desjardins du Qué., Confédn de, 2-70
    du Man., Fédn des, 2-70; Ont., 2-70
CALACS, Regroupement qué. des, 2-169
Calendar(s)
    Astronomical, 1-2
    Perpetual, 1-23
Calgary
    City Govt., 4-155
    Fdn., 2-208
    Sch. Districts, 9-1, 9-2
    Univ. of, 9-3
Calorifugeurs, Assn des, 2-197
Calmeadow, 2-33
Cambodian Assns., Fedn. of, 2-130
Cambrian College: Man., 9-16; Ont., AA & T, 9-32
Cambridge City Govt., 4-155
Camionnage
    Assn cdnne du, 2-188
    d'entreprise, Assn cdnne du, 2-189
    du Qué., Assn du, 2-189
Camosun College (B.C.), 9-8
Campaign 2000, 2-165
Campground Assns.: B.C., 2-184; Ont. (Private), 2-186
Camping
    Assn(s)., 2-149
    et de caravaning, Fédn qué. de, 2-152
    Committee, N.B., 2-152
    Magazines, 5-179
    du Qué., Assn des terrains de, 2-184
Campion College (Sask.), 9-54
Camps
    du Canada, Assn des, 2-149
    du Qué., Assn des, 2-149
Campus/Community Radio Assn., Ntl., 2-29
Canada
    Awards for Excellence, 1-95
    Centre for Mineral & Energy Tech., 3-82
    -China Friendship Assns., Fedn. of, 2-130
    Communication Group, 3-85
    Conseil des arts du, 3-55
    Council, 3-55; Awards, 1-96, 1-98, 1-104, 1-108, 1-111
    Day, 1-24
    Deposit Ins. Corp., 3-55
    Enquiries (Fed.), 3-85
    Government in/of, 3-43
    -Israel
        Cultural Fdn., 2-209
        Fdn. for Academic Exchanges, 2-129
    Labour Relations Bd. (Fed.), 3-55
    Lands Co. (Fed.), 3-55
    Man. Infrastructure Secretariat, 3-130

Canada (cont.)
    Mtge. & Housing Corp. (Fed.), 3-55
    N.B. Business Serv. Ctr., 3-134
    Order of, **15**, 1-26
    Pension Plan
        Div. (Fed.), 3-86
            Govt. Quick Ref., 3-30
    Place Corp., 3-56
    Ports Corp., 3-56
    Post Corp., 3-56
        Customer Service Info., 1-46
        Postal Rates & Info., 1-43
    West Fdn., 2-44
    World Youth,134
Canadian
    Anthem, 1-25
    Artists & Producers Profl. Relations Tribunal, 3-56
    Auto Workers Union, 2-203
    Awards, 1-92
    Banking Ombudsman, 7-1
    Bravery Decorations, **16**, 1-28
    Broadcasting Corp., 3-56
    Centre
        for Management Devel. (Fed.), 3-57
        for Occupational Health & Safety, 3-57
        on Substance Abuse, 3-57
    Chamber of Commerce, 7-24
    Clubs, Assn. of, 2-38
    Coast Guard, 3-67
    Commercial Corp., 3-57
    Consuls Abroad, 3-259
    Corps
        Assn., 2-126
        of Commissionaires, 2-126
    Dairy Commn., 3-57
    Delegations Abroad, 3-247
    Diplomats, 3-248
    Embassies Abroad, 3-259
    Environmental Assessment Agency, 3-65
    Flag, **1**
    Forces
        Base(s), 3-79
            Sch. in: Ont., 9-27; Qué., 9-45
        Commands, 3-79
        Stations, 3-79
    Government, 3-43 (*see also* Federal Govt.)
    Grain Commn., 3-57
    Heritage (Fed.), 3-58
        Navigation Canals, 1-64
    High Commns. Abroad, 3-259
    Honours List, 1-26
    Human Rights Commn., 3-59
    Imperial Bank of Commerce, 7-1
    Intergovernmental Conference Secretariat, 3-61
    International
        Devel. Agency, 3-61
        Grains Inst., 3-61
        Trade Tribunal, 3-61
    Judicial Council, 3-61
    Ministry, 3-46
    Missions Abroad, 3-247
    National
        Anthem, 1-25
        Rlwy. Co., 3-61
    Permanent
        Com. on Geographical Names, 3-61
        Missions Abroad, 3-247
    Polar Commn., 3-61
    Press, 2-145
    Radio-T.V. & Telecommunications Commn., 3-61
    -Scandinavian Fdn., 2-209
    Security Intelligence Service, 3-89
    Space Agency, 3-62
    Studies
        Assn. for, 2-45
        Inst. for, 2-188
        Intl. Council for, 2-156
        Magazines, *see* Scholarly Publications

Canadian
    Studies (cont.)
        Robarts Ctr. for (York Univ.), 9-32
    Tire Dealers Assn., 2-26
    Transp. Agency, 3-62
    Union Coll. (Univ. of Alta.), 9-3
    Western Bank, 7-1
    Wheat Bd., 3-62
Canadians
    Council of, 2-39
    & Society (Websites), 5-238
Canadienne-française
    Assns, 2-39
    pour l'avancement des sciences, Assn, 2-45
Canadiens, Le Conseil des, 2-39
Canado-Americaine Assn., 2-141
Canadore College, AA & T (Ont.), 9-32
Canal Soc., Cdn., 2-95
Canals, 1-64; Offices, 3-58
Canards illimités, 2-62
CANARIE Inc., 2-103
Cancer
    Action, Breast, 2-191
    Board, Alta., 3-101
    Clinics, *see* Special Treatment Ctrs.
    Fondation qué. du, 2-92
    Foundation
        B.C., 2-83
        Candlelighters Childhood, 2-90
        Govt. Bds., Commns., Fdns.: Ont., 3-180
    Information (B.C.), 3-116
    Insts.: National, 2-93; Ont., 2-93, 3-180
    Research
        Fund, Israel, 2-211
        Soc., 2-156
    Soc.
        Breast, 2-83
        Cdn., 2-84
    Treatment & Research Fdn., Man., 2-93 (*see also* Cancer, Govt. Commns., above)
Candlelighters Childhood Cancer Fdn., 2-90
CANCOPY, 2-138
CANDU Industries, Org. of, 2-124
Canin Cdn, Club, 2-22
Canine Assn., Cdn. Police, 2-22
CANMET (Fed.), 3-82
Canoe Assns., 2-149/150
    Alta. Whitewater, 2-149
    Wilderness, 2-153
Canoeing Assn(s)., Recreational, 2-151
Canoë-Kayak
    d'eau vive, Fédn de, 2-152
    de vitesse, Assn de, 2-150
Canola
    Council of Canada, 2-14
    Growers Assn., Sask., 2-15
    Prodrs. Commn., Alta., 2-12, 3-96
Canon(s)
    Forms of Address: (Anglican), 1-34; (R.C.), 1-35
    Law Soc., Cdn., 2-113
Canot-Camping, Fédn Qué. du, 2-151
Canotage, Assn cdnne de, 2-149; Récréatif, 2-151
CANSIM (Fed.), 3-89
Canterbury College (Windsor), 9-32
Cantons, Qué., 4-77
CanTRA, 2-178
Caoutchouc, Assn cdnne de l'industrie, 2-124
Cape Breton
    Regl. Municipality, 4-155
    Univ. College of, 9-23
    -Victoria Regl. Sch. Bd., 9-22
Capilano College (B.C.), 9-8
Capital
    Commns. (Govt.): B.C., 3-115; Ntl., 3-79
    Regl. Dist. Govt., B.C., 4-171
Capitale ntle, Commn de la, 3-79
Captioning Assns. (Closed), 2-29

Car Club of Canada, Antique & Classic, 2-23
Caravaning, Fédn qué. de camping et de, 2-152
Carbonization Research Assn., Cdn., 2-154
Cardinal, Forms of Address (R.C.), 1-34
Cardio-Pulmonary Technologists, Cdn. Assn. of, 2-83
Cardiologie, Soc. cdnne de, 2-85
Cardiology Technologists, Cdn. Soc. of, 2-89
Cardiovascular
    Nurses, Cdn. Council of, 2-136
    Soc., Cdn., 2-85
    & Thoracic Surgeons, Cdn. Soc. of, 2-89
CARE
    Canada, 2-108
    Productions, 2-166
Career(s)
    Academy (Nfld.), 9-20
    Colleges, Ntl. Assn. of, 2-53; Ont., 2-53
    Development
        Alta. Advanced Educ. & (Govt.), 3-94
        Dir. (N.W.T.), 3-151
        Fdn., Cdn., 2-166
        Inst(s): Man., 9-16; Ltd. (Sask.), 9-55
    Educators & Employers, Cdn. Assn. of, 2-56
    Information Assn., Cdn., 2-56
    Planning, Govt. Quick Ref., 3-7
    Plus (Nfld.), 9-20
    Support Services (Nfld.), 3-143
Caribana, 2-129
Caribbean
    -Central Amer. Policy Alternatives, Canada-, 2-107
    Centre for Research on Latin America & the (York Univ.), 2-156, 9-32
    Cultural Com., 2-129
    Magazines, 5-191
Cariboo Univ. College of the (B.C.), 9-9
Carleton (Ont.)
    Bd. of Educ., 9-24; R.C.S.S., 9-25
    Univ., 9-28
Carlton Trail Regl. College (Sask.), 9-54
Carnaval de Qué., 2-66
Carnivals, Winter, 1-91
Carpenters
    Joiners, Foresters & Industrial Wkrs., Ntl. Broth. of (Qué.), 2-201
    & Joiners of Amer., United Broth. of, 2-207
Carpentry Contractors Assn., Ont., 2-33
Carpet Inst., Cdn., 2-123
Carrefour cdn intl, 2-166
Carreleurs et métiers connexes, Union des, 2-207
Carrière
    et développement, Inst. (Qué.), 9-47
    Fond. cdnne pour l'avancement de la, 2-166
Cars, *see* Automobiles, Automotive
CARS Council, 2-26; Inst., 2-26
Cartoonists, Assn. of Cdn. Editorial, 2-190
Cartographer (B.C.), 3-114
Cartographic Assn., Cdn., 2-182
Cartographie, Assn qué. de, 2-182
Carton ondulé, Assn cdnne des fabricants de, 2-138
Cartothèques et archives cartographiques, Assn des, 2-116
Casey House Hospice, 2-17
Cassie Awards, 1-92
Casting Fedn., Cdn., 2-150
Catherine Booth Bible College (Man.), 9-15
Catholic
    Biblical Assn. of Canada, 2-7
    Bishops, Conference of: Cdn., 2-5; Ont., 2-5
    Charities of the Archdiocese of Toronto, 2-166
    Church
        Old Holy, 2-5
        Polish Ntl., 2-5
        Roman, 2-5; Forms of Address, 1-34
    Educ. Fdn. of Ont., 2-209
    Health Assn. of Canada, 2-90
    Hist'l Assn., Cdn., 2-95 (English); 2-98 (French)
    Magazines, *see* Religious Magazines

Catholic (cont.)
    Org. for Devel. & Peace, Cdn., 2-8
    Parent-Teacher Assns. of Ont., Fedn. of, 2-51
    Sch. Bds., *see* Educ., Bds. of; Parochial Schs.;
        Separate Schs.
    Sch. Trustees Assns.: Alta., 2-45; Cdn., 2-48
    Teachers
        Assn., Ont. English, 2-53
        Prov. Assn. of, 2-53
    Women's League of Canada, 2-192
Catholique(s)
    Assn
        des parents (Qué.), 2-6
        provinciale des enseignants, 2-53
    cdn de la santé, Assn., 2-90
    cdnne pour le développement et la paix, Org., 2-8
    Commn des écoles, *see* Separate Sch. Bds.
Cattle
    Breeders' Assn., Cdn., 2-19
    Commn., Alta., 3-96
    Mktg. Agencies: N.B., 3-134; Qué., 3-198
Cattlemen's Assn., Cdn., 2-19
Caucus Offices, *see* Legislative Assemblies
CAW Canada, 2-203
C.B., 1-30
CBC, 3-56
    Ombudsman, 3-56
    Radio Stns.: AM, 5-199; FM, 5-206
    TV Stns., 5-213
C.B.E., 1-30
CCOHS, 3-57
C.D. Howe Inst., 2-44
CDIC, 3-55
CEGEPS, 9-45
    Enseignant(e)s de, 2-196
    Fédn des, 2-51
CEIA, 2-60
Celiac Assn., Cdn., 2-85
Cell Biology, Cdn. Assn. for Anatomy, Neurobiology &, 2-162
Cellulose Insulation Mfrs. Assn. of Canada, 2-124
Celsius & Fahrenheit, 1-63
Celtic
    Arts
        Assn., Cdn., 2-24
        & Crafts, Gaelic College of (N.S.), 9-23
    Magazines, 5-191
Cement
    Assn., Cdn. Portland, 2-31
    Council, Cdn., 2-30
    Masons' Intl. Assn. of the US & Canada, 2-204
Cemeteries
    Ont. Assn. of, 2-77
    Regr., (B.C.), 3-109
Cemetery & Crematorium Assn. of B.C., 2-76
Censorship (Media), Govt. Quick Ref., 3-7
Census Figures, *see* Population Statistics (Fed.), 3-31
Cent-associés francophones, Cie de, 2-38
Centennial
    Centre Corp., Man., 3-123
    College, AA &T (Ont.), 9-33
Centrac College (Nfld.), 9-20
Centraide Canada Assns, 2-169/172
Central
    Amer. Policy Alternatives, Can.-Carib., 2-107
    & East European Studies, Intl. Council for, 2-156
Centrale de l'enseignement du Qué., 2-196
Centre(s)
    d'amitié autochtones, 2-134
    of Excellence (Ont.), 2-157
CEQ, 2-196
Ceramic(s)
    Magazines, 5-164
    Soc., Cdn., 2-190
Cercles canadiens, Assn des, 2-38
Cerebral Palsy
    Assn., Children's Rehab. &, 2-91
    Fdn., Grotto, 2-210

Cerebral Palsy (cont.)
    Ont. Fedn. for, 2-43
    Sports Assn., Cdn., 2-174
Certified
    Administrative Mgrs., Cdn. Inst. of, 2-121
    Exec. Accountants, Cdn. Assn. of, 2-8
    General Accountants Assn(s)., 2-9
    Management Consultants Insts., 2-121/122
Césarienne, Accouchement vaginal aprés, 2-36
CETAC-WEST, 2-61
CFBs & Detachments, 3-79
CGA-Canada, 2-9
CGIT Assn., Ntl., 2-37
C.H., 1-30
Chain Drug Stores, Cdn. Assn. of, 2-158
Challenged Students, Schools for, in: Ont., 9-27; Sask., 9-54
Chamber Music, Friends of, 6-40
Chambers
    of Commerce in: Alta., 7-24; B.C., 7-26; Cdn., 7-23;
        Intl., 7-23; Man., 7-28; N.B., 7-28; Nfld., 7-29;
        N.W.T., 7-29; N.S., 7-29; Ont., 7-30; P.E.I., 7-32;
        Prov. & Territorial, 7-24; Qué., 7-32; Sask., 7-34;
        Yukon, 7-35
    & Business Councils, Intl., 7-23
    of Mines, 7-35
Chambre des Communes, 3-45
Champignonnistes, Assn des, 2-14
Champs de bataille ntl, Commn des, 3-79
Chancellery, 3-43
Channels (Transp.), 1-64
Chaplaincy Servs. Ont., 3-180
Charitable Assistance Org., Cdn., 2-166
Charlesbourg, Ville de, Govt., 4-155 (& *see* Addenda)
Charlottetown City Govt., 4-146
Charolais Assn., Cdn., 2-20
Charpentiers-menuisiers, forestiers et travailleures d'usines, Fra. ntle des, 2-20
Charter Schools (Alta.), 9-2
Chartered
    Accountants Insts., 2-8, 9-34
    Banks, 7-1
    Business Valuators, Cdn. Inst. of, 2-34
    Secretaries & Admrs., Inst. of, 2-122
Charts, Govt. Quick Ref., 3-26
Chasse, de pêche & de piégeage, Comité conjoint de, 3-201
Chateauguay Valley English-Speaking People's Assn., 2-38
Châtelaine, École de Mode (Qué.), 9-47
Chaudronniers, Fra. ntle des, 2-201
Chauffage
    de la climatisation et de la réfrigération, Inst cdn de, 2-95
    L'Inst cdn de plomberie et de, 2-95
Chaussure(s) Assn
    des fournisseurs à l'industrie de la, 2-68
    des Manufacturiers de, 2-68
Checkers Fedn., Cdn. Intl., 2-150
Cheese Council, Intl., 2-188
Chefs
    & Cooks, Cdn. Fedn. of, 2-157
    cuisiniers et patissiers, Soc. des, 2-158
    d'entreprises, Conseil cdn des, 2-33
    de police, Assn cdnne des, 2-113
    de pompiers, Assn cdnne des, 2-159
    de service d'incendie du Qué., Assn des, 2-159
Chemical(s)
    Companies, Cdn., 7-40
    Distributors, Cdn. Assn. of, 2-35
    Engrg., Cdn. Soc. for, 2-35
    Govt. Quick Ref., 3-7
    Industry
        Assns., 2-35
        Magazines, 5-162
        Soc. of the, 2-36
    Inst. of Canada, 2-35

Chemical(s) (cont.)
    Physics, Ctr. for Interdisciplinary Studies in (U.W.O.), 9-31
    Process & Enviro. Tech., Institute for (NRC), 3-81
    Prodrs. Assn., Cdn., 2-35
    Reactor Engineering Ctr. (U.W.O.), 9-31
    Releases, *see* Emergency Measures/Response
    Science & Tech., Inst. for, 2-35
    Specialties Assn., Cdn. Mfrs. of, 2-35
    Tech., Cdn. Soc. for, 2-35
Chemins de fer
    du Canada, Assn des, 2-189
    nationaux du Canada, Compagnie des, 3-61
Chemistry
    Awards *see* Scientific Awards
    Cdn.
        Inst. for Research in Atmospheric, 2-162
        Soc. for, 2-35
    Shows, 1-75
Chemists
    Cdn. Assn. of Textile Colourists &, 2-67
    Oil & Colour, 2-35
Chênes, Commn scolaire des (Qué.), 9-42
Chercheurs, Fonds pour la formation de (Qué.), 3-201
Chess
    Assn.
        Cdn. Correspondence, 2-150
        Intl. Computer, 2-152
    Fedn. of Canada, 2-151; Qué., 2-152
Chevaux
    Assns d'éleveurs des, 2-19
    Soc. de promotion de l'industrie des courses de (Qué.), 3-198
Chèvres, La Soc. cdnne des éleveurs de, 2-20
Chez Ma Cousine, 2-17
CHICA Canada, 2-91
Chicken (*see also* Broiler; Poultry)
    Marketing Agency, Cdn., 2-142
    Marketing Bds./Commns. (Govt.): Alta., 3-96; B.C., 3-108; Cdn., 3-80; Man., 3-122; N.B., 3-134; Nfld., 3-144; N.S., 3-156; Ont., 3-170; Sask. 3-212
Chicoutimi
    Univ. du Qué. à, 9-47
    Ville de, Govt., 4-156
Chief
    Executives of Large Public Libraries (Ont.), 2-119
    Justice of Canada, 10-1
        Form of Address, 1-34
    Medical Examiners, *see* Coroners
Chiefs (of)
    Assembly of Manitoba, 2-132
    Ontario, 2-133
    Police Assns.: Atlantic, 2-113; Cdn., 2-113; Ont., 2-113; P.E.I., 2-115
    Union of B.C. Indian, 2-134
Chiens policiers, Assn cdnne de, 2-22
Chignecto-Central Regl. Sch. Bd. (N.S.), 9-22
Child
    Abuse Research & Educ. Productions Assn. of B.C., 2-166
    Care
        Advocacy Assn., 2-166
        Assn., Man., 2-37
        Br. (Ont.), 3-173
        Canada, Intl., 2-109
        Fedn., Cdn., 2-36
        Ont. Coalition for Better, 2-168
    Day Care Dirs. (Govt.): Man., 3-125; Sask., 3-220
    Evangelism Fellowship of Canada, 2-7
    & Family Service(s)
        Advocacy (Ont. Govt.), 3-173
        Brs./Divs. (Govt.): B.C., 3-119; Man., 3-125
        Review Bd., Ont., 3-174
    Find Assns., 2-36
    Haven Intl., 2-108
    Health
        Cdn. Inst. of, 2-87
        Dir. (Nfld.), 3-146

Child (cont.)
   Neurology Corp., Cdn. Assn. of, 2-83
   Service, Family & (B.C.), 3-119
   Therapists, Cdn. Assn. of Psychoanalytic, 2-125
   Welfare
      Bd. (Nfld.), 3-149
      Br. (Alta.), 3-100
      Govt. Quick Ref., 3-7
      League of Canada, 2-166
Childbirth
   Assns., 2-36
   By Choice Trust, 2-154
Childhood
   Assn., Holy, 2-7
   Cancer Fdn., Candlelighters, 2-90
   Educators Ont., Assn. of Early, 2-45
Children
   Alta. Orange Fdn. for, 2-208
   of Alcoholics
      Adult, 2-10
      Cdn. Assn. for, 2-10
   Assn(s). for
      Bright: Alta., 2-36; Man., 2-37; Ont., 2-36
      Gifted: B.C., 2-37; Nfld. & Lab., 2-37
      Vaccine Damaged, 2-41
   Cdn.
      Assn. for Young, 2-36
      Council for Exceptional, 2-36
      Feed the, 2-166
      Soc. for Prev. of Cruelty to, 2-166
   of the Covenant, 2-128
   with Disabilities, B.C. Lions Soc. for, 2-164
   End Physical Punishment of, 2-167
   Exhibitions, Shows & Events, 1-75
   & Families
      Alta. Assn. of Services for, 2-165
      Min. of (B.C.), 3-110
   Helping Children, 2-7
   Heritage of, 2-37
   Magazines, 5-179
   Music for Young, 6-40
   Orgs., 2-36
   Save the, 2-109
   Servs. Brs./Divs., see Children's Services
   Soc., Missing, 2-168
   & Television, Alliance for, 2-28
   & Youth
      Assns., 2-36
      Sask. Council on, 2-37
Children's
   Advocate, Alta., 3-99
   Aid Socs., Ont. Assn. of, 2-168
   Apparel Mfrs. Assn., 2-67
   Authors, Illustrators & Performers, Cdn. Soc. of, 2-194
   Book Ctr., Cdn., 2-144
   Charities, Ronald McDonald, 2-169
   Commr., (B.C.), 3-110
   Dance Theatre, Cdn., 6-42
   Exhibitions, Shows & Events, 1-75
   Fdn., Halifax, 2-210
   Fund, Christian, 2-7
   Intl. Summer Villages, 2-108
   Librarians, Cdn. Assn. of, 2-117
   Literature Awards & Prizes, see Literary Arts Awards
   Magazines, 5-179
   Mental Health Ctrs., Ont. Assn. of, 2-126
   Multimedia Fdn., Cdn., 2-103
   Oncology Care of Ont., 2-90
   Opera Chorus, Cdn., 6-39
   Psychiatric Research Inst., 2-125
   Rehab. & Cerebral Palsy Assn., 2-91
   Services Brs./Divs. (Govt.): Alta., 3-100; B.C., 3-119; Man., 3-125; N.W.T., 3-151; N.S., 3-157; Ont., 3-173; Yukon, 3-223
   Wish Fdn., 2-37
Chilliwack Sch. Dist. (B.C.), 9-6

Chimie
   atmosphérique, Inst cdn de la recherche en, 2-162
   du Canada, Inst de, 2-35
   Soc. cdnne de, 2-35
Chimique, Soc. cdnne
   du génie, 2-35
   de technologie, 2-35
Chimiques, Assn cdnne des
   distributeurs de produits, 2-35
   fabricants de produits, 2-35
   manufacturiers de spécialités, 2-35
Chimistes du Qué, Ordre des, 2-139
China
   Friendship Assns., Fedn. of Canada-, 2-130
   Govt., 3-226, 3-232
Chinchilla Breeders Assn., Ntl., 2-21
Chinese
   Cdn.
      Information
         & Community Services of Metro Toronto, 2-37
         Processing Profls., 2-103
      Intercultural Assn., 2-129
      Ntl. Council, 2-129
      Profls., Fedns. of, 2-130; Education Fdn., 2-210
   Era, see Epochs
   Govt.
      Depts./Agencies, 3-232
      Equivalency Table, 3-226
   Magazines, 5-191
   Medicine & Acupuncture Assn., 2-91
Chiropractic
   Assns., 2-85
   College, Cdn. Memorial, 9-34
   Educ., Council on, 2-91
   Science, College of, 2-91
Chiropracticiens du Qué., Assn des, 2-85
Chirurgie
   buccale et maxio-faciale, Assn cdnne de spécialistes en, 2-84
   cervico-faciale, Soc. cdnne, 2-90; Qué., 2-82
   infantile cdnne, Assn de la, 2-84
   plastique & reconstructive faciale, Académie cdnne de, 2-83
   vasculaire, Soc. cdnne de, 2-90
Chirurgiens
   cardiovasculaires et thoraciques, Soc. des, 2-89
   Collège des médecins et: N.-B., 2-92; royal des, 2-94
   Dentistes du Qué., Assn des, 2-40
   généraux cdnne, 2-83; Qué., 2-82
   plasticiens, Soc. cdnne des, 2-90
Choeur cdns, Assn des chefs de, 6-37
Choirs Awards & Prizes see Performing Arts
Chomedey de Laval, Commn Scolaire (Qué.), 9-42
Choral
   Awards, see Performing Arts
   Conductors, Assn. of Cdn., 6-37
   Fedn., Alta., 6-37; Ont., 6-40
   Soc., Bach Elgar, 6-39
Chorale Manitoba, Assn, 6-37
Chorales du Qué., Alliance des, 6-37
Choreographers Assn., Man. Indep., 6-43
Choreography Awards, see Performing Arts Awards
Chorus
   of Calgary, Festival, 6-40
   Cdn. Children's Opera, 6-39
Chrétien(ne)(s)
   et des juifs, Conseil cdn des, 2-7
   et missionaire, Alliance, 2-3
   Mouvement d'étudiant(e)s, 2-6
Christ
   Brethren in, 2-2
   Disciples of, 2-3
Christian
   Aid Mission, 2-7
   Booksellers Assn., 2-145
   Brethren Church (Qué.), 2-3
   Children's Fund of Canada, 2-7
   Church (Disciples of Christ), 2-3

Christian (cont.)
   Churches in Man., Assn. of, 2-6
   Farmers Fedn. of Ont., 2-14
   Fellowship, Inter-Varsity, 2-4
   Heritage Party, 2-141
   Holidays, 1-24
   Labour Assn. of Canada, 2-200
   & Missionary Alliance, 2-3
   Movement, Student, 2-6
   Record Servs. Inc., 2-42
   Reformed
      Church in N. Amer., 2-3
      World Relief Com., 2-7
   Schs., Ont. Alliance of, 2-51
   Schs. Lists of, see Private Schs.
   Science, 2-3
   Studies, Inst. for (Ont.), 3-40
   Temperance Union, Cdn. Woman's, 2-76
Christians & Jews, Cdn. Council of, 2-7
Christmas
   Craft Shows, see Crafts
   Day, 1-24
   Tree Growers Assn. of Ont., 2-75
Chronic
   Fatigue Syndrome Assn., 2-93; Group (Ont.), 2-91
   Pain Assn. of Canada, N. Amer., 2-93
CHUM Charitable Fdn., 2-209
Church
   Administration Magazines, 5-164
   Affiliated Schs. (Ont.), 9-34
   Army in Canada, 2-3
   Council on Justice & Corrections, 2-114
   Forms of Address, 1-34
   of God, 2-3; of Prophecy, 2-3
   History, Cdn. Soc. of, 2-96
   Holidays, 1-24
   of Jesus Christ of Latter-Day Saints, 2-3
      Reorganized, 2-5
   Library Assn. of Ont., 2-119
   of the Nazarene, 2-3
   Schools, Sask. Assn. of Indep., 2-52
Churches, 2-2
   Associated Gospel, 2-2
   Cdn. Council of, 2-7
   & Corp. Responsibility, Taskforce on the, 2-8
   Forum for Global Ministries, Cdn., 2-7; 9-34
Churchill
   Falls (Labrador) Corp. Ltd., 3-142
   (Sir Winston) Scholarship Fdn., 2-272
CIBC Bank, 7-1
CICA, 2-8
CIDA, 3-61
C.I.E., 1-30
CIM, 2-121
Ciment
   Conseil cdn du, 2-30
   Portland, Assn cdnne du, 2-31
Cinema
   Awards & Prizes, 1-93 (see also Culture & Visual Arts)
   Fédn profile des réalisateurs de télévision et de, 2-29
   indépendant, Alliance de la vidéo & du, 2-69
   Motion Picture Devel. Corp., Alta., 3-97
   Musée du, 2-69
   Régie du (Qué.), 3-199
   Supervisory Bd. (Qué.), 3-199
   et de télévision, Assn des réalisateurs de, 2-68
   & Television, Academy of Cdn., 2-68
Cinémas, Assn des propriétaires de, 2-69
Cinémathèque
   Ont., 2-67; québécoise, 2-69
Cinematographers, Cdn. Soc. of, 2-69
Cinq quilles, Assn cdnne des, 2-173
CIP, 5-1
Circulation Mgmt. Assn., Cdn., 2-144
Circulations Audit: Bd., 2-144; Bur., 2-11
Cirque, École ntle de (Qué.), 9-47
CISTI, 3-81

Cité collégiale, La (Ont.), 9-33
Cities
   & Clerks in: Alta., 4-1; B.C., 4-12; Man., 4-18; N.B., 4-24; Nfld., 4-29; N.S., 4-39; N.W.T., 4-37; Ont., 4-42; P.E.I., 4-74; Qué., 4-77; Sask., 4-134; Yukon, 4-152
   Major, in Canada, 4-153
   of N.B. Assn., 2-79
   & Towns, Population, 1-47, 4-1
Citizens
   Clearinghouse on Waste Mgmt., 2-62
   Coalition, Ntl., 2-35
   Inquiry (Govt.): Man., 3-128; Ont., 3-182
   Senior, *see* Senior Citizens
Citizenship
   Assns., 2-37
   Awards, 1-95
   B.C. Soc., 2-37
   & Cdn. Identity Sector (Fed.), 3-58
   Commn., Alta. Human Rights &, 3-101
   Councils, 2-37
   Fedn., Cdn., 2-37
   Govt. Depts.: Quick Ref., 3-8; Fed., 3-62; Man., 3-123; Ont. 3-172; Qué., 3-198
   & Immigration Canada (Fed.), 3-62
   Ontario Adv. Council on Multiculturalism &, 3-173
   Services (Alta.), 3-96
Citoyen(s)
   et de l'Immigration, Min. des Relations avec les (Qué.), 3-198
   Protecteur du (Qué.), 2-204
Citoyenneté
   Conseil Manitobain de la, 2-37
   et Immigration Canada, 3-62
City
   Clerks & Election Officers Assn. (Alta.), 2-79
   Farmer, 2-99
   Magazines, 5-179
Civic Holidays, 1-24
Civil
   Air Search & Rescue Assn., 2-55
   Aviation
      Org., Intl., 2-28, 3-247
      Tribunal, 3-91
   Defence, *see* Emergency Measures
   Engrg., Cdn. Soc. for, 2-59
   Law Divs. (Govt.): Alta., 3-77, 3-101; Nfld., 3-147; Ont., 3-171
   Lawyers' Assn., Alta. Govt., 2-113
   Liberties Assns., 2-102
      Cdn.-Muslim, 2-7
   Rights, *see* Human Rights
   Service
      Commns.: Man., 3-129; N.B., 3-136; Ont., 3-182
         (*see also* Public)
         War Veterans Assn., Dominion, 2-126
   Trial Lawyers' Assn., Alta., 2-113
Civilian Commn. on Police Services, Ont., 3-186
Civilisation(s)
   Musée cdn des, 6-1
   Musée de la (Qué.), 6-24
Civilization, Cdn. Museum of, 6-1
Civisme, Fédn cdnne du, 2-37
Claims & Indian Govt. Sector, 3-73
Clans & Scottish Socs., 2-130
Clarington, Municipality of, 4-156
Classical
   Assn. of Canada, 2-156
   & Medieval Numismatic Soc., 2-151
Claude St-Jean, Fdn, 2-81
Clay
   Brick Assn. of Canada, 2-32
   & Glass Assn., Ont., 2-191
Clean
   Energy, Planetary Assn. for, 2-57
   Environment
      Cdns. for a, 2-62
      Commn., Man., 3-125

Clean (cont.)
   N.S. Fdn., 2-62
   Water Agency, Ont., 3-178
Cleaning Trade Shows, 1-76
Cleanup, *see* Emergency Measures/Response
Clergy & Religious, Missionary Union of the, 2-5
Clerks of Assembly, *see* Legislative Assemblies
Clerks
   & Cities, 4-1
   & Election Officers Assn., City, 2-79
   at-the-Table in Canada, Assn. of, 2-79
   & Treasurers of Ont., Assn. of Municipal, 2-79
Climate
   Data, 1-65
   & Atmospheric Research Dir. (Fed.), 3-65
   Govt. Quick Ref., 3-8
Climatisation
   Assn ntle des travailleurs en, 2-197
   et de la réfrigération, Inst cdn du chauffage, de la, 2-95
Clinical
   Hypnosis, Ont. Soc. of, 2-94
   Immunology, Cdn. Soc. of Allergy &, 2-89
   Investigation, Cdn. Soc. for, 2-89
   Microbiology & Infectious Diseases, Cdn. Assn. for, 2-83
   Neurophysiologists, Cdn. Soc. of, 2-89
   Nurse Specialist Interest Group, Cdn., 2-136
   Pharmacology, Cdn. Soc. for, 2-89
Clock Collectors, Ntl. Assn. of Watch &, 2-152
Closed Captioning Assns., 2-29
Clothing (*see also* Fashion)
   & Accessories Magazines, 5-164
   Assns., 2-67
   Magazines, 5-164
   & Textile
      Import Info. (Fed.), 3-75
      Wkrs. Unions, Amal., 2-197
   Wkrs., Ntl. Fedn. of, 2-201
Clubs (*see also* Associations)
   Assn. of Cdn., 2-38
C.M.G., 1-30
CMHC, 3-55
CNEC Partners Intl., 2-108
CNIB, 2-42
CNR, 1-68, 3-61
Coaches Assn., Cdn. Swimming, 2-178
Coaching Assn. of Canada, 2-179
Coady Intl. Inst. (N.S.), 9-22
Coal
   Assn. of Canada, 2-128
   Branch (Fed.), 3-83
   Govt. Quick Ref., 3-8
Coast Guard, Cdn., 3-67
Coastal
   Computer Academy (Nfld.), 9-21
   Zone Devel. (Nfld.), 3-144
Coating(s)
   Assn., Cdn. Paint &, 2-31
   Magazines, 5-174
Coats of Arms, **1**
Cod Research Program, Northern (Fed.), 3-68
CODE, 2-108
Codevelopment Canada, 2-108
Coélique, Assn cdnne de la maladie, 2-85
Coeur, Fdn des maladies du, 2-92
Coffee
   Assn. of Canada, 2-73
   Vending Service Assn., Ont., 2-73
COFTM, 2-39
Cognitive
   & Computer Science Interuniv. Research Group, 2-104
   Science, Ctr. for (U.W.O.), 9-31
Coin Shows, *see* Hobbies Exhibitions
Colitis Fdn., Crohn's &, 2-91
Collectibles, *see* Antiques Shows
Collectifs, Fonds d'aide aux recours (Qué.), 3-204

Collection Agencies, Ont. Soc. of, 2-71
Collections d'entreprises, Assn des, 2-190
Collective Agreement Arbitration Bur. (B.C.), 3-117
College/Collège
   Conference Officers Assn., Cdn. Univ. &, 2-50
   Counselling Assn., Cdn. University &, 2-50
   Librarians, Alta. Assn. of, 2-116
   Relations Commn. (Ont.), 3-177
   of Teachers, Cdn., 2-48
   & University
      Food Services Assn., Cdn., 2-72
      Libraries, Cdn. Assn. of, 2-117
      Library Assn., Ont., 2-120
      Student Services, Cdn. Assn. of, 2-46
Colleges/Collèges
   Accreditation Bd., Private (Alta.), 3-95
   of Applied Arts & Tech. (*see* Community Colleges, for lists of)
      Council of Regents, Ont., 3-177
      Ont. Assn. of, 2-45
   d'arts appliquées et de tech. de l'Ont., Assn des, 2-45
   Assn. of
      Cdn.
         Bible, 2-45
         Community, 2-45
         Medical, 2-46
         Registrars of the Univs. &, 2-46
      Universities &, 2-46
   Athletic Assn., Cdn., 2-174
   Cdn. Service, 3-80
   Communautaires, Assn des, 2-45
   Community, *see* Community Colleges
   d'enseignement général et professionnel (Qué.), 9-45
   Fédn du personnel profl des, 2-196
   Ntl. Assn. of Career, 2-53
   Ont. Assn. of Career, 2-53
   Privées du Qué., Assn des, 2-45
   Public, Alta., 9-4
   & Social & Aboriginal Programs (B.C.), 3-108
   United World, 2-54
Collégial
   enseignement
      Commn d'évaluation de l' (Qué.), 3-201
      Sous-ministre adjoint (Qué.), 3-200
   Fédn autonome du, 2-200
Colour/Color
   in Art, Industry & Science, 2-59
   Chemists Assn., Oil &, 2-35
   Colourists & Chemists, Cdn. Assn. of Textile, 2-67
Columbia Academy of Radio, Television & Recording Arts (B.C.), 9-9
Columbus, Knights of, 2-35
Commemorative Medals, 1-31
Commerce (*see also* Chambers of Commerce)
   Assn cdnne du personnel enseignant en, 2-47
   autochtone, Conseil cdn pour le, 2-132
   Council, Electronic, 2-103
   Extérieur Tribunal cdn du, 3-61
   Facultés/Schs., Index to, 9-56
   Fédn du, 2-200
   International
      Affaires étrangères et du (Fed.), 3-68
      Conseil cdn pour le, 2-34
   Min. du (Qué.), 3-202
Commercial
   Accountants Guild, 2-9
   Appeals Commn., B.C., 3-110
   Arbitration
      Centres: B.C., 3-112; Qué. Ntl. & Intl., 2-110
      Commn., Inter-American, 2-111
      Insts., Intl. Fedn. of, 2-111
   Corp., Cdn., 3-57
   Counsellors (Cdn.) Abroad, 3-259
   Fisheries (Qué.), 3-197
   Reg'n Appeal Tribunal, Ont., 3-175
   Relations Min., Consumer & (Ont.), 3-174

Commercial (cont.)
   Travellers
      of Amer., United, 2-76
      Assn., N.W., 2-186
Commerciale(s)
   Corp., cdnne, 3-57
   École des hautes études de Montréal, 9-47
Commissionaires, Cdn. Corps of, 2-126
Commissioner
   for Fed. Judicial Affairs, 10-2
   of N.W.T., 3-150
   of Yukon, 3-221
Commissions scolaires (Qué.), 9-41
   Assn cdnne des, 2-49
   Fédn des enseignant(e)s de, 2-196
   du Qué.
      Assn des directeurs généraux des, 2-45
      Fédn des, 2-51
Commons, House of, *see* House of Commons; Parliament
Commonwealth
   Countries, 3-246
   Games Assn. of Canada, 2-179
   Honours, 1-29; Precedence of, 1-31
   Imports & Exports, 1-55
   of Learning, 2-51
   Literature & Lang. Studies, Cdn. Assn. for, 2-111
   Nations, 3-246
   Orders, Decorations & Medals, 1-29
   Press Union (Cdn. Sec.), 2-145
   Soc., Royal, 2-39
   War Graves Commn., 2-126
Communauté urbaine de (Qué.), 5-186
Communes, Chambre des, 3-45
Communicateurs municipaux du Qué., Assn des, 2-79
Communication
   Cdn. Network for Environmental Educ. &, 2-61
   Group, Canada, 3-85
   & Technical Wkrs. Union, Atlantic, 2-198
   Workers, Cdn. Union of, 2-207
Communications (*see also* Telecommunications)
   & Allied Wkrs., Cdn. Assn. of, 2-198
   Award(s) *see* Broadcasting & Film; Journalism
   Canadian
      Assn. of Photographers & Illustrators in, 2-140
      Women in, 2-192
   Cos., Cdn., 7-54
   Dept. (Qué.), 3-198
   Directory, 5-1
   Energy & Paperworkers Union of Canada, 2-200
   Exhibitions, Shows & Events, 1-76
   Fédn ntle des, 2-201
   Intl. Union
      Graphic, 2-201
      Transportation, 2-207
   Network(s) Govt.: Alta., 3-103; Sask., 3-213
   New Brunswick, 3-134
   Research Ctr. (Fed.), 3-76
   Soc. Intl. Interactive, 2-183
   Visual, *see* Advertising; Marketing; Sales
   Websites, 5-239
   Workers of America, 2-200
Communiste du Qué., Parti, 2-142
Communities Economic Devel. Fund (Man.), 3-130
Community
   Affairs (Govt.): N.W.T. (Dept.), 3-152; Yukon (Div.), 3-222
   Care
      B.C. Assn. of, 2-100
      Services, *see* Home Care Offices
   Churches, Cdn. Chapter of the Intl. Council of, 2-7
   Colleges
      Assn. of Cdn., 2-45
      Br. (N.S.), 3-158
      In (Lists of): Alta., 9-4; B.C., 9-8; Man., 9-16; N.B., 9-18; Nfld., 9-20; N.W.T., 9-21; N.S., 9-23; Ont., 9-32; P.E.I., 9-41; Qué., 9-45; Sask., 9-54; Yukon, 9-55

Community (cont.)
   Development
      Brs./Divs. (Govt.): B.C., 3-118; P.E.I., 3-189; Yukon, 3-222
      Dept. Alta., 3-96
   Economic Devel Institute, 2-44
   Health (*see also* Public Health)
      Accrediation, Ont. Council on, 2-93
      Brs./Divs (Govt.): B.C., 3-116; Man., 3-126; Nfld., 3-145; N.W.T., 3-151; Ont., 3-180
      Cdn. Assn. of Teachers of, 2-48
      Govt. Quick Ref., *see* Health Services, 3-19; Public Safety, 3-32
      Nurses Assn., 2-137
   & Hosp. Infection Control Assn., 2-91
   Info.
      Br. (Ont.), 3-172
      Ctrs. in Ont., Assn. of, 2-165
   Legal Educ. Assns., 2-114
   Living
      Assns. for, 2-41
      Brs./Divs. (Govt.): Man., 3-125; Sask., 3-220
      Servs. (B.C.), 3-119
   Mental Health Nurses Assn., 2-137
   Newspapers Assns., 2-144
   Planners Insts., 2-140
   Resources Mgmt. Program (Fed. Indian Affairs & Northern Devel.), 3-74
   Service Awards, *see* Public Affairs
   Services (Govt.): Quick Ref., 3-8; Alta., 3-96; B.C., 3-119; N.B., 3-136; N.W.T., 3-151; N.S., 3-157; Ont., 3-173; P.E.I., 3-191; Sask., 3-220; Yukon, 3-222
   & Social Services Min. (Ont.), 3-173
   Support
      Assn., Ont., 2-168
      Services
         Assn., Family & (Alta.), 2-167
         (Govt.), B.C., 3-119
         & Transportation Servs., Sask., 3-221
Comox Valley Sch. Dist. (B.C.), 9-8
Companies
   Br. (Ont.), 3-174
   Incorporation, Govt. Quick Ref., 3-22
   Major Canadian
      Agriculture & Fisheries, 7-40
      Chemicals, Biotechnology & Pharmaceuticals, 7-40
      Food & Beverage, 7-41
      Engineering & Contracting, 7-42
      Forestry & Paper, 7-43
      General Mfg., 7-43
      Industrial Mfg., 7-44
      Mining & Metals, 7-46
      Miscellaneous, 7-57
      Oil & Gas, 7-49
      Printing & Publishing, 7-51
      Retail Trade, Distribution, 7-51
      Service Industries, 7-53
      Telecommunications, Communications, Technology, 7-54
      Transp. & Utilities, 7-56
   Registrar, *see* Joint Stock Cos.
Comparative Literature
   Assn., Cdn., 2-111
   Ctr. for (U. of T.), 9-30
   & Intl. Educ. Soc., 2-51
Compassion Canada, 2-108
Compensation (*see also* Crimes; Criminal Injuries; Workers')
   Assn., Cdn., 2-110
   Employees' Union, 2-200
   Govt. Quick Ref., *see* Crimes Compensation, 3-10; Workers' Compensation, 3-40
Competition
   Law, Cdn. Assn. on, 2-113
   Policy, Bur. of (Fed.), 3-75

Composers
   Assn.
      of Cdn. Women, 2-191
      Manitoba, 6-40
   Authors & Music Publishers, Soc. of, 2-139
   Awards & Prizes, *see* Performing Arts
   Cdn. League of, 6-39
Composite Structures & Materials, Cdn. Assn. for, 2-58
Compositeurs
   et éditeurs de musique, Soc. cdnne des auteurs, 2-139
   du Qué., Soc. profl. des auteurs et des, 2-194
   Soc. des auteurs, recherchistes, documentalistes et, 2-206
Compositrices cdnnes, Assn des femmes, 2-191
Composting Council of Canada, 2-62
Comprehensive Auditing Fdn., Cdn., 2-8
Compressed
   Air & Gas Machinery Mfrs. Assn., 2-66
   Gas Assn., 2-78
   Gas Bd. of Examiners for (N.B.), 3-133
Comptabilité, Assn cdnne des professeurs de, 2-8
Comptables
   Agréés, 2-8; Ordre du Qué., 2-9
   d'assurance, Assn cdnne des, 2-9
   généraux licenciés, 2-9
   industriels, guilde des, 2-9
   en management
      accrédités du Qué., Ordre des, 2-10
   Soc. des, 2-9
Comptroller: Man (Div.), 3-125; N.B. (Office of) 3-134; P.E.I., 3-192
Compucollege Sch. of Business (Nfld.), 9-21
Compulsive Gambling, Cdn. Fdn. on, 2-166
Computational Studies of Intelligence, Cdn. Soc. for, 2-103
Computer(s) (*see also* Data Processing; Informatique)
   Academy, Coastal (Nfld.), 9-21
   -Aided Design Magazines, 5-164
   Assns., 2-103
   Chess Assn., Intl., 2-152
   Communications
      Inst. (Ont.), 9-35
      Soc., Cdn. Human-, 2-103
   Consultants, Assn. of Profl. (Ont.), 2-103
   Dealer Assn., Cdn., 2-103
   in Educ., Ctr. for Study of (York Univ.), 9-32
   Educators, Cdn. Community of, 2-103
   in Health, Cdn. Org. for Adv. of, 2-103
   Household, Statistics, 1-53
   Integrated Engineering, Ctr. for (U. of T.), 9-30
   Magazines, 5-164, 5-180
   Modems (Statistics), 1-53
   Multimedia Techn. Ctr. (Man.), 9-16
   Operations Mgmt., Assn. for, 2-103
   Orgs., 2-103
   Science
      Index to Faculties/Schs., 9-56
      Interuniv. Research Group, Cognitive &, 2-104
   Shows, 1-76
   Studies, Inst. for (Ont.), 9-35
   Systems Research Inst. (U. of T.), 9-30
Concerns, Canada, 2-10
Concessionnaires d'Automobiles du Qué., Corp. des, 2-26
Conciliation, Mediation &, Service (Fed.), 3-72
Concord College (Man.), 9-15
Concordia
   College (Alta.), 9-3
   Univ. (Qué.), 9-46
Concours
   Complet, 2-179
   de musique du Canada, 6-39
Concrete
   Assns., Ready Mixed, 2-31
   Block Assn., Ont., 2-33
   Canada, 2-32
   & Drain Contrs. Assn., Ont., 2-33
   Inst., Cdn. Prestressed, 2-31

Canadian Almanac & Directory 1997

Concrete (cont.)
  Masonry Prodrs. Assn., 2-30
  Pipe Assn., Cdn., 2-30; Ont., 2-33
Condition féminine Canada, 3-90
Condominium(s)
  Inst., Cdn., 2-101
  Mgrs. of Ont., Assn. of, 2-101
Conductors'
  Assn. of Cdn. Choral, 6-37
  Awards, see Performing Arts
Conestoga College, AA & T (Ont.), 9-33
Confectionery
  Distrs., Ntl. Assn. of Tobacco & (Qué.), 2-158
  Mfrs. Assn. of Canada, 2-73
  & Tobacco Wkrs. Intl. Union, 2-198
Confederation
  Centre Art Gallery & Museum (P.E.I.), 6-34
  College, AA & T (Ont.), 9-33
  Conferences, 1-25
  Fathers of, 1-25
  Governors Gen. of Canada Since, **2**
  Prov. entry dates: Alta., 3-92; B.C., 3-105; Man., 3-120; N.B., 3-131; Nfld., 3-140; N.S., 3-154; Ont., 3-164; P.E.I., 3-187; Qué., 3-193; Sask., 3-210
  of Regions Party of N.B., 2-141
Conference(s) (see also Conventions; Meetings)
  Banff Centre for (Alta.), 9-4
  Bd. of Canada, 2-44
  intergouvernementales cdn, sec des, 3-61
  Officers Assn., Cdn. Univ. & College, 2-50
  Planners, 1-68 (& see Addenda)
Confiserie, Assn ntl des distributeurs de tabac et, 2-158
Confiseries, Assn cdnne des fabricants de, 2-73
Conflict
  of Interest Commns. (Govt.): Quick Ref., 3-9; B.C., 3-111
  Resolution
    Cdn. Inst. for, 2-108
    La Marsh Research Program on Violence & (York Univ.), 9-32
    Office of (Fed.), 3-78
Congregational Christian Churches, 2-3
Congrès
  du Qué., Soc. du Centre des, 3-208
  des univs et collèges, Assn des coords de, 2-50
Congress Planners, see Conference Planners
Connexions Info. Sharing Services, 2-145
Conrad Grebel College (Waterloo), 9-31
Conseil
  des Cdns, 2-39
  exécutif (Qué.), 3-193
  privé, Bur. de, 3-43
  du Trésor du Canada, 3-91
Conseillers(ères)
  en consommation du Qué., Assn des, 2-38
  en management, Insts de, 2-121/122
  d'orientation, Corp. profl des, 2-56
  en relations industrielles du Qué., 2-111
  scolaires francophones du N.-B., Assn des, 2-45
Conseils scolaires
  Assn cdnne des commissions/, 2-49
  de l'Ont., Assn française des, 2-46
Conservancy of Canada, The Nature, 2-64
Conservation
  Assn., Ntl. Energy, 2-63
  of Atlantic Tunas, Intl. Commn. for, 3-248
  Authorities
    Ont., 3-184
    of Ont., Assn. of, 2-60
  Awards, see Environmental (see also Culture, Visual Arts & Architecture Awards)
  Canada, Soil, 2-65
  Centre de (Qué.), 3-199
  Councils: N.B., 2-62; Ont., 2-62
  Data Centre (Sask.), 3-215
  Dirs.: N.B., 3-139
  Districts, Man., 3-130
  de la faune du Qué., Synd. des agents de, 2-206

Conservation (cont.)
  Govt. Quick Ref., 3-9
  Inst., Cdn., 2-60, 3-58
  de la nature, Union qué. pour la, 2-135
  Officer (P.E.I.), 3-190
  & Prevention Div. (Ont.), 3-177
  Review Bd. (Ont.), 3-173
  Soc.
    Promoting Environmental, 2-65
    Sea Shepherd, 2-65
    Yukon, 2-65
  Tillage Soc., Alta., 2-12
Conservative
  Assns. (Progressive), 2-142
  Judaism, Cdn. Council for, 2-3
Conservatoires de musique et d'art dramatique du Qué., 3-199
Conservators, Cdn. Assn. of Profl., 2-190
Conservatory of Music, see Music
Consommateurs
  Assns, 2-38
  industriels d'électricité, Assn qué. des, 2-54
Consommation du Qué., Assn des conseillers en, 2-38
Constables
  du contrôle routiers de la Sûreté du Qué., Fra. des, 2-201
  spéciaux
    du gouvernement du Qué., Synd. des, 2-206
    d'Hydro-Qué., Fra. des, 2-201
Constabulary Public Complaints Commn., Royal Nfld., 3-148
Constance Lethbridge Rehabilitation Ctr., 2-42
Constellation College of Hospitality (Ont.), 9-35
Constituencies, see Electoral Dists.
Constitution (see also Fed./Prov. Relations)
  First Ministers' Conf. on Patriation of the, 1-25
  Govt. Quick Ref., 3-9
Constitutional
  Affairs ADM (Ont.), 3-180
  Law Brs./Divs. (Govt.): Alta., 3-101; Man., 3-128; N.W.T., 3-152; Ont., 3-171; Sask., 3-217
  Patriation (Participants), 1-25
  Relations (Sask.), 3-216
Constructeurs d'habitations, Assn cdnne des, 2-101; Qué., 2-101
Construction (see also, Building)
  Assn(s.), 2-30
    Cdn., 2-30
    Council of Ont., 2-32
  & Building Products, Trade Shows, 1-77
  Cdn. Inst. of Steel, 2-181
  Centre for Studies in (U.W.O), 9-31
  Commn de la (Qué.), 3-209
  Companies Bd., Que., 3-209
  Conseil prov. du Qué. des métiers de la, 2-32
  Côte-Nord, Synd., 2-206
  Council, Cdn. Steel, 2-181
  de Défense Canada, 3-64
  Exhibitions, Shows & Events, 1-77
  Fédn CSN, 2-200
  Govt. Quick Ref., 3-9
  Industries Br. (Fed.), 3-75
  Industry Panel (N.S.), 3-162
  Inst. for Research in (NRC), 3-81
  Labour Relations Assns., 2-111
  Magazines, 5-164
  Management Bur., 2-111
  Ntl. Assn. of Women in, 2-192
  Safety Assn. of Ont., 2-32
  Specifications Canada, 2-32
  Training Ctr., Atlantic (Nfld.), 9-20
  Trades Council of Ont., Prov. Bldg. &, 2-111
Consular
  Affairs (Fed.), 3-69
  Representatives
    in Canada, 3-248
    (Cdn.) Abroad, 3-259
Consultant Lobbyists, 7-35

Consulting
  Agrologists' Assn., Cdn., 2-13
  & Audit Canada (Fed.), 3-85
  Engrs. Assns., 2-57
Consumer(s)
  Affairs
    Brs./Divs. (Govt.): Alta., 3-103; N.B., 3-138; Ont., 3-174
    Office (Fed.), 3-75
    Profls. Cdn. Soc. of, 2-38
  Assns., 2-38
  & Commercial Relations: N.S. (Div.), 3-157; Ont. (Min.), 3-174
  Consultants, Assn. of (Qué.), 2-38
  & Corp. Affairs: (Man.), 3-122
  Depts. (Govt.): Man., 3-122; N.S., 3-156; Ont., 3-174
  Health Org. of Canada, 2-91
  Housing &, Dept. (N.S.), 3-156
  Magazines, 5-177
  Policy (Fed.), 3-75
  Price Index, 1-54
  Products Dir. (Fed.), 3-75
  Protection (Govt.): Quick Ref., 3-10; Sask. (Br.), 3-217
  Services (Govt.): B.C., 3-109; N.S., 3-156; P.E.I., 3-192; Yukon (Mgr.), 3-224
  & Trade Shows, 1-72
Contemporary
  Photography, Cdn. Museum of, 6-1
  Showcase, 6-37
Continental Geoscience Br. (Fed.), 3-82
Continuing
  Educ. (see also Education; Adult Education)
  Assn. for Univ., 2-46
Contracting Companies, Cdn., 7-42
Contractors (Construction), Assns., 2-30
Contreplaqué en bois dur, Assn cdnne du, 2-74
Contrôleur, Bur. du (N.B.), 3-134
Convention(s)
  Facilities, see Tourism
  Magazines, 5-165
  Planners, 1-68 (& see Addenda)
  & Visitors Assn., Ont., 2-186
Conversion Tables, Weights etc., 1-60
Conveyor Mfrs. Assn., Cdn., 2-65
Conviction Review Group (Fed.), 3-78
Cooks, Cdn. Fedn. of Chefs &, 2-157
Co-op, Atlantic, 2-14
Coopération
  Conseils: Ont., 2-108; Qué., 2-108
  internationale
    Centre cdn d'étude et de, 2-108
    Conseils: Cdn, 2-107; Man., 2-109; Ont., 2-109; Sask., 2-109
Co-operative
  Assn., Cdn., 2-13
  Career & Work Educ. Assn., 2-51
  & Credit Union Reg. (Man.), 3-123
  Education
    Assn., Ont., 2-53
    Cdn. Assn. for, 2-47
  Fédérée du Qué., 2-13
  Housing Assns. & Fedns., 2-101
  Loans Bd. of Ont., 3-169
  Wool Growers Ltd., 2-20
Co-operatives Brs./Divs. (Govt.): Man. 3-123; N.B., 3-138; Ont., 3-178
Copper & Brass Devel. Assn., Cdn., 2-127
Coptic Orthodox Church, 2-3
Copyright (see also Patents)
  Assns., 2-138
  Collective, 2-138
  Consumers, Cdn. Soc. of, 2-138
  Govt. Quick Ref., 3-30
  Inst., Cdn., 2-138
  Licensing Agency, Cdn., 2-13
  Registrar (Fed.), 3-75

Coquitlam
  City Govt., 4-156
  Sch. District, 9-6
Corée, Assn. cdnne des vétérans du, 2-127
Cork Wkrs. of America, United, 2-208
Corona Training Inst. (Nfld.), 9-21
Coroners (Govt.): Quick Ref., 3-10; Alta., 3-101; B.C., 3-110; Man., 3-126; N.B., 3-136; N.W.T., 3-151; N.S., 3-162; Ont., 3-186; P.E.I., 3-192; Qué., 3-207; Sask. 3-217; Yukon, 3-224
Corporate
  Affairs (Govt.): B.C., 3-113; Man., 3-122; Yukon, 3-224
  Art Collectors Assn., 2-190
  Counsel Assn., Cdn., (*see* Addenda)
  Directors, Inst. of, 2-122
  Growth, Cdn. Assn. for, 2-33
  -Higher Educ. Forum, 2-51
  Investment, Govt. Quick Ref., 3-23
  Relations Min. (B.C.), 3-114
  Responsibility, Taskforce on the Churches &, 2-8
  Secretaries, Cdn. Soc. of Corp., 2-121
  Secretary, Office of (Fed.), 3-75
  Services Brs./Divs. (Govt.): B.C., 3-113; Fed., 3-75
  Shareholder Services Assn., Cdn., 2-69
Corporations (*see also* Companies)
  Assn. of Cdn. Financial, 2-69
  in Support of Recycling, 2-64
Correctional
  Investigator (Fed.), 3-63
  Service(s) (*see also* Justice Depts.)
    Brs./Divs. (Govt.): Quick Ref., 3-10; Alta., 3-101; B.C., 3-109; Man., 3-128; N.B., 3-139; N.S., 3-162; Ont., 3-186; Qué., 3-207; Sask., 3-217; Yukon, 3-224
    Govt. Depts.: Fed., 3-63; Ont., 3-185 (*see also* Parole Bds.)
Correctionels
  Canada
    L'Enquêteur, 3-63
    Service, 3-63
  Serv., sous-ministre adjoint (Qué.), 3-207
Corrections
  Church Council on Justice &, 2-114
  Quick Ref., *see* Parole Bds., 3-30
Correspondence (*see also* Distance Educ.)
  Educ. in: B.C., 9-7; N.B., 9-17; N.S., 9-21
Corrosion Engrs., Ntl. Assn. of, 2-59
Corrugated
  Case Assn., Cdn., 2-138
  Converters, Assn. of Indep., 2-123
  Steel Pipe Inst., 2-182
Cosmetic, Toiletry & Fragrance Assn., Cdn., 2-123
Cosmetics
  Magazines, 5-165
  Trade Shows, 1-77
COSTI, 2-167
Cottagers' Assns., Fedn. of Ont., 2-151
Couchiching Inst. on Public Affairs, 2-121
Council of Cdns., 2-39
Councils, Major Cities, 4-153
Counselling
  Assn., Cdn. College & University, 2-50
  Foundation, 2-209
  & Guidance Assn., Cdn., 2-166
  & Referral & Educ. Ctr., Women's, 2-193
  Services of Alta., Native, 2-134
Counterpoint, 2-108
Counties in: B.C., 4-12, 4-17; N.B., 4-24; N.S., 4-39; Ont., 4-42, 4-73; Qué., 4-77
Country Music
  Assn., Cdn., 6-39
  Awards, 1-109
  Fdn., 6-40
County
  Clerks, *see* Counties
  Municipalities, Regl. (Qué.), 4-173
Courage, Star of, **16**, 1-28

Cour(s), Qué.
  d'Appel, 10-15
  Municipale, 10-17
  du Qué., 10-15
  Supérieure, 10-15
Courier Assn., Cdn., 2-187
Courses
  de chevaux, Soc. de promotion de l'industrie des (Qué.), 3-198
  Régie (Qué.), 3-208
Court(s)
  Admrs., Assn. of Cdn., 2-113
  Interpreters
    Assn. of Ont., 2-114
    & Translators, Assn. of Legal, 2-113
  Judges, Cdn. Assn. of Prov., 2-113; N.W.T., 2-115
  & Judges (*see also* Justice); in Alta., 10-2; B.C., 10-4; Fed., 10-1; Man., 10-6; N.B., 10-7; Nfld., 10-8; N.W.T., 10-8; N.S., 10-9; Ont., 10-10; P.E.I., 10-14; Qué., 10-15; Sask., 10-20; Yukon, 10-21 (& *see* Addenda)
  of Justice (Ont.), 10-10
  Martial Appeal Court, 10-2
  Métrage de Montréal, Festival intl de, 2-69
  Services Brs./Divs. (Govt.): Alta., 3-102; B.C., 3-110; Man., 3-128; N.B., 3-138; N.W.T., 3-152; N.S., 3-162; Ont., 3-171; Sask., 3-217; Yukon, 3-224
Courtepointe, Assn cdnne de la, 2-190
Courthouse Library Soc., B.C., 2-117
Courtiers
  d'annuités, Assn des, 2-104
  d'assurances, Assns des, 2-105
  en Douane, Soc. cdnne des, 2-34
  en imprimerie, Assn cdnne des, 2-11
  en valeurs mobilières, Assn cdnne des, 2-70
Couverture, Assn cdnne des entrepreneurs en, 2-32
Couvreurs
  Assn des maîtres, 2-32
  Assn ntle des ferblantiers et, 2-197
CPI, 1-54
CPP (Fed.), 3-86
Craft
  Council, Alta., 2-190
  & Design, N.B. College of, 9-18
  Devel. Br. (Nfld.), 3-149
  & Hobby Assn., Cdn., 2-190
Crafts (*see also* Hobbies)
  Assn(s)., 2-190; B.C., 2-190
  Awards, 1-96
  Council, Cdn., 2-190; Man., 2-191; N.S. Designer, 2-191; Ont., 2-191; P.E.I., 2-191; Qué, 2-190; Sask., 2-191
  Devel. Assn., Nfld. & Lab., 2-191
  Guild of Man., 2-190
  Magazines, *see* Hobbies
  Qué., Cdn. Guild of, 2-190
  Shows & Events, 1-77
Cranberry Mktg. Bd., B.C., 3-109
Crane Mfrs. Assn., Cdn., 2-65
Cream Mktg. Bds.: N.B., 3-134; Ont., 3-170
Creamerymen's Assn., Ont., 2-15
Creative Tech., Cdn. Ctr. for (Ont.), 2-58, 9-35
Credit
  agricole Canada. Soc. du, 3-66
  Assn. of Canada, 2-70
  Counselling Services
    Govt. Quick Ref., (*see* Debtors' Assistance), 3-11
    Ont. Assn. of, 2-71
  Institute, 2-70, 9-34
  Magazines, 5-165
  Management Assn., Cdn., 2-70
  Reporting Agencies, Regr. of (B.C.), 3-109
  Union(s) (*see also* Financial Insts.)
    Brs./Divs. (Govt.): Man., 3-123; N.B., 3-138; Ont., 3-178
    Central of Canada, 2-70
    Deposit Corps. (Govt.): Man., 3-123; Nfld., 3-143
    Institute, 2-70

CREDITEL of Canada Ltd., 2-70
Cree
  Hunters & Trappers Income Security Bd. (Qué.), 3-208
  Villages (Qué.), 4-77
Crees, Grand Council of the, 2-133
Crematorium Assn. of B.C., 2-76
Cricket Assn., Cdn., 2-174
Crime
  Prevention
    Bur., Insurance, 2-105
    Ntl., 3-77
  Writers of Canada, 2-194
Crimes Compensation, Govt. Quick Ref., 3-10
Criminal
  Code Review Bd. (Ont.), 3-172
  Court, *see* Provincial Court
  Injuries Compensation (Govt.): Quick Ref., 3-10; Alta., 3-102; Man., 3-128; Ont., 3-172
  Justice
    Assn., Cdn., 2-113
    Brs./Divs. (Govt.): Alta., 3-102; B.C., 3-110; Qué., 3-204
  Law Div. (Govt.), Ont., 3-172
  Lawyers Assn. (Ont.), 2-114
  Policy (Fed.), 3-77
Criminelles, Dir. (Qué.), 3-204
Criminologie
  Conseil des églises pour la justice et la, 2-114
  du Qué., Soc. de, 2-116
Criminology Centre of (U. of T.), 9-30
Crippled Children, Ont. Soc. for, 2-42
Cris
  Grand Conseil des, 2-133
  Office de la sécurité de revenu des chausseurs & piégeurs (Qué.), 3-208
Crisis Ctr.
  Eastman, 2-167
  Thompson, 2-169
Critical Care Nurses, Cdn. Assn. of, 2-135
Critic's
  Assn., Cdn. Theatre, 6-35; Awards, 6-65
  Intl. Assn of Art, 2-191
Criticism, Ctr. for the Study of Theory & (U.W.O.), 9-31
Critiques
  d'art, Assn intle des, 2-191
  Assn qué. des, 6-35
  de Théâtre du Canada, Assn des, 6-35
Croatian Magazines, 5-191
Crohn's & Colitis Fdn. of Canada, 2-91
Croix Rouge, Soc. cdnne de la, 2-55
Crop
  Improvement Assn., P.E.I. Soil &, 2-15
  Insurance Agencies (Govt.): B.C., 3-108; Man., 3-122; N.B., 3-134; Nfld., 3-144; N.S., 3-156; Ont., 3-169; Sask., 3-212
  Protection
    Inst. of Canada, 2-14
    Lab. (Sask.), 3-212
  Statistics, 1-56
  Tech., Dir. (Ont.), 3-169
Crops, *see* Field Crops
Cross
  Country
    Canada, 2-179
    Ski Assn., Cdn. Masters, 2-176
  of Valour, **16**, 1-28
Cross-cultural
  Communication Ctr., 2-38
  Magazines, *see* Multicultural Magazines
Crosse, Assn cdnne de, 2-176
Crossroads Intl., Cdn., 2-166
Crown
  Attorneys (*see also* Crown Counsel; Public Prosecutors)
    Assns.: Man., 2-115; Ont., 2-115
    Divs.: N.S., 3-162; P.E.I., 3-192

Canadian Almanac & Directory 1997

Crown
    Corporations
        Br. (Fed.), 3-67
        Council (Man.), 3-125
        & Privatization Br. (Fed.), 3-67
        Secretariat (B.C.), 3-112
    Counsel, Cdn. Assn. of, 2-113
    Investments Corp. of Sask., 3-213
    Lands (Govt. Agencies): B.C., 3-113; Man., 3-122; N.B., 3-139; Nfld., 3-145; N.S., 3-163 (see also Lands)
CRTC, 3-61
Cruelty
    to Animals, Socs. for Prev. of, 2-21
    to Children, Cdn. Soc. for Prev. of, 2-166
CSAE, 2-121
CSI - Sherbrooke, 2-108
CSIS, 3-89
Cuisiniers
    Fédn cdnne des chefs et, 2-157
    et patissiers, Soc. des chefs, 2-158
Culinary
    Art & Tech., Inst. of, 2-158
    Institute
        of Canada (P.E.I.), 9-41
        Cdn., 2-157
Cultivateurs, Synd. ntl des, 2-15
Cultural
    Affairs
        Cdn. Inst. of, 2-108
        (Govt.): Quick Ref., 3-3; N.B., 3-138; Nfld., 3-149; P.E.I. (Francophone), 3-190
    Alliance, Vancouver, 2-25
    Awards, 1-96
    Communities & Immigration Council (Qué.), 3-205
    Devel. & Heritage Sector (Fed.), 3-58
    Enterprise Devel. Commn., Arts & (Qué.), 3-199
    Exchange Soc., Sask., 2-98
    Execs., Assn. of, 2-120
    Facilities & Hist'l Resources (Alta.), 3-96
    Industries, Brs/Divs (Govt.), Fed., 3-58; Sask., 3-219
    Magazines, 5-180
    Orgs., Sask. Council of, 2-98
    Property
        Commn., Qué., 3-199
        Export Review Bd., Cdn., 3-58
    Soc. of The Deaf, Cdn., 2-42
Culture (see also Arts)
    Assns., 2-38
    Awards, 1-96 (see also Literary Arts, Performing Arts)
    Brs./Divs. (Govt.): Alta., 3-96; P.E.I., 3-190; Sask., 3-219
    Depts. (Govt.): Quick Ref., 3-3; B.C., 3-118; Fed., 3-58; Man., 3-123; N.B., 3-138; Nfld., 3-149; N.W.T., 3-151; N.S., 3-158; Ont., 3-172; Qué., 3-198
    Govt. Quick Ref., (see Arts) 3-3
    Magazines, 5-180
    Websites, 5-233
Culturel(les)
    Commn des biens (Qué.), 3-199
    Conseil des communautés (Qué.), 3-205
    Franco-manitobain: Assn, 2-38; Centre, 3-123
    des Franco-ontariennes, Union, 2-39
    Inst cdn des affaires, 2-108
    Soc. de développement des entreprises (Qué.), 2-39, 3-199
Cultures
    Inst cdn pour la protection des, 2-14
Culturisme amateur, Fédn de, 2-149
CUMBA, 2-40
Cumberland Regl. College (Sask.), 9-54
CUPE, 2-200
Curateur public du Qué., 3-200
Curling Assn(s.), Cdn., 2-174
    Nfld. & Lab., 2-179
Currency
    Govt. Quick Ref., 3-10

Currency (cont.)
    Museum of the Bank of Canada, 6-1
Current Events Magazines, 5-180
Curriculum Devel., Ont. Assn. for, 2-53
CUSO, 2-108
Custodial & Maintenance Assn., 2-200
Custody Review Bd., (Ont.), 3-174
Custom Engineered Machinery Mfrs. Assn., Cdn., 2-66
Customs
    Border Servs. (Fed.), 3-86
    Brokers, Cdn. Soc. of, 2-34
    Govt. Quick Ref., 3-10
    & Legislation Com., 2-187
    Offices, Regl. 1-41, 3-87
    Regulations, 1-39
Cutting Horse Assns., Cdn., 2-20
C.V.O., 1-3
CWB, 3-62
Cycling
    Assn., Cdn., 2-175
    Magazines, 5-17
Cypriot Fedn. of Canada, 2-130
Cyprus Hills Regl. College (Sask.), 9-54
Cystic Fibrosis Fdn., Cdn., 2-85; Que., 2-82
Cytology Cdn. Soc. of, 2-89
Czech (see also Tchèque)
    & Slovak Assn., 2-130

D

DAC Fdn. for People with Special Needs, 2-209
Daily
    Newspaper Assn., Cdn., 2-145
    Newspapers, see Newspapers
Dairy
    Agencies, Govt. Quick Ref., 3-11
    Bds./Commns. (Govt.): Quick Ref., 3-11; Alta., 3-96; Cdn., 3-57; N.S., 3-156
    Councils: Atlantic, 2-13; Ntl., 2-15; Ont., 2-15; Qué., 2-14
    Employees & Driver Salesmen, Alta. Broth. of, 2-196
    Farmer(s)
        of Canada, 2-13; of Ont., 2-14
        Publications, see Farm Publications
    & Food Industries Supply Assn., Cdn., 2-72
    Fdn., Sask., 2-15
    Industry
        Inspection Br. (Ont.), 3-169
        Statistics, 1-56
    Magazines, 5-165
    Nutrition Council of Alta., 2-14
    Producers Assn., P.E.I., 2-15
Dairying, Govt. Quick Ref., 3-11
Dairymen's Assn., N. Ont., 2-15
Dairyworld Foods, 2-14
Dalhousie Univ. (N.S.), 9-22
Dance (see also Music)
    Art, Anna Wyman, Sch. of (B.C.), 9-9
    Assn(s)., 6-41
    Awards & Prizes see also Performing Arts
    Cdn. Assn. for Health, Physical Education, Recreation &, 2-174
    Companies, 6-41
    Directory, 6-41
    Orgs., Cdn. Assn. of Profl., 6-41
    Teachers' Assn., Cdn., 6-42
Dancer Transition Resource Ctr., 6-42
Dangerous Goods (see also Hazardous Materials; Pesticide)
    Control (Govt.): Quick Ref., 3-11; Alta., 3-104
    Transp. of (Govt.): Quick Ref., 3-11; Fed., 3-91; N.B., 3-139; Ont., 3-187
Danish Assns. in Canada, Fedn. of, 2-130
Danse
    Moderne de Montréal, Ateliers de, 9-47
    Regroupement québécois de la, 6-44
Danseurs en Transition, Ctr de Ressources pour, 6-42

Database Assn. of Ont., 2-104
Daughters of the Empire, Imperial Order, 2-76
David Dunlop Observatory (U. of T.), 1-1, 9-30
Day Care
    Brs./Divs. (Govt.): Quick Ref., 3-11; Alta., 3-100; B.C., 3-119; Man., 3-125; Sask., 3-220
    & Homemaker Licensing Bd. (Nfld.), 3-149
De Havilland Moth Club of Canada, 2-28
Deaf (see also Hearing Impaired)
    Bob Rumball Ctr. for the, 2-41
    Canadian
        Assn. of the, 2-41
        Cultural Soc. of the, 2-42
    Man. Sch. for the, 9-15
    Provincial Sch. for the (B.C.), 9-7
    Sports Assns., 2-175
    Youth Canada, 2-42
Deafblind & Rubella Assn., Cdn., 2-85
Deafened Persons Assn., Cdn., 2-42
Deafness Research & Training Inst., Cdn., 2-42
Dean(s)
    Cdn. Fedn. of Business Sch., 2-48
    Council of Cdn. Law, 2-47
    & Directors of Home Economics & Related Areas in Cdn. Univs., 2-47
    of Educ., Ont. Assn. of, 2-53
    Forms of Address (Anglican Church), 1-34
    of Pharmacy, Assn. of, 2-46
    University, see Universities
Death
    Certificates, (Govt.): Quick Ref., 3-39; Alta., 3-103; B.C., 3-116; Man., 3-122; N.B., 3-136; Nfld., 3-145; N.W.T., 3-154; N.S., 3-157; Ont., 3-174; P.E.I., 3-191; Qué., 3-204; Sask., 3-215; Yukon, 3-223
    Leading Cause of, 1-49
    Statistics, 1-48
Debate Assn., Sask. Elocution &, 2-112
Debt Management Brs./Divs. (Govt.): N.B., 3-136; Nfld., 3-143; Sask., 3-215
Debtors' Assistance
    Dir. (B.C.), 3-109
    Govt. Quick Ref., 3-11
Decency, Cdns. for, 2-166
Décorateurs-ensembliers, Soc. des (Qué.), 2-107
Decorating
    Exhibitions, Shows & Events, 1-87
    Products Assn., Cdn., 2-123
Decorations
    Abbreviations, 1-32
    Bravery, **16**, 1-28
    Order of Precedence, 1-31
    pour Service méritore, **16**, 1-29
Decorative Arts, Cdn. Soc. of, 2-190
Decorators Assn. of B.C., Master Painters &, 2-32
Deeds Regrs. (Govt.): N.B., 3-136; N.S., 3-161; P.E.I., 3-192 (see also Property Reg'n.; Personal Property)
Defence
    Assns.
        Inst., Conf. of, 2-126
        Ntl. Network, 2-126
    Canada, Ntl., 3-79
    Construction Canada, 3-64
    Dept., Ntl. (Govt.), 3-79
    Govt. Quick Ref., 3-11
    Industries Br. (Fed. Govt.), 3-75
    Permanent Joint Bd. on (Canada-U.S.A.), 3-247
    Publications, see Military Publications
    Research & Educ. Ctr., 2-126
    Science Advisory Board (Ntl.), 3-79
Défense, ntl, 3-79
Déficiences, Conseil des Cdns avec, 2-42
Degrees, Abbreviations, 1-35
Delegations
    Abroad, Cdn., 3-259
    to Canada, 3-248
Delinquency, see Young Offenders
Delta
    Corp. of, Govt., 4-156; Sch. Dist., 9-6

Democratic Dev., Intl. Ctr. for Human Rights &, 2-102
Demographic Statistics, (Fed. Govt.), 3-89
Demonstration Schs. for Challenged Students in Ont., 9-27
Dene Nation, 2-133
Denominational
　Educ. Councils (Nfld.), 3-142
　Magazines, 5-187
Denominations, Religious, 2-2
Dentaires, Assn des facultés, 2-46
Dental
　Assistants Assn., Cdn., 2-40
　Assn(s)., 2-39
　　Cdn., 2-40
　Bds: Nfld., 2-40; N.S., 2-40
　Conventions, 1-78
　Council of P.E.I., Prov., 2-40
　Examining Bd., Ntl., 2-40
　Exhibitions, Shows & Events, 1-78
　Hygienists' Assn., Cdn., 2-40
　Lab. Conf., Commercial, 2-40
　Nurses & Assistants Assn. (Ont.), 2-40
　Research, Cdn. Assn. for, 2-39
　Surgeons
　　Colleges of, 2-40
　　Royal College of (Ont.), 2-41
　Technologists of Ont., College of, 2-40
Dentistes
　du Qué.
　　Assn. des chirurgiens, 2-40
　　Ordre des, 2-40
　et pharmaciens du Qué., Assn des conseils des médecins, 2-82
Dentistry
　Assn. of Cdn. Faculties of, 2-46
　Canada Fund, 2-40
　Cdn. Assn. of Public Health, 2-40
　Faculties/Schs., Index to, 9-56
　Magazines, 5-165
　Shows, 1-78
Dentists, Royal College of, 2-41
Denturist Assn(s.), 2-40
Denturologistes
　Assn des (Qué.), 2-39
　Ordre des (Qué.), 2-39
　Soc. des, (N.-B.), 2-40
Department Store Union, 2-206; Sask., 2-206
Dept. Stores, see Retail Trade, 7-51
Deposit Ins. Corp.: Canada, 3-55; Ont., 3-179
Dépôt(s)
　du Canada, Soc. d'assurance, 3-55
　et placement du Qué., Caisse de, 3-202
Depressive & Manic-Depressive Assn. of Ont., 2-125
Deputy Ministers (Govt.), Forms of Address, 6-75
Dermatologistes du Qué., Assn des, 2-82
Dermatology Assn., Cdn., 2-85
DES Action/Canada, 2-91
Design (see also Interior Design)
　Academies: Ont., 9-35; Qué., 9-47
　Alta. College of Art &, 9-4
　in Business, The Group for, 2-35
　Club of Canada, Advertising &, 2-11
　Emily Carr Inst. of Art & (B.C.), 9-9
　Exchange, 2-24
　Magazines, see Homes Magazines
　N.B. College of Craft &, 9-18
Designer(s)
　of Canada, Associated, 2-106
　Crafts Council, N.S., 2-191
　Industriels, Assns, 2-106/107
　d'intérieur, 2-107
　Interior, Assns. & Insts., 2-107
Desjardins
　Confédn des caisses populaires et d'économie, 2-70
　Fédn des cuisses d'économie, 2-70
　Fondation, 2-264
Dessinateurs éditoriaux, Assn cdnne des, 2-190

Détail, Conseil
　cdn du commerce de, 2-158
　qué. du commerce de, 2-158
Détaillants
　en alimentation du Qué., Assn des, 2-158
　en fourrures, Conseil des, 2-77
　de matérieux de const., Assn de, 2-32
　en quincaillerie, Assn cdnne des, 2-158
Detergent Assn., Soap &, 2-124
Developers Assn., Prospectors &, 2-128
Developing Countries, Aid to, see International Aid
Development (see also Community Devel.; Economic Devel.; Regl. Devel.; Rural Devel.)
　Agency, Cdn. Intl., 3-61
　Bank, Business, (Fed.), 3-55
　Corps.: Lower Churchill, 3-148; Man., 3-123; N.W.T., 3-153; Ont., 3-176
　Council, Northern Alta., 3-103
　Depts. (Govt.), see Economic Development
　Education
　　Inter-Church Com. for World, 2-110
　　Resource Assn., Intl., 2-109
　through Educ., Cdn. Org. for, 2-108
　Fund Corp., Sask., 3-215
　Institute
　　of Sask. (U. of Regina), 9-54
　　Urban, 2-141
　Intl. Assn. of Science & Tech. for, 2-163
　Management, Cdn. Inst. for, 2-140
　& Peace, 2-8
　Research Ctr., Intl., 3-77
　& Rural Renewal (Nfld.), 3-142
Développement
　Banque (Fed. Govt.), 3-55
　durable
　　Dir. gen. (Qué.), 3-201
　　Inst intle du, 2-63
　économique & tourisme, Dept. (N.B.), 3-134
　Inst Carrière et (Qué.), 9-47
　international
　　Agence cdnne de, 3-61
　　L'Assn cdnne d'études du, 2-107
　　Centre de recherches pour le, 3-77
　et la paix, Org. catholique cdnne pour le, 2-8
　régional (Qué.), Bur. féd. de, 3-66
　des regions, Sécrétariat au (Qué.), 3-20
　social, Conseil cdn de, 2-79
　urbain, Inst de, 2-202
Devis de construction Canada, 2-32
Devoir, Le (Qué.), 5-144
Dexter Cattle Assn., Cdn., 2-20
DFAIT, 3-68
DFO, 3-67
Diabète Québec, Assn, 2-82
Diabetes
　Assn., Cdn., 2-86
　Fdn., Juvenile, 2-92
Diagnostic Medical Sonographers, Cdn. Soc. of, 2-89
Die
　Casters Assn., Cdn., 2-123
　Stampers & Engravers Union of N. Amer., Intl. Plate Printers, 2-203
Diecasters, Indep. Union of Precision, 2-258
Dietetic Assn., Cdn., 2-85
Diététique du Qué., Assn des technicien(nes) en, 2-198
Diététistes
　Assn cdnne des, 2-86
　L'Ordre des (Ont.), 2-91
　du Qué.
　　profile des, 2-86
　　Synd. profl des, 2-206
Dietitians Assns., 2-86; College of (Ont.), 2-91
Diffusion, Office cdn de vérification de la, 2-144
Dindon, Office cdn de commercialisation du, 2-142
Dinosaur Prov. Park (Alta.), 6-2
Diocesan Theological College, Montréal, 3-54

Diplomatic
　Corps. Services (Fed.), 3-69
　Directory, 3-248
　Forms of Address, 1-35
　Reps.
　　in Canada, 3-248
　　(Cdn.) Abroad, 3-259
　　Govt. Quick Ref., 3-12
Direct
　Mktg. Assn., Cdn., 2-11
　Sellers Assn., 2-158
Directeurs/Directrices
　d'agence-vie, Assn des, 2-106
　d'Association, Soc. cdnne des, 2-121
　de bibliothèques
　　de N.-B., Conseil des, 2-119
　　publiques, Qué., 2-116; Montréal, 2-119
　de biologie, conseil universitaire des, 2-47
　et coordonnateurs de programmes de journalisme des univs cdnnes, 2-46
　d'éclairage de télévision, 2-29
　d'établissement d'enseignement, Fédn qué. des, 2-52
　d'établissements scolaires, Assn francophone intl des, 2-45
　d'expositions, Assn cdnne des, 2-66
　généraux
　　des commissions scolaires de Qué. assn des, 2-45
　　des municipalités du Qué., Assn des, 2-79
　de l'information en radio-télévision, Assn cdnne des, 2-29
　medias du Qué., Conseil des, 2-11
　de polices et pompiers, Assn des, 2-113
　de services de santé, Cdn des, 2-85
Directories, Magazines, 5-181
Directors
　Assn., Radio Television News, 2-29
　Guild of Canada, 2-69
　of Home Economics in Cdn. Univs., Deans &, 2-47
　Inst. of Corp., 2-122
　of Journalism Programs, Assn. of, 2-46
　Soc. of Television Lighting, 2-29
Disabilities
　Alta. Com. of Citizens with, 2-41
　B.C. Lions Soc. for Children with, 2-164
　Council of Cdns. with, 2-42
　Dir. (Sask. Labour), 3-218
　Employed Persons with, Statistics, 1-52
　Employment Servs. for Persons with, (N.B.), 3-133
　Persons with
　　Coord. Group (Fed.), 3-72
　　Premier's Council (Alta.), 3-101
　　Servs. to Persons, Dir. (Alta.), 3-100
　Schs. for Children, see Challenged Students
　Soc. for Manitobans with, 2-43
Disability
　Active Living Alliance for Cdns. with a, 2-172
　Issues
　　Adv. Council on, Ont., 3-173
　　Group (Ont.), 3-172
　Rights Council, Cdn., 2-42
Disabled (see also Handicapped; Handicapé(e)s)
　Alta. Rehab. Council for the, 2-42
　Assn. for the Neurologically, 2-41
　Cdn. Rehab. Council for the, 2-42
　Children, Qué., Soc. for, 2-43
　Equestrian Assn. for the, 2-179
　Nfld. Soc. for the Physically, 2-43
　People of Nfld./Lab., Consumer Org. of, 2-42
　Persons
　　Assns., 2-41
　　Cdn. Fdn. for Physically, 2-42
　　Commn., N.S., 3-157
　　Premier's Council on Status of (N.B.), 3-134
　　Servs. for, (Govt.): Quick Ref., 3-12; Fed. (Human Resources), 3-72; Qué. (Bureau des personnes handicapées), 3-207
　　Status of (Fed., Human Resources), 3-72

Disabled (cont.)
    P.E.I. Council of the, 2-43
    Québec March of Dimes for the, 2-43
    Rehab. Fdn. for the, (Ont.), 2-43
    Skiing Assns., 2-173/174
    Sport for (Ont.), 2-180
    Students, Ntl. Educl. Assn. of, 2-53
Disarmament (*see also* Peace; Nuclear)
    Cdn. Ambassador for, 3-69
    Coalition, Act for, 2-107
Disaster
    Assistance Bd., Man., 3-126
    & Emergency Programs (Alta.), 3-104
Disc Jockey Assn., Cdn., 6-39
Discrimination
    (Employment), Govt. Quick Ref., 3-12
    in the Workplace, Action Group Against, 2-55
Disease Control (Govt.): Alta., 3-100; Fed., 3-71; Nfld., 3-146
Dispatchers Assn., Cdn. Air Line, 2-198
Display Assn., Exhibit &, 2-66
Distance Education (*see also* Correspondence Education)
    Alta., 9-1
    Cdn. Assn. for, 2-47
    Brs./Divs. (Govt.): Alta., 3-98; B.C., 3-111; Man., 3-124; P.E.I., 3-191
Distances between major points in Canada, 1-66
    Solar, 1-14
Distillers, Assn. of Cdn., 2-72
Distillery, Wine etc. Wkrs. Intl. Union, 2-200
Distress Ctrs., Ont. Assn. of, 2-168
Distribution Cos., Cdn., 7-51
District(s)
    Local Gov't. (Man.), 4-23
    Municipalities, B.C., 4-12
    Ont., 4-72
    Regl. (B.C.), 4-17
Diver Training Ctr., Cdn. (Nfld.), 9-20
Diversification de l'économie de l'ouest Canada, 3-92
Diving Assn. Cdn., Amateur, 2-173
Divinity Colleges: Acadia (N.S.), 9-22; McMaster (Ont.), 9-29
Divorce
    Govt. Quick Ref., 3-12
    Grounds in Canada, 1-42
Dockyard Chargehands Assn., Fed. Govt., 2-200
Doctors' Assns., 2-80
Documentalistes etc., Soc. des auteurs, recherchistes, 2-206
Documentation, Assn pour l'avancement des sciences et des techniques de la, 2-117
Documents, Soc. cdnne pour l'analyse des, 2-119
Dog
    Licences, *see* Animal Control
    Orgs., W. Fedn. of Individuals &, 2-23
Dominican College (Ont.), 9-35
Dominion of Canada Rifle Assn., 2-151
Donkey & Mule Assn., Cdn., 2-20
Door
    & Hardware Inst., 2-124
    Mfrs. Assn., Cdn. Window &, 2-124
Dopage sportif, Centre cdn sur le, 2-174
Dossiers de santé, Assn cdnne interprofl du, 2-118
Douglas College (B.C.), 9-8
Doukhobor(s)
    Orthodox, 2-6
    Soc., Cdn., 2-129
Douleur, Soc. cdnne pour le traitement de la, 2-88
Down Syndrome Soc., Cdn., 2-86
Downtown Devel. Br. (N.B.), 3-138
Doyen(ne)s
    des écoles d'administration, Fédn cdnne des, 2-48
    des facultés de droit, 2-47
Drain Contrs. Assn., Ont. Concrete &, 2-42
Drainage Tribunal, Ont., 3-170

Drama
    Assns., 6-35
    Awards, *see* Broadcasting & Film; Literary Arts; Performing Arts
    in Education, Council of, 6-36
    for Pay Television, Fdn. to Underwrite, 2-210
Dramatique(s)
    Art, Conservatoire d' (Qué.), 3-199
    Centre des auteurs, 6-35
Draveurs, Commn scolaire des (Qué.), 9-42
Dreams Fdn. Canada, World of, 2-214
Dreamspeakers Festival Soc., 2-69
Drillers Assns., 2-44
Drilling
    Assn(s)., 2-44
    Contractors, Cdn. Assn. of Oilwell, 2-44
    Engrs., Cdn. Assn. of, 2-44
Drinking
    Age, Legal, 1-41
    /Driving Countermeasures (Govt.): Quick Ref., 3-12; N.S., 3-162; Ont., 3-171
Driver(s)
    Cdn. Racing, 2-176
    Control Bd. (Govt.), Yukon, 3-222
    Licences
        Div. (Man.), 3-126
        Govt. Quick Ref., 3-12
    Safety Council, Sask. Profl., 2-161
Driving, Drinking, *see* Drinking; Drunk
Droit(s)
    Assn
        cdnne des bibliothéques de, 2-117
        ntle de la femme et du, 2-192
    d'auteur, Soc. de perception de, 2-138
    canonique, Soc. cdnne de, 2-113
    de la concurrence, Assn cdnne d'étude du, 2-113
    Conseil des doyens des facultés de, 2-47
    de l'environnement, Assn cdnne, 2-61
    des handicapés, Centre de la défense des, 2-41
    humains
        Fondation cdnne des, 2-102
        Inst cdn des, 2-102
    international, Conseil cdn de, 2-113
    maritime, Assn cdnne de, 2-114
    de la personne
        de B'nai Brith, Ligue des, 2-102
        Commn des (Fed.), 3-60
        et du dével. démocratique, Centre intl des, 2-102
        Monument cdn pour les, 2-102
        au plan intl, Réseau des, 2-102
    des personnes handicapées, Conseil cdn des, 2-42
    de la politique de l'env., Inst cdn de, 2-61
    des ressources, Inst cdn du, 2-61
    et société, Assn cdnne de, 2-114
Drug(s) (*see also* Alcohol & Drug; Pharmaceuticals)
    Abuse
        Award, *see* Substance Abuse
        Commn., Alta. Alcohol &, 3-96
        Council on, 2-10
    Assn., Cdn. Wholesale, 2-139
    Concerns, Alcohol &, 2-10
    Dependency Servs. (Govt.): Nfld., 3-146; N.S., 3-160
    Dir. (Fed.), 3-71
    Education, Parent Resources Inst. for, 2-168
    -Free
        Sport, Cdn. Ctr. for, 2-174
        Workplace, Council for a, 2-10
    Govt. Quick Ref., 3-13
    Magazines, 5-165
    Mfrs. Assn., Cdn., 2-139
        Nonprescription, 2-139
    Parents Against, 2-10
    Programs Br. (Ont.), 3-180
    Purchasing (Fed. Govt.), 3-85
    Standards/Therapeutics Com., Man., 3-126
    Stores, Cdn. Assn. of, 2-158
Drugless Therapy, Bd. (Ont.), 3-180

Drunk Driving (*see also* Drinking/Driving Countermeasures)
    Against, 2-10
    Mothers Against, 2-10
Dry Cleaning Trade Shows *see* Cleaning Trade Shows
Ducks Unlimited, 2-62
Dufferin-Peel R.C.S.S. Bd. of Educ. (Ont.), 9-25
Dundas Valley Sch. of Art (Ont.), 9-34
Durham (Ont.)
    Bd. of Educ., 9-24; R.C.S.S., 9-26
    College, AA & T, 9-33
    Regl. Municipality of, Govt., 4-171
Dutch Magazines, 5-191
Duties, *see* Customs Regulations
DX Radio Club, Cdn. Intl., 2-150
Dying with Dignity, 2-167
Dyslexia Assn., Cdn., 2-86
Dystonia Medical Research Fdn., 2-91
Dystrophie musculaire, Assn cdnne de la, 2-93

E

Ear Bank, B.C., 2-83
Earls, 1-30
Early
    Childhood
        Educ. & Devel. Servs., The Inst. for (N.S.), 9-20
        Educators, Ont., Assn. for, 2-45
    Music: Calgary, 6-39; Vancouver, 6-40
Earnings, Average (Statistics), 1-53
Earth, 1-14
    Day Canada, 2-62
    Energy Assn., Cdn., 2-60
    Friends of the, 2-63
    Resources Research, Ctr. for (Memorial Univ.), 9-20
    Sciences Sector (Fed.), 3-82
    & Space Sciences, Ctr. for Research in (York Univ.), 9-32
Earthkeeping: Food & Agriculture in Christian Persp., 2-14
East
    European
        Countries, Cdn. Inst. for the Study of the Soviet Union &, 2-155
        Studies
            Ctr. for Russian & (U. of T.), 9-30
            Intl. Council for, 2-156
    Indian Magazines, 5-191
    Isle Shipyard Inc. (P.E.I.), 3-190
East York, Borough of, Govt., 4-156
Easter, 1-24
    Seal
        Research Inst., 2-42
        Societies, 2-42
Eastern
    Calendars, 1-2
    College of Applied Arts (Nfld.), 9-20
    Star, Order of the, 2-76
Eating Disorder Info. Ctr., Ntl., 2-93
Eaton Fdn., 2-209
Eau, Assn
    cdnne
        pour la qualité de l', 2-62
        sur la qualité de l', 2-60
    qué. des techniques de l', 2-60
Eaux
    embouteillées, Fédn cdnne des, 2-72
    potables et usées, Assn cdnne des, 2-62
    Soc. qué. d'assainissement des, 2-65, 3-197
    souterrainnes du Qué., Assn des, 2-44; Assn cdnne des, 2-44
Ecclesiastical
    Abbreviations, 1-35
    Forms of address, 1-34
Échanges, Soc. éducative de visites et d', 2-54
Échecs, Fédn
    cdnne des, 2-151
    qué. des, 2-152

Echo de l'ocean, 2-64
Éclairage de télévision, Soc. des directeurs d', 2-29
Éclaireurs pour le cancer dans l'enfance, Fdn des, 2-90
Eclipses, Sun & Moon, 1-22
École(s)
    d'Administration, Fédn cdnne des doyens des, 2-48
    Assn qué. du personnel de direction des, 2-46
    Forestières universitaires du Canada, Assn des, 2-46
    françaises de la communauté urbaine de Toronto Conseil des, 2-51
    d'optométrie du Canada, Assn des, 2-46
    privées
        Fédn cdnne des, 2-51
        Qué., 2-53
    de service social, Assn des, 2-46
    technique et professionnelle (Man.), 9-16
Ecological Reserves Advisory Com. (Man.), 3-130
Ecology (see also Environment(al); Conservation; Ecophilosophy; Naturalists; Nature; Pollution)
    Action Ctr., 2-62
    Ethics & Religion, Cdn. Coalition for, 2-60
    Magazines, see Environment Magazines
Eco-Network, Man., 2-61; Sask., 2-61
Economic
    Co-op & Devel., Org. for, 3-247
    Council, Atlantic Provs., 2-44, 3-131
    Developers
        Assn., 2-44
        Council of Ont., 2-45
    Development
        Agreement for Sustainable (P.E.I.), 3-190
        Authority, Alta., 3-97
        Bd. (Man.), 3-127
        Depts (Govt.): Alta., 3-97; Fed. (Industry), 3-74; Man. (Industry, etc.), 3-127; N.B., 3-134; Nfld., 3-142; N.W.T., 3-153; Ont., 3-175; P.E.I., 3-189; Qué. (Industrie, etc.), 3-202; Sask., 3-213; Yukon, 3-222
        Fund, Communities (Man.), 3-130
        Govt. Quick Ref., see Business Devel., 3-6
        Inst., Community, 2-44
        Nova Scotia Ctr. for Environmentally Sustainable, 2-64
        Profls Assn of Qué., 2-44
    Diversification Canada, Western, 3-92
    Educ., Cdn. Fdn. for, 2-49
    Innovation & Tech. Council (Man.), 3-128
    Justice, Ecum. Coalition for, 2-7
    Planning, Govt. Quick Ref., 4-15
    Recovery Commn. (Nfld.), 3-142
    Relations, Ctr. for the Study of Intl. (U.W.O.), 9-31
    Renewal Agency, N.S., 3-157
    Statistics, 1-54, 1-56
Economics
    Assn(s)., 2-44
        Cdn., 2-44
    Cdn. Assn. for Business, 2-44
    & Farm Mgmt., Cdn. Agric., 2-44
    Research Assn., Cdn. Health, 2-86
Économie
    Confédn des caisses populaires et d', 2-70
    Desjardins du Quebec, 2-70
    Familiale
        Assn cdnne d', 2-49
        du Qué., Fédn des assn coopératives, 2-70
    Fdn de l'assn cdnne d', 2-49
    rurale et de gestion agricole, Soc. cdnne d', 2-44
Économique
    des affaires, Assn cdnne de science, 2-44
    Assn
        cdnne d', 2-44; de développement, 2-44
        des profls en développement (Qué.), 2-44
    Centre de recherche et développement en, 2-44
    Fdn d'éducation, 2-49
Économistes qué., Assn des, 2-44
Economists
    Assn. of Ont. Land, 2-182
    Atlantic Assn. of Applied, 2-44

Economy
    & Environment, Yukon Council on, 3-221
    Round Tables on the Environment &, see Environment
    Statistics on the, 1-54, 1-56
Ecophilosophy Network, Cdn., 2-60
Ecosystem Conservation (Govt.): Fed. (Dir.), 3-65; Qué., 3-201
Écosystèmes, Dir. gén. de la connaissance des (Qué.), 3-201
Écran, Inst ntl des arts de l', 2-69
Écrivaines et écrivains, Union des, 2-194
Écrivains
    Awards, see Literary Arts Awards
    cdns, Soc. des, 2-194
    de langue française, Fédn intle des, 2-194
Ecumenical
    Coalition for Economic Justice, 2-7
    Council of Churches, Atl., 2-6
Ecumenism, Cdn. Ctr. for, 2-6
EDC, 3-66
EDI, 2-103
Edible Oil Foods, Inst. of, 2-73
Éditeurs
    anglophones du Qué., Assn des, 2-144
    cdns, Assn des, 2-144
    Awards (see Journalism; Literary Arts)
    de livres, Assn ntle des, 2-144
    de musique, Assn cdnne des, 2-145; Soc., 2-139
Editorial Cartoonists, Assn. of Cdn., 2-190
Editors
    Assn(s)., 2-193; of Canada, 2-194
    Awards (see Journalism; Literary Arts)
    Cdn. Soc. of Magazine, 2-194
Edmonton
    Art Gallery, 6-29
    City Govt., 4-156
    Community Fdn. 2-209
    Sch. Districts, 9-1, 9-2
Éducateurs
    de musique, Assn cdnne des, 6-39
    profls du N.-B., Assn des, 2-46
Éducatifs, Servs. (Govt.): N.B., 3-135; Qué., 3-200
Education
    des adultes
        Conseil intle d', 2-52
        Inst cdn d', 2-52
    Advanced (Govt.) see Advanced Education
    anglophone (Qué.), 3-200
    through Art, Cdn. Soc. for, 2-191
    Assn(s)., 2-45
        Cdn., 2-48
        Co-operative, Career & Work, 2-51
        for Media & Technology in, 2-46; Awards, 6-50
        Ont. Co-operative, 2-53
    Awards, 1-97
    Boards of: Alta. (Protestant Separate), 9-2; (Public), 9-1; (R.C. Separate), 9-2; B.C., 9-6; Man., 9-13; N.B., 9-17; Nfld., 9-19, (R.C.), 9-19; N.W.T., 9-21; N.S. 9-21; Ont., 9-24, (Protestant Separate), 9-27, (R.C. Separate), 9-25; P.E.I., 9-41; Qué., 9-41; Sask., 9-51; Yukon, 9-55
    Cdn.
        Assn.
            for Adult, 2-47
            of Business, 2-47
            for Co-operative, 2-47
            for Distance, 2-47
            of Fdns. of, 2-47
            for Pastoral Practice &, 2-47
            for the Promo. & Advancement of Science, 2-161
            for Teacher, 2-48
            for University Continuing, 2-46
        Bur. for Intl., 2-48
        Council for
            the Advancement of, 2-48
            Multicult. & Intercult., 2-48

Education
    Cdn. (cont.)
        Fdn. for Economic, 2-49
        Org. for Devel. through, 2-108
        Soc. for Study of, 2-50
            Higher, 2-50
    Centre
        d'animation de dével. et recherche en, 2-50
        National Co-operative, 2-51
        for the Study of Computers in (York Univ.), 9-32
    Commn., Maritimes Higher, 3-131
    & Communication, Cdn. Network for Environmental, 2-61
    Comparée et intle, Soc. cdnne d', 2-51
    Council(s)
        Denominational (Nfld.), 3-142
        of Drama in, 6-36
    Depts (Govt.): Quick Ref., 3-13; Alta., 3-97; B.C., 3-111; Man., 3-123; N.B., 3-135; Nfld., 3-142; N.W.T., 3-151; N.S. 3-158; Ont., 3-176; P.E.I., 3-190, 3-191; Qué., 3-200; Sask., 3-213; Yukon, 3-222
    à distance, assn cdnne de l', 2-47
    Foundations
        Atlantic Provs., 2-47
        Catholic, 2-209
        Fedn. of Chinese Cdn. Profls., 2-210
        Maritime Provs., 2-212
        OTA, 2-212
        française, Bur. de L' (Man.), 3-124
    Govt. Quick Ref., 3-13
    Group, Employment, Social Devel. & (Fed.), 3-72
    Index to Selected Faculties/Schs., 9-56
    International
        Assn.
            for Better Basic, 2-52
            for Publishing, 2-145
        Council for Adult, 2-52
    Internationale, Bur. cdn de, 2-48
    Labour Force Participation Statistics, 1-51
    de langue française, Assn cdnne d', 2-45
    Magazines, 5-165
    Manitoba
        Assn. for Bilingual, 2-52
        Parents for German, 2-53
    Ministries of, see Depts., above
    Ontario
        Assn. of Deans of, 2-53
        Inst. for Studies in, 9-35
    pastorales, Assn cdnne pour la pratique et l', 2-47
    Permanente dans les universités, 2-46
    Post-Secondary, see Post-Secondary Educ.
    Private, see Private Schs.
    Public Sch. Bds., see Bds. of Educ.
    Publications, 5-165
    du Québec, Fédn des proflles et profls de l', 2-196
    Reform, Coalition for, 2-51
    Relations Commn. (Ont.), 3-177
    Sask. Assn. for Multicultural, 2-54
    Secteur des services francophones d' (N.B.), 3-135
    Soc., Comparative & Intl., 2-51
    through Art, Cdn. Soc. for, 2-50; Ont., 2-191
    & Training
        (Govt. Agencies): Man., 3-123; Ont., 3-176
        Regl. Offices (Ont.), 9-24
    Websites, 5-242
    Wife Assault, 2-167
Educational
    Admin., Ont. Council for Leadership in, 2-53
    Assn. of Disabled Students, Ntl., 2-53
    Awards, 1-97
    Exchange Between Canada & the US, Fdn. for, 2-52
    Fdn., John Hart Hunter, 2-211
    Institutions Capital Financing Auth., B.C., 3-115
    Media Prodrs. & Distrs. Assn. of Canada, 2-51
    Orgs., 2-45
    Research
        Council, Ont., 2-53
        Officers, Assn. of (Ont.), 2-45

Canadian Almanac & Directory 1997

Educational (cont.)
  Scientific & Cultural Org., Mission of Canada to (UNESCO), 3-247
  Standards Inst., Cdn., 2-181
  Visits & Exchanges in Canada, Soc., 2-54
  Wkrs., Cdn. Union of, 2-199
Éducative de visites et d'échanges, Soc., 2-54
Educators
  Assn.
    Broadcast, 2-28
    of B.C., College Inst., 2-51
    of Business Teachers, 2-45
    Cdn.
      Music, 6-39
      Nurse, 2-136
    College Inst. (B.C.), 2-51
    of Early Childhood (Ont.), 2-45
    Music & Entertainment Industry, 6-40
    of N.B. Profl., 2-46
  Cdn. Community of Computer, 2-103
  Council of Outdoor (Ont.), 2-51
Égalité et d'emploi, Inst. d', 2-56
Egg
  Assns., 2-142
  Fund Bd. (Ont.), 3-170
  Marketing Agency, Cdn., 2-142
  Mktg. Bds./Comms. (Govt.): Alta., 3-96; B.C., 3-109; Cdn., 2-183, 3-80; Man., 3-122; N.B., 3-134; Nfld., 3-144; N.S., 3-156; Ont., 3-170; P.E.I., 3-189; Qué., 3-198; Sask. 3-212
  Processors Council, Cdn., 2-142
  Prodrs. Assns., 2-142/143
Église(s), 2-2
  baptistes françaises, Union d', 2-2
  Catholique, Soc. cdnne d'histoire de l', 2-98 (Française), 2-95 (Anglaise)
  communautaires, Section cdnne du conseil intl. des, 2-7
  Conseil cdn des, 2-7
  évangélique, Assn des, 2-2
  des frères chrétiens (Qué.), 2-3
  pour la justice et la criminologie, Conseil des, 2-114
  Réformée du Qué., 2-3
  Unie du Canada, 2-6
Egyptian Antiquities, Soc. for Study of, 2-157
Eighteenth Century Studies, Cdn. Soc. for, 2-155
Elderhostel Canada, 2-164
Election(s)
  Act, Fed., 1-41, 3-64
  B.C., 3-111
  Canada, 3-64
  Expenses, Govt. Quick Ref., 3-13
  Govt. Quick Ref., 3-13
  Man., 3-124
  N.W.T., 3-150
  N.S., 3-159
  Ont., 3-177
  Officers Assn., 2-79
  Offices/Officiers, see Electoral Officers
  P.E.I., 3-190
  du Qué., 3-201
  Regulations, 1-41
Electoral
  Districts, by City & Town, 4-1 (& see Addenda)
  Districts, Lists of (Govt.): Alta., 3-93; B.C., 3-106; Fed., 3-47; Man., 3-121; N.B., 3-132; Nfld., 3-141; N.W.T., 3-150; N.S., 3-155; Ont., 3-166; P.E.I., 3-187; Qué., 3-194; Sask., 3-211; Yukon, 3-221 (for number of eligible voters, see Population)
  Officers/Office(s) (Govt.): Quick Ref., 3-13; Alta., 3-98; B.C., 3-111; Fed., 3-64; Man., 3-124; N.B., 3-135; Nfld., 3-143; N.W.T., 3-150; N.S., 3-159; Ont., 3-177; P.E.I., 3-190; Qué., 3-201; Sask., 3-214; Yukon, 3-221
  Reform, Qué., 3-204
Électorale et parlementaire, Secrétariat à la réforme (Qué.), 3-204
Elector's Qualifications, 1-41

Electric
  Assn., Municipal, 2-143
  Railway. Hist'l Assn., Ont., 2-97
  Vehicle Assn. of Canada, 2-189
Electrical
  Contractors Assns., 2-54
  & Electronics Engrs., Inst. of, 2-55
  & Elevators Inspectors: Alta., 3-102; B.C., 3-118
  Equipment Magazines, 5-166
  Exhibitions, Shows & Events, 1-78
  Inspection (Govt.): Alta., 3-102; B.C., 3-118
  League(s), Cdn. Council of, 2-143; Ont., Man., 2-55
  Mfrs. Reps. Assn., Cdn., 2-54
  Power Systems Construction Assn., 2-54
  Trade Shows, 1-78
  Utilities Safety Assn. of Ont., 2-143
  Wkrs., Intl. Broth. of, 2-202; Interprov., 2-201
Électriciens du Qué., Corp des maîtres, 2-54
Électricité
  Assn qué. des consommateurs industriels, 2-54
  Fra. interprov. des ouvriers en, 2-201
Electricity
  Assns., 2-54
  Brs./ Divs. (Govt.): Alta., 3-98
Electro-Federation Canada, 2-54
Electronic
  & Appliance Service Assn., Cdn., 2-54
  Commerce Council, 2-103
  Data Interchange Council, 2-103
  Electrical, Salaried, Machine & Furniture Wkrs., Intl. Union of, 2-203
  Industry Assn. of Alta., 2-54
Electronics
  Assns., 2-54
  Electrical, Salaried, Machine & Furniture Wkrs., Intl. Union of, 2-203
  Engrs., Inst. of, Electrical &, 2-55
  Exhibitions, Shows & Events, 1-78
  Import Com., 2-188
  Info. Assn. of Man., 2-55
  Magazines, 5-166
  Marketers, Consumer, 2-54
Electrophysiologie médicale, Assn profl des technologues diplômes en, 2-82
Electroplaters & Surface Finishers Soc., Amer., 2-122
Electrostatics Research Ctr., Applied (U.W.O.), 9-31
Éléctrotechnologies, Cdn. Com. on, 2-54
Elémentaire du Qué., Assn des insts de niveaux préscolaire et, 2-46
Elevating Devices Safety Dir. (B.C.), 3-118
Elevator
  Constructors, Intl. Union of, 2-203
  & Escalator Assn., Ntl., 2-33
  Inspection (Govt.): Alta., 3-102; N.S., 3-162
Éleveurs, Assns des, 2-19
Eligible Voters, Number of, see Population
Elizabeth Fry Soc., 2-143
Elk Island Sch. Div. (Alta.), 9-1
Elks, B.P.O. (of Canada), 2-75
E.L.L. Sch. (Ont.), 9-35
Elocution & Debate Assn., Sask., 2-112
Élocution promédia, École de Radio et d' (Qué.), 9-47
Elsa Wild Animal Appeal of Canada, 2-62
Elvis in Canada Fan Club, 2-151
Embassies
  in Canada, 3-248
  (Cdn.), Abroad, 3-259
Emballage
  Assn cdnne de l', 2-138
  aux besoins des aînés, Conseil cdn pour l'adaptation de l', 2-138
Emballages de papier et de carton, Conseil de l'environnement des, 2-138
Embalmers' Assn., 2-76/77
Embroiderers' Assn. of Canada, 2-190
Emergency
  Assoc. Communications Teams, Radio, 2-55
  Health Servs. (Govt.): N.S., 3-160

Emergency (cont.)
  Measures (Govt.): Quick Ref., 3-13; Alta. (Pub. Security), 3-104; B.C., 3-118; Fed., 3-79; Man., 3-124; N.B., 3-138; Nfld., 3-148; N.W.T., 3-151; N.S., 3-159; Ont., 3-186; P.E.I., 3-190; Sask., 3-219; Yukon, 3-222 (see also Environmental Emergencies)
  Nurses Affiliation, Natl., 2-137
  Physicians, Cdn. Assn. of, 2-83
  Preparedness
    Canada, 3-79
    College, Cdn. (Ont.), 9-35
  Response
    Assns., 2-55
    Govt. Quick Ref., 3-13
  Services Magazines, 5-166
Emily Carr Inst. of Art & Design (B.C.), 9-9
Emmanuel College: Saskatoon, 9-54; Toronto, 9-31
Empaqueteurs de poisson du N.-B., Assn des, 2-72
Empire Club of Canada, 2-76
Emploi
  et des employeurs, Assn cdnne des spécialistes en, 2-56
  Inst. d'égalité et d', 2-56
Employed Persons with Disabilities (Statistics), 1-52
Employers'
  Advisor (Govt.) Ont., 3-181
  Advocate, N.B., 3-133
Employés(ées)
  de bureau, Synd. cdn de, 2-206
  de communications et travailleurs connexes, Assn cdnne des, 2-198
  généraux et du secteur public, Synd. ntl des, 2-203
  de production du Qué. et de l'Acadie, Synd. des, 2-206
  professionels
    et de bureau, Union intle des, 2-204
    et techniques, Synd. cdn des, 2-200
  en service social de la prov. du Qué., Assn des, 2-197
  de services publics, Fédn des, 2-200
  de téléphone, Assn cdnne des, 2-199
Employment (see also Labour)
  Assns., 2-55
  Bd., N.B. Labour &, 3-133
  Brs./Divs.: N.B., 3-133; Nfld., 3-142; Ont., 3-173
  Depts. (Govt.): Quick Ref., 3-14; B.C., 3-111; Fed. (Human Resources), 3-72; N.W.T., 3-151; Qué., 3-209
  Devel.
    Financing Auth., B.C. Housing &, 3-115
    Programs: (Man.), 3-124
  Discrimination, Govt. Quick Ref., 3-12
  Equity (Govt. Agencies/Commns.): Quick Ref., 3-12; B.C., 3-110; Ont., 3-181
  Govt. Quick Ref., 3-14
  Income Assistance Div. (Man.), 3-125
  Inst. of Equality &, 2-56
  & Investment, Min. (B.C.), 3-111
  by Occupation, 1-51
  Practices Br. (Ont.), 3-181
  & Regional Economic Devel. (Nfld.), 3-142
  Social Devel. & Educ. Group (Fed. Govt.), 3-72
  & Staffing Services Assn., 2-56
  Standards (Govt.): B.C., 3-117; Man., 3-129; N.B., 3-133; P.E.I., 3-192; Yukon, 3-224 (see also Labour Standards)
  Statistics, 1-51
  Support Servs. (N.S.), 3-157
End Physical Punishment of Children, 2-167
Endangered Species Advisory Com. (Man.), 3-130
Endocrinology & Metabolism, Cdn. Soc. of, 2-89
Endodontics, Cdn. Academy of, 2-39
Endometriosis Assn. of Canada, 2-91
Énergie
  Assn ntle pour la conservation de l', 2-63
  atomique
    du Canada ltée, 3-54
    Commn de contrôle de l', 3-54

Énergie (cont.)
 écolienne, Assn cdnne d', 2-56
 fluide, Assn cdnne d', 2-56
 du N.B., La Soc. d'. 3-139
 Office
  ntl de l', 3-80
  de répartition des approvisionnements d', 3-64
 Ressources naturelles et, Dept. (N.B.), 3-139
 Soc. planétaire pour l'assainissement de l', 2-57
 du Sol, Assn cdnne de l'énergie, 2-60
 Solaire, Soc. d', 2-57
 Sous-ministre adjoint (Qué.), 3-205
Energy
 AECB, 3-54
 AECL, 3-54
 Assn(s)., 2-56
  Cdn. Wind, 2-56
  Earth, 2-60
 Bds. (Govt.): Ntl., 3-80; Ont., 3-178
 Brs./Divs. (Govt.): B.C., 3-112; Nfld., 3-148; N.W.T., 3-153; N.S., 3-163; P.E.I., 3-189; Qué., 3-205; Yukon, 3-222
 of Canada, Atomic (Fed. Govt.), 3-54
 Cdn. Inst. of, 2-56
 Conservation
  Assn., Ntl., 2-63
  & Liaison Div. (Ont.), 3-178
 Control Bd., Atomic, 3-54
 Corps. (Govt.): Ont., 3-178; P.E.I., 3-190; Sask., 3-220; Yukon, 3-222
 Council of Canada, 2-56; 3-83
 Depts. (Govt.): Quick Ref., 3-14; Alta., 3-98; Man., 3-124; N.B., 3-139; Nfld., 3-148; Ont., 3-177; Sask., 3-214
 Efficiency (Govt.), Fed., 3-83
 Govt. Quick Ref., 3-14
 Inc., Sask., 4-231
 James Bay (Qué.), 3-202
 Mgmt. Br./Divs. (Govt.): Man., 3-124; N.W.T., 3-153
 Measurement, 1-62
 & Mines
  Branch (Yukon), 3-222
  Depts. (Govt.): Man., 3-124; Sask., 3-214
 Natural Resources &, Dept. (N.B.), 3-139
 Nuclear, Govt. Quick Ref., 3-28
 & Paperworkers Union of Canada, Communications &, 2-200
 Pathways Inc., 2-57
 Pipeline Assn., Cdn., 2-78
 Planetary Assn. for Clean, 2-57
 Probe Research Fdn., 2-57
 Research
  & Devel. Office for (Fed.), 3-83
  Inst.: Cdn., 2-56; Regina, 9-54
 Resources (Govt.): Quick Ref. 3-14; Fed., 3-83
 Sector (Fed.), 3-83
 Service Cos., Cdn. Assn. of, 2-56
 Soc., Solar, 2-57
 Supplies Allocation Bd. (Fed.), 3-64
 Tech., Canada Ctr. for, Mineral & (Fed.), 3-82, 3-84
 Technology Transfer, Wood, 2-57
 & Utilities Bd., Alta., 3-98
Enfance
 Accueil intl pour l', 2-108
 Assn cdnne pour la promotion des services de garde à l', 2-166
 Canada, Aide à l', 2-109
 Exceptionnelle, Conseil cdn de l', 2-36
 Fédn cdnne des services de garde à l', 2-36
 Ligue pour la protection de l', 2-166
Enfant(s)
 Assn(s.), 2-36
  cdnne pour les jeunes, 2-36
  de l'évangelisation des, 2-7
 doués et surdoués, Soc. pour enfants (Ont.), 2-36
 handicapés du Qué., Soc. pour les, 2-43
 Musique pour les jeunes, 6-40
 avec problèmes auditifs, Assn du Qué. pour, 2-41

Enfant(s) (cont.)
 Retour Canada, Réseau, 2-37
 et la télévision, Alliance pour l', 2-28
Engineering
 Assns., 2-57
  Cdn. Aboriginal Science &, 2-132
 Awards & Prizes, 1-111 (see also Educational Awards)
 Cdn. Inst. of Marine, 2-59
 Cdn. Soc.
  of Agricultural, 2-14
  for Chemical, 2-35
  for Civil, 2-59
  for Indus., 2-59
  for Mechanical, 2-59
  for Safety, 2-160
 Centre
  Chemical Reactor (U.W.O.), 9-31
  for Computer Integrated (U. of T.), 9-30
 Companies, Cdn., 7-42
 Faculties/Schs., Index to, 9-56
 Inst. of Canada, 2-59
 Inst. of Biomedical (U. of T.), 9-31
 Magazines, 5-166
 & Maintenance Assn., Plant, 2-59
 Management, Cdn. Soc. for, 2-59
 Research Council, Natural Sciences &, 3-84
 & Scientific Assns., Fedn. of, 2-201
 Society
  Audio, 2-28
  Cdn. Medical & Biological, 2-162
 Technicians & Technologists Socs., 2-58
 Women in Science &, 2-193
Engineers
 American Soc.
  of Heating, Refrigerating & Air Conditioning, 2-94
  of Mechanical, 2-57
  of Plumbing, 2-95
 Assn(s)., 2-57
  Aircraft
   Atlantic, 2-27
   Maintenance, 2-28
  of Consulting, 2-57
  Hospital (Alta.), 2-101
  Municipal, 2-59
  of Qué. Municipal, 2-57
 Awards, 1-111
 Bd. of Examiners of Stationary: N.B., 3-133; N.S., 3-
 Cdn.
  Assn.
   of Drilling, 2-44
   of Masters & Chief (Marine), 2-199
  Council of Profl., 2-58
  Soc. for Profl., 2-59
 Educ. & Development Inc., Operating (Nfld.), 9-21
 of the Govt. of Qué., Assn. of Profl., 2-198
 Inst. of
  Electrical & Electronics, 2-55
  Power, 2-59
 Intl. Fedn. of Profl. & Technical, 2-202
 Ntl. Soc. of Corrosion, 2-59
 Refrigeration Service, 2-95
 Soc. of
  Motion Picture & Television, 2-59
  Tribologists & Lubrication, 2-59
 Union of Operating, 2-255
 Western Assn. of Broadcast, 2-30
England (see United Kingdom)
English
 Alliance for Preservation of, 2-38
 As an Additional Language, Assn. of B.C. Teachers of, 2-45
 As a Living Language Private Sch. (Ont.), 9-35
 As a Second Language
  Teaching, 2-54
  in Qué., Soc. for the Promotion of the Teaching of, 2-54

English (cont.)
 Catholic Teachers' Assn., Ont., 2-53
 Language
  Literature, Qué. Soc. for the Promotion of, 2-112
  Publishers Assn., Qué., 2-144
 & Language Arts, Cdn. Council of Teachers of, 2-48
 Speaking
  People's Assn., Chateauguay Valley, 2-38
  Union of Canada, 2-39
Engrais du Qué., Assn des fabricants des, 2-35
Engravers Union of N. Amer., Intl. Plate Printers, Die Stampers &, 2-203
ENJEU, 2-63
L'Enquêteur correctionel Canada, 3-63
Enregistrement
 Académie cdnne des arts et des sciences de l', 6-39
 des animaux, Soc. cdnne d', 2-20
 Assn de l'industrie cdnne de l', 6-40
Enseignant(e)s
 Assn(s), 2-50
  cdnne pour la formation des, 2-48
 catholiques
  Assn prov. des, 2-53
  de langue anglaise, Assn des (Ont.), 2-53
 de cégeps, Fédn des, 2-196
 Collège cdn des, 2-48
 des Commns scolaires, Fédn des, 2-196
 des écoles
  publiques de l'Ont., Fédn des, 2-53
  secondaires de l'Ont., Fédn des, 2-53
 Fédn ntle des (du Qué.), 2-52
 Fédns, 2-50
 en français (Langue maternelle), Alliance cdnne des responsables et, 2-45
 franco-ontariens, Assn des, 2-46
 francophones du N.-B., Assn des, 2-50
 protestants du Qué., Assn des, 2-50
 retraités de l'Ont., 2-54
Enseignement
 de l'anglais (langue seconde), Soc. pour la promo. de l', 2-54
 collégial
  Commn d'évaluation de l' (Qué.), 3-201
  sous-ministre adjoint (Qué.), 3-200
 coopératif, Assn cdnne de l', 2-47
 Fédn
  du personnel des Etablissements privés d', 2-196
  qué. des directeurs(trices) d'établissements d', 2-52
 francophone à distance, Le Réseau d', 2-53
 Général, Collèges d', 9-45
 Privé, Commn consultative de l' (Qué.), 3-201
 Privés, Fédn des assns de l' (Qué.), 2-51
 du Qué., Centrale de l', 2-196; Fédns, 2-196
 Secondaire, Assn des insts d', 2-46
 Supérieur
  Assn cdnne contre le harcèlement sexuel en milieu d', 2-166
  et la recherche, Agence francophone pour, 2-45
  Soc. cdnne pour l'étude de l', 2-50
  & travail, Dept (N.B.), 3-132
Enterprise
 Bur., Women's, 2-193
 Cdn. Assn. of Family, 2-33
 Council, Pacific Corridor, 2-35
 Nfld. & Lab., Corp., 3-142
 P.E.I. Inc., 3-189
Entertainment
 Cdns. Concerned About Violence in, 2-166
 Industry Educators Assn., Music &, 6-40
 Magazines, 5-181
 Standards Br. (Ont.), 3-174
Entomological Soc. of Canada, 2-162
Entraîneurs, Assn cdnne des, 2-179
Entrepreneur(s)
 Awards, 1-94
 Cdn. Assn. of Women Execs. &, 2-191
 en construction du Qué., Assn des, 2-30

Canadian Almanac & Directory 1997

Entrepreneur(s) (cont.)
  en couverture, 2-32
  en mécanique, 2-32
  miniers, Assn des, 2-128
  de services en environnement du Qué., 2-60
  Women, 2-193
Entrepreneurship
  Fdn. for the Advancement of Cdn., 2-35
  Québécois, Académie de l', 9-47
Entreprise(s)
  et la Collectivité, Le Centre Cdn des relations entre, 2-33
  Conseil cdn des chefs d', 2-33
  Council, Pacific Corridor, 2-35
  culturelles, Soc. de dév. des, 2-39
  familiales, Assn. cdnne des, 2-33
  indépendante, Fédn cdnne de l', 2-34
  universités, Forum, 2-51
Enviro-Accès Inc., 2-63
Environment
  Ambassador for, 3-69
  Assn.
    of Ont., Water, 2-65
    Western Canada Water, 2-65
  Awards, 1-99
  Brs.: Nfld., 3-143
  Canada, 3-64
  Cdn. Council of Ministers of the, 2-60
  Cdns. for a Clean, 2-62
  Commn. Man., Clean, 3-125
  Conferences, 1-78
  Depts. (Govt.): Quick Ref., 3-15; Alta., 3-98; B.C., 3-112; Fed., 3-64; Man., 3-124; N.B., 3-135; Nfld., 3-143; N.W.T., 3-153; N.S., 3-159; Ont., 3-177; P.E.I. (Environmental Resources), 3-190; Qué., 3-201; Sask., 3-214
  & Energy
    Devel. Studies Fdn., Soc., 2-65
    Min. (Ont.), 3-177
  Exhibitions, Shows & Events, 1-78
  Fdn., Friends of the, 2-210
  Govt. Quick Ref., 3-15
  Indep. Assn. of Legal, Engrg. & Accounting Professionals for the, 2-63
  Industries Devel. Initiative (Man.), 3-127
  Industry
    Assns., 2-60
    Cdn. Council for Human Resources in the, 2-60
  James Bay Adv. Com. on, 4-213
  & Labour (Nfld.), 3-143
  Lands & Parks, Min. (B.C.), 3-112; Awards, 6-53
  Magazines, 5-181
  Networks, 2-61
  N.S. Business Council on the, 2-64
  & Plastics Inst. of Canada, 2-63
  Probe, 2-63
  Program (U.N.), 3-247
    Regional Office for North America, 2-65
  Reporting, State of (Govt.): B.C., 3-113; Fed., 3-65
  Round Tables (Govt.): Fed., 3-81; Man., 3-124; N.B., 3-135; Nfld., 3-143; N.S., 3-159; P.E.I., 3-190
  Trade Shows, 1-78
  Yukon Council on the Economy &, 3-221
Environmental
  Analytical Labs., Cdn. Assn. of, 2-60
  Appeal Bds. (Govt): Alta., 3-99; B.C., 3-113; Ont., 3-178
  Assessment
    Agency, Cdn., 3-65
    Board (Ont.), 3-178
    Brs./Divs. (Govt.): Alta., 3-99; B.C., 3-113; Nfld., 3-143; N.S., 3-159; Ont., 3-177; P.E.I., 3-190; Sask., 3-214; Yukon, 3-224
    Office (B.C.), 3-113
  Assn(s)., 2-59
    Cdn. Steel, 2-62
    Nfld. & Lab., 2-64
  Awards, 1-99

Environmental (cont.)
  Bill of Rights Office (Ont.), 3-177
  Biologists, Cdn. Soc. for, 2-61
  Centre, Alta., 3-99
  Coalition of P.E.I., 2-63
  Commissioner of Ont., 3-178
  Compensation Corp. (Ont.), 2-63
  Conservation
    Service (Fed.), 3-65
    Soc. Promoting, 2-65
  Cooperation, North American Commn. for, 3-84
  Council, Paper & Paperboard Packaging, 2-138
  Education
    & Communication, Cdn. Network for, 2-61
    Fort Whyte Centre for, 2-63
  Emergencies Br. (B.C.), 3-113
  Equip. Mfrs. Assn., Cdn., 2-66
  Health (Govt.): Alta., 3-100; Fed., 3-71; Nfld., 3-146
  Impact Assessment Brs./Divs. (Govt.): N.B., 3-135; P.E.I., 3-190
  Industries & Technologies Div. (N.S.), 3-159
  Industry Assn(s.), 2-60
  Investigations
    Cdn. Inst. for, 2-61
    Govt. Agencies: N.B., 3-135; Nfld., 3-143; Ont., 3-177
  Law
    Assn., Cdn., 2-61
    Centre (Alta.) Soc., 2-63
    & Policy, Cdn. Inst. for, 2-61
    Soc., Osgoode Hall, 2-64
  Liability Mgmt. Assn., Intl., 2-63
  Magazines, 5-181
  Management Div. (Man.), 3-124
  Managers' Assn., Sask., 2-61
  Medical Assn., Occupational &, 2-93
  Networks, 2-61
  Operations Div. (Man.), 3-124
  Policy & Stewardship, Inst. for, 2-63
  Protection
    Brs./Divs. (Govt.): B.C., 3-113; Fed., 3-65; N.W.T., 3-153; P.E.I., 3-190; Sask., 3-214; Yukon, 3-224
    Depts.: Alta., 3-98; B.C., 3-112
    Service (Fed. Govt.), 3-65
  Public Hearing Bd., Qué., 3-201
  Research
    Great Lakes Inst. for, 2-156
    Trust, Alta., 3-99
  Resources, Dept. (P.E.I.), 3-190
  Response Br., Rescue & (Cdn. Coast Guard), 3-68
  Sciences & Standards Div. (Ont.), 3-177
  Services Assn. of Alta., 2-60
  Soc., Sask., 2-64
  Standards Devel. Br. (Ont.), 3-177
  Studies, Inst. for (U. of T.), 9-30
  Support Servs., Div. (N.S.), 3-159
  Technology
    Advancement Dir. (Fed.), 3-65
    Corp., Cdn., 2-61
    Institute for Chemical Process & (NRC), 3-81
    Ont. Ctr. for, 2-64
  Trade Shows, 1-78
  Youth
    Alliance, 2-63
    Internship Program (Fed.), 3-72
Environmentally
  Responsible Tourism, Alta. League for, 2-184
  Sensitive, Parents of, 2-168
  Sound Packaging Coalition, 2-138
  Sustainable Economic Devel., N.S. Ctr. for, 2-64
Environments, Educ. & Devel. Fdn., Women &, 2-193
Environnement
  Assn cdnne des industries de l', 2-60
  Assn des entrepreneurs de services en, (Qué.), 2-63
  Bur. d'audiences publiques sur l' (Qué.), 3-201
  Canada, 3-64
  Depts. (Govt.): Fed., 3-64; N.B., 3-135; Qué., 3-201
  et l'économie see Tables rondes

Environnement (cont.)
  et de la Faune, Min. (Qué.), 3-201
  jeunesse, 2-63
  des lacs, Fédn des assns pour la protection de l', 2-63
  Réseau cdn de l', 2-61
  Tables rondes (Govt.): Ntle, 3-81; N.B., 3-143
Environnementale(s)
  Assn cdnne des laboratoires d'analyse, 2-60
  Centre pour l'avancement des technologies, 2-63
  commn Nord-Américaine de coopération, 3-84
  de la sidérurgie cdnne, 2-62
Épiciers indep., Fédn cdnne des, 2-72
Épilepsie, Assn qué. de, 2-91
Epilepsy
  Canada, 2-91
  Ont., 2-91
Episcopal Church, Ref'd, 2-5
EPOCH - Canada, 2-167
Epochs, 1-3
Equal Justice for All, 2-167
Equality & Employment, Inst. of, 2-56
Equator, Diameter, 1-14
Equestrian
  Assn. for the Disabled, 2-179
  Fedn., Cdn., 2-175
Equipment
  Assn(s)., 2-65
    Outdoor Power, 2-66
  Dealers' Assn., Ont. Retail Farm, 2-66
  Distrs., Cdn. Assn. of, 2-65
  Inst., Cdn. Farm & Industrial, 2-66
  Magazines: Electrical, 5-166; Office, 5-173; Rental, 5-175
  Mfrs. Assn.
    Environmental, 2-66
    Machinery &, 2-66
    Mining, 2-66
    Petroleum, 2-66
  & Operations Assn., Municipal, 2-66
Equitation thérapeutique, Assn cdnne d', 2-178
Equity
  Actors', 2-198
  Pay, see Pay Equity
Eras, 1-3
Erectors Assn., Ont., 2-33
Ergonomie, Assn cdnne d', 2-163
Ergothérapeutes
  Assn cdnne des, 2-84
  Ordre des (Qué.), 2-94
Erindale College (U. of T.), 9-31
Escadrilles cdnnes de plaisance, 2-151
Escalator Assn., Ntl. Elevator &, 2-33
Escrime, Fédn cdnne d', 2-175
Eskimos, see Inuit
Esperanto Assns., 2-112
ESSA/AESS, 2-200
Essais nondestructifs, Soc. cdnne pour, 2-181
Essential Servs. Council, Qué., 3-209
Esthétique, Soc. cdnne d', 2-155
Estonian
  Central Council in Canada, 2-128
  Evangelical Lutheran Church, 2-4
  Magazines, 5-192
Ethical Treatment of Food Animals, Cdns. for, 2-22
Ethics
  Ctr. for Practical (York Univ.), 9-32
  Commr., Alta., 3-99
  Counsellor, Office of (Fed.), 3-75
  & Human Values, Westminster Inst. for (U.W.O.), 9-31
  & Religion, Cdn. Coalition for Ecology, 2-60
Éthique commerciale, Bur. d', 2-33
Ethnic (see also Multicultural)
  Publications, 5-191
  Radio Broadcasters, Cdn. Assn. of, 2-29
  Studies Assn., Cdn., 2-48
Ethniques, Soc. cdnne des études, 2-48
Ethnocultural Council, Cdn., 2-129

Etobicoke (Ont.)
  Bd. of Educ., 9-24
  City Govt., 4-157
Étoile du courage, **16**, 1-28
Étrangères et du Commerce Intl, Affaires (Fed.), 4-68
Étude(s)
  africaines, Assn cdnne des, 2-47
  américaines, Assn d', 2-47
  asiatiques, Assn cdnne des, 2-47
  avancées, Assn cdnne des, 2-46
  Baha'ies, Assn d', 2-45
  bibliques, Soc. cdnne des, 2-50
  cdnnes, Assn d', 2-59; intl, 2-156
  centrales et est-européennes, Conseil intl d', 2-156
  classiques, Soc. cdnne des, 2-156
  et de coopération intl., Centre cdn., 2-108
  du dix-huitième siècle, Soc. cdnne d', 2-155
  de l'éduc., Soc. cdnne pour l', 2-50
  de l'enseignement supérieur, Soc. cdnne pour l', 2-50
  ethniques, Soc. cdnne d', 2-48
  fiscales, Assn cdnne d', 2-183
  humaines, Fédn cdnne des, 2-49
  mésopotamiens, Soc. cdnne des, 2-155
  patristiques, Assn cdnne des, 2-155
  nordiques, Assn universitaire cdnne d', 2-46
  stratégiques, Inst cdn d', 2-155
  théâtrales, Soc. qué. d'. 6-36
  ukrainiennes, Inst cdn d', 2-155
Etudiant(e)(s)
  Alliance cdnne des assns, 2-47
  chrétien(ne)s, Mouvement d', 2-6
  Fédn cdnne des, 2-49
  handicappés au niveau post-secondaire, Assn ntle des, 2-53
  et internes en pharmacie, Assn cdnne des, 2-139
  Serv. de placement (Qué.), 3-203
  des univs et collèges, Assn des services aux, 2-46
European
  Communities, Commn. to Canada, 3-247
  Trade Info. (Fed.), 3-69
Évaluateurs, Inst cdn des, 2-146
Evaluation
  Assns., 2-181
  Cdn. Assn. for Research in Nondestructive, 2-154
  -médias, 2-11
  pédagogique, Services d', 2-50
  de programmes, Soc. québécoise d', 2-181
  Soc., Cdn., 2-181
Evangelical
  Alliance Mission of Canada, 2-4
  Baptist Churches, Fellowship of, 2-4
  Church, Armenian, 2-2
  Covenant Church of Canada, 2-4
  Fellowship of Canada, 2-4
  Lutheran Church, 2-4
    Estonian, 2-4
  Mennonite
    Conf., 2-4
    Mission Conf., 2-4
Évangelique
  Alliance, 2-4
  Assn des églises, 2-2
Evangelisation des enfants, Assn d', 2-7
Evangelism Fellowship of Canada, Child, 2-7
Evening Stars, 1-15
Events
  Assns., 2-66
  Exhibitions, Shows &, 1-72
  & Festivals, 1-78
Évêques, Assemblées du Qué., 2-5
Evergreen Fdn., 2-63
Ex-Offenders Orgs., 2-143
Exceptional Children, The Cdn. Council for, 2-36
Exchange(s)
  Cdn. Assn. of Message, 2-183
  Soc. for Educ. Visits &, 2-54
  Stock, 7-9

Excise
  Duties & Taxes (Fed.), 3-86
  Offices Duties & Taxes Div. (Fed.), 3-87
  Taxes, *see* Customs Regulations
Executive
  Accountants, Cdn. Assn. of Certified, 2-8
  Councils (Govt.): Alta., 3-92; B.C., 3-106; Man., 3-120; N.B., 3-131; Nfld., 3-140; N.W.T., 3-150; N.S., 3-154; Ont., 3-165; P.E.I., 3-187; Qué., 3-193; Sask., 3-210; Yukon, 3-221
  Dept. of the (N.W.T.), 3-151
  Development (Fed. Agency), 3-57
  Forms of address, 1-33
  Govt. Quick Ref., 3-7
  Nurses, Academy of Cdn., 2-135
  Service Org., Cdn., 2-121
Executives
  Assn.
    Cdn. Food Service, 2-72
    of Cultural, 2-120
  Canadian
    College of Health Service, 2-85
    Soc. of Assn., 2-121
  & Entrepreneurs, Cdn. Assn. of Women, 2-191
  Inst. of Canada, Financial, 2-70
  Ntl. Soc. of Fundraising, 2-122
  of the Public Sector of Canada, Assn. of Profl., 2-120
Exercise Physiology, Cdn. Soc. for, 2-177
Exhibit & Display Assn., 2-66
Exhibition(s) (*see also* Festivals)
  Assn(s)., 2-66
    of N.S., 2-66
  Cdn. Assn. of Fairs &, 2-66
  Magazines, 5-176
  of Man., Prov., 2-67
  Sask. Assn. of Agricl. Socs. &, 2-15
  & Show Planners, 1-68 (& *see* Addenda)
  Shows & Events, List of, 1-72, 1-79
Expenditure(s)
  Average Household, 1-53
  Federal, 1-57
Experimental Farm, Central (Fed.), 3-52
Exploration
  Geochemists, Assn. of, 2-127
  Geological Servs. Div. (Sask.), 3-214
  Geophysicists, Cdn. Soc. of, 2-162
Explorationists, Nfld. & Lab., 2-128
Explosives Distrs. Assn., Cdn., 2-35
Export (*see also* Imports & Exports)
  agro-alimentaire du Qué., Club, 2-188
  of Cdn. Books, Assn. for, 2-144
  Clubs Canada, Fedn. of, 2-188
  Devel. Corp., 3-66
  Fedn., Cdn. Beef, 2-187
  & Import
    Permits Bur. (Fed.), 3-69
    (Statistics), 1-54, 1-55, 1-56
  Info. (Fed.), 3-69
Exportation(s)
  du livre cdn, Assn pour l', 2-144
  Soc. pour l'expansion des, 3-66
Exporters'
  Alliance of Manufacturers &, 2-122
  Cdn. Assn. of Fish, 2-71
Exposition(s)
  Assn(s.), 2-66
    Managers, Cdn. Assn. of, 2-66; Western, 2-67
    des professionels en (Qué.), 2-66
    Westerner, 2-67
  List of, 1-72
  Mgrs., Cdn. Assn. of, 2-66
Expropriation(s)
  Adv. Office, N.B., 3-138
  Compensation Bds. (Govt.): B.C., 3-110; N.S., 3-162
  Govt. Quick Ref., 3-15
Extension, Cdn. Soc. of, 2-14

External Affairs
  Govt. Quick Ref. *see* Intl. Affairs, 3-23
  & Intl. Trade Canada, *see* Foreign Affairs & Intl. Trade Canada
Extrusion Wkrs. Union, Indep. Cdn., 2-196
Eye Banks: B.C., 2-91; Ont., 2-91; Qué., 2-92
Eyesight Universal, Operation, 2-109

F

Fabricants Assns, 2-122
Facial Plastic & Reconstr. Surgery, Cdn. Academy of, 2-83
Facilitator, Office of the Prov. (Ont. Mun. Affairs), 3-183
Faculties/Schs., Index to selected, 9-56
Faculty Assns., 2-48
Fahrenheit & Celsius, 1-63
Faillite, Registraires de (Qué.), 10-15
Faim, Fdn cdnne contre la, 2-108
Fair(s)
  Assn., Royal Agricultural Winter, 2-67
  & Exhibitions, Cdn. Assn. of, 2-66
Fairview College (Alta.), 9-4
Faith for Canada, Soc. for Propagation of the, 2-8
Faiths, World Congress of, 2-8
Familiaux, Confédn des organismes, 2-167
Families
  Alta. Assn. of Servs. for Children &, 2-165
  Assn. of Canada, One Parent, 2-168
  B.C. Min. of Children &, 3-110
  Bereaved (Ont.), 2-165
  Magazines, 5-181
Famille(s)
  Assn cdnne de l'histoire des, 2-96
  L'Inst Vanier de la, 2-172
  monoparentales du Qué., Fédn des assns de, 2-167
  Sécrétariat à la (Qué.), 3-202
Family (*see also* Families)
  B.C. Council for the, 2-165
  Benefits (Govt.): Quick Ref., 3-15
  & Children's Servs.: N.S., 3-157; Yukon, 3-223
  Coalition Party of Ont., 2-141
  & Community Support Servs.
    Assn. of Alta., 2-167
    Brs./Divs. (Govt.): N.B., 3-136; Ont., 3-173
  Courts
    Alta. (Prov., Fam. & Youth Div.), 10-2
    B.C. (Prov., Fam. Div.), 10-5
    Man., Div., 10-6
    N.B. (Queen's Bench, Fam. Div.), 10-7
    Nfld. (Unified), 10-8
    N.W.T. (Territorial), 10-9
    N.S., 10-9
    Ont. (Provincial), 10-11
    P.E.I. (Trial Div.), 10-14
    Sask. (Queen's Bench, Prov. Div.), 10-20
  Economics Cooperative Assns. of Qué., Fedn. of, 2-70
  Enterprise, Cdn. Assn. of, 2-33
  Focus on the, 2-7
  History
    Assn. of Canada, 2-96
    Soc., Qué., 2-97; Alta., 2-95
    Socs., Cdn. Fedn. of Genealogical &, 2-95
  Income
    Average (Statistics), 1-53
    Plan (Sask.), 3-220
  Law
    Brs./Divs. (Govt.): Alta., 3-101; Fed., 3-78; Man., 3-128
    Judges' Assn., Ont., 2-115
  Mediation Canada, 2-167
  Medicine, Ctr. for Studies in (U.W.O.), 9-31
  Physicians, College of, 2-91
  Plan, Save a, 2-109
  Planning Assn., Natural, 2-154
  Resource Programs, Cdn. Assn. of, 2-117

Family (cont.)
    Secretariat (Qué.), 3-202
    Service
        Advocacy (Ont.), 3-173
        Assns., 2-167
    Services
        Brs./Divs. (Govt.): Alta. (Commn.), 3-100; B.C., 3-119; N.B., 3-136; Nfld., 3-149; Sask., 3-220; Yukon, 3-223
        Depts. (Govt.): Alta., 3-99; Man., 3-125
        Review Bd., Child & (Ont.), 3-174
        & Social Services, Dept. (Alta.), 3-99
    Support
        Dir. (N.W.T.), 3-152
        Plan (Ont.), 3-171
    Therapy, Alta. Assn. for Marriage &, 2-165; Ont., 2-168
    Vanier Inst. of the, 2-172
    Violence Prevention Brs./Divs. (Govt.): Alta., 3-100; Yukon, 3-224
    & Youth
        Law Policy Section (Fed.), 3-78
        Services Div. (Sask.), 3-220
Fanshawe College, AA & T (Ont.), 9-33
Fantasy Balloon Owners & Pilots Assn., 2-151
Farm
    Animal Council, Ont., 2-21
    Assistance Programs Br. (Ont.), 3-169
    Business
        Exhibitions, Shows & Events, 1-80
        Mgmt. Brs./Divs. (Govt.): Man., 3-122; N.B., 3-133; Nfld., 3-144; Ont., 3-169; P.E.I., 3-188
    Central Experimental (Fed.), 3-52
    Credit Corp. Canada, 3-66
    Exhibitions, Shows & Events, 1-80
    Family Advisor Program (Ont.), 3-170
    Finance Div. (Ont.), 3-169
    Implements
        Bd., Ont., 3-170
        & Supplies Magazines, 5-167
    Income Stabilization
        Admin. (Fed.), 3-53
        Bd., Ont., 3-170
    & Indust. Equip. Inst., Cdn., 2-66
    Land Security Bd. (Sask.), 3-218
    Lands Ownership Bd. (Man.), 3-122
    Loans:, Fed., 3-66; N.S., 3-156
    Machinery
        Bd., Man., 3-122
        Loans Act, N.B., 3-134
    Management Soc., Cdn. Agricultural Economics &, 2-44
    Mediation Bd. (Man.), 3-122
    Orgs. Accreditation Tribunal (Ont.), 3-170
    Practices
        Bd. (B.C.), 3-218
        on Bd. (Ont.), 3-170
    Products
        Appeal Tribunal, Ont., 3-170
        Corp. (Nfld.), 3-145
        Council, Ntl., 3-80
        Mktg. Commns. (Govt): N.B., 3-134; Ont., 3-170
        Statistics, 1-56
    Publications, 5-193
    Rehab. Admin., Prairie (Fed.), 3-54
    Safety Assn., 2-160
    Security Progs., Sask., 3-218
    Shows, 1-80
    Stress Unit (Sask.), 3-212
    Tax Rebate Appeal Bd., Ont., 3-170
    Tenure Arbitration Bd. (Sask.), 3-218
    Writers' Fedn. Cdn., 2-194
Farmer(s)
    Assistance Progs., Beginnning (Ont.), 3-170
    Assn(s)., 2-12
        Qué., 2-15
    Council, Atlantic, 2-13
    Establishment Loan Corp., Junior (Ont.), 3-170

Farmer(s) (cont.)
    Fedn., Christian (Ont.), 2-14
    Intl. Flying, 2-15
    Qué. Young, 2-15
    Union, Ntl., 2-15
Farming (see also Agriculture)
    Awards, 1-92
    Magazines, 5-167, 5-193
    Orgs., 2-12
Farmworkers Union, Cdn., 2-199
Fashion
    Apparel Mfrs. Guild, Qué., 2-68
    Assns., 2-67
    Exhibitions, Shows & Events, 1-81
    Exhibitors Inc., Ont. Fashion, 2-68
    Inst., Manitoba, 2-68
    Magazines, 5-181 (see also Clothing & Accessories)
    Market, Alta., 2-67
Fatality Review Bd. (Alta.), 3-102
FAT-COI, 2-195
Fathers of Confederation, 1-25
Faune(s)
    Assns, 2-62
    Environnement et de la, Min. de l' (Qué.), 3-201
    Fédn cdnne de la, 2-62; Qué., 2-62; N.-B., 2-62
    Fiducie pour la, 2-63
    Fondation de la (Qué.), 2-63, 3-202
    du Qué., Synd. des agents de conservation de la, 2-206
Fauteuil roulant
    Assn cdnne
        de Basketball en, 2-178
        des Sports en, 2-178
Feather of Hope Aboriginal Aids Prevention Soc., 2-18
Federal
    Cabinet, Forms of Address, 1-33
    Court of Canada, 10-1
    Electoral Dists.
        (across Canada), 4-1, & see Addenda
        (list of), 3-47, & see Addenda
    Finance Statistics, 1-57
    Government
        Agencies, 3-52
        of Canada, 3-43
        Depts., 3-52
        Dockyard Chargehands Assn., 2-200
        Lobbyists, see Consultant Lobbyists
        Hospitals in: Alta., 8-4; B.C., 8-10; Man., 8-13; Ont., 8-24; Sask., 8-54
    & Intergovt. Affairs, Alta., 3-100
    Judicial Affairs, Commr. for, 7-2
    Law Editors, 7-1
    Libraries, Council of, 2-119
    Office of Regl. Devel. Qué., 3-66
    -Prov. Relations (see also Intergovt. Affairs)
        Brs./Divs. (Govt): Man., 3-125; P.E.I., 3-190
        Depts., Govt. Quick Ref., 3-15
    Schs. see Native Schs.
    Superannuates Ntl. Assn., 2-79
Federalism Section, Cdn. (Alta.), 3-100
Federalists, World, 2-110
Federally Administered Schs.: Alta., 9-2; Man., 9-14; Qué., 9-44 (see also Native Schs.)
Feed
    Assn., Ont. Grain &, 2-15
    the Children, Cdn., 2-166
    Industry Assn., Cdn., 2-14
    Info. Centre, 2-14
    Mfrs. Assn., Qué., 2-13
Fellowships see Awards
Féminine
    condition (Govt.): Fed., 3-90; Qué., 3-198
    d'éducation et d'action sociale, Assn, 2-191
Feminist
    Assns., 2-191
    Magazines, 5-190
    Research (York Univ.), 9-32
        Ctr. for Women's Studies & (U.W.O.), 9-31

Femme
    Comité cdn d'action sur le statut de la, 2-192
    Congrès cdn pour la promotion des études chez la, 2-191
    Conseil du statut de la (Qué.), 3-198
    et du droit, Assn ntle de la, 2-191
Femmes
    d'affaires du Qué., 2-191
    cadres et entrepreneurs, 2-191
    du Canada, Le Conseil ntl des, 2-193
    cdnne-françaises, Fédn ntle des, 2-192
    cdnnes, Fdn des, 2-192
    de carrières libérales et commerciales, Fédn cdnne des clubs de, 2-192
    Chefs d'Entreprises, Les, 2-193
    en communication, Assn cdnne des, 2-192
    compositrices cdnnes, Assn des, 2-191
    diplômées des universités, Fédn des, 2-49
    Fonds d'action et d'éduc. juridiques pour les, 2-193
    immigrants et des femmes appartenant à une minorité visible, Org. ntle des, 2-38
    Inst cdn de recherches sur les, 2-155
    Médecins du Canada, Fédn des, 2-192
    musulmanes, Conseil des, 2-7
    du Qué., Fédn des, 2-192
    Réseau
        d'action et d'information pour les, 2-193
        ntl d'action-éducation des, 2-193
    en sciences et en génie, Corp des, 2-193
    Secrétariat à la condition (Qué.), 3-198
    du sport et de l'activité physique, Assn cdnne pour l'avancement des, 2-191
Fencing Fedn., Cdn., 2-175
Fenêtres, Assn cdnne des mfrs de portes et de, 2-124
Fer à cheval, Assn cdnne de, 2-152
Ferblantiers et couvreurs, Assn ntle des, 2-197
Ferries
    Corp., B.C., 3-112
    Office, Qué., 3-208
Ferroviaire Baie-Comeau-Hauterive, Soc. du port, 3-208
Ferroviaires, Conseil cdn des syndicats de métiers d'ateliers, 2-199
Ferry
    Corp. B.C., 3-112
    Line Ltd., Victoria, 3-112
    & Marine Wkrs. Union, B.C., 2-198
Fertility & Andrology Soc., Cdn., 2-154
Fertilizer Assns. & Insts., 2-35
Festival(s)
    & Anniversaries, Fixed & Movable, 1-24
    of the Arts Soc., B.C., 3-119
    Assn(s)., 2-66
    & Events, B.C. Assn. of, 2-66
    Fedn. of Cdn. Music, 2-66
    intl du court métrage de Montréal, 2-69
    List of, 1-72, 1-76
    Ontario, 2-67
    Soc. des fêtes et, 2-67
    Toronto Intl. Film, 2-67
Fêtes et festivals, Soc. des (Qué.), 2-67
Fibreboard Mfrs. Assn., Cdn., 2-123
Fibrose kystique, Fdn cdn de la, 2-85; Qué., 2-82
Fiction
    Awards & Prizes see Literary Arts
    Magazines, see Literary Magazines
Fiddle, see Music
FIDO, 2-23
Fiducie du Canada, Assn des compagnies de, 2-71
Field Hockey Assn.
    Canada, 2-179
    Cdn. Women's, 2-178
Fife House Fdn., 2-18
Figure Skating Assn., Cdn., 2-175
Fjord Horse Assn., Cdn., 2-20
Filles du Canada, Clubs des garçons et, 2-36
Filipino Magazines, 5-192

Film (*see also* Cinema; Motion Picture)
   Assn(s)., 2-68
      cdnne des distributeurs de, 2-69
      Ont., 2-69
   Awards, 1-93 (*see also* Educational; Performing Arts)
   Bd., Ntl., 3-80
   Centre, Cdn., 2-68
   Classification Bds./Commns. (Govt.): Quick Ref., 3-7; Alta., 3-96; B.C. (Appeal), 3-110, 2-118; Man., 3-123; Sask., 3-218 (*see also* Censorship)
   Craftspeople, Assn. of Cdn., 2-197
   Devel. Corps. (Govt.): N.S., 3-158; Ont., 3-173
   Distributors & Exporters, Cdn. Assn. of, 2-190
   Festival(s), 1-81
      Montréal Intl. Short, 2-69
      Society
         Greater Vancouver Intl., 2-67
         Moving Pictures Travelling Cdn., 2-69
      Toronto Intl., 2-67
   Inst., Cdn., 2-68
   Libraries, Govt. Quick Ref., 3-16
   Motion Picture Dev. Corp., Alta., 3-97
   Office ntl du, 3-80
   Production, Govt. Quick Ref., 3-16
   Review Bd., Ont., 3-175
   & Television
      Production Assn., Cdn., 2-68
      Women in, 2-30
   & Video
      Alliance, Indep., 2-69
      Festivals & Special Events, 1-81
Filmmakers'
   Co-op, Atlantic, 2-68
   Distribution Centre, Cdn., 2-68
Films et télévision, Assn des prodrs de (Qué.), 2-68
Finance(s)
   Assns., 2-69
   Canada, 3-66
   Depts. (Govt.): Quick Ref., 3-16; B.C., 3-114; Fed., 3-66; Man., 3-125; N.B., 3-135; Nfld., 3-143; N.W.T., 3-151; N.S., 3-159; Ont., 3-178; Qué., 3-202; Sask., 3-215; Yukon, 3-223 (*see also* Revenue; Treasury)
   Govt. Quick Ref., 3-16
   & Leasing Assn., Cdn., 2-69
   Magazines, 5-164, 5-179
   Officers
      Assn. of Ont., Municipal, 2-71
      Assn. of U.S. & Canada, Govt., 2-80
   Statistics, 1-57
   & Treasury Bd., Dept. (Nfld.), 3-143
Financement
   et de location, Assn cdnne de, 2-69
   Soc. gén. de, 3-203
Financial
   Accountants, Cdn. Inst. of, 2-9
   Admrs., Assn. of Public Serv., 2-198
   Aid Admrs., Student, 2-69
   Analysts, Cdn. Council of, 2-69
   Consultants, Cdn. Inst. of Chartered, 2-106
   Corporations, Assn. of Cdn., 2-69
   Education (Ont.), 9-34
   Executives Inst. 2-70
   Institutions, 7-1
      Commn., B.C., 3-115
      Dirs. (Govt.): Alta., 3-105; Qué., 3-203
      Govt. Quick Ref., 3-4
      Inspector Gen. (Qué.), 3-203
      Intl., Secretary of State, 3-67
      Supt. of (Fed.), 7-1, 3-77
   Mgmt. Bd. Secretariat (N.W.T.), 3-150
   Planners, Cdn. Assn. of, 2-69
   Planning, Cdn. Inst. of, 2-69, 9-34
   Post (Ont.), 5-139
   Publications, *see* Finance Magazines (*see also* Business Magazines)
   Sector Policy Br. (Fed.), 3-67
   Statistics, 1-57

Financière(s)
   Assn de planification fiscale et, 2-69
   Canada, Bur. du surintendant des institutions, 3-67
   Inspecteur gén. des Insts. (Qué.), 3-203
Financiers municipaux du Qué., Assn des cadres, 2-69
Financing Auth., Ont., 3-179
Fine Arts, *see* Arts
Finishes & Coatings Magazines, 5-174
Finnish
   -Cdn. Cultural Fedn., 2-130
   Magazines, 5-192
   Org. of Canada, 2-130
FIPRECAN, 2-160
Fire
   Chiefs Assns.: Cdn., 2-159; Ont., 2-160; Qué., 2-159
   College, Ont., 3-186
   Commrs. (*see* Fire Marshals)
   Fighters
      Assn., Ont., Profl., 2-204
      Cdn. Assn. of, 2-199
      Intl. Assn. of, 2-202
      Qué. Union of, 2-206
   Ins., Govt. Quick Ref., 3-21
   Mgmt. Dir. (Ont.), 3-184
   Marshals & Commrs.
      Assn. of Cdn., 2-159
      Govt. Offices: Quick Ref., 3-16; Alta., 3-102; B.C., 3-1185; Fed., 3-72; N.B., 3-138; Nfld., 3-148; N.S., 3-162; Ont., 3-186; P.E.I., 3-192; Qué., 3-208; Sask., 3-219; Yukon, 3-222
   Prevention
      Canada Assn., 2-160
      Govt. Quick Ref., 3-16
   Protection
      Assn., Ont. Industrial, 2-160
      Magazines, 5-167
   Safety Assn., Cdn., 2-159
Firearms
   Assn., Ntl., 2-152
   Control Task Group (Fed.), 3-78
   Officers (Govt.): Quick Ref., 3-17; Alta., 3-102; N.B., 3-140; N.S., 3-162; N.W.T., 3-152; Sask., 3-217; Yukon, 3-224
Firefighters
   Cdn. Assn. of, 2-199
   Prov. Fedn. of Ont., 2-205
   Qué. Union of, 2-206
Firemen & Oilers, Intl. Broth. of, 2-202
First
   Aid Attendants Assn. of B.C., Occupational, 2-55
   Ministers' Constitutional Conf. on Patriation of the Constitution, 1-25
   Nations
      AIDS
         Soc., Healing Our Spirit B.C., 2-18
         Task Force, Atlantic, 2-17
      Assembly of, 2-132
      Confederacy, 2-133
      Language Council, Sweetgrass, 2-112
      Schs., *see* Native Schs.
      of Man., Indian Council of, 2-133
      2-Spirited People of the, 2-132
   Night Celebrations, 1-82
Fiscal Policy & Economic Analysis Br. (Fed.), 3-67
Fiscale et financière, Assn de planification, 2-69
Fish
   Exporters, Cdn. Assn. of, 2-71
   & Game Assns., 2-62
   Mktg. Corp., Freshwater (Fed.), 3-70
   Packers Assns., 2-71/72
   Processor Assn., Qué., 2-71
   & Seafood Assns., 2-71
   & Wildlife (Govt.): Quick Ref., 3-17; Alta., 3-99; N.B., 3-139; Ont., 3-184; P.E.I., 3-190; Yukon, 3-225
Fisheries
   & Aquaculture (Govt.): N.B. (Dept.), 3-136; Nfld., 3-143; P.E.I. (Div.), 3-190

Fisheries (cont.)
   Assns., 2-71
   Brs./Divs. (Govt.): Alta., 3-99; B.C., 3-113; Man., 3-1299; N.W.T., 3-153; Sask., 3-214; Yukon, 3-225
   Companies, Cdn., 7-40
   Council of Canada, 2-71
   Commns., Intl., 3-247
   Conservation, Cdn. Ambassador for, 3-69
   Depts. (Govt.): Quick Ref., 3-17; B.C., 3-108; Fed., 3-673; N.B., 3-136; Nfld., 3-143; N.S., 3-159; P.E.I., 3-197; Qué., 3-197
   Devel. Inst.: N.B., 3-136; Nfld., 3-144
   Govt. Quick Ref., 3-17
   Innovation, Cdn. Centre for, 2-71
   Loans Bd. (N.S.), 3-160
   Magazines, 5-167
   Mgmt. Brs./Divs. (Govt.): Alta., 3-99; Fed., 3-68
   & Marine Inst. of Memorial Univ., (Nfld.), 9-20
   Museum of the Atlantic (NS), 6-13
   & Oceans Canada, 3-64
   Orgs., Intl., 3-247
   Prices Support Bd. (Fed.), 3-68
   Research Facilities (Fed.), 3-68
   Resource Conservation Council, 3-68
   Sch. of (N.B.), 3-136
   Statistics, 1-56
   Wildlife & Habitat Protection (B.C.), 3-113
Fishermen & Allied Wkrs. Union, 2-207
Fishermen's
   Assn., P.E.I., 2-72
   Publications, *see* Fisheries Magazines
Fishery, Task Force on Incomes & Adjustment in the Atlantic, 3-68
Fishing
   Assns., 2-71
   Exhibitions, Shows & Events, 1-82
   Industries, Venture Capital Investment (Qué.), 3-198
   Magazines, 5-182
   Resorts & Outfitters Assn., B.C., 2-149
Fitness
   Admin. Centre, Cdn. Sport &, 2-178
   Govt. Quick Ref. (*see* Recreation), 3-34
   & Lifestyle Research Inst., Cdn., 2-150
Fixed Link Bur. (P.E.I.), 3-189
Fixture Mfrs. Assn., Cdn. Lamp &, 2-123
Flag Assn., Cdn., 2-150
Flags & Coats of Arms, **1**
Flavour
   Fdn., Fresh for, 2-73
   Mfrs. Assn. of Canada, 2-73
Flax
   Council of Canada, 2-15
   Growers Western Canada, 2-15
Fleurs Canada Inc., 2-99
Flexible Foam Mfrs.' Assn., Cdn., 2-12
Flood(s) (*see also* Emergency Measures/Response)
   Mgmt. Dir. (Ont.), 3-184
Floor Covering
   Assn., Ntl., 2-124
   Magazines, 5-167
   Qué. Inst. of, 2-124
Flora & Fauna, Directory, 6-44
Floral
   Art, Cdn. Sch of (Man.), 9-16
   Emblems, **9**
Florists Magazines, 5-167
Flour Millers Assn., Ont., 2-73
Flowers
   Assns., 2-98
   Canada, 2-99
   Exhibitions, Shows & Events, 1-82
Fluid Power
   Assn., Cdn., 2-56
   Tech., Ctr. for (NRC), 3-81
Fly Fishing Canada, 2-152
Flying Farmers Intl., 2-15
FM Radio Stations, 5-206

Focus on the Family Assn., 2-7
Foi
　catholique (Qué. Educ.), 3-200
　Oeuvre pontificale de la propagation de, 2-8
　protestante (Qué. Educ.), 3-200
Foie, Fdn cdnne du, 2-87
Foire agricole royale d'hiver, 2-66
Foires et expositions, Assn cdnne des, 2-66
Folk
　Arts
　　Assns., 2-190
　　Councils: Cdn., 2-190; Ont. Multicultural, 2-191
　Dance Assn., Ont., 6-43
　Festivals, see Music Exhibitions, Shows & Events
　Fdn., Mariposa, 6-40
Folklore Canada Intl., 2-190
Foncier du Qué., Bur. de révision de l'évaluation, 3-197
Fonction publique
　Alliance de la, 2-205
　Assn proflle des cadres de la, 2-120
　Commn de la (Govt.): Fed., 3-84; Qué., 3-210
　Inst profl de la, 2-205
　du Qué., Synd. de la, 2-206
　des relations de travail dans la (Fed.), 3-84
　Synd. cdn de la, 2-200
Fondations, 2-208
Fonderies cdnnes, Assn des, 2-181
Fondements de l'éducation, Assn cdnne des, 2-47
Food (see also Agriculture, Nutrition)
　& Agric.
　　in Christian Persp., Earthkeeping, 2-14
　　Fisheries (Govt.): B.C., 3-108; Qué., 3-197
　　Min. (Sask.), 3-212
　Animals, Cdns. for Ethical Treatment of, 2-22
　Banks, Cdn. Assn. of, 2-165
　& Beverage
　　Assns., 2-72
　　Companies, Cdn., 7-41
　　Exhibitions, Shows & Events, 1-83
　　Magazines, 5-182
　Brokers Assn., Cdn., 2-72
　& Commercial Wkrs. Intl. Union, United, 2-207
　Companies, Cdn., 7-41
　Depts. (Govt.): Alta., 3-95; B.C., 3-108; Ont., 3-168; Qué., 3-197; Sask., 3-212
　Exhibitions, Shows & Events, 1-83
　& Fishing Industries Venture Capital Investment (Qué.), 3-198
　Govt. Quick Ref. (see Nutrition), 3-28
　Industries Supply Assn., Cdn. Dairy &, 2-72
　Industry
　　Assns., 2-72
　　Competitiveness Br. (Ont.), 3-169
　　Division (Ont.), 3-169
　Irradiation
　　Cdn. Coalition to Stop, 2-72
　　Consumers United to Stop, 2-73
　Inst. of Canada., 2-73
　Magazines, 5-182
　Marketing Bd., Agriculture & (Qué.), 3-198
　Processing Magazines, 5-167
　Processors Assns.: Ont., 2-73; Que., 2-72
　Production & Inspection Br. (Fed.), 3-53
　& Rural
　　Affairs, Agric., Dept. (Ont.), 3-168
　　Devel., Alta. Agric., 3-95
　Science & Tech., Cdn. Inst. of, 2-162
　Service
　　Assn., Cdn. College & Univ., 2-72
　　Execs. Assn. (Toronto), Cdn., 2-72
　Services Assns., 2-157
　Supervisors Assn., Cdn., 2-72
　Tech. Centre (P.E.I.), 3-190
　Terminal Bd., Ont., 3-170
Foods
　Cdn. Assn. of Specialty, 2-72
　Dir. (Fed. Health), 3-71
Foodservices Assn., Cdn. Restaurant &, 2-157

Football
　Assn., Cdn. Amateur, 2-179
　Hall of Fame, Cdn., 6-16
　League, Cdn., 2-175
　Players' Assn., Cdn., 2-199
Footwear
　Council, 2-68
　Exhibitions, Shows & Events, 1-83
　Importer, Cdn. Assn. of, 2-187
　Magazines, 5-167
Force, Measurement of, 1-62
Forage Commn., N.S. Grain &, 3-156
Foreign
　Aid Reform, Citizens for, 2-108
　Affairs
　　Govt. Quick Ref., see Intl. Affairs, 3-23
　　& Intl. Trade Canada (Fed.), 3-68
　Awards, 1-32
　Bank Subsidiaries, 7-2 (& see Addenda)
　Depts. & Agencies, 3-230
　Equivalency Tables, 3-226
　Imports & Exports, 1-54, 1-55, 1-56
　Investment, Govt. Quick Ref., see Investment, 3-23
　Language Magazines see Ethnic Magazines
　Service
　　Community Assn., 2-79
　　Officers, Profl. Assn. of, 2-204
Forensic
　Pathology Chief (Nfld.), 3-147
　Science(s)
　　Cdn. Soc. of, 2-162
　　Govt.: Ont., 3-186; Qué., 3-208
Forest(s)
　Alliance of B.C., 2-63
　Brs./Divs. (Govt.): Qué., 3-205; see also Forestry Brs./Divs.
　Engrg. Research Inst., 2-156
　Fire Mgmt. Dirs. (Govt): N.B., 3-139; P.E.I., 3-188; Sask., 3-214
　Improvement Assn. (P.E.I.), 2-74
　Industries
　　Assns.: Ont., 2-75; Qué., 2-74
　　Councils: B.C., 2-75; Cdn., 2-74
　　Magazines, 5-167
　Industry Exhibitions, Shows & Events, 1-83
　Insurance Fund, Agric. & (Qué.), 3-198
　Magazines, 5-167
　Management Network of Ctrs of Excellence, Sustainable, 2-75
　Mgmt. Brs./Divs. (Govt.): Nfld., 3-144; N.W.T., 3-153; Ont., 3-184
　Min. (B.C.), 3-115
　Pest Mgmt. Inst. (Fed.), 3-53
　Practices Code (B.C.), 3-115
　Products
　　Assns.: Alta., 2-74; N.B., 2-75; N.S., 2-75
　　Brs./Divs. (Govt.): Alta., 3-104; Nfld., 3-144
　　Commn., N.B., 3-139
　　Mktg. Bd., N.S. Primary, 3-163
　Protection
　　Assn., Nfld., 2-74
　　Dirs. (Govt.): Nfld., 3-144; N.S., 3-163
　　Ltd. (N.B.), 3-139
　　REXFOR, 3-206
　Ranger Sch., Maritime (N.B.), 9-18
　Renewal B.C., 3-115
　Research Inst., Ont., 3-184
　Resources
　　Govt.: Quick Ref., 3-17; Nfld., 3-144
　　Planning & Mensuration, Dir. (N.S.), 3-163
　Services (Govt.): Alta., 3-99; Cdn., 3-82
　Wardens, Jr., 2-75
Foresters
　Assns. of Profl.: B.C., 2-74; N.B., 2-74; Ont., 2-75
　of B.C., Consulting, 2-75
　Indep. Order of, 2-76
　Life Ins. Soc., Cdn., 2-105

Forestièr(e)(s)
　agréés du N.-B., Assn des, 2-74
　Assn des industries (Qué.), 2-74
　du Canada, 2-74
　Cdnne, Assn, 2-74; N.-B., 2-74
　Conseil cdn des industries, 2-74
　Fédn des travailleurs (Qué), 2-201
　Fonds d'Assurance-Prêts Agricoles & (Qué.), 3-198
　Institut du Canada, 2-74
　Ordre des ingénieurs (Qué.), 2-75
　Soc. de récupération, d'explor. et de dével., 3-206
　et travailleurs d'usines, Fra. ntle des charpentiers-menuisiers, 2-201
　universitaires, Assn des écoles, 2-46
Forestry
　Agric., Fisheries &, Dept. of (P.E.I.), 3-188
　Assn(s)., 2-74
　　Cdn., 2-74
　　Ntl. Aboriginal, 2-75
　Auth., Algonquin, 3-184
　Brs./Divs. (Govt.): Man., 3-129; Nfld., 3-144; N.S., 3-163; Sask., 3-214
　Cdn. Inst. of, 2-74
　Companies, Cdn., 7-43
　Depts. (Govt.): B.C., 3-115; Nfld., 3-144; P.E.I., 3-188
　Devel. (Alta.), 3-97
　Education, B.C., 2-74
　Exhibition Com., N.S., 2-75
　Exploitation, Qué., 3-206
　Faculties/Schs., Index to, 9-56
　Schs., Assn of Univ., 2-46
　& Wildlife Br. (Nfld.), 3-144
Forêt(s)
　Assn de santé et sécurité des industries de la (Qué.), 2-159
　Fédn des travailleurs du papier et de la, 2-201
　Réseau de Ctrs d'Excellence sur la Gestion Durable des, 2-75
　Sous-ministre adjoint (Qué.), 3-205
Formation
　des enseignants, Assn cdnne pour la, 2-48
　professionnelle, Assn cdnne de la, 2-50
Forms
　of Address, 1-33
　& Manuals Mgmt. Assn., 2-143
Fort Whyte Ctr. for Env. Educ., 2-63
Foster
　Parent Assns., B.C., Fedn. of, 2-165
　Parents Plan, 2-168
Foundations, 2-208
　of Educ., Cdn. Assn. of, 2-47
Foundry Assn., Cdn., 2-181
Foundrymen's Soc., Amer., 2-123
4-H Council, Cdn., 2-13
Four Arrows, 2-109
Fournisseurs d'hôtels et restaurants, Assn des, 2-157
Fourrure, Assns, Instituts et conseils, 2-77
Foursquare Gospel Church of Canada, 2-4
Fox Breeders Assn., Canada, 2-19
Foyer-école, Fédns des assns, 2-49
Fragrance Assn., Cdn., 2-123
Fraicheur égale saveur, Fdn, 2-73
Français
　Alliance cdnne des responsables et enseignants en français, 2-45
　Assn québécoise des professeurs de, 2-46
　Fédn cdnne pour l'alphabétisation en, 2-112
　Musée de l'Amerique, 6-24
　Office de la langue (Qué.), 3-200
Française(s)
　en Amérique, Conseil de la vie, 2-39
　Assemblée intle des parlementaires de langue, 2-38
　Assn(s)
　　cdnne
　　　d'éducation de langue, 2-45
　　　des rédacteurs agricoles de langue, 2-193
　　des juristes d'expression, Ont., 2-113; Sask., 2-113
　　de la radio et télévision de langue, 2-29

Française(s) (cont.)
    Conseil intl des radios-télévisions d'expression, 2-29
    Fédn intle des écrivains de langue, 2-194
    Union d'églises baptistes, 2-2
France
    -Canada Assn., 2-128
    Govt., 3-226, 3-233
    Tech. Press Agency, 2-188
Franchise Assn., Cdn. 2-34
Franco
    cdnne de la Sask., Assn culturelle, 2-39
    -manitobain(e)
        Assn culturelle, 2-38
        Centre Culturel, 3-123
        Soc., 2-39
    -ontarian(iens/iennes)
        Assn des enseignant(e)s, 2-46
        Conseil de l'éduc. (Ont.), 3-177
        d'histoire et de généalogie, Soc., 2-98
        de ressources pédagogiques, Centre, 2-51
        Union culturelle des, 2-39
    -yukonnaise, Assn, 2-39
Francophone(s)
    et acadienne, Fédn des communautés, 2-39
    Affairs Office of (Ont.), 3-179
    de l'Alberta, Fédn des parents, 2-52
    Assn
        intle des maires, 2-79
        de la presse, 2-193
    Centre (COFTM), 2-39
    Compagnie des cent-associés, 2-38
    Cultural Affairs (Govt.), P.E.I., 3-190
    à distance, Réseau d'enseignement, 2-53
    d'éduc., Div. des services, (N.B.), 3-133, 3-135
    pour l'enseignement supérieur et la recherche, Agence, 2-45
    Fédn des assns de parents (Ont.), 2-51
    Guides, 2-37
    intle des directeurs d'établissements scolaires, Assn, 2-46
    du N.-B., Assn des
        conseillers scolaires (N.B.), 2-45
        enseignant(e)s, 2-50
    de Terre-Neuve et du Labrador, Fédn des, 2-39
Francophonie Member Countries, 3-247
FRANTECH, 2-188
Fraser
    Inst., 2-45
    Valley, Univ. College of the, 9-9
Fraternal
    Assns., 2-75
    Magazines, 5-182
Fredericton
    City Govt., 4-157
    Fdn., 2-210
Free
    Methodist Church, 2-4
    Speech League, Cdn., 2-102
    Trade (see also NAFTA)
        Citizens Concerned About, 2-188
    Will Baptists, Atlantic Canada Assn. of, 2-2
Freedom of Info. (B.C.), 3-109
FreeNet, Ntl. Capital, 2-104
FreeNets, 5-232
Freestyle Ski, 2-175
Freight
    Carriers Assn. of Canada., 2-189
    Forwarders, 2-188
French
    Baccalauréat Programs, Schs. Offering (Qué.), 9-51
    Baptist Churches, Union of, 2-2
    Cdn. Parents for, 2-111
    as a First Language, Cdn. Assn. for the Teachers of, 2-45
    Govt.
        Depts./Agencies, 3-233
        Equivalency Table, 3-226
    Jurists Assn. (Sask.), 2-113

French (cont.)
    Language
        Bd. (Qué.), 3-200
        Coordination (Sask.), 3-216
        Council (Qué.), 3-200
        Education (Govt.): N.B., 3-135; N.S., 3-158; Ont., 3-1765; P.E.I., 3-190
        Radio Stations, AM, 5-199; FM, 5-206
        Sch.
            Bds. (Ont.), 9-27
            Council (Toronto), 2-51
        TV Stations, 5-213
Frequency Coord. System Assn., 2-183
Fresh for Flavour Fdn., 2-73
Freshwater
    Area of Canada, 1-63
    Fish Mktg. Corp., 3-70
    Inst., 3-68
Friedreich's Ataxia, Cdn. Assn. of, 2-81
Friends
    of the Earth, 2-63
    Hist'l Assn., Cdn., 2-96
    Religious Soc. of, 2-3
    Service Com., Cdn., 2-3
Friendship
    Centre(s)
        Cdn. Native, 2-133
        Ntl. Assn. of, 2-134
Frontenac Co. Bd. of Educ. (Ont.), 9-24
Fromages internationaux, Conseil cdn des, 2-188
Frontier College (Ont.), 9-35
Frontière intle, Commn de la (Fed.), 3-76
Frontiers Fdn., 2-167
Frossesse, Soc. intle pour l'étude de l'hypertension en, 2-36
Frost, low points, cities, 1-65
Fruit
    Growers Assns.: B.C., 2-13; N.S., 2-15; Ont., 2-15
    Industry Inspection Br. (Ont.), 3-169
    Mktg. Bds.: B.C., 3-108; Ont., 3-170
Fruiticulteurs et de maraîchers de l'Ont., L'Assn des, 2-15
Fruits & légumes
    Assn cdnne de la distribution de, 2-73
    Fédn des producteurs de, 3-198
Fuels (see also Coal; Oil; Electric Power; Nuclear)
    Assn., Cdn. Renewable, 2-56
Fulbright Program, The, 2-52
Fund
    Managers, Investment, 7-4
    Raising Execs., Cdn. Soc. of, 2-122
Funeral
    Advisory & Memorial Soc., 2-76
    Directors & Embalmers Assns., 2-76/77
    Service(s)
        Assn(s.), 2-76/77
        of Canada, 2-76
        Magazines, 5-167
        Trade Shows, 1-84
Fung Loy Kok Inst. of Taoism, 2-4
Fur
    Bearing Animals, Assn. for Prot. of, 2-77
    Council of Canada, 2-77; Retail, 2-77
    Industry, Govt. Quick Ref., 3-38
    Inst. of Canada, 2-77
    Mgmt. Supervisor (N.W.T.), 3-153
    Trade
        Assns., 2-77
        Magazines, 5-168
Furniture
    & Home Furnishing Publications, see Interior Design
    Manufacturers, Cdn. Council of, 2-123
    Publications, see Interior Design
    Shows, see Home Shows
    Workers, Intl. Union of, 2-203
Furriers Guild of Canada, 2-77
Fusion, 2-191

G

Gabriel Dumont Inst. of Native Studies (Sask.), 9-54
Gaelic College of Celtic Arts (N.S.), 9-23
Gaia Group, 2-63
Galleries Assns., 2-77
Galloway Assn., Cdn., 2-20
Galvanoplastes d'Amérique, Assn des, 2-122
Gambling, Cdn. Fdn. on Compulsive, 2-166
Game (see also Fish & Game)
    Assns., 2-62
    Farmers Assn., Sask., 2-15
    Farms, see Zoological Gardens
Games (see also Toys)
    Assn(s)., 2-149
        Commonwealth, 2-179
    Corporation, Qué. 2002 Winter, 2-180
    Council
        Canada, 2-173
        Cdn. Highland, 2-175
    Intl. Committee, Arctic Winter, 2-172
    Society, B.C., 3-119
    Toys &, Exhibitions, Shows, Events, 1-91
    World Univ., 2-181
Gaming
    Auth./Commns. (Govt.): Alta., 3-100; B.C., 3-115; N.S., 3-1576; Ont., 3-175; Qué., 3-208; Sask., 3-218
    Regs., Govt. Quick Ref., 3-25
Garbage, see Waste
Garçons et filles, Clubs des, 2-36
Garde à l'enfance
    Assn cdnne pour la promotion des services de, 2-166
Garden
    Shows, 1-82 (see also Home Shows)
    Supplies & Equipment Magazines, 5-168
Gardening
    Assns., 2-98
    Exhibitions, Shows & Events, 1-82
    Magazines, 5-182
Gardens, Botanical, 6-45
Garderie, Fédn des intervenantes en, 2-201
Gardes du corps du gouvernement du Qué., Assn prof des, 2-198
Garment
    Mfrs. Assn., of Western Canada, 2-68
    Workers of Amer., United, 2-207
GARROD Assn., 2-83
Gas (see also Oil; Petroleum)
    Assn(s)., 2-78
        Cdn., 2-56
        Compressed, 2-78
        Ont. Natural, 2-78
        Propane, 2-78
    Bd. of Examiners for Compressed (N.B.), 3-133
    Brs./Divs. (Govt.): Alta., 3-98; B.C., 3-118; Man., 3-124; Qué., 3-205
    Companies, Cdn., 7-49
    Machinery Mfrs. Assn., Compressed Air &, 2-66
    Natural, see Natural Gas
    Processors
        Assn., Cdn., 2-78
        Suppliers Assn., Cdn., 2-78
    Research Inst., Cdn., 2-56
    Trade Shows, see Petroleum Trade Shows
    Users Assn., Industrial, 2-78
Gastroenterology, Cdn. Assn. of, 2-83
Gatineau, Ville de, Govt., 4-157
Gay(s)
    Archives, Cdn. Lesbian &, 2-98
    Asian AIDS Project, 2-18
    & Lesbians Everywhere, Equality for, 2-98
    Rights in Ont., Coalition for Lesbian &, 2-98
Gaz
    Assn
        cdnne du, 2-56
        des consommateurs industriels de, 2-78
    naturel, Régie du (Qué.), 3-205
    propane, Assn cdnne du, 2-78
Gazette, The (Qué.), 5-144

G.B.E., 1-30
G.C., 1-29
G.C.B., 1-30
G.C.M.G., 1-30
Gear Products Mfrs. Assn., Cdn., 2-123
Gelbvieh Assn., Cdn., 2-20
Gem & Mineral Fedn. of Canada, 2-78
Gémeaux, Prix, 1-93
Gemini Awards, 1-93
Gemmological Assn., Cdn., 2-78
Gemmology, Cdn. Inst. of, 2-78
Gems, Assns., 2-78
Gendarmerie royale
    du Canada, 3-88
        Assn des anciens, 2-127
        comité externe d'examen de la, 3-88
        commn des plaintes du public contre la, 3-88
Genealogical
    Assns., 2-95; N.S., 2-96
    & Family History Socs., Cdn. Fedn. of, 2-95
    Inst. of the Maritimes, 2-96
    Socs.: B.C., 2-95; Jewish, 2-97; Man., 2-97; N.B., 2-97; Nfld./Lab., 2-97; Ont., 2-97; P.E.I., 2-97; Sask., 2-98
Généalogie
    Fédn québécoise des socs de, 2-96
    Soc. franco-ontarienne d'histoire et de, 2-98
Généalogique
    cdnne-française, Soc., 2-98
    de la N.-E., 2-96
Genealogy
    Assns., 2-95
    Magazines, 5-184
General
    Accountants Assns., Certified, 2-9
    Assembly, P.E.I., 3-187
    Church of the New Jerusalem, 2-4
    Hospitals in Canada, List of, 8-1
    Interest Magazines, 5-182
    Standards Bd., Cdn., 2-18, 3-85
    Surgeons, Cdn. Assn. of, 2-83
    Wkrs. Union, 2-201
Genesis Research Fdn., 2-210
Genetic Diseases Network, Cdn., 2-155
Geneticists, Cdn. College of Medical, 2-85
Genetics Soc. of Canada, 2-162
Génie
    chimique, Soc. cdnne du, 2-35
    civil, Soc. cdnne de, 2-59
    Conseil de recherches en sciences naturelles et en, du Canada, 3-84
    forestier, Inst cdn de recherches en, 2-156
    industriel, Soc. cdn de, 2-59
    mécanique, Soc. cdnne de, 2-59
    protéique, Réseau, 2-157
    rural, Soc. cdnne de, 2-14
Genie Awards, 1-93
Geochemists, Assn. of Exploration, 2-127
Geodetic Survey Div. (Fed.), 3-83
Geographers, Cdn. Assn. of, 2-47
Geographic
    Info.
        Data B.C., 3-113
        Corp., N.B., 3-136
        Section (Yukon), 3-225
    Sciences, College of (N.S.), 3-26
Geographical
    Names
        Agencies (Govt.): Canada, 3-61 ; Nfld., 3-145; Ont., 3-184; Qué., 3-200; Sask., 3-219
        Cdn. Permanent Com. on, 3-61
    Soc., Royal Cdn., 2-157
    Union, Intl., 2-157
Géographique(s)
    Comité permanent cdn des noms, 3-61
    Corp. d'info., N.B., 3-136

Geological
    Assn. of Canada, 2-163
    Services Brs./Divs. (Govt.): Quick Ref. 3-18; Man., 3-124; Sask., 3-214
    Surveys (Govt.): Alta., 3-104; Canada, 3-82; N.B., 3-139; Nfld., 3-148; Ont., 3-185; Yukon, 3-222
Geologists
    Assns., 2-58
    Cdn. Soc. of Petroleum, 2-78
    Govt.: Nfld., 3-148; N.W.T., 3-153; Yukon, 3-222
Geology
    Govt. Quick Ref., 3-18
    & Mines (Sask.), 3-214
Geomatics
    Canada (Fed.), 3-83
    Cdn. Inst. of, 2-182
    Ctrs. (Govt.): N.S., 3-161; P.E.I., 3-192
    Industry Assn. of Canada, 2-182
Geophysical Union, Cdn., 2-182
Geophysicists
    Assns., 2-58
    Cdn. Soc. of Exploration, 2-162
George Brown College, AA & T (Ont.), 9-33
George Cross, 1-29
Georgian College, AA & T (Ont.), 9-33
Geoscience
    Branch, Minerals & Continental, 3-82
    Centres (Fed.), 3-82
    Cos., Cdn. Assn. of, 2-161
    Council, Cdn., 2-162
    Info. Centre, Cdn., 3-82
Géoscientifique, Centre du Québec, 3-82
Geoscientists Assns., 2-58
Geotechnical
    Research Ctr. (U.W.O.), 9-31
    Soc., Cdn., 2-59
German
    -Cdn. Congress, 2-130
    Clubs, Central Org. of Sudetan-, 2-129
    Cultural Centres (Goethe Insts.), 2-130
    Educ., Man. Parents for, 2-53
    Govt.
        Depts./Agencies, 3-234
        Equivalency Table, 3-226
    Magazines, 5-192
    Wine Soc., 2-73
Germany, Govt., 3-226, 3-234
Gerontological Nursing Assn.: Cdn., 2-136; Ont., 2-137
Gerontology
    Cdn. Assn. on, 2-163
    Manitoba Assn. on, 2-164
Gestion
    des achats, Assn de, 2-122
    agricole, Soc. cdnne d'économie rurale et de, 2-44
    Centre cdn de, 3-57
    des déchets, Soc. ontarienne de, 2-64
    en ingéniere, Soc. cdnne de, 2-59
    Inst.
        cdn de, 2-121
        supérieur de, 2-56
    de personnel, Assn des entreprises en placement et, 2-56
    de la production et les stocks, Assn cdnne pour la, 2-123
    de la recherche, Assn cdnne de la, 2-155
    de trésorerie, Assn de, 2-71
Ghanaian-Cdns., Ntl. Council of, 2-131
Gideons Intl., 2-7
Gift(s)
    Exhibitions, Shows & Events, 1-84 (see also Crafts)
    Magazines, 5-168
    Packaging & Greeting Card Assn., 2-158
    & Tableware Assn., Cdn., 2-158
Gifted Children('s) Assns.: B.C., 2-37; Nfld./Lab., 2-37
Giftedness Québec, 2-37
Giller Prize, 1-106
Girl Guides of Canada, 2-37

Girls
    & Boys Clubs of Canada, 2-36
    in Training, Cdn., 2-37
Give the Gift of Literacy Fdn., 2-111
Glass
    Assn., Ont. Clay &, 2-191
    Magazines, 5-168
    Mfrs. Assn., Insulating, 2-124
    Moulders, Wkrs. Intl. Union, 2-201
    Wkrs. Intl. Union, Alum., Brick &, 2-197
Glenbow Museum, 6-2
Glendon College (York Univ.), 9-32
Glenn Gould Prize, 1-108
Global
    Analyses, Resource Centre for, 2-108
    Ministries, Cdn. Churches' Forum for, 2-7, 9-34
    Outreach Mission, 2-7
    Strategists, 2-109
    Survival, Physicians for, 2-109
Globe & Mail (Ont.), 5-139
Gloucester City Govt., 4-157
Go Kart Track Owners' Assn., Cdn., 2-150
GO Transit (Ont.), 3-187
Goat Soc., Cdn., 2-20
Goethe-Insts., 2-130
Golf
    Assns., 2-180; Cdn. Ladies, 2-176; Ont. Ladies', 2-179; P.E.I. Men's, 2-179; Royal Cdn., 2-180
    Fdn., Cdn., 2-175
    Industry Assn., Cdn., 2-175
    Magazines, see Sports & Recreation Magazines
    Supts. Assn., Cdn., 2-175
Golfers Assn., Cdn. Profl., 2-176
Golfeuses, Assn cdnne des, 2-176
Good
    Conduct Medals, 1-32
    Friday, 1-24
    Roads Assn., Ont., 2-189
Goodwill
    Rehab. Servs. Alta., 2-167
    Toronto, 2-167
Gospel
    Church, Foursquare, 2-4
    Churches, Associated, 2-2
    Missionary Union, 2-7
Gouverneur général du Canada, 3-43
Governance, Inst. on, 2-80
Government
    Assns., 2-79
    of Canada, 3-43
    Civil Lawyers Assn., Alta., 2-113
    Communications Office (B.C.), 3-116
    Depts. (Govt.): Alta., 3-94; B.C., 3-108; Fed., 3-52; Foreign, 3-230; Man., 3-121; N.B., 3-132; Nfld., 3-142; N.S., 3-156; Ont., 3-168; P.E.I., 3-188; Qué., 3-196; Sask., 3-212; Yukon, 3-222
    in Charge of Hospitals, 8-1
    in Charge of Libraries, 5-1
    Employees Unions: B.C., 2-198; Man., 2-204; N.B., 2-204; N.S., 2-204; Qué., 2-207; Sask., 2-204
    Equivalency Table, Foreign, 3-226
    Exhibitions, Shows & Events, 1-84
    Federal, 3-43
    Finance Officers Assn. of U.S. & Canada, 2-80
    Foreign, Equivalency Table, 3-226
    Forms of Address, 1-33
    Grants, Govt. Quick Ref., 3-19
    Info. Servs. (Govt.): Quick Ref., 3-18; Alta. (Public Affairs), 3-103; B.C. (Communic.), 3-115; Fed. (Enquiries), 3-85; Man., 3-128; N.B. (Communic.), 3-134; Nfld., 3-146; N.S., 3-157; Ont. (Citizens' Inquiry Serv.), 3-181; P.E.I. (Island Info.), 3-192; Qué. (Communic.), 3-209; Sask. (Media Servs.), 3-218; Yukon (Govt. Servs.), 3-223
    Leader, Yukon, 3-221
    Libraries Councils: Alta., 2-116; B.C., 2-119; Man., 2-119; N.S., 2-119; Ont., 2-120; Sask., 2-120

Government (cont.)
　Lobbyists see Consultant Lobbyists
　Magazines, 5-168
　Media Servs., Sask., 3-218
　Municipal, 4-1
　Public Works &, Canada, 3-85
　Publications (Fed.), 3-85
　Purchasing
　　Agents & Commns., see Purchasing
　　Quick Ref. (Govt.), 3-18
　Quick Ref., 3-1
　Reorganization Secretariat (Alta.), 3-100
　Services Depts. (Govt.): Alta., 3-103; B.C., 3-116; Fed., 3-85; Man., 3-125; N.B., 3-140; Nfld., 3-145; N.W.T., 3-152; N.S., 3-156; Ont., 3-181; Qué., 3-209; Sask., 3-218; Yukon, 3-223
Governor General, 3-43
　Flag of, **8**
　Form of Address, 1-33
Governor General's
　Awards, 1-104, 1-109, 1-110
　Performing Arts Fdn., 2-25
Governors Gen. since Confed'n., **2**
Graduate Studies
　Cdn. Assn. for, 2-46
　Ont. Council on, 2-53
Grain(s)
　Commns. (Govt.): Alta., 3-96; Cdn., 3-57; N.B., 3-134; N.S., 3-156
　Council, Cdn., 2-13
　Elevator Corp. (P.E.I.), 3-189
　& Feed Assn., Ont., 2-15
　Financial Protection Bd., Ont., 3-170
　Inst.
　　Cdn. Intl., 3-61
　　intl du Canada pour le, 3-61
　Mktg. Bd., N.S., 3-156
　Millers, Amer. Fedn. of, 2-197
　Policy Dir., Adaption & (Fed.), 3-53
　Research Fdn., Western, 2-16
　Services Union, 2-201
Grand
　Conseil des Cris, 2-133
　Lacs, Collège des (ont.), 9-33
　River Polytechnical Inst. (Ont.), 9-35
　Soc., 2-167
　Théâtre de Qué., Soc. du, 3-199
Grande Prairie Regl. College (Alta.), 9-4
Grandes Soeurs du Qué., Assn des, 2-164
Grandparents
　Requesting Access & Dignity, 2-167
　Soc. of B.C., Volunteer, 2-172
Grands
　Frères du Canada, 2-164; Qué., 2-164
　Lacs, Adm. de pilotage des (Fed.), 3-70
Grant MacEwan Community College (Alta.), 3-4
Grants, Govt. Quick Ref., 3-19
Grape
　Growers Assn. of B.C., 2-13
　Mktg. Bds. (Govt.): B.C., 3-109; Ont., 3-170
Graph Comm. Training Ctr., 2-143
Graphic(s)
　Arts (see also Printing)
　　Assns., 2-143
　　Exhibitions, Shows & Events, 1-84
　　Industries Assn., Sask., 2-184
　　Magazines, 5-168
　Communications Intl. Union, 2-201
　Designers of Canada, Soc. of, 2-143
　Industries Assn. of Alta., Printing &, 2-143
Graphiques du Qué., Assn des arts, 2-143
Graphistes, Soc. des, 2-143
Great Lakes
　Fishery Commn., 3-247
　Inst. for Environmental Research, 2-156
　Marine Heritage Fdn., 2-210
　Pilotage Auth. (Fed.), 3-70

Great Lakes (cont.)
　Pollution Prevention (Fed. Br.), 3-65; (Fed. Ctr.), 3-65
　Ports, Intl. Assn. of, 2-124
　Regional Water Quality Agreement, 3-77
Greater Toronto
　Area Office for the, 3-183
　Map, 4-175
Greater Vancouver
　Map, 4-174
　Regl. Govt., 4-171
Greater Victoria Sch. Dist., 9-6
Greek
　Magazines, 5-192
　Orthodox Church, 2-4
Green
　Industry Office (Ont.), 3-177
　Party, 2-141
Greenhouse
　Products Mktg. Bds., N.B., 3-134
　Vegetable Mktg. Bds.: N.S., 3-156; Ont., 3-170
GreenLEAP, 2-63
Greenpeace Canada, 2-63
Greenwich Time, 1-5
Greeting Card Assn., 2-158
Greffiers parlementaires, Assn des, 2-79
Gregorian Calendar, 1-2
Grey Panthers, Cdn., 2-163
Grignotines, Assn cdnne des fabricants de chips/, 2-73
Grocers, Cdn. Fedn. of Indep., 2-72
Grocery
　Distrs., Cdn. Council of, 2-72
　Products Mfrs. Assn. of Canada, 2-73
　Trade Magazines, 5-168
Grossesse, Accueil, 2-154
Grossistes en médicaments, Assn des, 2-139
Grotto Cerebral Palsy Fdn., 2-210
Ground Water Assns., 2-44
Groundwater Section (P.E.I.), 3-190
Group
　of 78, 2-109
　Psychotherapy Assn., Cdn., 2-125
Growers Assns., 2-12
Growth & Progress Statistics, 1-56
GST (Fed.), 3-86
Guard
　Assn., Cdn., 2-199
　Wkrs. of America, Intl. Union, United Plant, 2-203
Guelph
　City Govt., 4-157
　Univ. of, 9-30
Guernsey Assn., Cdn., 2-20
Guerre, Musée Cdn de la, 6-1
Guidance Assn., Cdn. Counselling &, 2-166
Guide
　Dogs for the Blind, Cdn., 2-42
　Outfitters Assn. of B.C., 2-152
Guides
　francophones du Canada, 2-37
　de montagne cdns, Assn des, 2-149
Gun(s), see Firearms
Gymnastics Fedn.
　Cdn., 2-175
　Cdn. Rhythmic Sportive, 2-176
Gynaecologists, Soc. of Obstetricians &, 2-94
Gynecologic Nurses, 2-137

H
Habitat
　Brs./Divs. (Govt.): Man., 3-130; P.E.I., 3-190
　faunique Canada, 2-65
　for Humanity, 2-7
　Protection, ADM (B.C.), 3-113
　(U.N.), 3-247
Habitation
　coopérative, Assns, 2-101
　Municipalités, culture &, Dept (N.B.), 3-138

Habitation (cont.)
　du Qué., Soc. d', 3-197
　et de rénovation urbaine, Assn cdnne d', 2-101
Hadassah-Wizo Org. of Canada, 2-192
Haemochromatosis Soc., Cdn., 2-86
Hail Assn., Sask. Municipal, 2-106
Hairdressers Assns.: B.C., 2-68; N.B., 2-68; N.S., 2-67
Hairdressing Exhibitions, Shows & Events, 1-84
Haldimand-Norfolk Regl. Mun. Govt., 4-171
Halibut Commn., Intl. Pacific, 3-248
nalieutiques, conseil pour le conservation des ressources, 3-68
Halifax
　City Govt., 4-157
　Fisheries Research Lab (Fed.), 3-68
　Regl. Municipal Govt., 4-171
　Sch. Bd., 9-22
Hall(s) of Fame
　Assn., Cdn. Agricl., 2-13
　Cdn. Football, 6-16
　Hockey, 6-16
Haltérophile cdnne, Fédn, 2-178
Haltérophilie du Qué., Fédn, 2-178
Halton
　Bd. of Educ. (Ont.), 9-24
　County Radial Rlwy., 2-97
　Regl. Mun. Govt., 4-171
Hamilton
　Art Gallery of, 6-32
　Bd. of Educ., 9-24
　City Govt., 4-158
　Community Fdn., 2-210
　-Wentworth
　　R.C.S.S. Bd. of Educ., 9-26
　　Regl. Mun. Govt., 4-171
Hamlets in: N.W.T., 4-37; Yukon, 4-152
Handbags & Accessories Assn., Luggage, Leathergoods &, 2-68
Handball
　Assn., Cdn., 2-175
　Fedn., Cdn. Team, 2-178
Handicap, Alliance de vie active pour les cdn(ne)s ayant un, 2-172
Handicapé(es)
　Assn
　　cdnne des sports pour skieurs, 2-173
　　qué. de loisir pour personnes, 2-41
　Bur. des personnes (Qué.), 3-207
　Centre de la défense des droits des, 2-41
　Conseil
　　cdn des droits des personnes, 2-42
　　du Premier ministre sur la cond. des pérsonnes, N.B., 3-134
　au niveau post-secondaire, Assn ntle des étudiants, 2-53
　Parade des dix-sous pour les: Conseil ntl, 2-42; Qué, 2-43
　Soc. pour les enfants, 2-43
Handicapped (see also Disabled)
　Advocacy Resource Centre for the, 2-41
　Assns., 2-41
　Persons
　　Office for (Qué.), 3-207
　　Qué. Leisure Assn. for, 2-41
Handwriting, Intl. Assn. of Master Penmen & Teachers of, 2-52
Hang Gliding Assn. of Canada, 2-152
Hansard, see Legislative Assemblies
Hanukah, 1-24
Harassment & Discrimination in the Workplace, Action Group Against, 2-55
Harbour
　Assn., Cdn. Port &, 2-124
　Commns. (Fed.), 3-91
Harbours
　& Ports Br. (Fed.), 3-91
　Small Craft, Br. (Fed. Fisheries), 3-68

Harcèlement
    sexuel en milieu d'enseignement, Assn cdn contre le, 2-166
    au travail, Groupe d'action contre le, 2-55
Hard of Hearing Assn., Cdn., 2-42
Hardware
    Assn., Cdn. Retail, 2-158
    Exhibitions, Shows & Events, 1-84
    & Housewares Mfrs. Assn., Cdn., 2-123
    Inst., Door &, 2-124
    Mfrs. Assn., Builders, 2-30
    Trade Magazines, 5-168
Hardwood Plywood Assn., Cdn, 2-74
Hare Krishna Movement, 2-4
Harmonies, Assn cdn des, 6-39
    du Qué., Fédn des, 6-39
Harmony Fdn. of Canada, 2-63
Harness Racing Commn., Maritime Prov., 3-131
Hastings Co. Bd. of Educ. (Ont.), 9-24
Hatcheries Assn., Ont., 2-143
Hatching Egg Mktg. Bd., Alta., 3-96 (*see also* Broiler)
Hautes études
    commerciales, École des (Qué.), 9-47
    Fédn intl des insts des, 2-52
Havres, Assn des ports et, 2-124
Hays Converter Assn., Cdn., 2-20
Hazardous (*see also* Dangerous Goods)
    Contaminants Br. (B.C.), 3-113
    Materials
        Brs./Divs. (Govt.): Alta., 3-104; Fed., 3-71; N.B., 3-135; N.W.T., 3-153; P.E.I., 3-190
        Govt. Quick Ref., 3-11
        Info. Review Commn. (Fed.), 3-71
    Waste(s), Govt. Quick Ref., 3-11
Head Librarians of N.B., Council of, 2-119
Healing
    Arts Radiation Protection Commn., Ont., 3-180
    Our Spirit, B.C. First Nations AIDS Project, 2-18
HEALNet, 2-92
Health
    Action Network Soc., 2-92
    Agencies, Assn. of Local Official, 2-82
    Assns., 2-80
        B.C., 2-83
        Catholic, 2-90
    Awards, 1-101
    Bds.
        Man., 3-126
        Secretariat, Ont., 3-180
    Canada (Fed.), 3-71
    Cdn.
        Council on Smoking &, 2-85
        Inst. of Child, 2-87
        Org. for Adv. of Computers in, 2-103
        Soc. for Intl., 2-90
    Care
        Assns, 2-80
        Auxilliaries, Assns., 2-100
        Awards, 1-101
        Cdn. Assn. for Quality in, 2-84
        Cdn. Inst. of, 2-87
        Centres in: Alta., 8-3; B.C., 8-10; Man., 8-12; N.B., 8-16; Nfld., 8-17; N.W.T., 8-19; N.S., 8-19; Qué., 8-37; Sask., 8-53; Yukon, 8-56
        Employees Union (Alta.), 2-201
        Facilities *see* Hospitals
        Guild, Cdn., 2-199
        Insurance, *see* Health Insurance, Govt. Br./Divs., below
        Magazines, 5-183
        Profls., Man. Assn. of, 2-203
        Public Relations Assn., 2-92
        Saint Elizabeth, 2-94
        Units, (Alta.), 8-1
    Centres, Assn. of Ont., 2-100
    Coalition, Cdn., 2-86
    & Community Services (Govt.): N.B., 3-136; P.E.I., 3-191

Health (cont.)
    Conferences, 1-84
    Councils
        Assn. of District (Ont.), 2-82
        Prov.: N.S., 3-160; Sask., 3-216
        Depts. (Govt.): Quick Ref., 3-19; Alta., 3-100; B.C., 3-116; Fed., 3-71; Man., 3-126; N.B., 3-136; Nfld., 3-145; N.W.T., 3-151; N.S., 3-160; Ont., 3-179; P.E.I., 3-190; Qué., 3-206; Sask., 3-215; Yukon, 3-223
    Economics Research Assn., Cdn., 2-86
    Education, Sch. of Physical & (U. of T.), 9-30
    Evidence Application & Linkage Network, 2-92
    Exhibitions, Shows & Events, 1-84
    Facilities (*see also* Hospitals)
        Cdn. Assn. of Social Work Admins. in, 2-100
    Food Assn., Cdn., 2-72
    Govt. Quick Ref., 3-19
    Industries Devel. (Man.), 3-127
    Insurance (*see also* Health Depts.)
        Assn., Cdn. Life &, 2-105
        Bd. (Qué.), 3-207
        Br./Divs. (Govt.): Quick Ref., 3-19; Man., 3-126; Nfld. Commn., 3-146; N.S., 3-160; Ont., 3-180; Sask., 3-215; Yukon, 3-223
    Institutional, Div. (Ont.), 3-180
    Libraries Assns., 2-118; Golden Horseshoe, 2-119
    Magazines, 5-183
    & Medical Awards, 1-101
    Ntl. Clearinghouse on Tobacco &, 2-93
    Occupational, *see* Occupational Health & Safety
    Org. of Canada, Consumer, 2-91
    Phys. Educ., Rec. & Dance, Cdn. Assn. for, 2-174
    Profls.
        Assns., Allied: Nfld./Lab., 2-197; Ont., 2-197
        & Technicians, Qué. Union of, 2-196
    Promotion Dirs.: Fed., 3-71; Nfld., 3-146; Ont., 3-180
    Public, *see* Public Health
    Publications, 5-183
    Record Assn., Cdn., 2-118
    Related Educ. in Ont., 9-34
    Research
        Cdns. for, 2-90
        Fund, Qué., 3-207
    & Safety (*see also* Occupational Health & Safety, Workplace Health & Safety)
        Assns., 2-158
        Cdn. Centre for, 2-85
    Sciences
        Assns.: Alta., 2-202; B.C., 2-204; Sask., 2-202
        Centre Fdn., 2-92
        Michener Inst. for Applied, 2-93
    Service Execs., Cdn. College of, 2-85
    Services
        Accreditation, Cdn. Council on, 2-100
        Govt. Quick Ref., 3-19
        Insurance Fund (Man.), 3-126
        Utilization & Research Commn., Sask., 3-216
    & Social Services
        Council, Yukon, 3-221
        Depts. (Govt.): N.W.T., 3-151; P.E.I., 3-190; Qué., 3-206; Yukon, 3-223
        Schs. Admin. by (Qué.), 9-45
        Staff, Fédn of (Qué.), 2-196
    Technology
        Assessment Cdn. Coord. Office for, 2-85
        Council (Qué.), 3-207
    Units, *see* Hospital Districts
    & Well-being, Ctr. for Studies in (U.W.O.), 9-31
    & Welfare Council (Qué.), 3-207
Healthcare (*see also* Health Care)
    Assns., 2-99; Cdn., 2-100
    Ont. Assn. of Dirs. of Volunteer Services in, 2-101
Healthy Communities Network, Cdn., 2-86
Hearing
    Aid Bd., Man., 3-123

Hearing (cont.)
    Assn.
        Cdn. Hard of, 2-42
        Speech & (N.S.), 2-43
        Speech Language (Alta.), 2-44
    Impaired (*see also* Deaf)
        Hockey Assn., Cdn., 2-175
        Schs. for: B.C., 9-7; Man., 9-15; N.S., 9-22; Ont., 9-27; Qué., 9-45
        Soc. Cdn., 2-42
Hearst, Collège Univ. de (Ont.), 9-29
Heart & Stroke Fdn. Canada, 2-92; Alta., 2-92
Heat
    Exchange Mfrs. Assn., Cdn., 2-123
    & Frost Insulators & Asbestos Wkrs., Intl. Assn. of, 2-202
Heating
    Assns., 2-94
    Cdn. Inst. of Plumbing &, 2-95
    Contractors' Assn., Indep. Plumbing, 2-95
    Exhibitions, Events & Shows, 1-84
    Magazines, 5-168
    Refrigerating & Air Conditioning
        Engineers, Amer. Soc. of, 2-94
        Inst. of Canada, 2-95
Heavy Construction Assns., 2-30
Hebdos du Qué., Les, 2-145
Hébergement
    Corp. d' (Qué.), 3-207
    de l'envol, 2-19
    en Qué., Ctrs d'accueil d', 8-40
    et de réadaptation, Confed. qué. des centres d', 2-100
Hebrew
    Culture Org., 2-130
    New Year, 1-24
Hegira
    Calendar of, 6-2
    Era, 1-3
Hellenique du Qué., Congrès, 2-130
Help
    the Aged, 2-164
    Fill a Dream Fdn., 2-211
Hematology Soc., Cdn., 2-86
Hemochromatosis Soc., Cdn., 2-86
Hemophilia Soc., Cdn., 2-86; Ont., 2-92
Henson College of Public Affairs & Continuing Educ. (Dalhousie), 9-22
Heraldry, 1-6; Soc. of Canada, 2-96
Hereditary Metabolic Diseases, Cdn. Assn. of Centres for the Mgmt. of, 2-83
Hereford Assn., Cdn., 2-20
Heritage (*see also* History)
    Assns., 2-95
    Awards *see* Culture
    Brs./Divs. (Govt.): B.C., 3-118; N.B., 3-138; N.S., 3-158; Ont., 3-172; P.E.I., 3-190; Sask., 3-219; Yukon, 3-225
    Canada, 2-96
    Cdn.
        Assn. for Sport, 2-174
        Fed. Dept., 3-58
        Navigation Canals, 1-64
        Soc. for Industrial, 2-96
        Warplane, 2-96
    Canadien du Québec, 2-96
    Centre Soc., Western, 2-98
    of Children of Canada, 2-37
    Consultants, Cdn. Assn. of Profl., 2-95
    Councils (Govt.) Man., 3-123
    Depts. (Govt.): Fed., 3-58; Man., 3-123
    Fedns.: Man., 2-97; Nova Scotian, 2-96
    Foundation
        of Nfld. & Lab., 2-96
        Ontario, 2-97, 3-173
        P.E.I. Museum &, 6-23, 2-97
        Sask., (Govt.), 3-219
    Fund, N. Ont., 3-185

Heritage (cont.)
    Grants Adv. Council (Man.), 3-123
    Industries Policy Br. (Ont.), 3-172
    Info. Network, Cdn. 2-96; 3-58
    Languages, Sask. Org. for, 2-112
    Resources, Govt. Quick Ref., 3-20
    Savings Trust Fund, Alta., 3-105
    Sector, Cultural Devel. & (Fed.), 3-58
    Soc., Sask. Architectural, 2-98
    Sites, Canada, 3-58
    Trust, B.C., 3-119
Herpetological Soc., Ont., 2-163
Herzberg Inst. of Astrophysics (NRC), 3-81
Herzing Career College (Man.), 9-16
High
    Blood Pressure Prev. & Control, Cdn. Coalition for, 2-85
    Commissions
        in Canada, 3-248
        (Cdn.), Abroad, 3-259
    Commissioners, Forms of Address, 1-35
    IQ Soc., 2-53
    School Athletic Assns.: Man., 2-179; Nfld./Lab., 2-179
Higher Education
    Cdn.
        Assn. Against Sexual Harassment in, 2-166
        Soc. for Study of, 2-50
    N.S. Council on, 3-158
    Training & Adult Learning (P.E.I.), 3-191
Highland
    Cattle Soc., Cdn., 2-20
    Games Council, Cdn., 2-175
Highway
    Operations Div. (P.E.I.), 3-193
    Programs (N.S.), 3-164
    Safety Brs./Divs. (Govt.): B.C., 3-119; P.E.I., 3-193
    Traffic
        Bd., Man., 3-127
        Controllers of the Québec Prov. Police, 2-201
    Transp. Bds.: N.W.T., 3-154; Ont., 3-187
Highways, Depts. (Govt.): B.C., 3-119; Man., 3-126; Sask., 3-216 (see also Transportation)
Hike Ontario, 2-152
Hikers of the Cdn Rockies, Sky Line, 2-153
Hiking
    Fedn. of Qué., Walking &, 2-152
    Trail Assns., Fedn. of Ont., 2-152
Hindu Calendar, 1-2
Hippodromes du Canada, 2-153
Hispanic Congress, Cdn., 2-129
Hispanists, Cdn. Assn. of, 2-47
Histoire
    de l'église, Soc. cdnne d', 2-96; Catholique, 2-95 (anglaise), 2-98 (française)
    de familles, Assn cdnne de, 2-96
    des familles du Qué., Soc. de l', 2-97
    Ferroviare, Assn cdnne d', 2-96
    et de généalogie, Soc. franco-ontarienne d', 2-98
    militaire, Commn cdnne d', 2-126
    nationale du Canada, Soc. d', 2-95
    orale, Soc. d', 2-96
    du Québec, Fédn des socs d', 2-96
    du travail, Comité cdn sur l', 2-110
Historic
    Resources Dirs. (Govt.): Man., 3-123; Nfld., 3-149
    Sites
        Brs./Divs. (Govt.): Alta., 3-96; Fed., 3-59; Yukon, 3-225 (see also Heritage)
        List of Ntl., 3-59
    Theatres' Trust, 2-96
    Vehicle Soc. of Ont., 2-23
Historical
    Assn(s)., 2-95
        B.C. Railway, 2-95
        Cdn., 2-96
        Catholic, 2-95 (English); 2-98 (French)
        Friends, 2-96

Historical
    Assn(s). (cont.)
        Railroad, 2-96
        Science & Tech., 2-162
        Ont. Electric Railway, 2-97
    Awards see Culture
    Fedn., B.C., 2-95
    High Schools, Sask. Assn. of, 2-52
    Microreproductions, Cdn. Inst. for, 2-96
    & Museums Assn., Yukon, 2-98
    Research Fdn., J. Douglas Ferguson, 2-97
    Resources
        Div. (Alta.), 3-96
        Fdn. (Alta.), 2-95
    Soc(s).: Alta., 2-97; Man., 2-97; N.B., 2-97; Nfld., 2-97; Royal N.S., 2-97; Ont., 2-97; Qué. (Literary &), 2-97
        Cdn. Aviation, 2-28
        Jewish, Toronto, 2-132
        Photographical, 2-140
Historique
    acadienne, 2-98
    du Canada, Soc., 2-96
    de Qué., 2-98
History
    Assn(s.), 2-95
        Bus., 2-95
        Family, 2-96
    Awards see Culture
    Cdn.
        Com. on Labour, 2-110
        Commn. of Military, 2-126
        Oral, 2-96
        Soc. of Church, 2-96
    Govt. Quick Ref., 3-20
    Magazines, 5-184
    McCord Museum of Cdn., 6-24
    of Medicine, 2-90
    of Nursing, Cdn. Assn. for the, 2-135
    & Philosophy of Science, 2-162
    & Tech., Inst. for (U. of T.), 9-31
    Pointe-à-Callière, Museum of Archaeology &, 6-24
    Soc.
        Alta. Family, 2-95
        Canada's Ntl., 2-95
        Ont. Black, 2-97
        Postal, 2-97
        Québec Family, 2-97
HIV
    Groups & socs., 2-16
    Policy Coord. (Fed.), 3-71
    Research, Cdn. Assn. for, 2-154
Hobbies (see also Crafts)
    Assns., 2-149
    Exhibitions, Shows & Events, 1-85
    Magazines, 5-184
Hobby Assn., Cdn. Craft &, 2-149
Hockey
    Assn(s).
        Ball, 2-174
        Cdn., 2-175
            Adult Recreational, 2-173
        Field, 2-179
        Hearing-Impaired, 2-175
        Ont. Minor, 2-179
    Canadian, 2-175
    Hall of Fame, 6-16
    sur gazon
        Assn cdnne féminine de, 2-178
        Canada, 2-179
    sur glace, Fédn québecoise de, 2-175
    League Players Assn., Ntl., 2-203
    Magazines, see Sports & Recreation
Hog Mktg. Bds. & Commns. (Govt.): B.C., 3-109; N.B., 3-134; Nfld., 3-145; P.E.I., 3-189
Holiday Exchange, World Homes, 2-187
Holidays, Standard, 1-24
Holistic Nurses Assn., Cdn., 2-136

Holland College (P.E.I.), 9-41
Holocaust Educ. & Memorial Centre (Toronto), 2-130
Holstein Assn. of Canada, 2-21
Holy Childhood Assn., 2-7
Home(s)
    Builders
        Assn., Cdn., 2-101
        Training, Atlantic (N.S.), 9-23
    Care
        Assn., Cdn., 2-101
        Offices in: Alta., 8-4; Man., 8-13; N.B., 8-16; Nfld., 8-18; Ont., 8-25; P.E.I., 8-33
    Computers (Statistics), 1-53
    Economics
        Assn., 2-49; Fdn., 2-49
        Deans & Dirs. of (Cdn. Univs.), 2-47
    Furnishings Publications, see Interior Design & Decor
    Inspectors, Cdn.
        Assn. of, 2-101
        Inst. of Profl., 2-147
    Magazines, 5-184
    & Sch. Fedns., 2-49
    Shows, 1-85
    Warranty Prog., Ont. New, 3-175
Homelink, 2-187
Homeopathic R&D, Cdn. Fdn. of, 2-86
Homosexuality
    Assns., 2-98
    & Religion, Council on, 2-98
Honey
    Council, Cdn., 2-14
    Mktg. Bd., Man., 3-122
    Packers Assn., Cdn., 2-14
    Prodrs. Fedn., Qué., 3-198
Hong Kong
    Govt.
        Depts./Agencies, 3-235
        Equivalency Table, 3-226
        Overseas Schs., 9-40
        Student Selection Office, B.C., 9-13
    Trade Devel. Council, 2-188
Honourable, use of title, 1-26
Honours
    Abbreviations, 1-32
    British & Commonwealth, 1-29
    Cdn., 1-26
HOPE Intl. Devel. Agency, 2-109
Hôpitaux (see also Hospitals)
    pédiatriques, Assn cdnne des, 2-100
    Privés, see Private Hospitals
    Psychiatriques, see Mental Hospitals
    du Qué., Assn des, 2-101
Horizons of Friendship, 2-109
Horse(s)
    Breeding Assns., 2-19
    Council of B.C., 2-22
    Exhibitions, Shows & Events, 1-86
    Magazines, 5-185
    Racing Commns., see Racing Commns.
    Trials Canada, 2-179
Horseshoe Canada Assn., 2-152
Horticultural
    Assns., 2-98; Alta., 2-98; Ont., 2-99; P.E.I., 2-99; Sask., 2-99
    Awards, see Agriculture & Farming
    Council, Cdn., 2-98
    Research Inst. (Ont.), 3-169
    Science, Cdn. Soc. for, 2-99
    Shows, see Flowers Exhibitions
Horticulture (see also Agriculture)
    et d'écologie du Qué., Fédn des socs d', 2-99
    Niagara Parks Botanical Gardens & Sch. of, 9-35
    ornementale, Fédn interdisciplinaire de l', 2-99
Hospital(s), 8-1
    Appeal Bd., Ont., 3-180

Canadian Almanac & Directory 1997

Hospital(s), (cont.)
   Assn(s)., 2-99
      of Cdn. Teaching, 2-99
      Auxiliaries Assns., 2-100
      Cdn. Assn. of Paediatric, 2-100
   Conventions & Shows, 1-86
   Depts., *see* Health Depts.
   Districts in: Alta., 8-1; B.C., 8-8; Man., 8-11; N.B., 8-15; Nfld., 8-17; N.S., 8-19; N.W.T., 8-18; Ont., 8-21; Qué., 8-34; Sask., 8-51
      Financing Authority, B.C. Regional, 3-115
   Employees' Union (B.C.), 2-202
   Engrs. Assn. of Alta., 2-101
   Federal
      in: Alta., 8-4; B.C., 8-10; Man., 8-13; Ont., 8-24; Sask., 8-54
      Govt., 3-71
   Govt.
      Depts. in charge of, 8-1
      Quick Ref., 3-20
   & Health
      In: Alta., 8-1; B.C., 8-8; Man., 8-11; N.B., 8-15; Nfld., 8-17; N.W.T., 8-18; N.S., 8-19; Ont., 8-21; P.E.I., 8-33; Qué., 8-34; Sask., 8-51; Yukon, 8-56
   Infection Control Assn., Community &, 2-91
   Libraries Assn., Ont., 2-120
   Magazines, 5-168
   Mental, *see* Mental Hospitals
   Pharmacists, Cdn. Soc. of, 2-139
   Private, *see* Private Hospitals
   Services Brs./Divs.: N.B., 3-136; Nfld., 3-146
   for Sick Children Fdn., 2-211
   & Treatment Ctr. Sch. Bds. in Ont., 9-27
Hospitaliers
   Centres (Qué.), 8-34
   et centres d'accueil privés du Qué., Assn des centres, 2-100
   Conseil des syndicats (de Montréal), 2-200
Hospitality (*see also* Food; Beverage)
   Constellation College of (Ont.), 9-35
   Fdn., Cdn., 2-72
   Industry, Exhibitions, Shows & Events, 1-86
Hostelling Intl., 2-185
Hostelry Inst., Ont., 2-186
Hotel(s) (*see also* Hospitality Industry)
   Assns., 2-185
   Employees & Restaurant Employees Intl. Union, 2-202
   Magazines, 5-169
   Mktg. & Sales Execs., Cdn., 2-185
Hôteliers
   Ottawa, 2-186
   du Qué., L'Assn des, 2-185
Hôtellerie du Qué., Inst de tourisme et d', 2-185
Hôtels et restaurants, Assn des fournisseurs d', 2-157
House of Assembly: Nfld., 3-141; N.S., 3-155 (*see also* Legislative Assemblies)
House of Commons, 3-45 (*see also* Parliament)
   Coms., 3-46
   Forms of Address, 1-33
   Members
      Alpha., 3-50
      By Constituency, 3-47
   Salaries, 3-47
House of Windsor, 3-245
Household
   Expenditure, Average (Statistics), 1-53
   Measures, 1-63
Housekeepers Assn., Cdn. Administrative, 2-100
Houseware(s)
   Exhibitions, Shows & Events, *see* Home Shows
   Magazines, 5-169
   Mfrs. Assn., Cdn., 2-123
Housing
   Assn(s)., 2-101
      Manufactured, Alta. & Sask., 2-102
      Ont. Non-Profit, 2-102
   Authority, Man., 3-127

Housing (cont.)
   Brs./Divs. (Govt.): Alta., 3-103; Sask., 3-219
   Corps. (Govt.): Quick Ref., 3-21; Alta., 3-103; Canada, 3-55; Nfld., 3-146; N.W.T., 3-151; Ont., 3-183; Qué., 3-197; Yukon, 3-223
   Depts. (Govt.): Quick Ref., 3-21; B.C., 3-117; Man., 3-127; N.B., 3-138; N.S., 3-160; Ont., 3-182
   & Employment Devel. Financing Auth., B.C., 3-115
   Fedns., Cooperative, 2-101
   Govt. Quick Ref., 3-21
   Inst., Cdn. Manufactured, 2-101
   Mgmt. Commn., B.C., 3-118
   Price Index, New, 1-53
   & Renewal
      Assn., Cdn., 2-101
      Corp., Man., 3-127
HRAI, 2-95
HRDC, 3-72
Huguenot Soc. of Canada, 2-97
Hull
   Ville de, Govt., 4-158
   Univ. du Qué. à, 9-47
Humaines Dével. des ressources (N.B.), 3-137
Human
   Devel., Inst. on (U. of T.), 9-31
   -Computer Communications Soc., Cdn., 2-103
   Factors Assn. of Canada, 2-163
   Nutrition, Ctr. for (U.W.O.), 9-31
   Resource(s) (*see also* Personnel)
      Assn(s)., 2-55
         Ont. Municipal, 2-80
      Council, Software, 2-104
      Dept. (Govt.): B.C., 3-116; N.S., 3-161
      Devel., Dept. (Govt.): Fed., 3-72; N.B., 3-137
      in the Environ. Industry, Cdn. Council for, 2-60
      Info. Systems Intl., Assn. for, 2-56
      Magazines, 5-169
      Profls. Assn. of Ont., 2-56; Qué., 2-55
   Rights
      Assns., 2-102
      Award, Alta., 6-58
      Bds./Commns. (Govt.): Quick Ref., 3-21; Alta., 3-101; B.C., 3-110; Cdn., 3-60; Man. 3-129; N.B., 3-133; Nfld., 3-146; N.S., 3-161; Ont., 3-173; P.E.I., 3-191; Sask., 3-218; Yukon, 3-224 (*see also* Ombudsmen; Bds. of Review)
      of B'nai B'rith, 2-102
      Cdn. Tribute to, 2-102
      & Citizenship Commn., Alta., 3-101
      & Civil Liberties Assns., 2-102
      Coalition, Vancouver Island, 2-102
      & Democratic Dev., Intl. Centre for, 2-102
      Fdn., Cdn., 2-102
      Govt. Quick Ref., 3-21 (*see also* Discrimination)
      Inst. of Canada, 2-102
      Movement, Macedonian, 2-102
      Network on Intl., 2-102
      & Race Relations, Canada Council on, 2-102
      Secretariat, Alta., 3-96
   Servs. in Alta., Assn of, 2-165
   Settlements Cdn. Mission to U.N. Centre for, 3-247
Humane
   Assn., Royal Cdn., 2-169
   Soc(s).: Cdn. Fedn. of, 2-21
   Trapping, Cdn. Assn. for, 2-77
Humanist Assn. of Canada, 2-156
Humanities
   Assn. of Canada, 2-156
   Cdn. Fedn. for, 2-49
   & Social Science Fedn., 2-52
Humber College, AA & T (Ont.), 9-33
HUME Fdn., 2-211
Humour, École ntle de l' (Qué.), 9-47
Hungarian
   -Cdn. Fedn., 2-130
   Magazines, 5-192
Hunger Fdn., Cdn., 2-108
Hunters, Ont. Fed. of Anglers &, 2-152

Hunting
   Fishing & Trapping Joint Com. (Qué.), 3-201
   Magazines, Fishing &, 5-182
Huntington
   Socs.: Canada, 2-92; Qué., 2-92
   Univ. (Ont.), 9-29
Huron College (Ont.), 9-31
Huronia Hist'l Adv. Council (Ont.), 3-176
Hydraulics Centre, Cdn., 3-81
Hydro
   Govt. Agencies: B.C., 3-116; Man., 3-127; Nfld., 3-146; Ont., 3-185; Qué., 3-202 (*see also* Power; Electric; Public Utilities)
   Profl. & Admin. Employees, Soc. of Ont., 2-206
   -Québec, 3-202
      Fraternité constables spéc. d', 2-201
      Synd. profl des ingénieurs d', 2-206
Hydrocéphalie du Qué., L'Assn de Spina-Bifida et, 2-94
Hydrographic
   Assn., Cdn., 2-162
   Service, Cdn., 3-68
Hydrology
   Br. (B.C.), 3-113
   Research Inst., Ntl., 3-65
Hygiène et sécurité au travail
   Centre cdn d', 3-57
   publique, Inst cdn des inspecteurs en, 2-87
   & de securité au travail, Ctr. cdn d', 2-85, 3-57
Hygienists' Assn., Cdn. Dental, 2-40
Hypertension
   artérielle, Coalition cdnne pour la prévention et le contrôle de l', 2-85
   in Pregnancy, Intl. Soc. for Study of, 2-36
   Soc., Cdn., 2-125
Hypnosis, Ont. Soc. of Clinical, 2-94
Hypnotism, Cdn. Inst. of, 2-87
Hypothèques et de logement, Soc. cdnne, 3-55

I

IAO Commercial & Residential Risk Services, 2-106
IAT (Qué.), 9-47
ICC, Cdn. Secretariat, 2-43
Iceland Fdn., Canada, 2-209
Icelandic
   Horse Fedn., Cdn., 2-20
   Magazines, 5-192
   Ntl. League, 2-130
ICOMOS Canada, 2-97
IDA, 2-70
Identity Sector, Citizenship & Cdn. (Fed.), 3-58
IDRC, 3-77
IEEE Canada, 2-55
Igloolik Research Ctr. (N.W.T.), 3-152
Ignatius College (Ont.), 9-35
IJC, 3-77
Illustrators
   Cdn. Soc. of Children's, 2-194
   in Communications, Cdn. Assn. of, 2-140
Image
   Mgmt. Soc., Cdn. Info. &, 2-103
   Processing & Pattern Recognition Soc., 2-103
IMAGINE (Cdn. Centre for Philanthropy), 2-166
Imaging Trade Assn., Cdn., 2-140
Immersion Teachers, Cdn. Assn. of, 2-45
Immeuble(s)
   Assn cdnne de l', 2-147; N.-B., 2-147
   Chambres d', 2-146
   Inst cdn de l', 2-148
Immigrant(s)
   Aid
      Jewish, 2-131
      Somali, 2-132
   Ont. Council of Agencies Serving, 2-38
   Services Org., Ottawa-Carleton, 2-38
   & Visible Minority Women
      Against Abuse, 2-192
      Ntl. Org. of, 2-38

Immigration
　Assns., 2-37
　Brs./Divs. (Govt.): B.C., 3-110; Man., 3-123; P.E.I., 3-189
　Bureau de révision (Qué.), 3-205
　Canada
　　Citizenship & (Fed.), 3-62
　　Citoyenneté et, 3-62
　Conseil des communautés culturelles & de l' (Qué.), 3-205
　Consultants. Org. of Profl., 2-38
　Depts.(Govt.): Quick Ref., 3-21; Fed., 3-62; Qué., 3-198
　Govt. Quick Ref., 3-21
　& Refugee Bd. (Fed.), 3-73
　et du statut de réfugié, Commn de (Fed.), 3-73
　Visas (Fed.), 3-63
Immobilière
　Chambres, 2-147
　du Qué., Fédn des, 2-147
　Socs.: Fed., 3-55; Qué., 3-210
Immunology, Cdn. Soc. of Allergy & Clinical, 2-89
Imperial
　Order Daughters of the Empire, 2-76
　Service Order, 1-31
Implant Assn., Cdn., 2-86
Implement Mfrs. Assn., Prairie, 2-66
Import(s)
　& Exports
　　Exhibitions, Shows & Events, 1-86
　　Govt. Quick Ref., 3-21
　　Magazines, 5-169
　　Statistics, 1-54, 1-55, 1-56
Importers Assn.
　Cdn., 2-187
　Regulated, 2-187
Imprimerie, Assn cdnne
　des courtiers en, 2-11
　de l', 2-143
Improvement Districts
　Alta., 4-11
　Assn. of Alta., Rural &, 2-80
In-Line & Roller Skating Assn., Cdn., 2-176
Incendie du Qué., Assn des chefs de service, 2-159
Incendies
　L'Assn cdnne des directeurs et commissaires des, 2-159
　Commissariat aux (Qué.), 3-208
Income
　Average Family (Statistics), 1-53
　Plan, Sask., 3-220
　Security
　　Bd., Cree Hunters & Trappers, 3-208
　　Brs./Divs. (Govt.): N.B., 3-137; Qué., 3-208; Sask., 3-220
　　Govt. Quick Ref., 3-21
　　Programs (Fed.), 3-72
　Support Brs./Divs. (Govt.): B.C., 3-119; Nfld., 3-149; N.S., 3-157
　Tax, see Taxation
Incorporation Regs., Govt. Quick Ref., 3-22
Indemnisation environnementale, Soc. d', 2-63
Independent
　Adjusters' Assn., Cdn., 2-105
　Assemblies of God, 2-4
　Business, Cdn. Fedn. of, 2-34
　Corrugated Converters, Assn. of, 2-123
　Grocers, Cdn. Fedn. of, 2-72
　Learning Centre, Ontario, 3-176
　List of, see Private Schs.
　Living Centres, Cdn. Assn. of, 2-41
　Record Production Assn., Cdn., 6-39
　Schools (see also Private Schs.)
　　Cdn. Assn. of, 2-47
　　& Colleges of Alta., Assn. of, 2-51
　　Conf. of (Ont.), 2-51
　　Fedns., 2-51
　　Inspector (B.C.), 3-111

Independent
　Schools (cont.)
　　Qué. Assn. of, 2-53
　　Study Program (Man.), 3-124
　Telephone Assn., Cdn., 2-183
　Unions, Cdn. Ntl. Fedn. of, 2-196
Indexing & Abstracting Soc. of Canada, 2-119
India, Ntl. Assn. of Cdns. of Origin in, 2-131
Indian
　Assn(s)., 2-132
　　of Alta., 2-133
　Calendar, 1-2
　Chiefs, Union of B.C., 2-134
　Claims Sector (Fed.), 3-73
　Commn. of Ont., 3-74
　Council of First Nations of Man., 2-133
　Cultural
　　Centre, Sask., 2-134
　　Education Centre., Man., 2-133
　Era, see Epochs
　Empire, Order of, 1-30
　Federated College (Sask.), 9-54
　Friendship Centres, 2-134
　Govt. Sector, Claims & (Fed.), 3-73
　Institute of Technologies, Sask., 3-64
　& Metis Affairs Secretariat, Sask., 3-216
　& Northern
　　Affairs Canada (Fed.), 3-73
　　Health Services (Fed.), 3-72
　Oil & Gas Canada (Fed.), 3-74
　(Saka) Era, 1-3
　Schools, see Native Schools
　Taxation Adv. Board (Fed.), 3-74
　Women's
　　Assn., Yukon, 2-134
　　Council, N.B., 2-134
Indians (see also Aboriginal Affairs)
　Assn. of Iroquois & Allied, 2-132
　Council for Yukon, 2-133
　Fedn. of Nfld., 2-133; Sask., 2-133
　Unions of, 2-134
Indiennes, affaires (Fed.), 3-73
Indigenous
　Govt., Inst. of (B.C.), 9-9
　Women's Collective of Man., 2-134
Indoor Air Quality & Climate, Intl. Soc. for, 2-63
Industrial
　Accident(s)
　　Council of Canada, Major, 2-160
　　Prevention Assn. (Ont.), 2-160
　　Victims Group of Ont., 2-160
　Accountants Guild, 2-9
　Aggregate, 1-57
　Archaeological Assn., Cdn. Steam Pres. &, 2-96
　Archaeology, Ont. Soc. of, 2-23
　Arts Assn., Cdn., 2-49
　Automation Magazines, 5-169
　Biotechnology Assn., 2-163
　Commercial & Inst. Accountants, Guild of, 2-9
　Design, Govt. Quick Ref., 3-22
　Designers, Assn(s)., 2-106/107
　Development
　　Bd., N.B., 3-135
　　Corp., Qué., 3-203
　　Govt. Quick Ref. see Business Devel.
　Disease Standards Panel, (Ont.), 3-181
　Engrg., Cdn. Soc. for, 2-59
　Environmental Engrg. Div. (Nfld.), 3-143
　Equip. Inst., Cdn. Farm &, 2-66
　Exhibitions, Shows & Events, 1-86
　Fire Protection Assn., Ont., 2-160
　Gas Users Assn., 2-78
　Heritage Canada, Cdn. Soc. for, 2-96
　Innovation Centre, Cdn., 2-123
　Magazines, 5-169
　Mktg. & Research Assn., 2-11
　Materials Inst. (NRC), 3-81
　Mechanics, Ntl. Assn. of, 2-197

Industrial (cont.)
　Orgs., Congress of (Amer.), 2-195
　Pollution Control Br. (N.S.), 3-159
　Relations
　　Assn., Cdn., 2-110
　　Ctrs.: Queens, 9-29; U. of T., 9-30
　　Govt. Offices: Quick Ref., N.B., 3-133; P.E.I., 3-192
　Research
　　Assistance Program (NRC), 3-81
　　Centre, Qué., 3-203
　　& Dev. Inst., 2-59
　Risks Insurers, Cdn., 2-105
　Roofing Contractors Assn., Ont., 2-32
　Safety (see also Occupational Health & Safety)
　　Magazines, 5-169
　Security, Cdn. Soc. for, 2-160
　Statistics, 1-57
　Sweetener Users, Cdn., 2-72
　Trade Shows, 1-86
　Training Apprenticeship & (P.E.I.), 3-191
　Transportation League, Cdn., 2-188
　Truck Assn. of Canada, 2-189
　Waste Br. (B.C.), 3-113
Industrie(s)
　Canada (Fed.), 3-74
　du commerce, de la science et de la tech., Min. de l' (Qué.), 3-202
Industriel(le)(s)
　Assn
　　cdnne de relations, 2-110
　　qué. pour le patrimoine, 2-95
　Centre de recherche (Qué.), 3-203
　& portuaire, Socs. du parc (Qué.), 3-203
　Soc. cdnne de l'héritage, 2-96
　Soc. de dévél. (Qué.), 3-203
Industry
　& Arts Academy (Nfld.), 9-21
　Assns., 2-122
　Canada (Fed.), 3-74
　Depts. (Govt.): Quick Ref., 3-22; Fed., 3-74; Man., 3-127; Nfld., 3-146; Qué., 3-202 (see also Economic Devel.; Trade)
　Devel. Man., 3-127
　Govt. Quick Ref., 3-22
　Product Price Index, 1-57
　& Science
　　Cdn. Soc. for Color in Art, 2-59
　　Policy (Fed.), 3-75
　Services Br. (Yukon), 3-225
　Technology & Forestry Devel. (Alta.), 3-97
　Trade
　　& Tech. Dept. (Nfld.), 3-146
　　& Tourism Dept. (Man.), 3-127
INFACT Canada, 2-36
Infant
　Deaths, Cdn. Fdn. for Study of, 2-86
　Feeding Action Coalition, 2-36
　Mortality, 1-48
Infantry Assn., Cdn., 2-126
Infection Control Assn., Com. & Hosp., 2-91
Infectious
　Disease Soc., Cdn., 2-86
　Diseases, Cdn. Assn. for Clinical Microbiology &, 2-83
Infertility Awareness Assn. Canada, 2-154
Infirmières/Infirmiers
　Assn des, 2-136
　autochtones du Canada, 2-132
　autorisés en service privé, Assn cdnne des, 2-136
　auxiliaires du Qué.
　　Alliance profile des, 2-197
　　Fédn des, 2-137
　　Ordre des, 2-136
　enseignantes, Assn des, 2-136
　Fédn ntle des synds, 2-203
　Fondation des, 2-137
　en gérontologie, Assn cdnne des, 2-136

Infirmières/Infirmiers (cont.)
　de néphrologie, 2-135
　en nursing cardiovasculaire, Conseil cdn des, 2-136
　en oncologie, Assn cdnne des, 2-136
　en orthopédie, Assn cdnne des, 2-137
　en pédiatrie, Assn cdnne des, 2-136
　du Qué.
　　Fédn des, 2-137
　　Ordre des, 2-137
　de sales d'opération, Assn des, 2-137
　en santé
　　communautaire, Assn cdnne des, 2-137
　　mentale, Fédn cdnne des, 2-136
　　respiratoire, Soc. cdnne des, 2-137
　　du travail, Assn cdnne des, 2-137
　en sidologie, Assn cdnne des, 2-136
　Soc. de protection des, 2-137
　en soins
　　aux brûlés, Assn cdnne des, 2-135
　　intraveineux, Assn cdnne des, 2-136
　　neurologiques, Assn cdnne des, 2-135
　　de phase aiguë, Assn cdnne des, 2-135
　Union qué. des, 2-138
　d'urgence, Affiliation des, 2-137
Inflation Rate, 1-54
Infographie, Inst de création artistique et de recherche en (Qué.), 9-47
Information
　Assn. of Man., Electronics &, 2-55
　Canada's Coalition for Public, 2-103
　Commissaire à l', 3-76
　Commr. of Canada, 3-76
　Géographie du NB, 3-136
　Govt. Services, see Government Information Services
　& Image Mgmt. Soc., Cdn., 2-103
　Highway Secretariats: N.B., 3-134; Qué., 3-199
　Management Directory, Communications &, 5-1
　Officer (Fed.), 3-76
　& Privacy Commr. (Govt.): Alta., 3-101; B.C., 3-117; Ont., 3-180; Sask., 3-216
　Processing
　　Profls., Chinese Cdn., 2-103
　　Security SIG, Cdn., 2-103
　　Soc., Cdn., 2-103
　Resource Mgmt. Assn. of Canada, 2-104
　Science
　　Amer. Soc. for, 2-116
　　Cdn. Assn. for, 2-117
　　Faculties/Schs., Index to, 9-56
　Services
　　Cdn. Assn. of Special Libraries &, 2-117
　　Govt., see Government Information Services
　　Man. (Govt.), 3-128
　Studies Ctr. for Research in (U.of T.), 9-30
　Systems, Intl. Assn for Human Resource, 2-56
　Technologies
　　Branch (Fed.), 3-76
　　Innovation, Centre for, 3-76
　Technology
　　Assns., 2-103
　　　of Canada, 2-104
　　　Ont. Library &, 2-120
　　Exploitation Br. (Fed.), 3-75
　　Faculties/Schs., Index to, 9-56
　　Inst. for (NRC), 3-81
　　Research Centre, 2-104
　& Telecommunications Initiative (Man.), 3-127
　Tech. Servs. Div. (B.C.), 3-114
Informatique
　Assn cdnne de l', 2-103
　cognitive des orgs, Groupe interuniversitaire de recherche en, 2-104
　juridique, Assn cdnnc pour l'avancement de l', 2-114
　Marsan, Collège d' (Qué.), 9-47
　de Québec, Inst d', 9-48
INFORUM Montréal World Trade Centre Inc., 2-188

Infrastructure
　Fed. Office of, 3-91
　& Policy (N.B.), 3-138
　Mgmt. (Alta.), 3-104
　Program, Canada
　　-Alta., 3-103
　　-Ont., 3-182
　　-P.E.I., 3-192
　　-Sask., 3-219
　Servs Br. (Man.), 3-130
Ingénieurs
　conseils
　　du Qué., Assn des, 2-57
　　du Canada, Assn des, 2-57
　forestiers du Qué., Ordre des, 2-75
　du Gouvernement du Qué., 2-198
　d'Hydro-Québec, Synd. profl des, 2-206
　Inst cdn des, 2-59
　municipaux du Qué., Assn des, 2-57
　professionnels, Conseil cdn des, 2-58
　du Qué., Ordre des, 2-58
Inhalothérapeutes, Assn profl des, 2-198
Injured
　Wkrs.
　　Alliance Cdn., 2-110
　　Union of Ont., 2-111
Injuries, Criminal, see Criminal Injuries
Ink Mfrs. Assn., Cdn. Printing, 2-143
Inland Fisheries Div. (N.S.), 3-160
Innis College (U. of T.), 9-31
Innovation(s)
　Corp., N.S., 3-158
　Ontario Corp., 3-176
INRS, 2-156; 9-47
Insolvency Practitioners Assn., 2-69
Inspector Gen., Office of (Fed.), 3-69
Inspiraplex, 2-94
Institutional
　Accountants Guild, 2-9
　Schs. (Man.), 9-15
Institutions Statistics (Fed.), 3-89
Instrument Soc. of Amer., 2-104
Insulating Glass Mfrs. Assn. of Canada, 2-124
Insulation
　Contractors Assn., B.C., 2-95
　Mfrs. Assn. of Canada, Cellulose, 2-124
Insulators
　& Asbestos Wkrs., Intl. Assn. of Heat & Frost, 2-202
　Assn. of Ont., Master, 2-32
Insurance
　Accountants Assn., Cdn., 2-9
　Adjustors Assn., Ont., 2-106
　Admrs. of Ont., Soc. of Public, 2-106
　Assn(s)., 2-104
　　Cdn.
　　　Bar, 2-113
　　　Life & Health, 2-105
　　　Mutual (Ont.), 2-106
　　　Nuclear, 2-106
　Automobile, Govt. Quick Ref., 3-3
　Autoplan (B.C.), 3-117
　Bds., Auto: Alta., 3-105; Qué., 3-208
　Brokers Assns., 2-105
　Bur. of Canada, 2-105
　Commn., Ont., 3-179
　Companies (& see Addenda)
　　Cdn. Assn. of Mutual, 2-104
　　List of, 7-13
　Conference, Toronto, 2-105
　Conventions, 1-87
　Corp.
　　of B.C. (Autoplan), 3-117
　　Canada Deposit, 3-55
　　Ont. Deposit, 3-179
　　Qué. Auto, 3-208
　　Sask. Govt., 3-216
　Council of B.C., 2-105, 3-115
　Crime Prevention Bur., 2-105

Insurance (cont.)
　Crop, see Crop Insurance
　Govt. Quick Ref., 3-22
　　Auto, 3-3
　　Health Care, 3-19
　　Life, Fire, 3-22
　　Unemployment, 3-38
　Institute(s), 2-106
　　of Canada, 2-106
　　Life, 2-106
　Magazines, 5-169
　Managers Assn., Life, 2-106
　Mgmt. Soc., Risk &, 2-106
　Medical Officers, Cdn. Life, 2-105
　Operations, Ctr. for Study of, 2-105
　Program (Fed.), 3-72
　Public (Man.), 3-128
　& Real Estate Div. (P.E.I.), 3-192
　Regulators, Cdn. Council of, 2-104
　Sask. Govt. (SGI), 3-216
　Soc., Cdn. Foresters Life, 2-105
　Statistics, Life, 1-57
　Supts. (Govt.): Quick Ref., 3-22; Alta., 3-105; Man., 3-122; N.B., 3-138; N.S., 3-157; P.E.I., 3-192; Qué., 3-203; Sask., 3-217; Yukon, 3-224
Insurers
　Adv. Org., 2-106
　Assn. of Cdn., 2-104
Integrated Sch. Bds. (Nfld.), 9-19
Intégration communautaire ou sociale, Assns, 2-41
Integrity
　Commn. on (Ont.), 3-180
　Vancouver, 2-98
Intellectual Property
　Govt. Quick Ref., 3-22
　Office, Cdn., 3-75
Intelligence
　Cdn. Soc. for Computational Study of, 2-103
　Review Com., Security, 3-88
　Service, Cdn., 3-89
Intelligent
　Sensing for Innovative Structure, 2-59
　Systems, Inst. for Robotics &, 2-156
Inter-Amer. Commercial Arbitration Commn., 2-111
Inter-Church
　Council of Canada, Women's, 2-193
　Fund for Intl. Devel., 2-211
Inter Pares, 2-109
Inter-Varsity Christian Fellowship, 2-4
Interactive
　Communication Soc., Intl., 2-183
　Multimedia Arts & Tech. Assn., 2-104
Intercultural
　Council, Man., 2-131
　Educ., Cdn. Council for Multicult., 2-48
Interculture Canada, 2-107
Interculturel de Montréal, Inst, 2-130
Intergouvernementales
　Affaires, (Govt.): Fed., 3-76; N.B., 3-137; Qué., 3-196
　Secrétariat des conférences, cdnnes, 3-61
Intergovernmental
　Affairs (Govt.): Alta., 3-100; Fed., 3-76; N.B., 3-137; Nfld., 3-141; N.W.T., 3-152; Ont., 3-180; Qué., 3-196; Sask., 3-216 (see also Fed.-Prov. Relations)
　Conference Secretariat, Cdn., 3-61
　Relations, Inst. for (Queen's Univ.), 9-29
Interior
　Alzheimer Fdn., 2-92
　Design
　　Assns., 2-106
　　Exhibitions, Shows & Events, 1-87
　　Magazines, 5-170
　Designers
　　of Canada, 2-106
　　Institutes, 2-107
　　of Ont., Assn. of Reg'rd, 2-107
Interministerial Women's Secretariat (P.E.I.), 3-191

Internal
　Auditors Inst., 2-9
　Medicine, Cdn. Soc. of, 2-90
International
　Affairs
　　Cdn. Inst. of, 2-108
　　Govt. Quick Ref., 3-23
　Agencies, 3-247
　Aid, Govt., Quick Ref., 3-23
　Atomic Energy Agency, 3-247
　Boundary Commn., 3-76
　Business
　　Brs./Divs. (Fed.): (Export Devel.), 3-66;
　　　(Finance), 3-69; (Foreign Affairs), 3-69
　　Cdn. Council for, 2-34
　　Councils, 7-23
　　Studies, Ctr. for (Nfld.), 9-20
　Centre of Winnipeg, 2-37
　Chambers of Commerce & Business Councils, 7-23
　Child
　　Care, 2-109
　　Haven, 2-108
　Civil Aviation Org., 3-247
　Commn. Medals, 1-31
　Co-operation
　　Assns., 2-107
　　Cdn. Council for, 2-107; Man., 2-109; Ont., 2-109;
　　　Sask., 2-109
　Development
　　Agency
　　　Cdn., 3-61
　　　HOPE, 2-109
　　Cdn. Assn. for the Study of, 2-107
　　Educ. Resources Assn., 2-109
　　Inter-Church Fund for, 2-211
　　Research Centre, 3-76
　Economic Relations, Ctr. for the Study of (U.W.O.), 9-31
　Education, Cdn. Bureau for, 2-48
　Finance Ctr. (B.C.), 3-112
　Fisheries Commns., 3-247
　Grains Inst., Cdn., 3-61
　Health, Cdn. Soc. for, 2-90
　Human Rights, Network on, 2-102
　Joint Commn., 3-77
　Labour Org., 3-247
　Law, Cdn. Council of, 2-113
　Maritime Ctr. (B.C.), 3-112
　Marketing, see Trade Reps.
　North Pacific Fisheries Commn., 3-248
　Organization Offices, 3-247
　PEN, 2-102
　Postal Rates, 1-45
　Relations
　　Assns., 2-107
　　Centre for (Queen's Univ.), 9-29
　　Min. of (Qué.), 3-204
　Relief Agency, 2-109
　Security Affairs, Political & (Fed.), 3-69
　Studies
　　Ctr. for (U. of T.), 9-30
　　& Cooperation, Cdn. Ctr. for, 2-108
　System of Units, 1-60
　Time Zones, 1-5
　Trade (see also Trade)
　　Assn., Cdn., 2-188
　　& Finance Br. (Fed. Finance), 3-67
　　Foreign Affairs &, Canada (Fed.), 3-68
　　Statistics, see Imports & Exports
　　Tribunal, Cdn., 3-61
　　Whaling Commn., 3-248
Internationale(s)
　Carrefour de solidarité, 2-108
　Commn. mixte, 3-77
　Min. des Relations (Qué.), 3-204
Internes & Residents
　Cdn. Assn. of, 2-83
　Profl. Assns. of, 2-205

Internet
　Service Providers, 5-230
　Website Directory, 5-233
Interns, see Internes
Interpreters
　Assn(s). 2-111; Ont., 2-114
　Council, Cdn. Translaters &, 2-111
　& Translators, Assn. of Legal Court, 2-113
Interprètes
　agréés du Qué., Ordre des, 2-112
　Conseil des traducteurs et, 2-111
　en langage visuel, Assn des, 2-111
　et des traducteurs judiciaires, Assn des, 2-113
Interstitial Cystitis Assn., 2-92
Interuniversity Athletic Union, 2-47
Interval & Transition Houses, Ont. Assn. of, 2-168
Intramural Rec. Assn., 2-150
Intraoculaires, Assn cdnne des implants, 2-86
Intravenous Nurses Assn., Cdn., 2-136
Inuit (see also Native; Aboriginal; First Nations)
　Art Fdn., 2-133
　Assn., Labrador, 2-133
　Broadcasting Corp., 5-198
　Tapirisat of Canada, 2-133
Inventors Assn. of Canada, 2-138
Inventory Control, Cdn. Assn. for Prod. &, 2-123
Investigation du Qué., Conseil des agences de securité et d', 2-160
Investigations Unit, Special (Ont. Att. Gen.), 3-171
Investissement, L'Inst des fonds d', 2-70
Investment(s) (see also Business & Finance)
　Assn., Pension, 2-71
　Brs./Divs. (Govt.): Alta., 3-97, 3-105; B.C., 3-112;
　　N.B. (Mgmt. Corp.), 3-136; N.S., 3-158, (Finance),
　　3-159; Ont., 3-175; P.E.I., 3-189; Sask., 3-213;
　　Yukon, 3-222
　Canada, 3-75
　Corp. Qué. Gen., 3-203
　Counsel Assn. of Ont., 2-70
　Dealers' Assn. of Canada, 2-70
　Employment &, Min. (B.C.), 3-111
　Fund(s)
　　Course, Cdn. (Ont.), 9-34
　　Inst. of Canada, 2-70
　　Mgrs., 7-4
　Govt. Quick Ref., 3-23
　Org., Social, 2-71
　& Trade Assn., Native, 2-134
Investors Assn. of Canada, 2-70
IODE, 2-76
Iona College (Windsor), 9-32
I.Q. Soc., High, 2-53
Iqualit Research Ctr. (N.W.T.), 3-152
Ireland Fund, 2-211
Iris Soc., Cdn., 2-98
Irish
　Cdn. Cultural Assn. N.B., 2-130
　Freedom Assn., 2-130
Iron
　Production, 1-56
　Steel & Industrial Wkrs. Union, 2-199
　Workers, Intl. Assn. of Bridge, Structural & Ornamental, 2-202
Iroquois & Allied Indians, Assn. of, 2-132
Irrigation
　Council, Alta. (Govt.), 3-96
　& Resource Mgmt. Div. (Alta.), 3-95
　Servs. (Sask.), 3-212
ISBN & ISMN, Cdn., 5-1
ISKCON Toronto, 2-4
Islam, Ahmadiyya Movement in, 2-2
Islamic
　Assns., Fed. of, 2-7
　Fdn. of Toronto, 2-130
　Heritage Assn., Cdn. Turkish, 2-129
　Holidays, 1-24
　Info. Fdn., 2-130
　Org., Cdn., 2-3

Island
　Info. Service (P.E.I.), 3-192
　Regulatory & Appeals Commn. (P.E.I.), 3-191
Islands Trust (B.C.), 3-118
Isolation thermique, Assn cdnne de l', 2-95
I.S.O., 1-31
Isolant de fibre de bois, Assn cdnne des manufacturiers d', 2-123
Israel
　Appeal of Canada, United, 2-132
　Cancer Research Fund, 2-211
　Fdn. for Academic Exchanges, Canada-, 2-129
　Inst. of Technology, 2-156
ISSN Canada, 5-1
ITAC, 2-104
Italian
　Cdn. Seniors Clubs, Fedn. of, 2-130
　Cdns., Ntl. Congress of, 2-131
　Cultural Inst., 2-130
　Govt.
　　Depts./Agencies, 3-236
　　Equivalency Table, 3-227
　Magazines, 5-192
　Pentecostal Church of Canada, 2-4
Italy
　Govt., 3-227, 3-236
　Sons of, 2-76
ITVA Canada, 2-29
IWA Canada, 2-203

J

J. Douglas Ferguson Historical Research Fdn., 2-97
Jack Miner Migratory Bird Fdn., 2-135
Jacks Inst., The (Man.), 9-16
Jails & Justice, Quaker Com. on, 2-143
Jamaican-Cdn. Assn., 2-130
James Bay
　Devel. (Qué.), 3-205
　Energy Soc. (Qué.), 3-202
　Environmental Advisory Com. (Qué.), 3-202
Jane Austen Soc. of N. Amer., 2-112
Japan
　Automobile Mfrs. Assn. Canada, 2-26
　Govt., 3-226, 3-237 (& see Addenda)
　Overseas Schs., 9-40
　Student Selection Office, B.C., 9-13
Japanese
　Automobile Dealers, Cdn. Assn. of, 2-26
　Cdn. Citizens' Assn., 2-130
　Cdns., Ntl. Assn. of, 2-131
　Era, see Epochs
　Govt.
　　Depts./Agencies, 3-237 (& see Addenda)
　　Equivalency Table, 3-226
　Magazines, 5-192
Jardin
　botanique de Montréal, Les Amis du, 2-98
　zoologique du Qué., 2-22
Jardiniers maraîchers du Qué., Assn des, 2-98
Jazz Soc., Edmonton, 6-40
JCI - Global Strategists, 2-109
JDF Canada, 2-92
Jean-Hamelin, Prix France-Qué., 6-59
Jehovah's Witnesses, 2-6
Jérôme-La Royer, Commn scolaire, 9-43
Jersey Cattle
　Assn. of Canada, 2-21
　Bur., World, 2-21
Jerusalem Centre for Public Affairs, 2-129
Jesuit
　Centre for Social Faith & Justice, 2-8
　Fathers & Brothers, 2-7
　Missions, Cdn., 2-8
Jesus
　Christ of Latter-Day Saints, Church of, 2-3
　　Reorganized, 2-5
　Soc. of, 2-7

Jeunes
  enfants
    L'Assn cdnne pour les, 2-36
    Musique pour les, 6-40
  entreprises du Canada, 2-37
  naturalistes, Les Cercles des, 2-135
  ruraux du Qué., Assn des, 2-13
Jeunesse
  Assns, 2-36
  Canada Monde, 2-107
  Cdnne-française, Fédn de la, 2-39
  Chambre de la (Qué.), 3-204
  Conseil N.B., 3-140
  Environnement, 2-63
  Fédn., 2-37; cdnne de la, 2-36
  J'écoute, 2-167
  Regroupement tourisme, 2-186
  sourde cdnne, 2-42
  Union intle pour les livres de, 2-145
Jeunesses musicales, 6-41
Jeux
  du Canada, Conseil des, 2-173
  du Commonwealth, 2-179
  de Highland, Conseil cdn des, 2-175
  d'hiver de Qué. 2002, 2-180
  mondiaux universitaires, 2-181
  olympiques spéciaux, 2-177
  récréatifs, Fédn qué. des, 2-152
  Régie (Qué.), 3-208
Jewellers
  Assn., Cdn., 2-78
  Corp., Qué., 2-78
  Inst., Cdn. (Ont.), 9-35
  Vigilance Canada, 2-78
Jewellery
  Appraisers Assn., 2-79
  Assns., 2-78
  Exhibitions, Shows & Events 1-84
  & Giftware Magazines, 5-170
Jewish
  Assn. for Devel., 2-131
  Calendar, 1-2
  Community
    Fdn. of Greater Montréal, 2-211
    Studies, Cdn. Centre for, 2-129
  Congress, Cdn., 2-129
  Era, see Epochs
  Fedn. of Greater Toronto, 2-131
  Forms of Address (Religious), 1-35
  Fdn. of Man., 2-211
  Genealogical Soc., 2-97
  Hist'l Soc., Toronto, 2-132
  Holidays, 1-24
  Immigrant Aid Services of Canada, 2-131
  Ntl. Fund, 2-131
  Publications, see Religious Magazines
  Research, Cdn. Inst. for, 2-129
  Students' Network, N. Amer., 2-53
  Studies, Centre for (York Univ.), 9-32
  War Veterans of Canada, 2-127
  Women
    Intl. of Canada, 2-192
    Ntl. Council of, 2-192
Jewry, Assn. of Soviet, 2-128
Jews, Cdn. Council of Christians &, 2-7
Job Protection Commn., B.C., 3-112
Jockey Club of Canada, 2-179; Ont., 2-179
John Gordon Home, 2-18
John Howard Soc., 2-143
John Milton Soc. for Blind, 2-43
John P. Robarts Research Inst. (U.W.O.), 9-31
Joiners of America, United Bro. of Carpenters &, 2-207
Joint
  Bd. on Defence (Canada-U.S.A.), 3-247
  Commn., Intl., 3-77
  Council, Ntl., 3-80
  Stock Cos., Regr. of (N.S.), 3-157
Jonquière, Ville de, Govt., 4-158

Jouet, Assn cdnne du, 2-124
Jouets, Conseil cdn d'évaluation des, 2-181
Journalism
  Awards, 1-102
  Fdn., Cdn., 2-194
  Magazines, 5-170
  Programs in Univ., Assn. of Dirs. of, 2-46
Journalistes
  La Guilde des, 2-204
  de ski, Assn cdnne des, 2-176
Journalists
  Assn., Automobile, 2-25
  Awards, 1-102
  Cdn. Assn. of, 2-193
Journals, see Scholarly Publications
Journaux régionaux du Qué., Assn des, 2-145
Journey Prize, 6-61
Jubilee Ctr. for Agricl. Research, 2-15
Judaea, Cdn. Young, 2-36
Judaism, Cdn. Council for
  Conservative, 2-3
  Reform, 2-3
Judaisme, l'Inst. cdn de recherche sur le, 2-129
Judge(s), 10-, & see Addenda (see also Courts; Justices)
  Advocate General (Fed. Defence), 3-79
  Assn.
    Ont., 2-115
    Ont. Family Law, 2-115
    of Man., Prov., 2-115
  Cdn. Assn. of Prov. Court, 2-113
  Forms of Address, 1-34
  N.W.T. Assn. of Prov. Court, 2-115
  Precedence, 6-34
Judiciaires
  Assn des interprètes et des traducteurs, 2-113
  Servs, Sous-ministre adjoint (Qué.), 3-204
Judicial
  Affairs Commr., Fed., 3-66, 10-2
  Council (Govt.): B.C., 3-110; Cdn., 3-61; N.W.T., 3-152; Yukon, 3-224
  Dists. & Centres: Alta., 10-3; B.C., 10-4; Man., 10-6; N.B., 10-7; Nfld., 10-8; N.S., 10-10; Ont., 10-10; Qué., 10-15; Sask., 10-20
  Inst., Ntl., 2-115
  Officers, P.E.I., 10-15
Judo Canada, 2-179
Judy Awards, 1-95
Juges
  des Cours Provinciales, Assn cdnne des, 2-113
  provinciaux des tribunaux criminels de l'Ont., Assn des, 2-115
Juif canadien, Congrès, 2-129
Juifs, Conseil cdn des chrétiens et des, 2-7
Juive, Centre cdn pour l'étude de la communauté, 2-129
Julian Calendar, 1-2
Jung (C.G.) Fdn. of the Ont. Assn. of Jungian Analysts, 2-209
Junior
  Achievement of Canada, 2-37
  Chamber, Cdn., 7-24
  Forest Wardens of Canada, 2-75
  Leagues, Fedn. of, 2-164
Juno Awards, 1-109
Jupiter, 1-14
Juridique(s)
  Affaires, Sous-ministre adjoint (Qué.), 3-204
  Cdn sur le VIH/SIDA, Réseau, 2-17
  Commn des services (Qué.), 3-204
  Fédn des professions, 2-114
  Soc. qué. d'information, 3-204
Juristes d'expression française, Assns: Ont., 2-113; Sask., 2-113
Jurists, Intl. Commn. of, 2-114
Justice(s)
  for All, Equal, 2-167
  Assn., Cdn. Criminal, 2-113
  Canada (Fed.), 3-77
  of Canada, Chief, 10-1

Justice(s) (cont.)
  Cdn.
    Ctr. for Law &, 2-7
    Inst. for Admin. of, 2-114
  Citizens for Public, 2-102
  & Corrections, Church Council on, 2-114
  Depts. (Govt.): Quick Ref., 3-23; Alta., 3-101; Fed., 3-77; Man., 3-128; N.B., 3-137; Nfld., 3-146; N.W.T., 3-152; N.S., 3-161; Qué., 3-203; Sask., 3-216; Yukon, 3-223 (see also Attorneys General)
  Govt. Quick Ref., 3-23
  Inst. of B.C., 9-9
  Ont.
    Court of (Gen. Div.), 10-10; (Prov. Div.), 10-11; (Admin.), 10-12
    Native Council on, 2-134
    Review Project, 3-171
  of the Peace Court, N.W.T., 10-9
  pénale, Assn cdnne de, 2-113
  Quaker Com. on Jails &, 2-143
  Research, Prairie (Sask.), 9-54
  Review Project (Ont.), 3-171
  Statistics, Cdn. Ctr. for, 3-90
  Ten Days for Global, 2-110
Juvenile(s) (see also Youth; Young Offenders)
  Diabetes Fdn., Canada, 2-92
  Products Assn., Cdn., 2-123

K

Kabalarian(s), Soc. of, 2-76
Kali-shiva AIDS Services, 2-18
Kamloops
  City Govt., 4-158
  Fdn., 9-6
  Sch. Dist., 3-7
Kanada Esperanto-Asocio, 2-112
Kanadan, Dhe Internasional Union for, 2-112
Karate Assn., Ntl., 2-179
Kativik
  Comité consultatif de l'environnement (Qué.), 3-201
  Environ. Adv. Com., 3-201
Kayak
  Assn. of B.C., Sea, 2-153
  Club, Yukon Canoe &, 2-151
  d'eau vive, Fédn. qué. de canoë, 2-152
Kayaking Assn. of B.C., Whitewater, 2-153
K.B.E., 1-30
K.C.B., 1-30
K.C.M.G., 1-30
K.C.V.O., 1-30
Keewatin Community College (Man.), 9-16
Kelowna City Govt., 4-158
Kelsey Inst. (Sask.), 9-54
Kemptville Agricl. College (Ont.), 9-34
Kendo Fedn., Cdn., 2-176
Kennel Club, Cdn., 2-22
Keyano College (Alta.), 9-4
Keyin Technical College (Nfld.), 9-21
Keystone Agricl. Prdrs., 2-13
Kidney Fdn. of Canada, 2-92
Kids
  First Parents Assn., 2-167
  Help
    Fdn., 2-37
    Phone, 2-167
Kilometre Road Distances, 1-66
Kinesiology Assn., Ont., 2-163
King's College
  Alta., 9-3; Ont., 9-31
  Univ. of (N.S.), 9-22
Kings Landing Historical Settlement, (N.B.), 6-11
Kingston City Govt., 4-159
Kinsmen & Kinette Clubs of Canada, 2-164
Kitchen Cabinet Assn., Cdn., 2-123

Canadian Almanac & Directory 1997

Kitchener
   City Govt., 4-159
   & Waterloo Community Fdn., 2-211
Kiwanis
   Intl., 2-164
   Music Festivals: N.S., 6-40; Toronto, 6-40
Klondike Days Assn., Edmonton, 2-66
Knighthood, Orders of, 1-30
Knights, 1-30
   of Columbus, 2-76
   Hospitallers, 2-76
   of Malta, 2-76
   of Pythias, 2-76
Knox College (Toronto), 9-31
Kodokan Black Belt Assn., Cdn., 2-179
Korea Veterans Assn. of Canada, 2-127
Korean
   Businessmen's Assn., Ont., 2-131
   Govt. (South), 3-227, 3-240
   Magazines, 5-192
KPMG Charitable Fdn., 2-211
Kwantlen University College, 9-8

L

La Leche League, 2-36
La Marsh Research Program on Violence & Conflict Resolution (York Univ.), 9-32
La Pocatière, Inst. de techn. agro-alimentaire de, 9-48
Labor
   Amer. Fedn. of, 2-195
   Zionist Alliance, 2-131
Laboratories
   Cdn. Assn. for Env. Analytical, 2-60
   Ont. Assn. of Medical, 2-101
Laboratory
   Animal Science, Cdn. Assn. for, 2-21
   Centre for Disease Control, (Fed.), 3-71
   Suppliers Assn., Cdn., 2-123
   Technologists
      Cdn. Soc. of, 2-90
      College of Medical (Ont.), 2-91
      Congress, see Medical Exhibitions
      Education (Ont.), 9-35
Laborers', Intl. Union of N. Amer., 2-203
Labour
   Adjustment Review Bd. (Fed.), 3-73
   Bds. (Govt.): Man., 3-129; N.B., 3-133
   Br./Div., N.B., 3-133
   Cdn. Fedn. of, 2-195
   Code, Canada, 3-55
   Congress, Cdn., 2-195
   Day, 1-24
   Depts. (Govt.): Quick Ref., 3-23; Alta., 3-102; B.C., 3-117; Fed. (Human Resources), 3-72; Man., 3-129; N.B., 3-132; Nfld., 3-143; N.S., 3-162; Ont., 3-180; Qué., 3-209; Sask., 3-218
   Federations, 2-195/196
   Force
      Development Bds. (Govt.): B.C., 3-117; Cdn., 3-73
      Statistics, 1-51
   Govt. Quick Ref., 3-23
   History, Cdn. Com. on, 2-110
   Info., Bur. of (Fed.), 3-72
   Legislation, Cdn. Assn. of Admrs. of, 2-110
   Magazines, 5-185
   & Manpower, Adv. Council, Qué., 3-209
   Market
      Policy: Fed., 3-72; Ont., 3-177
      & Productivity
         Ctr., Cdn., 2-34
         Commn., Public Sector (Ont.), 3-179
      Servs. (Fed.), 3-72
   Media, Cdn. Assn. of, 2-110
   Org., Intl., 3-247
   Program (Fed.), 3-72
   Publications, 5-185

Labour (cont.)
   Relations
      Assns., 2-110/111
      Bds. (Govt.): Alta., 3-102; B.C., 3-117; Canada, 3-55; Nfld., 3-143; N.S., 3-162; Ont., 3-181; P.E.I., 3-192; Sask., 3-218
      Employment &, Dept. (Nfld.), 3-143
   Servs. Div. (Man.), 3-129
   Standards Agencies (Govt.): Nfld., 3-143; N.W.T., 3-154; N.S., 3-162; Qué., 3-209; Sask., 3-218 (see also Employment Standards; Work Standards)
   Statistics (Fed.), 1-51, 3-89
   Unions, 2-195
Labourers' Assn., Interprov., 2-197
Labrador (see also Newfoundland)
   & Aboriginal Affairs Secretariat, 3-141
   College of Applied Arts, Tech. & Continuing Educ., 9-20
   Inst. of Northern Studies (Memorial Univ.), 9-20
Lacrosse Assn., Cdn., 2-176
Lacs, Fédn des assns pour la protection des, 2-63
Lactel, Groupe, 2-13
Lactière du Canada, Conseil ntl de l'industrie, 2-15
Ladies
   Golf Assn., Cdn., 2-179; Ont., 2-176
   Orange Benevolent Assn., 2-76
Laidlaw Fdn., 2-211
Lait
   Commn cdnne du, 3-57
   Fédn des producteurs de, (Qué.), 2-15, 3-198
Laitiers du Canada, Producteurs, 2-13
Laitière du Qué, Conseil de l'industrie, 2-14
Lake of the Woods Control Bd. (Man.), 3-130
Lakehead Univ. (Ont.), 9-28
Lakeland College (Alta.), 9-4
Lambton College AA & T (Ont.), 9-33
Lamp & Fixture Mfrs. Assn., Cdn., 2-123
Land(s)
   Allocations Appeal Bd., Sask., 3-212
   Area, Canada, 1-63
   Brs./Divs. (Govt.): Alta., 3-99; Man., 3-129; Nfld., 3-145; Yukon, 3-222
   Claims (Aboriginal Peoples), Govt.: Alta., 3-99; Fed., 3-73; B.C., 3-108; Yukon, 3-225
   Compensation Bd. (Alta.), 3-96
   Commr. (Ont.), 3-184
   Co., Canada, 3-55
   Corp., Ont., 3-182
   Crown, see Crown Lands
   Depts. (Govt.), Nfld., 3-145
   Economists, Assn. of Ont., 2-182
   Farm, see Farm Lands
   Forces (Ntl. Defence), 3-79
   Govt. Servs. & Lands (Nfld.), 3-145
   Information Centre (Man.), 3-129
   Mgmt. Brs./Divs. (Govt.): B.C., 3-113; N.S., 3-163; Sask., 3-214
   & Parks, Min. of Environment (B.C.), 3-112
   Reclamation Assn., Cdn., 2-61
   Registrars (Ont.), 3-174
   Resources, Govt. Quick Ref., 3-24
   Service (Alta.), 3-99
   Soc., Preservation of Agricl., 2-15
   Surveyors Assns., 2-182
   Titles Registrars (Govt.): Quick Ref., 3-24; Alta., 3-103; B.C., 3-110; Man., 3-128; Yukon, 3-224 (see also Property Registration; Deeds; Real Property Registration)
   & Trusts Servs. Sector (Fed. Indian & Northern Affairs), 3-74
   Value Appraisal Commn., Man., 3-126
   & Water Planning Sec. (N.B.), 3-135
Landlord & Tenant, Regs., Govt. Quick Ref., 3-25
Landlords Assn., Man., 2-102
Landrace Swine Breeders, Assn., Cdn., 2-20
Lands, see Land(s)

Landscape Architects
   Assns., 2-98/99
   Canada, 2-99
   Cdn. Soc. of, 2-99
Landscaping (see also Flowers, Gardening)
   Exhibitions, Shows & Events, 1-82
   Magazines, 5-170
Langara College (B.C.), 9-9
Langley
   Sch. Dist. (B.C.), 9-6
   District Govt., 4-159
Language
   Arts, Cdn. Council of Teachers of English &, 2-48
   Assns., 2-111
   Awards, see Culture (see also Educational Awards)
   Council, Sweetgrass First Nations, 2-112
   Educ. Centres in Ont., 9-35
   Interpreters, Assn. of Visual, 2-111
   Planning, Intl. Centre for Research on, 2-112
   Statistics, 1-50
   Studies, Cdn. Assn. for Commonwealth Lit. &, 2-111
   Teachers, Cdn. Assn. of Second, 2-48
   Workshop (Ont.), 9-35
Languages
   Awards, see Culture
   Commr. (Govt.): Fed., 3-84; N.W.T., 3-150
   of Instruction Commn. of Ont., 3-177
   Man. Assn. for Promotion of Ancestral, 2-112
   Sask. Org. for Heritage, 2-112
Langue(s)
   française
      Assemblée intle des parlementaires de, 2-38
      Assn
         cdnne d'éduc. de, 2-45
         cdnne de la radio et télévision de, 2-29
         cdnne des rédacteurs agricoles, 2-193
         des médecins de, 2-82
      Conseil de la (Qué.), 3-200
      Fédn intle des écrivains de, 2-194
      Office de la (Qué.), 3-200
   officielles, Commn aux (Fed.), 3-84
   seconde(s)
      Assn cdnne des professeurs de, 2-48
      Conseil des programmes de, 2-51
      au Qué., Soc. pour la promotion de l'enseignement de l'anglais, 2-54
Lao du Canada, Fédn des assns, 2-130
Large
   Public Libraries of Ont., Chief Execs. of, 2-119
   Urban Public Libraries, Council of Admrs. of, 2-119
LaSalle, Ville de, Govt., 4-159
Laser Class Assn., Intl. (N. Amer.), 2-152
Last Post Fund, 2-164
Latin America
   & Caribbean Centre for Research on, 2-156; (York Univ.), 9-32
   Resource Centre, Canada-, 2-107
   Secretary of State (Fed.), 3-69
Latin American
   Cdn. Business Assn., 2-188
   Working Group, 2-131
Latvian
   Business & Profl. Assn., Cdn., 2-129
   Magazines, 5-192
   Ntl. Fedn. in Canada, 2-129
Laubach Literacy Canada, 2-112
Laundry
   & Dry Cleaning Magazines, 5-170
   & Linen Inst., Cdn., 2-67
Laurentian
   Bank of Canada, 7-2
   Pilotage Auth., 3-78
   Univ. of Sudbury (Ont.), 9-29
Laurentides, Admin de pilotage des, 3-78
L'Autre Parole, 2-165
Laval
   Univ. (Qué.), 9-46
   Ville de, Govt., 4-159

Law (*see also* Civil Law, Commercial Law, Property Law, etc.)
  Assn(s)., 2-113
    Cdn.
      Environmental, 2-61
      Maritime, 2-114
    County of York, 2-114
  Awards, *see* Legal Awards
  Cdn.
    Assn. on Competition, 2-113
    Council on Intl., 2-113
    Inst. of Resources, 2-61
  Centre (Alta.), Environmental, 2-63
  Clerks of Ont., Inst. of, 2-114
  Courts Educ. Soc. of B.C., 3-110
  Deans, Council of Cdn., 2-47
  Editors, Fed., 10-1
  Enforcement
    Brs./Divs. (Govt.): Alta., 3-102; Man. (Agency), 3-129; N.B., 3-139; N.W.T., 3-152; Sask., 3-217
    Officers' Assn. (Ont.), Municipal, 2-115
  Faculties/Schs., Index to, 9-56
  Firms in: Alta., 10-22; B.C., 10-33; Canada, 10-22; Man., 10-43; N.B., 10-45; Nfld., 10-47; N.W.T., 10-47; N.S., 10-47; Ont., 10-49; P.E.I., 10-93; Qué., 10-93; Sask., 10-100; Yukon, 10-103
  Fdns.: Alta., 2-113, 3-102; B.C., 2-114; Cdn. Petroleum, 2-114; Man., 2-115; N.B., 2-115; Nfld., 2-114; N.S., 2-114; N.W.T., 2-115; Ont., 2-114; P.E.I., 2-114; Sask., 2-114; Yukon, 2-116, 3-224
  for the Future Fund, 2-211
  & Justice, Cdn. Ctr. for, 2-7
  Libraries, Cdn. Assn. of, 2-117; Montréal, 2-116
  Ntl. Assn. of Women & the, 2-192
  & Policy, Cdn. Inst. for Environmental, 2-61
  & Public Policy, Ctr. for Research on Public (York Univ.), 9-32
  Publications, *see* Legal Publications
  Reform
    Agencies of Canada, Fedn. of, 2-114
    Commns. (Govt.): B.C., 3-110; Man., 3-129; Ont., 3-172; Qué., 3-204; Sask. 3-217
  School, People's, 2-115
  & Soc. Assn., Cdn., 2-114
  Soc(s.), 2-114/115
    Cdn. Canon, 2-113
    Fedn. of, 2-114
    of Yukon, 3-224
Lawn Bowls Canada, 2-152
Lawrence College Inc. (Nfld.), 9-21
Lawyers, 10-22
  for Social Responsibility, 2-167
  Tech. for (Trade Show), 1-87
Le Gardeur, Commn scolaire de (Qué.), 9-42
Leadership in Educl. Admin., Ont. Council for, 2-53
Learner Assistance Div., 3-95
Learning
  Academy of: Man., 9-16; Nfld., 9-20
  Assn. of Ont., Rural, 2-54
  Commonwealth of, 2-51
  Disabilities, Assns., 2-52
  Enrichment Fdn., 2-52
  Inst. Advanced (Ont.), 9-35
  Ont. Council for University Lifelong, 2-53
  Opportunities for Women, Cdn. Congress for, 2-191
Leasing Assn., Cdn. Finance &, 2-69
Leather
  Magazines, 5-170
  Shows, *see* Fashion
Leathergoods, Handbags & Accessories Assn. of Canada, Luggage, 2-68
Legal
  Aid Agencies & Commns. (Govt.): Quick Ref., 3-25; Alta., 3-102; Man., 3-129; N.B., 3-138; Nfld., 3-148; N.S., 3-162; P.E.I., 3-192; Sask., 3-220; Yukon, 3-224
  Assns. & Law Socs., 2-113
  Awards, 1-103

Legal (cont.)
  Conventions, 1-87
  Court Interpreters Assn., 2-113
  Directory, 10-22
  Educ.
    & Action Fund, Women's, 2-193
    Assn., Community (Man.), 2-114; Sask. Public, 2-116
    Ont., Community, 2-114
    Soc. of Alta., 2-115; B.C., 2-114
    Socs., Public, 2-116
  Info. Assn.
    of Nfld., Public, 2-116
    of P.E.I., Community, 2-114
  Journals & Magazines, 5-170
  Medicine
    Cdn. College of, 2-85
    Lab., Qué., 3-208
  Network, Cdn. HIV/AIDS, 2-17
  Research Fdn. for, 2-114
  Services
    Brs./Divs. (Govt.): B.C., 3-110; N.B., 3-138; N.W.T. (Bd.), 3-152; N.S., 3-162; P.E.I., 3-192; Qué., 3-204; Yukon, 3-224
    Commn., Qué., 3-204
    Sector (Fed.), 3-77
    Soc.: B.C., 3-110; Yukon, 3-224
  Support Staff, Cdn. Assn. of, 2-113
  Tech., Cdn. Soc. for Adv. of, 2-114
Légale, Serv. de médecine (Qué.), 3-208
Legion, Royal Cdn., 2-127
Legislative
  Assemblies (Govt.): Quick Ref., 3-30; Alta., 3-93; B.C., 3-106; Man., 3-121; N.B., 3-131; Nfld., 3-141; N.W.T., 3-150; N.S., 3-155; Ont., 3-165; P.E.I., 3-187; Qué. (Ntl. Assembly), 3-194; Sask., 3-210; Yukon, 3-221
  Forms of Address, 1-33
  Servs., Br. (Fed.), 3-77
Legumes
  Assn cdnne la distribution de fruits et, 2-73
  Fédn des producteurs de (Qué.), 3-198
Leisure (*see also* Sports, Recreation)
  Assn. for Handicapped Persons, Qué., 2-41
  Craft Regs., Govt. Quick Ref., 3-25
  Ont. Research Council on, 2-152
Lending Services (Govt.), *see* Loan(s)
Length, Measurements, 1-62
Lent, 1-24
Lèpre, La Mission évangelique centre le, 2-93
Leprosy
  Mission Canada, 2-93
  Relief, 2-169
Lesbian & Gay
  Archives, Cdn., 2-98
  Rights of Ont., Coalition for, 2-98
Lesbians Everywhere, Equality for Gays &, 2-98
Leslie M. Frost Natural Resources Centre, 3-184
Lester B. Pearson College of the Pacific (B.C.), 9-9
Lethbridge
  City Govt., 4-160
  Community College, 9-4
  Univ. of, 9-3
Lettermail Rates, 1-45
Lettres, bibliothèques et arts, Dir. (Qué.), 3-199
Leukemia Research Fund, 2-157
Libano-cdnne, Fdn de l'amitié, 2-130
Liberal
  Parties & Assns., 2-141
  Party, Office of (Man.), 3-121
Libérations conditionnelles, Commn
  ntle des, 3-80
  qué. des, 3-208
Libertel de la Capitale Ntle, 2-104
Libertés civiles, Assn cdnne des, 2-102
Libraires du Qué., Assn des, 2-144
Librairie ancienne du Canada, Assn de la, 2-23
Librarians Assns., 2-116

Libraries, 5-1
  & Archives, Assn. of Cdn. Map, 2-116
  Assn(s.), 2-116
    of B.C. Govt., 2-119
    Health, 2-118
    Ont. Hospital, 2-120
    Special, 2-120
  Awards, 1-103
  Govt. Quick Ref, *see* Bibliographic Servs., 3-4
  Brs./Divs. (Govt.): Alta., 3-96; N.B., 3-138; Ont., 3-172; P.E.I., 3-190; Yukon, 3-222
  Cdn. Assn. of
    College & University, 2-117
    Law, 2-117
    Music, 2-117
    Public, 2-117
    Research, 2-117
    Special, 2-117
  Council
    Alta. Govt., 2-116
    of Federal, 2-119
    Man. Govt., 2-119
    N.S. Govt., 2-119
    Ont. Govt., 2-120
    Sask. Govt., 2-120
  Film (Govt. Quick Ref.), 3-18
  Govt. Depts. in Charge of, 5-1
  In: Alta., 5-2; B.C., 5-12; Man., 5-22; N.B., 5-28; Nfld., 5-31; N.W.T., 5-34; N.S., 5-35; Ont., 5-39; P.E.I., 5-84; Qué., 5-84; Sask., 5-105; Yukon, 5-112
  Legislative, *see* Legislative Assemblies
  in Occupational Safety & Health, 2-118
  Public, *see* Public Libraries
  Soc. of North America, Art, 2-116
  Special, *see* Special Libraries
Library
  Assn(s.), 2-116
    of Alta., 2-119
    Atlantic Provs., 2-117
    B.C., 2-117
    Cdn., 2-118
    Cdn. School, 2-119
    Church (Ont.), 2-119
    Manitoba, 2-119
    N.W.T., 2-119
    N.S., 2-119
    Ont., 2-120
    Qué., 2-116
    Sask., 2-120
  Awards, 1-104
  Bds. Assn. of: N.S., 2-119
  & Information Tech. Assn., Ont., 2-120
  National, 5-1
  of Parliament, 3-78
  Schools, Cdn. Council of, 2-118
  Science, Index to Faculties/Schs., 9-56
  Services (Govt.): Quick Ref., 3-4; Man., 3-123; Ont., 3-173
  Technicians Assns.: Alta., 2-116; Man., 2-119; Ont., 2-119; Sask., 2-120
  Trustees Assns.: B.C., 2-117; Cdn., 2-118; Man., 2-119; N.B., 2-119; Ont., 2-120; Sask., 2-120
Licence(s)
  Dog, *see* Animal Control
  Drivers' (Govt. Quick Ref.), 3-12
  Suspension Appeal Bds.: Man., 3-127; Ont., 3-187
Licensing Div., Driver & Vehicle (Man.), 3-126
Lieutenants Governor: Alta., 3-92; B.C., 3-105; Man., 3-120; N.B., 3-131; Nfld., 3-140; N.S., 3-154; Ont., 3-164; P.E.I., 3-187; Qué., 3-193; Sask., 3-210
  Boards of Review, *see* Boards of Review
  Forms of Address, 1-33
Life
  Alliance for, 2-154
  & Health Insurance Assn., Cdn., 2-105
  Insurance
    Govt. Quick Ref., 3-22
    Inst. of Canada, 2-105

Life
    Insurance (cont.)
        Mgrs. Assn. of Canada, 2-105
        Medical Officers Assn., Cdn., 2-105
        Soc., Cdn. Foresters, 2-105
        Statistics, 1-57
    Intermediaries Assn. (Qué.), 2-104
    League for (Man.), 2-154
    Saving Soc., Royal, 2-55
    Underwriters
        Assn. of Canada, 2-106
        Cdn. Inst. of Chartered, 2-106
Lifeboat Inst., Cdn., 2-55
Lifeforce Fdn., 2-212
Lifestyle Research Inst., Cdn. Fitness &, 2-150
Light Infantry Assn., Princess Patricia's Cdn., 2-127
Lighting
    Directors, Canada, Soc. of TV, 2-29
    Exhibitions, Shows & Events, 1-87
    Magazines, 5-171
Limousin Assn., Cdn., 2-20
Lincoln County Bd. of Educ. (Ont.), 9-24
Linen Inst., Cdn. Laundry &, 2-67
Linguistic Assn(s.), 2-111; Cdn., 2-111
Linguistique
    Assn cdnne de, 2-111
    Centre intl de recherche en aménagement, 2-112
    Secrétariat à la politique (Qué.), 3-200
Linoleum Workers of America, United, 2-208
Lionel Collectors Assn. of Canada, 2-152
Lionel Gelber Prize, 1-106
Lions
    Clubs Intl., 2-165
    Soc. for Children with Disabilities, B.C., 2-164
Liquor
    Appeal Bd., B.C., 3-110
    Bd. Employees Unions: Ont., 2-204; Qué., 2-206
    Bds., Corps. & Commns. (Govt.): Quick Ref., 3-25;
        Alta., 3-100; B.C., 3-110; Man., 3-123; N.B., 3-138;
        Nfld., 3-143; N.W.T., 3-154; N.S., 3-163; Ont., 3-
        175; P.E.I., 3-191; Qué., 3-208; Sask., 3-218;
        Yukon, 3-224
    Regulations, 1-41
Literacy
    Canada, Laubach, 2-112
    Devel. Council (Nfld.), 3-142
    Fdn.
        ABC Canada, 2-111
        Cdn. Give the Gift of, 2-111
    Minister
        Responsible (Fed.), 3-73
        of State, N.B., 3-135
    Movement for Cdn., 2-112
    Secretariat, Ntl., 3-72
    World, 2-113
Literary
    & Artistic Assn., Cdn., 2-111
    Awards & Prizes, 1-104 (see also Culture)
    & Hist'l Soc. of Qué., 2-97
    Magazines, 5-185 (see also Scholarly Publications)
    Manuscript Collection, 5-1
    Press Group, 2-145
    Translators Assn., 2-112
Literature
    Assn(s)., 2-111
        Cdn. Comparative, 2-111
    Awards, see Literary; Culture
    Centre for Comparative (U. of T.), 9-30
    & Lang. Studies, Cdn. Assn. for Commonwealth, 2-111
    Qué. Soc. for the Promo. of Eng. Lang., 2-112
    Research Serv., Cdn., 5-1
Lithuanian
    Cdn.
        Community, 2-129
        Fdn., 2-212
    Cdn. Roman Catholic Cultural Soc., 2-131
    Magazines, 5-192

Littéraire(s)
    et artistique cdnne, Assn, 2-111
    Assn des traducteurs, 2-112
    Fédn qué. du loisir, 2-194
Liver Fdn., Cdn., 2-87
Livestock (see also Agriculture)
    Assns., 2-19
    Financial Protection Bd., Ont., 3-170
    Incentives, N.B., 3-134
    Insurance Commn., N.S., 3-156
    Medicines Adv. Com., Ont., 3-170
    Owners' Compensation Bd. (Nfld.), 3-144
    Records Corp., Cdn., 2-20
    Statistics, 1-56
    Tech. Dir. (Ont.), 3-169
    & Veterinary Operations Br. (Sask.), 3-212
Livre(s)
    Assn
        ntle des éditeurs de, 2-144
        québécoise des salons du, 2-144
    cdn, Assn pour l'exportation du, 2-144
    Guilde cdnne des relieurs et des artisans du, 2-144
    de jeunesse, Union intle pour les, 2-145
Loan(s)
    Farm: Fed., 3-66; N.S., 3-156; Ont., 3-169; P.E.I., 3-189
    Fisheries: N.S., 3-160; P.E.I., 3-189
    Mortgage &, Cos., 7-4
    Small Business: Admin. (Fed.), 3-75; P.E.I., 3-189
    Statistics, 1-57
    & Trust Corps. Br. (Ont.), 3-178
Lobbyists, Consultant, 7-34
Local
    Government
        Administrators of Alta., 2-80
        Brs./Divs. (Govt.): Alta., 3-103; B.C., 3-118; Man.,
            3-130; N.B., 3-138; Ont., 3-161
        Districts, Man., 4-23
    Official Health Agencies, Assn. of, 2-82
Locks (Transp.), 1-64
Locomotive
    Engrs., Intl. Broth. of, 2-202
    Soc., Vintage, 2-23
Logement
    Régie du (Qué.), 3-197
    Soc. cdnne d'hyopthèques et de, 3-55
Logging
    Health & Safety Assn. Inc., Qué., 2-159
    Soc., Cdn. Well, 2-75
Logiciel, Conseil des ressources humaines du, 2-104
Logiciels, Alliance cdnne contre le vol de, 2-103
Logistics
    Exhibitions, Shows & Events, 1-87
    Inst., Cdn. Profl., 2-188
Lois et règlements, Dir. de la réfonte des (Qué.), 3-204
Loisir(s)
    et la danse, Assn cdnne pour la santé, l'éducation
        physique et les, 2-174
    Fdn. du personnel des éstablissements de, 2-196
    intramuros, Assn cdnne de, 2-150
    littéraire du Qué., 2-194
    /parcs, Assn cdnne des, 2-150
    pour personnes handicapées, Assn qué., 2-41
    Qué., Regroupement, 2-153
London (Ont.)
    Bd. of Educ., 9-24
    City Govt., 4-160
    Community Fdn., 2-212
Long Distance Riding Assn., Cdn., 2-150
Long Term Care (see also Acute Care Servs.)
    Assns., 2-100
Longshoremen's
    Assn., Intl., 2-202
    & Warehousemen's Union, Intl., 2-203
Longueuil
    Baron de, 1-30
    Ville de, Govt., 4-160
Loteries
    d'état, Assn Intle de, 2-70

Loteries (cont.)
    Soc. des (Qué.), 3-202
Lotteries
    Br., Alta. (Liquor & Gaming), 3-100
    Commn., P.E.I., 3-193
    Govt. Quick Ref., 3-25
    Intl. Assn. of State, 2-70
Lottery
    Appeal Bd. (Yukon), 3-224
    Collectors Soc., 2-152
    Corps.: Atlantic, 3-136; B.C., 3-115; Ont., 3-176;
        Qué., 3-202; Yukon, 3-222
Lovelight Intl. Fdn., 2-212
Low Vision Assn. of Ont., 2-43
Lower
    Churchill Devel. Corp. Ltd., 3-148
    Red River Valley Water Commn., 3-130
Loyalist College, AA & T (Ont.), 9-33
Loyalists Assn., United Empire, 2-98
LSC Language Studies Canada (Ont.), 9-35
Lubrication Engrs., Soc. of Tribologists &, 2-59
Luge Assn., Cdn., 2-176
Luggage
    Leathergoods, Handbags & Accessories Assn. of
        Canada, 2-68
    Shows, see Fashion
Lumber
    & Bldg. Materials Assn. of Ont., 2-32
    Bur., Maritime, 2-75
    Dealers Assn., Wholesale, 2-75
    Industries Publications, Forest &, 5-167
    Mfrs. Assns.: Cariboo, 2-74; Ont., 2-75; Qué., 2-74
    Standards Accred'n. Bd., Cdn., 2-74
Lumbermen's Assns.: Cdn., 2-74; Western Retail, 2-32
Lunar Tables, 1-8/13
Lung Assns., 2-87
Lupus Canada, 2-93
Luther College (Regina), 9-54
Lutheran
    Church, Evangelical, 2-4
        Estonian, 2-4
    Seminary, Waterloo (Wilfrid Laurier), 9-32
    Theological Seminary (Sask.), 9-54
    World Relief, Cdn., 2-7
Lutte
    amateur, Assn de, 2-173
    contre l'alcoolisme et les toxicomanies, Ctr. cdn, 3-57
Lyceum Club, 2-193

M

MacBride Museum (Yukon), 6-29
Macdonald College (McGill), 9-46
Macedonian
    Assn., Pan, 2-132
    Human Rights Movement, 2-102
    Magazines, 5-192
Machine(s)
    aratoires, Assn des marchands (Qué.), 2-65
    Assn sectorielle - Fabrication d'équipement de
        transport et, 2-159
    et des mécanismes, Commn cdnne pour la théorie
        des, 2-156
    Tool Distrs. Assn., Cdn., 2-66
Machinerie lourde
    Assn des propriétaires de, 2-65
    Union des opérateurs de, 2-207
Machinery
    Assns., 2-65
    & Equip. Mfrs. Assn. of Canada, 2-66
    Maintenance Magazines, 5-171
    Manufacturers' Assn.
        Cdn.
            Custom Engineered, 2-66
            Packaging & Printing, 2-66
            Pulp & Paper, 2-66
            Compressed Air & Gas, 2-66

Machinery (cont.)
    & Mfg. Exhibitions, Shows & Events, 1-87
    Underwriters' Assn., Cdn. Boiler &, 2-104
Machining Assn., Cdn. Tooling &, 2-124
Machinists & Aerospace Wkrs., Intl. Assn. of, 2-202
Mack Nursing Educ. Ctr. (Niagara College), 9-33
MacKenzie Art Gallery (Sask.), 6-34
Maçonnerie en béton, Assn cdnne des manufacturiers de, 2-30
Maçons, Synd. indép. des briqueteurs et des, 2-198
MADD Canada, 2-10
Magazine
    Awards, 1-103 (*see also* Journalism; Literary Arts)
    Editors, Cdn. Soc. of, 2-194
    Index, 5-148
    Publishers Assn., Cdn., 2-145
Magazines, 5-159 (*see also* Publications) (& *see* Addenda)
    Business, 5-159
    Canada (Assn.), 2-145
    Consumer, 5-177
    Ethnic, 5-191
    Farm, 5-193
    Index to, 5-148
    Scholarly, 5-195
    Trade Shows, 1-87
    University, 5-197
MAGFRAT Fdn., 2-212
Maggie's, 2-18
Magistrature
    Conseil de la: Cdn., 3-61; Qué., 3-204
    fédérale, Bur. de commissaire à la, 3-66
Magnetic Declination, 1-22
Mahatma Gandhi Cdn. Fdn. for World Peace, 2-109
Mail Users, Ntl. Assn. of Major, 2-11
Mailing Rates & Info., 1-43
Main d'oeuvre
    Conseil consultatif du travail et de la (Qué.), 3-209
    Soc. qué. de dével. de la ((Qué.), 3-209
Maine-Anjou Assn., Cdn., 2-20
Maintenance
    Assn., Custodial &, 2-200
    of Way Employees, Broth. of, 2-198
Maires francophones, Assn intle des, 2-79
Maison
    Amaryllis, 2-18
    d'Hérelle, 2-18
    Ludovic, 2-18
    du Parc, 2-18
Maîtres
    Couvreurs du Qué., Assn des, 2-32
    électriciens du Qué., Corp. des, 2-54
    photographes du Qué., 2-140
    de poste et adjoints, Assn cdnne des, 2-199
Major
    Cities & Towns, 4-153
    Industrial Accidents Council of Canada, 2-160
    League Baseball Players' Assn., 2-203
Makivik Corp., 2-133
Maladie(s)
    du coeur, Fdn des, 2-92
    génétiques, Réseau cdn sur les, 2-155
    infectieuses, Soc. cdnne de, 2-86
    inflammatoires de l'intestin, Fdn cdnne des, 2-91
    mentale, Fédn des familles et amis de la personne atteinte de, 2-125
    thyroidiennes, Fdn pour les, 2-94
Malaspina College, B.C., 9-9
Malaysia (Overseas Schs.), 9-40
Malentendants cdns, Assn des, 2-42
Malpractice Prevention Assn., Cdn., 2-88
Malta, Cdn. Assn., Sovereign Military Order of, 2-76
Maltese Cdn. Soc. of Toronto, 2-131
Malting Barley Research Inst., Brewing, 2-72
Man & Nature, Manitoba Museum of, 6-8
Management
    Accountants Socs., 2-9, 9-34

Management (cont.)
    Assn(s)., 2-120
    Cdn.
        Public Personnel, 2-121
        Research, 2-155
    Banff Centre for, 9-4
    Bds., Secretariat: N.W.T., 3-150; Ont., 3-181; Yukon, 3-223
    Cdn. Inst.
        of, 2-121
        for Development, 2-140
        for Organizations, 2-121
    Centre of AMA Intl., Cdn., 2-121
    Consultants, Insts. of Certified, 2-121/122
    Devel. Cdn. Centre for (Fed.), 3-57
    Faculties/Schs., Index to, 9-56
    Inst.
        of Profl., 2-122
        Western Cdn. (Sask.), 9-55
    & Profl. Employees Soc., 2-203
    Research, Ntl. Ctr. for (U.W.O.), 9-31
Managers, Cdn. Inst. of Certified Admin., 2-121
Mandataires, Dir. gén. (Qué.), 3-206
Manic Depressive Assn.
    of Metro Toronto, 2-125
    of Ont., Depressive &, 2-125
Manitoba
    Aquaria in, 6-45
    Archives in, 5-113
    Art Galleries in, 6-31
    Bds. of Trade in, 7-78
    Botanical Gardens in, 6-46
    Chambers of Commerce in, 7-28
    Chiefs, Assembly of, 2-132
    Cities & Towns in, 4-18
    Community Colleges in, 9-16
    Courts & Judges in, 10-6
    Education in, 9-13
    Federal Schs. in, 9-14
    Flag & Coat of Arms, **10**
    FreeNets, 5-233
    Government in, 3-120
    Hospitals in, 8-11
    Infrastructural Secretariat, Canada-, 3-130
    Institutional Schs., 9-15
    Law Firms in, 10-43
    Libraries in, 5-22
    Lobbyists in, 7-36
    Local Govt. Districts in, 4-23
    Meeting, Conference, & Event Planners in, 1-69
    Municipal Govt. in, 4-18
    Museums in, 6-8
    Native Schs. in, 9-14
    Newspapers in, 5-135
    Nursing Homes in, 8-13
    Online Service Providers, 5-231
    Private Schs. in, 9-16
    Sch. Divs. in, 9-13
    Universities in, 9-15
    Zoos in, 6-44
Manoeuvres interprov., Assn des, 2-197
Manpower (*see also* Labour; Employment; Unemployment)
    Adv. Council on Labour & (Qué.), 3-209
    Devel., Qué., 3-209
Manuals Mgmt. Assn., Forms &, 2-143
Manufactured Housing
    Assn., Alta. & Sask., 2-102
    Inst., Cdn., 2-101
Manufacturers (*see also* Industry)
    Assn(s)., 2-65, 2-122
        Automotive Parts, 2-25
    & Exporters, Alliance of, 2-122
Manufacturing
    Assns., 2-65, 2-122
    Companies, Cdn.
        General, 7-43
        Industrial, 7-44

Manufacturing (cont.)
    Exhibitions, Events & Shows, 1-87
    Govt. Quick Ref., *see* Industry
    & Processing Industries (Fed. Govt.), 3-75
    Statistics, 1-57
    Tech., Inst. for Advanced (NRC), 3-81
Manulife Bank of Canada, 7-2
Manutention du Qué., Assn de, 2-123
Many Island Pipe Lines Ltd., 3-220
Map(s)
    Branch (Alta.), 3-99
    Govt. Quick Ref., 3-26
    Libraries & Archives, Assn of Cdn., 2-116
    Magnetic Declination, 1-22
    Montréal, Communauté urbaine et région, 4-175
    Office, Canada, 3-83
    Ottawa-Carleton, Reg'l Municipality, 4-174
    Outaouais, Communauté urbaine et région, 4-174
    Star, 1-15
    Time Zones: Cdn., 1-3; U.S., 1-4; Intl., 1-5
    Toronto, Metro & region, 4-175
    Vancouver, Greater Reg'l Dist., 4-174
Maple
    Ridge Sch. Dist. (B.C.), 9-6
    Syrup
        Inst., Intl., 2-73
        Mktg. Bd., Qué., 3-198
        Prodrs.
            Assn Ont., 2-73
            of N.B., Cooperative of, 2-14
Mapping (*see also* Surveys & Mapping)
    Assns., 2-182
    Brs./Divs. (Govt.): Alta., 3-98; Fed., 3-83; Nfld., 3-148
    (*see also* Surveys & Mapping; Land Surveys; Legal Surveys Div.)
Maraîchers
    Fédn des producteurs du (Qué.), 3-198
    de l'Ont., L'Assn des fruitculteurs et des, 2-15
Marathon canadien de ski, 2-176
Marble Assn., Terrazzo Tile &, 2-33
March of Dimes, 2-42
Marchands des machines aratoires, Assn des, 2-65
Marche
    des dix sous, 2-42
    Fédn qué. de la, 2-152
Marché(s)
    Agricoles et alimentaires, Régie des (Qué.), 3-198
    de Capitaux (Qué.), 3-202
    du travail et de la productivité, Centre cdn du, 2-34
Marconi, Assn des ingénieurs et des scientifiques, 2-200
Marfan Assn., Cdn., 2-87
Marina Operators Assn., Ont., 2-152
Marine
    Aquaria, 6-45
    Atlantic Inc., 3-78
    Biosciences, Inst. for (NCR), 3-81
    Communications, Cdn. Ctr. for, 2-124
    Dealers Assn., Mid-Canada, 2-124
    Dynamics, Inst. for (NCR), 3-81
    Engrg., Cdn. Inst. of, 2-59
    Exhibitions, Shows & Events, 1-87
    Geosciences Br. (Fed. Govt.), 3-82
    Heritage Fdn., Great Lakes, 2-210
    Inst. of Memorial Univ., Fisheries & (Nfld.), 9-20
    Magazines, 5-176
    Manufacturers Assn., Ntl., 2-124
    marchande, Guilde de la, 2-199
    Navigation, Govt. Quick Ref., 3-26
    Navigational Servs. Br. (Cdn. Coast Guard), 3-67
    Officers Union, Cdn., 2-199
    Pilots Assn., 2-199
    Resources, Dir. (N.S.), 3-160
    Safety (Fed.), 3-91
    Science & Surveys, Bayfield Inst. for, 3-68
    Sciences, *see* Oceanography
    Trades Assns., 2-124
    Underwriters
        Assn. of B.C., 2-104; Cdn. Bd. of, 2-104

Canadian Almanac & Directory 1997

Marine (cont.)
    Wkrs.
        Fedn., 2-203
        Union, Ferry & (B.C.), 2-198
Mariners Assn., Cdn., 2-150
Marins cdns, Synd. Intl des, 2-206
Marionnettistes, Assn qué. des, 6-35
Mariposa Folk Fdn., 6-40
Maritime
    Boating Assn., 2-152
    Centre, Intl. (B.C.), 3-112
    Command (Ntl. Defence), 3-79
    Commerce, Chamber of, 7-24
    Conservatory of Music (N.S.), 9-23
    Employers Assn., B.C., 2-124
    Fédn., 2-189
    Fishermen's Union, 2-203
    Forest Ranger Sch. (N.B.), 9-18
    Higher Educ. Commn., 3-131
    Law
        Assn., Cdn., 2-114
        Sector, Admiralty & (Fed. Govt.), 3-77
    Lumber Bureau, 2-75
    Municipal Training & Devel. Bd., 3-131
    Museum of the Atlantic (N.S.), 6-13
    Premiers Council of, 3-131
    Provinces
        Educ. Fdn., 2-212, 3-131
        Harness Racing Commn., 3-131
        Higher Educ. Commn., 3-131
Market Gardeners Fedn., Qué., 3-198
Marketers
    Assn., Cdn. Print, 2-11
    Consumer Elecronics, 2-54
    Periodical, 2-145
Marketing
    Agency, N.S., 3-158
    Assn(s)., 2-10
        American, 2-11
        Cdn. Direct, 2-11
    Awards (see Advertising & Public Relations)
    Bds. of B.C., Council of, 3-109
    Bureau
        Newspaper, 2-11
        Radio, 2-12
    Cdn. Inst. of, 2-11
    Council, P.E.I., 3-189
    Dept. of Agric. & (N.S.), 3-156
    direct, Assn cdnne du, 2-11
    industriel, Assn cdnne de recherche et, 2-11
    Magazines, 5-159
    Mgmt. of Ont., Chartered Inst. of, 2-11
    Orgs., 2-10
    Practices Br. (Fed. Govt.), 3-75
    Programs, Ntl. (Agric.), 3-53
    Research
        Assn., Industrial, 2-11
        Orgs., Cdn. Assn. of, 2-11
        Soc., Profl., 2-12
Markham, Town of, Govt., 4-160
Marques, Inst. cdn. des brevets et, 2-138
Marquess, 1-30
Marquis Project, 2-109
Marriage
    Certificates (Govt.): Quick Ref., 3-39; Alta., 3-103; B.C., 3-116; Man., 3-122; N.B., 3-136; Nfld., 3-145; N.W.T., 3-154; N.S., 3-157; Ont., 3-174; P.E.I., 3-191; Qué., 3-204; Sask., 3-215; Yukon, 3-223
    & Family Therapy, Alta. Assn. for, 2-165; Ont. Assn. for, 2-168
    Regulations, 1-42
    Statistics, 1-50
Mars, Planet, 1-14
Marsan, Collège
    d'Informatique (Qué.), 9-47
    de Photographie (Qué.), 9-47
Masonic Fdns., 2-212

Masonry
    Contractors' Assn., Cdn., 2-31
    Producers Assn., Cdn. Concrete, 2-30
Masons
    Indep. Union, 2-198
    Royal Arch, 2-76
Masorti Judaism, Cdn. Fdn. for, 2-209
Mass, Measurement of, 1-62
Massage Therapist Alliance, Cdn., 2-87
Masseurs et massothérapeutes, Fédn qué. des, 2-92
Massey College (U. of T.), 9-31
Massothérapeutes, Alliance cdnne de, 2-92
Master
    Athlete Fedn., Cdn., 2-176
    Brewers' Assn. of The Americas, 2-73
    Insulators' Assn. of Ont., 2-32
    Painters & Decorators Assn. of B.C., 2-32
    Penmen & Teachers of Handwriting, Intl. Assn. of, 2-52
    Roofers Assn., Qué., 2-32
Masters
    Cross-Country Ski Assn., Cdn., 2-176
    Track & Field Assn., 2-176
MATCH Intl. Centre, 2-192
Materials Handling
    Assn. of Qué., 2-123
    & Distribution Magazines, 5-171
Mathematical Soc., Cdn., 2-155
Maurice Lamontagne Inst., 3-68
Maxillofacial Surgeons, Cdn. Assn. of Oral &, 2-84
Mayflower Descendants, Cdn. Soc. of, 2-96
Mayo Renewable Resources Council (Yukon), 3-225
Mayors
    Forms of Address, 1-34
    Major Cities, 4-153
Maytree Fdn., 2-212
MBA du Qué., Assn de, 2-120
McCord Museum of Cdn. History, 6-24
McGill Univ. (Qué.), 9-46
McLuhan
    Fdn., Herbert Marshall, 2-211
    Program in Culture & Tech. (U. of T.), 9-31
McMaster
    Divinity College (Ont.), 9-29
    Univ. (Ont.), 9-29
McMichael Cdn. Art Collection, 6-32
M.E. Assn. of Canada, Ont., 2-91
Measurement
    BBM Bur. of, 2-28
    Bureau
        Cdn. Outdoor, 2-11
        Print, 2-12
    Length, Area, Capacity, etc., 1-62
    Metric, see Weights & Measures
    Standards, Inst. for Ntl. (NCR), 3-81
Meat
    Council, Cdn., 2-72
    Importers Committee, Cdn., 2-187
    Industry Inspection Br. (Ont.), 3-169
    Packers & Processors, Ont. Indep., 2-73
    Science Assn., Cdn., 2-73
Mécaniciens industriels, Assn ntle des, 2-197
Mécanique, Assn des entrepreneurs en, 2-32
Mechanical
    Contractors Assns., 2-32
    Engrg. Cdn. Soc. for, 2-59
    Engrs., Amer. Soc. of, 2-57
    Wood-Pulps Network, 2-75
Médaille de la bravoure, **16**, 1-28
Medal of Bravery, **16**, 1-28
Medals, Precedence of, 1-31
MEDEC, 2-93
Médecine
    Académique, Inst cdn de, 2-86
    Assn des facultés de, 2-46
    chinoise et d'acupuncture, L'Assn de, 2-91
    Interne, Soc. cdnne de, 2-90
    Légale, see Légale médecine

Médecine (cont.)
    Nucléaire, Assn cdnne de, 2-84
    Physique et de réadaptation, Assn cdnne de, 2-84
    Sportive
        Académie cdnne de, 2-173
        Conseil cdn de la, 2-180
    transfusionnelle, Soc. cdnne de, 2-90
    du travail et de l'environnement, Assn cdnne de la, 2-93
Médecins
    Assns des, 2-80, 2-87
    biochimistes, Assn des, 2-83
    pour un Canada sans fumée, 2-10
    et chirugiens, Collège royal du, 2-94
    Collège des, 2-92
    dentistes et pharmaciens, Assn des conseils des, 2-82
    de famille, Collège des, 2-91
    Fédn des ordres des, 2-92
    du gouvernement du Qué., Synd. profl, 2-207
    de langue française, Assn des, 2-82
    microbiologistes, Assn cdnne des, 2-83
    omnipraticiens du Qué., 2-91
    ophtalmologistes du Qué., 2-82
    résidents du Qué., Fédn des, 2-201
    spécialistes du Qué., Fédn des, 2-92
    pour la Survie Mondiale, Assn des, 2-109
    du travail (Qué.), 2-82
    d'urgence, Assn cdnne des, 2-83
    vétérinaires, Ordre des, 2-28
Media(s)
    Assn., Cdn. Ski, 2-176
    Awards (see Broadcasting; Culture; Journalism; Literary Arts; Public Affairs)
    Cdn. Assn. of Labour, 2-110
    Censorship, Gov't Quick Ref., 3-7
    Directors' Council, Cdn., 2-11
    Guild, Cdn., 2-199
    Prodrs. & Distrs. Assn., Educational, 2-51
    du Qué., Conseil des dirs, 2-11
    Services (Sask. Govt.), 3-218
    Studies, Ctr. for Mass (U.W.O.), 9-31
    & Tech. in Educ., Assn. for, 2-46
Mediation
    Bds.: B.C., 3-112; Sask., 3-218
    Insts., Arbitration &, 2-110
    Services, (Govt.): Fed. (Human Resources), 3-72; Man., 3-129; Ont., 3-181
Mediawatch, 2-11
MedicAlert Fdn., 2-88
Medical(e)
    Assistance to Travellers, Intl. Assn. for, 2-92
    Assn(s).: 2-80; Cdn., 2-87; Qué., 2-87
    Awards, 1-101
    Biochemists, Cdn. Assn. of, 2-83
    & Biological Engrg. Soc., Cdn., 2-162
    Board, Nfld., 2-92
    Cdns pour la recherche, 2-90
    Care
        Commn., Nfld., 3-146
        Insurance (see also Health Insurance)
            Branch (Sask.), 3-215
            Govt. Quick Ref., 3-19
    Clinics, Cdn. Assn. of, 2-100
    Colleges, Assn. of Cdn., 2-46
    Conferences, 1-87
    Conseil, du Québec, 3-207
    Council
        of Canada, 2-93
        Qué., 3-207
        Yukon, 3-224
    Devices Canada, 2-93
    Examiners, see Coroners
    Exhibitions, Shows & Events, 1-87
    Fdn., Cdn., 2-88
    Geneticists, Cdn. College of, 2-85
    Health Dirs./Officers: Alta., 3-100; Man., 3-126; N.B., 3-137; N.W.T., 3-151
    Ins., Govt. Quick Ref., 3-19 (see also Health Ins.)

Canadian Almanac & Directory 1997

Medical(e) (cont.)
   Journals, 5-171
   Laboratories, Ont. Assn. of, 2-101
   Laboratory
      Technologists, College of, 2-91
      Technology Education (Ont.), 9-35
   Licensing Auths., Fedn. of, 2-92
   Magazines, 5-171, 5-183
   Malpractice Prevention Assn., Cdn., 2-88
   Microbiologists, Cdn. Assn. of, 2-83
   Mycology, Cdn. Soc. for, 2-90
   Officers Assn., Cdn. Life Insurance, 2-105
   Oncologists, Cdn. Assn. of, 2-83
   Orgs., 2-80
   Radiation
      Technologists, Cdn. Assn. of, 2-84
      Tech. Educ. (Ont.), 9-35
   Reform Group of Ont., 2-93
   Research
      Alta. Heritage Fdn. for, 2-81
      Council of Canada, 3-78
      Fdn., African Medical &, 2-81
   Secretaries Assn., Ont., 2-122
   Service Fdn., Man., 2-93
   Services
      Branch (Fed.), 3-71; P.E.I., 3-191
      Commn., B.C., 3-116
      Fdn., B.C., 2-83
      Inc., 2-157
      Plan, B.C., 3-116
   Soc(s). 2-87
      Educ. & Charitable Fund of the P.E.I., 2-209
   Specialists of Qué., Fedn. of 2-92
   Students, Cdn. Fedn. of, 2-86
   Technologists, Qué., 2-198
   Women, Fedn. of, 2-192
médicales Canada, Conseil de recherches, 3-78
Médicament(s)
   Assn cdnne de l'industrie du, 2-140
   Assn des grossistes en, 2-139
   brevetes, Conseil d'examen du prix des, 3-84
   sans ordonnance, Assn cdnne des fabricants de, 2-139
Medicare Dir. (N.B.), 3-137
Medicine
   Academy of, Ottawa, 2-80; Toronto, 2-81
   & Acupuncture Assn., Chinese, 2-91
   Awards, *see* Health & Medical
   Cdn.
      Academy of Sport, 2-173
      Assn. of Nuclear, 2-84
      College of Legal, 2-85
      Inst. of Academic, 2-86
      Soc.
         of Aerospace, 2-89
         for the History of, 2-90
         of Internal, 2-90
         for Transfusion, 2-90
   Centre for
      Offshore & Remote (Nfld.), 9-20
      Studies in Family (U.W.O.), 9-31
Medicine Hat College (Alta.), 9-4
Medicine
   Prices Review Bd. (Fed. Govt.), 3-84
   & Science Council, Sport, 2-180
Medieval
   Numismatic Soc., Classical &, 2-151
   Studies
      Ctr. for (U. of T.), 9-30
      Pontifical Inst. of, (U of T) 9-31
Mediterranean Inst., Cdn., 2-155
Medium Public Libraries of Ont., Admrs. of, 2-116
Meeting Professionals
   Intl., 2-35
   List of Cdn., 1-68 (& *see* Addenda)
Members, *see* Legislative Assemblies; House of Commons

Memorial
   Soc., Funeral Advisory &, 2-76
   Univ. of Nfld., 9-19
Mendel Art Gallery & Civil Conservatory (Sask.), 6-35
Mendelssohn Choir, Toronto, 6-41
Mennonite
   Bible College, Cdn. (Man.), 9-15
   Brethren Churches, Cdn. Conf. of, 2-2
   Central Committee, 2-4
   Conf.
      of Eastern Canada, 2-4
      Evangelical, 2-4
      Northwest, 2-4
   Fdn., 2-212
   Mission Conf., Evangelical, 2-4
Mennonites in Canada, Conf. of, 2-3
Mensa Canada Soc., 2-53
Men's Clothing Mfrs. Assn., 2-68
Mental
   Health
      Assn(s).: 2-125; Cdn., 2-125
      Bd./Com.: Alta. Prov., 2-101; Qué., 3-207
      Brs./Divs. (Govt.): Alta., 3-100; Man., 3-126; Nfld., 3-146; Ont., 3-180
      Centres, Ont. Assn. of Children's, 2-126
      Fdn., Ont., 3-180
      Fund, Ntl., 2-125
      Govt. Quick Ref. (*see* Health), 3-19
      Nurses
         Assn., Community, 2-137
         Cdn. Fedn. of, 2-136
      Patient Advocate (Alta.), 3-101
      Services (Govt.): Alta., 3-100; B.C., 3-116; Man., 3-126; N.B., 3-136; Nfld., 3-154; N.S., 3-160; N.W.T., 3-151; Sask., 3-216
      World Fedn. for, 2-126
   Hosps. & Community Care Facilities in: Alta., 8-5; B.C., 8-8; Man., 8-13; N.B., 8-16; Nfld., 8-17; N.S., 8-19; Ont., 8-25; Qué., 8-39; Sask., 8-54; Yukon, 8-56
Mentale du Qué., Com. de la santé, 3-207
Mentally Handicapped, Assns. for, 2-41
Merchandising (*see also* Trade)
   Assn., Cdn. Automatic, 2-11
   & Design, Intl. Academy of (Ont.), 9-35
Merchant
   Seaman Comp. Bd. (Fed.), 3-73
   Service Guild, Cdn., 2-199
Mercury, Planet, 1-14
Mercy Intl. Canada, 2-109
Meritorious Service Decorations, **16**, 1-29
Mesopotamian Studies, Cdn. Soc. for, 2-155
Message Exchanges, Cdn. Assn. of, 2-183
Metabolic Diseases, Cdn. Assn. of Centers for the Mgmt. of, 2-83
Metabolism, Cdn. Soc. of Endocrinology &, 2-89
Metal(s)
   Arts Guild, 2-191
   Assn., Architectural, 2-30
   Companies, Cdn., 7-46
   Govt. Quick Ref., 3-26
   Industries Assns., 2-181
   Sector (Fed.), 3-83
   Polishers, Buffers, Platers Intl. Union, 2-203
   Production Statistics, 1-56
Métallurgie
   Fédn de la, 2-201
   des mines et des produits chimique, Fédn démocratique de la, 2-200
Métallurgiques, Inst cdn des centres de service des produits, 2-182
Metallurgy & Petroleum, Cdn. Inst. of Mining, 2-127
Metalworking Magazines, 5-172
Meteor Showers, 1-15
Meteorological
   Centre, Cdn., 3-65
   & Oceanographic Soc., Cdn., 2-162

Meteorology (*see also* Climate)
   & Oceanography Br. (Fed. Govt.), 3-68
Meteors & Meteorites, 1-15
Methodist
   Church, Free, 2-4
   Episcopal Church, British, 2-2
Métiers d'art
   Conseil cdn des, 2-190
   Qué., Guilde cdnne des, 2-190; du Qué., 2-190
Metis
   & Aboriginal Assn., Ont., 2-133
   Affairs Secretariat, Indians & (Sask.), 3-216
   Assn., Lab., 2-133
   Fedns.: Man., 2-133; Pacific, 2-134
   Nations Alta., 2-133; B.C., 2-133; N.W.T., 2-133; Ont., 2-133; Sask. 2-133
   Ntl. Council, 2-133
   of Women, 2-133
   Settlement(s)
      Alta., 4-11
      Assns., Alta Fdn. of, 2-170
      Commn. (Alta.), 3-100
      General Council, 2-134
Metric Weights & Measures
   Govt. Quick Ref., 3-40
   Conversions, 1-62
Metro Toronto Language Sch., 9-35
Métropole, Min. de la (Que.), 3-204
Metropolitan
   Affairs, Min. of (Qué.), 3-204
   Areas Population, 1-47
   Separate Sch. Bd. (Ont.), 9-26
   Toronto
      Convention Centre Corp., 3-176
      Govt., 4-172
      Map, 4-175
Meubles, Conseil cdn des fabricants de, 2-123
Meuniers du Qué., Assn profl des, 2-13
Mexican Govt.
   Depts./Agencies, 3-237
   Equivalency Table, 3-227
Mexico
   Govt., 3-227, 3-237
Michener Inst. of Applied Health Sciences, 2-93
Micmac Native Friendship Centre, 2-134
Microbiologistes du Qué., Assn des, 2-161
Microbiologists, Cdn.
   Assn. of Medical, 2-83
   Cdn. Soc. of, 2-162
   College of, 2-161
Micronet, 2-157
Microreproductions, Cdn. Inst. for Hist'l, 2-96
Microscopical Soc. of Canada, 2-163
Microstructural Sciences, Inst. for (NRC), 3-81
Mid-Ocean Recording Studio (Man.), 9-16
Midwives Assns., 2-36
Miel, Conseil cdn du, 2-14
   du Qué., Fédn des producteurs de, 3-198
Migraine Fdn., 2-93
Mileage, Distance between major points in Canada, 1-66
Military
   Assns., 2-126
   Bases & Detachments, 3-79
   Schs., *see* Cdn. Forces Bases
   Collectors Club of Canada, 2-127
   Colleges, 3-80
      Royal (Ont.), 9-29
   Commands, 3-79
   Exhibitions, Shows & Events, 1-88
   History, Cdn. Commn. of, 2-126
   Inst., Royal Cdn., 2-127
   Magazines, 5-173
   Merit, Order of, **15**, 1-27
   Meritorious Serv. Decorations, **16**, 1-29
   Museums, Org. of, 2-78
   Rank Abbrevs., 1-35
   & United Services Insts. of Canada, Fedn. of, 2-127

Milk (see also Dairy; Dairying)
  Control Bd., Sask., 3-212
  Mktg. Bds. & Commns.: B.C., 3-109; Man., 3-122;
    N.B., 3-134; Nfld., 3-145; Ont., 3-170; Qué., 3-198
  Nova Scotia, 2-15
  Prices Review Commn., Man., 3-122
  Prodrs.
    Assn., B.C., 2-13; N.S., 2-15
    Mktg. Bds., see Mktg. Bds., above
    Soc., Alta., 2-12
  Production (Govt. Quick Ref., see Dairying), 3-11
Milking Shorthorn Soc., Cdn., 2-20
Mille-Îles, Commn scolaire des, 9-43
Millers Assn.
  Ntl., 2-73
  Ont. Flour, 2-73
Millwork Mfrs. Assn., 2-75
Mine(s)
  Accident
    Prevention Assn. of Man., 2-160
    Reporting System (B.C.), 3-112
  d'Amiante, Assn des, 2-127
  Assns., 2-127
  Brs./Divs. (Govt.): Man., 3-124; Nfld., 3-148; N.S., 3-163; Qué., 3-205; Yukon, 3-222
  Chambers of, 7-35
  Depts. (Govt.): Quick Ref., 3-26; Man., 3-124; Nfld., 3-148; N.W.T., 3-153; Ont., 3-185; Sask., 3-214
  Health & Safety Brs. (Govt.): N.S., 3-162; Sask., 3-218
  & Minerals, Assns., 2-127
  et des produits chimiques, Fédn démocratique de la métallurgie, des, 2-200
  sous-ministre adjoint (Qué.), 3-205
  Wkrs. of Amer., United, 2-208
Mineral(s)
  Analysts, Cdn., 2-127
  Brs./Divs. (Govt.): B.C., 3-112; Fed., 3-82; N.W.T., 3-153; N.S., 3-163; Ont., 3-185; P.E.I., 3-189; Sask., 3-214
  & Energy Tech., Canada Centre for, 3-82
  Exhibitions, Shows & Events, 1-88
  Exploration, Qué. (SOQUEM), 3-205
  Fedn. of Canada, Gem &, 2-78
  Production Statistics, 1-56
  Resources
    Assns, 2-127
    Brs./Divs. (Govt.): Alta., 3-98; Fed., 3-82; N.B., 3-139; Nfld., 3-148; N.W.T., 3-153; N.S., 3-163; Yukon, 3-222
  Revenue Br. (Sask.), 3-214
  Sector (Fed.), 3-83
  Tech. Br. (Fed.), 3-82
  Titles Br. (B.C.), 3-111
Mineralogical Assn. of Canada, 2-128
Mineralogy, Intl. Council for Applied, 2-128
Minerva Fdn., 2-212
Mines, see Mine(s)
Minière
  Assns: Qué., 2-128; N.-B., 2-128
  Soc. qué. d'exploration, 3-205
Minimum Wages, 1-52
  Bd., Sask., 3-218
  Govt. Quick Ref., 3-26
Mining
  Advisory Council on (B.C.), 3-112
  Assn(s).: 2-127; of Canada, 2-128
  Awards see Scientific Awards
  Bd., Man., 3-124
  Commr. (Ont.), 3-184
  Companies, Cdn., 7-46
  Contractors Assn., Cdn., 2-128
  Equip. Mfrs. Assn., Cdn., 2-66
  Exhibitions, Shows & Events, 1-88
  Govt. Quick Ref., 3-26
  Industry Research Org. of Canada, 2-155
  Magazines, 5-173
  Metallurgy, & Petroleum, Cdn. Inst. of, 2-127

Mining (cont.)
  & Minerals, Exhibitions, Shows & Events, 1-88
  Municipalities of Ont., Assn. of, 2-127
  Research Labs. (Fed.), 3-82
Ministers
  of the Environment, Cdn. Council of, 2-60
  Forms of Address: Govt., 1-33; Plenipotentiary, 1-35; Religious, 1-34
Ministry, The Cdn., 3-46
Mink Breeders Assns.: Can., 2-19; N.S., 2-21
Mint, Royal Cdn., 3-88
Miramichi Trades & Labour Union, 2-203
Missing Children's
  Network Canada, 2-37
  Soc. of Canada, 2-168
Mission
  Africa Inland, 2-6
  Global Outreach, 2-7
Missionaire, Alliance chrétienne, 2-3
Missionary
  Alliance, Christian &, 2-3
  Union of
    Canada, Gospel, 2-7
    the Clergy & Religious, 2-8
Missions
  Cdn. Jesuit, 2-8
  & Delegations Abroad, Cdn. Permanent, 3-247
  Fdn., Cdn. African, 2-6
Mississauga City Govt., 4-160
Mixte
  Conseil ntl, 3-80
  intle, Commn, 3-77
Mizrachi-Hapoel Hamizrachi Org. of Canada, 2-131
MLA, see Legislative Assemblies
Mobilization, Operation, 2-8
Mode Châtelaine, École de (Qué.), 9-47
Model Aeronautics Assn. of Canada, 2-152
Moderator of Canada, Forms of Address, 1-34
Mohammedan Era, see Epochs
Mohawk College (Ont.), 9-33; Fdn., 2-212
Molders, Pottery, Plastic & Allied Wkrs. Intl. Union, Glass, 2-201
Moldmakers, Cdn. Assn. of, 2-123
Molecular
  Biology, Cdn. Soc. of Biochemistry &, 2-162
  Sciences, Steacie Inst. for (NRC), 3-81
Molson Cos. Donations Fund, 2-212
Monarchist League of Canada, 2-97
Moncton
  City Govt., 4-161
  Univ. de, 9-18
Money in Circulation, 1-57
Monnaie
  Musée de la, 6-1
  royale cdnne, 3-88
Monoparentales du Qué., Fédn des assns de familles, 2-167
Monsignor, Forms of Address, 1-35
Montagne, Assn des guides de, 2-149
Montessori
  Inst., Toronto, 9-36
  Schs., see Private Schs.
Monteurs d'acier de structure, Fra. ntle des, 2-201
Montréal
  Ateliers de Danse Moderne de, 9-47
  Bank, 7-1
  La Bourse de, 7-10
  Carte régionale, 4-175
  Collège Technique de, 9-47
  Commn des écoles, 9-41
  Communauté urbaine de, 4-173; Carte/Map, 4-175
  Exchange, 7-10
  Map, Regional, 4-175
  Musée
    d'art contemporain de, 6-34
    des beaux arts de, 6-34
  Place des arts, 3-200
  Port of, Corp. (Fed.), 3-55

Montréal (cont.)
  Sch. Bds. in, 9-41
  Stock Exchange, 7-10
  Theological Colleges, 9-46
  Univ. de, 9-46
    Qué. à, 9-47
  Urban Community, 4-173
  Ville de, Govt., 4-161
Montréal-Nord, Ville de, Govt., 4-161
Monuments & Sites
  Canada, Intl. Council on, 2-97
  du Qué., Conseil des, 2-96
Moon
  Diameter of, 1-14
  Eclipses of, 1-22
  Tables, 1-8
Moose Jaw City Govt., 4-162
Mop Mfrs. Assn., Cdn., 2-123
Moped Industry Council, 2-189
Moravian Church, Cdn. District, 2-3
Morgan Horse Assn., Cdn., 2-20
Mormons, 2-3; 2-5
Mortgage
  Brokers Assn., Ont., 2-71
  Corp., Ont., 3-182
  & Housing Corps.: Alta., 3-110; Canada, 3-55
  & Loan Companies, 7-4
Motel(s) (see also Hotels; Hospitality Industry)
  Assns.: Alta., 2-186; Ont., 2-183; Ont. Hotel &, 2-185
  Campgrounds, Resorts Assn., B.C., 2-184
Mother(s)
  Against Drunk Driving, 2-10
  Magazines, Babies &, 5-178
  Superior, Forms of Address, 1-35
  Tongue Statistics, 1-50
Motion Picture (see also Film; Cinema)
  Appeal Bd., B.C., 3-110
  Assn., B.C., 2-68; Sask., 2-69
  Devel. Corp., Alta., 3-97
  Distrs. Assn., Cdn., 2-69
  Govt. Quick Ref., 3-16
  Industries Assn., Alta., 2-68
  & Television Engrs., Soc. of, 2-59
  Theatre Assns. of Canada, 2-69
Motoneige, Conseil cdn des orgs de, 2-150
Motoneigistes de Qué., Fédn des clubs de, 2-151
Motor
  Assns., 2-25
  Carrier(s) (see also Commercial Transport)
    Commn., B.C., 3-120
  Coach Assn., Western Canada, 2-189
  Dealers
    Assns., Alta., 2-27; B.C., 2-27; Man., 2-26, (see also Automobile)
    Regrs., see Motor Vehicles Dealers Regrs.
  Transport
    Admrs., Cdn. Council of, 2-188
    Assns., 2-188/189
    Bds.: Man., 3-127; Yukon, 3-222
  Truck(s)
    & Buses Magazines, 5-173
    Council, Private, 2-189
  Vehicle(s) (see also Drivers Licences; Transportation)
    Brs./Divs. (Govt.): B.C., 3-119; Man., 3-126; N.W.T., 3-154
    Dealers Regrs., B.C., 3-109
    Manufacturers' Assn., 2-27
    Registrars (Govt.): Alta., 3-103; Man., 3-126; N.B., 3-140; Nfld., 3-149; N.S., 3-157; P.E.I., 3-193; Yukon, 3-222
Motorcycle
  Assn., Cdn., 2-150
  Magazines see Automobile & Cycle Magazines
  & Moped Industry Council, 2-189
  Shows, see Automotive Exhibitions, Shows & Events
Motto (Canada), 1
Mouleurs sous pressions, Assn cdnne des, 2-123

Canadian Almanac & Directory 1997

Moutons, Soc. cdnne des Éleveurs de, 2-20
Mount
    Allison Univ., N.B., 9-18
    Royal College (Alta.), 9-4
    St. Bernard College, (N.S.), 9-22
    St. Vincent Univ., (N.S.), 9-22
Mountain
    Clubs of B.C., Fedn. of, 2-151
    Guides, Assn. of Cdn., 2-149
Movers Assn., Ont., 2-189
Moving
    Picture Machine Operators of the U.S. & Canada, Intl. Alliance of Theatrical Stage Employees &, 2-202
    Pictures Travelling Film Festival Soc., 2-69
MP/MPP, *see* House of Commons; Legislative Assembly
MS Society, 2-93
M.S.I. Fdn., 2-157
Mule Assn., Cdn. Donkey &, 2-20
Multi-material Recycling Inc. (OMMRI), Ont., 2-64
Multicultural
    Assns.: 2-128; NW Ont., 2-131; N.S., 2-131; Ont., 2-131
    Awards, *see* Citizenship & Bravery
    Council: N.B., 2-131; Sask., 2-131
    Educ., Sask. Assn. for, 2-54
    Festivals & Events, 1-88
    Grants Adv. Council (Man.), 3-123
    History Soc. of Ont., 2-131
    & Intercult. Educ., Cdn. Council for, 2-48
    Magazines, 5-192
    Resources Ctr. Inc., Man., 2-131
    Socs. & Service Agencies of B.C., Affil. of, 2-128
Multiculturalism (*see also* Intercultural)
    Assns., 2-128
    Brs.: B.C., 3-110; Sask., 3-219
    Commns/Councils (Govt.): Quick Ref., 3-27; Alta., 3-102; B.C., 3-110; Man., 3-123; N.B., 3-133; Ont., 3-173, (*see also* Communautés culturelles for Qué.)
    Ministerial Adv. Com. on (N.B.), 3-133
    Publications *see* Multicultural Publications
    Secretariat, Man. 3-123
    Secretary of State (Fed.), 3-58
Multifaith Action Soc., 2-8
Multilateral Trade Negotiations Br. (Fed. Govt.), 3-69
Multilingual Press Fedn., Cdn., 2-145
Multimedia
    Arts & Tech. Assn., Interactive, 2-104
    Fdn., Cdn. Children's, 2-103
Multiple
    Births Assn. of Canada, Parents of, 2-36
    Dwelling Standards Assn., 2-102
    Organ Retrieval & Exchange Prog., 2-93
    Sclerosis Soc. of Canada, 2-93
Municipal
    Admrs. Assns.: Alta. Rural, 2-79; Cdn., 2-79; Man., 2-80; N.B., 2-79; N.S., 2-79; Ont., 2-80; Sask., Rural, 2-80; Sask., Urban, 2-80
    Affairs. (Govt.): Quick Ref., 3-27; Alta., 3-102; B.C., 3-117; Man. (Northern), 3-130; (Urban Affairs), 3-131; N.B. (Municipalities etc.), 3-138; Nfld., 3-148; N.W.T., 3-152; N.S., 3-160; Ont., 3-182; P.E.I. (Prov. Affairs & Attorney General), 3-191; Qué., 3-196; Sask. (Mun. Govt.), 3-218; Yukon Div., 3-233
    Assessors of Ont., Inst. of, 2-102
    Assns.: N.E. Ont., 2-80; N.W. Ont., 2-80
    Bds.: Man., 3-130; Ont., 3-183; Sask., 3-219; Yukon, 3-222
    Chambers of Commerce, 7-23
    Clerks, Administrators, Secretaries, etc.: Alta., 4-1; B.C., 4-12; Man., 4-18; N.B., 4-24; Nfld., 4-29; N.W.T., 4-37; N.S., 4-39; Ont., 4-42; P.E.I., 4-74; Qué., 4-77; Sask., 4-134; Yukon, 4-152
    Clerks & Treas. of Ont., Assn. of, 2-79
    Commn., Qué., 3-197

Municipal (cont.)
    Courts (Qué.), 10-17
    Development, Govt. Quick Ref., 3-27
    Directory, 4-1
    Districts, Alta., 4-10
    Dists. & Counties Assn., Alta., 2-79
    Electric Assn., 2-143
    Employees Retirement Bd., Ont., 3-183
    Engrs. Assns.: Ont., 2-59; Qué., 2-57
    Equip. & Operations Assn. (Ont.), 2-66
    Finance
        N.S., 3-161
        Officers Assn. of Ont., 2-71
    Financing Corps. (Govt.): Alta., 3-105; Nfld., 3-143
    Govt., 4-1, 4-153
        Board, Alta., 3-103
    Hail Assn., Sask., 2-106
    Law Enforcement Officers Assn. (Ont.), 2-115
    Mgmt. Inst., Ont., 2-80
    Officers Assn. of B.C., 2-80
    Officers of Qué., Corp. of Chartered, 2-80
    & Prov. Affairs Dept. (Nfld.), 3-148
    Publications, *see* Government
    Recreation Assn., Ont., 2-152
    Recycling Coordinators, Assn. of, 2-60
    Social Services Assn., Ont., 2-168
    Tax Collectors of Ont., Assn. of, 2-183
    Training & Devel. Bd., Maritime, 3-131
    Waste Reduction Br. (B.C.), 3-113
    Water Assn., Ont., 2-143
Municipale, Commn (Qué.), 3-197
Municipalités
    de Comté (Qué.), 4-132
    culture et habitation, Dept. (N.B.), 3-138
    Fédn cdnne des, 2-79
    du N.-B., Assn des, 2-79; Union des, 2-80
    du Qué., 4-77
        Assn des directeurs généraux des, 2-79
        Union des, 2-80
    Rég. de comté & des mun. locales du Qué., Union des, 2-80
Municipalities
    Assns., Urban: Alta., 2-79; Sask., 2-80
    Culture & Housing, Dept. (N.B.), 3-138
    Fedns. of: Cdn., 2-79; Nfld./Lab., 2-80; Northern Ont., 2-79; P.E.I., 2-79
    In: Alta., 4-1; B.C., 4-12; Man., 4-18; N.B., 4-24; Nfld., 4-29; N.W.T., 4-37; N.S., 4-39; Ont., 4-42; P.E.I., 4-74; Qué., 4-77; Sask., 4-134; Yukon, 4-152
    Large, 4-153
    Man. Assn. of Urban, 2-80
    N.W.T. Assn. of, 2-80
    of Ont., Assn. of, 2-79
    Org. of Small Urban (Ont.), 2-80
    Sask. Assn. of Rural, 2-80
    Unions of: B.C., 2-80; Man., 2-80; N.B., 2-80; N.S., 2-80
Municipality Librarians of Ont., County & Regional, 2-119
Municipaux
    Agréés, Corp des officiers, 2-79
    Assn des
        administrateurs (N.-B.), 2-79
        cadres financiers, 2-69
        communicateurs, 2-79
        ingénieurs (Qué.), 2-57
        secrétaires et trésoriers (Ont.), 2-79
        urbanistes & des aménagistes, 2-79
    Corp. des secrétaires (Qué.), 2-79
Murray Grey Assn., Cdn., 2-20
Muscular Dystrophy Assn. of Canada, 2-93
Musée(s), 6-1
    d'art, Org. des directeurs des, 2-77
    cdns, Assn des, 2-77
    Fédn cdnne des amis de, 2-77
    militaires, L'Org. des, 2-78
    Québécois, Soc. des, 2-78
Muséologie, Dir. (Qué.), 3-199

Museum
    Assns., 2-77
    Brs./Divs. (Govt.): N.S., 3-158; Qué., 4-199
    & Heritage Fdn., P.E.I., 6-23, 2-97
Museums, 6-1
    Assn(s).: 2-77
        Yukon Hist'l &, 2-98
    Canada, ICOM, 2-77
    Cdn. Fedn. of Friends of, 2-77
    Directory of, 6-1
    Govt. Quick Ref., 3-27
    Intl. Council of, 2-77
    Org. of Military, 2-78
Mushroom
    Growers, Assn., Cdn., 2-14
    Mktg. Bd., B.C., 3-109
Music
    Academy, Nfld., 9-21
    Assns., 6-37
        Cdn. Country, 6-39
    Awards & Prizes (*see* Culture; Performing Arts)
    Canada, Youth &, 6-41
    Cdn.
        Bur. for Adv. of, 6-39
        Soc. for Traditional, 6-40
    Centre, Cdn., 6-39
    Competitions: Cdn., 6-39; Winnipeg, 6-41
    Conservatories: N.S., 9-23; Ont., 9-35; Qué., 3-199, 9-47; Sask., 9-54
    Country (Awards), 1-109
    Educators Assn., Cdn., 6-39
    & Entertainment Industry Educators Assn., 6-40
    Faculties/Schs., Index to, 9-57
    Festival(s), 1-88
        Adjudicators Assn., Cdn., 6-39
        Assn. of Greater Toronto, Kiwanis, 6-40
        Ntl., 6-40
        Fedns. & Assns. of 2-66
        N.S. Kiwanis, 6-40
    Foundation, Country, 6-40
    Friends of Chamber, 6-40
    Industries Assn. of Canada, 6-40
    Libraries, Cdn. Assn. of, 2-117
    Magazines, 5-186, 5-173
    N.B. Competitive Festival of, 6-40
    Orgs., 6-37
    Projects, Alliance for Cdn. New, 6-37
    Publishers Assn., Cdn., 2-145; Soc., 2-139
    Royal Conservatory of (Toronto), 9-35
    Schools in: Ont., 9-35; Qué., 9-47
    Shows & Events, 1-88
    Soc.
        Calgary Early, 6-39
        Cdn. Univ., 6-40
        Raag-Mala, 6-41
        Vancouver New, 6-41
    Therapy, Cdn. Assn. for, 6-39
    Trade Magazines, 5-173
    Western Bd. of, 6-41
    Women in, 2-193
    for Young Children, 6-40
Musicaction, 6-40
Musical
    Awards (*see* Performing Arts)
    Ensemble Guild, Ntl. Shevchenko, 6-40
    Heritage Soc., Cdn., 6-40
    Reproduction Rights Agency, 2-138
Musicians
    Awards, *see* Performing Arts
    Cdn. Amateur, 6-39
    Org. of Cdn. Symphony, 6-41
    of the U.S. & Canada, Amer. Fedn. of, 2-197
Musiciens
    amateurs du Canada, 6-39
    d'orchestras symphonique, L'Org. des, 6-41
Musique
    Assn cdnne des
        éducateurs de, 6-39

Musique
    Assn cdnne des (cont.)
        industries de la, 6-40
    cdnnne nouvelle, Alliance pour des projets de, 6-37
    Centre de, 6-39
    Concours de, 6-39
    Conservatoires de (Qué.), 3-199, 9-47
    École Supérieure de (Qué.), 9-47
    Festivals du, 1-88, 2-66
    pour les jeunes enfants, 6-40
    des universités cdnnes, Soc. de, 6-40
    Vincent d'Indy, École de (Qué.), 9-47
Muskoka Dist. Mun. Govt., 4-171
Muslim
    Calendar, 1-2
    Civil Liberties Assn., Cdn.-, 2-7
    Communities of Canada, Council of, 2-7
    Educ. & Welfare Fdn. of Canada, 2-131
    Women, Cdn. Council of, 2-7
    World League, 2-131
Mutual
    Fund Managers, 7-4
    Insurance
        Assn., Ont., 2-106
        Cos., Cdn. Assn. of, 2-104
Myalgic Encephalomyelitis
    Assn. of Canada, 2-93
    Group, (Ont.), 2-91
Myasthenia Gravis Fdn. of B.C., 2-93
Mycology, Cdn. Soc. for Medical, 2-90

N
Na'amat Canada, 2-192
NABS, 2-11
NAC, 2-192, 3-79
NACE Intl., 2-59
Nage synchronisée amateur, Assn cdnne de, 2-180
NAFTA
    Negotiator (Fed.), 3-69
    Secretariat, 3-84
Naissances
    Fédn du Qué pour le planning des, 2-154; du Canada, 2-154
    multiples du Canada, Assn de parents de, 2-36
N.A.I.T., 9-4
Names, Cdn. Soc for the Study of, 2-96
NAMMU, 2-11
Nanaimo
    City Govt., 4-162
    Sch. Dist., 9-6
Nancy's Very Own Fdn., 2-212
Narcolepsy, Cdn. Assn. for, see Sleep/Wake Disorders Canada
Narcotics (see also Drugs)
    Anonymous, 2-10
Naskapi Villages (Qué.), 4-77
Natation Canada, 2-180
National
    Academy of Canada, 2-157
    Adv. Council on Aging, 3-78
    Anthem, 1-25
    Archives, 5-112, 3-78
    Arts Centre, 3-79
    Assembly, Qué., 3-194
    Aviation Museum, 6-1
    Ballet of Canada, 6-43
    Bank of Canada, 7-1
    Battlefields Commn., 3-79
    Capital
        Commn., 3-79
        FreeNet, 2-130
    Citizens' Coalition, 2-35
    Debt, 1-57
    Defence: Govt. Quick Ref., 3-11; Fed., 3-79
    Energy Bd., 3-8
    Farm Products Council, 3-80
    Farmers Union, 2-15

National (cont.)
    Film Bd., 3-80
    Flag of Canada, **1**
    Gallery of Canada, The, 6-29
    Historic Sites, List of, 3-59
    Joint Council, 3-80
    Library of Canada, 5-1
    Measurement Standards (NRC), 3-81
    Museum of Science & Tech., 6-1
    Orders, 1-31
    Parks, List of, 3-59
    Parole Bd., 3-80
    Public Info. Canada (Al-Anon), 2-10
    Research Council, 3-80
    Round Table on the Environment & the Economy, 3-81
    Search & Rescue Secretariat, 3-81
    Security Studies, Ctr. for (Fed.), 3-89
    Transportation Agency of Canada, 3-62
Nations-Unies, Assn cdnne pour les, 2-110
Native (see also Aboriginal)
    Affairs Secretariat: Ont., 3-183; Qué., 3-196
    Alcoholism Council of Man., 2-134
    Alliance of Qué., 2-133
    Arts
        Festivals Assn., Intl., 2-133
        Fdn., 2-133
    Broth. of B.C., 2-204
    Business Inst. of Canada, 2-134
    Community Br. (Ont.), 3-172
    Council on Justice, Ont., 2-134
    Councils, 2-133
    Counselling Services of Alta., 2-134
    Devel. in Performing & Visual Arts, Assn for, 2-132
    Earth Performing Arts, 6-36
    Educ. (Govt.): Alta., 3-105; Man., 3-124
    Friendship Centre: Cdn., 2-133; Ntl. Assn. of, 2-134
    Investment & Trade Assn., 2-134
    Land Claims, see Land Claims
    Language(s) Ctr. for Research & Teaching of Cdn., (U.W.O.), 9-31
    Law Sector (Fed. Govt.), 3-77
    Magazines, 5-191
    Nations, United (B.C.), 2-133
    Peoples
        Cdn. Alliance in Solidarity with, 2-132
        Orgs., 2-132
        Schs.: in Alta., 9-2; Man., 9-14; N.B., 9-17; Nfld., 9-19; N.S., 9-22; Ont., 9-27; P.E.I., 9-41; Qué., 9-44; Sask., 9-54
    Services Div., Alta., 4-11
    Studies, Gabriel Dumont Inst. of (Sask.), 9-54
    Women's Assn. of Canada, 2-134
NATO, 3-247
Natural
    Gas
        Assn., Ont., 2-78
        Bd., Qué., 3-205
        Govt. Quick Ref., 3-29
    Health Sciences, Intl. Academy of (Ont.), 9-35
    Health Assn., Cdn., 2-88
    History
        Museum, Sask., see Royal Sask. Museum
        Socs.: Nfld./Lab., 2-135; P.E.I., 2-135; Sask., 2-135
    Products Mktg. Councils (Govt.): Man., 3-122; N.S., 3-156 (see also Farm Products; Agricultural Products; Agri-Food)
    Resources
        Canada, 3-81
        Conservation Bd., Alta., 3-99
        Depts. (Govt.): Quick Ref., 3-28; Fed., 3-81; Man., 3-129; N.B., 3-139; N.S., 3-163; Ont., 3-183; Qué., 3-205; (see also Energy; Environment; Forestry; Lands; Mines)
    Safety Assn., Ont., 2-160
    Service (Alta.), 3-99
    Sciences & Engrg. Research Council of Can., 3-84
    Tripartite Stabilization Program (Man.), 3-122

Naturalistes
    Les cercles des jeunes, 2-135
    du N.-B., Fédn des, 2-135
Naturalists
    Assns., 2-134
    Fedns. of, 2-135
    Soc., Man., 2-135
Nature
    Cdn. Museum of, 6-1
    Conservancy of Canada, 2-64
    Fedn., Cdn., 2-135
    Fonds mondial pour la, 2-65
    Magazines, Environment &, 5-181
    Man. Museum of Man &, 6-8
    Musée Cdnne de la, 6-1
    Sask., 2-135
    Union qué. pour la conservation de la, 2-135
Naturel, Régie du gaz (Qué.), 3-205
Naturelles, see Ressources Naturelles
Naturists, Fedn. of Cdn., 2-91
Naturopathic
    Assn., Cdn., 2-88; Ont., 2-93
    Medicine, Cdn. College of (Ont.), 9-34
    Practitioners, Alta. Assn. of, 2-81
Naturopathy, Bd. of Dirs. of Drugless Therapy (Ont.), 3-180
Nautical Research Soc., Cdn., 2-155
Naval
    Assn., Cdn., 2-126
    Benevolent Fund, Royal Cdn., 2-127
    Officers Assns. of Canada, 2-127
Navale
    Assn de la construction, 2-124
    Ligue, 2-127
Navigation
    Canals & Seaway, 1-64
    Govt. Quick Ref., 3-26
    Soc., Cdn., 2-124
Navy
    & Air Force Veterans, Army, 2-126
    League of Canada, 2-127
Nazarene
    Church of the, 2-3
    College, Cdn. (Man.), 9-15
NDE Inst. of Canada, 9-35
NDP, 2-142
    Office of the Leader, 3-46
Needlecraft Assn., Cdn. Sewing &, 2-67
Needletrades, Industrial & Textile Employees, Union of, 2-207
Negotiation
    Bd. (Ont.), 3-172
    Cdn. Intl. Inst. of Applied, 2-34
Neighbourhood Services, Cdn. Assn. of, 2-166
Neil Gray Memorial Fund, 2-10
Neonatal Nurses, 2-137
Nepean City Govt., 4-162
Néphrologues du Qué., Assn des, 2-82
Nephrology
    Cdn. Soc. of, 2-90
    Nurses & Technicians, Cdn. Assn. of, 2-135
Neptune, Planet, 1-14
Net Active Canada, see Addenda
Net Income Stabilization Admin. (Fed. Govt., Agric.), 3-53
Netball Assn., Cdn. Amateur, 2-173
Netherlandic Studies, Cdn. Assn. for Adv. of, 2-47
Netherlands Govt.
    Depts./Agencies, 3-238
    Equivalency Tables, 3-227
Networks (CBC), 3-66, (see also Radio; Television)
Neurobiology & Cell Biology, Cdn. Assn. for Anatomy, 2-162
Neurochirurgiens du Qué., Assn des, 2-82
Neurological
    Sciences, Cdn. Congress of, 2-161
    Soc., Cdn., 2-88
Neurologically Disabled, Assn. for, 2-41

Neurologues du Qué., Assn des, 2-82
Neurology Corp., Cdn. Assn. of Child, 2-83
Neuropathologists, Cdn. Assn. of, 2-84
Neurophysiologists, Cdn. Soc. of Clinical, 2-89
Neuroscience
    Network, 2-157
    Nurses, Cdn. Assn. of, 2-135
New Apostolic Church, 2-4
New Brunswick
    Aquaria in, 6-45
    Archives in, 5-113
    Art Galleries in, 6-31
    Boards of Trade in, 7-29
    Botanical Gardens in, 6-46
    Business Serv. Ctr., Canada-, 3-134
    Chambers of Commerce in, 7-29
    Cities & Towns in, 4-24
    Community Colleges in, 9-18
    Courts & Judges in, 10-7
    Education in, 9-17
    Flag & Coat of Arms, **10**
    FreeNets, 5-233
    Government in, 3-131
    Hospitals in, 8-15
    Law Firms in, 10-45
    Libraries in, 5-28
    Meeting, Conference, Exhibit & Event Planners in, 1-68
    Municipal Govt. in, 4-24
    Museums in, 6-11
    Native Schs. in, 9-17
    Newspapers in, 5-136
    Nursing Homes in, 8-16
    Post-Secondary Specialized Insts. in, 9-18
    Private Schs. in, 9-18
    School Districts, 9-17
    Univs. in, 9-18
    Zoos in, 6-44
New
    Caledonia, College of (B.C.), 9-8
    College (U. of T.), 9-31
    Democratic Party, 2-142
        Office of the Leader (Fed.), 3-46
    Housing Price Index, 1-53
    Jerusalem, General Church of the, 2-4
    Life League, 2-4
    Liskeard Agricl. College (Ont.), 9-34
    Music
        Projects, Alliance for Cdn., 6-37
        Soc., Vancouver, 6-41
    Year's
        Day, 1-24
        Eve Celebrations, see First Night
Newfoundland
    Aquaria in, 6-45
    Archives in, 5-113
    Art Galleries in, 6-31
    Boards of Trade, 7-25
    Botanical Gardens in, 6-46
    Chambers of Commerce in, 7-29
    Cities & Towns in, 4-29
    Community Colleges in, 9-20
    Courts & Judges in, 10-8
    Education in, 9-19
    Flag & Coat of Arms, **11**
    FreeNets, 5-233
    Government in, 3-140
    Hospitals in, 8-17
    & Labrador Enterprise, 3-142
    Law Firms in, 10-47
    Libraries in, 5-31
    Meeting, Conference, Exhibit & Event Planners in, 1-68
    Memorial Univ. of, 9-19
    Municipal Govt. in, 4-29
    Museums in, 6-12
    Native Schs. in, 9-19
    Newspapers in, 5-136

Newfoundland (cont.)
    Nursing Homes in, 8-18
    Post Secondary Insts. in, 9-20
    Private Schs. in, 9-21
    Sch. Bds. in, 9-19
    Univs. in, 9-19
    Zoos in, 6-44
Newman Fdn. of Toronto, 2-212
News
    Awards, 1-102
    Broadcasting Awards, 1-93
    Directors Assn., Radio TV, 2-29
    Magazines, 5-186
Newsletter Publishers Assn., 2-145
Newspaper(s), 5-130
    Assns.
        Alternative, 2-144
        Cdn.: Community, 2-144; Daily, 2-145
    Awards, 1-102
    Guild, 2-204
    In: Alta., 5-130; B.C., 5-132; Man., 5-135; N.B., 5-136; Nfld., 5-136; N.W.T., 5-137; N.S., 5-137; Ont., 5-138; P.E.I., 5-144; Qué., 5-144; Sask., 5-147; Yukon, 5-148
    Marketing Bur., 2-11
NFB, 3-80
NHL Players' Assn., 2-203
Niagara
    College AA & T (Ont.), 9-33
    Falls
        Bridge Commn., 3-184
        City Govt., 4-162
    Parks
        Commn., 3-176
        Sch. of Horticulture, 9-35
    Regl. Mun. Govt., 4-172
    South Bd. of Educ., 9-25
Nicaragua, Cdn. Action for, 2-107
Nickel Devel. Inst., 2-182
Night Skies, 1-15/21
Ninety-Nines, 2-28
Nipissing Univ., (Ont.), 9-29
Noix, Conseil cdn des, 2-73
Noms géographiques, com. permanent des, 3-61
Non-Destructive
    Evaluation, Cdn. Assn. for Research in, 2-154
    Testing, Cdn. Soc. for, 2-181
Nonprescription Drug Mfrs. Assn. of Canada, 2-139
Non-Profit Housing Assn., Ont., 2-102
Non-Smokers Rights Assn., 2-168
NORAD, 3-247
Noranda Fdn., 2-212
Nord-Américaine de coopération environmentale, commn, 3-84
Nord Canada, Affaires Indiennes et du, 3-73
Nord-Sud, Inst, 2-45
Nordic
    Combined Ski Canada, 2-179
    Ski Instructors, Cdn. Assn. of, 2-174
Normalisation, Assn cdnne de, 2-181
Norman Paterson Sch. of Intl. Affairs (Carleton Univ.), 9-28
Normandy Fdn., Cdn. Battle of, 2-126
Normes
    générales du Canada, Office des, 2-181
    de télévision par cable, Fdn des, 2-181
North
    American
        Aerospace Defense Command, 3-247
        Baptist: Coll. (Alta.), 9-3; Conf., Cdn., 2-4
        Commn. for Environmental Cooperation, 3-84
        Free Trade Agreement, see NAFTA
        Waterfowl Mgmt. Plan (Fed.), 3-65
    Atlantic
        Council, 3-247
        Salmon Conservation Org., 3-248
        Treaty Org., 3-247

North (cont.)
    Bay City Govt., 4-162
    Island College (B.C.), 9-9
    Pacific Fisheries Commn., Intl., 3-247
    -South Inst., 2-45
    Vancouver
        District of, Govt., 4-162
        Sch. Dist., 9-7
    -West
        Mounted Police Commemorative Assn., 2-97
        Regional College (Sask.), 9-55
    York (Ont.)
        Bd. of Educ., 9-25
        City Govt., 4-162
Northern
    Affairs
        Br. (Sask.), 3-219
        Canada, Indian &, 3-73
        Depts. (Govt.): Fed., 3-73; Man., 3-130
        Govt. Quick Ref., 3-3
        Sectoral Policy, 3-74
    Air Transp. Assn., 2-28
    Alberta
        Devel. Council, 3-103
        Inst. of Technology, 9-4
    B.C., Univ. of, 9-8
    Cod Research Program (Fed.), 3-68
    College AA & T (Ont.), 9-33
    Devel. (Govt.): Alta., 3-103; Ont., 3-185
    Health Servs., Indian &, 3-71
    Heritage Ctr., Prince of Wales (N.W.T.), 6-16
    Info. Network (Fed.), 3-73
    Lights College (B.C.), 9-9
    Ontario Heritage Fund Corp., 3-185
    Pipeline Agency, 3-84
    Studies, Assn. of Cdn. Univs. for, 2-46
    Villages: Qué., 4-77; Sask., 4-134
Northland, Ont., 3-185
Northlands College (Sask.), 9-55
Northumberland/Clarington Bd. of Educ. (Ont.), 9-25
Northwest
    Atlantic Fisheries
        Centre, 3-68
        Org., 3-247, 3-248
    Community College (B.C.), 9-9
    Mennonite Conference, 2-4
Northwest Territories
    Bds. of Educ., 9-21
    Chambers of
        Commerce, 7-29
        Mines, 7-35
    Cities & Towns in, 4-37
    Courts & Judges in, 10-8
    Education in, 9-21
    Flag & Coat of Arms, **14**
    Government of, 3-150
    Hospitals in, 8-18
    Law Firms in, 10-47
    Libraries in, 5-34
    Municipal Govt. in, 4-39
    Museums in, 6-16
    Newspapers in, 5-137
    Nursing Homes in, 8-19
    Post Secondary Insts. in, 9-21
Norway
    Fdn., Sons of, 2-213
    Govt., 3-227, 3-239
Norwegian Govt.
    Dept./Agencies, 3-239
    Equivalency Table, 3-227
Norwood Community Scholarship Fdn., 2-212
Notaires
    Chambre des (Qué.), 2-114
    Corp. de service des, 2-114
Notaries Public of B.C., Soc. of, 2-116
Nouveau
    Brunswick, see New Brunswick
    parti démocratique, 2-142

Nova Scotia
  Agric. College, 9-23
  Archives in, 5-113
  Art Galleries in, 6-31
  Bank of, 7-1
  Boards of Trade in, 7-29
  Chamber(s) of
    Commerce in, 7-29
    Mineral Resources, 7-35
  Cities & Towns in, 4-39
  Community Colleges, 9-23
  Courts & Judges in, 10-9
  Education in, 9-21
  Flag & Coat of Arms, **11**
  FreeNets, 5-233
  Government in, 3-154
  Hospitals in, 8-19
  Law Firms in, 10-47
  Libraries in, 5-35
  Lobbyists in, 7-36
  Meeting, Conference, Exhibit & Event Planners in, 1-68
  Municipal Govt. in, 4-39
  Museums in, 6-13
  Native Schs. in, 9-22
  Newspapers in, 5-137
  Nursing Homes, 8-20
  Online Service Providers in, 5-231
  Post Sec. & Spec. Insts. in, 9-23
  Private Schs., 9-23
  Sch. Bds. in, 9-21
  Teachers College, 9-23
  Univs. in, 9-22
  Zoos in, 6-45
Novelty & Prod. Wkrs., Intl. Union of Allied, 2-203
NRC, 3-80
NSERC, 3-84
Nuclear (*see also* Atomic)
  Assn., Cdn., 2-56
  Awareness Project, 2-57
  Div. (Govt.), 3-83
  Energy, Govt. Quick Ref., 3-28
  Insurance Assn. of Canada, 2-106
  Medicine, Cdn. Assn. of, 2-84
  Responsibility, Cdn. Coalition for, 2-56
  Soc., Cdn., 2-56
Numismatic
  Assns: Cdn., 2-150; Ont., 2-152
  Dealers, Cdn. Assn. of, 2-149
  Research Soc., Cdn., 2-155
  Soc., Classical & Medieval, 2-151
Nunavut
  Artic College (NWT), 9-21
  Environmental Scientist, Office of, 3-74
  Govt. Bds./Commns. (Fed.), 3-74
  Research Inst. (NWT), 3-152
  Tourism, 2-186
Nurse
  Administrators, Cdn. Assn. of, 2-135
  Educators Assn., Cdn., 2-136
Nursery Trades Assns., 2-99
Nurses'
  Academy of Cdn. Executive, 2-135
  Affiliation, Ntl. Emergency, 2-137
  in AIDS Care, Cdn. Assn. of, 2-136
  of Alta., United, 2-138
  Assn(s)., 2-135
    Aboriginal, 2-132
    of Alta., Staff, 2-138
    Cdn., 2-136
      Holistic, 2-136
      Intravenous, 2-136
      Occupational Health, 2-137
      Orthopaedic, 2-137
    Community
      Health, 2-137
      Mental Health, 2-137
    Ont., 2-137

Nurses'
  Assn(s (cont.)
    Operating Room, 2-137
    Psychiatric, 2-138
    St. Elizabeth Visiting, 2-138
  Cdn.
    Assn. of
      Burn, 2-135
      Critical Care, 2-135
      Nephrology, 2-135
      Neuroscience, 2-135
      Pediatric, 2-136
    Council of Cardiovascular, 2-136
    Fedn. of Mental Health, 2-136
  College of (Ont.), 2-137
  Fdn., Cdn., 2-137
  in Independent Practice, Cdn. Assn. of, 2-136
  & Nursing Assistants, Cdn. Assn. of Practical, 2-136
  in Oncology, Cdn. Assn. of, 2-136
  Protective Soc., Cdn., 2-137
  Publications, *see* Nursing Publications
  Registered, Assns., 2-136/137
  Respiratory Soc., Cdn., 2-137
  Union of Psychiatric, 2-138
  Unions: B.C., 2-135; Man., 2-137; Ntl. Fedn. of, 2-203; N.B., 2-137; Nfld./Lab., 2-137; N.S., 2-137; P.E.I., 2-138; Qué., 2-138; Sask., 2-138
  V.O.N., 2-138
Nursing
  Assistants
    Adv. Com. (Yukon), 3-224
    Assn(s)., 2-136
    Cdn. Assn. of Practical Nurses &, 2-136
    Programs (Ont.), 3-41
  Assns., 2-135
    Gerontological: Cdn., 2-136; Ont., 2-137
  Cdn. Assn.
    for the History of, 2-135
    of Univ. Schs. of, 2-47
  Educ. Ctr., Mack (Niagara Coll.), 9-33
  Faculties/Schs., Index to, 9-57
  Home(s)
    Assns., 2-100; Ont., 2-101
    Facilities in: Alta, 8-6; B.C., 8-10; Man., 8-13; N.B., 8-16; Nfld., 8-18; N.W.T., 8-19; N.S., 8-20; Ont., 8-25; P.E.I., 8-34; Qué., 8-40; Sask., 8-54
  Magazines, 5-173
  Stations in: Alta., 8-8; B.C., 8-11; Man., 8-15; Nfld., 8-18; Ont., 8-32; Yukon, 8-56
Nut
  Council, Cdn., 2-73
  Growers Soc. of, Ont., 2-16
Nutrition
  Ctr. for Human (U.W.O.), 9-31
  Council of Alta., Dairy, 2-14
  Govt. Quick Ref., 3-28
  Mgmt., Cdn. Soc. of, 2-90
  National Inst. of, 2-93
Nutritional Sciences, Cdn. Soc. for, 2-162
Nutritionists' Assns., 2-86

O

O Canada, 1-25
Oakville, Town of, Govt., 4-163
OBS (Fed.), 3-85
Observatories, 1-1
Obstetric Nurses, 2-137
Obstetricians & Gynaecologists, Soc. of, 2-94
Obstétriciens et gynécologues du Qué., Assn des, 2-82
Occupation, Employment by Detailed (Statistics), 1-51
Occupational
  Certification Bd., N.B. Apprenticeship &, 3-133
  & Environmental Medical Assn., 2-93
  First Aid Attendants Assn. of B.C., 2-55
  Health Nurses Assn., 2-137
  Servs. Br. (Fed.), 3-71

Occupational (cont.)
  Health & Safety (*see also* Workplace Health & Safety)
    Cdn. Centre for, 2-85, 3-57
    Govt. Agencies/Brs./Divs.: Quick Ref., 3-28; Alta., 3-102; Fed., 3-57; Man., 3-129; Nfld., 3-143; N.S., 3-162; Ont., 3-225; Qué., 3-209; Sask., 3-218; Yukon, 3-225
    Research Inst., Qué., 2-160
  Medical Assns.: Canada, 2-93; Qué., 2-82
  Safety, Govt. Quick Ref., 3-28
    & Health
      Cdn. Libraries in, 2-118
  Therapists
    Cdn. Assn. of, 2-84
    World Fedn. of, 2-94
  Therapy Fdn., Cdn., 2-88
  Training, Govt. Quick Ref., 3-29
Occupations Bd. (Qué.), 3-204
Ocean(s)
  Fisheries &, Canada, 3-67
  Engineering Research Ctr. (Memorial Univ.), 9-20
  Inst. of Canada, 2-163
  Pêches et, Canada, 3-67
  Sciences
    Centre (Memorial Univ.), 9-20
    Inst. of, 3-68
  Voice Intl., 2-64
Oceanographic Soc., Cdn., 2-162
Oceanography
  Bedford Inst. of, 3-68
  Govt. Quick Ref., 3-29
Oecuménique pour la justice économique, Coalition, 2-7
Oecumenisme, Centre cdn d', 2-6
Oeufs
  de comsommation, Fédn des producteurs d' (Qué.), 2-142, 3-198
  d'incubation Synd. des producteurs d' (Qué.), 3-198
  Office cdn de commercialisation des, 2-142
  et de volailles, Conseil cdn des transformateurs d', 2-142
Office
  Employees Union, Cdn., 2-206
  Equipment
    Exhibitions, Shows & Events, 1-89
    Magazines, 5-173
    Machine Dealers' Assn., Cdn., 2-158
  Products
    Assn., Cdn., 2-158
    Mfrs. Assn. of Canada, 2-124
  & Profl. Employees, Intl. Union of, 2-204
Official(s)
  Guardian: Ont., 3-171; Yukon, 3-224
  Languages
    Br. (Fed.), 3-58
    Govt. Quick Ref. (*see* Bilingualism), 3-5
  Office of
    Commr. of, 3-84
    N.W.T., 3-150
  Receivers (Bankruptcy), 10-21
Offshore
  Petroleum (Govt.): Canada-Nfld., 3-148; Canada-N.S., 3-163
  & Remote Medicine, Ctr. for (Memorial Univ.), 9-20
  Trade Assn. of N.S., 2-188
Oil
  Assns., 2-78
  & Colour Chemists Assn. Ont., 2-35
  Companies, Cdn., 7-49
  Foods, Inst. for Edible, 2-73
  & Gas (*see also* Petroleum)
    Brs./Divs. (Govt.): Fed., 3-83; N.W.T., 3-153
    Companies, Cdn., 7-49
    Exhibitions, Shows & Events, 1-89
    Exploration (SOQUIP), 3-206
    Magazines, 5-174
    Govt. Quick Ref., 3-29

Oil (cont.)
  Wkrs. Atlantic, 2-198; United, 2-207
Oilers, Intl. Broth. of Firemen &, 2-202
Oilwell Drilling Contr., Cdn. Assn. of, 2-44
OISE, 9-35
Okanagan
  Fdn., Central, 2-209
  Sch. Dist., Central, 9-6
  Univ. College, 9-9
  Valley Tree Fruit Auth. (Govt.), 3-108
Old
  Age Assistance, Govt. Quick Ref. (*see* Senior Citizens)
  Fort William Adv. Com. (Ont.), 3-176
  Holy Catholic Church, 2-5
  Order Amish Church, 2-5
Older
  Adult Centres' Assn. of Ont., 2-164
  Worker Adjustment Br. (Fed.), 3-72
Olds College (Alta.), 9-4
Olympic(s)
  Assn., Cdn., 2-176
  Special, 2-177
  Studies, Ctr. for (U.W.O.), 9-31
  Trust of Canada, 2-179
Ombudsman, Cdn. Banking, 7-1
Ombudsmen (Govt.): Quick Ref., 3-29; Alta., 3-103; B.C., 3-118; CBC, 3-56; Man., 3-130; N.B., 3-139; N.S., 3-163; Ont., 3-185; Qué., 3-204; Sask., 3-219
OMF Intl., 2-8
OMMRI, 2-64
Omnicom Profl. Language Services (Ont.), 9-35
Omnipraticiens du Qué., Fédn des médecins, 2-91
Oncologists, Cdn. Assn. of Medical, 2-83
Oncology
  Cdn.
    Assn. of Nurses in, 2-136
    Soc. of Surgical, 2-90
  Care of Ont., Children's, 2-90
One Parent Families Assn. of Canada, 2-168
One Voice - Seniors Network, 2-164
ONLINE, Operation (Nfld.), 3-146
Online Service Providers, 5-230 (& *see* Addenda)
Onomastique, Soc. cdnne d', 2-96
Ontario
  Agricultural Colleges in, 9-34
  Aquaria in, 6-46
  Archives in, 5-113
  Art
    Galleries in, 6-32
    Gallery of, 3-173
  Arts Council, 3-173
  Boards of Trade in, 7-30
  Botanical Gardens in, 6-46
  Centres of Excellence, 2-157
  Chambers of Commerce in, 7-30
  Cities & Towns in, 4-42
  College of Art, 9-34
  Colleges of Applied Arts & Tech. in, 9-32
  Counties & Districts in, 4-73/4
  Courts & Judges in, 10-10
  Devel. Corp., 3-176
  Education in, 9-23
  Flag & Coat of Arms, **12**
  FreeNets, 5-233
  Government in, 3-164
  Hospitals in, 8-21
  Hydro, 3-185
    Profl. & Admin. Employees, 2-206
  Inst. for Studies in Educ., 9-35
  Law Firms in, 10-49
  Libraries in, 5-39
  Lobbyists in, 7-36
  Meeting, Conference, Exhibit & Event Planners in, 1-68 (& *see* Addenda)
  Municipal Govt. in, 4-42
  Museums in, 6-16
  Native Schs. in, 9-27

Ontario (cont.)
  Newspapers in, 5-138
  Northland, 3-185
  Nursing Homes in, 8-25
  Online Service Providers in, 5-230
  Place Corp., 3-176
  Post Sec. & Spec. Insts. in, 9-34
  Private Schs. in, 9-36
  Regl. Mun. in, 4-74, 4-171
  Savings Office, 7-3
  Sch. Bds.: Public, 9-24; Separate, 9-25
  Science Centre, 6-16, 3-173
  Univs. in, 9-28
    Council of, 2-51
  Zoos in, 6-45
Open
  Bidding Serv. (Fed.), 3-85
  Learning Agency (B.C.), 3-111; 9-9
Opera
  Assns.: Calgary, 6-39; Edmonton, 6-40; Man., 6-40; Saskatoon, 6-41; Vancouver, 6-41
  Awards, *see* Performing Arts
  Chorus, Cdn. Children's, 6-39
  Company, Cdn., 6-40
  Cos. of Canada, Profl., 6-41
  Magazines, *see* Music Magazines
  de Montréal, 6-40
  Ontario, 6-41
  Victoria, Pacific, 6-41
Opérateurs de machinerie lourde, Union des, 2-207
Operating
  Engineers
    Cdn. Union of, 2-199
    Educ. & Development Inc. (Nfld.), 9-21
    Intl. Union of, 2-203
  Room Nurses Assn. of Canada, 2-137
Operation
  Eyesight Universal, 2-109
  Mobilization Canada, 2-8
  ONLINE (Nfld.), 3-146
Operational Research Soc., Cdn., 2-155
Operative Plasterers' & Cement Masons' Intl. Assn., 2-204
Ophtalmologistes du Qué., Assn des médecins, 2-82
Ophthalmological Soc., Cdn., 2-88
OPIRG, 2-157
Opportunities
  Agency, Atl. Canada, 3-54
  Corp., Sask., 3-213
Opportunity Co., Alta., 3-97
Opposition Offices & Leaders (Govt.): Alta., 3-93; B.C., 3-106; Fed., 3-46; Man., 3-121 N.B., 3-132; Nfld., 3-141; N.S., 3-155; Ont., 3-166; P.E.I., 3-187; Qué., 3-194; Sask., 3-210; Yukon, 3-221
Optical Magazines, 5-172
Optics Inst., Ntl., 2-59
Optique, Inst ntl d', 2-59
Optometrists Assns., 2-84
Optometry
  Assn. of Schools of, 2-46
  Publications, *see* Optical Publications
ORADIO, 2-27
Oral
  History Assn., Cdn., 2-96
  & Maxillofacial Surgeons, Cdn. Assn. of, 2-84
  Pathology, Cdn. Academy of, 2-39
  Radiology, Cdn. Academy of, 2-39
Orange Lodges, 2-76
Orchestras, 6-37
  Assn. of Cdn., 6-37
  Ontario, 6-41
  symphonique des jeunes de Montréal, 6-41
Orchid Soc., Southern Ont., 2-99
Order of
  the Bath, 1-30
  the British Empire, 1-30
  Canada, **15**, 1-26
  Excellence Council, Alta., 3-97

Order of (cont.)
  the Indian Empire, 1-30
  Military Merit, **15**, 1-27
  St. Michael & St. George, 1-30
Orders
  Benevolant, 2-75
  of Knighthood, 1-30
  Precedence, 1-31
Ordinariat militaire du Canada, 2-5
Ordinateur, Soc. cdnne pour l'étude d'intelligence par, 2-103
Organ
  Donors Canada, 2-94
  Retrieval & Exchange Prog., Multiple, 2-93
Organic
  Growers, Cdn., 2-14
  Trade Assn., 2-73
Organists, Royal Cdn. College of, 6-41
Organization Mgmt., Cdn. Inst. of, 2-121
Organizations 2-8
  Bur., Intl. (Fed.), 3-69
Orientation
  et de consultation, Soc. cdnne d', 2-166
  Corp. profl. des conseillers d', 2-56
Orienteering Fedn., Cdn., 2-150
Ornamental Plant Fdn., Cdn., 2-99
Ornithologists, Soc. of Cdn., 2-135
Orphans, Cdn. Fellowship for Romanian, 2-166
ORT
  Canada, 2-131
  Women's Cdn., 2-247
Orthesistes, Assn cdnne des prosthesistes et, 2-84
Orthodontists
  Cdn. Assn. of, 2-40
  Convention(s), *see* Dental Exhibitions, Shows & Events
Orthodox
  Antiochan, 2-2
  Church: in Amer., 2-5; Cdn., 2-3; Coptic, 2-3; Greek, 2-4; Romanian, 2-5; Serbian, 2-5; Ukranian, 2-6
  Churches, Patriarchal Parishes of the Russian, 2-5
  Dukhobors in Canada, 2-6
  Missionary Church, 2-5
Orthopaedic
  Assn., Cdn., 2-88
  Nurses Assn., Cdn., 2-137
  Technologists, Cdn. Soc. of, 2-90
Orthopédie du Qué., Assn, 2-82
Orthophonistes et audiologistes
  Assn. cdnne des, 2-84
  Ordre des (Qué.), 2-94
Orthoptic
  Council, Cdn., 2-88
  Soc., Cdn., 2-88
Orthotists, Cdn. Assn. of Prosthetists &, 2-84
Osgoode Hall
  Environmental Law Society, 2-64
  Law Sch. (York Univ.), 9-32
Oshawa City Govt., 4-163
Osteogenesis Imperfecta Soc., Cdn., 2-88
Osteopathic
  Aid Soc., Cdn., 2-88
  Assn., Cdn., 2-88
Osteoporosis Soc. of Canada, 2-94
Ostomy Assn., United, 2-94
Oto-rhino-laryngologie & de chirurgie cervico-faciale du Qué., Assn d', 2-82
Otolaryngology, Cdn. Soc. of, 2-90
Ottawa
  Bd. of Educ., 9-25
  -Carleton
    Community Fdn. of, 2-209
    Regl. Mun. Govt., 4-172; Map, 4-174
  City Govt., 4-163
  Congress Centre Corp., 3-176
  Map, Regional, 4-174
  Sch. of Art, 9-34
  Univ. of, 9-30

Our Lady of the Prairies Fdn., 2-213
Outaouais
   Communauté urbaine de l', 4-173; Carte/Map, 4-174
      Devel. Corp., 3-197
      Soc. d'aménagement de l' (Qué.), 3-197
Outdoor
   Advtg. Assn. of Canada, 2-12
   Educators of Ont., Council of, 2-51
   Measurement Bur., Cdn., 2-11
   Power Equip. Assn., Cdn., 2-66
   Recreation Br. (Yukon), 3-225
Outfitters Assn. of B.C., Fishing, 2-149; Guide, 2-152
Outillage municipal, Assn des profls à l', 2-65
Outrigger Racing Assn., Cdn., 2-150
Outward Bound: Ont., 2-153; Western Canada, 2-153, 9-9
Overseas
   Missionary Fellowship, 2-8
   Offices, Govt., *see* Foreign Offices
   Schs. (Ont.), 9-40
   Student Selection Offices, (B.C.), 9-13
Ovulation Method Billings, World Org., 2-154
Owens Art Gallery (N.B.), 6-31
Owners & Pilots Assn., Cdn., 2-28
Oxfam-Canada, 2-109

P

Pacific
   Asia Travel Assn., 2-186
   Biological Stn., 3-68
   Corridor Enterprise Council, 2-35
   Fisheries Orgs., 3-248
   Halibut Commn., Intl., 3-248
   Lester B. Pearson College of the (B.C.), 9-9
   Pilotage Auth. (Fed.), 3-84
   Salmon Commn., 3-248
   Studies, Joint Ctr. for Asia: U. of T., 9-31; York Univ., 9-32
   Univ. Libraries, Council of Prairie &, 2-119
Pacifique, Adm. de Pilotage du (Fed.), 3-84
Packaging
   Adv. Council, Cdn. Seniors, 2-138
   Assn(s)., 2-138
   Coalition, Environmentally Sound, 2-138
   Environmental Council, Paper & Paperboard, 2-138
   Exhibitions, Shows & Events, 1-89
   Magazines, 5-174
   & Printing Machinery Mfrs. Assn., Cdn., 2-66
PACT Communications Centre, 6-36
Paddle Sport BC, 2-153
Paddling Assn., Man., 2-150
Paediatric
   Fdn., Cdn., 2-88
   Hospitals, Cdn. Assn. of, 2-100
   Soc., Cdn., 2-88
   Surgeons, Cdn. Assn. of, 2-84
Paie, Assn cdnne de la, 2-70
Paiements, Assn cdnne des, 2-70
Pain
   Assn. of Canada, N. Amer. Chronic, 2-93
   Soc., Cdn., 2-88
Paint
   & Coatings Assn., Cdn., 2-31
   Magazines, 5-174
Painters'
   & Allied Trades
      Intl. Broth. of, 2-202
      Ntl. Assn. of (Qué.), 2-197
   & Decorators Assn. of B.C., 2-32
   in Water Colour, Cdn. Soc. of, 2-190
Painting Contractors Assn., Ont., 2-33
Paix
   Alliance cdnne pour la, 2-108
      Développement et, 2-8
      Fonds cdn pour la, 2-109
      Science et, 2-109
Pakistan Cdn. Friendship Soc., Progressive, 2-132

Pakistani
   Canadians, Ntl. Fedn. of, 2-132
   Magazines, 5-192
Paleontology, Royal Tyrrell Museum of, 6-2
Pallet
   & Container Assn., Cdn. Wood, 2-75
   Council, Cdn., 2-74
Palliative Care
   Assn., Cdn., 2-88
   Fdn., Jean Cameron, 2-211
Palliser Inst. (Sask.), 9-54
Palomino Horse Assn., Cdn., 2-20
Palynologists, Cdn. Assn. of, 2-161
Pan Macedonian Assn., 2-132
Panneaux
   de particules, Assn cdnne des, 2-74
   structural, Assn du, 2-33
PAPA, 2-25
Paper (*see also* Pulp & Paper)
   Box Mfrs. Assn., Cdn., 2-138
   Companies, Cdn., 7-43
   & Forest Wkrs., Fedn. of, 2-201
   Money Soc., Cdn., 2-150
   & Paperboard Packing Env. Council, 2-138
   Processing Trade Shows, 1-89
   Trade Assn., Cdn., 2-74
Paperboard Packaging Env. Council, 2-138
Paperworkers
   Independent, 2-202
   Intl. Union, United, 2-208
   Union of Canada, Communications, Energy &, 2-200
Papier
   et de la forêt, Fédn des travailleurs du, 2-201
   Synd. cdn des communications, de l'énergie et du, 2-200
PAPRICAN, 2-157
Parachuting Assn., Cdn. Sport, 2-151
Parades des dix sous, Qué., 2-43; Conseil Ntl de la, 2-42
Paragliding Assn., Hang Gliding &, 2-152
Paralympic Com., Cdn., 2-176
Paralysie cérébrale, Assn cdnne des sports de, 2-174
Paraplegia Fdn., Man., 2-93
Paraplegic Assn., B.C., 2-83, Cdn., 2-88
Parc(s)
   Assn cdnne des loisirs et, 2-150
   -autos du Qué. metropolitain, Soc., 3-210
   cdns, Partenaires des, 2-61
   Ntls, 3-59
   et des sites naturales, Soc. pour la protection des, 2-150
Parent
   Adv. Councils, B.C. Confed. of, 2-49
   & Child Health, Div. (Nfld.), 3-146
   Co-operative Preschools Intl., 2-53
   Council, Ont., 3-177; Man., 2-49
   Finders of Canada, 2-168
   Participation Preschools, Qué. Council of, 2-53
   Resources Inst. for Drug Education, 2-168
   -Teacher Assns. of Ont., Fedn. of, 2-51
Parenthood Fedn., Planned, 2-154
Parents
   Against Drugs, 2-10
   catholiques du Qué., Assn des, 2-6
   in Crisis Soc., B.C., 2-165
   of the Environmentally Sensitive, 2-168
   Fédn prov. des comités de (Man.), 2-52
   francophones de, Fédns: Alta., 2-52; Ont., 2-51
   for French, Cdn., 2-111
   for German Educ., 2-53
   of Multiple Births Assn. of Canada, 2-36
   de la Province de Qué., Fédn des comités de parents, 2-51
   -secours du Canada, Programme, 2-165
Parfums, Assn cdnne des cosmétiques, produits de toilette et, 2-123

Parishes, Qué., 4-77
Paritaire pour la santé et sécurité du travail, Assns, 2-159
Parkinson Fdn. of Canada, 2-94
Parkinson's Disease Assn., B.C., 2-83
Parkland Regional College (Sask.), 9-55
Parks
   Assn., Ont., 2-152
   Canada Sector (Fed.), 3-58
   Council, Ont., 3-184
   Depts. (Govt.): Quick Ref., 3-29; B.C., 3-112
   Brs./Divs. (Govt.): Alta., 3-99; Man., 3-129; N.B., 3-139; Nfld., 3-149; N.W.T., 3-153; N.S., 3-163; Ont., 3-184; P.E.I. (Tourism), 3-189; Qué., 3-201; Sask., 3-214; Yukon, 3-225
   Environment, Lands &, Min. (B.C.), 3-112
   Govt. Quick Ref., 3-29
   Ntl., List of, 3-59
   & Outdoor Recreation Dir. (Yukon), 3-225
   Partnership, Cdn., 2-61
   Pippy Park Commn. (Nfld.), 3-149
   /Recreation Assns., 2-150
   & Wilderness Soc., Cdn., 2-150
   & Wildlife Fdn., Recreation, Alta., 3-97
Parlement, Bibliothèque du, 3-79
Parlementaires de langue française, Assemblée intl des, 2-38
Parliament
   Cdn., 3-43
   Govt. Quick Ref., 3-30
   Library of, 3-79
   Members of, 3-47
      Forms of Address, 1-33
Parliamentary
   Centre, 2-188
   Librarians, Assn. of, 2-116
   Representation, 3-47
Paroisses, Qué., 4-77
Parole
   Boards (Govt.): Quick Ref., 3-30; B.C., 3-110; Ntl., 3-80; Ont., 3-186; Qué., 3-208
   Offices, Correctional Services (Fed.), 3-63
Parti
   communiste du Qué., 2-141
   Démocratique, Nouveau, 2-142
   Libéral, Qué., 2-141
   progressiste-conservateur, 2-142
   québécois, 2-142
   réformiste du Canada, 2-142
   socialiste du Canada, 2-142
   des travailleurs du Qué., 2-142
Particleboard Assn., Cdn., 2-74
Passover, 1-24
Passport(s)
   Affairs Br. (Fed.), 3-69
   Govt. Quick Ref., 3-30
   Info., 3-70
   Offices, 3-69
Pastoral Practice & Educ., Cdn. Assn. for, 2-47
Patent(s)
   Appeal Bd. (Fed.), 3-75
   Assns., 2-138
   Commr. (Fed. Govt.), 3-75
   Govt. Quick Ref., 3-30
   & Trademark Inst. of Canada, 2-138
Patented Medicine Prices Review Bd. (Fed.), 3-84
Pâtes et papiers
   Assn
      cdnne des, 2-75
      de santé et securité des, 2-159
   Inst. cdn de recherches sur les, 2-157
Pathologistes du Qué., Assn des, 2-82
Pathologists
   & Audiologists, Cdn. Assn. of Speech-Language, 2-84
   Cdn. Assn. of, 2-84
Patients Rights Assn., 2-102

Canadian Almanac & Directory 1997

Patinage
    artistique
        Assn cdnne de, 2-175
        du Qué., Fén de, 2-179
    -de vitesse amateur, Assn cdnne de, 2-173
Patissiers du Qué., Soc. des chefs, cuisiniers et, 2-158
Patriarchal Parishes of the Russian Orthodox Church, 2-5
Patrimoine
    Assn
        cdnne des consultants, 2-95
        qué. d'interprétation du, 2-95
    Cdn. (Fed.), 3-58
    franco-ontarien, Regroupement des orgs du, 2-97
    industriel, Assn qué. pour le, 2-95
    musical cdn, Soc. pour le, 6-40
    Réseau cdn d'info. sur le, 2-96
Patristic Studies, Cdn. Soc. of, 2-155
Patronat du Qué., Conseil du, 2-35
Patrouille cdnne de ski, 2-176
Pattern Recognition Soc., Cdn. Image Processing &, 2-103
Pavilion Corp., B.C., 3-118
Pay Equity
    B.C., see Employment Equity
    Commns. (Govt.): N.S., 3-163; Ont., 3-181
    Govt. Quick Ref., 3-30
Pay TV Services, 5-223
Payments Assn., Cdn., 2-70
Payroll Assn., Cdn., 2-70
PC Party, 2-142
    Office of the Leader (Fed.), 3-46
Pea & Bean Growers' Marketing Bd., N.S. Processing, 3-156
Peace
    Alliance, Cdn., 2-108
    Brigades Intl., 2-109
    Cdn. Catholic Org. for Devel. &, 2-8
    & Conflict Studies Program (U. of T.), 9-31
    Congress, Cdn., 2-108
    Devel. &, 2-8
    Science for, 2-109
Peacefund Canada, 2-109
Peacemakers, Project, 2-109
Peat
    Moss Assn., Cdn. Sphagnum, 2-14
    & Peatlands, Cdn. Soc. for, 2-61
Pêche(s)
    & Aquiculture commerciales (Qué.), 3-197
    Assn québécoise de l'industrie de la, 2-71
    Centre cdn d'innovations des, 2-71
    Conseil cdn des, 2-71
    Depts. (Govt.): Fed., 3-67; N.B., 3-136
    et Océans Canada, 3-67
    Office des prix des produits de la, 3-68
Pêcheries, & de l'alimentation, Min. de l'Agric. (Qué.) 3-197
Pêcheurs profls du Qué., Alliance des, 2-71
Pédagogiques
    Centre franco-ontarien de ressources, 2-51
    Conseil ontarien de recherches, 2-53
Pediatric (see also Paediatric)
    Hosps., Cdn. Assn. of, 2-100
    Nurses, Cdn. Assn. of, 2-136
Pédiatres du Qué., Assn des, 2-82
Pédiatrie
    La fdn cdnne de, 2-88
    Soc, cdnne de, 2-88
Pedigreed Seed Bd., P.E.I., 3-189
Peel (Ont.)
    Bd. of Educ., 9-25
    Regl. Mun. Govt., 4-172
P.E.I. see Prince Edward Island
Peintres
    en aquarelle, Soc. cdnne de, 2-190
    et métiers connexes, Assn ntle des, 2-197

Peinture
    du Qué., Conseil de la, 2-190
    et du revêtement, L'Assn cdnne de l'industrie de la, 2-31
Pelvic Inflammatory Disease Soc., 2-88
Pembina Inst. for Appropriate Devel., 2-64
PEN Canada, 2-102
Pen-Parents of Canada, 2-168
Penmen & Teachers of Handwriting, Intl. Assn. of Master, 2-52
Pension(s) (see also Superannuation)
    Advocates, Bur. of (Fed.), 3-92
    Appeals Bd., 10-2
    & Benefits Inst., Cdn., 2-70
    Bds. (Govt.): Alta., 3-105; Ont., 3-182; Qué., 3-208
    Brs./Divs. (Govt.): Alta., 3-102; N.B., 3-136; Nfld., 3-143; N.S., 3-159
    Commns. (Govt.): Man., 3-129; Ont., 3-179
    Govt. Quick Ref., 3-30
    Investment Assn. of Canada, 2-71
    Management, Assn. of Cdn., 2-69
    Supervisory Auths., Cdn. Assn. of, 2-69
    Supts. (Govt): Alta., 3-102; B.C., 3-117; Man., 3-129; N.B., 3-136; N.S., 3-159; Ont., 3-179; Sask., 3-217
    Veterans, 3-92
Pensioners
    Concerned, Cdn., 2-164
    & Senior Citizens
        Fedn., Ntl., 2-164
        Org., Alta. Prov., 2-163
Pentecost, Apostolic Church of, 2-2
Pentecostal
    Assemblies
        of Canada, 2-5
        of Newfoundland, 2-5
        Sch. Bd. (Nfld.), 9-19
    Bible College, Western, (B.C.), 9-10
    Church, Italian, 2-4
    College (Sask.) Central, 9-54
People
    First Soc. of Alta., 2-43
    Words & Change, 2-168
People's Law School, 2-115
Peptic Ulcer Research Fdn., Cdn., 2-88
Percheron Assn., Cdn., 2-20
Performers
    Awards, see Performing Arts
    Cdn. Soc. of Children's, 2-194
Performing
    Arts (see also Arts), 6-35
        Assn. for Native Devel. in, 2-132
        Awards, 1-08 (see also Culture Awards)
        Directory, 6-35
        Festivals, B.C., 2-66
        Fdn., Governor General's, 2-25
        Magazines, see Entertainment Magazines
        Publicists Assns., 2-25
        Rights Org. of Canada, see SOCAN
Perfusionnistes du Qué., Assn. des, 2-197
Perinatal Research Fdn., Molly Towell, 2-212
Periodical
    Council, Book &, 2-144
    Marketers of Canada, 2-145
    Writers Assn. of Canada, 2-194
Périodiques culturels qué., Soc. de dével., 2-146
Permanent
    Joint Bd. on Defence, 3-247
    Missions & Delegations Abroad, 3-247
Permis d'alcool, voir Liquor Bds.
Perpetual Calendar, 1-23
Personal
    Care Homes Program, Dir. (Nfld.), 3-146
    Property Regn. (Govt.): Alta., 3-103; B.C., 3-114; Ont., 3-174 (see also Deeds Regrs.)
Personnel (see also Human Resources)
    Mgmt. Assn., Cdn. Public, 2-121

Personnes handicapées
    Conseil du premier sour la condition (N.B.), 3-134
    Office des (Qué.), 3-207
Pest Mgmt.
    Regulatory Agency (Fed.), 3-72
    Soc., Cdn., 2-14
Pesticide(s)
    Adv.
        Com., Ont., 3-178
        Council, N.B., 3-135
    Control Officials, Cdn. Assn. of, 2-98
    Info. (Fed. Govt.), 3-71
    Mgmt. Br. (Govt.): N.B., 3-135; N.S., 3-159; P.E.I., 3-188
Pet(s)
    Food Assn. of Canada, 2-74
    Industry Joint Advisory Council, 2-22
    Trade Shows, 1-89
Pétanque, Fédn cdnne de, 2-151
Peterborough City Govt., 4-163
Petite taille, Assn qué. des personnes de, 2-165
Pétrole, Travailleurs unis du, 2-207
Petroleum (see also Oil & Gas; Natural Gas)
    Accountants Soc. of Canada, 2-9
    Assns., 2-78
    Bds., Offshore: Canada-Nfld., 3-148; Canada-N.S., 3-163
    Brs./Divs. (Govt.): Alta., 3-98; B.C., 3-112; Man., 3-124; N.W.T., 3-152; Sask., 3-214
    Cdn. Inst. of Mining, Metallurgy &, 2-127; Awards, 6-68
    Communication Fdn., 2-78
    Devel.,
        Agency (N.S.), 3-163
        Offshore & (Nfld.), 3-148
    Equip. Mfrs. Assn., Cdn., 2-66
    Geologists, Cdn. Soc. of, 2-78
    Geology Br. (B.C.), 3-112
    Industry Training Serv. (Alta.), 9-4
    Law Fdn., Cdn., 2-114
    Magazines, 5-174
    Producers, Cdn. Assn. of, 2-78
    Products
        Div. (N.W.T.), 3-152
        Inst., Cdn., 2-78
    Services Assn. of Canada, 2-78
    Society of CIM, 2-128
    Tax Soc., Cdn., 2-183
    Titles Br. (B.C.), 3-112
Pétroliers(ières)
    Assn cdnne des producteurs, 2-78
    Fdn des communications sur les ressources, 2-78
    Inst cdn des produits, 2-78
    Soc. qué. d'initiatives, 3-206
PFRA, 3-54
Pharmacare (B.C.), 3-116
Pharmaceutical(s) (see also Drugs)
    Assn(s)., 2-139; Cdn., 2-139
    Companies, Cdn., 7-40
    Exhibitions, Shows & Events, 1-89
    Manufacturers
        Assn. of Canada, 2-140
        Reps., Council for Accreditation of, 2-139
    Strategy, Ntl., 3-71
    Technology, Toronto Inst. of, 9-35
Pharmaciens
    Assn des conseils des médecins, dentistes et (Qué.), 2-82
    des établissements de santé du Qué., 2-82
    Ordre des, 2-139
    propriétaires, Assn qué. des, 2-139
    salariés, Assn profl des, 2-139
Pharmacists
    Assn(s)., 2-139; Ont., 2-139
    Cdn. Soc. of Hosp., 2-139
    Man. Soc. of, 2-139
Pharmacological Soc. of Canada, 2-162
Pharmacologie, Conseil consultatif de (Qué.), 3-207

Pharmacology
  Adv. Council on (Qué.), 3-207
  Cdn. Soc. for Clinical, 2-89
Pharmacy
  Assn(s)., 2-139
    B.C., 2-139
    of Deans of, 2-46
    of Faculties of, 2-139
    of N.S., 2-140
  Board, P.E.I., 2-140
  Cdn. Fdn. for, 2-86
  Council, Atlantic Provs., 2-139
  Examining Bd. of Canada, 2-140
  Faculties/Schs., Index to, 9-57
  Programs, The Cdn., Council for the Accreditation of, 2-85
  Registrars, Conf. of, 2-139
  Regulatory Authorities, Ntl. Assn. of, 2-139
  Students & Interns, Cdn. Assn. of, 2-139
Philanthropy, Cdn. Centre for, 2-166
Philatelic
  Exhibitions, see Hobbies Exhibitions
  Magazines, see Hobbies Magazines
  Research Fdn., The RPSC, 2-153
  Soc., Royal, 2-153
Philosophical Assn., Cdn., 2-155
Philosophy
  Inst. of Speculative, 2-156
  of Science
    Cdn. Soc. for the History &, 2-162
    & Tech., Inst. for History & (U. of T.), 9-31
  & Theology, Dominican College of (Ont.), 9-35
Phosphate Inst. of Canada, Potash &, 2-36
Photo
  Magazines, see Photography Magazines
  Marketing Assn. Intl., 2-140
Photographers
  Assns., 2-140
  of Canada, Profl., 2-140
  Gallery Soc., 2-140
  & Illustrators in Communication, Cdn. Assn. of, 2-140
Photographes
  et illustrateurs de publicité, Assn de, 2-140
  du Qué., Corp. des Maîtres, 2-140
Photographic Art, Ntl. Assn. for, 2-140
Photographical Historical Soc. of Canada, 2-140
Photographie Marsan, Collège de (Qué.), 9-47
Photography
  Assns., 2-140
  Awards see Journalism; Visual Arts
  Cdn. Museum of Contemporary, 6-1
  Magazines, 5-174, 5-187
Physiâtres du Qué., Assn des, 2-82
Physical
  Activity, Cdn. Assn. for Adv. of Women & Sport &, 2-191
  Educ., Rec. & Dance, Cdn. Assn. for, 2-174
  Medicine & Rehab., Cdn. Assn. of, 2-84
Physically
  Challenged, P.E.I. Recreation & Sports Assn. for the, 2-179
  Disabled
    Nfld. Soc. for, 2-43
    Persons, Cdn. Fdn. for, 2-42
Physician(s)
  for Aid & Relief, Cdn., 2-108
  Cdn. Assn. of Emergency, 2-83
  College of Family, 2-91
  Conferences, see Medical, 1-87
  for Global Survival, 2-109
  Services Inc. Fdn., 2-213
  for a Smoke-Free Canada, 2-10
  & Surgeons
    Colleges of, 2-92
    Royal College of, 2-94

Physiciens
  Assn cdnne des, 2-161
  en médecine, Collège cdn des, 2-161
Physicists
  Cdn. Assn. of, 2-161
  in Medicine, Cdn. College of, 2-161
Physics Awards, see Scientific
Physiological Soc., Cdn., 2-162
Physiologie de l'exercice, Soc. cdnne de, 2-177
Physiologists, Cdn. Soc. of Plant, 2-162
Physiothérapeutes
  Alliance des corporations profiles de, 2-81
  Corp. profile des (Qué.), 2-91
  & des thérapeutes en réadaptation physique du Qué, Synd. des, 2-206
Physiotherapists, College of (Ont.), 9-35
Physiotherapy
  Assn., Cdn., 2-88
  Div. of the Cdn. Physio. Assn., Sports, 2-180
  Regulatory Bds., Alliance of, 2-81
Phytopathological Soc., Cdn., 2-162
Pickering, Town of, Govt., 4-163
Picture Pioneers, Cdn., 2-69
P.I.D. Soc., Cdn., 2-88
Pierre Hénault, Centre, 2-17
Pigeon Union, Racing, 2-151
PIJAC Canada, 2-22
Pilotage
  Administration de: Atlantique, 3-54; Grands Lacs, 3-70; Laurentides, 3-78; Pacifique, 3-84
  Authorities: Atlantic, 3-54; Great Lakes, 3-70; Laurentian, 3-78; Ports & Habours (Fed. Govt. Transp.), 3-91; Pacific, 3-84
Pilots
  Assn.
    Cdn.
      Air Line, 2-198
      Owners &, 2-28
      Seaplane, 2-28
      Ultralight, 2-28
    International Women, 2-28
Pinto Horse Assn., Cdn., 2-20
Pinzgauer Assn., Cdn., 2-20
Pioneer Rwy. Assn., Alta., 2-95
Pipe
  Assn., Cdn. Concrete, 2-30; Ont. Concrete, 2-33
  Fitting Industry, United Assn. of Journeymen & Apprentices of the Plumbing &, 2-207
  Inst., Corrugated Steel, 2-182
  Line Contractors Assn. of Canada, 2-33
Pipe-line du Nord Canada, Adm. du, 3-84
Pipeline(s)
  Agency, Northern, 3-84
  Assn., Cdn. Energy, 2-78
  Govt. Quick Ref., 3-31
Pippy Park Commn. (Nfld.), 3-149
Pitch-in Canada, 2-64
Place du Canada, Corp., 3-56
Placement
  Agencies & Consultants, Assn. of Profl., 2-55
  et gestion de personnel, Assn des entreprises en, 2-56
  en personnel agences et conseillers, Assn de, 2-55
PLAN Intl. Canada, 2-168
Plaidoyer-Victimes, Assn qué, 2-165
Plains Research Ctr., Cdn. (U. of Regina), 9-54
Plaintes, Commissaires aux (Qué.), 3-207
Planetarium(s), 1-1
Planetary
  Assn. for Clean Energy, 2-57
  Configurations, 1-14
Planets, 1-14, 1-16/21; Symbols for, 1-15
Planification fiscale et financière, Assn de, 2-69
Planned Parenthood Fedn. of Can., 2-154
Planners
  Cdn. Assn. of Financial, 2-69
  Institutes, 2-140

Planning (see also Land Use)
  Assns., 2-140
  Cdn. Inst. of Financial, 2-69
  des naissances, Fédn du Qué. pour le, 2-154
  Programs, Assn. of Cdn. Univ., 2-46
  Technicians, Cdn. Assn. of Certified, 2-140
Plant
  Biotechnology Research Inst. (NRC), 3-81
  Engrg. & Maintenance Assn. of Canada, 2-59
  Fdn., Cdn. Ornamental, 2-99
  Guard Wkrs. of Amer., Intl. Union, United, 2-203
  Health Dir., Animal & (Fed.), 3-53
  Industry Brs./Divs. (Govt.): Alta., 3-95; Fed., 3-53; N.S., 3-156
  Physiologists, Cdn. Soc. of, 2-162
Plantes ornamentales, Fdn cdn des, 2-99
Plasterers & Cement Masons, Intl. Assn. of the U.S. & Canada, Operative, 2-204
Plastic(s)
  & Allied Wkrs. Intl. Union, 2-201
  Industry, Soc. of the, 2-124
  Institute
    of Canada, Env. &, 2-63
    Cdn., 2-123
  Magazines, 5-174
  & Reconstructive, Surgery, Cdn. Academy of Facial, 2-83
  & Rubber Exhibitions, Shows & Events, 1-89
  Surgeons, Cdn. Soc. of, 2-90
  Workers of America, United, 2-208
Plate Printers, Die Stampers & Engravers Union of N. Amer., Intl., 2-203
Play Therapy Inst., Cdn., 2-125
Playwrights
  Awards see Literary Arts Awards
  Ctr., Sask., 6-36
  Man. Assn. of, 6-36
  Network, Alta., 6-35
  Union of Canada, 6-36
PLEA B.C., 2-144, Sask., 2-144
Plebiscite Office (N.W.T.), 3-150
Plomberie et de chauffage, L'Inst cdn de, 2-95
Plongeon
  amateur, Assn cdnne du, 2-173
  du Qué., Fédn du, 2-179
Ploughshares, Project, 2-109
Plowing Org., Cdn., 2-14
Plowmen's Assn., Ont., 2-15
Plumbers, Pipefitters & Insulators, Ntl. Assn. of (Qué), 2-197
Plumbing
  Assns., 2-94
  Engineers, Amer. Soc. of, 2-95
  & Heating
    Cdn. Inst. of, 2-95
    Contractors' Assn., Indep., 2-95
  Inspectors Assn., Ont., 2-95
  Magazines, 5-168
  & Pipefitting Indust. of U.S. & Canada, United Assn. of Journcymen & Apprentices of the, 2-207
Pluto, Planet, 1-14
Plymouth Brethren, 2-3
Plywood Assn., Cdn. Hardwood, 2-74
Pneu du Qué., Assn des spécialistes du, 2-25
Podiatry Assn., Ont., 2-93
Poetry
  Awards & Prizes see Literary Arts Awards
  Magazines, see Literary Magazines; Scholarly Publications
Poets, League of Cdn., 2-194
Pointe-à-Callière, Museum of Archaeology & History, 6-24
Poison Control Centres, Cdn. Assn. of, 2-159
Poisson d'eau douce, Off. de commercialisation du, 3-70
Polaires, commn cdnne des affaires, 3-61
Polar
  Commn., Cdn., 3-61
  Continental Shelf Project, 3-83

Police
	Academy, Atlantic, (P.E.I.), 9-41
	Arbitration Commn., Ont., 3-186
	Assn(s).
		Alta. Fedn. of, 2-113
		Cdn., 2-114
			Ntl. Rlwys., 2-199
			Pacific, 2-199
		of N.S., 2-204
		Ont., 2-115
		Ont. Prov., 2-204
		Qué. Prov., 2-197
	Atlantic Assn. of Chiefs of, 2-113
	Boards, Cdn. Assn. of, 2-113
	Broth., of the Royal Nfld. Constabulary Assn., 2-204
	Cdn. Assn. of Chiefs of, 2-113
	Canine Assn., Cdn., 2-22
	College
		Cdn. (Ont.), 3-88, 9-35
		Ont., 3-186
	Commemorative Assn., North-West Mounted, 2-97
	Commns.: B.C., 3-110; N.B., 3-139; N.S., 3-162; Qué., 3-207; Sask., 3-218
	Complaints
		Commns.: Nfld., 3-148; Ont., 3-172
		Investigator, Sask., 3-218
	Ethics Commr., Qué., 3-207
	Govt. Quick Ref., 3-31
	Inst. de, Qué., 3-208
	Magazines, 5-174
	Officers, B.C. Fedn. of, 2-198
	Ont. Assn. of Chiefs of, 2-115
	Ont. Prov., 3-186
	P.E.I. Assn. of Chiefs of, 2-115
	RCMP, 3-88
	Services
		Boards, Ont. Assn. of, 2-115
		Ont. Civilian Commn. on, 3-186
	Sûreté du Qué., 3-208
Polices et pompiers du Qué., Assn des directeurs de, 2-113
Policière, Commissaire à la déontologie (Qué.), 3-207
Policiers
	Assn cdnne des, 2-114
	du Cdn Pacifique, Assn des, 2-199
	des chemins de fer nationaux, Assn des, 2-199
	de l'Ont., Assn des, 2-115
	Prov. du Qué., Assn des, 2-197
	du Qué., Fédn des, 2-201
Policing Services Brs./Divs. (Govt.): Quick Ref., 3-31; Alta., 3-102; N.S., 3-162; Ont., 3-186; Qué., 3-207; Yukon, 3-224
Policy
	Alternatives, Cdn. Centre for, 2-154
	Analysis, Inst. for (U. of T.), 2-45, 3-36
	Cdn. Inst. for Environmental Law &, 2-61
	& Stewardship, Inst. for Env., 2-63
Polish
	Alliance of Canada, 2-132
	Congress, Cdn., 2-129
	Magazines, 5-193
	Ntl. Catholic Church of Canada, 2-5
	Soc., Cdn., 2-129
Political
	Assns., 2-141
	& Intl. Security Affairs Br. (Fed. Govt.), 3-69
	Magazines, 5-187
	Science Assn., Cdn., 2-141
Pollution (see also Environment)
	Control
		Brs./Divs. (Govt.): Alta., 3-99; N.S., 3-159
		Equipment Assn., Ont., 2-64
	Prevention
		Awards, see Environmental Awards
		Brs./Divs. (Govt.): B.C., 3-113; Fed., 3-65
		Great Lakes (Fed.): Br., 3-65; Centre, 3-65
	Probe Fdn., 2-64

Polo
	Assn., Cdn., 2-176
	Water, 2-181
Polystyrene Recycling Assn., Cdn., 2-61
Polytechnic Univ., Ryerson, 9-29
Polytechnical Inst., Grand River, 9-35
Polytechnique, École (Montréal), 9-47
Pommes
	Fédn des producteurs de (Qué.), 3-198
	de terre
		Agence de la, N.B., 3-134
		Fédn des producteurs de (Qué.), 3-198
Pompiers
	Assn cdnne des, 2-199
	chefs de, 2-159
	Assn intle des, 2-202
	du Qué.
		Assn des directeurs de polices et, 2-113
		Synd. des, 2-206
	volontaires et permanents, Assn qué. des, 2-159
Pontifical(e)
	Inst. of Medieval Studies (U. of T.), 9-31
	de la progapation de la foi, Oeuvre, 2-8
Pony Club, Cdn., 2-176
Pool Inst., Ntl., 2-158
Population
	Census, 1-47
	Cities & Towns, 1-47, 4-1, 4-153
	Govt. Quick Ref., 3-31
	Historical Statistics, 1-58
	Metro. Areas, 1-47
	Municipalities, 4-1
	Provinces & Territories, 1-47
	Studies Ctr. (U.W.O.), 9-31
Porc(s)
	Conseil cdn du, 2-20
	Fédn des producteurs de (Qué.), 2-15
	inc., Centre de dével. du (Qué.), 3-198
Porcupine Caribou Mgmt. Bd., 3-74
Pork
	Council, Cdn., 2-20
	Devel. Centre Inc. (Qué.), 3-198
	Implementation Team (Sask.), 3-212
	Intl. Mktg. Group (Sask.), 3-212
	Producers Mktg. Bds./Commns. (Govt.): Alta, 3-96; Man., 3-122; N.S., 3-1565; Ont., 3-170; Sask., 3-212
Port(s)
	Corp (Fed.), 3-56
	Harbours (Fed.), 3-91
	& Harbour Assn., Cdn., 2-124
	Intl. Assn. of Great Lakes, 2-124
	of Montréal Corp. Inc., Old, 3-55
	Soc. cdnne des, 3-56
Portable Appliance Mfrs. Assn., 2-124
Portage la Prairie City Govt., 4-164
Portes, Assn cdnne des manufacturiers de fenêtres et de, 2-124
Portland Cement Assn., Cdn., 2-31
Portuaire, Socs. du parc industriel & (Qué.), 3-203
Portuguese
	Magazines, 5-193
	Social Service Centre, 2-38
Poseurs de systèmes intérieurs, union ntle des, 2-207
Positive (AIDS) Assns., 2-16
Post
	Corp., Canada, 3-56
	-MD Educ. Registry, Cdn., 2-88
	-Polio
		Awareness & Support Soc., B.C., 2-94
		Network (Man.), 2-9
	Secondary Educ.
		Brs./Divs.: B.C., 3-111; Ont., 3-177
		Dept. (Govt.), Sask., 3-219
		Programs, (Alta.), 3-95
		Schs., & Insts.: Alta., 9-4; B.C., 9-9; N.B., 9-18; Nfld., 9-20; N.W.T., 9-21; N.S., 9-23; Ont., 9-34; P.E.I., 9-41; Qué., 9-47; Sask., 9-55

Postal
	Abbreviations, Prov., 1-46
	History Soc. of Canada, 2-97
	Information, 1-43
	Officials, Assn. of, 2-198
	Rates, 1-45
	Revenue Statistics, 1-57
	Service, Govt. Quick Ref., 3-31
	Wkrs., Cdn. Union of, 2-199
Postaux, Assn ntle des grands usagers, 2-11
Postes
	Assn des officers des, 2-198
	Soc. cdnne des, 3-56
Postiers, Synd. des, 2-199
Postmasters & Assts. Assn., Cdn., 2-199
Potash & Phosphate Inst. of Canada, 2-36
Potato
	Chip Snack Food Assn., Cdn., 2-73
	Development & Marketing Council, N.B., 3-154
	Growers Assn., B.C., 2-13
	Mktg. Bds./Commns. (Govt.): Alta., 3-96; N.B., 3-134; N.S., 3-156; Ont., 3-170; P.E.I., 3-189
	Producers Assn. of N.S., Vegetable &, 2-16
Pottery, Plastic & Allied Wkrs. Intl. Union, Glass, Molders, 2-201
Poulets, Office cdn de commercialisation des, 2-142
Poultry
	Assns., 2-142
	Council, N.B., 2-142; Sask., 3-212
	& Egg Processors Council, Cdn., 2-142
	Mktg. Bds. (Govt.): P.E.I., 3-189; Qué., 3-198
Power
	Consumers, Assn. of Ont. Major, 2-56
	Corps. (Govt.): N.B., 3-139; N.W.T., 3-152; Tidal (N.S.) 3-164; Sask., 3-219; Twin Falls, 3-149 (see also Hydro; Electric)
	Engrs., Inst. of, 2-59
	Measurement of, 1-62
	& Power Plants Magazines, 5-174
	& Sail Squadrons, Cdn., 2-151
	Sask, 3-219
	Systems Construction Assn., Electrical, 2-54
Practical Nurses
	Assns., 2-136
	Fedn. of Ont., 2-138
Prairie
	Agricl. Machinery Inst. (Sask.), 3-212
	Assn. for Water Mgmt., 2-64
	Bible College & Graduate Sch. (Alta.), 9-4
	Farm Rehab. Admin. (Fed. Govt.), 3-54
	Implement Mfrs. Assn., 2-66
	Justice Research (U. of Regina), 9-54
	& Pacific University Libraries, Council of, 2-119
	Pools, 2-14
	Provinces Water Bd., 3-130
	West Regl. College (Sask.), 3-64
Precedence
	Cdn.
		Heads of Govt., 1-25
		Judges, 1-25
	of Orders, Decorations & Medals, Order of, 1-31
	Table of, 1-25
Precipitation at Cities, 1-65
Precision Diecasters, Indep. Union of, 2-202
Pregnancy, Intl. Soc. for Study of Hypertension in, 2-36
Pré-maternelles coops, Conseil qué. des, 2-53
Premier ministre: Cdn., 3-46; Qué., 3-193
Premières Nations, Assemblée des, 2-132
Premier's Councils: B.C. (Science), 3-112; Ont., 3-165
Premiers: Alta., 3-92; B.C., 3-106; Man., 3-120; N.B., 3-131; Nfld., 3-140; N.W.T., 3-150; N.S., 3-154; Ont., 3-164; P.E.I., 3-187; Qué., 3-193; Sask., 3-210
	Council of Maritime, 3-131
	Forms of Address, 1-33
Presbyterian
	Church, 2-5
	College of Montréal, 9-46

Preschools
    Intl., Parent Co-op., 2-53
    Parent Participation, Qué. Council of, 2-53
Préscolaire et elémentaire, Assn des institutions de niveaux, 2-46
Prescription Drug
    Program, Dir. (N.B.), 3-136
    Servs., Sask., 3-216
Presidents Assn. Canada, 2-122
Press
    Canadian, 2-145
        University, 2-145
    Club (Toronto), 2-187
    Council: Ont., 2-145; Man., 2-145
    Fdn., Cdn. Multilingual, 2-145
    Union, Commonwealth (Cdn. Section), 2-145
Presse
    cdnne, La, 2-145
    francophone, Assn de la, 2-193
    du Qué., 2-145
    universitaire cdnne, 2-145
Presses
    Assn. of Cdn. Univ., 2-144
    universitaires, Assn qué. des, 2-144
Prestressed Concrete Inst., Cdn., 2-31
Préventex, 2-159
Price Index: Consumer, 1-54; Mfg., 1-57
Prices (see also Statistics)
    Support Bd., Fisheries, 3-68
PRIDE Canada, 2-168
Priest, Forms of Address, 1-35
Primary Forest Products Mktg. Bd., N.S., 3-163
Prime Minister, Cdn., 3-46
    Deputy, Office of, 3-46
    Form of Address, 1-33
Prime Ministers since 1867, **4**
    Official Portraits, House of Commons, **6**
Prince Albert City Govt., 4-164
Prince Edward Island
    Aquarium, 6-45
    Archives in, 5-114
    Art Galleries in, 6-34
    Boards of Trade in, 7-32
    Botanical Gardens in, 6-46
    Chambers of Commerce in, 7-32
    Cities & Towns in, 4-74
    Courts & Judges in, 10-14
    Education in, 9-41
    Energy Corp., 3-190
    Flag & Coat of Arms, **12**
    Government in, 3-187
    Hospitals in, 8-33
    Law Firms in, 10-93
    Libraries in, 5-84
    Municipal Govt. in, 4-74
    Museums in, 6-23
    Native Schs. in, 9-41
    Newspapers in, 5-144
    Nursing Homes in, 8-34
    Post Sec. Schs. in, 9-41
    Private Schs. in, 9-41
    Sch. Bds. in, 3-41
    Univ. of, 9-41
Prince George
    City Govt., 4-164
    Sch. District, 9-7
Prince of Wales Northern Heritage Ctr. (N.W.T.), 6-16
Princess Patricia's Cdn. Light Infantry Assn., 2-127
Principals Assns.: Ont., 2-53, Cdn. Assn. of Principals, 2-48
Principaux des univs du Qué, Conf. des recteurs et des, 2-51
Print
    Marketers Assn., Cdn., 2-11
    Measurement Bur., 2-12
    Production Assn., Advertising Agency, 2-10

Printing (see also Graphic Arts)
    Assns., 2-143
    Equipment & Supply Dealers' Assn., 2-143
    & Graphics Industries Assn. of Alta., 2-143
    Industries
        Assn., Cdn., 2-143
        Council of, 2-143
    Ink Mfrs. Assn., Cdn., 2-143
    Machinery Mfrs. Assn., Cdn. Packaging &, 2-66
    Magazines, 5-174
    & Publishing Cos., Cdn., 7-51
    Services, Govt. (see also Queen's Printer)
        Canada Communications Group, 3-85
    Trades Assn., Intl. Allied, 2-202
Priorities & Planning Secretariat (N.S.), 3-163
Prison Guards, Union of (Qué.), 2-206
Prisoners
    Orgs., 2-143
    Rights
        Bds. of Review, Govt. Quick Ref., 3-5
        Group, 2-143
Prisons (see also Correctional Services; Corrections)
    Supt. of, Nfld., 3-147
Privacy (see also Access to Information; Information)
    Commrs. (Govt.): Alta., 3-101; B.C., 3-117; Canada, 3-84; Ont., 3-180; Sask., 3-216
    Govt. Quick Ref. (see Ombudsmen), 3-29
Private
    Campground Assn., Ont., 2-186
    Care, B.C. Assn. of, 2-100
    Colleges Accreditation Bd. (Alta.), 3-95
    Educ., Adv. Com. on, Qué., 3-201
    Hosps. in: Alta., 8-8; B.C., 8-11; Ont., 8-33; Qué., 8-50
    Investigators, Council of, 2-160
    Motor Truck Council of Canada, 2-189
    Schs. in: Alta., 9-4; B.C., 9-10; Man., 9-16; N.B., 9-18; Nfld., 9-21; N.S., 9-25; Ont., 9-36; P.E.I., 9-41; Qué., 9-48; Sask., 9-55
    Vocational Schs., Adv. Council (Alta.), 3-95
Privatization Br., Crown Corps. & (Fed.), 3-67
privé, Bureau du Conseil, 3-43
Privy Council, 3-43
    Forms of Address, 1-33
Prizes & Awards, 1-92
Pro-Life Soc. of B.C., 2-154
Pro Musica, Soc., 6-41
Proactive Mgmt. Group, 2-56
Probate Court: N.B., 10-8; N.S., 10-9
Probation
    Officers Assns. N.B., 2-115; Ont., 2-115
    Servs., Adult (Yukon), 3-224
Process Control Assn., 2-66
Procurement, see Purchasing
Produce
    Arbitration Bd., Ont., 3-170
    Mktg., Assn., Cdn., 2-73
Product
    Engrg. & Design, Magazines, 5-174
    Safety Br. (Fed. Govt.), 3-75
Production & Inventory Control, Cdn. Assn. for, 2-123
Productions
    animales du Qué., Conseil des, 3-189
    végétales du Qué., Conseil des, 3-189
Productivity Centre, Cdn. Market &, 2-34
Produits
    agricoles, Conseil ntl des, 3-80
    chimiques, Fédn démocratique de la métallurgie, des mines et des, 2-200
    manufacturés et de services, Synd. des travailleurs(euses) de, 2-207
Professeur(e)s
    de comptabilité, Assn cdnne des, 2-8
    et chargé(e)s de cours des universités, Fédn des, 2-196
    de danse, Assn cdnne des, 6-42
    de droit, Assn cdnne des, 2-113
    de l'État du Qué., Synd. des, 2-206
    de français, Assn québécoise des, 2-46

Professeur(e)s (cont.)
    d'immersion, Assn cdnne des, 2-45
    de langue seconde, Assn cdnne des, 2-48
    de Montréal, Alliance des, 2-196
    de santé communautaire, Assn cdnne des, 2-48
    d'université
        Assn cdnne des, 2-48
        Fédn qué. des, 2-48
Professional(s)
    Development Inst., 2-56
    Driver's Safety Council, Sask., 2-161
    Employees
        Assn. (B.C.), 2-205
        Soc., Mgmt. &, 2-203
    Forms of Address, 1-35
    Inst. of the Public Service, 2-205
    Management, Inst. of, 2-122
    & Technical Employees, Cdn. Union of, 2-200
    Women's Clubs, Cdn. Fedn. of, 2-192
Professionnel(le)(s)
    du gouvernement du Qué., Synd. de, 2-207
    salarié(es) et des cadres de Qué., Fédn des, 2-201
    et technique, Formation (Qué.), 3-200
Professions, Office des, Qué., 3-204
Programming Service, Cdn., 2-64
Progress Club, Cdn., 2-164
Progressiste-Conservateur du Canada, Parti, 2-142
Progressive
    Conservative
        Assns. & Parties, 2-142
        Office of the Leader (Fed.), 3-46
    Democratic Alliance Party (B.C.), Office of, 3-106
Project
    Management
        Institute, 2-122
        Orgs., Intl. Fedn. of, 2-122
    Peacemakers, 2-109
    Ploughshares, 2-109
Promotional Products Assn., 2-12
Propane
    Gas Assn. of Canada, 2-78
    Publications, see Gas Publications
Property (see also Real Estate; Crown Lands)
    Assessment Div. (Ont.), 3-179
    Insurance, Govt. Quick Ref., 3-21
    Mgmt.
        Brs./Divs. (Govt.): Alta., 3-104; Man., 3-125; Ont., 3-182; Sask., 3-219; Yukon, 3-223
        Corp., Sask., 3-219
    Publications, see Building Publications
    Registration Dirs. see also (Govt.): Man., 3-128; Ont., 3-174; P.E.I., 3-192; Sask., 3-217, 7-30 see also Deeds Regrs.
    Rights Div. (Man.), 3-128
    Standards Officers, Ont. Assn. of, 2-102
    Tax Assn., Cdn., 2-183
Propriétaires
    d'autobus du Qué., Assn des, 2-25
    de machinerie lourde du Qué., Assn des, 2-65
    du Qué., Assn des, 2-146
Prosecutions Div., Public: Man., 3-128; N.S., 3-162
Prosecutors (see also Crown Prosecutors; Public Prosecutors)
    Assn., Prov. (Ont.), 2-115
Prospecteurs du Qué., Assn des, 2-127
Prospectors & Developers Assns.: Can., 2-128; N.B., 2-128
Prosthetists & Orthotists, Cdn. Assn. of, 2-84
Prostitute's Safer Sex Project, 2-18
Protecteur du citoyen, Qué., 3-204
Protection
    -incendie, Assn ntle des travailleurs en, 2-197
    du territoire agricole, Commn (Qué.), 3-189
    de la vie privée du Canada, commn à la, 3-84
Protein Engrg. Network of Ctrs. of Excellence, 2-157
Protestant
    Separate Sch. Bds., see Separate Sch. Bds.
    Teachers of Qué., Prov. Assn. of, 2-50

Canadian Almanac & Directory 1997

Protestantes, Commn des ècoles, *see* Separate Sch. Bds.
Prothonotaries: N.S., 10-9; P.E.I., 10-15; Qué., 10-20
Protocol (Affairs of State) Divs./Offices (Govt.): Quick Ref., 3-32; Alta., 3-100; B.C., 3-114; Fed., 3-43, 3-69; N.B., 3-138; N.W.T., 3-150; N.S., 3-155; Ont., 3-175; P.E.I., 3-187; Qué., 3-205; Sask., 3-216
Protocole, Sous-ministre adjoint (Qué.), 3-205
Provincial
  Abbreviations (Postal), 1-46
  Affairs
    & Attorney General, Dept. (P.E.I.), 3-191
    Municipal &, Dept. (Nfld.), 3-148
  Birds, **9**
  Birth & Death Rates, 1-48
  Boards of Trade/Chambers of Commerce, 7-24
  Court Judges, Cdn. Assn. of, 2-113; N.W.T., 2-115
  Courts: Alta., 10-3; B.C., 10-5; Man., 10-7; N.B., 10-7; Nfld., 10-8; N.S., 10-9; Ont., 10-11; P.E.I., 10-15; Qué., 10-16; Sask., 10-20
  Decision Com. (Ont. Agric.), 3-170
  Electoral Districts, 4-1
  Employees, Alta. Union of, 2-204
  Facilitator, Office of (Ont.), 3-183
  Flags & Arms, **9**
  Floral Emblems, **9**
  Government Info. Services, Quick Ref., 3-18
  Holidays, 1-24
  Judges Assn. of Man., 2-115
  Legislature, Forms of address, 1-34
  Municipal &, Dept. of, Nfld., 3-148
  Museum of Alta., 6-2
  Orders, 1-31
  Parks, Govt. Agencies, *see* Parks
  Police
    Assn.: Ont., 2-204; Qué., 2-197
    Ontario, 3-186
    Sûreté du Qué., 3-208
  Populations, 1-47
  Prosecutors Assn. (Ont.), 2-115
  Relations, Fed.-, Govt. Quick Ref., 3-15
  & Territorial Boards of Trade/Chambers of Commerce, 7-24
  Treasury Dept. (P.E.I.), 3-192
PSAC, 2-205
Psoriasis
  Fdn., Cdn., 2-89
  Soc. of Canada, 2-94
Psychiatric
  Assn., Cdn., 2-125
  Hospitals, *see* Mental Hospitals
  Nurses
    Assns., 2-138
    Union of, 2-138
  Patient Advocate Office (Ont.), 3-180
  Research
    Fdn., Cdn., 2-125
    Inst., Children's, 2-125
Psychic
  Phenomena, Exhibitions, Shows & Events, 1-89
  Sciences, Intl. College of Spiritual & (Qué.), 9-48
Psychoanalytic
  Child Therapists, Cdn. Assn. of, 2-125
  Soc., Cdn., 2-125
Psychological Assn.: Cdn., 2-125; Ont., 2-126
Psychologues du Qué., Assn des, 2-125; Ordre des, 2-126
Psychomotor Learning & Sport Psychology, Cdn. Soc. for, 2-177
Psychotherapy Assn., Cdn. Group, 2-125
Public
  Admin.
    Assns., 2-79
    Awards, 1-103
    of Canada, Inst. of, 2-80
    Official Guardian & (Yukon), 3-224
    Sch. (Qué.), 9-47

Public (cont.)
  Affairs
    Assn. of Canada, 2-80
    Awards, 1-110
    Bur., Alta., 3-103
    Couchiching Inst., 2-121
  Appraisers, Intl. Inst. of, 2-147
  Buyers Assn., Ont., 2-35
  Colleges, Alta., 9-4
  Debt of Canada, 1-57
  Employees
    Assn., N.B., 2-204
    Cdn. Union of, 2-200
    Nfld. Assn. of, 2-204
    N.S. Union of, 2-204
  & General Employees, Ntl. Union of, 2-203
  Guardian, Office of (Alta.), 3-100
  Health
    Assn(s)., 2-89
      Cdn., 2-89
    Brs./Divs. (Govt.): N.B., 3-136; Nfld., 3-146; N.S., 3-160; Ont., 3-180; P.E.I., 3-191; Qué., 3-207
    Dentistry, Cdn. Assn. of, 2-40
    Govt. Quick Ref. (*see* Health), 3-19
    Inspectors, Cdn. Inst. of, 2-87
    Officers, *see* Medical Health Dirs./Officers
  Holidays, 1-24
  Hospitals, *see* Hospitals; Federal Hospitals
  Information Canada's Coalition for, 2-103
  Insurance
    Admrs., Soc. of (Ont.), 2-106
    Man., 3-128
  Interest
    Advocacy Centre, 2-115
    Research Group, Ont., 2-157
  Justice, Citizens for, 2-102
  Legal Educ. Assns. & Socs., 2-116
  Libraries
    Admrs. of Medium (Ont.), 2-116
    Assn(s)., 2-116
    Cdn. Assn. of, 2-117
    Council of Admins. of Large, Urban, 2-119
    in Alta., 5-2; B.C., 5-12; Man., 5-22; N.B., 5-28; Nfld., 5-31; N.W.T., 5-34; N.S., 5-35; Ont., 5-39; P.E.I., 5-84; Qué., 5-84; Sask., 5-105; Yukon, 5-112
    of Ont.
      Assn. of Small, 2-117
      Chief Execs. of Large, 2-119
  Library Assn., Ont., 2-120
  Personnel Mgmt. Assn., Cdn., 2-121
  Policy Inst. for Research on, 2-156
  -Private Partnerships, Cdn. Council for, 2-34
  & Private Rights Bd., Sask., 3-218
  Relations
    Assn. Canada, Health Care, 2-92
    Awards, 1-92
    Soc., Cdn., 2-121
  Safety Services, (Govt.): Quick Ref., 3-32; B.C., 3-110; N.B., 3-138; N.S., 4-162; Ont., 3-186; Yukon, 3-222
  School(s)
    Boards (*see also* Education; Bds. of Educ.)
      Assn., Ont., 2-53
    Div. (Yukon), 3-222
    Teachers' Fedn., Ont., 2-53
  Sector
    Employees, P.E.I., Union of, 2-204
    Labour Market & Productivity Commn. (Ont.), 3-179
  Security
    Dept. (Qué.), 3-207
    Div. (Alta.), 3-102
  Service(s) (*see also* Civil Service)
    Alliance of Canada, 2-205
    Assn. of Profl. Execs. of the, 2-120
    Commns. (Govt.): Canada, 3-84; Nfld., 3-148; Qué., 3-202; Sask., 3-219; Yukon, 3-224

Public
  Service(s) (cont.)
    Dept. (Govt.), N.W.T., 3-153
    Employee Relations (Govt.): Alta., 3-102; B.C., 3-115
    Employees Union (Ont.), 2-204
    Financial Administrators, Assn. of, 2-198
    Profl. Inst. of, 2-205
    Staff Relations Bd. (Fed. Govt.), 3-84
    Websites, 5-256
  Trustee (Govt.): Govt. Quick Ref., 3-32; Alta., 3-101; B.C., 3-110; Man., 3-128; N.W.T., 3-152; Ont., 3-171; P.E.I., 3-192; Qué., 3-200; Sask., 3-217
  Utilities
    Assn., 2-143
    Bds. & Commns. (*see also* Utilities): Govt. Quick Ref., 3-32; Man., 3-123; N.B., 3-140; Nfld., 3-149; N.W.T., 3-154 (*see* Regulatory & Appeals Commn. for P.E.I.)
  Utility Tribunals, Cdn. Assn. of Members of, 2-143
  Works
    Assn., Cdn., 2-143
    Depts. (Govt.): Quick Ref., 3-33; Alta., 3-103; Fed., 3-85; N.W.T., 3-152; N.S., 3-164; P.E.I., 3-193
    & Government Services Canada, 3-85
Publications, (*see* Magazines)
  Govt.
    Cdn. 3-85
    Quick Ref., 3-33
Publicité
  Club de Montréal, 2-12
  Fdn cdnne de la, 2-11
  Fdn cdnne de recherche en, 2-11
  par l'objet du Canada, Assn de la, 2-12
Publique
  Commn de la fonction: du Canada, 3-84; du Qué., 3-202
  École ntle d'admin (Qué.), 9-47
  Min. de la Sécurité (Qué.), 3-207
Publiques-privées, Le conseil cdn des socs, 2-34
Publishers
  Assn(s)., 2-143
    of Cdn., 2-144
      Magazine, 2-145 (& *see* Addenda)
      Music, 2-145
      Newsletter, 2-145
      Qué. English Lang., 2-144
  Awards, *see* Literary Arts Awards (*see also* Journalism Awards)
  Book (Cdn.), 5-115 (& *see* Addenda)
  Council, Cdn., 2-145
  Group, Sask., 2-146
  Magazines, list of, 5-159 (& *see* Addenda)
  Newspapers, list of, 5-130
Publishing
  Assns., 2-143
  Cos., Cdn., 7-51
  Educ., Intl. Assn. for, 2-145
  Industry Devel. Program, Book (Fed. Govt.), 3-58
  Publications, (*see* Printing Publications)
Pullett Prodrs. Mktg. Bd., N.S. Egg &, 3-156
Pulmonaire, Assns., 2-87
Pulp & Paper
  Assn., Cdn., 2-75
  Companies, Cdn., 7-43
  Employee Relations Forum, 2-111
  Health & Safety Assn., Qué., 2-159
  Machinery Mfrs. Assn., Cdn., 2-66
  Magazines, 5-175
  Processing, Exhibitions, Shows & Events, 1-89
  Research Inst. of Canada, 2-157
  & Woodworkers of Canada, 2-205
Pulse
  Crop Devel. Bd., Sask., 3-212
  Growers Commn., Alta., 3-96
Pump Mfrs. Assn., Cdn., 2-123
Puppetry Assn., Ont., 6-36

Purchasing
  Govt.: Quick Ref., 3-18; Alta., 3-103; B.C., 3-114; Fed., 3-85; Man., 3-125; N.B., 3-140; Nfld., 3-145; N.W.T., 3-153; N.S., 3-159; Ont. (Mgmt. Bd.), 3-181; P.E.I., 3-192; Qué., 3-209; Sask. (Prop. Mgmt.), 3-219; Yukon, 3-223 (*see also* Government Services; Supply & Services)
  Magazines, 5-175
  Mgmt. Assn. of Canada, 2-122
PWA coalitions & socs., 2-16
Pythias, Knights of, 2-76

Q

Quaker Com. on Jails & Justice, 2-143
Qualité, Assn de la, 2-33
Quality
  Council, Cdn., 2-34
  in Health care, Cdn. Assn. for, 2-84
  Inst., Natl., 2-35
Quantity Surveyors Cdn. Inst. of, 2-182
Quarter Horse Assn., Cdn., 2-20
Quarternary Assn., Cdn., 2-155
Québec
  Accueil et d'hébergement, Ctrs. d', 8-40
  Alliance, 2-38
  Aquaria in, 6-45
  Archives in, 5-114
  Art Galleries in, 6-34
  Bibliothèques, 5-84
  Botanical Gardens in, 6-46
  Bur. féd. de dévél. régl., 3-66
  CÉGEPS, 9-45
  Chambres de Commerce, 7-32
  Cities & Towns in, 4-77
  Committee for Canada, 2-141
  Commn scolaires, 9-41
  Communauté Urbaine de, 4-173
  Courts & Judges in, 10-15
  Education in, 9-41
  Fed. Office of Regl. Devel., 3-66
  Flag & Coat of Arms, **13**
  FreeNets, 5-233
  Government (Prov.), 3-193
  Hospitaliers, Ctrs., 8-34
  Hospitals in, 8-34
  -Labrador Fdn., 2-213
  Law Firms in, 10-93
  Libraries in, 5-84
  Lobbyists in, 7-39
  Meeting, Conference, Exhibit & Event Planners in, 1-71
  Municipal Govt., 4-77, 4-154
  Musée du, 6-24
  Museums in, 6-24
  Native Schs. in, 9-44
  Newspapers in, 5-144
  Nursing Homes in, 8-40
  Online Service Providers, 5-232
  Post Sec. & Spec. Insts. in, 9-47
  Private Schs. in, 9-48
  Regional Govts. in, 4-153
  Sch. Bds. in, 9-41
  Telephone, Synd. des agents de maîtrise de, 2-206
  Univ. du, 9-47
  Univs. in, 9-46
  Ville de, Govt., 4-164
  Winter Carnival, 2-85
  Zoos in, 6-45
Québécois
  Parti, 2-142
  pour le Canada, Comité, 2-141
Queen Elizabeth II, 3-245
  Accession of, 1-3
  Birthday of, 1-3
  Cdn. Research Fund (Govt.), 3-78
  & Royal Family, 3-245

Queen's
  Bench Courts: Alta., 10-3; Man., 10-6; N.B., 10-7; Sask., 10-20 (*see also* Supreme Court; Trial Div.; High Court)
  Birthday, 1-3
  College (Nfld.), 9-20
  Personal Cdn. Flag, **8**
  Printers: Alta., 3-103; B.C., 3-114; Federal, 3-85; N.B., 3-138; Nfld., 3-149; Ont., 3-182; P.E.I., 3-192; Sask., 3-217; Yukon, 3-223 (*see also* Printing Services, Govt.)
  Privy Council, 3-43
  Univ. (Ont.), 9-29
Quetico Fdn., 2-213
Quick Service Restaurant Council, 2-158
Quilles, Fédn des, 2-173; dix, 2-178
Quilters' Assn., Cdn., 2-190
Quincaillerie
  et articles ménagers, Assn cdnne des fabricants en, 2-123
  Assn cdnne des détaillants en, 2-158
  de bâtiment, Assn cdnne des fabricants de, 2-30
Quotidiens, Assn cdnne des, 2-145

R

Raag-Mala Music Soc., 6-41
Rabbis
  Cdn. Council of Reform, 2-3
  Forms of Address, 1-35
Race Relations
  Canada Council on Human Rights &, 2-102
  Ctr. for Research-Action on, 2-156
  Dir. (Govt.), Ont., 3-185
  Urban Alliance on, 2-132
Racetracks of Canada, 2-153
Racing
  Assn.
    Cdn. Outrigger, 2-150
    Vintage Automobile, 2-23
  Bds./Commns. (Govt.): Alta., 3-104; B.C., 3-115; Maritime (Harness), 3-131; Ont., 3-175; Qué., 3-198, 3-208
  Drivers Assn., Cdn., 2-176
  Form, Daily, 5-139
  Pigeon Union, Cdn., 2-151
Racism Secretariat, Ont. Anti-, 3-172
Racisme, Mouvement qué. pour combattre le, 2-168
Racquetball Assn., Cdn., 2-176
RADARSAT Program, 3-62
Radiation
  médicale, Assn cdnne des techniciens en, 2-84
  Protection Assn., Intl., 2-160
  Safety, Cdn. Inst. for, 2-160
  Technologists, Cdn. Assn. of Medical, 2-84
  Technology Educ. (Ont.), 9-35
Radio (*see also* Broadcasting)
  Advisory Board, 2-29
  Amateurs, 2-29
  Artists
    Alliance of Cdn. Cinema, TV &, 2-196
    American Fedn. of TV &, 2-197
  Assn.
    Ntl. Campus/Community, 2-29
    Ont. Vintage, 2-153
  Awards, 1-93, 1-102
  Broadcasters, Cdn. Assn. of Ethnic, 2-29
  Canada, Soc., 3-56
    Intl., 3-57
    Synd. des techniciens du réseau français de, 2-207
  Club, Cdn. Intl. DX, 2-150
  Competitions, 1-109
  Conseil consultatif cdn de la, 2-29
  et d'Élocution promédia (Qué.), 9-47
  Emergency Associated Communications Teams, 2-55
  étudiantes et communautaires, Assn ntle des, 2-29
  Govt. Quick Ref. (*see* Broadcasting), 3-5

Radio (cont.)
  Magazines, 5-175, 5-189
  Marketing Bur., 2-12
  Network Head Offices, 5-198
  North, CBC, 3-57
  Operators, Cdn. Assn. of Profl., 2-199
  Québec, 3-200
    Synd. des employés en radio-télédiffusion de, 2-196
  Stations
    AM, 5-199
    Awards, *see* Broadcasting
    FM, 5-206
  -télédiffusion de Radio-Qué., Synd. des employés, 2-196
  -Television
    Assn cdnne des directeurs de l'information en, 2-29
    cdnne, Assn pour les études sur la, 2-28
    du Qué., Soc. de, 3-200
    & Telecommunications Commn., 3-61
  & Television
    Assn. for Study of Cdn., 2-28
    de langue française, Assn cdnne de la, 2-29
    News Directors Assn., 2-29
    & Recording Arts, Columbia Academy of (B.C.), 9-9
Radioactive Waste & Radiation Div. (Fed.), 3-83
Radiodiffuseurs, Assn cdnne des, 2-29; Ethniques, 2-29
Radiodiffusion
  Assn cdnne des éducateurs en, 2-28
  et des telecommunications, Conseil de la, 3-61
Radiologie du Qué., Synd. profl des techniciens en, 2-207
Radiologistes due Qué., Assn des, 2-82
Radiologists, Cdn. Assn. of, 2-84
Radioprotection
  Assn intle de, 2-160
  Inst. Cdn de, 2-160
Radios-Télévisions d'expression française, Conseil intl des, 2-29
Rail
  Canada Traffic Controllers, Union of, 2-207
  Transportation, Govt. Quick Ref., 3-33
Railroad
  Companies, 1-67; CNR, 3-61; VIA, 3-92
  Hist'l Assn., Cdn., 2-96
Railway(s)
  Assn.
    Alta. Pioneer, 2-95
    West Coast, 2-98
  Assn. of Canada, 2-189
  BC Rail, 1-68, 3-112
  CNR, 1-68, 3-61
  Companies, 1-67
    Govt.: B.C., 3-112; CNR, 3-61; VIA, 3-92
  Halton County Radial, 2-97
  Hist'l Assn.: B.C., 2-95; Ont. Electric, 2-97
  Police Assn., CN, 2-199
  Resources, Alta., 3-104
  Safety (Fed.), 3-91
  Shopcraft Unions, Cdn. Council of, 2-199
  Statistics, 1-57
  VIA Rail, 1-68, 3-92
Rain, Acid *see* Acid Rain
Rainfall at Cities, 1-65
Rape Crisis Ctr., Ont. Coalition of, 2-168
Raquette, Assn cdnne de la, 2-149
RCMP, 3-88
  External Review Com., 3-88
  Public Complaints Commn., 3-88
  Training Academy, 3-88
REACT Canada, 2-55
Réadaptation
  Assn cdnne de médecine physique et de, 2-84
  Conf. qué. des centres d'hébergement et de, 2-100
  Constance-Lethbridge, Centre de, 2-42

Réadaptation (cont.)
　　physique du Qué., Synd. des physiothérapeutes et des thérapeutes en, 2-206
　　et du travail, Conseil cdn de la, 2-42
Reader's Digest Fdn., 2-213
Reading Assn., Intl., 2-112
Ready-mixed Concrete Assns., 2-31
REAP-Canada, 2-64
Real
　　Estate
　　　　Assessment Review Bd. (Qué.), 3-197
　　　　Assns. & Bds., 2-146; Alta., 2-146; B.C., 2-146; Cdn., 2-147; Man., 2-147; N.B., 2-147; Nfld., 2-147; N.S., 2-147; Ont., 2-147; P.E.I., 2-148; Sask., 2-148; Yellowknife, 2-148; Yukon, 2-148
　　　　Cos., Cdn. Inst. of Public, 2-147
　　　　Councils (Govt): B.C., 3-115; N.B., 3-138
　　　　Exhibitions, Shows & Events, 1-89
　　　　Govt. Quick Ref., 3-33
　　　　Inst. of Canada, 2-148
　　　　Magazines, 5-175
　　　　Servs. Brs./Divs. (Govt.): B.C., 3-113; Nfld., 3-145; Ont., 3-182; P.E.I., 3-192
　　Property
　　　　Assessment (P.E.I.), 3-192
　　　　Services (Fed.), 3-85
Realtors, 2-147
Realty
　　Corp., Ont., 3-182
　　Servs. (Fed.), 3-92
Réalisateurs(trices)
　　de cinéma et de télévision, Assn qué. des, 2-68
　　La Guide cdnne des, 2-69
　　de télévision et de cinéma, Fédn prflle des, 2-29
REAP Canada, 2-83
reBOOT Canada, 2-104
Receiver Gen. of Canada, 3-85
Receivers (Bankruptcy Act), 10-21
Recherche
　　Assn cdnne de la gestion de la, 2-155
　　sur les bactérioses, Réseau cdn de, 2-154
　　en biologie végétale, 2-63
　　sur le cancer, Soc. de, 2-156
　　et dével. en économique, Centre de, 2-44
　　en économie de la santé, Assn cdnne pour la, 2-86
　　en éducation
　　　　Assn ontarienne des agents de, 2-45
　　　　Centre d'animation de développement et de, 2-50
　　industrielle
　　　　Centre de (Qué.), 3-203
　　　　du Québec, Assn, 2-123
　　en informatique cognitive des orgs, 2-104
　　en marketing
　　　　Assn cdnne des orgs de, 2-11
　　　　Assn professionelle de, 2-12
　　médicale, Cdns pour la, 2-90
　　nautique, Soc. cdnne pour la, 2-155
　　opérationelle, Soc. cdnne de, 2-155
　　et de la productivité du N.B., Conseil de la, 3-139
　　en publicité, Fdn cdnne de, 2-11
　　en santé et en sécurité de travail, 2-160
　　scientifique, Inst ntl de la, 2-156, 9-47
　　sur le SIDA, Fdn cdnne de, 2-19
　　universitaire, Assn cdnne d'administrateurs de, 2-47
Recherches
　　avancées, La Fdn de l'inst cdn de, 2-155
　　sur les blessures de la route, Fond. de, 2-157
　　cliniques, Soc. cdnne des, 2-89
　　conseil ntl de, Canada, 3-80
　　dentaires, Assn cdnne de, 2-39
　　sur les femmes, Inst. cdn de, 2-155
　　gazières, Inst cdn des, 2-56
　　en génie forestier, Inst cdn de, 2-156
　　médicales Canada, Conseil de, 3-78
　　sur les pâtes et papiers, Inst cdn de, 2-157
　　politiques, Inst du, 2-156
　　et sauvetage, Secrétariat ntl de, 3-81

Recherches (cont.)
　　en sciences naturelles et en génie du Canada, conseil des, 3-84
　　en télécommunications, Inst cdn de, 2-183
　　théâtrales, Assn de, 6-35
　　urbaines et régionales, 2-140
Récherchistes, documentalistes et compositeurs, Soc. des, 2-206
Reconstructive Surgery, Cdn. Academy of Facial, Plastic &, 2-83
Record
　　Production Assn., Cdn. Indep., 6-39
　　Servs., Christian, 2-42
Recording
　　Arts
　　　　Columbia Academy (B.C.), 9-9
　　　　of Man., Sch. of, 9-16
　　　　& Sciences, Cdn. Academy of, 6-39
　　Industries Assn., Alta., 6-37
　　Industry Assn., Cdn., 6-40
　　Studio, Mid-Ocean (Man.), 9-16
Records
　　Fdn. to Assist Cdn. Talent on, 6-40
　　Mgrs. & Administrators, Assn. of, 2-120
　　Offices, Govt., see Archives
Recreation (see also Sport & Recreation)
　　Assn(s)., 2-149
　　　　Cdn.
　　　　　　Intramural, 2-150
　　　　　　Parks/, 2-150
　　　　Ont. Municipal, 2-152
　　Awards, 1-112
　　Brs./Divs. (Govt.): Alta., 3-96; B.C., 3-118; Man., 3-123; N.B., 3-138; N.S., 3-163; N.W.T., 3-152; Ont., 3-173; P.E.I., 3-190; Sask., 3-219; Yukon, 3-222
　　Centre Inc., Ont. Sports &, 2-179
　　Commn., N.S., 3-161
　　Council of B.C., Outdoor, 2-153
　　& Dance, Cdn. Assn. for Health, Phys. Ed., 2-174; Awards, 6-70
　　Depts. (Govt.): Quick Ref., 3-34; Nfld., 3-149; Ont., 3-172
　　Exhibitions, Shows & Events, 1-90
　　Facilities Assns.: B.C., 2-153; Ont., 2-152
　　Magazines, 5-176, 5-188
　　Parks & Wildlife Fdn., Alta., 3-97
　　Soc., Sask., 2-153
　　& Sports Assn. for the Physically Challenged, P.E.I., 2-179
　　Tourism, Culture &, Dept. (Nfld.), 3-149
　　Vehicle Dealers Assns., 2-27
Recreational
　　Aircraft Assn. Canada, 2-28
　　Canoeing Assn., Cdn., 2-151
　　Vehicle
　　　　Assn., Cdn., 2-185
　　　　Shows, see Automotive; Sports & Recreation
Recruiters Guild, Cdn., 2-56
Recteurs et principaux des univs. du Qué., Conf. des, 2-51
Récupérateurs du Qué., Assn des, 2-60
Récupération & de récyclage, Soc. qué. de, 3-202
RECYC-Québec, 3-202
Recycled Rubber Assn., N.A., 2-64
Recycling
　　Assn., Cdn. Polystyrene, 2-61
　　Awards, see Environmental
　　Coordinators, Assn. of Municipal, 2-60
　　Corps. in Support of, 2-64
　　Councils (Provs.), 2-64; Qué. (Govt.), 3-202
　　Industries, Cdn. Assn. of, 2-60
　　Section (N.B.), 3-135
Red Cross
　　Blood Transfusion Serv. Employees Assn., 2-199
　　Soc., Cdn., 2-55
Red Deer
　　City Govt., 4-164
　　College, 9-4

Red Deer (cont.)
　　Community Fdn., 2-213
Red Poll Cattle Assn., Cdn., 2-20
Red River Community College (Man.), 9-16
Rédacteurs
　　agricoles de langue française, Assn cdnne des, 2-193
　　-réviseurs, Assn cdnne des, 2-194
　　scientifiques, Assn cdnne des, 2-194
Redeemer College (Ont.), 9-34
Redressement d'entreprises, Assn cdnne de, 2-34
Reforestation, see Silviculture
Reform
　　Judaism, Cdn Council for, 2-3
　　Party of Canada, 2-142
　　　　Office of the: Leader (Fed.), 3-46; B.C., 3-106
　　Rabbis, Cdn. Council of, 2-3
Reformation & Renaissance Studies, Ctr. for (U. of T.), 9-30
Réforme électorale, Secrétariat (Qué.), 3-204
Reformed
　　Church
　　　　in Amer., Regl. Synod of Cda., 2-5
　　　　in N.Amer., Christian, 2-3
　　　　Episcopal Church, 2-5
　　　　World Relief Com., Christian, 2-7
Refrigerating
　　& Air Conditioning Engrs., Amer. Soc. of Heating, 2-94
　　Institute, 2-95
Refrigeration
　　& Air Conditioning Contrs. Assns., Cdn., 2-95; Ont., 2-95
　　climatisation et protection-incendie, Assn ntle des travailleurs en, 2-197
　　Serv. Engrs. Soc., 2-95
Refugee(s)
　　Bd., Immigration &, 3-73
　　Cdn. Council for, 2-166
　　Div. (Fed.), 3-63
　　Studies, Ctr. for (York Univ.), 9-32
　　U.N. High Commr. for, 3-247
Regent College (UBC), 9-8
Réfugié(s)
　　Commn de l'immigration et du statut de, 3-73
　　Conseil cdn pour les, 2-166
Régimes de retraite
　　Assn cdnne des orgs de contrôle des, 2-69
　　et d'assurances, Commn admin. des (Qué.), 3-210
Regina
　　City Govt., 4-165
　　Energy Research Inst., 9-54
　　Sch. Divisions, 9-53
　　Univ. of, 9-54
Regional
　　Affairs Secretariat (Qué), 3-200
　　County Muns., Qué., 4-77, 4-132
　　Courts (Ont.), 10-12
　　Delegates (Qué. Govt.), 3-194
　　Development
　　　　Corp., N.B., 3-139
　　　　Div., (B.C.), 3-118
　　　　Fed. Office of, 3-66
　　Dists.: B.C., 4-17, 4-171; Ont., 4-74, 4-171; Qué. 4-77, 4-173
　　Govt., Mun., 4-171
　　Municipalities, 4-171
　　Research, Intergov. Com. on Urban &, 2-140
Régionales, Secrétariat au développement des (Qué.), 3-200
Registered Retirement Savings Plans, Fund Mgrs., 7-4
Registraires des universités et collèges, Assn des, 2-60
Registrars
　　in Bankruptcy, see Brankruptcy
　　Court: Alta., 10-3; B.C., 10-4; Man., 10-6; N.B., 10-7; Nfld., 10-8; N.W.T., 10-8; N.S., 10-9; Ont., 10-10; P.E.I., 10-14; Qué., 10-19; Sask., 10-20
　　Gen., Govt. (Ont.), 3-174
　　of Univs. & Colleges, 2-46

Registrateurs, Cours (Qué.), 10-19
Registries, Brs./Divs. (Govt.): Alta., 3-103; B.C., 3-114; Ont., 3-174; Sask., 3-217
Regulatory & Appeals Commn., Island (P.E.I.), 3-191
Rehabilitation
   Appeal Bd. (Nfld.), 3-149
   Cdn. Assn. of Phys. Medicine &, 2-84
   Centres, Alta. Assn. of, 2-41
   & Cerebral Palsy Assn., Children's, 2-91
   Councils for Disabled, 2-42
   Fdn. of B.C., Kinsmen, 2-43
   Research Inst., Vocational &, 2-44
   des sites dégradés, Assn cdnne de, 2-61
   sociale du Qué, Assn des services de, 2-165
   & Work
      Cdn. Council on, 2-42
      Council, Ont., 2-43
REIC, 2-191
Reifel Bird Sanctuary, 2-135
Reimer Express Fdn., 2-213
Rein, La Fdn cdnne du, 2-92
Reinforcing Contractors Assn., Western, 2-182
Reinsurance Research Council, 2-106
Relationnistes du Qué., Soc. des, 2-122
Relations
   industrielles
      Assn cdnne des, 2-110
      du Qué., Ordre profl des conseillers en, 2-111
   publiques
      des orgs de la santé, L'Assn des, 2-92
      Soc. cdnne des, 2-121
   de travail dans la foncton publique, commn. (Fed.), 3-84
   du travail, Conseil cdn (Fed.), 3-55
Relève agricole, Fédn de la (Qué.), 3-198
Relief
   Agency, Intl., 2-109
   Cdn.
      Lutheran World, 2-7
      Physicians for Aid &, 2-108
Relieurs & des artisans du livre, Guilde cdnne des, 2-144
Religion
   Cdn. Coalition for Ecology, Ethics &, 2-60
   Council on Homosexuality &, 2-98
   Statistics, 1-50
   Websites, 5-258
Religious
   Conf., Cdn., 2-7
   Denominations, 2-2
   Forms of Address, 1-34
   Holidays, 1-24
   Magazines, 5-187
   Organizations, 2-6
   Schs., *see* Separate Schs.; Church Schs.
   Soc. of Friends, 2-3
Remembrance Day, 6-25
Remorquage, Soc. cdnne de, 2-26
Remote Sensing
   Centres for (Govt.): Canada, 3-82; N.W.T., 3-153
   Soc., Cdn., 2-59
   Surveys, Mapping &, (Fed.), 3-83
Rémunération, Assn cdnne de, 2-110
Renaissance Studies, Ctr. for Reformation & (U. of T.), 9-30
Renewable
   Fuels Assn., Cdn., 2-56
   Resources
      Brs/Divs.,: N.B., 3-139; N.S., 3-163
      Councils (Yukon), 3-225
      Govt. Depts.: N.W.T., 3-153; Yukon, 3-224
Renison College (Waterloo), 9-31
Rénovation urbaine, Assn cdnne d'habitation et de, 2-101
Renovators' Council, Cdn., 2-32
Renseignements de sécurité, surveillance des activités de, 3-88

Rent (*see also* Landlord & Tenant)
   Control, Govt., *see* Residential Tenancies
   Registry, Ont., 3-183
Rental
   Equipment Magazines, 5-175
   Exhibitions, Shows & Events, 1-89
   Housing Council of B.C., 2-102
Rentalsman, Office (Govt.): N.B., 3-138; Sask., 3-218
Rentes, Régie des (Qué.), 4-208
Reorganized Church of Jesus Christ of Latter Day Saints, 2-5
Reproductive Choice, Coalition for, 2-154
Rescue
   Assn., Civil Air Search &, 2-55
   Search &, *see* Search & Rescue
Research
   Admins., Cdn. Assn. of University, 2-47
   Assn(s)., 2-154
   Authority, Alta. Science &, 3-97
   Awards, *see* Scientific Awards
   Cdn. Inst. for Advanced (Ont.), 2-155, 9-35
   Centre(s)
      Intl., Devel., 3-77
      Pan Cdn. Network of, 3-76
   Council, Employees' Assn., 2-205
   Councils, Foundations (Govt.): Fed. (Ntl.), 3-80; (Medical), 3-78; N.B., 3-139; N.S., 3-158; Sask., 3-220
   & Development
      Inst., Industrial, 2-59
      Magazines, 5-175 (*see also* Scholarly Publications)
      Secretary of State for, 3-75
   Fdn.
      Cdn. Advertising., 2-11
      for Legal, 2-114
      Western Grains, 2-16
   Libraries, Cdn. Assn. of, 2-117
   Management Assn., Cdn., 2-155
   Medical Council (of Canada), 3-78
   Ntl. Council, 3-80
   Natural Sciences & Engrg. Council, 3-84
   in Nondestructive Evaluation, 2-154
   Orgs., Assn of Provincial, 2-154
   & Productivity Council, N.B., 3-139
   on Public Policy, Inst. for, 2-156
Researcher Training & Research Assistance Fund (Qué.), 3-201
Réseau Enfants retour Canada, 2-37
Resident(s)
   & Internes
      Cdn. Assn. of, 2-83
      Profl. Assns., 2-205
   Qué. Fedn. of, 2-201
Residential
   Tenancies Bds./Divs. (Govt.): B.C., 3-109; Man., 3-123; Nfld., 3-148; N.S., 3-161
   Treatment Concepts, Assn. for, 2-198
Resort Devel. Assn., Cdn., 2-185
Resorts Assns.: B.C., 2-184; Ont., 2-186
Resource(s)
   Centres, *see* Special Libraries
   Dept. (Govt.), N.W.T., 3-153; Yukon, 3-224
   Devel., Govt Quick Ref., 3-29
   Div. (Man.), 3-129
   Efficient Agricl. Production Canada, 2-64
   & Environment, Agricl. Groups Concerned About, 2-12
   Law, Cdn. Inst. of, 2-61
   Ltd., N.S., 3-163
   Management
      Dept. (Sask. Environment &), 3-214
      N.S. (Environment), 3-159
   Natural, *see* Natural Resources
   Railway, Alta., 3-104
   Recovery Fund Bd., N.S., 3-159
   Renewable (Govt. Dept.), Yukon, 3-224
   Water, *see* Water Resources

Resource(s) (cont.)
   Wildlife & Economic Devel. (Govt. Dept.), N.W.T., 3-153
Respiratory
   Health Network of Ctrs of Excellence, 2-94
   Soc., Cdn. Nurses, 2-137
   Therapists, Cdn. Soc. of, 2-90
Ressource(s)
   faunique, Dir. gén. (Qué.), 3-201
   humaines
      Assn, 2-55
         des profls. en, du Qué., 2-55
      cdnne des profls en systèmes de, 2-56
      Dével. des (Féd.), 3-77
      hydriques, Assn cdnne des, 2-62
      de l'industrie de l'environnement, Le Conseil cdn des, 2-60
      du logiciel, Conseil des, 2-104
   Inst cdn du droit des, 2-61
   naturelles (Govt. Depts.): Fed., 3-81; N.B., 3-139; Qué., 3-205
Restaurant(s) (*see also* Hospitality Industry)
   Assn(s)., 2-157
      des fournisseurs d'hôtels et, 2-157
   Employees Intl. Union, Hotel Employees &, 2-202
   & Foodservices Assns., 2-157/158
   Magazines, Hotels &, 5-169
   & Related Employees, Cdn. Union of, 2-200
   Suppliers Assn., Hotel & (Qué.), 2-157
Restaurateurs
   professionnels, Assn cdnne des, 2-190
   du Qué., Assn des, 2-157
Retail
   Assns., 2-157
   Building Supply Council, Cdn., 2-32
   Companies, Cdn., 7-51
   Council of Canada, 2-158
   Farm Equip. Dealers' Assn., Ont., 2-66
   Fur Council of Canada, 2-77
   Hardware Assn., Cdn., 2-158
   Lumbermen's Assn., Western, 2-32
   Magazines, 5-175
   Merchants Assns., 2-158
   Research Labs. of Canada, 2-231
   Travel Agents, Cdn. Assn. of, 2-184
   Wholesale
      & Department Store Union, 2-206
      Sask. Joint Bd., 2-206
      Union, 2-206
Retired
   Persons, Cdn. Assn. of, 2-163
   & Semi-Retired, Soc. for the, 2-164
Retirement Magazines, *see* Senior Citizens Magazines
Retraite
   Assn cdnne
      des orgs de contrôle des régimes de, 2-69
      des gestionnaires de fonds de, 2-71
      et des avantages sociaux, Inst cdn de la, 2-70
      d'assurances, Commn administrative des régions de (Qué.), 3-210
Retraités
   Assn cdnne des individus, 2-163
   concernés, Corp. cdnne des, 2-164
   fédéraux, Assn ntle des, 2-79
Retriever Club of Canada, Ntl., 2-22
Rett Syndrome Assn., Cdn., 2-89
Revenu (Govt.): Fed., 3-86; Qué., 3-206
Revenue
   Canada, 3-86
   Commrs., Bd. of (Sask.), 3-215
   Dept.: Fed., 3-86; Qué., 3-206
   Divs. (Govt.): B.C., 3-114; Sask., 3-215; Yukon, 3-223
Revêtement(s) de sol
   L'Assn cdnne de l'industrie de la peinture et du, 2-31
   Inst Qué. des, 2-124
   souples, Union ntle des poseurs de, 2-207
Rêves d'enfants, Fdn cdnne, 2-37

Review Bds. (Govt.): Quick Ref., 3-5; Alta., 3-102; B.C., 3-110; N.S., 3-164
Rheumatism Assn., Cdn., 2-89
Rhododendron Soc. of Canada, 2-99
Rhythmic Sportive Gymnastic Fedn., Cdn., 2-176
Richard III Soc. of Canada, 2-97
Richard Ivey Sch. of Business (U.W.O.), 9-31
Richmond
    City Govt., 4-165
    Sch. Dist., 9-7
Richmond Hill, Town of, Govt., 4-165
Ridgetown Agricl. College (Ont.), 9-34
Riding Assn.
    Cdn. Therapeutic, 2-178
    Long Distance, 2-150
Rifle Assn., Dominion of Canada, 2-151
Right to Die Soc., 2-169
Right to Life Assns., 2-154
Rights
    Agency, Cdn. Musical Reproduction, 2-138
    & Liberties Assns., 2-102
Rimouski, Univ. du Qué. à, 9-47
Ringette Canada, 2-180
Ringuette du Qué., Fédn Sportive de, 2-180
Risk & Insurance Mgmt. Soc., 2-106
River East Sch. Div. (Man.), 9-14
Road
    Builders Assns., 2-30
    Safety (Fed.), 3-91, *see* Hwy. Safety for provs.
Roads Assn., Ont. Good, 2-189
Robarts Ctr. for Cdn. Studies (York U.), 9-32
Robertson College Inc. (Man.), 9-16
Robotics & Intelligent Systems, Inst. for, 2-156
Rockies, College of the (B.C.), 9-8
Rodeo(s)
    Assn., Cdn. Profl., 2-176
    Exhibitions, Shows & Events, 1-89
Roeher Inst., 2-43
Roller
    Skating Assn., Cdn. In-Line &, 2-176
    Sports Canada, 2-153
Romagnola-Marchigiana Assn., Cdn., 2-20
Roman Catholic
    Church in Canada, 2-5
    Forms of Address, 1-34
    Separate Sch. Bds. *see* Separate Sch. Bds.
    Theological Seminaries (Ont.), 9-35
Romance & Mainstream, Writers Assn. for, 2-194
Romanian
    Orphans, Cdn. Fellowship for, 2-166
    Orthodox Church, 2-5
    Overseas Schs., 9-40
    World Congress, 2-132
Romark, 2-20
Ronald McDonald
    Children's Charities, 2-169
    House, 2-90
Roofing Contractors Assns., 2-32
Roosevelt Campobello Intl. Park Commn., 3-88
Rose Soc., Cdn., 2-99
R.O.S.E.S., Centre des, 2-17
Rotary Clubs in Canada, 2-165
Roulettes, Sports à, 2-153
Round
    Dance
        Assn., Toronto & Dist. Square &, 6-44
        Fedn., Square & (N.S.), 6-44
    Tables on the Environment & Economy *see* Environment
Routes, Assn qué. du transport et des, 2-241
Rowing Canada Aviron, 2-180
Royal
    Agricl. Winter Fair Assn., 2-67
    Arch Masons, 2-76
    Architectural Inst. of Canada, 2-24
    Astronomical Soc. of Canada, 2-163

Royal (cont.)
    Bank
        of Canada, 7-1
        Charitable Fdn., 2-213
    Botanical Gdns., 2-99; 3-173
    B.C. Museum, 6-4
    Cdn.
        Academy of Arts, 2-191
        Air Force Benevolent Fund, 2-127
        College of Organists, 6-41
        Geographical Soc., 2-157
        Golf Assn., 2-180
        Humane Assn., 2-169
        Institute, 2-157
        Legion, 2-127
        Military Inst., 2-127
        Mint, 3-88
        Mounted Police, 3-88
            External Review Committee, 3-88
            Public Complaints Commn., 3-88
            Veterans' Assn., 2-127
        Naval Benevolent Fund, 2-127
    Coat of Arms, **1**
    College
        of Dental Surgeons (Ont.), 2-41
        of Dentists, 2-41
        of Physicians & Surgeons, 2-94
    Commns. & Inquiries (Ont.), 3-172
    Commonwealth Soc., 2-39
    Conservatory of Music (Ont.), 9-35
    Family, 3-245
    Life Saving Soc. of Canada, 2-55
    Manitoba Winter Fair, 2-67
    Military College of Canada (Ont.), 9-29
    Nfld. Constabulary
        Commissioner, 3-146
        Complaints Commn., 3-148
        Police Broth. of, 2-204
        Public Complaints Commn., 3-157
    Nova Scotia Historical Soc., 2-97
    Ont. Museum, 6-16, 3-173
    Philatelic Soc., 2-153
    Royal Roads Univ. (B.C.), 9-7
    Saskatchewan Museum, 6-27
    Scottish Country Dancing Soc., 6-44
    Society
        of Canada, 2-157
        for the Encouragement of Arts, 2-157
    Tyrrell Museum of Palaeontology, 6-2
    Union Flag, **8**
    Victoria College (McGill Univ.), 9-46
    Victorian: Chain, 1-31; Order, 1-30
    Winnipeg Ballet, 6-44
RP Research Fdn., 2-94
RPSC Philatelic Research Fdn., 2-153
RRSP Fund Mgrs., 7-4
Rubber
    Assn.
        of Canada, 2-124
        N.A. Recycled, 2-64
    Cork, Linoleum & Plastic Wkrs. of Amer., United, 2-208
    Exhibitions, Shows & Events, 1-89
Rubella Assn., Cdn. Deaf-Blind &, 2-85
Rugby du Qué., Fédn de, 2-179
Rural
    Affairs, Agric., Food &, Dept. (Ont.), 3-168
    Development
        Depts. (Govt.): Alta., 3-95; Man., 3-130; N.B., 3-133; Nfld., 3-142
        Div., Ont., 3-169
    Dignity of Canada, 2-141
    & Improvement Districts (Alta.), Assn., 2-80
    Learning Assn. of Ont., 2-54
    Municipal Admrs. Assns.: Alta., 2-79; Sask., 2-80
    Municipalities, Sask. Assn. of, 2-80
    Municipalities in: Man., 4-18; N.S., 4-39; Sask., 4-148
    Population, 1-47

Rural (cont.)
    Renewal, Devel. & (Nfld.), 3-142
    Soc. cdnne de génie, 2-14
    Utilities (Alta.), 3-104
Ruraux du Qué., Assn des jeunes, 2-13
Russian
    Cdn. Cultural Aid Soc., 2-132
    Cdns., Fedn. of, 2-130
    & East European Studies, Ctr. for (U. of T.), 9-30
    Orthodox Church, 2-5
RV Dealers Assns., 2-27
Ryerson Polytechnic Univ., 9-29

S

Saanich, Corp. of, Govt., 4-165
SAFE KIDS Canada, 2-37
Safety (*see also* Public Safety)
    Assn.
        Cdn. Fire, 2-159
        Construction (Ont.), 2-32
        Farm, 2-160
        Ont. Natural Resources, 2-160
        Transportation (Ont.), 2-161
    Assns., 2-158
    Bd. of Canada, Transportation, 3-91
    Cdn. Inst. for Radiation, 2-160
    Councils: Alta, 2-158; B.C., 2-159; Canada, 2-159; Man. 2-160; N.B., 2-160; Nfld., 2-160; N.S., 2-160; Sask., 2-160
    Engineering, Cdn. Soc. of, 2-160
    Exhibitions, Shows & Events, 1-90
    League, Ont., 2-160; Qué., 2-160
    Occupational, *see* Occupational Health & Safety Profls., Assn. for Cdn. Reg'd., 2-159
    & Public Servs., Dept. of (N.W.T.), 3-153
Sages-femmes, Assns, 2-36
Sail (*see also* Boating)
    & Life Training Soc., 2-153
    Squadrons, Cdn. Power &, 2-151
Sailing Assn., B.C., 2-149
Saka Era, *see* Epochs
St. Andrew's
    Biological Stn., 3-68
    College: Man., 9-15; Sask., 9-54
Sainte Anne Université (N.S.), 9-23
St. Augustine's Seminary of Toronto, 9-35
St. Basil's College (Ont.), 9-35
St. Bernard College, Mount (N.S.), 9-22
Saint-Boniface, College universitaire de (Man.), 9-15
St. Catharines, City Govt., 4-165
St. Chad, College of Emmanuel & (Sask.), 9-54
St. Clair
    College AA & T (Ont.), 9-33
    Parkway Commn. (Ont.), 3-176
St. Elizabeth
    Health Care, 2-94
    Visiting Nurses Assn., 2-138
Ste-Foy, Ville de, Govt., 4-165
St. Francis Xavier Univ. (N.S.), 9-22
St-Hubert, Ville de, Govt., 4-166
St-Hyacinthe, Inst. de techn. agro-alimentaire, 9-48
Saint-Jean-Baptiste Soc., 2-39
St. Jerome's College, Univ. of (Waterloo), 9-31
Saint John City Govt., 4-166
St. John
    Ambulance, 2-55
    Baptist Day, 1-24
    of Jerusalem, Sovereign Order of, 2-76
St. John's
    College (Man.), 9-15
    City Govt., 4-166
    RC Sch. Dist. (Nfld.), 9-19
St. Joseph's College (Alta.), 9-3
St-Laurent
    Admin de la voie maritime du, 3-88
    Ville de, Govt., 4-166

St. Lawrence
    Centre, 3-65
    College (Ont.), 9-33
    Parks Commn. (Ont.), 3-176
    Seaway Auth. (Fed.), 3-88
St-Léonard, Ville de, Govt., 4-166
St. Leonard's Soc., 2-143
St. Mark's College (UBC), 9-8
Saint Mary's Univ. (N.S.), 9-22
St. Michael's College (U. of T.), 9-31
Saint Paul Univ. (Ont.), 9-30
St. Paul's
    College (Man.), 9-15
    R.C. Sch. Div. (Sask.), 9-53
    United College (Waterloo), 9-31
St. Peter the Apostle, Soc. of, 2-5
St. Peter's
    College (Sask.), 9-54
    Seminary (Ont.), 9-35
St. Stephen's College (Alta.), 9-3
St. Thomas More College (Sask.), 9-54
St. Thomas Univ. (N.B.), 9-18
St-Vincent de Paul, Soc., 2-169
St-Vincent Univ., Mount (N.S.), 9-22
Sainteté biblique, Mouvement de, 2-6
Saints'
    Church, 2-5
    Days, 1-24
S.A.I.T., 9-4
Salaries etc., Legislative: Alta., 3-93; B.C., 3-106; Fed., 3-47; Man., 3-121; N.B., 3-132; Nfld., 3-141; N.W.T., 3-150; N.S., 3-155; Ont., 3-166; P.E.I., 3-187; Qué., 3-194; Sask., 3-211; Yukon, 3-221
Salers Assn. of Canada, 2-21
Sales
    Assn., Cdn. Profl., 2-34
    Magazines, 5-159
    Reps., Cdn. Assn. of Wholesale, 2-29
    Taxes, Govt. Quick Ref., 3-34
Salles historiques, Soc. des, 2-96
Salmon
    Assn., N.S., 2-72
    Commns., Intl., 3-248
    Farmers Assn., B.C., 2-71
    Fedn., Atlantic, 2-71
    Growers Assn., N.B., 2-72
Salons du livre, Assn qué. des, 2-144
SALTS Sail & Life Training Soc., 2-153
Salutations, Correct, 1-33
Salvation Army, 2-5
Samaritan's Purse Canada, 2-169
Sancta Vetus Catholica Ecclesia Canadiensis, 2-5
Sanitarium Assn., Ntl., 2-101
Sanitation Supply Assn., Cdn., 2-123
Santé
    animale
        Assn cdnne des techniciens et technologistes en, 2-21
        La Fdn cdnne de la, 2-19
        Inst cdn de la, 2-21
    Assn
        cdnne
            pour la qualité dans les services de, 2-84
            pour la recherche en économie de la, 2-86
        catholique cdnne de la, 2-90
        des ctrs de (Ont.), 2-100
        et du bien-être, Le Conseil de la (Qué.), 3-207
    Bureaux de (Qué.), 8-34
    Canada, 3-71
    Centrale des profls de la, 2-200
    Ctrs de soins de (Qué.), 8-37
    Coalition cdnne de la, 2-86
    Collège cdn des dirs de services de, 2-85
    Communautaire, Assn cdnne des professeurs de, 2-48
    Conseil
        Cdn sur le tabagisme et la, 2-85
        d'évaluation des technologies de la (Qué.), 3-207

Santé (cont.)
    Depts.: Fed., 3-71; N.B., 3-136; Qué., 3-206
    l'education physique, le loisir et la danse, Assn cdnne pour la, 2-174
    Fonds de la recherche en (Qué.), 3-207
    infantile, Inst cdn de la, 2-87
    intl., Soc. cdnne pour la, 2-90
    mentale
        Assn cdnne pour la, 2-125
        Comité de la (Qué.), 3-207
        Fédn mondiale pour la, 2-126
    Office cdn de coordination de l'évaluation des technologies de la, 2-85
    publique
        Assn cdnne de, 2-89
        Sous-ministre adjoint (Qué.), 3-207
    Réseau
        cdn des communautés en, 2-86
        de liaison et d'application de l'info. sur la, 2-92
    Respiratoire, Réseau de ctrs d'excellence en, 2-94
    et de la securité du travail, Commn de la (Qué.), 3-207
    et securité
        des industries de la forêt, 2-159
        des pâtes et papiers du Qué., 2-159
        du travail
            Assns paritaires, 2-159
            Centre patronal de, 2-159
            du travail, Inst de recherche en, 2-160
    securité et l'indemnisation des accidents (N.-B.), 3-140
    et des services sociaux
        Fédn du personnel de la, 2-196
        Min. de la (Qué.), 3-206
        Schs. operated by, 9-45
    et Servs communautaires (N.B.), 3-136
    Synd. des profls & techniciens de la, 2-196
Sarnia City Govt., 4-166
SAS Users, Cdn. Assn. of, 2-103
Saskatchewan
    Aquaria in, 6-45
    Archives in, 5-115
    Art Galleries in, 6-34
    Boards of Trade in, 7-24, 7-34
    Botanical Gardens in, 6-47
    Chambers of Commerce in, 7-24, 7-34
    Cities & Towns in, 4-134
    Colleges in, 9-54
    Courts & Judges in, 10-20
    Education in, 9-51
    Flag & Coat of Arms, 6-32
    FreeNet, 5-233
    Government in, 3-210
    Hospitals in, 8-51
    Indian
        Federated College, 9-54
        Inst. of Technologies, 9-54
    Inst. of Applied Science & Tech., 9-54
    Law Firms in, 10-100
    Libraries in, 5-105
    Lobbyists in, 7-40
    Meeting, Conference, Exhibit & Event Planners, 1-72
    Municipal Govt. in, 4-134
    Museums in, 6-27
    Newspapers in, 5-147
    Nursing Homes in, 8-54
    Opportunities Corp., 3-213
    Private Schs. in, 9-55
    Regl. Colleges in, 9-54
    Rural Municipalities in, 4-148
    Sch. Divs. in, 9-51
    Universities in, 9-54
    Zoos in, 6-45
Saskatoon
    Academy of Learning, 9-55
    Child Ctr., 3-218
    City Govt., 4-167

Saskatoon (cont.)
    Fdn., 2-213
    Sch. Div., 9-53
SaskEnergy, 3-220
Saskeram Wildlife Mgmt. Area, 3-130
SaskPower, 3-219
SaskTel, 3-220
SaskWater, 3-220
Satellite Users Assn., Cdn., 2-29
Saturn, Planet, 1-14
Sault College of AA & T (Ont.), 9-33
Sault Ste. Marie, City Govt., 4-167
Saumon atlantique, Fédn du, 2-71
Saut
    de barils, Assn cdnne de, 2-191
    en ski Canada, 2-229
Sauvetage
    Canada, Soc. Royal de, 2-55
    recherches et, programme ntl., 3-81
Savants et scientifiques, Com. cdn des, 2-161
Save
    the Children-Canada, 2-109
    a Family Plan, 2-109
    Ont. Shipwrecks, 2-23
Savings
    Banks, 7-3
    Trust Fund, Alta. Heritage, 3-105
Savonniers cdns, Assn des, 2-124
Scaler's Act., Bd. of Examination under (N.B.), 3-139
Scandinavian Fdn., Cdn.-, 2-209
Scarborough (Ont.)
    Bd. of Education, 9-25
    City Govt., 4-167
    College (U. of T.), 9-31
SCDA, 2-121
Schizophrenia
    Fdn., Cdn., 2-125
    Soc. of Canada, 2-126
Scholarly Publications, 5-195
Scholars, Cdn. Com. of Scientists &, 2-161
Scholarship(s) (see also Awards)
    Assns., 2-154
    Trust Fdn., Cdn., 2-209
School(s) (see also Independent Schools, Private Schools)
    Administrators, Cdn. Assn. of, 2-121
    Athletic Assns.: Alta., 2-172; N.S., 2-179; Ont., 2-179
        P.E.I., 2-180
    Boards, see Education & Bds. of, for Lists of
        Assn(s)., 2-49; Ont. Public, 2-53
    Buildings Board (Alta.), 3-98
    Business
        Employees' Assn., N.B., 2-204
        Officials Assns.: Man., 2-53; Ont., 2-53
    Districts
        Capital Financing Authority, B.C., 3-115
        & Divisions, see Education & Bds. of Education
    Finance (Govt.): Alta., 3-98; B.C., 3-111; Man., 3-124
    Fedn. of Indep., 2-51
    Fdn. Audit Board, Alta., 3-98
    Home &, Fedns., 2-49
    Indep., List of, see Independent Schools
    Library Assns.: Cdn., 2-119; Man., 2-119; Ont., 2-120
    Private, List of, see Private Schools
    Programs Div. (Man.), 3-124
    Publications, University &, 5-197
    of Social Work, Cdn. Assn. of, 2-46
    Social Wkrs. & Attendance Counsellors, Cdn. Assn. of, 2-48
    Sports Fedn., Cdn., 2-176
    Superintendents, Man. Assn. of, 2-53
    Supervisors' Org., N.B., 2-204
    Trustees
        Assns., 2-49
        Catholic: Alta., 2-45; Cdn., 2-48
        Council, Ont., 2-53
        Ont. Separate, 2-53

SchoolNet, see Addenda
Science
    Alta. Fdn., 2-163
    Awards & Prizes, 1-111
    Cdn. Soc. for/of
        Colour in Art, Industry &, 2-59
        History & Philosophy of, 2-162
        the Weizmann Inst. of, 2-162
    Centre(s), 6-1
        Ont., 6-16, 3-173
    Conferences, 1-90
    Council of B.C., 3-112
    Education, Assn. for the Promo. & Advancement of, 2-161
    & Engineering
        Award, 1-111
        Cdn. Aboriginal, 2-132
        Res. Council, Natural (Fed.), 3-84
        Women in, 2-193
    Exhibitions, Shows & Events, 1-90
    Fellowship, Spiritual, 2-6
    Fdn., Youth, 2-163
    Govt. Depts.: Quick Ref., 3-34; Qué., 3-202
    Inst. of N.W.T., see Aurora Research Inst., 3-151
    Magazines, 5-175, 5-188 (see also Scholarly Publications)
    Min. de la (Qué.), 3-202
    North, 3-173
    Nova Scotian Inst. of, 2-163
    for Peace, 2-109
    Policy, Industry & (Fed.), 3-75
    Publications, 5-175, 5-188
    & Research Auth., Alta., 3-97
    Research & Devel. Secretary of State (Fed.), 3-75
    et de la technologie
        Conseil de la (Qué.), 3-203
        Min. de l'Industrie, de la Commerce (Qué.), 3-202
    & Technology
        Awards, 1-111
        Cdn. Inst. of Food, 2-162
        Councils (Govt.): B.C., 3-112; N.S. (Secretariat), 3-164; Qué., 3-203
        for Development, Intl. Assn. of, 2-163
        Div. (B.C.), 3-112
        Govt. Quick Ref., 3-34
        Historical Assn., Cdn., 2-162
        Industry, Commerce, Qué Min. of, 3-202
        Inst. for
            Chemical, 2-35
            History & Philosophy of (U. of T.), 9-31
        Magazines, 5-188
        Ntl. Adv. Council on, 3-75, 3-76
        Ntl. Museum of, 6-1
        Review Sec. (Fed.), 3-75
        Soc. for Cdn. Women in, 2-19
Sciences
    administratives du Canada, Assn des, 2-120
    Assn cdnne française pour l'avancement des, 2-45
    Atlantic Provs. Council on the, 2-161
    & Engrg. Research Council of Canada, Natural, 3-84
    naturelles et en génie du Canada, Conseil de recherches en, 3-84
    et de la Technologie, Musée ntl des, 6-1
    textiles, Inst. des, 2-163
Scientific
    Assns., 2-161
        Fedn. of Engrg. &, 2-201
    Awards, 1-111
    Research, Ntl. Inst. for (Qué.), 2-156, 9-47
    & Technical Info., Cdn. Inst. for (NRC), 3-81
Scientifique
    Affaires, Sous-ministre adjoint (Qué. Éduc.), 3-200
    Inst. ntl de la recherche, 2-156; 9-47
Scientists & Scholars, Cdn. Com. of, 2-161
Sclérose
    latérale amytrophique, Soc. cdnne, 2-81
    en plaques, Soc. cdnne, 2-93

Scolaires
    Assn
        des cadres (Qué.), 2-45
        francophone intl des directeurs d'établissements, 2-46
    Commissions (Qué.), 9-41
    Fédn des commissions (Qué.), 2-51
    francophones du N.-B., Assn des conseiller(e)s, 2-45
    de l'Ont., Assn française des conseils, 2-46
Scotiabank, 7-1
Scotland, Sons, of, 2-76
Scottish
    Clans in N.S., Fedn. of, 2-130
    Country Dancing Soc., Royal, 6-44
    Socs. of Canada, Clans &, 2-130
    Studies, Cdn. Assn. for, 2-48
Scouts Canada, 2-37
Screen Inst., Ntl., 2-69, 9-4
Sculptors Soc. of Canada, 2-191
Sculpture du Qué., Conseil de la, 2-190
Sea
    Kayak Assn. of B.C., 2-153
    Shepherd Conservation Soc., 2-65
Seafarers' Intl. Union of Canada, 2-206
Seafood Assns., 2-71
Sealant(s) & Waterproofing Assn., 2-33
Seamans Compensation Bd., Merchant, 3-73
Seaplane Pilots Assn., Cdn., 2-28
Search & Rescue
    Assn., Civil Air, 2-55
    Secretariat, Ntl., 3-81
Seasons, Dates of, 1-3
Seaway
    Auth., St. Lawrence, 3-88
    Transit, 1-64
Secan Assn., 2-16
Second Language(s)
    Programs, Council for, 2-51
    in Québec, Soc. for the Promo. of the Teaching of English as a, 2-54
    Teachers, Cdn. Assn. of, 2-48
    Teaching English as a, 2-54
Secondary Sch.
    Bds. in Ont., 9-27
    Teachers' Fedn., Ont., 2-53
Secours aux lépreux, 2-109
Secrétaires
    et administrateurs agréés au Canada, Inst des, 2-122
    municipaux du Qué., Corp. des, 2-79
    proflles du Qué., Fédn des, 2-121
    et trésoriers municipaux de l'Ont., Assn des, 2-79
Secretaries
    Assn., Ont. Medical, 2-122
    Cdn. Soc. of Corporate, 2-121
    Inst. of Chartered, 2-122
    International, Profl., 2-122
Secteur public, Synd. ntl des employés du, 2-203
Sécurité
    Assns, 2-158
    agrées, Assn des profls en, 2-159
    civile, Dir. gén. de la (Qué) 3-207
    Conseil cdn de la, 2-159
    fédérale des représentants de la, 2-160
    et d'investigation du Qué., Conseil des agences de, 2-160
    N.-B., Conseil de, 2-160
    publique, Min. de la (Qué.), 3-207
    du Qué., Ligue de, 2-160
    du revenu
        des chasseurs et piégeurs Cris, Office de la (Qué.), 3-208
        Min. de la (Qué.), 3-208
    dans les sports du Qué., Régie de la, 2-180
    Surveillance des activités de renseignements de, 3-88
    dans les transports de l'Ont., Assn de, 2-161
    des transports Canada, Bur. de la, 3-91

Securité (cont.)
    du travail
        Assns paritaire pour la santé et la, 2-159
        Ctr cdn d'hygiène et de, 2-85, 3-57
Securities (see also Banking; Financial Institutions)
    Admin. (Govt.): Quick Ref., 3-35; N.B., 3-138
    Commns. (Govt.): Alta., 3-105; B.C., 3-115; Man., 3-123; N.S., 3-162; Ont., 3-179; Sask., 3-218
    Commissions, Intl. Org. of, 2-70
    Inst., Cdn., 2-70, 9-34
    Regr.: Yukon, 3-224
Security
    Affairs Br., Political & Intl. (Fed.), 3-69
    Assn., Cdn. Alarm &, 2-159
    Bur., Intl. (Fed.), 3-69
    Cdn. Soc. for Industrial, 2-160
    Intelligence
        Review Com. (Fed.), 3-88
        Service, Cdn. (Fed.), 3-89
    Magazines, 5-175
    Officials, Fed. Assn. of, 2-160
    SIG, 2-103
Sedimentary & Marine Geosciences Br., (Fed.), 3-82
SEDS - Canada, 2-28
Seed
    Corn Mktg. Bd., Ont., 3-170
    Growers' Assn., Cdn., 2-14
    Mktg. Bd., P.E.I. Pedigreed, 3-189
    Potato Growers Assn., B.C., 2-13
    Trade Assn., Cdn., 2-14
SEEDS
    of Diversity, 2-99
    Fdn., 2-65
Self Employment Developers, Assn. of (Ont.), 2-55
Selkirk College (B.C.), 9-9
Semences, Assn cdnne
    du commerce des, 2-14
    des producteurs de, 2-14
Seminar Planners, see Conference Planners
Seminaries in: B.C., 9-10; Ont., 9-34, 9-35; Sask., 9-54
Sénat (Fed.), 3-44
Senate (Fed.), 3-44
    Forms of Address, 1-33
Send The Light, 2-8
Seneca College AA & T (Ont.), 9-33
Senior
    Ctrs, Cdn. Inst. of. 2-163
    Citizens (see also Aging; Seniors)
        Assns., 2-163
        Counsellors (B.C.), 3-119
        Exhibitions, Shows & Events, 1-90
        Fedn., N.B., 2-164; P.E.I., 2-164; Qué., 2-164
            Ntl. Pensioners &, 2-164
        Govt. Agencies for: Quick Ref., 3-35; B.C., 3-116; Man., 3-130; N.B., 3-136; N.S., 3-157; Ont., 3-173
        Magazines, 5-188
        Org., Atlantic Prov. Pensioners &, 2-163
        Orgs., Ont. Coalition for, 2-163
        Secretariats, see Govt. Agencies, above
        Services, Govt. Quick Ref., 3-35
        Sport & Recreation Assn., Alta., 2-163
    United, 2-164
Seniors
    Adv. Council for Alta., 3-97
    Brs./Divs. (Govt.): Quick Ref., 3-35; Alta., 3-96; Man., 3-130
    Clubs, Fedn. of Italian Cdn., 2-130
    Consumer Shows, 1-90
    Council (Qué.), 3-207
    Magazines, 5-188
    Man. Soc. of, 2-164
    Network (Canada), One Voice, 2-164
    Offices for (Govt.): B.C., 3-116; N.B., 3-136
    Ont. Assn. of Non-Profit Homes & Servs. for, 2-100
    Packaging Adv. Council, 2-138
Sensor & Control Tech. (NRC), 3-81
Sentencing Project Team (Fed. Justice), 3-78

Separate School
  Board(s)
    Protestant in: Alta., 9-2; Ont., 9-27; Qué., 9-41
    Roman Catholic in: Alta., 9-2; Nfld., 9-19; Ont., 9-25, 9-26; Qué., 9-41; Sask., 9-53 (see also Private Schools)
  Trustees Assn., Ont., 2-53
Sépultures de guerre du Commonwealth, Commission des, 2-126
Serbian
  Magazines, 5-193
  Ntl. Com., Cdn., 2-129
  Orthodox Church, 2-5
Serena Canada, 2-36
Serruriers de bâtiments, Fra. ntle des, 2-201
Servas Canada, 2-39
Service
  Clubs, 2-164
    Magazines, 5-182
  correctionnel
    Canada, 3-63
    du Qué., 3-204
  Employees Intl. Union, 2-206
  extérieur
    Assn de la communauté du, 2-79
    L'Assn profle des agents du, 2-204
  Industries Cos., Cdn., 7-53
  Medals, 1-31
  Social
    Assn des écoles de, 2-46
    Fond. cdnne du, 2-166
    Intl Canada, 2-167
    de la Prov. du Qué., Assn des employés en, 2-197
Services
  communautaires, santé et (N.-B.), 3-136
  correctionnels du Qué., Synd. des agents de la paix en, 2-206
  essentiels, Conseil des (Qué.), 3-209
  aux étudiants des universités et collèges du Canada, Assn des, 2-46
  gouvernementaux Canada, Travaux publics, 3-85
  publiques, Fédn des employé(es) de, 2-200
  de santé
    Assn cdnne pour la qualité dans les, 2-84
    Collège cdn des directeurs de, 2-86
    Conseil cdn d'agrément des, 2-100
  sociaux
    Fédn du personnel de la santé et des, 2-196
    en milieu de santé, Assn cdnne des administrateurs de, 2-100
    Min. de la santé et des (Qué.), 3-206
    des municipalités de l'Ont., Assn des, 2-168
  Supply & (see Supply & Services)
Seventh
  Day Adventist Church, 2-5
    Sch. Bds. (Nfld.), 9-19
  Step Soc., 2-143
Sewer & Watermain Contractors Assn., Ont., 2-33
Sewing & Needlecraft Assn., Cdn., 2-67
Sex
  Info & Educ. Council of Canada, 2-169
  Offender Programming (Fed.), 3-63
Sexologues du Qué., Assn des, 2-125
Sexual
  Assault Ctrs., Cdn. Assn. of, 2-166
    Harassment in Higher Educ., Cdn. Assn. Against, 2-166
Sexually Transmitted Disease Control, Govt. Quick Ref., 3-35
Sexuel, Ctrs d'aide et de lutte contre les agressions à caractère, 2-169
Sexuelles, Conseil du Canada d'information et éduc. 2-169
Shade Tree Council, Ont., 2-75
Shareholder Servs. Assn., Cdn. Corp., 2-69
Sharelife, 2-169
Shareowners Assn., Cdn., 2-101
Shaw Festival, 6-36

Sheep
  Breeders Assn., Cdn., 2-20
  Council, Canada, 2-19
  Mktg. Bds. & Commns. (Govt.): Alta., 3-96; Ont., 3-170; Qué., 3-198; Sask., 3-212
Sheet
  Metal
    Air Conditioning Contractors' Ntl. Assn., 2-182
    Air Handling Group, Ont., 2-182
    Workers
      Cdn. Council of, 2-206
      Intl. Assn., 2-206
    Steel Bldg. Inst., Cdn., 2-181
Shellfish Growers Assn., B.C., 2-71
Shelterbelt Ctr. (Fed.), 3-54
Sherbrooke
  Commn scolaire catholique de, 9-42
  Univ. de, 9-47
  Ville de, Govt., 4-167
Sheridan College of AA & T (Ont.), 9-34
Sheriffs: Man., 10-7; N.W.T., 10-9; N.S., 10-9; Ont., 10-14; Qué., 10-20; Yukon, 10-21
Shevchenko Musical Ensemble Guild, Ntl., 6-40
Shiatsu Sch. of Canada (Ont.), 9-35
Shipbuilding Assn., 2-124
Shipowners Assns.: Cdn., 2-188
Shippers' Council, Cdn., 2-188
Shipping
  Abbreviations, 1-39
  Amer. Bur. of, 2-188
  Assns., 2-188
  Fedn. of Canada, 2-189
  Magazines (Marine & Truck), 5-176
Shipwrecks, Save Ontario, 2-23
Shipyard(s)
  East Isle (P.E.I.), 3-190
  Gen. Wkrs. Fedn. of B.C., 2-206
Shire Horse Soc., Cdn., 2-22
Shoe (see also Footwear)
  Industry Suppliers Assn. of Canada, 2-68
  Mfrs. Assn. of Canada, 2-68
Shooting Fedn. of Canada, 2-153
Shorthorn
  Assn., Cdn., 2-20
  Soc., Cdn. Milking, 2-20
Show(s)
  & Events, Exhibitions, 1-72
  & Exhibitions Magazines, 5-176
  Planners, 1-68 (& see Addenda)
SI Units & Prefixes, 1-60
SIAS Intl. Art Soc., 2-191
Sickle Cell Soc., Cdn., 2-89
Sida
  Coalition des orgs communautaires qué. de lutte contre le, 2-17
  Comités et groupes, 2-16
  Fdn cdnne de recherche sur le, 2-19
  Soc. cdnne du, 2-16
Sidérurgie cdnne, Assn environnemental de la, 2-62
Sidérurgique cdnne, Assn pour le recherche dans l'industrie, 2-155
SIDS Fdn., 2-86
Sierra Clubs, 2-65
Sign Assn. of Canada, 2-12
Signs of Zodiac, 1-15
Sikh
  Fdn., 2-213
  Socs. of Canada, Fedn. of, 2-130
Silent
  Sports Assns., 2-175
  Voice Canada, 2-43
Silviculture Brs./Divs. (Govt.): B.C., 3-115; Nfld., 3-144; P.E.I., 3-188
Simcoe County Bd. of Educ. (Ont.), 9-25
Simmental Assn., Cdn., 2-21
Simon Fraser Univ. (B.C.), 9-7
Simulator Technologists, Cdn. Assn. of, 2-199

Singapore (Overseas Schs.), 9-40
Singers Awards, see Performing Arts
Single Parent Family Assns. of Qué., Fedn. of, 2-167
Sioniste cdnne, La Fédn, 2-129
Sir Sandford Fleming College of AA & T (Ont.), 9-34
Sir Wilfred Grenfell College (Nfld.), 9-20
Sirop d'érable
  du N.-B., Coop. des producteurs de, 2-14
  Inst Intl du, 2-73
Sites
  Canada, Intl. Council on Monuments &, 2-97
  du Qué., Conseil des monuments et, 2-96
Siting Task Force Secretariat (Mining, Fed.), 4-89
Skating Assn.
  Cdn. Amateur Speed, 2-173
  Cdn. Figure, 2-175
Ski
  Acrobatique, 2-175
  Assn.
    Cdn., 2-176
    Cdn. Masters Cross Country, 2-176
  Council, Cdn., 2-176
  de fond Canada, 2-179; Assn des maîtres en, 2-176
  Fdn., Vancouver, 2-214
  Freestyle, 2-175
  Industries Assn., Ntl., 2-179
  Instructors
    Alliance, Cdn., 2-176
    Cdn. Assn. of Nordic, 2-174
  Jumping Canada, 2-180
  Jumps Ltd., Thunder Bay, 3-173
  Magazines, see Sports & Recreation Magazines
  Marathon, Cdn., 2-176
  Media Assn., 2-176
  Nautique du Canada, 2-181
  Nordic Combined, 2-179
  Patrol System, Cdn., 2-176
  Resorts Assn., Ont., 2-186
  Saut en, 2-180
  Water, 2-181
Skiing, Cdn. Assn. for Disabled, 2-173
Skills
  Development (Govt.): B.C., 3-111; Qué., 3-200
  Training
    Education, Min. of (B.C.), 3-111
    Post-Secondary Educ. & (Sask.), 3-219
Sky
  Line Hikers of the Cdn. Rockies, 2-153
  Works Charitable Fdn., 2-213
Slavic Congress of Canada, 2-132
Slavists, Cdn. Assn. of, 2-48
Slavonic Assn., Cdn., 2-129
Sleep
  Soc., Cdn., 2-89
  /Wake Disorders Canada, 2-94
Slovak
  Assn., Czech &, 2-130
  Cdn. Ntl. Council, 2-132
  Heritage & Cultural Soc. of B.C., 2-132
  League, Cdn., 2-132
  Magazines, 5-193
Slovenian Christian Democratic Assn. of Canada, 2-132
SMAC, 2-9
Small
  Business
    Cdn. Org. of, 2-34
    Devel. Brs., (N.B.) 3-134
    Govt. (Dept.): B.C., 3-118; Quick Ref. (see Industry), 3-22
    Studies, P.J. Gardiner Inst. for (Nfld.), 3-23
    Tourism & Culture, Min. (B.C.), 3-118
  Claims Courts: Alta. (Prov. Ct.), 10-3; B.C. (Prov. Ct.), 10-5; N.W.T., 10-9; N.S., 10-10; Ont. (Gen. Div.), 10-10; P.E.I. (Supreme Ct., Trial Div.), 10-14; Qué., (Prov. Ct.), 10-16; Sask. (Prov. Ct.), 10-20
  Craft Harbours, 3-68

Canadian Almanac & Directory 1997

Small (cont.)
    Public Libraries of Ont., Assn. of, 2-117
    Urban Municipalities Org., Ont., 2-80
Smelter & Allied Wkrs., Cdn. Assn. of, 2-199
Smoke-Free Canada, Physicians for a, 2-10
Smoking & Health, Cdn. Council on, 2-85
Snowfall, Cities, 1-65
Snowmobile(s)
    Assns.: Alta., 2-149; Sask., 2-153
    Clubs, Ont. Fedn. of, 2-152
    Fedn., B.C., 2-149
    Govt. Quick Ref., *see* Leisure Craft
    Orgs., Cdn. Council of, 2-150
Snowmobilers Assns. N.S., 2-153
Snowshoe Assn., Cdn., 2-149
Soap & Detergent Assn., 2-124
Soaring Assn. of Canada, 2-153
Soccer Assns., 2-177
Social
    Affairs Commn., Qué., 3-204
    Assistance
        Programs (Ont.), 3-173
        Review Bd., (Ont.), 3-174
    Care Facilities Corp. (Qué.), 3-207
    Contract Implementation, Ont. Public Serv., 3-181
    Credit Party, B.C., 2-141
    Development
        Councils: Cdn., 2-79; Ont., 2-168
        Educ. Group, Employment (Fed.), 3-72
    & Economic Research, Inst. of (Memorial Univ.), 9-20
    Housing Corp., Alta., 3-103
    Investment Org., 2-71
    Justice in Canada, Inter-Church Assn. to Promote, 2-9
    Planning Councils: B.C. (& Research), 2-169;
        Edmonton, 2-167; Metro Toronto, 2-169; Ottawa-Carleton, 2-169; Winnipeg, 2-169
    Rehab. Agencies of Qué., Assn. of, 2-165
    Research
        Council, Qué., 3-207
        Inst. for (York Univ.), 9-32
    Response Assns., 2-165
    Responsibility, Lawyers for, 2-167
    Science Fedn. Humanities &, 2-52
    Service
        Canada, Intl., 2-167
        Employees of Qué., Assn. of, 2-197
    Services (*see also* Income Security)
        Appeal Bd. (Nfld.), 4-149
        Assn(s)., 2-165
        Ont. Municipal, 2-168
        Council, Yukon Health, 4-221
        Depts.: Govt. Quick Ref., 3-35; Alta. (Family &), 3-99; B.C., 3-119; Man. (Family Services), 3-125; N.B. (Human Resources), 3-137; Nfld., 3-149; N.W.T., 3-151; N.S. (Community Services), 3-157; Ont., 3-173; P.E.I., 3-190; Qué. (Santé etc.), 3-206; Sask., 3-220; Yukon, 3-223
    Statistics (Fed.), 3-89
    Welfare Appeals Bd. (N.B.), 3-137
    Work
        Admrs. in Health Facilities, Cdn. Assn. of, 2-100
        Cdn. Assn. of Schs. of, 2-46
        Faculties/Schs., Index to, 9-57
        Fdn., Cdn., 2-166
        Maritime Sch. of (Dalhousie), 9-22
    Worker(s)
        Advisory, Office of (Ont.), 3-181
        Assns: Alta., 2-165; B.C., 2-165; Cdn., 2-166;
            Man., 2-167; N.B., 2-168; Nfld., 2-168; N.S., 2-168
        & Attendance Counsellors, Cdn. Assn. of, 2-48
        Man. Inst. of Reg'rd., 2-167
Socialist Party of Canada, 2-142

Sociale(s)
    Commn des affaires (Qué.), 3-204
    Conseil qué. de la recherche, 3-207
Societies, 2-8
Sociology & Anthropology Assn., Cdn., 2-155
Softball Canada, 2-180
Soft Drink Assns., 2-73
Software
    Devel. Assn., Ont., 2-104
    Human Resource Council, 2-104
    Industry Assn. of N.S., 2-104
    Theft, Cdn Alliance Against, 2-103
Soil
    Conservation Canada, 2-65; Sask., 2-64
    & Crop Improvement Assn., P.E.I., 2-15
    & Land Mgmt. Div. (Nfld.), 3-144
    Science, Cdn. Soc. of, 2-162
Soils & Crops Br. (Man.), 3-122
Soins
    intensifs, Soc. cdnne de, 2-85
    à long terme, Assn cdnne de, 2-100
    palliatifs, Assn cdnne des, 2-88
    de santé, Assn cdnne des, 2-100
    et services
        communautaires, 2-100
        à domicile, Assn cdnne de, 2-101
Sol, Soc. cdnne de la science du, 2-162
Solar
    Energy Soc. of Canada, 2-57
    Industries Assn., Cdn., 2-56
    System, Elements of, 1-14
    Tables, 1-8/13
Soleil, Le (Qué.), 5-144
Soldiers Aid Commn. (Ont.), 3-174
Solicitors, *see also* Lawyers
    Servs. Br. (N.S.), 3-162
Solicitors General (Govt.): Quick Ref., 3-36; Fed., 3-88;
    N.B., 3-139; Ont., 3-185 (*see also* Sécurité publique, for Qué.)
    Correction Serv., Min. of (Ont.), 3-185
Solidarité intle, Carrefour de, 2-108
Solid Waste
    Assn. of N. Amer., 2-65
    Section (Govt.), P.E.I., 3-190
    & Recycling Section (N.B.), 3-135
Solliciteur général (Govt.): Fed., 3-88; N.B., 3-139
Sol, Soc. cdnne de la science du, 2-162
Sols Canada, Conservation des, 2-65
Somali Immigrant Aid Org., 2-132
Sommeil
    Eveil Canada, Affections du, 2-94
    Soc. cdnne du, 2-89
Sondages BBM, 2-28
Songwriters Assn. of Canada, 6-41
Sonographers, Cdn. Soc. of Diagnostic Med., 2-89
Sons of
    Italy, 2-76
    Norway Fdn., 2-213
    Scotland Benev. Assn., 2-76
SOQUEM, 4-205
SOQUIP, 4-206
Soroptimist Fdn. of Canada, 2-165
SOS Children's Village, B.C., 2-169; Canada, 2-169
Sourde cdnne, Jeunesse, 2-42
Sourds
    Assn des, 2-41
    Sports des, 2-175
    École orale de Montréal pour Les, 9-45
    du Qué., Coalition sida des, 2-17
Souris River Water Commn. (Man.), 3-130
Sous-titrage,
    Assn cdnne pour le, 2-29
    Regroupement québécois pour le, 2-29
South
    Asian
        AIDS Prevention, Alliance for, 2-17
        Studies, Ctr. for (U. of T.), 9-30
    Korean Govt.

South
    Korean (cont.)
        Depts./Agencies, 3-240
        Equivalency Table, 3-227
    Pacific Peoples Fdn., 2-132
Southeast Regl. College (Sask.), 9-55
Southern
    Alta. Inst. of Tech., 9-4
    Baptists, Cdn. Conv. of, 2-2
Southwest Regl. Sch. Bd. (N.S.), 9-22
Soutien, Fédn du personnel de, 2-196
Soviet
    Jewry in Canada, Assn. of, 2-128
    People, Cdn. Friends of, 2-108
    Union & Eastern European Countries, Cdn. Inst. for the Study of, 2-155
Soybean Mktg. Bd., Ont., 3-170
Spa & Pool Inst., Ntl., 2-158
Space
    Agency, Cdn., 3-62
    Govt. Quick Ref., 3-36
    Inst., Cdn. Aeronautics &, 2-28
    Science, Ctr. for Research in Earth & (York U.), 9-32
    Students for the Exploration & Devel. of, 2-36
    & Terrestrial Science, Inst. for, 2-163
Spanish Magazines, 5-193
Spatial(e)
    cdnne, Agence, 3-62
    Inst. aéronautique et, 2-28
SPCA's, 2-21
Speakers (Govt.): Alta., 3-93; B.C., 3-106; Fed. (House), 3-45; (Senate), 3-45; Man., 3-121; N.B., 3-131; Nfld., 3-141; N.W.T., 3-150; N.S., 3-155; Ont., 3-165; P.E.I., 3-187; Qué., 3-194; Sask., 3-210; Yukon, 3-221
SPEAQ, 2-69
Special
    Areas Bd., Alta., 3-103
    Care Assns., 2-10
    Events Soc., Intl., 2-67
    Libraries
        Assn., 2-120
        In: Alta., 5-7; B.C., 5-16; Man., 5-24; N.B., 5-29;
            Nfld., 5-32; N.W.T., 5-34; N.S., 5-36; Ont., 5-58;
            P.E.I., 5-84; Qué., 5-89; Sask., 5-108; Yukon, 5-112
        & Info. Servs., Cdn. Assn. of, 2-117
    Olympics Assns., 2-177
    Treatment Ctrs. in: Alta., 8-8; B.C. 8-11; Man., 8-15;
        N.B., 8-17; Nfld., 8-18; N.S., 8-20; Ont., 8-33; P.E.I.,
        8-34; Qué., 8-50; Sask., 8-56
    Waste Mgmt. Corp., Alta., 3-99
Specialty
    Foods, Cdn. Assn. of, 2-72
    & Pay Servs. (TV), 5-223
Spectroscopy Soc. of Canada, 2-163
Spectrum, Infor. Tech. & Telecommunications (Fed.), 3-76
Speculative Philosophy, Inst. of, 2-156
Speech
    Communicators Assn., Cdn., 2-42
    Fdn. of Ont., 2-43
    & Hearing Assn. of N.S., 2-43
    Language
        Hearing Assn. of Alta., 2-43
        Pathologists & Audiologists, Cdn. Assn. of, 2-84
Speed
    Measurement of, 1-63
    Skating Assn., Cdn. Amateur, 2-173
Sphagnum Peat Moss Assn., Cdn., 2-14
Spice Assn., Cdn., 2-73
Spills
    Action Ctr. (Ont.), 3-177
    Response Ctr. (Sask.), 3-214
Spina Bifida Assn. of Canada, 2-94
Spinal Research Org., Cdn., 2-90
Spiritual
    Communities of Christ, Union of, 2-6
    & Psychic Sciences, Intl. College of (Qué.), 9-48

Spiritual (cont.)
   Science Fellowship of Canada, 2-6
Sport(s) (see also Recreation)
   Administrators, Assn. of Ont., 2-172
   Assns., 2-172
   Automobile, Fédn cdnne du, 2-34
   Awards, 1-112
   Brs./Divs. (Govt.): N.B., 3-138; Nfld., 3-149; N.W.T., 3-152; Sask., 3-219; Yukon, 3-222
   Canada (Fed.), 3-58
   Cdn. Ctr. for Drug-Free, 2-174
   collégial, Assn cdnne du, 2-174
   Councils, 2-177/178; Cdn., 2-177
   for Disabled - Ont., 2-180
   Étudiant, Fédn qué. du, 2-179
   Exhibitions, Shows & Events, 1-90
   en fauteuil roulant, 2-178
   Fedn(s)., 2-227
      Cdn.
         Council of Prov./Territorial, 2-174
         School, 2-176
   Fishing Guides' Assn. Ont., 2-152
   & Fitness Admin. Ctr., Cdn., 2-178
   Govt. Quick Ref., see Recreation
   Heritage, Cdn. Assn. for, 2-174
   Magazines, 5-176, 5-188
   Medicine
      Cdn. Academy of, 2-173
      & Science Council of Canada, 2-180
   Parachuting Assn., Cdn., 2-151
   & Physical Activity, Cdn. Assn. for Adv. of Women &, 2-191
   Physiotherapy Div. of Cdn. Phys. Assn., 2-180
   Psychology, Cdn. Soc. for Psychomotor Learning &, 2-177
   Recreation, Parks & Wildlife Fdn., Alta., 3-97
   & Recreation
      Assn., Alta. Senior Citizens, 2-163
      Awards, 1-112
      Centre, Ont., 2-179
      Commn., N.S., 3-161
      Exhibitions, Shows & Events, 1-90
      Magazines, 5-176, 5-188
      Servs. Dir. (B.C.), 3-119
      Trade Shows, 1-90
Sporting Goods
   Assn., Cdn., 2-158
   Magazines, 5-176
Sportive
   Gym. Fedn., Rhythmic, 2-176
   interuniv. cdnne, Union, 2-47
Sports, see Sport(s) above
Sportsmen's Shows, see Sports & Recreation
Spring Begins, 1-3
Springboard, 2-143
Sprinkler Assn., Cdn. Automatic, 2-159
Square & Round Dance
   Assn., Toronto & Dist., 6-44
   Fedn. of N.S., 6-44
Squash Canada, 2-180
SRC, 4-62
Stabilization Prog., Ntl. Tripartite (Man.), 3-122
Stained Glass, Artists in, 2-190
Staff
   Nurses Assn. of Alta., 2-138
   Relations Bd., Public Serv. (Fed.), 3-84
   Union, Cdn., 2-199
Staffing
   & Classification Bd. (P.E.I.), 3-193
   Services Assn., Employment &, 2-56
Stagiaires post-MD en formation clinique, Système informatisé sur les, 2-88
Stamp(s)
   Collections (see also Philatelic)
      Magazines, see Hobbies Magazines
   Dealers Assn., Cdn., 2-151
   Exhibitions, Shows & Events, see Hobbies Exhibitions

Stampedes, see Rodeos
Standard Time Zones, 1-3
Standardbred Horse Soc., Cdn., 2-21
Standards
   Assns., 2-181
   Cdn., 2-181
   Bd., Cdn. Gen., 2-181; 3-85
   Councils
      Advertising, 2-11
      of Canada, 3-76
   Fdn., Cable TV, 2-181
   Govt. Quick Ref., 3-36
Standing/Cabinet/Legislative Committees: Alta., 3-93; B.C., 3-106; Man., 3-121; N.B., 3-132; Nfld., 3-141; N.S., 3-155; Ont., 3-165, 3-166; P.E.I., 3-187; Qué., 3-194; House of Commons, 3-46
Star of Courage, 16
Star Maps, 1-16/21
State of Environment Reporting (Fed.), 3-65
Stationary Engineers, Bds. of Examiners: N.B., 3-133; N.S., 3-163
Stationery, Magazines, 5-161
Statistical
   Information, 1-47
   Soc. of Canada, 2-163
Statistics (see also Vital Statistics)
   Canada, 3-89
      Regl. Ref. Ctrs., 3-90
   Govt. Agencies: Quick Ref., 3-36; B.C., 3-116; Fed., 3-89; Man., 3-123, 3-128; N.B., 3-136; N.W.T., 3-154; Qué., 3-202; Sask., 3-215; Yukon, 3-221
   Historical, 1-59
   Population, 4-1
Statistique
   Canada, 3-89
   du Qué., Bur. de la, 3-202
StatsCan see Statistics Canada
Status of Women
   Canada, 3-90
   Depts. (Govt.): Govt. Quick Ref., see Women's Issues; Fed., 3-90; Nfld., 3-149; N.W.T., 3-154; N.S., 3-163; P.E.I., 3-193; Qué., 3-198
Statut de la femme, Conseil du (Qué.), 3-198
Statutory Holidays, 1-24
Steacie Inst. for Molecular Science (NRC), 3-81
Steam Preservation & Industrial Archaeological Assn., Cdn., 2-96
Steel
   Bldg. Inst., Sheet, 2-181
   Can Recycling Council, 2-61
   Construction
      Cdn. Inst. of, 2-181
      Council, 2-181
   Corp., Sydney, 3-164
   Environmental Assn., Cdn., 2-62
   & Industrial Wkrs. Union, 2-199
   Industry
      Assns., 2-181
      Research Assn., 2-155
   Inst., Reinforcing, 2-182
   Pipe Inst., Corrugated, 2-182
   Prodrs. Assn., Cdn., 2-181
   Service Ctr. Inst., Cdn., 2-182
   Trade & Employment Congress, Cdn., 2-182
Steelworkers
   of Amer., United, 2-208
   Union, Indep. Cdn., 2-258
Stewardship, Inst. for Env. Policy &, 2-63
Stock
   Exchanges, 7-9
   Growers Assns.: Sask., 2-21; Western, 2-21
   Yards Bd., Ont., 3-170
Stoney Creek City Govt., 4-168
STOP, 2-65
Stores, Department & Chain, see Retailing
Strategic
   Mgmt., Intl. Soc. for, 2-141
   Studies, Cdn. Inst. of, 2-155

Strategis (Ind. Canada), 3-74
Stratford Festival Fdn., 6-36
Strathcona
   Fdn., Old, 2-212
   Trust, 2-214
Steacie Institute for Molecular Science (NRC), 3-81
Streetkids' Fdn., 2-169
Stress
   Cdn. Inst. of, 2-125
   Society for the Treatment & Study of, 2-126
   & Well-Being, Cdn. Ctr. for, 2-125
Strikes, Number of, 1-57
Stroke
   Fdns., Heart &, 2-92
   Recovery Assn. (Ont.), 2-94
Structural Board Assn., 2-33
Student
   Aid (Govt.): Quick Ref. 3-36; Fed., 3-72; Man., 3-121; Nfld., 3-142; N.S., 3-158; P.E.I., 3-191; Qué., 3-200 (see also Student Services)
   Christian Movement, 2-6
   Financial Aid Admins., Cdn. Assn. of, 2-69
   Guides, 5-197
   Placement Serv. (Qué.), 3-203
   Services
      Cdn. Assn. of College & Univ., 2-46
      Dirs. (Govt): B.C., 3-111; Man., 3-121; N.B., 3-133; Nfld., 3-142; N.S., 3-158; Qué., 3-200; Sask., 3-219
   Personnel, Assn. of Profl., 2-198
Students
   Cdn. Assn. of Pharmacy, 2-139
   Cdn. Fedn. of, 2-49
      Medical, 2-86
   for the Exploration & Devel. of Space, 2-28
   Finance Bd. (Alta.), 3-95
   Ntl. Educ. Assn. of Disabled, 2-53
   Network, N. Amer. Jewish, 2-53
   Services, Cdn. Fedn. of, 2-49
   Union of N.S., 2-54
Stuttering Treatment & Research, Inst. for, 2-156
Subsidies, Govt. Quick Ref., 3-19
Substance Abuse, Cdn. Ctr. on, 2-10, 3-57
Success/Angus Business Coll. (Man.), 9-16
Succession
   Duty (Govt.): Alta., 3-104
   to Throne, 3-246
Sucre, Inst cdn du, 2-73
Sudbury (Ont.)
   City Govt., 4-168
   Laurentian Univ., 9-29
   Nutrino Observatory (Queen's Univ.), 9-29
   Regl. Mun. Govt., 4-172
   University of, 9-29
Sudeten-German Clubs, Central Org. of, 2-129
Sugar
   Beet
      Growers' Mktg. Bd., Alta., 3-96
      Prodrs.' Assn., Cdn., 2-13
   Inst., Cdn., 2-73
Suicide
   Info. & Educ. Ctr., 2-169
   Prevention, Cdn. Assn. for, 2-125
   Support Prog., Survivors of, 2-126
Summer
   Begins, 1-3
   Villages
      Alta., 4-1
      Children's Intl., 2-108
Sun
   Azimuths, 1-7
   Dials, 6-9
   Diameter of, 1-14
   Distance of, 1-14
   Eclipses of, 1-22
   Rising, Setting, 1-6/13
Superannuated Teachers of Ont., 2-54
Superannuates Ntl. Assn., Federal, 2-79

Superannuation Commn., B.C., 3-115
Superintendent of
    Bankruptcy, 10-21
    Financial Insts. (Fed.), 7-1, 3-67
Supply
    Operations Serv. (Fed.), 3-85
    & Services
        Depts. (Govt.): Alta., 3-103; Fed. (Public Works
            & Govt. Servs.), 3-85; N.B., 3-140; Qué. (Govt.
            Services), 3-209
        Divs. (Govt.): Ont., 3-182; P.E.I., 3-192; Yukon, 3-223
Supreme Court (*see also* Queen's Bench Courts)
    of Canada, 10-1
    Provs.: B.C., 10-4; Nfld., 10-8; N.W.T., 10-8; N.S., 10-9; P.E.I., 10-14; Qué. (Superior), 10-15; Yukon, 10-21
Surdi-cécité et de la rubéole, Assn cdnne de la, 2-85
Surdité, Inst cdn de recherche et de formation sur la, 2-42
Sûreté
    industrielle, La Soc. cdnne de la, 2-160
    du Qué., 3-208
    Fra. des costables du contrôle routier, 2-201
Surface
    Finishers Soc., Amer. Electroplaters &, 2-122
    Rights Bds. (Govt.): Alta., 3-96; Man., 3-130; Sask., 3-218
    Science Western (U.W.O.), 9-31
    Transp. Tech., Ctr. for (NRC), 3-81
Surgeons
    Cdn.
        Assn. of
            General, 2-83
            Oral & Maxillofacial, 2-84
            Paediatric, 2-84
        Soc. of
            Cardiovascular & Thoracic, 2-89
            Plastic, 2-90
            Vascular, 2-90
    Colleges of, 2-92
    Conferences, *see* Medical Exhibitions
    Royal College of
        Dental, 2-41
        Physicians &, 2-94
Surgery
    Cdn. Academy of Facial, Plastic & Reconstructive, 2-83
    Head & Neck, Cdn. Soc., 2-90
Surgical Oncology, Cdn. Soc. of, 2-90
Surrey
    City Govt., 4-168
    Sch. Dist., 9-7
Surveillance des activités de renseignements de sécurité, 3-88
Surveyor(s)
    Assns., 2-182
    Cdn.
        Council of Land, 2-182
        Inst. of Quantity, 2-182
    Gen. Office of (Ont.), 3-184
Surveys & Mapping (Govt. Agencies): Quick Ref. (*see* Maps), 3-26; Alta., 3-98; Fed., 3-83; N.S., 3-163; (*see also* Land Surveys)
Sustainable
    Agriculture Assn., 2-16
    Development
        Award (Man.), 6-54
        Cdn. Intl. Inst. for, 2-63
        Dir. (Qué.), 3-201
        Economic Devel., Co-op. Agreement for (P.E.I.), 3-190
        Farming, 2-64
        Fisheries Network, 2-91
        Forest
            Mgmt. Network of Ctrs. of Excellence, 2-75
            Serv. (Fed.), 3-82
        Intl. Inst. for, 2-81

Sustainable (cont.)
    Land Mgmt Br. (Sask.), 3-214
    Production Br. (Sask.), 3-212
Swedish Magazines, 5-193
Sweetgrass First Nations Language Council, 2-112
Sweetener Users, Cdn. Industrial, 2-72
Swimming
    Assn., Cdn. Amateur Synchro., 2-180
    Canada, 2-180
    Coaches Assn., Cdn., 2-178
Swine Breeders Assns., 2-21
Swiss Govt.
    Depts./Agencies, 3-241
    Equivalency Table, 3-227
Switzerland
    Govt., 3-227, 3-241
    Overseas Schs., 9-41
Sydney
    City Govt., *see* Cape Breton Regl. Municipality
    Steel Corp., 3-164
Symbols & Abbreviations, Astronomical, 1-15
Symphony
    Musicians, Org. of, 6-41
    Orchestras, List of (& Socs.), 6-37
Synchro Canada, 2-180
Syndicalistes retraités, Assn des, 2-196
Syndicats
    affiliés, Fédn indép. des, 2-201
    cdns, Confédn des, 2-196
    démocratiques, Centrale des, 2-196
    de gestion agricole, Fédn des (Qué.), 3-198
    hospitaliers de Montréal, Conseil des, 2-200
    indépendants, Fédn cdnne des, 2-196
    nationaux, Confédn des, 2-196
Systems
    Corp., B.C., *see* Information Techn. Servs. Div., 3-114
    Inst., B.C. Advanced, 2-103
    Management, Assn. for, 2-103

T

Tabac
    et de la confiserie, Assn ntle des distributeurs de, 2-158
    Conseil cdn des fabricants des produits de, 2-124
    Offices des producteurs (Qué.), 3-198
    et la santé, Ctr ntl de doc. sur le, 2-93
Tabagisme et la santé, Conseil, 2-85
Table
    Ronde sur l'environnement et l'économie, Fed., 4-81
    Tennis Assn., Cdn., 2-151
Tableware Assn., Cdn., Gift &, 2-158
Tai Chi Soc., Taoist, 2-153
Taiwan
    Friendship Assn., Canada-, 2-107
    Govt.
        Depts./Agencies, 3-242
        Equivalency Table, 3-227
    Overseas Student Selection Office, (B.C.), 9-13
Tanners Assn., 2-124
Taoism, Fung Loy Kok Inst. of, 2-4
Taoist Tai Chi Soc. of Canada, 2-153
Tapirisat of Canada, Inuit, 2-133
Tarentaise Assn., Cdn., 2-21
Tariff(s) Programs (Fed. Revenue), 4-86
Tax
    Assn., Cdn. Property, 2-183
    Collectors of Ont., Assn. of Mun., 2-183
    Commr., N.S., 3-157
    Consultants, Cdn. Fedn. of, 2-183
    Court of Canada, 10-2
    Div. (Ont.), 3-179
    Fdn., Cdn., 2-183
    Policy Br. (Fed.), 3-67 (Finance); 3-86 (Revenue); Nfld., 3-143
    Soc., Cdn. Petroleum, 2-183

Taxation
    Assn(s)., 2-183
    Brs./Divs. (Govt.): Quick Ref., 3-34, 3-36; Alta. Treasury, 3-105; B.C. (Finance), 3-114; Fed. (Revenue), 3-86; Man. (Finance), 3-125; N.B. (Finance), 3-136; Nfld. (Finance), 3-143; N.W.T. (Finance), 3-151; N.S. (Finance), 3-159; Ont. (Finance), 3-178; P.E.I. (Treasury), 3-192; Qué. (Revenue), 3-206; Sask. (Finance), 3-215
    Cdn. Inst. of, 2-183
    Excise/GST, 3-86
    GST, 3-86
    Revenue Canada, 3-86
Taxicab Bd., Man., 3-127
Taxidermy, Cdn. College of (Man.), 9-16
Taxpayers
    Coalition, Niagara, 2-183
    Fedn., Cdn., 2-183; Ont., 2-183
TD Bank, 7-1
Tea
    Assn., 2-74
    Council of Canada, 2-74
Teacher
    Certification & Pensions, P.E.I., 3-190
    Education, Cdn. Assn. for, 2-48
    -Librarians' Assn., Yukon, 2-120
Teachers
    Assn(s)., 2-50
        Fedn. of Women, 2-52
        Franco-Ontarien, 2-46
    Awards, (*see* Education)
    Cdn. Assn.
        of Business Ed., 2-47
        of Immersion, 2-45
        of Law, 2-113
        of Second Language, 2-48
        of University, 2-48
    Cdn. College of, 2-48
    College, N.S., 9-23
    of Community Health, Cdn. Assn. of, 2-48
    Educ. (Ont.), 3-41
    of English
        as an Additional Lang., Assn. of B.C., 2-45
        Language Arts, Cdn. Council of, 2-48
    Fedn(s)., 2-50
        Cdn., 2-50
        Ont.: Pub. Sch., 2-53; Sec. Sch., 2-53
    of French as a First Language, Cdn. Assn. for the, 2-45
    of Handwriting, Intl. Assn. of Master Penmen &, 2-52
    Ntl. Fedn. of Québec, 2-52
    Pension Plan Bd., Ont., 3-177
    Prov. Assn. of Catholic (Qué.), 2-53; Protestant (Qué.), 2-50
    Publications, *see* Education Publications
    Socs., 2-50
    Superannuated (Ont.), 2-54
    of Technical Writing, Cdn. Assn. of, 2-48
    Unions, 2-50
Teaching
    Assns., 2-45
    Awards, (*see* Education)
    Congress, Qué., 2-196
    of English as a Second Language in Qué., 2-54
    Hospitals Assn. of Cdn., 2-99
    Publications, *see* Education
    Support Staff Union, 2-207
    Standards, Council on Alta., 3-98
Team Handball Fedn., Cdn., 2-178
Teamsters
    Canada, 2-207
    Intl. Broth. of, 2-202
Technical
    Asphalt Assn., Cdn., 2-59
    Awards, 1-111
    Employees, Cdn. Union of Profl., 2-200
    Industries, Nfld., & Lab. Alliance, 2-104

Technical (cont.)
   Info., Inst. for Scientific & (NRC), 3-81
   Schs. in: Alta., 9-4; B.C., 9-9; Nfld., 9-21; Sask., 9-54
      (*see also* Community Colleges)
   Standards Div. (Ont.), 3-174
   Univ. of N.S., 9-22
   & Vocational Insts., *see* Technical Schs. above
   Writing, Cdn. Assn. of Teachers of, 2-48
Technicians
   Assn(s)., 2-58
   & Technologists, Cdn. Council of, 2-58
Technion Soc., Cdn., 2-156
Technique(s)
   de Montréal, Collège, 9-47
   et professionnelle, École (Man.), 9-16
Technologie(s)
   avancée, Inst. de (Qué.), 9-47
   Conseil de la science et de la (Qué.), 3-203
   Dept. (Govt.), Qué., 3-202
   en éducation, Assn des média et de la, 2-46
   environnementales, Ctr pour l'avancement des, 2-63
   Industry Assn. of B.C., 2-104
   Musée ntl des sciences et de la, 6-1
   de pointe, Assn cdnne de, 2-57
   Sask. Indian Inst. of, 9-54
   supérieure, École de (Qué.), 9-47
   du Qué. Metropolitain, Parc, 3-203
Technologists' Assn(s)., 2-58
Technologistes
   agro-alimentaires, Assn des, 2-13
   de laboratoire, Soc. cdnne de, 2-90
   médicaux du Qué.
      Assn profl des, 2-198
      Ordre profl des, 2-94
   en orthopédie, Soc. cdnne des, 2-90
Technologues
   en cardiologie, Soc. cdnne des, 2-89
   diplômes en electrophysiologie médicale, Assn profl des, 2-82
   profiles, Corp. profile des (Qué.), 2-58
Technology
   Assessment, Cdn. Coord. Office for Health, 2-85
   Assns., 2-57
      Cdn. Advanced, 2-57
   Awards, 1-111
   Branch, Energy, Minerals & (P.E.I.) 3-189
   Cdn.
      Ctr for Creative (Ont.), 2-58, 9-35
      Soc. for the Advancement of Legal, 2-114
   Centrac College (Nfld.), 9-20
   Companies, Cdn., 7-54
   Council, Man. (Economic Innovation &), 3-128
   Depts. (Govt.): Govt. Quick Ref., 3-34; Nfld., 3-146; Qué., 3-202
   for Development, Intl. Assn. of Science &, 2-163
   in Educ., Assn. for Media &, 2-46
   Hist'l Assn., Cdn. Science &, 2-162
   Industries Assn., B.C., 2-57
   Institute(s): Alta., 9-4; B.C., 9-9; Ont., 9-35; Qué., 9-47
      for Chemical Science &, 2-35
   Israel Inst. of, 2-156
   Ntl.
      Adv. Council on Science &, 3-75
      Museum of Science &, 6-1
   Network, The Cdn., 2-154
   Northern Alta. Inst. of, 9-4
   & Science Secretariat (N.S.), 3-164
   & Social Devel., Ctr. for (U. of T.), 9-30
   Society
      Cdn. Air Cushion, 2-57
      for Cdn. Women in Science &, 2-193
   Southern Alta. Inst. for, 9-4
Tecumseh Community Dev. Corp., 2-134
Telebook Agency, Cdn., 2-145
Telecaster Com. of Canada, 2-29
Telecom Assn., Air Force, 2-183

Telecommunications
   Alliance, Cdn. Business, 2-183
   Assn(s)., 2-183
      Cdn. Wireless, 2-183
      Ont. Cable, 2-183
   Brs./Divs. (Govt.): Fed., 3-76; Qué., 3-210
   Commn. (CRTC), 3-61
   Companies, Cdn., 7-54
   Conseil de la radiodiffusion et des, 3-61
   Consultants Assn., Cdn., 2-183
   Employees Assn. of Man., 2-207
   Govt. Quick Ref., 3-37
   Initiative, Information & (Man.), 3-127
   Magazines, 5-176
   Régie des (Qué. Govt.), 3-199
   Regulation (CRTC), 3-61
   Research
      Cdn. Inst. for, 2-183
      Inst. of Ont., 2-183
   Saskatchewan, 3-220
   Suppliers, Assn. of Competitive, 2-183
   Union, Cdn. Overseas, 2-199
   Wkrs. Union, 2-207
Télédétection, Soc. cdnne de, 2-59
Télédiffuseurs, Le Comité des, 2-29
Téléfilm Canada, 3-90
TeleLearning Research Network, 2-59
Telemarketing
   Assn., Cdn., 2-11
   Industry Assn., 2-12
Telephone(s) (*see also* Telecommunications)
   Access Lines Statistics, 1-57
   Assn., Cdn. Indep., 2-183
   Employees' Assn., Cdn., 2-199
   Lines, Number of, 1-57
   System, Man., 3-131
Telescopes, Observatory, 1-1
Télé-Université (Qué.), 9-47
Television (*see also* Broadcasting; TV)
   Academy of Cdn. Cinema &, 2-68
   Alliance for Children &, 2-28
   Assn(s).
      of Canada, Intl. (ITVA), 2-29
      Cdn. Cable, 2-29
      des producteurs de films et (Qué.), 2-68
      québécoise des réalisateurs de cinéma et de, 2-68
      for Study of Cdn. Radio &, 2-28
   Awards & Prizes, *see* Broadcasting & Film, (*see also* Culture, Visual Arts)
   Bur. of Canada, 2-29
   Cable Companies, 5-223
   CBC, 3-56
   et de cinéma, Fédn profile des réalisateurs de, 2-29
   CRTC, 3-61
   Engrs., Soc. of Motion Picture &, 2-59
   Govt. Quick Ref., (*see* Broadcasting), 3-5
   de langue française, Assn cdnne de la radio et, 2-29
   Lighting Dirs., Soc. of, 2-29
   Magazines, 5-189
   Network Head Offices, 5-198
   News Directors' Assn., Radio, 2-29
   Production Assn., Cdn. Film &, 2-68
   & Radio Artists
      Alliance of Cdn., 2-196
      American Fedn. of, 2-197
   & Recording Arts, Columbia Academy of Radio (B.C.), 9-9
   Regulation (CRTC), 3-61
   Series Devel. Fdn., Cdn., 2-209
   Specialty & Pay, 5-223
   Standards Fdn., Cable, 2-181
   Stations, 5-213
   Women in Film &, 2-30
Temperance Union, Cdn. Women's Christian, 2-76
Temperatures
   Celsius & Fahrenheit, 1-63
   at Cities, 1-65
Ten Days for Global Justice, 2-110

Tenant(s)
   Assns., Fedn. of
      Metro Toronto, 2-101
      Ottawa-Carleton, 2-102
   Regulations, Govt. Quick Ref., 3-25
Tender Fruit
   Inst., Ont., 2-73
   Producers' Mktg Bd., (Ont.), 3-170
Tendering & Contracts (*see* Purchasing, Govt.)
Tennis
   Assns., 2-178; Table, 2-151
   Magazines, *see* Sports & Recreation Magazines
Tenpin Fedn., Cdn., 2-178
Teresa Group, 2-19
Terminologues du N.-B., 2-112
Terrains de camping, Assn des (Qué.), 2-184
Terrazzo Tile & Marble Assn. of Canada, 2-33
Terre(s)
   Les Ami(e)s de la, 2-63
   Jour de la, 2-62
   Sous-min. (Qué.), 3-205
Terrestrial Science, Inst. for Space &, 2-163
Territorial
   Bd. of Revision (N.W.T.), 3-152
   Chambers of Commerce, 7-24
   Courts: N.W.T., 7-8; Yukon, 7-22
   Electoral Divs., 4-37, 3-150
   Emblems, **14**
   Govts.: N.W.T., 3-150; Yukon, 3-150
TESL Canada Fedn., 2-54
Teslin Renewable Resources Council (Yukon), 3-225
Test Ctr., Cdn., 2-50
Testing
   Cdn. Soc. for Non-Destructive, 2-181
   & Standards, Assns., 2-181
Textile(s)
   Assns., 2-67
   Ctr des technologies, 2-67
   Colourists & Chemists, Cdn. Assn. of, 2-67
   Conseil des arts (Qué.), 2-190
   Fedn. of Canada, 2-68
   Fdn., Dominion, 2-209
   Inst., Cdn., 2-67
   Magazines, 5-176
   Processors, Serv. Trades, Health Care, Profl. & Technical Employees' Intl. Union, 2-207
   Science, Inst. of, 2-163
   Technology Ctr., 2-67
   et du vêtement, Fédn des synds du, 2-201
   Wkrs.
      of Amer., United, 2-208
      Unions, Amalgamated Clothing &, 2-197
Textual Scholarship, Ctr. for (U.W.O.), 9-31
Thalidomide Victims Assn. of Canada, 2-169
Thanatalogues du Qué., Corp. des, 2-76
Thanksgiving Day, 1-24
Thé, Assn du, 2-74; Conseil cdn du, 2-74
Théâtrales, Soc. qué. d'études, 6-36
Theatre
   Alliance Toronto, 6-37
   amateur, Assn qué. du, 6-35
   Assn(s)., 6-35
      Motion Picture, 2-69
      québécoise des critiques de, 6-35
   Awards & Prizes, *see* Educational; Literary Arts; Performing Arts
   Companies, 6-35
   Conseil québécois du, 6-35
   Critics Assn., Cdn., 6-35
   Directory, 6-35
   Exchange, Prairie, 6-36, 9-15
   Exhibitions, Shows & Events, *see* Arts Exhibitions
   Grand (Qué.), 3-199
   Institute, International, 6-36
   Magazines, *see* Entertainment Magazines
   Research, Assn. for Cdn., 6-35
   Sch., Ntl., 9-48
   Technology, Cdn. Inst. for, 6-35

Canadian Almanac & Directory 1997

Theatres
    Associés, 6-37
    Profl. Assn. of Cdn., 6-36
    Round Ont., Assn. of Summer, 6-35
    Trust, Historic, 2-96
    unis enfance jeunesse, 6-37
Theatrical Stage Employees & Moving Picture Machine Operators of the U.S. & Canada, Intl. Alliance of, 2-202
Theological
    College(s): B.C., 9-8; Ont., 9-29; Qué., 9-46; Sask., 9-54
    Seminaries (& Pre-Theol. Schs.): Ont., 9-34, 9-35; Sask., 9-54
    Soc., Cdn., 2-7
Theology, Schs. of: Atlantic, 9-22; Toronto (U. of T.), 9-31; -(Dominican College), 9-35; Vancouver, 9-10
Théorie des machines et des mécanismes, Commn cdnne pour la, 2-156
Theory & Criticism, Ctr. for Study of (U.W.O.), 9-31
Theosophical Soc. in Canada, 2-157
Thérapeutes
    en réadaptation physique du Qué., Synd. des physiothérapistes et des, 2-206
    respiratoires, Soc. cdnne des, 2-90
    du sport, Assn cdnne des, 2-84
Therapeutic(s)
    Com., Drug Standards & (Man.), 3-126
    Riding Assn., Cdn., 2-178
Therapy Insts., Art: Toronto, 9-36; Vancouver, 9-10
Thermal Insulation Assn. of Canada, 2-95
Third World Assistance, see International Aid
Thoracic
    Soc., Cdn., 2-87
    Surgeons, Cdn. Soc. of Cardiovascular &, 2-89
Thermal Tech. Ctr. (NRC), 3-81
Thorneloe Univ. (Ont.), 9-29
Thoroughbred Horse Soc., Cdn., 2-21
Thunder Bay
    City Govt., 4-168
    Ski Jumps Ltd., 3-173
Thyroid Fdn. of Canada, 2-94
Tibetan Assn., Cdn., 2-129
Tidal Power Corp. (N.S.), 3-164
Tile & Marble Assn. of Canada, Terrazzo, 2-33
Tilers, Ntl. Assn. of Tinsmiths &, 2-197
Tillage Soc., Alta. Conservation, 2-12
Timber
    Export Adv. Com. (B.C.), 3-115
    Mgmt. (Govt.): Quick Ref. (see Forest Resources), 3-17; B.C., 3-115; N.B., 3-139
Timbres de Pâques, Conseil Ntl des, 2-42
Time
    Standard, 1-3
    Zones, 1-3; Map (Canada), 1-3; (US) 1-4; Intl., 1-5
Tinsmiths & Tilers, Ntl. Assn. of, 2-197
Tir, Fédn de, 2-153
Tirage, Assn cdnne des chefs de, 2-144
Tire
    Recycling Mgmt. Bd. (Alta.), 3-99
    Specialists Assn., Qué., 2-25
Titles
    Correct, 1-26
    Land, see Land Titles
TLM Canada, 2-93
TMAC, 2-71
To Serve Canada, 2-39
Tobacco
    & Confectionery Distrs., Ntl. Assn. of (Qué.), 2-158
    & Health, Ntl. Clearinghouse on, 2-93
    Mktg. Bds.: N.B., 3-134; N.S., 3-156; Ont., 3-170; Qué., 3-198
    Mfrs. Council, Cdn., 2-124
    Workers Intl. Union, 2-198
Tobago Assns. in Canada, Natl. Council of, 2-131
Toiletry & Fragrance Assn., Cdn. Cosmetic, 2-123
Tomato Seedling Plant Mktg. Bd., Ont., 3-170
Tool Distrs. Assn., Cdn. Machine, 2-66

Tooling & Machining Assn., Cdn., 2-124
Topographic Info., Ctr. for (Fed.), 3-83
Topography see Maps & Charts
Toponymie, Commn de (Qué.), 3-200
Toronto (see also Metropolitan Toronto)
    Area, Office for the Greater, 3-183
    Art Therapy Inst., 9-36
    Arts Fdn. of Greater, 2-31
    Baptist Seminary, 9-34
    Bd. of Educ., 9-25
    City Govt., 4-168
    Community Fdn. for Greater, 2-209
    -Dominion Bank, 7-1
    Jewish Historical Soc., 2-132
    Language Sch., Metro, 9-35
    Map, Regional, 4-175
    Metro.
        Govt., 4-172
        Map, 4-175
        Separate Sch. Bd., 9-26
    Montessori Inst., 9-36
    Sch. of Theology (U. of T.), 9-31
    Stock Exchange, 7-11
    Univ. of, 9-30
Torture, Cdn. Ctr. for Victims of, 2-166
Tourbe & des tourbières, Soc. cdnne de la, 2-61
Tourette Syndrome Fdn. of Canada, 2-94
Tourism (see also Travel)
    Alta. League for Environmentally Responsible, 2-184
    Assn(s.), 2-183
        Cdn. Ntl. Aboriginal, 2-185
        Council of (B.C.), 2-158
    Brs./Divs. (Govt.): Alta., 3-97; B.C. 3-119; Fed., 3-75; N.W.T., 3-153; Nfld., 3-149; N.S., 3-158; Ont., 3-175; Sask., 3-213
    Canada, 3-75
    Depts. (Govt.): Quick Ref., 3-37; Alta., 3-97; B.C., 3-118; Man., 3-127; N.B., 3-134; Nfld., 3-149; Ont., 3-175; P.E.I., 3-189; Qué., 3-208; Yukon, 3-225
    Education Council, Alta., 3-97
    Exhibitions, Shows & Events, 1-91
    Govt. Quick Ref., 3-37
    Industry Assn(s)., Man., 2-187; N.B., 2-187; Nfld., 2-187; N.S., 2-187; N.W.T., 2-187; P.E.I., 2-187; Sask., 2-187; Yukon, 2-187
        of Canada, 2-186
    Industry, Trade &, Dept. (Man.), 3-127
    Initiative (Man.), 3-127
    Nunavut, 2-186
    Partnership Corp., Alta., 2-189, 3-97
    Research Inst., Cdn., 2-185
    Yukon, 3-225
Tourisme
    Dével. éconoomique &, Dept. (N.B.), 3-134
    et d'hôtellerie du Qué., Inst. de, 2-185
    Jeunesse, 2-186
    Québec, 3-208
    SDERS, 2-186
Tourist
    Info., Govt. Quick Ref., 3-37
    Org. Reps., Assn. of Ntl., 2-184
Touristiques
    Alliance cdnne des assns, 2-184
    Assn de l'industrie, 2-186
    régionales associées du Qué., Assns, 2-184
Towing Soc., Cdn., 2-26
Towns & Clerks in: Alta., 4-1; B.C., 4-12; Man., 4-18; N.B., 4-24; Nfld., 4-29; N.W.T., 4-37; N.S., 4-39; Ont., 4-42; P.E.I., 4-74; Qué., 4-77; Sask., 4-134; Yukon, 4-152
Townshippers Assn., 2-39
Townships: Ont., 4-42; Qué., 4-77
Toxic(s)
    Substances, see Dangerous Goods
    Waste Research Coalition, Ont., 2-64

Toxicology
    Ctr. for, 2-90
    Centres, Cdn Network of, 2-88
    Soc. of, 2-163
Toxicomanie(s)
    Ctr. cdn de lutte contre l'alcoolisme et les, 2-10, 3-57
    Fdn de la recherche sur la, 2-10
Toy(s)
    Assn., Cdn., 2-124
    Collectors' Soc., Cdn., 2-151
    & Games, Exhibitions, Shows & Events, 1-91
    Magazines, 5-176
    Store Assn., Indep., 2-158
    Testing Council, Cdn., 2-181
Track & Field Assn., Cdn. Masters, 2-176
Tract Soc., Cdn., 2-7
Trade(s)
    Admin. Br. (Fed.), 3-96
    Assn(s)., 2-187
        Cdn. Intl., 2-188
        Native Investment, 2-134
        of N.S., Offshore, 2-188
    Awards, 1-94
    Boards of, 7-23
    Brs./Divs. (Govt.): Alta., 3-97; N.W.T., 3-153; Sask., 3-189
    Centres: INFORUM Montréal World, 2-188; N.S., 3-158
    Certification, Apprenticeship &, N.W.T., 3-151
    Commissioner, Chief (Fed.), 3-69
    Depts. (Govt.): Quick Ref., 3-37; Fed., 3-68; Man., 3-127; Nfld., 3-146; Ont., 3-175 (se also Economic Devel.)
    Development
        Centre, N.S., 3-158
        Corp., B.C., 3-106
        Council, Hong Kong, 2-188
    Economic Devel. Trade &, Min. (Ont.), 3-175
    & Export Partnership, Sask., 3-213
    Foreign Affairs & Intl. (Fed. Dept.), 3-68
    Govt.
        Offices: Intl., 3-69; Ntl., 3-76
        Quick Ref., 3-37
    Info. (Fed.), 3-68
    International
        Brs./Divs. (Govt.): Alta., 3-100; Fed., 3-68
        Statistics, 1-54, 1-55
    & Investment Brs./Divs. (Govt.): B.C., 3-112; N.W.T., 3-153; Ont., 3-175
    Negotiations Br. Multilateral (Fed.), 3-69
    Shows, 1-72
    Statistics (Fed.), 1-54, 1-55, 4-89
    & Tech. Dept. of Industry (Nfld.), 3-146
    & Tourism
        Econ. Devel., Min. of (Ont.), 3-175
        Industry (Man.), 3-127
    Training Inst., Western (Sask.), 9-55
    Tribunal, Cdn. Intl., 3-61
    Union(s), 2-195; Magazines, 5-185
Trademark(s) (see also Patents; Copyright)
    Fed.
        Inst., Patent &, 2-138
        Opposition Bd., 3-75
        Regr. of (Fed.), 3-75
Trading
    Corp. Man., 3-128
    Partners
        Equivalency Table, 3-228
        Statistics, 1-54
Traditional Music, Cdn. Soc. for, 6-40
Traducteurs(trices)
    et interprètes, Assns, 2-111
    judiciares, 2-113
    littéraires, 2-112
Tradluctologie, Assn cdnne de, 2-111
Traffic (see also Highway Traffic)
    Council, Ont., 2-189
    Engineering, Dirs.: Man., 3-126; N.S., 3-164

Traffic (cont.)
    Injury Research Fdn. of Canada, 2-157
    Safety Bd. (Alta.), 3-104
    & Transportation, Cdn. Inst. of, 2-188
Trail Riders of the Cdn. Rockies, 2-153
Training (see also Apprenticeship; Occupational)
    Depts. (Govt.): B.C., 3-111; Man., 3-123; Ont., 3-176; P.E.I., 3-191; Sask., 3-219
    Inst., Ntl. (Man.), 9-16
    & Youth, Secretary of State (Fed.), 3-72
Traitement spécialisés, Ctrs de (see Special Treatment Ctrs.)
Trakehner Horse Soc., Cdn., 2-21
Transfusion Medicine, Cdn. Soc. for, 2-90
TransGas Ltd., Sask., 3-220
Transit
    Assn., Cdn. Urban, 2-189; Ont., 2-189
    B.C., 3-120
    GO, 3-187
    Union
        Amalgamated, 2-197
        Indep. Cdn., 2-202
Transitaires internationaux cdns, Assn des, 2-188
Transition Houses
    Ont. Assn. of Interval &, 2-168
    Soc. of (B.C./Yukon), 2-169
Translation
    Awards, see Literary Arts
    Services (Govt): Fed., 3-86; Man., 3-123; N.B., 3-140
    Studies, Cdn. Assn. for, 2-111
Translators
    Assn(s)., 2-111/112
        of Legal Court Interpreters &, 2-113
        Literary, 2-112
    Awards (see also Literary Arts)
    & Interpreters Council, Cdn., 2-111
Transplant(s), Soc. B.C., 2-83
Transport(s)
    Administrators, Cdn. Council of Motor, 2-188
    Bds.: Man., 3-127; N.W.T., 3-154; Ont., 3-187; Qué., 3-208 (see also Motor)
    Canada, 3-90
    du Canada
        Bur. de la sécurité des, 3-91
        Office des, 3-62
    Chartered Inst. of, 2-189
    Commn. (Qué.), 3-208
    Conseil de la recherche et du dével. en (Qué.), 3-108
    of Dangerous Goods, see Dangerous Goods
    Depts. (Govt.): Fed., 3-90; N.B., 3-140; Qué., 3-208
    entreposage, Assn sectorielle, 2-159
    et machines, Assn sectorielle, Fabrication d'équipement et, 2-159
    motorisé, Conseil cdn des admins en, 2-188
    et des routes, Assn qué. du, 2-188
    Sécurité des, Bur. (Fed.), 3-91
    Soc. qué. des, 3-208
    Statistics, 1-57
    Travailleurs unis des, 2-208
    2000 Canada, 2-189
    Wkrs. Union, Cdn., 2-199
Transportation (see also Automotive; Truck(s); Pilotage Auths.)
    Accident Investigation & Safety Board (Fed.), 3-91
    Adv. Council, Western, 2-189
    Agency: Ntl., 3-62; N.B., 3-140
    Assn(s)., 2-188; of Canada, 2-189
    Bd., Qué., 3-208
    Cdn. Inst. of Traffic &, 2-188
    Commn., Atlantic Provs., 2-188
    Communications Intl. Union, 2-207
    Companies, Cdn., 7-56
    of Dangerous Goods, see Dangerous Goods
    Depts. (Govt.): Quick Ref., 3-38; Alta., 3-104; B.C., 3-119; Fed., 3-90; Man., 3-126; N.B., 3-140; Nfld., 3-149; N.W.T., 3-154; N.S., 3-164; Ont., 3-186; P.E.I., 3-193; Qué., 3-208; Sask., 3-216; Yukon, 3-222

Transportation (cont.)
    Employees, Cdn. Union of, 2-200
    Exhibitions, Shows & Events, 1-91
    Financing Auth., B.C., 3-120
    Govt. Quick Ref., 3-38
    & Highways Min. (B.C.), 3-119
    League, Cdn. Industrial, 2-188
    Magazines, 5-176
    Policy Div. (Man.), 3-126
    & Public Works, Dept. (P.E.I.), 3-193
    Research
        & Devel. Council, Qué., 3-208
        Forum, Cdn., 2-188
    Safety (see also Hwy. Safety)
        Assn., Ont., 2-161
        Bd. of Canada, 3-91
        Br. (Alta.), 3-104
    Statistics, 1-57
    Trade Shows, 1-91
    Union, United, 2-208
    & Utilities Dept. (Alta.), 3-104
    Works, Servs. &, Dept. (Nfld.), 3-149
Trappers
    Fedn. of Canada, Aboriginal, 2-77
    Publications, see Fur Trade Publications
Trapping
    Cdn. Assn. for Humane, 2-77
    Publications, see Fur Trade Publications
    Regs., Govt. Quick Ref. (see Wildlife), 3-38
Trapshooting Assn., Cdn., 2-151
Travail
    Alliance cdnne des victimes d'accidents et de maladies de, 2-110
    Centre
        cdn d'hygiène et de sécurité au, 2-85; 3-57
        patronal de santé & sécurité du, 2-160
    Comité cdn sur l'histoire du, 2-110
    Commn
        des normes du (Qué.), 3-209
        de la santé et de la sécurité du (Qué.), 3-209
    Congrès du (Canada), 2-195
    Conseil cdn de la réadaptation et du, 2-42
        des Relations du Travail (Fed.), 3-55
    Enseignement superieur et (N.B.), 3-132
    Fédn
        Américaine du, 2-195
        cdnne du, 2-195
    Inst de recherche en santé et en sécurité de (Qué.), 2-160
    et de la main d'oeuvre, Conseil consultatif du (Qué.), 3-209
    Min. du, (Qué.), 3-209
    Relations de, Sous-ministre adjoint (Qué.), 3-209
Travailleurs(euses)
    de la boulangerie, de la confiserie et du tabac, 2-198
    en communication, Union cdnne des, 2-207
    forestiers du Qué., Fédn des, 2-201
    du papier et de la forêt, Fédn des, 2-201
    de produits manufacturiés et de services, 2-207
    du Qué.
        Fédn des, 2-195
        Parti des, 2-142
        sociaux, Assns, 2-165
            Ordre profile des (Qué.), 2-168
            des postes, Synd. des, 2-199
        unis du Qué., Synd. des, 2-207
Travaux publiques et services gouvernementaux Canada, 3-85
Travel
    Advisory (Fed.), 3-68
    Agents, Cdn. Assn. of Retail, 2-184
    Assn(s).
        Alliance of Cdn., 2-184
        Cdn. Business, 2-184
        Pacific Asia, 2-186
    Counsellors, Cdn. Inst., 2-185
    Depts., Govt., see Tourism
    Exhibitions, Shows & Events, 1-91

Travel (cont.)
    Magazines, 5-176, 5-190
    Orgs., 2-183
    Writers, Soc. of Amer., 2-194
Travellers
    Aid Soc. of Toronto, 2-187
    Assoc. Cdn., 2-184
    Assn., North West Commercial, 2-186
    Intl. Assn. for Medical Assistance to, 2-92
Traversiers, Soc. des (Qué.), 3-208
Treasurers of Ont., Assn of Municipal Clerks &, 2-79
Treasury
    Alberta, 3-104
    Bds. (Govt.): B.C., 3-114; Fed., 3-91; Man., 3-131; Nfld., 3-143; Sask., 3-213
    Brs./Divs. (Govt.): Alta., 3-104; B.C., 3-114; Man., 3-125; N.B., 3-136
    Management Assn. of Canada, 2-71
    Office of (Ont.), 3-179
    Prov. (Govt.): B.C., 3-114; P.E.I., 3-192
    Secretariats (Govt.): B.C., 3-120; Nfld., 3-141
Treated Wood, Cdn. Inst. of, 2-74
Treatment Ctrs. (see also Special Treatment (Ctrs.)
    Sch. Bds. in Ont., Hospitals &, 9-27
Treaty Negotiations
    Commn., B.C., 3-74
    Office (Fed.), 3-74
Trebas Inst.: B.C., 9-9; Ont., 9-36; Qué., 9-48
TREE Fdn. for Youth Dev., 2-214
Tree(s)
    Council, Ont. Shade, 2-75
    Fruit Mktg. Bd., B.C., 3-109
    Growers Assn. of Ont., Christmas, 2-75
Trent Univ. (Ont.), 9-30
Trésor, Conseil du (Govt.): Fed., 3-91; Qué., 3-209
Trésorerie, Assn de gestion de, 2-71
TRIAD Soc. for Truth in Adoption, 2-169
Trial Divs. (Courts): Fed., 10-1; N.B., 10-7; Nfld., 10-8; P.E.I., 10-14
Tribologists & Lubrication Engrs., Soc. of, 2-59
Tribology, Research Ctr. in (U.W.O.), 9-31
Tribute to Human Rights, Cdn., 2-102
Trillium
    Book Award, 1-106
    Fdn., Ont., 2-214, 3-173
Trinidad & Tobago Assns. of Canada, Ntl. Council of, 2-131
Trinity
    College (U. of T.), 9-31
    Western, Seminary, 9-8
    Western Univ. (B.C.), 9-7
        Theological Colleges of, 9-8
Troisième âge, Conseil consultatif ntl sur le, 3-78
Trois-Rivières, Univ. du Qué. à, 9-47
Trotting Assn., Cdn., 2-178
Troubles d'apprentissage, Assns, 2-52
Trout Farmers Assn., B.C., 2-71
Trowel Trades Cdn. Assn., 2-197
Truck(s) (see also Automotive)
    Assn., Industrial, 2-189
    Council of Canada, Private Motor, 2-189
    Shows, see Automotive Exhibitions, Shows & Events
Trucking Assns., 2-188/189
    Education Fdn., Ont., 2-212
Truelle, Assn cdnne des métiers de la, 2-197
Trust Companies
    Assn. of Canada, 2-71
    Br. (Ont.), 3-178
    in Canada, List of, 7-3
    Govt. Dirs., see Financial Institutions
Trustees see Public Trustees
    School, see School(s)
Tunas, Intl. Commn. for Conservation of Atlantic, 3-248
Tunnelling Assn. of Canada, 2-153

Canadian Almanac & Directory 1997

Turkey
   Marketing Agency, Cdn., 2-142
   Mktg. Bds./Commns. (Govt.): Alta., 3-96; B.C., 2-179, 3-109; Cdn., 3-80; Man., 3-122; N.B., 3-134; N.S., 3-156; Ont., 3-170; Sask., 3-213
Turkish
   Assns., Fedn. of Cdn., 2-130
   Islamic Heritage Assn., Cdn., 2-129
Turnaround Mgmt. Assn., Cdn., 2-34
Turner's Syndrome Soc., 2-94
Tuyauterie et calorifugeurs, Assn ntle des, 2-197
Tuyaux de
   béton, Assn cdnne des fabricants de, 2-30
   tôle ondulée, Inst pour, 2-182
TV (*see* Television)
TVB of Canada Inc., 2-29
TVOntario, 3-173
Twin Falls Power Corp. (Nfld.), 3-149
2-Spirited People of the First Nations, 2-132
Two/Ten Charity Trust, 2-214
Tyrrell Museum of Palaentology, Royal, 6-2

U

UBC, 3-9
UEL Assn., 2-98
Ukraine, Encyclopedia (U. of T.), 9-30
Ukrainian
   Cdn.
      Congress., 2-132
      Research Fdn., 2-132
   Cdns., Assn. of United, 2-128
   Charitable Trust, United, 2-214
   Immigrant Aid Soc., Cdn., 2-129
   Librarians Assn. of Canada, 2-120
   Magazines., 5-193
   National
      Aid Assn., 2-132
      Assn., 2-132
   Orthodox Church, 2-6
   Studies, Cdn. Inst. of, 2-155
ULSI, 2-157
Ultralight Pilots Assn. of Canada, 2-28
UN Assn. in Canada, 2-110
Underwater
   Archaeological Soc. B.C., 2-24
   Certification Inc., 2-172
Underwriters
   Assn.
      Cdn. Boiler & Machinery, 2-104
      Life, 2-106
      of B.C., Assn. of Marine, 2-104
      Cdn. Bd. of Marine, 2-104
   Laboratories of Canada, 2-106
Unemployment Insurance
   Div. (Fed.), 3-86
   Govt. Quick Ref., 3-38
UNEP, 3-247
UNESCO
   Cdn. Commn. for, 2-107; 3-247
   Cdn. Mission to, 3-247
   Clubs, Cdn. Assn. of, 2-107
UNICEF Com., Cdn., 2-169, 3-247
Unifarm, 2-14; Women of, 2-193
Unified Family Courts: Nfld., 10-8; Sask., 10-20
Union
   Coll., Cdn. (Alta.), 9-3
   Jack, **8**
   Retirees, Congress of, 2-196
Unions, 2-195
   Cdn. Ntl. Fedn. of Indep., 2-196
   Confedn.
      of Cdn., 2-196
      Ntl. Trade, 2-196
   Congress of Democratic, 2-196
Unitarian
   Church, 2-3
   Service Com. of Canada, 2-8

United
   Brethren Church in Canada, 2-6
   Church of Canada, 2-6
   Commercial Travelers of Amer., 2-76
   Empire Loyalists Assn., 2-98
   Israel Appeal, 2-132
   Kingdom
      Cdn. Diplomats in, 3-266
      Calendar, Civil, 1-3
      Dipl. Reps. to Canada, 3-258
      Govt.
         Depts./Agencies, 3-242
         Equivalency Table, 3-227
   Nations
      Assn. in Canada, 2-110, 3-247
      Cdn. Reps. to, 3-247
      Centre for Human Settlements, in Canada, 3-247
      Educational, Scientific & Cultural Org., 3-247
      Environment Prog., 2-65, 3-247
      High Commr. for Refugees, 3-247
      Medals, 1-31
      Permanent Missions Abroad, 3-247
   Ostomy Assn., 2-94
   Services Insts. of Canada, Fedn. of Military &, 2-127
   States
      Calendar, Civil, 1-2
      Govt.
         Depts./Agencies, 3-244
         Equivalency Table, 3-227
      Map, 1-4
      Postal Rates to (Cdn.), 1-45
      Time Zones, 1-4
      Trade Info. (Fed.), 3-69
   Theological College (Montréal), 9-46
   Way Assns., 2-169/172
   World Colleges, 2-70
Unity, Cdn. (Fed.), 3-77
Universitaires & scientifiques, Affaires, Sous-ministre adjoint (Qué.), 3-200
Université(s)
   et collèges du Canada, Assn des, 2-46
   Fédn
      du personnel profl des, 2-196
      des professeur(e)s et chargés de cours des, 2-196
   québécoise des professeur(e)s d', 2-48
   Qué., 3-53
   du Qué., Conf. des recteurs et principaux des, 2-51
Universities
   Aboriginal Programs Br. (B.C.), 3-111
   Assn. of Atlantic, 2-46
   & Colleges Assn.
      of Canada, 2-46
      Registrars of, 2-46
   Council of Ont., 2-51
   In: Alta., 9-3; B.C., 9-7; Man., 9-15; N.B., 9-18; Nfld., 9-19; N.S., 9-22; Ont., 9-28; P.E.I., 9-41; Qué., 9-46; Sask., 9-54
   for Northern Studies, Assn. of Cdn., 2-46
University (*see also* Universities)
   Affairs Branch (Qué.), 3-200
   Biology Chairs, Cdn. Council of, 2-47
   Business Officers, Cdn. Assn. of, 2-46
   & College
      Conference Officers Assn., Cdn., 2-50
      Counselling Assn., Cdn., 2-50
   Colleges: B.C., 9-9; Man., 9-15; N.S., 9-23; Ont., 9-31
   Continuing Educ. Assn., 2-46
   Faculty Assns., 2-48
   Food Serv. Assn., Cdn. College &, 2-72
   Forestry Schs., Assn. of, 2-46
   Games, World, 2-181
   Libraries (*see also* Special & College Libraries in each province, Section 1)
      Cdn. Assn. of College &, 2-117
      Council of Prairie & Pacific, 2-119
      Ont. Council of, 2-120
   Library Assn., Ont. College &, 2-120
   Lifelong Learning, Ont. Council for, 2-53

University (cont.)
   Music Soc., Cdn., 6-40
   Planning Programs, Assn. of Cdn., 2-46
   Presidents, Council of Western Cdn., 2-47
   Press, Cdn., 2-145
   Presses, Assn. of Cdn., 2-144
   Publications, 5-197
   Research Administrators, Cdn. Assn. of, 2-47
   Schs. of Nursing, Cdn. Assn. of, 2-47
   Service, World, 2-110
   Servs. Br. (Sask.), 3-219
   Student Servs., Cdn. Assn. of College &, 2-46
   Teachers, Cdn. Assn. of, 2-48
   Women, Cdn. Fedn. of, 2-49
UOA Canada, 2-94
Uranium Div. (Fed.), 3-83
Uranus, Planet, 1-14
Urbain du Canada, Inst, 2-140
Urban
   Affairs, Man., 3-131
   Agric., City Farmer, 2-99
   Alliance on Race Relations, 2-132
   & Community Studies, Ctr. for (U. of T.), 9-30
   Communities, Qué., 4-173
   Devel. Inst. of Canada, 2-141
   Inst., Cdn., 2-140
   Municipal Admrs. Assn. of Sask., 2-80
   Municipalities
      Assns: Alta., 2-79; Man., 2-80; Sask., 2-80
      Org. of Small (Ont.), 2-80
   Population, 1-47, 4-1
   & Regional Research, Intergovt. Com. on, 2-140
   Renewal (Govt. Quick Ref.), 3-38
   & Rural Planning Dir. (Nfld.), 3-148
   Studies, Inst. of, 2-156
   Transit
      Assn.: Cdn., 2-189; Ont., 2-189
   Transportation (Alta.), 3-104
Urbanistes
   et des aménagistes municipaux du Qué., Assn des, 2-79
   Inst cdn des, 2-140
   du Qué. Ordre des, 2-140
Urethane Mfrs. Assn., Cdn., 2-124
Urological Assn., Cdn., 2-90
USC Canada, 2-8
Used Car Dealers Assn. of Ont., 2-27
Utilities (*see also* Public Utilities)
   Assns., 2-143
   Bds./Commns. (Govt.): Alta. Energy &, 3-98; B.C., 3-120; N.S., 3-164; Yukon, 3-224
   Cos., Cdn., 7-56
   Dept., Alta. Transp. &, 3-104
   Safety Assn. of Ont., Electrical, 2-143
Utility
   Contractors Assn. of Ont., 2-143
   & Review Bd. (N.S.), 3-164
   Tribunals, Cdn. Assn. of Members of Public, 2-143

V

Vacances familles, 2-187
Vaccine Damaged Children, Assn. for, 2-41
Vadrouilles, Assn cdnne des fabricants de, 2-123
Vaginal Birth after Caesarian Canada, 2-36
Valeurs
   mobilières
      Assn cdnne des courtiers en, 2-70
      Commn des (Qué.), 3-202
      Inst cdn des, 2-70
      Org. intle des commissions de, 2-70
Valour, Cross of, 1-28
Valve Mfrs. Assn., Cdn., 2-124
Valuators, Cdn. Inst. of Chartered Business, 2-34
Vancouver
   Art
      Gallery, The, 6-30
      Therapy Inst., 9-10

Vancouver (cont.)
   City Govt., 4-168
   Community College, 9-9
   Cultural Alliance, 2-25
   Fdn., 2-214
   Map, Regional, 4-174
   Museum, The, 6-5
   Regional
      Dist. Govt., Greater, 4-171
      Map, 4-174
   Sch.
      Dist., 9-7; North, 9-7
      of Theology, 9-10
   Stock Exchange, 7-12
Vanier Inst. of the Family, 2-172
Variety
   Artists, Amer. Guild of, 2-197
   Clubs, 2-165
Vascular Surgery, Cdn. Soc. for, 2-90
Vaughan City Govt., 4-169
V.C., 1-29
Vegans for Animal Rights, Cdn., 2-22
Vegetable(s)
   Growers Assns.: Man., 2-16; N.S., 2-16; Ont., 2-15; P.E.I., 2-15
   Industry Inspection Br. (Ont.), 3-169
   Mktg. Bds. & Commns.(Govt.): Alta., 3-96; B.C., 3-109; Man., 3-122; N.S., 3-156; Ont., 3-170; Qué., 3-198; Sask., 3-213
Végétale(s)
   Inst de recherche en biologie, 2-63
   du Qué., Conseil des productions, 3-198
   Soc. cdnne de physiologie, 2-162
Vehicle(s)
   Assn.,
      Cdn. Recreational, 2-185
      Electric, 2-189
   Info. Ctr. of Canada, 2-27
   Licensing, see Driver Licensing
   Regs., Govt. Quick Ref., 3-25
Véhicules
   Recréatifs, Assn des commerçants de, 2-27
   tout terrain, Conseil cdn des dists de, 2-26
Velocity, Measurement of, 1-63
Vélo-Québec, 2-180
Vending
   Service Assn., Ont., Coffee &, 2-73
   & Vending Equipment Magazines, 5-177
Vente, Assn cdnne des professionnels de la, 2-34
Ventes en gros, Assn cdnne des reps de, 2-67
Venture Capital Cos., Assn. of Cdn., 2-69
Venus, Planet, 1-14
Verdun, Ville de, Govt., 4-169
Vérificateur(s)
   général (Govt.): Fed., 3-54; N.B., 3-134; Qué., 3-210
   internes, Inst des, 2-9
Vérification intégrée, Fdn cdnne pour la, 2-8
Vernon Sch. Dist. (B.C.), 9-7
Verti, Parti, 2-141
Vessel Mfrs. Assn., Cdn. Heat Exchange &, 2-123
Vêtement(s)
   Fédn
      cdnne du, 2-67
      ntle des travailleurs de l'industrie, 2-201
      des synds du textile et du, 2-201
   pour hommes, Assn des mfrs de, 2-68
   de mode du Qué., Guilde des mfrs de, 2-68
   du Qué., Inst des mfrs du, 2-68
Veteran(s)
   Affairs (Govt.): Quick Ref., 3-39; Fed., 3-92
   Appeal Bd. (Fed.), 3-92
   Army, Navy & Air Force, 2-126
   Assn(s)., 2-126
      Cdn. Council of War, 2-126
      Dominion Civil Serv. War, 2-126
      Ntl. Council of, 2-127
      Royal Cdn. Mounted Police, 2-127

Veteran(s) (cont.)
   of Canada
      Jewish War, 2-127
      Korea, 2-127
      Liaison Assn. of War, 2-127
Vétérinaires
   Assn cdnne des, 2-22
   du Qué., Ordre des médecins, 2-22
Veterinarians
   College of, Ont., 2-22
   Council of, 3-169
Veterinary
   College, Ont. (Guelph), 9-30
   Laboratory Servs. (Ont.), 3-169
   Magazines, 5-177
   Medical Assns., 2-22
   Medicine
      Confedn. of Cdn., of Faculties of Agric. &, 2-47
      Faculties/Schs., Index to, 9-57
   Science Orgs., 2-21
   Services (Govt.): B.C., 3-108; Man., 3-122; N.B., 3-134
Vexillologie, Assn cdnne de, 2-150
Via Rail Canada, 1-68, 3-92
Viandes du Canada, Conseil des, 2-72
Victim(s)
   Assistance, see also Criminal Injuries Compensation; Justice Depts.
   Com. (N.W.T.), 3-152
   Coord.'s Office (Sask.), 3-217
   Programs (Alta.), 3-102
   Services (Govt.): N.B., 3-139; N.W.T., 3-152; N.S., 3-162; Sask., 2-217
   of Torture, Cdn. Ctr. for, 2-166
   Witness
      Assistance Prog. (Man.), 3-128
      Services Coord. (Ont.), 3-172
Victoria
   City Govt., 4-169
   College (U. of T.), 9-31
   Cross, 1-29
   Day, 1-24
   (Ferry) Line Ltd., 3-112
   Fdn., 2-214
   Sch. Dist., Greater, 9-6
   Univ. of, 9-8
Victorian Order of Nurses, 2-138
Video
   Alliance, Indep. Film &, 2-69
   Distrs., Cdn. Assn. of, 2-68
   Festivals & Special Events, 1-81
   Magazines, 5-175, 5-189
Vie
   Alliance pour la, 2-154
   autonome, Assn cdnne des centres de, 2-41
   française en Amérique, Conseil de la, 2-39
   Ligue pour la, 2-154
   privée du Canada, Commn à la protection de la, 3-84
Vietnamese
   Buddhist Churches, Union of, 2-6
   Cdn. Fedn., 2-132
VIH, groupes, comités, centres, 2-16
Villages in: Alta., 4-1; B.C., 4-12; Man., 4-18; N.B., 4-24; Nfld. (Communities), 4-29; N.W.T., 4-37; N.S., 4-39; Ont., 4-42; P.E.I. (Communities), 4-74; Qué., 4-77; Sask., 4-134; Yukon, 4-152
Villes, Qué., 4-77
Vin cdn, Inst du, 2-73
Vincent d'Indy, École (Qué.), 9-47
Vintage
   Auto Racing Assn., 2-23
   Locomotive Soc., 2-23
   Radio Assn. Ont., 2-153
Viol, Assn cdnne des centres contre le, 2-166
Violence
   & Conflict Resolution, La Marsh Research Program on (York Univ.), 9-32
   in Entertainment, Cdns. Concerned about, 2-166

Violence (cont.)
   Govt. Quick Ref., 3-39
   Prevention
      Family (Alta.), 3-100
      Secretariat (Ont.), 3-172
      Unit (Yukon), 3-225
Violent Crime Initiatives (Alta.), 3-102
Visa Info., 3-63, 3-70
Viscounts, 6-40
Visible Minority Women
   Against Abuse, 2-192
   Ntl. Org. of Immigrants &, 2-38
Vision
   Assn. of Ont., Low, 2-43
   Inst. of Canada, 2-44
   Mondiale, 2-110
   Research, Ctr. for (York Univ.), 9-32
   TV, 2-8
Visitors Assns., Ont. Convention &, 2-186
Visons du Canada, Assn des éleveurs de, 2-19
Visual
   Art Assns., 2-190
   Arts
      Assn. for Native Dev. in, 2-132
      Awards, 1-96
      Faculties/Schs., Index to, 9-56
      N.S., 2-191; Ont., 2-191
   Language Interpreters, Assn. of, 2-111
   Media, Assn. for the Advancement of, 2-69
Visually Impaired (see also Blind)
   Schs. for: N.S., 9-22; Ont., 9-27
   Sports Assns., 2-174
Vital Statistics, 1-48 (see also Statistics)
   Govt. Agencies, 3-39 (see also Birth, Death & Marriage Certificates)
Vitrage isolant, Assn cdnne des manufacturiers de, 2-124
Vocational
   Assn., Cdn., 2-50
   College(s) & Insts., see Technical Schs.
   Education, see Technical Schs.
   & Rehab. Research Inst., 2-44
Voice of
   Business, 2-34
   Women, 2-193
Voie Maritime du Saint-Laurent, Admin de la, 3-88
La Voix, Le Réseau cdn des aîné(e)s, 2-164
Vol
   libre, Assn cdnne de, 2-152
   à voile, Assn cdnne de, 2-153
Volailles
   Conseil cdn des transformateurs d'oeufs et, 2-142
   Fédn des producteurs de (Qué.), 2-142, 3-198
Volleyball Assns., 2-180/181
Volume, Measurement of, 1-63
Voluntary Orgs., Coalition of Ntl., 2-166
Volunteer
   Bureaus/Ctrs., Ont. Assn. of, 2-168
   Grandparents Soc. of B.C., 2-172
   Servs. in Healthcare, Ont. Assn. of Dirs. of, 2-126
VON Canada, 2-138
Voters
   Number of (in Electoral Dists.), see Electoral Districts
   Qualifications, 1-41
Voyages, Assn
   des agents de (Qué.), 2-184
   cdnne
      des chargés de, 2-184; Montréal, 2-184
      des conseillers en, 2-185
Vuntut Renewable Resources Council (Yukon), 3-225

W

Wage Rates Index, see Industrial Aggregate
Wages, Minimum, 1-52; Govt. Quick Ref., 3-26
Walking & Hiking Fedn. of Qué., 2-152

War
  Amputations of Canada, 2-172
  Graves Commn., Commonwealth, 2-126
  Medals, 1-31
  Museum, Cdn., 6-1
  Veterans
    Assns.
      Cdn. Council of, 2-126
      Dominion Civil Servants, 2-126
      of Canada, Jewish, 2-127
    Liaison Assn. of, 2-127
Warehousemen's Union, Intl. Longshoremen's &, 2-203
Warplane Heritage, Cdn., 2-96
Wascana
  Centre Auth. (Sask.), 3-215
  Inst. (Sask.), 9-54
Waste(s)
  Assn. of N.A., Solid, 2-65
  Div., Action on, (Alta.), 3-99
  Hazardous (Govt. Quick Ref.), 3-11
  Management
    Assn.
      Air &, 2-59
      Ont., 2-64
    Citizens
      Clearinghouse on, 2-62
      Network on, 2-62
    Corp.
      Alta. Special Corp., 3-99
      Awards, 6-54
    Govt. Quick Ref., 3-39
  Radioactive Div. (Fed.), 3-83
  Reduction
    Adv. Com., Ont., 3-177
    Br. (Ont.), 3-177
    Council, Sask., 2-65
  Research Coalition, Ont. Toxic, 2-64
  Services Assn., Sask. Special, 2-78
  Treatment Magazines, 5-177
Wastewater (see also Water & Wastewater)
  Treatment, Qué., 3-197
Watch & Clock Collectors, Ntl. Assn. of, 2-152
Watch Tower Bible & Tract Soc., 2-6
Water
  Agency, Ont. Clean, 3-178
  Area, Canada (Fresh), 1-63
  Assn., Ont. Municipal, 2-143
  Bds., Nunavut, 3-74; N.W.T., 3-154; Prairie Provinces, 3-130
  Color, Cdn. Soc. of Painters in, 2-190
  Commns.: Lower Red River, 3-130; Souris River, 3-130
  Corp., Sask., 3-220
  Environment Assn. of Ont., 2-65; Western Canada, 2-65
  Management
    Divs. (Govt.): B.C., 3-113; Ont., 3-184
    Prairie Assn. for, 2-64
  Policy Office, (Fed.), 3-65
  Pollution, see Environment
  Polo Canada, 2-181
  Quality
    Agreement, Great Lakes, 3-77
    Assn., Cdn., 2-62
    Branch (B.C.), 3-113
    Cdn. Assn. on, 2-60
  Research Inst.: Ntl., 3-65; Sask. (U. of Regina), 9-54
  Resource(s) (see also Water Quality; Ecosystem Sciences)
    Assn., Cdn., 2-62
    Brs./Divs. (Govt.): Quick Ref., 3-40; Alta., 3-99; Man., 3-130; N.B., 3-135; Nfld., 3-143; N.S., 3-159; P.E.I., 3-190
  Services Bd., Man., 3-130
  Ski Canada, 2-181
  & Wastes Treatment Magazines, 5-177

Water (cont.)
  & Wastewater
    Assns.: B.C., 2-60; Cdn., 2-62; Western Canada, 2-65
    Section (N.B.), 3-135
  Well Assns., 2-44
Waterfowl
  & Furbearers Br. (P.E.I.), 3-190
  Mgmt. Plan, N. Amer. (Fed.), 3-65
  Soc., B.C., 2-135
Waterfront
  Devel. Corp. (N.S.), 3-158
  Industrial Parks (Qué.), 3-203
  Regeneration Trust (Ont.), 3-183
Waterloo
  City Govt., 4-169
  County Bd. of Educ. (Ont.), 9-25; R.C.S.S., 9-26
  Lutheran Seminary (Wilfrid Laurier), 9-32
  Regl. Mun., Govt., 4-173
  Univ. of, 9-31
Watermain Construction Assn., Ont. Sewer &, 2-33
Waterproofing Assn., Sealant &, 2-33
Weather
  Data, Cities, 1-65
  Govt. Quick Ref., 3-8, 3-40
  Services, Ntl., 3-65
Website Directory, 5-233
WEDC, 3-92
Weddings, see Bridal; Brides
WEED Fdn., 2-193
Week, The, 1-2
Weekly Newspaper(s) (see also Newspapers)
  Assns., 2-144
Weightlifting Fedn., Cdn., 2-178
Weights & Measures, 1-60
  Govt. Quick Ref., 3-40
Weizmann Inst. of Science, Cdn. Soc. for, 2-162
Welding
  Bur., Cdn., 2-32
  Magazines, 5-177
Welfare (see also Income Security; Social Services)
  Child, see Child Welfare
  Depts., see Social Services
Well
  Drilling Assns., 2-44
  Logging Soc., Cdn., 2-75
Welland Canal Locks, 1-64
Well-Being, Cdn. Ctr. for Stress &, 2-125
Wellington County Bd. of Educ. (Ont.), 9-25
Welsh Black Cattle Soc., Cdn., 2-21
Wesleyan Church of Canada, 2-6
West
  Coast Railway Assn., 2-98
Western
  Academy Broadcasting College (Sask.), 9-55
  Assn.
    Broadcast Engineers, 2-30
    of Exposition Mgrs., 2-67
  Barley Growers Assn., 2-16
  Canada
    Art Assn., 2-191
    Motor Coach Assn., 2-189
    Roadbuilders Assn., 2-31
    Water Environ. Assn., 2-65
    Water & Wastewater Assn., 2-65
    Wilderness Committee, 2-65
  Cdn.
    Management Inst. (Sask.), 9-55
    University Presidents, Council of, 2-47
    Wheat Growers Assn., 2-16
  Devel. Museum (Sask.), 6-27
  Economic Diversification Canada, 3-92
  Grains Research Fdn., 2-16
  Heritage Ctr. Soc., 2-98
  Ontario
    Breeders Inc., 2-21
    Univ. of, 9-31
  Pentecostal Bible College (B.C.), 9-10

Western (cont.)
  Stock Growers' Assn., 2-21
  Trade Training Inst. (Sask.), 9-55
  Transportation Advisory Council, 2-189
  Univ., Trinity (B.C.), 9-7
Westerner Exposition Assn., 2-67
Westminster Inst. for Ethics & Human Values (U.W.O.), 9-31
Westviking College of Applied Arts (Nfld.), 9-20
Wetland Conservation
  Corp., Sask., 3-215
  Council, North American, 3-65
Whaling Commn., Intl., 3-248
Wheat
  Bd., Cdn., 3-62
  Growers Assn., Western Cdn., 2-16
  Mktg. Bd., Ont., 3-170
  Pools: Alta., 2-13
Wheelchair
  Basketball Assn., Cdn., 2-178
  Sports Assn., Cdn., 2-178
Whitby, Town of, Govt., 4-169
Whitehorse
  City Govt., 4-169
Whitewater
  Canoe Assn., Alta., 2-149
  Kayaking Assn. of B.C., 2-153
Wholesale
  & Dept. Store Union, 2-206; Sask., 2-206
  Drug Assn., Cdn., 2-139
  Lumber Dealers Assn., 2-75
  Sales Reps., Cdn. Assn. of, 2-67
Wife Assault, Educ., 2-167
Wild Animal Appeal, Elsa, 2-62
Wilderness
  Assn., Alta., 2-60
  Canoe Assn., 2-153
  Com., Western Canada, 2-65
  School, Cdn. Outward Bound, 2-153
  Soc., Cdn. Parks &, 2-150
Wildflower Soc., Cdn., 2-99
Wildlife
  Brs./Divs. (Govt.): Quick Ref. 3-40; Alta., 3-99; B.C., 3-113; Cdn., 3-65; Man., 3-130; N.B., 3-139; Nfld., 3-144; N.W.T., 3-153; N.S., 3-163; P.E.I., 3-190; Sask., 3-214; Yukon, 3-225
  Com. on the Status of Endangered, 3-65
  Conservation
    Awards, see Environmental Awards
    Employees Union, Qué., 2-206
  Depts. (Govt.): N.W.T., 3-153; Qué., 3-201
  Directory, 6-44
  Fedn(s)., 2-62
    Cdn., 2-62
    Fdns.: Alta., 3-97; Cdn., 2-62; Qué. 3-202
  Fund, World, 2-65
  Habitat Canada, 2-65
  Mgmt. Area, Saskeram, 3-130
  Preservation Trust, 2-65
  Research Ctr., Ntl., 3-65
  Service, Cdn., 3-65
Wilfrid Laurier Univ. (Ont.), 9-32
Wind
  Energy Assn., Cdn., 2-56
  Tunnel Laboratory, Boundary Layer (U.W.O.), 9-31
Window & Door Mfrs. Assn., Cdn., 2-124
Windsor
  Art Gallery of, 6-32
  City Govt., 4-170
  House of, 3-245
  Univ. of, 9-31
Wine
  & Allied Wkrs. Intl. Union, Distillery, 2-200
  Council of Ont., 2-74
  Inst., Cdn., 2-73
  Soc., German, 2-73

Winnipeg
　Art Gallery, 6-31
　Ballet, Royal, 6-44
　City Govt., 4-170
　Fdn,, 2-273
　Sch. Div., 9-14
　Stock Exchange, 7-13
　Univ. of, 9-15
Winter
　Begins, 1-3
　Carnival (Qué.), 2-66
　Carnivals, 1-91
　Fair(s) (*see also* Agriculture)
　　Assn., Royal Agricl., 2-67
　　Royal Manitoba, 2-67
　Games, Arctic, 2-172; Qué., 2-180
Wireless Telecommunications Assn., Cdn., 2-183
Witness Asst. Program (Man.), 3-128
Wolf Damage Assessment Bd., Ont., 3-170
Womanpower, 2-193
Woman's Christian Temperance Union, Cdn., 2-76
Women
　Assns., 2-191
　Cdn.
　　Congress for Learning Opportunities for, 2-191
　　Council of Muslim, 2-7
　　Fedn. of University, 2-49
　　Research Inst. for Adv. of, 2-155
　in Communications, Cdn., 2-192
　Composers, Assn. of, 2-191
　Congress of Black, 2-192
　in Construction, Ntl. Assn. of, 2-192
　Entrepreneurs of Canada, 2-193
　& Environments Educ. & Devel. Fdn., 2-193
　Execs. & Entrepreneurs, Cdn. Assn. of, 2-191
　Exhibitions, Shows & Events, 1-92
　Fedn. of Medical, 2-192
　in Film & TV, 2-30
　Intl., Jewish, 2-192
　Labour Force Participation in, 1-52
　& the Law, Ntl. Assn. of, 2-192
　Métis Ntl. Council of, 2-133
　in Music, 2-193
　National
　　Action Com. on Status of, 2-192
　　Council of, 2-193
　　　Jewish, 2-192
　　Org. of Immigrants & Visible Minority, 2-38
　Pilots (Ninety-Nines), 2-28
　in Science
　　& Engrg. Corp., 2-193
　　& Tech., Soc. for Cdn., 2-193
　& Sport, & Phys. Activity, Cdn. Assn. for Adv. of, 2-191
　Status of, *see* Status of Women
　Teachers Assns. of Ont., Fedn. of, 2-52
　of Unifarm, 2-193
　Voice of, 2-193
　Voices of Positive, 2-19
Women's
　Art
　　Assn. of Canada, 2-193
　　Resource Ctr., 2-193
　Assn., Native, 2-134
　Clubs, Cdn. Fedn. of Bus. & Profl., 2-192
　Counselling & Referral & Educ. Ctr., 2-193
　Directorates (Govt.): Ont., 3-187; Yukon, 3-225
　Earnings (Statistics), 1-53
　Equality, B.C. Min. of, 3-120
　Enterprise Bur., 2-193
　Exhibitions, Shows & Events, 1-92
　& Feminist Magazines, 5-190
　Field Hockey Assn., 2-178
　Foundation, Cdn., 2-192
　Health (Govt.): B.C., 3-116; Fed., 3-71
　Insts., Federated, 2-192
　Inter-Church Council, 2-193
　Intl. League for Peace & Freedom, 2-193

Women's (cont.)
　Issues
　　Adv. Councils (Govt.): Alta., 3-105
　　Govt. Quick Ref., 3-40
　League, Catholic, 2-192
　Legal Educ. & Action Fund, 2-193
　Magazines, 5-190
　Network
　　Positive, 2-18
　　P.E.I., 2-193
　Research Ctr., 2-193
　Secretariats (Govt.): P.E.I., 3-191; Qué., 3-198; Sask., 3-221
　Studies & Feminist Research, Ctr. for (U.W.O.), 9-31
Wood
　Cdn. Inst. of Treated, 2-74
　Council, Cdn., 2-75
　Energy Technology Transfer, 2-57
　Exhibitions, Shows & Events, 1-92
　Pallet & Container Assn., Cdn., 2-75
　Preservers' Bur., Cdn., 2-75
Woodcarvers Assn., Ont., 2-191
Wooden Money Collectors, Cdn. Assn. of, 2-149
Woodland
　Cultural Ctr., 2-134
　Inst. (Sask.), 9-54
Wood-Pulps Network, 2-75
Woodsworth College (U. of T.), 9-31
Woodwork Mfrs. Assn.
　Architectural, 2-30
　Cdn., 2-75
Woodworkers
　Assn., Cariboo, 2-200
　of Canada, Pulp, Paper &, 2-205
Woodworking
　Exhibitions, Shows & Events, 1-92
　Magazines, 5-177
Wool
　Bur. of Canada, 2-68
　Growers, Cdn. Co-op., 2-20
　Mktg. Bds./Commns. (Govt.): Alta., 3-96; N.S., 3-156
WOOMB Canada Inc., 2-154
Words & Change, People, 2-215
Work
　Cdn. Council on Rehab. &, 2-42; Ont., 2-43
　Permits (Fed.), 3-70
　Standards (Alta.), 3-102
Worker Advisor Offices (Govt.): B.C., 3-117; Man., 3-129; Ont., 3-181 (*see also* Workers' Advocates)
Workers'
　Advocates (Govt.): N.B., 3-133; Sask., 3-218
　Alliance, Cdn. Injured, 2-110
　Assns., 2-195
　Compensation
　　Bds., Assn. of, 2-110
　　Bds. & Commns. (Govt.): Quick Ref. 3-41; Alta., 3-105; B.C., 3-117; Man., 3-131; Nfld., 3-149; N.W.T., 3-154; N.S., 3-164; Ont., 3-187; P.E.I., 3-193; Sask., 3-221; Yukon, 3-225 (for Qué., *see* Commn de la Santé et de la sécurité du travail)
　　Review Div. (Nfld.), 3-143
　Review Bd., B.C., 3-117
Workplace
　Health & Safety (Govt.): N.B., 3-140; Ont., 3-181
　Info. (Fed.), 3-72
　Safety Brs./Divs. (Govt.): Man., 3-129; Sask., 3-218
Works Services & Transportation Dept. (Nfld.), 3-149
World
　Congress of Faiths, 2-8
　Development, Cdn. Fdn. for, 2-108
　of Dreams Fdn. Canada, 2-214
　Federalists of Canada, 2-110
　Relief
　　Cdn. Lutheran, 2-7
　　Com., Christian Reformed, 2-7
　Trade
　　Centre, INFORUM Montréal, 2-188
　　& Convention Ctr., N.S., 3-158

World (cont.)
　University
　　Games, 2-181
　　Service of Canada, 2-110
　Vision Canada, 2-110
　Wildlife Fund, 2-65
　Youth, Canada, 2-107
Worldhomes Holiday Exchange, 2-187
Wrestling Assn., Cdn. Amateur, 2-173
Writers
　Alliance, Nfld./Lab., 2-194
　Assns., 2-193
　　Periodical, 2-194
　　for Romance & Mainstream, 2-194
　　Science, 2-194
　Awards & Prizes (*see* Literary Arts)
　Crime, 2-194
　Devel. Trust, 2-194
　Fedns.: B.C., 2-194; Cdn. Farm, 2-194; N.B., 2-195; N.S., 2-195
　Guilds: Alta., 2-194; Canada, 2-194; Man., 2-194; Sask., 2-194
　Soc. of Amer. Travel, 2-194
　Union of Canada, 2-194
WWF, 2-65
Wycliffe College (Toronto), 9-31

Y

Yacht Clubs, Council of B.C., 2-151
Yachting
　Assn., Cdn., 2-151
　Magazines, Boating &, 5-161
　Shows, *see* Boating Exhibitions
Yardbird Suite, 6-40
Yellowknife City Govt., 4-170
Yeux, Fond. de la Banque d'(Qué.), 2-115
Y.M.C.A. Canada, 2-153
Yoga Fellowship, Spiritualist, 2-6
Yom Kippur, 1-24
York
　City Govt., 4-170
　Law Assn., County of, 2-114
　Region Bd. of Educ. (Ont.), 9-25; R.C.S.S., 9-26
　Regional Mun., Govt., 4-173
　Univ. (Ont.), 9-32
Young
　Audiences, Cdn. Inst. of the Arts for, 2-25
　Children
　　Cdn. Assn. for, 2-36
　　Music for, 6-40
　Farmers, Qué., 2-15
　Judaea, Cdn., 2-36
　Men's Christian Assns., 2-153
　Offenders
　　Brs./Divs. (Govt.): Alta., 3-102; B.C., *see* Child & Youth Secretariat; N.B., 3-138; N.W.T., 3-152; Sask., 3-217 (*see also* Youth Correctional; Youth Corrections)
　　Govt. Quick Ref., 3-41
　People, Intl. Bd. on Books for, 2-145
　Women's Christian Assn., 2-153
Youth
　Alliance, Environmental, 2-63
　Assns., 2-36
　Bowling Council, Ntl., 2-228
　Canada World, 2-107
　Cdn. Esperanto, 2-112
　Correctional Servs. (Govt.): Man., 3-128; Nfld., 3-147
　Council of N.B., 3-140
　Courts: Alta., 10-3; B.C., 10-5; Man., 10-7; N.B., 10-7; Nfld., 10-8; N.W.T., 10-9; N.S., 10-9; Ont., 10-11; P.E.I., 10-15; Qué., 10-16; Sask., 10-20
　Deaf, 2-42
　Fedn., Progressive Conservative, 2-142
　Foundation, Cdn., 2-36
　Kaiser, 2-211

Canadian Almanac & Directory 1997

Youth (cont.)
   Law Policy Section (Fed.), 3-78
   Magazines, 5-191
   & Music Canada, 6-41
   Orchestras, 6-37
   Org., B'nai Brith, 2-36
   Outreach, Positive, 2-18
   Sask. Council on Children &, 2-37
   Science Fdn., 2-163
   Secretariats (Govt.): Man., 3-126; N.S., 3-161
   Secretary of State for Training & (Fed.), 3-72
   Service(s)
      Brs./Divs. (Govt.): Fed., 3-78; Sask., 3-220
      Govt. Quick Ref., 3-41
Yukon Territory
   Chambers of
      Commerce in, 7-24, 7-35
      Mines, 7-35
   Cities & Towns in, 4-152
   College, 3-222, 9-55

Communities, Assn. of, 2-79
Conservation Soc., 2-84
Courts & Judges, 10-21
Education in, 9-55
Energy Corp., 3-222
Flag & Coat of Arms, 6-33
Government in, 3-221
Hospitals in, 8-56
Law Firms in, 10-103
Libraries in, 5-112
Municipal Govt., 4-152
Museums in, 6-29
Newspapers in, 5-148
Post Secondary Educ. in, 9-55
Y.W.C.A., 2-153

Z

Zeller Family Fdn., 2-214
Zionist
   Alliance of Canada, Labor, 2-131
   Fedn., Cdn., 2-129
   Movement of Canada, Labor, 2-131
Zodiac, Signs of, 1-15
Zoning, Govt. Quick Ref., 3-41
ZOOCHECK Canada, 2-23
Zoological
   Gdns., 6-44
   Parks & Aquariums, Cdn. Assn. for, 2-21
   Soc. of Metro. Tor., 2-23
   Soc. of Montréal, 2-23
Zoologique
   de Qué., Soc., 2-23
   du Qué., Jardin, 2-22
Zoologists, Cdn. Soc. of, 2-22
Zoos, 6-44
Zootechnie, Soc. cdnne de, 2-22
Zoroastrian Calendar, 1-2

ABBREVIATIONS

Acc. (Accident)
Admin. (Administration)
Admrs. (Administrators)
Adv. (Advancement/Advisory)
Advtg. (Advertising)
Agric./Agricl. (Agriculture/Agricultural)
Alta. (Alberta)
ADM (Assistant Deputy Minister)
Amer. (America/American)
Asst. (Assistant)
Atty-Gen. (Attorney-General)
Auth. (Authority)
Br. (Branch)
B.C. (British Columbia)
Brdcstrs. (Broadcasters)
Broth. (Brotherhood)
Bur. (Bureau)
Cdn. (Canadian); cdn/cdnne (canadien/canadienne)
Cie (Compagnie)
Co./Cos. (Company/Companies)
Commn. (Commission)
Commr. (Commissioner)
Com. (Committee)
Conf. (Conference)
Const. (Construction)
Contrs. (Contractors)
Coord. (Coordinator/Coordination)
Corp./Corps. (Corporation/Corporations)
Dept./Depts. (Department/Departments)
Devel. (Development)
Dir./Dirs. (Director/Directors)
Distrs. (Distributors)
Dist. (District)

Div./Divs. (Division/Divisions)
Educ./Educl. (Education/Educational)
Engrg. (Engineering)
Engrs. (Engineers)
Exec./Execs. (Executive/Executives)
Fed. (Federal)
Fedn./Fedns. (Federation/Federations)
Fdn./Fdns. (Foundation/Foundations)
Fra. (Fraternité)
Gen. (General)
Govt. (Government)
Hist'l (Historical)
Hosp. (Hospital)
Inc. (Incorporated)
Indep. (Independent)
Info. (Information)
Insp. (Inspection)
Ins. (Insurance)
Inst. (Institute)
Intl. (International; intle internationale)
Ltd. (Limited); ltée (limitée)
Mgmt. (Management)
Mgr./Mgrs. (Manager/Managers)
Man. (Manitoba)
Mfrs./Mfg. (Manufacturers/Manufacturing)
Mktg. (Marketing)
Min. (Ministry/Ministre)
Mtge. (Mortgage)
Mun. (Municipal)
Ntl. (National); ntle (nationale)
N.B. (New Brunswick)
Nfld. (Newfoundland)
N. Amer. (North America/North American)

N.W.T (Northwest Territories)
N.S. (Nova Scotia)
Ont. (Ontario)
Org./Orgs. (Organization/Organizations)
P.E.I. (Prince Edward Island)
Prodrs. (Producers)
Profl./Profls. (Professional/Professionals)
Prof. (Professor)
Prov. (Provincial)
Qué. (Québec)
qué. (québécois(e))
Rlwy. (Railway)
Ref. (Reference)
Regl. (Regional)
Regr. (Registrar)
Reg'n (Registration)
Reg'rd (Registered)
Reg./Regs. (Regulation/Regulations)
Rehab. (Rehabilitation)
Rep./Reps. (Representative/Representatives)
Sask. (Saskatchewan)
Sch./Schs. (School/Schools)
Soc./Socs. (Society/Societies or société/sociétés)
Supt. (Superintendent)
Suprv. (Supervisor)
Susp. (Suspension)
Synd. (Syndicat)
Tech. (Technology)
Terrs. (Territories)
Transp. (Transport/Transportation)
Univ. (University/Université)

COPP CLARK PROFESSIONAL

ORDER FORM

ORDER BY PHONE:
TOLL-FREE 1-800-815-9417   IN TORONTO: (416) 597-1616

FAX THIS FORM TO (416) 597-1617
EMAIL: ORDERS@MAIL.CANADAINFO.COM

TO ORDER MAILING LISTS CALL AND ASK FOR A QUOTATION: (416) 597-1616, EXT 241

PLEASE SEND ME THE FOLLOWING DIRECTORIES: PHOTOCOPY THIS FORM FOR CONVENIENT ORDERING

QTY		TITLE	PRICE	TOTAL
	1.	CANADIAN ALMANAC & DIRECTORY 1997	$189.00	
	2.	CANADIAN ALMANAC & DIRECTORY 1997 ON CD-ROM	$299.00	
	3.	ASSOCIATIONS CANADA 1997/98	$267.50	
	4.	ASSOCIATIONS CANADA 1997/98 ON CD-ROM	$399.00	
	5.	CANADIAN ENVIRONMENTAL DIRECTORY 1996/97	$249.50	
	6.	CANADIAN ENVIRONMENTAL DIRECTORY 1996/97 ON CD-ROM	$389.00	
	7.	CANADIAN ENVIRONMENTAL BUSINESSLETTER	3 FREE ISSUES	
	8.	THE REGISTER OF CANADIAN HONOURS	$75.00	

	SUBTOTAL	
	SHIPPING ($6.75 PER TITLE)	
	ADD 7% GST	
	SUBTOTAL	
	ONTARIO BUYERS ADD 8% PST ON ITEMS 2 THROUGH 6	
	TOTAL	

PRICES ARE STATED IN CANADIAN DOLLARS.

☐ MAILING LISTS
Please call me with more information on mailing lists or send your full information kit. I am particularly interested in _____

☐ STANDING ORDER PLAN
By indicating a Standing Order you will receive copies of selected books annually on publication and SAVE 5% on all future editions.

SHIP TO:

NAME _____

TITLE/DEPT. _____

ORGANIZATION _____

ADDRESS _____

METHOD OF PAYMENT:

☐ CHEQUE/MONEY ORDER
Please find enclosed cheque payable to
Copp Clark Professional
in the amount shown as total above.

☐ CREDIT CARD
   ☐ VISA   ☐ AMEX   ☐ MASTERCARD

CARD NUMBER _____

EXPIRY DATE _____

SIGNATURE _____

☐ BILL MY COMPANY/ORGANIZATION

PO# IF APPLICABLE _____

CITY _____

PROV/POSTAL CODE _____

BUSINESS PHONE _____

FAX NUMBER _____

COPP CLARK PROFESSIONAL, 200 ADELAIDE STREET WEST, 3RD FLOOR, TORONTO, ONTARIO M5H 1W7

ADDENDA

Section 1
Page 1-70
Event Planners:
Bar Hodgson Productions Inc.'s phone number is 905/655-5403.
International Tradeshow Services Inc.'s URL is http://www.intltradeshows.com

Section 2
The following Associations are here listed in the Almanac for the first time:
The Canadian Corporate Counsel Association, #300, 20 Toronto St., Toronto ON M5C 2B8; 416/869-0522, Fax: 416/869-0946; Executive Director, Robert V.A. Jones, Q.C.
Net Active Canada, #1105, 7400, rue Sherbrooke ouest, Montréal PQ H4B 1R8; 514/481-9912, Email: jhs@well.com; URL: http://tdg.uoguelph.ca/~ipirg; Coordinator, John H. Stevenson
SchoolNet National Advisory Board, 235 Queen St. West, 8th Fl., Ottawa ON K1A 0H5; 613/993-5452; Fax: 613/941-1296, Toll Free: 1-800-461-5945, Email: schoolnet@ic.qc.ca; Chair, Byron James; Secretary, Doug Hall; Director, Elise Boisjoly

Section 3
Page 3-45
Peter Milliken replaces Bob Kilger as Deputy Chair, Committees of the Whole House. Bob Kilger becomes Chief Government Whip in the House of Commons.
Page 3-46
The URL for the Office of the Prime Minister has been changed to http://pm.gc.ca/
Page 3-102
Deputy Minister Robin Ford of Alberta Labour has retired.
Page 3-123
Ian G. Wright has been appointed President & CEO of the Manitoba Liquor Control Commission replacing Acting President Al Ahoff.
Page 3-187
Prince Edward Island held a general election on November 18th, 1996. Previously, on May 2, 1996, a new Election Act came into effect. One major change created by the new act was the elimination of the 16 dual member (Councillor & Assemblymen) ridings & the re-drawing of 27 new electoral districts. Each electoral district will now elect one member to the Legislative Assembly, decreasing the number of MLAs from 32 to 27. As a result of the election the party in power changed from the Liberal Party to the Progressive Conservative Party.
Unofficial election results are as follows:
1st - Andy Mooney, PC
2nd - Kevin MacAdam, PC
3rd - Michael Currie, PC
4th - Jim Bagnall, PC
5th - Pat Binns, PC
6th - Wilbur MacDonald, PC
7th - Pat Mella, PC
8th - Mildred A. Dover, PC
9th - Jamie Ballem, PC
10th - Elmer MacFadyen, PC
11th - Chester Gillan, PC
12th - Wayne Cheverie, Lib.
13th - Paul Connolly, Lib.
14th - Wes MacAleer, PC
15th - Don MacKinnon, PC
16th - Ron MacKinley, Lib.
17th - Norman MacPhee, PC
18th - Beth MacKenzie, PC
19th - Eric Hammill, PC
20th - Mitch Murphy, PC
21st - Greg Deighan, PC
22nd - Nancy Guptill, Lib.
23rd - Keith Milligan, Lib.
24th - Robert Maddix, Lib.
25th - Dr. Herb Dickieson, NDP
26th - Hector MacLeod, Lib.
27th - Robert J. Morrissey, Lib.
The party standings are as follows: Progressive Conservative (PC) 18, Liberal (Lib.) 8, New Democratic Party (NDP) 1; Total 27.
The Premier is Patrick Binns (PC). The Leader of the Opposition is Keith Milligan (Lib.).
Page 3-237
Under Government of Japan: a new Cabinet was appointed in mid-November 1996 following a national election. Prime Minister, Ryutaro Hashimoto; Chief of Cabinet Security, Seiroku Kajiyama. Ministers of: Agriculture, Forestry & Fisheries, Takao Fujimoto; Construction, Shizuka Kamei; Education, Takashi Kosugi; Foreign Affairs, Yukihiko Ikeda; Health & Welfare, Junichiro Koizumi; Home Affairs, Katsuhiko Shirakawa; International Trade & Industry, Shinji Sato; Justice, Isao Matsuura; Labour, Yutaka Okano; Posts & Telecommunications, Hisao Horinouchi; Transport, Makoto Koga. State Ministers: Defence: Fumio Kyuma; Economic Planning, Taro Aso; Environment, Michiko Ishii; Hokkei & Okinawa Development, Jitsuo Inagaki; Management Coordination, Kabun Muto; National Land, Kosuke Ito; Science & Technology, Riichiro Chikaoka.

Sections 3 & 4
Following is a revised list of electoral districts as will apply in the next federal election. (A list of present federal electoral districts is found on page 3-47; a list of present federal electoral districts by city & town is found on page 4-1.)

REPRESENTATION ORDER/DÉCRET DE REPRÉSENTATION
1996
New Electoral District Names/Nouveau nom des circonscriptions eléctorales

ALBERTA
Athabasca
Calgary Centre/Calgary-Centre
Calgary East/Calgary-Est
Calgary Northeast/Calgary-Nord-Est
Calgary-Nose Hill
Calgary Southeast/Calgary-Sud-Est
Calgary Southwest/Calgary-Sud-Ouest
Calgary West/Calgary-Ouest
Crowfoot
Edmonton East/Edmonton-Est
Edmonton North/Edmonton-Nord
Edmonton Southeast/Edmonton-Sud-Est
Edmonton Southwest/Edmonton-Sud-Ouest
Edmonton-Strathcona
Edmonton West/Edmonton-Ouest
Elk Island
Lakeland
Lethbridge
Macleod
Medicine Hat
Peace River
Red Deer
St. Albert
Wetaskiwin
Wild Rose
Yellowhead

BRITISH COLUMBIA/COLOMBIE-BRITANNIQUE
Burnaby-Douglas
Cariboo-Chilcotin
Delta-South Richmond
Dewdney-Alouette
Esquimalt-Juan de Fuca
Fraser Valley
Kamloops
Kelowna
Kootenay-Columbia
Langley-Matsqui
Nanaimo-Alberni
Nanaimo-Cowichan
New Westminster-Coquitlam-Burnaby
North Okanagan-Shuswap
North Vancouver
Okanagan-Coquihalla
Port Moody-Coquitlam
Prince George-Bulkley Valley
Prince George-Peace River
Richmond
Saanich-Gulf Islands
Skeena
South Surrey-White Rock-Langley
Surrey Central/Surrey-Centre
Surrey North/Surrey-Nord
Vancouver Centre/Vancouver-Centre
Vancouver East/Vancouver-Est
Vancouver Island North/Île de Vancouver-Nord
Vancouver Kingsway
Vancouver Quadra
Vancouver South-Burnaby/Vancouver-Sud-Burnaby
Victoria
West Kootenay-Okanagan
West Vancouver-Sunshine Coast

MANITOBA
Brandon-Souris
Charleswood-Assiniboine
Churchill
Dauphin-Swan River
Portage-Lisgar
Provencher
Saint Boniface/Saint-Boniface
Selkirk-Interlake
Winnipeg North/Winnipeg-Nord
Winnipeg North Centre/Winnipeg-Centre-Nord
Winnipeg South/Winnipeg-Sud
Winnipeg South Centre/Winnipeg-Centre-Sud
Winnipeg-St. Paul
Winnipeg-Transcona

NEW BRUNSWICK/NOUVEAU-BRUNSWICK
Acadie-Bathurst
Beauséjour
Charlotte
Fredericton
Fundy-Royal
Madawaska-Restigouche
Miramichi
Moncton
Saint John
Tobique-Mactaquac

ADDENDA-2

NEWFOUNDLAND/TERRE-NEUVE
Bonavista-Trinity-Conception
Burin-St. George's
Gander-Grand Falls
Humber-St. Barbe-Baie Verte
Labrador
St.- John's East/St. John's-Est
St. John's West/St. John's-Ouest

NORTHWEST TERRITORIES/TERRITOIRES DU NORD-OUEST
Nunavut
Western Arctic

NOVA SCOTIA/NOUVELLE-ÉCOSSE
Bras D'Or
Cumberland-Colchester
Dartmouth
Halifax
Halifax West/Halifax-Ouest
Kings-Hants
Pictou-Antigonish-Guysborough
Sackville-Eastern Shore
South Shore
Sydney-Victoria
West Nova

ONTARIO
Algoma
Barrie-Simcoe
Beaches-Woodbine
Bramalea-Gore-Malton
Brampton Centre/Brampton-Centre
Brampton West-Mississauga/Brampton-Ouest-Mississauga
Brant
Broadview-Greenwood
Bruce-Grey
Burlington
Cambridge
Davenport
Don Valley East/Don Valley-Est
Don Valley West/Don Valley-Ouest
Dufferin-Peel-Wellington-Grey
Durham
Eglinton-Lawrence
Elgin-Middlesex-London
Erie-Lincoln
Essex
Etobicoke Centre/Etobicoke-Centre
Etobicoke-Lakeshore
Etobicoke North/Etobicoke-Nord
Glengarry-Prescott-Russell
Gloucester-Carleton
Guelph-Wellington
Haldimand-Norfolk-Brant
Halton
Hamilton East/Hamilton-Est
Hamilton Mountain
Hamilton West/Hamilton-Ouest
Hastings-Frontenac-Lennox & Addington
Huron-Bruce
Kenora-Rainy River
Kent-Essex
Kingston & the Islands/Kingston et les Îles
Kitchener Centre/Kitchener-Centre
Kitchener-Waterloo
Lambton-Kent-Middlesex
Lanark-Carleton
Leeds-Grenville
London-Adelaide
London-Fanshawe
London West/London-Ouest
Markham
Mississauga Centre/Mississauga-Centre
Mississauga East/Mississauga-Est
Mississauga South/Mississauga-Sud
Mississauga West/Mississauga-Ouest
Nepean-Carleton
Niagara Centre/Niagara-Centre
Niagara Falls
Nickel Belt

Nipissing
Northumberland
Oak Ridges
Oakville
Oshawa
Ottawa Cenre/Ottawa-Centre
Ottawa South/Ottawa-Sud
Ottawa-Vanier
Ottawa West-Nepean/Ottawa-Ouest-Nepean
Oxford
Parkdale-High Park
Parry Sound-Muskoka
Perth-Middlesex
Peterborough
Pickering-Ajax-Uxbridge
Prince Edward-Hastings
Renfrew-Nipissing-Pembroke
Sarnia-Lambton
Sault Ste. Marie
Scarborough-Agincourt
Scarborough Centre/Scarborough-Centre
Scarborough East/Scarborough-Est
Scarborough-Rouge River
Scarborough Southwest/Scarborough-Sud-Ouest
Simcoe-Grey
Simcoe North/Simcoe-Nord
St. Catharines
St. Paul's
Stoney Creek
Stormont-Dundas
Sudbury
Thornhill
Thunder Bay-Atikokan
Thunder Bay-Nipigon
Timiskaming-Cochrane
Timmins-James Bay/Timmins-Baie James
Toronto Centre-Rosedale/Toronto-Centre-Rosedale
Trinity-Spadina
Vaughan-Aurora
Victoria-Haliburton
Waterloo-Wellington
Wentworth-Burlington
Whitby-Ajax
Willowdale
Windsor-St. Clair
Windsor West/Windsor-Ouest
York Centre/York-Centre
York North/York-Nord
York South-Weston/York-Sud-Weston
York West/York-Ouest

PRINCE EDWARD ISLAND/ÎLE-DU-PRINCE-ÉDOUARD
Cardigan
Egmont
Hillsborough
Malpeque

QUEBEC/QUÉBEC
Abitibi
Ahuntsic
Anjou-Rivière-des-Prairies
Argenteuil-Papineau
Beauce
Beauharnois-Salaberry
Beauport-Montmorency-Orléans
Bellechasse-Montmagny-L'Islet
Berthier-Montcalm
Bourassa
Brome-Missisquoi
Brossard-La Prairie
Chambly
Champlain
Charlesbourg
Charlevoix
Châteauguay
Chicoutimi
Compton-Stanstead
Drummond
Frontenac-Mégantic
Gaspé-Bonaventure-Îles-de-la-Madeleine

Gatineau
Hochelaga-Maisoneuve
Hull-Aylmer
Joliette
Jonquière
Kamouraska-Rivière-du-Loup-Témiscouata
Lachine-Notre-Dame-de-Grâce
Lac-Saint-Jean
Lac-Saint-Louis
LaSalle-Émard
Laurentides
Laurier-Sainte-Marie
Laval-Centre/Laval Centre
Laval-Est/Laval East
Laval-Ouest/Laval West
Lévis
Longueuil
Lotbinière
Louis-Hébert
Manicouagan
Matapédia-Matane
Mercier
Mont-Royal/Mount Royal
Outremont
Papineau-Saint-Denis
Pierrefonds-Dollard
Pontiac-Gatineau-Labelle
Portneuf
Québec
Québec-Est/Québec East
Repentigny
Richelieu
Richmond-Arthabaska
Rimouski
Roberval
Rosemont
Rouyn-Noranda-Témiscamingue
Saint-Eustache-Sainte-Thérèse
Saint-Hubert
Saint-Hyacinthe-Bagot
Saint-Jean
Saint-Lambert
Saint-Laurent-Cartierville
Saint-Léonard-Saint-Michel
Saint-Maurice
Shefford
Sherbrooke
Terrebonne-Blainville
Trois-Rivières
Vaudreuil
Verchères
Verdun-Saint-Henri
Westmount-Ville-Marie

SASKATCHEWAN
Battlefords-Lloydminster
Blackstrap
Churchill River/Rivière Churchill
Cypress Hills-Grasslands
Palliser
Prince Albert
Qu'Appelle
Regina-Arm River
Saskatoon-Humboldt
Saskatoon-Rosetown
Souris-Moose Mountain
Wanuskewin
Wascana
Yorkton-Melville

YUKON
Yukon

Section 4
Page 4-155
Ville de Charlesbourg: Maire: Ralph Mercier. Conseillers et Districts: 1) Clément Coulombe; 2) Jacques Mitchell; 3) Gilles Leduc; 4) Jacques Portelance; 5) Louisette Lachance; 6) André Gignac; 7) Claude Gosselin; 8) Guy Poirier; 9) Jean-Marie La-

liberté; 10) Régent Légaré; 11) Charles-Henri Verret.

Page 4-156

Corporation of Delta: Mayor: Beth Johnson. Councillors: Krista Engelland; George Hawksworth; Vicki Huntington; Lois Jackson; Wendy Jeske; R. Bruce McDonald.

Page 4-156

City of Edmonton: Bruce Thom replaces Richard Picherack as City Manager.

Page 4-158

City of Kamloops: Mayor: Clifford G. Branchflower. Councillors: Shirley O. Culver; Sharon E. Frissell; Russell S. Gerard; Patricia K. Kaatz; Joe N. Leong; Grant R. Robertson; Patricia A. Wallace; William H. Walton.

Page 4-158

City of Kelowna: Mayor: Walter Gray. Councillors: Andre Blanleil; Marion I. Bremner; Ron Cannan; Colin Day; Robert Douglas Hobson; Joe Leask; Smiley Nelson; Sharon Shepherd.

Page 4-162

City of Nanaimo: Mayor: Gary Richard Korpan. Councillors: Bill King; Jack Little; Paulette McCarthy; Blake McGuffie; Larry McNabb; Doug Rispin; Loyd Sherry.

Page 4-164

City of Prince George: Mayor: C. Kinsley. Councillors: Cliff Dezell; D. Goodkey; Don Grantham; Shirley Gratton; M. Krause; Anne Martin; Dan Rogers; Ronald Thiel.

Page 4-162

District of North Vancouver: Mayor: Don Bell. Councillors: Trevor Carolan; Ernis Crist; Glenys Deering-Robb; Janice Harris; Lisa Muri; Pat Munroe.

Page 4-165

City of Richmond: Mayor: Greg Halsey-Brandt. Councillors: Malcolm Brodie; Derek Dang; Lyn Greenhill; Ken Johnston; Kiichi Kumagai; Bill McNulty; Corisande Percival-Smith; Harold Steves.

Page 4-166

Ville de Saint Hubert: Maire: Michel Latendresse. Conseillers et Districts: 1) Jacques Thibault; 2) Carole Martin Chartré; 3) Suzanne Charbonneau; 4) Mario Boutin; 5) Jacques E. Poitras; 6) Monique Messier; 7) Yvan Laurin; 8) Jacques Lemire; 9) Roger Roy; 10) Jean-Guy Fortin; 11) Brian Taupier; 12) Lise Dutil; 13) Ronald Smith; 13) Marguerite Pearson Richard.

Page 4-168

City of Surrey: Mayor: Doug McCallum. Councillors: Edmund P. Caissie; Jeanne Eddington; J.E. Higginbotham; Marvin J. Hunt; Pam Lewin; Gary T. Robinson; Judy Villeneuve; Dianne Watts.

Page 4-168

City of Vancouver: Mayor: Philip Owen. Councillors: Don Bellamy; Nancy A. Chiavario; Jennifer Clarke; Alan Herbert; Lynne Kennedy; Daniel Lee; Don Lee; George J. Puil; Gordon Price; Sam Sullivan.

Page 4-169

City of Victoria: Mayor: Bob Cross. Councillors: Christopher M. Coleman; Bob Friedland; Bea Holland; Helen Hughes; Jane Lunt; Pamela Madoff; David McLean; Geoff Young.

Section 5
Page 5-115

Book Publishers:
Pannonia Books has moved to PO Box 716, Stn P, Toronto ON M5S 2Y4; 416/966-5156; Email: pannonia@interlog.com; URL: http://www.panbooks.com

Page 5-159:

Magazines:
Raddle Moon has moved to #518, 350 East 2 Ave., Vancouver BC V5J 4R8.

Contact has moved to Ceramic Contacts Inc., 429 - 12 St. NW, Calgary AB T2N 1X9; 403/270-3252; Email: btipton@cadvision; URL: http://www.idirect.com/~contact

Studies in Political Economy has moved to SR303, Carleton University, Ottawa ON, K1S 5B6; 613/520-2600, ext. 6625; Fax: 613/520-3981.

Page 5-230

Online Service Providers:
Lexicom Ltd., #60, 203 Lynnview Rd. SE, Calgary AB; 403/255-3615; Fax: 403/640-2138; Email: rae@lexi.net; URL: http//www.lexicom.ab.ca President, Michael Rae. Connection Speed to Internet: T1; Users' top connection speed: 33.6K; Number of phone lines: 13; Number of Users: 114

ViaNet, 361 Algonquin Blvd. West, Timmins ON; 705/268-5021; Fax: 705/264-6277; Email: helpme@vianet.on.ca; URL: http://www.vianet.on.ca

WBM Office Systems, 421 McDonald St., Regina SK; 306/721-2560; Fax: 306/721-2498; Email: webmaster@eagle.wbm.ca; URL: http://www.wbm

Page 5-244

The URL for the Office of the Prime Minister has changed to http://pm.gc.ca/

Section 7
Page 7-2:

Edward Speal has been appointed President/CEO for Paribas Bank of Canada.

Page: 7-13

Insurance Companies:
Balboa Life Insurance Company: The Chief Agent is A.W. Miles.

BCAA Isurance Corporation: Email: len.kelsey@bcaa.bc.ca; additional classes of insurance: Automobile, Fire, Property.

L'Industrielle-Alliance Compagnie d'Assurance sur la Vie: Raymond Garneau is Chair, President & CEO; Company Email: source@inalco.com

London & Midland General Insurance Company: The Vice-President/General Manager is A.W. Miles.

Page 7-38

Consultant Lobbyists:
Burstyn Jeffery Inc., of Toronto, have changed their address to: #1240, 155 University Ave., Toronto ON M5H 3B7; phone and fax remain the same.

Page 7-54

Major Canadian Companies (Telecommunications, Communications, Technology): Ivan Fecan is replacing Douglas Bassett as President/CEO of Baton Broadcasting Inc., as of December 18, 1996.

Section 10
Page 10-5:

B.C. Provincial Court Judges appointed: Wendy A. Young, Robin R. Smith, Suzanne K. MacGregor, Mark G. Takahashi

Page 10-14

P.E.I. Supreme Court: Trial Division. Justice Joseph A. Ghiz has died.

Page 10-67, 10-82

Law Firms:
Malach & Fiddler: 4 lawyers (Toronto office); 5 lawyers (Richmond Hill office).